BLACK'S LAW DICTIONARY

Definitions of the Terms and Phrases of American and English Jurisprudence, Ancient and Modern

By

HENRY CAMPBELL BLACK, M. A.

Author of Treatises on Judgments, Tax Titles, Intoxicating Liquors, Bankruptcy, Mortgages, Constitutional Law, Interpretation of Laws, Rescission and Cancellation of Contracts, Etc.

REVISED FOURTH EDITION

By

THE PUBLISHER'S EDITORIAL STAFF

ST. PAUL, MINN.
WEST PUBLISHING CO.
1968

Black's Law Dictionary 4th Ed. Rev.
12th Reprint—**1975**

PREFACE
REVISED FOURTH EDITION

THE sustained and growing popularity of BLACK'S LAW DICTIONARY since its appearance more than seventy five years ago is a striking tribute to the scholarship and learning of Henry Campbell Black, and to the essential soundness of the plan adopted by him for the compilation of a legal lexicon.

In accordance with the original plan of this work, consistently adhered to in all subsequent editions, the law student, confronted in his casebooks with reports from the Year Books, or with extracts from Glanvil, Bracton, Littleton, or Coke, will find in this dictionary an unusually complete collection of definitions of terms used in old English, European, and feudal law. The student will also find in this volume, on page 1795, a useful Table of British Regnal Years, listing the sovereigns of England for more than 900 years, together with the date of accession to the throne, and the length of reign.

BLACK'S LAW DICTIONARY has proven its value through the years to the busy practitioner, judge and law student who requires quick and convenient access to the meanings of legal terms and phrases found in statutes or judicial opinions, as well as to the special legal meanings of standard English words—meanings which frequently cannot be found in the ordinary English language dictionaries.

In the period of more than thirty five years since the publication of the Third Edition, the law has undergone substantial changes and developments. The vocabulary of the law has shown corresponding change and growth. A word, in the often quoted dictum of Mr. Justice Holmes, is "the skin of a living thought," and the words of statutes and judicial opinions reflect the contemporary thinking of legislators and jurists. In order adequately to represent this thinking in the fourth edition, a patient examination was made of the thousands of opinions handed down by the appellate courts each year. Some revisions and additions have been included in this Revised Fourth Edition.

Abbreviations of common words and phrases likely to be encountered by the user are explained in appropriate places throughout the main body of the work. A Table of Abbreviations of the titles of law reports, textbooks, and other legal literature is contained in the back of the volume and a Guide to Pronunciation is included in the front of the volume.

New features in this Revised Fourth Edition include the following:

Code of Professional Responsibility
Code of Judicial Conduct
An Outline of the Minimum Requirements for
Admission to Legal Practice in the United States

PREFACE—REVISED FOURTH EDITION

In order that BLACK'S LAW DICTIONARY should continue to be a handy one-volume work of ready reference, the enlarged contents of the Fourth Edition necessitated an improved typographical style. The type for the Fourth Edition was accordingly completely reset and arranged in wider columns, in a more attractive and readable manner.

The Publisher has drawn freely on its wide experience to make the present edition of BLACK'S LAW DICTIONARY superior to any of the earlier editions. It is confidently believed that this edition, both in content and format, sets new standards of excellence among law dictionaries.

THE PUBLISHER

ST. PAUL, MINN.
June, 1968

CONTENTS

	Page
Preface—Revised Fourth Edition	III
Front Matter	
Guide to Pronunciation	VII
Code of Professional Responsibility	XIII
Code of Judicial Conduct	LXIX
Minimum Requirements for Admission to Legal Practice in the United States	LXXVII
Text of Definitions	1
Back Matter	
Table of British Regnal Years	1795
Abbreviations	1797

GUIDE TO PRONUNCIATION

A NOTE ON PRONUNCIATION OF LATIN

One of the difficulties in pronouncing legal terms is that one commonly hears both the English system and the Roman system of pronouncing Latin words. Before 1900, the English pronunciation of Latin had developed for legal, medical, and other scientific terms. During the second half of the nineteenth century, scholars established that what is now known as the Roman pronunciation was used between 50 B.C. and 50 A.D. Nearly all schools in English-speaking countries adopted the Roman system of pronunciation. But by and large, the English pronunciation has persisted among lawyers, physicians, and scientists.

The main difference between the Roman and the English pronunciation of Latin is in the long sounds of a, e, and i. In English these sounds are ā, ē, and ī; in Roman, a is ä; e is ā; and i is ē.

The dominant usage among lawyers today is probably the English pronunciation, but the Roman system taught in the schools still has its influence. Lawyers who studied Latin in school often tend toward the Roman, and others often tend toward the English. Yet nearly all use both systems, or variations from both systems, to some extent.

For instance, many lawyers use the English pronunciation, rēz jo͞o′dĭ-kā′tȧ, but many lawyers prefer to say rāz jo͞o′dĭ-kä′tȧ—which is neither English nor Roman but a mixture. The Roman rās yo͞o′dĭ-cä-tȧ is seldom if ever heard. Probably all lawyers use the English hā′bē-ăs côr′pŭs or hā′bēz côr′pŭs; a lawyer who tries to get his client out of jail by asking for a writ of hä′bā-ăs côr′pŭs might not be understood. Yet the prevailing practice is probably to use the Roman ȧ-mē′cŭs cū′rē-ī, and not the English ȧ-mī′cŭs cū′rĭ-ē. One usually hears the mixture, sī′nē quä nōn; one seldom if ever hears the English sī′nē quā nŏn.

The following list is devoted mostly but not altogether to Latin words. For those words the English pronunciation is always in first place, followed by the Roman or a variation of the Roman whenever it is known to be widely used. The English pronunciation is never incorrect in the view of lexicographers, although local or general usage may often cause some lawyers to prefer a pronunciation other than the English. As the study of Latin in the schools declines still further, the English pronunciation is likely to continue to increase.

If a uniform system is ever achieved, it is much more likely to be the English than the Roman.

KEY TO PRONUNCIATION

Māke; chȧotic; câre; căt; ärt; ȧcross; ēat; ēvade; ĕbb; runnẽr; īce; hĭt; ōak; ōbey; ôrder; hŏt; fo͞od; fo͝ot; ūnit; ůnite; ûrge; ŭp; ɴ (French nasal, as in ensemble, äɴ säɴ′bl).

---

a fortiori	ā fôr′shĭ-ō′rī
a mensa et thoro	ā mĕn′sȧ ĕt thō′rō
a priori	ā′ prĭ-ō′rī; prī-ō′rī; ä′ prĭ-ō′rē
ab inconvenienti	ăb ĭn′cŏn-vē′nĭ-ĕn′tī
ab initio	ăb ĭn-ĭsh′ĭ-ō
actio in rem	ăk′shĭ-ō ĭn rĕm
ad idem	ăd ī′dĕm
affiant	ă-fī′ănt
agister	ȧ-jĭs′tẽr
aleatory	ā′lē-ȧ-tō′rĭ; -tẽr-ĭ
aliquot	ăl′ĭ-kwŏt
ambulatory	ăm′bů-lȧ-tō′rĭ
amicus curiae	ȧ-mī′kŭs kū′rĭ-ē; ȧ-mē′cŭs kū′rē-ī
animo revertendi	ăn′ĭ-mō rĕv′ẽr-tĕn′dī
animo testamenti	ăn′ĭ-mō tĕs′tȧ-mĕn′tī
appellant	ă-pĕl′ȧnt
appellate	ă-pĕl′ȧt
appellee	ăp′ĕ-lē′
assignee	ăs′ĭ-nē′
autre vie, pur	po͝or ōt′rē vē
bona fides	bō′nȧ fī′dēz
bona vacantia	bō′nȧ vȧ-kăn′shĭ-ȧ
capias	kā′pĭ-ăs; kăp′ĭ-ăs
casus belli	kā′sŭs bĕl′ī
casus foederis	kā′sŭs fĕd′ẽr-ĭs
casus fortuitus	kā′sŭs fôr-tū′ĭ-tŭs
casus omissus	kā′sŭs ō-mĭs′ŭs
causa causans	kô′zȧ kô′zănz; kou′zȧ kou′zănz
causa mortis	kô′zȧ môr′tĭs; kou′zȧ môr′tĭs
causa sine qua non	kô′zȧ sī′nē kwā nŏn′; kou′zȧ sī′nē kwä nōn
caveat emptor	kā′vē-ăt ĕmp′tôr; kă′vē-ăt
certiorari	sûr′shĭ-ō-râr′ī; -rä-rē
cestui que trust	sĕt′ĭ kȧ trŭst
chose	shōz

codicil	kŏd′ĭ-sĭl
consortium	kŏn-sôr′shĭ-ŭm
contra bonos mores	kŏn′trȧ bō′nōs mō′rēz
coram nobis	kō′răm nō′bĭs
corpus delicti	kôr′pŭs dē-lĭk′tī
corpus juris	kôr′pŭs jōō′rĭs
curtesy	kûr′tĕ-sĭ
cy-pres	sē′ prā′
damnum absque injuria	dăm′nŭm ăbs′kwē ĭn-jōō′rĭ-ȧ
de bene esse	dē bē′nē ĕs′ē
de facto	dē făk′tō
de jure	dē jōō′rē
de novo	dē nō′vō
del credere	dĕl krĕd′ĕr-ē; krē′dĕr-ē
delegatus non potest delegare	dĕl′ē-gā′tŭs nŏn pō′tĕst dĕl′ē-gā′rē
demesne	dē-mān′; -mēn′
demur	dē-mûr′
demurrer	dē-mûr′ĕr
descriptio personae	dē-skrĭp′shĭ-ō pĕr-sō′nē
detinue	dĕt′ĭ-nū
devise	dē-vīz′
devisee	dĕv′ĭ-zē′; dē-vīz′ē′
domicile	dŏm′ĭ-sĭl
dominium	dō-mĭn′ĭ-ŭm
donatio mortis causa	dō-nā′shĭ-ō môr′tĭs kô′zȧ; kou′zȧ
duces tecum	dū′sēs tē′kŭm
ejusdem generis	ē-jŭs′dĕm jĕn′ĕr-ĭs
eleemosynary	ĕl′ē-mŏs′ĭ-nĕr′ĭ; ĕl′ē-ē; -mŏz′ĭ-nĕr-ĭ
en ventre sa mere	äɴ väɴ′tr′ sȧ′ mâr′
enfeoff	ĕn-fĕf′; ĕn-fēf′
ex gratia	ĕks grā′shĭ-ȧ
ex parte	ĕks pär′tē
ex post facto	ĕks pōst făk′tō
exequatur	ĕk′sē-kwā′tĕr
expressio unius est exclusio alterius	ĕks-prĕsh′ĭ-ō ū′nĭ-ŭs ĕst ĕks-klōō′zhĭ-ō ăl-tē′rĭ-ŭs
facias	fā′shĭ-ăs
(scire facias)	sī′rē fā′shĭ-ăs
(fieri facias)	fī′ē-rī fā′shĭ-ăs
falsa demonstratio	făl′sȧ dĕm′ŏn-strā′shĭ-ō
feme covert	fĕm kŭv′ĕrt
feme sole	fĕm sōl

ferae naturae	fē′rē nȧ-tū′rē
force majeure	fôrs′ mȧ′zhûr′
forma pauperis, in	ĭn fôr′mȧ pô′pĕ-rĭs
functus officio	fŭngk′tŭs ŏ-fĭsh′ĭ-ō
gratis	grā′tĭs; gră′tĭs
gravamen	grȧ-vā′mĕn
habeas corpus	hā′bē-ās kôr′pŭs; hā′bēz
ignorantia juris	ĭg′nō-răn′shĭ-ȧ jo͞o′rĭs
imperium	ĭm-pē′rĭ-ŭm
imprimatur	ĭm′prĭ-mā′tẽr; -prī-
in esse	ĭn ĕs′ē
in extremis	ĭn ĕks-trē′mĭs
in fieri	ĭn fī′ē-rī
in futuro	ĭn fū-tū′rō
in limine	ĭn lĭm′ĭ-nē
in loco parentis	ĭn lō′kō pȧ-rĕn′tĭs
in pais	ĭn pā
in pari delicto	ĭn pā′rī dē-lĭc′tō; păr′ĭ
in pari materia	ĭn pā′rī mă-tē′rĭ-ȧ; pă′rĭ
in personam	ĭn pẽr-sō′năm
in praesenti	ĭn prē-zĕn′tī
in re	ĭn rē
in rem	ĭn rĕm
in toto	ĭn tō′tō
in transitu	ĭn trăn′sĭ-tū
indebitatus assumpsit	ĭn-dĕb′ĭ-tā′tŭs; ĭn-dĕb′ĭ-tä′tŭs; ă-sŭmp′sĭt; ă-sŭm′sĭt
indicia	ĭn-dĭsh′ĭ-ȧ
indictment	ĭn-dīt′mĕnt
inter partes	ĭn′tẽr pär′tēz
inter se	ĭn′tẽr sē′
inter vivos	ĭn′tẽr vī′vōs
intra vires	ĭn′trȧ vī′rēz
jura in re	jo͞o′rȧ ĭn rē
jus	jŭs
jus accrescendi	jŭs ăk′rē-sĕn′dī
jus civile	jŭs sĭ-vī′lē
jus gentium	jŭs jĕn′shĭ-ŭm
jus naturale	jŭs năt′ū-rā′lē
jus tertii	jŭs tûr′shĭ-ī
laches	lăch′ĕz
lessee	lĕs-ē′
lex domicilii	lĕks dŏm′ĭ-sĭl′ĭ-ī

lex fori	lĕks fō′rī
lex loci	lĕks lō′sī
lex situs	lĕks sī′tŭs
lien	lē′ĕn; lēn
locus standi	lō′kŭs stăn′dī
mala fides	mā′lȧ fī′dēz; mä′lȧ
mandamus	măn-dā′mŭs
mare clausum	mā′rē klô′sŭm; mä′rē klou′zŭm
mare liberum	mā′rē lĭb′ĕ-rŭm; mä′rē lē′bĕ-rŭm
mens rea	mĕnz rē-ȧ
mesne	mēn; mān
mutatis mutandis	mū-tā′tĭs mū-tăn′dĭs
ne exeat republica	nē ĕk′sē-ăt rē-pŭb′lĭ-kȧ
nihil est	nī′hĭl ĕst
nisi prius	nī′sī prī′ŭs
nolle prosequi	nŏl′ē prŏs′ē-kwī; prŏs′ē-kwĭ
non est factum	nŏn ĕst făk′tŭm
non obstante veredicto	nŏn ŏb-stăn′tē vĕr′ē-dĭk′tō
non sequitur	nŏn sĕk′wĭ-tēr
nudum pactum	nū′dŭm păk′tŭm
nulla bona	nŭl′ȧ bō′nȧ
nunc pro tunc	nŭngk′ prō′ tŭngk′
obiter dictum	ŏb′ĭ-tēr dĭk′tŭm; ōb′ĭ-tēr
obligatio	ŏb-lĭ-gā′shĭ-ō
obligee	ŏb′lĭ-jē′
obligor	ŏb′lĭ-gôr′; ŏb′lĭ-gôr
onus probandi	ō′nŭs prō-băn′dī
parens patriae	pā′rĕnz pā′trĭ-ē; pă′rĕnz păt′rē-ī
pari delicto	pā′rī dē-lĭk′tō; pă′rĭ
pari passu	pā′rī păs′ū; păr′ĭ păs′o͞o
particeps criminis	pär′tĭ-sĕps krĭm′ĭ-nĭs
pendente lite	pĕn-dĕn′tē lī′tē
persona non grata	pēr-sō′nȧ nŏn grā′tȧ
plene administravit	plē′nē ăd-mĭn′ĭ-strā′vĭt
poenitentiae, locus	lō′kŭs pĕn′ĭ-tĕn′shĭ-ē; -shē-ī
postea	pōst′ē-ȧ
praecipe	prĕs′ĭ-pē; prē′sĭ-pē
prima facie	prī′mȧ fā′shĭ-ē; fā′shē
profit a prendre	prŏf′ĭt ȧ präN′dr′
pro rata	prō rā′tȧ; rä′tȧ
publici juris	pŭb′lĭ-sī jo͞o′rĭs
qua	kwā; kwä
quaere	kwē′rē

quantum meruit	kwŏn′tŭm mĕr′o͞o-ĭt; mĕr′ū-ĭt
quantum valebat	kwŏn′tŭm vȧ-lē′băt
quare clausum fregit	kwā′rē klô′zŭm frē′jĭt; klou′zŭm
quasi	kwā′sī; kwä′sĭ
qui facit per alium facit per se	kwī fā′sĭt pĕr ā′lĭ-ŭm fā′sĭt pĕr sē
quia timet	kwī′ȧ tī′mĕt
quo warranto	kwō wŏ-răn′tō
ratio decidendi	rā′shĭ-ō dĕs′ĭ-dĕn′dī
rebus sic stantibus	rē′bŭs sĭk stăn′tĭ-bŭs
renvoi	rĕn-voi′; räɴ′vwä
res	rēz; rāz
res gestae	rēz jĕs′tē; rāz jĕs′tī
res inter alios acta	rēz ĭn′tĕr ā′lĭ-ōs ăk′tȧ
res ipsa loquitur	rēz ĭp′sȧ lŏk′wĭ-tĕr; rāz
res judicata	rēz jo͞o′dĭ-kā′tȧ; rāz jo͞o′dĭ-kä′tȧ
restitutio in integrum	rĕs′tĭ-tū′shĭ-ō ĭn ĭn′tē-grŭm
sans recours	säɴ rē-ko͞or′
scienter	sī-ĕn′tĕr
scire facias	sī′rē fā′shĭ-ăs
secus	sē′kŭs
semble	sĕm′b′l
seriatim	sēr′ĭ-ā′tĭm; sĕr′ĭ-
sine die	sī′nē dī′ē
sine qua non	sī′nē quā nŏn; sĭ′nĕ quä nōn
solatium	sō-lā′shĭ-ŭm
stare decisis	stā′rē dē-sī′sĭs; stä′rĕ
status quo	stā′tŭs kwō
sub judice	sŭb jo͞o′dĭ-sē
subpoena	sŭb-pē′nȧ; sŭ-pē′nȧ
subpoena duces tecum	sŭb-pē′nȧ; sŭ-pē′nȧ; dū′sēs tē′kŭm
suggestio falsi	sŭg-jĕs′chĭ-ō făl′sī
sui generis	sū′ī jĕn′ĕr-ĭs
sui juris	sū′ī jo͞o′rĭs
supersedeas	sū′pĕr-sē′dē-ăs
suppressio veri	sŭ-prĕsh′ĭ-ō vē′rī
tabula rasa	tăb′ū-lȧ rā′sȧ
ubi jus, ibi remedium	ū′bī jŭs, ī′bī rē-mē′dĭ-ŭm
ultra vires	ŭl′trȧ vī′rēz
uxor	ŭks′ôr
venue	vĕn′ū
vis major	vĭs mā′jôr
volenti non fit injuria	vō-lĕn′tī nŏn fĭt ĭn-jo͞o′rĭ-ȧ

CODE OF PROFESSIONAL RESPONSIBILITY *

Table of Contents

Page

PREAMBLE AND PRELIMINARY STATEMENT XVII

CANON 1. A LAWYER SHOULD ASSIST IN MAINTAINING THE INTEGRITY AND COMPETENCE OF THE LEGAL PROFESSION XIX

Ethical Considerations XIX

Disciplinary Rules XX

DR 1–101 Maintaining Integrity and Competence of the Legal Profession XX

DR 1–102 Misconduct XX

DR 1–103 Disclosure of Information to Authorities XXI

CANON 2. A LAWYER SHOULD ASSIST THE LEGAL PROFESSION IN FULFILLING ITS DUTY TO MAKE LEGAL COUNSEL AVAILABLE XXI

Ethical Considerations XXI

Recognition of Legal Problems XXI

Selection of a Lawyer: Generally XXIII

Selection of a Lawyer: Professional Notices and Listings ... XXIII

Financial Ability to Employ Counsel: Generally XXV

Financial Ability to Employ Counsel: Persons Able to Pay Reasonable Fees XXV

Financial Ability to Employ Counsel: Persons Unable to Pay Reasonable Fees XXVII

Acceptance and Retention of Employment XXVIII

Disciplinary Rules XXIX

DR 2–101 Publicity in General XXIX

DR 2–102 Professional Notices, Letterheads, Offices, and Law Lists XXIX

DR 2–103 Recommendation of Professional Employment . XXXII

DR 2–104 Suggestion of Need of Legal Services XXXIII

DR 2–105 Limitation of Practice XXXIII

DR 2–106 Fees for Legal Services XXXIV

DR 2–107 Division of Fees Among Lawyers XXXIV

DR 2–108 Agreements Restricting the Practice of a Lawyer XXXV

DR 2–109 Acceptance of Employment XXXV

DR 2–110 Withdrawal from Employment XXXV

CANON 3. A LAWYER SHOULD ASSIST IN PREVENTING THE UNAUTHORIZED PRACTICE OF LAW XXXVI

Ethical Considerations XXXVI

Disciplinary Rules XXXVIII

DR 3–101 Aiding Unauthorized Practice of Law XXXVIII

DR 3–102 Dividing Legal Fees with a Non-Lawyer XXXVIII

DR 3–103 Forming a Partnership with a Non-Lawyer ... XXXVIII

* Adopted by the American Bar Association at annual meeting in Dallas, Texas, on Aug. 12, 1969. Copyrighted by American Bar Association. Published with permission.

Page

CANON 4. A LAWYER SHOULD PRESERVE THE CONFIDENCES AND SECRETS OF A CLIENT XXXVIII

Ethical Considerations XXXVIII

Disciplinary Rules XXXIX
DR 4–101 Preservation of Confidences and Secrets of a Client XXXIX

CANON 5. A LAWYER SHOULD EXERCISE INDEPENDENT PROFESSIONAL JUDGMENT ON BEHALF OF A CLIENT XLI

Ethical Considerations XLI
Interests of a Lawyer That May Affect His Judgment XLI
Interests of Multiple Clients XLIII
Desires of Third Persons XLV

Disciplinary Rules XLVI
DR 5–101 Refusing Employment When the Interests of the Lawyer May Impair His Independent Professional Judgment XLVI
DR 5–102 Withdrawal as Counsel When the Lawyer Becomes a Witness XLVI
DR 5–103 Avoiding Acquisition of Interest in Litigation . XLVI
DR 5–104 Limiting Business Relations with a Client XLVII
DR 5–105 Refusing to Accept or Continue Employment if the Interests of Another Client May Impair the Independent Professional Judgment of the Lawyer .. XLVII
DR 5–106 Settling Similar Claims of Clients XLVII
DR 5–107 Avoiding Influence by Others Than the Client XLVII

CANON 6. A LAWYER SHOULD REPRESENT A CLIENT COMPETENTLY XLVIII

Ethical Considerations XLVIII

Disciplinary Rules XLIX
DR 6–101 Failing to Act Competently XLIX
DR 6–102 Limiting Liability to Client XLIX

CANON 7. A LAWYER SHOULD REPRESENT A CLIENT ZEALOUSLY WITHIN THE BOUNDS OF THE LAW XLIX

Ethical Considerations XLIX
Duty of the Lawyer to a Client LI
Duty of the Lawyer to the Adversary System of Justice .. LIV

Disciplinary Rules LVIII
DR 7–101 Representing a Client Zealously LVIII
DR 7–102 Representing a Client within the Bounds of the Law LVIII
DR 7–103 Performing the Duty of Public Prosecutor or Other Government Lawyer LIX
DR 7–104 Communicating with One of Adverse Interest . LIX
DR 7–105 Threatening Criminal Prosecution LIX
DR 7–106 Trial Conduct LIX
DR 7–107 Trial Publicity LX
DR 7–108 Communication with or Investigation of Jurors LXII
DR 7–109 Contact with Witnesses LXII
DR 7–110 Contact with Officials LXII

Page

CANON 8. A LAWYER SHOULD ASSIST IN IMPROVING THE LEGAL SYSTEM LXIII

Ethical Considerations LXIII

Disciplinary Rules LXIV
- DR 8–101 Action as a Public Official LXIV
- DR 8–102 Statements Concerning Judges and Other Adjudicatory Officers LXV

CANON 9. A LAWYER SHOULD AVOID EVEN THE APPEARANCE OF PROFESSIONAL IMPROPRIETY LXV

Ethical Considerations LXV

Disciplinary Rules LXVI
- DR 9–101 Avoiding Even the Appearance of Impropriety LXVI
- DR 9–102 Preserving Identity of Funds and Property of a Client LXVI

DEFINITIONS LXVII

*

AMERICAN BAR ASSOCIATION
CODE OF PROFESSIONAL RESPONSIBILITY
With Amendments to March 1, 1974

PREAMBLE AND PRELIMINARY STATEMENT

Preamble [1]

The continued existence of a free and democratic society depends upon recognition of the concept that justice is based upon the rule of law grounded in respect for the dignity of the individual and his capacity through reason for enlightened self-government.[2] Law so grounded makes justice possible, for only through such law does the dignity of the individual attain respect and protection. Without it, individual rights become subject to unrestrained power, respect for law is destroyed, and rational self-government is impossible.

Lawyers, as guardians of the law, play a vital role in the preservation of society. The fulfillment of this role requires an understanding by lawyers of their relationship with and function in our legal system.[3] A consequent obligation of lawyers is to maintain the highest standards of ethical conduct.

In fulfilling his professional responsibilities, a lawyer necessarily assumes various roles that require the performance of many difficult tasks. Not every situation which he may encounter can be foreseen,[4] but fundamental ethical principles are always present to guide him. Within the framework of these principles, a lawyer must with courage and foresight be able and ready to shape the body of the law to the ever-changing relationships of society.[5]

The Code of Professional Responsibility points the way to the aspiring and provides standards by which to judge the transgressor. Each lawyer must find within his own conscience the touchstone against which to test the extent to which his actions should rise above minimum standards. But in the last analysis it is the desire for the respect and confidence of the members of his profession and of the society which he serves that should provide to a lawyer the incentive for the highest possible degree of ethical conduct. The possible loss of that respect and confidence is the ultimate sanction. So long as its practitioners are guided by these principles, the law will continue to be a noble profession. This is its greatness and its strength, which permit of no compromise.

Preliminary Statement

In furtherance of the principles stated in the Preamble, the American Bar Association has promulgated this Code of Professional Responsibility, consisting of three separate but interrelated parts: Canons, Ethical Considerations, and Disciplinary Rules.[6] The Code is designed to be adopted by appropriate agencies both as an inspirational guide to the members of the profession and as a basis for disciplinary action when the conduct of a lawyer falls below the required minimum standards stated in the Disciplinary Rules.

Obviously the Canons, Ethical Considerations, and Disciplinary Rules cannot apply to non-lawyers; however, they do define the type of ethical conduct that the public has a right to expect not

---

1 The footnotes are intended merely to enable the reader to relate the provisions of this Code to the ABA Canons of Professional Ethics adopted in 1908, as amended, the Opinions of the ABA Committee on Professional Ethics, and a limited number of other sources; they are not intended to be an annotation of the views taken by the ABA Special Committee on Evaluation of Ethical Standards. Footnotes citing ABA Canons refer to the ABA Canons of Professional Ethics, adopted in 1908, as amended.

2 *Cf.* ABA Canons, Preamble.

3 "[T]he lawyer stands today in special need of a clear understanding of his obligations and of the vital connection between those obligations and the role his profession plays in society." *Professional Responsibility: Report of the Joint Conference*, 44 A.B.A.J. 1159, 1160 (1958).

4 "No general statement of the responsibilities of the legal profession can encompass all the situations in which the lawyer may be placed. Each position held by him makes its own peculiar demands. These demands the lawyer must clarify for himself in the light of the particular role in which he serves." *Professional Responsibility: Report of the Joint Conference*, 44 A.B.A.J. 1159, 1218 (1958).

5 "The law and its institutions change as social conditions change. They must change if they are to preserve, much less advance, the political and social values from which they derive their purposes and their life. This is true of the most important of legal institutions, the profession of law. The profession, too, must change when conditions change in order to preserve and advance the social values that are its reasons for being." Cheatham, *Availability of Legal Services: The Responsibility of the Individual Lawyer and the Organized Bar*, 12 U.C.L.A.L. Rev. 438, 440 (1965).

6 The Supreme Court of Wisconsin adopted a Code of Judicial Ethics in 1967. "The code is divided into standards and rules, the standards being statements of what the general desirable level of conduct should be, the rules being particular canons, the violation of which shall subject an individual judge to sanctions." In re Promulgation of a Code of Judicial Ethics, 36 Wis.2d 252, 255, 153 N.W. 2d 873, 874 (1967).

The portion of the Wisconsin Code of Judicial Ethics entitled "Standards" states that "[t]he following standards set forth the significant qualities of the ideal judge . . . ." *Id.*, 36 Wis.2d at 256, 153 N.W.2d at 875. The portion entitled "Rules" states that "[t]he court promulgates the following rules because the requirements of judi-

only of lawyers but also of their non-professional employees and associates in all matters pertaining to professional employment. A lawyer should ultimately be responsible for the conduct of his employees and associates in the course of the professional representation of the client.

The Canons are statements of axiomatic norms, expressing in general terms the standards of professional conduct expected of lawyers in their relationships with the public, with the legal system, and with the legal profession. They embody the general concepts from which the Ethical Considerations and the Disciplinary Rules are derived.

The Ethical Considerations are aspirational in character and represent the objectives toward which every member of the profession should strive. They constitute a body of principles upon which the lawyer can rely for guidance in many specific situations.[7]

The Disciplinary Rules, unlike the Ethical Considerations, are mandatory in character. The Disciplinary Rules state the minimum level of conduct below which no lawyer can fall without being subject to disciplinary action. Within the framework of fair trial,[8] the Disciplinary Rules should be uniformly applied to all lawyers,[9] regardless of the nature of their professional activities.[10] The Code makes no attempt to prescribe either disciplinary procedures or penalties [11] for violation of a Disciplinary Rule,[12] nor does it undertake to define standards for civil liability of lawyers for professional conduct. The severity of judgment against one found guilty of violating a Disciplinary Rule should be determined by the character of the offense and the attendant circumstances.[13] An enforcing agency, in applying the Disciplinary Rules, may find interpretive guidance in the basic principles embodied in the Canons and in the objectives reflected in the Ethical Considerations.

---

cial conduct embodied therein are of sufficient gravity to warrant sanctions if they are not obeyed . . . ." *Id.*, 36 Wis.2d at 259, 153 N.W.2d at 876.

7 "Under the conditions of modern practice it is peculiarly necessary that the lawyer should understand, not merely the established standards of professional conduct, but the reasons underlying these standards. Today the lawyer plays a changing and increasingly varied role. In many developing fields the precise contribution of the legal profession is as yet undefined." *Professional Responsibility: Report of the Joint Conference*, 44 A.B.A.J. 1159 (1958).

"A true sense of professional responsibility must derive from an understanding of the reasons that lie back of specific restraints, such as those embodied in the Canons. The grounds for the lawyer's peculiar obligations are to be found in the nature of his calling. The lawyer who seeks a clear understanding of his duties will be led to reflect on the special services his profession renders to society and the services it might render if its full capacities were realized. When the lawyer fully understands the nature of his office, he will then discern what restraints are necessary to keep that office wholesome and effective." *Id.*

8 "Disbarment, designed to protect the public, is a punishment or penalty imposed on the lawyer. . . . He is accordingly entitled to procedural due process, which includes fair notice of the charge." In re Ruffalo, 390 U.S. 544, 550, 20 L.Ed.2d 117, 122, 88 S.Ct. 1222, 1226 (1968), *rehearing denied*, 391 U.S. 961, 20 L.Ed.2d 874, 88 S.Ct. 1833 (1968).

"A State cannot exclude a person from the practice of law or from any other occupation in a manner or for reasons that contravene the Due Process or Equal Protection Clause of the Fourteenth Amendment. . . . A State can require high standards of qualification . . . but any qualification must have a rational connection with the applicant's fitness or capacity to practice law." Schware v. Bd. of Bar Examiners, 353 U.S. 232, 239, 1 L.Ed.2d 796, 801–02, 77 S.Ct. 752, 756 (1957).

"[A]n accused lawyer may expect that he will not be condemned out of a capricious self-righteousness or denied the essentials of a fair hearing." Kingsland v. Dorsey, 338 U.S. 318, 320, 94 L.Ed. 123, 126, 70 S.Ct. 123, 124–25 (1949).

"The attorney and counsellor being, by the solemn judicial act of the court, clothed with his office, does not hold it as a matter of grace and favor. The right which it confers upon him to appear for suitors, and to argue causes, is something more than a mere indulgence, revocable at the pleasure of the court, or at the command of the legislature. It is a right of which he can only be deprived by the judgment of the court, for moral or professional delinquency." Ex parte Garland, 71 U.S. (4 Wall.) 333, 378–79, 18 L.Ed. 366, 370 (1866).

See generally Comment, *Procedural Due Process and Character Hearings for Bar Applicants*, 15 Stan.L.Rev. 500 (1963).

9 "The canons of professional ethics must be enforced by the Courts and must be respected by members of the Bar if we are to maintain public confidence in the integrity and impartiality of the administration of justice." In re Meeker, 76 N.M. 354, 357, 414 P.2d 862, 864 (1966), *appeal dismissed*, 385 U.S. 449 (1967).

10 *See* ABA Canon 45.

"The Canons of this Association govern all its members, irrespective of the nature of their practice, and the application of the Canons is not affected by statutes or regulations governing certain activities of lawyers which may prescribe less stringent standards." ABA Comm. on Professional Ethics, *OPINIONS*, No. 203 (1940) [hereinafter each Opinion is cited as "*ABA Opinion*"].

Cf. ABA Opinion 152 (1936).

11 "There is generally no prescribed discipline for any particular type of improper conduct. The disciplinary measures taken are discretionary with the courts, which may disbar, suspend, or merely censure the attorney as the nature of the offense and past indicia of character may warrant." Note, 43 Cornell L.Q. 489, 495 (1958).

12 The Code seeks only to specify conduct for which a lawyer should be disciplined. Recommendations as to the procedures to be used in disciplinary actions and the gravity of disciplinary measures appropriate for violations of the Code are within the jurisdiction of the American Bar Association Special Committee on Evaluation of Disciplinary Enforcement.

13 "The severity of the judgment of this court should be in proportion to the gravity of the offenses, the moral turpitude involved, and the extent that the defendant's acts and conduct affect his professional qualifications to practice law." Louisiana State Bar Ass'n v. Steiner, 204 La. 1073, 1092–93, 16 So.2d 843, 850 (1944) (Higgins, J., concurring in decree).

"Certainly an erring lawyer who has been disciplined and who having paid the penalty has given satisfactory evidence of repentance and has been rehabilitated and restored to his place at the bar by the court which knows him best ought not to have what amounts to an order of permanent disbarment entered against him by a federal court solely on the basis of an earlier criminal record and without regard to his subsequent rehabilitation and present good character . . .. We think, therefore, that the district court should reconsider the appellant's appli-

CANON 1

A Lawyer Should Assist in Maintaining the Integrity and Competence of the Legal Profession

ETHICAL CONSIDERATIONS

EC 1-1 A basic tenet of the professional responsibility of lawyers is that every person in our society should have ready access to the independent professional services of a lawyer of integrity and competence. Maintaining the integrity and improving the competence of the bar to meet the highest standards is the ethical responsibility of every lawyer.

EC 1-2 The public should be protected from those who are not qualified to be lawyers by reason of a deficiency in education [1] or moral standards [2] or of other relevant factors [3] but who nevertheless seek to practice law. To assure the maintenance of high moral and educational standards of the legal profession, lawyers should affirmatively assist courts and other appropriate bodies in promulgating, enforcing, and improving requirements for admission to the bar.[4] In like manner, the bar has a positive obligation to aid in the continued improvement of all phases of pre-admission and post-admission legal education.

EC 1-3 Before recommending an applicant for admission, a lawyer should satisfy himself that the applicant is of good moral character. Although a lawyer should not become a self-appointed investigator or judge of applicants for admission, he should report to proper officials all unfavorable information he possesses relating to the character or other qualifications of an applicant.[5]

EC 1-4 The integrity of the profession can be maintained only if conduct of lawyers in violation of the Disciplinary Rules is brought to the attention of the proper officials. A lawyer should reveal voluntarily to those officials all unprivileged knowledge of conduct of lawyers which he believes clearly to be in violation of the Disciplinary Rules.[6] A lawyer should, upon request, serve on and assist committees and boards having responsibility for the administration of the Disciplinary Rules.[7]

EC 1-5 A lawyer should maintain high standards of professional conduct and should encourage fellow lawyers to do likewise. He should be temperate and dignified, and he should refrain from all

---

1 "[W]e cannot conclude that all educational restrictions [on bar admission] are unlawful. We assume that few would deny that a grammar school education requirement, before taking the bar examination, was reasonable. Or that an applicant had to be able to read or write. Once we conclude that *some* restriction is proper, then it becomes a matter of degree—the problem of drawing the line.

. . . . .

"We conclude the fundamental question here is whether Rule IV, Section 6 of the Rules Pertaining to Admission of Applicants to the State Bar of Arizona is 'arbitrary, capricious and unreasonable.' We conclude an educational requirement of graduation from an accredited law school is not." Hackin v. Lockwood, 361 F.2d 499, 503–04 (9th Cir. 1966), *cert. denied,* 385 U.S. 960, 17 L.Ed.2d 305, 87 S.Ct. 396 (1966).

2 "Every state in the United States, as a prerequisite for admission to the practice of law, requires that applicants possess 'good moral character.' Although the requirement is of judicial origin, it is now embodied in legislation in most states." Comment, *Procedural Due Process and Character Hearings for Bar Applicants,* 15 Stan.L.Rev. 500 (1963).

"Good character in the members of the bar is essential to the preservation of the integrity of the courts. The duty and power of the court to guard its portals against intrusion by men and women who are mentally and morally dishonest, unfit because of bad character, evidenced by their course of conduct, to participate in the administrative law, would seem to be unquestioned in the matter of preservation of judicial dignity and integrity." In re Monaghan, 126 Vt. 53, 222 A.2d 665, 670 (1966).

"Fundamentally, the question involved in both situations [*i.e.* admission and disciplinary proceedings] is the same—is the applicant for admission or the attorney sought to be disciplined a fit and proper person to be permitted to practice law, and that usually turns upon whether he has committed or is likely to continue to commit acts of moral turpitude. At the time of oral argument the attorney for respondent frankly conceded that the test for admission and for discipline is and should be the same. We agree with this concession." Hallinan v. Comm. of Bar Examiners, 65 Cal.2d 447, 453, 421 P.2d 76, 81, 55 Cal. Rptr. 228, 233 (1966).

3 "Proceedings to gain admission to the bar are for the purpose of protecting the public and the courts from the ministrations of persons unfit to practice the profession. Attorneys are officers of the court appointed to assist the court in the administration of justice. Into their hands are committed the property, the liberty and sometimes the lives of their clients. This commitment demands a high degree of intelligence, knowledge of the law, respect for its function in society, sound and faithful judgment and, above all else, integrity of character in private and professional conduct." In re Monaghan, 126 Vt. 53, 222 A.2d 665, 676 (1966) (Holden, C. J., dissenting).

4 "A bar composed of lawyers of good moral character is a worthy objective but it is unnecessary to sacrifice vital freedoms in order to obtain that goal. It is also important both to society and the bar itself that lawyers be unintimidated—free to think, speak, and act as members of an Independent Bar." Konigsberg v. State Bar, 353 U.S. 252, 273, 1 L.Ed.2d 810, 825, 77 S.Ct. 722, 733 (1957).

5 *See* ABA Canon 29.

6 ABA Canon 28 designates certain conduct as unprofessional and then states that: "A duty to the public and to the profession devolves upon every member of the Bar having knowledge of such practices upon the part of any practitioner immediately to inform thereof, to the end that the offender may be disbarred." ABA Canon 29 states a broader admonition: "Lawyers should expose without fear or favor before the proper tribunals corrupt or dishonest conduct in the profession."

7 "It is the obligation of the organized Bar and the individual lawyer to give unstinted cooperation and assistance to the highest court of the state in discharging its function and duty with respect to discipline and in purging the profession of the unworthy." *Report of the Special Committee on Disciplinary Procedures,* 80 A.B.A.Rep. 463, 470 (1955).

illegal and morally reprehensible conduct.[8] Because of his position in society, even minor violations of law by a lawyer may tend to lessen public confidence in the legal profession. Obedience to law exemplifies respect for law. To lawyers especially, respect for the law should be more than a platitude.

EC 1–6 An applicant for admission to the bar or a lawyer may be unqualified, temporarily or permanently, for other than moral and educational reasons, such as mental or emotional instability. Lawyers should be diligent in taking steps to see that during a period of disqualification such person is not granted a license or, if licensed, is not permitted to practice.[9] In like manner, when the disqualification has terminated, members of the bar should assist such person in being licensed, or, if licensed, in being restored to his full right to practice.

DISCIPLINARY RULES

DR 1–101 Maintaining Integrity and Competence of the Legal Profession.

(A) A lawyer is subject to discipline if he has made a materially false statement in, or if he has deliberately failed to disclose a material fact requested in connection with, his application for admission to the bar.[10]

(B) A lawyer shall not further the application for admission to the bar of another person known by him to be unqualified in respect to character, education, or other relevant attribute.[11]

DR 1–102 Misconduct.

(A) A lawyer shall not:

(1) Violate a Disciplinary Rule.

(2) Circumvent a Disciplinary Rule through actions of another.[12]

(3) Engage in illegal conduct involving moral turpitude.[13]

---

8 *Cf.* ABA Canon 32.

9 "We decline, on the present record, to disbar Mr. Sherman or to reprimand him—not because we condone his actions, but because, as heretofore indicated, we are concerned with whether he is mentally responsible for what he has done.

"The logic of the situation would seem to dictate the conclusion that, if he was mentally responsible for the conduct we have outlined, he should be disbarred; and, if he was not mentally responsible, he should not be permitted to practice law.

"However, the flaw in the logic is that he may have been mentally irresponsible [at the time of his offensive conduct] . . . ., and, yet, have sufficiently improved in the almost two and one-half years intervening to be able to capably and competently represent his clients. . . . .

"We would make clear that we are satisfied that a case has been made against Mr. Sherman, warranting a refusal to permit him to further practice law in this state unless he can establish his mental irresponsibility at the time of the offenses charged. The burden of proof is upon him.

"If he establishes such mental irresponsibility, the burden is then upon him to establish his present capability to practice law." In re Sherman, 58 Wash.2d 1, 6–7, 354 P.2d 888, 890 (1960), *cert. denied.* 371 U.S. 951, 9 L.Ed.2d 499, 83 S.Ct. 506 (1963).

10 "This Court has the inherent power to revoke a license to practice law in this State, where such license was issued by this Court, and its issuance was procured by the fraudulent concealment, or by the false and fraudulent representation by the applicant of a fact which was manifestly material to the issuance of the license." North Carolina ex rel. Attorney General v. Gorson, 209 N.C. 320, 326, 183 S.E. 392, 395 (1936), *cert. denied,* 298 U.S. 662, 80 L.Ed. 1387, 56 S.Ct. 752 (1936).

See also Application of Patterson, 318 P.2d 907, 913 (Or. 1957), *cert. denied,* 356 U.S. 947, 2 L.Ed.2d 822, 78 S.Ct. 795 (1958).

11 *See* ABA Canon 29.

12 In *ABA Opinion* 95 (1933), which held that a municipal attorney could not permit police officers to interview persons with claims against the municipality when the attorney knew the claimants to be represented by counsel, the Committee on Professional Ethics said:

"The law officer is, of course, responsible for the acts of those in his department who are under his supervision and control." *Opinion 85. In re Robinson,* 136 N.Y.S. 548 (affirmed 209 N.Y. 354–1912) held that it was a matter of disbarment for an attorney to adopt a general course of approving the unethical conduct of employees of his client, even though he did not actively participate therein.

". . . . 'The attorney should not advise or sanction acts by his client which he himself should not do.' *Opinion 75.*"

13 "The most obvious non-professional ground for disbarment is conviction for a felony. Most states make conviction for a felony grounds for automatic disbarment. Some of these states, including New York, make disbarment mandatory upon conviction for *any* felony, while others require disbarment only for those felonies which involve moral turpitude. There are strong arguments that some felonies, such as involuntary manslaughter, reflect neither on an attorney's fitness, trustworthiness, nor competence and, therefore, should not be grounds for disbarment, but most states tend to disregard these arguments and, following the common law rule, make disbarment mandatory on conviction for any felony." Note, 43 Cornell L.Q. 489, 490 (1958).

"Some states treat conviction for misdemeanors as grounds for automatic disbarment . . . . However, the vast majority, accepting the common law rule, require that the misdemeanor involve moral turpitude. While the definition of moral turpitude may prove difficult, it seems only proper that those minor offenses which do not affect the attorney's fitness to continue in the profession should not be grounds for disbarment. A good example is an assault and battery conviction which would not involve moral turpitude unless done with malice and deliberation." *Id. at 491.*

"The term 'moral turpitude' has been used in the law for centuries. It has been the subject of many decisions by the courts but has never been clearly defined because of the nature of the term. Perhaps the best general definition of the term 'moral turpitude' is that it imports an act of baseness, vileness or depravity in the duties which one person owes to another or to society in general, which is contrary to the usual, accepted and customary rule of right and duty which a person should follow. 58 C.J.S. at page 1201. Although offenses against revenue laws have been held to be crimes of moral turpitude, it has also been held that the attempt to evade the payment of taxes due to the government or any subdivision thereof, while wrong and unlawful, does not involve moral turpitude. 58 C.J.S. at page 1205." Comm. on Legal Ethics v. Scheer, 149 W.Va. 721, 726–27, 143 S.E.2d 141, 145 (1965).

(4) Engage in conduct involving dishonesty, fraud, deceit, or misrepresentation.

(5) Engage in conduct that is prejudicial to the administration of justice.

(6) Engage in any other conduct that adversely reflects on his fitness to practice law.[14]

DR 1-103 Disclosure of Information to Authorities.

(A) A lawyer possessing unprivileged knowledge of a violation of DR 1-102 shall report such knowledge to a tribunal or other authority empowered to investigate or act upon such violation.[15]

(B) A lawyer possessing unprivileged knowledge or evidence concerning another lawyer or a judge shall reveal fully such knowledge or evidence upon proper request of a tribunal or other authority empowered to investigate or act upon the conduct of lawyers or judges.[16]

CANON 2

A Lawyer Should Assist the Legal Profession in Fulfilling Its Duty to Make Legal Counsel Available

ETHICAL CONSIDERATIONS

EC 2-1 The need of members of the public for legal services [1] is met only if they recognize their legal problems, appreciate the importance of seeking assistance,[2] and are able to obtain the services of acceptable legal counsel.[3] Hence, important functions of the legal profession are to educate laymen to recognize their legal problems, to facilitate the process of intelligent selection of lawyers, and to assist in making legal services fully available.[4]

Recognition of Legal Problems

EC 2-2 The legal profession should assist laymen to recognize legal problems because such problems may not be self-revealing and often are not

---

"The right and power to discipline an attorney, as one of its officers, is inherent in the court. . . . This power is not limited to those instances of misconduct wherein he has been employed, or has acted, in a professional capacity; but, on the contrary, this power may be exercised where his misconduct outside the scope of his professional relations shows him to be an unfit person to practice law." In re Wilson, 391 S.W.2d 914, 917–18 (Mo. 1965).

[14] "It is a fair characterization of the lawyer's responsibility in our society that he stands 'as a shield,' to quote Devlin, J., in defense of right and to ward off wrong. From a profession charged with these responsibilities there must be exacted those qualities of truth-speaking, of a high sense of honor, of granite discretion, of the strictest observance of fiduciary responsibility, that have, throughout the centuries, been compendiously described as 'moral character' ". Schware v. Bd. of Bar Examiners, 353 U.S. 232, 247 L.Ed.2d 796, 806, 77 S.Ct. 752, 761 (1957) (Frankfurter, J., concurring).

"Particularly applicable here is Rule 4.47 providing that 'A lawyer should always maintain his integrity; and shall not willfully commit any act against the interest of the public; nor shall he violate his duty to the courts or his clients; *nor shall he, by any misconduct, commit any offense against the laws of Missouri or the United States of America, which amounts to a crime involving acts done by him contrary to justice, honesty, modesty or good morals*; nor shall he be guilty of any other misconduct whereby, for the protection of the public and those charged with the administration of justice, he should no longer be entrusted with the duties and responsibilities belonging to the office of an attorney.' " In re Wilson, 391 S.W.2d 914, 917 (Mo. 1965).

[15] *See* ABA Canon 29; *cf.* ABA Canon 28.

[16] *Cf.* ABA Canons 28 and 29.

[1] "Men have need for more than a system of law; they have need for a system of law which functions, and that means they have need for lawyers." Cheatham, *The Lawyer's Role and Surroundings*, 25 Rocky Mt.L.Rev. 405 (1953).

[2] "Law is not self-applying; men must apply and utilize it in concrete cases. But the ordinary man is incapable. He cannot know the principles of law or the rules guiding the machinery of law administration; he does not know how to formulate his desires with precision and to put them into writing; he is ineffective in the presentation of his claims." Cheatham, *The Lawyer's Role and Surroundings*, 25 Rocky Mt.L.Rev. 405 (1953).

[3] "This need [to provide legal services] was recognized by . . . Mr. [Lewis F.] Powell [Jr., President, American Bar Association, 1963–64], who said: 'Looking at contemporary America realistically, we must admit that despite all our efforts to date (and these have not been insignificant), far too many persons are not able to obtain equal justice under law. This usually results because their poverty or their ignorance has prevented them from obtaining legal counsel.' " Address by E. Clinton Bamberger, Association of American Law Schools 1965 Annual Meeting, Dec. 28, 1965, in Proceedings, Part II, 1965, 61, 63–64 (1965).

"A wide gap separates the need for legal services and its satisfaction, as numerous studies reveal. Looked at from the side of the layman, one reason for the gap is poverty and the consequent inability to pay legal fees. Another set of reasons is ignorance of the need for and the value of legal services, and ignorance of where to find a dependable lawyer. There is fear of the mysterious processes and delays of the law, and there is fear of overreaching and overcharging by lawyers, a fear stimulated by the occasional exposure of shysters." Cheatham, *Availability of Legal Services: The Responsibility of the Individual Lawyer and of the Organized Bar*, 12 U.C.L.A.L. Rev. 438 (1965).

[4] "It is not only the right but the duty of the profession as a whole to utilize such methods as may be developed to bring the services of its members to those who need them, so long as this can be done ethically and with dignity." *ABA Opinion* 320 (1968).

"[T]here is a responsibility on the bar to make legal services available to those who need them. The maxim, 'privilege brings responsibilities,' can be expanded to read, exclusive privilege to render public service brings responsibility to assure that the service is available to those in need of it." Cheatham, *Availability of Legal Services: The Responsibility of the Individual Lawyer and of the Organized Bar*, 12 U.C.L.A.L.Rev. 438, 443 (1965).

"The obligation to provide legal services for those actually caught up in litigation carries with it the obligation to make preventive legal advice accessible to all. It is among those unaccustomed to business affairs and fearful of the ways of the law that such advice is often most needed. If it is not received in time, the most valiant and skillful representation in court may come too late." *Professional Responsibility: Report of the Joint Conference*, 44 A.B.A.J. 1159, 1216 (1958).

timely noticed.[5] Therefore, lawyers acting under proper auspices should encourage and participate in educational and public relations programs concerning our legal system with particular reference to legal problems that frequently arise. Such educational programs should be motivated by a desire to benefit the public rather than to obtain publicity or employment for particular lawyers.[6] Examples of permissible activities include preparation of institutional advertisements [7] and professional articles for lay publications [8] and participation in seminars, lectures, and civic programs. But a lawyer who participates in such activities should shun personal publicity.[9]

EC 2–3 Whether a lawyer acts properly in volunteering advice to a layman to seek legal services depends upon the circumstances.[10] The giving of advice that one should take legal action could well be in fulfillment of the duty of the legal profession to assist laymen in recognizing legal problems.[11] The advice is proper only if motivated by a desire to protect one who does not recognize that he may have legal problems or who is ignorant of his legal rights or obligations. Hence, the advice is improper if motivated by a desire to obtain personal benefit,[12] secure personal publicity, or cause litigation to be brought merely to harass or injure another. Obviously, a lawyer should not contact

---

5 "Over a period of years institutional advertising of programs for the benefit of the public have been approved by this and other Ethics Committees as well as by the courts.

. . . .

"To the same effect are opinions of this Committee: *Opinion 179* dealing with radio programs presenting a situation in which legal advice is suggested in connection with a drafting of a will; *Opinions 205* and *227* permitting institutional advertising of lawyer referral plans; *Opinion 191* holding that advertising by lawyer members of a non-bar associated sponsored plan violated *Canon 27*. The Illinois Ethics Committee, in its *Opinion 201*, sustained bar association institutional advertising of a check-up plan

. . . .

"This Committee has passed squarely on the question of the propriety of institutional advertising in connection with a legal check-up plan. Informal Decision C–171 quotes with express approval the Michigan Ethics Committee as follows:

> As a public service, the bar has in the past addressed the public as to the importance of making wills, consulting counsel in connection with real estate transactions, etc. In the same way, the bar, as such, may recommend this program, provided always that it does it in such a way that there is not suggestion of solicitation on behalf of any individual lawyer."

ABA Opinion 307 (1962).

6 "We recognize a distinction between teaching the lay public the importance of securing legal services preventive in character and the solicitation of professional employment by or for a particular lawyer. The former tends to promote the public interest and enhance the public estimation of the profession. The latter is calculated to injure the public and degrade the profession.

. . . .

"Advertising which is calculated to teach the layman the benefits and advantages of preventive legal services will benefit the lay public and enable the lawyer to render a more desirable and beneficial professional service. . . ." *ABA Opinion* 179 (1938).

7 "[A bar association] may engage in a dignified institutional educational campaign so long as it does not involve the identification of a particular lawyer with the check-up program. Such educational material may point out the value of the annual check-up and may be printed in newspapers, magazines, pamphlets, and brochures, or produced by means of films, radio, television or other media. The printed materials may be distributed in a dignified way through the offices of persons having close dealings with lawyers as, for example, banks, real estate agents, insurance agents and others. They may be available in lawyers' offices. The bar association may prepare and distribute to lawyers materials and forms for use in the annual legal check-up." *ABA Opinion* 307 (1962).

8 "A lawyer may with propriety write articles for publications in which he gives information upon the law . . . ." ABA Canon 40.

"The newsletters, by means of which respondents are alleged to have advertised their wares, were sent to the officers of union clients represented by their firm. . . . They contain no reference to any cases handled by the respondents. Their contents are confined to rulings of boards, commissions and courts on problems of interest to labor union, together with proposed and completed legislation important to the Brotherhood, and other items which might affect unions and their members. The respondents cite Opinion 213 of the Committee on Professional Ethics and Grievances as permitting such practice. After studying this opinion, we agree that sending of newsletters of the above type to regular clients does not offend Canon 27." In re Ratner, 194 Kan. 362, 371, 399 P.2d 865, 872–73 (1965).

Cf. ABA Opinion 92 (1933).

9 *Cf. ABA Opinions* 307 (1962) and 179 (1938).

"There is no ethical or other valid reason why an attorney may not write articles on legal subjects for magazines and newspapers. The fact that the publication is a trade journal or magazine, makes no difference as to the ethical question involved. On the other hand, it would be unethical and contrary to the precepts of the Canons for the attorney to allow his name to be carried in the magazine or other publication . . . as a free legal adviser for the subscribers to the publication. Such would be contrary to *Canons 27* and *35* and Opinions heretofore announced by the Committee on Professional Ethics and Grievances. (See *Opinions 31, 41, 42,* and *56*)." *ABA Opinion* 162 (1936).

10 *See* ABA Canon 28.

11 This question can assume constitutional dimensions: "We meet at the outset the contention that 'solicitation' is wholly outside the area of freedoms protected by the First Amendment. To this contention there are two answers. The first is that a State cannot foreclose the exercise of constitutional rights by mere labels. The second is that abstract discussion is not the only species of communication which the Constitution protects; the First Amendment also protects vigorous advocacy, certainly of lawful ends, against governmental intrusion. . . .

. . . .

"However valid may be Virginia's interest in regulating the traditionally illegal practice of barratry, maintenance and champerty, that interest does not justify the prohibition of the NAACP activities disclosed by this record. Malicious intent was of the essence of the common-law offenses of fomenting or stirring up litigation. And whatever may be or may have been true of suits against governments in other countries, the exercise in our own, as in this case of First Amendment rights to enforce Constitutional rights through litigation, as a matter of law, cannot be deemed malicious." NAACP v. Button, 371 U.S. 415, 429, 439–40, 9 L.Ed.2d 405, 415–16, 422, 83 S.Ct. 328, 336, 341 (1963).

12 *See* ABA Canon 27.

a non-client, directly or indirectly, for the purpose of being retained to represent him for compensation.

EC 2–4 Since motivation is subjective and often difficult to judge, the motives of a lawyer who volunteers advice likely to produce legal controversy may well be suspect if he receives professional employment or other benefits as a result.[13] A lawyer who volunteers advice that one should obtain the services of a lawyer generally should not himself accept employment, compensation, or other benefit in connection with that matter. However, it is not improper for a lawyer to volunteer such advice and render resulting legal services to close friends, relatives, former clients (in regard to matters germane to former employment), and regular clients.[14]

EC 2–5 A lawyer who writes or speaks for the purpose of educating members of the public to recognize their legal problems should carefully refrain from giving or appearing to give a general solution applicable to all apparently similar individual problems,[15] since slight changes in fact situations may require a material variance in the applicable advice; otherwise, the public may be misled and misadvised. Talks and writings by lawyers for laymen should caution them not to attempt to solve individual problems upon the basis of the information contained therein.[16]

Selection of a Lawyer: Generally

EC 2–6 Formerly a potential client usually knew the reputations of local lawyers for competency and integrity and therefore could select a practitioner in whom he had confidence. This traditional selection process worked well because it was initiated by the client and the choice was an informed one.

EC 2–7 Changed conditions, however, have seriously restricted the effectiveness of the traditional selection process. Often the reputations of lawyers are not sufficiently known to enable laymen to make intelligent choices.[17] The law has become increasingly complex and specialized. Few lawyers are willing and competent to deal with every kind of legal matter, and many laymen have difficulty in determining the competence of lawyers to render different types of legal services. The selection of legal counsel is particularly difficult for transients, persons moving into new areas, persons of limited education or means, and others who have little or no contact with lawyers.[18]

EC 2–8 Selection of a lawyer by a layman often is the result of the advice and recommendation of third parties—relatives, friends, acquaintances, business associates, or other lawyers. A layman is best served if the recommendation is disinterested and informed. In order that the recommendation be disinterested, a lawyer should not seek to influence another to recommend his employment.[19] A lawyer should not compensate another person for recommending him, for influencing a prospective client to employ him, or to encourage future recommendations.[20]

Selection of a Lawyer: Professional Notices and Listings

EC 2–9 The traditional ban against advertising by lawyers, which is subject to certain limited exceptions, is rooted in the public interest. Competitive advertising would encourage extravagant, artful, self-laudatory [21] brashness in seeking business and

---

13 "The Canons of Professional Ethics of the American Bar Association and the decisions of the courts quite generally prohibit the direct solicitation of business for gain by an attorney either through advertisement or personal communication; and also condemn the procuring of business by indirection through touters of any kind. It is disreputable for an attorney to breed litigation by seeking out those who have claims for personal injuries or other grounds of action in order to secure them as clients, or to employ agents or runners, or to reward those who bring or influence the bringing of business to his office. . . . Moreover, it tends quite easily to the institution of baseless litigation and the manufacture of perjured testimony. From early times, this danger has been recognized in the law by the condemnation of the crime of common barratry, or the stirring up of suits or quarrels between individuals at law or otherwise." In re Ades, 6 F.Supp. 467, 474–75 (D. Mary. 1934).

14 "*Rule 2.*

"§a. . . .

"[A] member of the State Bar shall not solicit professional employment by

"(1) Volunteering counsel or advice except where ties of blood relationship or trust make it appropriate." Cal. Business and Professions Code § 6076 (West 1962).

15 "*Rule 18* . . . A member of the State Bar shall not advise inquirers or render opinions to them through or in connection with a newspaper, radio or other publicity medium of any kind in respect to their specific legal problems, whether or not such attorney shall be compensated for his services." Cal.Business and Professions Code § 6076 (West 1962).

16 "In any case where a member might well apply the advice given in the opinion to his individual affairs, the lawyer rendering the opinion [concerning problems common to members of an association and distributed to the members through a periodic bulletin] should specifically state that this opinion should not be relied on by any member as a basis for handling his individual affairs, but that in every case he should consult his counsel. In the publication of the opinion the association should make a similar statement." *ABA Opinion* 273 (1946).

17 "A group of recent interrelated changes bears directly on the availability of legal services. . . . [One] change is the constantly accelerating urbanization of the country and the decline of personal and neighborhood knowledge of whom to retain as a professional man." Cheatham, *Availability of Legal Services: The Responsibility of the Individual Lawyer and of the Organized Bar,* 12 U.C.L.A.L. Rev. 438, 440 (1965).

18 *Cf.* Cheatham, *A Lawyer When Needed: Legal Services for the Middle Classes,* 63 Colum.L.Rev. 973, 974 (1963).

19 *See* ABA Canon 27.

20 *See* ABA Canon 28.

21 " 'Self-laudation' is a very flexible concept; Canon 27 does not define it, so what course of conduct would be said to constitute it under a given state of facts would no doubt vary as the opinions of men vary. As a famous English judge said, it would vary as the length of the chancellor's foot. It must be in words and tone that will 'offend the traditions and lower the tone of our profession.' When it

thus could mislead the layman.[22] Furthermore, it would inevitably produce unrealistic expectations in particular cases and bring about distrust of the law and lawyers.[23] Thus, public confidence in our legal system would be impaired by such advertisements of professional services. The attorney-client relationship is personal and unique and should not be established as the result of pressures and deceptions.[24] History has demonstrated that public confidence in the legal system is best preserved by strict, self-imposed controls over, rather than by unlimited, advertising.

EC 2–10 Methods of advertising that are subject to the objections stated above [25] should be and are prohibited.[26] However, the Disciplinary Rules recognize the value of giving assistance in the selection process through forms of advertising that furnish identification of a lawyer while avoiding such objections. For example, a lawyer may be identified in the classified section of the telephone directory,[27] in the office building directory, and on his letterhead and professional card.[28] But at all times the permitted notices should be dignified and accurate.

EC 2–11 The name under which a lawyer conducts his practice may be a factor in the selection process.[29] The use of a trade name or an assumed name could mislead laymen concerning the identity, responsibility, and status of those practicing thereunder.[30] Accordingly, a lawyer in private practice should practice only under his own name, the name of a lawyer employing him, a partnership name composed of the name of one or more of the lawyers practicing in a partnership, or, if permitted by law, in the name of a professional legal corporation, which should be clearly designated as such. For many years some law firms have used a firm name retaining one or more names of deceased or retired partners and such practice is not improper if the firm is a bona fide successor of a firm in which the deceased or retired person was a member, if the use of the name is authorized by law or by contract, and if the public is not misled thereby.[31] However, the name of a partner

---

does this, it is 'reprehensible.' This seems to be the test by which 'self-laudation' is measured." State v. Nichols, 151 So.2d 257, 259 (Fla. 1963).

22 "Were it not for the prohibitions of . . . [Canon 27] lawyers could, and no doubt would be forced to, engage competitively in advertising of all kinds in which each would seek to explain to the public why he could serve better and accomplish more than his brothers at the Bar.

"Susceptible as we are to advertising the public would then be encouraged to choose an attorney on the basis of which had the better, more attractive advertising program rather than on his reputation for professional ability.

"This would certainly maim, if not destroy, the dignity and professional status of the Bar of this State." State v. Nichols, 151 So.2d 257, 268 (Fla. 1963) (O'Connell, J., concurring in part and dissenting in part).

23 *Cf.* ABA Canon 8.

24 "The prohibition of advertising by lawyers deserves some examination. All agree that advertising by an individual lawyer, if permitted, will detract from the dignity of the profession, but the matter goes deeper than this. Perhaps the most understandable and acceptable additional reasons we have found are stated by one commentator as follows:

" '1. That advertisements, unless kept within narrow limits, like any other form of solicitation, tend to stir up litigation, and such tendency is against the public interest.

" '2. That if there were no restrictions on advertisements, the least capable and least honorable lawyers would be apt to publish the most extravagant and alluring material about themselves, and that the harm which would result would, in large measure, fall on the ignorant and on those least able to afford it.

" '3. That the temptation would be strong to hold out as inducements for employment, assurances of success or of satisfaction to the client, which assurances could not be realized, and that the giving of such assurances would materially increase the temptation to use ill means to secure the end desired by the client.

" 'In other words, the reasons for the rule, and for the conclusion that it is desirable to prohibit advertising entirely, or to limit it within such narrow bounds that it will not admit of abuse, are based on the possibility and probability that this means of publicity, if permitted, will be abused.' Harrison Hewitt in a comment at 15 A.B.A.J. 116 (1929) reproduced in Cheatham, Cases and Materials on the Legal Profession (2d Ed., 1955), p. 525.

"Of course, competition is at the root of the abuses in advertising. If the individual lawyer were permitted to compete with his fellows in publicity through advertising, we have no doubt that Mr. Hewitt's three points, quoted above, would accurately forecast the result." Jacksonville Bar Ass'n v. Wilson, 102 So.2d 292, 294–95 (Fla. 1958).

25 *See* ABA Canon 27.

26 *Cf. ABA Opinions* 309 (1963) and 284 (1951).

27 *Cf. ABA Opinions* 313 (1964) and 284 (1951).

28 *See* ABA Canon 27.

29 *Cf. ABA Opinion* 303 (1961).

30 *See* ABA Canon 33.

31 *Id.*

"The continued use of a firm name by one or more surviving partners after the death of a member of the firm whose name is in the firm title is expressly permitted by the Canons of Ethics. The reason for this is that all of the partners have by their joint and several efforts over a period of years contributed to the good will attached to the firm name. In the case of a firm having widespread connections, this good will is disturbed by a change in firm name every time a name partner dies, and that reflects a loss in some degree of the good will to the building up of which the surviving partners have contributed their time, skill and labor through a period of years. To avoid this loss the firm name is continued, and to meet the requirements of the Canon the individuals constituting the firm from time to time are listed." *ABA Opinion* 267 (1945).

"Accepted local custom in New York recognizes that the name of a law firm does not necessarily identify the individual members of the firm, and hence the continued use of a firm name after the death of one or more partners is not a deception and is permissible. . . . The continued use of a deceased partner's name in the firm title is not affected by the fact that another partner withdraws from the firm and his name is dropped, or the name of the new partner is added to the firm name." *Opinion* No. 45, Committee on Professional Ethics, New York State Bar Ass'n, 39 N.Y.St.B.J. 455 (1967).

Cf. ABA Opinion 258 (1943).

who withdraws from a firm but continues to practice law should be omitted from the firm name in order to avoid misleading the public.

EC 2-12 A lawyer occupying a judicial, legislative, or public executive or administrative position who has the right to practice law concurrently may allow his name to remain in the name of the firm if he actively continues to practice law as a member thereof. Otherwise, his name should be removed from the firm name,[32] and he should not be identified as a past or present member of the firm; and he should not hold himself out as being a practicing lawyer.

EC 2-13 In order to avoid the possibility of misleading persons with whom he deals, a lawyer should be scrupulous in the representation of his professional status.[33] He should not hold himself out as being a partner or associate of a law firm if he is not one in fact,[34] and thus should not hold himself out as a partner or associate if he only shares offices with another lawyer.[35]

EC 2-14 In some instances a lawyer confines his practice to a particular field of law.[36] In the absence of state controls to insure the existence of special competence, a lawyer should not be permitted to hold himself out as a specialist [37] or as having special training or ability, other than in the historically excepted fields of admiralty, trademark, and patent law.[38]

EC 2-15 The legal profession has developed lawyer referral systems designed to aid individuals who are able to pay fees but need assistance in locating lawyers competent to handle their particular problems. Use of a lawyer referral system enables a layman to avoid an uninformed selection of a lawyer because such a system makes possible the employment of competent lawyers who have indicated an interest in the subject matter involved. Lawyers should support the principle of lawyer referral systems and should encourage the evolution of other ethical plans which aid in the selection of qualified counsel.

Financial Ability to Employ Counsel: Generally

EC 2-16 The legal profession cannot remain a viable force in fulfilling its role in our society unless its members receive adequate compensation for services rendered, and reasonable fees [39] should be charged in appropriate cases to clients able to pay them. Nevertheless, persons unable to pay all or a portion of a reasonable fee should be able to obtain necessary legal services,[40] and lawyers should support and participate in ethical activities designed to achieve that objective.[41]

Financial Ability to Employ Counsel: Persons Able to Pay Reasonable Fees

EC 2-17 The determination of a proper fee requires consideration of the interests of both client and lawyers.[42] A lawyer should not charge more than a reasonable fee,[43] for excessive cost of legal service would deter laymen from utilizing the legal system in protection of their rights. Furthermore, an excessive charge abuses the professional relationship between lawyer and client. On the other hand, adequate compensation is necessary in order to enable the lawyer to serve his client effectively and to preserve the integrity and independence of the profession.[44]

EC 2-18 The determination of the reasonableness of a fee requires consideration of all relevant circumstances,[45] including those stated in the Disciplinary Rules. The fees of a lawyer will vary according to many factors, including the time required, his experience, ability, and reputation, the

---

32 *Cf.* ABA Canon 33 and *ABA Opinion* 315 (1965).

33 *Cf. ABA Opinions* 283 (1950) and 81 (1932).

34 *See ABA Opinion* 316 (1967).

35 "The word 'associates' has a variety of meanings. Principally through custom the word when used on the letterheads of law firms has come to be regarded as describing those who are employees of the firm. Because the word has acquired this special significance in connection with the practice of the law the use of the word to describe lawyer relationships other than employer-employee is likely to be misleading." In re Sussman and Tanner, 241 Ore. 246, 248, 405 P.2d 355, 356 (1965).

According to *ABA Opinion* 310 (1963), use of the term "associates" would be misleading in two situations: (1) where two lawyers are partners and they share both responsibility and liability for the partnership; and (2) where two lawyers practice separately, sharing no responsibility or liability, and only share a suite of offices and some costs.

36 "For a long time, many lawyers have, of necessity, limited their practice to certain branches of law. The increasing complexity of the law and the demand of the public for more expertness on the part of the lawyer has, in the past few years—particularly in the last ten years—brought about specialization on an increasing scale." *Report of the Special Committee on Specialization and Specialized Legal Services*, 79 A.B.A.Rep. 582, 584 (1954).

37 "In varying degrees specialization has become the *modus operandi* throughout the legal profession. . . . American society is specialization conscious. The present Canons, however, do not allow lawyers to make known to the lay public the fact that they engage in the practice of a specialty. . . ." Tucker, *The Large Law Firm: Considerations Concerning the Modernization of the Canons of Professional Ethics*, 1965 Wis.L.Rev. 344, 348-49 (1965).

38 *See* ABA Canon 27.

39 *See* ABA Canon 12.

40 *Cf.* ABA Canon 12.

41 "If there is any fundamental proposition of government on which all would agree, it is that one of the highest goals of society must be to achieve and maintain equality before the law. Yet this ideal remains an empty form of words unless the legal profession is ready to provide adequate representation for those unable to pay the usual fees." *Professional Representation: Report of the Joint Conference*, 44 A.B.A.J. 1159, 1216 (1958).

42 *See* ABA Canon 12.

43 *Cf.* ABA Canon 12.

44 "When members of the Bar are induced to render legal services for inadequate compensation, as a consequence the quality of the service rendered may be lowered, the welfare of the profession injured and the administration of justice made less efficient." *ABA Opinion* 302 (1961). *Cf. ABA Opinion* 307 (1962).

45 *See* ABA Canon 12.

nature of the employment, the responsibility involved, and the results obtained. It is a commendable and long-standing tradition of the bar that special consideration is given in the fixing of any fee for services rendered a brother lawyer or a member of his immediate family.

EC 2–19 As soon as feasible after a lawyer has been employed, it is desirable that he reach a clear agreement with his client as to the basis of the fee charges to be made. Such a course will not only prevent later misunderstanding but will also work for good relations between the lawyer and the client. It is usually beneficial to reduce to writing the understanding of the parties regarding the fee, particularly when it is contingent. A lawyer should be mindful that many persons who desire to employ him may have had little or no experience with fee charges of lawyers, and for this reason he should explain fully to such persons the reasons for the particular fee arrangement he proposes.

EC 2–20 Contingent fee arrangements [47] in civil cases have long been commonly accepted in the United States in proceedings to enforce claims. The historical bases of their acceptance are that (1) they often, and in a variety of circumstances, provide the only practical means by which one having a claim against another can economically afford, finance, and obtain the services of a competent lawyer to prosecute his claim, and (2) a successful prosecution of the claim produces a *res* out of which the fee can be paid.[48] Although a lawyer generally should decline to accept employment on a contingent fee basis by one who is able to pay a reasonable fixed fee, it is not necessarily improper for a lawyer, where justified by the particular circumstances of a case, to enter into a contingent fee contract in a civil case with any client who, after being fully informed of all relevant factors, desires that arrangement. Because of the human relationships involved and the unique character of the proceedings, contingent fee arrangements in domestic relation cases are rarely justified. In administrative agency proceedings contingent fee contracts should be governed by the same considerations as in other civil cases. Public policy properly condemns contingent fee arrangements in criminal cases, largely on the ground that legal services in criminal cases do not produce a *res* with which to pay the fee.

EC 2–21 A lawyer should not accept compensation or any thing of value incident to his employment or services from one other than his client without the knowledge and consent of his client after full disclosure.[49]

EC 2–22 Without the consent of his client, a lawyer should not associate in a particular matter another lawyer outside his firm. A fee may properly be divided between lawyers [50] properly associated if the division is in proportion to the services performed and the responsibility assumed by each lawyer [51] and if the total fee is reasonable.

EC 2–23 A lawyer should be zealous in his efforts to avoid controversies over fees with clients [52] and should attempt to resolve amicably any differences on the subject.[53] He should not sue a client for a fee unless necessary to prevent fraud or gross imposition by the client.[54]

---

47 *See* ABA Canon 13; *see also* Mackinnon, Contingent Fees for Legal Services (1964) (A report of the American Bar Foundation).

"A contract for a reasonable contingent fee where sanctioned by law is permitted by *Canon 13*, but the client must remain responsible to the lawyer for expenses advanced by the latter. 'There is to be no barter of the privilege of prosecuting a cause for gain in exchange for the promise of the attorney to prosecute at his own expense.' (Cardozo, C. J. in Matter of Gilman, 251 N.Y. 265, 270–271.)" *ABA Opinion* 246 (1942).

48 *See* Comment, *Providing Legal Services for the Middle Class in Civil Matters: The Problem, the Duty and a Solution*, 26 U.Pitt.L.Rev. 811, 829 (1965).

49 *See* ABA Canon 38.

"Of course, as . . . [Informal Opinion 679] points out, there must be full disclosure of the arrangement [that an entity other than the client pays the attorney's fee] by the attorney to the client . . . ." *ABA Opinion* 320 (1968).

50 "Only lawyers may share in . . . a division of fees, but . . . it is not necessary that both lawyers be admitted to practice in the same state, so long as the division was based on the division of services or responsibility." *ABA Opinion* 316 (1967).

51 *See* ABA Canon 34.

"We adhere to our previous rulings that where a lawyer merely brings about the employment of another lawyer *but renders no service and assumes no responsibility in the matter*, a division of the latter's fee is improper. (*Opinions 18 and 153*).

"It is assumed that the bar, generally, understands what acts or conduct of a lawyer may constitute 'services' to a client within the intendment of *Canon 12*. Such acts or conduct invariably, if not always, involve 'responsibility' on the part of the lawyer, whether the word 'responsibility' be construed to denote the possible resultant legal or moral liability on the part of the lawyer to the client or to others, or the onus of deciding what should or should not be done in behalf of the client. The word 'services' in *Canon 12* must be construed in this broad sense and may apply to the selection and retainer of associate counsel as well as to other acts or conduct in the client's behalf." *ABA Opinion* 204 (1940).

52 *See* ABA Canon 14.

53 *Cf. ABA Opinion* 320 (1968).

54 *See* ABA Canon 14.

"Ours is a learned profession, not a mere money-getting trade. . . . Suits to collect fees should be avoided. Only where the circumstances imperatively require, should resort be had to a suit to compel payment. And where a lawyer does resort to a suit to enforce payment of fees which involves a disclosure, he should carefully avoid any disclosure not clearly necessary to obtaining or defending his rights." *ABA Opinion* 250 (1943).

But cf. ABA Opinion 320 (1968).

Financial Ability to Employ Counsel: Persons Unable to Pay Reasonable Fees

EC 2–24 A layman whose financial ability is not sufficient to permit payment of any fee cannot obtain legal services, other than in cases where a contingent fee is appropriate, unless the services are provided for him. Even a person of moderate means may be unable to pay a reasonable fee which is large because of the complexity, novelty, or difficulty of the problem or similar factors.[55]

EC 2–25 Historically, the need for legal services of those unable to pay reasonable fees has been met in part by lawyers who donated their services or accepted court appointments on behalf of such individuals. The basic responsibility for providing legal services for those unable to pay ultimately rests upon the individual lawyer, and personal involvement in the problems of the disadvantaged can be one of the most rewarding experiences in the life of a lawyer. Every lawyer, regardless of professional prominence or professional workload, should find time to participate in serving the disadvantaged. The rendition of free legal services to those unable to pay reasonable fees continues to be an obligation of each lawyer, but the efforts of individual lawyers are often not enough to meet the need.[56] Thus it has been necessary for the profession to institute additional programs to provide legal services.[57] Accordingly, legal aid offices,[58] lawyer referral services,[59] and other related programs have been developed, and others will be developed, by the profession.[60] Every lawyer should support all proper efforts to meet this need for legal services.[61]

---

55 "As a society increases in size, sophistication and technology, the body of laws which is required to control that society also increases in size, scope and complexity. With this growth, the law directly affects more and more facets of individual behavior, creating an expanding need for legal services on the part of the individual members of the society. . . . As legal guidance in social and commercial behavior increasingly becomes necessary, there will come a concurrent demand from the layman that such guidance be made available to him. This demand will not come from those who are able to employ the best of legal talent, nor from those who can obtain legal assistance at little or no cost. It will come from the large 'forgotten middle income class,' who can neither afford to pay proportionately large fees nor qualify for ultra-low-cost services. The legal profession must recognize this inevitable demand and consider methods whereby it can be satisfied. If the profession fails to provide such methods, the laity will." Comment, *Providing Legal Services for the Middle Class in Civil Matters: The Problem, the Duty and a Solution*, 26 U.Pitt.L.Rev. 811, 811–12 (1965).

"The issue is not whether we shall do something or do nothing. The demand for ordinary everyday legal justice is so great and the moral nature of the demand is so strong that the issue has become whether we devise, maintain, and support suitable agencies able to satisfy the demand or, by our own default, force the government to take over the job, supplant us, and ultimately dominate us." Smith, *Legal Service Offices for Persons of Moderate Means*, 1949 Wis.L.Rev. 416, 418 (1949).

56 "Lawyers have peculiar responsibilities for the just administration of the law, and these responsibilities include providing advice and representation for needy persons. To a degree not always appreciated by the public at large, the bar has performed these obligations with zeal and devotion. The Committee is persuaded, however, that a system of justice that attempts, in mid-twentieth century America, to meet the needs of the financially incapacitated accused through primary or exclusive reliance on the uncompensated services of counsel will prove unsuccessful and inadequate. . . . A system of adequate representation, therefore, should be structured and financed in a manner reflecting its public importance. . . . We believe that fees for private appointed counsel should be set by the court within maximum limits established by the statute." Report of the Att'y Gen's Comm. on Poverty and the Administration of Criminal Justice 41–43 (1963).

57 "At present this representation [of those unable to pay usual fees] is being supplied in some measure through the spontaneous generosity of individual lawyers, through legal aid societies, and—increasingly—through the organized efforts of the Bar. If those who stand in need of this service know of its availability and their need is in fact adequately met, the precise mechanism by which this service is provided becomes of secondary importance. It is of great importance, however, that both the impulse to render this service, and the plan for making that impulse effective, should arise within the legal profession itself." *Professional Responsibility: Report of the Joint Conference*, 44 A.B.A.J. 1159, 1216 (1958).

58 "Free legal clinics carried on by the organized bar are not ethically objectionable. On the contrary, they serve a very worthwhile purpose and should be encouraged." *ABA Opinion* 191 (1939).

59 "We are of the opinion that the [lawyer referral] plan here presented does not fall within the inhibition of the Canon. No solicitation for a particular lawyer is involved. The dominant purpose of the plan is to provide as an obligation of the profession competent legal services to persons in low-income groups at fees within their ability to pay. The plan is to be supervised and directed by the local Bar Association. There is to be no advertisement of the names of the lawyers constituting the panel. The general method and purpose of the plan only is to be advertised. Persons seeking the legal services will be directed to members of the panel by the Bar Association. Aside from the filing of the panel with the Bar Association, there is to be no advertisement of the names of the lawyers constituting the panel. If these limitations are observed, we think there is no solicitation of business by or for particular lawyers and no violation of the inhibition af *Canon 27*." *ABA Opinion* 205 (1940).

60 "Whereas the American Bar Association believes that it is a fundamental duty of the bar to see to it that all persons requiring legal advice be able to attain it, irrespective of their economic status . . . .

"Resolved, that the Association approves and sponsors the setting up by state and local bar associations of lawyer referral plans and low-cost legal service methods for the purpose of dealing with cases of persons who might not otherwise have the benefit of legal advice . . . ." *Proceedings of the House of Delegates of the American Bar Association*, Oct. 30, 1946, 71 A.B.A.Rep. 103, 109–10 (1946).

61 "The defense of indigent citizens, without compensation, is carried on throughout the country by lawyers representing legal aid societies, not only with the approval, but with the commendation of those acquainted with the work. Not infrequently services are rendered out of sympathy or for other philanthropic reasons, by individual lawyers who do not represent legal aid societies. There is nothing whatever in the Canons to prevent a lawyer

Acceptance and Retention of Employment

EC 2–26 A lawyer is under no obligation to act as adviser or advocate for every person who may wish to become his client; but in furtherance of the objective of the bar to make legal services fully available, a lawyer should not lightly decline proffered employment. The fulfillment of this objective requires acceptance by a lawyer of his share of tendered employment which may be unattractive both to him and the bar generally.[62]

EC 2–27 History is replete with instances of distinguished and sacrificial services by lawyers who have represented unpopular clients and causes. Regardless of his personal feelings, a lawyer should not decline representation because a client or a cause is unpopular or community reaction is adverse.[63]

EC 2–28 The personal preference of a lawyer to avoid adversary alignment against judges, other lawyers,[64] public officials, or influential members of the community does not justify his rejection of tendered employment.

EC 2–29 When a lawyer is appointed by a court or requested by a bar association to undertake representation of a person unable to obtain counsel, whether for financial or other reasons, he should not seek to be excused from undertaking the representation except for compelling reasons.[65] Compelling reasons do not include such factors as the repugnance of the subject matter of the proceeding, the identity[66] or position of a person involved in the case, the belief of the lawyer that the defendant in a criminal proceeding is guilty,[67] or the belief of the lawyer regarding the merits of the civil case.[68]

EC 2–30 Employment should not be accepted by a lawyer when he is unable to render competent service[69] or when he knows or it is obvious that the person seeking to employ him desires to institute or maintain an action merely for the purpose of harassing or maliciously injuring another.[70] Likewise, a lawyer should decline employment if the intensity of his personal feeling, as distinguished from a community attitude, may impair his effective representation of a prospective client. If a lawyer knows a client has previously obtained counsel, he should not accept employment in the matter unless the other counsel approves[71] or withdraws, or the client terminates the prior employment.[72]

EC 2–31 Full availability of legal counsel requires both that persons be able to obtain counsel and that lawyers who undertake representation complete the work involved. Trial counsel for a convicted defendant should continue to represent his client by advising whether to take an appeal and, if the appeal is prosecuted, by representing him through the appeal unless new counsel is substituted or withdrawal is permitted by the appropriate court.

---

from performing such an act, nor should there be." *ABA Opinion* 148 (1935).

62 *But cf.* ABA Canon 31.

63 "One of the highest services the lawyer can render to society is to appear in court on behalf of clients whose causes are in disfavor with the general public." *Professional Responsibility: Report of the Joint Conference*, 44 A.B.A.J. 1159, 1216 (1958).

One author proposes the following proposition to be included in "A Proper Oath for Advocates": "I recognize that it is sometimes difficult for clients with unpopular causes to obtain proper legal representation. I will do all that I can to assure that the client with the unpopular cause is properly represented, and that the lawyer representing such a client receives credit from and support of the bar for handling such a matter." Thode, *The Ethical Standard for the Advocate*, 39 Texas L.Rev. 575, 592 (1961).

"§ 6068. . . . It is the duty of an attorney:

. . . .

"(h) Never to reject, for any consideration personal to himself, the cause of the defenseless or the oppressed." Cal.Business and Professions Code § 6068 (West 1962). Virtually the same language is found in the Oregon statutes at Ore.Rev.Stats. Ch. 9 § 9.460(8).

See Rostow, *The Lawyer and His Client*, 48 A.B.A.J. 25 and 146 (1962).

64 *See* ABA Canons 7 and 29.

"We are of the opinion that it is not professionally improper for a lawyer to accept employment to compel another lawyer to honor the just claim of a layman. On the contrary, it is highly proper that he do so. Unfortunately, there appears to be a widespread feeling among laymen that it is difficult, if not impossible, to obtain justice when they have claims against members of the Bar because other lawyers will not accept employment to proceed against them. The honor of the profession, whose members proudly style themselves officers of the court, must surely be sullied if its members bind themselves by custom to refrain from enforcing just claims of laymen against lawyers." *ABA Opinion* 144 (1935).

65 ABA Canon 4 uses a slightly different test, saying, "A lawyer assigned as counsel for an indigent prisoner ought not to ask to be excused for any trivial reason . . . ."

66 *Cf.* ABA Canon 7.

67 *See* ABA Canon 5.

68 Dr. Johnson's reply to Boswell upon being asked what he thought of "supporting a cause which you know to be bad" was: "Sir, you do not know it to be good or bad till the Judge determines it. I have said that you are to state facts fairly; so that your thinking, or what you call knowing, a cause to be bad, must be from reasoning, must be from supposing your arguments to be weak and inconclusive. But, Sir, that is not enough. An argument which does not convince yourself, may convince the Judge to whom you urge it: and if it does convince him, why, then, Sir, you are wrong, and he is right." 2 Boswell, The Life of Johnson 47–48 (Hill ed. 1887).

69 "The lawyer deciding whether to undertake a case must be able to judge objectively whether he is capable of handling it and whether he can assume its burdens without prejudice to previous commitments. . . ." *Professional Responsibility: Report of the Joint Conference*, 44 A.B.A.J. 1158, 1218 (1958).

70 "The lawyer must decline to conduct a civil cause or to make a defense when convinced that it is intended merely to harass or to injure the opposite party or to work oppression or wrong." ABA Canon 30.

71 *See* ABA Canon 7.

72 *Id.*

"From the facts stated we assume that the client has discharged the first attorney and given notice of the discharge. Such being the case, the second attorney may properly accept employment. *Canon 7; Opinions 10, 130, 149.*" *ABA Opinion* 209 (1941).

EC 2–32 A decision by a lawyer to withdraw should be made only on the basis of compelling circumstances [73], and in a matter pending before a tribunal he must comply with the rules of the tribunal regarding withdrawal. A lawyer should not withdraw without considering carefully and endeavoring to minimize the possible adverse effect on the rights of his client and the possibility of prejudice to his client [74] as a result of his withdrawal. Even when he justifiably withdraws, a lawyer should protect the welfare of his client by giving due notice of his withdrawal,[75] suggesting employment of other counsel, delivering to the client all papers and property to which the client is entitled, cooperating with counsel subsequently employed, and otherwise endeavoring to minimize the possibility of harm. Further, he should refund to the client any compensation not earned during the employment.[76]

EC 2–33 Several Supreme Court decisions apparently give Constitutional protection to certain organizations which furnish certain legal services to their members under legal service plans which do not provide free choice in the selection of attorneys.* The basic tenets of the profession, according to EC 1–1 are independence, integrity and competence of the lawyer and total devotion to the interests of the client.** There is substantial danger that lawyers rendering services under legal service plans which do not permit the beneficiaries to select their own attorneys will not be able to meet these standards. The independence of the lawyer may be seriously affected by the fact that he is employed by the group and by virtue of that employment cannot give his full devotion to the interest of the member he represents. The group which employs the attorney will inevitably have the characteristic of a "lay intermediary" because of its control over the attorney inherent in the employment relationship. It is probably that attorneys employed by groups will be directed as to what cases they may handle and in the manner in which they handle the cases referred to them. It is also possible that the standards of the profession and quality of legal service to the public will suffer because consideration for economy rather than experience and competence will determine the attorneys to be employed by the group. An attorney interested in maintaining the historic traditions of the profession and preserving the function of a lawyer as a trusted and independent advisor to individual members of society should carefully consider the risks involved before accepting employment by groups under plans which do not provide their members with a free choice of counsel.

[73] *See* ABA Canon 44.

"I will carefully consider, before taking a case, whether it appears that I can fully represent the client within the framework of law. If the decision is in the affirmative, then it will take extreme circumstances to cause me to decide later that I cannot so represent him." Thode, *The Ethical Standard for the Advocate*, 39 Texas L.Rev. 575, 592 (1961) (from "A Proper Oath for Advocates").

[74] *ABA Opinion* 314 (1965) held that a lawyer should not disassociate himself from a cause when "it is obvious that the very act of disassociation would have the effect of violating *Canon 37*."

[75] ABA Canon 44 enumerates instances in which ". . . the lawyer may be warranted in withdrawing on due notice to the client, allowing him time to employ another lawyer."

[76] *See* ABA Canon 44.

*United Transportation Union v. State Bar of Michigan, 401 U.S. 576, 28 L.Ed.2d 339, 91 S.Ct. 1076 (1971); United Mine Workers v. Illinois State Bar Association, 389 U.S. 217, 19 L.Ed.2d 426, 88 S.Ct. 353 (1967); Brotherhood of Railroad Trainmen v. Virginia, 377 U.S. 1, 12 L.Ed.2d 89, 84 S.Ct. 1113 (1964); NAACP v. Button, 371 U.S. 415, 9 L.Ed.2d 405, 83 S.Ct. 328 (1963).

**"The very nature of the lawyer's profession necessitates the utmost good faith toward his client and the highest loyalty and devotion to his client's interest."; In Re Thomasson's Estate, 346 Mo. 911, 918, 144 S.W.2d 79, 80 (1940).

"The relation between attorney and client is highly fiduciary and of very delicate, exacting and confidential character, requiring very high degree of fidelity and good faith on attorney's part."; Laughlin v. Boatmen's Nat. Bank of St. Louis, 163 S.W.2d 761, 762 (1942).

"The relation of an attorney to his client is pre-eminently confidential. It demands on the part of the attorney undivided allegiance, a conspicuous degree of faithfulness and disinterestedness, absolute integrity and utter renunciation of every personal advantage conflicting in any way directly or indirectly with the interests of his client."; State Bar Association of Connecticut v. Connecticut Bank & Trust Co., 145 Conn. 222, 234, 140 A.2d 863, 864, 69 A.L.R.2d 394, 402 (1958).

DISCIPLINARY RULES

DR 2–101 Publicity in General.[77]

(A) A lawyer shall not prepare, cause to be prepared, use, or participate in the use of, any form of public communication that contains professionally self-laudatory statements calculated to attract lay clients; as used herein, "public communication" includes, but is not limited to, communication by means of television, radio, motion picture, newspaper, magazine, or book.

(B) A lawyer shall not publicize himself, or his partner, or associate, or any other lawyer affiliated with him or his firm, as a lawyer through newspaper or magazine advertisements, radio or television announcements, display advertisements in city or telephone directories, or other means of commercial publicity,[78] nor shall he authorize or permit others to do so in his behalf,[79] except that a lawyer

[77] *Cf.* ABA Canon 27; *see generally ABA Opinion* 293 (1957).

[78] *Cf. ABA Opinions* 133 (1935), 116 (1934), 107 (1934), 73 (1932), 59 (1931), and 43 (1931).

[79] "There can be no justification for the participation and acquiescence by an attorney in the development and publication of an article which, on its face, plainly amounts to a self-interest and unethical presentation of his achievements and capabilities." Matter of Connelly, 18 App.Div. 2d 466, 478, 240 N.Y.S.2d 126, 138 (1963).

recommended by, paid by, or whose legal services are furnished by, any of the offices or organizations enumerated in DR 2-103(D)(1) through (5) may authorize or permit or assist such organization to use such means of commercial publicity, which does not identify any lawyer by name, to describe the availability or nature of its legal services or legal service benefits. This rule does not prohibit limited and dignified identification of a lawyer as a lawyer as well as by name:[80]

(1) In political advertisements when his professional status is germane to the political campaign or to a political issue.

(2) In public notices when the name and profession of a lawyer are required or authorized by law or are reasonably pertinent for a purpose other than the attraction of potential clients.[81]

(3) In routine reports and announcements of a bona fide business, civic, professional, or political organization in which he serves as a director or officer.

(4) In and on legal documents prepared by him.

(5) In and on legal textbooks, treatises, and other legal publications, and in dignified advertisements thereof.

(6) In private communications by any of the offices or organizations enumerated in DR 2-103(D)(1) through (5), along with the biographical information permitted under DR 2-102(A)(6), in response to inquiries from a member or beneficiary of such office or organization.

(C) A lawyer shall not compensate or give any thing of value to representatives of the press, radio, television, or other communication medium in anticipation of or in return for professional publicity in a news item.[82]

DR 2-102 Professional Notices, Letterheads, Offices, and Law Lists.

(A) A lawyer or law firm shall not use professional cards, professional announcement cards, office signs, letterheads, telephone directory listings, law lists, legal directory listings, or similar professional notices or devices,[83] except that the following may be used if they are in dignified form:

(1) A professional card of a lawyer identifying him by name and as a lawyer, and giving his addresses, telephone numbers, the name of his law firm, and any information permitted under DR 2-105. A professional card of a law firm may also give the names of members and associates. Such cards may be used for identification[84] but may not be published in periodicals, magazines, newspapers,[85] or other media.[86]

(2) A brief professional announcement card stating new or changed associations or addresses, change of firm name, or similar matters pertaining to the professional office of a lawyer or law firm, which may be mailed to lawyers, clients, former clients, personal friends, and relatives.[87] It shall not state biographical data except to the extent reasonably necessary to identify the lawyer or to explain the change in his association, but it may state the immediate past position of the lawyer.[88] It may give the names and dates of predecessor firms in a continuing line of succession. It shall not state the

---

"An announcement of the fact that the lawyer had resigned and the name of the person to succeed him, or take over his work, would not be objectionable, either as an official communication to those employed by or connected with the administrative agency or instrumentality [that had employed him], or as a news release.

"But to include therein a statement of the lawyer's experience in and acquaintance with the various departments and agencies of the government, and a laudation of his legal ability, either generally or in a special branch of the law, is not only bad taste but ethically improper.

"It can have but one primary purpose or object: to aid the lawyer in securing professional employment in private practice by advertising his professional experience, attainments and ability." *ABA Opinion* 184 (1938).

Cf. ABA Opinions 285 (1951) and 140 (1935).

80 "The question is always . . . whether under the circumstance the furtherance of the professional employment of the lawyer is the primary purpose of the advertisement, or is merely a necessary incident of a proper and legitimate objective of the client which does not have the effect of unduly advertising him." *ABA Opinion* 290 (1956). *See ABA Opinion* 285 (1951).

81 *See ABA Opinions* 299 (1961), 290 (1956), 158 (1936), and 100 (1933); *cf. ABA Opinion* 80 (1932).

82 "*Rule 2.*

. . . .

"[A] member of the State Bar shall not solicit professional employment by . . . .

"(4) The making of gifts to representatives of the press, radio, television or any medium of communication in anticipation of or in return for publicity." Cal.Business and Professions Code § 6076 (West 1962).

83 *Cf. ABA Opinions* 233 (1941) and 114 (1934).

84 *See ABA Opinion* 175 (1938).

85 *See ABA Opinions* 260 (1944) and 182 (1938).

86 *But cf. ABA Opinions* 276 (1947) and 256 (1943).

87 *See ABA Opinion* 301 (1961).

88 "[I]t has become commonplace for many lawyers to participate in government service; to deny them the right, upon their return to private practice, to refer to their prior employment in a brief and dignified manner, would place an undue limitation upon a large element of our profession. It is entirely proper for a member of the profession to explain his absence from private practice, where such is the primary purpose of the announcement, by a brief and dignified reference to the prior employment.

". . . [A]ny such announcement should be limited to the immediate past connection of the lawyer with the government, made upon his leaving that position to enter private practice." *ABA Opinion* 301 (1961).

nature of the practice except as permitted under DR 2–105.[89]

(3) A sign on or near the door of the office and in the building directory identifying the law office. The sign shall not state the nature of the practice, except as permitted under DR 2–105.

(4) A letterhead of a lawyer identifying him by name and as a lawyer, and giving his addresses, telephone numbers, the name of his law firm, associates, and any information permitted under DR 2–105. A letterhead of a law firm may also give the names of members and associates,[90] **and names and dates relating to deceased and retired members.**[91] **A lawyer may be designated "Of Counsel" on a letterhead if he has a continuing relationship with a lawyer or law firm, other than as a partner or associate. A lawyer or law firm may be designated as "General Counsel" or by similar professional reference on stationery of a client if he or the firm devotes a substantial amount of professional time in the representation of that client.**[92] **The letterhead of a law firm may give the names and dates of predecessor firms in a continuing line of succession.**

(5) A listing of the office of a lawyer or law firm in the alphabetical and classified sections of the telephone directory or directories for the geographical area or areas in which the lawyer resides or maintains offices or in which a significant part of his clientele resides[93] **and in the city directory of the city in which his or the firm's office is located;**[94] **but the listing may give only the name of the lawyer or law firm, the fact he is a lawyer, addresses, and telephone numbers.**[95] **The listing shall not be in distinctive form**[96] **or type.**[97] **A law firm may have a listing in the firm name separate from that of its members and associates.**[98] **The listing in the classified section shall not be under a heading or classification other than "Attorneys" or "Lawyers",**[99] **except that additional headings or classifications descriptive of the types of practice referred to in DR 2–105 are permitted.**[100]

(6) A listing in a reputable law list[101] **or legal directory giving brief biographical and other informative data. A law list or directory is not reputable if its management or contents are likely to be misleading or injurious to the public or to the profession.**[102] **A law list is conclusively established to be reputable if it is certified by the American Bar Association as being in compliance with its rules and standards. The published data may include only the following: name, including name of law firm and names of professional associates; addresses**[103] **and telephone numbers; one or more fields of law in which the lawyer or law firm concentrates;**[104] **a**

---

89 *See ABA Opinion* 251 (1943).

90 "Those lawyers who are working for an individual lawyer or a law firm may be designated on the letterhead and in other appropriate places as 'associates'." *ABA Opinion* 310 (1963).

91 *See* ABA Canon 33.

92 *But see ABA Opinion* 285 (1951).

93 *See ABA Opinion* 295 (1959).

94 *But see ABA Opinion* 313 (1964) which says the Committee "approves a listing in the classified section of the city directory for lawyers only when the listing includes all lawyers residing in the community and when no charge is made therefor."

95 "The listing should consist only of the lawyer's name, address and telephone number." *ABA Opinion* 313 (1964).

96 "[A]dding to the regular classified listing a 'second line' in which a lawyer claims that he is engaged in a 'specialty' is an undue attempt to make his name distinctive." *ABA Opinion* 284 (1951).

97 "[Opinion 284] held that a lawyer could not with propriety have his name listed in distinctive type in a telephone directory or city directory. We affirm that opinion." *ABA Opinion* 313 (1964).

See ABA Opinions 123 (1934) and 53 (1931).

98 "[I]f a lawyer is a member of a law firm, both the firm, and the individual lawyer may be listed separately." *ABA Opinion* 313 (1964).

99 *See ABA Opinion* 284 (1951).

100 *See* Silverman v. State Bar of Texas, 405 F.2d 410, (5th Cir. 1968); *but see ABA Opinion* 286 (1952).

101 *Cf.* ABA Canon 43.

102 *Cf. ABA Opinion* 255 (1943).

103 "We are asked to define the word 'addresses' appearing in the second paragraph of Canon 27 . . . .

"It is our opinion that an address (other than a cable address) within the intendment of the canon is that of the lawyer's office or of his residence. Neither address should be misleading. If, for example, an office address is given, it must be that of a bona fide office. The residence address, if given, should be identified as such if the city or other place of residence is not the same as that in which the law office is located." *ABA Opinion* 249 (1942).

104 "[T]oday in various parts of the country Committees on Professional Ethics of local and state bar associations are authorizing lawyers to describe themselves in announcements to the Bar and in notices in legal periodicals and approved law lists as specialists in a great variety of things. Thus in the approved law lists or professional announcements there appear, in connection with the names of individual practitioners or firms, such designations as 'International Law, Public and Private'; 'Trial Preparation in Personal Injury and Negligence Actions'; 'Philippine War Damage Claims'; 'Anti-Trust'; 'Domestic Relations'; 'Tax Law'; 'Negligence Law'. It would seem that the ABA has given at least its tacit approval to this sort of announcement.

"It is important that this sort of description is not, in New York at least, permitted on letterheads or shingles or

statement that practice is limited to one or more fields of law; a statement that the lawyer or law firm specializes in a particular field of law or law practice but only if authorized under DR 2–105 (A)(4);[105] date and place of birth; date and place of admission to the bar of state and federal courts; schools attended, with dates of graduation, degrees, and other scholastic distinctions; public or quasi-public offices; military service; posts of honor; legal authorships; legal teaching positions; memberships, offices, committee assignments, and section memberships in bar associations; memberships and offices in legal fraternities and legal societies; technical and professional associations and societies; foreign language ability; names and addresses of references,[106] and, with their consent, names of clients regularly represented.[107]

(B) A lawyer in private practice shall not practice under a trade name, a name that is misleading as to the identity of the lawyer or lawyers practicing under such name, or a firm name containing names other than those of one or more of the lawyers in the firm, except that the name of a professional corporation or professional association may contain "P.C." or "P.A." or similar symbols indicating the nature of the organization, and if otherwise lawful a firm may use as, or continue to include in, its name, the name or names of one or more deceased or retired members of the firm or of a predecessor firm in a continuing line of succession.[108] A lawyer who assumes a judicial, legislative, or public executive or administrative post or office shall not permit his name to remain in the name of a law firm or to be used in professional notices of the firm during any significant period in which he is not actively and regularly practicing law as a member of the firm,[109] and during such period other members of the firm shall not use his name in the firm name or in professional notices of the firm.[110]

(C) A lawyer shall not hold himself out as having a partnership with one or more other lawyers unless they are in fact partners.[111]

(D) A partnership shall not be formed or continued between or among lawyers licensed in different jurisdictions unless all enumerations of the members and associates of the firm on its letterhead and in other permissible listings make clear the jurisdictional limitations on those members and associates of the firm not licensed to practice in all listed jurisdictions;[112] however, the same firm name may be used in each jurisdiction.

(E) A lawyer who is engaged both in the practice of law and another profession or business shall not so indicate on his letterhead, office sign, or professional card, nor shall he identify himself as a lawyer in any publication in connection with his other profession or business.

(F) Nothing contained herein shall prohibit a lawyer from using or permitting the use, in connection with his name, of an earned degree or title derived therefrom indicating his training in the law.

DR 2–103 Recommendation of Professional Employment.[113]

(A) A lawyer shall not recommend employment, as a private practitioner,[114] of himself, his partner, or associate to a non-lawyer who has not sought his advice regarding employment of a lawyer.[115]

---

elsewhere in communications to laymen. This is subject to the single exception that such announcement to laymen is permitted in the four traditional specialties, Admiralty, Patent, Copyright and Trade-mark." *Report of the Special Committee on Specialization and Specialized Legal Education*, 79 A.B.A.Rep. 582, 586 (1954).

105 This provision is included to conform to action taken by the ABA House of Delegates at the Mid-Winter Meeting, January, 1969.

106 *See* ABA Canon 43 and *ABA Opinion* 119 (1934); *but see ABA Opinion* 236 (1941).

107 *See* ABA Canon 27.

108 *See* ABA Canon 33; *cf. ABA Opinions* 318 (1967), 267 (1945), 219 (1941), 208 (1940), 192 (1939), 97 (1933), and 6 (1925).

109 *ABA Opinion* 318 (1967) held, "anything to the contrary in Formal Opinion 315 or in the other opinions cited notwithstanding" that: "Where a partner whose name appears in the name of a law firm is elected or appointed to high local, state or federal office, which office he intends to occupy only temporarily, at the end of which time he intends to return to his position with the firm, and provided that he is not precluded by holding such office from engaging in the practice of law and does not in fact sever his relationship with the firm but only takes a leave of absence, and provided that there is no local law, statute or custom to the contrary, his name may be retained in the firm name during his term or terms of office, but only if proper precautions are taken not to mislead the public as to his degree of participation in the firm's affairs."

Cf. ABA Opinion 143 (1935), New York County Opinion 67, and New York City Opinions 36 and 798; *but cf. ABA Opinion* 192 (1939) and Michigan Opinion 164.

110 *Cf.* ABA Canon 33.

111 *See ABA Opinion* 277 (1948); *cf.* ABA Canon 33 and *ABA Opinions* 318 (1967), 126 (1935), 115 (1934), and 106 (1934).

112 *See ABA Opinions* 318 (1967) and 316 (1967); *cf.* ABA Canon 33.

113 *Cf.* ABA Canons 27 and 28.

114 "We think it clear that a lawyer's seeking employment in an ordinary law office, or appointment to a civil service position, is not prohibited by . . . [Canon 27]." *ABA Opinion* 197 (1939).

115 "[A] lawyer may not seek from persons not his clients the opportunity to perform . . . a [legal] check-up." *ABA Opinion* 307 (1962).

(B) Except as permitted under DR 2-103(C), a lawyer shall not compensate or give anything of value to a person or organization to recommend or secure his employment [116] by a client, or as a reward for having made a recommendation resulting in his employment [117] by a client.

(C) A lawyer shall not request a person or organization to recommend or promote the use of his services or those of his partner or associate,[118] or any other lawyer affiliated with him or his firm, as a private practitioner, except that:

(1) He may request referrals from a lawyer referral service operated, sponsored, or approved by a bar association representative of the general bar of the geographical area in which the association exists and may pay its fees incident thereto.[119]

(2) He may cooperate with the legal service activities of any of the offices or organizations enumerated in DR 2-103 (D)(1) through (5) and may perform legal services for those to whom he was recommended by it to do such work if:

(a) The person to whom the recommendation is made is a member or beneficiary of such office or organizations; and

(b) The lawyer remains free to exercise his independent professional judgment on behalf of his client without direction or regulation by the organization or any person connected with it.

(D) A lawyer shall not knowingly assist a person or organization that furnishes, or pays for legal services to others, to promote the use of his services or those of his partner, or associate, or any other lawyer affiliated with him or his firm, as a private practitioner, except as permitted in DR 2-101(B). However, this does not prohibit a lawyer, or his partner, or associate, or any other lawyer affiliated with him or his firm, from being employed or paid by, or cooperating with, one of the following offices or organizations that promote the use of his services or those of his partner, or associate, or any other lawyer affiliated with him or his firm, as a private practitioner, if his independent professional judgment is exercised in behalf of his client without interference or control by any organization or other person:

(1) A legal aid office or public defender office:

(a) Operated or sponsored by a duly accredited law school.

(b) Operated or sponsored by a bona fide non-profit community organization.

(c) Operated or sponsored by a governmental agency.

(d) Operated, sponsored, or approved by a bar association representative of the general bar of the geographical area in which the association exists.[120]

(2) A military legal assistance office.

(3) A lawyer referral service operated, sponsored, or approved by a bar association representative of the general bar of the geographical area in which the association exists.[121]

(4) A bar association representative of the general bar of the geographical area in which the association exists [122] or an organization operated, sponsored or approved by such a bar association.

(5) Any other organization that furnishes, renders, or pays for legal services to its members or beneficiaries, provided the following conditions are satisfied:

(a) As to such organizations other than a qualified legal assistance organization:

(i) Such organization is not organized for profit and its primary purposes do not include the recommending, furnishing, rendering of or paying for legal services.

(ii) Said services must be only incidental and reasonably re-

---

116 *Cf. ABA Opinion* 78 (1932).

117 " 'No financial connection of any kind between the Brotherhood and any lawyer is permissible. No lawyer can properly pay any amount whatsoever to the Brotherhood or any of its departments, officers or members as compensation, reimbursement of expenses or gratuity in connection with the procurement of a case.' " In re Brotherhood of R. R. Trainmen, 13 Ill.2d 391, 398, 150 N.E. 2d 163, 167 (1958), *quoted in* In re Ratner, 194 Kan 362, 372, 399 P.2d 865, 873 (1965).
See ABA Opinion 147 (1935).

118 "This Court has condemned the practice of ambulance chasing through the media of runners and touters. In similar fashion we have with equal emphasis condemned the practice of direct solicitation by a lawyer. We have classified both offenses as serious breaches of the Canons of Ethics demanding severe treatment of the offending lawyer." State v. Dawson, 111 So.2d 427, 431 (Fla. 1959).

119 "Registrants [of a lawyer referral plan] may be required to contribute to the expense of operating it by a reasonable registration charge or by a reasonable percentage of fees collected by them." *ABA Opinion* 291 (1956).
Cf. ABA Opinion 227 (1941).

120 *Cf. ABA Opinion* 148 (1935).

121 *Cf. ABA Opinion* 227 (1941).

122 "If a bar association has embarked on a program of institutional advertising for an annual legal check-up and provides brochures and reprints, it is not improper to have these available in the lawyer's office for persons to read and take." *ABA Opinion* 307 (1962).
Cf. ABA Opinion 121 (1934).

lated to the primary purposes of such organization.

(iii) Such organization or its parent or affiliated organization does not derive a profit or commercial benefit from the rendition of legal services by the lawyer.

(iv) The member or beneficiary for whom the legal services are rendered, and not such organization, is recognized as the client of the lawyer in that matter.

(v) Any of the organization's members or beneficiaries is free to select counsel or his or her own choice, provided that if such independent selection is made by the client, then such organization, if it customarily provides legal services through counsel it pre-selects, shall promptly reimburse the member or beneficiary in the fair and equitable amount said services would have cost such organization if rendered by counsel selected by said organization.

(vi) Such organization is in compliance with all applicable laws, rules of court and other legal requirements that govern its operations.

(vii) The lawyer, or his partner, or associate, or any other lawyer affiliated with him or his firm, shall not have initiated such organization for the purpose, in whole or in part, of providing financial or other benefits to him or to them.

(viii) The articles of organization, by-laws, agreement with counsel, and the schedule of benefits and subscription charges are filed along with any amendments or changes within sixty days of the effective date with the court or other authority having final jurisdiction for the discipline of lawyers within the state, and within sixty days of the end of each fiscal year a financial statement showing, with respect to its legal service activities, the income received and the expenses and benefits paid or incurred are filed in the form such authority may prescribe.

(ix) Provided, however, that any non-profit organization which is organized to secure and protect Constitutionally guaranteed rights shall be exempt from the requirements of (v) and (viii).

(b) As to a qualified legal assistance organization (not described in DR 2-102(D)(1) through (4)):

(i) The primary purpose of such organization may be profit or non-profit and it may include the recommending, furnishing, rendering of or paying for legal services of all kinds.

(ii) The member or beneficiary, for whom the legal services are rendered, and not such organization, is recognized as the client of the lawyer in the matter.

(iii) Such organization is in compliance with all applicable laws, rules of court and other legal requirements that govern its operations.

(iv) The lawyer, or his partner, or associate, or any other lawyer affiliated with him or his firm, shall not have initiated such organization for the purpose, in whole or in part, of providing financial or other benefits to him or to them.

(E) A lawyer shall not accept employment when he knows or it is obvious that the person who seeks his services does so as a result of conduct prohibited under this Disciplinary Rule.

DR 2-104 Suggestion of Need of Legal Services.[124]

(A) A lawyer who has given unsolicited advice to a layman that he should obtain counsel or take legal action shall not accept employment resulting from that advice,[125] except that:

(1) A lawyer may accept employment by a close friend, relative, former client (if the advice is germane to the former employment), or one whom the lawyer reasonably believes to be a client.[126]

---

124 ABA Canon 28.

125 *Cf. ABA Opinions* 229 (1941) and 173 (1937).

126 "It certainly is not improper for a lawyer to advise his regular clients of new statutes, court decisions, and administrative rulings, which may affect the client's interests, provided the communication is strictly limited to such information. . . .

"When such communications go to concerns or individuals other than regular clients of the lawyer, they are thinly disguised advertisements for professional employment, and are obviously improper." *ABA Opinion* 213 (1941).

"It is our opinion that where the lawyer has no reason to believe that he has been supplanted by another lawyer, it is not only his right, but it might even be his duty to advise his client of any change of fact or law which might

(2) A lawyer may accept employment that results from his participation in activities designed to educate laymen to recognize legal problems, to make intelligent selection of counsel, or to utilize available legal services if such activities are conducted or sponsored by a qualified legal assistance organization.

(3) A lawyer who is recommended, furnished or paid by any of the offices or organizations enumerated in DR 2–103(D)(1) through (5) may represent a member or beneficiary thereof, to the extent and under the conditions prescribed therein. A lawyer whose legal services are currently being recommended, furnished or paid for by a legal assistance organization defined in DR 2–103(D)(5)(a) may not accept employment as a private practitioner from a member or beneficiary of such a legal assistance organization in any matter not covered by the benefits provided under the plan of such organization when such member or beneficiary has been his client under such plan.

(4) Without affecting his right to accept employment, a lawyer may speak publicly or write for publication on legal topics [127] so long as he does not emphasize his own professional experience or reputation and does not undertake to give individual advice.

(5) If success in asserting rights or defenses of his client in litigation in the nature of a class action is dependent upon the joinder of others, a lawyer may accept, but shall not seek, employment from those contacted for the purpose of obtaining their joinder.[128]

DR 2–105 Limitation of Practice.[129]

(A) A lawyer shall not hold himself out publicly as a specialist [130] or as limiting his practice,[131] except as permitted under DR 2–102(A)(6) or as follows:

(1) A lawyer admitted to practice before the United States Patent Office may use the designation "Patents," "Patent Attorney," or "Patent Lawyer," or any combination of those terms, on his letterhead and office sign. A lawyer engaged in the trademark practice may use the designation "Trademarks," "Trademark Attorney," or "Trademark Lawyer," or any combination of those terms, on his letterhead and office sign, and a lawyer engaged in the admiralty practice may use the designation "Admiralty," "Proctor in Admiralty," or "Admiralty Lawyer," or any combination of those terms, on his letterhead and office sign.[132]

(2) A lawyer may permit his name to be listed in lawyer referral service offices according to the fields of law in which he will accept referrals.

(3) A lawyer available to act as a consultant to or as an associate of other lawyers in a particular branch of law or legal service may distribute to other lawyers and publish in legal journals a dignified announcement of such availability,[133] but the announcement shall not contain a representation of special competence or experience.[134] The announcement shall not be distributed to lawyers more frequently than once in a calendar year, but it may be published periodically in legal journals.

(4) A lawyer who is certified as a specialist in a particular field of law or law practice by the authority having jurisdiction under state law over the subject of specialization by lawyers may hold himself out as such specialist but only in accordance with the rules prescribed by that authority.[135]

DR 2–106 Fees for Legal Services.[136]

(A) A lawyer shall not enter into an agreement for, charge, or collect an illegal or clearly excessive fee.[137]

---

defeat the client's testamentary purpose as expressed in the will.

"Periodic notices might be sent to the client for whom a lawyer has drawn a will, suggesting that it might be wise for the client to reexamine his will to determine whether or not there has been any change in his situation requiring a modification of his will." *ABA Opinion* 210 (1941).

Cf. ABA Canon 28.

127 *Cf. ABA Opinion* 168 (1937).

128 *But cf. ABA Opinion* 111 (1934).

129 *See* ABA Canon 45; *cf.* ABA Canons 27, 43, and 46.

130 *Cf. ABA Opinions* 228 (1941) and 194 (1939).

131 *See ABA Opinions* 251 (1943) and 175 (1938).

132 *See* ABA Canon 27; *cf. ABA Opinion* 286 (1952).

133 *Cf. ABA Opinion* 194 (1939).

134 *See* ABA Canon 46.

135 This provision is included to conform to action taken by the ABA House of Delegates at the Mid-Winter Meeting, January, 1969.

136 *See* ABA Canon 12.

137 The charging of a "clearly excessive fee" is a ground for discipline. State ex rel. Nebraska State Bar Ass'n. v. Richards, 165 Neb. 80, 90, 84 N.W.2d 136, 143 (1957).

"An attorney has the right to contract for any fee he chooses so long as it is not excessive (see Opinion 190), and this Committee is not concerned with the amount of such fees unless so excessive as to constitute a misappro-

(B) A fee is clearly excessive when, after a review of the facts, a lawyer of ordinary prudence would be left with a definite and firm conviction that the fee is in excess of a reasonable fee. Factors to be considered as guides in determining the reasonableness of a fee include the following:

(1) The time and labor required, the novelty and difficulty of the questions involved, and the skill requisite to perform the legal service properly.

(2) The likelihood, if apparent to the client, that the acceptance of the particular employment will preclude other employment by the lawyer.

(3) The fee customarily charged in the locality for similar legal services.

(4) The amount involved and the results obtained.

(5) The time limitations imposed by the client or by the circumstances.

(6) The nature and length of the professional relationship with the client.

(7) The experience, reputation, and ability of the lawyer or lawyers performing the services.

(8) Whether the fee is fixed or contingent.[138]

(C) A lawyer shall not enter into an arrangement for, charge, or collect a contingent fee for representing a defendant in a criminal case.[139]

DR 2–107 Division of Fees Among Lawyers.

(A) A lawyer shall not divide a fee for legal services with another lawyer who is not a partner in or associate of his law firm or law office, unless:

(1) The client consents to employment of the other lawyer after a full disclosure that a division of fees will be made.

(2) The division is made in proportion to the services performed and responsibility assumed by each.[140]

(3) The total fee of the lawyers does not clearly exceed reasonable compensation for all legal services they rendered the client.[141]

(B) This Disciplinary Rule does not prohibit payment to a former partner or associate pursuant to a separation or retirement agreement.

DR 2–108 Agreements Restricting the Practice of a Lawyer.

(A) A lawyer shall not be a party to or participate in a partnership or employment agreement with another lawyer that restricts the right of a lawyer to practice law after the termination of a relationship created by the agreement, except as a condition to payment of retirement benefits.[142]

(B) In connection with the settlement of a controversy or suit, a lawyer shall not enter into an agreement that restricts his right to practice law.

DR 2–109 Acceptance of Employment.

(A) A lawyer shall not accept employment on behalf of a person if he knows or it is obvious that such person wishes to:

(1) Bring a legal action, conduct a defense, or assert a position in litigation, or otherwise have steps taken for him, merely for the purpose of harassing or maliciously injuring any person.[143]

---

priation of the client's funds (see Opinion 27)." *ABA Opinion* 320 (1968).

Cf. ABA Opinions 209 (1940), 190 (1939), and 27 (1930) and State ex rel. Lee v. Buchanan, 191 So.2d 33 (Fla. 1966).

138 *Cf.* ABA Canon 13; *see generally* MacKinnon, Contingent Fees for Legal Services (1964) (A Report of the American Bar Foundation).

139 "Contingent fees, whether in civil or criminal cases, are a special concern of the law. . . .

"In criminal cases, the rule is stricter because of the danger of corrupting justice. The second part of Section 542 of the Restatement [of Contracts] reads: 'A bargain to conduct a criminal case . . . in consideration of a promise of a fee contingent on success is illegal. . . .'" Peyton v. Margiotti, 398 Pa. 86, 156 A.2d 865, 967 (1959).

"The third area of practice in which the use of the contingent fee is generally considered to be prohibited is the prosecution and defense of criminal cases. However, there are so few cases, and these are predominantly old, that it is doubtful that there can be said to be any current law on the subject. . . . In the absence of cases on the validity of contingent fees for defense attorneys, it is necessary to rely on the consensus among commentators that such a fee is void as against public policy. The nature of criminal practice itself makes unlikely the use of contingent fee contracts." MacKinnon, Contingent Fees for Legal Services 52 (1964) (A Report of the American Bar Foundation).

140 *See* ABA Canon 34 and *ABA Opinions* 316 (1967) and 294 (1958); *see generally ABA Opinions* 265 (1945), 204 (1940), 190 (1939), 171 (1937), 153 (1936), 97 (1933), 63 (1932), 28 (1930), 27 (1930), and 18 (1930).

141 "*Canon 12* contemplates that a lawyer's fee should not exceed *the value of the services* rendered. . . . . . .

"*Canon 12* applies, whether joint or separate fees are charged [by associate attorneys] . . . ." *ABA Opinion* 204 (1940).

142 "[A] general covenant restricting an employed lawyer, after leaving the employment, from practicing in the community for a stated period, appears to this Committee to be an unwarranted restriction on the right of a lawyer to choose where he will practice and inconsistent with our professional status. Accordingly, the Committee is of the opinion it would be improper for the employing lawyer to require the covenant and likewise for the employed lawyer to agree to it." *ABA Opinion* 300 (1961).

143 *See* ABA Canon 30.

"*Rule 13.* . . . A member of the State Bar shall not accept employment to prosecute or defend a case solely

(2) Present a claim or defense in litigation that is not warranted under existing law, unless it can be supported by good faith argument for an extension, modification, or reversal of existing law.

DR 2-110 Withdrawal from Employment.[144]

(A) In General.

(1) If permission for withdrawal from employment is required by the rules of a tribunal, a lawyer shall not withdraw from employment in a proceeding before that tribunal without its permission.

(2) In any event, a lawyer shall not withdraw from employment until he has taken reasonable steps to avoid foreseeable prejudice to the rights of his client, including giving due notice to his client, allowing time for employment of other counsel, delivering to the client all papers and property to which the client is entitled, and complying with applicable laws and rules.

(3) A lawyer who withdraws from employment shall refund promptly any part of a fee paid in advance that has not been earned.

(B) Mandatory withdrawal.

A lawyer representing a client before a tribunal, with its permission if required by its rules, shall withdraw from employment, and a lawyer representing a client in other matters shall withdraw from employment, if:

(1) He knows or it is obvious that his client is bringing the legal action, conducting the defense, or asserting a position in the litigation, or is otherwise having steps taken for him, merely for the purpose of harassing or maliciously injuring any person.

(2) He knows or it is obvious that his continued employment will result in violation of a Disciplinary Rule.[145]

(3) His mental or physical condition renders it unreasonably difficult for him to carry out the employment effectively.

(4) He is discharged by his client.

(C) Permissive withdrawal.[146]

If DR 2-110(B) is not applicable, a lawyer may not request permission to withdraw in matters pending before a tribunal, and may not withdraw in other matters, unless such request or such withdrawal is because:

(1) His client:

(a) Insists upon presenting a claim or defense that is not warranted under existing law and cannot be supported by good faith argument for an extension, modification, or reversal of existing law.[147]

(b) Personally seeks to pursue an illegal course of conduct.

(c) Insists that the lawyer pursue a course of conduct that is illegal or that is prohibited under the Disciplinary Rules.

(d) By other conduct renders it unreasonably difficult for the lawyer to carry out his employment effectively.

(e) Insists, in a matter not pending before a tribunal, that the lawyer engage in conduct that is contrary to the judgment and advice of the lawyer but not prohibited under the Disciplinary Rules.

(f) Deliberately disregards an agreement or obligation to the lawyer as to expenses or fees.

(2) His continued employment is likely to result in a violation of a Disciplinary Rule.

(3) His inability to work with co-counsel indicates that the best interests of the client likely will be served by withdrawal.

(4) His mental or physical condition renders it difficult for him to carry out the employment effectively.

(5) His client knowingly and freely assents to termination of his employment.

(6) He believes in good faith, in a proceeding pending before a tribunal, that the tribunal will find the existence of other good cause for withdrawal.

CANON 3

A Lawyer Should Assist in Preventing the Unauthorized Practice of Law

ETHICAL CONSIDERATIONS

EC 3-1 The prohibition against the practice of law by a layman is grounded in the need of the public for integrity and competence of those who undertake to render legal services. Because of the fiduciary and personal character of the lawyer-client relationship and the inherently complex nature of our legal system, the public can better be assured of the requisite responsibility and competence if the practice of law is confined to those

---

out of spite, or solely for the purpose of harassing or delaying another . . . .'' Cal.Business and Professions Code § 6067 (West 1962).

144 *Cf.* ABA Canon 44.

145 *See also* Code of Professional Responsibility, DR 5-102 and DR 5-105.

146 *Cf.* ABA Canon 4.

147 *Cf.* Anders v. California, 386 U.S. 738, 18 L.Ed.2d 493, 87 S.Ct. 1396 (1967), *rehearing denied*, 388 U.S. 924, 18 L.Ed.2d 1377, 87 S.Ct. 2094 (1967).

who are subject to the requirements and regulations imposed upon members of the legal profession.

EC 3-2 The sensitive variations in the considerations that bear on legal determinations often make it difficult even for a lawyer to exercise appropriate professional judgment, and it is therefore essential that the personal nature of the relationship of client and lawyer be preserved. Competent professional judgment is the product of a trained familiarity with law and legal processes, a disciplined, analytical approach to legal problems, and a firm ethical commitment.

EC 3-3 A non-lawyer who undertakes to handle legal matters is not governed as to integrity or legal competence by the same rules that govern the conduct of a lawyer. A lawyer is not only subject to that regulation but also is committed to high standards of ethical conduct. The public interest is best served in legal matters by a regulated profession committed to such standards.[1] The Disciplinary Rules protect the public in that they prohibit a lawyer from seeking employment by improper overtures, from acting in cases of divided loyalties, and from submitting to the control of others in the exercise of his judgment. Moreover, a person who entrusts legal matters to a lawyer is protected by the attorney-client privilege and by the duty of the lawyer to hold inviolate the confidences and secrets of his client.

EC 3-4 A layman who seeks legal services often is not in a position to judge whether he will receive proper professional attention. The entrustment of a legal matter may well involve the confidences, the reputation, the property, the freedom, or even the life of the client. Proper protection of members of the public demands that no person be permitted to act in the confidential and demanding capacity of a lawyer unless he is subject to the regulations of the legal profession.

EC 3-5 It is neither necessary nor desirable to attempt the formulation of a single, specific definition of what constitutes the practice of law.[2] Functionally, the practice of law relates to the rendition of services for others that call for the professional judgment of a lawyer. The essence of the professional judgment of the lawyer is his educated ability to relate the general body and philosophy of law to a specific legal problem of a client; and thus, the public interest will be better served if only lawyers are permitted to act in matters involving professional judgment. Where this professional judgment is not involved, non-lawyers, such as court clerks, police officers, abstracters, and many governmental employees, may engage in occupations that require a special knowledge of law in certain areas. But the services of a lawyer are essential in the public interest whenever the exercise of professional legal judgment is required.

EC 3-6 A lawyer often delegates tasks to clerks, secretaries, and other lay persons. Such delegation is proper if the lawyer maintains a direct relationship with his client, supervises the delegated work, and has complete professional responsibility for the work product.[3] This delegation enables a lawyer to render legal service more economically and efficiently.

EC 3-7 The prohibition against a non-lawyer practicing law does not prevent a layman from representing himself, for then he is ordinarily exposing only himself to possible injury. The purpose of the legal profession is to make educated legal representation available to the public; but anyone who does not wish to avail himself of such representation is not required to do so. Even so, the legal profession should help members of the public to recognize legal problems and to understand why it may be unwise for them to act for themselves in matters having legal consequences.

EC 3-8 Since a lawyer should not aid or encourage a layman to practice law, he should not practice law in association with a layman or other-

---

[1] "The condemnation of the unauthorized practice of law is designed to protect the public from legal services by persons unskilled in the law. The prohibition of lay intermediaries is intended to insure the loyalty of the lawyer to the client unimpaired by intervening and possibly conflicting interests." Cheatham, *Availability of Legal Services: The Responsibility of the Individual Lawyer and of the Organized Bar*, 12 U.C.L.A.L.Rev. 438, 439 (1965).

[2] "What constitutes unauthorized practice of the law in a particular jurisdiction is a matter for determination by the courts of that jurisdiction." *ABA Opinion* 198 (1939).

"In the light of the historical development of the lawyer's functions, it is impossible to lay down an exhaustive definition of 'the practice of law' by attempting to enumerate every conceivable act performed by lawyers in the normal course of their work." State Bar of Arizona v. Arizona Land Title & Trust Co., 90 Ariz. 76, 87, 366 P.2d 1, 8–9 (1961), *modified*, 91 Ariz. 293, 371 P.2d 1020 (1962).

[3] "A lawyer can employ lay secretaries, lay investigators, lay detectives, lay researchers, accountants, lay scriveners, nonlawyer draftsmen or nonlawyer researchers. In fact, he may employ nonlawyers to do any task for him except counsel clients about law matters, engage directly in the practice of law, appear in court or appear in formal proceedings a part of the judicial process, so long as it is he who takes the work and vouches for it to the client and becomes responsible to the client." *ABA Opinion* 316 (1967).

ABA Opinion 316 (1967) also stated that if a lawyer practices law as part of a law firm which includes lawyers from several states, he may delegate tasks to firm members in other states so long as he "is the person who, on behalf of the firm, vouched for the work of all of the others and, with the client and in the courts, did the legal acts defined by that state as the practice of law."

"A lawyer cannot delegate his professional responsibility to a law student employed in his office. He may avail himself of the assistance of the student in many of the fields of the lawyer's work, such as examination of case law, finding and interviewing witnesses, making collections of claims, examining court records, delivering papers, conveying important messages, and other similar matters. But the student is not permitted, until he is admitted to the Bar, to perform the professional functions of a lawyer, such as conducting court trials, giving professional advice to clients or drawing legal documents for them. The student in all his work must act as agent for the lawyer employing him, who must supervise his work and be responsible for his good conduct." *ABA Opinion* 85 (1932).

wise share legal fees with a layman.[4] This does not mean, however, that the pecuniary value of the interest of a deceased lawyer in his firm or practice may not be paid to his estate or specified persons such as his widow or heirs.[5] In like manner, profit-sharing retirement plans of a lawyer or law firm which include non-lawyer office employees are not improper.[6] These limited exceptions to the rule against sharing legal fees with laymen are permissible since they do not aid or encourage laymen to practice law.

EC 3-9 Regulation of the practice of law is accomplished principally by the respective states.[7] Authority to engage in the practice of law conferred in any jurisdiction is not per se a grant of the right to practice elsewhere, and it is improper for a lawyer to engage in practice where he is not permitted by law or by court order to do so. However, the demands of business and the mobility of our society pose distinct problems in the regulation of the practice of law by the states.[8] In furtherance of the public interest, the legal profession should discourage regulation that unreasonably imposes territorial limitations upon the right of a lawyer to handle the legal affairs of his client or upon the opportunity of a client to obtain the services of a lawyer of his choice in all matters including the presentation of a contested matter in a tribunal before which the lawyer is not permanently admitted to practice.[9]

DISCIPLINARY RULES

DR 3-101 Aiding Unauthorized Practice of Law.[10]

(A) A lawyer shall not aid a non-lawyer in the unauthorized practice of law.[11]

(B) A lawyer shall not practice law in a jurisdiction where to do so would be in violation of regulations of the profession in that jurisdiction.[12]

DR 3-102 Dividing Legal Fees with a Non-Lawyer.

(A) A lawyer or law firm shall not share legal fees with a non-lawyer,[13] except that:

(1) An agreement by a lawyer with his firm, partner, or associate may provide for the payment of money, over a reasonable period of time after his death, to his estate or to one or more specified persons.[14]

(2) A lawyer who undertakes to complete unfinished legal business of a deceased lawyer may pay to the estate of the de-

---

4 "No division of fees for legal services is proper, except with another lawyer . . . ." ABA Canon 34. Otherwise, according to *ABA Opinion* 316 (1967), "[t]he Canons of Ethics do not examine into the method by which such persons are remunerated by the lawyer. . . . They may be paid a salary, a per diem charge, a flat fee, a contract price, etc."

See ABA Canons 33 and 47.

5 "Many partnership agreements provide that the active partners, on the death of any one of them, are to make payments to the estate or to the nominee of a deceased partner on a pre-determined formula. It is only where the effect of such an arrangement is to make the estate or nominee a member of the partnership along with the surviving partners that it is prohibited by *Canon 34*. Where the payments are made in accordance with a pre-existing agreement entered into by the deceased partner during his lifetime and providing for a fixed method for determining their amount based upon the value of services rendered during the partner's lifetime and providing for a fixed period over which the payments are to be made, this is not the case. Under these circumstances, whether the payments are considered to be delayed payment of compensation earned but withheld during the partner's lifetime, or whether they are considered to be an approximation of his interest in matters pending at the time of his death, is immaterial. In either event, as Henry S. Drinker says in his book, Legal Ethics, at page 189: 'It would seem, however, that a reasonable agreement to pay the estate a proportion of the receipts for a reasonable period is a proper practical settlement for the lawyer's services to his retirement or death.' " *ABA Opinion* 308 (1963).

6 *Cf. ABA Opinion* 311 (1964).

7 "That the States have broad power to regulate the practice of law is, of course, beyond question." United Mine Workers v. Ill. State Bar Ass'n, 389 U.S. 217, 222 (1967).

"It is a matter of law, not of ethics, as to where an individual may practice law. Each state has its own rules." *ABA Opinion* 316 (1967).

8 "Much of clients' business crosses state lines. People are mobile, moving from state to state. Many metropolitan areas cross state lines. It is common today to have a single economic and social community involving more than one state. The business of a single client may involve legal problems in several states." *ABA Opinion* 316 (1967).

9 "[W]e reaffirmed the general principle that legal services to New Jersey residents with respect to New Jersey matters may ordinarily be furnished only by New Jersey counsel; but we pointed out that there may be multistate transactions where strict adherence to this thesis would not be in the public interest and that, under the circumstances, it would have been not only more costly to the client but also 'grossly impractical and inefficient' to have had the settlement negotiations conducted by separate lawyers from different states." In re Estate of Waring, 47 N.J. 367, 376, 221 A.2d 193, 197 (1966).

Cf. ABA Opinion 316 (1967).

10 Conduct permitted by the Disciplinary Rules of Canons 2 and 5 does not violate DR 3-101.

11 *See* ABA Canon 47.

12 It should be noted, however, that a lawyer may engage in conduct, otherwise prohibited by this Disciplinary Rule, where such conduct is authorized by preemptive federal legislation. *See* Sperry v. Florida, 373 U.S. 379, 10 L.Ed.2d 428, 83 S.Ct. 1322 (1963).

13 *See* ABA Canon 34 and *ABA Opinions* 316 (1967), 180 (1938), and 48 (1931).

"The receiving attorney shall not under any guise or form share his fee for legal services with a lay agency, personal or corporate, without prejudice, however, to the right of the lay forwarder to charge and collect from the creditor proper compensation for non-legal services rendered by the law [*sic*] forwarder which are separate and apart from the services performed by the receiving attorney." *ABA Opinion* 294 (1958).

14 *See ABA Opinions* 309 (1963) and 266 (1945).

ceased lawyer that proportion of the total compensation which fairly represents the services rendered by the deceased lawyer.

(3) A lawyer or law firm may include nonlawyer employees in a retirement plan, even though the plan is based in whole or in part on a profit-sharing arrangement.[15]

DR 3–103 Forming a Partnership with a Non-Lawyer.

(A) A lawyer shall not form a partnership with a non-lawyer if any of the activities of the partnership consist of the practice of law.[16]

CANON 4

A Lawyer Should Preserve the Confidences and Secrets of a Client

ETHICAL CONSIDERATIONS

EC 4–1 Both the fiduciary relationship existing between lawyer and client and the proper functioning of the legal system require the preservation by the lawyer of confidences and secrets of one who has employed or sought to employ him.[1] A client must feel free to discuss whatever he wishes with his lawyer and a lawyer must be equally free to obtain information beyond that volunteered by his client.[2] A lawyer should be fully informed of all the facts of the matter he is handling in order for his client to obtain the full advantage of our legal system. It is for the lawyer in the exercise of his independent professional judgment to separate the relevant and important from the irrelevant and unimportant. The observance of the ethical obligation of a lawyer to hold inviolate the confidences and secrets of his client not only facilitates the full development of facts essential to proper representation of the client but also encourages laymen to seek early legal assistance.

EC 4–2 The obligation to protect confidences and secrets obviously does not preclude a lawyer from revealing information when his client consents after full disclosure,[3] when necessary to perform his professional employment, when permitted by a Disciplinary Rule, or when required by law. Unless the client otherwise directs, a lawyer may disclose the affairs of his client to partners or associates of his firm. It is a matter of common knowledge that the normal operation of a law office exposes confidential professional information to nonlawyer employees of the office, particularly secretaries and those having access to the files; and this obligates a lawyer to exercise care in selecting and training his employees so that the sanctity of all confidences and secrets of his clients may be preserved. If the obligation extends to two or more clients as to the same information, a lawyer should obtain the permission of all before revealing the information. A lawyer must always be sensitive to the rights and wishes of his client and act scrupulously in the making of decisions which may involve the disclosure of information obtained in his professional relationship.[4] Thus, in the absence of consent of his client after full disclosure, a lawyer should not associate another lawyer in the handling of a matter; nor should he, in the absence of consent, seek counsel from another lawyer

---

15 *Cf. ABA Opinion* 311 (1964).

16 *See* ABA Canon 33; *cf. ABA Opinions* 239 (1942) and 201 (1940).

ABA Opinion 316 (1967) states that lawyers licensed in different jurisdictions may, under certain conditions, enter "into an arrangement for the practice of law" and that a lawyer licensed in State A is not, for such purpose, a layman in State B.

1 *See* ABA Canons 6 and 37 and *ABA Opinion* 287 (1953).

"The reason underlying the rule with respect to confidential communications between attorney and client is well stated in Mecham on Agency, 2d Ed., Vol. 2, § 2297, as follows: 'The purposes and necessities of the relation between a client and his attorney require, in many cases, on the part of the client, the fullest and freest disclosures to the attorney of the client's objects, motives and acts. This disclosure is made in the strictest confidence, relying upon the attorney's honor and fidelity. To permit the attorney to reveal to others what is so disclosed, would be not only a gross violation of a sacred trust upon his part, but it would utterly destroy and prevent the usefulness and benefits to be derived from professional assistance. Based upon considerations of public policy, therefore, the law wisely declares that all confidential communications and disclosures, made by a client to his legal adviser for the purpose of obtaining his professional aid or advice, shall be strictly privileged;—that the attorney shall not be permitted, without the consent of his client,—and much less will he be compelled—to reveal or disclose communications made to him under such circumstances.' " *ABA Opinion* 250 (1943).

"While it is true that complete revelation of relevant facts should be encouraged for trial purposes, nevertheless an attorney's dealings with his client, if both are sincere, and if the dealings involve more than mere technical matters, should be immune to discovery proceedings. There must be freedom from fear of revealment of matters disclosed to an attorney because of the peculiarly intimate relationship existing." Ellis-Foster Co. v. Union Carbide & Carbon Corp., 159 F.Supp. 917, 919 (D.N.J. 1958).

Cf. ABA Opinions 314 (1965), 274 (1946) and 268 (1945).

2 "While it is the great purpose of law to ascertain the truth, there is the countervailing necessity of insuring the right of every person to freely and fully confer and confide in one having knowledge of the law, and skilled in its practice, in order that the former may have adequate advice and a proper defense. This assistance can be made safely and readily available only when the client is free from the consequences of apprehension of disclosure by reason of the subsequent statements of the skilled lawyer." Baird v. Koerner, 279 F.2d 623, 629–30 (9th Cir. 1960).

Cf. ABA Opinion 150 (1936).

3 "Where . . . [a client] knowingly and after full disclosure participates in a [legal fee] financing plan which requires the furnishing of certain information to the bank, clearly by his conduct he has waived any privilege as to that information." *ABA Opinion* 320 (1968).

4 "The lawyer must decide when he takes a case whether it is a suitable one for him to undertake and after this decision is made, he is not justified in turning against his client by exposing injurious evidence entrusted to him. . . . [D]oing something intrinsically regrettable, because the only alternative involves worse consequences, is a necessity in every profession." Williston, Life and Law 271 (1940).

Cf. ABA Opinions 177 (1938) and 83 (1932).

if there is a reasonable possibility that the identity of the client or his confidences or secrets would be revealed to such lawyer. Both social amenities and professional duty should cause a lawyer to shun indiscreet conversations concerning his clients.

EC 4–3 Unless the client otherwise directs, it is not improper for a lawyer to give limited information from his files to an outside agency necessary for statistical, bookkeeping, accounting, data processing, banking, printing, or other legitimate purposes, provided he exercises due care in the selection of the agency and warns the agency that the information must be kept confidential.

EC 4–4 The attorney-client privilege is more limited than the ethical obligation of a lawyer to guard the confidences and secrets of his client. This ethical precept, unlike the evidentiary privilege, exists without regard to the nature or source of information or the fact that others share the knowledge. A lawyer should endeavor to act in a manner which preserves the evidentiary privilege; for example, he should avoid professional discussions in the presence of persons to whom the privilege does not extend. A lawyer owes an obligation to advise the client of the attorney-client privilege and timely to assert the privilege unless it is waived by the client.

EC 4–5 A lawyer should not use information acquired in the course of the representation of a client to the disadvantage of the client and a lawyer should not use, except with the consent of his client after full disclosure, such information for his own purposes.[5] Likewise, a lawyer should be diligent in his efforts to prevent the misuse of such information by his employees and associates.[6] Care should be exercised by a lawyer to prevent the disclosure of the confidences and secrets of one client to another,[7] and no employment should be accepted that might require such disclosure.

EC 4–6 The obligation of a lawyer to preserve the confidences and secrets of his client continues after the termination of his employment.[8] Thus a lawyer should not attempt to sell a law practice as a going business because, among other reasons, to do so would involve the disclosure of confidences and secrets.[9] A lawyer should also provide for the protection of the confidences and secrets of his client following the termination of the practice of the lawyer, whether termination is due to death, disability, or retirement. For example, a lawyer might provide for the personal papers of the client to be returned to him and for the papers of the lawyer to be delivered to another lawyer or to be destroyed. In determining the method of disposition, the instructions and wishes of the client should be a dominant consideration.

[5] *See* ABA Canon 11.

[6] *See* ABA Canon 37.

[7] *See* ABA Canons 6 and 37.

"[A]n attorney must not accept professional employment against a client or a former client which will, or even *may* require him to use confidential information obtained by the attorney in the course of his professional relations with such client regarding the subject matter of the employment . . . ." *ABA Opinion* 165 (1936).

[8] *See* ABA Canon 37.

"Confidential communications between an attorney and his client, made because of the relationship and concerning the subject-matter of the attorney's employment, are generally privileged from disclosure without the consent of the client, and this privilege outlasts the attorney's employment. *Canon 37.*" *ABA Opinion* 154 (1936).

[9] *Cf. ABA Opinion* 266 (1945).

DISCIPLINARY RULES

DR 4–101 Preservation of Confidences and Secrets of a Client.[10]

(A) "Confidence" refers to information protected by the attorney-client privilege under applicable law, and "secret" refers to other information gained in the professional relationship that the client has requested be held inviolate or the disclosure of which would be embarrassing or would be likely to be detrimental to the client.

(B) Except when permitted under DR 4–101(C), a lawyer shall not knowingly:

(1) Reveal a confidence or secret of his client.[11]

(2) Use a confidence or secret of his client to the disadvantage of the client.

(3) Use a confidence or secret of his client for the advantage of himself[12] **or of a third person,**[13] **unless the client consents after full disclosure.**

[10] *See* ABA Canon 37; *cf.* ABA Canon 6.

[11] "§ 6068 . . . It is the duty of an attorney: . . . .

"(e) To maintain inviolate the confidence, and at every peril to himself to preserve the secrets, of his client." Cal. Business and Professions Code § 6068 (West 1962). Virtually the same provision is found in the Oregon statutes. Ore.Rev.Stats. ch. 9, § 9.460(5).

"Communications between lawyer and client are privileged (Wigmore on Evidence, 3d. Ed., Vol. 8, §§ 2290–2329). The modern theory underlying the privilege is subjective and is to give the client freedom of apprehension in consulting his legal adviser (*ibid.*, § 2290, p. 548). The privilege applies to communications made in seeking legal advice for any purpose (*ibid.*, § 2294, p. 563). The mere circumstance that the advice is given without charge therefore does not nullify the privilege (*ibid.*, § 2303)." *ABA Opinion* 216 (1941).

"It is the duty of an attorney to maintain the confidence and preserve inviolate the secrets of his client . . . ." *ABA Opinion* 155 (1936).

[12] *See* ABA Canon 11.

"The provision respecting employment is in accord with the general rule announced in the adjudicated cases that a lawyer may not make use of knowledge or information acquired by him through his professional relations with his client, or in the conduct of his client's business, to his own advantage or profit (7 C.J.S., § 125, p. 958; Healy v. Gray, 184 Iowa 111, 168 N.W. 222; Baumgardner v. Hudson, D.C.App., 277 F. 552; Goodrum v. Clement, D.C.App., 277 F. 586)." *ABA Opinion* 250 (1943).

[13] *See ABA Opinion* 177 (1938).

(C) A lawyer may reveal:

(1) Confidences or secrets with the consent of the client or clients affected, but only after a full disclosure to them.[14]

(2) Confidences or secrets when permitted under Disciplinary Rules or required by law or court order.[15]

(3) The intention of his client to commit a crime[16] **and the information necessary to prevent the crime.**[17]

(4) Confidences or secrets necessary to establish or collect his fee[18] **or to defend himself or his employees or associates against an accusation of wrongful conduct.**[19]

(D) A lawyer shall exercise reasonable care to prevent his employees, associates, and others whose services are utilized by him from disclosing or using confidences or secrets of a client, except that a lawyer may reveal the information allowed by DR 4-101(C) through an employee.

---

14 "[A lawyer] may not divulge confidential communications, information, and secrets imparted to him by the client or acquired during their professional relations, unless he is authorized to do so by the client (People v. Gerold, 265 Ill. 448, 107 N.E. 165, 178; Murphy v. Riggs, 238 Mich. 151, 213 N.W. 110, 112; Opinion of this Committee, No. 91)." *ABA Opinion* 202 (1940).

Cf. ABA Opinion 91 (1933).

15 "A defendant in a criminal case when admitted to bail is not only regarded as in the custody of his bail, but he is also in the custody of the law, and admission to bail does not deprive the court of its inherent power to deal with the person of the prisoner. Being in lawful custody, the defendant is guilty of an escape when he gains his liberty before he is delivered in due process of law, and is guilty of a separate offense for which he may be punished. In failing to disclose his client's whereabouts as a fugitive under these circumstances the attorney would not only be aiding his client to escape trial on the charge for which he was indicted, but would likewise be aiding him in evading prosecution for the additional offense of escape.

"It is the opinion of the committee that under such circumstances the attorney's knowledge of his client's whereabouts is not privileged, and that he may be disciplined for failing to disclose that information to the proper authorities. . . ." *ABA Opinion* 155 (1936).

"We held in *Opinion* 155 that a communication by a client to his attorney in respect to the future commission of an unlawful act or to a continuing wrong is not privileged from disclosure. Public policy forbids that the relation of attorney and client should be used to conceal wrongdoing on the part of the client.

. . . . .

"When an attorney representing a defendant in a criminal case applies on his behalf for probation or suspension of sentence, he represents to the court, by implication at least, that his client will abide by the terms and conditions of the court's order. When that attorney is later advised of a violation of that order, it is his duty to advise his client of the consequences of his act, and endeavor to prevent a continuance of the wrongdoing. If his client thereafter persists in violating the terms and conditions of his probation, it is the duty of the attorney as an officer of the court to advise the proper authorities concerning his client's conduct. Such information, even though coming to the attorney from the client in the course of his professional relations with respect to other matters in which he represents the defendant, is not privileged from disclosure. . . ." *ABA Opinion* 156 (1936).

16 *ABA Opinion* 314 (1965) indicates that a lawyer must disclose even the confidences of his clients if "the facts in the attorney's possession indicate beyond reasonable doubt that a crime will be committed."

See ABA Opinion 155 (1936).

17 *See* ABA Canon 37 and *ABA Opinion* 202 (1940).

18 *Cf. ABA Opinion* 250 (1943).

19 *See* ABA Canon 37 and *ABA Opinions* 202 (1940) and 19 (1930).

"[T]he adjudicated cases recognize an exception to the rule [that a lawyer shall not reveal the confidences of his client], where disclosure is necessary to protect the attorney's interests arising out of the relation of attorney and client in which disclosure was made.

"The exception is stated in Mechem on Agency, 2d Ed., Vol. 2, § 2313, as follows: 'But the attorney may disclose information received from the client when it becomes necessary for his own protection, as if the client should bring an action against the attorney for negligence or misconduct, and it became necessary for the attorney to show what his instructions were, or what was the nature of the duty which the client expected him to perform. So if it became necessary for the attorney to bring an action against the client, the client's privilege could not prevent the attorney from disclosing what was essential as a means of obtaining or defending his own rights.'

"Mr. Jones, in his Commentaries on Evidence, 2d Ed., Vol. 5, § 2165, states the exception thus: 'It has frequently been held that the rule as to privileged communications does not apply when litigation arises between attorney and client to the extent that their communications are relevant to the issue. In such cases, if the disclosure of privileged communications becomes necessary to protect the attorney's rights, he is released from those obligations of secrecy which the law places upon him. He should not, however, disclose more than is necessary for his own protection. It would be a manifest injustice to allow the client to take advantage of the rule of exclusion as to professional confidence to the prejudice of his attorney, or that it should be carried to the extent of depriving the attorney of the means of obtaining or defending his own rights. In such cases the attorney is exempted from the obligations of secrecy.'" *ABA Opinion* 250 (1943).

CANON 5

A Lawyer Should Exercise Independent Professional Judgment on Behalf of a Client

ETHICAL CONSIDERATIONS

EC 5-1 The professional judgment of a lawyer should be exercised, within the bounds of the law, solely for the benefit of his client and free of compromising influences and loyalties.[1] Neither his

---

1 *Cf.* ABA Canon 35.

"[A lawyer's] fiduciary duty is of the highest order and he must not represent interests adverse to those of the client. It is also true that because of his professional responsibility and the confidence and trust which his client may legitimately repose in him, he must adhere to a high standard of honesty, integrity and good faith in dealing with his client. He is not permitted to take advantage of his position or superior knowledge to impose upon the client; nor to conceal facts or law, nor in any way deceive

personal interests, the interests of other clients, nor the desires of third persons should be permitted to dilute his loyalty to his client.

Interests of a Lawyer That May Affect His Judgment

EC 5–2 A lawyer should not accept proffered employment if his personal interests or desires will, or there is a reasonable probability that they will, affect adversely the advice to be given or services to be rendered the prospective client.[2] After accepting employment, a lawyer carefully should refrain from acquiring a property right or assuming a position that would tend to make his judgment less protective of the interests of his client.

EC 5–3 The self-interest of a lawyer resulting from his ownership of property in which his client also has an interest or which may affect property of his client may interfere with the exercise of free judgment on behalf of his client. If such interference would occur with respect to a prospective client, a lawyer should decline employment proffered by him. After accepting employment, a lawyer should not acquire property rights that would adversely affect his professional judgment in the representation of his client. Even if the property interests of a lawyer do not presently interfere with the exercise of his independent judgment, but the likelihood of interference can reasonably be foreseen by him, a lawyer should explain the situation to his client and should decline employment or withdraw unless the client consents to the continuance of the relationship after full disclosure. A lawyer should not seek to persuade his client to permit him to invest in an undertaking of his client nor make improper use of his professional relationship to influence his client to invest in an enterprise in which the lawyer is interested.

EC 5–4 If, in the course of his representation of a client, a lawyer is permitted to receive from his client a beneficial ownership in publication rights relating to the subject matter of the employment, he may be tempted to subordinate the interests of his client to his own anticipated pecuniary gain. For example, a lawyer in a criminal case who obtains from his client television, radio, motion picture, newspaper, magazine, book, or other publication rights with respect to the case may be influenced, consciously or unconsciously, to a course of conduct that will enhance the value of his publication rights to the prejudice of his client. To prevent these potentially differing interests, such arrangements should be scrupulously avoided prior to the termination of all aspects of the matter giving rise to the employment, even though his employment has previously ended.

EC 5–5 A lawyer should not suggest to his client that a gift be made to himself or for his benefit. If a lawyer accepts a gift from his client, he is peculiarly susceptible to the charge that he unduly influenced or overreached the client. If a client voluntarily offers to make a gift to his lawyer, the lawyer may accept the gift, but before doing so, he should urge that his client secure disinterested advice from an independent, competent person who is cognizant of all the circumstances.[3] Other than in

---

him without being held responsible therefor." Smoot v. Lund, 13 Utah 2d 168, 172, 369 P.2d 933, 936 (1962).

"When a client engages the services of a lawyer in a given piece of business he is entitled to feel that, until that business is finally disposed of in some manner, he has the undivided loyalty of the one upon whom he looks as his advocate and champion. If, as in this case, he is sued and his home attached by his own attorney, who is representing him in another matter, all feeling of loyalty is necessarily destroyed, and the profession is exposed to the charge that it is interested only in money." Grievance Comm. v. Rattner, 152 Conn. 59, 65, 203 A.2d 82, 84 (1964).

"One of the cardinal principles confronting every attorney in the representation of a client is the requirement of complete loyalty and service in good faith to the best of his ability. In a criminal case the client is entitled to a fair trial, but not a perfect one. These are fundamental requirements of due process under the Fourteenth Amendment. . . . The same principles are applicable in Sixth Amendment cases (not pertinent herein) and suggest that an attorney should have no conflict of interest and that he must devote his full and faithful efforts toward the defense of his client." Johns v. Smyth, 176 F.Supp. 949, 952 (E.D.Va.1959), *modified,* United States ex rel. Wilkins v. Banmiller, 205 F.Supp. 123, 128 n. 5 (E.D.Pa.1962), *aff'd,* 325 F.2d 514 (3d Cir. 1963), *cert. denied,* 379 U.S. 847, 13 L.Ed.2d 51, 85 S.Ct. 87 (1964).

[2] "Attorneys must not allow their private interests to conflict with those of their clients. . . . They owe their entire devotion to the interests of their clients." United States v. Anonymous, 215 F.Supp. 111, 113 (E.D. Tenn.1963).

"[T]he court [below] concluded that a firm may not accept any action against a person whom they are presently representing even though there is no relationship between the two cases. In arriving at this conclusion, the court cited an opinion of the Committee on Professional Ethics of the New York County Lawyers' Association which stated in part: 'While under the circumstances * * * there may be no actual conflict of interest * * * "maintenance of public confidence in the Bar requires an attorney who has accepted representation of a client to decline, while representing such client, any employment from an adverse party in any matter even though wholly unrelated to the original retainer." See Question and Answer No. 350, N.Y. County L. Ass'n, Questions and Answer No. 450 (June 21, 1956).' " Grievance Comm. v. Rattner, 152 Conn. 59, 65, 203 A.2d 82, 84 (1964).

[3] "Courts of equity will scrutinize with jealous vigilance transactions between parties occupying fiduciary relations toward each other. . . . A deed will not be held invalid, however, if made by the grantor with full knowledge of its nature and effect, and because of the deliberate, voluntary and intelligent desire of the grantor. . . . Where a fiduciary relation exists, the burden of proof is on the grantee or beneficiary of an instrument executed during the existence of such relationship to show the fairness of the transaction, that it was equitable and just and that it did not proceed from undue influence. . . . The same rule has application where an attorney engages in a transaction with a client during the existence of the relation and is benefited thereby. . . . Conversely, an attorney is not prohibited from dealing with his client or buying his property, and such contracts, if open, fair and honest, when deliberately made, are as valid as contracts between other parties. . . . [I]mportant factors in determining whether a transaction is fair include a showing by the fiduciary (1) that he made a full and frank

exceptional circumstances, a lawyer should insist that an instrument in which his client desires to name him beneficially be prepared by another lawyer selected by the client.[4]

EC 5–6 A lawyer should not consciously influence a client to name him as executor, trustee, or lawyer in an instrument. In those cases where a client wishes to name his lawyer as such, care should be taken by the lawyer to avoid even the appearance of impropriety.[5]

EC 5–7 The possibility of an adverse effect upon the exercise of free judgment by a lawyer on behalf of his client during litigation generally makes it undesirable for the lawyer to acquire a proprietary interest in the cause of his client or otherwise to become financially interested in the outcome of the litigation.[6] However, it is not improper for a lawyer to protect his right to collect a fee for his services by the assertion of legally permissible liens, even though by doing so he may acquire an interest in the outcome of litigation. Although a contingent fee arrangement[7] gives a lawyer a financial interest in the outcome of litigation, a reasonable contingent fee is permissible in civil cases because it may be the only means by which a layman can obtain the services of a lawyer of his choice. But a lawyer, because he is in a better position to evaluate a cause of action, should enter into a contingent fee arrangement only in those instances where the arrangement will be beneficial to the client.

EC 5–8 A financial interest in the outcome of litigation also results if monetary advances are made by the lawyer to his client.[8] Although this assistance generally is not encouraged, there are instances when it is not improper to make loans to a client. For example, the advancing or guaranteeing of payment of the costs and expenses of litigation by a lawyer may be the only way a client can enforce his cause of action,[9] but the ultimate liability for such costs and expenses must be that of the client.

EC 5–9 Occasionally a lawyer is called upon to decide in a particular case whether he will be a witness or an advocate. If a lawyer is both counsel and witness, he becomes more easily impeachable for interest and thus may be a less effective witness. Conversely, the opposing counsel may be handicapped in challenging the credibility of the lawyer when the lawyer also appears as an advocate in the case. An advocate who becomes a witness is in the unseemly and ineffective position of arguing his own credibility. The roles of an advocate and of a witness are inconsistent; the function of an advocate is to advance or argue the cause of another, while that of a witness is to state facts objectively.

EC 5–10 Problems incident to the lawyer-witness relationship arise at different stages; they relate either to whether a lawyer should accept employment or should withdraw from employment.[10] Regardless of when the problem arises, his decision is to be governed by the same basic considerations. It is not objectionable for a lawyer who is a potential witness to be an advocate if it is unlikely that he will be called as a witness because his testimony would be merely cumulative or if his testimony will relate only to an uncontested issue.[11] In the exceptional situation where it will be manifestly unfair to the client for the lawyer to refuse employment or to withdraw when he will likely be a witness on a contested issue, he may serve as advocate even though he may be a witness.[12] In making such decision, he should determine the personal or financial sacrifice of the client that may result from his refusal of employment or with-

disclosure of all the relevant information that he had; (2) that the consideration was adequate; and (3) that the principal had independent advice before completing the transaction." McFail v. Braden, 19 Ill.2d 108, 117–18, 166 N.E.2d 46, 52 (1960).

[4] See State ex rel. Nebraska State Bar Ass'n v. Richards, 165 Neb. 80, 94–95, 84 N.W.2d 136, 146 (1957).

[5] *See* ABA Canon 9.

[6] *See* ABA Canon 10.

[7] *See* Code of Professional Responsibility, EC 2–20.

[8] *See* ABA Canon 42.

[9] "*Rule 3a.* . . . A member of the State Bar shall not directly or indirectly pay or agree to pay, or represent or sanction the representation that he will pay, medical, hospital or nursing bills or other personal expenses incurred by or for a client, prospective or existing; provided this rule shall not prohibit a member:

"(1) with the consent of the client, from paying or agreeing to pay to third persons such expenses from funds collected or to be collected for the client; or

(2) after he has been employed, from lending money to his client upon the client's promise in writing to repay such loan; or

(3) from advancing the costs of prosecuting or defending a claim or action. Such costs within the meaning of this subparagraph (3) include all taxable costs or disbursements, costs or investigation and costs of obtaining and presenting evidence." Cal. Business and Professions Code § 6076 (West Supp.1967).

[10] "When a lawyer knows, prior to trial, that he will be a necessary witness, except as to merely formal matters such as identification or custody of a document or the like, neither he nor his firm or associates should conduct the trial. If, during the trial, he discovers that the ends of justice require his testimony, he should, from that point on, if feasible and not prejudicial to his client's case, leave further conduct of the trial to other counsel. If circumstances do not permit withdrawal from the conduct of the trial, the lawyer should not argue the credibility of his own testimony." *A Code of Trial Conduct: Promulgated by the American College of Trial Lawyers,* 43 A.B.A.J. 223, 224–25 (1957).

[11] *Cf.* Canon 19: "When a lawyer is a witness for his client, except as to merely formal matters, such as the attestation or custody of an instrument and the like, he should leave the trial of the case to other counsel."

[12] "It is the general rule that a lawyer may not testify in litigation in which he is an advocate unless circumstances arise which could not be anticipated and it is necessary to prevent a miscarriage of justice. In those rare cases where the testimony of an attorney is needed to protect his client's interests, it is not only proper but mandatory that it be forthcoming." Schwartz v. Wenger, 267 Minn. 40, 43–44, 124 N.W.2d 489, 492 (1963).

drawal therefrom, the materiality of his testimony, and the effectiveness of his representation in view of his personal involvement. In weighing these factors, it should be clear that refusal or withdrawal will impose an unreasonable hardship upon the client before the lawyer accepts or continues the employment.[13] Where the question arises, doubts should be resolved in favor of the lawyer testifying and against his becoming or continuing as an advocate.[14]

EC 5–11 A lawyer should not permit his personal interests to influence his advice relative to a suggestion by his client that additional counsel be employed.[15] In like manner, his personal interests should not deter him from suggesting that additional counsel be employed; on the contrary, he should be alert to the desirability of recommending additional counsel when, in his judgment, the proper representation of his client requires it. However, a lawyer should advise his client not to employ additional counsel suggested by the client if the lawyer believes that such employment would be a disservice to the client, and he should disclose the reasons for his belief.

EC 5–12 Inability of co-counsel to agree on a matter vital to the representation of their client requires that their disagreement be submitted by them jointly to their client for his resolution, and the decision of the client shall control the action to be taken.[16]

EC 5–13 A lawyer should not maintain membership in or be influenced by any organization of employees that undertakes to prescribe, direct, or suggest when or how he should fulfill his professional obligations to a person or organization that employs him as a lawyer. Although it is not necessarily improper for a lawyer employed by a corporation or similar entity to be a member of an organization of employees, he should be vigilant to safeguard his fidelity as a lawyer to his employer, free from outside influences.

Interests of Multiple Clients

EC 5–14 Maintaining the independence of professional judgment required of a lawyer precludes his acceptance or continuation of employment that will adversely affect his judgment on behalf of or dilute his loyalty to a client.[17] This problem arises whenever a lawyer is asked to represent two or more clients who may have differing interests, whether such interests be conflicting, inconsistent, diverse, or otherwise discordant.[18]

EC 5–15 If a lawyer is requested to undertake or to continue representation of multiple clients having potentially differing interests, he must weigh carefully the possibility that his judgment may be impaired or his loyalty divided if he accepts or continues the employment. He should resolve all doubts against the propriety of the representation. A lawyer should never represent in litigation multiple clients with differing interests,[19] and there are few situations in which he would be justified in representing in litigation multiple clients with potentially differing interests. If a lawyer accepted such employment and the interests did become actually differing, he would have to withdraw from employment with likelihood of resulting hardship on the clients; and for this reason it is preferable that he refuse the employment initially. On the other hand, there are many instances in which a lawyer may properly serve multiple clients having potentially differing interests in matters not involving litigation. If the interests vary only slightly, it is generally likely that

---

13 "The great weight of authority in this country holds that the attorney who acts as counsel and witness, in behalf of his client, in the same cause on a material matter, not of a merely formal character, and not in an emergency, but having knowledge that he would be required to be a witness in ample time to have secured other counsel and given up his service in the case, violates a highly important provision of the Code of Ethics and a rule of professional conduct, but does not commit a legal error in so testifying, as a result of which a new trial will be granted." Erwin M. Jennings Co. v. DiGenova, 107 Conn. 491, 499, 141 A. 866, 869 (1928).

14 "[C]ases may arise, and in practice often do arise, in which there would be a failure of justice should the attorney withhold his testimony. In such a case it would be a vicious professional sentiment which would deprive the client of the benefit of his attorney's testimony." Connolly v. Straw, 53 Wis. 645, 649, 11 N.W. 17, 19 (1881).

But see Canon 19: "Except when essential to the ends of justice, a lawyer should avoid testifying in court in behalf of his client."

15 *Cf.* ABA Canon 7.

16 *See* ABA Canon 7.

17 *See* ABA Canon 6; *cf. ABA Opinions* 261 (1944), 242 (1942), 142 (1935), and 30 (1931).

18 The ABA Canons speak of "conflicting interests" rather than "differing interests" but make no attempt to define such other than the statement in Canon 6: "Within the meaning of this canon, a lawyer represents conflicting interests when, in behalf of one client, it is his duty to contend for that which duty to another client requires him to oppose."

19 "Canon 6 of the Canons of Professional Ethics, adopted by the American Bar Association on September 30, 1937, and by the Pennsylvania Bar Association on January 7, 1938, provides in part that 'It is unprofessional to represent conflicting interests, except by express consent of all concerned given after a full disclosure of the facts. Within the meaning of this Canon, a lawyer represents conflicting interests when, in behalf of one client, it is his duty to contend for that which duty to another client requires him to oppose.' The full disclosure required by this canon contemplates that the possibly adverse effect of the conflict be fully explained by the attorney to the client to be affected and by him thoroughly understood. . . .

"The foregoing canon applies to cases where the circumstances are such that possibly conflicting interests may permissibly be represented by the same attorney. But manifestly, there are instances where the conflicts of interest are so critically adverse as not to admit of one attorney's representing both sides. Such is the situation which this record presents. No one could conscionably contend that the same attorney may represent both the plaintiff and defendant in an adversary action. Yet, that is what is being done in this case." Jedwabny v. Philadelphia Transportation Co., 390 Pa. 231, 235, 135 A.2d 252, 254 (1957), *cert. denied*, 355 U.S. 966, 2 L.Ed.2d 541, 78 S.Ct. 557 (1958).

the lawyer will not be subjected to an adverse influence and that he can retain his independent judgment on behalf of each client; and if the interests become differing, withdrawal is less likely to have a disruptive effect upon the causes of his clients.

EC 5-16 In those instances in which a lawyer is justified in representing two or more clients having differing interests, it is nevertheless essential that each client be given the opportunity to evaluate his need for representation free of any potential conflict and to obtain other counsel if he so desires.[20] Thus before a lawyer may represent multiple clients, he should explain fully to each client the implications of the common representation and should accept or continue employment only if the clients consent.[21] If there are present other circumstances that might cause any of the multiple clients to question the undivided loyalty of the lawyer, he should also advise all of the clients of those circumstances.[22]

EC 5-17 Typically recurring situations involving potentially differing interests are those in which a lawyer is asked to represent co-defendants in a criminal case, co-plaintiffs in a personal injury case, an insured and his insurer,[23] and beneficiaries of the estate of a decedent. Whether a lawyer can fairly and adequately protect the interests of multiple clients in these and similar situations depends upon an analysis of each case. In certain circumstances, there may exist little chance of the judgment of the lawyer being adversely affected by the slight possibility that the interests will become actually differing; in other circumstances, the chance of adverse effect upon his judgment is not unlikely.

EC 5-18 A lawyer employed or retained by a corporation or similar entity owes his allegiance to the entity and not to a stockholder, director, officer, employee, representative, or other person connected with the entity. In advising the entity, a lawyer should keep paramount its interests and his professional judgment should not be influenced by the personal desires of any person or organization. Occasionally a lawyer for an entity is requested by a stockholder, director, officer, employee, representative, or other person connected with the entity to represent him in an individual capacity; in such case the lawyer may serve the individual only if the lawyer is convinced that differing interests are not present.

EC 5-19 A lawyer may represent several clients whose interests are not actually or potentially differing. Nevertheless, he should explain any circumstances that might cause a client to question his undivided loyalty.[24] Regardless of the belief of a lawyer that he may properly represent multiple clients, he must defer to a client who holds the contrary belief and withdraw from representation of that client.

EC 5-20 A lawyer is often asked to serve as an impartial arbitrator or mediator in matters which involve present or former clients. He may serve in either capacity if he first discloses such present or former relationships. After a lawyer has undertaken to act as an impartial arbitrator or mediator, he should not thereafter represent in the dispute any of the parties involved.

Desires of Third Persons

EC 5-21 The obligation of a lawyer to exercise professional judgment solely on behalf of his client requires that he disregard the desires of others that might impair his free judgment.[25] The de-

---

20 "Glasser wished the benefit of the undivided assistance of counsel of his own choice. We think that such a desire on the part of an accused should be respected. Irrespective of any conflict of interest, the additional burden of representing another party may conceivably impair counsel's effectiveness.

"To determine the precise degree of prejudice sustained by Glasser as a result of the court's appointment of Stewart as counsel for Kretske is at once difficult and unnecessary. The right to have the assistance of counsel is too fundamental and absolute to allow courts to indulge in nice calculations as to the amount of prejudice arising from its denial." Glasser v. United States, 315 U.S. 60, 75–76, 86 L.Ed. 680, 702 S.Ct. 457, 467 (1942).

21 *See* ABA Canon 6.

22 *Id.*

23 *Cf. ABA Opinion* 282 (1950).

"When counsel, although paid by the casualty company, undertakes to represent the policyholder and files his notice of appearance, he owes to his client, the assured, an undeviating and single allegiance. His fealty embraces the requirement to produce in court all witnesses, fact and expert, who are available and necessary for the proper protection of the rights of his client. . . .

". . . The Canons of Professional Ethics make it pellucid that there are not two standards, one applying to counsel privately retained by a client, and the other to counsel paid by an insurance carrier." American Employers Ins. Co. v. Goble Aircraft Specialties, 205 Misc. 1066, 1075, 131 N.Y.S.2d 393, 401 (1954), *motion to withdraw appeal granted,* 1 App.Div.2d 1008, 154 N.Y.S.2d 835 (1956).

"[C]ounsel, selected by State Farm to defend Dorothy Walker's suit for $50,000 damages, was apprised by Walker that his earlier version of the accident was untrue and that actually the accident occurred because he lost control of his car in passing a Cadillac just ahead. At that point, Walker's counsel should have refused to participate further in view of the conflict of interest between Walker and State Farm. . . . Instead he participated in the ensuing deposition of the Walkers, even took an *ex parte* sworn statement from Mr. Walker in order to advise State Farm what action it should take, and later used the statement against Walker in the District Court. This action appears to contravene an Indiana attorney's duty 'at every peril to himself, to preserve the secrets of his client' . . . ." State Farm Mut. Auto Ins. Co. v. Walker, 382 F.2d 548, 552 (1967), *cert. denied,* 389 U.S. 1045, 19 L.Ed. 2d 837, 88 S.Ct. 789 (1968).

24 *See* ABA Canon 6.

25 *See* ABA Canon 35.

"Objection to the intervention of a lay intermediary, who may control litigation or otherwise interfere with the rendering of legal services in a confidential relationship, . . . derives from the element of pecuniary gain. Fearful of dangers thought to arise from that element, the courts of several States have sustained regulations aimed at these activities. We intimate no view one way or the other as to the merits of those decisions with respect to the particular arrangements against which they are disires of a third person will seldom adversely affect a lawyer unless that person is in a position to exert strong economic, political, or social pressures upon the lawyer. These influences are often subtle, and a lawyer must be alert to their existence. A lawyer subjected to outside pressures should make full disclosure of them to his client; [26] and if he or his client believes that the effectiveness of his representation has been or will be impaired thereby, the lawyer should take proper steps to withdraw from representation of his client.

EC 5–22 Economic, political, or social pressures by third persons are less likely to impinge upon the independent judgment of a lawyer in a matter in which he is compensated directly by his client and his professional work is exclusively with his client. On the other hand, if a lawyer is compensated from a source other than his client, he may feel a sense of responsibility to someone other than his client.

EC 5–23 A person or organization that pays or furnishes lawyers to represent others possesses a potential power to exert strong pressures against the independent judgment of those lawyers. Some employers may be interested in furthering their own economic, political, or social goals without regard to the professional responsibility of the lawyer to his individual client. Others may be far more concerned with establishment or extension of legal principles than in the immediate protection of the rights of the lawyer's individual client. On some occasions, decisions on priority of work may be made by the employer rather than the lawyer with the result that prosecution of work already undertaken for clients is postponed to their detriment. Similarly, an employer may seek, consciously or unconsciously, to further its own economic interests through the actions of the lawyers employed by it. Since a lawyer must always be free to exercise his professional judgment without regard to the interests or motives of a third person, the lawyer who is employed by one to represent another must constantly guard against erosion of his professional freedom.[27]

EC 5–24 To assist a lawyer in preserving his professional independence, a number of courses are available to him. For example, a lawyer should not practice with or in the form of a professional legal corporation, even though the corporate form is permitted by law,[28] if any director, officer, or stockholder of it is a non-lawyer. Although a lawyer may be employed by a business corporation with non-lawyers serving as directors or officers, and they necessarily have the right to make decisions of business policy, a lawyer must decline to accept direction of his professional judgment from any layman. Various types of legal aid offices are administered by boards of directors composed of lawyers and laymen. A lawyer should not accept employment from such an organization unless the board sets only broad policies and there is no interference in the relationship of the lawyer and the individual client he serves. Where a lawyer is employed by an organization, a written agreement that defines the relationship between him and the organization and provides for his independence is desirable since it may serve to prevent misunderstanding as to their respective roles. Although other innovations in the means of supplying legal counsel may develop, the responsibility of the lawyer to maintain his professional independence remains constant, and the legal profession must insure that changing circumstances do not result in loss of the professional independence of the lawyer.

DISCIPLINARY RULES

DR 5–101 Refusing Employment When the Interests of the Lawyer May Impair His Independent Professional Judgment.

(A) Except with the consent of his client after full disclosure, a lawyer shall not accept employment if the exercise of his professional judgment on behalf of his client will be or reasonably may be affected by his own financial, business, property, or personal interests.[29]

---

rected. It is enough that the superficial resemblance in form between those arrangements and that at bar cannot obscure the vital fact that here the entire arrangement employs constitutionally privileged means of expression to secure constitutionally guaranteed civil rights." NAACP v. Button, 371 U.S. 415, 441–42, 9 L.Ed.2d 405, 423–24, 83 S.Ct. 328, 342–43 (1963).

[26] *Cf.* ABA Canon 38.

[27] "Certainly it is true that 'the professional relationship between an attorney and his client is highly personal, involving an intimate appreciation of each individual client's particular problem.' And this Committee does not condone practices which interfere with that relationship. However, the mere fact the lawyer is actually paid by some entity other than the client does not affect that relationship, so long as the lawyer is selected by and is directly responsible to the client. See Informal Opinions 469 and 679. Of course, as the latter decision points out, there must be full disclosure of the arrangement by the attorney to the client. . . ." *ABA Opinion* 320 (1968).

"[A] third party may pay the cost of legal services as long as control remains in the client and the responsibility of the lawyer is solely to the client. Informal Opinions 469 ad [*sic*] 679. *See also Opinion* 237." *Id.*

[28] *ABA Opinion* 303 (1961) recognized that "[s]tatutory provisions now exist in several states which are designed to make [the practice of law in a form that will be classified as a corporation for federal income tax purposes] legally possible, either as a result of lawyers incorporating or forming associations with various corporate characteristics."

[29] *Cf.* ABA Canon 6 and *ABA Opinions* 181 (1938), 104 (1934), 103 (1933), 72 (1932), 50 (1931), 49 (1931), and 33 (1931).

"New York County [Opinion] 203. . . . [A lawyer] should not advise a client to employ an investment company in which he is interested, without informing him of this." Drinker, LEGAL ETHICS 956 (1953).

"In *Opinions* 72 and 49 this Committee held: The relations of partners in a law firm are such that neither the firm nor any member or associate thereof, may accept any professional employment which any member of the firm cannot properly accept.

"In *Opinion* 16 this Committee held that a member of a law firm could not represent a defendant in a criminal case which was being prosecuted by another member of

(B) A lawyer shall not accept employment in contemplated or pending litigation if he knows or it is obvious that he or a lawyer in his firm ought to be called as a witness, except that he may undertake the employment and he or a lawyer in his firm may testify:

(1) If the testimony will relate solely to an uncontested matter.

(2) If the testimony will relate solely to a matter of formality and there is no reason to believe that substantial evidence will be offered in opposition to the testimony.

(3) If the testimony will relate solely to the nature and value of legal services rendered in the case by the lawyer or his firm to the client.

(4) As to any matter, if refusal would work a substantial hardship on the client because of the distinctive value of the lawyer or his firm as counsel in the particular case.

DR 5-102 Withdrawal as Counsel When the Lawyer Becomes a Witness.[30]

(A) If, after undertaking employment in contemplated or pending litigation, a lawyer learns or it is obvious that he or a lawyer in his firm ought to be called as a witness on behalf of his client, he shall withdraw from the conduct of the trial and his firm, if any, shall not continue representation in the trial, except that he may continue the representation and he or a lawyer in his firm may testify in the circumstances enumerated in DR 5-101(B) (1) through (4).

(B) If, after undertaking employment in contemplated or pending litigation, a lawyer learns or it is obvious that he or a lawyer in his firm may be called as a witness other than on behalf of his client, he may continue the representation until it is apparent that his testimony is or may be prejudicial to his client.[31]

DR 5-103 Avoiding Acquisition of Interest in Litigation.

(A) A lawyer shall not acquire a proprietary interest in the cause of action or subject matter of litigation he is conducting for a client,[32] except that he may:

(1) Acquire a lien granted by law to secure his fee or expenses.

(2) Contract with a client for a reasonable contingent fee in a civil case.[33]

(B) While representing a client in connection with contemplated or pending litigation, a lawyer shall not advance or guarantee financial assistance to his client,[34] except that a lawyer may advance or guarantee the expenses of litigation, including court costs, expenses of investigation, expenses of medical examination, and costs of obtaining and presenting evidence, provided the client remains ultimately liable for such expenses.

DR 5-104 Limiting Business Relations with a Client.

(A) A lawyer shall not enter into a business transaction with a client if they have differing interests therein and if the client expects the lawyer to exercise his professional judgment therein for the protection of the client, unless the client has consented after full disclosure.

(B) Prior to conclusion of all aspects of the matter giving rise to his employment, a lawyer shall not enter into any arrangement or understanding with a client or a prospective client by which he acquires an interest in publication rights with respect to the subject matter of his employment or proposed employment.

DR 5-105 Refusing to Accept or Continue Employment if the Interests of Another Client May Impair the Independent Professional Judgment of the Lawyer.

(A) A lawyer shall decline proffered employment if the exercise of his independent professional judgment in behalf of a client will be or is likely to be adversely affected by the acceptance of the proffered employment,[35] or if it would be likely to involve him in representing differing interests, except to the extent permitted under DR 5-105(C).[36]

---

the firm who was public prosecuting attorney. The Opinion stated that it was clearly unethical for one member of the firm to oppose the interest of the state while another member represented those interests . . . . Since the prosecutor himself could not represent both the public and the defendant, no member of his law firm could either." *ABA Opinion* 296 (1959).

30 *Cf.* ABA Canon 19 and *ABA Opinions* 220 (1941), 185 (1938), 50 (1931), and 33 (1931); *but cf.* Erwin M. Jennings Co. v. DiGenova, 107 Conn. 491, 498-99, 141 A. 866, 868 (1928).

31 "This *Canon* [19] *of Ethics* needs no elaboration to be applied to the facts here. Apparently, the object of this precept is to avoid putting a lawyer in the obviously embarrassing predicament of testifying and then having to argue the credibility and effect of his own testimony. It was not designed to permit a lawyer to call opposing counsel as a witness and thereby disqualify him as counsel." Galarowicz v. Ward, 119 Utah 611, 620, 230 P.2d 576, 580 (1951).

32 ABA Canon 10 and *ABA Opinions* 279 (1949), 246 (1942), and 176 (1938).

33 *See* Code of Professional Responsibility, DR 2-106(C).

34 *See* ABA Canon 42; *cf. ABA Opinion* 288 (1954).

35 *See* ABA Canon 6; *cf. ABA Opinions* 167 (1937), 60 (1931), and 40 (1931).

36 *ABA Opinion* 247 (1942) held that an attorney could not investigate a night club shooting on behalf of one of the owner's liability insurers, obtaining the cooperation of the owner, and later represent the injured patron in an action against the owner and a different insurance com-

(B) A lawyer shall not continue multiple employment if the exercise of his independent professional judgment in behalf of a client will be or is likely to be adversely affected by his representation of another client, or if it would be likely to involve him in representing differing interests, except to the extent permitted under DR 5–105(C).[37]

(C) In the situations covered by DR 5–105(A) and (B), a lawyer may represent multiple clients if it is obvious that he can adequately represent the interest of each and if each consents to the representation after full disclosure of the possible effect of such representation on the exercise of his independent professional judgment on behalf of each.

(D) If a lawyer is required to decline employment or to withdraw from employment under a Disciplinary Rule, no partner or associate, or any other lawyer affiliated with him or his firm may accept or continue such employment.

DR 5–106 Settling Similar Claims of Clients.[38]

(A) A lawyer who represents two or more clients shall not make or participate in the making of an aggregate settlement of the claims of or against his clients, unless each client has consented to the settlement after being advised of the existence and nature of all the claims involved in the proposed settlement, of the total amount of the settlement, and of the participation of each person in the settlement.

DR 5–107 Avoiding Influence by Others Than the Client.

(A) Except with the consent of his client after full disclosure, a lawyer shall not:

(1) Accept compensation for his legal services from one other than his client.

(2) Accept from one other than his client any thing of value related to his representation of or his employment by his client.[39]

(B) A lawyer shall not permit a person who recommends, employs, or pays him to render legal services for another to direct or regulate his professional judgment in rendering such legal services.[40]

(C) A lawyer shall not practice with or in the form of a professional corporation or association authorized to practice law for a profit, if:

(1) A non-lawyer owns any interest therein,[41] except that a fiduciary representative of the estate of a lawyer may hold the stock or interest of the lawyer for a reasonable time during administration;

(2) A non-lawyer is a corporate director or officer thereof; [42] or

(3) A non-lawyer has the right to direct or control the professional judgment of a lawyer.[43]

CANON 6

A Lawyer Should Represent a Client Competently

ETHICAL CONSIDERATIONS

EC 6–1 Because of his vital role in the legal process, a lawyer should act with competence and proper care in representing clients. He should strive to become and remain proficient in his practice [1] and should accept employment only in mat-

---

pany unless the attorney obtain the "express consent of all concerned given after a full disclosure of the facts," since to do so would be to represent conflicting interests.

See ABA Opinions 247 (1942), 224 (1941), 222 (1941), 218 (1941), 112 (1934), 83 (1932), and 86 (1932).

[37] *Cf. ABA Opinions* 231 (1941) and 160 (1936).

[38] *Cf. ABA Opinions* 243 (1942) and 235 (1941).

[39] *See* ABA Canon 38.

"A lawyer who receives a commission (whether delayed or not) from a title insurance company or guaranty fund for recommending or selling the insurance to his client, or for work done for the client or the company, without either fully disclosing to the client his financial interest in the transaction, or crediting the client's bill with the amount thus received, is guilty of unethical conduct." *ABA Opinion* 304 (1962).

[40] *See* ABA Canon 35; *cf. ABA Opinion* 237 (1941).

"When the lay forwarder, as agent for the creditor, forwards a claim to an attorney, the direct relationship of attorney and client shall then exist between the attorney and the creditor, and the forwarder shall not interpose itself as an intermediary to control the activities of the attorney." *ABA Opinion* 294 (1958).

[41] "Permanent beneficial and voting rights in the organization set up to practice law, whatever its form, must be restricted to lawyers while the organization is engaged in the practice of law." *ABA Opinion* 303 (1961).

[42] "*Canon 33* . . . promulgates underlying principles that must be observed no matter in what form of organization lawyers practice law. Its requirement that no person shall be admitted or held out as a practitioner or member who is not a member of the legal profession duly authorized to practice, and amenable to professional discipline, makes it clear that any centralized management must be in lawyers to avoid a violation of this Canon." *ABA Opinion* 303 (1961).

[43] "There is no intervention of any lay agency between lawyer and client when centralized management provided only by lawyers may give guidance or direction to the services being rendered by a lawyer-member of the organization to a client. The language in *Canon 35* that a lawyer should avoid all relations which direct the performance of his duties by or in the interest of an intermediary refers to lay intermediaries and not lawyer intermediaries with whom he is associated in the practice of law." *ABA Opinion* 303 (1961).

[1] "[W]hen a citizen is faced with the need for a lawyer, he wants, and is entitled to, the best informed counsel he can obtain. Changing times produce changes in our laws and legal procedures. The natural complexities of law require continuing intensive study by a lawyer if he is to render his clients a maximum of efficient service. And, in so doing, he maintains the high standards of the legal profession; and he also increases respect and con-

ters which he is or intends to become competent to handle.

EC 6–2 A lawyer is aided in attaining and maintaining his competence by keeping abreast of current legal literature and developments, participating in continuing legal education programs,[2] concentrating in particular areas of the law, and by utilizing other available means. He has the additional ethical obligation to assist in improving the legal profession, and he may do so by participating in bar activities intended to advance the quality and standards of members of the profession. Of particular importance is the careful training of his younger associates and the giving of sound guidance to all lawyers who consult him. In short, a lawyer should strive at all levels to aid the legal profession in advancing the highest possible standards of integrity and competence and to meet those standards himself.

EC 6–3 While the licensing of a lawyer is evidence that he has met the standards then prevailing for admission to the bar, a lawyer generally should not accept employment in any area of the law in which he is not qualified.[3] However, he may accept such employment if in good faith he expects to become qualified through study and investigation, as long as such preparation would not result in unreasonable delay or expense to his client. Proper preparation and representation may require the association by the lawyer of professionals in other disciplines. A lawyer offered employment in a matter in which he is not and does not expect to become so qualified should either decline the employment or, with the consent of his client, accept the employment and associate a lawyer who is competent in the matter.[4]

EC 6–4 Having undertaken representation, a lawyer should use proper care to safeguard the interests of his client. If a lawyer has accepted employment in a matter beyond his competence but in which he expected to become competent, he should diligently undertake the work and study necessary to qualify himself. In addition to being qualified to handle a particular matter, his obligation to his client requires him to prepare adequately for and give appropriate attention to his legal work.

EC 6–5 A lawyer should have pride in his professional endeavors. His obligation to act competently calls for higher motivation than that arising from fear of civil liability or disciplinary penalty.

EC 6–6 A lawyer should not seek, by contract or other means, to limit his individual liability to his client for his malpractice. A lawyer who handles the affairs of his client properly has no need to attempt to limit his liability for his professional activities and one who does not handle the affairs of his client properly should not be permitted to do so. A lawyer who is a stockholder in or is associated with a professional legal corporation may, however, limit his liability for malpractice of his associates in the corporation, but only to the extent permitted by law.[5]

DISCIPLINARY RULES

DR 6–101 Failing to Act Competently.

(A) A lawyer shall not:

(1) Handle a legal matter which he knows or should know that he is not competent to handle, without associating with him a lawyer who is competent to handle it.

(2) Handle a legal matter without preparation adequate in the circumstances.

(3) Neglect a legal matter entrusted to him.[6]

---

fidence by the general public." Rochelle & Payne, *The Struggle for Public Understanding*, 25 Texas B.J. 109, 160 (1962).

"We have undergone enormous changes in the last fifty years within the lives of most of the adults living today who may be seeking advice. Most of these changes have been accompanied by changes and developments in the law. . . . Every practicing lawyer encounters these problems and is often perplexed with his own inability to keep up, not only with changes in the law, but also with changes in the lives of his clients and their legal problems.

"To be sure, no client has a right to expect that his lawyer will have all of the answers at the end of his tongue or even in the back of his head at all times. But the client does have the right to expect that the lawyer will have devoted his time and energies to maintaining and improving his competence to know where to look for the answers, to know how to deal with the problems, and to know how to advise to the best of his legal talents and abilities." Levy & Sprague, *Accounting and Law: Is Dual Practice in the Public Interest?*, 52 A.B.A.J. 1110, 1112 (1966).

[2] "The whole purpose of continuing legal education, so enthusiastically supported by the ABA, is to make it possible for lawyers to make themselves better lawyers. But there are no nostrums for proficiency in the law; it must come through the hard work of the lawyer himself. To the extent that that work, whether it be in attending institutes or lecture courses, in studying after hours or in the actual day in and day out practice of his profession, can be concentrated within a limited field, the greater the proficiency and expertness that can be developed." *Report of the Special Committee on Specialization and Specialized Legal Education*, 79 A.B.A.Rep. 582, 588 (1954).

[3] "If the attorney is not competent to skillfully and properly perform the work, he should not undertake the service." Degen v. Steinbrink, 202 App.Div. 477, 481, 195 N.Y.S. 810, 814 (1922), *aff'd mem.*, 236 N.Y. 669, 142 N.E. 328 (1923).

[4] *Cf. ABA Opinion* 232 (1941).

[5] *See ABA Opinion* 303 (1961); *cf.* Code of Professional Responsibility, EC 2–11.

[6] The annual report for 1967–1968 of the Committee on Grievances of the Association of the Bar of the City of New York showed a receipt of 2,232 complaints; of the 828 offenses against clients, 76 involved conversion, 49 involved "overreaching," and 452, or more than half of all such offenses, involved neglect. *Annual Report of the Committee on Grievances of the Association of the Bar of the City of New York*, N.Y.L.J., Sept. 12, 1968, at 4, col. 5.

DR 6–102 Limiting Liability to Client.

(A) A lawyer shall not attempt to exonerate himself from or limit his liability to his client for his personal malpractice.

CANON 7

A Lawyer Should Represent a Client Zealously Within the Bounds of the Law

ETHICAL CONSIDERATIONS

EC 7–1 The duty of a lawyer, both to his client [1] and to the legal system, is to represent his client zealously [2] within the bounds of the law,[3] which includes Disciplinary Rules and enforceable professional regulations.[4] The professional responsibility of a lawyer derives from his membership in a profession which has the duty of assisting members of the public to secure and protect available legal rights and benefits. In our government of laws and not of men, each member of our society is entitled to have his conduct judged and regulated in accordance with the law; [5] to seek

---

[1] "The right to be heard would be, in many cases, of little avail if it did not comprehend the right to be heard by counsel. Even the intelligent and educated layman has small and sometimes no skill in the science of law." Powell v. Alabama, 287 U.S. 45, 68–69, 77 L.Ed. 158, 170, 53 S.Ct. 55, 64 (1932).

[2] *Cf.* ABA Canon 4.

"At times . . . [the tax lawyer] will be wise to discard some arguments and he should exercise discretion to emphasize the arguments which in his judgment are most likely to be persuasive. But this process involves legal judgment rather than moral attitudes. The tax lawyer should put aside private disagreements with Congressional and Treasury policies. His own notions of policy, and his personal view of what the law should be, are irrelevant. The job entrusted to him by his client is to use all his learning and ability to protect his client's rights, not to help in the process of promoting a better tax system. The tax lawyer need not accept his client's economic and social opinions, but the client is paying for technical attention and undivided concentration upon his affairs. He is equally entitled to performance unfettered by his attorney's economic and social predilections." Paul, *The Lawyer as a Tax Adviser,* 25 Rocky Mt. L. Rev. 412, 418 (1953).

[3] *See* ABA Canons 15 and 32.

ABA Canon 5, although only speaking of one accused of crime, imposes a similar obligation on the lawyer: "[T]he lawyer is bound, by all fair and honorable means, to present every defense that the law of the land permits, to the end that no person may be deprived of life or liberty, but by due process of law."

"Any persuasion or pressure on the advocate which deters him from planning and carrying out the litigation on the basis of 'what, within the framework of the law, is best for my client's interest?' interferes with the obligation to represent the client fully within the law.

"This obligation, in its fullest sense, is the heart of the adversary process. Each attorney, as an advocate, acts for and seeks that which in his judgment is best for his client, within the bounds authoritatively established. The advocate does not *decide* what is just in this case—he would be usurping the function of the judge and jury—he acts for and seeks for his client that which he is entitled to under the law. He can do no less and properly represent the client." Thode, *The Ethical Standard for the Advocate,* 39 Texas L.Rev. 575, 584 (1961).

"The [Texas public opinion] survey indicates that distrust of the lawyer can be traced directly to certain factors. Foremost of these is a basic misunderstanding of the function of the lawyer as an advocate in an adversary system.

"Lawyers are accused of taking advantage of 'loopholes' and 'technicalities' to win. Persons who make this charge are unaware, or do not understand, that the lawyer is hired to win, and if he does not exercise every legitimate effort in his client's behalf, then he is betraying a sacred trust." Rochelle & Payne, *The Struggle for Public Understanding,* 25 Texas B.J. 109, 159 (1962).

"The importance of the attorney's undivided allegiance and faithful service to one accused of crime, irrespective of the attorney's personal opinion as to the guilt of his client, lies in Canon 5 of the American Bar Association Canon of Ethics.

"The difficulty lies, of course, in ascertaining whether the attorney has been guilty of an error of judgment, such as an election with respect to trial tactics, or has otherwise been actuated by his conscience or belief that his client should be convicted in any event. All too frequently courts are called upon to review actions of defense counsel which are, at the most, errors of judgment, not properly reviewable on habeas corpus unless the trial is a farce and a mockery of justice which requires the court to intervene. . . . But when defense counsel, in a truly adverse proceeding, admits that his conscience would not permit him to adopt certain customary trial procedures, this extends beyond the realm of judgment and strongly suggests an invasion of constitutional rights." Johns v. Smyth, 176 F.Supp. 949, 952 (E.D.Va.1959), *modified,* United States ex rel. Wilkins v. Banmiller, 205 F.Supp. 123, 128, n. 5 (E.D.Pa.1962), *aff'd,* 325 F.2d 514 (3d Cir. 1963), *cert. denied,* 379 U.S. 847, 13 L.Ed.2d 51, 85 S.Ct. 87 (1964).

"The adversary system in law administration bears a striking resemblance to the competitive economic system In each we assume that the individual through partisanship or through self-interest will strive mightily for his side, and that kind of striving we must have. But neither system would be tolerable without restraints and modifications, and at times without outright departures from the system itself. Since the legal profession is entrusted with the system of law administration, a part of its task is to develop in its members appropriate restraints without impairing the values of partisan striving. An accompanying task is to aid in the modification of the adversary system or departure from it in areas to which the system is unsuited." Cheatham, *The Lawyer's Role and Surroundings,* 25 Rocky Mt. L.Rev. 405, 410 (1953).

[4] "Rule 4.15 prohibits, in the pursuit of a client's cause, 'any manner of fraud or chicane'; Rule 4.22 requires 'candor and fairness' in the conduct of the lawyer, and forbids the making of knowing misquotations; Rule 4.47 provides that a lawyer 'should always maintain his integrity,' and generally forbids all misconduct injurious to the interests of the public, the courts, or his clients, and acts contrary to 'justice, honesty, modesty or good morals.' Our Commissioner has accurately paraphrased these rules as follows: 'An attorney does not have the duty to do all and whatever he can that may enable him to win his client's cause or to further his client's interest. His duty and efforts in these respects, although they should be prompted by his "entire devotion" to the interest of his client, must be within and not without the bounds of the law.' " In re Wines, 370 S.W.2d 328, 333 (Mo.1963).

See Note, 38 Texas L.Rev. 107, 110 (1959).

[5] "Under our system of government the process of adjudication is surrounded by safeguards evolved from centuries of experience. These safeguards are not designed merely to lend formality and decorum to the trial of causes. They are predicated on the assumption that to se-

any lawful objective[6] through legally permissible means;[7] and to present for adjudication any lawful claim, issue, or defense.

EC 7–2 The bounds of the law in a given case are often difficult to ascertain.[8] The language of legislative enactments and judicial opinions may be uncertain as applied to varying factual situations. The limits and specific meaning of apparently relevant law may be made doubtful by changing or developing constitutional interpretations, inadequately expressed statutes or judicial opinions, and changing public and judicial attitudes. Certainty of law ranges from well-settled rules through areas of conflicting authority to areas without precedent.

EC 7–3 Where the bounds of law are uncertain, the action of a lawyer may depend on whether he is serving as advocate or adviser. A lawyer may serve simultaneously as both advocate and adviser, but the two roles are essentially different.[9] In asserting a position on behalf of his client, an advocate for the most part deals with past conduct and must take the facts as he finds them. By contrast, a lawyer serving as adviser primarily assists his client in determining the course of future conduct and relationships. While serving as advocate, a lawyer should resolve in favor of his client doubts as to the bounds of the law.[10] In serving a client as adviser, a lawyer in appropriate circumstances should give his professional opinion as to what the ultimate decisions of the courts would likely be as to the applicable law.

Duty of the Lawyer to a Client

EC 7–4 The advocate may urge any permissible construction of the law favorable to his client, without regard to his professional opinion as to the likelihood that the construction will ultimately prevail.[11] His conduct is within the bounds of the law, and therefore permissible, if the position taken is supported by the law or is supportable by a good faith argument for an extension, modification, or reversal of the law. However, a lawyer is not justified in asserting a position in litigation that is frivolous.[12]

---

cure for any controversy a truly informed and dispassionate decision is a difficult thing, requiring for its achievement a special summoning and organization of human effort and the adoption of measures to exclude the biases and prejudgments that have free play outside the courtroom. All of this goes for naught if the man with an unpopular cause is unable to find a competent lawyer courageous enough to represent him. His chance to have his day in court loses much of its meaning if his case is handicapped from the outset by the very kind of prejudgment our rules of evidence and procedure are intended to prevent." *Professional Responsibility: Report of the Joint Conference,* 44 A.B.A.J. 1159, 1216 (1958).

6 "[I]t is . . . [the tax lawyer's] positive duty to show the client how to avail himself to the full of what the law permits. He is not the keeper of the Congressional conscience." Paul, *The Lawyer as a Tax Adviser,* 25 Rocky Mt.L.Rev. 412, 418 (1953).

7 *See* ABA Canons 15 and 30.

8 "The fact that it desired to evade the law, as it is called, is immaterial, because the very meaning of a line in the law is that you intentionally may go as close to it as you can if you do not pass it . . . . It is a matter of proximity and degree as to which minds will differ . . . ." Justice Holmes, in Superior Oil Co. v. Mississippi, 280 U.S. 390, 395–96, 74 L.Ed. 504, 508, 50 S.Ct. 169, 170 (1930).

9 "Today's lawyers perform two distinct types of functions, and our ethical standards should, but in the main do not, recognize these two functions. Judge Philbrick McCoy recently reported to the American Bar Association the need for a reappraisal of the Canons in light of the new and distinct function of counselor, as distinguished from advocate, which today predominates in the legal profession. . . .

". . . In the first place, any revision of the canons must take into account and speak to this new and now predominant function of the lawyer. . . . It is beyond the scope of this paper to discuss the ethical standards to be applied to the counselor except to state that in my opinion such standards should require a greater recognition and protection for the interest of the public generally than is presently expressed in the canons. Also, the counselor's obligation should extend to requiring him to inform and to impress upon the client a just solution of the problem, considering all interests involved." Thode, *The Ethical Standard for the Advocate,* 39 Texas L.Rev. 575, 578–79 (1961).

"The man who has been called into court to answer for his own actions is entitled to fair hearing. Partisan advocacy plays its essential part in such a hearing, and the lawyer pleading his client's case may properly present it in the most favorable light. A similar resolution of doubts in one direction becomes inappropriate when the lawyer acts as counselor. The reasons that justify and even require partisan advocacy in the trial of a cause do not grant any license to the lawyer to participate as legal advisor in a line of conduct that is immoral, unfair, or of doubtful legality. In saving himself from this unworthy involvement, the lawyer cannot be guided solely by an unreflective inner sense of good faith; he must be at pains to preserve a sufficient detachment from his client's interests so that he remains capable of a sound and objective appraisal of the propriety of what his client proposes to do." *Professional Responsibility: Report of the Joint Conference,* 44 A.B.A.J. 1159, 1161 (1958).

10 "[A] lawyer who is asked to advise his client . . . may freely urge the statement of positions most favorable to the client just as long as there is reasonable basis for those positions." *ABA Opinion 314 (1965).*

11 "The lawyer . . . is not an umpire, but an advocate. He is under no duty to refrain from making every proper argument in support of any legal point because he is not convinced of its inherent soundness. . . . His personal belief in the soundness of his cause or of the authorities supporting it, is irrelevant." *ABA Opinion* 280 (1949).

"Counsel apparently misconceived his role. It was his duty to honorably present his client's contentions in the light most favorable to his client. Instead he presumed to advise the court as to the validity and sufficiency of prisoner's motion, by letter. We therefore conclude that the prisoner had no effective assistance of counsel and remand this case to the District Court with instructions to set aside the Judgment, appoint new counsel to represent the prisoner if he makes no objection thereto, and proceed anew." McCartney v. United States, 343 F.2d 471, 472 (9th Cir. 1965).

12 "Here the court-appointed counsel had the transcript but refused to proceed with the appeal because he found no merit in it. . . . We cannot say that there was a finding of frivolity by either of the California courts or

EC 7-5 A lawyer as adviser furthers the interest of his client by giving his professional opinion as to what he believes would likely be the ultimate decision of the courts on the matter at hand and by informing his client of the practical effect of such decision.[13] He may continue in the representation of his client even though his client has elected to pursue a course of conduct contrary to the advice of the lawyer so long as he does not thereby knowingly assist the client to engage in illegal conduct or to take a frivolous legal position. A lawyer should never encourage or aid his client to commit criminal acts or counsel his client on how to violate the law and avoid punishment therefor.[14]

EC 7-6 Whether the proposed action of a lawyer is within the bounds of the law may be a perplexing question when his client is contemplating a course of conduct having legal consequence that vary according to the client's intent, motive, or desires at the time of the action. Often a lawyer is asked to assist his client in developing evidence relevant to the state of mind of the client at a particular time. He may properly assist his client in the development and preservation of evidence of existing motive, intent, or desire; obviously, he may not do anything furthering the creation or preservation of false evidence. In many cases a lawyer may not be certain as to the state of mind of his client, and in those situations he should resolve reasonable doubts in favor of his client.

EC 7-7 In certain areas of legal representation not affecting the merits of the cause or substantially prejudicing the rights of a client, a lawyer is entitled to make decisions on his own. But otherwise the authority to make decisions is exclusively that of the client and, if made within the framework of the law, such decisions are binding on his lawyer. As typical examples in civil cases, it is for the client to decide whether he will accept a settlement offer or whether he will waive his right to plead an affirmative defense. A defense lawyer in a criminal case has the duty to advise his client fully on whether a particular plea to a charge appears to be desirable and as to the prospects of success on appeal, but it is for the client to decide what plea should be entered and whether an appeal should be taken.[15]

EC 7-8 A lawyer should exert his best efforts to insure that decisions of his client are made only after the client has been informed of relevant considerations. A lawyer ought to initiate this decision-making process if the client does not do so. Advice of a lawyer to his client need not be confined to purely legal considerations.[16] A lawyer should advise his client of the possible effect of each legal alternative.[17] A lawyer should bring to bear upon this decision-making process the fullness of his experience as well as his objective viewpoint.[18] In assisting his client to reach a

---

that counsel acted in any greater capacity than merely as *amicus curiae* which was condemned in *Ellis, supra*. Hence California's procedure did not furnish petitioner with counsel acting in the role of an advocate nor did it provide that full consideration and resolution of the matter as is obtained when counsel is acting in that capacity. . . .

"The constitutional requirement of substantial equality and fair process can only be attained where counsel acts in the role of an active advocate in behalf of his client, as opposed to that of *amicus curiae*. The no-merit letter and the procedure it triggers do not reach that dignity. Counsel should, and can with honor and without conflict, be of more assistance to his client and to the court. His role as advocate requires that he support his client's appeal to the best of his ability. Of course, if counsel finds his case to be wholly frivolous, after a conscientious examination of it, he should so advise the court and request permission to withdraw. That request must, however, be accompanied by a brief referring to anything in the record that might arguably support the appeal. A copy of counsel's brief should be furnished the indigent and time allowed him to raise any points that he chooses; the court—not counsel—then proceeds, after a full examination of all the proceedings, to decide whether the case is wholly frivolous. If it so finds it may grant counsel's request to withdraw and dismiss the appeal insofar as federal requirements are concerned, or proceed to a decision on the merits, if state law so requires. On the other hand, if it finds any of the legal points arguable on their merits (and therefore not frivolous) it must, prior to decision, afford the indigent the assistance of counsel to argue the appeal." Anders v. California, 386 U.S. 738, 744, 18 L.Ed. 2d 493, 498, 87 S.Ct. 1396, 1399–1400 (1967), *rehearing denied,* 388 U.S. 924, 18 L.Ed.2d 1377, 87 S.Ct. 2094 (1967).

See Paul, *The Lawyer As a Tax Adviser*, 25 Rocky Mt. L.Rev. 412, 432 (1953).

[13] *See* ABA Canon 32.

[14] "For a lawyer to represent a syndicate notoriously engaged in the violation of the law for the purpose of advising the members how to break the law and at the same time escape it, is manifestly improper. While a lawyer may see to it that anyone accused of crime, no matter how serious and flagrant, has a fair trial, and present all available defenses, he may not co-operate in planning violations of the law. There is a sharp distinction, of course, between advising what can lawfully be done and advising how unlawful acts can be done in a way to avoid conviction. Where a lawyer accepts a retainer from an organization, known to be unlawful, and agrees in advance to defend its members when from time to time they are accused of crime arising out of its unlawful activities, this is equally improper."

"See also *Opinion 155.*" *ABA Opinion* 281 (1952).

[15] *See* ABA Special Committee on Minimum Standards for the Administration of Criminal Justice, *Standards Relating to Pleas of Guilty* pp. 69–70 (1968).

[16] "First of all, a truly great lawyer is a wise counselor to all manner of men in the varied crises of their lives when they most need disinterested advice. Effective counseling necessarily involves a thoroughgoing knowledge of the principles of the law not merely as they appear in the books but as they actually operate in action." Vanderbilt, *The Five Functions of the Lawyer: Service to Clients and the Public,* 40 A.B.A.J. 31 (1954).

[17] "A lawyer should endeavor to obtain full knowledge of his client's cause before advising thereon. . . . ." ABA Canon 8.

[18] "[I]n devising charters of collaborative effort the lawyer often acts where all of the affected parties are present as participants. But the lawyer also performs a similar function in situations where this is not so, as, for example, in planning estates and drafting wills. Here the instrument defining the terms of collaboration may affect persons not present and often not born. Yet here, too, the good lawyer does not serve merely as a legal conduit for his client's desires, but as a wise counselor, ex-

proper decision, it is often desirable for a lawyer to point out those factors which may lead to a decision that is morally just as well as legally permissible.[19] He may emphasize the possibility of harsh consequences that might result from assertion of legally permissible positions. In the final analysis, however, the lawyer should always remember that the decision whether to forego legally available objectives or methods because of non-legal factors is ultimately for the client and not for himself, In the event that the client in a non-adjudicatory matter insists upon a course of conduct that is contrary to the judgment and advice of the lawyer but not prohibited by Disciplinary Rules, the lawyer may withdraw from the employment.[20]

EC 7–9 In the exercise of his professional judgment on those decisions which are for his determination in the handling of a legal matter,[21] a lawyer should always act in a manner consistent with the best interests of his client.[22] However, when an action in the best interest of his client seems to him to be unjust, he may ask his client for permission to forego such action.[23]

EC 7–10 The duty of a lawyer to represent his client with zeal does not militate against his concurrent obligation to treat with consideration all persons involved in the legal process and to avoid the infliction of needless harm.

EC 7–11 The responsibilities of a lawyer may vary according to the intelligence, experience, mental condition or age of a client, the obligation of a public officer, or the nature of a particular proceeding. Examples include the representation of an illiterate or an incompetent, service as a public prosecutor or other government lawyer, and appearances before administrative and legislative bodies.

EC 7–12 Any mental or physical condition of a client that renders him incapable of making a considered judgment on his own behalf casts additional responsibilities upon his lawyer. Where an incompetent is acting through a guardian or other legal representative, a lawyer must look to such representative for those decisions which are normally the prerogative of the client to make. If a client under disability has no legal representative, his lawyer may be compelled in court proceedings to make decisions on behalf of the client. If the client is capable of understanding the matter in question or of contributing to the advancement of his interests, regardless of whether he is legally disqualified from performing certain acts, the lawyer should obtain from him all possible aid. If the disability of a client and the lack of a legal representative compel the lawyer to make decisions for his client, the lawyer should consider all circumstances then prevailing and act with care to safeguard and advance the interests of his client. But obviously a lawyer cannot perform any act or make any decision which the law requires his client to perform or make, either acting for himself if competent, or by a duly constituted representative if legally incompetent.

EC 7–13 The responsibility of a public prosecutor differs from that of the usual advocate; his duty is to seek justice, not merely to convict.[24] This special duty exists because: (1) the prosecutor represents the sovereign and therefore should use restraint in the discretionary exercise of governmental powers, such as in the selection of cases to prosecute; (2) during trial the prosecutor is not only an advocate but he also may make decisions normally made by an individual client, and those affecting the public interest should be fair to all; and (3) in our system of criminal justice the accused is to be given the benefit of all reasonable

---

perienced in the art of devising arrangements that will put in workable order the entangled affairs and interests of human beings." *Professional Responsibility: Report of the Joint Conference,* 44 A.B.A.J. 1159, 1162 (1958).

[19] *See.* ABA Canon 8.

"Vital as is the lawyer's role in adjudication, it should not be thought that it is only as an advocate pleading in open court that he contributes to the administration of the law. The most effective realization of the law's aims often takes place in the attorney's office, where litigation is forestalled by anticipating its outcome, where the lawyer's quiet counsel takes the place of public force. Contrary to popular belief, the compliance with the law thus brought about is not generally lip-serving and narrow, for by reminding him of its long-run costs the lawyer often deters his client from a course of conduct technically permissible under existing law, though inconsistent with its underlying spirit and purpose." *Professional Responsibility: Report of the Joint Conference,* 44 A.B.A.J. 1159, 1161 (1958).

[20] "My summation of Judge Sharswood's view of the advocate's duty to the client is that he owes to the client the duty to use all legal means in support of the client's case. However, at the same time Judge Sharswood recognized that many advocates would find this obligation unbearable if applicable without exception. Therefore, the individual lawyer is given the choice of representing his client fully within the bounds set by the law *or of telling his client that he cannot do so,* so that the client may obtain another attorney if he wishes." Thode, *The Ethical Standard for the Advocate,* 39 Texas L.Rev. 575, 582 (1961).

Cf. Code of Professional Responsibility, DR 2–110 (C).

[21] *See* ABA Canon 24.

[22] Thode, *The Ethical Standard for the Advocate,* 39 Texas L.Rev. 575, 592 (1961).

[23] *Cf. ABA Opinions* 253 (1946) and 178 (1938).

[24] *See* ABA Canon 5 and Berger v. United States, 295 U.S. 78, 79 L.Ed. 1314, 55 S.Ct. 629 (1935).

"The public prosecutor cannot take as a guide for the conduct of his office the standards of an attorney appearing on behalf of an individual client. The freedom elsewhere wisely granted to a partisan advocate must be severely curtailed if the prosecutor's duties are to be properly discharged. The public prosecutor must recall that he occupies a dual role, being obligated, on the one hand, to furnish that adversary element essential to the informed decision of any controversy, but being possessed, on the other, of important governmental powers that are pledged to the accomplishment of one objective only, that of impartial justice. Where the prosecutor is recreant to the trust implicit in his office, he undermines confidence, not only in his profession, but in government and the very ideal of justice itself." *Professional Responsibility: Report of the Joint Conference,* 44 A.B.A.J. 1159, 1218 (1958).

"The prosecuting attorney is the attorney for the state, and it is his primary duty not to convict but to see that justice is done." *ABA Opinion* 150 (1936).

doubts. With respect to evidence and witnesses, the prosecutor has responsibilities different from those of a lawyer in private practice: the prosecutor should make timely disclosure to the defense of available evidence, known to him, that tends to negate the guilt of the accused, mitigate the degree of the offense, or reduce the punishment. Further, a prosecutor should not intentionally avoid pursuit of evidence merely because he believes it will damage the prosecution's case or aid the accused.

EC 7–14 A government lawyer who has discretionary power relative to litigation should refrain from instituting or continuing litigation that is obviously unfair. A government lawyer not having such discretionary power who believes there is lack of merit in a controversy submitted to him should so advise his superiors and recommend the avoidance of unfair litigation. A government lawyer in a civil action or administrative proceeding has the responsibility to seek justice and to develop a full and fair record, and he should not use his position or the economic power of the government to harass parties or to bring about unjust settlements or results.

EC 7–15 The nature and purpose of proceedings before administrative agencies vary widely. The proceedings may be legislative or quasi-judicial, or a combination of both. They may be *ex parte* in character, in which event they may originate either at the instance of the agency or upon motion of an interested party. The scope of an inquiry may be purely investigative or it may be truly adversary looking toward the adjudication of specific rights of a party or of classes of parties. The foregoing are but examples of some of the types of proceedings conducted by administrative agencies. A lawyer appearing before an administrative agency,[25] regardless of the nature of the proceeding it is conducting, has the continuing duty to advance the cause of his client within the bounds of the law.[26] Where the applicable rules of the agency impose specific obligations upon a lawyer, it is his duty to comply therewith, unless the lawyer has a legitimate basis for challenging the validity thereof. In all appearances before administrative agencies, a lawyer should identify himself, his client if identity of his client is not privileged,[27] and the representative nature of his appearance. It is not improper, however, for a lawyer to seek from an agency information available to the public without identifying his client.

EC 7–16 The primary business of a legislative body is to enact laws rather than to adjudicate controversies, although on occasion the activities of a legislative body may take on the characteristics of an adversary proceeding, particularly in investigative and impeachment matters. The role of a lawyer supporting or opposing proposed legislation normally is quite different from his role in representing a person under investigation or on trial by a legislative body. When a lawyer appears in connection with proposed legislation, he seeks to affect the lawmaking process, but when he appears on behalf of a client in investigatory or impeachment proceedings, he is concerned with the protection of the rights of his client. In either event, he should identify himself and his client, if identity of his client is not privileged, and should comply with applicable laws and legislative rules.[28]

EC 7–17 The obligation of loyalty to his client applies only to a lawyer in the discharge of his professional duties and implies no obligation to adopt a personal viewpoint favorable to the interests or desires of his client.[29] While a lawyer must act always with circumspection in order that his conduct will not adversely affect the rights of a client in a matter he is then handling, he may take positions on public issues and espouse legal reforms he favors without regard to the individual views of any client.

EC 7–18 The legal system in its broadest sense functions best when persons in need of legal advice or assistance are represented by their own counsel. For this reason a lawyer should not communicate on the subject matter of the representation of his client with a person he knows to be represented in the matter by a lawyer, unless pursuant to law or rule of court or unless he has the consent of the lawyer for that person.[30] If one is not represented by counsel, a lawyer representing another may have to deal directly with the unrepresented person; in such an instance, a law-

---

25 As to appearances before a department of government, Canon 26 provides: "A lawyer openly . . . may render professional services . . . in advocacy of claims before departments of government, upon the same principles of ethics which justify his appearance before the Courts . . . ."

26 "But as an advocate before a service which itself represents the adversary point of view, where his client's case is fairly arguable, a lawyer is under no duty to disclose its weaknesses, any more than he would be to make such a disclosure to a brother lawyer. The limitations within which he must operate are best expressed in Canon 22 . . . ." *ABA Opinion* 314 (1965).

27 *See* Baird v. Koerner, 279 F.2d 623 (9th Cir. 1960).

28 *See* ABA Canon 26.

29 "Law should be so practiced that the lawyer remains free to make up his own mind how he will vote, what causes he will support, what economic and political philosophy he will espouse. It is one of the glories of the profession that it admits of this freedom. Distinguished examples can be cited of lawyers whose views were at variance from those of their clients, lawyers whose skill and wisdom make them valued advisers to those who had little sympathy with their views as citizens." *Professional Responsibility: Report of the Joint Conference*, 44 A.B.A.J. 1159, 1217 (1958).

"No doubt some tax lawyers feel constrained to abstain from activities on behalf of a better tax system because they think that their clients may object. Clients have no right to object if the tax adviser handles their affairs competently and faithfully and independently of his private views as to tax policy. They buy his expert services, not his private opinions or his silence on issues that gravely affect the public interest." Paul, *The Lawyer as a Tax Adviser*, 25 Rocky Mt.L.Rev. 412, 434 (1953).

30 *See* ABA Canon 9.

yer should not undertake to give advice to the person who is attempting to represent himself,[31] except that he may advise him to obtain a lawyer.

Duty of the Lawyer to the Adversary System of Justice

EC 7–19 Our legal system provides for the adjudication of disputes governed by the rules of substantive, evidentiary, and procedural law. An adversary presentation counters the natural human tendency to judge too swiftly in terms of the familiar that which is not yet fully known;[32] the advocate, by his zealous preparation and presentation of facts and law, enables the tribunal to come to the hearing with an open and neutral mind and to render impartial judgments.[33] The duty of a lawyer to his client and his duty to the legal system are the same: to represent his client zealously within the bounds of the law.[34]

EC 7–20 In order to function properly, our adjudicative process requires an informed, impartial tribunal capable of administering justice promptly and efficiently[35] according to procedures that command public confidence and respect.[36] Not only must there be competent, adverse presentation of evidence and issues, but a tribunal must be aided by rules appropriate to an effective and dignified process. The procedures under which tribunals operate in our adversary system have been prescribed largely by legislative enactments, court rules and decisions, and administrative rules. Through the years certain concepts of proper professional conduct have become rules of law applicable to the adversary adjudicative process. Many of these concepts are the bases for standards of professional conduct set forth in the Disciplinary Rules.

EC 7–21 The civil adjudicative process is primarily designed for the settlement of disputes between parties, while the criminal process is designed for the protection of society as a whole. Threatening to use, or using, the criminal process to coerce adjustment of private civil claims or controversies is a subversion of that process;[37] further, the person against whom the criminal process is so misused may be deterred from asserting his legal rights and thus the usefulness of the civil process in settling private disputes is impaired. As in all cases of abuse of judicial process, the improper use of criminal process tends to diminish public confidence in our legal system.

EC 7–22 Respect for judicial rulings is essential to the proper administration of justice; however, a litigant or his lawyer may, in good faith and within the framework of the law, take steps to test the correctness of a ruling of a tribunal.[38]

EC 7–23 The complexity of law often makes it difficult for a tribunal to be fully informed unless the pertinent law is presented by the lawyers in the cause. A tribunal that is fully informed on the applicable law is better able to make a fair and accurate determination of the matter before it. The adversary system contemplates that each lawyer will present and argue the existing law in the light most favorable to his client.[39] Where a lawyer knows of legal authority in the controlling jurisdiction directly adverse to the position of his client, he should inform the tribunal of its existence unless his adversary has done so; but, having made such disclosure, he may challenge its soundness in whole or in part.[40]

---

31 *Id.*

32 *See Professional Responsibility: Report of the Joint Conference*, 44 A.B.A.J. 1159, 1160 (1958).

33 "Without the participation of someone who can act responsibly for each of the parties, this essential narrowing of the issues [by exchange of written pleadings or stipulations of counsel] becomes impossible. But here again the true significance of partisan advocacy lies deeper, touching once more the integrity of the adjudicative process itself. It is only through the advocate's participation that the hearing may remain in fact what it purports to be in theory: a public trial of the facts and issues. Each advocate comes to the hearing prepared to present his proofs and arguments, knowing at the same time that his arguments may fail to persuade and that his proof may be rejected as inadequate. . . . The deciding tribunal, on the other hand, comes to the hearing uncommitted. It has not represented to the public that any fact can be proved, that any argument is sound, or that any particular way of stating a litigant's case is the most effective expression of its merits." *Professional Responsibility: Report of the Joint Conference,* 44 A.B.A.J. 1159, 1160–61 (1958).

34 *Cf.* ABA Canons 15 and 32.

35 *Cf.* ABA Canon 21.

36 *See Professional Responsibility: Report of the Joint Conference*, 44 A.B.A.J. 1159, 1216 (1958).

37 "We are of the opinion that the letter in question was improper, and that in writing and sending it respondent was guilty of unprofessional conduct. This court has heretofore expressed its disapproval of using threats of criminal prosecution as a means of forcing settlement of civil claims. . . .

"Respondent has been guilty of a violation of a principle which condemns any confusion of threats of criminal prosecution with the enforcement of civil claims. For this misconduct he should be severely censured." Matter of Gelman, 230 App.Div. 524, 527, 245 N.Y.S. 416, 419 (1930).

38 "An attorney has the duty to protect the interests of his client. He has a right to press legitimate argument and to protest an erroneous ruling." Gallagher v. Municipal Court, 31 Cal.2d 784, 796, 192 P.2d 905, 913 (1948).

"There must be protection, however, in the far more frequent case of the attorney who stands on his rights and combats the order in good faith and without disrespect believing with good cause that it is void, for it is here that the independence of the bar becomes valuable." Note, 39 Colum.L.Rev. 433, 438 (1939).

39 "Too many do not understand that accomplishment of the layman's abstract ideas of justice is the function of the judge and jury, and that it is the lawyer's sworn duty to portray his client's case in its most favorable light." Rochelle and Payne, *The Struggle for Public Understanding*, 25 Texas B.J. 109, 159 (1962).

40 "We are of the opinion that this Canon requires the lawyer to disclose such decisions [that are adverse to his client's contentions] to the court. He may, of course, after doing so, challenge the soundness of the decisions or present reasons which he believes would warrant the court in not following them in the pending case." *ABA Opinion* 146 (1935).

Cf. ABA Opinion 280 (1949) and Thode, *The Ethical Standard for the Advocate,* 39 Texas L.Rev. 575, 585–86 (1961).

EC 7-24 In order to bring about just and informed decisions, evidentiary and procedural rules have been established by tribunals to permit the inclusion of relevant evidence and argument and the exclusion of all other considerations. The expression by a lawyer of his personal opinion as to the justness of a cause, as to the credibility of a witness, as to the culpability of a civil litigant, or as to the guilt or innocence of an accused is not a proper subject for argument to the trier of fact.[41] It is improper as to factual matters because admissible evidence possessed by a lawyer should be presented only as sworn testimony. It is improper as to all other matters because, were the rules otherwise, the silence of a lawyer on a given occasion could be construed unfavorably to his client. However, a lawyer may argue, on his analysis of the evidence, for any position or conclusion with respect to any of the foregoing matters.

EC 7-25 Rules of evidence and procedure are designed to lead to just decisions and are part of the framework of the law. Thus while a lawyer may take steps in good faith and within the framework of the law to test the validity of rules, he is not justified in consciously violating such rules and he should be diligent in his efforts to guard against his unintentional violation of them.[42] As examples, a lawyer should subscribe to or verify only those pleadings that he believes are in compliance with applicable law and rules; a lawyer should not make any prefatory statement before a tribunal in regard to the purported facts of the case on trial unless he believes that his statement will be supported by admissible evidence; a lawyer should not ask a witness a question solely for the purpose of harassing or embarrassing him; and a lawyer should not by subterfuge put before a jury matters which it cannot properly consider.

EC 7-26 The law and Disciplinary Rules prohibit the use of fraudulent, false, or perjured testimony or evidence.[43] A lawyer who knowingly[44] participates in introduction of such testimony or evidence is subject to discipline. A lawyer should, however, present any admissible evidence his client desires to have presented unless he knows, or from facts within his knowledge should know, that such testimony or evidence is false, fraudulent, or perjured.[45]

EC 7-27 Because it interferes with the proper administration of justice, a lawyer should not suppress evidence that he or his client has a legal obligation to reveal or produce. In like manner, a lawyer should not advise or cause a person to secrete himself or to leave the jurisdiction of a tribunal for the purpose of making him unavailable as a witness therein.[46]

EC 7-28 Witnesses should always testify truthfully[47] and should be free from any financial inducements that might tempt them to do otherwise.[48] A lawyer should not pay or agree to pay a non-expert witness an amount in excess of reimbursement for expenses and financial loss incident to his being a witness; however, a lawyer may pay or agree to pay an expert witness a reasonable fee for his services as an expert. But in no event should a lawyer pay or agree to pay a contingent fee to any witness. A lawyer should exercise reasonable diligence to see that his client and lay associates conform to these standards.[49]

EC 7-29 To safeguard the impartiality that is essential to the judicial process, veniremen and jurors should be protected against extraneous influences.[50] When impartiality is present, public confidence in the judicial system is enhanced. There should be no extrajudicial communication with veniremen prior to trial or with jurors during trial by or on behalf of a lawyer connected with the case. Furthermore, a lawyer who is not connected with the case should not communicate with

---

41 *See* ABA Canon 15.

"The traditional duty of an advocate is that he honorably uphold the contentions of his client. He should not voluntarily undermine them." Harders v. State of California, 373 F.2d 839, 842 (9th Cir. 1967).

42 *See* ABA Canon 22.

43 *Id. Cf.* ABA Canon 41.

44 *See generally ABA Opinion* 287 (1953) as to a lawyer's duty when he unknowingly participates in introducing perjured testimony.

45 "Under any standard of proper ethical conduct an attorney should not sit by silently and permit his client to commit what may have been perjury, and which certainly would mislead the court and the opposing party on a matter vital to the issue under consideration. . . . . . .

"Respondent next urges that it was his duty to observe the utmost good faith toward his client, and therefore he could not divulge any confidential information. This duty to the client of course does not extend to the point of authorizing collaboration with him in the commission of fraud." In re Carroll, 244 S.W.2d 474, 474-75 (Ky. 1951).

46 *See* ABA Canon 5; *cf. ABA Opinion* 131 (1935).

47 *Cf.* ABA Canon 39.

48 "The prevalence of perjury is a serious menace to the administration of justice, to prevent which no means have as yet been satisfactorily devised. But there certainly can be no greater incentive to perjury than to allow a party to make payments to its opponents witnesses under any guise or on any excuse, and at least attorneys who are officers of the court to aid it in the administration of justice, must keep themselves clear of any connection which in the slightest degree tends to induce witnesses to testify in favor of their clients." In re Robinson, 151 App.Div. 589, 600, 136 N.Y.S. 548, 556-57 (1912), *aff'd*, 209 N.Y. 354, 103 N.E. 160 (1913).

49 "It will not do for an attorney who seeks to justify himself against charges of this kind to show that he has escaped criminal responsibility under the Penal Law, nor can he blindly shut his eyes to a system which tends to suborn witnesses, to produce perjured testimony, and to suppress the truth. He has an active affirmative duty to protect the administration of justice from perjury and fraud, and that duty is not performed by allowing his subordinates and assistants to attempt to subvert justice and procure results for his clients based upon false testimony and perjured witnesses." *Id.*, 151 App.Div. at 592, 136 N.Y.S. at 551.

50 *See* ABA Canon 23.

or cause another to communicate with a venireman or a juror about the case. After the trial, communication by a lawyer with jurors is permitted so long as he refrains from asking questions or making comments that tend to harass or embarrass the juror[51] or to influence actions of the juror in future cases. Were a lawyer to be prohibited from communicating after trial with a juror, he could not ascertain if the verdict might be subject to legal challenge, in which event the invalidity of a verdict might go undetected.[52] When an extrajudicial communication by a lawyer with a juror is permitted by law, it should be made considerately and with deference to the personal feelings of the juror.

EC 7-30 Vexatious or harassing investigations of veniremen or jurors seriously impair the effectiveness of our jury system. For this reason, a lawyer or anyone on his behalf who conducts an investigation of veniremen or jurors should act with circumspection and restraint.

EC 7-31 Communications with or investigations of members of families of veniremen or jurors by a lawyer or by anyone on his behalf are subject to the restrictions imposed upon the lawyer with respect to his communications with or investigations of veniremen and jurors.

EC 7-32 Because of his duty to aid in preserving the integrity of the jury system, a lawyer who learns of improper conduct by or towards a venireman, a juror, or a member of the family of either should make a prompt report to the court regarding such conduct.

EC 7-33 A goal of our legal system is that each party shall have his case, criminal or civil, adjudicated by an impartial tribunal. The attainment of this goal may be defeated by dissemination of news or comments which tend to influence judge or jury.[53] Such news or comments may prevent prospective jurors from being impartial at the outset of the trial[54] and may also interfere with the obligation of jurors to base their verdict solely upon the evidence admitted in the trial.[55]

---

51 "[I]t is unfair to jurors to permit a disappointed litigant to pick over their private associations in search of something to discredit them and their verdict. And it would be unfair to the public too if jurors should understand that they cannot convict a man of means without risking an inquiry of that kind by paid investigators, with, to boot, the distortions an inquiry of that kind can produce." State v. LaFera, 42 N.J. 97, 107, 199 A.2d 630, 636 (1964).

52 *ABA Opinion* 319 (1968) points out that "[m]any courts today, and the trend is in this direction, allow the testimony of jurors as to all irregularities in and out of the courtroom except those irregularities whose existence can be determined only by exploring the consciousness of a single particular juror, New Jersey v. Kociolek, 20 N.J. 92, 118 A.2d 812 (1955). Model Code of Evidence Rule 301. Certainly as to states in which the testimony and affidavits of jurors may be received in support of or against a motion for new trial, a lawyer, in his obligation to protect his client, must have the tools for ascertaining whether or not grounds for a new trial exist and it is not unethical for him to talk to and question jurors."

53 *Generally see* ABA Advisory Committee on Fair Trial and Free Press, Standards Relating to Fair Trial and Free Press (1966).

"[T]he trial court might well have proscribed extrajudicial statements by any lawyer, party, witness, or court official which divulged prejudicial matters . . . . See State v. Van Dwyne, 43 N.J. 369, 389, 204 A.2d 841, 852 (1964), in which the court interpreted Canon 20 of the American Bar Association's Canons of Professional Ethics to prohibit such statements. Being advised of the great public interest in the case, the mass coverage of the press, and the potential prejudicial impact of publicity, the court could also have requested the appropriate city and county officials to promulgate a regulation with respect to dissemination of information about the case by their employees. In addition, reporters who wrote or broadcast prejudicial stories, could have been warned as to the impropriety of publishing material not introduced in the proceedings. . . . In this manner, Sheppard's right to a trial free from outside interference would have been given added protection without corresponding curtailment of the news media. Had the judge, the other officers of the court, and the police placed the interest of justice first, the news media would have soon learned to be content with the task of reporting the case as it unfolded in the courtroom—not pieced together from extrajudicial statements." Sheppard v. Maxwell, 384 U.S. 333, 361–62, 16 L. E.2d 600, 619–20, 86 S.Ct. 1507, 1521–22 (1966).

"Court proceedings are held for the solemn purpose of endeavoring to ascertain the truth which is the *sine qua non* of a fair trial. Over the centuries Anglo-American courts have devised careful safeguards by rule and otherwise to protect and facilitate the performance of this high function. As a result, at this time those safeguards do not permit the televising and photographing of a criminal trial, save in two States and there only under restrictions. The federal courts prohibit it by specific rule. This is weighty evidence that our concepts of a fair trial do not tolerate such an indulgence. We have always held that the atmosphere essential to the preservation of a fair trial—the most fundamental of all freedoms—must be maintained at all costs." Estes v. State of Texas, 381 U.S. 532, 540, 14 L.Ed.2d 543, 549, 85 S.Ct. 1628, 1631–32 (1965), *rehearing denied*, 382 U.S. 875, 15 L.Ed.2d 118, 86 S.Ct. 18 (1965).

54 "Pretrial can create a major problem for the defendant in a criminal case. Indeed, it may be more harmful than publicity during the trial for it may well set the community opinion as to guilt or innocence. . . . The trial witnesses present at the hearing, as well as the original jury panel, were undoubtedly made aware of the peculiar public importance of the case by the press and television coverage being provided, and by the fact that they themselves were televised live and their pictures rebroadcast on the evening show." *Id.*, 381 U.S. at 536–37, 14 L.Ed.2d at 546–47, 85 S.Ct. at 1629–30.

55 "The undeviating rule of this Court was expressed by Mr. Justice Holmes over half a century ago in Patterson v. Colorado, 205 U.S. 454, 462 (1907):

> The theory of our system is that the conclusions to be reached in a case will be induced only by evidence and argument in open court, and not by any outside influence, whether of private talk or public print."

Sheppard v. Maxwell, 384 U.S. 333, 351, 16 L.Ed.2d 600, 614, 86 S.Ct. 1507, 1516 (1966).

"The trial judge has a large discretion in ruling on the issue of prejudice resulting from the reading by jurors of news articles concerning the trial. . . . Generalizations beyond that statement are not profitable, because each case must turn on its special facts. We have here the exposure of jurors to information of a character which

The release by a lawyer of out-of-court statements regarding an anticipated or pending trial may improperly affect the impartiality of the tribunal.[56] For these reasons, standards for permissible and prohibited conduct of a lawyer with respect to trial publicity have been established.

EC 7–34 The impartiality of a public servant in our legal system may be impaired by the receipt of gifts or loans. A lawyer,[57] therefore, is never justified in making a gift or a loan to a judge, a hearing officer, or an official or employee of a tribunal,[58] except as permitted by Section C(4) of Cannon 5 of the Code of Judicial Conduct, but a lawyer may make a contribution to the campaign fund of a candidate for judicial office in conformity with Section B(2) under Canon 7 of the Code of Judicial Conduct.

EC 7–35 All litigants and lawyers should have access to tribunals on an equal basis. Generally, in adversary proceedings a lawyer should not communicate with a judge relative to a matter pending before, or which is to be brought before, a tribunal over which he presides in circumstances which might have the effect or give the appearance of granting undue advantage to one party.[59] For example, a lawyer should not communicate with a tribunal by a writing unless a copy thereof is promptly delivered to opposing counsel or to the adverse party if he is not represented by a lawyer. Ordinarily an oral communication by a lawyer with a judge or hearing officer should be made only upon adequate notice to opposing counsel, or, if there is none, to the opposing party. A lawyer should not condone or lend himself to private importunities by another with a judge or hearing officer on behalf of himself or his client.

EC 7–36 Judicial hearings ought to be conducted through dignified and orderly procedures designed to protect the rights of all parties. Although a lawyer has the duty to represent his client zealously, he should not engage in any conduct that offends the dignity and decorum of proceedings.[60] While maintaining his independence, a lawyer should be respectful, courteous, and above-board in his relations with a judge or hearing officer before whom he appears.[61] He should avoid undue solicitude for the comfort or convenience of judge or jury and should avoid any other conduct calculated to gain special consideration.

EC 7–37 In adversary proceedings, clients are litigants and though ill feeling may exist between clients, such ill feeling should not influence a lawyer in his conduct, attitude, and demeanor towards opposing lawyers.[62] A lawyer should not make unfair or derogatory personal reference to opposing counsel. Haranguing and offensive tactics by lawyers interfere with the orderly administration of justice and have no proper place in our legal system.

EC 7–38 A lawyer should be courteous to opposing counsel and should accede to reasonable requests regarding court proceedings, settings, continuances, waiver of procedural formalities, and similar matters which do not prejudice the rights of his client.[63] He should follow local customs of courtesy or practice, unless he gives timely notice to opposing counsel of his intention not to do so.[64] A lawyer should be punctual in fulfilling all professional commitments.[65]

---

the trial judge ruled was so prejudicial it could not be directly offered as evidence. The prejudice to the defendant is almost certain to be as great when that evidence reaches the jury through news accounts as when it is a part of the prosecution's evidence. . . . It may indeed be greater for it is then not tempered by protective procedures." Marshall v. United States, 360 U.S. 310, 312–13, 3 L.Ed.2d 1250, 1252, 79 S.Ct. 1171, 1173 (1959).

"The experienced trial lawyer knows that an adverse public opinion is a tremendous disadvantage to the defense of his client. Although grand jurors conduct their deliberations in secret, they are selected from the body of the public. They are likely to know what the general public knows and to reflect the public attitude. Trials are open to the public, and aroused public opinion respecting the merits of a legal controversy creates a court room atmosphere which, without any vocal expression in the presence of the petit jury, makes itself felt and has its effect upon the action of the petit jury. Our fundamental concepts of justice and our American sense of fair play require that the petit jury shall be composed of persons with fair and impartial minds and without preconceived views as to the merits of the controversy, and that it shall determine the issues presented to it solely upon the evidence adduced at the trial and according to the law given in the instructions of the trial judge.

"While we may doubt that the effect of public opinion would sway or bias the judgment of the trial judge in an equity proceeding, the defendant should not be called upon to run that risk and the trial court should not have his work made more difficult by any dissemination of statements to the public that would be calculated to create a public demand for a particular judgment in a prospective or pending case." *ABA Opinion* 199 (1940).

Cf. Estes v. State of Texas, 381 U.S. 532, 544–45, 14 L. Ed.2d 543, 551, 85 S.Ct. 1628, 1634 (1965), *rehearing denied*, 381 U.S. 875, 15 L.Ed.2d 118, 86 S.Ct. 18 (1965).

56 *See* ABA Canon 20.

57 Canon 3 observes that a lawyer "deserves rebuke and denunciation for any device or attempt to gain from a Judge special personal consideration or favor."

See ABA Canon 32.

58 "*Judicial Canon 32* provides:

" 'A judge should not accept any presents or favors from litigants, or from lawyers practicing before him or from others whose interests are likely to be submitted to him for judgment.'

"The language of this Canon is perhaps broad enough to prohibit campaign contributions by lawyers, practicing before the court upon which the candidate hopes to sit. However, we do not think it was intended to prohibit such contributions when the candidate is obligated, by force of circumstances over which he has no control, to conduct a campaign, the expense of which exceeds that which he should reasonably be expected to personally bear!" *ABA Opinion* 226 (1941).

59 *See* ABA Canons 3 and 32.

60 *Cf.* ABA Canon 18.

61 *See* ABA Canons 1 and 3.

62 *See* ABA Canon 17.

63 *See* ABA Canon 24.

64 *See* ABA Canon 25.

65 *See* ABA Canon 21.

EC 7–39 In the final analysis, proper functioning of the adversary system depends upon cooperation between lawyers and tribunals in utilizing procedures which will preserve the impartiality of tribunals and make their decisional processes prompt and just, without impinging upon the obligation of lawyers to represent their clients zealously within the framework of the law.

DISCIPLINARY RULES

DR 7–101 Representing a Client Zealously.

(A) A lawyer shall not intentionally: [66]

(1) Fail to seek the lawful objectives of his client through reasonably available means [67] **permitted by law and the Disciplinary Rules, except as provided by DR 7–101(B). A lawyer does not violate this Disciplinary Rule, however, by acceding to reasonable requests of opposing counsel which do not prejudice the rights of his client, by being punctual in fulfilling all professional commitments, by avoiding offensive tactics, or by treating with courtesy and consideration all persons involved in the legal process.**

(2) Fail to carry out a contract of employment entered into with a client for professional services, but he may withdraw as permitted under DR 2–110, DR 5–102, and DR 5–105.

(3) Prejudice or damage his client during the course of the professional relationship [68] **except as required under DR 7–102(B).**

(B) In his representation of a client, a lawyer may:

(1) Where permissible, exercise his professional judgment to waive or fail to assert a right or position of his client.

(2) Refuse to aid or participate in conduct that he believes to be unlawful, even though there is some support for an argument that the conduct is legal.

DR 7–102 Representing a Client Within the Bounds of the Law.

(A) In his representation of a client, a lawyer shall not:

(1) File a suit, assert a position, conduct a defense, delay a trial, or take other action on behalf of his client when he knows or when it is obvious that such action would serve merely to harass or maliciously injure another.[69]

(2) Knowingly advance a claim or defense that is unwarranted under existing law, except that he may advance such claim or defense if it can be supported by good faith argument for an extension, modification, or reversal of existing law.

(3) Conceal or knowingly fail to disclose that which he is required by law to reveal.

(4) Knowingly use perjured testimony or false evidence.[70]

(5) Knowingly make a false statement of law or fact.

(6) Participate in the creation or preservation of evidence when he knows or it is obvious that the evidence is false.

(7) Counsel or assist his client in conduct that the lawyer knows to be illegal or fraudulent.

(8) Knowingly engage in other illegal conduct or conduct contrary to a Disciplinary Rule.

(B) A lawyer who receives information clearly establishing that:

(1) His client has, in the course of the representation, perpetrated a fraud upon a person or tribunal shall promptly call upon his client to rectify the same, and if his client refuses or is unable to do so, he shall reveal the fraud to the affected person or tribunal,[71] **except when the information is protected as a privileged communication.**

(2) A person other than his client has perpetrated a fraud upon a tribunal shall promptly reveal the fraud to the tribunal.[72]

DR 7–103 Performing the Duty of Public Prosecutor or Other Government Lawyer.[73]

(A) A public prosecutor or other government lawyer shall not institute or cause to be instituted criminal charges when he knows or it is obvious that the charges are not supported by probable cause.

(B) A public prosecutor or other government lawyer in criminal litigation shall make timely disclosure to counsel for the defendant, or to the defendant if he has no counsel, of the existence of evidence, known to the prosecutor or other government lawyer, that tends to negate the guilt of the accused, mitigate the degree of the offense, or reduce the punishment.

---

66 *See* ABA Canon 15.

67 *See* ABA Canons 5 and 15; *cf.* ABA Canons 4 and 32.

68 *Cf.* ABA Canon 24.

69 *See* ABA Canon 30.

70 *Cf.* ABA Canons 22 and 29.

71 *See* ABA Canon 41; *cf.* Hinds v. State Bar, 19 Cal.2d 87, 92–93, 119 P.2d 134, 137 (1941); *but see ABA Opinion* 287 (1953) and Texas Canon 38. *Also see* Code of Professional Responsibility, DR 4–101(C)(2).

72 *See* Precision Inst. Mfg. Co. v. Automotive M. M. Co., 324 U.S. 806, 89 L.Ed. 1381, 65 S.Ct. 993 (1945).

73 *Cf.* ABA Canon 5.

DR 7–104 Communicating With One of Adverse Interest.[74]

(A) During the course of his representation of a client a lawyer shall not:

(1) Communicate or cause another to communicate on the subject of the representation with a party he knows to be represented by a lawyer in that matter unless he has the prior consent of the lawyer representing such other party [75] or is authorized by law to do so.

(2) Give advice to a person who is not represented by a lawyer, other than the advice to secure counsel,[76] if the interests of such person are or have a reasonable possibility of being in conflict with the interests of his client.[77]

DR 7–105 Threatening Criminal Prosecution.

(A) A lawyer shall not present, participate in presenting, or theaten to present criminal charges solely to obtain an advantage in a civil matter.

DR 7–106 Trial Conduct.

(A) A lawyer shall not disregard or advise his client to disregard a standing rule of a tribunal or a ruling of a tribunal made in the course of a proceeding, but he may take appropriate steps in good faith to test the validity of such rule or ruling.

(B) In presenting a matter to a tribunal, a lawyer shall disclose: [78]

(1) Legal authority in the controlling jurisdiction known to him to be directly adverse to the position of his client and which is not disclosed by opposing counsel.[79]

(2) Unless privileged or irrelevant, the identities of the clients he represents and of the persons who employed him.[80]

(C) In appearing in his professional capacity before a tribunal, a lawyer shall not:

(1) State or allude to any matter that he has no reasonable basis to believe is relevant to the case or that will not be supported by admissible evidence.[81]

(2) Ask any question that he has no reasonable basis to believe is relevant to the case and that is intended to degrade a witness or other person.[82]

---

74 "*Rule 12.* . . . A member of the State Bar shall not communicate with a party represented by counsel upon a subject of controversy, in the absence and without the consent of such counsel. This rule shall not apply to communications with a public officer, board, committee or body." Cal.Business and Professions Code § 6076 (West 1962).

75 *See* ABA Canon 9; *cf. ABA Opinions* 124 (1934), 108 (1934), 95 (1933), and 75 (1932); *also see* In re Schwabe, 242 Or. 169, 174–75, 408 P.2d 922, 924 (1965).

"It is clear from the earlier opinions of this committee that *Canon 9* is to be construed literally and does not allow a communication with an opposing party, without the consent of his counsel, though the purpose merely be to investigate the facts. *Opinions 117, 95, 66,*" *ABA Opinion* 187 (1938).

76 *Cf. ABA Opinion* 102 (1933).

77 *Cf.* ABA Canon 9 and *ABA Opinion* 58 (1931).

78 *Cf.* Note, 38 Texas L.Rev. 107, 108–09 (1959).

79 "In the brief summary in the 1947 edition of the Committee's decisions (p. 17), *Opinion 146* was thus summarized: *Opinion 146*—A lawyer should disclose to the court a decision directly adverse to his client's case that is unknown to his adversary.

"We would not confine the Opinion to 'controlling authorities'—i.e., those decisive of the pending case—but, in accordance with the tests hereafter suggested, would apply it to a decision directly adverse to any proposition of law on which the lawyer expressly relies, which would reasonably be considered important by the judge sitting on the case.

. . . .

". . . The test in every case should be: Is the decision which opposing counsel has overlooked one which the court should clearly consider in deciding the case? Would a reasonable judge properly feel that a lawyer who advanced, as the law, a proposition adverse to the undisclosed decision, was lacking in candor and fairness to him? Might the judge consider himself misled by an implied representation that the lawyer knew of no adverse authority?" *ABA Opinion* 280 (1949).

80 "The authorities are substantially uniform against any privilege as applied to the fact of retainer or identity of the client. The privilege is limited to confidential communications, and a retainer is not a confidential communication, although it cannot come into existence without some communication between the attorney and the—at that stage prospective—client." United States v. Pape, 144 F.2d 778, 782 (2d Cir. 1944), *cert. denied,* 323 U.S. 752, 89 L.Ed.2d 602, 65 S.Ct. 86 (1944).

"To be sure, there may be circumstances under which the identification of a client may amount to the prejudicial disclosure of a confidential communication, as where the substance of a disclosure has already been revealed but not its source." Colton v. United States, 306 F.2d 633, 637 (2d Cir. 1962).

81 *See* ABA Canon 22; *cf.* ABA Canon 17.

"The rule allowing counsel when addressing the jury the widest latitude in discussing the evidence and presenting the client's theories falls far short of authorizing the statement by counsel of matter not in evidence, or indulging in argument founded on no proof, or demanding verdicts for purposes other than the just settlement of the matters at issue between the litigants, or appealing to prejudice or passion. The rule confining counsel to legitimate argument is not based on etiquette, but on justice. Its violation is not merely an overstepping of the bounds of propriety, but a violation of a party's rights. The jurors must determine the issues upon the evidence. Counsel's address should help them do this, not tend to lead them astray." Cherry Creek Nat. Bank v. Fidelity & Cas. Co., 207 App.Div. 787, 790–91, 202 N.Y.S. 611, 614 (1924).

82 *Cf.* ABA Canon 18.

"§ 6068. . . . It is the duty of an attorney:

. . . .

"(f) To abstain from all offensive personality, and to advance no fact prejudicial to the honor or reputation of a party or witness, unless required by the justice of the cause with which he is charged." Cal.Business and Professions Code § 6068 (West 1962).

(3) Assert his personal knowledge of the facts in issue, except when testifying as a witness.

(4) Assert his personal opinion as to the justness of a cause, as to the credibility of a witness, as to the culpability of a civil litigant, or as to the guilt or innocence of an accused;[83] but he may argue, on his analysis of the evidence, for any position or conclusion with respect to the matters stated herein.

(5) Fail to comply with known local customs of courtesy or practice of the bar or a particular tribunal without giving to opposing counsel timely notice of his intent not to comply.[84]

(6) Engage in undignified or discourteous conduct which is degrading to a tribunal.

(7) Intentionally or habitually violate any established rule of procedure or of evidence.

DR 7–107 Trial Publicity.[85]

(A) A lawyer participating in or associated with the investigation of a criminal matter shall not make or participate in making an extrajudicial statement that a reasonable person would expect to be disseminated by means of public communication and that does more than state without elaboration:

(1) Information contained in a public record.

(2) That the investigation is in progress.

(3) The general scope of the investigation including a description of the offense and, if permitted by law, the identity of the victim.

(4) A request for assistance in apprehending a suspect or assistance in other matters and the information necessary thereto.

(5) A warning to the public of any dangers.

(B) A lawyer or law firm associated with the prosecution or defense of a criminal matter shall not, from the time of the filing of a complaint, information, or indictment, the issuance of an arrest warrant, or arrest until the commencement of the trial or disposition without trial, make or participate in making an extrajudicial statement that a reasonable person would expect to be disseminated by means of public communication and that relates to:

(1) The character, reputation, or prior criminal record (including arrests, indictments, or other charges of crime) of the accused.

(2) The possibility of a plea of guilty to the offense charged or to a lesser offense.

(3) The existence or contents of any confession, admission, or statement given by the accused or his refusal or failure to make a statement.

(4) The performance or results of any examinations or tests or the refusal or failure of the accused to submit to examinations or tests.

(5) The identity, testimony, or credibility of a prospective witness.

(6) Any opinion as to the guilt or innocence of the accused, the evidence, or the merits of the case.

(C) DR 7–107(B) does not preclude a lawyer during such period from announcing:

(1) The name, age, residence, occupation, and family status of the accused.

(2) If the accused has not been apprehended, any information necessary to aid in his apprehension or to warn the public of any dangers he may present.

---

[83] "The record in the case at bar was silent concerning the qualities and character of the deceased. It is especially improper, in addressing the jury in a murder case, for the prosecuting attorney to make reference to his knowledge of the good qualities of the deceased where there is no evidence in the record bearing upon his character. . . . A prosecutor should never inject into his argument evidence not introduced at the trial." People v. Dukes, 12 Ill.2d 334, 341, 146 N.E.2d 14, 17–18 (1957).

[84] "A lawyer should not ignore known customs or practice of the Bar or of a particular Court, even when the law permits, without giving timely notice to the opposing counsel." ABA Canon 25.

[85] The provisions of Sections (A), (B), (C), and (D) of this Disciplinary Rule incorporate the fair trial-free press standards which apply to lawyers as adopted by the ABA House of Delegates, Feb. 19, 1968, upon the recommendation of the Fair Trial and Free Press Advisory Committee of the ABA Special Committee on Minimum Standards for the Administration of Criminal Justice.

Cf. ABA Canon 20; *see generally* ABA Advisory Committee on Fair Trial and Free Press, Standards Relating to Fair Trial and Free Press (1966).

"From the cases coming here we note that unfair and prejudicial news comment on pending trials has become increasingly prevalent. Due process requires that the accused receive a trial by an impartial jury free from outside influences. Given the pervasiveness of modern communications and the difficulty of effacing prejudicial publicity from the minds of the jurors, the trial courts must take strong measures to ensure that the balance is never weighed against the accused. And appellate tribunals have the duty to make an independent evaluation of the circumstances. Of course, there is nothing that prescribes the press from reporting events that transpire in the courtroom. But where there is a reasonable likelihood that prejudicial news prior to trial will prevent a fair trial, the judge should continue the case until the threat abates, or transfer it to another county not so permeated with publicity. . . . The courts must take such steps by rule and regulation that will protect their processes from prejudicial outside interferences. Neither prosecutors, counsel for defense, the accused, witnesses, court staff nor enforcement officers coming under the jurisdiction of the court should be permitted to frustrate its function. Collaboration between counsel and the press as to information affecting the fairness of a criminal trial is not only subject to regulation, but is highly censurable and worthy of disciplinary measures." Sheppard v. Maxwell, 384 U.S. 333, 362–63, 16 L.Ed.2d 600, 620, 86 S.Ct. 1507, 1522 (1966).

(3) A request for assistance in obtaining evidence.

(4) The identity of the victim of the crime.

(5) The fact, time, and place of arrest, resistance, pursuit, and use of weapons.

(6) The identity of investigating and arresting officers or agencies and the length of the investigation.

(7) At the time of seizure, a description of the physical evidence seized, other than a confession, admission, or statement.

(8) The nature, substance, or text of the charge.

(9) Quotations from or references to public records of the court in the case.

(10) The scheduling or result of any step in the judicial proceedings.

(11) That the accused denies the charges made against him.

(D) During the selection of a jury or the trial of a criminal matter, a lawyer or law firm associated with the prosecution or defense of a criminal matter shall not make or participate in making an extrajudicial statement that a reasonable person would expect to be disseminated by means of public communication and that relates to the trial, parties, or issues in the trial or other matters that are reasonably likely to interfere with a fair trial, except that he may quote from or refer without comment to public records of the court in the case.

(E) After the completion of a trial or disposition without trial of a criminal matter and prior to the imposition of sentence, a lawyer or law firm associated with the prosecution or defense shall not make or participate in making an extrajudicial statement that a reasonable person would expect to be disseminated by public communication and that is reasonably likely to affect the imposition of sentence.

(F) The foregoing provisions of DR 7–107 also apply to professional disciplinary proceedings and juvenile disciplinary proceedings when pertinent and consistent with other law applicable to such proceedings.

(G) A lawyer or law firm associated with a civil action shall not during its investigation or litigation make or participate in making an extrajudicial statement, other than a quotation from or reference to public records, that a reasonable person would expect to be disseminated by means of public communication and that relates to:

(1) Evidence regarding the occurrence or transaction involved.

(2) The character, credibility, or criminal record of a party, witness, or prospective witness.

(3) The performance or results of any examinations or tests or the refusal or failure of a party to submit to such.

(4) His opinion as to the merits of the claims or defenses of a party, except as required by law or administrative rule.

(5) Any other matter reasonably likely to interfere with a fair trial of the action.

(H) During the pendency of an administrative proceeding, a lawyer or law firm associated therewith shall not make or participate in making a statement, other than a quotation from or reference to public records, that a reasonable person would expect to be disseminated by means of public communication if it is made outside the official course of the proceeding and relates to:

(1) Evidence regarding the occurrence or transaction involved.

(2) The character, credibility, or criminal record of a party, witness, or prospective witness.

(3) Physical evidence or the performance or results of any examinations or tests or the refusal or failure of a party to submit to such.

(4) His opinion as to the merits of the claims, defenses, or positions of an interested person.

(5) Any other matter reasonably likely to interfere with a fair hearing.

(I) The foregoing provisions of DR 7–107 do not preclude a lawyer from replying to charges of misconduct publicly made against him or from participating in the proceedings of legislative, administrative, or other investigative bodies.

(J) A lawyer shall exercise reasonable care to prevent his employees and associates from making an extrajudicial statement that he would be prohibited from making under DR 7–107.

DR 7–108 Communication with or Investigation of Jurors.

(A) Before the trial of a case a lawyer connected therewith shall not communicate with or cause another to communicate with anyone he knows to be a member of the venire from which the jury will be selected for the trial of the case.

(B) During the trial of a case:

(1) A lawyer connected therewith shall not communicate with or cause another to communicate with any member of the jury.[86]

(2) A lawyer who is not connected therewith shall not communicate with or cause another to communicate with a juror concerning the case.

(C) DR 7–108(A) and (B) do not prohibit a lawyer from communicating with veniremen or jurors in the course of official proceedings.

---

[86] *See* ABA Canon 23.

(D) After discharge of the jury from further consideration of a case with which the lawyer was connected, the lawyer shall not ask questions of or make comments to a member of that jury that are calculated merely to harass or embarrass the juror or to influence his actions in future jury service.[87]

(E) A lawyer shall not conduct or cause, by financial support or otherwise, another to conduct a vexatious or harassing investigation of either a venireman or a juror.

(F) All restrictions imposed by DR 7-108 upon a lawyer also apply to communications with or investigations of members of a family of a venireman or a juror.

(G) A lawyer shall reveal promptly to the court improper conduct by a venireman or a juror, or by another toward a venireman or a juror or a member of his family, of which the lawyer has knowledge.

DR 7-109 Contact with Witnesses.

(A) A lawyer shall not suppress any evidence that he or his client has a legal obligation to reveal or produce.[88]

(B) A lawyer shall not advise or cause a person to secrete himself or to leave the jurisdiction of a tribunal for the purpose of making him unavailable as a witness therein.[89]

(C) A lawyer shall not pay, offer to pay, or acquiesce in the payment of compensation to a witness contingent upon the content of his testimony or the outcome of the case.[90] **But a lawyer may advance, guarantee, or acquiesce in the payment of:**

(1) Expenses reasonably incurred by a witness in attending or testifying.

(2) Reasonable compensation to a witness for his loss of time in attending or testifying.

(3) A reasonable fee for the professional services of an expert witness.

DR 7-110 Contact with Officials.[91]

(A) A lawyer shall not give or lend any thing of value to a judge, official, or employee of a tribunal, except as permitted by Section C(4) of Canon 5 of the Code of Judicial Conduct, but a lawyer may make a contribution to the campaign fund of a candidate for judicial office in conformity with Section B(2) under Canon 7 of the Code of Judicial Conduct.

(B) In an adversary proceeding, a lawyer shall not communicate, or cause another to communicate, as to the merits of the cause with a judge or an official before whom the proceeding is pending, except:

(1) In the course of official proceedings in the cause.

(2) In writing if he promptly delivers a copy of the writing to opposing counsel or to the adverse party if he is not represented by a lawyer.

(3) Orally upon adequate notice to opposing counsel or to the adverse party if he is not represented by a lawyer.

(4) As otherwise authorized by law,[92] **or by Section A(4) under Canon 3 of the Code of Judicial Conduct.**

CANON 8

A Lawyer Should Assist in Improving the Legal System

ETHICAL CONSIDERATIONS

EC 8-1 Changes in human affairs and imperfections in human institutions make necessary constant efforts to maintain and improve our legal system.[1] This system should function in a man-

[87] "[I]t would be unethical for a lawyer to harass, entice, induce or exert influence on a juror to obtain his testimony." *ABA Opinion* 319 (1968).

[88] *See* ABA Canon 5.

[89] *Cf.* ABA Canon 5.

"*Rule 15.* . . . . A member of the State Bar shall not advise a person, whose testimony could establish or tend to establish a material fact, to avoid service of process, or secrete himself, or otherwise to make his testimony unavailable." Cal.Business and Professions Code § 6076 (West 1962).

[90] *See* In re O'Keefe, 49 Mont. 369, 142 P. 638 (1914).

[91] *Cf.* ABA Canon 3.

[92] "*Rule 16.* . . . . A member of the State Bar shall not, in the absence of opposing counsel, communicate with or argue to a judge or judicial officer except in open court upon the merits of a contested matter pending before such judge or judicial officer; nor shall he, without furnishing opposing counsel with a copy thereof, address a written communication to a judge or judicial officer concerning the merits of a contested matter pending before such judge or judicial officer. This rule shall not apply to ex parte matters." Cal.Business and Professions Code § 6076 (West 1962).

[1] ". . . . [Another] task of the great lawyer is to do his part individually and as a member of the organized bar to improve his profession, the courts, and the law. As President Theodore Roosevelt aptly put it, 'Every man owes some of his time to the upbuilding of the profession to which he belongs.' Indeed, this obligation is one of the great things which distinguishes a profession from a business. The soundness and the necessity of President Roosevelt's admonition insofar as it relates to the legal profession cannot be doubted. The advances in natural science and technology are so startling and the velocity of change in business and in social life is so great that the law along with the other social sciences, and even human life itself, is in grave danger of being extinguished by new gods of its own invention if it does not awake from its lethargy. Vanderbilt, *The Five Functions of the Lawyer: Service to Clients and the Public,* 40 A.B.A.J. 31, 31–32 (1954).

ner that commands public respect and fosters the use of legal remedies to achieve redress of grievances. By reason of education and experience, lawyers are especially qualified to recognize deficiencies in the legal system and to initiate corrective measures therein. Thus they should participate in proposing and supporting legislation and programs to improve the system,[2] without regard to the general interests or desires of clients or former clients.[3]

EC 8–2 Rules of law are deficient if they are not just, understandable, and responsive to the needs of society. If a lawyer believes that the existence or absence of a rule of law, substantive or procedural, causes or contributes to an unjust result, he should endeavor by lawful means to obtain appropriate changes in the law. He should encourage the simplification of laws and the repeal or amendment of laws that are outmoded.[4] Likewise, legal procedures should be improved whenever experience indicates a change is needed.

EC 8–3 The fair administration of justice requires the availability of competent lawyers. Members of the public should be educated to recognize the existence of legal problems and the resultant need for legal services, and should be provided methods for intelligent selection of counsel. Those persons unable to pay for legal services should be provided needed services. Clients and lawyers should not be penalized by undue geographical restraints upon representation in legal matters, and the bar should address itself to improvements in licensing, reciprocity, and admission procedures consistent with the needs of modern commerce.

EC 8–4 Whenever a lawyer seeks legislative or administrative changes, he should identify the capacity in which he appears, whether on behalf of himself, a client, or the public.[5] A lawyer may advocate such changes on behalf of a client even though he does not agree with them. But when a lawyer purports to act on behalf of the public, he should espouse only those changes which he conscientiously believes to be in the public interest.

EC 8–5 Fraudulent, deceptive, or otherwise illegal conduct by a participant in a proceeding before a tribunal or legislative body is inconsistent with fair administration of justice, and it should never be participated in or condoned by lawyers. Unless constrained by his obligation to preserve the confidences and secrets of his client, a lawyer should reveal to appropriate authorities any knowledge he may have of such improper conduct.

EC 8–6 Judges and administrative officials having adjudicatory powers ought to be persons of integrity, competence, and suitable temperament. Generally, lawyers are qualified, by personal observation or investigation, to evaluate the qualifications of persons seeking or being considered for such public offices, and for this reason they have a special responsibility to aid in the selection of only those who are qualified.[6] It is the duty of lawyers to endeavor to prevent political considerations from outweighing judicial fitness in the selection of judges. Lawyers should protest earnestly against the appointment or election of those who are unsuited for the bench and should strive to have elected[7] or appointed thereto only those who are willing to forego pursuits, whether of a business, political, or other nature, that may interfere with the free and fair consideration of questions presented for adjudication. Adjudicatory of-

---

[2] *See* ABA Canon 29; *Cf.* Cheatham, *The Lawyer's Role and Surroundings*, 25 Rocky Mt.L.Rev. 405, 406–07 (1953).

"The lawyer tempted by repose should recall the heavy costs paid by his profession when needed legal reform has to be accomplished through the initiative of public-spirited laymen. Where change must be thrust from without upon an unwilling Bar, the public's least flattering picture of the lawyer seems confirmed. The lawyer concerned for the standing of his profession will, therefore, interest himself actively in the improvement of the law. In doing so he will not only help to maintain confidence in the Bar, but will have the satisfaction of meeting a responsibility inhering in the nature of his calling." *Professional Responsibility: Report of the Joint Conference*, 44 A.B.A.J. 1159, 1217 (1958).

[3] *See* Stayton, *Cum Honore Officium*, 19 Tex.B.J. 765, 766 (1956); *Professional Responsibility: Report of the Joint Conference*, 44 A.B.A.J. 1159, 1162 (1958); and Paul, *The Lawyer as a Tax Adviser*, 25 Rocky Mt.L.Rev. 412, 433–34 (1953).

[4] "There are few great figures in the history of the Bar who have not concerned themselves with the reform and improvement of the law. The special obligation of the profession with respect to legal reform rests on considerations too obvious to require enumeration. Certainly it is the lawyer who has both the best chance to know when the law is working badly and the special competence to put it in order." *Professional Responsibility: Report of the Joint Conference*, 44 A.B.A.J. 1159, 1217 (1958).

[5] "*Rule 14*. . . . A member of the State Bar shall not communicate with, or appear before, a public officer, board, committee or body, in his professional capacity, without first disclosing that he is an attorney representing interests that may be affected by action of such officer, board, committee or body." Cal.Business and Professions Code § 6076 (West 1962).

[6] *See* ABA Canon 2.

"Lawyers are better able than laymen to appraise accurately the qualifications of candidates for judicial office. It is proper that they should make that appraisal known to the voters in a proper and dignified manner. A lawyer may with propriety endorse a candidate for judicial office and seek like endorsement from other lawyers. But the lawyer who endorses a judicial candidate or seeks that endorsement from other lawyers should be actuated by a sincere belief in the superior qualifications of the candidate for judicial service and not by personal or selfish motives; and a lawyer should not use or attempt to use the power or prestige of the judicial office to secure such endorsement. On the other hand, the lawyer whose endorsement is sought, if he believes the candidate lacks the essential qualifications for the office or believes the opposing candidate is better qualified, should have the courage and moral stamina to refuse the request for endorsement." *ABA Opinion* 189 (1938).

[7] "[W]e are of the opinion that, whenever a candidate for judicial office merits the endorsement and support of lawyers, the lawyers may make financial contributions toward the campaign if its cost, when reasonably conducted, exceeds that which the candidate would be expected to bear personally." *ABA Opinion* 226 (1941).

ficials, not being wholly free to defend themselves, are entitled to receive the support of the bar against unjust criticism.[8] While a lawyer as a citizen has a right to criticize such officials publicly,[9] he should be certain of the merit of his complaint, use appropriate language, and avoid petty criticisms, for unrestrained and intemperate statements tend to lessen public confidence in our legal system.[10] Criticisms motivated by reasons other than a desire to improve the legal system are not justified.

EC 8–7 Since lawyers are a vital part of the legal system, they should be persons of integrity, of professional skill, and of dedication to the improvement of the system. Thus a lawyer should aid in establishing, as well as enforcing, standards of conduct adequate to protect the public by insuring that those who practice law are qualified to do so.

EC 8–8 Lawyers often serve as legislators or as holders of other public offices. This is highly desirable, as lawyers are uniquely qualified to make significant contributions to the improvement of the legal system. A lawyer who is a public officer, whether full or part-time, should not engage in activities in which his personal or professional interests are or foreseeably may be in conflict with his official duties.[11]

EC 8–9 The advancement of our legal system is of vital importance in maintaining the rule of law and in facilitating orderly changes; therefore, lawyers should encourage, and should aid in making, needed changes and improvements.

DISCIPLINARY RULES

DR 8–101 Action as a Public Official.

(A) A lawyer who holds public office shall not:

(1) Use his public position to obtain, or attempt to obtain, a special advantage in legislative matters for himself or for a client under circumstances where he knows or it is obvious that such action is not in the public interest.

(2) Use his public position to influence, or attempt to influence, a tribunal to act in favor of himself or of a client.

(3) Accept any thing of value from any person when the lawyer knows or it is obvious that the offer is for the purpose of influencing his action as a public official.

DR 8–102 Statements Concerning Judges and Other Adjudicatory Officers.[12]

(A) A lawyer shall not knowingly make false statements of fact concerning the qualifications of a candidate for election or appointment to a judicial office.

(B) A lawyer shall not knowingly make false accusations against a judge or other adjudicatory officer.

DR 8–103 Lawyer Candidate for Judicial Office.

(A) A lawyer who is a candidate for judicial office shall comply with the applicable provisions of Canon 7 of the Code of Judicial Conduct.

---

[8] *See* ABA Canon 1.

[9] "Citizens have a right under our constitutional system to criticize governmental officials and agencies. Courts are not, and should not be, immune to such criticism." Konigsberg v. State Bar of California, 353 U.S. 252, 269 (1957).

[10] "[E]very lawyer, worthy of respect, realizes that public confidence in our courts is the cornerstone of our governmental structure, and will refrain from unjustified attack on the character of the judges, while recognizing the duty to denounce and expose a corrupt or dishonest judge." Kentucky State Bar Ass'n v. Lewis, 282 S.W.2d 321, 326 (Ky. 1955).

"We should be the last to deny that Mr. Meeker has the right to uphold the honor of the profession and to expose without fear or favor corrupt or dishonest conduct in the profession, whether the conduct be that of a judge or not. . . . However, this Canon [29] does not permit one to make charges which are false and untrue and unfounded in fact. When one's fancy leads him to make false charges, attacking the character and integrity of others, he does so at his peril. He should not do so without adequate proof of his charges and he is certainly not authorized to make careless, untruthful and vile charges against his professional brethren." In re Meeker, 76 N.M. 354, 364–65, 414 P.2d 862, 869 (1966), *appeal dismissed*, 385 U.S. 449, 17 L.Ed.2d 510, 87 S.Ct. 613 (1967).

[11] "*Opinions 16, 30, 34, 77, 118* and *134* relate to *Canon 6*, and pass on questions concerning the propriety of the conduct of an attorney who is a public officer, in representing private interests adverse to those of the public body which he represents. The principle applied in those opinions is that an attorney holding public office should avoid all conduct which might lead the layman to conclude that the attorney is utilizing his public position to further his professional success or personal interests." *ABA Opinion* 192 (1939).

"The next question is whether a lawyer-member of a legislative body may appear as counsel or co-counsel at hearings before a zoning board of appeals, or similar tribunal, created by the legislative group of which he is a member. We are of the opinion that he may practice before fact-finding officers, hearing bodies and commissioners, since under our views he may appear as counsel in the courts where his municipality is a party. Decisions made at such hearings are usually subject to administrative review by the courts upon the record there made. It would be inconsistent to say that a lawyer-member of a legislative body could not participate in a hearing at which the record is made, but could appear thereafter when the cause is heard by the courts on administrative review. This is subject to an important exception. He should not appear as counsel where the matter is subject to review by the legislative body of which he is a member. . . . We are of the opinion that where a lawyer does so appear there would be conflict of interests between his duty as an advocate for his client on the one hand and the obligation to his governmental unit on the other." In re Becker, 16 Ill.2d 488, 494–95, 158 N.E.2d 753, 756–57 (1959).

Cf. ABA Opinions 186 (1938), 136 (1935), 118 (1934), and 77 (1932).

[12] *Cf.* ABA Canons 1 and 2.

CANON 9

A Lawyer Should Avoid Even the Appearance of Professional Impropriety

ETHICAL CONSIDERATIONS

EC 9–1 Continuation of the American concept that we are to be governed by rules of law requires that the people have faith that justice can be obtained through our legal system.[1] A lawyer should promote public confidence in our system and in the legal profession.[2]

EC 9–2 Public confidence in law and lawyers may be eroded by irresponsible or improper conduct of a lawyer. On occasion, ethical conduct of a lawyer may appear to laymen to be unethical. In order to avoid misunderstandings and hence to maintain confidence, a lawyer should fully and promptly inform his client of material developments in the matters being handled for the client. While a lawyer should guard against otherwise proper conduct that has a tendency to diminish public confidence in the legal system or in the legal profession, his duty to clients or to the public should never be subordinate merely because the full discharge of his obligation may be misunderstood or may tend to subject him or the legal profession to criticism. When explicit ethical guidance does not exist, a lawyer should determine his conduct by acting in a manner that promotes public confidence in the integrity and efficiency of the legal system and the legal profession.[3]

EC 9–3 After a lawyer leaves judicial office or other public employment, he should not accept employment in connection with any matter in which he had substantial responsibility prior to his leaving, since to accept employment would give the appearance of impropriety even if none exists.[4]

EC 9–4 Because the very essence of the legal system is to provide procedures by which matters can be presented in an impartial manner so that they may be decided solely upon the merits, any statement or suggestion by a lawyer that he can or would attempt to circumvent those procedures is detrimental to the legal system and tends to undermine public confidence in it.

EC 9–5 Separation of the funds of a client from those of his lawyer not only serves to protect the client but also avoids even the appearance of impropriety, and therefore commingling of such funds should be avoided.

EC 9–6 Every lawyer owes a solemn duty to uphold the integrity and honor of his profession; to encourage respect of the law and for the courts and the judges thereof; to observe the Code of Professional Responsibility; to act as a member of a learned profession, one dedicated to public service; to cooperate with his brother lawyers in supporting the organized bar through the devoting of his time, efforts, and financial support as his professional standing and ability reasonably permit; to conduct himself so as to reflect credit on the legal profession and to inspire the confidence, respect, and trust of his clients and of the public; and to strive to avoid not only professional impropriety but also the appearance of impropriety.[5]

DISCIPLINARY RULES

DR 9–101 Avoiding Even the Appearance of Impropriety.[6]

(A) A lawyer shall not accept private employment in a matter upon the merits of which he has acted in a judicial capacity.[7]

---

[1] "Integrity is the very breath of justice. Confidence in our law, our courts, and in the administration of justice is our supreme interest. No practice must be permitted to prevail which invites towards the administration of justice a doubt or distrust of its integrity." Erwin M. Jennings Co. v. DiGenova, 107 Conn. 491, 499, 141 A. 866, 868 (1928).

[2] "A lawyer should never be reluctant or too proud to answer unjustified criticism of his profession, of himself, or of his brother lawyer. He should guard the reputation of his profession and of his brothers as zealously as he guards his own." Rochelle and Payne, *The Struggle for Public Understanding*, 25 Texas B.J. 109, 162 (1962).

[3] *See* ABA Canon 29.

[4] *See* ABA Canon 36.

[5] "As said in Opinion 49 of the Committee on Professional Ethics and Grievances of the American Bar Association, page 134: 'An attorney should not only avoid impropriety but should avoid the appearance of impropriety.' " State ex rel, Nebraska State Bar Ass'n v. Richards, 165 Neb. 80, 93, 84 N.W.2d 136, 145 (1957).

"It would also be preferable that such contribution [to the campaign of a candidate for judicial office] be made to a campaign committee rather than to the candidate personally. In so doing, possible appearances of impropriety would be reduced to a minimum." *ABA Opinion* 226 (1941).

"The lawyer assumes high duties, and has imposed upon him grave responsibilities. He may be the means of much good or much mischief. Interests of vast magnitude are entrusted to him; confidence is reposed in him; life, liberty, character and property should be protected by him. He should guard, with jealous watchfulness, his own reputation, as well as that of his profession." People ex rel. Cutler v. Ford, 54 Ill. 520, 522 (1870), and also quoted in State Board of Law Examiners v. Sheldon, 43 Wyo. 522, 526, 7 P.2d 226, 227 (1932).

See ABA Opinion 150 (1936).

[6] *Cf.* Code of Professional Responsibility, EC 5–6.

[7] *See ABA* Canon 36.

"It is the duty of the judge to rule on questions of law and evidence in misdemeanor cases and examinations in felony cases. That duty calls for impartial and uninfluenced judgment, regardless of the effect on those immediately involved or others who may, directly or indirectly, be affected. Discharge of that duty might be greatly interfered with if the judge, in another capacity, were permitted to hold himself out to employment by those who are to be, or who may be, brought to trial in felony

(B) A lawyer shall not accept private employment in a matter in which he had substantial responsibility while he was a public employee.[8]

(C) A lawyer shall not state or imply that he is able to influence improperly or upon irrelevant grounds any tribunal, legislative body,[9] or public official.

DR 9–102 Preserving Identity of Funds and Property of a Client.[10]

(A) All funds of clients paid to a lawyer or law firm, other than advances for costs and expenses, shall be deposited in one or more identifiable bank accounts maintained in the state in which the law office is situated and no funds belonging to the lawyer or law firm shall be deposited therein except as follows:

(1) Funds reasonably sufficient to pay bank charges may be deposited therein.

(2) Funds belonging in part to a client and in part presently or potentially to the lawyer or law firm must be deposited therein, but the portion belonging to the lawyer or law firm may be withdrawn when due unless the right of the lawyer or law firm to receive it is disputed by the client, in which event the disputed portion shall not be withdrawn until the dispute is finally resolved.

(B) A lawyer shall:

(1) Promptly notify a client of the receipt of his funds, securities, or other properties.

(2) Identify and label securities and properties of a client promptly upon receipt and place them in a safe deposit box or other place of safekeeping as soon as practicable.

(3) Maintain complete records of all funds, securities, and other properties of a client coming into the possession of the lawyer and render appropriate accounts to his client regarding them.

(4) Promptly pay or deliver to the client as requested by a client the funds, securities, or other properties in the possession of the lawyer which the client is entitled to receive.

DEFINITIONS*

As used in the Disciplinary Rules of the Code of Professional Responsibility:

(1) "Differing interests" include every interest that will adversely affect either the judg-

---

cases, even though he did not conduct the examination. His private interests as a lawyer in building up his clientele, his duty as such zealously to espouse the cause of his private clients and to defend against charges of crime brought by law-enforcement agencies of which he is a part, might prevent, or even destroy, that unbiased judicial judgment which is so essential in the administration of justice.

"In our opinion, acceptance of a judgeship with the duties of conducting misdemeanor trials, and examinations in felony cases to determine whether those accused should be bound over for trial in a higher court, ethically bars the judge from acting as attorney for the defendants upon such trial, whether they were examined by him or by some other judge. Such a practice would not only diminish public confidence in the administration of justice in both courts, but would produce serious conflict between the private interests of the judge as a lawyer, and of his clients, and his duties as a judge in adjudicating important phases of criminal processes in other cases. The public and private duties would be incompatible. The prestige of the judicial office would be diverted to private benefit, and the judicial office would be demeaned thereby." *ABA Opinion* 242 (1942).

"A lawyer, who has previously occupied a judicial position or acted in a judicial capacity, should refrain from accepting employment in any matter involving the same facts as were involved in any specific question which he acted upon in a judicial capacity and, for the same reasons, should also refrain from accepting any employment which might reasonably appear to involve the same facts." *ABA Opinion* 49 (1931).

See ABA Opinion 110 (1934).

[8] *See ABA Opinions* 135 (1935) and 134 (1935); *cf.* ABA Canon 36 and *ABA Opinions* 39 (1931) and 26 (1930). *But see ABA Opinion* 37 (1931).

[9] "[A statement by a governmental department or agency with regard to a lawyer resigning from its staff that includes a laudation of his legal ability] carries implications, probably not founded in fact, that the lawyer's acquaintance and previous relations with the personnel of the administrative agencies of the government place him in an advantageous position in practicing before such agencies. So to imply would not only represent what probably is untrue, but would be highly reprehensible." *ABA Opinion* 184 (1938).

[10] *See* ABA Canon 11.

"*Rule 9.* . . . A member of the State Bar shall not commingle the money or other property of a client with his own; and he shall promptly report to the client the receipt by him of all money and other property belonging to such client. Unless the client otherwise directs in writing, he shall promptly deposit his client's funds in a bank or trust company . . . in a bank account separate from his own account and clearly designated as 'Clients' Funds Account' or 'Trust Funds Account' or words of similar import. Unless the client otherwise directs in writing, securities of a client in bearer form shall be kept by the attorney in a safe deposit box at a bank or trust company, . . . which safe deposit box shall be clearly designated as 'Clients' Account' or 'Trust Account' or words of similar import, and be separate from the attorney's own safe deposit box." Cal.Business and Professions Code § 6076 (West 1962).

"[C]ommingling is committed when a client's money is intermingled with that of his attorney and its separate identity lost so that it may be used for the attorney's personal expenses or subjected to claims of his creditors. . . . The rule against commingling was adopted to provide against the probability in some cases, the possibility in many cases, and the danger in all cases that such commingling will result in the loss of clients' money." Black v. State Bar, 57 Cal.2d 219, 225–26, 368 P.2d 118, 122, 18 Cal.Rptr. 518, 522 (1962).

* "Confidence" and "secret" are defined in DR 4–101(A)

ment or the loyalty of a lawyer to a client, whether it be a conflicting, inconsistent, diverse, or other interest.

(2) "Law firm" includes a professional legal corporation.

(3) "Person" includes a corporation, an association, a trust, a partnership, and any other organization or legal entity.

(4) "Professional legal corporation" means a corporation, or an association treated as a corporation, authorized by law to practice law for profit.

(5) "State" includes the District of Columbia, Puerto Rico, and other federal territories and possessions.

(6) "Tribunal" includes all courts and all other adjudicatory bodies.

(7) "A Bar association representative of the general bar of the geographical area in which the association exists" is a bar association, the membership of which is open to any lawyer in good standing in the geographical area and which has a membership at least equal to the lesser of three hundred members or twenty percent of the lawyers licensed to practice in the geographical area. A bar association of specialists as referred to in DR 2-105(A)(1) or (4) is "a bar association representative of the general bar" even though it does not meet the test of the preceding sentence.

(8) "Qualified legal assistance organization" is an organization described in DR 2-103(D)(1) through (4) or which recommends, furnishes, renders or pays for legal services to its members or beneficiaries under a plan operated, administered or funded by an insurance company or other organization which plan provides that the members or beneficiaries may select their counsel from lawyers representative of the general bar of the geographical area in which the plan is offered.

(9) "Lawyers representative of the general bar of the geographical area in which the plan is offered" are lawyers in good standing numbering not less than the greater of three hundred or twenty percent of those licensed to practice in the geographical area.

AMERICAN BAR ASSOCIATION CODE OF JUDICIAL CONDUCT *

CANON 1

A Judge Should Uphold the Integrity and Independence of the Judiciary

An independent and honorable judiciary is indispensable to justice in our society. A judge should participate in establishing, maintaining, and enforcing, and should himself observe, high standards of conduct so that the integrity and independence of the judiciary may be preserved. The provisions of this Code should be construed and applied to further that objective.

CANON 2

A Judge Should Avoid Impropriety and the Appearance of Impropriety in All His Activities

A. A judge should respect and comply with the law and should conduct himself at all times in a manner that promotes public confidence in the integrity and impartiality of the judiciary.

B. A judge should not allow his family, social, or other relationships to influence his judicial conduct or judgment. He should not lend the prestige of his office to advance the private interests of others; nor should he convey or permit others to convey the impression that they are in a special position to influence him. He should not testify voluntarily as a character witness.

Commentary

Public confidence in the judiciary is eroded by irresponsible or improper conduct by judges. A judge must avoid all impropriety and appearance of impropriety. He must expect to be the subject of constant public scrutiny. He must therefore accept restrictions on his conduct that might be viewed as burdensome by the ordinary citizen and should do so freely and willingly.

The testimony of a judge as a character witness injects the prestige of his office into the proceeding in which he testifies and may be misunderstood to be an official testimonial. This Canon, however, does not afford him a privilege against testifying in response to an official summons.

* The Code of Judicial Conduct was adopted by the House of Delegates of the American Bar Association on August 16, 1972.

CANON 3

A Judge Should Perform the Duties of His Office Impartially and Diligently

The judicial duties of a judge take precedence over all his other activities. His judicial duties include all the duties of his office prescribed by law. In the performance of these duties, the following standards apply:

A. Adjudicative Responsibilities.

(1) A judge should be faithful to the law and maintain professional competence in it. He should be unswayed by partisan interests, public clamor, or fear of criticism.

(2) A judge should maintain order and decorum in proceedings before him.

(3) A judge should be patient, dignified, and courteous to litigants, jurors, witnesses, lawyers, and others with whom he deals in his official capacity, and should require similar conduct of lawyers, and of his staff, court officials, and others subject to his direction and control.

Commentary

The duty to hear all proceedings fairly and with patience is not inconsistent with the duty to dispose promptly of the business of the court. Courts can be efficient and business-like while being patient and deliberate.

(4) A judge should accord to every person who is legally interested in a proceeding, or his lawyer, full right to be heard according to law, and, except as authorized by law, neither initiate nor consider *ex parte* or other communications concerning a pending or impending proceeding. A judge, however, may obtain the advice of a disinterested expert on the law applicable to a proceeding before him if he gives notice to the parties of the person consulted and the substance of the advice, and affords the parties reasonable opportunity to respond.

Commentary

The proscription against communications concerning a proceeding includes communications from lawyers, law teachers, and other persons who are not participants in the proceeding, except to the limited extent permitted. It does not preclude a judge from consulting with other judges, or with court personnel whose function is to aid the judge in carrying out his adjudicative responsibilities.

An appropriate and often desirable procedure for a court to obtain the advice of a disinterested expert on legal issues is to invite him to file a brief *amicus curiae.*

(5) A judge should dispose promptly of the business of the court.

Commentary

Prompt disposition of the court's business requires a judge to devote adequate time to his duties, to be punctual in attending court and expeditious in determining matters under submission, and to insist that court officials, litigants and their lawyers cooperate with him to that end.

(6) A judge should abstain from public comment about a pending or impending proceeding in any court, and should require similar abstention on the part of court personnel subject to his direction and control. This subsection does not prohibit judges from making public statements in the course of their official duties or from explaining for public information the procedures of the court.

Commentary

"Court personnel" does not include the lawyers in a proceeding before a judge. The conduct of lawyers is governed by DR7–107 of the *Code of Professional Responsibility.*

(7) A judge should prohibit broadcasting, televising, recording, or taking photographs in the courtroom and areas immediately adjacent thereto during sessions of court or recesses between sessions, except that a judge may authorize:

(a) the use of electronic or photographic means for the presentation of evidence, for the perpetuation of a record, or for other purposes of judicial administration;

(b) the broadcasting, televising, recording, or photographing of investitive, ceremonial, or naturalization proceedings;

(c) the photographic or electronic recording and reproduction of appropriate court proceedings under the following conditions:

(i) the means of recording will not distract participants or impair the dignity of the proceedings;

(ii) the parties have consented, and the consent to being depicted or recorded has been obtained from each witness appearing in the recording and reproduction;

(iii) the reproduction will not be exhibited until after the proceeding has been concluded and all direct appeals have been exhausted; and

(iv) the reproduction will be exhibited only for instructional purposes in educational institutions.

Commentary

Temperate conduct of judicial proceedings is essential to the fair administration of justice. The recording and reproduction of a proceeding should not distort or dramatize the proceeding.

B. Administrative Responsibilities.

(1) A judge should diligently discharge his administrative responsibilities, maintain professional competence in judicial administration, and facilitate the performance of the administrative responsibilities of other judges and court officials.

(2) A judge should require his staff and court officials subject to his direction and control to observe the standards of fidelity and diligence that apply to him.

(3) A judge should take or initiate appropriate disciplinary measures against a judge or lawyer for unprofessional conduct of which the judge may become aware.

Commentary

Disciplinary measures may include reporting a lawyer's misconduct to an appropriate disciplinary body.

(4) A judge should not make unnecessary appointments. He should exercise his power of appointment only on the basis of merit, avoiding nepotism and favoritism. He should not approve compensation of appointees beyond the fair value of services rendered.

Commentary

Appointees of the judge include officials such as referees, commissioners, special masters, receivers, guardians and personnel such as clerks, secretaries, and bailiffs. Consent by the parties to an appointment or an award of compensation does not relieve the judge of the obligation prescribed by this subsection.

C. Disqualification.

(1) A judge should disqualify himself in a proceeding in which his impartiality might reasonably be questioned, including but not limited to instances where:

(a) he has a personal bias or prejudice concerning a party, or personal knowledge of disputed evidentiary facts concerning the proceeding;

(b) he served as lawyer in the matter in controversy, or a lawyer with whom he previously practiced law served during such association as a lawyer concerning the matter, or the judge or such lawyer has been a material witness concerning it;

Commentary

A lawyer in a governmental agency does not necessarily have an association with other lawyers employed by that agency within the meaning of this subsection; a judge formerly employed by a governmental agency, however, should disqualify himself in a proceeding if his impartiality might reasonably be questioned because of such association.

(c) he knows that he, individually or as a fiduciary, or his spouse or minor child residing in his household, has a financial interest in the subject matter in controversy or in a party to the proceeding, or any other interest that could be substantially affected by the outcome of the proceeding;

(d) he or his spouse, or a person within the third degree of relationship to either of them, or the spouse of such a person:

(i) is a party to the proceeding, or an officer, director, or trustee of a party;

(ii) is acting as a lawyer in the proceeding;

Commentary

The fact that a lawyer in a proceeding is affiliated with a law firm with which a lawyer-relative of the judge is affiliated does not of itself disqualify the judge. Under appropriate circumstances, the fact that "his impartiality might reasonably be questioned" under Canon 3C(1), or that the lawyer-relative is known by the judge to have an interest in the law firm that could be "substantially affected by the outcome of the proceeding" under Canon 3C(1)(d)(iii) may require his disqualification.

(iii) is known by the judge to have an interest that could be substantially affected by the outcome of the proceeding;

(iv) is to the judge's knowledge likely to be a material witness in the proceeding;

(2) A judge should inform himself about his personal and fiduciary financial interests, and make a reasonable effort to inform himself about the personal financial interests of his spouse and minor children residing in his household.

(3) For the purposes of this section:

(a) the degree of relationship is calculated according to the civil law system;

Commentary

According to the civil law system, the third degree of relationship test would, for example, disqualify the judge if his or his spouse's father, grandfather, uncle, brother, or niece's husband were a party or lawyer in the proceeding, but would not disqualify him if a cousin were a party or lawyer in the proceeding.

(b) "fiduciary" includes such relationships as executor, administrator, trustee, and guardian;

(c) "financial interest" means ownership of a legal or equitable interest, however small, or a relationship as director, advisor, or other active participant in the affairs of a party, except that:

(i) ownership in a mutual or common investment fund that holds securities is not a "financial interest" in such securities unless the judge participates in the management of the fund;

(ii) an office in an educational, religious, charitable, fraternal, or civic organization is not a "financial interest" in securities held by the organization;

(iii) the proprietary interest of a policy holder in a mutual insurance company, of a depositor in a mutual savings association, or a similar proprietary interest, is a "financial interest" in the organization only if the outcome of the proceeding could substantially affect the value of the interest;

(iv) ownership of government securities is a "financial interest" in the issuer only if the outcome of the proceeding could substantially affect the value of the securities.

D. Remittal of Disqualification.

A judge disqualified by the terms of Canon 3C(1)(c) or Canon 3C(1)(d) may, instead of withdrawing from the proceeding, disclose on the record the basis of his disqualification. If, based on such disclosure, the parties and lawyers, independently of the judge's participation, all agree in writing that the judge's relationship is immaterial or that his financial interest is insubstantial, the judge is no longer disqualified, and may participate in the proceeding. The agreement, signed by all parties and lawyers, shall be incorporated in the record of the proceeding.

Commentary

This procedure is designed to minimize the chance that a party or lawyer will feel coerced into an agreement. When a party is not immediately available, the judge without violating this section may proceed on the written assurance of the lawyer that his party's consent will be subsequently filed.

CANON 4

A Judge May Engage in Activities to Improve the Law, the Legal System, and the Administration of Justice

A judge, subject to the proper performance of his judicial duties, may engage in the following quasi-judicial activities, if in doing so he does not

cast doubt on his capacity to decide impartially any issue that may come before him:

A. He may speak, write, lecture, teach, and participate in other activities concerning the law, the legal system, and the administration of justice.

B. He may appear at a public hearing before an executive or legislative body or official on matters concerning the law, the legal system, and the administration of justice, and he may otherwise consult with an executive or legislative body or official, but only on matters concerning the administration of justice.

C. He may serve as a member, officer, or director of an organization or governmental agency devoted to the improvement of the law, the legal system, or the administration of justice. He may assist such an organization in raising funds and may participate in their management and investment, but should not personally participate in public fund raising activities. He may make recommendations to public and private fund-granting agencies on projects and programs concerning the law, the legal system, and the administration of justice.

Commentary

As a judicial officer and person specially learned in the law, a judge is in a unique position to contribute to the improvement of the law, the legal system, and the administration of justice, including revision of substantive and procedural law and improvement of criminal and juvenile justice. To the extent that his time permits, he is encouraged to do so, either independently or through a bar association, judicial conference, or other organization dedicated to the improvement of the law.

Extra-judicial activities are governed by Canon 5.

CANON 5

A Judge Should Regulate His Extra-Judicial Activities to Minimize the Risk of Conflict with His Judicial Duties

A. Avocational Activities. A judge may write, lecture, teach, and speak on non-legal subjects, and engage in the arts, sports, and other social and recreational activities, if such avocational activities do not detract from the dignity of his office or interfere with the performance of his judicial duties.

Commentary

Complete separation of a judge from extra-judicial activities is neither possible nor wise; he should not become isolated from the society in which he lives.

B. Civic and Charitable Activities. A judge may participate in civic and charitable activities that do not reflect adversely upon his impartiality or interfere with the performance of his judicial duties. A judge may serve as an officer, director, trustee, or non-legal advisor of an educational, religious, charitable, fraternal, or civic organization not conducted for the economic or political advantage of its members, subject to the following limitations:

(1) A judge should not serve if it is likely that the organization will be engaged in proceedings that would ordinarily come before him or will be regularly engaged in adversary proceedings in any court.

Commentary

The changing nature of some organizations and of their relationship to the law makes it necessary for a judge regularly to reexamine the activities of each organization with which he is affiliated to determine if it is proper for him to continue his relationship with it. For example, in many jurisdictions charitable hospitals are now more frequently in court than in the past. Similarly, the boards of some legal aid organizations now make policy decisions that may have political significance or imply commitment to causes that may come before the courts for adjudication.

(2) A judge should not solicit funds for any educational, religious, charitable, fraternal, or civic organization, or use or permit the use of the prestige of his office for that purpose, but he may be listed as an officer, director, or trustee of such an organization. He should not be a speaker or the guest of honor at an organization's fund raising events, but he may attend such events.

(3) A judge should not give investment advice to such an organization, but he may serve on its board of directors or trustees even though it has the responsibility for approving investment decisions.

Commentary

A judge's participation in an organization devoted to quasi-judicial activities is governed by Canon 4.

C. Financial Activities.

(1) A judge should refrain from financial and business dealings that tend to reflect adversely on his impartiality, interfere with the proper performance of his judicial duties, exploit his judicial position, or involve him in frequent transactions with lawyers or persons likely to come before the court on which he serves.

***(2) Subject to the requirements of subsection (1), a judge may hold and manage investments, including real estate, and engage in other remunerative activity, but should not serve as an officer, director, manager, advisor, or employee of any business.**

Commentary

The Effective Date of Compliance provision of this Code qualifies this subsection with regard to a judge engaged in a family business at the time this Code becomes effective.

Canon 5 may cause temporary hardship in jurisdictions where judicial salaries are inadequate and judges are presently supplementing their income through commercial activities. The remedy, however, is to secure adequate judicial salaries.

[Canon 5C(2) sets the minimum standard to which a full-time judge should adhere. Jurisdictions that do not provide adequate judicial salaries but are willing to allow full-time judges to supplement their incomes through commercial activities may adopt the following substitute until such time as adequate salaries are provided:

***(2) Subject to the requirement of subsection (1), a judge may hold and manage investments, including real estate, and engage in other remunerative activity including the operation of a business.**

Jurisdictions adopting the foregoing substitute may also wish to prohibit a judge from engaging in certain types of businesses such as that of banks, public utilities, insurance companies, and other businesses affected with a public interest.]

(3) A judge should manage his investments and other financial interests to minimize the number of cases in which he is disqualified. As soon as he can do so without serious financial detriment, he should divest himself of investments and other financial interests that might require frequent disqualification.

(4) Neither a judge nor a member of his family residing in his household should accept a gift, bequest, favor, or loan from anyone except as follows:

(a) a judge may accept a gift incident to a public testimonial to him; books supplied by publishers on a complimentary basis for official use; or an invitation to the judge and his spouse to attend a bar-related function or activity devoted to the improvement of the law, the legal system, or the administration of justice;

(b) a judge or a member of his family residing in his household may accept ordinary social hospitality; a gift, bequest, favor, or loan from a relative; a wedding or engagement gift; a loan from a lending institution in its regular course of business on the same terms generally available to persons who are not judges; or a scholarship or fellowship awarded on the same terms applied to other applicants;

(c) a judge or a member of his family residing in his household may accept any other gift, bequest, favor, or loan only if the donor is not a party or other person whose interests have come or are likely to come before him, and, if its value exceeds $100, the judge reports it in the same manner as he reports compensation in Canon 6C.

Commentary

This subsection does not apply to contributions to a judge's campaign for judicial office, a matter governed by Canon 7.

(5) For the purposes of this section "member of his family residing in his household" means any relative of a judge by blood or marriage, or a person treated by a judge as a member of his family, who resides in his household.

(6) A judge is not required by this Code to disclose his income, debts, or investments, except as provided in this Canon and Canons 3 and 6.

Commentary

Canon 3 requires a judge to disqualify himself in any proceeding in which he has a financial interest, however small; Canon 5 requires a judge to refrain from engaging in business and from financial activities that might interfere with the impartial performance of his judicial duties; Canon 6 requires him to report all compensation he receives for activities outside his judicial office. A judge has the rights of an ordinary citizen, including the right to privacy of his financial affairs, except to the extent that limitations thereon are required to safeguard the proper performance of his duties. Owning and receiving income from investments do not as such affect the performance of a judge's duties.

(7) Information acquired by a judge in his judicial capacity should not be used or disclosed by him in financial dealings or for any other purpose not related to his judicial duties.

D. Fiduciary Activities. A judge should not serve as the executor, administrator, trustee, guardian, or other fiduciary, except for the estate, trust, or person of a member of his family, and then only if such service will not interfere with the proper performance of his judicial duties. "Member of his family" includes a spouse, child, grandchild, parent, grandparent, or other relative or person with whom the judge maintains a close familial relationship. As a family fiduciary a judge is subject to the following restrictions:

(1) He should not serve if it is likely that as a fiduciary he will be engaged in proceedings that would ordinarily come before him, or if the estate, trust, or ward becomes involved in adversary proceedings in the court on which he serves or one under its appellate jurisdiction.

Commentary

The Effective Date of Compliance provision of this Code qualifies this subsection with regard to a judge who is an executor, administrator, trustee, or other fiduciary at the time this Code becomes effective.

(2) **While acting as a fiduciary a judge is subject to the same restrictions on financial activities that apply to him in his personal capacity.**

Commentary

A judge's obligation under this Canon and his obligation as a fiduciary may come into conflict. For example, a judge should resign as trustee if it would result in detriment to the trust to divest it of holdings whose retention would place the judge in violation of Canon 5C(3).

E. Arbitration. A judge should not act as an arbitrator or mediator.

F. Practice of Law. A judge should not practice law.

G. Extra-judicial Appointments. A judge should not accept appointment to a governmental committee, commission, or other position that is concerned with issues of fact or policy on matters other than the improvement of the law, the legal system, or the administration of justice. A judge, however, may represent his country, state, or locality on ceremonial occasions or in connection with historical, educational, and cultural activities.

Commentary

Valuable services have been rendered in the past to the states and the nation by judges appointed by the executive to undertake important extra-judicial assignments. The appropriateness of conferring these assignments on judges must be reassessed, however, in light of the demands on judicial manpower created by today's crowded dockets and the need to protect the courts from involvement in extra-judicial matters that may prove to be controversial. Judges should not be expected or permitted to accept governmental appointments that could interfere with the effectiveness and independence of the judiciary.

CANON 6

A Judge Should Regularly File Reports of Compensation Received for Quasi-Judicial and Extra-Judicial Activities

A judge may receive compensation and reimbursement of expenses for the quasi-judicial and extra-judicial activities permitted by this Code, if the source of such payments does not give the appearance of influencing the judge in his judicial duties or otherwise give the appearance of impropriety, subject to the following restrictions:

A. Compensation. Compensation should not exceed a reasonable amount nor should it exceed what a person who is not a judge would receive for the same activity.

B. Expense Reimbursement. Expense reimbursement should be limited to the actual cost of travel, food, and lodging reasonably incurred by the judge and, where appropriate to the occasion, by his spouse. Any payment in excess of such an amount is compensation.

C. Public Reports. A judge should report the date, place, and nature of any activity for which he received compensation, and the name of the payor and the amount of compensation so received. Compensation or income of a spouse attributed to the judge by operation of a community property law is not extra-judicial compensation to the judge. His report should be made at least annually and should be filed as a public document in the office of the clerk of the court on which he serves or other office designated by rule of court.

CANON 7

A Judge Should Refrain from Political Activity Inappropriate to His Judicial Office

A. Political Conduct in General.

(1) **A judge or a candidate for election to judicial office should not:**

(a) **act as a leader or hold any office in a political organization;**

(b) **make speeches for a political organization or candidate or publicly endorse a candidate for public office;**

Commentary

A candidate does not publicly endorse another candidate for public office by having his name on the same ticket.

(c) **solicit funds for or pay an assessment or make a contribution to a political organization or candidate, attend political gatherings, or purchase tickets for political party dinners, or other functions, except as authorized in subsection A(2);**

(2) **A judge holding an office filled by public election between competing candidates, or a candidate for such office, may, only insofar as permitted by law, attend political gatherings, speak to such gatherings on his own behalf when he is a candidate for election or re-election, identify himself as a member of a political party, and contribute to a political party or organization.**

(3) **A judge should resign his office when he becomes a candidate either in a party primary or in a general election for a non-judicial office, except that he may continue to hold his judicial office while being a candidate for election to or serving as a delegate in a state constitutional convention, if he is otherwise permitted by law to do so.**

(4) **A judge should not engage in any other political activity except on behalf of measures to improve the law, the legal system, or the administration of justice.**

B. Campaign Conduct.

(1) A candidate, including an incumbent judge, for a judicial office that is filled either by public election between competing candidates or on the basis of a merit system election:

(a) should maintain the dignity appropriate to judicial office, and should encourage members of his family to adhere to the same standards of political conduct that apply to him;

(b) should prohibit public officials or employees subject to his direction or control from doing for him what he is prohibited from doing under this Canon; and except to the extent authorized under subsection B(2) or B(3), he should not allow any other person to do for him what he is prohibited from doing under this Canon;

(c) should not make pledges or promises of conduct in office other than the faithful and impartial performance of the duties of the office; announce his views on disputed legal or political issues; or misrepresent his identity, qualifications, present position, or other fact.

(2) A candidate, including an incumbent judge, for a judicial office that is filled by public election between competing candidates should not himself solicit or accept campaign funds, or solicit publicly stated support, but he may establish committees of responsible persons to secure and manage the expenditure of funds for his campaign and to obtain public statements of support for his candidacy. Such committees are not prohibited from soliciting campaign contributions and public support from lawyers. A candidate's committees may solicit funds for his campaign no earlier than [90] days before a primary election and no later than [90] days after the last election in which he participates during the election year. A candidate should not use or permit the use of campaign contributions for the private benefit of himself or members of his family.

Commentary

Unless the candidate is required by law to file a list of his campaign contributors, their names should not be revealed to the candidate.

[Each jurisdiction adopting this Code should prescribe a time limit on soliciting campaign funds that is appropriate to the elective process therein.]

(3) An incumbent judge who is a candidate for retention in or re-election to office without a competing candidate, and whose candidacy has drawn active opposition, may campaign in response thereto and may obtain publicly stated support and campaign funds in the manner provided in subsection B(2).

Compliance with the Code of Judicial Conduct

Anyone, whether or not a lawyer, who is an officer of a judicial system performing judicial functions, including an officer such as a referee in bankruptcy, special master, court commissioner, or magistrate, is a judge for the purpose of this Code. All judges should comply with this Code except as provided below.

A. Part-time Judge. A part-time judge is a judge who serves on a continuing or periodic basis, but is permitted by law to devote time to some other profession or occupation and whose compensation for that reason is less than that of a full-time judge. A part-time judge:

(1) is not required to comply with Canon 5C(2), D, E, F, and G, and Canon 6C;

(2) should not practice law in the court on which he serves or in any court subject to the appellate jurisdiction of the court on which he serves, or act as a lawyer in a proceeding in which he has served as a judge or in any other proceeding related thereto.

B. Judge Pro Tempore. A judge *pro tempore* is a person who is appointed to act temporarily as a judge.

(1) While acting as such, a judge *pro tempore* is not required to comply with Canon 5C(2), (3), D, E, F, and G, and Canon 6C.

(2) A person who has been a judge *pro tempore* should not act as a lawyer in a proceeding in which he has served as a judge or in any other proceeding related thereto.

C. Retired Judge. A retired judge who receives the same compensation as a full-time judge on the court from which he retired and is eligible for recall to judicial service should comply with all the provisions of this Code except Canon 5G, but he should refrain from judicial service during the period of an extra-judicial appointment not sanctioned by Canon 5G. All other retired judges eligible for recall to judicial service should comply with the provisions of this Code governing part-time judges.

Effective Date of Compliance

A person to whom this Code becomes applicable should arrange his affairs as soon as reasonably possible to comply with it. If, however, the demands on his time and the possibility of conflicts of interest are not substantial, a person who holds judicial office on the date this Code becomes effective may:

(a) continue to act as an officer, director, or non-legal advisor of a family business;

(b) continue to act as an executor, administrator, trustee, or other fiduciary for the estate or person of one who is not a member of his family.

MINIMUM REQUIREMENTS FOR ADMISSION TO LEGAL PRACTICE IN THE UNITED STATES *

This table contains information of educational and residence requirements reported in 1974. Full information and subsequent changes, if any, may be obtained by writing to the Clerk of the highest appellate Court or the Secretary of the Bar Board in each state. The compilation following does not reflect changes which may become effective on or after January 1, 1975.

* Originally published in the *Review of Legal Education*, Fall 1972 and reprinted with the permission of the American Bar Association 1973 and its Section of Legal Education and Admissions to the Bar.

MINIMUM REQUIREMENTS FOR ADMISSION TO LEGAL PRACTICE IN THE UNITED STATES

This table contains information of educational residence requirements reported September 1, 1970. Full information and subsequent changes, if any, may be obtained by writing to the Clerk of the highest appellate Court or the Secretary of the Bar Board in each state.

	Minimum amount of general education required before:		*Duration and distribution of period of law study if pursued:*			*Resident Requirements (for original applicants only, does not apply to lawyers seeking admission on comity for whom separate requirements are usually laid down)*
	Beginning period of law study	*Taking final examination*	*Wholly outside a law school*	*Partly in a law school*	*Wholly in a law school*	
American Bar Association Recommendations	Three years of resident study in a college for a 3-yrs. full-time or 2-yrs. for a 4-yrs. full-time law school study	....	Not permitted	At least the law school study recommended in the next column. No recommendation as to supplementary office work	Three years of full-time or "a longer course, equivalent in the number of working hours," of part-time study	
Alabama	96 semester hours or 144 quarter hours	....	Not permitted	No credit for office work	4 years from school approved by Board or if school is approved by A.B.A., 3 years	Bona fide residence at time of certification
Alaska	3 years college	....	Not permitted	Not permitted	Graduate of A.B.A. approved law school	30 days before exam
Arizona	3 years college	....	Not permitted	Not permitted	Graduate of an A.B.A. approved law school except for one who has practiced in another state at least 5 of last seven years immediately preceding application	
Arkansas	2 years college	....	Not permitted	Not permitted	Graduation from law school approved by A.B.A.	Bona fide residence at time of application
California	2 years approved college, or be 21 years of age and pass an educational equivalency examination or achieve admission to an accredited law school	....	4 years in California law office or California judge's chambers, or by correspondence. Must study aggregate of 3,456 hours and must take and pass first-year law students' examination at end of first year of law study	4 years. Any combination of study mentioned in preceding column and law school study	3 yrs. full-time and graduation or 4 yrs. part-time in accredited law school. 4 yrs. in unaccredited law school and must take and pass first year students' examination at end of first year of law study	None
Colorado	3 years regular college work in A.B.A. approved law school	....	Not permitted	Not permitted	Graduation as a full-time student or a part-time student under the standards adopted by the House of Delegates of the ABA on February 12, 1973	Bona fide residence for 1 mon. prior to examination and continuing until admission, except person admitted and practicing in another state, must become a resident prior to admission

Connecticut	College Degree (Consult Rules)	Bachelor's degree at an accredited college or university	Not permitted	Not permitted	"Pursued the study of law as a regular law student in residence at and obtained a bachelor of laws or equivalent degree from a law school accredited by the State Bar Examining Committee."	Bona fide intention to become resident
Delaware	Degree from college or university in a course approved by the Board of Examiners, or successful completion of examination approved by the Board of Examiners	....	Not permitted.	Not permitted	3 academic years and graduation from A.B.A. approved school or School of Jurisprudence, Oxford University or the School of Law at Cambridge University, England, plus 6 months clerkship	6 months for admission. Bona fide residence at time of bar exam
District of Columbia	....	....	Not permitted	Not permitted	Graduate of a law school approved by ABA at time of graduation	None
	3 years college or certified equivalent	....	No credit given for office study	....	Graduation from law school approved by A.B.A.	None
Florida	3 years college, or its equivalent	....	Not permitted	Not permitted	Graduate of law school approved by A.B.A. or member of A.A.L.S.	None
Georgia	2 yrs. college	....	Not permitted	Not permitted	LL.B or equivalent degree from a law school requiring classroom attendance for at least 3 academic years	All applicants must be residents of Georgia at the time of applying for the examination
Hawaii	3 years college	....	Not permitted	Not permitted	Graduate of A.B.A. approved law school or attorney admitted to practice in other jurisdiction(s) who is not a graduate of an approved school but who actively practiced in such jurisdiction(s) for 5 of 6 years immediately preceding application	3 mos. before admission
Idaho	3 years college	....	Not permitted	Not permitted	Graduate of law school approved by A.B.A.	Resident or intent to practice
Illinois	90 semester hours of acceptable college work	....	Not permitted	Not permitted	Graduate of law school approved by A.B.A.	None
Indiana	....	....	Not permitted	Not permitted	Graduate of law school approved by A.B.A.	Resident or intent to practice before admission

MINIMUM REQUIREMENTS FOR ADMISSION TO LEGAL PRACTICE IN THE UNITED STATES

	Minimum amount of general education required before:		*Duration and distribution of period of law study if pursued:*			*Resident Requirements (for original applicants only, does not apply to lawyers seeking admission on comity for whom separate requirements are usually laid down)*
	Beginning period of law study	*Taking final examination*	*Wholly outside a law school*	*Partly in a law school*	*Wholly in a law school*	
Iowa	3 years college	....	Not permitted	Not permitted	3 full years in an accredited law school and LL.B. or J.D. degree	Bona fide resident at time of application
Kansas	B.A., B.S. or higher degree	....	Not permitted	No provision	Applicant must show that his academic and law degrees have been earned during 14 academic semesters in accredited institutions, with not less than 6 semesters in an accredited college and 6 semesters in an accredited law school and the other 2 semesters in either one or the other of such institutions, as their curricula may provide	Resident of state, provided that non-residents graduating from an accredited law school in Kansas may take the first examination held after graduation
Kentucky	Satisfy A.B.A. requirements	....	Not permitted	Not permitted	LL.B degree from a law school approved by A.B.A. or by Assn. of American Law Schools	Resident or intent to practice
Louisiana	3 years college	....	Not permitted	Not permitted	Graduate of law school approved by A.B.A.	None
Maine	2 years college	....	Not permitted	Successful completion of 2/3 of requirement for graduation from A.B.A. approved law school followed by 1 year of law office study in Maine	Graduate from A.B.A. approved law school	None – Domicile of time of admission
Maryland	90 semester hours accredited college; see local rule for courses of study	....	Not permitted	Not permitted	A.B.A. approved law school	Domicile at application and admission
Massachusetts	Applicants shall have completed the work accepted for a bachelor's degree in a college approved by the board or otherwise have received an education equivalent thereto in its opinion	....	Not permitted	Not permitted	Graduation from approved 3-year full-time school or 4-year approved part-time school	None
Michigan	3 years college	....	Not permitted	Not permitted	3 years full-time law school, 4 years part-time law school	None, but applicant must satisfy Board that he intends in good faith to practice or teach law in State

Minnesota	Satisfy A.B.A. requirements	....	Not permitted	Not permitted	LL.B. or equivalent degree from A.B.A. approved school	Residence required at time of admission
Mississippi	2 years college	....	2 years office study. Approval of such study in advance	No rule	Graduation from A.B.A. approved school or Jackson School of Law	Bona fide residence on date of application
Missouri	3 years college	....	Not permitted	Not permitted	Registration required within 90 days after law study begun and LL.B. degree from a school approved by A.B.A.	Resident at admission
Montana	3 yrs. college or equiv.	....	Not permitted	Not permitted	Graduation from A.B.A. approved school	6 months prior to date of filing application and bona fide resident of the state
Nebraska	2 years in college	....	Not permitted	Not permitted	Graduate of law school approved by A.B.A.	Must be a resident
Nevada	3 years in accredited college for study in 3-yrs. full-time program. 2-years for study in 4-yrs. full-time program	....	Not permitted	Not permitted	Graduate of law school approved by A.B.A.	Bona fide resident by March 1 of the examination year and remain such until arrival of July examination
New Hampshire	3 years college	....	Not permitted	Not permitted	Graduate A.B.A. approved school	Resident at admission
New Jersey	3 years college	....	Not permitted	The law school study required in the next column and completion of an approved course in Skills and Methods unless permission is obtained to serve a nine-months' clerkship in lieu of taking the course	Graduate of A.B.A. approved law school	Domiciled at exam or declares intention to become domiciled or maintain principal office for practice of law in state
New Mexico	2 years college	....	Not permitted	Not permitted	Graduate of a law school approved by A.B.A.	90 days
New York	3 years college or equiv.	....	Not permitted	First year in approved law school, thereafter pursuing law office study for an aggregate total of four years	Successful completion of 3-year day school or 4-year evening course in an approved law school and graduation with LL.B. degree	6 months residence or 6 months full-time employment for certification
North Carolina	3/4 of the work required for a bachelor's degree at the university of the state in which the college or university is located	....	Not recognized	Not permitted	A law degree from a law school approved by the Council of the N.C. State Bar: or will receive a law degree within 60 days after the written exam: or applicant has successfully completed the courses required by the Council of the N.C. State Bar set out in Rule XI. Sec. 3	June 15th of year of exam
North Dakota	3 years college	....	Not permitted	Not permitted	Degree from A.B.A. approved school	Resident at time of admission

MINIMUM REQUIREMENTS FOR ADMISSION TO LEGAL PRACTICE IN THE UNITED STATES

	Minimum amount of general education required before:		*Duration and distribution of period of law study if pursued:*			*Resident Requirements (for original applicants only, does not apply to lawyers seeking admission on comity for whom separate requirements are usually laid down)*
	Beginning period of law study	*Taking final examination*	*Wholly outside a law school*	*Partly in a law school*	*Wholly in a law school*	
Ohio	Degree from accredited college	....	Not permitted	Not permitted	LL.B. degree from a school approved by A.B.A. or League of Ohio Law Schools and 10 hours of classroom instruction on legal ethics and professional responsibility	Resident at time of admission
Oklahoma	Bachelor's degree, minimum 120 credit hrs.	....	Not permitted	Not permitted	Registration required and graduation from school approved by A.B.A. or Board of Bar Examiners	Resident at exam
Oregon	....	....	Not permitted	Not permitted	Degree from school approved by A.B.A. or Supreme Court of Oregon	Resident or bona fide intention to become resident, expressed in affidavit at time of filing application but before being admitted. Affidavit of residence filed with the State Court Administrator, Supreme Court of Oregon, at time of admission
Pennsylvania	Satisfactory degree from an accredited college or education which in the opinion of the Board is equivalent to an undergraduate college education	....	Not permitted	Not permitted	Degree from A.B.A. approved school	At admission declare intent to prac. in PA
Puerto Rico	Bachelor's degree	....	Not permitted	Not permitted	Law degree from school approved by Superior Educational Council if pursued in P.R. or by A.B.A. if pursued outside of P.R.	1 yr. before app.
Rhode Island	....	....	Not permitted	Not permitted	Degree from approved law school plus 3 months office study, or plus completion of 6 week training course	3 months prior to admission
South Carolina	....	....	Not permitted	Not permitted	Degree from school approved by A.B.A. or Supreme Court of South Carolina	Bona fide resident on and from the first day of April of the year in which he takes the July examination or on and from the first day of November of the year next preceding the year in which he takes the February examination
South Dakota	....	....	Not permitted	Not permitted	Graduation from school approved by A.B.A.	Residence at time of application. Nonresident must give proof of intent to become citizen

Tennessee	Bachelor's degree from accredited college	....	Not permitted	Not permitted	Graduation from a school approved by A.B.A. or Board of Law Examiners	Bona fide intention to reside and practice in state. Licensed after establishing domicile and residence within State for at least two months
Texas	90 semester hours	....	Not permitted	36 months. Registration required	27 months full-time, 36 months part-time study in approved law school with credit for 50 semester hours	3 months
Utah	3 yrs. college	....	Not permitted	Not permitted	Graduation with LL.B. degree or its equivalent from a resident law school which requires for such degree a minimum of 6 years professional and academic study in an accredited institution	3 months prior to application
Vermont	3 years college	....	4 years after registration	4 years after registration. Credit given for law school study toward 4 year requirement	3 years if in a law school approved by Supreme Court	6 months for law school graduates. 6 months law office study for admission on motion or for out-of-state attorneys to appear for examination. Must be U.S. citizen in addition to 6 months residence
Virginia	3 years college	....	36 months of law study. Registration required	Credit allowed for law school toward three year requirement	Graduate school approved by A.B.A. or Board of Examiners	2 to 3 mos. before exam
Washington	4 years college	....	4 years law office study. Registration required	Study in a law school but not yielding a degree, followed by further study in school or in law office in state, in discretion of board	Graduate from an approved law school	Bona fide resident at time of admission
West Virginia	3 years accredited college	....	Not permitted	Not permitted	Degree from school fully approved by A.B.A.	30 days
Wisconsin	3 years college	....	Not permitted	Not permitted	Graduate of law school approved by A.B.A.	Residence at time of application
Wyoming	3 years college	....	Not permitted	1 year in approved law school. 2 years in law office study	3 years in approved law school	Bona fide resident of Wyoming may make application to take the Bar Examination but if Bar Examination passed, recommendation for admission will not be made to Supreme Court until applicant has been bona fide resident for six months

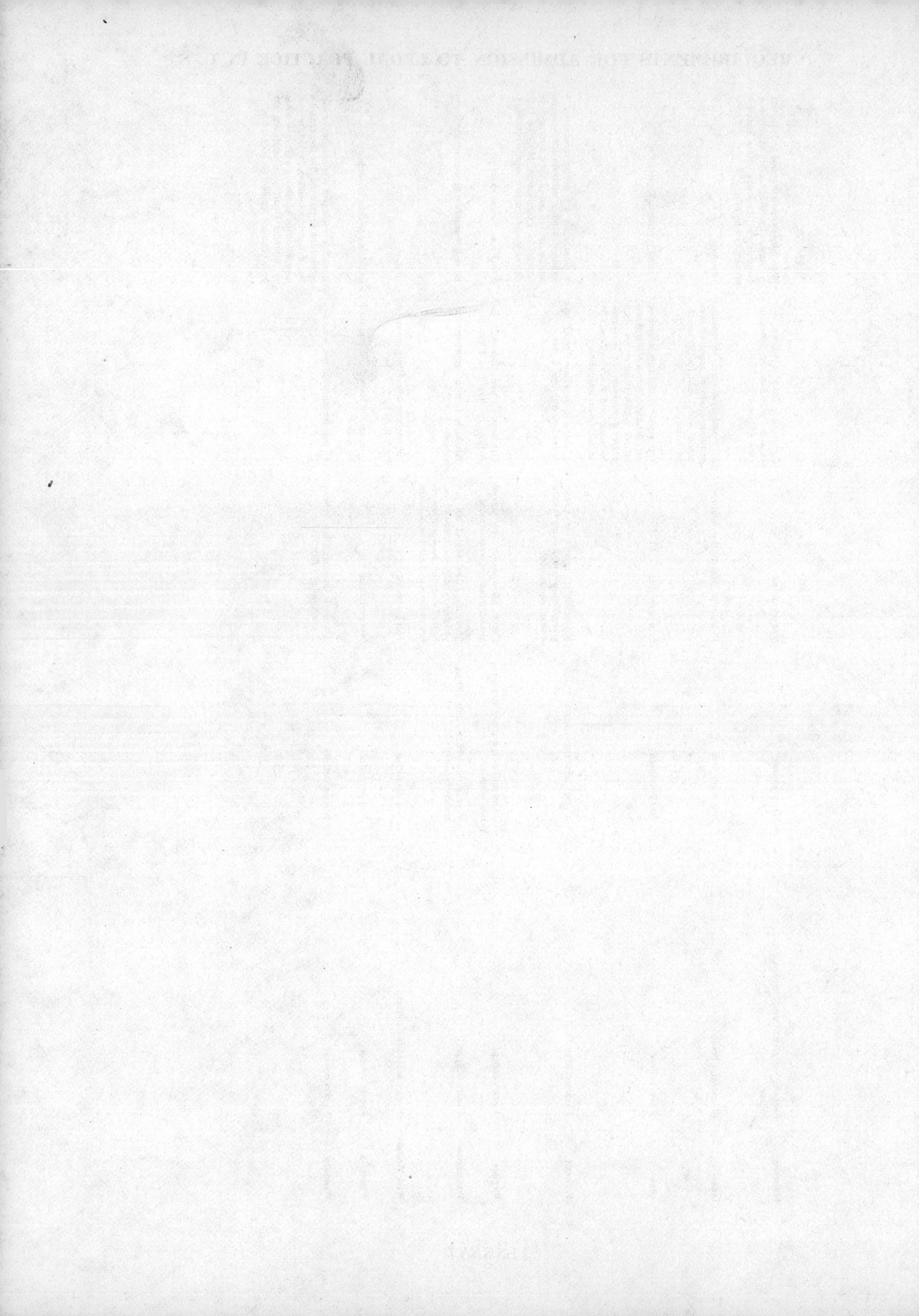

BLACK'S DICTIONARY OF LAW

FOURTH EDITION

Revised

A

A. The first letter in the English and most other alphabets derived from the Roman or Latin alphabet, which was one of several ancient Italian alphabets derived from the Greek, which was an adaptation of the Phœnician. The first letter in the Phœnician alphabet was called *aleph*, meaning "ox", which is also the meaning of the first letter in the Greek alphabet, *alpha*.

Alpha and the second letter of the Greek alphabet, *beta*, were combined to form "alphabet," which is largely the same in different languages. In Danish, Dutch, Polish and Swedish *alfabet;* in English, German and French, *alphabet;* in Italian, Portuguese and Spanish, *alfabeto;* in Russian, *alfabetŭ,* etc. This striking similarity shows borrowing, either mediately or immediately, from the same source.

A has several different forms, the most curious of which is little a and big A. All of our letters were first capitals, and remained so for a long time. Then small letters alone were used for centuries. Later capitals were used with small letters, largely for ornamental purposes. The ancient Egyptians had twenty a's to choose from, and it is said that a is the initial letter of about one-seventh of all Armenian words.

Nundinal Letters

A is also the first of the nundinal letters consisting of the first eight letters of the alphabet. These letters were repeated successively from the first to the last day of the year by the Romans and every ninth day was market day, when the country people came into the city to buy and sell and to attend to their private or religious affairs. However, no market day could coincide with the first day of January or the ninth day of the other months. The first market day of the year fell eight days from the preceding market day, which made the nundinal letter change every year, but if the nundinal letter for a given year was, for example, A, the market day always coincided with A, which was the ninth day from the preceding market day, both inclusive. No judgment could be pronounced, nor assemblies of the people held, on these days, but this was changed by the *lex Hortensia* in 246 B.C. Proposed laws were posted, and a vote could not be taken until three Roman weeks *(trinum nundinum)*, or 24 days, had elapsed. A judgment debtor had 30 days to satisfy judgment against him. If he failed to do so, he was seized and taken before the magistrate and if he could find no surety he was put in chains and held by the judgment creditor for 60 days, during which time the amount of his debt was proclaimed on three successive market days, and then if he failed, the XII Tables provided: "* * * *Tertiis nundinus partis secanto; si plus minusive secuerint, se fraude esto."* (On the third market day let him be cut into pieces; if any one [any creditor] cut more or less than his share, it shall not be a crime). Shylock, it will be remembered, had to cut just a pound of flesh and no more.

Dominical or Sunday Letters

A is also the first of the Dominical or Sunday letters, consisting of the first seven letters of the alphabet, which were introduced to replace the nundinal letters of the Romans. These letters, repeated successively from the first to the last day of the year, show the order of Sundays according to the Christian calendar. If the first day of January is on Sunday, all the rest of the days designated by A will also be Sundays. Since each common year ends on the same day of the week that it begins, the dominical letters change each year in retrogression. If the year is a leap year an adjustment is made either on the 25th or 29th of February. The dominical letters are used to determine the date of Easter but may also be used to determine the day of the week on which a given date falls in any year.

A as Symbol

Both as a symbol and as an abbreviation, A is used in every phase of human activity and learning. In law, commerce, manufacturing, engineering, printing, music, medicine, geometry, mathematics, physics, chemistry, logic, philosophy, aeronautics, artillery, etc., these devices, which are meaningless to the unitiated, simply could not be dispensed with. The Puritans first burned A on the forehead of the adulterer,—or at least on that of the adulteress!—and later fastened it on the sinner's clothing. The Roman judges used three wax-covered wooden tables. On one was inscribed A for *Absolvo* (I acquit); on the second C for *Condemno* (I condemn), and on the third N. L. for *Non liquet* (It is not clear). When a proposed law was to be voted on, Roman voters received two tablets, on one of which was inscribed A for *antiquo* (for the old law), and on the other U. R. for *Uti rogas* (as you ask). A is also the first of the letters employed by the Semites and the ancient Greeks as numeral signs. If the Greek *a* was accented above, it stood for 1; if below, it stood for 1000. The Romans also used A as a numeral sign before they adopted the letter D. If A was not accented, it stood for 500, but if accented thus, Ā, it stood for 5000.

The symbol @ is a graphic modification of the Latin *ad,* meaning "at" or "to". Some European railroads use A to designate first class railroad coaches. In European tourist guides A is used to designate places where there are hotels able to satisfy the wants of motorists. Mercantile agencies use A to indicate the highest commercial credit. A is also the highest mark given by teachers to pupils. Ship registries in United States, England, Germany and Norway use A to indicate the highest class of vessel.

In the record of American Shipping A1 stands for a first-class vessel of the highest seaworthiness, the lower degrees being expressed by A1½, etc., A3 being the lowest. In Lloyd's Register A1 means a first-class vessel. A printed in red means an over-aged vessel. Æ a third-class vessel. The broad A means an iron ship. The description of a ship as "A1" amounts to a warranty. Ollive v. Booker, 1 Exch. 423.

In ceramics A has various meanings. On fine old Sevres A alone shows that the piece was made in 1753, whereas AA shows that it was made in 1777. A is also used as a brand by certain breeders of bulls for the bull ring, as well as by manufacturers of fine Toledo swords. A denotes the first of a series, and is used to distinguish the first page of a folio from the second, which is marked b (Coke, Litt. 114a, 114b), as well as the first foot-note and the first section or subsection in statutes. It is also the name of the sixth note of the natural diatonic scale of C, or the first note of the relative minor scale. To this note all orchestral instruments are tuned. A also indicates the key in which many great pieces of music are composed. The money coined at the Paris mint is marked with an A, and it was long supposed that such coinage was superior to that of the provincial mints. This gave rise to the phrase *Etre marqué à l'A* (to be marked with an A) and was used to indicate a man of eminent rank or merit, just as we use A-1 or A to indicate excellence of either persons or commodities.

A is also used in numerous other phrases and proverbs. For example, *A word to the wise is sufficient.* This ordinarily admonitory proverb was held to be libellous in view of the context in which it was used. One who had sold out to his partner warned customers that the buyer was not responsible for his debts, since he was a minor, and that "a word to the wise is sufficient." The court said: "But when what was previously said is followed by the significant and proverbially precautionary words—'A word to the wise is sufficient,' the idea is at once conveyed that plaintiff, is wanting in honor and integrity as a business man, and that those who should deal with him would suffer loss." Hays v. Mather, 15 Ill.App. 30, 34. For the phrase, *from alpha to omega,* there is our *from A to Z* and *A to izzard,* and the German *von A bis Z,* which mean from beginning to end; completely; thoroughly; or in more modern slang, from soup to nuts. The German proverb *Wer A sagt, muṣ auch B sagen* is based on a profound knowledge of human nature, and translates, you can't say A without saying B; in for a penny, in for a pound. In other words, don't take the *first* step if you don't want to go the limit. Of a very ignorant or stupid person it has long been said that *He does not know great A from a bull's foot* or that he knows *ni A ni B* (neither A nor B). In *Birds of a feather flock together, a* means the same, or *a feather* means the same kind.

A as Abbreviation

As an abbreviation a, either alone or in combination with other letters, is used in all the arts and sciences as well in hundreds of non-technical ways. Its meaning as an abbreviation largely depends on context. In common usage, it may mean *about, accepted, acne, aged, answer, ante, area, amateur,* etc. It is also used for almost any name of a person beginning with A, as Alfred, Anna, etc. In chemistry it stands for argon. A note provided for "Int. @ 6% p. a." The court said: "The letter @ when used in a note, as it is here, is known and recognized among commercial people and businessmen as standing for 'at.'" Belford v. Beatty, 34 N.E. 254, 255, 145 Ill. 414, 418.

A is an abbreviation of *adversus* (against). *Versus* and its abbreviation v. are much oftener used in this sense, though the original Latin meaning of *versus* is toward; in the direction of.

Å, angstrom unit; the unit for measuring the length of light waves. The ultra violet rays of sunlight between 3130Å and 2900Å activate provitamins in the skin and certain foods, so as to produce the antirachitic substance known as vitamin D, which is also extracted from fish liver oils.

The Spelling of A

A was formerly spelt a-per-se, a ("a" by itself makes the word "a") of which A-per-se-A, A persey, and apersie were corruptions and synonymous with superior, chief, first, etc.

A in Latin and Law Latin

Anglo-American law abounds in Latin and French words and phrases, and the use of A in these languages is important to the English-speaking lawyer. In Latin "A" was used both as an abbreviation and as a symbol. For example "A" was an abbreviation for "Aulus," a praenomen, or the first of the usual three names of a person by which he was distinguished from others of the same family; also for "ante" in "a. d.," *ante diem* (before the day), and for "anno" (year) in a. u. c., *anno urbis conditae* (the year of the building of the city) and in *anno ab urbe condita* (from the year of the building of the city). As a preposition, the form was either Ā, ĀB or ABS. A was used before consonants; ab was usually used before vowels, but sometimes before consonants, whereas abs was used before "c" or "t." The meaning was "from," "away from," "on the side of," "at," "after," "since," "by," "by means of," "out of," "with reference to," "in regard of," "near by," and "along." For example, *A fronte* in front; *ab tergo,* from behind; *a puertitia,* from youth; *ab sole orbe,* from or at sunrise; *ab intestato,* without a will, intestate. In law Latin, "a" means "by," "with," "from," "in," "of," and "on," and AB means "by," "from," and "in". 1 C.J.S. p. 2.

A in French and Law French

In French À is a preposition, the meaning of which largely depends on context. It is usually translated as "into," "at," "to," "in," "by," "of," "with," "on," "from," "for," "under," "till," "within," "between," etc. It also changes into *au* and *aux* when combined with "the." A is also the third person, singular number, present tense, indicative mood of the verb *avoir,* (to have): *Il a* (he has). In law French "a" is used as a preposition meaning "at," "for," "in," "of," "on," "to," and "with." 1 C.J.S. p. 2.

A in Roman Criminal Law

Among the Romans this letter was used in criminal trials. The judges were furnished with small tables covered with wax, and each one inscribed on it the initial letter of his vote: A (absolvo) when he voted to acquit the accused; C (condemno) when he was for condemnation; and N L (non liquet), when the matter did not appear clearly, and he desired a new argument.

The letter A (i. e. antiquo, "for the old law") was inscribed upon Roman ballots under the Lex Tabellaria, to indicate a negative vote; Tayl.Civ. Law, 191, 192.

A as Indefinite Article

A is the form of the indefinite article that is used before consonants and initial consonant sounds, on being used before initial vowel sounds, as, for example, *a house, a year, a utility;* but *an oak, an ape* and *an hour,* because the h is silent. Formerly where the initial h of certain words was not accented, as historical, hypothetical, hotel, humble, etc., an was used, but now the h is no longer silent, and the best usage in both the United States and England is to use a before such words. *A hypothetical question, a historical monument, a hotel,* etc., are the correct forms.

The word "a" has varying meanings and uses. "A" means "one" or "any," but less emphatically than either. It may mean one where only one is intended, or it may mean any one of a great number. It is placed before nouns of the singular number, denoting an individual object or quality individualized. First Trust Joint Stock Land Bank of Chicago v. Armstrong, 222 Iowa 425, 269 N.W. 502, 506, 107 L.R.A. 873.

The article "a" is not necessarily a singular term; it is often used in the sense of "any" and is then applied to more than one individual object. Philadelphia & R. R. Co. v. Green & Flinn, 2 W.W. Harr.(Del.) 78, 119 A. 840, 846; In re Sanders, 54 Law J.Q.B. The article "a" is not generally used in a singular sense unless such an intention is clear from the language of the statute, 1 C.J.S., A, p. 1, but statute providing that parties to "a" reorganization shall be deemed a single employing unit referred to quality or nature of changes, rather than quantity, and meant not one or only one, but any, and fact that there had been more than one reorganization did not prevent statute from applying. Lindley v. Murphy, 387 Ill. 506, 56 N.E.2d 832, 838. So under a statute providing that the issuance of "a" certificate to one carrier should not bar a certificate to another over the same route, a certificate could be granted to more than two carriers over the same route. State ex rel. Crown Coach Co. v. Public Service Commission, 238 Mo.App. 287, 179 S.W.2d 123, 127. But the meaning depends on context. For example, in Workmen's Compensation Act, on, or in or about "a" railway, factory, etc., was held not to mean any railway, factory, etc., but *the* railway, factory, etc., of the employer. Francis v. Turner, [1900] 1 Q.B. 478; 69 L.J.Q.B. 182; 81 L.T. 770; 48 W.R. 228; 64 J.P. 53.

Insurance against loss occasioned by "a sea" did not limit insured to loss occasioned by a single wave, but covered losses occasioned by heavy waves during voyage. Snowden v. Guion, 101 N. Y. 458, 5 N.E. 322.

In State ex rel. Atty. Gen. v. Martin, 60 Ark. 343, 30 S. W. 421, 28 L.R.A. 153, the state Constitution provided for "a judge" in each circuit. Owing to increase in judicial business, the Legislature provided for an additional judge for the sixth circuit. It was contended that the statute was unconstitutional. The court said:

"Now, the adjective 'a,' commonly called the 'indefinite article,' and so called, too, because it does not define any particular person or thing, is entirely too indefinite, in the connection used, to define or limit the number of judges which the legislative wisdom may provide for the judicial circuits of the state. And it is perfectly obvious that its office and meaning was well understood by the framers of our constitution, for nowhere in that instrument do we find it used as a numerical limitation. It is insisted that if 'a' does not mean 'one,' and 'but one,' in the section quoted, then the way is open for a latitudinarian construction in the various other sections where it occurs.

"* * * So the question recurs as to the significance of the letter 'a,' for the convention must be taken to have meant what they have plainly said. It performs precisely the same office here as in every other section where it occurs. Section 6 of the article 7 says, 'A judge of the supreme court shall be learned in the law,' etc.; section 16 says, 'A circuit judge shall be learned in the law,' etc.; section 41, 'A justice of the peace shall be a qualified elector and a resident of the township,' etc. Does the word 'a' in these sections mean one, and only one, judge or justice? If so, which one? In the same section in which 'a judge' occurs we find, 'He shall be "a" conservator of the peace within the circuit.' Does 'a conservator' mean that he is to be the only conservator of the peace for the circuit? If so, this provision is plainly in conflict with others. See sections 4, 40. It is apparent that 'a' was used before the word 'judge' in the section under consideration because, according to our English idiom, the sentence could not have been euphoniously expressed without it. In some languages—the Latin and Russian, for instance—it would not have been used at all. It could have been omitted without in the least impairing the sense, and its use gave no additional force or meaning to the sentence. To use the illustration of the learned counsel for the state: If one orders 'a sack of flour, a ham, a horse, a ton of coal,' etc., it is understood he means but one. So it would be understood if he left off the 'a,' and said 'sack of flour, ham, horse, ton of coal,' the 'a' being used before the words beginning with the consonant sound simply to preserve the euphony. If the limitation is not in the word 'judge' without the 'a,' there is certainly no restriction with it. According to Mr. Webster, 'a' means 'one' or 'any,' but less 'emphatically than either.' It may mean one where only one is intended, or it may be any one of a great number. That is the trouble. Of itself, it is in no sense a term of limitation. If there were a dozen judges in any one circuit each would still be 'a judge' for that circuit. Mr. Webster also says, 'It is placed before nouns of the singular number, denoting an individual object, or quality individualized.' 'Quality' is defined as (1) 'the condition of being of such a sort as distinguished from others; (2) special or temporary character; profession, occupation.' Webst. Dict. The 'a' was so used here. The character, or profession, individualized, was that of a judge. The functions of the office to be performed were those of 'a judge,' not governor, sheriff, or constable. A review of the various other provisions of the constitution, supra, where the word 'a' occurs, shows that no absurd consequences, such as filling the offices in other departments with a multitudinous array of incumbents, could possibly result."

Where the law required the delivery of a copy of a notice to husband and a copy to wife, the sheriff's return that he had delivered "a copy" to husband and wife was insufficient. State v. Davis, Tex.Civ.App., 139 S.W.2d 638, 640.

In Lakeside Forge Co. v. Freedom Oil Works, 265 Pa. 528, 109 A. 216, 217, it was said:

"'A car or two' signifies an indefinite small number, and may include as many as seven. In that respect the expression is similar to 'a few.' It must be construed with reference to the subject matter, and is not necessarily confined to one or two. It is like the words 'in a day or two.'"

In Deutsch v. Mortgage Securities Co., 96 W.Va. 676, 123 S.E. 793, the deed contained a covenant against construction of flats or apartments and provided that no dwelling but "a one-family house" should be built on the lot. The grantee built two one-family dwelling houses; and it was held that he could properly do so.

"A" is sometimes read as "the." Bookham v. Potter, 37 L.J.C.P. 276; L.R. 3 C.P. 490; 16 W.R. 806; 18 L.T. 479, though the two terms are ordinarily distinguishable. Howell v. State, 138 S.E. 206, 164 Ga. 204. The grant of "a" right of sporting on land, gives only a concurrent right, but the grant of "the" right gives it exclusively. Sutherland v. Heathcote, [1892] 1 Ch. 475; 61 L.J. 248; 66 L.T. 210. And a license to fish with "a" rod and line does not justify the use of more than one rod and one line. Combridge v. Harrison, 72 L.T. 592; 64 L.J.M.C. 175; 59 J.P. 198.

Hinson v. Hinson, 176 N.C. 613, 97 S.E. 465, involved a will providing that son taking care of widow should receive $100 "a year." It was held that the quoted words were not synonymous with annually, but merely fixed the rate of compensation, and that there was no right to compensation until widow's death.

AAA. Agricultural Adjustment Act.

A. A. C. *Anno ante Christum,* the year before Christ.

A. A. C. N. *Anno ante Christum natum,* the year before the birth of Christ.

A AVER ET TENER. L. Fr. (L. Lat. *habendum et tenendum.*) To have and to hold. Co.Litt. §§ 523, 524. *A aver et tener a luy et a ses heires, a touts jours,*—to have and to hold to him and his heirs forever. Id. § 625. See Aver et Tener.

A. B. Able-bodied seaman. In English law a seaman is entitled to be rated A. B. when he has served at sea three years before the mast. In the United States the term "Able Seaman" is used. For the requirements of able seaman, see 46 U.S.C.A. § 672. Also *artium baccalaureus,* bachelor of arts. In England, generally written B. A.

A. B. A. American Bar Association.

A. B. A. J. American Bar Association Journal.

A BON DROIT. With good reason; justly; rightfully.

A. C., *Anno Christi,* the year of Christ.

A/C means account and is much used by bookkeepers. As used in a check, it has been held not a direction to the bank to credit the amount of the check to the person named, but rather a memorandum to identify the transaction in which the check was issued. Marsh v. First State Bank & Trust Co. of Canton, 185 Ill.App. 29, 32.

A CANCELLANDO. From cancelling. 3 Bl. Comm. 46.

A CANCELLIS. The Chancellor.

A CANCELLIS CURIAE EXPLODI. To be expelled from the bar of the court.

A CAPELLA OR A LA CAPELLA. In music, in the church style; also that the instruments are to play in unison with the vocal part, or that one part is to be played by a number of instruments.

A CAUSA DE CY. For this reason.

A. C. C. Agricultural Credit Corporation.

A CE. For this purpose.

A CEL JOUR. At this day.

A CŒLO USQUE AD CENTRUM. From the heavens to the center of the earth. Or more fully, *Cujus est solum ejus est usque ad coelum et ad inferos.* The owner of the soil owns to the heavens and also to the lowest depths. Or, *Cujus est solum est usque ad cœlum,*—the owner of the soil owns to the heavens. This doctrine has been questioned. Butler v. Frontier Telephone Co., 186 N.Y. 486, 79 N.E. 716, 11 L.R.A.,N.S., 920—and the flight of airplanes and recent oil and gas regulations undoubtedly have qualified the owner's dominion not only in the heavens but in the lowest depths. See American Digest System, Mines and Minerals, ⚷92, and Trespass, ⚷10.

A COMMUNI OBSERVANTIA NON EST RECEDENDUM. From common observance there should be no departure; there must be no departure from common usage. 2 Coke, 74; Co. Litt. 186*a*, 229*b*, 365*a*; Wing.Max. 752, max. 203. A maxim applied to the practice of the courts, to the ancient and established forms of pleading and conveyancing, and to professional usage generally. Id. 752–755. Lord Coke applies it to common professional opinion. Co.Litt. 186*a*, 364*b*.

A CONFECTIONE. From the making. Clayton's Case, 5 Coke, pt. II, la; Anonymous, 1 Ld. Raym. 480.

A CONFECTIONE PRAESENTIUM. From the making of the indentures. Clayton's Case, 5 Coke, pt. II, la.

A CONSILIIS. (Lat. *consilium,* advice.) Of counsel; a counsellor. The term is used in the civil law by some writers instead of *a responsis.* Spelman, "*Apocrisarius.*"

A CONTRARIO SENSU. On the other hand; in the opposite sense.

A CUEILLETTE. In French law. In relation to the contract of affreightment, signifies when the cargo is taken on condition that the master succeeds in completing his cargo from other sources. Arg.Fr.Merc.Law, 543.

A. D. *Anno Domini,* in the year of our Lord.

An information charging that act was committed on 4th day of August, "A. D. 190 ," alleged an impossible year "and it is quite evident that the last figure of the year was inadvertently omitted but what that figure was intended to be * * * cannot be inferred with any certainty." People v. Weiss, 168 Ill.App. 502, 504.

"The information alleges that the offense therein sought to be charged was committed 'on the 30th day of April, A. D. 19 .' There is no other allegation of time in the information, and it is in effect and for all practical purposes wholly wanting in any allegation as to time. The time alleged is impossible and in that respect the information is absurd. The objection is not merely technical, as that term is commonly used, but is substantial and fatal." People v. Wagner, 172 Ill.App. 84, 85

A DATO. From the date. Cro.Jac. 135. See *A Datu.*

A DATU. Law Latin. From the date. Anonymous, 1 Ld.Raym. 480; Haths v. Ash, 2 Salk. 413. See *A Dato.*

A DIE CONFECTIONIS. From the day of the making. Barwick's Case, 5 Coke 93b.

A DIE DATUS. From the day of the date. Hatter v. Ash, 1 Ld.Raym. 84; Anonymous, 1 Ld. Raym. 480; Seignorett v. Noguire, 2 Ld.Raym. 1241. Used in leases to determine the time or running of the estate, and when so used includes the day of the date. Doe v. Watkins, 1 Cowp. 189, 191. But *contra,* see Haths v. Ash, 2 Salk. 413.

A DIGNIORI FIERI DEBET DENOMINATIO. Denomination ought to be from the more worthy. The description (of a place) should be taken from the more worthy subject (as from a will). Fleta, lib. 4, c. 10, § 12.

A DIGNIORI FIERI DEBET DENOMINATIO ET RESOLUTIO. The title and exposition of a thing ought to be derived from, or given, or made with reference to, the more worthy degree, quality, or species of it. Wing.Max. 265, max. 75.

A. E. C. Atomic Energy Commission.

A FINE FORCE. Of pure necessity.

A FORCE. Of necessity.

A FORCE ET ARMIS. With force and arms.

A FORFAIT ET SANS GARANTIE. In French law. A formula used in indorsing commercial paper, and equivalent to "without recourse."

A FORTIORI. With stronger reason; much more. A term used in logic to denote an argument to the effect that because one ascertained fact exists, therefore another, which is included in it, or analogous to it, and which is less improbable, unusual, or surprising, must also exist.

A GRATIA. By grace; not of right.

A. H., *Anno Hegirae* (in the year of the hegira).

A ISSUE. At issue.

A JURE SUO CADUNT. They (for example, persons abandoning chattels) lose their right.

A JUSTITIA (QUASI A QUODAM FONTE) OMNIA JURA EMANANT. From justice, as a fountain, all rights flow. Brac. 2 *b*.

A LA GRANDE GREVAUNCE. To the great grievance.

A LARGE. Free; at large.

A LATERE. Lat. Collateral. Used in this sense in speaking of the succession to property. Bract. 20*b*, 62*b*. From, on, or at the side; collaterally. *A latere ascendit (jus).* The right ascends collaterally. Justices of the *Curia Regis* are described as *a latere regis residentes,* sitting at the side of the King; Bract. fol. 108*a*; 2 Reeve, Hist. Eng.L. 250.

In Civil Law and by Bracton, a synonym for *e transverso,* across. Bract. fol. 67*a*.

Applied also to a process or proceeding. Keilw. 159. Out of the regular or lawful course; incidentally or casually. Bract. fol. 42*b*; Fleta, lib. 3, c. 15, § 13.

From the side of; denoting closeness of intimacy or connection; as a court held before auditors *specialiter a latere regis destinatis.* Fleta, lib. 2, c. 2, § 4.

Apostolic; having full powers to represent the Pope as if he were present. Du Cange, *Legati, a latere;* 4 Bla.Com. 306.

A LIBELLIS. L. Lat. An officer who had charge of the *libelli* or petitions addressed to the sovereign. Calvin. A name sometimes given to a chancellor, (*cancellarius,*) in the early history of that office. Spelman, *"Cancellarius."*

A L'IMPOSSIBLE NUL N'EST TENU. No one is bound to do the impossible.

A LOUR FOY. In their allegiance.

A LUY ET A SES HEIRES A TOUTS JOURS. To him and to his heirs forever.

A. M. *Ante meridiem,* before noon. Only the abbreviation is ordinarily used. Orvik v. Casselman, 105 N.W. 1105, 15 N.D. 34. Also *artium magister,* master of arts. Also *annus mirabilis,* the wonderful year—1666, the year of the defeat of the Dutch fleet and of the great London fire. Also *anno mundi,* in the year of the world; that is, when the creation of the world is said to have taken place, 4004 B. C.

A. M. A. Agricultural Marketing Act.

A MA INTENT. On my action. Mitchell v. Reynolds, 1 Smith Lead.Cas. (7th Am. ed.) 516.

A MANIBUS. Lat. Royal scribe. Amanuensis.

A MANU SERVUS. Lat. A handservant; a scribe; a secretary.

A ME. (Lat. *ego,* I.) A term in feudal grants denoting direct tenure of the superior lord. 2 Bell, H.L.Sc. 133.

Unjustly detaining from me. He is said to withhold *a me* (from me) who has obtained possession of my property unjustly. Calvinus, Lex. To pay *a me,* is to pay from my money.

A MENSA ET THORO. Lat. From table and bed, but more commonly translated, from bed and board. A kind of divorce, which is rather a separation of the parties by law, than a dissolution of the marriage. 27 C.J.S., Divorce, § 160.

A MULTO FORTIORI. By far the stronger reason.

A NATIVITATE. From birth, or from infancy. Denotes that a disability, status, etc., is congenital. 3 Bla.Comm. 332; Reg.Orig. 266*b*.

A NON POSSE AD NON ESSE SEQUITUR ARGUMENTUM NECESSARIE NEGATIVE, LICET NON AFFIRMATIVE. A literal translation—From impossibility to non-existence the inference follows necessarily in the negative, though not in the affirmative—is as ambiguous as the original. It could be translated thus: The negative inference of non-existence necessarily follows from impossibility of existence, but the affirmative inference of existence cannot be drawn from mere possibility.

A. O. C. *Anno orbis conditi,* the year of the creation of the world.

À OUTRANCE. To the bitter end; to excess; to the utmost extent. Frequently incorrectly written by persons with only a smattering of French à l'outrance.

A PAIS. To the country; at issue.

A PALATIO. L. Lat. From *Palatium,* (a palace.) Counties palatine are hence so called. 1 Bl.Comm. 117. See Palatium.

A. P. C. Alien Property Custodian.

A. P. C. N. *Anno post Christum natum,* the year after the birth of Christ.

A PIRATIS AUT LATRONIBUS CAPTI LIBERI PERMANENT. Persons taken by pirates or robbers remain free. Dig. 49, 15, 19, 2; Gro. de J. B. lib. 3, c. 3, § 1.

A PIRATIS ET LATRONIBUS CAPTA DOMINUM NON MUTANT. Capture by pirates and robbers does not change title. Bynk. bk. 1, c. 17; 1 Kent, Comm. 108, 184. No right to booty vests in piratical captors; no right can be derived from them by recaptors to the prejudice of the original owners. 2 Wood.Lect. 428.

A POSTERIORI. Lat. From the effect to the cause; from what comes after. A term used in logic to denote an argument founded on experiment or observation, or one which, taking ascertained facts as an effect, proceeds by synthesis and induction to demonstrate their cause.

A. P. R. C. *Anno post Roman conditam,* year after the foundation of Rome.

A PRENDRE. L. Fr. To take; to seize. *Bref à prendre la terre,* a writ to take the land. Fet Ass. § 51. A right to take something out of the soil of another is a profit *à prendre,* or a right coupled with a profit. 1 Crabb, Real Prop. p. 125, § 115. Distinguished from an easement. 5 Adol. & E. 758. Sometimes written as one word, *apprendre, apprender.* See Profit à prendre.

Rightfully taken from the soil. 1 N. & P. 172; Waters v. Lilley, 4 Pick. (Mass.) 145, 16 Am.Dec. 333.

A PRIORI. Lat. From the cause to the effect; from what goes before. A term used in logic to denote an argument founded on analogy, or abstract considerations, or one which, positing a general principle or admitted truth as a cause, proceeds to deduce from it the effects which must necessarily follow.

A PROVISIONE VIRI. By the provision of man. 4 Kent, Comm. 55.

A QUO. Lat. From which. A court *a quo* (also written "a qua") is a court from which a cause has been removed. The judge *a quo* is the judge in such court. Clegg v. Alexander, 6 La. 339.

A term used, with the correlative *ad quem* (to which), in expressing the computation of time, and also of distance in space. Thus, *dies a quo,* the day from which and *dies ad quem,* the day to which, a period of time is computed. So, *terminus a quo,* the point or limit from which, and *terminus ad quem,* the point or limit to which, a distance or passage in space is reckoned.

A QUO INVITO ALIQUID EXIGI POTEST. From whom something may be exacted against his will.

A. R. *Anno Regni.* In the year of the reign; as A. R. V. R. 22, *(Anno Regni Victoriae Reginae vicesimo secundo)* in the twenty-second year of the reign of Queen Victoria.

A REMENAUNT. Forever.

A RENDRE. (Fr. to render, to yield.) That which is to be rendered, yielded, or paid. *Profits à rendre* comprehend rents and services. Ham. N.P. 192.

A RESCRIPTIS VALET ARGUMENTUM. An argument from rescripts [*i. e.* original writs in the register] is valid. Co.Litt. 11 *a.*

A RESPONSIS. L. Lat. In ecclesiastical law. One whose office it was to give or convey answers; otherwise termed *responsalis,* and *apocrisiarius.* One who, being consulted on ecclesiastical matters, gave answers, counsel, or advice; otherwise termed *a consiliis.* Spelman, *"Apocrisiarius."*

A RETRO. L. Lat. Behind; in arrear. *Et reditus proveniens indc à retro fuerit,* and the rent issuing therefrom be in arrear. Fleta, lib. 2, c. 55, § 2; c. 62, § 14.

A RUBRO AD NIGRUM. Lat. From the red to the black; from the rubric or title of a statute (which, anciently, was in *red* letters), to its body, which was in the ordinary *black.* Tray.Lat.Max.; Bell, *"Rubric;"* Erskine, Inst. 1, 1, 49.

A SAVOIR. To wit.

A SUMMO REMEDIO AD INFERIOREM ACTIONEM NON HABETUR REGRESSUS, NEQUE AUXILIUM. From (after using) the highest remedy, there can be no recourse (going back) to an inferior action, nor assistance, (derived from it.) Fleta, lib. 6, c. 1, § 2. A maxim in the old law of real actions, when there were grades in the remedies given; the rule being that a party who brought a writ of right, which was the highest writ in the law, could not afterwards resort or descend to an inferior remedy. Bract. 112*b*; 3 Bl.Comm. 193, 194.

A TEMPORE CUJUS CONTRARII MEMORIA NON EXISTET. From a time of which there is no memory to the contrary.

A TENERIS ANNIS. By reason of youth.

A TERME. For a or the term.

A TERME DE SA VIE. For the term of his life. U.B. 3 Edw. II, 55.

A TERME QUE N'EST MYE ENCORE PASSE. For a term that has not yet passed.

A TERME QUE PASSE EST. For a term that has passed.

À TORT. Without reason; unjustly; wrongfully.

À TORT ET À TRAVERS. Without consideration or discernment.

À TORT OU À DROIT. Right or wrong.

A VERBIS LEGIS NON EST RECENDENDUM. The words of a statute must not be departed from. 5 Coke 119; Wing.Max. 25. A court is not at liberty to disregard the letter of a statute, in favor of a supposed intention. 1 Steph.Comm. 71; Broom, Max. 268.

A VINCULO MATRIMONII. Lat. From the bond of matrimony. A term descriptive of a kind of divorce, which effects a complete dissolution of the marriage contract. See Divorce.

A B (fr. *Abba,* Syr., Father). The eleventh month of the Jewish civil year, and the fifth of the sacred year. It answers to the moon that begins in July, and consists of thirty days. On the 24th is observed a feast in memory of the abolishment of the Sadducean law, which required sons and daughters to be equal heirs and heiresses of their parents' estates. Brown's Dict. of Bible, John's Bib.Antiq. AB, at the beginning of English-Saxon names of places, is generally a contraction of abbot or abbey; whence it is inferred that those places once had an abbey there, or belonged to one elsewhere, as Abingdon in Berkshire. Blount's Law Gloss. Wharton's Law Lexicon.

AB. ABR. Abridgment.

AB ABUSU AD USUM NON VALET CONSEQUENTIA. A conclusion as to the use of a thing from its abuse is invalid. Broom, Max. 17.

AB ACTIS. Lat. An officer having charge of *acta,* public records, registers, journals, or minutes; an officer who entered on record the *acta* or proceedings of a court; a clerk of court; a notary or actuary. Calvin.Lex.Jurid. See *"Acta."* This, and the similarly formed epithets *à cancellis, à secretis, à libellis,* were also anciently the titles of a chancellor, (*cancellarius,*) in the early history of that office. Spelman, *"Cancellarius."*

AB AGENDO. Disabled from acting; unable to act; incapacitated for business or transactions of any kind.

AB ANTE. Lat. Before; in advance. Thus, a legislature cannot agree *ab ante* to any modification or amendment to a law which a third person may make. Allen v. McKean, 1 Sumn. 308, Fed. Cas.No.229 (college charter).

AB ANTECEDENTE. Lat. Beforehand; in advance. 5 M. & S. 110.

AB ANTIQUO. From old times; from ancient time; of old; of an ancient date. 3 Bl.Comm. 95.

AB ASSUETIS NON FIT INJURIA. From things to which one is accustomed (or in which there has been long acquiescence) no legal injury or wrong arises. If a person neglect to insist on his right, he is deemed to have abandoned it. Amb. 645; 3 Brown, Ch. 639; Jenk.Cent.Introd. vi.

AB EPISTOLIS. Lat. An officer having charge of the correspondence (*epistolæ*) of his superior or sovereign; a secretary. Calvin.; Spiegelius.

AB EXTRA. (Lat. *extra,* beyond, without.) From without. Lunt v. Holland, 14 Mass. 151.

AB INCONVENIENTI. From hardship, or inconvenience. An argument founded upon the hardship of the case, and the inconvenience or disastrous consequences to which a different course of reasoning would lead. Barber Asphalt Paving Co. v. Hayward, 248 Mo. 280, 154 S.W. 140.

AB INITIO. Lat. From the beginning; from the first act; entirely; as to all the acts done; in the inception. A party may be said to be a trespasser, an estate to be good, an agreement or deed to be void, or a marriage or act to be unlawful, *ab initio.* Plow. 6*a*, 16*a*; 1 Bl.Comm. 440; Hopkins v. Hopkins, 10 Johns. (N.Y.) 369.

Before. Contrasted in this sense with *ex post facto,* 2 Shars.Bla.Comm. 308; or with *postea,* Calvinus, Lex., *initium.*

Validity of insurance policy ab initio, In re Millers' & Manufacturers' Ins. Co., 97 Minn. 98, 106 N.W. 485; Unconstitutional statute as not void ab initio, State v. Poulin, 105 Me. 224, 74 A. 119, 24 L.R.A.,N.S., 408; physical incapacity, marriage not void ab initio, Bennett v. Bennett, 169 Ala. 618, 53 So. 986, L.R.A.1916C, 693.

AB INITIO MUNDI. Lat. From the beginning of the world. *Ab initio mundi usque ad hodiernum diem,* from the beginning of the world to this day. Y.B.M. 1 Edw. III, 24.

AB INTESTAT. Intestate. 2 Low.Can. 219. Merlin, Répert.

AB INTESTATO. Lat. In the civil law. From an intestate; from the intestate; in case of intestacy. *Hæreditas ab intestato,* an inheritance derived from an intestate. Inst. 2, 9, 6. *Successio ab intestato,* succession to an intestate, or in case of intestacy. Id. 3, 2, 3; Dig. 38, 6, 1. This answers to the descent or inheritance of real estate at common law. 2 Bl.Comm. 490, 516; Story, Confl.Laws, § 480. "Heir *ab intestato.*" 1 Burr. 420. The phrase *"ab intestato"* is generally used as the opposite or alternative of *ex testamento,* (from, by, or under a will.) *Vel ex testamento, vel ab intestato* [*hæreditates*] *pertinent,*—inheritances are derived either from a will or from an intestate, (one who dies without a will.) Inst. 2, 9, 6; Dig. 29, 4; Cod. 6, 14, 2.

AB INVITO. Unwillingly. Against one's will. By or from an unwilling party. A transfer ab invito is a compulsory transfer. See in invitum and invito.

AB JUDICATIO. A removal from court.

AB IRATO. Lat. By one who is angry. A devise or gift made by a man adversely to the interest of his heirs, on account of anger or hatred against them, is said to be made *ab irato.* A suit to set aside such a will is called an action *ab irato.* Merlin, Répert. *Ab irato.* Snell v. Weldon, 239 Ill. 279, 87 N.E. 1022.

AB OLIM. Of old.

AB OVO. The egg, hence from the beginning in allusion to old Roman custom of beginning a meal with eggs and ending with fruit, *ab ovo usque ad mala.* To begin with eggs and end with fruit. Also, at times in allusion to poets who began history of Trojan war with the egg from which Helen was said to have been hatched in contrast with Homer who plunged into the midst of things, or *in media res.*

AB URBE CONDITA. See A.U.C.

ABACIST or ABACISTA. A caster of accounts, an arithmetician.

ABACTION. A carrying away by violence.

ABACTOR. A stealer and driver away of cattle or beasts by herds or in great numbers at once, as distinguished from a person who steals a single animal or beast. Also called *abigeus,* q. v.

ABADENGO. In Spanish law. Land owned by an ecclesiastical corporation, and therefore exempt from taxation. In particular, lands or towns under the dominion and jurisdiction of an abbot. Escriche, Dicc. Raz.

ABALIENATE. To transfer interest or title.

ABALIENATIO. In Roman law. The perfect conveyance or transfer of property from one Roman citizen to another. This term gave place to the simple *alienatio,* which is used in the Digest and Institutes, as well as in the feudal law, and from which the English "alienation" has been formed. Inst. 2, 8, pr.; Id. 2, 1, 40; Dig. 50, 16, 28; Calvinus, Lex., *Abalienatio.*

ABALIENATION. In the Civil Law, a making over of realty, or chattels to another by due course of law.

ABAMITA. Lat. In the civil law. A great-great-grandfather's sister, (*abavi soror.*) Inst. 3, 6, 6; Dig. 38, 10, 3; Calvinus, Lex. Called *amita maxima.* Id. 38, 10, 10, 17. Called, in Bracton, *abamita magna.* Bract. fol. 68*b*.

ABANDON. To desert, surrender, forsake, or cede. To relinquish or give up with intent of never again resuming one's right or interest. Burroughs v. Pacific Telephone & Telegraph Co., 220 P. 152, 155, 109 Or. 404. To give up or to cease to use. Southern Ry. Co. v. Commonwealth, 105 S.E. 65, 67, 128 Va. 176. To give up absolutely; to forsake entirely; to renounce utterly; to relinquish all connection with or concern in; to desert. Commonwealth v. Louisville & N. R. Co., 258 S.W. 101, 102, 201 Ky. 670. It includes the intention, and also the external act by which it is carried into effect.

ABANDONEE. A party to whom a right or property is abandoned or relinquished by another. Applied to the insurers of vessels and cargoes. Lord Ellenborough, C.J., 5 Maule & S. 82; Abbott, J., Id. 87; Holroyd, J., Id. 89.

ABANDONMENT. The surrender, relinquishment, disclaimer, or cession of property or of rights. Stephens v. Mansfield, 11 Cal. 363 (land); Munsey v. Marnet Oil & Gas Co. (Tex.Civ.App.) 199 S.W. 686, 689 (oil lease); Shepard v. Alden, 201 N.W. 537, 539, 161 Minn. 135, 39 A.L.R. 1094 (bowling alleys); Union Grain & Elevator Co. v. McCammon Ditch Co., 240 P. 443, 445, 41 Idaho 216 (water rights).

The giving up of a thing absolutely, without reference to any particular person or purpose, as throwing a jewel into the highway; leaving a thing to itself, as a vessel at sea; vacating property with the intention of not returning, so that it may be appropriated by the next comer. 2 Bl. Comm. 9, 10; Judson v. Malloy, 40 Cal. 299, 310. Intention to forsake or relinquish the thing is an essential element, to be proved by visible acts. Sikes v. State, Tex.Cr.App., 28 S.W. 688; Jordan v. State, 107 Tex.Cr.R. 414, 296 S.W. 585, 586 (auto parts); Kunst v. Mabie, 72 W.Va. 202, 77 S.E. 987, 990 (uncut timber); Dow v. Worley, 126 Okl. 175, 256 P. 56, 60 (oil and gas lease); Duryea v. Elkhorn Coal & Coke Corporation, 123 Me. 482, 124 A. 206, 208.

The voluntary relinquishment of possession of thing by owner with intention of terminating his ownership, but without vesting it in any other person. Dober v. Ukase Inv. Co., 139 Or. 626, 10 P. 2d 356, 357. The relinquishing of all title, possession, or claim, or a virtual, intentional throwing away of property. Foulke v. New York Consol. R. Co., 228 N.Y. 269, 127 N.E. 237, 238, 9 A.L.R. 1384 (package in subway car).

Abandonment in law depends upon concurrence of intention to abandon and some overt act or failure to act which carries implication that owner neither claims nor retains any interest. Stinnett v. Kinslow, 238 Ky. 812, 38 S.W.2d 920, 922.

"Abandonment" includes both the intention to abandon and the external act by which the intention is carried into effect. In determining whether one has abandoned his property or rights, the intention is the first and paramount object of inquiry, for there can be no abandonment without the intention to abandon. Boatman v. Andre, 44 Wyo. 352, 12 P.2d 370, 373. Generally, "abandonment" can arise from a single act or from a series of acts. Holly Hill Lumber Co. v. Grooms, 16 S.E.2d 816, 821, 198 S.C. 118.

Time is not an essential element of "abandonment," although the lapse of time may be evidence of an intention to abandon, and where it is accompanied by acts manifesting such an intention, it may be considered in determining whether there has been an abandonment. Ullman ex rel. Eramo v. Payne, 127 Conn. 239, 16 A.2d 286, 287.

Mere nonuser is not necessarily an abandonment. Barnett v. Dickinson, 93 Md. 258, 48 A. 838 (home); Welsh v. Taylor, 134 N.Y. 450, 31 N.E. 896, 18 L.R.A. 535; Phillis v. Gross, 32 S.D. 438, 143 N.W. 373, 378 (contract for deed). See, however, Corkran, Hill & Co. v. A. H. Kuhlemann Co., 136 Md. 525, 111 A. 471, 474 (trademark). Distinguished from neglect: City of Vallezo v. Burrill, 64 Cal.App. 399, 221 P. 676 (pipe line).

"Abandonment" differs from surrender in that surrender requires an agreement, Noble v. Sturm, 210 Mich. 462, 178 N.W. 99, 103; and from forfeiture, in that forfeiture may be against the intention of the party alleged to have forfeited, Gila Water Co. v. Green, 29 Ariz. 304, 241 P. 307, 308.

In the Civil and French Law it is the act by which a debtor surrenders his property for the benefit of his creditors; Merlin, Répert. See Abandonment for Torts.

Actions, In General

Failure for indefinite period to prosecute action or suit, Morris v. Phifer State Bank, 90 Fla. 55, 105 So. 150, unless caused by an injunction, Barton v. Burbank, 138 La. 997, 71 So. 134. By statute in some states a definite time has been stated which will render a suit abandoned and subject to dismissal. Public Utilities Commission v. Smith, 298 Ill. 151, 131 N.E. 371, 375.

Failure to submit issue by instruction, Unterlachner v. Wells, 317 Mo. 181, 296 S.W. 755, 756; failure to perform conditions necessary to valid appeal or writ of error, Lewis v. Martin, 210 Ala. 401, 98 So. 635; Board of Public Instruction for Marion County v. Goodwin, 89 Fla. 379, 104 So. 779; failure to take issue upon garnishee's answer, Phelps v. Schmuck, 151 Kan. 521, 100 P.2d 67, 71.

Assignments of Error

Not argued. Meyer v. Hendrix, 311 Ill.App. 605, 37 N.E.2d 445, 446.

Not presented in brief. Roubay v. United States, C.C.A.Cal., 115 F.2d 49, 50.

Not supported by point, argument or authority. Cone v. Ariss, 13 Wash.2d 650, 126 P.2d 591, 593.

Bankrupt's Property

In re Mirsky, C.C.A.N.Y., 124 F.2d 1017.

Building Restrictions

Violations of restrictive covenant, Meyer v. Stein, 284 Ky. 497, 145 S.W.2d 105, 107.

ABANDONMENT

Cemeteries

No new burials and neglect of graves, Andrus v. Remmert, 136 Tex. 179, 146 S.W.2d 728, 730; casual use for farming purposes, In re Gundry, 294 Mich. 221, 292 N.W. 709, 711; disuse as to new interments, failure to cut grass or care for headstones, In re Board of Transportation of City of New York, 251 N.Y.S. 409, 413, 140 Misc. 557.

Children

Desertion or willful forsaking. Cannon v. State, 53 Ga.App. 264, 185 S.E. 364, 366.

Foregoing parental duties. Wright v. Fitzgibbons, Miss., 21 So.2d 709, 710.

Withdrawal or neglect of parental duties. In re Potter, 85 Wash. 617, 149 P. 23.

Relinquishment of parental claims. Glendinning v. McComas, 188 Ga. 345, 3 S.E.2d 562, 563.

Separation agreement committing custody of child to father. Gardner v. Hall, 132 N.J.Eq. 64, 26 A.2d 799, 809.

Separation from the child and failure to supply its needs. State v. Clark, 148 Minn. 389, 182 N.W. 452, 453.

Criminal offense, separation from child, and failure to supply its needs. Curtis v. State, 48 Ga.App. 135, 172 S.E. 99, 100.

Defeating recovery for wrongful death. In re Schiffrin's Estate, 272 N.Y.S. 583, 585, 152 Misc. 33.

Compensation Claims

Failure to file application for hearing. Hanks v. Southern Public Utilities Co., 210 N.C. 312, 186 S.E. 252.

Condemnation Proceedings

Dismissal of a petition. Will County v. Cleveland, 372 Ill. 111, 22 N.E.2d 929, 930.

Failure of commissioners to report, Kean v. Union County Park Commission, 129 N.J.Eq. 67, 18 A.2d 279, 280, or judgment determining invalidity. City of Los Angeles v. Abbott, Cal., 12 P.2d 19, 22; failure to pay moneys adjudged, Detroit International Bridge Co. v. American Seed Co., 228 N.W. 791, 795, 249 Mich. 289.

Construction Work

Cessation of operation and intent of owner and contractor to cease operations permanently, or at least for definite period, or some fair notice or knowledge of abandonment by lien claimant, actual or implied. Block v. Love, 136 Or. 685, 1 P.2d 588, 589.

Contracts

To constitute "abandonment" by conduct, action relied on must be positive, unequivocal, and inconsistent with the existence of the contract, Mood v. Methodist Episcopal Church South, Tex. Civ.App., 289 S.W. 461, 464. Abandonment is a matter of intent, Lohn v. Fletcher Oil Co., 38 Cal. App.2d 26, 100 P.2d 505, 507, and implies not only nonperformance, but an intent not to perform which may be inferred from acts which necessarily point to actual abandonment, Losei Realty Corporation v. City of New York, 254 N.Y. 41, 171 N.E. 899.

Copyrights

Common-law rights, Tamas v. 20th Century Fox Film Corporation, Sup., 25 N.Y.S.2d 899, 901; sale and delivery of uncopyrighted painting to state-owned public institution, Pushman v. New York Graphic Soc., Sup., 25 N.Y.S.2d 32, 34; copyrighted lectures not delivered to general public, but only to paying audiences and classes, National Institute for Improvement of Memory v. Nutt, D.C.Conn., 28 F.2d 132, 134.

Crops

Sharecropping tenant's willful failure to cultivate crops, Heaton v. Slaten, 25 Ala.App. 81, 141 So. 267, 268.

Ditches

Town's nonuser for a short period after permitting ditch to be blocked was insufficient. Foster v. Webster, Sup., 44 N.Y.S.2d 153, 156. Mere nonuser does not constitute. Musselshell Valley Farming & Livestock Co. v. Cooley, 86 Mont. 276, 283 P. 213, 218. After prescriptive right attached, water shortage in subsequent years rendering use of ditch unnecessary would not constitute. Bowman v. Bradley, 270 P. 919, 922, 127 Or. 45.

Domicile

Permanent removal from, Stafford v. Mills, 57 N.J.L. 570, 31 A. 1023.

Easements

To establish "abandonment" of an easement created by deed, there must be some conduct on part of owner of servient estate adverse to and inconsistent with existence of easement and continuing for statutory period, or nonuser must be accompanied by unequivocal and decisive acts clearly indicating an intent on part of owner of easement to abandon use of it. Richardson v. Tumbridge, 111 Conn. 90, 149 A. 241, 242.

Permanent cessation of use or enjoyment with no intention to resume or reclaim. Welsh v. Taylor, 134 N.Y. 450, 31 N.E. 896, 18 L.R.A. 535; Corning v. Gould, 16 Wend., N.Y., 531. Intention and completed act are both essential. Town of Orlando v. Stevens, 90 Okl. 2, 215 P. 1050, 1051; Goodman v. Brenner, 219 Mich. 55, 188 N.W. 377; bricking up of the openings for stairway and halls of adjoining buildings, Miller v. Teer, 220 N.C. 605, 18 S.E.2d 173, 178; where object of use of dedicated property wholly fails. Dallas County v. Miller, 140 Tex. 242, 166 S.W.2d 922. But mere nonuser is not sufficient. Smelcer v. Rippetoe, 24 Tenn.App. 516, 147 S.W.2d 109, 113, 114; O'Barr v. Duncan, 187 Ga. 642, 2 S.E.2d 82, 83; right of way acquired by grant. Burnham v. Mahoney, 222 Mass. 524, 111 N.E. 396, 398; Raleigh, C. & S. Ry. Co. v. McGuire, 171 N.C. 277, 88 S.E. 337, 339. Where owner of building had easement in adjoining wall, wrecking building preparatory to erection of a new building, did not cause loss of easement. Joel v. Publix-Lucas Theater, 193 Ga. 531, 19 S.E.2d 730, 736. And a mere temporary or occasional obstruction or use of an easement by the servient owner is not an "abandonment". Gerber v. Appel, Mo.App., 164 S.W.2d 225, 228. However nonuser of railroad crossing for more than 20 years, and conveyance of strips of land adjoining original right of way to railroad in fee simple, without reservation, constituted abandonment of easement in crossing. Cityco Realty Co. v. Philadelphia, B. & W. R. Co., 158 Md. 221, 148 A. 441, 444.

Employment

During Christmas holidays, notwithstanding a call at employer's office and discussing business, Stinson v. Dairymen's League Co-op. Ass'n, 186 A. 687, 688, 14 N.J.Misc. 671. Deviation from route, Loper v. Morrison, 145 P.2d 4, 23 Cal.2d 600; truck driver unnecessarily permitting passenger to drive, Ginther v. J. P. Graham Transfer Co., 33 A. 2d 923, 924, 348 Pa. 60. Contra where truck driver remained on driver's seat, directing operation of truck, and watched passenger's driving, Ginther v. J. P. Graham Transfer Co., 27 A.2d 712, 714, 149 Pa.Super. 635; and where truck driver became sick, Matzek v. United Storage & Trucking Co., 186 A. 193, 122 Pa.Super. 146. Truck drivers becoming intoxicated and remaining from work, Naylon v. State, Ct.Cl., 40 N.Y.S.2d 587, 590; Coal miner contrary to orders, riding on an empty car, Soroka v. Philadelphia & Reading Coal & Iron Co., 138 Pa.Super. 296, 10 A.2d.904, 907. But automobile driver's choosing longer route by paved highways to pick up a needed change of clothing at home did not constitute an "abandonment" of his employment. Mitchell v. Mitchell Drilling Co., 154 Kan. 117, 114 P.2d 841, 844.

Exceptions on Appeal

Not argued in brief, Currin v. Currin, 219 N.C. 815, 15 S.E.2d 279, 282. Not set out in brief, Star Mfg. Co. v. Atlantic Coast Line R. Co., 222 N.C. 330, 23 S.E.2d 32, 40. Not complaining of rulings on exceptions, Buckalew v. Brockner, La.App., 11 So.2d 720, 722. Failing to answer appeal to re-urge exception, John Myers Implement Co. v. De Boer, La.App., 9 So.2d 832, 833. Filing answers without insisting on decision on exceptions to jurisdiction ratione personæ, Weaver v. Mansfield Hardwood Lumber Co., La.App., 4 So.2d 781, 782.

Family

Where father during three or four months following his departure contributed only $32 to support of wife and three minor children, Howton v. Howton, 51 Cal.App.2d 323, 124 P.2d 837, 839. Contra where father helped to support family, In re Hess' Estate, 257 N.Y.S. 278, 282, 143 Misc. 335.

Franchises

Inferior service and lack of any service for few short intervals held insufficient to show "abandonment" of ferry franchise. McConnell v. Crittenden County, 250 Ky. 359, 63 S.W.2d 329.

Highways

Where public ceases to use street or highway under circumstances indicating intent to abandon, Grand Trunk Western R. Co. v. City of Flint, D. C.Mich., 55 F.2d 384, 386. But short sections of highway, discontinued by state highway commission upon relocating highway, were not abandoned. Mosteller v. Southern Ry. Co., 220 N.C. 275, 17 S.E.2d 133, 135. And cultivation of highway for short period by abutting landowners was not an "abandonment" of highway. Chicago & E. I. Ry. Co. v. Road Dist. No. 10, 353 Ill. 160, 187 N.E. 155, 157.

Homesteads

Removal with an intention never to return constitutes an "abandonment", and nothing less does. Farmers' State Bank of Georgetown v. Roberts, Tex.Civ.App., 59 S.W.2d 1089. Must be voluntary action, Wood v. Wood, 203 Ark. 344, 157 S.W.2d 36, 38. Temporary absence with intention to return, Brewer v. Brewer, 268 Ky. 625, 105 S.W.2d 582, 584. Absence of a design of permanent abandonment, Lanier v. Lanier, 95 Fla. 522, 116 So. 867, 868. Absence by necessity, Hinds v. Buck, 177 Tenn. 444, 150 S.W.2d 1071, 1072; sickness, In re Dunlap's Estate, 161 Or. 93, 87 P.2d 225, 229; advancing years and inability to care for selves, Gulf Production Co. v. Continental Oil Co., Tex., 132 S.W.2d 553, 573, 576; to rent to winter tourists, Collins v. Collins, 150 Fla. 374, 7 So. 443, 444. A deed with reservation of a life estate did not constitute "abandonment" of homestead. Arighi v. Rule & Sons, 41 Cal.App. 852, 107 P.2d 970, 972. Nor did filing of suit to partition land. Carr v. Langford, Tex.Civ.App., 144 S.W.2d 612, 613.

Husband

The act of a husband or wife who leaves his or her consort willfully, and with an intention of causing perpetual separation. People v. Cullen, 153 N.Y. 629, 47 N.E. 894, 44 L.R.A. 420.

Wife's leaving husband for a trip to Europe of less than two months against husband's wishes, did not constitute. In re Boesenberg's Estate, 37 N.Y.S.2d 194, 196, 179 Misc. 3.

Abandonment as cause for divorce must be willful and intentional without intention of returning, and without consent of spouse abandoned. Hickey v. Hickey, 152 Wash. 429, 277 P. 994, 995. Husband forcibly expelling wife from home, Tenorio v. Tenorio, 44 N.M. 89, 98 P.2d 838, 847. Refusal to talk to husband did not establish. Wyahllyeth v. Wyahllyeth, 182 Md. 663, 32 A.2d 380, 381. Wife refusing without good cause to accompany husband when moving, Ventrano v. Vetrano, 54 N.Y.S.2d 537, 539.

Word "abandoned," within statute providing that no wife who has abandoned husband shall have right of election to take against provisions of husband's will, has meaning ascribed thereto in matrimonial litigations, and carries no connotation of infidelity. Adultery of abandoned wife did not constitute "abandonment". In re Green's Estate, 280 N.Y.S. 692, 702, 155 Misc. 641.

A wife who told husband to get out of wife's home, and made no effort to effect a reconciliation, was not entitled to appointment as administratrix of his estate. In re Banaszak's Estate, 1 N.Y.S.2d 15, 164 Misc. 829.

Where husband paid wife living apart in caring for their child, she had not abandoned husband so as to preclude the recovery of an industrial pension for his death. Johnson v. Department of Labor and Industries of Washington, 3 Wash.2d 257, 100 P.2d 382, 385. But wife who had, prior to husband's death, left husband, resisted efforts toward a reconciliation, and instituted annulment proceedings, was not entitled to compensation for husband's death. La Fountain v. Industrial Accident Commission, 13 Cal.App.2d 130, 56 P.2d 257, 258.

Insured Property

A relinquishment or cession of property by the owner to the insurer of it, in order to claim as for a total loss. Chicago S. S. Lines v. U. S. Lloyds, C.C.A.Ill., 12 F.2d 733, 738.

The term is used only in reference to risks in navigation; but the principle is applicable in fire insurance, where there are remnants, and sometimes, also, under stipulations in life policies in favor of creditors. Cincinnati Ins. Co. v. Duffield, 6 Ohio St. 200, 67 Am.Dec. 339.

Inventions

The giving up of rights by inventor, as where he surrenders his idea or discovery or relinquishes the intention of perfecting his invention, and so throws it open to the public, or where he negligently postpones the assertion of his claims or fails to apply for a patent, and allows the public to use his invention. Electric Storage Battery Co. v. Shimadzu, Pa., 59 S.Ct. 675, 681, 307 U.S. 5, 613, 616, 83 L.Ed. 1071.

Disclaimer of claim of patent, Triumph Explosives v. Kilgore Mfg. Co., C.C.A.Md., 128 F.2d 444, 448; delaying 12 years after reducing shoe to practice before applying for patent, Salisbury v. Pediforme Shoe Co., D.C.N.Y., 31 F.Supp. 3, 7; omitting for many years to take any step to reinstate or renew rejected application, Na-Mac Products Corporation v. Federal Tool Corporation, C.C.A.Ill., 118 F.2d 167, 171; acquiescing in rejection of claims in patent application for device shown in later application for patent, Na-Mac Products Corporation v. Federal Tool Corporation, C.C.A.Ill., 118 F.2d 167, 171; Na-Mac Products Corporation v. Federal Tool Corporation, D.C.Ill., 36 F.Supp. 426, 430. But mere lapse of time before an inventor applies for a patent is not sufficient. Imperial Brass Mfg. Co. v. Bonney Forge & Tool Works, D.C.Pa., 38 F. Supp. 829, 832. Patent application was not filed until 2½ years after date of conception of invention, Chicago Rawhide Mfg. Co. v. National Motor Bearing Co., D.C.Cal., 50 F.Supp. 458, 460. Nor is disclosing invention to individuals with purpose of interesting them in production or manufacture. Pennington Engineering Co. v. Houde Engineering Corporation, D.C.N.Y., 43 F.Supp. 698, 706.

Leases in General

To constitute an "abandonment" of leased premises, there must be an absolute relinquishment of premises by tenant consisting of act and intention. Schnitzer v. Lanzara, 115 N.J.L. 332, 180 A. 234.

Closing up butcher shop with intention of giving up business and in removing all perishable merchandise, although tenant retained key and did not notify landlord of intention to vacate premises, held an "abandonment" and not a "surrender" of premises. Schnitzer v. Lanzara, 115 N. J.L. 332, 18 A. 234. Refusal by lessee of lessor's offer to reconstruct burned building, Girard Trust Co. v. Tremblay Motor Co., 291 Pa. 507, 140 A. 506, 512. But tenants surrendering premises pursuant to notice of forfeiture did not "abandon" premises. Becker v. Rute, 228 Iowa 533, 293 N.W. 18, 21.

Marriage

Withdrawal or denial of marital obligations without just cause, Reppert v. Reppert, Del.Super., 13 A.2d 705, 1 Terry 492.

Mineral Leases

"Abandonment" consists of an actual act of relinquishment, accompanied with the intent and purpose permanently to give up a claim and right of property. A distinction exists between "abandonment" and "surrender" which is the relinquishment of a thing or a property right thereto to another, which is not an essential element of abandonment. Distinction also exists between elements of "abandonment" and those of estoppel. Neither formal surrender of oil and gas lease nor release is necessary to effectuate "abandonment." Sigler Oil Co. v. W. T. Waggoner Estate, Tex.Civ. App., 276 S.W. 936, 938. Voluntary, intentional relinquishment of known right. Pure Oil Co. v. Sturm, 43 Ohio App. 105, 182 N.E. 875, 882.

Failing to start work under the lease for more than 40 years, Chapman v. Continental Oil Co., 149 Kan. 822, 89 P.2d 833, 834; breach of implied obligation to proceed with search and development of land with reasonable diligence, Wood v. Arkansas Fuel Oil Co., D.C.Ark., 40 F. Supp. 42, 45; no drilling on leased land for more than two years, and failure to pay rentals, Rehart v. Klossner, 48 Cal.App.2d 40, 119 P.2d 145, 147; drawing of casing from well with no intention of replacing it, Seaboard Oil Co. v. Commonwealth, 193 Ky. 629, 237 S.W. 48, 50. But there must be an intention by lessee to relinquish leased premises, Carter Oil Co. v. Mitchell, C.C.A.Okl., 100 F.2d 945, 950, 951; or an intention not to drill, Carter Oil Co. v. Mitchell, C.C.A.Okl., 100 F.2d 945, 950, 951. And ceasing of operations is not alone sufficient. Fisher v. Dixon, 188 Okl. 7, 105 P.2d 776, 777. Doing no substantial work for about one year immediately preceding suit to cancel lease, but remaining in possession and doing some work, Deace v. Stribling, Tex.Civ.App., 142 S.W.2d 564, 567; disconnection of well for a brief interval while well was being drilled to a greater depth, Cole v. Philadelphia Co., 345 Pa. 315, 26 A.2d 920, 923; abandoning work on unproductive well was not an abandonment of leased premises. Smith v. Tullos, 195 La. 400, 196 So. 912, 914.

Mining Claims

Relinquishment of a claim held by location without patent, where the holder voluntarily leaves his claim to be appropriated by the next comer, without any intention to retake or resume it, and regardless of what may become of it in the future. O'Hanlon v. Ruby Gulch Mining Co., 48 Mont. 65, 135 P. 913, 918. The term includes both the intention to abandon and the act by which the abandonment is carried into effect. Peachy v. Frisco Gold Mines Co., D.C.Ariz., 204 F. 659, 668.

Abandonment takes place whenever locator leaves claim without intention of holding it. Crane v. French, 39 Cal. App.2d 642, 104 P.2d 53, 60. But mere absence from claim, is not sufficient. Crane v. French, 39 Cal.App.2d 642, 104 P.2d 53, 60. And one co-owner's abandoning his interest is not an "abandonment" of entire claim. Crane v. French, 39 Cal.App.2d 642, 104 P.2d 53, 60.

Motions

Motion not called to court's attention until final hearing, Williams v. Smith, 149 Fla. 735, 6 So.2d 853, 854. Grounds not insisted on, Meador v. Nowell, 67 Ga.App. 564, 21 S.E.2d 312, 314; not argued in brief, In re Horton's Estate, 154 Kan. 269, 118 P. 2d 527, 531. Rulings not urged on appeal, Spears v. Brown Paper Mill Co., La.App., 9 So.2d 332, 334. Admitting sufficiency of evidence to sustain verdict, Copeland v. State, 66 Ga.App. 142, 17 S.E.2d 288, 289. But service of answer after making of motion to strike out portions of a complaint was not an "abandonment" of the motion. Russo v. Signode Steel Strapping Co., Sup., 37 N.Y.S.2d 166.

Office

Abandonment of a public office is a species of resignation, but differs from resignation in that resignation is a formal relinquishment, while abandonment is a voluntary relinquishment through nonuser. State v. Harmon, 115 Me. 268, 98 A. 804, 805.

It is not wholly a matter of intention, but may result from the complete abandonment of duties of such a continuance that the law will infer a relinquishment. Wilkinson v. City of Birmingham, 193 Ala. 139, 68 So. 999, 1002. It must be total, and under such circumstances as clearly to indicate an absolute relinquishment; and whether an officer has abandoned an office depends on his overt acts rather than his declared intention. Parks v. Ash, 168 Ga. 868, 149 S.E. 207, 209. It implies nonuser, but nonuser does not, of itself constitute abandonment. The failure to perform the duties pertaining to the office must be with actual or imputed intention on the part of the officer to abandon and relinquish the office. The intention may be inferred from the acts and conduct of the party, and is a question of fact. Abandonment may result from an acquiescence by the officer in his wrongful removal or discharge, but, as in other cases of abandonment, the question of intention is involved. McCall v. Cull, 51 Ariz. 237, 75 P.2d 696, 698.

Temporary absence is not ordinarily sufficient to constitute an "abandonment of office". State v. Green, 206 Ark. 361, 175 S.W.2d 575, 577. Responding to mandatory call for military service in emergency conditions, Caudel v. Prewitt, 296 Ky. 848, 178 S.W.2d 22, 25. And failure of former officers to assert right while decision of eligibility of elected successors was pending, was not an "abandonment" creating vacancy. State v. Levy Court of New Castle County, Del., 3 W.W.Harr. 554, 140 A. 642, 645.

Oil Wells

Where owner ceased working on well to work elsewhere to procure money to do further work on well, well was not abandoned. Jones v. Jos. Greenspon's Son Pipe Corporation, 313 Ill.App. 651, 40 N.E.2d 561.

Patents

There may be an abandonment of a patent, where the inventor dedicates it to the public use; and this may be shown by his failure to sue infringers, sell licenses, or otherwise make efforts to realize a personal advantage from his patent. Ransom v. New York, 4 Blatchf. 157, 20 Fed.Cas. 286.

Pleadings

The filing of a second amended complaint which was complete in itself and which did not reserve to itself any part of the original complaint or first amended complaint constituted an "abandonment" of the two former complaints. Seely v. Gilbert, 16 Wash.2d 611, 134 P.2d 710, 712. Cross-complainant by failing to take proper steps in trial court to have judgment that was silent on issues tendered by cross-complaint and answer thereto corrected did not thereby "abandon" cross-complaint. Brown v. National Life Ins. Co. of Washington County, Vt., 112 Ind.App. 684, 46 N.E. 2d 246, 249.

Prescriptive Rights

Non-use alone is insufficient. Burkman v. City of New Lisbon, 246 Wis. 547, 19 N.W.2d 311, 313; Smelcer v. Rippetoe, 24 Tenn.App. 516, 147 S.W.2d 109, 113, 114.

Privileges

Witness before grand jury who answered questions and immediately asked to retract answers, and thereupon asserted his privilege, did not "abandon" right to claim the privilege. United States v. Weisman, C.C.A.N.Y., 111 F.2d 260, 261.

Property

"Abandoned property" in a legal sense is that to which owner has relinquished all right, title, claim, and possession, with intention of not reclaiming it or resuming its ownership, possession or enjoyment. Jackson v. Steinberg, Or., 200 P.2d 376, 377, 378.

There must be concurrence of act and intent, that is, the act of leaving the premises or property vacant, so that it may be appropriated by the next comer, and the intention of not returning. Cohn v. San Pedro, L. A. & S. L. R. Co., 103 Cal.App. 496, 284 P. 1051, 1052. Relinquishment of all title, possession, or claim; a virtual intentional throwing away of property. Ex parte Szczygiel, Sup., 51 N.Y.S.2d 699, 702. Actual relinquishment, gas in pipe was not abandoned. Hein v. Shell Oil Co., 315 Ill.App. 297, 42 N.E.2d 949, 952. Nor was a sewing machine and phonograph left with landlady as security. Dickens v. Singer Sewing Mach. Co., 140 So. 296, 298, 19 La.App. 735.

Property for Special Purposes

Moving of church to erect drilling rig held not "abandonment of use for church purposes." Abandonment meant to wholly discontinue church use, and additional use was not sufficient. Skipper v. Davis, Tex.Civ.App., 59 S.W.2d 454, 457.

Merger of churches was not. Bridgeport-City Trust Co. v. Bridgeport Hospital, 120 Conn. 27, 179 A. 92, 94. Nor where intention was that nonconforming use as a fraternity house would be resumed. State ex rel. Morehouse v. Hunt, 235 Wis. 358, 291 N.W. 745, 751, 752. Nor mere cessation of a nonconforming use in zoned area for a reasonable period. Beyer v. Mayor and Council of Baltimore City, Md., 34 A.2d 765, 768, 769. Nor a discontinuance of a garage during war while owner served in army and on return postponed repossession for garage purposes due to city's using building. State v. Murray, 195 Wis. 657, 219 N.W. 271, 272. But removal of manufacturing equipment from manufacturing plant, was. Francisco v. City of Columbus, Ohio App., 31 N.E.2d 236, 243. And also disposing of all machinery, taking down smokestack and using property for storage purposes, notwithstanding vague intention of resuming slaughter house business. Beyer v. Mayor and City Council of Baltimore City, 182 Md. 444, 34 A.2d 765, 768, 769.

Dedicated use must wholly fail. Kirchen v. Remenga, 291 Mich. 94, 288 N.W. 344, 350, 351. Erection of buildings on park lands without objection of adjoining owners was not sufficient. Kirchen v. Remenga, 291 Mich. 94, 288 N.W. 344, 350, 351. Nor city's permitting a citizen's rock garden on small portion of street improvement tract. Kendrick v. City of St. Paul, 213 Minn. 283, 6 N.W.2d 449, 451. Nor diverting parkway to roadway. Ford v. City of Detroit, 273 Mich. 449, 263 N.W. 425, 426. Nor tearing down school building for salvaging material for erection of a waiting station for school children. McCullough v. Swifton Consol. School Dist., 202 Ark. 1074, 155 S.W.2d 353. Nor temporary disuse of school when land was offered for sale, later rescinded. Bernard v. Bowen, 214 N.C. 121, 198 S.E. 584.

Railroad Property

"Abandon" means to relinquish or give up with intent of never again resuming or claiming one's rights or interests in, to give up absolutely, to forsake entirely, to renounce utterly, to relinquish all connection with or concern in. Capital Transit Co. v. Hazen, 93 F.2d 250, 251, 68 App.D.C. 91. Abandonment did not mean a partial disuse with an intention to complete station on a contingency, but meant a final relinquishment, or giving up without intention of resuming. Wheeling & L. E. Ry. Co. v. Pittsburgh & W. V. Ry. Co., C.C.A.Ohio, 33 F.2d 390, 392. And to constitute an "abandonment" of right of way, there must be not only an actual relinquishment of the property, but an intention to abandon it. Abens v. Chicago, B. & Q. R. Co., 388 Ill. 261, 57 N.E.2d 883, 887.

Nonuser is a fact in determining it, but, though continued for years, is not conclusive. Arlington Realty Co. v. Keller, 105 N.J.Eq. 196, 147 A. 437, 438. Plowing up servient estate is not enough. Les v. Alibozek, 269 Mass. 153, 168 N.E. 919, 922, 66 A.L.R. 1094. Nor proposal to deliver and receive freight by motortrucks. New York Dock Ry. v Pennsylvania R. Co., D.C.Pa., 1 F.Supp. 20, 21. But failure to maintain and use that part of railroad on land conveyed constituted "abandonment." Atlantic Coast Line R. Co. v. Sweat, 177 Ga. 698, 171 S.E. 123, 129.

Remedies

Election of one of two inconsistent remedies, Lumber Mutual Casualty Ins. Co. of New York v. Friedman, 176 Misc. 703, 28 N.Y.S.2d 506, 509.

Rights in General

The relinquishment of a right. It implies some act of relinquishment done by the owner without regard to any future possession by himself, or by any other person, but with an intention to abandon. Dyer v. Sanford, 9 Metc., Mass., 395, 43 Am. Dec. 399.

It is properly confined to incorporeal hereditaments, since legal rights once vested must be divested according to law. But equitable rights may be abandoned. Great Falls Co. v. Worster, 15 N.H. 412; Cox v. Colossal Cavern Co., 210 Ky. 612, 276 S.W. 540; Inhabitants of School Dist. No. 4 v. Benson, 31 Me. 381, 52 Am.Dec. 618.

Ship and Freight

Act by which shipowner surrenders ship and freight to a trustee for benefit of claimants. See 46 U.S.C.A. § 185; Ohio Transp. Co. v. Davidson S. S. Co., 148 F. 185, 78 C.C.A. 319.

In France and other countries it is the surrender to a person having a claim arising out of a contract made with the master. American Transp. Co. v. Moore, 5 Mich. 368.

Taxing Power

Delegation of taxing power by legislature to city was not "abandonment of taxing power". Mouledoux v. Maestri, 197 La. 525, 2 So.2d 11, 16.

Trade-marks and Trade Names

There must be not only nonuser, but also an intent to abandon. Rockowitz Corset & Brassiere Corporation v. Madame X Co., 248 N.Y. 272, 162 N. E. 76, 78; Manz v. Philadelphia Brewing Co., D.C. Pa., 37 F.Supp. 79, 81. To give up use of trademarks permanently. Neva-Wet Corporation of America v. Never Wet Processing Corporation, 277 N.Y. 163, 13 N.E.2d 755, 761.

Disuse not sufficient in itself. Sherwood Co. v. Sherwood Distilling Co., 177 Md. 455, 9 A.2d 842, 845. Nor using owner's name. Bunte Bros. v. Standard Chocolates, D.C. Mass., 45 F.Supp. 478, 480. However, nonuser with extensive use by another is sufficient. Sherwood Co. v. Sherwood Distilling Co., 177 Md. 455, 9 A.2d 842, 845. But not where receiver continuously operated trade-mark licensee's property. American Dirigold Corporation v. Dirigold Metals Corporation. C.C.A.Mich., 125 F.2d 446, 454. Nor sale of all physical assets of manufacturing company by trustee in bankruptcy. Reconstruction Finance Corporation v. J. G. Menihan Corporation, D.C.N.Y., 28 F.Supp. 920, 923.

Trusts

State aid for hospital, with stipulation for beds for emergency cases, did not establish an "abandonment of trust". Noble v. First Nat. Bank of Anniston, 241 Ala. 85, 1 So.2d 289, 291.

Water Rights

"'Abandonment," as applied to water rights may be defined to be an intentional relinquishment of a known right. It is not based on a time element, and mere nonuser will not establish "abandonment" for any less time, at least, than statutory period, controlling element in "abandonment" being matter of intent. Hammond v. Johnson, 94 Utah 20, 66 P.2d 894, 899. To desert or forsake right. The intent and an actual relinquishment must concur. Central Trust Co. v. Culver, 23 Colo. App. 317, 129 P. 253, 254. Concurrence of relinquishment of possession, and intent not to resume it for beneficial use. Neither alone is sufficient. Osnes Livestock Co. v. Warren, 103 Mont. 284, 62 P.2d 206, 211.

Not using water when there was no water in creek because of another user's obstruction of flow and appropriation of all the water did not constitute. New Mexico Products Co. v. New Mexico Power Co., 42 N.M. 311, 77 P.2d 634, 641. Nor did milling company's permitting water's use by upper irrigators. Hutchinson v. Stricklin, 146 Or. 285, 28 P.2d 225, 230. Nor permitting upper appropriators to erect dam and store water. Irion v. Hyde, Mont., 81 P. 2d 353, 356. Nor change of place of use of decreed water right. Harris v. Chapman, 51 Idaho 283, 5 P.2d 733, 737. Nor failure to use all water to which entitled. Horse Creek Conservation Dist. v. Lincoln Land Co., 54 Wyo. 320, 92 P.2d 572, 577. Use of only enough water to water stock, because supply was insufficient to irrigate land. Federal Land Bank v. Morris, 112 Mont. 445, 116 P.2d 1007, 1010. But right to use a particular quantity of water may be abandoned by failure to apply such water to a beneficial use for an unreasonable period of time. Cundy v. Weber, 68 S.D. 214, 300 N.W. 17, 22.

Wife

Abandonment justifying divorce is a voluntary, unjustified, and final separation of one of married parties from the other, accompanied by an intention to terminate the marital relation, or an unjustified refusal to resume suspended cohabitation, as where husband left his wife because his children by former marriage could not live peaceably with second wife. Schwartz v. Schwartz, 158 Md. 80, 148 A. 259, 263.

Refusal by husband of request by sick wife without means of support, to return to home held "abandonment" as respects disorderly conduct. People v. Schenkel, 252 N.Y.S. 415, 418, 140 Misc. 843. Contra where separation agreement existed. People v. Gross, 291 N.Y.S. 597, 601, 161 Misc. 514. Where parties separated by agreement, and husband, in lieu of periodic payments for wife's support, made conveyance constituting valuable consideration, held not "abandonment" as respects husband's statutory right against wife's will. In re McCann's Estate, 281 N.Y.S. 445, 155 Misc. 763; or even if wife was justified in leaving husband on account of his cruel treatment, there must be a desertion without consent. In re Stolz' Estate, 260 N.Y.S. 906, 145 Misc. 799. But while there can be no "desertion" for divorce where parties are apart by consent, yet there may be an "abandonment" as respects separate maintenance, although the separation originated and continued by consent of parties. Pierson v. Pierson, 189 A. 391, 395,

15 N.J.Misc. 117. And as respects maintenance, husband's conduct rendering wife's condition unendurable constitutes "abandonment." Carder v. Carder, 227 Mo.App. 1005, 60 S.W.2d 706. Cruel treatment, Fallon v. Fallon, 111 N.J. Eq. 512, 162 A. 406, 408. Husband's refusal of wife's request to resume living with her, Clark v. Clark, 176 A. 81, 83, 13 N.J.Misc. 49; or refusal to receive wife at his residence, is an "abandonment" of her. Hockaday v. Hockaday, 182 La. 88, 161 So. 164. But not a husband's removal from wife's home after wife had instituted separation action, Kenneson v. Kenneson, 36 N.Y.S.2d 676, 685, 178 Misc. 832; or where husband moved out on command of wife's father. Anonymous v. Anonymous, 24 N.Y.S.2d 613, 618. Mere failure to support wife is not an abandonment within Divorce Act. Biddle v. Biddle, 104 N.J.Eq. 313, 145 A. 639, 640; but failing to provide wife with necessities, etc., is. Cooper v. Cooper, 176 Md. 695, 4 A.2d 714, 716. And convict sentenced for life did not abandon wife. In re Lindewall's Will, 18 N.Y.S.2d 281, 284, 259 App.Div. 196.

ABANDONMENT FOR TORTS. In the civil law. The relinquishment of a slave or animal who had committed a trespass to the person injured, in discharge of the owner's liability for such trespass or injury. Just. Inst. 4, 8, 9. A similar right exists in Louisiana. Fitzgerald v. Ferguson, 11 La.Ann. 396.

ABANDUN, ABANDUM, or ABANDONUM. Anything sequestered, proscribed, or abandoned. *Abandon, i. e., in bannum res missa,* a thing banned or denounced as forfeited or lost, whence to *abandon, desert,* or *forsake,* as lost and gone. Cunningham; Cowell.

ABARNARE. Lat. To discover and disclose to a magistrate any secret crime. *Leges Canuti,* cap. 10.

ABATABLE NUISANCE. A nuisance which is practically susceptible of being suppressed, or extinguished, or rendered harmless, and whose continued existence is not authorized under the law. Fort Worth & Denver City Ry. Co. v. Muncy, Tex. Civ.App., 31 S.W.2d 491, 494.

ABATAMENTUM. L. Lat. In old English law. An abatement of freehold; an entry upon lands by way of interposition between the death of the ancestor and the entry of the heir. Co. Litt. 277*a*; Yel. 151.

ABATARE. To abate. Yel. 151.

ABATE. To throw down, to beat down, destroy, quash. 3 Shars. Bla. Com. 168; Klamath Lumber Co. v. Bamber, 142 P. 359, 74 Or. 287. To do away with or nullify or lessen or diminish, In re Stevens' Estate, Cal.App., 150 P.2d 530, 534; to bring entirely down or demolish, to put an end to, to do away with, to nullify, to make void, Sparks Milling Co. v. Powell, 283 Ky. 669, 143 S.W.2d 75, 77.

See, also, Abatement; Abatement and Revival.

ABATEMENT. A reduction, a decrease, or a diminution. The Vestris, D.C.N.Y., 53 F.2d 847, 852.

A judgment afforded a defense by way of abatement. Panos v. Great Western Packing Co., Cal.App., 126 P.2d 889, 892.

Contracts

A reduction made by the creditor for the prompt payment of a debt due by the payor or debtor. Wesk. Ins. 7.

Debts

In equity, when equitable assets are insufficient to satisfy fully all the creditors, their debts must abate in proportion, and they must be content with a dividend, for *æquitas est quasi æqualitas.*

Freehold

The unlawful entry upon and keeping possession of an estate by a stranger, after the death of the ancestor and before the heir or devisee takes possession. Such an entry is technically called an "abatement," and the stranger an "abator." It is, in fact, a figurative expression, denoting that the rightful possession or freehold of the heir or devisee is overthrown by the unlawful intervention of a stranger. Abatement differs from intrusion, in that it is always to the prejudice of the heir or immediate devisee, whereas the latter is to the prejudice of the reversioner or remainder-man; and disseisin differs from them both, for to disseise is to put forcibly or fraudulently a person seised of the freehold out of possession. Brown v. Burdick, 25 Ohio St. 268. By the ancient laws of Normandy, this term was used to signify the act of one who, having an apparent right of possession to an estate, took possession of it immediately after the death of the actual possessor, before the heir entered. (Howard, Anciennes Lois des Francais, tome 1, p. 539.)

Legacies

A proportional diminution or reduction of the pecuniary legacies, when the funds or assets out of which such legacies are payable are not sufficient to pay them in full. Ward, Leg. p. 369, c. 6, § 7; 1 Story, Eq. Jur. § 555; 2 Bl. Comm. 512, 513; In re Hawgood's Estate, 37 S.D. 565, 159 N.W. 117, 123. Legacy accepted in lieu of dower. In re Hartman's Estate, 233 Iowa 405, 9 N.W.2d 359, 362.

Nuisance

The removal of a nuisance. 3 Bla. Comm. 5. See Nuisance.

Taxes and Duties

A drawback or rebate allowed in certain cases on the duties due on imported goods, in consideration of their deterioration or damage suffered during importation, or while in store. A diminution or decrease in the amount of tax imposed upon any person. Rogers v. Gookin, 198 Mass. 434, 85 N.E. 405 (real estate taxes); Central National Bank v. City of Lynn, 156 N.E. 42 (Shares in national banks) 259 Mass. 1.

As applied to taxation, it presupposes error or mistake in assessment. Gulf States Steel Co. v. U. S., C.C.A.Ala., 56 F.2d 43, 46.

Abatement of taxes relieves property of its share of the burdens of taxation after the assessment has been made and the tax levied. Sheppard v. Hidalgo County, 126 Tex. 550, 83 S.W.2d 649, 657.

ABATEMENT AND REVIVAL

Actions at Law

As used in reference to actions at law, word abate means that action is utterly dead and cannot be revived except by commencing a new action. First Nat. Bank v. Board of Sup'rs of Harrison County, 221 Iowa 348, 264 N.W. 281, 106 A.L.R. 566.

The overthrow of an action caused by the defendant's pleading some matter of fact tending to impeach the correctness of the writ or declaration, which defeats the action for the present, but does not debar the plaintiff from recommencing it in a better way. 3 Bla. Comm. 301; 1 Chit. Pl. (6th Lond. Ed.) 446; Guild v. Richardson, 6 Pick. (Mass.) 370; Wirtele v. Grand Lodge A. O. U. W., 111 Neb. 302, 196 N.W. 510. See Plea in Abatement.

To put a final end to suit, Dodge v. Superior Court in and for Los Angeles County, 139 Cal.App. 178, 33 P.2d 695, 696; overthrow of pending action apart from cause of action, Burnand v. Irigoyen, 56 Cal.App.2d 624, 133 P.2d 3, 6.

On plaintiff's death, Piukkula v. Pillsbury Astoria Flouring Mills Co., 150 Or. 304, 44 P.2d 162, 99 A.L.R. 259. Mere lapse of time between the death of a party and the taking of necessary steps to continue the action by or against the heir or personal representative does not work an abatement, Whaley v. Slater, 202 S.C. 182, 24 S.E.2d 266, 267.

Cause of Action

Destruction of cause of action. In re Thomasson, Mo., 159 S.W.2d 626, 628.

Chancery Practice

It differs from an abatement at law in this: that in the latter the action is entirely dead and cannot be revived; but in the former the right to proceed is merely suspended, and may be revived; F. A. Mfg. Co. v. Hayden & Clemons, C.C.A.Mass., 273 F. 374; Mutual Ben. Health & Accident Ass'n v. Teal, D.C.S.C., 34 F.Supp. 714, 716.

In England, declinatory pleas to the jurisdiction and dilatory to the persons were (prior to the judicature act) sometimes, by analogy to common law, termed "pleas in abatement."

Declinatory and dilatory pleas, see Story, Eq. Pl. § 708.

Death of one of parties, Geiger v. Merle, 360 Ill. 497, 196 N.E. 497, 502. Want of proper parties, 2 Tidd Pr. 932; Story, Eq.Pl. § 354; Witt v. Ellis, 2 Cold., Tenn., 38; petition for widow's allowance, In re Samson's Estate, 142 Neb. 556, 7 N.W.2d 60, 62, 144 A.L.R. 264.

ABATOR. In real property law, a stranger who, having no right of entry, contrives to get possession of an estate of freehold, to the prejudice of the heir or devisee, before the latter can enter, after the ancestor's death. Litt. § 397. In the law of torts, one who abates, prostrates, or destroys a nuisance.

ABATUDA. Anything diminished. *Moneta abatuda* is money clipped or diminished in value. Cowell; Dufresne.

ABAVIA. Lat. In the civil law. A great-great-grandmother. Inst. 3, 6, 4; Dig. 38, 10, 1, 6; Bract. fol. 68*b*.

ABAVITA. A great-great-grandfather's sister. Bract. fol. 68*b*. This is a misprint for *abamita* (q. v.). Burrill.

ABAVUNCULUS. Lat. In the civil law. A great-great-grandmother's brother (*avaviœ frater*). Inst. 3, 6, 6; Dig. 38, 10, 3; Calvinus, Lex. Called *avunculus maximus*. Id. 38, 10, 10, 17. Called by Bracton and Fleta *abavunculus magnus*. Bract. fol. 68*b*; Fleta, lib. 6, c. 2, § 19.

ABAVUS. Lat. In the civil law. A great-great-grandfather. Inst. 3, 6, 4; Dig. 38, 10, 1, 6; Bract. fol. 67*a*.

ABBACINARE. To blind by placing a burning basin or red-hot irons before the eyes. A form of punishment in the Middle Ages. Also spelt abacinare. The modern Italian is spelt with two b's, and means to blind. Abbacination. Blinding by placing burning basin or red-hot irons before the eyes. See Abbacinare.

ABBACY. The government of a religious house, and the revenues thereof, subject to an abbot, as a bishopric is to a bishop. Cowell. The rights and privileges of an abbot.

ABBEY. A monastery or nunnery for the use of an association of religious persons, having an abbot or abbess to preside over them.

ABBOT. A prelate in the 13th century who had had an immemorial right to sit in the national assembly. Taylor, Science of Jurispr. 287.

ABBOT, ABBAT. The spiritual superior or governor of an abbey. Feminine, *Abbess*.

ABBREVIATE OF ADJUDICATION. In Scotch law. An abstract of the decree of adjudication, and of the lands adjudged, with the amount of the debt. Adjudication is that diligence (execution) of the law by which the real estate of a debtor is adjudged to belong to his creditor in payment of a debt; and the abbreviate must be recorded in the register of adjudications.

ABBREVIATIO PLACITORUM. An abstract of ancient judicial records, prior to the Year Books. See Steph. Pl. (7th Ed.) 410.

ABBREVIATIONS. Shortened conventional expressions, employed as substitutes for names, phrases, dates, and the like, for the saving of space, of time in transcribing, etc. Abbott.

The abbreviations in common use in modern times consist of the initial letter or letters, syllable or syllables, of the word. Anciently, also, contracted forms of words, obtained by the omission of letters intermediate between the initial and final letters were much in use. These latter forms are now more commonly designated by the term *contraction*.

For Table of Abbreviations, see Appendix.

ABBREVIATIONUM ILLE NUMERUS ET SENSUS ACCIPIENDUS EST, UT CONCESSIO NON SIT INANIS. In abbreviations, such number and sense is to be taken that the grant be not made void. 9 Coke, 48.

ABBREVIATORS. In ecclesiastical law. Officers whose duty it is to assist in drawing up the Pope's briefs, and reducing petitions into proper form to be converted into papal bulls.

ABBROCHMENT, or ABBROACHMENT. The act of forestalling a market, by buying up at wholesale the merchandise intended to be sold there, for the purpose of selling it at retail. See Forestalling the Market.

ABBUTTALS. See Abuttals.

ABDICATION. The act of a sovereign in renouncing and relinquishing his government or throne, so that either the throne is left entirely vacant, or is filled by a successor appointed or elected beforehand.

Also, where a magistrate or person in office voluntarily renounces or gives it up before the time of service has expired.

The act of abdicating; giving up of office, power or authority, right or trust; renunciation. McCormick v. Engstrom, 119 Kan. 698, 241 P. 685, 688.

Abdication of rights to property may constitute an assignment. In re Johnston's Estate, 186 Wis. 599, 203 N.W. 376, 377.

It differs from resignation, in that resignation is made by one who has received his office from another and restores it into his hands, as an inferior into the hands of a superior; abdication is the relinquishment of an office which has devolved by act of law. It is said to be a renunciation, quitting, and relinquishing, so as to have nothing further to do with a thing, or the doing of such actions as are inconsistent with the holding of it. Chambers.

ABDITORIUM. An abditory or hiding place, to hide and preserve goods, plate or money. Jacob.

ABDUCTION. In criminal law. The offense of taking away a wife, child, or ward, by fraud and persuasion, or open violence. 3 Bl.Comm. 139-141; State v. Chisenhall, 106 N.C. 676, 11 S.E. 518 (female under 14); State v. Hopper, 186 N.C. 405, 119 S.E. 769, 772 (wife).

To take away surreptitiously by force in kidnapping. Doss v. State, 220 Ala. 30, 123 So. 231, 232, 68 A.L.R. 712.

The unlawful taking or detention of any female for purposes of marriage, concubinage, or prostitution. 4 Steph.Com. 84; People v. Crotty, 55 Hun, 611, 9 N.Y.S. 937. In many states this offense is created by statute and in most cases applies to females under a given age.

By statute in some states, abduction includes the withdrawal of a husband from his wife, as where another woman alienates his affection and entices him away and causes him to abandon his wife. Humphrey v. Pope, 122 Cal. 253, 54 P. 847.

ABEARANCE. Behavior; as a recognizance to be of good abearance signifies to be of good behavior. 4 Bl.Comm. 251, 256.

ABEREMURDER. (From Sax. *abere,* apparent, notorious; and *mord,* murder.) Plain or downright murder, as distinguished from the less heinous crime of manslaughter, or chance medley. Spelman; Cowell; Blount.

ABESSE. Lat. In the civil law. To be absent; to be away from a place. Said of a person who was *extra continentia urbis,* (beyond the suburbs of the city.)

ABET. A French word combined of two words "a" and "beter"—to bait or excite an animal. It includes knowledge of the wrongful purpose of the perpetrator and counsel and encouragement in the crime. People v. Terman, 4 Cal.App.2d 345, 40 P.2d 915, 916.

To encourage, incite, or set another on to commit a crime. This word is always applied to aiding the commission of a crime. To abet another to commit a murder is to command, procure, or counsel him to commit it, Old Nat. Brev. 21; Co. Litt. 475; to command, procure, counsel, encourage, induce, or assist, Short v. Commonwealth, 240 Ky. 477, 42 S.W.2d 696, 697; to encourage, counsel, induce, or assist, State v. Watts, Nev., 296 P. 26. To facilitate the commission of a crime, promote its accomplishment, or help in advancing or bringing it about. State v. Lord, 42 N.M. 638, 84 P.2d 80, 86. It includes knowledge of wrongful purpose of perpetrator. Daniels v. State, 58 Ga.App. 599, 199 S.E. 572, 577. State v. Kneedy, 232 Iowa 21, 3 N.W.2d 611, 615. People v. Stein, 55 Cal.App.2d 417, 130 P.2d 750, 751 (permitting wife to remain in house of prostitution).

See Abettor; Aid and Abet.

"Aid" and "abet" are nearly synonymous terms as generally used; but, strictly speaking, the former term does not imply guilty knowledge or felonious intent, whereas the word "abet" includes knowledge of the wrongful purpose and counsel and encouragement in the commission of the crime. Forgery, People v. Dole, 122 Cal. 486, 55 P. 581, 68 Am.St.Rep. 50; Raiford v. State, 59 Ala. 106; Violation of law against free passes, State v. Ankrom, 86 W.Va. 570, 103 S.E. 925, 927; Crime against nature, State v. Start, 65 Or. 178, 132 P. 512, 513; Robbery, People v. Powers, 293 Ill. 600, 127 N.E. 681, 682.

Instigate synonymous (malicious prosecution) Hughes v. Van Bruggen, 44 N.M. 534, 105 P.2d 494, 499.

"Abet" smacks more of technical terminology than does the word "aid", but it is almost synonymous with the word "aid". Assault and battery, Gentry v. State, 65 Ga. App. 100, 15 S.E.2d 464, 465.

ABETTATOR. L. Lat. In old English law. An abettor. Fleta, lib. 2, c. 65, § 7. See Abettor.

ABETTOR. In criminal law. An instigator, or setter on; one who promotes or procures a crime to be committed. Old Nat.Brev. 21. One who commands, advises, instigates, or encourages another to commit a crime; a person who, being present or in the neighborhood, incites another to commit a crime, and thus becomes a principal. See State v. Baldwin, 193 N.C. 566, 137 S.E. 590, 591.

Must have rendered assistance or encouragement to the perpetrator of the crime with knowledge of his felonious intent; offense of "aiding and abetting" being committed by person present who does some act or speaks some word aiding the actual perpetrator of the crime. Combs v. Commonwealth, 224 Ky. 653, 6 S.W.2d 1082, 1083. Must aid or commit some overt act or act of encouragement. Long v. Commonwealth, 288 Ky. 83, 155 S.W.2d 246, 247. One who so far participates in the commission of the offense as to be present for the purpose of assisting if necessary. State v. Epps, 213 N.C. 709, 197 S.E. 580, 583.

The distinction between abettors and accessories is the presence or absence at the commission of the crime. Cowell; Fleta, lib. 1, c. 34. Presence and participation are necessary to constitute a person an abettor. 4 Sharsw.Bla. Comm. 33; Bradley v. Commonwealth, 201 Ky. 413, 257 S. W. 11, 13. Common design to take life not necessary. State v. Lord, 42 N.M. 638, 84 P.2d 80, 86. Not essential that there should be a prearrangement or mutual understanding or concert of action. McKinney v. Commonwealth, 284 Ky. 16, 143 S.W.2d 745, 747, 748.

ABEYANCE. In the law of estates. In expectation, remembrance, and contemplation of law; the condition of a freehold when there is no person in being in whom it is vested.

In such cases the freehold has been said to be *in nubibus* (in the clouds), McKown v. McKown, 93 W.Va. 689, 117 S.E. 557, 559; *in pendenti* (in suspension); and *in gremio legis* (in the bosom of the law). Where there is a tenant of the freehold, the remainder or reversion in fee may exist for a time without any particular owner, in which case it is said to be in abeyance; Lyle v. Richards, 9 S. & R. Pa. 367; 3 Plowd. 29 *a, b,* 35 *a;* 1 Washb.R.P. 47.

Franchise of a corporation; Trustees of Dartmouth College v. Woodward, 4 Wheat. (U. S.) 691, 4 L.Ed. 629. Personal property as in case of a vessel captured at sea from its captors until it becomes invested with the character of a prize; 1 Kent, 102; 1 C.Rob.Adm. 139; 3 *id.* 97, n.; or the rights of property of a bankrupt, pending adjudication; Bank v. Sherman, 101 U.S. 403, 25 L.Ed. 866.

A condition of being undetermined. Fenn v. American Rattan & Reed Mfg. Co., 75 Ind.App. 146, 130 N.E. 129, 130. (Seller stating its inability to promise to deliver.)

Sales to third parties, of property acquired by county at tax sale, being held in "abeyance", means that certain rights or conditions are in expectancy. Willard v. Ward County, 72 N.D. 291, 6 N.W.2d 566, 568.

ABIATICUS, or AVIATICUS. L. Lat. In feudal law. A son's son; a grandson in the male line. Du Cange, *Avius;* Spelman; Lib.Feud., Baraterii, tit. 8, cited Id.

ABIDE. To accept the consequences of; to rest satisfied with; to wait for.

With reference to an order, judgment, or decree of a court, to perform, to execute. Jackson v. State, 30 Kan. 88, 1 P. 317. Where a statute provides for a recognizance "to *abide* the judgment of the court," one conditioned "to *await* the action of the court" is not sufficient; Wilson v. State, 7 Tex.App. 38. Defendant does not "abide the judgment" until costs of appeal are paid. Ex parte Tillery, 22 Ala.App. 193, 114 So. 15. And see State v. Gregory, 205 Iowa, 707, 216 N.W. 17, 19.

Defendant's presence in courtroom not a compliance with supersedeas bond conditioned to "abide final judgment," where there was no formal offer to surrender defendant into court's custody. American Surety Co. of New York v. State, 50 Ga.App. 777, 179 S.E. 407.

To abide and satisfy is used to express the execution or performance of a judgment or order by carrying it into complete effect, Erickson v. Elder, 34 Minn. 371, 25 N.W. 804, *Cf.* Woolfolk v. Jones, D.C.Va., 216 F. 807, 809.

Where costs are to abide final result, "abide" is synonymous with conform to. Getz v. Johnston, 145 Md. 426, 125 A. 689, 691.

To abide order respecting seized property, means to perform, obey, conform to. Cantor v. Sachs, 18 Del.Ch. 359, 162 A. 73, 84.

ABIDING BY. In Scotch law. A judicial declaration that the party abides by the deed on which he founds, in an action where the deed or writing is attacked as forged. Pat.Comp. It has the effect of pledging the party to stand the consequences of founding on a forged deed. Bell.

"Abide by" means to adhere to, to submit to, to obey, to accept the consequences of. Detroit Fidelity & Surety Co. v. U. S., C.C.A.Ohio, 36 F.2d 682, 683. (Recognizance)

To abide by an award means to await the award without revoking the submission. It does not mean to "acquiesce in" or "not dispute," in the sense of not being at liberty to contest the validity of the award when made, Hunt v. Wilson, 6 N.H. 36; Quimby v. Melvin, 35 N.H. 198; Weeks v. Trask, 81 Me. 127, 16 A. 413, 2 L.R.A. 532.

ABIDING CONVICTION. A definite conviction of guilt derived from a thorough examination of the whole case. Hopt v. Utah, 7 S.Ct. 614, 120 U.S. 439, 30 L.Ed. 708. A settled or fixed conviction. Davis v. State, 8 Ala.App. 147, 62 So. 1027, 1033. People v. Castro, 68 Cal.App.2d 491, 157 P.2d 25, 30.

ABIDING FAITH. Belief or confidence in the guilt of one accused of crime which remains or continues in the minds of the jury. Gray v. State. 56 Okl.Cr. 208, 38 P.2d 967, 970.

ABIGEATORES. See Abigeus.

ABIGEATUS. Lat. In the civil law. The offense of stealing or driving away cattle. See Abigeus.

ABIGEI. See Abigeus.

ABIGERE. Lat. In the civil law. To drive away. Applied to those who drove away animals with the intention of stealing them. Applied, also, to the similar offense of cattle stealing on the borders between England and Scotland. See Abigeus.

To drive out; to expel by force; to produce abortion. Dig. 47, 11, 4.

ABIGEUS. Lat. (Pl., *abigei,* or more rarely *abigeatores.*) In the civil law. A stealer of cattle; one who drove or drew away *(subtraxit)* cattle from their pastures, as horses or oxen from the herds, and made booty of them, and who followed this as a business or trade.

The term was applied also to those who drove away the smaller animals, as swine, sheep, and goats. In the latter case, it depended on the number taken, whether the offender was *fur* (a common thief) or *abigeus.* But the taking of a single horse or ox seems to have constituted the crime of *abigeatus.* And those who frequently did this were clearly *abigei,* though they took but an animal or two at a time. Dig. 47, 14, 3, 2. See Cod. 9, 37; Nov. 22, c. 15, § 1; 4 Bl.Comm. 239.

ABILITY. When the word is used in statutes, it is usually construed as referring to pecuniary ability, as in the construction of Tenterden's Act (*q. v.*); 1 M. & W. 101.

Contemplates earning capacity as well as property actually owned, to support abandoned wife; State v. Witham, 70 Wis. 473, 35 N.W. 934, Contra, Washburn v. Washburn, 9 Cal. 475.

The ability to buy, required in a purchaser as a condition to the broker's right to a commission, is the financial ability to meet the required terms of the sale, and does not mean solvency or ability to respond in damages for a breach of the contract. Stewart v. Sisk, 29 Ga.App. 17, 114 S.E. 71. See Able to Purchase.

A voter's "ability to read" within meaning of election statutes is satisfied if he can read in a reasonably intelligent manner sentences composed of words in common use and of average difficulty, although each word may not be always accurately pronounced, and "ability to write" is satisfied if he can by use of alphabetical signs express in a fairly legible way words of common use and average difficulty, though each word may not be accurately spelled. Williams v. Hays, 175 Ky. 170, 193 S.W. 1046, 1047. But the mere ability to write one's name and post office address, and nothing more, is insufficient. Murrel v. Allen, 180 Ky. 604, 203 S.W. 313, 314.

ABISHERING, or ABISHERSING. Quit of amercements. It originally signified a forfeiture or amercement, and is more properly *mishering, mishersing,* or *miskering,* according to Spelman. It has since been termed a liberty of freedom, because, wherever this word is used in a grant, the persons to whom the grant is made have the forfeitures and amercements of all others, and are themselves free from the control of any within their fee. Termes de la Ley, 7.

ABJUDICATIO. In old English law. The depriving of a thing by the judgment of a court; a putting out of court; the same as *forisjudicatio,* forjudgment, forjudger. Co.Litt. 100*a*, *b;* Townsh. Pl. 49. A removal from court. Calvinus, Lex.

Used to indicate an adverse decision in a writ of right: Thus, the land is said to be *abjudged* from one of the parties and his heirs. 2 Poll. & Maitl. 62.

ABJURATION. A renunciation or abandonment by or upon oath.

The oath by which any person holding office in England was formerly obliged to bind himself not to acknowledge any right in the Pretender to the throne of England; 1 Bla.Com. 368; 13 and 14 W. III, c. 6, repealed by 30 and 31 Vic. c. 59.

It also denotes an oath abjuring certain doctrines of the church of Rome.

ABJURATION OF ALLEGIANCE. A naturalized citizen of the United States, must declare that he doth renounce and *abjure* all allegiance and fidelity which he owes to any foreign prince, state, etc. 8 U.S.C.A. § 735.

ABJURATION OF THE REALM. In ancient English law. A renunciation of one's country, a species of self-imposed banishment, under an oath never to return to the kingdom unless by permission. 4 Bl.Comm. 332; Avery v. Everett, 110 N.Y. 317, 18 N.E. 148, 1 L.R.A. 264. See Abjure.

ABJURE. To renounce, or abandon, by or upon oath. See Abjuration.

A departure from the state without the intention of returning, and not a renunciation of one's country, upon an oath of perpetual banishment, as the term originally implied. Mead v. Hughes, 15 Ala. 148, 1 Am.Rep. 123.

ABLE-BODIED. As used in a statute relating to service in the militia, this term does not imply an absolute freedom from all physical ailment. It imports an absence of those palpable and visible defects which evidently incapacitate the person from performing the ordinary duties of a soldier. Darling v. Bowen, 10 Vt. 152. Ability to perform ordinary labor is not the test. Town of Marlborough v. Sisson, 26 Conn. 57.

ABLE SEAMAN. A grade of merchant seamen. 46 U.S.C.A. § 672.

ABLE TO EARN. The phrase in the Workmen's Compensation Act in reference to wages does not mean the maximum sum earned in any one week, but a fair average of the weekly wages which an employee is able to earn covering a sufficient period of time to determine his earning capacity. Reeves v. Dietz, 1 La.App. 501, 505. See also, Mt. Olive & Staunton Coal Co. v. Industrial Commission, 301 Ill. 521, 134 N.E. 16. Amount one is capable of earning if employed. Ferrara v. Clifton Wright Hat Co., 125 Conn. 140, 3 A.2d 842, 843.

Ability to obtain and hold employment means that the person referred to is either able or unable to perform the usual duties of whatever employment may be under consideration, in the manner that such duties are customarily performed by the average person engaged in such employment. Kinyon v. Kinyon, 230 Mo.App. 623, 71 S.W.2d 78, 82.

ABLE TO PURCHASE "Ability" in sales contracts, dependent on ability to purchase, usually means financial ability. Anderson v. Craig, 111 Mont. 182, 108 P.2d 205, 206; House v. Hornburg, Sup., 39 N.Y.S.2d 20, 22. Purchaser must have financial ability and legal capacity to acquire land. Campbell v. Hood, Tex.Com.App., 35 S.W.2d 93, 95, 85 A.L.R. 266.

Purchaser is able to purchase, as respects broker's right to commission, if he is financially able to command the necessary funds to close the deal within the time required. Hersh v. Garau, 218 Cal. 460, 23 P.2d 1022. Even though part of the money must be obtained on the purchased property itself. Pellaton v. Brunski, 69 Cal. App. 301, 231 P. 583, 584. But see Bateman v. Richard, 105 Okl. 272, 232 P. 443, 445; and Reynor v. Mackrill, 181 Iowa 210, 164 N.W. 335, 1 A.L.R. 523, holding that a person, to be able to purchase, must have the money for the cash payment, and not merely property on which he could raise it. See, also, Peters v. Mullins, 211 Ky. 123, 277 S.W. 316, 317. See Financially Able.

ABLEGATI. Papal ambassadors of the second rank, who are sent to a country where there is not a nuncio, with a less extensive commission than that of a nuncio. This title is equivalent to *envoy.*

ABLOCATIO. A letting out to hire, or leasing for money. Calvin. Sometimes used in the English form "ablocation."

ABMATERTERA. Lat. In the civil law. A great-great-grandmother's sister, *(abaviæ soror).* Inst. 3, 6, 6; Dig. 38, 10, 3. Called *matertera maxima.* Id. 38, 10, 10, 17. Called, by Bracton, *abmatertera magna.* Bract. fol. 68*b*.

ABNEPOS. Lat. A great-great-grandson. The grandson of a grandson or granddaughter. Calvinus, Lex.

ABNEPTIS. Lat. A great-great-granddaughter. The granddaughter of a grandson or granddaughter. Calvinus, Lex.

ABODE. One's home; habitation; place of dwelling; or residence. Ordinarily means "domicile." Hanson v. Williams, 170 Ga. 779, 154 S.E. 240, 242. Living place impermanent in character. Fowler v. Fowler, 156 Fla. 316, 22 So.2d 817, 818. Evans v. Evans, 141 Fla. 860, 194 So. 215, 217. The place where a person dwells. Dorsey v. Brigham, 177 Ill. 250, 52 N.E. 303, In re Erickson, 18 N.J.Misc. 5, 10 A.2d 142, 146.

Residence of a legal voter. Fry's Election Case, 71 Pa. 302, 10 Am.Rep. 698; Dale v. Irwin, 78 Ill. 181; Pope v. Board of Election Com'rs, 370 Ill. 196, 18 N.E.2d 214, 216. Fixed place of residence for the time being. Augustus Co., for Use of Bourgeois v. Manzella, 19 N.J.Misc. 29, 17 A.2d 68, 70; Hudson v. Birmingham Water Works Co., 238 Ala. 38, 189 So. 72, 73. For service of process, one's fixed place of residence for the time being. State ex rel. Merritt v. Heffernan, 142 Fla. 496, 195 So. 145, 147; Kurilla v. Roth, 132 N.J.L. 213, 38 A.2d 862, 864.

ABOGADO. Sp. An advocate. See Bozero.

ABOLISH. To do away with wholly; to annul. Webster. To dispense with. Alexander v. City of Lampasas, Tex.Civ.App., 275 S.W. 614, 616. Put an end to. Stretch v. Murphy, 166 Or. 439, 112 P. 2d 1018, 1021.

Imports absolute destruction, having its root in the Latin word "abolere," meaning to destroy utterly. Applies particularly to things of a permanent nature, such as institutions, usages, customs, as the abolition of slavery. Pondelick v. Passaic County, 111 N.J.Law 187, 168 A. 146, 147.

ABOLITION. The destruction, annihilation, abrogation, or extinguishment of anything. Peterson v. Pratt, 183 Iowa 462, 167 N.W. 101. Also the leave given by the sovereign or judges to a criminal accuser to desist from further prosecution. 25 Hen. VIII, c. 21.

In the Civil, French and German law, abolition is used nearly synonymously with pardon, remission, grace. Dig. 39, 4, 3, 3. There is, however, this difference: *grace* is the generic term; *pardon,* according to those laws, is the clemency which the prince extends to a man who has participated in a crime, without being a principal or accomplice; *remission* is made in cases of involuntary homicides, and self-defence. *Abolition* is used when the crime cannot be remitted. The prince then may, by letters of abolition, remit the punishment, but the infamy remains, unless letters of abolition have been obtained before sentence. *Encycl. de D'Alembert.*

Abolition of position or office, Rexstrew v. City of Huntington Park, Cal.App., 120 P.2d 136, 142. Positions of physicians and dentists, Lewin v. La Guardia, 22 N.Y.S.2d 409, 411, 175 Misc. 165. Lay-off of court attendant, Pondelick v. Passaic County, 111 N.J.L. 187, 168 A. 146, 147. Transfer not an abolition of office, Tremp v. Patten, 132 Conn. 120, 42 A.2d 834, 837.

ABORDAGE. Fr. In French commercial law. Collision of vessels.

ABORTIFACIENT. In medical jurisprudence. A drug or medicine capable of, or used for, producing abortion.

ABORTION. The expulsion of the fœtus at a period of utero-gestation so early that it has not acquired the power of sustaining an independent life. The unlawful destruction, or the bringing forth prematurely, of the human fœtus before the natural time of birth; State of Magnell, 51 A. 606, 3 Pennewill (Del.) 307. The act of bringing forth what is yet imperfect. Also the thing prematurely brought forth, or product of an untimely process. Sometimes loosely used for the offense of procuring a premature delivery; but strictly, the early delivering is the abortion; causing or procuring abortion is the full name of the offense. Wells v. New England Mut. L. Ins. Co., 191 Pa. 207, 43 A. 126, 53 L.R.A. 327.

Criminal miscarriage, Commonwealth v. Sierakowski, 154 Pa.Super. 321, 35 A.2d 790, 792; Mississippi State Board of Health v. Johnson, 197 Miss. 417, 19 So.2d 445, 448. "Abortion" and a "miscarriage produced by unlawful means" are synonymous, People v. Luckett, 23 Cal.App.2d 539, 73 P.2d 658, 659.

ABORTIONIST. One who criminally produces abortions, or one who follows business or practices of crime of producing abortions. State v. Guaraneri, 59 R.I. 173, 194 A. 589, 592, 593.

ABORTIVE TRIAL. A term descriptive of the result when a case has gone off, and no verdict has been pronounced, without the fault, contrivance, or management of the parties. Jebb & B. 51.

ABORTUS. Lat. The fruit of an abortion; the child born before its time, incapable of life.

ABOUT. Near in time, quantity, number, quality, or degree. Substantially, approximately, almost, or nearly. Odom v. Langston, 351 Mo. 609, 173 S.W.2d 826, 829. Testimony as to speed, Casto v. Hansen, 123 Or. 20, 261 P. 428, 429. Near, period of gestation of still born child, Life & Casualty Ins. Co. v. Walters, 190 Miss. 761, 198 So. 746, 748; Todd v. City of New York, City Ct., N.Y. 23 N.Y.S.2d 884, 888. Carrying burglar's tools in suitcase, Trousdale v. State, 168 Tenn. 210, 76 S.W. 2d 646, 647. Near the time. State ex rel. Nagle v. Leader Co., 97 Mont. 586, 37 P.2d 561, 564.

When used with reference to time, the term is of flexible significance, varying with the circumstances and the connection in which it is employed. Burlington Grocery Co. v. Heaphy's Estate, 98 Vt. 122, 126 A. 525, 528. But its use does not necessarily render time immaterial, nor make a contract one terminable at will. Costello v. Siems-Carey Co., 140 Minn. 208, 167 N.W. 551, 552. In a charter party, "about to sail" means just ready to sail. [1893] 2 Q.B. 274. And when it is said that one is "about" to board a street car, it means "in the act of." Fox v. Denver City Tramway Co., 57 Colo. 511, 143 P. 278, 280. With relation to quantity, the term suggests only an estimate of probable amount. Barkemeyer Grain & Seed Co. v. Hannant, 66 Mont. 120, 213 P. 208, 210. Its import is that the actual quantity is a near approximation to that mentioned, and it has the effect of providing against accidental variations. Norrington v. Wright, 6 S.Ct. 12, 115 U.S. 188, 29 L.Ed. 366. It may be given practically the same effect as the phrase more or less. Pierce v. Miller, 107 Neb. 851, 187 N.W. 105, 107; Cargo under vessel charter, Steamship Co. of 1912 v. C. H. Pearson & Son Hardwood Co., C.C.A. N.Y., 30 F.2d 770, 773. Contract for sale of electric energy, Merced Irr. Dist. v. San Joaquin Light & Power Corporation, 101 Cal.App. 153, 281 P. 415, 417. In a deed covers some slight or unimportant inaccuracy. Parrow v. Proulx, 111 Vt. 274, 15 A.2d 835, 838. Synonymous with "on" or "upon," as in offense of carrying concealed weapons. State v. Brunson, 162 La. 902, 111 So. 321, 323; Carriage of a pistol or revolver in a grip, satchel, or hand bag held in the hand or connected with the person, State v. Blazovitch, 88 W.Va. 612, 107 S.E. 291, or on the running board of an automobile, Armstrong v. State, 98 Tex.Cr.R. 335, 265 S.W. 701. Paulk v. State, 97 Tex.Cr.R. 415, 261 S.W. 779, 780. Near by, close at hand, convenient of access. Welch v. State, 97 Tex.Cr.R. 617, 262 S.W. 485; Brown v. U. S., 30 F.2d 474, 475, 58 App.D.C. 311. Weapon on shelf immediately behind defendant, who was seated in coupé type automobile. Hampton v. Commonwealth, 257 Ky. 626, 78 S.W.2d 748, 750. As to number, it merely implies an estimate of a particular lot or class and not a warranty. Holland v. Rock, 50 Nev. 340, 259 P. 415. In connection with distance or locality, the term is of relative significance, varying with the circumstances. Parker v. Town of Pittsfield, 88 Vt. 155, 92 A. 24, 26. Employee on an elevator is "about the premises". Lienau v. Northwestern Telephone Exch. Co., 151 Minn. 258, 186 N.W. 945, 946. Workman 200 feet from a factory was "about" the factory. Wise v. Central Dairy Co., 121 Kan. 258, 246 P. 501, 503. An automobile mechanic injured 17½ blocks from the employers' shop while making a road test of an automobile is not injured on, in, or about the employers' place of business. Iott v. Mosby, 126 Kan. 294, 268 P. 109. "About" in lease meaning in other parts of building. William A. Doe Co. v. City of Boston, 262 Mass. 458, 160 N.E. 262. Estimate of distance, Picharella v. Ovens Transfer Co., 135 Pa.Super. 112, 5 A.2d 408, 409. Estimate as to time, charter of vessel, Britain S. S. Co. v. Munson S. S. Line, D.C. N.Y., 25 F.2d 868, 869. Instruction regarding specified date, State v. Loahmann, Mo., 58 S.W.2d 309, 311. Courses and distances, Humble Oil & Refining Co. v. Luther, Tex. Civ.App., 40 S.W.2d 865, 867. Pistol under automobile seat. Commonwealth v. Nunnelley, 56 S.W.2d 689, 247 Ky. 109, 88 A.L.R. 805.

ABOUTISSEMENT. Fr. An abuttal or abutment. See Guyot, Répert. Univ. *"Aboutissans."*

ABOVE. Higher; superior. As, court above, plaintiff or defendant above. *Above all incumbrances* means in excess thereof; Williams v. McDonald, 42 N.J.Eq. 395, 7 A. 886. Principal; as distinguished from what is auxiliary or instrumental. 3 Bl.Comm. 291.

Bail to the action, or special bail, is otherwise termed bail *above*. 3 Bl.Comm. 291. Jurisdiction "above" the jurisdiction of justices of the peace. Synonymous with "without." Atlantic Coast Line R. Co. v. Nellwood Lumber Co., 21 Ga.App. 209, 94 S.E. 86, 87. Above high water means above a tide which might reasonably be expected to recur with some degree of frequency. Banks v. Wilmington Terminal Co., Del.Super., 24 A.2d 592, 598, 599, 601, 602, 2 Terry 489.

ABOVE CITED, or MENTIONED. Quoted before. A figurative expression taken from the ancient manner of writing books on scrolls, where whatever is mentioned or cited before in the same roll must be *above*. Encyc. Lond.

ABPATRUUS. Lat. A great-great-uncle; or, a great-great-grandfather's brother (*abavi frater*). Inst. 3, 6, 6; Dig. 38, 10, 3; Du Cange, Patruus. Called by Bracton and Fleta, *abpatruus magnus*. Bract. fol. 68*b;* Fleta, lib. 6, c. 2, § 17. It sometimes means uncle, and sometimes great-uncle.

ABRIDGE. To reduce or contract; usually spoken of written language.

Copyright Law

To epitomize; to reduce; to contract. It implies preserving the substance, the essence, of a work, in language suited to such a purpose. In making extracts there is no condensation of the author's language, and hence no abridgment. To abridge requires the exercise of the mind; it is not copying. Between a compilation and an abridgment there is a clear distinction. A compilation consists of selected extracts from different authors; an abridgment is a condensation of the views of one author. Story v. Holcombe, 4 McLean, 306, 310, Fed.Cas.No.13,497.

Practice

To shorten a declaration or count by taking away or severing some of the substance of it. Brooke, Abr., Com., Dig. *Abridgment;* 1 Viner, Abr. 109. See Abridgment.

ABRIDGMENT. Condensation; contraction. An epitome or compendium of another and larger work, wherein the principal ideas of the larger work are summarily contained.

Abridgments of the law are brief digests of the law, arranged alphabetically. (1 Steph.Comm. 51.) The term "digest" has now supplanted that of "abridgment." Sweet.

ABRIDGMENT OF DAMAGES. The right of the court to reduce the damages in certain cases. *Vide* Brooke, tit. "Abridgment."

ABROAD. In English chancery law, beyond the seas.

ABROGATE. To annul, repeal, or destroy; to annul or repeal an order or rule issued by a subordinate authority; to repeal a former law by legislative act, or by usage.

ABROGATION. The destruction or annulling of a former law, by an act of the legislative power, by constitutional authority, or by usage.

It stands opposed to *rogation*; and is distinguished from *derogation*, which implies the taking away only some part of a law; from *subrogation*, which denotes the adding a clause to it; from *dispensation*, which only sets it aside in a particular instance; and from *antiquation*, which is the refusing to pass a law. Encyc. Lond. Implied abrogation takes place when the new law contains provisions which are positively contrary to former laws, without expressly abrogating such laws. Bernard v. Vignaud, 10 Mart.O.S. La. 560; and also when the order of things for which the law has been made no longer exists. See Ex parte Lum Poy, D.C., 23 F.2d 690.

For "Express Abrogation," see that title.

ABSCOND. To go in a clandestine manner out of the jurisdiction of the courts, or to lie concealed, in order to avoid their process. Malvin v. Christoph, 54 Iowa, 562, 7 N.W. 6. To hide, conceal, or absent oneself clandestinely, with the intent to avoid legal process. Smith v. Johnson, 43 Neb. 754, 62 N.W. 217. Postponing limitations. Keck v. Pickens, 207 Ark. 757, 182 S.W.2d 873, 875. Fleeing from arresting or prosecuting officers of this state. Code Cr.Proc. art. 8. State v. Berryhill, 188 La. 549, 177 So. 663.

ABSCONDING DEBTOR. One who absconds from his creditors.

An absconding debtor is one who lives without the state, or who has intentionally concealed himself from his creditors, or withdrawn himself from the reach of their suits, with intent to frustrate their just demands. Thus, if a person departs from his usual residence, or remains absent therefrom, or conceals himself in his house, so that he cannot be served with process, with intent unlawfully to delay or defraud his creditors, he is an absconding debtor; but if he departs from the state or from his usual abode, with the intention of again returning, and without any fraudulent design, he has not absconded, nor absented himself, within the intendment of the law. Doughnut Corporation of America v. Tsakirides, 121 N.J.L. 136, 1 A.2d 467, 469. A party may abscond, and subject himself to the operation of the attachment law against absconding debtors, without leaving the limits of the state. Field v. Adreon, 7 Md. 209. A debtor who is shut up from his creditors in his own house is an absconding debtor. Ives v. Curtiss, 2 Root (Conn.) 133. Salzman v. Robinson, 10 N.J.Misc.R. 51, 157 A. 547, 548.

ABSENCE. The state of being absent, removed, or away from one's domicile, or usual place of residence. Maley v. Pennsylvania R. Co., 258 Pa. 73, 101 A. 911. Not present at particular time, opposite of appearance at a specified time. Hamilton v. Bernstein, 133 Kan. 229, 299 P. 581.

Absence is of a fivefold kind: (1) A *necessary absence*, as in banished or transported persons; this is entirely necessary. (2) *Necessary and voluntary*, as upon the account of the commonwealth, or in the service of the church. (3) A *probable absence*, according to the civilians, as that of students on the score of study. (4) *Entirely voluntary*, on account of trade, merchandise, and the like. (5) *Absence cum dolo et culpâ*, as not appearing to a writ, *subpœna*, citation, etc., or to delay or defeat creditors, or avoiding arrest, either on civil or criminal process. Ayliffe. Nonappearance to action, not merely that the party was not present in court vacating judgment. Strine v. Kaufman, 12 Neb. 423, 11 N.W. 867. In usual and natural signification, means physical absence. Inhabitants of Lanesborough v. Inhabitants of Ludlow, 250 Mass. 99, 145 N.E. 57, 58. Nonpresence, of official for service. Kurre v. American Indemnity Co. of Galveston, Tex., 223 Mo.App. 406, 17 S.W.2d 685, 688.

Presumption of Death Created

Intent to establish home at place last heard from not required. American Nat. Ins. Co. v. Garcia, Tex.Civ.App., 46 S.W.2d 1011, 1012. Away from a place to which one is expected to return. Woodmen of the World Life Ins. Soc. v. Cooper, Tex.Civ.App., 164 S.W.2d 729, 731.

In Scotch Law, want or default of appearance. A decree is said to be *in absence* where the defender (defendant) does not appear. Ersk. Inst. bk. 4, tit. 3, § 6.

ABSENT. Being away from; at a distance from; not in company with.

Paine v. Drew, 44 N.H. 306, where it was held that the word when used as an adjective referred only to the condition or situation of the person or thing spoken of at the time of speaking without reference to any prior condition or situation of the same person or thing, but when used as a verb implies prior presence. It has also been held to mean "not being in a particular place at the time referred to," and *not* to import prior presence. The term *absent defendants* does not embrace non-resident defendants but has reference to parties resident in the state, but temporarily absent therefrom. Wheeler v. Wheeler, 35 Ill. App. 123. See, however, Seimer v. James Dickinson Farm Mortg. Co., D.C.Ill., 299 F. 651, 658, holding that a foreign corporation is "absent" from the state, and limitation does not run in its favor. Commonwealth's attorney is "absent" when disqualified or disabled from performing functions of office. Northcutt v. Howard, 279 Ky. 219, 130 S.W.2d 70, 71, 72. A judge, disqualified to act. Dark Tobacco Growers' Co-op. Ass'n v. Wilson, 206 Ky. 550, 267 S.W. 1092, 1093. A deceased stockholder employee is not "absent" from duty, as respects sharing of profits, etc. Nichols v. Olympia Veneer Co., 135 Wash. 8, 236 P. 794, 796. Nonresident with office in state is not absent from state. Corash v. Texas Co., 35 N.Y.S.2d 334, 340, 264 App.Div. 292.

As a verb, "absent" means to take or withdraw to such a distance as to prevent intercourse; to depart from. People v. Day, 321 Ill. 552, 152 N.E. 495, 497.

ABSENT-MINDEDNESS. A state of mind in which the person affected fails to respond to the ordinary demands on his attention. Webster. See Racine Tire Co. v. Grady, 205 Ala. 423, 88 So. 337.

ABSENTE. Lat. Being absent; often used in the old reports of one of the judges not present at the hearing of a cause. 2 Mod. 14. *Absente Reo*, The defendant being absent.

ABSENTEE. One who dwells abroad; a landlord who resides in a country other than that from which he draws his rents. McCul. Pol. Econ.; 33 Brit. Quar. Rev. 455. One who is absent from his usual place of residence or domicile.

Foreign corporations, not filing declarations of domicile and names of agents. Palmer v. Avalon Oil Co., 10 La. App. 512, 120 So. 781, 782. In Louisiana law, one who has left his residence in a state leaving no one to represent him. Bartlett v. Wheeler, 31 La.Ann. 540; or who resides in another state but has property in Louisiana. Penn v. Evans, 28 La.Ann. 576. It has been also defined as one who has never been domiciled in the state and who resides abroad. Morris v. Bienvenu, 30 La.Ann. 878. One person cannot be both, at the same time, in the meaning of the law, a resident and an absentee. Spence v. Spence, 105 So. 28, 29, 158 La. 961.

ABSENTEES, or DES ABSENTEES. A parliament so called was held at Dublin, 10th May, 8 Hen. VIII. It is mentioned in letters patent 29 Hen. VIII.

ABSENTEM ACCIPERE DEBEMUS EUM QUI NON EST EO LOCI IN QUO PETITUR. We ought to consider him absent who is not in the place where he is demanded (or sought). Dig. 50, 16, 199.

ABSENTIA EJUS QUI REIPUBLICÆ CAUSÂ ABEST, NEQUE EI NEQUE ALII DAMNOSA ESSE DEBET. The absence of him who is away in behalf of the republic (on business of the state) ought not to be prejudicial either to him or to another. Dig. 50, 17, 140.

ABSOILE, ASSOIL, ASSOILE. To pardon; to deliver from excommunication. Staunford, Pl.Cr. 72; Kelham; Cowell.

ABSOLUTA SENTENTIA EXPOSITORE NON INDIGET. An absolute sentence or proposition (one that is plain without any scruple, or absolute without any saving) needs not an expositor. 2 Inst. 533.

ABSOLUTE. Complete; perfect; final; without any condition or incumbrance; as an absolute bond *(simplex obligatio)* in distinction from a conditional bond. Unconditional; complete and perfect in itself; without relation to or dependence on other things or persons. Instruction as to an "absolute" gift, Ketch v. Smith, 131 Okl. 263, 268 P. 715, 717. Irrevocable, final. Gift inter vivos by husband, President and Directors of Manhattan Co. v. Janowitz, 14 N.Y.S.2d 375, 382, 172 Misc. 290. Within limitation or restriction, Comford v. Cantrell, 177 Tenn. 553, 151 S.W.2d 1076, 1077.

An absolute estate is one that is free from all manner of condition or incumbrance; an estate in fee simple. Johnson v. McIntosh, 8 Wheat. 543, 5 L.Ed. 681; Fuller v. Missroon, 35 S.C. 314, 14 S.E. 714; Bradford v. Martin, 199 Iowa 250, 201 N.W. 574, 576; Middleton v. Dudding, Mo. Sup., 183 S.W. 443, 444. A rule is said to be absolute when on the hearing it is confirmed and made final. A conveyance is said to be absolute, as distinguished from a mortgage or other conditional conveyance. Gogarn v. Connors, 153 N.W. 1068, 188 Mich. 161. Absolute property is where a man hath solely and exclusively the right and also the occupation of movable chattels; distinguished from a qualified property, as that of a bailee. 2 Kent 347. An absolute owner is one in whom elements of titles of possession, right of possession, and right of property, are combined. Harris v. Southeast Portland Lumber Co., 123 Or. 549, 262 P. 243, 244. Absolute ownership exists when interest is so completely vested in insured that he cannot be deprived of it without his own consent. Norwich Union Fire Ins. Soc. v. Sawyer, 57 Ga.App. 739, 196 S.E. 223, 224. Absolute rights are such as appertain and belong to particular persons merely as individuals or single persons, as distinguished from relative rights, which are incident to them as members of society; 1 Sharsw.Bla.Com. 123; 1 Chit.Pr. 32. An absolute duty is one that is free from every restriction; unconditional; determined; not merely provisional; irrevocable. Broken telephone wires. Home Telephone Co. v. Weir, 101 N.E.1020, 1021, 53 Ind.App. 466; Railroad employee, Lehigh Valley R. Co. v. Beltz, C.C.A.N.Y., 10 F.2d 74, 77; Pedestrians, Scibilia v. City of Philadelphia, 279 Pa. 549, 124 A. 273, 275, 32 A.L.R. 981. An "absolute power of disposition," in the absence of statute, would be one by which the holder of the power might dispose of the property as fully and in the same manner as he might dispose of his individual estate acquired by his own efforts. In re Briggs' Will, 167 N.Y.S. 632, 635, 101 Misc. 191. In the law of insurance that is an *absolute interest* in property which is so completely vested in the individual that there could be no danger of his being deprived of it without his own consent. Libby Lumber Co. v. Pacific States Fire Ins. Co., 79 Mont. 166, 255 P. 340, 345, 60 A.L.R. 1. It may be used in the sense of vested. Hough v. Ins. Co., 29 Conn. 20, 76 Am.Dec. 581. *"Absolute control"* in Motor Vehicle Act does not require instant stoppage. Goff v. Clarksburg Dairy Co., 86 W.Va. 237, 103 S.E. 58, 60. As to absolute control of a mine, see People v. Boggess, 75 Cal.App. 499, 243 P. 478, 481; and of an estate, see Strickland v. Strickland, 271 Ill. 614, 111 N.E. 592, 594. Absolute veto is equivalent to "pocket veto". Okanogan, Methow, San Poelis (or San Poil), Nespelem, Colville, and Lake Indian Tribes or Bands of State of Washington v. United States, 49 S.Ct. 463, 279 U.S. 655, 73 L.Ed. 894, 64 A.L.R. 1434.

As to absolute "Conveyance," "Covenant," "Delivery," "Divorce," "Estate," "Gift," "Guaranty," "Interest," "Legacy," "Nuisance," "Nullity," "Obligation," "Property," "Rights," "Rule," "Sale," "Title," "Warrandice," see those titles.

ABSOLUTE LAW. The true and proper law of nature, immutable in the abstract or in principle, in theory, but not in application; for very often the object, the reason, situation, and other circumstances, may vary its exercise and obligation. 1 Steph.Comm. 21 *et seq.*

ABSOLUTELY. Completely; wholly; without qualification; without reference or relation to, or dependence upon, any other person, thing, or event. Thus, *absolutely void* means utterly void; Pearsoll v. Chapin, 44 Pa. 9. *Absolutely necessary* may be used to make the idea of necessity more emphatic; State v. Tetrick, 34 W.Va. 137, 11 S.E. 1002. An "absolutely necessary repair," within terms of Wisconsin St. 1925, § 85.02, prohibiting parking of vehicles except for making absolutely necessary repairs, includes repair of a punctured tire. Long v. Steffen, 194 Wis. 179, 215 N.W. 892, 893, 61 A.L.R. 1155. Independently or unconditionally, wholly or positively. Collins v. Hartford Accident & Indemnity Co., 178 Va. 501, 17 S.E.2d 413, 418.

"Absolutely void" is that which the law or nature of things forbids to be enforced at all, and that is "relatively void" which the law condemns as a wrong to individuals and refuses to enforce against them. Kyle v. Chaves, 42 N.Mex. 21, 74 P.2d 1030; Scudder v. Hart, 45 N.M. 76, 110 P.2d 536, 541.

A devise of property to have "absolutely" means without condition, exception, restriction, qualification or limitation, In re Darr's Estate, 206 N.W. 2, 3, 114 Neb. 116, and creates a fee-simple estate. In re Reynold's Estate, 94 Vt. 149, 109 A. 60, 63.

ABSOLUTION. In Canon Law, a juridical act whereby the clergy declare that the sins of such as are penitent are remitted. Among Protestants it is chiefly used for a sentence by which a person who stands excommunicated is released or freed from that punishment. Encyc. Brit.

In the Civil Law a sentence whereby a party accused is declared innocent of the crime laid to his charge.

In French Law, the dismissal of an accusation.

The term *acquitment* is employed when the accused is declared not guilty, and *absolution* when he is recognized as guilty but the act is not punishable by law or he is exonerated by some defect of intention or will. Merlin, Répert.

ABSOLUTISM. In politics. A system of government in which public power is vested in some person or persons, unchecked and uncontrolled by any law, institution, constitutional device, or coordinate body.

ABSOLVE. To set free, or release, as from obligation, debt, or responsibility. State ex rel. St. Louis Car Co. v. Hughes, 348 Mo. 125, 152 S.W.2d 193, 194.

ABSOLVITOR. In Scotch law. An acquittal; a decree in favor of the defender in any action.

ABSQUE. Without. Occurs in phrases taken from the Latin; such as those immediately following.

ABSQUE ALIQUO INDE REDENDO. Lat. Without reserving any rent therefrom; without rendering anything therefrom. A term used of a free grant by the crown. 2 Rolle, Abr. 502.

ABSQUE CONSIDERATIONE CURIÆ. In old practice. Without the consideration of the court; without judgment. Fleta, lib. 2, c. 47, § 13.

ABSQUE HOC. Without this. These are technical words of denial, used in pleading at common law by way of special traverse, to introduce the negative part of the plea, following the affirmative part or inducement. Martin v. Hammon, 8 Pa. 270. See, also, Traverse.

ABSQUE IMPETITIONE VASTI. Without impeachment of waste; without accountability for waste; without liability to suit for waste. A clause anciently often inserted in leases (as the equivalent English phrase sometimes is) signifying that the tenant or lessee shall not be liable to suit *(impetitio)* or challenged, or called to account, for committing waste. Co. Litt. 220*a*; Litt. § 352. See Waste.

ABSQUE TALI CAUSA. Lat. Without such cause. A form of replication, now obsolete, in an action *ex delicto* which works a general denial of the whole matter of the defendant's plea of *de injuria*. Gould, Pl. c. 7, § 10; Steph. Pl. 191.

ABSTENTION. In French law. Keeping an heir from possession; also tacit renunciation of a succession by an heir. Merl. Répert.

ABSTRACT, *n.* A less quantity containing the virtue and force of a greater quantity; an abridgment. Miller v. Kansas City Light & Power Co., C.C.A.Mo., 13 F.2d 723. A transcript is generally defined as a copy, and is more comprehensive than an abstract. Harrison v. Mfg. Co., 10 S.C. 278, 283. Summary or epitome, or that which comprises or concentrates in itself the essential qualities of a larger thing or of several things. Robbins Inv. Co. v. Robbins, 49 Cal.App. 2d 446, 122 P.2d 91, 92.

ABSTRACT, *v.* To take or withdraw from; as, to abstract the funds of a bank. Sprague v. State, 188 Wis. 432, 206 N.W. 69, 70.

ABSTRACT OF A FINE. In old conveyancing. One of the parts of a fine, being an abstract of the writ of covenant, and the concord, naming the parties, the parcels of land, and the agreement. 2 Bl.Comm. 351. More commonly called the "note" of the fine. See Fine; Concord.

ABSTRACT OF RECORD. A complete history in short, abbreviated form of the case as found in the record, complete enough to show that the questions presented for review have been properly reserved. State ex rel. Wallace State Bank v. Trimble, 308 Mo. 278, 272 S.W. 72, 73. Synopsis or summary of facts, rather than table of contents of transcript. Wing v. Brasher, 59 Mont. 10, 194 P. 1106, 1108. Abbreviated accurate and authentic history of proceedings. Brown v. Reichmann, 237 Mo.App. 136, 164 S.W.2d 201, 207.

ABSTRACT OF TITLE. A condensed history of the title to land, consisting of a synopsis or summary of the material or operative portion of all the conveyances, of whatever kind or nature, which in any manner affect said land, or any estate or interest therein, together with a statement of all liens, charges, or liabilities to which the same may be subject, and of which it is in any way material for purchasers to be apprised. Warv. Abst. § 2. Stevenson v. Polk, 71 Iowa, 278, 32 N.W. 340.

Record title, not extrinsic evidence thereof. Upton v. Smith, 166 N.W. 268, 183 Iowa 588. Showing a marketable title. Morgan v. W. A. Howard Realty Co., 68 Colo. 414, 191 P. 114, 115. An epitome of the record evidence of title. De Huy v. Osborne, 96 Fla. 435, 118 So. 161, 162. Including maps, plats, and other aids. Commissioners' Court of Madison County v. Wallace, 118 Tex. 279, 15 S.W.2d 535, 536. An epitome of the conveyances, transfers, and other facts relied on as evidence of title, together with all such facts appearing of record as may impair the title. State ex rel. Freeman v. Abstracters Board of Examiners, 99 Mont. 564, 45 P.2d 668, 670. Vangsness v. Bovill, 58 S.D. 228, 235 N.W. 601, 604. Memorandum or concise statement in orderly form of the substance of documents or facts appearing on public records which affect title to real property. State ex rel. Doria v. Ferguson, 145 Ohio St. 12, 60 N.E.2d 476, 478.

ABSTRACT QUESTION. One which does not rest upon existing facts or rights. Morris Plan Bank of Fort Worth v. Ogden, Tex.Civ.App., 144 S.W.2d 998, 1004.

ABSTRACTION. Taking from with intent to injure or defraud, "wrongful abstraction" is "unauthorized and illegal taking or withdrawing of funds, etc., and appropriation thereof to taker's benefit." Pacific Coast Adjustment Bureau v. Indemnity Ins. Co. of North America, 115 Cal. App. 583, 2 P.2d 218, 219.

For benefit of taker or of another with his consent. Austin v. Nieman, Tex.Civ.App., 3 S.W.2d 128, 129. Offense for bank officer, popular sense of word. Commonwealth v. Dauphinee, 121 Pa.Super. 565, 183 A. 807, 813. Under the National Bank Act, not necessarily the same as embezzlement, larceny, or misapplication of funds. Ferguson v. State, 80 Tex.Cr.R. 383, 189 S.W. 271, 273. State v. Hudson, 93 W.Va. 435, 117 S.E. 122, 126.

ABSURDITY. That which is both physically and morally impossible; and that is to be regarded as morally impossible which is contrary to reason, so that it could not be imputed to a man in his right senses. State v. Hayes, 81 Mo. 574, 585. Anything which is so irrational, unnatural, or inconvenient that it cannot be supposed to have been within the intention of men of ordinary intelligence and discretion. Black, Interp. Laws, 104; Graves v. Scales, 172 N.C. 915, 90 S.E. 439; obviously and flatly opposed to the manifest truth; inconsistent with the plain dictates of common sense; logically contradictory; nonsensical; ridiculous. Wade v. Empire Dist. Electric Co., 98 Kan. 366, 158 P. 28, 30.

ABUNDANS CAUTELA NON NOCET. Abundant or extreme caution does no harm. 11 Co. 6; Fleta, lib. 1, c. 28, § 1; 6 Wheat. 108. This principle is generally applied to the construction of instruments in which superfluous words have been inserted more clearly to express the intention.

ABUS DE CONFIANCE. Fraudulently misusing or spending to anybody's prejudice goods, cash, bills, documents, or contracts handed over for a special object. The Washington, D.C.N.Y., 19 F. Supp. 719, 722.

ABUSE, *n.* Everything which is contrary to good order established by usage. Merl. Répert. Departure from use; immoderate or improper use.

Action that would be necessary in ordinary affairs to make one guilty of an "abuse" connotes conduct of a different grade than what is meant when a court is said to have "abused its discretion." Beck v. Wings Field, Inc. C.C.A.Pa., 122 F.2d 114, 116.

Civil Law

The destruction of the substance of a thing in using it. See Abuse, *v.*

Corporate Franchise or Entity

The abuse or misuse of its franchises by a corporation signifies any positive act in violation of the charter and in derogation of public right, willfully done or caused to be done; the use of rights or franchises as a pretext for wrongs and injuries to the public. People v. Atlantic Ave. R. Co., 125 N.Y. 513, 26 N.E. 622.

Discretion

"Abuse of discretion" is synonymous with a failure to exercise a sound, reasonable, and legal discretion. Disbarment, Adair v. Pennewill, 153 A. 859, 860, 4 W.W.Harr.(Del.) 390. It is a strict legal term indicating that appellate court is simply of opinion that there was commission of an error of law in the circumstances. Refusing motion to amend pleadings, Tunstall v. Lerner Shops, 160 S.C. 557, 159 S.E. 386. Motions to consolidate actions, Bishop v. Bishop, 164 S.C. 493, 162 S.E. 756, 757. Vacating judgment, Detroit Fidelity & Surety Co. v. Foster, 171 S.C. 121, 169 S.E. 871, 881. And it does not imply intentional wrong or bad faith, or misconduct, nor any reflection on the judge but means the clearly erroneous conclusion and judgment—one is that clearly against logic and effect of such facts as are presented in support of the application or against the reasonable and probable deductions to be drawn from the facts disclosed upon the hearing; an improvident exercise of discretion; an error of law. New trial, State v. Draper, 83 Utah, 115, 27 P.2d 39. Setting aside of decree pro confesso. Ex parte Jones, 246 Ala. 433, 20 So.2d 859, 862.

A discretion exercised to an end or purpose not justified by and clearly against reason and evidence. Trimmer v. State, 142 Okl. 278, 286 P. 783, 786; Seaba v. State, 290 P. 1098, 1101, 144 Okl. 295. Unreasonable departure from considered precedents and settled judicial custom, constituting error of law. Beck v. Wings Field, Inc., C.C.A. Pa., 122 F.2d 114, 116, 117. The term is commonly employed to justify an interference by a higher court with the exercise of discretionary power by a lower court and is said by some authorities to imply not merely error of judgment, but perversity of will, passion, prejudice, partiality, or moral delinquency. The exercise of an honest judgment, however erroneous it may appear to be, is not an abuse of discretion. Stroup v. Raymond, 183 Pa. 279, 38 A. 626. Where a court does not exercise a discretion in the sense of being discreet, circumspect, prudent, and exercising cautious judgment, it is an abuse of discretion. State Board of Medical Examiners v. Spears, 79 Colo. 588, 247 P. 563, 565. Difference in judicial opinion is not synonymous with "abuse of judicial discretion" as respects setting aside verdict as against evidence. Belock v. State Mut. Fire Ins. Co., 106 Vt. 435, 175 A. 19, 22.

Distress

The using an animal or chattel distrained, which makes the distrainer liable as for a conversion.

Female Child

An injury to the genital organs in an attempt at carnal knowledge, falling short of actual penetration. Lee v. State, 246 Ala. 69, 18 So.2d 706, 707. But, according to other authorities, "abuse" is here equivalent to ravishment or rape. Palin v. State, 38 Neb. 862, 57 N.W. 743. Physical abuse. Montgomery v. State, 28 Ala.App. 442, 186 So. 589, 592.

Process

There is said to be an abuse of process when an adversary, through the malicious and unfounded use of some regular legal proceeding, obtains some advantage over his opponent. Wharton. Employment of process for doing an act clearly outside authority conveyed by express terms of writ. Shane v. Gulf Refining Co., 114 Pa.Super. 87, 173 A. 738, 740.

The gist of an action for "abuse of process" is improper use or perversion of process after it has been issued. Publix Drug Co. v. Breyer Ice Cream Co., 347 Pa. 346, 32 A.2d 413, 415. Holding of accused incommunicado before complying with warrant requiring accused to be taken before magistrate. People v. Crabb, 372 Ill. 347, 24 N.E.2d 46, 49. Warrant of arrest to coerce debtor. In re Williams, 233 Mo.App. 1174, 128 S.W.2d 1098, 1105. A malicious abuse of legal process occurs where the party employs it for some unlawful object, not the purpose which it is intended by the law to effect; in other words, a perversion of it. Lauzon v. Charroux, 18 R.I. 467, 28 A. 975. Vybiral v. Schildhauer, 265 N.W. 241, 244, 130 Neb. 433; Silverman v. Ufa Eastern Division Distribution, 236 N.Y.S. 18, 20, 135 Misc. 814. Thus, where the purpose of a prosecution for issuance of a check without funds was to collect a debt, the prosecution constituted an abuse of criminal process. Hotel Supply Co. v. Reid, 16 Ala.App. 563, 80 So. 137, 138. Regular and legitimate use of process, although with a bad intention, is not a malicious "abuse of process." Priest v. Union Agency, 174 Tenn. 304, 125 S.W.2d 142, 143. Action for "abuse of process" is distinguished from action for "malicious prosecution," in that action for abuse of process rests upon improper use of regularly issued process, while "malicious prosecution" has reference to wrong in issuance of process. Clikos v. Long, 231 Ala. 424, 165 So. 394, 396; McInnis v. Atlantic Inv. Corporation, 137 Or. 648, 4 P.2d 314, 315; Lobel v. Trade Bank of New York, 229 N.Y.S. 778, 781, 132 Misc. 643.

ABUSE, *v.* To make excessive or improper use of a thing, or to employ it in a manner contrary to the natural or legal rules for its use; to make an extravagant or excessive use, as to abuse one's authority.

In the civil law, the borrower of a chattel which, in its nature, cannot be used without consuming it, such as wine or grain, is said to abuse the thing borrowed if he uses it. It has been held to include misuse; Erie & North-East R. Co. v. Casey, 26 Pa. 287; to signify to injure, diminish in value, or wear away by improper use; *id.;* to be synonymous with injure; Dawkins v. State, 58 Ala. 376, 29 Am. Rep. 754.

ABUSIVE. Tending to deceive; practicing abuse; prone to ill treat by coarse, insulting words. U. S. v. Ault, D.C.Wash., 263 F. 800, 810. Using ill treatment, injurious, improper, hurtful, offensive, reproachful. People on Complaint of Wilson v. Sinclair, 149 N.Y.S. 54, 56, 86 Misc. 426.

ABUT. To reach, to touch. In old law, the ends were said to abut, the sides to adjoin. Cro. Jac. 184. And see Lawrence v. Killam, 11 Kan. 499, 511; Springfield v. Green, 120 Ill. 269, 11 N.E. 261. To take a new direction; as where a bounding line changes its course. Spelman, Gloss. *Abuttare.* To touch at the end; be contiguous; join at a border or boundary; terminate; to end at; to border on; to reach or touch with an end. Assessment of property, Hensler v. City of Anacortes, 140 Wash. 184, 248 P. 406, 407. The term "abutting" implies a closer proximity than the term "adjacent." Reversion of vacated park land,

City of Hutchinson v. Danley, 88 Kan. 437, 129 P. 163, 164. "Contiguous" synonymous, both conveying idea that lot borders on improvement. Reynard v. City of Caldwell, 55 Idaho 342, 42 P.2d 292, 296.

No intervening land. Johnson v. Town of Watertown, 131 Conn. 84, 38 A.2d 1, 4. Property at end of street sought to be vacated. Messinger v. City of Cincinnati, 36 Ohio App. 337, 173 N.E. 260, 262. Widen street, leaving free access to paved street, property within assessment statutes. Goodman v. City of Birmingham, 223 Ala. 199, 135 So. 336, 337. Though the usual meaning of the word is that the things spoken of do actually adjoin, "bounding and abutting" have no such inflexible meaning as to require lots assessed actually to touch the improvement; Cohen v. Cleveland, 43 Ohio St. 190, 1 N.E. 589.

ABUTMENTS. The walls of a bridge adjoining the land which support the end of the roadway and sustain the arches. The ends of a bridge, or those parts of it which touch the land. Board of Chosen Freeholders of Sussex County v. Strader, 18 N.J.Law, 108, 35 Am.Dec. 530. Support at either extreme end. City of New York v. New York Cent. R. Co., 48 N.Y.S.2d 189, 191, 183 Misc. 104.

ABUTTALS. Fr. The buttings or boundings of lands, showing to what other lands, highways, or places they belong or are abutting. Termes de la Ley; Cowell; Toml. It has been used to express the end boundary lines as distinguished from those on the sides, as "buttals and sidings"; Cro.Jac. 183.

ABUTTER. One whose property abuts, is contiguous, or joins at a border or boundary, as where no other land, road, or street intervenes.

ABUTTING OWNER. An owner of land which abuts or adjoins. The term usually implies that the relative parts actually adjoin, but is sometimes loosely used without implying more than close proximity. See Abut.

Where five-foot strip between property assessed for paving and street was conveyed to city but not used for street purposes, property assessed held not "abutting property," Davidson v. Salt Lake City, 81 Utah 203, 17 P.2d 234, 237. Property owners held "abutting property owners," subject to sewer assessment, notwithstanding street was widened from 40 to 50 feet when incorporated in state highway, and city bought the extra 5 feet on either side. Carey-Reed Co. v. Sisco, 251 Ky. 22, 64 S.W.2d 430, 433. Railroad in street was not "abutting owner". Town of Lenoir v. Carolina & N. W. Ry. Co., 194 N.C. 710, 140 S.E. 618, 619.

AC ETIAM. (Lat. And also.) The introduction of the statement of the real cause of action, used in those cases where it was necessary to allege a fictitious cause of action to give the court jurisdiction, and also the real cause in compliance with the statutes. It is sometimes written *acetiam*. 2 Stra. 922. See Bill of Middlesex under Bill, definition 2.

AC ETIAM BILLÆ. And also to a bill. See Ac Etiam.

AC SI. (Lat. As if.) Townsh. Pl. 23, 27. These words frequently occur in old English statutes. Lord Bacon expounds their meaning in the statute of uses: "The statute gives entry, not *simpliciter*, but with an ac si." Bac. Read. Uses, Works, iv. 195.

ACADEME. Place of academic study. Sisters of Mercy v. Town of Hooksett, 93 N.H. 301, 42 A.2d 222, 225.

ACADEMY. An institution of learning. An association of experts in some particular branch of art, literature, or science.

In its original meaning, an association formed for mutual improvement, or for the advancement of science or art; in later use, a species of educational institution, of a grade between the common school and the college. Academy of Fine Arts v. Philadelphia County, 22 Pa. 496; School holding rank between college and common school, U. S. ex rel. Jacovides v. Day, C.C.A.N.Y., 32 F.2d 542, 544; Sisters of Mercy v. Town of Hooksett, 93 N.H. 301, 42 A.2d 222, 225. See School.

ACAPTE. In French feudal law. A species of relief; a seignorial right due on every change of a tenant. A feudal right which formerly prevailed in Languedoc and Guyenne, being attached to that species of heritable estates which were granted on the contract of *emphyteusis*. Guyot, Inst. Feod. c. 5, § 12.

ACCEDAS AD CURIAM. (Lat. That you go to court.) An original writ out of chancery directed to the sheriff, for the purpose of removing a replevin suit from a Court Baron or a hundred court to one of the superior courts of law. It directs the sheriff *to go to the lower court*, and enroll the proceedings and send up the record. See Fitzh. Nat. Brev. 18; Dy. 169; 3 Bl. Comm. 34.

ACCEDAS AD VICE COMITEM. L. Lat. (You go to the sheriff.) A writ formerly directed to the coroners of a county in England, commanding them to go to the sheriff, where the latter had suppressed and neglected to return a writ of *pone*, and to deliver a writ to him requiring him to return it. Reg. Orig. 83. See Pone.

ACCELERATION. The shortening of the time for the vesting in possession of an expectant interest. Wharton. Hastening of the enjoyment of an estate which was otherwise postponed to a later period. Blackwell v. Virginia Trust Co., 177 Va. 299, 14 S.E.2d 301, 304.

If the life estate fails for any reason, the remainder is "accelerated". Elliott v. Brintlinger, 376 Ill. 147, 33 N.E. 2d 199, 201, 133 A.L.R. 1364. The word is also used in reference to contracts for payment of money in what is usually called an "acceleration clause" by which the time for payment of the debt is hastened or advanced because of breach of some condition such as failure to pay interest when due, McCormick v. Daggett, 162 Ark. 16, 257 S.W. 358; insolvency of the maker, Wright v. Seaboard Steel & Manganese Corporation, C.C.A.N.Y., 272 F. 807; or failure to keep mortgaged premises insured, Porter v. Schroll, 93 Kan. 297, 144 P. 216.

ACCEPT. To receive with approval or satisfaction; to receive with intent to retain. See Morris v. State, 102 Ark. 513, 145 S.W. 213, 214. Also, in the capacity of drawee of a bill, to recognize the draft, and engage to pay it when due. It is not equivalent to "acquiesce." Applett v. Empire Inv. Co., 99 Or. 533, 194 P. 461, 462. Admit and agree to; accede to or consent to; receive with approval; adopt; agree to. Rocha v. Hulen, 6 Cal.App.2d 245, 44 P.2d 478, 482, 483. Street committee's and city engineer's reports. City of Morehead v. Blair, 243 Ky. 84, 47 S.W.2d 741, 742. Means something more than to receive, meaning to adopt, to agree to carry out provisions. Assignee of lease, Pickler v. Mershon, 212 Iowa, 447, 236 N.W. 382, 385; Central State Bank v. Herrick, 214 Iowa 379, 240 N.W. 242, 246. Renewal health and accident policy premiums, Prescott v. Mutual Ben. Health and Accident Ass'n, Fla., 183 So. 311, 314, 119 A.L.R. 525.

ACCEPTANCE. The taking and receiving of anything in good part, and as it were a tacit agreement to a preceding act, which might have been defeated or avoided if such acceptance had not been made. Brooke, Abr. The act of a person to whom a thing is offered or tendered by another, whereby he receives the thing with the intention of retaining it, such intention being evidenced by a sufficient act. Ætna Inv. Corporation v. Chandler Landscape & Floral Co., 227 Mo.App. 17, 50 S.W.2d 195, 197.

The exercise of power conferred by an offer by performance of some act. In re Larney's Estate, 266 N.Y.S. 564, 148 Misc. 871.

Bills of Exchange

An engagement to pay the bill in money when due. 4 East 72; Hunt v. Security State Bank, 91 Or. 362, 179 P. 248, 251.

The act by which the person on whom a bill of exchange is drawn (called the "drawee") assents to the request of the drawer to pay it, or, in other words, engages, or makes himself liable, to pay it when due. Bell-Wayland Co. v. Bank of Sugden, 95 Okl. 67, 218 P. 705. It may be by parol or in writing, and either general or special, absolute or conditional; and it may be impliedly, as well as expressly, given. 3 Kent, Comm. 83, 85; Story, Bills, §§ 238, 251. Telegram directing drawer to draw draft. Hoffer v. Eastland Nat. Bank, Tex.Civ.App., 169 S.W.2d 275, 278. Certification at request of the payee or holder. Welch v. Bank of Manhattan Co., 35 N.Y.S.2d 894, 895, 264 App.Div. 906. But the usual and regular mode of acceptance is by the drawee's writing across the face of the bill the word "accepted," and subscribing his name; after which he is termed the *acceptor*. Story, Bills, § 243.

Contracts

Compliance by offeree with terms and conditions of offer would constitute an "acceptance". Davis & Clanton v. C. I. T. Corporation, 190 S.C. 151, 2 S.E.2d 382, 383.

Qualifications or conditions make a "counteroffer," not an "acceptance." Cohn v. Penn Beverage Co., 313 Pa. 349, 169 A. 768, 769. Bullock v. McKeon, 104 Cal.App. 72, 285 P. 392, 395.

Deed

Act by which vendee vests himself with title to the property. Hardin v. Kazee, 238 Ky. 526, 38 S.W.2d 438.

Insurance

In a contract of insurance, the "acceptance" occurs when insurer agrees to accept application and to issue policy. Acacia Mut. Life Ass'n v. Berry, 54 Ariz. 208, 94 P.2d 770, 772. Delay or inaction on the part of an insurer cannot constitute an "acceptance". French American Banking Corporation v. Fireman's Fund Ins. Co., D.C.N.Y., 43 F.Supp. 494, 498. More than mere mental resolution or determination on part of insurer to accept application. Must be communicated to applicant. Limbaugh v. Monarch Life Ins. Co., Springfield, Mass., Mo.App., 84 S.W.2d 208, 212.

Marine Insurance

The acceptance of an abandonment by the underwriter is his assent, either express or to be implied from the surrounding circumstances, to the sufficiency and regularity of the abandonment. Rap. & Law.

Sales

An acceptance implies, not only the physical fact of receiving the goods, but also the intention of retaining them. Illinois Fuel Co. v. Mobile & O. R. Co., 319 Mo. 899, 8 S.W.2d 834, 841.

Retaining and using goods. Ohio Electric Co. v. Wisconsin-Minnesota Light & Power Co., 161 Wis. 632, 155 N. W. 112, 113. Pressure tanks, Dunck Tank Works v. Sutherland, 236 Wis. 83, 294 N.W. 510, 513. Coal stokers used for 15 months before request for removal, United States v. Lux Laundry Co., C.C.A.Ind., 118 F.2d 848, 849. Where goods are expressly rejected, receipt does not mean acceptance. State Board of Administration v. Roquemore, 218 Ala. 120, 117 So. 757, 760. The acceptance of goods sold under a contract which would be void by the statute of frauds without delivery and acceptance involves something more than the act of the vendor in the delivery. It requires that the vendee should also act, and that his act should be of such a nature as to indicate that he receives and accepts the goods delivered as his property. He must receive and retain the articles delivered, intending thereby to assume the title to them, to constitute the acceptance mentioned in the statute. Rodgers v. Phillips, 40 N.Y. 524. See, also, Snow v. Warner, 10 Metc. (Mass.) 132, 43 Am.Dec. 417. There must be some unequivocal act, with intent to take possession as owner. Vacuum Ash & Soot Conveyor Co. v. Huyler's, 101 N.J.Law, 147, 127 A. 203, 204. Title and possession must be in unrestricted control of buyer so as not to permit of recall or rescission. Mellen Produce Co. v. Fink, 225 Wis. 90, 273 N.W. 538. Mere words are insufficient to establish "delivery and receipt." Mellen Produce Co. v. Fink, 225 Wis. 90, 273 N.W. 538, 542.

The following are the principal varieties of acceptances:

Absolute. An express and positive agreement to pay the bill according to its tenor.

Conditional. An engagement to pay the bill on the happening of a condition. Todd v. Bank of Kentucky, 3 Bush (Ky.) 628. A "conditional acceptance" is in effect a statement that the offeree is willing to enter into a bargain differing in some respects from that proposed in the original offer. The conditional acceptance is, therefore, itself a counter offer. Hoskins v. Michener, 33 Idaho, 681, 197 P. 724. Morris F. Fox & Co. v. Lisman, 208 Wis. 1, 237 N.W. 267, 271. Worley v. Holding Corporation, 348 Ill. 420, 181 N.E. 307, 309.

Express. An undertaking in direct and express terms to pay the bill; an absolute acceptance.

Implied. An undertaking to pay the bill inferred from acts of the drawee of a character which fairly warrant such an inference. In case of a bilateral contract, "acceptance" of an offer need not be expressed, but may be shown by any words or acts indicating the offeree's assent to the proposed bargain. Prescott v. Mutual Ben. Health and Accident Ass'n, 133 Fla. 510, 183 So. 311, 315, 119 A.L.R. 525. Frederick Raff Co. v. Murphy, 110 Conn. 234, 147 A. 709, 711. Tenant for several months continued to occupy storeroom and paid rentals, C. R. Anthony Co. v. Stroud, 189 Okl. 104, 114 P.2d 177, 178. Landlord's reletting leased premises after default in rent, In re Lear Shoe Co., Sup., 22 N.Y.S.2d 778, 782. Taking possession, exercise of ownership and dominion and failure to complain to seller, Bell v. Main, D.C.Pa., 49 F.Supp. 689, 692.

Partial. An acceptance varying from the tenor of the bill. An acceptance to pay part of the amount for which the bill is drawn, 1 Strange 214, or to pay at a different time, 14 Jur. 806; Hatcher v. Stolworth, 25 Miss. 376; or at a different place, 4 M. & S. 462, would be partial. For some examples of what do and what do not constitute conditional acceptances, see Heaverin v. Donnell, 7 Smedes & M. (Miss.) 245, 45 Am.Dec. 302; Campbell v. Pettengill, 7 Greenl. (Me.) 126, 20 Am.Dec. 349; Ensign v. Clark Bros. Cutlery Co., 195 Mo.App. 584, 193 S.W. 961, 962. Provisions respecting cutting of timber etc. on optioned land, did not destroy the "acceptance". Bastian v. United States, C. C.A.Ohio, 118 F.2d 777, 779. Would be in named place for purpose of entering into option, Ackerman v. Carpenter, 113 Vt. 77, 29 A.2d 922, 925. Counter proposition to option. Tholl Oil Co. v. Miller, 197 La. 976, 3 So.2d 97, 98. Conditional, qualified acceptance, Moore Bros. v. Kirkpatrick, Tex.Civ.App., 172 S.W.2d 135, 137.

Qualified. One either conditional or partial, and which introduces a variation in the sum, time, mode, or place of payment.

Supra protest. An acceptance by a third person, after protest of the bill for non-acceptance by the drawee, to save the honor of the drawer or some particular indorser. A general acceptance is an absolute acceptance precisely in conformity with the tenor of the bill itself, and not qualified by any statement, condition, or change. Todd v. Bank of Kentucky, 3 Bush (Ky.) 628. A special acceptance is the qualified acceptance of a bill of exchange, as where it is accepted as payable at a particular place "and not elsewhere." Rowe v. Young, 2 Brod. & B. 180. See Trade Acceptance.

ACCEPTANCE AU BESOIN. Fr. In French law. Acceptance in case of need; an acceptance by one on whom a bill is drawn *au besoin,* that is, in case of refusal or failure of the drawee to accept. Story, Bills, §§ 65, 254, 255.

ACCEPTARE.

Civil Law

Lat. To accept; to assent; to assent to a promise made by another. Gro. de J. B. lib. 2, c. 11, § 14.

Pleading

To accept. *Acceptavit,* he accepted. 2 Strange, 817. *Non acceptavit,* he did not accept. 4 Man. & G. 7.

ACCEPTEUR PAR INTERVENTION. In French law. Acceptor of a bill for honor.

ACCEPTILATION. In the civil and Scotch law. A release made by a creditor to his debtor of his debt, without receiving any consideration. Ayl. Pand. tit. 26, p. 570. It is a species of donation, but not subject to the forms of the latter, and is valid unless in fraud of creditors. Merl. Répert.

The verbal extinction of a verbal contract, with a declaration that the debt has been paid when it has not; or the acceptance of something merely imaginary in satisfaction of a verbal contract. Sanders' Just. Inst. (5th Ed.) 386.

ACCEPTOR. The person who accepts a bill of exchange, (generally the drawee,) or who engages to be primarily responsible for its payment. Nissenbaum v. State, 38 Ga.App. 253, 143 S.E. 776, 777.

ACCEPTOR SUPRA PROTEST. One who accepts a bill which has been protested, for the honor of the drawer or any one of the indorsers.

ACCESS. Approach; or the means, power, or opportunity of approaching. Sometimes importing the occurrence of sexual intercourse, Jackson v. Jackson, 182 Okl. 74, 76 P.2d 1062, 1066; otherwise as importing opportunity of communication for that purpose as between husband and wife.

In real property law, the term "access" denotes the right vested in the owner of land which adjoins a road or other highway to go and return from his own land to the highway without obstruction. Cobb v. Commissioners of Lincoln Park, 202 Ill. 427, 67 N.E. 5, 6, 8. "Access" to property does not necessarily carry with it possession. People v. Brenneauer, 166 N.Y.S. 801, 806, 101 Misc. 156. A deed, however, which conveys land and "also the right of access to the adjoining park and use of spring on same," may be deemed to convey not merely the right to pass through the park in order to reach the spring, but to convey a right of entry into the park as a park and by implication, the right to the use and enjoyment of the park. Gœtz v. Knoxville Power & Light Co., 154 Tenn. 545, 290 S.W. 409, 414.

The right of "access" as applied to a private wharf on public lands merely means that there may not be built an obstruction separating the lands from the navigable highway. City of Oakland v. Hogan, 41 Cal.App.2d 333, 106 P. 2d 987, 995.

The right of "access to public records" includes not only a legal right of access but a reasonable opportunity to avail oneself of the same. American Surety Co. of New York v. Sandberg, D.C.Wash., 225 F. 150, 155.

Canon Law

The right to some benefice at some future time.

ACCESS (EASEMENT OF). An "easement of access" is the right which an abutting owner has of ingress to and egress from his premises, in addition to the public easement in the street. State Highway Board v. Baxter, 167 Ga. 124, 144 S.E. 796, 800; Lang v. Smith, 113 Pa.Super. 559, 173 A. 682, 683. "Access to an underground sewer" means more than a right to open the surface to make repairs, and implies the right of connection by branches. Heyman v. Biggs, 150 N.Y.S. 246, 247, 164 App.Div. 430.

ACCESSARY. See Accessory.

ACCESSIO. In Roman law. An increase or addition; that which lies next to a thing, and is supplementary and necessary to the principal thing; that which arises or is produced from the principal thing; an "accessory obligation" *(q. v.).* Calvinus, Lex. Jurid.

One of the modes of acquiring property, being the extension of ownership over that which grows from, or is united to, an article which one already possesses. Mather v. Chapman, 40 Conn. 382, 397, 16 Am.Rep. 46.

Accessio includes both accession and accretion as used in the common law. See Adjunctio.

ACCESSION. Coming into possession of a right or office; increase; augmentation; addition.

The right to all which one's own property produces, whether that property be movable or immovable; and the right to that which is united to it by accession, either naturally or artificially. 2 Kent, 360; 2 Bl.Comm. 404; Franklin Service Stations v. Sterling Motor Truck Co. of N. E., 50 R.I. 336, 147 A. 754, 755.

Riparian owners' right to abandoned river beds and rights of alluvion by accretion and reliction, Manry v. Robison, 122 Tex. 213, 56 S.W.2d 438, 443, 444.

A principle derived from the civil law, by which the owner of property becomes entitled to all which it produces, and to all that is added or united to it, either naturally or artificially, (that is, by the labor or skill of another,) even where such addition extends to a change of form or materials; and by which, on the other hand, the possessor of property becomes entitled to it, as against the original owner, where the addition made to it by his skill and labor is of greater value than the property itself, or where the change effected in its form is so great as to render it impossible to restore it to its original shape. Twin City Motor Co. v. Rouzer Motor Co., 197 N.C. 371, 148 S.E. 461, 463. In Blackwood Tire & Vulcanizing Co. v. Auto Storage Co., 133 Tenn. 515, 182 S.W. 576, L.R.A.1916E, 254, Ann.Cas.1917C, 1168, this principle was applied in favor of the conditional seller who, on nonpayment, retook the automobile sold, together with tire casings which the buyer had fitted thereto. Valley Chevrolet Co. v. O. S. Stapley Co., 50 Ariz. 417, 72 P.2d 945.

International Law

The absolute or conditional acceptance by one or several states of a treaty already concluded between other sovereignties. Merl. Répert. It may be of two kinds: *First,* the formal entrance of a third state into a treaty so that such state becomes a party to it; and this can only be with the consent of the original parties. *Second,* a state may accede to a treaty between other states solely for the purpose of guarantee, in which case, though a party, it is affected by the treaty only as a guarantor. 1 Oppenheim, Int.L. sec. 532. See Adhesion.

Also, the commencement or inauguration of a sovereign's reign.

ACCESSION, DEED OF. In Scotch law. A deed executed by the creditors of a bankrupt or insolvent debtor, by which they approve of a trust given by their debtor for the general behoof, and bind themselves to concur in the plans proposed for extricating his affairs. Bell, Dict.

ACCESSORIUM NON DUCIT, SED SEQUITUR SUUM PRINCIPALE. Co. Litt. 152*a*, 389*a*. That which is the accessory or incident does not lead, but follows, its principal.

ACCESSORIUS SEQUITUR NATURAM SUI PRINCIPALIS. An accessary follows the nature of his principal. 3 Inst. 139. One who is accessary to a crime cannot be guilty of a higher degree of crime than his principal.

ACCESSORY. Anything which is joined to another thing as an ornament, or to render it more perfect, or which accompanies it, or is connected with it, as an incident, or as subordinate to it, or which belongs to or with it; for example, the halter of a horse, the frame of a picture, the keys of a house.

Adjunct or accompaniment. Louis Werner Saw Mill Co. v. White, 205 La. 242, 17 So.2d 264, 270.

A sale of land carried with it the standing timber as an "accessory." Woollums v. Hewitt, 142 La. 597, 77 So. 295, 296.

Automobile Accessories

Articles primarily adapted for use in motor vehicles, under revenue acts. Universal Battery Co. v. U. S., Ct.Cl., 50 S.Ct. 422, 423, 281 U.S. 580, 74 L.Ed. 1051.

Criminal Law

Contributing to or aiding in the commission of a crime. One who, without being present at the commission of a felonious offense, becomes guilty of such offense, not as a chief actor, but as a participator, as by command, advice, instigation, or concealment; either before or after the fact or commission; a *particeps criminis.* 4 Bl.Comm. 35; Cowell.

One who is not the chief actor in the offense, nor present at its performance, but in some way concerned therein, either *before* or *after* the act committed. State v. Thomas, 136 A. 475, 477, 105 Conn. 757. One who aids and abets another. People v. Smith, 260 N.W. 911, 271 Mich. 553. Commands or counsels another. United States v. Peoni, C.C.A.N.Y., 100 F.2d 401, 402.

An "accessory" to a crime is always an "accomplice." People v. Ah Gee, 37 Cal.App. 1, 174 P. 371, 373. In certain crimes, there can be no accessories; all who are concerned are principals. These are (according to many authorities) treason, and all offenses below the degree of felony: 4 Bla.Comm. 35; Com. v. McAtee, 8 Dana (Ky.) 28; Williams v. State, 12 Smedes & M. (Miss.) 58.

Accessory Before the Fact

One who, being absent at the time a crime is committed, yet assists, procures, counsels, incites, induces, encourages, engages, or commands another to commit it. 4 Steph. Comm. 90, note n. People v. Owen, 241 Mich. 111, 216 N.W. 434. United States v. Pritchard, D.C.S.C., 55 F.Supp. 201, 203; rape, Clayton v. State, 244 Ala. 10, 13 So.2d 420, 422.

Murder, Wells v. State, 94 Ga. 70, 20 S.E.2d 580, 582. Distilling, State v. Lackmann, Mo., 12 S.W. 2d 424, 425.

Accessory During the Fact

One who stands by without interfering or giving such help as may be in his power to prevent the commission of a criminal offense. Farrell v. People, 8 Colo.App. 524, 46 P. 841.

Accessory After the Fact

One who, having full knowledge that a crime has been committed, conceals it from the magistrate, and harbors, assists, or protects the person charged with, or convicted of, the crime. Vernon's Ann.C.C.P. art. 53.

All persons who, after the commission of any felony, conceal or aid the offender, with knowledge that he has committed a felony, and with intent that he may avoid or escape from arrest, trial, conviction, or punishment, are accessories.

Comp.Laws N.D.1913, § 9219; Rev.Code S.D.1919, § 3595.

An accessory *after the fact* is a person who, knowing a felony to have been committed by another, receives, relieves, comforts or assists the felon, in order to enable him to escape from punishment, or the like. Buck v. Commonwealth, 116 Va. 1031, 83 S.E. 390, 393. Knowledge, or denial of knowledge, of perpetration of crime, or silence does not make one an "accessory after the fact." Commonwealth v. Giacobbe, 341 Pa. 187, 19 A.2d 71, 75. Cantu v. State, 135 S.W.2d 705, 710, 141 Tex.Cr.R. 99. But affirmative action by false testimony or otherwise usable by accused to escape punishment constitutes one "accessory" as to his testimony. Fisher v. State, 34 S.W.2d 293, 294, 117 Tex.Cr.R. 552; false statements to sheriff relative to defendant's connection with homicide in order to evade arrest, Littles v. State, 111 Tex.Cr.R. 500, 14 S.W.2d 853, 854.

Aiders and Abettors Distinguished

The concept of an "accessory before the fact" presupposes a prearrangement to do the criminal act, and to constitute one an "aider and abettor" he must be on the ground and by his presence aid, encourage or incite the principal. Morei v. United States, C.C.A.Ohio, 127 F.2d 827, 830, 831.

Principal Distinguished

"Principal in the second degree," as distinguished from "accessory before the fact," is one who aids in commission of felony by being either actually or constructively present, aiding, and abetting commission of felony, when perpetrated. Neumann v. State, 116 Fla. 98, 156 So. 237, 239.

ACCESSORY ACTION. In Scotch practice. An action which is subservient or auxiliary to another. Of this kind are actions of "proving the tenor," by which lost deeds are restored; and actions of "transumpts," by which copies of principal deeds are certified. Bell, Dict.

ACCESSORY CONTRACT. In the civil law. A contract which is incident or auxiliary to another or principal contract; such as the engagement of a surety. Poth. Obl. pt. 1, c. 1, § 1, art. 2.

A principal contract is one entered into by both parties on their own accounts, or in the several qualities they assume. An accessory contract is made for assuring the performance of a prior contract, either by the same parties or by others; such as suretyship, mortgage, and pledge. Blaisdell v. Coe, 83 N.H. 167, 139 A. 758, 65 A.L.R. 626.

ACCESSORY OBLIGATION.

Civil Law

An obligation which is incident to another or principal obligation; the obligation of a surety. Poth. Obl. pt. 2, c. 1, § 6.

Scotch Law

Obligations to antecedent or primary obligations, such as obligations to pay interest, etc. Ersk. Inst. lib. 3, tit. 3, § 60.

See, further, Obligation.

ACCESSORY TO ADULTERY. Implies more than connivance, which is merely knowledge with consent. A conniver abstains from interference; an accessory directly commands, advises, or procures the adultery. 20 & 21 Vict. c. 85, §§ 29, 31.

ACCIDENT. The word "accident" is derived from the Latin verb "accidere" signifying "fall upon, befall, happen, chance." In an etymological sense anything that happens may be said to be an accident and in this sense, the word has been defined as befalling; a change; a happening; an incident; an occurrence or event. In its most commonly accepted meaning, or in its ordinary or popular sense, the word may be defined as meaning a fortuitous circumstance, event, or happening, an event happening without any human agency, or if happening wholly or partly through human agency, an event which under the circumstances is unusual and unexpected by the person to whom it happens; an unusual, fortuitous, unexpected, unforeseen or unlooked for event, happening or occurrence; an unusual or unexpected result attending the operation or performance of a usual or necessary act or event; chance or contingency; fortune; mishap; some sudden and unexpected event taking place without expectation, upon the instant, rather than something which continues, progresses or develops; something happening by chance; something unforeseen, unexpected, unusual, extraordinary or phenominal, taking place not according to the usual course of things or events, out of the range of ordinary calculations; that which exists or occurs abnormally, or an uncommon occurrence; the word may be employed as denoting a calamity, casualty, catastrophe, disaster, an undesirable or unfortunate happening; any unexpected personal injury resulting from any unlooked for mishap or occurrence; any unpleasant or unfortunate occurrence, that causes injury, loss, suffering or death; some untoward occurrence aside from the usual course of events. Adams v. Metropolitan Life Ins. Co., 136 Pa.Super. 454, 7 A.2d 544, 547; without known or assignable cause, Ramsay v. Sullivan Mining Co., 51 Idaho 366, 6 P.2d 856, 858.

In its proper use the term excludes negligence; Dallas Ry. & Terminal Co. v. Allen, Tex.Civ.App., 43 S.W.2d 165, 170; that is, an accident is an event which occurs without the fault, carelessness, or want of proper circumspection of the person affected, or which could not have been avoided by the use of that kind and degree of care necessary to the exigency and in the circumstances in which he was placed. Brown v. Kendall, 6 Cush. (Mass.) 292; essential requirement being that happening be one to which human fault does not contribute, Hogan v. Kansas City Public Service Co., 322 Mo. 1103, 19 S.W.2d 707, 713, 65 A.L.R. 129; happening of an event without any human agency, Terry v. Woodmen Accident Co., 225 Mo.App. 1223, 34 S.W.2d 163, 164. It has been said, moreover, that the word "accident" does not have a settled legal signification; Klopfenstein v. Union Traction Co., 112 Kan. 770, 212 P. 1097, 1098; and that in its ordinary meaning it does not negative the idea of negligence on the part of the person whose physical act caused the occurrence. Campbell v. Jones, 73 Wash. 688, 132 P. 635, 636. Not merely inevitable casualty or the act of providence, or what is technically called vis major, or irresistible force. Gardner v. State, 1 N.Y. S.2d 994, 997, 166 Misc. 113.

See Act of God.

Automobiles

The word "accident" as used in automobile liability policy requiring notice of any "accident" to be given to the insurer as a condition precedent to liability means an untoward and unforeseen occurrence in the operation of the automobile which results in injury to the person or property of another. Ohio Casualty Ins. Co. v. Marr, C.C. A.Okl., 98 F.2d 973, 975.

Connotes event which occurs without one's foresight or expectation, and does not exclude negligence. American Indemnity Co. v. Jamison, Tex.Civ.App., 62 S.W.2d 197; without intention or design, Rothman v. Metropolitan Casualty Ins. Co., 134 Ohio St. 241, 16 N.E.2d 417, 421, 117 A.L.R. 1169.

The word "accident", requiring operator of vehicle to stop immediately in case of accident, contemplates any situation occurring on the highway wherein he so operates his automobile as to cause injury to the property or person of another using the same highway. State v. Masters, 106 W.Va. 46, 144 S.E. 718, 719.

Equity

Such an unforeseen event, misfortune, loss, act, or omission as is not the result of any negligence or misconduct in the party. Engler v. Knoblaugh, 131 Mo.App. 481, 110 S.W. 16.

Unforeseen and undesigned event, productive of disadvantage. Wharton. Surprise is used interchangeably. State ex rel. Hartley v. Innes, 137 Mo.App. 420, 118 S.W. 1168.

Occurrence, not the result of negligence or misconduct of the party seeking relief in relation to a contract, as was not anticipated by the parties when the same was entered into, and which gives an undue advantage to one of them over another in a court of law. White & Hamilton Lumber Co. v. Foster, 157 Ga. 493, 122 S.E. 29, 30.

Insurance Contracts

An accident within accident insurance policies is an event happening without any human agency, or, if happening through such agency, an event which, under circumstances, is unusual and not expected by the person to whom it happens. Sizemore v. National Casualty Co., 108 W.Va. 550, 151 S.E. 841.

Sudden and instant happening, referable to definite and fixed period of time. Jackson v. Employers' Liability Assur. Corporation, 248 N.Y.S. 207, 210, 139 Misc. 686.

May be inflicted intentionally and maliciously by one not the agent of the insured, if unintentional on the part of the insured. Goodwin v. Continental Casualty Co., 175 Okl. 469, 53 P.2d 241, 243.

A more comprehensive term than "negligence," and in its common signification the word means an unexpected happening without intention or design. Sontag v. Galer, 279 Mass. 309, 181 N.E. 182, 183.

Accidental injury or death is an unintended and undesigned result arising from acts done, while injury or death by "accidental means" is a result arising from acts unintentionally done. Adams v. Metropolitan Life Ins. Co., 136 Pa.Super. 454, 7 A.2d 544, 547.

Maritime Law and Marine Insurance

"Accidents of navigation" or "accidents of the sea" are such as are peculiar to the sea or to usual navigation or the action of the elements, which do not happen by the intervention of man, and are not to be avoided by the exercise of proper prudence, foresight, and skill. The G. R. Booth, 19 S.Ct. 9, 171 U.S. 450, 43 L.Ed. 234. See also Perils of the Sea.

Practice

That which ordinary prudence could not have guarded against. Cupples v. Zupan, 35 Idaho 458, 207 P. 328, 329. An event happening unexpectedly and without fault; an undesigned and unforeseen occurrence of an afflictive or unfortunate character; a casualty or mishap. Allen v. State, 13 Okl.Cr. 533, 165 P. 748; Baird v. Kensal Light & Power Co., 246 N.W. 279, 282, 63 N.D. 88; drunkenness of juror during recess required discharge of jury. Fetty v. State, 119 Neb. 619, 230 N.W. 440, 442.

Workmen's Compensation

Term "accident," within Workmen's Compensation Act, has been defined as a befalling; an event that takes place without one's foresight or expectation; an undesigned, sudden, and unexpected event; chance; contingency; often, an undesigned and unforeseen occurrence of an afflictive or unfortunate character; casualty; mishap; as, to die by an accident. Its synonyms are chance, contingency, mishap, mischance, misfortune, disaster, calamity, catastrophe. Term "accidental" has been defined as happening by chance, or unexpectedly; taking place not according to the usual course of things; casual; fortuitous; as, an accidental visit. Its synonyms are undesigned, unintended, chance, unforeseen, unexpected, unpremeditated; accessory, collateral, secondary, subordinate; extrinsic, extraneous, additional, adscititious, dependent, conditional. Indian Territory Illuminating Oil Co. v. Williams, 157 Okl. 80, 10 P.2d 1093, 1094.

With or without negligence. Great Atlantic & Pacific Tea Co. v. Sexton, 242 Ky. 266, 46 S.W.2d 87, 88.

Not technical legal term. Arquin v. Industrial Commission, 349 Ill. 220, 181 N.E. 613, 614.

ACCIDENTAL. Happening by chance, or unexpectedly; taking place not according to usual course of things; casual; fortuitous. Morris v. New York Life Ins. Co., C.C.A.Md., 49 F.2d 62, 63; Murphy v. Travelers Ins. Co., Neb., 2 N.W.2d 576, 578, 579.

ACCIDENTAL KILLING. One resulting from an act which is lawful and lawfully done under a reasonable belief that no harm is possible;—distinguished from "involuntary manslaughter," which is the result of an unlawful act, or of a lawful act done in an unlawful way. Rowe v. Commonwealth, 206 Ky. 803, 268 S.W. 571, 573.

ACCIDENTAL VEIN. See Vein.

ACCIDERE. Lat. To fall; fall in; come to hand; happen. Judgment is sometimes given against an executor or administrator to be satisfied out of assets *quando acciderint; i. e.,* when they shall come to hand. See Quando Acciderint.

ACCION. In Spanish law. A right of action; also the method of judicial procedure for the recovery of property or a debt. Escriche, Dic. Leg. 49. Wilder v. Lambert, 91 Tex. 510, 44 S.W. 281, 284.

ACCIPERE QUID UT JUSTITIAM FACIAS, NON EST TAM ACCIPERE QUAM EXTORQUERE. To accept anything as a reward for doing justice is rather extorting than accepting. Lofft, 72.

ACCIPITARE. To pay relief to lords of manors. *Capitali domino accipitare, i. e.,* to pay a relief, homage, or obedience to the chief lord on becoming his vassal. Fleta, lib. 2, c. 50.

ACCOLA.

Civil Law

One who inhabits or occupies land near a place, as one who dwells by a river, or on the bank of a river. Dig. 43, 13, 3, 6.

Feudal Law

A husbandman; an agricultural tenant; a tenant oi a manor. Spelman. A name given to a class of villeins in Italy. Barr. St. 302.

ACCOMENDA. In maritime law. A contract between the owner of goods and the master of a ship, by which the former intrusts the property to the latter to be sold by him on their joint account.

In such case, two contracts take place: First, the contract called *mandatum,* by which the owner of the property gives the master power to dispose of it; and the contract of partnership, in virtue of which the profits are to be divided between them. One party runs the risk of losing his capital; the other, his labor. If the sale produces no more than first cost, the owner takes all the proceeds. It is only the profits which are to be divided. Emerig.Mar. Loans, § 5.

ACCOMMODATED PARTY. One to whom the credit of the accommodation party is loaned, and is not necessarily the payee, since the inquiry always is as to whom did the maker of the paper loan his credit as a matter of fact. Wilhoit v. Seavall, 121 Kan. 239, 246 P. 1013, 1015, 48 A.L.R. 1273; not third person who may receive advantage, State v. Banta, 148 Okl. 239, 299 P. 479, 483. First Nat. Bank v. Boxley, 129 Okl. 159, 264 P. 184, 186, 64 A.L.R. 588.

ACCOMMODATION. An arrangement or engagement made as a favor to another, not upon a consideration received; something done to oblige, usually spoken of a loan of money or commercial paper; also a friendly agreement or composition of differences. Abbott; Sales v. Martin, 173 Ky. 616, 191 S.W. 480, 482. The word implies no consideration. William D. Seymour & Co. v. Castell, 160 La. 371, 107 So. 143, 145.

"While a party's intent may be to aid a maker of note by lending his credit, if he seeks to accomplish thereby legitimate objects of his own, and not simply to aid maker, the act is not for 'accommodation.'" Bazer v. Grimmett, 16 La.App. 613, 135 So. 54, 56.

ACCOMMODATION ACCEPTANCE. The acceptance of accommodation paper.

ACCOMMODATION BILL OR NOTE. See Accommodation Paper.

ACCOMMODATION INDORSEMENT. See Indorsement.

ACCOMMODATION INDORSER. A party who places his name to a note without consideration for purpose of benefiting or accommodating some other party. Stubbins Hotel Co. v. Bassbarth, 43 N.D. 191, 174 N.W. 217, 218; McDaniel v. Altoona State Bank, 126 Kan. 719, 271 P. 394.

ACCOMMODATION LANDS. Land bought by a builder or speculator, who erects houses thereon, and then leases portions thereof upon an improved ground-rent.

ACCOMMODATION MAKER. One who puts his name to a note without any consideration with the intention of lending his credit to the accommodated party. In re Chamberlain's Estate, Cal. App., 109 P.2d 449, 454.

In this connection "without consideration" means "without consideration to the accommodating party directly." Warren Nat. Bank, Warren, Pa., v. Suerken, 45 Cal.App. 736, 188 P. 613, 614. One who receives no part of the proceeds, which are used exclusively for another maker's benefit, as in discharging his own personal obligation. Backer v. Grummett, 39 Cal.App. 101, 178 P. 312, 313. Must not receive any benefit or consideration directly or indirectly, and transaction must be one primarily for the benefit of the payee. First Trust Co. of Lincoln v. Anderson, 135 Neb. 397, 281 N.W. 796, 798; Void of present or anticipated personal profit, gain, or advantage. Robertson v. City Nat. Bank of Bowie, 120 Tex. 226, 36 S.W.2d 481, 483.

Incidental benefit to party insufficient. Morrison v. Painter, Mo.App., 170 S.W.2d 965, 970.

ACCOMMODATION NOTE. One to which accommodating party has put his name, without consideration, to accommodate some other party, who is to issue it and is expected to pay it. Brown Carriage Co. v. Dowd, 155 N.C. 307, 71 S.E. 721, 724; Farmers Loan & Trust Co. v. Brown, 182 Iowa, 1044, 165 N.W. 70, 73.

ACCOMMODATION PAPER. An accommodation bill or note is one to which the accommodating party, be he acceptor, drawer, or indorser, has put his name, without consideration, for the purpose of benefiting or accommodating some other party who desires to raise money on it, and is to provide for the bill when due. Miller v. Larned, 103 Ill. 562; Crothers v. National Bank of Chesapeake City, 158 Md. 587, 149 A. 270, 272; Hickox v. Hickox, Tex.Civ.App., 151 S.W.2d 913, 917.

Must be executed for the purpose of loaning credit, and incidental benefit to party is insufficient. Morrison v. Painter, Mo.App., 170 S.W.2d 965, 970.

ACCOMMODATION PARTY. One who has signed an instrument as maker, drawer, acceptor, or indorser without receiving value therefor, and for purpose of lending his name to some other person as means of securing credit. Bachman v. Junkin, 129 Neb. 165, 260 N.W. 813.

The term does not include one who, for the accommodation of the maker, guaranteed the payment of a note. Noble v. Beeman-Spaulding-Woodward Co., 65 Or. 93, 131 P. 1006, 1010.

Indorser, Myrtilles, Inc., v. Johnson, 124 Conn. 177, 199 A. 115, 117; president and directors of bank, Davis v. Holt, Federal Deposit Ins. Corporation, Intervenor, Mo.App., 154

S.W.2d 595, 597; apparent comaker. McLendon v. Lane, 51 Ga.App. 409, 180 S.E. 746; to make note look better for payee bank, Pirtle v. Johnson, 145 Kan. 8, 64 P.2d 2, 4.

ACCOMMODATION ROAD. A road opened for benefit of certain individuals to go from and to their homes, for service of their lands, and for use of some estates exclusively. Civ.Code La. art. 706.

ACCOMMODATION TRAIN. One designed to accommodate local travel by stopping at most stations. Gray v. Chicago, M. & St. P. R. Co., 189 Ill. 400, 59 N.E. 950, 951. In another aspect it is a train designed to carry passengers as well as freight. White v. Ill. Cent. R. Co., 99 Miss. 651, 55 So. 593, 595.

ACCOMMODATION WORKS. Works which a railway company is required to make and maintain for the accommodation of the owners or occupiers of land adjoining the railway; *e. g.*, gates, bridges, culverts, fences, etc. 8 Vict. c. 20, § 68.

ACCOMMODATUM. The same as *commodatum, q. v.*

ACCOMPANY. To go along with. Webster's Dict. To go with or attend as a companion or associate, to occur in association with. United States v. Lee, C.C.A.Wis., 131 F.2d 464, 466.

The word has been defined judicially in cases involving varied facts; thus, a boy driver was held not accompanying the team when he was runnning to stop it. Willis v. Semmes, 111 Miss. 589, 71 So. 865, 866. A motion based on answer already deposited with the clerk of court is accompanied with copy of answer. Los Angeles County v. Lewis, 179 Cal. 398, 177 P. 154, 155. An automobile driver under sixteen is not accompanied by an adult person unless the latter exercises supervision over the driver. Rush v. McDonnell, 214 Ala. 47, 106 So. 175, 179. An unlicensed driver is not accompanied by a licensed driver unless the latter is near enough to render advice and assistance. Hughes v. New Haven Taxicab Co., 87 Conn. 416, 87 A. 721.

ACCOMPLICE. In criminal law. A person who knowingly, voluntarily, and with common intent with the principal offender unites in the commission of a crime. State v. Keithley, 83 Mont. 177, 271 P. 449, 451, People v. Frahm, 107 Cal.App. 253, 290 P. 678, 682, State v. Coroles, 74 Utah, 94, 277 P. 203, 204. One who is in some way concerned or associated in commission of crime; partaker of guilt; one who aids or assists, or is an accessory. McLendon v. U. S., C.C.A.Mo., 19 F.2d 465, 466. Equally concerned in the commission of crime. Fryman v. Commonwealth, 289 Ky. 540, 159 S.W. 2d 426, 429.

An "accomplice" is one who is guilty of complicity in crime charged, either by being present and aiding or abetting in it, or having advised and encouraged it, though absent from place when it was committed, though mere presence, acquiescence, or silence, in the absence of a duty to act, is not enough, no matter how reprehensible it may be, to constitute one an accomplice. State v. Arnold, 84 Mont. 348, 275 P. 757, 760; presence unnecessary. King v. State, 135 Tex.Cr.R. 378, 120 S.W.2d 590, 592. Knowledge and concealment not sufficient. Wallis v. State, Okl. Cr.App., 292 P. 1056, 1057.

Falsely denying having knowledge of crime not of itself sufficient. Tipton v. State, 126 Tex.Cr.R. 439, 72 S.W.2d 290, 293.

Thief and receiver of stolen property ordinarily not "accomplices". People v. Lima, 25 Cal.2d 573, 154 P.2d 698, 700, 701.

Giver of bribe is an "accomplice". Turner v. State, 58 Ga.App. 775, 199 S.E. 837, 839, Contra, State v. Emory, 55 Idaho 649, 46 P.2d 67, 70.

As specifically applied to witnesses for the state and the necessity for corroborating them, "accomplice" includes all persons connected with the offense by an unlawful act or omission either before, at the time of, or after the commission of the offense, whether such witness was present or participated in the crime or not. Chandler v. State, 89 Tex.Cr.R. 309, 230 S.W. 1002, 1003.

Mere presence is insufficient. Snowden v. State, 27 Ala. App. 14, 165 So. 410.

Suborned witness is an "accomplice". People v. Nicosia, 4 N.Y.S.2d 35, 37, 166 Misc. 597. Contra. State v. De Vaughn, 2 Cal.App.2d 572, 39 P.2d 223, 224.

Receiver of bribe not "accomplice" of giver. People v. Martin, 114 Cal.App. 392, 300 P. 130, 132.

The term includes all the *participes criminis*, Darden v. State, 12 Ala.App. 165, 68 So. 550, 551, whether they are considered, in strict legal propriety, as principals in the first or second degree, or merely as accessories before or after the fact. In re Rowe, 23 C.C.A. 103, 77 F. 161; Luck v. State, 125 Tex.Cr.R. 152, 67 S.W.2d 302. But in Kentucky it has been held that "accomplice" does not include an accessory after the fact. See, however, Commonwealth v. Barton, 153 Ky. 465, 156 S.W. 113, 114. And the same rule has been announced elsewhere. State v. Lyons, 144 Minn. 348, 175 N.W. 689, 691. A feigned accomplice has been defined as one who co-operates with view of aiding justice to detect a crime. State v. Verganadis, 50 Nev. 1, 248 P. 900, 903; Decoy not "accomplice". U. S. v. Becker, C.C.A.N.Y., 62 F.2d 1007, 1009.

Liquor control board inspector, Magee v. State, 135 Tex. Cr.R. 381, 120 S.W.2d 248, 249.

ACCORD, *n.* A satisfaction agreed upon between the party injuring and the party injured which, when performed, is a bar to all actions upon this account. Kromer v. Heim, 75 N.Y. 576, 31 Am. Rep. 491; Buob v. Feenaughty Machinery Co., 191 Wash. 477, 71 P.2d 559, 564. An agreement to accept, in extinction of an obligation, something different from or less than that to which the person agreeing to accept is entitled. Whepley Oil Co. v. Associated Oil Co., 6 Cal.App.2d 94, 44 P.2d 670, 677.

Substitution of an agreement between the party injuring and the party injured, in view of the original obligation. Barbarich v. Chicago, M., St. P. & P. Ry. Co., 92 Mont. 1, 9 P.2d 797, 799.

It may arise both where the demand itself is unliquidated or in dispute, and where the amount and nature of the demand is undisputed, and it is agreed to give and take less than the demand. J. F. Morgan Paving Co. v. Carroll, 211 Ala. 121, 99 So. 640, 641.

"Payment," as distinguished from accord, means full satisfaction. State v. Tyler County State Bank, Tex.Com. App., 277 S.W. 625, 627, 42 A.L.R. 1347.

See Accord and Satisfaction; Compromise and Settlement.

ACCORD, *v.* In practice. To agree or concur, as one judge with another. "I accord." Eyre, C. J., 12 Mod. 7. "The rest accorded." 7 Mod. 361.

ACCORD AND SATISFACTION. An agreement between two persons, one of whom has a right of action against the other, that the latter should do or give, and the former accept, something in satisfaction of the right of action different from, and usually less than, what might be legally enforced.

When the agreement is executed, and satisfaction has been made, it is called "accord and satisfaction." Rogers v. Spokane, 9 Wash. 168, 37 P. 300.

It is discharge of contract, or of disputed claim arising either from contract or from tort, by substitution of agreement between parties in satisfaction of such contract or disputed claim and execution of the agreement. Nelson v. Chicago Mill & Lumber Corporation, C.C.A.Ark., 76 F.2d 17, 100 A.L.R. 87.

"Accord and satisfaction" results where there is assent to acceptance of payment in compromise of dispute, or in extinguishment of liability uncertain in amount, or where payment, coupled with condition whereby use of money will be wrongful if condition is ignored, is accepted. Hudson v. Yonkers Fruit Co., 258 N.Y. 168, 179 N.E. 373. Regardless of whether claim is liquidated or unliquidated. May Bros. v. Doggett, 155 Miss. 849, 124 So. 476, 478.

Settlement of claims under insurance policies. Lehaney v. New York Life Ins. Co., 307 Mich. 125, 11 N.W.2d 830, 832.

Accepted amount tendered by insurer as cash surrender value of policies. Greenberg v. Metropolitan Life Ins. Co., 379 Ill. 421, 41 N.E.2d 495, 497, 140 A.L.R. 775.

See, also, Sierra & San Francisco Power Co. v. Universal Electric & Gas Co., 197 Cal. 376, 241 P. 76, 80.

More recently, a broader application of the doctrine has been made, where one promise or agreement is set up in satisfaction of another. Continental Nat. Bank v. McGeoch, 92 Wis. 286, 66 N.W. 606.

An "accord and satisfaction arises" where parties, by a subsequent agreement, have satisfied the former one, and the latter agreement has been executed. The execution of a new agreement may itself amount to a satisfaction, where it is so expressly agreed by the parties; and without such agreement, if the new promise is founded on a new consideration, in which case the taking of the new consideration amounts to the satisfaction of the former contract.

A dispute or controversy is not an essential element of some forms of accord and satisfaction, as an accord and satisfaction of a liquidated claim by the giving and acceptance of a smaller sum and some additional consideration, such as new security, payment of the debt before due, payment by a third person, or where property or personal services are accepted from an insolvent debtor in satisfaction. Burgamy v. Holton, 165 Ga. 384, 141 S.E. 42, 47.

"Composition settlement" contemplates agreement not only between debtor and creditors, but also among creditors, whereas "accord and satisfaction" is agreement between debtor and single creditor. Russell v. Douget, La.App., 171 So. 501, 502.

"Novation" is a species of "accord and satisfaction". Munn v. Town of Drakesville, 226 Iowa 1040, 285 N.W. 644, 648.

See Acceptance; Composition; Compromise; Novation.

ACCORDANCE. Agreement; harmony; concord; conformity. Webster, Dict.; City and County of San Francisco v. Boyd, 22 Cal.2d 685, 140 P.2d 666, 668.

An act done in accordance with a purpose once formed is not necessarily an act done in pursuance of such purpose, for the purpose may have been abandoned before the act was done. State v. Robinson, 20 W.Va. 713, 742. A charter providing that a city's power of taxation shall be exercised "in accordance with" the state Constitution and laws means in a manner not repugnant to or in conflict or inconsistent therewith. City of Norfolk v. Norfolk Landmark Pub. Co., 95 Va. 564, 28 S.E. 959, 960. The words "in accordance with this act" as used in N. M. Laws 1899, c. 22, § 25, dealing with validity of tax titles, was not improperly interpreted as meaning "under this act." Straus v. Foxworth, 231 U.S. 162, 34 S.Ct. 42, 44, 58 L.Ed. 168.

ACCORDANT. Fr. and Eng. Agreeing; concurring. "Baron Parker, *accordant*," Hardr. 93; "Holt, C. J., *accordant*," 6 Mod. 299; "Powys, J., *accord*," "Powell, J., *accord*," Id. 298.

ACCOUCHEMENT. The act of a woman in giving birth to a child. The fact of the accouchement, which may be proved by the direct testimony of one who was present, as a physician or midwife, is often important evidence in proving parentage.

ACCOUNT. A detailed statement of the mutual demands in the nature of debt and credit between parties, arising out of contracts or some fiduciary relation. Portsmouth v. Donaldson, 32 Pa. 202, 72 Am.Dec. 782.

A statement in writing, of debts and credits, or of receipts and payments; a list of items of debts and credits, with their respective dates. Rensselaer Glass Factory v. Reid, 5 Cow., N.Y., 593.

An "account" is defined as a statement of pecuniary transactions; a record or course of business dealings between parties; a list or statement of monetary transactions, such as payments, losses, sales, debits, credits, etc., in most cases showing a balance or result of comparison between items of an opposite nature; and is not held to include a liability for unliquidated damages resulting from the breach of an entire contract, expressing only an entire consideration. Harnischfeger Sales Corporation v. Pickering Lumber Co., C.C.A.Mo., 97 F.2d 692, 695.

The word is sometimes used to denote the balance, or the right of action for the balance, appearing due upon a statement of dealings; as where one speaks of an assignment of accounts; but there is a broad distinction between an account and the mere balance of an account, resembling the distinction in logic between the premises of an argument and the conclusions drawn therefrom. A balance is but the conclusion or result of the debit and credit sides of an account. It implies mutual dealings, and the existence of debt and credit, without which there could be no balance. McWilliams v. Allan, 45 Mo. 574.

A generic term, difficult to define, having various meanings, depending somewhat upon the surrounding circumstances and the connection in which it is used. Wolcott & Lincoln v. Butler, 155 Kan. 105, 122 P.2d 720, 722, 141 A.L.R. 356.

Flexible in meaning, meaning valuation; worth; value. Ex parte Means, 200 Ala. 378, 76 So. 294; may refer either to past or future indebtedness, Semel v. Braun, 157 N.Y. S. 907, 908, 94 Misc. 238; an itemized account, Brooks v. International Shoe Co., 132 Ark. 386, 200 S.W. 1027.

Closed

An account to which no further additions can be made on either side, but which remains still open for adjustment and set-off, which distinguishes it from an account stated. Mandeville v. Wilson, 5 Cranch 15, 3 L.Ed. 23.

Current

An open or running or unsettled account between two parties; the antithesis of an account stated. See Watson v. Gillespie, 200 N.Y.S. 191, 198, 205 App.Div. 613; Caffarelli Bros. v. Lyons Bros. Co., Tex.Civ.App., 199 S.W. 685, 686; Continental Casualty Co. v. Easley, Tex.Civ.App., 290 S.W. 251, 253.

An "account current" is an active checking account, through which credit and debit items are constantly passing. In re Fricke's Will, 202 N.Y.S. 906, 912, 122 Misc. 427.

All items must constitute one demand. Meyers v. Barrett & Zimmerman, 196 Minn. 276, 264 N.W. 769, 773.

Duties

Duties payable by the English customs and inland revenue act, 1881, (44 Vict. c. 12, § 38,) on a *donatio mortis causa*, or on any gift, the donor of which dies within three months after making it, or on joint property voluntarily so created, and taken by survivorship, or on property taken under a voluntary settlement in which the settlor had a life-interest.

Mutual

Accounts comprising mutual credits between the parties; or an existing credit on one side which constitutes a ground for credit on the other, or where there is an understanding that mutual debts shall be a satisfaction or set-off *pro tanto* between the parties. McConnell v. Arkansas Coffin Co., 172 Ark. 87, 287 S.W. 1007.

Open

An account which has not been finally settled or closed, but is still running or open to future adjustment or liquidation. Open account, in legal as well as in ordinary language, means an indebtedness subject to future adjustment, and which may be reduced or modified by proof. James v. Lederer-Strauss & Co., 32 Wyo. 377, 233 P. 137, 139.

An open account can become an account stated only by the debtor's admission of liability, or failure to deny liability for a reasonable time after receipt of account. Brooks v. White, 187 N.C. 656, 122 S.E. 561.

Payable

"Accounts payable" are contract obligations owing by a person on open account. West Virginia Pulp & Paper Co. v. Karnes, 120 S.E. 321, 322, 137 Va. 714; State Tax Commission v. Shattuck, 38 P.2d 631, 639, 44 Ariz. 379.

Public

The accounts kept by officers of the nation, state, or kingdom, of the receipt and expenditure of the revenues of the government.

Rendered

An account made out by the creditor, and presented to the debtor for his examination and acceptance. When accepted, it becomes an account stated. Freeland v. Cocke, 17 Va. (3 Munf.) 352.

Settled

One in which the balance has been in fact paid, thereby differing from an account stated. See Dempsey v. McGinnis, 219 S.W. 148, 150, 203 Mo. App. 494.

Stated

The settlement of an account between the parties, with a balance struck in favor of one of them; an account rendered by the creditor, and by the debtor assented to as correct, either expressly, or by implication of law from the failure to object. Preston v. La Belle View Corporation, 212 N.W. 286, 288, 192 Wis. 168.

Monthly statements rendered by bank without depositor's objection, Pierce & Gamet v. Live Stock Nat. Bank, 213 Iowa 1388, 239 N.W. 580, 583.

Unperformed promise of one party to pay a stated sum. Hammond Lumber Co. v. Richardson Building & Lumber Co., 209 Cal. 82, 285 P. 851, 853.

An agreement between parties who have had previous transactions of a monetary character that all the items of the account representing such transactions, and the balance struck, are correct, together with a promise, express or implied, for the payment of such balance. Pelavin v. Fenton, Davis & Boyle, 255 Mich. 680, 239 N.W. 268, 269.

No particular form is necessary; it may be oral, written, partly oral and partly written. Murphy v. Smith, 26 Ariz. 394, 226 P. 206, 208. An account stated is not ordinarily recognized in Virginia and West Virginia, except as between merchant and merchant, and principal and agent, with mutual accounts. Price Hill Colliery Co. v. Pinkney, 96 W.Va. 74, 122 S.E. 434, 436. This was also a common count in a declaration upon a contract under which the plaintiff might prove an absolute acknowledgment by the defendant of a liquidated demand of a fixed amount, which implies a promise to pay on request. It might be joined with any other count for a money demand. The acknowledgment or admission must have been made to the plaintiff or his agent. Wharton.

ACCOUNT, or ACCOUNT RENDER. In practice. "Account," sometimes called "account render," was a form of action at common law against a person who by reason of some fiduciary relation (as guardian, bailiff, receiver, etc.) was bound to render an account to another, but refused to do so. Portsmouth v. Donaldson, 32 Pa. 202, 72 Am.Dec. 782; Peoples Finance & Thrift Co. of Visalia v. Bowman, 137 P.2d 729, 731, 58 Cal.App.2d 729.

"Action of account" is common-law action to compel person to render account for property or money of another. Dahlberg v. Fisse, 328 Mo. 213, 40 S.W.2d 606, 609. Equitable in nature. Gaines Bros. Co. v. Gaines, 188 Okl. 300, 108 P.2d 177, 179.

In England, this action early fell into disuse; and as it is one of the most dilatory and expensive actions known to the law, and the parties are held to the ancient rules of pleading, and no discovery can be obtained, it never was adopted to any great extent in the United States. But in some states this action was employed, chiefly because there were no chancery courts in which a bill for an accounting would lie. The action is peculiar in the fact that two judgments are rendered, a preliminary judgment that the defendant do account with the plaintiff (*quod computet*) and a final judgment (*quod recuperet*) after the accounting for the balance found due. Field v. Brown, 146 Ind. 293, 45 N.E. 464, 16 Blatchf. 178.

ACCOUNT-BOOK. A book kept by a merchant, trader, mechanic, or other person, in which are entered from time to time the transactions of his trade or business. Greenl. Ev. §§ 115–118.

Volumes bound or sewed together in which accounts are regularly kept, and excluding collections of loose and indeterminate memoranda. W. T. Raleigh Co. v. Rotenberry, 174 Miss. 319, 164 So. 5, 6. May now include modern book of detachable leaves, but leaves must be of such appropriate uniformity of material as reasonably to constitute leaves of account book in which they are contained. W. T. Raleigh Co. v. Rotenberry, 174 Miss. 319, 164 So. 5, 6.

ACCOUNT COMPUTATIO. The primary idea of "account computatio", whether in proceedings of courts of law or equity, is some matter of debt and credit, or demand in nature thereof. Coleman v. Kansas City, 351 Mo. 254, 173 S.W.2d 572, 576.

ACCOUNT FOR. To pay over the money to the person entitled thereto. U. S. v. Rehwald, D.C. Cal., 44 F.2d 663.

ACCOUNT IN BANK. See Bank Account.

ACCOUNTABLE. Subject to pay; responsible; liable. Where one indorsed a note "A. C. accountable," it was held that, under this form of indorsement, he had waived demand and notice. Furber v. Caverly, 42 N.H. 74.

ACCOUNTABLE RECEIPT. An instrument acknowledging the receipt of money or personal property, coupled with an obligation to account for or pay or deliver the whole or some part of it to some person. State v. Riebe, 7 N.W. 262, 27 Minn. 315.

ACCOUNTANT. One who keeps accounts; a person skilled in keeping books or accounts; an expert in accounts or bookkeeping. See U. S. ex rel. Liebmann v. Flynn, D.C.N.Y., 16 F.2d 1006, 1007; Frazer v. Shelton, 150 N.E. 696, 701, 320 Ill. 253.

One competent to design and control systems of accounts. Roberts v. Hosking, 95 Mont. 562, 28 P.2d 199, 201.

A person who renders an account: an executor, guardian, etc.

ACCOUNTANT GENERAL, or ACCOMPTANT GENERAL. An officer of the court of chancery, appointed by act of parliament to receive all money lodged in court, and to place the same in the Bank of England for security. 12 Geo. I. c. 32; 1 Geo. IV, c. 35; 15 & 16 Vict. c. 87, §§ 18–22, 39. See Daniell, Ch.Pr. (4th Ed.) 1607 et seq. The office, however, has been abolished by 35 & 36 Vict. c. 44, and the duties transferred to her majesty's paymaster general.

ACCOUNTANTS, CHARTERED. Persons skilled in the keeping and examination of accounts, who are employed for the purpose of examining and certifying to the correctness of accounts of corporations and others. British Commonwealth equivalent of Certified Public Accountant.

ACCOUNTING. An act or system of making up or settling accounts; a statement of account, or a debit and credit in financial transactions. Kansas City v. Burns, 137 Kan. 905, 22 P.2d 444.

Rendition of an account, either voluntarily or by order of a court. Buxton v. Edwards, 134 Mass. 567, 578. In the latter case, it imports a rendition of a judgment for the balance ascertained to be due. Apple v. Smith, 106 Kan. 717, 190 P. 8, 10. The term may include payment of the amount due. Pyatt v. Pyatt, 46 N.J.Eq. 285, 18 A. 1048.

ACCOUNTS RECEIVABLE. Contract obligations owing to a person on open account. West Virginia Pulp & Paper Co. v. Karnes, 137 Va. 714, 120 S.E. 321, 322; charge accounts, Haverfield Co. v. Evatt, 143 Ohio St. 58, 54 N.E.2d 149, 152, installment balances, Duke Power Co. v. Hillsborough Tp., Somerset County, 20 N.J.Misc. 240, 26 A.2d 713, 725.

ACCOUPLE. To unite; to marry. *Ne unques accouple*, never married.

ACCREDIT. In international law. (1) To acknowledge; to receive as an envoy in his public character, and give him credit and rank accordingly. Burke. (2) To send with credentials as an envoy. Webst.Dict. This latter use is now the accepted one.

ACCREDITED LAW SCHOOL. "An accredited law school" and a "law school approved by this court," are synonymous. Ex parte State Board of Law Examiners of Florida, 141 Fla. 706, 193 So. 753.

ACCREDITED REPRESENTATIVE. As respects service of process, representative having general authority to act. Rorick v. Stilwell, 101 Fla. 4, 133 So. 609, 615.

ACCREDULITARE. L. Lat. In old records. To purge an offense by oath. Blount; Whishaw.

ACCRESCERE. In the civil and old English law. To grow to; to increase; to pass to, and become united with, as soil to land *per alluvionem*. Dig. 41, 1, 30, pr. The term is used in speaking of islands which are formed in rivers by deposit; Calvinus, Lex.; 3 Kent 428. It is used in a related sense in the common-law phrase *jus accrescendi*, the right of survivorship; 1 Washb.R.P. 426.

Pleading

To commence; to arise; to accrue. *Quod actio non accrevit infra sex anos*, that the action did not accrue within six years; 3 Chit.Pl. 914.

ACCRETION. The act of growing to a thing; usually applied to the gradual and imperceptible accumulation of land by natural causes, as out of the sea or a river.

Civil Law

The right of heirs or legatees to unite or aggregate with their shares or portions of the estate the portion of any co-heir or legatee who refuses to accept it, fails to comply with a condition, becomes incapacitated to inherit, or dies before the testator. Anderson v. Lucas, 204 S.W. 989, 993, 140 Tenn. 336. Under a deed of trust: Miller v. Douglass, 192 Wis. 486, 213 N.W. 320, 322.

Mortgages

As used in a mortgage on cattle, with all increase thereof and accretions thereto, the word "accretions" is not confined to the results of natural growth, but includes the additions of parts from without, i. e., of cattle subsequently added to the herd. Stockyards Loan Co. v. Nichols, C.C.A.Okl., 243 F. 511, 513, 1 A.L.R. 547.

Realty

Addition of portions of soil, by gradual deposition through the operation of natural causes, to that already in possession of owner. St. Louis, etc., R. Co. v. Ramsey, 53 Ark. 314, 13 S.W. 931, 8 L.R.A. 559, 22 Am.St.Rep. 195; 51 L.R.A. 425, n.; Willett v. Miller, 176 Okl. 278, 55 P.2d 90, 92. Along banks of navigable or unnavigable stream. Smith v. Whitney, 105 Mont. 523, 74 P.2d 450, 453, change in river boundary, Hancock v. Moore, Tex.Civ.

App., 137 S.W.2d 45, 51, 52. Tideland artificially filled was not an "accretion". City of Newport Beach v. Fager, 39 Cal.App.2d 23, 102 P.2d 438, 442.

Accretion of land is of two kinds: By *alluvion, i. e.*, by the washing up of sand or soil, so as to form firm ground; or by *dereliction*, as when the sea shrinks below the usual water-mark. The term "alluvion" is applied to deposit itself, while "accretion" denotes the act. However, the terms are frequently used synonymously. Katz v. Patterson, 135 Or. 449, 296 P. 54, 55. In determining whether change in course of river is by "accretion" or "avulsion," test is not whether witnesses might see from time to time that progress has been made, but whether witnesses could perceive change while it was going on. Goins v. Merryman, 183 Okl. 155, 80 P.2d 268, 270. Land uncovered by gradual subsidence of water is not an "accretion" but a "reliction." Independent Stock Farm v. Stevens, 128 Neb. 619, 259 N.W. 647, 648.

Trust Property

Receipts other than those ordinarily considered as income; and ordinary cash dividends, the sole income, were not accretions. Doty v. C. I. R., C.C.A.1, 148 F.2d 503, 505.

See Accrue; Avulsion; Alluvion; Reliction.

ACCROACH. To encroach; to exercise power without due authority. In French law, to delay. Whishaw.

To attempt to exercise royal power. 4 Bl.Comm. 76. A knight who forcibly assaulted and detained one of the king's subjects till he paid him a sum of money was held to have committed treason, on the ground of accroachment. 1 Hale, P.C. 80.

ACCROCHER. Fr. To delay; retard; put off. *Accrocher un procès*, to stay the proceedings in a suit.

ACCRUAL, CLAUSE OF. See Accruer, Clause of.

ACCRUAL BASIS. A method of keeping accounts which shows expenses incurred and income earned for a given period, although such expenses and income may not have been actually paid or received in cash. Orlando Orange Groves Co. v. Hale, 119 Fla. 159, 161 So. 284.

Right to receive and not the actual receipt determines inclusion of amount in gross income. When right to receive an amount becomes fixed, right accrues. H. Liebes & Co. v. Commissioner of Internal Revenue, C.C.A.9, 90 F.2d 932, 937. Obligations payable to or by taxpayer are treated as if discharged when incurred. H. Liebes & Co. v. Commissioner of Internal Revenue, C.C.A.9, 90 F.2d 932, 936. Entries are made of credits and debits when liability arises, whether received or disbursed. Insurance Finance Corporation v. Commissioner of Internal Revenue, C.C.A.3, 84 F.2d 382. Books showing sales by accounts receivable and purchases by accounts payable, and set up inventories at beginning and end of year. Consolidated Tea Co. v. Bowers, D.C.N.Y., 19 F.2d 382.

ACCRUE. Derived from the Latin, "ad" and "creso," to grow to. In past tense, in sense of due and payable; vested. It means to increase; to augment; to come to by way of increase; to be added as an increase, profit, or damage. Hartsfield Co. v. Shoaf, 184 Ga. 378, 191 S.E. 693, 695. Acquired; fell due; made or executed; matured; occurred; received; vested; was created; was incurred. H. Liebes & Co. v. Commissioner of Internal Revenue, C.C.A.9, 90 F.2d 932, 936. To attach itself to, as a subordinate or accessory claim or demand arises out of, and is joined to, its principal. Lifson v. Commissioner of Internal Revenue, C.C.A.8, 98 F.2d 508.

Produce of money lent. "Interest accrues to principal." Weiss v. Commissioners of Land Office, 182 Okl. 39, 75 P.2d 1142, 1144. Costs accrue to a judgment.

The term is also used of independent or original demands, and then means to arise, to happen, to come into force or existence; to vest; as in the phrase, "The right of action did not *accrue* within six years." Amy v. Dubuque, 98 U.S. 470, 476, 25 L.Ed. 228. To become a present right or demand; to come to pass. H. Liebes & Co. v. Commissioner of Internal Revenue, C.C.A.9, 90 F.2d 932, 936.

It is distinguished from sustain: Adams v. Brown, 4 Litt. (Ky.) 7; and from owing: Gross v. Partenheimer, 159 Pa. 556, 28 A. 370; Fay v. Holloran, 35 Barb. (N. Y.) 295; it is also distinguished from arise: State v. Circuit Court of Waushara County, 165 Wis. 387, 162 N.W. 436, 437.

Cause of Action

A cause of action "accrues" when a suit may be maintained thereon. Dillon v. Board of Pension Com'rs of City of Los Angeles, 18 Cal.2d 427, 116 P.2d 37, 39, 136 A.L.R. 800. Whenever one person may sue another. Hensley v. Conway, Tex.Civ.App., 29 S.W.2d 416, 418.

Cause of action "accrues," on date that damage is sustained and not date when causes are set in motion which ultimately produce injury. City of Philadelphia v. Lieberman, C.C.A.Pa., 112 F.2d 424, 428. Date of injury. Fredericks v. Town of Dover, 125 N.J.L. 288, 15 A.2d 784, 787. When actual damage has resulted. National Lead Co. v. City of New York, C.C.A.N.Y., 43 F.2d 914, 916. As soon as contract is breached. Wichita Nat. Bank v. United States Fidelity & Guaranty Co., Tex.Civ.App., 147 S.W.2d 295, 297.

Contracts

The word accrued, as used in reference to contracts in which process may be sent out of the country to be served, has reference to the place where the contract was made and executed. Phelps v. McGee, 18 Ill. 155, 158.

Taxation

Income "accrues" to taxpayer when there arises to him a fixed or unconditional right to receive it. Franklin County Distilling Co. v. Commissioner of Internal Revenue, C.C.A.6, 125 F.2d 800, 804, 805. But not unless there is a reasonable expectancy that the right will be converted into money or its equivalent. Swastika Oil & Gas Co. v. Commissioner of Internal Revenue, C.C.A.6, 123 F.2d 382, 384.

Where taxpayer makes returns on accrual basis, item "accrues" when all events occur which fix amount payable and determine liability of taxpayer. Hudson Motor Car Co. v. U. S., Ct.Cl., 3 F. Supp. 834, 847.

Tax "accrues" for deduction when all events have occurred which fix amount of tax and determine liability of taxpayer for it, although there has not yet been assessment or maturity. Elmhirst v. Duggan, D.C.N.Y., 14 F.Supp. 782, 784.

Estate tax "accrued," immediately on death, though not payable until one year thereafter. Ewbank v. U. S., C.C.A.Ind., 50 F.2d 409.

ACCRUED COMPENSATION. Awarded compensation, due and payable. Wood Coal Co. v. State Compensation Com'r, 119 W.Va. 581, 195 S.E. 528, 529.

ACCRUED DEPRECIATION. The lessened service value of the utility plant due to its consumption in furnishing service. Wisconsin Telephone Co. v. Public Service Commission, 232 Wis. 274, 287 N.W. 122, 152. Portion of useful service life which has expired. State ex rel. City of St. Louis v. Public Service Commission, 341 Mo. 920, 110 S. W.2d 749, 768.

ACCRUED RIGHT. As used in Constitution, a matured cause of action, or legal authority to demand redress. Morley v. Hurst, 174 Okl. 2, 49 P. 2d 546, 548.

ACCRUER (or ACCRUAL), CLAUSE OF. An express clause, frequently occurring in the case of gifts by deed or will to persons as tenants in common, providing that upon the death of one or more of the beneficiaries his or their shares shall go to the survivor or survivors. Brown. The share of the decedent is then said to *accrue* to the others.

ACCRUING. Inchoate; in process of maturing. That which will or may, at a future time, ripen into a vested right, an available demand, or an existing cause of action. Hartsfield Co. v. Shoaf, 184 Ga. 378, 191 S.E. 693, 695. Arising by way of increase, growth or profit. It connotes continuing growth, increase or augmentation. Globe Indemnity Co. v. Bruce, C.C.A.Okl., 81 F.2d 143, 153.

ACCRUING COSTS. Costs and expenses incurred after judgment.

ACCRUING INTEREST. Running or accumulating interest, as distinguished from accrued or matured interest; interest daily accumulating on the principal debt but not yet due and payable. Gross v. Partenheimer, 159 Pa. 556, 28 A. 370.

ACCRUING RIGHT. One that is increasing, enlarging, or augmenting. Richards v. Land Co., 54 F. 209, 4 C.C.A. 290.

ACCT. An abbreviation for "account," of such universal and immemorial use that the courts will take judicial notice of its meaning. Heaton v. Ainley, 108 Iowa, 112, 78 N.W. 798.

ACCUMULATED PROFITS. Earned surplus or undivided profits. Flint v. Commissioner of Corporations and Taxation, 43 N.E.2d 789, 791, 792, 312 Mass. 204.

Include profits earned and invested. Commissioner of Corporations and Taxation v. Filoon, 310 Mass. 374, 38 N.E.2d 693, 698, 700.

And they take into account losses, as well as gains. Commissioner of Corporations and Taxation v. Church, Mass., 61 N.E.2d 143, 145.

ACCUMULATED SURPLUS. In statutes relative to the taxation of corporations, this term refers to the fund which the company has in excess of its capital and liabilities. Trenton Iron Co. v. Yard, 42 N.J.Law, 357; People's F. Ins. Co. v. Parker, 34 N.J.Law, 479, 35 N.J.Law, 575. See Earnings.

ACCUMULATIONS. Increase by continuous or repeated additions, or, if taken literally, means either profit accruing on sale of principal assets, or increase derived from their investment, or both. In re Wells' Will, 300 N.Y.S. 1075, 1078, 165 Misc. 385.

Adding of interest or income of a fund to principal pursuant to provisions of a will or deed, preventing its being expended. In re Watson's Will, 258 N.Y.S. 755, 144 Misc. 213.

When an executor or other trustee masses the rents, dividends, and other income which he receives, treats it as a capital, invests it, makes a new capital of the income derived therefrom, invests that, and so on, he is said to accumulate the fund, and the capital and accrued income thus procured constitute *accumulations*. Hussey v. Sargent, 116 Ky. 53, 75 S.W. 211, In re Rogers' Estate, 179 Pa. 609, 36 A. 340. See Perpetuity.

ACCUMULATIVE. That which accumulates, or is heaped up; additional. Said of several things heaped together, or of one thing added to another.

ACCUMULATIVE JUDGMENT. Where a person has already been convicted and sentenced, and a second or additional judgment is passed against him, the execution of which is postponed until the completion of the first sentence, such second judgment is said to be *accumulative*.

As to accumulative "Legacy," see that title.

ACCUMULATIVE LEGACY. A second, double or additional legacy; a legacy given in addition to another given by the same instrument, or by another instrument.

ACCUMULATIVE SENTENCE. A sentence, additional to others, imposed on a defendant who has been convicted upon an indictment containing several counts, each of such counts charging a distinct offense, or who is under conviction at the same time for several distinct offenses; one of such sentences to begin at the expiration of another. Carter v. Mclaughry, 183 U.S. 365, 22 S. Ct. 181, 46 L.Ed. 236; State v. Hamby, 126 N.C. 1066, 35 S.E. 614; Braudon v. Mackey, 122 Kan. 207, 251 P. 176, 177.

ACCUSARE NEMO SE DEBET, NISI CORAM DEO. No one is bound to accuse himself, except before God. See Hardres, 139.

ACCUSATION. A formal charge against a person, to the effect that he is guilty of a punishable offense, laid before a court or magistrate having jurisdiction to inquire into the alleged crime. Coplon v. State, 15 Ala.App. 331, 73 So. 225, 228. See Accuse.

"Accusation" is equivalent of "information" at common law which is mere allegation of prosecuting officer by whom it is preferred. Sutton v. State, 54 Ga.App. 349, 188 S.E. 60, 62.

ACCUSATOR POST RATIONABILE TEMPUS NON EST AUDIENDUS, NISI SE BENE DE OMISSIONE EXCUSAVERIT. Moore, 817. An accuser ought not to be heard after the expiration of a reasonable time, unless he can account satisfactorily for the delay.

ACCUSATORY PART. The "accusatory part" of an indictment is that part where the offense is named. Deaton v. Commonwealth, 220 Ky. 343, 295 S.W. 167, 168.

ACCUSE. To bring a formal charge against a person, to the effect that he is guilty of a crime or punishable offense, before a court or magistrate having jurisdiction to inquire into the alleged crime. People v. Frey, 112 Mich. 251, 70 N W. 548.

In its popular sense "accusation" applies to all derogatory charges or imputations, whether or not they relate to a punishable legal offense, and however made, whether orally, by newspaper, or otherwise. People v. Braman, 30 Mich. 460. But in legal phraseology, it is limited to such accusations as have taken shape in a prosecution. United States v. Patterson, 150 U.S. 65, 14 S.Ct. 20, 37 L.Ed. 999.

ACCUSED. "Accused" is the generic name for the defendant in a criminal case, and is more appropriate than either "prisoner" or "defendant." 1 Car. & K. 131.

The person against whom an accusation is made: one who is charged with a crime or misdemeanor. See People v. Braman, 30 Mich. 468. The term cannot be said to apply to a defendant in a civil action; Castle v. Houston, 19 Kan. 417, 37 Am.Rep. 127; and see Mosby v. Ins. Co., 31 Gratt. (Va.) 629.

ACCUSER. The person by whom an accusation is made.

ACCUSTOMED. Habitual; often used; synonymous with usual; Farwell v. Smith, 16 N.J.Law, 133.

ACEPHALI. The levelers in the reign of Hen. I., who acknowledged no head or superior. Leges H. 1; Cowell. Also certain ancient heretics, who appeared about the beginning of the sixth century, and asserted that there was but one substance in Christ, and one nature. Wharton; Gibbon, Rom. Emp. ch. 47.

ACEQUIA. A ditch, channel, or canal, through which water, diverted from its natural course, is conducted, for use in irrigation or other purposes; public ditches. Comp.L.N.Mex. tit. 1, c. 1, § 6 (Comp.St.1929, §§ 151–401).

ACHAT, also ACHATE, ACHATA, ACHET. In French law. A purchase or bargain. Cowell.

It is used in some of our law-books, as well as *achetor*, a purchaser, which in some ancient statutes means purveyor. Stat. 36 Edw. III; Merlin, Répert.

ACHERSET. In old English law. A measure of grain, conjectured to have been the same with our quarter, or eight bushels. Cowell.

ACHIEVE SUBJECT MATTER. The English equivalent for patentability. Mesta Mach. Co. v. Federal Machine & Welder Co., C.C.A.Pa., 110 F. 2d 479, 480.

ACKNOWLEDGE. To own, avow, or admit; to confess; to recognize one's acts, and assume the responsibility therefor.

ACKNOWLEDGMENT. To "acknowledge" is to admit, affirm, declare, testify, avow, confess, or own as genuine. Favello v. Bank of America Nat. Trust & Savings Ass'n, 24 Cal.App.2d 342, 74 P.2d 1057, 1058.

Child

An avowal or admission that the child is one's own; recognition of a parental relation, either by a written agreement, verbal declarations or statements, by the life, acts, and conduct of the parties, or any other satisfactory evidence that the relation was recognized and admitted. In re Spencer, Sur., 4 N.Y.S. 395; In re Hunt's Estate, 33 N.Y.S. 256, 86 Hun, 232.

Parents formally acknowledged child during ceremony in which both marriage and baptism took place. Cormier v. Cormier, 185 La. 968, 171 So. 93, 97, 98. Letter to registrar of college where child was student. In re Horne's Estate, 149 Fla. 710, 7 So.2d 13, 16.

The "public acknowledgment" of paternity, under Civ. Code Cal. § 230, is the opposite of private acknowledgment, and means the same kind of acknowledgment a father would make of his legitimate child. In re Baird's Estate, 193 Cal. 225, 223 P. 974, 994.

Generally

Implying obligation or incurring responsibility. Weyerhaeuser Timber Co. v. Marshall, C.C.A. Wash., 102 F.2d 78, 81.

Act of a person who avows or admits the truth of certain facts which, if established, will entail a civil liability upon him. Thus, the debtor's *acknowledgment* of the creditor's demand or right of action will toll the statute of limitations. Ft. Scott v. Hickman, 112 U.S. 150, 163, 5 Sup.Ct. 56, 28 L.Ed. 636; Letters, Leffek v. Luedeman, 95 Mont. 457, 27 P.2d 511, 91 A.L.R. 286; Lincoln-Alliance Bank & Trust Co. v. Fisher, 286 N.Y.S. 722, 247 App.Div. 465; payments. Erskine v. Upham, 56 Cal.App.2d 235, 132 P.2d 219, 224, 225. McMahan v. Dorchester Fertilizer Co., 184 Md. 155, 40 A.2d 313, 314.

Testator's statement to attesting witness. Anthony v. College of the Ozarks, 207 Ark. 212, 180 S.W.2d 321, 324.

Instruments

Formal declaration before authorized official, by person who executed instrument, that it is his free act and deed. Jemison v. Howell, 161 So. 806, 230 Ala. 423, 99 A.L.R. 1511. The certificate of the officer on such instrument that it has been so acknowledged. Williford v. Davis, 106 Okl. 208, 232 P. 828, 831.

Money

A sum paid in some parts of England by copyhold tenants on the death of their lords, as a recognition of their new lords, in like manner as money is usually paid on the attornment of tenants. Called a fine by Blackstone; 2 Bla.Com. 98.

Separate Acknowledgment

An acknowledgment of a deed or other instrument, made by a married woman, on her examination by the officer separate and apart from her husband. Hutchinson v. Stone, 79 Fla. 157, 84 So. 151, 154.

ACOLYTE. An inferior church servant, who, next under the sub-deacon, follows and waits upon the priests and deacons, and performs the offices of lighting the candles, carrying the bread and wine, and paying other servile attendance. Spelman; Cowell.

ACQUAINTED. Having personal knowledge of. Kelly v. Calhoun, 95 U.S. 710, 24 L.Ed. 544. Acquaintance expresses less than familiarity; In re Carpenter's Estate, 94 Cal. 406, 29 P. 1101. It is "familiar knowledge"; Wyllis v. Haun, 47 Iowa, 614; Chauvin v. Wagner, 18 Mo. 531.

"Acquaintance" expresses less than familiarity; familiarity less than intimacy. Acquaintance springs from occasional intercourse, familiarity from daily intercourse, intimacy from unreserved intercourse; acquaintance, having some knowledge, familiarity, from long habit, intimacy, by close connection. Atkins Corporation v. Tourny, 6 Cal.2d 206, 57 P.2d 480, 483. To be "personally acquainted with," and to "know personally," are equivalent terms; Kelly v. Calhoun, 95 U.S. 710, 24 L.Ed. 544. When used with reference to a paper to which a certificate or affidavit is attached, it indicates a substantial knowledge of the subject-matter thereof. Bohan v. Casey, 5 Mo. App. 101.

ACQUEREUR. In French and Canadian law. One who acquires title, particularly to immovable property, by purchase.

ACQUEST. An estate acquired newly, or by purchase. 1 Reeve, Eng.Law, 56.

ACQUÊTS. In the civil law. Property which has been acquired by purchase, gift, or otherwise than by succession. Immovable property which has been acquired otherwise than by succession. Merl. Répert.

Profits or gains of property, as between husband and wife. Civil Code La. art. 2402. The profits of all the effects of which the husband has the administration and enjoyment, either of right or in fact, of the produce of the joint industry of both husband and wife, and of the estates which they may acquire during the marriage, either by donations made jointly to them both, or by purchase, or in any other similar way, even though the purchase be only in the name of one of the two, and not of both. See Community; Conquêts.

ACQUIESCE. To give an implied consent to a transaction, to the accrual of a right, or to any act, by one's mere silence, or without express assent or acknowledgment., Scott v. Jackson, 89 Cal. 258, 26 P. 898.

ACQUIESCENCE. Conduct recognizing the existence of a transaction, and intended, in some extent at least, to carry the transaction, or permit it to be carried, into effect; it is some act, not deliberately intended to ratify a former transaction known to be voidable, but recognizing the transaction as existing, and intended, in some extent at least, to carry it into effect, and to obtain or claim the benefits resulting from it, and thus differs from "confirmation," which implies a deliberate act, intended to renew and ratify a transaction known to be voidable. De Boe v. Prentice Packing & Storage Co., 172 Wash. 514, 20 P.2d 1107, 1110.

Passive compliance or satisfaction; distinguished from avowed consent on the one hand, and, on the other, from opposition or open discontent. Paul v. Western Distributing Co., 142 Kan. 816, 52 P.2d 379, 387. Acquiescence from which assent may be reasonably inferred. Frank v. Wilson & Co., 24 Del.Ch. 237, 9 A.2d 82, 86. Equivalent to assent inferred from silence with knowledge or from encouragement and presupposes knowledge and assent. Andrew v. Rivers, 207 Iowa 343, 223 N.W. 102, 105. Imports tacit consent, concurrence, acceptance or assent. Natural Soda Products Co. v. City of Los Angeles, Cal.App., 132 P.2d 553, 563. A silent appearance of consent. Worcester, Dict. Darnell v. Bidwell, 115 Me. 227, 98 A. 743, 745, 5 A.L.R. 1320. Failure to make any objections. Scott v. Jackson, 89 Cal. 258, 26 P. 898. Submission to an act of which one had knowledge. See Pence v. Langdon, 99 U.S. 578, 25 L.Ed. 420. It imports full knowledge. Rabe v. Dunlap, 51 N.J.Eq. 40, 25 A. 959. Knowledge without objection. Indiana Harbor Belt R. Co. v. Jones, 220 Ind. 139, 41 N.E.2d 361, 363.

It is to be distinguished from avowed consent, on the one hand, and from open discontent or opposition, on the other.

It arises where a person who knows that he is entitled to impeach a transaction or enforce a right neglects to do so for such a length of time that, under the circumstances of the case, the other party may fairly infer that he has waived or abandoned his right. Norfolk & W. R. Co. v. Perdue, 40 W.Va. 442, 21 S.E. 755.

Acquiescence and *laches* are cognate but not equivalent terms. The former is a submission to, or resting satisfied with, an existing state of things, while laches implies a neglect to do that which the party ought to do for his own benefit or protection. Hence laches may be evidence of acquiescence. Laches imports a merely passive assent, while acquiescence implies active assent. In re Wilbur's Estate, 334 Pa. 45, 5 A.2d 325, 331. "Acquiescence" relates to inaction during performance of an act while "laches" relates to delay after act is done. Bay Newfoundland Co. v. Wilson & Co., 24 Del.Ch. 30, 4 A.2d 668, 671, 673. "Acquiescence" is synonymous with "abandonment"; Sclawr v. City of St. Paul, 132 Minn. 238, 156 N.W. 283, 284, and is distinguished from "admission"; Saunders v. Busch-Everett Co., 138 La. 1049, 71 So. 153, 154; and from "ratification" and "estoppel in pais"; Marion Sav. Bank v. Leahy, 200 Iowa 220, 204 N.W. 456, 458; but see Murray v. Smith, 152 N.Y.S. 102, 108, 166 App.Div. 528; differs from "confirmation", in that confirmation implies a deliberate act, intended to renew and ratify a transaction known to be voidable, Bauer v. Dotterer, 202 Ark. 1055, 155 S.W.2d 54, 57. A form of "equitable estoppel", Schmitt v. Wright, 317 Ill.App. 384, 46 N.E.2d 184, 192.

See Admission; Confession; Ratification.

ACQUIESCENCE, ESTOPPEL BY. Acquiescence is a species of estoppel. Bankers' Trust Co. v. Rood, 211 Iowa, 289, 233 N.W. 794, 802, 73 A.L.R. 1421.

An estoppel arises where party aware of his rights sees other party acting upon mistaken notion of his rights. Minear v. Keith Furnace Co., Iowa, 239 N.W. 584, 587. Injury accruing from one's acquiescence in another's action to his prejudice creates "estoppel". Lebold v. Inland Steel Co., C.C.A.Ill., 125 F.2d 369, 375; Passive conduct on the part of one who has knowledge of the facts may be basis of estoppel. Winslow v. Burns, 47 N.M. 29, 132 P.2d 1048, 1050.

It must appear that party to be estopped was bound in equity and good conscience to speak and that party claiming estoppel relied upon acquiescence and was misled thereby to change his position to his prejudice. Sherlock v. Greaves, 106 Mont. 206, 76 P.2d 87, 91.

Acquiescence in a judgment in order to constitute an estoppel must be unqualified. Messer v. Henlein, 72 N.D. 63, 4 N.W.2d 587, 589. One who stands by while his property is sold is "estopped" from setting up title against purchaser. Meadows v. Hampton Live Stock Commission Co., 55 Cal.App.2d 634, 131 P.2d 591, 592, 593.

The doctrine is applicable only where there is some element of turpitude or neglect. City of Lafayette v. Keen, 113 Ind.App. 552, 48 N.E.2d 63, 70.

ACQUIETANDIS PLEGIIS. A writ of justices, formerly lying for the surety against a creditor who refuses to acquit him after the debt has been satisfied. Reg. of Writs 158; Cowell; Blount.

ACQUIRE. To gain by any means, usually by one's own exertions; to get as one's own; to obtain by search, endeavor, practice, or purchase; receive or gain in whatever manner; come to have. Clarno v. Gamble-Robinson Co., 190 Minn. 256, 251 N.W. 268, 269.

In law of contracts and of descents, to become owner of property; to make property one's own. Crutchfield v. Johnson & Latimer, 243 Ala. 73, 8 So.2d 412. To gain ownership of. Commissioner of Insurance v. Broad Street Mut. Casualty Ins. Co., 312 Mass. 261, 44 N.E.2d 683, 684. Broad meaning including both purchase and construction; acquisition being the act of getting or obtaining something which may be already in existence, or may be brought into existence through means employed to acquire it. Ronnow v. City of Las Vegas, 57 Nev. 332, 65 P.2d 133, 140. Sometimes used in the sense of "procure," Jolly v. McCoy, 36 Cal.App. 479, 172 P. 618, 619. It does not necessarily mean that title has passed. Godwin v. Tuttle, 70 Or. 424, 141 P. 1120, 1122. Includes taking by devise. U. S. v. Merriam, 263 U.S. 179. 44 S.Ct. 69, 70 68 L.Ed. 240, 29 A.L.R. 1547.

ACQUIRED. To get, procure, secure, acquire. Jones v. State, 126 Tex.Cr.R. 469, 72 S.W.2d 260, 263.

Coming to an intestate in any other way than by gift, devise, or descent from a parent or the ancestor of a parent. In re Miller's Will, 2 Lea (Tenn.) 54.

ACQUIRED RIGHTS. Those which a man does not naturally enjoy, but which are owing to his own procurement, as sovereignty, or the right of commanding, or the right of property. Borden v. State, 11 Ark. 519, 527, 44 Am.Dec. 217.

ACQUIRER TAX. German estate inheritance legacy tax, not true inheritance or legacy tax, imposed upon recipient, and not affecting executors. In re Gotthelf's Will, 273 N.Y.S. 247, 152 Misc. 309.

ACQUISITION. The act of becoming the owner of certain property; the act by which one acquires or procures the property in anything. State ex rel. Fisher v. Sherman, 135 Ohio St. 458, 21 N.E.2d 467, 470. Used also of the thing acquired. Hartigan v. City of Los Angeles, 170 Cal. 313, 149 P. 590, 592. Taking with, or against, consent. Scribner v. Wikstrom, 93 N.H. 17, 34 A.2d 658, 660. Especially a material possession obtained by any means. Jones v. State, 126 Tex.Cr.R. 469, 72 S.W.2d 260, 263.

Original acquisition is that by which a man secures a property in a thing which is not at the time he acquires it, and in its then existing condition, the property of any other individual. It may result from occupancy; 2 Kent, 289; accession; 2 Kent, 293; intellectual labor—namely, for inventions, which are secured by patent rights; and for the authorship of books, maps, and charts, which is protected by copyrights; 1 Bouv.Inst. 508, n.

Derivative acquisitions are those which are procured from others. Goods and chattels may change owners by act of law in the cases of forfeiture, succession, marriage, judgment, insolvency, and intestacy; or by act of the parties, as by gift or sale.

An acquisition may result from the act of the party himself, or those who are in his power acting for him, as his children while minors; Gale v. Parrot, 1 N.H. 28. See Dig. 41. 1. 53; Inst. 2. 9. 3.

See Accession.

ACQUIT. To set free, release or discharge as from an obligation, burden or accusation. Commonwealth v. Benson, 94 Pa.Super. 10, 15. To absolve, one from an obligation or a liability; or to legally certify the innocence of one charged with crime. Dolloway v. Turrill, 26 Wend.N.Y. 383, 400.

ACQUIT À CAUTION. The certificate proving receipt of security that goods shipped from one French port to another shall not be sent to a foreign country. Argles, Fr.Merc.Law, 543.

ACQUIT BACK. In mineral deed, vested in the grantee the title to such mineral rights as grantor had at time of execution of deed, where grantor had received his title from grantee and the expression was intended to reconvey such title. Allen v. Boykin, 199 Miss. 417, 24 So.2d 748, 750.

ACQUITMENT. See Absolution.

ACQUITTAL.

Contracts

A release, absolution, or discharge from an obligation, liability, or engagement.

According to Lord Coke, there are three kinds of acquittal, namely: by deed, when the party releases the obligation; by prescription; by tenure; Co. Litt. 100 *a*.

Crimes

The legal and formal certification of the innocence of a person who has been charged with crime; a deliverance or setting free a person from a charge of guilt.

In a narrow sense, it is the absolution of a party accused on a trial before a traverse jury. Thomas v. De Graffenreid, 2 Nott & McC. (S. C.) 143. Properly speaking, however, one is not acquitted by the jury but by the judgment of the court. People v. Rogers, 170 N.Y.S. 86, 87, 102 Misc. 437. And he may be legally acquitted by a judgment rendered otherwise than in pursuance of a verdict, as where he is discharged by a magistrate because of the insufficiency of the evidence, or the indictment is dismissed by the court or a nol. pros. entered. State v. Hart, 90 N.J. Law 261, 101 A. 278. But compare State v. Smith, 170 N.C. 742; 87 S.E. 98, 99.

"Nol. pros." not equivalent of "acquittal." Bolton v. State, 166 Miss. 290, 146 So. 453, 454. The unnecessary discharge of the jury without the consent of the accused after it has been sworn may constitute an acquittal. Riley v. Commonwealth, 190 Ky. 204, 227 S.W. 146, 147. Acquittal discharges from guilt, pardon only from punishment. Younger v. State, 2 W.Va. 579, 98 Am.Dec. 791.

It may occur even though the question of guilt or innocence has never been submitted to a jury, as where a defendant, having been held under an indictment or information, is discharged because not brought to trial within the time provided by the Criminal Code. State v. Taylor, 130 Kan. 813, 288 P. 731, 732.

Acquittals in fact are those which take place when the jury, upon trial, finds a verdict of not guilty.

Acquittals in law are those which take place by mere operation of law; as where a man has been charged merely as an assessory, and the principal has been acquitted. 2 Co.Inst. 364. Ccmpare State v. Walton, 186 N.C. 485, 119 S.E. 886, 888.

See Jeopardy; Autrefois Acquit; Convict.

Feudal Law

The obligation on the part of a mesne lord to protect his tenant from any claims, entries or molestations by lords paramount arising out of the services due to them by the mesne lord. See Co.Litt. 100*a*.

ACQUITTANCE. A written discharge, whereby one is freed from an obligation to pay money or perform a duty. It differs from a *release* in not requiring to be under seal. Pothier, Oblig. n. 781. See Milliken v. Brown, 1 Rawle (Pa.) 391.

This word, though perhaps not strictly speaking synonymous with "receipt," includes it. A receipt is one form of an acquittance; a discharge is another. A receipt in full is an acquittance, and a receipt for a part of a demand or obligation is an acquittance *pro tanto*. State v. Shelters, 51 Vt. 104, 31 Am.Rep. 679.

ACQUITTED. Released; absolved; purged of an accusation; judicially discharged from accusation; released from debt, etc. Includes both civil and criminal prosecutions. Dolloway v. Turrill, 26 Wend. (N.Y.) 383, 399. See Acquittal.

ACRE. A quantity of land containing 160 square rods of land, in whatever shape. Serg. Land Laws Pa. 185; Cro.Eliz. 476, 665; 6 Coke 67; Poph. 55; Co.Litt. 5*b*.

Originally the word "acre" *(acer, aker,* or Sax, *æcer)* was not used as a measure of land, or to signify any determinate quantity of land, but to denote any open ground, *(latum quantumvis agrum,)* wide champaign, or field; which is still the meaning of the German *acker*, derived probably from the same source, and is preserved in the names of some places in England, as Castle Acre, South Acre, etc. Burrill. Originally a strip in the fields that was ploughed in the forenoon. Maitland, Domesday and Beyond, 387.

ACRE FOOT. 325,850 gallons, or the amount of water which will cover one acre one foot in depth. Rowles v. Hadden, Tex.Civ.App., 210 S.W. 251, 258.

ACRE RIGHT. "The share of a citizen of a New England town in the common lands. The value of the acre right was a fixed quantity in each town, but varied in different towns. A 10-acre lot or right in a certain town was equivalent to 113 acres of upland and 12 acres of meadow, and a certain exact proportion was maintained between the acre right and salable lands." Messages, etc., of the Presidents, Richardson, X, 230.

ACREFIGHT, or ACRE. A camp or field fight; a sort of duel, or judicial combat, anciently fought by single combatants, English and Scotch, between the frontiers of the two kingdoms with sword and lance. Called "campfight," and the combatants "champions," from the open "acre" or *field* that was the stage of trial. Cowell.

ACROMIAL PROCESS. A point in the region of the shoulder about where the arm joins or fits into the shoulder blade. Muskogee Electric Traction Co. v. Mueller, 39 Okl. 63, 134 P. 51, 52.

ACROSS. From side to side. Transverse to the length of. Hannibal & St. J. R. Co. v. Packet Co., 8 S.Ct. 874, 125 U.S. 260, 31 L.Ed. 731; but see Appeal of Bennett's Branch Imp. Co., 65 Pa. 242. It may mean over, Brown v. Meady, 10 Me. 391, 25 Am.Dec. 248; or "upon and along," Mt. Vernon Telephone Co. v. Franklin Farmers' Co-op. Telephone Co., 113 Me. 46, 92 A. 934, 935, Ann.Cas. 1917B, 649; or "upon," Jefferson County v. Louisville & I. R. Co., 160 S.W. 502, 504, 155 Ky. 810; or "within," Quanah, A. & P. Ry. Co. v. Cooper, Tex.Civ.App., 236 S.W. 811, 812. See Comstock v. Van Deusen, 5 Pick. (Mass.) 163, where a grant of a right of way *across* a lot of land was held not to mean a right to enter at one side, go partly across and come out at a place on the same side. And compare Brooklyn Heights R. Co. v. Steers, 106 N.E. 919, 920, 213 N.Y. 76; but see Holley v. State, 9 Ala.App. 33, 63 So. 738.

ACT, *v.* In Scotch practice. To do or perform judicially; to enter of record. Surety "acted in the Books of Adjournal." 1 Broun, 4.

ACT, *n.* Denotes affirmative; expression of will, purpose; carries idea of performance; primarily that which is done or doing; exercise of power, or effect of which power exerted is cause; a performance; a deed. Brown v. Standard Casket Mfg. Co., 234 Ala. 512, 175 So. 358, 364.

In its most general sense, this noun signifies something done voluntarily by a person; the exercise of an individual's power; an effect produced in the external world by an exercise of the power of a person objectively, prompted by intention, and proximately caused by a motion of the will. Herman v. Pan American Life Ins. Co., 183 La. 1045, 165 So. 195, 200. In a more technical sense, it means something done voluntarily by a person, and of such a nature that certain legal consequences attach to it. Jefferson Standard Life Ins. Co. v. Myers, Tex.Com.App., 284 S.W. 216, 218. Thus a grantor acknowledges the conveyance to be his "*act* and deed," the terms being synonymous. It may denote something done by an individual, as a private citizen, or as an officer; or by a body of men, as a legislature, a council, or a court of justice; including not merely physical acts, but also decrees, edicts, laws, judgments, resolves, awards, and determinations. Some general laws made by the Congress of the United States are styled joint resolutions, and these have the same force and effect as those styled acts. But see Decher v. Vaughan, 209 Mich. 565, 177 N.W. 388, 392. Carries idea of performance. Edmonds v. Shirley, 22 Ala.App. 398, 116 So. 303.

An instrument in writing to verify facts. Webster, Dict.

It is used in this sense of the published acts of assembly, congress, etc. In a sense approaching this, it has been held in trials for treason that letters and other written documents were *acts;* 1 Fost.Cr.Cas. 198; 2 Stark. 116.

Act indicates the intention. 8 Co. 146*b*; Broom, Max. 301.

Civil Law

An *act* is a writing which states in a legal form that a thing has been said, done, or agreed. Merl. Répert.

Acts under private signature are those which have been made by private individuals under their hands.

Private acts are those made by private persons as registers in relation to their receipts and expenditures, schedules, acquittances, and the like.

Public acts are those which have a public authority, and which have been made before public officers, are authorized by a public seal, have been made public by the authority of a magistrate, or which have been extracted and been properly authenticated from public records.

Legislation

A written law, formally ordained or passed by the legislative power of a state, called in England an "act of parliament," and in the United States an "act of congress," or of the "legislature;" a statute. People v. Tiphaine, 3 Parker, Cr.R. (N.Y.) 241; United States v. Smith, 27 Fed.Cas. 1167.

The words *bill* and *law* are frequently used synonymously with *act*, People v. City of Buffalo, 161 N.Y.S. 706, 712, 175 App.Div. 218, but incorrectly; Sedgwick County Com'rs v. Bailey, 13 Kan. 600; a bill being only the draft or form of the act presented to the legislature but not enacted; Southwark Bank v. Com., 26 Pa. 446. "Act" does not include ordinances or regulations made by local authorities, or even statutes having only a local application; People v. City of Buffalo, 157 N.Y.S. 938, 940, 93 Misc. 275; although sometimes used interchangeably with "measure" and "law"; Whittemore v. Terral, 140 Ark. 493, 215 S.W. 686, 687. Generally, the word refers to entire statute enacted, rather than to a section. Board of Trustees of Firemen's Relief and Pension Fund of City of Muskogee v. Templeton, 184 Okl. 281, 86 P.2d 1000, 1002.

Acts are either public or private. Public acts (also called general acts, or general statutes, or statutes at large) are those which relate to the community generally, or establish a universal rule for the governance of the whole body politic. Private acts (formerly called special, Co. Litt. 126*a*) are those which relate either to particular persons (personal acts) or to particular places (local acts), or which operate only upon specified individuals or their private concerns. Unity v. Burrage, 103 U.S. 454, 26 L.Ed. 465. Public acts are those which concern the whole community and of which courts of law are bound to take judicial notice. Sasser v. Martin, 101 Ga. 447, 29 S.E. 278.

A "special" or "private" act is one operating only on particular persons and private concerns; a "local act" is one applicable only to a particular part of the legislative jurisdiction. Trumper v. School Dist. No. 55 of Musselshell County, 55 Mont. 90, 173 P. 946, 947.

To denote an avowal of criminal acts, or the concession of the truth of a criminal charge, the word "confession" seems more appropriate.

Practice

Anything done by a court and reduced to writing; a decree, judgment, resolve, rule, order, or other judicial proceeding. In Scotch law, the orders and decrees of a court, and in French and German law, all the records and documents in an action, are called "acts."

Scotch Practice

An abbreviation of *actor,* (proctor or advocate, especially for a plaintiff or pursuer,) used in records. *"Act.* A. *Alt.* B." an abbreviation of *Actor,* A. *Alter,* B.; that is, for the pursuer or plaintiff, A., for the defender, B. 1 Broun, 336, note.

ACT BOOK. In Scotch practice. The minute book of a court. 1 Swin. 81.

ACT IN PAIS. An act done out of court, and not a matter of record. A deed or an assurance transacted between two or more private persons in the country, that is, according to the old common law, upon the very spot to be transferred, is matter *in pais.* 2 Bl.Comm. 294.

ACT OF ATTAINDER. A legislative act, attainting a person. See Attainder.

ACT OF BANKRUPTCY. Any act which renders a person liable to be proceeded against as a bankrupt, or for which he may be adjudged bankrupt.

These acts are usually defined and classified in statutes on the subject. Duncan v. Landis, C.C.A.Pa., 106 Fed. 839, 45 C.C.A. 666; In re Chapman, D.C., 99 Fed. 395. Such as: insolvency or suffering or permitting a creditor to obtain a preference, Von Segerlund v. Dysart, C.C.A.Cal., 137 F.2d 755, 758, 761; appointment of a receiver, United States v. Emory, 62 S.Ct. 317, 319, 314 U.S. 423, 86 L.Ed. 315; hindering, delaying or defrauding creditors, In re Thompson, D.C.La., 28 F.Supp. 707, 710; failure to discharge a lien, In re Flushing Queensboro Laundry, C.C.A.N.Y., 90 F.2d 601. Permitting creditor to obtain any levy, attachment, judgment, or other lien, In re Day, D.C.Md., 22 F.Supp. 946, 949; assignment for benefit of creditors, In re Roy, D. C.N.H., 46 F.Supp. 952, 954; or a written admission of one's inability to pay his debts, In re Turner, D.C.Ky., 51 F. Supp. 740, 743.

ACT OF CURATORY. In Scotch law. The act extracted by the clerk, upon any one's acceptance of being curator. Forb.Inst. pt. 1, b. 1, c. 2, tit. 2. 2 Kames, Eq. 291. Corresponding with the order for the appointment of a guardian, in English and American practice.

ACT OF ELIZABETH. See Act of Supremacy.

ACT OF GOD. An act occasioned exclusively by violence of nature without the interference of any human agency. It means a natural necessity proceeding from physical causes alone without the intervention of man. It is an act, event, happening, or occurrence, a disaster and effect due to natural causes and inevitable accident, or disaster; a natural and inevitable necessity which implies entire exclusion of all human agency which operates without interference or aid from man and which results from natural causes and is in no sense attributable to human agency. It is an accident which could not have been occasioned by human agency but proceeded from physical causes alone. Short v. Kerr, 104 Ind.App. 118, 9 N.E.2d 114, 118.

In the civil law, *vis major.* Any misadventure or casualty is said to be caused by the "act of God" when it happens by the direct, immediate, and exclusive operation of the forces of nature, uncontrolled or uninfluenced by the power of man and without human intervention, and is of such a character that it could not have been prevented or escaped from by any amount of foresight or prudence, or by any reasonable degree of care or diligence, or by the aid of any appliances which the situation of the party might reasonably require him to use. Inevitable accident, or casualty; any accident produced by any physical cause which is irresistible, such as lightning, tempests, perils of the seas, an inundation, or earthquake; and also the sudden illness or death of persons. People v. Tubbs, 37 N.Y. 586; Central of Georgia Ry. Co. v. Hall, 124 Ga. 322, 52 S.E. 679, 4 L.R.A.,N.S., 898, 110 Am.St.Rep. 170, 4 Ann.Cas. 128. Story, Bailm. §§ 25, 511; 2 Bl.Comm. 122. Inevitable accident or casualty. Noel Bros. v. Texas & P. Ry. Co., 16 La.App. 622, 133 So. 830, 832; not preventable by human care, skill, or foresight, but resulting from natural causes, The Empress of France, D.C.N.Y., 49 F.2d 291. Misfortunes and accidents arising from inevitable necessity which human prudence could not foresee or prevent. Pleasure Beach Park Co. v. Bridgeport Dredge & Dock Co., 116 Conn. 496, 165 A. 691, 692. Limited, v. Lehigh Valley R. Co., D.C.N.Y., 254 F. 351, 353, a landside in the Panama Canal, Gans S. S. Line v. Wilhelmsen, C.C. A.N.Y., 275 F. 254, 261, and changes in the styles of wearing apparel, Rosenblatt v. Winstanley, Mo.App., 186 S.W. 542, 543, are not "acts of God"; otherwise, however, as to a strike, accompanied with violence and intimidation, see Southern Cotton Oil Co. v. Louisville & N. R. Co., 15 Ga.App. 751, 84 S.E. 198, 199.

The term is sometimes defined as equivalent to inevitable accident; Neal v. Saunderson, 2 Sm. & M. (Miss.) 572, 41 Am.Dec. 609; Central of Georgia Ry. Co. v. Council Bros., 36 Ga.App. 573, 137 S.E. 569, 570 (see, however, Cannon v. Hunt, 113 Ga. 509, 38 S.E. 983; Harmony Grove Telephone Co. v. Potts, 24 Ga.App. 178, 100 S.E. 236, but incorrectly, as there is a distinction between the two; Alaska Coast Co. v. Alaska Barge Co., 79 Wash. 216, 140 P. 334, 335. Bolton v. Burnett, 5 Blackf. (Ind.) 222.

See Inevitable Accident; Perils of the Sea.

ACT OF GOVERNMENT. The usual name of Cromwell's Constitution vesting the supreme power in a Protector and two houses of Parliament, passed March 25, 1657.

ACT OF GRACE. In Scotch law. A term applied to the act of 1696, c. 32, by which it was provided that where a person imprisoned for a civil debt is so poor that he cannot aliment [maintain] himself, and will make oath to that effect, it shall be in the power of the magistrates to cause the creditor by whom he is incarcerated to provide an aliment for him, or consent to his liberation; which, if the creditor delay to do for 10 days, the magistrate is authorized to set the debtor at liberty. Bell. The term is often used to designate a general act of parliament, originating with the crown, such as has often been passed at the commencement of a new reign, or the coming of age or marriage of a sovereign, or at the close of a period of civil troubles, declaring pardon or amnesty to numerous offenders. Abbott.

ACT OF HONOR. When a bill has been protested, and a third person wishes to take it up, or accept it, for honor of one or more of the parties, the notary draws up an instrument, evidencing the transaction, called by this name.

ACT OF INDEMNITY. A statute by which those who have committed illegal acts which subject them to penalties are protected from the consequences of such acts.

ACT OF INSOLVENCY. Within the meaning of the national currency act, an act which shows a bank to be insolvent, such as nonpayment of its circulating notes, bills of exchange, or certificates of deposit; failure to make good the impairment of capital, or to keep good its surplus or reserve; in fact, any act which shows that the bank is unable to meet its liabilities as they mature, or to perform those duties which the law imposes for the purpose of sustaining its credit. Hayden v. Chemical Nat. Bank, C.C.A.N.Y., 84 Fed. 874, 28 C.C.A. 548; Kullman & Co. v. Woolley, C.C.A. Miss., 83 F.2d 129, 132; Garvin v. Chadwick Realty Corporation, 212 Ind. 499, 9 N.E.2d 268, 271.

ACT OF LAW. The operation of fixed legal rules upon given facts or occurrences, producing consequences independent of the design or will of the parties concerned; as distinguished from "act of parties." Also an act performed by judicial authority which prevents or precludes a party from fulfilling a contract or other engagement. Metcalf v. State, 57 Okl. 64, 156 P. 305, 306, L.R.A. 1916E, 595.

ACT OF PARLIAMENT. A statute, law, or edict, made by the British sovereign, with the advice and consent of the lords spiritual and temporal, and the commons, in parliament assembled. Acts of parliament form the *leges scriptæ, i. e.*, the written laws of the kingdom.

ACT OF PROVIDENCE. An accident against which ordinary skill and foresight could not guard. McCoy v. Danley, 20 Pa. 91, 57 Am.Dec. 680. Equivalent to "act of God," see *supra*.

ACT OF SALE. In Louisiana law. An official record of a sale of property, made by a notary who writes down the agreement of the parties as stated by them, and which is then signed by the parties and attested by witnesses. Hodge v. Palms, Mich., 117 Fed. 396, 54 C.C.A. 570.

ACT OF SETTLEMENT. The statute (12 & 13 Wm. III, c. 2) limiting the crown to the Princess Sophia of Hanover, and to the heirs of her body being Protestants. 1 Bla.Com. 128; 2 Steph.Com. 290. One clause of it made the tenure of judges' office for life or good behavior independent of the crown.

ACT OF STATE. An act done by the sovereign power of a country, or by its delegate, within the limits of the power vested in him. An act of state cannot be questioned or made the subject of legal proceedings in a court of law.

ACT OF SUPREMACY. An act of 26 Hen. VIII. c. 1, and also 1 Eliz. c. 1, which recognized the king as the only supreme head on earth of the Church of England having full power to correct all errors, heresies, abuses, offenses, contempts and enormities. The oath, taken under the act, denies to the Pope any other authority than that of the Bishop of Rome.

ACT OF UNIFORMITY. In English law. The statute of 13 & 14 Car. II. c. 4, enacting that the book of common prayer, as then recently revised, should be used in every parish church and other place of public worship, and otherwise ordaining a uniformity in religious services, etc. 3 Steph. Comm. 104.

ACT OF UNION. The statutes uniting England and Wales, 27 Hen. VIII, c. 26, confirmed by 34 & 35 Hen. VIII, c. 26; England and Scotland, 5 Anne. c. 8; Great Britain and Ireland, 39 & 40 Geo. III, c. 67. 1 Bl.Comm. 97.

The act uniting the three lower counties (now Delaware) to the province of Pennsylvania, passed at Upland, Dec. 7, 1682, is so called.

ACT ON PETITION. A form of summary proceeding formerly in use in the high court of admiralty, in England, in which the parties stated their respective cases briefly, and supported their statements by affidavit. 2 Dod.Adm. 174, 184; 1 Hagg.Adm. 1, note.

ACTA DIURNA. Lat. In the Roman law. Daily acts or chronicles; the public registers or journals of the daily proceedings of the senate, assemblies of the people, courts of justice, etc. Supposed to have resembled a modern newspaper. Brande. Thus: I do not find the thing published in the *acta diurna* (daily records of affairs); Tacitus, Ann. 3, 3; Ainsworth, Lex.; Smith, Lex.

ACTA EXTERIORA INDICANT INTERIORA SECRETA. 8 Coke, 146*b*. External acts indicate undisclosed thoughts.

ACTA IN UNO JUDICIO NON PROBANT IN ALIO NISI INTER EASDEM PERSONAS. Things done in one action cannot be taken as evidence in another, unless it be between the same parties. Tray.Lat.Max. 11.

ACTA PUBLICA. Lat. Things of general knowledge and concern; matters transacted before certain public officers. Calvinus, Lex.

ACTE. In French law, denotes a document, or formal, solemn writing, embodying a legal attestation that something has been done, corresponding to one sense or use of the English word "act."

Actes de naissance are the certificates of birth, and must contain the day, hour, and place of birth, together with the sex and intended christian name of the child, and the names of the parents and of the witnesses. *Actes de mariage* are the marriage certificates, and contain names, professions, ages, and places of birth and domicile of the two persons marrying, and of their parents; also the consent of these latter, and the mutual agreements of the intended husband and wife to take each other for better and worse, together with the usual attestations. *Actes de décès* are the certificates of death, which are required to be drawn up before any one may be buried. *Les actes de l'état civil* are public documents. Brown.

ACTE AUTHENTIQUE. A deed executed with certain prescribed formalities, in the presence of a notary, mayor, *greffier, huissier,* or other functionary qualified to act in the place in which it is drawn up. Argles, Fr.Merc.Law, 50.

ACTE DE FRANCISATION. The certificate of registration of a ship, by virtue of which its French nationality is established.

ACTE D'HÉRITIER. Act of inheritance. Any action or fact on the part of an heir which manifests his intention to accept the succession; the acceptance may be express or tacit. Duverger.

ACTE EXTRAJUDICIAIRE. A document served by a *huissier,* at the demand of one party upon another party, without legal proceedings.

ACTING. The word "acting" means doing duty for another; officiating; holding a temporary rank or position or performing services temporarily; as, an acting captain, manager, president. Pellecchia v. Mattia, 121 N.J.L. 21, 1 A.2d 28. Performing; operating. See Meyer v. Johnston, 64 Ala. 603, 665.

An acting trustee is one who takes upon himself to perform some or all of the trusts mentioned in a will. Sharp v. Sharp, 2 Barn. & Ald. 415.

ACTING OFFICER. The phrase "acting officer" is used to designate, not an appointed incumbent, but merely a locum tenens, who is performing the duties of an office to which he himself does not claim title. State ex rel. Gossett v. O'Grady, 137 Neb. 824, 291 N.W. 497, 501; State Bank of Williams v. Gish, 167 Iowa, 526, 149 N.W. 600, 601.

"*Acting* Supervising Architect." Fraser v. United States, 16 Ct.Cl. 514. An acting executor is one who assumes to act as executor for a decedent, not being the executor legally appointed or the executor in fact. Morse v. Allen, 99 Mich. 303, 58 N.W. 327.

ACTIO. Lat. In the civil law. An action or suit; a right or cause of action. It should be noted that this term means both the proceeding to enforce a right in a court and the right itself which is sought to be enforced.

The first sense here given is the older one. Justinian, following Celsus, gives the well-known definition: *Actio nihil aliud est quam jus persequendi in judicio quod sibi debetur,* which may be thus rendered: An action is simply the *right* to enforce one's demands in a court of law. See Pollock, Expansion of C. L. 92.

ACTIO AD EXHIBENDUM. An action for the purpose of compelling a defendant to exhibit a thing or title in his power. It was preparatory to another action, which was always a real action in the sense of the Roman law; that is, for the recovery of a thing, whether it was movable or immovable. Merl.Quest.tome i, 84.

ACTIO ÆSTIMATORIA; ACTIO QUANTI MINORIS. Two names of an action which lay in behalf of a buyer to reduce the contract price proportionately to the defects of the object, not to cancel the sale; the *judex* had power, however, to cancel the sale. Hunter, Rom.Law, 332, 505.

ACTIO ARBITRARIA. Action depending on the discretion of the judge. In this, unless defendant would make amends to plaintiff as dictated by the judge in his discretion, he was liable to be condemned. Hunter, Rom.Law, 825, 987.

ACTIO BONÆ FIDEI. (Lat.: An action of good faith.) A class of actions in which the judge might at the trial *ex officio,* take into account any equitable circumstances that were presented to him affecting either of the parties to the action. 1 Spence, Eq.Jur. 210, 218.

ACTIO CALUMNIÆ. An action to restrain defendant from prosecuting a groundless proceeding or trumped-up charge against plaintiff. Hunter, Rom.Law, 859, 1020. An action for malicious prosecution. So.Afr.Leg.Dict.

ACTIO CIVILIS. In the common law. A civil action, as distinguished from a criminal action.

Bracton divides personal actions into *criminalia et civilia,* according as they grow out of crimes or contracts. Bract. fol. 101*b*. *Actiones civiles* are those forms of remedies which were established under the rigid system of the civil law, the *jus civilis.* See Actio Honoraria.

ACTIO COMMODATI. Included several actions appropriate to enforce the obligations of a borrower or a lender. Hunter, Rom.Law, 305.

ACTIO COMMODATI CONTRARIA. An action by the borrower against the lender, to compel the execution of the contract. Poth. *Prêt à Usage,* n. 75.

ACTIO COMMODATI DIRECTA. An action by a lender against a borrower, the principal object of which is to obtain a restitution of the thing lent. Poth. *Prêt à Usage,* nn. 65, 68.

ACTIO COMMUNI DIVIDUNDO. An action to procure a judicial division of joint property. Hunter, Rom.Law, 194. It was analogous in its object to proceedings for partition in modern law.

ACTIO CONDICTIO INDEBITATI. An action by which the plaintiff recovers the amount of a sum of money or other thing he paid by mistake. Poth. Promutuum, n. 140; Merl. Répert.

ACTIO CONFESSORIA. An affirmative petitory action for the recognition and enforcement of a servitude. So called because based on plaintiff's affirmative allegation of a right in defendant's land. Distinguished from an *actio negatoria,* which was brought to repel a claim of defendant to a servitude in plaintiff's land. Mackeld. Rom. Law, § 324.

ACTIO CONTRARIO. Counter action or cross action.

ACTIO CRIMINALIS. Criminal action.

ACTIO DAMNI INJURIA. The name of a general class of actions for damages, including many species of suits for losses caused by wrongful or negligent acts. The term is about equivalent to our "action for damages."

ACTIO DE DOLO MALO. An action of fraud; an action which lay for a defrauded person against the defrauder and his heirs, who had been enriched by the fraud, to obtain the restitution of the thing of which he had been fraudulently deprived, with all its accessions (*cum omni causa;*) or, where this was not practicable, for compensation in damages. Mackeld.Rom.Law, § 227.

ACTIO DE PECULIO. An action concerning or against the *peculium,* or separate property of a party.

ACTIO DE PECUNIA CONSTITUTA. An action for money engaged to be paid; an action which lay against any person who had engaged to pay money for himself, or for another without any formal stipulation. Inst. 4, 6, 9; Dig. 13, 5; Cod. 4, 18.

ACTIO DE TIGNO JUNCTO. An action by the the owner of material built by another into his building.

If so used in good faith double their value could be recovered; if in bad faith, the owner could recover suitable damage for the wrong, and recover the property when the building came down. So. Afr. Leg. Dict.

ACTIO DEPOSITI CONTRARIA. An action which the depositary has against the depositor, to compel him to fulfil his engagement towards him. Poth. *Du Dépôt,* n. 69.

ACTIO DEPOSITI DIRECTA. An action which is brought by the depositor against the depositary, in order to get back the thing deposited. Poth. *Du Dépôt,* n. 60.

ACTIO DIRECTA. A direct action; an action founded on strict law, and conducted according to fixed forms; an action founded on certain legal obligations which from their origin were accurately defined and recognized as actionable. See Actio Utilis.

ACTIO EMPTI. An action employed in behalf of a buyer to compel a seller to perform his obligations or pay compensation; also to enforce any special agreements by him, embodied in a contract of sale. Hunter, Rom.Law, 332, 505.

ACTIO EX CONDUCTO. An action which the bailor of a thing for hire may bring against the bailee, in order to compel him to redeliver the thing hired.

ACTIO EX CONTRACTU. In the civil and common law. An action of contract; an action arising out of, or founded on, contract. 3 Bl.Comm. 117.

ACTIO EX DELICTO. In the civil and common law. An action of tort; an action arising out of fault, misconduct, or malfeasance. Inst. 4, 6, 15; 3 Bl.Comm. 117. *Ex maleficio* is the more common expression of the civil law; which is adopted by Bracton. Inst. 4, 6, 1; Bract. fols. 102, 103.

ACTIO EX LOCATO. An action upon letting; an action which the person who let a thing for hire to another might have against the hirer. Dig. 19, 2; Cod. 4, 65.

ACTIO EX STIPULATU. An action brought to enforce a stipulation.

ACTIO EXERCITORIA. An action against the *exercitor* or employer of a vessel.

ACTIO FAMILIÆ ERCISCUNDÆ. An action for the partition of an inheritance. Inst. 4, 6, 20; Id. 4, 17, 4. Called, by Bracton and Fleta, a mixed action, and classed among actions arising *ex quasi contractu.* Brac. fol. 100*b*; Bract. fols. 443 *b*, 444; Fleta, lib. 2, c. 60, § 1.

ACTIO FURTI. An action of theft; an action founded upon theft. Inst. 4, 1, 13–17; Bract. fol. 444. This could be brought only for the penalty attached to the offense, and not to recover the thing stolen, for which other actions were provided. Inst. 4, 1, 19. An appeal of larceny. The old process by which a thief can be pursued and the goods vindicated. 2 Holdsw.Hist.Eng.L. 202.

ACTIO HONORARIA. An honorary, or prætorian action. Dig. 44, 7, 25, 35. *Actiones honorariæ* are those forms of remedies which were gradually introduced by the prætors and ædiles, by virtue of their equitable powers, in order to prevent the failure of justice which too often resulted from the employment of the *actiones civiles.* These were found so beneficial in practice that they eventually supplanted the old remedies, of which in the time of Justinian hardly a trace remained. Mackeldey, Civ.L. § 194; 5 Savigny, System.

ACTIO IN FACTUM. In action adapted to the particular case, having an analogy to some *actio in jus,* the latter being founded on some subsisting acknowledged law. 1 Spence, Eq.Jur. 212. The origin of these actions is similar to that of actions on the case at common law.

ACTIO IN PERSONAM.

Admiralty Law

An action directed against the particular person who is to be charged with the liability. It is distinguished from an *actio in rem,* which is a suit directed against a specific *thing* (as a vessel) irrespective of the ownership of it, to enforce a claim or lien upon it, or to obtain, out of the thing or out of the proceeds of its sale, satisfaction for an injury alleged by the claimant.

Civil Law

An action against the person, founded on a personal liability; an action seeking redress for the violation of a *jus in personam* or right available against a particular individual.

ACTIO IN REM. In the civil and common law. An action *for a thing;* an action for the recovery of a thing possessed by another. Inst. 4, 6, 1. An action for the enforcement of a right (or for redress for its invasion) which was originally available against all the world, and not in any special sense against the individual sued, until he violated it. See In Rem.

ACTIO JUDICATI. An action instituted, after four months had elapsed after the rendition of judgment, in which the judge issued his warrant to seize, first, the movables, which were sold within eight days afterwards; and then the immovables, which were delivered in pledge to the creditors, or put under the care of a curator, and if, at the end of two months, the debt was not paid, the land was sold. Dig. 42, 1; Cod. 8, 34.

According to some authorities, if the defendant then utterly denied the rendition of the former judgment, the plaintiff was driven to a new action, conducted like any other action, which was called *actio judicati,* and which had for its object the determination of the question whether such a judgment had been rendered. The exact meaning of the term is by no means clear. See Savigny, Syst. 305, 411; 3 Ortolan, Just. § 2033.

ACTIO LEGIS AQUILIÆ. An action under the Aquilian law; an action to recover damages for maliciously or injuriously killing or wounding the slave or beast of another, or injuring in any way a thing belonging to another. Otherwise called *damni injuriæ actio.*

ACTIO MANDATI. Included actions to enforce contracts of mandate or obligations arising out of them. Hunter, Rom.Law, 316.

ACTIO MIXTA. A mixed action; an action brought for the recovery of a thing, or compensation for damages, and also for the payment of a penalty: partaking of the nature both of an *actio in rem* and *in personam.* Inst. 4, 6, 16, 18, 19, 20; Mackeld.Rom.Law, § 209.

ACTIO NEGATORIA (or NEGATIVA). An action brought to repel a claim of the defendant to a servitude in the plaintiff's land. Mackeld.Rom. Law, § 324. See Actio Confessoria.

ACTIO NEGOTIORUM GESTORUM. Included actions between principal and agent and other parties to an engagement, whereby one person undertook the transaction of business for another.

ACTIO NON. In pleading. The Latin name of that part of a special plea which follows next after the statement of appearance and defense, and declares that the plaintiff "ought not to have or maintain his aforesaid action thereof against" the defendant (in Latin, *actionem non habere debet*). 1 Chit.Plead. 531; 2 *id.* 421; Stephens, Plead. 394.

ACTIO NON ACCREVIT INFRA SEX ANNOS. The name of the plea of the statute of limitations, when the defendant alleges that the plaintiff's action has not accrued within six years.

ACTIO NON DATUR NON DAMNIFICATO. An action is not given to one who is not injured. Jenk.Cent. 69.

ACTIO NON FACIT REUM, NISI MENS SIT REA. An act does not make one guilty, unless the intention be bad. Lofft, 37.

ACTIO NON ULTERIUS. In English pleading. A name given to the distinctive clause in the plea to the *further maintenance* of the action, introduced in place of the plea *puis darrein continuance;* the averment being that the plaintiff ought not *further (ulterius)* to have or maintain his action. Steph.Pl. 64, 65, 401.

ACTIO NOXALIS. A noxal action; an action which lay against a master for a crime committed or injury done by his slave; and in which the master had the alternative either to pay for the damage done or to deliver up the slave to the complaining party. Inst. 4, 8, pr.; Heinecc.Elem. lib. 4, tit. 8. So called from *noxa,* the offense or injury committed. Inst. 4, 8, 1.

ACTIO PERPETUA. An action without limitation period.

ACTIO PERSONALIS. In the civil and common law. A personal action.

The ordinary term for this kind of action in the civil law is *actio in personam, (q. v.,)* the word *personalis* being of only occasional occurrence. Inst. 4, 6, 8, *in tit.;* Id. 4, 11, pr. 1. Bracton, however, uses it freely, and hence the *personal action* of the common law. Bract. fols. 102*a,* 159*b.* See Action.

ACTIO PERSONALIS MORITUR CUM PERSONA. A personal right of action dies with the person. Noy, Max. 14.

The maxim was originally applied to almost every form of action, whether arising out of contract or tort, but the common law was modified by the Statute of 4 Edward the III. Momand v. Twentieth-Century Fox Film Corporation, D.C.Okl., 37 F.Supp. 649, 652.

ACTIO PIGNORATITIA. An action of pledge; an action founded on the contract of pledge (*pignus*). Dig. 13, 7; Cod. 4, 24.

ACTIO PŒNALIS. Called also *actio ex delicto.* An action in which a penalty was recovered of the delinquent.

Actiones pœnales and *actiones mixtæ* comprehended cases of injuries, for which the civil law permitted redress by private action, but which modern civilization universally regards as crimes; that is, offenses against society at large, and punished by proceedings in the name of the state alone. Thus, theft, receiving stolen goods, robbery, malicious mischief, and the murder or negligent homicide of a slave (in which case an injury to property was involved), gave rise to private actions for damages against the delinquent. Inst. 4, 1. *De obligationibus quæ ex delicto nascuntur; id.* 2. *De bonis vi raptis; id.* 3. *De lege Aquilia.* And see Mackeldey, Civ.L. § 196; 5 Savigny, System, § 210.

Actio pœnalis in hæredem non datur, nisi forte ex damno locupletior hæres factus sit. A penal action is not given against an heir, unless, indeed, such heir is benefited by the wrong.

ACTIO PRÆJUDICIALIS. A preliminary or preparatory action. An action instituted for the determination of some preliminary matter on which other litigated matters depend, or for the determination of some point or question arising in another or principal action; and so called from its being *determined before, (prius,* or *præ judicari.)*

ACTIO PRÆSCRIPTIS VERBIS. A form of action which derived its force from continued usage or the *responsa prudentium,* and was founded on the unwritten law. 1 Spence, Eq.Jur. 212. The distinction between this action and an *actio in factum* is said to be, that the latter was founded not on usage or the unwritten law, but by analogy to or on the equity of some subsisting law; 1 Spence, Eq.Jur. 212.

ACTIO PRÆTORIA. A prætorian action; one introduced by the prætor, as distinguished from the more ancient *actio civilis, (q. v.)* Inst. 4, 6, 3; Mackeld.Rom.Law, § 207.

ACTIO PRO SOCIO. An action of partnership. An action brought by one partner against his associates to compel them to carry out the terms of the partnership agreement. Story, Partn., Bennett ed. § 352; Pothier, Contr. de Société, n. 34.

ACTIO PUBLICIANA. An action which lay for one who had lost a thing of which he had *bona fide* obtained possession, before he had gained a property in it, in order to have it restored, under color that he had obtained a property in it by prescription. Inst. 4, 6, 4; Heinecc. Elem. lib. 4, tit. 6, § 1131; Halifax, Anal. b. 3, c. 1, n. 9. It was an honorary action, and derived its name from the prætor Publicius, by whose edict it was first given. Inst. 4, 6, 4.

ACTIO QUÆLIBET IT SUA VIA. Every action proceeds in its own way. Jenk.Cent. 77.

ACTIO QUOD JUSSU. An action given against a master, founded on some business done by his slave, acting under his *order, (jussu.)* Inst. 4, 7, 1; Dig. 15, 4; Cod. 4, 26.

ACTIO QUOD METUS CAUSA. An action granted to one who had been compelled by unlawful force, or fear *(metus causa)* that was not groundless, *(metus probabilis* or *justus,)* to deliver, sell, or promise a thing to another. Bract. fol. 103*b*; Mackeld.Rom.Law, § 226.

ACTIO REALIS. A real action. The proper term in the civil law was *rei vindicatio.* Inst. 4, 6, 3.

ACTIO REDHIBITORIA. An action to cancel a sale in consequence of defects in the thing sold.

It was prosecuted to compel complete restitution to the seller of the thing sold, with its produce and accessories, and to give the buyer back the price, with interest, as an equivalent for the restitution of the produce. Hunter, Rom.Law, 332. See Redhibitory Action.

ACTIO RERUM AMOTARUM. An action for things removed; an action which, in cases of divorce, lay for a husband against a wife, to recover things carried away by the latter, in contemplation of such divorce. Dig. 25, 2; Id. 25, 2, 25, 30. It also lay for the wife against the husband in such cases. Dig. 25, 2, 7, 11; Cod. 5, 21.

ACTIO RESCISSORIA. An action for restoring plaintiff to a right or title which he has lost by prescription, in a case where the equities are such that he should be relieved from the operation of the prescription. Mackeld.Rom.Law, § 226.

An action to rescind a prescriptive title by one who was entitled to exemption from the prescription law, as a minor, etc.

ACTIO SERVIANA. An action which lay for the lessor of a farm, or rural estate, to recover the goods of the lessee or farmer, which were pledged or bound for the rent. Inst. 4, 6, 7.

ACTIO STRICTI JURIS. An action of strict right. The class of civil law personal actions, which were adjudged only by the strict law, and in which the judge was limited to the precise language of the formula, and had no discretionary power to regard the *bona fides* of the transaction. See Inst. 4, 6, 28; Gaius, iii. 137; Mackeld. Rom.Law, § 210; 1 Spence, Eq.Jur. 218.

ACTIO TEMPORALIS. An action which must be brought within a limited time. See **Limitation.**

ACTIO TUTELÆ. Action founded on the duties or obligations arising on the relation analogous to that of guardian and ward.

ACTIO UTILIS. A beneficial action or equitable action. An action founded on equity instead of strict law, and available for those who had equitable rights or the beneficial ownership of property.

Actions are divided into *actiones directæ* or *utiles.* The former are founded on certain legal obligations which from their origin were accurately defined and recognized as actionable. The latter were formed analogically in imitation of the former. They were permitted in legal obligations for which the *actiones directæ* were not originally intended, but which resembled the legal obligations which formed the basis of the direct action. Mackeld.Rom.Law, § 207.

ACTIO VENDITI. An action employed in behalf of a seller, to compel a buyer to pay the price, or perform any special obligations embodied in a contract of sale. Hunter, Rom.Law, 332.

ACTIO VI BONORUM RAPTORUM. An action for goods taken by force; a species of mixed action, which lay for a party whose goods or movables *(bona)* had been taken from him by force, (*vi,*) to recover the things so taken, together with a penalty of triple the value. Inst. 4, 2; Inst. 4, 6, 19. Bracton describes it as lying *de rebus mobilibus vi ablatis sive robbatis,* (for movable things taken away by force, or robbed.) Brac. fol. 103*b*.

ACTIO VULGARIS. A legal action; a common action. Sometimes used for *actio directa*. Mackeld.Rom.Law, § 207.

ACTION. Conduct; behavior; something done; the condition of acting; an act or series of acts.

French Commercial Law

Stock in a company, or shares in a corporation.

Practice

The legal and formal demand of one's right from another person or party made and insisted on in a court of justice. Smith-Webster Co. v. John, C.C.A.Pa., 259 F. 549, 551; Dinsmore v. Barker, 61 Utah, 332, 212 P. 1109; Shaw v. Lone Star Building & Loan Ass'n, Tex.Civ.App., 40 S.W. 2d 968, 969. Pursuit of right in court, without regard to form of procedure. Ginzberg v. Wyman, 272 Mass. 499, 172 N.E. 614, 615. Form of suit given by law for recovery of that which is one's due. Co.Litt. 284*b*, 285*a*; Peterson v. A. Guthrie & Co., D.C.Wash., 3 F.Supp. 136, 138. Judicial means of enforcing a right. Code Ga. 1882, § 3151 (Civ.Code 1926, § 5507). Judicial remedy for the enforcement or protection of a right. White v. White, 98 Ind.App. 587, 186 N.E. 349, 351.

An ordinary proceeding in a court of justice by which one party prosecutes another for the enforcement or protection of a right, the redress or prevention of a wrong, or the punishment of a public offense. Code Civ.Proc.S.D.1903, § 12 (Comp.Laws 1929, § 2091); Missionary Soc. v. Ely, 47 N.E. 537, 56 Ohio St. 405.

Cross-action, White v. St. Louis Post Offices Corporation, 348 Mo. 961, 156 S.W.2d 695, 698, and counterclaim, Webster v. Freeman, 27 Cal.App.2d 5, 80 P.2d 497, 499, are actions but not set off, Kress v. Central Trust Co. of Rochester, 283 N.Y.S. 467, 471, 246 App.Div. 76.

It includes all the formal proceedings in a court of justice attendant upon the demand of a right made by one person of another in such court, including an adjudication upon the right and its enforcement or denial by the court.

Proceedings held actions: Disbarment, In re Wilcox, 90 Kan. 646, 135 P. 995; probating will, Simpson v. Simpson, 273 Ill. 90, 112 N.E. 276, 277; will contest, Byrne v. Byrne, Mo.Sup., 181 S.W. 391, 392; workmen's compensation, Pigeon v. Employers' Liability Assur. Corporation, 216 Mass. 51, 102 N.E. 932, 935, Ann.Cas.1915A, 737; criminal prosecution, Mason v. U. S., C.C.A.Ill., 1 F.2d 279, 280; mandamus, People v. Lueders, 287 Ill. 107, 122 N.E. 374, 375; naturalization, In re Fordiani, 98 Conn. 435, 120 A. 338, 341.

Proceedings held not actions: attachment, State v. Superior Court of Spokane County, 110 Wash. 49, 187 P. 708; arbitration, Temple v. Riverland Co., Tex.Civ.App., 228 S. W. 605, 609; criminal prosecution, U. S. v. Cleveland, D.C. Ala., 281 F. 249, 253; Wynn v. Commonwealth, 198 Ky. 644, 249 S.W. 783, 784; writ of citation, McClelland v. State, 101 Ohio St. 42, 127 N.E. 409, 410; certiorari, Campbell, v. Common Council of City of Watertown, 46 S.D. 574, 195 N.W. 442; mandamus, De Leyer v. Britt, 212 N.Y. 565, 106 N.E. 57; child's support, Head v. Fuller, 122 Me. 15, 118 A. 714, 715; drainage, Richardson County v. Drainage Dist. No. 2 of Richardson County, 96 Neb. 169, 147 N.W. 205, 206; condemnation, State v. Superior Court for Ferry County, 145 Wash. 576, 261 P. 110, 111.

Scotch Law

A suit or judicial proceeding.

Suit Distinguished

Strictly applied, action does not usually refer to chancery practice. City of Beckley v. Craighead, 125 W.Va. 484, 24 S.E.2d 908, 911. But terms "action" and "suit" are now nearly, if not entirely, synonymous. (3 Bl.Comm. 3, 116, et passim.) Elmo v. James, Tex.Civ.App., 282 S.W. 835, 839; Coleman v. Los Angeles County, 180 Cal. 714, 182 P. 440. Or, if there be a distinction, it is that the term "action" is generally confined to proceedings in a court of law, while "suit" is equally applied to prosecutions at law or in equity. McBride v. University Club, 112 Ohio St. 69, 146 N.E. 804, 805; Guarantee Trust & Banking Co. v. Dickson, 148 Ga. 311, 96 S.E. 561, 562; Niantic Mills Co. v. Riverside & O. Mills, 19 R.I. 34, 31 A. 432; Ulshafer v. Stewart, 71 Pa. 170. Formerly, however, an *action* was considered as terminating with the giving of judgment, the execution forming no part of it. (Litt. § 504; Co.Litt. 289*a*.) A *suit* included the execution. (Litt. § 291*a*.) So, an action is termed by Lord Coke, "the *right* of a *suit*." (2 Inst. 40.) Burrill.

Types of Actions

Actions are called, in common-law practice, *ex contractu* when they are founded on a contract; *ex delicto* when they arise out of a tort. Nelson v. Great Northern R. Co., 28 Mont. 297, 72 Pac. 642; Van Oss v. Synon, 85 Wis. 661, 56 N.W. 190.

If a cause of action arises from a breach of promise, the action is "ex contractu," and, if it arises from breach of duty growing out of contract, it is "ex delicto." Tort or trespass is none the less such because it incidentally involves breach of contract. Berning v. Colodny & Colodny, 103 Cal.App. 188, 284 P. 496, 498.

As to class or representative actions. See Class Or Representative Action.

As to the distinction between a *revocatory action* and an *action in simulation,* see Chapman v. Irwin, 157 La. 920, 103 So. 263, 265.

Civil actions are such as lie in behalf of persons to enforce their rights or obtain redress of wrongs in their relation to individuals.

Common law actions are such as will lie, on the particular facts, at common law, without the aid of a statute.

Criminal actions are such as are instituted by the sovereign power, for the purpose of punishing or preventing offenses against the public.

Local action. See Local Action.

Mixed actions partake of twofold nature of real and personal actions, having for their object the demand and restitution of real property and also personal damages for a wrong sustained. 3 Bl.Comm. 118; Hall v. Decker, 48 Me. 257. Mixed actions are those which are brought for the specific recovery of lands, like real actions, but comprise, joined with this claim, one for damages in respect of such property; such as the action of waste, where, in addition to the recovery of the place wasted, the demandant claims damages; the writ of entry, in which, by statute, a demand of mesne profits may be joined; and dower, in which a claim for detention may be included. 48 Me. 255. In the civil law, an action in which some specific thing was demanded, and also some personal obligation claimed to be performed; or, in other words, an action which proceeded both *in rem* and *in personam*. Inst. 4, 6, 20.

Penal actions are such as are brougnt, either by the state or by an individual under permission of a statute, to enforce a penalty imposed by law for the commission of a prohibited act.

Personal action. In civil law, an action *in personam*. It seeks to enforce an obligation imposed on the defendant by his contract or delict; that is, it is the contention that he is bound to transfer some dominion or to perform some service or to repair some loss. Gaius, bk. 4, § 2. In common law. An action brought for the recovery of some debt or for damages for some personal injury, in contradistinction to the old real actions, which related to real property only. See 3 Bl.Comm. 117. Boyd v. Cronan, 71 Me. 286; Doe v. Waterloo Min. Co., C.C.Cal., 43 F. 219; Osborn v. Fall River, 140 Mass. 508, 5 N.E. 483. An action which can be brought only by the person himself who is injured, and not by his representatives.

Popular actions, in English usage, are those actions which are given upon the breach of a penal statute, and which any man that will may sue on account of the king and himself, as the statute allows and the case requires. Because the action is not given to one especially, but generally to any that will prosecute, it is called "action popular;" and, from the words used in the process, *(qui tam pro domino rege sequitur quam pro se ipso,* who sues as well for the king as for himself,) it is called a *qui tam* action. Tomlins.

Real actions. At common law, one brought for the specific recovery of lands, tenements, or hereditaments. Steph.Pl. 3; Crocker v. Black, 16 Mass. 448; Hall v. Decker, 48 Me. 256; Doe v. Waterloo Min. Co., C.C.Cal., 43 F. 220; Mathews v. Sniggs, 75 Okl. 108, 182 P. 703, 708. They are *droitural* when they are based upon the right of property, and *possessory* when based upon the right of possession. They are either writs of right; writs of entry upon disseisin (which lie in the per, the per et cui, or the post), intrusion, or alienation; writs ancestral possessory, as mort d'ancestor, aiel, besaiel, cossinage, or nuper obiit. Com.Dig. *Actions* (D 2). The former class was divided into *droitural,* founded upon demandant's own seisin, and *ancestral droitural* upon the demandant's claim in respect of a mere right descended to him from an ancestor. Possessory actions were divided in the same way—as to the demandant's own seisin and as to that of his ancestor. Among the civilians, real actions, otherwise called "vindications," were those in which a man demanded something that was his own. They were founded on dominion, or *jus in re*. The real actions of the Roman law were not, like the real actions of the common law, confined to real estate, but they included personal, as well as real, property. Wharton.

Statutory actions are such as can only be based upon the particular statutes creating them.

Transitory actions are those founded upon a cause of action not necessarily referring to or arising in any particular locality. Their characteristic feature is that the right of action follows the person of the defendant. Brown v. Brown, 155 Tenn. 530, 296 S.W. 356, 358. Actions are "transitory" when the transactions relied on might have taken place anywhere, and are "local" when they could not occur except in some particular place; the distinction being in the nature of the subject of the injury, and not in the means used or the place at which the cause of action arises. Brady v. Brady, 161 N.C. 324, 77 S.E. 235, 236, 44 L.R.A.,N.S., 279; Taylor v. Sommers Bros. Match Co., 35 Idaho, 30, 204 P. 472, 474, 42 A.L.R. 189. The test of whether an action is local or transitory is whether the injury is done to a subject-matter which, in its nature, could not arise beyond the locality of its situation, in contradistinction to the subject causing the injury. Mattix v. Swepston, 127 Tenn. 693, 155 S.W. 928, 929. Actions triable where defendant resides are termed "transitory" and those triable where the subject-matter is situated are termed "local." State v. District Court of Swift County, 164 Minn. 433, 205 N.W. 284, 285.

See Cause of Action.

ACTION EX CONTRACTU. An action for breach of promise set forth in a contract, express or implied. Bristol v. Sun Vacuum Stores, 181 Misc. 522, 42 N.Y.S.2d 501, 504; McCullough v. The American Workmen, 200 S.C. 84, 20 S.E.2d 640, 644.

ACTION EX DELICTO. An action arising from a breach of duty growing out of contract. Berning v. Colodny & Colodny, 103 Cal.App. 188, 284 P. 496, 498; Federal Life Ins. Co. v. Maxam, 70 Ind.App. 266, 117 N.E. 801, 806.

ACTION FOR ACCOUNTING. Action in equity based on inadequacy of legal remedy and particularly applicable to mutual and complicated accounts and where confidential or fiduciary relationship exists. Dahlberg v. Fisse, 328 Mo. 213, 40 S.W.2d 606, 609. To adjust mutual accounts and to strike a balance. Cline v. McKee, 186 Okl. 366, 98 P.2d 25, 27.

ACTION FOR MONEY HAD AND RECEIVED. One in assumpsit based upon promise to repay implied by law, and in respect of limitation is a stated or liquidated account. Mutual Building & Loan Ass'n v. Watson, 226 Ala. 526, 147 So. 817, 818.

Where one person has received money or its equivalent under such circumstances that in equity and good conscience he ought not to retain it and in justice it belongs to another. Interstate Life & Accident Co. v. Cook, 19 Tenn.App. 290, 86 S.W.2d 887, 891.

ACTION FOR POINDING. An action by a creditor to obtain a sequestration of the rents of land and the goods of his debtor for the satisfaction of the debt, or to enforce a distress.

ACTION IN PERSONAM, IN REM. See In Personam, In Rem.

ACTION OF ABSTRACTED MULTURES. An action for multures or tolls against those who are thirled to a mill, *i. e.*, bound to grind their corn at a certain mill, and fail to do so. Bell.

ACTION OF ADHERENCE. See Adherence.

ACTION OF A WRIT. A phrase used when a defendant pleads some matter by which he shows that the plaintiff had no cause to have the writ sued upon, although it may be that he is entitled to another writ or action for the same matter. Cowell.

ACTION OF ASSIZE. A real action which proves the title of the demandant, merely by showing his ancestor's possession. Sherman v. Dilley, 3 Nev. 21, 26, citing 5 Chit.Bl. 184.

ACTION OF ASSUMPSIT. See Assumpsit.

ACTION OF BOOK DEBT. A form of action for the recovery of claims, such as are usually evidenced by a book-account; this action is principally used in Vermont and Connecticut. Newton v. Higgins, 2 Vt. 366.

ACTION ON CONTRACT. An action brought to enforce rights whereof the contract is the evidence, and usually the sufficient evidence. Kokusai Kisen Kabushiki Kaisha v. Argos Mercantile Corporation, C.C.A.N.Y., 280 F. 700, 701.

ACTION ON THE CASE. A species of personal action of very extensive application, otherwise called "trespass on the case," or simply "case," from the circumstance of the plaintiff's whole *case or cause of complaint* being set forth at length in the original writ by which formerly it was always commenced. 3 Bl.Comm. 122. Wallace v. Wilmington & N. R. Co., 8 Houst. (Del.) 529, 18 A. 818.

In its most comprehensive signification it includes *assumpsit* as well as an action in form *ex delicto;* at present when it is mentioned it is usually understood to mean an action in form *ex delicto.* It is founded on the common law or upon acts of Parliament, and lies generally to recover damages for torts not committed with force, actual or implied; or having been occasioned by force where the matter affected was not tangible, or the injury was not immediate but consequential; or where the interest in the property was only in reversion, in all of which cases trespass is not sustainable; 1 Chit.Pl. 132. In the progress of judicial contestation it was discovered that there was a mass of tortious wrongs unattended by direct and immediate force, or where the force, though direct, was not expended on an existing right of present enjoyment, for which the then known forms of action furnished no redress. The action on the case was instituted to meet this want. And wrongs which will maintain an action on the case are frequently committed in the nonobservance of duties, which are but the implication of contract obligation, duties of requisite skill, fidelity, diligence, and a proper regard for the rights of others, implied in every obligation to serve another. If the cause of action arises from a breach of promise, the action is "ex contractu"; but if the cause of action arises from a breach of duty growing out of the contract, it is in form ex delicto and case. When there is a contract, either express or implied, from which a common-law duty results, an action on the case lies for the breach of that duty. Bently-Beale, Inc. v. Wesson Oil & Snowdrift Sales Co., 231 Ala. 562, 165 So. 830, 832. See Assumpsit.

ACTION QUASI IN REM. An action brought against persons which only seeks to subject certain property of those persons to discharge of claims asserted and judgment therein is only conclusive between parties and their privies. Tobin v. McClellan, 225 Ind. 335, 75 N.E.2d 149, 151.

ACTION REDHIBITORY. See Redhibitory Action.

ACTION TO QUIET TITLE. One in which plaintiff asserts his own estate and declares generally that defendant claims some estate in the land, without defining it, and avers that the claim is without foundation, and calls on defendant to set forth the nature of his claim, so that it may be determined by decree.

It differs from a "suit to remove a cloud," in that plaintiff therein declares on his own title, and also avers the source and nature of defendant's claim, points out its defect, and prays that it may be declared void as a cloud on plaintiff's estate. Manning v. Gregoire, 97 Or. 394, 192 P. 406, 407. The apparent difference between an action to restore a lost instrument and one to quiet title is that, in the former, ordinarily both the titles of plaintiff and defendant are deraigned in the complaint, which must disclose that, notwithstanding an apparent interest of defendant the property belongs to plaintiff; and in the latter action the complaint need only allege the ultimate fact of plaintiff's interest and defendant's outstanding claim. Nicholson v. Nicholson, 67 Mont. 517, 216 P. 328, 329, 31 A.L.R. 548. See, also, Slette v. Review Pub. Co., 71 Mont. 518, 230 P. 580, 581. It embraces every sort of a claim whereby the plaintiff might be deprived of his property or his title clouded or its value depreciated, or whereby the plaintiff might be incommoded or damnified by assertion of an outstanding title already held or to grow out of the adverse pretension. Bank of American Nat. Trust & Savings Ass'n v. Town of Atherton, 60 Cal.App.2d 268, 140 P.2d 678, 680.

ACTIONABLE. That for which an action will lie, furnishing legal ground for an action.

ACTIONABLE FRAUD. Deception practiced in order to induce another to part with property or surrender some legal right; a false representation made with an intention to deceive; may be committed by stating what is known to be false or by professing knowledge of the truth of a statement which is false, but in either case, the essential ingredient is a falsehood uttered with intent to deceive. Sawyer v. Prickett, 19 Wall. 146, 22 L. Ed. 105.

To constitute "actionable fraud," it must appear that defendant made a material representation; that it was false; that when he made it he knew it was false, or made it recklessly without any knowledge of its truth and as a positive assertion; that he made it with intention that it should be acted on by plaintiff; that plaintiff acted in reliance on it; and that plaintiff thereby suffered injury. Blair v. McCool, 136 Or. 139, 295 P. 950, 952. Essential elements are representation, falsity, scienter, deception, and injury. Cobb v. Cobb, 211 N.C. 146, 189 S.E. 479, 482.

ACTIONABLE MISREPRESENTATION. A false statement respecting a fact material to the contract and which is influential in procuring it. Wise v. Fuller, 29 N.J.Eq. 257.

ACTIONABLE NEGLIGENCE. The breach or nonperformance of a legal duty, through neglect or carelessness, resulting in damage or injury to another. Fidelity & Casualty Co. v. Cutts, 95 Me. 162, 49 Atl. 673.

It is failure of duty, omission of something which ought to have been done, or doing of something which ought not to have been done, or which reasonable man, guided by considerations which ordinarily regulate conduct of human affairs, would or would not do. Goff v. Emde, 32 Ohio App. 216, 167 N.E. 699, 700. Essential elements are failure to exercise due care, injury, or damage, and proximate cause. Rountree v. Fountain, 203 N.C. 381, 166 S.E. 329, 330.

ACTIONABLE NUISANCE. Anything wrongfully done or permitted which injures or annoys another in the enjoyment of his legal rights. Miller v. City of Dayton, 70 Ohio App. 173, 41 N.E.2d 728, 730.

Anything injurious to health, or indecent, or offensive to the senses, or an obstruction to the free use of property so as to interfere with the comfortable enjoyment of life or property. Cooper v. Overton, 102 Tenn. 211, 52 S.W. 183, 45 L.R.A. 591.

ACTIONABLE TORT. To constitute an "actionable tort," there must be a legal duty, imposed by statute or otherwise, owing by defendant to the one injured, and in the absence of such duty damage caused is "injury without wrong" or "damnum absque injuria." Coleman v. California Yearly Meeting of Friends Church, 27 Cal.App.2d 579, 81 P.2d 469, 470.

ACTIONABLE WORDS. In law of libel and slander, such words as naturally imply damage. Dahm v. O'Connell, 161 N.Y.S. 909, 911, 96 Misc. 582.

Per Quod

Words actionable only on allegation and proof of special damage. Knapp v. Post Printing & Publishing Co., 111 Colo. 492, 144 P.2d 981, 984.

Words not actionable per se upon their face, but only in consequence of extrinsic facts showing circumstances under which they were said or the damages resulting to slandered party therefrom. Smith v. Mustain, 210 Ky. 445, 276 S.W. 154, 155, 44 A.L.R. 386. Not injurious on their face in their usual and natural signification, but only so in consequence of extrinsic facts and requiring innuendo. Piplack v. Mueller, 97 Fla. 440, 121 So. 459.

Per Se

Words in themselves libelous. Knapp v. Post Printing & Publishing Co., 111 Colo. 492, 144 P.2d 981, 984.

Words which law presumes must actually, proximately, and necessarily damage defendant for which general damages are recoverable and whose injurious character is a fact of common notoriety, established by the general consent of men, necessarily importing damage. Ellsworth v. Martindale-Hubbell Law Directory, 66 N.D. 578, 268 N.W. 400, 407. Words themselves opprobrious; susceptible only of opprobrious meaning. Fite v. Oklahoma Pub. Co., 146 Okl. 150, 293 P. 1073, 1075. Importing a charge of some punishable crime or some offensive disease, imputing moral turpitude, or tending to injure a party in his trade or business. Barnes v. Trundy, 31 Me. 321; Lemons v. Wells, 78 Ky. 117; Mayrant v. Richardson, 1 Nott & McC. 347, 9 Am.Dec. 707. Tending to injure one's reputation, thereby exposing him to public hatred, contempt or ridicule, tending to degrade or lower him. Hodges v. Cunningham, 160 Miss. 576, 135 So. 215, 217. Such words are actionable without allegation of special damages. Kluender v. Semann, 203 Iowa 68, 212 N.W. 326, 327. See also Libelous per se.

ACTIONABLE WRONG. Committed when a responsible person has neglected to use a reasonable degree of care for protection of another person from such injury as under existing circumstances should reasonably have been foreseen as a proximate consequence of that negligence. Chadwick v. Bush, 174 Miss. 75, 163 So. 823, 824.

ACTIONARE. L. Lat. (From *actio,* an action.) In old records. To bring an action; to prosecute, or sue. Thorn's Chron.; Whishaw.

ACTIONARY. A foreign commercial term for the proprietor of an *action* or share of a public company's stock; a stockholder.

ACTIONES LEGIS. In the Roman law, legal or lawful action; actions of or at law,) *legitimæ actiones.*) Dig. 1, 2, 2, 6.

ACTIONES NOMINATÆ. (Lat. named actions). In the English chancery, writs for which there were precedents. The statute of Westminster, 2, c. 24, gave chancery authority to form new writs *in consimili casu;* hence the action on the case.

ACTIONS. (Fr.) Shares of corporate stock. Compare Actionary.

ACTIONS ORDINARY. In Scotch law, all actions which are not rescissory. Ersk.Inst. 4, 1, 18.

ACTIONS RESCISSORY. In Scotch law, these are either (1) actions of proper improbation for declaring a writing false or forged; (2) actions of reduction-improbation for the production of a writing in order to have it set aside or its effect ascertained under the certification that the writing if not produced shall be declared false or forged; and (3) actions of simple reduction, for declaring a writing called for null until produced. Ersk.Princ. 4, 1, 5.

ACTIONUM GENERA MAXIME SUNT SERVANDA. The kinds of actions are especially to be preserved. Lofft 460.

ACTIVE. That is in action; that demands action; actually subsisting; the opposite of passive. An active debt is one which draws interest. An active trust is a confidence connected with a duty. An active use is a present legal estate.

ACTIVE CONCEALMENT. This implies a purpose or design accomplished by words or acts, while passive concealment consists in mere silence where there is a duty to speak. Vendt v. Duenke, Mo.App., 210 S.W.2d 692, 699.

Concealment becomes a fraud where it is effected by misleading and deceptive talk, acts, or conduct, where it is accompanied by misrepresentations, or where, in addition to a party's silence, there is any statement, word, or act on his part which tends affirmatively to a suppression of the truth. Such conduct is designated active concealment. Equitable Life Ins. Co. of Iowa v. Halsey, Stuart & Co., C.C.A.Ill., 112 F.2d 302, 309.

ACTIVE NEGLIGENCE. A term of extensive meaning obviously embracing many occurrences that would fall short of willful wrongdoing, or of crass negligence, for example, all inadvertent acts causing injury to others, resulting from failure to exercise ordinary care, likewise all acts the effects of which are misjudged or unforeseen, through want of proper attention, or reflection, and hence the term covers the acts of willful wrongdoing and also those which are not of that character. Cohen v. Noel, Tenn.App., 104 S.W.2d 1001, 1005.

ACTIVE SERVICE. "Active service" in army does not necessarily mean actual service, but means service performed at direction of superior officer or officers while receiving emoluments to which soldier is entitled. United States v. Woodworth, D.C.Mass., 36 F.Supp. 645, 646.

ACTIVE TRUST. See Trust.

ACTIVITY. A recreational "activity" is a physical or gymnastic exercise, an agile performance, such as dancing. McClure v. Board of Education of City of Visalia, 38 Cal.App. 500, 176 P. 711, 712.

ACTON BURNEL, STATUTE OF. In English law, a statute, otherwise called *Statutum Mercatorum* or *de Mercatoribus* the statute of the merchants, made at a parliament held at the castle or village of Acton Burnel in Shropshire, in the 11th year of the reign of Edward I. 2 Reeves, Eng. Law, 158–162. It was a statute for the collection of debts, the earliest of its class, being enacted in 1283. A further statute for the same object, and known as De Mercatoribus, was enacted 13 Edw. I. (c. 3.). See Statute Merchant.

ACTOR.

Old European Law

A patron, proctor, advocate, or pleader; one who acted for another in legal matters; one who represented a party and managed his cause. An attorney, bailiff, or steward; one who managed or acted for another. The Scotch "doer" is the literal translation.

Roman Law

One who acted for another; one who attended to another's business; a manager or agent. A slave who attended to, transacted, or superintended his master's business or affairs, received and paid out moneys, and kept accounts. Burrill.

The word has a variety of closely-related meanings, very nearly corresponding with manager. Thus, *actor dominæ*, manager of his master's farm; *actor ecclesiæ*, manager of church property; *actores provinciarum*, tax-gatherers, treasurers, and managers of the public debt.

Actor ecclesiæ.—An advocate for a church; one who protects the temporal interests of a church. *Actor villæ* was the steward or head-bailiff of a town or village. Cowell.

Plaintiff or complainant. In a civil or private action the plaintiff was often called by the Romans *"petitor;"* in a public action *(causa publica)* he was called *"accusator."* The defendant was called *"reus,"* both in private and public causes; this term, however, according to Cicero, (*De Orat.* ii. 43,) might signify either party, as indeed we might conclude from the word itself. In a private action, the defendant was often called *"adversarius,"* but either party might be called so.

Also, the term is used of a party who, for the time being, sustains the burden of proof, or has the initiative in the suit.

Actor qui contra regulam quid adduxit, non est audiendus. A plaintiff (or pleader) is not to be heard who has advanced anything against authority, (or against the rule.)

Actor sequitur forum rei. According as *rei* is intended as the genitive of *res*, a thing, or *reus*, a defendant, this phrase means: The plaintiff follows the forum of the property in suit, or the forum of the defendant's residence. Branch, Max. 4. Home, Law Tr. 232; Story, Confl.L. § 325 *k*; 2 Kent 462.

ACTORE NON PROBANTE REUS ABSOLVITUR. When the plaintiff does not prove his case the defendant is acquitted (or absolved). Hob. 103.

ACTORI INCUMBIT ONUS PROBANDI. The burden of proof rests on the plaintiff, (or on the party who advances a proposition affirmatively.) Hob. 103.

ACTORNAY. In old Scotch law, an attorney. Skene.

ACTRIX. Lat. A female actor; a female plaintiff. Calvinus, Lex.

ACTS OF COURT. Legal memoranda made in the admiralty courts in England, in the nature of pleas.

ACTS OF POSSESSION. To constitute adverse possession, acts of possession must be such as, if seen by the party whose claim is sought to be divested, would apprise him that the party doing the acts claimed the ownership of the property. Crosby v. City of Greenville, 183 Mich. 452, 150 N.W. 246, 248.

ACTS OF SEDERUNT. In Scotch law, ordinances for regulating the forms of proceeding, before the court of session, in the administration of justice, made by the judges, who have the power by virtue of a Scotch act of parliament passed in 1540. Ersk. Prin. § 14.

ACTUAL. Real; substantial; existing presently in act, having a valid objective existence as opposed to that which is merely theoretical or possible. Ciaccio v. Hartman, 170 La. 949, 129 So. 540. Opposed to potential, possible, virtual, conceivable, theoretical, hypothetical, or nominal. American Ins. Co. of Newark, N. J., v. Seminole County Board of Education, 51 Ga.App. 808, 181 S.E. 783, 786. Something real, in opposition to constructive or speculative; something existing in act. Astor v. Merritt, 4 S.Ct. 413, 111 U.S. 202, 28 L. Ed. 401. Existing in act, fact, or reality. Guarisco v. Massachusetts Bonding & Insurance Co., 4 N.Y.S.2d 788, 792, 167 Misc. 875.

It is used as a legal term in contradistinction to virtual or constructive as of possession or occupation; Cleveland v. Crawford, 7 Hun (N.Y.) 616; or an actual settler, which implies actual residence; McIntyre v. Sherwood, 82 Cal. 139, 22 Pac. 937. An actual seizure means nothing more than seizure, since there was no fiction of constructive seizure before the act; L.R. 6 Exch. 203.

Actually is opposed to seemingly, pretendedly, or feignedly, as *actually engaged in farming* means really, truly, in fact; In re Strawbridge & Mays, 39 Ala. 367; Ayer & Lord Tie Co. v. Commonwealth, 208 Ky. 606, 271 S.W. 693, 694.

As to actual "Bias," "Damages," "Delivery," "Fraud," "Malice," "Notice," "Occupation," "Ouster," "Possession," "Residence," "Seisin," "Total Loss," see those titles.

ACTUAL AUTHORITY. In the law of agency, such authority as a principal intentionally confers on the agent, or intentionally or by want of ordinary care allows the agent to believe himself to possess. National Cash Register Co. v. Wichita Frozen Food Lockers, Tex.Civ.App., 172 S.W.2d 781, 787. Includes both express and implied authority. Grismore v. Consolidated Products Co., 232 Iowa 328, 5 N.W.2d 646, 651.

ACTUAL BIAS. See Bias.

ACTUAL CASH VALUE. The fair or reasonable cash price for which the property could be sold in the market, in the ordinary course of business, and not at forced sale; the price it will bring in a fair market after reasonable efforts to find a purchaser who will give the highest price. Peavy-Wilson Lumber Co. v. Jackson, 161 La. 669, 109 So. 351, 352. What property is worth in money, allowing for depreciation. Glens Falls Ins. Co. of New York v. Garner, 229 Ala. 39, 155 So. 533, 536. Ordinarily, "actual cash value," "fair market price," and "market value" are synonymous terms. Butler v. Ætna Ins. Co. of Hartford, Conn., 64 N.D. 764, 256 N.W. 214, 218.

ACTUAL CHANGE OF POSSESSION. In statutes of frauds, an open, visible, and unequivocal change of possession, manifested by the usual outward signs, as distinguished from a merely formal or constructive change. Stevens v. Irwin, 15 Cal. 503, 76 Am.Dec. 500.

ACTUAL COST. The actual price paid for goods by a party, in the case of a real *bona fide* purchase, and not the market value of the goods. Ogunquit Village Corporation v. Inhabitants of Wells, 123 Me. 207, 122 A. 522, 524.

"Actual cost" has no common-law significance, and it is without any well-understood trade or technical meaning. It is a general or descriptive term which may have varying meanings according to the circumstances in which it is used. It imports the exact sum expended or loss sustained rather than the average or proportional part of the cost. Its meaning may be restricted to overhead or extended to other items. State v. Northwest Poultry & Egg Co., 203 Minn. 438, 281 N.W. 753, 755.

ACTUAL DELIVERY. See Delivery.

ACTUAL EVICTION. An actual expulsion of the tenant out of all or some part of the demised premises; a physical ouster or dispossession from the very thing granted or some substantial part thereof. Cauley v. Northern Trust Co., 315 Ill. App. 307, 43 N.E.2d 147, 155, 315.

An arbitrary and willful interference with tenant's rights by landlord is essential. Kusche v. Sabin, City Ct., New Rochelle, 6 N.Y.S.2d 771, 773. Deprivation of beneficial enjoyment of property in whole or in part or exclusion from some portion of demised premises. Kusche v. Sabin, City Ct., New Rochelle, 6 N.Y.S.2d 771, 773. Dispossession by process of law, Stanton v. Conley, 278 N.Y.S. 275, 277, 244 App.Div. 84. Expulsion or exclusion from demised premises. Liberal Savings & Loan Co. v. Frankel Realty Co., 137 Ohio St. 489, 30 N.E.2d 1012, 1017, physical expulsion by landlord. General American Life Ins. Co. v. North American Mfg. Co., 320 Ill.App. 488, 51 N.E.2d 619, wrongful entry on premises by lessor is necessary. Title & Trust Co. v. Durkheimer Inv. Co., 155 Or. 427, 63 P.2d 909.

ACTUAL FRAUD. See Fraud.

ACTUAL LOSS. One resulting from the real and substantial destruction of the property insured.

ACTUAL MARKET VALUE. In custom laws, the price at which merchandise is freely offered for sale to all purchasers; the price which the manufacturer or owner would have received for merchandise, sold in the ordinary course of trade in the usual wholesale quantities. United States v. Sischo, D.C.Wash., 262 F. 1001, 1011.

ACTUAL NOTICE. See Notice.

ACTUAL POSSESSION. See Possession.

ACTUAL PRACTICE. Active, open and notorious engagement in business, vocation or profession as opposed to casual, occasional or clandestine practice. State ex rel. Laughlin v. Washington State Bar Ass'n, 26 Wash.2d 914, 176 P.2d 301, 309.

ACTUAL RESIDENCE. The abode, where one actually lives, not mere naked legal residence. In Re McGrath, 243 App.Div. 803, 278 N.Y.S. 135.

ACTUAL SALE. Lands are "actually sold" at a tax sale, so as to entitle the treasurer to the statutory fees, when the sale is completed; when he has collected from the purchaser the amount of the bid. Miles v. Miller, 5 Neb. 272.

ACTUAL VALUE. "Actual value" to be awarded in condemnation proceeding is price that would probably result from negotiations between willing seller and willing buyer. State v. Hoblitt, 87 Mont. 403, 288 P. 181, 185. "Actual value," "market value," "fair value," and the like may be used as convertible terms. Kerr v. Clinchfield Coal Corporation, 169 Va. 149, 192 S.E. 741, 744. "Saleable value," "actual value," "cash value," and others used in directions to tax assessing officers, all mean the same thing. In re Lang Body Co., C.C.A.Ohio, 92 F.2d 338, 340.

ACTUAL VIOLENCE. An assault with actual violence is an assault with physical force put in action, exerted upon the person assailed. The term violence is synonymous with physical force, and the two are used interchangeably in relation to assaults. Tanner v. State, 24 Ga.App. 132, 100 S.E. 44.

ACTUARIUS. In Roman law, a notary or clerk. One who drew the acts or statutes, or who wrote in brief the public acts.

An officer who had charge of the public baths; an officer who received the money for the soldiers, and distributed it among them; a notary.

An *actor*, which see. Du Cange.

ACTUARY. In English ecclesiastical law, a clerk that registers the acts and constitutions of the lower house of convocation; or a registrar in a court christian.

Also an officer appointed to keep savings banks accounts; the computing officer of an insurance company; a person skilled in calculating the value of life interests, annuities, and insurances. Champagne v. Unity Industrial Life Ins. Co., La. App., 161 So. 52, 53.

ACTUM. Lat. A deed; something done.

ACTUS. In the civil law, an act or action. *Non tantum verbis, sed etiam actu;* not only by words, but also by act. Dig. 46, 8. 5.

A species of right of way, consisting in the right of driving cattle, or a carriage, over the land subject to the servitude. Inst. 2, 3, pr. It is sometimes translated a "road," and included the kind of way termed *"iter,"* or path. Lord Coke, who adopts the term *"actus"* from Bracton, defines it a foot and horse way, vulgarly called "pack and prime way;" but distinguishes it from a cart-way. Co.Litt. 56*a*; Boyden v. Achenbach, 79 N.C. 539.

In old English law, an act of parliament; a statute. 8 Coke 40. A distinction, however, was sometimes made between *actus* and *statutum*. *Actus parliamenti* was an act made by the lords and commons; and it became *statutum*, when it received the king's consent. Barring.Obs.St. 46, note *b*.

Actus curiæ neminem gravabit. An act of the court shall prejudice no man. Jenk.Cent. 118. Where a delay in an action is the act of the court, neither party shall suffer for it.

Actus Dei nemini est damnosus. The act of God is hurtful to no one. 2 Inst. 287. That is, a person cannot be prejudiced or held responsible for an accident occurring without his fault and attributable to the "act of God." See Act of God.

Actus Dei nemini facit injuriam. The act of God does injury to no one. 2 Bl.Comm. 122. A thing which is inevitable by the act of God, which no industry can avoid, nor policy prevent, will not be construed to the prejudice of any person in whom there was no laches. Broom, Max. 230.

Actus inceptus, cujus perfectio pendet ex voluntate partium, revocari potest; si autem pendet ex voluntate testiæ personæ, vel ex contingenti, revocari non potest. An act already begun, the completion of which depends on the will of the parties, may be revoked; but if it depend on the will of a third person, or on a contingency, it cannot be revoked. Bac.Max. reg. 20.

Actus judiciarius coram non judice irritus habetur, de ministeriali autem a quocunque provenit ratum esto. A judicial act by a judge without jurisdiction is void; but a ministerial act, from whomsoever proceeding, may be ratified. Lofft, 458.

Actus legis nemini est damnosus. The act of the law is hurtful to no one. An act in law shall prejudice no man. 2 Inst. 287.

Actus legis nemini facit injuriam. The act of the law does injury to no one. 5 Coke, 116.

Actus legitimi non recipiunt modum. Acts required to be done by law do not admit of qualification. Hob. 153; Branch, Princ.

Actus me invito factus non est meus actus. An act done by me, against my will, is not my act. Branch, Princ.

Actus non facit reum, nisi mens sit rea. An act does not make [the doer of it] guilty, unless the mind be guilty; that is, unless the intention be criminal. 3 Inst. 107. The intent and the act must both concur to constitute the crime. Lord Kenyon, C. J., 7 Term 514; Broom, Max. 306.

Actus repugnus non potest in esse produci. A repugnant act cannot be brought into being, *i. e.*, cannot be made effectual. Plowd. 355.

Actus servi in iis quibus opera ejus communiter adhibita est, actus domini habetur. The act of a servant in those things in which he is usually employed, is considered the act of his master. Lofft, 227.

A. D. An abbreviation of Anno Domini meaning in the year of our Lord. Commonwealth v. Traylor, 20 Ky.Law Rep. 97, 98, 45 S.W. 356.

AD. Lat. At; by; for; near; on account of; to; until; upon; with relation to or concerning.

AD ABUNDANTIOREM CAUTELAM. L. Lat. For more abundant caution. 2 How. State Tr. 1182. Otherwise expressed, *ad cautelam ex superabundanti.* Id. 1163.

AD ADMITTENDUM CLERICUM. For the admitting of the clerk. A writ in the nature of an execution, commanding the bishop to admit his clerk, upon the success of the latter in a *quare impedit.*

AD ALIUD EXAMEN. To another tribunal; belonging to another court, cognizance, or jurisdiction.

AD ALIUM DIEM. At another day. A common phrase in the old reports. Yearb. P. 7 Hen. VI. 13.

AD ASSISAS CAPIENDAS. To take assises; to take or hold the assises. Bract. fol. 110*a*; 3 Bl. Comm. 185, 352. *Ad assisam capiendam;* to take an assise. Bract. fol. 110*b*.

AD AUDIENDAM CONSIDERATIONEM CURIÆ. To hear the judgment of the court. Bract. 383 *b*.

AD AUDIENDUM ET DETERMINANDUM. To hear and determine. St. Westm. 2, cc. 29, 30. 4 Bla.Com. 278.

AD BARRAM. To the bar; at the bar. 3 How. State Tr. 112.

AD BARRAM EVOCATUS. Called to the bar. 1 Ld.Raym. 59.

AD CAMPI PARTEM. For a share of the field or land, for champert. Fleta, lib. 2, c. 36, § 4.

AD CAPTUM VULGI. Adapted to the common understanding.

AD COLLIGENDUM. For collecting; as an administrator or trustee *ad colligendum.* 2 Kent 414.

AD COLLIGENDUM BONA DEFUNCTI. For collecting the goods of the deceased. See Administration of Estates.

AD COMMUNE NOCUMENTUM. To the common nuisance. Broom & H.Com. 196.

AD COMMUNEM LEGEM. At common law, the name of a writ of entry (now obsolete) brought by the reversioners after the death of the life tenant, for the recovery of lands wrongfully alienated by him.

AD COMPARENDUM. To appear. *Ad comparendum, et ad standum juri,* to appear and to stand to the law, or abide the judgment of the court. Cro.Jac. 67.

AD COMPUTUM REDDENDUM. To render an account. St.Westm. 2, c. 11.

AD CULPAM. Until misbehavior.

AD CURIAM. At a court. 1 Salk. 195. To court. *Ad curiam vocare,* to summon to court.

AD CUSTAGIA. At the costs. Toullier; Cowell; Whishaw.

AD CUSTUM. At the cost. 1 Bl.Comm. 314.

AD DAMNUM. In pleading. "To the damage." The technical name of that clause of the writ or declaration which contains a statement of the plaintiff's money loss, or the damages which he claims. Vincent v. Life Ass'n, 75 Conn. 650, 55 Atl. 177.

AD DEFENDENDUM. To defend. 1 Bl.Comm. 227.

AD DIEM. At a day; at the day. Townsh.Pl. 23. *Ad alium diem.* At another day. Y.B. 7 Hen. VI, 13. *Ad certum diem,* at a certain day. 2 Strange, 747. *Solvit ad diem;* he paid at or on the day. 1 Chit.Pl. 485.

AD EA QUÆ FREQUENTIUS ACCIDUNT JURA ADAPTANTUR. Laws are adapted to those cases which most frequently occur. 2 Inst. 137; Broom, Max. 43.

Laws are adapted to cases which frequently occur. A statute, which, construed according to its plain words, is, in all cases of ordinary occurrence, in no degree inconsistent or unreasonable, should not be varied by construction in every case, merely because there is one possible but highly improbable case in which the law would operate with great severity and against our notions of justice. The utmost that can be contended is that the construction of the statute should be varied in that particular case, so as to obviate the injustice. 7 Exch. 549; 8 Exch. 778.

AD EFFECTUM. To the effect, or end. Co.Litt. 204*a*; 2 Crabb, Real Prop. p. 802, § 2143. *Ad effectum sequentem,* to the effect following. 2 Salk. 417.

AD EVERSIONEM JURIS NOSTRI. To the overthrow of our right. 2 Kent 91.

AD EXCAMBIUM. For exchange; for compensation. Bract. fol. 12*b*, 37*b*.

AD EXHÆREDATIONEM. To the disherison, or disinheriting; to the injury of the inheritance. 3 Bl.Comm. 288.

Formal words in the old writ of waste, which calls upon the tenant to appear and show cause why he hath committed waste and destruction in the place named, *ad exhæredationem,* etc.; Fitzherbert, Nat.Bev. 55.

AD EXITUM. At issue; at the end (of the pleadings.) Steph.Pl. 24.

AD FACIENDUM. To do. Co.Litt. 204*a*. *Ad faciendum, subjiciendum et recipiendum;* to do, submit to, and receive. *Ad faciendam juratamillam;* to make up that jury. Fleta, lib. 2, c. 65, § 12.

AD FACTUM PRÆSTANDUM. In Scotch law, a name descriptive of a class of obligations marked by unusual severity. A debtor *ad fac. præs.* is denied the benefit of the act of grace, the privilege of sanctuary, and the *cessio bonorum;* Erskine, Inst. lib. 3, tit. 3, § 62; Kames, Eq. 216.

AD FEODI FIRMAM. To fee farm. Fleta, lib. 2, c. 50, § 30.

AD FIDEM. In allegiance. 2 Kent, Comm. 56. Subjects born *ad fidem* are those born in allegiance.

AD FILUM AQUÆ. To the thread of the water; to the central line, or middle of the stream. *Usque ad filum aquæ,* as far as the thread of the stream. Bract. fol. 208*b*; 235*a*. A phrase of frequent occurrence in modern law; of which *ad medium filum aquæ (q. v.)* is another form, and etymologically more exact.

AD FILUM VIÆ. To the middle of the way; to the central line of the road. Parker v. Inhabitants of Framingham, 8 Metc. (Mass.) 260.

AD FINEM. Abbreviated *ad fin.* To the end. It is used in citations to books, as a direction to read from the place designated to the end of the chapter, section, etc. *Ad finem litis,* at the end of the suit.

AD FIRMAM. To farm. Derived from an old Saxon word denoting rent. *Ad firmam noctis* was a fine or penalty equal in amount to the estimated cost of entertaining the king for one night. Cowell. *Ad feodi firmam,* to fee farm. Spelman.

AD FUNDANDAM JURISDICTIONEM. To make the basis of jurisdiction. [1905] 2 K.B. 555.

AD GAOLAS DELIBERANDAS. To deliver the gaols; to empty the gaols. Bract. fol. 109*b*. *Ad gaolam deliberandam;* to deliver the gaol; to make gaol delivery. Bract. fol. 110*b*.

AD GRAVAMEN. To the grievance, injury, or oppression. Fleta, lib. 2, c. 47, § 10.

AD HOC. For this; for this special purpose.

An attorney ad hoc, or a guardian or curator ad hoc, is one appointed for a special purpose, generally to represent the client or infant in the particular action in which the appointment is made. Bienvenu v. Insurance Co., 33 La.Ann. 212.

AD HOMINEM. To the person. A term used in logic with reference to a personal argument.

AD HUNC DIEM. At this day. 1 Leon. 90.

AD IDEM. To the same point, or effect. *Ad idem facit,* it makes to or goes to establish the same point. Bract. fol. 27*b*.

AD INDE. Thereunto. *Ad inde requisitus,* thereunto required. Townsh.Pl. 22.

AD INFINITUM. Without limit; to an infinite extent; indefinitely.

AD INQUIRENDUM. To inquire; a writ of inquiry; a judicial writ, commanding inquiry to be made of anything relating to a cause pending in court. Cowell.

AD INSTANTIAM. At the instance. 2 Mod. 44. *Ad instantiam partis,* at the instance of a party. Hale, Com.Law, 28.

AD INTERIM. In the meantime. An officer *ad interim* is one appointed to fill a temporary vacancy, or to discharge the duties of the office during the absence or temporary incapacity of its regular incumbent.

AD JUDICIUM. To judgment; to court. *Ad judicium provocare;* to summon to court; to commence an action; a term of the Roman law. Dig. 5, 1, 13, 14.

AD JUNGENDUM AUXILIUM. To joining in aid; to join in aid. See Aid Prayer.

AD JURA REGIS. To the rights of the king; a writ which was brought by the king's clerk, presented to a living against those who endeavored to eject him, to the prejudice of the king's title. Reg. Writs 61.

AD LARGUM. At large: as, title at large; assize at large. See Dane, Abr. c. 144, art. 16, § 7. Also at liberty; free, or unconfined. *Ire ad largum,* to go at large. Plowd. 37.

At large; giving details, or particulars; *in extenso.* A special verdict was formerly called a verdict at large. Plowd. 92.

AD LIBITUM. At pleasure. 3 Bla.Com. 292.

AD LITEM. For the suit; for the purposes of the suit; pending the suit. A guardian *ad litem* is a guardian appointed to prosecute or defend a suit on behalf of a party incapacitated by infancy or otherwise.

AD LUCRANDUM VEL PERDENDUM. For gain or loss. Emphatic words in the old warrants of attorney. Reg. Orig. 21, et seq. Sometimes expressed in English, "to lose and gain." Plowd. 201.

AD MAJOREM CAUTELAM. For greater security. 2 How.State Tr. 1182.

AD MANUM. At hand; ready for use. *Et querens sectam habeat ad manum;* and the plaintiff immediately have his suit ready. Fleta, lib. 2, c. 44, § 2.

AD MEDIUM FILUM AQUÆ. To the middle thread of the stream. See Ad Filum Aquæ.

AD MEDIUM FILUM VIÆ. To the middle thread of the way.

AD MELIUS INQUIRENDUM. A writ directed to a coroner commanding him to hold a second inquest. See 45 Law J.Q.B. 711.

AD MORDENDUM ASSUETUS. Accustomed to bite. Cro.Car. 254. A material averment in declarations for damage done by a dog to persons or animals. 1 Chit.Pl. 388; 2 Chit.Pl. 597.

AD NOCUMENTUM. To the nuisance, or annoyance; to the hurt or injury. Fleta, lib. 2, c. 52, § 19. *Ad nocumentum liberi tenementi sui,* to the nuisance of his freehold. Formal words in the old assise of nuisance. 3 Bl.Comm. 221.

AD OFFICIUM JUSTICIARIORUM SPECTAT, UNICUIQUE CORAM EIS PLACITANTI JUSTITIAM EXHIBERE. It is the duty of justices to administer justice to every one pleading before them. 2 Inst. 451.

AD OMISSA VEL MALE APPRETIATA. With relation to omissions or wrong interpretations. 3 Ersk.Inst. 9, § 36.

AD OPUS. To the work. See 21 Harv.L.Rev. 264, citing 2 Poll. & Maitl. 232 *et seq.;* Use.

AD OSTENDENDUM. To show. Formal words in old writs. Fleta, lib. 4, c. 65, § 12.

AD OSTIUM ECCLESIÆ. At the door of the church. One of the five species of dower formerly recognized by the English law. 1 Washb.Real Prop. 149; 2 Bl.Comm. 132.

AD PIOS USUS. Lat. For pious (religious or charitable) uses or purposes. Used with reference to gifts and bequests.

AD PROSEQUENDAM. To prosecute. 11 Mod. 362.

Ad proximum antecedens fiat relatio nisi impediatur sententiâ. Relative words refer to the nearest antecedent, unless it be prevented by the context. Jenk.Cent. 180; Brown v. Brown, Del., 3 Terry 157, 29 A.2d 149, 153.

AD PUNCTUM TEMPORIS. At the point of time. Sto.Bailm. § 263.

AD QUÆRIMONIAM. On complaint of.

AD QUAESTIONEM FACTI NON RESPONDENT JUDICES, AD QUAESTIONEM JURIS NON RESPONDENT JURATORES. Means that juries must answer to questions of fact and judges to questions of law. Ex parte United States, C.C.A. Wis., 101 F.2d 870, 874.

AD QUEM. To which.

A term used in the computation of time or distance, as correlative to *a quo;* denotes the end or terminal point. See A Quo.

The *terminus a quo* is the point of beginning or departure; the *terminus ad quem,* the end of the period or point of arrival.

AD QUESTIONES FACTI NON RESPONDENT JUDICES; AD QUESTIONES LEGIS NON RESPONDENT JURATORES. Judges do not answer questions of fact; juries do not answer questions of law. 8 Coke, 308; Co.Litt. 295.

AD QUÆSTIONES LEGIS JUDICES, ET NON JURATORES, RESPONDENT. Judges, and not jurors, decide questions of law. 7 Mass. 279.

AD QUOD CURIA CONCORDAVIT. To which the court agreed. Yearb.P. 20 Hen. VI. 27.

AD QUOD DAMNUM. The name of a writ formerly issuing from the English chancery, commanding the sheriff to make inquiry "to what damage" a specified act, if done, will tend.

It is a writ which ought to be sued before the king grants certain liberties, as a fair, market or such like, which may be prejudicial to others, and thereby it should be inquired whether it will be a prejudice to grant them, and to whom it will be prejudicial, and what prejudice will come thereby. Termes de la Ley.

There is also another writ of *ad quod damnum*, if any one will turn a common highway and lay out another way as beneficial. Termes de la Ley.

The writ of *ad quod damnum* is a common-law writ, in the nature of an original writ, issued by the prothonotary, and in condemnation proceedings is returnable to and subject to confirmation of the Superior Court. Elbert v. Scott, Del., 5 Boyce 1, 90 A. 587.

AD QUOD NON FUIT RESPONSUM. To which there was no answer.

A phrase used in the reports, where a point advanced in argument by one party was not denied by the other; or where a point or argument of counsel was not met or notice by the court; or where an objection was met by the court, and not replied to by the counsel who raised it. 3 Coke, 9; 4 Coke, 40.

AD RATIONEM PONERE. To cite a person to appear. A technical expression in the old records of the Exchequer, signifying, to put to the bar and interrogate as to a charge made; to arraign on a trial.

AD RECOGNOSCENDUM. To recognize. Fleta, lib. 2, c. 65, § 12. Formal words in old writs.

AD RECTE DOCENDUM OPORTET, PRIMUM INQUIRERE NOMINA, QUIA RERUM COGNITIO A NOMINIBUS RERUM DEPENDET. In order rightly to comprehend a thing, inquire first into the names, for a right knowledge of things depends upon their names. Co.Litt. 68.

AD RECTUM. (L. Lat.) To right. To do right. To meet an accusation. To answer the demands of the law. *Habeant eos ad rectum.* They shall render themselves to answer the law, or to make satisfaction. Bract. fol. 124 *b*.

AD REPARATIONEM ET SUSTENTATIONEM. For repairing and keeping in suitable condition.

AD RESPONDENDUM. For answering; to make answer; words used in certain writs employed for bringing a person before the court to make answer in defense in a proceeding, as in *habeas corpus ad respondendum* and *capias ad respondendum, q. v.*

AD SATISFACIENDUM. To satisfy. The emphatic words of the writ of *capias ad satisfaciendum*, which requires the sheriff to *take* the person of the defendant *to satisfy* the plaintiff's claim.

AD SECTAM. At the suit of. Commonly abbreviated to *ads.*

Used in entering and indexing the names of cases, where it is desired that the name of the defendant should come first. Thus, "B. *ads.* A." indicates that B. is defendant in an action brought by A., and the title so written would be an inversion of the more usual form "A. *v.* B."

AD STUDENDUM ET ORANDUM. For studying and praying; for the promotion of learning and religion. A phrase applied to colleges and universities. 1 Bl.Comm. 467.

AD TERMINUM ANNORUM. For a term of years.

AD TERMINUM QUI PRÆTERIT. For a term which has passed. Words in the Latin form of the writ of entry employed at common law to recover, on behalf of a landlord, possession of premises, from a tenant holding over after the expiration of the term for which they were demised. See Fitzh. Nat.Brev. 201.

AD TRISTEM PARTEM STRENUA EST SUSPICIO. Suspicion lies heavy on the unfortunate side.

AD TUNC ET IBIDEM. In pleading, the Latin name of that clause of an indictment containing the statement of the subject-matter "then and there being found."

AD ULTIMAN VIM TERMINORUM. To the most extended import of the terms; in a sense as universal as the terms will reach. 2 Eden, 54.

AD USUM ET COMMODUM. To the use and benefit.

AD VALENTIAM. To the value. See Ad Valorem.

AD VALOREM. According to value. Powell v. Gleason, Ariz., 74 P.2d 47, 50, 114 A.L.R. 838.

Duties are either *ad valorem* or *specific;* the former when the duty is laid in the form of a percentage on the value of the property; the latter where it is imposed as a fixed sum on each article of a class without regard to its value. The term *ad valorem* tax means a tax or duty upon the value of the article or thing subject to taxation. Arthur v. Johnston, 185 S.C. 324, 194 S.E. 151, 154.

AD VENTREM INSPICIENDUM. To inspect the womb. A writ for the summoning of a jury of matrons to determine the question of pregnancy.

AD VIM MAJOREM VEL AD CASUS FORTUITUS NON TENETUR QUIS, NISI SUA CULPA INTERVENERIT. No one is held to answer for the effects of a superior force, or of accidents, unless his own fault has contributed. Fleta, lib. 2, c. 72, § 16.

AD VITAM. For life. Bract. fol. 13*b*. *In feodo, vel ad vitam;* in fee, or for life. Id.

AD VITAM AUT CULPAM. For life or until fault. Words descriptive of a tenure of office "for life or good behavior," equivalent to *quamdiu bene se gesserit.*

AD VOLUNTATEM. At will. Bract. fol. 27*a*. *Ad voluntatem domini,* at the will of the lord.

AD WARACTUM. To fallow. Bract. fol. 228*b*. See Waractum.

ADAPTED. Capable of use. People v. Dorrington, 221 Mich. 571, 191 N.W. 831, 832. Indicates that the object referred to has been made suitable; has been made to conform to; has been made fit by alteration. Raynor v. United States, C.C.A.Ind., 89 F.2d 469, 471.

ADAWLUT. Corrupted from *Adalat,* justice, equity; a court of justice. The terms "Dewanny Adawlut" and "Foujdarry Adawlut" denote the civil and criminal courts of justice in India. Wharton.

ADCORDABILIS DENARII. Money paid by a vassal to his lord upon the selling or exchanging of a feud. Enc. Lond.

ADD. To unite; attach; annex; join. Board of Com'rs of Hancock County v. State, 119 Ind. 473, 22 N.E. 10.

ADDENDUM. A thing that is added or to be added; a list or section consisting of added material.

ADDICERE. Lat. In the civil law, to adjudge or condemn; to assign, allot, or deliver; to sell. In the Roman law, *addico* was one of the three words used to express the extent of the civil jurisdiction of the prætors.

ADDICT. As defined in Acts 1894, No. 157, one who has acquired the habit of using spirituous liquors or narcotics to such an extent as to deprive him of reasonable self-control. Interdiction of Gasquet, 147 La. 722, 85 So. 884, 888.

ADDICTIO. In the Roman law, the giving up to a creditor of his debtor's person by a magistrate; also the transfer of the (deceased) debtor's goods to one who assumes his liabilities.

Additio probat minoritatem. An addition [to a name] proves or shows minority or inferiority. 4 Inst. 80; Wing.Max. 211, max. 60. That is, if it be said that a man has a fee tail, it is less than if he has the fee.

This maxim is applied by Lord Coke to courts, and terms of law; *minoritas* being understood in the sense of difference, inferiority, or qualification. Thus, the style of the king's bench is *coram rege,* and the style of the court of chancery is *coram domino rege in cancellaria;* the addition showing the difference. 4 Inst. 80. By the word "fee" is intended *fee-simple,* fee-tail not being intended by it, unless there be added to it the *addition* of the word "tail." 2 Bl.Comm. 106; Litt. § 1.

ADDITION. Implies physical contact, something added to another. Structure physically attached to or connected with building itself. Mack v. Eyssell, 332 Mo. 671, 59 S.W.2d 1049; Washington Loan & Trust Co. v. Hammond, 51 App.D.C. 260, 278 F. 569, 571.

Extension; increase; augmentation. Meyering v. Miller, 330 Mo. 885, 51 S.W.2d 65, 66.

That which has become united with or a part of. Judge v. Bergman, 258 Ill. 246, 101 N.E. 574, 576.

French Law

A supplementary process to obtain additional information. Guyot, Répert.

Insurance

The word "addition," as applied to buildings, usually means a part added or joined to a main building. Agnew v. Sun Ins. Office, 167 Wis. 456, 167 N.W. 829. It may also apply to buildings appurtenant to some other building though not actually in physical contact therewith. Taylor v. Northwestern Nat. Ins. Co., 34 Cal.App. 471, 167 P. 899. Not limited to structures physically a part of the main building. Gertner v. Glens Falls Ins. Co., 184 N.Y.S. 669, 670, 193 App.Div. 836.

Liens

Within the meaning of the mechanic's lien law, an "addition" to a building must be a lateral addition. Lake & Risley Co. v. Still, 7 N.J.Misc. 47, 144 A. 110. It must occupy ground without the limits of the building to which it constitutes an addition, so that the lien shall be upon the building formed by the addition and the land upon which it stands. Updike v. Skillman, 27 N.J.L. 132. See also, Lamson v. Maryland Casualty Co., 196 Iowa 1185, 194 N.W. 70, 71.

An alteration in a former building, by adding to its height, or to its depth, or to the extent of its interior accommodations, is merely an "alteration," and not an "addition." Putting a new story on an old building is not an addition. Updike v. Skillman, 27 N.J.L. 132. See, also, Lamson v. Maryland Casualty Co., 196 Iowa 1185, 194 N.W. 70, 71.

Did not include new livestock acquired by mortgagor after execution of mortgage. American State Bank of Watertown v. Boyle, 212 Minn. 293, 4 N.W.2d 108, 109.

Name

Whatever is added to a man's name by way of title or description. Cowell.

In English law, there are four kinds of *additions,*—additions of *estate,* such as yeoman, gentleman, esquire; additions of *degree,* or names of dignity, as knight, earl, marquis, duke; additions of *trade,* mystery, or occupation, as scrivener, painter, mason, carpenter; and additions of *place* of residence, as London, Chester, etc. The only additions recognized in American law are those of mystery and residence.

At common law there was no need of addition in any case; 2 Ld.Raym. 988; it was required only by stat. 1 Hen. V. c. 5, in cases where process of outlawry lies. In all other cases it is only a description of the person, and common reputation is sufficient; 2 Ld.Raym. 849.

ADDITIONAL. This term embraces the idea of joining or uniting one thing to another, so as thereby to form one aggregate. Ex parte Boddie, 200 S.C. 379, 21 S.E.2d 4, 8.

"Additional security" imports a security, which, united with or joined to the former one, is deemed to make it, as an aggregate, sufficient as a security from the beginning. State v. Hull, 53 Miss. 626; Searcy v. Cullman County, 196 Ala. 287, 71 So. 664, 665.

ADDITIONAL BURDEN. See Eminent Domain.

ADDITIONAL INSURED. A person using another's automobile, which is covered by liability policy containing statutory omnibus clause, only when insured's permission is expressly or impliedly given for particular use. Stewart v. City of Rio Vista, 72 Cal.App.2d 279, 164 P.2d 274, 275.

Driver chosen by friend to whom automobile was entrusted by husband who had possession with direct permission of wife in whose name record title lay was not additional insured. Fox v. Crawford, Ohio App., 80 N.E.2d 187, 189.

Where driver of automobile at time it struck pedestrian was using automobile for his own purpose after having received permission from owner only to get automobile started and return automobile to owner's home, driver was not additional insured. Howe v. Farmers Auto. Inter-Insurance Exchange, Wash., 202 P.2d 464, 472.

ADDITIONAL LEGACY. See Legacy.

ADDITIONAL SERVITUDE. The imposition of a new and additional easement or servitude on land originally taken by eminent domain proceedings, a use of a different character, for which owner of property is entitled to compensation. S. D. Childs & Co. v. City of Chicago, 198 Ill.App. 590, 593; Williams v. Meridan Light & Ry. Co., 110 Miss. 174, 69 So. 596, 597.

ADDITIONAL WORK. Of nature involved in modifications and changes, not independent project. Maryland Casualty Co. v. City of South Norfolk, C.C.A.Va., 54 F.2d 1032, 1037. Work which results from a change or alteration in plans concerning work which has to be done under a contract, while "extra work" relates to work which is not included within the contract itself. De Martini v. Elade Realty Corp., Co.Ct., 52 N.Y.S.2d 487, 489.

ADDITIONALES. In the law of contracts. Additional terms or propositions to be added to a former agreement.

ADDITUR. The power of trial court to assess damages or increase amount of an inadequate award made by jury verdict, as condition of denial of motion for new trial, with consent of defendant whether or not plaintiff consents to such action. Dorsey et al. v. Barba et al., 226 P.2d 677.

ADDLED. Stupid, muddled, foolish. Windham v. State, 93 Tex.Cr.R. 477, 248 S.W. 51, 54.

ADDLED PARLIAMENT. The parliament which met in 1614. It sat for but two months and none of its bills received the royal assent. Taylor, Jurispr. 359.

ADDONE, Addonne. L. Fr. Given to. Kelham.

ADDRESS. Place where mail or other communications will reach person. Munson v. Bay State Dredging & Contracting Co., 314 Mass. 485, 50 N.E.2d 633, 636. Generally a place of business or residence.

Equity

Part of a bill wherein is given the appropriate and technical description of the court in which the bill is filed.

Legislation

A formal request addressed to the executive by one or both branches of the legislative body, requesting him to perform some act.

It is provided as a means for the removal of judges deemed unworthy, though the causes of removal would not warrant impeachment. It is not provided for in the Constitution of the United States; and even in those states where the right exists it is exercised but seldom.

Offense

Not synonym of hazard, but an antonym, and, as respects gaming and devices, means skillful management, dexterity, or adroitness. In re Wigton, 151 Pa.Super. 337, 30 A.2d 352, 355.

ADDRESS TO THE CROWN. When the royal speech has been read in Parliament, an address in answer thereto is moved in both houses. Two members are selected in each house by the administration for moving and seconding the address. Since the commencement of the session 1890–1891, it has been a single resolution expressing their thanks to the sovereign for his gracious speech.

ADDUCE. To present, bring forward, offer, introduce. Used particularly with reference to evidence. Tuttle v. Story County, 56 Iowa 316, 9 N.W. 292.

Broader in its signification than the word "offered." Beatty v. O'Connor, 106 Ind. 81, 5 N.E. 880; Brown v. Griffin, 40 Ill.App. 558.

ADEEM. To take away, recall, or revoke. To satisfy a legacy by some gift or substituted disposition, made by the testator, in advance. Tolman v. Tolman, 85 Me. 317, 27 Atl. 184. Woodburn Lodge No. 102, I. O. O. F., v. Wilson, 148 Or. 150, 34 P.2d 611, 614. See Ademption.

If the identical thing bequeathed is not in existence, or has been disposed of, the legacy is "adeemed" and the legatee's rights are gone. Lange v. Lange, 127 N.J.Eq. 315, 12 A.2d 840, 843; Welch v. Welch, 147 Miss. 728, 113 So. 197, 198.

ADELANTADO. In Spanish law, the military and political governor of a frontier province. This office has long since been abolished. Also a president or president judge; a judge having jurisdiction over a kingdom, or over certain provinces only. So called from having authority over the judges of those places. Las Partidas, pt. 3, tit. 4, l. 1.

ADELING, or ATHELING. Noble; excellent. A title of honor among the Anglo-Saxons, properly belonging to the king's children. Spelman.

ADEMPTIO. Lat. In the civil law, a revocation of a legacy; an ademption. Inst. 2, 21, pr. Where it was expressly transferred from one person to another, it was called *translatio.* Inst. 2, 21, 1; Dig. 34, 4.

ADEMPTION. Extinction or withdrawal of legacy by testator's act equivalent to revocation or indicating intention to revoke. Tagnon's Adm'x v. Tagnon, 253 Ky. 374, 69 S.W.2d 714.

Removal. Lewis v. Hill, 387 Ill. 542, 56 N.E.2d 619, 621. Testator's giving to a legatee that which he has provided in his will, or his disposing of that part of his estate so bequeathed in such manner as to make it impossible to carry out the will. Hurley v. Schuler, 296 Ky. 118, 176 S.W.2d 275, 276. Revocation, recalling, or cancellation, of a legacy, according to the apparent intention of the testator, implied by the law from acts done by him in his life, though such acts do not amount to an express revocation of it. Burnham v. Comfort, 108 N.Y. 535, 15 N.E. 710.

The act by which the testator pays to his legatee, in his life-time, a general legacy which by his will he had proposed to give him at his death, 1 Rop.Leg. p. 365; and the act by which a specific legacy has become inoperative on account of the testator having parted with the subject. Dillender v. Wilson, 228 Ky. 758, 16 S.W.2d 173, 174.

See Advancement.

ADEO. Lat. So, as. *Adeo plene et integre,* as fully and entirely. 10 Coke, 65.

ADEQUATE. Sufficient; proportionate; equally efficient; equal to what is required; suitable to the case or occasion; satisfactory. Nagle v. City of Billings, 77 Mont. 205, 250 P. 445, 446. Equal to some given occasion or work. Nissen v. Miller, 44 N.M. 487, 105 P.2d 324, 326. Commensurate; it does not mean average or graduation. Vandermade v. Appert, 125 N.J.Eq. 366, 5 A.2d 868, 871.

ADEQUATE CARE. Such care as a man of ordinary prudence would himself take under similar circumstances to avoid accident; care proportionate to the risk to be incurred. Wallace v. Wilmington & N. R. Co., 8 Houst. (Del.) 529, 18 Atl. 818.

ADEQUATE CAUSE. Sufficient cause for a particular purpose. Pennsylvania & N. Y. Canal & R. Co. v. Mason, 109 Pa. 296, 58 Am.Rep. 722.

In criminal law, adequate cause for the passion which reduces a homicide committed under its influence from the grade of murder to manslaughter, means such cause as would commonly produce a degree of anger, rage, resentment, or terror, in a person of ordinary temper, sufficient to render the mind incapable of cool reflection. Insulting words or gestures, or an assault and battery so slight as to show no intention to inflict pain or injury, or an injury to property unaccompanied by violence are not adequate causes. Vollintine v. State, 77 Tex.Cr.R. 522, 179 S.W. 108; Berry v. State, 157 S.W.2d 650, 652, 143 Tex.Cr.R. 67. See Adequate Provocation.

ADEQUATE COMPENSATION. Just value of property taken under power of eminent domain, payable in money. Buffalo, etc., R. Co. v. Ferris, 26 Tex. 588. Market value of property when taken. Louisiana Highway Commission v. Guidry, 176 La. 389, 146 So. 1, 5. It includes interest. Texarkana & Ft. S. Ry. Co. v. Brinkman, Tex.Civ.App., 288 S.W. 852, 853. It may include the cost or value of the property to the owner for the purposes for which he designed it. Elbert County v. Brown, 16 Ga.App. 834, 86 S.E. 651, 656.

Such only as puts injured party in as good a condition as he would have been in if injury had not been inflicted. Town of Winchester v. Cox, 129 Conn. 106, 26 A.2d 592, 597.

ADEQUATE CONSIDERATION. One which is equal, or reasonably proportioned, to the value of that for which it is given. 1 Story, Eq.Jur. §§ 244–247. One which is not so disproportionate as to shock our sense of that morality and fair dealing which should always characterize transactions between man and man. U. S. Smelting, Refining & Milling Co. v. Utah Power & Light Co., 197 P. 902, 905, 58 Utah, 168. Fair and reasonable under circumstances. Boulenger v. Morison, 88 Cal.App. 664, 264 P. 256, 259. Reasonably just and equitable. Laguna Land & Water Co. v. Greenwood, 92 Cal.App. 570, 268 P. 699, 700.

ADEQUATE OR REASONABLE FACILITIES. Such railroad facilities as might be fairly demanded, with regard to size of place, extent of demand for transportation, cost of furnishing additional accommodation asked for, and to all other facts which would have bearing upon question of convenience and cost. Kurn v. State, 175 Okl. 379, 52 P.2d 841, 843.

ADEQUATE PREPARATION. Embraces full consultation with accused, interviews with witnesses, study of facts and law, and determination of character of defense to be made and policy to be followed during trial. Nelson v. Commonwealth, 295 Ky. 641, 175 S.W.2d 132, 133.

ADEQUATE PROVOCATION. An adequate provocation to cause a sudden transport of passion that may suspend the exercise of judgment and exclude premeditation and a previously formed design is one that is calculated to excite such anger as might obscure the reason or dominate the volition of an ordinary reasonable man. Commonwealth v. Webb, 252 Pa. 187, 97 A. 189, 191.

ADEQUATE REMEDY. One vested in the complainant, to which he may at all times resort at his own option, fully and freely, without let or hindrance. Wheeler v. Bedford, 7 A. 22, 54 Conn. 244; State ex rel. Heimov v. Thomson, 131 Conn. 8, 37 A.2d 689, 692. Suitable, proportionate, or sufficient. Fischer v. Damm, 36 Ohio App. 515, 173 N.E. 449, 451.

A remedy which is plain and complete and as practical and efficient to the ends of justice and its prompt administration as the remedy in equity. Farmers & Traders Bank v. Kendrick, 341 Mo. 571, 108 S.W.2d 62, 64.

A remedy that affords complete relief with reference to the particular matter in controversy, and is appropriate to the circumstances of the case. State v. Huwe, 103 Ohio St. 546, 134 N.E. 456, 459. A remedy to be adequate, precluding resort to mandamus, must not only be one placing relator in statu quo, but must itself enforce in some way performance of the particular duty. State v. Erickson, 104 Conn. 542, 133 A. 683, 686. Must reach end intended, and actually compel performance of duty in question. Buchanan v. Buchanan, 124 Va. 255, 6 S.E.2d 612, 620. Must be plain, accurate, certain, speedy, specific, and appropriate to the particular circumstances, and must also be equally as convenient, beneficial, and effective as the remedy by mandamus. Simpson v. Williams Rural High School Dist., Tex.Civ.App., 153 S.W.2d 852, 856.

ADESSE. In the civil law; to be present; the opposite of *abesse.* Calvin.

ADEU. Without day, as when a matter is finally dismissed by the court. *Alez adeu,* go without day. Y. B. 5 Edw. II. 173. See Adieu.

ADFERRUMINATIO. In the civil law, the welding together of iron; a species of *adjunctio,* (*q. v.*). Called also *ferruminatio.* Mackeld.Rom.Law, § 276; Dig. 6, 1, 23, 5.

ADHERENCE. In Scotch law, the name of a form of action by which the mutual obligation of marriage may be enforced by either party. Bell. It corresponds to the English action for the restitution of conjugal rights. Wharton.

ADHERING. Joining, leagued with, cleaving to; as, "adhering to the enemies of the United States."

"Adhering" consists in giving to the United States the loyalty due from a citizen. United States v. Stephan, D.C. Mich., 50 F.Supp. 738, 741.

Any intentional act furthering hostile designs of enemies of the United States, or an act which intentionally strengthens or tends to strengthen enemies of the United States, or which weakens or tends to weaken power of the United States to resist and attack such enemies, constitutes "adhering" to such enemies. United States v. Haupt, D.C. Ill., 47 F.Supp. 836, 839.

Rebels, being citizens, are not "enemies," within the meaning of the constitution; hence a conviction for treason, in promoting a rebellion, cannot be sustained under that branch of the constitutional definition which speaks of "adhering to their enemies, giving them aid and comfort." United States v. Greathouse, 2 Abb.U.S. 364, Fed.Cas.No. 15,254.

ADHESION. The entrance of another state into an existing treaty with respect only to a part of the principles laid down or the stipulations agreed to. Opp.Int.L. § 533.

Properly speaking, by adhesion the third state becomes a party only to such parts as are specifically agreed to, and by accession it accepts and is bound by the whole treaty. See Accession.

ADHIBERE. In the civil law, to apply; to employ; to exercise; to use. *Adhibere diligentiam,* to use care. *Adhibere vim,* to employ force.

ADIATION. A term used in the laws of Holland for the application of property by an executor. Wharton.

ADIEU. L. Fr. Without day. A common term in the Year Books, implying final dismissal from court.

ADIPOCERE. A waxy substance (chemically margarate of ammonium or ammoniacal soap) formed by the decomposition of animal matter protected from the air but subjected to moisture; in medical jurisprudence, the substance into which a human cadaver is converted which has been buried for a long time in a saturated soil or has lain long in water.

ADIRATUS. Lost; strayed; a price or value set upon things stolen or lost, as a recompense to the owner. Cowell.

ADIT. In mining law, an entrance or approach; a horizontal excavation used as an entrance to a mine, or a vent by which ores and water are carried away; an excavation "in and along a lode," which in statutes of Colorado and other mining states is made the equivalent of a discovery shaft. Electro-Magnetic M. & D. Co. v. Van Auken, 9 Colo. 204, 11 P. 80.

ADITUS. An approach; a way; a public way. Co.Litt. 56*a*.

ADJACENT. Lying near or close to; sometimes, contiguous; neighboring. Ex parte Jeffcoat, 108 Fla. 207, 146 So. 827. *Adjacent* implies that the two objects are not widely separated, though they may not actually touch, Harrison v. Guilford County, 218 N.C. 718, 12 S.E.2d 269, while *adjoining* imports that they are so joined or united to each other that no third object intervenes. Wolfe v. Hurley, D.C.La., 46 F.2d 515, 521.

A word of flexible meaning, depending upon context and subject matter. U. S. v. Denver & R. G. Ry. Co., D.C. Colo., 31 F. 886; Johnston v. Davenport Brick & Tile Co., D.C.Iowa, 237 F. 668, 669.

Suburbs of city not within limits of another municipality though a long strip of land 10 feet wide connected the property with city limits. Lefler v. City of Dallas, Tex. Civ.App., 177 S.W.2d 231, 235.

ADJECTIVE LAW. The aggregate of rules of procedure or practice. As opposed to that body of law which the courts are established to administer, (called "substantive law,") it means the rules according to which the substantive law is administered. That part of the law which provides a method for enforcing or maintaining rights, or obtaining redress for their invasion. Maurizi v. Western Coal & Mining Co., 321 Mo. 378, 11 S.W.2d 268, 272. Holl.Jur. 61,238.

ADJOINING. The word in its etymological sense, means touching or contiguous, as distinguished from lying near to or adjacent. Broun v. Texas & N. O. R. Co., Tex.Civ.App., 295 S.W. 670, 674; Plainfield-Union Water Co. v. Inhabitants of City of Plainfield, 84 N.J.Law, 634, 87 A. 448, 450. To be in contact with; to abut upon. State ex rel. Boynton v. Bunton, 141 Kan. 103, 40 P.2d 326, 328. And the same meaning has been given to it when used in statutes. City of New York v. Alheidt, 151 N.Y.S. 463, 464, 88 Misc. 524. See Adjacent.

ADJOURN. To put off; defer; postpone. To postpone action of a convened court or body until another time specified, or indefinitely, the latter being usually called to adjourn *sine die.* Bispham v. Tucker, 2 N.J.L. 253; Reynolds v. Cropsey, 241 N.Y. 389, 150 N.E. 303. To suspend or recess during a meeting which continues in session. Byrd v. Byrd, 193 Miss. 249, 8 So.2d 510, 512.

Suspending business for a time, delaying. Probably, without some limitation, it would, when used with reference to a sale on foreclosure, or any judicial proceeding, properly include the fixing of the time to which the postponement was made. Waldrop v. Kansas City Southern Ry. Co., 131 Ark. 453, 199 S.W. 369, 371, L.R.A.1918B, 1081.

ADJOURNAL. A term applied in Scotch law and practice to the records of the criminal courts. The original records of criminal trials were called "bukis of adiornale," or "books of adjournal," few of which are now extant. An "act of adjournal" is an order of the court of justiciary entered on its minutes.

ADJOURNAMENTUM EST AD DIEM DICERE SEU DIEM DARE. An adjournment is to appoint a day or give a day. 4 Inst. 27. Hence the formula "*eat sine die.*"

ADJOURNATUR. L. Lat. It is adjourned. A word with which the old reports very frequently conclude a case. 1 Ld.Raym. 602; 1 Show. 7; 1 Leon. 88.

A continuation of the same meeting, and at such adjourned meeting the governing body can do any act which might have been done if no adjournment had taken place, and limitations imposed on governing body as regards action at original meeting obtain at adjourned meeting. Vogel v. Parker, 118 N.J.L. 521, 193 A. 817, 818. One ordered by board at regular meeting, and which is to convene after termination of such regular meeting and prior to next regular meeting. Byrd v. Byrd, 193 Miss. 249, 8 So.2d 510, 513.

ADJOURNED SUMMONS. A summons taken out in the chambers of a judge, and afterwards taken into court to be argued by counsel.

ADJOURNED TERM. In practice, a continuance, by adjournment, of a regular term. Harris v. Gest, 4 Ohio St. 473; Kingsley v. Bagby, 2 Kan. App. 23, 41 P. 991. Distinguished from an "additional term," which is a distinct term. Harris v. Gest, 4 Ohio St. 473; Kingsley v. Bagby, 2 Kan. App. 23, 41 P. 991. A continuation of a previous or regular term; the same term prolonged, wherein power of court over business which has been done, and the entries made at the regular term, continues. Van Dyke v. State, 22 Ala. 57; Carter v. State, 14 Ga.App. 242, 80 S.E. 533, 534.

ADJOURNMENT. A putting off or postponing of business or of a session until another time or place; the act of a court, legislative body, public meeting, or officer, by which the session or assembly is dissolved, either temporarily or finally, and the business in hand dismissed from consideration, either definitely or for an interval. If the adjournment is final, it is said to be *sine die*. See Johnson City v. Tennessee Eastern Electric Co., 133 Tenn. 632, 182 S.W. 587, 589.

In the civil law a calling into court; a summoning at an appointed time. Due Cange.

ADJOURNMENT DAY. A further day appointed by the judges at the regular sittings at *nisi prius* to try issue of fact not then ready for trial.

ADJOURNMENT DAY IN ERROR. In English practice, a day appointed some days before the end of the term at which matters left undone on the affirmance day are finished. 2 Tidd, Pr. 1176.

ADJOURNMENT IN EYRE. The appointment of a day when the justices in eyre mean to sit again. Cowell; Spelman.

ADJOURNMENT SINE DIE. An adjournment without setting a time for another meeting or session. See Sine Die.

ADJUDGE. To pass on judicially, to decide, settle, or decree, or to sentence or condemn. People v. Rave, 364 Ill. 72, 3 N.E.2d 972, 975.

Judgment of a court of competent jurisdiction; equivalent of convicted and sentenced. In re Tarlo's Estate, 315 Pa. 321, 172 A. 139, 140. Implies a judicial determination of a fact, and the entry of a judgment. Department of Banking v. Hedges, 136 Neb. 382, 286 N.W. 277, 283. Does not mean the same as *deemed* contra, under statute, State v. District Court, 64 Mont. 181, 208 P. 952, 955. Blaufus v. People, 69 N.Y. 107, 25 Am.Rep. 148. Predicated only of an act of the court. Searight v. Com., 13 S. & R. Pa. 301. Compare Drinkhouse v. Van Ness, 202 Cal. 359, 260 P. 869, 874; People ex rel. Strohsahl v. Strohsahl, 222 N.Y.S. 319, 324, 221 App.Div. 86.

ADJUDICATAIRE. In Canadian law, a purchaser at a sheriff's sale. See 1 Low.Can. 241; 10 Low. Can. 325.

ADJUDICATE. To settle in the exercise of judicial authority. To determine finally. Synonymous with *adjudge* in its strictest sense. United States v. Irwin, 8 S.Ct. 1033, 127 U.S. 125, 32 L.Ed. 99; Street v. Benner, 20 Fla. 700.

ADJUDICATEE. In French and civil law, the purchaser at a judicial sale. Brent v. New Orleans, 6 So. 793, 41 La.Ann. 1098.

ADJUDICATIO. In the civil law, an adjudication. The judgment of the court that the subject-matter is the property of one of the litigants; confirmation of title by judgment. Mackeld.Rom.Law, § 204.

ADJUDICATION. The giving or pronouncing a judgment or decree in a cause; also the judgment given. People ex rel. Argus Co. v. Hugo, 168 N.Y. S. 25, 27, 101 Misc. 481. Or the entry of a decree by a court in respect to the parties in a case. Samuel Goldwyn, Inc., v. United Artists Corporation, C.C.A.Del., 113 F.2d 703, 706.

It implies a hearing by a court, after notice, of legal evidence on the factual issue involved. Genzer v. Fillip, Tex.Civ.App., 134 S.W.2d 730, 732. The equivalent of a "determination." Campbell v. Wyoming Development Co., 55 Wyo. 347, 100 P.2d 124, 132. And contemplates that the claims of all the parties thereto have been considered and set at rest. Miller v. Scobie, 152 Fla. 328, 11 So.2d 892, 894. The term is principally used in bankruptcy proceedings, the adjudication being the order which declares the debtor to be a bankrupt. First Nat. Bank v. Pothuisje, 217 Ind. 1, 25 N.E.2d 436, 438, 130 A.L.R. 1238.

French Law

A sale made at public auction and upon competition. Adjudications are voluntary, judicial, or administrative. Duverger.

Scotch Law

A species of diligence, or process for transferring the estate of a debtor to a creditor, carried on as an ordinary action before the court of session. A species of judicial sale, redeemable by the debtor. A decreet of the lords of session, adjudging and appropriating a person's lands, hereditaments, or any heritable right to belong to his creditor, who is called the "adjudger," for payment or performance. Bell; Ersk.Inst. c. 2, tit. 12, §§ 39–55; Forb.Inst. pt. 3, b. 1, c. 2, tit. 6.

Adjudication contra hæreditatem jacentem. When a debtor's heir apparent renounces the succession, any creditor may obtain a decree *cognitionis causâ*, the purpose of which is that the amount of the debt may be ascertained so that the real estate may be adjudged.

Adjudication in bankruptcy. See Bankruptcy.

Adjudication in implement. An action by a grantee against his grantor to compel him to complete the title.

ADJUNCT. Something added to another. New York Trust Co. v. Carpenter, C.C.A.Ohio, 250 F. 668, 672.

An additional judge sometimes appointed in the Court of Delegates, *q. v.*

ADJUNCTIO. In the civil law, adjunction; a species of *accessio,* whereby two things belonging to different proprietors are brought into firm connection with each other; such as interweaving, (*intertextura*); welding together, (*adferruminatio*); soldering together, (*applumbatura*); painting, (*pictura*); writing, (*scriptura*); building, (*inadificatio*); sewing, (*satio*); and planting, (*plantatio*). Inst. 2, 1, 26–34; Dig. 6, 1, 23; Mackeld.Rom.Law, § 276. See Accessio.

ADJUNCTION. In civil law, the attachment or union permanently of a thing belonging to one person to that belonging to another. This union may be caused by *inclusion,* as if one man's diamond be set in another's ring, or by *soldering, sewing, construction, writing,* or *painting.*

The common law implicitly adopts the civil law doctrines. See 2 Bla.Com. 404. See Accession.

One associated with another in a subordinate or an auxiliary manner; an associate.

ADJUNCTS. Additional judges sometimes appointed in the Court of Delegates, *q. v.* See Shelford, Lun. 310; 1 Hagg.Eccl.Rep. 384; 2 Id. 84; 3 id. 471.

ADJUNCTUM ACCESSORIUM. An accessory or appurtenance.

ADJURATION. A swearing or binding upon oath.

ADJUST. To settle or arrange; to free from differences or discrepancies; to bring to satisfactory state so that parties are agreed, as to adjust amount of loss by fire. Western Loggers' Machinery Co. v. National Union Fire Ins. Co., 136 Or. 549, 299 P. 311, 312. Controversy to property or estate, In re Sidman's Estate, 278 N.Y.S. 43, 154 Misc. 675. To bring to proper relations; to settle; Jeff Davis County v. Davis, Tex.Civ.App., 192 S.W. 291, 295. To determine and apportion an amount due. Flaherty v. Insurance Co., 46 N.Y.S. 934, 20 App.Div. 275. Accounts are adjusted when they are settled and a balance struck. Townes v. Birchett, 12 Leigh Va. 173, 201. It is sometimes used in the sense of pay. See Lynch v. Nugent, 80 Iowa, 422, 46 N.W. 61. When used in reference to a liquidated claim, Combination Oil & Gas Co. v. Brady, Tex.Civ.App., 96 S.W.2d 415, 416.

ADJUSTED COST BASIS. For income tax purposes, original cost plus additions to capital less depreciation results in the "adjusted cost basis." Herder v. Helvering, 106 F.2d 153, 162, 70 App.D.C. 287.

ADJUSTER. One appointed to adjust a matter, to ascertain or arrange or settle. Commercial Credit Co. v. Macht, 89 Ind.App. 59, 165 N.E. 766. One who makes any adjustment or settlement. Popa v. Northern Ins. Co., 192 Mich. 237, 158 N.W. 945, 946, or who determines the amount of a claim, as a claim against an insurance company. Samchuck v. Insurance Co. of North America, 99 Or. 565, 194 P. 1095. He is a special agent for the person or company for whom he acts. Bond v. National Fire Ins. Co., 77 W.Va. 736, 88 S.E. 389, 394; Howe v. State Bar of California, 212 Cal. 222, 298 P. 25, 27. Compare Manheim v. Standard Fire Ins. Co. of Hartford, Conn., 84 Wash. 16, 145 P. 992.

ADJUSTMENT. An arrangement; a settlement. Henry D. Davis Lumber Co. v. Pacific Lumber Agency, 220 P. 804, 805, 127 Wash. 198.

In the law of insurance, the adjustment of a loss is the ascertainment of its amount and the ratable distribution of it among those liable to pay it; the settling and ascertaining the amount of the indemnity which the assured, after all allowances and deductions made, is entitled to receive under the policy, and fixing the proportion which each underwriter is liable to pay. Marsh.Ins. 4th Ed. 499; 2 Phil.Ins. §§ 1814, 1815; New York v. Insurance Co., 39 N.Y. 45, 100 Am.Dec. 400; Whipple v. Insurance Co., 11 R. I. 139.

ADJUTANT GENERAL. The term "civil adjutant general" is used as one of convenience merely to designate state adjutant general who has not been officially recognized by War Department. People v. Newlon, 77 Colo. 516, 238 P. 44, 47.

ADJUVARI QUIPPE NOS, NON DECIPI, BENEFICIO OPORTET. We ought to be favored, not injured by that which is intended for our benefit. (The species of bailment called "loan" must be to the advantage of the borrower, not to his detriment.) Story, Bailm. § 275. See 8 El. & Bl. 1051.

ADLAMWR. In Welsh law, a proprietor who, for some cause, entered the service of another proprietor, and left him after the expiration of a year and a day. He was liable to the payment of 30 pence to his patron. Wharton.

ADLEGIARE. To purge one's self of a crime by oath.

ADMANUENSIS. A person who swore by laying his hands on the book.

ADMEASUREMENT. Ascertainment by measure; measuring out; assignment or apportionment by measure, that is, by fixed quantity or value, by certain limits, or in definite and fixed proportions.

ADMEASUREMENT OF DOWER. In practice, a remedy which lay for the heir on reaching his majority to rectify an assignment of dower made during his minority, by which the doweress had received more than she was legally entitled to. 2 Bl.Comm. 136; Gilb. Uses, 379.

The remedy is of rare occurrence. Jones v. Brewer, 1 Pick. (Mass.) 314; McCormick v. Taylor, 2 Ind. 336. In some of the states the statutory proceeding enabling a widow to compel the assignment of dower is called "admeasurement of dower."

ADMEASUREMENT OF PASTURE. In English law, a writ which lay between those that have common of pasture appendant, or by vicinage, in cases where any one or more of them surcharges the common with more cattle than they ought. Bract. fol. 229*a;* 1 Crabb, Real Prop. p. 318, § 358. The remedy is now abolished in England; 3 Sharsw.Bla.Com. 239, *n.;* and in the United States; 3 Kent 419.

ADMEASUREMENT, WRIT OF. It lay against persons who usurped more than their share, in the two following cases: Admeasurement of dower, and admeasurement of pasture. Termes de la Ley.

ADMENSURATIO. In old English law, admeasurement. Reg.Orig. 156, 157.

ADMEZATORES. In old Italian law, persons chosen by the consent of contending parties, to decide questions between them. Literally, mediators. Spelman.

ADMINICLE. Used as an English word in the statute of 1 Edw. IV, c. 1, in the sense of aid, or support.

In civil law, imperfect proof. Merl. Répert. See Adminiculum.

In Scotch law, an aid or support to something else. A collateral deed or writing, referring to another which has been lost, and which it is in general necessary to produce before the tenor of the lost deed can be proved by parol evidence. Ersk.Inst. b. 4, tit. 1, § 55.

ADMINICULAR. Auxiliary or subordinate to. "The murder would be *adminicular* to the robbery," (*i. e.,* committed to accomplish it.) The Marianna Flora, 3 Mason, 121, Fed.Cas.No.9080.

ADMINICULAR EVIDENCE. Auxiliary or supplementary evidence; such as is presented for the purpose of explaining and completing other evidence. (Chiefly used in ecclesiastical law)

ADMINICULATE. To give adminicular evidence.

ADMINICULATOR. An officer in the Romish church, who administered to the wants of widows, orphans, and afflicted persons. Spelman.

ADMINICULUM. Lat. An adminicle; a prop or support; an accessory thing. An aid or support to something else, whether a right or the evidence of one. It is principally used to designate evidence adduced in aid or support of other evidence, which without it is imperfect. Brown.

ADMINISTER. To manage or conduct. Glocksen v. Holmes, 299 Ky. 626, 186 S.W.2d 634, 637. To discharge the duties of an office; to take charge of business; to manage affairs; to serve in the conduct of affairs, in the application of things to their uses; to settle and distribute the estate of a decedent. Hunter v. City of Louisville, 208 Ky. 562, 271 S.W. 690, 691.

Also, to give, as an oath; to direct or cause to be taken. Gilchrist v. Comfort, 34 N.Y. 239; Brinson v. State, 89 Ala. 105, 8 So. 527; State v. Van Wormer, 103 Kan. 309, 173 P. 1076, 1081.

To apply, as medicine or a remedy; to give, as a dose or something beneficial or suitable. Barfield v. State, 71 Okl.Cr. 195, 110 P.2d 316, 317. To cause or procure a person to take some drug or other substance into his or her system; to direct and cause a medicine, poison, or drug to be taken into the system. State v. Jones, 4 Pennewill (Del.) 109, 53 Atl. 861; McCaughey v. State, 156 Ind. 41, 59 N.E. 169.

Neither fraud nor deception is a necessary ingredient in the act of administering poison. To force poison into the stomach of another; to compel another by threats of violence to swallow poison; to furnish poison to another for the purpose and with the intention that the person to whom it is delivered shall commit suicide therewith, and which poison is accordingly taken by the suicide for that purpose; or to be present at the taking of poison by a suicide, participating in the taking thereof, by assistance, persuasion, or otherwise,—each and all of these are forms and modes of "administering" poison. Blackburn v. State, 23 Ohio St. 146.

ADMINISTRATION. Managing or conduct of an office or employment; the performance of the executive duties of an institution, business, or the like. Webb v. Frohmiller, 52 Ariz. 128, 79 P.2d 510.

In public law, the administration of government means the practical management and direction of the executive department, or of the public machinery or functions, or of the operations of the various organs of the sovereign; direction or oversight of any office, service, or employment. Greene v. Wheeler, C.C.A.Wis., 29 F.2d 468, 469. The term "administration" is also conventionally applied to the whole class of public functionaries, or those in charge of the management of the executive department. House v. Creveling, 147 Tenn. 589, 250 S.W. 357, 358.

ADMINISTRATION EXPENSE. "Administrative expenses" imply disbursements incidental to the management of the estate for which credit would be allowed on a voucher. In re Hooker's Estate, 18 N.Y.S.2d 107, 112, 173 Misc. 515. Those deductible in computing estate tax are merely charges which are proper deductions and in ordinary course of administration will ultimately be allowed. Bourne v. U. S., Ct.Cl., 2 F.Supp. 228, 231.

ADMINISTRATION OF ESTATES. Supervision by an executor or administrator. Peterson v. Demmer, D.C.Tex., 34 F.Supp. 697, 700. Management of estate by independent executrix. Palfrey v. Harborth, Tex.Civ.App., 158 S.W.2d 326, 327. Normally involves the collection, management, and distribution of estate, including legal proceedings necessary to satisfy claims of creditors, next of kin, legatees, or whatever other parties may have any claim to property of a deceased person. Hawley v. Hawley, 114 F.2d 745, 748, 72 App.D.C. 376.

The management and settlement of the estate of an intestate, or of a testator who has no executor, performed under the supervision of a court, by a person duly qualified and legally appointed, and usually involving (1) the collection of the decedent's assets; (2) payment of debts and claims against him and expenses; (3) distributing the remainder of the estate among those entitled thereto.

The term is applied broadly to denote the management of an estate by an executor, and also the management of estates of minors, lunatics, etc., in those cases where trustees have been appointed by authority of law to take charge of such estates in place of the legal owners. Bouvier; Crow v. Hubard, 62 Md. 565.

Administration is principally of the following kinds, viz.:

Ad colligendum bona defuncti. To collect the goods of the deceased. Special letters of administration granted to one or more persons, authorizing them to *collect* and preserve the goods of the deceased, are so called. 2 Bl.Comm. 505; 2 Steph.Comm. 241. These are otherwise termed "letters *ad colligendum,*" and the party to whom they are granted, a "collector."

An administrator *ad colligendum* is the mere agent or officer of the court to collect and preserve the goods of the deceased until some one is clothed with authority to administer them, and cannot complain that another is appointed administrator in chief. Flora v. Mennice, 12 Ala. 836.

Ancillary administration is auxiliary and subordinate to the administration at the place of the decedent's domicile; it may be taken out in any foreign state or country where assets are locally situated, and is merely for the purpose of collecting such assets and paying debts there.

Cum testamento annexo. Administration with the will annexed. Administration granted in cases where a testator makes a will, without naming any executors; or where the executors who are named in the will are incompetent to act, or refuse to act; or in case of the death of the executors, or the survivor of them. 2 Bl.Comm. 503, 504.

De bonis non. Administration of the goods not administered. Administration granted for the purpose of administering such *of the goods* of a deceased person as were *not administered* by the former executor or administrator. Tucker v. Horner, 10 Phila.Pa. 122.

De bonis non cum testamento annexo. That which is granted when an executor dies leaving a part of the estate unadministered. Clemens v. Walker, 40 Ala. 189.

Durante absentia. That which is granted during the absence of the executor and until he has proved the will.

Durante minori ætate. Where an infant is made executor; in which case administration with will annexed is granted to another, during the minority of such executor, and until he shall attain his lawful age to act. See Godo. 102.

Foreign administration. That which is exercised by virtue of authority properly conferred by a foreign power.

Pendente lite. Administration during the suit. Administration granted during the pendency of a suit touching the validity of a will. 18 N.J.Law, 15, 20.

Public administration is such as is conducted (in some jurisdictions) by an officer called the public administrator, who is appointed to administer in cases where the intestate has left no person entitled to apply for letters.

General administration. The grant of authority to administer upon the entire estate of a decedent, without restriction or limitation, whether under the intestate laws or with the will annexed. Clemens v. Walker, 40 Ala. 198.

Special administration. Authority to administer upon some few particular effects of a decedent, as opposed to authority to administer his whole estate. In re Senate Bill, 12 Colo. 193, 21 P. 482.

Letters of Administration. The instrument by which an administrator or administratrix is authorized by the probate court, surrogate, or other proper officer, to have the charge and administration of the goods and chattels of an intestate. See Mutual Ben. L. Ins. Co. v. Tisdale, 91 U.S. 243, 23 L.Ed. 314.

ADMINISTRATION SUIT. In English practice, a suit brought in chancery, by any one interested, for administration of a decedent's estate, when there is doubt as to its solvency. Stimson.

ADMINISTRATIVE. Connotes of or pertains to administration, especially management, as by managing or conducting, directing, or superintending, the execution, application, or conduct of persons or things. Fluet v. McCabe, Mass., 299 Mass. 173, 12 N.E.2d 89, 93. Particularly, having the character of executive or ministerial action. Mauritz v. Schwind, Tex.Civ.App., 101 S.W.2d 1085, 1090. In this sense, administrative functions or acts are distinguished from such as are judicial. People v. Austin, 46 N.Y.Supp. 526, 20 App.Div. 1. Synonymous with "executive." Sheely v. People, 54 Colo. 136, 129 P. 201, 202; Saint v. Allen, 126 So. 548, 555, 169 La. 1046. An administrative act concerns daily affairs as distinguished from permanent matters. People v. Graham, 70 Colo. 509, 203 P. 277, 278.

ADMINISTRATIVE ACTS. Acts of an officer which are to be deemed as acts of administration, and are commonly called "administrative acts" and classed among those governmental powers properly assigned to the executive department, are those acts which are necessary to be done to carry out legislative policies and purposes already declared by the legislative body or such as are devolved upon it by the organic law of its existence. Ex parte McDonough, 27 Cal.App.2d 155, 80 P.2d 485, 487.

ADMINISTRATIVE AGENCY. An agency of the sovereign power charged with administering particular legislation. Examples are compensation and industrial commissions, Joseph H. Weiderhoff, Inc., v. Neal, D.C.Mo., 6 F.Supp. 798, 799; Federal Trade Commission, Hastings Mfg. Co. v. Federal Trade Commission, 153 F.2d 253, certiorari denied 66 S.Ct. 1344, 328 U.S. 853, 90 L.Ed. 1626; tax commissions, First State Bank of Mountainair v. State Tax Commission, 59 P.2d 667, 40 N.M. 319; public service commissions, New York Cent. R. Co. v. Public Service Commission, 7 N.E. 2d 957, 212 Ind. 329; and the like.

ADMINISTRATIVE BOARD. The term is very broad and includes bodies exercising varied functions, some of which involve orders made or other acts done ex parte or without full hearing as to the operative facts, while others are done only after such a notice and hearing, and the functions of the former kind are plainly "administrative" and those of the latter are "quasi judicial". Beaverdale Memorial Park v. Danaher, 127 Conn. 175, 15 A.2d 17, 21.

"Administrative boards" differ from "courts" in that boards frequently represent public interests entrusted to boards, whereas courts are concerned with litigating rights of parties with adverse interests. Rommell v. Walsh, 15 A.2d 6, 9, 127 Conn. 16.

ADMINISTRATIVE DISCRETION. "Administrative discretion" means that the doing of acts or things required to be done may rest, in part at least, upon considerations not entirely susceptible of proof or disproof and at times which considering the circumstances and subject-matter cannot be supplied by the Legislature, and a statute confers such discretion when it refers a commission or officer to beliefs, expectations, or tendencies instead of facts for the exercise of the powers conferred. Culver v. Smith, Tex.Civ.App., 74 S. W.2d 754, 757.

ADMINISTRATIVE LAW. That branch of public law which deals with the various organs of the sovereign power considered as in motion, and prescribes in detail the manner of their activity, being concerned with such topics as the collection of the revenue, the regulation of the military and naval forces, citizenship and naturalization, sanitary measures, poor laws, coinage, police, the public safety and morals, etc. See Holl.Jur. 305–307.

ADMINISTRATIVE OFFICER. Politically and as used in constitutional law, an officer of the executive department of government, and generally one of inferior rank; legally, a ministerial or executive officer, as distinguished from a judicial officer. People v. Salsbury, 134 Mich. 537, 96 N.W. 936.

One who performs mere ministerial or administrative functions. In re Gold, C.C.A.N.J., 93 F.2d 676, 680. Officers that are neither judicial nor legislative; executive officers, Spivey v. State, 104 P.2d 263, 277, 69 Okl.Cr. 397. Such as: The clerk of circuit court, State ex rel. and to Use of City of St. Louis v. Priest, 348 Mo. 37, 152 S.W.2d 109, 112. Receivers in bank liquidation proceedings, People ex rel. Nelson v. Crawford State Sav. Bank, 310 Ill.App. 533, 34 N.E.2d 872. State highway commissioner, Strobel Steel Const. Co. v. Sterner, 125 N.J.L. 622, 18 A.2d 28, 29.

ADMINISTRATIVE REMEDY. One not judicial, but provided by commission or board created by legislative power. Kansas City Southern R. Co. v. Ogden Levee Dist., C.C.A.Ark., 15 F.2d 637, 642. Against wrongful assessment of benefits by a levee district. Board of Directors of St. Francis Levee Dist. v. St. Louis-San Francisco Ry. Co., C.C.A.Ark., 74 F.2d 183, 188.

ADMINISTRATOR, in the most usual sense of the word, is a person to whom letters of administration, that is, an authority to administer the estate of a deceased person, have been granted by the proper court. A representative of limited authority, whose duties are to collect assets of estate, pay its debts, and distribute residue to those entitled. Smith v. White's Estate, 108 Vt. 473, 188 A. 901, 904. A technical trustee. In re Watkins' Estate, Vt., 41 A.2d 180, 188.

He resembles an executor, but, being appointed by the court, and not by the deceased, he has to give security for the due administration of the estate, by entering into a bond with sureties, called the administration bond. Smith v. Gentry, 16 Ga. 31; Collamore v. Wilder, 19 Kan. 78; Gormley v. Watson, 177 Ga. 763, 171 S.E. 280, 281.

By the law of Scotland the father is what is called the "administrator-in-law" for his children. As such, he is *ipso jure* their tutor while they are pupils, and their curator during their minority. The father's power extends over whatever estate may descend to his children, unless where that estate has been placed by the donor or grantor under the charge of special trustees or managers. This power in the father ceases by the child's discontinuing to reside with him, unless he continues to live at the father's expense; and with regard to daughters, it ceases on their marriage, the husband being the legal curator of his wife. Bell.

Civil Law

A manager or conductor of affairs, especially the affairs of another, in his name or behalf. A manager of public affairs in behalf of others. Calvin. A public officer, ruler, or governor. Nov. 95, gl.; Cod. 12, 8.

Domestic

One appointed at the place of the domicile of the decedent; distinguished from a foreign or an ancillary administrator.

Foreign

One appointed or qualified under the laws of a foreign state or country, where the decedent was domiciled.

Public

An official provided for by statute in some states to administer upon the property of intestates in certain cases. See Rocca v. Thompson, 32 S.Ct. 207, 223 U.S. 317, 56 L.Ed. 453.

ADMINISTRATOR CUM TESTAMENTO ANNEXO. See Cum Testamento Annexo.

ADMINISTRATOR DE BONIS NON. "Administrators de bonis non administratis" are, as the term signifies, persons appointed by the court of probate to administer on the effects of a decedent which have not been included in a former administration. Paul v. Butler, 129 Kan. 244, 282 P. 732, 734.

Where will is set aside as void, administrator subsequently appointed is not "administrator de bonis non," but administrator of entire estate with power to attack nominated executor's report. Douglas' Adm'r v. Douglas' Ex'r, 48 S.W.2d 11, 14, 243 Ky. 321.

ADMINISTRATOR WITH WILL ANNEXED. One appointed administrator of deceased's estate after executors named in will refused to act. In re Kenney's Estate, 41 N.M. 576, 72 P.2d 27, 29, 113 A.L.R. 403.

ADMINISTRATRIX. A woman who administers, or to whom letters of administration have been granted.

ADMINISTRAVIT. Lat. He has administered. Used in the phrase *plene administravit,* which is the name of a plea by an executor or administrator to the effect that he has "fully administered" (lawfully disposed of) all the assets of the estate that have come to his hands.

ADMIRAL. Title of high naval officers; they are of various grades,—rear admiral, vice-admiral, admiral, admiral of the fleet, the last named being the highest. But by Act of Jan. 24, 1873 (17 Stat. 418), certain grades ceased to exist when the offices became vacant.

In old English law, a high officer or magistrate that had the government of the king's navy, and the hearing of all causes belonging to the sea. Cowell.

In European law, an officer who presided over the *admiralitas,* or *collegium ammiralitatis.* Locc. de Jur.Mar. lib. 2, c. 2, § 1.

ADMIRALITAS. L. Lat. Admiralty; the admiralty, or court of admiralty.

In European law, an association of private armed vessels for mutual protection and defense against pirates and enemies

ADMIRALTY. A court which has a very extensive jurisdiction of maritime causes, civil and criminal, controversies arising out of acts done upon or relating to the sea, and questions of prize.

It is properly the successor of the consular courts, which were emphatically the courts of merchants and sea-going persons, established in the principal maritime cities on the revival of commerce after the fall of the Western Empire, to supply the want of tribunals that might decide causes arising out of maritime commerce.

Also, the system of jurisprudence relating to and growing out of the jurisdiction and practice of the admiralty courts.

American Law

A tribunal exercising jurisdiction over all maritime contracts, torts, injuries, or offenses. Panama R. Co. v. Johnson, 44 S.Ct. 391, 264 U.S. 375, 68 L.Ed. 748.

"Admiralty" does not extend to all navigable waters, but is limited to the ocean, navigable rivers running into the ocean, and the Great Lakes and their connections. The Frank G. Fobert, D.C.N.Y., 32 F.Supp. 214, 216.

The jurisdiction of the admiral, and the administration of the admiralty law proper—the local maritime law—as it became a judicial function, has passed into the hands of the courts. Renew v. U. S., D.C.Ga., 1 F.Supp. 256, 259.

English Law

The court of the admiral, perhaps erected by Edward III, 3 Bla.Comm. 69, or as early as the time of Henry I.

The building where the lords of the admiralty transact business.

ADMIRALTY, FIRST LORD OF THE. The normal head of the executive department of state which presides over the naval forces of the kingdom is the lord high admiral, but in practice the functions of the great office are discharged by several Lords Commissioners, of whom one, being the chief, is called the "First Lord," and is a member of the Cabinet. He is assisted by other lords, called Sea Lords, and by various secretaries.

ADMISSIBLE. Pertinent and proper to be considered in reaching a decision. Used with reference to the issues to be decided in any judicial proceeding.

As applied to evidence, the term means that it is of such a character that the court or judge is bound to receive it; that is, allow it to be introduced.

ADMISSION.

Bail

The order of a competent court or magistrate that a person accused of crime be discharged from actual custody upon the taking of bail. People v. Solomon, 15 Pac. 4, 5 Utah, 277.

Admitting to bail is a judicial act to be performed by a court or judicial officer, Trevathan v. Mutual Life Ins. Co. of New York, 166 Or. 515, 113 P.2d 621, 624; and by "allowing bail" or "admitting to bail" is not meant the formal justification, subscription, or acknowledgment by the sureties, the term first mentioned relating to the order determining that the offense is bailable and fixing the amount of undertaking, and "taking the bail" meaning the final acceptance or approval of it by the court. Clatsop County v. Wuopio, 95 Or. 30, 186 P. 547.

English Ecclesiastical Law

The act of the bishop, who, on approval of the clerk presented by the patron, after examination, declares him fit to serve the cure of the church to which he is presented, by the words *"admitto te habilem,"* I admit thee able. 1 Crabb, Real Prop. p. 138, § 123.

Immigration Laws

Authorities accepting alien seaman into body of our inhabitants as possible resident. U. S. ex rel. Georgas v. Day, C.C.A.N.Y., 43 F.2d 917, 919.

Membership in Corporation

The act of a corporation or company by which an individual acquires the rights of a member of such corporation or company.

Practice as Attorney at Law

The act by which attorneys and counsellors become recognized as officers of the court and are allowed to practice.

Testimony or Evidence

Admission or concession by a party in pleading or as evidence. See Admissions.

ADMISSIONALIS. In European law. An usher. Spelman.

ADMISSIONS. Confessions, concessions or voluntary acknowledgments made by a party of the existence of certain facts. Roosevelt v. Smith, 40 N.Y.S. 381, 17 Misc. 323. More accurately regarded, they are statements by a party, or some one identified with him in legal interest, of the existence of a fact which is relevant to the cause of his adversary. Brooks v. Sessoms, 171 S.E. 222, 223, 47 Ga.App. 554. They are against the interest of the party making them. Little Fay Oil Co. v. Stanley, 90 Okl. 265, 217 P. 377, 378.

It is not essential that an "admission" be contrary to interest of party at time it is made; it is enough if it be inconsistent with position which party takes either in pleadings or at trial. Harvey v. Provandie, 83 N.H. 236, 141 A. 136, 140.

The term "admission" is usually applied to civil transactions and to those matters of fact in criminal cases which do not involve criminal intent, while the term "confession" is generally restricted to acknowledgments of guilt. People v. Sourisseau, 62 Cal.App.2d 917, 145 P.2d 916, 923. State v. Lindsey, 26 N.M. 526, 194 P. 877, 878.

An "admission" as applied in criminal cases is the avowal of a fact or of circumstances from which guilt may be inferred, but only tending to prove the offense charged, and not amounting to a confession of guilt. Theis v. State, Ga., 164 S.

E. 456, 457. A statement by defendant of fact or facts pertinent to issues tending, in connection with proof of other facts or circumstances, to prove guilt, but which is, of itself, insufficient to authorize conviction. Commonwealth v. Elliott, 292 Pa. 16, 140 A. 537, 538. Does not include statements which are part of the res gestæ. State v. Clark, 102 Mont. 432, 58 P.2d 276, 278.

Direct, called also *express,* admissions are those which are made in direct terms.

Implied admissions are those which result from some act or failure to act of the party. Part payment of a debt is an admission of liability to pay debt. Hart v. Deshong, Del., 1 Terry 218, 8 A.2d 85, 87. Defendants' failure to specifically deny their signatures to notes, "admission" that they signed the acknowledgments. Háas v. Johnson, 203 La. 697, 14 So.2d 606, 608. Undenied accusations were implied "admission". State v. Postal, 215 Minn. 427, 10 N.W.2d 373, 378.

Incidental admissions are those made in some other connection, or involved in the admission of some other fact.

Judicial admissions are those made in court by a person's attorney for the purpose of being used as a substitute for the regular legal evidence of the facts at the trial. Martin v. State, 46 Okl.Cr. 411, 287 P. 424. Such as are made voluntarily by a party, which appear of record in the proceedings of the court. Formal acts done by a party or his attorney in court on the trial of a cause for the purpose of dispensing with proof by the opposing party of some fact claimed by the latter to be true. Wiley v. Rutland R. Co., 86 Vt. 504, 86 A. 808, 810. Concession by defendant that she had executed a bill of sale for the automobile to intervener to secure an indebtedness was an "admission in judicio" by defendant against her title to the automobile. McDay v. Long, 63 Ga.App. 421, 11 S.E.2d 395, 399. But opening statements of counsel are not, technically, "admissions." Wilkey v. State ex rel. Smith, 238 Ala. 595, 192 So. 588, 591. See Acquiescence; Quasi-Admissions; True Admission.

Pleading

The acknowledgment or recognition by one party of the truth of some matter alleged by the opposite party, made in a pleading, the effect of which is to narrow the area of facts or allegations required to be proved by evidence. Connecticut Hospital v. Brookfield, 69 Conn. 1, 36 A. 1017.

An allegation not denied is deemed not controverted, and silence of pleader is usually treated as an admission against him for purpose of the action. Doughty v. Pallissard, 3 N.Y.S.2d 452, 453, 167 Misc. 55. Generally pleadings must be regarded as "judicial admissions", rather than ordinary "admissions". Hughes v. Fort Worth Nat. Bank, Tex.Civ.App., 164 S.W.2d 231, 232.

In *confession and avoidance,* admission of truth of opposite party's pleading is made.

Express admissions may be made of matters of fact only. See Confession and Avoidance.

In Equity. Partial admissions are those which are delivered in terms of uncertainty, mixed up with expianatory or qualifying circumstances.

Plenary admissions are those which admit the truth of the matter without qualification, whether it be asserted as from information and belief or as from actual knowledge. See Burrell v. Hackley, C.C.N.Y., 35 F. 833.

"Admissions against interest" are any statements made by or attributable to a party to an action, which constitute admissions against his interest and tend to establish or disprove any material fact in the case. Kellner v. Whaley, 148 Neb. 259, 27 N.W.2d 183, 189.

ADMIT. To allow, receive, or take; to suffer one to enter; to give possession; to license. Gregory v. United States, 17 Blatchf. 325, 10 Fed.Cas. 1195. Confess. Provident Life & Accident Ins. Co. v. Fodder, 99 Ind.App. 556, 193 N.E. 698, 700. Unequivocal acknowledgment of guilt. Ex parte Tozier, D.C.Me., 2 F.2d 268, 269. See Admission; Admissions.

ADMITTANCE. In English law, the act of giving possession of a copyhold estate. It is of three kinds: (1) Upon a voluntary grant by the lord, where the land has escheated or reverted to him. (2) Upon surrender by the former tenant. (3) Upon descent, where the heir is tenant on his ancestor's death. 2 Bla.Comm. 366.

ADMITTENDO CLERICO. An old English writ issuing to the bishop to establish the right of the Crown to make a presentation to a benefice. A writ of execution upon a right of presentation to a benefice being recovered in *quare impedit,* addressed to the bishop or his metropolitan, requiring him to admit and institute the clerk or presentee of the plaintiff. Reg.Orig. 33*a*.

ADMITTENDO IN SOCIUM. A writ for associating certain persons, as knights and other gentlemen of the county, to justices of assize on the circuit. Reg.Orig. 206.

ADMIXTURE. A substance formed by mixing; state of being mixed; act of mixing.

ADMONISH. To caution or advise. People v. Pennington, 267 Ill. 45, 107 N.E. 871, 872. To counsel against wrong practices, or to warn against danger of an offense. Ft. Smith Light & Traction Co. v. Hendrickson, 126 Ark. 377, 189 S. W. 1064, 1067.

ADMONITION. A reprimand from a judge to a person accused, on being discharged, warning him of the consequences of his conduct, and intimating to him that, should he be guilty of the same fault for which he has been admonished, he will be punished with greater severity. Merlin, *Répert.* The admonition was authorized as a species of punishment for slight misdemeanors. In ecclesiastical law, this is the lightest form of punishment.

Any authoritative oral communication or statement by way of advice or caution by the court to the jury respecting their duty or conduct as jurors, the admissibility or nonadmissibility of evidence, or the purpose for which any evidence admitted may be considered by them. Miller v. Noell, 193 Ky. 659, 237 S.W. 373, 374.

ADMONITIO TRINA. The threefold warning given to a prisoner who stood mute, before he was subjected to *peine forte et dure* (*q. v.*). 4 Bl.Comm. 325; 4 Steph.Comm. 391.

ADMORTIZATION. The reduction of property of lands or tenements to mortmain, in the feudal customs.

ADM'R. Ths abbreviation will be judicially presumed to mean "administrator." Moseley v. Mastin, 37 Ala. 216, 221.

ADNEPOS. The son of a great-great-grandson. Calvinus, Lex.

ADNEPTIS. The daughter of a great-great-granddaughter. Calvinus, Lex.

ADNICHILED. Annulled, canceled, made void. 28 Hen. VIII.

ADNIHILARE. In old English law, to annul; to make void; to reduce to nothing; to treat as nothing; to hold as or for nought.

ADNOTATIO. In the civil law, the subscription of a name or signature to an instrument. Cod. 4, 19, 5, 7.

A rescript *(q. v.)* of the prince or emperor, signed with his own hand, or sign-manual. Cod. 1, 19, 1. "In the imperial law, casual homicide was excused by the indulgence of the emperor, signed with his own sign-manual, *annotatione principis*." 4 Bl.Comm. 187.

ADOBE. Earth. In arid or desert regions, an alluvial or playa clay from which bricks are made for construction of houses, called "adobe" houses. See Sweeney v. Jackson County, 93 Or. 96, 178 P. 365, 376.

ADOLESCENCE. That age which follows puberty and precedes the age of majority. It commences for males at fourteen, and for females at twelve years, and continues until twenty-one years complete.

ADOPT. To accept, appropriate, choose, or select; to make that one's own (property or act) which was not so originally.

To adopt a route for the transportation of the mail means to take the steps necessary to cause the mail to be transported over that route. Rhodes v. U. S., Dev.Ct.Cl. 47. To adopt a contract is to accept it as binding, notwithstanding some defect which entitles the party to repudiate it. Thus, when a person affirms a voidable contract, or ratifies a contract made by his agent beyond his authority, he is sometimes said to adopt it. Sweet. Strictly, however, the word "adopt" should be used to apply to void transactions, while the word "ratify" should be limited to the final approval of a voidable transaction by one who theretofore had the optional right to relieve himself from its obligations. United German Silver Co. v. Bronson, 92 Conn. 266, 102 A. 647, 648. "Adoption" of a contract by one not a party thereto is of the nature of a novation. Edwards v. Heralds of Liberty, 263 Pa. 548, 107 A. 324, 326. See Affirm.

To accept, consent to, and put into effective operation; as in the case of a constitution, constitutional amendment, ordinance, or by-law. Real v. People, 42 N.Y. 282; People v. Norton, 59 Barb. (N.Y.) 191. A Code. City of Albany v. Nix, 21 Ala.App. 164, 106 So. 199, 200. Statements in an application appearing above insured's signature. Republic Mut. Ins. Co. v. Wilson, 66 Ohio App. 522, 35 N.E.2d 467, 468.

To take into one's family the child of another and give him or her the rights, privileges, and duties of a child and heir. State v. Thompson, 13 La.Ann. 515; Abney v. De Loach, 84 Ala. 393.

Adoption of children was a thing unknown to the common law, but was a familiar practice under the Roman law and in those countries where the civil law prevails, as France and Spain. Butterfield v. Sawyer, 187 Ill. 598, 58 N.E. 602, 52 L.R.A. 75, 79 Am.St.Rep. 246. Creature of the law, and statutory requirements must be strictly carried out. Owles v. Jackson, 199 La. 940, 7 So.2d 192, 194.

To accept an alien as a citizen or member of a community or state and invest him with corresponding rights and privileges, either (in general and untechnical parlance) by naturalization, or by an act equivalent to naturalization, as where a white man is "adopted" by an Indian tribe. Hampton v. Mays, 4 Ind.T. 503, 69 S.W. 1115.

ADOPTION. The taking and receiving as one's own that to which he bore no prior relation, colorable or otherwise. Davies v. Lahann, C.C.A.N.M., 145 F.2d 656, 659. The act of one who takes another's child into his own family, treating him as his own, and giving him all the rights and duties of his own child. See In re Chambers' Estate, 183 N.Y.S. 526, 528, 112 Misc. 551. In manner provided by and with consequences specified in statute. Fisher v. Robison, 329 Pa. 305, 198 A. 81, 82. A juridicial act creating between two persons certain relations, purely civil, of paternity and filiation. 6 Demol. § 1; Grimes v. Grimes, 207 N.C. 778, 178 S.E. 573. The relation thereby created is a statutory status, not a contractual relation. Caruso v. Caruso, 13 N.Y.S.2d 239, 241, 175 Misc. 290. Though legal adoption may confer on person adopted rights of actual relationship of child, simple "adoption" extends only to his treatment as member of the household. Shepherd v. Sovereign Camp, W.O.W., 166 Va. 488, 186 S.E. 113, 116. See, also, Adopt.

Adoption, properly speaking, refers only to persons who are strangers in blood, In re Lund's Estate, Cal.App., 148 P.2d 709, 711. And is not synonymous with "legitimation," which refers to persons of the same blood. Blythe v. Ayres, 96 Cal. 532, 31 P. 915, 19 L.R.A. 40. But this distinction is not always observed. In re Presly's Estate, 113 Okl. 160, 240 P. 89, 90. It is a relationship artificially created by statute. Borner v. Larson, 70 N.D. 313, 293 N.W. 836, 839.

ADOPTION BY PUBLIC ACKNOWLEDGMENT. See Legitimate.

ADOPTIVE ACT. An act of legislation which comes into operation within a limited area upon being adopted, in manner prescribed therein, by the inhabitants of that area.

ADOPTIVUS. Lat. Adoptive. Applied both to the parent adopting, and the child adopted. Inst. 2, 13, 4; Inst. 3, 1, 10–14.

ADPROMISSOR. In the civil and Scotch law, a guarantor, surety, or cautioner; a peculiar species of *fidejussor;* one who adds his own promise to the promise given by the-principal debtor, whence the name.

ADQUIETO. Payment. Blount.

ADRECTARE. To set right, satisfy, or make amends.

ADRHAMIRE. In old European law, to undertake, declare, or promise solemnly; to pledge; to pledge one's self to make oath. Spelman.

ADRIFT. Sea-weed, between high and low watermark, which has not been deposited on the shore, and which during flood-tide is moved by each rising and receding wave, is *adrift,* although the bottom of the mass may touch the beach. Anthony v. Gifford, 2 Allen (Mass.) 549.

ADROGATION. In the civil law, the adoption of one who was *impubes;* that is, if a male, under fourteen years of age; if a female, under twelve. Dig. 1, 7, 17, 1.

ADS. An abbreviation for *ad sectam (q. v.)*, meaning "at the suit of." Bowen v. Sewing Mach. Co., 86 Ill. 11.

ADSCENDENTES. Lat. In the civil law, ascendants. Dig. 23, 2, 68; Cod. 5, 5, 6.

ADSCRIPTI. See Adscriptus.

ADSCRIPTI GLEBÆ. Slaves who served the master of the soil, who were annexed to the land, and passed with it when it was conveyed. Calvinus, Lex.

In Scotland, as late as the reign of George III., laborers in collieries and salt works were bound to the coal-pit or salt work in which they were engaged, in a manner similar to that of the *adscripti* of the Romans. Bell. These *servi adscripti* (or *adscriptitii*) *glebæ* held the same position as the *villeins regardant* of the Normans; 2 Bla.Com. 93. See 1 Poll. & Mait. 372.

ADSCRIPTITII. Lat. A species of serfs or slaves. See 1 Poll. & Mait. 372.

Those persons who were enrolled and liable to be drafted as legionary soldiers. Calvinus, Lex.

ADSCRIPTUS. In the civil law, added, annexed, or bound by or in writing; enrolled, registered; united, joined, annexed, bound to, generally. *Servus colonæ adscriptus,* a slave annexed to an estate as a cultivator. Dig. 19, 2, 54, 2. *Fundus adscriptus,* an estate bound to, or burdened with a duty. Cod. 11, 2, 3.

ADSESSORES. Side judges. Assistants or advisers of the regular magistrates, or appointed as their substitutes in certain cases. Calvinus, Lex. See Assessor.

ADSTIPULATOR. In Roman law, an accessory party to a promise, who received the same promise as his principal did, and could equally receive and exact payment; or he only stipulated for a part of that for which the principal stipulated, and then his rights were coextensive with the amount of his own stipulation. One who supplied the place of a procurator at a time when the law refused to allow stipulations to be made by procuration. Sandars, Just.Inst. (5th Ed.) 348.

ADULT.

Civil Law

A male infant who has attained the age of fourteen; a female infant who has attained the age of twelve. Dom.Liv.Prel. tit. 2, § 2, n. 8.

Common Law

One who has attained the legal age of majority, generally 21 years, though in some states women are legally "adults" at 18. Schenault v. State, 10 Tex.App. 410; Lucas v. United States Fidelity & Guaranty Co., 174 A. 712, 713, 113 N.J.Law, 491.

ADULTER. Lat. One who corrupts; one who seduces another man's wife. *Adulter solidorum.* A corruptor of metals; a counterfeiter. Calvinus. Lex.

ADULTERA. In the civil law, an adulteress; a woman guilty of adultery. Dig. 48, 5, 4, pr.; Dig. 48, 5, 15, 8.

ADULTERATION. The act of corrupting or debasing; the act of mixing something impure or spurious with something pure or genuine, or an inferior article with a superior one of the same kind. State v. Norton, 24 N.C. 40. The term is generally applied to the act of mixing up with food or drink intended to be sold other matters of an inferior quality, and usually of a more or less deleterious quality. Grosvenor v. Duffy, 121 Mich. 220, 80 N.W. 19, though the artificially colored poppy seeds were not deleterious and had the same food value as the naturally colored seeds. U. S. v. Two Bags, Each Containing 110 Pounds, Poppy Seeds, C.C.A.Ohio, 147 F.2d 123, 127.

ADULTERATOR. Lat. A corrupter. In the civil law. A forger; a counterfeiter. *Adulteratores monetæ,* counterfeiters of money. Dig. 48, 19, 16, 9.

ADULTERINE. Begotten in an adulterous intercourse. Those are not deemed adulterine who are begotten of a woman openly married through ignorance of a former wife being alive. In the Roman and canon law, adulterine bastards were distinguished from such as were the issue of two unmarried persons, and the former were treated with more severity, not being allowed the *status* of natural children, and being ineligible to holy orders.

ADULTERINE BASTARDS. The offspring of adulterous relations. Kotzke v. Kotzke's Estate, 205 Mich. 184, 171 N.W. 442, 443. See, also, Adulterous Bastards.

ADULTERINE GUILDS. Traders acting as a corporation without a charter, and paying a fine annually for permission to exercise their usurped privileges. Smith, Wealth Nat. b. 1, c. 10.

ADULTERIUM. A fine anciently imposed for the commission of adultery.

ADULTEROUS BASTARDS. Those produced by an unlawful connection between two persons, who at the time when the child was conceived, were, either of them or both, connected by marriage with some other person. Civil Code La. art. 182.

ADULTERY. Voluntary sexual intercourse of a married person with a person other than the offender's husband or wife. Franzetti v. Franzetti, Tex.Civ.App., 120 S.W.2d 123, 127.

In some states, however, as was also true under the Roman and Jewish law, this crime is committed only when the *woman* is married to a third person; the unlawful commerce of a married man with an unmarried woman not being of the grade of adultery. Com. v. Call, 21 Pick. Mass. 509, 32 Am.Dec. 284, and note; Com. v. Elwell, 2 Metc. 190, 39 Am.Dec. 398. In other jurisdictions, both parties are guilty of adultery, even though only one of them is married. Goodwin v. State, 70 Tex.Cr.R. 600, 158 S.W. 274, 275. In some jurisdictions, also, a distinction is made between double and single adultery, the former being committed where both parties are married to other persons, the latter where one only is so married. Hunter v. U. S., 1 Pin.Wis. 91, 39 Am.Dec. 277.

Open and Notorious Adultery

To constitute living in open and notorious adultery, the parties must reside together publicly in the face of society, as if conjugal relations existed between them, and their so living and the fact that they are not husband and wife must be known in the community. McCullough v. State, 107 Tex.Cr.R. 258, 296 S.W. 530.

ADVANCE, *v.* To pay money or render other value before it is due; to furnish something before an equivalent is received; to loan; to furnish capital in aid of a projected enterprise, in expectation of return from it. Powell v. Allan, 70 Cal. App. 663, 234 P. 339, 344. To supply beforehand; to furnish on credit or before goods are delivered or work done; to furnish as a part of a stock or fund; to pay money before it is due; to furnish money for a specific purpose understood between the parties, the money or sum equivalent to be returned; furnishing money or goods for others in expectation of reimbursement; money or commodities furnished on credit; a loan, or gift or money advanced to be repaid conditionally; may be equivalent to "pay." In re Altman's Will, Sur., 6 N.Y.S.2d 972, 975.

An agreement to "advance" money for personal property implies a loan with property as pledge, rather than a payment of purchase money in sale. Shelley v. Byers, 73 Cal. App. 44, 238 P. 177, 182.

ADVANCE PAYMENT. Payments made in anticipation of a contingent or fixed future liability. Smith v. Unity Industrial Life Ins. Co., La.App., 13 So.2d 129, 132.

ADVANCEMENT. Money or property given by a parent to his child or, sometimes, presumptive heir, or expended by the former for the latter's benefit, by way of anticipation of the share which the child will inherit in the parent's estate and intended to be deducted therefrom. It is the latter circumstance which differentiates an advancement from a gift or a loan. Brewer's Adm'r v. Brewer, 181 Ky. 400, 205 S.W. 393, 396; In re Allen's Estate, 207 Pa. 325, 56 A. 928.

A perfect and irrevocable gift. In re Wiese's Estate, 222 Iowa 935, 270 N.W. 380, 382. Passing title in lifetime of donor. Burkhart v. Lowery, 115 Ind.App. 445, 59 N.E.2d 732, 734; but which must be accounted for by donee on distribution of donor's estate. In re Beier's Estate, 205 Minn. 43, 284 N.W. 833, 835, 836, 837, 838. "Advancement," unlike "ademption" (q. v.), applies only to cases of intestacy. Ellard v. Ferris, 91 Ohio St. 339, 110 N.E. 476, 479. An "advancement by portion," within the meaning of the statute, is a sum given by a parent to establish a child in life, (as by starting him in business,) or to make a provision for the child, (as on the marriage of a daughter). L. R. 20 Eq. 155. See Ademption; Gift.

ADVANCES. Moneys paid before or in advance of the proper time of payment; money or commodities furnished on credit; a loan or gift, or money advanced to be repaid conditionally. Powder Co. v. Burkhardt, 97 U.S. 110, 24 L.Ed. 973.

This word, when taken in its strict legal sense, does not mean gifts, (advancements,) and does mean a sort of loan; and, when taken in its ordinary and usual sense, it includes both loans and gifts,—loans more readily, perhaps, than gifts. Landrum & Co. v. Wright, 11 Ala.App. 406, 66 So. 892.

Payments advanced to the owner of property by a factor or broker on the price of goods which the latter has in his hands, or is to receive, for sale.

"Loans" are repayable at maturity, while "advances" are not repaid by party receiving them, but are covered by proceeds of consigned goods. People ex rel. James Talcott, Inc., v. Goldfogle, 211 N.Y.S. 122, 123, 213 App.Div. 719.

ADVANTAGE. Any state, condition, circumstance, opportunity, or means specially favorable to success, prosperity, interest, reputation, or any desired end. Duvall v. State, 92 Ind.App. 134, 166 N.E. 603, 604. Preference or priority. United States v. Preston, 4 Wash. 446, Fed.Cas.No.16,087.

ADVANTAGIUM. In old pleading, an advantage. Co.Ent. 484; Townsh.Pl. 50.

ADVENA. In Roman law, one of foreign birth, who has left his own country and settled elsewhere, and who has not acquired citizenship in his new locality; often called *albanus.* Du Cange.

ADVENT. A period of time recognized by the English common and ecclesiastical law, beginning on the Sunday that falls either upon St. Andrew's day, being the 30th of November, or the next to it, and continuing to Christmas day. Wharton.

ADVENTITIOUS. That which comes incidentally, fortuitously, or out of the regular course. "Adventitious value" of lands, see Central R. Co. v. State Board of Assessors, 49 N.J.Law, 1, 7 A. 306.

ADVENTITIUS. Lat. Fortuitous; incidental; coming from an unusual source. *Adventitia bona* are goods which fall to a man otherwise than by inheritance. *Adventitia dos* is a dowry or portion given by some friend other than the parent.

ADVENTURA. An adventure. 2 Mon.Angl. 615; Townsh.Pl. 50. Flotson, jetson, and lagon are styled *adventuræ maris,* (adventures of the sea.) Hale, De Jure Mar. pt. 1, c. 7.

ADVENTURE. A hazardous and striking enterprise, a bold undertaking in which hazards are to be met and issue hangs upon unforeseen events. Bond v. O'Donnell, 205 Iowa, 902, 218 N.W. 898, 902, 63 A.L.R. 901.

Generally

Adventure, bill of. In mercantile law, a writing signed by a merchant, stating that the property in goods shipped in his name belongs to another, to the adventure or chance of which the person so named is to stand, with a covenant from the merchant to account to him for the produce.

Gross adventure. In maritime law, a loan on bottomry. So named because the lender, in case of a loss, or expense incurred for the common safety, must contribute to the *gross* or general average.

Joint adventure. A commercial or maritime enterprise undertaken by several persons jointly; a limited partnership,—not limited in the statutory sense as to the liability of the partners, but as to its scope and duration. Lobsitz v. E. Lissberger Co., 168 App.Div. 840, 154 N.Y.S. 556, 557. A special partnership. McDaniel v. State Fair of Texas, Tex.Civ.App., 286 S.W. 513, 517. An association of two or more persons to carry out a single business enterprise for profit, for which purpose they combine their property, money, effects, skill, and knowledge. Forman v. Lumm, 214 App.Div. 579, 212 N.Y.S. 487. A special combination of two or more persons, where, in some specific adventure, a profit is jointly sought, without any actual partnership or corporate designation. Griffin v. Reilly, Tex.Civ.App., 275 S.W. 242, 246.

It is ordinarily, but not necessarily, limited to a single transaction, Forbes v. Butler, 66 Utah, 373, 242 P. 950, 956, which serves to distinguish it from a partnership, Barry v. Kern, 184 Wis. 266, 199 N.W. 77, 78. But the business of conducting it to a successful termination may continue for a number of years. Elliott v. Murphy Timber Co., 117 Or. 387, 244 P. 91, 93, 48 A.L.R. 1043. There is no real distinction between a "joint adventure" and what is termed a "partnership for a single transaction." Atlas Realty Co. v. Galt, 153 Md. 586, 139 A. 285, 286. A "joint adventure," while not identical with a partnership, is so similar in its nature and in the relations created thereby that the rights of the parties as between themselves are governed practically by the same rules that govern partnerships. Goss v. Lanin, 170 Iowa 57, 152 N.W. 43, 45.

Marine Insurance

A very usual word in policies of marine insurance, and everywhere used as synonymous, or nearly so, with "perils." It is often used by the writers to describe the enterprise or voyage as a "marine adventure" insured against. Moores v. Louisville Underwriters, C.C.Tenn., 14 Fed. 233.

Mercantile Law

Sending goods abroad under charge of a supercargo or other agent, at the risk of the sender, to be disposed of to the best advantage for the benefit of the owners.

The goods themselves so sent.

ADVENTURER. One who undertakes uncertain or hazardous actions or enterprises. It is also used to denote one who seeks to advance his own interests by unscrupulous designs on the credulity of others. It has been held that to impute that a person is an adventurer is a libel; 18 L.J.C.P. 241.

ADVERSARIA. (From Lat. *adversa,* things remarked or ready at hand.) Rough memoranda, common-place books.

ADVERSARY. A litigant-opponent, the opposite party in a writ or action.

ADVERSARY PROCEEDING. One having opposing parties; contested, as distinguished from an *ex parte* application; one of which the party seeking relief has given legal warning to the other party, and afforded the latter an opportunity to contest it. Excludes an adoption proceeding. Platt v. Magagnini, 187 P. 716, 718, 110 Wash. 39.

ADVERSE. Opposed; contrary; in resistance or opposition to a claim, application, or proceeding. Having opposing interests; having interests for the preservation of which opposition is essential. In re National Lock Co., D.C.Ill., 9 F.Supp. 432, 433.

As to adverse "Claim," "Enjoyment," "User," "Verdict," "Witness," see those titles.

ADVERSE INTEREST. The "adverse interest" of a witness, so as to permit cross-examination by the party calling him, must be so involved in the event of the suit that a legal right or liability will be acquired, lost, or materially affected by the judgment, and must be such as would be promoted by the success of the adversary of the party calling him. Dinger v. Friedman, 279 Pa. 8, 123 A. 641, 643. On petition in bankruptcy court for removal of trustee's attorney, attorney has an interest adverse to trustee. In re Mallow Hotel Corporation, D.C.Pa., 18 F.Supp. 15, 17.

ADVERSE PARTY. An "adverse party" entitled to notice of appeal is every party whose interest in relation to the judgment or decree appealed from is in conflict with the modification or reversal sought by the appeal.

Every party interested in sustaining the judgment or decree. Harrigan v. Gilchrist, 121 Wis. 127, 99 N.W. 909. All parties appearing against losing party unless reversal of case will not be to party's detriment. Shea v. Shea, Iowa, 264 N.W. 590. Any party who would be prejudicially affected by a modification or reversal of the judgment appealed from. Great Falls Nat. Bank v. Young, 67 Mont. 328, 215 P. 651, 652. One who has interest in opposing object sought to be accomplished by appeal. In re Baxter's Estate, 94 Mont. 257, 22 P.2d 182. Party to record, whose interest in subject-matter of appeal is adverse to, reversal or modification of judgment or order appealed from. MacDonald v. Superior Court in and for City and County of San Francisco, 101 Cal.App. 423, 281 P. 672, 673. A party who, by the pleadings, is arrayed on the opposite side. Merrill v. St. Paul City Ry. Co., 170 Minn. 332, 212 N.W. 533. The other party to the action. Highland v. Hines, 80 N.H. 179, 116 A. 347, 349. A party to the record for, or against, whom judgment is sought. Merchants' Supply Co. v. Hughes' Ex'rs, 139 Va. 212, 123 S.E. 355, 356. "Opposite" party synonymous. In re Wah-shah-she-me-tsa-he's Estate, 111 Okl. 177, 239 P. 177, 178. And term is not necessarily confined to plaintiffs as against defendants, or vice versa. Arwood v. Hill's Adm'rs, 135 Va. 235, 117 S.E. 603, 605. But a defaulting defendant is not an "adverse party"; Holt v. Empey, 32 Idaho, 106, 178 P. 703; nor is one who is named as a party but is not served; Kissler v. Moss, 26 Idaho, 516, 144 P. 647. Compare Fergen v. Lonie, 50 S.D. 328, 210 N.W. 102, 103 (garnishment debtor not served in garnishment proceeding).

ADVERSE POSSESSION. A method of acquisition of title by possession for a statutory period under certain conditions. Lowery v. Garfield County, Mont., 208 P.2d 478, 486. It has been described as the statutory method of acquiring title to land by limitation. Field v. Sosby, Tex.Civ. App., 226 S.W.2d 484, 486.

The possession must be actual, Ortiz v. Pacific States Properties, Cal.App., 215 P.2d 514, 516;

adverse, Flanery v. Greene, 158 S.W.2d 413, 415, 289 Ky. 244; under claim of right, Thomas v. Durchslag, Ill., 90 N.E.2d 200, 204, 404 Ill. 581; continuous, Davis v. Federal Land Bank of Columbia, 13 S.E.2d 417, 419, 219 N.Car. 248; open Wilberforce University v. College of Ed. and Indus. Arts at Wilberforce University, 90 N.E.2d 172, 173, 86 Ohio App. 121; notorious, Edie v. Coleman, 141 S.W.2d 238, 242, 243, 235 Mo.App. 1289; exclusive, Laudati v. State, 30 N.Y.S.2d 267, 270, and hostile, Singley v. Dempsey, 42 So.2d 609, 612, 252 Ala. 677. Although color of title is not essential, Roesch v. Gerst, 138 P.2d 846, 851, 852, 18 Wash.2d 294, it is of great evidentiary value in establishing adverse possession, Lincoln v. Mills, 2 So.2d 809, 811, 191 Miss. 512.

Adverse possession depends on intent of occupant to claim and hold real property in opposition to all the world, Sertic v. Roberts, 136 P.2d 248, 171 Ore. 121; and also embodies the idea that owner of or persons interested in property have knowledge of the assertion of ownership by the occupant, Field v. Sosby, Tex.Civ.App., 226 S.W.2d 484, 486.

Payment of taxes alone is not sufficient in itself to establish adverse possession, Blitch v. Sapp, 194 So. 328, 330, 142 Fla. 166. It is mandatory that the element of continuous possession exist for the full statutory period, Wells v. Tietge, 9 N.W.2d 180, 182, 143 Neb. 230.

ADVERSUS. In the civil law, against, *(contra.)* *Adversus bonos mores,* against good morals. Dig. 47, 10, 15.

Adversus extraneos vitiosa possessio prodesse solet. Prior possession is a good title of ownership against all who cannot show a better. D. 41. 2. 53; Salmond, Jurispr. 638.

ADVERTISE. To give notice to, inform or notify, give public notice of, announce publicly, notice or observe. People v. Hopkins, 263 N.Y.S. 290, 147 Misc. 12. To advise, announce, apprise, command, give notice of, inform, make known, publish. People v. Montague, 274 N.W. 347, 351, 280 Mich. 610. On call to the public attention by any means whatsoever; Commonwealth v. Allison, 227 Mass. 57, 116 N.E. 265, 266.

It includes publication by hand bills, signs, bill boards, sound trucks and radio, Rust v. Missouri Dental Board, 348 Mo. 616, 155 S.W.2d 80, 83; or in a newspaper, or by means of placards, or other written public notices; Nichols v. Nichols, 192 Ala. 206, 68 So. 186, 187. It is merely identification and description, apprising of quality and place, Rast v. Van Deman & Lewis Co., 240 U.S. 342, 36 S.Ct. 370, 377, 60 L.Ed. 679. And "advertising purposes" are not limited to matters of vocation, or even avocation, but include advertisements essentially for unselfish purposes, Almind v. Sea Beach Ry. Co., 141 N.Y.S. 842, 843, 157 App.Div. 230.

ADVERTISEMENT. Notice given in a manner designed to attract public attention. Edwards v. Lubbock County, Tex., 33 S.W.2d 482, 484. Information communicated to the public, or to an individual concerned, as by handbills or the newspaper. First Nat. Corporation v. Perrine, 99 Mont. 454, 43 P.2d 1073, 1077.

A sign-board, erected at a person's place of business, giving notice that lottery tickets are for sale, Com. v. Hooper, 5 Pick.Mass. 42.

ADVERTISEMENTS OF QUEEN ELIZABETH. Certain articles or ordinances drawn up by Archbishop Parker and some of the bishops in 1564, at the request of Queen Elizabeth, the object of which was to enforce decency and uniformity in the ritual of the church. The queen subsequently refused to give her official sanction to these advertisements, and left them to be enforced by the bishops under their general powers. Phillim.Ecc. Law, 910; 2 Prob.Div. 276; 354.

ADVICE. View; opinion; the counsel given by lawyers to their clients; an opinion expressed as to wisdom of future conduct. Hughes v. Van Bruggen, 44 N.M. 534, 105 P.2d 494, 496.

The word has several different meanings, among others, as follows: Information or notice given; intelligence;—usually information communicated by letter;—Chiefly as to drafts or bills of exchange; as, a letter of advice.—Advice implies real or pretended knowledge, often professional or technical, on the part of the one who gives it. Provident Trust Co. v. National Surety Co., D.C.Pa., 44 F.Supp. 514, 515.

The instruction usually given by one merchant or banker to another by letter, informing him of shipments made to him, or of bills or drafts drawn on him, with particulars of date, or sight, the sum, and the payee. Bills presented for acceptance or payment are frequently dishonored for *want of advice.*

Letter of advice is a communication from one person to another, advising or warning the latter of something which he ought to know, and commonly apprising him beforehand of some act done by the writer which will ultimately affect the recipient. Chit. Bills, 162.

ADVISARE, ADVISARI. Lat. To consult, deliberate, consider, advise; to be advised. Occurring in the phrase *curia advisari vult,* which see (usually abbreviated *cur. adv. vult,* or *C. A. V.,*) the court wishes to be advised, or to consider of the matter.

ADVISE. To give an opinion or counsel, or recommend a plan or course of action; also to give notice. Long v. State, 23 Neb. 33, 36 N.W. 310. To encourage. Voris v. People, 75 Colo. 574, 227 P. 551, 553. "Inform" or "acquaint." Ericson v. Steiner, 119 Cal.App. 305, 6 P.2d 298, 300.

It is different in meaning from "instruct" or "persuade." Hughes v. Van Bruggen, 44 N.M. 534, 105 P.2d 494, 497. Where a statute authorizes the trial court to *advise* the jury to acquit, the court has no power to *instruct* the jury to acquit. The court can only counsel, and the jury are not bound by the advice. People v. Horn, 70 Cal. 17, 11 P. 470. "Advise" imports that it is discretionary or optional with the person addressed whether he will act on such advice or not. State v. Downing, 23 Idaho, 540, 130 P. 461, 462.

ADVISED. Prepared to give judgment, after examination and deliberation. "The court took time to be advised." 1 Leon. 187.

ADVISEDLY. With deliberation; intentionally. 15 Moore P.C. 147.

ADVISEMENT. Consideration; deliberation; consultation. Drainage Dist. No. 1 of Lincoln

County v. Suburban Irr. Dist., 139 Neb. 460, 298 N.W. 131, 134. The consultation of a court, after the argument of a cause by counsel, and before delivering their opinion. In re Hohorst, 150 U.S. 662, 14 S.Ct. 221, 37 L.Ed. 1211.

ADVISORY. Counselling, suggesting, or advising, but not imperative or conclusive. A verdict on an issue out of chancery is advisory. Watt v. Starke, 101 U.S. 252, 25 L.Ed. 826. Not binding on chancellor. Merritt v. Palmer, 289 Ky. 141, 158 S.W.2d 163, 165.

ADVISORY OPINION. A formal opinion by judge or judges or a court or a law officer upon a question of law submitted by a legislative body or a governmental official, but not actually presented in a concrete case at law. Douglas Oil Co. v. State, Tex.Civ.App., 81 S.W.2d 1064, 1077.

Merely opinion of judges or court, which adjudicates nothing and is binding on no one, in exercise of wholly non or extra-judicial function. The expression ordinarily connotes the practice which existed in England from very early times of extra-judicial consultation of the judges by the Crown and the House of Lords. Douglas Oil Co. v. State, Tex.Civ.App., 81 S.W.2d 1064, 1077.

ADVOCACY. The act of pleading for, supporting, or recommending active espousal. Gitlow v. People of State of New York, 45 S.Ct. 625, 626, 268 U.S. 652, 69 L.Ed. 1138.

ADVOCARE. Lat. To defend; to call to one's aid; to vouch; to warrant.

ADVOCASSIE. L. Fr. The office of an advocate; advocacy. Kelham.

ADVOCATA. In old English law, a patroness; a woman who had the right of presenting to a church. Spelman.

ADVOCATE, *v.* To speak in favor of; defend by argument. Ex parte Bernat, D.C.Wash., 255 F. 429, 432. To support, vindicate, or recommend publicly. Butash v. State, 212 Ind. 492, 9 N.E.2d 88, 90. Not for an educational purpose, but to disseminate controversial "propaganda," which means plan for publication of doctrine or system of principles. Leubuscher v. Commissioner of Internal Revenue, C.C.A., 54 F.2d 998, 999.

ADVOCATE, *n.* One who assists, defends, or pleads for another; one who renders legal advice and aid and pleads the cause of another before a court or a tribunal, a counselor. Haverty Furniture Co. v. Foust, 174 Tenn. 203, 124 S.W.2d 694, 697.

A person learned in the law, and duly admitted to practice, who assists his client with advice, and pleads for him in open court. Holthouse.

An assistant; adviser; a pleader of causes.

Derived from *advocare,* to summon to one's assistance; *advocatus* originally signified an assistant or helper of any kind, even an accomplice in the commission of a crime; Cicero, *Pro Cœcina,* c. 8; Livy, lib. ii. 55; iii. 47; Tertullian, *De Idolatr.* cap. xxiii.; Petron. *Satyric.* cap. xv. Secondarily, it was applied to one called in to assist a party in the conduct of a suit; Inst. 1, 11, D. 50, 13. *de extr. cogn.* Hence, a pleader, which is its present signification.

Civil and Ecclesiastical Law

An officer of the court, learned in the law, who is engaged by a suitor to maintain or defend his cause.

Generally

—Advocate general. The adviser of the crown in England on questions of naval and military law.

—Lord Advocate. The principal crown lawyer in Scotland, and one of the great officers of state of Scotland. It is his duty to act as public prosecutor; but private individuals injured may prosecute upon obtaining his concurrence. He is assisted by a solicitor general and four junior counsel, termed "advocates-depute." He has the power of appearing as public prosecutor in any court in Scotland, where any person can be tried for an offense, or in any action where the crown is interested. Wharton.

—Queen's advocate. A member of the College of Advocates, appointed by letters patent, whose office is to advise and act as counsel for the crown in questions of civil, canon, and international law. His rank is next after the solicitor general.

ADVOCATI. Lat. In Roman law, patrons; pleaders; speakers.

ADVOCATI ECCLESIÆ. Advocates of the church.

A term used in the ecclesiastical law to denote the patrons of churches who presented to the living on an avoidance. This term was also applied to those who were retained to argue the cases of the church. These were of two sorts: those retained as pleaders to argue the cases of the church and attend to its law-matters; and advocates, or patrons of the advowson. Cowell; Spelman, Gloss.

ADVOCATI FISCI. In civil law, those chosen by the emperor to argue his cause whenever a question arose affecting his revenues. 3 Bla. Comm. 27. Advocates of the fisc, or revenue; fiscal advocates, *(qui causam fisci egissent.)* Cod. 2, 9, 1; Cod. 2, 7, 13. Answering, in some measure, to the king's counsel in English law.

ADVOCATIA. In the civil law, the quality, function, privilege, or territorial jurisdiction of an advocate.

The functions, duty, or privilege of an advocate. Du Cange, *Advocatia.*

ADVOCATION. In Scotch law, a process by which an action may be carried from an inferior to a superior court before final judgment in the former.

ADVOCATIONE DECIMARUM. A writ which lay for tithes, demanding the fourth part or upwards, that belonged to any church.

ADVOCATOR. In old practice, one who called on or vouched another to warrant a title; a voucher. *Advocatus;* the person called on, or vouched; a vouchee. Spelman; Townsh.Pl. 45.

In Scotch practice, an appellant. 1 Broun, R. 67.

ADVOCATUS. A pleader; a narrator. Bracton, 412 *a*, 372 *b*.

In the civil law, an advocate; one who managed or assisted in managing another's cause before a judicial tribunal. Called also *"patronus."* Cod. 2, 7, 14. But distinguished from *causidicus.* Id. 2, 6, 6.

ADVOCATUS DIABOLI. In ecclesiastical law, the devil's advocate; the advocate who argues against the canonization of a saint.

Advocatus est, ad quem pertinet jus advocationis alicujus ecclesiæ, ut ad ecclesiam, nomine proprio, non alieno, possit præsentare. A patron is he to whom appertains the right of presentation to a church, in such a manner that he may present to such a church in his own name, and not in the name of another. Co.Litt. 119.

ADVOUTRER. In old English law, an adulterer. Beaty v. Richardson, 56 S.C. 173, 34 S.E. 73, 46 L.R.A. 517.

ADVOUTRY. In old English law, adultery between parties both of whom were married. Hunter v. U. S., 1 Pin. (Wis.) 91, 39 Am.Dec. 277. Or the offense by an adulteress of continuing to live with the man with whom she committed the adultery. Cowell; Termes de la Ley. Sometimes spelled "advowtry." See Advoutrer.

ADVOWEE, or AVOWEE. The person or patron who has a right to present to a benefice. Fleta, lib. 5, c. 14.

ADVOWEE PARAMOUNT. The sovereign, or highest patron.

ADVOWSON. In English ecclesiastical law, the right of presentation to a church or ecclesiastical benefice; the right of presenting a fit person to the bishop, to be by him admitted and instituted to a certain benefice within the diocese, which has become vacant. 2 Bl.Comm. 21; Co.Litt. 119*b*, 120*a*. The person enjoying this right is called the "patron" *(patronus)* of the church, and was formerly termed *"advocatus,"* the advocate or defender, or in English, *"advowee."* Id.; 1 Crabb, Real Prop. p. 129, § 117.

When there is no patron, or he neglects to exercise his right within six months, it is called a *lapse,* and a title is given to the ordinary to collate to a church: when a presentation is made by one who has no right, it is called a *usurpation.*

Advowsons are of different kinds.

Advowson appendant is an advowson annexed to a manor, and passing with it, as incident or appendant to it, by a grant of the manor only, without adding any other words. 2 Bl.Comm. 22; Co.Litt. 120, 121; 1 Crabb, Real Prop. p. 130, § 118.

Advowson collative. Where the bishop happens himself to be the patron, in which case (presentation being impossible, or unnecessary) he does by one act, which is termed *"collation,"* or conferring the benefice, all that is usually done by the separate acts of presentation and institution. 2 Bl.Comm. 22, 23; 1 Crabb, Real Prop. p. 131, § 119.

Advowson donative exists where the patron has the right to put his clerk in possession by his mere gift, or deed of donation, without any presentation to the bishop, or institution by him. 2 Bl.Comm. 23; 1 Crabb, Real Prop. p. 131, § 119.

Advowson in gross is an advowson separated from the manor, and annexed to the person. 2 Bl.Comm. 22; Co. Litt. 120; 1 Crabb, Real Prop. p. 130, § 118; 3 Steph. Comm. 116.

Advowson presentative is the usual kind of advowson, where the patron has the right of *presentation* to the bishop, or ordinary, and moreover to demand of him to institute his clerk, if he finds him canonically qualified. 2 Bl.Comm. 22; 1 Crabb, Real Prop. p. 131, § 119.

ADVOWTRY. See Advoutry.

ÆDES. Lat. In the civil law, a house, dwelling, temple, place of habitation, whether in the city or country. Dig. 30, 41, 5. In the country everything upon the surface of the soil passed under the term *"ædes."* Du Cange; Calvin.

ÆDIFICARE. Lat. In civil and old English law, to make or build a house; to erect a building. Dig. 45, 1, 75, 7.

Ædificare in tuo proprio solo non licet quod alteri noceat. 3 Inst. 201. To build upon your own land what may injure another is not lawful.

A proprietor of land has no right to erect an edifice on his own ground, interfering with the due enjoyment of adjoining premises, as by overhanging them, or by throwing water from the roof and eaves upon them, or by obstructing ancient lights and windows. Broom, Max. 369.

Ædificatum solo solo cedit. What is built upon land belongs to or goes with land. Broom, Max. 172; Co.Litt. 4*a*.

Ædificia solo cedunt. Buildings belong to [go with] the soil. Fleta, lib. 3, c. 2, § 12.

ÆDILE. In Roman law, an officer who attended to the repairs of the temples and other public buildings; the repairs and cleanliness of the streets; the care of the weights and measures; the providing for funerals and games; and to regulating the prices of provisions. Ainsworth, Lex.; Smith, Lex.; Du Cange.

ÆDILITUM EDICTUM. In the Roman law, the Ædilitian Edict.

An edict providing remedies for frauds in sales, the execution of which belonged to the curule ædiles. Dig. 21, 1. See Cod. 4, 58. That provision by which the buyer of a diseased or imperfect slave, horse, or other animal was relieved at the expense of the vendor who had sold him as sound knowing him to be imperfect. Calvinus, Lex.

ÆFESN. In old English law, the remuneration to the proprietor of a domain for the privilege of feeding swine under the oaks and beeches of his woods.

ÆGROTO. Lat. Being sick or indisposed. A term used in some of the older reports. "Holt *ægroto.*" 11 Mod. 179.

ÆGYLDE. Uncompensated, unpaid for, unavenged. From the participle of exclusion, *a, æ,* or *ex,* (Goth.,) and *gild,* payment, requital. Anc. Inst.Eng.

ÆL. A Norman French term signifying "grandfather." It is also spelled *"aieul"* and *"ayle."* Kelham.

ÆQUIOR EST DISPOSITIO LEGIS QUAM HOMINIS. The disposition of the law is more equitable than that of man. 8 Coke, 152.

ÆQUITAS. In the civil law, equity, as opposed to *strictum* or *summum jus, (q. v.)*. Otherwise called *æquum, æquum bonum, æquum et bonum, æquum et justum*. Calvin.

Referring to the use of this term, Prof. Gray says (Nature and Sources of the Law 290): "Austin and Maine take *æquitas* as having an analogous meaning to equity; they apply the term to those rules which the prætors introduced through the Edict in modification of the *jus civile*, but it seems to be an error to suppose that *æquitas* had this sense in the Roman Law." He quotes Prof. Clark (Jurisprudence 367) as doubting "whether *æquitas* is ever clearly used by the Roman jurists to indicate simply a *department* of Law" and expresses the opinion that an examination of the authorities more than justifies his doubt. *Æquitas* is opposed to *strictum jus* and varies in meaning between reasonable modification of the letter and substantial justice. It is to be taken as a frame of mind in dealing with legal questions and not as a source of law.

See Æquum et Bonum.

Æquitas agit in personam. Equity acts upon the person. 4 Bouv.Inst. n. 3733.

Æquitas est correctio legis generaliter latæ, qua parte deficit. Equity is the correction of that wherein the law, by reason of its generality, is deficient. Plowd. 375.

Æquitas est correctio quædam legi adhibita, quia ab eâ abest aliquid propter generalem sine exceptione comprehensionem. Equity is a certain correction applied to law, because on account of its general comprehensiveness, without an exception, something is absent from it. Plowd. 467.

Æquitas est perfecta quædam ratio quæ jus scriptum interpretatur et emendat; nulla scriptura comprehensa, sed solum in verâ ratione consistens. Equity is a certain perfect reason, which interprets and amends the written law, comprehended in no writing, but consisting in right reason alone. Co.Litt. 24*b*.

Æquitas est quasi æqualitas. Equity is as it were equality; equity is a species of equality or equalization. Co.Litt. 24.

Æquitas ignorantiæ opitulatur, oscitantiæ non item. Equity assists ignorance, but not carelessness.

Æquitas non facit jus, sed juri auxiliatur. Equity does not make law, but assists law. Lofft, 379.

Æquitas nunquam contravenit legis. Equity never counteracts the laws.

Æquitas sequitur legem. Equity follows the law. 5 Barb.N.Y. 277, 282.

Æquitas supervacua odit. Equity abhors superfluous things. Lofft, 282.

Æquitas uxoribus, liberis, creditoribus maxime favet. Equity favors wives and children, creditors most of all.

ÆQUUM ET BONUM. "The Roman conception involved in '*æquum et bonum*' or '*æquitas*' is identical with what we mean by 'reasonable' or nearly so."

"On the whole, the natural justice or 'reason of the thing' which the common law recognizes and applies does not appear to differ from the 'law of nature' which the Romans identified with *jus gentium*, and the medieval doctors of the civil and common law boldly adopted as being divine law revealed through man's natural reason." Sir F. Pollock, Expans. of C. L. 111, citing [1902] 2 Ch. 661, where *jus naturale* and *æquum et bonum* were taken to have the same meaning.

Æquum et bonum est lex legum. What is equitable and good is the law of laws. Hob. 224.

ÆQUUS. Lat. Equal; even. A provision in a will for the division of the residuary estate *ex æquus* among the legatees means equally or evenly. Archer v. Morris, 47 Atl. 275, 61 N.J.Eq. 152.

ÆRA, or ERA. A fixed point of chronological time, whence any number of years is counted; thus, the Christian era began at the birth of Christ, and the Mohammedan era at the flight of Mohammed from Mecca to Medina. The derivation of the word has been much contested. Wharton.

ÆRARIUM. Lat. In the Roman law. The treasury, *(fiscus.)* Calvin.

AËRIAL NAVIGATION. See Aeronautics.

AERODROME. A term originally applied by Professor Langley to his flying machine but now used in the same sense as "airport" *(q. v.)*.

AERONAUT. This term under some statutes includes every person who, being in or upon an airship or anything attached thereto, undertakes to direct its ascent, course, or descent in the air, or the ascent, course, or descent in the air of anything attached to such airship.

Under the Uniform Aeronautics Act it includes aviator, pilot, baloonist, and every other person having any part in the operation of aircraft while in flight. See Aeronautics.

AERONAUTIC ACTIVITY. The term is broad enough to cover what is ordinarily incident to an airplane trip. The aeronautic activities of one who takes such a trip do not begin or end with the actual flight, but include his presence or movements in or near to the machine incidental to beginning or concluding the trip. Blonski v. Bankers' Life Co., 209 Wis. 5, 243 N.W. 410.

Insured killed when struck by propeller after emerging from airplane at end of flight, Day v. Equitable Life Assur. Soc. of U. S., C.C.A.Colo., 83 F.2d 147, 148. To a contrary effect: Tierney v. Occidental Life Ins. Co., 89 Cal.App. 779, 265 P. 400.

AERONAUTIC EXPEDITION. Traveling as passenger in airplane operated in regular passenger service was engaging in "aeronautic expedition" under life policy. Gibbs v. Equitable Life Assur. Soc. of U. S., 256 N.Y. 208, 176 N.E. 144. Contra. King v. Equitable Life Assur. Soc. of United States, 232 Iowa 541, 5 N.W.2d 845, 846, 155 A.L.R.

1022. Pleasure trip in airplane over airport on pleasant day was not "aeronautic expedition" under life policy. Day v. Equitable Life Assur. Soc. of U. S., C.C.A.Colo., 83 F.2d 147, 149.

AERONAUTIC OPERATION. Passenger on regularly scheduled airplane trip engaged in "aeronautic operation," within life policy. Day v. Equitable Life Assur. Soc. of U. S., C.C.A.Colo., 83 F.2d 147, 148. Did not include casual trip in airplane; "aeronautic operations" signifying more than occasional venture. Gits v. New York Life Ins. Co., C.C.A.Ill., 32 F.2d 7, 10. Nor a pleasure flight in airplane. Day v. Equitable Life Assur. Soc. of U. S., C.C.A.Colo., 83 F.2d 147, 148.

AERONAUTICS. The science, art or practice of sailing in the air; aerial navigation; the branch of aerostatics which treats of floating in or navigating the air as in an airship or airplane. Massachusetts Protective Ass'n v. Bayersdorfer, C.C.A. Ohio, 105 F.2d 595, 597. Operation of aircraft. Equitable Life Assur. Soc. of United States v. Dyess, 194 Ark. 1023, 109 S.W.2d 1263, 1265.

It is divided into two branches: aerostation, dealing with machines which, like balloons, are lighter than air; and aviation, dealing with artificial flight by machines which are heavier than air. Bew v. Travelers' Ins. Co., 95 N.J.Law, 533, 112 A. 859, 860, 14 A.L.R. 983.

A passenger in an airplane, whether he takes part in its operation or not, "participates in aeronautics" within the meaning of an insurance policy. Meredith v. Business Men's Acc. Ass'n of America, 213 Mo.App. 688, 252 S.W. 976, 977. Contra as to a transport airplane passenger who could not pilot an airplane, had no knowledge of flying, and at time of accident was traveling on private business. Gregory v. Mutual Life Ins. Co. of New York, C.C.A.Ark., 78 F.2d 522, 524. As to an insured, who was a fare-paying passenger on a commercial transport plane over an established route while plane was wholly under the control of others. Bayersdorfer v. Massachusetts Protective Ass'n, D.C.Ohio, 20 F.Supp. 489, 492. A father riding with son as guest in airplane purchased by father for son. Day v. Equitable Life Assur. Soc. of U. S., C.C.A.Colo., 83 F.2d 147, 149. And where insured after alighting from a flight, in bending over to avoid a wire, was struck by the propeller of the aeroplane. Tierney v. Occidental Life Ins. Co. of California, 89 Cal.App. 779, 265 P. 400, 401.

See, also, Aircraft; Airship; Airport; Airway; Aviation.

AEROPLANE. See Aircraft; Hydro-Aeroplane; Seaplane.

AEROSTATICS. "Aerostatics" is divided into two main branches; aerostation dealing, properly, with machines, which, like balloons, are lighter than air, and aviation dealing with the problem of artificial flight by means of flying machines, which, like birds, are heavier than air. Swasey v. Massachusetts Protective Ass'n, C.C.A.Ariz., 96 F.2d 265, 266.

AEROSTATION. See Aerostatics, and Aeronautics, note.

ÆS. Lat. In the Roman law, money, (literally, brass;) metallic money in general, including gold. Dig. 9, 2, 2, pr.; Dig. 9, 2, 27, 5; Dig. 50, 16, 159.

ÆS ALIENUM. A civil law term signifying a debt. Literally translated, the money of another; the civil law considered borrowed money as the property of another, as distinguished from *æs suum,* one's own money.

ÆS SUUM. One's own money. In the Roman law, debt; a debt; that which others owe to us, *(quod alii nobis debent.)* Dig. 50, 16, 213.

ÆSNECIA. In old English law, Esnecy; the right or privilege of the eldest born. Spelman; Glanv. lib. 7, c. 3; Fleta, lib. 2, c. 66, §§ 5, 6.

ÆSNECIUS. See Anecius; Aesnecia.

ÆSTHETIC. Relating to that which is beautiful or in good taste. People v. Wolf, 216 N.Y.S. 741, 744, 127 Misc. 382. Pertaining to the beautiful. Hav-A-Tampa Cigar Co. v. Johnson, 149 Fla. 148, 5 So.2d 433, 440.

ÆSTIMATIO CAPITIS. Lat. The value of a head.

In Saxon law, the estimation or valuation of the head: the price or value of a man. The price to be paid for taking the life of a human being. By the laws of Athelstan, the life of every man not excepting that of the king himself, was estimated at a certain price, which was called the *were,* or *æstimatio capitis.* Crabb, Eng.Law, c. 4.

ÆTAS. Lat. In the civil law. Age.

ÆSTIMATIO PRÆTERITI DELICTI EX POSTREMO FACTO NUNQUAM CRESCIT. The weight of a past offense is never increased by a subsequent fact. Bacon.

ÆTAS INFANTIÆ (also written infantili) **PROXIMA.** The age next to infancy; the first half of the period of childhood *(pueritia,)* extending from seven years to ten and a half. Inst. 3, 20, 9; 4 Bl.Comm. 22. See Age.

ÆTAS LEGITIMA. Lawful age; the age of twenty-five. Dig. 3, 5, 27, pr.; Id. 26, 2, 32, 2; Id. 27, 7, 1, pr.

ÆTAS PERFECTA. Complete age; full age; the age of twenty-five. Dig. 4, 4, 32; Id. 22, 3, 25, 1.

ÆTAS PRIMA. The first age; infancy, *(infantia).* Cod. 6, 61, 8, 3.

ÆTAS PUBERTATI PROXIMA. The age next to puberty; the last half of the period of childhood *(pueritia),* extending from ten and a half years to fourteen, in which there might or might not be criminal responsibility according to natural capacity or incapacity. Inst. 3, 20, 9; 4 Bl.Comm. 22. See Age.

ÆTATE PROBANDA. A writ which inquired whether the king's tenant holding in chief by chivalry was of full age to receive his lands. It was directed to the escheater of the county. Now disused.

ÆTHELING. In Saxon law, a noble; generally a prince of the blood.

AFFAIR. (Fr.). A law suit.

The term frequently refers to an amour; intrigue; liaison.

AFFAIRS. An inclusive term, bringing within its scope and meaning anything that a person may do. Walker v. United States, C.C.A.Mo., 93 F.2d 383, 391.

A person's concerns in trade or property; business. Bragaw v. Bolles, 51 N.J.Eq. 84, 25 A. 947. That which is done or to be done. Wicks v. City and County of Denver, 61 Colo. 266, 156 P. 1100, 1103. A corporation's borrowing money, and methods of obtaining loans. Cameron v. First Nat. Bank, Tex.Civ.App., 194 S.W. 469, 470. Person and estate of alleged incompetent. State ex rel. Bevan v. Williams, 316 Mo. 665, 291 S.W. 481, 482. General operations carried on by an employer. Gocs v. Thomas E. Coale Coal Co., 142 Pa.Super. 479, 16 A.2d 720, 723.

AFFECT. To act upon; influence; change; enlarge or abridge; often used in the sense of acting injuriously upon persons and things. Ryan v. Carter, 93 U.S. 84, 23 L.Ed. 807; Tyler v. Wells, 2 Mo.App. 538; Holland v. Dickerson, 41 Iowa 373; Meurer v. Hooper, Tex.Civ.App., 271 S.W. 172, 177. Does not mean to impair. Harris v. Friend, 24 N.M. 627, 175 P. 722, 725. To lay hold of or attack (as a disease does); to act, or produce an effect upon; to impress or influence (the mind or feelings); to touch. State v. Hurd, 5 Wash.2d 308, 105 P.2d 59, 61, 62. Acted upon, influenced, concerned. In re National Lock Co., D.C.Ill., 9 F. Supp. 432, 433. Implies an indirect relation. Chapman v. Home Ice Co., D.C.Tenn., 43 F.Supp. 424, 428.

AFFECTED WITH A PUBLIC INTEREST. Affirmatively, phrase means that a business or property must be such or be so employed as to justify the conclusion that it has been devoted to a public use, and its use thereby in effect granted to the public. Negatively, it does not mean that a business is affected with a public interest merely because it is large or because the public are warranted in having a feeling of concern in respect of its maintenance. H. Earl Clack Co. v. Public Service Commission of State of Montana, 94 Mont. 488, 22 P.2d 1056.

A business given a virtual monopoly in its field or where the public adapt their business or conduct to the methods used by it. Western Buse Telephone Co. v. Northwestern Bell Telephone Co., 188 Minn. 524, 248 N.W. 220, 229. The business must affect the prosperity of a large part of the members of the body politic. Ex parte Kazas, 22 Cal.App. 2d 161, 70 P.2d 962, 967. This phrase means something more than "quasi public," or "not strictly private," and similar phrases employed as a basis for upholding police regulations. A business is not affected with a public interest merely because the public derives benefit, accommodation, ease or enjoyment from its existence or operation, such as admissions to places of amusement or entertainment. Tyson & Bro.-United Theatre Ticket Offices v. Banton, 273 U.S. 418, 47 S.Ct. 426, 429, 71 L.Ed. 718, 58 A.L.R. 1236.

Businesses. Three classes of such businesses: (1) Those carried on under the authority of a public grant or privilege expressly or impliedly imposing an affirmative duty of rendering public service demanded by the public, such as common carriers and public utilities; (2) occupations regarded as exceptional, the public interest attaching to which has been recognized from earliest times and has survived the period of arbitrary laws by Parliament or colonial legislatures for regulating trades and callings, such as inns, cabs, and grist mills; (3) businesses which, though not public at their inception, have become such by devoting their business to a public use, thereby granting the public an interest in that use and subjecting themselves to public regulation to extent of that interest, although the property continues to belong to its private owner, and to be entitled to protection accordingly, as public warehouses for storage of grain, banks, and insurance companies. Rohrer v. Milk Control Board, 121 Pa.Super. 281, 184 A. 133, 138.

AFFECTIO TUA NOMEN IMPONIT OPERI TUO. Your disposition (or motive, intention) gives name (or character) to your work or act. Bract. fol. 2*b*, 101*b*.

AFFECTION. The making over, pawning, or mortgaging of a thing to assure the payment of a sum of money, or the discharge of some other duty or service. Crabb, Technol.Dict.

In a medical sense, an abnormal bodily condition. A local "affection" is not a local disease within the meaning of an insurance policy, unless the affection has sufficiently developed to have some bearing on the general health. Cady v. Fidelity & Casualty Co. of New York, 134 Wis. 322, 113 N.W. 967, 971, 17 L.R.A.,N.S., 260.

AFFECTUS. Disposition; intention, impulse or affection of the mind. One of the causes for a challenge of a juror is *propter affectum,* on account of a suspicion of *bias* or favor. 3 Bl.Comm. 363; Co.Litt. 156.

AFFECTUS PUNITUR LICET NON SEQUATUR EFFECTUS. The intention is punished although the intended result does not follow. 9 Coke, 55.

AFFEER. To assess, liquidate, appraise, fix in amount.

Account

To confirm it on oath in the exchequer. Cowell; Blount; Spelman.

Amercement

To establish the amount which one amerced in a court-leet should pay. See Amercement.

AFFEERORS. Persons who, in court-leets, upon oath, settle and moderate the fines and amercements imposed on those who have committed offenses arbitrarily punishable, or that have no express penalty appointed by statute. They are also appointed to moderate fines, etc., in courts-baron. Cowell.

AFFERMER. L. Fr. To let to farm. Also to make sure, to establish or confirm. Kelham.

AFFIANCE. To assure by pledge. A plighting of troth between man and woman. Littleton, § 39.

An agreement by which a man and woman promise each other that they will marry together. Pothier, *Traité du Mar,* n. 24. Co.Litt. 34 *a.* See Dig. 23, 1, 1; Code, 5. 1. 4.

AFFIANT. The person who makes and subscribes an affidavit. The word is used, in this sense, interchangeably with "deponent." But the latter term should be reserved as the designation of one who makes a deposition.

AFFIDARE. To swear faith to; to pledge one's faith or do fealty by making oath. Cowell. Used of the mutual relation arising between landlord and tenant; 1 Washb.R.P. 19; 1 Bla.Com. 367; Termes de la Ley, *Fealty.* Affidavit is of kindred meaning.

AFFIDARI. To be mustered and enrolled for soldiers upon an oath of fidelity.

AFFIDATIO. A swearing of the oath of fidelity or of fealty to one's lord, under whose protection the quasi-vassal has voluntarily come. Brown.

AFFIDATIO DOMINORUM. An oath taken by the lords in parliament.

AFFIDATUS. One who is not a vassal, but who for the sake of protection has connected himself with one more powerful. Spelman; 2 Bl.Comm. 46.

AFFIDAVIT. A written or printed declaration or statement of facts, made voluntarily, and confirmed by the oath or affirmation of the party making it, taken before an officer having authority to administer such oath. Cox v. Stern, 170 Ill. 442, 48 N.E. 906, 62 Am.St.Rep. 385; Hays v. Loomis, 84 Ill. 18. A statement or declaration reduced to writing, and sworn to or affirmed before some officer who has authority to administer an oath or affirmation. Shelton v. Berry, 19 Tex. 154, 70 Am.Dec. 326, and In re Breidt, 84 N.J.Eq. 222, 94 A. 214, 216.

A written or printed declaration or statement of facts, made voluntarily, and confirmed by the oath or affirmation of the party making it, taken before an officer having authority to administer such oath. June v. School Dist. No. 11, Southfield Tp., 283 Mich. 533, 278 N.W. 676, 677, 116 A.L.R. 581. Any voluntary ex parte statement reduced to writing and sworn to or affirmed before some person legally authorized to administer oath or affirmation, made without notice to adverse party and without opportunity to cross-examine. Kirk v. Hartlieb, 193 Ark. 37, 97 S.W.2d 434, 435, 436. The word sometimes includes "depositions." U. S. v. Kaplan, D.C.Ga., 286 F. 963, 970.

"Affidavits" are of two kinds; those which serve as evidence to advise the court in the decision of some preliminary issue or determination of some substantial right, and those which merely serve to invoke the judicial power. Worthen v. State, 189 Ala. 395, 66 So. 686, 688.

AFFIDAVIT OF DEFENSE. An affidavit stating that the defendant has a good defense to the plaintiff's action on the merits. The statements required in such an affidavit vary considerably in the different states where they are required. Called also an affidavit of merits *(q. v.)*, as in Massachusetts.

AFFIDAVIT OF DEMAND. "Affidavit of demand" filed under Code section to obtain judgment for want of affidavit of defense held not equivalent of "declaration." Penn Central Light & Power Co. v. Central Eastern Power Co., 6 W. W.Harr. 74, 171 A. 332.

AFFIDAVIT OF MERITS. One setting forth that the defendant has a meritorious defense (substantial and not technical) and stating the facts constituting the same. Palmer v. Rogers, 70 Iowa 381, 30 N.W. 645. Represents that, on the substantial facts of the case, justice is with the affiant. Wendel v. Wendel, 58 S.D. 438, 236 N.W. 468, 469.

AFFIDAVIT OF SERVICE. An affidavit intended to certify the service of a writ, notice, or other document.

AFFIDAVIT TO HOLD TO BAIL. An affidavit required in many cases before the defendant in a civil action may be arrested. Such an affidavit must contain a statement, clearly and certainly expressed, by some one acquainted with the fact, of an indebtedness from the defendant to the plaintiff, and must show a distinct cause of action; 1 Chit.Pl. 165.

AFFILARE. L. Lat. To put on record; to file or affile. *Affiletur,* let it be filed. 8 Coke, 160. *De recordo affilatum,* affiled of record. 2 Ld. Raym. 1476.

AFFILE. A term employed in old practice, signifying to put on file. 2 Maule & S. 202. In modern usage it is contracted to *file.*

AFFILIATE. Signifies a condition of being united, being in close connection, allied, or attached as a member or branch. Johanson v. Riverside County Select Groves, 4 Cal.App.2d 114, 40 P.2d 530, 534.

"Affiliate with" is defined as to receive on friendly terms; to associate with; to be intimate with; to sympathize with; to consort with; and to connect or associate one's self with. Wolck v. Weedin, C.C.A.Wash., 58 F.2d 928, 930. But "affiliated" does not bear construction that one of affiliated organizations is in all particulars identical with or covered by parent organization with which it may be said to be affiliated. People v. Horiuchi, 114 Cal.App. 415, 300 P. 457, 460.

AFFILIATION. Imports less than membership in an organization, but more than sympathy, and a working alliance to bring to fruition the proscribed program of a proscribed organization, as distinguished from mere co-operation with a proscribed organization in lawful activities, is essential. Bridges v. Wixon, Cal., 326 U.S. 135, 65 S.Ct. 1443, 1447, 89 L.Ed. 2103.

It includes an element of dependability upon which the organization can rely which, though not equivalent to membership duty, rests upon course of conduct that could not be abruptly ended without giving at least reasonable cause for charge of breach of good faith. U. S. ex rel. Kettunen v. Reimer, C.C.A.N.Y., 79 F.2d 315, 317.

The act of imputing or determining the paternity of a bastard child, and the obligation to maintain it.

Corporations

Actual control of corporations by same interests is insufficient; legally enforceable control of stock of corporations by same interests being required. Island Petroleum Co. v. Commissioner of Internal Revenue, C.C.A., 57 F.2d 992, 994. Commences with acquisition of corporation from owners outside of group and ends with disposal of all properties or stock to those outside group. Hernandez v. Charles Ilfeld Co., C.C.A.N.M., 66 F.2d 236, 238.

Ecclesiastical Law

A condition which prevented the superior from removing the person affiliated to another convent. Guyot, Répert.

French Law

A species of adoption which exists by custom in some parts of France. The person affiliated succeeded equally with other heirs to the property acquired by the deceased to whom he had been affiliated, but not to that which he inherited.

AFFINAGE. A refining of metals. Blount.

AFFINES. In the civil law, connections by marriage, whether of the persons or their relatives. Calvinus, Lex.

Neighbors, who own or occupy adjoining lands. Dig. 10, 1, 12.

From this word we have affinity, denoting relationship by marriage; 1 Bla.Com. 434. The singular, *affinis*, is used in a variety of related significations—a boundary; Du Cange; a partaker or sharer, *affinis culpæ* (an aider or one who has knowledge of a crime); Calvinus, Lex.

AFFINIS MEI AFFINIS NON EST MIHI AFFINIS. One who is related by marriage to a person related to me by marriage has no affinity to me. Shelf.Mar. & Div. 174.

AFFINITAS. Lat. In the civil law, affinity; relationship by marriage. Inst. 1, 10, 6.

AFFINITAS AFFINITATIS. Remote relationship by marriage. That connection between parties arising from marriage which is neither consanguinity nor affinity. Davidson v. Whitehill, 87 Vt. 499, 89 A. 1081, 1085. This term signifies the connection between the kinsmen of the two persons married, as, for example, the husband's brother and the wife's sister. Erskine, Inst. 1. 6. 8.

AFFINITY. A close agreement; relation; spiritual relation or attraction held to exist between certain persons. State ex inf. Norman v. Ellis, 325 Mo. 154, 28 S.W.2d 363, 367. Relation which one spouse because of marriage has to blood relatives of the other. State v. Hooper, 140 Kan. 481, 37 P.2d 52.

Degrees of relationship by affinity are computed as are degrees of relationship by consanguinity. The doctrine of affinity grew out of the canonical maxim that marriage makes husband and wife one. The husband has the same relation, by affinity, to his wife's blood relatives as she has to them by consanguinity and vice versa. State v. Hooper, 140 Kan. 481, 37 P.2d 52.

Affinity is distinguished into three kinds: (1) *Direct*, or that subsisting between the husband and his wife's relations by blood, or between the wife and the husband's relations by blood; (2) *secondary*, or that which subsists between the husband and his wife's relations by marriage; (3) *collateral*, or that which subsists between the husband and the relations of his wife's relations. Wharton.

In a larger sense, consanguinity or kindred. Co.Litt. 157*a*.

Quasi Affinity

In the civil law, the affinity which exists between two persons, one of whom has been betrothed to a kinsman of the other, but who have never been married.

AFFIRM. To ratify, make firm, confirm, establish, reassert. Cowell; Ashby v. Peters, 128 Neb. 338, 258 N.W. 639, 644, 99 A.L.R. 843.

In the practice of appellate courts, to *affirm* a judgment, decree, or order, is to declare that it is valid and right, and must stand as rendered below; to ratify and reassert it; to concur in its correctness and confirm its efficacy. Boner v. Fall River County Bank, 25 Wyo. 260, 168 P. 726, 727.

Contracts

Ratify and accept voidable contract. Cf. Adopt.

Pleading

To allege or aver a matter of fact; to state it affirmatively; the opposite of *deny* or *traverse*.

Practice

To make affirmation; to make a solemn and formal declaration or asseveration that an affidavit is true, that the witness will tell the truth, etc., this being substituted for an oath in certain cases. Also, to give testimony on affirmation.

AFFIRMANCE. In practice. The confirming, or ratifying of a former law, or judgment. Cowell; Blount.

The confirmation and ratification by an appellate court of a judgment, order, or decree of a lower court brought before it for review. See Affirm, note.

The ratification or confirmation of a voidable contract or act by the party who is to be bound thereby.

The term is in accuracy to be distinguished from *ratification*, which is a recognition of the validity or binding force as against the party ratifying, of some act performed by another person; and from *confirmation*, which would seem to apply more properly to cases where a doubtful authority has been exercised by another in behalf of the person ratifying; but these distinctions are not generally observed with much care.

AFFIRMANCE DAY GENERAL. In the English court of exchequer, a day appointed by the judges of the common pleas, and barons of the exchequer, to be held a few days after the beginning of every term for the general affirmance or reversal of judgments. 2 Tidd, Pr. 1091.

AFFIRMANT. A person who testifies on affirmation, or who affirms instead of taking an oath. See Affirmation. Used in affidavits and depositions which are *affirmed*, instead of sworn to in place of the word "deponent."

AFFIRMANTI, NON NEGANTI INCUMBIT PROBATIO. The [burden of] proof lies upon him who affirms, not upon one who denies. Steph. Pl. 84.

AFFIRMANTIS EST PROBARE. He who affirms must prove. Porter v. Stevens, 9 Cush., Mass., 535.

AFFIRMATION. In practice, a solemn and formal declaration or asseveration that an affidavit is true, that the witness will tell the truth, etc., this being substituted for an oath in certain cases.

A solemn religious asseveration in the nature of an oath. 1 Greenl.Ev. § 371.

Quakers, as a class, and other persons who have conscientious scruples against taking an oath, are allowed to make affirmation in any mode which they may declare to be binding upon their consciences, in confirmation of the truth of testimony which they are about to give. 1 Atk. 21, 46; Cowp. 340, 389; 1 Leach Cr.Cas. 64; 1 Ry. & M. 77.

AFFIRMATION OF FACT. A statement concerning a subject-matter of a transaction which might otherwise be only an expression of opinion but which is affirmed as an existing fact material to the transaction, and reasonably induces the other party to consider and rely upon it, as a fact. Stone v. McCarty, 64 Cal.App. 158, 220 P. 690, 694.

AFFIRMATIO UNIUS EXCLUSIO EST ALTERIUS. The affirmance of one thing is the exclusion of the other. State v. Evans, 214 La. 472, 38 So.2d 140, 147.

AFFIRMATIVE. That which declares positively; that which avers a fact to be true; that which establishes; the opposite of negative.

The party who, upon the allegations of pleadings joining issue, is under the obligation of making proof, in the first instance, of matters alleged, is said to hold the affirmative, or, in other words, to sustain the burden of proof. Abbott.

As to affirmative "Damages," "Plea," "Proof," "Warranty," see those titles.

AFFIRMATIVE ACTION. The "affirmative action" which the National Labor Relations Board is authorized to take to effectuate the policies of the National Labor Relations Act is action to make effective the redress of rights conferred upon employees by the act. National Labor Relations Board v. National Casket Co., C.C.A.2, 107 F.2d 992, 998.

It is broad, but is not unlimited, is remedial not punitive, and is to be exercised in aid of the Board's authority to restrain violations and as a means of removing or avoiding the consequences of violations. National Labor Relations Board v. Fansteel Metallurgical Corporation, 306 U.S. 240, 59 S.Ct. 490, 497, 83 L.Ed. 627, 123 A.L.R. 599.

It is not disciplinary. National Labor Relations Board v. Leviton Mfg. Co., C.C.A.2, 111 F.2d 619, 621.

AFFIRMATIVE AUTHORIZATION. Something more than authority by mere implication. White, Gratwick & Mitchell v. Empire Engineering Co., 125 Misc. 47, 210 N.Y.S. 563, 572.

AFFIRMATIVE CHARGE. The general "affirmative charge" is an instruction to the jury that, whatever the evidence may be, defendant cannot be convicted under the count in the indictment to which the charge is directed. Coker v. State, 18 Ala.App. 550, 93 So. 384, 386.

AFFIRMATIVE DEFENSE. In code pleading. New matter constituting a defense; new matter which, assuming the complaint to be true, constitutes a defense to it. Carter v. Eighth Ward Bank, 33 Misc. 128, 67 N.Y.S. 300.

AFFIRMATIVE EASEMENT. An "affirmative easement" is one which gives to the owner of the dominant tenement the right to use the servient tenement, or to do some act thereon which would otherwise be unlawful. Clements v. Taylor, Tex. Civ.App., 184 S.W.2d 485, 487.

AFFIRMATIVE PREGNANT. In pleading, an affirmative allegation implying some negative in favor of the adverse party. Fields v. State, 134 Ind. 46, 32 N.E. 780.

AFFIRMATIVE PROOF. Such evidence of the truth of matters asserted as tends to establish them, regardless of character of evidence offered. Glass v. Newport Clothing Co., 110 Vt. 368, 8 A.2d 651, 654.

AFFIRMATIVE RELIEF. Relief, benefit, or compensation which may be due and granted to defendant. Garner v. Hannah, 6 Duer, N.Y., 262. Relief for which defendant might maintain an action independently of plaintiff's claim and on which he might proceed to recovery, although plaintiff abandoned his cause of action or failed to establish it. Southwestern Surety Ins. Co. v. Walser, 77 Okl. 240, 188 P. 335, 336.

AFFIRMATIVE STATUTE. A statute couched in affirmative or mandatory terms. 1 Bl.Comm. 142.

One which directs the doing of an act, or declares what shall be done; as a *negative* statute is one which prohibits a thing from being done, or declares what shall not be done. Blackstone describes affirmative acts of parliament as those "wherein justice is directed to be done according to the law of the land." 1 Bl.Comm. 142.

AFFIRMATIVE WARRANTY. Affirms existence of a fact at time policy is entered into, while promissory warranty requires that something be done or not done after policy has taken effect. Sentinel Life Ins. Co. v. Blackmer, C.C.A.Colo., 77 F.2d 347, 350.

AFFIX. Fix or fasten in any way, to attach physically. Penn v. Dyba, 115 Cal.App. 67, 1 P.2d 461, 464. To attach to, inscribe, or impress upon, as a signature, a seal, a trade-mark. Pen.Code N.Y. § 367. To attach, add to, or fasten upon, permanently, as in the case of fixtures annexed to real estate.

A thing is deemed to be affixed to land when it is attached to it by the roots, as in the case of trees, vines, or shrubs; or imbedded in it, as in the case of walls; or permanently resting upon it, as in the case of buildings; or permanently attached to what is thus permanent, as by means of cement, plaster, nails, bolts, or screws. Miller v. Waddingham, 3 Cal.Unrep.Cas. 375, 25 Pac. 688, 11 L.R.A. 510; Tolle v. Vandenberg, 44 Okl. 780, 146 P. 212, 213.

AFFIXING. Securely attached. Mechanics' Nat. Bank of Trenton v. Newman, 137 Misc. 587, 244 N.Y.S. 529, 531.

AFFIXUS. In the civil law, affixed, fixed, or fastened to.

AFFLICTION. A distress of mind or body; that which causes continuing anguish or suffering.

AFFORARE. To set a price or value on a thing. Blount.

AFFORATUS. Appraised or valued, as things vendible in a market. Blount.

AFFORCE. To add to; to increase; to strengthen; to add force to.

AFFORCE THE ASSIZE. In old English practice, a method of securing a verdict, where the jury disagreed, either by confining them without meat and drink, or, more anciently, by adding other jurors to the panel, to a limited extent, until twelve could be found who were unanimous. Bract. fol. 185*b*, 292*a*; Fleta, lib. 4, c. 9, § 2; 2 Reeve, Hist.Eng.Law, 267.

AFFORCIAMENTUM. In old English law, a fortress or stronghold, or other fortification. Cowell.

The calling of a court upon a solemn or extraordinary occasion. Id.

AFFOREST. To convert land into a forest in the legal sense of the word.

AFFORESTATION. The turning of a part of a country into forest or woodland or subjecting it to forest law, *q. v.*

AFFOUAGE. In French law, the right of the inhabitants of a commune or section of a commune to take from the forest the fire-wood which is necessary for their use. Duverger.

AFFRANCHIR. L. Fr. To set free. Kelham.

AFFRANCHISE. To liberate; to make free.

AFFRAY. The fighting of two or more persons in some public place to the terror of the people. Wallace v. Commonwealth, 207 Ky. 122, 268 S.W. 809, 813.

Where two or more persons voluntarily or by agreement engage in any fight, or use any blows or violence towards each other in an angry or quarrelsome manner, in any public place to the disturbance of others.

Words are insufficient, but if one person, by such abusive language toward another as is calculated and intended to bring on a fight, induces the other to strike him, both are guilty of "affray." State v. Maney, 194 N.C. 34, 138 S.E. 441, 442.

It differs from a riot in not being premeditated. Hawk. P.C. bk. 1, c. 65, § 3; 4 Bl.Comm. 146; 1 Russ.Crimes, 271.

AFFRECTAMENTUM. Affreightment; a contract for the hire of a vessel. From the Fr. *fret,* which, according to Cowell, meant tons or tonnage. *Affreightamentum* was sometimes used. Du Cange.

AFFREIGHTMENT. A contract of affreightment is a contract with a ship-owner to hire his ship, or part of it, for the carriage of goods. The Fred Smartley, Jr., C.C.A.Va., 100 F.2d 971, 973.

Such a contract generally takes the form either of a charter-party or of a bill of lading. Bramble v. Culmer, 78 Fed. 501, 24 C.C.A. 182. A contract to transport goods constitutes a contract of "affreightment," although there is towage service connected therewith. The Independent, D.C.La., 37 F.Supp. 106, 111.

In French law, freighting and affreighting are distinguished. The owner of a ship freights it, *(le frete;)* he is called the freighter, *(freteur;)* he is the letter or lessor, *(locateur, locator.)* The merchant affreights *(affrete)* the ship, and is called the affreighter, *(affreteur;)* he is the hirer, *(locataire, conductor.)* Emerig. Tr. des Ass. c. 11, § 3.

AFFRETEMENT. Fr. In French law, the hiring of a vessel; affreightment *(q. v.).* Called also *nolissement.* Ord.Mar. liv. 1, tit. 2, art. 2; Id. liv. 3, tit. 1, art. 1.

AFFRI. In old English law, plow cattle, bullocks or plow horses. *Affri,* or *afri carucæ;* beasts of the plow. Spelman.

AFFRONT. An insult or indignity; assault, insololence.

AFORESAID. Before, or already said, mentioned, or recited; premised. Plowd. 67. Alabama Great Southern R. Co. v. Smith, 191 Ala. 643, 68 So. 56, 57. Foresaid is used in Scotch law.

Although the words "preceding" and "aforesaid" generally mean next before, and "following" means next after, yet a different signification will be given to them if required by the context and the facts of the case. Simpson v. Robert, 35 Ga. 180.

AFORETHOUGHT. In criminal law, deliberate; planned; premeditated; prepense. State v. Fiske, 63 Conn. 388, 28 A. 572. See Malice Aforethought; Premeditation; 4 Bla.Com. 199; Respublica v. Mulatto Bob, 4 Dall., Pa., 146, 1 L.Ed. 776; U. S. v. Cornell, 2 Mas. 91, Fed.Cas.No.14,868.

"Aforethought" as used in the law of murder means thought of beforehand and for any length of time, however short, before the doing of the act, and is synonymous with premeditation. State v. Smith, 26 N.M. 482, 194 P. 869, 872.

AFRICAN DESCENT. Persons of African nativity or of "African descent" within the meaning of the Naturalization Act, as amended by Act July 14, 1870 (8 U.S.C.A. § 703 note), are members of the negro races of Africa or their descendants by intermixture with races constituting free white persons, the negro races referred to being those from which the emancipated slaves in the United States descend. Ex parte Shahid, D.C.S.C., 205 F. 812, 815.

AFTER. Later, succeeding, subsequent to, inferior in point of time or of priority or preference.

Subsequent in time to. Cheney v. National Surety Corporation, 256 App.Div. 1041, 10 N.Y.S.2d 706. At. Hyman Bros. Box & Label Co. v. Industrial Accident Commission, 180 Cal. 423, 181 P. 784, 786. On and after New York Trust Co. v. Portland Ry. Co., 197 App.Div. 422, 189 N.Y.S. 346, 348. "At the end of" or "as soon as," and in computation of time, is generally understood in sense of excluding day of date mentioned. Taylor v. National Life & Accident Ins. Co., Tex.Civ.App., 63 S.W.2d 1082, 1083. But the words "after the filing" as used in sections 63 and 68 of the Bankruptcy Act (11 U.S.C.A. §§ 103, 108) do not mean the day after that of filing, but refer to the very instant of filing if ascertainable. In re Ledbetter, D.C.Ga., 267 F. 893, 896. A note payable generally "after date," is payable on demand. Love v. Perry, 19 Ga.App. 86, 90 S.E. 978, 979.

AFTER-ACQUIRED. Acquired after a particular date or event. Thus, a judgment is a lien on after-acquired realty, *i. e.,* land acquired by the debtor after entry of the judgment. Hughes v. Hughes, 152 Pa. 590, 26 A. 101.

AFTER ACQUIRED TITLE. Doctrine under which title acquired by grantor who previously attempted to convey title to land which he did not in fact own, inures automatically to benefit of prior grantees. Perkins v. White, Miss., 43 So.2d 897, 899; Morris v. Futischa, 194 Okl. 224, 148 P.2d 986, 987.

AFTER-BORN CHILD. A statute making a will void as to after-born children means physical birth, and is not applicable to a child legitimated by the marriage of its parents. Appeal of McCulloch, 113 Pa. 247, 6 A. 253. See En Ventre Sa Mere; Posthumous Child.

AFTER-DISCOVERED. Discovered or made known after a particular date or event.

AFTER-DISCOVERED EVIDENCE. See Evidence.

AFTER SIGHT. This term as used in a bill payable so many days after sight, means after legal sight; that is, after legal presentment for acceptance. The mere fact of having seen the bill or known of its existence does not constitute legal "sight." Mitchell v. Degrand, 17 Fed.Cas. 494.

AFTERMATH. A second crop of grass mown in the same season; also the right to take such second crop. See 1 Chit.Gen.Pr. 181.

"Aftermath" as used in the manufacture of window glass means the colder glass remaining on and in molten bath after drawing of glass cylinder. Okmulgee Window Glass Co. v. Window Glass Mach. Co., C.C.A.Okl., 265 F. 626, 630.

AFTERNOON. May mean the whole time from noon to midnight, or it may mean the earlier part of that time as distinguished from evening. Clevenger v. Carl B. King Drilling Co., Tex.Civ. App., 62 S.W.2d 1001. But ordinarily means that part of day between noon and evening. Buttrick v. Woman's Hospital Aid Ass'n, 87 N.H. 194, 177 A. 416, 418.

AFTERTHOUGHT. A thought composed after the event and with deliberation. A devise to escape difficulty.

AFTERWARD, AFTERWARDS. Subsequent in point of time; synonymous with "thereafter," Lamoutte v. Title Guaranty & Surety Co., 165 App. Div. 573, 151 N.Y.S. 148, 154, or with "then," Boyce v. Mosely, 102 S.C. 361, 86 S.E. 771, 772.

AGAINST. Adverse to; contrary, Cram v. Meagher, 113 Vt. 463, 35 A.2d 855, In re Dean's Estate, 350 Mo. 494, 166 S.W.2d 529, 533. Signifies discord or conflict; opposed to; without the consent of; in contact with. Palmer v. Superior Mfg. Co., D.C. N.Y., 203 F. 1003, 1005, Clemens v. Perry, Tex.Civ. App., 29 S.W.2d 529, 533. Sometimes meaning "upon," which is almost, if not altogether, synonymous with word "on." Northern Pac. Ry. Co. v. Gas Development Co., 103 Mont. 214, 62 P.2d 204, 205. Denoting manifestation of raped woman's utmost reluctance and greatest resistance. State v. Egner, 317 Mo. 457, 296 S.W. 145, 146.

AGAINST THE EVIDENCE. Means "against the weight of the evidence." Cram v. Meagher, 113 Vt. 463, 35 A.2d 855.

AGAINST THE FORM OF THE STATUTE. Technical words which must be used in framing an indictment for a breach of the statute prohibiting the act complained of. The Latin phrase is *contra forman statuti, q. v.* State v. Murphy, 15 R.I. 543, 10 A. 585.

AGAINST THE PEACE. A technical phrase used in alleging a breach of the peace. See Contra Pacem. State v. Tibbetts, 86 Me. 189, 29 A. 979.

AGAINST THE WEIGHT OF THE EVIDENCE. "Contrary to the evidence". Russell v. Pilger, 113 Vt. 537, 37 A.2d 403, 411.

AGAINST THE WILL. Technical words which must be used in framing an indictment for robbery from the person, rape and some other offenses. Whittaker v. State, 50 Wis. 521, 7 N.W. 431, 36 Am.St.Rep. 856.

AGALMA. An impression or image of anything on a seal. Cowell.

AGARD. L. Fr. An award. *Nul fait agard;* no award made.

AGARDER. L. Fr. To award, adjudge, or determine; to sentence, or condemn.

AGE. The length of time during which a person has lived; the time at which one attains full personal rights and capacities. In law the term signifies those periods in the lives of persons of both sexes which enable them to do certain acts which, before they had arrived at those periods, they were prohibited from doing. 2 C.J.S., p. 1013.

As used in particular statutes, the term implies disability and, by definition, has been applied to all minors under a certain age and to others disabled by old age. Hampton v. Ewert, C.C.A.Okl., 22 F.2d 81, 87.

Age and schooling certificate. Collings-Taylor Co. v. American Fidelity Co., 96 Ohio St. 123, 117 N.E. 158.

Age fixed by law. Johnson v. Travelers' Ins. Co., 147 Or. 345, 32 P.2d 587.

Age of consent. Ex parte Hutchens, 296 Mo. 331, 246 S.W. 186, 189.

Age of legal consent. Johnson v. Alexander, 39 Cal.App. 177, 178 P. 297; Fisher v. Bernard, 65 Vt. 663, 27 A. 316.

Age of majority. Gates v. Shaffer, 72 Wash. 451, 130 P. 896.

Age of maturity. Commercial Bank & Trust Co. v. Noble, 112 So. 691, 146 Miss. 552.

Age of twenty-one years. Vanderbilt v. Eidman, 196 U.S. 480, 25 S.Ct. 331, 49 L.Ed. 563.

Legal Age. See Legal Age.

Legal school age. Inhabitants of Needham v. Wellesley, 139 Mass. 372, 31 N.E. 732.

AGE, *Awe, Aive.* **L. Fr. Water. Kelham.**

AGE PRAYER. A suggestion of nonage, made by an infant party to a real action, with a prayer that the proceedings may be deferred until his full age. It is now abolished. St. 11 Geo. IV.; 1 Wm. IV. c. 37, § 10; 1 Lil.Reg. 54; 3 Bl.Comm. 300.

AGENCY. Includes every relation in which one person acts for or represents another by latter's authority, Saums v. Parfet, 270 Mich. 165, 258 N.W. 235, where one person acts for another, either in the relationship of principal and agent, master and servant, or employer or proprietor and independent contractor, Gorton v. Doty, 57 Idaho 792, 69 P.2d 136, 139.

Properly speaking, agency relates to commercial or business transactions. Humble Oil & Refining Co. v. Bell, Tex.Civ.App., 172 S.W.2d 800,

803, and frequently is used in connection with an arrangement which does not in law amount to an agency, as where the essence of an arrangement is bailment or sale, as in the case of a sale agency exclusive in certain territory. State Compensation Ins. Fund v. Industrial Accident Commission, 216 Cal. 351, 14 P.2d 306, 310.

It also designates a place at which business of company or individual is transacted by an agent. Johnson Freight Lines v. Davis, 170 Tenn. 177, 93 S.W.2d 637, 639.

The relation created by express or implied contract or by law, whereby one party delegates the transaction of some lawful business with more or less discretionary power to another, who undertakes to manage the affair and render to him an account thereof. State ex rel. Cities Service Gas Co. v. Public Service Commission, 337 Mo. 809, 85 S.W.2d 890, 894. Or where one person confides the management of some affair, to be transacted on his account, to other party. 1 Liverm. Prin. & Ag. 2. Or one party is authorized to do certain acts for, or in relation to the rights or property of the other. But means more than tacit permission, and involves request, instruction, or command. Klee v. U. S., C.C.A.Wash., 53 F.2d 58, 61. Being the consensual relation existing between two persons, by virtue of which one is subject to other's control. Tarver, Steele & Co. v. Pendleton Gin Co., Tex.Civ.App., 25 S.W.2d 156, 159.

Actual agency. Exists where the agent is really employed by the principal. Weidenaar v. N. Y. Life Ins. Co., 36 Mont. 592, 94 P. 1, 6.

Agency by estoppel. One created by operation of law and established by proof of such acts of the principal as reasonably lead to the conclusion of its existence. Sigel-Campion Live Stock Commission Co. v. Ardohain, 71 Colo. 410, 207 P. 82, 83. Arises where principal, by negligence in failing to supervise agent's affairs, allows agent to exercise powers not granted to him, thus justifying others in believing agent possesses requisite authority. Reifsnyder v. Dougherty, 301 Pa. 328, 152 A. 98, 100. Though principal have no notice of agent's conduct, Dispatch Printing Co. v. National Bank of Commerce, 109 Minn. 440, 124 N.W. 236, 50 L.R.A.,N.S., 74.

Agency of necessity. A term sometimes applied to the kind of implied agency which enables a wife to procure what is reasonably necessary for her maintenance and support on her husband's credit and at his expense, when he fails to make proper provision for her necessities. Bostwick v. Brower, 49 N.Y.S. 1046, 22 Misc. 709.

Deed of agency. A revocable and voluntary trust for payment of debts. Wharton.

Exclusive agency. Defined as an agreement by owner that during life of contract he will not sell property to a purchaser procured by another agent, which agreement does not preclude owner himself from selling to a purchaser of his own procuring, while a contract giving a broker "exclusive sale" is more than such exclusive agency, and is an agreement by the owner that he will not sell the property during the life of the contract to any purchaser not procured by the broker in question. Harris v. McPherson, 97 Conn. 164, 115 A. 723, 724, 24 A.L.R. 1530; Harris & White v. Stone, 137 Ark. 23, 207 S.W. 443, 444.

General agency. That which exists when there is a delegation to do all acts connected with a particular trade, business or employment. Hinkson v. Kansas City Life Ins. Co., 93 Or. 473, 183 P. 24, 29. It implies authority on the part of the agent to act without restriction or qualification in all matters relating to the business of his principal. Schwartz v. Maryland Casualty Co., 82 N.H. 177, 131 A. 352, 353.

Implied agency. One created by act of parties and deduced from proof of other facts. Sigel-Campion Live Stock Commission Co. v. Ardohain, 71 Colo. 410, 207 P. 82, 83. It is an actual agency, proved by deductions or inferences from other facts, and third party need have no knowledge of the principal's acts, nor have relied on them. Kentucky-Pennsylvania Oil & Gas Corporation v. Clark, 247 Ky. 438, 57 S.W.2d 65.

Ostensible agency. One which exists where the principal intentionally or by want of ordinary care causes a third person to believe another to be his agent who is not really employed by him. Weidenaar v. N. Y. Life Ins. Co., 36 Mont. 592, 94 P. 1, 6. See, also, Agency by Estoppel.

AGENCY COUPLED WITH INTEREST. Interest in continued existence of power or authority to act with reference to business, where secured by contract and based on consideration moving from agent to principal looking to exercise of power as means of reimbursement, creates "agency coupled with an interest." Bowling v. National Convoy & Trucking Co., 101 Fla. 634, 135 So. 541, 544. Agent must have an interest or estate in the thing to be disposed of or managed under the power. Eduardo Fernandez Y Compania v. Longino & Collins, 199 La. 343, 6 So.2d 137, 142, 143.

AGENCY RELATIONSHIP. An employment for purpose of representation in establishing legal relations between principal and third persons. Blabon v. Hay, 269 Mass. 401, 169 N.E. 268, 271.

AGENDA. Memoranda of things to be done, as items of business or discussion to be brought up at a meeting; a program consisting of such items. Webster. Baton Rouge Bldg. Trades Council v. T. L. James & Co., 201 La. 749, 10 So.2d 606, 619.

AGENESIA. In medical jurisprudence, impotentia generandi; sexual impotence; incapacity for reproduction, existing in either sex, and whether arising from structural or other causes.

AGENFRIDA. Sax. The true master or owner of a thing. Spelman.

AGENHINA. In Saxon law, a guest at an inn, who, having stayed there for three nights, was then accounted one of the family. Cowell.

AGENS. Lat. An agent, a conductor, or manager of affairs. Distinguished from *factor,* a workman. A plaintiff. Fleta, lib. 4, c. 15, § 8.

AGENT. A person authorized by another to act for him, one intrusted with another's business. Downs v. Delco-Light Co., 175 La. 242, 143 So. 227. One who represents and acts for another under the contract or relation of agency, *q. v.* Fowler v. Cobb, Mo.App., 232 S.W. 1084. A business representative, whose function is to bring about, modify, affect, accept performance of, or terminate contractual obligations between principal and third persons. Saums v. Parfet, 270 Mich. 165, 258 N.W. 235. One who undertakes to transact some business, or to manage some affair, for another, by the authority and on account of the latter, and to render an account of it. 1 Livermore, Ag. 67. See Co.Litt. 207; 1 B. & P. 316; Thomas B. Jeffrey Co. v. Lockridge, 173 Ky. 282, 190 S.W. 1103, 1105. One who acts for or in place of another by authority from him; a substitute, a deputy, appointed by principal with power to do the things which principal may do. Stephenson v. Golden, 279 Mich. 710, 276 N.W. 849. One who deals not only with things, as does a servant, but with persons, using his own discretion as to means, and frequently establishing contractual relations between his principal and third persons. Rendleman v. Niagara Sprayer Co., D.C.Ill., 16 F.2d 122, 124. See, also, State v. Bond, 94 W.Va. 255, 118 S.E. 276, 279.

Agent and patient. A phrase indicating the state of a person who is required to do a thing, and is at the same time the person to whom it is done; as, when a man is indebted to another, and he appoints him his executor, required to pay the debt in his capacity of executor, and entitled to receive it in his own right. Termes de la Ley.

Apparent agent or ostensible agent. One whom the principal, either intentionally or by want of ordinary care, induces third persons to believe to be his agent, though he has not, either expressly or by implication, conferred authority on him. Ware v. Home Mut. Ins. Ass'n of Iowa, 135 Neb. 329, 281 N.W. 617, 620. A person who, whether or not authorized, reasonably appears to third person, because of manifestations of another, to be authorized to act as agent for such other. Hansche v. A. J. Conroy, Inc., 222 Wis. 553, 269 N.W. 309, 312.

Diplomatic agent. A person employed by a sovereign to manage his private affairs, or those of his subjects in his name, at the court of a foreign government. Wolff, Inst. Nat. § 1237.

General agency business. One not engaged as agent for single firm or person, but holding himself out to public as being engaged in business of being agent. Comer v. State Tax Commission of New Mexico, 41 N.M. 403, 69 P.2d 936.

General agent. One employed in his capacity as a professional man or master of an art or trade, or one to whom the principal confides his whole business or all transactions or functions of a designated class; or he is a person who is authorized by his principal to execute all deeds, sign all contracts, or purchase all goods, required in a particular trade, business, or employment. See Story, Ag. § 17; Thompson v. Michigan Mut. Life Ins. Co., 56 Ind.App. 502, 105 N.E. 780, 782; Little v. Minneapolis Threshing Mach. Co., 166 Iowa 651, 147 N.W. 872, 873. One empowered to transact all business of principal at any particular time or any particular place, a general manager. Abuc Trading & Sales Corporation v. Jennings, 151 Md. 392, 135 A. 166, 173. An agent to manage buildings and lease and collect the rents, Daniel v. Pappas, C.C.A.Okl., 16 F.2d 880, 883. An agent empowered to enter into contracts without consulting insurer, notwithstanding restriction of his territory, London & Lancashire Ins. Co. v. McWilliams, 215 Ala. 481, 110 So. 909, 910.

Local agent. One appointed to act as the representative of a corporation and transact its business generally (or business of a particular character) at a given place or within a defined district. See Frick Co. v. Wright, 23 Tex. Civ.App. 340, 55 S.W. 608; Moore v. Freeman's Nat. Bank, 92 N.C. 594.

Managing agent. A person who is invested with general power, involving the exercise of judgment and discretion, as distinguished from an ordinary agent or employee, who acts in an inferior capacity, and under the direction and control of superior authority, both in regard to the extent of the work and the manner of executing the same. Reddington v. Mariposa Land & Min. Co., 19 Hun, N.Y., 405; Taylor v. Granite State Prov. Ass'n, 32 N.C. 992, 136 N.Y. 343, 32 Am.St.Rep. 749. One who has exclusive supervision and control of some department of a corporation's business, the management of which requires of such person the exercise of independent judgment and discretion, and the exercise of such authority that it may be fairly said that service of summons upon him will result in notice to the corporation. Federal Betterment Co. v. Reeves, 73 Kan. 107, 84 P. 560, 4 L.R.A.,N.S., 460; Hatinen v. Payne, 150 Minn. 344, 185 N.W. 386, 387. As used in section 4274, Wilson's Statutes of Oklahoma 1903, Ann., an agent whose agency extends to all the transactions of the corporation within the state; one who has or is engaged in the management of the business of the corporation, in distinction from the management of a local or particular branch or department of said business. Waters Pierce Oil Co. v. Foster, 52 Okl. 412, 153 P. 169, 171.

Mercantile agents. Agents employed for the sale of goods or merchandise are called "mercantile agents," and are of two principal classes,—brokers and factors *(q. v.)*; a factor is sometimes called a "commission agent," or "commission merchant." Russ. Merc. Ag. 1.

Practice of the House of Lords and Privy Council. In appeals, solicitors and other persons admitted to practice in those courts in a similar capacity to that of solicitors in ordinary courts, are technically called "agents." Macph. Priv. Coun. 65.

Private agent. An agent acting for an individual in his private affairs; as distinguished from a *public* agent, who represents the government in some administrative capacity.

Public agent. An agent of the public, the state, or the government; a person appointed to act for the public in some matter pertaining to the administration of government or the public business. See Story, Ag. § 302; Whiteside v. United States, 93 U.S. 254, 23 L.Ed. 882.

Real-estate agent. Any person whose business it is to sell, or offer for sale, real estate for others, or to rent houses, stores, or other buildings, or real estate, or to collect rent for others. Act July 13, 1866, c. 184, § 9, par. 25; 14 St. at Large, 118. Carstens v. McReavy, 1 Wash.St. 359, 25 P. 471.

A special agent is one employed to conduct a particular transaction or piece of business for his principal or authorized to perform a specified act. Hinkson v. Kansas City Life Ins. Co., 93 Or. 473, 183 P. 24, 29; Pettijohn v. St. Paul Fire & Marine Ins. Co., 100 Kan. 482, 164 P. 1096, 1097; Hoffman v. Marano, 71 Pa.Super.Ct. 26, 28.

AGENTES ET CONSENTIENTES PARI PŒNA PLECTENTUR. Acting and consenting parties are liable to the same punishment. 5 Coke, 80.

AGER. Lat. A field; land generally. A portion of land inclosed by definite boundaries. Municipality No. 2 v. Orleans Cotton Press, 18 La. 167, 36 Am.Dec. 624. In old English law, an acre *(q. v.)*. Spelman.

AGGER. Lat. In the civil law, a dam, bank or mound. Cod. 9, 38; Townsh.Pl. 48.

AGGRAVATED ASSAULT. The term has no technical and definite common law meaning. In re Burns, C.C.Ark., 113 F. 987; People v. Ochotski, 115 Mich. 601, 73 N.W. 889. The term is one which is employed to describe an assault which has, in addition to the mere intent to commit it, another object which is also criminal, Brimhall v. State, 31 Ariz. 522, 255 P. 165, 53 A.L.R. 231; or to include all those species of assault which, for various reasons, have come to be regarded as more heinous than common assault, State v. Jones, 133 S.C. 167, 130 S.E. 747; or which have been made the subject of special legislative provisions, Daffan v. State, Tex.Cr.App., 21 S.W.2d 301 and Njecick v. State, 178 Wis. 94, 189 N.W. 147.

An assault where the means or instrument used to accomplish the injury is highly dangerous or where assailant has some ulterior and malicious motive in committing assault other than a mere desire to punish injured person. Strickbine v. State, 201 Ark. 1031, 148 S.W.2d 180, 181, 182; when committed with a deadly weapon under circumstances not amounting to an intent to murder, Myers v. State, 72 Tex.Cr.R. 630, 163 S.W. 432; or when the instrument or means used is such as inflicts disgrace upon the person assaulted, Cirul v. State, 83 Tex.Cr.R. 8, 200 S.W. 1088; Scott v. State, 73 Tex.Cr.R. 622, 166 S.W. 729, 730 (indecent and improper fondling of the person). In Arizona, aggravated assault is different from simple assault only by infliction of serious bodily injury, Brimhall v. State, 31 Ariz. 522, 255 P. 165, 166, 53 A.L.R. 231.

AGGRAVATING. Passenger ejected from plane. Delta Air Corporation v. Porter, 70 Ga.App. 152, 27 S.E.2d 758, 762.

AGGRAVATION. Any circumstance attending the commission of a crime or tort which increases its guilt or enormity or adds to its injurious consequences, but which is above and beyond the essential constituents of the crime or tort itself.

Matter of aggravation, correctly understood, does not consist in acts of the same kind and description as those constituting the gist of the action, but in something done by the defendant, on the occasion of committing the trespass, which is, to some extent, of a different legal character from the principal act complained of. Hathaway v. Rice, 19 Vt. 107. So on an indictment for murder the prisoner may be convicted of manslaughter, for the averment of malice aforethought is merely matter of aggravation. Co.Litt. 282 *a*.

In pleading, the introduction of matter into the declaration which tends to increase the amount of damages, but does not affect the right of action itself. Steph.Pl. 257; 12 Mod. 597.

AGGRAVATION OF THE DISABILITY. Refers to the course or progress of the workman's condition resulting from the specific injury for which an award or arrangement of compensation has been made. Keefer v. State Industrial Accident Commission, 171 Or. 405, 135 P.2d 806, 809.

AGGREGATE. Entire number, sum, mass, or quantity of something; amount; complete whole, and one provision under will may be the aggregate if there are no more units to fall into that class. In re Curley's Will, 151 Misc. 664, 272 N.Y.S. 489. Composed of several; consisting of many persons united together; a combined whole. 1 Bl.Comm. 469.

AGGREGATE CORPORATION. See Corporation.

AGGREGATES. Name for materials consisting largely of rock, gravel and sand used for construction and surfacing of highways or, as a component part, in forming concrete for such construction. Pioneer Gravel Equipment Mfg. Co. v. Diamond Iron Works, C.C.A.Minn., 72 F.2d 161.

AGGREGATIO MENTIUM. The meeting of minds. The moment when a contract is complete. A supposed derivation of the word "agreement," *q. v.*

AGGREGATION. In law of patents, it means that the elements of a claimed combination are incapable of co-operation to produce a unitary result, and in its true sense does not need prior art patents to support it. National Popsicle Corporation v. Harvey, D.C.Pa., 6 F.Supp. 784, 786.

It does not imply mechanical interaction of parts, but only union of all elements of invention to realize single purpose. Simplex Piston Ring Co. of America v. Horton-Gallo-Creamer Co., C.C.A.Conn., 61 F.2d 748, 750. A combination which merely brings together two or more functions to be availed of independently of each other does not represent "invention" but constitutes mere "aggregation." Hemming v. S. S. Kresge Co., D.C.Conn., 24 F.Supp. 981, 983. The assembly of old elements, in a device in which each performs the same function in the same way as it did when used alone, without mutuality of action, interaction, or co-operation, is mere "aggregation" not involving invention. In re Smith, 57 App.D.C. 204, 19 F.2d 678, 679.

AGGRESSOR. One who first employs hostile force. Penn v. Henderson, 174 Or. 1, 146 P.2d 760, 766. The party who first offers violence or offense. He who begins a quarrel or dispute, either by threatening or striking another. See Wilkie v. State, 33 Okl.Cr. 225, 242 P. 1057, 1059.

AGGRIEVED. Having suffered loss or injury; damnified; injured.

AGGRIEVED PARTY. One whose legal right is invaded by an act complained of, or whose pecuniary interest is directly affected by a decree or judgment. Glos v. People, 259 Ill. 332, 102 N.E. 763, 766, Ann.Cas.1914C, 119. See next topic. One whose right of property may be established or divested. McFarland v. Pierce, 151 Ind. 546, 45 N.E. 706. The word "aggrieved" refers to a substantial grievance, a denial of some personal or property right, or the imposition upon a party of a burden or obligation. Roullard v. McSoley, 54 R.I. 232, 172 A. 326, 327. Injured in a legal sense. In re Donnelly's Estate, 55 S.D. 426, 226 N.W. 563, 565.

Adoption, Appeal of Cummings, 126 Me. 111, 136 A. 662, 663; disbarment, State v. Hunter, 152 Tenn. 233, 276 S.W. 639, 640; bar association, State v. Huddleston, 173 Ark. 686, 293 S.W. 353, 358; *contra*, disciplinary proceedings; In re Dolphin, 240 N.Y. 89, 147 N.E. 538, 539; lunacy inquisition, Commonwealth v. Davidson, 269 Pa. 218, 112 A. 115. One against whom error has been committed, Kinealy v. Macklin, 67 Mo. 95. Or one against whom an appealable order or judgment has been entered. Ely v. Frisbie, 17 Cal. 260. Any party having an interest recognized by law in the subject-matter, which interest is injuriously affected by judgment. Hornbeck v. Richards, 80 Mont. 27, 257 P. 1025, 1026. A complainant who has received less than the relief demanded, or a defendant who has not been accorded the full amount of his set-off or counterclaim. Blanchard v. Neill, 83 N.J.Eq. 446, 91 A. 811. See, also, Kondas v. Washoe County Bank, 50 Nev. 181, 254 P. 1080, 1081. One under necessity of answering or replying to irrelevant and redundant matter in a pleading. Shea v. Kiely, Sup., 167 N.Y.S. 570, 572.

AGILD. In Saxon law, free from penalty, not subject to the payment of *gild*, or *weregild;* that is, the customary fine or pecuniary compensation for an offense. Spelman; Cowell.

AGILER. In Saxon law, an observer or informer.

AGILLARIUS. L. Lat. In old English law, a hayward, herdward, or keeper of the herd of cattle in a common field. Cowell.

AGIO. In commercial law, a term used to express the difference in point of value between metallic and paper money, or between one sort of metallic money and another. McCul.Dict.

An Italian word for accommodation.

AGIOTAGE. A speculation on the rise and fall of the public debt of states, or the public funds. The speculator is called *"agioteur."*

AGIST. In ancient law it meant to take in and give feed to the cattle of strangers in the king's forest, and to collect the money due for the same to the king's use. Spelman; Cowell.

In modern law it means to take in cattle to feed, or pasture, at a certain rate of compensation. Bank of Tehama County v. Federal Realty Co., 2 Cal.2d 333, 40 P.2d 507, 509. See Agistment.

AGISTATIO ANIMALIUM IN FORESTA. The drift or numbering of cattle in the forest.

AGISTER. See Agistor.

AGISTERS, or GIST TAKERS. Officers appointed to look after cattle, etc. See Williams, Common, 232.

AGISTMENT. The taking and feeding of other men's cattle in the king's forest, or on one's own land, at a certain rate. Bank of Tehama County v. Federal Realty Co., 2 Cal.2d 333, 40 P.2d 507, 509. Also the profit or recompense for such pasturing of cattle. Williams v. Miller, 68 Cal. 290, 9 Pac. 166. A species of bailment. Patchen-Wilkes Stock Farm Co. v. Walton, 166 Ky. 705, 179 S.W. 823.

In canon law it is a composition or mean rate at which some right or due might be reckoned.

There is also agistment of *sea-banks,* where lands are charged with a tribute to keep out the sea; and *terræ agistatæ* are lands whose owners must keep up the sea-banks. Holthouse.

Tithe of Agistment was a small tithe paid to the rector or vicar on cattle or other produce of grass lands. It was paid by the occupier of the land and not by the person who put in his cattle to graze. Rawle, Exmoor 31.

AGISTOR. One who takes in horses or other animals to pasture at certain rates. Story, Bailm. § 443; Cox v. Chase, 99 Kan. 740, 163 P. 184, 186. An officer who had the charge of cattle pastured for a certain stipulated sum in the king's forest and who collected the money paid for them.

AGITATOR. One who stirs up; excites; ruffles; perturbs. One who incessant advocates a social change.

Labor agitator. One actively engaged in promoting the interests of the laboring men. The term does not imply the use of unlawful or improper means. Wabash R. Co. v. Young, 69 N.E. 1003, 1005, 1006, 162 Ind. 102, 4 L.R.A., N.S., 1091.

Seditious agitator. A disturber of the public peace, a subverter of just laws, and a bad citizen. Wilkes v. Shields, 64 N.W. 921, 62 Minn. 426, 427.

AGNATES. In the law of descents, relations by the father, or on the father's side. This word is used in the Scotch law, and by some writers as an English word, corresponding with the Latin *agnati, (q. v.)* Ersk.Inst. b. 1, tit. 7, § 4.

AGNATI. In Roman law, the term included all the cognates who trace their connection exclusively through males.

A table of *cognates* is formed by taking each lineal ancestor in turn and including all his descendants of both sexes in the tabular view. If, then, in tracing the various branches of such a genealogical table or tree, we stop whenever we come to the name of a female, and pursue that particular branch or ramification no further, all who remain after the descendants of women have been excluded are *agnates,* and their connection together is agnatic relationship. Maine, Anc. Law, 142.

All persons are agnatically connected together who are under the same *patria potestas,* or who have been under it, or who might have been under it if their lineal ancestor had lived long enough to exercise his empire. Maine, Anc. Law, 144.

The *agnate family* consisted of all persons living at the same time, who would have been subject to the *patria potestas* of a common ancestor, if his life had been continued to their time. Hadl.Rom.Law, 131.

Cognates were all persons who could trace their blood to a single ancestor or ancestress, and agnates were those cognates who traced their connection exclusively through males. Maine, Anc. Law. Between *agnati* and *cognati* there is this difference: that, under the name of agnati, *cognati* are included, but not *è converso;* for instance, a father's brother, that is, a paternal uncle, is both *agnatus* and *cognatus,* but a mother's brother, that is, a maternal uncle, is a *cognatus* but not *agnatus.* (Dig. 38, 7, 5, pr.) Burrill.

AGNATIC. [From *agnati, q. v.*] Derived from or through males. 2 Bl.Comm. 236.

AGNATIO. In the civil law, relationship on the fathers' side; the relationship of *agnati;* agnation. *Agnatio a patre est.* Inst. 3, 5, 4; Id. 3, 6, 6.

AGNATION. Kinship by the father's side. See Agnates; Agnati.

AGNOMEN. Lat. An additional name or title; a nickname. A name or title which a man gets by some action or peculiarity; the last of the four names sometimes given a Roman. Thus, Scipio *Africanus,* (the African,) from his African victories. Ainsworth; Calvinus, Lex. See Nomen.

AGNOMINATION. A surname; an additional name or title; agnomen.

AGNUS DEI. Lat. Lamb of God. A piece of white wax, in a flat, oval form, like a small cake, stamped with the figure of a lamb, and consecrated by the pope. Cowell.

AGONY. Violent physical pain or mental distress. City of Chicago v. McLean, 133 Ill. 148, 24 N.E. 527, 8 L.R.A. 765.

AGRAPHIA. See Aphasia.

AGRARIAN. Relating to land, or to a division or distribution of land; as an agrarian law.

AGRARIAN LAWS. In Roman law, laws for the distribution among the people, by public authority, of the lands constituting the public domain, usually territory conquered from an enemy.

In common parlance the term is frequently applied to laws which have for their object the more equal division or distribution of landed property; laws for subdividing large properties and increasing the number of landholders.

AGRARIUM. A tax upon or tribute payable out of land.

AGREAMENTUM. In old English law, agreement; an agreement. Spelman.

AGREE. To concur; come into harmony; give mutual assent; unite in mental action; exchange promises; make an agreement; arrange; to settle. Mickleson v. Gypsy Oil Co., 110 Okl. 117, 238 P. 194, 198. Consent. Smith v. Jones, 185 Ga. 236, 194 S.E. 556, 560. Harmonize or reconcile. "You will *agree* your books." 8 Coke, 67. Concur or acquiesce in; approve or adopt. *Agreed, agreed* *to,* are frequently used in the books, (like *accord,*) to show the concurrence or harmony of cases. *Agreed per curiam* is a common expression. Usually implies some contractual undertaking. In re Gray's Estate, 160 Misc. 710, 290 N.Y.S. 603, 605. To grant or covenant, as when a grantor agrees that no building shall be erected on an adjoining lot; Hogan v. Barry, 143 Mass. 538, 10 N. E. 253; or a mortgagor agrees to cause all taxes to be paid; Mackay v. Truchon, 171 Mo.App. 42, 153 S.W. 502, 503.

AGRÉÉ. In French law, a person authorized to represent a litigant before the Tribunals of Commerce. If such person be a lawyer, he is called an *avocat-agréé.* Coxe, Manual of French Law.

AGREEANCE. In Scotch law, agreement; an agreement or contract.

AGREED. Settled or established by agreement.

This word in a deed creates a covenant.

It is a technical term, synonymous with "contracted," McKisick v. McKisick, Meigs Tenn. 433. It means, *ex vi termini,* that it is the agreement of both parties. Aikin v. Albany, V. & C. R. Co., 26 Barb.N.Y. 298.

AGREED CASE. Stipulations signed by litigants' attorneys, constituted an "agreed case". In re Davis Bros. Stone Co., 245 Wis. 130, 13 N.W.2d 512, 515.

Evidence presented by stipulation that stated facts constituted entire evidence is not an "agreed case". Struble-Werneke Motor Co. v. Metropolitan Securities Corporation, 93 Ind.App. 416, 178 N.E. 460, 462. Nor is an agreed statement of facts on which a case is submitted in lieu of evidence. Byers v. Essex Inv. Co., 281 Mo. 375, 219 S.W. 570, 571; Reddick v. Board of Com'rs of Pulaski County, 14 Ind.App. 598, 41 N.E. 834.

AGREED ORDER. The only difference between an agreed order and one which is made in the due course of the proceedings in an action is that in the one case it is agreed to, and in the other it is made as authorized by law. Claflin v. Gibson, 21 Ky.Law Rep. 337, 51 S.W. 439.

AGREED STATEMENT OF FACTS. A statement of facts, agreed on by the parties as true and correct, to be submitted to a court for a ruling on the law of the case. United States Trust Co. v. New Mexico, 183 U.S. 535, 22 Sup.Ct. 172, 46 L.Ed. 315. See Case Stated.

Where testimony was contradictory, stipulation relating to testimony did not constitute an "agreed state of facts". McPherson v. State Industrial Accident Commission, 169 Or. 190, 127 P.2d 344, 346.

AGREEMENT. A coming or knitting together of minds; a coming together in opinion or determination; the coming together in accord of two minds on a given proposition; in law a concord of understanding and intention between two or more parties with respect to the effect upon their relative rights and duties, of certain past or future facts or performances; the consent of two or more persons concurring respecting the transmission of some property, right, or benefits, with the view of contracting an obligation, a mutual obligation. Bac.Abr.; Rocha v. Hulen, 6 Cal.App.2d 245, 44 P.2d 478, 482.

The act of two or more persons, who unite in expressing a mutual and common purpose, with the view of altering their rights and obligations. The union of two or more minds in a thing done or to be done; a mutual assent to do a thing. Com. Dig. "Agreement," A 1. See Aggregatio Mentium. Carter v. Prairie Oil & Gas Co., 58 Okl. 365, 160 P. 319, 322. A compact between parties who are thereby subjected to the obligation or to whom the contemplated right is thereby secured. People v. Mills, 160 Misc. 730, 290 N.Y.S. 48, 52.

Although often used as synonymous with "contract," Douglass v. W. L. Williams Art Co., 143 Ga. 846, 85 S.E. 993, it is a wider term than "contract" (Anson, Cont. 4.) An agreement might not be a contract, because not fulfilling some requirement. And each of a series of mutual stipulations or constituent clauses in a contract might be denominated an "agreement." The meaning of the contracting parties is their agreement. Whitney v. Wyman, 101 U.S. 396, 25 L.Ed. 1050. *"Agreement"* is seldom applied to specialties. Pars.Cont. 6.

"Agreement" is not synonymous with "promise" or "undertaking." It signifies a mutual contract, on consideration. Andrews v. Pontue, 24 Wend.N.Y. 285; Wain v. Warlters, 5 East, 10; wherein parties must have a distinct intention common to both, and without doubt or difference. Blake v. Mosher, 11 Cal.App.2d 532, 54 P.2d 492, 494.

The writing or instrument which is evidence of an agreement.

Classification

Conditional agreements, the operation and effect of which depend upon the existence of a supposed state of facts, or the performance of a condition, or the happening of a contingency.

Executed agreements, which have reference to past events, or which are at once closed and where nothing further remains to be done by the parties.

Executory agreements are such as are to be performed in the future. They are commonly preliminary to other more formal or important contracts or deeds, and are usually evidenced by memoranda, parol promises, etc.

Express agreements are those in which the terms and stipulations are specifically declared and avowed by the parties at the time of making the agreement.

Implied agreement. (1) Implied in fact. One inferred from the acts or conduct of the parties, instead of being expressed by them in written or spoken words. Baltimore Mail S. S. Co. v. U. S., C.C.A.Md., 76 F.2d 582, 585. (2) Implied in law; more aptly termed a constructive or quasi contract. One where, by fiction of law, a promise is imputed to perform a legal duty, as to repay money obtained by fraud or duress. Baltimore Mail S. S. Co. v. U. S., C.C.A.Md., 76 F.2d 582, 585. One inferred by the law where the conduct of the parties with reference to the subject-matter is such as to induce the belief that they intended to do that which their acts indicate they have done. Baltimore & O. R. Co. v. U. S., 261 U.S. 592, 43 S.Ct. 425, 67 L.Ed. 816; Cuneo v. De Cuneo, 24 Tex.Civ.App. 436, 59 S.W. 284.

Parol agreements. Such as are either by word of mouth or are committed to writing, but are not under seal. The common law draws only one great line, between things under seal and not under seal. Wharton.

In agreement means in conformity, or harmony with. Brown Real Estate Co. v. Lancaster County, 110 Neb. 665, 194 N.W. 897, 898.

AGREEMENT FOR INSURANCE. An agreement often made in short terms preliminary to the filling out and delivery of a policy with specific stipulations.

AGREEMENT NOT TO BE PERFORMED WITHIN A YEAR. An agreement that necessarily must require more than year for performance. Marble

v. Town of Clinton, Mass., 9 N.E.2d 522, 524, 111 A.L.R. 1101. Incapable of performance within one year. Street v. Maddux, Marshall, Moss & Mallory, 58 App.D.C. 42, 24 F.2d 617, 619.

AGREEMENT OF SALE; AGREEMENT TO SELL. An agreement of sale may imply not merely an obligation to sell, but an obligation on the part of the other party to purchase (cf. Loud v. St. Louis Union Trust Co., 313 Mo. 552, 281 S.W. 744, 755) while an agreement to sell is simply an obligation on the part of the vendor or promisor to complete his promise of sale; Treat v. White, 181 U.S. 264, 21 Sup.Ct. 611, 45 L.Ed. 853. It is a contract to be performed in future, and, if fulfilled, results in a sale; it is preliminary to sale and is not the sale. Callender v. Crossfield Oil Syndicate, 84 Mont. 263, 275 P. 273, 276.

AGREEMENT TO SELL LAND. A contract to be performed in future which if fulfilled results in sale. In re Frayser's Estate, 401 Ill. 364, 82 N.E. 2d 633, 638.

AGREER. Fr. In French marine law, to rig or equip a vessel. Ord. Mar. liv. 1, tit. 2, art. 1.

AGREZ. Fr. In French marine law, the rigging or tackle of a vessel. Ord. Mar. liv. 1, tit. 2, art. 1; Id. tit. 11, art. 2; Id. liv. 3, tit. 1, art. 11.

AGRI. Arable lands in common fields.

AGRI LIMITATI.

In Roman law, lands belonging to the state by right of conquest, and granted or sold in plots. Sandars, Just.Inst., 5th Ed., 98.

In modern civil law, lands whose boundaries are strictly limited by the lines of government surveys. Hardin v. Jordan, 140 U.S. 371, 11 Sup. Ct. 808, 35 L.Ed. 428.

AGRICULTURAL. Pertaining to, or dealing with, agriculture; also, characterized by or engaged in farming as the leading pursuit. Oak Woods Cemetery Ass'n v. Murphy, 383 Ill. 301, 50 N.E.2d 582, 587.

AGRICULTURAL CHEMISTRY. A study of products of the soil, especially foods, their nutritive value, their intensive production, study of composition of soil, chemical methods of fertilization, prevention or amelioration of plant diseases, extinction of insects and other detriments to agriculture, and in general study of animal and plant life with relation to the science of chemistry. In re Frasch's Estate, 125 Misc.Rep. 381, 211 N.Y.S. 635, 638.

AGRICULTURAL COMMODITIES. Generally synonymous with agricultural or farm products, and not including agricultural implements, Bowles v. Rock, D.C.Neb., 55 F.Supp. 865, 868; or commercial fertilizer and ground and crushed limestone, Stiver v. Holley, 215 Ind. 9, 17 N.E.2d 831, 832.

AGRICULTURAL EMPLOYMENT. Farm labor synonymous, and includes all farm work and work incidental thereto. Smythe v. Phœnix, 63 Idaho 585, 123 P.2d 1010, 1012.

AGRICULTURAL HOLDING. Land cultivated for profit in some way. Within the meaning of the English Agricultural Holdings act of 1883, the term will not include natural grass lands. Such lands are pastoral holdings. 32 S.J. 630.

AGRICULTURAL LABOR. Services performed on farm, for owner or tenant. California Employment Commission v. Butte County Rice Growers Ass'n, Cal., 154 P.2d 892, 894. Broader in meaning than farming or farm labor and includes one engaged in horticulture. St. Louis Rose Co. v. Unemployment Compensation Commission, 348 Mo. 1153, 159 S.W.2d 249, 250, and maintenance work and similar service in employer's farm packing house. Latimer v. United States, D.C.Cal., 52 F.Supp. 228, 234, 235, 236, 237. The science and art of production of plants and animals useful to man. Murphy v. Mid-West Mushroom Co., 350 Mo. 658, 168 S.W.2d 75, 77, 78.

AGRICULTURAL LANDS. A term used merely to distinguish rural from urban or other properties. Eisenzimmer v. Bell, 75 N.D. 733, 32 N.W. 2d 891, 893.

Land may be assessable as "agricultural land" though it be covered by native timber and underbrush, grass, and weeds. Milne v. McKinnon, 32 S.D. 627, 144 N.W. 117, 118. The term is synonymous with land "agricultural in character." State v. Stewart, 58 Mont. 1, 190 P. 129, 131.

AGRICULTURAL LIEN. A statutory lien in some states to secure money or supplies advanced to an agriculturist to be expended or employed in the making of a crop and attaching to that crop only. Jones-Phillips Co. v. McCormick, 174 N.C. 82, 93 S.E. 449, 452.

AGRICULTURAL PRODUCT. Things which have a situs of their production upon the farm and which are brought into condition for uses of society by labor of those engaged in agricultural pursuits as contradistinguished from manufacturing or other industrial pursuits. In re Rodgers, Neb., 134 Neb. 832, 279 N.W. 800, 803.

That which is the direct result of husbandry and the cultivation of the soil. The product in its natural unmanufactured condition. Getty v. Milling Co., 40 Kan. 281, 19 P. 617. It has been held not to include beef cattle; Davis & Co. v. City of Macon, 64 Ga. 128, 37 Am.Rep. 60; but to include forestry products; Northern Cedar Co. v. French, 131 Wash. 394, 230 P. 837, 846.

AGRICULTURAL PURSUITS. Every process and step taken and necessary to the completion of a finished farm product. Big Wood Canal Co. v. Unemployment Compensation Division of Industrial Accident Board, 61 Idaho 247, 100 P.2d 49, 51.

AGRICULTURAL SOCIETY. One for promoting agricultural interests, such as improvement of land, implements, and brands of cattle. Crete Mills v. Nebraska State Board of Agriculture, 132 Neb. 244, 271 N.W. 684, 688; or for giving agricultural fairs; Town of West Hartford v. Connecticut Fair Ass'n, 88 Conn. 627, 92 A. 432.

AGRICULTURAL WORKER. Tasks incidental to agricultural activities all are within the scope of the employment of an "agricultural worker." Melendez v. Johns, Ariz., 76 P.2d 1163, 1167.

AGRICULTURE. The art or science of cultivating the ground, including the harvesting of crops, and in a broad sense, the science or art of production of plants and animals useful to man, including in a variable degree, the preparation of these products for man's use. In the broad sense, it includes farming, horticulture, forestry, together with such subjects as butter, cheese, making sugar, etc. Sancho v. Bowie, C.C.A.Puerto Rico, 93 F.2d 323, 324.

The cultivation of soil for food products or any other useful or valuable growths of the field or garden: tillage, husbandry; also, by extension, farming, including any industry practiced by a cultivator of the soil in connection with such cultivation, as breeding and rearing of stock, dairying, etc. The science that treats of the cultivation of the soil. Stand. Dict.; State v. Stewart, 58 Mont. 1, 190 P. 129, 131.

"Agriculture" refers to the field or farm with all its wants, appointments, and products, as distinguished from "horticulture," which refers to the garden, with its less important though varied products. Dillard v. Webb, 55 Ala. 468.

AGUSADURA. In ancient customs, a fee, due from the vassals to their lord for sharpening their plowing tackle.

AHTEID. In old European law, a kind of oath among the Bavarians. Spelman. In Saxon law. One bound by oath, *q. d.* "oathtied." From *ath,* oath, and *tied.* Id.

AID. To support, help, assist, or strengthen. Hines v. State, 16 Ga.App. 411, 85 S.E. 452, 454. Act in cooperation with. Cornett v. Commonwealth, 198 Ky. 236, 248 S.W. 540, 542.

Supplement the efforts of another. Anderson v. Board of Medical Examiners, 117 Cal.App. 113, 3 P.2d 344, 346.

A person "aids" when being present at the time and place he does some act to render aid to the actual perpetration of the crime, though he takes no direct share in its commission. State v. Johnson, 220 N.C. 773, 18 S.E.2d 358, 360.

This word must be distinguished from its synonym "encourage," the difference being that the former connotes active support and assistance. Although it may not import necessary criminality in the act furthered. See Abet.

AID AND ABET. Help, assist, or facilitate the commission of a crime, promote the accomplishment thereof, help in advancing or bringing it about, or encourage, counsel, or incite as to its commission. State v. Lord, 42 N.M. 638, 84 P.2d 80, 86.

Implies knowledge. Winning v. Board of Dental Examiners, 114 Cal.App. 658, 300 P. 866, 868.

At common law it consisted in being present at the time and place, and doing some act to render aid to the actual perpetrator of the crime, though without taking a direct share in its commission. See 4 Bl.Comm. 34; State v. Tally, 102 Ala. 25, 15 So. 722.

It comprehends all assistance rendered by words, acts, encouragement, support, or presence, actual or constructive, to render assistance if necessary. Johnson v. State, 21 Ala.App. 565, 110 So. 55; State v. Davis, 191 Iowa, 720, 183 N.W. 314, 316. But it is not sufficient that there is a mere negative acquiescence not in any way made known to the principal malefactor. People v. Barnes, 311 Ill. 559, 143 N.E. 445, 447. See Accessory; Abettor; Aider and Abettor.

AID AND ASSIST. The words "aided and assisted," as used in the statute prohibiting the sale of intoxicating liquors, as regards the condemnation or confiscation of vehicles, implies either knowledge on the part of the owner that the vehicle was being used for unlawful transportation, or such negligence or want of care as to charge him with such knowledge or notice. In re Gattina, 203 Ala. 517, 84 So. 760.

AID AND COMFORT. Help; support; assistance; counsel; encouragement.

As an element in the crime of treason (see Constitution of the United States, art. 3, § 3), the giving of "aid and comfort" to the enemy may consist in a mere attempt. It is not essential to constitute the giving of aid and comfort that the enterprise commenced should be successful and actually render assistance. Young v. United States, 97 U.S. 39, 62, 24 L.Ed. 992. An act which intentionally strengthens or tends to strengthen enemies of the United States, or which weakens or tends to weaken power of the United States to resist and attack such enemies. United States v. Haupt, D.C.Ill., 47 F.Supp. 836, 839. Any intentional act furthering hostile designs of enemies of the United States. United States v. Haupt, D.C.Ill., 47 F.Supp. 836, 839.

AID BOND. See Bond.

AID OF THE KING. The king's tenant prays this, when rent is demanded of him by others.

AID PRAYER. In English practice, a proceeding formerly made use of, by way of petition in court, praying in aid of the tenant for life, etc., from the reversioner or remainderman, when the title to the inheritance was in question. It was a plea in suspension of the action. 3 Bl.Comm. 300.

AID SOCIETIES. See Benefit Societies.

AIDER. One who is actually or constructively present at the commission of the offense and is a "principal". State v. Bachmeyer, 247 Wis. 294, 19 N.W.2d 261, 263.

Mere proof of a defendant's presence at the time of the commission of a criminal act is not sufficient to render him an "aider". Gentry v. State, 65 Ga.App. 100, 15 S.E. 2d 464, 465.

AIDER AND ABETTOR. One who assists another in the accomplishment of a common design or purpose; he must be aware of, and consent to, such design or purpose. Peats v. State, 213 Ind. 560, 12 N.E.2d 270, 277.

One who advises, counsels, procures, or encourages another to commit a crime, himself being guilty of some overt act or advocacy or encouragement of his principal, actually or constructively present when crime is committed, and participating in commission thereof by some act, deed, word, or gesture, Turner v. Commonwealth, 268 Ky. 311, 104 S.W.2d 1085, and sharing the criminal intent of the principal. State v. Reedy, 97 W.Va. 549, 127 S.E. 24, 28. But one who incites or instigates the commission of a felony when he is neither actually nor constructively present is an "aider, abettor, or procurer" within the meaning of a statute. Neal v. State, 104 Neb. 56, 175 N.W. 669, 670.

AIDER BY VERDICT. The healing or remission, by a verdict rendered, of a defect or error in pleading which might have been objected to before verdict.

The presumption of the proof of all facts necessary to the verdict as it stands, coming to the aid of a record in which such facts are not distinctly alleged.

AIDING AN ESCAPE. Any overt act, intended and useful to assist attempted or completed departure of prisoner from lawful custody before his discharge by due process of law. State v. Navarro, 131 Me. 345, 163 A. 103, 104.

AIDS. In feudal law, originally mere benevolences granted by a tenant to his lord, in times of distress; but at length the lords claimed them as of right.

They were principally three: (1) To ransom the lord's person, if taken prisoner; (2) to make the lord's eldest son and heir apparent a knight; (3) to give a suitable portion to the lord's eldest daughter on her marriage. Abolished by 12 Car. II, c. 24.

Also, extraordinary grants to the crown by the house of commons, which were the origin of the modern system of taxation. 2 Bl.Comm. 63, 64.

A *reasonable aid* was a duty claimed by the lord of the fee of his tenants, holding by knight service, to marry his daughter, etc. Cowell.

AIEL (spelled also *Ayel, Aile, Ayle,* and *Aieul*). L. Fr. A grandfather.

A writ which lieth where the grandfather was seized in his demesne as of fee of any lands or tenements in fee simple the day that he died, and a stranger abateth or entereth the same day and dispossesseth the heir. Fitzh.Nat.Brev. 222; Termes de la Ley; 3 Bla.Com. 186; 2 Poll. & Maitl. 57. See Abatement of Freehold.

AIELESSE. A Norman French term signifying "grandmother." Kelham.

AILE. A corruption of the French word *aieul,* grandfather. See Aiel.

AILMENT. Commonly means indisposition of body or mind, a slight illness. Mutual Life Ins. Co. of New York v. Burton, 167 Tenn. 606, 72 S. W.2d 778, 781.

But within meaning of an application for a benefit certificate, it is something which substantially impairs the health of the applicant, materially weakens the vigor of his constitution, or seriously deranges his vital functions, thereby excluding chronic rheumatism. National Americans v. Ritch, 121 Ark. 185, 180 S.W. 488, 489. And in life insurance application does not include mere temporary indisposition, which, though requiring medical treatment, is readily remediable. Zogg v. Bankers' Life Co. of Des Moines, Iowa, C.C.A.W.Va., 62 F.2d 575, 578. Nor passing discomfort. Washington Fidelity Nat. Ins. Co. v. Lacey, 45 Ohio App. 104, 186 N.E. 751, 754. However, it covers disorders which could not properly be called diseases. Cromeens v. Sovereign Camp W. O. W., Mo.App., 247 S.W. 1033, 1034.

AIM A WEAPON. To point it intentionally. Edwards v. State, 28 Ga.App. 466, 111 S.E. 748. "Aim" denotes direction toward some minute point in an object, while "point" implies direction toward the whole object. Buchanan v. State, 25 Okl.Cr. 198, 219 P. 420, 423.

AINESSE. In French feudal law, the right or privilege of the eldest born; primogeniture; esnecy. Guyot, Inst.Feud. c. 17.

AIR. That fluid transparent substance which surrounds our globe. Bank v. Kennett, 101 Mo.App. 370, 74 S.W. 474.

AIR BASE. See Base.

AIR CONDITION. To render a room, building, office, hotel or the like reasonably comfortable by circulating air which is maintained at a predetermined temperature by either warming or cooling it. Magee Laundry & Cleaners v. Harwell Appliance Co., 184 Miss. 435, 185 So. 571, 572.

AIR COURSES. As applied to the operation of coal mines, passages for conducting air. Ricardo v. Central Coal & Coke Co., 100 Kan. 95, 163 P. 641, 643. See Airway.

AIRCRAFT. Any contrivance used, or designed for navigation of or flight in the air, except a parachute or other contrivance designed for such navigation but used primarily as safety equipment. 49 U.S.C.A. §§ 171–184.

As defined in the Uniform Aeronautics Act, the term includes balloon, airplane, hydroplane and every other vehicle used for navigation through the air. See Aeronautics; Airship; Hydro-Aeroplane.

AIRE. In old Scotch law, the court of the justices itinerant, corresponding with the English *eyre,* (*q. v.*) Skene de Verb. Sign. voc. *Iter.*

AIRPLANE. See Aeronautics; Hydro-Aeroplane; Aircraft; Airship.

AIRPORT. Landing and taking off place for air planes. City of Mobile v. Lartigue, 23 Ala.App. 479, 127 So. 257, 260.

With its beacons, landing fields, runways, and hangars, it is analogous to a harbor with its lights, wharves, and docks; the one is the landing place and haven of ships that navigate the water, the other of those that navigate the air. Coleman v. City of Oakland, 110 Cal.App. 715, 295 P. 59, 61. And includes all land, buildings, structures or other improvements, necessary or convenient in the establishment and operation of an airport. Moore v. Gordon, Tex.Civ.App., 122 S.W.2d 239, 242.

Any locality either of water or land which is adapted for the landing and taking off of aircraft and which provides facilities for shelter, supply, and repair of aircraft, or a place used regularly for receiving or discharging passengers or cargo by air. 49 U.S.C.A. §§ 171–184. City of Wichita v. Clapp, 125 Kan. 100, 263 P. 12, 63 A.L.R. 478.

AIRSHIP. Under some statutes it includes every kind of vehicle or structure intended for use as a means of transporting passengers or goods, or both, in the air. As defined by the International Flying Convention of 1919, an airship means an aircraft using gas lighter than air as a means of support and having means of propulsion.

See Aeronautics; Aircraft; Hydro-Aeroplane.

AIRT AND PAIRT. In old Scotch criminal law, accessary; contriver and partner. 1 Pitc.Crim. Tr. pt. 1, p. 133; 3 How.State Tr. 601. Now written *art and part,* (*q. v.*)

AIRWAY. Applies to air routes for either airplanes or seaplanes and is a material or permanent way through the air laid out with precision and care that an engineer adopts in choosing the course of and laying down a roadway. City of Wichita v. Clapp, 125 Kan. 100, 263 P. 12, 14, 63 A.L.R. 478.

In English law, a passage for the admission of air into a mine. 24 & 25 Vict. c. 97, § 28. See Air Courses.

AISIAMENTUM (spelled also *Esamentum, Aismentum*). In old English law, an easement. Spelman.

AISNE or EIGNE. In old English law, the eldest or first born.

AJOURNMENT. In French law, the document pursuant to which an action or suit is commenced, equivalent to the writ of summons in England. Actions, however, are in some cases commenced by *requête* or petition. Arg.Fr.Merc.Law, 545.

AJUAR. In Spanish law, paraphernalia. The jewels and furniture which a wife brings in marriage.

AJUTAGE (spelled also *Adjutage*). A conical tube used in drawing water through an aperture, by the use of which the quantity of water drawn is much increased.

AKIN. In old English law. Of kin. "Next-a-kin." 7 Mod. 140.

AL. L. Fr. At the; to the. *Al barre*; at the bar. *Al huis d'esglise;* at the church door.

ALÆ ECCLESIÆ. The wings or side aisles of a church. Blount.

ALANERARIUS. A manager and keeper of dogs for the sport of hawking; from *alanus*, a dog known to the ancients. A falconer. Blount.

ALARM LIST. The list of persons liable to military watches, who were at the same time exempt from trainings and musters. See Prov.Laws 1775–76, c. 10, § 18; Const.Mass. c. 11, § 1, art. 10; Pub.St.Mass.1882, p. 1287.

ALBA FIRMA. In old English law, white rent; rent payable in silver or white money, as distinguished from that which was anciently paid in corn or provisions, called black mail, or black rent; *reditus nigri.* Spelman; Reg.Orig. 319*b*.

ALBACEA. In Spanish law, an executor or administrator; one who is charged with fulfilling and executing that which is directed by the testator in his testament or other last disposition. Emeric v. Alvarado, 64 Cal. 529, 2 Pac. 418, 433.

ALBANAGIUM. In old French law, the state of alienage; of being a foreigner or alien.

ALBANUS. In old French law, a stranger, alien, or foreigner.

ALBINATUS. In old French law, the state or condition of an alien or foreigner.

ALBINATUS JUS. In old French law, the *droit d'aubaine* in France, whereby the king, at an alien's death, was entitled to all his property, unless he had peculiar exemption. Repealed in June, 1791.

ALBUM BREVE. A blank writ; a writ with a blank or omission in it.

ALBUS LIBER. The white book; an ancient book containing a compilation of the law and customs of the city of London.

ALCABALA. In Spanish law, a duty of a certain per cent. paid to the treasury on the sale or exchange of property.

ALCAIDE. Sp. Jailer, warden, governor of a fortress.

ALCALDE. The name of a judicial officer in Spain, and in those countries which have received their laws and institutions from Spain. His functions somewhat resembled those of mayor in small municipalities on the continent, or justice of the peace in England and most of the United States. Castillero v. U. S., 2 Black, 17, 194, 17 L.Ed. 360.

ALCOHOLIC BEVERAGE. The term is distinguished from the term "intoxicating liquor," in that a beverage may be alcoholic in that it contains some alcohol, and yet not be intoxicating as defined in National Prohibition Act. Premier-Pabst Sales Co. v. McNutt, D.C.Ind., 17 F.Supp. 708, 714.

Beer. Liquor Control Commission v. McGillis, 91 Utah, 586, 65 P.2d 1136, 1141. Ethyl alcohol, within tax statute. H. O. Hurley Co. v. Martin, 267 Ky. 182, 101 S.W.2d 657, 660. It is immaterial whether the liquor is suitable or desirable for beverage purposes, if it is prohibited by law and is in fact used as a beverage. Powell v. State, 179 Md. 399, 18 A.2d 587, 590, 591. But it must be drinkable. McChristy v. State, 138 Tex.Cr.R. 26, 133 S.W.2d 976, 977.

ALCOHOLIC LIQUORS. "Alcoholic, spirituous and malt liquors" mean intoxicating liquors which can be used as a beverage, and which, when drunk to excess, will produce intoxication. Howard v. Acme Brewing Co., 143 Ga. 1, 83 S.E. 1096, 1097, Ann. Cas.1917A, 91; F. W. Woolworth Co. v. State, 72 Okl.Cr. 125, 113 P.2d 399, 403.

The term includes raw alcohol. C. J. Lincoln Co. v. State, 122 Ark. 204, 183 S.W. 173, 174. Beer, ale, or wine in Selective Service Act, § 12 (50 U.S.C.A. § 226 note). U. S. v. Kinsel, D.C., 263 F. 141, 142. And lemon and vanilla extracts, made or used for beverage purposes, containing alcohol. Brandon v. State, 24 Ala.App. 289, 134 So. 890, 891. But not specially denatured alcohol. M. H. McCarthy & Co. v. Doran, D.C.Mass., 43 F.2d 659, 661. See Intoxicating Liquor.

ALCOHOLISM. In medical jurisprudence, the pathological effect (as distinguished from physiological effect) of excessive indulgence in intoxicating liquors.

A morbid condition resulting from the inordinate or excessive use of alcoholic beverages. Cochran v. Commissioner of Internal Revenue, C.C.A.4, 78 F.2d 176, 178.

It is *acute* when induced by excessive potations at one time or in the course of a single debauch. An attack of delirium tremens and alcoholic homicidal mania are examples of this form. It is *chronic* when resulting from the long-continued use of spirits in less quantities, as in the case of dipsomania.

ALCOVE ROOM. An "alcove room," within Tenement House Law N. Y. § 65, is a room with an alcove. People on Complaint of Hickey v. Whitelow, Mag.Ct.N.Y., 166 N.Y.S. 141, 148.

ALDERMAN. A judicial or administrative magistrate.

See Aldermannus.

Originally the word was synonymous with "elder" or "senator," but was also used to designate an earl, and even a king.

In American cities, one of a board of municipal officers next in order to the mayor. State v. Waterman, 95 Conn. 414, 111 A. 623, 624; Board of Lights and Waterworks v. Dobbs, 151 Ga. 53, 105 S.E. 611, 612. The aldermen are generally a legislative body, having limited judicial powers as a body, as in matters of internal police regulation, laying out and repairing streets, constructing sewers, and the like; though in many cities they hold separate courts, and have magisterial powers to a considerable extent.

In English law, an associate to the chief civil magistrate of a corporate town or city.

The word would seem to have been rather an appellation of honor, originally, than a distinguishing mark of office. Spelman Gloss.

ALDERMANNUS. L. Lat. An alderman.

ALDERMANNUS CIVITATIS VEL BURGI. Alderman of a city or borough, from which the modern office of alderman has been derived. T. Raym. 435, 437.

ALDERMANNUS COMITATUS. The alderman of the county. According to Spelman, he held an office intermediate between that of an earl and a sheriff. According to other authorities, he was the same as the earl. 1 Bl.Comm. 116.

ALDERMANNUS HUNDREDI SEU WAPENTACHII. Alderman of a hundred or wapentake. Spelman.

ALDERMANNUS REGIS. Alderman of the king. So called, either because he received his appointment from the king or because he gave the judgment of the king in the premises allotted to him.

ALDERMANNUS TOTIUS ANGLIÆ. Alderman of all England. An officer among the Anglo-Saxons, supposed by Spelman to be the same with the chief justiciary of England in later times. Spelman.

ALE-CONNER. In old English law, an officer appointed by the court-leet, sworn to look to the assise and goodness of ale and beer within the precincts of the leet. Kitch. Courts, 46; Whishaw. And to look to the assise of bread. Cowell.

This officer is still continued in name, though the duties are changed or given up; 1 Crabb, Real Prop. 501.

ALE-HOUSE. A place where ale is sold to be drunk on the premises where sold.

ALE SILVER. A rent or tribute paid annually to the lord mayor of London, by those who sell ale within the liberty of the city.

ALE-STAKE. A maypole or long stake driven into the ground, with a sign on it for the sale of ale. Cowell.

ALEA. Lat. In the civil law, a game of chance or hazard. Dig. 11, 5, 1. See Cod. 3, 43. The chance of gain or loss in a contract.

ALEATOR. Lat. (From *alea, q. v.,* meaning dice). In the civil law, a gamester; one who plays at games of hazard. Dig. 11, 5; Cod. 3, 43.

ALEATORY CONTRACT. A mutual agreement, of which the effects, with respect both to the advantages and losses, whether to all the parties or to some of them, depend on an uncertain event. Losecco v. Gregory, 108 La. 648, 32 So. 985.

Contracts in which promise by one party is conditioned on fortuitous event. Southern Surety Co. v. MacMillan Co., C.C.A.Okl., 58 F.2d 541, 549.

A contract, the obligation and performance of which depend upon an uncertain event, such as insurance, engagements to pay annuities, and the like.

A contract is aleatory or hazardous when the performance of that which is one of its objects depends on an uncertain event. It is certain when the thing to be done is supposed to depend on the will of the party, or when in the usual course of events it must happen in the manner stipulated.

ALER A DIEU. L. Fr. In old practice. To be dismissed from court; to go quit. Literally, "to go to God."

ALER SANS JOUR. In old practice, a phrase used to indicate the final dismissal of a case from court without continuance. "To go without day."

ALEU. Fr. In French feudal law, an allodial estate, as distinguished from a feudal estate or benefice.

ALFET. A cauldron into which boiling water was poured, in which a criminal plunged his arm up to the elbow, and there held it for some time, as an ordeal. Du Cange.

ALFRED'S CODE. See Dombec, Domboc.

ALGARUM MARIS. Probably a corruption of *Laganum maris, lagan* being a right, in the middle ages, like *jetsam* and *flotsam,* by which goods thrown from a vessel in distress became the property of the king, or the lord on whose shores they were stranded. Spelman; Jacob; Du Cange.

ALGO. Span. In Spanish law, property. White, Nov.Recop. b. 1, tit. 5, c. 3, § 4.

ALIA. Lat. Other things.

ALIA ENORMIA. Other wrongs. The name given to a general allegation of injuries caused by the defendant with which the plaintiff in an action of trespass under the common-law practice concluded his declaration. Archb.Crim.Pl. 694.

ALIAMENTA. A liberty of passage, open way, water-course, etc., for the tenant's accommodation. Kitchen.

ALIAS. Lat. Otherwise; equivalent of "alias dictus" or "otherwise called", indicating one was called by one or the other of two names, Commonwealth v. Liebowitz, 143 Pa.Super. 75, 17 A.2d 719, 721; at another time; in another manner; formerly.

ALIAS DICTUS. "Otherwise called." Antone v. State, 49 Ariz. 168, 65 P.2d 646, 649, (shorter and more usual form, *alias;* see Kennedy v. People, 39 N.Y. 245). Known by both those names, and is called one or the other. People v. Mellon, 171 Misc. 171, 11 N.Y.S.2d 786, 790. A fictitious name assumed by a person is colloquially termed an "*alias.*" State v. Melson, 161 La. 423, 108 So. 794, 795.

ALIAS EXECUTION. One issued after first has been returned without having accomplished its purpose. Richards-Conover Hardware Co. v. Sharp, 150 Kan. 506, 95 P.2d 360, 364.

ALIAS SUBPOENA. One issued after the first has been returned without having accomplished its purpose. Richards-Conover Hardware Co. v. Sharp, 150 Kan. 506, 95 P.2d 360, 364.

ALIAS SUMMONS. A summons issued when original has not produced its effect because defective in form or manner of service, and when issued, which supersedes the first writ. Mansur v. Pacific Mut. Life Ins. Co. of California, 136 Mo. App. 726, 118 S.W. 1193, 1194; McGuire v. Montvale Lumber Co., 190 N.C. 806, 131 S.E. 274, 275.

ALIAS TAX WARRANT. One issued after the first has been returned without having accomplished its purpose. Richards-Conover Hardware Co. v. Sharp, 150 Kan. 506, 95 P.2d 360, 364.

ALIAS WRIT. A second writ. Ditmar v. Beckham, Tex.Civ.App., 77 S.W.2d 893, 894.

At common law "alias" as applied to an execution or fieri facias referred to new writ issued after original fieri facias was returned unproductive, but under the Code the term applies to an execution issued in lieu of a lost original. U-Driv-It System of Macon v. Lyles, 71 Ga.App. 70, 30 S.E.2d 111, 114. A writ issued where one of the same kind has already been issued in the same cause without having been effective. Schmidt v. Schmidt, 108 Mont. 246, 89 P.2d 1020, 1021. It is used of all species of writs.

Historically, the word "alias" refers to a former command of the same sort, and it was part of a Latin sentence meaning, "We command you as we have before (sicut alias) commanded you." Schmidt v. Schmidt, 108 Mont. 246, 89 P.2d 1020, 1021.

ALIAS WRIT OF EXECUTION. One issued after the first has been returned without having accomplished its purpose. Richards-Conover Hardware Co. v. Sharp, 150 Kan. 506, 95 P.2d 360, 364.

ALIBI. Lat. In criminal law, elsewhere; in another place. State v. Hubbard, 351 Mo. 143, 171 S.W.2d 701, 706.

Means that at time of commission of crime charged in indictment defendant was at different place so remote or distant or under such circumstances that he could not have committed offense. State v. Parsons, 206 Iowa 390, 220 N.W. 328, 330. It is a physical circumstance and derives its entire potency as a defense from fact that it involves the physical impossibility of guilt of accused. Gregg v. State, 69 Okl.Cr. 103, 101 P.2d 289, 296. Strictly it is not a defense though usually called such in criminal procedure. State v. Norman, 103 Ohio St. 541, 134 N.E. 474.

ALIEN. *n.* A foreigner; one born abroad.

A person who owes allegiance to a foreign government. De Cano v. State, 7 Wash.2d 613, 110 P.2d 627, 631, 633.

In this country is a person born out of the United States and unnaturalized under our Constitution and laws, 2 Kent, Comm. 50. Caparell v. Goodbody, 132 N.J.Eq. 559, 29 A.2d 563, 569. In England, one born out of the allegiance of the king.

A native born Filipino living in the United States but not admitted to United States citizenship was an "alien". United States v. Gancy, D.C.Minn., 54 F.Supp. 755, 758, 759. But term for immigration purposes would not apply to a Filipino seeking to enter the Territory of Hawaii or to a Filipino lawfully admitted to Hawaii who seeks entry therefrom into the United States. Id. Nor to citizens of the Philippine Islands of the Filipino race. De Cano v. State, 7 Wash.2d 613, 110 P.2d 627, 631, 633.

As to the effect of marriage on the status of women, whether they were originally aliens or citizens of the United States, see 8 U.S.C.A. §§ 9-368; U. S. ex rel. Ulrich v. Kellogg, 58 App.D.C. 360, 30 F.2d 984, 985, 71 A.L.R. 1210. Petition of Peterson, D.C.Wash., 33 F.Supp. 615, 616. Johansen v. Staten Island Shipbuilding Co., 272 N.Y. 140, 5 N.E.2d 68, 70. In re Pezzi, D.C.Cal., 29 F.2d 999, 1001.

ALIEN or ALIENE. *v.* To transfer or make over to another; to convey or transfer the property of a thing from one person to another; to alienate. Usually applied to the transfer of lands and tenements. Co.Litt. 118; Cowell.

ALIEN AMY. In international law, alien friend. An alien who is the subject or citizen of a foreign government at peace with our own.

ALIEN AND SEDITION LAWS. Acts of congress of July 6 and July 14, 1798. See Whart. State Tr. 22.

ALIEN ENEMY. In international law, an alien who is the subject or citizen of some hostile state or power. See Dyer, *2b;* Co.Litt. 129*b*. A person who, by reason of owing a permanent or temporary allegiance to a hostile power, becomes, in time of war, impressed with the character of an enemy. See 1 Kent, Comm. 74; 2 Id. 63; Bell v. Chapman, 10 Johns., N.Y., 183; Dorsey v. Brigham, 177 Ill. 250, 52 N.E. 303, 42 L.R.A. 809. Subjects of a foreign state at war with United States. Caparell v. Goodbody, 132 N.J.Eq. 559, 29 A.2d 563, 569.

Whether or not a person is an alien enemy depends, not on his nationality, but on the place in which he voluntarily resides or carries on business. Porter v. Freudenberg, [1915] 1 K.B. 857. See, also, Noble v. Great American Ins. Co., 194 N.Y.S. 60, 66, 200 App.Div. 773.

ALIEN FRIEND. Subjects of a foreign state at peace with the United States. Caparell v. Goodbody, 132 N.J.Eq. 559, 29 A.2d 563, 569, 570. Or citizen; an *alien amy.* Techt v. Hughes, 229 N.Y. 222, 128 N.E. 185, 186, 11 A.L.R. 166.

ALIEN NÉE. An alien born, *i. e.,* a person who has been born an alien.

ALIENA NEGOTIA EXACTO OFFICIO GERUNTUR. The business of another is to be conducted with particular attention. Jones, Bailm. 83; First Nat. Bank of Carlisle v. Graham, 79 Pa. 118, 21 Am.Rep. 49.

ALIENABLE. Proper to be the subject of alienation or transfer.

ALIENAGE. The condition or state of an alien.

ALIENATE. To convey; to transfer the title to property. Co.Litt. 118*b*. *Alien* is very commonly used in the same sense. 1 Washb. Real Prop. 53.

"Sell, *alienate*, and dispone" are the formal words of transfer in Scotch conveyances of heritable property. Bell.

The term has a technical legal meaning, and any transfer of real estate, short of a conveyance of the title, is not an alienation of the estate. Masters v. Insurance Co., 11 Barb., N.Y., 630. See, also, Nichols & Shepard Co. v. Dunnington, 118 Okl. 231, 247 P. 353, 355. But the word has been defined as to convey or transfer to another as title, property, or right, to part voluntarily with ownership of property, and, in widest sense, property is alienated when transferred from one person to another in any way; but generally alienating is restricted to transfer of title to property by act of owner, as distinguished from transfer effected entirely by operation of law. Delfelder v. Poston, 42 Wyo. 176, 293 P. 354, 361.

ALIENATIO LICET PROHIBEATUR, CONSENSU TAMEN OMNIUM, IN QUORUM FAVOREM PROHIBITA EST, POTEST FIERI, ET QUILIBET POTEST RENUNCIARE JURI PRO SE INTRODUCTO. Although alienation be prohibited, yet, by the consent of all in whose favor it is prohibited, it may take place; for it is in the power of any man to renounce a law made in his own favor. Co.Litt. 98.

ALIENATIO REI PRÆFERTUR JURI ACCRESCENDI. Alienation is favored by the law rather than accumulation. Co.Litt. 185.

ALIENATION. In real property law, the transfer of the property and possession of lands, tenements, or other things, from one person to another. Termes de la Ley.

The term is particularly applied to absolute conveyances of real property. Conover v. Mutual Ins. Co., 1 N.Y. 290, 294. The voluntary and complete transfer from one person to another. Rich v. Doneghey, 71 Okl. 204, 177 P. 86, 89, 3 A.L.R. 352; Chouteau v. Chouteau, 49 Okl. 105, 152 P. 373, 376. Disposition by will. *Contra*, Postlethwaite v. Edson, 102 Kan. 619, 171 P. 769, 773, L.R.A.1918D, 983. Leases, especially of Indians' allotted lands. Bailey v. King, 57 Okl. 528, 157 P. 763, 764; Ashton v. Noble, 65 Okl. 45, 162 P. 784, 785; Williams v. Hylan, 215 N.Y.S. 101, 106, 126 Misc.Rep. 807. Every mode of passing realty by the act of the party, as distinguished from passing it by the operation of law. Rathbun v. Allen, 63 R.I. 109, 7 A.2d 273, 275. But the term is inapplicable to mortgages. Worthington v. Tipton, 24 N.M. 89, 172 P. 1048, 1049.

The act by which the title to real estate is voluntarily resigned by one person to another and accepted by the latter, in the forms prescribed by law. Cf. In re Ehrhardt, U.S.D.C., 19 F.2d 406, 407 (bankruptcy proceedings).

It is said to signify the wrongful transfer of property to another or the wrongful conversion of property for which an action of trover was maintainable at common law. Sauls v. Whitman, 171 Okl. 113, 42 P.2d 275, 280.

In medical jurisprudence, a generic term denoting the different kinds or forms of mental aberration or derangement.

ALIENATION IN MORTMAIN. See Amortization; Mortmain.

ALIENATION OF AFFECTIONS. The robbing of husband or wife of the conjugal affection, society, fellowship, and comfort which inheres in the normal marriage relation. Young v. Young, 236 Ala. 627, 184 So. 187, 190.

Loss of consortium between spouses from wrongful acts of others. Young v. Young, 236 Ala. 627, 184 So. 187, 190. The deprivation of one spouse of the right to the aid, comfort, assistance, and society of the other spouse in family relationships. Hargraves v. Ballou, 47 R.I. 186, 131 A. 643, 645.

ALIENATION OFFICE. In English practice, an office for the recovery of fines levied upon writs of covenant and entries.

ALIENEE. One to whom an alienation, conveyance, or transfer of property is made. See Alienor.

ALIENI GENERIS. Lat. Of another kind. 3 P. Wms. 247.

ALIENI JURIS. Lat. Under the control, or subject to the authority, of another person; *e. g.*, an infant who is under the authority of his father or guardian; a wife under the power of her husband. The term is contrasted with Sui Juris, (*q. v.*).

ALIENIGENA. One of foreign birth; an alien. 7 Coke, 31.

ALIENISM. The state, condition, or character of an alien. 2 Kent, Comm. 56, 64, 69.

ALIENIST. One who has specialized in the study of mental diseases. State v. Reidell, 9 Houst., Del., 470, 14 A. 550, 552. Persons qualified by experience, knowledge, and previous opportunities to express opinion as to defendant's mental condition at a particular time. People v. Norton, 138 Cal.App. 70, 31 P.2d 809, 810.

ALIENOR. He who makes a grant, transfer of title, conveyance, or alienation. Correlative of *alienee*.

ALIENUS. Lat. Another's; belonging to another; the property of another. *Alienus homo*, another's man, or slave. Inst. 4, 3, pr. *Aliena res*, another's property. Bract. fol. 13*b*.

ALIGNMENT. The act of laying out or adjusting a line. The state of being so laid out or adjusted. The ground plan of a railway or other road or work as distinguished from its profile or gradients. Village of Chester v. Leonard, 68 Conn. 495, 37 A. 397. An adjustment to a line. Harner v. Monongalia County Court, 80 W.Va. 626, 92 S.E. 781, 785.

ALIKE. Similar to another. The term is not synonymous with "identical," which means "exactly the same." Carn v. Moore, 74 Fla. 77, 76 So. 337, 340.

ALIMENT. In Scotch law, to maintain, support, provide for; to provide with necessaries. As a noun, maintenance, support; an allowance from the husband's estate for the support of the wife. Paters. Comp. §§ 845, 850, 893.

In civil law, food and other things necessary to the support of life; money allowed for the purpose of procuring these. Dig. 50, 16, 43.

In common law, to supply with necessaries. Purcell v. Purcell, 3 Edw.Ch.N.Y. 194.

ALIMENTA. Lat. In the civil law, aliments; things necessary to sustain life; means of support, including food, (*cibaria,*) clothing, (*vestitus,*) and habitation, (*habitatio.*) Dig. 34, 1, 6.

ALIMENTOS. The Spanish term for support and maintenance. Escriche Diccionario.

ALIMONY. Comes from Latin "alimonia" meaning sustenance, and means, therefore, the sustenance or support of the wife by her divorced husband and stems from the common-law right of the wife to support by her husband. Eaton v. Davis, 176 Va. 330, 10 S.E.2d 893, 897. Derived from Latin word "alere," meaning to nourish or sustain. Allowances which husband by court order pays wife for maintenance while they are separated or after they are divorced. Merriman v. Hawbaker, D.C.Ill., 5 F.Supp. 432, 433. Or pending a suit for divorce. And see Bowman v. Worthington, 24 Ark. 522; Lynde v. Lynde, 64 N.J.Eq. 736, 52 A. 694, 58 L.R.A. 471. But in its strictly legal sense relates to the provisions made pendente lite. Warne v. Warne, 36 S.D. 573, 156 N. W. 60, 62. Compare Emerson v. Emerson, 120 Md. 584, 87 A. 1033, 1035, holding that in the absence of statute, in case of an absolute divorce the duty to support ceases and with it the right to alimony.

Generally it is restricted to money unless otherwise authorized by statute. Lloyd v. Lloyd, 183 Ga. 751, 189 S.E. 903, 904. But it may be such an allowance out of husband's estate. Davis v. Davis, 61 Okl. 275, 161 P. 190, 191. Equally applicable to all allowances, whether annual or in gross. Burrows v. Purple, 107 Mass. 432.

It may continue during the joint lives of husband and wife, or so long as they live apart. Cohen v. Cohen, Md., 174 Md. 61, 197 A. 564, 565, 566. But is essentially a different thing from a division of the property of the parties. Mesler v. Jackson, Circuit Judge, 188 Mich. 195, 154 N.W. 63, 65. Not being an "estate", nor the separate property of wife. Cizek v. Cizek, 69 Neb. 797, 99 N.W. 28.

It does not partake of nature of damages or penalty for husband's misconduct. Kennard v. Kennard, 87 N.H. 320, 179 A. 414, 419. Nor is it founded on contract, express or implied, but on husband's natural and legal duty to support wife. Smith v. Smith, D.C.N.Y., 7 F.Supp. 490, 491.

In its broad sense, it means also an award for the support of a child or children. Schafer v. Schafer, 193 N.Y.S. 43, 44, 118 Misc.Rep. 254; Brown v. Brown, 222 Mass. 415, 111 N.E. 42, 43. And it includes provision for an education. Floyd v. Floyd, 91 Fla. 910, 108 So. 896, 898.

Alimony in gross, or in a lump sum, is in the nature of a final property settlement, and hence in some jurisdictions is not included in the term "alimony," which in its strict or technical sense contemplates money payments at regular intervals. Parmly v. Parmly, 125 N.J.Eq. 545, 5 A.2d 789, 791; 27 C.J.S. Divorce, § 235, p. 965.

Alimony pendente lite is an allowance made pending a suit for divorce or separate maintenance including a reasonable allowance for preparation of the suit as well as for support. Davis v. Davis, 15 Wash.2d 297, 130 P.2d 355, 359. Or pending an appeal. Robinson v. Robinson, N.J. Err. & App., 92 A. 94, 96, L.R.A.1915B, 1071.

Permanent alimony is a provision for the support and maintenance of a wife during her lifetime. In re Spencer, 83 Cal. 460, 23 P. 395, 17 Am.St.Rep. 266.

ALIO INTUITU. Lat. In a different view; under a different aspect. 4 Rob.Adm. & Pr. 151. With another view or object; with respect to another case or condition. 7 East, 558; 6 M. & S. 231. See Diverso Intuitu.

ALIQUID CONCEDITUR NE INJURIA REMANEAT IMPUNITA, QUOD ALIAS NON CONCEDERETUR. Something is (will be) conceded, to prevent a wrong remaining unredressed, which otherwise would not be conceded. Co.Litt. 197*b*.

ALIQUID POSSESSIONIS ET NIHIL JURIS. Somewhat of possession, and nothing of right, (but no right).

A phrase used by Bracton to describe that kind of possession which a person might have of a thing as a guardian, creditor, or the like; and also that kind of possession which was granted for a term of years, where nothing could be demanded but the usufruct. Bract. fols. 39*a*, 160*a*.

ALIQUIS NON DEBET ESSE JUDEX IN PROPRIA CAUSA, QUIA NON POTEST ESSE JUDEX ET PARS. A person ought not to be judge in his own cause, because he cannot act as judge and party. Co.Litt. 141; 3 Bl.Comm. 59.

ALIQUOT. Strictly, contained in something else an exact number of times. But as applied to resulting trusts, "aliquot" is treated as meaning fractional. Fox v. Shanley, 94 Conn. 350, 109 A. 249, 251. And means any definite interest. Hinshaw v. Russell, 280 Ill. 235, 117 N.E. 406, 408.

ALITER. Otherwise; as otherwise held or decided.

ALIUD EST CELARE, ALIUD TACERE. To conceal is one thing; to be silent is another. Lord Mansfield, 3 Burr. 1910.

ALIUD EST DISTINCTIO, ALIUD SEPARATIO. Distinction is one thing; separation is another. It is one thing to make things distinct, another thing to make them separable.

ALIUD EST POSSIDERE, ALIUD ESSE IN POSSESSIONE. It is one thing to possess; it is another to be in possession. Hob. 163.

ALIUD EST VENDERE, ALIUD VENDENTI CONSENTIRE. To sell is one thing; to consent to a sale (seller) is another thing. Dig. 50, 17, 160.

ALIUD EXAMEN. A different or foreign mode of trial. 1 Hale, Com.Law, 38.

ALIUNDE. Lat. From another source; from elsewhere; from outside.

Evidence aliunde. Evidence from outside, from another source. In certain cases a written instrument may be explained by evidence *aliunde,* that is, by evidence drawn from sources exterior to the instrument itself, *e. g.,* the testimony of a witness to conversations, admissions, or preliminary negotiations.

Evidence aliunde (i. e., from without the will) may be received to explain an ambiguity in a will. 1 Greenl. Ev. § 291.

ALIUNDE RULE. A verdict may not be impeached by evidence of juror unless foundation for introduction thereof is first made by competent evidence aliunde, or from some other source. State v. Adams, 141 Ohio St. 423, 48 N.E.2d 861, 863, 146 A.L.R. 509.

ALIUS. Lat. Other. The neuter form is *aliud,* something else; another thing.

ALIVE. As respects birth, it means that child shall have an independent life of its own for some period, even momentarily, after birth. Evidenced by respiration or other indications of life, such as beating of heart and pulsation of arteries. Fleming v. Sexton, 172 N.C. 250, 90 S.E. 247, 249. Cf. Hydrostatic Test. Or heart tones in response to artificial respiration, or pulsation of umbilical cord after being severed. In re Stuertz' Estate, 124 Neb. 149, 245 N.W. 412, 413.

In respect of estate matters, a child en ventre sa mere is "born" and "alive" for all purposes for his benefit. In re Holthausen's Will, 175 Misc. 1022, 26 N.Y.S.2d 140, 143.

ALL. Means the whole of—used with a singular noun or pronoun, and referring to amount, quantity, extent, duration, quality, or degree. The whole number or sum of—used collectively, with a plural noun or pronoun expressing an aggregate. Every member of individual component of; each one of—used with a plural noun. In this sense, all is used generically and distributively. "All" refers rather to the aggregate under which the individuals are subsumed than to the individuals themselves. State v. Hallenberg-Wagner Motor Co., 341 Mo. 771, 108 S.W.2d 398, 401. See Both.

ALL AMERICAN. Indicative of supremacy, superiority, and distinction in the athletic world. R. W. Eldridge Co. v. Southern Handkerchief Mfg. Co., D.C.S.C., 23 F.Supp. 179, 182, 184, 185.

ALL AND SINGULAR. All without exception. A comprehensive term often employed in conveyances, wills, and the like, which includes the aggregate or whole and also each of the separate items or components. McClaskey v. Barr, C.C., 54 Fed. 798.

ALL CASES AT LAW. Within constitutional guaranty of jury trial, refers to common law actions as distinguished from causes in equity and certain other proceedings. Breimhorst v. Beckman, 227 Minn. 409, 35 N.W.2d 719, 734.

ALL DISABILITY. Includes both total and partial disability caused by a permanent injury to the leg or arm, or resulting from or relating to the permanent injury, and embraces not only all incapacity to labor, directly or indirectly arising from such permanent injury, but likewise cases of no incapacity at all. Bausch v. Fidler, 277 Pa. 573, 121 A. 507. Includes pain, annoyance, inconveniences, disability to work, and everything incident to the permanent injury. Vanaskie v. Stevens Coal Co., 133 Pa.Super. 457, 2 A.2d 531, 532.

ALL FAULTS. A sale of goods with "all faults" covers, in the absence of fraud on the part of the vendor, all such faults and defects as are not inconsistent with the identity of the goods as the goods described. Whitney v. Boardman, 118 Mass. 242.

ALL FOURS. Two cases or decisions which are alike in all material respects, and precisely similar in all the circumstances affecting their determination, are said to be or to run on "all fours."

ALL THE ESTATE. The name given in England to the short clause in a conveyance or other assurance which purports to convey "all the estate, right, title, interest, claim, and demand" of the grantor, lessor, etc., in the property dealt with. Dav.Conv. 93.

ALL THE MEMBERS. The provision of a church constitution that "all the members" can discharge their parish priest means that all shall have opportunity to participate, but not that all members must attend the meeting or vote in the affirmative for the discharge of the priest. Stryjewski v. Panfil, 269 Pa. 568, 112 A. 764, 765.

ALL-ADDENDUM. As respects patent on a tooth gearing, "all-addendum" and "all-dedendum" mean that the working faces of the teeth of one element are outside, and those of the other element inside, their respective "pitch circles" which refers to circles passing through the pitch point and coaxial with the axes of rotation of the intermeshing gear wheels. In re Cook, Cust. & Pat. App., 103 F.2d 909, 911.

ALLEGANS CONTRARIA NON EST AUDIENDUS. One alleging contrary or contradictory things (whose statements contradict each other) is not to be heard. 4 Inst. 279. Applied to the statements of a witness.

ALLEGANS SUAM TURPITUDINEM NON EST AUDIENDUS. One who alleges his own infamy is not to be heard. 4 Inst. 279.

ALLEGARI NON DEBUIT QUOD PROBATUM NON RELEVAT. That ought not to be alleged which, if proved, is not relevant. 1 Ch.Cas. 45.

ALLEGATA. In Roman law, a word which the emperors formerly signed at the bottom of their rescripts and constitutions; under other instruments they usually wrote *signata* or *testata.* Encyc. Lond.

ALLEGATA ET PROBATA. Lat. Things alleged and proved. The allegations made by a party to a suit, and the proof adduced in their support. Crump v. State, 30 Ala.App. 241, 4 So.2d 188, 189.

ALLEGATIO CONTRA FACTUM NON EST ADMITTENDA. An allegation contrary to the deed (or fact) is not admissible.

ALLEGATION. The assertion, declaration, or statement of a party to an action, made in a pleading, setting out what he expects to prove. Mathews v. Underpinning & Foundation Co., 17 N.J.Misc. 79, 4 A.2d 788, 789.

A material allegation in a pleading is one essential to the claim or defense.

In ecclesiastical law, the statement of the facts intended to be relied on in support of the contested suit.

In English ecclesiastical practice the word seems to designate the pleading as a whole: the three pleadings are known as the allegations; and the defendant's plea is distinguished as the defensive, or sometimes the responsive, allegation, and the complainant's reply as the rejoining allegation.

ALLEGATION OF FACT. Generally narration of transaction by stating details according to their legal effect, and statement of right or liability flowing from certain facts is conclusion of law. Maylender v. Fulton County Gas & Electric Co., 131 Misc. 514, 227 N.Y.S. 209, 217.

ALLEGATION OF FACULTIES. A statement made by the wife of the property of her husband, in order to obtain alimony. Wright v. Wright, 3 Tex. 168. See Faculties.

ALLEGE. To state, recite, assert, or charge; to make an allegation. To affirm, assert, or declare. State v. Hostetter, Mo.Sup., 222 S.W. 750, 754.

ALLEGED. Stated; recited; claimed; asserted; charged. Lynn v. Nichols, 122 Misc.Rep. 170, 202 N.Y.S. 401, 406.

ALLEGIANCE. Obligation of fidelity and obedience to government in consideration for protection that government gives. U. S. v. Kuhn, D.C.N.Y., 49 F.Supp. 407, 414.

The citizen or subject owes an absolute and permanent allegiance to his government or sovereign until he becomes a citizen or subject of another government or another sovereign. The alien owes a local and temporary allegiance during period of his residence. U. S. v. Wong Kim, Ark., 169 U.S. 649, 18 Sup.Ct. 456, 42 L.Ed. 890.

"The tie or *ligamen* which binds the subject [or citizen] to the king [or government] in return for that protection which the king [or government] affords the subject, [or citizen."] 1 Bl.Comm. 366. It consists in "a true and faithful obedience of the subject due to his sovereign," 7 Coke, 4*b*, and is a comparatively modern corruption of ligeance *(ligeantia)*, which is derived from liege *(ligius)*, meaning absolute or unqualified. It signified originally liege fealty, i. e. absolute and unqualified fealty. 18 L.Q.Rev. 47.

In Norman French, alleviation; relief; redress. Kelham.

Acquired allegiance, is that binding a naturalized citizen.

Local or actual allegiance, is that measure of obedience due from a subject of one government to another government, within whose territory he is temporarily resident. From this are excepted foreign sovereigns and their representatives, naval and armed forces when permitted to remain in or pass through the country or its waters.

Natural allegiance. In English law, that kind of allegiance which is due from all men born within the king's dominions, immediately upon their birth, which is intrinsic and perpetual, and cannot be divested by any act of their own. 1 Bl.Comm. 369; 2 Kent, Comm. 42. In American law, the allegiance due from citizens of the United States to their native country, and also from naturalized citizens, and which cannot be renounced without the permission of government, to be declared by law. 2 Kent, Comm. 43–49.

It is said to be due to the king in his political, not his personal, capacity; L. R. 17 Q. B. D. 54, quoted in U. S. v. Wong Kim, Ark., 169 U.S. 663, 18 Sup.Ct. 456, 42 L.Ed. 890; and so in the United States "it is a political obligation" depending not on ownership of land, but on the enjoyment of the protection of government; Wallace v. Harmstad, 44 Pa. 492; and it "binds the citizen to the observance of all laws" of his own sovereign; Adams v. People, 1 N.Y. 173.

ALLEGIARE. To defend and clear one's self; to wage one's own law. An archaic word which simply means to define or justify by due course of law. State v. Hostetter, Mo., 222 S.W. 750.

ALLEGING DIMINUTION. The allegation in an appellate court, of some error in a subordinate part of the *nisi prius* record. See Diminution.

ALLEN CHARGE. An instruction advising jurors to have deference for each other's views, that they should listen, with a disposition to be convinced, to each other's argument, deriving its name from the case of Allen v. United States, 164 U.S. 492, 17 S.Ct. 154, 41 L.Ed. 528, wherein the instruction was approved. Coupe v. United States, 72 App.D.C. 86, 113 F.2d 145, 149; Green v. U. S., 309 F.2d 852. Variously called dynamite charge, shotgun instruction, third degree instruction.

ALLERGY. A susceptibility to disease. Vogt v. Ford Motor Co., Mo.App., 138 S.W.2d 684, 688.

ALLEVIARE. L. Lat. In old records, to levy or pay an accustomed fine or composition; to redeem by such payment. Cowell.

ALLEY. A narrow way designed for the special accommodation of the property it reaches. Atchison, T. & S. F. Ry. Co. v. City of Chanute, 95 Kan. 161, 147 P. 836, 837; Wooldridge v. Pacific Coast Coal Co., Wash., 155 P.2d 1001, 1003.

ALLIANCE. The relation or union between persons or families contracted by intermarriage; affinity.

In international law, a union or association of two or more states or nations, formed by league or treaty, for the joint prosecution of a war (offensive alliance), or for their mutual assistance and protection in repelling hostile attacks (defensive alliance). The league or treaty by which the association is formed. The act of confederating, by league or treaty, for the purposes mentioned.

The term is also used in a wider sense, embracing unions for objects of common interest to the contracting parties, as the "Holy Alliance" entered into in 1815 by Prussia, Austria and Russia for the purpose of counteracting the revolutionary movement in the interest of political liberalism.

ALLISION. The running of one vessel into or against another, as distinguished from a collision, *i. e.*, the running of two vessels against each other. But this distinction is not very carefully observed.

ALLOCABLE. Synonymous with "distributable". In analyzing accounts, the breaking down of a lump sum charged or credited to one account into several parts to be charged or credited to other accounts. Fleming v. Commissioner of Internal Revenue, C.C.A.Tex., 121 F.2d 7, 9.

ALLOCATE. Power to allocate critical materials included power to distribute, to assign, to allot. Gallagher's Steak House v. Bowles, C.C.A.N.Y., 142 F.2d 530, 534. To ration or withhold from private consumption. State ex rel. Guide Management Corp. v. Alexander, 223 Ind. 221, 59 N.E.2d 169, 172.

ALLOCATION. An allowance made upon an account in the English exchequer. Cowell. Placing or adding to a thing. Encyc. Lond.

Assignment or allotment. Jacobson v. Bowles, D.C.Tex., 53 F.Supp. 532, 534.

ALLOCATIONE FACIENDA. In old English practice, a writ for allowing to an accountant such sums of money as he hath lawfully expended in his office; directed to the lord treasurer and barons of the exchequer upon application made. Jacob.

ALLOCATO COMITATU. In old English practice, in proceedings in outlawry, when there were but two county courts holden between the delivery of the writ of *exigi facias* to the sheriff and its return, a special *exigi facias*, with an *allocato comitatu* issued to the sheriff in order to complete the proceedings. See Exigent.

ALLOCATUR. Lat. It is allowed. A word formerly used to denote that a writ or order was allowed.

A word denoting the allowance by a master or prothonotary of a bill referred for his consideration, whether touching costs, damages, or matter of account. Lee, Dict.

A special allocatur is the special allowance of a writ (particularly a writ of error) which is required in some particular cases.

ALLOCATUR EXIGENT. A species of writ anciently issued in outlawry proceedings, on the return of the original writ of exigent. 1 Tidd, Pr. 128. See Exigent.

ALLOCUTION. Formality of court's inquiry of prisoner as to whether he has any legal cause to show why judgment should not be pronounced against him on verdict of conviction. Archb.Crim. Pl. 173; State v. Pruitt, Mo., 169 S.W.2d 399, 400.

ALLOCUTUS. See Allocution.

ALLODARII. Owners of allodial lands. Owners of estates as large as a subject may have. Co. Litt. 1; Bac. Abr. *"Tenure,"* A.

ALLODIAL. Free; not holden of any lord or superior; owned without obligation of vassalage or fealty; the opposite of feudal. Barker v. Dayton, 28 Wis. 384; Wallace v. Harmstad, 44 Pa. 499.

ALLODIUM. Land held absolutely in one's own right, and not of any lord or superior; land not subject to feudal duties or burdens.

An estate held by absolute ownership, without recognizing any superior to whom any duty is due on account thereof. 1 Washb.Real Prop. 16. McCartee v. Orphan Asylum, 9 Cow., N.Y., 511, 18 Am.Dec. 516.

ALLOGRAPH. A writing or signature made for a person by another; opposed to autograph.

ALLONGE. A piece of paper annexed to a bill of exchange or promissory note, on which to write endorsements for which there is no room on the instrument itself. Pardessus, n. 343; Story, Prom. Notes, §§ 121, 151; Fountain v. Bookstaver, 141 Ill. 461, 31 N.E. 17; Bergmann v. Puhl, 195 Wis. 120, 217 N.W. 746, 748, 56 A.L.R. 915.

ALLOPATHIC PRACTICE. The ordinary method of practicing medicine as adopted and taught by the great body of physicians. Bradbury v. Bardin, 34 Conn. 452, 453, 35 Conn. 577. Also, and more properly, that method of combatting disease by the use of remedies producing effects different from those of the disease being treated;—opposed to homeopathy.

ALLOT. To apportion, distribute; to divide property previously held in common among those entitled, assigning to each his ratable portion, to be held in severalty; to set apart specific property, a share of a fund, etc., to a distinct party. Millet v. Bilby, 110 Okl. 241, 237 P. 859, 861.

In the law of corporations, to allot shares, debentures, etc., is to appropriate them to the applicants or persons who have applied for them; this is generally done by sending to each applicant a letter of allotment, informing him that a certain number of shares have been allotted to him. Sweet.

ALLOTMENT. A share or portion; that which is allotted; apportionment, division; the distribution of shares in a public undertaking or corporation. Reuter v. Reuter's Succession, 206 La. 474, 19 So.2d 209, 212. Assignment. Pace v. Eoff, Tex. Com.App., 48 S.W.2d 956, 963. Partition; the distribution of land under an inclosure act. The term ordinarily and commonly used to describe land held by Indians after allotment, and before the issuance of the patent in fee that deprives the land of its character as Indian country. Estes v. U. S., C.C.A., 225 F. 980, 981; Harris v. Grayson, 90 Okl. 147, 216 P. 446, 449. See Allottee.

ALLOTMENT CERTIFICATE. A document issued to an applicant for shares in a company or public loan announcing the number of shares allotted or assigned and the amounts and due dates of the calls or different payments to be made on the same. An "allotment certificate," when issued to an enrolled member of the Five Civilized Tribes of the Indian Territory, is an adjudication of the special tribunal empowered to decide the question that the party to whom it issues is entitled to the land, and it is a conveyance of the right to this title to the allottee. Bowen v. Carter, 42 Okl. 565, 144 P. 170, 173.

ALLOTMENT NOTE. In English law, a writing by a seaman, whereby he makes an assignment of part of his wages in favor of his wife, father or mother, grandfather or grandmother, brother or sister. Mozley & Whitley.

ALLOTMENT SYSTEM. Designates the practice in England of dividing land in small portions for cultivation by agricultural laborers and other cottagers at their leisure, and after they have performed their ordinary day's work. Wharton.

ALLOTMENT WARDEN. By the English general inclosure act, 1845, § 108, when an allotment for the laboring poor of a district has been made on an inclosure under the act, the land so allotted is to be under the management of the incumbent and church warden of the parish, and two other persons elected by the parish, and they are to be styled "the allotment wardens" of the parish. Sweet.

ALLOTTEE. One to whom an allotment is made, who receives a ratable share under an allotment; a person to whom land under an inclosure act or shares in a public undertaking are allotted.

An "allottee," as the word is used in the act of April 21, 1904 (chapter 1402, 33 Stat. 189-204), is one, generally an Indian, freedman, or adopted citizen of a tribe of Indians, to whom a tract of land out of a common holding has been given by, or under the supervision of, the United States. Lynch v. Franklin, 37 Okl. 60, 130 P. 599, 600. The word does not include such allottee's heirs. Bradley v. Goddard, 45 Okl. 77, 145 P. 409, 410.

ALLOW. The word has no rigid or precise meaning, but its import varies according to circumstances or context in connection with which it is used. It may mean bestow, assign, to any one as his right or due, to accord, or to imply discretion, or unqualified and definite promise to do some specified thing. Dunlop Sand & Gravel Corporation v. Hospelhorn, 172 Md. 279, 191 A. 701, 706. To approve of, accept as true, approve, admit, concede, adopt, or fix. Headford Bros. & Hitchins Foundry Co. v. Associated Manufacturers Corporation of America, 224 Iowa 1364, 278 N.W. 624, 628. To grant something as a deduction or an addition; to abate or deduct; as, to allow a sum for leakage. Pittsburgh Brewing Co. v. Commissioner of Internal Revenue, C.C.A.3, 107 F.2d 155, 156. To grant, or permit; as to allow an appeal or a marriage; to allow an account or claim. Also to give a fit portion out of a larger property or fund. Thurman v. Adams, 82 Miss. 204, 33 So. 944. To sanction, either directly or indirectly, as opposed to merely suffering a thing to be done. People v. Duncan, 22 Cal.App. 430, 134 P. 797, 798; to acquiesce in. Luckie v. Diamond Coal Co., 41 Cal.App. 468, 183 P. 178, 181; Curtis & Gartside Co. v. Pigg, 39 Okl. 31, 134 P. 1125, 1129. To suffer, to tolerate; Gregory v. U. S., 17 Blatchf. 325, Fed.Cas.No.5,803; to fix; Hinds v. Marmolejo, 60 Cal. 229. To substitute. Glenn v. Glenn, 41 Ala. 571. Intent in wills; and an equivalent of I will; Ramsey v. Hanlon, C.C. Pa., 33 F. 425.

ALLOWANCE. A deduction, an average payment, a portion assigned or allowed; the act of allowing. See Stone v. State, 197 Ala. 293; 72 So. 536, 537; Sawyer v. U. S., C.C.A., 10 F.2d 416, 421. For "Family," see that title.

In army terminology, ordinarily refers to extra and special items in addition to regular compensation. United States v. Jackson, S.C., 302 U.S. 628, 58 S.Ct. 390, 392, 82 L.Ed. 488.

As distinguished from a "salary," which is a fixed compensation, decreed by authority and for permanence, and is paid at stated intervals, and depends upon time, and not the amount of the services rendered, "allowance" is a variable quantity. Blaine County v. Pyrah, 32 Idaho, 111, 178 P. 702, 703.

Not synonymous with "alimony". Warne v. Warne, 36 S.D. 573, 156 N.W. 60, 62.

Special allowances. In English practice, in taxing the costs of an action as between party and party, the taxing officer is, in certain cases, empowered to make special allowances; *i. e.*, to allow the party costs which the ordinary scale does not warrant. Sweet.

ALLOWANCE PENDENTE LITE. In the English chancery division, where property which forms the subject of proceedings is more than sufficient to answer all claims in the proceedings, the court may allow to the parties interested the whole or part of the income, or (in the case of personalty) part of the property itself. St. 15 & 16 Vict. c. 86, § 57; Daniell, Ch.Pr. 1070.

ALLOWED CLAIM. Against an estate it is a debt or charge which is valid in law and entitled to enforcement. Commissioner of Internal Revenue v. Lyne, C.C.A.1, 90 F.2d 745, 747.

ALLOY. An inferior or cheaper metal mixed with gold or silver in manufacturing or coining. As respects coining, the amount of alloy is fixed by law, and is used to increase the hardness and durability of the coin.

A compound of two or more metals. Treibacher-Chemische Werke Gesellschaft mit Beschränkter Haftung v. Roessler & Hasslacher Chemical Co., C.C.A.N.Y., 219 F. 210, 211. A mixture or combination of metals while in state of fusion. Pittsburgh Iron & Steel Foundries Co. v. Seaman-Sleeth Co., D.C.Pa., 236 F. 756, 757; Treibacher Chemische Werke Gesellschaft mit Beschränkter Haftung v. Roessler & Hasslacher Chemical Co., D.C.N.Y., 214 F. 410, 412.

ALLOYNOUR. L. Fr. One who conceals, steals, or carries off a thing privately. Britt. c. 17. See Eloigne.

ALLUVIO MARIS. Lat. In the civil and old English law, the washing up of the sea; the soil thus formed; formation of soil or land from the sea; maritime increase. Hale, Anal. § 8. "*Alluvio maris* is an increase of the land adjoining, by the projection of the sea, casting up and adding sand and slubb to the adjoining land, whereby it is increased, and for the most part by insensible degrees." Hale, de Jure Mar. pt. 1, c. 6.

ALLUVION. That increase of the earth on a shore or bank of a stream or the sea, by the force of the water, as by a current or by waves, which is so gradual that no one can judge how much is added at each moment of time. Inst. 1, 2, t. 1, § 20. Ang. Water Courses, 53. Jefferis v. East Omaha Land Co., 134 U.S. 178, 10 Sup.Ct. 518, 33 L.Ed. 872. Willett v. Miller, 176 Okl. 278, 55 P.2d 90, 92. "Accretion" denotes the act. However, the terms are frequently used synonymously. Katz v. Patterson, 135 Or. 449, 296 P. 54, 55. Avulsion is sudden and perceptible. St. Clair County v. Lovingston, 23 Wall. 46, 23 L.Ed. 59. See Accretion; Avulsion.

ALLY. A nation which has entered into an alliance with another nation. 1 Kent, Comm. 69.

A citizen or subject of one of two or more allied nations. Siemund v. Schmidt, Mun.Ct.N.Y., 168 N.Y.S. 935.

ALMANAC. A publication, in which is recounted the days of the week, month, and year, both common and particular, often distinguishing the fasts, feasts, terms, etc., from the common days by proper marks, pointing out also the several changes of the moon, tides, eclipses, etc.

ALMARIA. The archives, or, as they are sometimes styled, muniments of a church or library.

ALMESFEOH. In Saxon law, alms-fee; alms-money. Otherwise called "Peter-pence." Cowell.

ALMOIN. Alms; a tenure of lands by divine service. See Frankalmoigne.

ALMONER. One charged with the distribution of alms. The office was first instituted in religious houses and although formerly one of importance is now in England almost a sinecure.

ALMOXARIFAZGO. In Spanish law, a general term, signifying both export and import duties, as well as excise.

ALMS. Charitable donations. Any species of relief bestowed upon the poor. That which is given by public authority for the relief of the poor.

ALMS FEE. Peter-pence (or Peter's pence), which see.

ALMSHOUSE. A house for the publicly supported paupers of a city or county. People v. City of New York, 36 Hun, N.Y., 311. In England an almshouse is not synonymous with a work-house or poorhouse, being supported by private endowment.

It may be a public institution kept up by public revenues, or it may be an institution maintained by private endowment and contributions, where the indigent, sick, and poor are cared for without cost to themselves. State Board of Control v. Buckstegge, 18 Ariz. 277, 158 P. 837, 839.

ALNAGER, or ULNAGER. A sworn officer of the king whose duty it was to look to the assise of woolen cloth made throughout the land, and to the putting on the seals for that purpose ordained, for which he collected a duty called "alnage." Cowell; Termes de la Ley.

ALNETUM. In old records, a place where alders grow, or a grove of alder trees. Doomsday Book; Co.Litt. 4*b*.

ALOD, Alode, Alodes, Alodis. L. Lat. In feudal law, old forms of *alodium* or *allodium (q. v.)*.

A term used in opposition to *feodum* or *fief*, which means property, the use of which was bestowed upon another by the proprietor, on condition that the grantee should perform certain services for the grantor, and upon the failure of which the property should revert to the original possessor. See 1 Poll. & Maitl. 45.

ALODIAN. Sometimes used for allodial, but not well authorized. Cowell.

ALODIARII. See Allodarii.

ALONE. Apart from others; singly; sole. Salem Capital Flour Mills Co. v. Water-Ditch & Canal Co., C.C.Or., 33 Fed. 154.

ALONG. Lengthwise of, implying motion or at or near, distinguished from across. Nicolai v. Wisconsin Power & Light Co., 227 Wis. 83, 277 N.W. 674, 678. By, on, up to, or over, according to the subject-matter and context. State v. Downes, 79 N.H. 505, 112 A. 246; Sioux City Bridge Co. v. Miller, C.C.A., 12 F.2d 41, 48. The term does not necessarily mean touching at all points; Com. v. Franklin, 133 Mass. 569; nor does it necessarily imply contact, Watts v. City of Winfield, 101 Kan. 470, 168 P. 319, 321.

ALSO. Besides; as well; in addition; likewise; in like manner; similarly; too; withal. West Jersey Trust Co. v. Hayday, 124 N.J.Eq. 85, 199 A. 407, 411. Some other thing; including; further; furthermore; in the same manner; moreover; nearly the same as the word "and" or "likewise." Schilling v. Central California Traction Co., 1 P. 2d 53, 55, 115 Cal.App. 30.

The word imports no more than "item" and may mean the same as "moreover"; but not the same as "in like manner"; Evans v. Knorr, 4 Rawle (Pa.) 68; nor is it synonymous with "other," City of Ft. Smith v. Gunter, 106 Ark. 371, 154 S.W. 181, 183. It may be (1) the beginning of an entirely different sentence, or (2) a copulative carrying on the sense of the immediately preceding words into those immediately succeeding. Stroud, Jud. Dict., citing 1 Jarm. 497 n.; 1 Salk. 239; Security State Bank v. Jones, 121 Kan. 396, 247 P. 862, 863.

ALT. In Scotch practice, an abbreviation of *Alter*, the other; the opposite party; the defender. 1 Broun, 336, note.

ALTA PRODITIO. L. Lat. In old English law, high treason. 4 Bl.Comm. 75. See High Treason.

ALTA VIA. L. Lat. In old English law, a highway; the highway. 1 Salk. 222. *Alta via regia;* the king's highway; "the king's high street." Finch, Law, b. 2, c. 9.

ALTARAGE. In ecclesiastical law, offerings made on the altar; all profits which accrue to the priest by means of the altar. Ayliffe, Parerg. 61.

ALTENHEIM. A German word meaning "home for old people." German Pioneer Verein v. Meyer, 70 N.J.Eq. 192, 63 A. 835.

ALTER. To make a change in; to modify; to vary in some degree; to change some of the elements or ingredients or details without substituting an entirely new thing or destroying the identity of the thing affected. Davis v. Campbell, 93 Iowa, 524, 61 N.W. 1053. To change partially. Cross v. Nee, D.C.Mo., 18 F.Supp. 589, 594. To change in one or more respects, but without destruction of existence or identity of the thing changed; to increase or diminish. Kraus v. Kraus, 301 Ill.App. 606, 22 N.E.2d 862. See Alteration; Change.

To change may import the substitution of an entirely different thing, while to alter is to operate upon a subject-matter which continues objectively the same while modified in some particular. To "amend" implies that the modification made in the subject improves it, which is not necessarily the case with an alteration. See Ex parte Woo Jan, D.C.Ky., 228 F. 927, 940.

But "alter" is sometimes used synonymously with "change," Board of Sup'rs of Yavapai County v. Stephens, 20 Ariz. 115, 177 P. 261, 264, and with "enlarge," City of Jamestown v. Pennsylvania Gas Co., C.C.A.N.Y., 1 F.2d 871, 883.

The other; the opposite party. See Alt.

ALTER EGO. Second self. 3 C.J.S. Alter Ego.

Theory that subordinate or servient corporation may be controlled by superior or dominant corporation, so that dominant corporation may be held liable for subordinate corporation's negligence. Barnes v. Liebig, 146 Fla. 219, 1 So.2d 247, 253.

To establish the "alter ego" doctrine, it must be shown that the stockholders disregarded the entity of the corporation, made corporation a mere conduit for the transaction of their own private business, and that the separate individualities of the corporation and its stockholders in fact ceased to exist. Sefton v. San Diego Trust & Savings Bank, Cal.App., 106 P.2d 974, 984.

The doctrine of "alter ego" does not create assets for or in corporation, but it simply fastens liability on the individual who uses the corporation merely as an instrumentality in conducting his own personal business, and that liability springs from fraud perpetrated not on the corporation, but on third persons dealing with corporation. Garvin v. Matthews, 193 Wash. 152, 74 P.2d 990, 992.

A new corporation taking over all of mortgaged assets of old corporation in exchange for all of old corporation's capital stock and continuing to operate business formerly operated by old corporation was "alter ego" of old corporation so as to be obligated to pay annual patent royalty which old corporation was required to pay, notwithstanding that old corporation retained title to mortgaged assets. Dummer v. Wheeler Osgood Sales Corp., 198 Wash. 381, 88 P.2d 453, 458.

ALTERATION. Variation; changing; making different. A change of a thing from one form or state to another; making a thing different from what it was without destroying its identity. Paye v. City of Grosse Pointe, 279 Mich. 254, 271 N.W. 826, 827. See Alter.

As applied to *buildings,* it is a change or substitution in a substantial particular of one part of a building for a building different in that particular; a change or changes within the superficial limits of an existing structure; an installation that becomes an integral part of the building and changes its structural quality; a substantial change therein; a varying or changing the form or nature of such building without destroying its identity. Paye v. City of Grosse Pointe, 279 Mich. 254, 271 N.W. 826, 827.

Alteration of *highway* means change of course of existing highway, leaving it substantially the same highway as before, but with its course in some respects changed. Huening v. Shenkenberg, 208 Wis. 177, 242 N.W. 552, 553.

An alteration is an act done upon the *instrument* by which its meaning or language is changed. If what is written upon or erased from the instrument has no tendency to produce this result, or to mislead any person, it is not an alteration. Oliver v. Hawley, 5 Neb. 444.

An alteration is said to be *material* when it affects, or may possibly affect, the rights of the persons interested in the document.

Language different in legal effect, or change in rights, interests, or obligations of parties. Bank of Moberly v. Meals, 316 Mo. 1158, 295 S.W. 73, 77; Commercial Credit Co. v. Giles, Tex.Civ.App., 207 S.W. 596, 598. It introduces some change into instrument's terms, meaning, language, or details. See U. S. v. Sacks, 257 U.S. 37, 42 S.Ct. 38, 39, 66 L.Ed. 118. Strictly speaking, it is some material change on face of instrument by one of the parties thereto without consent of the other, Johnston v. DePuy, 15 N.J.Misc. 94, 188 A. 742, 743; since a mutual agreement of parties concerned creates a new agreement. Leake, Cont. 430. If performed by a mere stranger, it is more technically described as a *spoliation* or *mutilation.* Knox v. Horne, Tex.Civ.App., 200 S.W. 259, 260; Bercot v. Velkoff, 111 Ind. App. 323, 41 N.E.2d 686, 692. The term is not properly applied to any change which involves the substitution of a practically new document. Kempner v. Simon, 195 N.Y.S. 333, 334, 119 Misc.Rep. 60. And it should in strictness be reserved for the designation of changes in form or language, and not used with reference to modifications in matters of substance. The term is also to be distinguished from "defacement." Too, if what is done simply takes away what was given before, or a part of it under a *will,* it is a revocation; but if it gives something in addition or in substitution, then it is an alteration. Appeal of Miles, 68 Conn. 237, 36 A. 39, 36 L.R.A. 176.

ALTERCATION. Warm contentions in words, dispute carried on with heat or anger, controversy, wrangle, wordy contest. Ivory v. State, 128 Tex.Cr.R. 408, 81 S.W.2d 696, 698.

ALTERIUS CIRCUMVENTIO ALII NON PRÆBET ACTIONEM. The deceiving of one person does not afford an action to another. Dig. 50, 17, 49.

ALTERNAT. A usage among diplomatists by which the rank and places of different powers, who have the same right and pretensions to precedence, are changed from time to time, either in a certain regular order or one determined by lot. In drawing up treaties and conventions, for example, it is the usage of certain powers to alternate, both in the preamble and the signatures, so that each power occupies, in the copy intended to be delivered to it, the first place. Wheat.Int. Law, § 157.

ALTERNATE LEGACY. See Legacy.

ALTERNATIM. L. Lat. Interchangeably. Litt. § 371; Townsh.Pl. 37.

ALTERNATIVA PETITIO NON EST AUDIENDA. An alternative petition or demand is not to be heard. 5 Coke, 40.

ALTERNATIVE. One or the other of two things; giving an option or choice; allowing a choice between two or more things or acts to be done. See Malone v. Meres, 91 Fla. 709, 109 So. 677, 693.

ALTERNATIVE CONTRACT. A contract whose terms allow of performance by the doing of either one of several acts at the election of the party from whom performance is due. Crane v. Peer, 43 N.J.Eq. 553, 4 A. 72.

ALTERNATIVE JUDGMENT. See Judgment.

ALTERNATIVE OBLIGATION. An obligation allowing the obligor to choose which of two things he will do, the performance of either of which will satisfy the instrument. A promise to deliver a certain thing or to pay a specified sum of money is an example of this kind of obligation.

ALTERNATIVE PLEADING. A pleading alleging substantive facts so disjunctively that it cannot be determined upon which of them the pleader intends to rely as basis for recovery. Groover v. Savannah Bank & Trust Co., 186 Ga. 476, 198 S.E. 217, 219.

ALTERNATIVE RELIEF. The term "alternative," as used in Equity Rule 25 (see Fed.Rules Civ.Proc. rule 8, 28 U.S.C.A.), allowing relief to be stated and sought in alternative forms, means mutually exclusive. Boyd v. New York & H. R. Co., D.C.N.Y., 220 F. 174, 179.

ALTERNATIVE REMAINDERS. Remainders in which disposition of property is made in alternative, one to take effect only in case the other does not, and in substitution of it. Riddle v. Killian, 366 Ill. 294, 8 N.E.2d 629, 634.

ALTERNATIVE REMEDY. Where a new remedy is created in addition to an existing one, they are called "alternative" if only one can be enforced; but if both, "cumulative."

ALTERNATIVE WRIT. A writ commanding the person against whom it is issued to do a specified thing, or show cause to the court why he should not be compelled to do it. Allee v. McCoy, 2 Marv., Del., 465, 36 A. 359. Under the common-law practice, the first *mandamus* is an alternative writ; 3 Bla.Com. 111; but in modern practice this writ is often dispensed with and its place is taken by a rule to show cause. See Mandamus.

ALTERNIS VICIBUS. L. Lat. By alternate turns; at alternate times; alternately. Co.Litt. 4*a*; Shep.Touch. 206.

ALTERUM NON LÆDERE. Not to injure another. This maxim, and two others, *honeste vivere*, and *suum cuique tribuere, (q. v.,)* are considered by Justinian as fundamental principles upon which all the rules of law are based. Inst. 1, 1, 3.

ALTERUTER. Lat. One of two; either.

ALTIUS NON TOLLENDI. In the civil law, a servitude due by the owner of a house, by which he is restrained from building beyond a certain height. Dig. 8, 2, 4; Sandars, Just.Inst. 119.

ALTIUS TOLLENDI. In the civil law, a servitude which consists in the right, to him who is entitled to it, to build his house as high as he may think proper. In general, however, every one enjoys this privilege, unless he is restrained by some contrary title. Sandars, Just.Inst. 119.

ALTO ET BASSO. High and low. This phrase is applied to an agreement made between two contending parties to submit all matters in dispute, *alto et basso,* to arbitration. Cowell.

ALTUM MARE. L. Lat. In old English law, the high sea, or seas. Co.Litt. 260*b*. The deep sea. *Super altum mare,* on the high seas. Hob. 212*b*.

ALUMNUS. A child which one has nursed; a foster-child. Dig. 40, 2, 14.

Also a graduate from a school, college, or other institution of learning.

ALVEUS. The bed or channel through which the stream flows when it runs within its ordinary channel. Calvinus, Lex.

Alveus derelictus, a deserted channel. Mackeld. Rom.Law, § 274.

AMALGAMATION. Union of different races, or diverse elements, societies, or corporations, so as to form a homogeneous whole or new body; interfusion; intermarriage; consolidation; coalescence; as, the amalgamation of stock. Stand. Dict.

To join in a single body two or more associations, organizations, or corporations. Peterson v. Evans, 288 Ill.App. 623, 6 N.E.2d 520.

In England it is applied to the merger or consolidation of two incorporated companies or societies.

The word has no definite meaning; it involves the blending of two concerns into one; 1904, 2 Ch. 268.

AMALPHITAN CODE OR TABLE. A collection of sea-laws, compiled about the end of the eleventh century, by the people of Amalphi.

It consists of the laws on maritime subjects, which were or had been in force in countries bordering on the Mediterranean; and was for a long time received as authority in those countries. Azuni; Wharton. It became a part of the law of the sea; The Scotia, 14 Wall., U.S., 170, 20 L.Ed. 822. See Code.

AMANUENSIS. One who writes on behalf of another that which he dictates.

AMBACTUS. A messenger; a servant sent about; one whose services his master hired out. Spelman.

AMBASCIATOR. A person sent about in the service of another; a person sent on a service, A word of frequent occurrence in the writers of the middle ages. Spelman.

AMBASSADOR. In international law, a public officer, clothed with high diplomatic powers, commissioned by a sovereign prince or state to transact the international business of his government at the court of the country to which he is sent.

The commissioner who represents one country in the seat of government of another. He is a public minister, which, usually, a consul is not. Brown. A person sent by one sovereign to another, with authority, by letters of credence, to treat on affairs of state. Jacob. The personal representatives of the head of the state which sends them, entitled to special honors and special privileges and having varied duties; mouthpiece of communications, government informant, and protector of citizens of his country. Russian Government v. Lehigh Valley R. Co., D.C.N.Y., 293 F. 133. See Letter of Credence; Minister.

A distinction was formerly made between Ambassadors *Extraordinary,* who were sent to conduct special business or to remain for an indeterminate period, and Ambassadors *Ordinary,* who were sent on permanent missions; but this distinction is no longer observed.

AMBER, or AMBRA. In old English law, a measure of four bushels.

AMBIDEXTER. Skillful with both hands; one who plays on both sides. Applied anciently to an attorney who took pay from both sides, and subsequently to a juror guilty of the same offense. Cowell.

AMBIGUA RESPONSIO CONTRA PROFERENTEM EST ACCIPIENDA. An ambiguous answer is to be taken against (is not to be construed in favor of) him who offers it. 10 Coke, 59.

AMBIGUIS CASIBUS SEMPER PRÆSUMITUR PRO REGE. In doubtful cases, the presumption always is in behalf of the crown. Lofft, Append. 248.

AMBIGUITAS. Lat. From *ambiguus,* doubtful, uncertain, obscure. Ambiguity; uncertainty of meaning.

Ambiguitas latens, a latent ambiguity; *ambiguitas patens,* a patent ambiguity. See Ambiguity.

AMBIGUITAS CONTRA STIPULATOREM EST. Doubtful words will be construed most strongly against the party using them.

AMBIGUITAS VERBORUM LATENS VERIFICATIONE SUPPLETUR; NAM QUOD EX FACTO ORITUR AMBIGUUM VERIFICATIONE FACTI TOLLITUR. A latent ambiguity in the language may be removed by evidence; for whatever ambiguity arises from an extrinsic fact may be explained by extrinsic evidence. Bac.Max.Reg. 23. Said to be "an unprofitable subtlety; inadequate and uninstructive." Prof. J. B. Thayer in 6 Harv. L. 417.

AMBIGUITAS VERBORUM PATENS NULLA VERIFICATIONE EXCLUDITUR. A patent ambiguity cannot be cleared up by extrinsic evidence (or is never holpen by averment). Lofft, 249; Bacon, Max. 25.

AMBIGUITY. Doubtfulness; doubleness of meaning. Chapman v. Metropolitan Life Ins. Co., 172 S.C. 250, 173 S.E. 801, 803. Duplicity, indistinctness, or uncertainty of meaning of an expression used in a written instrument. Arkansas Amusement Corporation v. Kempner, C.C.A.Ark., 57 F. 2d 466, 472. Want of clearness or definiteness; difficult to comprehend or distinguish; of doubtful import. Business Men's Assur. Ass'n v. Read, Tex.Civ.App., 48 S.W.2d 678, 680. For "Extrinsic Ambiguity," see that title.

Ambiguity of language is to be distinguished from unintelligibility and inaccuracy, for words cannot be said to be ambiguous unless their signification seems doubtful and uncertain to persons of competent skill and knowledge to understand them. Story, Contr. 272. It does not include uncertainty arising from the use of peculiar words, or of common words in a peculiar sense. Wig. Wills, 174; In re Milliette's Estate, 206 N.Y.S. 342, 349, 123 Misc.Rep. 745. It is *latent* where the language employed is clear and intelligible and suggests but a single meaning, but some extrinsic fact or extraneous evidence creates a necessity for interpretation or a choice among two or more possible meanings, as where a description apparently plain and unambiguous is shown to fit different pieces of property. Logue v. Von Almen, 379 Ill. 208, 40 N.E.2d 73, 82, 140 A.L.R. 251. A *patent* ambiguity is that which appears on the face of the instrument, and arises from the defective, obscure, or insensible language used. Carter v. Holman, 60 Mo. 504; Stokeley v. Gordon, 8 Md. 505; Carroll v. Cave Hill Cemetery Co., 172 Ky. 204, 189 S.W. 186, 190.

AMBIGUITY UPON THE FACTUM. An ambiguity in relation to the very foundation of the instrument itself, as distinguished from an ambiguity in regard to the construction of its terms.

The term is applied, for instance, to a doubt as to whether a testator meant a particular clause to be a part of the will, or whether it was introduced with his knowledge, or whether a codicil was meant to republish a former will, or whether the residuary clause was accidentally omitted. Eatherly v. Eatherly, 1 Cold., Tenn., 461, 465, 78 Am.Dec. 499.

AMBIGUUM PACTUM CONTRA VENDITOREM INTERPRETANDUM EST. An ambiguous contract is to be interpreted against the seller.

AMBIGUUM PLACITUM INTERPRETARI DEBET CONTRA PROFERENTEM. An ambiguous plea ought to be interpreted against the party pleading it. Co.Litt. 303*b*.

AMBIT. A boundary line, as going around a place; an exterior or inclosing line or limit. Ellicott v. Pearl, 10 Pet., U.S., 412, 442, 9 L.Ed. 475.

The limits or circumference of a power or jurisdiction; the line circumscribing any subject-matter. As to the ambit of a port, see Leonis Steamship Co., Ltd., v. Rank, Ltd., [1907] 1 K.B. 344, 352; Pyman Bros. v. Dreyfus Bros. & Co. [1890] 24 Q.B.D. 152, 155.

AMBITUS. In the Roman law, a going around; a path worn by going around. A space of at least two and a half feet in width, between neighboring houses, left for the convenience of going around them. Calvin.

The procuring of a public office by money or gifts; the unlawful buying and selling of a public office. Inst. 4, 18, 11; Dig. 48, 14.

AMBLOTIC. Having the power to cause abortion; anything used to produce abortion.

AMBULANCE. A vehicle for the conveyance of the sick or wounded. In time of war they are considered neutral and must be respected by the belligerents. Oppenheim, Int.L. 126.

AMBULANCE CHASER. A lawyer or his agent who follows up accidents in the streets and tries to induce the injured person to sue for damages. Kelley v. Boyne, 239 Mich. 204, 214 N.W. 316, 318, 53 A.L.R. 273.

A popular name for one who solicits negligence cases for an attorney. In re Newell, 160 N.Y.S. 275, 278, 174 App. Div. 94. One seeking out persons and directing them to an attorney in consideration of a percentage of the recovery. In re Mitgang, 385 Ill. 311, 52 N.E.2d 807, 816.

AMBULANCE CHASING. A term descriptive of the practice of some attorneys, on hearing of a personal injury which may have been caused by the negligence or wrongful act of another, of at once seeking out the injured person with a view to securing authority to bring action on account of the injury. Chunes v. Duluth, W. & P. Ry. Co., D.C.Minn., 298 F. 964. Laymen's acquainting themselves with occurrence of accidents and approaching injured persons or their representatives with a view toward soliciting employment for an attorney in the litigation arising from the accident State ex rel. Wright v. Hinckle, 137 Neb. 735, 291 N.W. 68, 72.

AMBULATORIA EST VOLUNTAS DEFUNCTI USQUE AD VITÆ SUPREMUM EXITUM. The will of a deceased person is ambulatory until the latest moment of life. Dig. 34, 4, 4.

AMBULATORY. (Lat. *ambulare,* to walk about). Movable; revocable; subject to change.

Ambulatoria voluntas (a changeable will) denotes the power which a testator possesses of altering his will during his life-time. Hattersley v. Bissett, 50 N.J.Eq. 577, 25 Atl. 332.

Courts. The court of king's bench in England was formerly called an ambulatory court, because it followed the king's person, and was held sometimes in one place and sometimes in another. So, in France, the supreme court or parliament was originally ambulatory. 3 Bl.Comm. 38, 39, 41.

A *sheriff's return* has been said to be ambulatory until it is filed. Wilmot, J., 3 Burr. 1644.

AMBUSH. The noun "ambush" means (1) the act of attacking an enemy unexpectedly from a concealed station; (2) a concealed station, where troops or enemies lie in wait to attack by surprise, an ambuscade; (3) troops posted in a concealed place for attacking by surprise. The verb "ambush" means to lie in wait, to surprise, to place in ambush. Dale County v. Gunter, 46 Ala. 118, 142, referred to in Darneal v. State, 14 Okl.Cr. 540, 174 P. 290, 292, 1 A.L.R. 638.

AMELIORATING WASTE. An act of lessee, though technically constituting waste, yet in fact resulting in improving instead of doing injury to land. J. H. Bellows Co. v. Covell, 28 Ohio App. 277, 162 N.E. 621, 622.

AMELIORATIONS. Betterments; improvements. 6 Low.Can. 294; 9 Id. 503.

AMENABLE. Subject to answer to the law; accountable; responsible; liable to punishment. Pickelsimer v. Glazener, 173 N.C. 630, 92 S.E. 700, 704.

Also means tractable, that may be easily led or governed; formerly applied to a wife who is governable by her husband. Cowell.

AMEND. To improve. To change for the better by removing defects or faults. Cross v. Nee, D.C. Mo., 18 F.Supp. 589, 594. To change, correct, revise. Texas Co. v. Fort, 168 Tenn. 679, 80 S.W.2d 658, 660.

AMENDE HONORABLE. An apology.

In old English law, it was a penalty imposed upon a person by way of disgrace or infamy, as a punishment for any offense, or for the purpose of making reparation for any injury done to another, as the walking into church in a white sheet, with a rope about the neck and a torch in the hand, and begging the pardon of God, or the king, or any private individual, for some delinquency.

A punishment somewhat similar to this, which bore the same name, was common in France for offenses against public decency or morality. It was abolished by the law of the 25th of September, 1791; Merlin, Répert. In 1826 it was re-introduced in cases of sacrilege and was finally abolished in 1830.

AMENDMENT. A change, ordinarily for the better. Musher v. Perera, 162 Md. 44, 158 A. 14, 15. An amelioration of the thing without involving the idea of any change in substance or essence. Van Deusen v. Ruth, 343 Mo. 1096, 125 S.W.2d 1, 3.

Any writing made or proposed as an improvement of some principal writing. Ex parte Woo Jan, D.C.Ky., 228 F. 927, 941; Couch v. Southern Methodist University, Tex.Civ.App., 290 S.W. 256, 260.

In *legislation,* it is a modification or alteration proposed to be made in a bill on its passage, or an enacted law; also such modification or change when made. Brake v. Callison, C.C.Fla., 122 Fed. 722; State v. MacQueen, 82 W.Va. 44, 95 S.E. 666, 668.

It is to be distinguished from a "substitute for a bill." In re Ross, 86 N.J.Law, 387, 94 A. 304, 306. It is an alteration in the law already existing, leaving some part of the original still standing. State ex inf. Crain ex rel. Peebles v. Moore, 339 Mo. 492, 99 S.W.2d 17, 19. To effect an improvement or better carry out the purpose for which statute was framed. State ex rel. Foster v. Evatt, 144 Ohio St. 65, 56 N.E.2d 265, 282. And it includes additions to, as well as corrections of, matters already treated. Christian Feigenspan, Inc., v. Bodine, D.C.N.J., 264 F. 186, 190. See, also, State v. Fulton, 99 Ohio St. 168, 124 N.E. 172, 175.

In *practice* it is the correction of error committed in progress of a cause. Lintott v. McCluskey, 105 N.J.Eq. 354, 148 A. 161, 164. The correction of an error committed in any process, pleading, or proceeding at law, or in equity, and which is done either of course, or by the consent of parties, or upon motion to the court in which the proceeding is pending. 3 Bl.Comm. 407, 448; 1 Tidd, Pr. 696. Hardin v. Boyd, 113 U.S. 756, 5 Sup.Ct. 771, 28 L. Ed. 1141.

An amendment to a pleading, as distinguished from a "supplemental pleading" *(q. v.),* has reference to facts existing at the time of the commencement of the action. Fisher v. Bullock, 198 N.Y.S. 538, 540, 204 App.Div. 523. And it is the correction of some error or mistake in a pleading already before the court. Pantaleo v. Colt's Patent Fire Arms Mfg. Co., D.C.N.Y., 13 F.Supp. 989, 990.

AMENDS. A satisfaction given by a wrongdoer to the party injured, for a wrong committed. 1 Lil.Reg. 81.

AMENITY. In real property law, such circumstances, in regard to situation, outlook, access to a water course, or the like, as enhance the pleasantness or desirability of an estate for purposes of residence, or contribute to the pleasure and enjoyment of the occupants, rather than to their indispensable needs.

In England, upon the building of a railway or the construction of other public works, "amenity damages" may be given for the defacement of pleasure grounds, the impairment of riparian rights, or other destruction of or injury to the amenities of the estate.

In the law of *easements,* an "amenity" consists in restraining the owner from doing that with and on his property which, but for the grant or covenant, he might lawfully have done; sometimes called a "negative easement" as distinguished from that class of easements which compel the owner to suffer something to be done on his property by another. Equitable Life Assur. Soc. v. Brennan, 30 Abb.N.C. 260, 24 N.Y.Supp. 784, 788. A restrictive covenant. South Buffalo Stores v. W. T. Grant Co., 274 N.Y.S. 549, 555, 153 Misc. 76.

AMENS. See Demens.

AMENTIA. Insanity; idiocy. See Insanity.

AMERALIUS. L. Lat. A naval commander, under the eastern Roman empire, but not of the highest rank; the origin, according to Spelman, of the modern title and office of admiral. Spelman.

AMERCE. To impose an amercement or fine; to punish by a fine or penalty.

AMERCEMENT. A pecuniary penalty, in the nature of a fine, imposed upon a person for some fault or misconduct, he being "in mercy" for his offense. It was assessed by the peers of the delinquent, or the affeerors, or imposed arbitrarily at the discretion of the court or the lord. Goodyear v. Sawyer, C.C.Tenn., 17 Fed. 9.

The difference between *amercements* and *fines* is as follows: The latter are certain, and are created by some statute; they can only be imposed and assessed by courts of record; the former are arbitrarily imposed. Termes de la Ley, 40.

The word "amercement" has long been especially used of a mulct or penalty, imposed by a court upon its own officers for neglect of duty, or failure to pay over moneys collected. In particular, the remedy against a sheriff for failing to levy an execution or make return of proceeds of sale is, in several of the states, known as "amercement." In others, the same result is reached by process of attachment. Abbott. Stansbury v. Mfg. Co., 5 N.J.Law, 441.

AMERCEMENT ROYAL. In Great Britain a penalty imposed on an officer for a misdemeanor in his office.

AMERICAN. Pertaining to the western hemisphere or in a more restricted sense to the United States. See Beardsley v. Selectmen of Bridgeport, 53 Conn. 493, 3 A. 557, 55 Am.Rep. 152. It was assumed in Life Photo Film Corp. v. Bell, 90 Misc.Rep. 469, 154 N.Y.S. 763, 764, that the term "American" included all classes of citizens, native and naturalized, irrespective of where they originally came from.

AMERICAN AGENCY SYSTEM. Its purport is that upon termination of an insurance agency, if the agent's financial obligations to the insurer are paid in full, all rights in the expiration data of existing insurance procured by the agent belong to him. Woodruff v. Auto Owners Ins. Co., 300 Mich. 54, 1 N.W.2d 450, 453.

AMERICAN CLAUSE. In marine insurance, a proviso in a policy to the effect that, in case of any subsequent insurance, the insurer shall nevertheless be answerable for the full extent of the sum subscribed by him, without right to claim contribution from subsequent underwriters. American Ins. Co. v. Griswold, 14 Wend., N.Y., 399.

AMERICAN EXPERIENCE TABLE OF MORTALITY. A series of tables dealing with life insurance, costs and values, varying according to the age of the insured, the period during which the policy has been in force, and the term of the particular policy. Horton v. Atlantic Life Ins. Co., 187 S.C. 155, 197 S.E. 512, 514, 116 A.L.R. 788.

AMEUBLISSEMENT. In French law, a species of agreement which by a fiction gives to immovable goods the quality of movable. Merl. Répert.; 1 Low.Can. 25, 58.

AMI; AMY. A friend; as *alien ami,* an alien belonging to a nation at peace with us; *prochein ami,* a next friend suing or defending for an infant, married woman, etc.

AMICABLE. Friendly; mutually forbearing; agreed or assented to by parties having conflicting interests or a dispute; as opposed to hostile or adversary.

AMICABLE ACTION. An action brought and carried on by the mutual consent and arrangement of the parties, to obtain judgment of court on a doubtful question of law, the facts being usually settled by agreement. Lord v. Veazie, 8 How. 251, 12 L.Ed. 1067. See Case Stated.

AMIABLES COMPOSITEURS. See Amicable Compounders.

AMICABLE COMPOUNDERS. In Louisiana law and practice, amicable compounders are arbitrators authorized to abate something of the strictness of the law in favor of natural equity.

AMICABLE SCIRE FACIAS TO REVIVE A JUDGMENT. A written agreement, signed by the person to be bound by the revival, in the nature of a writ of scire facias with a confession of judgment thereon, which must be duly docketed, but which requires no judicial action on the part of the court, and which has the force and effect of a judgment rendered upon an adverse or contested writ of scire facias. Second Nat. Bank, for Use of Federal Reserve Bank of Philadelphia, v. Faber, 332 Pa. 124, 2 A.2d 747, 749.

AMICUS CURIÆ. Lat. A friend of the court.

A by-stander (usually a counsellor) who interposes and volunteers information upon some matter of law in regard to which the judge is doubtful or mistaken, Fort Worth & D. C. Ry. Co. v. Greathouse, Tex.Civ.App., 41 S.W.2d 418, 422; or upon a matter of which the court may take judicial cognizance. The Claveresk, C.C.A.N.Y., 264 F. 276, 279; In re Perry, 83 Ind.App. 456, 148 N.E. 163, 165. Implies friendly intervention of counsel to remind court of legal matter which has escaped its notice, and regarding which it appears to be in danger of going wrong. Blanchard v. Boston & M. R., 86 N.H. 263, 167 A. 158, 160.

Also a person who has no right to appear in a suit but is allowed to introduce argument, authority, or evidence to protect his interests. Ladue v. Goodhead, 181 Misc. 807, 44 N.Y.S.2d 783, 787.

AMIRAL. Fr. In French maritime law, admiral. Ord. de la Mar. liv. 1, tit. 1, § 1.

AMITA. Lat. An aunt on the father's side. *Amita magna.* A great-aunt on the father's side. *Amita major.* A great-great aunt on the father's side. *Amita maxima.* A great-great-great aunt, or a great-great-grandfather's sister. Calvinus, Lex.

AMITINUS. The child of a brother or sister; a cousin; one who has the same grandfather, but different father and mother. Calvinus, Lex.

AMITTERE. Lat. In the civil and old English law, to lose. Hence the old Scotch "amitt."

AMITTERE CURIAM. To lose the court; to be deprived of the privilege of attending the court.

AMITTERE LEGEM TERRÆ. To lose the protection afforded by the law of the land.

AMITTERE LIBERAM LEGEM. To lose one's frank-law.

A term having the same meaning as *amittere legem terræ, (q. v.)* He who lost his law lost the protection extended by the law to a freeman, and became subject to the same law as thralls or serfs attached to the land.

To lose the privilege of giving evidence under oath in any court; to become infamous, and incapable of giving evidence. Glanville 2. If either party in a wager of battle cried "craven" he was condemned *amittere liberam legem;* 3 Bla.Com. 340.

AMNESIA. Loss of memory.

AMNESTY. A sovereign act of oblivion for past acts, granted by a government to all persons (or to certain persons) who have been guilty of crime or delict, generally political offenses,—treason, sedition, rebellion,—and often conditioned upon their return to obedience and duty within a prescribed time.

A general pardon or proclamation of such pardon from subjects' offenses against the government; while usually exerted in behalf of certain classes of persons, subject to trial, but not convicted, it is not confined to such cases. Commonwealth v. Hamburg Magistrate, 104 Pa.Super. 221, 158 A. 629, 631.

A declaration of the person or persons who have newly acquired or recovered the sovereign power in a state, by which they pardon all persons who composed, supported, or obeyed the government which has been overthrown.

The word "amnesty" properly belongs to international law, and is applied to treaties of peace following a state of war, and signifies there the burial in oblivion of the particular cause of strife, so that that shall not be again a cause for war between the parties; and this signification of "amnesty" is fully and poetically expressed in the Indian custom of burying the hatchet. And so amnesty is applied to rebellions which by their magnitude are brought within the rules of international law. It means only "oblivion," and never is a grant. Knote v. U. S., 10 Ct.Cl. 407.

Amnesty is the abolition and forgetfulness of the offense; pardon is forgiveness. Knote v. U. S., 95 U.S. 149, 152, 24 L.Ed. 442. The first is usually addressed to crimes against the sovereignty of the state, to political offenses; the second condones infractions of the peace of the state. Burdick v. United States, 236 U.S. 79, 35 S.Ct. 267, 271, 59 L.Ed. 476.

Express amnesty is one granted in direct terms.

Implied amnesty is one which results when a treaty of peace is made between contending parties. Vattel, 1, 4, c. 2, § 20.

AMONG. Mingled with or in the same group or class. Dwight Mfg. Co. v. Word, 200 Ala. 221, 75 So. 979, 983, Genung v. Best, 100 N.J.Eq. 250, 135 A. 514, 516. Intermingled with. Eddings v. Southern Dairies, D.C.S.C., 42 F.Supp. 664, 666.

Commerce *among* the states cannot stop at the external boundary line of each state. Gibbons v. Ogden, 9 Wheat. 194, 6 L.Ed. 23; Ft. Smith & W. R. Co. v. Blevins, 35 Okl. 378, 130 P. 525, 529. Where property is directed by will to be distributed *among* several persons, it cannot be all given to one, nor can any of the persons be wholly excluded from the distribution. Hudson v. Hudson, 6 Munf., Va., 352.

"Among" is sometimes held to be equivalent to "between"; Hick's Estate, 134 Pa. 507, 19 A. 705; Records v. Fields, 155 Mo. 314, 55 S.W. 1021. But "among" implies more than two objects as differentiated with "between." St. Louis Union Trust Co. v. Little, 320 Mo. 1058, 10 S.W.2d 47, 53.

AMORTISE. See Amortize.

AMORTISSEMENT. (Fr.) The redemption of a debt by a sinking fund.

AMORTIZATION. An alienation of lands or tenements in mortmain. The reduction of the property of lands or tenements to mortmain.

In its modern sense, amortization is the operation of paying off bonds, stock, a mortgage, or other indebtedness, commonly of a state or corporation, by installments, or by a sinking fund. An "amortization plan" for the payment of an indebtedness is one where there are partial payments of the principal, and accrued interest, at stated periods for a definite time, at the expiration of which the entire indebtedness will be extinguished. Bystra v. Federal Land Bank of Columbia, 82 Fla. 472, 90 So. 478, 480; Applestein v. Royalty Realty Corporation, 181 Md. 171, 28 A.2d 830, 831.

AMORTIZE. To alien lands in mortmain.

To destroy, kill, or deaden. Elliott v. U. S., D.C.Me., 16 F.2d 164, 165. See Amortization.

AMOTIO. In the civil law, a moving or taking away. "The slightest *amotio* is sufficient to constitute theft, if the *animus furandi* be clearly established." 1 Swint. 205. See Amotion.

AMOTION. A putting or turning out; dispossession of lands. Ouster is an *amotion* of possession. 3 Bl.Comm. 199, 208.

A moving or carrying away; the wrongful taking of personal chattels. Archb.Civil Pl.Introd. c. 2, § 3.

In *corporation law,* the act of removing an officer, or official representative, of a corporation from his office or official station, before the end of the term for which he was elected or appointed, but without depriving him of membership in the body corporate. In this last respect the term differs from "disfranchisement," or expulsion. Richards v. Clarksburg, 30 W.Va. 491, 4 S.E. 774; In re Koch, 257 N.Y. 318, 178 N.E. 545, 546.

AMOUNT. The effect, substance, or result; the total or aggregate sum. Hilburn v. Railroad Co., 23 Mont. 229, 58 P. 551.

The sum of principal and interest. McCabe v. Cary's Ex'rs, 135 Va. 428, 116 S.E. 485, 491. But see In re Stoneman, Sur., 146 N.Y.S. 172, 175 (interest excluded). See, also, Candelaria v. Gutierrez, 28 N.M. 434, 213 P. 1037, holding that the "amount of judgment" within a statute requiring a bond for supersedeas does not include interest or costs.

AMOUNT COVERED. In insurance, the amount that is insured, and for which underwriters are liable for loss under a policy of insurance.

AMOUNT IN CONTROVERSY. The damages claimed or relief demanded; the amount claimed or sued for. Glenwood Light & Water Co. v. Mutual Light, Heat & Power Co., 239 U.S. 121, 36 S.Ct. 30, 60 L.Ed. 174; Smith v. Giles, 65 Tex. 341; Wabash Ry. Co. v. Vanlandingham, C.C.A.Mo., 53 F.2d 51.

Value of property. Peterson v. Sucro, C.C.A.N.C., 93 F.2d 878, 114 A.L.R. 890. Value of the property interest in trade-name. Beneficial Industrial Loan Corporation v. Kline, C.C.A.Iowa, 132 F.2d 520, 525. Value of the object sought to be gained by the suit. Boesenberg v. Chicago Title & Trust Co., C.C.A.Ill., 128 F.2d 245, 246. Aggregate amount of all causes of action properly joined in action at law. Firestone Tire & Rubber Co. v. Brent, D.C.N.Y., 2 F.Supp. 425, 426. Contra. Plaintiffs' claims could not be aggregated for jurisdictional purposes. Independence Shares Corporation v. Deckert, C.C.A.Pa., 108 F.2d 51, 53.

AMOUNT IN DISPUTE. Value in money of the relief prayed for. Finley v. Smith, Mo.App., 170 S.W.2d 166, 170; or sought but denied, Bushnell v. Mississippi & Fox River Drainage Dist. of Clark County, 340 Mo. 811, 102 S.W.2d 871, 873, and includes value of thing in contest where a thing, instead of an amount, is in dispute. Noel Estate v. Louisiana Oil Refining Corporation, La.App., 170 So. 272, 273.

AMOUNT OF LOSS. In insurance, the diminution, destruction, or defeat of the value of, or of the charge upon, the insured subject to the assured, by the direct consequence of the operation of the risk insured against, according to its value in the policy, or in contribution for loss, so far as its value is covered by the insurance.

AMOUNT TO. To reach in the aggregate, to rise to or reach by accumulation of particular sums or quantities. Peabody v. Forest Preserve District of Cook County, 320 Ill. 454, 151 N.E. 271, 274.

AMOVE. To remove from a post or station. 3 C.J.S. p. 1059.

AMOVEAS MANUS. Lat. That you remove your hands.

After office found, the king was entitled to the things forfeited, either lands or personal property; the remedy for a person aggrieved was by "petition," or *"monstrans de droit,"* or *"traverses,"* to establish his superior right. Thereupon a writ issued, *quod manus domini regis amoveantur.* 3 Bl.Comm. 260.

AMPARO. In Spanish-American law, a document issued to a claimant of land as a protection to him, until a survey can be ordered, and the title of possession issued by an authorized commissioner. Trimble v. Smither's Adm'r, 1 Tex. 790.

AMPLIATION. Action of judge in merely deferring the cause for further examination constitutes "ampliation," practice in such instances being for judge to make the usual notation of non liquet. Sonnier v. Sonnier, 14 La.App. 588, 130 So. 133, 135.

In *civil law,* a deferring of judgment until a cause be further examined. Calvin.; Cowell. An order for the rehearing of a cause on a day appointed, for the sake of more ample information. Halifax, Anal. b. 3, c. 13, n. 32.

In this case, the judges pronounced the word *amplius,* or by writing the letters N. L. for *non liquet (q. v.),* signifying that the cause was not clear. It is very similar to the common-law practice of entering *cur. adv. vult* in similar cases.

In *French law,* a duplicate of an acquittance or other instrument. A notary's copy of acts passed before him, delivered to the parties.

AMPLIUS. In the Roman law, more; further; more time.

A word which the prætor pronounced in cases where there was any obscurity in a cause, and the *judices* were uncertain whether to condemn or acquit; by which the case was deferred to a day named. Adam, Rom. Ant. 287.

AMPUTATION OF RIGHT HAND. An ancient punishment for a blow given in a superior court; or for assaulting a judge sitting in the court.

AMUSEMENT. Pastime; diversion; enjoyment.

A pleasurable occupation of the senses, or that which furnishes it. Young v. Board of Trustees of Broadwater County High School, 90 Mont. 576, 4 P.2d 725, 726.

AMY. See Ami; Prochein Ami.

AN. The English indefinite article. Equivalent to "one" or "any"; seldom used to denote plurality. Kaufman v. Superior Court, 115 Cal. 152, 46 Pac. 904.

AN ET JOUR. Fr. Year and day; a year and a day.

AN, JOUR, ET WASTE. In feudal law, year, day, and waste. A forfeiture of the lands to the crown incurred by the felony of the tenant, after which time the land escheats to the lord. Termes de la Ley, 40. See Year, Day, and Waste.

ANACRISIS. In the civil law, an investigation of truth, interrogation of witnesses, and inquiry made into any fact, especially by torture.

ANÆSTHESIA. In medical jurisprudence. (1) Loss of sensation, or insensibility to pain, general or local, induced by the administration or application of certain drugs such as ether, nitrous oxide gas, or cocaine. (2) Defect of sensation, or more or less complete insensibility to pain, existing in various parts of the body as a result of certain diseases of the nervous system.

ANAGRAPH. A register, inventory, or commentary.

ANALOGOUS. Derived from the Greek ana, up, and logos, ratio. Means bearing some resemblance. Irving v. Kerlow Steel Flooring Co., D.C. N.J., 25 F.Supp. 901, 902.

If elements and purposes of one art are so related and similar to those of another as to make an appeal to one skilled in such art, the two arts are "analogous". Copeman Laboratories Co. v. General Plastics Corp., C.C.A.Ill., 149 F.2d 962, 963.

ANALOGY. In logic. Identity or similarity of proportion.

Where there is no precedent in point, in cases on the same subject, lawyers have recourse to cases on a different subject-matter, but governed by the same general principle. This is reasoning by analogy. Wharton.

The similitude of relations which exist between things compared. See Smith v. State, 63 Ala. 58.

"Analogy" does not mean identity, but implies a difference. Sturm v. Ulrich, C.C.A.Okl., 10 F.2d 9, 11.

ANALYTICAL JURISPRUDENCE. A theory and system of jurisprudence wrought out neither by inquiring for ethical principles or the dictates of the sentiments of justice nor by the rules which may be actually in force, but by analyzing, classifying and comparing various legal conceptions. See Jurisprudence.

ANAPHRODISIA. In medical jurisprudence, impotentia cœundi; frigidity; incapacity for sexual intercourse existing in either man or woman, and in the latter case sometimes called "dyspareunia."

ANARCHIST. One who professes and advocates the doctrines of anarchy, *q. v.* And see Cerveny v. Chicago Daily News Co., 139 Ill. 345, 28 N.E. 692, 13 L.R.A. 864. In the immigration statutes, it includes, not only persons who advocate the overthrow of organized government by force, but also those who believe in the absence of government as a political ideal, and seek the same end through propaganda. Ex parte Caminita, D.C.N.Y., 291 F. 913, 915.

ANARCHY. Absence of government; state of society where there is no law or supreme power; lawlessness or political disorder; destructive of and confusion in, government. People v. Mintz, 106 Cal.App. 725, 290 P. 93, 98.

At its best it pertains to a society made orderly by good manners rather than law, in which each person produces according to his powers and receives according to his needs, and at its worst, the word pertains to a terroristic resistance of all present government and social order. State v. Schleifer, 102 Conn. 708, 130 A. 184, 188.

Criminal anarchy as the doctrine that organized government should be overthrown by force, or by assassination of executive officers, or by any unlawful means. See People v. Gitlow, 183 N.Y.S. 846, 847, 111 Misc.Rep. 641, and 15 Rep. Am. Bar Assn. 210.

ANATHEMA. An ecclesiastical punishment by which a person is separated from the body of the church, and forbidden all intercourse with the members of the same.

It differs from excommunication, which simply forbids the person excommunicated from going into the church and taking the communion with the faithful.

ANATHEMATIZE. To pronounce anathema upon; to pronounce accursed by ecclesiastical authority; to excommunicate. See Anathema.

ANATOCISM. In the civil law, repeated or doubled interest; compound interest; usury. Cod. 4, 32, 1, 30.

ANCESTOR. One from whom a person lineally descended or may be descended; a progenitor. Russell v. Roberts, 54 Ohio App. 441, 7 N.E.2d 811, 814.

A former possessor; the person last seised. Termes de la Ley; 2 Bl.Comm. 201. A deceased person from whom another has inherited land. Bailey v. Bailey, 25 Mich. 185; McCarthy v. Marsh, 5 N.Y. 275.

For example, a child may be the "ancestor" of his parent, and an infant brother, the "ancestor" of an adult brother. Embraces collaterals as well as lineals. Purcell v. Sewell, 223 Ala. 73, 134 So. 476, 480. Correlative of "heir." In re Long's Estate, 180 Okl. 28, 67 P.2d 41, 43, 110 A.L.R. 1002.

The term differs from "predecessor," in that it is applied to a natural person and his progenitors, while the latter is applied also to a corporation and those who have held *offices* before those who now fill them. Co. Litt. 78*b*. "Ancestor" may embrace both lineals and collaterals, Cornell v. Child, 170 App.Div. 240, 156 N.Y.S. 449, 452, or both testator and testatrix, Pfaffenberger v. Pfaffenberger, 189 Ind. 507, 127 N.E. 766, 767; it may also be limited to mean immediate ancestor, In re Simpson's Estate, Sur., 144 N.Y.S. 1099, 1101.

ANCESTRAL. Relating to ancestors, or to what has been done by them; as *homage ancestral (q. v.).* Derived from ancestors.

Ancestral estates are such as are transmitted by descent, and not by purchase. 4 Kent. Comm. 404. Brown v. Whaley, 58 Ohio St. 654, 49 N.E. 479, 65 Am.St.Rep. 793. Or such as are acquired either by descent or by operation of law. Gray v. Chapman, 122 Okl. 130, 243 P. 522, 525. Realty which came to the intestate by descent or devise from a now dead ancestor or by deed of actual gift from a living one, there being no other consideration than that of blood. In re Long's Estate, 180 Okl. 28, 67 P.2d 41, 50, 110 A.L.R. 1002. Real estate coming to distributee by descent, gift, or devise from any kinsman. Ward v. Ives, 91 Conn. 12, 98 A. 337, 339. Allotments to members of Indian tribes or their heirs have been treated as an ancestral estate. Sims v. Brown, 46 Okl. 767, 149 P. 876, 877; McDougal v. McKay, 237 U.S. 372, 35 S.Ct. 605, 607, 59 L.Ed. 1001.

ANCHOR. A measure containing ten gallons.

The instrument used by which a vessel or other body is held. See Walsh v. Dock Co., 77 N.Y. 448; Reid v. Ins. Co., 19 Hun, N.Y., 284.

ANCHOR WATCH. A watch, consisting of a small number of men, (from one to four,) kept constantly on deck while the vessel is riding at single anchor, to see that the stoppers, painters, cables, and buoy-ropes are ready for immediate use. The Lady Franklin, 2 Lowell, 220, Fed.Cas. No.7,984. The lookout intrusted to one or two men when a vessel is at anchor. O'Hara v. Luckenbach S. S. Co., 269 U.S. 364, 46 S.Ct. 157, 160, 70 L.Ed. 313.

ANCHORAGE. In English law, a prestation or toll for every anchor cast from a ship in a port; and sometimes, though there be no anchor. Hale, de Jure Mar. pt. 2, c. 6. See 1 W.Bl. 413 et seq.; 4 Term. 262.

ANCIENT. Old; that which has existed from an indefinitely early period, or which by age alone has acquired certain rights or privileges accorded in view of long continuance.

ANCIENT DEED. A deed 30 years old and shown to come from a proper custody and having nothing suspicious about it. Davis v. Wood, 161 Mo. 17, 61 S.W. 695.

ANCIENT DEMESNE. Manors which in the time of William the Conqueror were in the hands of the crown, and are so recorded in the Domesday Book. Fitzh.Nat.Brev. 14, 56; Baker v. Wich, 1 Salk. 56.

Also a species of copyhold, which differs, however, from common copyholds in certain privileges, but yet must be conveyed by surrender, according to the custom of the manor.

There are three sorts: (1) Where the lands are held freely by the king's grant; (2) customary freeholds, which are held of a manor in ancient demesne, but not at the lord's will, although they are conveyed by surrender, or deed and admittance; (3) lands held by copy of court-roll at the lord's will, denominated copyholds of base tenure.

Tenure in *ancient demesne* may be pleaded in abatement to an action of ejectment. Rust v. Roe, 2 Burr. 1046.

ANCIENT DOCUMENTS. See Ancient Writings.

ANCIENT HOUSE. One which has stood long enough to acquire an easement of support against the adjoining land or building. 3 Kent, Comm. 437; 2 Washb.Real Prop. 74, 76.

In England this term is applied to houses or buildings erected before the time of legal memory, (Cooke, Incl. Acts, 35, 109,) that is, before the reign of Richard I., although practically any house is an ancient messuage if it was erected before the time of living memory, and its origin cannot be proved to be modern.

ANCIENT LIGHTS. Lights or windows in a house, which have been used in their present state, without molestation or interruption, for twenty years, and upwards.

To these the owner of the house has a right by prescription or occupancy, so that they cannot be obstructed or closed by the owner of the adjoining land which they may overlook. Wright v. Freeman, 5 Har. & J., Md., 477; Story v. Odin, 12 Mass. 160, 7 Am.Dec. 81.

ANCIENT READINGS. Readings or lectures upon the ancient English statutes, formerly regarded as of great authority in law. Litt. § 481; Co. Litt. 280.

ANCIENT RECORDS. See Ancient Writings.

ANCIENT RENT. The rent reserved at the time the lease was made, if the building was not then under lease. Orby v. Lord Mohun, 2 Vern. 542.

ANCIENT SERJEANT. In English law, the eldest of the queen's serjeants.

ANCIENT STREET. The doctrine is not based upon fact that streets have existed for a long time, but is invoked when it appears that common grantor owning land comprising street in question as well as property in question and other lots has given deeds to lots bounding them by street, thereby not only dedicating the street to public use but at same time creating private easements in the street, which cannot be taken without compensation. Dwornick v. State, 251 App.Div. 675, 297 N.Y.S. 409, 411.

ANCIENT WALL. A wall built to be used, and in fact used, as a party-wall, for more than twenty years, by the express permission and continuous acquiescence of the owners of the land on which it stands. Eno v. Del Vecchio, 4 Duer, N. Y., 53, 63. Schneider v. 44–84 Realty Corporation, 169 Misc. 249, 7 N.Y.S.2d 305, 309.

ANCIENT WATER COURSE. A water course is "ancient" if the channel through which it naturally runs has existed from time immemorial independent of the quantity of water which it discharges. Earl v. De Hart, 12 N.J.Eq. 280, 72 Am. Dec. 395.

ANCIENT WRITINGS. Documents bearing on their face every evidence of age and authenticity, of age of 30 years, and coming from a natural and reasonable official custody. Hartzell v. U. S., C. C.A.Iowa, 72 F.2d 569, 579.

These are presumed to be genuine without express proof, when coming from the proper custody. Jones v. Scranton Coal Co., 274 Pa. 312, 118 A. 219. Bonds more than 50 years old are admissible as ancient documents, where they are on their face free from suspicion as to their authenticity, come from the proper source, and are accompanied by some corroborating evidence. Smythe v. Inhabitants of New Providence Tp., Union County, N. J., C.C.A.N.J., 263 F. 481. Only the original copy of a deed, not the record copy, can be considered as an ancient document. Laclede Land & Improvement Co. v. Goodno, Mo. Sup., 181 S.W. 410, 413.

ANCIENTS. In English law, gentlemen of the inns of court and chancery.

In Gray's Inn the society consists of benchers, ancients, barristers, and students under the bar; and here the ancients are of the oldest barristers. In the Middle Temple, those who had passed their readings used to be termed "ancients." The Inns of Chancery consist of ancients and students or clerks; from the ancients a principal or treasurer is chosen yearly. Wharton.

The *Council of Ancients* was the upper Chamber of the French legislature under the constitution of 1795, consisting of 250, each required to be at least forty years old.

ANCIENTY. Eldership; seniority. Used in the statute of Ireland, 14 Hen. VIII. Cowell.

ANCILLA. Lat. A handmaid, an auxiliary, a subordinate. Manley v. Standard Oil Co. of Tex., D.C.Tex., 8 F.R.D. 354, 356.

ANCILLARY. Aiding; attendant upon; describing a proceeding attendant upon or which aids another proceeding considered as principal. In re Stoddard, 238 N.Y. 147, 144 N.E. 484, 486. Auxiliary or subordinate. Johnson v. Thomas, D.C. Tex., 16 F.Supp. 1019.

ANCILLARY ADMINISTRATION. Administration in state where decedent has property and which is other than where decedent was domiciled. First Nat. Bank v. Blessing, 231 Mo.App. 288, 98 S.W.2d 149, 151.

ANCILLARY ATTACHMENT. One sued out in aid of an action already brought, its only office being to hold the property attached under it for the satisfaction of the plaintiff's demand. Templeton v. Mason, 107 Tenn. 625, 65 S.W. 25.

ANCILLARY BILL OR SUIT. One growing out of and auxiliary to another action or suit, either at law or in equity, such as a bill for discovery, or a proceeding for the enforcement of a judgment, or to set aside fraudulent transfers of property. Coltrane v. Templeton, Va., 45 C.C.A. 328, 106 F. 370. One growing out of a prior suit in the same court, dependent upon and instituted for the purpose either of impeaching or enforcing the judgment or decree in a prior suit. Hume v. New York, C.C.A.N.Y., 255 F. 488, 491; Caspers v. Watson, C.C.A.Ill., 132 F.2d 614, 615.

ANCILLARY JURISDICTION. "Ancillary jurisdiction" of federal court generally involves either proceedings which are concerned with pleadings, processes, records or judgments of court in principal case or proceedings which affect property already in court's custody. Cooperative Transit Co. v. West Penn Electric Co., C.C.A.W.Va., 132 F.2d 720, 723. The ancillary process must be to aid, enjoin, or regulate original suit and prevent relitigation in other courts of issues heard and adjudged in such suit. O'Brien v. Richtarsic, D.C. N.Y., 2 F.R.D. 42, 44.

ANCILLARY PROCEEDING. One subordinate to or in aid of another primary action. Schram v. Roney, D.C.Mich., 30 F.Supp. 458, 461.

ANCILLARY RECEIVER. One appointed in aid of, and in subordination to, a foreign receiver for purpose of collecting and taking charge of assets, as of insolvent corporation, in the jurisdiction where he is appointed. In re Stoddard, 242 N.Y. 148, 151 N.E. 159, 164, 45 A.L.R. 622.

ANCIPITIS USUS. Lat. In international law, of doubtful use; the use of which is doubtful; that may be used for a civil or peaceful, as well as military or warlike, purpose. Gro. de Jure B. lib. 3, c. 1, § 5, subd. 3; 1 Kent, Comm. 140.

AND. A conjunction connecting words or phrases expressing the idea that the latter is to be added to or taken along with the first. Grand Trunk Western Ry. Co. v. Thrift Co., 68 Ind.App. 198, 116 N.E. 756, 759. Added to, together with, joined with, Business Men's Building & Loan Ass'n v. Tumulty, 13 N.J.Misc. 638, 180 A. 772. As well as. Porter v. Moores, 4 Heisk., Tenn., 16. Including. Finch v. Hunter, 148 Ark. 482, 230 S. W. 553, 554. "And also," Carter v. Keesling, 130 Va. 655, 108 S.E. 708, 713. Sometimes construed as "or." Land & Lake Ass'n v. Conklin, 182 App. Div. 546, 170 N.Y.S. 427, 428.

It expresses a general relation or connection, a participation or accompaniment in sequence, having no inherent meaning standing alone but deriving force from what comes before and after. In its conjunctive sense the word is used to conjoin words, clauses, or sentences, expressing the relation of addition or connection, and signifying that something is to follow in addition to that which proceeds and its use implies that the connected elements must be grammatically co-ordinate, as where the elements preceding and succeeding the use of the words refer to the same subject matter. While it is said that there is no exact synonym of the word in English, it has been defined to mean "along with", "also", "and also", "as well as", "besides", "together with". Oliver v. Oliver, 286 Ky. 6, 149 S.W.2d 540, 542.

When expression "and/or" is used, that word may be taken as will best effect the purpose of the parties as gathered from the contract taken as a whole, or, in other words, as will best accord with the equity of the situation. Bobrow v. U. S. Casualty Co., 231 App.Div. 91, 246 N.Y.S. 363, 367.

The symbol "&c" indicates things of like character, with the things enumerated just before it. Fleck v. Harmstad, 304 Pa. 302, 155 A. 875, 878, 77 A.L.R. 874. It has been recognized as "sanctioned by age and good use." Brown v. State, 16 Tex.App. 245. And was constantly used by Lord Coke without a suggestion from any quarter that it is not English; Berry v. Osborn, 28 N.H. 279.

ANDROCHIA. In old English law, a dairy-woman. Fleta, lib. 2, c. 87.

ANDROGYNUS. A hermaphrodite.

ANDROLEPSY. The taking by one nation of the citizens or subjects of another, in order to compel the latter to do justice to the former. Wolffius, § 1164; Moll. de Jure Mar. 26.

ANDROMANIA. Nymphomania. 44 C.J.S. Insane Persons § 2, p. 19.

ANDROPHONOMANIA. Homicidal insanity.

ANECIUS. L. Lat. Spelled also *æsnecius, enitius, æneas, eneyus,* Fr. *aisne.* The eldest-born; the first-born; senior, as contrasted with the *puis-né* (younger). Spelman.

ANEURISM, or ANEURYSM. A sac formed by the dilatation of the weakened walls of an artery, usually resulting in a soft pulsating tumor. 3 Words and Phrases, Perm. Ed.

ANEW. To try a case or issue "anew" or "de novo" implies that the case or issue has been heard before. Gaiser v. Steele, 25 Idaho, 412, 137 P. 889, 890.

ANGARIA. A term used in the Roman law to denote a forced or compulsory service exacted by the government for public purposes; as a forced rendition of labor or goods for the public service; in particular, the right of a public officer to require the service of vehicles or ships. See Dig. 50, 4, 18, 4.

In *feudal law,* any troublesome or vexatious personal service paid by the tenant or villein to his lord. Spelman.

In *maritime law,* a forced service *(onus)* imposed on a vessel for public purposes; an impressment of a vessel. Locc. de Jure Mar. lib. 1, c. 5, §§ 1–6. See Angary, Right Of.

ANGARY, RIGHT OF. In international law, formerly the right *(jus angariæ)* claimed by a belligerent to seize merchant vessels in the harbors of the belligerent and to compel them, on payment of freight, to transport troops and supplies to a designated port. 2 Opp. 446.

At the present day, the right of a belligerent to appropriate, either for use, or for destruction in case of necessity, neutral property temporarily located in his own territory or in that of the other belligerent. The property may be of any description whatever, provided the appropriation of it be for military or naval purposes.

ANGEL. An ancient English coin, of the value of ten shillings sterling. Jacob.

ANGER. A strong passion of the mind excited by real or supposed injuries; not synonymous with "heat of passion," "malice," or "rage or resentment," because these are all terms of wider import and may include anger as an element or as an incipient stage. Hoffman v. State, 97 Wis. 571, 73 N.W. 51.

ANGILD. In Saxon law, the single value of a man or other thing; a single weregild *(q. v.)*; the compensation of a thing according to its single value or estimation. Spelman. The double gild or compensation was called *"twigild,"* the triple, *"trigild,"* etc. Id. See Angylde.

When a crime was committed, before the Conquest, the angild was the money compensation that the person who had been wronged was entitled to receive. Maitl. Domesday Book & Beyond 274.

ANGINA PECTORIS. Violent paroxysm of pain arising frequently from some disease of the coronary arteries, and is manifestation of disease rather than recognized disease in itself. Foster v. Borough of State College, 124 Pa.Super. 492, 189 A. 786, 789.

ANGLESCHERIA. In old English law, Englishery; the fact of being an Englishman.

ANGLIÆ JURA IN OMNI CASU LIBERTATIS DANT FAVOREM. The laws of England in every case of liberty are favorable, (favor liberty in all cases.) Fortes. c. 42.

ANGLICE. In English, a term formerly used in pleading when a thing is described both in Latin and English, inserted immediately after the Latin and as an introduction of the English translation.

ANGLING. Derived from noun "angle," meaning a fishhook; tackle for catching fish, consisting of a line, hook, and bait, with or without a rod. Catching fish by rod, line and hook, or by line and hook. State v. Mears, 213 Ind. 257, 12 N.E.2d 343, 344.

ANGLO-INDIAN. An Englishman domiciled in the Indian territory of the British crown.

ANGORA GOAT. A more or less degenerate goat, known as the "Cape Angora," produced by breeding the original Angora with the Cape Colony goat, whose hair is shown to be dealt in, used, and known as mohair, is an "Angora goat" within the meaning of that expression in Schedule K, par. 305, Tariff Act of 1913. U. S. v. Beadenkopf Co., 8 Ct.Cust.App. 283, 284.

ANGUISH. Extreme pain of body or mind; excruciating distress. Carson v. Thompson, Mo. App., 161 S.W.2d 995, 1000. Agony, but, as used in law, particularly mental suffering or distress of great intensity. Cook v. Railway Co., 19 Mo.App. 334. It is not synonymous with inconvenience, annoyance, or harassment. Western Union Telegraph Co. v. Stewart, 16 Ala.App. 502, 79 So. 200, 201.

ANGYLDE. In Saxon law, the rate fixed by law at which certain injuries to person or property were to be paid for; in injuries to the person, it seems to be equivalent to the "were," *i. e.*, the price at which every man was valued. It seems also to have been the fixed price at which cattle and other goods were received as currency, and to have been much higher than the market price, or *ceapgild.* Wharton. See Angild.

ANHLOTE. In old English law, a single tribute or tax, paid according to the custom of the country as scot and lot.

ANIENS, or ANIENT. Null, void, of no force or effect. Fitzh.Nat.Brev. 214. See Anniented.

ANIMAL. Any animate being which is endowed with the power of voluntary motion. An animate being, not human. Bernardine v. City of New York, 182 Misc. 609, 44 N.Y.S.2d 881, 883.

Domestic animals are tame as distinguished from wild; living in or near the habitations of man or by habit or special training in association with man. Thurston v. Carter, 112 Me. 361, 92 A. 295, L.R.A.1915C, 359.

Domitæ are those which have been tamed by man; domestic.

Feræ naturæ are those which still retain their wild nature.

Mansuetæ naturæ are those gentle or tame by nature, such as sheep and cows.

ANIMALS OF A BASE NATURE. Animals in which a right of property may be acquired by reclaiming them from wildness, but which, at common law, by reason of their base nature, are not regarded as possible subjects of a larceny. 3 Inst. 109; 1 Hale, P.C. 511, 512.

Some animals which are now usually tamed come within this class, as dogs and cats; and others which, though wild by nature and often reclaimed by art and industry, clearly fall within the same rule, as bears, foxes, apes, monkeys, ferrets, and the like; 1 Hawk.Pl.Cr. 33, § 36; 4 Bla.Com. 236; 2 East, Pl.Cr. 614. See 1 Wms.Saund. 84, note 2.

ANIMALIA FERA, SI FACTA SINT MANSUETA ET EX CONSUETUDINE EUNT ET REDEUNT, VOLANT ET REVOLANT, UT CERVI, CYGNI, ETC., EO USQUE NOSTRA SUNT, ET ITA INTELLIGUNTUR QUAMDIU HABUERUNT ANIMUM REVERTENDI. Wild animals, if they be made tame, and are accustomed to go out and return, fly away and fly back, as stags, swans, etc., are considered to belong to us so long as they have the intention of returning to us. 7 Coke, 16.

ANIMO. Lat. With intention, disposition, design, will. *Quo animo*, with what intention. *Animo cancellandi*, with intention to cancel. 1 Pow.Dev. 603. *Furandi*, with intention to steal. 4 Bl.Comm. 230; 1 Kent, Comm. 183. *Lucrandi*, with intention to gain or profit. 3 Kent, Comm. 357. *Manendi*, with intention to remain. 1 Kent, Comm. 76. *Morandi,* with intention to stay, or delay. *Republicandi,* with intention to republish. 1 Pow.Dev. 609. *Revertendi,* with intention to return. 2 Bl. Comm. 392. *Revocandi,* with intention to revoke. 1 Pow.Dev. 595. *Testandi,* with intention to make a will. See Animus and the titles which follow it.

ANIMO ET CORPORE. By the mind, and by the body; by the intention and by the physical act. Dig. 50, 17, 153; Id. 41, 2, 3, 1; Fleta, lib. 5, c. 5, §§ 9, 10

ANIMO FELONICO. With felonious intent. Hob. 134.

ANIMUS. Lat. Mind; intention; disposition; design; will. *Animo (q. v.),* with the intention or design. These terms are derived from the civil law.

ANIMUS AD SE OMNE JUS DUCIT. It is to the intention that all law applies. Law always regards the intention.

ANIMUS CANCELLANDI. The intention of destroying or canceling, (applied to wills).

ANIMUS CAPIENDI. The intention to take or capture. 4 C.Rob.Adm. 126, 155.

ANIMUS DEDICANDI. The intention of donating or dedicating.

ANIMUS DEFAMANDI. The intention of defaming. The phrase expresses the malicious intent which is essential in every case of verbal injury to render it the subject of an action for libel or slander.

ANIMUS DERELINQUENDI. The intention of abandoning. 4 C.Rob.Adm. 216. Rhodes v. Whitehead, 27 Tex. 304, 84 Am.Dec. 631.

ANIMUS DIFFERENDI. The intention of obtaining delay.

ANIMUS DONANDI. The intention of giving. Expressive of the intent to give which is necessary to constitute a gift.

ANIMUS ET FACTUM. To constitute a change of domicile, there must be an "animus et factum"; the "factum" being a transfer of the bodily presence, and the "animus" the intention of residing permanently or for indefinite period. Hayward v. Hayward, 65 Ind.App. 440, 115 N.E. 966, 970. See Animus Manendi.

ANIMUS ET FACTUS. Intention and act; will and deed. Used to denote those acts which become effective only when accompanied by a particular intention.

ANIMUS FURANDI. Intent to steal, or to feloniously deprive the owner permanently of his property. Jones v. Commonwealth, 172 Va. 615, 1 S.E. 2d 300, 301.

ANIMUS HOMINIS EST ANIMA SCRIPTI. The intention of the party is the soul of the instrument. 9 Bulst. 67; Pitm. Prin. & Sur. 26. In order to give life or effect to an instrument, it is essential to look to the intention of the individual who executed it.

ANIMUS LUCRANDI. The intention to make a gain or profit.

ANIMUS MANENDI. The intention of remaining; intention to establish a permanent residence. 1 Kent, Comm. 76. This is the point to be settled in determining the domicile or residence of a party. Id. 77. See Animus et Factum.

ANIMUS MORANDI. The intention to remain, or to delay.

ANIMUS POSSIDENDI. The intention of possessing.

ANIMUS QUO. The intent with which.

ANIMUS RECIPIENDI. The intention of receiving.

ANIMUS RECUPERANDI. The intention of recovering. Locc. de Jure Mar. lib. 2, c. 4, § 10.

ANIMUS REPUBLICANDI. The intention to republish.

ANIMUS RESTITUENDI. The intention of restoring. Fleta, lib. 3, c. 2, § 3.

ANIMUS REVERTENDI. The intention of returning.

A man retains his domicile if he leaves it *animo revertendi.* In re Miller's Estate, 3 Rawle (Pa.) 312, 24 Am.Dec. 345; 4 Bl.Comm. 225; 2 Russ.Crimes, 18; Poph. 42, 52; 4 Coke, 40. Also, a term employed in the civil law, in expressing the rule of ownership in tamed animals.

ANIMUS REVOCANDI. The intention to revoke.

ANIMUS SIGNANDI. Intention to sign instrument as and for a will. Hamlet v. Hamlet, 183 Va. 453, 32 S.E.2d 729, 732.

ANIMUS TESTANDI. Intention or serious purpose to make will. In re Kemp's Will, Del., 7 W. W.Harr. 514, 186 A. 890, 894.

ANKER. A measure containing ten gallons.

ANN. In Scotch law, half a year's stipend, over and above what is owing for the incumbency, due to a minister's relict, or child, or next of kin, after his decease. Whishaw.

ANNA. In East Indian coinage, a piece of money, the sixteenth part of a rupee.

ANNALES. Lat. Annuals; a title formerly given to the Year Books.

In old records. Yearlings; cattle of the first year. Cowell.

ANNALS. Masses said in the Romish church for the space of a year or for any other time, either for the soul of a person deceased, or for the benefit of a person living, or for both. Aylif. Parerg.

ANNALY. In Scotch law, to alienate; to convey.

ANNATES. In ecclesiastical law, first-fruits paid out of spiritual benefices to the Pope, so called because the value of one year's profit was taken as their rate.

ANNEX. Derived from the Latin "annectere," meaning to tie or bind to. To attach, and often, specifically, to subjoin. In re Annexation to City of Easton of Tract of Land in Williams Tp., Northampton County, 139 Pa.Super. 146, 11 A.2d 662, 664. To add to; to unite. The word expresses the idea of joining a smaller or subordinate thing with another, larger, or of higher importance. Waterbury Lumber & Coal Co. v. Asterchinsky, 87 Conn. 316, 87 A. 739, 740, Ann.Cas. 1916B, 613. To consolidate, as school districts. Evans v. Hurlburt, 117 Or. 274, 243 P. 553, 554. To make an integral part of something larger.

It implies physical connection or physically joined to, yet physical connection may be dispensed with, and things may be annexed without being in actual contact, when reasonably practicable. Elliott Common School Dist. No. 48 v. County Board of School Trustees, Tex.Civ.App., 76 S.W.2d 786, 789.

In the law relating to *fixtures*, the expression "annexed to the freehold" means fastened to or connected with it; mere juxtaposition, or the laying of an object, however heavy, on the freehold, does not amount to annexation. Merritt v. Judd, 14 Cal. 64.

ANNEXATION. The act of attaching, adding, joining, or uniting one thing to another; generally spoken of the connection of a smaller or subordinate thing with a larger or principal thing.

The attaching an illustrative or auxiliary document to a deposition, pleading, deed, etc., is called "annexing" it. So the incorporation of newly-acquired territory into the national domain, as an integral part thereof, is called "annexation," as in the case of the addition of Texas to the United States.

In the law relating to *fixtures*: *Actual annexation* includes every movement by which a chattel can be joined or united to the freehold. *Constructive annexation* is the union of such things as have been holden parcel of the realty, but which are not actually annexed, fixed, or fastened to the freehold. Shep.Touch. 469; Amos & F. Fixt. 2.

Scotch Law

The union of lands to the crown, and declaring them inalienable. Also the appropriation of the church-lands by the crown, and the union of lands lying at a distance from the parish church to which they belong, to the church of another parish to which they are contiguous.

ANNI ET TEMPORA. Lat. Years and terms. An old title of the Year Books.

ANNI NUBILES. A woman's marriageable years. The age at which a girl becomes by law fit for marriage; the age of twelve.

ANNICULUS. A child a year old. Calvinus, Lex.

ANNICULUS TRECENTESIMO SEXAGESIMO-QUINTO DIE DICITUR, INCIPIENTE PLANE NON EXACTO DIE, QUIA ANNUM CIVILITER NON AD MOMENTA TEMPORUM SED AD DIES NUMERAMUR. We call a child a year old on the three hundred and sixty-fifth day, when the day is fairly begun but not ended, because we calculate the civil year not by moments, but by days. Dig. 50, 16, 134; Id. 132; Calvin.

ANNIENTED. Made null, abrogated, frustrated, or brought to nothing. Litt. c. 3, § 741. Cf. Aniens.

ANNIVERSARY. An annual day, in old ecclesiastical law, set apart in memory of a deceased person. Also called "year day" or "mind day." Spelman.

As applied to an insurance policy, "anniversary" means yearly recurring date of the policy, Mid-Continent Life Ins. Co. v. Skye, 113 Okl. 184, 240 P. 630, 632, or perhaps the date of the delivery thereof, Jefferson Standard Life Ins. Co. v. Baker, Tex.Civ.App., 260 S.W. 223, 225.

ANNO DOMINI. In the year of the Lord. Commonly abbreviated A. D. The computation of time, according to the Christian era, dates from the birth of Christ.

ANNONA. Barley; corn; grain; food; a yearly contribution of food, of various kinds, for support.

Annona porcum, acorns; *annona frumentum hordeo admixtum*, corn and barley mixed; *annona panis*, bread without reference to the amount. Du Cange; Spelman, Gloss.; Cowell.

The term is used in the old English law, and also in the civil law quite generally, to denote anything contributed by one person towards the support of another.

ANNONÆ CIVILES. A species of yearly rents issuing out of certain lands, and payable to certain monasteries.

ANNOTATIO. In the civil law, the sign-manual of the emperor; a rescript of the emperor, signed with his own hand. It is distinguished both from a rescript and pragmatic sanction, in Cod. 4, 59, 1.

ANNOTATION. A remark, note, or commentary on some passage of a book, intended to illustrate its meaning. Webster.

In the *civil law*, an imperial rescript (see Rescript) signed by the emperor. The answers of the prince to questions put to him by private persons respecting some doubtful point of law. Also summoning an absentee. Dig. 1, 5. And the designation of a place of deportation. Dig. 32, 1, 3.

ANNOUNCED. A decision is "announced," preventing nonsuit, when court's conclusion on issue tried is made known from bench or by any publication, oral or written, even if judgment has not been rendered. Ex parte Alabama Marble Co., 216 Ala. 272, 113 So. 240, 242.

ANNOYANCE. Discomfort; vexation. Not synonymous with anguish, inconvenience, or harassment. Western Union Telegraph Co. v. Stewart, 16 Ala.App. 502, 79 So. 200, 201. "Annoyance and inconvenience" relate as much to physical as to mental conditions. Chicago, I. & L. Ry. Co. v. Ader, 184 Ind. 235, 110 N.E. 67, 69. It includes feeling of imposition and oppression Alabama Water Service Co. v. Wakefield, 231 Ala. 112, 163 So. 626.

ANNUA NEC DEBITUM JUDEX NON SEPARAT IPSUM. A judge (or court) does not divide annuities nor debt. 8 Coke, 52; 1 Salk. 36, 65. Debt and annuity cannot be divided or apportioned by a court.

ANNUA PENSIONE. An ancient writ to provide the king's chaplain, if he had no preferment, with a pension. Reg.Orig. 165, 307.

ANNUAL. Of or pertaining to year; returning every year; coming or happening yearly. Payne v. Gypsy Oil Co., 129 Okl. 18, 263 P. 138, 140. Occurring or recurring once in each year; continuing for the period of a year; accruing within the space of a year; relating to or covering the events or affairs of a year. State v. McCullough, 3 Nev. 224. Once a year, without signifying what time in year. Rolerson v. Standard Life Ins. Co., Tex.Civ.App., 244 S.W. 845, 846.

ANNUAL AMOUNT. The annual amount of contribution at the rate at which deceased was contributing to support of partial dependents, at the time of his injury, regardless of whether that rate had existed for a year or more or for less than a year. Spreckles Sugar Co. v. Industrial Acc. Commission, 186 Cal. 256, 199 P. 8.

ANNUAL ASSAY. An annual trial of the gold and silver coins of the United States, to ascertain whether the standard fineness and weight of the coinage is maintained. See Rev.St.U.S. § 3547 (31 U.S.C.A. § 363).

ANNUAL AVERAGE EARNINGS. Include both the earnings from a seasonal occupation and also the actual earnings for the remainder of the year from whatever occupation they may have been received, provided the nonseasonal income is limited to employments of the same class and is measured by the wages of the injured employee, or those similarly employed, as the facts may require, whenever the feature of nonseasonal employment is involved Dicaro v. Fitzgibbon, 249 App.Div. 38, 291 N.Y.S. 764, 767.

ANNUAL DEPRECIATION. The annual loss, not restored by current maintenance, which is due to all the factors causing the ultimate retirement of the property. These factors embrace wear and tear, decay, inadequacy, and obsolescence. The annual loss in service value not restored by current maintenance and incurred in connection with the consumption or prospective retirement of property in the course of service from causes known to be in current operation, and whose effect can be forecast with a reasonable approach to accuracy. State v. Hampton Water Works Co., 91 N.H. 278, 18 A.2d 765, 770.

ANNUAL PENSION. In Scotch law, a yearly profit or rent.

ANNUAL RENT. In Scotch law, yearly interest on a loan of money.

ANNUAL SALARY. Does not refer to salary by calendar years, but by the years of incumbent's term, according to time of year when term commences, and salary must be calculated for year as a whole. State ex rel. Harvey v. Linville, 318 Mo. 698, 300 S.W. 1066, 1067.

ANNUAL VALUE. The net yearly income derivable from a given piece of property; its fair rental value for one year, deducting costs and expenses; the value of its use for a year.

ANNUALLY. In annual order or succession; yearly, every year, year by year. Upham v. Shattuck, 151 Kan. 966, 101 P.2d 901, 903. At end of each and every year during a period of time. Patterson v. McNeeley, 16 Ohio St. 348. Imposed once a year, computed by the year. People ex rel. Mutual Trust Co. v. Westchester County v. Miller, 177 N.Y. 51, 69 N.E. 124, 125.

ANNUITANT. The recipient of an annuity; one who is entitled to an annuity.

ANNUITIES OF TIENDS. In Scotch law, annuities of tithes; 10*s*. out of the boll of tiend wheat, 8*s*. out of the boll of beer, less out of the boll of rye, oats, and peas, allowed to the crown yearly of the tiends not paid to the bishops, or set apart for other pious uses.

ANNUITY. A yearly payment of money for life or years. State ex rel. Chamberlain v. Johnstone, 65 N.D. 727, 262 N.W. 193. Or in fee, and chargeable only on the person of the grantor. Co.Litt. 144*b*. A fixed sum, granted or bequeathed, payable periodically but not necessarily annually. Wilkin v. Board of Com'rs of Oklahoma County, 77 Okl. 88, 186 P. 474, 475; Fate v. Fate, 295 Ill. App. 271, 14 N.E.2d 890, 892. A legacy payable by installments. In re Beach's Estate, 203 N.Y.S. 492, 494, 122 Misc.Rep. 261. Also, the right to receive such periodical amount. Daniel v. Life Ins. Co. of Virginia, Tex.Civ.App., 102 S.W.2d 256, 259.

It is distinguished from an "income," in that the latter is interest or profits to be earned. Grand Rapids Trust Co. v. Herbst, 220 Mich. 321, 190 N.W. 250, 252. Too, it is chargeable on the person merely, and so far personalty; while a rent-charge is something reserved out of realty, or fixed as a burden upon an estate in land. 2 Bl.Comm. 40; Rolle, Abr. 226; Horton v. Cook, 10 Watts (Pa.) 127, 36 Am.Dec. 151.

The contract of *annuity* is that by which one party delivers to another a sum of money, and agrees not to reclaim it so long as the receiver pays the rent agreed upon. This annuity may be either perpetual or for life. See Succession of Vidalat, 155 La. 1005, 99 So. 801, 802.

The name of an action, now disused, (L. Lat. *breve de annuo redditu,*) which lay for the recovery of an annuity. Reg.Orig. 158*b;* Bract. fol. 203*b*; 1 Tidd, Pr. 3.

ANNUITY POLICY. An insurance policy providing for monthly payments to insured to begin at fixed date and continue through insured's life. Hamilton v. Penn Mut. Life Ins. Co., 196 Miss. 345, 17 So.2d 278, 280.

ANNUITY-TAX. An impost levied annually in Scotland for the maintenance of the ministers of religion.

ANNUL. To reduce to nothing; annihilate; obliterate; to make void or of no effect; to nullify; to abolish; to do away with. Ex parte Mitchell, 123 W.Va. 283, 14 S.E.2d 771, 774. To cancel; destroy; abrogate. To annul a judgment or judicial proceeding is to deprive it of all force and operation, either *ab initio* or prospectively as to future transactions. In re Morrow's Estate, 204 Pa. 484, 54 A. 342.

It is not a technical word and there is nothing which prevents the idea from being expressed in equivalent words; Woodson v. Skinner, 22 Mo. 24.

ANNULMENT. Act of annulling; act of making void retrospectively as well as prospectively. Deihl v. Jones, 170 Tenn. 217, 94 S.W.2d 47, 48.

Action for divorce is distinguished from one for annulment, in that "divorce action" is predicated on valid marriage and decree terminates relationship from date thereof, while "annulment" destroys existence of void or voidable marriage and everything appertaining thereto from the beginning. Wigder v. Wigder, 14 N.J.Misc. 880, 188 A. 235, 236.

ANNULUS. Lat. In old English law, a ring; the ring of a door. *Per haspam vel annulum hostii exterioris;* by the hasp or ring of the outer door. Fleta, lib. 3, c. 15, § 5.

ANNULUS ET BACULUS. (Lat. ring and staff.) The investiture of a bishop was *per annulum et baculum,* by the prince's delivering to the prelate a ring and pastoral staff, or crozier. 1 Bl.Comm. 378; Spelman.

ANNUM, DIEM, ET VASTUM. See Year, Day, and Waste.

ANNUS. Lat. In civil and old English law, a year; the period of three hundred and sixty-five days. Dig. 40, 7, 4, 5; Calvin.; Bract. fol. 359*b*.

ANNUS DELIBERANDI. In Scotch law, a year of deliberating; a year to deliberate. The year allowed by law to the heir to deliberate whether he will enter and represent his ancestor. It commences on the death of the ancestor, unless in the case of a posthumous heir, when the year runs from his birth. Bell.

ANNUS, DIES, ET VASTUM. In old English law, year, day, and waste. See Year, Day, and Waste.

ANNUS EST MORA MOTUS QUO SUUM PLANETA PERVOLVAT CIRCULUM. A year is the duration of the motion by which a planet revolves through its orbit. Dig. 40, 7, 4, 5; Calvin.; Bract. 359*b*.

ANNUS ET DIES. A year and a day.

ANNUS INCEPTUS PRO COMPLETO HABETUR. A year begun is held as completed. Tray. Lat.Max. 45.

ANNUS LUCTUS. The year of mourning. It was a rule among the Romans, and also the Danes and Saxons, that widows should not marry *infra annum luctûs,* (within the year of mourning.) Cod. 5, 9, 2; 1 Bl.Comm. 457.

ANNUS UTILIS. A year made up of available or serviceable days. Brissonius; Calvin. In the plural, *anni utiles* signifies the years during which a right can be exercised or a prescription grow. In prescription, the period of incapacity of a minor, etc., was not counted; it was no part of the *anni utiles.*

ANNUUS REDITUS. A yearly rent; annuity. 2 Bl.Comm. 41; Reg.Orig. 158*b*.

ANOMALOUS. Deviating from common rule; irregular; exceptional; abnormal. Palmer v. Palmer, Woolf & Gray, 183 La. 458, 164 So. 245, 247. Unusual; not conforming to rule, method, or type.

ANOMALOUS INDORSER. A stranger to a note, who indorses it after its execution and delivery but before maturity, and before it has been indorsed by the payee. Buck v. Hutchins, 45 Minn. 270, 47 N.W. 808.

ANOMALOUS PLEA. One which is partly affirmative and partly negative. Baldwin v. Elizabeth, 42 N.J.Eq. 11, 6 A. 275; Potts v. Potts, N.J.Ch., 42 A. 1055.

ANON., AN., A. Abbreviations for anonymous.

ANONYMOUS. Nameless; wanting a name or names. A publication, withholding the name of the author, is said to be anonymous. An anonymous letter is one that has no name signed. Belk v. State, 102 Tex.Cr.R. 561, 278 S.W. 842.

Cases are sometimes reported anonymously, *i. e.,* without giving the names of the parties. Abbreviated to *"Anon."*

An anonymous society in the Mexican code is one which has no firm name and is designated by the particular designation of the object of the undertaking.

ANOTHER. Additional. Harelson v. South San Joaquin Irr. Dist., 20 Cal.App. 324, 128 P. 1010, 1011. Distinct or different. Hammell v. State, 198 Ind. 45, 152 N.E. 161, 163; Ex parte Lyman, D.C.Wash., 202 F. 303, 304.

ANOTHER ACTION PENDING. See Auter Action Pendant.

ANOYSANCE. Annoyance; nuisance. Cowell; Kelham.

ANSEL, ANSUL, or AUNCEL. In old English law, an ancient mode of weighing by hanging scales or hooks at either end of a beam or staff, which, being lifted with one's finger or hand by the middle, showed the equality or difference between the weight at one end and the thing weighed at the other. Termes de la Ley, 66.

ANSWER. As a verb, the word denotes an assumption of liability, as to "answer" for the debt or default of another.

Pleading

Strictly speaking, it is a pleading by which defendant in suit at law endeavors to resist the plaintiff's demand by an allegation of facts, either denying allegations of plaintiff's complaint or confessing them and alleging new matter in avoidance, which defendant alleges should prevent recovery on facts alleged by plaintiff. In re Herle's Will, 173 Misc. 879, 19 N.Y.S.2d 263, 265.

In chancery pleading, the term denotes a defense in writing, made by a defendant to the allegations contained in a bill or information filed by the plaintiff against him.

In pleading, under the Codes of Civil Procedure, the answer is the formal written statement made by a defendant setting forth the grounds of his defense; corresponding to what, in actions under the common-law practice is called the "plea." But as used in a statute providing that defendant must appear and answer the petition, "answer" refers to any sort of pleading filed by defendant. State ex rel. Oliver Hast Auction Co. v. Grimm, 197 Mo.App. 566, 196 S.W. 1019, 1021. Cross-complaint. Celina Mut. Casualty Co. v. Baldridge, 213 Ind. 193, 12 N.E.2d 258, 260. Counterclaim. Long v. Mutual Trust Life Ins. Co., 191 Minn. 163, 253 N.W. 762. Motion to quash service of summons. Phillips v. Manufacturers Trust Co., C.C.A.Idaho, 101 F.2d 723, 727. Objections by contestants to petition for probate of will. In re Swim's Will, 258 N.Y.S. 458, 144 Misc. 206. Objections to executor's final report. Meier v. Union Trust Co. of Indianapolis, 93 Ind.App. 457, 176 N.E. 42, 51. Demurrer. Evans v. Superior Court in and for Los Angeles County, 14 Cal.App.2d 743, 59 P.2d 159, 160, contra. Mariner v. Milisich, 45 Nev. 193, 200 P. 478.

In Massachusetts, the term denotes the statement of the matter intended to be relied upon by the defendant in avoidance of the plaintiff's action, taking the place of special pleas in bar, and the general issue, except in real and mixed actions. Pub.St.Mass.1882, p. 1287.

In matrimonial suits in the (English) probate, divorce, and admiralty division, an answer is the pleading by which the respondent puts forward his defense to the petition. Browne, Div. 223.

Under the old admiralty practice in England, the defendant's first pleading was called his "answer." Williams & B.Adm.Jur. 246.

Frivolous answer. See Sham Answer, *infra*.

An *irrelevant answer* is one that has no substantial relation to the controversy;—distinguishable from a sham answer. Rosatti v. Common School Dist. No. 96 of Cass County, 53 N.D. 268, 205 N.W. 678, 679.

A *sham answer* is one sufficient on its face but so clearly false that it presents no real issue to be tried. Bank of Richards, Mo., v. Sheasgreen, 153 Minn. 363, 190 N.W. 484. One good in form, but false in fact and not pleaded in good faith. Burkhalter v. Townsend, 139 S.C. 324, 138 S.E. 34, 36. A frivolous answer, on the other hand, is one which on its face sets up no defense, although it may be true in fact.

A *voluntary answer*, in chancery, was an answer put in by a defendant, when plaintiff had filed no interrogatories which required to be answered. Hunt, Eq.

Practice

A reply to interrogatories; an affidavit in answer to interrogatories. The declaration of a fact by a witness after a question has been put, asking for it.

ANTAPOCHA. In the Roman law, a transcript or counterpart of the instrument called *"apocha"* (*q. v.*), signed by the debtor and delivered to the creditor. Calvin.

ANTE. Lat. Before. Usually employed in old pleadings as expressive of time, as *præ* (before) was of place, and *coram* (before) of person. Townsh.Pl. 22.

Occurring in a report or a text-book, it is used to refer the reader to a previous part of the book.

ANTE EXHIBITIONEM BILLÆ. Before the exhibition of the bill. Before suit begun.

ANTE-FACTUM, or ANTE-GESTUM. Done before. A Roman law term for a previous act, or thing done before.

ANTE JURAMENTUM. See Antejuramentum.

ANTE LITEM MOTAM. At time when declarant had no motive to distort truth. In re Hayden's Estate, 176 Misc. 1078, 29 N.Y.S.2d 852, 856. Before suit brought, before controversy instituted. Also, before the controversy arose. Corbett v. Hawes, 187 N.C. 653, 122 S.E. 478, 479.

ANTE MORTEM INTEREST. Interests existing only prior to, and not after, transferor's death. Cairins v. Martin, 130 N.J.Eq. 313, 22 A.2d 415, 419.

ANTE NATUS. Born before. A person born before another person or before a particular event.

The term is particularly applied to one born in a country before a revolution, change of government or dynasty, or other political event, such that the question of his rights, *status*, or allegiance will depend upon the date of his birth with reference to such event. In England, the term commonly denotes one born before the act of union with Scotland; in America, one born before the declaration of independence. Its opposite is *post natus*, one born after the event.

ANTEA. Lat. Formerly; heretofore.

ANTECEDENT. Prior in point of time. Turner v. State, 84 Tex.Cr.R. 267, 206 S.W. 689.

ANTECEDENT CREDITORS. Those whose debts are created before the debtor makes a transfer not lodged for record. Stone v. Keith, 218 Ky. 11, 290 S.W. 1042, 1043.

ANTECESSOR. An ancestor (*q. v.*).

ANTEDATE. To affix an earlier date; to date an instrument as of a time before the time it was written.

ANTEJURAMENTUM. In Saxon law, a preliminary or preparatory oath (called also *"præjuramentum,"* and *"juramentum calumniæ,"* (*q. v.*), which both the accuser and accused were required to make before any trial or purgation; the accuser swearing that he would prosecute the criminal, and the accused making oath on the very day that he was to undergo the ordeal that he was innocent of the crime with which he was charged. Whishaw.

ANTENATI. See Ante Natus.

ANTENNA. In wireless telegraphy, the wire in the air on the tall mast is called the "antenna." National Electric Signaling Co. v. Telefunken Wireless Telegraph Co. of United States, C.C.A. N.Y., 221 F. 629, 631. A wire, or a combination of wires, supported in the air for directly transmitting electric waves into space, or receiving them therefrom. Webster, Dict.

ANTENUPTIAL. Made or done before a marriage.

ANTENUPTIAL CONTRACT. A contract made before marriage. Agreement in contemplation of marriage, Hewett v. Gott, 294 P. 897, 901, 132 Kan. 168, called a marriage contract.

ANTENUPTIAL SETTLEMENTS. Contracts or agreements between a man and woman before marriage, but in contemplation and generally in consideration of marriage, whereby the property rights and interests of either the prospective husband or wife, or both of them, are determined, or where property is secured to either or both of them, or to their children. In re Carnevale's Will, 248 App.Div. 62, 289 N.Y.S. 185, 188.

ANTHRACITE COAL. "Anthracite coal" differs from bituminous coal in the amount of fixed carbon, the amount of volatile matter, color, luster, and structural character. The percentage of fixed carbon in anthracite coal is much higher and the percentage of volatile matter is much lower than in bituminous coal. Anthracite coal is hard, compact and is comparatively clean and free from dust and is commonly termed "hard coal," and burns with practically no smoke. Commonwealth v. Hudson Coal Co., 287 Pa. 64, 134 A. 413, 414.

ANTHRACNOSE. A disease of watermelons caused by parasitic fungus capable of puncturing and invading tissues of rind and sometimes of pulp within fruit. S. L. Shepard & Co. v. Agwilines, Inc., C.C.A.S.C., 130 F.2d 67, 69.

ANTHRACOSIS. A type of pneumoconiosis due to inhalation of coal dust. Allen v. Shell Petroleum Corporation, 146 Kan. 67, 68 P.2d 651, 657.

ANTHRAX. Also called splenic fever, carbuncular fever, malignant pustule, charbon, and woolsorters' disease. An acute, infectious disease of animals, especially cattle, swine, and sheep, and transmissible to human beings. Century Dict.; Bacon v. United States Mut. Acc. Ass'n, 123 N.Y. 304, 25 N.E. 399, 400, 9 L.R.A. 617.

ANTHROPOMETRY. In criminal law and medical jurisprudence. The measurement of the human body; a system of measuring the dimensions of the human body, both absolutely and in their proportion to each other, the facial, cranial, and other angles, the shape and size of the skull, etc., for purposes of comparison with corresponding measurements of other individuals, and serving for the identification of the subject in cases of doubtful or disputed identity. It was largely adopted after its introduction in France in 1883, but fell into disfavor as being costly and as liable to error. It has given place to the "finger print" system devised by Francis Galton. See Bertillon System.

ANTI MANIFESTO. A term used in international law to denote a proclamation or manifesto published by one of two belligerent powers, alleging reasons why the war is defensive on its part.

ANTI–TRUST ACTS. Federal and state statutes to protect trade and commerce from unlawful restraints and monopolies. U. S. v. Knight Co., 15 S.Ct. 249, 156 U.S. 1, 39 L.Ed. 325; U. S. v. New York Great Atlantic & Pacific Tea Co., C.C.A.Tex., 137 F.2d 459. See, also, Restraint of Trade.

Clayton Act, Oct. 15, 1914 as amended, 15 U.S.C.A. §§ 12–27, 44; 18 U.S.C.A. § 412; 28 U.S.C.A. §§ 381–383, 386–390; 29 U.S.C.A. § 52.

Sherman Anti-Trust Act, July 2, 1890, as amended, 15 U.S.C.A. §§ 1–7, 15 note.

ANTICHRESIS. In the civil law. A species of mortgage, or pledge of immovables. An agreement by which the debtor gives to the creditor the income from the property which he has pledged, in lieu of the interest on his debt. Guyot, Répert; Marquise De Portes v. Hurlbut, 44 N.J.Eq. 517, 14 A. 891. It is analogous to the Welsh mortgage of the common law. In the French law, if the income was more than the interest, the debtor was entitled to demand an account of the income, and might claim any excess.

A debtor may give as security for his debt any immovable which belongs to him, the creditor having the right to enjoy the use of it on account of the interest due, or of the capital if there is no interest due; this is called "antichresis." Civ. Code Mex. art. 1927.

By the law of Louisiana, there are two kinds of pledges,—the pawn and the antichresis. A pawn relates to movables, and the antichresis to immovables. The antichresis must be reduced to writing; and the creditor thereby acquires the right to the fruits, etc., of the immovables, deducting yearly their proceeds from the interest, in the first place, and afterwards from the principal of his debt. He is bound to pay taxes on the property, and keep it in repair, unless the contrary is agreed. The creditor does not become the proprietor of the property by failure to pay at the agreed time, and any clause to that effect is void. He can only sue the debtor, and obtain sentence for sale of the property. The possession of the property is, however, by the contract, transferred to the creditor. La.Civil Code, Arts. 3176–3181; Livingston v. Story, 11 Pet. 351, 9 L.Ed. 746.

The "antichresis" is an antiquated contract, and has been resorted to in Louisiana in but a few instances. Harang v. Ragan, 134 La. 201, 63 So. 875, 877. Essential element of contract, Conklin v. Caffall, 179 So. 434, 437, 438, 439, 189 La. 301.

ANTICIPATION. Act of doing or taking a thing before its proper time, Wilmington Trust Co. v. Wilmington Trust Co., 25 Del.Ch. 193, 15 A.2d 665, 668, 669. To do, take up, or deal with, before another; to preclude or prevent by prior action; to be before in doing, State ex rel. Todd v. Thomas, 127 Neb. 891, 257 N.W. 265, 96 A.L.R. 1470.

In conveyancing, the act of assigning, charging, or otherwise dealing with income before it becomes due.

In patent law, a person is said to have been anticipated when he patents a contrivance already known within the limits of the country granting the patent. Topliff v. Topliff, 12 S.Ct. 825, 145 U.S. 156, 36 L.Ed. 658.

An unsuccessful attempt to achieve a particular purpose is not "anticipation". Swan Carburetor Co. v. Nash Motors Co., D.C.Md., 25 F.Supp. 24, 34. The test being whether patentee has added anything of value to the sum of human knowledge, whether he has made the world's work easier, cheaper, and safer, so that return to prior art would be a retrogression. Butler v. Burch Plow Co., C.C.A.Cal., 23 F.2d 15, 24. But invention is not "anticipated" by accidental, incidental or unintentional use of some of its features, unless the benefits or ensuing results from such use are appreciated or recognized. Balaban v. Polyfoto Corporation, D.C.Del., 47 F.Supp. 472, 477, 478.

In law of negligence, "anticipation" is not confined to expectation. Kenney v. Wong Len, 81 N.H. 427, 128 A. 343, 344. But compare Hardy v. Missouri Pac. R. Co., C.C.A.Ark., 266 F. 860, 863, 36 A.L.R. 1. It means probability not possibility as applied to duty to anticipate consequences of conduct attacked as negligent. Empire Dist. Electric Co. v. Harris, C.C.A.Mo., 82 F.2d 48, 52.

ANTICIPATORY BREACH OF CONTRACT. See Breach of Contract.

ANTIGRAPHUS. In Roman law. An officer whose duty it was to take care of tax money. A comptroller.

ANTIGRAPHY. A copy or counterpart of a deed.

ANTINOMIA. In Roman law. A real or apparent contradiction or inconsistency in the laws. Merl. Répert. Conflicting laws or provisions of law; inconsistent or conflicting decisions or cases.

ANTINOMY. A term used in logic and law to denote a real or apparent inconsistency or conflict between two authorities or propositions; same as *antinomia* (*q. v.*).

ANTIQUA CUSTUMA. In English law. Ancient custom. An export duty on wool, woolfells, and leather, imposed during the reign of Edw. I. It was so called by way of distinction from an increased duty on the same articles, payable by foreign merchants, which was imposed at a later period of the same reign and was called *"custuma nova."* 1 Bl.Comm. 314.

ANTIQUA STATUTA. Also called *"Vetera Statuta."* English statutes from the time of Richard I. to Edward III. 1 Reeve, Eng.Law, 227. See Nova Statuta.

ANTIQUARE. In Roman law. To restore a former law or practice; to reject or vote against a new law; to prefer the old law. Those who voted against a proposed law wrote on their ballots the letter "A," the initial of *antiquo*, I am for the old law. Calvin.

ANTIQUUM DOMINICUM. In old English law. Ancient demesne.

ANTITHETARIUS. In old English law. A man who endeavors to discharge himself of the crime of which he is accused, by retorting the charge on the accuser. He differs from an approver in this: that the latter does not charge the accuser, but others. Jacob.

ANTRUSTIO. In early feudal law. A confidential vassal. A term applied to the followers or dependents of the ancient German chiefs, and of the kings and counts of the Franks. Burrill.

ANUELS LIVRES. L. Fr. The Year Books. Kelham.

ANY. Some; one out of many; an indefinite number. State v. Pierson, 204 Iowa 837, 216 N. W. 43, 44. One indiscriminately of whatever kind or quantity. Federal Deposit Ins. Corporation v. Winton, C.C.A.Tenn., 131 F.2d 780, 782. One or some (indefinitely). Slegel v. Slegel, 135 N.J.Eq. 5, 37 A.2d 57, 58. "Any" does not necessarily mean only one person, but may have reference to more than one or to many. Doherty v. King, Tex.Civ. App., 183 S.W.2d 1004, 1007. As a synonym for "some". Kayser v. Occidental Life Ins. Co. of California, 234 Iowa 310, 12 N.W.2d 582, 587.

It is often synonymous with "either", State v. Antonio, 3 Brev. (S.C.) 562; Carr-Lowry Lumber Co. v. Martin, 144 Miss. 106, 109 So. 849, 850. And is given the full force of "every" or "all", Glen Alden Coal Co. v. City of Scranton, 282 Pa. 45, 127 A. 307, 308; Southern Ry. Co. v. Gaston County, 200 N.C. 780, 158 S.E. 481. Its generality may be restricted by the context, Drainage Dist. No. 1 of Bates County v. Bates County, Mo.Sup., 216 S.W. 949, 953. Thus, the giving of a right to do some act "at any time" is commonly construed as meaning within a reasonable time. Paulson v. Weeks, 80 Or. 468, 157 P. 590, 592, Ann.Cas. 1918D, 741. And the words "any other" following the enumeration of particular classes are to be read as "other such like," and include only others of like kind or character. Southern Ry. Co. v. Columbia Compress Co., C.C.A.S.C., 280 F. 344, 348.

ANYTHING. Sometimes used colloquially in the sense of whatever. Pittsburgh Plate Glass Co. v. H. Neuer Glass Co., C.C.A.Ohio, 253 F. 161, 164.

AORTA. The large artery of the body, about one and a half inches in diameter, through which blood is carried away from heart to be ultimately distributed to various parts of body. It is composed of three layers, an inner coat called the "intima," a middle coat called the "media," and an outer coat called the "adventia." Woelfle v. Connecticut Mut. Life Ins. Co. of Hartford, Conn., 234 Mo.App. 135, 112 S.W.2d 865, 870.

APANAGE. In old French law. A provision of lands or feudal superiorities assigned by the kings of France for the maintenance of their younger sons. An allowance assigned to a prince of the reigning house for his proper maintenance out of the public treasury. 1 Hallam, Mid. Ages, pp. ii, 88; Wharton.

APARTMENT. A part of a house occupied by a person, while the rest is occupied by another, or others. As to the meaning of this term, see People v. St. Clair, 38 Cal. 137.

APARTMENT HOTEL. Generally understood to apply to those houses which contain nonhousekeeping apartments without a kitchen or cooking facilities, wherein the proprietor furnishes a restaurant for feeding the occupants of the different apartments. Waitt Const. Co. v. Chase, 188 N.Y. S. 589, 591, 197 App.Div. 327. A covenant prohibiting erection of an "apartment house" does not prohibit an apartment hotel containing one, two, and three room suites without kitchens or kitchenettes. Griswold Realty & Holding Corporation v. West End Avenue & Seventy-Fifth St. Corporation, 209 N.Y.S. 764, 766, 125 Misc. 30.

APARTMENT HOUSE. A building arranged in several suites of connecting rooms, each suite designed for independent housekeeping, but with certain mechanical conveniences, such as heat, light, or elevator services, in common to all families occupying the building. Konick v. Champneys, 108 Wash. 35, 183 P. 75, 77, 6 A.L.R. 459. Sometimes called a flat or flat house. Lignot v. Jaekle, 72 N.J.Eq. 233, 65 A. 221. It comes within the prohibition of a restrictive building covenant forbidding buildings designed for any purpose other than a private dwelling house. Taylor v. Lambert, 279 Pa. 514, 124 A. 169, 170. But it is not a "hotel." Satterthwait v. Gibbs, 288 Pa. 428, 135 A. 862, 864. A house for two families has been held to be an "apartment house" within a restrictive covenant. Austin v. Richardson, Tex.Com. App., 288 S.W. 180, 181.

An "apartment house" is not a hotel, but is a building used as a dwelling for several families, each living separate and apart. Peirce v. Kelner, 304 Pa. 509, 156 A. 61, 62. It is not a number of private dwellings, built one on another, but a collection of dwellings. A place for housing a number of people grouped in families assigned to different sections in the same structure. Fox v. Sumerson, 338 Pa. 545, 13 A.2d 1, 2.

APARTMENT HOUSE HI-JACKER. One who takes possession of an insolvent or abandoned apartment house business, collects as much rent as possible in advance and pays no bills of any kind, thus seriously affecting, if not destroying, the good will of the business Thompson v. Dubois, 215 Cal. 577, 11 P.2d 862, 863.

APATISATIO. An agreement or compact. Du Cange.

APERTA BREVIA. Open, unsealed writs.

APERTUM FACTUM. An overt act.

APERTURA TESTAMENTI. In the civil law. A form of proving a will, by the witnesses acknowledging before a magistrate their having sealed it.

APEX. The summit or highest point of anything; the top; *e. g.*, in mining law, "apex of a vein." See Larkin v. Upton, 12 S.Ct. 614, 144 U.S. 19, 36 L.Ed. 330. An "apex" is all that portion of a terminal edge of a mineral vein from which the vein has extension downward in the direction of the dip. Stewart Mining Co. v. Ontario Mining Co., 35 S.Ct. 610, 614, 237 U.S. 350, 59 L.Ed. 989. Or it is the juncture of two dipping limbs of a fissure vein. Jim Butler Tonopah Mining Co. v. West End Consol. Mining Co., 38 S.Ct. 574, 576, 247 U. S. 450, 62 L.Ed. 1207.

The apex of ore vein or lode is ascent along line of its dip or outcropping, beyond which it extends no further to surface of land. Brugger v. Lee Yim, 12 Cal.App.2d 38, 55 P.2d 564, 571.

APEX JURIS. The summit of the law; a legal subtlety; a nice or cunning point of law; close technicality; a rule of law carried to an extreme point, either of severity or refinement A term used to denote a stricter application of the rules of law than is indicated by the phrase *summum jus (q. v.)*.

APEX RULE. In mining law. The mineral laws of the United States give to the locator of a mining claim on the public domain the whole of every vein the apex of which lies within his surface exterior boundaries, or within perpendicular planes drawn downward indefinitely on the planes of those boundaries; and he may follow a vein which thus apexes within his boundaries, on its dip, although it may so far depart from the perpendicular in its course downward as to extend outside the vertical side-lines of his location; but he may not go beyond his end-lines or vertical planes drawn downward therefrom. This is called the apex rule. Rev.St.U.S. § 2322 (30 U.S.C.A. § 26); Stewart Mining Co v. Ontario Mining Co., 23 Idaho, 724, 132 P. 787, 792.

APHASIA. In medical jurisprudence. Loss of the faculty or power of articulate speech; a condition in which the patient, while retaining intelligence and understanding and with the organs of speech unimpaired, is unable (in "motor aphasia") to utter articulate words, or unable to vocalize the particular word which is in his mind and which he wishes to use, or utters words different from those he believes himself to be speaking, or (in "sensory aphasia" or apraxia) is unable to understand spoken or written language. *Sensory aphasia* includes *word blindness* and *word deafness,* visual and auditory aphasia. *Motor aphasia* often includes *agraphia,* or the inability to write words of the desired meaning. The seat of the disease is in the brain, but it is not a form of insanity.

APHONIA. In medical jurisprudence. Loss of the power of articulate speech in consequence of morbid conditions of some of the vocal organs. It may be incomplete, in which case the patient can whisper. It is to be distinguished from congenital dumbness, and from temporary loss of voice through extreme hoarseness or minor affections of the vocal cords, as also from aphasia, the latter being a disease of the brain without impairment of the organs of speech.

APICES JURIS NON SUNT JURA [JUS]. Extremities, or mere subtleties of law are not rules of law [are not law]. Co.Litt. 304*b*; 10 Coke, 126; Wing.Max. 19, max. 14; Broom, Max. 188. Legal principles must not be carried to their extreme consequences, regardless of equity and good sense. Salmond, Jurispr. 639. See Apex Juris.

APICES LITIGANDI. Extremely fine points, or subtleties of litigation. Nearly equivalent to the modern phrase "sharp practice." "It is unconscionable in a defendant to take advantage of the *apices litigandi,* to turn a plaintiff around and make him pay costs when his demand is just." Per Lord Mansfield, in 3 Burr. 1243.

APNŒA. In medical jurisprudence. Want of breath; difficulty in breathing; partial or temporary suspension of respiration; specifically, such difficulty of respiration resulting from over-oxygenation of the blood, and in this distinguished from "asphyxia" (*q. v.*), which is a condition resulting from a deficiency of oxygen in the blood due to suffocation or any serious interference with normal respiration. The two terms were formerly (but improperly) used synonymously.

APOCHA (also *Apoca*). Lat. In the civil law. A writing acknowledging payments; acquittance. It differs from acceptilation in this: that acceptilation imports a complete discharge of the former obligation whether payment be made or not; *apocha,* discharge only upon payment being made. Calvin. See Antapocha.

APOCHÆ ONERATORIÆ. In old commercial law. Bills of lading.

APOCRISARIUS. In civil law. A messenger; an ambassador.

In ecclesiastical law. One who answers for another. An officer whose duty was to carry to the emperor messages relating to ecclesiastical matters, and to take back his answer to the petitioners. An officer who gave advice on questions of ecclesiastical law. An ambassador or legate of a pope or bishop. Spelman.

A messenger sent to transact ecclesiastical business and report to his superior; an officer who had charge of the treasury of a monastic edifice; an officer who took charge of opening and closing the doors. Du Cange; Spelman; Calvinus, Lex.

APOCRISARIUS CANCELLARIUS. In the civil law. An officer who took charge of the royal seal and signed royal dispatches.

Called, also, *secretarius, consiliarius* (from his giving advice); *referendarius; a consiliis* (from his acting as counsellor); *a responsis,* or *responsalis.*

APOGEAN TIDES. When moon is farthest from earth, its tide-producing power is diminished and tides at such time exhibit a decreased rise and fall, and such tides are called "apogean tides." Miller v. Bay-To-Gulf, 141 Fla. 452, 193 So. 425, 428.

APOGRAPHIA. In civil law. An examination and enumeration of things possessed; an inventory. Calvinus, Lex.

APOPLEXY. In medical jurisprudence. The failure of consciousness and suspension of voluntary motion from suspension of the functions of the cerebrum.

The group of symptoms arising from rupture of a minute artery and consequent hemorrhage into the substance of the brain or from the lodgment of a minute clot in one of the cerebral arteries.

The symptoms consist usually of sudden loss of consciousness, muscular relaxation, lividity of the face and slow stertorous respiration, lasting from a few hours to several days. Death frequently ensues. If consciousness returns, there is found paralysis of some of the voluntary muscles, very frequently of the muscles of the face, arm, and leg upon one side, giving the symptom of hemiplegia. There is usually more or less mental impairment, which presents no uniform character, but varies indefinitely.

By apoplexy is meant a break or rupture of a blood vessel in the brain, not produced by any external cause. Robinson v. Ætna Life Ins. Co., Tex.Com.App., 276 S.W. 900, 902.

APOSTACY (also spelled *Apostasy*). In English law. The total renunciation of Christianity, by embracing either a false religion or no religion at all. This offense can take place only in such as have once professed the Christian religion. 4 Bl.Comm. 43; 4 Steph.Comm. 231.

APOSTATA. In civil and old English law. An apostate; a deserter from the faith; one who has renounced the Christian faith. Cod. 1, 7; Reg.Orig. 71*b*.

APOSTATA CAPIENDO. An obsolete English writ which issued against an apostate, or one who had violated the rules of his religious order. It was addressed to the sheriff, and commanded him to deliver the defendant into the custody of the abbot or prior. Reg.Orig. 71, 267; Jacob; Wharton.

APOSTILLE, Appostille. L. Fr. An addition; a marginal note or observation. Kelham.

APOSTLES. In English admiralty practice. A term borrowed from the civil law, denoting brief dismissory letters granted to a party who appeals from an inferior to a superior court, embodying a statement of the case and a declaration that the record will be transmitted.

This term is still sometimes applied in the admiralty courts of the United States to the papers sent up or transmitted on appeals.

APOSTOLI. In civil law. Certificates of the inferior judge from whom a cause is removed, directed to the superior. Dig. 49, 6. See Apostles.

Those sent as messengers. Spelman, Gloss.

APOSTOLUS. A messenger; an ambassador, legate, or nuncio. Spelman.

APOTHECA. In the civil law. A repository; a place of deposit, as of wine, oil, books, etc. Calvin.

APOTHECARY. Any person who keeps a shop or building where medicines are compounded or prepared according to prescriptions of physicians, or where medicines are sold. Com. v. Fuller, 2 Walk. (Pa.) 550.

In England and Ireland an apothecary is a member of an inferior branch of the medical profession and is licensed by the Apothecaries Company to practice medicine as well as to sell drugs.

The term "druggist" properly means one whose occupation is to buy and sell drugs without compounding or preparing them. The term therefore has a much more limited and restricted meaning than the word "apothecary," and there is little difficulty in concluding that the term "druggist" may be applied in a technical sense to persons who buy and sell drugs. State v. Donaldson, 41 Minn. 74, 42 N. W. 781.

APP. CT. Appellate Court.

APPARATOR. A furnisher or provider. Formerly the sheriff, in England, had charge of certain county affairs and disbursements, in which capacity he was called *"apparator comitatus"* (apparator for the county), and received therefor a considerable emolument. Cowell.

APPARATUS. An outfit of tools, utensils, or instruments adapted to accomplishment of any branch of work or for performance of experiment or operation. McClintock & Irvine Co. v. Ætna Explosives Co., 260 Pa. 191, 103 A. 622, 623, Ann. Cas.1918E, 1078. A group or set of organs concerned in performance of single function. First State Bank of Perkins v. Pulliam, 112 Okl. 22, 239 P. 595, 596. A generic word of the most comprehensive significance which may mean implements and an equipment of things provided, and adapted as a means to some end. Bruce v. Sibeck, 25 Cal.App.2d 691, 78 P.2d 741, 743.

As used in statutes granting exemption from execution, etc., "apparatus" means a complex device or machine designed for the accomplishment of a special purpose; a complex instrument or appliance, mechanical or chemical, for a specific action or operation; machinery; mechanism; as a newspaper printing press, Harris v. Townley, Tex. Civ.App., 161 S.W. 5; or four pool tables, Harris v. Todd, Tex.Civ.App., 158 S.W 1189; but not a threshing outfit, Comer v. Powell, Tex.Civ.App., 189 S.W. 88, 91; nor a well-drilling rig, consisting of boiler, engine, and other parts of complicated machinery, Thresher v. McEvoy, Tex.Civ. App., 193 S.W. 159, 160. In re Willis, D.C.Tex., 292 F. 872, 873, it was said that the term "apparatus" is practically synonymous with "tools."

APPAREL. The term is said to derive from two sources, "apparel" from the Latin "ad," meaning to, and "par," meaning equal, to point out the means by which outwardly one keeps even or in line with his group or class. In re Steimes' Estate, 270 N.Y.S. 339, 150 Misc. 279 (a will case).

APPARENT. That which is obvious, evident, or manifest; what appears, or has been made manifest; appearing to the eye or mind. Walker v. John Smith, T., 199 Ala. 514, 74 So. 451, 453; In respect to facts involved in an appeal or writ of error, that which is stated in the record. An error discovered by close scrutiny of the entire evidence is not "apparent." Stewart v. McAllister, Tex.Civ.App., 209 S.W. 704, 706.

"Apparent" means "open to view," "capable of being easily understood," "evident," "seeming," rather than "true" or "real," "synonymous with," "likely," "probable," or "obvious" and as meaning primarily, "capable of being seen or easily seen," "open to view," "visible to the eye," "within sight or view," and, secondarily, "clear or manifest to the understanding," "plain," "evident," "obvious," "known," "palpable," "indubitable," while "indubitable" has been defined as meaning "certain" or "unquestionable," which is synonymous with "sure." Stevenson v. State, Del., 1 Terry 268, 8 A.2d 914, 915 (in statute requiring driver to stop after automobile accident).

The word "apparent" within rule that use of realty must be apparent to create easement by implication on severance of unity of ownership of dominant and servient tenements does not necessarily mean "visible", but means that easement's indicia, careful inspection of which by person ordinarily conversant with subject would disclose such use, must be plainly visible. Romanchuk v. Plotkin, 215 Minn. 156, 9 N.W.2d 421, 425.

APPARENT AGENCY. See Agency.

APPARENT AUTHORITY. In the law of agency, such authority as the principal knowingly permits the agent to assume, or which he holds the agent out as possessing; such authority as he appears to have by reason of the actual authority which he has; such authority as a reasonably prudent man, using diligence and discretion, in view of the principal's conduct, would naturally suppose the agent to possess. Iowa Loan & Trust Co. v. Seaman, 203 Iowa 310, 210 N.W. 937, 940; Kissell v. Pittsburgh, Ft. W. & C. Ry. Co., 194 Mo.App. 346, 188 S.W. 1118, 1121; Brager v. Levy, 122 Md. 554, 90 A. 102, 104; Atto v. Saunders, 77 N.H. 527, 93 A. 1037, 1039; Campbell Paint & Varnish Co. v. Ladd Furniture & Carpet Co., Tex.Civ.App., 83 S.W.2d 1095, 1097; Humble Oil & Refining Co. v. Wood, Tex.Civ.App., 94 S.W.2d 573, 574.

It includes the power to do whatever is usually done and necessary to be done in order to carry into effect the principal power conferred. Oliver v. United States Fidelity & Guaranty Co., 176 N.C. 598, 97 S.E. 490, 491. Such authority as a principal intentionally or by want of ordinary care causes or allows third person to believe that agent possesses. Fireman's Fund Indemnity Co. v. Longshore Beach and Country Club, Inc., 127 Conn. 493, 18 A.2d 347, 349.

It is not actual authority and may often be authority not actually possessed by agent, but is such as principal holds agent out as possessing. Northwestern Mut. Life Ins. Co. v. Steckel, 216 Iowa 1189, 250 N.W. 476; Herbert v. Langhoff, La.App., 164 So. 262, 266.

"Apparent authority" of an agent must be determined by what the principal does, rather than by acts of the agent. Grismore v. Consolidated Products Co., 232 Iowa 328, 5 N.W.2d 646, 651.

It must be traceable to the principal and cannot be established solely by acts and conduct of agent, and principal is only liable for the appearance of authority caused by him. Storms v. United Grain & Millworkers' Union, 64 Ohio App. 19, 27 N.E.2d 781, 783.

APPARENT DANGER. As used with reference to the doctrine of self-defense in homicide, means such overt actual demonstration, by conduct and acts, of a design to take life or do some great personal injury, as would make the killing apparently necessary to self-preservation. Modesett v. Emmons, Tex.Com.App., 292 S.W. 855, 856.

Under a statute providing that it shall not be a defense to an action for injuries to an employee that the dangers inherent or apparent in the employment contributed to the injury, an "apparent danger" is one the existence of which the employee has knowledge, actual or constructive. Standard Steel Car Co. v. Martinecz, 66 Ind.App. 672, 113 N.E. 244, 248.

APPARENT DEFECTS. In a thing sold, are those which can be discovered by simple inspection. Code La. art. 2497 (Civil Code, § 2521). See, also, Woolley v. Ablah, 119 Kan. 380, 240 P. 266, 269.

APPARENT EASEMENT. See Easement.

APPARENT HEIR. In English law. One whose right of inheritance is indefeasible, provided he outlive the ancestor. 2 Bl.Comm. 208. See, also, Heir Apparent. In Scotch law. He is the person to whom the succession has actually opened. He is so called until his regular entry on the lands by service or infeftment on a precept of *clare constat.*

APPARENT NECESSITY. In actions under the Alabama Homicide Act, "apparent necessity" which will justify killing in self-defense must be such as to impress a reasonable man of its presence and imminence, and must so impress defendant at the time of the fatal shot. Drummond v. Drummond, 212 Ala. 242, 102 So. 112, 114.

APPARITIO. In old practice. Appearance; an appearance. *Apparitio in judicio,* an appearance in court. Bract. fol. 344. *Post apparitionem,* after appearance. Fleta, lib. 6, c. 10, § 25.

APPARITOR. An officer or messenger employed to serve the process of the spiritual courts in England and summon offenders. Cowell.

In the civil law. An officer who waited upon a magistrate or superior officer, and executed his commands. Calvin.; Cod. 12, 53–57.

APPARLEMENT. In old English law. Resemblance; likelihood; as apparlement of war. St. 2 Rich. II. st. 1, c. 6; Cowell.

APPARURA. In old English law the apparura were furniture, implements, tackle, or apparel. *Carucarum apparura,* plow-tackle. Cowell.

APPEAL. In civil practice. The complaint to a superior court of an injustice done or error committed by an inferior one, whose judgment or decision the court above is called upon to correct or reverse.

The removal of a cause from a court of inferior to one of superior jurisdiction, for the purpose of obtaining a review and retrial. Hall v. Kincaid, 64 Ind.App. 103, 115 N.E. 361, 365. Lea County State Bank v. McCaskey Register Co., 39 N.M. 454, 49 P.2d 577, 579.

In general terms a resort to an upper court or tribunal. State ex rel. School Dist. No. 8 v. Lensman, 108 Mont. 118, 88 P.2d 63, 65. A rehearing by a superior court on both law and fact, a process of civil law origin, and the usual and appropriate mode of review for cases originating in a court of equity. Sohland v. Baker, 15 Del.Ch. 431, 141 A. 277, 283, 58 A.L.R. 693.

The word "appeal" has no absolutely fixed and definite meaning but may be used to denote the review by a court of the action of some board or administrative officer. In re Determination of Relative Rights to Use of Waters of Deschutes River, 108 P.2d 276, 281, 282, 165 Or. 435. An "appeal" is a creature of statute, not a constitutional or inherent right. Carilli v. Hersey, 303 Mass. 82, 20 N.E.2d 492, 495. It is merely a continuation of original lawsuit. Bowersock v. Missouri Valley Drainage Dist. of Holt County, 237 Mo.App. 346, 168 S.W.2d 479, 481. Patterson v. Old Dominion Trust Co., 149 Va. 597, 140 S.E. 810, 813. It has become a term of general application in law, with meaning depending on statutory provisions respecting appellate procedure. Cino v. Driscoll, 130 N.J.L. 535, 34 A.2d 6, 8.

Appeal is sometimes used to denote the nature of appellate jurisdiction, as distinguished from original jurisdiction, without any particular regard to the mode by which a cause is transmitted to a superior jurisdiction. Dorris Motor Car Co. v. Colburn, 307 Mo. 137, 270 S.W. 339, 346. "Appeal" has no conclusive meaning, and it is necessary in each instance to look to the particular act giving an appeal, to determine powers to be exercised by the appellate court. McCauley v. Imperial Woolen Co., 261 Pa. 312, 104 A. 617, 620.

The fundamental difference between an "appeal" and an action to "review" is that in the case of appeal the tribunal by which the first determination was made is not a party to the proceeding to review, while, in an action to review, the tribunal which made the determination is a party to the proceeding to review. Milwaukee County v. Industrial Commission, 228 Wis. 94, 279 N.W. 655, 657, 658.

An "appeal" in equity is a trial de novo. Simmons v. Stern, C.C.A.N.M., 9 F.2d 256, 259.

"Appeal" may also be used to denote the act of invoking another judicial forum for the trial. Newell v. Kalamazoo Circuit Judge, 215 Mich. 153, 183 N.W. 907, 908. See Appealed. As used in statutes authorizing taxpayers or parties to condemnation proceedings to appeal, the term often has its nontechnical sense meaning to "apply for" or "ask." Purcell Bank & Trust Co. of Purcell v. Byars, 66 Okl. 70, 167 P. 216, 218.

An "appeal" is a step in a judicial proceeding, and in legal contemplation there can be no appeal where there has been no decision by a judicial tribunal. Two things are essential to an appeal in its proper sense: First, the decision of a judicial tribunal, and, second, a superior court invested with authority to review the decision of the inferior tribunal. People ex rel. Nelson Bros. Storage & Furniture Co. v. Fisher, 273 Ill. 228, 25 N.E.2d 785, 787.

"Appeal" differs from trial in that it is a review on original record after that has been made in accordance with well-recognized principles of judicial procedure. Koukly v. Weber, 277 N.Y.S. 39, 154 Misc. 659.

In criminal practice. A formal accusation made by one private person against another of having committed some heinous crime. 4 Bl. Comm. 312.

Appeal was also the name given to the proceeding in English law where a person, indicted of treason or felony, and arraigned for the same, confessed the fact before plea pleaded, and *appealed,* or accused others, his accomplices in the same crime, in order to obtain his pardon. In this case he was called an "approver" or "prover," and the party appealed or accused, the "appellee." 4 Bl.Comm. 330. Appeals have been abolished by statute.

Cross Appeal

Where both parties to a judgment appeal therefrom, the appeal of each is called a "cross-appeal" as regards that of the other. 3 Steph.Comm. 581.

Legislation

The act by which a member of a legislative body who questions the correctness of a decision of the presiding officer, or "chair," procures a vote of the body upon the decision.

Old French Law

A mode of proceeding in the lords' courts, where a party was dissatisfied with the judgment of the peers, which was by accusing them of having given a false or malicious judgment, and offering to make good the charge by the duel or combat. This was called the "appeal of false judgment." Montesq. Esprit des Lois, liv. 28, c. 27.

Writ of Error Distinguished

The distinction between an appeal and a writ of error is that an appeal is a process of civil law origin, and removes a cause entirely, subjecting the facts, as well as the law, to a review and revisal; but a writ of error is of common law origin, and it removes nothing for re-examination but the law. Cunningham v. Neagle, 10 S.Ct. 658, 135 U.S. 1, 34 L.Ed. 55; Buessel v. U. S., C.C.A. Conn., 258 F. 811, 814. The present tendency is to ignore the distinction between "writ of error" and "appeal," and, when found in modern statutes, the meaning given "appeal" must be gathered from the language of the statute itself. Widgins v. Norfolk & W. Ry. Co., 142 Va. 419, 128 S.E. 516, 518.

APPEAL BOND. The bond given on taking an appeal, by which the appellant and his sureties are bound to pay damages and costs if he fails to prosecute the appeal with effect. Omaha Hotel Co. v. Kountze, 2 S.Ct. 911, 107 U.S. 378, 27 L.Ed. 609. A general purpose of appeal bonds is to discourage vexatious and frivolous appeals. State v. Coletti, 102 Kan. 523, 170 P. 995, 997. To protect those interested in the judgment. Richmond v. Williamson, 16 Wash.2d 194, 132 P.2d 1031, 1033.

The sole and only purpose of "appeal bond" is to stay issuance of execution until cause can be passed upon and disposed of by appellate court. State ex rel. Gnekow v. U. S. Fidelity & Guaranty Co., Mo.App., 150 S.W.2d 581, 584.

APPEAL IN FORMA PAUPERIS. A privilege given indigent person to prosecute an appeal, otherwise and independently allowable, without payment of fees and costs incident to such prosecution. Millslagle v. Olson, C.C.A.Neb., 130 F.2d 212, 213. See, also, In Forma Pauperis.

APPEALED. In a sense not strictly technical, this word may be used to signify the exercise by a party of the right to remove a litigation from one forum to another; as where he removes a suit involving the title to real estate from a justice's court to the common pleas. Lawrence v. Souther, 8 Metc.(Mass.) 166.

APPEAR. In practice. To be properly before a court; as a fact or matter of which it can take notice. To be in evidence; to be proved. "Making it *appear* and proving are the same thing." Freem. 53. Coming into court by a party to a suit, whether plaintiff or defendant. Madison v. State, 31 Ala.App. 602, 20 So.2d 541, 542; Bennett v. Rodgers, 205 Mo.App. 458, 225 S.W. 101. See Appearance.

Frequently used in judicial proceedings as meaning "clear to the comprehension" when applied to matters of opinion or reasoning, and "satisfactorily or legally known or made known", when used in reference to facts of evidence. Blackshear v. Liberty Mut. Ins. Co., 26 S.E.2d 793, 804, 69 Ga.App. 790. Facts "appear" when the evidence from which facts may be found is introduced, and presumptions disappear when facts appear. Christiansen v. Hilber, 282 Mich. 403, 276 N.W. 495, 497.

APPEAR OF RECORD. A substitution of trustee under deed of trust "appears of record" in the office of the chancery clerk, by being actually spread at large on the record. King v. Jones, 121 Miss. 319, 83 So. 531.

APPEARANCE. In practice. A coming into court as party to a suit, whether as plaintiff or defendant. Stephens v. Ringling, 102 S.C. 333, 86 S.E. 683, 685. The formal proceeding by which a defendant submits himself to the jurisdiction of the court. Flint v. Comly, 95 Me. 251, 49 A. 1044. The voluntary submission to a court's jurisdiction. Pacilio v. Scarpati, 300 N.Y.S. 473, 478, 165 Misc. 586; Braman v. Braman, 258 N.Y.S. 181, 186, 236 App.Div. 164.

"Appearance" is the act of appearing, coming, or being in sight, becoming visible or clear to apprehension of the mind, of being known as subject of observation or comprehension, or as a thing proved, of being obvious or manifest. Hallack & Howard Lumber Co. v. Bagly, 100 Colo. 402, 68 P.2d 442, 443.

Appearance anciently meant an actual coming into court, either in person or by attorney. Appearance may be made by the party in person or by his agent. Everett Ry., Light & Power Co. v. U. S., D.C.Wash., 236 F. 806, 808. But *in criminal cases* the personal appearance of the accused in court is often necessary.

An appearance may be either *general* or *special;* the former is a simple and unqualified or unrestricted submission to the jurisdiction of the court, the latter a submission to the jurisdiction for some specific purpose only, not for all the purposes of the suit. Louisville & N. R. Co. v. Industrial Board of Illinois, 282 Ill. 136, 118 N.E. 483, 485. A special appearance is for the purpose of testing the sufficiency of service or the jurisdiction of the court; a general appearance is made where the defendant waives defects of service and submits to the jurisdiction. State v. Huller, 23 N.M. 306, 168 P. 528, 534, 1 A.L.R. 170.

An appearance may also be either *compulsory* or *voluntary,* the former where it is compelled by process served on the party, the latter where it is entered by his own will or consent, without the service of process, though process may be outstanding. 1 Barb.Ch.Pr. 77. It is said to be *optional* when entered by a person who intervenes in the action to protect his own interests, though not joined as a party; it occurs in chancery practice, especially in England; *conditional,* when coupled with conditions as to its becoming or being taken as a general appearance; *gratis,* when made by a party to the action, but before the service of any process or legal notice to appear; *de bene esse,* when made provisionally or to remain good only upon a future contingency; or when designed to permit a party to a proceeding to refuse to submit his person to the jurisdiction of the court unless it is finally determined that he has forever waived that right. Farmers Trust Co. v. Alexander, 334 Pa. 434, 6 A.2d 262, 265; *subsequent,* when made by a defendant after an appearance has already been entered for him by the plaintiff; *corporal,* when the person is physically present in court.

An answer constitutes an "appearance." Wieser v. Richter, 247 Mich. 52, 225 N.W. 542, 543. A party who answers, consents to a continuance, goes to trial, takes an appeal, or does any other substantial act in a cause, although he has not been served with summons, is deemed to have entered his "appearance" unless he objects and preserves his protests to the jurisdiction of his person. Robinson v. Bossinger, 195 Ark. 445, 112 S.W.2d 637, 640. Acts of an attorney in prosecuting an action on behalf of his client constitute an "appearance." Pacilio v. Scarpati, 300 N.Y.S. 473, 165 Misc. 586.

Appearance by Attorney

This term and "appearance by counsel" are distinctly different, the former being the substitution of a legal agent for the personal attendance of the suitor, the latter the attendance of an advocate without whose aid neither the party attending nor his attorney in his stead could safely proceed; and an appearance by attorney does not supersede the appearance by counsel. Mercer v. Watson, 1 Watts (Pa.) 351. See In re Ford's Estate, 163 N.Y.S. 960, 98 Misc. 100.

Appearance Day

The day for appearing; that on which the parties are bound to come into court. Cruger v. McCracken (Tex.Civ.App.) 26 S.W. 282. Compare City of Decatur v. Barteau, 260 Ill. 612, 103 N.E. 601, 602.

Appearance Docket

A docket kept by the clerk of the court, in which appearances are entered, containing also a brief abstract of all the proceedings in the cause. See McAdams v. Windham, 191 Ala. 287, 68 So. 51, 52.

Notice of Appearance

A notice given by defendant to a plaintiff that he appears in the action in person or by attorney.

APPEARAND HEIR. In Scotch law. An apparent heir. See Heir Apparent.

APPELLANT. The party who takes an appeal from one court or jurisdiction to another. Used broadly or nontechnically, the term includes one who sues out a writ of error. Widgins v. Norfolk & W. Ry. Co., 142 Va. 419, 128 S.E. 516, 518.

APPELLATE. Pertaining to or having cognizance of appeals and other proceedings for the judicial review of adjudications.

Word "appellate" has a general meaning, and it has a specific meaning indicating the distinction between original jurisdiction and appellate jurisdiction. Woodruff v. Bell, 143 Kan. 110, 53 P.2d 498, 499.

APPELLATE COURT. A court having jurisdiction of appeal and review; a court to which causes are removable by appeal, *certiorari*, or error; a reviewing court, and, except in special cases where original jurisdiction is conferred, not a "trial court" or court of first instance. Sanborn v. Pacific Mut. Life Ins. Co., 42 Cal.App.2d 99, 108 P.2d 458, 461; Jackson v. Chesapeake & O. Ry. Co., 179 Va. 642, 20 S.E.2d 489, 493.

APPELLATE JURISDICTION. The power and authority to take cognizance of a cause and proceed to its determination, not in its initial stages, but only after it has been finally decided by an inferior court, *i. e.*, the power of review and determination on appeal, writ of error, certiorari, or other similar process. Jurisdiction on appeal; jurisdiction to revise or correct the proceedings in a cause already instituted and acted upon by an inferior court, or by a tribunal having the attributes of a court. Illinois Cent. R. Co. v. Dodd, 105 Miss. 23, 61 So. 743, 49 L.R.A.,N.S., 565. The term includes proceedings in error. Miami County v. City of Dayton, 92 Ohio St. 179, 110 N.E. 726, 727.

If court's jurisdiction is appellate, it has no authority to determine a question in an action originally instituted in it. Rogers v. Leahy, 296 Ky. 44, 176 S.W.2d 93, 95, 149 A. L.R. 1267.

Exercise of "appellate jurisdiction" involves power not only to correct errors in judgment under review, but to make such disposition of causes as justice may require in order that a correct principle of decision, arising since judgment appealed from, and having a bearing upon the right disposition of the cause, may be passed on by trial court, whose judgment will be vacated and cause remanded for further proceeding to that end in proper cases. Yates v. St. Johns Beach Development Co., 122 Fla. 141, 165 So. 384, 385.

APPELLATIO. Lat. An appeal.

APPELLATOR. An old law term having the same meaning as "appellant" *(q. v.)*.

In the civil law, the term was applied to the judge ad quem, or to whom an appeal was taken. Calvin.

APPELLEE. The party in a cause against whom an appeal is taken; that is, the party who has an interest adverse to setting aside or reversing the judgment. Slayton v. Horsey, 97 Tex. 341, 78 S.W. 919. Sometimes also called the "respondent."

In a nontechnical sense, "appellee" may include a defendant in writ of error. Widgins v. Norfolk & W. Ry. Co., 142 Va. 419, 128 S.E. 516, 518.

In old English law. Where a person charged with treason or felony pleaded guilty and turned approver or "king's evidence," and accused another as his accomplice in the same crime, in order to obtain his own pardon, the one so accused was called the "appellee." 4 Bl.Comm. 330.

APPELLO. Lat. In the civil law. I appeal. The form of making an appeal *apud acta*. Dig. 49, 1, 2.

APPELLOR. In old English law. A criminal who accuses his accomplices, or who challenges a jury. See Approver.

APPEND. To add or attach. American Cannel Coal Co. v. Indiana Cotton Mills, 78 Ind.App. 115, 134 N.E. 891, 893.

APPENDAGE. Something added as an accessory to or the subordinate part of another thing. American Cannel Coal Co. v. Indiana Cotton Mills, 78 Ind.App. 115, 134 N.E. 891, 893.

An "appendage" for a schoolhouse includes a well on the school premises. Schofield v. School Dist. No. 113, Labette County, 105 Kan. 343, 184 P. 480, 481, 7 A.L.R. 788. But "appendages" of a railroad do not include Liberty bonds pledged to indemnify a surety on its appeal bond, or cash which was not indispensable to enjoyment of the property nor to its operation. Jackman v. St. Louis & H. R. Co., 304 Mo. 319, 263 S.W. 230, 231.

APPENDANT. A thing annexed to or belonging to another thing and passing with it; a thing of inheritance belonging to another inheritance which is more worthy; as an advowson, common, etc., which may be appendant to a manor, common of fishing to a freehold, a seat in a church to a house, etc. It differs from appurtenance, in that appendant must ever be by prescription, *i. e.*, a personal usage for a considerable time, while an appurtenance may be created at this day; for if a grant be made to a man and his heirs, of common in such a moor for his beasts levant or couchant upon his manor, the commons are appurtenant to the manor, and the grant will pass them. Meek v. Breckenridge, 29 Ohio St. 648. See Appurtenance.

APPENDITIA. The appendages or appurtenances of an estate or house, dwelling, etc.; thus, *pent-houses* are the *appenditia domus*. Cowell.

APPENDIX. A printed volume, used on an appeal to the English house of lords or privy council, containing the documents and other evidence presented in the inferior court and referred to in the cases made by the parties for the appeal. Answering in some respects to the "paper-book" or "case" in American practice.

APPENSURA. Payment of money by weight instead of by count. Cowell.

APPERTAIN. To belong to; to have relation to; to be appurtenant to. Chattel mortgages, Ferguson v. Steen, Tex.Civ.App., 293 S.W. 318, 320; landlord and tenant, State v. Bodden, 166 Wis. 219, 164 N.W. 1009, 1011. To be used in connection with (sales contract), McVeety v. Hayes, 111 Wash. 457, 191 P. 401, 402. See, also, Appurtenance; Appurtenant.

APPERTAINING. Connected with in use or occupancy. It does not necessarily import contiguity, as does "adjoining," and is therefore not synonymous with it: Miller v. Mann, 55 Vt. 475, 479. Peculiar to (sale of goods), Herndon v. Moore, 18 S.C. 339.

APPLE CIDER VINEGAR. Vinegar made from evaporated apples by treating them with a certain percentage of water squeezed out again as apple juice. People v. Douglas Packing Co., 236 N.Y. 1, 139 N.E. 759, 760.

APPLIANCE. Refers to machinery and all instruments used in operating it, and is to be distinguished from word "materials," which includes everything of which anything is made. Things applied to or used as a means to an end. Roberts v. City of Los Angeles, 61 P.2d 323, 330, 7 Cal.2d 477. An "appliance" is a mechanical thing, a device or apparatus. One Black Mule v. State, 204 Ala. 440, 85 So. 749.

The term has been applied to a railroad track, Hines v. Kelley, Tex.Civ.App., 226 S.W. 493, 496; motor tracks in a coal mine, Jaggie v. Davis Colliery Co., 75 W.Va. 370, 84 S.E. 941; an automobile, Ross v. Tabor, 53 Cal.App. 605, 200 P. 971, 973; a telephone lineman's safety belt, Boone v. Lohr, 172 Iowa 440, 154 N.W. 591, 592; and a plank on which a painting foreman was working, Peterson v. Beck, 27 Cal.App. 571, 150 P. 788, 789; but not, however, to a station water tank, rope, or scaffold used thereon, by a painter, McFarland v. Chesapeake & O. Ry. Co., 177 Ky. 551, 197 S.W. 944, 947; nor to a moving picture machine, Balcom v. Ellintuch & Yarfitz, 179 App.Div. 548, 166 N.Y.S. 841, 842; nor the steps of a caboose, Cincinnati, N. O. & T. P. Ry. Co. v. Goldston, 163 Ky. 42, 173 S.W. 161, 162.

APPLICABLE. Fit, suitable, pertinent, or appropriate. Thomas v. City of Huntington, 80 Ind. App. 476, 141 N.E. 358, 359. Brought into actual contact with. People v. Buffalo Cold Storage Co., 185 N.Y.S. 790, 794, 113 Misc. 479.

When a constitution or court declares that the common law is in force in a particular state so far as it is *applicable*, it is meant that it must be applicable to the habits and conditions of the community, as well as in harmony with the genius, the spirit, and the objects of their institutions. Wagner v. Bissell, 3 Iowa 402.

When a constitution prohibits the enactment of local or special laws in all cases where a general law would be *applicable*, a general law should always be construed to be applicable, in this sense, where the entire people of the state have an interest in the subject. But where only a portion of the people are affected, as in locating a county-seat, it will depend upon the facts and circumstances of each particular case whether such a law would be applicable. Evans v. Job, 8 Nev. 322.

APPLICABLE LOCAL LAW. Term used to determine the persons who come within the term heirs and is the law which would be used to ascertain the heirs of the designated ancestor if he had owned the property and had died intestate. Restatement, Property, § 305e.

APPLICANT. An applicant, as for letters of administration, is one who is entitled thereto, and who files a petition asking that letters be granted. Jerauld v. Chambers, 44 Cal.App. 771, 187 P. 33.

APPLICARE. Lat. In old English law. To fasten to; to moor (a vessel). Anciently rendered, "to apply." Hale, de Jure Mar.

APPLICATIO EST VITA REGULÆ. Application is the life of a rule. 2 Bulst. 79.

APPLICATION. A putting to, placing before, preferring a request or petition to or before a person. The act of making a request for something. In re Meyer, 166 N.Y.S. 505, 100 Misc. 587. A written request to have a certain quantity of land at or near a certain specified place. Biddle v. Dougal, 5 Bin. (Pa.) 151. A petition. Scott v. Strobach, 49 Ala. 477, 489. Gardner v. Goodner Wholesale Grocery Co., 113 Tex. 423, 256 S.W. 911, 913. The use or disposition made of a thing. A bringing together, in order to ascertain some relation or establish some connection; as the *application* of a rule or principle to a case or fact.

Insurance

The preliminary request, declaration, or statement made by a party applying for an insurance policy, such as one on his life, or against fire. Whipple v. Prudential Ins. Co. of America, 222 N.Y. 30, 118 N.E. 211, 212.

An "application" is no more than proposition to insurance company and must be accepted before there can be meeting of minds required to form binding contract.

Brouster v. John Hancock Mut. Life Ins. Co., Mo.App., 171 S.W.2d 775, 777; Kronjaeger v. Travelers Ins. Co., 124 W.Va. 730, 22 S.E.2d 689, 692.

Payments

Appropriation of a payment to some particular debt; or the determination to which of several demands a general payment made by a debtor to his creditor shall be applied.

Mere uncommunicated intention or belief on part of debtor as to application of payment to creditor is not such an appropriation as constitutes "application" by him. Delaware Dredging Co. v. Tucker Stevedoring Co., C.C.A.Pa., 25 F.2d 44, 46.

Purchase Money

The disposition made of the funds received by a trustee on a sale of real estate held under the trust.

APPLY. To make a formal request or petition, usually in writing, to a court, officer, board, or company, for the granting of some favor, or of some rule or order, which is within his or their power or discretion. For example, to apply for an injunction, for a pardon, for a policy of insurance, or for a receiver. In re Bucyrus Road Machinery Co., C.C.A.Ohio, 10 F.2d 333, 334.

To use or employ for a particular purpose; to appropriate and devote to a particular use, object, demand, or subject-matter. Thus, to apply payments to the reduction of interest. Foley v. Hastings, 107 Conn. 9, 139 A. 305, 306. See Appropriate.

To put, use, or refer, as suitable or relative; to co-ordinate language with a particular subject-matter; as to apply the words of a statute to a particular state of facts.

The word "apply" is used in connection with statutes in two senses. When construing a statute, in describing the class of persons, things, or functions which are within its scope; as that the statute does not "apply" to transactions in interstate commerce. When discussing the use made of a statute, in referring to the process by which the statute is made operative; as where the jury is told to "apply" the statute of limitation if they find that the cause of action arose before a given date. Brandeis, J., dissenting in Dahnke-Walker Milling Co. v. Bondurant, 42 S.Ct. 106, 110, *n.*, 257 U.S. 282, 66 L.Ed. 239.

APPOINT. To designate, ordain, prescribe, nominate. People v. Fitzsimmons, 68 N.Y. 519; Rhodes v. City of Tacoma, 97 Wash. 341, 166 P. 647. To allot, set apart. Heisler v. Robbins, 17 Ariz. 429, 153 P. 771, 772. To fix, constitute, or ordain, prescribe, settle, also to assign authority to a particular use, task or office, allot, designated. Lambach v. Anderson, 228 Iowa 1173, 293 N.W. 505, 510.

"Appoint" is used where exclusive power and authority is given to one person, officer, or body to name persons to hold certain offices. State v. Doss, 102 W.Va. 162, 134 S.E. 749. It is usually distinguished from "elect," meaning to choose by a vote of the qualified voters of the city. State ex rel. Smith v. Bowman, 184 Mo.App. 549, 170 S.W. 700, 701. But the distinction is not invariably observed. Schaffner v. Shaw, 191 Iowa 1047, 180 N.W. 853, 854.

APPOINTEE. A person who is appointed or selected for a particular purpose; as the appointee under a power is the person who is to receive the benefit of the power.

"Appointed" and "elected" are used interchangeably. Van Cleve v. Wallace, 216 Minn. 500, 13 N.W.2d 467, 469.

APPOINTMENT. The designation of a person, by the person or persons having authority therefor, to discharge the duties of some office or trust. In re Nicholson's Estate, 104 Colo. 561, 93 P.2d 880, 884. See, also, Power of Appointment.

The exercise of a right to designate the person or persons who are to take the use of real estate. 2 Washb.Real Prop. 302; Merchants' Loan & Trust Co. v. Patterson, 308 Ill. 519, 139 N.E. 912, 919. The act of a person in directing the disposition of property, by limiting a use, or by substituting a new use for a former one, in pursuance of a power granted to him for that purpose by a preceding deed, called a "power of appointment;" also the deed or other instrument by which he so conveys. Where the power embraces several permitted objects, and the appointment is made to one or more of them, excluding others, it is called "exclusive."

Appointment may signify an appropriation of money to a specific purpose. Harris v. Clark, 3 N.Y. 93, 119, 51 Am.Dec. 352. See Illusory Appointment. It may also mean the arranging of a meeting. Spears v. State, 89 Tex.Cr.R. 459, 232 S.W. 326, 328.

Office or Public Function

The selection or designation of a person, by the person or persons having authority therefor, to fill an office or public function and discharge the duties of the same. State v. Braman, 173 Wis. 596, 181 N.W. 729, 730.

The term "appointment" is to be distinguished from "election." The former is an executive act. Election means that the person is chosen by a principle of selection in the nature of a vote, participated in by the public generally or by the entire class of persons qualified to express their choice in this manner. Mono County v. Industrial Acc. Commission, 175 Cal. 752, 167 P. 377, 378.

"Election" to office usually refers to vote of people, whereas "appointment" relates to designation by some individual or group. Board of Education of Boyle County v. McChesney, 235 Ky. 692, 32 S.W.2d 26, 27.

APPOINTOR. The person who appoints, or executes a power of appointment; as *appointee* is the person to whom or in whose favor an appointment is made. 1 Steph.Comm. 506, 507; 4 Kent, Comm. 316.

One authorized by the donor, under the statute of uses, to execute a power. 2 Bouv.Inst. n. 1923.

The appointor is the instrument of the donor of the power, and the appointee takes under the original will or instrument which creates the trust, and not from the donee of the power. Barret v. Berea College, 48 R.I. 258, 137 A. 145, 147.

APPORT. L. Fr. In old English law. Tax; tallage; tribute; imposition; payment; charge; expenses. Kelham.

APPORTION. To divide and distribute proportionally. School Dist. No. 3, Platte County, v. School Dist. No. 2, Platte County, 29 Wyo. 80, 210 P. 562.

APPORTIONMENT. The division, partition, or distribution of a subject-matter in proportionate parts. Hunt v. Callaghan, 32 Ariz. 235, 257 P. 648, 649. The division of rights or liabilities among several persons entitled or liable to them in accordance with their respective interests. Valley Nat. Bank of Phœnix v. Apache County, 57 Ariz. 459, 114 P.2d 883, 886.

Contracts

The allowance, in case of a severable contract, partially performed, of a part of the entire consideration proportioned to the degree in which the contract was carried out.

Corporate Shares

The *pro tanto* division among the subscribers of the shares allowed to be issued by the charter, where more than the limited number have been subscribed for. Haight v. Day, 1 Johns.Ch., N.Y., 18.

Incumbrances

Where several persons are interested in an estate, apportionment, as between them, is the determination of the respective amounts which they shall contribute towards the removal of the incumbrance.

Rent

The allotment of their shares in a rent to each of several parties owning it. The determination of the amount of rent to be paid when the tenancy is terminated at some period other than one of the regular intervals for the payment of rent. Gluck v. Baltimore, 81 Md. 315, 32 A. 515, 48 Am. St.Rep. 515.

Representatives

The determination upon each decennial census of the number of representatives in congress which each state shall elect, the calculation being based upon the population. See Const.U.S. art. 1, § 2; Amend. 14, § 2.

Right of Common

A division of the right of common between several persons, among whom the land to which, as an entirety, it first belonged has been divided.

Taxes

The apportionment of a tax consists in a selection of the subjects to be taxed, and in laying down the rule by which to measure the contribution which each of these subjects shall make to the tax. Barfield v. Gleason, 111 Ky. 491, 63 S.W. 964.

APPORTS EN NATURE. In French law. That which a partner brings into the partnership other than cash; for instance, securities, realty or personalty, cattle, stock, or even his personal ability and knowledge. Argl.Fr.Merc.Law, 545.

APPORTUM. In old English law. The revenue, profit, or emolument which a thing brings to the owner. Commonly applied to a corody or pension. Blount.

APPOSAL OF SHERIFFS. The charging them with money received upon their account in the exchequer. St. 22 & 23 Car. II.; Cowell.

APPOSER. An officer in the exchequer, clothed with the duty of examining the sheriffs in respect of their accounts. Usually called the "foreign apposer." Termes de la Ley. The office is now abolished.

APPOSTILLE, or APOSTILLE. In French law, an addition or annotation made in the margin of a writing. Merl. Répert.

APPRAISAL. A valuation or an estimation of value of property by two disinterested persons of suitable qualifications. Jacobs v. Schmidt, 231 Mich. 200, 203 N.W. 845, 846.

APPRAISE. In practice. To fix or set a price or value upon; to fix and state the true value of a thing, and, usually, in writing. Vincent v. German Ins. Co., 120 Iowa, 272, 94 N.W. 458. To value property at what it is worth. Tax Commission of Ohio v. Clark, 20 Ohio App. 166, 151 N.E. 780, 781.

To "appraise" money means to count. In re Hollinger's Estate, 259 Pa. 72, 102 A. 409.

APPRAISEMENT. A just and true valuation of property. A valuation set upon property under judicial or legislative authority. Cocheco Mfg. Co. v. Strafford, 51 N.H. 482. A valuation or estimation of the value of property. Littlehead v. Sheppard, 123 Okl. 29, 251 P. 60, 62.

An "arbitration" presupposes a controversy or difference to be decided, and the arbitrators proceed in a judicial way. On the other hand, an appraisal or valuation is generally a mere auxiliary feature of a contract of sale, the purpose of which is not to adjudicate a controversy but to avoid one. Thompson v. Newman, 36 Cal.App. 248, 171 P. 982, 983.

APPRAISER. A person appointed by competent authority to make an appraisement, to ascertain and state the true value of goods or real estate.

The title of "appraiser" carries with it a significance that he is to be the judge of the evidence he desires submitted to him on the question of valuation, in cases fairly treated by him. In re Gibert's Estate, 160 N.Y.S. 213, 214, 96 Misc. 401.

General Appraisers

Appraisers appointed under an act of congress to afford aid and assistance to the collectors of customs in the appraisement of imported merchandise. Gibb v. Washington, 10 Fed.Cas. 288.

Merchant Appraisers

Where the appraisement of an invoice of imported goods made by the revenue officers at the custom house is not satisfactory to the importer, persons may be selected (under this name) to make a definitive valuation; they must be merchants engaged in trade. Oelberman v. Merritt, C.C.N.Y., 19 Fed. 408; s. c., 8 Sup.Ct. 151, 123 U.S. 356, 31 L.Ed. 164.

APPRECIABLE. Capable of being estimated, weighed, judged of, or recognized by the mind; capable of being perceived or recognized by the senses; perceptible but not a synonym of substantial. Fisher v. Los Angeles Pacific Co., 21 Cal. App. 677, 132 P. 767, 769; Stodder v. Rosen Talking Mach. Co., 247 Mass. 60, 141 N.E. 569, 571.

As used in a decree enjoining operation of a cotton oil mill in such manner as to throw out lint in "appreciable" quantities, "appreciable" may be practically synonymous with unreasonable. Buckeye Cotton Oil Co. v. Ragland, C. C.A.Miss., 11 F.2d 231, 234.

APPRECIATE. To estimate justly; to set a price or value on. Holmes v. Connell's Estate, 207 Mich. 663, 175 N.W. 148, 149; Brace v. Black, 125 Ill. 33, 17 N.E. 66. When used with reference to the nature and effect of an act, "appreciate" may be synonymous with "know" or "understand." Western Indemnity Co. v. MacKechnie, Tex.Civ.App., 214 S.W. 456, 460.

APPRECIATION IN VALUE. Appreciation in the value of property has reference to the so-called unearned increment, and does not include that added value of the property made by extensions and permanent improvements. People ex rel. Adirondack Power & Light Corporation v. Public Service Commission, 193 N.Y.S. 186, 189, 200 App.Div. 268.

APPREHEND. To take hold of, whether with the mind, and so to conceive, believe, fear, dread, Trogdon v. State, 133 Ind. 1, 32 N.E. 725; or actually and bodily, and so to take a person on a criminal process; to seize; to arrest, Hogan v. Stophlet, 179 Ill. 150, 53 N.E. 604, 44 L.R.A. 809. To understand. Golden v. State, 25 Ga. 527, 531. To be conscious or sensible of. Collins v. Liddle, 67 Utah, 242, 247 P. 476, 479.

APPREHENSIO. Lat. In the civil and old English law. A taking hold of a person or thing; apprehension; the seizure or capture of a person. Calvin.

One of the varieties or subordinate forms of *occupatio*, or the mode of acquiring title to things not belonging to any one.

APPREHENSION.

In Practice

The seizure, taking, or arrest of a person on a criminal charge. The term "apprehension" is applied exclusively to criminal cases, and "arrest" to both criminal and civil cases. People v. Martin, 188 Cal. 281, 205 P. 121, 123, 21 A.L.R. 1399.

Civil Law

A physical or corporal act, *(corpus,)* on the part of one who intends to acquire possession of a thing, by which he brings himself into such a relation to the thing that he may subject it to his exclusive control; or by which he obtains the physical ability to exercise his power over the thing whenever he pleases. One of the requisites to the acquisition of judicial possession, and by which, when accompanied by intention, *(animus,)* possession is acquired. Mackeld.Rom.Law, §§ 248, 249, 250.

APPRENDRE. A fee or profit taken or received. Cowell.

APPRENTICE. A person, usually a minor, bound in due form of law to a master, to learn from him his art, trade, or business, and to serve him during the time of his apprenticeship. 1 Bl.Comm. 426. City of St. Louis v. Bender, 248 Mo. 113, 154 S.W. 88, 89, 44 L.R.A.,N.S., 1072.

APPRENTICE EN LA LEY. An ancient name for students at law, and afterwards applied to counsellors, *apprentici ad barras*, from which comes the more modern word "barrister." In some of the ancient law-writers the terms apprentice and barrister are synonymous. Co. 2d Inst. 214; Eunomus, Dial. 2, § 53, p. 155.

APPRENTICESHIP. A contract by which one person, usually a minor, called the "apprentice," is bound to another person, called the "master," to serve him during a prescribed term of years in his art, trade, or business, in consideration of being instructed by the master in such art or trade, and (commonly) of receiving his support and maintenance from the master during such term.

The term during which an apprentice is to serve.

The *status* of an apprentice; the relation subsisting between an apprentice and his master.

APPRENTICIUS AD LEGEM. An apprentice to the law; a law student; a counsellor below the degree of serjeant; a barrister. See Apprentice en la Ley.

APPRIZING. In Scotch law. A form of process by which a creditor formerly took possession of the estates of the debtor in payment of the debt due. It is now superseded by adjudications.

APPROACH. To come nearer in space. Lawrence v. Goodwill, 44 Cal.App. 440; Weber v. Greenebaum, 270 Pa. 382, 113 A. 413, 414.

Thus, an "approaching" street car is one coming near to, in point of time and place. Ruffin Coal & Transfer Co. v. Rich, 214 Ala. 622, 108 So. 600, 602.

APPROACH, RIGHT OF. In international law. The right of a ship of war, upon the high sea, to draw near to another vessel for the purpose of ascertaining the nationality of the latter. The Marianna Flora, 11 Wheat., U.S., 43, 44, 6 L.Ed. 405. Kent understood it to be equivalent to the right of visit. 1 Kent, Comm. 153. And at present the right of approach has no existence apart from the right of visit.

APPROACHES. A way, passage, or avenue by which a place or building can be approached; an access. State ex rel. Washington Toll Bridge Authority v. Yelle, 197 Wash. 110, 84 P.2d 688, 691; State v. Zangerle, 43 Ohio App. 30, 182 N.E. 644, 646.

Comprising the necessary traffic arteries and adjustment of a bridge to develop its maximum traffic capacity. State ex rel. Washington Toll Bridge Authority v. Yelle, 197 Wash. 110, 84 P.2d 688, 691, 692, 694; including embankments, grades, or structures of any sort serving as a passage or way. Starrett v. Inhabitants of Town of Thomaston, 126 Me. 205, 137 A. 67, 70. That part of the roadway which is essential to make the bridge accessible and convenient for public use. With respect to bridge or viaduct; In re Rosedale Ave. in City of New York, 162 N.Y.S. 877, 885, 175 App.Div. 864.

APPROBATE AND REPROBATE. In Scotch law. To approve and reject; to attempt to take advantage of one part, and reject the rest. Bell.

Equity suffers no person to *approbate and reprobate* the same deed. 1 Kames, Eq. 317; 1 Bell, Comm. 146. The doctrine of *approbate and reprobate* is the English doctrine of election.

APPROPRIATE. To make a thing one's own; to make a thing the subject of property; to exercise dominion over an object to the extent, and for the purpose, of making it subserve one's own proper use or pleasure. People v. Ashworth, 222 N.Y.S. 24, 27, 220 App.Div. 498. To prescribe a particular use for particular moneys; to designate or destine a fund or property for a distinct use, or for the payment of a particular demand. McKenzie Const. Co. v. City of San Antonio, Tex., 50 S.W.2d 349, 352; Jennings v. Kinsey, 308 Mo. 265, 271 S.W. 786, 787. Also used in the sense of distribute.

In this sense it may denote the act of an executor or administrator who distributes the estate of his decedent among the legatees, heirs, or others entitled, in pursuance of his duties and according to their respective rights; to take away from one to whom a chattel belongs, and to devote it to the exclusive use and benefit of him who appropriates it. Davis v. Perkins, 178 Ga. 195, 172 S.E. 562, 565; or properly used in this sense to denote the acquisition of property and a right of exclusive enjoyment in those things which before were without an owner or were *publici juris.* People v. Lammerts, 164 N.Y. 137, 58 N.E. 22.

APPROPRIATE PROCESS. A subpoena, subpoena duces tecum, or order to appear and produce books and records and testify within Internal Revenue Code providing that the Commissioner of Internal Revenue may ask the District Court by appropriate process to compel attendance, testimony or production of books, papers or other data. In re Wolrich, D.C.N.Y., 84 F.Supp. 481, 482.

APPROPRIATION. The act of appropriating or setting apart; prescribing the destination of a thing; designating the use or application of a fund. State v. Erickson, 93 Mont. 466, 19 P.2d 227, 229; McKenzie Const. Co. v. City of San Antonio, Tex.Civ.App., 50 S.W.2d 349, 352.

Public Law

The act by which the legislative department of government designates a particular fund, or sets apart a specified portion of the public revenue or of the money in the public treasury, to be applied to some general object of governmental expenditure, or to some individual purchase or expense. Blaine County Inv. Co. v. Gallet, 35 Idaho, 102, 204 P. 1066, 1067. Authority given by Legislature to proper officers to apply distinctly specified sum from designated fund out of treasury in given year for specified object or demand against state. State ex rel. Murray v. Carter, 167 Okl. 473, 30 P.2d 700, 702.

An element of the definition of "appropriation" is that the money appropriated be out of the general revenues of the state. Black and White Taxicab Co. v. Standard Oil Co., 25 Ariz. 381, 218 P. 139, 144. An "expenditure" is the expending, a laying out of money, disbursement, and is not the same as an "appropriation," the setting apart or assignment to a particular person or use. Grout v. Gates, 97 Vt. 434, 124 A. 76, 80; Suppiger v. Eniking, 60 Idaho 292, 91 P.2d 362, 364, 365.

A specific appropriation is an act of the legislature by which a named sum of money has been set apart in the treasury, and devoted to the payment of a particular demand. Stratton v. Green, 45 Cal. 149.

Appropriation of land. The act of selecting, devoting, or setting apart land for a particular use or purpose, as where land is appropriated for public buildings, military reservations, or other public uses. McSorley v. Hill, 2 Wash.St. 638, 27 Pac. 552; Jackson v. Wilcox, 2 Ill. 360. Taking of private property for public use in the exercise of the power of eminent domain. N. Ward Co. v. Board of Street Com'rs of City of Boston, 217 Mass. 381, 104 N.E. 965, 966. In this sense it may refer merely to physical occupation and contemplate payment prior thereto, in contra-distinction to "taking," referring to a legal taking and presupposing payment after damages are due. Keller v. City of Bridgeport, 101 Conn. 669, 127 A. 508, 511.

Appropriation of payments. The application of a payment to the discharge of a particular debt.

Thus, if a creditor has two distinct debts due to him from his debtor, and the latter makes a general payment on account, without specifying at the time to which debt he intends the payment to apply, it is optional for the creditor to *appropriate* (apply) the payment to either of the two debts he pleases. Gwin v. McLean, 62 Miss. 121; Martin v. Draher, 5 Watts (Pa.) 544.

Appropriation of water. An appropriation of water flowing on the public domain consists in the capture, impounding, or diversion of it from its natural course or channel and its actual application to some beneficial use private or personal to the appropriator, to the entire exclusion (or exclusion to the extent of the water appropriated) of all other persons. To constitute a valid appropriation, there must be an intent to apply the water to some beneficial use existing at the time or contemplated in the future, a diversion from the natural channel by means of a ditch or canal, or some other open physical act of taking possession of the water, and an actual application of it within a reasonable time to some useful or beneficial purpose. In re Water Rights in Silvies River, 115 Or. 27, 237 P. 322, 336; In re Manse Spring and Its Tributaries, Nye County, 60 Nev. 280, 108 P.2d 311, 314; State of Neb. v. State of Wyo., U.S.Neb. & Wyo., 65 S.Ct. 1332, 1349, 325 U.S. 589, 89 L.Ed. 1815.

It follows water to its original source whether through surface or subterranean streams or through percolation,

Justesen v. Olsen, 40 P.2d 802, 809, 86 Utah 158; and entitles appropriator to continuing right to use water to extent of appropriation, but not beyond that reasonably required and actually used. State of Arizona v. State of California, Ariz. & Cal., 56 S.Ct. 848, 852, 298 U.S. 558, 80 L.Ed. 1331.

English Ecclesiastical Law

The perpetual annexing of a benefice to some spiritual corporation either sole or aggregate, being the patron of the living. 1 Bl.Comm. 384; 3 Steph.Comm. 70-75; 1 Crabb, Real Prop. p. 144, § 129.

Where the annexation is to the use of a lay person, it is usually called an "impropriation" *(q. v.)*. 1 Crabb, Real Prop. p. 145, § 130. There have been no appropriations since the dissolution of monasteries.

APPROPRIATION BILL. A measure before a legislative body authorizing the expenditure of public moneys and stipulating the amount, manner, and purpose of the various items of expenditure. State ex rel. Finnegan v. Dammann, 220 Wis. 143, 264 N.W. 622, 624.

APPROPRIATOR. One who makes an appropriation; as, an appropriator of water. Lux v. Haggin, 69 Cal. 255, 10 Pac. 736.

English Ecclesiastical Law

A spiritual corporation entitled to the profits of a benefice.

APPROVAL. The act of confirming, ratifying, sanctioning, or consenting to some act or thing done by another. Rooney v. South Sioux City, 111 Neb. 1, 195 N.W. 474, 475. "Approval" implies knowledge and exercise of discretion after knowledge. State v. Duckett, 133 S.C. 85, 130 S.E. 340, 342; McCarten v. Sanderson, 111 Mont. 407, 109 P.2d 1108, 1112, 132 A.L.R. 1229.

The act of a judge or magistrate in sanctioning and accepting as satisfactory a bond, security, or other instrument which is required by law to pass his inspection and receive his approbation before it becomes operative.

APPROVE. To be satisfied with; to confirm, ratify, sanction, or consent to some act or thing done by another; to sanction officially; to ratify; to confirm; to pronounce good; think or judge well of; admit the propriety or excellence of; be pleased with. Western Hospital Ass'n v. Industrial Accident Board, 51 Idaho 334, 6 P.2d 845, 848; MacNeill v. Maddox, 194 Ga. 802, 22 S.E.2d 653, 654; Board of Education of City of Hutchinson v. Reno Community High School, 124 Kan. 175; 257 P. 957, 959; Tibbens v. Clayton, D.C. Okl., 288 F. 393, 394. Distinguishable from "authorize," meaning to permit a thing to be done in future. Gray v. Gill, 210 N.Y.S. 658, 660, 125 Misc. 70.

To take to one's proper and separate use. To improve; to enhance the value or profits of anything. To inclose and cultivate common or waste land.

To *approve common* or waste land is to inclose and convert it to the purposes of husbandry, which the owner might always do, provided he left common sufficient for such as were entitled to it. 3 Kent, Comm. 406.

Old Criminal Law

To accuse or prove; to accuse an accomplice by giving evidence against him.

APPROVED INDORSED NOTES. Notes indorsed by another person than the maker, for additional security, the indorser being satisfactory to the payee. Mills v. Hunt, 20 Wend., N.Y., 431.

APPROVEMENT. At ancient common law a practice of criminal prosecutions by which a person accused of treason or felony was permitted to exonerate himself by accusing others and escaping prosecution himself. Lee v. State, 115 Fla. 30, 155 So. 123; Guthrie v. Commonwealth, 171 Va. 461, 198 S.E. 481, 482, 119 A.L.R. 683.

The custom existed only in capital cases, and consisted in the accused, called "approver", being arraigned and permitted to confess before plea and appeal or accuse another as his accomplice of the same crime in order to obtain his pardon.

APPROVER. L. Fr. To approve or prove; to vouch. Kelham.

APPROVER. An accomplice in crime who accuses others of the same offense, and is admitted as a witness at the discretion of the court to give evidence against his companions in guilt. He is vulgarly called "King's Evidence."

One who confesses himself guilty of felony and accuses others of the same crime to save himself from punishment. Myers v. People, 26 Ill. 175. By the old law, if he failed to convict those he accused he was at once hung. Lee v. State, 115 Fla. 30, 155 So. 123. See, also, Antithetarius.

In old English law. Certain men sent into the several counties to increase the farms (rents) of hundreds and wapentakes, which formerly were let at a certain value to the sheriff. Cowell.

Bailiffs of lords in their franchises. Sheriffs were called the king's "approvers" in 1 Edw. III, st. 1, c. 1. Termes de la Ley, 49.

Approvers in the Marches were those who had license to sell and purchase beasts there.

APPROXIMATE. Used in the sense of an estimate merely, meaning more or less, but about and near the amount, quantity, or distance specified. Stockburger v. Brooker, 33 Ga.App. 676, 127 S.E. 663. Near to; about; a little more or less; close. Texas Employers' Ins. Ass'n v. Fitzgerald, Tex. Civ.App., 292 S.W. 925, 927. Fiesel v. Bennett, 225 Iowa 98, 280 N.W. 482, 484. "Approximately" is very nearly synonymous with "proximately," P. B. Arnold Co. v. Buchanan, 60 Ind.App. 626, 111 N.E. 204, 207; meaning very nearly, but not absolutely. Sandberg v. Margold Realty Corporation, 247 N.Y.S. 139, 141, 231 App.Div. 241.

APPROXIMATION. Equitable doctrine by which precise terms of charitable trust can be varied under certain circumstances. Heustess v. Huntingdon College, 242 Ala. 272, 5 So.2d 777, 779, 780; applicable solely to charitable trusts and employed only where on failure of trust the court finds a general charitable intent. Waterbury Trust Co. v. Porter, 131 Conn. 206, 38 A.2d 598, 603.

APPRUARE. To take to one's use or profit. Cowell.

APPULSUS. In the civil law. A driving to, as of cattle to water. Dig. 8, 3, 1, 1.

APPURTENANCE. That which belongs to something else; an adjunct; an appendage; something annexed to another thing more worthy as principal, and which passes as incident to it, as a right of way or other easement to land; an outhouse, barn, garden, or orchard, to a house or messuage. Cohen v. Whitcomb, 142 Minn. 20, 170 N.W. 851, 852; Alwes v. Richheimer, 185 Ark. 535, 47 S.W.2d 1084, 1085; Joplin Waterworks Co. v. Jasper County, 327 Mo. 964, 38 S.W.2d 1068, 1076. An article adapted to the use of the property to which it is connected, and which was intended to be a permanent accession to the freehold. Szilagy v. Taylor, 63 Ohio App. 105, 25 N.E.2d 360, 361.

An article may become an "appurtenance to realty" without physical attachment. Metropolitan Life Ins. Co. v. Jensen, 69 S.D. 225, 9 N.W.2d 140, 141.

APPURTENANT. Belonging to; accessory or incident to; adjunct, appended, or annexed to; answering to *accessorium* in the civil law. 2 Steph. Comm. 30 note. McClintic-Marshall Co. v. Ford Motor Co., 254 Mich. 305, 236 N.W. 792, 795; Being employed in leases for the purpose of including any easements or servitudes used or enjoyed with the demised premises. Riddle v. Littlefield, 53 N.H. 508, 16 Am.Rep. 388.

A thing is "appurtenant" to something else only when it stands in relation of an incident to a principal, and is necessarily connected with the use and enjoyment of the latter. Catterall v. Pulis, 137 Okl. 86, 278 P. 292, 294.

A thing is deemed to be incidental or *appurtenant* to land when it is by right used with the land for its benefit, as in the case of a way, or water-course, or of a passage for light, air, or heat from or across the land of another. Mattix v. Swepston, 127 Tenn. 693, 155 S.W. 928, 930.

Land cannot be appurtenant to land. Hurley v. Liberty Lake Co., 112 Wash. 207, 192 P. 4, 5; except in case of land under water. In re Eastern Boulevard in Borough of the Bronx, City of New York, 243 N.Y.S. 57, 61, 230 App. Div. 52.

APRAXIA. See Aphasia.

APROVECHAMIENTO. In Spanish law. Approvement, or improvement and enjoyment of public lands. As applied to pueblo lands, it has particular reference to the commons, and includes not only the actual enjoyment of them but a right to such enjoyment. Hart v. Burnett, 15 Cal. 530, 566.

APT. Fit; suitable; appropriate.

APT TIME. Apt time sometimes depends upon *lapse* of time; as, where a thing is required to be done at the first term, or within a given time, it cannot be done afterwards. But the phrase more usually refers to the *order* of proceedings, as fit or suitable. Holmes Electric Co. v. Carolina Power & Light Co., 150 S.E. 621, 623, 197 N.C. 766.

APT WORDS. Words proper to produce the legal effect for which they are intended; sound technical phrases.

APTA VIRO. Fit for a husband; marriageable; a woman who has reached marriageable years.

APUD ACTA. Among the acts; among the recorded proceedings. In the civil law, this phrase is applied to appeals taken orally, in the presence of the judge, at the time of judgment or sentence. Credit Co., Ltd., v. Arkansas Cent. Ry. Co., 9 S. Ct. 107, 108, 128 U.S. 258, 32 L.Ed. 448.

AQUA. In the civil and old English law. Water; sometimes a stream or water-course.

AQUA ÆSTIVA. In Roman law. Summer water; water that was used in summer only. Dig. 43, 20, 1, 3, 4.

AQUA CEDIT SOLO. Water follows the land. A sale of land will pass the water which covers it. 2 Bl.Comm. 18; Co.Litt. 4.

AQUA CURRENS. Running water.

AQUA CURRIT ET DEBET CURRERE, UT CURRERE SOLEBAT. Water runs, and ought to run, as it has used to run. A running stream should be left to flow in its natural channel, without alteration or diversion, Goble v. Louisville & N. R. Co., 187 Ga. 243, 200 S.E. 259, 261; that water is the common and equal property of every one through whose domain it flows. Elmore v. Ingalls, 17 So.2d 674, 245 Ala. 481.

AQUA DULCIS, or FRISCA. Fresh water. Reg. Orig. 97; Bract. fols. 117, 135.

AQUA FONTANEA. Spring water. Fleta, lib. 4, c. 27, § 8.

AQUA PROFLUENS. Flowing or running water. Dig. 1, 8, 2.

AQUA QUOTIDIANA. In Roman law. Daily water; water that might be drawn at all times of the year, *(qua quis quotidie possit uti, si vellet)*. Dig. 43, 20, 1–4.

AQUA SALSA. Salt water.

AQUÆ DUCTUS. In the civil law. A servitude which consists in the right to carry water by means of pipes or conduits over or through the estate of another. Dig. 8, 3, 1; Inst. 2, 3.

AQUÆ HAUSTUS. In the civil law. A servitude which consists in the right to draw water from the fountain, pool, or spring of another. Inst. 2, 3, 2; Dig. 8, 3, 1, 1.

AQUÆ IMMITTENDÆ. A civil law easement or servitude, consisting in the right of one whose house is surrounded with other buildings to cast waste water upon the adjacent roofs or yards. Similar to the common law easement of drip. Bellows v. Sackett, 15 Barb. (N.Y.) 96.

AQUAGIUM. A canal, ditch, or water course running through marshy grounds. A mark or gauge placed in or on the banks of a running stream, to indicate the height of the water, was called *"aquagaugium."* Spelman.

AQUATIC RIGHTS. Rights which individuals have to the use of the sea and rivers, for the purpose of fishing and navigation, and also to the soil in the sea and rivers.

AQUILIAN LAW. See Lex Aquilia.

ARABANT. They plowed. A term of feudal law, applied to those who held by the tenure of plowing and tilling the lord's lands within the manor. Cowell.

ARABLE LAND. That which is fit for plowing or tillage, and thus is distinguishable from swamp land, which is land that is too wet for cultivation. 6 C.J.S. p. 143; McCarter v. Sooy Oyster Co., 75 A. 211, 215, 78 N.J.Law, 394.

ARAHO. In feudal law. To make oath in the church or some other holy place. All oaths were made in the church upon the relics of saints, according to the Ripuarian laws. Cowell; Spelman.

ARALIA. Plowlands. Land fit for the plow. Denoting the character of land, rather than its condition. Spelman.

ARATOR. A plowman; a farmer of arable land.

ARATRUM TERRÆ. In old English law. A plow of land; a plowland; as much land as could be tilled with one plow (or by a single "arator" or plowman). Whishaw.

ARATURA TERRÆ. The plowing of land by the tenant, or vassal, in the service of his lord. Whishaw.

ARATURIA. Land suitable for the plow; arable land. Spelman.

ARBITER. A person chosen to decide a controversy; an arbitrator, referee. A person bound to decide according to the rules of law and equity, as distinguished from an arbitrator, who may proceed wholly at his own discretion, so that it be according to the judgment of a sound man. Cowell.

In the Roman law. A judge invested with a discretionary power. A person appointed by the prætor to examine and decide that class of causes or actions termed *"bonæ fidei,"* and who had the power of judging according to the principles of equity, *(ex æquo et bono;)* distinguished from the *judex, (q. v.,)* who was bound to decide according to strict law. Inst. 4, 6, 30, 31.

According to Mr. Abbott, the distinction is as follows: "Arbitrator" is a technical name of a person selected with reference to an established system for friendly determination of controversies, which, though not judicial, is yet regulated by law; so that the powers and duties of the arbitrator, when once he is chosen, are prescribed by law, and his doings may be judicially revised if he has exceeded his authority. "Arbiter" is an untechnical designation of a person to whom a controversy is referred, irrespective of any law to govern the decision; and is the proper word to signify a referee of a question outside of or above municipal law. But it is elsewhere said that the distinction between arbiters and arbitrators is not observed in modern law. Russ.Arb. 112.

ARBITRAGE. Transactions of bankers and mercantile houses by which stocks or bills are bought in one market and sold in another for the sake of the profit arising from a difference in price in the two markets.

ARBITRAMENT. The award or decision of arbitrators upon a matter of dispute, which has been submitted to them. Termes de la Ley.

ARBITRAMENT AND AWARD. A plea to an action brought for the same cause which had been submitted to arbitration and on which an award had been made. Wats.Arb. 256.

ARBITRAMENTUM ÆQUUM TRIBUIT CUIQUE SUUM. A just arbitration renders to every one his own. Noy, Max. 248.

ARBITRARILY. See Arbitrary.

A finding that certain orders were "arbitrarily" given by an engineer in charge of a public improvement did not amount to a finding that they were given in bad faith, fraudulently, or through ignorance or incompetency. First Savings & Trust Co. v. Milwaukee County, 158 Wis. 207, 148 N.W. 22, 33.

ARBITRARINESS. Conduct or acts based alone upon one's will, and not upon any course of reasoning and exercise of judgment. Garman v. Myers, 183 Okl. 141, 80 P.2d 624, 626.

ARBITRARY. Means in an "arbitrary" manner, as fixed or done capriciously or at pleasure; without adequate determining principle; not founded in the nature of things; nonrational; not done or acting according to reason or judgment; depending on the will alone; absolutely in power; capriciously; tyrannical; despotic; Corneil v. Swisher County, Tex.Civ.App., 78 S.W.2d 1072, 1074. Without fair, solid, and substantial cause; that is, without cause based upon the law. U. S. v. Lotempio, D.C.N.Y., 58 F.2d 358, 359; not governed by any fixed rules or standard. People ex rel. Hultman v. Gilchrist, 188 N.Y.S. 61, 65, 114 Misc. 651.

ARBITRARY GOVERNMENT. The difference between a free and an arbitrary government is that in the former limits are assigned to those to whom the administration is committed, but the latter depends on the will of the departments or some of them. Kamper v. Hawkins, 1 Va.Cas. 20, 23.

ARBITRARY POWER. Power to act according to one's own will; especially applicable to power conferred on an administrative officer, who is not furnished any adequate determining principle. Fox Film Corporation v. Trumbull, D.C.Conn., 7 F.2d 715, 727.

ARBITRARY PUNISHMENT. That punishment which is left to the decision of the judge, in distinction from those defined by statute.

ARBITRATION. The submission for determination of disputed matter to private unofficial persons selected in manner provided by law or agreement. Stockwell v. Equitable Fire & Marine Ins. Co., 25 P.2d 873, 134 Cal.App. 534. The substitution of their award or decision for judgment of a court. In re Curtis-Castle Arbitration, 64 Conn. 501, 30 A. 769, 42 Am.St.Rep. 200; Atlantic Fruit

Co. v. Red Cross Line, D.C.N.Y., 276 F. 319; Red Cross Line v. Atlantic Fruit Co., 44 S.Ct. 274, 264 U.S. 109, 68 L.Ed. 582.

Compulsory arbitration is that which occurs when the consent of one of the parties is enforced by statutory provisions. Wood v. City of Seattle, 23 Wash. 1, 62 Pac. 135, 52 L.R.A. 369.

Voluntary arbitration is by mutual and free consent of the parties.

The *submission* is an agreement by which parties agree to submit their differences to the decision of a referee or arbitrators. It is sometimes termed a reference. 3 M. & W. 816; McManus v. McCulloch, 6 Watts (Pa.) 357; Stewart v. Cass, 16 Vt. 663, 42 Am.Dec. 534; Howard v. Sexton, 4 N.Y. 157. As to "final submission," see In re Gitt, 125 N.Y.S. 369, 140 App.Div. 382. In a wide sense, "arbitration" may embrace the whole method of thus settling controversies, and include all the various steps. But in a more strict use, the term denotes only the submission and hearing, the decision being separately spoken of, and called an "award." An award is the judgment or decision of arbitrators or referees on a matter submitted to them. It is also the writing containing such judgment. Cowell; *Termes de la Ley;* Jenk. 137. See Award.

As distinguished from appraisal, an arbitration presupposes a controversy or a difference to be tried and decided. On the other hand, an appraisal or valuation is generally a mere auxiliary feature, as of a contract of sale, the purpose of which is not to adjudicate a controversy but to avoid one. Toledo S. S. Co. v. Zenith Transp. Co., 184 F. 391, 106 C.C.A. 501.

ARBITRATION CLAUSE. A clause inserted in a contract providing for compulsory arbitration in case of dispute as to rights or liabilities under it; ineffectual if it purports to oust the courts of jurisdiction entirely. See Perry v. Cobb, 88 Me. 435, 34 A. 278, 49 L.R.A. 389.

ARBITRATION OF EXCHANGE. This takes place where a merchant pays his debts in one country by a bill of exchange upon another.

The business of buying and selling exchange (bills of exchange) between two or more countries or markets, and particularly where the profits of such business are to be derived from a calculation of the relative value of exchange in the two countries or markets, and by taking advantage of the fact that the rate of exchange may be higher in the one place than in the other at the same time.

ARBITRATOR. A private, disinterested person, chosen by the parties to a disputed question, for the purpose of hearing their contention, and giving judgment between them; to whose decision (award) the litigants submit themselves either voluntarily, or, in some cases, compulsorily, by order of a court. Fudickar v. Insurance Co., 62 N.Y. 399.

"Referee" is of frequent modern use as a synonym of arbitrator, but is in its origin of broader signification and less accurate than arbitrator.

ARBITRIOS. In Spanish and Mexican law. Taxes imposed by municipalities on certain articles of merchandise, to defray the general expenses of government, in default of revenues from "propios" *(q. v.)*, i. e., lands owned by the municipality, or the income of which was legally set apart for its support. Sometimes used in a wider sense, as meaning the resources of a town, including its privileges in the royal lands as well as the taxes. Escriche Dict.; Sheldon v. Milmo, 90 Tex. 1, 36 S.W. 413.

ARBITRIUM. The decision of an arbiter, or arbitrator; an award; a judgment.

ARBITRIUM EST JUDICIUM. An award is a judgment. Jenk.Cent. 137.

ARBITRIUM EST JUDICIUM BONI VIRI, SECUNDUM ÆQUUM ET BONUM. An award is the judgment of a good man, according to justice. 3 Bulst. 64.

ARBOR. Lat. A tree; a plant; something larger than an herb; a general term including vines, osiers, and even reeds. The mast of a ship. Brissonius. Timber. Ainsworth; Calvinus, Lex.

In a technological sense, "arbor" denotes the core consisting of an iron pipe over which is spread a thin coating of damp sand and which is inserted in the mold used in casting iron pipe. Casey-Hedges Co. v. Gates, 139 Tenn. 63, 201 S.W. 760, 761, L.R.A.1918B, 184.

ARBOR CIVILIS. A genealogical tree. Coke, Inst.

ARBOR CONSANGUINITATIS. A table, formed in the shape of a tree, showing the genealogy of a family. See the *arbor civilis* of the civilians and canonists. Hale, Com.Law, 335.

ARBOR DUM CRESCIT, LIGNUM DUM CRESCERE NESCIT. [That which is] a tree while it grows, [is] wood when it ceases to grow. Cro. Jac. 166; Hob. 77*b*, in marg.

ARBOR FINALIS. In old English law. A boundary tree; a tree used for making a boundary line. Bract. fols. 167, 207*b*.

ARCA. Lat. In the civil law. A chest or coffer; a place for keeping money. Dig. 30, 30, 6; Id. 32, 64. Brissonius.

ARCANA IMPERII. State secrets. 1 Bl.Comm. 337.

ARCARIUS. In civil and old English law. A treasurer; a keeper of public money. Cod. 10, 70, 15; Spelman.

ARCHAIONOMIA. A collection of Saxon laws, published during the reign of Queen Elizabeth, in the Saxon language, with a Latin version by Lambard.

ARCHBISHOP. In English ecclesiastical law. The chief of the clergy in his province, having supreme power under the king or queen in all ecclesiastical causes. He has also his own diocese, in which he exercises episcopal jurisdiction, as in his province he exercises archiepiscopal authority. In England he is addressed as *Most Reverend.*

ARCHDEACON. A dignitary of the Anglican church who has ecclesiastical jurisdiction immediately subordinate to that of the bishop, either throughout the whole of his diocese or in some particular part of it. He is a ministerial officer; 1 Bla.Com. 383. He is addressed as *Venerable.*

ARCHDEACON'S COURT. In English ecclesiastical law. A court held before a judge appointed by the archdeacon, and called his official. Its jurisdiction comprises the granting of probates and administrations, and ecclesiastical causes in general, arising within the archdeaconry. It is the most inferior court in the whole ecclesiastical polity of England. 3 Bl.Comm. 64; 3 Steph.Comm. 430.

ARCHDEACONRY. A division of a diocese, and the circuit of an archdeacon's jurisdiction.

ARCHERY. In feudal law. A service of keeping a bow for the lord's use in the defense of his castle. Co.Litt. 157.

ARCHES COURT. In English ecclesiastical law. A court of appeal belonging to the Archbishop of Canterbury, the judge of which is called the "Dean of the Arches," because his court was anciently held in the church of Saint Mary-le-Bow, (*Sancta Maria de Arcubus,*) so named from the steeple, which is raised upon pillars built archwise. 3 Bl.Comm. 64.

The court was formerly held in the hall belonging to the College of Civilians, commonly called "Doctors' Commons." It is now held in Westminster Hall. Its proper jurisdiction is only over the thirteen peculiar parishes belonging to the archbishop in London, but, the office of Dean of the Arches having been for a long time united with that of the archbishop's principal official, the Judge of the Arches, in right of such added office, it receives and determines appeals from the sentences of all inferior ecclesiastical courts within the province.

ARCHETYPE. The original from which a copy is made.

ARCHICAPELLANUS. L. Lat. In old European law. A chief or high chancellor, (*summus cancellarius*). Spelman.

ARCHITECT. One who makes plans and specifications for a building and superintends its construction. Payne v. De Vaughn, 77 Cal.App. 399, 246 P. 1069, 1071; Stephens County v. J. N. McCammon, Inc., 122 Tex. 148, 52 S.W.2d 53; Sugarman Contracting Co. v. Phœnix Finance System, Iowa, 243 N.W. 369, 370. Also one who plans and constructs landscape work. State v. McIlhenny, 201 La. 78, 9 So.2d 467, 470.

ARCHIVES. The Rolls; any place where ancient records, charters, and evidences are kept. In libraries, the private depository. Cowell; Spelman.

The derivative meaning of the word (now the more common) denotes the writings themselves thus preserved; thus we say the archives of a college, of a monastery, a public office, etc. Texas M. Ry. Co. v. Jarvis, 69 Tex. 537, 7 S.W. 210.

ARCHIVIST. The custodian of archives.

ARCIFINIOUS. (Lat., *arcifinius* or *arcifinalis*; Fr., *arcifinie.*) Pertaining to landed estates having natural boundaries, such as woods, mountains, or rivers. The owners of such estates, unlike the owners of "agri limitati" (*q. v.*), have the right of alluvion. Smith v. St. Louis Public Schools, 30 Mo. 290, 303.

Also, having a frontier forming a natural defense. Twiss, Law of Nations, II. 215.

ARCTA ET SALVA CUSTODIA. Lat. In strict (or close) and safe custody or keeping. When a defendant is arrested on a *capias ad satisfaciendum,* (*ca. sa.,*) he is to be kept *arcta et salva custodi.* 3 Bl.Comm. 415.

ARDENT SPIRITS. Spirituous or distilled liquors. State v. Centennial Brewing Co., 55 Mont. 500, 179 P. 296, 297; Christian v. Commonwealth, 132 Va. 616, 111 S.E. 130.

Synonymous with "spirituous liquors" (*q. v.*) and, sometimes, with intoxicating liquors generally, though the term is properly applied only to liquors obtained by distillation, such as rum, whisky, brandy, and gin. 48 C.J.S. p. 139; Sarlls v. U. S., 14 S.Ct. 720, 721, 152 U.S. 570, 572, 38 L.Ed. 556.

ARDOUR. In old English law. An incendiary; a house burner.

ARE, *n.* A surface measure in the French law, in the form of a square, equal to 1076.441 square feet.

AREA. A surface, a territory, a region. Fleming v. Farmers Peanut Co., C.C.A.Ga., 128 F.2d 404, 406. Any plane surface, also the inclosed space on which a building stands, the sunken space or court giving ingress and affording light to the basement of a building, a particular extent of surface. State v. Armstrong, 97 Neb. 343, 149 N. W. 786, 788, Ann.Cas.1917A, 554. An inclosed yard or opening in a house; an open place adjoining a house. 1 Chit.Pr. 176. The site of a house; a site for building; the space where a house has stood. The ground on which a house is built, and which remains after the house is removed. Brissonius; Calvin.

In the civil law. A vacant space in a city; a place not built upon. Dig. 50, 16, 211.

"Area" in geometry means the superficial contents of any figure. State v. City of Polytechnic, Tex.Civ.App., 194 S.W. 1136, 1140.

AREAL GEOLOGY. That branch of geology which pertains to the distribution, position, and form of the areas of the earth's surface, occupied by different sorts of rock or different geologic formations, and to the making of geologic maps. Lewis v. Carr, 49 Nev. 366, 246 P. 695, 696.

AREAWAY. As used in an ordinance regulating the construction of areaways under any sidewalk, "areaway" was equivalent to cellar or room under the sidewalk. State v. Armstrong, 97 Neb. 343, 149 N.W. 786, 788, Ann.Cas.1917A, 554.

ARENALES. In Spanish law. Sandy beaches; or grounds on the banks of rivers. White, Recop. b. 2, tit. 1, c. 6.

ARENDATOR. A farmer or renter; in some provinces of Russia, formerly one who farmed the public rents or revenues; a "crown arendator" is one who rents an estate belonging to the crown.

ARENIFODINA. In the civil law. A sandpit. Dig. 7, 1, 13, 5.

ARENTARE. Lat. To rent; to let out at a certain rent. Cowell. *Arentatio.* A renting.

AREOPAGITE. In ancient Greek law. A lawyer or chief judge of the Areopagus in capital matters in Athens; a tribunal so called after a hill or slight eminence, in a street of that city dedicated to Mars, where the court was held in which those judges were wont to sit. Wharton.

ARERE. L. Fr. Behind; in arrear; back; again. Adams Gloss.

ARETRO. In arrear; behind. Also written *a retro.*

ARG. An abbreviation of *arguendo.*

ARGENT. In heraldry. Silver.

ARGENTARIUS (*pl.,* **Argentarii**). In the Roman law, a money lender or broker; a dealer in money; a banker. *Argentarium,* the instrument of the loan, similar to the modern word "bond" or "note."

ARGENTARIUS MILES. A money porter in the English exchequer, who carries the money from the lower to the upper exchequer to be examined and tested. Spelman.

ARGENTEUS. An old French coin, answering nearly to the English shilling. Spelman.

ARGENTUM. Silver; money.

ARGENTUM ALBUM. Bullion; uncoined silver; common silver coin; silver coin worn smooth. Cowell; Spelman.

ARGENTUM DEI. God's money; God's penny; money given as earnest in making a bargain. Cowell.

ARGUENDO. In arguing; in the course of the argument. A statement or observation made by a judge as a matter of argument or illustration, but not directly bearing upon the case at bar, or only incidentally involved in it, is said (in the reports) to be made *arguendo,* or in the abbreviated form, *arg.*

ARGUMENT. An effort to establish belief by a course of reasoning.

In rhetoric and logic, an inference drawn from premises, the truth of which is indisputable, or at least highly probable.

The argument of a demurrer, special case, appeal, or other proceeding involving a question of law, consists of the speeches of the opposed counsel; namely, the "opening" of the counsel having the right to begin, (*q. v.,*) the speech of his opponent, and the "reply" of the first counsel. It answers to the trial of a question of fact. Sweet. But the submission of printed briefs may technically constitute an argument. State v. California Min. Co., 13 Nev. 209. Also, the opening statement to a jury is part of the argument. State v. McCaskill, 173 Iowa 563, 155 N.W. 976, 977.

ARGUMENTATIVE. By way of reasoning. In pleading. Indirect; inferential. Steph.Pl. 179.

A pleading is so called in which the statement on which the pleader relies is implied instead of being expressed, or where it contains, in addition to proper statements of facts, reasoning or arguments upon those facts and their relation to the matter in dispute, such as should be reserved for presentation at the trial.

ARGUMENTATIVE INSTRUCTION. An instruction which singles out or unduly emphasizes a particular issue, theory, or defense, or one which tends to invade the province of the jury with regard to the weight, probative effect, or sufficiency of the evidence or the inferences to be drawn therefrom. See 64 C.J. §§ 594, 601.

ARGUMENTUM A COMMUNITER ACCIDENTIBUS IN JURE FREQUENS EST. An argument drawn from things commonly happening is frequent in law. Broom Max. 44.

ARGUMENTUM A DIVISIONE EST FORTISSIMUM IN JURE. An argument from division [of the subject] is of the greatest force in law. Co. Litt. 213*b;* 6 Coke 60.

ARGUMENTUM A MAJORI AD MINUS NEGATIVE NON VALET; VALET E CONVERSO. An argument from the greater to the less is of no force negatively; affirmatively (or conversely) it is. Jenk.Cent. 281.

ARGUMENTUM A SIMILI VALET IN LEGE. An argument from a like case (from analogy) is good in law. Co.Litt. 191.

ARGUMENTUM AB AUCTORITATE EST FORTISSIMUM IN LEGE. An argument from authority is the strongest in the law. "The book cases are the best proof of what the law is." Co. Litt. 254*a.*

ARGUMENTUM AB IMPOSSIBILI VALET IN LEGE. An argument drawn from an impossibility is forcible in law. Co.Litt. 92*a.*

ARGUMENTUM AB INCONVENIENTI. An argument arising from the inconvenience which the proposed construction of the law would create.

Where the constitutionality of a statute is concerned, it is only when the question is close and doubtful that this doctrine will be applied and consideration taken of the consequences of declaring the statute unconstitutional. Calhoun County v. Early County, 205 Ga. 169, 52 S.E.2d 854; Smith v. City Council of Augusta, 203 Ga. 511, 47 S.E.2d 582, 587.

ARGUMENTUM AB INCONVENIENTI EST VALIDUM IN LEGE; QUIA LEX NON PERMITTIT ALIQUOD INCONVENIENS. An argument drawn from what is inconvenient is good in law, because the law will not permit any inconvenience. Co.Litt. 66*a,* 258.

ARGUMENTUM AB INCONVENIENTI PLURIMUM VALET [EST VALIDUM] IN LEGE. An argument drawn from inconvenience is of the greatest weight [is forcible] in law. Co.Litt. 66*a,*

97*a*, 152*b*, 258*b*; Broom, Max. 184. If there be in any deed or instrument equivocal expressions, and great inconvenience must necessarily follow from one construction, it is strong to show that such construction is not according to the true intention of the grantor; but where there is no equivocal expression in the instrument, and the words used admit only of one meaning, arguments of inconvenience prove only want of foresight in the grantor. 3 Madd. 540; 7 Taunt. 496.

ARIBANNUM. In feudal law. A fine for not setting out to join the army in obedience to the summons of the king.

ARIERBAN, or ARRIERE-BAN. An edict of the ancient kings of France and Germany, commanding all their vassals, the noblesse, and the vassals' vassals, to enter the army, or forfeit their estates on refusal. Spelman. See, also, Arrier Ban.

ARIMANNI. A mediæval term for a class of agricultural owners of small allodial farms, which they cultivated in connection with larger farms belonging to their lords, paying rent and service for the latter, and being under the protection of their superiors. Military tenants holding lands from the emperor. Spelman.

ARISE. To spring up, originate, to come into being or notice, to become operative, sensible, visible, or audible; to present itself. Bergin v. Temple, 111 Mont. 539, 111 P.2d 286, 289, 290, 133 A.L.R. 1115; Lane v. Travelers Ins. Co. of Hartford, Conn., 230 Iowa 973, 299 N.W. 553, 555.

"Accrue" not synonymous; the latter term means to result, to add, to acquire, to receive, to benefit, Roques v. Continental Casualty Co., 17 La.App. 465, 135 So. 51, 52.

A case "arises" under the Constitution or a law of the United States, so as to be within the jurisdiction of a federal court, whenever its correct decision depends on the construction of either. Cleveland, C., C. & St. L. Ry. Co. v. Hirsch, C.C.A.Ohio, 204 F. 849, 851; Blease v. Safety Transit Co., C.C.A.S.C., 50 F.2d 852, 854.

A cause of action or suit "arises", so as to start running of limitation, when party has a right to apply to proper tribunal for relief. Washington Security Co. v. State, 9 Wash.2d 197, 114 P.2d 965, 967, 135 A.L.R. 1330; and it arises at time when and place where act is unlawfully omitted or committed. State ex rel. Birnamwood Oil Co. v. Shaughnessy, 243 Wis. 306, 10 N.W.2d 292, 295.

ARISING OUT OF AND IN THE COURSE OF OWN EMPLOYMENT. Workmen's Compensation Acts provide for compensating an employee whose injury is one "arising out of and in the course of the employment." These words describe an injury directly and naturally resulting in a risk reasonably incident to the employment. Thomas v. Proctor & Gamble Mfg. Co., 104 Kan. 432, 179 P. 372, 374, 6 A.L.R. 445; Trudenich v. Marshall, D.C.Wash., 34 F.Supp. 486, 488. They mean that there must be some causal connection between the conditions under which the employee worked and the injury which he received. Amicucci v. Ford Motor Co., 308 Mich. 151, 13 N.W.2d 241.

The words "arising out of employment" refer to the origin of the cause of the injury, while "course of employment" refer to the time, place, and circumstances under which the injury occurred. Walker v. Hyde, 43 Idaho, 625, 253 P. 1104, 1105. See, further, Course; Watson v. Pitcairn, Mo.App., 139 S.W.2d 552, 554; Ervin v. Industrial Commission, 364 Ill. 56, 4 N.E.2d 22, 25.

ARISTOCRACY. A government in which a class of men rules supreme; a form of government which is lodged in a council composed of select members or nobles, without a monarch, and exclusive of the people.

A privileged class of the people; nobles and dignitaries; people of wealth and station.

ARISTO-DEMOCRACY. A form of government where the power is divided between the nobles (or the more powerful) and the people.

ARLES. Earnest. Used in Yorkshire in the phrase "Arles-penny." Cowell. In Scotland it has the same signification. Bell.

ARM OF THE SEA. A portion of the sea projecting inland, in which the tide ebbs and flows. 5 Coke, 107. It is considered as extending as far into the interior of a country as the water of fresh rivers is propelled backwards by the ingress of the tide. Adams v. Pease, 2 Conn. 484; U. S. v. Grush, 5 Mason, 290, Fed.Cas.No.15,268; Ex parte Byers, D.C.Mich., 32 Fed. 404. See Fauces Terræ.

ARMA. Lat. Arms; weapons, offensive and defensive; armor; arms or cognizances of families.

ARMA DARE. To dub or make a knight.

ARMA IN ARMATOS SUMERE JURA SINUNT. The laws permit the taking up of arms against armed persons. 2 Inst. 574.

ARMA MOLUTA. Sharp weapons that cut, in contradistinction to such as are blunt, which only break or bruise. Fleta, lib. 1, c. 33, par. 6.

ARMA REVERSATA. Reversed arms, a punishment for a traitor or felon. Cowell.

ARMATA VIS. In the civil law. Armed force. Dig. 43, 16, 3; Fleta, lib. 4, c. 4.

ARMED. Furnished or equipped with weapons of offense or defense. People ex rel. Griffin v. Hunt, 270 N.Y.S. 248, 254, 150 Misc. 163.

A vessel is "armed" when she is fitted with a full armament for fighting purposes. Murray v. The Charming Betsy, 2 Cranch, 121, 2 L.Ed. 208.

ARMED FORCE. As used in statutes authorizing peace officers to summon an "armed force" to aid them, this term may refer to a military organization, but this is not necessarily so, and, depending on the context, it may mean only a posse comitatus (*q. v.*). Chapin v. Ferry, 28 P. 754, 756, 3 Wash. 386, 15 L.R.A. 116.

ARMED NEUTRALITY. An attitude of neutrality between belligerents which the neutral state is prepared to maintain by armed force if necessary.

ARMED PEACE. A situation in which two or more nations, while actually at peace with each other, are armed for possible or probable hostilities.

ARMIGER. An armor-bearer; an esquire. A title of dignity belonging to gentlemen authorized to bear arms. Cowell. In its earlier meaning, a servant who carried the arms of a knight. A tenant by scutage; a servant or valet; applied, also, to the higher servants in convents. Spelman.

ARMING ONE'S SELF. Equipping one's self with a weapon or weapons. Simmons v. State, 87 Tex. Cr.R. 270, 220 S.W. 554.

ARMISCARA. An ancient mode of punishment, which was to carry a saddle at the back as a token of subjection. Spelman.

ARMISTICE. A suspending or cessation of hostilities between belligerent nations or forces for a considerable time. Dooley v. Johnson, 133 Cal. App. 459, 24 P.2d 540.

The term cannot properly be applied to agreements between a government on one side and rioters, brigands, and banditti on the other. O'Neill v. Central Leather Co., 87 N.J.L. 552, 94 A. 789, 790, L.R.A.1917A, 276.

An armistice differs from a mere "suspension of arms" *(q. v.)* in that the latter is concluded for very brief periods and for local military purposes only, whereas an armistice not only covers a longer period, but is agreed upon for political purposes. It is said to be *general* if it relates to the whole area of the war, and *partial* if it relates to only a portion of that area. Partial armistices are sometimes called truces *(q. v.)* but there is no hard and fast distinction.

ARMORIAL BEARINGS. In English law. A device depicted on the (now imaginary) shield of one of the nobility, of which gentry is the lowest degree. The criterion of nobility is the bearing of arms, or armorial bearings, received from ancestry.

ARMORUM APPELLATIONE, NON SOLUM SCUTA ET GLADII ET GALEÆ, SED ET FUSTES ET LAPIDES CONTINENTUR. Under the name of arms are included, not only shields and swords and helmets, but also clubs and stones. Co.Litt. 162.

ARMORY. A building where arms, ammunition, and instruments of war are stored. Comp.Laws 1929, §§ 692, 3395. Grosse Ile v. Saunders, 262 Mich. 451, 247 N.W. 912, 913.

ARMS. Anything that a man wears for his defense, or takes in his hands, or uses in his anger, to cast at or strike at another. Co.Litt. 161*b*, 162*a*; State v. Buzzard, 4 Ark. 18.

Arms, or coat of arms, signifies *insignia, i. e.,* ensigns of honor, such as were formerly assumed by soldiers of fortune, and painted on their shields to distinguish them; or nearly the same as armorial bearings *(q. v.).*

ARMS, LAW OF. That law which gives precepts and rules concerning war; how to make and observe leagues and truce, to punish offenders in the camp, and such like. Cowell; Blount. Now more commonly called the "law of war." See, also, War.

ARMY. The armed forces of a nation intended for military service on land.

An "army" is a body of men whose business is war, while the "militia" is a body of men composed of citizens occupied temporarily in the pursuit of civil life, but organized by discipline and drill, and called into the field for temporary military service when the exigencies of the country require it. And see Brown v. Soldiers' Bonus Board, 44 R.I. 483, 116 A. 280, 281.

—Regular army. The permanent military establishment, which is maintained both in peace and war according to law. 10 U.S.C.A. § 3; State v. Moorhead, 102 Neb. 276, 167 N.W. 70, 71.

AROMATARIUS. A word formerly used for a grocer. 1 Vent. 142.

AROUND. In the vicinity of. Hawkins v. First National Bank, Tex.Civ.App., 175 S.W. 163, 164.

Thus, sheep branded "O" on the hip or side may be within a mortgage covering sheep described as branded "O" around the hip bone.

ARPEN, Arpent, Arpennus. A measure of land of uncertain quantity mentioned in Domesday and other old books; by some called an "acre," by others "half an acre," and by others a "furlong." Spelman; Cowell; Blount. Quoted in McMillan v. Aiken, 205 Ala. 35, 88 So. 135, 143.

A French measure of land, containing one hundred square perches, of eighteen feet each, or about an acre. But the quantity varied in different provinces. Spelman. An "arpent" is a land measure varying in dimension from .84 of an acre to 1.04 acres and to 1.28 acres, accordingly as the arpent meant is an arpent de Paris, an arpent commun, or an arpent d'ordonnance. Troll v. City of St. Louis, 257 Mo. 626, 168 S.W. 167, 171. In Louisiana, the terms "arpent" and "acre" are sometimes used interchangeably; but there is a considerable difference, the arpent being the square of 192 feet and the acre of 209 and a fraction. Randolph v. Sentilles, 110 La. 419, 34 So. 587.

ARPENTATOR. A measurer or surveyor of land. Cowell; Spelman.

ARRA. In the civil law. Earnest; earnest-money; evidence of a completed bargain. Used of a contract of marriage, as well as any other. Spelled, also, *Arrha, Arrhœ, Arrœ,* Calvin. Cf. Arles.

ARRAIGN. In criminal practice. To bring a prisoner to the bar of the court to answer the matter charged upon him in the indictment. Ex parte Jeffcoat, 109 Fla. 207, 146 So. 827, 828. The arraignment *(q. v.)* of a prisoner consists of calling upon him by name, and reading to him the indictment, (in the English tongue,) and demanding of him whether he be guilty or not guilty, and entering his plea. State v. Voelpel, 213 Iowa 702, 239 N.W. 677, 679.

In old English law. To order, or set in order; to conduct in an orderly manner; to prepare for trial. *To arraign an assise* was to cause the tenant to be called to make the plaint, and to set the cause in such order as the tenant might be enforced to answer thereunto. Litt. § 442; Co. Litt. 262*b*.

ARRAIGNMENT. See Arraign.

ARRAIGNS, CLERK OF. In English law. An assistant to the clerk of assise.

ARRAMEUR. In old French law. An officer employed to superintend the loading of vessels, and the safe stowage of the cargo. 1 Pet.Adm.Append. XXV.

ARRANGEMENT. A setting in order. 1 El. & Bl. 540. Plan for corporate reorganization proposing to effect a composition or extension of time with reference to corporation's unsecured debts. John Hancock Mut. Life Ins. Co. v. Casey, C.C.A. Mass., 141 F.2d 104, 107.

ARRANGEMENT, DEED OF. A term used in England to express an assignment for the benefit of creditors.

ARRAS. In Spanish law. The donation which the husband makes to his wife, by reason or on account of marriage, and in consideration of the *dote,* or portion, which he receives from her. Miller v. Dunn, 62 Mo. 219. The property contributed by the husband *ad sustinenda onera matrimonii* (for bearing the expenses).

ARRAY. The whole body of jurors summoned to attend a court, as they are *arrayed* or arranged on the panel. Dane, Abr. Index; 1 Chit.Crim.Law, 536; Com.Dig. "Challenge," B. Durrah v. State, 44 Miss. 789. A ranking, or setting forth in order; the order in which jurors' names are ranked in the panel containing them. Co.Litt. 156*a;* 3 Bl.Comm. 359.

ARRAYER. An English military officer in the early part of the fifteenth century. His duties were similar to those of the modern Lord Lieutenant of a county.

ARREARS, or ARREARAGES. Money unpaid at the due time, as rent behind; the remainder due after payment of a part of an account; money in the hands of an accounting party. Board of Education of Glen Ellyn Tp. High School Dist. No. 87 v. Boger, 291 Ill. 191, 125 N.E. 768, 770. Indebtedness. State ex rel. City of South Euclid v. Zangerle, 145 Ohio St. 433, 62 N.E.2d 160, 162.

In arrear (arrears). Overdue and unpaid. Hollingsworth v. Willis, 64 Miss. 157, 8 So. 170. Behind in the payment of that which is due. Grand Court of Texas Independent Order of Calanthe v. Johns, Tex.Civ.App., 181 S.W. 869, 870.

ARRECT. To accuse or charge with an offense. *Arrectati,* accused or suspected persons.

ARRENDAMIENTO. In Spanish law. The contract of letting and hiring an estate or land, (*heredad.*) White, Recop. b. 2, tit. 14, c. 1.

ARRENT. In old English law. To let or demise at a fixed rent. Particularly used with reference to the public domain or crown lands; as where a license was granted to inclose land in a forest with a low hedge and a ditch, under a yearly rent, or where an encroachment, originally a purpresture, was allowed to remain on the fixing and payment of a suitable compensation to the public for its maintenance.

ARREST. To deprive a person of his liberty by legal authority. Taking, under real or assumed authority, custody of another for the purpose of holding or detaining him to answer a criminal charge or civil demand. Ex parte Sherwood, 29 Tex.App. 334, 15 S.W. 812. Physical seizure of person by arresting officer or submission to officer's authority and control is necessary to constitute an "arrest." Thompson v. Boston Pub. Co., 285 Mass. 344, 189 N.E. 210, 213. It is a restraint, however slight, on another's liberty to come and go. Turney v. Rhodes, 42 Ga.App. 104, 155 S.E. 112. It is the taking, seizing or detaining the person of another, touching or putting hands upon him in the execution of process, or any act indicating an intention to arrest. U. S. v. Benner, Bald. 234, 239, Fed.Cas.No.14,568; State v. District Court of Eighth Judicial Dist. in and for Cascade County, 70 Mont. 378, 225 P. 1000, 1001; Hoppes v. State, 105 P.2d 433, 439, 70 Okl.Cr. 179.

As used in Bankruptcy Act, § 9 (11 USCA § 27), arrest includes "imprisonment." Ex parte Harrison, D.C.Mass., 272 F. 543, 544.

One of the means which the law gives the creditor to secure the person of his debtor while the suit is pending, or to compel him to give security for his appearance after judgment. La.Code Prac. art. 210.

As ordinarily used, the terms arrest and attachment coincide in meaning to some extent; though in strictness, as a distinction, an arrest may be said to be the act resulting from the service of an attachment. And in the more extended sense which is sometimes given to attachment, including the act of taking, it would seem to differ from arrest in that it is more peculiarly applicable to a taking of property, while *arrest* is more commonly used in speaking of persons.

Arrest is also applied in some instances to a seizure and detention of personal chattels, especially of ships and vessels; thus, in admiralty actions a ship or cargo is *arrested* when the marshal has served the writ in an action *in rem.* Pelham v. Rose, 9 Wall. 103, 19 L.Ed. 602.

Civil Practice

The apprehension of a person by virtue of a lawful authority to answer the demand against him in a civil action. Gentry v. Griffith, 27 Tex. 462.

Criminal Cases

The apprehending or detaining of the person in order to be forthcoming to answer an alleged or suspected crime. Ex parte Sherwood, 29 Tex.App. 334, 15 S.W. 812.

The word *arrest* is said to be more properly used in civil cases, and *apprehension* in criminal. Thus, a man is arrested under a *capias ad respondendum,* and apprehended under a warrant charging him with larceny.

Malicious Arrest

An arrest made willfully and without probable cause, but in the course of a regular proceeding.

Parol Arrest

One ordered by a judge or magistrate from the bench, without written complaint or other proceedings, of a person who is present before him, and which is executed on the spot; as in case of breach of the peace in open court.

Rearrest

Right of an officer to take without warrant one forcibly freeing himself after arrest. Gross v.

State, 186 Ind. 581, 117 N.E. 562, 1 A.L.R. 1151, or escaping in any manner, Hefler v. Hunt, 120 Me. 10, 112 A. 675, or violating parole, Massey v. Cunningham, 169 Ark. 410, 275 S.W. 737, or failing to respond to bond for appearance, Porter v. Garmony, 148 Ga. 261, 96 S.E. 426.

Second Arrest

The "second arrest" forbidden after discharge on habeas corpus means an imprisonment based on the same information and not under a new information followed by a lawful warrant. State v. Riley, 109 Minn. 437, 124 N.W. 13. See, also, Stair v. Heska Amone Congregation, 128 Tenn. 190, 159 S.W. 840, 841.

Warrant of Arrest

A written order issued and signed by a magistrate, directed to a peace officer or some other person specially named, and commanding him to arrest the body of a person named in it, who is accused of an offense. Brown v. State, 109 Ala. 70, 20 So. 103.

ARREST OF INQUEST. Pleading in arrest of taking the inquest upon a former issue, and showing cause why an inquest should not be taken.

ARREST OF JUDGMENT. The act of staying a judgment, or refusing to render judgment in an action at law and in criminal cases, after verdict, for some matter intrinsic appearing on the face of the record, which would render the judgment, if given, erroneous or reversible. 3 Bl. Comm. 393; 3 Steph.Comm. 628; 2 Tidd, Pr. 918; Speer v. Pierce, 18 Tenn.App. 351, 77 S.W.2d 77, 78; State v. Ferguson, 165 Tenn. 61, 52 S.W.2d 140.

It is the fact that a motion in arrest of judgment is based on some defect on the face of the record or pleadings which aids in distinguishing it from a motion for a new trial. Maddox Coffee Co. v. McHan, 22 Ga.App. 198, 95 S. E. 736. It differs also from a motion to set aside a judgment, in that a motion in arrest of judgment must be made during the term when the judgment was rendered. Love v. National Liberty Ins. Co., 157 Ga. 259, 121 S.E. 648, 650. A motion in arrest of judgment is practically a demurrer, People v. Cordosco, 77 Cal.App. 780, 246 P. 461, 462, and has been abolished in some jurisdictions. State v. Sharp, Mo.Sup., 300 S.W. 501.

ARRESTANDIS BONIS NE DISSIPENTUR. In old English law. A writ which lay for a person whose cattle or goods were taken by another, who during a contest was likely to make away with them, and who had not the ability to render satisfaction. Reg.Orig. 126.

ARRESTANDO IPSUM QUI PECUNIAM RECEPIT. In old English law. A writ which issued for apprehending a person who had taken the king's prest money to serve in the wars, and then hid himself in order to avoid going.

ARRESTATIO. In old English law. An arrest *(q. v.)*.

ARRESTEE. In Scotch law. The person in whose hands, the movables of another, or a debt due to another, are arrested by the creditor of the latter by the process of *arrestment.* 2 Kames, Eq. 173, 175.

If, in contempt of the arrestment, he make payment of the sum or deliver the goods arrested to the common debtor, he is not only liable criminally for breach of the arrestment, but he must pay the debt again to the arrester; Erskine, Inst. 3, 6, 6.

ARRESTER. In Scotch law. One who sues out and obtains an arrestment of his debtor's goods or movable obligations. Erskine, Inst. 3. 6. 1.

ARRESTMENT. In Scotch law. Securing a criminal's person till trial, or that of a debtor till he give security *judicio sisti.* The order of a judge, by which he who is debtor in a movable obligation to the arrester's debtor is prohibited to make payment or delivery till the debt due to the arrester be paid or secured. Erskine, Inst. 3. 6. 1; 1. 2. 12.

ARRESTMENT JURISDICTIONIS FUNDANDÆ CAUSÂ. In Scotch law. A process to bring a foreigner within the jurisdiction of the courts of Scotland. The warrant attaches a foreigner's goods within the jurisdiction, and these will not be released unless caution or security be given.

ARRESTO FACTO SUPER BONIS MERCATORUM ALIENIGENORUM. In old English law. A writ against the goods of aliens found within this kingdom, in recompense of goods taken from a denizen in a foreign country, after denial of restitution. Reg.Orig. 129. The ancient civilians called it *"clarigatio,"* but by the moderns it is termed *"reprisalia."*

ARRET. Fr. A judgment, sentence, or decree of a court of competent jurisdiction.

The term is derived from the French law, and is used in Canada and Louisiana.

Saisie arrêt is an attachment of property in the hands of a third person. Code Pr.La. art. 209; 2 Low.Can. 77; 5 Low.Can. 198, 218. See "Saisie."

ARRETTED. Convened before a judge and charged with a crime.

Ad rectum malefactorem is, according to Bracton, to have a malefactor forthcoming to be put on his trial.

Imputed or laid to one's charge; as, no folly may be *arretted* to one under age. Bracton, 1. 3, tr. 2, c. 10; Cunningham, Dict.; Cowell.

ARRHABO. In the civil law. Earnest; money given to bind a bargain. Calvin.

ARRHÆ. In the civil law. Money or other valuable things given by the buyer to the seller, for the purpose of evidencing the contract; earnest. See Arra; Pot-de-vin.

Arrhœ sponsalitiœ were the earnest or present given by one betrothed to the other at the betrothal.

ARRIAGE AND CARRIAGE. In English and Scotch law. Indefinite services formerly demandable from tenants, but prohibited by statute, (20 Geo. II, c. 50, §§ 21, 22.) Holthouse; Ersk.Inst. 2, 6, 42.

ARRIER BAN. In feudal law. A second summons to join the lord, addressed to those who had neglected the first. A summons of the inferiors or vassals of the lord. Spelman, Gloss. See, also, Arierban.

ARRIERE FIEF, or FEE. In feudal law. A fief or fee dependent on a superior one; an inferior fief granted by a vassal of the king, out of the fief held by him. Montesq. Esprit des Lois, liv. 31, cc. 26, 32.

ARRIERE VASSAL. In feudal law. The vassal of a vassal.

ARRIVAL. In marine insurance, arrival of a vessel means an arrival for purposes of business, requiring an entry and clearance and stay at the port so long as to require some of the acts connected with business, and not merely touching at a port for advices, or to ascertain the state of the market, or being driven in by an adverse wind and sailing again as soon as it changes. F. S. Royster Guano Co. v. U. S., C.C.A.Va., 18 F.2d 469, 470.

"A vessel arrives at a port of discharge when she comes, or is brought, to a place where it is intended to discharge her, and where is the usual and customary place of discharge. When a vessel is insured to one or two ports, and sails for one, the risk terminates on her arrival there. If a vessel is insured to a particular port of discharge, and is destined to discharge cargo successively at two different wharves, docks, or places, within that port, each being a distinct place for the delivery of cargo, the risk ends when she has been moored twenty-four hours in safety at the first place. But if she is destined to one or more places for the delivery of cargo, and delivery or discharge of a portion of her cargo is necessary, not by reason of her having reached any destined place of delivery, but as a necessary and usual nautical measure, to enable her to reach such usual and destined place of delivery, she cannot properly be considered as having arrived at the usual and customary place of discharge, when she is at anchor for the purpose only of using such means as will better enable her to reach it. If she cannot get to the destined and usual place of discharge in the port because she is too deep, and must be lightered to get there, and, to aid in prosecuting the voyage, cargo is thrown overboard or put into lighters, such discharge does not make that the place of arrival; it is only a stopping-place in the voyage. When the vessel is insured to a particular port of discharge, arrival within the limits of the harbor does not terminate the risk, if the place is not one where vessels are discharged and voyages completed. The policy covers the vessel through the port navigation, as well as on the open sea, until she reaches the destined place." Simpson v. Insurance Co., Holmes, 137, Fed.Cas.No.12,886.

"Arrival of ship," within meaning of bills of lading requiring claims to be filed, must be construed, where misdelivery is charged, as meaning date when cargo is discharged or offered for delivery. The Cardiganshire, D.C. Cal., 9 F.2d 416, 420. "Arrival" within the immigration laws means compliance with the requirements entitling an alien to entry. See 8 USCA §§ 106, 380. In re Kempson, D. C.Wash., 14 F.2d 668, 669.

ARRIVE. To come to a particular place; to reach a particular or certain place. Thompson v. U. S., 1 Brock. 411, Fed.Cas.No.13,985; 8 B. & C. 119.

The words "arrive" and "enter" are not always synonymous; there certainly may be an arrival without an actual entry or attempt to enter. United States v. Open Boat, 5 Mason, 120, 132, Fed.Cas.No.15,967. And where a vessel from a foreign port, laden with liquors, anchored within four leagues of the coast, and the master without a permit therefor allowed part of the cargo to be taken away, with the intention of so disposing of the entire cargo, the vessel had "arrived" within the meaning of Tariff Act 1922, § 586 (19 USCA § 488). The Cherie, C.C.A.Me., 13 F.2d 992, 993.

ARROGATION. In the civil law. The adoption of a person who was of full age or *sui juris*. 1 Browne, Civil & Adm.Law, 119; Dig. 1, 7, 5; Inst. 1, 11, 3. Reinders v. Koppelmann, 68 Mo. 497, 30 Am.Rep. 802.

ARRONDISSEMENT. In France, one of the subdivisions of a department.

ARSÆ ET PENSATÆ. Burnt and weighed. A term formerly applied to money tested or assayed by fire and by weighing.

ARSENALS. Store-houses for arms; dock-yards, magazines, and other military stores.

ARSER IN LE MAIN. Fr. Burning in the hand. The punishment by burning or branding the left thumb of lay offenders who claimed and were allowed the benefit of clergy, so as to distinguish them in case they made a second claim of clergy. 5 Coke, 51; 4 Bl.Comm. 367; *Termes de la Ley.*

ARSON. At common law, the malicious burning of the house or outhouse of another. 4 Bla.Com. 220; Thacker v. Commonwealth, 219 Ky. 789, 294 S.W. 491, 492; State v. Berry, 188 La. 612, 177 So. 684, 686; Commonwealth v. Cooper, 264 Mass. 378, 162 N.E. 733, 734.

At common law burning buildings other than dwelling houses is not arson. Sawyer v. State, 100 Fla. 1603, 132 So. 188, 193. Part of building ignited sufficient to establish corpus delicti. State v. Caliendo, 4 A.2d 837, 840, 136 Me. 514.

At common law it must be the house of another. 1 Bish. Cr.Law, § 389; State v. Beckwith, Me., 198 A. 739, 742. But it is now an offense to burn one's own house under the statutes of New Hampshire, Arkansas, California, and other states. State v. Blumenthal, 136 Ark. 532, 203 S.W. 36, 37, L.R.A.1918E, 482.

Whether "house" or "dwelling house" be used in statute defining the crime may be of importance in determining whether occupancy is or is not an element. 1 Hale, P.C. 566, 567; Commonwealth v. Barney, 64 Mass. (10 Cush.) 478. Some states have expressly eliminated occupancy as an element, State v. Snover, 101 N.J.Law, 543, 126 A. 850; P.L. 1919, p. 257; while others have made it a distinction between degrees of the crime, People v. Abrams, 174 Cal. 172, 162 P. 395, 396.

In several states, this crime is divided into arson in the first, second, and third degrees, the first degree including the burning of an inhabited dwelling-house in the nighttime; the second degree, the burning (at night) of a building other than a dwelling-house, but so situated with reference to a dwelling-house as to endanger it; the third degree, the burning of any building or structure not the subject of arson in the first or second degree, or the burning of property, his own or another's with intent to defraud or prejudice an insurer thereof. State v. Jessup, 42 Kan. 422, 22 P. 627.

ARSURA. The trial of money by heating it after it was coined. The loss of weight occasioned by this process. A pound was said to *burn* so many pence *(tot ardere denarios)* as it lost by the fire. Spelman. The term is now obsolete.

ART. Systematic application of knowledge or skill in effecting a desired result; also an employment, occupation or business requiring such knowledge or skill; a craft; as industrial arts.

Jones Bros. Co. v. Underkoffler, D.C.Pa., 16 F.Supp. 729, 730; Miller v. State, 9 Okl.Cr. 255, 131 P. 717, 718, L.R.A.1915A, 1088. A principle put in practice and applied to some art, machine, manufacture, or composition of matter. Earle v. Sawyer, 4 Mason, 1, Fed.Cas.No.4,247.

In the law of patents, this term means a useful art or manufacture which is beneficial and which is described with exactness in its mode of operation. Such an art can be protected only in the mode and to the extent thus described. Jacobs v. Baker, 7 Wall. 297, 19 L.Ed. 200. It is synonymous with process or method when used to produce a useful result, and may be either a force applied, a mode of application, or the specific treatment of a specific object, and must produce physical effects. Emmett v. Metals Processing Corporation, C.C.A.Ariz., 118 F.2d 796, 798.

—**Prior Art.** In patent law, something that a man skilled in the art may by diligence discover. Davis-Bournonville Co. v. Alexander Milburn Co., C.C.A. N.Y., 1 F.2d 227, 231.

In seduction cases, "art" means the skillful and systematic arrangement of means for the attainment of a desired end. Hayes v. State, 19 Ala. App. 241, 96 So. 647.

ART, WORDS OF. Words used in a technical sense; words scientifically fit to carry the sense assigned them.

ART AND PART. In Scotch law. The offense committed by one who aids and assists the commission of a crime, but who is not the principal or chief actor in its actual commission. An accessory. A principal in the second degree. Paters. Comp.

ART MUSEUM. A building containing works of art. In re Everson's Will, 52 N.Y.S.2d 395, 399, 268 App.Div. 425.

ARTESIAN BASIN. A body of water more or less compact, moving through soils with more or less resistance. Justesen v. Olsen, 40 P.2d 802, 810, 86 Utah, 158.

ARTESIAN WELL. A well bored through impermeable strata into a subterranean body of water which, being under pressure, rises naturally to the surface. Loosely, any deep bored well. 6 C.J.S. p. 773.

ARTHEL, ARDHEL, or ARDDELIO. To avouch; as if a man were taken with stolen goods in his possession he was allowed a lawful *arthel, i. e.,* vouchee, to clear him of the felony; but provision was made against it by 28 Hen. VIII, c. 6. Blount.

ARTICLE. A separate and distinct part of an instrument or writing comprising two or more particulars; one of several things presented as connected or forming a whole. Carter v. Railroad Co., 126 N.C. 437, 36 S.E. 14. A particular object or substance, a material thing or a class of things. People v. Epstean, 170 N.Y.S. 68, 73, 102 Misc. 476. Material or tangible object. Gayer v. Whelan, 59 Cal.App.2d 255, 138 P.2d 763, 768. "Thing" of value. Gayer v. Whelan, 59 Cal.App.2d 255, 138 P.2d 763, 768.

In English ecclesiastical law. A complaint exhibited in the ecclesiastical court by way of libel. The different parts of a libel, responsive allegation, or counter allegation in the ecclesiastical courts. 3 Bl.Comm. 109.

In Scotch practice. A subject or matter; competent matter. "Article of dittay." 1 Broun, 62. A "point of dittay." 1 Swint. 128, 129.

ARTICLED CLERK. In English law. A clerk bound to serve in the office of a solicitor in consideration of being instructed in the profession. This is the general acceptation of the term; but it is said to be equally applicable to other trades and professions. Reg. v. Reeve, 4 Q.B. 212.

ARTICLES. 1. A connected series of propositions; a system of rules. The subdivisions of a document, code, book, etc. A specification of distinct matters agreed upon or established by authority or requiring judicial action.

2. A statute; as having its provisions articulately expressed under distinct heads. Several of the ancient English statutes were called "articles," (*articuli.*)

3. A system of rules established by legal authority; as *articles* of war, *articles* of the navy, *articles* of faith. (See *infra.*)

4. A contractual document executed between parties, containing stipulations or terms of agreement; as *articles* of agreement, *articles* of partnership.

5. A naval term meaning employment contract. South Chicago Coal & Dock Co. v. Bassett, C.C.A. Ill., 104 F.2d 522, 526.

6. In chancery practice. A formal written statement of objections filed by a party, after depositions have been taken, showing ground for discrediting the witnesses.

7. In ecclesiastical law. A complaint in the form of a libel exhibited to an ecclesiastical court. See Article.

ARTICLES APPROBATORY. In Scotch law. That part of the proceedings which corresponds to the answer to the charge in an English bill in chancery. Paters. Comp.

ARTICLES IMPROBATORY. In Scotch law. Articulate averments setting forth the facts relied upon. Bell. That part of the proceedings which corresponds to the charge in an English bill in chancery to set aside a deed. Paters. Comp. The answer is called "articles approbatory."

ARTICLES, LORDS OF. A committee of the Scottish parliament, which, in the mode of its election, and by the nature of its powers, was calculated to increase the influence of the crown, and to confer upon it a power equivalent to that of a negative before debate. This system appeared inconsistent with the freedom of parliament, and at the revolution the convention of estates declared it a grievance, and accordingly it was suppressed by Act 1690, c. 3. Wharton.

ARTICLES OF AGREEMENT. A written memorandum of the terms of an agreement.

It is a common practice for persons to enter into articles of agreement, preparatory to the execution of a formal deed, whereby it is stipulated that one of the parties shall convey to the other certain lands, or release his right to them, or execute some other disposition of them.

When persons form voluntary associations for religious, literary, social, or other purposes, and adopt rules by which to regulate their conduct and measure their rights, by the provisions of which members may be admitted and expelled, such rules are articles of agreement, to which all who have become members are parties, and by which they must be governed in their relations to the associations. Brown v. Harris County Medical Soc., Tex.Civ.App., 194 S. W. 1179, 1180.

ARTICLES OF ASSOCIATION, OR OF INCORPORATION. Articles subscribed by the members of a joint-stock company or corporation organized under a general law, and which create the corporate union between them. Such articles are in the nature of a partnership agreement, and commonly specify the form of organization, amount of capital, kind of business to be pursued, location of the company, etc. Articles of association are to be distinguished from a charter, in that the latter is a grant of power from the sovereign or the legislature.

ARTICLES OF CONFEDERATION. The name of the instrument embodying the compact made between the thirteen original states of the Union, before the adoption of the present constitution.

ARTICLES OF FAITH. In English law. The system of faith of the Church of England, more commonly known as the "Thirty-Nine Articles."

ARTICLES OF IMPEACHMENT. A formal written allegation of the causes for impeachment; answering the same office as an indictment in an ordinary criminal proceeding.

ARTICLES OF INCORPORATION. The instrument by which a private corporation is formed and organized under general corporation laws. People v. Golden Gate Lodge, 128 Cal. 257, 60 P. 865. See Articles of Association.

ARTICLES OF PARTNERSHIP. A written agreement by which the parties enter into a copartnership upon the terms and conditions therein stipulated.

ARTICLES OF RELIGION. In English ecclesiastical law. Commonly called the "Thirty-Nine Articles;" a body of divinity drawn up by the convocation in 1562, and confirmed by James I.

ARTICLES OF ROUP. In Scotch law. The terms and conditions under which property is sold at auction.

ARTICLES OF SET. In Scotch law. An agreement for a lease. Paters. Comp.

ARTICLES OF THE CLERGY. The title of a statute passed in the ninth year of Edward II. for the purpose of adjusting and settling the great questions of cognizance then existing between the ecclesiastical and temporal courts. 2 Reeve, Hist. Eng.Law, 291–296.

ARTICLES OF THE NAVY. A system of rules prescribed by act of parliament for the government of the English navy; also, in the United States, there are articles for the government of the navy.

ARTICLES OF THE PEACE. A complaint made or exhibited to a court by a person who makes oath that he is in fear of death or bodily harm from some one who has threatened or attempted to do him injury. The court may thereupon order the person complained of to find sureties for the peace, and, in default, may commit him to prison. 4 Bl.Comm. 255.

ARTICLES OF UNION. In English law. Articles agreed to, A. D. 1707, by the parliaments of England and Scotland, for the union of the two kingdoms. They were twenty-five in number. 1 Bl. Comm. 96.

ARTICLES OF WAR. Codes framed for the government of a nation's army or navy.

ARTICULATE ADJUDICATION. In Scotch law. Where the creditor holds several distinct debts, a separate adjudication for each claim is thus called.

ARTICULATED PLEADING. The stating in separate paragraphs, separately numbered, of each material fact of the petition. Newspaper Feature Service v. Southern Pub. Co., 140 La. 702, 73 So. 777.

ARTICULATELY. Article by article; by distinct clauses or articles; by separate propositions.

ARTICULI. Lat. Articles; items or heads. A term applied to some old English statutes, and occasionally to treatises.

ARTICULI CLERI. "Articles of the clergy" (*q. v.*). See Circumspecte Agatis.

ARTICULI DE MONETA. Articles concerning money, or the currency. The title of a statute passed in the twentieth year of Edward I. 2 Reeve, Hist.Eng.Law, 228; Crabb, Eng.Law (Amer. Ed.) 167.

ARTICULI MAGNÆ CHARTÆ. The preliminary articles, forty-nine in number, upon which the *Magna Charta* was founded.

ARTICULI SUPER CHARTAS. Articles upon the charters. The title of a statute passed in the twenty-eighth year of Edward I. st. 3, confirming or enlarging many particulars in *Magna Charta*, and the *Charta de Foresta*, and appointing a method for enforcing the observance of them, and for the punishment of offenders. 2 Reeve, Hist. Eng.Law, 103, 233.

ARTICULO MORTIS. (Or more commonly *in articulo mortis.*) At the point of death; in the article of death, which means at the moment of death; in the last struggle or agony. Succession of Villa, 132 La. 714, 61 So. 765, 770.

ARTIFICE. An ingenius contrivance or device of some kind, and, when used in a bad sense, it corresponds with trick or fraud. United States v. Corlin, D.C.Cal., 44 F.Supp. 940, 943. It implies craftiness and deceit, and imports some element of moral obliquity. Davis v. Boston Elevated Ry. Co., 235 Mass. 482, 126 N.E. 841, 845; Finch v. Gibson, 140 Tenn. 134, 203 S.W. 759, 761.

A representation contrary to a well-known fact, such as a representation that pregnancy will not result from natural sexual intercourse, will not constitute artifice, deception, or promises.

ARTIFICER. One who buys goods in order to reduce them, by his own art or industry, into other forms, and then to sell them. Lansdale v. Brashear, 3 T.B.Mon. (Ky.) 335.

One who is actually and personally engaged or employed to do work of a mechanical or physical character, not including one who takes contracts for labor to be performed by others. Ingram v. Barnes, 7 El. & Bl. 135; Chawner v. Cummings, 8 Q.B. 321.

One who is master of his art, and whose employment consists chiefly in manual labor. Wharton; Cunningham.

ARTIFICIAL. Is in opposition to the word "natural". California Casualty Indemnity Exchange v. Industrial Accident Commission of California, 13 Cal.2d 529, 90 P.2d 289; Created by art, or by law; existing only by force of or in contemplation of law.

ARTIFICIAL FORCE. In patent law. A natural force so transformed in character or energies by human power as to possess new capabilities of action; this transformation of a natural force into a force practically new involves a true inventive act. Wall v. Leck, 60 Fed. 555, 13 C.C.A. 630.

ARTIFICIAL MEMBER OF BODY. A substitute for, and not a mere aid to, a natural part, organ, limb, or other separable part of body. California Casualty Indemnity Exchange v. Industrial Accident Commission, Cal.App., 82 P.2d 1115, 1116.

ARTIFICIAL PERSONS. Persons created and devised by human laws for the purposes of society and government, as distinguished from natural persons. Corporations are examples of artificial persons. 1 Bl.Comm. 123. Chapman v. Brewer, 43 Neb. 890, 62 N.W. 320, 47 Am.St.Rep. 779.

ARTIFICIAL PRESUMPTIONS. Also called "legal presumptions;" those which derive their force and effect from the law, rather than their natural tendency to produce belief. 3 Starkie, Ev. 1235. Gulick v. Loder, 13 N.J.Law, 72, 23 Am.Dec. 711.

ARTIFICIAL SUCCESSION. The succession between predecessors and successors in a corporation aggregate or sole. Thomas v. Dakin, 22 Wend. (N.Y.) 100.

ARTIFICIAL WATER COURSE. See Water Course.

ARTIFICIALLY. Technically; scientifically; using terms of art. A will or contract is described as "artificially" drawn if it is couched in apt and technical phrases and exhibits a scientific arrangement.

ARTIFICIALLY DEVELOPED WATER. "Artificially developed water," to which one may acquire right superior to adjudicated rights of earlier appropriators of natural waters of stream into which he turns it, is water produced and contributed by him, which would not have reached stream if left to flow in accordance with natural laws. C.L. § 1766. In re Nix, 45 P.2d 176, 178, 96 Colo. 540.

ARTISAN. One skilled in some kind of mechanical craft or art; a skilled mechanic. O'Clair v. Hale, 25 Misc.Rep. 31; Warner Memorial University v. Ritenour, Tex.Civ.App., 56 S.W.2d 236, 237.

As used in lien statutes, the term includes the architect, Kansas City Southern Ry. Co. v. Wallace, 38 Okl. 233, 132 P. 908, 911, 46 L.R.A.,N.S., 112, but not a subcontractor, Huffman v. McDonald, Tex.Civ.App., 261 S.W. 146, 147. An optometrist is not an "artisan." Swanz v. Clark, 71 Mont. 385, 229 P. 1108.

ARURA. An old English law term, signifying a day's work in plowing.

ARVIL-SUPPER. A feast or entertainment made at a funeral in the north of England; *arvil bread* is bread delivered to the poor at funeral solemnities, and *arvil, arval,* or *arfal,* the burial or funeral rites. Cowell.

AS or **A/S** or **A/s.** Account sales; also after sight, at sight.

AS. Lat. In the Roman and civil law. A pound weight; and a coin originally weighing a pound, (called also *"libra"*) divided into twelve parts, called *"unciæ."*

The parts were reckoned (as may be seen in the law, *Servum de hæredibus,* Inst. lib. xiii. *Pandect*) as follows: *uncia,* 1 ounce; *sextans,* 2 ounces; *triens,* 3 ounces; *quadrans,* 4 ounces; *quincunx,* 5 ounces; *semis,* 6 ounces; *septunx,* 7 ounces; *bes,* 8 ounces; *dodrans,* 9 ounces; *dextans,* 10 ounces; *deunx,* 11 ounces.

Any integral sum, subject to division in certain proportions.

Frequently applied in the civil law to inheritances; the whole inheritance being termed "as," and its several proportionate parts *"sextans," "quadrans,"* etc. Burrill.

The term "as," and the multiples of its *unciæ,* were also used to denote the rates of interest. 2 Bl.Comm. 462, note *m.*

AS. Used as an adverb, etc., means like, similar to, of the same kind, in the same manner, in the manner in which. Van Pelt v. Hilliard, 75 Fla. 792, 78 So. 693, 697, L.R.A.1918E 639; Price v. Skylstead, 69 Mont. 453, 222 P. 1059, 1060. It may also have the meaning of because, since, or it being the case that; State v. Rudman, 126 Me. 177, 136 A. 817, 819; in the character or under the name of; State v. Blue, 134 La. 561, 64 So. 411, 414; when; Shane Bros. & Wilson Co. v. Barrett,

71 Ind.App. 313, 124 N.E. 780, 781; With significance of in degree, to that extent, so far. Snyder and Blankfard Co., v. Farmers Bank of Tifton, 178 Md. 601, 16 A.2d 837, 841.

AS AGAINST; AS BETWEEN. These words contrast the relative position of two persons, with a tacit reference to a different relationship between one of them and a third person. For instance, the temporary bailee of a chattel is entitled to it *as between* himself and a stranger, or *as against* a stranger; reference being made by this form of words to the rights of the bailor. Wharton.

AS FAR AS HUMAN CARE AND FORESIGHT WILL GO. Means for utmost care and diligence of very cautious persons, and makes one responsible for even slightest neglect. Kline v. Santa Barbara Consol. Ry. Co., 90 P. 125, 127, 150 Cal. 741.

AS IS. A sale of goods by sample "as is" requires that the goods be of the kind and quality represented, even though they be in a damaged condition. Schwartz v. Kohn, Sup., 155 N.Y.S. 547, 548. Use of expression in sales agreement that goods are sold "as is" implies that buyer is taking delivery of goods in some way defective and upon express condition that he must trust to his own examination. Roby Motors Co. v. Cade, La.App., 158 So. 840, 841.

AS LONG AS. The phrase "as long as life doth last," in a will, is tantamount to "forever." In re Brown, 119 Kan. 402, 239 P. 747.

AS OF COURSE. Under a statute providing that an attachment will be dissolved, "as of course," upon defendant's entering his appearance and filing his answer, the quoted words mean when asked by defendant. Pitman v. West, 198 Mo.App. 92, 199 S.W. 756, 757.

AS PER. "As per" is a sort of law and business term which is hardly susceptible of literal translation, but which is commonly understood to mean, "in accordance with," or "in accordance with the terms of," or "as by the contract authorized." Continental Bank & Trust Co. v. Times Pub. Co., 142 La. 209, 76 So. 612, 617, L.R.A.1918B, 632.

AS SOON AS. This term has a relative meaning according to the thing which is to be done. Eichelbaum & Smith v. Bishop, 75 Pa.Super.Ct. 528, 529. It often denotes merely a reasonable time; Childers v. Brown, 81 Or. 1, 158 P. 166, 168, Ann. Cas.1918D, 170; and it may be the equivalent of "whenever"; People v. Merhige, 180 N.W. 418, 422, 212 Mich. 601. Sometimes it means immediately. Columbia Digger Co. v. Rector, D.C.S.D., 215 F. 618, 630.

AS SOON AS MAY BE. Promptly and with due diligence; as soon as was reasonably possible; within a reasonable time; as soon as possible; forthwith; as soon as they conveniently can. George A. Fuller Co. v. Jersey City, 21 N.J.Misc. 38, 29 A.2d 720, 722.

AS SOON AS POSSIBLE. When used with reference to the time of performing some act, such as the shipment of goods, these words mean merely within a reasonable time. Birmingham Paper Co. v. Holder, 24 Ga.App. 630, 101 S.E. 692; National Cash Register Co. v. McCann, 140 N.Y.S. 916, 920, 80 Misc. 165 ("as soon as possible" requires a much more speedy fulfillment than within a reasonable time).

AS SOON AS PRACTICABLE. Means reasonable time. Callaway v. Central Surety & Insurance Corporation, C.C.A.Tex., 107 F.2d 761, 762; London Guarantee & Accident Co. v. Shafer, D.C.Ohio, 35 F.Supp. 647, 649; London Guarantee & Accident Co. v. Shafer, D.C.Ohio, 32 F.Supp. 905, 908; Unverzagt v. Prestera, 13 A.2d 46, 48, 339 Pa. 141.

These words are not synonymous with "as soon as possible"; they mean ordinarily as soon as reasonably can be expected. Texas Employers' Ins. Ass'n v. Mumniey, Tex. Civ.App., 200 S.W. 251, 253; or "in due time", Texas Employers' Ins. Ass'n v. Mummey, Tex.Civ.App., 200 S.W. 251, 252. But the words have also been construed as practically synonymous with speedily. Roberson v. Weaver, 145 Ga. 620, 89 S.E. 769, 772.

AS SPEEDILY AS POSSIBLE. Means within reasonable time or without unreasonable delay, having regard to all the circumstances of the case and the things to be done. Tatum v. Levi, 117 Cal. App. 83, 3 P.2d 963, 967.

AS SUCH. When used to give some example of a rule, is never exclusive of other cases which that rule is made to embrace. Dinnat v. Succession of Lewis, 8 La.App. 820, 821.

ASCEND. To go up; to pass up or upwards; to go or pass in the ascending line. 4 Kent, Comm. 393, 397.

ASCENDANTS. Persons with whom one is related in the ascending line; one's parents, grandparents, great-grandparents, etc.

ASCENDIENTES. In Spanish law. Ascendants; ascending heirs; heirs in the ascending line. Schm.Civil Law, 259.

ASCENT. Passage upwards; the transmission of an estate from the ancestor to the heir in the ascending line. See 4 Kent, Comm. 393, 397.

ASCERTAIN. To fix; to render certain or definite; to estimate and determine; to clear of doubt or obscurity. Pughe v. Coleman, Tex.Civ.App., 44 S.W. 578. To insure as a certainty. United States v. Foster, C.C.A.Iowa, 131 F.2d 3, 7. To find out by investigation, U. S. v. Carver, 43 S.Ct. 181, 182, 260 U.S. 482, 67 L.Ed. 361. Sometimes it means to "assess", Commonwealth v. Deford Co., 137 Va. 542, 120 S.E. 281, 285; or to "hear, try, and determine," In re Higgins' Estate, 143 N.Y.S. 552, 556, 81 Misc. 579.

ASCERTAINED AS AFORESAID. Manner theretofore prescribed. State ex rel. Walker v. Harrington, Del., 30 A.2d 688, 693, 3 Terry 246.

ASCRIPTITIUS (or ASCRIPTICIUS). In Roman law. A foreigner who had been registered and naturalized in the colony in which he resided. Cod. 11, 47.

A man bound to the soil but not a slave. 2 Holdsw.Hist.E.L. 217. See Adscriptitii.

ASCUN, or ASCUNS. L. Fr. Any; any one; some. Adams Gloss.

ASESINATO. In Spanish law, murder. The term is said to be derived from the "assassins" of Syria. Escriche Diccionario. The offense corresponds closely to the common-law crime of murder in the first degree. U. S. v. Alias, 18 Philippine 453, 455; U. S. v. Pico, 18 Philippine 386, 388.

ASEXUALIZATION. See Vasectomy.

ASIDE. On one side; apart. *To set aside.* To annul; to make void. State v. Primm, 61 Mo. 171.

ASK. In an affidavit wherein affiant asks that a cause be reinstated and set down for trial, "asks" is practically synonymous with "moves." Harris v. Chicago House-Wrecking Co., 314 Ill. 500, 145 N.E. 666, 669.

ASPECT. View; object; possibility. Implies the existence of alternatives. Used in the phrases "bill with a double aspect" and "contingency with a double aspect."

ASPERSIONS. "Aspersions" may mean the making of calumnious report or may mean nothing more than criticism or censure. Fitts v. Davis, 269 F. 1018, 1019, 50 App.D.C. 234.

ASPHALT. A brown to black, solid bituminous substance occurring native at the Dead Sea, in Trinidad, and elsewhere, and also obtained as a residue from petroleum, coal tar, lignite tar, etc., and consists chiefly of a mixture of hydrocarbons and varies from hard and brittle to plastic forms. Asphalt Revetment Co. v. United States, 48 F. Supp. 520, 523, 98 Ct.Cl. 289.

ASPHYXIA. Apparent death, suspended animation, in living organism due to deficiency of oxygen and excess of carbon dioxide in the blood. Levinson v. Reliance Life Ins. Co. of Pittsburgh, Pa., 184 Md. 453, 41 A.2d 485, 487. Safe Deposit & Trust Co. of Baltimore v. New York Life Ins. Co., D.C.Md., 14 F.Supp. 721, 723.

ASPHYXIA CARBONICA. A suffocation from inhalation of coal gas, water gas, or carbon monoxide. Levinson v. Reliance Life Ins. Co. of Pittsburgh, Pa., Md., 184 Md. 453, 41 A.2d 485, 487.

ASPHYXIATION. A state of asphyxia. Stone v. Physicians Casualty Ass'n of America, 130 Neb. 769, 266 N.W. 605, 607.

ASPIRIN. A coal tar product commonly kept in drug stores and sold for medicinal purposes. It is not a proprietary or patent medicine, but is a drug or medicine, within a statute prohibiting retailing by one not a registered pharmacist. State v. Zotalis, 172 Minn. 132, 214 N.W. 766, 767. People v. Garcia, 1 Cal.App.2d 761, 32 P.2d 445, 447. State v. Jewett Market Co., 209 Iowa, 567, 228 N.W. 288, 289.

ASPORTATION. The removal of things from one place to another. The carrying away of goods; one of the circumstances requisite to constitute the offense of larceny. 4 Bl.Comm. 231. Rex v. Walsh, 1 Moody, Cr.Cas. 14, 15. Any appreciable changing of the location of the property involved with felonious intent. People v. Ashworth, 222 N.Y.S. 24, 27, 220 App.Div. 498; Banks v. State, 133 Ark. 169, 202 S.W. 43.

To constitute "asportation," the thing taken must have been in entire or absolute possession of taker. Adams v. Commonwealth, 153 Ky. 88, 154 S.W. 381, 44 L.R.A.,N.S., 637. But goods need not be removed from owner's premises, but act of thief in putting property into sack which he carries is sufficient. 21 Okl.St.Ann. § 1701. Brinkley v. State, 60 Okl.Cr. 106, 61 P.2d 1023, 1025. The slightest removal of goods from the place where the owner placed them or wanted them to be is sufficient. Driggers v. State, 118 So. 20, 21, 96 Fla. 232.

ASPORTAVIT. He carried away. Sometimes used as a noun to denote a carrying away. An "*asportavit* of personal chattels." 2 H.Bl. 4.

ASSACH. In old Welsh law. An oath made by compurgators. Brown.

ASSART. In English law. The offense committed in the forest, by pulling up the trees by the roots that are thickets and coverts for deer, and making the ground plain as arable land. It differs from waste, in that waste is the cutting down of coverts which may grow again, whereas assart is the plucking them up by the roots and utterly destroying them, so that they can never afterward grow. This is not an offense if done with license to convert forest into tillage ground. Consult *Manwood's Forest Laws,* pt. I, p. 171. Wharton. See Essarter.

ASSART RENTS. Rents paid to the Crown for assarted lands.

ASSASSINATION. Murder committed for hire, without provocation or cause of resentment given to the murderer by the person upon whom the crime is committed. Ersk.Inst. 4, 4, 45. A murder committed treacherously or by stealth or surprise, or by lying in wait. Sorrell v. State, 135 Tex.Cr.R. 535, 120 S.W.2d 1058, 1059.

ASSATH. An ancient custom in Wells, by which a person accused of crime could clear himself by the oaths of three hundred men. It was abolished by St. 1 Hen. V. c. 6. Cowell; Spelman.

ASSAULT. An intentional, unlawful offer of corporal injury to another by force, or force unlawfully directed toward person of another, under such circumstances as create well-founded fear of imminent peril, coupled with apparent present ability to execute attempt, if not prevented. State v. Staw, 97 N.J.L. 349, 116 A. 425; Naler v. State, 148 So. 880, 25 Ala.App. 486.

Intention to harm is of the essence, Raefeldt v. Koenig, 152 Wis. 459, 140 N.W. 56, 57, L.R.A.1918E, 1052; but general malevolence or recklessness is sufficient, State v. Fine, 324 Mo. 194, 23 S.W.2d 7, 10; hence striking intentionally, or by driving machine in reckless disregard of human life and safety is sufficient. Webb v. State, 68 Ga.App. 466, 23 S.E.2d 578, 580. It implies repulsion, or at least want of consent. People v. Dong Pok Yip, 164 Cal. 143, 127 P. 1031,

1032; hence operation without consent is assault. Dicenzo v. Berg, 340 Pa. 305, 16 A.2d 15, 16. Assault must have been unwarranted, but it need not have been committed in anger. McGovern v. Weis, 39 N.Y.S.2d 115, 118, 265 App. Div. 367; hence self-defense is not "assault". City of Gaffney v. Putnam, 197 S.C. 237, 15 S.E.2d 130, 131. Mere words, although provoking or insulting, are insufficient; Western Union Telegraph Co. v. Hill, C.C.A.Ala., 67 F.2d 487; Dahlin v. Fraser, 206 Minn. 476, 288 N.W. 851, 852.

In some jurisdictions degrees of the offense are established, as first degree, State v. Laughlin, Mont., 73 P.2d 718, 721; second degree, State v. Reynolds, 94 Wash. 270, 162 P. 358, 359; and third degree, State v. Steele, 83 Wash. 470, 145 P. 581; State v. Laughlin, 105 Mont. 490, 73 P.2d 718, 721.

Aggravated Assault

One committed with the intention of committing some additional crime; or one attended with circumstances of peculiar outrage or atrocity. This class includes assault with a dangerous or deadly weapon; Brinkley v. State, 82 Tex.Cr.R. 150, 198 S.W. 940; assault upon infants or females, if it create a sense of shame; Wren v. State, 27 Ariz. 491, 232 P. 398; and assault of lust, meaning an assault, less than felonious, with intent to have improper sexual connection; State v. Eslick, Mo.App., 216 S.W. 974, 975.

ASSAULT WITH INTENT TO COMMIT MANSLAUGHTER. An unlawful assault committed in such manner and with such means as would have resulted in commission of crime of manslaughter if person assaulted had then and there died from effects of assault. Lassiter v. State, 98 Fla. 370, 123 So. 735; State v. Crutcher, 1 N.W.2d 195, 199, 231 Iowa 418.

ASSAULT WITH INTENT TO COMMIT MURDER. To constitute this assault and specific intent to kill, actuated by malice aforethought, must concur. Perez v. State, 114 Tex.Cr.R. 473, 22 S.W.2d 309, 310; Griffin v. State, 177 S.E. 511, 50 Ga.App. 213.

ASSAULT WITH INTENT TO COMMIT RAPE. Is constituted by the existence of the facts which bring the offense within the definition of an assault, coupled with an intention to commit the crime of rape. Steptoe v. State, 133 Tex.Cr.R. 194, 115 S.W.2d 916, 917; State v. Jackson, 200 La. 432, 8 So.2d 285, 286.

ASSAULT WITH INTENT TO COMMIT ROBBERY. Involves an assault as well as an intent to commit robbery. Foss v. State, 36 Ohio App. 417, 173 N.E. 296, 297.

Secret Assault

Under a North Carolina statute, to warrant conviction for malicious, "secret assault," state must prove all essential elements of crime, namely, malice, use of deadly weapon in secret manner, with intent to kill. State v. Kline, 190 N.C. 177, 129 S.E. 417, 418.

It is not essential, however, that the person assaulted be unconscious of the presence of his adversary, though the purpose of such adversary must not be known. State v. Oxendine, 187 N.C. 658, 122 S.E. 568, 571.

Simple Assault

One committed with no intention to do any other injury. An offer or attempt to do bodily harm which falls short of an actual battery; an offer or attempt to beat another, but without touching him; for example, a blow delivered within striking distance, but which does not reach its mark. Norton v. State, 14 Tex. 393. Also, sometimes, the use of physical violence upon another, without circumstances of aggravation. Ratcliff v. State, 106 Tex.Cr.R. 37, 289 S.W. 1072, 1074. "Simple assault and battery" is an unlawful act of violent injury to another, unaccompanied by any circumstances of aggravation. State v. Jones, 133 S.C. 167, 130 S.E. 747, 751. And see State v. Staw, 97 N.J.L. 349, 116 A. 425.

ASSAY. The proof or trial, by chemical experiments, of the purity or fineness of metals,—particularly of the precious metals, gold and silver. West v. State, 140 Tex.Cr.R. 493, 145 S.W.2d 580, 584.

A trial of weights and measures by a standard; as by the constituted authorities, clerks of markets, etc. Reg.Orig. 280.

A trial or examination of certain commodities, as bread, cloths, etc. Cowell; Blount. See Annual Assay.

ASSAY OFFICE. The staff of persons by whom (or the building or department in which) the process of assaying gold and silver, required by government, incidental to maintaining the coinage, is conducted.

ASSAYER. One whose business it is to make assays of the precious metals. West v. State, 140 Tex.Cr.R. 493, 145 S.W.2d 580, 584.

ASSAYER OF THE KING. An officer of the royal mint, appointed by St. 2 Hen. VI. c. 12, who received and tested the bullion taken in for coining; also called *"assayator regis."* Cowell; Termes de la Ley.

ASSECURARE. To assure, or make secure by pledges, or any solemn interposition of faith. Cowell; Spelman.

ASSECURATION. In European law. Assurance; insurance of a vessel, freight, or cargo. Ferrière.

ASSECURATOR. In maritime law. An insurer, *(aversor periculi.)* Locc. de Jure Mar. lib. 2, c. 5, § 10.

ASSEDATION. In Scotch law. An old term, used indiscriminately to signify a lease or feu-right. Bell; Ersk.Inst. 2, 6, 20.

ASSEMBLAGE. A collection of persons. Also the act of coming together. State v. Breen, 110 Kan. 817, 205 P. 632, 633. Public address upon public grounds. In re Whitney, 57 Cal.App.2d 167, 134 P.2d 516, 521.

ASSEMBLE. When applied to a machine, "assemble" means to collect or gather together the parts and place them in their proper relation to each other to constitute the machine. Citizens' Nat. Bank v. Bucheit, 14 Ala.App. 511, 71 So. 82, 38.

ASSEMBLY. The concourse or meeting together of a considerable number of persons at the same place. Also the persons so gathered.

Popular assemblies are those where the people meet to deliberate upon their rights; these are guaranteed by the constitution. Const.U.S.Amend. art. 1.

Political assemblies are those required by the constitution and laws: for example, the general assembly.

The lower or more numerous branch of the legislature in many of the states is also called the "Assembly" or "House of Assembly," but the term seems to be an appropriate one to designate any political meeting required to be held by law.

ASSEMBLY GENERAL. The highest ecclesiastical court in Scotland, composed of a representation of the ministers and elders of the church, regulated by Act 5th Assem. 1694.

ASSEMBLY, UNLAWFUL. In criminal law. The assembling of three or more persons together to do an unlawful act, who separate without actually doing it, or making any motion towards it. 3 Inst. 176; 4 Bl.Comm. 146. It differs from a riot or rout, because in each of the latter cases there is some act done besides the simple meeting. 1 Bish.Crim.Law, § 535; 2 Bish.Crim.Law, §§ 1256, 1259.

ASSENT. Compliance; approval of something done; a declaration of willingness to do something in compliance with a request. Norton v. Davis, 83 Tex. 32, 18 S.W. 430; Appeal of Pittsburgh, 115 Pa. 4, 7 A. 778; To approve, ratify and confirm. People v. Consolidated Indemnity and Ins. Co., 233 App.Div. 74, 251 N.Y.S. 566, 569. It implies a conscious approval of facts actually known, as distinguished from mere neglect to ascertain facts. White-Wilson-Drew Co. v. Lyon-Ratcliff Co., C.C.A.Ill., 268 F. 525, 526. Sometimes it is equivalent to "authorize." Hagerla v. Mississippi River Power Co., D.C.Iowa, 202 F. 776, 783. In the sense of the law is a matter of overt acts, not of inward unanimity in motives, design or the interpretation of words. Triboro Coach Corporation v. New York State Labor Relations Board, 261 App.Div. 636, 27 N.Y.S.2d 83, 85.

"Assent" is an act of understanding, while "consent" is an act of the will or feelings. Klundby v. Hogden, 202 Wis. 438, 232 N.W. 858, 860, 73 A.L.R. 648. It means passivity or submission which does not include consent. Perryman v. State, 63 Ga.App. 819, 12 S.E.2d 388, 390.

Express Assent

That which is openly declared.

Implied Assent

That which is presumed by law.

Mutual Assent

The meeting of the minds of both or all the parties to a contract; the fact that each agrees to all the terms and conditions, in the same sense and with the same meaning as the others. Insurance Co. v. Young, 23 Wall. 107, 23 L.Ed. 152.

ASSERT. To state as true; declare; maintain. To assert against another has probably a *prima facie* meaning of a contradiction of him, but the context or circumstances may show that it connotes a criminatory charge; 7 L.J.Ex. 268.

ASSERTORY COVENANT. One which affirms that a particular state of facts exists; an affirming promise under seal.

ASSERTORY OATH. See Oath.

ASSESS. To ascertain; fix the value of. State ex rel. Ambrose v. Trimble, 304 Mo. 533, 263 S.W. 840, 842. In re Calhoun Beach Holding Co., 205 Minn. 582, 287 N.W. 317, 322. To fix the amount of the damages or the value of the thing to be ascertained. New Orleans Terminal Co. v. Dixie Rendering, La.App., 179 So. 98, 100. To impose a pecuniary payment upon persons or property; People v. Priest, 169 N.Y. 435, 62 N.E. 568. To ascertain, adjust, and settle the respective shares to be contributed by several persons toward an object beneficial to them all, in proportion to the benefit received.

In connection with taxation of property, means to make a valuation and appraisal of property, usually in connection with listing of property liable to taxation, and implies the exercise of discretion on the part of officials charged with duty of assessing, including the listing or inventory of property involved, determination of extent of physical property, and placing of a value thereon. Montana-Dakota Power Co. v. Weeks, D.C.N.D., 8 F.Supp. 935, 936. To tax. Johnson City v. Clinchfield R. Co., 163 Tenn. 332, 43 S.W.2d 386, 387.

To adjust or fix the proportion of a tax which each person, of several liable to it, has to pay; to apportion a tax among several; to distribute taxation in a proportion founded on the proportion of burden and benefit. Seymour v. Peters, 67 Mich. 415, 35 N.W. 62. To calculate the rate and amount of taxes. Flanigan v. Police Jury of Jackson Parish, 145 La. 613, 82 So. 722, 726.

"Assess" is sometimes used as synonymous with "levy"; Lehigh Valley R. Co. v. State Board of Taxes and Assessment, 101 N.J.Law, 298, 128 A. 432, 433; and is sometimes distinguished therefrom; City of Portland v. Portland Ry. Light & Power Co., 80 Or. 271, 156 P. 1058, 1064.

ASSESSED. Is equivalent to imposed. Town of Brandon v. Harvey, 105 Vt. 435, 168 A. 708, 710. To value or appraise. Abrams v. City and County of San Francisco, 48 Cal.App.2d 1, 119 P.2d 197, 199.

ASSESSED VALUATION. Value on each unit of which a prescribed amount must be paid as property taxes. In re Calhoun Beach Holding Co., 205 Minn. 582, 287 N.W. 317, 322.

ASSESSMENT. In a general sense, the process of ascertaining and adjusting the shares respectively to be contributed by several persons towards a common beneficial object according to the benefit received.

Taxation

The listing and valuation of property for the purpose of apportioning a tax upon it, either according to value alone or in proportion to benefit received. Also determining the share of a tax to be paid by each of many persons; or apportioning the entire tax to be levied among the different taxable persons, establishing the proportion due from each. Town of Albertville v. Hooper, 196 Ala. 642, 72 So. 258. Northwestern Imp. Co. v. Henneford, 184 Wash. 502, 51 P.2d 1083, 1085. Iowa Nat. Bank. v. Stewart, 214 Iowa 1229, 232 N.W. 445, 451. It fixes the liability of the taxpayer and ascertains the facts and furnishes the data for the proper preparation of the tax rolls. Dallas Joint Stock Land Bank of Dallas v. State, Tex.Civ.App., 118 S.W.2d 941, 942.

"Assessment" and "levy" are frequently used interchangeably. Huyler v. Huyler's, 44 N.Y.S.2d 255, 257. Though properly speaking it does not include the levy of taxes. Commissioner of Internal Revenue v. Patrick Cudahy Family Co., C.C.A.7, 102 F.2d 930, 932. Assessment is also popularly used as synonym for taxation in general, the authorative imposition of a rate or duty to be paid, but in its technical signification it is only taxation for a special purpose or local improvement, local taxation, as distinguished from general taxation; taxation on principle of apportionment according to the relation between burden and benefit; whole taxes are impositions for purpose of general revenue. Collister v. Kovanda, 51 Ohio App. 43, 199 N.E. 477, 478; Home Owners' Loan Corporation v. Tyson, 133 Ohio St. 184, 12 N.E.2d 478, 480; Atlantic Coast Line R. Co. v. Town of Ahoskie, 192 N.C. 258, 134 S.E. 653, 654.

An assessment is doubtless a tax, but the term implies something more; it implies a tax of a particular kind, predicated upon the principle of equivalents, or benefits, which are peculiar to the persons or property charged therewith, and which are said to be assessed or appraised, according to the measure or proportion of such equivalents; whereas a simple tax is imposed for the purpose of supporting the government generally, without reference to any special advantage which may be supposed to accrue to the persons taxed. Taxes must be levied, without discrimination, equally upon all the subjects of property; whilst assessments are only levied upon lands, or some other specific property, the subjects of the supposed benefits; to repay which the assessment is levied. In re Walker River Irr. Dist., 44 Nev. 321, 195 P. 327, 330.

Corporations

Installments of the money subscribed for shares of stock, called for from the subscribers by the directors, from time to time as the company requires money, are called "assessments," or, in England, "calls." Water Co. v. Superior Court, 92 Cal. 47, 28 Pac. 54, 27 Am.St.Rep. 91; Spangler v. Railroad Co., 21 Ill. 278; Stewart v. Publishing Co., 1 Wash.St. 521, 20 Pac. 605. While the terms "call" and "assessment" are generally used synonymously, the latter term applies with peculiar aptness to contributions above the par value of stock or the subscription liability of the stockholders; Porter v. Northern Fire & Marine Ins. Co., 36 N.D. 199, 161 N.W. 1012, 1014; whereas "call" or "installments" means action of the board of directors demanding payment of all or portion of unpaid subscriptions; Seyberth v. American Commander Min. & Mill. Co., 42 Idaho, 254, 245 P. 392, 395.

It has been said, however, that the superadded liability of stockholders to creditors, is not in a true sense an "assessment," but is a "statutory liability." Leach v. Arthur Sav. Bank, 203 Iowa, 1052, 213 N.W. 772, 773.

Damages

Fixing the amount of damages to which the successful party in a suit is entitled after an interlocutory judgment has been taken; also the name given to the determination of the sum which a corporation proposing to take lands for a public use must pay in satisfaction of the demand proved or the value taken.

Insurance

An apportionment made in general average upon the various articles and interests at risk, according to their value at the time and place of being in safety, for contribution for damage and sacrifices purposely made, and expenses incurred for escape from impending common peril. 2 Phil. Ins. c. xv.

A sum specially levied in mutual benefit insurance upon a fixed and definite plan within the limit of the company's or society's fundamental law of organization to pay losses, or losses and expenses incurred, being to a certain degree substantially the equivalent of premiums. Beaver State Merchants' Mut. Fire Ins. Ass'n v. Smith, 97 Or. 579, 192 P. 798, 800. The periodical demands made by a mutual insurance company, under its charter and by-laws, upon the makers of premium notes, are also denominated "assessments." Hill v. Insurance Co., 129 Mich. 141, 88 N.W. 392. Meaning "premiums," Ancient Order of United Workmen of Kansas v. Hobbs, 136 Kan. 708, 18 P.2d 561, 562; and being the consideration for the insurance contracts. Downing v. School Dist. of City of Erie, 297 Pa. 474, 147 A. 239, 240.

Mining

"Assessment" as applied to labor on mining claims is universally understood to mean the annual labor required by Rev.St.U.S. § 2324 (30 U.S.C.A. § 28), in order to hold the right to the possession of the claim after a discovery and complete location has been made. Smith v. Union Oil Co., 166 Cal. 217, 135 P. 966, 969. See Assessment Work.

ASSESSMENT ASSOCIATION. This term, as defined by the Nebraska insurance laws, does not include an insurance company which requires the payment of a fixed premium in advance and provides benefits not in any degree dependent upon the collection of assessments from other members, and which does not provide for the levying of extra assessments, if necessary. Western Life & Accident Co. of Colorado v. State Ins. Board of Nebraska, 101 Neb. 152, 162 N.W. 530.

ASSESSMENT COMPANY. In life insurance. A company in which a death loss is met by levying an assessment on the surviving members of the association. National Ben. Ass'n v. Clay, 162 Ky. 409, 172 S.W. 922, 923.

ASSESSMENT CONTRACT. One wherein the payment of the benefit is in any manner or degree dependent on the collection of an assessment levied on persons holding similar contracts. Folkens v. Insurance Co., 98 Mo.App. 480, 72 S.W. 720.

ASSESSMENT DISTRICT. In taxation. Any subdivision of territory, whether the whole or part of any municipality, in which by law a separate assessment of taxable property is made by the officers elected or appointed therefor. Rev. Stat.Wis.1898, § 1031 (St.1931, § 70.04).

ASSESSMENT FOR BENEFITS. A burden levied under the power of taxation. Jackson v. City of Lake Worth, 156 Fla. 452, 23 So.2d 526, 528.

See Tax. Cooper Union for Advancement of Science and Art v. City of New York, 272 App. Div. 438, 71 N.Y.S.2d 204, 207.

ASSESSMENT FUND. The assessment fund of a mutual benefit association is the balance of the assessments, less expenses, out of which beneficiaries are paid. Kerr v. Ben. Ass'n, 39 Minn. 174, 39 N.W. 312, 12 Am.St.Rep. 631.

ASSESSMENT INSURANCE. Exists when benefit to be paid is dependent upon collection of such assessments as may be necessary for paying the amounts to insured. Keen v. Bankers Mut. Life Co., 230 Mo.App. 1072, 93 S.W.2d 85, 90.

ASSESSMENT LABOR. These words in Act Feb. 12, 1903 (30 U.S.C.A. § 102), providing that such labor on oil claims may be done on one of a group of contiguous claims refers to the annual labor required of the locator of a mineral claim after discovery by Rev.St. § 2324 (30 U.S.C.A. § 28), and not to work before discovery. Union Oil Co. of California v. Smith, 39 S.Ct. 308, 311, 249 U.S. 337, 63 L.Ed. 635. See Assessment, under the heading "In Mining."

ASSESSMENT LIST. The list furnished by the assessor to the board of equalization. Adsit v. Park, 144 La. 934, 81 So. 430, 434.

ASSESSMENT PERIOD. Means taxable period. Johnson City v. Clinchfield R. Co., 163 Tenn. 332, 43 S.W.2d 386, 387.

ASSESSMENT ROLL. In taxation. The list or roll of taxable persons and property, completed, verified, and deposited by the assessors, not as it appears after review and equalization. Brady v. Weissenstein, 260 Mich. 678, 245 N.W. 798, 799.

ASSESSMENT WORK. Under the mining laws of the United States, the holder of an unpatented mining claim on the public domain is required, in order to hold his claim, to do labor or make improvements upon it to the extent of at least one hundred dollars in each year.. Rev.St.U.S. § 2324 (30 U.S.C.A. § 28). This is commonly called by miners "doing assessment work."

ASSESSOR. An officer chosen or appointed to appraise, value, or assess property.

The assessing power, and not merely the county assessor. Board of Com'rs of San Miguel County v. Floaten, 66 Colo. 540, 181 P. 122.

A person learned in some particular science of industry, who sits with the judge on the trial of a cause requiring such special knowledge and gives his advice.

In England it is the practice in admiralty business to call in assessors, in cases involving questions of navigation or seamanship. They are called "nautical assessors" *(q. v.)*, and are always Brethren of the Trinity House.

Civil and Scotch Law

Persons skilled in law, selected to advise the judges of the inferior courts. Bell; Dig. 1, 22; Cod. 1, 51.

ASSETS. The word, though more generally used to denote everything which comes to the representatives of a deceased person, yet is by no means confined to that use, but has come to signify everything which can be made available for the payment of debts, whether belonging to the estate of a deceased person or not. Hence we speak of the assets of a bank or other monied corporation, the assets of an insolvent debtor, and the assets of an individual or private copartnership; and we always use this word when we speak of the means which a party has, as compared with his liabilities or debts. Pelican v. Rock Falls, 81 Wis. 428, 51 N.W. 871.

Bankruptcy

The property or effects of a bankrupt or insolvent, applicable to the payment of his debts.

The term "assets" includes all property of every kind and nature, chargeable with the debts of the bankrupt, that comes into the hands of and under the control of the signee; and the value thereof is not to be considered a less sum than that actually realized out of said property, and received by the assignee for it. In re Taggert, 16 N.B.R. 351, Fed.Cas.No.13,725; Progressive Building & Loan Co. v. Hall, C.C.A.Va., 220 F. 45, 46.

Commercial Law

The aggregate of available property, stock in trade, cash, etc., belonging to a merchant or mercantile company.

The term "assets," as applied to a bank, is broad enough to cover anything which is or may be available to pay creditors; but, as usually understood, it refers to the tangible property of the corporation, and not to the liability of stockholders contingent upon insolvency. Hill v. Smathers, 173 N.C. 642, 92 S.E. 607, 609; Deariso v. Mobley, 38 Ga.App. 313, 143 S.E. 915, 920. But when the individual liability of stockholders has been enforced by the superintendent of banks, funds collected by him thereunder are "assets." Bennett v. Wilkes County, 164 Ga. 790, 139 S.E. 566, 568.

But on other hand stockholders' voluntary assessment to relieve bank or for betterment of stock. Thomson v. Holt, 345 Mo. 296, 132 S.W.2d 974, 977; bank stockholders' liability, Farmers & Merchants Bank of Morgantown v. Bank of Masontown, 123 W.Va. 451, 15 S.E.2d 569, 572; and bank directors' contribution to special bond account to make good shrinkage in regular bond were held to be assets. Asher v. West End Bank, 345 Mo. 89, 131 S.W.2d 549, 551.

Probate Law

Property of a decedent available for the payment of debts and legacies; the estate coming to the heir or personal representative which is chargeable, in law or equity, with the obligations which such heir or representative is required, in his representative capacity, to discharge.

In an accurate and legal sense, all the personal property of the deceased which is of a salable nature, and may be converted into ready money, is deemed *assets*. But the word is not confined to such property; for all other property of the deceased, real or personal, tangible or intangible, legal or equitable, which can be made available for or can be appropriated to payment of debts, is, in a large sense, assets. Trust Co. v. Earle, 110 U.S. 710, 4 Sup.Ct. 231, 28 L.Ed. 301; Condo v. Barbour, 101 Ind.App. 483, 200 N.E. 76; Tapp v. Stuart, D.C.Okl., 6 F.Supp. 577, 578.

General

—Assets entre mains. L. Fr. Assets in hand; assets in the hands of executors or administrators, applicable for the payment of debts. Termes de la Ley; 2 Bl.Comm. 510; 1 Crabb, Real Prop. 23; Favorite v. Booher, 17 Ohio St. 557.

—Assets per descent. That portion of the ancestor's estate which descends to the heir, and which is sufficient to charge him, as far as it goes, with the specialty debts of his ancestors. 2 Williams, Ex'rs, 1011.

—Equitable assets. Equitable assets are all assets which are chargeable with the payment of debts or legacies in equity, and which do not fall under the description of legal assets. 1 Story, Eq.Jur. § 552. Those portions of the property which by the ordinary rules of law are exempt from debts, but which the testator has voluntarily charged as assets, or which, being non-existent at law, have been created in equity. Adams, Eq. 254, et seq.

They are so called because they can be reached only by the aid and instrumentality of a court of equity, and because their distribution is governed by a different rule from that which governs the distribution of legal assets. 2 Fonbl. Eq. b. 4, pt. 2, c. 2, § 1, and notes; Story, Eq. Jur. § 552.

—Legal assets. See Legal Assets.

—Personal assets. Chattels, money, and other personal property belonging to a bankrupt, insolvent, or decedent estate, which go to the assignee or executor.

—Quick assets. This term was used in a corporation credit statement merely to distinguish liquid assets from those permanently invested in the business, like real estate and machinery, and included amounts charged against officers for return of part of salaries paid them in a previous year, in accordance with the agreement of employment. In re American Knit Goods Mfg. Co., C.C.A.N.Y., 173 F. 480, 97 C.C.A. 486.

—Real assets. Lands or real estate in the hands of an heir, chargeable with the payment of the debts of the ancestor. 2 Bl.Comm. 244, 302.

ASSEVERATION. An affirmation; a positive assertion; a solemn declaration. This word is seldom, if ever, used for a declaration made under oath, but denotes a declaration accompanied with solemnity or an appeal to conscience, whereas by an oath one appeals to God as a witness of the truth of what one says.

ASSEWIARE. To draw or drain water from marsh grounds. Cowell.

ASSIGN, *v.* To make over or set over to another. North Tex. Nat. Bank v. Thompson, Tex.Civ.App., 23 S.W.2d 494, 499. To appoint, allot, select, or designate for a particular purpose, or duty.

Thus, in England, justices are said to be "*assigned* to take the assises," "*assigned* to hold pleas," "*assigned to* make gaol delivery," "*assigned* to keep the peace," etc. St. Westm. 2, c. 30; Reg. Orig. 68, 69; 3 Bl.Comm. 58, 59, 353; 1 Bl. Comm. 351.

To transfer persons, as a sheriff is said to assign prisoners in his custody.

Conveyancing

To transfer; as to assign property, or some interest therein. Cowell; 2 Bl.Comm. 326; North Texas Nat. Bank v. Thompson, Tex.Civ.App., 23 S.W.2d 494, 499; To transfer the title or ownership, as of choses in action. Burkett v. Doty, 176 Cal. 89, 167 P. 518, 520.

Practice

To point at, or point out; to set forth, or specify; to mark out or designate; to particularize; as to *assign errors* on a writ of error; to *assign breaches* of a covenant. 2 Tidd, Pr. 1168; 1 Tidd, 686; Commercial Standard Ins. Co. v. Noack, Tex. Civ.App., 45 S.W.2d 798, 801.

ASSIGNABILITY. "Survivability" convertible term. People ex rel. Rude v. La Salle County, 310 Ill.App. 541, 34 N.E.2d 865, 867. City of Milwaukee v. Boynton Cab Co., 201 Wis. 581, 231 N.W. 597, 598.

ASSIGNABLE. That may be assigned or transferred; transferable; negotiable, as a bill of exchange. Comb. 176; Story, Bills, § 17.

ASSIGNATION. In French law. A writ of summons.

In Scotch law. A term equivalent to assignment.

ASSIGNATION HOUSE. A bawdyhouse. State v. Bragg, Mo.App., 220 S.W. 25, 26. See, also, People v. Arcega, 49 Cal.App. 239, 193 P. 264, 266. A house resorted to for prostitution. State v. Hesselmeyer, 343 Mo. 797, 123 S.W.2d 90, 99.

ASSIGNATUS UTITUR JURE AUCTORIS. An assignee uses the right of his principal; an assignee is clothed with the rights of his principal. Wing.Max. 56; 1 Exch. 32; 18 Q.B. 878.

ASSIGNAY. In Scotch law. An assignee.

ASSIGNEE. A person to whom an assignment is made; grantee. Nolan v. City of New York, 39 N.Y.S.2d 360, 363, 179 Misc. 1011. Ely v. Com'rs, 49 Mich. 17, 12 N.W. 893, 13 N.W. 784. The term is commonly used in reference to personal property; but it is not incorrect, in some cases, to apply it to realty, *e. g.*, "assignee of the reversion."

Assignee in fact is one to whom an assignment has been made in fact by the party having the right. Tucker v. West, 31 Ark. 643. One to whom an assignment has been made. Michigan Trust Co. v. Chaffee, D.C.N.D., 44 F.Supp. 848, 850.

Assignee in law is one in whom the law vests the right; as an executor or administrator.

Old Law

A person deputed or appointed by another to do any act, or perform any business. Blount. An *assignee*, however, was distinguished from a *deputy*, being said to occupy a thing in his own right, while a deputy acted in right of another. Cowell.

ASSIGNEE FOR THE BENEFIT OF CREDITORS. One to whom, under an insolvent or bankrupt law, the whole estate of a debtor is transferred to be administered for the benefit of creditors; he is a trustee for the creditors who stands in the shoes of an assignor, and can assert no claim to property which assignor could not. Slater v. Oriental Mills, 18 R.I. 352, 27 A. 443, 444; Textor v. Orr, 86 Md. 392, 38 A. 939, 940.

ASSIGNMENT. A transfer or making over to another of the whole of any property, real or personal, in possession or in action, or of any estate or right therein. Bostrom v. Bostrom, 60 N.D. 792, 236 N.W. 732, 734. It includes transfers of all kinds of property, Higgins v. Monckton, 28 Cal.App.2d 723, 83 P.2d 516, 519. But is ordinarily limited to transfers of choses in action and to rights in or connected with property, as distinguished from the particular item of property. In re Beffa's Estate, 54 Cal.App. 186, 201 P. 616, 617. It is generally appropriate to the transfer of equitable interests. Kavanaugh v. Cohoes Power & Light Corporation, 187 N.Y.S. 216, 228, 114 Misc. 590.

To constitute valid "assignment," there must be perfected transaction between parties intended to vest in assignee present right in thing assigned. In re Lynch's Estate, 272 N.Y.S. 79, 85, 151 Misc. 549. It is contract, and is subject to same requisites as to validity as other contracts, such as proper parties, mutual assent, consideration, and legal subject-matter. Hutsell v. Citizens' Nat. Bank, 166 Tenn. 598, 64 S.W.2d 188.

The transfer of the interest one has in *lands* and *tenements;* more particularly applied to the unexpired residue of a term or estate for life or years; Cruise, Dig. tit. xxxii. (Deed) c. vii, § 15; 1 Steph.Com. 507.

The distinction between an "assignment" and a "sublease" is that an assignment transfers the entire unexpired term. Sandford v. Ambassador Restaurant Co., 247 N.Y.S. 655, 657, 139 Misc. 3.

The deed by which the transfer is made. Humphrey v. Coquillard Wagon Works, 37 Okl. 714, 132 P. 899, 902, 49 L.R.A.,N.S., 600.

A transfer of the title to a bill, note, or check.

An assignment at common law differs from an indorsement in that by an assignment the assignor passed title to the assignee but did not subject himself to any contractual liability, whereas an indorser, in addition to passing title, impliedly contracts to pay note at maturity on demand and notice on maker's failure to so do. Johnson v. Beickey, 64 Utah, 43, 228 P. 189, 191.

In patent law, the transfer of the entire interest in a patented invention or of an undivided portion of such entire interest as to every section of the United States. Rob.Pat. § 762. It differs from grant in relation to the territorial area to which they relate. A grant is the transfer of the exclusive right in a specific part of the United States. It is an exclusive sectional right. A license is a transfer of a less or different interest than either the interest in a whole patent or an undivided part of such whole interest or an exclusive sectional interest. Littlefield v. Perry, 21 Wall. 205, 22 L.Ed. 577.

A license is distinguished from an assignment and a grant in that the latter transfers the monopoly as well as the invention, while a license transfers only the invention and does not affect the monopoly otherwise than by estopping the licensor from exercising his prohibitory powers in derogation of the privileges conferred by him upon the licensee. Rob. Pat. § 806. See Pope Mfg. Co. v. Mfg. Co., 144 U.S. 248, 12 S.Ct. 641, 36 L.Ed. 423.

—Assignment for benefit of creditors. An assignment in trust made by insolvent and other debtors for the payment of their debts. These are usually regulated by state statutes. Woodard v. Morrissey, 115 Kan. 511, 223 P. 306, 307.

The distinctive test between an "assignment" and a sale, where another creditor is to be paid off, is that in the former case such other creditor is to receive some of the property or its proceeds, and in the latter the creditor to whom title is passed takes for himself the whole property, stipulating to pay the other creditor out of his own means and not out of the property or its proceeds. Silver & Goldstein v. Chapman, 163 Ga. 604, 136 S.E. 914, 919.

—Assignment of account. Transfer to assignee giving him a right to have moneys when collected applied to payment of his debt. Nanny v. H. E. Pogue Distillery Co., 56 Cal.App.2d 817, 133 P.2d 686, 688.

—Assignment of dower. The act by which the share of a widow in her deceased husband's real estate is ascertained and set apart to her. Bettis v. McNider, 137 Ala. 588, 34 So. 813, 97 Am.St.Rep. 59.

—Assignment of error. See Error.

—Assignment pro tanto. Where an order is drawn upon a third party and made payable out of a particular fund then due or to become due to the drawer, the delivery of the order to the payee operates as an assignment pro tanto of the fund. Doyle v. East New York Sav. Bank, 44 N.Y.S.2d 318, 323.

Under Mechanics' Lien Law a workman or materialman who serves on owner a stop notice becomes an assignee pro tanto of debt due from owner to contractor. Commonwealth Roofing Co. v. Riccio, 81 N.J.Eq. 486, 87 A. 114, 115.

Check drawn on a bank operates as an assignment pro tanto of depositor's funds in favor of holder. Nat. Bank of America v. Indiana Banking Co., 114 Ill. 483, 2 N.E. 401.

—Assignment with preferences. An assignment for the benefit of creditors, with directions to the assignee to prefer a specified creditor or class of creditors, by paying their claims in full before the others receive any dividend, or in some other manner. More usually termed a "preferential assignment."

—Foreign assignment. An assignment made in a foreign country, or in another state. 2 Kent, Comm. 405, *et seq.*

—General assignment. An assignment made for the benefit of *all* the assignor's creditors, instead of a few only; or one which transfers the *whole* of his estate to the assignee, instead of a part only. Royer Wheel Co. v. Fielding, 101 N.Y. 504, 5 N.E. 431.

—Voluntary assignment. An assignment for the benefit of his creditors made by a debtor voluntarily; as distinguished from a compulsory assignment which takes place by operation of law in proceedings in bankruptcy or insolvency. Presumably it means an assignment of a debtor's property in trust to pay his debts generally, in distinction from a transfer of property to a particular creditor in payment of his demand, or to a conveyance by way of collateral security or mortgage. Dias v. Bouchaud, 10 Paige (N.Y.) 445.

ASSIGNOR. A person who assigns a right, whether or not he is the original owner thereof. Restatement, Contracts, § 149(2).

ASSIGNS. Assignees; those to whom property shall have been transferred. Now seldom used except in the phrase, in deeds, "heirs, administrators, and assigns." Stannard v. Marboe, 159 Minn. 119, 198 N.W. 127. It generally comprehends all those who take either immediately or remotely from or under the assignor, whether by conveyance, devise, descent, or act of law. Ferrell v. Deverick, 100 S.E. 850, 853, 85 W.Va. 1.

ASSISA. In old English and Scotch law. An assise; a kind of jury or inquest; a writ; a sitting of a court; an ordinance or statute; a fixed or specific time, number, quantity, quality, price, or weight; a tribute, fine, or tax; a real action; the name of a writ. See Assise.

ASSISA ARMORUM. Assise of arms. A statute or ordinance requiring the keeping of arms for the common defense. Hale, Com.Law, c. 11.

ASSISA CADERE. To fail in the assise; *i. e.,* to be nonsuited. Cowell; 3 Bl.Comm. 402.

ASSISA CADIT IN JURATUM. The assise falls (turns) into a jury; hence to submit a controversy to trial by jury.

ASSISA CONTINUANDA. An ancient writ addressed to the justices of assise for the continuation of a cause, when certain facts put in issue could not have been proved in time by the party alleging them. Reg.Orig. 217.

ASSISA DE CLARENDON. The assise of Clarendon. A statute or ordinance passed in the tenth year of Henry II., by which those that were accused of any heinous crime, and not able to purge themselves, but must abjure the realm, had liberty of forty days to stay and try what succor they could get of their friends towards their sustenance in exile. Bract. fol. 136; Co.Litt. 159*a*; Cowell.

ASSISA DE FORESTA. Assise of the forest; a statute concerning orders to be observed in the royal forests.

ASSISA DE MENSURIS. Assise of measures. A common rule for weights and measures, established throughout England by Richard I., in the eighth year of his reign. Hale, Com.Law, c. 7.

ASSISA DE NOCUMENTO. An assise of nuisance; a writ to abate or redress a nuisance.

ASSISA DE UTRUM. An obsolete writ, which lay for the parson of a church whose predecessor had alienated the land and rents of it.

ASSISA FRISCÆ FORTIÆ. Assise of fresh force, which see.

ASSISA MORTIS D'ANCESTORIS. Assise of mort d'ancestor, which see.

ASSISA NOVÆ DISSEYSINÆ. Assise of novel disseisin, which see.

ASSISA PANIS ET CEREVISIÆ. Assise of bread and ale, or beer. The name of a statute passed in the fifty-first year of Henry III., containing regulations for the sale of bread and ale; sometimes called the "statute of bread and ale." Co.Litt. 159*b*; 2 Reeve, Hist.Eng.Law, 56; Cowell; Bract. fol. 155.

ASSISA PROROGANDA. An obsolete writ, which was directed to the judges assigned to take assises, to stay proceedings, by reason of a party to them being employed in the king's business. Reg.Orig. 208.

ASSISA ULTIMÆ PRÆSENTATIONIS. Assise of darrein presentment, (*q. v.*).

ASSISA VENALIUM. The assise of salable commodities, or of things exposed for sale.

ASSISE, or ASSIZE. An ancient species of court, consisting of a certain number of men, usually twelve, who were summoned together to try a disputed cause, performing the functions of a jury, except that they gave a verdict from their own investigation and knowledge and not upon evidence adduced. From the fact that they sat together, (*assideo,*) they were called the "assise." See Bract. 4, 1, 6; Co.Litt. 153*b*, 159*b*. A court composed of an assembly of knights and other substantial men, with the baron or justice, in a certain place, at an appointed time. Grand Cou. cc. 24, 25.

The verdict or judgment of the jurors or recognitors of assise. 3 Bl.Comm. 57, 59.

In modern English law, the name "assises" or "assizes" is given to the court, time, or place where the judges of assise and *nisi prius,* who are sent by special commission from the crown on circuits through the kingdom, proceed to take indictments, and to try such disputed causes issuing out of the courts at Westminster as are then ready for trial, with the assistance of a jury from the particular county; the regular sessions of the judges at *nisi prius*.

Anything reduced to a certainty in respect to time, number, quantity, quality, weight, measure, etc. Spelman.

An ordinance, statute, or regulation. Spelman gives this meaning of the word the first place among his definitions, observing that *statutes* were in England called "assises" down to the reign of Henry III.

A species of writ, or real action, said to have been invented by Glanville, chief justice to Henry II., and having for its object to determine the right of possession of lands, and to recover the possession. 3 Bl.Comm. 184, 185.

The whole proceedings in court upon a writ of assise. Co.Litt. 159*b*. The verdict or finding of the jury upon such a writ. 3 Bl.Comm. 57.

—Assise of Clarendon. See Assisa.

—Assise of darrein presentment. A writ of assise which formerly lay when a man or his ancestors under whom he claimed presented a clerk to a benefice, who was instituted, and afterwards, upon the next avoidance, a stranger presented a clerk and thereby disturbed the real patron. 3 Bl.Comm. 245; St. 13 Edw. I. (Westm. 2) c. 5. It has given way to the remedy by *quare impedit*.

—Assise of fresh force. In old English practice. A writ which lay by the usage and custom of a city or borough, where a man was disseised of his lands and tenements in such city or borough. It was called "fresh force," because it was to be sued within forty days after the party's title accrued to him. Fitzh.Nat.Brev. 7 C.

—Assise of mort d'ancestor. A real action which lay to recover land of which a person had been deprived on the death of his ancestor by the abatement or intrusion of a stranger. 3 Bl.Comm. 185; Co.Litt. 159*a*. It was abolished by St. 3 & 4 Wm. IV, c. 27.

—Assise of Northhampton. A re-enactment and enlargement (1176) of the Assise of Clarendon. 1 Holdsw.Hist.E.L. 21.

—Assise of novel disseisin. A writ of assise which lay for the recovery of lands or tenements, where the claimant had been lately disseised.

—Assise of nuisance. A writ of assise which lay where a nuisance had been committed to the complainant's freehold; either for abatement of the nuisance or for damages.

—Assise of the forest. A statute touching orders to be observed in the king's forests. Manwood, 35.

—Assise of utrum. A writ of assise which lay for a parson to recover lands which his predecessor had improperly allowed the church to be deprived of. 3 Bla.Com. 257.

An assise for the trial of the question of whether land is a lay fee, or held in frankalmoigne. 1 Holdsw.Hist.E.L. 21.

—Assise rents. The certain established rents of the freeholders and ancient copyholders of a manor; so called because they are *assised*, or made precise and certain.

—Grand assize. A peculiar species of trial by jury, introduced in the time of Henry II., giving the tenant or defendant in a writ of right the alternative of a trial by battel, or by his peers. Abolished by 3 & 4 Wm. IV, c. 42, § 13. See 3 Bl. Comm. 341. See Battel.

ASSISER. An assessor; juror; an officer who has the care and oversight of weights and measures.

ASSISORS. In Scotch law. Jurors; the persons who formed that kind of court which in Scotland was called an "assise," for the purpose of inquiring into and judging divers civil causes, such as perambulations, cognitions, molestations, purprestures, and other matters; like jurors in England. Holthouse.

ASSIST. To help; aid; succor; lend countenance or encouragement to; participate in as an auxiliary. People v. Hayne, 83 Cal. 111, 23 Pac. 1, 7 L.R.A. 348, 17 Am.St.Rep. 211. To contribute effort in the complete accomplishment of an ultimate purpose intended to be effected by those engaged. People v. Thurman, 62 Cal.App. 147, 216 P. 394, 395.

ASSISTANCE. Imports voluntary participation in wrongful acts of promotors. Peterson v. Hopson, 29 N.E.2d 140, 148, 306 Mass. 597.

ASSISTANCE, or (ASSISTANTS) COURT OF. See Court of Assistants.

ASSISTANCE OF COUNSEL. Sixth Amendment to Federal Constitution, guaranteeing accused in criminal prosecution "assistance of counsel" for his defense, means effective assistance. U.S.C.A. Const. Amend. 6. Thomas v. District of Columbia, 90 F.2d 424, 428, 67 App.D.C. 179. As distinguished from bad faith, sham, mere pretense or want of opportunity for conferences and preparation. Beckett v. Hudspeth, C.C.A.Kan., 131 F.2d 195, 196.

ASSISTANCE, WRIT OF. See Writ of Assistance.

ASSISTANT. A deputy, agent, or employee; as, an assistant assessor. Pryor Brown Transfer Co. v. Gibson, 154 Tenn. 260, 290 S.W. 33, 35, 51 A.L.R. 193. One who stands by and aids or helps another, and is not an agent. Wells-Dickey Co. v. Embody, 82 Mont. 150, 266 P. 869, 874. Ordinarily refers to employee whose duties are to help his superior, to whom he must look for authority to act. State ex rel. Dunn v. Ayers, 112 Mont. 120, 113 P.2d 785, 788.

ASSISTANT JUDGE. A judge of the English court of general or quarter sessions in Middlesex. He differs from the other justices in being a barrister of ten years' standing, and in being salaried. St. 7 & 8 Vict. c. 71; 22 & 23 Vict. c. 4; Pritch. Quar.Sess. 31.

ASSISTANT TEACHER. An "assistant teacher," meaning a classroom teacher of a subject, is not a "laboratory assistant," meaning a helper of a teacher who does no teaching. People ex rel. Becker v. Board of Education of City of New York, Sup., 162 N.Y.S. 643, 648.

ASSISUS. Rented or farmed out for a specified assise; that is, a payment of a certain assessed rent in money or provisions.

ASSITHMENT. Weregild (*q. v.*) or compensation by a pecuniary mulct. Cowell.

ASSIZE. In the practice of the criminal courts of Scotland, the fifteen men who decide on the conviction or acquittal of an accused person are called the "assize," though in popular language, and even in statutes, they are called the "jury." Wharton. See Assise.

ASSIZES. Sessions of the justices or commissioners of assize. These assizes are held twice in each year in each of the various shires of England, with some exceptions, for the trial of matters of fact in issue in both civil and criminal cases. They still retain the ancient name in popular language, though the commission of assize is no longer issued. See Assise.

ASSIZES DE JERUSALEM. A code of feudal jurisprudence prepared by an assembly of barons and lords A. D. 1099, after the conquest of Jerusalem. It was compiled principally from the laws and customs of France.

ASSOCIATE. Signifies confederacy or union for a particular purpose, good or ill. Weir v. United States, C.C.A.Ind., 92 F.2d 634, 638, 114 A.L.R. 481; Means "also". Smith v. Maine, 260 N.Y.S. 409, 145 Misc. 521.

An officer in each of the English courts of common law, appointed by the chief judge of the court, and holding his office during good behavior, whose duties were to superintend the entry of causes, to attend the sittings of *nisi prius,* and there receive and enter verdicts, and to draw up the posteas and any orders of *nisi prius.* The associates are now officers of the Supreme Court of Judicature, and are styled "Masters of the Supreme Court." Wharton.

A person associated with the judges and clerk of assise in the commission of general jail delivery. Mozley & Whitley.

The term is frequently used of the judges of appellate courts, other than the presiding judge or chief justice.

ASSOCIATES IN OFFICE. "Associates in office" are those who are united in action; who have a common purpose; who share the responsibility or authority and among whom is reasonable equality; those who are authorized by law to perform the duties jointly or as a body. Barton v. Alexander, 27 Idaho 286, 148 P. 471, 474, Ann.Cas. 1917D, 729.

ASSOCIATION. The act of a number of persons in uniting together for some special purpose or business. The persons so joining. It is a word of vague meaning used to indicate a collection of persons who have joined together for a certain object. U. S. v. Martindale, D.C.Kan., 146 F. 280, 284; In re Sautter's Estate, 142 Neb. 42, 5 N.W.2d 263, 268; W. R. Roach & Co. v. Harding, 348 Ill. 454, 181 N.E. 331, 336. An unincorporated society; a body of persons united and acting together without a charter, but upon the methods and forms used by incorporated bodies for the prosecution of some common enterprise. Clark v. Grand Lodge of Brotherhood of Railroad Trainmen, 328 Mo. 1084, 43 S.W.2d 404, 408. It is not a legal entity separate from the persons who compose it. Meinhart v. Contresta, Sup., 194 N.Y.S. 593, 594.

A confederacy or union for particular purposes, good or ill. Johnson's Dict.

In that sense "association" is a generic term and may indifferently comprehend a voluntary confederacy, which is a partnership dissoluble by the persons who formed it, or a corporate confederacy, deriving its existence from a confederacy, and dissoluble only by the law." Campbell v. Floyd, 153 Pa. 84, 25 A. 1033, 1036.

A body of persons invested with some, yet not full, corporate rights and powers, but will not include the state. State v. Taylor, 7 S.D. 533, 64 N.W. 548.

"Association" and "society" are convertible terms. Kribs v. United Order of Foresters, 191 Mo.App. 524, 177 S.W. 766, 769. Also often used as synonymous with "company". Law v. Crist, 41 Cal.App.2d 862, 107 P.2d 953, 955.

It is fundamentally a large partnership, from which it differs, in that it is not bound by the acts of the individual partners, but only by those of its manager or trustee; and that shares in it are transferable, and that it is not dissolved by the retirement, death, or bankruptcy of its individual members. In re Lloyds of Texas, D.C.Tex., 43 F.2d 383, 385.

A "business trust" is an "association" when it has a continuing entity throughout trust period, centralized management, continuity of trust uninterrupted by death among beneficial owners, means for transfer of beneficial interests, and limitation of personal liabilities of participants to property embarked in undertaking. Fletcher v. Clark, D.C.Wyo., 57 F.Supp. 479, 480.

"Association" has been held to include a common-law business or Massachusetts trust. Tracy v. Banker, 170 Mass. 266, 49 N.E. 308, 39 L.R.A. 508.

Articles of association. See Articles.

English Law

A writ directing certain persons (usually the clerk and his subordinate officers) to associate themselves with the justices and sergeants for the purpose of taking the assizes. 3 Bla.Comm. 59.

National Banking Associations

The statutory title of corporations organized for the purpose of carrying on the business of banking under the laws of the United States. Rev.St.U.S. § 5133 (12 USCA § 21).

ASSOCIÉ EN NOM. In French law. In a *société en commandité* an *associé en nom* is one who is liable for the engagements of the undertaking to the whole extent of his property. This expression arises from the fact that the names of the *associés* so liable figure in the firm-name or form part of the *société en nom collectif.* Arg.Fr.Merc.Law, 546.

ASSOIL. (Spelled also *assoile, absoile, assoilyie.*) To absolve; acquit; to set free; to deliver from excommunication. St. 1 Hen. IV, c. 7; Cowell.

ASSOILZIE. In Scotch law. To acquit the defendant in an action; to find a criminal not guilty.

ASSUME. To pretend. To undertake; engage; promise. 1 Ld.Raym. 122; 4 Coke, 92; Hopkins v. Erskine, 118 Me. 276, 107 A. 829, 830. To take to or upon one's self. Springer v. De Wolf, 194 Ill. 218, 62 N.E. 542, 56 L.R.A. 465, 88 Am.St.Rep. 155; Anicker v. Doyle, 84 Okl. 62, 202 P. 281, 284; Bell Telephone Co. of Pennsylvania v. Public Service Commission of Pennsylvania, 119 Pa.Super. 292, 181 A. 73, 74. Also taking up, receiving, adopting, taking to oneself, or to put on deceitfully, take appearance of, affect, or outwardly seem. Nickell v. State, 205 Wis. 614, 238 N.W. 508, 510. To take on, become bound as another is bound, or put oneself in place of another as to an obligation or liability. Texas Employers' Ins. Ass'n v. Texas & P. Ry. Co., Tex.Civ.App., 129 S.W.2d 746, 749.

ASSUMED RISK. See Assumption of Risk.

ASSUMPSIT. Lat. He undertook; he promised.

A promise or engagement by which one person assumes or undertakes to do some act or pay something to another. It may be either oral or in writing, but is not under seal. It is *express* if the promisor puts his engagement in distinct and definite language; it is *implied* where the law infers a promise (though no formal one has passed) from the conduct of the party or the circumstances of the case. Dukes v. Rogers, 67 Ga. App. 661, 21 S.E.2d 295, 297.

Practice

A form of action which lies for the recovery of damages for the non-performance of a parol or simple contract; or a contract that is neither of record nor under seal. 7 Term. 351; Ballard v. Walker, 3 Johns. Cas. (N.Y.) 60. A liberal and equitable action, applicable to almost every case where money has been received which in equity and good conscience ought to be refunded; express promise is not necessary to sustain action, but it may be maintained whenever anything is received or done from the circumstances of which the law implies a promise of compensation. Armour & Co. v. Whitney & Kemmerer, Inc., 164 Va. 12, 178 S.E. 889, 98 A.L.R. 596.

Express assumpsit. See Express Assumpsit

Special assumpsit is an action of assumpsit brought upon an express contract or promise.

General (common or indebitatus) assumpsit is an action of assumpsit brought upon the promise or contract implied by law in certain cases. It is founded upon what the law terms an implied promise on the part of defendant to pay what, in good conscience, he is bound to pay to plaintiff. Tr. and Ha. Pr. 1490; Ruse v. Williams, 14 Ariz. 445, 130 P. 887, 888, 45 L.R.A.,N.S., 923.

The action of *assumpsit* differs from *trespass* and *trover,* which are founded on a tort, not upon a contract; from *covenant* and *debt,* which are appropriate where the ground of recovery is a sealed instrument, or special obligation to pay a fixed sum; and from *replevin,* which seeks the recovery of specific property, if attainable, rather than of damages.

ASSUMPSIT FOR MONEY HAD AND RECEIVED. Is of equitable character and lies, in general, whenever defendant has received money which in equity and good conscience he ought to pay to plaintiff. Henderson v. Koenig, 192 Mo. 690, 91 S.W. 88, 91.

ASSUMPSIT ON QUANTUM MERUIT. When a person employs another to do work for him, without any agreement as to his compensation, the law implies a promise from the employer to the workman that he will pay him for his services as much as he may deserve or merit. In such case, the plaintiff may suggest in his declaration that the defendant promised to pay him as much as he reasonably deserved, and then aver that his trouble was worth such a sum of money, which the defendant has omitted to pay. This is called an "assumpsit on quantum meruit". Travis v. Kennedy, Tex.Civ.App., 66 S.W.2d 444, 446.

ASSUMPTION. The act of conceding or taking for granted. Gordon v. Schellhorn, 95 N.J.Eq. 563, 123 A. 549, 552.

The term is substantially synonymous with "inference," "probability," and "presumption." Ohio Bldg. Safety Vault Co. v. Industrial Board of Illinois, 277 Ill. 96, 115 N.E. 149, 154.

The act or agreement of assuming or taking upon one's self; the undertaking or adoption of a debt or obligation primarily resting upon another, as where the purchaser of real estate "assumes" a mortgage resting upon it, in which case he adopts the mortgage debt as his own and becomes personally liable for its payment. Lenz v. Railroad Co., 111 Wis. 198, 86 N.W. 607; Bell Telephone Co. of Pennsylvania v. Public Service Commission of Pennsylvania, 119 Pa.Super. 292, 181 A. 73, 75.

The difference between the purchaser of land assuming a mortgage on it and simply buying subject to the mortgage, is that in the former case he makes himself personally liable for the payment of the mortgage debt, while in the latter case he does not. Hancock v. Fleming, 103 Ind. 533, 3 N.E. 254. When he takes the conveyance subject to the mortgage, he is bound only to the extent of the property. Brichetto v. Raney, 76 Cal.App. 232, 245 P. 235, 241. Where one "assumes" a lease, he takes to himself the obligations, contracts, agreements, and benefits to which the other contracting party was entitled under the terms of the lease. Cincinnati, etc., R. Co. v. Indiana, etc., R. Co., 44 Ohio St. 287, 314, 7 N.E. 152.

ASSUMPTION OF INDEBTEDNESS. Means for one person to bind himself to pay debt incurred by another. Pawnee County Excise Board v. Kurn, 187 Okl. 110, 101 P.2d 614, 618.

ASSUMPTION OF RISK. Exists where none of fault for injury rests with plaintiff, but where plaintiff assumes consequences of injury occurring through fault of defendant, third person, or fault of no one. Rodgers v. Stoller, 284 Ky. 108, 143 S.W.2d 1047, 1048. It is based upon the maxim "volenti non fit injuria," which means that to which a person assents is not regarded in law as an injury. Poole v. Lutz & Schmidt, 273 Ky. 586, 117 S.W.2d 575, 576. And predicated upon knowledge and consent. Kansas City Southern Ry. Co. v. Diggs, 205 Ark. 150, 167 S.W.2d 879, 883. While more generally used as between master and servant, courts do not confine it to such relationship. Adams' Adm'r v. Callis & Hughes, 253 Ky. 382, 69 S.W.2d 711, 712.

Doctrine held applicable in action by automobile guest passenger. Gill v. Arthur, 69 Ohio App. 386, 43 N.E.2d 894, 899. But held not applicable in automobile collision cases generally. Schubring v. Weggen, 234 Wis. 517, 291 N.W. 788, 789, 790, 791.

In some jurisdictions, doctrine confined to master and servant relation. Dowse v. Maine Cent. R. R., 91 N.H. 419, 20 A.2d 629, 631; Parker v. Grand Trunk Western R. Co., 261 Mich. 293, 246 N.W. 125, 126; West Texas Utilities Co. v. Reuner, Tex., 32 S.W.2d 264, 270. A term or condition in a contract of employment, either express or implied from the circumstances of the employment, by which the employee agrees that dangers of injury ordinarily or obviously incident to the discharge of his duty in the particular employment shall be at his own risk. Parker v. City of Wichita, 150 Kan. 249, 92 P.2d 86, 89; Wisconsin & Arkansas Lumber Co. v. Otts, 178 Ark. 283, 10 S.W.2d 364, 365; Southern Pac. Co. v. McCready, C.C.A.Cal., 47 F.2d 673, 675. It has reference to dangers that are normally and necessarily incident to the occupation, which are deemed to be assumed by workmen of mature years, whether they are actually aware of them or not. Chesapeake & O. Ry. Co. v. Cochran, C.C.A.W.Va., 22 F.2d 22, 25.

It is founded upon the knowledge of the servant either actual or constructive, as to the hazards to be encountered and his consent to take the chance of danger. Schuppenies v. Oregon Short Line R. Co., 38 Idaho, 672, 225 P. 501, 505. But it does not include the risks from the negligence of the master, or the gross negligence of his superior servant. Burton Const. Co. v. Metcalfe, 162 Ky. 366, 172 S.W. 698, 702; "Contributory negligence" is not synonymous with assumption of risk. Dolese Bros. Co. v. Kahl, C.C.A.Iowa, 203 F. 627, 630. "Assumed risk" is founded upon the knowledge of the employee, either actual or constructive, of the risks to be encountered, and his consent to take the chance of injury therefrom. Contributory negligence implies misconduct, the doing of an imprudent act by the injured party, or his dereliction in failing to take proper precaution for his personal safety. The doctrine of assumed risk is founded upon contract, while contributory negligence is solely matter of conduct. Wheeler v. Tyler, 129 Minn. 206, 152 N.W. 137.

ASSUMPTION OF SKILL. The doctrine known as the "assumption of skill" on the part of the master sometimes makes the knowledge implied against the master relative to the safety of the place of work, and the nature, constituents, and general characteristics of the things used in the business, superior to that implied against the servant, especially where the servant is inexperienced. Hines v. Little, 26 Ga.App. 136, 105 S.E. 618.

ASSURANCE. A pledge, guaranty, or surety. National Watch Co. v. Weiss, 163 N.Y.S. 46, 47, 98 Misc. 453. A declaration tending to inspire full confidence. Texas & N. O. Ry. Co. v. New, Tex.Civ.App., 95 S.W.2d 170, 175. A making secure; insurance.

The term was formerly of very frequent use in the modern sense of insurance, particularly in English maritime law, and still appears in the policies of some companies, but is otherwise seldom seen of late years. There seems to be a tendency, however, to use *assurance* for the contracts of life insurance companies, and *insurance* for risks upon property.

In conveyancing. A deed or instrument of conveyance. The legal evidences of the transfer of property are in England called the "common assurances" of the kingdom, whereby every man's estate is *assured* to him, and all controversies, doubts, and difficulties are either prevented or removed. 2 Bl.Comm. 294. State v. Farrand, 8 N.J.Law, 335.

ASSURANCE, FURTHER, COVENANT FOR. See Covenant for Further Assurance.

ASSURE. To make certain and put beyond doubt. Armour & Co. v. New York, N. H. & H. R. Co., 41 R.I. 361, 103 A. 1031, 1033. To declare solemnly; to assure to any one with design of inspiring belief or confidence; to declare, aver, avouch, assert, or asseverate. Chanin v. Chevrolet Motor Co., C.C.A.Ill., 89 F.2d 889, 891. Used interchangeably with insure in insurance law; in real property documents it means a warranty; and in business documents, generally, it means a pledge or security. Utilities Engineering Institute v. Kafad, 58 N.Y.S.2d 743, 745, 185 Misc. 1035.

ASSURED. A person who has been insured by some insurance company, or underwriter, against losses or perils mentioned in the policy of insurance. Brockway v. Insurance Co., C.C.Pa., 29 Fed. 766.

Thus where a wife insures her husband's life for her own benefit and he has no interest in the policy, she is the "assured" and he the "insured."

The person for whose benefit the policy is issued and to whom the loss is payable, not necessarily the person on whose life or property the policy is written. Insurance Co. v. Luchs, 2 S.Ct. 949, 108 U.S. 498, 27 L.Ed. 800. Ordinarily synonymous with insured. Thompson v. Northwestern Mut. Life Ins. Co., 161 Iowa, 446, 143 N.W. 518.

ASSURED CLEAR DISTANCE AHEAD. Requires driver keep automobile under such control that he can stop in distance that he can clearly see, the distance varying with circumstances. Lauerman v. Strickler, 141 Pa.Super. 240, 14 A.2d 608, 610; Smiley v. Arrow Spring Bed Co., 138 Ohio St. 81, 33 N.E.2d 3, 5, 6, 7, 9, 133 A.L.R. 960.

ASSURER. An insurer against certain perils and dangers; an underwriter; and indemnifier.

ASSYTHEMENT. In Scotch law. Damages awarded to the relative of a murdered person from the guilty party, who has not been convicted and punished. Paters. Comp.

ASTIPULATION. A mutual agreement, assent, and consent between parties; also a witness or record.

ASTITRARIUS HÆRES. An heir apparent who has been placed, by conveyance, in possession of his ancestor's estate during such ancestor's lifetime. Co.Litt. 8.

ASTITUTION. An arraignment (*q. v.*).

ASTRARIUS. In old English law. A householder; belonging to the house; a person in actual possession of a house.

ASTRARIUS HÆRES. Where the ancestor by conveyance hath set his heir apparent and his family in a house in his lifetime. Cunningham, L. Dict.

ASTRER. In old English law. A householder, or occupant of a house or hearth.

ASTRICT. In Scotch law. To assign to a particular mill.

ASTRICTION TO A MILL. A servitude by which grain growing on certain lands or brought within them must be carried to a certain mill to be ground, a certain multure or price being paid for the same. Jacob.

ASTRIHILTET. In Saxon law. A penalty for a wrong done by one in the king's peace. The offender was to replace the damage twofold. Spelman.

ASTRUM. A house, or place of habitation. Bract. fol. 267*b*; Cowell.

ASYLUM. A sanctuary, or place of refuge and protection, where criminals and debtors found shelter, and from which they could not be taken without sacrilege. Cromie v. Institution of Mercy, 3 Bush (Ky.) 391.

Shelter; refuge; protection from the hand of justice. The word includes not only place, but also shelter, security, protection.

A fugitive from justice, who has committed a crime in a foreign country, "seeks an asylum" at all times when he claims the use of the territories of the United States. In re De Giacomo, 12 Blatchf. 395, Fed.Cas.No.3,747. Every sovereign state has the right to offer an asylum to fugitives from other countries, but there is no corresponding right on the part of the alien to claim asylum. In recent years this right of asylum has been voluntarily limited by most states by treaties providing for the extradition *(q. v.)* of fugitive criminals.

In time of war, a place of refuge in neutral territory for belligerent war-ships.

An institution for the protection and relief of unfortunates, as asylums for the poor, for the deaf and dumb, or for the insane. Lawrence v. Leidigh, 58 Kan. 594, 50 P. 600, 62 Am.St.Rep. 631. The term may also include a hospital constructed and maintained by the United States government for the treatment of soldiers and exsoldiers. Kemp v. Heebner, 77 Colo. 177, 234 P. 1068, 1069.

AT. A term of considerable elasticity of meaning, and somewhat indefinite. As used to fix a time, it does not necessarily mean eo instante or the identical time named, or even a fixed definite moment. Barnett v. Strain, 151 Ga. 553, 107 S.E. 530, 532; In re Clark's Estate, 61 P.2d 1221, 1222, 17 Cal.App.2d 323; And may mean on the same day, Perry v. Gross, 172 Cal. 468, 156 P. 1031, 1032. But "at" may often express simply nearness and proximity, and consequently may denote a reasonable time. Smeltzer v. Atlanta Coach Co., 44 Ga.App. 53, 160 S.E. 665, 666. Primarily, "at" means "near" or "near to," and involves the idea of proximity. Chesapeake & O. Ry. Co. v. Hill, 215 Ky. 222, 284 S.W. 1047, 1048, 48 A.L.R. 327; "At" a village or city may mean "near." Howell v. State, 164 Ga. 204, 138 S.E. 206, 209; Board of Trustees of Albany College v. Monteith, 64 Or. 356, 130 P. 633, 636. Depending on the context, "at" may be equivalent to "in"; Millikan v. Security Trust Co., 187 Ind. 307, 118 N.E. 568; Fayette County Board of Education v. Tompkins, 212 Ky. 751, 280 S.W. 114, 116; "toward"; State v. Cunningham, 107 Miss. 140, 65 So. 115, 117, 51 L.R.A. (N.S.) 1179; "after"; Davis v. Godart, 131 Minn. 221, 154 N.W. 1091, 1092; "not later than"; Smith v. Jacksonville Oil Mill Co., 21 Ga.App. 679, 94 S.E. 900, 901; or be equivalent to the words on, by, about, under, over, through, from, to, etc.

AT ARM'S LENGTH. Beyond the reach of personal influence or control.

Parties are said to deal "at arm's length" when each stands upon the strict letter of his rights, and conducts the business in a formal manner, without trusting to the other's fairness or integrity, and without being subject to the other's control or overmastering influence.

AT BAR. Before the court. "The case at bar," etc. Dyer, 31.

AT ISSUE. Whenever the parties come to a point in the pleadings which is affirmed on one side and denied on the other, they are said to be at an issue. Willard v. Zehr, 215 Ill. 154, 74 N.E. 107, 108.

AT LARGE. Not limited to any particular place, district, person, matter, or question; open to discussion or controversy; not precluded. Free; unrestrained; not under corporal control; as a ferocious animal so free from restraint as to be liable to do mischief. Fully; in detail; in an extended form.

A congressman at large is one who is elected by the electors of an entire state.

AT LAW. According to law; by, for, or in law; particularly in distinction from that which is done in or according to equity; or in titles such as sergeant at law, barrister at law, attorney or counsellor at law. Hooker v. Nichols, 116 N.C. 157, 21 S.E. 208.

AT LEAST. In deed of trust covenant specifying amount of fire insurance, means at lowest estimate, at smallest concession or claim, in smallest or lowest degree, at smallest number. Browne v. Franklin Fire Ins. Co., 225 Mo.App. 665, 37 S.W.2d 977, 979.

AT ONCE. In contracts of various kinds the phrase is construed as synonymous with "immediately" and "forthwith," where the subject-matter is the giving of notice. The use of such term does not ordinarily call for instantaneous action, but rather that notice shall be given within such time as is reasonable in view of the circumstances. George v. Aetna Casualty and Surety Co., 121 Neb. 647, 238 N.W. 36, 39. Likewise, contracts or statutes requiring the performance of a particular act "at once" are usually held to mean simply within a reasonable time. Arizona Power Co. v. State, 19 Ariz. 114, 166 P. 275, 277. An order to "ship at once" is synonymous with "as soon as possible". Myers v. Hardin, 208 Ark. 505, 186 S.W.2d 925, 928.

AT SEA. Out of the limits of any port or harbor on the sea-coast. U. S. v. Symonds, 7 S.Ct. 411, 120 U.S. 46, 30 L.Ed. 557.

AT WAR. Death of seaman from Pearl Harbor Attack as occurring while nation was "at war". Rosenau v. Idaho Mut. Ben. Ass'n, 65 Idaho 408, 145 P.2d 227, 232.

AT ANY TIME. Grant of time without limit. Haworth v. Hubbard, 220 Ind. 611, 44 N.E.2d 967, 970, 144 A.L.R. 887. Period of time limited by circumstances. Imes v. Globe Oil & Refining Co., 84 P.2d 1106, 1107, 1108, 184 Okl. 79. Within a reasonable time. Haworth v. Hubbard, 220 Ind. 611, 44 N.E.2d 967, 970, 144 A.L.R. 887.

AT ANY TIME PRIOR TO. Synonymous with "not later than". Hughes v. United States, C.C.A. Tenn., 114 F.2d 285, 287.

AT THE COURTHOUSE DOOR. In proximity of courthouse door. At place provided for posting of legal notices in courthouse. Matson v. Federal Farm Mortg. Corporation, Tex.Civ.App., 151 S.W.2d 636, 640, 641.

AT THE END OF THE WILL. The words "at the end of the will" within statute providing that every will shall be subscribed by testator at the end of the will mean the end of the language and not paper on which it is written. In re Golden's Will, 300 N.Y.S. 737, 738, 165 Misc. 205; In re Hildreth's Will, 36 N.Y.S.2d 938, 939, 940.

AT TIME CAUSE OF ACTION ACCRUES. Is sometimes applied to present enforcible demand, but more often simply means to arise or come into existence. Stone v. Phillips, 142 Tex. 216, 176 S.W.2d 932, 933.

ATAMITA. In the civil law. A great-great-great-grandfather's sister.

ATAVIA. In the civil law. A great-grandmother's grandmother.

ATAVUNCULUS. The brother of a great-grandfather's grandmother, or a great-great-great-grandfather's brother.

ATAVUS. The male ascendant in the fifth degree. The great-grandfather's or great-grandmother's grandfather; a fourth grandfather.

The ascending line of lineal ancestry runs thus: *Pater, Avus, Proavus, Abavus, Atavus, Tritavus.* The seventh generation in the ascending scale will be *Tritavi-pater,* and the next above it *Proavi-atavus.*

ATHA. (Spelled also *Atta, Athe, Atte.*) In Saxon law. An oath; the power or privilege of exacting and administering an oath. Spelman.

ATHEIST. One who does not believe in the existence of a God. Gibson v. Insurance Co., 37 N.Y. 584.

ATIA. Hatred or ill-will. See De Odio et Atia.

ATILIAN LAW. See Lex Atilia.

ATILIUM. The tackle or rigging of a ship; the harness or tackle of a plow. Spelman.

ATINIAN LAW. See Lex Atinia.

ATMATERTERA. A great-grandfather's grandmother's sister, (*ataviæ soror;*) called by Bracton "*atmatertera magna.*" Bract. fol. 68*b*.

ATOMIZE. To reduce to atoms or atom-like particles; pulverize; spray. In re Preble, Cust. & Pat.App., 45 F.2d 1007, 1009; Stearns-Roger Mfg. Co. v. Greenawalt, C.C.A.Colo., 62 F.2d 1033, 1039.

ATPATRUUS. The brother of a great-grandfather's grandfather.

ATRAVESADOS. In maritime law. A Spanish term signifying athwart, at right angles, or abeam; sometimes used as descriptive of the position of a vessel which is "lying to." The Hugo, D.C.N.Y., 57 F. 403, 410.

ATROCIOUS ASSAULT AND BATTERY. An assault by maiming and wounding. State v. Staw, 97 N.J.Law, 349, 116 A. 425.

ATROCITY. A word implying conduct that is outrageously or wantonly wicked, criminal, vile, cruel; extremely horrible and shocking. State v. Wyman, 56 Mont. 600, 186 P. 1, 3.

ATROPINE. A drug employed for purposes of dilating the eye so as to put the small muscles inside the eye at rest and to prevent adhesions of the iris and lens. De Zon v. American President Lines, C.C.A.Cal., 129 F.2d 404, 406.

ATS. At suit of.

ATTACH. To bind, fasten, tie, or connect, to make fast or join, and its antonyms are separate, detach, remove. State v. Modern Box Makers, 217 Minn. 41, 13 N.W.2d 731, 733. To take or apprehend by commandment of a writ or precept. Buckeye Pipe-Line Co. v. Fee, 62 Ohio St. 543, 57 N.E. 446, 78 Am.St.Rep. 743.

It differs from *arrest,* because it takes not only the body, but sometimes the goods, whereas an arrest is only against the person; besides, he who attaches keeps the party attached in order to produce him in court on the day named, but he who arrests lodges the person arrested in the custody of a higher power, to be forthwith disposed of. Fleta, lib. 5, c. 24. See Attachment.

In a broad sense, "attach" indicates any seizure of property for the purpose of bringing it within the custody of the court, and is not limited to a seizure on mesne process. In re Clark, D.C.Mich., 11 F.2d 540, 541.

ATTACHÉ. A person attached to an embassy, to the suite of an ambassador, or to a foreign legation. One connected with an office, *e. g.*, a public office. Noel v. Lewis, 35 Cal.App. 658, 170 P. 857, 859.

ATTACHED. A term describing the physical union of two otherwise independent structures or objects, or the relation between two parts of a single structure, each having its own function. National Brake & Electric Co. v. Christensen, C.C.A.Wis., 229 F. 564, 570. As applied to buildings, the term is often synonymous with "annexed." Williams Mfg. Co. v. Insurance Co. of North America, 93 Vt. 161, 106 A. 657, 659.

The word "attached," in an affidavit of service of a notice, used to designate a notice appearing on the reverse side of the affidavit, is improper. Wood v. Yearous, 159 Iowa, 211, 140 N.W. 362, 364.

ATTACHIAMENTA. L. Lat. Attachment.

ATTACHIAMENTA BONORUM. A distress formerly taken upon goods and chattels, by the legal *attachiators* or bailiffs, as security to answer an action for personal estate or debt.

ATTACHIAMENTA DE PLACITUS CORONÆ. Attachment of pleas of the crown. Jewison v. Dyson, 9 Mees. & W. 544.

ATTACHIAMENTA DE SPINIS ET BOSCIS. A privilege granted to the officers of a forest to take to their own use thorns, brush, and windfalls, within their precincts. Kenn.Par.Antiq. 209.

ATTACHIAMENTUM. L. Lat. An attachment.

ATTACHING CREDITOR. See Creditor.

ATTACHMENT. The act or process of taking, apprehending, or seizing persons or property, by virtue of a writ, summons, or other judicial order, and bringing the same into the custody of the law; used either for the purpose of bringing a person before the court, of acquiring jurisdiction over the property seized, to compel an appearance, to furnish security for debt or costs, or to arrest a fund in the hands of a third person who may become liable to pay it over. Also the writ or other process for the accomplishment of the purposes above enumerated, this being the more common use of the word. A remedy ancillary to an action by which plaintiff is enabled to acquire a lien upon property or effects of defendant for satisfaction of judgment which plaintiff may obtain. First Nat. Bank & Trust Co. of Vermillion v. Kirby, 62 S.D. 489, 253 N.W. 616; Lipscomb v. Rankin, Tex.Civ.App., 139 S.W.2d 367, 369. Though sometimes called an ancillary or auxiliary proceeding, it is in all essential respects, a suit. Farmers State Bank of Lexington v. Lemmer, 130 Neb. 211, 264 N.W. 415, 416.

The purpose is to take defendant's property into legal custody, so that it may be applied on defendant's debt to plaintiff when established. John Deere Plow Co. of St. Louis v. L. D. Jennings, Inc., 203 S.C. 426, 27 S.E.2d 571, 572; Union Bank & Trust Co. v. Edwards, 281 Ky. 693, 137 S.W.2d 344, 348.

At common law, "attachment" was procedure whereby sheriff was commanded to attach a defendant who, after being personally served, disobeyed original writ of summons, by keeping certain of his goods which he would forfeit if he did not appear, or by making him find securities who would be amerced if he continued his nonappearance, and, if after such attachment he still neglected to appear, he would not only forfeit this security, but was compellable by a writ of distringas infinite. Grimmett v. Barnwell, 184 Ga. 461, 192 S.E. 191, 194, 116 A.L.R. 257.

Execution and attachment distinguished. See Execution.

Persons

A writ issued by a court of record, commanding the sheriff to bring before it a person who has been guilty of contempt of court, either in neglect or abuse of its process or of subordinate powers. 3 Bl.Comm. 280; 4 Bl.Comm. 283; Commonwealth v. Shecter, 250 Pa. 282, 95 A. 468, 470.

Property

A species of mesne process, by which a writ is issued at the institution or during the progress of an action, commanding the sheriff to seize the property, rights, credits, or effects of the defendant to be held as security for the satisfaction of such judgment as the plaintiff may recover. It is principally used against absconding, concealed, or fraudulent debtors. U. S. Capsule Co. v. Isaacs, 23 Ind.App. 533, 55 N.E. 832.

To Give Jurisdiction

Where the defendant is a non-resident, or beyond the territorial jurisdiction of the court, his goods or land within the territory may be seized upon process of attachment; whereby he will be compelled to enter an appearance, or the court acquires jurisdiction so far as to dispose of the property attached. This is sometimes called "foreign attachment." Megee v. Beirne, 39 Pa. 50; Bray v. McClury, 55 Mo. 128. In such a case, the proceeding becomes in substance one in rem against the attached property. St. John v. Parsons, 54 Ohio App. 420, 7 N.E.2d 1013, 1014.

Domestic and Foreign

In some jurisdictions it is common to give the name "domestic attachment" to one issuing against a resident debtor, (upon the special ground of fraud, intention to abscond, etc.,) and to designate an attachment against a non-resident, or his property, as "foreign." Longwell v. Hartwell, 30 A. 495, 164 Pa. 533; David E. Kennedy, Inc. v. Schleindl, 290 Pa. 38, 137 A. 815, 816, 53 A.L.R. 1020.

But the term "foreign attachment" more properly belongs to the process otherwise familiarly known as "garnishment." It was a peculiar and ancient remedy open to creditors within the jurisdiction of the city of London, by which they were enabled to satisfy their own debts by attaching or seizing the money or goods of the debtor in the hands of a third person within the jurisdiction of the city. Welsh v. Blackwell, 14 N.J.Law, 346. This power and process survive in modern law, in all common-law jurisdictions, and are variously denominated "garnishment," "trustee process," or "factorizing." Raiguel v. McConnell, 25 Pa. 362, 363. A "foreign attachment" is a mesne process issued to compel a foreign debtor to appear to the suit of his creditor, while "attachment execution" is a final process issued for the purpose of enforcing a judgment already obtained. Williams v. Ricca, 324 Pa. 33, 187 A. 722, 723.

ATTACHMENT EXECUTION. A name given in some states to a process of garnishment for the satisfaction of a judgment. As to the judgment debtor it is an execution; but as to the garnishee it is an original process—a summons commanding him to appear and show cause, if any he has, why the judgment should not be levied on the goods and effects of the defendant in his hands. Sniderman v. Nerone, 7 A.2d 496, 499, 136 Pa.Super. 381.

ATTACHMENT OF PRIVILEGE. In English law. A process by which a man, by virtue of his privilege, calls another to litigate in that court to which he himself belongs, and who has the privilege to answer there. A writ issued to apprehend a person in a privileged place. *Termes de la Ley.*

ATTACHMENT OF THE FOREST. One of the three courts formerly held in forests. The highest court was called "justice in eyre's seat;" the middle, the "swainmote;" and the lowest, the "attachment." Manwood, 90, 99.

ATTAIN. To reach or come to by progression or motion; to arrive at; as, to attain a ripe old age. Watkins v. Metropolitan Life Ins. Co., 156 Kan. 27, 131 P.2d 722, 723.

ATTAINDER. That extinction of civil rights and capacities which takes place whenever a person who has committed treason or felony receives sentence of death for his crime. 1 Steph.Com. 408; 1 Bish.Cr.L. § 641; State v. Hastings, 37 Neb. 96, 55 N.W. 781.

The effect of "attainder" upon such felon is, in general terms, that all his estate, real and personal, is forfeited. Caldwell v. Hill, 179 Ga. 417, 176 S.E. 381, 386, 98 A.L.R. 1124. It differs from conviction, in that it is *after* judgment, whereas conviction is upon the verdict of guilty, but *before* judgment pronounced, and may be quashed upon some point of law reserved, or judgment may be arrested. The consequences of attainder are forfeiture of property and corruption of blood. 4 Bl.Comm. 380. At the common law, attainder resulted in three ways, viz.: *by confession, by verdict,* and *by process* or *outlawry.* The first case was where the prisoner pleaded guilty at the bar, or having fled to sanctuary, confessed his guilt and abjured the realm to save his life. The second was where the prisoner pleaded not guilty at the bar, and the jury brought in a verdict against him. The third, when the person accused made his escape and was outlawed. Coke, Litt. 391.

In England, by statute 33 & 34 Vict. c. 23, attainder upon conviction, with consequent corruption of blood, forfeiture, or escheat, is abolished. In the United States, the doctrine of attainder is now scarcely known, although during and shortly after the Revolution acts of attainder were passed by several of the states. The passage of such bills is expressly forbidden by the constitution.

Bill of Attainder

A legislative act, directed against a designated person, pronouncing him guilty of an alleged crime, (usually treason,) without trial or conviction according to the recognized rules of procedure, and passing sentence of death and attainder upon him.

"Bills of attainder," as they are technically called, are such special acts of the legislature as inflict capital punishments upon persons supposed to be guilty of high offenses, such as treason and felony, without any conviction in the ordinary course of judicial proceedings. If an act inflicts a milder degree of punishment than death, it is called a "bill of pains and penalties," but both are included in the prohibition in the Federal constitution. Losier v. Sherman, 157 Kan. 153, 138 P.2d 272, 273; State v. Graves, 352 Mo. 1102, 182 S.W.2d 46, 54.

ATTAINT. Attainted, stained, or blackened.

In old English practice. A writ which lay to inquire whether a jury of twelve men had given a false verdict, in order that the judgment might be reversed. 3 Bl.Comm. 402; Bract. fol. 288*b*–292; Fleta, 1, 5, c. 22, § 8.

This inquiry was made by a grand assise or jury of twenty-four persons, usually knights, and, if they found the verdict a false one, the judgment was that the jurors should become infamous, should forfeit their goods and the profits of their lands, should themselves be imprisoned, and their wives and children thrust out of doors, should have their houses razed, their trees extirpated, and their meadows plowed up, and that the plaintiff should be restored to all that he lost by reason of the unjust verdict. 3 Bl.Comm. 404; Co.Litt. 294*b*.

ATTAINT D'UNE CAUSE. In French law. The gain of a suit.

ATTEMPT.

In Civil Matters

In statutes and in cases other than criminal prosecutions an "attempt" ordinarily means an intent combined with an act falling short of the thing intended. In re Bergland's Estate, 180 Cal. 629, 182 P. 277, 283, 5 A.L.R. 1363. It may be described as an endeavor to do an act, carried beyond mere preparation, but short of execution. Columbian Ins. Co. of Indiana v. Modern Laundry, C.C.A.Minn., 277 F. 355, 358, 20 A.L.R. 1159.

In Criminal Law

An effort or endeavor to accomplish a crime, amounting to more than mere preparation or planning for it, which, if not prevented, would have resulted in the full consummation of the act attempted, but which, in fact, does not bring to pass the party's ultimate design. Dooley v. State, 27 Ala.App. 261, 170 So. 96, 98.

Acts amounting to mere preparation for commission of crime, if unaccompanied by some overt act toward actual commission, do not amount to an "attempt" and cannot be punished as such. People v. Lombard, 131 Cal.App. 525, 21 P.2d 955. Implies an intent and an actual effort to carry out or consummate the intent or purpose. Dooley v. State, 27 Ala.App. 261, 170 So. 96, 97, 98.

To constitute an act of attempt, the act must possess four characteristics: First, it must be a step toward a punishable offense; second, it must be apparently (but not necessarily in reality) adapted to the purpose intended; third, it must come dangerously near to success; fourth, it must not succeed. State v. Ainsworth, 146 Kan. 665, 72 P.2d 962.

ATTENDANT, *n.* One who owes a duty or service to another, or in some sort depends upon him. Termes de la Ley. One who follows and waits upon another.

ATTENDANT, *adj.* Accompanying, or connected with. Fletcher v. Winnfield Bottling Works, 160 La. 261, 107 So. 103, 104.

ATTENDANT TERMS. In English law, terms, (usually mortgages,) for a long period of years, which are created or kept outstanding for the purpose of *attending* or waiting upon and protecting the inheritance. 1 Steph.Comm. 351.

A phrase used in conveyancing to denote estates which are kept alive, after the objects for which they were originally created have ceased, so that they might be deemed merged or satisfied, for the purpose of protecting or strengthening the title of the owner. Abbott.

ATTENDED BY A PHYSICIAN. As used in application for insurance, requires an attendance with reference to some disease of a serious character, affecting sound bodily health and does not refer to a mere temporary indisposition or an ailment trivial in its nature. Houston v. Metropolitan Life Ins. Co., 232 Mo.App. 195, 97 S.W.2d 856, 861.

ATTENTAT. Lat. He attempts.

In the civil and canon law. Anything wrongfully innovated or *attempted* in a suit by an inferior judge (or judge *a quo*) pending an appeal. 1 Addams, 22, note; Shelf.Mar. & Div. 562; Ayliffe, Parerg. 100.

ATTENTION. Consideration; notice. The phrase "your bill shall have attention" was held to be ambiguous and not to amount to an acceptance of the bill. 2 B. & Ald. 113.

ATTERMINARE. In old English law. To put off to a succeeding term; to prolong the time of payment of a debt. Stat.Westm. 2, c. 4; Cowell; Blount.

ATTERMINING. In old English law. A putting off; the granting of a time or term, as for the payment of a debt. Cowell.

ATTERMOIEMENT. In canon law. A making terms; a composition, as with creditors. 7 Low.C. 272, 306.

ATTEST. To bear witness to; to bear witness to a fact; to affirm to be true or genuine; to act as a witness to; to certify; to certify to the verity of a copy of a public document; formally by signature; to make solemn declaration in words or writing to support a fact; to signify by subscription of his name that the signer has witnessed the execution of the particular instrument. Lindsey v. Realty Trust Co., Tex.Civ.App., 75 S.W.2d 322, 324; City Lumber Co. of Bridgeport v. Borsuk, 131 Conn. 640, 41 A.2d 775, 778.

Also the technical word by which, in the practice in many of the states, a certifying officer gives assurance of the genuineness and correctness of a copy. Thus, an "attested" copy of a document is one which has been examined and compared with the original, with a certificate or memorandum of its correctness, signed by the persons who have examined it. Gerner v. Mosher, 58 Neb. 135, 78 N.W. 384, 46 L.R.A. 244.

ATTESTATION. The act of witnessing an instrument in writing, at the request of the party making the same, and subscribing it as a witness. In re Jones' Estate, 101 Wash. 128, 172 P. 206, 207. The act of witnessing the execution of a paper and subscribing the name of the witness in testimony of such fact. In re Carlson's Estate, 156 Or. 597, 68 P.2d 119, 121.

Execution and *attestation* are clearly distinct formalities; the former being the act of the party, the latter of the witnesses only. *Subscription* differs from *attestation*, in that the former is the mere manual or mechanical act of signing—the act of the hand, whereas the latter signifies the mental act of bearing witness to—the act of the senses. In re Smith's Estate, 130 Neb. 739, 266 N.W. 611, 613.

ATTESTATION CLAUSE. That clause wherein the witnesses certify that the instrument has been executed before them, and the manner of the execution of the same.

In wills. A certificate certifying as to facts and circumstances attending execution of will. In re Bragg's Estate, 106 Mont. 132, 76 P.2d 57, 62.

ATTESTATION OF WILL. Act of witnessing performance of statutory requirements to valid execution. Davis v. Davis, Tex.Civ.App., 45 S.W.2d 240, 241; Zaruba v. Schumaker, Tex.Civ.App., 178 S.W.2d 542, 543.

There is some authority to the effect that there may be a perfect attestation without subscription, on the theory that attestation is mental, and subscription is mechanical. In re Chambers' Estate, 187 Wash. 417, 60 P.2d 41, 44.

ATTESTED COPY. See Attest.

ATTESTING WITNESS. One who signs his name to an instrument, at the request of the party or parties, for the purpose of proving and identifying it. In re McDonough's Estate, 193 N.Y.S. 734, 736, 201 App.Div. 203.

ATTESTOR. One who attests or vouches for.

ATTESTOR OF A CAUTIONER. In Scotch practice. A person who attests the sufficiency of a cautioner, and agrees to become *subsidiarie* liable for the debt. Bell.

ATTILE. In old English law. The rigging or furniture of a ship. Jacob, L.Dict. Rigging; tackle. Cowell.

ATTINCTA. L. Lat. An attaint, stain, or blackening; a conviction or finding of guilty of some offense. Adams Gloss.

ATTORN. To turn over; to transfer to another money or goods; to assign to some particular use or service. Hemminger v. Klaprath, 15 N.J. Misc. 163, 189 A. 363, 364. To consent to the transfer of a rent or reversion. To agree to become tenant to one as owner or landlord of an estate previously held of another, or to agree to recognize a new owner of a property or estate and promise payment of rent to him. Hurley v. Stevens, 220 Mo.App. 1057, 279 S.W. 720, 722.

Feudal Law

To turn over; to transfer to another money or goods; to assign to some particular use or service. 2 Bla.Comm. 288; 1 Spence, Eq.Jur. 137.

Where a lord aliened his seigniory, he might, with the consent of the tenant, and in some cases without, *attorn* or transfer the homage and service of the latter to the alienee or new lord. Bract. fols. 81*b*, 82.

ATTORNARE. Lat. To attorn; to transfer or turn over; to appoint an attorney or substitute.

ATTORNARE REM. To turn over money or goods, *i. e.*, to assign or appropriate them to some particular use or service.

ATTORNATO FACIENDO VEL RECIPIENDO. An obsolete writ, which commanded a sheriff or steward of a county court or hundred court to receive and admit an attorney to appear for the person that owed suit of court. Fitz.N.B. 156, 349.

ATTORNATUS. One who is attorned, or put in the place of another; a substitute; hence, an attorney. 7 C.J.S. p. 694.

ATTORNATUS FERE IN OMNIBUS PERSONAM DOMINI REPRESENTAT. An attorney represents the person of his master in almost all respects. Adams Gloss., citing Bract. fol. 342.

ATTORNE. L. Fr. In old English law. An attorney. Britt. c. 126.

ATTORNEY. In the most general sense this term denotes an agent or substitute, or one who is appointed and authorized to act in the place or stead of another. Nardi v. Poinsatte, D.C.Ind., 46 F.2d 347, 348. An agent, or one acting on behalf of another. Sherts v. Fulton Nat. Bank of Lancaster, 342 Pa. 337, 21 A.2d 18.

One who is put in place, stead, and turn of another to manage his matters of law. Kaufman v. Jurczak, 102 N.J.Eq. 66, 139 A. 716. An agent employed by party to case to manage it for him. McLyman v. Miller, 52 R.I. 374, 161 A. 111, 112.

When used with reference to the proceedings of courts, or the transaction of business in the courts, the term always means "attorney at law" *(q. v.)* unless a contrary meaning is clearly indicated. In re Morse, 98 Vt. 85, 126 A. 550, 551, 36 A.L.R. 527.

"Lawyer" and "attorney" are synonymous. People v. Taylor, 56 Colo. 441, 138 P. 762, 763.

—Attorney ad hoc. See Ad Hoc.

—Attorney at large. In old practice. An attorney who practiced in all the courts. Cowell.

—Attorney at law. An advocate, counsel, or official agent employed in preparing, managing, and trying cases in the courts. An officer in a court of justice, who is employed by a party in a cause to manage it for him. In re Bergeron, 220 Mass. 472, 107 N.E. 1007, 1008, Ann.Cas.1917A, 549.

In English law. A public officer belonging to the superior courts of common law at Westminster, who conducted legal proceedings on behalf of others, called his clients, by whom he was retained; he answered to the solicitor in the courts of chancery, and the proctor of the admiralty, ecclesiastical, probate, and divorce courts. An attorney was almost invariably also a solicitor. It is now provided by the judicature act, 1873, § 87, that solicitors, attorneys, or proctors of, or by law empowered to practice in, any court the jurisdiction of which is by that act transferred to the high court of justice or the court of appeal, shall be called "solicitors of the supreme court." Wharton.

The term "attorney at law," as used in the United States, usually includes "barrister," "counsellor," and "solicitor," in the sense in which those terms are used in England. In some states, as well as in the United States supreme court, "attorney" and "counsellor" are distinguishable, the former term being applied to the younger members of the bar, and to those who carry on the practice and formal parts of the suit, while "counsellor" is the adviser, or special counsel retained to try the cause. Rap. & L.

—Attorney in fact. A private attorney authorized by another to act in his place and stead, either for some particular purpose, as to do a particular act, or for the transaction of business in general, not of a legal character. This authority is conferred by an instrument in writing, called a "letter of attorney," or more commonly a "power of attorney." Treat v. Tolman, C.C.A.N.Y., 113 F. 893, 51 C.C.A. 522; Massachusetts Bonding & Insurance Co. v. Bankers' Surety Co., 96 Ind.App. 250, 179 N.E. 329, 334.

This term is employed to designate persons who act under a special agency, or a special letter of attorney, so that they are appointed *in factum,* for the deed, or special act to be performed; but in a more extended sense it includes all other agents employed in any business, or to do any act or acts *in pais* for another. Bacon, Abr. *Attorney;* Story, Ag. § 25.

—Attorney of record. Attorney whose name must appear somewhere in permanent records or files of case, or on the pleadings or some instrument filed in the case, or on appearance docket. Delaney v. Husband, 64 N.J.L. 275, 45 A. 265. Person whom the client has named as his agent upon whom service of papers may be made. Reynolds v. Reynolds, 21 Cal.2d 580, 134 P.2d 251, 254.

—Attorney of the wards and liveries. In English law. This was the third officer of the duchy court. Bac.Abr. "Attorney."

—Attorney's certificate. In English practice, a certificate of the commissioners of stamps that the attorney therein named has paid the annual tax or duty. This must be renewed yearly; and the penalty for practising without such certificate is fifty pounds; Stat. 37 Geo. III. c. 90, §§ 26, 28, 30. See also 7 & 8 Vict. c. 73, §§ 21-26; 16 & 17 Vict. c. 63.

—Attorney's lien. See Attorney's Lien.

—Letter of attorney. A power of attorney; a written instrument by which one person constitutes another his true and lawful attorney, in order that the latter may do for the former, and in his place and stead, some lawful act. People v. Smith, 112 Mich. 192, 70 N.W. 466, 67 Am.St.Rep. 392. An instrument of writing, appointing an attorney in fact for an avowed purpose and setting forth his powers and duties. Mullins v. Commonwealth, 179 Ky. 71, 200 S.W. 9, 11. It is, in effect, a mere contract of agency. Filtsch v. Bishop, 118 Okl. 272, 247 P. 1110, 1111. A *general* power authorizes the agent to act generally in behalf of the principal. A *special* power is one limited to particular acts.

—Power of attorney. Commonly meant the instrument by which authority of one person to act in place and stead of another as attorney in fact is set forth. In re Katz' Estate, 274 N.Y.S. 202, 152 Misc. 757.

—Public attorney. A name sometimes given to an attorney at law, as distinguished from a *private* attorney, or attorney in fact.

ATTORNEY GENERAL.

English Law

The chief law officer of the realm, being created by letters patent, whose office is to exhibit informations and prosecute for the crown in matters criminal, and to file bills in the exchequer in any matter concerning the king's revenue. 3 Bla. Comm. 27; Termes de la Ley; Wilentz v. Hendrickson, 133 N.J.Eq. 447, 33 A.2d 366, 374.

American Law

The attorney general of the United States is the head of the department of justice, appointed by the president, and a member of the cabinet. He appears in behalf of the government in all cases in the supreme court in which the government is interested, and gives his legal advice to the president and heads of departments upon questions submitted to him. Act of Sept. 24, 1789 (5 U.S.C.A. §§ 291, 303, 309).

He is the chief law officer of the federal and state governments with the duty of representing the sovereign, national or state. Johnson v. Commonwealth, ex rel. Meredith, 291 Ky. 829, 165 S.W.2d 820, 826.

In each state also there is an attorney general, or similar officer, who appears for the people, as in England the attorney general appears for the crown. State v. District Court, 22 Mont. 25, 55 Pac. 916; He is the chief law officer of the state and head of the legal department. People v. Newcomer, 284 Ill. 315, 120 N.E. 244, 247; Darling Apartment Co. v. Springer, 22 A.2d 397, 403, 25 Del. 420, 137 A.L.R. 803.

ATTORNEY GENERAL'S BILL. An indictment presented to grand jury by leave of court without prior complaint before magistrate and holding for court. Commonwealth v. Wilson, 134 Pa. Super. 222, 4 A.2d 324, 327.

ATTORNEY'S LIEN. The right of an attorney at law to hold or retain in his possession the money or property of a client until his proper charges have been adjusted and paid. It requires no equitable proceeding for its establishment. Sweeley v. Sieman, 123 Iowa, 183, 98 N.W. 571. Also a lien on funds in court payable to the client, or on a judgment or decree or award in his favor, recovered through the exertions of the attorney, and for the enforcement of which he must invoke the equitable aid of the court. Fowler v. Lewis, 36 W. Va. 112, 14 S.E. 447.

Charging lien. An attorney's lien, for his proper compensation, on the fund or judgment which his client has recovered by means of his professional aid and services. Goodrich v. McDonald, 112 N.Y. 157, 19 N.E. 649; In re Craig, 157 N.Y.S. 310, 311, 171 App.Div. 218. It is a specific lien covering only the services rendered by an attorney in the action in which the judgment was obtained, whereas a retaining lien is a general lien for the balance of the account between the attorney and his client, and applies to the property of the client which may come into the attorney's possession in the course of his employment. In re Heinsheimer, 143 N.Y.S. 895, 896, 159 App.Div. 33.

Retaining lien. The lien which an attorney has upon all his client's papers, deeds, vouchers, etc., which remain in his possession, entitling him to retain them until satisfaction of his claims for professional services. In re Wilson, D.C.N.Y., 12 F. 239; It is a general lien. Roxana Petroleum Co. v. Rice, 109 Okl. 161, 235 P. 502, 507.

ATTORNEYSHIP. The office of an agent or attorney.

ATTORNMENT. In feudal and old English law. A turning over or transfer by a lord of the services of his tenant to the grantee of his seigniory.

Attornment is the act of a person who holds a leasehold interest in land, or estate for life or years, by which he agrees to become the tenant of a stranger who has acquired the fee in the land, or the remainder or reversion, or the right to the rent or services by which the tenant holds. Snyder v. Bernstein Bros., 201 Iowa, 931, 208 N.W. 503, 504. It is an act by which a tenant acknowledges his obligation to a new landlord. Del-New Co. v. James, 167 A. 747, 748, 111 N.J.L. 157.

And requires an overt act by the tenant. Hemminger v. Klaprath, 189 A. 363, 15 N.J.Misc. 163.

The doctrine of attornment grew out of the peculiar relations existing between the landlord and his tenant under the feudal law, and the reasons for the rule never had any existence in this country, and is inconsistent with our laws, customs and institutions. Beyond its application to estop a tenant from denying the title of his landlord, it can serve but little, if any, useful purpose. Perrin v. Lepper, 34 Mich. 292.

ATTRACTIVE AGENCIES DOCTRINE. See Attractive Nuisance Doctrine. Schock v. Ringling Bros. and Barnum & Bailey Combined Shows, 5 Wash. 599, 105 P.2d 838, 843.

ATTRACTIVE INSTRUMENTALITIES DOCTRINE. See Attractive Nuisance Doctrine. Schock v. Ringling Bros. and Barnum & Bailey Combined Shows, 5 Wash.2d 599, 105 P.2d 838, 843.

ATTRACTIVE NUISANCE DOCTRINE. The doctrine is that one maintaining on his premises a condition, instrumentality, machine or other agency, which is dangerous to young children because of their inability to appreciate peril and may reasonably be expected to attract them to premises, owes duty to exercise reasonable care to protect them against dangers of such attraction. Schock v. Ringling Bros. and Barnum & Bailey Combined Shows, 5 Wash.2d 599, 105 P.2d 838, 843.

The doctrine, is that person who has an instrumentality, agency, or condition upon his own premises, or who creates such condition on the premises of another, or in a public place, which may reasonably be apprehended to be a source of danger to children, is under a duty to take such precautions as a reasonably prudent man would take to prevent injury to children of tender years whom he knows to be accustomed to resort there, or who may, by reason of something there which may be expected to attract them, come there to play. Atlantic Coast Line R. Co. v. O'Neal, 48 Ga.App. 706, 172 S.E. 740, 741. It does not apply to natural condition or common dangers existing in order of nature, McCall v. McCallie, 48 Ga.App. 99, 171 S.E. 843, 844, applies only in favor of children of tender years, too young to appreciate danger. Drew v. Lett, 95 Ind.App. 89, 182 N.E. 547, 548. Requires that the attraction be visible from a public place or a place where children have a right to be. Rokicki v. Polish Nat. Alliance of United States of North America, 314 Ill.App. 380, 41 N.E.2d 300.

AU BESOIN. Fr. In case of need. *"Au besoin chez Messieurs —— à ——."* "In case of need, apply to Messrs. —— at ——". A phrase sometimes used in the direction of a bill of exchange, pointing out the person to whom application may be made for payment in case of failure or refusal of the drawee to pay. Story, Bills § 65.

AUBAINE. See Droit d'Aubaine.

AUCTION. A public sale of land or goods, at public outcry, to the highest bidder. Perry Trading Co. v. City of Tallahassee, 128 Fla. 424, 174 So. 854, 857, 111 A.L.R. 463.

A sale by auction is a sale by public outcry to the highest bidder on the spot. Barber Lumber Co. v. Gifford, 25 Idaho, 654, 139 P. 557, 560.

While auction is very generally defined as a sale to the *highest* bidder, and this is the usual meaning, there may be a sale to the *lowest* bidder, as where land is sold for non-payment of taxes to whomsoever will take it for the shortest term; or where a contract is offered to the one who will perform it at the lowest price. And these appear fairly included in the term "auction." Abbott.

Dutch Auction

A method of sale by auction which consists in the public offer of the property at a price beyond its value, and then gradually lowering the price until some one becomes the purchaser. Crandall v. State, 28 Ohio St. 482.

Public Auction

A sale of property at auction, where any and all persons who choose are permitted to attend and offer bids. The phrase imports a sale to the highest and best bidder with absolute freedom for competitive bidding. State v. Miller, 52 Mont. 562, 160 P. 513, 515.

Though this phrase is frequently used, it is doubtful whether the word "public" adds anything to the force of the expression, since "auction" itself imports publicity. If there can be such a thing as a private auction, it must be one where the property is sold to the highest bidder, but only certain persons, or a certain class of persons, are permitted to be present or to offer bids.

AUCTIONARIÆ. Catalogues of goods for public sale or auction.

AUCTIONARIUS. A seller; a regrator; a retailer; one who bought and sold; an auctioneer, in the modern sense. Spelman, Gloss. One who buys poor, old, worn-out things to sell again at a greater price. Du Cange.

AUCTIONEER. A person authorized or licensed by law to sell lands or goods of other persons at public auction; one who sells at auction. City of Chicago v. Ornstein, 323 Ill. 258, 154 N.E. 100, 52 A.L.R. 489; One who sells goods at public auction for another on commission, or for a recompense. State ex rel. Danziger v. Recorder of Mortgages for Parish of Orleans, 206 La. 259, 19 So.2d 129, 132.

Auctioneers differ from *brokers*, in that the latter may both buy and sell, whereas auctioneers can only sell; also brokers may sell by private contract only, and auctioneers by public auction only. Auctioneers can only sell goods for ready money, but factors may sell upon credit. Wilkes v. Ellis, 2 H.Bl. 557; Steward v. Winters, 4 Sandf.Ch. (N. Y.) 590.

AUCTOR. In the Roman law. An auctioneer.

In the civil law. A grantor or vendor of any kind.

In old French law. A plaintiff. Kelham.

AUCTORITAS. In the civil law. Authority.

In old European law. A diploma, or royal charter. A word frequently used by Gregory of Tours and later writers. Spelman.

AUCTORITATES PHILOSOPHORUM, MEDICORUM, ET POETARUM, SUNT IN CAUSIS ALLEGANDÆ ET TENENDÆ. The opinions of philosophers, physicians, and poets are to be alleged and received in causes. Co.Litt. 264.

AUCUPIA VERBORUM SUNT JUDICE INDIGNA. Catching at words is unworthy of a judge. Hob. 343. Applied in State v. Flemming, 66 Me. 142, 151, 22 Am.R. 552.

AUDI ALTERAM PARTEM. Hear the other side; hear both sides. No man should be condemned unheard. Broom, Max. 113; L.R. 2 P.C. 106; Lowry v. Inman, 46 N.Y. 119; Shaw v. Stone, 1 Cush. (Mass.) 243.

AUDIENCE. In international law. A hearing; interview with the sovereign. The king or other chief executive of a country grants an audience to a foreign minister who comes to him duly accredited; and, after the recall of a minister, an "audience of leave" ordinarily is accorded to him.

AUDIENCE COURT. In English law. A court belonging to the Archbishop of Canterbury, having jurisdiction of matters of form only, as the confirmation of bishops, and the like. This court has the same authority with the Court of Arches, but is of inferior dignity and antiquity. The Dean of the Arches is the official auditor of the Audience court. The Archbishop of York has also his Audience court.

AUDIENDO ET TERMINANDO. A writ or commission to certain persons to appease and punish any insurrection or great riot. Fitzh.Nat.Brev. 110.

AUDIT, *n.* The process of auditing accounts; the hearing and investigation had before an auditor. People v. Barnes, 114 N.Y. 317, 20 N.E. 609; An official examination of an account or claim, comparing vouchers, charges, and fixing the balance. Williams v. Tompkins, Tex.Civ.App., 42 S.W.2d 106, 110.

AUDIT, *v.* To hear; to examine an account; and in a broad sense it includes its adjustment or allowance, disallowance, or rejection. New York Catholic Protectory v. Rockland County, 144 N.Y. S. 552, 556, 159 App.Div. 455. An audience; a hearing; an examination in general; a formal or official examination and authentication of accounts, with witnesses, vouchers, etc. Green-Boots Const. Co. v. State Highway Commission, 165 Okl. 288, 25 P.2d 783.

Sometimes restricted to a mere mathematical calculation or process, but, in its generally accepted sense, includes an investigation and weighing of the evidence and deciding of whether entries in books are true and correct. Lumber Mut. Casualty Ins. Co. of New York v. Horowitz, 1 N.Y.S.2d 191, 193, 165 Misc. 506.

AUDITA QUERELA. The name of a writ constituting the initial process in an action brought by a judgment defendant to obtain relief against the consequences of the judgment, on account of some matter of defense or discharge, arising since its rendition and which could not be taken advantage of otherwise. Barnett v. Gitlitz, 290 Ill.App. 212, 8 N.E.2d 517, 520. May also lie for matters arising before judgment where defendant had no opportunity to raise such matters in defense. Louis E. Bower, Inc., v. Silverstein, 298 Ill.App. 145, 18 N.E.2d 385, 387.

In some states, where the same relief may be obtained by motion, the remedy by motion has superseded the ancient remedy.

AUDITOR. A public officer whose function is to examine and pass upon the accounts and vouchers of officers who have received and expended public money by lawful authority. An officer who examines accounts and verifies the accuracy of the statements therein. Hicks v. Davis, 100 Kan. 4, 163 P. 799.

General

Auditor of the imprest. Any of several officers in the English exchequer, who formerly had the charge of auditing the accounts of the customs, naval and military expenses, etc., now performed by the commissioners for auditing public accounts. Jacob.

Auditor of the receipts. An officer of the English exchequer. 4 Inst. 107.

State auditor. An officer whose business is to examine and certify accounts and claims against the state and to keep an account between the state and its treasurer. State v. Jorgenson, 29 N.D. 173, 150 N.W. 565, 567.

English Law

An officer or agent of the crown, or of a private individual, or corporation, who examines periodically the accounts of under officers, tenants, stewards, or bailiffs, and reports the state of their accounts to his principal.

Practice

An officer (or officers) of the court, assigned to state the items of debit and credit between the parties in a suit where accounts are in question, and exhibit the balance. Campbell v. Crout, 3 R.I. 60.

AUGMENTATION. The increase of the crown's revenues from the suppression of religious houses and the appropriation of their lands and revenues. Also the name of a court (now abolished) erected 27 Hen. VIII., to determine suits and controversies relating to monasteries and abbey-lands. The court was dissolved in the reign of Mary, but the office of augmentations remained long after. Cowell.

A share of the great tithes temporarily granted to the vicars by the appropriators, and made perpetual by statute 29 Car. II. c. 8. The word is used in a similar sense in the Canadian law.

AUGUSTA LEGIBUS SOLUTA NON EST. The empress or queen is not privileged or exempted from subjection to the laws. 1 Bl.Comm. 219; Dig. 1, 3, 31.

AULA. In old English law. A hall, or court; the court of a baron, or manor; a court baron. Spelman.

This word was employed in mediæval England along with *curia;* it was used of the meetings of the lord's men held there in the same way that the word *court* was used. McIlwain, High Court of Parl. 30.

AULA ECCLESIÆ. A nave or body of a church where temporal courts were anciently held.

AULA REGIS. (Called also *Aula Regia.*) The king's hall or palace. The chief court of England in early Norman times. It was established by William the Conqueror in his own hall. It was composed of the great officers of state, resident in the palace, and followed the king's household in all his expeditions. See, also, Curia Regis.

AULIC. Pertaining to a royal court.

AULIC COUNCIL. In the old German empire, the personal council of the emperor, and one of the two supreme courts of the empire which decided without appeal. It was instituted about 1502, was modified in 1654, and ceased to exist on the extinction of the German Empire in 1806. The title was also given to the Council of State of the former Emperor of Austria. Cent.Dict.

AULNAGE. See Alnager.

AULNAGER. See Alnager.

AUMEEN. In Indian law. Trustee; commissioner; a temporary collector or supervisor, appointed to the charge of a country on the removal of a zemindar, or for any other particular purpose of local investigation or arrangement.

AUMIL. In Indian law. Agent; officer; native collector of revenue; superintendent of a district or division of a country, either on the part of the government zemindar or renter.

AUMILDAR. In Indian law. Agent; the holder of an office; an intendant and collector of the revenue, uniting civil, military, and financial powers under the Mohammedan government.

AUMONE, SERVICE IN. Where lands are given in alms to some church or religious house, upon condition that a service or prayers shall be offered at certain times for the repose of the donor's soul. Britt. 164.

AUNCEL WEIGHT. In English law. An ancient mode of weighing, described by Cowell as "a kind of weight with scales hanging, or hooks fastened to each end of a staff, which a man, lifting up upon his forefinger or hand, discerneth the quality or difference between the weight and the thing weighed."

AUNT. The sister of one's father or mother, and a relation in the third degree, correlative to niece or nephew. See 2 Comyn, Dig. 474; Dane, Abr. c. 126, a. 3, § 4.

AURA EPILEPTICA. In medical jurisprudence, a term used to designate the sensation of a cold vapor frequently experienced by epileptics before the loss of consciousness occurs in an epileptic fit. Aurentz v. Anderson, 3 Pittsb.R.(Pa.) 311.

AURES. A Saxon punishment by cutting off the ears, inflicted on those who robbed churches, or were guilty of any other theft.

AURUM REGINÆ. Queen's gold. A royal revenue belonging to every queen consort during her marriage with the king.

AUSTRALIAN BALLOT. An official ballot on which the names of all the candidates are printed. Its use is accompanied by safeguards designed to maintain secrecy in voting. The so-called Australian ballot laws, widely adopted in various forms in the United States, have generally been sustained by the courts. 29 C.J.S. p. 224.

AUSTRALIAN WOOL. A fine grade of wool grown in Australia. Federal Trade Commission v. Winsted Hosiery Co., 42 S.Ct. 384, 385, 258 U.S. 483, 66 L.Ed. 729.

AUTER, Autre. L. Fr. Another; other. See Autre.

AUTHENTIC. Genuine; true; real; pure; reliable; trustworthy; having the character and authority of an original; duly vested with all necessary formalities and legally attested; competent, credible, and reliable as evidence. Downing v. Brown, 3 Colo. 590; Woods v. Jastremski, 201 La. 1092, 11 So.2d 4, 8.

AUTHENTIC ACT. In the civil law. An act which has been executed before a notary or public officer authorized to execute such functions, or which is testified by a public seal, or has been rendered public by the authority of a competent magistrate, or which is certified as being a copy of a public register. Nov. 73, c. 2; Cod. 7, 52, 6, 4, 21; Dig. 22, 4; Mossler Acceptance Co. v. Osborne, La. App., 14 So.2d 492, 493.

AUTHENTICATION. In the law of evidence. The act or mode of giving authority or legal authenticity to a statute, record, or other written instrument, or a certified copy thereof, so as to render it legally admissible in evidence. Voloshin v. Ridenour, C.C.A.Canal Zone, 299 F. 134. Verifications of judgments. Collette v. Hanson, 174 A. 466, 467, 133 Me. 146.

An attestation made by a proper officer by which he certifies that a record is in due form of law, and that the person who certifies it is the officer appointed so to do. Acts done with a view of causing an instrument to be known and identified.

AUTHENTICS. In the civil law. A Latin translation of the Novels of Justinian by an anonymous author; so called because the Novels were translated *entire,* in order to distinguish it from the epitome made by Julian. 1 Mackeldey, Civ. Law, § 72. A collection of extracts made from the Novels by a lawyer named Irnier, which he inserted in the code at the places to which they refer. These extracts have the reputation of not being correct. Merlin, *Répert. Authentique.*

AUTHENTICUM. In the civil law. An original instrument or writing; the original of a will or other instrument, as distinguished from a copy. Dig. 22, 4, 2; Id. 29, 3, 12.

AUTHOR. One who produces, by his own intellectual labor applied to the materials of his composition, an arrangement or compilation new in itself. Lithographic Co. v. Sarony, 4 S.Ct. 279, 111 U.S. 53, 28 L.Ed. 349.

A beginner or mover of anything; hence efficient cause of a thing; creator; originator; a composer, as distinguished from an editor, translator or compiler. Remick Music Corp. v. Interstate Hotel Co. of Neb., D.C.Neb., 58 F.Supp. 523, 531.

AUTHORITIES. Citations to statutes, precedents, judicial decisions, and text-books of the law, made on the argument of questions of law or the trial of causes before a court, in support of the legal positions contended for, or adduced to fortify the opinion of a court or of a text writer upon any question.

AUTHORITY. Permission. People v. Howard, 31 Cal.App. 358, 160 P. 697, 701. Control over, jurisdiction. State v. Home Brewing Co. of Indianapolis, 182 Ind. 75, 105 N.E. 909, 916. Often synonymous with power. State v. District Court of Eighth Judicial Dist. in and for Natrona County, 33 Wyo. 281, 238 P. 545, 548. The power delegated by a principal to his agent. Clark v. Griffin, 95 N.J.Law, 508, 113 A. 234, 235. The lawful delegation of power by one person to another. Rucks-Brandt Const. Co. v. Price, 165 Okl. 178, 23 P.2d 690, 692. Power of agent to affect legal relations of principal by acts done in accordance with principal's manifestations of consent to agent. In re Fitzpatrick's Estate, Sur., 17 N.Y.S.2d 280, 288.

General

Authority by estoppel. Not actual, but apparent only, being imposed on the principal because his conduct has been such as to mislead, so that it would be unjust to let him deny it. Moore v. Switzer, 78 Colo. 63, 239 P. 874, 875. See Apparent Authority.

Authority coupled with an interest. Authority given to an agent for a valuable consideration, or which forms part of a security. See Unger v. Newlin Haines Co., 94 N.J.Eq. 458, 120 A. 331, 335.

Apparent authority. That which, though not actually granted, the principal knowingly permits the agent to exercise, or which he holds him out as possessing. L. E. Mumford Banking Co. v. Farmers' & Merchants' Bank of Kilmarnock, 116 Va. 449, 82 S.E. 112, 118. See Authority by Estoppel.

Express authority. That given explicitly, either in writing or orally. See Express Authority.

General authority. That which authorizes the agent to do everything connected with a particular business. Story, Ag. § 17. It empowers him to bind his principal by all acts within the scope of his employment; and it cannot be limited by any private direction not known to the party dealing with him. Paley, Ag. 199.

Implied authority. Actual authority circumstantially proved. Koivisto v. Bankers' & Merchants' Fire Ins. Co., 148 Minn. 255, 181 N.W. 580, 582. That which the principal intends his agent to possess, and which is implied from the principal's conduct. Moore v. Switzer, 78 Colo. 63, 239 P. 874, 875. It includes only such acts as are incident and necessary to the exercise of the authority expressly granted. Coulson v. Stevens, 122 Miss. 797, 85 So. 83, 85.

Limited authority. Such authority as the agent has when he is bound by precise instructions.

Naked authority. That arising where the principal delegates the power to the agent wholly for the benefit of the former.

Special authority. That which is confined to an individual transaction. Whitehead v. Tuckett, 15 East, 400, 408. Such an authority does not bind the principal, unless it is strictly pursued. Paley, Ag. 202.

Unlimited authority. That possessed by an agent when he is left to pursue his own discretion.

Governmental Law

Legal power; a right to command or to act; the right and power of public officers to require obedience to their orders lawfully issued in the scope of their public duties.

In the English law relating to public administration, an authority is a body having jurisdiction in certain matters of a public nature.

AUTHORITY OF THE COURT. The official power of the court. In re Bassett, 15 N.Y.S.2d 737, 745, 172 Misc. 613.

AUTHORITY TO EXECUTE A DEED. Must be given by deed. Blood v. Goodrich, 9 Wend. (N.Y.) 68, 75, 24 Am.Dec. 121.

AUTHORIZE. To empower; to give a right or authority to act. Board of Com'rs of Sedgwick County v. Toland, 121 Kan. 109, 245 P. 1019, 1021. To clothe with authority, warrant, or legal power. Arkansas & Memphis Ry. Bridge & Terminal Co. v. State, 174 Ark. 420, 295 S.W. 378, 380. To permit a thing to be done in the future. Gray v. Gill, 210 N.Y.S. 658, 660, 125 Misc. 70. It has a mandatory effect or meaning, implying a direction to act. Quality Building & Securities Co. v. Bledsoe, 125 Cal.App. 493, 14 P.2d 128, 132.

"Authorized" is sometimes construed as equivalent to "permitted"; Crecelius v. Chicago, M. & St. P. Ry. Co., 274 Mo. 671, 205 S.W. 181, 186; and sometimes as equivalent to "directed"; U. S. Sugar Equalization Board v. P. De Ronde & Co., C. C.A.Del., 7 F.2d 981, 986; or to similar mandatory language. Catron v. Marron, 19 N.M. 200, 142 P. 380, 382. The word indicates merely possessed of authority; that is, possessed of legal or rightful power, the synonym of which is "competency." Doherty v. Kansas City Star Co., 143 Kan. 802, 57 P.2d 43, 45.

AUTO ACORDADO. In Spanish colonial law. An order emanating from some superior tribunal, promulgated in the name and by the authority of the sovereign. Schm.Civil Law, 93.

AUTO LIVERY SERVICE. The business of furnishing for hire an automobile with a chauffeur, the car to be driven where the hirer directs. The term is also applied to the business of leasing driverless cars. See Collette v. Page, 44 R.I. 26, 114 A. 136, 18 A.L.R. 74.

See Automobile; Drive it Yourself Cars.

AUTO-OPTIC EVIDENCE. An exhibit of a thing offered before jury as evidence to be seen through jury's own eyes. Johnson v. State, 139 Tex.Cr.R. 279, 139 S.W.2d 579, 581. See, also, Autoptic Proference.

AUTO STAGE. A motor vehicle used for the purpose of carrying passengers, baggage, or freight on a regular schedule of time and rates. State v. Ferry Line Auto Bus Co., 99 Wash. 64, 168 P. 893, 894. See Automobile.

AUTOCRACY. The name of an unlimited monarchical government. A government at the will of one man, (called an "autocrat,") unchecked by constitutional restrictions or limitations.

AUTOGRAPH. One's handwriting.

AUTOGRAPHIC. Self-writing or self-recording. In re Autographic Register Co., Cust. & Pat.App., 39 F.2d 718.

AUTOMATIC. Having inherent power of action or motion; self-acting or self-regulating; mechanical. American Roll Gold Leaf Co. v. W. H. Coe Mfg. Co., C.C.A.R.I., 212 F. 720, 724.

AUTOMATISM. In medical jurisprudence, this term is applied to actions or conduct of an individual apparently occurring without will, purpose, or reasoned intention on his part; a condition sometimes observed in persons who, without being actually insane, suffer from an obscuration of the mental faculties, loss of volition or of memory, or kindred affections. "Ambulatory automatism" describes the pathological impulse to purposeless and irresponsible wanderings from place to place often characteristic of patients suffering from loss of memory with dissociation of personality.

AUTOMOBILE. A vehicle for the transportation of persons or property on the highway, carrying its own motive power and not operated upon fixed tracks. Blashfield's Cyclopedia of Automobile Law, vol. 1, c. 1, § 2.

A wheeled vehicle propelled by gasoline, steam, or electricity. Stanley v. Tomlin, 143 Va. 187, 129 S.E. 379, 382. A self-propelled vehicle suitable for use on a street or roadway. State v. Freels, 136 Tenn. 483, 190 S.W. 454; A vehicle designed mainly for the transportation of persons, equipped with an internal combustion, hydrocarbon vapor engine furnishing the motive power and forming a structural portion thereof. American-La France Fire Engine Co. v. Riordan, C.C.A.N.Y., 6 F.2d 964, 967. It is generic term, covering both trucks and passenger cars. Wiese v. Polzer, 212 Wis. 337, 248 N.W. 113, 116.

For "Auto Stage," "Family Automobile Doctrine," "Family Car Doctrine," and "Family Purpose Doctrine," see those titles.

Etymologically, the term might include any self-propelled vehicle, as an electric street car, or a motor boat, but in popular and legal usage it is confined to a vehicle for the transportation of persons or property on terrestrial highways, carrying its own motive power and not operated upon fixed tracks. Bethlehem Motors Corporation v. Flynt, 178 N.C. 399, 100 S.E. 693, 694. Synonymous with "motor vehicle." State v. Ferry Line Auto Bus Co., 99 Wash. 64, 168 P. 893, 894. "Car" as substitute or synonym. Monroe's Adm'r v. Federal Union Life Ins. Co., 251 Ky. 570, 65 S.W.2d 680, 681.

Taxicabs included. Navy Gas & Supply Co. v. Schoech, 105 Colo. 374, 98 P.2d 860, 864, 126 A.L.R. 1225. Trolley vehicles or trolley busses excluded. City of Dayton v. De Brosse, 62 Ohio St. 232, 23 N.E.2d 647, 650.

AUTOMOBILE GUEST. A person who is received and entertained in the automobile of another. Chanson v. Morgan's Louisiana & T. R. & S. S. Co., 18 La.App. 602, 136 So. 647, 649. Linn v. Nored, Tex.Civ.App., 133 S.W.2d 234, 237.

AUTONOMY. The political independence of a nation; the right (and condition) of power of self-government; the negation of a state of political influence from without or from foreign powers. Lieber, Civ.Lib.; Green v. Obergfell, 121 F.2d 46, 57, 73 App.D.C. 298.

AUTOPSY. The dissection of a dead body for the purpose of inquiring into the cause of death. Pub. St.Mass.1882, p. 1288. Sudduth v. Insurance Co., C.C.Ky., 106 F. 823. A post mortem examination to determine the cause, seat, or nature of a disease. E. O. Painter Fertilizer Co. v. Boyd, 93 Fla. 354, 114 So. 444, 445.

AUTOPTIC PROFERENCE. Proffering or presenting in open court of articles for observation or inspection of the tribunal. Kabase v. State, 31 Ala.App. 77, 12 So.2d 758, 764.

AUTRE. Fr. Another.

AUTRE ACTION PENDANT. In pleading. Another action pending. A species of plea in abatement. 1 Chit.Pl. 454.

AUTRE DROIT. In right of another, *e. g.*, a trustee holds trust property in right of his *cestui que trust.* A *prochein amy* sues in right of an infant. 2 Bl.Comm. 176.

AUTRE VIE. Another's life. A person holding an estate for or during the life of another is called a tenant *"pur autre vie,"* or *"pur terme d'autre vie."* Litt. § 56; 2 Bl.Comm. 120. See Estate Pur Autre Vie.

AUTREFOIS. L. Fr. At another time; formerly; before; heretofore.

AUTREFOIS ACQUIT. Fr. Formerly acquitted. In criminal law. The name of a plea in bar to a criminal action, stating that the defendant has been once already indicted and tried for the same alleged offense and has been acquitted. Simco v. State, 9 Tex.App. 348; State v. Bilton, 156 S.C. 324, 153 S.E. 269, 272.

AUTREFOIS ATTAINT. In criminal law. Formerly attainted. A plea that the defendant has already been attainted for one felony, and therefore cannot be criminally prosecuted for another. 4 Bl.Comm. 336; 12 Mod. 109; R. & R. 268. This is not a good plea in bar in the United States, nor in England in modern law. 1 Bish.Cr.L. § 692; Singleton v. State, 71 Miss. 782, 16 So. 295, 42 Am. St.Rep. 488.

AUTREFOIS CONVICT. Fr. Formerly convicted. In criminal law. A plea by a criminal in bar to an indictment that he has been formerly convicted of the same crime. 4 Bl.Comm. 336; 4 Steph.Comm. 404.

AUXILIARY. Aiding; attendant on; ancillary *(q. v.)*; as, an auxiliary bill in equity, an auxiliary receiver. Buckley v. Harrison, 31 N.Y.S. 1001, 10 Misc. 683; Bowman v. Stark, Tex.Civ.App., 185 S.W. 921, 924. Synonymous with "subsidiary." Baker v. Fenley, 128 S.W.2d 295, 298, 233 Mo.App. 998.

AUXILIATOR. Lat. Helper or assistant; the word is closely related to the English word auxiliary. Esta Co. v. Burke, D.C.Pa., 257 F. 743, 746.

AUXILIUM. In feudal and old English law. Aid; compulsory aid, hence a tax or tribute; a kind of tribute paid by the vassal to his lord, being one of the incidents of the tenure by knight's service. Spelman; Fitzh.Nat.Brev. 62.

AUXILIUM AD FILIUM MILITEM FACIENDUM ET FILIAM MARITANDAM. An ancient writ which was addressed to the sheriff to levy compulsorily an aid towards the knighting of a son and the marrying of a daughter of the tenants *in capite* of the crown.

AUXILIUM CURIÆ. In old English law. A precept or order of court citing and convening a party, at the suit and request of another, to warrant something. Kenn.Par.Ant. 477.

AUXILIUM REGIS. In English law. The king's aid or money levied for the royal use and the public service, as taxes granted by parliament. A subsidy paid to the king. Spelman.

AUXILIUM VICE COMITI. An ancient duty paid to sheriffs. Cowell.

AVAIL OF MARRIAGE. In feudal law. The right of marriage, which the lord or guardian in chivalry had of disposing of his infant ward in matrimony. A guardian in socage had also the same right, but not attended with the same advantage. 2 Bl.Comm. 88.

In Scotch law. A certain sum due by the heir of a deceased ward vassal, when the heir became of marriageable age. Ersk.Inst. 2, 5, 18.

AVAILABILITY FOR WORK. Within Unemployment Compensation Law requires no more than availability for suitable work which claimant has no good cause for refusing. Hagadone v. Kirkpatrick, 66 Idaho 55, 154 P.2d 181, 182.

AVAILABLE. Suitable; usable. Lively v. American Zinc Co. of Tennessee, 137 Tenn. 261, 191 S.W. 975, 979; Having sufficient force or efficacy; effectual. Pittsburgh, C., C. & St. L. Ry. Co. v. Broderick, 56 Ind.App. 58, 102 N.E. 887, 891.

AVAILABLE MEANS. This phrase, among mercantile men, is a term well understood to be anything which can readily be converted into money; but it is not necessarily or primarily money itself. McFadden v. Leeka, 48 Ohio St. 513, 28 N.E. 874; Benedict v. Huntington, 32 N.Y. 224; Brigham v. Tillinghast, 13 N.Y. 218.

AVAILS. Profits, proceeds, or use. In re Coughlin's Estate, 53 N.D. 188, 205 N.W. 14, 16; Cordes v. Harding, 27 Cal.App. 474, 150 P. 650, 651. With reference to wills, it means the *corpus* or proceeds of the estate after the payment of the debts. 1 Amer. & Eng.Enc.Law, 1039. See Allen v. De Witt, 3 N.Y. 279; McNaughton v. McNaughton, 34 N.Y. 201.

AVAL. In French law. The guaranty of a bill of exchange; so called because usually placed at the foot or bottom *(aval)* of the bill. Story, Bills, §§ 394, 454. 11 Harv.L.Rev. 55.

In Canadian law. The act of subscribing one's signature at the bottom of a promissory note or of a bill of exchange; properly an act of suretyship, by the party signing, in favor of the party to whom the note or bill is given. 1 Low.Can. 221; 9 Low.Can. 360.

AVANTURE. L. Fr. Chance; hazard; mischance.

AVARIA, AVARIE. Average; the loss and damage suffered in the course of a navigation. Poth. Mar.Louage, 105.

AVENAGE. A certain quantity of oats paid by a tenant to his landlord as rent, or in lieu of some other duties. Jacob, L.Dict.

AVENTURE, or ADVENTURE. A mischance causing the death of a man, as where a person is suddenly drowned or killed by any accident, without felony. Co.Litt. 391; Whishaw.

AVENUE. Any broad passageway, bordered on each side by trees. Greene v. Helme, 94 Vt. 392, 111 A. 557, 559. It may be synonymous with "street" but not with "boulevard." City of St. Louis v. Breuer, Mo.Sup., 223 S.W. 108, 110.

"Street," "avenue," "road," "public road," "county road," and "public highway" are used indiscriminately in legislation and judicial decisions. "Street" or "avenue" commonly applies to a public highway in a village, town, or city and "road" to a suburban highway, but there may be "roads" in a city or town and "streets" and "avenues" in the country. City of Spokane v. Spokane County, 179 Wash. 130, 36 P.2d 311, 313.

AVER. L. Fr. To have.

Aver et tener. In old conveyancing. To have and to hold.

AVER, *v.* In pleading. To declare or assert; to set out distinctly and formally; to allege.

In old pleading. To avouch or verify. Litt. § 691; Co.Litt. 362*b*. To make or prove true; to make good or justify a plea.

AVER, *n.* In old English and French. Property; substance, estate and particularly live stock or cattle; hence a working beast; a horse or bullock. Cowell; Kelham.

Aver corn. A rent reserved to religious houses, to be paid in corn. Corn drawn by the tenant's cattle. Cowell.

Aver land. In feudal law. Land plowed by the tenant for the proper use of the lord of the soil. Blount.

Aver penny. Money paid towards the king's averages or carriages, and so to be freed thereof. Termes de la Ley.

Aver silver. A custom or rent formerly so called. Cowell.

AVERA. A day's work of a ploughman, formerly valued at eight pence. Jacob, L.Dict.

AVERAGE. A mean proportion, medial sum or quantity, made out of unequal sums or quantities. Brisendine v. Skousen Bros., 48 Ariz. 416, 62 P.2d 326, 329, 112 A.L.R. 1089; Long v. Ottumwa Ry. & Light Co., 162 Iowa, 11, 142 N.W. 1008, 1015.

In ordinary usage the term signifies the mean between two or more quantities, measures, or numbers. If applied to something which is incapable of expression in terms of measure or amount, it signifies that the thing or person referred to is of the ordinary or usual type.

Average charges. "Average charges for toll and transportation" are understood to mean, and do mean, charges made at a mean rate, obtained by dividing the entire receipts for toll and transportation by the whole quantity of tonnage carried, reduced to a common standard of tons moved one mile. Hersh v. Railway Co., 74 Pa. 190.

Average prices. Such as are computed on all the prices of any articles sold within a certain period or district.

General average (also called "gross") consists of expense purposely incurred, sacrifice made, or damage sustained for the common safety of the vessel, freight, and cargo, or the two of them, at risk, and is to be contributed for by the several interests in the proportion of their respective values exposed to the common danger, and ultimately surviving, including the amount of expense, sacrifice, or damage so incurred in the contributory value. Star of Hope v. Annan, 9 Wall. 203, 19 L. Ed. 638; *Lex Rhodia,* Dig. 14, 2, 1.

"General average" is a contribution by the several interests engaged in a maritime venture to make good the loss of one of them for the voluntary sacrifice of a part of the ship or cargo to save the residue of the property and the lives of those on board, or for extraordinary expenses necessarily incurred for the common benefit and safety of all. California Canneries Co. v. Canton Ins. Office, 25 Cal.App. 303, 143 P. 549, 553. The law of general average is part of the maritime law, and not of the municipal law, and applies to maritime adventures only. Ralli v. Troop, 157 U.S. 386, 15 S.Ct. 657, 39 L.Ed. 742.

Gross average. More commonly called "general average" *(q. v.).* Where loss or damage occurs to a vessel or its cargo at sea, *average* is the adjustment and apportionment of such loss between the owner, the freight, and the cargo, in proportion to their respective interests and losses, in order that one may not suffer the whole loss, but each contribute ratably. Coster v. Insurance Co., 2 Wash.C.C. 51, 6 Fed.Cas. 611.

Particular average is a loss happening to the ship, freight, or cargo which is not to be shared by contribution among all those interested, but must be borne by the owner of the subject to which it occurs. It is thus called in contradistinction to *general* average. Bargett v. Insurance Co., 3 Bosw. (N.Y.) 395.

Petty average denotes such charges and disbursements as, according to occurrences and the custom of every place, the master necessarily furnishes for the benefit of the ship and cargo, either at the place of loading or unloading, or on the voyage; such as the hire of a pilot for conducting a vessel from one place to another, towage, light money, beaconage, anchorage, bridge toll, quarantine and such like. Park, Ins. 100; Le Guidon, c. 5, a. 13; Weyt, de A. 3, 4; Weskett, art. Petty Av.; 2 Phill.Ins. § 1269, n. 1; 2 Arnould, Mar.Ins. 927.

Simple average is the same as "particular average" *(q. v.).*

In maritime law. Loss or damage accidentally happening to a vessel or to its cargo during a voyage. Also a small duty paid to masters of ships, when goods are sent in another man's ship, for their care of the goods, over and above the freight.

In old English law. A service by horse or carriage, anciently due by a tenant to his lord. Cowell. A labor or service performed with working cattle, horses, or oxen, or with wagons and carriages. Spelman.

Stubble, or remainder of straw and grass left in corn-fields after harvest. In Kent it is called *"gratten,"* and in other parts *"roughings."*

AVERIA. In old English law. A term applied to working cattle, such as horses, oxen, etc.

AVERIA CARRUCÆ. Beasts of the plow. 3 Bla. Comm. 9; 4 Term, 566.

AVERIIS CAPTIS IN WITHERNAM. A writ granted to one whose cattle were unlawfully distrained by another and driven out of the county in which they were taken, so that they could not be replevied by the sheriff. Reg.Orig. 82.

AVERIUM. Lat. Goods; property. A beast of burden. Spelman, Gloss.

AVERMENT. In pleading. A positive statement of facts, in opposition to argument or inference. 1 Chit.Pl. 320; Bacon, Abr. *Pleas,* B.

Averments were formerly said to be general and particular; but only particular averments are found in modern pleading. 1 Chit.Pl. 277.

Immaterial and *impertinent averments* (which are synonymous, 5 D. & R. 209) are those which need not be made, and, if made, need not be proved. Williamson v. Allison, 2 East, 446; Panton v. Holland, 17 Johns. (N.Y.) 92, 8 Am.Dec. 369.

Negative averments are those in which a negative is used.

Particular averments are the assertions of particular facts.

Unnecessary averments are statements of matters which need not be alleged, but which, if alleged, must be proved. Carth. 200.

In old pleading. An offer to prove a plea, or pleading. The concluding part of a plea, replication, or other pleading, containing new affirmative matter, by which the party offers or declares himself "ready to *verify.*"

AVERRARE. In feudal law. A duty required from some customary tenants, to carry goods in a wagon or upon loaded horses. Jacob, L.Dict.

AVERSIO. In the civil law. An averting or turning away. A term applied to a species of sale in gross or bulk.

Letting a house altogether, instead of in chambers. 4 Kent, Comm. 517.

AVERSIO PERICULI. A turning away of peril. Used of a contract of insurance. 3 Kent, Comm. 263.

AVERUM. Goods, property, substance; a beast of burden. Spelman.

AVET. A term used in the Scotch law, signifying to abet or assist. Tomlin, Dict.

AVIA. In the civil law. A grandmother. Inst. 3, 6, 3.

AVIATICUS. In the civil law. A grandson.

AVIATION. The art of flying, especially the management of airplanes; the act, art or science of flying by mechanical means, especially with machines heavier than air. Massachusetts Protective Ass'n v. Bayersdorfer, C.C.A.Ohio, 105 F. 2d 595, 597; Spychala v. Metropolitan Life Ins. Co., 339 Pa. 237, 13 A.2d 32, 33.

AVIATION, ENGAGED IN. The phrase "engaged in aviation" within the meaning of an insurance policy denotes the act of flying in the air in a machine heavier than air, whether piloting or riding as a passenger. Masonic Acc. Ins. Co. v. Jackson, Ind.App., 147 N.E. 156. See Aeronautics.

AVIZANDUM. In Scotch law. To make *avizandum* with a process is to take it from the public court to the private consideration of the judge. Bell.

AVOCAT. Fr. An advocate; a barrister.

AVOCATION. A calling away, a diversion, suggesting idea of smaller affairs of life, or occasional employments as distinguished from one's ordinary or principal occupation. Bullitt v. Delaware Bus Co., Del., 180 A. 519, 522, 7 W.W.Harr. 62; a subordinate or occasional occupation. Mutual Life Ins. Co. of New York v. Enecks, 41 Ga. App. 644, 154 S.E. 198, 199.

AVOID. To annul; cancel; make void; to destroy the efficacy of anything. To evade; escape. Graves v. Apt, 233 Mass. 587, 124 N.E. 432, 433. But it has no sinister meaning, and does not imply subterfuge or artifice in escape. Booth v. Scott, 276 Mo. 1, 205 S.W. 633, 639.

AVOIDABLE CONSEQUENCES, DOCTRINE OF. Doctrine imposes duty on person injured to minimize damages. Reavis v. Raylor, Tex.Civ.App., 162 S.W.2d 1030, 1037; Lips v. Opp, 96 P.2d 865, 867, 150 Kan. 745.

AVOIDANCE. A making void, useless, empty, or of no effect; annulling, cancelling; escaping or evading.

English Ecclesiastical Law

The term describes the condition of a benefice when it has no incumbent.

Parliamentary Language

Avoidance of a decision signifies evading or superseding a question, or escaping the coming to a decision upon a pending question. Holthouse.

Pleading

The allegation or statement of new matter, in opposition to a former pleading, which, admitting the facts alleged in such former pleading, shows cause why they should not have their ordinary legal effect. Mahaiwe Bank v. Douglass, 31 Conn. 175. See Confession and Avoidance.

AVOIRDUPOIS. The name of a system of weights (sixteen ounces to the pound) used in weighing articles other than medicines, metals, and precious stones; so named in distinction from the Troy weight.

AVOUCHER. The calling upon a warrantor of lands to fulfill his undertaking. See Voucher.

AVOUÉ. In French and Canadian law. A barrister, advocate, solicitor, or attorney. An officer charged with representing and defending parties before the tribunal to which he is attached. Duverger.

AVOW. In pleading. To acknowledge and justify an act done. 3 Bla.Comm. 150. To make an avowry. Tleeta, 1.1, c. 4, Cunningham, Dict. See Avowry; Justification.

For example, when replevin is brought for a thing distrained, and the party taking claims that he had a right to make the distress, he is said to avow. Newell Mill Co. v. Muxlow, 115 N.Y. 170, 21 N.E. 1048.

AVOWAL. An open declaration. Purpose is to enable the court to know what the witness would have stated in answer to the question propounded, and to inform the court what the interrogator would prove contrary to the testimony given at the trial. Fennell v. Frisch's Adm'r., 192 Ky. 535, 234 S.W. 198 (1921); Robertson v. Commonwealth, 269 Ky. 317, 107 S.W.2d 292 (1937). See Clay, Kentucky Practice, Rule 43.10. Fed.R.Civ.P. 43(c).

AVOWANT. One who makes an avowry.

AVOWEE. In ecclesiastical law. An advocate of a church benefice.

AVOWRY. A pleading in the action of replevin, by which the defendant *avows*, that is, acknowledges, the taking of the distress or property complained of, where he took it in his own right, and sets forth the reason of it; as for rent in arrear, damage done, etc. 3 Bl.Comm. 149; 1 Tidd Pr. 645. L. A. W. Acceptance Corporation v. Chernick, 143 A. 783, 784, 49 R.I. 434.

Avowry is the setting forth, as in a declaration, the nature and merits of the defendant's case, showing that the distress taken by him was lawful, which must be done with such sufficient authority as will entitle him to a *retorno habendo*. Wilhem v. Boyd, 172 Md. 79, 190 A. 823, 826.

An avowry must be distinguished from a *justification*. The former species of plea admits the plaintiff's ownership of the property, but alleges a right in the defendant sufficient to warrant him in taking the property and which still subsists. A justification, on the other hand, denies that the plaintiff had the right of property or possession in the subject-matter, alleging it to have been in the defendant or a third person, or avers a right sufficient to warrant the defendant in taking it, although such right has not continued in force to the time of making answer. See 2 W.Jones, 25.

AVOWTERER. In English law. An adulterer with whom a married woman continues in adultery. Termes de la Ley.

AVOWTRY. In old English law. Adultery. Termes de la Ley.

AVULSION. The removal of a considerable quantity of soil from the land of one man, and its deposit upon or annexation to the land of another, suddenly and by the perceptible action of water. 2 Washb.Real Prop. 452; Wharton. Rees v. McDaniel, 115 Mo. 145, 21 S.W. 913; Schwartzstein v. B. B. Bathing Park, 197 N.Y.S. 490, 492, 203 App. Div. 700; Conkey v. Knudsen, 143 Neb. 5, 8 N.W. 2d 538, 542.

A sudden abandonment of an old channel and the creation of a new one. Harper v. Holston, 119 Wash. 436, 205 P. 1062, 1064.

Where running streams are the boundaries between states, the same rule applies as between private proprietors, and, if the stream from any cause, natural or artificial, suddenly leaves its old bed and forms a new one by the process known as "avulsion," the resulting change of channel works no change of boundary, which remains in the middle of the old channel though no water may be flowing in it and irrespective of subsequent changes in the new channel. State of Arkansas v. State of Tennessee, 246 U.S. 158, 38 S.Ct. 301, 304, 62 L.Ed. 638, L.R.A.1918D, 258; Stull v. U. S., C.C.A.Neb., 61 F.2d 826, 830.

To constitute "avulsion," rather than "accretion," so as to preclude change in boundary between riparian owners, it is not necessary that soil washed away be identifiable; it being sufficient that change is so sudden that owner of land washed away is able to point out approximately as much land added to opposite bank as he had washed away. 60 Okl.St.Ann. §§ 335, 336. Goins v. Merryman, 183 Okl. 155, 80 P.2d 268.

See Accretion; Alluvion; Reliction.

AVUNCULUS. In the civil law. A mother's brother. 2 Bl.Comm. 230. *Avunculus magnus,* a great-uncle. *Avunculus major,* a great-grandmother's brother. *Avunculus maximus,* a great-great-grandmother's brother. See Dig. 38, 10, 10; Inst. 3, 6, 2.

AVUS. In the civil law. A grandfather. Inst. 3, 6, 1.

AWAIT. Used in old statutes to signify a lying in wait, or waylaying.

AWARD, *v.* To grant, concede, or adjudge to. To give or assign by sentence or judicial determination. Hobson v. Superior Court of Tulare County, 69 Cal.App. 60, 230 P. 456, 457. Thus, a jury *awards* damages; the court *awards* an injunction. Starkey v. Minneapolis, 19 Minn. 206 (Gil. 166). One *awards* a contract to a bidder. Jackson v. State, 194 Ind. 130, 142 N.E. 1, 2, (holding that a finding that a contract was "awarded to" a bidder meant it was entered into with all required legal formalities).

AWARD, *n.* The decision or determination rendered by arbitrators or commissioners, or other private or extrajudicial deciders, upon a controversy submitted to them; also the writing or document embodying such decision. Keiser v. Berks County, 253 Pa. 167, 97 A. 1067, 1068.

Under Workmen's Compensation Acts, the term may be used in the above sense, as signifying a decision or determination of the Industrial Board, or some equivalent body. Frankfort General Ins. Co. v. Conduitt, 74 Ind.App. 584, 127 N.E. 212, 215. It may also be used to refer to the amount of compensation fixed by the board, an "award" being an amount fixed by arbitration. Odrowski v. Swift & Co., 99 Kan. 163, 162 P. 268, 269. Hence, a compensation agreement, which is not approved by the Industrial Board, is not an award. Bruce v. Stutz Motor Car Co. of America, 83 Ind.App. 257, 148 N.E. 161, 162.

A judgment, sentence, or final decision. Higginbotham v. State, 20 Ala.App. 159, 101 So. 166. A finding or judgment based upon an appraisement. Riddell v. Rochester German Ins. Co. of New York, 36 R.I. 240, 89 A. 833, 835. See Arbitration.

AWAY-GOING CROP. A crop sown before the expiration of a tenancy, which cannot ripen until after its expiration to which, however, the tenant is entitled. Broom, Max. 412; Miller v. Gray, Tex. Civ.App., 108 S.W.2d 265, 267, 268.

AWM. Also *aum* or *awme.* In old English statutes. A measure of wine, or vessel containing forty gallons.

AWN-HINDE. See Third-Night-Awn-Hinde.

AXIOM. In logic. A self-evident truth; an indisputable truth.

AXMINSTER. The trade-name of a certain kind of rug. The term now generally includes the machine-made product as well as the handmade. Beuttell & Sons v. U. S., 8 Ct.Cust.App. 409, 412.

AYANT CAUSE. In French law, and also in Louisiana, this term signifies one to whom a right has been assigned, either by will, gift, sale, exchange, or the like; an assignee. An *ayant cause* differs from an heir who acquires the right by inheritance. 8 Toullier, n. 245.

AYLE. See Aiel.

AYRE. In old Scotch law. Eyre; a circuit or iter.

AYUNTAMIENTO. In Spanish law. A congress of persons; the municipal council of a city or town. 1 White, Coll. 416; Friedman v. Goodwin, 9 Fed.Cas. 818; Strother v. Lucas, 12 Pet. 442, 9 L.Ed. 1137, notes.

AZURE. A term used in heraldry, signifying blue.

B

B. The second letter of the English alphabet; is used to denote the second of a series of pages, notes, etc.; the subsequent letters, the third and following numbers.

B. C. An abbreviation for "before Christ," "bail court," "bankruptcy cases," and "British Columbia."

B. D. S. A. Business and Defense Services Administration.

B. E. An abbreviation for "Baron of the Court of Exchequer."

B. F. An abbreviation for *bonum factum,* a good or proper act, deed, or decree; signifies "approved."

B. L. S. Bureau of Labor Statistics.

B. R. An abbreviation for *Bancus Regis,* (King's Bench,) or *Bancus Reginæ* (Queen's Bench.) It is frequently found in the old books as a designation of that court. In more recent usage, the initial letters of the English names are ordinarily employed, *i. e.,* K. B. or Q. B.

B. S. *Bancus Superior,* that is, upper bench.

B— S—. Designation of statements of another as b— s— carried the implications that they were absurd and fanciful. People v. Nitti, 312 Ill. 73, 143 N.E. 448, 456.

BABBITT. To line or furnish with "babbitt metal," which is a soft white anti-friction metal, of varying compositions, or any of several alloys similarly used. Ingersol v. National Sash & Door Factory, 134 La. 19, 63 So. 609, 610.

"BABY ACT." A plea of infancy, interposed for the purpose of defeating an action upon a contract made while the person was a minor, is vulgarly called "pleading the baby act." By extension, the term is applied to a plea of the statute of limitations.

BACHELERIA. In old records. Commonalty or yeomanry, in contradistinction to baronage.

BACHELOR. One who has taken the first degree (baccalaureate) in the liberal arts and sciences, or in law, medicine, or divinity, in a college or university.

A man who has never been married.

A kind of inferior knight; an esquire.

BACK, *v.* To indorse; to sign on the back; to sign generally by way of acceptance or approval. Where a warrant issued in one county is presented to a magistrate of another county and he signs it for the purpose of making it executory in his county, he is said to "back" it. 4 Bl.Comm. 291. This custom prevails in England, Scotland, and some of the United States. So an indorser of a note or bill is colloquially said to "back" it. Seabury v. Hungerford, 2 Hill (N.Y.) 80.

BACK, *adv.* To the rear; backward; in a reverse direction. Also, in arrear.

BACK CARRY. In forest law, the crime of having, on the back, game unlawfully killed. See Backbear.

BACK LANDS. A term of no very definite import, but generally signifying lands lying back from (not contiguous to) a highway or a water course. See Ryerss v. Wheeler, 22 Wend. (N.Y.) 150.

BACK TAXES. Those assessed for a previous year or years and remaining due and unpaid from the original tax debtor. M. E. Church v. New Orleans, 107 La. 611, 32 So. 101.

BACKADATION. See Backwardation.

BACKBEAR. In forest law. Carrying on the back. One of the cases in which an offender against vert and venison might be arrested, as being taken with the mainour, or manner, or found carrying a deer off on his *back.* Manwood; Cowell.

BACKBEREND (also Backberende). Sax. Bearing upon the back or about the person. Applied to a thief taken with the stolen property in his immediate possession. Bract. 1, 3, tr. 2, c. 32. Used with *handhabend,* having in the hand.

BACKBOND. A bond of indemnification given to a surety.

In Scotch law. A deed attaching a qualification or condition to the terms of a conveyance or other instrument. This deed is used when particular circumstances render it necessary to express in a separate form the limitations or qualifications of a right. Bell. The instrument is equivalent to a declaration of trust in English conveyancing.

BACKING. Indorsement; indorsement by a magistrate. Gondas v. Gondas, 99 N.J.Eq. 473, 134 A. 615, 617.

BACKING A WARRANT. See Back.

BACK-SEAT DRIVER. A highly nervous passenger whether sitting in rear or by driver, who by unwarranted advice and warnings interferes in careful operation of automobile. Winters v. York Motor Express Co., 116 Pa.Super. 421, 176 A. 812, 815.

BACKSIDE. In English law. A term formerly used in conveyances and also in pleading; it imports a yard at the back part of or behind a house, and belonging thereto.

BACKWARDATION (also called Backadation). In the language of the stock exchange, this term signifies a consideration paid for delay in the delivery of stock contracted for, when the price is lower for time than for cash. Dos Passos, Stock-Brok. 270.

BACKWARDS. In a policy of marine insurance, the phrase "forwards and backwards at sea" means from port to port in the course of the voyage, and not merely from one terminus to the other and back. 1 Taunt. 475.

BACKWATER. Water in a stream which, in consequence of some dam or obstruction below, is detained or checked in its course, or flows back. Webster v. North Poudre Irr. Co., 74 Colo. 565, 223 P. 36. Water caused to flow backward from a steam-vessel by reason of the action of its wheels or screw.

BACULUS. A rod, staff, or wand, used in old English practice in making livery of seisin where no building stood on the land, (Bract. 40;) a stick or wand, by the erection of which on the land involved in a real action the defendant was summoned to put in his appearance; this was called *"baculus nuntiatorius."* 3 Bl.Comm. 279.

BAD. Vicious, evil, wanting in good qualities; the reverse of good. Davis v. Pennsylvania Co. for Insurances on Lives and Granting Annuities, 337 Pa. 456, 12 A.2d 66, 68. Defective, faulty, inferior, or imperfect. Kniffley v. Reid, 152 S.W. 2d 615, 616, 287 Ky. 212. The technical word for unsoundness in pleading.

BAD BEHAVIOR. Where a judgment in a criminal case has been suspended on condition of good behavior, the term "good behavior" means conduct that is authorized by law, and "bad behavior" means conduct such as the law will punish. State v. Hardin, 183 N.C. 815, 112 S.E. 593, 594.

BAD DEBT. Generally speaking, one which is uncollectible.

BAD FAITH. The opposite of "good faith," generally implying or involving actual or constructive fraud, or a design to mislead or deceive another, or a neglect or refusal to fulfill some duty or some contractual obligation, not prompted by an honest mistake as to one's rights or duties, but by some interested or sinister motive. State v. Griffin, 100 S.C. 331, 84 S.E. 876, 877; Penn Mut. L. Ins. Co. v. Mechanics' Savings Bank & Trust Co., C.C.A.Tenn., 73 F. 653, 19 C.C.A. 316, 38 L.R.A. 33, 70; Spiegel v. Beacon Participations, 297 Mass. 398, 8 N.E.2d 895, 907.

BAD MOTIVE. Intentionally doing a wrongful act knowing at the time that it is wrongful. Luhmann v. Schaefer, Mo.App., 142 S.W.2d 1088, 1090; Davis v. Nash Central Motors, Mo.App., 332 S.W. 2d 475, 480.

BAD PLACE. Under a contract requiring the employer to timber all bad places in the mine unless caused by the miner's negligence, a "bad place" was a place in the roof which could not be made reasonably safe by the ordinary propping usually done by the miner himself. W. G. Duncan Coal Co. v. Thompson's Adm'r, 157 Ky. 304, 162 S.W. 1139, 1140.

BAD TITLE. One which conveys no property to the purchaser of the estate; one which is so radically defective that it is not marketable, and hence such that a purchaser cannot be legally compelled to accept it. Heller v. Cohen, 15 Misc. 378, 36 N.Y.S. 668.

BADGE. A mark or cognizance worn to show the relation of the wearer to any person or thing; the token of anything; a distinctive mark of office or service.

BADGE OF FRAUD. A term used relatively to the law of fraudulent conveyances made to hinder and defraud creditors. It is defined as a fact tending to throw suspicion upon a transaction, and calling for an explanation. Bump, Fraud.Conv. 31; Phelps v. Samson, 113 Iowa, 145, 84 N.W. 1051. It is a suspicious circumstance that overhangs a transaction, or appears on the face of the papers. Toone v. Walker, 115 Okl. 289, 243 Pa. 147, 148. A circumstance which does not alone prove fraud, but which warrants inference of fraud, especially where there is a concurrence of many such badges. Brennecke v. Riemann, Mo., 102 S.W.2d 874, 877, 109 A.L.R. 1214.

Recognized "badges of fraud" include fictitious consideration, false statements as to consideration, transactions different from usual course of doing business, transfer of all of a debtor's property, insolvency, confidential relationship of parties, and transfers in anticipation of suit or execution. Hendrix v. Goldman, Mo., 92 S.W.2d 733, 736.

BADGER. In old English law. One who made a practice of buying corn or victuals in one place, and carrying them to another to sell and make profit by them.

BAG. A sack or satchel. A certain and customary quantity of goods and merchandise in a sack. Wharton. An uncertain quantity of goods and merchandise, from three to four hundred. Jacob.

BAGA. In English law. A bag or purse. Thus there is the petty-bag-office in the common-law jurisdiction of the court of chancery, because all original writs relating to the business of the crown were formerly kept in a little sack or bag, *in parvâ bagâ.* 1 Madd.Ch. 4.

BAGAVEL. The citizens of Exeter had granted to them by charter from Edward I. the collection of a certain tribute or toll upon all manner of wares brought to that city to be sold, toward the paving of the streets, repairing of the walls, and maintenance of the city, which was commonly called bagavel, bethugavel and chippinggavel. Antiq. of Exeter.

BAGGAGE. In the law of carriers, this term comprises such articles of personal convenience or necessity as are usually carried by passengers for their personal use. It includes whatever the passenger takes with him for his personal use or convenience according to the habits or wants of the particular class to which he belongs, either with reference to the immediate necessities or ultimate purpose of the journey. Texas & P. Ry. Co. v. Bryant, Tex.Civ.App., 11 S.W.2d 659, 660

Thus, jewelry suitable to the condition in life of the passenger and intended for personal use on the journey is "baggage." Missouri Pac. R. Co. v. Pugh, 157 Ark. 383, 248 S.W. 897. But it is not baggage where carried by a traveler for the use of another or for the purpose of business or sale. Illinois Cent. R. Co. v. Fontaine, 217 Ky. 211, 289 S.W. 263, 266, 52 A.L.R. 1064.

A multitude of objects have been held to be baggage; *e. g.*, razors in a trunk checked by a male passenger, San Antonio & A. P. Ry. Co. v. Green, Tex.Civ.App., 170 S.W. 110, 111, and a thimble carried in her trunk by the mother of two small children, Louisville & N. R. Co. v. Hestle, 200 Ala. 137, 75 So. 885, 887. Other articles have been held not to be baggage, such as stocks and bonds, Jandorf v. Pullman Co., 171 N.Y.S. 321, 322, 104 Misc. 79; a gun and gun case, not connected with the purpose of the trip, House v. Chicago & N. W. Ry. Co., 32 S.D. 209, 142 N.W. 736, 738; and an article for use in housekeeping after the end of a passenger's journey, Louisville & N. R. Co. v. Fletcher, 194 Ala. 257, 69 So. 634, 635.

BAGGAGE CAR. A closed car in a passenger train used to transport the property of the passengers. Ward v. Gulf, M. & N. R. Co., 23 Tenn.App. 533, 134 S.W.2d 917.

BAGGAGE CAR SERVICE. A service rendered in such car in connection with the transportation of passengers by a passenger train movement or its equivalent. Ward v. Gulf, M. & N. R. Co., 23 Tenn.App. 533, 134 S.W.2d 917, 923.

BAHADUM. A chest or coffer. Fleta.

BAIL, *v.* To procure the release of a person from legal custody, by undertaking that he shall appear at the time and place designated and submit himself to the jurisdiction and judgment of the court.

To deliver the defendant to persons who, in the manner prescribed by law, become security for his appearance in court. To set at liberty a person arrested or imprisoned, on security being taken for his appearance on a day and a place certain, which security is called "bail," because the party arrested or imprisoned is delivered into the hands of those who bind themselves for his forthcoming, (that is, become bail for his due appearance when required,) in order that he may be safely protected from prison. Wharton. Stafford v. State, 10 Tex.App. 49.

To procure release of one charged with an offense by insuring his future attendance in court and compelling him to remain within jurisdiction of court. Manning v. State ex rel. Williams, 190 Okl. 65, 120 P.2d 980, 981.

The object of "bail" in civil cases is either directly or indirectly to secure payment of a debt or performance of other civil duties, while in criminal cases object is to secure appearance of principal before the court when his presence is needed. Johnson v. Shaffer, 64 Ohio App. 236, 28 N.E.2d 765, 767. In its more ancient signification, the word includes the delivery of property, real or personal, by one person to another.

BAIL, *n.* The surety or sureties who procure the release of a person under arrest, by becoming responsible for his appearance at the time and place designated. Those persons who become sureties for the appearance of the defendant in court.

—Bail above or bail to the action. See Special bail, *infra.*

—Bail absolute. Sureties whose liability is conditioned upon the failure of the principal to duly account for money coming to his hands as administrator, guardian, etc.

—Bail below, or bail to the sheriff. See Bail to the sheriff or bail below, *infra.*

—Bail bond. A bond executed by a defendant who has been arrested, together with other persons as sureties, naming the sheriff, constable, or marshal as obligee, in a penal sum proportioned to the damages claimed or penalty denounced, conditioned that the defendant shall duly appear to answer to the legal process in the officer's hands, or shall cause special bail to be put in, as the case may be.

An obligation signed by the accused with sureties, conditioned that the same shall be void on the performance by the accused of such acts as he is required to perform. State v. Wilson, 265 Mo. 1, 175 S.W. 603, 605.

Its purpose is to secure the presence of the one charged in court when his presence is required in order to answer to the charge. State v. Clark, 234 Iowa 338, 11 N.W.2d 722. In criminal cases, a bail bond is a contract under seal, which, from its nature, requires sureties or bail, and therefore differs from a "recognizance," which is a debt or obligation of record, acknowledged before some court or magistrate authorized to take it, with condition to do some particular act, and which need not be executed by the parties. State v. Bradsher, 189 N.C. 401, 127 S.E. 349, 351, 38 A.L.R. 1102. But under the law of Connecticut, "recognizance" and "bail" are interchangeable. National Surety Co. v. Nazzaro, 239 Mass. 341, 132 N.E. 49, 50.

—Bail common. A fictitious proceeding, intended only to express the appearance of a defendant, in cases where special bail is not required. It is put in in the same form as special bail, but the sureties are merely nominal or imaginary persons, as John Doe and Richard Roe. 3 Bl.Comm. 287.

—Bail court. In English law and practice. An auxiliary court of the court of queen's bench at Westminster, wherein points connected more particularly with pleading and practice are argued and determined. Holthouse; Wharton, Law Dict. 2d Lond. ed. It has been abolished.

—Bail dock. Formerly at the Old Bailey, in London, a small room taken from one of the corners of the court, and left open at the top, in which certain malefactors were placed during trial. Cent. Dict.

—Bail in error. That given by a defendant who intends to bring a writ of error on the judgment and desires a stay of execution in the meantime.

—Bail piece. A formal entry or memorandum of the recognizance or undertaking of special bail in civil actions, which, after being signed and acknowledged by the bail before the proper officer, is filed in the court in which the action is pending. 3 Bl.Comm. 291; Worthen v. Prescott, 60 Vt. 68, 11 Atl. 690.

—Bail to the action or bail above. Special bail (*q. v.*).

—Bail to the sheriff or bail below. Persons who undertake that a defendant arrested upon mesne process in a civil action shall duly appear to answer the plaintiff; such undertaking being in the form of a bond given to the sheriff, termed a "bail bond" (*q. v.*). 3 Bl.Comm. 290; 1 Tidd, Pr. 221. Sureties who bind themselves to the sheriff to secure the defendant's appearance, or his putting in bail to the action on the return-day of the writ.

"Bail to the sheriff was originally designed to temporarily liberate the defendant from close custody, and to place means in the sheriff's hands to insure the defendant's appearance to answer at the return of the writ. * * * The appearance which was contemplated was not, however, necessarily an actual appearance in person, but by putting in new bail, called bail to the action, special bail, or bail above. This special bail, or bail above, was by recognizance, which was matter of record, and an act of appearance, and by it the bail were bound that if the defendant should be condemned he should pay or render himself a prisoner, and if he did not, that they would pay the condemnation. The undertaking of the bail to the sheriff, or bail below, was wholly different, and was adapted to the specific exigency. It was in the form of a bond to the sheriff, and was conditioned for the defendant's appearance at the return of the writ, which meant putting in and perfecting bail above." De Myer v. McGonegal, 32 Mich. 120, 124.

—Civil bail. That taken in civil actions.

—Common bail. Fictitious sureties formally entered in the proper office of the court. See Bail common, *supra.*

—Special bail. Responsible sureties who undertake as bail above. Persons who undertake jointly and severally in behalf of a defendant arrested on mesne process in a civil action that, if he be condemned in the action, he shall pay the costs and condemnation, (that is, the amount which may be recovered against him,) or render himself a prisoner, or that they will pay it for him. 3 Bl. Comm. 291; 1 Tidd, Pr. 245; Sellon, Pr. 137. See Bail to the sheriff or bail below, *supra.*

—Straw bail. Nominal or worthless bail. Irresponsible persons, or men of no property, who make a practice of going bail for any one who will pay them a fee therefor, and who originally, as a mark of their purpose, wore straw in their shoes.

BAIL. Fr. In French and Canadian law. A lease of lands. See Merlin, Répert. *Bail.*

—Bail à cheptel. A contract by which one of the parties gives to the other cattle to keep, feed and care for, the borrower receiving half the profit of increase, and bearing half the loss. Duverger.

—Bail à ferme. A contract of letting lands.

—Bail à longues années. A lease for more than nine years; the same as bail emphyteotique (see infra) or an emphyteutic lease.

—Bail à loyer. A contract of letting houses.

—Bail à rente. A contract partaking of the nature of the contract of sale, and that of the contract of lease; it is translative of property, and the rent is essentially redeemable. Clark's Heirs v. Christ's Church, 4 La. 286; Poth. Bail à Rente, 1, 3.

—Bail emphyteotique. An emphyteutic lease; a lease for a term of years with a right to prolong indefinitely; practically equivalent to an alienation. 5 Low. C. 381; 6 Low. C. 58. See Emphyteusis.

BAILABLE. Capable of being bailed; admitting of bail; authorizing or requiring bail.

BAILABLE ACTION. One in which the defendant is entitled to be discharged from arrest only upon giving bond to answer.

BAILABLE OFFENSE. One for which the prisoner may be admitted to bail.

BAILABLE PROCESS. Such as requires the officer to take bail, after arresting the defendant. That under which the sheriff is directed to arrest the defendant and is required by law to discharge him upon his tendering suitable bail as security for his appearance. A *capias ad respondendum* is bailable; not so a *capias ad satisfaciendum.*

BAILEE. In the law of contracts. One to whom goods are bailed; the party to whom personal property is delivered under a contract of bailment. Hotels Statler Co. v. Safier, 103 Ohio St. 638, 134 N.E. 460, 462, 22 A.L.R. 1190. A species of agent to whom something movable is committed in trust for another. Cowart v. State, 16 Ala.App. 119, 75 So. 711, 713; Smith v. State, 78 Okl.Cr. 375, 148 P.2d 206, 208.

BAILEE POLICIES. Floating policies which cover goods while in possession of warehouse without particular description in the policy. Gillespie v. Federal Compress & Warehouse Co., 265 S.W.2d 21, 27, 37 Tenn.App. 476.

BAILIE. In the Scotch law. (1) A magistrate having inferior criminal and civil jurisdiction, similar to that of an alderman, (*q. v.*;) (2) an officer appointed to confer infeoffment, (*q. v.*;) a bailiff, (*q. v.*;) a server of writs. Bell.

BAILIFF. One to whom some authority, care, guardianship, or jurisdiction is delivered, committed, or intrusted; one who is deputed or appointed to take charge of another's affairs; an overseer or superintendent; a keeper, protector, or guardian; a steward. Spelman. A sheriff's officer or deputy. 1 Bl.Comm. 344. A court attendant, sometimes called a tipstaff.

A magistrate, who formerly administered justice in the parliaments or courts of France, answering to the English sheriffs as mentioned by Bracton.

A person acting in a ministerial capacity who has by delivery the custody and administration of lands or goods for the benefit of the owner or bailor, and is liable to render an account thereof. Co.Litt. 271; Story, Eq.Jur. § 446; West v. Weyer, 18 N.E. 537, 46 Ohio St. 66, 15 Am.St.Rep. 552.

—Bailiff-errant. A bailiff's deputy.

—Bailiffs of franchises. In English law. Officers who perform the duties of sheriffs within liberties or privileged jurisdictions, in which formerly the king's writ could not be executed by the sheriff. Spelman.

—Bailiffs of hundreds. In English law. Officers appointed over hundreds, by the sheriffs, to collect fines therein, and summon juries; to attend the judges and justices at the assises and quarter sessions; and also to execute writs and process in the several hundreds. 1 Bl.Comm. 345; 3 Steph. Comm. 29; Bract. fol. 116.

—Bailiffs of manors. In English law. Stewards or agents appointed by the lord (generally by an authority under seal) to superintend the manor, collect fines, and quit rents, inspect the buildings, order repairs, cut down trees, impound cattle trespassing, take an account of wastes, spoils, and misdemeanors in the woods and demesne lands, and do other acts for the lord's interest. Cowell.

—High bailiff. An officer attached to an English county court. His duties are to attend the court when sitting; to serve summonses; and to execute orders, warrants, writs, etc. St. 9 & 10 Vict. c. 95, § 33; Poll.C.C.Pr. 16. He also has similar duties under the bankruptcy jurisdiction of the county courts.

—Special bailiff. A deputy sheriff, appointed at the request of a party to a suit, for the special purpose of serving or executing some writ or process in such suit.

BAILIVIA. In old law. A bailiff's jurisdiction, a bailiwick; the same as *bailium*. Spelman. See Bailiwick.

In old English law. A liberty, or exclusive jurisdiction, which was exempted from the sheriff of the county, and over which the lord of the liberty appointed a bailiff with such powers within his precinct as an under-sheriff exercised under the sheriff of the county. Whishaw.

BAILIWICK. A bailivia.

BAILLEUR DE FONDS. In Canadian law. The unpaid vendor of real estate. 1 Low. C. 1, 6; 9 Low. C. 497.

BAILLI. In old French law. One to whom judicial authority was assigned or delivered by a superior.

BAILMENT. A delivery of goods or personal property, by one person to another, in trust for the execution of a special object upon or in relation to such goods, beneficial either to the bailor or bailee or both, and upon a contract, express or implied, to perform the trust and carry out such object, and thereupon either to redeliver the goods to the bailor or otherwise dispose of the same in conformity with the purpose of the trust. Fulcher v. State, 32 Tex.Cr.R. 621, 25 S.W. 625.

A delivery of goods for some purpose, upon a contract, express or implied, that after the purpose has been fulfilled they shall be redelivered to the bailor, or otherwise dealt with according to his direction, or kept until reclaimed. In re George L. Nadell & Co., 294 Mich. 150, 292 N.W. 684, 686. A delivery of something of a personal nature by one party to another to be held according to the purpose or object of the delivery and to be returned or delivered over when that purpose is accomplished. Hardin v. Grant. Tex.Civ.App., 54 S.W.2d 189, 190; Hogan v. O'Brien, 206 N.Y.S. 831, 833, 123 Misc. 865. The term "bailment" is derived from the French word "bailler," meaning "to deliver." It imports a delivery of personal property by one person to another in trust for a specific purpose, with a contract, expressed o implied, that the trust shall be faithfully executed and the property returned or duly accounted for when the specific purpose is accomplished or kept until bailor claims it. Commonwealth v. Polk, 256 Ky. 100, 75 S.W.2d 761, 764.

According to Story, the contract does not necessarily imply an undertaking to redeliver the goods. On the other hand, Blackstone, although his definition does not include the return, speaks of it in all his examples of bailments as a duty of the bailee; and Kent says that the application of the term to cases in which no return or redelivery to the owner or his agent is contemplated, is extending the definition of the term beyond its ordinary acceptation in English law. A consignment to a factor would be a bailment for sale, according to Story; while according to Kent it would not.

Classification

Sir William Jones has divided bailments into five sorts, namely: *Depositum*, or deposit; *mandatum*, or commission without recompense; *commodatum*, or loan for use without pay; *pignori acceptum*, or pawn; *locatum*, or hiring, which is always with reward. This last is subdivided into *locatio rei*, or hiring, by which the hirer gains a temporary use of the thing; *locatio operis faciendi*, when something is to be done to the thing delivered; *locatio operis mercium vehendarum*, when the thing is merely to be carried from one place to another. Jones, Bailm. 36.

Lord Holt divided bailments thus:

(1) *Depositum*, or a naked bailment of goods, to be kept for the use of the bailor.

(2) *Commodatum*. Where goods or chattels that are useful are lent to the bailee *gratis*, to be used by him.

(3) *Locatio rei*. Where goods are lent to the bailee to be used by him for hire.

(4) *Vadium*. Pawn or pledge.

(5) *Locatio operis faciendi*. Where goods are delivered to be carried, or something is to be done about them, for a reward to be paid to the bailee.

(6) *Mandatum*. A delivery of goods to somebody who is to carry them, or do something about them, *gratis*. 2 Ld. Raym. 909.

Another division, suggested by Bouvier as being a better general division for practical purposes, is as follows: *First*, those bailments which are for the benefit of the bailor, or of some person whom he represents; *second*, those for the benefit of the bailee, or some person represented by him; *third*, those which are for the benefit of both parties.

In General

—Bailment for hire. A contract in which the bailor agrees to pay an adequate recompense for the safe-keeping of the thing intrusted to the custody of the bailee, and the bailee agrees to keep it and restore it on the request of the bailor, in the same condition substantially as he received it, excepting injury or loss from causes for which he is not responsible.

—Bailment for mutual benefit. One in which the parties contemplate some price or compensation in return for benefits flowing from the bailment, necessarily involving an express or implied agreement or undertaking to that effect. Armored Car Service, Inc. v. First Nat. Bank of

Miami, Fla.App., 114 So.2d 431, 434. For example, delivery of automobile to one who, for a consideration, undertakes to repair it. Fox Chevrolet Sales, Inc. v. Middleton, to Use of Farm Bureau Mut. Auto. Ins. Co., 99 A.2d 731, 732, 203 Md. 158, 43 A.L.R.2d 399.

—Actual bailment. One which exists where there is either (a) an "actual delivery," consisting in giving to the bailee or his agent the real possession of the chattel, or (b) a "constructive delivery," consisting of any of those acts which, although not truly comprising real possession of the goods transferred, have been held by legal construction equivalent to acts of real delivery. Wentworth v. Riggs, 159 App.Div. 899, 143 N.Y.S. 955, 956.

—Constructive bailment. One arising where the person having possession of a chattel holds it under such circumstances that the law imposes upon him the obligation to deliver it to another. Wentworth v. Riggs, 159 App.Div. 899, 143 N.Y.S. 955, 956. See, also, Involuntary bailment, *infra*.

—Gratuitous bailment. Another name for a depositum or naked bailment, which is made only for the benefit of the bailor and is not a source of profit to the bailee. Foster v. Essex Bank, 17 Mass. 499, 9 Am.Dec. 168.

—Involuntary bailment. One arising by the accidental leaving of personal property in the possession of any person without negligence on the part of its owner. Grossman Co. v. White, 52 Okl. 117, 152 P. 816, 817

A "bailment" is created by the element of lawful possession and the duty to act for the thing as the property of another, whether such possession is based on contract in the ordinary sense or not. Foulke v. New York Consol. R. Co., 228 N.Y. 269, 127 N.E. 237, 239, 9 A.L.R. 1384. See Constructive bailment, *supra*.

—Lucrative bailment. One which is undertaken upon a consideration and for which a payment or recompense is to be made to the bailee, or from which he is to derive some advantage. Prince v. Alabama State Fair, 106 Ala. 340, 17 So. 449, 28 L.R.A. 716.

—Bailment lease. A legal method by which one desiring to purchase an article but unable to pay therefor at the time, may secure possession thereof with the right to use and enjoy it as long as he pays stipulated rentals and becomes absolute owner after completing such installment payments, on payment of an additional sum which may be nominal. In re Robinson, D.C.Pa., 40 F. Supp. 320, 322, 323.

Bailments as Distinguished from Other Transactions

—Chattel mortgages. A radical distinction between a bailment and a chattel mortgage is that, by a mortgage, the title is transferred to the mortgagee, subject to be revested by performance of the condition, but, in case of a bailment, the bailor retains the title and parts with the possession for a special purpose. Walker v. Staples, 5 Allen (Mass.) 34.

—Debt. The distinction between an obligation to restore the specific thing received, or of returning others of equal value, is the distinction between a "bailment" and a "debt." Alamitos Land Co. v. Texas Co., 11 Cal.App.2d 614, 54 P.2d 489, 491.

—Exchanges. An agreement by which A is to let B have a horse, in consideration that B will let A have another horse, creates an exchange, not a bailment. Austin v. Seligman, C.C.N.Y., 21 Blatchf. 506, 18 Fed. 519.

—Partnerships. Where animals are delivered to be taken care of for a certain time, and at the expiration of that time the same number of animals is to be returned, and any increase is to be enjoyed by both parties, there is a bailment, not a partnership. Simmons v. Shaft, 91 Kan. 553, 138 P. 614, 615.

—Sales. The test of a bailment is that the identical thing is to be returned in the same or in some altered form; if another thing of equal value is to be returned, the transaction is a sale. Sturm v. Boker, 14 S.Ct. 99, 150 U.S. 312, 37 L.Ed. 1093; Borman v. U. S., C.C.A.N.Y., 262 F. 26, 29.

Conditional sale. Contemplates that at some time the title shall pass to the purchaser and that he shall pay the purchase price, while a "bailment" contemplates that the title shall not pass to the bailee, but remain in the bailor, and that the property shall be returned to the bailor. Vermont Acceptance Corporation v. Wiltshire, 103 Vt. 219, 153 A. 199, 200, 73 A.L.R. 792.

—Trusts. The passing of the legal title from the owner to the party to whom personal property is delivered distinguishes a "trust" from a bailment. National Cattle Loan Co. v. Ward, 113 Tex. 312, 255 S.W. 160, 164; McIntyre v. Smith, 154 Md. 660, 141 A. 405, 410.

BAILOR. The party who *bails* or delivers goods to another, in the contract of bailment. McGee v. French, 49 S.C. 454, 27 S.E. 487; Story, Bailm. §§ 74, 388.

BAIR-MAN. In old Scotch law. A poor insolvent debtor, left bare and naked, who was obliged to swear in court that he was not worth more than five shillings and fivepence.

BAIRN'S PART. In Scotch law. Children's part; a third part of the defunct's free movables, debts deducted, if the wife survive, and a half if there be no relict. See Legitim.

BAIRNS. In Scotch law. A known term, used to denote one's whole issue. Ersk.Inst. 3, 8, 48. But it is sometimes used in a more limited sense. Bell.

BAIT. To attack with violence; to provoke and harass. 2 A. & E. Encyc. 63; L.R. 9 Q.B. 380.

BAITING ANIMALS. In English law. Procuring them to be worried by dogs. Punishable on summary conviction, under 12 & 13 Vict. c. 92, § 3.

BAKER. In its ordinary use respecting a bakery business, a generic term including in its scope different services connected with the bakery business, such as doing shop service in putting bread in boxes. Futopolus v. Midland Casualty Co., 174 Wis. 208, 182 N.W. 845, 847.

BAKERY. Any place used for the purpose of mixing, compounding, or baking for sale or for purposes of a restaurant, bakery or hotel, any bread, biscuit, pretzels, crackers, buns, rolls, macaroni, cake, pies, or any food products of which flour or meal is a principal ingredient. Continental Baking Co. v. Campbell, 176 Okl. 218, 55 P.2d 114, 116.

BAKING POWDER. A mixture in dry form of certain alkali and acid substances, combined with a filler; when moistened and heated, as in baking dough, a chemical reaction occurs, liberating carbonic gas, which "raises" or leavens the bread. Royal Baking Powder Co. v. Emerson, C.C.A.Ark., 270 F. 429, 436.

BALÆNA. A large fish, called by Blackstone a "whale." Of this the king had the head and the queen the tail as a perquisite whenever one was taken on the coast of England. 1 Bl.Comm. 222; Prynne, Ann.Reg. 127.

BALANCE. An equality between the sums total of the two sides of an account, or the excess on either side. Jones v. Marrs, 114 Tex. 62, 263 S.W. 570, 574.

The conclusion or result of the debit and credit sides of an account. It implies mutual dealings, and the existence of debt and credit, without which there could be no balance. Thillman v. Shadrick, 69 Md. 528, 16 Atl. 138. The amount remaining due from one person to another on a settlement of the accounts involving their mutual dealings; the difference between the two sides (debit and credit) of an account.

Often used in the sense of residue or remainder, and, in a general sense, may be defined as what remains or is left over. Commercial Discount Co. v. Holland, 107 Cal.App. 83, 289 P. 906, 908.

—Balance of convenience. A term descriptive of a rule for determining in a doubtful case what decree should be made; for example, whether an injunction should be granted. Cohen v. City of Houston, Tex.Civ.App., 176 S.W. 809, 814. It pertains to a test to determine what order will with the least inconvenience to either party assure the victorious one the fruits of his decree. Town of Williams v. Iowa Falls Electric Co., 185 Iowa, 493, 170 N.W. 815.

—Balance of power. In international law. A distribution and an opposition of forces, forming one system, so that no state shall be in a position, either alone or united with others, to impose its will on any other state or interfere with its independence. Ortolan.

—Balance sheet. A statement made by merchants and others to show the true state of a particular business.

When it is desired to ascertain the exact state of a merchant's business, or other commercial enterprise, at a given time, all the ledger accounts are closed up to date and balances struck; and these balances, when exhibited together on a single page, and so grouped and arranged as to close into each other and be summed up in one general result, constitute the "balance-sheet." Eyre v. Harmon, 92 Cal. 580, 28 P. 779.

—General balance. Sometimes used to signify the difference which is due to a party claiming a lien on goods in his hands for work or labor done, or money expended in relation to those and other goods of the debtor. 3 B. & P. 485; 3 Esp. 268; McWilliams v. Allan, 45 Mo. 573.

—Net balance. In commercial usage, the balance of the proceeds, as from a sale of stock, after deducting the expenses incident to the sale. Evans v. Waln, 71 Pa. 74.

BALCANIFER, or BALDAKINIFER. The standard-bearer of the Knights Templar.

BALCONIES. Small galleries of wood or stone on the outside of houses. In London, the erection of them is regulated by the building acts.

BALDIO. In Spanish law. Waste land; land that is neither arable nor pasture. White New Recop. b. 2, tit. 1, c. 6, § 4, and note. Unappropriated public domain, not set apart for the support of municipalities. Sheldon v. Milmo, 90 Tex. 1, 36 S.W. 415.

BALE. A pack or certain quantity of goods or merchandise, wrapped or packed up in cloth and corded round very tightly, marked and numbered with figures corresponding to those in the bills of lading for the purpose of identification. Wharton.

A bale of cotton is a certain quantity of that commodity compressed into a cubical form, so as to occupy less room than when in bags. 2 Car. & P. 525. Penrice v. Cocks, 2 Miss. 229.

A standard package of merchantable lint cotton, separated from the seed by the first process of a cotton gin, weighing approximately 500 pounds, and classifiable under one of the recognized market grades. Wichita Falls Compress Co. v. W. L. Moody & Co., Tex.Civ.App., 154 S.W. 1032, 1045.

BALISE. Fr. In French marine law. A buoy.

BALIUS. In the civil law. A teacher; one who has the care of youth; a tutor; a guardian. Du Cange; Spelman.

BALIVA. (Spelled also *Balliva;* equivalent to *Balivatus, Balivia*). L. Lat. In old English law. A bailiwick; the jurisdiction of a sheriff; the whole district within which the trust of the sheriff was to be executed. Cowell; 3 Bla.Com. 283.

BALIVO AMOVENDO. See Ballivo Amovendo.

BALL-HOOTING. In lumbering, a term designating a process of sliding log down a mountain side. Bradford v. English, 190 N.C. 742, 130 S.E. 705.

BALLAST. That which is used for trimming a ship to bring it down to a draft of water proper and safe for sailing. Great Western Ins. Co. v. Thwing, 13 Wall. 674, 20 L.Ed. 607.

There is considerable analogy between *ballast* and *dunnage.* Dunnage is placed under the cargo to keep it from being wetted by water getting into the hold, or between the different parcels to keep them from bruising and injuring each other. Great Western Ins. Co. v. Thwing, 13 Wall. 674, 20 L.Ed. 607.

BALLASTAGE. A toll paid for the privilege of taking up ballast from the bottom of a port or harbor. This arises from the property in the soil. 2 Chitty, Comm.Law 16.

BALLIUM. A fortress or bulwark; also bail. Cunningham.

BALLIVO AMOVENDO. An ancient writ to remove a bailiff from his office for want of sufficient land in the bailiwick. Reg.Orig. 78.

BALLOON. See Aeronaut; Aeronautics; Aircraft.

BALLOON MORTGAGE. A mortgage providing for specific payments at stated regular intervals, and final payment of more than twice any of the periodic payments. Bellman v. Yarmark Enterprises, Inc., Fla.App., 180 So.2d 663, 665.

BALLOT. Derived from ballotta, a round bullet, a voice or lot, means act of voting, usually in secret, by balls or by written or printed tickets or slips of paper; the system of voting by balls or tickets, or by any device for casting or recording votes, as by voting machine. Norris v. Mayor and City Council of Baltimore, 192 A. 531, 535, 172 Md. 667. Also piece of paper on which the voter gives expression to his choice. Sawyer Stores v. Mitchell, 103 Mont. 148, 62 P.2d 342, 348.

A slip of paper bearing the names of the offices to be filled at the particular election and the names of the candidates for whom the elector desires to vote, or containing a particular question of administration or public policy on which the voter is asked to express his views. It may be printed, or written, or partly printed and partly written, and is deposited by the voter in a "ballot box" which is in the custody of the officers holding the election. Denny v. Pratt, 104 Conn. 396, 133 A. 107, 108.

Used as a symbol of secrecy, while "viva voce" is used as a symbol of publicity. Day v. Walker, 124 Neb. 500, 247 N.W. 350, 351.

The whole amount of votes cast.

Joint Ballot

In parliamentary practice, an election or vote by ballot participated in by the members of both houses of a legislative assembly sitting together as one body, the result being determined by a majority of the votes cast by the joint assembly thus constituted, instead of by concurrent majorities of the two houses. See State v. Shaw, 9 S.C. 144.

Official Ballot

Depending on its use in local statutes, this term has a varied meaning. It may refer to a ballot which has been furnished by the clerk; Cain v. Garvey, Tex.Civ.App., 187 S.W. 1111, 1116; or it may contemplate that a ballot must have been printed under the supervision of a designated member of the electoral board, sealed by the board, and by resolution declared to be one of the official ballots for the election to be held; Xippas v. Commonwealth, 141 Va. 497, 126 S.E. 207, 209.

Mutilated Ballot

One from which the name of the candidate is cut out. Murray v. Waite, 113 Me. 485, 94 A. 943, 945, Ann.Cas.1918A, 1128. One which is destitute or deprived of some essential or valuable part; greatly shortened. Stubbs v. Moursund, Tex.Civ. App., 222 S.W. 632, 634.

BALLOT-BOX. A case usually made of wood for receiving ballots.

BALLOTTEMENT. Fr. In medical jurisprudence. A test for pregnancy by palpation with the finger inserted in the vagina to the mouth of the uterus. The tip of the finger being quickly jerked upward, the fœtus, if one be present, can be felt rising upward and then settling back against the finger.

BALNEARII. In the Roman law. Those who stole the clothes of bathers in the public baths. 4 Bl.Comm. 239.

BAN.

In Old English and Civil Law

A proclamation; a public notice; the announcement of an intended marriage. Cowell. An excommunication; a curse, publicly pronounced. A proclamation of silence made by a crier in court before the meeting of champions in combat. Cowell. A statute, edict, or command; a fine, or penalty. An expanse; an extent of space or territory; a space inclosed within certain limits; the limits or bounds themselves. Spelman. An open field; the outskirts of a village. A privileged space or territory around a town, monastery, or other place.

French Law

The right of announcing the time of mowing, reaping, and gathering the vintage, exercised by certain seignorial lords. Guyot, Repert. Univ.

Old European Law

A military standard; a thing unfurled, a banner. Spelman. A summoning to a standard; a calling out of a military force; the force itself so summoned; a national army levied by proclamation.

BANAL. In Canadian and old French law. Pertaining to a *ban* or privileged place; having qualities or privileges derived from a *ban*. Thus, a banal mill is one to which the lord may require his tenant to carry his grain to be ground.

BANALITY. In Canadian law. The right by virtue of which a lord subjects his vassals to grind at his mill, bake at his oven, etc. Used also of the region within which this right applied. Guyot, Repert. Univ.; 1 Low.C. 31; 3 Low.C. 1.

BANC. Bench; the place where a court permanently or regularly sits; the seat of judgment; as, *banc le roy*, the king's bench; *banc le common pleas*, the bench of common pleas.

The full bench, full court. A "sitting *in banc*" is a meeting of all the judges of a court, usually for the purpose of hearing arguments on demurrers, points reserved, motions for new trial, etc., as distinguished from the sitting of a single judge at the assises or at *nisi prius* and from trials at bar. Cowell.

BANCI NARRATORES. In old English law. Advocates; countors; serjeants. Applied to advocates in the common pleas courts. 1 Bl.Comm. 24; Cowell.

BANCO. Ital. A seat or bench of justice; also, in commerce, a word of Italian origin signifying a bank. Also a small tract of land on opposite side of river from country to which it belongs, and so existing by virtue of an avulsive change in the river. San Lorenzo Title & Improvement Co. v. City Mortgage Co., Tex.Civ.App., 48 S.W.2d 310, 314. See, also, Banc.

BANCUS. L. Lat. In old English law and practice. A bench or seat in the king's hall or palace. Fleta, lib. 2, c. 16, § 1.

A high seat, or seat of distinction; a seat of judgment, or tribunal for the administration of justice.

Often used for the court itself; thus, the English court of common pleas was formerly called *Bancus*. Viner, Abr. *Courts* (M).

A sitting *in banc;* the sittings of a court with its full judicial authority, or in full form, as distinguished from sittings at *nisi prius*. Cowell; Spelman.

A stall, bench, table, or counter, on which goods were exposed for sale. Cowell.

BANCUS REGINÆ. The queen's bench. See Queen's Bench.

BANCUS REGIS. The king's bench; the supreme tribunal of the king after parliament. 3 Bl.Comm. 41.

In Banco Regis. In or before the court of king's bench.

BANCUS SUPERIOR. The upper bench. The king's bench was so called during the Protectorate.

BAND. In old Scotch law. A proclamation calling out a military force.

BANDIT. An outlaw; a man *banned,* or put under a ban; a brigand or robber. *Banditti,* a band of robbers.

BANE. A malefactor. Bract. l. 1, t. 8, c. 1.

Also a public denunciation of a malefactor; the same with what was called *"hutesium,"* hue and cry. Spelman.

BANERET, or BANNERET. In English law. A knight made in the field, by the ceremony of cutting off the point of his standard, and making it, as it were, a banner. Knights so made are accounted so honorable that they are allowed to display their arms in the royal army, as barons do, and may bear arms with supporters. They were sometimes called *"vexillarii."* Wharton.

A degree of honor next after a baron's, when conferred by the king; otherwise, it ranks after a baronet. 1 Bla.Comm. 403.

BANI. Deodands (*q. v.*).

BANISHMENT. In criminal law. A punishment inflicted upon criminals, by compelling them to quit a city, place, or country for a specified period of time, or for life. Cooper v. Telfair, 4 Dall. 14, 1 L.Ed. 721; People v. Potter, 1 Park.Cr.R. (N.Y.) 54. Synonymous with exilement and imports a compulsory loss of one's country. 3 P. Wms. 38.

It is inflicted principally upon political offenders, "transportation" being the word used to express a similar punishment of ordinary criminals. Banishment, however, merely forbids the return of the person banished before the expiration of the sentence, while transportation involves the idea of deprivation of liberty after the convict arrives at the place to which he has been carried. Rap. & L.

BANISTER AND RAILING. These words, in the New York Tenement House Law, § 35, mean a balustrade, consisting of balusters or supports, upon which is placed a railing commonly placed on the outer or open edge of a stairway. Cahill v. Kleinberg, 233 N.Y. 255, 135 N.E. 323.

BANK. A bench or seat; the bench of justice; the bench or tribunal occupied by the judges; the seat of judgment; a court. The full bench, or full court; the assembly of all the judges of a court.

A "sitting *in bank*" is a meeting of all the judges of a court, usually for the purpose of hearing arguments on demurrers, points reserved, motions for new trial, and other law points, as distinguished from the sitting of a single judge at the assises or at *nisi prius* and from trials at bar to determine facts. 3 Bla.Comm. 28, n. But in this sense, *banc* is perhaps the more usual form of the word. "Sitting in bank" is also described as an official meeting of four of the judges of a common-law court. Wharton, Lex.

Bank le Roy. The king's bench. Finch, 198.

An acclivity; an elevation or mound of earth, especially that which borders the sides of a water course.

The land adjacent to a river. Graham v. Knight, Tex. Civ.App., 240 S.W. 981, 983.

That part of a stream which retains the water. Dawson County v. Phelps County, 94 Neb. 112, 142 N.W. 697, 699.

The elevation of land which confines the waters of a stream in their natural channel when they rise the highest and do not overflow the banks. Department of Health of New Jersey v. Chemical Co. of America, 90 N.J.Eq. 425, 107 A. 164, 166. A water-washed and relatively permanent elevation or acclivity at the outer line of a river bed which separates the bed from the adjacent upland, and serves to confine the waters within the bed and to preserve the course of the river. State of Oklahoma v. State of Texas, 43 S.Ct. 221, 260 U.S. 606, 67 L.Ed. 428; Horton v. Niagara, Lockport & Ontario Power Co., 247 N.Y.S. 741, 745, 231 App.Div. 386. The land lying between the edge of the water of a stream at its ordinary low stage and the line which the edge of the water reaches in its ordinary high stage. Wemple v. Eastham, 150 La. 247, 90 So. 637, 638. An elevation of land which confines the waters of a stream when they rise out of the bed. Neither the line of ordinary high-water mark, nor of ordinary low-water mark, nor of a middle stage of water can be assumed as the line dividing the bed from the banks. Banks are fast land, on which vegetation appropriate to such land in the particular locality grows wherever the bank is not too steep to permit such growth, and bed is soil of a different character, and having no vegetation, or only such as exists, when commonly submerged in water. State v. Nolegs, 139 P. 943, 946, 40 Okl. 479. On the borders of navigable streams, where there are levees established according to law, the levees form the "banks of the river." Ward v. Board of Levee Com'rs of Orleans Levee Dist., 152 La. 158, 92 So. 769, 772.

An institution, of great value in the commercial world, empowered to receive deposits of money, to make loans, and to issue its promissory notes, (designed to circulate as money, and commonly called "bank-notes" or "bank-bills,") or to perform any one or more of these functions. State v. Wagner, 202 Iowa, 739, 210 N.W. 901, 902; People v. Bartow, 6 Cow.N.Y. 290; Dearborn v. Northwestern Savings Bank, 42 Ohio St. 617; In re Prudence Co., D.C.N.Y., 10 F.Supp. 33, 36.

An institution, usually incorporated with power to issue its promissory notes intended to circulate as money (known as bank notes); or to receive the money of others on general deposit, to form a joint fund that shall be used by the institution, for its own benefit, for one or more of the purposes of making temporary loans and discounts; of dealing in notes, foreign and domestic bills of exchange, coin, bullion, credits, and the remission of money; or with both these powers, and with the privileges, in addition to these basic powers, of receiving special deposits and making collections for the holders of negotiable paper, if the institution sees fit to engage in such business. State of Kansas ex rel. Boynton v. Hayes, C.C.A.Kan., 62 F.2d 597, 600. The term "bank" is usually restricted in its application to an incorporated body; while a private individual making it his business to conduct banking operations is generally denominated a "banker." Hobbs v. Bank, C.C.A. N.Y., 101 F. 75, 41 C.C.A. 205; Wells, Fargo & Co. v. Northern Pac. R. Co., C.C.Or., 23 F. 469.

The house or place where the business of banking is carried on.

Banks in the commercial sense are of three kinds, viz.: (1) of deposit; (2) of discount; (3) of circulation. Strictly speaking, the term "bank" implies a place for the deposit of money, as that is the most obvious purpose of such an institution. Originally the business of banking consisted only in receiving deposits, such as bullion, plate, and the like, for safe-keeping until the depositor should see fit to draw it out for use, but the business, in the progress of events, was extended, and bankers assumed to discount bills and notes, and to loan money upon mortgage, pawn, or other security, and, at a still later period, to issue notes of their own, intended as a circulating currency and a medium of exchange, instead of gold and silver. Modern bankers frequently exercise any two or even all three of those functions, but it is still true that an institution prohibited from exercising any more than one of those functions is a bank, in the strictest commercial sense. Oulton v. German Sav. & L. Soc., 17 Wall. 118, 21 L.Ed. 618; Millikan v. Security Trust Co., 118 N.E. 568, 569, 187 Ind. 307; Rev.St.U.S. § 3407 (12 USCA § 561).

—**Bank-account.** A sum of money placed with a bank or banker, on deposit, by a customer, and subject to be drawn out on the latter's check. The statement or computation of the several sums deposited and those drawn out by the customer on checks, entered on the books of the bank and the depositor's passbook. Gale v. Drake, 51 N.H. 84.

—**Bank bill.** Same as bank note. Eastman v. Com., 4 Gray (Mass.) 416. See Bank note, *infra*.

—**Bank book.** A book kept by a customer of a bank, showing the state of his account with it. See Pass-book.

—**Bank cashier.** A chief executive officer and general agent through whom financial operations of bank are conducted. Hamilton Nat. Bank of Chattanooga, Tenn., v. Lerman, 229 Ala. 363, 157 So. 75.

—**Bank charges.** This term in an action on a bill of exchange is equivalent to expenses of noting and may be especially endorsed as a liquidated demand; [1893] 1 Q.B. 318.

—**Bank check.** See Check.

—**Bank credit.** A credit with a bank by which, on proper security given to the bank, a person receives liberty to draw to a certain extent agreed upon. In Scotland also called a cash account. Cent. Dict.

—**Bank depositor.** One who delivers to or leaves with a bank a sum of money subject to his order. Wharton v. Poughkeepsie Sav. Bank, 31 N.Y.S.2d 311, 313, 262 App.Div. 598.

—**Bank draft.** A check, draft, or other order for payment of money, drawn by an authorized officer of a bank upon either his own bank or some other bank in which funds of his bank are deposited. Polotsky v. Artisans Sav. Bank, Del., 180 A. 791, 792, 7 W.W.Harr. 142.

—**Bank note.** A promissory note issued by a bank or banker authorized to do so, payable to bearer on demand, and intended to circulate as money. Townsend v. People, 4 Ill. 328; Low v. People, 2 Park.Cr.R. (N.Y.) 37. See, also, Banker's note.

In the early history of banks, their notes were generally denominated bills of credit. Briscoe v. Bank of the Commonwealth of Kentucky, 11 Pet. 257, 9 L.Ed. 709.

—**Bank stock.** Shares in the capital of a bank; shares in the property of a bank. In England the term is applied chiefly to the stock of the Bank of England.

—**Bank teller.** See Teller.

—**Bank in failing condition.** Under some statutes, an insolvent bank. Hanson v. State, 160 Ark. 329, 254 S.W. 691, 694.

—**Bank of circulation.** One which issues bank notes payable to bearer. Dunn v. State, 13 Ga. App. 314, 79 S.E. 170, 171. See Bank of issue, *infra*.

—**Bank of deposit.** A savings bank or any other bank which receives money on deposit. Dunn v. State, 13 Ga.App. 314, 79 S.E. 170, 171.

—**Bank of discount.** One which lends money on collateral or by means of discounts of commercial paper. Dunn v. State, 13 Ga.App. 314, 79 S.E. 170, 171.

—**Bank of issue.** One which, pursuant to authority conferred by its charter, issues its own notes intended to circulate as money. Millikan v. Security Trust Co., 187 Ind. 307, 118 N.E. 568, 569.

—**Joint-stock banks.** In English law. Joint-stock companies for the purpose of banking. They are regulated, according to the date of their incorporation, by charter, or by 7 Geo. IV, c. 46; 7 & 8 Vict. cc. 32, 113; 9 & 10 Vict. c. 45, (in Scotland and Ireland;) 20 & 21 Vict. c. 49; and 27 & 28 Vict. c. 32; or by the "Joint-Stock Companies Act, 1862," (25 & 26 Vict. c. 89.) Wharton.

—**Savings bank.** An institution in the nature of a bank, formed or established for the purpose of receiving deposits of money, for the benefit of the persons depositing, to accumulate the produce of so much thereof as shall not be required by the depositors, their executors or administrators, at compound interest, and to return the whole or any part of such deposit, and the produce thereof, to the depositors, their executors or administrators, deducting out of such produce so much as shall be required for the necessary expenses attending the management of such institution, but deriving no benefit whatever from any such deposit or the produce thereof. Grant, Banks, 546; Bulakowski v. Philadelphia Sav. Fund Soc., 270 Pa. 538, 113 A. 553, 554. They differ from the ordinary banks of discount and deposit in not being engaged in business for profit. Commercial Trust Co. of New Jersey v. Hudson County Board of Taxation, 86 N.J.Law, 424, 92 A. 263, 265.

BANK HOLIDAY OF 1933. Presidential Proclamations No. 2039, issued March 6, 1933, and No. 2040, issued March 9, 1933, temporarily suspended banking transactions by member banks of the Federal Reserve System. Normal banking functions were resumed on March 13, subject to certain restrictions. The first proclamation, it was held, had no authority in law until the passage on March 9, 1933, of a ratifying act (12 U.S.C.A. § 95b). Anthony v. Bank of Wiggins, 183 Miss. 885, 184 So. 626. The present law forbids member banks of the Federal Reserve System to transact banking business, except under regulations of the Secretary of the Treasury, during an emergency proclaimed by the President. 12 U.S.C.A. § 95.

BANK NIGHT. A device by which a theater provides a registration book which any person over eighteen years of age, whether a patron of the theater or not, may sign. The book is placed in the lobby or outside the doors of the theater and no charge is made for registration nor need one who does so buy a ticket to the theater. A number is given to each name. On stated occasions, the numbers representing all the names registered are placed in a container on the stage of the theater and one number is drawn. The name of the person having that registration number is announced both inside and outside the theater and on coming forward within a certain time, he receives a sum of money which the theater provides from its own funds. If the person whose number is drawn is outside the theater, he is permitted to enter and claim the award without paying the admission. If he does not come forward within the time set, the money is added to the sum to be awarded on the next bank night. Under the plan, various safeguards are thrown about the operation to insure fairness in the allotment of the money. State v. Dorau, 124 Conn. 160, 198 A. 573, 574. If not a *lottery*, a bank night is at least a *gift enterprise*. Barker v. State, 56 Ga. App. 705, 193 S.E. 605, 609. But it is generally considered to be a *lottery*. State ex rel. Hunter v. Fox Beatrice Theatre Corporation, 133 Neb. 392, 275 N.W. 605, 606; Furst v. A. & G. Amusement Co., 128 N.J.L. 311, 25 A.2d 892, 893; Commonwealth v. Lund, 142 Pa.Super. 208, 15 A.2d 839, 846.

BANKABLE PAPER. In mercantile law. Notes, checks, bank bills, drafts, and other securities for money, received as cash by the banks. The term does not necessarily mean discountable paper, but paper of such high credit that, if the time of payment was reasonable and the banks had loanable funds, they would ordinarily discount it. Edward P. Allis Co. v. Madison Electric Light, Heat & Power Co., 9 S.D. 459, 70 N.W. 650, 652.

National bank notes are received as bankable money without regard to the locality of the bank issuing them. U.S.Rev.Stat. § 5133 (12 USCA § 21); Veazie Bank v. Fenno, 8 Wall. 533, 19 L.Ed. 482.

BANKER. A private person who keeps a bank; one who is engaged in the business of banking. People v. Doty, 80 N.Y. 228; Auten v. Bank, 19 S.Ct. 628, 174 U.S. 125, 43 L.Ed 920.

Individual Banker

Under some statutes, an individual banker, as distinguished from a "private banker" (*q. v.*), is a person who, having complied with the statutory requirements, has received authority from the state to engage in the business of banking, while a private banker is a person engaged in banking without having any special privileges or authority from the state. Perkins v. Smith, 116 N.Y. 441, 23 N.E. 21.

Private Banker

One who carries on the business of banking without being incorporated. State of Missouri v. Angle, C.C.A.Mo., 236 F. 644, 650; Herzog v. Transatlantic Trust Co., Sup., 172 N.Y.S. 394, 395. One who carries on the business of banking by receiving money on deposit with or without interest, by buying and selling bills of exchange, promissory notes, gold or silver coin, bullion, uncurrent money, bonds or stock, or other securities, and by loaning money without being incorporated. State ex rel. Barker v. Sage, 267 Mo. 493, 184 S.W. 984, 988. See Individual banker, *supra*.

BANKER'S ACCEPTANCE. A draft or bill of exchange of which the acceptor is a bank or banker engaged generally in the business of granting bankers' acceptance credits. Atterbury v. Bank of Washington Heights of City of New York, 241 N.Y. 231, 149 N.E. 841, 843.

BANKER'S LIEN. A lien which a banker has by virtue of which he can appropriate any money or property in his possession belonging to a customer to the extinguishment of any matured debt of such customer to the bank, provided such property or money has not been charged, with the knowledge of the bank, with the subservience of a special burden or purpose, or does not constitute a trust fund of which the banker has notice. American Surety Co. of New York v. Bank of Italy, 63 Cal.App. 149, 218 P. 466, 468.

BANKER'S NOTE. A commercial instrument resembling a bank note in every particular except that it is given by a private banker or unincorporated banking institution. 6 Mod. 29; 3 Chit. Comm.Law 590.

BANKEROUT. O. Eng. Bankrupt; insolvent; indebted beyond the means of payment.

BANKING. The business of receiving money on deposit, loaning money, discounting notes, issuing notes for circulation, collecting money on notes deposited, negotiating bills, etc. Bank v. Turner, 154 Ind. 456, 57 N.E. 110.

The business of banking, as defined by law and custom, consists in the issue of notes payable on demand intended to circulate as money when the banks are banks of issue; in receiving deposits payable on demand; in discounting commercial paper; making loans of money on collateral security; buying and selling bills of exchange; negotiating loans, and dealing in negotiable securities issued by the government, state and national, and municipal and other corporations. Mercantile Bank v. New York, 121 U.S. 138, 156, 7 S.Ct. 826, 30 L.Ed. 895; In re Prudence Co., D. C.N.Y., 10 F.Supp. 33, 36.

Having a place of business where deposits are received and paid out on checks and where money is loaned on security is the substance of the "business of banking." Marvin v. Kentucky Title Trust Co., 218 Ky. 135, 291 S.W. 17, 18, 50 A.L.R. 1337; State of Kansas ex rel. Boynton v. Hayes, C.C.A.Kan., 62 F.2d 597, 600.

BANKING A DEAL. Means making to one who wishes to consummate a deal a loan of money on collateral for a consideration which may consist of interest, a fee, or a part of the securities or property involved in the deal. Cray, McFawn & Co. v. Hegarty, Conroy & Co., D.C.N.Y., 27 F.Supp. 93, 99.

BANKING GAME. Gambling game at which money is bet or hazarded. State v. Singley, 195 La. 519, 197 So. 218, 219.

BANKING HOURS. A term which, in addition to the regular hours, includes time to allow presentment, after closing, to the bank returning a check, if such presentment is necessary in fact. Columbia-Knickerbocker Trust Co. v. Miller, 156 App. Div. 810, 142 N.Y.S. 440, 445.

BANKRUPT. Originally and strictly, a trader who secretes himself or does certain other acts tending to defraud his creditors. 2 Bl.Comm. 471; Shor v. McGregor, C.C.A.Tex., 108 F.2d 421, 423. In a looser sense, an insolvent person; a broken-up or ruined trader. Everett v. Stone, 3 Story, 453, Fed.Cas.No.4,577.

In the English law there were two characteristics which distinguished bankrupts from insolvents: the former must have been a *trader* and the object of the proceedings *against*, not *by*, him. As used in American law, the distinction between a bankrupt and an insolvent is not generally regarded. Sturges v. Crowninshield, 4 Wheat. 122, 4 L.Ed. 529; 2 Kent, 390; McCormick v. Pickering, 4 N.Y. 283. On the continent of Europe, however, the distinction still exists. Holtz.Enc. *voc. sig.* Bankerott.

A person who has committed an act of bankruptcy; one who has done some act or suffered some act to be done in consequence of which, under the laws of his country, he is liable to be proceeded against by his creditors for the seizure and distribution among them of his entire property. Ashby v. Steere, 2 Woodb. & M. 347, 2 Fed. Cas. 15; In re Scott, 21 Fed.Cas. 803; U. S. v. Pusey, 27 Fed.Cas. 632. For "Examination of bankrupt", see Examination.

The term includes one against whom involuntary petition has been filed. United States v. Agresti, C.C.A.N.Y., 130 F.2d 152, 153, 154.

A person who, by the formal decree of a court, has been declared subject to be proceeded against under the bankruptcy laws, or entitled, on his voluntary application, to take the benefit of such laws. See Bankruptcy Act July 1, 1898, c. 541, § 1, 30 Stat. 544 (11 USCA § 1).

BANKRUPT LAW. A law for benefit and relief of creditors and their debtors in cases in which the latter are unable or unwilling to pay their debts. Campbell v. Alleghany Corporation, C.C. A.Md., 75 F.2d 947, 951.

A bankrupt law is distinguished from the ordinary law between debtor and creditor, as involving these three general principles: (1) A summary and immediate seizure of all the debtor's property; (2) a distribution of it among the creditors in general, instead of merely applying a portion of it to the payment of the individual complainant; and (3) the discharge of the debtor from future liability for the debts then existing.

The leading distinction between a bankrupt law and an insolvent law, in the proper technical sense, consists in the character of the persons upon whom it is designed to operate,—the former contemplating as its objects bankrupts only, that is, traders of a certain description; the latter, insolvents in general, or persons unable to pay their debts. This has led to a marked separation between the two systems, in principle and in practice, which in England has always been carefully maintained, although in the United States it has of late been disregarded. A bankrupt law, moreover, in its proper sense, is a remedy intended primarily for the benefit of creditors; it is set in motion at their instance, and operates upon the debtor against his will, (*in invitum,*) although in its result it effectually discharges him from his debts. An insolvent law, on the other hand, is chiefly intended for the benefit of the debtor, and is set in motion at his instance, though possibly less effective as a discharge in its final result. Sturges v. Crowninshield, 4 Wheat. 194, 4 L.Ed. 529; Vanuxen v. Hazlehursts, 4 N.J.Law, 192, 7 Am.Dec. 582; Adams v. Storey, 1 Paine, 79, 1 Fed.Cas. 142; Kunzler v. Kohaus, 5 Hill (N.Y.) 317.

The only substantial difference between a strictly bankrupt law and an insolvent law lies in the circumstance that the former affords relief upon the application of the creditor, and the latter upon the application of the debtor. Martin v. Berry, 37 Cal. 222.

BANKRUPTCY. The state or condition of one who is a bankrupt; amenability to the bankrupt laws; the condition of one who has committed an act of bankruptcy, and is liable to be proceeded against by his creditors therefor, or of one whose circumstances are such that he is entitled, on his voluntary application, to take the benefit of the bankrupt laws.

The term is used in a looser sense as synonymous with "insolvency,"—inability to pay one's debts; the stopping and breaking up of business because the trader is broken down, insolvent, ruined. Phipps v. Harding, C.C.A.Wis., 70 Fed. 468, 17 C.C.A. 203, 30 L.R.A. 513.

It constitutes a branch of equity jurisprudence. In re Flour Mills of America, D.C.Mo., 27 F.Supp. 559, 560. Its purpose is to secure finally to creditors distribution of value of at least part of debtor's assets and to bankrupt discharge from his debts, to end that creditors may be paid as much as may be and that bankrupt may have new start in life. In re Jones, D.C.Mo., 10 F.Supp. 165, 167.

Insolvency means a simple inability to pay as debts should become payable, whereby the debtor's business would be broken up; bankruptcy means the particular legal *status*, to be ascertained and declared by a judicial decree. In re Black, 2 Ben. 196, Fed.Cas.No.1,457.

The proceedings taken under the bankrupt law, against a person (or firm or company) to have him adjudged a bankrupt, and to have his estate administered for the benefit of the creditors, and divided among them. That branch of jurisprudence, or system of law and practice, which is concerned with the definition and ascertainment of acts of bankruptcy and the administration of bankrupts' estates for the benefit of their creditors and the absolution and restitution of bankrupts.

Act of Bankruptcy. See Act.

Adjudication of Bankruptcy

The judgment or decree of a court having jurisdiction, that a person against whom a petition in bankruptcy has been filed, or who has filed his voluntary petition, be ordered and adjudged to be a bankrupt.

Bankruptcy Courts. Courts for the administration of the bankrupt laws.

Bankruptcy Proceedings

This term includes all proceedings in a federal court having jurisdiction in bankruptcy, founded on a petition in bankruptcy and either directly or collaterally involved in the adjudication and discharge of the bankrupt and the collection and administration of his estate. Kidder v. Horrobin, 72 N.Y. 167. See, also, Proceedings in bankruptcy. Steps in administration of estate in bankruptcy court within summary jurisdiction of bankruptcy court. (Bankr.Act, § 24a, b, 11 U.S.C.A. § 47(a) (b). Childs v. Ultramares Corporation, C.C.A. N.Y., 40 F.2d 474, 477.

Controversies Arising in Bankruptcy Proceedings. See Proceedings in bankruptcy.

Extension. See Extension.

Involuntary Bankruptcy. See Voluntary bankruptcy, *infra.*

Voluntary Bankruptcy

Bankruptcy (in the sense of proceedings taken under the bankruptcy law) is either voluntary or involuntary; the former where the proceeding is initiated by the debtor's own petition to be adjudged a bankrupt and have the benefit of the law. In re Murray, D.C.Iowa, 96 F. 600; Metsker v. Bonebrake, 2 Sup.Ct. 351, 108 U.S. 66, 27 L.Ed. 654, the latter where he is forced into bankruptcy on the petition of a sufficient number of his creditors.

See Bankrupt; Bankrupt Law.

Bankruptcy Rule

Allows claim only for amount of debt, less value of security. In re Baker, 333 Pa. 273, 3 A.2d 785, 786.

BANLEUCA. (Same as the French *banlieue*). An old law term, signifying a space or tract of country around a city, town, or monastery, distinguished and protected by peculiar privileges. Spelman.

BANLIEU, or BANLIEUE. In French and Canadian law. The same as *banleuca (q. v.).*

BANNER. A small flag bearing a device or symbol and intended to be carried or waved. L.R. 2 P.C. 387. The term includes a canvas, parti-colored or bearing party words and stretched across a street. 4 O'M. & H. 179.

BANNERET. See Baneret.

BANNI, or BANNITUS. In old law, one under a ban, *(q. v.;)* an outlaw or banished man. Britt. cc. 12, 13; Calvin.

BANNI NUPTIARUM. L. Lat. In old English law. The bans of matrimony.

BANNIMUS. Lat. We ban or expel. The form of expulsion of a member from the University of Oxford, by affixing the sentence in some public places, as a promulgation of it. Cowell.

BANNIRE AD PLACITA, AD MOLENDINUM. To summon tenants to serve at the lord's courts, to bring corn to be ground at his mill.

BANNITIO. Banishment; expulsion by a ban or public proclamation. Adams Gloss.

BANNITUS. See Banni.

BANNS OF MATRIMONY. Public notice or proclamation of a matrimonial contract, and the intended celebration of the marriage of the parties in pursuance of such contract. Cowell; 1 Bla. Comm. 439; Pothier, *Du Mariage* p. 2, c. 2.

Such announcement is required by the English law to be made in a church or chapel, during service, on three consecutive Sundays before the marriage is celebrated. The object is to afford an opportunity for any person to interpose an objection if he knows of any impediment or other just cause why the marriage should not take place. The publication of the banns may be dispensed with by procuring a special license to marry.

BANNUM. A ban *(q. v.).*

BANNUS. In old English law. A proclamation. *Bannus regis;* the king's proclamation, made by the voice of a herald, forbidding all present at the trial by combat to interfere either by motion or word, whatever they might see or hear. Bract. fol. 142.

BANQUE. Fr. A bench; the table or counter of a trader, merchant, or banker. *Banque route;* a broken bench or counter; bankrupt.

BANS OF MATRIMONY. See Banns of Matrimony.

BANYAN. In East Indian law. A Hindoo merchant or shop-keeper. The word is used in Bengal to denote the native who manages the money concerns of a European, and sometimes serves him as an interpreter.

BAR. A partition or railing running across a court-room, intended to separate the general public from the space occupied by the judges, counsel, jury, and others concerned in the trial of a cause. In the English courts it is the partition behind which all outer-barristers and every member of the public must stand. Solicitors, being officers of the court, are admitted within it; as are also queen's counsel, barristers with patents of precedence, and serjeants, in virtue of their ranks. Parties who appear in person also are placed within the bar on the floor of the court.

A particular part of the court-room; for example, the place where prisoners stand at their trial, hence the expression "prisoner at the bar."

The court, in its strictest sense, sitting in full term. The presence, actual or constructive, of the court. Thus, a trial *at bar* is one had before the full court, distinguished from a trial had before a single judge at *nisi prius*. So the "case at bar" is the case now before the court and under its consideration; the case being tried or argued.

In another sense, the whole body of attorneys and counsellors, or the members of the legal profession, collectively, who are figuratively called the "bar," from the place which they usually occupy in court. They are thus distinguished from the "bench," which term denotes the whole body of judges.

In the practice of legislative bodies, the outer boundary of the house; therefore, all persons, not being members, who wish to address the house, or are summoned to it, appear *at the bar* for that purpose.

In the law of contracts, an impediment, obstacle, or preventive barrier.

Thus, relationship within the prohibited degrees is a *bar* to marriage. In this sense also we speak of the "bar of the statute of limitations."

That which defeats, annuls, cuts off, or puts an end to.

Thus, a provision "in bar of dower" is one which has the effect of defeating or cutting off the dower-rights which the wife would otherwise become entitled to in the particular land.

In pleading, a special plea, constituting a sufficient answer to an action at law; so called because it *barred, i. e.,* prevented, the plaintiff from further prosecuting it with effect, and, if established by proof, defeated and destroyed the action altogether. Now called a special "plea in bar." It may be further described as a plea or peremptory exception of a defendant to destroy the plaintiff's action. City of San Antonio v. Johnson, Tex.Civ.App., 186 S.W. 866. See Plea in bar.

A barrier or counter over which liquors and food are passed to customers, hence the portion of the room behind the counter where the liquors for sale are kept. Hinton v. State, 137 Tex.Cr.R. 352, 129 S.W.2d 670, 673.

BAR ASSOCIATION. An association of members of the bar. Such associations have been organized in most states. The first was in Mississippi in 1825, but it is not known to have had a continued existence. An association of Grafton and Coos counties in New Hampshire had an existence before 1800, and probably a more or less continuous life since then, having finally merged into a state association. Similar associations exist in many of the counties in various states.

—Bar integration. See Integrated Bar.

BAR FEE. In English law. A fee taken by the sheriff, time out of mind, for every prisoner who is acquitted. Bac.Abr. "Extortion." Abolished by St. 14 Geo. III. c. 26; 55 Geo. III. c. 50; 8 & 9 Vict. c. 114.

BAR ROOM. A place where intoxicating liquors are sold to be drunk on the same premises. City of Spokane v. Baughman, 103 P. 14, 17, 54 Wash. 315.

A room containing a bar or counter at which liquors are sold, or a room with a bar where liquors and refreshments are served. Mustard v. Elwood, C.C.A.Alaska, 223 F. 225, 226.

The words "bar" and "bar room" have a more restrictive meaning than "saloon," and mean a place from which intoxicating liquors are to be sold. Greil Bros. Co. v. Mabson, 179 Ala. 444, 60 So. 876, 877, 43 L.R.A.,N.S., 664.

BAR SINISTER. A term popularly though erroneously used for *baton,* a mark of illegitimacy. Webster.

BARAGARIA. Span. A concubine, whom a man keeps alone in his house, unconnected with any other woman. Las Partidas, pt. 4, tit. 14.

BARAT. See Berat.

BARATRIAM COMMITTIT QUI PROPTER PECUNIAM JUSTITIAM BARACTAT. He is guilty of barratry who for money sells justice. Bell. (This maxim, however, is one pertaining more to the meaning of "barratry" as used in Scotch law than to its common-law meaning. See Barratry.)

BARBANUS. In old Lombardic law. An uncle, *(patruus.)*

BARBAROUS. As used in a divorce statute, it implies a merciless and savage disposition, taking pleasure in suffering, without pity, and with an evil and malicious will. Hansell v. Hansell, 15 Pa.Co.Ct.R., 514, 515.

BARBER. One who makes a business of shaving and trimming beards and cutting and dressing hair. Dellacorte v. Gentile, 98 N.J.Eq. 194, 129 A. 739, 740.

The term has been held to include a woman, who, being employed in a beauty parlor serving women customers exclusively, cut a woman's hair in the style of bobbed hair. State v. Leftwich, 142 Wash. 329, 253 P. 448, 449, 59 A.L.R. 539. But it has also been thought that the proprietor of a "hairdressing and beauty parlor," the important features of whose business included cutting hair, massaging, clipping hair with barber clippers, singeing the hair, giving tonics, shampooing, and manicuring, but not shaving the face, was not a "barber" within a statute subjecting barbers to examination and regulation. Keith v. State Barber Board, 112 Kan. 834, 212 P. 871, 872, 31 A.L.R. 432.

In England in former times, barbers also practiced surgery and dentistry, but by 32 Hen. VIII, c. 42, barbers, although they were thereby incorporated with the surgeons of London, were not to practice surgery, except the drawing of teeth.

BARBICANAGE. In old European law. Money paid to support a barbican or watchtower.

BARBITTS. L. Fr. (Modern Fr. *brebis.*) Sheep.

BARE. Naked; without a covering; unaccompanied.

BARE OR MERE LICENSEE. One whose presence on premises is merely tolerated; while a "licensee" or "invitee" is one who is on the premises by invitation, express or implied. Chicago, R. I. & P. Ry. Co. v. McCleary, 175 Okl. 347, 53 P.2d 555, 557.

BARE PATENT LICENSE. A grant of authority to make, use or vend patented product throughout the United States or in a given part thereof, with no right of exclusion. 35 U.S.C.A. § 47. Innis, Speiden & Co. v. Food Machinery Corporation, D. C.Del., 2 F.R.D. 261, 263.

BARE TRUSTEE. One whose trust is to convey, and the time has arrived for a conveyance by him; or a trustee to whose office no duties were originally attached, or who, although such duties were originally attached to his office, would, on the requisition of his *cestuis que trust*, be compellable in equity to convey the estate to them or by their direction. Christie v. Ovington, 1 Ch.Div. 279, 281.

BAREBONES PARLIAMENT. A parliament summoned by Cromwell in 1653.

BARET. L. Fr. A wrangling suit. Britt. c. 92; Co.Litt. 368*b*.

BARGAIN. A mutual undertaking, contract, or agreement.

A contract or agreement between two parties, the one to sell goods or lands, and the other to buy them. Bank v. Archer, 16 Miss. 192.

As a verb, to sell for cash, or on terms, rather than to trade or exchange. In re Wellings' Estate, 197 Cal. 189, 240 P. 21, 24.

"If the word 'agreement' imports a mutual act of two parties, surely the word 'bargain' is not less significative of the consent of two. In a popular sense, the former word is frequently used as declaring the engagement of one only. A man may agree to pay money or to perform some other act, and the word is then used synonymously with 'promise' or 'engage.' But the word 'bargain' is seldom used, unless to express a mutual contract or undertaking." Packard v. Richardson, 17 Mass. 131, 9 Am.Dec. 123.

—Bargain money. These words in a contract for the sale of land have much the same significance as earnest money. Morgan v. Forbes, 236 Mass. 480, 128 N.E. 792, 793.

—Catching bargain. A bargain by which money is loaned, at an extortionate or extravagant rate, to an heir or any one who has an estate in reversion or expectancy, to be repaid on the vesting of his interest; or a similar unconscionable bargain with such person for the purchase outright of his expectancy. See Edler v. Frazier, 174 Iowa, 46, 156 N.W. 182, 187. That kind of fraud often perpetrated upon young, inexperienced, or ignorant people. Provident Life & Trust Co. v. Fletcher, C.C.A.N.Y., 258 F. 583, 586.

See Unconscionable Bargain

BARGAIN AND SALE. In conveyancing. The transferring of the property of a thing from one to another, upon valuable consideration, by way of sale. Shep.Touch. (by Preston,) 221.

A contract or bargain by the owner of land, in consideration of money or its equivalent paid, to sell land to another person, called the "bargainee," whereupon a use arises in favor of the latter, to whom the seisin is transferred by force of the statute of uses. Laing v. McClung, 103 W. Va. 341, 137 S.E. 744, 745.

The proper and technical words to denote a bargain and sale are "bargain and sell;" but any other words that are sufficient to raise a use upon a valuable consideration are sufficient. 2 Wood.Conv. 15; Jackson ex dem. Hudson v. Alexander, 3 Johns. (N.Y.) 484, 3 Am.Dec. 517.

The expression "bargain and sale" is also applied to transfers of personalty, in cases where there is first an executory agreement for the sale, (the bargain,) and then an actual and completed sale.

BARGAIN OR CONTRACT IN RESTRAINT OF TRADE. Any bargain or contract which purports to limit in any way right of either party to work or to do business. Stoia v. Miskinis, 298 Mich. 105, 298 N.W. 469, 474.

BARGAINEE. The grantee of an estate in a deed of bargain and sale. The party to a bargain to whom the subject-matter of the bargain or thing bargained for is to go.

BARGAINOR. The person who makes a bargain. The party to a bargain who is to receive the consideration and perform the contract by delivery of the subject-matter.

BARGE. Name originally applied to a small sailing vessel but afterwards came into general use for a flat bottomed boat used for carrying goods on inland waterways. Barges are usually towed or fitted with some kind of engine. The Sakito Maru, D.C.Cal., 41 F.Supp. 769, 778.

BARK. It is sometimes figuratively used to denote the mere words or letter of an instrument, or outer covering of the ideas sought to be expressed, as distinguished from its inner substance or essential meaning. "If the *bark* makes for them, the pith makes for us." Bacon.

BARLEYCORN. In linear measure. The third of an inch.

BARMOTE COURTS. Courts held in certain mining districts belonging to the Duchy of Lancaster, for regulation of the mines, and for deciding questions of title and other matters relating thereto. 3 Steph.Comm. 347, note b.

BARN. A covered building for securing productions of the earth. Washington v. Arizona, 46 Ariz. 446, 52 P.2d 476, 478.

It may be both a cornhouse and a stable; State v. Smith, 28 Iowa 565, 568; and has been used interchangeably with stable; Saylor v. Commonwealth, 22 Ky.L.Rep. 472, 57 S. W. 614, 615.

BARNARD'S INN. An inn of chancery. See Inns of Chancery.

BARO. In old law, a man, whether slave or free. In later usage, a freeman or freedman; a strong man; a good soldier; a hired soldier; a vassal; a baron; a feudal tenant or client. A man of dignity and rank; a knight. A magnate in the church. A judge in the exchequer *(baro scaccarii).* The first-born child. A husband.

The word is said by Spelman to have been used more frequently in the last sense; Spelman, Gloss.

BARON. A lord or nobleman; the most general title of nobility in England. 1 Bl.Comm. 398, 399. A particular degree or title of nobility, next to a viscount. The lowest title in Great Britain. A judge of the court of exchequer. 3 Bl.Comm. 44; Cowell. A freeman. Co.Litt. 58*a*. Also a vassal holding directly from the king. A husband; occurring in this sense in the phrase *"baron et feme,"* husband and wife.

The term has essentially the same meanings as *Baro (q. v.).*

BARON COURT. See Court-Baron.

BARON ET FEME. Man and woman; husband and wife. Spelman, Gloss.; 1 Bla.Comm. 442.

A wife being under the protection and influence of her *baron,* lord, or husband, is styled a *"feme-covert," (fœmina viro cooperta,)* and her state of marriage is called her "coverture." Cummings v. Everett, 82 Me. 260, 19 A. 456.

BARONS OF THE CINQUE PORTS. Members of parliament from these ports, viz.: Sandwich, Romney, Hastings, Hythe, and Dover. Winchelsea and Rye have been added. See Cinque Ports.

BARONS OF THE EXCHEQUER. The six judges of the court of exchequer in England, of whom one is styled the "chief baron;" answering to the justices and chief justice of other courts.

BARONAGE. In English law. The collective body of the barons, or of the nobility at large. Spelman.

BARONES SCACCARII. See Barons of the Exchequer.

BARONET. An English name or hereditary title of dignity or rank (but not a title of nobility, being next below that of baron), established in 1611 by James I. It is created by letters patent, and descends to the male heir. Spelman.

BARONY. The dignity of a baron; a species of tenure; the territory or lands held by a baron. Spelman; 2 Holdsw.Hist.Eng.L. 159.

In Scotland, a large freehold estate, even though the proprietor is not a baron. See Barony of Land, *infra.*

BARONY OF LAND. In England, a quantity of land amounting to 15 acres. In Ireland, a subdivision of a county.

BARRA, or BARRE. In old practice. A plea in bar. The bar of the court. A barrister.

BARRATOR. One who commits barratry. See Barretor.

BARRATROUS. Fraudulent; having the character of barratry.

BARRATRY. In criminal law. Also spelled "Barretry." The offense of frequently exciting and stirring up quarrels and suits, either at law or otherwise. 4 Bla.Com. 134; State v. Batson, 220 N.C. 411, 17 S.E.2d 511, 512, 513.

Common barratry is the practice of exciting groundless judicial proceedings. Pen.Code Cal. § 158; Lucas v. Pico, 55 Cal. 128; Com. v. McCulloch, 15 Mass. 229; Ex parte McCloskey, 82 Tex.Cr.R. 531, 199 S.W. 1101, 1102.

In maritime law. An act committed by the master or mariners of a vessel, for some unlawful or fraudulent purpose, contrary to their duty to the owners, whereby the latter sustain injury. It may include negligence, if so gross as to evidence fraud. Hansen v. Barnard, C.C.A.N.Y., 270 F. 163, 166.

Some fraudulent act of the master or mariners, tending to their own benefit, to the prejudice of the owner of the vessel, without his privity or consent. Kendrick v. Delafield, 2 Caines N.Y. 67.

A generic term, which includes many acts of various kinds and degrees. It comprehends any unlawful, fraudulent, or dishonest act of the master or mariners, and every violation of duty by them arising from gross and culpable negligence contrary to their duty to the owner of the vessel, and which might work loss or injury to him in the course of the voyage insured. A mutiny of the crew, and forcible dispossession by them of the master and other officers from the ship, is a form of barratry. Greene v. Pacific Mut. Ins. Co., 9 Allen, Mass., 217.

In Scotch law. The crime committed by a judge who receives a bribe for his judgment. Skene; Brande.

See Champerty.

BARRED. Obstructed by a bar; subject to hindrance or obstruction by a bar or barrier which, if interposed, will prevent legal redress or recovery; as, when it is said that a claim or cause of action is "barred by the statute of limitations." Wilson v. Knox County, 132 Mo. 387, 34 S.W. 45, 477.

BARREL. A measure of capacity, equal (in England) to 36 imperial gallons. The standard United States measure, except as to barrels of petroleum, equals 31½ gallons. Pope v. Joschke, Tex.Civ. App., 228 S.W. 986, 987.

In agricultural and mercantile parlance, as also in the inspection laws, the term means, *prima facie,* not merely a certain quantity, but, further, a certain state of the article; namely, that it is in a cask. State v. Moore, 33 N.C. 72.

BARREN MONEY. In the civil law. A debt which bears no interest.

BARRENNESS. Sterility; the incapacity to bear children.

BARRETOR. In criminal law. A common mover, exciter, or maintainer of suits and quarrels either in courts or elsewhere in the country; a disturber of the peace who spreads false rumors and calumnies, whereby discord and disquiet may grow among neighbors. Co.Litt. 368.

Common Barretor

One who frequently excites and stirs up groundless suits and quarrels, either at law or otherwise. State v. Batson, 220 N.C. 411, 17 S.E.2d 511, 512, 513.

BARRETRY. In criminal law. The act or offense of a barretor, *(q. v.;)* usually called "common barretry." 4 Steph.Comm. 262. See Barratry.

BARRICADE. An obstruction or block to prevent passage. Schawe v. Leyendecker, Tex.Civ.App., 269 S.W. 864, 866; Crowley v. City of Raymond, 198 Wash. 432, 88 P.2d 858, 859.

BARRIER. A fence. Page Steel & Wire Co. v. Smith Bros. Hardware Co., C.C.A.Ohio, 64 F.2d 512.

In mining law and the usage of miners, a wall of coal left between two mines.

BARRISTER. In English law. An advocate; a counsellor learned in the law who has been admitted to plead at the bar, and who is engaged in conducting the trial or argument of causes.

To be distinguished from the *attorney,* who draws the pleadings, prepares the testimony, and conducts matters out of court. In re Rickert, 66 N.H. 207, 29 Atl. 559, 24 L. R.A. 740.

See King's Counsel.

Inner Barrister

A serjeant or king's counsel who pleads within the bar.

Junior Barrister

A barrister under the rank of queen's counsel. Also the junior of two counsel employed on the same side in a case. Mozley & Whitley.

Outer or Utter Barrister

One who pleads "outer" or without the bar.

Such barristers were so called because they sat "uttermost on the forms of the benchers which they call the bar." 29 L.Q.R. 25. They are distinguished from benchers, or those who have been readers, and are allowed to plead within the bar, as are the king's counsel.

Utter Barrister

The same as "Outer barrister," *supra.*

Vacation Barrister

A counsellor newly called to the bar, who is to attend for several long vacations the exercises of the house.

BART. The usual abbreviation for *Baronet (q. v.).*

BARTER. A contract by which parties exchange goods or commodities for other goods. Finker v. Boyer, 331 Mo. 1242, 56 S.W.2d 372.

It differs from *sale,* in this: that in the latter transaction goods or property are always exchanged for money. Guerreiro v. Peile, 3 Barn. & Ald. 617; Cooper v. State, 37 Ark. 418; Meyer v. Rousseau, 47 Ark. 460, 2 S.W. 112. In a sale there is a fixed price; in a barter there is not. Speigle v. Meredith, 4 Biss. 120, Fed.Cas.No.13,227.

This term is not applied to contracts concerning land, but to such only as relate to goods and chattels. Speigle v. Meredith, 4 Biss. 123, Fed.Cas.No.13,227.

It sometimes signifies a corrupt transaction. In re Troy, 43 R.I. 279, 111 A. 723, 724.

BARTON. In old English law. The demesne land of a manor; a farm distinct from the mansion.

Sometimes it is used for the manor house itself; and in some places for out houses and fold yards. In the statute 2 & 3 Edw. 6, c. 12, Barton lands and demesne lands are used as synonymous. Cowell.

BAS. Fr. Low; inferior; subordinate.

BAS CHEVALIERS. In old English law. Low, or inferior knights, by tenure of a base military fee, as distinguished from *barons* and *bannerets,* who were the chief or superior knights. Cowell; Kennett, Paroch.Ant.; Blount.

BAS VILLE. In French law. The suburbs of a town.

BASAL FRACTURE. A fracture of the skull beginning at the base of the skull to the rear and left extending to the top of the skull. Marland Refining Co. v. McClung, 102 Okl. 56, 226 P. 312, 313.

BASE, *adj.* Low; inferior; servile; of subordinate degree; impure, adulterated, or alloyed.

—Base animal. See Animal.

—Base bullion. Base silver bullion is silver in bars mixed to a greater or less extent with alloys or base materials. Hope Min. Co. v. Kennon, 3 Mont. 44.

—Base coin. Debased, adulterated, or alloyed coin. Gabe v. State, 6 Ark. 540; Cohens v. Virginia, 6 Wheat. 333, 5 L.Ed. 257.

—Base court. In English law. An inferior court, that is, not of record, as the court baron. Cunningham; Kitch. 95, 96; Cowell.

—Base estate. The estate which "base tenants" *(q. v.)* have in their land. Cowell.

—Base fee. In English law. An estate or fee which has a qualification subjoined thereto, and which must be determined whenever the qualification annexed to it is at an end. 2 Bl.Comm. 109. Wiggins Ferry Co. v. Railroad Co., 94 Ill. 93; Scobey v. Beckman, 111 Ind.App. 574, 41 N.E.2d 847, 850.

It is a fee for the reason that it may last forever if the contingency does not happen, but debased because its duration depends upon collateral circumstances which qualify it. McIntyre v. Dietrich, 128 N.E. 321, 322, 294 Ill. 126; sometimes called a conditional fee; Citizens' Electric Co. v. Susquehanna Boom Co., 113 A. 559, 561, 270 Pa. 517; a determinable fee; Penick v. Atkinson, 77 S.E. 1055, 1057, 139 Ga. 649, 46 L.R.A.,N.S., 284, Ann.Cas.1914B, 842; or a qualified fee; In re Douglass' Estate, 143 N.W. 299, 302, 94 Neb. 280, Ann.Cas.1914D, 447. Burche v. Neal, 149 S.E. 611, 612, 107 W.Va. 559.

—Base infeftment. In Scotch law. A disposition of lands by a vassal, to be held of himself.

—Base right. In Scotch law. A subordinate right; the right of a subvassal in the lands held by him. Bell.

—Base services. In feudal law. Such services as were unworthy to be performed by the nobler men, and were performed by the peasants and those of servile rank. 2 Bla.Comm. 62; 1 Washb. R.P. 25.

—Base tenants. Tenants who performed to their lords services in villenage; tenants who held at the will of the lord, as distinguished from *frank* tenants, or freeholders. Cowell.

—Base tenure. A tenure by villenage, or other customary service, as distinguished from tenure by military service; or from tenure by free service. Cowell.

BASE, *n.* Bottom, foundation, groundwork, that on which a thing rests. Webster.

The locality on which a military or naval force relies for supplies or from which it initiates operations. Webster. For example: air base; military base; marine base; naval base; submarine base.

—Base Hospital. See Hospital.

—Air Base. A military or naval establishment forming a center of supporting activities for the military or naval air arm; a training center for air corps personnel; a place where equipment and supplies of the air corps are kept. The term is included in the word *fort.* Greenville Baseball v. Bearden, 200 S.C. 363, 20 S.E.2d 813, 816.

—Submarine Base. A naval base for the housing, repair and maintenance of submarines, for keeping supplies; a place where personnel is trained; a place from which operations are initiated.

BASED UPON. Means an initial or starting point for calculation. State ex rel. Snidow v. State Board of Equalization, 93 Mont. 19, 17 P.2d 68.

BASEBALL. A game of skill within the criminal offense of betting on such a game. Mace v. State, 58 Ark. 79, 22 S.W. 1108.

When played by professionals for profit, it is a performance of worldly employment and business within the Sunday Law of Pennsylvania. Commonwealth v. American Baseball Club of Philadelphia, 290 Pa. 136, 138 A. 497, 53 A.L.R. 1027.

BASEMENT. A floor partly beneath the surface of the ground but distinguished from a cellar by being well lighted and fitted for living purposes. In England the ground floor of a city house.

BASIC OR PIONEER PATENT. One discovered in new field and recognized by scientific world or industry as startling, unexpected, and unprophesied. Northwest Engineering Corporation v. Keystone Driller Co., C.C.A.Wis., 70 F.2d 13, 16.

BASILEUS. A Greek word, meaning "king." A title assumed by the emperors of the Eastern Roman Empire. It is used by Justinian in some of the Novels; and is said to have been applied to the English kings before the Conquest. See 1 Bl. Comm. 242.

BASILICA. The name given to a compilation of Roman and Greek law, prepared about A.D. 880 by the Emperor Basilius, and published by his successor, Leo the Philosopher. It was written in Greek, was mainly an abridgment of Justinian's *Corpus Juris,* and comprised sixty books, only a portion of which are extant. It remained the law of the Eastern Empire until the fall of Constantinople, in 1453.

BASILS. In old English law. A kind of money or coin abolished by Henry II.

BASIN. When speaking of a large river, ordinarily means or includes the entire area drained by the main stream and its tributaries. City of Tulsa v. Peacock, 181 Okl. 383, 74 P.2d 359, 360.

In admiralty law and marine insurance. A part of the sea inclosed in rocks. U. S. v. Morel, 13 Am.Jur. 286, 26 Fed.Cas. 1,310.

BASIS. Fundamental principle; groundwork; support; foundation; the foundation or groundwork of anything; that upon which anything may rest or the principal component parts of a thing. Tolmie v. San Diego Fruit & Produce Co., 57 Idaho 631, 68 P.2d 61, 64. State v. Kansas City & M. Ry. & Bridge Co., 106 Ark. 248, 153 S.W. 614, 616.

BASKET TENURE. In feudal law. Lands held by the service of making the king's baskets.

BASOCHE. Fr. An association of the "Clercs du Parlement" of Paris, supposed to have been instituted in 1302. It judged all civil and criminal matters that arose among the clerks and all actions brought against them. Hist. for Ready Reference.

BASSA, BASSO, or BASSUS. L. Lat. Low. Adams Gloss.

BASSA TENURA. See Base Fee.

BASSE JUSTICE. In feudal law. Low justice; the right exercised by feudal lords of personally trying persons charged with trespasses or minor offenses.

BASSET. A card game resembling faro. It was invented in Venice, and was widely popular in Europe from about 1650 to 1800.

BASTARD. An illegitimate child; a child born of an unlawful intercourse, and before the lawful marriage of its parents. Pettus v. Dawson, 82 Tex. 18, 17 S.W. 714.

A child born after marriage, but under circumstances which render it impossible that the husband of his mother can be his father. State v. Coliton, 73 N.D. 582, 17 N.W.2d 546, 548, 549, 156 A.L.R. 1403.

A child is not a bastard if born after marriage, although begotten before. 1 Bla.Com. 455, 456; 8 East, 210; State v. Herman, 35 N.C. 502.

One begotten and born out of lawful wedlock. Ex parte Newsome, 212 Ala. 168, 102 So. 216, 218.

This definition, which is substantially the same as Blackstone's, is open to the objection that it does not include with sufficient certainty those cases where children are born during wedlock but are not the children of the mother's husband.

Such children as are not born either in lawful wedlock or within a competent time after its determination. In re Paterson's Estate, 34 Cal.App.2d 305, 93 P.2d 825, 827.

One born of an illicit union. Civ.Code La. arts. 27, 197.

The term also includes a child born of parents while in a state of slavery, inasmuch as the parents were under disability to contract marriage. Cole v. Taylor, 132 Tenn. 92, 177 S.W. 61, 65.

In Louisiana, "bastards," as distinguished from "natural children," are illegitimate children who have not been acknowledged by their parents. "Natural children" are those who have been acknowledged by both or either of their parents. Briggs v. McLaughlin, 134 La. 133, 63 So. 851, 852.

—Bastard eigné. In old English law. Bastard elder. If a child was born of an illicit connection, and afterwards the parents intermarried and had another son, the elder was called bastard eigné, or, as it is now spelled, ainé, and the second son was called puisné, or since born, or sometimes he was called mulier puisné. 2 Bla.Comm. 248.

—Special bastard. One born of parents before marriage, the parents afterward intermarrying. 3 Bl.Comm. 335.

By the civil and Scotch law, as well as by the statute law prevailing in over half of the states of the Union, the child would then be legitimated.

BASTARDA. A female bastard. Calvinus, Lex.; Fleta, lib. 5, c. 5, § 40.

BASTARDIZE. To declare one a bastard, as a court does. To give evidence to prove one a bastard. A mother (married) cannot bastardize her child.

BASTARDUS NON POTEST HABERE HÆREDEM NISI DE CORPORE SUO LEGITIME PROCREATUM. A bastard can have no heir unless it be one lawfully begotten of his own body. Tray. Lat.Max. 51.

BASTARDUS NULLIUS EST FILIUS, AUT FILIUS POPULI. A bastard is nobody's son, or the son of the people.

BASTARDY. The offense of begetting a bastard child. The condition of a bastard. Dinkey v. Com., 17 Pa. 129, 55 Am.Dec. 542.

BASTARDY PROCESS. The method provided by statute of proceeding against the putative father to secure a proper maintenance for the bastard.

It is of a special character in nature of civil action. In re Mitchell, 189 Okl. 51, 113 P.2d 979, 980.

BASTON. In old English law, a baton, club, or staff. A term applied to officers of the wardens of the prison called the "Fleet," because of the staff carried by them. Cowell; Spelman; Termes de la Ley. See Justices of Trail-Baston.

BATABLE-GROUND. Land that is in controversy, or about the possession of which there is a dispute, as the lands which were situated between England and Scotland before the Union. Skene.

BATAILLE. In old English law. Battel; the trial by combat or *duellum*.

BATH, KNIGHTS OF THE. See Knights of the Bath.

BATIMENT. In French marine law. A vessel or ship.

BATONNIER. The chief of the French bar in its various centres, who presides in the council of discipline. Arg.Fr.Merc.Law, 546.

BATTEL. Trial by combat; wager of battel. See Wager of Battel.

BATTERY. Any unlawful beating, or other wrongful physical violence or constraint, inflicted on a human being without his consent. Goodrum v. State, 60 Ga. 511.

A willful and unlawful use of force or violence upon the person of another. Long v. Rogers, 17 Ala. 540. An unlawful touching of the person of another by the aggressor himself, or any other substance put in motion by him. Kirland v. State, 43 Ind. 153, 13 Am.Rep. 386; Commonwealth v. Remley, 257 Ky. 209, 77 S.W.2d 784. The consummation of an unlawful assault. State v. Hamburg, Del., 143 A. 47, 48. The slightest touching of another, or of his clothes or anything else attached to his person, if done in a rude, insolent, or angry manner. Booher v. Trainer, 172 Mo.App. 376, 157 S.W. 848, 850; Commonwealth v. Gregory, 132 Pa. Super. 507, 1 A.2d 501, 503.

The actual offer to use force to the injury of another person is *assault;* the use of it is *battery,* which always includes an assault; hence the two terms are commonly combined in the term "assault and battery." Harris v. State, 15 Okl.Cr. 369, 177 P. 122, 123.

A surgical operation is a technical "battery" regardless of its result, and is excusable only when there is express or implied consent by the patient. Bonner v. Moran, 126 F.2d 121, 122, 75 U.S.App.D.C. 156, 139 A.L.R. 1366.

—Assault and Battery of a High and Aggravated Nature. An unlawful act of violent injury to the person of another, accompanied by circumstances of aggravation, such as the use of deadly weapon, great disparity between the ages and physical conditions of the parties, or the purposeful infliction of shame and disgrace. State v. Jones, 133 S.C. 167, 130 S.E. 747, 751.

—Simple Battery. One not accompanied by circumstances of aggravation, or not resulting in grievous bodily injury.

BATTONIER. In French and Canadian law. A member of the bar selected as the head of the bar.

BATTURE. According to Richelet and the French Academy, a marine term, used to denote a bottom of sand, stone, or rock, mixed together, and rising towards the surface of the water; as a technical word and also in common parlance, an elevation of the bed of a river, under the surface of the water. The term is, however, sometimes used to denote the same elevation of the bank, when it has risen above the surface of the water, or is as high as the land on the outside of the bank. Conkey v. Knudsen, 143 Neb. 5, 8 N.W.2d 538, 541.

In this latter sense it is synonymous with "alluvion." It means, in common-law language, land formed by accretion. Producers' Oil Co. v. Hanszen, 132 La. 691, 61 So. 754.

The term is used in Louisiana, and is applied principally to certain portions of the bed of the Mississippi river which are uncovered at time of low water but are covered annually at time of ordinary high water. Boyce Cottonseed Oil Mfg. Co. v. Board of Com'rs of Red River, Atchafalaya & Bayou Bœuf Levee Dist., 160 La. 727, 107 So. 506, 508.

BAUXITE. An earth containing aluminum in sufficient quantities to make it worth working for the extraction of alumina. American Bauxite Co. v. Board of Equalization of Saline County, 119 Ark. 362, 177 S.W. 1151, 1152. United States v. Aluminum Co. of America, D.C.N.Y., 44 F.Supp. 97, 109.

BAWD. One who procures opportunities for persons of opposite sexes to cohabit in an illicit manner; who may be, while exercising the trade of a bawd, perfectly innocent of committing in his or her own proper person the crime either of adultery or of fornication. See Dyer v. Morris, 4 Mo. 216.

BAWDY-HOUSE. A house of ill fame; a house of prostitution; a brothel. A house or dwelling maintained for the convenience and resort of persons desiring unlawful sexual connection. Davis v. State, 2 Tex.App. 427; State v. Porter, 38 Ark. 638; People v. Buchanan, 1 Idaho 689. An assignation house. State v. Bragg, Mo.App., 220 S.W. 25, 26. A disorderly house. Putman v. State, 9 Okl.Cr. 535, 132 P. 916, 921, 46 L.R.A.,N.S., 593.

To constitute a bawdy-house, the house must be "resorted to" or "frequented," that is to say, used a number of times, by lewd people of both sexes. State v. Seba, Mo. App., 200 S.W. 300; but need not be inhabited or resorted to by more than one woman for purpose of prostitution. Trent v. Commonwealth, 181 Va. 338, 25 S.E.2d 350, 351.

BAY. A pond-head made of a great height to keep in water for the supply of a mill, etc., so that the wheel of the mill may be turned by the water rushing thence, through a passage or flood-gate. St. 27 Eliz. c. 19. (This is generally called a fore-bay.)

A bending or curving of the shore of the sea or of a lake, so as to form a more or less inclosed body of water. State v. Town of Gilmanton, 14 N.H. 477. An opening into the land, or an arm of the sea, where the water is shut in on all sides except at the entrance. Mayo v. New York Cent. R. Co., 263 N.Y. 277, 189 N.E. 217, 218.

BAYGALL. A low-lying wet land matter with vegetable fibres and often with gallberry and other thick-growing bushes. McNeal v. Carter, 191 Ga. 441, 12 S.E.2d 332, 333.

BAY WINDOW. A window projecting from the wall of a building so as to form a recess or bay within, and, properly speaking, rising from the ground or basement, with straight sides only; but the term is also ordinarily applied to such projecting windows with curved sides, properly called bow windows, and also to projecting windows supported from the building, above the ground, properly called oriel windows. Hieronimus v. Moran, 272 Ill. 254, 111 N.E. 1022, 1023.

BAYLEY. In old English law. Bailiff. This term is used in the laws of the colony of New Plymouth, Mass., A.D. 1670, 1671. Burrill.

BAYOU. A species of creek or stream common in Louisiana and Texas. An outlet from a swamp, pond, or lagoon, to a river, or the sea. See Surgett v. Lapice, 8 How. 48, 70, 12 L.Ed. 982.

BEACH. This term, in its ordinary signification, when applied to a place on tide waters means the space between ordinary high and low water mark; East Hampton v. Kirk, 6 Hun (N.Y.) 257; or the space over which the tide usually ebbs and flows. It is a term not more significant of a sea margin than "shore." Niles v. Patch, 13 Gray (Mass.) 257; Hodge v. Boothby, 48 Me. 68.

In common parlance designates that portion of shore consisting generally of sand and pebbles, resulting usually from the action of water, as distinct from the upland, to which it often extends above normal high-water mark. Borden v. Town of Westport, 112 Conn. 152, 151 A. 512, 515.

Beach is synonymous with "shore," "strand," or "flats." Littlefield v. Littlefield, 28 Me. 180.

The term may also include the sandy shore above mean high water which is washed by storms and exceptionally high tides. Newkirk v. Sherwood, 94 A. 982, 984, 89 Conn. 598.

To "beach" a ship is to run it upon the beach or shore; this is frequently found necessary in case of a fire, leak, etc.

See Foreshore; Sea-Shore.

Public Beach

One left by the state or others claiming it open to the common use of the public, which the unorganized public and each of its members have a right to use while it remains such. Brower v. Wakeman, 88 Conn. 8, 89 A. 913, 914.

BEACON. A light-house, or sea-mark, formerly used to alarm the country, in case of the approach of an enemy, but now used for the guidance of ships at sea, by night, as well as by day.

BEACONAGE. Money paid for the maintenance of a beacon or signal-light. Comyns, Dig. *Navigation* (H).

BEADLE. In English ecclesiastical law. An inferior parish officer, who is chosen by the vestry, and whose business is to attend the vestry, to give notice of its meetings, to execute its orders, to attend upon inquests, and to assist the constables. Wharton. See, also, Bedel.

BEAMS AND BALANCE. Instruments for weighing goods and merchandise.

BEAR. To support, sustain, or carry; to give rise to, or to produce, something else as an incident or auxiliary. See Stevenson v. Mellor, 252 Pa. 219, 97 A. 393, 394; to render, to manage, or direct, or to conduct; to carry on, or maintain;

to be answerable for, and to defray. Teeter v. Mid-West Enterprise Co., 174 Okl. 644, 52 P.2d 810, 812.

BEAR ARMS. To carry arms as weapons and with reference to their military use, not to wear them about the person as part of the dress. Aymette v. State, 2 Humph. (Tenn.) 158.

As applied to fire-arms, includes the right to load and shoot them, and to use them as such things are generally used. Hill v. State, 53 Ga. 480.

BEAR INTEREST. To generate interest, so that the instrument or loan spoken of shall produce or yield interest at the rate specified by the parties or granted by law. Slaughter v. Slaughter, 21 Ind. App. 641, 52 N.E. 995.

BEARER. One who bears, carries, or holds a thing. Defined by the Negotiable Instruments Act as the person in possession of a bill or note which is payable to bearer. Miller v. People's Sav. Bank, 193 Mo.App. 498, 186 S.W. 547, 550.

When a check, note, draft, etc., is payable to "bearer," it imports that the contents thereof shall be payable to any person who may present the instrument for payment. Thompson v. Perrine, 106 U.S. 589, 1 S.Ct. 564, 568, 27 L. Ed. 298.

BEARERS. In old English law. Such as bear down or oppress others; maintainers. Cowell.

BEARING DATE. Disclosing a date on its face; having a certain date. Words frequently used in pleading and conveyancing to introduce the date which has been put upon an instrument. See 2 Greenl.Ev. § 160; 2 Dowl. & L. 759.

BEAST. An animal; a domestic animal; a quadruped, such as may be used for food or in labor or for sport; *e. g.*, a cow; Taylor v. State, 6 Humph. (Tenn.) 285; a horse; Winfrey v. Zimmerman, 8 Bush (Ky.) 587; and a hog; State v. Enslow, 10 Iowa, 115; but a dog was held not to be; U. S. v. Gideon, 1 Minn. 292 (Gil. 226); but see Morewood v. Wakefield, 133 Mass. 241.

BEASTS OF THE CHASE. In English law. Properly, the buck, doe, fox, martin, and roe, but in a common and legal sense extending likewise to all the beasts of the forest, which beside the others are reckoned to be the hind, hare, bear, and wolf, and, in a word, all wild beasts of venery or hunting. Co.Litt. 233; 2 Bla.Comm. 39.

BEASTS OF THE FOREST. In English law. The hart, hind, hare, boar, and wolf. Co.Litt. 233*a*. See Beasts of the Chase.

BEASTS OF THE PLOW. An old term for animals employed in the operations of husbandry, including horses. Somers v. Emerson, 58 N.H. 49.

BEASTS OF THE WARREN. In English law. Hares, coneys, and roes. Co.Litt. 233; 2 Bla. Comm. 39.

BEASTGATE. In Suffolk, England, imports land and common for one beast. Bennington v. Goodtitle, 2 Strange, 1084; Rosc.Real Act. 485.

BEAT, *v.* To strike or hit repeatedly, as with blows. Regina v. Hale, 2 Car. & K. 327; Com. v. McClellan, 101 Mass. 35; Com. v. McClellan, 101 Mass. 35.

In the criminal law and the law of torts, with reference to assault and battery, the term includes any unlawful physical violence offered to another. See Battery.

To beat, in a legal sense, is not merely to whip, wound, or hurt, but includes any unlawful imposition of the hand or arm. Goodrum v. State, 60 Ga. 511; Yarbrough v. State, 17 Ga.App. 828, 88 S.E. 710, 711.

BEAT, *n.* In some of the southern states (as Alabama, Mississippi, South Carolina) the principal legal subdivision of a county, corresponding to towns or townships in other states; or a voting precinct. Eaton v. State, 20 Ala.App. 110, 101 So. 94, 95.

BEATING OF THE BOUNDS. An ancient custom in England by which, once a year, the minister, etc., of a parish walked about its boundaries to preserve a recollection of them. Cent.Dict. (Perambulation).

BEAUPLEADER. (L. Fr. fair pleading). A writ of prohibition directed to the sheriff or another, directing him not to take a fine for beaupleader.

There was anciently a fine imposed called a fine for beaupleader, which is explained by Coke to have been originally imposed for bad pleading. Coke, 2d Inst. 123. The statute of Marlebridge (52 Hen. III.) c. 11, enacts, that neither in the circuit of justices, nor in counties, hundreds, or courts-baron, any fines shall be taken for *fair pleading;* namely, for not pleading fairly or aptly to the purpose. Upon this statute this writ was ordained, directed to the sheriff, bailiff, or him who shall demand the fine; and it is a prohibition or command not to do it. Cowell; Co. 2d Inst. 122; Crabb, Eng.Law 150.

BEAUTY CULTURE. Generally, the means employed to improve personal appearance, is an occupation operating directly on the person. Hoff v. State, Del.Super., 197 A. 75, 78, 81.

BECAUSE OF. For. Kelly v. State Personnel Board of California, 31 Cal.App.2d 443, 88 P.2d 264, 266.

BECAUSE OF EMPLOYMENT. In this phrase as used in the Workmen's Compensation Act, excepting an employer from liability for the willful act of a third person directed against an employee because of his employment, the words "because of" are not synonymous with "caused by" but with "on account of," or "by reason of." Saucier's Case, 122 Me. 325, 119 A. 860, 861.

BECOME. To pass from one state to another; to enter into some state or condition.

Hence one who is a member of a particular organization at the time of the enactment of a statute making it a felony to "become" a member of such an organization cannot be said to be within the purview of the act. State v. Laundy, 103 Or. 443, 204 P. 958, 963.

BED. The hollow or channel of a water course; the depression between the banks worn by the regular and usual flow of the water.

Soil only which the water occupies sufficiently long and continuously to wrest it from vegetation and destroy its value for agricultural purposes. State ex rel. O'Connor v. Sorenson, 271 N.W. 234, 236, 222 Iowa 1248.

The land that is covered by the water in its ordinary low stage. Wemple v. Eastham, 150 La. 247, 90 So. 637, 638.

That portion of its soil which is alternately covered and left bare as there may be an increase or diminution in the supply of water, and which is adequate to contain it at its average and mean state during an entire year. Maufrais v. State, 142 Tex. 559, 180 S.W.2d 144, 147.

Area extending between the opposing banks measured from the foot of the banks from the top of the water at its ordinary stage, including sand bars which may exist between the foot of said banks as thus defined. Town of Refugio v. Heard, Tex.Civ.App., 95 S.W.2d 1008, 1010.

It includes the lands below ordinary high water mark. United States v. Chicago, M., St. P. & P. R. Co., 61 S.Ct. 772, 775, 312 U.S. 592, 313 U.S. 543, 85 L.Ed. 1064.

Bed of navigable lake extends to high water mark. Miami Corporation v. State, 186 La. 784, 173 So. 315.

Also, the right of cohabitation or marital intercourse; as in the phrase "divorce from bed and board," or *a mensa et thoro*.

BED OF JUSTICE. In old French law. The seat or throne upon which the king sat when personally present in parliament; hence it signified the parliament itself.

BED-ALE or BID-ALE. A friendly assignation for neighbors to meet and drink at the house of newly married persons or other poor people and then for the guests to contribute to the housekeepers. Cowell. See Bidal.

BEDDING. Covers practically everything, that is to say, mattresses, springs, cots, couches, quilts, cushions, and also the bed itself. Baltimore Bedding Corporation v. Moses, 182 Md. 229, 34 A.2d 338, 340.

BEDEHOUSE. A hospital or almshouse for bedesmen or poor people who prayed for their founders and benefactors. Cunningham.

BEDEL. In English law. A crier or messenger of court, who summons men to appear and answer therein. Cowell. A herald to make public proclamations. Cent. Dict.

An officer of the forest, similar to a sheriff's special bailiff. Cowell.

A collector of rents for the king. Plowd. 199, 200.

An inferior officer in a parish or liberty, or in an institution, such as the Blue Coat School in London.

A subordinate officer of a university who walked with a mace before one of the officers on ceremonial occasions and performed other minor duties ordinarily. See Beadle.

BEDELARY. The jurisdiction of a bedel, as a bailiwick is the jurisdiction of a bailiff. Co.Litt. 234*b*; Cowell.

BEDEREPE. A service which certain tenants were anciently bound to perform, as to reap their landlord's corn at harvest. Said by Whishaw to be still in existence in some parts of England. Blount; Cowell; Whishaw.

BEDEWERI. Those which we now call *banditti;* profligate and excommunicated persons. Cunningham.

BEDLAM. A corruption of *Bethlehem.* The hospital of St. Mary of Bethlehem in London, originally a priory, founded about 1247, but used from about 1400 as an asylum for the insane.

BEEF. Used frequently to mean an animal of the cow species and not beef prepared for market. A beef or one beef is an expression frequently used to designate an animal fit for use as beef, instead of designating it as a steer, a heifer, an ox, or a cow. Davis v. State, 40 Tex. 135.

BEER. A liquor compounded of malt and hops, differing from ales, not so much in its ingredients as in its processes of fermentation.

A brewed liquor made of grain, especially barley, flavored with hops, which has undergone fermentation and contains alcohol. State v. Lynch, 5 Boyce (Del.) 569, 96 A. 32. An alcoholic beverage resulting from the fermentation of cereals or other starchy substances. U. S. v. Standard Brewery, D.C.Md., 260 F. 486, 487.

In its ordinary sense, it denotes a beverage which is intoxicating; Moffitt v. People, 59 Colo. 406, 149 P. 104, 107; Hoskins v. Commonwealth, 171 Ky. 204, 188 S.W. 348, 349; and is within the fair meaning of the words "strong or spirituous liquors," used in the statutes on this subject. Maier v. State, 2 Tex.Civ.App. 296, 21 S.W. 974.

But also held that "liquor," in common parlance, does not ordinarily mean "beer." Lea v. State, 181 S.W.2d 351, 353, 181 Tenn. 378.

Any liquor, whether intoxicating or not, made by the usual process of making beer, although fermentation is arrested to reduce the percentage of alcohol. Brown v. State, 17 Ariz. 314, 152 P. 578, 582.

BEER-HOUSE; BEER-SHOP. In English law. A place where beer is sold to be consumed on the premises; as distinguished from a "beer-shop," which is a place where beer is sold to be consumed off the premises. 16 Ch.Div. 721.

BEFORE. Prior to; preceding. In the presence of; under the official purview of; as in a magistrate's jurat, "*before* me personally appeared," etc. State v. Murnane, 172 Minn. 401, 215 N.W. 863.

Thus, an acknowledgment made to an officer over a telephone wire by one who is not present with the officer, is not an acknowledgment "before" the officer. Hutchinson v. State, 79 Fla. 157, 84 So. 151, 154.

In the absence of any statutory provision governing the computation of time, the authorities are uniform that, where an act is required to be done a certain number of days or weeks *before* a certain other day upon which another act is to be done, the day upon which the first act is done is to be excluded from the computation, and the whole number of days or weeks must intervene before the day fixed for doing the second act. Ward v. Walters, 63 Wis. 44, 22 N.W. 844.

When used as a preposition, does not indicate a period of time as do the prepositions "for," "during," and "throughout," but merely an event or act preceding in time, or earlier than, or previously to, the time mentioned. First Nat. Corporation v. Perrine, 43 P.2d 1073, 1077, 99 Mont. 454.

BEG. To solicit alms or charitable aid. The act of a cripple in passing along the sidewalk and silently holding out his hand and receiving money from passers-by is "begging for alms," within the meaning of a statute which uses that phrase. In re Haller, 3 Abb.N.C.,N.Y., 65.

BEGA. A land measure used in the East Indies. In Bengal it is equal to about a third part of an acre.

BEGET. See Begotten.

BEGGAR. One who lives by begging charity, or who has no other means of support than solicited alms.

BEGIN. To originate; to come into existence; to start; to institute; to initiate; to commence. People ex rel. Northchester Corporation v. Miller, 31 N.Y.S.2d 586, 587, 263 App.Div. 83.

BEGOTTEN. "To be begotten" means the same as "begotten," embracing all those whom the parent shall have begotten during his life, *quos procreaverit*. Cox v. Newby, 85 S.E. 369, 370, 101 S.C. 193. The term is peculiarly and chiefly applicable to a father. Swain v. Bowers, 91 Ind. App. 307, 158 N.E. 598, 601.

BEGUM. In India. A lady, princess, woman of high rank.

BEGUN. In a statute providing that nothing contained in it should affect prosecutions "begun" under any existing act, the word "begun" means both those which have already been begun and those which may hereafter be begun. Lang v. U. S., C.C.A.Ill., 133 F. 201, 66 C.C.A. 255.

BEHALF. Benefit, support, defence, or advantage.

A witness testifies on "behalf" of the party who calls him, notwithstanding his evidence proves to be adverse to that party's case. Richerson v. Sternburg, 65 Ill. 274. See, further, 12 Q.B. 693; 18 Q.B. 512.

BEHAVIOR. Manner of having, holding, or keeping one's self; manner of behaving, whether good or bad; conduct; manners; carriage of one's self, with respect to propriety and morals; deportment. Webster. State v. Roll, 1 Ohio Dec. 284; Schneiderman v. United States, Cal., 63 S.Ct. 1333, 1340, 320 U.S. 118, 87 L.Ed. 1796.

Surety to be of good *behavior* is a larger requirement than surety to keep the peace. Dalton, c. 122; 4 Burns, Just. 355. See Good Behavior.

BEHETRIA. In Spanish law. Lands situated in districts and manors in which the inhabitants had the right to select their own lords.

BEHOOF. Use; benefit; profit; service; advantage. It occurs in conveyances, *e. g.*, "to his and their use and behoof." Stiles v. Japhet, 84 Tex. 91, 19 S.W. 450.

BEING STRUCK. Collision, or striking together of two objects, one of which may be stationary. Davilla v. Liberty Life Ins. Co., 114 Cal.App. 308, 299 P. 831, 834.

BELIEF. A conviction of the truth of a proposition, existing subjectively in the mind, and induced by argument, persuasion, or proof addressed to the judgment. Keller v. State, 102 Ga. 506, 31 S.E. 92. Latrobe v. J. H. Cross Co., D.C.Pa., 29 F.2d 210, 212. A conclusion arrived at from external sources after weighing probability. Ex parte State ex rel. Attorney General, 100 So. 312, 313, 211 Ala. 1.

Conviction of the mind, arising not from actual perception or knowledge, but by way of inference, or from evidence received or information derived from others.

A conviction of the truth of a given proposition or an alleged fact resting upon grounds insufficient to constitute positive knowledge. Boone v. Merchants' & Farmers' Bank, D.C.N.C., 285 F. 183, 191.

With regard to things which make not a very deep impression on the memory, it may be called "belief." "Knowledge" is nothing more than a man's firm belief. The difference is ordinarily merely in the degree; to be judged of by the court, when addressed to the court; by the jury, when addressed to the jury. Hatch v. Carpenter, 9 Gray (Mass.) 274.

Knowledge is an assurance of a fact or proposition founded on perception by the senses, or intuition; while "belief" is an assurance gained by evidence, and from other persons. Brooks v. Sessoms, 47 Ga.App. 554, 171 S.E. 222, 224.

"Suspicion" is weaker than "belief," since suspicion requires no real foundation for its existence, while "belief" is necessarily based on at least assumed facts. Pen. Code, § 836, subd. 3. Cook v. Singer Sewing Mach. Co., 32 P.2d 430, 431, 138 Cal.App. 418.

BELLIGERENCY. In international law. The status of *de facto* statehood attributed to a body of insurgents, by which their hostilities are legalized.

Before they can be recognized as belligerents they must have some sort of political organization and be carrying on what in international law is regarded as legal war. There must be an armed struggle between two political bodies, each of which exercises *de facto* authority over persons within a determined territory, and commands an army which is prepared to observe the ordinary laws of war. Moore, Int. Law Dig. I, 196; Dana's Wheaton, note 15, page 35; In re Jones, 71 W.Va. 567, 77 S.E. 1029, 45 L.R.A.,N.S., 1030, Ann.Cas.1914C, 31.

Quality of being belligerent; status of a belligerent; act or state of waging war; warfare. Webster's New Int. Dict.

BELLIGERENT. In international law. As an adjective, it means engaged in lawful war. As a noun, it designates either of two nations which are actually in a state of war with each other, as well as their allies actively co-operating, as distinguished from a nation which takes no part in the war and maintains a strict indifference as between the contending parties, called a "neutral." U. S. v. The Ambrose Light, D.C.N.Y., 25 F. 412; Johnson v. Jones, 44 Ill. 151, 92 Am.Dec. 159.

BELLIGERENTS. A body of insurgents who by reason of their temporary organized government are regarded as conducting lawful hostilities. Also, militia, corps of volunteers, and others, who although not part of the regular army of the state, are regarded as lawful combatants provided they observe the laws of war. See Ex parte Toscano, D.C.Cal., 208 F. 938. See, also, Belligerency.

Bello parta cedunt reipublicæ. Things acquired in war belong or go to the state. 1 Kent, Comm. 101; 5 C.Rob.Adm. 173, 181; The Joseph, 1 Gall. 558, Fed.Cas.No.7,533. The right to all captures vests primarily in the sovereign. A fundamental maxim of public law. Cited 2 Russ. & M. 56.

BELLUM. Lat. In public law. War. An armed contest between nations; the state of those who forcibly contend with each other. *Jus belli,* the law of war.

BELONG. To appertain to; to be the property of. Property "belonging" to a person has two general meanings: (1) ownership; People ex rel. Gill v. Lake Forest University, 367 Ill. 103, 10 N.E.2d 667, 671; and (2) less than ownership, *i. e.,* less than an unqualified and absolute title, such as the absolute right of user. City and County of San Francisco v. McGovern, 28 Cal.App. 491, 152 P. 980, 984.

A road may be said with perfect propriety to belong to a man who has the right to use it as of right although the soil does not belong to him; 31 L.J.Ex. 227.

When used in public and private statutes, and especially when used in reference to inhabitancy, the poor, etc., designates the place of a person's legal settlement, and not merely his place of residence. City of Bridgeport v. Town of Greenwich, 165 A. 797, 116 Conn. 537.

BELONGING. That which is connected with a principal or greater thing; an appendage, an appurtenance; also ownership. Church of the Holy Faith v. State Tax Commission, 39 N.M. 403, 48 P.2d 777, 779.

BELONGINGS. That which belongs to one; property; possessions;—a term properly used to express ownership. In a will. Ford's Adm'r v. Wade's Adm'r, 242 Ky. 18, 45 S.W.2d 818, 820.

BELOW. In practice. Inferior; of inferior jurisdiction, or jurisdiction in the first instance. The court from which a cause is removed for review is called the "court *below.*"

Preliminary; auxiliary or instrumental.

Bail to the sheriff is called "bail *below,*" as being preliminary to and intended to secure the putting in of bail above, or special bail. See Bail.

BENCH. A seat of judgment or tribunal for the administration of justice; the seat occupied by judges in courts; also the court itself, or the aggregate of the judges composing a court, as in the phrase "before the full bench."

The judges taken collectively, as distinguished from counsellors and advocates, who are called the bar.

The term, indicating originally the seat of the judges, came to denote the body of judges taken collectively, and also the tribunal itself, as the King's Bench.

In English ecclesiastical law. The aggregate body of bishops.

BENCH LEGISLATION. See *Judge-made law* under the title Judge.

BENCH WARRANT. Process issued by the court itself, or "from the bench," for the attachment or arrest of a person; either in case of contempt, or where an indictment has been found, or to bring in a witness who does not obey the *subpœna.* So called to distinguish it from a warrant, issued by a justice of the peace, alderman, or commissioner. Oxford v. Berry, 204 Mich. 197, 170 N.W. 83, 87.

BENCHERS. In English law. Seniors in the Inns of Court, intrusted with their government, and usually, but not necessarily, king's counsel, elected by co-optation, and having the entire management of the property of their respective inns.

BENE. Lat. Well; in proper form; legally; sufficiently.

BENEDICTA EST EXPOSITIO QUANDO RES REDIMITUR À DESTRUCTIONE. 4 Coke, 26. Blessed is the exposition when anything is saved from destruction. It is a laudable interpretation which gives effect to the instrument, and does not allow its purpose to be frustrated.

BENEFICE. In ecclesiastical law. In its technical sense, this term includes ecclesiastical preferments to which rank or public office is attached, otherwise described as ecclesiastical dignities or offices, such as bishoprics, deaneries, and the like; but in popular acceptation, it is almost invariably appropriated to rectories, vicarages, perpetual curacies, district churches, and endowed chapelries. 3 Steph.Comm. 77.

"Benefice" is a term derived from the feudal law, in which it signified a permanent stipendiary estate, or an estate held by feudal tenure. 4 Bl.Comm. 107.

BÉNÉFICE. Fr. In French law. A benefit or advantage, and particularly a privilege given by the law rather than by the agreement of the parties.

BÉNÉFICE DE DISCUSSION. Benefit of discussion. The right of a guarantor to require that the creditor should exhaust his recourse against the principal debtor before having recourse to the guarantor himself.

BÉNÉFICE DE DIVISION. Benefit of division; right of contribution as between co-sureties.

BÉNÉFICE D'INVENTAIRE. A term which corresponds to the *beneficium inventarii* of Roman law, and substantially to the English law doctrine that the executor properly accounting is only liable to the extent of the assets received by him.

BÉNÉFICIAIRE. The person in whose favor a promissory note or bill of exchange is payable; or any person in whose favor a contract of any description is executed. Arg.Fr.Merc.Law. 547.

BENEFICIAL. Tending to the benefit of a person; yielding a profit, advantage, or benefit; enjoying or entitled to a benefit or profit. This term is applied both to estates (as a "beneficial interest") and to persons (as "the beneficial owner"). Kolb v. Landes, 277 Ill. 440, 115 N.E. 539, 541; In re Williams' Will, 50 Mont. 142, 145 P. 957, 959.

BENEFICIAL OR BENEVOLENT ASSOCIATION. A voluntary association for mutual assistance in time of need and sickness, and for the care of families of deceased members. Lafferty v. Supreme Council Catholic Mut. Ben. Ass'n, 259 Pa. 452, 103 A. 280, 281; but also held to include incorporated organizations. State v. Texas

Mut. Life Ins. Co. of Texas, Tex.Civ.App., 51 S.W. 2d 405, 410.

Another name for a "benefit society;" "benevolent society," and "fraternal" or "friendly society." State v. Texas Mut. Life Ins. Co. of Texas, Tex.Civ.App., 51 S.W.2d 405, 410.

BENEFICIAL ENJOYMENT. The enjoyment which a man has of an estate in his own right and for his own benefit, and not as trustee for another. 11 H.L.Cas. 271.

BENEFICIAL ESTATE. An estate in expectancy is one where the right to the possession is postponed to a future period, and is "beneficial" where the devisee takes solely for his own use or benefit, and not as the mere holder of the title for the use of another. In re Seaman's Estate, 147 N.Y. 69, 41 N.E. 401.

BENEFICIAL INTEREST. Profit, benefit, or advantage resulting from a contract, or the ownership of an estate as distinct from the legal ownership or control. People v. Schaefer, 266 Ill. 334, 107 N.E. 617, 619; Christiansen v. Department of Social Security, 15 Wash.2d 465, 131 P.2d 189, 191, 192.

When considered as designation of character of an estate, is such an interest as a devisee, legatee, or donee takes solely for his own use or benefit, and not as holder of title for use and benefit of another. People v. Northern Trust Co., 330 Ill. 238, 161 N.E. 525, 528.

BENEFICIAL POWER. In New York law and practice. A power which has for its object the donee of the power, and which is to be executed solely for his benefit; as distinguished from a trust power, which has for its object a person other than the donee, and is to be executed solely for the benefit of such person. Jennings v. Conboy, 73 N.Y. 234; In re New York Life Ins. & Trust Co., Sur., 139 N.Y.S. 695, 705; People, by Van Schaick v. New York Title & Mortgage Co., 270 N.Y.S. 473, 150 Misc. 488.

BENEFICIAL USE. The right to use and enjoy property according to one's own liking or so as to derive a profit or benefit from it, including all that makes it desirable or habitable, as light, air, and access; as distinguished from a mere right of occupancy or possession. Reining v. Railroad Co., Super.Ct., 13 N.Y.Supp. 240.

Such right to enjoyment of property where legal title is in one person while right to such use or interest is in another. Christiansen v. Department of Social Security, 15 Wash.2d 465, 131 P.2d 189, 191.

BENEFICIARY. One for whose benefit a trust is created; a *cestui que trust.* 195 N.E. 557, 564, 97 A.L.R. 1170. A person having the enjoyment of property of which a trustee, executor, etc., has the legal possession. The person to whom a policy of insurance is payable. Parrott Estate Co. v. McLaughlin, D.C.Cal., 12 F.Supp. 23, 25; Odom v. Prudential Ins. Co. of America, 173 Or. 435, 145 P.2d 480, 482. One receiving benefit or advantage, or one who is in receipt of benefits, profits, or advantage. Bauer v. Myers, C.C.A.Kan., 244 F. 902, 908. For "Favored Beneficiary," see that title.

BENEFICIARY ASSOCIATION. See Beneficial or Benevolent Association.

BENEFICIARY HEIR. In the law of Louisiana. One who has accepted the succession under the benefit of an inventory regularly made. Civ.Code La. art. 883. Also, one who may accept the succession with benefit of inventory. Succession of Galiano, La.App., 195 So. 377, 379.

BENEFICIO PRIMA, or PRIMO [ECCLESIASTICO HABENDO]. In English law. An ancient writ, which was addressed by the king to the lord chancellor, to bestow the benefice that should first fall in the royal gift, above or under a specified value, upon a person named therein. Reg.Orig. 307.

BENEFICIUM.

In Early Feudal Law

A benefice; a permanent stipendiary estate; the same with what was afterwards called a "fief," "feud," or "fee." 3 Steph.Comm. 77, note *i*; Spelman. It originally meant a "benefaction" from the king, usually to a noble.

In the Civil Law

A benefit or favor; any particular privilege. Dig. 1, 4, 3; Cod. 7, 71; Mackeld.Rom.Law, § 196.

A general term applied to ecclesiastical livings. 4 Bl.Comm. 107; Cowell.

In General

—Beneficium abstinendi. In Roman law. The power of an heir to abstain from accepting the inheritance. Sandars, Just.Inst. (5th Ed.) 214.

—Beneficium cedendarum actionum. In Roman law. The privilege by which a surety could, before paying the creditor, compel him to make over to him the actions which belonged to the stipulator, so as to avail himself of them. Sandars, Just. Inst. (5th Ed.) 332, 351.

—Beneficium clericale. Benefit of clergy (*q. v.*).

—Beneficium competentiæ. In Scotch law. The privilege of competency. A privilege which the grantor of a gratuitous obligation was entitled to, by which he might retain sufficient for his subsistence, if, before fulfilling the obligation, he was reduced to indigence. Bell. In the civil law. The right which an insolvent debtor had, among the Romans, on making cession of his property for the benefit of his creditors, to retain what was required for him to live honestly according to his condition. 7 Toullier, n. 258.

A defendant's privilege of being condemned only in an amount which he could pay without being reduced to a state of destitution. Sand. Justinian iv. vi. 37.

—Beneficium divisionis. In civil and Scotch law. The privilege of one of several co-sureties (cautioners) to insist upon paying only his *pro rata* share of the debt. Bell; La.Civ.Code, arts. 3045–3051.

—Beneficium inventarii. See Benefit of Inventory.

—Beneficium ordinis. In civil and Scotch law. The privilege of order. The privilege of a surety to require that the creditor should first proceed against the principal and exhaust his remedy against him, before resorting to the surety. Bell.

—Beneficium separationis. In the civil law. The right to have the goods of an heir separated from those of the testator in favor of creditors.

BENEFICIUM INVITO NON DATUR. A privilege or benefit is not granted against one's will. Adams Gloss.

BENEFICIUM NON DATUM NISI PROPTER OFFICIUM. Hob. 148. A remuneration [is] not given, unless on account of a duty performed.

BENEFICIUM NON DATUR NISI OFFICII CAUSA. A benefice is not granted except on account or in consideration of duty. Adams Gloss.

BENEFICIUM PRINCIPIS DEBET ESSE MANSURUM. The benefaction of a prince ought to be lasting. Adams Gloss.

BENEFIT. Advantage; profit; fruit; privilege; advantage. Fitch v. Bates, 11 Barb. (N.Y.) 473; Ferrigino v. Keasbey, 93 Conn. 445, 106 A. 445, 447; In re Krause's Estate, 173 Wash. 1, 21 P.2d 268; a pecuniary advantage or profit; gain; account; interest; the whole benefit and entire beneficial interest. Bird v. Newcomb, 170 Va. 208, 196 S.E. 605, 608.

In the Workmen's Compensation Act, the term "benefits" is used of an award to be granted when an injury results in death, and is distinguished from "compensation," which is to be granted when an injury results in incapacity or disability. Di Cicco v. Industrial Commission of Ohio, 11 Ohio App. 271, 273.

In Contracts

When it is said that a valuable consideration for a promise may consist of a benefit to the promisor, "benefit" means that the promisor has, in return for his promise, acquired some legal right to which he would not otherwise have been entitled. Irving v. Irwin, 24 P.2d 215, 216, 133 Cal. App. 374. Woolum v. Sizemore, 267 Ky. 384, 102 S.W.2d 323, 324.

"Benefit" is not limited to pecuniary gains, nor to any particular kind of advantage; it refers to what is advantageous, whatever promotes prosperity or happiness, what enhances the value of the property or rights of citizens as contradistinguished from what is injurious. Hooper v. Merchants' Bank & Trust Co., 130 S.E. 49, 52, 190 N. C. 423.

In Eminent Domain

It is a rule that, in assessing damages for private property taken or injured for public use, "special benefits" may be set off against the amount of damage found, but not "general benefits." Within the meaning of this rule, general benefits are such as accrue to the community at large, to the vicinage, or to all property similarly situated with reference to the work or improvement in question; while special benefits are such as accrue directly and solely to the owner of the land in question and not to others. Brand v. Union Elevated R. Co., 101 N.E. 247, 249, 258 Ill. 133, Ann.Cas.1914B, 473, L.R.A.1918A, 878.

In Taxation

With reference to an assessment for a drainage ditch, a benefit is anything that will make land more valuable for tillage or more desirable for a residence or more valuable in the general market. Watson v. Armstrong, 180 Ind. 49, 102 N.E. 273.

BENEFIT ASSOCIATION. See Benefit Societies.

BENEFIT BUILDING SOCIETY. The original name for what is now more commonly called a "building society" *(q. v.)*.

BENEFIT CERTIFICATE. A written obligation to pay the person therein named the amount specified upon the conditions therein stipulated. Green v. Grand United Order of Odd Fellows, Tex.Civ. App., 163 S.W. 1068, 1070.

Also a term usually applied to policies issued by fraternal and beneficiary societies. Chandler v. New York Life Ins. Co., 194 Ark. 6, 104 S.W.2d 1060, 1061.

BENEFIT OF BARGAIN RULE. Under such rule a defrauded purchaser may recover the difference between the real and the represented value of the property purchased regardless of the fact that the actual loss suffered might have been less. Stewart v. Potter, 44 N.M. 460, 104 P.2d 736, 739.

BENEFIT OF CESSION. In the civil law. The release of a debtor from future imprisonment for his debts, which the law operates in his favor upon the surrender of his property for the benefit of his creditors. Poth.Proc.Civil, pt. 5, c. 2, § 1.

BENEFIT OF CLERGY. In its original sense, the phrase denoted the exemption which was accorded to clergymen from the jurisdiction of the secular courts, or from arrest or attachment on criminal process issuing from those courts in certain particular cases. Afterwards, it meant a privilege of exemption from the punishment of death accorded to such persons as were *clerks*, or who could read. This privilege of exemption from capital punishment was anciently allowed to clergymen only, but afterwards to all who were connected with the church, even to its most subordinate officers, and at a still later time to all persons who could read, (then called "clerks,") whether ecclesiastics or laymen. It does not appear to have been extended to cases of high treason, nor did it apply to mere misdemeanors. The privilege was claimed after the person's conviction, by a species of motion in arrest of judgment, technically called "praying his clergy." As a means of testing his clerical character, he was given a psalm to read, (usually, or always, the fifty-first,) and, upon his reading it correctly, he was turned over to the ecclesiastical courts, to be tried by the bishop or a jury of twelve clerks. These heard him on oath, with his witnesses and compurgators, who attested their belief in his innocence. This privilege operated greatly to mitigate the extreme rigor of the criminal laws, but was found to involve such gross abuses that parliament began to enact that certain crimes should be felonies "without benefit of clergy," and finally, by St. 7 Geo. IV. c. 28, § 6, it was altogether abolished. The act of congress of April 30, 1790, c. 9, § 31, 1 Stat. 119, provided that there should be no benefit of clergy for any capital crime against the United States, and, if this privilege formed a part of the common law of the several states before the Revolution, it no longer exists.

BENEFIT OF COUNSEL. The guaranty of "benefit of counsel" to accused, given in the Georgia Bill of Rights of Const. art. 1, § 1, par. 5, means more than the mere appointment by the court of counsel to represent the accused and implies also that such counsel be given a reasonable time for preparation to properly represent the accused at the trial. Reliford v. State, 140 Ga. 777, 79 S.E. 1128, 1129. Sheppard v. State, 165 Ga. 460, 141 S.E. 196, 198.

BENEFIT OF DISCUSSION. In the civil law. The right which a surety has to cause the property of the principal debtor to be applied in satisfaction of the obligation in the first instance. Civ.Code La. arts. 3045–3051. In Scotch law. That whereby the antecedent heir, such as the heir of line in a pursuit against the heir of tailzie, etc., must be first pursued to fulfill the defunct's deeds and pay his debts. This benefit is likewise competent in many cases to cautioners.

BENEFIT OF DIVISION. Same as *beneficium divisionis (q. v.)*.

BENEFIT OF INVENTORY. In the civil law. The privilege which the heir obtains of being liable for the charges and debts of the succession, only to the value of the effects of the succession, by causing an inventory of these effects within the time and manner prescribed by law. Civil Code La. art. 1032.

BENEFIT OF ORDER. See Beneficium Ordinis.

BENEFIT SOCIETIES. Under this and several similar names, in various states, corporations exist to receive periodical payments from members, and hold them as a fund to be loaned or given to members needing pecuniary relief. Such are beneficial societies of Maryland, fund associations of Missouri, loan and fund associations of Massachusetts, mechanics' associations of Michigan, protection societies of New Jersey. Friendly societies in Great Britain are a still more extensive and important species belonging to this class. Comm. v. Equitable Ben. Ass'n, 137 Pa. 412, 18 A. 1112.

BENERTH. A feudal service rendered by the tenant to his lord with plow and cart. Cowell.

BENEVOLENCE. The doing of a kind or helpful action towards another, under no obligation except an ethical one.

The love of humanity; the desire to promote its prosperity or happiness. The term includes acts of well-wishing towards others, for the promotion of general happiness, and plans actuated by love of others and a desire for their well-being. In re Peabody's Estate, 208 N.Y.S. 664, 671, 124 Misc. 338. Also beneficent; doing well.

It is a broader term than "charity" which it includes, and with which it is frequently used synonymously. "Charity" in its legal sense implies giving without consideration or expectation of return, and "benevolence" applies to any act which is prompted by or has for its object the well-being of others. State v. Texas Mut. Life Ins. Co. of Texas, Tex.Civ.App., 51 S.W.2d 405, 410.

In public law. Nominally a voluntary gratuity given by subjects to their king, but in reality a tax or forced loan. Cowell; 1 Bla.Comm. 140.

BENEVOLENT. Philanthropic; humane; having a desire or purpose to do good to men; intended for the conferring of benefits, rather than for gain or profit; loving others and actively desirous of their well being. In re Altman's Estate, 149 N.Y.S. 601, 605, 87 Misc. 255.

This word is certainly more indefinite, and of far wider range, than "charitable" or "religious;" it would include all gifts prompted by good-will or kind feeling towards the recipient, whether an object of charity or not. The natural and usual meaning of the word would so extend it. It has no legal meaning separate from its usual meaning. "Charitable" has acquired a settled limited meaning in law, which confines it within known limits. But in all the decisions in England on the subject it has been held that a devise or bequest for benevolent objects, or in trust to give to such objects, is too indefinite, and therefore void. Suter v. Hilliard, 132 Mass. 413, 42 Am.Rep. 444;

This word, as applied to objects or purposes, may refer to those which are in their nature charitable, and may also have a broader meaning and include objects and purposes not charitable in the legal sense of that word. Acts of kindness, friendship, forethought, or good-will might properly be described as benevolent. It has therefore been held that gifts to trustees to be applied for "benevolent purposes" at their discretion, or to such benevolent purposes as they could agree upon, do not create a public charity. But where the word is used in connection with other words explanatory of its meaning, and indicating the intent of the donor to limit it to purposes strictly charitable, it has been held to be synonymous with, or equivalent to, "charitable." Suter v. Hilliard, 132 Mass. 412, 42 Am.Rep. 444;

BENEVOLENT ASSOCIATIONS. Those having a philanthropic or charitable purpose, as distinguished from such as are conducted for profit; specifically, "benefit associations" or "beneficial associations." Methodist Episcopal Church Baraca Club v. City of Madison, 167 Wis. 207, 167 N. W. 258, L.R.A.1918D, 1124.

BENEVOLENT CORPORATION. One that ministers to all; the purpose may be anything that promotes the mental, physical, or spiritual welfare of man. Society of Helpers of Holy Souls v. Law, 267 Mo. 667, 186 S.W. 718, 725; with respect to exemption from succession tax. Corbin v. American Industrial Bank & Trust Co., 95 Conn. 50, 110 A. 459, 461. The term may include a corporation to which a bequest is made to be used in the improvement of the social, physical, and economic condition of the employees of a business corporation. In re Altman's Estate, 149 N.Y.S. 601, 605, 87 Misc. 255.

BENEVOLENT SOCIETY. Benevolent association. Spring Park Ass'n v. Rosedale Park Amusement Co., 216 Ala. 549, 114 So. 43, 44. In English law, "benevolent societies" are societies established and registered under the Friendly Societies Act, 1875, for any charitable or benevolent purposes.

BENEVOLENTIA REGIS HABENDA. The form in ancient fines and submissions to purchase the king's pardon and favor in order to be restored to place, title or estate. Paroch.Antiq. 172.

BENHURST. In Berkshire, a remedy for the inhabitants thereof to levy money recovered against them on the statute of hue and cry. 39 Eliz. c. 25.

BENIGNE FACIENDÆ SUNT INTERPRETATIONES CHARTARUM, UT RES MAGIS VALEAT QUAM PEREAT; ET QUÆ LIBET CONCESSIO FORTISSIME CONTRA DONATOREM INTERPRETANDA EST. Liberal interpretations are to be made of deeds, so that the purpose may rather stand than fall; and every grant is to be taken most strongly against the grantor. Hayes v. Kershow, 1 Sandf.Ch. (N.Y.) 258, 268.

BENIGNE FACIENDÆ SUNT INTERPRETATIONES, PROPTER SIMPLICITATEM LAICORUM, UT RES MAGIS VALEAT QUAM PEREAT; ET VERBA INTENTIONI, NON E CONTRA, DEBENT INSERVIRE. Constructions [of written instruments] are to be made liberally, on account of the simplicity of the laity, [or common people,] in order that the thing [or subject-matter] may rather have effect than perish, [or become void]; and words must be subject to the intention, not the intention to the words. 2 Bla.Com. 379; 1 Bulstr. 175; Krider v. Lafferty, 1 Whart. (Pa.) 315.

BENIGNIOR SENTENTIA IN VERBIS GENERALIBUS SEU DUBIIS, EST PRÆFERENDA. The more favorable construction is to be placed on general or doubtful expressions. 2 Kent 557.

BENIGNIUS LEGES INTERPRETANDÆ SUNT QUO VOLUNTAS EARUM CONSERVETUR. Laws are to be more liberally interpreted, in order that their intent may be preserved. Dig. 1, 3, 18.

BENZINE. A crude petroleum distillate. George K. Hale Mfg. Co. v. Hafleigh & Co., C.C.A.Pa., 52 F.2d 714, 718.

BEQUEATH. To give personal property by will to another. Fielding v. Alkire, 124 Kan. 592, 261 P. 597, 599. It therefore is distinguishable from "devise," which is properly used of realty. Stubbs v. Abel, 114 Or. 610, 233 P. 852, 857; Fleck v. Harmstad, 155 A. 875, 876, 304 Pa. 302, 77 A.L.R. 874.

But if the context clearly shows the intention of the testator to use the word "bequeath" as synonymous with "devise," it may be held to pass real property. Stubbs v. Abel, 114 Or. 610, 233 P. 852, 859.

BEQUEST. A gift by will of personal property; a legacy. In re Fratt's Estate, 60 Mont. 526, 199 P. 711, 714; In re Wood's Estate, 6 N.W.2d 846, 848, 232 Iowa 1004; Disposition of realty in will is termed "devise." Grand Island Trust Co. v. Snell, 249 N.W. 293, 125 Neb. 148.

The term does not mean a "gift" in the narrow sense of a voluntary act of charity or good will, but ordinarily means a testamentary disposition of the testator's personalty. First Presbyterian Church of Mt. Vernon v. Dennis, 178 Iowa, 1352, 161 N.W. 183, 185, L.R.A.1917C, 1005. It is not necessarily limited to a gratuity, and may include a recompense. U. S. v. Merriam, 44 S.Ct. 69, 70, 263 U.S. 179, 68 L.Ed. 240, 29 A.L.R. 1547.

"Bequest" and "devise" are often used synonymously. In re McGovern's Estate, 77 Mont. 182, 250 P. 812, 817.

Conditional Bequest

One the taking effect or continuing of which depends upon the happening or non-occurrence of a particular event. Merrill v. College, 74 Wis. 415, 43 N.W. 104.

Executory Bequest

The bequest of a future, deferred, or contingent interest in personalty.

Residuary Bequest

A gift of all the remainder of the testator's personal estate, after payment of debts and legacies, etc.

Specific Bequest

One whereby the testator gives to the legatee all his property of a certain class or kind; as all his pure personalty.

BERAT. Also *barat.* A warrant or patent of dignity or privilege given by an Oriental monarch. Cent. Dict.

BERBIAGE. A rent paid for the pasturing of sheep. Wharton.

BERCARIA. In old English law, a sheepfold; also a place where the bark of trees was laid to tan.

BERCARIUS, or BERCATOR. A shepherd.

BEREWICHA, or BEREWICA. In old English law. A term used in Domesday for a village or hamlet belonging to some town or manor.

BERG. A rock (Cent. Dict.); a hill (Wharton); in South Africa, a mountain (Webster).

BERGHMAYSTER. An officer having charge of a mine. A bailiff or chief officer among the Derbyshire miners, who, in addition to his other duties, executes the office of coroner among them. Blount; Cowell.

BERGHMOTH, or BERGHMOTE. The ancient name of the court now called "barmote," *(q. v.).*

BERIA, BERIE, or BERRY. A plain; a large open field. Wharton. See Berra.

BERM BANK. A ledge at the bottom of a cutting or bank, as of a creek, to catch earth that may roll down the slope, or to strengthen the bank. Miller v. State, 149 N.Y.S. 788, 789, 164 App.Div. 522.

BERNET. In Saxon law. Burning; the crime of house burning, now called "arson." Cowell; Blount.

BERRA. In old law. A plain; open heath. Cowell.

BERRY, or BURY. A villa or seat of habitation of a nobleman; a dwelling or mansion house; a sanctuary.

BERTILLON SYSTEM. A method of anthropometry *(q. v.)*, used chiefly for the identification of criminals and other persons, consisting of the taking and recording of a system of numerous, minute, and uniform measurements of various parts of the human body, absolutely and in relation to each other, the facial, cranial, and other angles, and of any eccentricities or abnormalities noticed in the individual.

BERTON. A large farm; the barn-yard of a large farm.

BES. Lat. In the Roman law. A division of the *as*, or pound, consisting of eight *unciœ*, or duodecimal parts, and amounting to two-thirds of the *as*. 2 Bl.Comm. 462 note *m*.

Two-thirds of an inheritance. Inst. 2, 14, 5.

Eight per cent. interest. 2 Bl.Comm. ubi supra.

BESAILE, BESAYLE. The great-grandfather, *proavus*. 1 Bl.Comm. 186.

BESAYEL, Besaiel, Besayle. In old English law. A writ which lay where a great-grandfather died seised of lands and tenements in fee-simple, and on the day of his death a stranger abated, or entered and kept out the heir. Reg.Orig. 226; Fitzh. Nat.Brev. 221 D; 3 Bl.Comm. 186.

BESIDES. In addition to; moreover; also; likewise. State v. State Road Commission, 100 W.Va. 531, 131 S.E. 7, 10.

In provisions in a will for children "besides" an eldest son, no children take unless there be a son. 4 Dr. & War. 235.

BESEECH. To entreat; to emplore. Tiencken v. Zerbst, 196 S.C. 438, 13 S.E.2d 483, 484.

BESOIN. Fr. Need. See Au Besoin.

BESOT. To stupefy, to make dull or senseless, to make to dote; and "to dote" is to be delirious, silly, or insane. Gates v. Meredith, 7 Ind. 440, 441.

BESS. A well-known contraction of "Elizabeth." H. R. & C. Co. v. Smith, 208 N.Y.S. 396, 400, 212 App.Div. 173.

BESSEMERIZING. A process by which copper relatively pure is obtained from matte. Peirce-Smith Converter Co. v. United Verde Copper Co., D.C.Del., 293 F. 108, 109.

BEST. Of the highest quality; of the greatest usefulness for the purpose intended. For example:

The "best bid" of interest by a prospective depositary of school funds would not necessarily be the highest bid, but, looking to the solvency of the bidder, the bond tendered, and all the circumstances surrounding the transaction, the safety and preservation of the school fund, the "best bid" might be the lowest bid. Donna Independent School Dist. v. First State Bank of Donna, Tex.Civ.App., 227 S.W. 974, 975.

Where one covenants to use his "best endeavors," there is no breach if he is prevented by causes wholly beyond his control and without any default on his part. 7 H. & N. 92.

The "best interests" of a child whose custody is in question has reference more particularly to the moral welfare than to mere comforts, benefits, or advantages that wealth can give. Jones v. Moore, 61 Utah, 383, 213 P. 191, 194. The "best interests" of an estate mean the greatest or most advantage or usefulness to such estate. Stockyards Nat. Bank of South Omaha v. Bragg, 67 Utah, 60, 245 P. 966, 971.

BEST EVIDENCE. Primary evidence, as distinguished from secondary; original, as distinguished from substitutionary; the best and highest evidence of which the nature of the case is susceptible, not the highest or strongest evidence which the nature of the thing to be proved admits of. See, also, Primary Evidence.

A written instrument is itself always regarded as the primary or best possible evidence of its existence and contents; a copy, or the recollection of a witness, would be secondary evidence. Manhattan Malting Co. v. Sweteland, 14 Mont. 269, 36 P. 84.

"Best evidence" or "primary evidence" includes the best evidence which is available to a party and procurable under the existing situation, and all evidence falling short of such standard, and which in its nature suggests there is better evidence of the same fact, is "secondary evidence." Best v. Equitable Life Assur. Soc., Mo.App., 299 S.W. 118, 120.

The best evidence of a fact is the testimony of a person who knows. State v. Normandale, 154 La. 523, 97 So. 798, 799 (mother could testify to the date of her daughter's birth, as against an objection that the baptismal certificate or the registry was the best evidence).

"Best evidence rule". Is that highest available degree of proof must be produced. Cheadle v. Bardwell, 95 Mont. 299, 26 P.2d 336. It means that no evidence which is merely substitutionary in its nature shall be received so long as original evidence can be had; Pettit v. Campbell, Tex.Civ. App., 149 S.W.2d 633, 635, 636; that contents of document must be proved by producing document itself. Nunan v. Timberlake, 85 F.2d 407, 410, 66 App.D.C. 150.

BESTIA. A beast, as a being without reason; —opposed to man; while animal, a living being, includes man also. Adams Gloss., citing Just. Inst., 2, 1, 12.

BESTIAE CARUCAE. Beasts of the plow. Adams Gloss., citing Fleta, IV, c. 17, § 14.

BESTIALITY. A sexual connection between a human being and a brute of the opposite sex. State v. Poole, 122 P.2d 415, 416, 59 Ariz. 44.

At common law the term "crime against nature" embraced both "sodomy" and "bestiality", State v. Poole, 122 P.2d 415, 416, 59 Ariz. 44. See Sodomy.

BESTOW. To give, grant, confer, or impart; not necessarily limited in meaning to "devise." Tillett v. Nixon, 180 N.C. 195, 104 S.E. 352, 355.

BET. An agreement between two or more persons that a sum of money or other valuable thing, to which all jointly contribute, shall become the sole property of one or some of them on the happening in the future of an event at present uncertain, or according as a question disputed between them is settled in one way or the other. Coulter v. State, 122 Tex.Cr.R. 9, 53 S.W.2d 477, 480.

A contract by which two or more parties agree that a sum of money, or other thing, shall be paid or delivered to one of them on the happening or not happening of an uncertain event. Grooms v. Knox, 25 Ala.App. 185, 142 So. 582.

In a "bet" or "wager" money belongs to the persons posting it, each of whom has a chance to win it, but, in the case of a "purse" or "premium," money belongs to the person offering it, who has no chance to win it, but is certain to lose it. Toomey v. Penwell, 76 Mont. 166, 245 P. 943, 945, 45 A.L.R. 993.

Bet and wager are synonymous terms. Woodcock v. McQueen, 11 Ind. 16; Shumate v. Com., 15 Grat. (Va.) 660.

BETHLEHEM. See Bedlam.

BETTING BOOK. A book kept for registering bets on the result of a race as operated on race track. In a broader sense, the "betting book" is that book which enables the professional bettor to carry on his business, and to promote a race, and it includes the book, the making book and the bookmaker. State v. Austin, 142 La. 384, 76 So. 809, 810; People v. Semmler, 345 Ill. 272, 178 N.E. 100, 101.

BETRAYAL. A "betrayal," as of a professional secret on the part of a physician, signifies a wrongful disclosure in violation of the trust imposed by the patient. Simonsen v. Swenson, 104 Neb. 224, 177 N.W. 831, 832, 9 A.L.R. 1250.

BETROTHED. One who has exchanged promises to marry. The term may be synonymous with "intended wife." Mace v. Grand Lodge, A. O. U. W. of Massachusetts, 234 Mass. 299, 125 N.E. 569.

BETROTHMENT, BETROTHAL. Mutual promise of marriage; the plighting of troth; a mutual promise or contract between a man and woman competent to make it, to marry at a future time.

BETTER DESCRIBED. More fully delineated or more fully pictured or painted. Katzin v. Kruvant, 99 N.J.Eq. 619, 133 A. 516, 517.

BETTER EQUITY. See Equity.

BETTERMENT. An improvement put upon an estate which enhances its value more than mere repairs. The improvement may be either temporary or permanent. People v. Klee, 282 Ill. 440, 118 N.E. 754, 757.

Also applied to denote the additional value which an estate acquires in consequence of some public improvement, as laying out or widening a street, etc., Chase v. Sioux City, 86 Iowa, 603, 53 N.W. 333.

BETTERMENT ACTS. Statutes which provide that a bona fide occupant of real estate making lasting improvements in good faith shall have a lien upon the estate recovered by the real owner to the extent that his improvements have increased the value of the land. Also called "occupying claimant acts." Jones v. Hotel Co., 86 F. 386, 30 C.C.A. 108.

BETWEEN. A space which separates. Hobson v. Postal Telegraph-Cable Co., 161 Tenn. 419, 32 S.W.2d 1046. Strictly applicable only with reference to two things, but this may be understood as including cases in which a number of things are discriminated collectively as two wholes, or as taken in pairs, or where one thing is set off against a number of others. In re McShane's Will, 286 N.Y.S. 680, 682, 158 Misc. 777. Sometimes used synonymously with "among". In re Moore's Estate, 157 Pa.Super. 296, 43 A.2d 359.

As a measure or indication of distance, this word has the effect of excluding the two termini. Morris & E. R. Co. v. Central R. Co., 31 N.J.Law, 212.

If an act is to be done "between" two certain days, it must be performed before the commencement of the latter day. In computing the time in such a case, both the days named are to be excluded. Hodges v. Filstrup, 94 Fla. 943, 114 So. 521, 522. But a clause in a contract of sale to the effect that the purchaser could require the vendor to repurchase between the fifth and sixth year from a certain date means during the sixth year. Van Demark v. California Home Extension Ass'n, 43 Cal.App. 685, 185 P. 866, 868.

In case of a devise to A. and B. "between them," these words create a tenancy in common. Lashbrook v. Cock, 2 Mer. 70.

Between equal equities the law must prevail. This is hardly of general application.

BEVERAGE. A liquor or liquid for drinking. Burnstein v. U. S., C.C.A.Cal., 55 F.2d 599, 603. Especially pleasant or refreshing drink, or a habitual one. Tennant v. F. C. Whitney & Sons, 133 Wash. 581, 234 P. 666, 670.

This term is properly used to distinguish a sale of liquors to be drunk for the pleasure of drinking, from liquors to be drunk in obedience to a physician's advice, Falstaff Corporation v. Allen, D.C.Mo., 278 F. 643, 645; or from a liquid which it is possible to swallow, but which is not reasonably palatable or fit for drinking, Tennant v. F. C. Whitney & Sons, 133 Wash. 581, 234 P. 666. Thus, it is held that pure alcohol is not a "beverage" but a violent irritant. Chas. L. Joy & Co. v. Carlson, 28 Idaho 445, 154 P. 640, 641.

This term sometimes has a narrower meaning signifying a drink artificially prepared. Climax Dairy Co. v. Mulder, 78 Colo. 407, 242 P. 666, 669. United States v. Robason, D.C.Kan., 38 F.Supp. 991, 992.

BEWARED. O. Eng. Expended. Before the Britons and Saxons had introduced the general use of money, they traded chiefly by exchange of wares. Wharton.

BEYOND A REASONABLE DOUBT. In evidence means fully satisfied, entirely convinced, satisfied to a moral certainty; State v. Harris, 28 S.E.2d 232, 237, 223 N.C. 697; and phrase is the equivalent of the words clear, precise and indubitable. Ferguson Packing Co. v. Mihalic, 99 Pa.Super. 158, 162.

An accused's guilt must be established "beyond a reasonable doubt," which means that facts proven must, by virtue of their probative force, establish guilt. People ex rel. Schubert v. Pinder, 9 N.Y.S.2d 311, 312, 170 Misc. 345.

BEYOND SEA. Beyond the limits of the kingdom of Great Britain and Ireland; outside the United States; out of the state.

Beyond sea, beyond the four seas, beyond the seas, and out of the realm, are synonymous. Prior to the union of the two crowns of England and Scotland, on the accession of James I., the phrases "beyond the four seas," "beyond the seas," and "out of the realm," signified out of the limits of the realm of England. Pancoast's Lessee v. Addison, 1 Har. & J. (Md.) 350, 2 Am.Dec. 520.

In Pennsylvania, it has been construed to mean "without the limits of the United States," which approaches the literal signification. Ward v. Hallam, 2 Dall. 217, 1 L.Ed. 355. The same construction has been given to it in Missouri. Keeton's Heirs v. Keeton's Adm'r, 20 Mo. 530. See Ang.Lim. §§ 200, 201.

BIAS. Inclination; bent; prepossession; a preconceived opinion; a predisposition to decide a cause or an issue in a certain way, which does not leave the mind perfectly open to conviction. Maddox v. State, 32 Ga. 587, 79 Am.Dec. 307; Pierson v. State, 18 Tex.App. 558. To incline to one side. Yarbrough v. Mallory, 225 Ala. 579, 144 So. 447, 448. Condition of mind, which sways judgment and renders judge unable to exercise his functions impartially in particular case. Evans v. Superior Court in and for Los Angeles County, 107 Cal.App. 372, 290 P. 662, 665.

As used in law regarding disqualification of judge, refers to mental attitude or disposition of the judge toward a party to the litigation, and not to any views that he may entertain regarding the subject matter involved. State ex rel. Mitchell v. Sage Stores Co., 157 Kan. 622, 143 P.2d 652, 655.

Actual bias consists in the existence of a state of mind on the part of the juror which satisfies the court, in the exercise of a sound discretion, that the juror cannot try the issues impartially and without prejudice to the substantial rights of the party challenging. People v. Wells, 100 Cal. 227, 34 P. 718.

BIBLE. See Family Bible.

BICAMERAL SYSTEM. A term applied by Jeremy Bentham to the division of a legislative body into two chambers, as in the United States government.

BID. An offer by an intending purchaser to pay a designated price for property which is about to be sold at auction. U. S. v. Vestal, D.C.N.C., 12 F. 59. Payne v. Cave, 3 Term, 149; Eppes v. Railroad Co., 35 Ala. 56. See Chilling a sale.

An offer to perform a contract for work and labor or supplying materials at a specified price.

Similarly, an offer to do any of various other acts, as the payment by a bank of a particular rate of interest for the privilege of becoming a depositary of county funds. Casey v. Independence County, 109 Ark. 11, 159 S.W. 24, 25, Ann. Cas.1915C, 1008. A "bid" for bonds is no more nor less than a proposition. Joint School Dist. No. 132 in Major County and Alfalfa County v. Dabney, 127 Okl. 234, 260 P. 486, 491.

—Bid in. Property sold at auction is said to be "bid in" by the owner or an incumbrancer or some one else who is interested in it, when he attends the sale and makes the successful bid.

—Bid off. One is said to "bid off" a thing when he bids for it at an auction sale, and it is knocked down to him in immediate succession to the bid and as a consequence of it. Eppes v. Railroad Co., 35 Ala. 56; Doudna v. Harlan, 45 Kan. 484, 25 Pac. 883.

—Bidder. One who makes a bid. One who offers to pay a specified price for an article offered for sale at a public auction. Webster v. French, 11 Ill. 254. As to "Responsible bidder" see that title.

—Biddings. Offers of a designated price for goods or other property put up for sale at auction.

—By-bidding. In the law relating to sales by auction, this term is equivalent to "puffing." The practice consists in making fictitious bids for the property, under a secret arrangement with the owner or auctioneer, for the purpose of misleading and stimulating other persons who are bidding in good faith.

—Competitive bidding. "Competitive bidding" means that the council must by due advertisement give opportunity for everyone to bid, but does not mean that more than one bid must be submitted. Blanton v. Town of Wallins, 218 Ky. 295, 291 S.W. 372, 375. The term means bidding upon the same undertaking, upon the same material items in the subject-matter, upon the same thing. Leininger v. Ward, 126 Okl. 114, 258 P. 863, 864.

—Upset bid. A bid made after a judicial sale, but before the successful bid at the sale has been confirmed, larger or better than such successful bid, and made for the purpose of upsetting the sale and securing to the "upset bidder" the privilege of taking the property at his bid or competing at a new sale. Yost v. Porter, 80 Va. 858.

BIDAL, or BIDALL. An invitation of friends to drink ale at the house of some poor man, who hopes thereby to be relieved by charitable contribution. It is something like "house-warming," *i. e.*, a visit of friends to a person beginning to set up housekeeping. Wharton. See Bed-Ale.

"There was an antient Custom called a *Bid-Ale* * * * when any honest Man decayed in his Estate, was set up again by the liberal Benevolence and Contributions of Friends at a Feast, to which those Friends were bid or invited. It was most used in the West of England, and in some Counties called a Help Ale." Brand's Pop. Antiq. (1777), p. 339, *note*.

BIELBRIEF. Germ. In European maritime law. A document furnished by the builder of a vessel, containing a register of her admeasurement, particularizing the length, breadth, and dimensions of every part of the ship.

It sometimes also contains the terms of agreement between the party for whose account the ship is built, and the ship-builder. It has been termed in English the "grand bill of sale;" in French, *"contrat de construction ou de la vente d'un vaisseau,"* and corresponds in a great degree with the English, French, and American "register," *(q. v.,)* being an equally essential document to the lawful ownership of vessels. Jac. Sea Laws, 12, 13, and note. In the Danish law, it is used to denote the contract of bottomry.

BIENES. Sp. In Spanish law. Goods; property of every description, including real as well as personal property; all things (not being persons) which may serve for the uses of man. Larkin v. U. S., 14 Fed.Cas. 1154.

—Bienes comunes. Common property; those things which, not being the private property of any person, are open to the use of all, such as the air, rain, water, the sea and its beaches. Lux v. Haggin, 69 Cal. 255, 315, 10 Pac. 707.

—Bienes ganaciales. A species of community in property enjoyed by husband and wife, the property being divisible equally between them on the dissolution of the marriage; does not include what they held as their separate property at the time of contracting the marriage. Welder v. Lambert, 91 Tex. 510, 44 S.W. 281.

—Bienes publicos. Those things which, as to property, pertain to the people or nation, and, as to their use, to the individuals of the territory or district, such as rivers, shores, ports, and public roads. Lux v. Haggin, 69 Cal. 315, 10 P. 707.

BIENNIALLY. This term, in a statute, signifies, not duration of time, but a period for the happening of an event; once in every two years. People v. Tremain, 9 Hun (N.Y.) 576; People v. Kilbourn, 68 N.Y. 479.

BIENS. In English law. Property of every description, except estates of freehold and inheritance. Sugd.Vend. 495; Co.Litt. 119*b*.

In French law. This term includes all kinds of property, real and personal. *Biens* are divided into *biens meubles,* movable property; and *biens immeubles,* immovable property. The distinction between movable and immovable property is recognized by the continental jurists, and gives rise, in the civil as well as in the common law, to many important distinctions as to rights and remedies. Story, Confl.Laws, § 13, note 1. Castle v. Castle, C.C.A.Hawaii, 267 F. 521, 523.

BIGA, or BIGATA. A cart or chariot drawn with two horses, coupled side to side; but it is said to be properly a cart with two wheels, sometimes drawn by one horse; and in the ancient records it is used for any cart, wain, or wagon. Jacob.

BIGAMUS. In the civil law. A man who was twice married; one who at different times and successively has married two wives. 4 Inst. 88. One who has two wives living. One who marries a widow.

Used in ecclesiastical matters as a reason for denying benefit of the clergy. *Termes de la Ley.*

BIGAMUS SEU TRIGAMUS, ETC., EST QUI DIVERSIS TEMPORIBUS ET SUCCESSIVÈ DUAS SEU TRES UXORES HABUIT. 4 Inst. 88. A bigamus or trigamus, etc., is one who at different times and successively has married two or three wives.

BIGAMY. The criminal offense of willfully and knowingly contracting a second marriage (or going through the form of a second marriage) while the first marriage, to the knowledge of the offender, is still subsisting and undissolved. Scoggins v. State, 32 Ark. 213; People v. Manfredonio, 191 N.Y.S. 748, 117 Misc. 632, 39 N.Y.Cr.R. 41.

The state of a man who has two wives, or of a woman who has two husbands, living at the same time. State v. Lindsey, 26 N.M. 526, 194 P. 877. Farewell v. Commonwealth, 189 S.E. 321, 323, 167 Va. 475.

The offense of having a plurality of wives at the same time is commonly denominated "polygamy;" but the name "bigamy" has been more frequently given to it in legal proceedings. 1 Russ.Crimes, 185.

The use of the word "bigamy" to describe this offense is well established by long usage, although often criticized as a corruption of the true meaning of the word. Polygamy is suggested as the correct term, instead of bigamy, to designate the offense of having a plurality of wives or husbands at the same time, and has been adopted for that purpose in the Massachusetts statutes. But as the substance of the offense is marrying a second time, while having a lawful husband or wife living, without regard to the number of marriages that may have taken place, bigamy seems not an inappropriate term. The objection to its use urged by Blackstone (4 Bl.Comm. 163) seems to be founded not so much upon considerations of the etymology of the word as upon the propriety of distinguishing the ecclesiastical offense termed "bigamy" in the canon law, and which is defined below, from the offense known as "bigamy" in the modern criminal law. The same distinction is carefully made by Lord Coke, (4 Inst. 88.) But, the ecclesiastical offense being now obsolete, this reason for substituting polygamy to denote the crime here defined ceases to have weight. Abbott.

In the canon law, the term denoted the offense committed by an ecclesiastic who married two wives successively. It might be committed either by marrying a second wife after the death of a first or by marrying a widow.

BIGOT. An obstinate person, or one that is wedded to an opinion, in matters of religion, etc.

BILAGINES. By-laws of towns; municipal laws.

BILAN. A term used in Louisiana, derived from the French. A book in which bankers, merchants, and traders write a statement of all they owe and all that is due them; a balance-sheet. See Dauphin v. Soulie, 3 Mart. (N.S.) 446.

BILANCIIS DEFERENDIS. In English law. An obsolete writ addressed to a corporation for the carrying of weights to such a haven, there to weigh the wool anciently licensed for transportation. Reg.Orig. 270.

BILATERAL CONTRACT. A term, used originally in the civil law, but now generally adopted, denoting a contract in which both the contracting parties are bound to fulfill obligations reciprocally towards each other; as a contract of sale, where one becomes bound to deliver the thing sold, and the other to pay the price of it. Montpelier Seminary v. Smith, 69 Vt. 382, 38 A. 66. A contract executory on both sides, National Surety Co. v. City of Atlanta, 102 S.E. 175, 176, 24 Ga.App. 732, and one which includes both rights and duties on each side, Crane Ice Cream Co. v. Terminal Freezing & Heating Co., 147 Md. 588, 128 A. 280, 282, 39 A.L.R. 1184. One containing mutual promises between parties; each party being both promisor and promisee. Aden v. Dalton, 341 Mo. 454, 107 S.W.2d 1070, 1073.

"Every convention properly so called consists of a promise or mutual promises proffered and accepted. Where one only of the agreeing parties gives a promise, the convention is said to be 'unilateral.' Wherever mutual promises are proffered and accepted, there are, in strictness, two or more conventions. But where the performance of either of the promises is made to depend on the performance of the other, the several conventions are commonly deemed one convention and the convention is then said to be 'bilateral.'" Aust.Jur. § 308.

See, also, Contract.

BILBOES. A device used for punishment at sea, similar to the stocks (*q. v.*) on land.

BILGED. In admiralty law and marine insurance. That state or condition of a vessel in which water is freely admitted through holes and breaches made in the planks of the bottom, occasioned by injuries, whether the ship's timbers are broken or not. Peele v. Insurance Co., 3 Mason, 27, 39, 19 Fed.Cas. 103.

BILINE. A word used by Britton in the sense of "collateral." *En line biline,* in the collateral line. Britt, c. 119.

BILINGUIS. Of a double language or tongue; that can speak two languages. A term applied in the old books to a jury composed partly of Englishmen and partly of foreigners, which, by the English law, an alien party to a suit is, in certain cases, entitled to; more commonly called a "jury *de medietate linguæ.*" 3 Bl.Comm. 360; 4 Steph. Comm. 422.

BILL. A formal declaration, complaint, or statement of particular things in writing.

As a legal term, this word has many meanings and applications, the more important of which are enumerated below.

1. A formal written statement of complaint to a court of justice

In the ancient practice of the court of king's bench, the usual and orderly method of beginning an action was by a *bill,* or original bill, or plaint. This was a written statement of the plaintiff's cause of action, like a declaration or complaint, and always alleged a trespass as the ground of it, in order to give the court jurisdiction. 3 Bl.Comm. 43.

In Scotch law, every summary application in writing, by way of petition to the Court of Session, is called a "bill." Cent. Dict.

—Bill chamber. In Scotch law. A department of the court of session in which petitions for suspension, interdict, etc., are entertained. It is equivalent to sittings in chambers in the English and American practice. Paters. Comp.

—Bill of privilege. In old English law. A method of proceeding against attorneys and officers of the court not liable to arrest. 3 Bl.Comm. 289.

—Bill of proof. In English practice. The name given, in the mayor's court of London, to a species of intervention by a third person laying claim to the subject-matter in dispute between the parties to a suit.

2. A species of writ

A formal written declaration by a court to its officers, in the nature of process.

—Bill of Middlesex. An old form of process similar to a *capias,* issued out of the court of king's bench in personal actions, directed to the sheriff of the county of Middlesex, (hence the name,) and commanding him to take the defendant and have him before the king at Westminster on a day named, to answer the plaintiff's complaint.

3. A formal written petition

To a superior court for action to be taken in a cause already determined, or a record or certified account of the proceedings in such action or some portion thereof, accompanying such a petition.

—Bill of advocation. In Scotch practice. A bill by which the judgment of an inferior court is appealed from, or brought under review of a superior. Bell.

—Bill of certiorari. A bill, the object of which is to remove a suit in equity from some inferior court to the court of chancery, or some other superior court of equity, on account of some alleged incompetency of the inferior court, or some injustice in its proceedings. Story, Eq.Pl. (5th Ed.) § 298.

—Bill of evidence. Stenographer's transcript of testimony heard at trial and may be considered on appeal as bill of exceptions. Spencer v. Commonwealth, 250 Ky. 370, 63 S.W.2d 288.

—Bill of exceptions. A formal statement in writing of the objections or exceptions taken by a party during the trial of a cause to the decisions, rulings, or instructions of the trial judge, stating the objection, with the facts and circumstances on which it is founded, and, in order to attest its accuracy, signed and sealed by the judge; the object being to put the controverted rulings or decisions upon the record for the information of the appellate court. Buessel v. U. S., C.C.A.Conn., 258 Fla. 811, 815.

It is designed to preserve and make a part of the record proceedings not otherwise of record. Yott v. Yott, 100 N. E. 902, 903, 257 Ill. 419; It is only that part of the proceedings not embraced in the judgment roll. When the ends of justice require it, the terms "bill of exceptions" and "statement of case" are regarded as synonymous; Shawnee Commercial College v. Aydelotte, 38 P.2d 579, 581, 170 Okl. 15.

"Bill of exceptions" and "transcripts of evidence," however, are clearly distinguishable. The latter may contain no objection or exception, and nothing other than the evidence introduced on the trial; the former is, strictly speaking, only a record which points out alleged errors committed below in relation to evidence as well as other things. Broadway & Newport Bridge Co. v. Commonwealth, 173 Ky. 165, 190 S.W. 715, 719.

4. In equity practice

A formal written complaint, in the nature of a petition, addressed by a suitor in chancery to the chancellor or to a court of equity or a court having equitable jurisdiction, showing the names of the parties, stating the facts which make up the case and the complainant's allegations, averring that the acts disclosed are contrary to equity, and praying for process and for specific relief, or for such

relief as the circumstances demand. Sharon v. Sharon, 67 Cal. 185, 7 P. 456.

—Bill for a new trial. A bill in equity in which the specific relief asked is an injunction against the execution of a judgment rendered at law, and a new trial in the actic. on account of some fact which would render it inequitable to enforce the judgment, but which was not available to the party on the trial at law, or which he was prevented from presenting by fraud or accident, without concurrent fraud or negligence on his own part.

—Bill for foreclosure. One which is filed by a mortgagee against the mortgagor, for the purpose of having the estate sold, thereby to obtain the sum mortgaged on the premises, with interest and costs. 1 Madd.Ch.Pr. 528.

—Bill for fraud. The object and effect of it, even if the fraud consists of want of notice, are to vacate the former decree, not to retry the case. Caldwell v. Huffstutter, 173 Tenn. 225, 116 S.W.2d 1017, 1019.

—Bill in aid of execution. A bill to set aside encumbrances or conveyances therein specified as fraudulent. Pape v. Pareti, 42 N.E.2d 361, 364, 315 Ill.App. 1; Dean v. Torrence, 299 N.W. 793, 796, 299 Mich. 24.

—Bill in nature of a bill of review. A bill in equity, to obtain a re-examination and reversal of a decree, filed by one who was not a party to the original suit, nor bound by the decree.

—Bill in nature of a bill of revivor. Where, on the abatement of a suit, there is such a transmission of the interest of the incapacitated party that the title to it, as well as the person entitled, may be the subject of litigation in a court of chancery, the suit cannot be continued by a mere bill of revivor, but an original bill upon which the title may be litigated must be filed. This is called a "bill in the nature of a bill of revivor." It is founded on privity of estate or title by the act of the party. And the nature and operation of the whole act by which the privity is created is open to controversy. Story, Eq.Pl. §§ 378–380; 2 Amer. & Eng.Enc.Law, 271.

—Bill in nature of a supplemental bill. A bill filed when new parties, with new interests, arising from events happening since the suit was commenced, are brought before the court; wherein it differs from a supplemental bill, which is properly applicable to those cases only where the same parties or the same interests remain before the court. Story, Eq.Pl. (5th Ed.) § 345 et seq.

—Bill in nature of interpleader. See Bill of Interpleader.

—Bill of conformity. One filed by an executor or administrator, who finds the affairs of the deceased so much involved that he cannot safely administer the estate except under the direction of a court of chancery. This bill is filed against the creditors, generally, for the purpose of having all their claims adjusted, and procuring a final decree settling the order of payment of the assets. 1 Story, Eq.Jur. § 440.

—Bill of discovery. A proceeding by a party against an adversary for discovery of facts within adversary's knowledge, or discovery of documents, writings, or other things within his possession or power, to be used either offensively or defensively in a pending or contemplated action. Dallas Joint Stock Land Bank v. Rawlins, Tex.Civ.App., 129 S.W.2d 485, 486; First Nat. Bank v. Dade-Broward Co., 171 So. 510, 125 Fla. 594.

In aid of action at law is equitable remedy to enable litigant to obtain, prior to trial, such information as is in exclusive possession of adverse party and is necessary to establishment of complainant's case. Yorkshire Worsted Mills v. National Transit Co., 325 Pa. 427, 190 A. 897, 898.

—Bill of information. Where a suit is instituted on behalf of the crown or government, or of those of whom it has the custody by virtue of its prerogative, or whose rights are under its particular protection, the matter of complaint is offered to the court by way of information by the attorney or solicitor general, instead of by petition. Where a suit immediately concerns the crown or government alone, the proceeding is purely by way of information, but, where it does not do so immediately, a relator is appointed, who is answerable for costs, etc., and, if he is interested in the matter in connection with the crown or government, the proceeding is by information and bill. Informations differ from bills in little more than name and form, and the same rules are substantially applicable to both. 3 Bl.Comm. 261.

—Bill of interpleader. The name of a bill in equity to obtain a settlement of a question of right to money or other property adversely claimed, in which the party filing the bill has no interest, although it may be in his hands, by compelling such adverse claimants to litigate the right or title between themselves, and relieve him from liability or litigation. Republic Casualty Co. v. Fischmann, 99 N.J.Eq. 758, 134 A. 179, 180.

—Bill of peace. One which is filed when a person has a right which may be controverted by various persons, at different times, and by different actions. Smith v. Cretors, 164 N.W. 338, 340, 181 Iowa 189.

—Bill of review. One which is brought to have a decree of the court reviewed, corrected, or reversed. Dodge v. Northrop, 85 Mich. 243, 48 N.W. 505. It is in the nature of a writ of error. Rubin v. Midlinsky, 327 Ill. 89, 158 N.E. 395.

It is equitable procedure to procure explanation, alteration, or reversal of final decree by court which rendered it. People v. Sterling, 357 Ill. 354, 192 N.E. 229, 234.

The object of a "bill of review" and of a bill in nature of a bill of review in the old chancery practice was to procure a reversal, modification, or explanation of a decree in a former suit. Barz v. Sawyer, 159 Iowa 481, 141 N.W. 319, 321.

A "bill of review," or a bill in the nature of a bill of review, are of three classes; those for error appearing on the face of the record, those for newly discovered evidence, and those for fraud impeaching the original transaction. Moore v. Shook, 276 Ill. 47, 114 N.E. 592, 593. Such bills are peculiar to courts of equity at common law. Satterwhite v. State, 149 Ark. 147, 231 S.W. 886, 887.

—Bill of revivor. One which is brought to continue a suit which has abated before its final consummation, as, for example, by death, or marriage of a female plaintiff. Brooks v. Laurent, C.C.A. Fla., 98 F. 647, 39 C.C.A. 201.

—Bill of revivor and supplement. One which is a compound of a supplemental bill and bill of revivor, and not only continues the suit, which has abated by the death of the plaintiff, or the like, but supplies any defects in the original bill arising from subsequent events, so as to entitle the party to relief on the whole merits of his case. Westcott. Bowie v. Minter, 2 Ala. 411.

—Bill quia timet. A bill invoking the aid of equity "because he fears," that is, because the complainant apprehends an injury to his property rights or interests, from the fault or neglect of another. Bisp.Eq. § 568; 2 Story, Eq.Jur. § 826.

Such bills are entertained to guard against possible or prospective injuries, and to preserve the means by which existing rights may be protected from future or contingent violations; differing from injunctions, in that the latter correct past and present or imminent and certain injuries. De Carli v. O'Brien, 41 P.2d 411, 416, 150 Or. 35, 97 A.L.R. 693.

—Bill to carry a decree into execution. One which is filed when, from the neglect of parties or some other cause, it may become impossible to carry a decree into execution without the further decree of the court. Hind, Ch.Pr. 68; Story, Eq.Pl. § 42.

—Bill to perpetuate testimony. A bill in equity filed in order to procure the testimony of witnesses to be taken as to some matter not at the time before the courts, but which is likely at some future time to be in litigation. Story, Eq.Pl. (5th Ed.) § 300 et seq.

—Bill to quiet possession and title. Also called a bill to remove a cloud on title (q. v.), and though sometimes classed with bills *quia timet* or for the cancellation of void instruments, they may be resorted to in other cases when the complainant's title is clear and there is a cloud to be removed; Maguire v. City of Macomb, 293 Ill. 441, 127 N.E. 682, 686.

—Bill to suspend a decree. One brought to avoid or suspend a decree under special circumstances.

—Bill to take testimony de bene esse. One which is brought to take the testimony of witnesses to a fact material to the prosecution of a suit at law which is actually commenced, where there is good cause to fear that the testimony may otherwise be lost before the time of trial. 2 Story, Eq.Jur. § 1813, n.

—Cross-bill. One which is brought by a defendant in a suit against a plaintiff in or against other defendants in the same suit, or against both, touching the matters in question in the original bill. Story, Eq.Pl. § 389; Mitf.Eq.Pl. 80.

It is a bill brought by a defendant against a plaintiff, or other parties in a former bill depending, touching the matter in question in that bill. It is usually brought either to obtain a necessary discovery of facts in aid of the defense to the original bill, or to obtain full relief to all parties in reference to the matters of the original bill. It is to be treated as a mere auxiliary suit. Kidder v. Barr, 35 N. H. 251; Blythe v. Hinckley, C.C.Cal., 84 F. 234. A species of pleading, used for the purpose of obtaining a discovery necessary to the defense, or to obtain some relief founded on the collateral claims of the party defendant to the original suit. Tison v. Tison, 14 Ga. 167. Also, if a bill of exchange or promissory note be given in consideration of another bill or notice, it is called a "cross" or "counter" bill or note. Landon v. Public Utilities Commission of Kansas, D.C.Kan., 234 F. 152, 167.

—Supplemental bill. A bill to bring before the court matters arising after the filing of the original bill or not then known to complainant. Puget Sound Power & Light Co. v. City of Seattle, C.C. A.Wash., 5 F.(2d) 393. See Bill in nature of a supplemental bill.

5. In legislation and constitutional law

The word means a draft of an act of the legislature before it becomes a law; a proposed or projected law. A draft of an act presented to the legislature, but not enacted. Hubbard v. Lowe, D. C.N.Y., 226 F. 135, 137. Also a special act passed by a legislative body in the exercise of a *quasi* judicial power. Scudder v. Smith, 331 Pa. 165, 200 A. 601, 604.

The word "bill" may mean the bill as it is first introduced in one of the houses of the legislature, or it may refer to it at any time in any of its stages until finally passed. People v. Brady, 262 Ill. 578, 105 N.E. 1, 4. An *act* is the appropriate term for it, after it has been acted on by, and passed by, the legislature. Herbring v. Brown, 92 Or. 176, 180 P. 328, 330. Thus, bills of attainder, bills of pains and penalties, are spoken of.

—Bill of attainder. See Attainder.

—Bill of indemnity. In English law. An act of parliament, passed every session until 1869, but discontinued in and after that year, as having been rendered unnecessary by the passing of the promissory oaths act, 1868, for the relief of those who have unwittingly or unavoidably neglected to take the necessary oaths, etc., required for the purpose of qualifying them to hold their respective offices. Wharton.

—Bill of pains and penalties. A special act of the legislature which inflicts a punishment, less than death, upon persons supposed to be guilty of treason or felony, without any conviction in the ordinary course of judicial proceedings.

It differs from a bill of attainder in this: that the punishment inflicted by the latter is death.

—Private bill. One dealing only with a matter of private personal or local interest. Lowell, Gov. of Eng. 266.

All legislative bills which have for their object some particular or private interest are so termed, as distinguished from such as are for the benefit of the whole community, which are thence termed "public bills." People v. Chautauqua County, 43 N.Y. 17.

—Private bill office. See Private.

—Private member's bill. One of a public nature introduced by a private member;—distinguished from a private bill, which is one dealing only with a matter of private personal or local interest. Lowell, Gov. of Eng. 266.

6. A solemn and formal legislative declaration of popular rights and liberties

Promulgated on certain extraordinary occasions, as the famous Bill of Rights in English history.

—Bill of rights. A formal and emphatic legislative assertion and declaration of popular rights and liberties usually promulgated upon a change of government; particularly the statute 1 W. & M. St. 2, c. 2. Also the summary of the rights and liberties of the people, or of the principles of constitutional law deemed essential and fundamental, contained in many of the American state constitutions. Hamill v. Hawks, C.C.A.Okl., 58 F.2d 41, 47. That portion of Constitution guaranteeing rights and privileges to the individual. Brown v. State, 219 Ind. 251, 37 N.E.2d 73, 77, 137 A.L.R. 679.

7. In the law of contracts

An obligation; a deed, whereby the obligor acknowledges himself to owe to the obligee a certain sum of money or some other thing. It may be indented or poll, and with or without a penalty.

—Bill obligatory. A bond absolute for the payment of money. It is called also a "single bill," and differs from a promissory note only in having a seal. See Bill penal. Bank v. Greiner, 2 Serg. & R. (Pa.) 115.

—Bill of debt. An ancient term including promissory notes and bonds for the payment of money. Com.Dig. "Merchant," F. 2.

—Bill penal. A written obligation by which a debtor acknowledges himself indebted in a certain sum, and binds himself for the payment thereof, in a larger sum, called a "penalty." Bonds with conditions have superseded such bills in modern practice. They are sometimes called bills obligatory, and are properly so called; but every bill obligatory is not a bill penal. Comyns, Dig. *Obligations,* D; Cro.Car. 515. See 2 Ventr. 106, 198.

—Bill single. A written promise to pay to a person or persons named a stated sum at a stated time, without any condition. When under seal, as is usually the case, it is sometimes called a "bill obligatory," *(q. v.)* It differs from a "bill penal," *(q. v.)* in that it expresses no penalty.

8. In commercial law

A written statement of the terms of a contract, or specification of the items of a transaction or of a demand; also a general name for any item of indebtedness, whether receivable or payable.

Accounts for goods sold, services rendered, or work done. Newman v. San Antonio Traction Co., Tex.Civ.App., 155 S.W. 688, 690.

As a verb, as generally and customarily used in commercial transactions, "bill" is synonymous with "charge" or "invoice." George M. Jones Co. v. Canadian Nat. R. Co., D.C.Mich., 14 F.2d 852, 855.

—Bill-book. In mercantile law. A book in which an account of bills of exchange and promissory notes, whether payable or receivable, is stated.

—Bill-head. A printed form on which merchants and traders make out their bills and render accounts to their customers.

—Bill of lading. In common law. The written evidence of a contract for the carriage and delivery of goods sent by sea for a certain freight. Mason v. Lickbarrow, 1 H.Bl. 359. A written memorandum, given by the person in command of a merchant vessel, acknowledging the receipt on board the ship of certain specified goods, in good order or "apparent good order," which he undertakes, in consideration of the payment of freight, to deliver in like good order (dangers of the sea excepted) at a designated place to the consignee therein named or to his assigns. Devato v. Barrels, D.C.N.Y., 20 Fed. 510.

The term is often applied to a similar receipt and undertaking given by a carrier of goods by land. A bill of lading is an instrument in writing, signed by a carrier or his agent, describing the freight so as to identify it, stating the name of the consignor, the terms of the contract for carriage, and agreeing or directing that the freight be delivered to the order or assigns of a specified person at a specified place. See Civil Code Cal. § 2126a; Aman v. Dover & Southbound R. Co., 179 N.C. 310, 102 S.E. 392, 393; Rudin v. King-Richardson Co., 143 N.E. 198, 201, 311 Ill. 513. It is receipt for goods, contract for their carriage, and is documentary evidence of title to goods. Schwalb v. Erie R. Co., 293 N.Y.S. 842, 846, 161 Misc. 743.

A *clean* bill of lading is one which contains nothing in the margin qualifying the words in the bill of lading itself. 61 Law T. 330; Creery v. Holly, 14 Wend. (N.Y.) 26; Sayward v. Stevens, 3 Gray (Mass.) 97.

An *order* bill of lading is one in which it is stated that goods are consigned to order of any person named therein. F. L. Shaw Co. v. Coleman, Tex.Civ.App., 236 S.W. 178, 180.

A *straight* bill of lading is one in which it is stated that goods are consigned to a specified person. Atlantic Coast Line R. Co. v. Roe, 91 Fla. 762, 109 So. 205, 207.

A *through* bill of lading is one by which a railroad contracts to transport over its own line for a certain distance carloads of merchandise or stock, there to deliver the same to its connecting lines to be transported to the place of destination at a fixed rate per carload for the whole distance. Gulf, C. & S. F. R. Co. v. Vaughn, 4 Willson, Ct. App.Tex. § 182, 16 S.W. 775.

—Bill of parcels. A statement sent to the buyer of goods, along with the goods, exhibiting in detail the items composing the parcel and their several prices, to enable him to detect any mistake or omission; an invoice.

—Bill of sale. In contracts. A written agreement, formerly limited to one under seal, by which one person assigns or transfers his right to or interest in goods and personal chattels to another. Wilson v. Voche, 172 S.E. 672, 48 Ga.App. 173. An instrument by which, in particular, the property in ships and vessels is conveyed. Young v. Stone, 70 N.Y.S. 558, 61 App.Div. 364. See Grand bill of sale, *infra*.

—Bill payable. In a merchant's accounts, all bills which he has accepted, and promissory notes which he has made, are called "bills payable," and are entered in a ledger account under that name, and recorded in a book bearing the same title. See West Virginia Pulp & Paper Co. v. Karnes, 137 Va. 714, 120 S.E. 321, 322.

—Bill receivable. In a merchant's accounts, all notes, drafts, checks, etc., payable to him, or of which he is to receive the proceeds at a future date, are called "bills receivable," and are entered in a ledger-account under that name, and also noted in a book bearing the same title. State v. Robinson, 57 Md. 501. Miami Coal Co. v. Fox, 203 Ind. 99, 176 N.E. 11, 16, 79 A.L.R. 333.

—Bill rendered. A bill of items rendered by a creditor to his debtor; an "account rendered," as distinguished from "an account stated." Hill v. Hatch, 11 Me. 455.

—Grand bill of sale. In English law. The name of an instrument used for the transfer of a ship while she is at sea. An expression which is understood to refer to the instrument whereby a ship was originally transferred from the builder to the owner, or first purchaser. 3 Kent, Comm. 133.

9. In the law of negotiable instruments

A promissory obligation for the payment of money.

Standing alone or without qualifying words, the term is understood to mean a bank note, United States treasury note, or other piece of paper circulating as money. Green v. State, 28 Tex.App. 493, 13 S.W. 785.

—Bill of credit. In constitutional law. A bill or promissory note issued by the government of a state or nation, upon its faith and credit, designed to circulate in the community as money, and redeemable at a future day. Hale v. Huston, 44 Ala. 138, 4 Am.Rep. 124. In mercantile law. A license or authority given in writing from one person to another, very common among merchants, bankers, and those who travel, empowering a person to receive or take up money of their correspondents abroad.

—Bill of exchange. A written order from A. to B., directing B. to pay to C. a certain sum of money therein named. Byles, Bills, 1. An open (that is, unsealed) letter addressed by one person to another directing him, in effect, to pay, absolutely and at all events, a certain sum of money therein named, to a third person, or to any other to whom that third person may order it to be paid, or it may be payable to bearer or to the drawer himself. 1 Daniel, Neg.Inst. 27.

An unconditional order in writing addressed by one person to another, signed by the person giving it, requiring the person to whom it is addressed to pay on demand or at a fixed or determinable future time a sum certain in money to order or to bearer. Clayton Town-Site Co. v. Clayton Drug Co., 147 P. 460, 20 N.M. 185; Smythe v. Sanders, 101 So. 435, 436, 136 Misc. 382; Sometimes called a "trade acceptance." Jones v. Revere Preserving Co., 247 Mass. 225, 142 N.E. 70, 71.

A "check" differs from a "bill of exchange" in that it is always drawn on a deposit whereas a bill is not. Wilson v. Buchenau, D.C.Cal., 43 F.Supp. 272, 275.

—Domestic bill of exchange. A bill of exchange drawn on a person residing in the same state with the drawer; or dated at a place in the state, and drawn on a person living within the state. It is the residence of the drawer and drawee which must determine whether a bill is domestic or foreign. Ragsdale v. Franklin, 25 Miss. 143. See, also, Inland bill of exchange.

—Foreign bill of exchange. A bill of exchange drawn in one state or country, upon a foreign state or country. See Story, Bills, § 22; 3 Kent, Comm. 94, note.

A bill of exchange drawn in one country upon another country not governed by the same homogeneous laws, or not governed throughout by the same municipal laws. A bill of exchange drawn in one of the United States upon a person residing in another state is a foreign bill.

—Inland bill of exchange. One of which the drawer and drawee are residents of the same state or country. Miller v. American Gold Mining Co., 3 Alaska, 1. See Domestic bill of exchange.

10. In maritime law

The term is applied to contracts of various sorts, but chiefly to bills of lading and to bills of adventure.

—Bill of adventure. A written certificate by a merchant or the master or owner of a ship, to the effect that the property and risk in goods shipped on the vessel in his own name belong to another person, to whom he is accountable for the proceeds alone.

—Bill of gross adventure. In French maritime law. Any written instrument which contains a contract of bottomry, *respondentia,* or any other kind of maritime loan. There is no corresponding English term. Hall, Marit. Loans, 182, n.

—Bill of health. An official certificate, given by the authorities of a port from which a vessel clears, to the master of the ship, showing the state of the port, as respects the public health, at the time of sailing, and exhibited to the authorities of the port which the vessel next makes, in token that she does not bring disease.

If the bill alleges that no contagious or infectious disease existed, it is called a "clean" bill; if it admits that one was suspected or anticipated, or that one actually prevailed, it is called a "touched" or a "foul" bill.

11. In revenue law and procedure

The term is given to various documents filed in or issuing from a custom house, principally of the sorts described below.

—Bill of entry. An account of the goods entered at the custom-house, both incoming and outgoing. It must state the name of the merchant exporting or importing, the quantity and species of merchandise, and whither transported, and whence.

—Bill of sight. When an importer of goods is ignorant of their exact quantity or quality, so that he cannot make a perfect entry of them, he may give to the customs officer a written description of them, according to the best of his information and belief. This is called a "bill of sight."

—Bill of store. In English law. A kind of license granted at the custom-house to merchants, to carry such stores and provisions as are necessary for their voyage, custom free. Jacob.

—Bill of sufferance. In English law. A license granted at the custom-house to a merchant, to suffer him to trade from one English port to another, without paying custom. Cowell.

12. In criminal law

A bill of indictment, see *infra*.

—Bill of appeal. An ancient, but now abolished, method of criminal prosecution. See Battel.

—Bill of indictment. A formal written document accusing a person or persons named of having committed a felony or misdemeanor, lawfully laid before a grand jury for their action upon it. State v. Ray, Rice (S.C.) 4, 33 Am.Dec. 90. See Presentment.

If the grand jury decide that a trial ought to be had, they indorse on it "a true bill;" if otherwise, "not a true bill" or "not found."

13. In common-law practice

An itemized statement or specification of particular details, especially items of cost or charge.

—Bill of costs. A certified, itemized statement of the amount of costs in an action or suit. Doe v. Thompson, 22 N.H. 219.

By the English usage, this term is applied to the statement of the charges and disbursements of an attorney or solicitor incurred in the conduct of his client's business, and which might be taxed upon application, even though not incurred in any suit. Thus, conveyancing costs might be taxed. Wharton.

—Bill of particulars. In practice. A written statement or specification of the particulars of the demand for which an action at law is brought, or of a defendant's set-off against such demand, (including dates, sums, and items in detail,) furnished by one of the parties to the other, either voluntarily or in compliance with a judge's order for that purpose. 1 Tidd, Pr. 596–600; 2 Archb.Pr. 221; Ferguson v. Ashbell, 53 Tex. 250; Baldwin v. Gregg, 13 Metc. (Mass.) 255.

It is designed to aid the defendant in interposing the proper answer and in preparing for trial, by giving him detailed information regarding the cause of action stated in the complaint. Wetmore v. Goodwin Film & Camera Co., (D.C.) 226 F. 352, 353. It is neither a pleading nor proof of the facts therein contained, Nilson v. Ebey Land Co., 90 Wash. 295, 155 P. 1036, and is not for the purpose of discovering evidence, nor to find what plaintiff knows, but what he claims, Intermountain Ass'n of Credit Men v. Milwaukee Mechanics' Ins. Co., 44 Idaho 491, 258 P. 362, 363. A bill of particulars is not designed to uphold an insufficient indictment, but to give accused fair notice of what he is called on to defend. Clary v. Commonwealth, 163 Ky. 48, 173 S.W. 171, 173. People v. Bain, 359 Ill. 455, 195 N.E. 42.

14. In English law

A draft of a patent for a charter, commission, dignity, office, or appointment.

Such a bill is drawn up in the attorney general's patent bill office, is submitted by a secretary of state for the King's signature, when it is called the "King's bill," and is then countersigned by the secretary of state and sealed by the privy seal, and then the patent is prepared and sealed. Sweet.

For Exchequer Bills, see that title.

BILL OF MORTALITY. A written statement or account of the number of deaths which have occurred in a certain district within a given time.

BILLA. L. Lat. A bill; an original bill.

BILLA CASSETUR, or QUOD BILLA CASSETUR. (That the bill be quashed.) In practice. The form of the judgment rendered for a defendant on a plea in abatement, where the proceeding is *by bill;* that is, where the suit is commenced by *capias,* and not by original writ. 2 Archb.Pr.K.B. 4.

BILLA EXCAMBII. A bill of exchange.

BILLA EXONERATIONIS. A bill of lading.

BILLA VERA. (A true bill.) In old practice. The indorsement anciently made on a bill of indictment by a grand jury, when they found it sufficiently sustained by evidence. 4 Bl.Comm. 306.

BILLBOARD. An erection annexed to the land in the nature of a fence for the purpose of posting advertising bills and posters. Randall v. Atlanta Advertising Service, 159 Ga. 217, 125 S.E. 462, 463; Cochrane v. McDermott Advertising Agency, 6 Ala.App. 121, 60 So. 421, 422.

BILLET. A soldier's quarters in a civilian's house; or the ticket which authorizes him to occupy them.

In French law. A bill or promissory note. *Billet à ordre,* a bill payable to order. *Billet à vue,* a bill payable at sight. *Billet de complaisance,* an accommodation bill. *Billet de change,* an engagement to give, at a future time, a bill of exchange, which the party is not at the time prepared to give. Story, Bills, § 2, n.

BILLETA. In old English law. A bill or petition exhibited in parliament. Cowell.

BILLIARD TABLES. This term includes "pool tables" as used in statutes, since "pool tables" are billiard tables with pockets. Village of Atwood v. Otter, 296 Ill. 70, 129 N.E. 573, 578.

BILLY. A small bludgeon that may be carried in the pocket; a club; especially, a policeman's club. Cent. Dict.; Webster, New Intl. Dict.

BI-METALLIC. Pertaining to, or consisting of, two metals used as money at a fixed relative value.

BI-METALLISM. The legalized use of two metals in the currency of a country at a fixed relative value.

BIND. To obligate; to bring or place under definite duties or legal obligations, particularly by a bond or covenant; to affect one in a constraining or compulsory manner with a contract or a judgment. Stone v. Bradbury, 14 Me. 193.

So long as a contract, an adjudication, or a legal relation remains in force and virtue, and continues to impose duties or obligations, it is said to be *"binding."* A man is *bound* by his contract or promise, by a judgment or decree against him, by his bond or covenant, by an estoppel, etc.

BIND OUT. To place one under a legal obligation to serve another; as to *bind out* an apprentice.

BINDER. The memorandum of an agreement for insurance, intended to give temporary protection pending investigation of the risk and issuance of a formal policy. Seiderman v. Herman Perla Inc., 268 N.Y. 188, 197 N.E. 190, 191.

A verbal contract of insurance in præsenti, of which the insurance agent makes a memorandum, temporary in its nature, Norwich Union Fire Ins. Society v. Dalton, Tex. Civ.App., 175 S.W. 459, 460; thus constituting a short method of issuing a temporary policy to continue until execution of the formal one, Sherri v. National Surety Co., 243 N.Y. 266, 153 N.E. 70, 71. Carew, Shaw & Bernasconi v. General Casualty Co. of America, 189 Wash. 329, 65 P.2d 689, 695.

A "binder" as used in marine insurance is an application for insurance made on behalf of the proposed insured and approved by the insurer or his agent. Muller v. Globe & Rutgers Fire Ins. Co. of City of New York, C.C.A.N.Y., 246 F. 759, 760.

BINDING INSTRUCTION. One in which jury is told if they find certain conditions to be true to find for plaintiff or defendant, as case might be. Scott-Burr Stores Corporation v. Foster, 197 Ark. 232, 122 S.W.2d 165, 169.

BINDING OVER. The act by which a court or magistrate requires a person to enter into a recognizance or furnish bail to appear for trial, to keep the peace, to attend as a witness, etc.

BINDING RECEIPT OR SLIP. Is a limited acceptance of an application for insurance given by an authorized agent pending the ascertainment of the company's willingness to assume the burden of the proposed risk, the effect of which is to protect the applicant until the company acts upon the application, and, if it declines to accept the burden, the binding effect of the slip ceases eo instante. Hallauer v. Fire Ass'n of Philadelphia, 83 W.Va. 401, 98 S.E. 441, 443; Seiderman v. Herman Perla, Inc., 268 N.Y. 188, 197 N.E. 190, 191.

BINOCULAR VISION. The vision of the two eyes acting together, used in determining depth, width, distance, and comparative placing of different objects; distinguished from "field vision," meaning the general vision used in catching in sight, and following and locating objects. Gigleo v. Dorfman & Kimiavsky, 106 Conn. 401, 138 A. 448, 450.

BIPARTITE. Consisting of, or divisible into, two parts. A term in conveyancing descriptive of an instrument in two parts, and executed by both parties.

BIRRETUM, BIRRETUS. A cap or coif used formerly in England by judges and serjeants at law. Spelman.

BIRTH. The act of being born or wholly brought into separate existence. Wallace v. State, 10 Tex. App. 270.

BIS. Lat. Twice.

BIS DAT QUI CITO DAT. He pays twice who pays promptly.

BIS IDEM EXIGI BONA FIDES NON PATITUR; ET IN SATISFACTIONIBUS NON PERMITTITUR AMPLIUS FIERI QUAM SEMEL FACTUM EST. Good faith does not suffer the same thing to be demanded twice; and in making satisfaction [for a debt or demand] it is not allowed to be done more than once. 9 Coke, 53.

BISAILE (also BESAILE, BESAYEL, BESAIEL, BESAYLE). The father of one's grandfather or grandmother.

BISANTIUM, BESANTINE, BEZANT. An ancient coin, first issued at Constantinople; it was of two sorts,—gold, equivalent to a ducat, valued at 9s. 6d.; and silver, computed at 2s. They were both current in England. Wharton.

BI-SCOT. In old Engish law. A fine imposed for not repairing banks, ditches, and causeways.

BISHOP. In English law. An ecclesiastical dignitary, being the chief of the clergy within his diocese, subject to the archbishop of the province in which his diocese is situated. Most of the bishops are also members of the House of Lords.

BISHOP'S COURT. In English law. An ecclesiastical court, held in the cathedral of each diocese, the judge whereof is the bishop's chancellor, who judges by the civil canon law; and, if the diocese be large, he has his commissaries in remote parts, who hold consistory courts, for matters limited to them by their commission.

BISHOPRIC. In ecclesiastical law. The diocese of a bishop, or the circuit in which he has jurisdiction; the office of a bishop. 1 Bl.Comm. 377–382.

BISSEXTILE. The day which is added every fourth year to the month of February, in order to make the year agree with the course of the sun.

By statute 21 Hen. III., the 28th and 29th of February count together as one day. This statute is in force in some of the United States. Porter v. Holloway, 43 Ind. 35; Harker v. Addis, 4 Pa. 515.

BITING RULE. When first taker of conveyed property under writing submitted for construction is initially conveyed a fee title, it is then incompetent and invalid to modify, qualify, or reduce thereafter the apparent fee title of the first taker so as to reduce it to a life estate, and any gift over after death of first taker is void. Hanks v. McDanell, 210 S.W.2d 784, 786, 307 Ky. 243, 17 A.L.R.2d 1.

BITULITHIC. Designating a kind of paving the main body of which consists of broken stone cemented together with bitumen or asphalt. Washburn v. Board of Com'rs of Shawnee County, 103 Kan. 169, 172 P. 997, 998. Bituminous macadam means bitulithic pavement. Washburn v. Board of Com'rs of Shawnee County, 103 Kan. 169, 172 P. 997, 998. See Bitumen.

BITUMEN. Mineral pitch; black, tarry substance used in cements, in construction of pavements, etc., and by extension, the term includes any one of natural hydrocarbons, including hard, solid, brittle varieties called asphalt, semi-solid maltha and mineral tars, oily petroleums, and light volatile naphthas. Western Willite Co. v. Trinidad Asphalt Mfg. Co., C.C.A.Mo., 16 F.2d 446, 448.

BITUMINOUS COAL. Bituminous coal is much less hard than anthracite; it is dusty and dirty and is commonly termed "soft coal." Bituminous coal burns with more or less smoke while anthracite coal burns with practically no smoke. As the fuel ratio of bituminous coal rises the coal is more soft; as the fuel ratio of anthracite coal rises the coal is more hard. Commonwealth v. Hudson Coal Co., 287 Pa. 64, 134 A. 413, 414. See Anthracite coal.

BITUMINOUS MACADAM. Bitulithic pavement. Washburn v. Board of Com'rs of Shawnee County, 103 Kan. 169, 172 P. 997, 998. See Bitulithic.

BLACK ACRE and WHITE ACRE. Fictitious names used by the old writers to distinguish one parcel of land from another, to avoid ambiguity, as well as the inconvenience of a fuller description.

BLACK ACT. The statute 9 Geo. I. c. 22, so called because it was occasioned by the outrages committed by persons with their faces blacked or otherwise disguised, who appeared in Epping Forest, near Waltham, in Essex, and destroyed the deer there, and committed other offenses. Repealed by 7 & 8 Geo. IV, c. 27.

BLACK ACTS. Old Scotch statutes passed in the reigns of the Stuarts and down to the year 1586 or 1587, so called because printed in black letter. Bell.

BLACK BOOK OF HEREFORD. In English law. An old record frequently referred to by Cowell and other early writers.

BLACK BOOK OF THE ADMIRALTY. A book of the highest authority in admiralty matters, generally supposed to have been compiled during the reign of Edward III. with additions of a later date. It contains the laws of Oleron, a view of crimes and offenses cognizable in the admiralty, and many other matters. See De Lovio v. Boit, 2 Gall. 404, Fed.Cas.No.3,776.

BLACK BOOK OF THE EXCHEQUER. The name of an ancient book kept in the English exchequer, containing a collection of treaties, conventions, charters, etc.

BLACK CAP. The head-dress worn by the judge in pronouncing the sentence of death. It is part of the judicial full dress, and is worn by the judges on occasions of especial state. Wharton.

BLACK CODE. A name given collectively to the body of laws, statutes, and rules in force in various southern states prior to 1865, which regulated the institution of slavery, and particularly those forbidding their reception at public inns and on public conveyances. Civil Rights Cases, 3 S.Ct. 18, 109 U.S. 3, 27 L.Ed. 835.

BLACK GAME. In English law. Heath fowl, in contradistinction to red game, as grouse.

BLACK LIQUOR. A term used in the paper pulp industry. It denotes a residual liquor coming from the digesters in which wood chips are cooked. Babcock & Wilcox Co. v. North Carolina Pulp Co., D.C.Del., 35 F.Supp. 215, 221.

BLACK MARIA. A closed wagon or van in which prisoners are carried to and from the jail, or between the court and the jail.

BLACK MAT CABARETTA. A cross between a goatskin and a skin of some other animal. J. H. Stockamore Leather Co. v. Duane Shoe Co., 187 N.Y.S. 258, 195 App.Div. 947.

BLACK MUSLIM. An organization of American Negroes, founded in Detroit in 1930 by an American Negro calling himself Mohammad Elijah. To the traditional Koran the founders added the doctrine of Black Supremacy and proclaimed the desirability of maintaining (or regaining) the purity of the black race. 62 Col.L.Rev. 1488 (1962); 75 Harv.L.Rev. 837 (1962); State v. Cubbage (Del.), 210 A.2d 555 (1965).

BLACK RENTS. In old English law. Rents reserved in work, grain, provisions, or baser money than silver, in contradistinction to those which were reserved in *white* money or silver, which were termed "white rents," (*reditus albi,*) or blanch farms. Tomlins; Whishaw. See Blackmail.

BLACK-ROD, GENTLEMAN USHER OF. In England, the title of a chief officer of the king, deriving his name from the *Black Rod* of office, on the top of which reposes a golden lion, which he carries. During the session of Parliament he attends on the peers, summons the Commons to the House of Lords; and to his custody all peers impeached for any crime or contempt are first committed.

BLACK WARD. A subvassal, who held ward of the king's vassal.

BLACKJACK. A short bludgeon consisting of a heavy head, as of metal, on an elastic shaft or with a flexible handle; a bludgeon-like weapon consisting of a lead slug attached to a leather thong; a small leather-covered club or billy weighted at the head and having an elastic shaft. 5 Words and Phrases, Perm. Ed.

As a card game, another name for *vingt-et-un* (twenty-one); also, a variety of hearts in which the jack of spades counts as ten hearts. Webster, New Intl. Dict.

BLACKLEG. A person who gets his living by frequenting race-courses and places where games of chance are played, getting the best odds, and giving the least he can, but not necessarily cheating. That is not indictable either by statute or at common law. Barnett v. Allen, 3 Hurl. & N. 379.

In a later case it has been thought that "blackleg" ordinarily means a swindler, but does not mean a "scab" or strike breaker, and that its use may be libelous per se. United Mine Workers of America v. Cromer, 159 Ky. 605, 167 S.W. 891, 892.

BLACKLIST. A list of persons marked out for special avoidance, antagonism, or enmity on the part of those who prepare the list or those among whom it is intended to circulate; as where a trades-union "blacklists" workmen who refuse to conform to its rules, or where a list of insolvent or untrustworthy persons is published by a commercial agency or mercantile association. Quoted and relied on in Dick v. Northern Pac. Ry. Co., 86 Wash. 211, 150 P. 8, 12, Ann.Cas.1917A, 638, holding that this word is a generic term having no such well-defined meaning in law as to make its use in a pleading a definite charge of any specific misconduct against a person so charged. Cleary v. Great Northern Ry. Co., 147 Minn. 403, 180 N.W. 545, 546; Masters v. Lee, 39 Neb. 574, 58 N.W. 222; Mattison v. Railway Co., 2 Ohio N.P. 279.

BLACKMAIL. In one of its original meanings, this term denoted a tribute paid by English dwellers along the Scottish border to influential chieftains of Scotland, as a condition of securing immunity from raids of marauders and border thieves.

Also, rents payable in cattle, grain, work, and the like. Such rents were called "blackmail," (*reditus nigri,*) in distinction from white rents, (*blanche firmes,*) which were rents paid in silver. See Black rents.

The extortion of money by threats or overtures towards criminal prosecution or the destruction of a man's reputation or social standing.

In common parlance, the term is equivalent to and synonymous with, "extortion,"—the exaction of money, either for the performance of a duty, the prevention of an injury, or the exercise of an influence. It supposes the service to be unlawful, and the payment involuntary. Not infrequently it is extorted by threats, or by operating upon the fears or the credulity, or by promises to conceal, or offers to expose, the weaknesses, the follies, or the crimes of the victim. Mitchell v. Sharon, C.C.Cal., 51 F. 424; In re Mills, 104 Wash. 278, 176 P. 556, 562. "Blackmail" has a broader meaning than the New York statutory crime of blackmail, and denotes extortion in any mode by means of intimidation, as the extortion of money by threats of accusation or exposure, or of unfavorable criticism in the press. Guenther v. Ridgway Co., 156 N.Y.S. 534, 535, 170 App.Div. 725.

BLACKSMITH SHOP. A place to which the people of a community resort for the purpose of having machinery and tools repaired and iron work done. State v. Shumaker, 103 Kan. 741, 175 P. 978, 979.

BLADA. In old English law. Growing crops of grain of any kind. Spelman. All manner of annual grain. Cowell. Harvested grain. Bract. 217*b;* Reg.Orig. 94*b*, 95.

BLADARIUS. In old English law. A cornmonger; meal-man or corn-chandler; a bladier, or engrosser of corn or grain. Blount.

BLANC SEIGN. In Louisiana, a paper signed at the bottom by him who intends to bind himself, give acquittance, or compromise, at the discretion of the person whom he intrusts with such *blanc seign,* giving him power to fill it with what he may think proper, according to agreement. Musson v. U. S. Bank, 6 Mart.O.S. (La.) 718.

BLANCH HOLDING. An ancient tenure of the law of Scotland, the duty payable being trifling, as a penny or a pepper-corn, etc., if required; similar to free and common socage.

BLANCHE FIRME. White rent; a rent reserved, payable in silver.

BLANCUS. In old law and practice. White; plain; smooth; blank.

BLANK. A space left unfilled in a written document, in which one or more words or marks are to be inserted to complete the sense. Angle v. Insurance Co., 92 U.S. 337, 23 L.Ed. 556.

Also a skeleton or printed form for any legal document, in which the necessary and invariable words are printed in their proper order, with blank spaces left for the insertion of such names, dates, figures, additional clauses, etc., as may be necessary to adapt the instrument to the particular case and to the design of the party using it.

BLANK ACCEPTANCE. An acceptance of a bill of exchange written on the paper before the bill is made, and delivered by the acceptor.

BLANK BAR. Also called the "common bar." The name of a plea in bar which in an action of trespass is put in to oblige the plaintiff to assign the certain place where the trespass was committed. It was most in practice in the common bench. See Cro.Jac. 594.

BLANK BONDS. Scotch securities, in which the creditor's name was left blank, and which passed by mere delivery, the bearer being at liberty to put in his name and sue for payment. Declared void by Act 1696, c. 25.

BLANK INDORSEMENT. The indorsement of a bill of exchange or promissory note, by merely writing the name of the indorser, without mentioning any person to whom the bill or note is to be paid; called "blank," because a blank or space is left *over* it for the insertion of the name of the indorsee, or of any subsequent holder. Otherwise called an indorsement "in blank." 3 Kent, Comm. 89; Story, Prom. Notes, § 138.

BLANKET. In tariff acts: A heavy cover for a bed or a horse, with a thick, soft nap on both sides. Riley & Co. v. U. S., 8 Ct.Cust.App. 116, 118.

BLANKET POLICY. See Insurance—Blanket Policy.

BLANKS. A kind of white money, (value 8d.,) coined by Henry V. in those parts of France which were then subject to England; forbidden to be current in that realm by 2 Hen. VI. c. 9. Wharton.

BLASARIUS. An incendiary.

BLASPHEMY.

In English Law

Blasphemy is the offense of speaking matter relating to God, Jesus Christ, the Bible, or the Book of Common Prayer, intended to wound the feelings of mankind or to excite contempt and hatred against the church by law established, or to promote immorality. Sweet.

In American Law

Any oral or written reproach maliciously cast upon God, His name, attributes, or religion. Com. v. Kneeland, 20 Pick. (Mass.) 213; Young v. State, 10 Lea (Tenn.) 165; People v. Ruggles, 8 Johns. (N.Y.) 290, 5 Am.Dec. 335; Updegraph v. Com., 11 Serg. & R. (Pa.) 406.

In general, blasphemy may be described as consisting in speaking evil of the Deity with an impious purpose to derogate from the divine majesty, and to alienate the minds of others from the love and reverence of God.

It is purposely using words concerning God calculated and designed to impair and destroy the reverence, respect, and confidence due to Him as the intelligent creator, governor, and judge of the world. It embraces the idea of detraction, when used towards the Supreme Being, as "calumny" usually carries the same idea when applied to an individual. It is a willful and malicious attempt to lessen men's reverence of God by denying His existence, or His attributes as an intelligent creator, governor, and judge of men, and to prevent their having confidence in Him as such. Com. v. Kneeland, 20 Pick. (Mass.) 211, 212.

The use of this word is, in modern law, exclusively confined to sacred subjects; but *blasphemia* and *blasphemare* were anciently used to signify the reviling by one person of another. Nov. 77, c. 1, § 1; Spelman.

BLASTING. Practice or occupation of rending heavy masses, especially of rock, by means of explosives, as in oil well drilling, quarrying, etc. Seismic Explorations v. Dobray, Tex.Civ.App., 169 S.W.2d 739, 742.

BLEACHERS. A relatively low-priced seat for a spectator at sports or games, or the section or structure (originally roofless) containing such seats. Lowden v. Jefferson County Excise Board, 122 P.2d 991, 992, 190 Okl. 276; Zeitz v. Cooperstown Baseball Centennial, N.Y.Sup., 29 N.Y.S.2d 56, 57.

BLEES. In old English law. Grain; particularly corn.

BLENCH, BLENCH HOLDING. See Blanch Holding.

BLENDED FUND. In England, where a testator directs his real and personal estate to be sold, and disposes of the proceeds as forming one aggregate, this is called a "blended fund."

BLENDED PRICE. As applied to milk, a price paid to producers based upon a pool average weighted by the volume of milk disposed of, according to different types of utilization. Queensboro Farm Products v. State, 24 N.Y.S.2d 413, 417, 175 Misc. 574.

BLETA. An old name for peat or combustible earth dug up and dried for burning. Wharton.

BLIND. The condition of one who is deprived of the faculty of seeing.

A voter is not "blind" within the meaning of Ky. St. § 1475, authorizing clerk to mark ballot for blind person, if he has left his spectacles at home, but a person so devoid of sight that he cannot see pencil mark made by clerk is "blind." Smith v. Jones, 221 Ky. 546, 299 S.W. 170, 171. One who by accident lost all vision except enough to enable him to recognize a form without distinguishing its outlines is "blind" within the Workmen's Compensation Act. Industrial Commission of Colorado v. Johnson, 64 Colo. 461, 172 P. 422, 423.

BLIND CAR. On railroads, one on which there is neither steps nor platform at the ends. Helm v. Hines, 109 Kan. 48, 196 P. 426.

BLIND CORNER. One where the building extends to the property line. Mobile Light & R. Co. v. Gadik, 211 Ala. 582, 100 So. 837, 838.

BLIND NAILING. "Blind nailing," in a contract relating to the interior finish of a house, means driving the nails in with a nail set, and concealing them with putty and paint. Sterling Engineering and Construction Co. v. Berg, 161 Wis. 280, 152 N.W. 851, 852.

BLIND TIGER. A place where intoxicants are sold on the sly, and contrary to the law. Town of Ruston v. Fountain, 118 La. 53, 42 So. 644; City of Shreveport v. Maroun, 134 La. 490, 64 So. 388, 389. A "tippling-house." Calhoun v. Bell, 136 La. 149, 66 So. 761, 762, Ann.Cas.1916D, 1165.

BLIND WAGON. Such as one used for moving furniture and the like, is one without the name or address of the owner of it thereon. Mike Berniger Moving Co. v. O'Brien, Mo.App., 240 S.W. 481, 483.

BLINDCRAFT. A natural descriptive term identifying in a broad sense work of the blind, conveying the idea of the blind performing deftly at any of the various skills or trades to which their talents are applied or leaving the suggestion of dexterity and skill of the blind as well as their handiwork itself. San Francisco Ass'n for Blind v. Industrial Aid for Blind, D.C.Mo., 58 F.Supp. 995, 1001.

BLINKS. In old English law. Boughs broken down from trees and thrown in a way where deer are likely to pass. Jacob.

BLOCK. A square or portion of a city or town inclosed by streets, whether partially or wholly occupied by buildings or containing only vacant lots. Also used synonymous with "square." Weeks v. Hetland, 202 N.W. 807, 812, 813, 52 N.D. 351. The platted portion of a city surrounded by streets. Cravens v. Putnam, 101 Kan. 161, 165 P. 801, 802. The term need not, however, be limited to blocks platted as such, but may mean an area bounded on all sides by streets or avenues. St. Louis-San Francisco R. Co. v. City of Tulsa, Okl., C.C.A.Okl., 15 F.2d 960, 963. It must be surrounded on at least three sides by streets, which must be marked on the ground, and not simply indicated as such on a plat. Seested v. Dickey, 318 Mo. 192, 300 S.W. 1088, 1098.

BLOCK BOOK SYSTEM. An abstract of property assessed for taxes and also of property unrendered and of which owners were unknown, together with maps and plats. Southern Surety Co. v. Lafferty, Tex.Civ.App., 43 S.W.2d 460, 463.

BLOCK-BOOKING. The practice of licensing or offering for license one motion picture feature or group of features on condition that exhibitor will also license another feature or group of features released by distributor during a given period. U. S. v. Paramount Pictures, N.Y., 68 S.Ct. 915, 928, 334 U.S. 131, 92 L.Ed. 1260.

BLOCK-HOLER. One who follows up the miner to blast or throw down large rocks left in the process of mining in a "stope." Mesich v. Tamarack Mining Co., 184 Mich. 363, 151 N.W. 564, 566.

BLOCK OF SURVEYS. In Pennsylvania land law. Any considerable body of contiguous tracts surveyed in the name of the same warrantee, without regard to the manner in which they were originally located; a body of contiguous tracts located by exterior lines, but not separated from each other by interior lines. Morrison v. Seaman, 183 Pa. 74, 38 A. 710.

BLOCK TO BLOCK RULE. The "block to block rule" for assessing the benefits for the opening of a new street is, the assessment against the lots in each block of the cost of acquiring the lands in that block. In re St. Raymona Ave. in City of New York, 162 N.Y.S. 185, 188, 175 App.Div. 518.

BLOCKADE. In international law. A marine investment or beleaguering of a town or harbor. A sort of circumvallation round a place by which all foreign connection and correspondence is, as far as human power can effect it, to be cut off. 1 C.Rob.Adm. 151.

It is not necessary, however, that the place should be invested by land, as well as by sea, in order to constitute a legal blockade; and, if a place be blockaded by sea only, it is no violation of belligerent rights for the neutral to carry on commerce with it by inland communications. 1 Kent, Comm. 147.

The actual investment of a port or place by a hostile force fully competent, under ordinary circumstances, to cut off all communication therewith, so arranged or disposed as to be able to apply its force to every point of practicable access or approach to the port or place so invested. The Olinde Rodrigues, D.C.S.C., 91 Fed. 274; Id., 19 S.Ct. 851, 174 U.S. 510, 43 L.Ed. 1065; The Peterhoff, 5 Wall. 50, 18 L.Ed. 564; Grinnan v. Edwards, 21 W.Va. 347.

It is called a "blockade *de facto*" when the usual notice of the blockade has not been given to the neutral powers by the government causing the investment, in consequence of which the blockading squadron has to warn off all approaching vessels.

Pacific Blockade

A means of coercion short of war, usually adopted by the joint action of several nations.

An instance of it occurred when Great Britain and Germany united to prevent the slave traffic and stop the importation of arms on the east coast of Africa. Snow, Int. Law 79. In 1827 Greece was blockaded by France, Russia, and Great Britain; in 1850 the Greek ports were blockaded by Great Britain, and again in 1855 by the combined fleets of the five Great Powers. In 1887 the Institute of International Law unanimously declared in favor of the legality of pacific blockade, subject to certain conditions. See 21 L. Mag. & Rev. 285; 2 Oppen. §§ 40-49.

Paper Blockade

The state of a line of coast proclaimed to be under blockade in time of war, when the naval force on watch is not sufficient to repel a real attempt to enter.

Public Blockade

A blockade which is not only established in fact, but is notified, by the government directing it, to other governments; as distinguished from a *simple* blockade, which may be established by a naval officer acting upon his own discretion or under direction of superiors, without governmental notification. The Circassian, 2 Wall. 150, 17 L. Ed. 796.

Simple Blockade

One established by a naval commander acting on his own discretion and responsibility, or under the direction of a superior officer, but without governmental orders or notification. The Circassian, 2 Wall. 150, 17 L.Ed. 796.

BLOCKAGE. Recognition in the field of taxation of fact that in some instances a large block of stock cannot be marketed and turned into cash as readily as a few shares. Citizens Fidelity Bank & Trust Co. v. Reeves, Ky., 259 S.W.2d 432, 433.

BLOCKAGE RULE. Process of determining value of large blocks of corporate stock for gift and estate tax purposes, based on the postulate that a large block of stock cannot be marketed as readily and as advantageously in price as can a few shares. Montclair Trust Co. v. Zink, Prerog., 57 A.2d 372, 376, 380, 141 N.J.Eq. 401.

BLOCKHEAD. A term importing want of natural cleverness, and slowness and obstinacy of mind.

BLOOD. Kindred; consanguinity; family relationship; relation by descent from a common ancestor. Swasey v. Jaques, 144 Mass. 135, 10 N.E. 758, 59 Am.Rep. 65.

A person may be said to be "of the blood" of another who has any, however small a portion, of the blood derived from a common ancestor, Miller v. Grimes, 262 Pa. 226, 105 A. 92, thus including half blood as well as whole blood, Gardner's Estate v. Gardner, 42 Utah, 40, 129 P. 360, 361. All persons are of the blood of an ancestor who may, in the absence of other and nearer heirs, take by descent from that ancestor. Cornell v. Child, 156 N.Y.S. 449, 452, 170 App.Div. 240.

Half-Blood

A term denoting the degree of relationship which exists between those who have the same father or the same mother, but not both parents in common.

Mixed Blood

A person is "of mixed blood" who is descended from ancestors of different races or nationalities; but particularly, in the United States, the term denotes a person one of whose parents (or more remote ancestors) was a negro. U. S. v. First Nat. Bank of Detroit, Minn., 234 U.S. 245, 34 S.Ct. 846, 848, 58 L.Ed. 1298.

Whole Blood

Kinship by descent from the same father and mother; as distinguished from *half* blood, which is the relationship of those who have one parent in common, but not both.

BLOOD FEUD. Avenging the slaughter of kin on the person who slaughtered him, or on his belongings.

Whether the Teutonic or the Anglo-Saxon law had a legal right of blood feud has been disputed, but in Alfred's day it was unlawful to begin a feud until an attempt had been made to exact the price of the life *(weregild, q. v.)*.

BLOOD MONEY. A weregild, or pecuniary mulct paid by a slayer to the relatives of his victim. Also used, in a popular sense, as descriptive of money paid by way of reward for the apprehension and conviction of a person charged with a capital crime.

BLOOD STAINS, TESTS FOR. See Precipitin Test.

BLOODHOUNDS. Dogs remarkable for their sense of smell and ability to follow a scent or track a human being. Pedigo v. Com., 103 Ky. 41, 44 S.W. 143, 42 L.R.A. 432, 82 Am.St.Rep. 566.

It has been held that to permit evidence that a hound has tracked an alleged criminal, it must be shown that it had been trained in that work.

BLOODWIT. An amercement for bloodshed. Cowell. The privilege of taking such amercements. Skene. A privilege or exemption from paying a fine or amercement assessed for bloodshed. Cowell.

BLOODY HAND. In forest law. The having the hands or other parts bloody, which, in a person caught trespassing in the forest against venison, was one of the four kinds of circumstantial evidence of his having killed deer, although he was not found in the act of chasing or hunting. Manwood.

BLOWING WATER. By a ship is throwing water in the hold back and forth and forcing it through crevices in the ceiling and coming in contact with the cargo. The Charles Rohde, D.C.Md., 8 F.2d 506.

BLUDGEON. Part of a boy's baseball bat, the upper end of which had been broken off, has been held to be a bludgeon within a statute relating to the carrying of any concealed instrument. People v. McPherson, 220 N.Y. 123, 115 N.E. 515, 516. Contra as to an iron bar, twenty inches long and three-eighths to one-half inch in diameter. People v. Visarities, 222 N.Y.S. 401, 403, 220 App.Div. 657.

BLUE. As applied to a cow, generally denoting either a modified shade of black, or black with white intermingled, or dark gray, dove, or slate color, which, in contrast with some decided color or with white, suggests and somewhat resembles blue. Graham v. State, 16 Ga.App. 221, 84 S.E. 981, 983.

BLUE LAWS. A supposititious code of severe laws for the regulation of religious and personal conduct in the colonies of Connecticut and New Haven; hence any rigid Sunday laws or religious regulations. The assertion by some writers of the existence of the blue laws has no other basis than the adoption, by the first authorities of the New Haven colony, of the Scriptures as their code of law and government, and their strict application of Mosaic principles. Century Dict.

BLUE NOTES. Notes accepted by a life insurance company for the amount of premiums on the policy, which provide for the continuance of the policy in force until the due date of the notes. Robnett v. Cotton States Life Ins. Co., 148 Ark. 199, 230 S.W. 257, 258.

"Extension notes" in insurance parlance. O'Dell v. American Nat. Ins. Co., Mo.App., 107 S.W.2d 108, 110.

BLUE SKY LAW. A popular name for acts providing for the regulation and supervision of investment companies, for the protection of the community from investing in fraudulent companies. A law intended to stop the sale of stock in fly by night concerns, visionary oil wells, distant gold mines, and other like fraudulent exploitations. Dinsmore v. National Hardwood Co., 234 Mich. 436, 208 N.W. 701.

BLUFF. A high, steep bank, as by a river, the sea, a ravine, or a plain, or a bank or headland with a broad, steep face. Columbia City Land Co. v. Ruhl, 70 Or. 246, 141 P. 208, 210.

BLUMBA. A certifying metal tag attached to kosher meat. People on Complaint of Waller v. Jacob Branfman & Son, 263 N.Y.S. 629, 632, 147 Misc. 290.

BLUNDER. As applied in cases of ordinary negligence is the want of or absence of ordinary care, a failure to do what should have been done or the doing of that which should not have been done, resulting in the happening of an event or injury which could have and should have been foreseen and avoided by use of such care as a reasonably prudent person would have exercised under the same or similar circumstances. Loyd v. Pierce, Tex.Civ.App., 89 S.W.2d 1035, 1038.

BLUNDERBUSS. A firearm intended to shoot objects at close quarters, without exact aim. Moline v. Kotch, 213 Minn. 326, 6 N.W.2d 462.

BOARD. An official or representative body organized to perform a trust or to execute official or representative functions or having the management of a public office or department exercising administrative or governmental functions. Commissioners of State Ins. Fund v. Dinowitz, 39 N.Y. S.2d 34, 38, 179 Misc. 278.

A committee of persons organized under authority of law in order to exercise certain authorities, have oversight or control of certain matters, or discharge certain functions of a magisterial, representative, or fiduciary character. Thus, "board of aldermen," "board of health," "board of directors," "board of works."

Also lodging, food, entertainment, furnished to a guest at an inn or boarding house.

When used with reference to prisoners, as a basis for the sheriff's fee, board may be equivalent to "necessary food." Pacific Coal Co. v. Silver Bow County, 79 Mont. 323, 256 P. 386.

"Board," as a verb, means to receive food for a reasonable compensation, either with or without lodging. In re Doubleday, 159 N.Y.S. 947, 949, 173 App.Div. 739; Wofford v. Hooper, 149 Tenn. 250, 259 S.W. 549.

To "board" a train may mean simply to "enter" it. St. Louis, I. M. & S. Ry. Co. v. Williams, 117 Ark. 329, 175 S.W. 411, 412.

BOARD MEASURE. This term, in a contract of sale of lumber for a specified price per thousand feet, literally implies a measurement of lumber having the dimensions of length, width, and thickness, according to the number of cubic inches; but it may be subject to explanation according to the particular circumstances. Paepcke-Leicht Lumber Co. v. Talley, 106 Ark. 400, 153 S.W. 833, 836.

BOARD OF ALDERMEN. The governing body of a municipal corporation. Oliver v. Jersey City, 63 N.J.Law, 96, 42 A. 782. See Aldermen.

BOARD OF AUDIT. A tribunal provided by statute in some states, to adjust and settle the accounts of municipal corporations. Osterhoudt v. Rigney, 98 N.Y. 222.

BOARD OF CIVIL AUTHORITY. In Vermont, in the case of a city this term includes the mayor and aldermen and justices residing therein; in the case of a town, the selectmen and town clerk and the justices residing therein; in the case of a village, the trustees or bailiffs and the justices residing therein. Vt.St.1894, 19, 59 (G.L. 70).

BOARD OF DIRECTORS. The governing body of a private corporation.

Bank's "board of directors" within statute requiring their consent means all directors. Code 1923, § 3412. McLemore v. State, 26 Ala.App. 228, 157 So. 455, 457.

"Township board" and "board of directors" as interchangeable terms. State ex rel. Kent v. Olenhouse, 324 Mo. 49, 23 S.W.2d 83, 85.

BOARD OF EDUCATION. An agency of the state for government and management of a school district. McCurdy v. Board of Education of City of Bloomington, 359 Ill. 188, 194 N.E. 287. The agency to which state delegates power and duty of controlling schools in school district. Charles B. Saxon, Inc., v. Board of Education of Union Free School Dist. No. 1 of Town of Catskill, 168 Misc. 209, 4 N.Y.S.2d 757. Public municipal corporation, Gustafson v. Wethersfield Tp. High School Dist. 191, 319 Ill.App. 255, 49 N.E.2d 311, 312.

BOARD OF EQUALIZATION. See Equalization.

BOARD OF FIRE UNDERWRITERS. Unincorporated voluntary associations composed exclusively of persons engaged in business of fire insurance, for consolidation and co-operation in matters affecting the business. Childs v. Insurance Co., 66 Minn. 393, 69 N.W. 141, 35 L.R.A. 99.

BOARD OF HEALTH. A board or commission with certain powers and duties relative to preservation and improvement of the public health. Gaines v. Waters, 64 Ark. 609, 44 S.W. 353. A term descriptive of an official body. Fisher v. Kelly, 289 N.Y. 161, 44 N.E.2d 413, 416. The "Department of Health" of a city having a commissioner of health as its single executive head, was a "Board of Health". Fisher v. Kelly, 264 App. Div. 596, 36 N.Y.S.2d 497, 499.

BOARD OF MEDICAL EXAMINERS. A board exercising certain powers in respect to licensing osteopathic physicians and surgeons. Jordt v. California State Board of Education, 35 Cal.App.2d 591, 96 P.2d 809, 811.

BOARD OF PARDONS. A board to investigate applications for executive clemency and to make reports and recommendations thereon to the governor.

BOARD OF PUBLIC WORKS. Common council of city in taking action respecting street improvements and making assessments. City of Crown Point v. Newcomer, 204 Ind. 589, 185 N.E. 440, 441.

BOARD OF REVIEW. A quasi judicial body to hear evidence tending to show errors in an assessment roll and to decide whether the assessor's valuation is correct. State v. Williams, 160 Wis. 648, 152 N.W. 450, 451.

BOARD OF SPECIAL INQUIRY. An instrument of executive power, made up of subordinates of the commissioner of immigration with administrative duties. Pearson v. Williams, 202 U.S. 281, 26 S.Ct. 608, 50 L.Ed. 1029.

BOARD OF SUPERVISORS. An organized committee, or body of officials, constituting part of the county government, with special charge of the county revenues.

BOARD OF THE TOWN. The board of education of a school district is a "board of the town."

Charles B. Saxon, Inc., v. Board of Education of Union Free School Dist. No. 1 of Town of Catskill, 168 Misc. 209, 4 N.Y.S.2d 757.

BOARD OF TRADE. An organization for the advancement and protection of business interests. Retailers Credit Ass'n of Alameda County v. Commissioner of Internal Revenue, C.C.A.9, 90 F.2d 47, 51, 111 A.L.R. 152. An organization of merchants, manufacturers, etc., of a city, for furthering its commercial interests, advancing its prosperity, etc. In England, an administrative department of government, for the consideration of matters relating to trade and foreign plantations.

BOARD OF WORKS. A board for the better local management of the English metropolis having the care and management of grounds and gardens; the superintendence of drainage; the regulation of street traffic and of the buildings of the metropolis. Brown.

BOARDER. One who makes a special contract for food with or without lodging. Berkshire Woollen Co. v. Proctor, 7 Cush., Mass., 424; One who boards at a boarding house or school. Atlantic City v. Le Beck, 125 N.J.L. 373, 15 A.2d 653, 654. One who has food and lodging for an agreed price, usually under a contract intended to continue for a considerable period of time. Ullman v. State, 1 Tex.App. 220, 28 Am.Rep. 405.

A guest, as distinguished from boarder, comes and remains without any bargain for *time,* and may go away when he pleases. Stewart v. McCready, 24 How.Prac., N.Y., 62; In re Doubleday, 173 App.Div. 739, 159 N.Y.S. 947, 949.

BOARDING HOUSE. A house where the business of keeping boarders generally is carried on, and which is held out by the owner or keeper as a place where boarders are kept; one for the accommodation of those who enter under contract for entertainment at a certain rate for a certain period of time, as for a week or month, at a rate of compensation agreed on; a house kept principally for the residence of permanent boarders. Singelakis v. Davidson, 117 N.J.L. 332, 188 A. 443, 444. A sort of public house, partaking in some degree of the character of an inn or restaurant. Baddour v. City of Long Beach, 279 N.Y. 167, 18 N.E.2d 18, 21, 124 A.L.R. 1003. A *quasi* public house, where boarders are generally and habitually kept, and which is held out and known as a place of entertainment of that kind. Cady v. McDowell, 1 Lans., N.Y. 486; Friedrich Music House v. Harris, 200 Mich. 421, 166 N.W. 869, L.R.A.1918D, 400.

A house occupied for carrying on the business of keeping boarders, although while prosecuting the business and as a means of prosecuting it, the occupant and his wife and children live in the house. Trainor v. Le Beck, 101 N.J.Eq. 823, 139 A. 16, 17. A boarding-house and an inn or hotel differs in, that in a boarding-house the guest is under an express contract, while in an inn there is no express agreement. Willard v. Reinhardt, 2 E. D. Smith, N. Y., 148; McIntosh v. Schops, 92 Or. 307, 180 P. 593. An innkeeper is also bound to receive a guest when he presents himself. 2 El. & Bl. 144; McClaugherty v. Cline, 128 Tenn. 605, 163 S.W. 801. A "boarding-house" is also less public in character. State v. Brown, 112 Kan. 814, 212 P. 663, 664, 31 A.L.R. 338. See, also, Talbott v. Southern Seminary, 131 Va. 576, 109 S.E. 440, 19 A.L.R. 534. A "rooming house" differs from a "boarding-house" only in that the latter furnishes meals. City of Independence v. Richardson, 117 Kan. 656, 232 P. 1044, 1046. A boarding school, however, is not a boarding-house within a lien statute. Talbott v. Southern Seminary, 131 Va. 576, 109 S.E. 440, 441, 19 A.L.R. 534.

BOARIUS, *adj.* Lat. Relating to neat cattle. See Bovarius.

BOAT. A small open vessel, or water craft, usually moved by oars or rowing.

It is commonly distinguished in law from a ship or vessel, by being of smaller size and without a deck. The Saxon, D.C.S.C., 269 F. 639, 641. But "boat" and "vessel" are often used synonymously. Southern Pac. Co. v. Jensen, 244 U.S. 205, 37 S.Ct. 524, 527, 61 L.Ed. 1086, L.R.A. 1918C, 451. And see State v. Hutchins, 79 N.H. 132, 105 A. 519, 521, 2 A.L.R. 1685 ("boats and rafts" held broad enough to cover all water craft, not merely small rowboats). The verb "boat" means to go in a boat. Chappell v. Commercial Casualty Ins. Co., 120 W.Va. 262, 197 S.E. 723, 724.

International rule that sailing vessels shall keep out of way of sailing vessels or boats fishing with nets or lines or trawls does not apply to craft 55 feet long equipped with machinery powerful enought to handle a trawl which would ordinarily be decked over, would have living accommodations for crew, etc. International Rules, art. 26, 33 U.S.C.A. § 111. The Virginia and Joan, C.C.A.Mass., 86 F.2d 259, 261. Seaplanes equipped with pontoons or hulls having hydroplaning surfaces are "hydroplane boats" though provided with wings. Fauber v. United States, Ct. Cl., 37 F.Supp. 415, 435.

BOATABLE. A term applied in some states to minor rivers and streams capable of being navigated in small boats, skiffs, or launches, though not by steam or sailing vessels. New England Trout, etc., Club v. Mather, 68 Vt. 338, 35 A. 323, 33 L.R.A. 569.

A "boatable stream" is one of common passage as a high way. Boutwell v. Champlain Realty Co., 89 Vt. 80, 94 A. 108, 111, Ann.Cas.1918A, 726.

BOATING. Conveyance by a boat, of whatever kind, of persons or freight. Bosworth v. Nelson, 172 Ga. 612, 158 S.E. 306, 307.

BOATSWAIN. A seaman who superintends the work of the crew. South Atlantic S. S. Co. of Delaware v. Munkacsy, Del., 7 W.W.Harr. 580, 187 A. 600, 604. The foreman of sailors. McCauley v. Pacific Atlantic S. S. Co., 167 Or. 80, 115 P.2d 307, 308.

BOB-TAIL DRIVER. A person collecting and delivering laundry without being subject to complete control of employer. Ring v. City Dry Cleaners, Fla., 152 Fla. 622, 12 So.2d 593, 594.

BOBTAILED CABOOSE. One with a door in the front end and without any platform. St. Louis Southwestern Ry. Co. of Texas v. Johnson, Tex. Civ.App., 249 S.W. 1092.

BOBTAILS. Persons who conduct stores or establishments of their own where patrons may bring articles to be laundered. Schwartz v. Laundry & Linen Supply Drivers' Union, Local 187, 339 Pa. 353, 14 A.2d 438, 439.

BOC. In Saxon law. A book or writing; a deed or charter. *Boc land,* deed or charter land. *Land boc,* a writing for conveying land; a deed or charter; a land-book. The *land-bocs,* or evidences of title, corresponding to modern deeds, were destroyed by William the Conqueror.

BOC HORDE. A place where books, writings, or evidences were kept, generally in monasteries. Cowell.

BOC LAND. In Saxon law. Allodial lands held by deed or other written evidence of title.

BOCERAS. Sax. A scribe, notary, or chancellor among the Saxons.

BODILY. Pertaining to or concerning the body; of or belonging to the body or the physical constitution; not mental but corporeal. Electric R. Co. v. Lauer, 21 Ind.App. 466, 52 N.E. 703; Provident Life & Accident Ins. Co. v. Campbell, 18 Tenn. App. 452, 79 S.W.2d 296.

Under a health insurance policy the words "bodily disease or illness" have been held to embrace insanity. American Nat. Ins. Co. v. Denman, Tex.Civ.App., 260 S.W. 226, 227; Syphilis and insanity caused by syphilis. Magill v. Travelers Ins. Co., C.C.A.Mo., 133 F.2d 709, 712.

Bodily Harm

Any touching of the person of another against his will with physical force, in an intentional, hostile, and aggressive manner, or a projecting of such force against his person. People v. Moore, 50 Hun, 356, 3 N.Y.Supp. 159. Any impairment of physical condition of another's body or physical pain or illness, but does not include minute disturbance of nerve centers caused by fear, shock or other emotions. Clark v. Associated Retail Creditmen of Washington, 70 App.D.C. 183, 105 F.2d 62, 64.

Bodily Heirs

Heirs begotten or borne by the person referred to; lineal descendants. Turner v. Hause, 199 Ill. 464, 65 N.E. 445; Righter v. Forrester, 1 Bush, Ky., 278.

Progeny or issue, including children, grandchildren, and other lineal descendants. Matthews v. Matthews, 214 N.C. 204, 198 S.E. 663, 665. Children synonymous. Murdock v. Deal, 208 N.C. 754, 182 S.E. 466. Heirs of body synonymous, Williamson v. Cox, 218 N.C. 177, 10 S.E.2d 662, 666. Adopted child as included in words "bodily heirs", Leeper v. Leeper, 347 Mo. 442, 147 S.W.2d 660, 663, 133 A.L.R. 586. Words of limitation, Kinnaird v. Farmers' & Merchants' Bank, 249 Ky. 661, 61 S.W.2d 291.

Bodily Infirmity

A settled disease or ailment that would probably result to some degree in general impairment of physical health and vigor. Travelers' Ins. Co. of Hartford, Conn., v. Byers, 123 Cal.App. 473, 11 P.2d 444, 446; Ross v. First American Ins. Co., 125 Neb. 329, 250 N.W. 75, 79. An ailment or disorder of an established and settled character. Maremont v. Lawyers Mut. Ben. Ass'n, 294 Ill. App. 605, 13 N.E.2d 849; Ross v. First American Ins. Co., 125 Neb. 329, 250 N.W. 75, 79; something that amounts to inroad on physical health or impairment of bodily or mental powers. McClure v. World Ins. Co., 126 Neb. 676, 254 N.W. 393; Gyulai v. Prudential Ins. Co. of America, 135 Pa. Super. 73, 4 A.2d 824, 826.

Bodily Injury

Any physical or corporeal injury; not necessarily restricted to injury to the trunk or main part of the body as distinguished from the head or limbs. State Life Ins. Co. v. Allison, C.C.A.Ala., 269 F. 93, 94, 14 A.L.R. 412; Ross v. International Travelers Ass'n, Tex.Civ.App., 283 S.W. 621. A physical injury only. United States Fidelity & Guaranty Co. v. Shrigley, D.C.Ark., 26 F.Supp. 625, 628. A cut, bruise, or wound. Chase v. Business Men's Assur. Co. of America, C.C.A.Utah, 51 F.2d 34, 36. A localized abnormal condition of the living body. King v. Travelers Ins. Co., 123 Conn. 1, 192 A. 311. An injury caused by external violence. Brannaker v. Prudential Ins. Co. of America, 236 Mo.App. 239, 150 S.W.2d 498, 502. Burns v. Employers' Liability Assur. Corporation, Limited, of London, England, 134 Ohio St. 222, 16 N.E.2d 316, 321, 117 A.L.R. 733.

"Bodily injuries" and "personal injuries" are not synonymous. Malone v. Costa, 151 Fla. 144, 9 So.2d 275, 277. "Bodily injury" and "personal injury" may be used as equivalent terms. Cormier v. Hudson, 284 Mass. 231, 187 N.E. 625, 626. American Fidelity & Casualty Co. v. Mahon, 170 Md. 573, 185 A. 330, 332, 105 A.L.R. 1200.

Bodily Member

An ear is not embraced in the term "member". Lumbermens Mut. Casualty Co. v. Cook, 69 Ga. App. 131, 25 S.E.2d 67, 71.

Great Bodily Harm

An injury of a greater and more serious kind than battery. Shires v. Boggess, 72 W.Va. 109, 77 S.E. 542, 545. Equivalent to "maim." State v. Foster, 281 Mo. 618, 220 S.W. 958, 959.

Great Bodily Injury

An injury of a more grave and serious character than an ordinary battery, but one which cannot be definitely defined. State v. Ockij, 165 Iowa, 237, 145 N.W. 486, 487; Hallett v. State, 109 Neb. 311, 190 N.W. 862, 863.

BODMERIE, BODEMERIE, BODDEMEREY. Belg. and Germ. Bottomry *(q. v.)*.

BODY. A person. Used of a natural body, or of an artificial one created by law, as a corporation.

The main part of the human body; the trunk. Walker v. State, 34 Fla. 167, 16 So. 80, 43 Am.St. Rep. 186. The term may, however, embrace all members of the person, Louisville Ry. Co. v. Veith, 157 Ky. 424, 163 S.W. 217; including the head, Franklin v. State, 33 Ohio Cir.Ct.R. 21, 22.

Also the main part of an instrument; in deeds it is spoken of as distinguished from the recitals and other introductory parts and signatures; in *affidavits,* from the title and jurat.

A collection of laws; that is, the embodiment of the laws in one connected statement or collection, called a "body of laws" *(q. v.)*.

A cement mixer assembled on a truck, Consolidated Rock Products Co. v. Carter, 54 Cal.App.2d 519, 129 P.2d

455, 457. The Workmen's Benefit Fund of the United States of America. In re Workmen's Benefit Fund of United States, 38 N.Y.S.2d 429, 431, 265 App.Div. 176.

BODY CORPORATE. A corporation public or private.

School districts, Commonwealth v. School Dist. of Pittsburgh, Allegheny County, 343 Pa. 394, 23 A.2d 496. State Building Commission, Utah State Building Commission, for Use and Benefit of Mountain States Supply Co., v. Great American Indemnity Co., 105 Utah 11, 140 P.2d 763, 767.

BODY EXECUTION. An "execution" for confinement of defendant, Hershey v. People, 91 Colo. 113, 12 P.2d 345, 347.

A "body execution" is an "execution" which directs that, in accordance with the provisions therein set forth, the body of the defendant therein named be committed to jail. Ex parte Thompson, 111 Vt. 7, 9 A.2d 107, 110.

BODY HEIRS. Sometimes words of purchase. Brown v. Boone, 129 Kan. 786, 284 P. 436, 437.

BODY OF A COUNTY. A county at large, as distinguished from any particular place within it. A county considered as a territorial whole. State v. Arthur, 39 Iowa, 632; People v. Dunn, 31 App. Div. 139, 52 N.Y.Supp. 968.

BODY OF AN INSTRUMENT. The main and operative part; the substantive provisions, as distinguished from the recitals, title, jurat, etc.

BODY OF LAWS. An organized and systematic collection of rules of jurisprudence.

BODY OF THE OFFENSE. When applied to any particular offense, means that the particular crime charged has actually been committed by some one. Barrett v. State, 57 Okl. 259, 47 P.2d 613, 617.

BODY POLITIC OR CORPORATE. A social compact by which the whole people covenants with each citizen, and each citizen with the whole people, that all shall be governed by certain laws for the common good, Uricich v. Kolesar, 54 Ohio App. 309, 7 N.E.2d 413, 414. A term applied to a corporation. County. Bazzoli v. Larson, 40 Ohio App. 321, 178 N.E. 331, 332; Lindburg v. Bennett, 117 Neb. 66, 219 N.W. 851, 855. Municipality. Middle-States Utilities Co. v. City of Osceola, 1 N.W.2d 643, 645, 231 Iowa 462; Lindburg v. Bennett, 117 Neb. 66, 219 N.W. 851, 855. School district. Patrick v. Maybank, 198 S.C. 262, 17 S.E.2d 530, 534.

State or nation or public associations, Utah State Building Commission, for Use and Benefit of Mountain States Supply Co., v. Great American Indemnity Co., 105 Utah 11, 140 P.2d 763, 767.

BOILARY. Water arising from a salt well belonging to a person who is not the owner of the soil.

BOILER. Insurance policies defining a boiler as a receptacle in which steam is generated, including the stop valve nearest the boiler, have been held not to include a nipple screwed into the outlet of the stop valve, Cambria Coal Mining Co. v. Travelers' Indemnity Co., 144 Tenn. 469, 234 S.W. 323, 324, nor the whistle pipe above the whistle valve, Norfolk & W. Ry. Co. v. Royal Indemnity Co., D.C.Pa., 257 F. 849, 850; nor damage by gas explosion in fire box and chimney, Hartford Steam Boiler Inspection & Insurance Co. v. Kleinman, Tex.Civ.App., 293 S.W. 894, 895.

Under the Boiler Inspection Act Feb. 17, 1911, § 2, 45 U.S.C.A. § 23, a locomotive cab is an appurtenance to the boiler, Brown v. Lehigh Valley R. Co., 108 Misc. 384, 177 N.Y.S. 618, 619; and a bell ringer is a part or appurtenance of a locomotive and tender, Hines v. Smith, C.C.A.Ill., 275 F. 766, 767; but not a so-called trail car similar to a flat car, used exclusively in switching cars or trains onto a transfer boat, for the purpose of preventing the great weight of the locomotive from being placed on the apron or approaches of the transfer boat, Alabama & V. Ry. Co. v. Ware, 129 Miss. 315, 92 So. 161, 162.

BOILS. A policy, providing for the payment of indemnity in the event the insured suffered from "boils," is clear and explicit, and does not cover disability occasioned by a disease designated as "ischio-rectal abscess." Midland Casualty Co. v. Mason, 55 Okl. 93, 154 P. 1171, 1172. A localized inflammatory swelling of the skin. Beck v. State, 29 Ala.App. 410, 197 So. 42, 43.

BOIS, or BOYS. L. Fr. Wood; timber; brush.

BOLHAGIUM, or BOLDAGIUM. A little house or cottage. Blount.

BOLT. The desertion by one or more persons from the political party to which he or they belong; the permanent withdrawal before adjournment of a portion of the delegates to a political convention. Rap. & L.

A mass or block of wood from which anything may be cut or formed. St. Louis, I. M. & S. R. Co. v. J. F. Hasty & Sons, 255 U.S. 252, 41 S.Ct. 269, 270, 65 L.Ed. 614.

BOLTING. In English practice. A term formerly used in the English inns of court, but more particularly at Gray's Inn, signifying the private arguing of cases, as distinguished from *mooting*, which was a more formal and public mode of argument. Cowell; Tomlins; Holthouse.

BOMBAY REGULATIONS. Regulations passed for the presidency of Bombay, and the territories subordinate thereto. They were passed by the governors in council of Bombay until the year 1834, when the power of local legislation ceased, and the acts relating thereto were thenceforth passed by the governor general of India in council. Mozley & Whitley.

BON. Fr. In old French law, a royal order or check on the treasury, invented by Francis I. *Bon pour mille livres,* good for a thousand livres. Step.Lect. 387.

In modern law. The name of a clause (*bon pour* ———, good for so much) added to a cedule or promise, where it is not in the handwriting of the signer, containing the amount of the sum which he obliges himself to pay. Poth.Obl. part 4, ch. 1, art. 2, § 1.

BONA. Lat. *n.* Goods; property; possessions. In the Roman law, this term was used to designate all species of property, real, personal, and mixed, but was more strictly applied to real estate. In modern civil law, it includes both personal property (technically so called) and chattels real, thus corresponding to the French *biens (q. v.)*. In the common law, its use was confined to the description of movable goods. Tisdale v. Harris, 20 Pick. (Mass.) 13.

Bona Confiscata

Goods confiscated or forfeited to the imperial *fisc* or treasury. 1 Bl.Comm. 299.

Bona et Catalla

Goods and chattles. Movable property. This expression includes all personal things that belong to a man. 16 Mees. & W. 68.

Bona Felonum

In English law. Goods of felons; the goods of one convicted of felony. 5 Coke, 110.

Bona Forisfacta

Goods forfeited.

Bona Fugitivorum

In English law. Goods of fugitives; the proper goods of him who flies for felony. 5 Coke, 109*b*.

Bona Immobilia

Lands. Castle v. Castle, C.C.A.Haw., 267 F. 521, 522.

Bona Mobilia

In the civil law. Movables. Castle v. Castle, C.C.A. Haw., 267 F. 521, 522. Those things which move themselves or can be transported from one place to another, and not permanently attached to a farm, heritage, or building.

Bona Notabilia

Notable goods; property worthy of notice, or of sufficient value to be accounted for. 2 Bl.Comm. 509; Rolle, Abr. 908. Moore v. Jordan, 36 Kan. 271, 13 P. 337, 59 Am. Rep. 550.

Bona Paraphernalia

In the civil law. The separate property of a married woman other than that which is included in her dowry; more particularly, her clothing, jewels, and ornaments. Whiton v. Snyder, 88 N.Y. 303.

Bona Peritura

Goods of a perishable nature; such goods as an executor or trustee must use diligence in disposing of and converting them into money.

Bona Utlagatorum

Goods of outlaws; goods belonging to persons outlawed.

Bona Vacantia

Vacant, unclaimed, or stray goods. Those things in which nobody claims a property, and which belonged, under the common law, to the finder, except in certain instances, when they were the property of the king. 1 Bl.Comm. 298.

Bona Waviata

In English law. Waived goods: goods stolen and *waived*, that is, thrown away by the thief in his flight, for fear of being apprehended, or to facilitate his escape; and which go to the sovereign. 5 Coke, 109*b*; 1 Bl.Comm. 296.

BONA. Lat. *adj.* Good. Used in numerous legal phrases of which the following are the principal:

Bona Fides

Good faith; integrity of dealing; honesty; sincerity; the opposite of *mala fides* and of *dolus malus*.

Bona Gestura

Good abearance or behavior.

Bona Gratia

In the Roman law. By mutual consent; voluntarily. A term applied to a species of divorce where the parties separated by mutual consent; or where the parties renounced their marital engagements without assigning any cause, or upon mere pretexts. Tayl. Civil Law, 361 362; Calvin.

Bona Memoria

Good memory. Generally used in the phrase *sanæ mentis et bonæ memoriæ*, of sound mind and good memory, as descriptive of the mental capacity of a testator.

Bona Patria

In the Scotch law. An assize or jury of good neighbors. Bell.

BONA FIDE. In or with good faith; honestly, openly, and sincerely; without deceit or fraud. M. Lowenstein & Sons v. British-American Mfg. Co., C.C.A.Conn., 7 F.2d 51, 53; Fairfield Holding Corporation v. Souther, 258 Mass. 540, 155 N.E. 639, 640. Truly; actually; without simulation or pretense. Innocently; in the attitude of trust and confidence; without notice of fraud, etc. Real, actual, genuine, and not feigned. Bridgeport Mortgage & Realty Corporation v. Whitlock, 128 Conn. 57, 20 A.2d 414, 416.

The phrase "*bona fide*" is sometimes used ambiguously; thus, the expression "*bona fide* holder for value" (see that title, *infra*) may either mean a holder for real value, as opposed to a holder for pretended value, or it may mean a holder for real value without notice of any fraud, etc. Byles, Bills, 121.

Bona Fide Contract Carriers

Genuine contract carriers without deceit or fraud. Infantino v. Pennsylvania Public Utility Commission, 146 Pa.Super. 245, 22 A.2d 108, 109; Puhl v. Pennsylvania Public Utility Commission, 139 Pa.Super. 152, 11 A.2d 508, 511.

Bona Fide Holder for Value

An innocent or "bona fide holder for value" of negotiable paper is one who has taken it in good faith for a valuable consideration in the ordinary course of business and when it was not overdue. McCamant v. McCamant, Tex.Civ.App., 187 S.W. 1096, 1099. "Holder in due course" as equivalent for expression "bona fide holder for value without notice." Drumm Const. Co. v. Forbes, 305 Ill. 303, 137 N.E. 225, 226, 26 A.L.R. 764; Bank of California v. National City Co., 138 Wash. 517, 244 P. 690, 691; Bruce v. Citizens' Nat. Bank of Lineville, 185 Ala. 221, 64 So. 82, 84; Weller v. Meadows, Mo.App., 272 S.W. 85, 90. One who receives negotiable paper in payment of antecedent obligations without notice of prior equities. W. Horace Williams Co. v. Vandaveer, Brown & Stoy, Tex.Civ.App., 84 S.W.2d 333, 340.

Bona Fide Judgment Creditor

One who in good faith, without fraud or collusion, recovers a judgment for money honestly due him. Rochester Trust Co. v. White, 243 Pa. 469, 90 A. 127, 129.

Bona Fide Mortgagee

Essential elements of status are good faith, valuable consideration, and absence of notice. Companaro v. Gondolfo, C.C.A.N.J., 60 F.2d 451, 452. To constitute "bona fide mortgagee" there must be an absence of notice and payment of, or fixed liability for the consideration. Cambridge Production Credit Ass'n v. Patrick, 140 Ohio St. 521, 45 N.E.2d 751, 755, 144 A.L.R. 323.

Bona Fide Operation

Substantial, as distinguished from incidental, sporadic, or infrequent service. Goncz v. Interstate Commerce Commission, D.C.Mass., 48 F.Supp. 286, 288.

Bona Fide Possessor

One who not only supposes himself to be the true proprietor of the land, but who is ignorant that his title is contested by some other person claiming a better right to it. Whitehead v. Barker, 288 Mich. 19, 284 N.W. 629, 631.

Bona Fide Possessor Facit Fructus Consumptos Suos

By good faith a possessor makes the fruits consumed his own. Tray. Lat. Max. 57.

Bona Fide Purchaser

A purchaser in good faith for valuable consideration and without notice. Neal v. Holt, Tex.Civ.App., 69 S.W.2d 603, 609. A purchaser for a valuable consideration paid or parted with in the belief that the vendor had a right to sell, and without any suspicious circumstances to put him on inquiry. Merritt v. Railroad Co., 12 Barb., N. Y., 605. One who acts without covin, fraud, or collusion; one who, in the commission of or connivance at no fraud, pays full price for the property, and in good faith, honestly, and in fair dealing buys and goes into possession. Sanders v. McAffee, 42 Ga. 250. One who at time of purchase advances a new consideration, surrenders some security, or does some other act which leaves him in a worse position if his purchase should be set aside. Kelly v. Grainey, 113 Mont. 520, 129 P.2d 619, 626. Title, possession, and want of notice, either actual or constructive, as the essential factors. Taylor v. Lindenmann, 211 Iowa, 1122, 235 N.W. 310, 312. Payment of consideration prior to notice of adverse claim as essential. The J. Oswald Boyd, D.C.Mich., 53 F.Supp. 103, 106. Payment of valuable consideration, good faith, absence of purpose to take unfair advantage of third persons, and absence of actual or constructive notice of outstanding rights of others as the essential elements. Luschen v. Stanton, 192 Okl. 454, 137 P.2d 567, 570. "Innocent purchaser for value" and "bona fide purchaser" as synonymous. Felts v. Whitaker, Tex. Civ.App., 129 S.W.2d 682, 690.

Bona Fide Residence

Residence with domiciliary intent, i. e., a home in which the party actually lives. Alburger v. Alburger, 138 Pa.Super. 339, 10 A.2d 888, 890.

BONA FIDES EXIGIT UT QUOD CONVENIT FIAT. Good faith demands that what is agreed upon shall be done. Dig. 19, 20, 21; Id. 19, 1, 50; Id. 50, 8, 2, 13.

BONÆ FIDEI NON CONGRUIT DE APICIBUS JURIS DISPUTARE. It is unbecoming to (or incompatible with) good faith to discuss (insist upon) the extreme subtleties of the law. A maxim which may be more freely rendered as meaning, "To insist on extreme subtleties of law is an encouragement to fraud." Adams. Gloss.

BONA FIDES NON PATITUR UT BIS IDEM EXIGATUR. Good faith does not allow us to demand twice the payment of the same thing. Dig. 50, 17, 57; Broom, Max. 338, note; Perine v. Dunn, 4 Johns.Ch., N.Y., 143.

BONÆ FIDEI. In the civil law. Of good faith; ir good faith.

BONÆ FIDEI CONTRACTS. In civil and Scotch law. Those contracts in which equity may interpose to correct inequalities, and to adjust all matters according to the plain intention of the parties. 1 Kames, Eq. 200.

BONÆ FIDEI EMPTOR. A purchaser in good faith. One who either was ignorant that the thing he bought belonged to another or supposed that the seller had a right to sell it. Dig. 50, 16, 109. See Id. 6, 2, 7, 11.

BONÆ FIDEI POSSESSOR. A possessor in good faith. One who believes that no other person has a better right to the possession than himself. Mackeld.Rom.Law, § 243.

BONÆ FIDEI POSSESSOR IN ID TANTUM QUOD SESE PERVENERIT TENETUR. A possessor in good faith is liable only for that which he himself has obtained (or that which has come to him). 2 Inst. 285.

BONANZA. Enormous profit for miner in placer mine. Ballagh v. Williams, 50 Cal.App.2d 10, 122 P.2d 343, 344.

BOND. A certificate or evidence of a debt. State v. Merchants Nat. Bank of Mobile, 230 Ala. 661, 162 So. 270; First State Bank of Kansas City v. Bone, 122 Kan. 493, 252 P. 250, 254. A contract. Cusack v. McGrain, 136 Ohio St. 27, 23 N.E.2d 633, 635. A debt on which interest is paid. Commissioner of Internal Revenue v. H. P. Hood & Sons, C.C.A.1, 141 F.2d 467, 469. A deed whereby the obligor obliges himself, his heirs, executors and administrators, to pay a certain sum of money to another at a day appointed. Gural v. Engle, 128 N.J.L. 252, 25 A.2d 257, 260; Commonwealth, for Use of Fayette County v. Perry, 330 Pa. 355, 199 A. 204, 206. A mere promise to pay. Deppe v. Lufkin, C.C.A.Mass., 116 F.2d 483, 486. A specialty or sealed instrument and not merely a written instrument. Forrest v. Hawkins, 169 Va. 470, 194 S.E. 721, 722. A written obligation. Davis v. Phipps, 191 Ark. 298, 85 S.W.2d 1020, 1023, 100 A.L.R. 1110; Covington Virginian v. Woods, 182 Va. 538, 29 S.E.2d 406; Code Miss.1930, § 1365. An instrument which is not necessarily under seal. Carson, Pirie, Scott & Co. v. Duffy-Powers, Inc., D.C.N.Y., 9 F.Supp. 199, 201; Code Miss.1930, § 1365. An instrument with a clause, with a sum fixed as a penalty, binding the parties to pay the same, conditioned, however, that the payment of the penalty may be avoided by the performance by some one or more of the parties of certain acts. In re Fitch, 3 Redf.Sur., N.Y., 459. And see Stifel Estate Co. v. Cella, 220 Mo.App. 657, 291 S.W. 515, 518. Any contractual funding device. Leon County v. State, 122 Fla. 505, 165 So. 666. Debentures. First State Bank of Kansas City v. Bone, 122 Kan. 493, 252 P. 250, 254. Obligation to pay interest embodied in bonds as included in word "bonds." Eisiminger v. Elliott, Colo., 103 Colo. 216, 84 P.2d 823, 825.

In old Scotch law. A bond-man; a slave. Skene.

Bonds are either single (simple) or double, (conditional.) A *single* bond is one in which the obligor binds himself, his heirs, etc., to pay a certain sum of money to another person at a specified day. A *double* (or conditional) bond is one to which a condition is added that if the obligor does or forbears from doing some act the obligation shall be void. Formerly such a condition was sometimes contained in a separate instrument, and was then called a "defeasance."

Word "bond" in a statute means negotiable bonds. Royal Oak Drain. Dist., Oakland County v. Keefe, C.C.A. Ohio, 87 F.2d 786. Word "bonds" in statute held applicable to a single bond. Lien Law N.Y. § 231. In re Downtown Athletic Club of New York City, D.C.N.Y., 18 F.Supp. 712, 715.

As a verb, to place under the conditions of a bond; specif.: to convert into a debt secured by bonds. State ex rel. Pittman Bros. Const. Co. v. Watson, 199 La. 623, 6 So.2d 709, 712. To give bond for, as for duties on goods; to secure payment of duties, by giving bond. *Bonded,* secured by bond. Bonded goods are those for the duties on which bonds are given.

Bond and Disposition in Security

In Scotch law. A bond and mortgage on land.

Bond and Mortgage

A species of security, consisting of a bond conditioned for the repayment of a loan of money, and a mortgage of realty to secure the performance of the stipulations of the bond. Meigs v. Bunting, 141 Pa. 233, 21 A. 588, 23 Am.St. Rep. 273.

A bond and mortgage are distinct and separate securities. In re Maroney's Estate, 311 Pa. 336, 166 A. 914, 915. "Bond" is primarily contract to pay while "mortgage" is separate contract to secure payment. Mendelson v. Realty Mortg. Corporation, 257 Mich. 442, 241 N.W. 154, 155.

Investment in certificates of participation in bonds and mortgages as within statute authorizing investment in "bonds and mortgages". In re Smith, 279 N.Y. 479, 18 N.E.2d 666, 670.

Bond Creditor

A creditor whose debt is secured by a bond.

Bond for Deed

An agreement to make title in the future or an executory or incomplete sale. Ingram v. Smith, 62 Ga.App. 335, 7 S.E.2d 922, 926. An agreement to buy and sell real estate on small monthly payments. Galverina v. Ben L. Lewis Corporation, La.App., 165 So. 29.

Bond for Title

An agreement to make title in the future or an executory or incomplete sale. Ingram v. Smith, 62 Ga.App. 335, 7 S.E.2d 922, 926. White v. Stokes, 67 Ark. 184, 53 S.W. 1060. In re Phœnix Planing Mill, D.C.Ga., 250 F. 899, 903. It is not a conveyance of legal title but only a contract to convey and may ripen into an equitable title upon payment of the consideration. Faddell v. Taylor, Tex.Com.App., 239 S.W. 931, 932.

Bond Issue

Delivery of instruments as covered by term. Vans Agnew v. Fort Myers Drainage Dist., C.C.A.Fla., 69 F.2d 244, 245.

Bond of Indebtedness

Instruments containing promise to pay sum certain under seal and issued in series in nature of corporate securities. Bellefield Co. v. Heiner, D.C.Pa., 26 F.2d 292, 293. A temporary bond in registered form issued by public service corporation. Wisconsin Public Service Corporation v. United States, D.C.Wis., 40 F.Supp. 327, 330.

Bond of Such Ordinary

Bond that the ordinary gives for the faithful performance of duties as clerk. Jones v. Reed, 58 Ga.App. 72, 197 S.E. 665, 668.

Bond Tenants

In English law. Copyholders and customary tenants are sometimes so called. 2 Bl.Comm. 148.

Bond with Surety

Bond executed without surety but accompanied by certified check as substitute. Clinch Valley Lumber Corporation v. Hagan Estates, Inc., 167 Va. 1, 187 S.E. 440, 441.

Bonds of State or Public Corporation

State's or city's general obligation bonds. City of Los Angeles v. Agardy, 1 Cal.2d 76, 33 P.2d 834, 835.

Claim Bond

Primarily in nature of forthcoming bond. Sanders v. Farrier, Tex.Civ.App., 271 S.W.2d 293, 298.

Corporate Bonds

See Corporate Bonds.

Forthcoming Bond

A bond conditioned that a certain article shall be forthcoming at a certain time or when called for. See Claim bond.

General Mortgage Bond

A bond secured upon an entire corporate property, parts of which are subject to one or more prior mortgages.

Heritable Bond

In Scotch law, a bond for a sum of money to which is joined a conveyance of land or of heritage, to be held by the creditor in security of the debt.

Income Bonds

Bonds on which interest is payable only when earned and after payment of interest upon prior mortgages.

Indemnity Bond

See Indemnity Bond.

Liability Bond

One which is intended to protect the assured from liability for damages or to protect the persons damaged by injuries occasioned by the assured as specified, when such liability should accrue, and be imposed by law, as by a court, as distinguished from an indemnity bond, whose purpose is only to indemnify the assured against actual loss by way of reimbursement for moneys paid or which must be paid. Fenton v. Poston, 114 Wash. 217, 195 P. 31, 33.

Lloyd's Bond

A bond issued for work done or goods delivered and bearing interest.

Municipal Bond

See Municipal bonds.

Official Bond

A bond given by a public officer, conditioned that he shall well and faithfully perform all the duties of the office. The term is sometimes made to include the bonds of executors, guardians, trustees, etc.

Railroad Aid Bonds

Bonds issued by municipal corporations to aid in the construction of railways.

Redelivery Bond

A statutory bond given by a person in whose possession attached property is found in order to regain possession of the property. Burnham-Munger-Root Dry Goods Co. v. Strahl, 102 Neb. 142, 166 N.W. 266.

Simple Bond

At common law, a bond without penalty; a bond for the payment of a definite sum of money to a named obligee on demand or on a day certain. Burnside v. Wand, 170 Mo. 531, 71 S.W. 337, 62 L.R.A. 427.

Single Bond

A deed whereby the obligor obliges himself, his heirs, executors, and administrators, to pay a certain sum of money to the obligee at a day named, without terms of defeasance.

Straw Bond

A bond upon which is used either the names of fictitious persons or those unable to pay the sum guaranteed; generally applied to insufficient bail bonds, improperly taken.

BONDAGE. Slavery; involuntary personal servitude; captivity. In old English law, villenage, villein tenure. 2 Bl.Comm. 92.

BONDED INDEBTEDNESS. Indebtedness lawfully contracted for corporate purposes, payable from taxes on all property within municipality. Bolton v. Wharton, 163 S.C. 242, 161 S.E. 454, 460.

BONDED WAREHOUSE. See Warehouse System.

BONDSMAN. A surety; one who has entered into a bond as surety. The word seems to apply especially to the sureties upon the bonds of officers, trustees, etc., while *bail* should be reserved for the sureties on recognizances and bail-bonds. Haberstich v. Elliott, 189 Ill. 70, 59 N.E. 557.

BONES GENTS. L. Fr. In old English law. Good men (of the jury).

BONI HOMINES. In old European law. Good men; a name given in early European jurisprudence to the tenants of the lord, who judged each other in the lord's courts. 3 Bl.Comm. 349.

BONI JUDICIS EST AMPLIARE JURISDICTIONEM. It is the part of a good judge to enlarge (or use liberally) his remedial authority or jurisdiction. 1 C.B.N.S. 255; 4 Bingh.N.C. 233; 4 Scott N.R. 229.

BONI JUDICIS EST AMPLIARE JUSTITIAM. It is the duty of a good judge to enlarge or extend justice. 1 Burr. 304.

BONI JUDICIS EST JUDICIUM SINE DILATIONE MANDARE EXECUTIONI. It is the duty of a good judge to cause judgment to be executed without delay. Co.Litt. 289.

BONI JUDICIS EST LITES DIRIMERE, NE LIS EX LITE ORITUR, ET INTEREST REIPUBLICÆ UT SINT FINES LITIUM. It is the duty of a good judge to prevent litigations, that suit may not grow out of suit, and it concerns the welfare of a state that an end be put to litigation. 4 Coke, 15*b*; 5 Coke, 31*a*.

BONIFICATION. The remission of a tax, particularly on goods intended for export, having the same effect as a bonus or drawback. A device enabling a commodity to be exported and sold in the foreign market as if it had not been taxed. U. S. v. Passavant, 169 U.S. 16, 18 S.Ct. 219, 42 L. Ed. 644.

BONIS CEDERE. In the civil law. To make a transfer or surrender of property, as a debtor did to his creditors. Cod. 7, 71.

BONIS NON AMOVENDIS. A writ addressed to the sheriff, when a writ of error has been brought, commanding that the person against whom judgment has been obtained be not suffered to remove his goods till the error be tried and determined. Reg. Orig. 131.

BONITARIAN OWNERSHIP. In Roman law. A species of equitable title to things, as distinguished from a title acquired according to the strict forms of the municipal law; the property of a Roman citizen in a subject capable of quiritary property, acquired by a title not known to the civil law, but introduced by the prætor, and protected by his *imperium* or supreme executive power, *e. g.*, where *res mancipi* had been transferred by mere tradition. Poste's Gaius Inst. 187. See Quiritarian Ownership.

BONO ET MALO. A special writ of jail delivery, which formerly issued of course for each particular prisoner. 4 Bl.Comm. 270.

BONUM DEFENDENTIS EX INTEGRA CAUSA; MALUM EX QUOLIBET DEFECTU. The success of a defendant depends on a perfect case; his loss arises from some defect. 11 Coke, 68*a*.

BONUM NECESSARIUM EXTRA TERMINOS NECESSITATIS NON EST BONUM. A good thing required by necessity is not good beyond the limits of such necessity. Hob. 144.

BONUS. A consideration or premium paid by a company for a charter or other franchise or privilege. Com. v. Transp. Co., 107 Pa. 112; for privilege of carrying on corporate business, United Gas Improvement Co. v. Burnet, C.C.A.3, 64 F.2d 957, 958. A consideration for what is received, and advantage or benefit given in return for a benefit received, or an inducement for conferring a benefit. Church v. Winship, 175 La. 816, 144 So. 585, 586. "A definite sum to be paid at one time, for a loan of money for a specified period, distinct from and independently of the interest." Association v. Wilcox, 24 Conn. 147. A gratuity to which the recipient has no right to make a demand. Walling v. Plymouth Mfg. Corporation, C.C.A.Ind., 139 F.2d 178, 182. A premium or extra or irregular remuneration in consideration of offices performed or to encourage their performance. Willkie v. Commissioner of Internal Revenue, C.C.A.6, 127 F.2d 953, 956. A premium paid to a grantor or vendor. An advance royalty. Sneed v. Commissioner of Internal Revenue, C.C.A.Tex., 119 F.2d 767, 770. An "arbitrary award" given without reference to qualifications for position. Thomas v. Kern, 280 N.Y. 236, 20 N.E.2d 738, 740. An extra consideration given for what is received, or something given in addition to what is ordinarily received by, or strictly due, the recipient. La Juett v. Coty Mach. Co., 153 Misc. 410, 275 N.Y.S. 822. An increase in salary or wages in contracts of employment. Attorney General v. City of Woburn, 317 Mass. 465, 58 N.E.2d 746, 747. An offer to employees to procure efficient and faithful service. Roberts v. Mays Mills, 184 N.C. 406, 114 S.E. 530, 532, 28 A. L.R. 338; Duffy Bros. v. Bing & Bing, 217 App. Div. 10, 215 N.Y.S. 755, 758. Any premium or advantage. Consideration or down payment for mineral lease or transfer of oil lands. State Nat. Bank of Corpus Christi v. Morgan, Tex.Civ.App., 123 S.W.2d 1036, 1038; In re Levy, 185 Okl. 477, 94 P.2d 537, 539; Gift in recognition of officer's past successful direction of corporate affairs. Thomas v. Commissioner of Internal Revenue, C.C.A.La., 135 F.2d 378, 379. "Interest" for the purpose of the usury law. Bowen v. Mt. Vernon Sav. Bank, 70 App.D.C. 273, 105 F.2d 796, 797.

The word "bonus" may in its natural import imply a gift or gratuity. Carson v. Olcott, 105 Or. 259, 209 P. 610, 611. No distinction may be made between a soldier's "bonus" given for past service and a "pension," the one being a reward for past military services payable at once, and the other such a reward payable in installments. People v. Westchester County Nat. Bank of Peekskill, 231 N.Y. 465, 132 N.E. 241, 243, 15 A.L.R. 1344.

BONUS JUDEX SECUNDUM ÆQUUM ET BONUM JUDICAT, ET ÆQUITATEM STRICTO JURI PRÆFERT. A good judge decides according to what is just and good, and prefers equity to strict law. Co.Litt. 34.

BONUS STOCK. Technically, stock issued to the purchasers of bonds as an inducement to them to purchase bonds or loan money. California Trona Co. v. Wilkinson, 20 Cal.App. 694, 130 P. 190, 194.

BONY. Slate and other refuse from mine. Maksimshuk v. Union Collieries Co., 128 Pa.Super. 86, 193 A. 669, 671, 672, 673.

BOODLE. Usually applied to designate the money held to be paid or paid as a bribe for corrupt official action. Boehmer v. Detroit Free Press Co., 94 Mich. 7, 9, 53 N.W. 822, 823, 34 Am.St.Rep. 318.

BOODLING. In the slang of the day, corrupt legislative practices and corrupt influences affecting legislation. Julian v. Kansas City Star Co., 209 Mo. 35, 107 S.W. 496, 501.

BOOK. An assembly or concourse of ideas expressed in words. U. S. v. One Obscene Book Entitled "Married Love", D.C.N.Y., 48 F.2d 821, 823. A literary composition which is printed; a printed composition bound in a volume. Scoville v. Toland, 21 Fed.Cas. 864. The largest subdivisions of a treatise or other literary composition.

A bound volume consisting of sheets of paper, not printed, containing manuscript entries; such as a merchant's account-books, dockets of courts, etc. A manuscript as a "book". In re Beecher's Estate, 17 Pa.C.C.R. 161; 8 L.J.Ch. 105. "Financial statement" of bank "book". State v. Cloutier, 181 La. 222, 159 So. 330.

Minute book of bank as "book." Lewis v. U. S., C.C.A. Okl., 22 F.2d 760, 764. Papers prepared in the progress of a cause, though entirely written, and not at all in the book form, such as demurrer-books, error-books, paper-books, etc. Photographs as books. Marietta Mfg. Co. v. Hedges-Walsh-Weidner Co., 9 W.W.Harr. 511, 2 A.2d 922, 927. Records made on loose sheets as book. Town of Bennington v. Booth, 101 Vt. 24, 140 A. 157, 159, 57 A.L.R. 156. X-ray pictures as books. Whetsel v. Shaw, 343 Pa. 182, 22 A.2d 751, 753.

In copyright law, the term may include a pamphlet, a magazine, a collection of blank forms, or a single sheet of music or of ordinary printing. U. S. v. Bennett, 24 Fed. Cas. 1,093; M. Witmark & Sons v. Standard Music Roll Co., N.J., 221 F. 376, 380, 137 C.C.A. 184. A term which distinguishes writings from such other copyrightable subjects. Sebring Pottery Co. v. Steubenville Pottery Co., D.C.Ohio, 9 F.Supp. 384, 386.

Book Account

A detailed statement, in the nature of debits and credits between persons; an account or record of debit and credit kept in a book. Taylor v. Horst, 52 Minn. 300, 54 N.W. 734; Wright v. Loaiza, 177 Cal. 605, 171 P. 311. A book in which a detailed history of business transactions is entered; a record of goods sold or services rendered; a statement in detail of the transactions between parties. Tillson v. Peters, 41 Cal.App.2d 671, 107 P.2d 434, 438.

Entire account between parties at time action is commenced. Gardner v. Rutherford, 57 Cal.App.2d 874, 136 P.2d 48, 52. Entries on loose pages. Foothill Ditch Co. v. Wallace Ranch Water Co., 25 Cal.App.2d 555, 78 P.2d 215, 220.

Book Debt

The words "book debt" include goods sold and delivered, and work, labor, and services performed, the evidence of which consists of entries in an original book. Hamill v. O'Donnell, 2 Miles, Pa., 102.

Book of Acts

A term applied to the records of a surrogate's court. 8 East, 187.

Book of Adjournal

In Scotch law. The original records of criminal trials in the court of justiciary.

Book of Original Entries

A book in which a merchant enters from day to day a record of his transactions. McKnight v. Newell, 207 Pa. 562, 57 A. 39. A book kept for charging goods sold and delivered, in which the entries are made contemporaneously with the delivery of the goods. United Grocery Co. v. J. M. Dannelly & Son, 93 S.C. 580, 77 S.E. 706, Ann.Cas. 1914D, 489. A book in which a detailed history of business transactions is entered. Nicola v. U. S., C.C.A.Pa., 72 F.2d 780, 783.

Distinguished from such books as a ledger. But see Cassil v. Carter, 98 Okl. 49, 223 P. 685, 686. Workmen's slips for repairs done on automobiles, although not bound in book form. H. W. Emeny Auto Co. v. Neiderhauser, 175 Iowa 219, 157 N.W. 143, 144.

Book of Rates

An account or enumeration of the duties or tariffs authorized by parliament. 1 Bl.Comm. 316.

Book of Responses

In Scotch law. An account which the directors of the chancery kept to enter all non-entry and relief duties payable by heirs who take precepts from chancery.

Book Value

As applied to stock, the value shown by deducting liabilities and other matters required to be deducted from assets, Elhard v. Rott, 36 N.D. 221, 162 N.W. 302; Gurley v. Woodbury, 177 N.C. 70, 97 S.E. 754, 756; the value determined by net profits or deficit, Davis v. Coshnear, 129 Me. 334, 151 A. 725, 727. The value found by adding to par value the plus value of surplus, In re Fisher's Estate, 344 Pa. 607, 26 A.2d 192, 196. As applied to finance, the value of anything as shown in books of account. Davis v. Coshnear, 129 Me. 334, 151 A. 725, 727.

"Book value" of a business is based upon actual costs of a stock of merchandise and accounts on hand less depreciation. Mills v. Rich, 249 Mich. 489, 229 N.W. 462, 463. "Book value" of building and loan stock is proportionate amount of net assets applicable. Thirteenth Ward Building & Loan Ass'n of Newark v. Weissberg, 115 N.J.Eq. 487, 170 A. 662, 665, 98 A.L.R. 134.

Bookland

In English law. Land, also called "charter-land," which was held by deed under certain rents and free services, and differed in nothing from free socage land. 2 Bl.Comm. 90.

Books

All the volumes which contain authentic reports of decisions in English courts, from the earliest times to the present, are called, *par excellence*, "The Books." Wharton.

Books of Account

Books in which merchants, traders, and business men generally keep their accounts. Colbert v. Piercy, 25 N.C. 80. Entries made in the regular course of business. Nicola v. U. S., C.C.A.Pa., 72 F.2d 780, 783. Entries on loose leaves or cards. 12 Okl.St.Ann. § 501. Maney v. Cherry, 170 Okl. 469, 41 P.2d 82, 83. Serial, continuous, and permanent memorials of business and affairs. Cudahy Packing Co. v. U. S., C.C.A.Ill., 15 F.2d 133, 136. Broderick v. Adamson, 159 Misc. 634, 288 N.Y.S. 688, 696.

Pad slips, cash register items, and adding machine slips, pinned together and preserved. Home Ins. Co. v. Flewellen, Tex.Civ.App., 221 S.W. 630, 631. A diary. State v. Coffey, 8 Wash.2d 504, 112 P.2d 989, 991. A ledger of accounts. In re Anderson, D.C.N.Y., 35 F.Supp. 717, 719. A memorandum. Brett v. Dean, 239 Ala. 675, 196 So. 881, 883. A pay-roll book. Hirsch v. Automatic Canteen Co. of America, 296 Ill.App. 47, 15 N.E.2d 888.

Books of Bank

Stock books of bank. Broderick v. Adamson, 159 Misc. 634, 288 N.Y.S. 688, 696.

Books of Corporations

"Books, records, and papers" of corporations as interchangeable terms. Birmingham News v. State, 207 Ala. 440, 93 So. 25, 26. Whatever is kept as written evidence of official doings and business transactions. First Nat. Bank of Colorado Springs v. Holt, Mo.App., 158 S.W.2d 229, 231.

Books of Tax Receiver

Tax digests, copies of which must be placed in hands of state revenue commissioner, tax collector, etc. Cady v. State, 198 Ga. 99, 31 S.E.2d 38, 43.

Face of Book

See Face of Book.

Office Book

See Office.

Reference Books

Books to refer to. State v. Innes, 89 Kan. 168, 130 P. 677, 679.

BOOKED. Engaged, destined, bound to promise or pledge oneself to make an engagement. Mente & Co. v. Heller, 99 N.J.Law, 475, 123 A. 755, 756.

BOOKING CONTRACT. A contract made by agents who procure contracts for appearance of acts and actors in theaters. Hart v. B. F. Keith Vaudeville Exchange, C.C.A.N.Y., 12 F.2d 341, 342, 47 A.L.R. 775.

BOOKMAKER. A professional betting man, especially one connected with the turf. City of Portland v. Duntley, Or., 203 P.2d 640, 644.

BOOKMAKING. Originally, the collection of sheets of paper or other substances on which entries could be made, either written or printed. People ex rel. Lichtenstein v. Langan, 196 N.Y. 260, 89 N.E. 921, 922, 25 L.R.A.,N.S., 479, 17 Ann. Cas. 1081. The term now commonly denotes the recording or registering of bets or wagers on any trial or contest of speed or power of endurance or selling pools. People of State of New York v. Bennett, C.C.N.Y., 113 Fed. 515, 516. A species of betting on horse races. Ex parte Hernan, 45 Tex.Cr.R. 343, 77 S.W. 225, 226. The bets are booked or a record kept of them in a book. Spies v. Rosenstock, 87 Md. 14, 39 A. 268, 269.

BOOKMAKING ESTABLISHMENT. Where wagers are made on horse races being run at tracks in various parts of United States. Albright v. Karston, 206 Ark. 307, 176 S.W.2d 421, 422.

BOOM. An inclosure formed by piers and a chain of spars to collect or store logs or timber. Powers' Appeal, 125 Pa. 175, 17 A. 254, 11 Am.St.Rep. 882; Gasper v. Heimbach, 59 Minn. 102, 60 N.W. 1080. Spars or logs and chains or other fixtures used to keep them in place. Rollins v. Clay, 33 Me. 132, 138.

BOOM COMPANY. A company formed to improve streams for floating of logs by booms and other contrivances, and to run, drive, boom and raft logs.

BOOMAGE. A charge on logs for use of a boom in collecting, storing, or rafting them. Lumber Co. v. Thompson, 83 Miss. 499, 35 So. 828. A right of entry on riparian lands to fasten booms and boom sticks. Farrand v. Clarke, 63 Minn. 181, 65 N.W. 361.

BOON DAYS. In English law. Certain days in the year (sometimes called "due days") on which tenants in copyhold were obliged to perform corporal services for the lord. Whishaw.

BOOSTED FIRE. A fire wherein some inflammable substance other than that of which the building was constructed or which it contained contributed to its burning and spreading. State v. Lytle, 214 Minn. 171, 7 N.W.2d 305, 309.

BOOT, or BOTE. An old Saxon word, equivalent to "estovers."

BOOTHAGE. See Bothagium.

BOOTING, or BOTING, CORN. Certain rent corn, anciently so called. Cowell.

BOOTLEGGER. A seller of whisky. Medlock v. State, 79 Tex.Cr.R. 322, 185 S.W. 566, 568. One engaged in unlawful disposition of liquor. Hathaway v. Benton, 172 Iowa 299, 154 N.W. 474, 476. One who sells liquor on the sly. Knothe v. State, 115 Neb. 119, 211 N.W. 619, 621.

BOOTLEGGING. A popular designation for the use, possession, or transportation of liquor in violation of the law, Commonwealth v. Cicere, 282 Pa. 492, 128 A. 446, 448, importing the peddling and illegal sales of intoxicating liquor, Lamar v. State, 190 Ind. 235, 130 N.E. 114.

BOOTSTRAP DOCTRINE. The decision of a court on a special as well as a general appearance that it has jurisdiction is not subject of collateral attack but is res judicata. Peri v. Groves, 183 Misc. 579, 50 N.Y.S.2d 300, 308.

BOOTY. Property captured from the enemy in war, on land. U. S. v. Bales of Cotton, 28 Fed. Cas. 302.

BOOZE. Intoxicating liquor. Tennant v. F. C. Whitney & Sons, 133 Wash. 581, 234 P. 666, 669.

BORD. An old Saxon word, signifying a cottage; a house; a table.

BORD-BRIGCH. In Saxon law. A breach or violation of suretyship; pledge-breach, or breach of mutual fidelity.

BORD-HALFPENNY. A customary small toll paid to the lord of a town for setting up boards, tables, booths, etc., in fairs or markets.

BORDAGE. In old English law. A species of base tenure, by which certain "bord lands" were anciently held in England; the service was that of keeping the lord in small provisions.

BORDARIA. A cottage.

BORDARII, or BORDIMANNI. In old English law. Tenants of a less servile condition than the *villani,* who had a bord or cottage, with a small parcel of land, on condition they should supply the lord with small provisions. Spelman.

BORDER WARRANT. A process granted by a judge ordinary, on either side of the border between England and Scotland, for arresting the person or effects of a person living on the opposite side, until he find security, *judicio sisti.* Bell.

BORDEREAU. In French law. A note enumerating the purchases and sales which may have been made by a broker or stockbroker. This name is also given to the statement given to a banker with bills for discount or coupons to receive. Arg.Fr.Merc.Law, 547. A detailed statement of account; a summary of an instrument.

BORDLANDS. The demesnes which the lords keep in their hands for the maintenance of their board or table. Cowell. Also lands held in bordage. Lands which the lord gave to tenants on condition of supplying him with small provisions, etc.

BORDLODE. A service anciently required of tenants to carry timber out of the woods of the lord to his house; or it is said to be the quantity of food or provision which the *bordarii* or bordmen paid for their bordlands. Jacob.

BORDSERVICE. A tenure of bordlands.

BOREL-FOLK. Country people; derived from the French *bourre,* (Lat. *floccus,)* a lock of wool, because they covered their heads with such stuff. Blount.

BORG. In Saxon law. A pledge, pledge giver, or surety. The name given among the Saxons to the head of each family composing a tithing or decennary, each being the pledge for the good conduct of the others. Also the contract or engagement of suretyship; and the pledge given.

BORGBRICHE. A breach or violation of suretyship, or of mutual fidelity. Jacob.

BORGESMON. In Saxon law. The name given to the head of each family composing a tithing.

BORGH OF HAMHALD. In old Scotch law. A pledge or surety given by the seller of goods to the buyer, to make the goods forthcoming as his own proper goods, and to warrant the same to him. Skene.

BORN. A child *en ventre sa mère.* Merrill v. Winchester, 120 Me. 203, 113 A. 261, 264. If an infant is born dead or at such an early stage of pregnancy as to be unable to live, it is to be considered as never born. Marsellis v. Thalhimer, 2 Paige, Ch., N.Y., 35.

BORN ALIVE. Where child, although it never cried, breathed and its heart beat some minutes, it was "born alive." Sanford v. Getman, 124 Misc. 80, 206 N.Y.S. 865. A child never heard to cry, but whose heart beats could be heard, though no respiration could be induced, was "born alive." In re Union Trust Co., 89 Misc. 69, 151 N.Y.S. 246, 253.

BORN OUT OF WEDLOCK. Children whose parents are not, and have not been, married to each other regardless of marital status of either parent with respect to another. State v. Coliton, 73 N.D. 582, 17 N.W.2d 546, 549, 552, 156 A.L.R. 1403.

BORN OUTSIDE THE UNITED STATES. Where, at time of birth of children born in the United States, their father was a duly accredited diplomatic representative of the French Republic to the United States, they became subject to the jurisdiction of France, and were "born outside of the United States" within the naturalization provisions of section 315 of the Nationality Act of 1940, 8 U.S.C.A. § 715. In re Thenault, D.C.D.C., 47 F. Supp. 952, 953.

BOROUGH.

In English Law

A town, a walled town. Co.Litt. 108*b*. A town of note or importance; a fortified town. Cowell. An ancient town. Litt. 164. A corporate town that is not a city. Cowell. An ancient town, corporate or not, that sends burgesses to parliament. Co.Litt. 109*a;* 1 Bl.Comm. 114, 115. A city or other town sending burgesses to parliament. 1 Steph.Comm. 116. In its more modern English acceptation, a town or city or place organized for government.

A parliamentary borough is a town which returns one or more members to parliament.

In Scotch Law

A corporate body erected by the charter of the sovereign, consisting of the inhabitants of the territory erected into the borough. Bell.

In American Law

In Pennsylvania, Connecticut and New Jersey, a part of a township having a charter for municipal purposes. Southport v. Ogden, 23 Conn. 128. See, also, 1 Dill.Mun.Corp. § 41, n.

A territorial fraction of a city having certain powers with reference to local concerns. Crose v. City of Los Angeles, 175 Cal. 774, 167 P. 386, 387. "Village" and "borough" as duplicate or cumulative names of the same thing. Brown v. State, 18 Ohio St. 496.

Borough Courts

In English law. Private and limited tribunals, held by prescription, charter, or act of parliament, in particular districts for the convenience of the inhabitants, that they may prosecute small suits and receive justice at home.

Borough English

A custom prevalent in some parts of England, by which the youngest son inherits the estate in preference to his older brothers. 1 Bl.Comm. 75.

The custom is said by Blackstone to have been derived from the Saxons, and to have been so called in distinction from the Norman rule of descent; 2 Bla.Comm. 83.

Borough Fund

In English law. The revenues of a municipal borough from rents and produce of its land, houses, and stocks and supplemented where necessary by a borough rate.

Borough-Heads

Borough-holders, bors-holders, or burs-holders.

Borough-Reeve

The chief municipal officer in towns unincorporated before the municipal corporations act, 5 & 6 Wm. IV, c. 76.

Borough Sessions

Courts of limited criminal jurisdiction, established in English boroughs under the municipal corporations act.

Pocket Borough

A borough entitled to send a representative to parliament, in which a single individual could entirely control the election.

BORRASCA. Absence of profit, or not enough profit to pay the cost of operation, of a placer mine. Ballagh v. Williams, 50 Cal.App.2d 10, 122 P.2d 343, 344.

BORROW. To solicit and receive from another any article of property or thing of value with the intention and promise to repay or return it or its equivalent.

Strictly speaking, borrowing implies a gratuitous loan. Carter-Mullaly Transfer Co. v. Angell, Tex.Civ.App., 181 S.W. 237, 238. But money may be "borrowed" on an agreement to pay interest for its use. Legal Tender Cases, 110 U.S. 421, 4 S.Ct. 122, 28 L.Ed. 204. Though the word is often used in the sense of returning the thing borrowed *in specie,* where money is borrowed, the identical money loaned is not to be returned. In a broad sense the term means a contract for the use of money. State v. School Dist., 13 Neb. 88, 12 N.W. 812. The term may be used to express the idea of receiving something from another for one's own use, to appropriate. Finch v. McClellan, 77 Ind. App. 533, 130 N.E. 13, 15. The word "loan" is the correlative of "borrow." U. S. v. Warn, D.C.Idaho, 295 F. 328, 330. The term when used in connection with lending an automobile chauffeur does not imply that the owner surrenders control over him. Hooper v. Brawner, 148 Md. 417, 129 A. 672, 677. Compare Henderson v. State, 75 Fla. 464, 78 So. 427, 428, holding that an indictment alleging that defendant "did borrow" a shotgun sufficiently alleged that defendant received the shotgun into his possession. The right to borrow money as applied to a municipal corporation is a power to create indebtedness. Jones v. Board of Education of Guilford County, 185 N.C. 303, 117 S.E. 37, 40.

Agreement by building and loan association, in purchasing residence property on which it had a first mortgage, to assume a second mortgage. Gardner v. Johns, 64 Ohio App. 229, 28 N.E.2d 691, 694.

"Borrow" has been held the reciprocal action with "to lend". Bank of United States v. Drapkin & Goldberg Const. Co., City Ct., N.Y., 11 N.Y.S.2d 334, 336. Dirt taken from plots of ground near sides of highway embankment. State v. Smith, 167 La. 301, 119 So. 56, 61. Earth brought from outside highway location and used for embankments. Barry v. Duffin, 290 Mass. 398, 195 N.E. 511, 514.

BORROW PIT. A pit or bank from which material is taken for use in filling or embanking. Haynes v. Jones, 91 Ohio St. 197, 110 N.E. 469, 470.

BORROWE. In old Scotch law. A pledge.

BORROWED CAPITAL. Moneys due by corporation to another corporation used as its capital. State v. Banana Selling Co., 185 La. 668, 170 So. 30, 32.

Amount standing on books to personal credit of stockholders credited without restriction or limitation on stockholders as to manner or time of payment to them of respective accounts. Weed & Bro. v. U. S., Ct.Cl., 38 F.2d 935, 940. Dividends declared by corporation but not paid during taxable year. Bulger Block Coal Co. v. U. S., Ct.Cl., 48 F.2d 675, 677; Southport Mill v. Commissioner of Internal Revenue, C.C.A.La., 26 F.2d 17. Payment of losses sustained by corporation by its principal stockholder. State v. Mayer Sugar & Molasses Co., 204 La. 742, 16 So.2d 251, 253.

BORROWED MONEY OR PROPERTY. Notes and bonds given in payment of assets. Coal Co. v. United States, C.C.A.W.Va., 137 F.2d 948, 953. Credit by bank to payee's account of amount of customer's notes taken in lieu of cash. Department of Treasury (Gross Income Tax Division) v. Advance Paint Co., 222 Ind. 294, 53 N.E.2d 59. Profits loaned by partners to partnership. Nye v. U. S., C.C.A.Mass., 84 F.2d 457, 462.

BORROWER. He to whom a thing is lent at his request.

Under usury statute, one having the use of money by forbearance of his creditor, or any person who secures the use of money in any way upon an excessive consideration, Law, Clark & Co. v. Mitchell, 200 Ala. 565, 76 So. 923, 924; the party who is bound by original contract to pay loan, Faber v. Siegel, 286 N.Y.S. 974, 158 Misc. 722; the purchaser of land subject to usurious mortgage and subsequent mortgagees, Hatch v. Baker, 249 N.Y.S. 215, 217, 139 Misc. 717; the indorser of note who received no part of money advanced and who was mere surety, Faber v. Siegel, 286 N.Y.S. 974, 158 Misc. 722.

BORROWING POWER. Signifies only an unfunded indebtedness. Bond v. Cowan, 272 Mich. 296, 261 N.W. 331.

BORROWINGS. Checks by bank against second bank and honored while items deposited by former were in process of collection. Guaranty by bank of transaction where another bank issued letter of credit for first bank's customer. Indebtedness represented by notes given by bank when borrowing money. Overdrafts by bank maintaining checking account with another bank. Schramm v. Bank of California Nat. Ass'n, 143 Or. 546, 20 P.2d 1093, 1096.

BORSHOLDER. In Saxon law. The borough's ealder, or headborough.

BOSCAGE. In English law. The food which wood and trees yield to cattle; browsewood mast, etc. Spelman. An ancient duty of wind-fallen wood in the forest. Manwood.

BOSCARIA. Wood-houses, or ox-houses.

BOSCUS. Wood; growing wood of any kind, large or small, timber or coppice. Cowell; Jacob.

BOSTON CREAM PIE. Two layers of sponge cake with a layer of a sort of cream custard. Lohse v. Coffey, D.C.Mun.App., 32 A.2d 258, 259.

BOTE, BOT. In old English law. A recompense or compensation, or profit or advantage. Also reparation or amends for any damage done. Necessaries for the maintenance and carrying on of husbandry. An allowance; the ancient name for estovers.

House-bote is a sufficient allowance of wood from off the estate to repair or burn in the house, and sometimes termed "fire-bote;" *plow-bote* and *cart-bote* are wood to be employed in making and repairing all instruments of husbandry; and *hay-bote* or *hedge-bote* is wood for repairing of hays, hedges, or fences. The word also signifies reparation for any damage or injury done, as *man-bote,* which was a compensation or amends for a man slain, etc.

BOTELESS. In old English law. Without amends; without the privilege of making satisfaction for a crime by a pecuniary payment; without relief or remedy. Cowell.

BOTH. The one and the other; the two without the exception of either. Lower Indian Creek Drainage and Levee Dist. of Cass County v. Vallery, 343 Ill. 49, 174 N.E. 842, 843. All of two, United States v. Bachman, D.C.Pa., 246 F. 1009, 1011. The term likewise has a meaning which excludes more than two mentioned subject matters. In re Turner's Estate, 171 Misc. 78, 11 N.Y. S.2d 800, 802.

"Either," may mean "both." Kibler v. Parker, 191 Ark. 475, 86 S.W.2d 925, 926.

Both Real and Personal

Use in will to indicate all of testatrix' property. Hoffman v. Hoffman, 61 Ohio App. 371, 22 N.E.2d 652, 654.

BOTHA. In old English law. A booth, stall, or tent to stand in, in fairs or markets. Cowell.

BOTHAGIUM, or BOOTHAGE. Customary dues paid to the lord of a manor or soil, for the pitching or standing of booths in fairs or markets.

BOTHNA, or BUTHNA. In old Scotch law. A park where cattle are inclosed and fed. Bothna also signifies a barony, lordship, etc. Skene.

BOTILER OF THE KING. An officer who provided the king's wines. By virtue of his office, he might choose, out of every ship laden with wines, one cask before the mast, and one behind. 25 Edw. III, st. 5, c. 21. Wharton. *Cf.* Butlerage.

BOTTELLARIA. A buttery or cellar, in which bottles or butts of wine and other liquors are deposited. Wharton.

BOTTLE. An open mouthed vessel, with a neck with an aperture which may be closed, capable of containing liquids. Fieldcrest Dairies v. City of Chicago, D.C.Ill., 35 F.Supp. 451, 452.

BOTTOM HOLE CONTRACT. When operator drills a well to a certain depth, the owners or persons for whom the well is drilled will pay a certain sum. Barnett v. Kemerer, 179 Okl. 588, 66 P.2d 1053, 1055.

BOTTOM LAND. As used in a contract to convey means low land formed by alluvial deposits along the river, low-lying ground, a dale, valley, or intervale. Lexington & E. Ry. Co. v. Williams, 183 Ky. 343, 209 S.W. 59, 62.

BOTTOMAGE. L. Fr. Bottomry.

BOTTOMRY. In maritime law. A contract by which the owner of a ship borrows for the use, equipment, or repair of the vessel, and for a definite term, and pledges the ship (or the keel or *bottom* of the ship, *pars pro toto*) as security; it being stipulated that if the ship be lost in the specified voyage, or during the limited time, by any of the perils enumerated, the lender shall lose his money. Carrington v. The Pratt, 18 How. 63, 15 L.Ed. 267; Braynard v. Hoppock, 7 Bosw.N.Y. 157.

A contract by which a ship or its freightage is hypothecated as security for a loan, which is to be repaid only in case the ship survives a particular risk, voyage, or period. Civ.Code Cal. § 3017. The contract usually in form a bond.

When the loan is not made on the ship, but on the goods on board, and which are to be sold or exchanged in the course of the voyage, the borrower's personal *responsibility* is deemed the principal security for the performance of the contract, which is therefore called *"respondentia."*

BOTTOMRY BOND. The instrument embodying the contract or agreement of bottomry. A contract for a loan on the bottom of the ship, at an extraordinary interest, upon maritime risks, to be borne by the lender for a voyage, or for a definite period. The Grapeshot, 9 Wall. 135, 19 L.Ed. 651.

BOTULISM. Food poisoning caused by a toxin which is produced by Clostridium (bacillus) botulinum. Armour & Co. v. Leasure, 177 Md. 393, 9 A.2d 572, 575.

BOUCHE. Fr. The mouth. An allowance of provision. *Avoir bouche à court;* to have an allowance at court; to be in ordinary at court; to have meat and drink scotfree there. Blount; Cowell.

BOUCHE OF COURT, or BUDGE OF COURT. A certain allowance of provision from the king to his knights and servants, who attended him on any military expedition.

BOUGH OF A TREE. In feudal law. A symbol which gave seisin of land, to hold of the donor *in capite.*

BOUGHT. The word "bought" implies a completed transaction, a vesting of the right of title to and possession of the property sold, Bull v. Morrison, Tex.Civ.App., 241 S.W. 561, 562, and also imports a valuable consideration, Grimes v. State, 32 Ga. App. 541, 123 S.E. 918.

BOUGHT AND SOLD NOTES. A note of the sale by a broker employed to buy and sell goods is called a "sold note," and a like note to the seller is called a "bought note." Avondale Mills v. Benchley Bros., 244 Mass. 153, 138 N.E. 586, 589.

BOULEVARD. The word originally indicated a bulwark or rampart, and afterwards applied to a public walk or road on the site of a demolished fortification, and is now employed in same sense as public drive. A street or highway with park-like appearance; or one specially designed for pleasure walking or driving. Newbold v. Brotzge, 209 Ky. 218, 272 S.W. 755, 756; Chaplin v. Kansas City, 259 Mo. 479, 168 S.W. 763, 765. A wide street, or a street encircling a town, with sides or center for shade trees, etc. State ex rel. Copland v. City of Toledo, 75 Ohio App. 378, 62 N.E.2d 256, 258. It is adapted and set apart for purposes of ornament, exercise, and amusement. See, also, Avenue. A "public way", City of Medford v. Metropolitan District Commission, 303 Mass. 537, 22 N.E.2d 110, 111.

It is not technically a street, avenue, or highway. Howe v. Lowell, 171 Mass. 575, 51 N.E. 536; Park Com'rs v. Farber, 171 Ill. 146, 49 N.E. 427. "Street" and "boulevard" may be interchangeable. City of Fargo v. Gearey, 33 N.D. 64, 156 N.W. 552, 555.

BOUNCER. A term used to designate persons employed to preserve the peace in establishments such as night clubs and other places of amusement where people indulge in dancing, drinking and in gambling. Moore v. Blanchard, La.App., 35 So.2d 667, 669.

BOUND. As an *adjective,* denotes the condition of being constrained by the obligations of a bond or a covenant.

In the law of shipping, "bound to" or "bound for" denotes that the vessel spoken of is intended or designed to make a voyage to the place named. U. S. v. Bengochea, C.C.A.Fla., 279 F. 537, 541.

"Bound" and "concluded" as synonymous. McKinnon v. Chenoweth, 176 Or. 74, 155 P.2d 944, 954.

As a *noun,* denotes a limit or boundary, or a line inclosing or marking off a tract of land. In the phrase "metes and bounds," denotes the natural or artificial marks which indicate their beginning and ending. "Bound" may signify the limit itself, and "boundary" designate a visible mark which indicates the limit. "Bound" and "duty" as synonymous. Essenpreis v. Elliott's Department Store Co., Mo.App., 37 S.W.2d 458, 462.

BOUND BAILIFFS. In English law. Sheriffs' officers are so called, from their being usually *bound* to the sheriff in an obligation with sureties, for the due execution of their office. 1 Bl.Comm. 345, 346.

BOUNDARY. Every separation, natural or artificial, which marks the confines or line of division of two contiguous estates. Civ.Code La. art. 826. Limits or marks of enclosures if possession be without title, or the boundaries or limits stated in title deed if possession be under a title. Snelling v. Adair, 196 La. 624, 199 So. 782, 787.

"At the entrance" and "at the boundary" as synonymous. McGough v. Hendrickson, 58 Cal.App.2d 60, 136 P. 2d 110, 114. Banks or confines at ordinary high water as boundary of water course. Beck v. Kulesza, 4 W.W.Harr., Del., 559, 156 A. 346, 349. Meander line as "boundary". United States v. Elliott, C.C.A.Okl., 131 F.2d 720, 724.

Boundary Suit

Trespass to try title in which every matter in dispute would be determined by determination of boundary line. Southern Pine Lumber Co. v. Whiteman, Tex.Civ.App., 104 S.W.2d 635, 637.

Case of Boundary

One where the location of the boundary is the determining question of the entire case. West Lumber Co. v. Goodrich, 113 T. 14, 223 S.W. 183, 191; Maxfield v. E. L. Sterling & Sons, 110 Tex. 212, 217 S.W. 937.

Natural Boundary

Any formation or product of nature which may serve to define and fix one or more of the lines inclosing an estate or piece of property. See Peuker v. Canter, 62 Kan. 363, 63 P. 617.

Private Boundary

An artificial boundary set up to mark the beginning or direction of a boundary line.

Public Boundary

A natural boundary; a natural object or land-mark used as a boundary or as a beginning point for a boundary line.

BOUNDED TREE. A tree marking or standing at the corner of a field or estate.

BOUNDERS. In American law. Visible marks or objects at the ends of the lines drawn in surveys of land, showing the courses and distances. Burrill.

BOUNDS. The external or limiting lines, either real or imaginary, of any object or space; that which limits or circumscribes. Stone v. Waukegan, C.C.A. 7, 205 F. 495, 496.

Contract as meant by "bounds". City of Elkins v. Stickley, 114 W.Va. 103, 170 S.E. 902, 903. Edges of road as "bounds of the highway". Decker v. Roberts, 126 Conn. 478, 12 A.2d 541, 543. Trespass committed by a person who excavates minerals under-ground beyond boundary of his land as "working out of bounds."

BOUNTY. A gratuity, or an unusual or additional benefit conferred upon, or compensation paid to, a class of persons. Iowa v. McFarland, 110 U.S. 471, 4 S.Ct. 210, 28 L.Ed. 198; In re Hoag, D.C. N.Y., 227 F. 478, 479. A premium given or offered to enlisted men to induce enlistment into public service. Abbe v. Allen, 39 How.Prac., N.Y., 488.

An amount appropriated by Congress to repay the city for rental value of land taken for navy yard during Civil War as not a bounty. Moyers v. City of Memphis, 135 Tenn. 263, 186 S.W. 105, 113, Ann.Cas.1918C, 854.

Bounty is the appropriate term where services or action of many persons are desired, and each who acts upon the offer may entitle himself to the promised gratuity. Reward is more proper in the case of a single service, which can be only once performed, and therefore will be earned only by the person or co-operative persons who succeed while others fail. Ingram v. Colgan, 106 Cal. 113, 38 P. 315, 28 L.R.A. 187, 46 Am.St.Rep. 221. Bonus, suggests the idea of a gratuity to induce a money transaction between individuals. Abbott.

Bounty Lands

Portions of the public domain given or donated as a bounty for services rendered, chiefly for military service. See 43 U.S.C.A. § 791.

Bounty of Queen Ann

A name given to a royal charter, which was confirmed by 2 Anne, c. 11, whereby all the revenue of first-fruits and tenths was vested in trustees, to form a perpetual fund for the augmentation of poor ecclesiastical livings. Wharton.

BOURDON TUBE. A pressure-responsive device comprising a hollow tubular member. James P. Marsh Corporation v. United States Gauge Co., D. C.Ill., 42 F.Supp. 998, 1001.

BOURG.

In old French law. An assemblage of houses surrounded with walls; a fortified town or village.

In old English law. A borough, a village.

BOURGEOIS. The inhabitant of a *bourg*. A person entitled to the privileges of a municipal corporation; a burgess. A member of the middle classes. People v. Gitlow, 234 N.Y. 132, 136 N.E. 317, 322.

BOURSE. Fr. An exchange; a stock-exchange.

BOURSE DE COMMERCE. In the French law. An aggregation, sanctioned by government, of merchants, captains of vessels, exchange agents, and courtiers, the two latter being nominated by the government, in each city which has a *bourse*. Brown.

BOUSSOLE. In French marine law. A compass; the mariner's compass.

BOUWERYE. Dutch. In old New York law. A farm; a farm on which the farmer's family resided.

BOUWMEESTER (also BOUWMASTER). Dutch. In old New York law. A farmer.

BOVARIUS, *adj.* Lat. Relating to horned cattle. The Forum Bovarium was the cattle market at Rome, near the Circus Maximus. It had a large brazen statue of an ox.

BOVATA TERRÆ. As much land as one ox can cultivate. Said by some to be thirteen, by others eighteen, acres in extent. Skene; Spelman; Co. Litt. 5*a*. See Carucata.

BOVINE. From the Latin "bos," meaning cow or bull. "Neat cattle" are animals belonging to the genus "bos," a term not embracing horses, sheep, goats, or swine. "Cattle" as generally used in the Western States means "neat cattle"; it includes cows, bulls, and steers, but not horses, mares, geldings, colts, mules, jacks, or jennies, goats, hogs, sheep, shoats, or pigs. State v. District Court of Fifth Judicial Dist. in and for Nye County, 42 Nev. 218, 174 P. 1023, 1025.

BOW-BEARER. An under-officer of the forest, whose duty it was to oversee and true inquisition make, as well of sworn men as unsworn, in every bailiwick of the forest; and of all manner of trespasses done, either to vert or venison, and cause them to be presented, without any concealment, in the next court of attachment, etc. Cromp. Jur. 201.

BOWIE KNIFE. A long knife shaped like a dagger but having only one edge. Knox v. State, 157 Tenn. 120, 6 S.W.2d 318, 319. A butcher knife, Mireles v. State, 80 Tex.Cr.R. 648, 192 S.W. 241, 242; a "dirk," Bivens v. State, 133 Tex.Cr.R. 604, 113 S.W.2d 921.

BOWYERS. Manufacturers of bows and shafts. An ancient company of the city of London.

BOX. A construction of permanent, fixed dimensions and size. Lyon, Inc., v. Clayton & Lambert Mfg. Co., D.C.Del., 13 F.Supp. 331, 333.

BOX DOLLY. A vehicle which has but one wheel, a wide cylindrical drum in the center of it, and is shaped like a box, the lower part of which extends down as far as the axis of the drum. The Rosalie Mahony, D.C.Wash., 218 F. 695, 697.

BOX STEP. A passenger car step. Hill v. Minneapolis, St. Paul, & S. S. M. Ry. Co., 160 Minn. 484, 200 N.W. 485, 486.

BOX STRAPPING. Metal strips intended to reinforce the ends of heavy wooden packing cases to prevent them from breaking open. Stanley Works v. Twisted Wire & Steel Co., C.C.A.N.Y., 256 F. 98, 99.

BOXED WEIGHT BASIS. According to weight at time of packing and after wrapping. Swift & Co. v. Wallace, C.C.A.7, 105 F.2d 848, 861.

BOXING BOUT. A contest of skill between two participants. Fischer v. City of Cleveland, 42 Ohio App. 75, 181 N.E. 668, 670.

BOXING OF PINE TREES. As equivalent to "hanging of cups upon timber." Howard v. State, 17 Ala.App. 9, 81 So. 345, 346.

BOY. Legitimate child. In re Dragoni, 53 Wyo. 143, 79 P.2d 465, 468. Male child. Hinerman v. Hinerman, 85 W.Va. 349, 101 S.E. 789, 790.

BOYCOTT. A conspiracy or confederation to prevent the carrying on of business, or to injure the business of any one by preventing potential customers from doing business with him or employing the representatives of said business, by threats, intimidation, coercion, etc. Dick v. Northern Pac. Ry. Co., 86 Wash. 211, 150 P. 8, 12, Ann.Cas.1917A, 638; Hailey v. Brooks, Tex.Civ.App., 191 S.W. 781, 783.

Intimidation and coercion as essential elements. Smythe Neon Sign Co. v. Local Union No. 405 of International Brotherhood of Electrical Workers of Cedar Rapids, 226 Iowa 191, 284 N.W. 126, 130. Labor union members' voluntary determination to refrain from working in erection of materials not bearing union label. Frank Schmidt Planing Mill Co. v. Mueller, Mo.App., 154 S.W.2d 610, 614, 615. Labor union's promulgation of rule prohibiting members from handling and erecting work not bearing union label, Crescent Planing Mill Co. v. Mueller, 234 Mo.App. 1243, 123 S.W.2d 193, 196. The word does not necessarily import illegality, Smythe Neon Sign Co. v. Local Union No. 405 of International Brotherhood of Electrical Workers of Cedar Rapids, 226 Iowa 191, 284 N.W. 126, 130.

Primary Boycott

That which occurs when an organized union of employees, by concerted action, ceases dealing with a former employer. Pierce v. Stablemen's Union, Local No. 8760, 156 Cal. 70, 103 P. 325, 327.

Secondary Boycott

A combination to exercise coercive pressure on customers, actual or prospective, to cause them to withhold or withdraw their patronage. Duplex Printing Press Co. v. Deering, 254 U.S. 443, 41 S. Ct. 172, 176, 65 L.Ed. 349, 16 A.L.R. 196. An act which, when committed in concert, may cause such injury to the public, or be so useless or unfair that these conditions will be decisive as to whether such act is permissible or forbidden. Justin Seubert, Inc., v. Reiff, 98 Misc. 402, 164 N. Y.S. 522, 526.

BOYD RULE. In a corporate reorganization, no junior security may be given participation without providing a new consideration therefor, unless all securities senior to it have received full equivalent of their rights against the estate. Phelan v. Middle States Oil Corp., D.C.N.Y., 124 F.Supp. 728, 781.

BOYLE'S LAW. The principle that as the pressure of gas increases at a fixed temperature, the volume decreases in inverse proportion, or the product of the pressure and volume is a constant quantity. Huntington Development & Gas Co. v. Topping, 115 W.Va. 364, 176 S.E. 424, 425.

BOZERO. In Spanish law. An advocate; one who pleads the causes of others, or his own, before courts of justice, either as plaintiff or defendant. Called also *abogado*.

BRABANT. A variety of the old coin known as a crocard. See Crockards.

BRABANTER. A mercenary soldier or bandit who figured in the Anglo-French wars of the 11th and 13th centuries, and who came from the old duchy of Brabant, now partly comprised in the provinces of Brabant in Belgium and of North Brabant in the Netherlands. Cent. Dict.

BRACERY. The statute of 32 Hen. VIII, c. 9, to prevent the buying and selling of pretended rights or titles, is commonly called "the Bill of Bracery and buying of titles." Cain v. Monroe, 23 Ga. 82, 86, 89, 94; Webb v. Camp, 26 Ga. 354, 357. See Buying Titles.

BRACHIUM MARIS. An arm of the sea.

BRACINUM. A brewing; the whole quantity of ale brewed at one time, for which *tolsestor* was paid in some manors. *Brecina,* a brewhouse.

BRAHMIN, BRAHMAN, or BRAMIN. In Hindu law. A divine; a priest; the first Hindu caste.

BRAIN INJURY. A "concussion" as "brain injury". Le Francois v. Hobart College, Sup., 31 N.Y.S.2d 200, 204.

BRAKE. An effective "brake" consists of the "brake shoe," and the "brake drum." Davis Sewing Mach. Co. v. New Departure Mfg. Co., C.C.A. Ohio, 217 F. 775, 780.

BRANCH. An offshoot, lateral extension, or subdivision. Any member or part of a body or system; a department. Northern Indiana Land Co. v. Carlin, 139 Ind. 324, 127 N.E. 197, 201.

A branch of a family stock is a group of persons related by descent from a common ancestor, and related to the main stock by the fact that that common ancestor descends from the original founder or progenitor. Certificate given by the Trinity House to pilots who have passed an examination. Houston Pilots v. Goodwin, Tex.Civ.App., 178 S.W.2d 308, 311. "Group", "wing", "faction", "party" or "section" and "branch" as synonymous. In re McKean's Estate, 152 Pa.Super. 613, 33 A.2d 51, 52.

BRANCH OF A RIVER. "Branch," as distinguished from a channel of a river, may have two or more separate channels; "channel" meaning primarily the bed. United States v. Hutchings, D.C.Okl., 252 F. 841, 844.

BRANCH OF THE SEA. This term, as used at common law, included rivers in which the tide ebbed and flowed. Arnold v. Mundy, 6 N.J.Law, 86, 10 Am.Dec. 356.

BRANCH PILOT. One possessing a license, commission, or certificate of competency issued by the proper authority and usually after an examination. Dean v. Healy, 66 Ga. 503; State v. Follett, 33 La. Ann. 228. Holder of certificate given by the Trinity House to pilots who have passed an examination. Houston Pilots v. Goodwin, Tex.Civ.App., 178 S.W.2d 308, 311.

BRANCH RAILROAD. A lateral extension of a main line; a road connected with or issuing from a main line. Biles v. Railroad Co., 5 Wash. 509, 32 Pac. 211; Blanton v. Railroad Co., 86 Va. 618, 10 S.E. 925. Feeder lines, Union Pac. R. Co. v. Anderson, 167 Or. 687, 120 P.2d 578, 588.

BRAND. To stamp; to mark, either with a hot iron or with a stencil plate. Dibble v. Hathaway, 11 Hun, N.Y., 575. And see Miles v. Vermont Fruit Co., 98 Vt. 1, 124 A. 559, 563.

BRANDING. An ancient mode of punishment by inflicting a mark on an offender with a hot iron. A recognized punishment for some military offenses. Marking of cattle for the purpose of identification.

BRANDY. Product from distilling wine or the fermented juice of any fruit. Chicago, B. & Q. R. Co. v. California Wine Co., 313 Ill.App. 498, 40 N. E.2d 624, 627.

BRANKS. An instrument formerly used in some parts of England for the correction of scolds; a scolding bridle.

BRASIATOR. A maltster, a brewer.

BRASIUM. Malt.

BRASS KNUCKLES or KNUCKS. A weapon worn on the hand for the purposes of offense or defense, so made that in hitting with the fist considerable damage is inflicted. It is called "brass knuckles" because it was originally made of brass. The term is now used as the name of the weapon without reference to the metal of which it is made; Patterson v. State, 3 Lea, Tenn., 575.

BRAWL. A clamorous or tumultuous quarrel in a public place, to the disturbance of the public peace.

In English law, specifically, a noisy quarrel or other uproarious conduct creating a disturbance in a church or churchyard. 4 B.Comm. 146; 4 Steph.Comm. 253.

"Tumults" and "brawls" as substantially identical. State v. Perkins, 42 N.H. 464.

BREACH. The breaking or violating of a law, right, or duty, either by commission or omission.

This name is sometimes given to that part of the declaration which alleges the violation of the defendant's promise or duty, immediately preceding the *ad damnum* clause.

Expenditure by administrator of proceeds of policy pending appeal from award of proceeds to administrator as "breach" of obligation of faithful administration. State ex rel. and to Use of Gnekow v. United States Fidelity & Guaranty Co., 349 Mo. 528, 163 S.W.2d 86, 90.

BREACH OF CLOSE. The unlawful or unwarrantable entry on another person's soil, land, or close. 3 Bl.Comm. 209.

BREACH OF CONTRACT. Failure, without legal excuse, to perform any promise which forms the whole or part of a contract. Friedman v. Katzner, 139 Md. 195, 114 A. 884, 886. Prevention or hindrance by party to contract of any occurrence or performance requisite under the contract for the creation or continuance of a right in favor of the other party or the discharge of a duty by him. Sharp v. Williams, 141 Fla. 1, 192 So. 476, 480. Unequivocal, distinct and absolute refusal to perform agreement. R. T. Clark & Co. v. Miller, 154 Miss. 233, 122 So. 475, 481. Violation of obligation. Russell v. Stephens, 191 Wash. 314, 71 P.2d 30, 31.

Anticipatory Breach

A breach committed before there is a present duty of performance, and is the outcome of words evincing intention to refuse performance in the future. King Features Syndicate v. Valley Broadcasting Co., D.C.Tex., 42 F.Supp. 107, 108.

Acquiescence by other party as necessary, Cerruti v. Burdick, 130 Conn. 284, 33 A.2d 333, 335. Clear and unequivocal, renunciation of contract and refusal to perform as essential, Kimel v. Missouri State Life Ins. Co., C.C.A. Kan., 71 F.2d 921, 923. Party to contract putting it out of his power to perform as breach, Assembly, Inc., v. Giller, 134 Misc. 657, 236 N.Y.S. 308, 313. Positive statement that promissor will not or cannot substantially perform contractual duties as breach, Hawkinson v. Johnston, C.C.A. Mo., 122 F.2d 724, 729, 730.

Bankruptcy as "anticipatory breach", In re Robertson, D.C.Ark., 41 F.Supp. 665, 668.

Doctrine is that party denying liability destroys contract so far as able. Pollack v. Pollack, Tex.Com.App., 46 S.W. 2d 292, 293.

Continuing Breach

Such breach occurs where the state of affairs, or the specific act, constituting the breach, endures for a considerable period of time, or is repeated at short intervals.

Constructive Breach

Such breach takes place when the party bound to perform disables himself from performance by some act, or declares, before the time comes, that he will not perform. Jordan v. Madsen, 69 Utah, 112, 252 P. 570, 573; The Adamello, D.C.Va., 19 F.2d 388, 389.

BREACH OF COVENANT. The nonperformance of any covenant agreed to be performed, or the doing of any act covenanted not to be done. Holthouse.

BREACH OF DUTY. In a general sense, any violation or omission of a legal or moral duty. More particularly, the neglect or failure to fulfill in a just and proper manner the duties of an office or fiduciary employment. Every violation by a trustee of a duty which equity lays upon him, whether willful and fraudulent, or done through negligence or arising through mere oversight or forgetfulness, is a breach of duty. Hivick v. Hemme, 118 Okl. 167, 247 P. 692, 693.

BREACH OF POUND. The breaking any pound or place where cattle or goods distrained are deposited, in order to take them back. 3 Bl.Comm. 146.

BREACH OF PRISON. The offense of actually and forcibly breaking a prison or gaol, with intent to escape. 4 Chit.Bl. 130, notes; 4 Steph. Comm. 255. The escape from custody of a person lawfully arrested on criminal process.

BREACH OF PRIVILEGE. An act or default in violation of the privilege of either house of parliament, of congress, or of a state legislature.

BREACH OF PROMISE. Violation of a promise; chiefly used as an elliptical expression for "breach of promise of marriage."

BREACH OF THE PEACE. A violation or disturbance of the public tranquillity and order. The offense of breaking or disturbing the public peace by any riotous, forcible, or unlawful proceeding. 4 Bl.Comm. 142, *et seq.;* People v. Bartz, 53 Mich. 493, 19 N.W. 161. "Breach of the peace" is a generic term, State v. Reichman, 135 Tenn. 653, 188 S.W. 225, 228, Ann.Cas.1918B, 889, and includes all violations of public peace or order and acts tending to a disturbance thereof, City of St. Louis v. Slupsky, 254 Mo. 309, 162 S.W. 155, 157, 49 L.R. A.,N.S., 919. One who commits a breach of the peace is guilty of disorderly conduct, but not all disorderly conduct is necessarily a "breach of the peace." Garvin v. City of Waynesboro, 15 Ga.App. 633, 84 S.E. 90, 91; City of Seattle v. Franklin, 191 Wash. 297, 70 P.2d 1049, 1051.

A *constructive* breach of the peace is an unlawful act which, though wanting the elements of actual violence or injury to any person, is yet inconsistent with the peaceable and orderly conduct of society. An *apprehended* breach of the peace is caused by the conduct of a man who threatens another with violence or physical injury, or who goes about in public with dangerous and unusual weapons in a threatening or alarming manner, or who publishes an aggravated libel upon another, etc.

BREACH OF TRUST. Any act done by a trustee contrary to the terms of his trust, or in excess of his authority and to the detriment of the trust; or the wrongful omission by a trustee of any act required of him by the terms of the trust. Also the wrongful misappropriation by a trustee of any fund or property which had been lawfully committed to him in a fiduciary character. Every violation by a trustee of a duty which equity lays upon him, whether willful and fraudulent, or done through negligence, or arising through mere oversight and forgetfulness, is a "breach of trust." The term, therefore, includes every omission and commission in carrying out the trust according to its terms, of care and diligence in protecting and investing the trust property, and of using perfect good faith. H. B. Cartwright & Bro. v. United States Bank & Trust Co., 23 N.M. 82, 167 P. 436, 453. A violation by the trustee of any duty which he owes to the beneficiary. Bruun v. Hanson, C.C.A.Idaho, 103 F.2d 685, 699.

BREACH OF TRUST WITH FRAUDULENT INTENT. Larceny after trust. State v. Owings, 205 S.C. 314, 31 S.E.2d 906, 907.

BREACH OF WARRANTY. In real property law and the law of insurance. The failure or falsehood of an affirmative promise or statement, or the nonperformance of an executory stipulation. Stewart v. Drake, 9 N.J.Law, 139. Failure of insured to disclose trivial and temporary disorders. Franklin Life Ins. Co. v. Critz, C.C.A.Miss., 109 F.2d 417. As used in the law of sales, "breach of warranty," unlike fraud, does not involve guilty knowledge, Anglo-California Trust Co. v. Hall, 211 P. 991, 993, 61 Utah, 223, and rests on contract, Oelwein Chemical Co. v. Baker, 204 Iowa, 66, 214 N.W. 595, 596. Falsity of statements incorporated into fidelity bond. City Bank & Trust Co. v. Commercial Casualty Co., La.App., 176 So. 27, 30.

BREAD ACTS. Laws providing for the sustenance of persons kept in prison for debt.

BREAK. "Break" may be used in a broad sense, as in seller's covenant in contract of sale of auto, to indicate a weakness, impairment, or destruction of parts, however caused. American Locomotive Co. v. National Wholesale Grocery Co., 226 Mass. 314, 115 N.E. 404, 405, L.R.A.1917D, 1125.

BREAK A LEG. Pertaining to a broken bone anywhere between ankle and hip, with possible exception of patella, 100% American Local Mut. Life & Accident Ass'n of El Paso v. Work, Tex. Civ.App., 289 S.W. 1020.

BREAK AND TAKE. Sale of merchandise or amusement where customer pays for a chattel and a chance for another unpaid for chattel, the ticket being the opportunity for fortuitous selection of a differentiated article. Minter v. Federal Trade Commission, C.C.A.3, 102 F.2d 69, 73.

BREAKAGE. Odd cents retained by race track promoter out of amounts due on wagers. Wise v. Delaware Steeplechase & Race Ass'n, Del.Super., 2 Terry 182, 18 A.2d 419, 421, 423.

BREAKDOWN SERVICE. As applied to an electric public service corporation is primarily a service for emergency and is used in case the electric plant of the customer breaks down; it is also used when very little electricity is required, as upon holidays and Sundays, and also at the peak of the service when a maximum current is required during the day. People ex rel. New York Edison Co. v. Public Service Commission for First Dist., 191 App.Div. 237, 181 N.Y.S. 259, 261.

BREAKING. Forcibly separating, parting, disintegrating, or piercing any solid substance.

In the law as to housebreaking and burglary, it means the tearing away or removal of any part of a house or of the locks, latches, or other fastenings intended to secure it, or otherwise exerting force to gain an entrance, with the intent to commit a felony; or violently or forcibly breaking out of a house, after having unlawfully entered it, in the attempt to escape. Sims v. State, 136 Ind. 358, 36 N.E. 278; Melton v. State, 24 Tex.App. 287, 6 S.W. 303. Actual "breaking" involves application of some force. Rains v. Commonwealth, 293 Ky. 429, 169 S.W.2d 41, 44, the action of accused must have been such as would, without additional effort, have made an entry possible. Armour v. State, 72 Okl.Cr. 44, 112 P.2d 1116, 1119, but there is no requirement that there be shown violence, a latch lifted, or a bolt drawn. People v. Viola, 264 App.Div. 38, 34 N.Y.S.2d 1018, 1020. The term in indictment, information or instruction implies force. State v. Stuart, 316 Mo. 150, 289 S.W. 822, 824; Humphrey v. State, 110 Tex.Cr.R. 62, 7 S.W.2d 576, 577; McFarland v. Commonwealth, 227 Ky. 411, 13 S.W.2d 277, 278. The slightest force is sufficient, as the lifting or opening of a latch, Dennis v. State, 71 Tex.Cr.R. 162, 158 S.W. 1008, 1010; State v. Gendusa, 193 La. 59, 190 So. 332, 339; or the raising of a window, Hollis v. State, 69 Tex.Cr.R. 286, 153 S.W. 853, 854; State v. Chappell, 185 S.C. 111, 193 S.E. 924, 925; or the opening of a door, State v. Lapoint, 87 Vt. 115, 88 A. 523, 47 L.R.A.,N.S., 717; Gibson v. Commonwealth, 204 Ky. 704, 265 S.W. 339, 345; Yeargin v. State, 54 Okl.Cr. 34, 14 P.2d 431, 432; Kidd v. Commonwealth, 273 Ky. 300, 116 S.W.2d 636, 638; or the opening of unfastened transom. State v. Chappell, 185 S.C. 111, 193 S.E. 924; or entry with a key or by manipulating hasp from outside, McGilveray v. State, 111 Tex.Cr.R. 256, 12 S.W.2d 585; or turning of knob of door, State v. Edell, 7 W.W.Harr. Del., 404, 183 A. 630. But entry by open door, window, or other opening does not constitute "breaking", George v. State, 183 Miss. 327, 184 So. 67, 68. Breaking lock securing pump handle on gasoline tank releasing handle is sufficient "breaking". Chaney v. State, 25 Ala.App. 141, 142 So. 103.

As an element of the crime of burglary breaking may be either actual or constructive. Davis v. Commonwealth, 132 Va. 521, 110 S.E. 356. Entering a building by a chimney is a constructive breaking. State v. Hart, 94 S.C. 214, 77 S.E. 862.

BREAKING A CASE. The expression by the judges of a court, to one another, of their views of a case, in order to ascertain how far they are agreed, and as preliminary to the formal delivery of their opinions. "We are breaking the case, that we may show what is in doubt with any of us." Holt, C. J., addressing Dolbin, J., 1 Show. 423.

BREAKING A CLOSE. An unlawful entry upon land. Littleton v. Roberts, 181 S.C. 303, 187 S.E. 349, 350.

Wrongdoer need only set in motion some dangerous agency which in itself, though quite distant from wrongdoer, inflicts wrong. Western Union Telegraph Co. v. Bush, 191 Ark. 1085, 89 S.W.2d 723, 725, 103 A.L.R. 367.

BREAKING BULK. The offense committed by a bailee (particularly a carrier) in opening or unpacking the chest, parcel, or case containing goods intrusted to his care, and removing the goods and converting them to his own use.

BREAKING DOORS. Forcibly removing the fastenings of a house, so that a person may enter.

BREAKING INTO. Breaking with burglarious intent. State v. Hefflin, 338 Mo. 236, 89 S.W.2d 938, 946, 103 A.L.R. 1301.

BREAKING JAIL. The act of a prisoner in effecting his escape from a place of lawful confinement.

BREAKING OF ARRESTMENT. In Scotch law. The contempt of the law committed by an arrestee who disregards the arrestment used in his hands, and pays the sum or delivers the goods arrested to the debtor. The breaker is liable to the arrester in damages. See Arrestment.

BREAST OF THE COURT. A metaphorical expression signifying the conscience, discretion, or recollection of the judge.

During the term of a court, the record is said to remain "in the breast of the judges of the court and in their remembrance." Co.Litt. 260*a*; 3 Bl.Comm. 407. When we say that the record is in the "breast of the court" to be changed during the term, we only mean that the proceedings attested by it have not yet obtained that irrevocable character which places them beyond the power of the court after the term. Willson v. Ice, 78 W.Va. 672, 90 S.E. 272, 275.

BREATH. In medical jurisprudence. The air expelled from the lungs at each expiration.

BREATHING. Expansion and contraction, under the influence of changing temperatures, of materials used in cables for transmission of high-tension electric currents. Electric Cable Joint Co. v. Brooklyn Edison Co., N.Y., 292 U.S. 69, 54 S.Ct. 586, 587, 78 L.Ed. 1131.

BREDWITE. In Saxon and old English law. A fine, penalty, or amercement imposed for defaults in the assise of bread. Cowell.

BREED. Produce (offspring) by hatching or gestation; to hatch. Miller Hatcheries v. Boyer, C.C.A.Iowa, 131 F.2d 283, 287.

BREHON. In old Irish law. A judge. 1 Bl. Comm. 100. Brehons, (*breitheamhuin,*) judges.

BREHON LAW. The name given to the ancient system of law of Ireland as it existed at the time of its conquest by Henry II.

BRENAGIUM. A payment in bran, which tenants anciently made to feed their lords' hounds.

BREPHOTROPHI. In the civil law. Persons appointed to take care of houses destined to receive foundlings.

BRETHREN. This word, in a will, may include sisters, as well as brothers, of the person indicated; it is not necessarily limited to the masculine gender. Terry v. Brunson, 1 Rich.Eq., S.C., 78.

BRETHREN OF TRINITY HOUSE. See Elder Brethren.

BRETTS AND SCOTTS, LAWS OF THE. A code or system of laws in use among the Celtic tribes of Scotland down to the beginning of the fourteenth century, and then abolished by Edward I. of England.

BRETTWALDA. In Saxon law. The ruler of the Saxon heptarchy.

BREVE. L. Lat. A writ. An original writ.

A writ or precept of the king issuing out of his courts. A writ by which a person is summoned or attached to answer an action, complaint, etc., or whereby anything is commanded to be done in the courts, in order to justice, etc. Skene.

BREVE DE RECTO. A writ of right, or license for a person ejected out of an estate, to sue for the possession of it.

BREVE INNOMINATUM. A writ making only a general complaint, without the details or particulars of the cause of action.

BREVE ITA DICITUR, QUIA REM DE QUA AGITUR, ET INTENTIONEM PETENTIS, PAUCIS VERBIS BREVITER ENARRAT. A writ is so called because it briefly states, in few words, the matter in dispute, and the object of the party seeking relief. 2 Inst. 39.

BREVE JUDICIALE DEBET SEQUI SUUM ORIGINALE, ET ACCESSORIUM SUUM PRINCIPALE. Jenk.Cent. 292. A judicial writ ought to follow its original, and an accessory its principal.

BREVE JUDICIALE NON CADIT PRO DEFECTU FORMÆ. Jenk.Cent. 43. A judicial writ fails not through defect of form.

BREVE NOMINATUM. A named writ. A writ stating the circumstances or details of the cause of action, with the time, place, and demand, very particularly.

BREVE ORIGINALE. An original writ; a writ which gave *origin* and commencement to a suit.

BREVE PERQUIRERE. To purchase a writ or license of trial in the king's courts by the plaintiff.

BREVE TESTATUM. A written memorandum introduced to perpetuate the tenor of the conveyance and investiture of lands. 2 Bl.Comm. 307. In Scotch law. A similar memorandum made out at the time of the transfer, attested by the *pares curiæ* and by the seal of the superior. Bell.

BREVET.

In military law. A commission by which an officer is promoted to the next higher rank, but without conferring a right to a corresponding increase of pay.

In French law. A privilege or warrant granted by the government to a private person, authorizing him to take a special benefit or exercise an exclusive privilege. Thus a *brevet d'invention* is a patent for an invention.

BREVIA. Lat. The plural of *breve*.

BREVIA ADVERSARIA. Adversary writs; writs brought by an adversary to recover land. 6 Coke, 67.

BREVIA AMICABILIA. Amicable or friendly writs; writs brought by agreement or consent of the parties.

BREVIA ANTICIPANTIA. At common law. Anticipating or preventive writs. Six were included in this category, viz.: Writ of *mesne; warrantia chartæ; monstraverunt; audita querela; curia claudenda;* and *ne injuste vexes*. Peters v. Linenschmidt, 58 Mo. 466.

BREVIA DE CURSU. Writs of course. Formal writs issuing as of course.

BREVIA FORMATA. Certain writs of approved and established form which were granted of course in actions to which they were applicable, and which could not be changed but by consent of the great council of the realm. Bract. fol. 413*b*.

BREVIA JUDICIALIA. Judicial writs. Auxiliary writs issued from the court during the progress of an action, or in aid of the judgment.

BREVIA MAGISTRALIA. Writs occasionally issued by the *masters* or clerks of chancery, the form of which was varied to suit the circumstances of each case. Bract. fol. 413*b*.

BREVIA SELECTA. Choice or selected writs or processes. Often abbreviated to Brev. Sel.

BREVIA, TAM ORIGINALIA QUAM JUDICIALIA, PATIUNTUR ANGLICA NOMINA. 10 Coke, 132. Writs, as well original as judicial, bear English names.

BREVIA TESTATA. The name of the short memoranda early used to show grants of lands out of which the deeds now in use have grown. Jacob.

BREVIARIUM ALARICIANUM. A compilation of Roman law made by order of Alaric II., king of the Visigoths, in Spain, and published for the use of his Roman subjects in the year 506. It is also known as *Lex Romana Visigothorum*. It became the principal, if not the only, representative of Roman law among the Franks.

BREVIARIUM ANIANI. Another name for the Brevarium Alaricianum, (*q. v.*) Anian was the referendery or chancellor of Alaric, and was commanded by the latter to authenticate, by his signature, the copies of the breviary sent to the *comites*. Mackeld. Rom. Law, § 68.

BREVIATE. A brief; brief statement, epitome, or abstract. A short statement of contents, accompanying a bill in parliament. Holthouse. The name is usually applied to the famous brief of Mr. Murray (afterwards Lord Mansfield) for the complainant in the case of Penn v. Lord Baltimore, 1 Ves. 444.

BREVIBUS ET ROTULIS LIBERANDIS. A writ or mandate to a sheriff to deliver to his successor the county, and appurtenances, with the rolls, briefs, remembrance, and all other things belonging to his office. Reg.Orig. 295.

BREWER. One who manufactures fermented liquors, for sale, from malt, wholly or in part, or from any substitute therefor. U. S. v. Wittig, 28 Fed.Cas. 745.

BRIBE. Anything of value; any gift, advantage or emolument; any price, reward or favor. State v. Douglas, 70 S.D. 203, 16 N.W.2d 489, 496. Any money, goods, right in action, property, thing of value, or any preferment, advantage, privilege or emolument, or any promise or undertaking to give any, asked, given, or accepted, with a corrupt intent to induce or influence action, vote, or opinion of person in any public or official capacity. People v. Van de Carr, 87 App.Div. 386, 84 N.Y.S. 461; People v. Ward, 110 Cal. 369, 42 P. 894; Williams v. State, 188 Ind. 283, 123 N.E. 209, 213. It is a gift, not necessarily of pecuniary value, bestowed to influence the conduct of the receiver, and must be of substantial value to him. People v. Hyde, 156 App.Div. 618, 141 N.Y.S. 1089, 1093.

Payment of corporate funds by director and executive officer of the corporation to officials of labor union to prevent ruinous strikes which union officials were under no legal duty to call as "bribe". Hornstein v. Paramount Pictures, Sup., 37 N.Y.S.2d 404, 412.

BRIBERY. The offering, giving, receiving, or soliciting of any thing of value to influence action as official or in discharge of legal or public duty. Allen v. State, 63 Okl.Cr. 16, 72 P.2d 516, 519. The corrupt tendering or receiving of a price for official action. State v. London, 194 Wash. 458, 78 P.2d 548, 554, 115 A.L.R. 1255. The receiving or offering any undue reward by or to any person concerned in the administration of public justice or a public officer to influence his behavior in office. Walsh v. People, 65 Ill. 65, 16 Am.Rep. 569; State v. Harrah, 101 W.Va. 300, 132 S.E. 654, 655, 4 Bl.Comm. 139, and note. The taking or giving a reward for public office. Brown.

Acceptance by public officer of compensation for doing legal duty, Ex parte Montgomery, 244 Ala. 91, 12 So.2d 314, 317; agreement by public official to refrain from performing official act or to corruptly perform act contrary to rules of honesty essential, Selvidge v. State, 126 Tex.Cr.R. 489, 72 S.W.2d 1079, 1080; Attempt to bribe officer engaged in making an unlawful arrest, Sugarman v. State, 173 Md. 52, 195 A. 324, 326; Attempted bribery as included in term, Coleman v. State ex rel. Mitchell, 132 Fla. 845, 182 So. 627, 628; Coleman v. State ex rel. Mitchell, 132 Fla. 845, 182 So. 627, 628; "extortion" and "bribery" mutually exclusive, People v. Feld, 262 App.Div. 909, 28 N.Y.S.2d 796, 797; involuntary payments insufficient, Hornstein v. Paramount Pictures, Sup., 37 N.Y.S.2d 404, 413; unlawful concert of one or more persons acting with one or more other persons essential, People v. Keyes, Cal.Sup., 284 P. 1105; voluntary giving of something of value to influence performance of official duty as essence, Hornstein v. Paramount Pictures, Sup., 37 N.Y.S.2d 404, 413.

At common law, the gist of the offense was the tendency to prevert justice, People v. Peters, 265 Ill. 122, 106 N.E. 513, 515, Ann.Cas.1916A, 813; the offering, giving, receiving or soliciting of anything of value to influence action as a public official, Coleman v. State ex rel. Mitchell, Fla., 182 So. 627, 628; corrupt agreement induced by offer of reward, Osborn v. State, 160 Tenn. 594, 28 S.W.2d 47, 48; The term now extends to many classes of officers and is not confined to judicial officers; it applies both to the actor and receiver, and extends to voters, cabinet ministers, legislators, sheriffs, and other classes. 2 Whart.Crim. Law, § 1858. In re Crum, 55 N.D. 876, 215 N.W. 682, 688, 55 A.L.R. 220; State v. McGraw, 142 La. 417, 76 So. 822. All persons whose official conduct is connected with the administration of the government are subjects, Commonwealth v. Benedict, 114 Pa.Super. 183, 173 A. 850, 851; persons acting under color of title to office, though not an officer de jure, are subjects, Ex parte Covell, 63 Okl. 256, 74 P.2d 626, 631; but it has also been held that the person charged to have been bribed must be an officer, de facto or de jure, or among the governmental administrative personnel. State v. London, 194 Wash. 458, 78 P.2d 548, 115 A.L.R. 1255.

BRIBERY AT ELECTIONS. The offense committed by one who gives or promises or offers money or any valuable inducement to an elector, in order to corruptly induce the latter to vote in a particular way or to abstain from voting, or as a reward to the voter for having voted in a particular way or abstained from voting.

BRIBOUR. One that pilfers other men's goods; a thief.

BRICOLIS. An engine by which walls were beaten down. Blount.

BRIDEWELL. In England. A house of correction.

BRIDGE. A structure erected over a river, creek, stream, ditch, ravine, obstruction in highway or other place to facilitate the passage and for benefit of travelers.

The term includes both arches and abutments; Bardwell v. Town of Jamaica, 15 Vt. 438; Andrew B. Hendryx Co. v. City of New Haven, 104 Conn. 632, 134 A. 77, 79; as well as approaches; 71 L.T. 430; McGee v. Jones County, 161 Iowa, 296, 142 N.W. 957, 959, 48 L.R.A.,N.S., 141; In re Park Lane South in City of New York, 206 App.Div. 269, 200 N.Y.S. 555, 557; *contra,* under a statute, City of Stamford v. Town of Stamford, 100 Conn. 434, 124 A. 26, 27. The term likewise includes fills or embankments, Havird v. Richmond County, 47 Ga.App. 580, 171 S.E. 220; Morgan County v. Glass, 139 Ga. 415, 77 S.E. 583; appurtenances necessary to its proper use, Lumley v. Pollard, 61 Ga.App. 681, 7 S.E.2d 308, 313; culverts; Central Bridge & Const. Co. v. Saunders County, 106 Neb. 484, 184 N.W. 220, 223; *contra,* Village of Marissa v. Jones, 327 Ill. 180, 158 N.E. 389, 394; viaducts; In re City of Boston, 221 Mass. 468, 109 N.E. 389, 392; but not a railway viaduct, designed only for the passage of engines and cars; Bridge Proprietors v. Land & Improvement Co., 1 Wall. 116, 17 L.Ed. 571; nor does the term include a drain under a bridge; Ellis v. Floyd County, 24 Ga.App. 717, 102 S.E. 181; nor a franchise or contract to build a bridge; New Orleans Pontchartrain Bridge Co. v. Louisiana Public Service Commission, 162 La. 874, 111 So. 265, 266; nor piping and water boxes and culverts for drainage purposes across public roads, Montgomery County v. Seaboard Air Line Ry. Co., 41 Ga. App. 130, 152 S.E. 261, 262; nor flood walls, Jefferson County Fiscal Court v. Jefferson County ex rel. Grauman, 278 Ky. 68, 128 S.W.2d 230, 232, 233; nor an elevated roadway or causeway of reinforced concrete, resting upon concrete piers or columns. Rumsey v. Department of Labor and Industries, 192 Wash. 538, 74 P.2d 214, 216.

"Bridges" and "culverts" are not synonymous. Protest of Evans, 153 Okl. 191, 4 P.2d 1030, 1031.

Bridges are either public or private. Public bridges are such as form a part of the highway, common, according to their character as foot, horse, or carriage bridges, to the public generally, with or without toll. State v. Street, 117 Ala. 203, 23 So. 807; Bonneville County v. Bingham County, 24 Idaho, 1, 132 P. 431, 433; they are bridges across a creek, river, or other natural body of water, etc., erected for the accommodation of the public, In re Walnut St. Bridge in City of Des Moines, 220 Iowa 55, 261 N.W. 781, 782. A private bridge is one which is not open to the use of the public generally, and does not form part of the highway. Rex v. Bucks County, 12 East, 192. Such a bridge will not be considered a public bridge although it may be occasionally used by the public. Thompson v. R. Co., 3 Sandf.Ch., N.Y., 625; 1 Rolle, Abr. 368, *Bridges,* pl. 2; 2 Inst. 701; 1 Salk. 359.

BRIDGE OVER A PUBLIC WAY. A bridge upon which railroad runs above highway. Boston & M. R. R. v. Worcester County Com'rs, 300 Mass. 415, 15 N.E.2d 455, 457.

BRIDGE UNDER A PUBLIC WAY. A bridge for travelers to use as part of a highway crossing railroad over level thereof. Boston & M. R. R. v. Worcester County Com'rs, 300 Mass. 415, 15 N.E. 2d 455.

BRIDGE-MASTERS. Persons chosen by the citizens, to have the care and supervision of bridges, and having certain fees and profits belonging to their office, as in the case of London Bridge.

BRIDLE ROAD. In the location of a private way laid out by the selectmen, and accepted by the town, a description of it as a "bridle road" does not confine the right of way to a particular class of animals or special mode of use. Flagg v. Flagg, 16 Gray, Mass., 175.

BRIEF. A written document; a letter; a writing in the form of a letter. A summary, abstract, or epitome. A condensed statement or epitome of some larger document, or of a series of papers, facts and circumstances, or propositions.

In American practice. A written or printed document, prepared by counsel to serve as the basis for an argument upon a cause in an appellate court, and usually filed for the information of the court. It embodies the points of law which the counsel desires to establish, together with the arguments and authorities upon which he rests his contention. A brief, within a rule of court requiring counsel to furnish briefs, before argument, implies some kind of statement of the case for the information of the court. Gardner v. Stover, 43 Ind. 356. A "brief" is the vehicle of counsel to convey to the appellate court the essential facts of his client's case, a statement of the questions of law involved, the law he would have applied, and the application he desires made of it by the court. Bell v. Germain, 12 Cal.App. 375, 107 P. 630. The brief of evidence in connection with an auditor's report is considered a "brief" though it may embody the stenographic report of the testimony in full. McKenzie v. Perdue, 67 Ga.App. 202, 19 S.E.2d 765, 774.

In Ecclesiastical law. A papal rescript sealed with wax. See Bull.

In English practice. A document prepared by the attorney, and given to the barrister, before the trial of a cause, for the instruction and guidance of the latter. It contains, in general, all the information necessary to enable the barrister to successfully conduct their client's case in court, such as a statement of the facts, a summary of the pleadings, the names of the witnesses, and an outline of the evidence expected from them, and any suggestions arising out of the peculiarities of the case.

In Scotch law. Brief is used in the sense of "writ," and this seems to be the sense in which the word is used in very many of the ancient writers.

Brief a l'evesque

A writ to the bishop which, in *quare impedit,* shall go to remove an incumbent, unless he recover or be presented *pendente lite.* 1 Keb. 386.

Brief of Title

A methodical epitome of all the patents, conveyances, incumbrances, liens, court proceedings, and other matters affecting the title to real estate.

Brief Out of the Chancery

In Scotch law. A writ issued in the name of the sovereign in the election of tutors to minors, the cognoscing of lunatics or of idiots, and the ascertaining the widow's terce; and sometimes in dividing the property belonging to heirs-portioners. In these cases only brieves are now in use. Bell.

Brief Papal

In ecclesiastical law. The pope's letter upon matters of discipline.

Printed Brief

Typewritten brief is a written and not a "printed brief." Waterman Lumber & Supply Co. v. Holmes, Tex.Civ.App., 161 S.W. 70.

BRIEFLY. Concisely; in a few words; pertaining to a short or abridged statement. Boynton Real Estate Co. v. Woodbridge Tp., 94 N.J.Law, 226, 109 A. 514, 515.

BRIEVE. In Scotch law. A writ. 1 Kames, Eq. 146.

BRIGA. In old European law. Strife, contention, litigation, controversy.

BRIGANDINE. A coat of mail or ancient armour, consisting of numerous jointed scale-like plates, very pliant and easy for the body, mentioned in 4 & 5 P. & M. c. 2.

BRIGBOTE. In Saxon and old English law. A tribute or contribution towards the repairing of bridges. See Bote.

BRINE. A solution 4 per cent. salt is brine, within the meaning of the provision of paragraph 488, Free List, Tariff Act of 1913, for "fruits in brine." Amerman & Patterson v. U. S., 12 Ct.Cust.App. 117, 118.

BRING. To convey to the place where the speaker is or is to be, to bear from a more distant to a nearer place, to make to come, procure, produce, draw to, to convey, carry or conduct, move. Frederick v. Great Northern Ry. Co., 207 Wis. 234, 240 N.W. 387, 390. The doing of something effectual; the bringing of someone to account, or the accomplishment of some definite purpose. Landrum v. Fulton, 47 Ohio App. 376, 191 N.E. 917, 918.

BRING ABOUT. To procure, implies completion. Jackson v. Thompson, Tex.Civ.App., 74 S.W.2d 1055, 1057.

BRING INTO. To import, U. S. v. Gully, D.C.N.Y., 9 F.2d 959; to introduce, Sturgeon v. State, 17 Ariz. 513, 154 P. 1050, 1055, L.R.A.1917B, 1230.

BRING SUIT. To "bring" an action or suit has a settled customary meaning at law, and refers to the initiation of legal proceedings in a suit. Lake & Co. v. King County, 4 Wash.2d 651, 104 P.2d 599, 601. A suit is "brought" at the time it is commenced. Hames v. Judd, Com.Pl., 9 N.Y.Supp. 743, 30 St.R. 666, 16 Daly 110; Goldenberg v. Murphy, 108 U.S. 162, 2 Sup.Ct. 388, 27 L.Ed. 686; Buecker v. Carr, 60 N.J.Eq. 300, 47 Atl. 34. "Brought" and "commenced" in statutes of limitations are commonly deemed to have been used interchangeably. Hannaman v. Gordon, Tex.Com. App., 261 S.W. 1006, 1008. Under such statutes, the suit may be "brought," when the summons subsequently served is issued. Mill Creek & Minehill Nav. & R. Co. v. United States, D.C.Pa., 246 F. 1013, 1016. Under a statute providing that no action shall be "brought or maintained", "brought" applies to actions not yet instituted. Bruenn v. North Yakima School Dist. No. 7, Yakima County, 101 Wash. 374, 172 P. 569, 571. "Institute and prosecute" and "bring suit" as synonymous. Traders & General Ins. Co. v. Spillers, Tex.Civ.App., 88 S.W.2d 738, 740.

BRING UP. Nurse, rear, and educate child until full age. In re Bamber's Estate, 147 Misc. 712, 265 N.Y.S. 798.

BRINGING ACTION TO TRIAL. Motion to reset case for trial as "bringing action to trial". Craghill v. Ford, 127 Cal.App. 661, 16 P.2d 343, 346.

BRINGING ERROR. Writ of error is considered as brought at time it is filed in court which renders judgment. Girard Fire & Marine Ins. Co. v. Commonwealth Building & Loan Ass'n, C.C.A. Tex., 32 F.2d 736.

BRINGING MONEY INTO COURT. The act of depositing money in the custody of a court or of its clerk or marshal, for the purpose of satisfying a debt or duty, or to await the result of an interpleader. Dirks v. Juel, 59 Neb. 353, 80 N.W. 1045.

BRIS. In French maritime law. Literally, breaking; wreck. Distinguished from *naufrage, (q. v.)*.

BRISTOL BARGAIN. In English law. A contract by which A. lends B. £1,000 on good security, and it is agreed that £500, together with interest, shall be paid at a time stated; and, as to the other £500, that B., in consideration thereof, shall pay to A. £100 *per annum* for seven years. Wharton.

BRITISH COLUMBIA. The territory on the north-west coast of North America, once known by the designation of "New Caledonia." Its government is provided for by 21 & 22 Vict. c. 99. Vancouver Island is united to it by the 29 & 30 Vict. c. 67. See 33 & 34 Vict. c. 66.

BRITISH SUBJECT. Any person owing permanent allegiance to crown. U. S. ex rel. Graber v. Karnuth, C.C.A.N.Y., 30 F.2d 242, 243.

BRITISH THERMAL UNIT. The amount of heat required to raise a pound of water one degree Fahrenheit. Shawnee Gas & Electric Co. v. Corporation Commission of Oklahoma, 111 Okl. 13, 237 P. 844.

BROAD INTERPRETATION. That interpretation of Constitution or statute which, brushing aside minor objections and trivial technicalities, effectuates intent of act. In re Senate Resolution No. 2 Concerning Constitutionality of House Bill No. 6, 94 Colo. 101, 31 P.2d 325, 332.

BROCAGE. The wages, commission, or pay of a broker (also called "brokerage"). Also the avocation or business of a broker.

BROCARD. In old English law. A legal maxim. "Brocardica Juris," the title of a small book of legal maxims, published at Paris, 1508.

BROCARIUS, BROCATOR. In old English and Scotch law. A broker; a middleman between buyer and seller; the agent of both transacting parties. Bell; Cowell.

BROCELLA. In old English law. A wood, a thicket or covert of bushes and brushwood. Cowell; Blount.

BROKEN. Impoverishment. Walsh v. Kennedy, 115 Mont. 551, 147 P.2d 425, 430.

BROKEN STOWAGE. In maritime law. That space in a ship which is not filled by her cargo.

BROKER. An agent employed to make bargains and contracts for a compensation. Story, Ag. § 28; Payne v. Ponder, 139 Ga. 283, 77 S.E. 32, 34. A dealer in securities issued by others. White v. Financial Guarantee Corporation, 13 Cal.App.2d 93, 56 P.2d 550, 553. A middleman or negotiator between parties. San Jacinto Life Ins. Co. v. Brooks, Tex.Civ.App., 274 S.W. 648, 650; Messick v. Johnson, 155 Okl. 139, 8 P.2d 28, 30; Gile v. Tsutakawa, 109 Wash. 366, 187 P. 323, 326; Civil Code La. art. 3016. A person dealing with another for sale of property. Davis v. Chipman, 210 Cal. 609, 293 P. 40, 44. A person whose business it is to bring buyer and seller together. Keys v. Johnson, 68 Pa. 42. The term extends to almost every branch of business, to realty as well as personalty. Richmond Mortgage & Loan Corporation v. Rose, 142 Va. 342, 128 S.E. 604, 605.

A voyage is called a "broker" where no fish are caught on a fishing voyage or from some other reason there are no proceeds from a fish auction. The Dirigo First, D.C.Mass., 60 F.Supp. 675.

For distinction between "commission merchant" and "broker," see Commission Merchant. For "Factor" and "broker" as synonymous or distinguishable, see Factor.

Ordinarily, the term is applied to one acting for others but is applicable to one in business of negotiating purchases or sales for himself. McCornick & Co., Bankers, v. Tolmie Bros., 42 Idaho 1, 243 P. 355, 358; Johnson v. Winslow, 155 Misc. 170, 279 N.Y.S. 147.

A "broker" is an agent with special and limited authority. Stephenson v. Golden, 279 Mich. 710, 276 N.W. 849, 858; Portsmouth Cotton Oil Refining Corp. v. Madrid Cotton Oil Co., 200 Ala. 634, 77 So. 8, 9. A middleman, as distinguished from a broker, is employed merely to bring the parties together when each desires to exchange his property for that of the other, or where one desires to sell and the other to purchase and his services are not rendered as the agent of either party; but a "broker" is the agent of a party, employed to procure a customer or to effect the sale or exchange. Tracey v. Blake, 229 Mass. 57, 118 N.E. 271, 272.

Brokers are of many kinds, the most important being enumerated and defined as follows:

Exchange Broker

See Exchange Broker.

Merchandise Brokers

Buyers and sellers of goods and negotiators between buyer and seller, but without having the custody of the property.

Money-Broker

A money-changer; a scrivener or jobber; one who lends or raises money to or for others.

Note Brokers

Negotiators of the discount or sale of commercial paper.

Pawnbrokers

Lenders of money on goods deposited with them in pledge, taking high rates of interest.

Real Estate Brokers

Persons who procure the purchase or sale of land, acting as intermediary between vendor and purchaser, and who negotiate loans on real-estate security, manage and lease estates, etc. Latta v. Kilbourn, 150 U.S. 524, 14 S.Ct. 201, 37 L.Ed. 169; Abraham v. Wasaff, 111 Okl. 138, 239 P. 138, 140. A broker employed in negotiating the sale, purchase, or exchange of lands on a commission contingent on success. Oregon Home Builders v. Montgomery Inv. Co., 94 Or. 349, 184 P. 487, 491. A person engaged in business to such an extent that it is his vocation or partial vocation. Morris v. O'Neill, 239 Mich. 663, 215 N.W. 8, 9; Kolb v. Burkhardt, 148 Md. 539, 129 A. 670, 672.

Ship-Brokers

Who transact business between the owners of ships and freighters or charterers, and negotiate the sale of vessels.

Stock Brokers

Brokers employed to buy and sell for their principals stocks, bonds, government securities, etc. The term "broker" applies as well to a broker on the Board of Trade as to one on the Stock Exchange. Cutler v. Pardridge, 182 Ill.App. 350, 358.

BROKERAGE. The wages or commissions of a broker; also, his business or occupation.

BROKERAGE CONTRACT. A contract of agency, whereby broker is employed to make contracts of kind agreed upon in name and on behalf of his principal, and for which he is paid an agreed commission. Nolen's Adm'r v. Robinson, 213 Ky. 752, 281 S.W. 1034, 1036; Hardesty v. Martin Ebersbach Co., C.C.A.Ohio, 294 F. 5, 6. A unilateral contract wherein the principal makes an offer which is interpreted as promise to pay broker a commission in consideration of his producing a buyer ready, able, and willing to buy the property on the principal's terms. In re Cowan's Estate, Sur., 13 N.Y.S.2d 374, 376.

BROSSUS. Bruised, or injured with blows, wounds, or other casualty. Cowell.

BROTHEL. A bawdy-house; a house of ill fame; a common habitation of prostitutes. United States v. Casey, D.C.Ohio, 247 F. 362, 364.

BROTHER. One person is a brother "of the whole blood" to another, the former being a male, when both are born from the same father and mother. He is a brother "of the half blood" to that other (or half-brother) when the two are born to the same father by different mothers or by the same mother to different fathers.

The term may embrace half brothers. Thompson v. Smith, 102 Okl. 150, 227 P. 77, 80; Darson v. Moore, 163 Miss. 705, 142 So. 447, 452. It may be deemed to embrace only a blood brother. Droney v. U. S., D.C.D.C., 59 F. Supp. 154, 155

In the civil law, the following distinctions are observed: Two brothers who descend from the same father, but by different mothers, are called "consanguine" brothers. If they have the same mother, but are begotten by different fathers, they are called "uterine" brothers. If they have both the same father and mother, they are denominated brothers "germane."

BROTHER-IN-LAW. A wife's brother or a sister's husband. There is not any relationship, but only affinity, between brothers-in-law. Farmers' L. & T. Co. v. Iowa Water Co., C.C., 80 Fed. 469. See State v. Foster, 112 La. 533, 36 So. 554. Two men are not brothers-in-law from the circumstance merely of having married sisters. Cruce v. State, 87 Fla. 406, 100 So. 264, 265.

BROTHERHOOD AND GUESTLING, COURT OF. The Brotherhood was a conference of seven towns (*i. e.*, the Cinque Ports and two other ancient towns) as to the provision of the necessary ships and as to arranging for the herring sale at Yarmouth, and for other such purposes. The Guestling was rather a wider meeting, at which not merely the Brotherhood, but deputies from other associated towns were present for the discussion of subjects of common interest to all.

BROUGHT. Taken; carried. United States v. Townsend, D.C.N.Y., 219 F. 761, 762. Past tense of "bring." Frederick v. Great Northern Ry. Co., 207 Wis. 234, 240 N.W. 387, 390, 80 A.L.R. 984.

A proceeding is not "brought" as regards defendant until process has been issued from an appropriate court in good faith intending or making an effort to serve it. City of Revere v. Special Judge of Dist. Court of Chelsea, 262 Mass. 393, 160 N.E. 431, 433. A writ of error is not "brought" until it is filed or lodged in the court, or with the clerk of the court, which rendered the judgment. U. S. v. Shaffer, D.C.Wash., 278 F. 549, 551.

BROUGHT IN QUESTION UPON THE RECORD. The constitutionality of an act is "brought in question upon the record" when it is clearly questioned by the allegation of any pleading, or by any other formal objection filed in the case. Brosco v Frost, 63 R.I. 1, 6 A.2d 705, 706.

BROUGHT TO THE ATTENTION OF. Equivalent to the expression "made known to." State v. Sullivan, 159 La. 589, 105 So. 631, 636.

BROUGHT TO TRIAL. An action is not brought to trial until the trial is commenced. Miller & Lux v. Superior Court of California in and for Merced County, 192 Cal. 333, 219 P. 1006, 1009.

BROWN DECREE. A decree which terminates marriage without specifying in whose favor issue as to grounds for divorce was decided. Spector v. Spector, 382 P.2d 659, 666, 94 Ariz. 175.

BRUARIUM. In old English law. A heath ground; ground where heath grows. Spelman.

BRUGBOTE. See Brigbote.

BRUILLUS. In old English law. A wood or grove; a thicket or clump of trees in a park or forest. Cowell.

BRUISE. In medical jurisprudence. A contusion; an injury upon the flesh of a person with a blunt or heavy instrument, without solution of continuity, or without breaking the skin. Shadock v. Road Co., 79 Mich. 7, 44 N.W. 158. See Contusion.

BRUKBARN. In old Swedish law. The child of a woman conceiving after a rape, which was made legitimate. Literally, the child of a struggle. Burrill.

BRUSHING. Digging of space in middle of bottom of mine entry or room neck in which to lay track. Schillings v. Big Creek Coal Co., Mo.App. 277 S.W. 964, 965.

BRUTUM FULMEN. An empty noise; an empty threat. A judgment void upon its face which is in legal effect no judgment at all, and by which no rights are divested, and from which none can be obtained, and neither binds nor bars anyone. Dollert v. Pratt-Hewit Oil Corporation, Tex.Civ.App., 179 S.W.2d 346, 348.

BS. Impurities in crude oil. Crude Oil Contracting Co. v. Insurance Co. of North America, C.C.A.Okl., 118 F.2d 476.

B.T.U. "British Thermal Units." Bennett v. Piscitello, 170 Misc. 177, 9 N.Y.S.2d 69, 71.

BUBBLE. An extravagant or unsubstantial project for extensive operations in business or commerce, generally founded on a fictitious or exaggerated prospectus, to ensnare unwary investors. Companies formed on such a basis or for such purposes are called "bubble companies." The term is chiefly used in England.

BUBBLE ACT. The statute 6 Geo. I. c. 18 (1719), "for restraining several extravagant and unwarrantable practices herein mentioned," prompted by the collapse of the "South Sea Project." It was mostly repealed by the statute 6 Geo. IV. c. 91.

BUCK SWAMPER. An employee of lumber company to mark timber and brush in a wooded area to be cut later for the formation of a road. Demasters v. State Compensation Com'r, 112 W.Va. 498, 165 S.E. 667.

BUCKET SHOP. An office or place (other than a regularly incorporated or licensed exchange) where persons engage in pretended buying and selling of commodities. Connor v. Black, 119 Mo. 126, 24 S.W. 184; Gatewood v. North Carolina, 203 U.S. 531, 27 S.Ct. 167, 51 L.Ed. 305.

BUCKETING. Receipt of orders to purchase and sell stock without intention of executing orders and without execution of orders. Kaiser v. Butchart, 200 Minn. 545, 274 N.W. 680, 683, 113 A.L.R. 847.

BUCK'S EXTENSION PROCESS. Some uniform, continuous force or pull applied to leg or foot below break to overcome natural contraction of muscles of thigh. Sweet v. Douge, 145 Wash. 142, 259 P. 25. See Counterextension.

BUCKSTALL. A toil, net, or snare, to take deer. 4 Inst. 306.

BUDGET. A balance sheet or statement of estimated receipts and expenditures. Appalachian Electric Power Co. v. City of Huntington, 115 W. Va. 588, 177 S.E. 431, 433; a plan or method whereby expenditures are controlled. Kistler v. Carbon County, 154 Pa.Super. 299, 35 A.2d 733, 735; An estimate. Board of Sup'rs of Chesterfield County v. Chesterfield County School Board, 182 Va. 266, 28 S.E.2d 698, 703.

A name given in England to the statement annually presented to parliament by the chancellor of the exchequer, containing the estimates of the national revenue and expenditure.

BUDGET SYSTEM. A system by which income and expenditure for definite period are balanced. Rowe v. Stanley County, 52 S.D. 516, 219 N.W. 122, 123.

BUFFER. A contrivance to mitigate the shock by cars coming together rather than a safety appliance; an elastic apparatus for deadening the jar caused by the collision of bodies. George v. Atchison, T. & S. F. Ry. Co., 102 Kan. 774, 178 P. 403, 404.

"Agency," "adjunct," "branch," "instrumentality," "dummy," "tool" and "buffer" as synonymous. Lowendahl v. Baltimore & O. R. Co., 247 App.Div. 144, 287 N.Y.S. 62, 74.

BUFFET. A public place for lunch or light refreshments. McCormick v. Brennan, 224 Ill.App. 251, 254.

BUG. Vibrating horizontal arm for the semi-automatic production of code dots, as distinguished from the Morse key. Vibroplex Co. v. J. H. Bunnell & Co., D.C.N.Y., 13 F.2d 528.

BUGGERY. A carnal copulation against nature; a man or a woman with a brute beast, a man with a man, or man unnaturally with a woman. 3 Inst. 58; 12 Coke, 36. Ausman v. Veal, 10 Ind. 356, 71 Am.Dec. 331; Com. v. J., 21 Pa.Co.Ct.R. 626. This term is often used interchangeably with "sodomy"; but even when so used, it does not necessarily include the act called "fellatio" or "fellation." State v. Murry, 136 La. 253, 66 So. 963, 964. See Sodomy.

BUILD. To construct and raise anew. Attorney General ex rel. Gibson v. Board of Sup'rs of Montcalm County, 141 Mich. 590, 104 N.W. 792, 794. To form by uniting materials into a regular structure. United States v. Blair, C.C.N.Y., 190 F. 372, 374. The term may also be employed in the sense of obtain, secure, or acquire. Verner v. Muller, 89 S.C. 545, 72 S.E. 393.

"Build" is not synonymous with amend, repair, or maintain. State v. White, 16 R.I. 591, 18 A. 179; Hutchinson v. City of Olympia, 2 Wash.T. 314, 5 P. 606, 608. But it has been held that a grant of power to build a railroad, or a requirement that certain persons shall build bridges, may include the power or duty of maintenance or repair. Central R. Co. v. Collins, 40 Ga. 582, 624; Franklin County Com'rs v. White Water Valley Canal Co., 2 Ind. 162, 163.

BUILDER. One whose occupation is the building or erection of structures, the controlling and directing of construction, or the planning, constructing, remodeling and adapting to particular uses buildings and other structures. Turner v. Haar, 114 Mo. 335, 21 S.W. 737, 738. One who puts a structure into permanent form. Kansas City Southern Ry. Co. v. Wallace, 38 Okl. 233, 132 P. 908, 911, 46 L.R.A.,N.S., 112. One who builds. Hopkins v. Department of Labor and Industries, 190 Wash. 251, 67 P.2d 872, 875. The term may be synonymous with "contractor." State v. Clark, 43 Wash. 664, 86 P. 1067. It may also designate a shipwright, a mason, etc., and likewise an architect. Savannah & C. R. Co. v. Callahan, 49 Ga. 506, 511. *Contra*, as to "architect," People ex rel. v. Lower, 251 Ill. 527, 96 N.E. 346, 347, 36 L.R.A. 1203.

BUILDING. An edifice. State v. Ornelas, 42 N.M. 17, 74 P.2d 723, 725; People v. Chase, 117 Cal.App.Supp. 775, 1 P.2d 60, 61; A structure. State v. Ornelas, 42 N.M. 17, 74 P.2d 723, 725. A fabric built or constructed. State v. Ornelas, 42 N.M. 17, 74 P.2d 723, 725. That which is built. Brown v. Sikes, 188 S.C. 288, 198 S.E. 854, 856; People v. Chase, 117 Cal.App.Supp. 775, 1 P.2d 60, 61.

A fabric or edifice designed to stand more or less permanently. Brown v. Sikes, 188 S.C. 288, 198 S.E. 854, 856; a fabric, structure, or edifice, designed for the habitation of men or animals or for the shelter of property. People v. Gillespie, 344 Ill. 290, 176 N.E. 316, 318. A structure or edifice erected by man, composed of stone, wood, brick, marble or other proper substance, and intended for use or convenience. State v. Crouse, 117 Me. 363, 104 A. 525, 526; Sacks v. Legg, 219 Ill.App. 144, 147; Rabb v. W. P. Ellison, Inc., 89 N.J.Law, 416, 99 A. 119, 120. A structure or edifice inclosing a space within its walls, and usually, but not necessarily, covered with a roof. State v. Elliott, 198 Iowa 71, 199 N.W. 270, 271; Netter v. Scholtz, 282 Ky. 493, 138 S.W.2d 951, 953.

"Erecting" as synonym. Board of Com'rs of Guadalupe County v. State, 43 N.M. 409, 94 P.2d 515, 516, 520; "premises" as synonym. Everett v. Patrons' & Farmers' Mut. Fire Ins. Co. of Jackson County, 222 Mo.App. 1010, 7 S.W. 2d 463, 468.

The term generally, though not always, implies the idea of a habitation for the permanent use of man, or an erection connected with his permanent use. Rouse v. Catskill & N. Y. Steamboat Co., 13 N.Y.S. 126, 127, 35 N.Y.St.Rep. 491; It imports tangibility, Wells Fargo & Co. v. Jersey City, D.C.N.J., 207 F. 871, 876, and may include the land on which it stands, as well as adjacent land, Thomas v. Long, 182 Iowa, 859, 166 N.W. 287, 288; Dallas Land & Loan Co. v. Garrett, Tex.Civ.App., 276 S.W. 471, 473; Freedman v. S. S. Kresge Co., 290 Mass. 114, 194 N.E. 829, 830. It includes many different kinds of structures and edifices. Great Eastern Casualty Co. v. Blackwelder, 21 Ga.App. 586, 94 S.E. 843, 844. The identity or difference of meaning of the words "building," "improvement" and "structure" depends upon context in connection with which they are used. Lanier v. Lovett, 25 Ariz. 54, 213 P. 391, 394.

A ship as building within gambling statute. People v. Chase, 117 Cal.App.Supp. 775, 1 P.2d 60, 61.

BUILDING A FIRE. "Kindling a fire" and "building a fire" are equivalent. State v. Merrill, 132 Me. 103, 167 A. 172, 173.

BUILDING AND LOAN ASSOCIATION. An organization for the purpose of accumulating a fund by subscriptions and savings of its members to assist them in building or purchasing for themselves dwellings or real estate by the loan to them of the requisite money. McCauley v. Association, 97 Tenn., 13 Pickle, 421, 37 S.W. 212, 213, 35 L.R.A. 244; Rhodes v. Missouri Savings & Loan Co., 173 Ill. 621, 50 N.E. 998, 1000, 43 L.R.A. 93. A juristic person organized by government to accomplish certain ends, which may be public or quasi public. Hopkins Federal Savings & Loan Ass'n v. Cleary, Wis., 296 U.S. 315, 56 S.Ct. 235, 80 L.Ed. 251, 100 A.L.R. 1403. Quasi public corporations chartered to encourage thrift and promote ownership of homes. Hopkins Federal Savings & Loan Ass'n v. Cleary, Wis., 296 U.S. 315, 56 S.Ct. 235, 237, 241, 80 L.Ed. 251, 100 A.L.R. 1403.

A private corporation designed for the purpose of accumulating into its treasury, by means of the gradual payment by its members of their stock subscriptions in periodical installments, a fund to be invested from time to time in advances made to such shareholders on their stock as may apply for this privilege on approved security, the borrowing members paying interest and a premium for this preference in securing an advancement over other members, and continuing to pay the regular installments on their stock in addition, all of which funds, together with payments made by the nonborrowing members, including fines, forfeitures, and other like revenues, go into the common fund until it, with the profits thereon, aggregates the face value of all the shares in the association, the legal effect of which is to extinguish the liability incurred for the loans and advancements, and to distribute to each nonborrowing member the par value of his stock. Washington Nat. Building, Loan & Investment Ass'n v. Stanley, 38 Or. 319, 63 P. 489, 492, 84 Am.St.Rep. 793. See, also, Wilkinson v. Mutual Bldg. & Sav. Ass'n, C.C.A. Wis., 13 F.2d 997, 998.

BUILDING IS COVERED. The words ordinarily mean that the property shall be insured in the standard form of insurance from that instant for a reasonable time until either the policy or policies can be written out, or their issuance approved or disapproved or some other temporary impediment to the complete formal contract of insurance can be removed. Shumway v. Home Fire & Marine Ins. Co. of California, 301 Mass. 391, 17 N.E.2d 212, 214.

BUILDING LEASE. A lease of land for a long term of years, usually 99, at a rent called a "ground rent," the lessee covenanting to erect certain edifices thereon according to specification, and to maintain the same, etc., during the term.

BUILDING LIEN. The statutory lien of a material-man or contractor for the erection of a building. June v. Doke, 35 Tex.Civ.App. 240, 80 S.W. 406.

BUILDING LINE. A line established by municipal authority, to secure uniformity of appearance in the streets of the city, drawn at a certain uniform distance from the curb or from the edge of the sidewalk, and parallel thereto, upon which the fronts of all buildings on that street must be placed, or beyond which they are not allowed to project. See Tear v. Freebody, 4 C.B.,N.S., 263.

As used in a city charter authorizing the establishment of a "building line" along boulevards, the term means a mark of division or demarkation; an outline or contour; a limit or boundary;—not a straight line. City of St. Louis v. Handlan, 242 Mo. 88, 145 S.W. 421, 422, 423. As to the meaning of the term in town and city plats, see Simpson v. Mikkelsen, 196 Ill. 575, 63 N.E. 1036, 1037.

BUILDING LOAN AGREEMENT. An agreement by which one undertakes to advance to another money to be used primarily in erection of buildings. York Mortg. Corporation v. Clotar Const. Corporation, 254 N.Y. 128, 172 N.E. 265, 269.

BUILDING MATERIAL. Material used in construction work. Wood Preserving Corporation v. State Tax Commission, 235 Ala. 438, 179 So. 254, 255. Material essential to erection or construction of house or other structure, Mutual Lumber Co. v. Sheppard, Tex.Civ.App., 173 S.W.2d 494, 497, 498, 500.

BUILDING OR STRUCTURE USED AS CHURCH. A building wholly dedicated to purposes of religious worship. Miles v. McKinney, 174 Md. 551, 199 A. 540, 547, 117 A.L.R. 207.

BUILDING PERMIT. A permit to erect a building. Commissioners of Easton v. Covey, 74 Md. 262, 22 A. 266; Commonwealth v. Devlin, 305 Pa. 440, 158 A. 161, 163.

BUILDING RESTRICTIONS. Covenants creating easement running with land in each deed containing restrictions. Strauss v. J. C. Nichols Land Co., 327 Mo. 205, 37 S.W.2d 505, 508.

BUILDING SITE. As used in contract, for filling of the "building site" to grade, term contemplated the entire lot. Myevre v. Liberty Realty & Securities Co., 156 La. 496, 100 So. 694, 696.

BUILDING SOCIETY. An association in which the subscriptions of the members form a capital stock or fund out of which advances may be made to members desiring them, on mortgage security.

BUL. In the ancient Hebrew chronology, the eighth month of the ecclesiastical, and the second of the civil year. It has since been called *"Marshevan,"* and answers to our October.

BULK. Unbroken packages. Merchandise which is neither counted, weighed, nor measured. See Texas & P. Ry. Co. v. Gate City Fertilizer Co., Tex.Civ.App., 176 S.W. 868, 869.

Bulk is said of that which is neither counted, weighed, nor measured. A sale by the bulk is the sale of a quantity such as it is, without measuring, counting, or weighing. Civil Code La. art. 3556, par. 6.

When used in relation to sale of goods by sample, "bulk" means the whole quantity of goods sold, which is supposed to be fairly represented by the sample. American Paper Products Co. v. Morton Salt Co., Mo.App., 279 S.W. 761, 763. This is the meaning which the word has as used in Uniform Sales Act Pa. § 14, P.L. c. 543; 69 P.S. § 123, F. A. D. Andrea, Inc., v. Dodge, C.C.A.Pa., 15 F.2d 1003, 1005.

BULK SALES ACTS. A class of statutes designed to prevent the defrauding of creditors by secret sale in bulk of all or substantially all of a merchant's stock of goods. A. J. Long Cigar & Grocery Co. v. Harvey, 33 Ga.App. 236, 125 S.E. 870; Wolfe v. Bellfair Hat Co., Sup., 47 N.Y.S.2d 908, 910.

BULK WINDOWS. "Bulk windows" include show windows as well as bay windows, sometimes called "bow windows," within a statute conferring on cities the power to regulate certain obstructions in the street. City of Baltimore v. Nirdlinger, 131 Md. 600, 102 A. 1014, 1019.

BULL. In ecclesiastical law. An instrument granted by the pope of Rome, and sealed with a seal of lead, containing some decree, commandment, or other public act, emanating from the pontiff. Bull, in this sense, corresponds with edict or letters patent from other governments. Cowell; 4 Bl.Comm. 110; 4 Steph.Comm. 177, 179.

There are three kinds of apostolical rescripts—the *brief,* the *signature,* and the *bull;* which last is most commonly used in legal matters.

This is also a cant term of the Stock Exchange, meaning one who speculates for a rise in the market.

BULL AND BOAR. These animals, by the ancient custom of some places, were required to be kept by the parson for the use of his parishioners, in consideration of his having tithes of calves and pigs. 1 Rolle Abr. 559.

BULLDOZER. A blade, the arms of which are fastened to a tractor and hold the blade in front of the tractor. Eldredge v. Sargent, 150 Kan. 824, 96 P.2d 870, 871.

BULL-HEADED. Headstrong, obstinate, stupidly stubborn. Enloe v. Southern Ry. Co., 179 N.C. 83, 101 S.E. 556, 558.

BULL PEN. A certain place of confinement at a penitentiary. State v. Kelley, 118 Or. 397, 247 P. 146, 148.

BULLA. A seal used by the Roman emperors, during the lower empire; it was of four kinds,—gold, silver, wax, and lead.

BULLET. Synonymous with "shot," meaning a projectile, particularly a solid ball or bullet that is not intended to fit the bore of a piece. Green v. Commonwealth, 122 Va. 862, 94 S.E. 940, 941.

BULLETIN. An officially published notice or announcement concerning the progress of matters of public importance. In France, the registry of the laws.

BULLETIN DES LOIS. In France, the official sheet which publishes the laws and decrees; this publication constitutes the promulgation of the law or decree.

BULLION. Gold and silver intended to be coined.

The term is usually applied to a quantity of these metals ready for the mint, but as yet lying in bars, plates, lumps, or other masses; but it may also include ornaments or dishes of gold and silver, or foreign coins not current as money, when intended to be descriptive of its adaptability to be coined, and not of other purposes to which it may be put. Thalheim v. State, 38 Fla. 169, 20 So. 938. The term may import money. Emery Bird Thayer Dry Goods Co. v. Williams, C.C.A.Mo., 98 F.2d 166, 171.

BULLION FUND. A fund of public money maintained in connection with the mints, for the purpose of purchasing precious metals for coinage, and also of enabling the mint to make returns of coins to private depositors of bullion without waiting until such bullion is actually coined.

BUM–BAILIFF. A person employed to dun one for a debt; a bailiff employed to arrest a debtor. Probably a vulgar corruption of "bound-bailiff" *(q. v.)*.

BUNCO GAME. Any trick, artifice, or cunning calculated to win confidence and to deceive, whether by conversation, conduct, or suggestion. State v. Ferrato, 72 Wash. 112, 129 P. 898, 899.

BUNDA. In old English law. A bound, boundary, border, or limit (*terminus, limes*).

BUNDLE, *v.* To sleep on the same bed without undressing; applied to the custom of a man and woman, especially lovers, thus sleeping. A. & E. Ency. This custom is adverted to in Seagar v. Sligerland, 2 Caines, N.Y., 219, and Hollis v. Wells, 3 Clark, Pa., 169.

BUOY. In maritime law. A piece of wood or cork, or a barrel, raft, or other thing, made secure and floating upon a stream or bay, intended as a guide and warning to mariners, by marking a spot where the water is shallow, or where there is a reef or other danger to navigation, or to mark the course of a devious channel. Buoys are regulated by federal legislation; see 14 U.S.C.A. § 87.

BURDEN. A burden, as on interstate commerce, means anything that imposes either a restrictive or onerous load upon such commerce. State of Missouri v. Kansas Natural Gas Co., D.C.Mo., 282 F. 341, 345.

Where the Railroad Commission ordered construction of a viaduct carrying a street over railroad tracks, construction and operation of street car tracks on the viaduct was not an "additional burden," and did not entitle abutting owners to damages. In eminent domain or condemnation proceedings see In re Ely Ave. in City of New York, 88 Misc. 320, 150 N.Y.S. 698, 701.

BURDEN OF PROOF. (Lat. *onus probandi.*) In the law of evidence. The necessity or duty of affirmatively proving a fact or facts in dispute on an issue raised between the parties in a cause. Willett v. Rich, 142 Mass. 356, 7 N.E. 776, 56 Am. Rep. 684; People v. McCann, 16 N.Y. 58, 69 Am. Dec. 642, 15 How.Pr. 503.

The term "burden of proof" is not to be confused with "*prima facie* case." Kendall v. Brownson, 47 N.H. 200; Carver v. Carver, 97 Ind. 511, or with expressions referring to a similar idea, such as the "burden of evidence," Hyer v. C. E. Holmes & Co., 12 Ga.App. 837, 79 S.E. 58, 60, or "the burden of proceeding," Mason v. Geist, Mo.App., 263 S.W. 236, 237, or the burden of going forward with the evidence, First Nat. Bank v. Ford, 30 Wyo. 110, 216 P. 691, 694, 31 A.L.R. 1441.

It is frequently said, however, to have two distinct meanings: (1) the duty of producing evidence as the case progresses, and (2) the duty to establish the truth of the claim by preponderance of the evidence, and though the former may pass from party to party, the latter rests throughout upon the party asserting the affirmative of the issue. Sellers v. Kincaid, 303 Ill. 216, 135 N.E. 429, 433; Stofer v. Dunham, Mo.App., 208 S.W. 641, 644.

Again "burden of proof" is sometimes used to refer merely to the rule of practice fixing the order of proof, as distinguished from the "preponderance of the evidence" meaning the weight of evidence. Thompson v. Dyson, 120 Kan. 591, 244 P. 867, 868.

BUREAU. An office for the transaction of business. A name given to the several departments of the executive or administrative branch of government, or their divisions. In re Strawbridge, 39 Ala. 375; In re McLaughlin, 124 Misc. 766, 210 N.Y.S. 68, 72.

As applied to a division of an administrative department, the term may include the operating force. People v. Coffin, 202 Ill.App. 100.

BUREAUCRACY. A system in which the business of government is carried on in departments, each under the control of a chief, in contradistinction from a system in which the officers of government have a co-ordinate authority.

BURG, BURGH. A term anciently applied to a castle or fortified place; a borough (*q. v.*). Spelman.

BURGAGE. A name anciently given to a dwelling-house in a borough town. Blount.

BURGAGE–HOLDING. A tenure by which lands in royal boroughs in Scotland were held of the sovereign. The service was watching and warding, and was done by the burgesses within the territory of the borough, whether expressed in the charter or not.

BURGAGE–TENURE. In English law. One of the three species of free socage holdings; a tenure whereby houses and lands which were formerly the site of houses, in an ancient borough, are held of some lord by a certain rent. There are a great many customs affecting these tenures, the most remarkable of which is the custom of Borough English. See Litt. § 162; 2 Bl.Comm. 82.

BURGATOR. One who breaks into houses or inclosed places, as distinguished from one who committed robbery in the open country. Spelman.

BURGBOTE. In old English law. A term applied to a contribution towards the repair of castles or walls of defense, or of a borough.

BURGENSES. In old English law. Inhabitants of a *burgus* or borough; burgesses. Fleta, lib. 5, c. 6, § 10.

BURGERISTH. A word used in Domesday, signifying a breach of the peace in a town. Jacob.

BURGESS. In English law. An inhabitant or freeman of a borough or town; a person duly and legally admitted a member of a municipal corporation. Spelman; 3 Steph.Comm. 188, 189. A magistrate of a borough. Blount. An elector or voter; a person legally qualified to vote at elections. The word in this sense is particularly defined by the statute 5 & 6 Wm. IV. c. 76, §§ 9, 13. 3 Steph.Comm. 192. A representative of a borough or town, in parliament. Co.Litt. 109*a*; 1 Bl.Comm. 174.

In American law. The chief executive officer of a borough, bearing the same relation to its government and affairs that the *mayor* does to those of a city; so used in Pennsylvania. In Connecticut boroughs the *board of burgesses* corresponds to the township board or board of trustees in some other states, or to the common council of a city. Cent. Dict.

BURGESS ROLL. A roll, required by the St. 5 & 6 Wm. IV. c. 76, to be kept in corporate towns or boroughs, of the names of burgesses entitled to certain new rights conferred by that act.

BURGH-BRECHE. A fine imposed on the community of a town, for a breach of the peace, etc.

BURGH ENGLISH. See Borough English.

BURGH ENGLOYS. Borough English (*q. v.*).

BURGHMAILS. Yearly payments to the crown of Scotland, introduced by Malcolm III., and resembling the English fee-farm rents.

BURGHMOTE. In Saxon law. A court of justice held semi-annually by the bishop or lord in a *burg*, which the thanes were bound to attend without summons.

BURGLAR. One who commits burglary. One who breaks into a dwelling-house in the nighttime with intent to commit a felony. O'Connor v. Press Pub. Co., 34 Misc. 564, 70 N.Y.Supp. 367. See Burglary.

BURGLARIOUSLY. In pleading. A technical word which must be introduced into an indictment for burglary at common law. Lewis v. State, 16 Conn. 34; Reed v. State, 14 Tex.App. 665.

BURGLARITER. L. Lat. (Burglariously.) In old criminal pleading. A necessary word in indictments for burglary.

BURGLARY. The breaking and entering the house of another in the nighttime, with intent to commit a felony therein, whether the felony be actually committed or not. Soders v. State, 81 Tex.Cr.R. 506, 195 S.W. 1146, 1147; Hunter v. State, 29 Ind. 80; State v. Allen, 186 N.C. 302, 119 S.E. 504, 506; State v. Hodgdon, 89 Vt. 148, 94 A. 301, 302.

The common-law definition has been much modified by statute in several of the states. Pen.Code Cal. § 459; People v. Mendelson, 264 Ill. 453, 106 N.E. 249, 251, L.R.A. 1915C, 627; State v. Dunlap, 103 N.J.Law, 209, 136 A. 510; Burglary of private residence at night is "nighttime burglary" and not ordinary "burglary." Shaffer v. State, 137 Tex.Cr.R. 476, 132 S.W.2d 263. Commission in nighttime is not essential. People v. Glickman, 377 Ill. 360, 36 N.E.2d 720, 722, 723; State v. Williams, 189 La. 355, 179 So. 452. Entry in the nighttime without breaking, or breaking and entering in the daytime constitutes "burglary." State v. Williams, 189 La. 355, 179 So. 452.

Intended commission of some other offense is essential. Commonwealth v. Doran, 145 Pa.Super. 173, 20 A.2d 815, 816.

Entry into a house made in an unusual place with intent to commit a felony or theft is a "burglary by breaking." Harroll v. State, 135 Tex.Cr.R. 65, 117 S.W.2d 103.

See Breaking.

BURGLARY IN THE FIRST DEGREE. Unlawful and intentional breaking and unlawful and intentional entry in nighttime into dwelling house presently occupied, with intent to commit felony. State v. Madden, 212 N.C. 56, 192 S.E. 859, 860. Burglary committed "between sunset and sunrise". People v. Helsley, 41 Cal.App.2d 935, 108 P.2d 97, 98.

BURGOMASTER. The title given in Germany to the chief executive officer of a borough, town, or city; corresponding to our "mayor."

BURGUNDIAN LAW. See Lex Burgundionum.

BURGWHAR. A burgess (*q. v.*).

BURH. A fastness. The hill-top that has been fortified as a burh. Very often it has given its name to a neighboring village; it is the future *borough*. The entrenchment around a great man's house was a burh. See Maitland, Domesday and Beyond, 183.

BURIAL. Act of burying a deceased person, sepulture, interment, act of depositing a dead body in the earth, in a tomb or vault, or in the water; the act of interring the human dead. Brady v. Presnell, 204 N.C. 659, 169 S.E. 278, 280. See Lay v. State, 12 Ind.App. 362, 39 N.E. 768.

BURIAL INSURANCE. A contract based on legal consideration whereby obligor undertakes to furnish obligee or one of latter's relatives at death burial reasonably worth fixed sum. Sisson v. Prata Undertaking Co., 49 R.I. 132, 141 A. 76.

BURIAL PLACE. A portion of ground set apart for or occupied by grave, or as a grave or graveyard. Code 1932, § 9052. Leaphart v. Harmon, 186 S.C. 362, 195 S.E. 628, 629.

BURIAL PURPOSES. Continuing care, preservation, and ornamentation of the place of interment as included in term. People v. Rosehill Cemetery Co., 371 Ill. 510, 21 N.E.2d 766, 770.

BURKING, BURKISM. Murder committed with the object of selling the cadaver for purposes of dissection, particularly and originally, by suffocating or strangling the victim.

BURLAW COURTS. Courts consisting of neighbors selected by common consent to act as judges in determining disputes between neighbor and neighbor.

BURLAWS. In Scotch law. Laws made by neighbors elected by common consent in the burlaw courts. Skene.

BURLESQUE. A plotless musical entertainment consisting of a series of unrelated episodes and dances, all with the purpose of depicting or suggesting sexual subjects or objects. Bonserk Theatre Corporation v. Moss, Sup., 34 N.Y.S.2d 541, 549.

BURN, *n.* A hurt, injury, or effect caused by burning. Webster, Dict.

A "first-degree burn" varies from redness to a blister. A "second-degree burn" results where the skin is charred or killed. Murphy v. Ludowici Gas & Oil Co., 96 Kan. 321, 150 P. 581, 582.

BURN, *v.* To consume with fire. See Hiatt v. Travelers' Ins. Co., 197 Iowa 153, 197 N.W. 3, 4, 33

A.L.R. 655; Pacific Creosoting Co. v. Thames & Mersey Marine Ins. Co., D.C.Wash., 210 F. 958, 959.

"Burning," outside of laboratories and certain workshops, is a process of oxidation, which, if sufficiently violent, heats the elements involved to incandescence, and, if combustible gases are given off, there is a flame. Scully v. Bremer County Farmers' Mut. Fire Ins. Ass'n, 215 Iowa 368, 245 N.W. 280, 282.

The verb "to burn," in an indictment for arson, is to be taken in its common meaning of "to consume with fire." Hester v. State, 17 Ga. 130. To constitute a "burning" essential to arson, there must be a wasting or destruction of the fibers or texture of the wood, no matter how small in extent. People v. Oliff, 361 Ill. 237, 197 N.E. 777, 780; it is not necessary that the building should be consumed or materially injured and it is sufficient if fire is actually communicated to any part thereof, however small. State v. Mutschler, 55 N.D. 120, 212 N.W. 832, 833; charring is burning. State v. Pisano, 107 Conn. 630, 141 A. 660, 661.

BURNED OUT OF SIGHT. Merchandise is "burned out of sight" when burned to an ash or into such small particles that it might be washed away by water or swept into débris. Hyland v. Millers Nat. Ins. Co., D.C.Cal., 58 F.2d 1003, 1007.

BURNING FLUID. As used in policies of insurance, this term does not mean any fluid which will burn, but it means a recognized article of commerce, called by that name, and which is a different article from naphtha or kerosene. Putnam v. Insurance Co., C.C.N.Y., 4 Fed. 764; Wheeler v. Insurance Co., 6 Mo.App. 235.

BURNING IN THE HAND. In old English criminal law, laymen, upon being accorded the benefit of clergy, were burned with a hot iron in the brawn of the left thumb, in order that, being thus marked, they could not again claim their clergy. 4 Bl.Comm. 367. This practice was finally abolished by Stat. 19 Geo. III. c. 74; though before that time the burning was often done with a cold iron.

BURNT COTTON. Cotton which has been on fire, and which has not been subsequently repicked and rebaled. Southern Ry. Co. v. Pettit, C.C.A. Tenn., 257 F. 663, 664.

BURROCHIUM. A burroch, dam, or small wear over a river, where traps are laid for the taking of fish. Cowell.

BURROWMEALIS. In Scotch law. A term used to designate the rents paid into the king's private treasury by the burgesses or inhabitants of a borough.

BURSA. Lat. A purse.

BURSAR. A treasurer of a college.

BURSARIA. The exchequer of collegiate or conventual bodies; or the place of receiving, paying, and accounting by the bursars. Also stipendiary scholars, who live upon the burse, fund, or joint-stock of the college.

BURYING ALIVE. In English law. The ancient punishment of sodomites, and those who contracted with Jews. Fleta, lib. 1, c. 27, § 3.

BURYING-GROUND. A place set apart for the interment of the dead; a cemetery. Appeal Tax Court v. Academy, 50 Md. 353.

BUS. A vehicle which serves passenger public, but does not operate upon fixed tracks. Patillo v. State, 120 Tex.Cr.R. 568, 47 S.W.2d 847.

BUSCARL. In Saxon and old English law. Seamen or marines. Spelman.

BUSHEL. A dry measure, containing four pecks, eight gallons, or thirty-two quarts. But the dimensions of a bushel, and the weight of a bushel of grain, etc., vary in the different states in consequence of statutory enactments. Richardson v. Spafford, 13 Vt. 245; Milk v. Christie, 1 Hill, N.Y., 106; Hockin v. Cooke, 4 Term, 316.

BUSHIDO. *Jap.* The unwritten code of conduct of the *Samurai* demanding loyalty to superiors only, simplicity of living and military valor. Treachery and brutality against one's enemies, and self-sacrifice, blind loyalty and unquestioning obedience to one's superiors are cardinal characteristics of the code. 1945 Report of the Tenney Joint Fact-Finding Committee on Un-American Activities to the California Legislature, p. 49.

BUSINESS. The term "business" has no definite or legal meaning. Connor v. City of University Park, Tex.Civ.App., 142 S.W.2d 706, 715; it may be an uncertain one. In re Frey's Will, 154 Misc. 421, 277 N.Y.S. 269, 272.

The term may mean or embrace:

Activity, Norman v. Southwestern R. Co., 42 Ga.App. 812, 157 S.E. 531, 533; In re Frey's Will, 277 N.Y.S. 269, 272, 154 Misc. 421; activity of some continuity, regularity and permanency, means of material being and livelihood, Board of Sup'rs of Amherst County v. Boaz, 176 Va. 126, 10 S.E.2d 498, 499. Activity or enterprise for gain, benefit, advantage or livelihood, Union League Club v. Johnson, Cal. App., 108 P.2d 487, 490. Activity which benefits corporation's organizers or members, O'Neil v. United Producers & Consumers Co-op., 57 Ariz. 295, 113 P.2d 645, 648; affairs, Sills v. Sorenson, 192 Wash. 318, 73 P.2d 798, 802, Industrial Fibre Co. v. State, 31 Ohio App. 347, 166 N.E. 418, 419; any particular occupation or employment, Industrial Fibre Co. v. State, 31 Ohio App. 347, 166 N.E. 418, 419; automobile liability policy excepting liability to insured's chauffeurs while engaged in his "business," anything in which insured desired to concern himself. Dickey v. General Accident Fire & Life Assur. Corporation Limited of Perth, Scotland, 328 Pa. 541, 195 A. 875; barter, Wills v. National Mineral Co., 176 Okl. 193, 55 P.2d 449, 453; busyness, Snell v. Commissioner of Internal Revenue, C.C.A.Fla., 97 F.2d 891, 892; calling, Gardner v. Trustees of Main St. M. E. Church of Ottumwa, Iowa, 244 N.W. 667, 669, Morgan v. Salt Lake City, 78 Utah 403, 3 P.2d 510, 513; capacity by which results are reached, Norman v. Southwestern R. Co., 42 Ga.App. 812, 157 S.E. 531, 533; In re Frey's Will, 277 N.Y.S. 269, 272, 154 Misc. 421; commercial or industrial establishment or enterprise, Westor Theatres v. Warner Bros. Pictures, D.C.N.J., 41 F.Supp. 757, 761; concern, Industrial Fibre Co. v. State, 31 Ohio App. 347, 166 N.E. 418, 419; constant or continuous or habitual employment or occupation, Burk v. United States, C.C.A.Ala., 134 F.2d 879, 881; efforts of men to improve their economic conditions and satisfy their desires, People ex rel. Atty. Gen. v. Jersin, 101 Colo. 406, 74 P.2d 668, 670; employment, Industrial Fibre Co. v. State, 31 Ohio App. 347, 166 N.E. 418, 419; employment, occupation, or profession engaged in for gain or livelihood, Mergenthaler Linotype Co. v. McNamee, 123 Neb. 71, 249 N.W. 92, 93; employment occupying substantial portion of time and attention, Walsh v. Industrial Commission, 345 Ill. 366, 178 N.E. 82, 83; energy by which results are reached, Norman v. Southwestern R. Co., 42

Ga.App. 812, 157 S.E. 531, 533; In re Frey's Will, 277 N.Y.S. 269, 272, 154 Misc. 421; enterprise in which person engaged shows willingness to invest time and capital on future outcome, Doggett v. Burnet, 62 App.D.C. 103, 65 F.2d 191, 194; every legitimate avocation in life by which honest support for family may be obtained, Postal Savings & Loan Ass'n v. Powell, Tex.Civ.App., 47 S.W.2d 343, 352; every step in a long, complicated financial or commercial transaction, Business Management Corporation v. Department of Industrial Relations, Cal.App., 123 P.2d 142, 143; everything about which a person can be employed, Higgins v. Commissioner of Internal Revenue, 312 U.S. 212, 61 S.Ct. 475, 478, 85 L.Ed. 783; exchange of things of value, Wills v. National Mineral Co., 176 Okl. 193, 55 P.2d 449, 453; family car doctrine, any benefit which may inure to the owner, Donn v. Kunz, Ariz., 79 P.2d 965, 968; good will, In re Frey's Will, 277 N.Y.S. 269, 272, 154 Misc. 421, In re Weber's Estate, 261 Pa. 561, 104 A. 735, 737; intercourse of a commercial character, Karnuth v. U. S., on Petition of Albro, for Cook, N. Y., 279 U.S. 231, 49 S.Ct. 274, 278, 73 L.Ed. 677; mercantile transactions in general, Industrial Fibre Co. v. State, 31 Ohio App. 347, 166 N.E. 418, 419; occupation, Industrial Fibre Co. v. State, 31 Ohio App. 347, 166 N.E. 418, 419, Morgan v. Salt Lake City, 78 Utah 403, 3 P.2d 510, 513; occupation connected with operation or details of barter, trade, industry or commerce, Bankers' Holding Corporation v. Maybury, 161 Wash. 681, 297 P. 740, 743, 75 A.L.R. 1237; occupation or duty which requires attention as a business, Taylor v. Seney, 52 Ohio App. 79, 3 N.E.2d 374, 376; opportunities, Norman v. Southwestern R. Co., 42 Ga.App. 812, 157 S.E. 531, 533, In re Frey's Will, 277 N.Y.S. 269, 272, 154 Misc. 421; ordinary vocation, Ostlie v. H. F. Dirks & Son, 189 Minn. 34, 248 N.W. 283; professions, Connor v. City of University Park, Tex.Civ.App., 142 S.W.2d 706, 715; property, In re Frey's Will, 277 N.Y.S. 269, 272, 154 Misc. 421; In re Weber's Estate, 261 Pa. 561, 104 A. 735, 737; pursuit, Morgan v. Salt Lake City, 78 Utah 403, 3 P.2d 510, 513; regular profession, trade or occupation, Bordo v. Grayek, 136 Pa.Super. 124, 7 A.2d 142, 144; right or occasion of making one's self busy, Industrial Fibre Co. v. State, 31 Ohio App. 347, 166 N.E. 418, 419; sale, Wills v. National Mineral Co., 176 Okl. 193, 55 P.2d 449, 453; that which habitually busies or occupies or engages the time, attention, labor, and effort of men as a principal serious concern or interest or for livelihood or profit, Curley v. New England Trust Co., 221 Mass. 384, 109 N.E. 171, 174, Massolini v. Driscoll, 114 Conn. 546, 159 A. 480, 482; trade, Connor v. City of University Park, Tex.Civ. App., 142 S.W.2d 706, 715, Morgan v. Salt Lake City, 78 Utah 403, 3 P.2d 510, 513; transaction, Industrial Fibre Co. v. State, 31 Ohio App. 347, 166 N.E. 418, 419; occasional, single or isolated activities do not constitute business, Vandervort v. Industrial Commission of Wisconsin, 203 Wis. 362, 234 N.W. 492, 493; Goddard v. Chaffee, 2 Allen, Mass., 395, 79 Am.Dec. 796. But see Industrial Commission v. Hammond, 77 Colo. 414, 236 P. 1006, 1008.

Definition of "business" is not dependent on whether enterprise is profitable or has prospects of being profitable. Doggett v. Burnet, 62 App.D.C. 103, 65 F.2d 191, 193.

Labor, business, and work are not synonyms.

Business Affected with Public Interest

One so employed as to justify conclusion that it has been devoted to public use, and its use thereby in effect granted to public. Williams v. Standard Oil Co. of Louisiana, Tenn., 278 U.S. 235, 49 S.Ct. 115, 116, 73 L.Ed. 287, 60 A.L.R. 596.

Business Agent

Agent having some general supervision over general affairs. Rorick v. Stilwell, 101 Fla. 4, 133 So. 609, 615.

Business Compulsion

Species of duress. Marrazzo v. Orino, Wash., 194 Wash. 364, 78 P.2d 181, 186.

Business Corporation

A corporation organized for the purpose of carrying on a business for profit. City of St. Louis v. Smith, 325 Mo. 471, 30 S.W.2d 729, 731.

Business Course

A course such as is usually taught by business or commercial schools and colleges. Union Nat. Bank v. Kirby, 189 Ark. 369, 72 S.W.2d 229, 230.

Business Done in State

Business begun and completed or ended in state. Clark v. Atlantic Pipe Line Co., Tex.Civ.App., 134 S.W.2d 322, 328.

Business Enterprise

Investment of capital, labor and management in an undertaking for profit; one of the recognized attributes is centralized management and control. Helvering v. Jewel Mining Co., C.C.A.8, 126 F.2d 1011, 1015.

Business Gains

Gains from sale, exchange, or other disposition of property used in business. Fackler v. Commissioner of Internal Revenue, C.C.A.6, 133 F.2d 509, 512.

Business Hours

In general those hours during which persons in the community generally keep their places open for the transaction of business. Casalduc v. Diaz, C.C.A.Puerto Rico, 117 F.2d 915, 916.

In respect to the time of presentment and demand of bills and notes, business hours generally range through the whole day down to the hours of rest in the evening, except when the paper is payable at a bank or by a banker; Cayuga County Bank v. Hunt, 2 Hill, N.Y., 635. See Lunt v. Adams, 17 Me. 230.

An order allowing a stockholder to examine the books of a corporation "during business hours" does not mean that such examination be carried on throughout the entire business day, nor in the nighttime. Breslauer v. S. Franklin & Co., 205 Ill.App. 372, 374.

Business League

An association is a business league if persons thereof have some common business interest. Underwriters' Laboratories v. Commissioner of Internal Revenue, C.C.A.7, 135 F.2d 371, 374.

Business Losses

Losses from sale, exchange, or other disposition of property used in trade or business. Fackler v. Commissioner of Internal Revenue, C.C.A.6, 133 F.2d 509, 512.

Business Name

Trade-name, business name and commercial name as synonymous. Plum v. Siekmann, 135 Neb. 101, 280 N.W. 264, 268.

Business of Peddling

Business of one relying on present solicitation of chance patrons for purchases of uncertain quantities and making concurring deliveries. National Baking Co. v. Zabel, 227 Wis. 93, 277 N.W. 691, 693.

Business of Public Character

Business wherein person engaged expressly or impliedly holds himself out as engaged in business of supplying his product or service to public as a class or to limited portion of public. Masgai v. Public Service Commission of Pennsylvania, 124 Pa.Super. 370, 188 A. 599, 600.

Business of Same Nature

Business of like character. Rahoutis v. Unemployment Compensation Commission, 171 Or. 93, 136 P.2d 426, 434.

Business of Similar Nature

Business of analogous nature. Bedford v. Johnson, 102 Colo. 203, 78 P.2d 373, 376.

Business of the Community

A business in which a husband is engaged is prima facie the business of the community. Bird v. Steele, 74 Wash. 68, 132 P. 724, 725.

Business Pertaining to His Occupation

Duty pertaining to his occupation as synonym. Doherty v. American Employers' Ins. Co. of Boston, Mass., 112 N.J.Law, 52, 169 A. 652, 653.

Business Situs

A situs acquired for tax purposes by one who has carried on a business in the state more or less permanent in its nature. Endicott, Johnson & Co. v. Multnomah County, 96 Or. 679, 190 P. 1109, 1111. A situs arising when notes, mortgages, tax sale certificates and the like are brought into the state for something more than a temporary purpose, and are devoted to some business use there and thus become incorporated with the property of the state for revenue purposes. Lockwood v. Blodgett, 106 Conn. 525, 138 A. 520, 525. A situs arising where possession and control of property right has been localized in some independent business or investment away from owner's domicile so that its substantial use and value primarily attach to and become an asset of the outside business. State v. Atlantic Oil Producing Co., 174 Okl. 61, 49 P.2d 534, 538.

Business Trust

As distinguished from a joint-stock company, a pure "business trust" is one in which the managers are principals, and the shareholders are cestuis que trust. Betts v. Hackathorn, 159 Ark. 621, 252 S.W. 602, 604, 31 A.L.R. 847. The essential attribute is that property is placed in the hands of trustees who manage and deal with it for use and benefit of beneficiaries. Morriss v. Finkelstein, Mo.App., 127 S.W.2d 46, 49. A "Massachusetts trust" or "common law trust," In re Conover's Estate, 295 Ill.App. 443, 14 N.E.2d 980, 985.

Business Visitor

One who is invited or permitted to enter or remain upon the premises of another for a purpose directly or indirectly connected with the business dealings between them, Kurre v. Graham Ship by Truck Co., 136 Kan. 356, 15 P.2d 463, 465. One who comes on land at occupant's instance for purposes connected with purpose, business, or otherwise, for which occupant uses land, Haefeli v. Woodrich Engineering Co., 255 N.Y. 442, 175 N.E. 123, 125.

Farming Business

See Farming Business.

Private Business or Enterprise

One in which capital, time, attention, labor, and intelligence have been invested for gain and profit for private benefit, purposes and use. Green v. Frazier, 44 N.D. 395, 176 N.W. 11, 17.

Public Business

An element is that the business by its nature must be such that the public must use the same, or the commodities bought and sold in such manner as to affect the community at large as to supply, price, etc. Consumers' Light & Power Co. v. Phipps, 120 Okl. 223, 251 P. 63, 64.

BUSONES COMITATUS. In old English law. The barons of a county.

BUSSA. A term used in the old English law, to designate a large and clumsily constructed ship.

BUT. Except, except that, on the contrary, or, and also, yet, still. State v. Marsh, 108 Neb. 267, 187 N.W. 810, 812; Rickman v. Commonwealth, 195 Ky. 715, 243 S.W. 929.

BUTANE. Highly explosive and inflammable substance. Ohio Casualty Ins. Co. v. Callaway, D.C. Okl., 45 F.Supp. 586, 588.

BUTCHER. One who slaughters animals or dresses their flesh for market; a dealer in meat. Broadway v. Cope, 208 N.C. 85, 179 S.E. 452; Provo City v. Provo Meat & Packing Co., 49 Utah 528, 165 P. 477, 479, Ann.Cas.1918D, 530.

BUTLERAGE. A privilege formerly allowed to the king's butler, to take a certain part of every cask of wine imported by an alien; the part of the cask thus taken.

Called also prisage; 2 Bulstr. 254. Anciently, it might be taken also of wine imported by a subject. 1 Bla.Com. 315; *Termes de la Ley;* Cowell.

See, also, Botiler of the King.

BUTLER'S ORDINANCE. In English law. A law for the heir to punish waste in the life of the ancestor.

"Though it be on record in the parliament book of Edward I., yet it never was a statute, nor ever so received; but only some constitution of the king's council, or lords in parliament, which never obtained the strength or force of an act of parliament." Hale, Hist. Eng. Law, p. 18.

BUTT. A measure of liquid capacity, equal to one hundred and eight gallons; also a measure of land.

BUTTALS. The bounding lines of land at the end; abuttals, which see.

BUTTE. A hill. State v. Jefferson Island Salt Mining Co., 183 La. 304, 163 So. 145.

BUTTED AND BOUNDED. A phrase sometimes used in conveyancing, to introduce the boundaries of lands. See Butts and Bounds.

BUTTER. A dairy product manufactured exclusively from pure, unadulterated milk or cream, or both, with or without salt or coloring matter. Pardy v. Boomhower Grocery Co., 178 App.Div. 347, 164 N.Y.S. 775, 776; a product which should contain not less than 80 per centum by weight of milk fat. U. S. v. Centralia Dairy Co., D.C.Wash., 60 F.2d 141, 142.

BUTTER FAT. The natural fat of milk. Wiseman v. Affolter, 192 Ark. 509, 92 S.W.2d 388, 389.

BUTTS. In old English law. Short pieces of land left unplowed at the *ends* of fields, where the plow was turned about (otherwise called "headlands") as sidelings were similarly unplowed pieces on the sides. Burrill; Cowell. Also a place where bowmen meet to shoot at a mark.

BUTTS AND BOUNDS. A phrase used in conveyancing, to describe the end lines or circumscribing lines of a certain piece of land. The phrase "metes and bounds" has the same meaning.

The angles or points where these lines change their direction. Cowell; Spelman, Gloss. See Abuttals.

BUTTY. A local term in the north of England, for the associate or deputy of another; also of things used in common.

BUY. To acquire the ownership of property by giving an accepted price or consideration therefor; or by agreeing to do so; to acquire by the payment of a price or value; to purchase. Webster. To obtain something for a price, usually money. In re Troy, 43 R.I. 279, 111 A. 723, 724. As applied to prohibition law, means to possess. Slaughter v. State, 23 Ala.App. 390, 128 So. 129.

BUY IN. To purchase, at public sale, property which is one's own or which one has caused or procured to be sold.

BUYER. One who buys; a purchaser, particularly of chattels.

BUYER 60 CONTRACT. A contract wherein purchaser not wishing to pay for stock purchased outright buys it at a price in excess of the market and is allowed 60 days' time to pay for stock. Herrlein v. Tocchini, 128 Cal.App. 612, 18 P.2d 73, 75.

BUYING LONG. Purchase of stocks now with the expectation of selling them for a profit in the future. Henderson v. Usher, 125 Fla. 709, 170 So. 846, 851.

BUYING TITLES. The purchase of the rights or claims to real estate of a person who is not in possession of the land or is disseised. Void, and an offense, at common law and by 32 Hen. VIII, c. 9. This rule has been generally adopted in the United States, and is affirmed by statute in some states; 3 Washb.R.P. *596. Hinman v. Hinman, 4 Conn. 575; Helms v. May, 29 Ga. 124; Wash v. McBrayer, 1 Dana, Ky., 566; Bush v. Cooper, 26 Miss. 599, 59 Am.Dec. 270. But in other states, such a purchase is valid. Fetrow v. Merriwether, 53 Ill. 279; Hall's Lessee v. Ashby, 9 Ohio, 96, 34 Am. Dec. 424.

See, also, Bracery.

BY. Before a certain time, Rankin v. Woodworth, 3 Pen. & W., Pa., 48. Beside. Close to. In. In close proximity. In consequence of. Not later than a certain time, Fanta v. Maddex, 80 Cal.App. 513, 252 P. 630, 633; Scheuer & Tiego v. Benedict, 173 Wis. 241, 181 N.W. 129, 12 A.L.R. 1166. On or before a certain time, J. C. Engelman Land Co. v. La Blanco Agr. Co., Tex.Civ.App., 220 S.W. 653, 655. Through the means, act, agency or instrumentality of, Carroll v. Industrial Commission of Colorado, 69 Colo. 473, 195 P. 1097, 19 A.L.R. 107; Stevenson v. Lee Moor Contracting Co., 45 N.M. 354, 115 P.2d 342, 349. To. Under. With. The word may be used as exclusive, use preceding signature as indicating signature officially, and not personally. Pennsylvania Co. for Insurances on Lives and Granting Annuities v. Wallace, 346 Pa. 532, 31 A.2d 71, 77.

BY AN ACQUITTANCE FOR THE LAST PAYMENT ALL OTHER ARREARAGES ARE DISCHARGED. Noy, 40.

BY-BIDDER. One employed by the seller or his agent to bid on property with no purpose to become a purchaser, so that bidding thereon may be stimulated in others who are bidding in good faith. Osborn v. Apperson Lodge, Free and Accepted Masons, No. 195, of Louisa, Ky., 213 Ky. 533, 281 S.W. 500, 502, 46 A.L.R. 117.

BY-BIDDING. See Bid.

BY BILL, BY BILL WITHOUT WRIT. In practice. Terms anciently used to designate actions commenced by original *bill,* as distinguished from those commenced by original *writ,* and applied in modern practice to suits commenced by *capias ad respondendum.* 1 Arch.Pr. pp. 2, 337; 3 Bla. Comm. 285, 286. See Harkness v. Harkness, 5 Hill, N.Y., 213. The usual course of commencing an action in the King's Bench was by a bill of Middlesex. In an action commenced *by bill* it is not necessary to notice the form or nature of the action. 1 Chit.Pl. 283.

BY COLOR OF OFFICE. Acts done "by color of office" are where they are of such a nature that office gives no authority to do them. State v. National Surety Co., 162 Tenn. 547, 39 S.W.2d 581, 583.

BY ESTIMATION. In conveyancing. A term used to indicate that the quantity of land as stated is estimated only, not exactly measured; it has the

the same meaning and effect as the phrase "more or less." Hays v. Hays, 126 Ind. 92, 25 N.E. 600, 11 L.R.A. 376. It is said that the meaning of these words has never been precisely ascertained by judicial decision. See Sugden, Vend. 231; Noble v. Googins, 99 Mass. 234.

BY GOD AND MY COUNTRY. In old English criminal practice. The established formula of reply by a prisoner, when arraigned at the bar, to the question, "Culprit, how wilt thou be tried?"

BY LAW. By statutory law, Board of Education of Union Free School Dist. No. Six of Town of Greenburgh v. Town of Greenburgh, 277 N.Y. 193, 13 N.E.2d 768, 770. By state-wide legislation, and not ordinance, U. S. Fidelity & Guaranty Co. v. Guenther, C.C.A.Ohio, 31 F.2d 919, 920.

BY-LAW MEN. In English law. The chief men of a town, representing the inhabitants. In an ancient deed, certain parties are described as "yeomen and *by-law men.*" 6 Q.B. 60. They appear to have been men appointed for some purpose of limited authority by the other inhabitants, under by-laws of the corporation appointing.

BY-LAWS. Regulations, ordinances, rules or laws adopted by an association or corporation or the like for its government. The word has also been used to designate the local laws or municipal statutes of a city or town. See Kilgour v. Gratto, 224 Mass. 78, 112 N.E. 489, 490. But of late the tendency is to employ the word "ordinance" exclusively for this class of enactments, reserving "by-law" for the rules adopted by private corporations.

In England the term *by-law* includes any order, rule or regulation made by any local authority or statutory corporation subordinate to Parliament; 1 Odgers, C.L. 91.

A resolution is not necessarily a by-law though a by-law may be in the form of a resolution. Peck v. Elliott, C.C.A. Tenn., 24 C.C.A. 425, 79 Fed. 10, 38 L.R.A. 616; Bagley v. Oil Co., 201 Pa. 78, 50 A. 760, 56 L.R.A. 184. Distinction between a by-law and a regulation, if any, discussed, Compton v. Van Volkenburgh, 34 N.J.Law, 135.

BY OPERATION OF LAW. Effected by some positive legal rule or amendment. Terminals & Transportation Corporation v. State, 169 Misc. 703, 8 N.Y.S.2d 282, 284.

BY-PASSING. As used in a contract for the construction of a subway, requiring the by-passing of all gas pipes whose service cannot be temporarily dispensed with, "by-passing" means the temporary cutting out of the gas mains under the street and laying of substituted temporary overhead gas pipes until all danger in using the original pipes is passed. Degnon Contracting Co. v. City of New York, 202 App.Div. 390, 196 N.Y.S. 63, 64.

BY REASON OF. Because of. Freeman v. Bennett, Tex.Civ.App., 195 S.W. 238, 241. By means, acts, or instrumentality of. State v. Kaufman, 50 S.D. 645, 211 N.W. 691, 692.

BY THE BY (also *Bye*). Incidentally; without new process. A term used in former English practice to denote the method of filing a declaration against a defendant who was already in the custody of the court at the suit of a different plaintiff or of the same plaintiff in another cause. It is no longer allowed; Archbold, New Pr. 293.

BY VIRTUE OF. By force of, by authority of, by reason of. Phillips v. Houston Nat. Bank, Houston, Tex., C.C.A.Tex., 108 F.2d 934, 936. Because of, through, or in pursuance of. State ex rel. and to Use of Jasper County v. Gass, 317 Mo. 744, 296 S.W. 431, 432. Money received by an officer by virtue of his office is money which that officer received under the law of his office, and not in violation thereof. Hollingsworth v. State, 73 Fla. 44, 75 So. 612, 614.

BYE-BIL-WUFFA. In Hindu law. A deed of mortgage or conditional sale.

BYRLAWS. See Burlaws.

BYROAD. The statute law of New Jersey recognizes three different kinds of roads: A public road, a private road, and a byroad. A byroad is a road used by the inhabitants, and recognized by statute, but not laid out. Such roads are often called "driftways." They are roads of necessity in newly-settled countries. Van Blarcom v. Frike, 29 N.J.Law, 516. See, also, Stevens v. Allen, 29 N.Y.Law, 68. An obscure or neighborhood road in its earlier existence, not used to any great extent by the public, yet so far a public road that the public have of right free access to it at all times. Wood v. Hurd, 34 N.J.Law, 89.

BYSTANDER. One who stands near; a chance looker-on; hence one who has no concern with the business being transacted. Baker v. State, 79 Tex. Cr.R. 510, 187 S.W. 949, 952; One present but not taking part, looker-on, spectator, beholder, observer. Music v. De Long, 209 Iowa, 1068, 229 N. W. 673, 676.

Under statutes relating to summoning of bystanders to complete jury panel, "bystanders" may be held to mean qualified talesmen summoned by sheriff from county at large. Commonwealth v. Sacco, 255 Mass. 369, 151 N.E. 839, 847. The term means qualified electors, not necessarily persons present in court. Bennett v. State, 161 Ark. 496, 257 S.W. 372, 373.

Under statutes authorizing "bystanders" to certify bill of exceptions, parties to the suit and their attorneys, Walker v. State, 88 Tex.Cr.R. 389, 227 S.W. 308, 312; and also witnesses in the case, McConnell v. McCord, 170 Ark. 839, 281 S.W. 384, as well as persons not present at the trial, are not bystanders, Buck v. St. Louis Union Trust Co., 267 Mo. 644, 185 S.W. 208, 211. Though jurors are not "bystanders" in the ordinary meaning of that term, they can sign a bystanders' bill of exceptions to acts and comments by the court and the argument of attorneys thereon. Alamo Iron Works v. Prado, Tex.Civ.App., 220 S.W. 282, 291.

C

C. The third letter of the alphabet.

The letter is used as an abbreviation of many words of which it is the initial letter, such as cases, civil, circuit; as a numeral, in like manner with that use of A and B; and to designate the *third* of a series of propositions, sections, etc.

It was used among the Romans to denote condemnation, being the initial letter of *condemno,* I condemn. Tayl. Civil Law, 192.

The initial letter of the word *"Codex,"* used by some writers in citing the Code of Justinian. Tayl. Civil Law, 24.

C.—CT.—CTS. These abbreviations stand for "cent" or "cents," and any one of them, placed at the top or head of a column of figures, sufficiently indicates the denomination of the figures below. Jackson v. Cummings, 15 Ill. 453; Linck v. Litchfield, 141 Ill. 469, 31 N.E. 123.

C. A. B. Civil Aeronautics Board.

C. A. F. Under "c. a. f." provision in sale contract, freight figures substantially only as a part of the purchase price, not as a reservation of title, and the situation is similar to a "c. i. f." contract. Madeirense Do Brasil S/A v. Stulman-Emrick Lumber Co., C.C.A.N.Y., 147 F.2d 399, 402; cost and freight allowed to point of destination, being the equivalent of shipment F. O. B. from point of origin. Farris & Co. v. William Schluderberg, T. J. Kurdle Co., 142 Fla. 765, 196 So. 184.

C. A. V. An abbreviation for *curia advisari vult,* the court will be advised, will consider, will deliberate.

C. B. In reports and legal documents, an abbreviation for common bench. Also an abbreviation for chief baron.

C. C. Various terms or phrases may be denoted by this abbreviation; such as circuit court, (or city or county court;) criminal cases, (or crown or civil or chancery cases;) civil code; chief commissioner; and *cepi corpus,* I have taken his body.

C. C.; B. B. I have taken his body; bail bond entered. See Capias ad Respondendum.

C. C. P. An abbreviation for Code of Civil Procedure; also for court of common pleas.

C. C. & C. I have taken his body and he is held.

C. F. & I. Also written "c. f. i." Letters used in contracts for *cost, freight and insurance,* indicating that the price fixed covers not only cost but freight and insurance to be paid by the seller; Benj. Sales, § 887; L.R. 8 Ex. 179; 7 H. & N. 574; Mee v. McNider, 109 N.Y. 500, 502, 17 N.E. 424.

C. I. A. Central Intelligence Agency.

C. I. F. Also written "c. i. f." These letters in contracts of sale indicate, as does the expression "c. f. i." or "C. F. & I." (*q. v.*), that the price fixed covers the cost of goods, insurance, and freight. National Wholesale Grocery Co. v. Mann, 251 Mass. 238, 146 N.E. 791, 793; A. Klipstein & Co. v. Dilsizian, C.C.A.N.Y., 273 F. 473, 475; Columbus Bagging & Tie Co. v. Steel Union Co., 43 Ga. App. 126, 158 S.E. 459, 460.

C. J. An abbreviation for chief justice; also for circuit judge.

C. L. An abbreviation for civil law.

C. L. P. Common law procedure, in reference to the English acts so entitled.

C. O. D. "Collect on delivery." These letters import the carrier's liability to return to the consignor either the goods or the charges. U. S. Exp. Co. v. Keefer, 59 Ind. 267; Express Co. v. Wolf, 79 Ill. 434; Danciger v. American Express Co., 192 Mo.App. 172, 179 S.W. 797, 798. The carrier accepts a check instead of cash at its own peril. Joseph Mogul, Inc., v. C. Lewis Lavine, Inc., 220 App.Div. 287, 221 N.Y.S. 391, 393.

C. P. An abbreviation for common pleas.

C. P. A. Certified Public Accountant.

C. R. An abbreviation for *curia regis;* also for chancery reports.

C. S. C. Civil Service Commission.

C. T. A. An abbreviation for *cum testamento annexo,* in describing a species of administration.

C. & F. The term "c. & f." means that the sale price includes in a lump sum "cost" and "freight" to named destination, and either requires seller to prepay freight or permits buyer, after having paid actual charges, to deduct them from the price. Madeirense Do Brasil S/A v. Stulman-Emrick Lumber Co., C.C.A.N.Y., 147 F.2d 399, 402.

CA. SA. An abbreviation of *capias ad satisfaciendum, q. v.*

CABAL. A small association for the purpose of intrigue; an intrigue. This name was given to that ministry in the reign of Charles II. formed by Clifford, Ashley, Buckingham, Arlington, and Lauderdale, who concerted a scheme for the restoration of popery. The initials of these five names form the word "cabal;" hence the appellation. Hume, Hist.Eng. ix. 69.

CABALIST. In French commercial law. A factor or broker.

CABALLARIA. Pertaining to a horse. It was a feudal tenure of lands, the tenant furnishing a horseman suitably equipped in time of war, or when the lord had occasion for his service.

CABALLERIA. In Spanish law. An allotment of land acquired by conquest, to a horse soldier. A quantity of land, varying in extent in different provinces. In those parts of the United States which formerly belonged to Spain, it is a lot of one hundred feet front, two hundred feet depth, and equivalent to five peonias. 2 White, New Recop. 49; Strother v. Lucas, 12 Pet. 444, 9 L.Ed. 1137, note; Escriche, Dicc. Raz.

CABALLERO. In Spanish law. A knight. So called on account of its being more honorable to go on horseback (*à caballo*) than on any other beast.

CABANA. Cabin or small house. Godson v. Town of Surfside, 150 Fla. 614, 8 So.2d 497, 500.

CABARET. A room where musical entertainment is permitted in connection with restaurant business. People v. Liquorman, 171 Misc. 535, 13 N.Y.S.2d 410, 411.

CABINET. The advisory board or council of a king or other chief executive. The select or secret council of a prince or executive government; so called from the apartment in which it was originally held. Webster

CABINET COUNCIL. In English law. A private and confidential assembly of the most considerable ministers of state, to concert measures for the administration of public affairs; first established by Charles I. Wharton.

CABLE. A large and strong rope or chain. An assembly of wires held together in some way. Triangle Conduit & Cable Co. v. National Electric Products Corporation, D.C.Del., 56 F.Supp. 979, 981.

The term "cable railroad" in a city charter has been held to imply street railroads. City of Denver v. Mercantile Trust Co. of New York, C.C.A.Colo., 201 F. 790, 802.

CABLE TRANSFER. A credit for a sum of money payable at the place indicated. Oshinsky v. Taylor, Sup., 172 N.Y.S. 231, 232.

CABLISH. Brush-wood, or more properly windfall-wood.

CABOOSE CAR. A car attached to the rear of a freight train, fitted up for the accommodation of the conductor, brakeman, and chance passengers. Mammoth Cave R. Co. v. Commonwealth, 176 Ky. 747, 197 S.W. 406, 407.

CABOTAGE. A nautical term from the Spanish, denoting strictly navigation from cape to cape along the coast without going out into the open sea. In International Law, cabotage is identified with *coasting-trade* so that it means navigating and trading along the coast between the ports thereof.

CACHEPOLUS, or CACHERELLAS. An inferior bailiff, or catchpoll. Jacob.

CACHET, LETTRES DE. Letters issued and signed by the kings of France, and countersigned by a secretary of state, authorizing the imprisonment of a person. Abolished during the revolution of 1789. See Lettres de Cachet.

CACICAZGOS. In Spanish-American law. Property entailed on the *caciques*, or heads of Indian villages, and their descendants. Schm.Civil Law, 309.

CADASTRE. Sp. An official statement of the quantity and value of real property in any district, made for the purpose of justly apportioning the taxes payable on such property. Strother. v. Lucas, 12 Pet. 410, 428, note, 9 L.Ed. 1137.

CADASTU. In French law. An official statement of the quantity and value of realty made for purposes of taxation; same as *cadastre, (q. v.)*.

CADAVER. A dead human body; a corpse. *Cadaver nullius in bonis*, no one can have a right of property in a corpse. 3 Co.Inst. 110, 2 Bl. Comm. 429; Griffith v. Railroad Co., 23 S.C. 32, 55 Am.Rep. 1.

CADAVEROUS. Pale, wan or ghastly appearance. Commonwealth v. Caldutte, 136 Pa.Super. 52, 7 A.2d 121, 123.

CADERE. Lat. To end; cease; fail; as in phrases such as *cadit actio*, (or *breve*,) the action (or writ) fails; *cadit assisa*, the assise abates; *cadit quœstio*, the discussion ends, there is no room for further argument; *cadere ab actione* (literally, to fall from an action), to fail in an action; *cadere in partem*, to become subject to a division.

To be changed; to become; to be turned into. *Cadit assisa in juratum*, the assise is changed into a jury. Calvinus, Lex.

CADET. Students in the military academy at West Point are styled "cadets;" students in the naval academy at Annapolis, "cadet midshipmen."

In England. A younger brother; the younger son of a gentleman; particularly applied to a volunteer in the army, waiting for some post. Jacob.

CADI. A Turkish civil magistrate.

CADIT. Lat. It falls, abates, fails, ends, ceases. See Cadere.

CADUCA. In the civil law. Property of an inheritable quality; property such as descends to an heir. Also the lapse of a testamentary disposition or legacy. Also an escheat; escheated property.

CADUCARY. Relating to or of the nature of escheat, forfeiture, or confiscation. 2 Bl.Comm. 245.

CÆDUA. In the civil and old common law. Kept for cutting; intended or used to be cut. A term applied to wood.

CÆSAR. In the Roman law. A cognomen in the Gens Julia, which was assumed by the successors of Julius. Tayl. Civil Law, 31.

CÆSAREAN (also spelled **Caesarian**) **OPERATION.** A surgical operation whereby the fœtus is taken from the mother, with a view to save the lives of both, or either of them. Wharton.

CÆTERUS. Lat. Other; another; the rest.

CÆTERIS PARIBUS. Other things being equal.

CÆTERIS TACENTIBUS. The others being silent; the other judges expressing no opinion. Comb. 186.

CÆTERORUM. When a limited administration has been granted, and all the property cannot be administered under it, administration *cœterorum* (as to the residue) may be granted.

CAFE. A place where meals and drinks are served to the public generally or to selected portions of the public. In re Bowers, D.C.Cal., 33 F. Supp. 965, 966.

The word as ordinarily and popularly used means a restaurant or house for refreshments. Proprietors' Realty Co. v. Wohltmann, 95 N.J.Law, 303, 112 A. 410. The terms "restaurant" and "café" are substantially synonymous. State v. Shoaf, 179 N.C. 744, 102 S.E. 705, 9 A.L.R. 426.

CAHIER. In old French law. A list of grievances prepared for deputies in the states-general. A petition for the redress of grievances enumerated.

CAHOOTS. Partnership, teaming up, or combining efforts. City of Abilene v. Luhn, Tex.Civ.App., 65 S.W.2d 370, 371.

CAIN, or CANE. In Scotch law. Rent paid in kind, as in poultry, eggs, etc.; hence, any tax, tribute, or duty. Cent. Dict.

CAIRNS' ACT. An English statute for enabling the court of chancery to award damages. 21 & 22 Vict. c. 27. Repealed as having been superseded by the Judicature Act of 1873.

CAISSON DISEASE. A dizziness accompanied with partial paralysis of the limbs, caused by too rapid reduction of air pressure to which men have been accustomed. Williams v. Missouri Bridge & Iron Co., 212 Mich. 150, 180 N.W. 357, 358. A condition caused by excessive air pressure wherein gas emboli or bubbles in the tissues of the body may induce severe pain and paralysis, Cannella v. Gulf Refining Co. of Louisiana, La.App., 154 So. 406, 413.

CALABOOSE. A term used vulgarly, and occasionally in judicial proceedings and law reports, to designate a jail or prison, particularly a town or city jail or lock-up. Supposed to be a corruption of the Spanish *calabozo,* a dungeon. See Gilham v. Wells, 64 Ga. 194.

CALAMITY. A state of deep distress or misfortune, produced by some adverse circumstance or event; misery; any great misfortune or cause of loss or misery; usually an event or disaster that produces extensive evil. City of Muskegon Heights v. Danigelis, 253 Mich. 260, 235 N.W. 83, 84, 73 A.L.R. 696.

CALAMUS. Lat. A reed; cane; hence, a reed pen; reed-pipe; arrow; small rod, etc. Harper, Lat. Dict. Also, an ancient Greek measure of length of 10 feet. Cent. Dict.

CALCETUM, CALCEA. A causeway, or common hard-way, maintained and repaired with stones and rubbish.

CALCULATE. To compute mathematically; in its broader significance, to intend, to purpose, or to design. State v. Smith, 57 Mont. 349, 188 P. 644, 648.

CALCULATED. An act may produce a certain effect, whether intended or not; fitted, adapted, or suited. Polly v. People, 107 Colo. 6, 108 P.2d 220, 223. Likely or intended. State v. Wyman, 56 Mont. 600, 186 P. 1, 5; Pouchan v. Godeau, 167 Cal. 692, 140 P. 952, 953.

CALE. In old French law. A punishment of sailors, resembling the modern "keelhauling."

CALEFAGIUM. In old law. A right to take fuel yearly. Cowell; Blount.

CALENDAR. The established order of the division of time into years, months, weeks, and days; or a systematized enumeration of such arrangement; an almanac. Rives v. Guthrie, 46 N.C. 86; Sculley v. Red Lodge-Rosebud Irr. Dist., 83 Mont. 282, 272 P. 543, 552.

Calendar Days

A calendar day contains 24 hours but "calendar days" may be synonymous with "working days." Sherwood v. American Sugar Refining Co., C.C. A.N.Y., 8 F.2d 586, 588. The time from midnight to midnight, Lanni v. Grimes, 173 Misc. 614, 18 N. Y.S.2d 322, 327. So many days reckoned according to the course of the calendar.

Calendar Month

One of the months of the year as enumerated in the calendar. Daley v. Anderson, 7 Wyo. 1, 48 P. 840, 75 Am.St.Rep. 870.

Calendar Week

A block of seven days registered on calendar beginning with Sunday and ending with Saturday. Sonoma County v. Sanborn, 1 Cal.App.2d 26, 36 P.2d 419, 422. Term may consist of any seven days of given month. Sonoma County v. Sanborn, 1 Cal.App.2d 26, 36 P.2d 419, 422.

Calendar Year

The period from January 1 to December 31, inclusive. Byrne v. Bearden, 27 Ga.App. 149, 107 S. E. 782, 783; Application of Title Guarantee & Trust Co., 183 Misc. 490, 48 N.Y.S. 374, 375. Ordinarily calendar year means 365 days except leap year, and is composed of 12 months varying in length. Shaffner v. Lipinsky, 194 N.C. 1, 138 S.E. 418, 419; United States, for Use of Strona v. Bussey, D.C.Cal., 51 F.Supp. 996, 999.

"Calendar year preceding election" means year beginning January 1 and ending December 31. People v. Milan, 89 Colo. 556, 5 P.2d 249, 253.

Calendar of Causes

A list of the causes instituted in the particular court, and now ready for trial, drawn up before beginning of the term. It is sometimes called the "trial list," or "docket."

Calendar of Prisoners

In English practice. A list kept by the sheriffs containing the names of all the prisoners in their custody, with the several judgments against each in the margin. Staundef.P.C. 182; 4 Bl.Comm. 403.

Special Calendar

A calendar or list of causes, containing those set down specially for hearing, trial, or argument.

CALENDS. Among the Romans the first day of every month, being spoken of by itself, or the very day of the new moon, which usually happen together. And if *pridie,* the day before, he added to it, then it is the last day of the foregoing month, as *pridie calend. Septemb.* is the last day of August. If any number be placed with it, it signifies that day in the former month which comes so much before the month named, as the tenth calends of October is the 20th day of September; for if one reckons backwards, beginning at October, that 20th day of September makes the 10th day before October. In March, May, July, and October, the calends begin at the sixteenth day, but in other months at the fourteenth; which calends must ever bear the name of the month following, and be numbered backwards from the first day of the said following months. Jacob. See Rives v. Guthrie, 46 N.C. 87.

CALENDS, GREEK. A metaphorical expression for a time never likely to arrive, inasmuch as the Greeks had no calends.

CALF. As used in an exemption statute, should be construed to include an animal sucking a cow that is being milked, even though the animal be a yearling. Kiggins v. Henne & Meyer Co., Tex. Civ.App., 199 S.W. 494, 496.

CALICHE ROCK. A substance containing calcium carbonate like that found in ordinary limestone. Board of Com'rs of Roosevelt County v. Good, 44 N.M. 495, 105 P.2d 470, 472.

CALL, *n.*

Contract Language

As used in contract, means demand for payment of, especially by formal notice. Keyes v. Kimmel, 9 N.J.Misc.R. 604, 155 A. 19, 20.

Conveyancing

A visible natural object or landmark designated in a patent, entry, grant, or other conveyance of lands, as a limit or boundary to the land described, with which the points of surveying must correspond. Also the courses and distances designated. King v. Watkins, C.C.Va., 98 Fed. 922. See, also, Kentucky Union Co. v. Shepherd, 192 Ky. 447, 234 S.W. 10, 13.

Corporation Law

A demand by directors upon subscribers for shares for payment of a portion or installment; in this sense, it is capable of three meanings: (1) The resolution of the directors to levy the assessment; (2) its notification to the persons liable to pay; (3) the time when it becomes payable. Railway Co. v. Mitchell, 4 Exch. 543; Hatch v. Dana, Ill., 101 U.S. 205, 25 L.Ed. 885; Stewart v. Pub. Co., 1 Wash.St. 521, 20 P. 605.

Although the terms "call" and "assessment" are often used synonymously, the latter term applies with peculiar aptness to contributions above the par value of stock or the subscription liability of the stockholders. Porter v. Northern Fire & Marine Ins. Co., 36 N.D. 199, 161 N.W. 1012, 1014. See Assessment.

Dealings in Futures

Deposit of more margin. Fenner v. Tucker, 213 N.C. 419, 196 S.E. 357, 359.

Dealings in Securities or Grain

Option or right to demand a certain amount of securities or grain at a fixed price at or within certain time agreed on. Colston v. Burnet, 61 App. D.C. 192, 59 F.2d 867, 868; Dillon, Read & Co. v. Hoey, D.C.N.Y., 45 F.Supp. 475, 477.

English Law

The election of students to the degree of barrister at law, hence the ceremony or epoch of election, and the number of persons elected.

Mutual Act or Benefit Association Certificate

Official declaration that payment is required or demand for payment. Pasley v. Brady Mut. Life Ass'n, Tex.Civ.App., 2 S.W.2d 278, 279.

CALL, *v.* To summon or demand by name; to demand the presence and participation of a number of persons by calling aloud their names, either in a pre-arranged and systematic order or in a succession determined by chance.

Terms "called" and "sold" as equivalent. In re Gyllstrom's Will, 15 N.Y.S.2d 801, 808, 172 Misc. 655.

Call of the House

A call of the names of members of a legislative body in pursuance of a resolution requiring attendance of members.

Calling a Summons

In Scotch practice. See this described in Bell, Dict.

Calling an Election

Commonly construed as including, or as being synonymous with, the giving of notice of the election. State v. Hall, 73 Or. 231, 144 P. 475, 478; People v. Gough, 260 Ill. 542, 103 N.E. 685, 686.

Calling the Docket

The public calling of the docket or list of causes at commencement of term of court for setting a time for trial or entering orders of continuance, default, nonsuit, etc. Blanchard v. Ferdinand, 132 Mass. 391.

Calling the Jury

Successively drawing out of a box the names of the jurors on the panels annexed to the *nisi prius* record, and calling them over in the order in which they are so drawn.

Calling the Plaintiff

A formal method of causing a nonsuit to be entered. When a plaintiff or his counsel, seeing that sufficient evidence has not been given to maintain the issue, withdraws, the crier is ordered to call or demand the plaintiff, and if neither he, nor any person for him appear, he is nonsuited. The phrase "let the plaintiff be called" is to be explained by reference to this practice. See 3 Bla. Comm. 376; 2 C. & P. 403; Porter v. Perkins, 5 Mass. 236, 4 Am.Dec. 52.

Calling to Testify

Under certain statutes, when adversary takes the witness' deposition, Allen v. Pollard, 109 Tex. 536, 212 S.W. 468; Clayton v. Ogden State Bank, 82 Utah 564, 26 P.2d 545, 548; or when he files interrogatories to the witness stating that his deposition will be taken in answer thereto, Wyatt v. Chambers, Tex.Civ.App., 182 S.W. 16, 18.

Calling to the Bar

In English practice. Conferring the dignity or degree of barrister at law upon a member of one of the inns of court. Holthouse. "Calls to the bench and bar are to be made by the most ancient, being a reader, who is present at supper on call night." 1 Black Books of Lincoln's Inn. 339.

Calling Upon a Prisoner

When a prisoner has been found guilty on an indictment, the clerk of the court addresses him and calls upon him to say why judgment should not be passed upon him.

CALL PATENT. One whose corners are all stakes, or all but one, or whose lines were not run out and marked at time. Combs v. Combs, 238 Ky. 362, 38 S.W.2d 243, 244.

CALLABLE. Option to pay before maturity on call. In re Opinions of the Justices, 231 Ala. 152, 164 So. 572, 578.

CALLABLE BONDS. Bonds which may be called for payment before their maturity. Fales v. Multnomah County, 119 Or. 127, 248 P. 151, 152.

CALLED UPON TO PAY. Compelled or required to pay. Taylor v. Coon, 79 Wis. 76, 48 N.W. 123, 128.

CALLERS. Persons employed by a motor carrier to unload truck or trailer bodies and advise checker of nature of items of freight unloaded. Cream v. M. Moran Transp. Lines, D.C.N.Y., 57 F.Supp. 212, 216.

CALLING. A business, occupation, or trade. Gray v. Board of County Com'rs of Sedgwick County, 101 Kan. 195, 165 P. 867, 868, L.R.A.1918F, 182. One's usual occupation, vocation, or business. Crook v. Commonwealth, 147 Va. 593, 136 S.E. 565, 567, 50 A.L.R. 1043. A profession, Ex parte Galusha, 184 Cal. 697, 195 P. 406, 407; C. D. Shamburger Lumber Co. v. Delavan, Tex.Civ.App., 106 S.W.2d 351, 355, 356.

CALPES. In Scotch law. A gift to the head of a clan, as an acknowledgment for protection and maintenance.

CALUMNIA.

In the civil law calumny, malice, or ill design; a false accusation; a malicious prosecution. Lanning v. Christy, 30 Ohio St. 115, 27 Am.Rep. 431.

In the old common law. A claim, demand, challenge to jurors.

CALUMNIÆ JURAMENTUM. In the old canon law. An oath similar to the *calumniœ jusjurandum,* (*q. v.*).

CALUMNIÆ JUSJURANDUM. The oath of (against) calumny. An oath imposed upon the parties to a suit that they did not sue or defend with the intention of calumniating, (*calumniandi animo,*) *i. e.*, with a malicious design, but from a firm belief that they had a good cause. Inst. 4, 16. The object was to prevent vexatious and unnecessary suits. It was especially used in divorce cases, though of little practical utility; Bish. Marr. & Div. § 353; 2 Bish.Marr.Div. & Sep. § 264. A somewhat similar provision is to be found in the requirement made in some states that the defendant shall file an affidavit of merits.

CALUMNIATOR. In the civil law. One who accused another of a crime without cause; one who brought a false accusation. Cod. 9, 46.

CALUMNY. Defamation; slander; false accusation of a crime or offense. See Calumnia.

CALVIN'S CASE. Calvin v. Smith, 7 Rep. 1; 2 S.T. 559, decided in 1608, in which it was held that persons born in Scotland after the accession of James I to the crown of England in 1603 were not aliens but were capable of inheriting land in England. Wharton.

CALVO DOCTRINE. The doctrine stated by the Argentine jurist, Carlos Calvo, that a government is not bound to indemnify aliens for losses or injuries sustained by them in consequence of domestic disturbances or civil war, where the state is not at fault, and that therefore foreign states are not justified in intervening, by force or otherwise, to secure the settlement of claims of their citizens on account of such losses or injuries. Such intervention, Calvo says, is not in accordance with the practice of European States towards one another, and is contrary to the principle of state sovereignty. 3 Calvo §§ 1280, 1297. The Calvo Doctrine is to be distinguished from the Drago Doctrine (*q. v.*).

See 18 Green Bag 377.

CALYPSO SONG. A song distinguished by a certain form, rhythm, and narrative style, apparently indigenous to the Island of Trinidad. Baron v. Leo Feist, Inc., D.C.N.Y., 78 F.Supp. 686, 687.

CAMARA. In Spanish law. A treasury. Las Partidas, pt. 6, tit. 3, 1, 2.

The exchequer. White, New Recop. b. 3, tit. 8, c. 1.

CAMBELLANUS, or CAMBELLARIUS. A chamberlain. Spelman.

CAMBER. Ship's camber is convex arc of vessel's deck from side to side. The Indien, C.C.A.Cal., 71 F.2d 752, 757.

CAMBIALE JUS. The law of exchange.

CAMBIATOR. In old English law. An exchanger. *Cambiatores monetæ,* exchangers of money; money-changers.

CAMBIO. In Spanish law. Exchange. Schm. Civil Law, 148.

CAMBIPARTIA. Champerty; from *campus,* a field, and *partus,* divided. Spelman.

CAMBIPARTICEPS. A champertor.

CAMBIST. In mèrcantile law. A person skilled in exchanges; one who trades in promissory notes or bills of exchange; a broker.

CAMBIUM. In the civil law. Change or exchange. A term applied indifferently to the exchange of land, money, or debts. Du Cange.

Cambium reale or *manuale* was the term generally used to denote the technical common-law exchange of lands; *cambium locale, mercantile,* or *trajectitium,* was used to designate the modern mercantile contract of exchange, whereby a man agrees, in consideration of a sum of money paid him in one place, to pay a like sum in another place. Poth. *de Change,* n. 12; Story, Bills, § 2, et seq.

CAMERA. In old English law. A chamber, room, or apartment; a judge's chamber; a treasury; a chest or coffer. Also, a stipend payable from vassal to lord; an annuity. See In Camera.

CAMERA REGIS. In old English law. A chamber of the king; a place of peculiar privileges especially in a commercial point of view. The city of London was so called. Year Book, p. 7, Hen. VI, 27; Burrill, Law Dic.

CAMERA SCACCARII. The old name of the exchequer chamber.

CAMERA STELLATA. The star chamber (*q. v.*).

CAMERALISTICS. The science of finance or public revenue, comprehending the means of raising and disposing of it.

CAMERARIUS. A chamberlain; a keeper of the public money; a treasurer. Spelman Gloss. *Cambellarius;* 1 Perr. & D. 243. Also a bailiff or receiver.

CAMINO. In Spanish law. A road or highway. Las Partidas, pt. 3, tit. 2, l. 6.

CAMOUFLAGE. The art of disguising or concealing the nature of objects. Palmer v. Commonwealth, 240 Ky. 175, 41 S.W.2d 936, 938.

CAMP. The ground or spot on which huts, tents, are erected for shelter; single hut or shelter; to camp; to encamp; to lodge in a camp. Jones v. State, 64 Ga.App. 376, 13 S.E.2d 462, 465.

CAMPAIGN. All the things and necessary legal and factual acts done by a candidate and his adherents to obtain a majority or plurality of the votes to be cast; running for office, or candidacy for office. Norris v. United States, C.C.A.Neb., 86 F.2d 379, 382. Any organized effort to promote a cause or to secure some definite result with any group of persons. State ex rel. Green v. City of Cleveland, Ohio App., 33 N.E.2d 35, 36.

CAMPANA. In old European law. A bell. Spelman.

CAMPANA BAJULA. A small handbell used in the ceremonies of the Romish church; and, among Protestants, by sextons, parish clerks, and criers. Cowell.

CAMPANARIUM, CAMPANILE. A belfry, bell tower, or steeple; a place where bells are hung. Spelman; Townsh.Pl. 191, 213.

CAMPARTUM. A part of a larger field or ground, which would otherwise be in gross or in common. See Champert; Champerty.

CAMPBELL'S (LORD) ACTS. English statutes, for amending the practice in prosecutions for libel, 9 & 10 Vict. c. 93; also 6 & 7 Vict. c. 96, providing for compensation to relatives in the case of a person having been killed through negligence; also 20 & 21 Vict. c. 83, in regard to the sale of obscene books, etc.

CAMPERS. A share; a champertor's share; a champertous division or sharing of land.

CAMPERTUM. A cornfield; a field of grain. Blount; Cowell; Jacob; Whishaw.

CAMPFIGHT. In old English law. The fighting of two champions or combatants in the field; the judicial combat, or *duellum.* 3 Inst. 221.

CAMPUM PARTERE. To divide the land. See Champerty.

CAMPUS. (Lat. A field.)

In old European law. An assembly of the people anciently held in the open air, in some *plain.*

In feudal and old English law. A field, or plain. The field, ground, or lists marked out for the combatants in the *duellum,* or trial by battle. Burrill, Law Dict.

CAMPUS MAII. The field of May. An anniversary assembly of the Saxons, held on May-day, when they confederated for the defense of the kingdom against all its enemies.

CAMPUS MARTII. The field of March. See Champ de Mars.

CAN. As a noun, a contraption in which employees are lowered to the floor of a mine. Eagle-Picher Mining & Smelting Co. v. Coffey, 186 Okl. 214, 97 P.2d 48, 49.

CAN. As a verb, to be enabled by law; to have a right to, Bailey Realty & Loan Co. v. Bunting, 31 Ala.App. 450, 19 So.2d 607, 608. To put in a can or cans, to preserve by putting in sealed cans, to tin, Henry v. Markesan State Bank, C.C.A.Minn., 68 F.2d 554, 557; is often interpreted as the equivalent of "may." The Pantorium v. McLaughlin, 116 Neb. 61, 215 N.W. 798, 799. See Cannot.

CANA. A Spanish measure of length varying (in different localities) from about five to seven feet.

CAÑADA. Sp. Valley. Benavides v. State, Tex. Civ.App., 214 S.W. 568, 572.

CANADIAN JUMPER. A term applied to a nervous person who jumps when another touches him, shouting at the same time, or when anything thrown hits him, or when a loud noise is made. Goupiel v. Grand Trunk Ry. Co., 94 Vt. 337, 111 A. 346, 347.

CANAL. An artificial ditch or trench in the earth, for confining water to a defined channel, to be used for purposes of transportation. See Bishop v. Seeley, 18 Conn. 394; Hubbard v. Dunne, 276 Ill. 598, 115 N.E. 210, 215; Guinan v. Boston, Cape Cod & New York Canal Co., C.C.A.N.Y., 1 F.2d 239.

It includes the banks; it has reference to the excavation or channel as a receptacle for the water; it is an artificial thing. Kennedy v. Indianapolis, 103 U.S. 604, 26 L.Ed. 550. As used in statute concerning right of way over public lands for irrigation, it embraces whole project including reservoir. U. S. v. Big Horn Land & Cattle Co., C.C.A.Colo., 17 F.2d 357, 364; Johnson Irr. Co. v. Ivory, 46 Wyo. 221, 24 P.2d 1053, 1056.

CANCEL. To obliterate; to strike or cross out; to destroy the effect of an instrument by defacing, obliterating, expunging, or erasing it; to revoke or recall. Ellsworth College v. Carleton, 178 Iowa 845, 160 N.W. 222, 223; Reliance Life Ins. Co. v. Thayer, 84 Okl. 238, 203 P. 190, 192. To annul or destroy, make void or invalid, or set aside. Irwin v. State Brokerage Co., 82 Ind.App. 687, 147 N.E. 531, 532; In re Crawford's Will, 80 Misc. 615, 142 N.Y.S. 1032, 1033; Clegg v. Schvaneveldt, 79 Utah 195, 8 P.2d 620, 621. To rescind or abandon. Pearson v. Brown, 27 Cal.App. 125, 148 P. 956, 958. To repeal, surrender, or waive. Greib v. Dullea, 66 Cal.App.2d 986, 153 P.2d 581, 590. To terminate. Schwartz v. Van Winkle, Sup., 47 N.Y.S.2d 264, 265.

The term is sometimes equivalent to "discharge" or "pay." Auburn City Bank v. Leonard, 40 Barb., N.Y., 119; Debes v. Texas Nat. Bank of Beaumont, Tex.Civ.App., 92 S.W.2d 476, 479.

Courts of equity frequently cancel instruments which have answered the end for which they were created, or instruments which are void or voidable, in order to prevent them from being vexatiously used against the person apparently bound by them. Snell, Eq. 498.

See Cancellation.

CANCELLARIA. Chancery; the court of chancery. *Curia cancellaria* is also used in the same sense. See 4 Bl.Comm. 46; Cowell.

CANCELLARII ANGLIÆ DIGNITAS EST, UT SECUNDUS A REGE IN REGNO HABETUR. The dignity of the chancellor of England is that he is deemed the second from the sovereign in the kingdom. 4 Inst. 78.

CANCELLARIUS. A chancellor; a scrivener, or notary. A janitor, or one who stood at the door of the court and was accustomed to carry out the commands of the judges. Du Cange.

In early English law, the keeper of the king's seal. In this sense only, the word chancellor seems to have been used in the English law; 3 Bla.Comm. 46. See 15 Harv.L. Rev. 109; 4 Co.Inst. 78; Dugdale Orig. Jur. fol. 34; and generally Selden, Discourses; Inderwick, King's Peace; 3 Steph.Com. 346; 1 Poll. & Maitl. 172; 1 Stubbs, Const. Hist. 381; Campbell, Lives of the Lord Chancellors, vol: 1; Holdsw. Hist. E. L.; Pollock, Expans. of C. L.

CANCELLATION. Abandonment of contract. State ex rel. Pacific Mut. Life Ins. Co. v. Larson, 152 Fla. 729, 12 So.2d 896, 897. Act of crossing out a writing, Plaut v. Shirley, 200 Ky. 619, 255 S.W. 273, 274; In re Parsons' Will, 119 Misc. 26, 195 N.Y.S. 742, 745; Culp v. First Commercial Sav. Bank of Constantine, 288 Mich. 646, 286 N.W. 113, 114; act which manifests an intent to annul and puts the instrument in condition where its invalidity appears on its face, In re Akers' Will, 74 App.Div. 461, 77 N.Y.Supp. 643; Baldwin v. Howell, 45 N.J.Eq. 519, 15 A. 236; In re Tremain's Will, Surr., 7 N.Y.S.2d 781, 790; Annulment or abrogation, Golden v. Fowler, 26 Ga. 464, Winton v. Spring, 18 Cal. 455, Sanborn v. Ballonfonte, 98 Cal.App. 482, 277 P. 152, 155; defacement or mutilation of instrument, Worcester Bank & Trust Co. v. Ellis, 292 Mass. 88, 197 N.E. 637, 639. Reduction by insurer of amount of insurance, Gill v. Fidelity Phenix Fire Ins. Co., D.C.Ky., 5 F.Supp. 1, 2; Suspension of insurance policy, Federal Land Bank of Omaha v. Farmers' Mut. Ins. Ass'n of Adams and Adjoining Counties, 217 Iowa 1098, 253 N.W. 52. Termination, Otterbein v. Babor & Comeau Co., 272 N.Y. 149, 5 N.E.2d 71, 72, 107 A.L.R. 1510; words of revocation written across instrument, In re Semler's Will, 176 Misc. 687, 28 N.Y. S.2d 390, 392, 393.

Cancellation is properly distinguished from obliteration. Townshend v. Howard, 86 Me. 285, 29 A. 1077. Spoliation may amount to a cancellation. Cancellation does not revoke unless done with that intention. In re Woods' Will, Sur., 11 N.Y.Supp. 157.

CANCELLATURA. In old English law. A canceling. Bract. 398*b*.

CANCELLI. The rails or lattice work or balusters inclosing the bar of a court of justice or the communion table. Also the lines drawn on the face of a will or other writing, with the intention of revoking or annulling it.

CANDIDATE. One who seeks or offers himself, or is put forward by others, for an office, privilege, or honor. Starkweather v. Hoss, 126 Or. 630, 270 P. 768, 770; State ex rel. Ranney v. Corey, Ohio App., 47 N.E.2d 799, 800; it is not necessary that he should have been nominated. Leonard v. Com., 112 Pa. 624, 4 A. 224. A nominee, State ex rel. Van Schoyck v. Board of Com'rs of Lincoln County, 46 N.M. 472, 131 P.2d 278, 284. Under a presidential primary law, a person receiving the approval of the required number of petitioners may be deemed a candidate even contrary to his wishes. McCamant v. Olcott, 80 Or. 246, 156 P. 1034, 1038, L.R.A.1916E, 706.

CANDLEMAS-DAY. In English law. A festival appointed by the church to be observed on the second day of February in every year, in honor of the purification of the Virgin Mary, being forty days after her miraculous delivery. At this festival, formerly, the Protestants went, and the Papists now go, in procession with lighted candles; they also consecrate candles on this day for the service of the ensuing year. It is the fourth of the four cross quarter-days of the year. Wharton.

CANE. In Scotch law. The same as *cain* (*q. v.*).

CANFARA. In old records. A trial by hot iron, formerly used in England. Whishaw.

CANNOT. Denotes that one is not able (to do some act). Southern Pac. Co. v. Frye & Bruhn, 82 Wash. 9, 143 P. 163, 165. But the term is often equivalent to "shall not." Bragg v. Hatfield, 124 Me. 391, 130 A. 233, 234.

CANON.

A Dignitary of the English Church

A dignitary of the English church, being a prebendary or member of a cathedral chapter. All members of chapters except deans are now entitled *canons*, in England. 2 Steph.Comm. 11th ed. 687, n.; 1 Bla.Comm. 382.

A Law, Rule, etc.

A law, rule, or ordinance in general, and of the church in particular. An ecclesiastical law or statute. A rule of doctrine or discipline. The term is generally applied to designate the ordinances of councils and decrees of popes.

A System or Aggregation of Correlated Rules

A system or aggregation of correlated rules, whether of statutory origin or otherwise, relating to and governing a particular department of legal science or a particular branch of the substantive law.

Canon law. A body of ecclesiastical jurisprudence. In England, according to Blackstone, there is a kind of national canon law. 1 Bl. Comm. 82. The canon law is contained in two principal parts,—the decrees or ecclesiastical constitutions made by the popes and cardinals; and the decretals or canonical epistles written by the pope, or by the pope and cardinals, at the suit of one or more persons. As the decrees set out the origin of the canon law, and the rights, dignities, and decrees of ecclesiastical persons, with their manner of election, ordination, etc., so the decretals contain the law to be used in the ecclesiastical courts. Jacob. The canon law forms no part of the law of England, unless it has been brought into use and acted on there; 11 Q.B. 649. See generally Encycl.Br., *sub voce,* Canon Law; Maitland, Canon Law; Jenks' Teutonic Law; 1 Sel. Essays on Anglo-Amer.Leg.Hist. 46; Ayliffe, Par.Jur.Can. Ang.; Preface to Burn, Eccl.Law, Tyrwhitt ed. 22; Hale, Civ.L. 26; Bell's Case of a Putative Marriage, 203; *Dict. du Droit Canonique;* Stair, Inst. b. 1, t. 1, 7; 1 Poll. & Maitl. 90.

Canon religiosorum. In ecclesiastical records. A book wherein the religious of every greater convent had a fair transcript of the rules of their order, frequently read among them as their local statutes. Kennett, Gloss.; Cowell.

Canons of construction. The system of fundamental rules and maxims which are recognized as governing the construction or interpretation of written instruments. In re Clarke, 174 App.Div. 736, 161 N.Y.S. 484, 487.

Canons of descent. The legal rules by which inheritances are regulated, and according to which estates are transmitted by descent from the ancestor to the heir.

Canons of inheritance. The legal rules by which inheritances are regulated, and according to which estates are transmitted by descent from the ancestor to the heir. 2 Bl.Comm. 208.

In Civil, Spanish, and Mexican Law an annual charge or rent; an emphyteutic rent.

In Old English records. A prestation, pension, or customary payment.

CANONICAL. Pertaining to, or in conformity to, the canons of the church.

CANONICAL DISABILITY. Incurable physical impotency or incapacity for copulation. D. v. D., Del.Super., 2 Terry 263, 20 A.2d 139, 141.

CANONICAL OBEDIENCE. That duty which a clergyman owes to the bishop who ordained him, to the bishop in whose diocese he is beneficed, and also to the metropolitan of such bishop. Wharton.

CANONICUS. In old English law. A canon. Fleta, lib. 2, c. 69, § 2.

CANONIST. One versed and skilled in the canon law; a professor of ecclesiastical law.

CANONRY. In English ecclesiastical law. An ecclesiastical benefice, attaching to the office of canon. Holthouse.

CANT. In the civil law. A method of dividing property held in common by two or more joint owners. It may be avoided by the consent of all of those who are interested, in the same manner that any other contract or agreement may be avoided. Hayes v. Cuny, 9 Mart.O.S. (La.) 87. See Licitacion.

CANTEL, or CANTLE. A lump, or that which is added above measure; also a piece of anything, as "cantel of bread," or the like. Blount.

CANTERBURY, ARCHBISHOP OF. In English ecclesiastical law. The primate of all England; the chief ecclesiastical dignitary in the church. His customary privilege is to crown the kings and queens of England. Has also, by 25 Hen. VIII, c. 21, the power to grant dispensations. Wharton.

CANTRED. A district comprising a hundred villages; a hundred. A term used in Wales in the same sense as "hundred" is in England. Cowell; Termes de la Ley.

CANUM. In feudal law. A species of duty or tribute payable from tenant to lord, usually consisting of produce of the land.

CANVASS. The act of examining and counting the returns of votes cast at a public election. Bowler v. Eisenhood, 1 S.Dak. 577, 48 N.W. 136, 12 L.R.A. 705; In re Stewart, 24 App.Div. 201, 48 N.Y.S. 957.

CANVASSER. Any of certain persons, as officers of a state, county, or district, intrusted with the duty of examining the returns of votes cast at an election. See Canvass.

One who, in a given town, city, or county, goes from house to house in an effort to take orders for goods; in this sense, to be distinguished from traveling salesmen. City of El Dorado Springs v. Highfill, 268 Mo. 501, 188 S.W. 68.

CAP. In mining, a square piece of plank or block wedged between the top of posts or props and the roof of the mine. Big Branch Coal Co. v. Wrenchie, 160 Ky. 668, 170 S.W. 14, 16.

CAP BOARD. Board about fourteen inches long and about four inches wide which is placed on top of a pillar in mines to prevent pillar from breaking through slate when weight comes against it. Hall v. Proctor Coal Co., 236 Ky. 813, 34 S.W.2d 425, 426.

CAP OF MAINTENANCE. One of the regalia or ornaments of state belonging to the sovereigns of England, before whom it is carried at the coronation and other great solemnities. Caps of maintenance are also carried before the mayors of several cities in England. Enc.Lond.

CAPABLE. Susceptible; competent; qualified; fitting; possessing legal power or capacity. United States v. Sischo, D.C.Wash., 262 F. 1001, 1005. Able, fit or adapted for. U. S. v. Sischo, C.C.A. Wash., 270 F. 958, 961; State v. Wharton, 132 Kan. 409, 295 P. 656, 658. "Capable of contracting" as meaning legally capable, not mentally capable. Szwed v. Morris & Co., 187 Mo.App. 510, 174 S.W. 146, 148.

CAPACITY. A word having many meanings, dependent on its relationship to the subject-matter. Campbell v. Cornish, 163 Okl. 213, 22 P.2d 63.

It may mean: ability; actual production of an oil well, Helis v. Ward, D.C.La., 20 F.Supp. 514, 517; an intelligent perception and understanding of the dispositions made of property, etc., In re Null's Estate, 302 Pa. 64, 153 A. 137, 139. Qualification: size, space, or compass, strength, power or force, Campbell v. Cornish, 163 Okl. 213, 22 P.2d 63; sound mind, Chambers v. Winn, Tex.Civ.App., 133 S.W.2d 279, 282; the attribute of persons which enables them to perform civil or juristic acts. Sargent v. Burdett, 96 Ga. 111, 22 S.E. 667; 2 Com.Dig. 294.

"Capacity to sue" consists in right to come into court, Braden v. Neal, 132 Kan. 387, 295 P. 678, 680.

"Public capacity" of municipal property is such capacity as all the people of the state are alike interested in. Board of Com'rs of Woodward County v. Willett, 49 Okl. 254, 152 P. 365, 366, L.R.A.1916E, 92.

CAPAX DOLI. Lat. Capable of committing crime, or capable of criminal intent. The phrase describes the condition of one who has sufficient intelligence and comprehension to be held criminally responsible for his deeds.

CAPAX NEGOTII. Competent to transact affairs; having business capacity.

CAPE. In English practice. A judicial writ, now abolished, touching a plea of lands or tenements.

It was divided into *cape magnum*, or the *grand cape*, which lay before appearance to summon the tenant to answer the default, and also over to the demandant and *cape parvum*, or *petit cape*, after appearance or view granted, summoning the tenant to answer the default only. Termes de la Ley; 3 Steph.Comm. 606, note; Fleta, l. 6, c. 55, § 40; 2 Wms.Saund. 45 *c, d;* Rosc. Real Act. 165, et seq. It was called a "cape," from the word with which it commenced, and a "grand cape" (or *cape magnum*) to distinguish it from the *petit cape*, which lay after appearance.

CAPE AD VALENTIAM. A species of *cape magnum.*

CAPELLA. In old records. A box, cabinet, or repository in which were preserved the relics of martyrs. Spelman. A small building in which relics were preserved; an oratory or chapel. Id.

In old English law. A chapel. Fleta, lib. 5, c. 12, § 1; Spelman; Cowell.

CAPERS. Vessels of war owned by private persons, and different from ordinary privateers only in size, being smaller. Beawes, Lex Merc. 230.

CAPIAS. Lat. "That you take." The general name for several species of writs, the common characteristic of which is that they require the officer to take the body of the defendant into custody; they are writs of attachment or arrest.

In English practice, the process on an indictment when the person charged is not in custody, and in cases not otherwise provided for by statute. 4 Steph.Comm. 383.

Capias Ad Audiendum Judicium

A writ issued, in a case of misdemeanor, after the defendant has appeared and is found guilty, to bring him to hear judgment if he is not present when called. 4 Bl.Comm. 368.

Capias Ad Computandum

In the action of account render, after judgment of *quod computet,* if the defendant refuses to appear personally before the auditors and make his account, a writ by this name may issue to compel him. The writ is now disused. See Thesaurus Brevium, 38; Coke, Entries, 46, 47, Rastell, Entries, 14 b. 15.

Capias Ad Respondendum

A judicial writ, (usually simply termed a *"capias,"* and commonly abbreviated to *ca. resp.*) by which actions at law were frequently commenced; and which commands the sheriff to *take* the defendant, and him safely keep, so that he may have his body before the court on a certain day, to *answer* the plaintiff in the action. 3 Bl.Comm. 282; 1 Tidd, Pr. 128. It notifies defendant to defend suit and procures his arrest until security for plaintiff's claim is furnished. Null v. Staiger, 333 Pa. 370, 4 A.2d 883, 885.

Capias Ad Satisfaciendum

A writ of execution, (usually termed, for brevity, a *"ca. sa.,"*) which commands the sheriff to *take* the party named, and keep him safely, so that he may have his body before the court on a certain day, *to satisfy* the damages or debt and damages in certain actions. It deprives the party taken of his liberty until he makes the satisfaction awarded. 3 Bl.Comm. 414, 415; 2 Tidd, Pr. 993, 1025; Litt. § 504; Co.Litt. 289*a*; Strong v. Linn, 5 N.J.Law, 803. As a rule it lay in all cases where a *capias ad respondendum* lay. It was a very common form of execution; but its efficiency has been destroyed by statutes.

Capias Extendi Facias

A writ of execution issuable in England against a debtor to the crown, which commands the sheriff to "take" or arrest the body, and "cause to be extended" the lands and goods of the debtor. Man.Exch.Pr. 5.

Capias in Withernam

A writ, in the nature of a reprisal, which lies for one whose goods or cattle, taken under a distress, are removed from the county, so that they cannot be replevied, commanding the sheriff to seize other goods or cattle of the distrainor of equal value.

Capias Pro Fine

(That you take for the fine or in mercy.) Formerly, if the verdict was for the defendant, the plaintiff was adjudged to be amerced for his false claim; but, if the verdict was for the plaintiff, then in all actions *vi et armis,* or where the defendant, in his pleading, had falsely denied his own deed, the judgment contained an award of a *capiatur pro fine;* and in all other cases the defendant was adjudged to be amerced. The insertion of the *misericordia* or of the *capiatur* in the judgment is now unnecessary. Wharton; 8 Coke, 60; 11 Coke, 43; Co.Litt. 131; 3 Bl.Comm. 398; 5 Mod. 285. A writ in all respects an execution for collection of fine. Board of Councilmen of City of Frankfort v. Rice, 249 Ky. 771, 61 S.W.2d 614, 615.

Capias Utlagatum

(You take the outlaw.) In English practice. A writ which lies against a person who has been *outlawed* in an action, by which the sheriff is commanded to *take* him, and keep him in custody until the day of the return, and then present him to the court, there to be dealt with for his contempt. Reg.Orig. 138*b*; 3 Bl.Comm. 284.

CAPIATUR PRO FINE. (Let him be taken for the fine.) In English practice. A clause inserted at the end of old judgment records in actions of debt, where the defendant denied his deed, and it was found against him upon his false plea, and the jury were troubled with the trial of it. Cro. Jac. 64. See Capias pro Fine.

CAPITA. Heads, and, figuratively, entire bodies, whether of persons or animals. Spelman.

Persons individually considered, without relation to others, (polls;) as distinguished from *stirpes* or stocks of descent. The term in this sense, making part of the common phrases, *in capita, per capita,* is derived from the civil law. Inst. 3, 1, 6.

CAPITA, PER. By heads; by the poll; as individuals. In the distribution of an intestate's personalty, the persons legally entitled to take are said to take *per capita,* that is, equal shares, when they claim, each in his own right, as in equal degree of kindred; in contradistinction to claiming by right of representation, or *per stirpes.*

CAPITAL, *n.* The word may have different meanings when used in different connections. Commissioner of Corporations and Taxation v. Filoon, 310 Mass. 374, 38 N.E.2d 693, 699, 700, 705.

It may mean: actual property or estate, People v. Com'rs of Taxes, 23 N.Y. 192; State ex rel. Corinne Realty Co. v. Becker, 320 Mo. 908, 8 S.W.2d 970, 972. Aggregate of property, Southern Package Corporation v. State Tax Commission, 195 Miss. 864, 15 So.2d 436; all capital invested plus surplus or undivided profits, W. A. Gordon & Co. v. Lines, D.C.La., 25 F.2d 894, 895; amount, or value, of property up to par value of paid up issued shares or stated value of no-par shares, Randall v. Bailey, 23 N.Y.S.2d 173, 182; assets, Pace v. Pace Bros. Co., 91 Utah, 149, 63 P.2d 590, 591. Capital stock, Security State Bank v. Breen, 277 N.W. 497, 500, 65 S.D. 640; condemnation award, In re Wacht's Estate, 32 N.Y.S.2d 871, 903, 904; contributions by partners, M. & C. Creditors Corporation v. Pratt, 17 N.Y.S.2d 240, 258, 259, 172 Misc. 695. Dividends earned before creation of trust, Hubley's Guardian Ad Litem v. Wolfe, 259 Ky. 574, 82 S.W.2d 830, 834, 101 A.L.R. 1359; dividends received by trustee stockholder in liquidation of corporation, Anderson v. Bean, 272 Mass. 432, 172 N.E. 647, 651, 72 A.L.R. 959; extraordinary dividends paid on reducing value of stock, In re Sears' Will, 26 N.Y.S.2d 912, 915, 176 Misc. 242. Fund, Civ.Code, art. 148. French v. Wolf, 181 La. 733, 160 So. 396, Webb v. Armistead, C.C.Va., 26 F. 70; gain from sale of realty, United States v. National City Bank of New York, D.C.N.Y., 21 F.Supp. 791, 794; means contributed by share owners, Parkinson v. State Bank of Millard County, 84 Utah, 278, 35 P.2d 814, 820, 94 A.L.R. 1112; money invested at interest; money required of partners by agreement, M. & C. Creditors Corporation v. Pratt, 17 N.Y.S.2d 240, 258, 259, 172 Misc. 695; money which one adventures in an undertaking; paid-up issued shares of stock, Newfield v. Stieglitz, D.C.N.Y., 47

F.Supp. 885, 886; place where legislative department holds its sessions and where chief offices of the executive are located; political and governmental metropolis; preferred stock received as dividend, Burns v. Hines, 298 Ill.App. 563, 19 N.E.2d 382, 392; principal sum of a fund of money; proceeds of sale or exchange of capital of trust property, In re Clarke's Will, 204 Minn. 574, 284 N.W. 876, 879; property, Putnam v. U. S., C.C.A.Mass., 149 F.2d 721, 726; repayment of a debt, Philadelphia Nat. Bank v. Rothensies, D.C.Pa., 43 F.Supp. 923, 925; seat of government; stock dividends, Gray v. Hemenway, 268 Mass. 515, 168 N.E. 102, 103; subscribed, paid-up capital, Child v. Ogden State Bank, 81 Utah, 464, 20 P.2d 599, 607, 88 A.L.R. 1284; sum formed when profits apportioned to building and loan association shares coalesce with dues paid, In re Sixth Ward Building & Loan Ass'n of Newark, 134 N.J.Eq. 98, 34 A.2d 292, 295; sum total of corporate stock, Haggard v. Lexington Utilities Co., 260 Ky. 261, 84 S.W.2d 84, 87; surplus used as capital, Feeders' Supply Co. v. Commissioner of Internal Revenue, C.C.A.8, 31 F.2d 274, 276; unamortized debt discount and expense, State Tax Commission v. Mississippi Power & Light Co., 194 Miss. 260, 11 So.2d 828, 829.

In political economy, that portion of the produce of industry existing in a country, which may be made directly available, either for the support of human existence, or the facilitating of production.

The term does not embrace temporary loans. Bailey v. Clark, 21 Wall. 286, 22 L.Ed. 651. But see Bridgewater Mfg. Co. v. Funkhouser, 115 Va. 476, 79 S.E. 1074, 1075.

Income is the fruit of capital; capital is the source of income. Carter v. Rector, 88 Okl. 12, 210 P. 1035, 1037.

As to what is moneyed capital in a federal act respecting state taxation of national bank stock, see First Nat. Bank v. Chapman, 173 U.S. 214, 19 S.Ct. 407, 43 L.Ed. 669.

CAPITAL, *adj.* Affecting or relating to the head or life of a person; entailing the ultimate penalty. Principal; leading; chief; as "capital burgess." 10 Mod. 100.

Capital Assets

All capital invested plus surplus or undivided profits. Williams v. McGowan, D.C.N.Y., 58 F. Supp. 692, 694, 695; Assets of a permanent or fixed nature or employed in carrying on business or trade. Rathborne v. Collector of Revenue, 196 La. 795, 200 So. 149, 153, 154; goodwill, Williams v. McGowan, D.C.N.Y., 58 F.Supp. 692, 694, 695, Commissioner of Internal Revenue v. Shapiro, C.C.A.6, 125 F.2d 532, 535, 536; property acquired and held for profit or investment for more than two years. Sommers v. Commissioner of Internal Revenue, C.C.A.10, 63 F.2d 551, 553; title to property held for profit. Jones' Estate v. Commissioner of Internal Revenue, C.C.A.Tex., 127 F.2d 231, 232.

Capital Case or Crime

One in or for which death penalty may, but need not necessarily, be inflicted, Lee v. State, 31 Ala.App. 91, 13 So.2d 583, 587.

Capital Expenditure

Cost of construction made with expectation of existence for an indefinite period, E. W. Edwards & Son v. Clarke, D.C.N.Y., 29 F.Supp. 671, 672, 673; expenditure in nature of an investment for the future, Marin Union Junior College Dist. v. Gwinn, 106 Cal.App. 12, 288 P. 799, 800.

Capital Gains

Additions to principal, Holcombe v. Ginn, 296 Mass. 415, 6 N.E.2d 351, 108 A.L.R. 1134; gains from sale of capital assets in excess of appraisal values or costs, In re Talbot's Will, 170 Misc. 138, 9 N.Y.S.2d 806, 810.

Capital Impairment

Reduction of assets of corporation below aggregate of outstanding shares of capital stock. Ashman v. Miller, C.C.A.Mich., 101 F.2d 85, 90.

Capital Increase

An increase not attributable to earnings. In re Lueders' Estate, 337 Pa. 155, 10 A.2d 415, 417.

Capital Investment

Acquisition price of a "capital asset", Commissioner of Internal Revenue v. Rowan Drilling Co., C.C.A.Tex., 130 F.2d 62, 64, 65; capital stock, surplus and undivided profits, O'Connor v. Bankers Trust Co., 159 Misc. 920, 289 N.Y.S. 252, 276; money spent to increase an asset. Peerless Stages v. Commissioner of Internal Revenue, C.C.A.9, 125 F.2d 869, 871.

Capital Outlay

Money expended in acquiring, equipping, and promoting an enterprise. Rideout v. Eich, 105 Cal.App. 597, 288 P. 450, 454.

Capital Punishment

Punishment of death. Ex parte Herndon, 18 Okl.Cr. 68, 192 P. 820, 19 A.L.R. 804, State v. Johnston, 83 Wash. 1, 144 P. 944, 945.

Capital Recovery

Collection of charged-off bad debt where reserve account system is used. National Bank of Tulsa v. Oklahoma Tax Commission, Okl., 145 P.2d 768, 771, 772.

Capital Stock

The term has various meanings.

It may mean: amount fixed by charter to be subscribed and paid in or secured to be paid in by shareholders. State ex rel. Corinne Realty Co. v. Becker, 320 Mo. 908, 8 S.W.2d 970, 971. Amount of stock that corporation may issue. Schwemer v. Fry, 212 Wis. 88, 249 N.W. 62, 90 A.L.R. 308; amount subscribed, contributed or secured to be paid in. Haggard v. Lexington Utilities Co., 260 Ky. 261, 84 S.W. 2d 84, 87; Person v. Board of State Tax Com'rs, 184 N.C. 499, 115 S.E. 336, 346; capital, Central Illinois Public Service Co. v. Swartz, 284 Ill. 108, 119 N.E. 990, 992; Louisville & N. R. Co. v. Bosworth, D.C.Ky., 209 F. 380, 411; corporate assets or property, Bates v. Daley's Inc., 5 Cal. App.2d 95, 42 P.2d 706, 709; evidence of rights in property. Southern Package Corporation v. State Tax Commission, 195 Miss. 864, 15 So.2d 436; fund employed in carrying on business or enterprise, Chicago, M., St. P. & P. R. Co. v. Harmon, 89 Mont. 1, 295 P. 762, 769; liability of the corporation to its shareholders, after creditors' claims have been liquidated, Department of Treasury of Indiana v. Crowder, 214 Ind. 252, 15 N.E.2d 89, 91; valuation of the corporation as a business enterprise, Commonwealth v. Columbia Gas & Electric Corporation, 336 Pa. 209, 8 A.2d 404, 410.

Capital Stock Tax

Tax on privilege of doing business, Wisconsin Cent. Ry. Co. v. U. S., Ct.Cl., 41 F.2d 870, 885.

Capital Surplus

Property paid into corporation by shareholders in excess of capital stock liability. Commissioner of Corporations and Taxation v. Filoon, 310 Mass. 374, 38 N.E.2d 693, 699, 700.

CAPITALE. A thing which is stolen, or the value of it. Blount.

CAPITALE VIVENS. Live cattle. Blount.

CAPITALIS. In old English law. Chief; principal; at the *head*. A term applied to persons, places, judicial proceedings, and some kinds of property.

CAPITALIS BARO. In old English law. Chief baron. *Capitalis baro scaccarii domini regis*, chief baron of the exchequer. Townsh.Pl. 211.

CAPITALIS CUSTOS. Chief warden or magistrate; mayor. Fleta, lib. 2, c. 64, § 2.

CAPITALIS DEBITOR. The chief or principal debtor, as distinguished from a surety, (*plegius*.)

CAPITALIS DOMINUS. Chief lord. Fleta, lib. 1, c. 12, § 4; Id. c. 28, § 5.

CAPITALIS JUSTICIARIUS. The chief justiciary; the principal minister of state, and guardian of the realm in the king's absence.

This office originated under William the Conqueror; but its power was greatly diminished by *Magna Charta*, and finally distributed among several courts by Edward I. Spelman; 3 Bl.Comm. 38.

CAPITALIS JUSTICIARIUS AD PLACITA CORAM REGE TENENDA. Chief justice for holding pleas before the king. The title of the chief justice of the king's bench, first assumed in the latter part of the reign of Henry III. 2 Reeve, Eng. Law, 91, 285.

CAPITALIS JUSTICIARIUS BANCI. Chief justice of the bench. The title of the chief justice of the (now) court of common pleas, first mentioned in the first year of Edward I. 2 Reeve, Eng.Law, 48.

CAPITALIS JUSTICIARIUS TOTIUS ANGLIÆ. Chief justice of all England. The title of the presiding justice in the court of *aula regis*. 3 Bl.Comm. 38; 1 Reeve, Eng.Law, 48.

CAPITALIS PLEGIUS. A chief pledge; a head borough. Townsh.Pl. 35.

CAPITALIS REDITUS. A chief rent.

CAPITALIS TERRA. A head-land. A piece of land lying at the head of other land.

CAPITALIST. One exclusively dependent on accumulated property, whether denoting a person of large wealth or one having an income from investments. Elliott v. Frankfort Marine, Accident & Plate Glass Ins. Co. of Frankfort-on-the-Main, Germany, 172 Cal. 261, 156 P. 481, 483, L.R.A. 1916F, 1026. The word has no legal meaning. In re Green's Estate, 109 Misc. 112, 178 N.Y.S. 353, 361.

CAPITALIZATION METHOD. A method of measuring values of realty for purpose of determining values of mortgages by expertly estimating the gross income which property should throw off, and separately the expenses reasonably required to carry it, and thus arriving at a fair estimate of net income and using a capitalization figure or factor, expertly chosen. Depreciation must be taken into consideration in use of such method. In re New York Title & Mortgage Co. (Series B-K), 21 N.Y.S.2d 575, 594, 595.

CAPITALIZE. In one sense, to convert a periodical payment into a sum in hand. Brown v. Erie R. Co., 87 N.J.Law, 487, 91 A. 1023, 1026, Ann.Cas. 1917C, 496.

CAPITANEUS. A tenant *in capite*. He who held his land or title directly from the king himself. A captain; a naval commander. This latter use began A. D. 1264. Spelman, Gloss. *Capitaneus, Admiralius*. A commander or ruler over others, either in civil, military, or ecclesiastical matters.

CAPITARE. In old law and surveys. To head, front, or abut; to touch at the head, or end.

CAPITATIM. Lat. By the head; by the poll; severally to each individual.

CAPITATION TAX. A poll tax. A tax or imposition upon the person. Leedy v. Bourbon, 12 Ind. App. 486, 40 N.E. 640; Hattiesburg Grocery Co. v. Robertson, 126 Miss. 34, 88 So. 4, 5, 25 A.L.R. 748. It is a very ancient kind of tribute, and answers to what the Latins called "*tributum*," by which taxes on persons are distinguished from taxes on merchandise, called "*vectigalia*." Wharton.

CAPITE. Lat. By the head.

Tenure *in capite* was an ancient feudal tenure, whereby a man held lands of the king immediately. It was of two sorts,—the one, principal and general, or of the king as the source of all tenure; the other, special and subaltern, or of a particular subject. It is now abolished. Jacob. As to distribution *per capita*, see Capita, per.

CAPITE MINUTUS. In the civil law. One who had suffered *capitis diminutio*, one who lost *status* or legal attributes. See Dig. 4, 5.

CAPITIS DIMINUTIO. In Roman law. A diminishing or abridgment of personality; a loss or curtailment of a man's *status* or aggregate of legal attributes and qualifications.

CAPITIS DIMINUTIO MAXIMA. The highest or most comprehensive loss of *status*. This occurred when a man's condition was changed from one of freedom to one of bondage, when he became a slave. It swept away with it all rights of citizenship and all family rights.

CAPITIS DIMINUTIO MEDIA. A lesser or medium loss of status. This occurred where a man lost his rights of citizenship, but without losing his liberty. It carried away also the family rights.

CAPITIS DIMINUTIO MINIMA. The lowest or least comprehensive degree of loss of *status*. This occurred where a man's family relations alone were changed. It happened upon the arrogation of a person who had been his own master, (*sui juris,*) or upon the emancipation of one who had been under the *patria potestas.* It left the rights of liberty and citizenship unaltered. See Inst. 1, 16, pr.; 1, 2, 3; Dig. 4, 5, 11; Mackeld.Rom.Law, § 144.

CAPITITIUM. A covering for the head, mentioned in St. 1 Hen. IV. and other old statutes, which prescribe what dresses shall be worn by all degrees of persons. Jacob.

CAPITULA. Collections of laws and ordinances drawn up under heads of divisions. Spelman. The term is used in the civil and old English law, and applies to the ecclesiastical law also, meaning chapters or assemblies of ecclesiastical persons. Du Cange. The *Royal and Imperial Capitula* were the edicts of the Frankish Kings and Emperors.

CAPITULA CORONÆ. Chapters of the crown. Chapters or heads of inquiry, resembling the *capitula itineris (infra)* but of a more minute character.

CAPITULA DE JUDÆIS. A register of mortgages made to the Jews. 2 Bl.Comm. 343; Crabb, Eng.Law, 130, et seq.

CAPITULA ITINERIS. Articles of inquiry which were anciently delivered to the justices in eyre when they set out on their circuits. These schedules were designed to include all possible varieties of crime. 2 Reeve, Eng.Law, p. 4, c. 8.

CAPITULA RURALIA. Assemblies or chapters, held by rural deans and parochial clergy, within the precinct of every deanery; which at first were every three weeks, afterwards once a month, and subsequently once a quarter. Cowell.

CAPITULARY. In French law. A collection and code of the laws and ordinances promulgated by the kings of the Merovingian and Carlovingian dynasties.

Any orderly and systematic collection or code of laws.

In ecclesiastical law. A collection of laws and ordinances orderly arranged by divisions. A book containing the beginning and end of each Gospel which is to be read every day in the ceremony of saying mass. Du Cange.

CAPITULATION. In military law. The surrender of a fort, fortified town, or army in the field to a besieging or opposing army; the treaty or agreement between the commanding officers which embodies the terms and conditions on which the surrender is made.

In international law. *Capitulations* is the name used for treaty engagements between the Turkish government and the principal states of Europe by which subjects of the latter, residents in the territory of the former, were exempt from the laws of the places where they dwelt. 1 Kinglake, Invasion of Crimea 116.

"The 'usages of the Franks' begin in what are known in international law as 'the capitulations,' granting rights of exterritoriality to Christians residing or traveling in Mohammedan countries. * * * By these * * * capitulations a usage was established that Franks [a generic name for all participants in such privileges], being in Turkey, whether domiciled or temporarily, should be under the jurisdiction, civil and criminal, of their respective ministers and consuls." Dainese v. United States, 15 Ct.Cl. 64.

In the civil law. An agreement by which the prince and the people, or those who have the right of the people, regulate the manner in which the government is to be administered. Wolffius, § 989.

CAPITULI AGRI. Head-fields; lands lying at the head or upper end of furrows, etc.

CAPITULUM. Lat. A leading division of a book or writing; a chapter; a section. Tert.Adv.Jud. 9, 19. Abbreviated, Cap.

CAPITULUM EST CLERICORUM CONGREGATIO SUB UNO DECANO IN ECCLESIA CATHEDRALI. A chapter is a congregation of clergy under one dean in a cathedral church. Co.Litt. 98.

CAPPA. In old records. A cap. *Cappa honoris,* the cap of honor. One of the solemnities or ceremonies of creating an earl or marquis.

CAPPER. A decoy or lure for purpose of swindling. Barron v. Board of Dental Examiners of California, 109 Cal.App. 382, 293 P. 144, 145.

CAPRICIOUS DISBELIEF. A willful, deliberate disbelief of an apparently trustworthy witness. Popilock v. Piernikoski, 161 Pa.Super. 587, 56 A. 2d 326, 328.

CAPTAIN. A head-man; commander; commanding officer.

The captain of a war-vessel is the officer first in command. In the United States navy, the rank of "captain" is intermediate between that of "commander" and "commodore." The governor or controlling officer of a vessel in the merchant service is usually styled "captain" by the inferior officers and seamen, but in maritime business and admiralty law is perhaps more commonly designated as "master." In foreign jurisprudence his title is often that of "patron." In the United States army (and the militia) the captain is the commander of a company of soldiers, one of the divisions of a regiment. The term is also used to designate the commander of a squad of municipal police.

The "captain of the watch" on a vessel is a kind of foreman or overseer and is an officer within statutes regulating conduct of officers to seamen. U. S. v. Trice, D.C.Tenn., 30 Fed. 491.

CAPTATION. In French law. The act of one who succeeds in controlling the will of another, so as to become master of it; used in an invidious sense. Succession of Schlumbrecht, 138 La. 173, 70 So. 76, 79.

It was formerly applied to the first stage of the hypnotic or mesmeric trance.

CAPTATOR. A person who obtains a gift or legacy through artifice. See Captation.

CAPTIO. In old English law and practice. A taking or seizure; arrest; receiving; holding of court.

CAPTION. In Practice. That part of a legal instrument, as a commission, indictment, etc., which shows where, when, and by what authority it is taken, found, or executed. U. S. v. Beebe, 2 Dak. 292, 11 N.W. 505.

When used with reference to an indictment, caption signifies the style or preamble or commencement of the indictment; when used with reference to a commission, it signifies the certificate to which the commissioners' names are subscribed, declaring when and where it was executed. Brown. The caption is not a part of the indictment, Brown v. Hudspeth, C.C.A.Kan., 103 F.2d 958, 959, but is the formal history of its finding, and is to be distinguished from the introductory portion. Harrington v. U. S., C.C.A. Iowa, 267 F. 97, 100. Caption of indictment is entry of record showing when and where court is held, who presided, venire and indorsements, and who were summoned and sworn as grand jurors. Williams v. State, 20 Ala.App. 26, 100 So. 573, 574.

The caption of a pleading, deposition, or other paper connected with a case in court, is the heading or introductory clause which shows the names of the parties, name of the court, number of the case on the docket or calendar, etc. Quoted with approval in St. Louis Lightning Rod Co. v. Johnson, 18 Ga.App. 190, 89 S.E. 169, 170. The terms "title" and "caption" are synonymous. Id. The caption of depositions should state the title of the cause, the names of the parties, and at whose instance the depositions are taken; Knight v. Nichols, 34 Me. 208. See Waskern v. Diamond, 1 Hemp. 701, Fed.Cas.No.17,248. Generally, the title or caption is not part of the pleading, unless expressly made so by reference in the body thereof. Jackson v. Ashton, 8 Pet. 148, 8 L.Ed. 898.

Also signifies a taking, seizure, or arrest of a person. 2 Salk. 498. The word in this sense is now obsolete in English law.

In Scotch law. Caption is an order to incarcerate a debtor who has disobeyed an order, given to him by what are called "letters of horning," to pay a debt or to perform some act enjoined thereby. Bell.

CAPTIVES. Prisoners of war. As in the goods of an enemy, so also in his person, a sort of qualified property may be acquired, by taking him a prisoner of war, at least till his ransom be paid. 2 Bl.Comm. 402.

CAPTOR. In international law. One who takes or seizes property in time of war; one who takes the property of an enemy. In a stricter sense, one who takes a prize at sea. 2 Bl.Comm. 401; 1 Kent, Comm. 86, 96, 103. Consult Oakes v. U. S., 174 U.S. 778, 19 S.Ct. 864, 43 L.Ed. 1169. The term also designates a belligerent who has captured the person of an enemy.

CAPTURE. In international law. The taking or wresting of property from one of two belligerents by the other. Also a taking of property by a belligerent from an offending neutral.

In some cases, this is a mode of acquiring property. Thus every one may, as a general rule, on his own land, or on the sea, capture any wild animal, and acquire a qualified ownership in it by confining it, or absolute ownership by killing it. 2 Steph.Comm. 79.

Capture, in technical language, is a taking by military power; a seizure is a taking by civil authority. U. S. v. Athens Armory, 35 Ga. 344, Fed.Cas.No.14,473.

The sequestering of alien enemy property under vesting orders by the alien property custodian is in the nature of a "capture". Crowley v. Allen, D.C.Cal., 52 F.Supp. 850, 852.

CAPUT. A head; the head of a person; the whole person; the life of a person; one's personality; *status*; civil condition.

At common law. A head. *Caput comitatis*, the head of the county; the sheriff; the king. Spelman. A person; a life. The upper part of a town. Cowell. A castle. Spelman.

Capitis æstimatio. In Saxon law. The estimation or value of the head, that is, the price or value of a man's life.

Caput anni. The first day (or beginning) of the year.

Caput baroniæ. The castle or chief seat of a baron.

Caput jejunii. The beginning of the Lent fast, *i. e.*, Ash Wednesday.

Caput loci. The head or upper part of a place.

Caput lupinum. In old English law. A wolf's head. An outlawed felon was said to be *caput lupinum*, and might be knocked on the head like a wolf. 4 Bla.Comm. 320, 284.

Caput mortuum. A dead head; dead; obsolete.

Caput portus. In old English law. The head of a port. The town to which a port belongs, and which gives the denomination to the port, and is the head of it. Hale de Jure Mar. pt. 2, (*de portubus maris,*) c. 2.

Caput, principium, et finis. The head, beginning, and end. A term applied in English law to the king, as head of parliament. 4 Inst. 3; 1 Bl. Comm. 188.

In civil law. It signified a person's civil condition or *status*, and among the Romans consisted of three component parts or elements,—*libertas*, liberty; *civitas*, citizenship; and *familia*, family.

CAPUTAGIUM. In old English law. Head or poll money, or the payment of it. Cowell; Blount; Spelman, Gloss.

CAPUTIUM. In old English law. A head of land; a headland. Cowell.

CAR. A vehicle primarily intended for transportation of persons or freight, Hall v. Federal Life Ins. Co., Mo.App., 71 S.W.2d 762, 764; a vehicle moved on wheels, Burrus v. Continental Life Ins. Co., 225 Mo.App. 1129, 40 S.W.2d 493, 494.

The term may include a vehicle adapted to running on the rails of a railroad. State v. Tardiff, 111 Me. 552, 90 A. 424, 425, L.R.A.1915A, 817; a hand car, Boyd v. Missouri Pac. Ry. Co., 249 Mo. 110, 155 S.W. 13, 17, Ann.Cas.1914D, 37; a locomotive, U. S. v. Philadelphia & R. Ry. Co., D.C. Pa., 223 F. 215, 216; a tender and locomotive, Pennell v. Philadelphia & Reading Railway Co., 231 U.S. 675, 34 S.Ct. 220, 58 L.Ed. 430; an automobile. Monroe's Adm'r v. Federal Union Life Ins. Co., 251 Ky. 570, 65 S.W.2d 680, 681.

Car Load

The quantity usually contained in an ordinary car used for transporting the particular commodity involved. Ward v. Cotton Seed Products Co., 193 Ala. 101, 69 So. 514, 515.

General Service Cars

Cars serviceable as flat or gondola cars and also as dump cars. National Dump Car Co. v. Pullman Co., C.C.A.Ill., 228 F. 122, 124.

CAR TRUST CERTIFICATES, OR SECURITIES. A class of investment securities based upon the conditional sale or hire of railroad cars or locomotives with a reservation of title or lien in the vendor or bailor until the property is paid for. See Fidelity Trust Co. v. Lederer, D.C.Pa., 276 F. 51; Commonwealth v. Philadelphia Rapid Transit Co., 287 Pa. 190, 134 A. 455.

CARABUS. In old English law. A kind of raft or boat. Spelman.

CARAT. A measure of weight for diamonds and other precious stones, equivalent to three and one-sixth grains Troy, though divided by jewelers into four parts called "diamond grains." Also a standard of fineness of gold, twenty-four carats being conventionally taken as expressing absolute purity, and the proportion of gold to alloy in a mixture being represented as so many carats.

CARBON COPY. A copy, as of a letter, produced by placing a sheet of carbon paper between two sheets of letter paper, so that the same impression produces both the letter and the carbon copy. Engles v. Blocker, 127 Ark. 385, 192 S.W. 193, 195. See, also, Copy.

CARBONIC ACID. See Choke damp.

CARCAN. In French law. An instrument of punishment, somewhat resembling a pillory. It sometimes signifies the punishment itself. Biret, Vocab.

CARCANUM. A gaol; a prison.

CARCARE. In old English law. To load; to load a vessel; to freight.

CARCATUS. Loaded; freighted, as a ship.

CARCEL-AGE. Gaol-dues; prison-fees.

CARCER. A prison or gaol. Strictly, a place of detention and safe-keeping, and not of punishment. Co.Litt. 620.

CARCER AD HOMINES CUSTODIENDOS, NON AD PUNIENDOS, DARI DEBET. A prison should be used for keeping persons, not for punishing them. Co.Litt. 260*a*. See Dig. 48. 19. 8. 9.

CARCER NON SUPPLICII CAUSÂ SED CUSTODIÆ CONSTITUTUS. A prison is ordained not for the sake of punishment, but of detention and guarding. Lofft, 119.

CARDINAL. In ecclesiastical law. A dignitary of the court of Rome, next in rank to the pope. There are cardinal bishops, cardinal priests, and cardinal deacons. See Fleury, *Hist. Ecclés.* liv. xxxv. n. 17, li. n. 19; Thomassin, part. ii. liv. i. c. 53, part. iv. liv. i. cc. 79, 80; Loiseau, *Traité des Ordres*, c. 3, n. 31; André *Droit Canon.*

CARDS. In criminal law. Small papers or pasteboards of an oblong or rectangular shape, on which are printed figures or points, used in playing certain games. See State v. Lewis, 12 Wis. 434.

CARE. Attention, Seaman v. State, 106 Ohio St. 177, 140 N.E. 108, 111, Lustenberger v. Boston Casualty Co., Mass., 14 N.E.2d 148, 151, 115 A.L.R. 1055; charge, Emery v. Wheeler, 152 A. 624, 626, 129 Me. 428, Lustenberger v. Boston Casualty Co., Mass., 14 N.E.2d 148, 151, 115 A.L.R. 1055; custody, Madison v. State, 163 Tenn. 198, 42 S.W.2d 209, Fox West Coast Theatres v. Union Indemnity Co., 167 Wash. 319, 9 P.2d 78, 81; diligence; discretion; heed, caution, concern, Northern Indiana Power Co. v. West, 218 Ind. 321, 32 N.E.2d 713, 720; inclination, wish or disposition, Stella v. Downyflake Restaurant, 126 Conn. 441, 11 A.2d 848, 849; maintenance, Stafford v. Stovall, 109 Okl. 234, 235 P. 238, 239; management, Seaman v. State, 106 Ohio St. 177, 140 N.E. 108, 111; opposite of negligence or carelessness, Raymond v. Portland R. Co., 100 Me. 529, 62 A. 602, 605, 3 L.R.A.,N.S., 94; oversight, Emery v. Wheeler, 129 Me. 428, 152 A. 624, 626, Madison v. State, 163 Tenn. 198, 42 S.W.2d 209; prudence, Quanah, A. & P. Ry. Co. v. Eblen, Tex.Civ.App., 55 S.W.2d 1060, 1063; regard, Lustenberger v. Boston Casualty Co., Mass., 14 N.E.2d 148, 151, 115 A.L.R. 1055, Arnold v. United States, C.C.A.Colo., 94 F.2d 499, 505; safekeeping, preservation, security, Fox West Coast Theatres v. Union Indemnity Co., 167 Wash. 319, 9 P.2d 78, 81; to cause to have care; to trouble; to care for; to regard. Arnold v. United States, C.C.A.Colo., 94 F.2d 499, 505; vigilance; watchfulness.

There are three degrees of care which are frequently recognized, corresponding (inversely) to the three degrees of negligence, viz.: slight care, ordinary care, and great care.

Slight care is such as persons of ordinary prudence usually exercise about their own affairs of slight importance. 25 Okl.St.Ann. § 4. Or it is that degree of care which a person exercises about his own concerns, though he may be a person of less than common prudence or of careless and inattentive disposition. Litchfield v. White, 7 N.Y. 442, 57 Am.Dec. 534; Bank v. Guilmartin, 93 Ga. 503, 21 S.E. 55, 44 Am.St.Rep. 182.

Ordinary care is that degree of care which persons of ordinary care and prudence are accustomed to use and employ, under the same or similar circumstances. Gunn v. Railroad Co., 36 W.Va. 165, 14 S.E. 465, 32 Am.St.Rep. 842; Railroad Co. v. Howard, 79 Ga. 44, 3 S.E. 426; Liston v. Reynolds, 69 Mont. 480, 223 P. 507, 509; Pauls Valley Compress & Storage Co. v. Harris, 62 Okl. 103, 162 P. 216, 218. Or it is that degree of care which may reasonably be expected from a person in the party's situation, that is, reasonable care. Neal v. Gillett, 1855, 23 Conn. 443.

Reasonable care is such a degree of care, precaution, or diligence as may fairly and properly be expected or required, having regard to the nature of the action, or of the subject-matter, and the circumstances surrounding the transaction. See Johnson v. Hudson River R. Co., 6 Duer, N.Y., 646; Appel v. Eaton & Price Co., 97 Mo.App. 428, 71 S.W. 741; Illinois Cent. R. Co. v. Noble, 142 Ill. 578, 32 N.E. 684. It is such care as an ordinarily prudent person would exercise under the conditions existing at the time he is called upon to act. Midland Valley R. Co. v. Bell, C.C.A.Okl., 242 F. 803, 808; Loverage v. Carmichael, 164 Minn. 76, 204 N.W. 921, 922. Substantially synonymous with ordinary or due care. Kucera v. Grigsby, 24 Ohio

App. 457, 156 N.E. 249, 250; Wiley v. Rutland R. Co., 86 Vt. 504, 86 A. 808, 811.

Great care is such as persons of ordinary prudence usually exercise about affairs of their own which are of great importance; or it is that degree of care usually bestowed upon the matter in hand by the most competent, prudent, and careful persons having to do with the particular subject. Railway Co. v. Smith, 87 Tex. 348, 28 S.W. 520; Telegraph Co. v. Cook, Cal., 61 F. 628, 9 C.C.A. 680.

A high degree of care is not the legal equivalent of reasonable care. Gallatty v. Central R. of New Jersey, 86 N.J.Law, 416, 92 A. 279, 280. It is that degree of care which a very cautious, careful, and prudent person would exercise under the same or similar circumstances. Bryning v. Missouri, K. & T. Ry. Co. of Texas, Tex.Civ.App., 167 S.W. 826, 827; a degree of care commensurate with the risk of danger. New Jersey Fidelity & Plate Glass Ins. Co. v. Lehigh Valley R. Co., 92 N.J.Law, 467, 105 A. 206, 207.

Highest degree of care and utmost degree of care have substantially the same meaning. Brogan v. Union Traction Co., 76 W.Va. 698, 86 S.E. 753, 756. "Highest degree of care" only requires the care and skill exacted of persons engaged in the same or similar business. Birmingham Ry., Light & Power Co. v. Cockrell, 10 Ala.App. 578, 65 So. 704. It means the highest degree required by law where human safety is at stake, and the highest degree known to the usage and practice of very careful, skillful, and diligent persons engaged in the same business by similar means or agencies. Birmingham Ry., Light & Power Co. v. Barrett, 179 Ala. 274, 60 So. 262, 264.

This division into three degrees of care, however, does not command universal assent. Raymond v. Portland R. Co., 100 Me. 529, 62 A. 602, 605, 3 L.R.A.,N.S., 94; Pomroy v. Bangor & Aroostook R. Co., 102 Me. 497, 67 A. 561, 562.

CARELESS. Synonymous with "negligent," the latter being probably the better word in pleadings. Delmore v. Kansas City Hardwood Flooring Co., 90 Kan. 29, 133 P. 151, 47 L.R.A.,N.S., 1220. Absence of ordinary or proper care, Pelfrey v. Commonwealth, 247 Ky. 484, 57 S.W.2d 474. Reckless, Stout v. Gallemore, 138 Kan. 385, 26 P.2d 573, 577.

CARELESSLY. Without care. Seago v. Paul Jones Realty Co., 185 Mo.App. 292, 170 S.W. 372, 373. Negligently; denoting the absence of ordinary care. Jones v. Commonwealth, 213 Ky. 356, 281 S.W. 164, 167.

CARENA. A term used in the old ecclesiastical law to denote a period of forty days.

CARENCE. In French law. Lack of assets; insolvency.

A *procès-verbal de carence* is a document setting out that the *huissier* attended to issue execution upon a judgment, but found nothing upon which to levy. Arg.Fr. Merc.Law, 547.

CARETA (spelled, also, *Carreta* and *Carecta*). A cart; a cart-load.

CARETORIUS, or CARECTARIUS. A carter. Blount.

CARGA. In Spanish law. An incumbrance; a charge. White, New Recop. b. 2, tit. 13, c. 2, § 2.

CARGAISON. In French commercial law. Cargo; lading.

CARGARE. In old English law. To charge. Spelman.

CARGO. In mercantile law. The load or lading of a vessel; the goods, merchandise, or whatever is conveyed in a ship or other merchant vessel. Seamans v. Loring, 21 Fed.Cas. 920; Thwing v. Insurance Co., 103 Mass. 401, 4 Am.Rep. 567.

While "cargo" is primarily the load of the ship, it may have a varying meaning. Pennsylvania Sugar Co. v. Czarnikow-Rionda Co., C.C.A.Pa., 245 F. 913, 915. The term may be applied in such a sense as to include passengers, as well as freight, but in a technical sense it designates goods only. Wolcott v. Eagle Ins. Co., 4 Pick., Mass., 429. Thus, we say, A cargo of emigrants. See 7 M. & G. 729, 744; Davison v. Von Lingen, 113 U.S. 49, 5 S.Ct. 346, 28 L.Ed. 885.

CARIAGIUM. In old English law. Carriage; the carrying of goods or other things for the king.

CARISTIA. Dearth, scarcity, dearness. Cowell.

CARK. In old English law. A quantity of wool, whereof thirty make a sarplar. (The latter is equal to 2,240 pounds in weight.) St. 27 Hen. VI. c. 2. Jacob.

CARLISLE TABLES. Life and annuity tables, compiled at Carlisle, England, about 1780. Used by actuaries, etc.

CARMACK ACT. An act of Congress, June 29, 1906, 49 U.S.C.A. § 20(11, 12), amending the Hepburn Act. It supersedes all state regulations; Chicago, B. & Q. R. Co. v. Miller, 226 U.S. 513, 33 S.Ct. 155, 57 L.Ed. 323.

CARMEN. In the Roman law. Literally, a verse or song. A formula or form of words used on various occasions, as of divorce. Tayl.Civil Law, 349.

CARNAL. Pertaining to the body, its passions and its appetites; animal; fleshly; sensual; impure; sexual. People v. Battilana, 52 Cal.App.2d 685, 126 P.2d 923, 928.

CARNAL ABUSE. An act of debauchery of the female sexual organs by those of the male which does not amount to penetration;—the offense commonly called statutory rape consists of carnal abuse. State v. Huggins, 84 N.J.Law, 254, 87 A. 630, 633. An injury to the genital organs in an attempt at carnal knowledge, falling short of actual penetration. Snyder v. State, 92 Ohio St. 167, 110 N.E. 644, 645. Carnal knowledge of a female child of tender age includes abuse. Dawkins v. State, 58 Ala. 376, 29 Am.Rep. 754.

CARNAL KNOWLEDGE. Coitus; copulation; the act of a man in having sexual bodily connection with a woman; sexual intercourse. State v. Normandale, 154 La. 523, 97 So. 798, 800; Patton v. State, 105 Tex.Cr.R. 128, 287 S.W. 51, 52. There is "carnal knowledge" if there is the slightest penetration of the sexual organ of the female by the sexual organ of the male. It is not necessary that the vagina be entered or that the hymen be ruptured; the entering of the vulva or labia is sufficient. State v. Huggins, 84 N.J.Law, 254, 87 A. 630, 633.

CARNALITER. In old criminal law. Carnally. *Carnaliter cognovit*, carnally knew. Technical words in indictments for rape, and held essential. 1 Hale, P.C. 637–639.

CARNALLY KNEW. In pleading. A technical phrase in an indictment to charge the defendant with the crime of rape. Some authorities suggest that the words "carnally knew" are included in the term "rapuit" and are therefore unnecessary; 2 Hawk.P.C. c. 25, § 56; 2 Stark.Cr.Pl. 431, n. (*e*); at least in states in which the statutes do not designate the crime by the words "did ravish and carnally know"; 1 Hale, P.C. 628, 632; 3 Russell, Cr. (6th ed.) 230. See Noble v. State, 22 Ohio St. 545; Dawkins v. State, 58 Ala. 378, 29 Am.Rep. 754.

CARNO. In old English law. An immunity or privilege. Cowell.

CAROOME. In English law. A license by the lord mayor of London to keep a cart.

CARPEMEALS. Cloth made in the northern parts of England, of a coarse kind, mentioned in 7 Jac. I. c. 16. Jacob.

CARRERA. In Spanish law. A carriage-way; the right of a carriage-way. Las Partidas, pt. 3, tit. 31, l. 3.

CARRIAGE. A vehicle used especially for the transportation of persons either for pleasure or business, and drawn by horses or other draught animals over the ordinary streets and highways of the country; not including cars used exclusively upon railroads or street railroads expressly constructed for the use of such cars. Snyder v. North Lawrence, 8 Kan. 84; Cream City R. Co. v. Chicago, etc., R. Co., 63 Wis. 93, 23 N.W. 425, 53 Am.Rep. 267.

The act of carrying, or a contract for transportation of persons or goods.

As used in exemption statutes, includes an automobile, Patten v. Sturgeon, C.C.A.Okl., 214 F. 65, 67, Hammond v. Pickett, Tex.Civ.App., 158 S.W. 174, 175, and it includes motor vehicles under various other circumstances. Ansell v. City of Boston, 254 Mass. 208, 150 N.E. 167, 168; State v. Jarvis, 89 Vt. 239, 95 A. 541, 543.

In admiralty, "carriage" includes ability to lift a cargo and hold it afloat, and does not necessarily involve any translation of the vessel from one place to another. The Jungshoved, D.C.N.Y., 272 F. 122, 124.

The business of carriage is that arising under contracts by which a person obligates himself, for an agreed price, to transport, or have transported, an object of some kind, to a designated place. Kocke v. Garnier, 15 La.App. 461, 131 So. 198, 199.

The contract of carriage is a contract for the conveyance of property, persons, or messages, from one place to another. Civ.Code Cal. § 2085; Comp.Laws N.D.1913, § 6185; Comp.Laws S.D.1929, § 1108.

As to "carriage by land or water" within the Illinois Workmen's Compensation Act, see Stevens v. Illinois Cent. R. Co., 306 Ill. 370, 137 N.E. 859, 861; Mattoon Clear Water Co. v. Industrial Commission, 291 Ill. 487, 126 N.E. 168, 169.

CARRICLE, or CARRACLE. A ship of great burden.

CARRIER. One undertaking to transport persons or property, Windham v. Pace, 192 S.E. 271, 6 S.E.2d 270, 274; or one employed in or engaged in the business of carrying goods for others for hire. Roeske v. Lamb, 39 N.M. 111, 41 P.2d 522, 523.

In common speech, "carriers" means transportation systems as distinguished from corporations owning or operating them. Virginian Ry. Co. v. Mullens, 271 U.S. 220, 46 S.Ct. 526, 529, 70 L.Ed. 915. And this is its meaning as used in the Federal Control Act, § 10. Missouri Pac. R. Co. v. Ault, 256 U.S. 554, 41 S.Ct. 593, 65 L.Ed. 1087; Birmingham Trust & Savings Co. v. Atlanta, B. & A. Ry. Co., D.C.Ga., 271 F. 731, 739 (Transportation Act). An electric railway that is part of the "general steam-railroad system" is a "carrier" subject to the Railway Labor Act, Sprague v. Woll, C.C.A.Ill., 124 F.2d 767, 769.

A school bus acts as a "carrier." Leach v. School Dist. No. 322 of Thurston County, 197 Wash. 384, 85 P.2d 666, 667.

Carriers are either common or private. Standard Oil Co. v. Public Service Commission of Wisconsin, 217 Wis. 563, 259 N.W. 598.

Common carriers are those that hold themselves out or undertake to carry persons or goods of all persons indifferently, or of all who choose to employ it, Merchants Parcel Delivery v. Pennsylvania Public Utility Commission, 150 Pa.Super. 120, 28 A.2d 340, 344; Burnett v. Riter, Tex.Civ. App., 276 S.W. 347, 349; or those whose occupation or business is transportation of persons or things for hire or reward, In re Rodgers, Neb., 279 N.W. 800, 803, 804.

Common carriers of passengers are those that undertake to carry all persons indifferently who may apply for passage, so long as there is room, and there is no legal excuse for refusal. Lazor v. Banas, 114 Pa.Super. 425, 174 A. 817, 819; Anderson v. Fidelity & Casualty Co. of New York, 100 Misc. 411, 166 N.Y.S. 640, 642.

Private carriers are those who transport or undertake to transport in a particular instance for hire or reward. Allen v. Sackrider, 37 N.Y. 341; Columbus-Cincinnati Trucking Co. v. Public Utilities Commission, 141 Ohio St. 228, 47 N.E.2d 623, 625, 626.

For "Extension", see that title.

CARRIER'S LIEN. The right to hold the consignee's cargo until payment is made for the work of transporting it. Sommers Const. Co. v. Atlantic Coast Line R. Co., 62 Ga.App. 23, 7 S.E.2d 429, 431.

CARROTED FUR. Fur that has been treated by a solution of nitrate of mercury, so as to remove the water-repellant substance covering the fibers, making them more pliable and more easily to interlock with other fibers of fur, or of wool. Matteawan Mfg. Co. v. Emmons Bros. Co., C.C.A. Mass., 253 F. 372, 375.

CARRUCA. See Caruca.

CARRY. To bear, bear about, sustain, transport, remove, or convey. To have or bear upon or about one's person, as a watch or weapon;—locomotion not being essential. State v. Nieto, 101 Ohio St. 409, 130 N.E. 663, 665. Compare Heaton v. State, 130 Tenn. 163, 169 S.W. 750. As applied to insurance, means "possess" or "hold." San Francisco Realty Co. v. Linnard, 98 Cal.App. 33, 276 P. 368, 370.

CARRY A MEMBER. To pay the assessments against a sick or indigent member, as of a beneficial association, the payment being made by the other members or the local lodge or camp on his behalf. Bennett v. Sovereign Camp, Woodmen of the World, Tex.Civ.App., 168 S.W. 1023, 1026.

CARRY AN ELECTION. For a candidate to be elected, or a measure carried, at an election, he or it must receive a majority or a plurality of the legal votes cast. McKinney v. Barker, 180 Ky. 526, 203 S.W. 303, 304, L.R.A.1918E, 581.

CARRY ARMS OR WEAPONS. To wear, bear, or carry them upon the person or in the clothing or in a pocket, for the purpose of use, or for the purpose of being armed and ready for offensive or defensive action in case of a conflict with another person. State v. Carter, 36 Tex. 89; State v. Murray, 39 Mo.App. 128.

CARRY COSTS. A verdict is said to carry costs when the party for whom the verdict is given becomes entitled to the payment of his costs as incident to such verdict.

CARRY ON TRADE OR BUSINESS. To conduct, prosecute or continue a particular avocation or business as a continuous operation or permanent occupation. The repetition of acts may be sufficient. Lichtenstein v. State, 34 Ga.App. 138, 128 S.E. 704; Ledgerwood v. Dashiell, Tex.Civ.App., 177 S.W. 1010, 1012; Martin v. Bankers' Trust Co., 18 Ariz. 55, 156 P. 87, 90, Ann.Cas.1918E, 1240; Territory v. Harris, 8 Mont. 140, 19 P. 286; Hutchings v. Burnet, 61 App.D.C. 109, 58 F.2d 514. To hold one's self out to others as engaged in the selling of goods or services. Helvering v. Highland, C.C.A.4, 124 F.2d 556, 561.

CARRY PASSENGERS FOR A CONSIDERATION. Transportation of persons under such conditions that operator owes them duty of carrier for hire. Cartos v. Hartford Accident & Indemnity Co., 160 Va. 505, 169 S.E. 594, 597.

CARRY STOCK. To provide funds or credit for its payment for the period agreed upon from the date of purchase. Saltus v. Genin, 16 N.Y.Super. Ct. 260. And see Pickering v. Demerritt, 100 Mass. 421.

CARRY THE IRON. See *Fire Ordeal* under the title Ordeal.

CARRYING AWAY. In criminal law. The act of removal or asportation, by which the crime of larceny is completed, and which is essential to constitute it. Gettinger v. State, 13 Neb. 308, 14 N.W. 403.

CART. In its ordinary and primary acceptation, a carriage with two wheels; yet it may mean a carriage in general, Favers v. Glass, 22 Ala. 624, 58 Am.Dec. 272; but not an automobile, Whitney v. Welnitz, 153 Minn. 162, 190 N.W. 57, 28 A.L.R. 68. The vehicle in which criminals are taken to execution.

CART BOTE. Wood or timber which a tenant is allowed by law to take from an estate, for the purpose of repairing instruments, (including necessary vehicles,) of husbandry. 2 Bl.Comm. 35. See Bote.

CARTA.

In old English law. A charter, or deed. Any written instrument.

In Spanish law. A letter; a deed; a power of attorney. Las Partidas, pt. 3, tit. 18, 1. 30.

CARTA MERCATORIA. A grant (1303) to certain foreign merchants, in return for custom duties, of freedom to deal wholesale in all cities and towns of England, power to export their merchandise, and liberty to dwell where they pleased, together with other rights pertaining to speedy justice; 1 Holdsw.Hist.E.L. 311.

CARTE. In French marine law. A chart.

CARTE BLANCHE. A white sheet of paper; an instrument signed, but otherwise left blank. A sheet given to an agent, with the principal's signature appended, to be filled up with any contract or engagement as the agent may see fit. Hence, metaphorically, unlimited authority.

CARTEL.

In Trade and Commerce

A combination of producers of any product joined together to control its production, sale, and price, and to obtain a monopoly in any particular industry or commodity. Also, an association by agreement of companies or sections of companies having common interests, designed to prevent extreme or unfair competition and allocate markets, and to promote the interchange of knowledge resulting from scientific and technical research, exchange of patent rights, and standardization of products. U. S. v. National Lead Co., D.C. N.Y., 63 F.Supp. 513.

State of War

An agreement between two hostile powers for the delivery of prisoners or deserters, or authorizing certain non-hostile intercourse between each other which would otherwise be prevented by the state of war; for example, agreements for intercommunication by post, telegraph, telephone, railway. II Op. 282.

Duel

A written challenge to a duel.

CARTULARY. A place where papers or records are kept.

In the plural: Ancient English records containing documents and legal proceedings—the muniments of title of the great landowners, and other miscellaneous documents. 2 Holdsw.Hist.E.L. 273. See 1 Poll. & Maitl. p. xxii.

CARUCA, or CARUA. A plow. A four-wheeled carriage. A team for a plow, or four oxen abreast. See Carucata.

CARUCAGE. In old English law. A kind of tax or tribute anciently imposed upon every plow, (*carue* or plow-land,) for the public service. Spelman. The act of plowing.

CARUCATA, CARUCATE. A certain quantity of land used as the basis for taxation. A cartload. As much land as may be tilled by a single plow in a year and a day. Skene, *de verb, sig.* A plow land of one hundred acres. Ken. Gloss. The quantity varies in different counties from sixty to one hundred and twenty acres. Whart. See Littleton, Ten. cclxii; 2 Holdsw.Hist.E.L. 56; Maitl. Domesday Book and Beyond 395; 1 L.J.R. 96. Also, a team of cattle, or a cart-load. See Bovata terræ.

CARUCATARIUS. One who held lands in *carvage*, or plow-tenure. Cowell.

CARUE. A carve of land; plow-land. Britt. c. 84.

CARVAGE. The same as carucage, (*q. v.*) Cowell.

CARVE. In old English law. A carucate or plow-land.

CAS FORTUIT. Fr. In the law of insurance. A fortuitous event; an inevitable accident.

CASATA. In old English law. A house with land sufficient for the support of one family. Otherwise called *"hida,"* a hide of land, and by Bede, *"familia."* Spelman.

CASATUS. A vassal or feudal tenant possessing a *casata;* that is, having a house, household, and property of his own.

CASE.

Action, Cause, Suit, or Controversy

A general term for an action, cause, suit, or controversy, at law or in equity; a question contested before a court of justice; an aggregate of facts which furnishes occasion for the exercise of the jurisdiction of a court of justice. Quoted with approval in Kelly v. Roetzel, 64 Okl. 36, 165 P. 1150, 1153. See, also, Gebhard v. Sattler, 40 Iowa, 156; Martin v. Hunter, 1 Wheat. 352, 4 L.Ed. 97. A controversy that is litigated. City of Akron v. Roth, 88 Ohio St. 456, 103 N.E. 465, 467. A cause of action. Strother v. Union Pac. R. Co., D.C.Mo., 220 F. 731, 732; Colla v. Carmichael U-Drive Autos, 111 Cal.App. 378, 294 P. 378, 380.

The word "case" or "cause" means a judicial proceeding for the determination of a controversy between parties wherein rights are enforced or protected, or wrongs are prevented or redressed. Ex parte Chesser, 93 Fla. 590, 112 So. 87, 90; any proceeding judicial in its nature, McCarthy v. Clancy, 110 Conn. 482, 148 A. 551, 557.

Case of actual controversy. The phrase in Federal Declaratory Judgment Act connotes controversy of justiciable nature, excluding advisory decree on hypothetical facts. John P. Agnew & Co., Inc. v. Hoage, App.D.C., 69 App.D.C. 116, 99 F.2d 349, 351.

Case sufficient to go to a jury. A case that has proceeded upon sufficient proof to that stage where it must be submitted to jury and not decided against the state as a matter of law. State v. McDonough, 129 Conn. 483, 29 A.2d 582, 584.

Cases and controversies. This term, as used in the constitution of the United States, embraces claims or contentions of litigants brought before the court for adjudication by regular proceedings established for the protection or enforcement of rights, or the prevention, redress, or punishment of wrongs; and whenever the claim or contention of a party takes such a form that the judicial power is capable of acting upon it, it has become a case or controversy. Interstate Commerce Com'n v. Brimson, 154 U.S. 447, 14 Sup.Ct. 1125, 38 L.Ed. 1047. These two terms are to be distinguished; for there may be a "separable controversy" within a "case," which may be removed from a state court to a federal court, though the case as a whole is not removable. Snow v. Smith, C.C.Va., 88 Fed. 658. The term "controversies", if distinguishable from "cases", is so in that it is less comprehensive than the term "cases" and includes only suits of a civil nature, Smith v. Blackwell, C.C.A.S.C., 115 F.2d 186, 188.

Applications and Special Proceedings

The word "case" may include application for divorce, applications for the establishment of highways, applications for orders of support of relatives, and other special proceedings unknown to the common law. S. D. Warren Co. v. Fritz, 138 Me. 279, 25 A.2d 645, 648.

Box or Container

A box or container, as for cans or bottles filled with milk or other liquid goods. Ex parte Reineger, 184 Cal. 97, 193 P. 81, 83.

Event, Happening, etc.

In ordinary usage, the word "case" means "event," "happening," "situation," "circumstances." Highfield v. Delaware Trust Co., Del.Super., 188 A. 919, 922.

Form of Action

A form of action which lies to recover damages for injuries for which the more ancient forms of action will not lie. Steph.Pl. 15. An abbreviated form of the title "trespass on the case," *q. v.* Munal v. Brown, C.C.Colo., 70 F. 968. See, also, Wadleigh v. Katahdin Pulp & Paper Co., 116 Me. 107, 100 A. 150, 151. Action where injury is merely consequential. Mawson v. Vess Beverage Co., Mo.App., 173 S.W.2d 606, 612, 613.

Grand Jury Inquiry

As used in statute authorizing a challenge to an individual grand juror, any matter that might become subject of inquiry by grand jury. People v. Prior, 268 App.Div. 717, 54 N.Y.S.2d 150, 153.

Statement of Facts

A statement of the facts involved in a transaction or series of transactions, drawn up in writing in a technical form, for submission to a court or judge for decision or opinion. Under this meaning of the term are included a "case made" for a motion for new trial, a "case reserved" on the trial of a cause, an "agreed case" for decision without trial, etc.

Case agreed on. A formal written enumeration of the facts in a case, assented to by both parties as correct and complete, and submitted to the court by their agreement, in order that a decision may be rendered without a trial, upon the court's conclusions of law upon the facts as stated.

Case for motion. In English divorce and probate practice, when a party desires to make a motion, he must file, among other papers, a case for motion, containing an abstract of the proceedings in the suit or action, a statement of the circumstances on which the motion is founded, and the prayer or nature of the decree or order desired. Browne, Div. 251; Browne, Prob.Pr. 295.

Case-made. A statement of facts in relation to a disputed point of law, agreed to by both parties and submitted to the court without a preceding action. This is found only in the Code states. See De Armond v. Whitaker, 99 Ala. 252, 13 So. 613; A complete record of each successive action of the trial court at the trial, including testimony. In re Opinion of the Judges, 29 Okl.Cr. 27, 232 P. 121, 122. A "case-made" consists of those things which transpired in court during the trial, and which are not a part of the record. Jones v. State, 9 Okl.Cr. 189, 130 P. 1178.

Case on appeal. In American practice. Before the argument in the appellate court of a case brought there for review, the appellant's counsel prepares a document or brief, bearing this name, for the information of the court, detailing the testimony and the proceedings below. In English practice. The "case on appeal" is a printed statement prepared by each of the parties to an appeal to the house of lords or the privy council, setting out methodically the facts which make up his case, with appropriate references to the evidence printed in the "appendix." The term also denotes a written statement, prepared and transmitted by an inferior court or judge raising a question of law for the opinion of a superior court.

Case reserved. A statement in writing of the facts proved on the trial of a cause, drawn up and settled by the attorneys and counsel for the respective parties under the supervision of the judge, for the purpose of having certain points of law, which arose at the trial and could not then be satisfactorily decided, determined upon full argument before the court in *banc*. This is otherwise called a "special case;" and it is usual for the parties, where the law of the case is doubtful, to agree that the jury shall find a general verdict for the plaintiff, subject to the opinion of the court upon such a case to be made, instead of obtaining from the jury a special verdict. 3 Bl.Comm. 378; 3 Steph.Comm. 621; Steph.Pl. 92, 93; 1 Burrill, Pr. 242, 463.

Case stated. In practice. An agreement in writing, between a plaintiff and defendant, that the facts in dispute between them are as therein agreed upon and set forth. 3 Sharsw.Bla.Comm. 453, n.; 6 Term, 313. A case agreed upon. A statement of all the facts of a case, with the names of the witnesses, and a detail of the documents which are to support them. A statement of agreed facts. Caissie v. City of Cambridge, 317 Mass. 346, 58 N.E.2d 169. An auditor's report. Hanifin v. C. & R. Const. Co., 313 Mass. 651, 48 N.E.2d 913, 918. A brief. As to the distinction between submission on a case stated and a submission merely on agreed facts, see Frati v. Jannini, 226 Mass. 430, 115 N.E. 746, 747.

Case to move for new trial. In practice. A case prepared by the party against whom a verdict has been given, upon which to move the court to set aside the verdict and grant a new trial.

Supplementary Proceedings

The word "cases" in section providing that "act shall apply in all cases now pending or hereafter instituted in which the final decree of divorce was recorded prior to the effective date of this act", is synonym of "supplementary proceedings". Chiapetta v. Jordan, 16 So.2d 641, 644, 153 Fla. 788.

CASE LAW. The aggregate of reported cases as forming a body of jurisprudence, or the law of a particular subject as evidenced or formed by the adjudged cases, in distinction to statutes and other sources of law.

CASE SYSTEM. A method of teaching or studying the science of the law by a study of the cases historically, or by the inductive method. It was introduced in the Law School of Harvard University in 1869–70 by Christopher C. Langdell, Dane Professor of Law.

CASEMENT. A window sash opening on hinges affixed to the upright side of the frame, and includes wooden as well as steel construction. Johnson Metal Products Co. v. Lundell-Eckberg Mfg. Co., D.C.N.Y., 18 F.Supp. 572, 574.

CASH. Money or its equivalent; usually ready money. Kerlin v. Young, 159 Ga. 95, 125 S.E. 204, 207; Britain v. Rice, Tex.Civ.App., 204 S.W. 254, 256.

Money in hand, either in current coin or other legal tender, or in bank bills or checks paid and received as money. Dunlap v. Whitmer, 133 La. 317, 62 So. 938, 943, Ann.Cas. 1915C, 990. Bank deposits, In re Feist's Will, 170 Misc. 497, 10 N.Y.S.2d 506, 508; Lane v. Railey, 280 Ky. 319, 133 S.W.2d 74, 79, 80. Bank notes or sight drafts, Lane v. Railey, 280 Ky. 319, 133 S.W.2d 74, 79, 80. Bank's deposit certificate. Bingham v. Montcalm County, 251 Mich. 651, 232 N.W. 348, check, Van Decar v. Streeter, 136 Misc. 206, 240 N.Y.S. 492, 497. Commercial paper. Commercial Credit Corporation v. Third & Lafayette Streets Garage, 131 Misc. 786, 228 N.Y.S. 166, 168. Currency, coin, specie. Lane v. Railey, 280 Ky. 319, 133 S.W.2d 74, 79, 80. Whatever can be used as money without being converted into another form. That which circulates as money, including bank bills. Hooper v. Flood, 54 Cal. 221; Dazel v. Landry, 21 Nev. 291, 30 Pac. 1064; United States v. Williams, D.C. Wash., 282 F. 324, 325. The term may include currency, municipal orders, warrants, or scrip. Arkansas Public Utilities Co. v. Incorporated Town of Heber Springs, 151 Ark. 249, 235 S.W. 999, 1001. It is frequently used as an antonym of "credit." Parrish v. American Ry. Employees' Pub. Corporation, 83 Cal.App. 298, 256 P. 590, 591; State v. Woodward, 208 Ala. 31, 93 So. 826.

CASH ACCOUNT. A record, in bookkeeping, of all cash transactions; an account of moneys received and expended.

CASH BOOK. In bookkeeping, an account book in which is kept a record of all cash transactions, or all cash received and expended.

The object of the cash book is to afford a constant facility to ascertain the true state of a man's cash. Pardessus, n. 87.

CASH CONTRACT. A "cash contract," as of a municipal corporation, is one not creating a debt within the constitution. Jeffersonville v. Cotton State Belting Supply Co., 30 Ga.App. 470, 118 S.E. 442.

CASH DISCOUNT. A deduction from billed price which seller allows for payment within a certain time. Leonard v. U. S., Ct.Cl., 7 F.Supp. 295, 297.

CASH MARKET VALUE. "Fair market value", "reasonable market value" or "fair cash market value" as synonymous. Housing Authority of Birmingham Dist. v. Title Guarantee Loan & Trust Co., 243 Ala. 157, 8 So.2d 835, 837. For "Fair Cash Market Value," see that title.

CASH NOTE. In England. A bank-note of a provincial bank or of the Bank of England.

CASH PRICE. A price payable in cash at the time of sale of property, in opposition to a barter or a sale on credit.

CASH SALE. A sale for money in hand. Steward v. Scudder, 24 N.J.Law, 101; Bass v. Green & Yates, 201 Ala. 515, 78 So. 869. A sale conditioned on payment concurrent with delivery. Weyerhaeuser Timber Co. v. First Nat. Bank, 150 Or. 172, 43 P.2d 1078, 1081. See, further, Sale.

CASH SURRENDER VALUE. The "cash surrender value" of a life policy is the reserve less a surrender charge. Guggenheim v. Rasquin, U.S. N.Y., 312 U.S. 254, 61 S.Ct. 507, 508, 85 L.Ed. 813.

CASH VALUE. The cash value of an article or piece of property is the price which it would bring at private sale (as distinguished from a forced or auction sale) the terms of sale requiring the payment of the whole price in ready money, with no deferred payments. Tax Com'rs v. Holliday, 150 Ind. 216, 49 N.E. 14, 42 L.R.A. 826; Cummings v. Bank, 101 U.S. 162, 25 L.Ed. 903. For "Fair Cash Value," see that title.

Actual value or market value, Fort Worth & D. N. Ry. Co. v. Sugg, Tex.Civ.App., 68 S.W.2d 570, 572; Yeoman Mut. Life Ins. Co. v. State Board of Assessment, 229 Iowa 220, 294 N.W. 330, 334. Clear market value or fair market value. In re Ryerson's Estate, 239 Wis. 120, 300 N.W. 782, 784. Price property will bring on sale by one desiring, but not compelled, to sell to one desiring, but not compelled, to purchase. Insurance Co. of North America v. McGraw, 255 Ky. 839, 75 S.W.2d 518, 520. Saleable value, In re Lang Body Co., C.C. A.Ohio, 92 F.2d 338, 340. Usual selling price at private sale and not at a forced or auction sale. Volunteer State Life Ins. Co. v. Union Title Guarantee Co., 175 La. 183, 143 So. 43, value at which property would be taken in payment of just debt from solvent debtor. Bank of Fairfield v. Spokane County, 173 Wash. 145, 22 P.2d 646, 652.

CASHIER, *v.* In military law. To deprive a military officer of his rank and office.

CASHIER, *n.* An officer of a moneyed institution, or commercial house, or bank, who is intrusted with, and whose duty it is to take care of, the cash or money of such institution or bank. A custodian of the money of a bank, mercantile house, and the like. Miller v. State, 88 Tex.Cr. R. 69, 225 S.W. 379, 381, 12 A.L.R. 597.

The cashier of a bank is its chief executive officer. Pemiscot County Bank v. Central-State Nat. Bank, 132 Tenn. 152, 177 S.W. 74, 75; Bank of Commerce of Chanute v. Sams, 96 Kan. 437, 152 P. 28, 29. He is its chief financial agent, through whom its principal financial dealings are conducted; Brown v. Mt. Holly Nat. Bank, 288 Pa. 478, 136 A. 773, 775; and is peculiarly that agency authorized to make loans and collections, whose special duty it is to give direction to and further the stockholders' interests; People's Bank of Calhoun v. Harry L. Winter, Inc., 161 Ga. 898, 132 S.E. 422, 424.

He receives and pays out its moneys, collects and pays its debts, and receives and transfers its commercial securities. Tellers and other subordinate officers may be appointed, but they are under his direction, and are, as it were, the arms by which designated portions of his various functions are discharged. Merchants' Nat. Bank v. State Nat. Bank, 10 Wall. 650, 19 L.Ed. 1008.

CASHIERED. Dismissal with ignominy or dishonor, or in disgrace. Metropolis Co. v. Croasdell, 145 Fla. 455, 199 So. 568, 569.

CASHIER'S CHECK. See Check.

CASHLITE. An amercement or fine; a mulct.

CASING-HEAD GAS. Natural gas from an oil well, saturated with oil vapors or gasoline. 58 C.J.S. p. 26.

—Casing-head gasoline. Sometimes called natural gasoline. It is produced from casing-head gas by compression or separation of the gases which come from oil wells. 58 C.J.S. p. 21.

CASKET. In one sense, a coffin. Ware v. State, 31 Ga.App. 554, 121 S.E. 251.

CASSARE. To quash; to render void; to break. Du Cange.

CASSATION. In French law. Annulling; reversal; breaking the force and validity of a judgment. A decision emanating from the sovereign authority, by which a decree or judgment in the court of last resort is broken or annulled. Merl. Repert.

CASSATION, COURT OF. (Fr. *cour de cassation.*) The highest court in France; so termed from possessing the power to quash (*casser*) the decrees of inferior courts. It is a court of appeal in criminal as well as civil cases.

CASSETUR BILLA. (Lat. That the bill be quashed.) In practice. The form of the judgment for the defendant on a plea in abatement, where the action was commenced by bill, (*billa.*) 3 Bl.Comm. 303; Steph.Pl. 128, 131. The form of an entry made by a plaintiff on the record, after a plea in abatement, where he found that the plea could not be confessed and avoided, nor traversed, nor demurred to; amounting in fact to a discontinuance of the action. 2 Archb.Pr.K.B. 3, 236; 1 Tidd, Pr. 683.

CASSETUR BREVE. (Lat. That the writ be quashed.) In practice. The form of the judgment for the defendant on a plea in abatement, where the action was commenced by original writ (*breve*). 3 Bl.Comm. 303; Steph.Pl. 107, 109.

A judgment sometimes entered against a plaintiff at his request when, in consequence of allegations of the defendant, he can no longer prosecute his suit with effect. 5 Term 634.

CASSOCK, or CASSULA. A garment worn by a priest.

CAST, *v.* In old English practice. To allege, offer, or present; to proffer by way of excuse (as to "cast an essoin").

This word is now used as a popular, rather than a technical, term, in the sense of to overcome, overthrow, or defeat in a civil action at law. It also means to deposit formally or officially. Maddox v. Board of State Canvassers, Mont., 149 P.2d 112, 115; Port of Palm Beach Dist. v. State, 156 Fla. 99, 22 So.2d 581, 582. It is also used in connection with the imposition upon a party litigant of costs in the suit: as, A. is "cast" for the costs of the case.

CAST AWAY. To cast away a ship is to do such an act upon or in regard to it as causes it to perish or be lost, so as to be irrecoverable by ordinary means. The term is synonymous with "destroy," which means to unfit a vessel for service beyond the hope of recovery by ordinary means. U. S. v. Vanranst, 28 Fed.Cas. 360.

CASTEL, or CASTLE. A fortress in a town; the principal mansion of a nobleman. 3 Inst. 31.

CASTELLAIN. In old English law. The lord, owner, or captain of a castle; the constable of a fortified house; a person having the custody of one of the crown mansions; an officer of the forest.

CASTELLANUS. A castellain; the keeper or constable of a castle. Spelman.

CASTELLARIUM, CASTELLATUS. In old English law. The precinct or jurisdiction of a castle. Blount.

CASTELLORUM OPERATIO. In Saxon and old English law. Castle work. Service and labor done by inferior tenants for the building and upholding of castles and public places of defense. One of the three necessary charges, (*trinoda necessitas,*) to which all lands among the Saxons were expressly subject. Cowell. Towards this some gave their personal service, and others, a contribution of money or goods. 1 Bla.Comm. 263.

CASTIGATORY. An engine used to punish women who have been convicted of being common scolds. It is sometimes called the trebucket, tumbrel, ducking-stool, or cucking-stool. U. S. v. Royall, 27 Fed.Cas. 907.

CASTING VOTE. Where the votes of a deliberative assembly or legislative body are equally divided on any question or motion, it is the privilege of the presiding officer to cast one vote (if otherwise he would not be entitled to any vote) on either side, or to cast one additional vote, if he has already voted as a member of the body. This is called the "casting vote." Brown v. Foster, 88 Me. 49, 33 A. 662, 31 L.R.A. 116.

CASTLEGUARD. In feudal law. An imposition anciently laid upon such persons as lived within a certain distance of any castle, towards the maintenance of such as watched and warded the castle.

CASTLEGUARD RENTS. In old English law. Rents paid by those that dwelt within the precincts of a castle, towards the maintenance of such as watched and warded it.

CASTRENSIS. In the Roman law. Relating to the camp or military service.

Castrense peculium, a portion of property which a son acquired in war, or from his connection with the camp. Dig. 49, 17.

CASTRUM. Lat.

In Roman law. A camp.

In old English law. A castle. Bract. fol. 69*b*. A castle, including a manor. 4 Coke, 88.

CASU CONSIMILI. In old English law. A writ of entry, granted where tenant by the curtesy, or tenant for life, alienated in fee, or in tail, or for another's life, which was brought by him in reversion against the party to whom such tenant so alienated to his prejudice, and in the tenant's lifetime. Termes de la Ley. See Consimili Casu.

CASU PROVISO. Lat. In the case provided for. A writ of entry framed under the provisions of the statute of Gloucester (6 Edw. I.) c. 7, which lay for the benefit of the reversioner when a tenant in dower aliened in fee or for life.

CASUAL. Accidental, Gray v. Greenwood, 32 A. 2d 347, 350, 21 N.J.Misc. 137; Texas & N. O. R. Co. v. Owens, Tex.Civ.App., 54 S.W.2d 848, 853; Sonnenberg v. Berg's Market, 227 Mo.App. 391, 55 S.W.2d 494; by chance, Texas & N. O. R. Co. v. Owens, Tex.Civ.App., 54 S.W.2d 848, 853; coming by chance, Lawrenz v. Langford Electric Co., 206 Minn. 315, 288 N.W. 727, 731; Norris v. Koenig, Mo.App., 183 S.W.2d 160, 162; fortuitous, Sonnenberg v. Berg's Market, 227 Mo.App. 391, 55 S.W.2d 494, 495. Happening or coming to pass without design and without being foreseen or expected. Root v. Topeka Ry. Co., 96 Kan. 694, 153 P. 550; Ranson-Rooney Co. v. Overseas Ry., 17 La.App. 205, 134 So. 765, 768; impermanent, Board of Sup'rs of Amherst County v. Boaz, 176 Va. 126, 10 S.E.2d 498, 500; incidental, Mason v. Wampler, 89 Ind.App. 483, 166 N.E. 885, 886, Coffin v. Hook, Ind.App., 45 N.E.2d 369, 372; indeterminate, Texas & N. O. R. Co. v. Owens, Tex.Civ.App., 54 S.W.2d 848, 853; irregular, Gardner v. Trustees of Main St. M. E. Church of Ottumwa, 217 Iowa, 1390, 250 N.W. 740; liable to happen, subject to chance or accident, Coffin v. Hook, 112 Ind.App. 549, 45 N.E. 2d 369, 372; occasional, Cardillo v. Mockabee, 70 App.D.C. 16, 102 F.2d 620, 622; uncertain, Coffin v. Hook, 112 Ind.App. 549, 45 N.E.2d 369, 372; unexpected, Gray v. Greenwood, 21 N.J.Misc. 137, 32 A.2d 347, 350; Texas & N. O. R. Co. v. Owens, Tex.Civ.App., 54 S.W.2d 848, 853; unforeseen, Texas & N. O. R. Co. v. Owens, Tex.Civ.App., 54 S.W. 2d 848, 853; Lawrenz v. Langford Electric Co., 206 Minn. 315, 288 N.W. 727, 731; unpremeditated, Lawrenz v. Langford Electric Co., 206 Minn. 315, 288 N.W. 727, 731; without regularity, Norris v. Koenig, Mo.App., 183 S.W.2d 160, 162; Sonnenberg v. Berg's Market, 227 Mo.App. 391, 55 S.W.2d 494.

CASUAL BETTOR. An occasional and irregular bettor who is not guilty of crime of engaging in betting and gambling organized and carried on as a systematic business. Bamman v. Erickson, 288 N.Y. 133, 41 N.E.2d 920, 922.

CASUAL DEFICENCY OF REVENUE. An unforeseen or unexpected deficiency, or an insufficiency of funds to meet some unforeseen and necessary expense. Atlanta Distributing Terminals v. Board of Com'rs etc., of Fulton County, 177 Ga. 250, 170 S.E. 52, 56.

CASUAL DEFICIT. A deficit happening by chance or accident and without design. State Budget Commission v. Lebus, 244 Ky. 700, 51 S.W.2d 965.

CASUAL EJECTOR. In practice. The nominal defendant in an action of ejectment. French v. Robb, 67 N.J.Law, 260, 51 A. 509, 57 L.R.A. 956.

CASUAL EMPLOYEE. Though courts have refrained from defining "casual employee" as such term is used in the Workmen's Compensation Act, the test in the particular case is whether service rendered or work done, rather than contract of hiring, is of casual nature; infrequency of employment or its duration being immaterial. Hygeia Ice & Coal Co. v. Schaeffer, 152 Md. 231, 136 A. 548, 551.

As regards whether an employee is a "casual" employee the word "casual" means something happening without design and unexpectedly. Ward v. Ocean Forest Club, 188 S.C. 233, 198 S.E. 385.

CASUAL EMPLOYMENT. Employment at uncertain times or irregular intervals. Johnson v. Wisconsin Lumber & Supply Co., 203 Wis. 304, 234 N.W. 506, 507, 72 A.L.R. 1279; employment by chance, fortuitously, and for no fixed time, Boyd v. Philmont Country Club, 129 Pa.Super. 135, 195 A. 156, 157, 158; employment casual and not in usual course of trade, business, occupation or profession of employer. Kunkler v. Mauck, 108 Ind.App. 98, 27 N.E.2d 97, 99. Employment for short time and limited and temporary purpose, Moore v. Clarke, 171 Md. 39, 187 A. 887, 894, 107 A.L.R. 924; fortuitous and irregular employment. McCabe v. Timothy Shanahan & Son, 147 Pa.Super. 491, 24 A.2d 16, 18; occasional, irregular or incidental employment, Maguire v. Valley Forge Military Academy, 116 Pa.Super. 495, 176 A. 865, 867.

The test is the nature of the work or an analysis of the contract of employment. State Farm Mut. Automobile Ins. Co. v. Brooks, D.C.Mo., 43 F.Supp. 870, 872; or whether the employment is necessary to carry out the employer's business in usual way. Thompson v. G. Correale & Sons, 130 N.J.L. 431, 33 A.2d 578, 579; or the scope of the contract of employment or the continuity of employment. Cochrane v. William Penn Hotel, Hartford Accident & Indemnity Co., Intervener, 140 Pa.Super. 323, 13 A.2d 875, 877; "Casual" means occasional; incidental; happening at uncertain times; not stated or regular; its antonyms being regular; systematic; periodic; certain, Pooler's Case, 122 Me. 11, 118 A. 590, 591; Dial v. Coleman's Lunch, 217 Iowa, 945, 251 N.W. 33; happening or coming to pass without design and without being foreseen or expected, accidental, fortuitous, coming by chance, coming without regularity, Tokash v. General Baking Co., 349 Mo. 767, 163 S.W.2d 554, 556; The term refers to nature of employment and not to length. Parks v. E. M. Carmell Co., 168 Tenn. 385, 79 S.W.2d 285, 287.

CASUAL EVIDENCE. A phrase used to denote all such evidence as happens to be adducible of a fact or event, but which was not prescribed by statute or otherwise arranged beforehand to be the evidence of the fact or event. Brown.

CASUAL PAUPER. A poor person who, in England, applies for relief in a parish other than that of his settlement. The ward in the work-house to which they are admitted is called the "casual ward."

CASUAL POOR. In English law. Those who are not settled in a parish. Such poor persons as are suddenly taken sick, or meet with some accident, when away from home, and who are thus providentially thrown upon the charities of those among whom they happen to be. Force v. Haines, 17 N.J.Law, 405.

CASUALTY. Accident; event due to sudden, unexpected or unusual cause; event not to be foreseen or guarded against; inevitable accident; misfortune or mishap; that which comes by chance or without design. A loss from such an event or cause; as by fire, shipwreck, lightning, etc. Story, Bailm. § 240; Gill v. Fugate, 117 Ky. 257, 78 S.W. 191; Farmers Co-op. Soc. No. 1 of Quanah v. Maryland Casualty Co., Tex.Civ.App., 135 S.W.2d 1033, 1036; Matheson v. Commissioner of Internal Revenue, C.C.A., 54 F.2d 537, 539; Stieffen v. Darling, 158 Va. 375, 163 S.E. 353, 354.

Chance; accident; contingency; also that which comes without design or without being foreseen. Bennett v. Howard, 175 Ky. 797, 195 S.W. 117, 118, L.R.A.1917E, 1075; United States v. Rogers, C.C.A. Cal., 120 F.2d 244, 246.

—Casualties of superiority. In Scotch law. Payments from an inferior to a superior, that is, from a tenant to his lord, which arise upon uncertain events, as opposed to the payment of rent at fixed and stated times. Bell.

—Casualties of wards. In Scotch law. The mails and duties due to the superior in wardholdings.

CASUS. Lat. Chance; accident; an event; a case; a case contemplated.

CASUS BELLI. An occurrence giving rise to or justifying war.

CASUS FŒDERIS. In international law. The case of the treaty. The particular event or situation contemplated by the treaty, or stipulated for, or which comes within its terms. Grotius, b. 2, c. 25; Vattel, b. 2, c. 12, § 168; 1 Kent, 49. In commercial law. The case or event contemplated by the parties to an individual contract or stipulated for by it, or coming within its terms.

CASUS FORTUITUS. An inevitable accident, a chance occurrence, or fortuitous event. A loss happening in spite of all human effort and sagacity. 3 Kent, Comm. 217, 300; The Majestic, 166 U.S. 375, 17 S.Ct. 597, 41 L.Ed. 1039.

CASUS FORTUITUS NON EST SPERANDUS, ET NEMO TENETUR DEVINARE. A fortuitous event is not to be expected, and no one is bound to foresee it. 4 Coke, 66.

CASUS FORTUITUS NON EST SUPPONENDUS. A fortuitous event is not to be presumed. Hardr. 82, arg.

CASUS MAJOR. In the civil law. A casualty; an extraordinary casualty, as fire, shipwreck, etc. Dig. 44, 7, 1, 4.

CASUS OMISSUS. A case omitted; an event or contingency for which no provision is made; particularly a case not provided for by the statute on the general subject, and which is therefore left to be governed by the common law. 5 Co. 38; 11 East 1; Broom, Max. 46.

CASUS OMISSUS ET OBLIVIONI DATUS DISPOSITIONI JURIS COMMUNÍS RELINQUITUR. A case omitted and given to oblivion (forgotten) is left to the disposal of the common law. 5 Coke, 38. A particular case, left unprovided for by statute, must be disposed of according to the law as it existed prior to such statute. Broom, Max. 46; 1 Exch. 476.

CASUS OMISSUS PRO OMISSO HABENDUS EST. A case omitted is to be held as (intentionally) omitted. Tray.Lat.Max. 67.

CAT. A domestic animal that catches mice; a well known domesticated carnivorous mammal kept to kill mice and rats and as a house pet. Thurston v. Carter, 112 Me. 361, 92 A. 295, L.R.A. 1915C, 359.

An instrument with which criminals are flogged. It consists of nine lashes of whipcord, tied to a wooden handle, and is frequently called cat-o-nine-tails. It is used where the whipping-post is retained as a mode of punishment and was formerly resorted to in the navy.

CATALLA. In old English law. Chattels. The word among the Normans primarily signified only beasts of husbandry, or, as they are still called, "cattle," but, in a secondary sense, the term was applied to all movables in general, and not only to these, but to whatever was not a fief or feud. Wharton.

CATALLA JUSTE POSSESSA AMITTI NON POSSUNT. Chattels justly possessed cannot be lost. Jenk.Cent. 28.

CATALLA OTIOSA. Dead goods or chattels, as distinguished from animals. Idle cattle, that is, such as were not used for working, as distinguished from beasts of the plow; called also *animalia otiosa.* Bract. fols. 217, 217*b;* 3 Bl.Comm. 9.

CATALLA REPUTANTUR INTER MINIMA IN LEGE. Chattels are considered in law among the least (or minor) things. Jenk.Cent. 52.

CATALLIS CAPTIS NOMINE DISTRICTIONIS. An obsolete writ that lay where a house was within a borough, for rent issuing out of the same, and which warranted the taking of doors, windows, etc., by way of distress.

CATALLIS REDDENDIS. For the return of the chattels; an obsolete writ that lay where goods delivered to a man to keep till a certain day were not upon demand redelivered at the day. Reg. Orig. 39.

CATALLUM. A chattel. Most frequently used in the plural form, *catalla (q. v.).* Cowell; Du Cange.

CATALS. Goods and chattels. See Catalla.

CATANEUS. A tenant *in capite.* A tenant holding immediately of the crown. Spelman.

CATASCOPUS. An old name for an archdeacon.

CATASTROPHE. A notable disaster; a more serious calamity than might ordinarily be understood from the term "casualty." Reynolds v. Board of Com'rs of Orleans Levee Dist., 139 La. 518, 71 So. 787, 791.

CATCH TIME CHARTER. One under which compensation is paid for the time the boat is actually used. Schoonmaker-Conners Co. v. New York Cent. R. Co., D.C.N.Y., 12 F.2d 314, 315.

CATCHING BARGAIN. See Bargain.

CATCHINGS. Things caught, and in the possession, custody, power, and dominion of the party, with a present capacity to use them for his own purposes. The term includes blubber, or pieces of whale flesh cut from the whale, and stowed on or under the deck of a ship. A policy of insurance upon outfits, and catchings substituted for the outfits, in a whaling voyage, protects the blubber. Rogers v. Insurance Co., 1 Story, 603; Fed.Cas.No. 12,016; 4 Law Rep. 297.

CATCHLAND. Land in Norfolk, so called because it is not known to what parish it belongs, and the minister who first seizes the tithes of it, by right of preoccupation, enjoys them for that year. Cowell.

CATCHPOLL. A name formerly given to a sheriff's deputy, or to a constable, or other officer whose duty it is to arrest persons. He was a sort of serjeant. The word is not now in use as an official designation. Minshew.

CATER COUSIN. (From Fr. *Quatrecousin.*) A cousin in the fourth degree; hence any distant or remote relative. Bla.Law Tracts 6.

CATHEDRAL. In English ecclesiastical law. A tract set apart for the service of the church. The church of the bishop of the diocese, in which is his *cathedra,* or throne, and his special jurisdiction; in that respect the principal church of the diocese.

CATHEDRAL PREFERMENTS. In English ecclesiastical law. All deaneries, archdeaconries, and canonries, and generally all dignities and offices in any cathedral or collegiate church, below the rank of a bishop.

CATHEDRATIC. In English ecclesiastical law. A sum of 2*s.* paid to the bishop by the inferior clergy; but from its being usually paid at the bishop's *synod,* or visitation, it is commonly named *synodals.* Wharton.

CATHOLIC CREDITOR. In Scotch law. A creditor whose debt is secured on all or several distinct parts of the debtor's property. Bell.

CATHOLIC EMANCIPATION ACT. The statute of 10 Geo. IV, *c.* 7, by which Roman Catholics were restored, in general, to the full enjoyment of all civil rights, except that of holding ecclesiastical offices, and certain high appointments in the state. 3 Steph.Comm. 109.

CATONIANA REGULA. In Roman law. The rule which is commonly expressed in the maxim, *Quod ab initio non valet tractu temporis non convalebit,* meaning that what is at the beginning void by reason of some technical (or other) legal defect will not become valid merely by length of time. The rule applied to the institution of *hæredes,* the bequest of legacies, and such like. The rule is not without its application also in English law; *e. g.,* a married woman's will (being void when made) is not made valid merely because she lives to become a widow. Brown.

CATTLE. A generic term for domestic quadrupeds; animals used by man for labor or food. In its primary sense, it embraces horses, mares, geldings, foals, or fillies, asses, and mules, as well as animals of the ox kind or bovine species. Bell v. Erie R. Co., 183 App.Div. 608, 171 N.Y.S. 341, 343. The term may also include goats, swine, and sheep. Ash Sheep Co. v. U. S., 252 U.S. 159, 40 S.Ct. 241, 243, 64 L.Ed. 507. Calves running with their mothers are cattle. Peterson v. Citizens' Bank of Stuart, 117 Neb. 327, 220 N.W. 575, 577.

In the narrower, popular sense, animals of the bovine genus. State v. Eaglin, 148 La. 75, 86 So. 658, 659; Gragg v. State, 112 Neb. 732, 201 N.W. 338, 340. This is the sense in which the term is generally used in the western United States, and it is said further that it is not generally, but may be, taken to mean calves, or animals younger than yearlings. State v. District Court of Fifth Judicial Dist. in and for Nye County, 42 Nev. 218, 174 P. 1023, 1025.

CATTLE GATE. In English law. A customary proportionate right of pasture enjoyed in common with others. 34 E. L. & Eq. 511; 1 Term 137. A right to pasture cattle in the land of another. It is a distinct and several interest in the land, passing by lease and release. 13 East, 159; 5 Taunt. 811.

CATTLEGUARD. A device to prevent cattle from straying along a railroad-track at a highway-crossing. Heskett v. Railway Co., 61 Iowa, 467, 16 N.W. 525; True v. Maine Cent. R. Co., 113 Me. 375, 94 A. 183, 184.

CATTLE PASS. As used in a statute, a narrow passage way under a railroad track high and wide enough to admit the passage of a cow, horse, or ox to and from a pasture. True v. Maine Cent. R. Co., 113 Me. 375, 94 A. 183, 184.

CATTLE RANGE. Under a statute, a range the usual and customary use of which has been for cattle. State v. Butterfield, 30 Idaho 415, 165 P. 218, 219.

CATTLE RUSTLING. Stealing of bovine cattle, Galeppi v. C. Swanston & Son, 107 Cal.App. 30, 290 P. 116, 119.

CAUCASIAN. Pertaining to the white race, to which belong the greater part of European nations and those of western Asia. Rice v. Gong Lum, 139 Miss. 760, 104 So. 105, 110. The term is inapplicable to denote families or stocks inhabiting Europe, and speaking either the so-called Aryan or Semitic languages. Ex parte Shahid, D.C.S.C., 205 F. 812, 814.

CAUCUS. A meeting of the legal voters of any political party assembled for the purpose of choosing delegates or for the nomination of candidates for office.

CAUDA TERRÆ. A land's end, or the bottom of a ridge in arable land. Cowell.

CAULCEIS. Highroads or ways pitched with flint or other stones.

CAUPO. In the civil law. An innkeeper. Dig. 4, 9, 4, 5.

CAUPONA. In the civil law. An inn or tavern. Inst. 4, 5, 3.

CAUPONES. In the civil law. Innkeepers. Dig. 4, 9; Id. 47, 5; Story, Ag. § 458.

CAURSINES. Italian merchants who came into England in the reign of Henry III., where they established themselves as money lenders, but were soon expelled for their usury and extortion. Cowell; Blount.

CAUSA.

In General

Lat. A cause, reason, occasion, motive, or inducement.

As Preposition

Used with the force of a preposition, it means by virtue of, on account of. Also with reference to, in contemplation of. *Causa mortis,* in anticipation of death.

Condition, etc.

A condition; a consideration; motive for performing a juristic act. Used of contracts, and found in this sense in the Scotch law also. Bell.

In the Civil Law and in Old English Law

The word signified a source, ground, or mode of acquiring property; hence a title; one's title to property. Thus, *"titulus est justa causa possidendi id quod nostrum est;"* title is the lawful ground of possessing that which is ours. 8 Coke, 153. See Mackeld.Rom.Law, §§ 242, 283.

In Old English Law

A cause; a suit or action pending. *Causa testamentaria,* a testamentary cause. *Causa matrimonialis,* a matrimonial cause. Bract. fol. 61.

In Old European Law

Any movable thing or article of property.

See "Cause."

CAUSA CAUSÆ EST CAUSA CAUSATI. The cause of a cause is the cause of the thing caused. 12 Mod. 639. The cause of the cause is to be considered as the cause of the effect also. Freem. 329.

CAUSA CAUSANS. The immediate cause; the last link in the chain of causation.

CAUSA CAUSANTIS, CAUSA EST CAUSATI. The cause of the thing causing is the cause of the effect. 4 Camp. 284; Marble v. City of Worcester, 4 Gray, Mass., 398.

CAUSA DATA ET NON SECUTA. In the civil law. Consideration given and not followed, that is, by the event upon which it was given. The name of an action by which a thing given in the view of a certain event was reclaimed if that event did not take place. Dig. 12, 4; Cod. 4, 6.

CAUSA ECCLESIÆ PUBLICIS ÆQUIPARATUR; ET SUMMA EST RATIO QUÆ PRO RELIGIONE FACIT. The cause of the church is equal to public cause; and paramount is the reason which makes for religion. Co.Litt. 341.

CAUSA ET ORIGO EST MATERIA NEGOTII. The cause and origin is the substance of the thing; the cause and origin of a thing are a material part of it. The law regards the original act. 1 Coke, 99; Wing.Max. 41, Max. 21.

CAUSA HOSPITANDI. For the purpose of being entertained as a guest. 4 Maule & S. 310.

CAUSA JACTITATIONIS MARITAGII. A form of action which anciently lay against a party who boasted or gave out that he or she was married to the plaintiff, whereby a common reputation of their marriage might ensue. 3 Bla.Comm. 93. See Jactitation of Marriage.

CAUSA LIST. See Cause List.

CAUSA MATRIMONII PRÆLOCUTI. A writ lying where a woman has given lands to a man in fee-simple with the intention that he shall marry her, and he refuses so to do within a reasonable time, upon suitable request. Cowell. Now obsolete. 3 Bla.Comm. 183, n.

CAUSA MORTIS. In contemplation of approaching death.

CAUSA MORTIS DONATIO. See Donatio Mortis Causa.

CAUSA PATET. The reason is open, obvious, plain, clear, or manifest. A common expression in old writers. Perk. c. 1, §§ 11, 14, 97.

CAUSA PROXIMA. The immediate, nearest, or latest cause. The efficient cause; the one that necessarily sets the other causes in operation. Insurance Co. v. Boon, 95 U.S. 117, 130, 24 L.Ed. 395.

CAUSA PROXIMA NON REMOTA SPECTATUR. An efficient adequate cause being found, it must be considered the true cause unless some other independent cause is shown to have intervened between it and the result. Mead v. Chickasha Gas & Electric Co., 137 Okl. 74, 278 P. 286, 291. The immediate (or direct), not the remote, cause, is looked at, or considered. 12 East, 648; 3 Kent, Comm. 302; Memphis & C. R. Co. v. Reeves, 10 Wall. 191, 19 L.Ed. 909; L. R. 1 C. P. 320; 4 Am. L.Rev. 201. For a distinction, however, between immediate and proximate cause, see "Cause."

CAUSA REI. In the civil law. Things accessory or appurtenant. The accessions, appurtenances, or fruits of a thing; comprehending all that the claimant of a principal thing can demand from a defendant in addition thereto, and especially what he would have had, if the thing had not been withheld from him. Inst. 4, 17, 3; Mackeld. Rom.Law, § 166.

CAUSA REMOTA. A remote or mediate cause; a cause operating indirectly by the intervention of other causes.

CAUSA SCIENTIÆ PATET. The reason of the knowledge is evident. A technical phrase in Scotch practice, used in depositions of witnesses.

CAUSA SINE QUA NON. A necessary or inevitable cause; a cause without which the effect in question could not have happened. Hayes v. Railroad Co., 111 U.S. 228, 4 S.Ct. 369, 28 L.Ed. 410. A cause without which the thing cannot be. With reference to negligence, it is the cause without which the injury would not have occurred. Fisher v. Butte Electric Ry. Co., 72 Mont. 594, 235 P. 330, 332.

CAUSA TURPIS. A base (immoral or illegal) cause or consideration.

CAUSA VAGA ET INCERTA NON EST CAUSA RATIONABILIS. 5 Coke, 57. A vague and uncertain cause is not a reasonable cause.

CAUSÆ DOTIS, VITÆ, LIBERTATIS, FISCI SUNT INTER FAVORABILIA IN LEGE. Causes of dower, life, liberty, revenue, are among the things favored in law. Co.Litt. 341.

CAUSAM NOBIS SIGNIFICES QUARE. A writ addressed to a mayor of a town, etc., who was by the king's writ commanded to give seisin of lands to the king's grantee, on his delaying to do it, requiring him to show cause why he so delayed the performance of his duty. Blount; Cowell.

CAUSARE. In the civil and old English law. To be engaged in a suit; to litigate; to conduct a cause.

CAUSATOR. A litigant; one who takes the part of the plaintiff or defendant in a suit.

In old European law. One who manages or litigates another's cause. Spelman.

CAUSE, *v.* To be the cause or occasion of; to effect as an agent; to bring about; to bring into existence; to make. La Page v. U. S., C.C.A. Minn., 146 F.2d 536, 538, 156 A.L.R. 965; Huffman v. U. S., C.C.A.Colo., 259 F. 35, 38; Shea v. U. S., C.C.A.Ohio, 251 F. 440, 447. To induce; to compel. Hill v. Montgomery, 352 Mo. 147, 176 S.W. 2d 284, 287.

CAUSE, *n.* (Lat. *causa.*) Each separate antecedent of an event, Griffin v. Anderson Motor Service Co., 227 Mo.App. 855, 59 S.W.2d 805, 808.

Means, Metropolitan Life Ins. Co. v. Funderburk, Tex.Civ.App., 81 S.W.2d 132, 137. Motive, In re Canal Bank & Trust Co.'s Liquidation, 178 La. 575, 152 So. 297, 298. Probable cause, State v. Brockman, 231 Wis. 634, 283 N.W. 338, 340. Producing cause, Traders & General Insurance Co. v. Ray, Tex.Civ.App., 128 S.W.2d 80, 84. Sum of antecedents of an event, Burns v. Eminger, 84 Mont. 397, 276 P. 437, 442; Griffin v. Anderson Motor Service Co., 227 Mo.App. 855, 59 S.W.2d 805, 808. That which produces an effect; whatever moves, impels or leads. Weinberg v. Richardson, 291 Ill. App. 618, 10 N.E.2d 893; Merlo v. Public Service Co. of Northern Illinois, 381 Ill. 300, 45 N.E.2d 665, 675; State v. Craig, 161 S.C. 232, 159 S.E. 559, 560. The origin or foundation of a thing, as of a suit or action; a ground of action. State v. Dougherty, 4 Or. 203.

As used with reference to the removal of an officer or employee, "cause" means a just, not arbitrary, cause; one relating to a material matter, or affecting the public interest. Brokaw v. Burk, 89 N.J.Law, 132, 98 A. 11, 12; a cause relating to and affecting administration of office and of substantial nature directly affecting public's rights and interests, State ex rel. Rockwell v. State Board of Education, 213 Minn. 184, 6 N.W.2d 251, 260, 143 A.L.R. 503.

Conduct indicating unworthy or illegal motives or improper administration of power, Voorhees v. Kopler, 239 App.Div. 83, 265 N.Y.S. 532, 533; Tappan v. Helena Federal Savings & Loan Ass'n of Helena, Ark., 193 Ark. 1023, 104 S.W.2d 458, 459; Zurich General Accident & Liability Ins. Co. v. Kinsler, 12 Cal.2d 98, 81 P.2d 913, 915; misfeasance or nonfeasance, Schoonover v. City of Viroqua, 244 Wis. 615, 12 N.W.2d 912, 914; As used in fraternal benefit society by-law authorizing suspension of subordinate council and dissolution of its charter, "cause," means legal cause or just cause, a substantial, reasonable, or just cause. Wichita Council No. 120 of Security Ben. Ass'n v. Security Ben. Ass'n, 138 Kan. 841, 28 P.2d 976, 979, 94 A.L.R. 629.

"Cause" and "consequence" are correlative terms. Kelsey v. Rebuzzini, 87 Conn. 556, 89 A. 170, 171, 52 L.R.A., N.S., 103; In re Benson, 178 Okl. 299, 62 P.2d 962, 965.

Clause for termination of employment for "any cause" held to refer to cause justifying termination for employee's breach of contract, not arbitrarily. Parsil v. Emery, 242 App.Div. 653, 272 N.Y.S. 439, 440.

Statute permitting an award to be set aside for "cause" means for good cause or some such cause as fraud or surprise, Elsenpeter v. Potvin, 213 Minn. 129, 5 N.W.2d 499, 501.

In Civil and Scotch Law

The consideration of a contract, that is, the inducement to it, or motive of the contracting party for entering into it. Dig. 2, 14, 7; Toullier, liv. 3, tit. 3, c. 2, § 4; 1 Abb. 28; Bell, Dict.

The civilians use the term "cause," in relation to obligations, in the same sense as the word "consideration" is used in the jurisprudence of England and the United States. It means the motive, the inducement to the agreement,—*id quod inducet ad contrahendum.* Mouton v. Noble, 1 La.Ann. 192. But see Ames, 3 Sel.Essays in Anglo-Amer.Leg.Hist. 279; Poll.Contr. 74.

Used also in the civil law in the sense of *res* (a thing). *Non porcellum, non agnellum nec alia causa* (not a hog, not a lamb, nor other thing). Du Cange.

In Pleading

Reason; motive; matter of excuse or justification. See 8 Co. 67; 11 East 451; 1 Chit.Pl. 585.

In Practice

A suit, litigation, or action. Any question, civil or criminal, litigated or contested before a court of justice.

As used in venue statute, "cause" means "cause of action", which means the right which a party has to institute a judicial proceeding. Bergin v. Temple, 111 Mont. 539, 111 P.2d 286, 289, 133 A.L.R. 1115.

Cause imports a judicial proceeding entire, and is nearly synonymous with *lis* in Latin, or suit in English. "Case" not infrequently has a more limited signification, importing a collection of facts, with the conclusion of law thereon. See Shirts v. Irons, 47 Ind. 445; Erwin v. U. S., D.C. Ga., 37 Fed. 470, 2 L.R.A. 229. But "cause" and "case" are often synonymous. Zilz v. Wilcox, 190 Mich. 486, 157 N.W. 77, 80; Schmalz v. Arnwine, 118 Or. 300, 246 P. 718, 719; Cheney v. Richards, 130 Me. 288, 155 A. 642, 644.

A distinction is sometimes taken between "cause" and "action." Burrill observes that a cause is not, like an action or suit, said to be commenced, nor is an action, like a cause, said to be tried. But, if there is any substantial difference between these terms, it must lie in the fact that "action" refers more peculiarly to the *legal procedure* of a controversy; "cause" to its *merits* or the state of facts involved. Thus, we cannot say "the *cause* should have been replevin." Nor would it be correct to say "the plaintiff pleaded his own *action.*"

As to "Probable Cause" and "Proximate Cause," see those titles. As to challenge "for cause," see "Challenge."

CAUSE-BOOKS. Books kept in the central office of the English supreme court, in which are entered all writs of summons issued in the office. Rules of Court, v 8.

CAUSE LIST. In English practice. A printed roll of actions, to be tried in the order of their entry, with the names of the solicitors for each litigant. Similar to the calendar of causes, or docket, used in American courts.

CAUSE OF ACTION. A "cause of action" may mean one thing for one purpose and something different for another. Venezuelan Meat Export Co. v. U. S., D.C.Md., 12 F.Supp. 379, 383; U. S. v. Memphis Cotton Oil Co., Ct.Cl., 288 U.S. 62, 53 S. Ct. 278, 280, 77 L.Ed. 619.

It may mean: accident, Maryland Casualty Co. v. Gerlaske, C.C.A.Tex., 68 F.2d 497, 499; act causing injury, Fiscus v. Kansas City Public Service Co., 153 Kan. 493, 112 P.2d 83, 85; action, Wattman v. St. Luke's Hospital Ass'n, 314 Ill.App. 244, 41 N.E.2d 314, 319; averment of facts sufficient to justify a court in rendering a judgment, Mobley v. Smith, 24 Ala.App. 553, 138 So. 551; Vickers v. Vickers, 45 Nev. 274, 202 P. 31, 32; breach of contract or agreement, Press v. Davis, Tex.Civ.App., 118 S.W.2d 982, 989, 990; breach of duty. Shapiro v. McCarthy, 279 Mass. 425, 181 N.E. 842, 844; case, Colla v. Carmichael U-Drive Autos, 111 Cal.App. 378, 294 P. 378, 380; claim, Bishop v. Jensen, 212 Wis. 30, 248 N.W. 771, 772; East Side Mill & Lumber Co. v. Southeast Portland Lumber Co., 155 Or. 367, 64 P.2d 625, 627, 628; concept of law of remedies. Rooney v. Maczko, 315 Pa. 113, 172 A. 151, 153; U. S. v. Memphis Cotton Oil Co., Ct.Cl., 288 U.S. 62, 53 S.Ct. 278, 280, 77 L.Ed. 619; concurrence of the facts giving rise to enforceable claim, United States v. Standard Oil Co. of California, D.C.Cal., 21 F.Supp. 645, 660; contract, Stone Fort Nat. Bank of Nacogdoches v. Forbess, 126 Tex. 568, 91 S.W.2d 674; demand, State v. Vincent, 152 Or. 205, 52 P.2d 203, 206; every fact which it is necessary to establish to support right or obtain judgment, Beale v. Cherryhomes, Tex.Civ.App., 21 S.W.2d 65, 66; Dublin Mill & Elevator Co. v. Cornelius, Tex.Civ.App., 5 S.W.2d 1027, 1028; fact, or a state of facts to which law, sought to be enforced against a person or thing, applies. Gulf, C. & S. F. Ry. Co v. Cities Service Co., D.C.Del., 270 F. 994, 995; Condor Petroleum Co. v. Greene, Tex.Civ.App., 164 S.W.2d 713, 718; Burns v. Duncan, 23 Tenn.App. 374, 133 S.W.2d 1000, 1004; facts constituting wrong, Whalen v. Strong, 230 App.Div. 617, 246 N.Y.S. 40, 45; facts which give rise to one or more relations of right-duty between two or more persons, Elliott v. Mosgrove, 162 Or. 507, 93 P.2d 1070, 1072, 1073, 1076; failure to perform legal obligation to do, or refrain from performance of, some act, In re Canfield's Will, 165 Misc. 66, 300 N.Y.S. 502; ground on which an action may be maintained or sustained, ground or reason for an action, East Side Mill & Lumber Co. v. Southeast Portland Lumber Co., 155 Or. 367, 64 P.2d 625, 627, 628. Juncture of wrong and damage, City of Newport v. Rawlings, 289 Ky. 203, 158 S.W.2d 12, 14; legal duty and breach of duty, Alford v. Zeigler, 65 Ga.App. 294, 16 S.E.2d 69, 74; legal liability arising out of facts, White v. Nemours Trading Corporation, D.C.Mass., 290 F. 250, 252; legal obligation, Hartford Accident & Indemnity Co. v. Clegg, 103 Utah 414, 135 P.2d 919, 922, 923; legal right in plaintiff and duty in defendant and violation or breach of right or duty, Evans v. Williams, 291 Ky. 484, 165 S.W.2d 52, 54; legal right of action. Inhabitants of Town of Milo v. Milo Water Co., 129 Me. 463, 152 A. 616, 617; legal right violated, Howard v. Brown, 172 Okl. 308, 44 P.2d 959, 961; legal wrong threatened or committed, Connor v. Williams, 187 S.C. 119, 197 S.E. 211, 214; matter for which action may be brought, Ex parte Teeters, 130 Or. 631, 280 P. 660, 662; Williams v. City of Dallas, Tex.Civ.App., 52 S.W.2d 373, 375; negligent act or acts, Cox v. Wilkes-Barre R. Corporation, 334 Pa. 568, 6 A.2d 538, 539; obligation, United States v. Standard Oil Co. of California, D.C.Cal., 21 F.Supp. 645, 660; occurrence which gives rise to litigation, Maryland Casualty Co. v. Gerlaske, C.C.A.Tex., 68 F.2d 497, 499; particular matter for which suit is brought, Severance v. Heyl & Patterson, 115 Pa.Super. 36, 174 A. 787, 789; power to enforce obligation, Woods v. Cook, 14 Cal.App.2d 560, 58 P.2d 965, 966; primary right and corresponding duty and delict or wrong, Vasu v. Kohlers, Inc., 145 Ohio St. 321, 61 N.E.2d 707, 714; redressible wrong, Meshek v. Cordes, 164 Okl. 40, 22 P.2d 921, 926; or breach of duty by defendant, Skalowski v. Joe Fisher, Inc., 152 S.C. 108, 149 S.E. 340, 344, 65 A.L.R. 1427; American Nat. Ins. Co. v. Warnock, Tex.Civ.App., 143 S.W.2d 624, 628; right of action or right of recovery, Williams v. City of Dallas, Tex.Civ.App., 52 S.W. 2d 373, 375; Graham v. Scripture, 26 How.Prac., N.Y., 501; right to bring suit, Viers v. Webb, 76 Mont. 38, 245 P. 257, 259; Grenada Bank v. Petty, 174 Miss. 415, 164 So. 316, 318; right to enforce obligations, Woods v. Cook, 14 Cal.App.2d 560, 58 P.2d 965, 966; right to prosecute an action with effect, Travelers' Ins. Co. v. Louis Padula Co., 224 N.Y. 397, 121 N.E. 348, 350; right to recover something from another, Universal Oil Products Co. v. Standard Oil Co. of Indiana, D.C.Mo., 6 F.Supp. 37, 39; right to relief in court, Kittinger v. Churchill Evangelistic Ass'n, 239 App.Div. 253, 267 N.Y.S. 719, 722; Mulligan v. Bond & Mortgage Guarantee Co., 193 App.Div. 741, 184 N.Y.S. 429, 431; subject matter of the controversy, Johnson v. Jordan, D.C.Okl., 22 F.Supp. 286, 289; subject-matter on which plaintiff grounds his right of recovery, Zelen v. Domestic Industries, 131 Neb. 123, 267 N.W. 352, 354; East Side Mill & Lumber Co. v. Southeast Portland Lumber Co., 155 Or. 367, 64 P.2d 625, 627, 628; that which creates necessity for bringing action, Brevick v. Cunard S. S. Co., 63 N.D. 210, 247 N.W. 373, 375; that which produces or effects result complained of, Jacobson v. Mutual Ben. Health & Accident Ass'n, 73 N.D. 108, 11 N.W.2d 442, 445, 446; unlawful violation of a right. Keith v. Texas & P. R. Co., 14 La.App. 290, 129 So. 190, 194; violation or invasion of right, East Side Lumber & Coal Co. v. Barfield, 193 Ga. 273, 18 S.E.2d 492, 496; wrong committed or threatened, Criswell v. Criswell, 101 Neb. 349, 165 N.W. 302.

It may sometimes mean a person having a right of action. Thus, where a legacy is left to a married woman, and she and her husband bring an action to recover it, she is called in the old books the "meritorious cause of action." 1 H.Bl. 108.

A distinction may be taken between "cause of action" and "right of action." Elliott v. Chicago, M. & St. P. Ry. Co., 35 S.D. 57, 150 N.W. 777, 779. The cause of action is distinct from the "remedy." Tonn v. Inner Shoe Tire Co., Tex.Civ.App., 260 S.W. 1078, 1080. And the cause of action may exist, though the remedy does not. Chandler v. Horne, 23 Ohio App. 1, 154 N.E. 748, 750.

Cause of action is not synonymous with chose in action. Bank of Commerce v. Rutland & W. R. Co., 10 How.Prac., N.Y., 1. But under a Montana statute, if the relief sought is the recovery of money or other personal property, the cause of action is designated a "thing in action." State v. District Court of Tenth Judicial Dist. in and for Fergus County, 74 Mont. 355, 240 P. 667, 669.

CAUSE OF INJURY. That which actually produces it, Anderson v. Byrd, 133 Neb. 483, 275 N. W. 825, 826.

CAUSE SUIT TO BE BROUGHT. Commence or begin, State v. Osen, 67 N.D. 436, 272 N.W. 783, 784.

CAUSES CÉLÈBRES. Celebrated cases. A work containing reports of the decisions of interest and importance in French courts in the seventeenth and eighteenth centuries.

Secondarily a single trial or decision is often called a *"cause célèbre,"* when it is remarkable on account of the parties involved or the unusual, interesting, or sensational character of the facts.

CAUSEWAY. A raised roadbed through low lands; it differs from a levee. Board of Sup'rs of Quitman County v. Carrier Lumber & Mfg. Co., 103 Miss. 324, 60 So. 326, 327. See, also, Coleman-Fulton Pasture Co. v. Aransas County, Tex.Civ. App., 180 S.W. 312, 313.

CAUSIDICUS. In the civil law. A speaker or pleader; one who argued a cause *ore tenus*. See "Advocate."

CAUTELA. Lat. Care; caution; vigilance; prevision.

CAUTI JURATORIA. See "Caution Juratory."

CAUTIO. In the Civil and French law. Security given for the performance of any thing; bail; a bond or undertaking by way of surety. Also the person who becomes a surety.

In Scotch law. A pledge, bond, or other security for the performance of an obligation, or completion of the satisfaction to be obtained by a judicial process. Bell, Dict.; 6 Mod. 162.

CAUTIO FIDEJUSSORIA. Security by means of bonds or pledges entered into by third parties. Du Cange.

CAUTIO MUCIANA. Security given by an heir or legatee, to obtain immediate possession of inheritance or legacy, for observance of a condition annexed to the bequest, where the act which is the object of the condition is one which he must avoid committing during his whole life, *e. g.*, that he will never marry, never leave the country, never engage in a particular trade, etc. See Mackeld. Rom.Law, § 705.

CAUTIO PIGNORATITIA. Security given by pledge, or deposit, as plate, money, or other goods.

CAUTIO PRO EXPENSIS. Security for costs, charges, or expenses.

CAUTIO USUFRUCTUARIA. Security, which tenants for life give, to preserve the property rented free from waste and injury. Ersk.Inst. 2, 9, 59.

CAUTION. In Scotch law, and in admiralty law. Surety; security; bail; an undertaking by way of surety. 6 Mod. 162. See Cautio. See also Prudence; Cautious.

To warn, exhort, to take heed, or give notice of danger. Arnold v. United States, C.C.A.Colo., 94 F.2d 499, 501.

CAUTION JURATORY. In Scotch law. Security given by oath. That which a suspender swears is the best he can afford in order to obtain a suspension. Ersk.Pract. 4, 3, 6.

CAUTIONARY. In Scotch law. An instrument in which a person binds himself as surety for another.

CAUTIONARY JUDGMENT. Where an action in tort was pending and the plaintiff feared the defendant would dispose of his real property before judgment, a cautionary judgment was entered with a lien on the property; Seisner v. Blake, 13 Pa.Co.Ct.R. 333; so in an action on a note against a religious association, where it was alleged that the defendant was endeavoring to sell its real estate before judgment on the note; Witmer & Dundore v. Port Treverton Church, 17 Pa.Co.Ct.R. 38.

CAUTIONE ADMITTENDA. In English ecclesiastical law. A writ that lies against a bishop who holds an excommunicated person in prison for contempt, notwithstanding he offers sufficient caution or security to obey the orders and commandment of the church for the future. Reg.Orig. 66; Cowell.

CAUTIONER. In Scotch law. A surety; a bondsman. One who binds himself in a bond with the principal for greater security. He is still a cautioner whether the bond be to pay a debt, or whether he undertake to produce the person of the party for whom he is bound. Bell.

CAUTIONNEMENT. In French law. The same as becoming surety in English law.

CAUTIONRY. In Scotch law. Suretyship.

CAUTIOUS. Careful; prudent. Horton v. New York Cent. R. Co., 205 App.Div. 763, 200 N.Y.S. 365, 366.

The terms "cautious" and "prudent" may be used interchangeably in defining negligence. Malcolm v. Mooresville Cotton Mills, 191 N.C. 727, 133 S.E. 7, 9. But "cautious" differs from "prudent" in suggesting the idea of timidity, with its secondary meaning as overprudent; fearful. People v. Anderson, 58 Cal.App. 267, 208 P. 324, 325. See Prudence.

CAVEAT. Lat. Let him beware.

An intimation to a judge or officer notifying him to suspend a proceeding until merits of the caveat are determined. In re Phillips' Estate, 293 Pa. 351, 143 A. 9. A formal notice or warning given by a party interested to a court, judge, or ministerial officer against the performance of certain acts within his power and jurisdiction. This process may be used in the proper courts to prevent (temporarily or provisionally) the proving of a will or the grant of administration, or to arrest the enrollment of a decree in chancery when the party intends to take an appeal, to prevent the grant of letters patent, etc. It is also used, in the American practice, as a kind of equitable process, to stay the granting of a patent for lands. Ex parte Crafts, 28 S.C. 281, 5 S.E. 718; In re McCahan's Estate, 221 Pa. 188, 70 A. 711; See, also, 1 Burn, Eccl.Law 19, 263; Nelson, Abr.; Dane, Abr.; Ayliffe, *Parerg.;* 3 Bla. Comm. 246; 2 Chit.Pr. 502, note *b;* 3 Redf.Wills 119; Poph. 133; 1 Sid. 371.

In patent law. A formal written notice to officers of the patent-office, requiring them to refuse letters patent on a particular invention or device to any other person, until the party filing the caveat (called the "caveator") shall have an opportunity to establish his claim to priority of invention. The practice was abolished by act of June 25, 1910, c. 414, § 1, 36 Stat. 843.

CAVEAT ACTOR. Let the doer, or actor, beware.

CAVEAT EMPTOR. Let the buyer beware (or take care). Kellogg Bridge Co. v. Hamilton, 110 U.S. 108, 116, 3 S.Ct. 537, 28 L.Ed. 86.

This maxim summarizes the rule that a purchaser must examine, judge, and test for himself, Miller v. Tiffany, 1 Wall. 309, 17 L.Ed. 540; Hargous v. Stone, 5 N.Y. 82; Humphrey v. Baker, 71 Okl. 272, 176 P. 896; the purchaser at sheriff's sales must inform himself of extent of judgment debtor's title, Brightwell v. First Nat. Bank, C.C.A.Fla., 109 F.2d 271, 273; the purchaser takes risk of quality and condition unless he protects himself by a warranty or there has been a false representation, State ex rel. Jones Store Co. v. Shain, Mo., 179 S.W.2d 19, 20. There is no warranty of title. McKnight v. Johnson, 236 Ky. 763, 34 S.W.2d 239, 240.

CAVEAT EMPTOR, QUI IGNORARE NON DEBUIT QUOD JUS ALIENUM EMIT. Hob. 99. Let a purchaser beware, who ought not to be ignorant that he is purchasing the rights of another. Let a buyer beware; for he ought not to be ignorant of what they are when he buys the rights of another. Broom, Max. 768; Co.Litt. 132 *a*; 3 Taunt. 439; Sugd. V. & P. 328; 1 Story, Eq.Jur. ch. 6.

CAVEAT TO WILL. A demand that will be produced and probated in open court. An attack on validity of alleged will. Whitehurst v. Abbott, 225 N.C. 1, 33 S.E.2d 129, 132.

CAVEAT VENDITOR.

In Roman law. A maxim, or rule, casting the responsibility for defects or deficiencies upon the *seller* of goods. See Hargous v. Stone, 5 N.Y. 73.

In English and American Jurisprudence. *Caveat venditor* is sometimes used as expressing, in a rough way, the rule which governs all those cases of sales to which *caveat emptor* does not apply.

CAVEAT VIATOR. Let the wayfarer beware. Broom, Max. 387, n.; 10 Exch. 774. This phrase has been used as a concise expression of the duty of a traveler on the highway to use due care to detect and avoid defects in the way. Cornwell v. Com'rs, 10 Exch. 771, 774.

CAVEATOR. One who files a caveat.

CAVENDUM EST A FRAGMENTIS. Beware of fragments. Bac.Aph. 26.

CAVERE. Lat. In the civil and common law. To take care; to exercise caution; to take care or provide for; to provide by law; to provide against; to forbid by law; to give security; to give caution or security on arrest.

CAVERS. Persons stealing ore from mines in Derbyshire, punishable in the berghmote or miners' court; also officers belonging to the same mines. Wharton.

CAYA. In old English law. A quay, kay, key, or wharf. Cowell.

CAYAGIUM. In old English law. Cayage or kayage; a toll or duty anciently paid the king for landing goods at a quay or wharf. The barons of the Cinque Ports were free from this duty. Cowell.

CEAP. A bargain; anything for sale; a chattel; also cattle, as being the usual medium of barter. Sometimes used instead of ceapgild, (*q. v.*).

CEAPGILD. Payment or forfeiture of an animal. An ancient species of forfeiture. Cowell.

CEASE. To stop; to become extinct; to pass away; to come to an end. MacDonald v. Ætna Indemnity Co., 90 Conn. 226, 96 A. 926, 927; Martin v. Gray, 193 Ark. 32, 97 S.W. 439, 441. Suspend or forfeit. Marks v. La Guardia, Sup., 31 N.Y.S.2d 336, 350. A cessation of activity. Huasteca Petroleum Co. v. Cia de Navegacao Lloyd Brasileiro, D.C.N.Y., 297 F. 318, 321; In re Simpson, 62 Cal.App. 549, 217 P. 789, 790.

City of Macon v. Bunch, 156 Ga. 27, 118 S.E. 769, held that a city detective, by being kept in jail for 31 days to answer an indictment, did not cease to perform the duties of his office so as to cause a vacancy therein.

CEASE TO DO BUSINESS. A going concern ceases to do business when it sells all its property, plant, assets of all kinds, including cash, and the buyer takes possession. Van Oss v. Premier Petroleum Co., 113 Me. 180, 93 A. 72, 77.

CEDE. To yield up; to assign; to grant. Generally used to designate the transfer of territory from one government to another. Goetze v. United States, C.C.N.Y., 103 Fed. 72; Baltimore v. Turnpike Road, 80 Md. 535, 31 A. 420.

CEDENT. In Scotch law. An assignor. One who transfers a chose in action. Kames, Eq. 43.

CEDO. I grant. The word ordinarily used in Mexican conveyances to pass title to lands. Mulford v. Le Franc, 26 Cal. 88, 108.

CEDULA.

In old English law. A schedule.

In Spanish law. An act under private signature, by which a debtor admits the amount of the debt, and binds himself to discharge the same on a specified day or on demand. Also the notice or citation affixed to the door of a fugitive criminal requiring him to appear before the court where the accusation is pending.

CEDULE. In French law. The technical name of an act under private signature. Campbell v. Nicholson, 3 La.Ann. 458.

CELATION. In medical jurisprudence. Concealment of pregnancy or delivery.

CELDRA. In old English law, a chaldron. In old Scotch law, a measure of grain, otherwise called a "chalder." See 1 Kames, Eq. 215.

CELEBRATION OF MARRIAGE. The formal act by which a man and woman take each other for husband and wife, according to law; the solemnization of a marriage. The term is usually applied to a marriage ceremony attended with ecclesiastical functions. See Pearson v. Howey, 11 N.J. Law, 19.

CELIBACY. The condition or state of life of an unmarried person.

CELLERARIUS. A butler in a monastery; sometimes in universities called "manciple" or "caterer."

CEMETERY. A graveyard; burial ground. Peterson v. Stolz, Tex.Civ.App., 269 S.W. 113, 117; Village of Villa Park v. Wanderer's Rest Cemetery Co., 316 Ill. 226, 147 N.E. 104, 105. Place or area set apart for interment of the dead. City of Wichita v. Schwertner, 130 Kan. 397, 286 P. 266, 268, Damon v. State, Tex.Com.App., 52 S.W.2d 368, 370.

Term includes not only lots for depositing the bodies of the dead, but also avenues, walks, and grounds for shrubbery and ornamental purposes. Ex parte Adlof, 86 Tex. Cr.R. 13, 215 S.W. 222, 223. Town of Blooming Grove v. Roselawn Memorial Park Co., 231 Wis. 492, 286 N.W. 43, 45. A place of burial, differing from a churchyard by its locality and incidents. Wharton. See Winters v. State, 9 Ind. 174; Cemetery Ass'n v. New Haven, 43 Conn. 243, 21 Am.Rep. 643.

Six or more human bodies being buried at one place constitutes the place a cemetery.

CEMETERY WORK. Platting, grading, planting, beautifying, and maintaining a tract of land in such manner as to render it a proper place for sepulture of the dead, and to preserve it as such. Rosedale Cemetery Ass'n v. Industrial Accident Commission of California, 37 Cal.App. 706, 174 P. 351, 352.

CENDULÆ. Small pieces of wood laid in the form of tiles to cover the roof of a house; shingles. Cowell.

CENEGILD. In Saxon law. An expiatory mulct or fine paid to the relations of a murdered person by the murderer or his relations. Spelman.

CENELLÆ. In old records. Acorns.

CENNINGA. A notice given by a buyer to a seller that the things which had been sold were claimed by another, in order that he might appear and justify the sale. Blount; Whishaw. But the exact significance of this term is somewhat doubtful. Spelman, Gloss.

CENS. In French Canadian law. An annual tribute or due reserved to a seignior or lord, and imposed merely in recognition of his superiority. Guyot, Inst. c. 9. The *cens* varies in amount and in mode of payment. 2 Low.C. 40. See Censive; Censitaire.

CENSARIA. In old English law. A farm, or house and land let at a standing rent. Cowell.

CENSARII. In old English law. Farmers, or such persons as were liable to pay a census, (tax.) Blount; Cowell.

CENSERE. In the Roman law. To ordain; to decree. Dig. 50, 16, 111.

CENSITAIRE. In Canadian law. A tenant by *cens, (q. v.)*

CENSIVE. In Canadian law. Tenure by *cens, (q. v.)*

CENSO. In Spanish and Mexican law. An annuity. A ground rent. The right which a person acquires to receive a certain annual pension, for the delivery which he makes to another of a determined sum of money or of an immovable thing. Civ.Code Mex. art. 3206. See Schm.Civil Law, 149, 309; White, New Recop. bk. 2, c. 7, § 4.

CENSO AL QUITAR. A redeemable annuity; otherwise called "censo redimible." Trevino v. Fernandez, 13 Tex. 630.

CENSO CONSIGNATIVO. A *censo (q. v.)* is called *"consignativo"* when he who receives the money assigns for the payment of the pension (annuity) the estate the fee in which he reserves. Civ.Code Mex. art. 3207.

CENSO ENFITEUTICO. In Spanish and Mexican law. An emphyteutic annuity. That species of *censo* (annuity) which exists where there is a right to require of another a certain canon or pension annually, on account of having transferred to that person forever certain real estate, but reserving the fee in the land. The owner who thus transfers the land is called the *"censualisto,"* and the person who pays the annuity is called the *"censatario."* Hall, Mex.Law, § 756; Hart v. Burnett, 15 Cal. 557.

CENSO RESERVATIO. In Spanish and Mexican law. The right to receive from another an annual pension by virtue of having transferred land to him by full and perfect title. Trevino v. Fernandez, 13 Tex. 655.

CENSORSHIP. The denial of right of "freedom of the press" and of right of "freedom of speech", and of all those rights and privileges which are had under a free government. Esquire, Inc., v. Walker, D.C.D.C., 55 F.Supp. 1015, 1020.

CENSUALES. In old European law. A species of *oblati* or voluntary slaves of churches or monasteries; those who, to procure the protection of the church, bound themselves to pay an annual tax or quit-rent only of their estates to a church or monastery.

CENSUERE. In Roman law. They have decreed. The term of art, or technical term for the judgment, resolution, or decree of the senate. Tayl. Civil Law, 566.

CENSUMETHIDUS, or CENSUMORTHIDUS. A dead rent, like that which is called "mortmain." Blount; Cowell.

CENSURE. In ecclesiastical law. A spiritual punishment.

It consists in withdrawing from a baptized person (whether belonging to the clergy or the laity) a privilege which the church gives him, or in wholly expelling him from the Christian communion. The principal varieties of censures are admonition, degradation, deprivation, excommunication, penance, sequestration, suspension. Phillim. Ecc.Law, 1367.

A custom observed in certain manors in Devon and Cornwall, where all persons above the age of sixteen years are cited to swear fealty to the lord, and to pay 11d. per poll, and 1d. per annum.

CENSUS. The official counting or enumeration of people of a state, nation or district, Huntington v. Cast, 149 Ind. 255, 48 N.E. 1025; Republic v. Paris, 10 Hawaii, 581; Vale Independent Consol. School Dist. No. 2 of Butte County v. School Dist. No. 71 of Meade County, 54 S.D. 207, 222 N.W. 948. It is a finding of the population and not an "estimate." State ex rel. Reynolds v. Jost, 265 Mo. 51, 175 S.W. 591, 597, Ann.Cas.1917D, 1102.

In Roman law. A numbering or enrollment of the people, with a valuation of their fortunes.

In old European law. A tax, or tribute; a toll. Montesq. Esprit des Lois, liv. 30, c. 14.

CENSUS REGALIS. In English law. The annual revenue or income of the crown.

CENT. A coin of the United States, the least in value of those now minted. It is the hundredth part of a dollar. Its weight is 48 gr., and it is composed of ninety-five per centum of copper and of five per centum of tin and zinc in such proportions as shall be determined by the Director of the Mint. Act of Feb. 12, 1873, § 16. See Rev.Stat. § 3515, 31 U.S.C.A. § 317.

CENTAL. A weight of 100 pounds avoirdupois, used at Liverpool for corn. Cent.Dict. Usually called *hundredweight* in the United States.

CENTENA. A hundred. A district or division containing originally a hundred freemen, established among the Goths, Germans, Franks, and Lombards, for military and civil purposes, and answering to the Saxon "hundred." Spelman; 1 Bl.Comm. 115.

Also, in old records and pleadings, a hundred weight.

CENTENARII. Petty judges, under-sheriffs of counties, that had rule of a hundred, (*centena,*) and judged smaller matters among them. 1 Vent. 211.

CENTENI. The principal inhabitants of a *centena,* or district composed of different villages, originally in number a hundred, but afterwards only called by that name.

CENTER. This term is often used, not in its strict sense of a geographical or mathematical center, but as meaning the middle or central point or portion of anything. Bass v. Harden, 160 Ga. 400, 128 S.E. 397, 400; Hill v. Ralph, 165 Ark. 524, 265 S.W. 57, 58; Darnell v. Ransdall, Mo.App., 277 S.W. 372, 373.

The center of a section of land is the intersection of a straight line from the north quarter corner to the south quarter corner with a straight line from the east quarter corner to the west quarter corner. Lunz v. Sandmeier's Estate, 172 Minn. 338, 215 N.W. 426. Similarly, the center of a street intersection refers to the point where the center lines of the two streets cross. Thrush v. Lingo Lumber Co., Tex.Civ.App., 262 S.W. 551, 552. The edges of the hardened surface of a road constitute the "bounds of the highway" in determining "center" of highway at an intersection. Decker v. Roberts, 126 Conn. 478, 12 A.2d 541, 543. The center of the main channel of a river, is the middle of broad and distinctly defined bed of main river. Hill City Compress Co. v. West Kentucky Coal Co., 155 Miss. 55, 122 So. 747, 748.

CENTESIMA. In Roman law. The hundredth part.

Usuriæ centesimæ. Twelve per cent. per annum; that is, a hundredth part of the principal was due each month, —the month being the unit of time from which the Romans reckoned interest. 2 Bl.Comm. 462, note.

CENTIME. The name of a denomination of French money, being the one-hundredth part of a franc.

CENTRAL CRIMINAL COURT. Since 1834, an English court, having jurisdiction for the trial of crimes and misdemeanors committed in London and certain adjoining parts of Kent, Essex, and Sussex, and of such other criminal cases as may be sent to it out of the king's bench superseded the "Old Bailey."

CENTRAL OFFICE. The central office of the supreme court of judicature in England is the office established in pursuance of the recommendation of the legal departments commission in order to consolidate certain offices. It is divided into departments. Sweet.

CENTRAL STATION. A plant at which electric current is generated to supply consumers. People ex rel. Taylor v. Walsh, 140 Misc. 25, 248 N.Y.S. 753, 757.

CENTRAL TRAFFIC CONTROL. A system of railroad operation for directing the movement of trains by signals controlled from a central point. Van Schaick v. McCarthy, C.C.A.Colo., 116 F.2d 987, 990.

CENTRAL VISION. The exact and clear vision of the thing one looks directly at. Baugh v. Glassell-Rogers Drilling Co., La.App., 190 So. 130, 132.

CENTRALIZATION. The system of government in a country where management of local matters is in the hands of functionaries appointed by the ministers of state, paid by the state, and in constant communication and under the constant control and inspiration of the ministers of state, and where the funds of the state are largely applied to local purposes. Wharton.

CENTUMVIRI. In Roman law. The name of an important court consisting of a body of one hundred and five judges. 3 Bla.Comm. 515.

CENTURY. One hundred. A body of one hundred men. The Romans were divided into *centuries* as the English were divided into hundreds.

Also a cycle of one hundred years.

CEORL. In Anglo Saxon law. A class of freemen personally free, but possessing no landed property. Guizot, Rep.Govt.

A tenant at will of free condition, who held land of the thane on condition of paying rent or services. Cowell.

A freeman of inferior rank occupied in husbandry. Spelman.

Under the Norman rule, this term, as did others which denoted workmen, especially those which applied to the conquered race, became a term of reproach, as is indicated by the popular signification of churl. Cowell; 1 Poll. & Maitl. 8; 2 *id.* 458.

CEPI. Lat. I have taken. This word was of frequent use in the returns of sheriffs when they were made in Latin, and particularly in the return to a writ of *capias.*

The full return (in Latin) to a writ of *capias* was commonly made in one of the following forms: *Cepi corpus,* I have taken the body, i. e., arrested the body of the defendant: *Cepi corpus et bail,* I have taken the body and released the defendant on a bail-bond; *Cepi corpus et committitur,* I have taken the body and he has been committed (to prison); *Cepi corpus et est in custodia,* I have taken the defendant and he is in custody; *Cepi corpus et est languidus,* I have taken the defendant and he is sick, i. e., so sick that he cannot safely be removed from the place where the arrest was made; *Cepi corpus et paratum habeo,* I have taken the body and have it (him) ready, i. e., in custody and ready to be produced when ordered.

CEPIT.

In civil practice. He took. This was the characteristic word employed in (Latin) writs of trespass for goods taken, and in declarations in trespass and replevin.

Replevin *in the cepit* is a form of replevin which is brought for carrying away goods merely. Wells, Repl. § 53; Ford v. Ford, 3 Wis. 399.

In criminal practice. A technical word necessary in an indictment for larceny. The charge must be that the defendant took the thing stolen with a felonious design. Bac.Abr. "Indictment," G, 1.

CEPIT ET ABDUXIT. He took and led away. The emphatic words in writs in trespass or indictments for larceny, where the thing taken was a living chattel, *i. e.,* an animal.

CEPIT ET ASPORTAVIT. He took and carried away. Applicable in a declaration in trespass or an indictment for larceny where the defendant has carried away goods without right. 4 Bl. Comm. 231.

CEPIT IN ALIO LOCO. In pleading. A plea in replevin, by which the defendant alleges that he took the thing replevied in another place than that mentioned in the declaration. 1 Chit.Pl. 490; Rast.Entr. 554, 555; Morris, Repl. 141; Wells Repl. § 707.

CEPPAGIUM. In old English law. The stumps or roots of trees which remain in the ground after the trees are felled. Fleta, lib. 2, c. 41, § 24.

CERA, or CERE. In old English law. Wax; a seal.

CERA IMPRESSA. Lat. An impressed seal.

It may include an impression made on wafers or other adhesive substances capable of receiving an impression, or even paper. Pierce v. Indseth, 106 U.S. 546, 1 S.Ct. 418, 27 L.Ed. 254.

CERAGRUM. In old English law. A payment to provide candles in the church. Blount.

CEREVISA. In old English law. Ale or beer.

CERT MONEY. In old English law. Head money or common fine. Money paid yearly by the residents of several manors to the lords thereof, for the certain keeping of the leet, *(pro certo letæ;)* and sometimes to the hundred. Blount; 6 Coke, 78; Cowell.

CERTA DEBET ESSE INTENTIO, ET NARRATIO, ET CERTUM FUNDAMENTUM, ET CERTA RES QUÆ DEDUCITUR IN JUDICIUM. The design and narration ought to be certain, and the foundation certain, and the matter certain, which is brought into court to be tried. Co.Litt. 303*a*.

CERTA RES. In old English law. A certain thing. Fleta, lib. 2, c. 60, §§ 24, 25.

CERTAIN. Ascertained; precise; identified; definitive; clearly known; unambiguous; or, in law, capable of being identified or made known, without liability to mistake or ambiguity, from data already given. Losecco v. Gregory, 108 La. 648, 32 So. 986; White v. Wadhams, 204 Mich. 381, 170 N.W. 60, 62. Not specifically named; indeterminate, indefinite; one or some. Wilhite v. Armstrong, 328 Mo. 1064, 43 S.W.2d 422, 423. Some among possible others, In re Mineral Lac Paint Co., D.C.Pa., 17 F.Supp. 1, 2. That which may be made certain. Brown v. City of Shreveport, La. App., 15 So.2d 234, 236; Singer v. Campbell, 217 Ky. 830, 290 S.W. 667, 668; Civ.Code La. art. 3556; Lee v. Pearson, La.App., 143 So. 516, 518.

CERTAIN SERVICES. In feudal and old English law. Such services as were stinted (limited or defined) in quantity, and could not be exceeded on any pretense; as to pay a stated annual rent, or to plow such a field for three days. 2 Bl.Comm. 61.

CERTAINTY. Absence of doubt. Bennett v. McKrell, Tex.Civ.App., 125 S.W.2d 701, 707.

In Pleading

Distinctness; clearness of statement; particularity.

Such precision and explicitness in the statement of alleged facts that the pleader's averments and contention may be readily understood by the pleader on the other side, as well as by the court and jury. State v. Burke, 151 Mo. 143, 52 S.W. 226.

This word is technically used in pleading in two different senses, signifying either distinctness, or particularity, as opposed to undue generality.

Certainty is said to be of three sorts: (1) *Certainty to a common intent* is such as is attained by using words in their ordinary meaning, but is not exclusive of another meaning which might be made out by argument or inference. See 2 H.Bla. 530; Andr.Steph.Pl. 384. (2) *Certainty to a certain intent in general* is that which allows of no misunderstanding if a fair and reasonable construction is put upon the language employed, without bringing in facts which are possible, but not apparent. 1 Wms. Saund. 49; Fuller v. Hampton, 5 Conn. 423. (3) *Certainty to a certain intent in particular* is the highest degree of technical accuracy and precision. Co.Litt. 303; 2 H.Bl. 530; State v. Parker, 34 Ark. 158, 36 Am.Rep. 5; Lawes, Pl. 54. These definitions, which have been adopted from Coke, have been subjected to severe criticism, but are of some utility in drawing attention to the different degrees of exactness and fulness of statement required in different instances. 13 East, 112; 3 Maule & S. 14; People v. Dunlap, 13 Johns., N.Y., 437.

In Contracts

The quality of being specific, accurate, and distinct. As to uncertainty of contract, see Davie v. Min. Co., 93 Mich. 491, 53 N.W. 625, 24 L.R.A. 357; Van Schaick v. Van Buren, 70 Hun, 575, 24 N.Y.S. 306.

A thing is certain when its essence, quality, and quantity are described, distinctly set forth, etc. Dig. 12, 1, 6. It is uncertain when the description is not that of an individual object, but designates only the kind. Civ.Code La. art. 3556, par. 7; 5 Coke, 121.

In Determining Negotiability of Instrument

That is certain which may be rendered certain; a commercial, and not mathematical, certainty. Gerrish v. Atlantic Ice & Coal Co., C.C.A.Ga., 80 F. 2d 648, 650.

CERTIFICANDO DE RECOGNITIONE STAPULÆ. In English law. A writ commanding the mayor of the staple to certify to the lord chancellor a statute-staple taken before him where the party himself detains it, and refuses to bring in the same. There is a like writ to certify a statute-merchant, and in divers other cases. Reg.Orig. 148, 151, 152.

CERTIFICATE. A document in use in the English customhouse. No goods can be exported *by certificate*, except foreign goods formerly imported, on which the whole or a part of the customs paid on importation is to be drawn back. Wharton.

A ticket. Hall v. U. S., D.C.Cal., 10 F.Supp. 739, 740.

A warrant. Graham v. State, 123 Tex.Cr.R. 121, 57 S.W.2d 850, 854.

A written assurance, or official representation, that some act has or has not been done, or some event occurred, or some legal formality been complied with.

A written assurance made or issuing from some court, and designed as a notice of things done therein, or as a warrant or authority, to some other court, judge, or officer. People v. Foster, 27 Misc.Rep. 576, 58 N.Y.S. 574; U. S. v. Ambrose, 108 U.S. 336, 2 S.Ct. 682, 27 L.Ed. 746. A statement of some fact in a writing signed by the party certifying. Nowell v. Mayor and Council of Monroe, 177 Ga. 648, 171 S.E. 136, 141. A declaration in writing. Ballen & Friedman v. Bank of Krenlin, 37 Okl. 112, 130 P. 539, 540, 44 L.R.A.,N.S., 621. A "certificate" by a public officer is a statement written and signed, but not necessarily or customarily sworn to, which is by law made evidence of the truth of the facts stated for all or for certain purposes. State v. Abernethy, 190 N.C. 768, 130 S.E. 619, 620.

A writing by which testimony is given that a fact has or has not taken place. Laclede Land & Improvement Co. v. Morten, 183 Mo.App. 637, 167 S.W. 658.

CERTIFICATE FOR COSTS. In English practice. A certificate or memorandum drawn up and signed by the judge before whom a case was tried, setting out certain facts the existence of which must be thus proved before the party is entitled, under the statutes, to recover costs.

CERTIFICATE INTO CHANCERY. In English practice. This is a document containing the opinion of the common-law judges on a question of law submitted to them for their decision by the chancery court.

CERTIFICATE LANDS. In Pennsylvania, in the period succeeding the revolution, lands set apart in the western portion of the state, which might be bought with the certificates which the soldiers of that state in the revolutionary army had received in lieu of pay. Cent. Dict.

CERTIFICATE OF ACKNOWLEDGMENT. The certificate of a notary public, justice of the peace, or other authorized officer, attached to a deed, mortgage, or other instrument, setting forth that the parties thereto personally appeared before him on such a date and acknowledged the instrument to be their free and voluntary act and deed. Read v. Loan Co., 68 Ohio St. 280, 67 N.E. 729, 62 L.R.A. 790. A verification of the act of the maker of an instrument. Thane v. Dallas Joint Stock Land Bank of Dallas, Tex.Civ.App., 129 S.W.2d 795, 799.

CERTIFICATE OF ASSIZE. A writ granted for the re-examination or retrial of a matter passed by assize before justices. Fitzh.Nat.Brev. 181. It is now entirely obsolete. 3 Bla.Comm. 389. Consult, also, Comyns, Dig. *Assize* (B, 27, 28).

CERTIFICATE OF DEPOSIT. A written acknowledgment by a bank or banker of a deposit with promise to pay to depositor, to his order, or to some other person or to his order, Wheelock v. Cantley, 227 Mo.App. 102, 50 S.W.2d 731, 734; Mariland Finance Corporation v. People's Bank of Keyser, 99 W.Va. 230, 128 S.E. 294, 295. A bank's promissory note, Dickenson v. Charles, 173 Va. 393, 4 S.E.2d 351, 353.

Documents showing deposits in building and loan association in form of passbooks or any other appropriate written recital. Alter v. Security Building & Loan Co. of Defiance, 58 Ohio App. 114, 16 N.E.2d 228, 233.

CERTIFICATE OF DONATION. A permit or right granted certificate holder to enter upon land belonging to state to make improvements required by law. Young v. Pumphrey, 191 Ark. 98, 83 S.W. 2d 84, 86.

CERTIFICATE OF EVIDENCE. Practically synonymous with bill of exceptions. Yott v. Yott, 257 Ill. 419, 100 N.E. 902, 903.

CERTIFICATE OF HOLDER OF ATTACHED PROPERTY. A certificate required by statute, in some states, to be given by a third person who is found in possession of property subject to an attachment in the sheriff's hands, setting forth the amount and character of such property and the nature of the defendant's interest in it. Code Civil Proc.N.Y. § 650, Civil Practice Act, § 918.

CERTIFICATE OF INCORPORATION. The instrument by which a private corporation is formed, under general statutes, executed by several persons as incorporators and filed in some designated public office as evidence of corporate existence. This is properly distinguished from a "charter," which is a direct legislative grant of corporate existence and powers to named individuals.

CERTIFICATE OF INDEBTEDNESS. An obligation sometimes issued by corporations having practically the same force and effect as a bond, though not usually secured on any specific property. Christie v. Duluth, 82 Minn. 202, 84 N.W. 754. It may, however, create a lien on all the property of the corporation issuing it, superior to the rights of general creditors. Jefferson Banking Co. v. Trustees of Martin Institute, 146 Ga. 383, 91 S.E. 463, 466.

CERTIFICATE OF INTEREST. An instrument evidencing a fractional or percentage interest in oil and gas production. People v. Sidwell, 27 Cal. 2d 121, 162 P.2d 913, 915.

CERTIFICATE OF OCCUPANCY. A paper certifying that premises complied with provisions of zoning ordinance. Frank J. Durkin Lumber Co. v. Fitzsimmons, 106 N.J.Law, 183, 147 A. 555, 557.

CERTIFICATE OF PREFERRED STOCK. Certificate that person is registered holder of designated number of shares of preferred capital stock. Cring v. Sheller Wood Rim Mfg. Co., 98 Ind.App. 310, 183 N.E. 674, 677.

CERTIFICATE OF PUBLIC CONVENIENCE AND NECESSITY. A license or permit to use highways for stated purposes. Railroad Commission of Texas v. Southwestern Greyhound Lines, Tex.Civ.App., 92 S.W.2d 296, 301, 302.

CERTIFICATE OF PURCHASE. A certificate issued by public officer to successful bidder at a judicial sale (such as a tax sale), which will entitle him to a deed upon confirmation of sale by the court, or (as the case may be) if the land is not redeemed within the time limited. Lightcap v. Bradley, 186 Ill. 510, 58 N.E. 221.

CERTIFICATE OF REGISTRY. In maritime law. A certificate of the registration of a vessel according to the registry acts, for the purpose of giving her a national character. 3 Steph.Comm. 274; 3 Kent, Comm. 139–150.

CERTIFICATE OF SALE. The same as "certificate of purchase," *supra.*

CERTIFICATE OF STOCK. A certificate of a corporation or joint-stock company that named person is owner of designated number of shares of stock. Gibbons v. Mahon, 136 U.S. 549, 10 S.Ct. 1057, 34 L.Ed. 525; Edwards v. Wabash Ry. Co., C.C.A.N.Y., 264 F. 610, 613. A written instrument stating or acknowledging that named person is owner of designated number of shares of stock. It is merely written evidence of ownership of stock, and of the rights and liabilities resulting from such ownership. It is merely a paper representation of an incorporeal right, and stands on the footing similar to that of other muniments of title. Whitehead v. Gormley, 116 Okl. 287, 245 P. 562, 565, 47 A.L.R. 171; Misenheimer v. Alexander, 162 N.C. 226, 78 S.E. 161, 164; Home for Destitute Crippled Children v. Boomer, 308 Ill.App. 170, 31 N.E.2d 812, 820; Warren v. New Jersey Zinc Co., N.J.Ch., 116 N.J.Eq. 315, 173 A. 128, 132.

CERTIFICATE SENT TO 1 B. Notation reading "Certificate Sent to 1 B" meant that certificate was to be sent to single beneficiary if war risk insurance application should be accepted. McCormack v. U. S., C.C.A.N.Y., 66 F.2d 519, 521.

CERTIFICATE, TRIAL BY. A mode of trial now little in use; it is resorted to in cases where the fact in issue lies out of the cognizance of the court, and the judges, in order to determine the question, are obliged to rely upon the solemn averment or information of persons in such a station as affords them the clearest and most competent knowledge of the truth. Brown.

CERTIFICATION. In Scotch practice. This is the assurance given to a party of the course to be followed in case he does not appear or obey the order of the court.

CERTIFICATION OF ASSIZE. In English practice. A writ anciently granted for the re-examining or retrial of a matter passed by assize before justices, now entirely superseded by the remedy afforded by means of a new trial. See Certificate of Assize.

CERTIFICATS DE COUTUME. In French law. Certificates given by a foreign lawyer, establishing the law of the country to which he belongs upon one or more fixed points. These certificates can be produced before the French courts, and are received as evidence in suits upon questions of foreign law. Arg.Fr.Merc.Law, 548.

CERTIFIED CARRIERS. Carriers using highways of state to whom certificates of public convenience and necessity have been issued. People v. Henry, 131 Cal.App. 82, 21 P.2d 672.

CERTIFIED CHECK. A depositor's check recognized and accepted by bank officer as valid appropriation of the amount specified and as drawn against funds held by bank.

The usual method of certification is for cashier or teller to write across face of check, over his signature, statement that it is good when properly indorsed. See McAdoo v. Farmers' State Bank of Zenda, 106 Kan. 662, 189 P. 155, 156; Bathgate v. Exchange Bank of Chula, 199 Mo.App. 583, 205 S.W. 875, 876.

The certification of a check is a statement of fact, amounting to an estoppel of the bank to deny liability. Bank of Bay Biscayne v. Ball, 99 Fla. 745, 128 So. 491, 492. A warranty that sufficient funds are on deposit and have been set aside. World Exchange Bank v. Commercial Casualty Ins. Co., 255 N.Y. 1, 173 N.E. 902, 904. It means that bank holds money to pay check and is liable to pay it to proper party. Sundial Const. Co. v. Liberty Bank of Buffalo, 277 N.Y. 137, 13 N.E.2d 745, 746.

CERTIFIED COPY. A copy of a document or record, signed and certified as a true copy by the officer to whose custody the original is intrusted. People v. Foster, 27 Misc. 576, 58 N.Y.Supp. 574; Ehrlich v. Mulligan, 104 N.J.Law, 375, 140 A. 463, 465, 57 A.L.R. 596.

CERTIFIED PUBLIC ACCOUNTANT. A trained accountant who examines the books of accounts of corporations and others and reports upon them.

CERTIFY. To testify in writing; to make known or establish as a fact. Smith v. Smith, Ind.App., 110 N.E. 1013, 1014. To vouch for a thing in writing. State ex inf. Carnahan ex rel. Webb v. Jones, 266 Mo. 191, 181 S.W. 50, 52. To give a certificate, or to make a declaration about a writing. Ainsa v. Mercantile Trust Co. of San Francisco, 174 Cal. 504, 163 P. 898, 901. To warrant. Ettman v. Federal Life Ins. Co., D.C.Mo., 48 F. Supp. 578, 580.

CERTIORARI. Lat. (To be informed of, to be made certain in regard to.) The name of a writ of review or inquiry. Leonard v. Willcox, 101 Vt. 195, 142 A. 762, 766; Nissen v. International Brotherhood of Teamsters, Chauffeurs, Stablemen & Helpers of America, 229 Iowa 1028, 295 N.W. 858.

Certiorari is an appellate proceeding for re-examination of action of inferior tribunal or as auxiliary process to enable appellate court to obtain further information in pending cause. Shapleigh Hardware Co. v. Brumfield, 159 Miss. 175, 130 So. 98. A writ directed only to an inferior tribunal, Stewart v. Johnston, C.C.A.Cal., 97 F.2d 548. It is a discretionary writ, Lennon v. School Dist. No. 11, Greer County, 189 Okl. 37, 113 P.2d 382, 384. Issued only for good cause on showing negativing laches in prosecuting appeal, In re Snelgrove, 208 N.C. 670, 182 S.E. 335, 336. It is available for review of official, judicial or quasi judicial actions. State v. Canfield, 166 Minn. 414, 208 N.W. 181; People ex rel. Elmore v. Allman, 382 Ill. 156, 46 N.E.2d 974, 975. It brings into superior court the record of the administrative or inferior judicial tribunal for inspection, Murphy v. Cuesta, Rey & Co., 381 Ill. 162, 45 N.E.2d 26, 28. It lies as a substitute for an appeal, Pue v. Hood, 222 N.C. 310, 22 S.E.2d 896, 898. To correct errors of law, Dube v. Mayor of City of Fall River, 308 Mass. 12, 30 N.E.2d 817, 818; to restrain excesses of jurisdiction, Stacy v. Mayor of City of Haverhill, 317 Mass. 188, 57 N.E.2d 564. To review erroneous or unwarranted acts or proceedings, State ex rel. Allen v. Rose, 123 Fla. 544, 167 So. 21, 24. To review questions of law, Public Welfare Commission v. Civil Service Commission, 289 Mich. 101, 286 N.W. 173, 175. Where circumstances are so exceptional that an immediate review is in interest of justice, Vingi v. Read, 68 R.I. 484, 29 A.2d 637, 639; where judgment is a miscarriage of justice or will result in substantial injury to legal rights, Goodkind v. Wolkowsky, 151 Fla. 62, 9 So.2d 553, 562; or where applicant for writ lost right of appeal through no fault of his own, McCain v. Collins, 204 Ark. 521, 164 S.W.2d 448, 451. It lies to determine whether inferior tribunal acted within or abused or exceeded jurisdiction, Brundage v. O'Berry, 101 Fla. 320, 134 So. 520, 521; Pierce v. Green, 229 Iowa 22, 294 N.W. 237, 253, 131 A.L.R. 335; or proceeded illegally, Board of Zoning Appeals of City of Indianapolis v. Waintrup, 99 Ind.App. 576, 193 N.E. 701, 705; or proceeded regularly, In re Revocation of Restaurant

Liquor License No. R-8981, Issued to John Mami, 144 Pa.Super. 285, 19 A.2d 549, 552; or whether judgment is prejudicial and materially harmful, Jacksonville American Pub. Co. v. Jacksonville Paper Co., 143 Fla. 835, 197 So. 672, 674. It performs the office of the common-law writ of error, Berry v. Recorder's Court of Town of West Orange, 124 N.J.L. 385, 11 A.2d 743, 745. Limited review only is involved in the writ, Brundage v. O'Berry, 101 Fla. 320, 134 So. 520, 521. Quashal of record or proceeding is the only relief available, State ex rel. St. Louis County v. Evans, 346 Mo. 209, 139 S.W.2d 967, 969.

Originally, and in English practice, an original writ commanding judges or officers of inferior courts to certify or to return records or proceedings in a cause for judicial review of their action. Jacob; Ashworth v. Hatcher, 98 W.Va. 323, 128 S.E. 93. For other common-law definitions, see F. N. B. 554 A; Bac.Abr. 162, 168, citing 4 Burr. 2244; In re Dance, 2 N.D. 184, 49 N.W. 733, 33 Am.St.Rep. 768.

In Florida the writs of "certiorari" in use are the common-law writs, the statutory writ to review judgments of civil courts of record, the rule certiorari to review interlocutory appeals in equity, the rule certiorari for supplying omitted parts of records on appeals or writs of error, and writs of certiorari issued to review quasi judicial judgments or orders of quasi judicial bodies or officers. Kilgore v. Bird, 149 Fla. 570, 6 So.2d 541, 544, 545.

In Massachusetts it is a writ by the supreme judicial court commanding inferior tribunal to certify and return its records in a particular case that any errors or irregularities which appear in the proceedings may be corrected. Pub.St.Mass.1882, p. 1288; Coolidge v. Bruce, 249 Mass. 465, 144 N.E. 397.

In Texas, the ordinary office of writ of "certiorari" is to perfect the record on appeal. Rev.St.1925, art. 932. Zamora v. Garza, Tex.Civ.App., 117 S.W.2d 165.

In somes states the writ has been abolished by statute so far as the common-law name is concerned, but the remedy is preserved under the new name of "writ of review"; Southwestern Telegraph & Telephone Co. v. Robinson, Tex., 1 C.C.A. 91, 48 F. 771.

CERTIORARI, BILL OF. In English chancery practice. An original bill praying relief. It was filed for the purpose of removing a suit pending in some inferior court of equity into the court of chancery, on account of some alleged incompetency or inconvenience.

CERTIORARI FACIAS. Cause to be certified. The command of a writ of certiorari.

CERTUM EST QUOD CERTUM REDDI POTEST. That is certain which can be rendered certain. Co.Litt. 45 *b*, 96 *a*, 142 *a*; 2 Bla.Comm. 143; 2 M. & S. 50; 3 Term 463; 3 M. & K. 353; President, etc., of Lechmere Bank v. Boynton, 11 Cush., Mass., 380.

CERURA. A mound, fence, or inclosure.

CERVISARII. In Saxon law. Tenants who were bound to supply drink for their lord's table. Cowell.

CERVISIA. Ale, or beer. Sometimes spelled *"cerevisia."*

CERVISIARIUS. In old records. An alehouse keeper. A beer or ale brewer. Blount; Cowell.

CERVUS. Lat. A stag or deer.

CESAREVITCH, CESAREWITCH. Originally, a title introduced in Russia in 1799 by Paul I (1754–1801) for his second son, the Grand Duke Constantine. Afterward the title of the czar's eldest son, or the heir apparent to the Russian throne. 6 New Internatl.Encyc. 420.

CESAREVNA. In Imperial Russia, the title of the wife of the cesarevitch, or heir apparent. 6 New Internatl.Encyc. 420.

CESIONARIO. In Spanish law. An assignee. White, New Recop. b. 3, tit. 10, c. 1, § 3.

CESS, *v.* In old English law. To cease, stop, determine, fail.

CESS, *n.* An assessment or tax. In Ireland, it was anciently applied to an exaction of victuals, at a certain rate, for soldiers in garrison.

CESSA REGNARE, SI NON VIS JUDICARE. Cease to reign, if you wish not to adjudicate. Hob. 155.

CESSANTE CAUSA, CESSAT EFFECTUS. The cause ceasing, the effect ceases. Broom, Max. 160; 1 Exch. 430.

CESSANTE RATIONE LEGIS, CESSAT ET IPSA LEX. The reason of the law ceasing, the law itself also ceases. Broom, Max. 159; 4 Co. 38; Appeal of Cummings, 11 Pa. 273; Nice's Appeal, 54 Pa. 201. See Dig. 35, 1, 72, 6.

CESSANTE STATU PRIMITIVO, CESSAT DERIVATIVUS. When the primitive or original estate determines, the derivative estate determines also. 8 Coke, 34; Broom, Max. 495; 4 Kent 32.

CESSARE. L. Lat. To cease, stop, or stay.

CESSAVIT PER BIENNIUM. In practice. An obsolete writ, which could formerly have been sued out when the defendant had for two years *ceased* or neglected to perform such service or to pay such rent as he was bound to do by his tenure, and had not upon his lands sufficient goods or chattels to be distrained. Fitzh.Nat.Brev. 208. It also lay where a religious house held lands on condition of performing certain spiritual services which it failed to do. 3 Bl.Comm. 232. Emig v. Cunningham, 62 Md. 460.

CESSE. (1) An assessment or tax; (2) a tenant of land was said to *cesse* when he neglected or *ceased* to perform the services due to the lord. Co.Litt. 373*a*, 380*b*.

CESSER. Neglect; a ceasing from, or omission to do, a thing. 3 Bl.Comm. 232. The determination of an estate. 1 Coke, 84; 4 Kent, Comm. 33, 90, 105, 295. The determination or ending of a term, annuity, etc. Sweet.

As to the cesser clause in a charter party, see Steamship Rutherglen Co. v. Howard Houlder & Partners, N.Y., 122 C.C.A. 166, 203 F. 848; The Marpesia, C.C.A.N.Y., 292 F. 957, 973.

CESSER, PROVISO FOR. A provision in a settlement creating long terms that when the trusts are satisfied, the term should cease and determine. Sweet. This proviso generally expresses three events: (1) The trusts never arising; (2) their becoming unnecessary or incapable of taking effect; (3) the performance of them. Sugd.Vend. (14th Ed.) 621–623.

CESSET EXECUTIO. (Let execution stay.) In practice. A stay of execution; or an order for such stay; the entry of such stay on record. 2 Tidd, Pr. 1104.

CESSET PROCESSUS. (Let process stay.) A stay of proceedings entered on the record. See 2 Dougl. 627; 11 Mod. 231. Formal order for stay of process or proceedings, Brooks v. Super Service, 183 Miss. 833, 183 So. 484.

CESSIO. Lat. A cession; a giving up, or relinquishment; a surrender; an assignment.

CESSIO BONORUM. In Roman law. Cession of goods. A surrender, relinquishment, or assignment of all his property and effects made by an insolvent debtor for the benefit of his creditors. The term is commonly employed in modern continental jurisprudence to designate a bankrupt's assignment of property to be distributed among his creditors, and is used in the same sense by some English and American writers, but here rather as a convenient than as a strictly technical term. See 2 Bl.Comm. 473; Dig. 2, 4, 25; 48, 19, 1; Nov. 4. 3; La.Civ.Code art. 2166 (Civ.Code, art. 2170); Sturges v. Crowninshield, 4 Wheat. 122, 4 L.Ed. 529.

CESSIO IN JURE. In Roman law. A fictitious suit, in which the person who was to acquire the thing claimed (*vindicabat*) the thing as his own, the person who was to transfer it acknowledged the justice of the claim, and the magistrate pronounced it to be the property (*addicebat*) of the claimant. Sandars' Just.Inst., 5th Ed., 89, 122.

CESSION. The act of ceding; a yielding or giving up; surrender; relinquishment of property or rights.

In the Civil Law

An assignment. The act by which a party transfers property to another. The surrender or assignment of property for the benefit of one's creditors. See Cessio Bonorum.

In Ecclesiastical Law

A giving up or vacating a benefice, by accepting another without a proper dispensation. 1 Bl. Comm. 392; Latch. 234; Cowell.

In Public Law

The assignment, transfer, or yielding up of territory by one state or government to another. Municipality of Ponce v. Church, 210 U.S. 310, 28 S.Ct. 737, 52 L.Ed. 1068.

CESSION DES BIENS. In French law. The voluntary or compulsory surrender which a debtor in insolvent circumstances makes of all his goods to his creditors.

CESSION OF GOODS. The surrender of property; the relinquishment that a debtor makes of all his property to his creditors, when he finds himself unable to pay his debts. Civil Code La. art. 2170.

CESSIONARY. In Scotch law. An assignee. Bell.

CESSIONARY BANKRUPT. One who gives up his estate to be divided among his creditors.

CESSMENT. An assessment, or tax.

CESSOR. One who ceases or neglects so long to perform a duty that he thereby incurs the danger of the law. O. N. B. 136.

CESSURE. L. Fr. A receiver; a bailiff. Kelham.

C'EST ASCAVOIR. L. Fr. That is to say, or to-wit. Generally written as one word, *cestascavoir, cestascavoire.*

C'EST LE CRIME QUI FAIT LA HONTE, ET NON PAS L'ÉCHAFAUD. Fr. It is the offense which causes the shame, and not the scaffold.

CESTUI, CESTUY. He. Used frequently in composition in law French phrases.

CESTUI QUE TRUST. He who has a right to a beneficial interest in and out of an estate the legal title to which is vested in another. 2 Washb. Real Prop. 163. The person who possesses the equitable right to property and receives the rents, issues, and profits thereof, the legal estate of which is vested in a trustee. Bernardsville Methodist Episcopal Church v. Seney, 85 N.J.Eq. 271, 96 A. 388, 389; Moore v. Shifflett, 187 Ky. 7, 216 S.W. 614, 616. Beneficiary of trust, Ulmer v. Fulton, 129 Ohio St. 323, 195 N.E. 557, 564, 97 A.L.R. 1170.

CESTUI QUE USE. He for whose use and benefit lands or tenements are held by another. The *cestui que use* has the right to receive the profits and benefits of the estate, but the legal title and possession (as well as the duty of defending the same) reside in the other. 2 Bla.Comm. 330; 2 Washb. Real Prop. 95.

CESTUI QUE VIE. He whose life is the measure of the duration of an estate. 1 Washb. Real Prop. 88. The person for whose life any lands, tenements, or hereditaments are held.

CESTUY QUE DOIT INHERITER AL PÈRE DOIT INHERITER AL FILS. He who would have been heir to the father of the deceased shall also be heir of the son. Fitzh. Abr. "Descent," 2; 2 Bl. Comm. 239, 250.

CF. An abbreviated form of the Latin word *confer,* meaning "compare." Directs the reader's attention to another part of the work, to another volume, case, etc., where contrasted, analogous, or explanatory views or statements may be found.

CH. This abbreviation most commonly stands for "chapter," or "chancellor," but it may also mean "chancery," or "chief."

CHACE. L. Fr. A chase or hunting ground.

CHACEA. In old English law. A station of game, more extended than a park, and less than a forest; also the liberty of chasing or hunting within a certain district; also the way through which cattle are driven to pasture, otherwise called a "droveway." Blount.

CHACEA EST AD COMMUNEM LEGEM. A chase is by common law. Reg.Brev. 806.

CHACEABLE. L. Fr. That may be chased or hunted.

CHACER. L. Fr. To drive, compel, or oblige; also to chase or hunt.

CHACURUS. L. Lat. A horse for the chase, or a hound, dog, or courser.

CHAFEWAX. An officer in the English chancery whose duty was to prepare wax to seal the writs, commissions, and other instruments thence issuing. The office was abolished by St. 15 & 16 Vict. c. 87, § 23.

CHAFFERS. An ancient term for goods, wares, and merchandise; hence the word *chaffering*, which is yet used for buying and selling, or beating down the price of an article. The word is used in Stat. 3 Edw. III. c. 4.

CHAFFERY. Traffic; the practice of buying and selling.

CHAIN. A measure used by engineers and surveyors, being twenty-two yards in length.

CHAIN OF TITLE. Successive conveyances, or other forms of alienation, affecting a particular parcel of land, arranged consecutively, from the government or original source of title down to the present holder. Capper v. Poulsen, 321 Ill. 480, 152 N.E. 587, 588; Maturi v. Fay, 96 N.J.Eq. 472, 126 A. 170, 173; Havis v. Thorne Inv. Co., Tex.Civ. App., 46 S.W.2d 329, 332.

CHAIN STORE. A store in a group of stores, one or more of which is located within the state, under the same management, supervision, or ownership. Lee v. Herndon, 151 Fla. 657, 10 So.2d 305, 306.

CHAIRMAN. A name given to the presiding officer of an assembly, public meeting, convention, deliberative or legislative body, board of directors, committee, etc.

CHAIRMAN OF COMMITTEES OF THE WHOLE HOUSE. In English parliamentary practice. In the commons, this officer, always a member, is elected by the house on the assembling of every new parliament. When the house is in committee on bills introduced by the government, or in committee of ways and means, or supply, or in committee to consider preliminary resolutions, it is his duty to preside.

CHALDRON, CHALDERN, or CHALDER. Twelve sacks of coals, each holding three bushels, weighing about a ton and a half. In Wales they reckon 12 barrels or pitchers a ton or chaldron, and 29 cwt. of 120 lbs. to the ton. Wharton.

A measure of capacity, equal to fifty-eight and two-thirds cubic feet, nearly. Cowell.

CHALLENGE, *v.* To object or except to; to prefer objections to a person, right, or instrument; to formally call into question the capability of a person for a particular function, or the existence of a right claimed, or the sufficiency or validity of an instrument; to call or put in question; to put into dispute; to render doubtful.

CHALLENGE, *n.* A request by one person to another to fight a duel. Ivey v. State, 12 Ala. 276; Hawk.Pl.Cr. b. 1, c. 3, § 3; State v. Farrier, 8 N.C. 487; 2 Bish.Cr.Law, § 312.

An objection or exception.

The objection or exception may be:

1. Against a person who presents himself at the polls as a voter, in order that his right to cast a ballot may be inquired into.

2. Against legal documents, as a declaration, count, or writ. But this use of the word is now obsolescent. See, however, Adkins v. Wayne County Court, 94 W.Va. 460, 119 S.E. 284, 285.

3. Taken to the personal qualification of a judge or magistrate about to preside at the trial of a cause; as on account of personal interest, his having been of counsel, bias, etc. See Bank of North America v. Fitzsimons, 2 Binn., Pa., 454; Pearce v. Affleck, 4 *id.* 349.

4. Taken to the jurors summoned and returned for the trial of a cause, People v. Travers, 88 Cal. 233, 26 P. 88. See 2 Poll. & Maitl. 619, 646; Co.Litt. 155*b*.

Challenge for Cause

A challenge to a juror for which some cause or reason is alleged. Termes de la Ley; Bl.Comm. 353. Thus distinguished from a peremptory challenge. Turner v. State, 114 Ga. 421, 40 S.E. 308; Cr. Code N. Y. § 374.

Challenge Propter Affectum

A challenge on account of bias or partiality or prejudice. State v. Sawtelle, 66 N.H. 488, 32 A. 831.

Challenge Propter Defectum

A challenge on account of some legal disqualification, such as infancy or alienage.

Challenge Propter Delictum

A challenge on account of crime; that is, disqualification arising from the conviction of an infamous crime. Co.Litt. 155 *b et seq.;* State v. Levy, 187 N.C. 581, 122 S.E. 386, 389.

Challenge Propter Honoris Respectum

A challenge on account of party's social rank.

Challenge to the Array

An exception to the whole panel in which the jury are *arrayed*, or set in order by the sheriff in his return, upon account of partiality, or some default in the sheriff, coroner, or other officer who arrayed the panel or made the return. 3 Bl.Comm. 359; Co.Litt. 155*b;* Moore v. Guano Co., 130 N.C. 229, 41 S.E. 293; Durrah v. State, 44 Miss. 789. A challenge to the form and manner of making up the panel. Cobb v. Atlanta Coach Co., 46 Ga.App. 633, 168 S.E. 126, 127. A challenge that goes to illegality of drawing, selecting, or impaneling array. Lake v. State, 100 Fla. 386, 129 So. 833, 834.

Challenge to the Favor

A challenge based on circumstances of suspicion, as acquaintance, and the like. 3 Bl.Comm. 363; 4 Bl.Comm. 353; State v. Sawtelle, 66 N.H. 488, 32 A. 831; Cobb v. Atlanta Coach Co., 46 Ga.App. 633, 168 S.E. 126, 127.

Challenge to the Panel

The same as a challenge to the array, supra. See Pen. Code Cal. § 1058; Pate v. State, 15 Okl.Cr. 90, 175 P. 122, 123.

Challenge to the Poll

A challenge made to an individual juror. State v. Carlino, 99 N.J.Law, 292, 122 A. 830, 831; Cobb v. Atlanta Coach Co., 46 Ga.App. 633, 168 S.E. 126, 127.

General Challenge

A species of challenge for cause, being an objection to a particular juror, to the effect that the juror is disqualified from serving in any case. Pen. Code Cal. § 1071.

Peremptory Challenge

In criminal practice. A species of challenge which the prosecution or the prisoner is allowed to have against a certain number of jurors, without assigning any cause. Lewis v. U. S., 146 U.S. 370, 13 S.Ct. 136, 36 L.Ed. 1011; Turpin v. State, 55 Md. 462; Leary v. Railway Co., 69 N.J.Law, 67, 54 A. 527.

Principal Challenge

A challenge of a juror for a cause which carries with it, *prima facie*, evident marks of suspicion either of malice or favor; as that a juror is of kin to either party within the ninth degree; that he has an interest in the cause, etc. 3 Bl.Comm. 363. A species of challenge to the array made on account of partiality or some default in the sheriff or his under-officer who arrayed the panel. 4 Bla.Comm. 353; Co.Litt. 156 *a, b*. A challenge based on alleged facts from which, if proven to be true, incapacity to serve is conclusively presumed. Cobb v. Atlanta Coach Co., 46 Ga.App. 633, 168 S.E. 126, 127. A challenge for principal cause. Butler v. Greensboro Fire Ins. Co., 196 N.C. 203, 145 S.E. 3, 4.

CHALLENGE TO FIGHT. A summons or invitation, given by one person to another, to engage in a personal combat; a request to fight a duel. A criminal offense. See Steph.Crim.Dig. 40; 3 East, 581; State v. Perkins, 6 Blackf.Ind. 20.

CHAMBER. A room or apartment in a house. A private repository of money; a treasury. A compartment; a hollow or cavity. Proudfit Loose Leaf Co. v. Kalamazoo Loose Leaf Binder Co., C.C.A.Mich., 230 F. 120, 131. Also used to designate a court, a commission, or an association of persons habitually meeting together in an apartment, *e. g.*, the "star chamber," "chamber of deputies," "chamber of commerce."

CHAMBER BUSINESS. A term applied to all such judicial business as may properly be transacted by a judge at his chambers or elsewhere, as distinguished from such as must be done by the court in session. In re Neagle, C.C.Cal., 39 Fed. 855, 5 L.R.A. 78.

CHAMBER OF ACCOUNTS. In French law. A sovereign court, of great antiquity, in France, which took cognizance of and registered the accounts of the king's revenue; nearly the same as the English court of exchequer. Enc. Brit.

CHAMBER OF COMMERCE. An association (which may or may not be incorporated) comprising the principal merchants, manufacturers, and traders of a city, designed for convenience in buying, selling and exchanging goods, and to foster the commercial and industrial interests of the place. Similar societies are known by various names, as, Board of Trade, etc. A board or association to promote the commercial interests of a locality, county, or the like, or a society of a city who meet to promote the general trade and commerce of the place. Retailers Credit Ass'n of Alameda County v. Commissioner of Internal Revenue, C.C.A.9, 90 F.2d 47, 51, 111 A.L.R. 152.

CHAMBER SURVEYS. In Pennsylvania, false and fraudulent pretenses of surveys of public lands by surveyors. Schraeder Min. & Mfg. Co. v. Packer, 129 U.S. 688, 9 S.Ct. 385, 32 L.Ed. 760.

CHAMBER, WIDOW'S. A portion of the effects of a deceased person, reserved for the use of his widow, and consisting of her apparel, and the furniture of her bed-chamber, is called in London the "widow's chamber." 2 Bl.Comm. 518.

This custom in London of reserving her apparel and furniture for the widow of a freeman was abolished by 19 & 20 Vict. c. 94.

CHAMBERDEKINS, or CHAMBER DEACONS. In old English law. Certain poor Irish scholars, clothed in mean habit, and living under no rule; also beggars banished from England. 1 Hen. V. cc. 7, 8. Wharton.

CHAMBERLAIN. Keeper of the chamber. Originally the chamberlain was the keeper of the treasure chamber (*camera*) of the prince or state; otherwise called "treasurer." Cowell.

The name of several high officers of state in England, as the lord great chamberlain of England, lord chamberlain of the household, chamberlain of the exchequer. Cowell; Blount.

The word is also used in some American cities as the title of an officer corresponding to "treasurer."

CHAMBERLARIA. Chamberlainship; the office of a chamberlain. Cowell.

CHAMBERS.

In Practice

The private room or office of a judge; any place in which a judge hears motions, signs papers, or does other business pertaining to his office, when he is not holding a session of court. Business so transacted is said to be done "in chambers." Quoted with approval in Chapman v. Chattooga Oil-Mill Co., 22 Ga.App. 446, 96 S.E. 579, 580. See, also, Atchison, T. & S. F. Ry. Co. v. Long, 122 Okl. 86, 251 P. 486, 491; Hoskins v. Baxter, 64 Minn. 226, 66 N.W. 969; In re Verdigris Conservancy Dist., 131 Kan. 214, 289 P. 966, 968. The term is also applied, in England, to the private office of a barrister.

In International Law

Portions of the sea cut off by lines drawn from one promontory to another, or included within lines extending from the point of one cape to the next, situate on the sea-coast of the same nation, and which are claimed by that nation as asylums for merchant vessels, and exempt from the operations of belligerents.

CHAMBERS OF THE KING. See King's Chambers.

CHAMBIUM. In old English law. Change, or exchange. Bract. fols. 117, 118.

CHAMBRE DEPEINTE. A name anciently given to St. Edward's chamber, called the "Painted Chamber," destroyed by fire with the houses of parliament.

CHAMFER. A small gutter, furrow, or groove; the slope or bevel produced by cutting off the edge of anything which was originally right angled. Syracuse Chilled Plow Co. v. Robinson, C.C.N.Y., 35 F. 502, 503.

CHAMOTTE. A clay which has been burned to an extent which deprives it of further shrinkage on being again subjected to heat. Panzl v. Battle Island Paper & Pulp Co., D.C.N.Y., 132 F. 607, 609. As used in the arts, see Id., C.C.A.N.Y., 138 F. 48, 50.

CHAMP DE MAI. (Lat. *Campus Maii.*) The field or assembly of May. The national assembly of the Franks, held in the month of May.

CHAMP DE MARS. (Lat. *Campus Martii.*) The field or assembly of March. The national assembly of the Franks, held in the month of March, in the open air.

CHAMPART. In French law. The grant of a piece of land by the owner to another, on condition that the latter would deliver to him a portion of the crops. 18 Toullier, n. 182.

CHAMPERT.

In old English law. A share or division of land; champerty.

In old Scotch law. A gift or bribe, taken by any great man or judge from any person, for delay of just actions, or furthering of wrongous actions, whether it be lands or any goods movable. Skene.

CHAMPERTOR. In criminal law. One who makes or brings pleas or suits, or causes them to be moved or brought, either directly or indirectly, and sues them at his proper costs, upon condition of having a part of the gains or of the land in dispute. One guilty of champerty. St. 33 Edw. I, c. 2; In re Aldrich, 86 Vt. 531, 86 A. 801, 802.

CHAMPERTOUS. Of the nature of champerty; affected with champerty.

The conveyance of land which is in the adverse possession of another is "champertous". Reynolds v. Thomas Forman Co., 295 Ky. 41, 174 S.W.2d 132, 134.

CHAMPERTY. A bargain by a stranger with a party to a suit, by which such third person undertakes to carry on the litigation at his own cost and risk, in consideration of receiving, if successful, a part of the proceeds or subject sought to be recovered. Small v. Mott, 22 Wend., N.Y., 405; Gilman v. Jones, 87 Ala. 691, 5 So. 785, 7 So. 48, 4 L.R.A. 113; Jamison Coal & Coke Co. v. Goltra, C.C.A.Mo., 143 F.2d 889, 895, 154 A.L.R. 1191. An agreement between owner of claim and volunteer that latter may collect claim at his own expense and divide proceeds. Gibson v. Gillespie, 4 W.W. Harr. (Del.) 331, 152 A. 589, 593.

The purchase of an interest in a thing in dispute, with the object of maintaining and taking part in the litigation. 7 Bing. 378.

"Maintenance" consists in maintaining, supporting, or promoting the litigation of another. "Champerty" is a bargain to divide the proceeds of litigation between the owner of the liquidated claim and a party supporting or enforcing the litigation. Draper v. Zebec, 219 Ind. 362, 37 N.E.2d 952, 956.

CHAMPION. A person who fights a combat in his own cause, or in place of another. The person who, in the trial by battel, fought either for the tenant or demandant. 3 Bl.Comm. 339; Bracton, l. 4, t. 2, c. 12.

A person who engages in any contest; a combatant; a fighter; one who acts or speaks in behalf of a person, or a cause; defender; an advocate. Egan v. Signal Pub. Co., 140 La. 1069, 74 So. 556, 558.

CHAMPION OF THE KING OR QUEEN. An ancient officer, whose duty it was at the coronation to challenge "that, if any man shall deny the king's title to the crown, he is there ready to defend it in single combat." Wharton.

CHANCE. Absence of explainable or controllable causation; accident; fortuity; hazard; result or issue of uncertain and unknown conditions or forces; risk; unexpected, unforeseen, or unintended consequence of an act. The opposite of intention, design, or contrivance.

But it has been held that there is a wide difference between *chance* and *accident*. Harless v. U. S., Morris, Iowa, 169, 173.

CHANCE BARGAIN. The entering into a contract for better or worse, accompanied by the taking of chances as to the true facts and situation of the thing or article bargained about. Marr v. Lawson, 290 Ky. 342, 161 S.W.2d 42, 44.

CHANCE-MEDLEY. In criminal law. A sudden affray. This word is sometimes applied to any kind of homicide by misadventure, but in strictness it is applicable to such killing only as happens in defending one's self. 4 Bl.Comm. 184.

CHANCE VERDICT. See Verdict.

CHANCEL. In ecclesiastical law. The part of a church in which the communion table stands; it belongs to the rector or the impropriator. 2 Broom & H. Comm. 420.

CHANCELLOR. In American law, this is the name given in some states to the judge (or the presiding judge) of a court of chancery.

In England, besides being the designation of the chief judge of the court of chancery, the term is used as the title of several judicial officers attached to bishops or other high dignitaries and to the universities. The title is also used in some of the dioceses of the Protestant Episcopal Church in the United States to designate a member of the legal profession who gives advice and counsel to the bishop and other ecclesiastical authorities.

In Scotland, this title is given to the foreman of an assize or jury. Bisph.Eq. 7.

An officer bearing this title is to be found in some countries of Europe, and is generally invested with extensive political authority.

Chancellor of a Cathedral

In English ecclesiastical law. One of the *quatuor personæ*, or four chief dignitaries of the cathedrals of the old foundation.

Chancellor of a Diocese

In ecclesiastical law, the officer appointed to assist a bishop in matters of law, and to hold his consistory courts for him. 1 Bl.Comm. 382; 2 Steph.Comm. 672.

Chancellor of a University

In English law. The official head of a university.

Chancellor of the Duchy of Lancaster

In English law. An officer before whom, or his deputy, the court of the duchy chamber of Lancaster is held. Hob. 77; 3 Bl.Comm. 78.

Chancellor of the Exchequer

In English law. A high officer of the crown, who formerly sat in the exchequer court. Cowell. In modern times his duties are such as pertain to a minister of state charged with the management of the national revenue and expenditure. 2 Steph.Com. 467.

Chancellor of the Order of the Garter and Other Military Orders

In England, an officer who seals the commissions and the mandates of the chapter and assembly of the knights, keeps the register of their proceedings, and delivers their acts under the seal of their order.

Chancellor, the Lord High

In England, the highest judicial functionary in the kingdom.

He exercises many functions and powers over and above the jurisdiction which he exercises in his judicial capacity in the supreme court of judicature, of which he is the head. Wharton.

Vice-Chancellor

In English law. A judge of the court of chancery, acting as assistant to the lord chancellor, and holding a separate court. 3 Steph.Comm. 418.

CHANCELLOR'S COURTS IN THE TWO UNIVERSITIES. In English law. Courts of local jurisdiction, resembling borough courts, in and for the two universities of Oxford and Cambridge in England. 3 Bl.Comm. 83; Odgers, C.L. 1030; 12 East, 12; 13 East, 635; 15 East, 634; 10 Q.B. 292.

CHANCER. To adjust according to principles of equity, as would be done by a court of chancery. Cent. Dict.

The practice arose in parts of New England when the courts, without equity jurisdiction, were compelled to act upon equitable principles. See Lewiston v. Gagne, 89 Me. 395, 36 A. 629, 56 Am.St.Rep. 432; In re Appel, Mass., 90 C.C.A. 172, 163 F. 1002, 20 L.R.A.,N.S., 76.

CHANCERY. Equity; equitable jurisdiction; a court of equity; the system of jurisprudence administered in courts of equity. Kenyon v. Kenyon, 3 Utah, 431, 24 P. 829. See Court of Chancery.

CHANGE. As a noun. An alteration; a modification or addition; substitution of one thing for another. Exchange of money against money of a different denomination. Also small coin. Also an abbreviation of *exchange*.

As a verb. Alter; cause to pass from one place to another; exchange; make different; put one thing in place of another; vacate.

CHANGE OF BENEFICIARY. A divesting of beneficial interest held by one person and a vesting of that interest in another. Goldman v. Moses, 287 Mass. 393, 191 N.E. 873, 874.

CHANGE OF DOMICILE. Change of abode or residence and intention to remain. In re Fischer's Estate, 151 Misc. 74, 271 N.Y.S. 101. Shenton v. Abbott, 178 Md. 526, 15 A.2d 906, 908, 909.

CHANGE OF GRADE. Usually understood as an elevation or depression of the surface of a street, or a change of the natural contour of its face so as to facilitate travel over it. McCabe v. City of New York, 155 App.Div. 262, 140 N.Y.S. 127, 131.

It is essential that there shall have been a previously established grade and that a new grade be physically made. Gas Engine & Power Co. v. City of New York, 166 App.Div. 297, 151 N.Y.S. 310, 313; Berglar v. University City, Mo.App., 190 S.W. 620, 623.

CHANGE OF LOCATION. Removal from old to new location. Weber County v. Ritchie, 98 Utah 272, 96 P.2d 744.

CHANGE OF VENUE. Properly speaking, the removal of a suit begun in one county or district to another county or district for trial, though the term is also sometimes applied to the removal of a suit from one court to another court of the same county or district. Felts v. Railroad Co., 195 Pa. 21, 45 A. 493; State v. Wofford, 119 Mo. 375, 24 S. W. 764.

CHANGER. An officer formerly belonging to the king's mint, in England, whose business was chiefly to *exchange* coin for bullion brought in by merchants and others.

CHANNEL. The bed in which the main stream of a river flows, rather than the deep water of the stream as followed in navigation. Bridge Co. v. Dubuque County, 55 Iowa, 558, 8 N.W. 443. See The Oliver, D.C.Va., 22 F. 849; Iowa v. Illinois, 147 U.S. 1, 13 S.Ct. 239, 37 L.Ed. 55.

But the term is sometimes used to designate the customary and traveled fairway. The Arlington, C.C.A.N.Y., 19 F.2d 285, 286, 54 A.L.R. 101. It may also be used as a generic term applicable to any water course, whether a river, creek, slough, or canal. McKissick Cattle Co. v. Alsaga, 41 Cal.App. 380, 182 P. 793, 797. The "channel" of a river is to be distinguished from a "branch." U. S. v. Hutchings, D.C.Okl., 252 F. 841, 844.

Main Channel

That bed of the river over which the principal volume of water flows. St. Louis & St. P. Packet Co. v. Keokuk & H. Bridge Co., C.C.Iowa, 31 F. 757. Compare State of Oklahoma v. State of Texas, 258 U.S. 574, 42 S.Ct. 406, 414, 66 L.Ed. 771.

The main channel of a navigable stream, called for as a boundary between states, means the "thalweg," or deepest and most navigable channel as it then existed. Whiteside v. Norton, C.C.A.Minn., 205 F. 5, 9.

Natural Channel

The channel of a stream as determined by the natural conformation of the country through which it flows. See Larrabee v. Cloverdale, 131 Cal. 96, 63 P. 143. The floor or bed on which the water flows, and the banks on each side thereof as carved out by natural causes. Pima Farms Co. v. Proctor, 30 Ariz. 96, 245 P. 369, 372.

CHANTER. The chief singer in the choir of a cathedral. Mentioned in 13 Eliz. c. 10.

CHANTRY. A church or chapel endowed with lands for the maintenance of priests to say mass daily for the souls of the donors. Termes de la Ley; Cowell.

CHAPEL. A place of worship; a lesser or inferior church, sometimes a part of or subordinate to another church. Webster. Rex v. Nixon, 7 Car. & P. 442; In re Atkinson's Will, 120 Misc. 186, 197 N.Y.S. 831, 832.

Chapel of Ease

In English ecclesiastical law. A chapel built in aid of original church for parishioners who had fixed their residence at some distance. 3 Steph. Comm. 151.

Free Chapels

So called from their freedom or exemption from all ordinary jurisdiction.

Private Chapels

Chapels owned by private persons, and used by themselves and their families. 2 Steph.Comm. 745.

Proprietary Chapels

In English law. Those belonging to private persons who have purchased or erected them with a view to profit or otherwise.

Public Chapels

In English law, chapels founded later than the church for parishioners who fixed their residence at a distance; and chapels so circumstanced were described as "chapels of ease." 3 Steph.Comm. (7th Ed.) 745.

CHAPELRY. The precinct and limits of a chapel. The same thing to a chapel as a parish is to a church. Cowell; Blount; Termes de la Ley.

CHAPERON. A hood or bonnet anciently worn by the Knights of the Garter; also a little escutcheon fixed in the forehead of horses drawing a hearse at a funeral. Wharton.

CHAPITRE. A summary of matters to be inquired of or presented before justices in eyre, justices of assise, or of the peace, in their sessions. Also articles delivered by the justice in his charge to the inquest. Brit. c. iii.

CHAPLAIN. An ecclesiastic who performs divine service in a chapel; but it more commonly means one who attends upon a king, prince, or other person of quality, for the performance of clerical duties in a private chapel. 4 Coke, 90. A clergyman officially attached to a ship of war, to an army, (or regiment,) or to some public institution, for the purpose of performing divine service. Webster.

CHAPMAN. An itinerant vendor of small wares. A trader who trades from place to place. Say. 191, 192.

CHAPTER. In ecclesiastical law. A congregation of ecclesiastical persons in a cathedral church, consisting of canons, or prebendaries, whereof the dean is the head, all subordinate to the bishop. And they are termed *"capitulum,"* as a kind of head, instituted not only to assist the bishop but also anciently to rule and govern the diocese in the time of vacation. Burn, Dict.; Coke, Litt. 103.

CHARACTER. Class or division to which claim belongs, Jackson State Nat. Bank of Jackson, Miss., v. Merchants' Bank & Trust Co. of Jackson, Miss., 177 La. 975, 149 So. 539, 541.

The aggregate of the moral qualities which belong to and distinguish an individual person; the general result of the one's distinguishing attributes.

That moral predisposition or habit, or aggregate of ethical qualities, which is believed to attach to a person, on the strength of the common opinion and report concerning him. A person's fixed disposition or tendency, as evidenced to others by his habits of life, through the manifestation of which his general reputation for the possession of a character, good or otherwise, is obtained. Keith v. State, 127 Tenn. 40, 152 S.W. 1029, 1030.

The estimate attached to an individual or thing the community. Biddle v. Riley, 118 Ark. 206, 176 S.W. 134, 137, L.R.A.1915F, 992; Rogers v. State, 126 Tex.Cr.R. 39, 70 S.W.2d 188, 189; H. L. Shaffer & Co. v. Prosser, 99 Colo. 335, 62 P.2d 1161, 1163. The opinion generally entertained of a person derived from the common report of the people who are acquainted with him. Smith v. State, 88 Ala. 73, 7 So. 52; State v. Turner, 36 S.C. 534, 15 S.E. 602.

Although "character" is often used in the sense of "reputation," Garrison v. State, 217 Ala. 322, 116 So. 705; Commonwealth v. Harvie, 345 Pa. 516, 28 A.2d 926, 927; the terms are distinguishable, State v. Taylor, 267 Mo. 41, 183 S.W. 299, 301; Commonwealth v. Webb, 252 Pa. 187, 97 A. 189, 192.

Though, in a subjective sense, character, general character, and general report or reputation are the same. Powers v. Leach, 26 Vt. 278; and though general character has always been proved by proving general reputation. Leverich v. Frank, 6 Or. 213. See, also, Richardson v. State, 94 Tex.Cr.R. 616, 253 S.W. 273, 277. "Character" is what a man is, and "reputation" is what he is supposed to be. State v. Pickett, 202 Iowa, 1321, 210 N.W. 782, 783. "Character" depends on attributes possessed, and "reputation" on attributes which others believe one to possess. Bills v. State, 187 Ind. 721, 119 N.E. 465. The former signifies reality and the latter merely what is accepted to be reality at present. State v. Leabo, 120 Or. 160, 249 P. 363.

CHARBON. Another name for anthrax (*q. v.*).

CHARGE, *v.* To impose a burden, duty, obligation, or lien; to create a claim against property; to claim; to demand; to accuse; to instruct a jury on matters of law. To impose a tax, duty, or trust. Ex parte Horn, D.C.Wash., 292 F. 455, 457. In commercial transactions, to bill or invoice. George M. Jones Co. v. Canadian Nat. Ry. Co., D. C.Mich., 14 F.2d 852, 855.

A jury is "charged" with duty of trying prisoner (or, as otherwise expressed, with his fate or his "deliverance") as soon as they are impaneled and sworn; this is a different matter from "charging" the jury in the sense of giving them instructions. Tomasson v. State, 112 Tenn. 596, 79 S.W. 803. And see Keith v. Commonwealth, 197 Ky. 362, 247 S.W. 42, 44.

To load, as a firearm. People v. Limeberry, 298 Ill. 355, 131 N.E. 691, 696.

CHARGE, *n.* An incumbrance, lien, or claim; a burden or load; an obligation or duty; a liability; an accusation. Darling v. Rogers, 22 Wend. (N. Y.) 491. Custody. Randazzo v. U. S., C.C.A.Mo.,

300 F. 794, 797; In re Boulware's Will, 258 N.Y.S. 522, 144 Misc. 235. Price. Aiken Mills v. United States, D.C.S.C., 53 F.Supp. 524, 526. Rate. Borough of Mechanicsburg v. Valley Rys., 109 Pa. Super. 48, 165 A. 541, 542.

Conversion of electrical energy into chemical energy within a cell or storage battery. Elliott Works v. Frisk, D.C.Iowa, 58 F.2d 820, 822.

In Common-law Practice

The final address by judge to jury before verdict, in which he sums up the case, and instructs jury as to the rules of law which apply to its various issues, and which they must observe. The term also applies to the address of court to grand jury, in which the latter are instructed as to their duties.

In Contracts

An obligation. Com.Dig. "Rent," c. 6; 2 Ball & B. 223; Termes de la Ley. An undertaking to keep the custody of another person's goods. State v. Clark, 86 Me. 194, 29 A. 984.

In Criminal Law

An accusation or oral charge. People v. Ross, 235 Mich. 433, 209 N.W. 663, 666; Haggard v. First Nat. Bank of Mandan, 72 N.D. 434, 8 N.W.2d 5, 9. A formal complaint, information, or indictment. People v. Lepori, 35 Cal.App. 60, 169 P. 692, 694. A count. State v. Thornton, 142 La. 797, 77 So. 634, 636; State v. Pucketty, 39 N.M. 511, 50 P.2d 964, 965. Accused or arraigned. Code Cr.Proc. § 57. People v. Hickox, 10 N.Y.S.2d 318, 320, 170 Misc. 354.

In Equity Pleading

An allegation in the bill of matters which disprove or avoid a defense which it is alleged the defendant is supposed to pretend or intend to set up. Story, Eq.Pl. § 31; Cooper, Eq.Pl. 11; 1 Dan.Ch.Pr. 372, 1883, n.; 11 Ves.Ch. 574.

In Equity Practice

A written statement presented to a master in chancery by a party of the items with which the opposite party should be debited or should account for, or of the claim of the party making it. A charge may embrace the whole liabilities of the accounting party. Hoff.Mast. 36.

In Scotch Law

The command of the king's letters to perform some act; as a *charge* to enter heir. Also a messenger's execution, requiring a person to obey the order of the king's letters; as a *charge* on letters of horning, or a *charge* against a superior. Bell.

In the Law of Wills

A responsibility or liability imposed by the testator upon a devisee personally, or upon the land devised. Potter v. Gardner, 12 Wheat. 498, 6 L.Ed. 706; Boal v. Metropolitan Museum of Art of City of New York, C.C.A.N.Y., 298 F. 894, 908. A pecuniary burden. In re Clark's Will, 37 N.Y.S.2d 522, 523, 179 Misc. 75.

A devise for beneficial enjoyment of devisee subject to payment of a sum of money or performance of a particular duty. Howells State Bank v. Pont, 113 Neb. 181, 202 N.W. 457, 459.

General Charge

The charge or instruction of the court to the jury upon the case, as a whole, or upon its general features and characteristics.

Public Charge

A person whom it is necessary to support at public expense by reason of poverty, insanity and poverty, disease and poverty, or idiocy and poverty. Wallis v. U. S., ex rel. Mannara, C.C.A.N.Y., 273 F. 509, 511. As used in Immigration Act Feb. 5, 1917, § 19, 8 U.S.C.A. § 155, one who produces a money charge on, or an expense to, the public for support and care. Ex parte Kichmiriantz, D.C.Cal., 283 F. 697, 698. As so used, the term is not limited to paupers or those liable to become such, but includes those who will not undertake honest pursuits, or who are likely to become periodically the inmates of prisons. Ex parte Horn, D.C. Wash., 292 F. 455, 457. But see Ng Fung Ho v. White, C.C.A.Cal., 266 F. 765, 769.

Special Charge

A charge or instruction given by the court to the jury, upon some particular point or question involved in the case, and usually in response to counsel's request for such instruction.

CHARGE AND DISCHARGE. Under former equity practice, in taking an account before a master, a written statement of items for which plaintiff asked credit and a counter-statement, exhibiting claims or demands defendant held against plaintiff.

CHARGÉ DES AFFAIRES, or CHARGÉ D'AFFAIRES. The title of a diplomatic representative of inferior rank. In re Baiz, 135 U.S. 403, 10 S.Ct. 854, 34 L.Ed. 222; Du Pont v. Pichon, 4 Dall. 321, 1 L.Ed. 851.

CHARGE-OFF. Anything manifesting intent to eliminate an item from assets. Rubinkam v. Commissioner of Internal Revenue, C.C.A.7, 118 F.2d 148, 149.

CHARGE-SHEET. A paper kept at a police-station to receive each night the names of the persons brought and given into custody, the nature of the accusation, and the name of the accuser in each case. Wharton.

CHARGE TO ENTER HEIR. In Scotch law. A writ commanding a person to enter heir to his predecessor within forty days, otherwise an action to be raised against him as if he had entered.

CHARGEABLE. This word, in its ordinary acceptation, as applicable to the imposition of a duty or burden, signifies capable of being charged, subject to be charged, liable to be charged, or proper to be charged. Gilfillan v. Chatterton, 38 Minn. 335, 37 N.W. 583.

CHARGEANT. Weighty; heavy; penal; expensive. Kelham.

CHARGES. The expenses which have been incurred, or disbursements made, in connection with a contract, suit, or business transaction. Spoken of an action, it is said that the term includes more than what falls under the technical description of "costs."

Instructions. Standard v. Texas Pacific Coal & Oil Co., Tex.Civ.App., 47 S.W.2d 443, 447.

CHARGING LIEN. A lien is a charging lien where the debt is a charge upon the specific property although it remains in the debtor's possession. See, also, Attorney's Lien.

CHARGING ORDER. See Order.

CHARITABLE. Having the character or purpose of a charity (*q. v.*).

The term is sometimes deemed to be synonymous with "eleemosynary," Hamburger v. Cornell University, 166 N.Y.S. 46, 48, 99 Misc. 564; with "benevolent," In re Dol's Estate, 182 Cal. 159, 187 P. 428, 431; with "beneficent," People v. Thomas Walters Chapter of Daughters of American Revolution, 311 Ill. 304, 142 N.E. 566.

CHARITABLE BEQUEST. A bequest is charitable if its aims and accomplishments are of religious, educational, political, or general social interest to mankind and if the ultimate recipients constitute either the community as a whole or an unascertainable and indefinite portion thereof. In re Henderson's Estate, 17 Cal.2d 853, 112 P.2d 605, 607, 609. See, also, Charity.

CHARITABLE CORPORATION. One that freely and voluntarily ministers to the physical needs of those pecuniarily unable to help themselves. In re Rockefeller's Estate, 177 App.Div. 786, 165 N.Y.S. 154, 158. One which, by its powers, or usage, is charged with administering charitable relief. In re Beekman's Estate, 196 App.Div. 681, 188 N.Y.S. 178, 179. One organized for the purpose, among other things, of promoting the welfare of mankind at large, or of a community, or of some class from a part of it indefinite as to number of individuals. In re Dol's Estate, 186 Cal. 64, 198 P. 1039.

CHARITABLE GIFT. See Charity.

CHARITABLE HOSPITAL OR SANITARIUM. One maintained for gratuitous treatment of sick and needy. Moss v. Youngblood, 187 Ga. 188, 200 S.E. 689, 694. One not maintained for a gain, profit or private advantage. In re Farmers' Union Hospital Ass'n of Elk City, 190 Okl. 661, 126 P.2d 244, 246. One operated by means of contributions, Bedford v. Colorado Fuel & Iron Corporation, 102 Colo. 538, 81 P.2d 752, 759, 760. One when charges collected are no more than needed for maintenance. Gundry v. R. B. Smith Memorial Hospital Ass'n, 293 Mich. 36, 291 N.W. 213, 214, 215. One when income from patients able to pay is used for maintenance or extension of facilities devoted to charitable purposes. Benton County v. Allen, 170 Or. 481, 133 P.2d 991, 992, 993, 995. One which does not deny treatment to persons unable to pay though it charges those able to pay. Commissioner of Internal Revenue v. Battle Creek, C.C.A. Fla., 126 F.2d 405, 406.

CHARITABLE INSTITUTION. One supported in whole or in part at public expense or by charity. City of Vicksburg v. Vicksburg Sanitarium, 117 Miss. 709, 78 So. 702. One for the relief of a certain class of persons, either by alms, education, or care. Utica Trust & Deposit Co. v. Thompson, 87 Misc. 31, 149 N.Y.S. 392, 398. One administering a public or private charity; an eleemosynary institution. St. Albans Hospital v. Town of Enosburg, 96 Vt. 389, 120 A. 97, 99. One performing service of public good or welfare without profit. Society of Cincinnati v. Exeter, 92 N.H. 348, 31 A.2d 52, 55.

CHARITABLE ORGANIZATION. One which has no capital stock and no provision for making dividends and profits, but derives its funds mainly from public and private charity, and holds them in trust for the objects and purposes expressed in its charter. Congregational Sunday School & Publishing Soc. v. Board of Review, 290 Ill. 108, 125 N.E. 7, 9. One conducted not for profit, but for promotion of welfare of others. Stearns v. Association of Bar of City of New York, 154 Misc. 71, 276 N.Y.S. 390.

CHARITABLE SCHOOL OR EDUCATIONAL INSTITUTION. A college preparatory school operated without profit some of whose students paid no tuition, College Preparatory School for Girls of Cincinnati v. Evatt, 144 Ohio St. 408, 59 N.E.2d 142, 145. One devoted to public education without private gain. Southern Methodist University v. Clayton, 142 Tex. 179, 176 S.W.2d 749, 750. One supported wholly or in part by public subscriptions or endowment, New York University v. Taylor, 251 App.Div. 444, 296 N.Y.S. 848, 849; or by private charity. Bodenheimer v. Confederate Memorial Ass'n, D.C.Va., 5 F.Supp. 526, 528.

CHARITABLE SOCIETY. An educational institution is a charitable society. In re Cooper's Estate, 229 Iowa 921, 295 N.W. 448, 454.

CHARITABLE USES OR PURPOSES. Originally those enumerated in the statute 43 Eliz. c. 4, and afterwards those which, by analogy, come within its spirit and purpose. Boyle, Char. 17. See, also, Charity.

CHARITABLE TRUST. A fiduciary relationship subjecting holder of property to deal with it for a charitable purpose. In re White's Estate, 340 Pa. 92, 16 A.2d 394, 396, 397. A trust for benefit of public or of some portion thereof. Delaware Trust Co. v. Fitzmaurice, Del.Ch., 31 A.2d 383, 388. Its characteristics are the expression of a definite charitable purpose and the indefiniteness of the beneficiaries. Woodcock v. Wachovia Bank & Trust Co., 214 N.C. 224, 199 S.E. 20.

A cemetery corporation is a "charitable trust". De Geeter v. Wolklin, 133 N.J.Eq. 510, 42 A.2d 561, 562. So, too, a Christian church. Burgie v. Muench, 65 Ohio App. 176, 29 N.E.2d 439, 440.

CHARITY. The word "charity" may be used in a subjective or an objective sense.

It may mean or apply to:

Accomplishment of some social interest, In re Tollinger's Estate, 349 Pa. 393, 37 A.2d 500, 501, 502. Act or feeling of benevolence, Southern Methodist Hospital and Sanatorium of Tucson v. Wilson, 51 Ariz. 424, 77 P.2d 458. Advancement of purposes beneficial to public, Rabinowitz v. Wollman, 174 Md. 6, 197 A. 566, 568. All good affections men ought to bear towards each other. Morice v. Bishop of Durham, 9 Ves. 399. All which aids man and seeks to improve his condition. Waddell v. Young Women's Christian Ass'n, 133 Ohio St. 601, 15 N.E.2d 140, 142. Almsgiving, In re Rathbone's Estate, 11 N.Y.S.2d 506, 527, 170 Misc. 1030. Amelioration of persons in unfortunate circumstances, Second Nat. Bank v. Second Nat. Bank, 171 Md. 547, 190 A. 215, 111 A.L.R. 711. An institution founded by a gift and intended for public use as a hospital, library, school, or museum, Southern Methodist Hospital and Sanatorium of Tucson v. Wilson, 51 Ariz. 424, 77 P.2d 458, 460, 461. Any purpose in which the public has an interest, Collins v. Lyon, Inc., 181 Va. 230, 24 S.E.2d 572, 580. Any purpose of general benefit untainted by motives of private gain. Stearns v. Association of Bar of City of New York, 276 N.Y.S. 390, 395, 154 Misc. 71. Any scheme or effort to better the condition of society or any considerable part thereof. Tharpe v. Central Georgia Council of Boy Scouts of America, 185 Ga. 810, 196 S.E. 762, 764, 116 A.L.R. 373. Assistance to persons in establishing. Bruce v. Young Men's Christian Ass'n, 51 Nev. 372, 277 P. 798, 799; assistance to the needy. Benefit of handcraftsmen. Benefit of an indefinite number of persons, Morgan v. National Trust Bank of Charleston, 331 Ill. 182, 162 N.E. 888, 890. Benefit of minister. In re Edge's Estate, 288 N.Y.S. 437, 440, 159 Misc. 505. Benevolence, philanthropy, and good will. Santa Fe Lodge No. 460, B. P. O. E., v. Employment Sec.

Commission, 49 N.M. 149, 159 P.2d 312, 315. Benevolent or philanthropic, Beckwith v. Parish, 69 Ga. 569; Price v. Maxwell, 28 Pa. 23. Dissemination of knowledge; Christian love, Boruch v. SS. Peter & Paul's Orthodox Russian Church, 111 N.J.L. 116, 166 A. 723. Conferring advantages of a social character. La Societe Francaise De Bienfaisance Mutuelle v. California Employment Commission, 56 Cal.App.2d 534, 133 P.2d 47, 51, 52. Eleemosynary, Collier v. Lindley, 203 Cal. 641, 266 P. 526, 528. General public use which extends to the rich as well as to the poor. Hamilton v. Corvallis General Hospital Ass'n, 146 Or. 168, 30 P.2d 9, 14. Gift for benefit of indefinite number, St. Louis Union Trust Co. v. Burnet, C.C.A., 59 F.2d 922, 926. Gift to the general public use. Maretick v. South Chicago Community Hospital, 297 Ill.App. 488, 17 N.E.2d 1012, 1014. Gift without consideration or expectation of return, State v. Texas Mut. Life Ins. Co. of Texas, Tex.Civ.App., 51 S.W.2d 405, 410. Improvement of man. Boston Symphony Orchestra v. Board of Assessors of City of Boston, Mass., 1 N.E.2d 6, 9. Improvement of spiritual, mental, social and physical conditions. Andrews v. Young Men's Christian Ass'n of Des Moines, 226 Iowa 374, 284 N.W. 186, 192. Lessening burdens of government. Stork v. Schmidt, 129 Neb. 311, 261 N.W. 552, 554. Physical, mental or moral betterment, In re Tollinger's Estate, 349 Pa. 393, 37 A.2d 500, 501, 502. Promotion of government or municipal purposes, Powers v. First Nat. Bank, Tex.Civ.App., 137 S.W.2d 839, 842. Promotion of happiness of man. Old Colony Trust Co. v. Welch, D.C.Mass., 25 F.Supp. 45, 48. Promotion of philanthropic and humanitarian purposes. Jackson v. Phillips, 14 Allen, Mass., 556. Promotion of well-doing and well-being of social man. Krause v. Peoria Housing Authority, 370 Ill. 356, 19 N.E.2d 193, 199. Promotion or fostering science, education, enlightenment, benefit, of mankind, Irwin v. Swinney, D.C.Mo., 44 F.2d 172, 174. Property held for public purposes. St. Louis Union Trust Co. v. Burnet, C.C.A.8, 59 F.2d 922, 927. Public benefit, convenience, utility, or comfort, Camp v. Presbyterian Soc. of Sackets Harbor, 173 N.Y.S. 581, 584, 105 Misc. 139. Reclamation of criminals. Relief of persons in unfortunate circumstances, Second Nat. Bank v. Second Nat. Bank, 171 Md. 547, 190 A. 215, 111 A.L.R. 711. Religious, educational, benevolent, and humanitarian objects. In re Jordan's Estate, 329 Pa. 427, 197 A. 150. Services accorded to the needy. Unselfish things as are wont to be done by those who are animated by love. Bok v. McCaughn, C.C.A.Pa., 42 F.2d 616, 619. What is done out of good will and a desire to add to the improvement of moral, mental, and physical welfare of public. Old Colony Trust Co. v. Welch, D.C.Mass., 25 F.Supp. 45, 48. Whatever is given for love of God or love of your neighbor, free from every consideration that is personal, private, or selfish. Vidal v. Girard, 2 How. 128, 11 L.Ed. 205, appr. Price v. Maxwell, 28 Pa. 35. Whatever proceeds from sense of moral duty or feeling of kindness and humanity for relief or comfort of another, Doyle v. Railroad Co., 118 Mass. 195, 198, 19 Am. Rep. 431. Uncertainty regarding beneficiaries is distinct feature. Goode's Adm'r v. Goode, 238 Ky. 620, 38 S.W.2d 691, 694.

Foreign Charity

One created or endowed in a state or country foreign to that of the domicile of the benefactor. Taylor's Ex'rs v. Trustees of Bryn Mawr College, 34 N.J.Eq. 101.

Public Charity

A charity wherein the benefit is conferred on indefinite persons composing the public or some part of the public. Continental Illinois Nat. Bank & Trust Co. v. Harris, 359 Ill. 86, 194 N.E. 250, 253.

A gift to be applied consistently with existing laws for the benefit of an indefinite number of persons, by bringing their minds under the influence of education or religion, by relieving their bodies from disease, suffering, or constraint, or by assisting them to establish themselves in life, or by erecting and maintaining public buildings or works, or otherwise lessening the burdens of government. Robinson v. Crutcher, 277 Mo. 1, 209 S.W. 104, 105.

A "purely public charity" which Legislature may exempt from taxation is a charity indiscriminately dispensed to some portion or group of public where ends accomplished are wholly benevolent and are accomplished without profit or gain and, the beneficiaries are saved from becoming burdens upon society and the state. City of Houston v. Scottish Rite Benev. Ass'n, 111 Tex. 191, 230 S.W. 978, 981.

Pure Charity

One which is entirely gratuitous, and which dispenses its benefits without any charge or pecuniary return whatever. See In re Lenox's Estate, Sur., 9 N.Y.S. 895, 31 St.R. 959; Kentucky Female Orphan School v. Louisville, 100 Ky. 470, 36 S.W. 921, 40 L.R.A. 119.

CHARLATAN. One who pretends to more knowledge or skill than he possesses; a "quack." Brinkley v. Fishbein, C.C.A.Tex., 110 F.2d 62, 64.

CHARLEY. A familiar nickname or substitute for "Charles." Carroll v. State, 24 Okl.Cr. 26, 215 P. 797, 798.

CHARRE OF LEAD. A quantity consisting of 36 pigs of lead, each pig weighing about 70 pounds.

CHART. The word "chart," as used in the copyright law, does not include sheets of paper exhibiting tabulated or methodically arranged information. Taylor v. Gilman, C.C.N.Y., 24 Fed. 632.

CHARTA.

In Old English Law

A charter or deed; an instrument written and sealed; the formal evidence of conveyances and contracts. Also any signal or token by which an estate was held.

The term came to be applied, by way of eminence, to such documents as proceeded from the sovereign, granting liberties or privileges, and either where the recipient of the grant was the whole nation, as in the case of *Magna Charta,* or a public body, or private individual, in which case it corresponded to the modern word "charter."

In the Civil Law

Paper, suitable for the inscription of documents or books; hence, any instrument or writing. See Dig. 32, 52, 6; Nov. 44, 2.

Charta Communis

In old English law. An indenture; a common or mutual charter or deed; one containing mutual covenants, or involving mutuality of obligation; one to which both parties might have occasion to refer, to establish their respective rights. Bract. fols. 33*b*, 34.

Charta Cyrographata (or Chyrographata)

In old English law. A chirographed charter; a charter executed in two parts, and cut through the middle, *(scinditur per medium,)* where the word *"cyrographum,"* or *"chirographum,"* was written in large letters. Bract. fol. 34; Fleta, lib. 3, c. 14, § 3. See Chirograph.

Charta De Foresta

A collection of the laws of the forest, made in the 9th Hen. III, and said to have been originally a part of *Magna Charta.*

The *charta de foresta* was called the Great Charter of the woodland population, nobles, barons, freemen, and slaves, loyally granted by Henry III. early in his reign (A.D.1217). Inderwick, King's Peace 159; Stubb's Charters 847. There is a difference of opinion as to the *original* charter of the forest similar to that which exists respecting the true and original Magna Carta *(q. v.)*, and for the same reason, viz., that both required repeated confirmation by the kings, despite their supposed inviolability. This justifies the remark of recent historians as to the great charter that "this theoretical sanctity and this practical insecurity are shared with 'the Great Charter of Liberties' by the Charter of the Forest which was issued in 1217." 1 Poll. & Maitl. 158. It is asserted with great positiveness by Inderwick that no forest charter was ever granted by King John, but that Henry III. issued the charter of 1217 (which he puts in the third year of the reign, which, however, only commenced Oct. 28, 1216), in pursuance of the promises of his father; and Lord Coke, referring to it as a charter on which the lives and liberties of the woodland population depended, says that it was confirmed at least thirty times between the death of John and that of Henry V.; 4 Co.Inst. 303.

Webster, under the title Magna Charta, says that the name is applied to the charter granted in the 9th Hen. III. and confirmed by Edw. I. Prof. Maitland, in speaking of Magna Carta, refers to "the sister-charter which defined the forest law" as one of the four documents which, at the death of Henry III., comprised the written law of England. 1 Soc. England 410. Edward I. in 1297 confirmed "the charter made by the common consent of all the realm in the time of Henry III. to be kept in every point without breach." Inderwick, King's Peace 160; Stubb's Charters 486. The Century Dictionary refers to this latter charter of Edw. I. as *the* Charter of the Forest; but it was, as already shown, only a confirmation of it, and a comparison of the authorities leaves little if any doubt that the date was as above stated and the history as here given. Its provisions may be found in Stubb's Charters and they are summarized by Inderwick, in his work above cited.

Charta De Una Parte

A deed-poll; a deed of one part. Formerly used to distinguish a *deed poll*—that is, an agreement made by one party only—from a deed *inter partes*. Co.Litt. 229.

Charta Partita

(Literally, a deed divided.) A charter-party. 3 Kent, Comm. 201.

CHARTA DE NON ENTE NON VALET. A deed of a thing not in being is not valid. Co.Litt. 36.

CHARTA NON EST NISI VESTIMENTUM DONATIONIS. A deed is nothing else than the vestment of a gift. Co.Litt. 36.

CHAUSSÉE. Fr. A levee of earth, made to retain the water of a river or pond; a levee made in low, wet, and swampy places to serve as a road. Armas v. New Orleans, 3 La. 86, 99.

CHARTÆ LIBERTATUM. The charters (grants) of liberties. These are *Magna Charta* and *Charta de Foresta*.

CHARTARUM SUPER FIDEM, MORTUIS TESTIBUS, AD PATRIAM DE NECESSITUDINE RECURRENDUM EST. Co.Litt. 36. The witnesses being dead, the truth of charters must of necessity be referred to the country, *i. e.*, a jury.

CHARTE. Fr. A chart, or plan, which mariners use at sea.

CHARTE-PARTIE. Fr. In French marine law. A charter-party.

CHARTEL. A variant of "cartel" (*q. v.*).

CHARTER, *v.* In mercantile law. To hire or lease a vessel for a voyage. Thus, a "chartered" is distinguished from a "seeking" ship. 7 East, 24.

CHARTER, *n.* An instrument emanating from the sovereign power, in the nature of a grant, either to the whole nation, or to a class or portion of the people, or to a colony or dependency, and assuring to them certain rights, liberties, or powers. Such was the "Great Charter" or "*Magna Charta,*" and such also were the charters granted to certain of the English colonies in America. See Story, Const. § 161; 1 Bla.Comm. 108.

A charter differs from a constitution, in that the former is granted by the sovereign, while the latter is established by the people themselves.

A city's organic law. Hudson Motor Car Co. v. City of Detroit, 282 Mich. 69, 275 N.W. 770, 773, 113 A.L.R. 1472.

An act of a legislature creating a corporation, or creating and defining the franchise of a corporation. Baker v. Smith, 41 R.I. 17, 102 A. 721, 723; Bent v. Underdown, 156 Ind. 516, 60 N.E. 307. Also a corporation's constitution or organic law; Schultz v. City of Phœnix, 18 Ariz. 35, 156 P. 75, 76; C. J. Kubach Co. v. McGuire, 199 Cal. 215, 248 P. 676, 677; that is to say, the articles of incorporation taken in connection with the law under which the corporation was organized; Chicago Open Board of Trade v. Imperial Bldg. Co., 136 Ill.App. 606; In re Hanson's Estate, 38 S.D. 1, 159 N.W. 399, 400. The authority by virtue of which an organized body acts. Ryan v. Witt, Tex. Civ.App., 173 S.W. 952, 959. A contract between the state and the corporation, between the corporation and the stockholders, and between the stockholders and the state. Bruun v. Cook, 280 Mich. 484, 273 N.W. 774, 777.

In Old English Law

A deed or other written instrument under seal; a conveyance, covenant, or contract. Cowell; Spelman; Co.Litt. 6; 1 Co. 1; F.Moore 687.

In Old Scotch Law

A disposition made by a superior to his vassal, for something to be performed or paid by him. 1 Forb.Inst. pt. 2, b. 2, c. 1, tit. 1. A writing which contains the grant or transmission of the feudal right to the vassal. Ersk.Inst. 2, 3, 19.

Blank Charter

A document given to the agents of the crown in the reign of Richard II. with power to fill up as they pleased.

Charter of Pardon

In English law. An instrument under the great seal, by which a pardon is granted to a man for a felony or other offense.

Charter of the Forest

See Charta de foresta.

Charter Rolls

Ancient English records of royal charters, granted between the years 1199 and 1516.

CHARTER-HOUSE. Formerly a convent of Carthusian monks in London; now a college founded and endowed by Thomas Sutton. The governors of the charter-house are a corporation aggregate without a head, president, or superior, all the members being of equal authority. 3 Steph. Comm. (7th Ed.) 14, 97.

CHARTER-LAND. In English law. Otherwise called "book-land." Property held by deed under certain rents and free services. It, in effect, differs nothing from the free socage lands, and hence have arisen most of the freehold tenants, who hold of particular manors, and owe suit and service to the same. 2 Bl.Comm. 90.

CHARTER-PARTY. A contract by which a ship, or some principal part thereof, is let to a merchant for the conveyance of goods on a determined voyage to one or more places. Fish v. Sullivan, 40 La.Ann. 193, 3 So. 730; Vang v. Jones & Laughlin Steel Corporation, D.C.Pa., 7 F.Supp. 475, 478.

A specific and express contract by which the owner lets a vessel or some particular part thereof to another person for a specified time or use. Jones & Laughlin Steel Corporation v. Vang, C.C.A.Pa., 73 F.2d 88, 91.

A written agreement by which a ship-owner lets the whole or a part to a merchant for the conveyance of goods in consideration of payment of freight. Maude & P. Mer. Shipp. 227; Parker v. Washington Tug & Barge Co., 85 Wash. 575, 148 P. 896, 898. 3 Kent Comm. 201.

The contract by which a ship owner may either let the capacity or burden of the ship, continuing the employment of the owner's master, crew, and equipments, or may surrender the entire ship to the charterer, who then provides them himself. The master or part owner may be a charterer. Civil Code Cal. § 1959; Civil Code Dak. § 1127.

"A charter party may be a contract for the lease of the vessel, or for a special service to be rendered by the owner of the vessel. Where, as is very frequently the case, the shipowner undertakes to carry a cargo, to be provided by the charterer, on a designated voyage, the arrangement is * * * a mere contract of affreightment." United States v. Hvoslef, 237 U.S. 1, 35 S.Ct. 459, 460, 59 L.Ed. 813, Ann. Cas.1916A, 286.

CHARTERED SHIP. A ship hired or freighted; a ship which is the subject-matter of a charter-party.

CHARTERER. In mercantile law. One who charters (*i. e.*, hires or engages) a vessel for a voyage; a freighter. 2 Steph.Comm. 184; 3 Kent, Comm. 137; Turner v. Cross, 83 Tex. 218, 18 S.W. 578, 15 L.R.A. 262.

CHARTIS REDDENDIS. (For returning the charters.) An ancient writ which lay against one who had charters of feoffment intrusted to his keeping and refused to deliver them. Reg.Orig. 159.

CHARTOPHYLAX. In old European law. A keeper of records or public instruments; a chartulary; a registrar. Spelman.

CHARUE. In old English law. A plow. *Bestes des charues;* beasts of the plow.

CHASE. The liberty or franchise of hunting, one's self, and keeping protected against all other persons, beasts of the chase within a specified district, without regard to the ownership of the land. 2 Bl.Comm. 414–416.

The act of acquiring possession of animals *feræ naturæ* by force, cunning, or address.

A privileged place for preservation of deer and beasts of the forest. It is commonly less than a forest and of larger compass than a park. Every forest is a chase, but every chase is not a forest. It differs from a park in that it is not inclosed, yet it must have certain metes and bounds. Manwood, 49: *Termes de la Ley.*

Common Chase

In old English law. A place where all alike were entitled to hunt wild animals.

CHASSIS. As applied to a motor car, the rectangular metal framework, as distinguished from its body and seats, but including its accessories for propulsion, as the tanks, motor, etc., and general running gear. Kansas City Automobile School Co. v. Holcker-Elberg Mfg. Co., Mo.App., 182 S.W. 759, 761.

CHASTE. Never voluntarily having had unlawful sexual intercourse. Marchand v. State, 113 Neb. 87, 201 N.W. 890, 891. An unmarried woman who has had no carnal knowledge of men. New v. State, 141 Tex.Cr.R. 536, 148 S.W.2d 1099, 1101.

One who falls from virtue and afterwards reforms is chaste within the meaning of the seduction statutes. Wood v. State, 48 Ga. 288, 15 Am.Rep. 664; People v. Weinstock, 27 N.Y.Cr.R. 53, 140 N.Y.S. 453, 456.

CHASTE CHARACTER. Denoting purity of mind and innocence of heart;—not limited merely to unlawful sexual intercourse. State v. Wilcoxen, 200 Iowa, 1250, 206 N.W. 260, 261.

As used in statutes, means actual personal virtue. It may include the character of one who was formerly unchaste but is reformed. Boak v. State, 5 Iowa, 430; People v. Nelson, 153 N.Y. 90, 46 N.E. 1040, 60 Am.St.Rep. 592.

CHASTITY. Purity; continence.

It means that virtue which prevents the unlawful intercourse of the sexes; the state of purity or abstinence from unlawful sexual connection. People v. Kehoe, 123 Cal. 224, 55 P. 911, 69 Am.St.Rep. 52; actual personal virtue and character, and not a mere external reputation for chastity. People v. Weinstock, 27 N.Y.Cr.R. 53, 140 N.Y.S. 453, 457. See Chaste.

CHATTEL. An article of personal property; any species of property not amounting to a freehold or fee in land. People v. Holbrook, 13 Johns., N.Y., 94; U. S. v. Sischo, C.C.A.Wash., 270 F. 958, 961. A thing personal and movable. Castle v. Castle, C.C.A.Haw., 267 F. 521, 522. Things which in law are deemed personal property, they are divisible into chattels real and chattels personal.

The term "chattels" is a more comprehensive one than "goods," as it includes animate as well as inanimate property. 2 Chit.Bl.Comm. 383, note. In a devise, however, they may be of the same import. Shep.Touch. 447; 2 Fonbl.Eq. 335.

Chattel Interest

An interest in corporeal hereditaments less than a freehold. 2 Kent, Comm. 342.

Personal Chattels

Movable things. 2 Bl.Comm. 387; 2 Kent, 340; Co.Litt. 48*a*; 4 Co. 6; In re Gay, 5 Mass. 419; Miller v. Hirschmann, 170 Md. 145, 183 A. 259, 263.

Evidences of debt are chattels personal. Greene Line Terminal Co. v. Martin, 122 W.Va. 483, 10 S.E.2d 901, 906.

Real Chattels

Such as concern, or savor of, the realty, such as leasehold estates; interests issuing out of, or annexed to, real estate; such chattel interests as devolve after the manner of realty. Mozley & Whitley; 2 Bl.Comm. 386; In re Dalton's Estate, 183 Iowa, 1013, 168 N.W. 332, 334; Intermountain Realty Co. v. Allen, 60 Idaho 228, 90 P.2d 704, 706, 122 A.L.R. 647; Keystone Pipe & Supply Co. v. Crabtree, 174 Okl. 562, 50 P.2d 1086, 1088. An interest in real estate less than freehold, Lincoln Nat. Bank & Trust Co. of Fort Wayne v. Nathan, 215 Ind. 178, 19 N.E.2d 243, 249.

CHATTEL MORTGAGE. A mortgage on chattels. O'Connor v. Hassett, 207 Iowa, 155, 222 N.W. 530. A transfer of some legal or equitable right in personal property or creation of a lien thereon as security for payment of money or performance of some other act, Miller v. Eagle, Star & British Dominions Ins. Co., Limited, of London, England, United States Branch, New York, 146 S.C. 123, 143 S.E. 663, 666; Columbia Cas. Co. v. Sodini, 159 Kan. 478, 156 P.2d 524, 528; Anglo-American Mill Co. v. First Nat. Bank, 76 Colo. 57, 230 P. 118, 120; subject to defeasance on performance of the conditions. Personal Finance Co. of Providence v. Henley-Kimball Co., R.I., 1 A.2d 121, 124, 117 A.L.R. 1476; Thomas, Mortg. 427.

An instrument of sale of personalty conveying title to mortgagee with terms of defeasance; and, if the terms of redemption are not complied with, then, at common law, the title becomes absolute. Stewart v. Slater, 6 Duer (N. Y.) 99; In re Packard Press, C.C.A.N.Y., 5 F.2d 633, 635. A bill of sale with a defeasance clause incorporated in it. Monongahela Ins. Co. v. Batson, 111 Ark. 167, 163 S.W. 510, 511; Bank of Dillon v. Murchison, C.C.A.4, 213 F. 147, 151.

An absolute pledge, to become an absolute interest if not redeemed at a fixed time. Cortelyou v. Lansing, 2 Caines, Cas., N.Y., 200, per Kent, Ch.

A conditional sale of chattel as security for debt or performance of some other obligation. Jones, Chat. Mortg. § 1. Allen v. Steiger, 17 Colo. 552, 31 P. 226; Adler, Salzman & Adler v. Ammerman Furniture Co., 100 Conn. 223, 123 A. 268, 269.

A pledge is distinguished from a chattel mortgage in that in a mortgage, the title is transferred; in a pledge, the possession. Jones, Mortg. § 4; Security Trust Co. v. Edwards, 90 N.J.Law, 558, 101 A. 384, 385, L.R.A.1917F, 273; Thompson v. Dolliver, 132 Mass. 103; Thoen v. First Nat. Bank, 199 Minn. 47, 271 N.W. 111, 113; In pledge, the pawnee has only a special property in the thing deposited. Evans v. Darlington, 5 Blackf., Ind., 320.

A conditional sale is distinguished from a chattel mortgage in that the purchaser has merely a right to purchase, and no debt or obligation exists on the part of the vendor. Weathersly v. Weathersly, 40 Miss. 462, 90 Am.Dec. 344; Gomez v. Kamping, 4 Daly, N.Y., 77. In mortgage, title passes; in conditional sale possession is transferred and title retained. Kettwig v. Aero Inv. Co., 191 Minn. 500, 254 N.W. 629.

CHATTEL REAL. All interests in real estate of lesser dignity than a freehold estate, and which lesser estates or interest descended under the rules for devaluation of personal property and not as freehold or fee simple estates. Intermountain Realty Co. v. Allen, 60 Idaho 228, 90 P.2d 704, 705, 122 A.L.R. 647.

CHAUD-MEDLEY. A homicide committed in the heat of an affray and while under the influence of passion; it is thus distinguished from *chance-medley,* which is the killing of a man in a casual affray in self-defense. 4 Bl.Comm. 184. It has been said, however, that the distinction is of no great importance. See 1 Russ.Crimes, 660.

CHAUFFEUR. An operator who directly or indirectly receives compensation for operating motor vehicle. Turner v. State, 226 Ala. 269, 146 So. 601. Operators who drive jitneys in cities and towns for hire, Day v. Bush, 18 La.App. 682, 139 So. 42, 44. Person employed or paid to operate, drive and attend car. People v. Fulton, 96 Misc. 663, 162 N.Y.S. 125, 126; Des Moines Rug Cleaning Co. v. Automobile Underwriters, 215 Iowa 246, 245 N.W. 215, 217; State v. Depew, Md., 175 Md. 274, 1 A.2d 626, 627.

Test whether person is a chauffeur is whether he operated motor vehicle in whole or part-time employment, whether he was at such time an employee, servant, agent, or independent contractor, and whether he was paid for his service. Maryland Casualty Co. v. Cronholm, D.C.Tex., 32 F.Supp. 375, 377.

CHAUMPERT. A kind of tenure mentioned in a patent of 35 Edw. III. Cowell; Blount.

CHAUNTRY RENTS. Money paid to the crown by the servants or purchasers of chauntry-lands. See Chantry.

CHEAT, *v.* To deceive and defraud. State v. Mastin, 277 Mo. 495, 211 S.W. 15, 18; Moore v. State, 92 Ind.App. 150, 168 N.E. 202, 203. It necessarily implies a fraudulent intent. Clolinger v. Callahan, 204 Ky. 33, 263 S.W. 700, 702.

The words "cheat and defraud" usually mean to induce a person to part with the possession of property by reason of intentionally false representations relied and acted upon by such person to his harm. Antonio Pepe Co. v. Apuzzo, 98 Conn. 807, 120 A. 681, 682; They include not only the crime of false pretenses, but also all civil frauds. Hinshaw v. State, 188 Ind. 147, 122 N.E. 418, 419. They include all tricks, devices, artifices, or deceptions used to deprive another of property or other right. State v. Parker, 114 Conn. 354, 158 A. 797, 800.

CHEAT, *n.* Swindling; defrauding. "Deceitful practices in defrauding or *endeavoring* to defraud another of his known right, by some *willful device,* contrary to the plain rules of common honesty." Hawk.P.C. b. 2, c. 23, § 1. "The fraudulent obtaining the property of another by any deceitful and illegal practice or token (short of felony) which affects or may affect the public." Steph.Crim. Law, 93.

Cheats, punishable at common law, are such cheats (not amounting to felony) as are effected by deceitful or illegal symbols or tokens which may affect the public at large, and against which common prudence could not have guarded. 2 Whart.Crim.Law, § 1116; 2 East, P.C. 818; Von Mumm v. Frash, C.C.N.Y., 56 F. 836; State v. Parker, 43 N.H. 85.

CHEATERS, or ESCHEATORS, were officers appointed to look after the king's escheats, a duty which gave them great opportunities of fraud and oppression, and in consequence many complaints were made of their misconduct. Hence it seems that a *cheater* came to signify a fraudulent person, and thence the verb to *cheat* was derived. Wharton.

CHECK, *v.* To control or restrain; to hold within bounds. To verify or audit; to verify, guard, or examine the work of another. Marsh v. State, 125

Ark. 282, 188 S.W. 815, 816; State v. Hearn, 115 Ohio St. 340, 154 N.E. 244, 245. Particularly used with reference to the control or supervision of one department, bureau, office, or person over another.

As used in initiative statute, to compare names of signer of petition against official registration list. Halgren v. Welling, 91 Utah, 16, 63 P.2d 550, 554.

CHECK, *n.* A commercial device intended for use as a temporary expedient for actual money, and generally designed for immediate payment, and not for circulation. Kennedy v. Jones, 140 Ga. 302, 78 S.E. 1069, 1070, Ann.Cas.1914D, 355; Merchants' Nat. Bank v. Bank, 10 Wall. 647, 19 L.Ed. 1008.

A draft for payment of money. Wright v. Loring, 351 Ill. 584, 184 N.E. 865, 866. An order for payment of money. Glennan v. Rochester Trust & Safe Deposit Co., 209 N.Y. 12, 102 N.E. 537, 539, 52 L.R.A.,N.S., 302, Ann.Cas.1915A, 441; Weiss v. Fenwick, 111 N.J.Eq. 385, 162 A. 609, 611; Anderson v. National Bank of Tacoma, 146 Wash. 520, 264 P. 8, 10. A request to pay money, Standard Factors Corporation v. Manufacturers Trust Co., 182 Misc. 701, 50 N.Y. S.2d 10, 13.

A draft or order upon a bank or banking-house, purporting to be drawn upon a deposit of funds, for the payment at all events of a certain sum of money to a certain person therein named, or to him or his order, or to bearer, and payable instantly on demand. 2 Daniel, Neg.Inst. § 1566; Bank v. Wheaton, 4 R.I. 33; Economy Fuse & Mfg. Co. v. Standard Electric Mfg. Co., 359 Ill. 504, 194 N.E. 922, 924.

A bill of exchange drawn on a bank payable on demand. Commercial & Savings Bank Co. of Bellafontaine, Ohio, v. Citizens' Nat. Bank of Franklin, 68 Ind.App. 417, 120 N.E. 670, 674; Bell-Wayland Co. v. Bank of Sugden, 95 Okl. 67, 218 P. 705, 706; Thomas v. Berger, 118 Pa.Super. 422, 180 A. 32. A check differs from an ordinary bill of exchange in that it is drawn on a bank or bankers, and is payable immediately on presentment, without days of grace; it is payable immediately on presentment, and no acceptance as distinct from payment is required; it is supposed to be drawn upon a previous deposit of funds, and is an absolute appropriation of so much money in the hands of the bankers to the holder of the check. Merchants' Nat. Bank v. State Nat. Bank, 10 Wall. 647, 19 L.Ed. 1008; People v. Compton, 123 Cal. 403, 56 P. 44.

The term "check," within the ordinary meaning of that term, includes "draft," the only distinction being that in a draft the drawer is a bank, while in the ordinary check the drawer is an individual. Leach v. Mechanics' Sav. Bank, 202 Iowa, 899, 211 N.W. 506, 508, 50 A.L.R. 388.

A check is a contract. Deal v. Atlantic Coast Line R. Co., 225 Ala. 533, 144 So. 81, 82, 86 A.L.R. 455; Roff v. Crenshaw, Cal.App., 159 P.2d 661, 662.

Cashier's Check

One issued by an authorized officer of a bank directed to another person, evidencing that the payee is authorized to demand and receive upon presentation from the bank the amount of money represented by the check. State v. Tyler County State Bank, Tex.Com.App., 277 S.W. 625, 627, 42 A. L.R. 1347. A form of a check by which the bank lends its credit to the purchaser of the check, the purpose being to make it available for immediate use in banking circles. Duke v. Johnson, 127 Wash. 601, 221 P. 321, 322. A bill of exchange drawn by a bank upon itself, and accepted by the act of issuance. Anderson v. Bank of Tupelo, 135 Miss. 351, 100 So. 179; In its legal effect, it is the same as a certificate of deposit, certified check or draft. Montana-Wyoming Ass'n of Credit Men v. Commercial Nat. Bank of Miles City, 80 Mont. 174, 259 P. 1060, 1061. An acknowledgment of a debt drawn by bank upon itself. In re Liquidation of State Bank of Binghamton, 152 Misc. 579, 274 N.Y.S. 41.

Crossed Check

A check crossed with two lines, between which are either the name of a bank or the words "and company," in full or abbreviated. In the former case, the banker on whom it is drawn must not pay the money for the check to any other than the banker named; in the latter case, he must not pay it to any other than a banker. 2 Steph.Comm. 118, note *c*. And see 7 Exch. 389; [1903] A.C. 240; Farmers' Bank v. Johnson, King & Co., 134 Ga. 486, 68 S.E. 85, 30 L.R.A.,N.S., 697.

Forged Check

A check on which the maker's name is forged—not one which has forged indorsements. Kleinman v. Chase Nat. Bank of City of New York, 124 Misc. 173, 207 N.Y.S. 191, 193. See, also, International Union Bank v. National Surety Co., 245 N.Y. 368, 157 N.E. 269, 270. A check which is created as a result of a criminal act of forgery. Samples v. Milton County Bank, 34 Ga.App. 248, 129 S.E. 170.

Memorandum Check

A check given by a borrower to a lender, for the amount of a short loan, with the understanding that it is not to be presented at the bank, but will be redeemed by the maker himself when the loan falls due. This understanding is evidenced by writing the word *"Mem."* on the check. This is not unusual among merchants. See U. S. v. Isham, 17 Wall. 502, 21 L.Ed. 728; Franklin Bank v. Freeman, 16 Pick., Mass., 539; Story, Pr.Notes § 499.

Traveler's Check

See that title.

CHECK-BOOK. A book containing blank checks on a particular bank or banker.

CHECK-OFF SYSTEM. Deduction by employer from pay of employees of sums and payment of such sums to union. Pacific Mills v. Textile Workers' Union of America, Local No. 254, 197 S.C. 330, 15 S.E.2d 134, 136, 135 A.L.R. 497; Local 60 of Industrial Union of Marine and Shipbuilding Workers of America v. Welin Davit and Boat Corporation, 133 N.J.Eq. 551, 33 A.2d 708, 709; Borderland Coal Corporation v. International Organization of United Mine Workers of America, D. C.Ind., 275 F. 871, 873.

CHECK-ROLL. In English law. A list or book, containing the names of such as are attendants on, or in the pay of, the queen or other great personages, as their household servants.

CHECKER. The old Scotch form of exchequer.

CHECKERBOARD SYSTEM. This term, with reference to entries on lands, means one entry built on another, and a third on the second. Sequatchie & South Pittsburg Coal & Iron Co. v. Tennessee Coal, Iron & R. Co., 131 Tenn. 221, 174 S.W. 1122.

CHEFE. In Anglo-Norman law. Were or weregild; the price of the head or person, *(capitis pretium.)*

CHEMERAGE. In old French law. The privilege or prerogative of the eldest. A provincial term derived from *chemier, (q. v.)* Guyot, Inst.

CHEMIER. In old French law. The eldest born. A term used in Poitou and other places. Guyot, Inst.

CHEMIN. Fr. The road wherein every man goes; the king's highway. Called in law Latin *via regia*. Termes de la Ley; Cowell; Spelman, Gloss.

CHEMIS. In old Scotch law. A chief dwelling or mansion house.

CHEQUE. A variant of check (*q. v.*).

CHEROKEE NATION. One of the civilized Indian tribes. See Indians; Indian Tribe.

CHEVAGE. A sum of money paid by villeins to their lords in acknowledgment of their bondage.

It was exacted for permission to marry, and also permission to remain without the dominion of the lord. When paid to the king, it was called subjection. *Termes de la Ley;* Co.Litt. 140 *a;*. Spelman, Gloss.

Chevage seems also to have been used for a sum of money yearly given to a man of power for his countenance and protection as a chief or leader. Termes de la Ley; Cowell.

CHEVANTIA. In old records. A loan or advance of money upon credit. Cowell.

CHEVISANCE. An agreement or composition; an end or order set down between a creditor or debtor; an indirect gain in point of usury, etc.; also an unlawful bargain or contract. Wharton.

CHEVITIÆ. In old records. Pieces of ground, or *heads* at the end of plowed lands. Cowell.

CHEZE. A homestead or homesfall which is accessory to a house.

CHICANE. Swindling; shrewd cunning. The use of tricks and artifice.

CHICKASAW NATION. One of the civilized Indian tribes. See Indians; Indian Tribe.

CHIEF. One who is put above the rest. Principal; leading; head; eminent in power or importance; the best or most important or valuable of several; paramount; of leading importance.

Declaration in chief is a declaration for the principal cause of action. 1 Tidd, Pr. 419.

Examination in chief is the first examination of a witness by the party who produces him. 1 Greenl.Ev. § 445.

Tenant in chief. See "Chief, tenant in," *infra.*

CHIEF BARON. The presiding judge of the English court of exchequer; answering to the chief justice of other courts. 3 Bl.Comm. 44; 3 Steph. Comm. 401.

CHIEF CLERK. The principal clerical officer of a bureau or department, who is generally charged, subject to the direction of his superior officer, with the superintendence of the administration of the business of the office.

CHIEF JUDGE. In some states, the presiding judge, as in the New York Court of Appeals and the Maryland Court of Appeals. The term is also used in 1 Tyler (Vt.) with "assistant" judge for the puisne. It is likewise applied to the judge of the London bankruptcy court. In general, the term is equivalent to "presiding justice" or "presiding magistrate." Bean v. Loryea, 81 Cal. 151, 22 P. 513.

CHIEF JUSTICE. The presiding, eldest, or principal judge of a court of justice.

CHIEF JUSTICE OF ENGLAND. The presiding judge in the king's bench division of the high court of justice, and, in the absence of the lord chancellor, president of the high court, and also an *ex officio* judge of the court of appeals. The full title is "Lord Chief Justice of England."

CHIEF JUSTICE OF THE COMMON PLEAS. In England. The presiding judge in the court of common pleas, and afterwards in the common pleas division of the high court of justice, and one of the *ex officio* judges of the high court of appeal.

CHIEF JUSTICIAR. In old English law. A high judicial officer and special magistrate, who presided over the *aula regis* of the Norman kings, and who was also the principal minister of state, the second man in the kingdom, and, by virtue of his office, guardian of the realm in the king's absence. 3 Bl.Comm. 38.

CHIEF LORD. The immediate lord of the fee, to whom the tenants were directly and personally responsible. Burton, R.P. 317.

CHIEF MAGISTRATE. The head of the executive department of government of a nation, state, or municipal corporation. McIntire v. Ward, 3 Yeates, Pa., 424.

CHIEF OFFICE. Office of paramount importance or the leading office. City of Newark v. New Jersey Inv. Co., 18 N.J.Misc. 182, 11 A.2d 730, 731.

CHIEF PLEDGE. The borsholder, or chief of the borough. Spelman.

CHIEF RENTS. In English law. Were the annual payments of freeholders of manors; and were also called "quit-rents," because by paying them the tenant was freed from all other rents or services. 2 Bl.Comm. 42.

CHIEF, TENANT IN. In English feudal law. All the land in the kingdom was supposed to be holden mediately or immediately of the king, who was styled the "Lord Paramount," or "Lord Above All;" and those that held immediately under him, in right of his crown and dignity, were called his tenants "*in capite*" or "in chief," which was the most honorable species of tenure, but at the same time subjected the tenant to greater and more burdensome services than inferior tenures did. Brown. One who held directly of the king. 1 Washb.R.P. *19.

CHIEFRIE. In feudal law. A small rent paid to the lord paramount.

CHILD. See Children.

CHILDREN. Progeny

Child of tender age or years

Such a child must be less than 14 years old. Barnhill's Adm'r v. Mt. Morgan Coal Co., D.C.Ky., 215 F. 608, 610. A minor more than 15 years of age is not included within the meaning of the term. Paulk & Fossil v. Lee, 31 Ga.App. 629, 121 S.E. 845.

Child's Part

A "child's part," which a widow, by statute in some states, is entitled to take in lieu of dower or the provision made for her by will, is a full share to which a child of the decedent would be entitled, subject to the debts of the estate and the cost of administration up to and including distribution. Benedict v. Wilmarth, 46 Fla. 535, 35 So. 84.

Illegitimate Child

A bastard (*q. v.*).

Legitimate Child

One born in lawful wedlock.

Natural Child

A bastard (*q. v.*); a child born out of lawful wedlock. But in a statute declaring that adopted shall have all the rights of "natural" children, the word "natural" was used in the sense of "legitimate." Barns v. Allen, 9 Am.Law Reg., O.S., 747. In Louisiana. Illegitimate children who have been acknowledged by the father. Civ.Code La. art. 202. In the civil law. A child by natural relation or procreation; a child by birth, as distinguished from a child by adoption. Inst. 1, 11, pr.; Id. 3, 1, 2; Id. 3, 8 pr. See, also, Conner v. Parsley, 192 Ky. 827, 234 S.W. 972, 974; Middletown Trust Co. v. Gaffey, 96 Conn. 61, 112 A. 689, 691.

A child by concubinage, in contradistinction to a child by marriage. Cod. 5, 27.

Posthumous Child

One born after the father's death.

Quasi Posthumous Child

In the civil law. One who, born during the life of his grandfather, or other male ascendant, was not his heir at the time he made his testament, but who by the death of his father became his heir in his life-time. Inst. 2, 13, 2; Dig. 28, 3, 13.

The word "child" in statutes often means either child or children. Cunningham v. Dunn, 84 W.Va. 593, 100 S.E. 410, 411. See Children.

"Children" is ordinarily a word of description, limited to persons standing in the same relation, and has the same effect as if all the names were given. Rowley v. Currie, 94 N.J.Eq. 606, 120 A. 653, 656.

The words "child or children," in their usual sense, are words of purchase. Phillips v. Mercantile Trust Co. of Baltimore, 195 A. 394, 395, 173 Md. 290; Kelly v. Kelly, 176 Ark. 548, 3 S.W.2d 305; Deener v. Watkins, 191 Ark. 776, 87 S.W.2d 994, 995; they may, however, be used as words of limitation, Bonds v. Hutchison, 199 S.C. 197, 18 S.E.2d 661, 662, 663; Crawford v. Withrow, 314 Pa. 497, 171 A. 894, 895; Young v. Munsey Trust Co., 72 App.D.C. 73, 111 F.2d 514, 515.

The terms "child" or "children" may include or apply to:

Adopted children, Dyer v. Lane, 202 Ark. 571, 151 S.W.2d 678, 680; Ex parte Cline, 213 Ala. 599, 105 So. 686, 687; Ryan v. Foreman, 262 Ill. 175, 104 N.E. 189; but some decisions hold that adopted children are not included in absence of manifest intention, Savells v. Brown's Guardian, 187 Ky. 134, 218 S.W. 462, 463; Melek v. Curators of University of Missouri, 213 Mo.App. 572, 250 S.W. 614, 615; for cases holding that "child" or "children" does not include adopted children, see Everitt v. LaSpeyre, 195 Ga. 377, 24 S.E.2d 381, 383; Moffet v. Cash, 346 Ill. 287, 178 N.E. 658, 659; In re Sandford's Estate, 160 Misc. 898, 290 N.Y.S. 959, 960; Adult child, Mindlin v. Consolidated Taxpayers Mut. Ins. Co., 173 Misc. 961, 19 N.Y.S.2d 340, 342; State ex rel. Buerk v. Calhoun, 330 Mo. 1172, 52 S.W.2d 742, 83 A.L.R. 1393; after-born child, Westport Paper-Board Co. v. Staples, 127 Conn. 115, 15 A.2d 1, 5; contra, Albers v. Donovan, 371 Ill. 458, 21 N.E.2d 563, 565; all lineal descendants. Boston Safe Deposit & Trust Co. v. Park, 307 Mass. 255, 29 N.E.2d 977, 980; blood relations. In re Fletcher's Estate, 103 Pa.Super. 69, 157 A. 810, 811; child by second marriage, Nelson v. Estill, 175 Ga. 526, 165 S.E. 820, 823; child that would inherit from an intestate parent, In re Gossett's Estate, 46 N.M. 344, 129 P.2d 56, 58, 60, 142 A.L.R. 1441; child en ventre sa mere, Valley Nat. Bank v. Hartford Accident & Indemnity Co., 57 Ariz. 276, 113 P.2d 359, 361: Thomson v. Elliott, 152 Misc. 188, 273 N.Y.S. 898; children born in wedlock, Bell v. Phyn, 7 Ves. 458; In re Silva's Estate, 32 Ariz. 573, 261 P. 40, 41. Children by former marriage, In re Freisinger's Will, 263 App. Div. 970, 33 N.Y.S.2d 196, 197; children by various marriages of parent named, McMullen v. Block, Tex.Civ.App., 168 S.W.2d 667, 670; children in first degree. In re Brown's Estate, 133 Misc. 587, 233 N.Y.S. 426, 430; Children regardless of age, Citizens' Bank of Lancaster v. Foglesong, 326 Mo. 581, 31 S.W.2d 778, 783; correlative of "parent;" descendant or descendants of first degree, Benners v. First Nat. Bank of Birmingham, 247 Ala. 74, 22 So.2d 435, 442; first degree descendants, Spencer v. Title Guarantee Loan & Trust Co., 222 Ala. 485, 132 So. 730, 731; first generation of offspring. New York Life Ins. Co. v. Beebe, D.C.Md., 57 F.Supp. 754, 757.

Grandchildren, Holbrook v. Shepard, 245 N.Y. 618, 157 N.E. 882; Tucker v. Tucker, 259 Ky. 361, 82 S.W.2d 458, 459, 460; Cherokee Brick Co. v. Bishop, 156 Tenn. 168, 299 S.W. 770; but, ordinarily, grandchildren are not included, Lowrey v. Le Flore, 48 Okl. 235, 149 P. 1112, 1114, Ann. Cas.1918E, 1001; Sabit v. Safe Deposit & Trust Co. of Baltimore, 184 Md. 24, 40 A.2d 231, 238; In re Blodgett's Will, 250 App.Div. 324, 294 N.Y.S. 358, 366; as used in deeds or wills especially, the term "children" will not be construed to mean grandchildren, unless a strong case of intention or context requires it. Greenfield v. Lauritson, 306 Ill. 279, 137 N.E. 818, 819; Davis v. Mitchell, Tenn. App., 178 S.W.2d 889, 904; In re Reed's Estate, 342 Pa. 54, 19 A.2d 365, 366.

Heirs or heirs of the body, Beall v. Beall, 331 Ill. 28, 162 N.E. 152, 154; Schwarz v. Rabe, 129 Kan. 430, 283 P. 642, 643; Conover v. Code, 184 Ind. 604, 112 N.E. 7, 12; Darragh v. Barmore, Tex.Com.App., 242 S.W. 714, 718; but the intention to use "children" in the sense of "heirs" must be made clear. Farrell v. Faries, Del., 22 A.2d 380, 384, 385. So, too, the term "heirs" may mean "children," Albers v. Donovan, 371 Ill. 458, 21 N.E.2d 563, 565; Lane v. Citizen's & Southern Nat. Bank, 195 Ga. 828, 25 S.E.2d 800, 804; but the intention to so use the word must be manifest. Welles v. Pape, 63 Ohio App. 432, 27 N.E.2d 169, 172; For cases holding that "heirs" does not mean "children" see Erwin Nat. Bank v. Riddle, 18 Tenn.App. 561, 79 S.W.2d 1032, 1038; Triplett v. Triplett, 332 Mo. 870, 60 S.W.2d 13, 15.

Illegitimate children, State ex rel. Herbert v. Hocking Valley Mining Co., 73 Ohio App. 483, 57 N.E.2d 236, 238; In re Anonymous, 165 Misc. 62, 300 N.Y.S. 292; but other decisions have held that the terms exclude illegitimate children, Bank of Montclair v. McCutcheon, 107 N.J.Eq. 564, 152 A. 379, 380; Jacobs v. United States, C.C.A.La., 112 F.2d 51; Gee v. Commonwealth, 263 Ky. 808, 94 S.W.2d 17, 19; illegitimate children that have been acknowledged or adopted, Weyerhaeuser Timber Co. v. Marshall, C.C.A. Wash., 102 F.2d 78, 81; Jenkins v. City of Los Angeles, 60 Cal.App.2d 50, 40 P.2d 45, 46; Hastings v. Rathbone, 194 Iowa, 177, 188 N.W. 960, 962, 23 A.L.R. 392; immediate offspring or progeny, McQueen v. Stephens, Tex.Civ.App., 100 S.W.2d 1053, 1055; In re Conant's Estate, 144 Misc. 743, 259 N.Y.S. 885; infant offspring. In re Berg's Estate, 72 N.D. 52, 4 N.W.2d 575, 580, 140 A.L.R. 1332. Issue, Woodley v. Howse, 133 Kan. 639, 3 P.2d 475, 476; Hodge v. Lovell's Trustee, 262 Ky. 509, 90 S.W.2d 683, 686. So too, "issue" may mean "children." Pierson v. Jones, 108 N.J.Eq. 453, 155 A. 541, 542; In re Morningstar's Will, 143 Misc. 620, 257 N.Y.S. 240, 249. Legitimate children, Dunlavy v. Lowrie, 372 Ill. 622, 25 N.E.2d 67, 71; Town of Plymouth v. Hey, 285 Mass. 357, 189 N.E. 100, 101; Middleton v. Luckenbach S. S. Co., C.C.A.N.Y., 70 F.2d 326, 328;

legitimated child, Brown v. Shwinogee, 128 Okl. 149, 261 P. 920, 921; living children, In re Schuette's Estate, 138 Neb. 568, 293 N.W. 421, 422; Ward v. Ward, 176 Ga. 849, 169 S.E. 120, 121, 122; male or female, Turner v. Metropolitan Life Ins. Co., 56 Cal.App.2d 862, 133 P.2d 859, 861; Curtis v. Safe Deposit & Trust Co. of Baltimore, 178 Md. 360, 13 A.2d 546, 548; married child, Killian v. Burnham, 191 Okl. 248, 130 P.2d 538, 539; In re Drye, 250 Mich. 210, 229 N.W. 623, 625; minor or minors. Walsh v. Walsh, Cal.App., 106 P.2d 763, 764; State v. Flath, 59 N.D. 121, 228 N.W. 847, 849; "natural-born children." In re Corr's Estate, 338 Pa. 337, 12 A.2d 76, 78; natural offspring of parentage, In re Wait's Estate, Sur., 42 N.Y.S.2d 735, 738, 739; offspring of either sex and of any age, Morris v. Williams, Tex.Civ.App., 92 S.W.2d 541, 544; opposite of "adult," Miller v. Finegan, 26 Fla. 29, 7 So. 140, 6 L.R.A. 813; Potter v. Golden Rule Grocery Co., 169 Tenn. 240, 84 S.W.2d 364, 365; person under age of 18 years, State v. Flath, 59 N.D. 121, 228 N.W. 847, 848; person under age of majority, Wade v. State, 24 Ala.App. 176, 132 So. 71, 72; posthumous child, Travelers Ins. Co. v. Dudley, 180 Tenn. 191, 173 S.W.2d 142, 144; posthumous, illegitimate child, Morgan v. Susino Const. Co., 130 N.J.L. 418, 33 A.2d 607, 610.

Contra, Gierak v. Lehigh & Wilkes-Barre Coal Co., 101 Pa.Super. 397, 399; Staker v. Industrial Commission of Ohio, 127 Ohio St. 13, 186 N.E. 616; quick child, Guiffrida v. State, 61 Ga.App. 595, 7 S.E.2d 34, 35; sons and daughters, Kimberlin v. Hicks, 150 Kan. 449, 94 P.2d 335, 340; Stepchildren, Newark Paving Co. v. Klotz, 85 N.J.Law, 432, 91 A. 91, 92; Travelers Ins. Co. v. E. I. Du Pont De Nemours & Co., Del., 1 Terry 285, 9 A.2d 88, 91.

CHILDWIT. In Saxon law. The right which a lord had of taking a fine of his bondwoman gotten with child without his license. Termes de la Ley.

The custom in Essex county, England, whereby every reputed father of a bastard child was obliged to pay a small fine to the lord. Cowell.

CHILLING A SALE. The act of bidders or others who combine or conspire to suppress fair competition at a sale, for the purpose of acquiring the property at less than its fair value. Vette v. Hackman, 292 Mo. 138, 237 S.W. 802, 805.

CHILTERN HUNDREDS. In English law. The offices of steward or bailiff of His Majesty's three Chiltern Hundreds of Stoke, Desborough, and Bonenham; or the steward of the Manor of Northsted. Chiltern Hundreds is an appointment under the hand and seal of the Chancellor of the Exchequer. May, Parl.Pr. 642.

The stewardship of the Chiltern Hundreds is a nominal office in the gift of the crown, usually accepted by members of the house of commons desirous of vacating their seats. By law a member once duly elected to parliament is compelled to discharge the duties of the trust conferred upon him, and is not enabled at will to resign it. But by statute, if any member accepts any office of profit from the crown, (except officers in the army or navy accepting a new commission,) his seat is vacated. If, therefore, any member wishes to retire from the representation of the county or borough by which he was sent to parliament, he applies to the lords of the treasury for the stewardship of one of the Chiltern Hundreds, which having received, and thereby accomplished his purpose, he again resigns the office. Brown.

CHIMIN. In old English law. A road, way, highway. It is either the king's highway (*chiminus regis*) or a private way. The first is that over which the subjects of the realm, and all others under the protection of the crown, have free liberty to pass, though the property in the soil itself belong to some private individual; the last is that in which one person or more have liberty to pass over the land of another, by prescription or charter. Wharton. See Chemin.

CHIMINAGE. A toll for passing on a way through a forest; called in the civil law *"pedagium."* Cowell. See Co.Litt. 56 *a*; Spelman, Gloss.; Termes de la Ley; Baldwin's Ed. of Britton, 63.

CHIMINUS. The way by which the king and all his subjects and all under his protection have a right to pass, though the property of the soil of each side where the way lieth may belong to a private man. Cowell.

CHIMNEY MONEY, or HEARTH MONEY. A tax upon chimneys or hearth; an ancient tax or duty upon houses in England, now repealed. See Hearth Money; Fuage.

CHIPPINGAVEL. In old English law. A tax upon trade; a toll imposed upon traffic, or upon goods brought to a place to be sold; a toll for buying and selling. Whishaw; Blount.

CHIRGEMOT, CHIRCHGEMOT. (Also spelled Chirgemote, Chirchgemote, Circgemote, Kirkmote.) In Saxon law. An ecclesiastical assembly or court. Spelman. A synod or meeting in a church or vestry. 4 Inst. 321; Blount; Spelman, Gloss.; Hen. I. cc. 4, 8; Cunningh.Law Dict.

CHIROGRAPH. In Civil and Canon law. An instrument written out and subscribed by the hand of the party who made it, whether the king or a private person. Du Cange; Cowell.

In old English law. A deed or indenture; also the last part of a fine of land, called more commonly, perhaps, the foot of the fine. Cruise, Dig. t. 35, c. 2, s. 52.

An instrument of gift or conveyance attested by the subscription and crosses of the witnesses, which was in Saxon times called *"chirographum,"* and which, being somewhat changed in form and manner by the Normans, was by them styled *"charta."* Anciently when they made a chirograph or deed which required a counterpart, as we call it, they engrossed it twice upon one piece of parchment contrariwise, leaving a space between, in which they wrote in capital letters the word "chirograph," and then cut the parchment in two through the middle of the word, giving a part to each party. Cowell; 2 Bla.Comm. 296. See, also, Charta cyrographata.

In Scotch law. A written voucher for a debt. Bell.

CHIROGRAPHA. In Roman law. Writings emanating from a single party, the debtor.

CHIROGRAPHER OF FINES. In English law. The title of the officer of the common pleas who engrossed fines in that court so as to be acknowledged into a perpetual record. Cowell.

CHIROGRAPHUM. In Roman law. A handwriting; that which was written with a person's own hand. An obligation which a person wrote or subscribed with his own hand; an acknowledgment of debt, as of money received, with a promise to repay. An evidence or voucher of debt; a security for debt. Dig. 26, 7, 57, pr. A right of action for debt.

CHIROGRAPHUM APUD DEBITOREM REPERTUM PRÆSUMITUR SOLUTUM. An evidence of debt found in the debtor's possession is presumed to be paid. Halk.Max. 20; Bell, Dict. See 14 M. & W. 379.

CHIROGRAPHUM NON EXTANS PRÆSUMITUR SOLUTUM. An evidence of debt not existing is presumed to have been discharged. Tray. Lat.Max. 73.

CHIROPODIST. One who treats diseases or malformations of the hands or feet, especially a surgeon for the feet, hands, and nails; a cutter or extractor of corns and callosities. State v. Armstrong, 38 Idaho 493, 225 P. 491, 33 A.L.R. 835.

CHIROPODY. The art of removing corns and callouses. State v. Armstrong, 38 Idaho 493, 225 P. 491, 493, 33 A.L.R. 835.

CHIROPRACTIC, CHIROPRACTICS. A system of healing that treats disease by manipulation of the spinal column. Joyner v. State, 181 Miss. 245, 179 So. 573, 575, 115 A.L.R. 954. A system of therapeutic treatment, through adjusting of articulations of human body, particularly those of the spine. Walkenhorst v. Kesler, 92 Utah 312, 67 P.2d 654, 662. The specific science that removes pressure on the nerves by the adjustment of the spinal vertebrae. State v. Boston, 226 Iowa 429, 284 N.W. 143, 144.

CHIROPRACTOR. One who practices the system of chiropractic. Cummings v. State, 214 Ala. 209, 106 So. 852, 854. One professing a system of manipulations which aims to cure disease by the mechanical restoration of displaced or subluxated bones, especially the vertebræ, to their normal relation. Board of Medical Examiners of State of Utah v. Freenor, 47 Utah, 430, 154 P. 941, 942, Ann. Cas.1917E, 1156.

CHIRURGEON. The ancient denomination of a surgeon.

CHIVALRY. In feudal law. Knight-service Tenure in chivalry was the same as tenure by knight-service. 2 Bl.Comm. 61, 62.

CHIVALRY, COURT OF. See Court of Chivalry.

CHIVALRY, TENURE BY. Tenure by knight-service. Co.Litt.

CHOATE LIEN. Lien which is perfected so that nothing more need be done to make it enforcible. Identity of lienor, property subject to lien and amount of lien are all established. Walker v. Paramount Engineering Co., C.A.Mich., 353 F.2d 445, 449; U. S. v. City of New Britain, Conn., Conn., 74 S.Ct. 367, 369, 347 U.S. 81, 98 L.Ed. 520. The lien must be definite and not mere ascertainable in the future by taking further steps. Gower v. State Tax Commission, 295 P.2d 162, 207 Or. 288.

CHOKE DAMP. A common name for carbonic acid;—so called from its extinguishing of flame and animal life. Wells' Adm'r v. Sutherland Coal & Coke Co., 116 Va. 1003, 83 S.E. 384, 385.

CHOP-CHURCH. A word mentioned in 9 Hen. VI. c. 65, by the sense of which it was in those days a kind of trade, and by the judges declared to be lawful. But Brooke, in his abridgment, says it was only permissible by law. It was, without doubt, a nickname given to those who used to change benefices, as to "chop and change" is a common expression. Jacob.

CHOPS. The mouth of a harbor. Pub.St.Mass. 1882, p. 1288.

CHORAL. In ancient times a person admitted to sit and worship in the choir; a chorister.

CHOREPISCOPUS. In old European law. A rural bishop, or bishop's vicar. Spelman; Cowell.

CHOSE. Fr. A thing; an article of personal property. A chose is a chattel personal, (Williams, Pers.Prop. 4,) and is either in action or in possession. See Chose in Action and Chose in Possession, *infra*.

Chose local. A local thing; a thing annexed to a place, as a mill. Kitchin, fol. 18; Cowell; Blount.

Chose transitory. A thing which is movable, and may be taken away or carried from place to place. Cowell; Blount.

CHOSE IN ACTION. A personal right not reduced into possession, but recoverable by a suit at law. North Carolina Bank & Trust Co. v. Williams, 160 S.E. 484, 485, 201 N.C. 464. A right to personal things of which the owner has not the possession, but merely a right of action for their possession. 2 Bl.Comm. 389, 397; 1 Chit.Pr. 99. The phrase includes all personal chattels which are not in possession; 11 App.Cas. 440; Powers v. Fisher, 279 Mich. 442; 272 N.W. 737, 739; and all property in action which depends entirely on contracts express or implied; Castle v. Castle, C.C.A. Hawaii, 267 F. 521, 523. A right to receive or recover a debt, demand, or damages on a cause of action *ex contractu* or for a tort or omission of a duty. Comyns, Dig. *Biens*. Moran v. Adkerson, 168 Tenn. 372, 79 S.W.2d 44, 45. Pickering v. Peskind, 43 Ohio App. 401, 183 N.E. 301, 303. A right to recover by suit a personal chattel. Garford Motor Truck Co. v. Buckson, 4 W.W.Harr. 103, 143 A. 410, 411. Assignable rights of action ex contractu and perhaps ex delicto. Coty v. Cogswell, 100 Mont. 496, 50 P.2d 249, 250. Personalty to which the owner has a right of possession in future, or a right of immediate possession, wrongfully withheld. And see Tumy v. Mayer, 289 Ill. 458, 124 N.E. 661, 662.

CHOSE IN POSSESSION. A personal thing of which one has possession. A thing in possession, as distinguished from a thing in action. Vawter v. Griffin, 40 Ind. 601. See Chose in Action. Taxes and customs, if paid, are a chose in possession; if unpaid, a chose in action. 2 Bl.Comm. 408.

CHOSEN FREEHOLDERS. Under the municipal organization of the state of New Jersey, each county has a board of officers, called by this name, composed of representatives from the cities and townships within its limits, and charged with administering the revenues of the county. They correspond to the "county commissioners" or "supervisors" in other states.

CHOUT. In Hindu law. A fourth, a fourth part of the sum in litigation. The "Mahratta chout" is a fourth of the revenues exacted as tribute by the Mahrattas.

CHOW SUM. A Chinese name for ginseng roots which have been dried and treated with sugar and honey, such treatment having the purpose and effect of enhancing their value commercially but not therapeutically. Tong & Co. v. U. S., 12 Ct. Cust.App. 32, 33.

CHRENECRUDA. Under the Salic law. This was a ceremony performed by a person who was too poor to pay his debt or fine, whereby he applied to a rich relative to pay it for him. It consisted (after certain preliminaries) in throwing green herbs upon the party, the effect of which was to bind him to pay the whole demand.

CHRISTIAN. Pertaining to Jesus Christ or the religion founded by him; professing Christianity. As a noun, it signifies one who accepts and professes to live by the doctrines and principles of the Christian religion; it does not include Mohammedans, Jews, pagans, or infidels. State v. Buswell, 40 Neb. 158, 58 N.W. 728, 24 L.R.A. 68. One who believes or professes or is assumed to believe in Jesus Christ, and the truth as taught by Him. Conway v. Third Nat. Bank & Trust Co., 118 N.J.Eq. 61, 177 A. 113, 116.

CHRISTIAN NAME. The baptismal name as distinct from the surname. Stratton v. Foster, 11 Me. 467. The name which is given one after his birth or at baptism, or is afterward assumed by him in addition to his family name. Badger Lumber Co. v. Collinson, 97 Kan. 791, 156 P. 724, 725.

A Christian name may consist of a single letter. Wharton; People v. Reilly, 257 Ill. 538, 101 N.E. 54, Ann.Cas. 1914A, 1112. There is no presumption that letters are not themselves Christian names, and where a letter or letters appear before a surname they are treated, in the absence of any showing to the contrary, as the Christian name. Riley v. Litchfield, 168 Iowa, 187, 150 N.W. 81, 82, Ann.Cas. 1917B, 172.

CHRISTIANITATIS CURIA. The court Christian. An ecclesiastical court, as opposed to a civil or lay tribunal. Cowell. See, also, Court Christian.

CHRISTIANITY. The religion founded and established by Jesus Christ. Hale v. Everett, 53 N. H. 9, 54, 16 Am.Rep. 82; People v. Ruggles, 8 Johns. (N.Y.) 297, 5 Am.Dec. 335.

CHRISTMAS DAY. A festival of the Christian church, observed on the 25th of December, in memory of the birth of Jesus Christ.

CHROME YELLOW. A metal largely used as a yellow pigment. It is an active poison. U. S. v. R. C. Boeckel & Co., C.C.A.Mass., 221 F. 885, 888.

CHROMO. A chromolithograph;—a picture produced from drawings on stones, each color being represented by a different stone. Stecher Lithographic Co. v. Dunston Lithograph Co., D.C.N.Y., 233 F. 601, 602.

CHRONIC. With reference to diseases, of long duration, or characterized by slowly progressive symptoms; deep-seated and obstinate, or threatening a long continuance;—distinguished from acute. Golden v. Lerch Bros., 211 Minn. 30, 300 N.W. 207, 211.

CHURCH. In its most general sense, the religious society founded and established by Jesus Christ, to receive, preserve, and propagate his doctrines and ordinances.

It may also mean a body of communicants gathered into church order, Stebbins v. Jennings, 10 Pick. (Mass.) 193; body or community of Christians, united under one form of government by the profession of the same faith, and the observance of the same ritual and ceremonies, McNeilly v. First Presbyterian Church in Brookline, 243 Mass. 331, 137 N.E. 691, 694; building, Combined Congregations of District of Columbia v. Dent, 140 F.2d 9, 10, 78 U.S.App. D.C. 254; congregation, Trustees of Pencader Presbyterian Church in Pencader Hundred v. Gibson, Del., 22 A.2d 782, 787, 788; organization for religious purposes, Williams v. Williams, 215 N.C. 739, 3 S.E.2d 334, 338; place where persons regularly assemble for worship, Stubbs v. Texas Liquor Control Board, Tex.Civ.App., 166 S.W.2d 178, 180; religious society or body, In re Werner's Will, Sur., 181 N. Y.S. 433, 434; society of persons who profess the Christian religion, Church of the Holy Faith v. State Tax Commission, 39 N.M. 403, 48 P.2d 777, 784.

In English ecclesiastical law. An institution established by the law of the land in reference to religion. 3 Steph. Comm. 54. The word "church" is said to mean, in strictness, not the material fabric, but the cure of souls and the right of tithes. 1 Mod. 201.

A congregational church is a voluntary association of Christians united for discipline and worship, connected with, and forming a part of, some religious society, having a legal existence. Anderson v. Brock, 3 Me. 248.

Church Building Acts

Statutes passed in England in and since the year 1818, to extend the accommodation afforded by the national church. 3 Steph.Comm. 152–164.

Church Discipline Act

The statute 3 & 4 Vict. c. 86, containing regulations for trying clerks in holy orders charged with offenses against ecclesiastical law, and for enforcing sentences pronounced in such cases. Phillim. Ecc.Law, 1314.

Church of England

A distinct branch of Christ's church, it is also an institution of the state of which the sovereign is the supreme head. Wharton. Pawlet v. Clark, 9 Cranch 292, 3 L.Ed. 735.

Church Property

Within constitutional exemption from taxation, it means property used for religious worship and instruction. Church of the Holy Faith v. State Tax Commission, 39 N.M. 403, 48 P.2d 777, 784.

Church Rate

In English law. A sum assessed for the repair of parochial churches by the representatives of the parishioners in vestry assembled. Wharton.

Church Reeve

A church warden; an overseer of a church. Now obsolete. Cowell.

Church-Scot

In old English law. Customary obligations paid to the parish priest; from which duties the religious sometimes purchased an exemption for themselves and their tenants.

Church Wardens

A species of ecclesiastical officers who are intrusted with the care and guardianship of the church building and property. See 3 Steph.Comm. 90; 1 Bla.Comm. 394; Cowell; Terrett v. Taylor, 9 Cranch, 43, 3 L.Ed. 650.

Church-Yard

See Cemetery.

Community Church

A name signifying a federation of churches retaining their separate identity and distinctive doctrines. Christian Church of Vacaville v. Crystal, 78 Cal.App. 1, 247 P. 605, 608.

CHURCHESSET. In old English law. A certain portion or measure of wheat, anciently paid to the church on St. Martin's day; and which, according to Fleta, was paid as well in the time of the Britons as of the English. Fleta, lib. 1, c. 47, § 28.

CHURL. In Saxon law. A freeman of inferior rank, chiefly employed in husbandry. 1 Reeve, Eng.Law, 5. A tenant at will of free condition, who held land from a thane, on condition of rents and services. Cowell. See Ceorl.

CI. Fr. So; here. *Ci Dieiu Vous eyde,* so help you God. *Ci devant,* heretofore. *Ci bien,* as well.

CIBARIA. Lat. In the civil law. Food; victuals. Dig. 34, 1.

CICATRIX. In medical jurisprudence. A scar; the mark left in the flesh or skin after the healing of a wound, and having the appearance of a seam or of a ridge of flesh.

CIDER. Formerly, any liquor made of fruit juices; now, the juice of apples either before or after fermentation. People v. Tretneck, 22 N.Y.S. 2d 720, 721, 175 Misc. 41; People v. McCoy, 217 Mich. 575, 187 N.W. 338.

Cider vinegar. Vinegar made from apple cider. People v. Douglas Packing Co., 194 N.Y.S. 633, 635, 118 Misc. 775.

Hard cider. Fermented cider, a strong, spirituous, and intoxicating drink. Monroe Cider Vinegar & Fruit Co. v. Riordan, D.C.N.Y., 274 F. 736, 737; People v. Emmons, 144 N.W. 479, 481, 178 Mich. 126, Ann.Cas.1915D, 425.

Sweet cider. Cider before fermentation, or cider in which fermentation has been prevented—cider not yet become hard. U. S. v. Dodson, D.C.Cal., 268 F. 397, 403. A nonalcoholic beverage composed of the expressed juice of apples. Monroe Cider Vinegar & Fruit Co. v. Riordan, C.C.A.N.Y., 280 F. 624, 626.

CINQUE PORTS. Certain important ports or havens on the south-east coast of England, towards France. 3 Bl.Comm. 79. Their representatives in parliament and inhabitants were termed barons. Brande; Cowell; Termes de la Ley. And see Round, Feudal England 563.

The 18 & 19 Vict. c. 48, (amended by 20 & 21 Vict. c. 1,) abolished jurisdiction and authority of the lord warden of the Cinque Ports.

CIPHER. Ordinarily, a secret or disguised written communication, unintelligible to one without a key. As applied to telegrams, a "cipher" message is one that is unintelligible. Western Union Telegraph Co. v. Geo. F. Fish, Inc., 148 Md. 210, 128 A. 14, 16.

CIPPI. An old English law term for the stocks, an instrument in which the wrists or ankles of petty offenders were confined.

CIRCADA. A tribute anciently paid to the bishop or archbishop for visiting churches. Du Fresne.

CIRCA. Lat. About; around; also, concerning; with relation to. Commonly used before a given date when the exact time is not known; as, *circa* 1800. Abbreviated *circ.* or *c.*

CIRCAR. In Hindu law. Head of affairs; the state or government; a grand division of a province; a headman. A name used by Europeans in Bengal to denote the Hindu writer and accountant employed by themselves, or in the public offices. Wharton.

CIRCUIT. A division of the country, appointed for a particular judge to visit for the trial of causes or for the administration of justice. See 3 Bla. Comm. 58; State v. Mappus, 107 S.C. 345, 92 S.E. 1053.

Circuits, as the term is used in England, may be otherwise defined to be the periodical progresses of the judges of the superior courts of common law, through the several counties of England and Wales, for the purpose of administering civil and criminal justice. 3 Bla.Comm. 57; 3 Steph.Comm. 321.

CIRCUIT COURTS. Courts whose jurisdiction extends over several counties or districts, and of which terms are held in the various counties or districts to which their jurisdiction extends.

In several of the states, the name given to a tribunal, the territorial jurisdiction of which may comprise several counties or districts, and whose sessions are held in such counties or districts alternately. These courts usually have general original jurisdiction. Renshaw v. Reynolds, 317 Mo. 484, 297 S.W. 374, 376.

The name of a former system of courts of the United States, invested with general original jurisdiction of such matters and causes as are of Federal cognizance, except the matters specially delegated to the district courts. 1 Kent, Comm. 301-303.

CIRCUIT COURTS OF APPEALS. See Courts of Appeals.

CIRCUIT JUDGE. The judge of a circuit court. Crozier v. Lyons, 72 Iowa 401, 34 N.W. 186.

CIRCUIT JUSTICE. In federal law and practice. The justice of the supreme court who is allotted to a given circuit. 28 U.S.C.A. § 42.

CIRCUIT PAPER. In English practice. A paper containing a statement of the time and place at which the several assises will be held, and other statistical information connected with the assises. Holthouse.

CIRCUITUS EST EVITANDUS; ET BONI JUDICIS EST LITES DIRIMERE, NE LIS EX LITE ORIATUR. 5 Coke, 31. Circuity is to be avoided; and it is the duty of a good judge to determine litigations, lest one lawsuit arise out of another. Co.Litt. 384 *a*; Wing.Max. 179; Broom, Max. 343; 15 M. & W. 208; 5 Exch. 829.

CIRCUITY OF ACTION. A complex, indirect, or roundabout course of legal proceeding, making two or more actions necessary in order to effect that adjustment of rights between all the parties concerned in the transaction which, by a more direct course, might have been accomplished in a single suit. Fellows v. Fellows, 4 Cow. (N.Y.) 682, 15 Am.Dec. 412.

CIRCULAR INSANITY. Maniac depressive psychosis. Turley v. Turley, 374 Ill. 571, 30 N.E.2d 64, 65.

CIRCULAR LETTER OF CREDIT. A letter authorizing one person to pay money or extend credit to another on the credit of the writer. Pines v. United States, C.C.A.Iowa, 123 F.2d 825, 828.

CIRCULAR NOTES. Instruments similar to "letters of credit." They are drawn by resident bankers upon their foreign correspondents, in favor of persons traveling abroad. Brown.

CIRCULATED. A thing is "circulated" when it passes, as from one person or place to another, or spreads, as a report or tale. Willard v. State, 129 Tex.Cr.R. 384, 87 S.W.2d 269, 270.

CIRCULATION. As used in statutes providing for taxes on the circulation of banks, this term includes all currency or circulating notes or bills, or certificates or bills intended to circulate as money. U. S. v. Wilson, 106 U.S. 620, 2 S.Ct. 85, 27 L. Ed. 310. As used in newspaper and magazine publishing businesses, a body of subscribers and an established advertising clientele. Meredith Pub. Co. v. Commissioner of Internal Revenue, C.C.A., 64 F.2d 890, 893. Reading of libelous document with defendant's consent in hearing of others. Myre v. State, 126 Tex.Cr.R. 157, 70 S.W.2d 428.

Circulating medium. This term is more comprehensive than the term "money," as it is the medium of exchanges, or purchases and sales, whether it be gold or silver coin or any other article.

CIRCULATORY HEATING SYSTEM. One in which the heating box, being outside the room to be heated, heats a body of air in passing over it, which body of air is then conducted to the room to be heated, thus indirectly accomplishing the result;—distinguished from a "radiating" or direct system, in which the heating body or box is in the room intended to be heated. Pelton v. Williams, C.C.A.Ohio, 235 F. 131, 132.

CIRCUMDUCTION. In Scotch law. A closing of the period for lodging papers, or doing any other act required in a cause. Paters. Comp.

CIRCUMDUCTION OF THE TERM. In Scotch practice. The sentence of a judge, declaring the time elapsed within which a proof ought to have been led, and precluding the party from bringing forward any further evidence. Bell.

CIRCUMFERENTIAL. Etymologically inclusive of spiral. See George W. Todd & Co. v. J. Whitaker Mfg. Co., D.C.Pa., 226 F. 791, 794.

CIRCUMSPECTE AGATIS. The title of a statute passed 13 Edw. I (1285) and so called from the initial words of it, the object of which was to ascertain the boundaries of ecclesiastical jurisdiction in some particulars, or, in other words, to regulate the jurisdiction of the ecclesiastical and temporal courts. 2 Reeve, Eng.Law, 215, 216. See, however, 2 Holdsw.Hist.E.L. 246. And see Articles of the clergy.

CIRCUMSTANCES. Attendant facts. Pope v. Reading Co., 304 Pa. 326, 156 A. 106, 109. The surroundings at the commission of an act.

The terms "circumstance" and "fact" are, in many applications, synonymous; but the true distinction of a circumstance is its *relative* character. "Any fact may be a circumstance with reference to any other fact." 1 Benth. Jud.Evid. 42, note; Id. 142. "Circumstances" are minor facts, Pulliam v. State, 196 Ga. 782, 28 S.E.2d 139, 147; related or accessory facts, occurrences or things which stand around, or about, which attend upon, which closely precede or follow, which surround and accompany, which depend upon, or which support or qualify a principal fact or event, Salter v. State, 163 Ga. 80, 135 S.E. 408, 409.

As used in a statute for an allowance for the wife in a divorce action, having regard to the "circumstances" of the parties, it includes practically everything which has a legitimate bearing on present and prospective matters relating to the lives of both parties. Lamborn v. Lamborn, 80 Cal.App. 494, 251 P. 943, 945.

The "circumstances of the transaction itself," as used in the doctrine of dying declarations, are the circumstances or facts leading up to, causing, or attending the homicide, and are not confined to occurrences at the very time thereof. Pendleton v. Commonwealth, 131 Va. 676, 109 S.E. 201, 209.

Thrift, integrity, good repute, business capacity, and stability of character, for example, are "circumstances" which may be very properly considered in determining the question of "adequate security." Martin v. Duke, 5 Redf. Sur. (N.Y.) 600.

CIRCUMSTANTIAL EVIDENCE. The term includes all evidence of indirect nature. Milligan v. State, 109 Fla. 219, 147 So. 260, 263.

It is direct evidence as to facts deposed to but indirect as to the factum probandum, Brown v. State, 126 Tex.Cr.R. 449, 72 S.W.2d 269, 270; evidence of facts or circumstances from which the existence or nonexistence of fact in issue may be inferred. People v. Steele, 37 N.Y.S.2d 199, 200, 179 Misc. 587; Wolff v. Employers Fire Ins. Co., 282 Ky. 824, 140 S.W.2d 640, 645, 130 A.L.R. 682; Scott v. State, 57 Ga.App. 489, 195 S.E. 923, 924; inferences drawn from facts proved, Hatfield v. Levy Bros., 18 Cal.2d 798, 117 P. 2d 841, 845; preponderance of probabilities, Hercules Powder Co., v. Nieratko, 113 N.J.L. 188, 173 A. 606, 610; process of decision by which court or jury may reason from circumstances known or proved, to establish by inference the principal fact, People v. Taddio, 292 N.Y. 488, 55 N.E. 2d 749, 750.

It means that existence of principal facts is only inferred from circumstances. Twin City Fire Ins. Co. v. Lonas, 255 Ky. 717, 75 S.W.2d 348, 350.

When the existence of the principal fact is deduced from evidentiary by a process of probable reasoning, the evidence and proof are said to be presumptive. Best, Pres. 246; Id. 12. All presumptive evidence is circumstantial because necessarily derived from or made up of *circumstances*, but all circumstantial evidence is not presumptive. Burrill.

The proof of various facts or circumstances which usually attend the main fact in dispute, and therefore tend to prove its existence, or to sustain, by their consistency, the hypothesis claimed. Or as otherwise defined, it consists in reasoning from facts which are known or proved to establish such as are conjectured to exist.

CIRCUMSTANTIBUS, TALES DE. See Tales.

CIRCUMVENTION. In Scotch law. Any act of fraud whereby a person is reduced to a deed by decreet. It has the same sense in the civil law. Dig. 50, 17, 49, 155. And see Oregon v. Jennings, 7 S.Ct. 124, 119 U.S. 74, 30 L.Ed. 323.

CIRCUS. A large inclosure with one end rounded for races, a show in which feats of horsemanship, tumbling, strength, etc., are exhibited. Zucarro v. State, 82 Tex.Cr.R. 1, 197 S.W. 982, 985, L.R.A. 1918B, 354.

CIRIC. In Anglo-Saxon and old English law, a church.

CIRIC–BRYCE. Any violation of the privileges of a church.

CIRIC SCEAT. Church-scot, or shot; an ecclesiastical due, payable on the day of St. Martin, consisting chiefly of corn.

CIRLISCUS. A ceorl (*q. v.*).

CISTA. A box or chest for the deposit of charters, deeds, and things of value.

CITACION. In Spanish law. Citation; summons; an order of a court requiring a person against whom a suit has been brought to appear and defend within a given time.

It is synonymous with the term *emplazamiento* in the old Spanish law, and the *in jus vocatio* of the Roman law.

CITATIO. Lat. A citation or summons to court.

CITATIO AD REASSUMENDAM CAUSAM. A summons to take up the cause. A process, in the civil law, which issued when one of the parties to a suit died before its determination, for the plaintiff against the defendant's heir, or for the plaintiff's heir against the defendant, as the case might be; analogous to a modern bill of revivor, which is probably borrowed from this proceeding.

CITATIO EST DE JURI NATURALI. A summons is by natural right. Cases in Banco Regis Wm. III. 453.

CITATION. A writ issued out of a court of competent jurisdiction, commanding a person therein named to appear on a day named and do something therein mentioned, or show cause why he should not. Proctor, Prac. Sheldon v. Sheldon, 100 N.J.Eq. 24, 134 A. 904, 907. An order or summons by which a defendant is directed or notified to appear. Adams v. Citizens Bank, 136 So. 107, 109, 17 La.App. 422; Burrage v. Hunt Production Co., Tex.Civ.App., 114 S.W.2d 1228, 1239. The act by which a person is so summoned or cited.

It is usually original process in any proceeding where used, and in such respect is analogous to a writ of capias or summons at law and subpœna in chancery. Gondas v. Gondas, 99 N.J.Eq. 473, 134 A. 615, 618.

As the act of the court through its proper officer commanding the appearance of defendant at the time and place named to answer to plaintiff's petition, it has the dignity of official character and weight of superior authority. Moran Oil & Gas Co. v. Anderson, Tex.Civ.App., 223 S.W. 1031, 1032. It is used in this sense, in American law, in the practice upon writs of error from the United States supreme court, and in the proceedings of courts of probate in many of the states. Durfee v. Durfee, 293 Mass. 472, 200 N.E. 395, 397; Schwartz v. Lake, 109 La. 1081, 34 So. 96.

It is also the name of the process used in the English ecclesiastical, probate, and divorce courts to call the defendant or respondent before them. 3 Bl.Comm. 100; 3 Steph. Comm. 720. And in Scotch practice it is the calling of a party to an action done by an officer of the court under a proper warrant; the service of a writ or bill of summons. Paters. Comp.

CITATION OF AUTHORITIES. The reading, or production of, or reference to, legal authorities and precedents, (such as constitutions, statutes, reported cases, and elementary treatises,) in arguments to courts, or in legal text-books, to establish or fortify the propositions advanced.

CITATIONS, LAW OF. In Roman law. An act of Valentinian, passed A. D. 426, providing that the writings of only five jurists, viz., Papinian, Paul, Gaius, Ulpian, and Modestinus, should be quoted as authorities. The majority was binding on the judge. If they were equally divided the opinion of Papinian was to prevail; and in such a case, if Papinian was silent upon the matter, then the judge was free to follow his own view of the matter. Brown.

CITATIONES NON CONCEDANTUR PRIUSQUAM EXPRIMATUR SUPER QUA RE FIERI DEBET CITATIO. Citations should not be granted before it is stated about what matter the citation is to be made. (A maxim of ecclesiastical law.) 12 Coke, 44.

CITE. L. Fr. City; a city. *Cite de Loundr'*, city of London.

CITE. To summon; to command the presence of a person; to notify a person of legal proceedings against him and require his appearance thereto. See In re Eno's Estate, 180 N.Y.S. 889, 890, 111 Misc. 69. To read or refer to legal authorities, in an argument to a court or elsewhere, in support of propositions of law sought to be established.

CITIZEN. A member of a free city or jural society, (*civitas,*) possessing all the rights and privileges which can be enjoyed by any person under its constitution and government, and subject to the corresponding duties. "Citizens" are members of community inspired to common goal, who, in associated relations, submit themselves to rules of conduct for the promotion of general welfare and conservation of individual as well as collective rights. In re McIntosh, D.C.Wash., 12 F. Supp. 177.

The term appears to have been used in the Roman government to designate a person who had the freedom of the city, and the right to exercise all political and civil privileges of the government. There was also, at Rome, a partial citizenship, including civil, but not political rights. Complete citizenship embraced both. Thomasson v. State, 15 Ind. 451; 17 L.Q.Rev. 270; 1 Sel.Essays in Anglo-Amer. L.H. 578.

A member of a nation or body politic of the sovereign state or political society who owes allegiance, Luria v. U. S., 34 S.Ct. 10, 19, 231 U.S. 9, 58 L.Ed. 101; U. S. v. Polzin, D.C.Md., 48 F.Supp. 476, 479.

A member of the civil state entitled to all its privileges. Cooley, Const.Lim. 77. One of the sovereign people. A constituent member of the sovereignty synonymous with the people. Scott v. Sandford, 19 How. 404, 15 L.Ed. 691.

In American Law

One who, under the constitution and laws of the United States, or of a particular state, is a member of the political community, owing allegiance and being entitled to the enjoyment of full civil rights. Amy v. Smith, 1 Litt. (Ky.) 331; Minor v. Happersett, 21 Wall. 162, 22 L.Ed. 627.

All persons born or naturalized in the United States, and subject to the jurisdiction thereof, are citizens of the United States and of the state wherein they reside. Amend. XIV, Const.U.S.; Nyman v. Erickson, 100 Wash. 149, 170 P. 546, 547.

The term may include or apply to an elector qualified to vote in an election, Belmont v. Town of Gulfport, 97 Fla. 688, 122 So. 10; children of alien parents born in United States, Von Schwerdtner v. Piper, D.C.Md., 23 F.2d 862, 863; U. S. v. Minoru Yasui, D.C.Or., 48 F.Supp. 40, 54; children of American citizens born outside United States, Hoaland v. Attorney General of United States, D.C.Md., 42 F.Supp. 13, 22; Indians, United States v. Hester, C.C.A. Okl., 137 F.2d 145, 147; State v. McAlhaney, 220 N.C. 387, 17 S.E.2d 352, 354; national banks, American Surety Co. v. Bank of California, C.C.A.Or., 133 F.2d 160, 162; Ezzell v. First Nat. Banks, 218 Ala. 462, 119 So. 2, 3; negroes and whites, United States v. Ellis, D.C.S.C., 43 F.Supp. 321, 324; nonresident who has qualified as administratrix of estate of deceased resident, Williams' Code Tenn. § 8236. Hunt v. Noll, C.C.A.Tenn., 112 F.2d 288, 289; persons entitled to privileges and immunities conferred upon same terms upon which they are conferred upon other citizens, Austin v. United States, D.C.Ill., 40 F.Supp. 777, 778.

The terms "citizen" and "citizenship" are distinguishable from "resident" or "inhabitant." Jeffcott v. Donovan, C.C.A.Ariz., 135 F.2d 213, 214; and from "domicile," Wheeler v. Burgess, 263 Ky. 693, 93 S.W.2d 351, 354; First Carolinas Joint Stock Land Bank of Columbia v. New York Title & Mortgage Co., D.C.S.C., 59 F.2d 350, 351. The words "citizen" and "citizenship," however, usually include the idea of domicile, Delaware, L. & W. R. Co. v. Petrowsky, C.C.A.N.Y., 250 F. 554, 557; citizen inhabitant and resident often synonymous, Jonesboro Trust Co. v. Nutt, 118 Ark. 368, 176 S.W. 322, 324; Edgewater Realty Co. v. Tennessee Coal, Iron & Railroad Co., D.C.Md., 49 F. Supp. 807, 809; and citizenship and domicile are often synonymous. Messick v. Southern Pa. Bus Co., D.C.Pa., 59 F.Supp. 799, 800.

A corporation is a citizen of state under whose laws it is created and a nonresident of every other state. Jackson Securities & Investment Co. v. State, 241 Ala. 288, 2 So.2d 760, 764. It is not a citizen within meaning of federal constitution declaring citizens of each state entitled to privileges and immunities of citizens in the several states or within Fourteenth Amendment prohibiting states from abridging privileges and immunities of citizens of United States, J. D. L. Corporation v. Bruckman, 11 N.Y. S.2d 741, 746, 171 Misc. 3; but see In re Thermiodyne Radio Corporation, D.C.Del., 26 F.2d 713, 714; nor within statute authorizing citizens of United States to prosecute appeal to Circuit Court of Appeals without prepaying costs or giving security, Atlantic S. S. Corporation v. Kelley, C.C.A.Fla., 79 F.2d 339, 340; nor within statute authorizing permission to citizens to sue in forma pauperis, Quittner v. Motion Picture Producers & Distributors of America, C.C.A.2, 70 F.2d 331, 332; nor within statute requiring suit in district wherein either plaintiff or defendant resides, Standard Stoker Co. v. Lower, D.C.Md., 46 F.2d 678, 684; Sutherland v. U. S., C.C.A.Neb., 74 F.2d 89, 92. Insurance companies, incorporated under state law, are "citizens of this state" within statute requiring foreign insurance companies to file bonds for payment of their obligations to such citizens. Republic Ins. Co. v. Cunningham, Tex.Civ.App., 62 S.W.2d 339, 343. The term "citizen" will not be construed to include a corporation, unless the general purpose and import of the statutory or constitutional provision seems to require it. St. Louis & S. F. R. Co. v. State, 120 Ark. 182, 179 S.W. 342, 343, Ann.Cas.1917C, 873; Jennings v. Idaho Ry., Light & Power Co., 26 Idaho, 703, 146 P. 101, 102, L.R.A.1915D, 115, Ann.Cas.1916E, 359.

Neither a corporation nor a partnership is a citizen of the United States entitled to immunity from service of summons by substituted service, Western Mut. Fire Ins. Co. v. Lamson Bros. & Co., D.C.Iowa, 42 F.Supp. 1007, 1012.

Filipinos are not citizens of United States. De Cano v. State, 7 Wash.2d 613, 110 P.2d 627, 631; People v. Cordero, 50 Cal.App.2d 146, 122 P.2d 648, 649; but see holding that Filipinos are within provision of Neutrality Act defining "citizen" as including any individual owing allegiance to the United States. Suspine v. Compania Transatlantica Centroamericana, S. A., D.C.N.Y., 37 F.Supp. 268, 271.

A state cannot be a citizen. Query v. 206 Cases of Assorted Liquor, D.C.S.C., 49 F.Supp. 693, 695.

But a state and the federal government each has citizens of its own, and the same person may be at the same time a citizen of the United States and a citizen of a state. The government of the United States can neither grant nor secure to its citizens rights or privileges which are not expressly or by implication placed under its jurisdiction. All that cannot be so granted or secured are left to the exclusive protection of the states. U. S. v. Cruikshank, 92 U.S. 542, 23 L.Ed. 588.

With reference to the jurisdiction and power of federal courts and removal of actions a citizen of the District of Columbia is not a "citizen of a state", Neild v. District of Columbia, 110 F.2d 246, 249, 71 App.D.C. 306; Glaeser v. Acacia Mut. Life Ass'n, D.C.Cal., 55 F.Supp. 925, 926; a corporation is a citizen of the state where it is organized, and a foreign corporation does not become a citizen of another state where it is authorized to carry on business, Van Buren v. Connecticut Gen. Life Ins. Co., D.C.Mass., 42 F.Supp. 279, 280; a municipal subdivision, such as county, city, town, or school district, is a citizen, Siegel v. City of Detroit, Department of Street Railways, D.C.Mich., 52 F.Supp. 669; Pettibone v. Cook County, Minn., C.C.A. Minn., 120 F.2d 850, 852; a national bank is a citizen of state where it has its principal place of business, American Surety Co. of New York v. Bank of California, D.C.Or., 44 F.Supp. 81, 83; Atwood v. National Bank of Lima, C.C.A. Ohio, 115 F.2d 861, 862; a state is not a citizen, Board of Health of Township of Hillside v. Mundet Cork Corporation, 126 N.J.Eq. 100, 8 A.2d 105, 106, 107; State of North Dakota v. National Milling & Cereal Co., C.C.A.N.D., 114

F.2d 777, 779; State Highway Commission of Wyoming v. Utah Const. Co., (Wyo.) 49 S.Ct. 104, 106, 278 U.S. 194, 73 L.Ed. 262; a turnpike commission is a citizen, Hunkin-Conkey Const. Co. v. Pennsylvania Turnpike Commission, D.C.Pa., 34 F.Supp. 26, 28; an association is not a citizen, Rife v. Lumber Underwriters, C.C.A.Tenn., 204 F. 32, 35; Village Mills Co. v. Houston Oil Co. of Texas, Tex.Civ. App., 186 S.W. 785, 788; domicile and citizen are synonmous in federal courts, Earley v. Hershey Transit Co., D.C. Pa., 55 F.Supp. 981, 982; inhabitant, resident and citizen are synonymous, Standard Stoker Co. v. Lower, D.C.Md., 46 F.2d 678, 683.

In English Law

An inhabitant of a city. 1 Rolle, 138. The representative of a city, in parliament. 1 Bl.Comm. 174.

The word "subject" is used to designate an inhabitant of the *country,* or one amenable to the laws of the nation.

CITIZENSHIP. The *status* of being a citizen (*q. v.*).

CITY.

In England

An incorporated town or borough which is or has been the see of a bishop. Co.Litt. 108; 1 Bl. Comm. 114; Cowell; 1 Steph.Comm. 115. State v. Green, 126 N.C. 1032, 35 S.E. 462.

There is said, however, to be no necessary connection between a city and a see. Oxford Dict., citing Freeman.

A large town incorporated with certain privileges. The inhabitants of a city. The citizens. Worcester.

In America

A municipal corporation; Streat v. Vermilya, 268 Mich. 1, 255 N.W. 604, 606; also the territory within the corporate limits. Municipal Power Transmission Co. v. City of Lyndon, 127 Kan. 59, 272 P. 158, 160.

A large town or municipal corporation, State v. Haynes, 175 Ark. 645, 300 S.W. 380, 382; a political entity or subdivision for governmental purposes, Nolan v. Jones, 215 Ky. 238, 284 S.W. 1054, 1056; a public institution for self-government, Loeb v. City of Jacksonville, 101 Fla. 429, 134 So. 205, 207; a public corporation for public purposes, Chase v. Inhabitants of Town of Litchfield, 134 Me. 122, 182 A. 921, 924.

A state agency for carrying on local government. Hudson Motor Car Co. v. City of Detroit, 282 Mich. 69, 275 N. W. 770, 773, 113 A.L.R. 1472; a voluntary association or corporation. State ex rel. McQueen v. Brandon, 244 Ala. 62, 12 So.2d 319, 322; Leviton v. Board of Education of City of Chicago, 374 Ill. 594, 30 N.E.2d 497, 500.

The fundamental distinction between town and city organization is that in the former all the qualified inhabitants meet together to deliberate and vote as individuals, each in his own right, while in the latter all municipal functions are performed by deputies; the one being direct, the other representative. In re Opinion of the Justices, 229 Mass. 601, 119 N.E. 778, 781.

The word "city," however, is often used to include an incorporated town. Noble v. State, 112 Tex.Cr.R. 676, 18 S. W.2d 619, 620; and to include villages, People v. City of Chicago, 349 Ill. 304, 182 N.E. 419, 431. It has also been held that, under statutes, the term includes all municipal corporations and corporate authorities, such as a board of park commissioners; People v. Kesner, 321 Ill. 230, 151 N. E. 481, 483; but that it does not include a village; Village of Depue v. Banschbach, 273 Ill. 574, 113 N.E. 156, 159.

In Medieval History

In the Middle Ages in Germany, fortified places in the enjoyment of market-jurisdiction.

The German as well as the French cities are a creation of the Middle Ages; there was an organic connection with the Roman town-system. Schröder, Lehrbuch des Deutchen Rechtsgeschichte 588.

CITY COUNCIL. The name of a group of municipal officers constituting primarily a legislative and administrative body, but which is often charged with judicial or quasi judicial functions, as when sitting on charges involving the removal of an officer for cause. Rutter v. Burke, 89 Vt. 14, 93 A. 842, 849.

CITY ELECTION. Any election in a city at which people of the city may vote, Wing v. Ryan, 6 N. Y.S.2d 825, 829, 255 App.Div. 163.

CITY OF LONDON COURT. A court having a local jurisdiction within the city of London. It is to all intents and purposes a county court, having the same jurisdiction and procedure.

CITY REAL ESTATE. Property owned and used for municipal purposes. McSweeney v. Bazinet, 55 N.Y.S.2d 558, 561, 269 App.Div. 213.

CITY WARRANT. A command of council to treasurer to pay amount. State v. McCarthy, 282 P. 1045, 1048, 86 Mont. 100.

CIUDADES. Sp. In Spanish law, cities; distinguished from towns (pueblos) and villages (villas.) Hart v. Burnett, 15 Cal. 537.

CIVIC. Pertaining to a city or citizen, or to citizenship. Cleveland Opera Co. v. Cleveland Civic Opera Ass'n, 22 Ohio App. 400, 154 N.E. 352, 353.

CIVIC ENTERPRISE. A project or undertaking in which citizens of a city co-operate to promote the common good and general welfare of the people of the city. James McCord Co. v. Citizens' Hotel Co., Tex.Civ.App., 287 S.W. 906, 908.

CIVIL. Originally, pertaining or appropriate to a member of a *civitas* or free political community; natural or proper to a *citizen.* Also, relating to the community, or to the policy and government of the citizens and subjects of a state.

The word is derived from the Latin civilis, a citizen. Byers v. Sun Savings Bank, 41 Okl. 728, 139 P. 948, 949, 52 L.R.A.,N.S., 320, Ann.Cas.1916D, 222. In law, it has various significations. In contradistinction to *barbarous* or *savage,* it indicates a state of society reduced to order and regular government. In contradistinction to *criminal,* it indicates the private rights and remedies of men. It is also used in contradistinction to *military, ecclesiastical, natural,* or *foreign.* Story, Const. § 791; 1 Bla.Comm. 6, 125, 251; Montesquieu, Sp. of Laws, b. 1, c. 3; Rutherforth, Inst. b. 2, c. 2; *id.* c. 3; *id.* c. 8, p. 359; Heineccius, Elem. Jurisp.Nat. b. 2, ch. 6.

A prisoner's statutory obligation to pay for his keep and maintenance is civil. Auditor General v. Hall, 300 Mich. 215, 1 N.W.2d 516, 518, 139 A.L.R. 1022.

As to civil "Commotion," "Conspiracy," "Contempt," "Corporations," "Death," "Injury," "Liberty," "Obligation," "Officer," "Possession," "Remedy," "Rights," and "War," see those titles. See, also, the following titles beginning with "Civil."

CIVIL ACTION.

In general

An action wherein an issue is presented for trial formed by averments of complaint and denials of answer or replication to new matter, White v. White, 98 Ind.App. 587, 186 N.E. 349, 351; an adversary proceeding for declaration, enforcement, or protection of a right, or redress, or prevention of a wrong, People v. Barker, 29 Cal.App. 2d Supp. 766, 77 P.2d 321, 323; Lee v. Lang, 140 Fla. 782, 192 So. 490, 491; Johnston v. State, 212 Ind. 375, 8 N.E. 590, 592. Every action other than a criminal action, City of Neenah v. Krueger, 206 Wis. 473, 240 N.W. 402, 404; Gillson v. Vendome Petroleum Corporation, D.C.La., 35 F.Supp. 815, 819.

Both actions at law and actions in equity. Klepinger v. Rhodes, 140 F.2d 697, 698, 78 U.S.App.D.C. 340.

In the Civil Law

A personal action which is instituted to compel payment, or the doing of some other thing which is purely civil. Pothier, Introd. *Gen. aux Cont.* 110.

At Common Law

One which seeks the establishment, recovery, or redress of private and civil rights. One brought to recover some civil right, or to obtain redress for some wrong not being a crime or misdemeanor. Wheeling Traction Co. v. Pennsylvania Co., D.C.Ohio, 1 F.2d 478, 479.

Civil suits relate to and affect only individual rights whereas criminal prosecutions involve public wrongs. Cancemi v. People, 18 N.Y. 128. They include all cases, both at law and in equity, which cannot legally be denominated "criminal cases." Fenstermacher v. State, 19 Or. 504, 25 P. 142; Welford v. Havard, 127 Miss. 83, 89 So. 812, 813.

In Code Practice

The one form of action for enforcement or protection of private rights and prevention or redress of private wrongs. Code N.Y. § 69. It may also be brought for the recovery of a penalty or forfeiture.

"Civil action" implies adversary parties and an issue, and is designed for the recovery or vindication of a civil right or the redress of some civil wrong. Bopst v. Williams, 287 Mo. 317, 229 S.W. 796, 798. It is a generic term, and does not necessarily imply jury trial. State Board of Medical Examiners v. Macy, 92 Wash. 614, 159 P. 801, 804.

CIVIL BILL COURT. A tribunal in Ireland with a jurisdiction analogous to that of the county courts in England. The judge of it is also chairman of quarter sessions (where the jurisdiction is more extensive than in England), and performs the duty of revising barrister. Wharton.

CIVIL DAMAGE ACTS. Acts which provide in certain cases an action for damages to one injured because of the furnishing of liquor. Tarwater v. Atlantic Co., 176 Tenn. 510, 144 S.W.2d 746, 747.

CIVIL DAY. See the title Day.

CIVIL ENFORCEMENT PROCEEDING. The penalty actions under Emergency Price Control Act. Bowles v. Barde Steel Co., 177 Or. 421, 164 P.2d 692, 715, 162 A.L.R. 328.

CIVIL INFORMATION. A legal proceeding in chancery, older than the court of equity. Wilson v. State Water Supply Commission, 84 N.J.Eq. 150, 93 A. 732, 733.

CIVIL INQUEST. A proceeding to determine whether an individual is a criminal sexual psychopathic person within statute providing for confinement and treatment of such persons. People v. Chapman, 301 Mich. 584, 4 N.W.2d 18, 26.

CIVIL LAW. "Civil Law," "Roman Law" and "Roman Civil Law" are convertible phrases, meaning the same system of jurisprudence.

That rule of action which every particular nation, commonwealth, or city has established peculiarly for itself; more properly called "municipal" law, to distinguish it from the "law of nature," and from international law. See Bowyer, Mod. Civil Law, 19; Sevier v. Riley, 189 Cal. 170, 244 P. 323, 325.

That division of municipal law which is occupied with the exposition and enforcement of civil rights as distinguished from criminal law.

The system of jurisprudence held and administered in the Roman empire, particularly as set forth in the compilation of Justinian and his successors,—comprising the Institutes, Code, Digest, and Novels, and collectively denominated the "*Corpus Juris Civilis*,"—as distinguished from the common law of England and the canon law.

The word "civil," as applied to the laws in force in Louisiana, before the adoption of the Civil Code, is not used in contradistinction to the word "criminal," but must be restricted to the Roman law. It is used in contradistinction to the laws of England and those of the respective states. Jennison v. Warmack, 5 La. 493.

CIVIL LIABILITY. The amenability to civil action as distinguished from amenability to criminal prosecution. Com. v. Shimpeno, 160 Pa.Super. 104, 50 A.2d 39, 43. A sum of money assessed either as general, special or liquidated damages, either single, double or treble for violation such as overcharges. Lewis v. Anderson, D.C.Cal., 72 F.Supp. 119, 123.

CIVIL LIST. In English public law. An annual sum granted by parliament, at the commencement of each reign, for the expense of the royal household and establishment, being a provision made for the crown out of the taxes in lieu of its proper patrimony. 2 Steph.Comm. 591; 1 Bl.Comm. 332.

CIVIL NUISANCE. At common law, anything done to hurt or annoyance of lands, tenements, or hereditaments of another. Brownsey v. General Printing Ink Corporation, 118 N.J.L. 505, 193 A. 824, 826.

CIVIL OBLIGATION. One which binds in law, and may be enforced in a court of justice. Pothier, Obl. 173, 191.

CIVIL OFFICE. An office, not merely military in its nature, that pertains to the exercise of the powers or authority of civil government. State ex rel. Landis v. Futch, 122 Fla. 837, 165 So. 907, 909. Requisites are continuity, creation and definition of powers and duties by Constitution or Legislature, or their authority, possession of governmental power, and independence unless controlled by superior officers. State ex rel. McIntosh v. Hutchinson, 187 Wash. 61, 59 P.2d 1117, 1118, 105 A.L.R. 1234.

CIVIL OFFICER. See Officer.

CIVIL POSSESSION. See Possession.

CIVIL RESPONSIBILITY. The liability to be called upon to respond to an action at law for an injury caused by a delict or crime, as opposed to criminal responsibility, or liability to be proceeded against in a criminal tribunal.

CIVIL RIGHTS. See Right.

CIVIL SERVICE. This term properly includes all functions under the government, except military functions. In general it is confined to functions in the great administrative departments of state. People v. Cram, 61 N.Y.S. 858, 29 Misc. 359. But in enlarged sense means all service rendered to and paid for by state, nation, or political subdivisions thereof, except that pertaining to naval or military affairs. Long v. Wells, 186 Ga. 602, 198 S.E. 763, 768.

CIVIL SERVICE REFORM. Substitution of business principles and methods for spoils system in conduct of civil service, especially in matter of appointments. Ward v. Leche, 189 La. 113, 179 So. 52, 55.

CIVIL SIDE. When the same court has jurisdiction of both civil and criminal matters, proceedings of the first class are often said to be on the civil side; those of the second, on the criminal side.

CIVIL TOWNSHIP. A legal subdivision of the county for governmental purposes. Appeal of Trustees of Iowa College, 185 Iowa 434, 170 N.W. 813, 814.

CIVIL YEAR. See Year.

CIVILIAN. One who is skilled or versed in the civil law. A doctor, professor, or student of the civil law. Also a private citizen, as distinguished from such as belong to the army and navy or (in England) the church.

CIVILIS. Lat. Civil, as distinguished from criminal. *Civilis actio*, a civil action. Bract. fol. 101*b*.

CIVILISTA. In old English law. A civil lawyer, or civilian. Dyer, 267.

CIVILITER. Civilly. In a person's civil character or position, or by civil (not criminal) process or procedure. This term is used in distinction or opposition to the word *"criminaliter,"*—criminally,—to distinguish civil actions from criminal prosecutions. 2 East, 104.

CIVILITER MORTUUS. Civilly dead; dead in the view of the law. The condition of one who has lost his civil rights and capacities, and is accounted dead in law. Rasor v. Rasor, 173 S.C. 365, 175 S.E. 545.

CIVILIZATION.

In Practice

A law; an act of justice, or judgment which renders a criminal process civil; performed by turning an information into an inquest, or the contrary. Wharton.

In Public Law

A term which covers several states of society; it is relative, and has no fixed sense, but implies an improved and progressive condition of the people, living under an organized government. Roche v. Washington, 19 Ind. 56, 81 Am.Dec. 376. It consists not merely in material achievements, in accomplishment and accumulation of wealth, or in advancement in culture, science, and knowledge, but also in doing of equal and exact justice. Stiglitz v. Schardien, 239 Ky. 799, 40 S.W.2d 315, 321.

CIVIS. Lat. In the Roman law. A citizen; as distinguished from *incola,* (an inhabitant;) origin or birth constituting the former, domicile the latter. Code, 10, 40, 7. And see U. S. v. Rhodes, 27 Fed.Cas. 788.

CIVITAS. Lat. In the Roman law. Any body of people living under the same laws; a state. *Jus civitatis,* the law of a state; civil law. Inst. 1, 2, 1, 2. *Civitates fœderatæ,* towns in alliance with Rome, and considered to be free. Butl.Hor.Jur. 29.

Citizenship; one of the three *status,* conditions, or qualifications of persons. Mackeld.Rom.Law, § 131.

A term in the Anglo-Saxon land books, commonly applied to Worcester, Canterbury and other such places, which are both bishop's sees and the head places of large districts. Maitland, Domesday and Beyond 183. See 17 L.Q.R. 274. Oxford Dict. *s. v. City.*

See City.

CLAIM, *n.* A broad, comprehensive word, Wheeler v. Equitable Life Assur. Soc. of United States, 211 Minn. 474, 1 N.W.2d 593, 596.

CLAIM, *v.* To demand as one's own; to assert, Hill v. Henry, 66 N.J.Eq. 150, 57 Atl. 555. To state; to urge; to insist.

It may embrace or apply to a call, In re Heim's Estate, 3 N.Y.S.2d 134, 138, 166 Misc. 931; a demand, Moulding-Brownell Corporation v. E. C. Delfosse Const. Co., 291 Ill. App. 343, 9 N.E.2d 459, 461, a pretense; a right or title, Orenberg v. Thecker, 143 F.2d 375, 377, 79 U.S.App.D.C. 149; Lawrence v. Miller, 2 N.Y. 245, 254; an account, In re Stratman's Estate, 231 Iowa 480, 1 N.W.2d 636, 642; an action on account, Coleman v. Kansas City, 351 Mo. 254, 173 S.W.2d 572, 576; an assertion, Ritter v. Albuquerque Gas & Electric Co., 47 N.M. 329, 142 P.2d 919, 922; both the principal amount of judgment and interest thereon, Powell v. Link, C.C.A.Va., 114 F.2d 550, 554; cause of suit or cause of action, Jacobson v. Mutual Ben. Health & Accident Ass'n, 73 N.D. 108, 11 N.W.2d 442, 446; challenge of property or ownership of a thing which is wrongfully withheld, Douglas v. Beasley, 40 Ala. 147; Prigg v. Pennsylvania, 16 Pet. 615, 10 L.Ed. 1060; challenge of something as right, Uintah State Bank v. Ajax, 77 Utah, 455, 297 P. 434, 438. Claims ex delicto as well as ex contractu, Williams v. Williams, 217 Ind. 581, 29 N.E.2d 557, 558. Debt, Tanner v. Best's Estate, 40 Cal.App.2d 442, 104 P.2d 1084, 1087. But not all valid "claims" are "debts," State Banking Co. v. Hinton, 178 Ga. 68, 172 S.E. 42, 47, 91 A.L.R. 596; existing right, Mellus v. Potter, 91 Cal.App. 700, 267 P. 563, 564; judgment, Jennings v. Loucks, 297 N.Y.S. 893, 896, 163 Misc. 791; legal capability to require a positive or negative act of another person, Kocourek, Jural Relations, 2d Ed., 7; legal claim, right. In re Heinemann's Will, 201 Wis. 484, 230 N.W. 698, 700; means by or through which claimant obtains possession or enjoyment of privilege or thing, Lawrence v. Miller, 2 N.Y. 245, 254; valid claim,

Tennessee Consol. Coal Co. v. Commissioner of Internal Revenue, C.C.A.6, 117 F.2d 452, 454.

In patent law, specification by applicant for patent of particular things in which he insists his invention is novel and patentable; the clause in application in which applicant defines precisely what his invention is. Westinghouse Electric & Mfg. Co. v. Metropolitan Electric Mfg. Co., C.C.A.N.Y., 290 F. 661, 664.

Under Compensation Acts, a claim for which an amount of compensation may be deducible. Texas Employers Ins. Ass'n v. Booth, Tex.Civ.App., 113 S.W.2d 231, 241.

A demand for compensation, Georgia Casualty Co. v. Ward, Tex.Civ.App., 220 S.W. 380, 381; or for payment of medical expenses, Schmidt v. City of Lincoln, 137 Neb. 546, 290 N.W. 250, 253; A notice that claimant is claiming compensation and benefits, Kaplan v. Kaplan Knitting Mills, 248 N.Y. 10, 161 N.E. 204, 206; A provision that no claim for compensation shall be assignable before payment, covers both claims and awards. Pacific Electric R. Co. v. Commonwealth Bonding & Casualty Ins. Co., 55 Cal.App. 704, 204 P. 262, 263.

Under land laws, tract of land taken up by a preemptioner or other settler (and also his possession of it). Railroad Co. v. Abink, 14 Neb. 95, 15 N.W. 317.

Under mechanic's lien law of some states, a demand put on record by a mechanic or material-man against a building for work or material contributed to its erection.

Under statute authorizing the courts to order a bill of particulars of the "claim" of either party, "claim" is coextensive with "case," and embraces all causes of action and all grounds of defense, the pleas of both parties, and pleas in confession and avoidance, no less than complaints and counter-claims. Orvis v. Jennings, 6 Daly (N.Y.) 446.

When applied to estate of decedent, asserted but unadjudicated obligation, In re Franks' Estate, 277 N.Y.S. 573, 154 Misc. 472; debt or demand of a pecuniary nature, Tinkham v. Tinkham, 112 Ind.App. 532, 45 N.E.2d 357, 360; debts already due and unmatured debts, Roth v. Ravich, 111 Conn. 649, 151 A. 179, 180, 74 A.L.R. 364.

Within statute concerning presentation of false claim to political unit or officer, one which upon its face purports to be charge for which county would be liable. State ex rel. Welling v. Third Judicial District Court in and for Salt Lake County, 87 Utah 416, 49 P.2d 950, 952.

Within World War Veterans' Act any physical writing which furnishes the desired information, Cable v. United States, C.C.A.Ill., 104 F.2d 541, 545; assertion of a present claim demand, Werner v. United States, C.C.A.N.Y., 86 F. 2d 113; Cannon v. United States, D.C.Pa., 45 F.Supp. 106, 108.

An adverse claim is one set up by a stranger to goods upon which the sheriff has levied an execution or attachment. It is also applied to claims to real property.

For "Counter-claim" and "False Claim," and "False or Fraudulent Claim," see those titles.

CLAIM ACCRUED. Damage accrued. Megerell v. State, Ct.Cl., 46 N.Y.S.2d 685, 688; Edlux Const. Corporation v. State, 300 N.Y.S. 509, 511, 252 App. Div. 373.

CLAIM BOND. A bond primarily in the nature of a forthcoming bond. Liability can be based thereon when the court adjudges the failure of the claimant in trial of right of property to establish his right to it. Sanders v. Farrier, Tex.Civ. App., 271 S.W. 293, 298.

CLAIM JUMPING. The location on ground, knowing it to be excess ground, within the staked boundaries of another mining claim initiated prior thereto, because law governing manner of making location had not been complied with, so that location covers the workings of the prior locators. Nelson v. Smith, 42 Nev. 302, 176 P. 261, 265.

CLAIM PROPERTY BOND. A bond filed by a defendant in cases of replevin and of execution to procure return of goods. Snyder v. Frankenfield, 4 Pa.Dist.R. 767; Weaver v. Lawrence, 1 Dall. 156, 1 L.Ed. 79; 1 Dall.U.S. (4th Ed. by Brightly) 156, 157, note.

CLAIM AND DELIVERY. Action at law for recovery of specific personal chattels wrongfully taken and detained, with damages which the taking or detention has caused; a modification of common-law action of replevin. Railroad Co. v. Gila County, 8 Ariz. 292, 71 P. 913; Farmers & Depositors Bank v. Taylor, 290 Ky. 774, 162 S.W.2d 764, 765.

CLAIM IN EQUITY. In English practice. In simple cases, the summary proceeding by claim was sometimes adopted. This summary practice was created by orders 22d April, 1850. See Smith, Ch. Pr. 664. By Consolid.Ord.1860, viii, r. 4, claims were abolished. Wharton.

CLAIM OF COGNIZANCE OR OF CONUSANCE. An intervention by a third person, claiming jurisdiction or demanding judicature in cause, which plaintiff has commenced out of the claimant's court. Now obsolete. 2 Wils. 409; 2 Bl.Comm. 350, note; 3 Bl.Comm. 298.

CLAIM OF LIBERTY. In English practice. A suit or petition to the queen, in the court of exchequer, to have liberties and franchises confirmed there by the attorney general.

CLAIM OF OWNERSHIP, RIGHT AND TITLE. As regards adverse possession, claim of land as one's own to hold it for oneself. Peters v. Gilund, Tex.Civ.App., 186 S.W.2d 1019, 1020. Claim of right, claim of title and claim of ownership are synonymous. Ewing v. Tanner, 193 S.E. 243, 247, 184 Ga. 773; City of Rock Springs v. Sturm, 39 Wyo. 494, 273 P. 908, 911. Claimant's intention to claim in hostility to real owner, Bowden-Gazzam Co. v. Hogan, 22 Wash.2d 27, 154 P.2d 285, 289, 290. Color of title and claim of title are synonymous. Sullivan v. Neel, 105 Mont. 253, 73 P.2d 206, 208; Walton v. Sikes, 165 Ga. 422, 141 S.E. 188, 190. Intention of disseisor to appropriate and use land as his own, irrespective of any semblance of color, or right, or title. Marion Inv. Co. v. Virginia Lincoln Furniture Corporation, 171 Va. 170, 198 S.E. 508, 513, 118 A.L.R. 939.

CLAIMANT. As used in escheat proceeding, persons interested in the estate as heirs. In re Peers' Estate, 234 Iowa 403, 12 N.W.2d 894, 895. As used in statute regarding processing tax refunds, one from whom tax has been collected. Upchurch Packing Co. v. United States, D.C.Ga., 53 F.Supp. 791, 793. One who claims or asserts a right, demand or claim though sometimes "claimant" has a more restricted meaning. Weisgerber v. Workmen's Compensation Bureau, 70 N.D. 165, 292 N.W. 627, 630, 128 A.L.R. 1482.

In admiralty practice. A person who lays claim to property seized on a libel *in rem,* and is authorized and admitted to defend the action. The Conqueror, 17 S.Ct. 510, 166 U.S. 110, 41 L.Ed. 937; Thirty Hogsheads of Sugar, Bentzon, Claimant v. Boyle, 9 Cranch, 191, 3 L.Ed. 701.

CLAIMANT ADJUSTER. One who will obtain, secure, enforce, or establish a right, claim, or demand for an individual against an insurance company. Wilkey v. State ex rel. Smith, 244 Ala. 568, 14 So.2d 536, 543.

CLAM. Lat. In the civil law. Covertly; secretly.

CLAM FACTUM ID VIDETUR ESSE, QUOD QUISQUE, QUUM CONTROVERSIAM HABERET, HABITURUMVE SE PUTARET, FECIT. That appears to be covertly (secretly) done, which anyone did, when he had a legal dispute, or thought he would have one. Adams Gloss.

CLAM, VI, AUT PRECARIO. A technical phrase of the Roman law, meaning by force, stealth, or importunity.

CLAM DELINQUENTES MAGIS PUNIUNTUR QUAM PALAM. 8 Coke, 127. Those sinning secretly are punished more severely than those sinning openly.

CLAMEA ADMITTENDA IN ITINERE PER ATTORNATUM. An ancient writ by which the king commanded the justices in eyre to admit the claim by attorney of a person who was in the royal service, and could not appear in person. Reg.Orig. 19.

CLAMOR. In old English law. A claim or complaint; an outcry; clamor.

In the civil law. A claimant. A debt; anything claimed from another. A proclamation; an accusation. Du Cange.

CLANDESTINE. Secret; hidden; concealed. The "clandestine importation" of goods is a term used in English statutes as equivalent to "smuggling." Keck v. U. S., 19 S.Ct. 254, 172 U.S. 434, 43 L.Ed. 505. A clandestine marriage is (legally) one contracted without observing the conditions precedent prescribed by law, such as publication of bans, procuring a license, or the like. Hay v. State, 68 Fla. 458, 67 So. 107.

CLAP. Vulgar name for gonorrhea. Sally v. Brown, 220 Ky. 576, 295 S.W. 890, 891.

CLARE CONSTAT. (It clearly appears.) In Scotch law. The name of a precept for giving seisin of lands to an heir; so called from its initial words. Ersk.Inst. 3, 8, 71.

CLAREMETHEN. In old Scotch law. The warranty of stolen cattle or goods; the law regulating such warranty. Skene.

CLARENDON, ASSIZE OF. A statute (1166) the principal feature of which was an improvement of judicial procedure in the case of criminals. It was a part of the same scheme of reform as the Constitution of Clarendon. See James C. Carter, The Law, etc., 65.

CLARENDON, CONSTITUTIONS OF. Certain statutes made in the reign of Henry II. of England, at a parliament held at Clarendon, (A. D. 1164,) by which the king checked the power of the pope and his clergy, and greatly narrowed the exemption they claimed from secular jurisdiction. 4 Bl.Comm. 422; Fitz Stephen 27; 2 Lingard 59; 1 Hume 382; Wilkins 321; 1 Poll. & M. 430–440, 461; 2 *id.* 196.

CLARIFICATIO. Lat. In old Scotch law. A making clear; the purging or clearing (clenging) of an assise. Skene.

CLASS. The order or rank according to which persons or things are arranged or assorted.

Also a body of persons uncertain in number, Weaver v. Liberty Trust Co., 183 A. 544, 548, 170 Md. 212; a group of persons, things, qualities, or activities, having common characteristics or attributes. Inter-County Rural Electric Co-op. Corporation v. Reeves, 294 Ky. 458, 171 S.W.2d 978, 982. Also grade, Commonwealth ex rel. Margiotti v. Sutton, 327 Pa. 337, 193 A. 250, 252. Also same descriptive properties. Cheek-Neal Coffee Co. v. Hal Dick Mfg. Co., Cust. & Pat.App., 40 F.2d 106, 107.

CLASS ACTION. An action brought on behalf of other persons similarly situated. Mitchell v. Wright, D.C.Ala., 62 F.Supp. 580, 582; Calabrese v. Chiumento, D.C.N.J., 3 F.R.D. 435, 437.

CLASS GIFT. A gift of aggregate sum to body of persons, uncertain in number at time thereof, to be ascertained at future time, Hepburn v. Winthrop, 83 F.2d 566, 570, 65 App.D.C. 309, 105 A.L.R. 310.

CLASS LEGISLATION. Legislation limited in operation to certain persons or classes of persons, natural or artificial, or to certain districts of territory or state, Vardaman v. McBee, 198 Miss. 251, 21 So.2d 661, 664. Legislation operating upon portion of particular class of persons or things. Shaw v. Fox, 246 Ky. 342, 55 S.W.2d 11.

The term is applied to enactments which divide the people or subjects of legislation into classes, with reference either to the grant of privileges or the imposition of burdens, upon an arbitrary, unjust, or invidious principle, or which make arbitrary discriminations between those persons or things coming within the same class. Leuthold v. Brandjord, 100 Mont. 96, 47 P.2d 41, 45; People v. Marcello, Mag.Ct.N.Y., 25 N.Y.S.2d 533, 537, 538, 539.

CLASS or REPRESENTATIVE ACTION. One in which one or more members of a class sue either for themselves or for themselves and other members of a class. Huester v. Gilmour, D.C.Pa., 13 F. Supp. 630, 631; City of Dallas v. Armour & Co., Tex.Civ.App., 216 S.W. 222, 224. The plaintiff in a representative action before judgment is, as a rule, *dominus litis,* (*q. v.,*) and may discontinue or compromise the action as he pleases. Sweet.

CLASS REPRESENTATION. Where members of class sue or are sued on behalf of other members judgment is conclusive for and against those members of class thus represented, in absence of fraud or collusion. Barnes v. Fort, 181 S.W.2d 881, 884, 181 Tenn. 522; Grand International Brotherhood of Locomotive Engineers v. Mills, 43 Ariz. 379, 31 P.2d 971, 982.

CLASS SUIT. See Class or Representative Action.

CLASSIARIUS. A seaman or soldier serving at sea.

CLASSICI. In the Roman law. Persons employed in servile duties on board of vessels. Cod. 11, 12.

CLASSIFICATION. A grouping into classes. Davison v. Parke Austin & Lipscomb, 19 N.Y.S.2d 117, 121, 173 Misc. 782.

It is the grouping of things in speculation or practice because they agree with one another in certain particulars and differ from other things in those particulars. Southern Package Corporation v. State Tax Commission, 164 So. 45, 47, 174 Miss. 212; Anderson v. Board of Public Instruction of Hillsborough County, 102 Fla. 695, 136 So. 334. The putting together of like subjects or facts under common designation. Tuttle v. Board of Education of Salt Lake City, 77 Utah, 270, 294 P. 294, 299.

The word may have two meanings, one primarily signifying a division required by statutes, fundamental and substantial, and the other secondary, signifying an arrangement or enumeration adopted for convenience only. In re Wichita Falls & Southern Ry. Co., D.C.Tex., 30 F.Supp. 750, 751.

In the practice of the English chancery division, where in an administration action, it appears to the judge (or chief clerk) that any of the parties form a class having the same interest, he may require them to be represented by one solicitor, to prevent expense of each attending by separate solicitors. In practice the term is also applied to the directions given by the chief clerk as to which of the parties are to attend on each of the accounts and inquiries directed by the judgment. Sweet.

CLASSIFICATION OF RISKS. Term in fire insurance to the nature and situation of the articles insured, and in accident insurance to the occupation of the applicant. Hopkins v. Connecticut General Life Ins. Co., 225 N.Y. 76, 121 N.E. 465, 467.

CLASSIFIED. Grouped in classes. People v. Johnson, 42 Cal.App.2d Supp. 827, 109 P.2d 770, 774.

CLASSIFIED CIVIL SERVICE. The primary meaning is that there be classification, while secondary meaning is mere arrangement or enumeration in schedule of titles of positions. Matter of Merriweather v. Roberts, 274 N.Y.S. 188, 190, 152 Misc. 57.

CLASSIFY. Group. Breslav v. New York & Queens Electric Light & Power Co., 291 N.Y.S. 932, 935, 249 App.Div. 181; Esquire, Inc., v. Walker, D.C.D.C., 55 F.Supp. 1015, 1021.

CLAUSE. A single paragraph or subdivision of a legal document, such as a contract, deed, will, constitution, or statute. Sometimes a sentence or part of a sentence. Bee Line Transp. Co. v. Connecticut Fire Ins. Co. of Hartford, C.C.A.N.Y., 76 F.2d 759, 760.

CLAUSE IRRITANT. In Scotch law. By this clause, in a deed or settlement, the acts or deeds of a tenant for life or other proprietor, contrary to the conditions of his right, become null and void; and by the "resolutive" clause such right becomes resolved and extinguished. Bell.

CLAUSE POTESTATIVE. In French law. The name given to the clause whereby one party to a contract reserves to himself the right to annul it.

CLAUSE ROLLS. In English law. Rolls which contain all such matters of record as were committed to close writs; these rolls are preserved in the Tower.

CLAUSULA. A clause; a sentence or part of a sentence in a written instrument or law.

CLAUSULA DEROGATIVA. A clause in a will which provides that no will subsequently made is to be valid. The latter would still be valid, but there would be ground for suspecting undue influence. Grotius.

CLAUSULA GENERALIS DE RESIDUO NON EA COMPLECTITUR QUÆ NON EJUSDEM SINT GENERIS CUM IIS QUÆ SPECIATIM DICTA FUERANT. A general clause of remainder does not embrace those things which are not of the same kind with those which had been specially mentioned. Lofft, Appendix, 419.

CLAUSULA GENERALIS NON REFERTUR AD EXPRESSA. 8 Coke, 154. A general clause does not refer to things expressed.

CLAUSULA QUÆ ABROGATIONEM EXCLUDIT AB INITIO NON VALET. A clause [in a law] which precludes its abrogation is void from the beginning. Bac.Max. 77.

CLAUSULA VEL DISPOSITIO INUTILIS PER PRÆSUMPTIONEM REMOTAM, VEL CAUSAM EX POST FACTO NON FULCITUR. A useless clause or disposition [one which expresses no more than the law by intendment would have supplied] is not supported by a remote presumption, [or foreign intendment of some purpose, in regard whereof it might be material,] or by a cause arising afterwards, [which may induce an operation of those idle words.] Bac.Max. 82, regula 21.

CLAUSULÆ INCONSUETÆ SEMPER INDUCUNT SUSPICIONEM. Unusual clauses [in an instrument] always induce suspicion. 3 Coke, 81.

CLAUSUM. Lat. Close, closed up, sealed. Inclosed, as a parcel of land.

In old English law. Close. Closed.

A writ was either *clausum* (close) or *apertum* (open). Grants were said to be by *literæ patentæ* (open grant) or *literæ clausæ* (close grant); 2 Bla.Comm. 346. Occurring in the phrase *quare clausum fregit* (Rucker v. McNeely, 4 Blackf. [Ind.] 181), it denotes in this sense only realty in which the plaintiff has some exclusive interest, whether for a limited or unlimited time or for special or for general purposes; 1 Chit.Pl. 174; Austin v. Sawyer, 9 Cow. (N.Y.) 39; 6 East, 606.

CLAUSUM FREGIT. L. Lat. (He broke the close.) In pleading and practice. Technical words formerly used in certain actions of trespass, and still retained in the phrase *quare clausum fregit* (*q. v.*).

CLAUSUM PASCHIÆ. In English law. The morrow of the *utas*, or eight days of Easter; the end of Easter; the Sunday after Easter-day. 2 Inst. 157.

CLAUSURA. In old English law. An inclosure. *Clausura heyæ*, the inclosure of a hedge. Cowell.

CLAVES CURIÆ. The keys of the court. They were the officers of the Scotch courts, such as clerk, doomster, and serjeant. Burrill.

CLAVES INSULÆ. In Manx law. The keys of the Island of Man, or twelve persons to whom all ambiguous and weighty causes are referred.

CLAVIA. In old English law. A club or mace; tenure *per serjeantiam claviæ*, by the serjeanty of the club or mace. Cowell.

CLAVIGERATUS. A treasurer of a church.

CLAWA. A close, or small inclosure. Cowell.

CLEAN. Irreproachable; innocent of fraud or wrongdoing; free from defect in form or substance; free from exceptions or reservations. It is a very elastic adjective, however, and is particularly dependent upon context. Clampitt v. St. Louis Southwestern R. Co. of Texas, Tex.Civ.App., 185 S.W. 342, 344.

CLEAN BILL OF HEALTH. One certifying that no contagious or infectious disease exists, or certifying as to healthy conditions generally without exception or reservation.

CLEAN BILL OF LADING. One without exception or reservation as to the place or manner of stowage of the goods, and importing that the goods are to be (or have been) safely and properly stowed under deck. The Delaware, 14 Wall. 596, 20 L.Ed. 779; The St. Johns N. F., C.C.A. N.Y., 272 F. 673, 674. One which contains nothing in the margin qualifying the words in the bill of lading itself. The Isla de Panay, C.C.A.N.Y., 292 F. 723, 730; Thomas Roberts & Co. v. Calmar S. S. Corp., D.C.Pa., 59 F.Supp. 203, 209.

CLEAN HANDS. Equitable relief may be denied on ground of deceit or impurity of motive, O'Brien v. Hamill, 264 N.Y.S. 557, 147 Misc. 709; fraud or wilful misconduct, Eresch v. Braecklein, C.C.A. Kan., 133 F.2d 12, 14; Margolis v. Burke, Sup., 53 N.Y.S.2d 157, 161, 162; unjust and unfair conduct, Dutch Maid Bakeries v. Schleicher, 58 Wyo. 374, 131 P.2d 630, 634; unlawful or inequitable conduct, Rhodes v. Miller, 179 So. 430, 432, 189 La. 288; Lodati v. Lodati, 52 N.Y.S.2d 119, 120, 268 App. Div. 1003; wrongdoing, Dales v. Muir, 351 Pa. 187, 40 A.2d 476, 477.

The maxim is confined to misconduct in relation to or connected with the matter in litigation. Teuscher v. Grogg, 136 Okl. 129, 276 P. 753, 760, 66 A.L.R. 143; Hartman v. Cohn, 350 Pa. 41, 38 A.2d 22, 25. It is inapplicable where to withhold relief would offend public morals more than to grant relief, Furman v. Furman, 34 N.Y.S.2d 699, 704, 178 Misc. 582; and where result will be to leave property in hands of one having no claim thereto or require further litigation, Harrell v. Allen, 183 Va. 722, 33 S.E.2d 222, 226. The act must prejudicially affect defendant, Wiley v. Wiley, 59 Cal.App.2d 840, 139 P.2d 950, 951. But it has been held that application of maxim is not limited to a case where the iniquitous action is one of which the moving party may personally complain. Leo Feist, Inc. v. Young, D.C.Wis., 46 F.Supp. 622, 628.

CLEAN OIL. Oil which has 3 per cent. or less by volume of water and sediment. Alamitos Land Co. v. Shell Oil Co., 3 Cal.2d 396, 44 P.2d 573, 575.

CLEAN WATER. Water that is not filthy or polluted. U. S. v. Durst, D.C.W.Va., 59 F.Supp. 891, 894.

CLEAR. Obvious; beyond reasonable doubt; perspicuous; plain.

Free from all limitation, qualification, question, or shortcoming. Condorodis v. Kling, 33 Ohio App. 452, 169 N.E. 836, 838. Ex parte Williams, 128 Tex.Cr.R. 148, 79 S.W.2d 325, 326; Free from incumbrance, obstruction, burden, limitation, etc., Frank v. Murphy, 64 Ohio App. 501, 29 N.E. 2d 41, 43; Plain, evident, free from doubt or conjecture, also unincumbered, free from deductions or drawbacks, Ketch v. Smith, 131 Okl. 263, 268 P. 715, 717. That which can be seen without dimness, Bremner v. Marc Eidlitz & Son, 118 Conn. 666, 174 A. 172, 174.

CLEAR AND CONVINCING PROOF. Generally, this phrase and its numerous variations mean proof beyond a reasonable, *i. e.*, a well-founded doubt. Southwestern Bell Telephone Co. v. City of San Antonio, Tex., D.C.Tex., 4 F.Supp. 570, 573. Some cases give a less rigorous, but somewhat uncertain, meaning, *viz.*, more than a preponderance but less than is required in a criminal case. O'Briant v. Lee, 212 N.C. 793, 195 S.E. 15, 20.

A higher degree of proof than weight of the evidence. Snyderwine v. McGrath, 343 Pa. 245, 22 A.2d 644, 647. Independent facts and circumstances which are, in opinion of court and jury, strong, Wright v. Austin, Tex.Civ.App., 175 S.W.2d 281, 284; it shall be found that witnesses are credible, that they distinctly remember facts to which they testify, that they narrate details exactly, and that their statements are true, McDonnell v. General News Bureau, C.C.A.Pa., 93 F.2d 898, 901. The degree of proof which will produce in the mind of the court a firm belief or conviction. In re Chappell, Ohio App., 33 N.E.2d 393, 397. Evidence that convinced a presumably unbiased and unprejudiced jury, Pegues v. Dilworth, 134 Tex. 169, 132 S.W.2d 582, 586. Proof sufficient to convince ordinarily prudent minded people. Rowland v. Holt, 253 Ky. 718, 70 S.W.2d 5, 9. The proof need not be conclusive. Hobart v. Hobart Estate Co., 26 Cal.2d 412, 159 P.2d 958, 976.

CLEAR AND PRESENT DANGER. Immediately serious violence is expected or is advocated or past conduct furnishes reason to believe such advocacy is contemplated. United States v. Korner, D.C.Cal., 56 F.Supp. 242, 248.

CLEAR ANNUAL VALUE. The net yearly value to the possessor of the property, over and above taxes, interest on mortgages, and other charges and deductions. Shelton v. Campbell, 109 Tenn. 690, 72 S.W. 112.

CLEAR ANNUITY. The devise of an annuity "clear" means an annuity free from taxes (Hodgworth v. Crawley, 2 Atk. 376) or free or clear of legacy or inheritance taxes. In re Bispham's Estate, 24 Wkly.Notes Cas. (Pa.) 79.

CLEAR CHANCE. A chance is a clear chance if exercise of vigilance would have discovered helpless peril and avoided the injury. Leinbach v. Pickwick Greyhound Lines, 138 Kan. 50, 23 P.2d 449, 456, 92 A.L.R. 1.

CLEAR DAYS. If a certain number of clear days be given for the doing of any act, the time is to be reckoned exclusively, as well of the first day as the last. Hodgins v. Hancock, 14 Mees. & W. 120; State v. Marvin, 12 Iowa 502.

CLEAR EVIDENCE OR PROOF. Evidence which is positive, precise and explicit, which tends directly to establish the point to which it is adduced and is sufficient to make out a prima facie case. Reynolds v. Blaisdell, 23 R.I. 16, 49 A. 42.

It necessarily means a clear preponderance. It may mean no more than a fair preponderance of proof but may be construed as requiring a higher degree of proof. It may convey the idea, under emphasis, of certainty. It may be understood as meaning beyond doubt. The expression is equivocal and mischievous. Aubin v. Duluth St. Ry. Co., 169 Minn. 342, 211 N.W. 580, 583.

CLEAR LEGAL RIGHT. A right inferable as a matter of law from uncontroverted facts. Federal Land Bank of Springfield v. Pickard, 9 N.Y.S. 2d 696, 707, 169 Misc. 753.

CLEAR MARKET PRICE. Fair market price. In re Spitly's Estate, 124 Cal.App. 642, 13 P.2d 385, 386.

CLEAR MARKET VALUE. With regard to inheritance tax, highest price obtainable. In re Nicklas' Estate, 132 N.J.L. 450, 41 A.2d 122, 124; net value, Hamlen v. Martin, 128 N.J.Eq. 393, 16 A.2d 457, 459; sum which property would bring on a fair sale by a willing seller not obliged to sell to a willing buyer not obliged to buy, or fair market value, or cash value, In re Ryerson's Estate, 239 Wis. 120.

CLEAR RESIDUE. Addition of income from funds, used to pay decedent's debts, administration expenses, and general legacies, to residue of estate. In re Foster's Will, 256 N.Y.S. 383, 385, 143 Misc. 191.

CLEAR TITLE. Good title, Clark v. Ray, Tex. Civ.App., 96 S.W.2d 808, 813; marketable title, Gantt v. Harper, 82 Mont. 393, 267 P. 296, 298; contra, Frank v. Murphy, 64 Ohio App. 501, 29 N.E. 2d 41, 43; one free from incumbrance, obstruction, burden, or limitation. Frank v. Murphy, 64 Ohio App. 501, 29 N.E.2d 41, 43.

For a clear deed, see Rohr v. Kindt, 3 Watts & S. (Pa.) 563, 39 Am.Dec. 53; clear of expense; 2 Ves. & B. 341; clear of assessments; Peart v. Phipps, 4 Yeates (Pa.) 386; clear bill of lading; William Zoller Co. v. Hartford Fire Ins. Co., 272 Pa. 386, 116 A. 359, 362. See, also, Clean Bill of Lading.

CLEAR TITLE OF RECORD. Freedom from apparent defects, grave doubts, and litigious uncertainties; such title as a reasonably prudent person, with full knowledge, would accept. Tull v. Milligan, 173 Okl. 131, 48 P.2d 835, 842.

CLEAR VALUE. With regard to net value after payment of debts and expenses of administration, Bouse v. Hutzler, 180 Md. 682, 26 A.2d 767, 769, 141 A.L.R. 843; sum which, after deducting amount necessary for payment of such taxes, yielded the amount of the specific legacies where will directed that taxes should not be deducted from legacies. Bouse v. Hutzler, 180 Md. 682, 26 A.2d 767, 769, 141 A.L.R. 843.

CLEARANCE. In Maritime law. The right of a ship to leave port. The act of clearing or leaving port. The certificate issued by the collector of a port evidencing the power of the ship to leave port. Hamburg-American Steam Packet Co. v. U. S., C.C.A.N.Y., 250 F. 747, 759. Worcester, Dict.

In contract for exhibition of motion pictures, the interval of time between conclusion of exhibition in one theater and commencement of exhibition at another theater. Waxmann v. Columbia Pictures Corporation, D.C.Pa., 40 F.Supp. 108, 111.

CLEARANCE CARD. A letter given to an employee by his employer, at the time of his discharge or end of service, showing the cause of such discharge or voluntary quittance, the length of time of service, his capacity, and such other facts as would give to those concerned information of his former employment. Cleveland, C., C. & St. L. R. Co. v. Jenkins, 174 Ill. 398, 51 N.E. 811, 62 L.R.A. 922, 66 Am.St.Rep. 296.

CLEARING. The departure of a vessel from port, after complying with the customs and health laws and like local regulations.

In mercantile law. A method of making exchanges and settling balances, adopted among banks and bankers.

CLEARING–HOUSE. A device or an association, usually unincorporated, for adjustment and payment of daily balances between banks in a city. Andrew v. Farmers' & Merchants' Sav. Bank of Moravia, 215 Iowa 1336, 245 N.W. 226, 229.

CLEARING LOAN. One made to a bond dealer while an issue of bonds are being sold. In re Stone's Will, 211 Wis. 518, 248 N.W. 446, 447.

CLEARING TITLE. Acts or proceedings necessary to render title marketable. Johnston v. Cox, 114 Fla. 243, 154 So. 206.

CLEARINGS. Method of making exchanges and settling balances among banks and bankers. Andrew v. Farmers' & Merchants' Sav. Bank of Moravia, 215 Iowa 1336, 245 N.W. 226, 228.

CLEARLY. Visible, unmistakable, in words of no uncertain meaning. Johnson v. Grady County, 50 Okl. 188, 150 P. 497.

Beyond a question or beyond a reasonable doubt, Johnson v. Grady County, 50 Okl. 188, 150 P. 497, 502; honestly, straightforwardly, and frankly, Huntington Securities Corporation v. Busey, C.C.A.Ohio, 112 F.2d 368, 370; plainly, Huntington Securities Corporation v. Busey, C.C.A.Ohio, 112 F.2d 368, 370; without obscurity, without obstruction, without entanglement or confusion, without uncertainty. Commonwealth v. Scovern, 292 Pa. 26, 140 A. 611, 614.

CLEARLY ERRONEOUS. Findings when based upon substantial error in proceedings or misapplication of law, Kauk v. Anderson, C.C.A.N.D., 137 F.2d 331, 333; or when unsupported by substantial evidence, or contrary to clear weight of evidence or induced by erroneous view of the law. Gasifier Mfg. Co. v. General Motors Corporation, C.C.A. Mo., 138 F.2d 197, 199; Smith v. Porter, C.C.A. Ark., 143 F.2d 292, 294.

CLEARLY EXPRESSED IN TITLE. Title must so express subject that lawmakers and people may not be left in doubt as to matters treated. Home Insurance Co. of New York v. Dahmer, 167 Misc. 893, 150 So. 650, 651.

CLEARLY PROVED. Preponderance of the evidence. Olson v. Union Oil Co. of California, Cal. App., 25 Cal.App.2d 627, 78 P.2d 446, 447.

Proof sufficient to satisfy mind of finder of facts that its weight is such as to cause a reasonable person to accept the fact as established. In re Frihauf, 58 Wyo. 479, 135 P. 2d 427, 433.

CLEARLY REFLECTS THE INCOME. Any method of accounting which clearly reflects a reasonable allowance for depreciation. Chicago & N. W. R. Co. v. Commissioner of Internal Revenue, C.C. A.7, 114 F.2d 882, 885.

CLEMENT'S INN. An inn of chancery. See Inns of Chancery.

CLEMENTINES. In canon law. The collection of decretals or constitutions of Pope Clement V., made by order of John XXII., his successor, who published it in 1317.

CLENGE. In old Scotch law. To clear or acquit of a criminal charge. Literally, to cleanse or clean.

CLEP AND CALL. In old Scotch practice. A solemn form of words prescribed by law, and used in criminal cases, as in pleas of wrong and unlaw.

CLERGY. The whole body of clergymen or ministers of religion. Also an abbreviation for "benefit of clergy." See Benefit of Clergy.

Regular clergy. Monks who lived *secundum regulas* (according to the *rules*) of their respective houses or societies were so denominated in old English Law in contradistinction to the parochial clergy, or "secular" clergy. 1 Chit. Bl. 387, note.

CLERGYABLE. In old English law. Allowing of, or entitled to, the benefit of clergy (*privilegium clericale*). Used of persons or crimes. 4 Bla. Com. 371. See Benefit of Clergy.

CLERGYMAN. Spiritual representative of church. In re Swenson, 183 Minn. 602, 237 N.W. 589, 591.

CLERICAL. Pertaining to clergymen; or pertaining to the office or labor of a clerk.

CLERICAL ERROR. Generally, a mistake in writing or copying. 1 L.Raym. 183; Los Angeles Shipbuilding & Dry Dock Corporation v. Los Angeles County, 22 Cal.App.2d 418, 71 P.2d 282; Franklin v. State, 240 Ala. 57, 197 So. 58, 59.

It may include error apparent on face of instrument, record, indictment or information. In re Goldberg's Estate, 10 Cal.2d 709, 76 P.2d 508, 512; error in respect of matters of record, Shotwell v. State, 135 Tex.Cr.R. 366, 120 S.W.2d 97; errors, mistakes, or omissions by clerk, writer, counsel, or judge which are not the result of exercise of judicial function; Pacific Finance Corporation of California v. La Monte, 64 Idaho 438, 133 P.2d 921, 922; Wilson v. City of Fergus Falls, 181 Minn. 329, 232 N.W. 322, 323; failure of clerk to enter order, Keller v. Cleaver, 67 P.2d 131, 133, 20 Cal.App.2d 364; omission in statutory provision, Craig v. State, 164 S.W.2d 1007, 1008, 204 Ark. 798; order fixing tax rate below statutory rate, In re Jagnow's Estate, 266 N.Y.S. 785, 788, 148 Misc. 657; placing of case on calendar without notice, New England Furniture & Carpet Co. v. Willcuts, D.C.Minn., 55 F.2d 983, 987; purported order incongruous and irrelevant to surrounding recitals, Carpenter v. Pacific Mut. Life Ins. Co. of California, 14 Cal.2d 704, 96 P.2d 796, 799; signature by judge to judgment which does not express judicial desire or intention, Bastajian v. Brown, 19 Cal.2d 209, 120 P.2d 9, 12.

CLERICAL MISPRISION. Mistake or fraud perpetrated by clerk of court which is susceptible of demonstration by face of record, or a clerical error, which is an error by clerk in transcribing or otherwise apparent on the face of the record. Ballew v. Fowler, 285 Ky. 149, 147 S.W.2d 65, 66. But see Newman v. Ohio Valley Fire & Marine Ins. Co., 221 Ky. 616, 299 S.W. 559, 560.

CLERICAL TONSURE. The having the head shaven, which was formerly peculiar to clerks, or persons in orders, and which the coifs worn by serjeants at law are supposed to have been introduced to conceal. 1 Bl.Comm. 24, note *t*; 4 Bl. Comm. 367.

CLERICALE PRIVILEGIUM. In old English law. The clerical privilege; the privilege or benefit of clergy.

CLERICI DE CANCELLARIA; CLERICI DE CURSU. Clerks of the chancery. See Cursitors.

CLERICI NON PONANTUR IN OFFICIIS. Co. Litt. 96. Clergymen should not be placed in offices; *i. e.*, in secular offices. See Lofft, 508.

CLERICI PRÆNOTARII. The six clerks in chancery. 2 Reeve, Eng.Law, 251.

CLERICO ADMITTENDO. See Admittendo Clerico.

CLERICO CAPTO PER STATUTUM MERCATORUM. A writ for the delivery of a clerk out of prison, who was taken and incarcerated upon the breach of a statute merchant. Reg.Orig. 147.

CLERICO CONVICTO COMMISSO GAOLÆ IN DEFECTU ORDINARII DELIBERANDO. An ancient writ, that lay for the delivery to his ordinary of a clerk convicted of felony, where the ordinary did not challenge him according to the privilege of clerks. Reg.Orig. 69.

CLERICO INFRA SACROS ORDINES CONSTITUTO, NON ELIGENDO IN OFFICIUM. A writ directed to those who had thrust a bailiwick or other office upon one in holy orders, charging them to release him. Reg.Orig. 143.

CLERICUS. In old English law. A clerk or priest; a person in holy orders; a secular priest; a clerk of a court. An officer of the royal household, having charge of the receipt and payment of moneys, etc. Fleta enumerates several of them, with their appropriate duties; as *clericus coquinæ*, clerk of the kitchen; *clericus panetr' et butelr'*, clerk of the pantry and buttery. Lib. 2, cc. 18, 19. In Roman law. A minister of religion in the Christian church; an ecclesiastic or priest. Cod. 1, 3; Nov. 3, 123, 137. A general term, including bishops, priests, deacons, and others of inferior order. Brissonius. Also of the amanuenses of the judges or courts of the king. Du Cange.

CLERICUS ET AGRICOLA ET MERCATOR, TEMPORE BELLI, UT ORET, COLAT, ET COMMUTET, PACE FRUUNTUR. 2 Inst. 58. Clergymen, husbandmen, and merchants, in order that they may preach, cultivate, and trade, enjoy peace in time of war.

CLERICUS MERCATI. In old English law. Clerk of the market. 2 Inst. 543.

CLERICUS NON CONNUMERETUR IN DUABUS ECCLESIIS. 1 Rolle. A clergyman should not be appointed to two churches.

CLERICUS PAROCHIALIS. In old English law. A parish clerk.

CLERIGOS. In Spanish law. Clergy; men chosen for the service of God. White, New Recop. b. 1, tit. 5, ch. 4.

CLERK. One who sells goods, waits on customers, or engages in clerical work such as bookkeeping, copying, transcribing, letter writing, tabulating, etc., a stenographer, etc., Appeal of Walker, 294 Pa. 385, 144 A. 288, 289; In re Goldman Stores, D.C.La., 3 F.Supp. 936, 937.

In New England, used to designate a corporation official who performs some of the duties of a secretary. As used in statute service on clerk of corporation, some general officer of the corporation, Baker v. New York Cent. R. Co., 16 N.Y.S.2d 78, 79, 258 App.Div. 854.

A person employed in a public office, or as an officer of a court, whose duty is to keep records or accounts. In re Allen, N.J.Sup., 95 A. 215, 216; Crawford v. Roloson, 254 Mass. 163, 149 N.E. 707, 709. See Clerk of Court.

A person serving a practicing solicitor under binding articles in England, for the purpose of being admitted to practice as a solicitor. Under exemption provision of Civil Service Law a private or confidential clerk of elective judicial officer. Neary v. O'Connor, 18 N.Y.S.2d 634, 637, 173 Misc. 696.

A person in holy orders; a clergyman; an individual attached to the ecclesiastical state, and who has the clerical tonsure. See 4 Bl.Comm. 366, 367.

CLERK OF ARRAIGNS. In English law. An assistant to the clerk of assise. His duties are in the crown court on circuit.

CLERK OF ASSISE. In English law. Officers who officiate as associates on the circuits. They record all judicial proceedings done by the judges on the circuit.

CLERK OF COURT. An officer of a court of justice who has charge of the clerical part of its business, who keeps its records and seal, issues process, enters judgments and orders, gives certified copies from the records, etc. Ross v. Heathcock, 57 Wis. 89, 15 N.W. 9; Gordon v. State, 2 Tex. App. 154. An assistant whose principal duty is to make correct memorial of court's orders and directions. People's Ditch Co. v. Foothill Irr. Dist., 123 Cal.App. 251, 11 P.2d 86, 88.

CLERK OF ENROLLMENTS. In English law. The former chief officer of the English enrollment office, (*q. v.*) He now forms part of the staff of the central office.

CLERK OF THE CROWN IN CHANCERY. See Crown Office in Chancery.

CLERK OF THE HOUSE OF COMMONS. An officer of the English house of commons appointed by the crown. He makes entries, remembrances, and journals of the things done and passed in the house. He signs all orders of the house, indorses the bills sent or returned to the lords, and reads whatever is required to be read in the house. He has the custody of all records and other documents. May, Parl.Pr. 236.

CLERK OF THE MARKET. The overseer or superintendent of a public market. In old English law, he was a *quasi* judicial officer, having power to settle controversies arising in the market between persons dealing there. Called *"clericus mercati."* 4 Bl.Comm. 275.

CLERK OF THE PARLIAMENTS. One of the chief officers of the house of lords. He is appointed by the crown, by letters patent. On entering office he makes a declaration to make true entries and records of the things done and passed in the parliaments, and to keep secret all such matters as shall be treated therein. May, Parl.Pr. 238.

CLERK OF THE PEACE. In English law. An officer whose duties are to officiate at sessions of the peace, to prepare indictments, and to record the proceedings of the justices, and to perform a number of special duties in connection with the affairs of the county.

CLERK OF THE PETTY BAG. See Petty Bag Office.

CLERK OF THE PRIVY SEAL. These officers attend the lord privy seal, or, in absence of the lord privy seal, the principal secretary of state. Their duty is to write and make out all things that are sent by warrant from the signet to the privy seal, and which are to be passed to the great seal; and also to make out privy seals (as they are termed) upon any special occasion of his majesty's affairs. Cowell.

CLERK OF THE SIGNET. An officer, in England, whose duty it is to attend on the king's principal secretary, who has the custody of the privy signet, as well for the purpose of sealing his majesty's private letters, as also grants which pass his majesty's hand by bill signed. Cowell.

CLERK OF THE TABLE. An official of the British House of Commons who advises the speaker on all questions of order.

CLERKS OF INDICTMENTS. Officers attached to the central criminal court in England, and to each circuit. They prepare and settle indictments against offenders, and assist the clerk of arraigns.

CLERKS OF RECORDS AND WRITS. Officers formerly attached to the English court of chancery, whose duties consisted principally in sealing bills of complaint and writs of execution, filing affidavits, etc. By the judicature (officers') act, 1879, they have been transferred to the central office of the supreme court, under the title of "Masters of the Supreme Court," and the office has been abolished. Sweet.

CLERKS OF SEATS. In the principal registry of the probate division of the English high court, they discharge the duty of preparing and passing the grants of probate and letters of administration, take bonds from administrators, receive *caveats* against a grant being made, etc. Sweet.

CLERKSHIP. The period which must be spent by a law-student in the office of a practising attorney before admission to the bar. 1 Tidd Pr. 61, et seq. In re Dunn, 43 N.J.Law, 359, 39 Am.Rep. 600.

In old English practice. The art of drawing pleadings and entering them on record in Latin, in the ancient court hand; otherwise called "skill of pleading in actions at the common law."

CLIENS. Lat. In the Roman law. A client or dependent. One who depended upon another as his patron or protector, adviser or defender, in suits at law and other difficulties. Dionys. ii. 10; Adams, Rom.Ant. 33.

CLIENT. A person who employs or retains an attorney, or counsellor, to appear for him in courts, advise, assist, and defend him in legal proceedings, and to act for him in any legal business. McCreary v. Hoopes, 25 Miss. 428; McFarland v. Crary, 6 Wend., N.Y., 297; Cross v. Riggins, 50 Mo. 335. It should include one who disclosed confidential matters to attorney while seeking professional aid, whether attorney was employed or not. Sitton v. Peyree, 117 Or. 107, 241 P. 62, 64.

CLIENTELA. In old English law. Clientship, the state of a client; and, correlatively, protection, patronage, guardianship.

CLIFFORD'S INN. An inn of chancery. See Inns of Chancery.

CLINICAL TESTS. Observations made of patient by physician or surgeon without the aid of instruments, apparatus or chemical examinations for the discovery of the existence or progress of disease or the patient's condition. Peterson v. Widule, 157 Wis. 641, 147 N.W. 966, 970, 52 L.R.A., N.S., 778.

CLIPPED SOVEREIGNTY. In the relations of the several states of the United States to other nations, the states have what is termed a clipped sovereignty. Anderson v. N. V. Transandine Handelmaatschappij, Sup., 28 N.Y.S.2d 547, 552.

CLITO. In Saxon law. The son of a king or emperor. The next heir to the throne; the Saxon adeling. Spelman.

CLOERE. A jail; a prison or dungeon.

CLOSE, *v.* To finish, terminate, complete, wind up; as, to "close" an account, a bargain, an estate, or public books, such as tax books. Bilafsky v. Abraham, 183 Mass. 401, 67 N.E. 318.

To shut up, so as to prevent entrance or access by any person; as in statutes requiring saloons to be "closed" at certain times, which further implies an entire suspension of business, Texas Co. v. Texarkana Mach. Shops, Tex.Civ.App., 1 S.W. 2d 928, 931.

CLOSE, *n.* A portion of land, as a field, inclosed, as by a hedge, fence, or other visible inclosure, 3 Bl.Comm. 209, or by an invisible ideal boundary founded on limit of title.

The interest of a person in any particular piece of ground, whether actually inclosed or not. Meade v. Watson, 67 Cal. 591, 8 Pac. 311.

In practice. The word means termination; winding up. Thus the close of the pleadings is where the pleadings are finished, *i. e.*, when issue has been joined.

CLOSE, *adj.* In practice. Closed or sealed up. A term applied to writs and letters, as distinguished from those that are open or patent.

CLOSE COPIES. Copies of legal documents which might be written closely or loosely at pleasure; as distinguished from *office* copies.

CLOSE CORPORATION. See Corporation.

CLOSE-HAULED. In admiralty law, this nautical term means the arrangement or trim of a vessel's sails when she endeavors to make a progress in the nearest direction possible towards that point of the compass from which the wind blows. But a vessel may be considered as close-hauled, although she is not quite so near to the wind as she could possibly lie. Chadwick v. Packet Co., 6 El. & Bl. 771.

CLOSE JAIL EXECUTION. A body execution which has indorsed in or upon it the statement that the defendant ought to be confined in close jail. Ex parte Thompson, 111 Vt. 7, 9 A.2d 107.

CLOSE MOLDS. Molds in two parts, called the drag and the case (or cope) forming together a two-part flask, one part being placed over the other and each being impressed with one half of the matrix or pattern. Cole v. U. S., C.C.A.Colo., 269 F. 250, 252.

CLOSE ROLLS. Rolls containing the record of the close writs (*literæ clausæ*) and grants of the king, kept with the public records. 2 Bl. Comm. 346.

CLOSE SEASON. The season of the year or period of time in which the taking of particular game or fish is prohibited, or in which all hunting or fishing is forbidden by law. State v. Theriault, 70 Vt. 617, 41 A. 1030, 43 L.R.A. 290, 67 Am.St.Rep. 695. *Cf.* Fence-Month.

CLOSE TO. Near; very near; immediately adjoining. Govier v. Brechler, 159 Wis. 157, 149 N. W. 740, 742.

CLOSE WRIT. See Writ.

CLOSED COURT. A term sometimes used to designate the Common Pleas Court of England when only serjeants could argue cases, which practice persisted until 1833.

CLOSED SEASON. The same as "close season" (*q. v.*).

CLOSED SHOP. Such shop exists where worker must be member of union as condition precedent to employment. Miners in General Group v. Hix, 123 W.Va. 637, 17 S.E.2d 810, 813.

CLOSED SHOP CONTRACT. A contract requiring employer to hire only union members and to discharge non-union members and requiring that employees, as a condition of employment, remain union members. Silva v. Mercier, Cal.App., 187 P.2d 60, 64.

CLOTHING WOOL. Short-stapled wool prepared by carding, as distinguished from "combing wool," which is long-stapled wool prepared by combing. U. S. v. Stone & Downer Co., 12 Ct.Cust.App. 557, 558.

CLOTURE. The procedure in deliberative assemblies whereby debate is closed.

Introduced in the English parliament in the session of 1882.

It is generally effected by moving the previous question. See Roberts, Rules of Order §§ 20, 58*a*.

CLOUD ON TITLE. An outstanding claim or incumbrance which, if valid, would affect or impair the title of the owner of a particular estate, and on its face has that effect, but can be shown by extrinsic proof to be invalid or inapplicable to the estate in question. A conveyance, mortgage, judgment, tax-levy, etc., may all, in proper cases, constitute a cloud on title. Parker v. Vallerand, 136 Me. 519, 8 A.2d 594; Anderson v. Guenther, 144 Or. 446, 25 P.2d 146.

It is not necessary in West Virginia that claim be valid on its face. Gardner v. Buckeye Savings & Loan Co., 108 W.Va. 673, 152 S.E. 530, 532.

CLOUGH. A valley. Also an allowance for the turn of the scale, on buying goods wholesale by weight.

CLUB. A voluntary, incorporated or unincorporated association of persons for purposes of a social, literary, or political nature, or the like. A club is not a partnership. 2 Mees. & W. 172.

Unincorporated Members' Club. A society of persons each of whom contributes to the fund out of which the expenses of conducting the society are paid. Van Pelt v. Hilliard, 75 Fla. 792, 78 So. 693, 695, L.R.A.1918E, 639.

Unincorporated Proprietary Club. One the property and funds of which belong to a proprietor who usually conducts the club with a view to profit. Van Pelt v. Hilliard, 75 Fla. 792, 78 So. 693, 695.

CLUB-LAW. Rule of violence; regulation by force; the law of arms.

CLUTCH. A device introduced in the transmission, some place between the mechanism in which power is created and the mechanism to which it is applied, and which serves to make and break the connection between the two. Eclipse Mach. Co. v. Harley Davidson Motor Co., C.C.A.Pa., 252 F. 805, 806.

CLYPEUS, or CLIPEUS. In old English law. A shield; metaphorically one of a noble family. *Clypei prostrati,* noble families extinct. Mat. Paris, 463.

C/O. A symbol meaning "care of." International Store Co. v. Barnes, Mo.App., 3 S.W.2d 1039, 1041.

CO. A prefix meaning with, in conjunction, joint, jointly, unitedly, and not separately, *e. g.*, co-trustees, co-executors, co-brokers. Brandenburger & Marx v. Heimberg, Mun.Ct.N.Y., 34 N.Y.S.2d 935, 938.

Also an abbreviation for "county," (Gilman v. Sheets, 78 Iowa 499, 43 N.W. 299.) and for "company," (Railroad Co. v. People, 155 Ill. 299, 40 N.E. 599). It may also indicate a partnership (Jennette v. Coppersmith, 176 N.C. 82, 97 S.E. 54, 55).

COACH. Coach is a generic term. It is a kind of carriage, and is distinguished from other vehicles, chiefly, as being a covered box, hung on leathers, with four wheels. Turnpike Co. v. Neil, 9 Ohio 12; Turnpike Co. v. Frink, 15 Pick. (Mass.) 444. A term applied both to vehicles traveling over roads and upon rails. Bruce Transfer Co. v. Johnston, 287 N.W. 278, 280, 227 Iowa 50.

COADJUTOR. An assistant, helper, or ally; particularly a person appointed to assist a bishop who from age or infirmity is unable to perform his duty. Olcott v. Gabert, 86 Tex. 121, 23 S.W. 985. Also an overseer, (coadjutor of an executor,) and one who disseises a person of land not to his own use, but to that of another.

CO-ADMINISTRATOR. One who is a joint administrator with one or more others.

COADUNATIO. A uniting or combining together of persons; a conspiracy. 9 Coke, 56.

CO-ADVENTURER. One who takes part with others in an adventure or in a venture or business undertaking attended with risk. McRee v. Quitman Oil Co., 16 Ga.App. 12, 84 S.E. 487; Easter Oil Corporation v. Strauss, Tex.Civ.App., 52 S.W.2d 336, 344.

COAL NOTE. A species of promissory note, formerly in use in the port of London, containing the phrase "value received in coals." By the statute 3 Geo. II. c. 26, §§ 7, 8, these were to be protected and noted as inland bills of exchange. But this was repealed by the statute 47 Geo. III. sess. 2, c. 68, § 28.

COALITION. In French law. An unlawful agreement among several persons not to do a thing except on some conditions agreed upon; particularly, industrial combinations, strikes, etc.; a conspiracy.

CO-ASSIGNEE. One of two or more assignees of the same subject-matter.

COAST, *v.* To slide down hill upon snow or ice as on a sled; to ride, glide or move by or as by the force of gravity as on a bicycle without pedaling. Samuelson v. Sherrill, 225 Iowa 421, 280 N.W. 596, 599.

COAST, *n.* The edge or margin of a country bounding on the sea.

The term includes small islands and reefs naturally connected with the adjacent land, and rising above the surface of the water, but not shoals perpetually covered by water. U. S. v. Pope, 28 Fed.Cas. 630; Hamilton v. Menifee, 11 Tex. 751.

This word is particularly appropriate to the edge of the sea, while "shore" may be used of the margins of inland waters.

COAST GUARD. In English law. A body of officers and men raised and equipped by the commissioners of the admiralty for the defense of the coasts of the realm, and for the more ready manning of the navy in case of war or sudden emergency, as well as for the protection of the revenue against smugglers. Mozley & Whitley.

COAST WATERS. Tide waters navigable from the ocean by sea-going craft, the term embracing all waters opening directly or indirectly into the ocean and navigable by ships coming in from the ocean of draft as great as that of the larger ships which traverse the open seas. The Britannia, 153 U.S. 130, 14 S.Ct. 795, 38 L.Ed. 660; The Victory, D.C.Va., 63 F. 636; The Garden City, D.C.N.Y., 26 F. 773.

COASTER. A vessel plying exclusively between domestic ports, and usually engaged in domestic trade; not including pleasure yachts. Belden v. Chase, 150 U.S. 674, 14 S.Ct. 264, 37 L.Ed. 1218.

COASTING. Sliding down hill or incline on sled or car or riding bicycle, without working the pedals; Samuelson v. Sherrill, 225 Iowa 421, 280 N.W. 596, 599. Movement of sled or vehicle by momentum due to previously exerted force or force of gravity. Tyne v. B. F. Goodrich Co., 297 N.Y.S. 425, 428, 252 App.Div. 24; Bryant v. Market St. Ry. Co., Cal.App., 158 P.2d 18, 22.

COASTING TRADE. In maritime law. Commerce and navigation between different places along the coast of the United States. Commercial intercourse between different districts in different states, different districts in same state, or different places in same district, on sea-coast or on navigable river. Shannon v. Streckfus Steamers, 131 S.W.2d 833, 836, 279 Ky. 649.

COASTWISE. Vessels "plying coastwise" are those engaged in domestic trade, or plying between port and port in the United States. San Francisco v. California Steam Nav. Co., 10 Cal. 504; Petition of Canadian Pac. Ry. Co., D.C.Wash., 278 F. 180, 202.

COAT ARMOR. Heraldic ensigns, introduced by Richard I. from the Holy Land, where they were first invented. Originally painted on shields of the Christian knights who went to the Holy Land during the crusades, to identify them. Wharton.

COBRA-VENOM REACTION. In medical jurisprudence. A method of serum-diagnosis of insanity from hæmolysis by injections of venom of cobras or other serpents.

COCKBILL. To place the yards of a ship at an angle with the deck. Pub.St.Mass.1882, p. 1288.

COCKET. In English law. A seal belonging to the custom-house, or rather a scroll of parchment, sealed and delivered by the officers of the custom-house to merchants, as a warrant that their merchandises are entered; likewise a sort of measure. Fleta, lib. 2, c. ix.

COCKPIT. A name which used to be given to the judicial committee of the privy council, the council-room being built on the old cockpit of Whitehall Place.

COCKSETUS. A boatman; a cockswain. Cowell.

COCOTTE. A woman who leads a fast life, one who gives herself up for money. Also a poached egg. Rovira v. Boget, 240 N.Y. 314, 148 N.E. 534, 535.

CODE. A collection, compendium or revision of laws. Chumbley v. People's Bank & Trust Co., 60 S.W.2d 164, 166, 166 Tenn. 35. A complete system of positive law, scientifically arranged, and promulgated by legislative authority. Abbott; a system of rules. Wilentz v. Crown Laundry Service, 172 A. 331, 332, 116 N.J.Eq. 40. Any systematic body of law. Wall v. Close, 14 So.2d 19, 26, 203 La. 345.

A "Code" implies compilation of existing laws, systematic arrangement into chapters, subheads, table of contents, and index, and revision to harmonize conflicts, supply omissions, and generally clarify and make complete body of laws designed to regulate completely subjects to which they relate. Gibson v. State, 214 Ala. 38, 106 So. 231, 235.

The collection of laws and constitutions made by order of the Emperor Justinian is distinguished by the appellation of "The Code," by way of eminence. See Code of Justinian.

A *code* is to be distinguished from a *digest.* Digests of statutes consist of a collection of existing statutes, while a code is promulgated as one new law covering the whole field of jurisprudence.

Code civil. The code which embodies the civil law of France.

It was promulgated in 1804. When Napoleon became emperor, the name was changed to "Code Napoléon," by which it is still often designated, though it is now officially styled by its original name of "Code Civil."

Code de commerce. A French code, enacted in 1807, as a supplement to the Code Napoléon, regulating commercial transactions, the laws of business, bankruptcies, and the jurisdiction and procedure of the courts dealing with these subjects.

Code de procédure civil. That part of the Code Napoléon which regulates the system of courts, their organization, civil procedure, special and extraordinary remedies, and the execution of judgments.

Code d'instruction criminelle. A French code, enacted in 1808, regulating criminal procedure.

Code Napoléon. See Code Civil.

Code noir. Fr. The black code. A body of laws which formerly regulated the institution of slavery in the French colonies.

Code of Justinian. The Code of Justinian *(Codex Justinianeus)* was a collection of imperial constitutions, compiled, by order of that emperor, by a commission, and promulgated A. D. 529. It comprised twelve books, and was the first of the four compilations of law which make up the *Corpus Juris Civilis.* This name is often met in a connection indicating that the entire *Corpus Juris Civilis* is intended, or, sometimes, the *Digest;* but its use should be confined to the *Codex.*

Code pénal. The penal or criminal code of France, enacted in 1810.

CODEX. Lat. A code or collection of laws; particularly the Code of Justinian. Also a roll or volume, and a book written on paper or parchment.

CODEX GREGORIANUS. A collection of imperial constitutions made by Gregorius, a Roman jurist of the fifth century, about the middle of the century. It contained the constitutions from Hadrian down to Constantine. Mackeld.Rom.Law, § 63.

CODEX HERMOGENIANUS. A collection of imperial constitutions made by Hermogenes, a jurist of the fifth century. It was nothing more than a supplement to the Codex Gregorianus, (supra,) containing the constitutions of Diocletian and Maximilian. Mackeld.Rom.Law, § 63.

CODEX JUSTINIANEUS. A collection of imperial constitutions, made by a commission of ten persons appointed by Justinian, A.D. 528.

CODEX REPETITÆ PRÆLECTIONIS. The new code of Justinian; or the new edition of the first or old code, promulgated A.D. 534, being the one now extant. Mackeld.Rom.Law, § 78. Tayl.Civil Law, 22.

CODEX THEODOSIANUS. A code compiled by the emperor Theodosius the younger, A.D. 438. 1 Bl.Comm. 81.

It was a collection of all the imperial constitutions then in force. It was the only body of civil law publicly received as authentic in the western part of Europe till the twelfth century, the use and authority of the Code of Justinian being during that interval confined to the East. 1 Bl.Comm. 81.

CODEX VETUS. The old code. The first edition of the Code of Justinian; now lost. Mackeld. Rom.Law, § 70.

CODICIL. A supplement or an addition to a will; it may explain, modify, add to, subtract from, qualify, alter, restrain or revoke provisions in will. In re Phelps' Will, 232 N.Y.S. 418, 421, 133 Misc. 450; Butler University v. Danner, 114 Ind.App. 236, 50 N.E.2d 928, 932; In re Cazaurang's Estate, 42 Cal.App.2d 796, 110 P.2d 138; Blackford v. Anderson, 226 Iowa 1138, 286 N.W. 735, 743; Adams v. Foley, 360 Ohio App. 295, 173 N.E. 197, 198.

Usually it does not supersede or totally revoke the will. Holcomb v. Holcomb, 159 So. 564, 566, 173 Miss. 192; but is part of the will, Knebelkamp v. Acosta, 114 S.W.2d 737, 739, 272 Ky. 506; Succession of Patterson, 188 La. 635, 177 So. 692, 694; Simmons v. Gunn, 156 Va. 305, 157 S.E. 573, 574; and may confirm, reexecute, revive or republish the will, Des Portes v. Des Portes, 157 S.C. 407, 154 S.E. 426, 429; In re Warne's Estate, 302 Pa. 386, 153 A. 688, 690; United States v. Moore, 197 Ark. 664, 124 S.W.2d 807, 809. It must be executed with same solemnity as a will. Adams v. Foley, 36 Ohio App. 295, 173 N.E. 197, 198.

CODICILLUS. In the Roman law. A codicil; an informal and inferior kind of will, in use among the Romans.

CODIFICATION. Process of collecting and arranging the laws of a country or state into a code, *i. e.*, into a complete system of positive law, scientifically ordered, and promulgated by legislative authority.

COEMPTIO. One of the modes in which marriage was contracted among the Romans. Adams, Rom.Ant. 501.

CO-EMPTION. The act of purchasing the whole quantity of any commodity. Wharton.

CO-EQUAL. To be or become equal to; to have the same quantity, the same value, the same degree or rank, or the like, with; to be commensurate with. State ex rel. Com'rs of Land Office v. Board of Com'rs of Nowata County, 166 Okl. 78, 25 P.2d 1074, 1077.

COERCE. Compelled to compliance; constrained to obedience, or submission in a vigorous or forcible manner. Fluharty v. Fluharty, 8 W.W.Harr. 487, 193 A. 838, 840.

COERCION. Compulsion; constraint; compelling by force or arms. Fluharty v. Fluharty, Del. Super., 8 W.W.Harr. 487, 193 A. 838, 840; Santer v. Santer, 115 Pa.Super. 7, 174 A. 651, 652.

It may be actual, direct, or positive, as where physical force is used to compel act against one's will, or implied, legal or constructive, as where one party is constrained by subjugation to other to do what his free will would refuse. Metro-Goldwyn-Mayer Distributing Corporation v. Cocke, Tex.Civ.App., 56 S.W.2d 489; Fluharty v. Fluharty, 8 W. W.Harr. 487, 193 A. 838, 840. It may be actual or threatened exercise of power possessed, or supposedly possessed. In re New York Title & Mortgage Co., 271 N.Y.S. 433, 150 Misc. 827; Weir v. McGrath, D.C.Ohio, 52 F.2d 201, 203.

As used in testamentary law, any pressure by which testator's action is restrained against his free will in the execution of his testament. Max Ams Mach. Co. v. International Ass'n of Machinists, Bridgeport Lodge, No. 30, 92 Conn. 297, 102 A. 706, 709; Hughes v. Leonard, 66 Colo. 500, 181 P. 200, 203, 5 A.L.R. 817.

Duress and coercion are not synonymous though their meanings often shade into one another. McKenzie-Hague Co. v. Carbide & Carbon Chemicals Corporation, C.C.A. Minn., 73 F.2d 78, 85.

CO-EXECUTOR. One who is a joint executor with one or more others. See, also, Joint Executors.

COFFEE-HOUSE. A house of entertainment where guests are supplied with coffee and other refreshments, and sometimes with lodging. Century Dict. A coffee-house is not an inn. Thompson v. Lacy, 3 Barn. & Ald. 283; Com. v. Woods, 4 Ky.Law Rep. 262; Potson v. City of Chicago, 304 Ill. 222, 136 N.E. 594, 596.

COFFERER OF THE QUEEN'S HOUSEHOLD. In English law. A principal officer of the royal establishment, next under the controller, who, in the countinghouse and elsewhere, had a special charge and oversight of the other officers, whose wages he paid.

COGITATIONIS PŒNAM NEMO PATITUR. No one is punished for his thoughts. Dig. 48, 19, 18.

COGNAC. A distilled brandy, containing more than one-half of 1 per centum of alcohol. Benson v. U. S., C.C.A.Tex., 10 F.2d 309, 310.

COGNATES. (Lat. *cognati.*) Relations by the mother's side, or by females. Mackeld.Rom.Law, § 144. A common term in Scotch law. Ersk.Inst. 1, 7, 4.

COGNATI. Lat. In the civil law. Cognates; relations by the mother's side. 2 Bl.Comm. 235. Relations in the line of the mother. Hale, Com. Law, c. xi. Relations by or through females.

COGNATIO. Lat.

In the civil law. Cognation. Relationship, or kindred generally. Dig. 38, 10, 4, 2; Inst. 3, 6, pr.

Relationship through females, as distinguished from *agnatio,* or relationship through males. *Agnatio a patre sit, cognatio a matre.* Inst. 3, 5, 4. See Agnatio.

In Canon law. Consanguinity, as distinguished from affinity. 4 Reeve, Eng.Law, 56–58. Consanguinity, as including affinity. Id.

COGNATION. In the civil law. Signifies generally the kindred which exists between two persons who are united by ties of blood or family, or both.

Civil cognation is that which proceeds alone from the ties of families, as the kindred between the adopted father and the adopted child.

Mixed cognation is that which unites at the same time the ties of blood and family, as that which exists between brothers the issue of the same lawful marriage. Inst. 3. 6; Dig. 38. 10.

Natural cognation is that which is alone formed by ties of blood; such is the kindred of those who owe their origin to an illicit connection, either in relation to their ascendants or collaterals.

COGNATUS. Lat. In the civil law. A relation by the mother's side; a cognate.

A relation, or kinsman, generally.

COGNITIO.

In old English law. The acknowledgment of a fine; the certificate of such acknowledgment.

In the Roman law. The judicial examination or hearing of a cause.

COGNITIONES. Ensigns and arms, or a military coat painted with arms. Mat.Par. 1250.

COGNITIONIBUS MITTENDIS. In English law. A writ to a justice of the common pleas, or other, who has power to take a fine, who, having taken the fine, defers to certify it, commanding him to certify it. Now abolished. Reg.Orig. 68.

COGNITIONIS CAUSÆ. In Scotch practice. A name given to a judgment or decree pronounced by a court, ascertaining the amount of a debt against the estate of a deceased landed proprietor, on cause shown, or after a due investigation. Bell.

COGNITOR. In the Roman law. An advocate or defender in a private cause; one who defended the cause of a person who was present. Calvin. Lex.Jurid.

COGNIZABLE. Capable of being tried or examined before a designated tribunal, State v. Wilmot, 51 Idaho 233, 4 P.2d 363, 364; within jurisdiction of court or power given to court to adjudicate controversy. Samuel Goldwyn, Inc. v. United Artists Corporation, C.C.A.Del., 113 F.2d 703, 707.

COGNIZANCE. Jurisdiction, or the exercise of jurisdiction, or power to try and determine causes; judicial examination of a matter, or power and authority to make it. Clarion County v. Hospital, 111 Pa. 339, 3 A. 97.

Judicial notice or knowledge; the judicial hearing of a cause; acknowledgment; confession; recognition.

Claim of cognizance or of conusance. See Claim of Cognizance or of Conusance.

Judicial cognizance. See Judicial.

The term also applies to a power granted by the king to a city or town to hold pleas within it. 11 East, 543; 1 W. Bla. 454; 3 Bla.Com. 298. An acknowledgment by defendant or deforciant in fine that the land belongs to, or is the right of, the complainant, 12 Ad. & El. 259. An answer in replevin, by which defendant acknowledges taking of the goods and want of title, but justifies on ground that the taking was by command of one entitled to the property. Lawes, Pl. 35; 2 Bla.Com. 350. Inhabitants of Sturbridge v. Winslow, 21 Pick., Mass., 87; Noble v. Holmes, 5 Hill, N.Y., 194.

COGNIZEE. The party to whom a fine was levied. 2 Bl.Comm. 351.

COGNIZOR. In old conveyancing. The party levying a fine. 2 Bl.Comm. 350, 351.

COGNOMEN.

In English law. A surname. A name added to the *nomen* proper, or name of the individual; a name descriptive of the family.

In Roman law. A man's family name.

The first name *(prœnomen)* was the proper name of the individual; the second *(nomen)* indicated the *gens* or tribe to which he belonged; while the third *(cognomen)* denoted his family or house. The *agnomen* was added on account of some particular event, as a further distinction. Vicat. See Cas. *temp.* Hardw. 286; 6 Co. 65.

COGNOMEN MAJORUM EST EX SANGUINE TRACTUM, HOC INTRINSECUM EST; AGNOMEN EXTRINSECUM AB EVENTU. 6 Coke, 65. The cognomen is derived from the blood of ancestors, and is intrinsic; an agnomen arises from an event, and is extrinsic.

COGNOVIT. Defendant has confessed judgment and justice of claim, Dyer v. Johnson, Tex.Civ. App., 19 S.W.2d 421, 422. Written authority of debtor and his direction for entry of judgment against him. Blott v. Blott, 227 Iowa 1108, 290 N.W. 74, 76.

COGNOVIT ACTIONEM. (He has confessed the action.) A defendant's written confession of action against him. It is usually upon condition; is supposed to be given in court; and impliedly authorizes plaintiff's attorney to sign judgment and issue execution. Mallory v. Kirkpatrick, 54 N.J. Eq. 50, 33 A. 205.

COHABIT or COHABITATION. Dwelling together. Hunt v. Hunt, 172 Miss. 732, 161 So. 119, 121, Johnson v. Commonwealth, 152 Va. 965, 146 S.E. 289, 291. Intercourse together as husband and wife. State v. Hoffman, 68 N.D. 610, 282 N.W. 407, 409. Living, or abiding or residing together as man and wife. Jones v. State, 182 Tenn. 60, 184 S.W.2d 167, 169; State v. Barlow, 107 Utah 292, 153 P.2d 647, 651; In re Miller's Estate, 182 Okl. 534, 78 P.2d 819, 827.

It may mean copulation or sexual intercourse, Bracksmayer v. Bracksmayer, Sup., 22 N.Y.S.2d 110, 112; as in divorce statutes, Varnell v. Varnell, 182 S.W.2d 466, 467, 207 Ark. 711; De Berry v. De Berry, 115 W.Va. 604, 177 S. E. 440, 441; or promiscuous and casual relations, as in pandering statute, Boykin v. U. S., 130 F.2d 416, 421, 76 U.S.App.D.C. 147. But in some circumstances occasional acts of sexual intercourse may be insufficient proof. Cutrer v. State, 154 Miss. 80, 121 So. 106, 107.

COHABITING IN STATE OF ADULTERY OR FORNICATION. Living together as husband and wife. Martin v. State, 89 Ind.App. 107, 165 N.E. 763.

Proof must establish at least one act of sexual intercourse, or facts from which such act may reasonably be inferred. Warner v. State, 202 Ind. 479, 175 N.E. 661, 663, 74 A.L.R. 1357.

COHÆREDES UNA PERSONA CENSENTUR, PROPTER UNITATEM JURIS QUOD HABENT. Co.Litt. 163. Co-heirs are deemed as one person, on account of the unity of right which they possess.

COHÆRES. Lat. In civil and old English law. A co-heir, or joint heir.

COHAN RULE. Where part of expenditures by taxpayers are of deductible nature as ordinary and necessary business expense are unidentifiable, 50% of expenditures are allowed as deduction. Poletti v. C. I. R., C.A.Mo., 351 F.2d 345, 349.

CO-HEIR. One of several to whom an inheritance descends.

CO-HEIRESS. A joint heiress. A woman who has an equal share of an inheritance with another woman.

COHERER. In wireless telegraphy, the "detector" or "coherer" and "wave responsive device" is a device by which the electromagnetic waves cause the indicator to respond. National Electric Signaling Co. v. Telefunken Wireless Telegraph Co. of United States, C.C.A.N.Y., 221 F. 629, 631.

COHUAGIUM. A tribute made by those who meet promiscuously in a market or fair. Du Cange.

COIF. A title given to serjeants at law, who are called "serjeants of the coif," from the coif they wear on their heads. The use of this coif at first was to cover the clerical tonsure, many of the practicing serjeants being clergymen who had abandoned their profession. It was a thin linen cover, gathered together in the form of a skull or helmet; the material being afterwards changed into white silk, and the form eventually into the black patch at the top of the forensic wig, which is now the distinguishing mark of the degree of serjeant at law. (Cowell; Foss, Judg.; 3 Steph. Comm. 272, note.) Brown.

COIN, *v.* To fashion pieces of metal into a prescribed shape, weight, and degree of fineness, and stamp them with prescribed devices, by authority of government, in order that they may circulate as money, Legal Tender Cases, 12 Wall. 484, 20 L. Ed. 287; Thayer v. Hedges, 22 Ind. 301; Hague v. Powers, 39 Barb.(N.Y.) 466, or to invent words or phrases.

COIN, *n.* Pieces of gold, silver, or other metal, fashioned into a prescribed shape, weight, and degree of fineness, and stamped, by authority of government, with certain marks and devices, and put into circulation as money at a fixed value, Com. v. Gallagher, 16 Gray, Mass., 240; Latham v. U. S., 1 Ct.Cl. 150; Borie v. Trott, 5 Phila., Pa., 403, or any metal disc, State v. Kelleher, 127 A. 503, 504, 2 W.W.Harr., Del., 559.

Strictly speaking, coin differs from money, as the species differs from the genus. Money is any matter, whether metal, paper, beads, shells, etc., which has currency as a medium in commerce. Coin is a particular species, always made of metal, and struck according to a certain process called "coinage." Wharton.

COINAGE. The process or the function of coining metallic money; also the great mass of metallic money in circulation. Meyer v. Roosevelt, 25 How. Prac., N.Y., 105; U. S. v. Otey, C.C.Or., 31 F. 70.

COINSURANCE. A relative division of risk between the insurer and the insured, dependent upon the relative amount of the policy and the actual value of the property insured, and taking effect only when the actual loss is partial and less than the amount of the policy; the insurer being liable to the extent of the policy for a loss equal to or in excess of that amount. Buse v. National Ben Franklin Ins. Co. of Pittsburg, Pa., 160 N.Y. S. 566, 568, 96 Misc. 229.

COITUS. Sexual intercourse; carnal copulation; coition.

COJUDICES. Lat. In old English law. Associate judges having equality of power with others.

COKE. Partially consumed bituminous coal, from which the volatile constituents have been burned away, or partly graphitized carbon, whose fiber has been affected by escaping and burning gases, so that it is lighter than coal, although its substance is hard and dense. Mitchell v. Connellsville Central Coke Co., C.C.A.Pa., 231 F. 131, 137; Otto Coking Co. v. Koppers Co., C.C.A.Del., 258 F. 122, 131.

COKE'S INSTITUTES. See Institutes.

COLD BLOOD. Used in common parlance to designate a willful, deliberate, and premeditated homicide. Skeggs v. State, 24 Ala.App. 307, 135 So. 431, 432.

COLD WATER ORDEAL. The trial which was anciently used for the common sort of people, who, having a cord tied about them under their arms, were cast into a river; if they sank to the bottom until they were drawn up, which was in a very short time, then were they held guiltless; but such as did remain upon the water were held culpable, being, as they said, of the water rejected and kept up. Wharton.

COLIBERTUS. In feudal law. One who, holding in free socage, was obliged to do certain services for the lord. A middle class of tenants between servile and free, who held their freedom of tenure on condition of performing certain services. Said to be the same as the *conditionales.* Cowell.

COLLAPSIBLE CORPORATION. In income tax law, for purpose of determining whether gain from the sale or exchange of stock is gain from the sale or exchange of a capital asset or gain from the sale or exchange of property which is not a capital asset, a corporation formed or availed of principally for the manufacture, construction, or production of property, or for the holding of stock in a corporation so formed or availed of, with a view to the sale or exchange of stock by its shareholders, or a distribution to its shareholders, prior to the realization by such corporation of a substantial part of the net income to be derived from such property, and the realization by such shareholders of gain attributable to such property. 26 U.S.C.A. § 117.

COLLATERAL. By the side; at the side; attached upon the side. Not lineal, but upon a parallel or diverging line. Additional or auxiliary; supplementary; co-operating; accompanying as a secondary fact, or acting as a secondary agent; related to, complementary; accompanying as a co-ordinate, City Investment & Loan Co. v. Wichita Hardware Co., Tex.Civ.App., 57 S.W.2d 222, 223; collateral security, Pepper v. Beville, 100 Fla. 97, 129 So. 334, 337.

As to collateral "Consanguinity," "Descent," "Estoppel," "Guaranty," "Issue," "Limitation," "Negligence," "Power," "Proceeding," and "Warranty," see those titles.

COLLATERAL ACT. In old practice. The name "collateral act" was given to any act (except the payment of money) for the performance of which a bond, recognizance, etc., was given as security.

COLLATERAL ANCESTORS. A phrase sometimes used to designate uncles and aunts, and other collateral antecessors, who are not strictly ancestors. Banks v. Walker, 3 Barb.Ch. (N.Y.) 438, 446.

COLLATERAL ASSURANCE. That which is made over and above the principal assurance or deed itself.

COLLATERAL or INDIRECT ATTACK. On a judicial proceeding, an attempt to avoid, defeat, or evade it, or deny its force and effect, in some incidental proceeding not provided by law for the express purpose of attacking it. May v. Casker, 188 Okl. 448, 110 P.2d 287, 290. On a judgment, any proceeding in which the integrity of a judgment is challenged, except those made in the action wherein the judgment is rendered or by appeal. Edward Thompson Co. v. Thomas, 49 F.2d 500, 60 App.D.C. 118; In re Peterson's Estate, 12 Wash.2d 686, 123 P.2d 733, 751.

An attempt to impeach the judgment by matters dehors the record in an action other than that in which it was rendered; an attempt to avoid, defeat, or evade it, or deny its force and effect in some incidental proceeding not provided by law for the express purpose of attacking it; any proceeding which is not instituted for the express purpose of annulling, correcting, or modifying such decree, or an objection, incidentally raised in the course of a proceeding, which presents an issue collateral to the issues made by the pleadings. Trustees of Somerset Academy v. Picher, C.C.A. Me., 90 F.2d 741, 743.

COLLATERAL ESTOPPEL. The collateral determination of a question by a court having general jurisdiction of the subject. Small v. Haskins, 26 Vt. 209.

Conclusiveness of judgment in prior action where subsequent action is upon a different cause of action. Babcock v. Babcock, 63 Cal.App.2d 94, 146 P.2d 279, 281.

Where complaint in a divorce action alleged that there was no community property, and divorce decree found that all allegations of complaint were true and sustained by evidence, the decree was a conclusive determination that husband's insurance policies were not community property, and under the doctrine of "collateral estoppel" divorced wife was estopped from litigating that issue upon husband's death. Maxwell v. Maxwell, 66 Cal.App.2d 549, 152 P.2d 530, 532.

COLLATERAL FACTS. Such as are outside the controversy, or are not directly connected with the principal matter or issue in dispute. Summerour v. Felker, 102 Ga. 254, 29 S.E. 448; Garner v. State, 76 Miss. 515, 25 So. 363; Jones v. State, 70 Ga.App. 431, 28 S.E.2d 373, 386.

COLLATERAL FRAUD. See Fraud.

COLLATERAL IMPEACHMENT. See Collateral Attack.

COLLATERAL INHERITANCE TAX. A tax levied upon the collateral devolution of property by will or under the intestate law. Perfection Tire & Rubber Co. v. Kellogg-Mackay Equipment Co., 194 Iowa 523, 187 N.W. 32, 33.

COLLATERAL KINSMEN. Those who descend from one and the same common ancestor, but not from one another.

COLLATERAL LINE. See Descent.

COLLATERAL PROMISE. A promise merely super-added to the promise of another, he remaining primarily liable. Fairbanks v. Barker, 115 Me. 11, 97 A. 3, 5; Miller v. Davis, 168 Ky. 661, 182 S.W. 839, 840.

COLLATERAL SECURITY. A security given in addition to the direct security, and subordinate to it, intended to guaranty its validity or convertibility or insure its performance; so that, if the direct security fails, the creditor may fall back upon the collateral security. Butler v. Rockwell, 23 P. 462, 14 Colo. 125; McCormick v. Bank, C.C.Ind., 57 F. 110; Perfection Tire & Rubber Co. v. Kellogg-Mackay Equipment Co., 194 Iowa 523, 187 N.W. 32, 33; Barbin v. Moore, 85 N.H. 362, 159 A. 409, 415, 83 A.L.R. 62.

Collateral security, in bank phraseology, means some security additional to the personal obligation of the borrower. Shoemaker v. Bank, 2 Abb., U.S., 423, Fed.Cas.No.12,-801, or pledge of negotiable paper, shares of corporate stock, and the like. Turner v. Commercial Savings Bank, 17 Ga.App. 631, 87 S.E. 918; A. H. Averill Machinery Co. v. Bain, 50 Mont. 512, 148 P. 334.

COLLATERAL UNDERTAKING. "Collateral" and "original" have become the technical terms whereby to distinguish promises that are within, and such as are not within, the statute of frauds. Elder v. Warfield, 7 Har. & J., Md., 391; Turner v. Commercial Savings Bank, 17 Ga.App. 631, 87 S. E. 918.

COLLATERALIS ET SOCII. The ancient title of masters in chancery.

COLLATIO BONORUM. Lat. In the civil law. The obligation on successors to an inheritance to return to the common inheritance gifts received from the ancestor during his lifetime. In re Farmers' Loan & Trust Co., 163 N.Y.S. 961, 967, 99 Misc. 420; In re Farmers' Loan & Trust Co., 168 N.Y.S. 952, 956, 181 App.Div. 642. A joining together or contribution of goods into a common fund.

This occurs where a portion of money, advanced by the father to a son or daughter, is brought into *hotchpot*, in order to have an equal distributory share of his personal estate at his death. See Collation.

COLLATIO SIGNORUM. In old English law. A comparison of marks or seals. A mode of testing the genuineness of a seal, by comparing it with another known to be genuine. Adams. See Bract. fol. 389*b*.

COLLATION. It is the bringing into the estate of an intestate an estimate of the value of advancements made by the intestate to his or her children in order that the whole may be divided in accordance with the statute of descents. In re Howlett's Estate, 275 Mich. 596, 267 N.W. 743, 744.

It is synonymous with "hotchpot." Moore v. Freeman, 50 Ohio St. 592, 35 N.E. 502.

Civil Law

The collation of goods is the supposed or real return to the mass of the succession which an heir makes of property which he received in advance of his share or otherwise, in order that such property may be divided together with the other effects of the succession. Civ.Code La. art. 1227; Miller v. Miller, 105 La. 257, 29 So. 802; Succession of Thompson, 9 La.Ann. 96.

The fundamental basis of doctrine is legal presumption that ancestor intended absolute equality among his descendants in final distribution of his property, that donation by him during his lifetime to any one of them was merely advancement d'hoirie or advance on donee's hereditary share to establish him in life or for some other useful purpose, and that ancestor intended to reestablish equality among his descendants in final partition of his estate. Le Blanc v. Volker, La.App., 198 So. 398, 401.

Ecclesiastical Law

The act by which the bishop who has the bestowing of a benefice gives it to an incumbent. 2 Bla.Com. 22.

Practice

The comparison of a copy with its original to ascertain its correctness; or the report of the officer who made the comparison.

COLLATION OF SEALS. When upon the same label one seal was set on the back or reverse of the other. Wharton.

COLLATION TO A BENEFICE. In ecclesiastical law. This occurs where the bishop and patron are one and the same person, in which case the bishop cannot present the clergyman to himself, but does, by the one act of collation or conferring the benefice, the whole that is done in common cases both by presentation and institution. 2 Bl.Comm. 22.

COLLATIONE FACTÂ UNI POST MORTEM ALTERIUS. A writ directed to justices of the common pleas, commanding them to issue their writ to the bishop, for the admission of a clerk in the place of another presented by the crown, where there had been a demise of the crown during a suit; for judgment once passed for the king's clerk, and he dying before admittance, the king may bestow his presentation on another. Reg. Orig. 31.

COLLATIONE HEREMITAGII. In old English law. A writ whereby the king conferred the keeping of an hermitage upon a clerk. Reg.Orig. 303, 308.

COLLECT. To gather together; to bring scattered things (assets, accounts, articles of property) into one mass or fund; to assemble.

To collect a debt or claim is to obtain payment or liquidation of it, either by personal solicitation or legal proceedings. Isler v. National Park Bank of New York, 239 N.Y. 462, 147 N.E. 66, 68.

COLLECT ON DELIVERY. See C. O. D.

COLLECTIBLE. Debts, obligations, demands, liabilities that one may be made to pay by means of legal process. Shanahan v. State, 142 Md. 616, 121 A. 636, 640.

COLLECTION AGENCY. A concern which collects all kinds of claims for others. McCarthy v. Hughes, 36 R.I. 66, 88 A. 984, 985, Ann.Cas.1915D, 26.

COLLECTION OF ILLEGAL FEES. Collection by public official of fees in excess of those fixed by law for certain services. Parker v. Morgan, 48 Utah 405, 160 P. 764, 765.

COLLECTIVE BARGAINING. As contemplated by National Labor Relations Act is a procedure looking toward making of collective agreements between employer and accredited representatives of employees concerning wages, hours, and other conditions of employment, and requires that parties deal with each other with open and fair minds and sincerely endeavor to overcome obstacles existing between them to the end that employment relations may be stabilized and obstruction to free flow of commerce prevented. National Labor Relations Act § 8(5), 29 U.S.C.A. § 158(5). Rapid Roller Co. v. National Labor Relations Board, C.C.A.7, 126 F.2d 452, 460.

The essence of "collective bargaining" is the freedom of choice of employees in selection of their bargaining representative. National Labor Relations Act § 1 et seq., 29 U.S.C.A. § 151 et seq. National Labor Relations Board v. American Rolling Mill Co., C.C.A.6, 126 F.2d 38, 41.

"Collective bargaining," within provision of National Labor Relations Act providing that a refusal to bargain collectively should be an unfair labor practice, does not require employer to reach an agreement, but does require sincere negotiations with representatives of employees. National Labor Relations Act § 8(5), 29 U.S.C.A. § 158(5). National Labor Relations Board v. Biles Coleman Lumber Co., C.C.A.9, 98 F.2d 18, 22.

COLLECTIVE BARGAINING AGREEMENT. Agreement between an employer and a labor union which regulates terms and conditions of employment. Railway Mail Ass'n v. Murphy, 44 N.Y.S. 2d 601, 605, 608, 180 Misc. 868; McNeil v. Peoples Life Ins. Co., D.C.Mun.App., 43 A.2d 293, 294. See, also, "Collective Labor Agreement" and "Trade Agreement."

COLLECTIVE LABOR AGREEMENT. Also called "trade agreement". Bargaining agreement as to wages and conditions of work entered into by groups of employees, usually organized into a brotherhood or union on one side and groups of employers or corporations on the other side. Brisbin v. E. L. Oliver Lodge No. 335 of Brotherhood of Railway Clerks, 134 Neb. 517, 279 N.W. 277, 283; Rentschler v. Missouri Pac. R. Co., 126 Neb. 493, 253 N.W. 694, 696, 95 A.L.R. 1.

It becomes a binding contract when it is adopted into and made a part of the individual contract of each employee, and a breach of its terms will give rise to a cause of action by either party.

COLLECTOR. One appointed to receive taxes or other impositions: as, collector of taxes, collector of militia fines, etc. A person appointed by a private person to collect the credits due him.

COLLECTOR OF DECEDENT'S ESTATE. A person temporarily appointed by the probate court to collect rents, assets, interest, bills receivable, etc., of a decedent's estate, and act for the estate in all financial matters requiring immediate settlement. Such collector is usually appointed when there is protracted litigation as to the probate of the will, or as to the person to take out administration, and his duties cease as soon as an executor or administrator is qualified.

COLLECTOR OF THE CUSTOMS. An officer of the United States, appointed for the term of four years. Act May 15, 1820, § 1; 3 Story, U.S.Laws, 1790 (19 U.S.C.A. § 5). Rev.Stat.U.S. § 2613 (19 U.S.C.A. § 5). His general duties are defined in § 2621 (19 U.S.C.A. § 33).

COLLECTION. Indorsement "for collection." See For Collection.

COLLEGA. In the civil law. One invested with joint authority. A colleague; an associate.

COLLEGATARIUS. Lat. In the civil law. A colegatee. Inst. 2, 20, 8.

COLLEGATARY. A co-legatee; a person who has a legacy left to him in common with other persons.

COLLEGE. An organized assembly or collection of persons, established by law, and empowered to co-operate for the performance of some special function or for the promotion of some common object, which may be educational, political, ecclesiastical, or scientific in its character.

The assemblage of the cardinals at Rome is called a "college." So, in the United States, the body of presidential electors is called the "electoral college."

In the most common use of the word, it designates an institution of learning (usually incorporated) which offers instruction in the liberal arts and humanities and in scientific branches, but not in the technical arts or those studies preparatory to admission to the professions. Com. v. Banks, 198 Pa. 397, 48 A. 277; Chegaray v. New York, 13 N.Y. 229. Also applied to all kinds of institutions from universities, or departments thereof to "business colleges," "barber colleges," etc. State v. Erickson, 75 Mont. 429, 244 P. 287, 291.

In England, it is a civil corporation, company or society of men, having certain privileges, and endowed with certain revenues, founded by royal license. An assemblage of several of these colleges is called a "university." Wharton.

COLLEGIA. In the civil law. The guild of a trade.

COLLEGIALITER. In a corporate capacity. 2 Kent, Comm. 296.

COLLEGIATE CHURCH. In English ecclesiastical law. A church built and endowed for a society or body corporate of a dean or other president, and secular priests, as canons or prebendaries in the said church; such as the churches of Westminster, Windsor, and others. Cowell.

COLLEGIUM. Lat. In the civil law. A word having various meanings; *e. g.*, an assembly, society, or company; a body of bishops; an army; a class of men. But the principal idea of the word was that of an association of individuals of the same rank and station, or united for the pursuit of some business or enterprise. Sometimes, a corporation, as in the maxim "tres faciunt collegium" (1 Bl.Comm. 469), though the more usual and proper designation of a corporation was "universitas."

COLLEGIUM AMMIRALITATIS. The college or society of the admiralty.

COLLEGIUM EST SOCIETAS PLURIUM CORPORUM SIMUL HABITANTIUM. Jenk.Cent. 229. A college is a society of several persons dwelling together.

COLLEGIUM ILLICITUM. One which abused its right, or assembled for any other purpose than that expressed in its charter.

COLLEGIUM LICITUM. An assemblage or society of men united for some useful purpose or business, with power to act like a single individual. 2 Kent, Comm. 269.

COLLIDE. To strike or dash against; to come into collision; to clash. Collins v. Leahy, Mo. App., 102 S.W.2d 801, 809.

COLLIERY. This term is sufficiently wide to include all contiguous and connected veins and seams of coal which are worked as one concern, without regard to the closes or pieces of ground under which they are carried, and apparently also the engines and machinery in such contiguous and connected veins. MacSwin. Mines, 25. Carey v. Bright, 58 Pa. 85.

It includes every operation and work, both under and above ground, used or to be used to mine and prepare coal. Moore v. Stevens Coal Co., 315 Pa. 564, 173 A. 661, 662.

COLLIGENDUM BONA DEFUNCTI. See Ad Colligendum, etc.

COLLISION. Striking together of two objects, one of which may be stationary. Davilla v. Liberty Life Ins. Co., 114 Cal.App. 308, 299 P. 831, 834. Act or instance of colliding; state of having collided. Guenther v. American Indem. Co., 246 Wis. 478, 17 N.W.2d 570, 571.

Maritime Law

The act of ships or vessels striking together.

In its strict sense, collision means the impact of two vessels both moving, and is distinguished from *allision*, which designates the striking of a moving vessel against one that is stationary. But collision is used in a broad sense, to include allision, and perhaps other species of encounters between vessels, or a vessel and other floating, though non-navigable, objects. Wright v. Brown, 4 Ind. 97, 58 Am.Dec. 622; London Assur. Co. v. Companhia De Moagens, 68 F. 258, 15 C.C.A. 379; Lehigh & Wilkes-Barre Coal Co. v. Globe & Rutgers Fire Ins. Co., C.C.A.N.Y., 6 F.2d 736, 738, 43 A.L.R. 215.

The term is not inapplicable to cases where a stationary vessel is struck by one under way, strictly termed "allision"; or where one vessel is brought into contact with another by swinging at anchor. And even an injury received by a vessel at her moorings, in consequence of being violently rubbed or pressed against by a second vessel lying alongside of her, in consequence of a collision against such second vessel by a third one under way, may be compensated for, under the general head of "collision," as well as an injury which is the direct result of a "blow," properly so called. The Moxey, Abb.Adm. 73, Fed.Cas.No. 9,894.

Automobile Insurance Law

The term denotes the act of colliding; striking together; violent contact. Long v. Royal Ins. Co., 180 Wash. 360, 40 P.2d 132, 133, 105 A.L.R. 1423. The term implies an impact or sudden contact of a moving body with an obstruction in its line of motion, whether both bodies are in motion or one stationary and the other, no matter which, in motion. St. Paul Fire & Marine Ins. Co. v. American Compounding Co., 211 Ala. 593, 100 So. 904, 906, 35 A.L.R. 1018; Rea v. Motors Ins. Corporation, 48 N.M. 9, 144 P.2d 676, 678, 679, 681.

But liability depends on what the automobile collides with and, of course, the cause of the collision and the terms of the policy. Liability has been sustained where collision was with embankment, Pred v. Employers' Indemnity Corporation, 112 Neb. 161, 198 N.W. 864, 866, 35 A.L.R. 1003; and also denied, Fox v. Interstate Exch., 182 Wis. 28, 195 N.W. 842. Liability has also been denied where collision was with earth, after automobile had gone over an embankment, Continental Casualty Co. v. Paul, 209 Ala. 166, 95 So. 814, 815, 30 A.L.R. 802 (*contra* Polstein v. Pacific Fire Ins. Co., 203 N.Y.S. 362, 122 Misc. 194); and with stump after skidding off the road, Ploe v. International Indemnity Co., 128 Wash. 480, 223 P. 327, 328, 35 A.L.R. 999. Liability has been sustained for damages caused by collision with sides of rut, Wood v. Southern Casualty Co., Tex.Civ.App., 270 S.W. 1055, 1057; and both sustained and denied where body or frame of automobile collided with the road through the breaking of an axle or other cause, Young v. New Jersey Ins. Co., D.C.Mont., 284 F. 492, 493; Great American Mut. Indemnity Co. v. Jones, 111 Ohio St. 84, 144 N.E. 596, 35 A.L.R. 1023; Great Eastern Casualty Co. v. Solinsky, 150 Tenn. 206, 263 S.W. 71, 74, 35 A.L.R. 1007. Liability has been sustained where elevator containing automobile fell, Freiberger v. Globe Indemnity Co., 199 N.Y.S. 310, 311, 205 App.Div. 116; National Fire Ins. Co of Hartford, Conn., v. Elliott, C.C.A. Mo., 7 F.2d 522, 527, 42 A.L.R. 1121; where standing car ran over precipice, St. Paul Fire & Marine Ins. Co. v. American Compounding Co., 211 Ala. 593, 100 So. 904, 906, 35 A.L.R. 1018; where scoop of steamshovel loading autotruck fell on latter, Universal Service Co. v. American Ins. Co., 213 Mich. 523, 181 N.W. 1007, 14 A.L.R. 183; but denied where second floor of garage fell upon automobile, O'Leary v. St. Paul Fire & Marine Ins. Co., Tex.Civ.App., 196 S.W. 575. This subject is fully discussed in Blashfield, Cyc. of Automobile Law and Prac., Perm.Ed., §§ 3691–3698.

COLLISION CLAUSE. An additional provision for insurance, on the margin of the policy, covering the contingency of a collision of the insured vessel with another vessel and the liability of the insured for the injury to such other vessel. Fireman's Fund Ins. Co. v. Globe Nav. Co., C.C.A. Wash., 236 F. 618, 631. Also known as "running down" clause.

COLLISTRIGIUM. The pillory.

COLLOBIUM. A hood or covering for the shoulders, formerly worn by serjeants at law.

COLLOCATION. In French law. The arrangement or marshaling of the creditors of an estate in the order in which they are to be paid according to law. Merl. Répert.

COLLOQUIUM. One of the usual parts of the declaration in an action for slander. It is a general averment that the words complained of were spoken "of and concerning the plaintiff," or concerning the extrinsic matters alleged in the inducement, and its office is to connect the whole publication with the previous statement. Van Vechten v. Hopkins, 5 Johns., N.Y., 220, 4 Am.Dec. 339; Lukehart v. Byerly, 53 Pa. 421; Express Pub. Co. v. Wilkins, Tex.Civ.App., 218 S.W. 614, 616; Kee v. Armstrong, Byrd & Co., 75 Okl. 84, 182 P. 494, 498, 5 A.L.R. 1349.

An averment that the words in question are spoken of or concerning some usage, report, or fact which gives to words otherwise indifferent the peculiar defamatory meaning assigned to them. Carter v. Andrews, 16 Pick., Mass., 6; Moore v. Leverett, Tex.Civ.App., 33 S.W.2d 838, 842.

COLLUSION. Is an agreement between two or more persons to defraud a person of his rights by the forms of law, or to obtain an object forbidden by law. It implies the existence of fraud of some kind, the employment of fraudulent means, or of lawful means for the accomplishment of an unlawful purpose. May Hosiery Mills v. United States District Court in and for Dist. of Montana, C.C.A. Mont., 64 F.2d 450, 454.

A secret combination, conspiracy, or concert of action between two or more persons for fraudulent or deceitful purpose. W. E. Bowen Improvement Co. v. Van Hafften, 209 Mo.App. 629, 238 S.W. 147, 149; Daly v. Haight, 156 N.Y.S. 538, 541, 170 App.Div. 469.

A secret arrangement between two or more persons, whose interests are apparently conflicting, to make use of the forms and proceedings of law in order to defraud a third person, or to obtain that which justice would not give them, by deceiving a court or its officers. Railroad Co. v. Gay, 86 Tex. 571, 26 S.W. 599, 25 L.R.A. 52; Balch v. Beach, 119 Wis. 77, 95 N.W. 132. A secret agreement between two persons that one should institute a suit against the other, in order to obtain the decision of a judicial tribunal for some sinister purpose. In re Insull Utility Investments, D.C.Ill., 6 F.Supp. 653, 655.

In divorce proceedings, collusion is an agreement between husband and wife that one of them shall commit, or appear to have committed, or be represented in court as having committed, acts constituting a cause of divorce, for the purpose of enabling the other to obtain a divorce. But it also means connivance or conspiracy in initiating or prosecuting the suit, as where there is a compact for mutual aid in carrying it through to a decree. Beard v. Beard, 65 Cal. 354, 4 P. 229; Pohlman v. Pohlman, 60 N.J.Eq. 28, 46 A. 658; McCauley v. McCauley, 88 N.J.Eq. 392, 103 A. 20, 23. Rosenzweig v. Rosenzweig, 246 N.Y.S. 231, 233, 231 App.Div. 13.

COLLUSIVE ACTION. An action not founded upon an actual controversy between the parties to it, but brought for purpose of securing a determination of a point of law for the gratification of curiosity or to settle rights of third persons not parties. It will not be entertained. City and County of San Francisco v. Boyd, 22 Cal.2d 685, 140 P.2d 666, 669, 670.

COLLYBISTA. In the civil law. A money-changer; a dealer in money.

COLLYBUM. In the civil law. Exchange.

COLNE. In Saxon and old English law. An account or calculation.

COLONUS. In old European law. A husbandman; an inferior tenant employed in cultivating the lord's land. A term of Roman origin, corresponding with the Saxon ceorl. 1 Spence, Ch. 51.

COLONY. A dependent political community, consisting of a number of citizens of the same country who have emigrated therefrom to people another, and remain subject to the mother-country. U. S. v. The Nancy, 3 Wash.C.C. 287, Fed.Cas.No.15,854.

A settlement in a foreign country possessed and cultivated, either wholly or partially, by immigrants and their descendants, who have a political connection with and subordination to the mother-country, whence they emigrated. In other words, it is a place peopled from some more ancient city or country. Wharton.

Colonial Office

In the English government, this is the department of state through which the sovereign appoints colonial governors, etc., and communicates with them. Until the year 1854, the secretary for the colonies was also secretary for war.

Colonial Laws

In America, this term designates the body of law in force in the thirteen original colonies before the Declaration of Independence. In England, the term signifies the laws enacted by Canada and the other present British colonies.

COLOR. An appearance, semblance, or *simulacrum,* as distinguished from that which is real. A *prima facie* or apparent right. Hence, a deceptive appearance; a plausible, assumed exterior, concealing a lack of reality; a disguise or pretext. Railroad Co. v. Allfree, 64 Iowa 500, 20 N.W. 779; Broughton v. Haywood, 61 N.C. 383; Wilt v. Bueter, 186 Ind. 98, 111 N.E. 926, 929.

In pleading. Ground of action admitted to subsist in the opposite party by the pleading of one of the parties to an action, which is so set out as to be apparently valid, but which is in reality legally insufficient.

A term of the ancient rhetoricians, and early adopted into the language of pleading. It was an apparent or *prima facie* right; and the meaning of the rule that pleadings in confession and avoidance should give color was that they should confess the matter adversely alleged, to such an extent, at least, as to admit some apparent right in the opposite party, which required to be encountered and avoided by the allegation of new matter. Color was either express, *i. e.,* inserted in the pleading, or implied, which was naturally inherent in the structure of the pleading. Steph.Pl. 233; Merten v. Bank, 5 Okl. 585, 49 P. 913. Wheeler v. Nickels, 168 Or. 604, 126 P.2d 32, 36.

The word also means the dark color of the skin showing the presence of negro blood; and hence it is equivalent to African descent or parentage. Johnson v. Board of Education of Wilson County, 166 N.C. 468, 82 S.E. 832, 834, L.R.A.1915A, 828.

COLOR OF AUTHORITY. That semblance or presumption of authority sustaining the acts of a public officer which is derived from his apparent title to the office or from a writ or other process in his hands apparently valid and regular. State v. Oates, 86 Wis. 634, 57 N.W. 296, 39 Am.St.Rep. 912.

COLOR OF LAW. The appearance or semblance, without the substance, of legal right. State v. Brechler, 185 Wis. 599, 202 N.W. 144, 148.

COLOR OF OFFICE. An act unjustly done by the countenance of an office, being grounded upon corruption, to which the office is as a shadow and color. Plow. 64. Day v. National Bond & Investment Co., Mo.App., 99 S.W.2d 117, 119.

A claim or assumption of right to do an act by virtue of an office, made by a person who is legally destitute of any such right. Feller v. Gates, 40 Or. 543, 67 P. 416, 56 L.R.A. 630, 91 Am.St.Rep. 492; Citizens' Bank of Colquitt v. American Surety Co. of New York, 174 Ga. 852, 164 S.E. 817; Pontiac Trust Co. v. Newell, 266 Mich. 490, 254 N.W. 178, 181.

Such person must be at least officer *de factor*. Burrall v. Acker, 23 Wend., N.Y., 606, 35 Am.Dec. 582; Day v. National Bond & Investment Co., Mo.App., 99 S.W.2d 117, 119. See, also, Colore Officil.

COLOR OF TITLE. The appearance, semblance, or *simulacrum* of title. Also termed "apparent title." Any fact, extraneous to the act or mere will of the claimant, which has the appearance, on its face, of supporting his claim of a present title to land, but which, for some defect, in reality falls short of establishing it. Howth v. Farrar, C.C.A. Tex., 94 F.2d 654, 658; Saltmarsh v. Crommelin, 24 Ala. 352.

Anything in writing purporting to convey title to the land, which defines the extent of the claim, it being immaterial how defective or imperfect the writing may be, so that it is a sign, semblance, or color of title. Theisen v. Qualley, 42 S.D. 367, 175 N.W. 556, 557. A title that is imperfect, but not so obviously so that it would be apparent to one not skilled in the law. Ipock v. Gaskins, 161 N.C. 673, 77 S.E. 843, 847.

A writing upon its face professing to pass title but which does not, either through want of title in the grantor or a defective mode of conveyance. Philbin v. Carr, 75 Ind.App. 560, 129 N.E. 19, 24; Glass v. Lynchburg Shoe Co., 212 N.C. 70, 192 S.E. 899.

That which the law considers *prima facie* a good title, but which, by reason of some defect, not appearing on its face, does not in fact amount to title. An absolute nullity, as a void deed, judgment, etc., will not constitute color of title. Causey v. White, 143 Ga. 7, 84 S.E. 58; Stearns Coal & Lumber Co. v. Boyatt, 168 Ky. 111, 181 S.W. 962, 964. That which is title in appearance but not in reality. Fitschen Bros. Commercial Co. v. Noyes' Estate, 76 Mont. 175, 246 P. 773, 779; Boland v. Heck, 179 Okl. 403, 65 P.2d 1213, 1215.

"Any instrument having a grantor and grantee, and containing a description of the lands intended to be conveyed, and apt words for their conveyance, gives color of title to the lands described. Such an instrument purports to be a conveyance of the title, and because it does not, for some reason, have that effect, it passes only color or the semblance of a title." Brooks v. Bruyn, 35 Ill. 392.

"Color of title" is not synonymous with "claim of title." To constitute "color of title" there must be a paper title to give color to the adverse possession, whereas, a "claim of title" may be shown wholly by parol. Walton v. Sikes, 165 Ga. 422, 141 S.E. 188, 190.

COLORABLE. That which has or gives color. That which is in appearance only, and not in reality, what it purports to be. Counterfeit, feigned, having the appearance of truth. Ellis v. Jones, 73 Colo. 516, 216 P. 257, 258.

COLORABLE ALTERATION. One which makes no real or substantial change, but is introduced only as a subterfuge or means of evading the patent or copyright law.

COLORABLE CAUSE OR INVOCATION OF JURISDICTION. With reference to actions for malicious prosecution, a "colorable cause or invocation of jurisdiction" means that a person, apparently qualified, has appeared before a justice and made a complaint under oath and in writing, stating some facts which in connection with other facts constitute a criminal offense or bear a similitude thereto. Hotel Supply Co. v. Reid, 16 Ala. App. 563, 80 So. 137, 138.

COLORABLE CLAIM. In bankruptcy law, a claim made by one holding the property as an agent or bailee of the bankrupt; a claim in which as a matter of law, there is no adverseness. In re B'um, C.C.A.Wis., 202 F. 883, 884; In re Western Rope & Mfg. Co., C.C.A.Okl., 298 F. 926, 927.

COLORABLE IMITATION. In the law of trademarks, this phrase denotes such a close or ingenious imitation as to be calculated to deceive ordinary persons.

COLORABLE PLEADING. The practice of giving *color* in pleading.

COLORABLE TRANSACTION. One presenting an appearance which does not correspond with the reality, and, ordinarily, an appearance intended to conceal or to deceive. Osborn v. Osborn, 102 Kan. 890, 172 P. 23, 24.

COLORE OFFICII. Lat. By color of office. Officer's acts unauthorized by officer's position, though done in form that purports that acts are done by reason of official duty and by virtue of office. Richards v. American Surety Co. of New York, 48 Ga.App. 102, 171 S.E. 924. See, also, Color of Office.

COLORED. By common usage in America, this term, in such phrases as "colored persons," "the colored race," "colored men," and the like, is used to designate negroes or persons of the African race, including all persons of mixed blood descended from negro ancestry. Collins v. Oklahoma State Hospital, 76 Okl. 229, 184 P. 946, 949, 7 A.L.R. 895; Theophanis v. Theophanis, 244 Ky. 689, 51 S.W.2d 957.

But where a state Constitution provided for separate schools for the white and colored races, the term "white race" was held to be limited to the Caucasian race, and the term "colored races" to embrace all other races. Rice v. Gong Lum, 139 Miss. 760, 104 So. 105, 107.

It has also been held that there is no legal technical signification to the phrase "colored person" which the courts are bound judicially to know. Pauska v. Daus, 31 Tex. 74.

COLPICES. Young poles, which, being cut down, are made levers or lifters. Blount.

COLPINDACH. In old Scotch law. A young beast or cow, of the age of one or two years; in later times called a "cowdash."

COLT. An animal of the horse species, whether male or female, not more than four years old. Russ. & R. 416; Mallory v. Berry, 16 Kan. 295; Pullen v. State, 11 Tex.App. 91.

COM. An abbreviation for "company," exactly equivalent to "Co." Keith v. Sturges, 51 Ill. 142.

COMBARONES. In old English law. Fellow-barons; fellow-citizens;—the citizens or freemen of the Cinque Ports being anciently called "barons;" the term "*combarones*" is used in this sense in a grant of Henry III. to the barons of the port of Fevresham. Cowell.

COMBAT. A forcible encounter between two or more persons; a battle; a duel. Trial by battle.

Mutual Combat

One into which both the parties enter willingly or voluntarily; it implies a common intent to fight, but not necessarily an exchange of blows. Aldridge v. State, 59 Miss. 250; Tate v. State, 46 Ga. 158; State v. Moss, 24 N.M. 59, 172 P. 199; Findley v. State, 125 Ga. 583, 54 S.E. 106.

COMBATERRÆ. A valley or piece of low ground between two hills. Kennett, Gloss.

COMBE. A small or narrow valley.

COMBINATION. A conspiracy, or confederation of men for unlawful or violent deeds. See Deupree v. Thornton, 97 Neb. 812, 151 N.W. 305, 307, L.R.A.1917C, 65.

In patent law. A union of different elements. A patent may be taken out for a new combination of existing machines. Stevenson Co. v. McFassell, C.C.A.Pa., 90 F. 707, 33 C.C.A. 249; Moore v. Schaw, C.C.Cal., 118 F. 602; Moody v. Fiske, 2 Mas. 112, Fed.Cas.No.9,745.

In patent law. A composition of old or new elements, and it is patentable, if it produces new and useful results, though all its constituents were well known and in common use before it was made, provided the results are a product of the combination, and not a mere aggregate of several results. U. S. Industrial Chemical Co. v. Theroz Co., C.C.A.Md., 25 F.2d 387, 391.

The distinction between a "combination" and an "aggregation" lies in the presence or absence of mutuality of action; a "combination" essentially requiring that there be some joint operation performed by its elements, producing a result due to their joint and cooperating action, while in an "aggregation" there is a mere adding together of separate contributions, each operating independently of the other. Ball v. Coker, C.C.A.S.C., 210 F. 278, 282; Mead Morrision Mfg. Co. v. Exeter Mach. Works, D.C.Pa., 215 F. 731.

COMBINATION IN RESTRAINT OF TRADE. A trust, pool, or other association of two or more individuals or corporations having for its object to monopolize the manufacture or traffic in a particular commodity, to regulate or control the output, restrict the sale, establish and maintain the price, stifle or exclude competition, or otherwise to interfere with the normal course of trade under conditions of free competition. Northern Securities Co. v. U. S., 193 U.S. 197, 24 S.Ct. 436, 48 L.Ed. 679; U. S. v. Knight Co., 156 U.S. 1, 15 S.Ct. 249, 39 L.Ed. 325.

COMBINED CARBON. As used in the metallurgy of iron and steel, carbon in union with some one or more metallic constituents in the iron alloy. Pittsburgh Iron & Steel Foundries Co. v. Seaman-Sleeth Co., C.C.A.Pa., 248 F. 705, 707.

COMBING WOOL. A long-stapled wool, usually combed, employed in the manufacture of worsteds. Stone & Downer Co. v. U. S., 12 Ct.Cust.App. 62, 63; U. S. v. Stone & Downer Co., 12 Ct.Cust.App. 557. See Clothing Wool.

COMBUSTIBLE. Capable of undergoing combustion; apt to catch fire; inflammable. Hebrlee v. Hawley, 112 Kan. 398, 211 P. 129, 131.

COMBUSTIO. Burning. In old English law. The punishment inflicted upon apostates.

COMBUSTIO DOMORUM. Houseburning; arson. 4 Bl.Comm. 272.

COMBUSTIO PECUNIÆ. Burning of money; the ancient method of testing mixed and corrupt money, paid into the exchequer, by melting it down.

COME. To present oneself; to appear in court. In modern practice, though such presence may be constructive only, the word is still used to indicate participation in the proceedings. Horner v. O'Laughlin, 29 Md. 472. Melfi v. Barney, R.I., 121 A. 67, 68.

Thus, a pleading may begin, "Now *comes* the defendant," etc. In case of a default, the technical language of the record is that the party "*comes* not, but makes default."

COMES, *v.* A word used in a pleading to indicate the defendant's presence in court. See Come.

COMES, *n.* Lat. A follower, companion, or attendant; a count or earl.

COMES AND DEFENDS. This phrase, anciently used in the language of pleading, and still surviving in some jurisdictions, occurs at the commencement of a defendant's plea or demurrer; and of its two verbs the former signifies that he appears in court, the latter that he defends the action.

COMFORT. Benefit, consolation, contentment, ease, enjoyment, happiness, pleasure, or satisfaction. National Surety Co. v. Jarrett, 95 W.Va. 420, 121 S.E. 291.

COMFORTABLE SPEED. As applied to railway trains, is a speed which has been developed by experience and observation to mean that speed at which you can run a train around a curve, and the passengers will not feel any uncomfortable or unpleasant lurch in going around the curve. Chesapeake & O. Ry. Co. v. Tanner, 165 Va. 406, 182 S.E. 239.

COMINUS. Lat. Immediately; hand-to-hand; in personal contact.

COMITAS. Lat. Courtesy; civility; comity. An indulgence or favor granted another nation, as a mere matter of indulgence, without any claim of right made. *Comitas inter communitates;* or *comitas inter gentes;* comity between communities or nations; comity of nations. 2 Kent, Comm. 457.

COMITATU COMMISSO. A writ or commission, whereby a sheriff is authorized to enter upon the charges of a county. Reg.Orig. 295.

COMITATU ET CASTRO COMMISSO. A writ by which the charge of a county, together with the keeping of a castle, is committed to the sheriff.

COMITATUS. In old English law. A county or shire; the body of a county. The territorial jurisdiction of a *comes, i. e.*, count or earl. 1 Bla. Comm. 116. An earldom. 1 Ld.Raym. 13. The county court, a court of great antiquity and of great dignity in early times. 1 Spence, Eq.Jur. 42,

66. Also, the retinue or train of a prince or high governmental official. Spelman. The retinue which accompanied a Roman proconsul to his province. Du Cange. The personal following of professional warriors. Taylor, Jurispr. 216.

COMITES. Counts or earls. Attendants or followers. Persons composing the retinue of a high functionary.

Persons who are attached to the suite of a public minister. As to their privileges, see Respublica v. De Longchamps, 1 Dall. (Pa.) 117, 1 L.Ed. 59; U. S. v. Benner, Baldw. 240, Fed.Cas.No.14,568.

COMITES PALEYS. Counts or earls palatine; those who had the government of a county palatine.

COMITIA. In Roman law. An assembly, either (1) of the Roman curiæ, in which case it was called the *"comitia curiata vel calata"*; or (2) of the Roman centuries, in which case it was called the *"comitia centuriata"* (called also *comitia majora*); or (3) of the Roman tribes, in which case it was called the *"comitia tributa."* Only patricians were members of the first *comitia*, and only plebians of the last; but the *comitia centuriata* comprised the entire populace, patricians and plebians both, and was the great legislative assembly passing the *leges*, properly so called, as the senate passed the *senatus consulta*, and the *comitia tributa* passed the *plebiscita*. Under the *Lex Hortensia*, 287 B.C., the *plebiscitum* acquired the force of a *lex*. Brown.

COMITISSA. In old English law. A countess; an earl's wife.

COMITIVA. In old English law. The dignity and office of a *comes* (count or earl); the same with what was afterwards called *"comitatus."*

Also a companion or fellow-traveler; a troop or company of robbers. Jacob.

COMITY. Courtesy; complaisance; respect; a willingness to grant a privilege, not as a matter of right, but out of deference and good will. Dow v. Lillie, 26 N.D. 512, 144 N.W. 1082, 1088, L.R.A. 1915D, 754; Cox v. Terminal R. Ass'n of St. Louis, 331 Mo. 910, 55 S.W.2d 685.

Comity of Nations

(Lat. *comitas gentium*)

The most appropriate phrase to express the true foundation and extent of the obligation of the laws of one nation within the territories of another. Story, Confl.Laws, § 38. That body of rules which states observe towards one another from courtesy or mutual convenience, although they do not form part of international law. Holtz. Enc. *s. v.* Hilton v. Guyot, 159 U.S. 113, 16 S.Ct. 139, 40 L.Ed. 95; People v. Rushworth, 294 Ill. 455, 128 N.E. 555, 558; Second Russian Ins. Co. v. Miller, C.C.A.N.Y., 297 F. 404, 409.

It is derived altogether from the voluntary consent of the latter; and it is inadmissible when it is contrary to its known policy, or prejudicial to its interests. In the silence of any positive rule affirming or denying or restraining the operation of foreign laws, courts of justice presume the tacit adoption of them by their own government, unless repugnant to its policy, or prejudicial to its interests. It is not the comity of the courts, but the comity of the nation, which is administered and ascertained in the same way, and guided by the same reasoning, by which all other principles of the municipal law are ascertained and guided.

The recognition which one nation allows within its territory to the legislative, executive, or judicial acts of another nation, having due regard both to international duty and convenience and to the rights of its own citizens or of other persons who are under the protection of its laws. State ex rel. National Surety Corporation v. Price, 129 Neb. 433, 261 N.W. 894.

"The use of the word 'comity' as expressing the basis of jurisdiction has been criticized. It is, however, a mere question of definition. The principles lying behind the word are recognized. * * * The truth remains that jurisdiction depends upon the law of the forum, and this law in turn depends upon the public policy disclosed by the acts and declarations of the political departments of the government." Russian Socialist Federated Soviet Republic v. Cibrario, 235 N.Y. 255, 139 N.E. 259, 260.

Judicial Comity

The principle in accordance with which the courts of one state or jurisdiction will give effect to the laws and judicial decisions of another, not as a matter of obligation, but out of deference and respect. Franzen v. Zimmer, 35 N.Y.S. 612, 90 Hun 103; Stowe v. Bank, C.C.Me., 92 F. 96; Strawn Mercantile Co. v. First Nat. Bank, Tex. Civ.App., 279 S.W. 473, 474; Bobala v. Bobala, 68 Ohio App. 63, 33 N.E.2d 845, 849.

There is no statute or common-law rule by which one court is bound to abide by the decisions of another court of equal rank. It does so simply for what may be called comity among judges. There is no common law or statutory rule to oblige a court to bow to its own decisions; it does so on the ground of judicial comity. (1884) 9 P.D. 98, per Brett, M. R.

Of such a use of the word, however, Dicey says: "The term 'comity' * * * is open to the charge of implying that the judge, when he applies foreign law to a particular case, does so as a matter of caprice or favor."

Comity is not a rule of law, but one of practice, convenience and expediency. It is something more than mere courtesy, which implies only deference to the opinion of others, since it has a substantial value in securing uniformity of decision, and discouraging repeated litigation of the same question. But its obligation is not imperative. Comity persuades; but it does not command. It declares not how a case shall be decided, but how it may with propriety be decided. Mast, Foos & Co. v. Mfg. Co., 177 U.S. 485, 488, 20 S.Ct. 708, 44 L.Ed. 856; National Electric Signaling Co. v. Telefunken Wireless Telegraph Co. of United States, C.C.A.N.Y., 221 F. 629, 632; Lauer v. Freudenthal, 96 Wash. 394, 165 P. 98, 99.

Comity of States

Simply a phrase designating the practice by which the courts of one state follow the decision of another on a like question, though not bound by law of precedents to do so. Larrick v. Walters, 39 Ohio App. 363, 177 N.E. 642, 645.

COMMA. A point used to mark the smallest structural divisions of a sentence, or a rhetorical punctuation mark indicating the slightest possible separation in ideas or construction. Travelers' Ins. Co. v. Pomerantz, 124 Misc. 250, 207 N.Y.S. 81, 86.

COMMAND. An order, imperative direction, or behest. State v. Mann, 2 N.C. 4; Barney v. Hayes.

11 Mont. 571, 29 P. 282, 28 Am.St.Rep. 495. As applied to a fortress, "command" means actual control of the garrison for military purposes. As applied to a ship, it means actual control of the crew for nautical purposes. Hamilton v. U. S., C. C.A.Va., 268 F. 15, 19.

The term "instance," as used with reference to doing an act at one's instance, does not imply the same degree of obligation to obey as does "command." Feore v. Trammel, 104 So. 808, 813, 213 Ala. 293.

COMMANDEMENT. In French law. A writ served by the *huissier* pursuant to a judgment or to an executory notarial deed. Its object is to give notice to the debtor that if he does not pay the sum to which he has been condemned by the judgment, or which he engaged to pay by the notarial deed, his property will be seized and sold. Arg.Fr.Merc.Law, 550.

COMMANDER IN CHIEF. By article 2, § 2, of the constitution it is declared that the president shall be commander in chief of the army and navy of the United States. The term implies supreme control of military operations during the progress of a war, not only on the side of strategy and tactics, but also in reference to the political and international aspects of the war. See Fleming v. Page, 9 How. 603, 13 L.Ed. 276; Prize Cases, 2 Black, 635, 17 L.Ed. 459; Swaim v. U. S., 28 Ct. Cl. 173.

COMMANDERY. In old English law. A manor or chief messuage with lands and tenements thereto appertaining, which belonged to the priory of St. John of Jerusalem, in England; he who had the government of such a manor or house was styled the "commander," who could not dispose of it, but to the use of the priory, only taking thence his own sustenance, according to his degree. The manors and lands belonging to the priory of St. John of Jerusalem were given to Henry the Eighth by 32 Hen. VIII. c. 20, about the time of the dissolution of abbeys and monasteries; so that the name only of commanderies remains, the power being long since extinct. Wharton.

COMMANDITAIRES. Special partners; partners *en commandité*. See Commandité.

COMMANDITÉ. In French law. A partnership in which some furnish money, and others furnish their skill and labor in place of capital.

A special or limited partnership, where the contract is between one or more persons who are general partners, and jointly and severally responsible, and one or more other persons who merely furnish a particular fund or capital stock, and thence are called "*commanditaires*," or "*commenditaires*," or "partners *en commandité*;" the business being carried on under the social name or firm of the general partners only, composed of the names of the general or complementary partners, the partners in *commandité* being liable to losses only to the extent of the funds or capital furnished by them. Story, Partn. § 78; 3 Kent, Comm. 34. The term includes a partnership containing dormant rather than special partners. Story, Partn. § 109.

COMMANDMENT.

An authoritative order of a judge or magisterial officer.

In criminal law. The act or offense of one who commands another to transgress the law, or do anything contrary to law, as theft, murder, or the like. Particularly applied to the act of an accessary before the fact, in inciting, procuring, setting on, or stirring up another to do the fact or act. 2 Inst. 182.

COMMARCHIO. A boundary; the confines of land.

COMMENCE. To perform the first act of. Robinson v. Gordon Oil Co., 258 Mich. 643, 242 N.W. 795, 796. To institute. State v. Murphy, 120 Kan. 350, 243 P. 288, 289. To demand something by the institution of process in a court of justice. Ledonne v. Commerce Ins. Co. of Glen Falls, N.Y., 307 Pa. 1, 160 A. 612.

To commence an action or suit is to demand something by the institution of process in a court of justice. Cohens v. Virginia, 6 Wheat. 408, 5 L.Ed. 257.

To "bring" a suit is an equivalent term; an action is "commenced" when it is "brought," and vice versa. Goldenberg v. Murphy, 108 U.S. 162, 2 S.Ct. 388, 27 L.Ed. 686; Hannaman v. Gordon, Tex.Com.App., 261 S.W. 1006, 1007.

An action is "commenced" within the meaning of the statute of limitations as soon as the summons is signed and sealed in good faith, for the purpose of immediate service, and that purpose is not afterwards abandoned. Wilson v. Clear, 85 N.J.L. 474, 89 A. 1031. Compare Glenn v. Payne, 153 Tenn. 240, 280 S.W. 1019, 1021. Owen v. City of Eastland, 124 Tex. 419, 78 S.W.2d 178, 179.

A suit in a court of record is "commenced", so as to save suit from bar of statute of limitations, when the petition is filed, even though process is not issued until the period of limitation has run, since plaintiff has done all he can toward commencement of the suit. Mo.St.Ann. § 724, p. 940. City of St. Louis v. Miller, 235 Mo.App. 987, 145 S.W.2d 504, 505.

A suit in equity is not commenced until the issuance of a subpœna followed by a bona fide effort to serve it. U. S. v. Scheurman, D.C.Idaho, 218 F. 915, 919.

To commence drilling operations within the meaning of an oil and gas lease has reference to the first movement of the drill in penetrating the ground. Solberg v. Sunburst Oil & Gas Co., 73 Mont. 94, 235 P. 761, 763. But see Terry v. Texas Co., Tex.Civ.App., 228 S.W. 1019, holding that a lessee, by placing timbers for the erection of a derrick, together with machinery, including a boiler, on the ground where an oil well was to be drilled, complied with a provision requiring him to "commence to drill." But compare Lauderdale Power Co. v. Perry, 202 Ala. 394, 80 So. 476, 480.

Criminal prosecution is "commenced" within statute of limitations when complaint is filed with magistrate in good faith and warrant issued. Hicks v. State, 54 Okl.Cr. 431, 23 P.2d 219.

Commencement of building or improvement, within the meaning of Lien Law, is the visible commencement of actual operations on the ground for the erection of the building, which every one can readily recognize as commencement of a building, and which is done with intention to continue the work until building is completed. Security Stove & Mfg. Co. v. Sellards, 133 Kan. 747, 3 P.2d 481, 482, 76 A.L.R. 1397.

COMMENCEMENT OF A DECLARATION. That part of the declaration which follows the venue and precedes the circumstantial statement of the cause of action.

It formerly contained a statement of the names of the parties, and the character in which they sue or are sued, if any other than their natural capacity; of the mode in which the defendant had been brought into court, and a brief statement of the form of action. In modern practice, however, in most cases, it contains little else then the names and character of the parties.

COMMENDA. In French law. The delivery of a benefice to one who cannot hold the legal title, to keep and manage it for a time limited and render an account of the proceeds. Guyot, Rép.Univ.

In Mercantile Law. An association in which the management of the property was intrusted to individuals. Troub.Lim.Partn. c. 3, § 27.

COMMENDA EST FACULTAS RECIPIENDI ET RETINENDI BENEFICIUM CONTRA JUS POSITIVUM À SUPREMÂ POTESTATE. Moore, 905. A commendam is the power of receiving and retaining a benefice contrary to positive law, by supreme authority.

COMMENDAM. In ecclesiastical law. The appointment of a suitable clerk to hold a void or vacant benefice or church living until a regular pastor be appointed. Hob. 144; Latch, 236.

In Commercial Law. A species of limited partnership. The limited partnership (or *Société en commandité*) of the French law has been introduced into the Code of Louisiana under the title of "Partnership *in Commendam.*" Civil Code La. art. 2810 (Civ.Code, art. 2839). See Mitchell, in 3 Sel.Essays, Anglo-Amer.L.H. 183; Commandité; Société.

COMMENDATIO. In the civil law. Commendation, praise, or recommendation, as in the maxim "simplex commendatio non obligat," meaning that mere recommendation or praise of an article by the seller of it does not amount to a warranty of its qualities. 2 Kent, Comm. 485.

COMMENDATION. In feudal law. The act by which an owner of alodial land placed himself and his land under the protection of a lord, so as to constitute himself his vassal or feudal tenant.

COMMENDATORS. Secular persons upon whom ecclesiastical benefices were bestowed, as in Scotland; called so because the benefices were commended and intrusted to their supervision. They are merely trustees.

COMMENDATORY. He who holds a church living or preferment *in commendam.*

COMMENDATORY LETTERS. In ecclesiastical law. Such as are written by one bishop to another on behalf of any of the clergy, or others of his diocese traveling thither, that they may be received among the faithful, or that the clerk may be promoted, or necessaries administered to others, etc. Wharton.

COMMENDATUS. In feudal law. One who intrusts himself to the protection of another. Spelman. A person who, by voluntary homage, put himself under the protection of a superior lord. Cowell.

COMMENT. The expression of the judgment passed upon certain alleged facts by a person who has applied his mind to them, and who while so commenting assumes that such allegations of fact are true. The assertion of a fact is not a "comment." Horn v. State, 106 Tex.Cr.R. 190, 292 S. W. 227, 228.

COMMENT UPON THE EVIDENCE. Means that trial judge is prohibited from conveying to jury trial judge's personal opinion as to the truth or falsity of any evidence, but prohibition does not prohibit judges from giving counsel reasons for rulings on questions presented during progress of trial, or prohibit them in all cases from stating, when necessary, the facts upon which they base their conclusions. State v. Brown, 19 Wash. 2d 195, 142 P.2d 257, 259, 260.

COMMERCE. The exchange of goods, productions, or property of any kind. Jeu Jo Wan v. Nagle, C.C.A.Cal., 9 F.2d 309, 310.

Intercourse by way of trade and traffic between different peoples or states and the citizens or inhabitants thereof, including not only the purchase, sale, and exchange of commodities, but also the instrumentalities and agencies by which it is promoted and the means and appliances by which it is carried on, and the transportation of persons as well as of goods, both by land and by sea. Brennan v. Titusville, 14 S.Ct. 829, 153 U.S. 289, 38 L. Ed. 719; Railroad Co. v. Fuller, 17 Wall. 568, 21 L.Ed. 710; Hoke v. United States, 33 S.Ct. 281, 283, 227 U.S. 308, 57 L.Ed. 523, 43 L.R.A.,N.S., 906, Ann.Cas.1913E, 905. Also interchange of ideas, sentiments, etc., as between man and man. U. S. v. Eason Oil Co., D.C.Okl., 8 F.Supp. 365, 368.

Commerce, in its simplest signification, means an exchange of goods; but in the advancement of society, labor, transportation, intelligence, care and various mediums of exchange, become commodities and enter into commerce; the subject, the vehicle, the agent, and their various operations become the objects of commercial regulation. Lorenzetti v. American Trust Co., D.C.Cal., 45 F.Supp. 128, 132.

"Commerce" is not traffic alone, but is intercourse between nations and parts of nations in all its branches. Blumenstock Bros. Advertising Agency v. Curtis Pub. Co., 252 U.S. 436, 40 S.Ct. 385, 387, 64 L.Ed. 649.

The words "commerce" and "trade" are often used interchangeably; but, strictly speaking, commerce relates to intercourse or dealings with foreign nations, states, or political communities, while trade denotes business intercourse or mutual traffic within the limits of a state or nation, or the buying, selling, and exchanging of articles between members of the same community. Hooker v. Vandewater, 4 Denio, N.Y., 353, 47 Am.Dec. 258; Jacob; Wharton.

—Commerce among the states. Transportation from one state to another, and also all commercial intercourse between the different states, and all component parts of such intercourse. Dahnke-Walker Milling Co. v. Bondurant, 257 U.S. 282, 42 S.Ct. 106, 108, 66 L.Ed. 239.

—Commerce with foreign nations. Commerce between citizens of the United States and citizens or subjects of foreign governments; commerce which, either immediately or at some stage of its progress, is extraterritorial. U. S. v. Holliday, 3 Wall. 409, 18 L.Ed. 182; Veazie v. Moor, 14 How. 573, 14 L.Ed. 545; Lord v. Steamship Co., 102 U.S. 544, 26 L.Ed. 224. The same as "foreign commerce," which see *infra*.

Power of Congress to regulate "commerce with foreign nations" comprehends every species of commercial intercourse. U.S.C.A.Const. art. 1, § 8, cl. 3. Board of Trustees of University of Illinois v. U. S., Cust. & Pat.App., 53 S.Ct. 509, 289 U.S. 48, 77 L.Ed. 1025.

—Commerce with Indian tribes. Commerce with individuals belonging to such tribes, in the nature of buying, selling, and exchanging commodities, without reference to the locality where carried on, though it be within the limits of a state. U. S. v. Holliday, 3 Wall. 407, 18 L.Ed. 182; U. S. v. Cisna, 25 Fed.Cas. 424.

—Domestic commerce. Commerce carried on wholly within the limits of the United States, as distinguished from foreign commerce. Also, commerce carried on within the limits of a single state, as distinguished from interstate commerce. Louisville & N. R. Co. v. Tennessee R. R. Com'n, C.C. Tenn., 19 Fed. 701.

—Foreign commerce. Commerce or trade between the United States and foreign countries. Com. v. Housatonic R. Co., 143 Mass. 264, 9 N.E. 547; Foster v. New Orleans, 94 U.S. 246, 24 L.Ed. 122. The term is sometimes applied to commerce between ports of two sister states not lying on the same coast, *e. g.*, New York and San Francisco.

—Internal commerce. Such as is carried on between individuals within the same state, or between different parts of the same state. Lehigh Val. R. Co. v. Pennsylvania, 145 U.S. 192, 12 S.Ct. 806, 36 L.Ed. 672; Steamboat Co. v. Livingston, 3 Cow. (N.Y.) 713. Now more commonly called "intrastate" commerce.

—International commerce. Commerce between states or nations entirely foreign to each other. Louisville & N. R. Co. v. Tennessee R. R. Com'n, C.C.Tenn., 19 F. 701.

—Interstate commerce. Such as is carried on between different states of the Union or between points lying in different states. See Interstate Commerce.

—Intrastate commerce. Such as is begun, carried on, and completed wholly within the limits of a single state. Contrasted with "interstate commerce" (*q. v.*). State v. Reed, 53 Mont. 292, 163 P. 477, 479, Ann.Cas.1917E, 783. And see Southern Pac. Co. v. State, 19 Ariz. 20, 165 P. 303, 306.

COMMERCIA BELLI. War contracts. Contracts between nations at war, or their subjects.

Agreements entered into by belligerents, either in time of peace to take effect in the event of war, or during the war itself, by which arrangement is made for non-hostile intercourse. They may take the form of armistices, truces, capitulations, cartels, passports, safe-conducts, safeguards. 1 Kent 159; 2 Opp. 274.

Contracts between citizens of one belligerent and those of another, or between citizens of one belligerent and the other belligerent. They may take the form of ransom bills (*q. v.*), bills of exchange drawn by prisoners of war, or receipts for requisitions. 1 Kent 104.

COMMERCIAL. Relating to or connected with trade and traffic or commerce in general. "Zante Currents", C.C.Cal., 73 F. 189. Occupied with commerce. Bowles v. Co-Operative G. L. F. Farm Products, D.C.N.Y., 53 F.Supp. 413, 415.

COMMERCIAL AGENCY. The same as a "mercantile" agency. In re United States Mercantile Reporting, etc., Co., 4 N.Y.S. 916, 52 Hun, 611. See Mercantile.

COMMERCIAL AGENT. An officer in the consular service of the United States, of rank inferior to a consul. Also used as equivalent to "commercial broker," see *infra*.

COMMERCIAL BROKER. One who negotiates the sale of merchandise without having the possession or control of it, being distinguished in the latter particular from a commission merchant. Adkins v. Richmond, 98 Va. 91, 34 S.E. 967, 47 L.R.A. 583, 81 Am.St.Rep. 705.

COMMERCIAL CORPORATION. One engaged in commerce in the broadest sense of that term; hence including a railroad company. Sweatt v. Railroad Co., 23 Fed.Cas. 530.

COMMERCIAL COURT. A name applied in English practice to the trial of commercial causes in London and Liverpool before judges of the High Court. It is said to be "a mere piece of convenience in the arrangement of business." [1895] 2 Ch. 491.

COMMERCIAL DOMICILE. See Domicile.

COMMERCIAL ESTABLISHMENT. A place where commodities are exchanged, bought or sold. State ex rel. Kansas City Power & Light Co. v. Smith, 342 Mo. 75, 111 S.W.2d 513, 515.

COMMERCIAL FRUSTRATION. Excuse of party from performance if contract depends on existence of given person or thing and such person or thing perishes, and if contract is rendered impossible by act of God, the law, or other party. Wood v. Bartolino, 48 N.M. 175, 146 P.2d 883, 885, 890.

In theory it amounts to no more than a condition or term of a contract which the law implies to take the place of a covenant that it is assumed would have been inserted by the parties had the contingency which arose occurred to them at the time they made the contract. Lloyd v. Murphy, Cal.App., 142 P.2d 939, 942, 943. And doctrine is predicated upon premise of giving relief in a situation where parties could not reasonably protect themselves by terms of a contract against happening of subsequent events. Berline v. Waldschmidt, 159 Kan. 585, 156 P.2d 865, 867. Hence doctrine has no application where events were reasonably foreseeable and controllable by the parties.

COMMERCIAL INSOLVENCY. Inability of a businessman to pay his debts as they become due in the regular and ordinary course of business. Willing v. Eveloff, C.C.A.Pa., 94 F.2d 344, 346.

COMMERCIAL INSURANCE. See Insurance.

COMMERCIAL LAW. A phrase used to designate the whole body of substantive jurisprudence applicable to the rights, intercourse, and relations of persons engaged in commerce, trade, or mercantile pursuits. It is not a very scientific or accurate term. As foreign commerce is carried on by means of shipping, the term has come to be used occasionally as synonymous with "maritime law;" but, in strictness, the phrase "commercial law" is wider, and includes many transactions or legal questions which have nothing to do with shipping or its incidents. Watson v. Tarpley, 18 How. 521, 15 L.Ed. 509; Williams v. Gold Hill Min. Co., C.C.Cal., 96 F. 464.

COMMERCIAL LETTER OF CREDIT. See Letter of Credit under the title Credit.

COMMERCIAL MARK. In French law. A trademark is specially or purely the mark of the manufacturer or producer of the article, while a "commercial" mark is that of the dealer or merchant who distributes the product to consumers or the trade. La Republique Francaise v. Schultz, C.C. N.Y., 57 F. 41.

COMMERCIAL PAPER. Bills of exchange, promissory notes, bank-checks, and other negotiable instruments for the payment of money, which, by their form and on their face, purport to be such instruments as are, by the law-merchant, recognized as falling under the designation of "commercial paper." In re Hercules Mut. L. Assur. Soc., 6 Ben. 35, 12 Fed.Cas. 12. Negotiable paper given in due course of business, whether the element of negotiability be given it by the law-merchant or by statute. In re Sykes, D.C.Ill., 5 Biss. 113, Fed. Cas.No.13,708; Martin v. McAvoy, 130 Wash. 641, 228 P. 694; Postal Telegraph Cable Co. v. Citizens' Nat. Bank, C.C.A.N.J., 228 F. 601, 604.

COMMERCIAL PARTNERSHIP. A "commercial and trading partnership" is one that buys and sells;—distinguished from one of employment and occupation. Reid v. Linder, 77 Mont. 406, 251 P. 157, 161.

COMMERCIAL RAILROADS. A term used to embrace those railroads intended to carry all freight and passenger traffic between one town or place and another, and usually not constructed upon streets and highways except for short distances;—distinguished from street railways. Anhalt v. Waterloo, C. F. & N. Ry. Co., 166 Iowa, 479, 147 N.W. 928, 931.

COMMERCIAL TRAVELER. A drummer; a traveling salesman who simply exhibits samples of goods kept for sale by his principal, and takes orders from purchasers for such goods, which goods are afterwards to be delivered by the principal to the purchasers, and payment for the goods is to be made by the purchasers to the principal on such delivery. McKindly v. Dunham, 55 Wis. 515, 13 N.W. 485, 42 Am.Rep. 740.

An agent who sells by sample and on credit, is not intrusted with the possession of the goods to be sold, has no implied authority to receive payment, and payment to whom will not discharge the purchaser. Butler v. Dorman, 68 Mo. 302, 30 Am.Rep. 795; Seiple v. Irwin, 30 Pa. 513; Kornemann v. Monaghan, 24 Mich. 36.

COMMERCIUM. Lat. In the civil law. Commerce; business; trade; dealings in the nature of purchase and sale; a contract.

COMMERCIUM JURE GENTIUM COMMUNE ESSE DEBET, ET NON IN MONOPOLIUM ET PRIVATUM PAUCORUM QUÆSTUM CONVERTENDUM. 3 Inst. 181. Commerce, by the law of nations, ought to be common, and not converted to monopoly and the private gain of a few.

COMMINALTY. The commonalty or the people.

COMMINATORIUM. In old practice. A clause sometimes added at the end of writs, admonishing the sheriff to be faithful in executing them. Bract. fol. 398.

COMMINGLE. To put together in one mass. Pfau v. State, 148 Ind. 539, 47 N.E. 927, 929.

COMMINUTED FRACTURE. One in which the bones have been somewhat crushed. Sang v. City of St. Louis, 262 Mo. 454, 171 S.W. 347, 349.

COMMISE. In old French law. Forfeiture; the forfeiture of a fief; the penalty attached to the ingratitude of a vassal. Guyot, Inst.Feod. c. 12.

COMMISSAIRE. In French law. A person who receives from a meeting of shareholders a special authority, viz., that of checking and examining the accounts of a manager or of valuing the *apports en nature, (q. v.)* The name is also applied to a judge who receives from a court a special mission, *e. g.*, to institute an inquiry, or to examine certain books, or to supervise the operations of a bankruptcy. Arg.Fr.Merc.Law, 551.

COMMISSAIRES-PRISEURS. In French law. Auctioneers, who possess the exclusive right of selling personal property at public sale in the towns in which they are established; and they possess the same right concurrently with notaries, *greffiers*, and *huissiers*, in the rest of the arrondissement. Arg.Fr.Merc.Law, 551.

COMMISSARIA LEX. A principle of the Roman law relative to the forfeiture of contracts. See Commissoria Lex.

COMMISSARIAT. The whole body of officers who make up the commissaries' department of an army.

COMMISSARY.

In ecclesiastical law. One who is sent or delegated to execute some office or duty as the representative of his superior; an officer of the bishop, who exercises spiritual jurisdiction in distant parts of the diocese. 1 Holdsw.Hist.L. 369.

In military law. An officer whose principal duties are to supply an army with provisions and stores. As to the rank and duties of such officers in the United States army, see 10 U.S.C.A. § 71 et seq.

COMMISSARY COURT. A Scotch ecclesiastical court of general jurisdiction, held before four commissioners, members of the Faculty of Advocates, appointed by the crown.

COMMISSION. A warrant or authority or letters patent, issuing from the government, or one of its departments, or a court, empowering a person or persons named to do certain acts, or to exercise jurisdiction, or to perform the duties and exercise the authority of an office, (as in the case of an officer in the army or navy.) Bledsoe v. Colgan, 138 Cal. 34, 70 P. 924.

Also, in private affairs, it signifies the authority or instructions under which one person transacts business or negotiates for another.

In a derivative sense, a body of persons to whom a commission is directed. A board or committee officially appointed and empowered to perform certain acts or exercise certain jurisdiction of a public nature or relation; as a "commission of assise."

Civil Law

A species of bailment, being an undertaking, without reward, to do something in respect to an article bailed; equivalent to "mandate."

Commercial Law

The recompense or reward of an agent, factor, broker, or bailee, when the same is calculated as a percentage on the amount of his transactions or on the profit to the principal. In this sense, however, the word occurs perhaps more frequently in the plural. Gray v. Stern, 85 Wash. 645, 149 P. 26, 28. Jackson v. Stanfield, 137 Ind. 592, 37 N.E. 14, 23 L.R.A. 588. Sinclair Coal Co. v. Pittsburg and Ashland Coal and Dock Co., 178 Minn. 114, 226 N.W. 206, 208. But the term may mean simply a compensation; Smith v. Starke, 196 Mich. 311, 162 N.W. 998, 999; and does not necessarily imply a mere per centum valuation; Jenkins v. Locke-Paddon Co., 30 Cal.App. 52, 157 P. 537.

Also, a compensation to an administrator for the faithful discharge of his duties. In re Jula's Estate, 3 N.J.Misc. 976, 130 A. 733, 735.

Criminal Law

Doing or perpetration; the performance of an act. Groves v. State, 116 Ga. 516, 42 S.E. 755, 59 L.R.A. 598.

Practice

An authority or writ issuing from a court, in relation to a cause before it, directing and authorizing a person or persons named to do some act or exercise some special function; usually to take the depositions of witnesses.

COMMISSION DAY. In English practice. The opening day of the assises.

COMMISSION DE LUNATICO INQUIRENDO. The same as a commission of lunacy, (see *infra.*) In re Misselwitz, 177 Pa. 359, 35 A. 722.

COMMISSION DEL CREDERE. In commercial law. Where an agent of a seller undertakes to guaranty to his principal the payment of the debt due by the buyer. Story, Ag. 28.

The phrase *"del credere"* is borrowed from the Italian language, in which its signification is equivalent to our word "guaranty" or "warranty."

COMMISSION GOVERNMENT. A method of municipal government in which the legislative power is in the hands of a few persons. State v. Ure, 91 Neb. 31, 135 N.W. 224. Gardner v. Board of Park Directors, 35 Cal.App. 597, 170 P. 672, 673 (mayor held not a "commissioner").

COMMISSION MERCHANT. A term which is synonymous with "factor." It means one who receives goods, chattels, or merchandise for sale, exchange, or other disposition, and who is to receive a compensation for his services, to be paid by the owner, or derived from the sale, etc., of the goods. State v. Thompson, 120 Mo. 12, 25 S.W. 346. One whose business is to receive and sell goods for a commission, being intrusted with the possession of the goods to be sold, and usually selling in his own name. Hughes v. Young, 17 Tenn.App. 24, 65 S.W.2d 858, 864.

Factors are frequently called "commission merchants", and it is said that there is no difference in the meaning of these terms, the latter being perhaps more commonly used in America. Thompson v. Woodruff, 7 Cold. 410; Duguid v. Edwards, 50 Barb., N.Y., 288; Lyon v. Alvord, 18 Conn. 80.

A commission merchant or factor differs from a broker in that he may buy and sell in his own name without disclosing his principal and has the goods in his possession; while the broker can only buy or sell in the name of his principal, and has no possession of the goods sold. Slack v. Tucker, 23 Wall. 321, 330, 23 L.Ed. 143; Perkins v. State, 50 Ala. 154, 156. A commission merchant has a lien upon the goods for his charges, advances, and commissions, while the broker has no control of the property and is responsible only for bad faith. A commission merchant or factor has a special property in the goods. Sutton v. Kiel Cheese & Butter Co., 155 Ky. 465, 159 S.W. 950, 951. A "factor" or "commission merchant" is one who has the actual or technical possession of goods or wares of another for sale, while a "merchandise broker" is one who negotiates the sale of merchandise without having it in his possession or control, being simply an agent with very limited powers. Hughes v. Young, 17 Tenn.App. 24, 65 S.W.2d 858, 864.

See, also, Factor.

COMMISSION OF ANTICIPATION. In English law. An authority under the great seal to collect a tax or subsidy before the day.

COMMISSION OF APPRAISEMENT AND SALE. Where property has been arrested in an admiralty action *in rem* and ordered by the court to be sold, the order is carried out by a commission of appraisement and sale; in some cases (as where the property is to be released on bail and the value is disputed) a commission of appraisement only is required. Sweet.

COMMISSION OF ARRAY. In English law. A commission issued to send into every county officers to muster or set in military order the inhabitants. The introduction of commissions of lieutenancy, which contained, in substance, the same powers as these commissions, superseded them. 2 Steph.Comm. (7th Ed.) 582.

COMMISSION OF ASSIZE. In English practice. A commission which formerly issued from the king, appointing certain persons as commissioners or judges of assize to hold the assizes in association with discreet knights during those years in which the justices in eyre did not come. A commission issued to judges of the high court or court of appeal, authorizing them to sit at the assizes for the trial of civil actions.

COMMISSION OF BANKRUPT. A commission or authority formerly granted by the lord chancellor to such persons as he should think proper, to examine the bankrupt in all matters relating to his trade and effects, and to perform various other important duties connected with bankruptcy matters. But now, under St. 1 & 2 Wm. IV. c. 56, § 12, a fiat issues instead of such commission.

COMMISSION OF CHARITABLE USES. This commission issues out of chancery to the bishop and others, where lands given to charitable uses are misemployed, or there is any fraud or dispute concerning them, to inquire of and redress the same, etc.

COMMISSION OF DELEGATES. When any sentence was given in any ecclesiastical cause by the archbishop, this commission, under the great seal, was directed to certain persons, usually lords, bishops, and judges of the law, to sit and hear an appeal of the same to the king, in the court of chancery. But latterly the judicial committee of the privy council has supplied the place of this commission. Brown.

COMMISSION OF LUNACY. A commission issuing from a court of competent jurisdiction, authorizing an inquiry to be made into the mental condition of a person who is alleged to be a lunatic.

A writ issued out of chancery, or such court as may have jurisdiction of the case, directed to a proper officer, to inquire whether a person named therein is a lunatic or not. In re Moore, 68 Cal. 281, 9 P. 164.

COMMISSION OF PARTITION. In the former English equity practice, this was a commission or authority issued to certain persons, to effect a division of lands held by tenants in common desiring a partition; when the commissioners reported, the parties were ordered to execute mutual conveyances to confirm the division. Commissioners appointed to make partition are in the nature of arbitrators. Clough v. Cromwell, 250 Mass. 324, 145 N.E. 473, 474.

COMMISSION OF REBELLION. In English law. An attaching process, formerly issuable out of chancery, to enforce obedience to a process or decree; abolished in August, 1841.

COMMISSION OF REVIEW. In English ecclesiastical law. A commission formerly sometimes granted in extraordinary cases, to revise the sentence of the court of delegates. 3 Bl.Comm. 67. Now out of use, the privy council being substituted for the court of delegates, as the great court of appeal in all ecclesiastical causes. 3 Steph. Comm. 432.

COMMISSION OF THE PEACE. In English law. A commission from the crown, appointing certain persons therein named, jointly and severally, to keep the *peace*, etc. Justices of the peace are always appointed by special commission under the great seal, the form of which was settled by all the judges, A. D. 1590, and continues with little alteration to this day. 1 Bl.Comm. 351; 3 Steph. Comm. 39, 40.

COMMISSION OF TREATY WITH FOREIGN PRINCES. Leagues and arrangements made between states and kingdoms, by their ambassadors and ministers, for the mutual advantage of the kingdoms in alliance. Wharton.

COMMISSION OF UNLIVERY. In an action in the English admiralty division, where it is necessary to have the cargo in a ship unladen in order to have it appraised, a commission of unlivery is issued and executed by the marshal. Williams & B. Adm. Jur. 233.

COMMISSION TO EXAMINE WITNESSES. In practice. A commission issued out of the court in which an action is pending, to direct the taking of the depositions of witnesses who are beyond the territorial jurisdiction of the court.

COMMISSION TO TAKE ANSWER IN CHANCERY. In English law. A commission issued when defendant lives abroad to swear him to such answer. 15 & 16 Vict. c. 86, § 21. Obsolete. See Jud. Acts, 1873, 1875.

COMMISSION TO TAKE DEPOSITIONS. A written authority issued by a court of justice, giving power to take the testimony of witnesses who cannot be personally produced in court. Tracy v. Suydam, 30 Barb. (N. Y.) 110.

COMMISSIONED OFFICERS. In the United States army and navy and marine corps, those of or above the rank of second lieutenant. Davis, Mil. L. 26. Those who hold their rank and office under commissions issued by the president, as distinguished from non-commissioned officers (in the army, including sergeants, corporals, etc.) and warrant officers (in the navy, including boatswains, gunners, etc.) and from privates or enlisted men. Stephens v. Civil Service Commission of New Jersey, 101 N.J.Law 192, 127 A. 808, 811. See Babbitt v. U. S., 16 Ct.Cl. 202.

COMMISSIONER. A person to whom a commission is directed by the government or a court. State v. Banking Co., 14 N.J.L. 437; In re Canter, 81 N.Y.S. 338, 40 Misc. 126.

In the governmental system of the United States, this term denotes an officer who is charged with the administration of the laws relating to some particular subject-matter, or the management of some bureau or agency of the government. Such are the commissioners of education, of patents, of pensions, of fisheries, of the general land-office, of Indian affairs, etc.

In the state governmental systems, also, and in England, the term is quite extensively used as a designation of various officers having a similar authority and similar duties.

In the commission form of municipal government, the term is applied to any of the several officers constituting the commission. Gardner v. Board of Park Directors, 35 Cal.App. 597, 170 P. 672, 673.

—**Commissioners of bail.** Officers appointed to take recognizances of bail in civil cases.

—**Commissioners of bankrupts.** The name given, under the former English practice in bankruptcy, to the persons appointed under the great seal to execute a commission of bankruptcy (*q. v.*).

—**Commissioners of circuit courts.** Officers appointed by and attached to the former circuit courts of the United States, performing functions partly ministerial and partly judicial. In re Com'rs of Circuit Court, C.C.N.C., 65 F. 317. Their office was abolished by the Act of May 28, 1896 (34 Stat. 184) and they have been succeeded by "United States commissioners." See that title.

—**Commissioners of deeds.** Officers empowered by the government of one state to reside in another state, and there take acknowledgments of deeds and other papers which are to be used as evidence or put on record in the former state.

—**Commissioners of highways.** Officers appointed in each county or township, in many of the states, with power to take charge of the altering, opening, repair, and vacating of highways within such county or township.

—**Commissioner of patents.** The title given by law to the head of the patent office. See 35 USCA § 2.

—**Commissioners of sewers.** In English law. Commissioners appointed under the great seal, and constituting a court of special jurisdiction; which is to overlook the repairs of the banks and walls of the seacoast and navigable rivers, or, with consent of a certain proportion of the owners and occupiers, to make new ones, and to cleanse such rivers, and the streams communicating therewith. St. 3 & 4 Wm. IV. c. 22, § 10; 3 Steph. Comm. 442.

—**Commissioner of woods and forests.** An officer created by act of parliament of 1817, to whom was transferred the jurisdiction of the chief justices of the forest. Inderwick, The King's Peace.

—**County commissioners.** See County.

COMMISSIONS. The compensation or reward paid to a factor, broker, agent, bailee, executor, trustee, receiver, etc., usually calculated as a percentage on the amount of his transactions or the amount received or expended. See Commission.

COMMISSIVE. Caused by or consisting in acts of commission, as distinguished from neglect, sufferance, or toleration; as in the phrase "commissive waste," which is contrasted with "permissive waste." See Waste.

COMMISSORIA LEX. In Roman law. A law according to which a seller might stipulate that he should be freed from his obligation, and might rescind the sale, if the purchase price were not paid at the appointed time. Also a law by which a debtor and his pledgee might agree that, if the debtor did not pay at the day appointed, the pledge should become the absolute property of the creditor. This, however, was abolished by a law of Constantine. Cod. 8, 35, 3. See Dig. 18, 3; Mackeld. Rom.Law, §§ 447, 461; 2 Kent, Comm. 583.

COMMIT. To perpetrate, as a crime; to perform, as an act. Groves v. State, 116 Ga. 516, 42 S.E. 755, 59 L.R.A. 598.

To send a person to prison by virtue of a lawful authority, for any crime or contempt, or to an asylum, workhouse, reformatory, or the like, by authority of a court or magistrate. People v. Beach, 122 Cal. 37, 54 P. 369.

To deliver a defendant to the custody of the sheriff or marshal, on his surrender by his bail. 1 Tidd, Pr. 285, 287.

COMMITMENT. In practice. The warrant or *mittimus* by which a court or magistrate directs an officer to take a person to prison. Authority for holding in prison one convicted of crime. Ex parte Haynes, 98 Tex.Cr.R. 609, 267 S.W. 490, 493. A process directed to a ministerial officer by which a person is to be confined in prison, usually issued by a court or magistrate. People ex rel. Wojek v. Henderson, 235 N.Y.S. 173, 178, 134 Misc. 228.

A warrant which does not direct an officer to commit a party to prison but only to receive him into custody and safely keep him for further examination, is not a commitment. Gilbert v. U. S., 23 Ct.Cl. 218.

The act of sending a person to prison by means of such a warrant or order. Allen v. Hagan, 170 N.Y. 46, 62 N.E. 1086.

A proceeding for the restraining and confining of insane persons for their own and the public's protection. Vance v. Ellerbe, 150 La. 388, 90 So. 735, 740.

COMMITTED IN PRESENCE OF OFFICER. Under statutes authorizing arrest without warrant, when facts and circumstances occurring within officer's observation, in connection with what, under circumstances, may be considered as common knowledge, give him probable cause to believe or reasonable grounds to suspect that such is the case. Noce v. Ritchie, 109 W.Va. 391, 155 S.E. 127, 128.

COMMITTEE. A person, or an assembly or board of persons, to whom the consideration, determination, or management of any matter is committed or referred, as by a court. Lloyd v. Hart, 2 Pa. 473, 45 Am.Dec. 612; Farrar v. Eastman, 5 Me.

345; Blaisdell v. Inhabitants of Town of York, 110 Me. 500, 87 A. 361, 370.

An individual or body to whom others have delegated or committed a particular duty, or who have taken on themselves to perform it in the expectation of their act being confirmed by the body they profess to represent or act for. 15 Mees. & W. 529.

The term is especially applied to the person or persons who are invested, by order of the proper court, with the guardianship of the person and estate of one who has been adjudged a lunatic.

In parliamentary law. A portion of a legislative body, comprising one or more members, who are charged with the duty of examining some matter specially referred to them by the house, or of deliberating upon it, and reporting to the house the result of their investigations or recommending a course of action.

A committee may be appointed for one special occasion, or it may be appointed to deal with all matters which may be referred to it during a whole session or during the life of the body. In the latter case, it is called a "standing committee." It is usually composed of a comparatively small number of members, but may include the whole house.

Joint committee. A joint committee of a legislative body comprising two chambers is a committee consisting of representatives of each of the two houses, meeting and acting together as one committee.

Secret committee. A secret committee of the house of commons is a committee specially appointed to investigate a certain matter, and to which secrecy being deemed necessary in furtherance of its objects, its proceedings are conducted with closed doors, to the exclusion of all persons not members of the committee. All other committees are open to members of the house, although they may not be serving upon them. Brown.

COMMITTING MAGISTRATE. An inferior judicial officer who is invested with authority to conduct the preliminary hearing of persons charged with crime, and either to discharge them for lack of sufficient prima facie evidence or to commit them to jail to await trial or (in some jurisdictions) to accept bail and release them thereon. The term is said to be synonymous with "examining court." State v. Rogers, 31 N.M. 485, 247 P. 828, 833.

COMMITTITUR. In practice. An order or minute, setting forth that the person named in it *is committed* to the custody of the sheriff.

COMMITTITUR PIECE. In English law. An instrument in writing on paper or parchment, which charges a person, already in prison, in execution at the suit of the person who arrested him. 2 Chit.Archb.Pr. (12th Ed.) 1208.

COMMIXTIO, or COMMIXTION. In the civil law. The mixing together or confusion of things, dry or solid, belonging to different owners, as distinguished from *confusio,* which has relation to liquids. *Lec. Elém. du Dr. Rom.* §§ 370, 371; Story, Bailm. § 40; 1 Bouvier, Inst. n. 506.

COMMODATE. Where property is loaned gratuitously by owner for sole benefit, accommodation, and use of borrower, and specific thing loaned is to be returned. The Pegeen, D.C.Cal., 14 F.Supp. 748, 751. See, also, Commodatum.

COMMODATI ACTIO. Lat. In the civil law. An action of loan; an action for a thing lent. An action given for the recovery of a thing loaned, *(commodatum,)* and not returned to the lender. Inst. 3, 15, 2; Id. 4, 1, 16.

COMMODATO. In Spanish law. A contract by which one person lends gratuitously to another some object not consumable, to be restored to him in kind at a given period; the same contract as *commodatum (q. v.).*

COMMODATUM. A contract by which one of the parties binds himself to return to the other certain personal chattels which the latter delivers to him to be used by him without reward; loan for use. Slack v. Bryan, 299 Ky. 132, 184 S.W.2d 873, 876.

A gratuitous loan of goods to be temporarily used by the bailee, and returned in specie. Hanes v. Shapiro & Smith, 168 N.C. 24, 84 S.E. 33, 35. He who lends to another a thing for a definite time, to be enjoyed and used under certain conditions, without any pay or reward, is called *"commodans;"* the person who receives the thing is called *"commodatarius,"* and the contract is called *"commodatum."* It differs from *locatio* and *conductio,* in this: that the use of the thing is gratuitous. Dig. 13, 6; Inst. 3, 2, 14; Story, Bailm. § 221. Coogs v. Bernard, 2 Ld.Raym. 909; Adams v. Mortgage Co., 82 Miss. 263, 34 So. 482, 17 L.R.A.,N.S., 138, 100 Am.St.Rep. 633; World's Columbian Exposition Co. v. Republic of France, C.C.A. Ill., 96 F. 693, 38 C.C.A. 483.

COMMODITIES. Those things which are useful or serviceable, particularly articles of merchandise movable in trade. American League Baseball Club of Chicago v. Chase, 149 N.Y.S. 6, 15, 86 Misc. 441.

Goods, wares, and merchandise of any kind; movables; articles of trade or commerce. Queen Ins. Co. v. State, 86 Tex. 250, 24 S.W. 397, 22 L.R.A. 483. Movable articles of value; things that are bought and sold. United States v. Sischo, D.C. Wash., 262 F. 1001, 1005. See, also, Commodity.

This word is a broader term than merchandise, and, in referring to commerce may include almost any article of movable or personal property. Pound v. Lawrence, Tex. Civ.App., 233 S.W. 359, 361; Shuttleworth v. State, 35 Ala. 415; State v. Henke, 19 Mo. 225.

Labor has been held not to be a commodity. Rohlf v. Kasemeier, 140 Iowa 182, 118 N.W. 276, 23 L.R.A., N.S., 1285. But it has been held that the supplying of telephone service is the supplying of a commodity of commerce; McKinley Telephone Co. v. Cumberland Telephone Co., 152 Wis. 359, 140 N.W. 38, 39; and it has also been thought that the privilege of receiving property by will or intestate succession is a commodity subject to the Massachusetts excise law; Dana v. Dana, 226 Mass. 297, 115 N.E. 418, 419.

COMMODITIES CLAUSE. A clause in the act of Congress, June 29, 1906 (49 USCA § 1 (8), providing that it shall be unlawful for any railroad company to transport commodities (excepting timber and its manufactured products) manufactured, mined or produced by it, or under its authority, or which it may own in whole or in part, or in which it may have any interest, direct or indirect, except such articles or commodities as may be necessary and intended for its use in its business. U. S. v. R. Co., 31 S.Ct. 387, 220 U.S. 257, 55 L.Ed. 458.

COMMODITY. In the most comprehensive sense, convenience, accommodation, profit, benefit, advantage, interest, commodiousness.

In the commercial sense, any movable or tangible thing that is produced or used as the subject of barter or sale. People v. Epstean, 170 N.Y.S. 68, 79, 102 Misc. 476. See Commodities.

COMMODITY RATE. With reference to railroads, a rate which applies to a specific commodity alone;—distinguished from a "class rate," meaning a single rate which applies to a number of articles of the same general character. Norfolk Southern R. Co. v. Freeman Supply Corporation, 145 Va. 207, 133 S.E. 817, 818.

COMMODORE. A grade in the United States navy, superior to a captain. Omitted from the active list. Act of March 3, 1899, c. 413, 30 Stat. 1004. See 34 USCA § 1.

COMMODUM EX INJURIÂ SUÂ NEMO HABERE DEBET. No person ought to have advantage from his own wrong. Jenk.Cent. 161; Finch, Law, b. 1, c. 3, n. 62.

COMMON, *n.* An incorporeal hereditament which consists in a profit which one man has in connection with one or more others in the land of another. Trustees v. Robinson, 12 Serg. & R. (Pa.) 31; Thomas v. Inhabitants of Marshfield, 10 Pick. (Mass.) 364; 3 Kent 403; United States v. 1,010.8 Acres, More or Less, Situate in Sussex County, Del., D.C.Del., 56 F.Supp. 120, 132, 134.

In English law, is an incorporeal right which lies in grant, originally commencing on some agreement between lords and tenants, which by time has been formed into prescription, and continues good, although there be no deed or instrument to prove the original contract. 4 Coke, 37; 1 Crabb, Real Prop. p. 258, § 268.

Common, or a right of common, is a right or privilege which several persons have to the produce of the lands or waters of another. Van Rensselaer v. Radcliff, 10 Wend., N.Y., 647, 25 Am.Dec. 582.

Also an uninclosed piece of land set apart for public or municipal purposes, in many cities and villages of the United States. Newell v. Hancock, 67 N.H. 244, 35 A. 253. United States v. 1,010.8 Acres, More or Less, Situate in Sussex County, Del., D.C.Del., 56 F.Supp. 120, 122, 134.

—Common appendant. A right annexed to the possession of arable land, by which the owner is entitled to feed his beasts on the lands of another, usually of the owner of the manor of which the lands entitled to common are a part. 2 Bl.Comm. 33; Van Rensselaer v. Radcliff, 10 Wend. (N.Y.) 648.

—Common appurtenant. A right of feeding one's beasts on the land of another, (in common with the owner or with others,) which is founded on a grant, or a prescription which supposes a grant. 1 Crabb, Real Prop. p. 264, § 277.

This kind of common arises from no connection of tenure, and is against common right; it may commence by grant within time of memory, or, in other words, may be created at the present day; it may be claimed as annexed to any kind of land, and may be claimed for beasts not commonable, as well as those that are. 2 Bl.Comm. 33; Van Rensselaer v. Radcliff, 10 Wend., N.Y., 649.

—Common because of vicinage is where the inhabitants of two townships which lie contiguous to each other have usually intercommoned with one another, the beasts of the one straying mutually into the other's fields, without any molestation from either. 2 Bl.Comm. 33; Co. Litt. 122*a;* 4 Co. 38*a;* 10 Q.B. 581, 589, 604; Smith v. Floyd, 18 Barb. (N.Y.) 523.

This is, indeed, only a permissive right, intended to excuse what, in strictness, is a trespass in both, and to prevent a multiplicity of suits, and therefore either township may inclose and bar out the other, though they have intercommoned time out of mind.

—Common in gross, or at large. A species of common which is neither appendant nor appurtenant to *land,* but is annexed to a man's *person,* being granted to him and his heirs by deed; or it may be claimed by prescriptive right, as by a parson of a church or the like corporation sole. 2 Bl.Comm. 34. It is a separate inheritance, entirely distinct from any other landed property, vested in the person to whom the common right belongs. 2 Steph.Comm. 6; Mitchell v. D'Olier, 68 N.J.L. 375, 53 A. 467, 59 L.R.A. 949.

—Common of digging. Common of digging, or common in the soil, is the right to take for one's own use part of the soil or minerals in another's land; the most usual subjects of the right are sand, gravel, stones, and clay. It is of a very similar nature to common of estovers and of turbary. Elton, Com. 109.

—Common of estovers. A liberty of taking necessary wood for the use or furniture of a house or farm from off another's estate, in common with the owner or with others. 2 Bl.Comm. 35. It may be claimed, like common of pasture, either by grant or prescription. 2 Steph.Comm. 10; Plowd. 381; Van Rensselaer v. Radcliff, 10 Wend. (N.Y.) 648.

—Common of fishery. The same as Common of piscary. See *infra.*

—Common of fowling. In some parts of the country a right of taking wild animals (such as conies or wildfowl) from the land of another has been found to exist; in the case of wildfowl, it is called a "common of fowling." Elton, Com. 118.

—Common of pasture. The right or liberty of pasturing one's cattle upon another man's land. It may be either appendant, appurtenant, in gross, or because of vicinage. Van Rensselaer v. Radcliff, 10 Wend. (N.Y.) 647.

—Common of piscary. The right or liberty of fishing in another man's water, in common with the owner or with other persons. 2 Bl.Comm. 34. A liberty or right of fishing in the water covering the soil of another person, or in a river running through another's land. 3 Kent, Comm. 409. Hardin v. Jordan, 11 S.Ct. 808, 140 U.S. 371, 35 L.Ed. 428. It is quite different from a common fishery, with which, however, it is frequently confounded. See Fishery.

—**Common of shack.** A species of common by vicinage prevailing in the counties of Norfolk, Lincoln, and Yorkshire, in England; being the right of persons occupying lands lying together in the same common field to turn out their cattle after harvest to feed promiscuously in that field. 2 Steph.Comm. 6, 7; 5 Coke, 65; 1 B. & Ald. 710.

—**Common of turbary.** In its modern sense the right of taking peat or turf from the waste land of another, for fuel in the commoner's house. Williams, Common, 187; Van Rensselaer v. Radcliff, 10 Wend. (N.Y.) 647; 4 Co. 37; 3 Atk. 189, Noy, 145; 7 East, 127.

—**Common sans nombre.** Common without number, that is, without *limit* as to the *number* of cattle which may be turned on; otherwise called "common without stint." Bract. fols. *53b, 222b;* 2 Steph.Comm. 6, 7; 2 Bl.Comm. 34. United States v. 1,010.8 Acres, More or Less, Situate in Sussex County, Del., D.C.Del., 56 F.Supp. 120, 133.

—**Common, tenants in.** See Tenants in Common.

—**Common without stint.** Another name for Common sans nombre. See *supra.*

COMMON, *adj.* Usual, ordinary, accustomed; shared among several; owned by several jointly. Koen v. State, 35 Neb. 676, 53 N.W. 595, 17 L.R.A. 821. Belonging or pertaining to many or to the majority; generally or prevalent, of frequent or ordinary occurrence or appearance; familiar by reason of frequency. Webb v. New Mexico Pub. Co., 47 N.M. 279, 141 P.2d 333, 335. Also, usual, customary, and habitual, professed, or confessed, and used indefinitely in various terms implying illegal or criminal conduct, such as common scold, common thief, etc. Levine v. State, 166 A. 300, 302, 110 N.J.L. 467.

As to common "Bail," "Barretor," "Carrier," "Chase," "Condedit," "Council," "Counts," "Day," "Debtor," "Diligence," "Drunkard," "Error," "Fishery," "Highway," "Informer," "Inn," "Intendment," "Intent," "Jury," "Labor," "Nuisance," "Occupant," "Property," "School," "Scold," "Seal," "Seargeant," "Stock," "Traverse," "Vouchee," "Wall," see those titles.

—**Common appearance.** That which could be filed by the plaintiff, who could enter a rule on the defendant to plead, where the defendant, after due service of process on him, had removed from the jurisdiction without having entered an appearance, or could not be found. 12 Geo. II., c. 29; 1 Troub. & Haly, Pr. 159; Bender v. Ryan, 9 Wkly. Notes Cas. (Pa.) 144.

—**Common assurances.** The several modes or instruments of conveyance established or authorized by the law of England. Called "common" because thereby *every man's* estate is assured to him. 2 Bl.Comm. 294. The legal evidences of the translation of property, whereby every person's estate is assured to him, and all controversies, doubts, and difficulties are either prevented or removed. Wharton.

—**Common causes or suits.** A term anciently used to denote civil actions, or those depending between subject and subject, as distinguished from *pleas of the crown.* Dallett v. Feltus, 7 Phila. (Pa.) 627.

—**Common condidit.** See Condedit.

—**Common danger.** "Common danger" which gives a right to contribution in general average does not mean equal danger; hence, the fact that a part of the cargo of a stranded steamship is of a kind which is in little danger of injury does not relieve it of the liability to contribute. Willcox, Peck & Hughes v. American Smelting & Refining Co., D.C.N.Y., 210 F. 89, 91.

—**Common design.** In criminal law. Community of intention between two or more persons to do an unlawful act. State v. Hill, 273 Mo. 329, 201 S.W. 58, 60.

—**Common enterprise.** See Joint enterprise.

—**Common fine.** In old English law. A certain sum of money which the residents in a leet paid to the lord of the leet, otherwise called "head silver," "cert money," *(q. v.,)* or *"certum letœ."* Termes de la Ley; Cowell; Fleta; Wharton. A sum of money paid by the inhabitants of a manor to their lord, towards the charge of holding a court leet. Bailey, Dict.

—**Common form.** A will is said to be proved in common form when the executor proves it on his own oath; as distinguished from "proof by witnesses," which is necessary when the paper propounded as a will is disputed. Hubbard v. Hubbard, 7 Or. 42; Sutton v. Hancock, 118 Ga. 436, 45 S.E. 504.

—**Common hall.** A court in the city of London, at which all the citizens, or such as are free of the city, have a right to attend.

—**Common learning.** Familiar law or doctrine. Dyer, 27*b*, 33.

—**Common liquor dealer.** In Florida, one who, being charged with unlawfully engaging in and carrying on the business of a dealer in liquors, has been before convicted of a like offense and duly sentenced therefor. Thomas v. State, 74 Fla. 200, 76 So. 780. See, also, Common thief, *infra.*

—**Common peril.** See Common danger, *supra.*

—**Common place.** Common pleas. The English court of common pleas is sometimes so called in the old books.

—**Common prayer.** The liturgy, or public form of prayer prescribed by the Church of England to be used in all churches and chapels, and which the clergy are enjoined to use under a certain penalty.

—**Common repute.** The prevailing belief in a given community as to the existence of a certain fact or aggregation of facts. Brown v. Foster, 41 S. C. 118, 19 S.E. 299.

—Common right. A term applied to rights, privileges, and immunities appertaining to and enjoyed by all citizens equally and in common, and which have their foundation in the common law. Co. Inst. 142*a;* Spring Valley Waterworks v. Schottler, 62 Cal. 106.

—Common seller. A common seller of any commodity (particularly under the liquor laws of many states) is one who sells it frequently, usually, customarily, or habitually; in some states, one who is shown to have made a certain number of sales, either three or five. State v. O'Conner, 49 Me. 596; State v. Nutt, 28 Vt. 598; Moundsville v. Fountain, 27 W.Va. 194; Com. v. Tubbs, 1 Cush. (Mass.) 2.

—Common sense. Sound practical judgment; that degree of intelligence and reason, as exercised upon the relations of persons and things and the ordinary affairs of life, which is possessed by the generality of mankind, and which would suffice to direct the conduct and actions of the individual in a manner to agree with the behavior of ordinary persons.

—Common service. That service in which are engaged (with reference to the fellow-servant rule) all those who enter into the service of a common master, except those who become heads of and vested with absolute control of separate departments or branches of a great and diversified business. Union Pac. R. Co. v. Marone, C.C.A. Neb., 246 F. 916, 923.

The term, in its broadest and most obvious sense, would include all activities prosecuted in the business of the master which have for their purpose the attainment of one common end: nevertheless, an employee, invested with the duty of overseeing, directing, and controlling workmen, is not a fellow servant with respect to the discharge of those duties, but is a representative of the master. Funk v. Fulton Iron Works Co., 311 Mo. 77, 277 S.W. 566, 569.

—Common thief. One who by practice and habit is a thief; or, in some states, one who has been convicted of three distinct larcenies at the same term of court. Stevens v. Com., 4 Metc. (Mass.) 364.

—Common use. This phrase, as used in an anti-trust law extending to contracts affecting the prices of articles or commodities in "common use," describes articles used by the people in general; such articles or commodities as are in general use or used to a great extent in the homes of the people; the articles which are produced to be sold to the people, to be consumed and used by the people in general, and to be found for sale in all the marts of trade. People v. Epstean, 102 Misc. 476, 170 N.Y.S. 68, 75. It suggests the opposite of casual use. Geis v. State, 126 Md. 265, 94 A. 909, 910.

—Common victualer. The keeper of a restaurant or public eating house, where the food sold is eaten on the premises. Commonwealth v. Meckel, 221 Mass. 70, 108 N.E. 917.

—Common weal. The public or common good or welfare.

—Common woman. One who is low, inferior, vulgar, or coarse; also, one who is unchaste. But the term does not necessarily impute unchastity. Daniel v. Moncure, 58 Mont. 193, 190 P. 983, 985.

COMMON BAR. In pleading. (Otherwise called "blank bar.") A plea to compel the plaintiff to assign the particular place where the trespass has been committed. Steph.Pl. 256.

COMMON BENCH. The ancient name for the English court of common pleas. Its original title appears to have been simply "The Bench," but it was designated "Common Bench" to distinguish it from the "King's Bench," and because in it were tried and determined the causes of *common* persons, *i. e.,* causes between subject and subject, in which the crown had no interest.

COMMON ENEMY DOCTRINE. Recognized as to surface waters in but a few states, under which no natural easement or servitude exists in favor of the superior or higher land as to mere surface water, or such as falls or accumulates by rains or the melting of snow; and the proprietor of the inferior or lower tenement or estate may at his option lawfully obstruct or hinder the flow of such water thereon, and in so doing may turn back or off of his own lands, and onto and over the lands of other proprietors, such water, without liability by reason of such obstruction or diversion. Miller v. Letzerich, 121 Tex. 248, 49 S.W.2d 404, 411, 85 A.L.R. 451.

COMMON HUMANITY DOCTRINE. Where a passenger becomes sick or is injured while en route, carrier owes duty under "common humanity doctrine" to render to passenger such reasonable care and attention as common humanity would dictate. Alabama Great S. R. Co. v. Taylor, 190 Miss. 69, 199 So. 310, 312.

COMMON KNOWLEDGE. Is what court may declare applicable to action without necessity of proof. It is knowledge that every intelligent person has. Strain v. Isaacs, 59 Ohio App. 495, 18 N.E.2d 816, 825. It includes matters of learning, experience, history, and facts of which judicial notice may be taken. Shelley v. Chilton's Adm'r, 236 Ky. 221, 32 S.W.2d 974, 977.

COMMON LAW. As distinguished from the Roman law, the modern civil law, the canon law, and other systems, the common law is that body of law and juristic theory which was originated, developed, and formulated and is administered in England, and has obtained among most of the states and peoples of Anglo-Saxon stock. Lux v. Haggin, 69 Cal. 255, 10 P. 674.

As distinguished from law created by the enactment of legislatures, the common law comprises the body of those principles and rules of action, relating to the government and security of persons and property, which derive their authority solely from usages and customs of immemorial antiquity, or from the judgments and decrees of the courts recognizing, affirming, and enforcing such usages and customs; and, in this sense, particularly the ancient unwritten law of England. 1 Kent, Comm. 492. Western Union Tel. Co. v. Call Pub. Co., 21 S.Ct. 561, 181 U.S. 92, 45 L.Ed. 765; Barry v. Port Jervis, 72 N.Y.S. 104, 64 App. Div. 268; U. S. v. Miller, D.C.Wash., 236 F. 798, 800.

As distinguished from equity law, it is a body of rules and principles, written or unwritten, which are of fixed and immutable authority, and which must be applied to controversies rigorously and in their entirety, and cannot be modified to suit the peculiarities of a specific case, or colored by any judicial discretion, and which rests confessedly upon custom or statute, as distinguished from any claim to ethical superiority. Klever v. Seawall, C.C.A.Ohio, 65 F. 395, 12 C.C.A. 661.

As distinguished from ecclesiastical law, it is the system of jurisprudence administered by the purely secular tribunals.

As concerns its force and authority in the United States, the phrase designates that portion of the common law of England (including such acts of parliament as were applicable) which had been adopted and was in force here at the time of the Revolution. This, so far as it has not since been expressly abrogated, is recognized as an organic part of the jurisprudence of most of the United States. Industrial Acceptance Corporation v. Webb, Mo.App., 287 S.W. 657, 660.

The "common law" of England, which is the rule of decision in all courts of Montana, in so far as it is not repugnant to the Constitution of the United States or the Constitution or laws of that state, means that body of jurisprudence as applied and modified by the courts of this country up to the time it was adopted in Montana. Herrin v. Sutherland, 74 Mont. 587, 241 P. 328, 330, 42 A.L.R. 937. See, also, Norvell-Wilder Hardware Co. v. McCamey, Tex. Civ.App., 290 S.W. 772, 773; Fletcher v. Los Angeles Trust & Savings Bank, 182 Cal. 177, 187 P. 425, 427.

The common law of England, adopted by Pol. Code Cal. § 4468, does not refer solely to the lex non scripta, the common law unmodified by statute, but contemplates the whole body of jurisprudence as it stood, influenced by statute at the time when the Code section was adopted, and also embraces equity. Martin v. Superior Court of California in and for Alameda County, 176 Cal. 289, 168 P. 135, 136, L.R.A.1918B, 313.

In a wider sense than any of the foregoing, the "common law" may designate all that part of the positive law, juristic theory, and ancient custom of any state or nation which is of general and universal application, thus marking off special or local rules or customs.

For "Federal Common Law," see that title.

As a compound adjective "common-law" is understood as contrasted with or opposed to "statutory," and sometimes also to "equitable" or to "criminal." See examples below.

COMMON-LAW ACTION. A civil suit, as distinguished from a criminal prosecution or a proceeding to enforce a penalty or a police regulation; not necessarily an action which would lie at common law. Kirby v. Railroad Co., C.C.Iowa, 106 F. 551; U. S. v. Block, 24 Fed.Cas. 1,174.

COMMON-LAW ASSIGNMENTS. Such forms of assignments for the benefit of creditors as were known to the common law, as distinguished from such as are of modern invention or authorized by statute. Ontario Bank v. Hurst, C.C.A.Mich., 103 F. 231, 43 C.C.A. 193.

COMMON-LAW CHEAT. The obtaining of money or property by means of a false token, symbol, or device; this being the definition of a cheat or "cheating" at common law. State v. Renick, 33 Or. 584, 56 Pac. 275, 44 L.R.A. 266, 72 Am.St.Rep. 758.

COMMON-LAW CONTEMPT. A name sometimes applied to proceedings for contempt which are criminal in their nature, as distinguished from those which are intended as purely civil remedies ordinarily arising out of the alleged violation of some order entered in the course of a chancery proceeding. People v. Samuel, 199 Ill.App. 294, 297; People v. Buconich, 199 Ill.App. 410, 412.

COMMON-LAW COURTS. In England, those administering the common law. Equitable L. Assur. Soc. v. Paterson, 41 Ga. 364, 5 Am.Rep. 535.

COMMON-LAW CRIME. One punishable by the force of the common law, as distinguished from crimes created by statute. In re Greene, C.C. Ohio, 52 F. 104.

COMMON-LAW JURISDICTION. Jurisdiction of a court to try and decide such cases as were cognizable by the courts of law under the English common law; the jurisdiction of those courts which exercise their judicial powers according to the course of the common law. U. S. v. Power, 27 Fed.Cas. 607.

COMMON-LAW LARCENY. See Larceny.

COMMON-LAW LIEN. One known to or granted by the common law, as distinguished from statutory, equitable, and maritime liens; also one arising by implication of law, as distinguished from one created by the agreement of the parties. The Menominie, D.C.Minn., 36 F. 197; Tobacco Warehouse Co. v. Trustee, 117 Ky. 478, 78 S.W. 413, 64 L.R.A. 219.

It is a right extended to a person to retain that which is in his possession belonging to another, until the demand or charge of the person in possession is paid or satisfied. Whiteside v. Rocky Mountain Fuel Co., C.C.A.Colo., 101 F.2d 765, 769; Goldwater v. Mendelson, 8 N.Y.S. 627, 629, 170 Misc. 422.

COMMON-LAW MARRIAGE. One not solemnized in the ordinary way, but created by an agreement to marry, followed by cohabitation; a consummated agreement to marry, between persons legally capable of making marriage contract, per verba de præsenti, followed by cohabitation. Collins v. Hoag and Rollins, 121 Neb. 716, 238 N.W. 351.

There must be a public and continued recognition of such relation by the parties as distinguished from occasional or incidental recognition. Whitaker v. Shenault, Tex.Civ. App., 172 S.W. 202, 203.

COMMON-LAW MORTGAGE. One possessing the characteristics or fulfilling the requirements of a mortgage at common law; not known in Louisiana, where the civil law prevails; but such a mortgage made in another state and affecting lands in Louisiana, will be given effect there as a "conventional" mortgage, affecting third persons after due inscription. Gates v. Gaither, 46 La.Ann. 286, 15 So. 50.

COMMON-LAW PROCEDURE ACTS. Three acts of parliament, passed in the years 1852, 1854, and 1860, respectively, for the amendment of the procedure in the common-law courts. The common-law procedure act of 1852 is St. 15 & 16 Vict. c. 76; that of 1854, St. 17 & 18 Vict. c. 125; and that of 1860, St. 23 & 24 Vict. c. 126. Mozley & Whitley.

COMMON-LAW REMEDY. This phrase, within the meaning of U. S. Judicial Code 1911, § 256 (Act March 3, 1911, c. 231, 36 Stat. 1100, see Historical and Revision Notes under 28 U.S.C.A. § 1333), was not limited to remedies in the common-law courts, but embraced all methods of enforcing rights and redressing injuries known to the common or statutory law. Kennerson v. Thames Towboat Co., 89 Conn. 367, 94 A. 372, 375, L.R.A. 1916A, 436. See, also, Northern Pacific S. S. Co. v. Industrial Acc. Commission of California, 174 Cal. 346, 163 P. 199, 202. See Notes of Decisions under 28 U.S.C.A. § 1333.

The "right of a common-law remedy," saved to suitors in actions maritime in their nature arising under charter parties by U. S. Judicial Code 1911, § 24, par. 3 (see Historical and Revision Notes under 28 U.S.C.A. § 1333) did not include attempted changes by the states in the substantive admiralty law, but did include all means, other than proceedings in admiralty, which may be employed to enforce the right or to redress the injury involved, and included remedies in pais, as well as proceedings in court; judicial remedies conferred by statute, as well as those existing in the common law; remedies in equity, as well as those enforceable in a court of law. Red Cross Line v. Atlantic Fruit Co., 44 S.Ct. 274, 277, 264 U.S. 109, 68 L.Ed. 582.

COMMON-LAW TRADE-MARK. One appropriated under common-law rules, regardless of statutes. Stratton & Terstegge Co. v. Stiglitz Furnace Co., 258 Ky. 678, 81 S.W.2d 1, 3.

COMMON-LAW WIFE. A woman who was party to a "common-law marriage," as above defined; or one who, having lived with a man in a relation of concubinage during his life, asserts a claim, after his death, to have been his wife according to the requirements of the common law. In re Brush, 49 N.Y.S. 803, 25 App.Div. 610.

COMMON LAWYER. A lawyer learned in the common law.

COMMON NIGHTWALKER. See Night Walkers.

COMMON NUISANCE. A danger or damage threatening the public. Canfield v. Quayle, 10 N.Y.S.2d 781, 784, 170 Misc. 621.

COMMON OPINION IS GOOD AUTHORITY IN LAW. Co.Litt. 186*a*; Bank of Utica v. Mersereau, 3 Barb.Ch. (N.Y.) 528, 577, 49 Am.Dec. 189.

COMMON PLEAS. The name of a court of record having general original jurisdiction in civil suits.

COMMON PLEAS, THE COURT OF. See Court of Common Pleas.

COMMON RECOVERY. In conveyancing. A species of common assurance, or mode of conveying lands by matter of record, formerly in frequent use in England. It was in the nature and form of an action at law, carried regularly through, and ending in a *recovery* of the lands against the tenant of the freehold; which recovery, being a supposed adjudication of the right, bound all persons, and vested a free and absolute fee-simple in the recoverer. 2 Bl.Comm. 357. Christy v. Burch, 25 Fla. 942, 2 So. 258. Common recoveries were abolished by the statutes 3 & 4 Wm. IV. c. 74.

They were resorted to when the object was to create an absolute bar of estates tail, and of the remainders and reversions expectant on the determination of such estates. 2 Bla.Comm. 357. Though it has been used in some of the states, this form of conveyance is practically obsolete, easier and less expensive modes of making conveyances having been substituted. Frost v. Cloutman, 7 N.H. 9, 26 Am.Dec. 723.

COMMONABLE. Entitled to common. Commonable beasts are either beasts of the plow, as horses and oxen, or such as manure the land, as kine and sheep. Beasts not commonable are swine, goats, and the like. Co. Litt. 122*a*; 2 Bl.Comm. 33.

COMMONALTY. The great body of citizens; the mass of the people, excluding the nobility.

The body of people composing a municipal corporation, excluding the corporate officers.

The body of a society or corporation, as distinguished from the officers. 1 Perr. & D. 243.

Charters of incorporation of the various tradesmen's societies, etc., in England are usually granted to the master, wardens, and commonalty of such corporation.

COMMONANCE. The commoners, or tenants and inhabitants, who have the right of common or commoning in open field. Cowell.

COMMONERS. In English law. Persons having a right of *common.* So called because they have a right to pasture on the waste, in common with the lord. 2 H.Bl. 389.

COMMONS. The class of subjects in Great Britain exclusive of the royal family and the nobility. They are represented in parliament by the house of commons.

Part of the demesne land of a manor, (or land the property of which was in the lord,) which, being uncultivated, was termed the "lord's waste," and served for public roads and for common of pasture to the lord and his tenants. 2 Bl.Comm. 90.

Squares; pleasure grounds and spaces or open places for public use or public recreation owned by towns;—in modern usage usually called "parks." Jones v. City of Jackson, 104 Miss. 449, 61 So. 456, 457.

COMMONS, HOUSE OF. See House of Commons.

COMMONTY. In Scotch law. Land possessed in common by different proprietors, or by those having acquired rights of servitude. Bell.

COMMONWEALTH. The public or common weal or welfare. This cannot be regarded as a technical term of public law, though often used in political science. It generally designates, when so employed, a republican frame of government,—one in which the welfare and rights of the entire mass of people are the main consideration, rather than the privileges of a class or the will of a monarch; or it may designate the body of citizens living under such a government.

Sometimes it may denote the corporate entity, or the government, of a jural society (or state) possessing powers of self-government in respect of its immediate concerns, but forming an integral part of a larger government, (or nation.) State v. Lambert, 28 S.E. 930, 44 W.Va. 308.

In this latter sense, it is the official title of several of the United States (as Pennsylvania, Massachusetts, Virginia, and Kentucky), and would be appropriate to them all. In the former sense, the word was used to designate the English government during the protectorate of Cromwell.

See Government; Nation; State.

COMMORANCY. The dwelling in any place as an inhabitant; which consists in usually lying there. 4 Bl.Comm. 273. In American law it is used to denote a mere temporary residence. Pullen v. Monk, 82 Me. 412, 19 A. 909; Gilman v. Inman, 85 Me. 105, 26 A. 1049.

COMMORANT. Staying or abiding; dwelling temporarily in a place. One residing in a particular town, city, or district. Barnes, 162.

COMMORIENTES. Several persons who perish at the same time in consequence of the same calamity.

COMMORTH, or COMORTH. A contribution which was gathered at marriages, and when young priests said or sung the first masses. Prohibited by 26 Hen. VIII. c. 6. Cowell.

COMMOTE. Half a cantred or hundred in Wales, containing fifty villages. Also a great seignory or lordship, and may include one or divers manors. Co. Litt. 5.

COMMOTION. A "civil commotion" is an insurrection of the people for general purposes, though it may not amount to rebellion where there is a usurped power. 2 Marsh.Ins. 793; Boon v. Insurance Co., 40 Conn. 584; Grame v. Assur. Soc., 5 S.Ct. 150, 112 U.S. 273, 28 L.Ed. 716; Spruill v. Insurance Co., 46 N.C. 127.

A civil commotion is an uprising among a mass of people which occasions a serious and prolonged disturbance and infraction of civil order not attaining the status of war or an armed insurrection; it is a wild and irregular action of many persons assembled together. Hartford Fire Ins. Co., Hartford, Conn. v. War Eagle Coal Co., C.C.A.W.Va., 295 F. 663, 665. The term refers to political disorders, not to an economic disturbance. The Poznan, D.C.N.Y., 276 F. 418, 427.

COMMUNE, *adj.* Lat. See Communis.

COMMUNE, *n.* A self-governing town or village. The name given to the committee of the people in the French revolution of 1793; and again, in the revolutionary uprising of 1871, it signified the attempt to establish absolute self-government in Paris, or the mass of those concerned in the attempt. In old French law, it signified any municipal corporation. And in old English law, the commonalty or common people. 2 Co.Inst. 540.

COMMUNE CONCILIUM. The King's Council. See Privy Council.

COMMUNE CONCILIUM REGNI. The common council of the realm. One of the names of the English parliament. See Communitas Regni Angliæ.

COMMUNE FORUM. The common place of justice. The seat of the principal courts, especially those that are fixed.

COMMUNE PLACITUM. In old English law. A common plea or civil action, such as an action of debt.

COMMUNE VINCULUM. A common or mutual bond. Applied to the common stock of consanguinity, and to the feodal bond of fealty, as the common bond of union between lord and tenant. 2 Bl.Comm. 250; 3 Bl.Comm. 230.

COMMUNI CUSTODIA. In English law. An obsolete writ which anciently lay for the lord, whose tenant, holding by knight's service, died, and left his eldest son under age, against a stranger that entered the land, and obtained the ward of the body. Reg. Orig. 161.

COMMUNI DIVIDUNDO. In the civil law. An action which lies for those who have property in common, to procure a division. It lies where parties hold land in common but not in partnership. Calvin.

COMMUNIA. In old English law. Common things, *res communes.* Such as running water, the air, the sea, and sea shores. Bract. fol. 7*b*.

COMMUNIA PLACITA. In old English law. Common pleas or actions; those between one subject and another, as distinguished from pleas of the crown.

COMMUNIA PLACITA NON TENENDA IN SCACCARIO. An ancient writ directed to the treasurer and barons of the exchequer, forbidding them to hold pleas between common persons (*i. e.*, not debtors to the king, who alone originally sued and were sued there) in that court, where neither of the parties belonged to the same. Reg. Orig. 187.

COMMUNIÆ. In feudal law on the continent of Europe, this name was given to towns enfranchised by the crown, about the twelfth century, and formed into free corporations by grants called "charters of community."

COMMUNIBUS ANNIS. In ordinary years; on the annual average.

COMMUNICATE. To bestow, convey, make known, recount, impart; to give by way of information. Whitford v. North State Life Ins. Co., 163 N.C. 223, 79 S.E. 501, 502, Ann.Cas.1915B, 270; Prevost v. Morgenthau, 106 F.2d 330, 334, 70 App. D.C. 306.

COMMUNICATION. Information given, the sharing of knowledge by one with another; conference; consultation or bargaining preparatory to making a contract. Intercourse; connection. Also, the Masonic equivalent for the word "meeting." State v. Goodwyn, 83 W.Va. 255, 98 S.E. 577.

Something said by one person to another;—so used in a statute providing that neither a party nor his or her spouse shall be examined as a witness as to personal transactions or communications between witness and persons since deceased. Secor v. Siver, 188 Iowa, 1126, 161 N.W. 769, 772, 176 N.W. 981.

"Transactions and communications," within statute declaring inadmissible testimony of interested witness concerning transactions and communications between himself and deceased person, embrace every variety of affairs which conform to the subject of negotiation, interviews, or actions between two persons, and include every method by which one person can derive impressions or information from the conduct, condition or language of another. Bright v. Virginia & Gold Hill Water Co., C.C.A.Nev., 270 F. 410, 413.

The act of communicating;—so used in a statute declaring that no husband or wife shall be compelled to disclose any confidential communication made by one to the other during marriage. Whitford v. North State Life Ins. Co., 163 N.C. 223, 79 S.E. 501, 502, Ann.Cas.1915B, 270. In a broader sense, the word embraces all knowledge upon the part of either obtained by reason of the marriage relations, and which but for the confidence growing out of such relation would not have been known. Prudential Ins. Co. of America v. Pierce's Adm'r, 270 Ky. 216, 109 S.W.2d 616, 617.

As used in a statute providing that an attorney cannot, without the consent of his client, be examined as to any communication made by the client, "communication" is not restricted to mere words but includes acts as well. Ex parte McDonough, 170 Cal. 230, 149 P. 566, 567, L.R.A. 1916C, 593, Ann.Cas.1916E, 327.

French Law

The production of a merchant's books, by delivering them either to a person designated by the court, or to his adversary, to be examined in all their parts, and as shall be deemed necessary to the suit. Arg. Fr. Merc. Law, 552.

—Confidential communications. These are certain classes of communications, passing between persons who stand in a confidential or fiduciary relation to each other, (or who, on account of their relative situation, are under a special duty of secrecy and fidelity,) which the law will not permit to be divulged, or allow them to be inquired into in a court of justice, for the sake of public policy and the good order of society. Examples of such privileged relations are those of husband and wife and attorney and client. Hatton v. Robinson, 14 Pick.Mass. 416, 25 Am.Dec. 415; Parker v. Carter, 4 Munf.Va. 287, 6 Am.Dec. 513; Parkhurst v. Berdell, 110 N.Y. 386, 18 N.E. 123, 6 Am.St.Rep. 384.

—Privileged communication. In the law of evidence. A communication made to a counsel, solicitor, or attorney, in professional confidence, and which he is not permitted to divulge; otherwise called a "confidential communication." 1 Starkie, Ev. 185.

In the law of libel and slander. A defamatory statement made to another in pursuance of a duty, political, judicial, social, or personal, so that an action for libel or slander will not lie, though the statement be false, unless in the last two cases actual malice be proved in addition. Bacon v. Railroad Co., 66 Mich. 166, 33 N.W. 181; 5 E. & B. 347.

When a communication is fairly made by one in the discharge of a public or private duty, legal, moral, or social, of perfect or imperfect obligation, or in the conduct of his own affairs, to one who has a corresponding interest to receive such communication, it is "privileged," International & G. N. Ry. Co. v. Edmundson, Tex.Com.App., 222 S.W. 181, 183, if made in good faith and without actual malice, Baker v. Clark, 186 Ky. 816, 218 S.W. 280, 285. A "privileged communication" is one made in good faith, upon any subject-matter in which the party communicating has an interest, or in reference to which he has, or honestly believes he has, a duty, and which contains matter which, without the occasion upon which it is made, would be defamatory and actionable. Peak v. Taubman, 251 Mo. 390, 158 S.W. 656, 663. In a "privileged communication" the words used, if defamatory and libelous, are excused, while in "fair comment" the words are not a defamation of plaintiff and not libelous. Van Lonkhuyzen v. Daily News Co., 203 Mich. 570, 170 N.W. 93, 99.

Privileged communications are either (1) absolutely privileged, or (2) conditionally or qualifiedly privileged. Grantham v. Wilkes, 135 Miss. 777, 100 So. 673. An "absolutely privileged communication" is one made in the interest of the public service or the due administration of justice, and is practically limited to legislative and judicial proceedings and other actions of state. Grantham v. Wilkes, 135 Miss. 777, 100 So. 673. By an "absolutely privileged" publication is not to be understood a publication for which the publisher is in no wise responsible, but it means a publication in respect of which, by reason of the occasion upon which it is made, no remedy can be had in a civil action for slander or libel, Peterson v. Cleaver, 105 Neb. 438, 181 N.W. 187, 189, 15 A.L.R. 447, even though the words are published maliciously and with knowledge of their falsity, Spencer v. Looney, 116 Va. 767, 82 S.E. 745, 747. A "qualifiedly privileged communication" is a slanderous statement uttered in good faith upon a proper occasion and from a proper motive based upon an honest belief that it is true, but, unlike communications wholly privileged, the defendant has the burden of proving want of malice or ill will. Peak v. Taubman, 251 Mo. 390, 158 S.W. 656, 665. A communication "qualifiedly privileged" is one which is prima facie privileged only, and in which the privilege may be lost by proof of malice in the publication. Spencer v. Looney, 116 Va. 767, 82 S.E. 745, 747. A communication made in good faith upon any subject-matter in which the party communicating has an interest or in reference to which he has a duty, either legal, moral, or social, if made to a person having a corresponding interest or duty, is "qualifiedly privileged." Peterson v. Cleaver, 105 Neb. 438, 181 N.W. 187, 189, 15 A.L.R. 447; Massee v. Williams, C.C.A.Tenn., 207 F. 222, 230; German-American Ins. Co. v. Huntley, 62 Okl. 39, 161 P. 815, 818.

COMMUNINGS. In Scotch law. The negotiations preliminary to entering into a contract.

COMMUNIO BONORUM. In the civil law. A community of goods.

COMMUNION OF GOODS. In Scotch law. The right enjoyed by married persons in the movable goods belonging to them. Bell.

COMMUNIS, COMMUNE, *adj.* Lat. Common.

COMMUNIS ERROR FACIT JUS. Common error makes law. 4 Inst. 240; Noy, Max. p. 37, max. 27. Common error goeth for a law. Finch, Law, b. 1, c. 3, no. 54. Common error sometimes passes current as law. Broom, Max. 139, 140.

What was at first illegal is presumed, when repeated many times, to have acquired the force of usage; and then it would be wrong to depart from it. 1 Ld.Raym. 42; 6 Cl. & F. 172; 3 M. & S. 396; Goodman v. Eastman, 4 N.H. 458; Kent v. Kent, 2 Mass. 357; Davey v. Turner, 1 Dall. 13, 1 L.Ed. 15. The converse of this maxim is *communis error non facit jus.* A common error does not make law. 4 Inst. 242; 3 Term 725; 6 Term 564.

COMMUNIS OPINIO. Common opinion; general professional opinion. According to Lord Coke (who places it on the footing of observance or usage), common opinion is good authority in law. Co. Litt. 186*a*.

COMMUNIS PARIES. In the civil law. A common or party wall. Dig. 8, 2, 8, 13.

COMMUNIS RIXATRIX. In old English law. A common scold, (*q. v.*) 4 Bl.Comm. 168.

COMMUNIS SCRIPTURA. In old English law. A common writing; a writing common to both parties; a chirograph. Glan. lib. 8, c. 1.

COMMUNIS STIPES. A common stock of descent; a common ancestor.

COMMUNISM. A system of social organization in which goods are held in common, the opposite of the system of private property; communalism, any theory or system of social organization involving common ownership of agents of production of industry, the latter of which theories is referred to in the popular use of the word "communism" while the scientific usage sometimes conforms to the first alone and sometimes alternates between the first and second; also the principles and theories of the Communist Party, especially in Soviet Russia. Feinglass v. Reinecke, D.C.Ill., 48 F.Supp. 438, 440.

Any theory or system of social organization involving common ownership of the agents of production, and some approach to equality in the distribution of the products of industry. Webster, Dict. A system by which the state controls the means of production and the distribution and consumption of industrial products. Cent.Dict.

An equality of distribution of the physical means of life and enjoyment as a transition to a still higher standard of justice that all should work according to their capacity and receive according to their wants. 1 Mill, Pol.Ec. 248.

COMMUNIST. A supporter of the Paris Commune; in 1871 Communard; a member of the Communist Party in any country, especially Soviet Russia; one who belives in communism. Feinglass v. Reinecke, D.C.Ill., 48 F.Supp. 438, 440, 441.

Communist International. See Third International.

COMMUNIST PARTY. A semipolitical party of recent years representing the Socialist radical wing and holding of the tenets and beliefs of Communism. It has quite generally seceded from the Socialists, organizing in many countries but chiefly in Russia. Garriga v. Richfield, 20 N.Y.S. 2d 544, 547, 174 Misc. 315.

COMMUNITAS REGNI ANGLIÆ. The general assembly of the kingdom of England. One of the ancient names of the English parliament. 1 Bl. Comm. 148. See, also, Commune Concilium Regni.

COMMUNITY. Neighborhood; vicinity, synonymous with locality. Conley v. Valley Motor Transit Co., C.C.A.Ohio, 139 F.2d 692, 693. People who reside in a locality in more or less proximity. State ex inf. Thompson ex rel. Kenneppe v. Scott, 304 Mo. 664, 264 S.W. 369, 370. A society or body of people living in the same place, under the same laws and regulations, who have common rights, privileges, or interests. In re Huss, 126 N.Y. 537, 27 N.E. 784, 12 L.R.A. 620; Sacred Heart Academy of Galveston v. Karsch, 122 S.W.2d 416, 417, 173 Tenn. 618.

It connotes a congeries of common interests arising from associations—social, business, religious, governmental, scholastic, recreational. Lukens Steel Co. v. Perkins, 107 F.2d 627, 631, 70 App.D.C. 354.

The term "community," as used in a statute providing that communities may be incorporated for the purpose of supplying inhabitants with water, should be construed to include all the inhabitants of a district having a community of interest in obtaining for themselves in common a water supply for domestic use. Hamilton v. Rudeen, 112 Or. 268, 224 P. 92, 93.

In connection with the rule requiring, for purposes of impeachment, a knowledge of the character of the witness in the community or neighborhood in which he resides, the term "community" means, generally, where the person is well known and has established a reputation. Craven v. State, 22 Ala.App. 39, 111 So. 767, 769.

Civil Law

A corporation or body politic. Dig. 3, 4.

French Law

A species of partnership which a man and a woman contract when they are lawfully married to each other. See, also, Community Property, *infra.*

Conventional community is that which is formed by express agreement in the contract of marriage.

By this contract the legal community which would otherwise subsist may be modified as to the proportions which each shall take, and as to the things which shall compose it.

Legal community is that which takes place by virtue of the contract of marriage itself.

The French system of community property was known as the dotal system, and the Spanish as the ganancial system. The conquest of Mexico by the Spaniards and their acquisition of the Florida territory resulted in the introduction on American soil of the Spanish system, which now prevails, usually in a somewhat modified form, in Texas, California, Nevada, Arizona, Washington, Idaho, New Mexico, Porto Rico, and the Philippines. Ballinger, Com.Property, § 6; Chavez v. McKnight, 1 N.M. 147. The Louisiana Code has, with slight modifications, adopted the dotal system of the Code Nepoléon as regards the separate rights of husband and wife, but as to their common property, it retained the essential features of the Spanish ganancial system.

COMMUNITY ACCOUNT. A bank account consisting of separate and community funds commingled in such manner that neither can be distinguished from the other. Smith v. Buss, 135 Tex. 566, 144 S.W.2d 529, 532.

COMMUNITY DEBT. One chargeable to the community (of husband and wife) rather than to either of the parties individually. Calhoun v. Leary, 6 Wash. 17, 32 P. 1070.

COMMUNITY HOUSE. A house occupied by two or more families. Fox v. Sumerson, 338 Pa. 545, 13 A.2d 1, 2.

COMMUNITY OF INTEREST. Term as applied to relation of joint adventure means interest common to both or all parties, that is, mixture or identity of interest in venture wherein each and all are reciprocally concerned and from which each and all derive material benefit and sustain a mutual responsibility. Carboneau v. Peterson, 1 Wash.2d 347, 95 P.2d 1043, 1055.

COMMUNITY OF PROFITS. This term, as used in the definition of a partnership, (to which a community of profits is essential,) means a proprietorship in them as distinguished from a personal claim upon the other associate, a property right in them from the start in one associate as much as in the other. Moore v. Williams, 26 Tex.Civ. App. 142, 62 S.W. 977.

COMMUNITY PROPERTY. Property owned in common by a husband and wife as a kind of marital partnership. Coleman v. Coleman, Tex.Civ. App., 293 S.W. 695, 699. Property acquired by husband and wife, or either, during marriage, when not acquired as the separate property of either. In re Lux's Estate, 114 Cal. 73, 45 P. 1023; Mitchell v. Mitchell, 80 Tex. 101, 15 S.W. 705; Ames v. Hubby, 49 Tex. 705; Holyoke v. Jackson, 3 Wash.T. 235, 3 P. 841; Civ. Code Cal. § 687.

This partnership or community consists of the profits of all the effects of which the husband has the administration and enjoyment, either of right or in fact, of the produce of the reciprocal industry and labor of both husband and wife, and of the estates which they may acquire during the marriage, either by donations made jointly to them both, or by purchase, or in any other similar way, even although the purchase be only in the name of one of the two, and not of both, because in that case the period of time when the purchase is made is alone attended to, and not the person who made the purchase. Rev.Civ.Code La. arts. 2402, 2404; Brown v. Cobb, 10 La. 172; Barnes v. Thompson, 154 La. 1036, 98 So. 657, 658.

COMMUTATION. Alteration; change; substitution; the act of substituting one thing for another. Steinacher v. Swanson, 131 Neb. 439, 268 N.W. 317, 321.

Criminal Law

The change of a punishment from a greater to a less; as from hanging to imprisonment. People v. Jenkins, 325 Ill. 372, 156 N.E. 290, 292. Fehl v. Martin, 155 Or. 455, 64 P.2d 631, 632.

Although both a pardon and a commutation are granted by the sovereign power; Goben v. State, 32 Okl.Cr. 237, 240 P. 1085, 1087; a "commutation" means merely a change of punishment, while a "pardon" avoids or terminates punishment for crime; Lupo v. Zerbest, C.C.A.Ga., 92 F.2d 362, 364. A pardon bears no relation to the term of punishment, and must be accepted or it is nugatory; commutation removes no stain, restores no civil privilege, and may be effected without the consent and against the will of the prisoner. In re Charles, 115 Kan. 323, 222 P. 606, 608; Chapman v. Scott, D.C.Conn., 10 F.2d 156, 159.

"Commutation" is also distinguishable from a "reprieve" or "respite," meaning simply the withholding of a sentence for an interval of time, a postponement of execution, or a temporary suspension of execution. State v. District Court of Eighteenth Judicial Dist. in and for Blaine County, 73 Mont. 541, 237 P. 525, 527.

Civil Law

The conversion of the right to receive a variable or periodical payment into the right to receive a fixed or gross payment; a substitution of one sort of payment for another, or of money payment in lieu of a performance of a compulsory duty or labor. Commutation may be effected by private agreement, but it is usually done under a statute. Steinacher v. Swanson, 131 Neb. 439, 268 N.W. 317, 321.

COMMUTATION OF TAXES. Payment of a designated lump sum (permanent or annual) for the privilege of exemption from taxes, or the settlement in advance of a specific sum in lieu of an ad valorem tax. Cotton Mfg. Co. v. New Orleans, 31 La.Ann. 440.

COMMUTATION OF TITHES. Signifies the conversion of tithes into a fixed payment in money.

COMMUTATION TICKET. A railroad ticket giving the holder the right to travel at a certain rate for a limited number of trips (or for an unlimited number within a certain period of time) for a less amount than would be paid in the aggregate for so many separate trips. Interstate Commerce Com'n v. Baltimore & O. R. Co., C.C.Ohio, 43 F. 56.

COMMUTATIVE CONTRACT. In civil law. One in which each of the contracting parties gives and receives an equivalent; *e. g.*, the contract of sale. Pothier, Obl. n. 13; State ex rel. Waterman v. J. S. Waterman and Co., 178 La. 340, 151 So. 422, 426. See Contract.

COMMUTATIVE JUSTICE. See Justice.

COMPACT, *n.* An agreement; a contract. Green v. Biddle, 8 Wheat. 1, 92, 5 L.Ed. 547. Usually applied to conventions between nations or sovereign states.

A contract between parties, which creates obligations and rights capable of being enforced, and contemplated as such between the parties, in their distinct and independent characters. Story, Const. b. 3, c. 3; Rutherf.Inst. b. 2, c. 6, § 1.

A mutual consent of parties concerned respecting some property or right that is the object of the stipulation, or something that is to be done or forborne. Chesapeake & O. Canal Co. v. Baltimore & O. R. Co., 4 Gill & J., Md., 1.

COMPACT, *adj.* Closely or firmly united or packed, as the particles of solid bodies; firm; solid; dense; as a compact texture in rocks; also, lying in a narrow compass or arranged so as to economize space; having a small surface or border in proportion to contents or bulk; close; as, a compact estate; a compact order or formation of troops. Wails v. Board of Commissioners of Okmulgee County, 156 Okl. 165, 9 P.2d 946, 948. Concentrated, or near to. Webster v. Toulon Tp. High School Dist. No. 4, 313 Ill. 541, 145 N.E. 118, 121; State v. Tindell, 210 P. 619, 621, 112 Kan. 256.

COMPACT SCHOOL DISTRICT. One so closely united and so nearly adjacent to the school building that all the students residing in the district may conveniently travel from their homes to the school building and return the same day in a reasonable length of time and with a reasonable degree of comfort. People ex rel. Tudor v. Vance, 29 N.E.2d 673, 675, 374 Ill. 415; People ex rel. Frailey v. McNeely, 32 N.E.2d 608, 610, 376 Ill. 64.

COMPANAGE. All kinds of food, except bread and drink. Spelman.

COMPANIES CLAUSES CONSOLIDATION ACT. An English statute, (8 Vict. c. 16,) passed in 1845, which consolidated the clauses of previous laws still remaining in force on the subject of public companies. It is considered as incorporated into all subsequent acts authorizing the execution of undertakings of a public nature by companies, unless expressly excepted by such later acts. Its purpose is declared by the preamble to be to avoid repeating provisions as to the constitution and management of the companies, and to secure greater uniformity in such provisions. Wharton.

COMPANION OF THE GARTER. One of the knights of the Order of the Garter.

COMPANIONS. In French law. A general term, comprehending all persons who compose the crew of a ship or vessel. Poth. Mar. Cont. no. 163.

COMPANULATE. This term, used to describe the shape of the cover of a lunch-box containing a thermos bottle, means bell-shaped. American Can Co. v. Goldee Mfg. Co., D.C.N.Y., 290 F. 523, 527.

COMPANY. A society or association of persons, in considerable number, interested in a common object, and uniting themselves for the prosecution usually of some commercial or industrial undertaking, or other legitimate business. Mills v. State, 23 Tex. 303; Smith v. Janesville, 52 Wis. 680, 9 N.W. 789.

The proper signification of the word "company," when applied to persons engaged in trade, denotes those united for the same purpose or in a joint concern. It is so commonly used in this sense, or as indicating a partnership, that few persons accustomed to purchase goods at shops, where they are sold by retail, would misapprehend that such was its meaning. Palmer v. Pinkham, 33 Me. 32.

The term is not identical with "partnership," although every unincorporated society is, in its legal relations, a partnership. In common use a distinction is made, the name "partnership" being reserved for business associations of a limited number of persons (usually not more than four or five) trading under a name composed of their individual names set out in succession; while "company" is appropriated as the designation of a society comprising a larger number of persons, with greater capital, and engaged in more extensive enterprises, and trading under a title not disclosing the names of the individuals. Attorney General v. Mercantile Marine Ins. Co., 121 Mass. 525.

Sometimes the word is used to represent those members of a partnership whose names do not appear in the name of the firm. See 12 Toullier, 97.

A number of persons united for performing or carrying on anything jointly. In re Tidewater Coal Exchange, C.C.A.N.Y., 280 F. 638, 643.

Thus, the term is not necessarily limited to a trading or commercial body, but may include an unincorporated organization to promote fraternity among its members and provide mutual aid and protection through the payment of death benefits. In re Order of Sparta, D.C.Pa., 238 F. 437.

"Company" is a generic and comprehensive word, which may include individuals, partnerships, and corporations. Asbury v. Town of Albemarle, 162 N.C. 247, 78 S.E. 146, 148, 44 L.R.A.,N.S., 1189; Ellerson v. Grove, C.C.A.N.C., 44 F.2d 493, 497. But not a municipality. City of Los Angeles, Cal., v. Eighth Judicial District Court, 58 Nev. 1, 67 P.2d 1019, 1023.

The word is sometimes applicable to a single individual. Harger v. Harger, 144 Ark. 375, 222 S.W. 736, 739. But compare Wood v. Wood, 78 Or. 181, 151 P. 969, 970, L.R.A. 1916C, 251, Ann.Cas.1918A, 226.

Joint Stock Company

An association of individuals for purposes of profit, possessing a common capital contributed by the members composing it, such capital being commonly divided into shares of which each member possesses one or more, and which are transferable by the owner. Shelf. Jt. St. Co. 1. One having a joint stock or capital, which is divided into numerous transferable shares, or consists of transferable stock. Lindl. Partn. 6. A partnership whereof the capital is divided, or agreed to be divided, into shares so as to be transferable without the express consent of the co-partners. Pars. Part. § 435. A *quasi* partnership, invested by statutes in England and many of the states with some of the privileges of a corporation. See Pennsylvania v. Mining Co., 10 Wall. 556, 19 L. Ed. 998; L.R. 4 Eq. 695. It lies midway between a corporation and a copartnership. Rocky Mountain Stud Farm Co. v. Lunt, 46 Utah, 299, 151 P. 521, 527.

A "joint-stock company" is an entirely different organization from a "corporation," although it has many of the same characteristics and is often not improperly called a quasi corporation, especially under particular statutes, but in Kentucky it is still what it was at common law, namely, a hybrid midway between a corporation and a partnership, that is, it had directors and officers, articles of association, a common capital divided into shares which represented the interests of the members and are transferable without the consent of the other members so that the death of a member does not dissolve the company—but, on the other hand, each member was liable for the debts of the concern, so that such company had characteristics of both a corporation and a partnership. Roller v. Madison, 172 Ky. 693, 189 S.W. 914, 915.

Limited Company

A company in which the liability of each shareholder is limited by the number of shares he has taken, so that he cannot be called on to contribute beyond the amount of his shares. In England, the memorandum of association of such company may provide that the liability of the directors, manager, or managing director thereof shall be unlimited. 30 & 31 Vict. c. 131; 1 Lindl. Partn. 383; Mozley & Whitley.

Public Company

In English law. A business corporation; a society of persons joined together for carrying on some commercial or industrial undertaking.

COMPARABLE ACCOMMODATION. Within the rule that it is the rent generally prevailing on the freeze date for comparable accommodations in a defense-rental area that determines rent that may be charged, two accommodations are "comparable" if they are sufficiently similar to be regarded by an expert as of substantially equal rental value or if they are sufficiently similar so that an expert taking as a standard the rent prevailing for one and making allowances for such differences as would be reflected in rental value would be able to determine the appropriate corresponding rent for the other. Sirianni v. Bowles, Em.App., 148 F.2d 343, 344.

COMPARATIO LITERARUM. In the civil law. Comparison of writings, or handwritings. A mode of proof allowed in certain cases.

COMPARATIVE. Proceeding by the method of comparison; founded on comparison; estimated by comparison.

COMPARATIVE INTERPRETATION. That method of interpretation which seeks to arrive at the meaning of a statute or other writing by comparing its several parts and also by comparing it as a whole with other like documents proceeding from the same source and referring to the same general subject. Glenn v. York County, 6 Rich. (S.C.) 412.

COMPARATIVE JURISPRUDENCE. The study of the principles of legal science by the comparison of various systems of law.

COMPARATIVE NEGLIGENCE. That doctrine in the law of negligence by which the negligence of the parties is compared, in the degrees of "slight," "ordinary," and "gross" negligence, and a recovery permitted, notwithstanding the contributory negligence of the plaintiff, when the negligence of the plaintiff is slight and the negligence of the defendant gross, but refused when the plaintiff has been guilty of a want of ordinary care, thereby contributing to his injury, or when the negligence of the defendant is not gross, but only ordinary or slight, when compared, under the circumstances of the case, with the contributory negligence of the plaintiff. 3 Amer. & Eng. Enc. Law, 367. St. Louis & S. F. R. Co. v. Elsing, 37 Okl. 333, 132 P. 483, 486.

Where negligence by both parties is concurrent and contributes to injury, recovery is not barred under such doctrine, but plaintiff's damages are diminished proportionately, provided his fault is less than defendant's, and that, by exercise of ordinary care, he could not have avoided consequences of defendant's negligence after it was or should have been apparent. Rogers v. McKinley, 48 Ga.App. 262, 172 S.E. 662, 664.

COMPARISON OF HANDWRITING. A comparison by the juxtaposition of two writings, in order, by such comparison, to ascertain whether both were written by the same person.

A method of proof resorted to where the genuineness of a written document is disputed; it consists in comparing the handwriting of the disputed paper with that of another instrument which is proved or admitted to be in the writing of the party sought to be charged, in order to infer, from their identity or similarity in this respect, that they are the work of the same hand. Johnson v. Insurance Co., 105 Iowa, 273, 75 N.W. 101.

COMPARATIVE RECTITUDE. Doctrine wherein relief by divorce is granted to the party least in fault when both have shown grounds for divorce. Blankenship v. Blankenship, 51 Nev. 356, 276 P. 9, 10, 63 A.L.R. 1127.

Doctrine does not apply in Nevada.

COMPASCUUM. Belonging to commonage *Jus compascuum,* the right of common of pasture.

COMPASS, THE MARINER'S. An instrument used by mariners to point out the course of a ship at sea. It consists of a magnetized steel bar called the "needle," attached to the under side of a card, upon which are drawn the points of the compass, and supported by a fine pin, upon which it turns freely in a horizontal plane.

COMPASSING. Imagining or contriving, or plotting. In English law, "compassing the king's death" is treason. 4 Bl.Comm. 76.

COMPATERNITAS. In the canon law. A kind of spiritual relationship contracted by baptism.

COMPATERNITY. Spiritual affinity, contracted by sponsorship in baptism.

COMPATIBILITY. As applied to offices, such relation and consistency between the duties of two offices that they may be held and filled by one person.

COMPEAR. In Scotch law. To appear.

COMPEARANCE. In Scotch practice. Appearance; an appearance made for a defendant; an appearance by counsel. Bell.

COMPEL. To force. Temple Lumber Co. v. Living, Tex.Civ.App., 289 S.W. 746, 749. To oblige. Texas Electric Ry. v. Jones, Tex.Civ.App., 231 S. W. 823, 824.

In an allegation that plaintiff was compelled to pay license taxes, the word "compel" does not necessarily import elements of compulsory payment. Singer Sewing Mach. Co. v. Teasley, 198 Ala. 673, 73 So. 969, 971; Sinnott v. District Court in and for Clarke County, 201 Iowa, 292, 207 N.W. 129, 131.

As to compelling a person to testify against himself, see State v. Backstrom, 117 Kan. 111, 230 P. 306, 308; U. S. v. Cooper, D.C.Iowa, 288 F. 604, 609; U. S. v. Kallas, D.C. Wash., 272 F. 742, 751; U. S. v. Monia, Ill., 317 U.S. 424, 63 S.Ct. 409, 411, 87 L.Ed. 376.

COMPELLATIVUS. An adversary or accuser.

Compendia sunt dispendia. Co. Litt. 305. Abbreviations (or abridgments) are detriments.

COMPENDIUM. An abridgment, synopsis, or digest.

COMPENSABLE DEATH. Within Workmen's Compensation Acts is one which results to employee from injury by accident arising out of and in course of employment. Slade v. Willis Hosiery Mills, 209 N.C. 823, 184 S.E. 844, 845.

COMPENSABLE INJURY. Within Workmen's Compensation Acts is an injury for which compensation is payable, and date of such an injury is not time of the accident or occurrence causing injury, but the time when the right to compensation accrues. S. G. Taylor Chain Co. v. Marianowski, 182 N.E. 584, 585, 95 Ind.App. 120. Muehlhausen Spring Co. v. Szewczyk, 104 Ind.App. 161, 8 N.E.2d 104, 106.

COMPENSACION. In Spanish law. Compensation; set-off. The extinction of a debt by another debt of equal dignity between persons who have mutual claims on each other.

COMPENSATIO. Lat. In the civil law. Compensation, or set-off. A proceeding resembling a set-off in the common law, being a claim on the part of the defendant to have an amount due to him from the plaintiff deducted from his demand. Dig. 16, 2; Inst. 4, 6, 30, 39; 3 Bl.Comm. 305.

COMPENSATIO CRIMINIS. (Set-off of crime or guilt.) In practice. The compensation or set-off of one crime against another; the plea of recrimination in a suit for a divorce; that is, that the complainant is guilty of the same kind of offense with which the respondent is charged. See 1 Hagg.Cons. 144; 1 Hagg.Eccl. 714; Wood v. Wood, 2 Paige, Ch. (N.Y.) 108, 2 D. & B. 64; Bishop, Marr. & D. §§ 393, 394.

COMPENSATION. Indemnification; payment of damages; making amends; making whole; giving an equivalent or substitute of equal value; that which is necessary to restore an injured party to his former position; consideration or price of a privilege purchased; equivalent in money for a loss sustained; equivalent given for property taken or for an injury done to another; giving back an equivalent in either money which is but the measure of value, or in actual value otherwise conferred; recompense in value; recompense or reward for some loss, injury, or service, especially when it is given by statute; remuneration for the injury directly and proximately caused by a breach of contract or duty; remuneration or satisfaction for injury or damage of every description; that return which is given for something else. An act which a court orders to be done, or money which a court or other tribunal orders to be paid, by a person whose acts or omissions have caused loss or injury to another, in order that thereby the person damnified may receive equal value for his loss, or be made whole in respect of his injury. Railroad Co. v. Denman, 10 Minn. 280 (Gil. 208); Hughson Condensed Milk Co. v. State Board of Equalization, 23 Cal.App.2d 281, 73 P.2d 290, 292. For "Extra Compensation" and "Fair and Reasonable Compensation", see these titles.

"Compensation" is a misleading term, and is used merely for lack of a word more nearly expressing the thought of the law which permits recovery for an imponderable and intangible thing for which there is no money equivalent. Stutsman v. Des Moines City Ry. Co., 180 Iowa, 524, 163 N.W. 580, 585.

The word "compensation," as used in Workmen's Compensation Acts, means the money relief afforded an injured employee or his dependents according to the scale established and for the persons designated in the act, and not the compensatory damages recoverable in an action at law for a wrong done or a contract broken. Christensen v. Morse Dry Dock & Repair Co., 214 N.Y.S. 732, 740, 216 App.Div. 274.

As used in Workmen's Compensation Acts, "compensation" is distinguishable from "benefits"; the former applying to an allowance where the employee is only injured, and the latter applying in case of death. Terry v. General Electric Co., 232 N.Y. 120, 133 N.E. 373, 374. The term "compensation" may include funeral benefits. Donoho v. Atlantic Basin Iron Works, 206 N.Y.S. 494, 495, 210 App. Div. 535. But see Barber v. Estey Organ Co., 100 Vt. 72, 135 A. 1, 2; Industrial Commission v. Hammond, 77 Colo. 414, 236 P. 1006, 1008.

Also that equivalent in money which is paid to the owners and occupiers of lands taken or injuriously affected by the exercise of the power of eminent domain. Louisiana and F. Plank Road Co. v. Pickett, 25 Mo. 535, 539; Oregon Short Line R. Co. v. Fox, 28 Utah 311, 78 P. 800, 801.

In the constitutional provision for "just compensation" for property taken under the power of eminent domain, this term means a payment in money. Any benefit to the remaining property of the owner, arising from public works for which a part has been taken, cannot be considered as compensation. Railroad Co. v. Burkett, 42 Ala. 83.

As compared with consideration and damages, compensation, in its most careful use, seems to be between them. Consideration is amends for something given by consent, or by the owner's choice. Damages is amends exacted from a wrong-doer for a tort. Compensation is amends for something which was taken without the owner's choice, yet without commission of a tort. Thus, one should say, consideration for land sold; compensation for land taken for a railway; damages for a trespass. But such distinctions are not uniform. Land damages is a common expression for compensation for lands taken for public use. Abbott.

"Compensation" is distinguishable from "damages," inasmuch as the former may mean the sum which will remunerate an owner for land actually taken, while the latter signifies an allowance made for injury to the residue; but such distinction is not ordinarily observed. Faulkner v. City of Nashville, 154 Tenn. 145, 285 S.W. 39, 43.

The remuneration or wages given to an employee or, especially, to an officer. Salary, pay, or emolument. Christopherson v. Reeves, 44 S.D. 634, 184 N.W. 1015, 1019; Higgins v. Glenn, 65 Utah, 406, 237 P. 513, 515.

The ordinary meaning of the term "compensation," as applied to officers, is remuneration, in whatever form it may be given, whether it be salaries and fees, or both combined. State v. Bland, 91 Kan. 160, 136 P. 947, 949. It is broad enough to include other remuneration for official services; State ex rel. Emmons v. Farmer, 271 Mo. 306, 196 S.W. 1106, 1108; such as mileage or traveling expenses; Leckenby v. Post Printing & Publishing Co., 65 Colo. 443, 176 P. 490, 492; and also the repayment of amounts expended. Compare, however, People v. Chapman, 225 N.Y. 700, 122 N.E. 240; McCoy v. Handlin, 35 S.D. 487, 153 N.W. 361, 371, L.R.A.1915E, 858, Ann.Cas.1917A, 1046.

But the term is not necessarily synonymous with "salary." See People v. Wemple, 115 N.Y. 302, 22 N.E. 272; Com. v. Carter, 21 Ky.L.Rep. 1509, 55 S.W. 701; Crawford County v. Lindsay, 11 Ill.App. 261; Kilgore v. People, 76 Ill. 548.

A "reasonable compensation" is that which will fairly compensate the laborer when the character of the work and the effectiveness and ability entering into the service are considered. Chapman v. A. H. Averill Machinery Co., 28 Idaho, 121, 152 P. 573, 575.

Compensation is not synonymous with "pension," which is ordinarily a gratuity from the government or some of its subordinate agencies in recognition of, but not in payment for, past services. Dickey v. Jackson, 181 Iowa 1155, 165 N.W. 387, 389.

The Civil, Scotch, and French Law

Recoupment; set-off. The meeting of two debts due by two parties, where the debtor in the one debt is the creditor in the other; that is to say, where one person is both debtor and creditor to another, and therefore, to the extent of what is due to him, claims allowance out of the sum that he is due. Bell; 1 Kames, Eq. 395, 396.

In order for "compensation" to take place, the two debts must exist simultaneously and have as their object the payment of a sum of money or a certain quantity of consumable things of one and the same kind, and the debts must be equally liquidated and demandable. Blanchard v. Bank of Morgan City & Trust Co., La.App., 185 So. 120, 122.

Compensation is of three kinds.—legal, or by operation of law; compensation by way of exception; and by reconvention. Stewart v. Harper, 16 La.Ann. 181; Blanchard v. Cole, 8 La. 158; 8 Dig. 16, 2; Code, 4, 31; Inst. 4, 6, 30; Burge, Suret. b. 2, c. 6, p. 181; La.Civ. Code, arts. 2203–2208 (Civ.Code, arts. 2207–2211).

Criminal Law

Recrimination. See Compensatio Criminis; Recrimination.

"Commutation" and "compensation" in statutes providing for reduction of sentence for good behavior are used interchangeably. Ryan v. Lawes, 278 N.Y.S. 608, 154 Misc. 572.

COMPENSATION PERIOD. The period fixed by the Workmen's Compensation Act during which the injured party is to receive compensation, unless the board reduces the period by correspondingly increasing the amount of weekly compensation. Southern Casualty Co. v. Boykin, Tex.Civ. App., 298 S.W. 639, 640.

COMPENSATORY DAMAGES. See Damages.

COMPERENDINATIO. In the Roman law. The adjournment of a cause, in order to hear the parties or their advocates a second time; a second hearing of the parties to a cause. Calvin.

COMPERTORIUM. In the civil law. A judicial inquest made by delegates or commissioners to find out and relate the truth of a cause. Wharton.

COMPERUIT AD DIEM. A plea in bar of an action of debt on a bail bond that the defendant appeared at the day required. For forms, see 5 Wentworth 470; Lilly, Entr. 114; 2 Chit. Pl. 527. See, generally, Comyns, Dig. *Pleader* (2 W. 31); 7 B. & C. 478.

COMPETE. To contend emulously, to strive for the position for which another is striving, to contend in rivalry. People v. Chew, 67 Colo. 394, 179 P. 812, 813; Commonwealth v. Shenandoah River Light & Power Corporation, 135 Va. 47, 115 S.E. 695, 698. See Competition.

COMPETENCY. In the law of evidence. The presence of those characteristics, or the absence of those disabilities, which render a witness legally fit and qualified to give testimony in a court of justice;—applied, in the same sense, to documents or other written evidence.

Competency differs from credibility. The former is a question which arises before considering the evidence given by the witness; the latter concerns the degree of credit to be given to his story. The former denotes the personal qualification of the witness; the latter his veracity. A witness may be competent, and yet give incredible testimony; he may be incompetent, and yet his evidence, if received, be perfectly credible. Competency is for the court; credibility for the jury. Yet in some cases the term "credible" is used as an equivalent for "competent." Thus, in a statute relating to the execution of wills, the term "credible witness" is held to mean one who is entitled to be examined and to give evidence in a court of justice; not necessarily one who is personally worthy of belief, but one who is not disqualified by imbecility, interest, crime, or other cause. 1 Jarm.Wills, 124; Smith v. Jones, 68 Vt. 132, 34 A. 424; Com. v. Holmes, 127 Mass. 424, 34 Am.Rep. 391.

In French law. The right in a court to exercise jurisdiction in a particular case.

COMPETENT. Duly qualified; answering all requirements; having sufficient ability or authority; possessing the requisite natural or legal qualifications; able; adequate; suitable; sufficient; capable; legally fit. Levee Dist. v. Jamison, 176 Mo. 557, 75 S.W. 679; In re Fichter's Estate, 279 N.Y. S. 597, 600, 155 Misc. 399. See, also, Incompetency.

A testator may be said to be "competent," if he has mental capacity to understand the nature of his act, to understand and recollect the nature and situation of his property and his relations to persons having claims on his bounty and whose interests are affected by his will. In re Smith's Estate, 200 Cal. 152, 252 P. 325, 328.

When generally applied to arbitrators, the term does not mean "expert." Home Ins. Co. v. Walter, Tex.Civ.App., 230 S.W. 723, 724.

COMPETENT AND OMITTED. In Scotch practice. A term applied to a plea which might have been urged by a party during the dependence of a cause, but which had been omitted. Bell.

COMPETENT AUTHORITY. As applied to courts and public officers, this term imports jurisdiction and due legal authority to deal with the particular matter in question. Mitchel v. U. S., 9 Pet. 735, 9 L.Ed. 283; Charles v. Charles, 41 Minn. 201, 42 N.W. 935.

COMPETENT EVIDENCE. That which the very nature of the thing to be proven requires, as, the production of a writing where its contents are the subject of inquiry. 1 Greenl.Ev. § 2; Hill v. Hill, 216 Ala. 435, 113 So. 306, 308; Goltra v. Penland, 45 Or. 254, 77 P. 129, 133. Also, generally, admissible or relevant, as the opposite of "incompetent." Ryan v. Town of Bristol, 63 Conn. 261, 27 A. 309, 312.

COMPETENT COURT. A court, either civil or criminal, having lawful jurisdiction. People ex rel. Fisher v. Morhous, 49 N.Y.S.2d 110, 116, 183 Misc. 51.

COMPETENT WITNESS. One who is legally qualified to be heard to testify in a cause. People v. Compton, 123 Cal. 403, 56 P. 44; Bank of Uvalde, Tex.Civ.App., 60 S.W.2d 888, 889. See Competency.

As used in the statute relating to the execution of wills, the term means a person who, at the time of making the attestation, could legally testify in court to the facts which he attests by subscribing his name to the will. In re Wiese's Estate, 98 Neb. 463, 153 N.W. 556, L.R.A.1915E, 832.

COMPETITION. Rivalry. People ex rel. Broderick v. Goldfogle, 123 Misc. 399, 205 N.Y.S. 870, 877. The play of contending forces ordinarily engendered by an honest desire for gain. U. S. v. American Linseed Oil Co., 43 S.Ct. 607, 611, 262 U.S. 371, 67 L.Ed. 1035. The effort of two or more parties, acting independently, to secure the custom of a third party by the offer of the most favorable terms. It is the struggle between rivals for the same trade at the same time; the act of seeking or endeavoring to gain what another is endeavoring to gain at the same time. Lipson v. Socony Vacuum Corporation, C.C.A.Mass., 87 F.2d 265, 270.

As used in a statute taxing moneyed capital competing with national banks, "competition" means a condition of business rivalry which arises when moneyed capital is devoted with reasonable continuity and regularity to operations having for their primary and characteristic purpose, as distinguished from some incidental operations or details, the transaction of some branch of business which may be carried on by national banks, and it is not necessary that this employment shall bring capital into competition with all of such branches. People ex rel. Pratt v. Goldfogle, 242 N.Y. 277, 151 N.E. 452, 461. The term involves the idea of struggling to obtain the same thing. First Nat. Bank v. City of Hartford, 187 Wis. 290, 203 N.W. 721, 729. See, also, First Nat. Bank v. City of Hartford, 47 S.Ct. 462, 466, 273 U.S. 548, 71 L.Ed. 767, 59 A.L.R. 1.

Unity of object with diversity of method is the essence of competition. Continental Securities Co. v. Interborough Rapid Transit Co., D.C.N.Y., 207 F. 467, 470.

Scotch Practice

The contest among creditors claiming on their respective diligences, or creditors claiming on their securities. Bell.

Unfair Competition in Trade

See Unfair.

COMPETITIVE CIVIL SERVICE EXAMINATION. Examination which conforms to measures or standards which are sufficiently objective to be capable of being challenged and reviewed by other examiners of equal ability and experience. Fink v. Finegan, 270 N.Y. 356, 1 N.E.2d 462, 464.

COMPETITIVE BIDDING. Requires that all bidders be placed on a plane of equality, and that they bid upon the same terms and conditions. State Highway Commission of Kentucky v. King, 259 Ky. 414, 82 S.W.2d 443.

COMPETITIVE TRAFFIC. Traffic which, as to any one carrier, originates at a point served also by another carrier, which other carrier handles the traffic at equal line-haul rates from origin to destination. Northern Pac. Ry. Co. v. United States, D.C.Minn., 41 F.Supp. 439, 441.

COMPETITORS. Persons endeavoring to do the same thing and each offering to perform the act, furnish the merchandise, or render the service better or cheaper than his rival. Continental Securities Co. v. Interborough Rapid Transit Co., D.C. N.Y., 207 F. 467, 470.

COMPILATION. A literary production composed of the works of others and arranged in a methodical manner.

A compilation consists of selected extracts from different authors; an abridgment is a condensation of the views of one author. Story v. Holcombe, 4 McLean 306, 314, Fed. Cas.No.13,497.

COMPILE. To copy from various authors into one work. Story v. Holcombe, 23 Fed.Cas. 171, 174. See Compilation.

Such a collection of statutes differs from a code in this, that none of the laws so compiled derives any new force or undergoes any modification in its relation to other statutes *in pari materia* from the fact of the compilation, while a code is a re-enactment of the whole body of the positive law and is to be read and interpreted as one entire and homogeneous whole.

COMPILED STATUTES. A collection of the statutes existing and in force in a given state, all laws and parts of laws relating to each subject-matter being brought together under one head, and the whole arranged systematically in one book, either under an alphabetical arrangement or some other plan of classification. Railway Co. v. State, 31 S.E. 531, 104 Ga. 831; Black, Interp. Laws, p. 363; Fidelity and Columbia Trust Co. v. Meek, 294 Ky. 122, 171 S.W.2d 41, 44.

COMPLAINANT. In practice. One who applies to the courts for legal redress; one who exhibits a bill of complaint. This is the proper designation of one suing in equity, though "plaintiff" is often used in equity proceedings as well as at law. Benefit Ass'n v. Robinson, 147 Ill. 138, 35 N.E. 168.

One who instigates prosecution or who prefers accusation against suspected person. State v. Snyder, 93 N.J.L. 18, 107 A. 167, 168.

COMPLAINT. In civil practice. In those states having a Code of Civil Procedure, the complaint is the first or initiatory pleading on the part of the plaintiff in a civil action. It corresponds to the declaration in the common-law practice. Code N.Y. § 141; McMath v. Parsons, 26 Minn. 246, 2 N.W. 703. Its purpose is to give defendant information of all material facts on which plaintiff relies to support his demand. Fox v. Cosgriff, 64 Idaho 448, 133 P.2d 930, 932.

The complaint shall contain: (1) The title of the cause, specifying the name of the court in which the action is brought, the name of the county in which the trial is required to be had, and the names of the parties to the action, plaintiff and defendant. (2) A plain and concise statement of the facts constituting a cause of action, without unnecessary repetition; and each material allegation shall be distinctly numbered. (3) A demand of the relief to which the plaintiff supposes himself entitled. If the recovery of money be demanded, the amount thereof must be stated. Code N.C.1883, § 233 (C.S. § 506).

Cross-complaint. In code practice. Whenever the defendant seeks affirmative relief against any party, relating to or depending upon the contract or transaction upon which the action is brought, or affecting the property to which the action relates, he may, in addition to his answer, file at the same time, or by permission of the court subsequently, a cross-complaint. The cross-complaint must be served upon the parties affected thereby, and such parties may demur or answer thereto as to the original complaint. Standley v. Insurance Co., 95 Ind. 254; Harrison v. McCormick, 69 Cal. 616, 11 P. 456; Bank v. Ridpath, 29 Wash. 687, 70 P. 139. This is allowed when a defendant has a cause of action against a co-defendant, or a person not a party to the action, and affecting the subject-matter of the action. The only real difference between a complaint and a cross-complaint is that the first is filed by the plaintiff and the second by the defendant. Both contain a statement of the facts, and each demands affirmative relief upon the facts stated. The difference between a counter-claim and a cross-complaint is that in the former the defendant's cause of action is against the plaintiff; and the latter, against a co-defendant, or one not a party to the action; White v. Reagan, 32 Ark. 290.

In criminal law. A charge, preferred before a magistrate having jurisdiction, that a person named (or an unknown person) has committed a specified offense, with an offer to prove the fact, to the end that a prosecution may be instituted. It is a technical term, descriptive of proceedings before a magistrate. Hobbs v. Hill, 157 Mass. 556, 32 N.E. 862; In some instances "complaint" is interchangeable with "information." State v. Stafford, 26 Idaho, 381, 143 P. 528, 530; State v. Ritzler, 17 Ohio App. 394, 395. And is often used interchangeably with "affidavit." Hebebrand v. State, 129 Ohio St. 574, 196 N.E. 412, 415.

COMPLETE, *v.* To finish; accomplish that which one starts out to do. Ries v. Williams, 190 Ky. 596, 228 S.W. 40, 41.

COMPLETE, *adj.* Full; entire; including every item or element of the thing spoken of, without omissions or deficiencies; as, a "complete" copy, record, schedule, or transcript. Bailey v. Martin, 119 Ind. 103, 21 N.E. 346.

Perfect; consummate; not lacking in any element or particular; as in the case of a "complete legal title" to land, which includes the possession, the right of possession, and the right of property. Dingey v. Paxton, 60 Miss. 1054; Ehle v. Quackenboss, 6 Hill N. Y. 537; Versailles Tp. v. Ulm, 152 Pa.Super. 384, 33 A.2d 265, 267.

COMPLETE AND PERMANENT LOSS OF USE OF RIGHT ARM. Inability to use in any gainful activity. Bell & Zoller Mining Co. v. Industrial Commission, 322 Ill. 395, 153 N.E. 580, 582.

COMPLETE DETERMINATION OF CAUSE. Determination of every issue so as to render decree or judgment res judicata. Consolidated Gas Co. of New York v. Newton, D.C.N.Y., 256 F. 238, 244.

COMPLETE FRACTURE OF ARM. Breaking of only one bone in forearm, insufficient. Columbia Mut. Life Assur. Co. v. Penn, 97 So. 673, 133 Miss. 266.

COMPLETE IN ITSELF. Of a legislative act, covering entire subject; not amendatory. Minier v. Burt County, 95 Neb. 473, 145 N.W. 977, 979.

COMPLETE LOSS OF SIGHT. A destruction of ability to perceive, distinguish, and recognize objects to such extent that what remains will not confer any of benefits of sight or vision to practical and useful extent. Mulcahey v. Brotherhood of Ry. Trainmen, 229 Mo.App. 610, 79 S.W.2d 759, 765.

COMPLETE PAYMENT. On a contract, the final payment. Robinson v. U. S., C.C.A.N.Y., 251 F. 461, 466.

COMPLETED. Finished; nothing substantial remaining to be done; state of a thing that has been created, erected, constructed or done substantially according to contract. Fox & Co. v. Roman Catholic Bishop of the Diocese of Baker City, 107 Or. 557, 215 P. 178, 179; Taylor Bros. v. Gill, 259 P. 236, 238, 126 Okl. 293, 54 A.L.R. 979; Bayou Meto Drainage Dist. of Lonoke County v. Ingram, 165 Ark. 318, 264 S.W. 947, 949.

COMPLETED OIL WELL. A well finished or sunk to the depth necessary to find oil, or to such a depth as, in the absence of oil, precludes a probability of finding it at a further depth. Howard v. Hughes, 294 Mich. 533, 293 N.W. 740, 743.

COMPLETION. The finishing or accomplishing in full of something theretofore begun; substantial performance of what one has agreed to do; state in which no essential element is lacking. Flad v. Murphysboro & S. I. R. Co., C.C.A.Ill., 283 F. 386, 390.

COMPLICATED. Consisting of many parts or particulars not easily severable in thought; hard to understand or explain; involved, intricate, confused. Niemes v. Niemes, 97 Ohio St. 145, 119 N.E. 503, 505.

COMPLICATED FRACTURE. One where flesh and ligaments get between parts of broken bones, causing suppuration and preventing union of such parts. Sang v. City of St. Louis, 262 Mo. 454, 171 S.W. 347, 349.

COMPLICE. One who is united with others in an ill design; an associate; a confederate; an accomplice.

COMPLY. To yield, to accommodate, or to adapt oneself to, to act in accordance with. Dragwa v. Federal Labor Union No. 23070, 41 A.2d 32, 36, 136 N.J.Eq. 172.

COMPOS MENTIS. Sound of mind. Having use and control of one's mental faculties.

COMPOS SUI. Having the use of one's limbs, or the power of bodily motion. *Si fuit ita compos sui quod itinerare potuit de loco in locum,* if he had so far the use of his limbs as to be able to travel from place to place. Bract. fol. 14*b*.

COMPOSED OF. Formed of; consisting of. Hoskins Mfg. Co. v. General Electric Co., D.C.Ill., 212 F. 422, 428.

COMPOSITE WORK. Within Copyright Act means work to which a number of authors have contributed distinguishable parts. Copyright Act of 1909, § 24, 17 U.S.C.A. § 24. Shapiro, Bernstein & Co. v. Bryan, C.C.A.N.Y., 123 F.2d 697, 699.

COMPOSITIO MENSURARUM. The ordinance of measures. The title of an ancient ordinance, not printed, mentioned in the statute 23 Hen. VIII, c. 4; establishing a standard of measures. 1 Bl. Comm. 275.

COMPOSITIO ULNARUM ET PERTICARUM. The statute of ells and perches. The title of an English statute establishing a standard of measures. 1 Bl.Comm. 275.

COMPOSITION. An agreement, made upon a sufficient consideration, between an insolvent or embarrassed debtor and his creditors, whereby the latter, for the sake of immediate or sooner payment, agree to accept a dividend less than the whole amount of their claims, to be distributed *pro rata,* in discharge and satisfaction of the whole. Bank v. McGeoch, 92 Wis. 286, 66 N.W. 606; Pioneer Minerals Corporation v. Larabic Bros. Bankers, 99 Mont. 358, 43 P.2d 884, 886.

"Composition" should be distinguished from "accord." The latter properly denotes an arrangement between a debtor and a single creditor for a discharge of the obligation by a part payment or on different terms. The former designates an arrangement between a debtor and the whole body of his creditors (or at least a considerable proportion of them) for the liquidation of their claims by the dividend offered.

Ancient Law

Among the Franks, Goths, Burgundians, and other barbarous peoples, this was the name given to a sum of money paid, as satisfaction for a wrong or personal injury, to the person harmed, or to his family if he died, by the aggressor. It was originally made by mutual agreement of the parties, but afterwards established by law, and took the place of private physical vengeance.

COMPOSITION CHIPS. In the metal trade, "composition chips" or "turnings" are chips without aluminum. Ehrlich v. United Smelting & Aluminum Co., 252 Mass. 12, 147 N.E. 20.

COMPOSITION DEED. An agreement embodying the terms of a composition between a debtor and his creditors.

COMPOSITION IN BANKRUPTCY. An arrangement between a bankrupt and his creditors, whereby the amount he can be expected to pay is liquidated, and he is allowed to retain his assets, upon condition of his making the payments agreed upon. Fisher Supply Co. v. Northwestern Gravel Co., 216 Iowa 909, 249 N.W. 664, 666, 667.

The difference between a common-law "composition with creditors" and a "composition in bankruptcy" is that in a composition with creditors the creditors voluntarily release the principal debtor and therefore release co-debtors, while in the case of a bankruptcy composition the discharge is by operation of law and not by act of the creditors who assent to the composition. Barker v. Ackers, 29 Cal.App.2d 162, 84 P.2d 264, 271.

COMPOSITION OF MATTER. In patent law, a substance composed of two or more different substances, without regard to form. A mixture or chemical combination of materials. Jacobs v. Baker, 7 Wall. 295, 19 L.Ed. 200.

COMPOSITION OF TITHES, OR REAL COMPOSITION. This arises in English ecclesiastical law, when an agreement is made between the owner of lands and the incumbent of a benefice, with the consent of the ordinary and the patron, that the lands shall, for the future, be discharged from payment of tithes, by reason of some land or other real recompense given in lieu and satisfaction thereof. 2 Bl.Comm. 28; 3 Steph.Comm. 129.

COMPOTARIUS. In old English law. A party accounting. Fleta, lib. 2, c. 71, § 17.

COMPOUND, *v.* To compromise; to effect a composition with a creditor; to obtain discharge from a debt by the payment of a smaller sum. Bank v. Malheur County, 45 P. 781, 30 Or. 420, 35 L.R.A. 141. To put together as elements, ingredients, or parts, to form a whole, to combine, to unite; to form or make up as a composite product by combining different elements, ingredients, or parts, as to combine a medicine. Department of Treasury of Indiana v. Ridgely, 211 Ind. 9, 4 N.E.2d 557, 561, 108 A.L.R. 1067.

COMPOUND, *n.* A combination of two or more elements or things by means of human agency; an artificial or synthetic product. Monticelli Bros. v. U. S., 8 Ct.Cust.App. 21, 24.

COMPOUND INTEREST. Interest upon interest, *i. e.,* when the interest of a sum of money is added to the principal, and then bears interest, which thus becomes a sort of secondary principal. Camp v. Bates, 11 Conn. 487; Woods v. Rankin, 2 Heisk. (Tenn.) 46; U. S. Mortg. Co. v. Sperry, C. C.Ill., 26 F. 730; American Brake Shoe & Foundry Co. v. Interborough Rapid Transit Co., D.C.N.Y., 26 F.Supp. 954, 955.

COMPOUND LARCENY. See Larceny.

COMPOUNDER. In Louisiana. The maker of a composition, generally called the "amicable compounder."

COMPOUNDING A FELONY. The offense committed by a person who, having been directly injured by a felony, agrees with the criminal that he will not prosecute him, on condition of the latter's making reparation, or on receipt of a reward or bribe not to prosecute.

The offense of taking a reward for forbearing to prosecute a felony; as where a party robbed takes his goods again, or other amends, upon an agreement not to prosecute. Rieman v. Morrison, 106 N.E. 215, 217, 264 Ill. 279.

COMPRA Y VENTA. In Spanish law. Purchase and sale.

COMPREMESSO. In Italian. The instrument whereby parties agree to submit to arbitration a dispute between them. The equivalent of "compromissum" under the Roman Law, the principles of which have been carried into the common law and are to be found in agreements of accord and satisfaction and compromise and settlement. Castelli v. Tolibia, 83 N.Y.S.2d 554, 562.

COMPRINT. A surreptitious printing of another book-seller's copy of a work, to make gain thereby, which was contrary to common law, and is illegal. Wharton.

COMPRISE. To comprehend; include; contain; embrace; cover. Hoskins Mfg. Co. v. General Electric Co., D.C.Ill., 212 F. 422, 428.

COMPRIVIGNI. In the civil law. Children by a former marriage, (individually called *"privigni,"* or *"privignœ"*) considered relatively to each other.

Thus, the son of a husband by a former wife, and the daughter of a wife by a former husband, are the *comprivigni* of each other. Inst. 1, 10, 8.

COMPROMISE. An arrangement arrived at, either in court or out of court, for settling a dispute upon what appears to the parties to be equitable terms, having regard to the uncertainty they are in regarding the facts, or the law and the facts together. Colburn v. Groton, 66 N.H. 151, 28 A. 95, 22 L.R.A. 763; Isaacs v. Wishnick, 136 Minn. 317, 162 N.W. 297; Joyner v. City of Seattle, 144 Wash. 641, 258 P. 479, 481. A settlement of differences by mutual concessions or an adjustment of matters in dispute by mutual concessions. Forker v. Berkes, 111 Ind.App. 92, 38 N.E.2d 296, 299; In re Cusimano's Will, 22 N.Y.S.2d 677, 680, 681, 174 Misc. 1068.

It is essential to a compromise that there be mutual concessions or yielding of opposing claims. Scott v. Scott, 131 Okl. 144, 268 P. 245, 248; Hutson v. McConnell, 139 Okl. 240, 281 P. 760, 763.

In the civil law. An agreement whereby two or more persons mutually bind themselves to refer their legal dispute to the decision of a designated third person, who is termed "umpire" or "arbitrator." Dig. 4, 8; Mackeld. Rom. Law, § 471.

OFFER OF COMPROMISE. See Offer, *n.*

COMPROMISE VERDICT. One which is reached only by the surrender of conscientious convictions on one material issue by some jurors in return for a relinquishment of matters in their like settled opinion on another issue, and the result is one which does not hold the approval of the entire panel. North British & Mercantile Ins. Co. v. Parnell, 53 Ga.App. 178, 185 S.E. 122, 126.

COMPROMISSARII SUNT JUDICES. Jenk. Cent. 128. Arbitrators are judges.

COMPROMISSARIUS. In the civil law. An arbitrator.

COMPROMISSUM. A submission to arbitration.

COMPROMISSUM AD SIMILITUDINEM JUDICIORUM REDIGITUR. A compromise is brought into affinity with judgments. Strong v. Strong, 9 Cush. (Mass.) 571.

COMPTE ARRÊTÉ. Fr. An account stated in writing, and acknowledged to be correct on its face by the party against whom it is stated. Paschal v. Union Bank of Louisiana, 9 La.Ann. 484.

COMPTER. In Scotch law. An accounting party.

COMPTROLLER. A public officer of a state or municipal corporation, charged with certain duties in relation to the fiscal affairs of the same, principally to examine and audit the accounts of collectors of the public money, to keep records, and report the financial situation from time to time. There are also officers bearing this name in the treasury department of the United States. Beneficial Loan Soc. of New Orleans v. Straus, La. App., 148 So. 85, 87.

Comptroller in bankruptcy. An officer in England, whose duty it is to receive from the trustee in each bankruptcy his accounts and periodical statements showing the proceedings in the bankruptcy, and also to call the trustee to account for any misfeasance, neglect, or omission in the discharge of his duties. Robs.Bankr. 13; Bankr.Act 1869, § 55.

Comptrollers of the Hanaper. In English law. Officers of the court of chancery; their offices were abolished by 5 & 6 Vict. c. 103.

State comptroller. A supervising officer of revenue in a state government, whose principal duty is the final auditing and settling of all claims against the state. State v. Doron, 5 Nev. 413.

COMPULSA. A judicially attested copy of a testimonio. State v. Balli, Tex.Civ.App., 173 S.W.2d 522, 527.

COMPULSION. Constraint; objective necessity; duress. Forcible inducement to the commission of an act. Navigation Co. v. Brown, 100 Pa. 346. The act of compelling or the state of being compelled; the act of driving or urging by force or by physical or moral constraint; subjection to force. Fluharty v. Fluharty, Del.Super., 193 A. 838, 840.

The "compulsion" which will excuse a criminal act must be present, imminent and impending and of such a nature as to induce a well-grounded apprehension of death or serious bodily harm. Browning v. State, 31 Ala.App. 137, 13 So.2d 54, 56.

To constitute "compulsion" or "coercion" rendering payment involuntary, there must be some actual or threatened exercise of power possessed, or supposedly possessed, by payee over payer's person or property, from which payer has no means of immediate relief except by advancing money. Wake Development Co. v. O'Leary, 118 Cal.App. 131, 4 P.2d 802, 803.

COMPULSORY, *n.* In ecclesiastical procedure, a compulsory is a kind of writ to compel the attendance of a witness, to undergo examination. Phillim. Ecc. Law, 1258.

COMPULSORY, *adj.* Involuntary; forced; coerced by legal process or by force of statute.

COMPULSORY ARBITRATION. That which takes place where the consent of one of the parties is enforced by statutory provisions. Wood v. Seattle, 62 P. 135, 23 Wash. 1, 52 L.R.A. 369.

COMPULSORY NONSUIT. An involuntary nonsuit. See Nonsuit.

COMPULSORY PAYMENT. One not made voluntarily, but exacted by duress, threats, the enforcement of legal process, or unconscionably taking advantage of another. Singer Sewing Mach. Co. v. Teasley, 73 So. 969, 971, 198 Ala. 673.

COMPULSORY PROCESS. Process to compel the attendance in court of a person wanted there as a witness or otherwise; including not only the ordinary subpœna, but also a warrant of arrest or attachment if needed. State v. Nathaniel, 52 La.Ann. 558, 26 So. 1008.

It means such coercive means as the courts, by virtue of their inherent powers or sanction of the law, are permitted to employ, Greene v. Ballard, 174 Ky. 808, 192 S.W. 841, 845; and includes right to have subpœna served, as well as issued (Const. § 11). Fugate v. Commonwealth, 202 Ky. 509, 260 S.W. 338, 340.

COMPULSORY SALE OR PURCHASE. A term sometimes used to characterize the transfer of title to property under the exercise of the power of eminent domain. In re Barre Water Co., 62 Vt. 27, 20 A. 109, 9 L.R.A. 195; United States v. Certain Parcels of Land in City of San Diego, San Diego County, D.C.Cal., 44 F.Supp. 936, 937.

COMPURGATOR. One of several neighbors of a person accused of a crime, or charged as a defendant in a civil action, who appeared and swore that they believed him on his oath. 3 Bl.Comm. 341.

COMPUTING SCALE. A balance having an indicator apparatus so arranged that, within the limits of weights and prices for which it is contrived, one glance at a printed card, which is a part thereof, shows not only the weight of the article, but its price at a given rate per pound. Standard Computing Scale Co. v. Farrell, D.C.N.Y., 242 F. 87.

COMPUTO. Lat. To compute, reckon, or account. Used in the phrases *insimul computassent*, "they reckoned together," (see Insimul;) *plene computavit*, "he has fully accounted," (see Plene;) *quod computet*, "that he account," (see Quod Computet.)

COMPUTATION. The act of computing, numbering, reckoning, or estimating. The account or estimation of time by rule of law, as distinguished from any arbitrary construction of the parties. Cowell.

COMPUTUS. A writ to compel a guardian, bailiff, receiver, or accountant to yield up his accounts. It is founded on the statute Westm. 2, c. 12; Reg. Orig. 135.

COMTE. Fr. A count or earl. In the ancient French law, the *comte* was an officer having jurisdiction over a particular district or territory, with functions partly military and partly judicial.

CON. *Adj.* A slang or cant abbreviation for confidence, as a *con* man or a *con* game. Webster.

CON. *Prep.* With. Calef v. Calef, 54 Me. 365, 92 Am.Dec. 549.

CON-. A prefix meaning with, together. Webster.

CON BUENA FE. In Spanish law. With (or in) good faith.

CONACRE. In Irish practice. The payment of wages in land, the rent being worked out in labor at a money valuation. Wharton.

CONATUS QUID SIT, NON DEFINITUR IN JURE. 2 Bulst. 277. What an attempt is, is not defined in law.

CONCEAL. To hide; secrete; withhold from the knowledge of others; to withdraw from observation; to withhold from utterance or declaration; to cover or keep from sight. Hopper v. Hopkins, 162 Md. 448, 160 A. 166, 167.

The synonyms of conceal are "to hide; disguise, dissemble; secrete." To hide is generic; "conceal" is simply not to make known what we wish to secrete; disguise or dissemble is to conceal by assuming some false appearance; to secrete is to hide in some place of secrecy. A man may conceal facts, disguise his sentiments, dissemble his feelings, or secrete stolen goods. Darneal v. State, 14 Okl.Cr. 540, 174 P. 290, 292, 1 A.L.R. 638.

The word "conceal," according to the best lexicographers, signifies to withhold or keep secret mental facts from another's knowledge, as well as to hide or secrete physical objects from sight or observation. Gerry v. Dunham, 57 Me. 339.

CONCEALED. Not synonymous with "lying in wait." If a person conceals himself for the purpose of shooting another unawares, he is lying in wait; but a person may, while concealed, shoot another without committing the crime of murder. People v. Miles, 55 Cal. 207.

The term "concealed weapons" means weapons willfully or knowingly covered or kept from sight. Owen v. State, 31 Ala. 387.

CONCEALERS. In old English law. Such as find out concealed lands; that is, lands privily kept from the king by common persons having nothing to show for them. They are called "a troublesome, disturbant sort of men; turbulent persons." Cowell.

CONCEALMENT. A withholding of something which one knows and which one, in duty, is bound to reveal. Dolcater v. Manufacturers & Traders Trust Co., D.C.N.Y., 25 F.Supp. 637, 641; Strauss v. Dubuque Fire & Marine Ins. Co. of Dubuque, Iowa, 132 Cal.App. 283, 22 P.2d 582.

The terms "misrepresentation" and "concealment" have a known and definite meaning in the law of insurance. Misrepresentation is the statement of something as fact which is untrue in fact, and which the assured states, knowing it to be not true, with an intent to deceive the underwriter, or which he states positively as true, without knowing it to be true, and which has a tendency to mislead, such fact in either case being material to the risk. Concealment is the designed and intentional withholding of any fact material to the risk, which the assured, in honesty and good faith, ought to communicate to the underwriter; mere silence on the part of the assured, especially as to some matter of fact which he does not consider it important for the underwriter to know, is not to be considered as such concealment. If the fact so untruly stated or purposely suppressed is not material, that is, if the knowledge or ignorance of it would not naturally influence the judgment of the underwriter in making the contract, or in estimating the degree and character of the risk, or in fixing the rate of the premium, it is not a "misrepresentation" or "concealment," within the clause of the conditions annexed to policies. Daniels v. Insurance Co., 12 Cush. (Mass.). 416, 59 Am.Dec. 192; Sun Ins. Office, Limited, of London v. Mallick, 160 Md. 71, 153 A. 35, 43.

CONCEALMENT MAY BE BASIS OF ESTOPPEL. Lo Bue v. Porazzo, 48 Cal.App.2d 82, 119 P.2d 346, 348. Elements of such estoppel are concealment of material facts with knowledge thereof, ignorance thereof on part of person to whom representations are made, or from whom facts are concealed, intention that such person shall act thereon, and action induced thereby on his part. Rhoads v. Rhoads, Mo., 119 S.W.2d 247, 252; Rosser v. Texas Co., 173 Okl. 309, 48 P. 2d 327, 330.

The doctrine of "estoppel by concealment and suppression" applies only where there has been reduction to practice of invention. Bogoslowsky v. Huse, 142 F.2d 75, 76, 31 C.C.P.A.(Patents) 1034.

CONCEALMENT OF CAUSE OF ACTION. To constitute it so as to prevent running of limitations, some trick or artifice must be employed to prevent inquiry or elude investigation, or to mislead and hinder party who has a cause of action from obtaining information, and acts relied on must be of an affirmative character and fraudulent. Middleton v. Pruden, 57 Ga.App. 555, 196 S.E. 259, 262.

CONCEDER. Fr. In French law. To grant. See Concession.

CONCEDO. Lat. I grant. A word used in old Anglo-Saxon grants, and in statutes merchant.

CONCEPTION. The beginning of pregnancy, (*q. v.*).

CONCEPTUM. In the civil law. A theft *(furtum)* was called *"conceptum,"* when the thing stolen was searched for, and found upon some person in the presence of witnesses. Inst. 4, 1, 4.

CONCERN. To pertain, relate, or belong to; be of interest or importance to; have connection with; to have reference to; to involve; to affect the interest of. People v. Photocolor Corporation, 281 N.Y.S. 130, 156 Misc. 47.

CONCERNING, CONCERNED. Relating to; pertaining to; affecting; involving; being substantially engaged in or taking part in. U. S. v. Fulkerson, D.C.Cal., 74 F. 631; May v. Brown, 3 Barn. & C. 137; People v. Marty, 59 Cal.App. 503, 210 P. 964, 965.

CONCERT OF EUROPE. The union between the chief powers of Europe for purposes of concerted action in matters affecting their mutual interests. It is sometimes called the *Primacy of the Great Powers.* It has existed under various forms from the time of the Congress of Vienna, in 1815.

CONCERT-ROOM. A place in which musical, as distinguished from dramatic, performances are usually given. People ex rel. McShane v. Keller, 161 N.Y.S. 132, 138, 96 Misc. 92.

CONCERTED ACTION (or PLAN). Action that has been planned, arranged, adjusted, agreed on and settled between parties acting together pursuant to some design or scheme. State v. Jessup & Moore Paper Co., 4 Boyce (Del.) 248, 88 A. 449, 451; Rock Creek Oil Corporation v. Moore, Tex. Civ.App., 41 S.W.2d 501, 504.

CONCESSI. Lat. I have granted. At common law, in a feoffment or estate of inheritance, this word does not imply a warranty; it only creates a covenant in a lease for years. Co.Litt. 384*a*. Koch v. Hustis, 113 Wis. 599, 87 N.W. 834; Vaughan's Argument in Vaughan 126; Butler's note, Co. Litt. 384. But see 1 Freem. 339, 414.

CONCESSIMUS. Lat. We have granted. A term used in conveyances, the effect of which was to create a joint covenant on the part of the grantors. 5 Co. 16; Bacon, Abr. *Covenant.*

CONCESSIO. In old English law. A grant. One of the old common assurances, or forms of conveyance.

CONCESSIO PER REGEM FIERI DEBET DE CERTITUDINE. 9 Coke, 46. A grant by the king ought to be made from certainty.

CONCESSIO VERSUS CONCEDENTEM LATAM INTERPRETATIONEM HABERE DEBET. A grant ought to have a broad interpretation (to be liberally interpreted) against the grantor. Jenk. Cent. 279.

CONCESSION. A grant; ordinarily applied to the grant of specific privileges by a government; French and Spanish grants in Louisiana. Western M. & M. Co. v. Peytona Coal Co., 8 W.Va. 446. A voluntary grant, or a yielding to a claim or demand; rebate; abatement. U. S. v. P. Koenig Coal Co., D.C.Mich., 1 F.2d 738, 740; Williams v. Belvedere Hotel Co., 137 Md. 665, 113 A. 335, 337, 14 A.L.R. 622.

CONCESSIT SOLVERE. He granted and agreed to pay. In English law. An action of debt upon a simple contract. It lies by custom in the mayor's court, London, and Bristol city court.

CONCESSOR. In old English law. A grantor.

CONCESSUM. Accorded; conceded. This term, frequently used in the old reports, signifies that the court admitted or assented to a point or proposition made on the argument.

CONCESSUS. A grantee.

CONCILIABULUM. A council house.

CONCILIATION. In French law. The formality to which intending litigants are subjected in cases brought before the *juge de paix.* The judge convenes the parties and endeavors to reconcile them. Should he not succeed, the case proceeds. In criminal and commercial cases, the preliminary of conciliation does not take place. Arg. Fr. Merc. Law, 552.

CONCILIUM. Lat. A council.

Roman Law

A meeting of a section of the people to consider and decide matters especially affecting itself. Launspach, State and Family in Early Rome 70. Also argument in a cause, or the sitting of the court to hear argument; a motion for a day for the argument of a cause; a day allowed to a defendant to present his argument; an imparlance. State ex rel. Stueve v. Reynolds, 266 Mo. 12, 178 S.W. 468, 470.

CONCILIUM ORDINARIUM. In Anglo-Norman times. An executive and residuary judicial committee of the *Aula Regis, (q. v.)*.

CONCILIUM REGIS. An ancient English tribunal existing during the reigns of Edward I. and Edward II., to which was referred cases of extraordinary difficulty. Co.Litt. 304.

CONCIONATOR. In old records. A common council man; a freeman called to a legislative hall or assembly. Cowell.

CONCLUDE. To finish; determine; to estop; to prevent.

CONCLUDED. Ended; determined; estopped; prevented from.

CONCLUSION. The end; the termination; the act of finishing or bringing to a close. The conclusion of a declaration or complaint is all that part which follows the statement of the plaintiff's cause of action. The conclusion of a plea is its final clause, in which the defendant either "puts himself upon the country" (where a material averment of the declaration is traversed and issue tendered) or offers a verification, which is proper where new matter is introduced. State v. Waters, 1 Mo.App. 7.

Trial Practice

It signifies making the final or concluding address to the jury or the court. The act of a man by which he has confessed a matter or thing which he can no longer deny.

This is, in general, the privilege of the party who has to sustain the burden of proof.

CONCLUSION AGAINST THE FORM OF THE STATUTE. The proper form for the conclusion of an indictment for an offense created by statute is the technical phrase "against the form of the statute in such case made and provided;" or, in Latin, *contra formam statuti.*

CONCLUSION OF FACT. An inference drawn from the subordinate or evidentiary facts. Maeder Steel Products Co. v. Zanello, 109 Or. 562, 220 P. 155, 158. Reed v. Woodmen of the World, 94 Mont. 374, 22 P.2d 819, 822.

CONCLUSION OF LAW. Within the rule that pleadings should contain only facts, and not conclusions of law, this means a proposition not arrived at by any process of natural reasoning from a fact or combination of facts stated, but by the application of the artificial rules of law to the facts pleaded. Levins v. Rovegno, 71 Cal. 273, 12 P. 161.

CONCLUSION TO THE COUNTRY. In pleading. The tender of an issue to be tried by jury. Co. Litt. 126 *a*; 1 Saund. 103; 1 Chit. Pl. 592; Com. Dig. *Pleader,* E, 32.

CONCLUSIVE. Shutting up a matter; shutting out all further evidence; not admitting of explanation or contradiction; putting an end to inquiry; final; irrefutable; decisive. Edwards v. Shreveport Creosoting Co., 207 La. 699, 21 So.2d 878. Beyond question or beyond dispute; manifest; plain; clear; obvious; visible; apparent; indubitable; palpable; and "notorious." Covington County v. Fite, 120 Miss. 421, 82 So. 308, 309.

As to conclusive "Presumption," and "Proof," see those titles.

CONCLUSIVE EVIDENCE. That which is incontrovertible, either because the law does not permit it to be contradicted, or because it is so strong and convincing as to overbear all proof to the contrary and establish the proposition in question beyond any reasonable doubt. Thompson Lumber Co. v. Interstate Commerce Commission (Com.Ct.) 193 F. 648, 682.

CONCORD. In the old process of levying a fine of lands, the concord was an agreement between the parties (real or feigned) in which the deforciant (or he who keeps the other out of possession) acknowledges that the lands in question are the right of complainant; and, from the acknowledgment or admission of right thus made, the party who levies the fine is called the "cognizor," and the person to whom it is levied the "cognizee." 2 Bl.Comm. 350.

The term also denotes an agreement between two persons, one of whom has a right of action against the other, settling what amends shall be made for the breach or wrong; a compromise or an accord.

Old Practice

An agreement between two or more, upon a trespass committed, by way of amends or satisfaction for it. Plowd. 5, 6, 8.

CONCORDARE LEGES LEGIBUS EST OPTIMUS INTERPRETANDI MODUS. To make laws agree with laws is the best mode of interpreting them. Halk. Max. 70.

CONCORDAT. In public law. A compact or convention between two or more independent governments.

An agreement made by a temporal sovereign with the pope, relative to ecclesiastical matters.

In French law. A compromise effected by a bankrupt with his creditors, by virtue of which he engages to pay within a certain time a certain proportion of his debts, and by which the creditors agree to discharge the whole of their claims in consideration of the same. Arg. Fr. Merc. Law, 553.

CONCORDIA. Lat. In old English law. An agreement, or concord. Fleta, lib. 5, c. 3, § 5. The agreement or unanimity of a jury. *Compellere ad concordiam.* Fleta, lib. 4, c. 9, § 2.

CONCORDIA DISCORDANTIUM CANONUM. The harmony of the discordant canons. A collection of ecclesiastical constitutions made by

Gratian, an Italian monk, A.D. 1151; more commonly known by the name of "*Decretum Gratiani.*"

CONCORDIA PARVÆ RES CRESCUNT ET OPULENTIA LITES. 4 Inst. 74. Small means increase by concord and litigations by opulence.

CONCUBARIA. A fold, pen, or place where cattle lie. Cowell.

CONCUBEANT. Lying together, as cattle.

CONCUBINAGE. A species of loose or informal marriage which took place among the ancients, and is yet in use in some countries. See Concubinatus.

The act or practice of cohabiting, in sexual commerce, without the authority of law or a legal marriage. Succession of Lannes, 187 La. 17, 174 So. 94, 98.

The words *concubinage* and *prostitution* have no common law meaning, but in their popular sense cover all cases of lewd intercourse; People v. Cummons, 56 Mich. 544, 23 N.W. 215.

An exception against a woman suing for dower, on the ground that she was the concubine, and not the wife, of the man of whose land she seeks to be endowed. Britt. c. 107.

CONCUBINATUS. In Roman law. An informal, unsanctioned, or "natural" marriage, as contradistinguished from the *justæ nuptiæ,* or *justum matrimonium,* the civil marriage.

CONCUBINE. (1) A woman who cohabits with a man to whom she is not married. State v. Dusin, 125 Kan. 400, 264 P. 1043, 1044. (2) A sort of inferior wife, among the Romans, upon whom the husband did not confer his rank or quality.

CONCUR. To agree; accord; act together; consent. In the practice of appellate courts, a "concurring opinion" is one filed by one of the judges or justices, in which he agrees with the conclusions or the result of another opinion filed in the case (which may be either the opinion of the court or a dissenting opinion) though he states separately his views of the case or his reasons for so concurring. State v. Pierce, 175 Wash. 461, 27 P.2d 1083.

In Louisiana law. To join with other claimants in presenting a demand against an insolvent estate.

CONCURATOR. In the civil law. A joint or co-curator, or guardian.

CONCURRENCE. In French law. The possession, by two or more persons, of equal rights or privileges over the same subject-matter.

CONCURRENCE DELOYALE. A term of the French law nearly equivalent to "unfair trade competition;" and used in relation to the infringement of rights secured by trade-marks, etc. It signifies a dishonest, perfidious, or treacherous rivalry in trade, or any manœuvre calculated to prejudice the good will of a business or the value of the name of a property or its credit or renown with the public, to the injury of a business competitor. Simmons Medicine Co. v. Mansfield Drug Co., 93 Tenn. 84, 23 S.W. 165.

CONCURRENT. Running together; having the same authority; acting in conjunction; agreeing in the same act or opinion; pursuit of same course; contributing to the same event; contemporaneous. Brinkman v. Morgan, C.C.A.Kan., 253 F. 553, 554. Co-operating, accompanying, conjoined, associated, concomitant, joint and equal, existing together, and operating on the same subject. Rose v. Sprague, 248 Ky. 635, 59 S.W.2d 554, 556. United in agreement. State ex rel. School Dist. No. 8, v. Lensman, 108 Mont. 118, 88 P.2d 63, 68.

As to concurrent "Cause," "Covenants," "Insurance," "Lease," "Negligence," "Resolution," and "Writs," see those titles.

CONCURRENT JURISDICTION. The jurisdiction of several different tribunals, each authorized to deal with the same subject-matter at the choice of the suitor. Cashman v. Vickers, 69 Mont. 516, 223 P. 897, 898.

CONCURRENT LIENS. Maritime liens are concurrent when they are of the same rank, and for supplies or materials or services in preparation for the same voyage, or if they arise on different bottomry bonds to different holders for advances at the same time for the same repairs. The J. W. Tucker, D.C.N.Y., 20 F. 132.

CONCURRENT POWER. Political powers exercised independently in the same field of legislation by both federal and state governments. State ex rel. School Dist. No. 8, v. Lensman, 108 Mont. 118, 88 P.2d 63, 68.

CONCURSO. In the law of Louisiana, the name of a suit or remedy to enable creditors to enforce their claims against an insolvent or failing debtor. Schroeder v. Nicholson, 2 La. 355. Litigation or opportunity of litigation between various creditors, each claiming adversely to one another to share in a fund or an estate, object being to assemble in one accounting all claimants on the fund. Seal v. Gano, 160 La. 636, 107 So. 473, 474.

CONCURSUS. In the civil law. (1) A running together; a collision, as *concursus creditorum,* a conflict among creditors. Graphic Arts Bldg. Co. v. Union Indemnity Co., 163 La. 1, 111 So. 470, 471; Miller v. Bonner, 163 La. 332, 111 So. 776, 778; (2) A concurrence, or meeting, as *concursus actionum,* concurrence of actions.

A proceeding in Louisiana similar to interpleader. See Louisiana Molasses Co. v. Le Sassier, 52 La.Ann. 2070, 28 So. 217.

CONCUSS. In Scotch law. To coerce.

CONCUSSIO. In the civil law. The offense of extortion by threats of violence. Dig. 47, 13.

CONCUSSION. In the civil law. The unlawful forcing of another by threats of violence to give something of value. It differs from robbery, in this: That in robbery the thing is taken by force, while in concussion it is obtained by threatened violence. Heinec.Elem. § 1071.

In medical jurisprudence. Concussion of the brain is a jarring of the brain substance, by a fall, blow, or other external injury, without laceration of its tissue, or with only microscopical laceration. Mathews v. Hayne, La.App., 188 So. 462, 468.

CONDEDIT. In ecclesiastical law. The name of a plea entered by a party to a libel filed in the ecclesiastical court, in which it is pleaded that the deceased made the will which is the subject of the suit, and that he was of sound mind. 2 Eng. Ecc. R. 438; 6 Eng. Ecc. R. 431.

CONDEMN. To find or adjudge guilty. 3 Leon. 68. To adjudge or sentence. 3 Bl.Comm. 291. To adjudge (as an admiralty court) that a vessel is a prize, or that she is unfit for service. 1 Kent, Comm. 102; 5 Esp. 65. To set apart or expropriate property for public use, in the exercise of the power of eminent domain. State v. Sayer, 43 S.D. 45, 177 N.W. 807, 809.

CONDEMNATION. In admiralty law. The judgment or sentence of a court having jurisdiction and acting *in rem,* by which (1) it is declared that a vessel which has been captured at sea as a prize was lawfully so seized and is liable to be treated as prize; or (2) that property which has been seized for an alleged violation of the revenue laws, neutrality laws, navigation laws, etc., was lawfully so seized, and is, for such cause, forfeited to the government; or (3) that the vessel which is the subject of inquiry is unfit and unsafe for navigation. Gallagher v. Murray, 9 Fed.Cas. 1087.

In the civil law. A sentence or judgment which condemns some one to do, to give, or to pay something, or which declares that his claim or pretensions are unfounded. Lockwood v. Saffold, 1 Ga. 72; State v. Harr, 24 Tenn.App. 298, 143 S.W.2d 893, 895.

In real property law. The process by which property of a private owner is taken for public use, without his consent, but upon the award and payment of just compensation, being in the nature of a forced sale and condemner stands toward owner as buyer toward seller. Atlanta, K. & N. R. Co. v. Southern Ry. Co., C.C.A.Tenn., 131 F. 666, 66 C.C.A. 601; Jones v. Oklahoma City, 192 Okl. 470, 137 P.2d 233, 237, 155 A.L.R. 375.

A "condemnation proceeding" is a special proceeding at law to determine in a single action the damages done by the taking, but it is not a civil action, or a civil process within the meaning of the statutes relating to civil process. In re New Haven Water Co., 86 Conn. 361, 85 A. 636, 638. The law authorizing it must be strictly construed, and every condition and requirement must be shown to have been complied with. Richter v. Rodgers, 327 Mo. 543, 37 S.W.2d 523, 528.

CONDEMNATION MONEY. In practice. The damages which the party failing in an action is adjudged or *condemned* to pay; sometimes simply called the "condemnation."

As used in an appeal bond, this phrase means the damages which should be awarded against the appellant by the judgment of the court. It does not embrace damages not included in the judgment. Thomas v. Gethman, 91 Okl. 42, 215 P. 731, 732.

CONDESCENDENCE. In the Scotch law. A part of the proceedings in a cause, setting forth the facts of the case on the part of the pursuer or plaintiff.

CONDICTIO. In Roman law. A general term for actions of a personal nature, founded upon an obligation to give or do a certain and defined thing or service. It is distinguished from *vindicatio rei,* which is an action to vindicate one's right of property in a thing by regaining (or retaining) possession of it against the adverse claim of the other party.

CONDICTIO CERTI. An action which lies upon a promise to do a thing, where such promise or stipulation is certain, *(si certa sit stipulatio.)* Inst. 3, 16, pr.; Id. 3, 15, pr.; Dig. 12, 1; Bract. fol. 103*b*.

CONDICTIO EX LEGE. An action arising where the law gave a remedy, but provided no appropriate form of action. Calvin.

CONDICTIO INDEBITATI. An action which lay to recover anything which the plaintiff had given or paid to the defendant, by mistake, and which he was not bound to give or pay, either in fact or in law.

CONDICTIO REI FURTIVÆ. An action which lay to recover a thing stolen, against the thief himself, or his heir. Inst. 4, 1, 19.

CONDICTIO SINE CAUSA. An action which lay in favor of a person who had given or promised a thing without consideration, *(causa.)* Dig. 12, 7; Cod. 4, 9.

CONDITIO. Lat. A condition.

CONDITIO BENEFICIALIS, QUÆ STATUM CONSTRUIT, BENIGNE SECUNDUM VERBORUM INTENTIONEM EST INTERPRETANDA; ODIOSA AUTEM, QUÆ STATUM DESTRUIT, STRICTE SECUNDUM BERBORUM PROPRIETATEM ACCIPIENDA. 8 Coke, 90. A beneficial condition, which creates an estate, ought to be construed favorably, according to the intention of the words; but a condition which destroys an estate is odious, and ought to be construed strictly according to the letter of the words.

CONDITIO DICITUR, CUM QUID IN CASUM INCERTUM QUI POTEST TENDERE AD ESSE AUT NON ESSE, CONFERTUR. Co. Litt. 201. It is called a "condition," when something is given on an uncertain event, which may or may not come into existence.

CONDITIO ILLICITA HABETUR PRO NON ADJECTÂ. An unlawful condition is deemed as not annexed.

CONDITIO PRÆCEDENS ADIMPLERI DEBET PRIUS QUAM SEQUATUR EFFECTUS. Co. Litt. 201. A condition precedent must be fulfilled before the effect can follow.

CONDITION. A future and uncertain event upon the happening of which is made to depend the existence of an obligation, or that which subordinates the existence of liability under a contract to a certain future event. Standard Surety & Casualty Co. v. Wynn, Tex.Civ.App., 172 S.W.2d 789, 792; Barber Asphalt Paving Co. v. St. Louis Cypress Co., 121 La. 152, 46 So. 193, 197.

Civil Law

The rank, situation, or degree of a particular person in some one of the different orders of society.

An agreement or stipulation in regard to some uncertain future event, not of the essential nature of the transaction, but annexed to it by the parties, providing for a change or modification of their legal relations upon its occurrence. Mackeld. Rom. Law, § 184.

Classification. Conditions are of the following several kinds:

The *casual* condition is that which depends on chance, and is in no way in the power either of the creditor or of the debtor. Civ.Code La. art. 2023.

A *mixed* condition is one that depends at the same time on the will of one of the parties and on the will of a third person, or on the will of one of the parties and also on a casual event. Civ.Code La. art. 2025.

The *potestative* condition is that which makes the execution of the agreement depend on an event which it is in the power of the one or the other of the contracting parties to bring about or to hinder. Civ.Code La. art. 2024.

A *resolutory* or *dissolving* condition is that which, when accomplished, operates the revocation of the obligation, placing matters in the same state as though the obligation had not existed. It does not suspend the execution of the obligation. It only obliges the creditor to restore what he has received in case the event provided for in the condition takes place. Civ.Code La. art. 2045; Moss v. Smoker, 2 La.Ann. 991.

A *suspensive* condition is that which depends, either on a future and uncertain event, or on an event which has actually taken place, without its being yet known to the parties. In the former case, the obligation cannot be executed till after the event; in the latter, the obligation has its effect from the day on which it was contracted, but it cannot be enforced until the event be known. Civ.Code La. art. 2043; New Orleans v. Railroad Co., 18 S.Ct. 875, 171 U.S. 312, 43 L.Ed. 178; Moss v. Smoker, 2 La.Ann. 991. A condition which prevents a contract from going into operation until it has been fulfilled.

Common Law

The rank, situation, or degree of a particular person in some one of the different orders of society; or his *status* or situation, considered as a juridical person, arising from positive law or the institutions of society. Thill v. Pohlman, 76 Iowa, 638, 41 N.W. 385.

A clause in a contract or agreement which has for its object to suspend, rescind, or modify the principal obligation, or, in case of a will, to suspend, revoke, or modify the devise or bequest; a qualification, restriction, or limitation modifying or destroying the original act with which it is connected; an event, fact, or the like that is necessary to the occurrence of some other, though not its cause; a prerequisite. Towle v. Remsen, 70 N.Y. 303.

A *modus* or quality annexed by him that hath an estate, or interest or right to the same, whereby an estate, etc., may either be defeated, enlarged, or created upon an uncertain event. Co.Litt. 201*a*.

A qualification or restriction annexed to a conveyance of lands, whereby it is provided that in case a particular event does or does not happen, or in case the grantor or grantee does or omits to do a particular act, an estate shall commence, be enlarged, or be defeated. Anderson v. Palladine, 39 Cal.App. 256, 178 P. 553, 554.

An "estate on condition" arises where an estate is granted, either in fee simple or otherwise, with an express qualification annexed, whereby the estate granted shall either commence, be enlarged, or be defeated, upon performance or breach of such qualification or condition. Hall v. Quinn, 190 N.C. 326, 130 S.E. 18, 20. Moe v. Gier, 116 Cal.App. 403, 2 P.2d 852, 855.

In insurance parlance, the printed conditions on the inside of the policy which serve generally as a limitation of risk or of liability or impose various conditions requiring compliance by the insured. Federal Intermediate Credit Bank of Baltimore v. Globe & Rutgers Fire Ins. Co., D.C. Md., 7 F.Supp. 56, 68.

Mode or state of being; state or situation; essential quality; property; attribute. Consolidated Arizona Smelting Co. v. Egich, 22 Ariz. 543, 199 P. 132, 134.

Classification. The different kinds of conditions known to the common law may be arranged and described as follows:

Express and implied conditions are also called by the older writers, respectively, *conditions in deed* (or in fact, the Law French term being *conditions en fait*) and *conditions in law*. Co. Litt. 201*a*.

They are either *express* or *implied*, the former when incorporated in express terms in the deed, contract, lease, or grant; the latter, when inferred or presumed by law, from the nature of the transaction or the conduct of the parties, to have been tacitly understood between them as a part of the agreement, though not expressly mentioned. 2 Crabb, Real Prop. p. 792; Bract. fol. 47; Civ.Code La. art. 2026; Raley v. Umatilla County, 15 Or. 172, 13 P. 890, 3 Am.St.Rep. 142.

They are *possible* or *impossible;* the former when they admit of performance in the ordinary course of events; the latter when it is contrary to the course of nature or human limitations that they should ever be performed.

They are *lawful* or *unlawful*; the former when their character is not in violation of any rule, principle, or policy of law; the latter when they are such as the law will not allow to be made.

They are *consistent* or *repugnant;* the former when they are in harmony and concord with the other parts of the transaction; the latter when they contradict, annul, or neutralize the main purpose of the contract. Repugnant conditions are also called "insensible."

They are *affirmative* or *negative;* the former being a condition which consists in doing a thing; as provided that the lessee shall pay rent, etc., and the latter being a condition which consists in not doing a thing; as provided that the lessee shall not alien, etc. Shep. Touch. 118.

They are *precedent* or *subsequent.* A condition precedent is one which must happen or be performed before the estate to which it is annexed can vest or be enlarged; or it is one which is to be performed before some right dependent thereon accrues, or some act dependent thereon is performed. Federal Land Bank of Louisville v. Luckenbill, 213 Ind. 616, 13 N.E.2d 531, 533. A "condition precedent" is one that is to be performed before the agreement becomes effective, and which calls for the happening of some event or the performance of some act after the terms of the contract have been agreed on, before the contract shall be binding on the parties. Rogers v. Maloney, 85 Or. 61, 165 P. 357, 358; Mercer-Lincoln Pine Knob Oil Co. v. Pruitt, 191 Ky. 207, 229 S.W. 374. A condition subsequent is one annexed to an estate already vested, by the performance of which such estate is kept and continued, and by the failure or non-performance of which it is defeated; or it is a condition referring to a future event, upon the happening of which the obligation becomes no longer binding upon the other party, if he chooses to avail himself of the condition. Co. Litt. 201; Carroll v. Carroll's Ex'r, 248 Ky. 386, 58 S.W.2d 670, 672.

Conditions may also be *positive* (requiring that a specified event shall happen or an act be done) and *restrictive* or *negative,* the latter being such as impose an obligation not to do a particular thing, as, that a lessee shall not alien or sub-let or commit waste, or the like. Shep. Touch. 118.

They may be *single, copulative,* or *disjunctive.* Those of the first kind require the performance of one specified thing only; those of the second kind require the performance of divers acts or things; those of the third kind require the performance of one of several things. Shep. Touch. 118.

Conditions may also be *independent, dependent,* or *mutual.* They belong to the first class when each of the two conditions must be performed without any reference to the other; to the second class when the performance of one condition is not obligatory until the actual performance of the other; and to the third class when neither party need perform his condition unless the other is ready and willing to perform his, or, in other words, when the mutual covenants go to the whole consideration on both sides and each is precedent to the other. Huggins v. Daley, W.Va., 99 F. 609, 40 C.C.A. 12, 48 L.R.A. 320.

The following varieties may also be noted: A condition *collateral* is one requiring the performance of a collateral act having no necessary relation to the main subject of the agreement. A *compulsory* condition is one which expressly requires a thing to be done, as, that a lessee shall pay a specified sum of money on a certain day or his lease shall be void. Shep. Touch. 118. *Concurrent* conditions are those which are mutually dependent and are to be performed at the same time. Milwaukee Land Co. v. Ruesink, 50 Mont. 489, 148 P. 396, 401. A condition *inherent* is one annexed to the rent reserved out of the land whereof the estate is made, or rather, to the estate in the land, in respect of rent. Shep. Touch. 118.

French Law

The following peculiar distinctions are made: (1) A condition is *casuelle* when it depends on a chance or hazard; (2) a condition is *potestative* when it depends on the accomplishment of something which is in the power of the party to accomplish; (3) a condition is *mixte* when it depends partly on the will of the party and partly on the will of others; (4) a condition is *suspensive* when it is a future and uncertain event, or present but unknown event, upon which an obligation takes or fails to take effect; (5) a condition is *resolutoire* when it is the event which undoes an obligation which has already had effect as such. Brown.

Synonyms Distinguished

A "condition" is to be distinguished from a *limitation,* in that the latter may be to or for the benefit of a stranger, who may then take advantage of its determination, while only the grantor, or those who stand in his place, can take advantage of a condition. Hoselton v. Hoselton, 166 Mo. 182, 65 S.W. 1005; and in that a limitation ends the estate without entry or claim, which is not true of a condition. It also differs from a *conditional limitation.* In determining whether, in the case of estates greater than estates for years, the language constitutes a "condition" or a "conditional limitation," the rule applied is that, where an estate is so expressly limited by the words of its creation that it cannot endure for any longer time than until the condition happens on which the estate is to fail, this is limitation, but when the estate is expressly granted on condition in deed, the law permits it to endure beyond the time of the contingency happening, unless the grantor takes advantage of the breach of condition, by making entry. Lonas v. Silver, 195 N.Y. S. 214, 215, 201 App.Div. 383; Yarbrough v. Yarbrough, 151 Tenn. 221, 269 S.W. 36, 38. It differs also from a *covenant,* which can be made by either grantor or grantee, while only the grantor can make a condition (Co. Litt. 70); De Grasse v. Verona Mining Co., 185 Mich. 514, 152 N.W. 242, 246; The chief distinction between a condition subsequent in a deed and a covenant pertains to the remedy in event of breach, which, in the former case, subjects the estate to a forfeiture, and in the latter is merely a ground for recovery of damages. Bartell v. Senger, 160 Md. 685, 155 A. 174, 176. A *charge* is a devise of land with a bequest out of the subject-matter, and a charge upon the devisee personally, in respect of the estate devised, gives him an estate on condition. A condition also differs from a *remainder;* for, while the former may operate to defeat the estate before its natural termination, the latter cannot take effect until the completion of the preceding estate.

CONDITIONAL. That which is dependent upon or granted subject to a condition.

As to conditional "Acceptance," "Appearance," "Bequest," "Contract," "Delivery," "Devise," "Fee," "Guaranty," "Judgment," "Legacy," "Limitation," "Obligation," "Pardon," "Privilege," and "Sale," see those titles.

CONDITIONAL CREDITOR. In the civil law. A creditor having a future right of action, or having a right of action in expectancy. Dig. 50, 16, 54.

CONDITIONAL INDORSEMENT. See Indorsement.

CONDITIONAL STIPULATION. In the civil law. A stipulation to do a thing upon condition, as the happening of any event.

CONDITIONALLY PRIVILEGED COMMUNICATION. One made in good faith on any subject matter in which the person publishing has an interest, or in reference to which he has a duty, if made to a person having a corresponding interest or duty, even though it contains matter which otherwise would be actionable. Cook v. East Shore Newspapers, 327 Ill.App. 559, 64 N.E.2d 751, 760.

The essential elements of a "conditionally privileged communication" are good faith, an interest to be upheld, a statement limited in its scope to such purpose, a proper occasion, and publication in a proper manner to proper persons. Cook v. East Shore Newspaper, 327 Ill.App. 559, 64 N.E. 2d 751.

CONDITIONES QUÆLIBET ODIOSÆ; MAXIME AUTEM CONTRA MATRIMONIUM ET COMMERCIUM. Any conditions are odious, but especially those which are against [in restraint of] marriage and commerce. Lofft, Appendix, 644.

CONDITIONS OF SALE. The terms upon which sales are made at auction; usually written or printed and exposed in the auction room at the time of sale.

CONDOMINIA. In the civil law. Co-ownerships or limited ownerships, such as *emphyteusis, superficies, pignus, hypotheca, ususfructus, usus,* and *habitatio.* These were more than mere *jura in re alienâ,* being portion of the *dominium* itself, although they are commonly distinguished from the *dominium* strictly so called. Brown.

CONDOMINIUM. System of separate ownership of individual units in multiple-unit building. Susskind v. 1136 Tenants Corp., 251 N.Y.S.2d 321, 327, 43 Misc.2d 588.

CONDONACION. In Spanish law. The remission of a debt, either expressly or tacitly.

CONDONATION. The conditional remission or forgiveness, by means of continuance or resumption of marital cohabitation, by one of the married parties, of a known matrimonial offense committed by the other, that would constitute a cause of divorce; the condition being that the offense shall not be repeated. Pain v. Pain, 37 Mo.App. 115; Betz v. Betz, 25 N.Y.Super.Ct. 696; State v. Manos, 204 N.C. 52, 167 S.E. 493; Thum v. Thum, 105 Colo. 352, 98 P.2d 279, 280.

"Condonation," to constitute valid defense in divorce action, must be free, voluntary, and not induced by duress or fraud; "condonation" means pardon of offense, voluntary overlooking or implied forgiveness by treating offender as if offense had not been committed. Panther v. Panther, 147 Okl. 131, 295 P. 219, 221. The term is also sometimes applied to forgiveness of a past wrong, fault, injury, or breach of duty in other relations, as, for example, in that of master and servant. Leatherberry v. Odell, C.C. N.C., 7 F. 648. Also, antenuptial unchastity is capable of "condonation." Wesley v. Wesley, 181 Ky. 135, 204 S.W. 165, 166.

CONDONE. To make condonation of.

CONDUCE. To contribute to as a result. Board of Com'rs of Mercer County v. Deitsch, 94 Ohio St. 1, 113 N.E. 745, 747.

CONDUCT, *v.* To manage; direct; lead; have direction; carry on; regulate; do business. Wichita Film & Supply Co. v. Yale, 194 Mo.App. 60, 184 S.W. 119, 121; State v. Mahfouz, 181 La. 23, 158 So. 609; Scholz v. Leuer, 7 Wash.2d 76, 109 P.2d 294, 301.

CONDUCT, *n.* Personal behavior; deportment; mode of action; any positive or negative act. Kelly v. State, 151 Md. 87, 133 A. 899, 904; Lamborn v. New York Cotton Exch., 197 N.Y.S. 57, 60, 203 App.Div. 565.

CONDUCT, ESTOPPEL BY. An estoppel exists where a man by his own acts or acceptance is concluded from saying the truth. Menzenberger v. American State Bank, 101 Ind.App. 600, 198 N. E. 819. See, also, Equitable Estoppel.

The doctrine does not apply to an agreement which is illegal. Miller v. California Roofing Co., 55 Cal.App.2d 136, 130 P.2d 740, 745.

Elements or essentials of estoppel are acts done which cannot be contravened without fraud or gross misconduct, Tradesmens Nat. Bank of New Haven v. Minor, 190 A. 270, 272, 122 Conn. 419; change of position to injury of party claiming benefit of estoppel, Mundt v. Mallon, 106 Mont. 244, 76 P.2d 326, 329; Thompson v. Hudgens, 159 S.E. 807, 811, 161 S.C. 450; false representation or concealment, Marshall v. Wilson, 175 Or. 506, 154 P.2d 547, 553; Hamilton v. Northeast Mut. Ins. Ass'n, Mo.App., 116 S.W.2d 159, 163; ignorance of facts of one claiming right of estoppel, McCarthy v. Union Pac. Ry. Co., 58 Wyo. 308, 131 P.2d 326, 330, 332; inducement to do or forbear doing, something one would not, or would, otherwise have done, O'Brien v. U. S., C.C.A.Ind., 51 F.2d 674, 678; intent to have other party act or conduct calculated to mislead, Woodmen of the World Life Ins. Soc. v. Greathouse, 242 Ala. 532, 7 So.2d 89, 91; Marshall v. Wilson, 175 Or. 506,

154 P.2d 547, 553; knowledge of party sought to be estopped, McLearn v. Hill, 276 Mass. 519, 177 N.E. 617, 619, 77 A.L.R. 1039; misleading of person claiming estoppel, Dodd v. Rotterman, 161 N.E. 756, 761, 330 Ill. 362; State v. Abernathy, 159 Tenn. 175, 17 S.W.2d 17, 19; prejudice to party claiming estoppel, Combs v. Salyer, 165 S.W.2d 40, 43, 291 Ky. 592; Burlington Sav. Bank of Burlington, Vt., v. Rockwell, C.C.A.Idaho, 31 F.2d 27, 29; reliance upon conduct of one sought to be estopped, Wiedersum v. Atlantic Cement Products, 25 N.Y.S.2d 496, 501, 261 App.Div. 305; State v. Smith, 135 Neb. 423, 281 N.W. 851, 856; representation or concealment of material facts, City Dairy Co. v. Uservo, Inc., 101 Ind.App. 375, 199 N.E. 457.

CONDUCT MONEY. In English practice. Money paid to a witness who has been subpœnaed on a trial, sufficient to defray the reasonable expenses of going to, staying at, and returning from the place of trial. Lush, Pr. 460; Archb. New Pr. 639.

CONDUCTI ACTIO. In the civil law. An action which the hirer *(conductor)* of a thing might have against the letter, *(locator.)* Inst. 3, 25, pr. 2.

CONDUCTIO. In the civil law. A hiring. Used generally in connection with the term *locatio,* a letting. *Locatio et conductio,* (sometimes united as a compound word, *"locatio-conductio,"*) a letting and hiring. Inst. 3, 25; Bract. fol. 62, c. 28; Story, Bailm. §§ 8, 368.

CONDUCTOR. In the civil law. A hirer.

CONDUCTOR OPERARUM. In the civil law. A person who engages to perform a piece of work for another, at a stated price.

CONDUCTUS. A thing hired.

CONE. In geology. Area built up by a stream, near the mouth of a canyon of boulders, small stones, gravel, sand and other detritus. Haack v. San Fernando Mission Land Co., 177 Cal. 140, 169 P. 1021, 1022.

CONE AND KEY. In old English law. A woman at fourteen or fifteen years of age may take charge of her house and receive *cone* and *key;* that is, keep the accounts and keys. Cowell. Said by Lord Coke to be *cover* and *keye,* meaning that at that age a woman knew what in her house should be kept under lock and key. 2 Inst. 203.

CONFARREATIO. In Roman law. A sacrificial rite resorted to by marrying persons of high patrician or priestly degree, for the purpose of clothing the husband with the *manus* over his wife; the civil modes of effecting the same thing being *coemptio,* (formal,) and *usus mulieris,* (informal.) Brown.

CONFECTIO. The making and completion of a written instrument. 5 Coke, 1.

CONFEDERACY.

Criminal Law

The association or banding together of two or more persons for the purpose of committing an act or furthering an enterprise which is forbidden by law, or which, though lawful in itself, becomes unlawful when made the object of the confederacy. State v. Crowley, 41 Wis. 284, 22 Am.Rep. 719; Watson v. Navigation Co., 52 How.Prac. (N.Y.) 353. *Conspiracy* is a more technical term for this offense. The act of two or more who combine together to do any damage or injury to another, or to do any unlawful act. Jacob. State v. Crowley, 41 Wis. 284, 22 Am.Rep. 719.

Equity Pleading

An improper combination alleged to have been entered into between the defendants to a bill in equity.

International Law

A league or agreement between two or more independent states whereby they unite for their mutual welfare and the furtherance of their common aims. The term may apply to a union so formed for a temporary or limited purpose, as in the case of an offensive and defensive alliance; but it is more commonly used to denote that species of political connection between two or more independent states by which a central government is created, invested with certain powers of sovereignty, (mostly external,) and acting upon the several component states as its units, which, however, retain their sovereign powers for domestic purposes and some others. See Federal Government.

CONFEDERATION. A league or compact for mutual support, particularly of princes, nations, or states. Such was the colonial government during the Revolution.

CONFERENCE. A meeting of several persons for deliberation, for the interchange of opinion, or for the removal of differences or disputes. Thus, a meeting between a counsel and solicitor to advise on the cause of their client.

In the practice of legislative bodies, when the two houses cannot agree upon a pending measure, each appoints a committee of "conference," and the committees meet and consult together for the purpose of removing differences, harmonizing conflicting views, and arranging a compromise which will be accepted by both houses.

French Law

A concordance or identity between two laws or two systems of laws.

International Law

A personal meeting between the diplomatic agents of two or more powers, for the purpose of making statements and explanations that will obviate the delay and difficulty attending the more formal conduct of negotiations.

CONFESS. To admit as true; to assent to; to concede. Guydon v. Taylor, 115 Ind.App. 685, 60 N.E.2d 750, 751. To admit the truth of a charge or accusation. Usually spoken of charges of tortious or criminal conduct.

CONFESSING ERROR. A plea to an assignment of error, admitting the same.

CONFESSIO. Lat. A confession. *Confessio in judicio,* a confession made in or before a court.

CONFESSIO FACTA IN JUDICIO OMNI PROBATIONE MAJOR EST. A confession made in court is of greater effect than any proof. Jenk. Cent. 102.

CONFESSION. In criminal law. A voluntary statement made by a person charged with the commission of a crime or misdemeanor, communicated to another person, wherein he acknowledges himself to be guilty of the offense charged, and discloses the circumstances of the act or the share and participation which he had in it. Spicer v. Com., 21 Ky.L.Rep. 528, 51 S.W. 802. State v. Gibson, 69 N.D. 70, 284 N.W. 209, 214, 215, 219; Sango v. State, 52 Okl.Cr. 359, 5 P.2d 400, 401; Edwards v. State, Okl.Cr.App., 288 P. 359, 361. Also the act of a prisoner, when arraigned for a crime or misdemeanor, in acknowledging and avowing that he is guilty of the offense charged.

"Confession" comprises whole criminal charge; whereas, "admission" relates only to particular fact or circumstance covered thereby. State v. Davis, 212 Iowa 131, 235 N.W. 759, 761.

Classification

Confessions are divided into judicial and extrajudicial. The former are such as are made before a magistrate or court in the due course of legal proceedings; they include confessions made in preliminary examinations before magistrates. Mularkey v. State, 199 Wis. 269, 225 N.W. 933, 934. The latter are such as are made by a party elsewhere than in court or before a magistrate, 1 Greenl. Ev. § 216, State v. Corey, 182 Minn. 48, 233 N.W. 590, 591; Foster v. State, 79 Okl.Cr. 183, 152 P.2d 929, 932; Louette v. State, 152 Fla. 495, 12 So.2d 168, 172; whether to an official or non-official person, Prather v. State, 76 Okl.Cr. 385, 137 P.2d 249, 252. One made by the party out of court, or to any person, official or otherwise, when made not in the course of a judicial examination or investigation. State v. Stevenson, 98 Or. 285, 193 P. 1030, 1032.

An *implied* confession is where the defendant, in a case not capital, does not plead guilty but indirectly admits his guilt by placing himself at the mercy of the court and asking for a light sentence. 2 Hawk. P. C. p. 469; State v. Conway, 20 R.I. 270, 38 A. 656. An *indirect* confession is one inferred from the conduct of the defendant. An *involuntary* confession is one induced by hope, promise, fear, violence, torture, or threat. Lyons v. State, 77 Okl.Cr. 197, 138 P.2d 142, 148; Lyons v. State, 140 P.2d 248. People v. Tielke, 259 Ill. 88, 102 N.E. 229, 231. A *naked* confession is an admission of the guilt of the party, but which is not supported by any evidence of the commission of the crime. A *relative* confession, in the older criminal law of England, "is where the accused confesseth and appealeth others thereof, to become an approver," (2 Hale, P. C. c. 29,) or in other words to "turn king's evidence." This is now obsolete, but something like it is practiced in modern law, where one of the persons accused or supposed to be involved in a crime is put on the witness stand under an implied promise of pardon. State v. Willis, 71 Conn. 293, 41 A. 820. A *simple* confession is merely a plea of guilty. State v. Willis, 71 Conn. 293, 41 A. 820. A *voluntary* confession is one made spontaneously by a person accused of crime, free from the influence of any extraneous disturbing cause, and in particular, not influenced, or extorted by violence, threats, or promises. State v. Clifford, 86 Iowa, 550, 53 N.W. 299, 41 Am.St.Rep. 518.

No confession induced by official threat of prosecution is voluntary. Cannan v. U. S., C.C.A.Tex., 19 F.2d 823, 824; State v. Dolan, 86 N.J.L. 192, 90 A. 1034, 1035.

It need not be spontaneous nor proceed wholly at maker's suggestion, but may be set in motion by external causes, so long as such influences are not what the law deems improper. People v. Vinci, 295 Ill. 419, 129 N.E. 193, 195.

For *extrajudicial* confession, see, also, the title Extrajudicial.

CONFESSION AND AVOIDANCE. A plea in confession and avoidance is one which avows and confesses the truth of the averments of fact in the declaration, either expressly or by implication, but then proceeds to allege new matter which tends to deprive the facts admitted of their ordinary legal effect, or to obviate, neutralize, or *avoid* them. Bavarian Brewing Co. v. Retkowski, 113 A. 903, 907, 1 W.W.Harr. (Del.) 225; Brown v. Jones, 137 Or. 520, 3 P.2d 768, 769.

CONFESSION OF DEFENSE. In English practice. Where defendant alleges a ground of defense arising since the commencement of the action, the plaintiff may deliver confession of such defense and sign judgment for his costs up to the time of such pleading, unless it be otherwise ordered. Jud. Act 1875, Ord. XX, r. 3.

CONFESSION OF JUDGMENT. See Judgment.

CONFESSO, BILL TAKEN PRO. In equity practice. An order which the court of chancery makes when the defendant does not file an answer, that the plaintiff may take such a decree as the case made by his bill warrants.

CONFESSOR. An ecclesiastic who receives auricular confessions of sins from persons under his spiritual charge, and pronounces absolution upon them. The secrets of the confessional are not privileged communications at common law, but this has been changed by statute in some states. See 1 Greenl. Ev. §§ 247, 248.

CONFESSORIA ACTIO. Lat. In the civil law. An action for enforcing a servitude. Mackeld. Rom. Law, § 324.

CONFESSUS IN JUDICIO PRO JUDICATO HABETUR, ET QUODAMMODO SUA SENTENTIÂ DAMNATUR. 11 Coke, 30. A person confessing his guilt when arraigned is deemed to have been found guilty, and is, as it were, condemned by his own sentence.

CONFIDE. A synonym of the word "trust," and means to put into one's trust or keeping. Burch v. McMillin, Tex., 15 S.W.2d 86, 90.

CONFIDENCE. Trust; reliance; ground of trust. In the construction of wills, this word is considered peculiarly appropriate to create a trust.

"It is as applicable to the subject of a trust, as nearly a synonym, as the English language is capable of. Trust is a confidence which one man reposes in another, and confidence is a trust." Appeal of Coates, 2 Pa. 133.

CONFIDENCE GAME. Obtaining of money or property by means of some trick, device, or swindling operation in which advantage is taken of the confidence which the victim reposes in the swindler. People v. Mutchler, 309 Ill. 207, 140 N.E. 820, 822, 35 A.L.R. 339; Roll v. People, 243 P. 641, 643, 78 Colo. 589; People v. Epstein, 338 Ill. 631, 170 N.E. 678, 679. For distinction between false pretenses and confidence game, see False Pretenses.

One obtaining property by unlawful means, other than by fraudulently obtaining and then abusing victim's confidence, is not guilty of obtaining property by means of "confidence game." Bomareto v. People, 111 Colo. 99, 137 P.2d 402, 404.

CONFIDENTIAL. Intrusted with the confidence of another or with his secret affairs or purposes; intended to be held in confidence or kept secret.

CONFIDENTIAL COMMUNICATIONS. See Communication.

CONFIDENTIAL CREDITOR. This term has been applied to the creditors of a failing debtor who furnished him with the means of obtaining credit to which he was not entitled, involving in loss the unsuspecting and fair-dealing creditors. Gay v. Strickland, 112 Ala. 567, 20 So. 921.

CONFIDENTIAL RELATION. A fiduciary relation. These phrases are used as convertible terms. It is a peculiar relation which exists between client and attorney, principal and agent, principal and surety, landlord and tenant, parent and child, guardian and ward, ancestor and heir, husband and wife, trustee and *cestui que trust*, executors or administrators and creditors, legatees, or distributees, appointer and appointee under powers, and partners and part owners. In these and like cases, the law, in order to prevent undue advantage from the unlimited confidence or sense of duty which the relation naturally creates, requires the utmost degree of good faith in all transactions between the parties. Shell Petroleum Corporation v. Pratt, D.C.Kan., 22 F.Supp. 304, 305, 306. It is not confined to any specific association of parties. It appears when the circumstances make it certain that the parties do not deal on equal terms, but on the one side there is an overmastering influence, or, on the other, weakness, dependence, or trust, justifiably reposed. The mere existence of kinship does not, of itself, give rise to such relation. In re Null's Estate, 302 Pa. 64, 153 A. 137. It covers every form of relation between parties wherein confidence is reposed by one in another, and former relies and acts upon representations of the other and is guilty of no derelictions on his own part. Peckham v. Johnson, Tex.Civ.App., 98 S.W.2d 408, 416.

The term "confidential relations," within the exception to the rule that misrepresentations of law will not work an estoppel, is not confined to the strict fiduciary relationship existing between those having definite, well-recognized legal relations of trust and confidence, but extends to every possible case in which a fiduciary relation exists as a fact, though it may be a moral, social, domestic, or merely personal relation, and need not be a legal one. Robbins v. Law, 48 Cal.App. 555, 192 P. 118, 120; Hitchcock v. Tackett, 208 Ky. 803, 272 S.W. 52, 54.

CONFINEMENT. Confinement may be by either a moral or a physical restraint, by threats of violence with a present force, or by physical restraint of the person. Ex parte Snodgrass, 43 Tex. Cr.R. 359, 65 S.W. 1061.

Restraint by sickness in childbirth; lying-in for delivery of child, or possibly because of advanced pregnancy. Rose v. Commonwealth Beneficial Ass'n, 86 A. 673, 674, 4 Boyce (Del.) 144.

Solitary Confinement

See Solitary Confinement.

CONFIRM. To complete or establish that which was imperfect or uncertain; to ratify what has been done without authority or insufficiently. Railway Co. v. Ransom, 15 Tex.Civ.App. 689, 41 S.W. 826. Vermont Shade Roller Co. v. Burlington Traction Co., 102 Vt. 489, 150 A. 138, 142. To make firm or certain; to give new assurance of truth or certainty; to put past doubt. State ex rel. Sherrill v. Milam, 113 Fla. 491, 153 So. 100.

CONFIRMARE EST ID FIRMUM FACERE QUOD PRIUS INFIRMUM FUIT. Co. Litt. 295. To confirm is to make firm that which was before infirm.

CONFIRMARE NEMO POTEST PRIUS QUAM JUS EI ACCIDERIT. No one can confirm before the right accrues to him. 10 Coke, 48.

CONFIRMAT USUM QUI TOLLIT ABUSUM. He confirms the use [of a thing] who removes the abuse [of it]. Moore, 764.

CONFIRMATIO. The conveyance of an estate, or the communication of a right that one hath in or unto lands or tenements, to another that hath the possession thereof, or some other estate therein, whereby a voidable estate is made sure and unavoidable, or whereby a particular estate is increased or enlarged. Shep. Touch. 311; 2 Bl. Comm. 325.

CONFIRMATIO CHARTARUM. Lat. Confirmation of the charters. A statute passed in the 25 Edw. I., whereby the Great Charter is declared to be allowed as the common law; all judgments contrary to it are declared void; copies of it are ordered to be sent to all cathedral churches and read twice a year to the people; and sentence of excommunication is directed to be as constantly denounced against all those that, by word or deed or counsel, act contrary thereto or in any degree infringe it. 1 Bl.Comm. 128.

CONFIRMATIO CRESCENS. An enlarging confirmation; one which enlarges a rightful estate. Shep. Touch. 311.

CONFIRMATIO DIMINUENS. A diminishing confirmation. A confirmation which tends and serves to diminish and abridge the services whereby a tenant doth hold, operating as a release of part of the services. Shep. Touch. 311.

CONFIRMATIO PERFICIENS. A confirmation which makes valid a wrongful and defeasible title, or makes a conditional estate absolute. Shep. Touch. 311.

CONFIRMATIO EST NULLA UBI DONUM PRÆCEDENS EST INVALIDUM. Moore, 764; Co. Litt. 295. Confirmation is void where the preceding gift is invalid.

CONFIRMATIO OMNES SUPPLET DEFECTUS, LICET ID QUOD ACTUM EST AB INITIO NON VALUIT. Co. Litt. 295*b*. Confirmation supplies all defects, though that which had been done was not valid at the beginning.

CONFIRMATION. A contract or written memorandum thereof, by which that which was infirm, difficult of proof, void, imperfect, or subject to be avoided is ratified, rendered valid and binding, made firm and unavoidable. Schifferdecker v. Busch, 225 N.Y.S. 106, 111, 130 Misc. 625.

It implies a deliberate act, intended to renew and ratify a transaction known to be voidable. Bauer v. Dotterer, 202 Ark. 1055, 155 S.W.2d 54, 57.

A conveyance of an estate or right *in esse*, whereby a voidable estate is made sure and unavoidable, or whereby a particular estate is increased. Co. Litt. 295*b*. Beetem v. Garrison, 129 Md. 664, 99 A. 897, 900.

English Ecclesiastical Law

The ratification by the archbishop of the election of a bishop by dean and chapter under the king's letter missive prior to the investment and consecration of the bishop by the archbishop. 25 Hen. VIII. c. 20.

CONFIRMATION OF SALE. The confirmation of a judicial sale by the court which ordered it is a signification in some way (usually by the entry of an order) of the court's approval of the terms, price, and conditions of the sale. Johnson v. Cooper, 56 Miss. 618; Hyman v. Smith, 13 W.Va. 765.

CONFIRMAVI. Lat. I have confirmed. The emphatic word in the ancient deeds of confirmation. Fleta, lib. 3, c. 14, § 5.

CONFIRMEE. The grantee in a deed of confirmation.

CONFIRMOR. The grantor in a deed of confirmation.

CONFISCABLE. Capable of being confiscated or suitable for confiscation; liable to forfeiture. Camp v. Lockwood, 1 Dall. (Pa.) 393, 1 L.Ed. 194.

CONFISCARE. In civil and old English law. To confiscate; to claim for or bring into the fisc, or treasury. Bract. fol. 150.

CONFISCATE. To appropriate property to the use of the state. To adjudge property to be forfeited to the public treasury; to seize and condemn private forfeited property to public use. City of Portsmouth v. Public Utilities Commission, 108 Ohio St. 272, 140 N.E. 604, 606; Moscow Fire Ins. Co. of Moscow, Russia, v. Bank of New York & Trust Co., 294 N.Y.S. 648, 663, 161 Misc. 903.

Formerly, it appears, this term was used as synonymous with "forfeit," but at present the distinction between the two terms is well marked. Confiscation supervenes upon forfeiture. The person, by his act, forfeits his property; the state thereupon appropriates it, that is, confiscates it. Hence, to confiscate property implies that it has first been forfeited; but to forfeit property does not necessarily imply that it will be confiscated.

CONFISCATEE. One whose property has been seized and sold under a confiscation act, *e. g.*, for unpaid taxes. See Brent v. New Orleans, 41 La. Ann. 1098, 6 So. 793.

CONFISCATION. The act of confiscating; or of condemning and adjudging to the public treasury.

"Confiscation" is to be distinguished from "condemnation" as prize. The former is the act of the sovereign against a rebellious subject; the latter is the act of a belligerent against another belligerent. Confiscation may be effected by such means, summary or arbitrary, as the sovereign, expressing its will through lawful channels, may please to adopt. Condemnation as prize can only be made in accordance with principles of law recognized in the common jurisprudence of the world. Both are proceedings *in rem*, but confiscation recognizes the title of the original owner to the property, while in prize the tenure of the property is qualified, provisional, and destitute of absolute ownership. Winchester v. U. S., 14 Ct.Cl. 48.

CONFISCATORY RATES. For utility are rates which do not afford net return sufficient to preserve utility's property and to attract capital necessary to enable utility to discharge its public duties. Wichita Gas Co. v. Public Service Commission of Kansas, D.C.Kan., 2 F.Supp. 792, 799. Rates which do not afford a reasonable return on value of property at time it is used in public service. State v. Tri-State Telephone and Telegraph Co., 204 Minn. 516, 284 N.W. 294, 305.

CONFISCATION ACTS. Certain acts of congress, enacted during the progress of the civil war (1861 and 1862) in the exercise of the war powers of the government and meant to strengthen its hands and aid in suppressing the rebellion, which authorized the seizure, condemnation, and forfeiture of "property used for insurrectionary purposes." Semmes v. U. S., 91 U.S. 27, 23 L.Ed. 193.

CONFISCATION CASES. The name given to a group of fifteen cases decided by the United States supreme court in 1868, on the validity and construction of the confiscation acts of congress. Reported in 7 Wall. 454, 19 L.Ed. 196.

CONFISK. An old form of *confiscate*.

CONFITENS REUS. An accused person who admits his guilt.

CONFLICT OF LAWS. Inconsistency or difference between the municipal laws of different states or countries, arising in the case of persons who have acquired rights or a *status*, or made contracts, or incurred obligations, within the territory of two or more jurisdictions. Hence, that branch of jurisprudence, arising from the diversity of the laws of different nations, states or jurisdictions, in their application to rights and remedies, which reconciles the inconsistency, or decides which law or system is to govern in the particular case, or settles the degree of force to be accorded to the law of another jurisdiction, (the acts or rights in question having arisen under it,) either where it varies from the domestic law, or where the domestic law is silent or not exclusively applicable to the case in point. In this sense it is often called "private international law," a term adopted by Westlake, by Woolsey, Internatl. Law (5th Ed.) § 73, and others, and characterized as "handy and manageable," but at bottom inaccurate, by Dicey, Conflict of Laws, Moore's Ed. 12, who points out that the defect of the name "Conflict of Laws" is that the supposed conflict is fictitious and never really takes place, and that the expression has the further radical defect of concealing from view the circumstance that the question by the law of what country a given transaction shall be governed is often too plain to admit of doubt. If, he says, the term applies to the conflict in the mind of a judge as to which of two systems of law should govern a given case, this amounts simply to saying that the term "conflict of laws" may be used as an inaccurate equivalent for the less objectionable phrase "choice of laws." Taylor, Jurisprudence, 611, after considering the opinion of many writers, concludes that the term "private international law" is subject to many objections. Holland, Jurisprudence, 410, considers it "wholly indefensible," as does Gray, Nature, etc., of the Law, 124. Pollock, First Book of Jurispr. 99, prefers the German term—Internationales Privatrecht.

CONFLICT OF PRESUMPTIONS. In this conflict certain rules are applicable, viz.: (1) Special take precedence of general presumptions; (2) constant of casual ones; (3) presume in favor of innocence; (4) of legality; (5) of validity; and, when these rules fail, the matter is said to be at large. Brown.

CONFLICTING EVIDENCE. It has been said that there is not, in a legal sense, a conflict of evidence unless there is a possibility that men of ordinary reason and fairness would feel justified in drawing different conclusions from the evidence before them. Seeley v. Osborne, 220 N.Y. 416, 116 N.E. 97.

CONFORMITY. Correspondence in form, manner, or use; agreement; harmony; congruity. Reasonover v. Reasonover, 122 Tex. 512, 58 S.W. 2d 817, 819.

English Ecclesiastical Law

Adherence to the doctrines and usages of the Church of England.

CONFORMITY ACT, or STATUTE. A term used to designate Act June 1, 1872, c. 255, § 5, 17 Stat. 197, whence was derived Rev. St. U. S. § 914 providing that the practice, pleadings, and forms and modes of proceeding in civil causes, other than equity and admiralty causes, in the federal district courts shall conform, as near as may be, to those existing in like causes in the courts of the state within which such district courts are held. Since the adoption of the Federal Rules of Civil Procedure, 28 U.S.C.A., the Conformity Act is no longer effective. De Rosmo v. Feeny, 1941, 38 F. Supp. 834; Hydraulic Press Mfg. Co. v. Williams, White & Co., C.C.A.Ill.1947, 165 F.2d 489.

CONFORMITY, BILL OF. See Bill of Conformity.

CONFRAIRIE. Fr. In old English law. A fraternity, brotherhood, or society. Cowell.

CONFRERES. Brethren in a religious house; fellows of one and the same society. Cowell.

CONFRONTATION. In criminal law, the act of setting a witness face to face with the prisoner, in order that the latter may make any objection he has to the witness, or that the witness may identify the accused. State v. Behrman, 114 N.C. 797, 19 S.E. 220, 25 L.R.A. 449.

The constitutional right of confrontation does not mean merely that witnesses are to be made visible to the accused, but imports the constitutional privilege to cross-examine them. State v. Crooker, 123 Me. 310, 122 A. 865, 866, 33 A.L.R. 821.

CONFUSIO. In the civil law. The inseparable intermixture of property belonging to different owners; it is properly confined to the pouring together of fluids, but is sometimes also used of a melting together of metals or any compound formed by the irrecoverable commixture of different substances.

It is distinguished from *commixtion* by the fact that in the latter case a separation may be made, while in a case of *confusio* there cannot be. 2 Bl.Comm. 405.

CONFUSION. This term, as used in the civil law and in compound terms derived from that source, means a blending or intermingling, and is equivalent to the term "merger" as used at common law. Palmer v. Burnside, 1 Woods, 182 Fed. Cas. No. 10,685.

CONFUSION OF BOUNDARIES. The title of that branch of equity jurisdiction which relates to the discovery and settlement of conflicting, disputed, or uncertain boundaries.

CONFUSION OF DEBTS. A mode of extinguishing a debt, by the concurrence in the same person of two qualities or adverse rights to the same thing which mutually destroy each other. This may occur in several ways, as where the creditor becomes the heir of the debtor, or the debtor the heir of the creditor, or either accedes to the title of the other by any other mode of transfer. Woods v. Ridley, 11 Humph. (Tenn.) 198.

CONFUSION OF GOODS. The inseparable intermixture of property belonging to different owners; properly confined to the pouring together of fluids, but used in a wider sense to designate any indistinguishable compound of elements belonging to different owners. The term "confusion" is applicable to a mixing of chattels of one and the same general description, differing thus from "accession," which takes place where various materials are united in one product. Confusion of goods arises wherever the goods of two or more persons are so blended as to have become undistinguishable. 1 Schouler, Pers. Prop. 41. Barker v. Stearns Coal & Lumber Co., 291 Ky. 184, 163 S.W.2d 466, 471.

CONFUSION OF RIGHTS. A union of the qualities of debtor and creditor in the same person. The effect of such a union is, generally, to extinguish the debt. 1 Salk. 306; Cro. Car. 551; 1 Ld. Raym. 515. 5 Term 381; Comyns, Dig. *Baron et Feme* (D); Baylor University v. Bradshaw, Tex. Civ.App., 52 S.W.2d 1094, 1101.

CONFUSION OF TITLES. A civil-law expression, synonymous with "merger," as used in the common law, applying where two titles to the same property unite in the same person. Palmer v. Burnside, 1 Woods, 179, Fed. Cas. No. 10,685.

CONFUTE. To prove to be false, defective, or invalid. Wiley v. Baker, 219 Mich. 629, 190 N.W. 273, 278.

CONGÉ. Fr. In French law. Permission, leave, license; a passport or clearance to a vessel; a permission to arm, equip, or navigate a vessel.

CONGÉ D'ACCORDER. Leave to accord. A permission granted by the court, in the old process of levying a fine, to the defendant to agree with the plaintiff. *Termes de la Ley;* Cowell. See Licentia Concordandi; 2 Bla.Comm. 350.

CONGÉ D'EMPARLER. Leave to imparl. The privilege of an imparlance, (*licentia loquendi.*) 3 Bl.Comm. 299.

CONGÉ D'ESLIRE. Also spelled congé d'élire, congé délire. Cowell; *Termes de la Ley;* 1 Bla. Comm. 379, 382. A permission or license from the British sovereign to a dean and chapter to elect a bishop, in time of vacation; or to an abbey or priory which is of royal foundation, to elect an abbot or prior.

CONGEABLE. L. Fr. Lawful; permissible; allowable. "Disseisin is properly where a man entereth into any lands or tenements where his entry is not *congeable,* and putteth out him that hath the freehold." Litt. § 279. See Ricard v. Williams, 7 Wheat. 107, 5 L.Ed. 398.

CONGILDONES. In Saxon law. Fellow-members of a guild.

CONGIUS. An ancient measure containing about a gallon and a pint. Cowell.

CONGREGATE. To come together; to assemble; to meet. Board of Health of City of Paterson v. Clayton, 93 N.J.L. 64, 106 A. 813, 814.

CONGREGATION. An assembly or gathering; specifically, an assembly or society of persons who together constitute the principal supporters of a particular parish, or habitually meet at the same church for religious exercises. Laird v. State, 69 Tex.Cr.R. 553, 155 S.W. 260, 262.

Ecclesiastical Law

Certain bureaus at Rome, where ecclesiastical matters are attended to.

CONGREGATIONAL SYSTEM OF CHURCH ORGANIZATION. Where the local organization is the governing body and is sufficient unto itself. Doughty v. Herr, 97 Ind.App. 427, 185 N.E. 657, 658.

CONGRESS. In International Law. An assembly of envoys, commissioners, deputies, etc., from different sovereignties who meet to concert measures for their common good, or to adjust their mutual concerns.

In American Law. The legislative assembly of the United States, composed of the senate and house of representatives (*q. v.*). U. S. Const. art. 1, § 1.

CONGRESSMAN. Strictly, a member of the Congress of the United States. But there is a strong tendency in popular usage to apply this term only to a member of the House of Representatives, as distinguished from a senator. State v. Kopriva, 49 N.D. 1040, 194 N.W. 704, 705.

CONGRESSUS. The extreme practical test of the truth of a charge of impotence brought against a husband by a wife. It is now disused. Causes Célèbres, 6, 183.

CONJECTIO. In the civil law of evidence. A throwing together. Presumption; the putting of things together, with the inference drawn therefrom.

CONJECTIO CAUSÆ. In the civil law. A statement of the case. A brief synopsis of the case given by the advocate to the judge in opening the trial. Calvin.

CONJECTURAL CHOICE, RULE OF. Where all theories of causation rest only on conjecture, no jury question is presented. Cummings v. Grand Trunk Western R. Co., 127 N.W.2d 842, 844, 372 Mich. 695.

CONJECTURE. A slight degree of credence, arising from evidence too weak or too remote to cause belief. Weed v. Scofield, 73 Conn. 670, 49 A. 22; 1 Mascardus, *De Prob.* quæst. 14, n. 14. Supposition or surmise. The idea of a fact, suggested by another fact; as a possible cause, concomitant, or result. Burrill, Circ. Ev. 27. An idea or notion founded on a probability without any demonstration of its truth; an idea or surmise inducing a slight degree of belief founded upon some possible, or perhaps probable fact of which there is no positive evidence. Oklahoma City v. Wilcoxson, 173 Okl. 433, 48 P.2d 1039, 1043. An explanation consistent with but not deducible as a reasonable inference from known facts or conditions. Southern Ry. Co. v. Dickson, 211 Ala. 481, 100 So. 665, 669. In popular use, synonymous with "guess." Fedorawicz v. Citizens' Electric Illuminating Co., 246 Pa. 141, 92 A. 124, 125.

Also, the bringing together of the circumstances, as well as the result obtained. Reynolds v. Maryland Casualty Co., 274 Mo. 83, 201 S.W. 1128, 1133.

CONJOINT ROBBERY. Where the act is committed by two or more persons. Patterson v. State, 78 Okl.Cr. 244, 147 P.2d 179, 184.

CONJOINTS. Persons married to each other. Story, Confl. Laws, § 71; Wolffius, *Droit de la Nat.* § 858.

CONJUDEX. In old English law. An associate judge. Bract. 403.

CONJUGAL. Of or belonging to marriage or the married state; suitable or appropriate to the married state or to married persons; matrimonial; connubial. Swanson v. Swanson, 20 A.2d 617, 618, 128 Conn. 128, 135 A.L.R. 849.

CONJUGAL RIGHTS. Matrimonial rights; the right which husband and wife have to each other's society, comfort, and affection.

CONJUGIUM. One of the names of marriage, among the Romans. Tayl. Civil Law, 284.

CONJUNCT. In Scotch law. Joint.

CONJUNCTA. In the civil law. Things joined together or united; as distinguished from *disjuncta,* things disjoined or separated. Dig. 50, 16, 53.

CONJUNCTIM. Lat. In old English law. Jointly. Inst. 2, 20, 8.

CONJUNCTIM ET DIVISIM. L. Lat. In old English law. Jointly and severally.

CONJUNCTIO. In the civil law. Conjunction; connection of words in a sentence. See Dig. 50, 16, 29, 142.

CONJUNCTIO MARITI ET FEMINÆ EST DE JURE NATURÆ. The union of husband and wife is of the law of nature.

CONJUNCTIVE. Connecting in a manner denoting union.

A grammatical term for particles which serve for joining or connecting together. Thus, the word "and" is called a "conjunctive," and "or" a "disjunctive," conjunction.

CONJUNCTIVE DENIAL. Where several material facts are stated conjunctively in the complaint, an answer which undertakes to deny their averments as a whole, conjunctively stated, is called a "conjunctive denial." Doll v. Good, 38 Cal. 287.

CONJUNCTIVE OBLIGATION. See Obligation.

CONJURATIO. In Old English Law. A swearing together; an oath administered to several together; a combination or confederacy under oath. Cowell.

In Old European Law. A compact of the inhabitants of a commune, or municipality, confirmed by their oaths to each other and which was the basis of the commune. Steph. Lect. 119.

CONJURATION. In old English law. A plot or compact made by persons combining by oath to do any public harm. Cowell.

The offense of having conference or commerce with evil spirits, in order to discover some secret, or effect some purpose. Cowell.

Classed by Blackstone with witchcraft, enchantment, and sorcery, but distinguished from each of these by other writers. 4 Bl.Comm. 60; Cowell. Cooper v. Livingston, 19 Fla. 693; Mozley & W. Law Dict.

CONJURATOR. In old English law. One who swears or is sworn with others; one bound by oath with others; a compurgator; a conspirator.

CONNECT. To join or fasten together as by something intervening; to associate as in occurrence or in idea; to combine; to unite or link together, as in an electrical circuit; to establish a bond or relation between; to meet or make connections for transference of passengers or change of means of communication. City of Independence v. Board of Com'rs of Montgomery County, 140 Kan. 661, 38 P.2d 105.

CONNECTED. Joined; united by junction, by an intervening substance or medium, by dependence or relation, or by order in a series. State v. Patterson, 95 S.C. 463, 79 S.E. 309, 310.

With reference to buildings, the term does not generally denote such a close union as is implied by the word "attached" or "annexed," but rather signifies the connection effected by a flume: Plattsburg Gas & Electric Co. v. Miller, 206 N.Y.S. 42, 45, 123 Misc. 651; or by piping or telephone connections; Williams Mfg. Co. v. Insurance Co. of North America, 93 Vt. 161, 106 A. 657, 659.

A counterclaim, to be "connected" with the subject of the action, must be directly connected, so that the parties could be supposed to have foreseen and contemplated it in their mutual acts. Haberle-Crystal Spring Brewing Co. v. Handrahan, 165 N.Y.S. 251, 255, 100 Misc. 163; Placerville Gold Mining Co. v. Beal, 168 Cal. 682, 144 P. 748, 749.

As used in the Act to Regulate Commerce (Act Feb. 4, 1887, c. 104, § 15, 24 Stat. 384), as amended by Act June 29, 1906, c. 3591, § 4, 34 Stat. 589 (49 USCA § 15), "connected with" transportation means "a part of" transportation. New York Cent. & H. R. R. Co. v. General Electric Co., 146 N.Y.S. 322, 327, 83 Misc. 529.

CONNECTION. The state of being connected or joined; union by junction, by an intervening substance or medium, by dependence or relation, or by order in a series. State v. Patterson, 95 S.C. 463, 79 S.E. 309, 310. Annernen v. Penn, Cust. & Pat.App., 69 F.2d 653, 654.

A contract for a connection between railroads means a physical joining of the rails so as to permit trains to pass from one set of rails to the other. Philip A. Ryan Lumber Co. v. Ball, Tex.Civ.App., 197 S.W. 1037, 1038. See, also, State v. Babcock, 161 Minn. 80, 200 N.W. 843, 844; Raynor v. New York & L. I. Traction Co., 149 N.Y.S. 151, 155, 86 Misc. 201.

CONNECTIONS. Relations by blood or marriage, but more commonly the relations of a person with whom one is connected by marriage. In this sense, the relations of a wife are "connections" of her husband. The term is vague and indefinite. See Storer v. Wheatley, 1 Pa. 507.

CONNEXITÉ. In French law. This exists when two actions are pending which, although not identical as in *lis pendens,* are so nearly similar in object that it is expedient to have them both adjudicated upon by the same judges. Arg. Fr. Merc. Law, 553.

CONNIVANCE. The secret or indirect consent or permission of one person to the commission of an unlawful or criminal act by another. State v. Gesell, 124 Mo. 531, 27 S.W. 1101. A winking at; voluntary blindness; an intentional failure to discover or prevent the wrong; forbearance or passive consent. Pierce v. Crisp, 260 Ky. 519, 86 S.W.2d 293, 296.

The corrupt consent of one party to the commission of the acts of the other constituting the cause of divorce. Dennis v. Dennis, 36 A. 34, 68 Conn. 186, 34 L.R.A. 449, 57 Am.St.Rep. 95; Manville v. Manville, Mo.App., 81 S.W.2d 382, 388.

A corrupt intent is essential. Ratcliff v. Ratcliff, 221 Mo.App. 944, 288 S.W. 794, 796. But see Leavitt v. Leavitt, 229 Mass. 196, 118 N.E. 262, and 33 L.J.Mat.Cas. 161.

Connivance differs from condonation, though the same legal consequences may attend it. Connivance necessarily involves criminality on the part of the individual who connives; condonation may take place without imputing the slightest blame to the party who forgives the injury. Connivance must be the act of the mind before the offense has been committed; condonation is the result of a determination to forgive an injury which was not known until after it was inflicted. Turton v. Turton, 3 Hagg.Eccl. 350.

Connivance differs, also, from collusion: the former is generally collusion for a particular purpose, while the latter may exist without connivance. 3 Hagg.Eccl. 130.

CONNIVE. To co-operate secretly with, or to have a secret or clandestine understanding with. People v. Munday, 293 Ill. 191, 127 N.E. 364, 368. To take part or co-operate privily with another, to aid or abet. People v. Munday, 215 Ill.App. 356, 377. To look upon with secret favor; it implies both knowledge and assent, either active or passive. State v. Furth, 82 Wash. 665, 144 P. 907, 910.

CONNOISSEMENT. In French law. An instrument, signed by the master of a ship or his agent, containing a description of the goods loaded on a ship, the persons who have sent them, the persons to whom they were sent, and the undertaking to transport them;—similar to the English and American bill of lading. Guyot, *Répert. Univ.; Ord. de la Marine,* l. 3, t. 3, art. 1.

CONNUBIUM. In the civil law. Marriage. Among the Romans, a lawful marriage as distinguished from "concubinage" (*q. v.*), an inferior marriage.

CONOCIAMENTO. In Spanish law. A recognizance. White, New Recop. b. 3, tit. 7, c. 5, § 3.

CONOCIMIENTO. In Spanish law. A bill of lading. In the Mediterranean ports it is called *"poliza de cargamiento."*

CONPOSSESSIO. In modern civil law. A joint possession. Mackeld. Rom. Law, § 245.

CONQUEREUR. In Norman and old English law. The same as "conqueror" (*q. v.*).

CONQUEROR. In old English and Scotch law. The first purchaser of an estate; he who first brought an estate into his family, or into the family owning it. 2 Bl.Comm. 242, 243.

CONQUEST. In feudal law. Conquest; acquisition by purchase; any method of acquiring the ownership of an estate other than by descent. Also an estate acquired otherwise than by inheritance.

In international law. The acquisition of the sovereignty of a country by force of arms, exercised by an independent power which reduces the vanquished to the submission of its empire. Castillero v. U. S., 2 Black, 109, 17 L.Ed. 360; American Ins. Co. v. Canter, 1 Pet. 511, 7 L.Ed. 242.

In Scotch law. Purchase. Bell.

CONQUESTOR. Conqueror. The title given to William of Normandy.

CONQUÊTS. In French law. The name given to every acquisition which the husband and wife, jointly or severally, make during the conjugal community. Thus, whatever is acquired by the husband and wife, either by his or her industry or good fortune, inures to the extent of one-half for the benefit of the other. Merl. Repert. *"Conquêt"*; Merl. *Quest., "Conquêt."* Picotte v. Cooley, 10 Mo. 312. In Louisiana, these gains are called *acquêts.*

CONQUISITIO. In feudal and old English law. Acquisition. 2 Bl.Comm. 242.

CONQUISITOR. In feudal law. A purchaser, acquirer, or conqueror. 2 Bl.Comm. 242, 243.

CONSANGUINEUS. Lat. A person related by blood; a person descended from the same common stock.

CONSANGUINEUS EST QUASI EODEM SANGUINE NATUS. Co. Litt. 157. A person related by consanguinity is, as it were, sprung from the same blood.

CONSANGUINEUS FRATER. In civil and feudal law. A half-brother by the father's side, as distinguished from *frater uterinus,* a brother by the mother's side. 2 Bla.Comm. 231.

CONSANGUINITY. Kinship; blood relationship; the connection or relation of persons descended from the same stock or common ancestor. 2 Bl. Comm. 202; Rector v. Drury, 3 Pin. (Wis.) 298; Sweezey v. Willis, 1 Brad.Surr.R. (N.Y.) 495.

Consanguinity is distinguished from "affinity," which is the connection existing in consequence of a marriage, between each of the married persons and the kindred of the other. Sizemore v. Commonwealth, 210 Ky. 637, 276 S.W. 524, 525.

Lineal and Collateral Consanguinity

Lineal consanguinity is that which subsists between persons of whom one is descended in a direct line from the other, as between son, father, grandfather, great-grandfather, and so upwards in the direct ascending line; or between son, grandson, great-grandson, and so downwards in the direct descending line. Collateral consanguinity is that which subsists between persons who have the same ancestors, but who do not descend (or ascend) one from the other. Thus, father and son are related by lineal consanguinity, uncle and nephew by collateral consanguinity. 2 Bl.Comm. 203; Capps v. State, 87 Fla. 388, 100 So. 172, 173.

CONSCIENCE. The moral sense; the faculty of judging the moral qualities of actions, or of discriminating between right and wrong; particularly applied to one's perception and judgment of the moral qualities of his own conduct, but in a wider sense, denoting a similar application of the standards of morality to the acts of others. The sense of right and wrong inherent in every person by virtue of his existence as a social entity; good conscience being a synonym of equity. Van Graafieland v. Wright, 286 Mo. 414, 228 S.W. 465, 469. In law, especially the moral rule which requires probity, justice, and honest dealing between man and man, as when we say that a bargain is "against conscience" or "unconscionable," or that the price paid for property at a forced sale was so inadequate as to "shock the conscience." This is also the meaning of the term as applied to the jurisdiction and principles of decision of courts of chancery, as in saying that such a court is a "court of conscience," that it proceeds "according to conscience," or that it has cognizance of "matters of conscience." See 3 Bl.Comm. 47–56; People v. Stewart, 7 Cal. 143; Miller v. Miller, 187 Pa. 572, 41 A. 277.

As an element of equitable jurisdiction it is not the private opinion of an individual court, but is rather to be regarded as a metaphorical term, designating the common standard of civil right and expediency combined, based upon general principles and limited by established doctrines, to which the court appeals and by which it tests the conduct and rights of suitors. National City Bank of New York v. Gelfert, 284 N.Y. 13, 29 N.E.2d 449, 452.

CONSCIENCE OF THE COURT. When an issue is sent out of chancery to be tried at law, to "inform the conscience of the court," the meaning is that the court is to be supplied with exact and dependable information as to the unsettled or disputed questions of fact in the case, in order that it may proceed to decide it in accordance with the principles of equity and good conscience in the light of the facts thus determined. Watt v. Starke, 101 U.S. 252, 25 L.Ed. 826.

CONSCIENCE, COURTS OF. Courts, not of record, constituted by act of parliament in the city of London, and other towns, for the recovery of small debts; otherwise and more commonly called "Courts of Requests." 3 Steph.Comm. 451.

CONSCIENCE, RIGHT OF. As used in some constitutional provisions, this phrase is equivalent to religious liberty or freedom of conscience. Com. v. Lesher, 17 Serg. & R. (Pa.) 155; State v. Cummings, 36 Mo. 263.

CONSCIENTIA DICITUR A CON ET SCIO, QUASI SCIRE CUM DEO. 1 Coke, 100. Conscience is called from *con* and *scio,* to know, as it were, with God.

CONSCIENTIA REI ALIENI. In Scotch law. Knowledge of another's property; knowledge that a thing is not one's own, but belongs to another. He who has this knowledge, and retains possession, is chargeable with "violent profits."

CONSCIENTIOUS OBJECTOR. One who, by reason of religious training and belief, is conscientiously opposed to participation in war. Selective Training & Service Act of 1940, § 5(g), 50 U.S.C.A. App., § 305(g). U. S. v. Kauten, C.C.A. N.Y., 133 F.2d 703.

One conscientiously opposed on religious grounds to participation in war need not be a member of a religious sect whose creed forbids participation in war to be entitled to classification as a conscientious objector. U. S. v. Bowles, C.C.A.N.J., 131 F.2d 818. It is sufficient if he has a conscientious scruple against war in any form. U. S. ex rel. Phillips v. Downer, C.C.A.N.Y., 135 F.2d 521, 524, 525.

CONSCIENTIOUS SCRUPLE. A conscientious scruple against taking an oath, serving as a juror in a capital case, doing military duty, or the like, is an objection or repugnance growing out of the fact that the person believes the thing demanded of him to be morally wrong, his conscience being the sole guide to his decision; it is thus distinguished from an "objection on principle," which is dictated by the reason and judgment, rather than the moral sense, and may relate only to the propriety or expediency of the thing in question. People v. Stewart, 7 Cal. 143.

CONSCRIPTION. Drafting into the military service of the state; compulsory military service falling upon all male subjects evenly, within or under certain specified ages. Kneedler v. Lane, 45 Pa. 267. Certain classes, however, may be exempt, and drafted men are sometimes released upon furnishing acceptable substitutes or by the payment of a sum of money. Davis, Mil. Law 51.

CONSECRATE. In ecclesiastical law. To dedicate to sacred purposes, as a bishop by imposition of hands, or a church or churchyard by prayers, etc. Consecration is performed by a bishop or archbishop.

CONSECRATIO EST PERIODUS ELECTIONIS; ELECTIO EST PRÆAMBULA CONSECRATIONIS. 2 Rolle, 102. Consecration is the termination of election; election is the preamble of consecration.

CONSECUTIVE. Successive; succeeding one another in regular order. Walsworth v. Casassa, 219 Mass. 200, 106 N.E. 847; to follow in uninterrupted succession. People v. Hirschbein, 60 P.2d 532, 16 Cal.App.2d 458.

CONSEDO. Sp. A term used in conveyances under Mexican law, equivalent to the English word "grant." Mulford v. Le Franc, 26 Cal. 103.

CONSEIL D'ÉTAT. Council of state. One of the oldest of French institutions, its origin dating back to 1302. It decides or advises upon state questions and measures proposed for legislation, submitted to it by the President of the Republic, by the members of the Cabinet, and by Parliament. Coxe, Manual of French Law.

CONSEIL DE FAMILLE. In French law. A family council. Certain acts require the sanction of this body. For example, a guardian can neither accept nor reject an inheritance to which the minor has succeeded without its authority, (Code Nap. 461;) nor can he accept for the child a gift *inter vivos* without the like authority, (Code Nap. 463.)

CONSEIL DE PRUDHOMMES. In French law. One of a species of trade tribunals, charged with settling differences between masters and workmen. They endeavor, in the first instance, to conciliate the parties. In default, they adjudicate upon the questions in dispute. Their decisions are final up to 200*f*. Beyond that amount, appeals lie to the tribunals of commerce. Arg. Fr. Merc. Law, 553.

CONSEIL JUDICIAIRE. In French law. When a person has been subjected to an interdiction on the ground of his insane extravagance, but the interdiction is not absolute, but limited only, the court of first instance, which grants the interdiction, appoints a council, called by this name, with whose assistance the party may bring or defend actions, or compromise the same, alienate his estate, make or incur loans, and the like. Brown.

CONSENSUAL CONTRACT. A term derived from the civil law, denoting a contract founded upon and completed by the mere consent of the contracting parties, without any external formality or symbolic act to fix the obligation.

CONSENSUAL MARRIAGE. Marriage resting simply on consent per verba de præsenti, between competent parties. Such marriage is valid. Fisher v. Fisher, 250 N.Y. 313, 165 N.E. 460, 461, 61 A.L.R. 1523. See, also, Common-law Marriage.

CONSENSUS AD IDEM. An agreement of parties to the same thing; a meeting of minds.

CONSENSUS EST VOLUNTAS PLURIUM AD QUOS RES PERTINET, SIMUL JUNCTA. Lofft, 514. Consent is the conjoint will of several persons to whom the thing belongs.

CONSENSUS FACIT LEGEM. Consent makes the law. (A contract is law between the parties agreeing to be bound by it.) Branch, Princ.

CONSENSUS, NON CONCUBITUS, FACIT NUPTIAS VEL MATRIMONIUM, ET CONSENTIRE NON POSSUNT ANTE ANNOS NUBILES. 6 Coke, 22. Consent, and not cohabitation (or coition), constitutes nuptials or marriage, and persons cannot consent before marriageable years. 1 Bl.Comm. 434; Co. Litt. 33*a*; Dig. 50, 17, 30. See 10 Cl. & F. 534; Broom, Max. 505.

CONSENSUS TOLLIT ERROREM. Co. Litt. 126. Consent (acquiescence) removes mistake. 2 Inst. 123; Rogers v. Cruger, 7 Johns. (N.Y.) 611; Kuhler v. Hoover, 4 Pa. 335; Wilkinson's Appeal, 65 Pa. 190.

CONSENSUS VOLUNTAS MULTORUM AD QUOS RES PERTINET, SIMUL JUNCTA. Consent is the united will of several interested in one subject-matter. Davis, 48; Branch, Princ.

CONSENT. A concurrence of wills. Voluntarily yielding the will to the proposition of another; acquiescence or compliance therewith. Twin Ports Oil Co. v. Pure Oil Co., D.C.Minn., 26 F.Supp. 366, 371. Agreement; the act or result of coming into harmony or accord. Glantz v. Gabel, 66 Mont. 134, 212 P. 858, 860.

Consent is an act of reason, accompanied with deliberation, the mind weighing as in a balance the good or evil on each side. 1 Story, Eq.Jur. § 222; Lervick v. White Top Cabs, La.App., 10 So.2d 67, 73. It means voluntary agreement by a person in the possession and exercise of sufficient mentality to make an intelligent choice to do something proposed by another. People v. Kangiesser, 44 Cal. App. 345, 186 P. 388, 389. It supposes a physical power to act, a moral power of acting, and a serious, determined, and free use of these powers. Fonblanque, Eq. b. 1, c. 2, s. 1; New Jersey Mfrs' Casualty Ins. Co., 148 A. 790, 791, 106 N.J.L. 238. Consent is implied in every agreement. It is an act unclouded by fraud, duress, or sometimes even mistake. Heine v. Wright, 76 Cal.App. 338, 244 P. 955, 956.

There is a difference between consenting and submitting. Every consent involves a submission; but a mere submission does not necessarily involve consent. 9 Car. & P. 722.

"Consent" is an active acquiescence as distinguished from "assent," meaning a silent acquiescence. People v. Lowe, 205 N.Y.S. 77, 78, 209 App.Div. 498. "Consent" means an active circumstance of concurrence; "assent" is a passive act of concurrence before another does the act charged. Perryman v. State, 63 Ga.App. 819, 12 S.E.2d 388, 390. But the two terms may be used interchangeably. Bartlett v. Sundin, 169 N.Y.S. 391, 393, 182 App.Div. 117.

"Consent" is sometimes synonymous merely with "waiver." Dahlquist v. Denver & R. G. R. Co., 52 Utah, 438, 174 P. 833, 844. See, also, Seegmiller v. Day, C.C.A.Ill., 249 F. 177, 178; Toledo Fence & Post Co. v. Lyons, C.C.A.Ohio, 290 F. 637, 640.

As used in the law of rape "consent" means consent of the will, and submission under the influence of fear or terror cannot amount to real consent. Hallmark v. State, 22 Okl. Cr. 422, 212 P. 322, 328. There must be an exercise of intelligence based on knowledge of its significance and moral quality and there must be a choice between resistance and assent. State v. Schwab, 109 Ohio St. 532, 143 N. E. 29, 31. And if woman resists to the point where further resistance would be useless or until her resistance is overcome by force or violence, submission thereafter is not "consent". People v. McIlvain, 130 P.2d 131, 135, 55 Cal. App.2d 322.

See Assent.

Consent decree. See Decree.

Consent judgment. See Judgment.

Express Consent. That directly given, either *viva voce* or in writing. It is positive, direct, unequivocal consent, requiring no inference or implication to supply its meaning. Pacific Nat. Agricultural Credit Corporation v. Hagerman, 40 N.M. 116, 55 P.2d 667, 670.

Express or Implied Consent. Under motor vehicle liability insurance law providing that policy should cover any person responsible for operation of insured vehicle with insured's express or implied consent, words "express or implied consent" primarily modify not the word "operation", but the word "responsible", and imply possession of vehicle with consent of owner and responsibility to him. Hurley v. Flanagan, 313 Mass. 567, 48 N.E.2d 621, 624.

Implied Consent. That manifested by signs, actions, or facts, or by inaction or silence, which raise a presumption that the consent has been given. Avery v. State, 12 Ga.App. 562, 77 S.E. 892. See State v. Horton, 247 Mo. 657, 153 S.W. 1051, 1053; White v. White, 84 N.J.Eq. 512, 95 A. 197, 199.

CONSENT RULE. An entry of record by the defendant, confessing the lease, entry, and ouster by the plaintiff, in an action of ejectment. A superseded instrument, in which a defendant in an action of ejectment specified for what purpose he intended to defend, and undertook to confess not only the fictitious lease, entry, and ouster, but that he was in possession. See Ad.Eject. 233.

CONSENTIBLE LINES. See Line.

CONSENTIENTES ET AGENTES PARI PŒNA PLECTENTUR. They who consent to an act, and they who do it, shall be visited with equal punishment. 5 Coke 80.

CONSENTIRE MATRIMONIO NON POSSUNT INFRA [ANTE] ANNOS NUBILES. Parties cannot consent to marriage within the years of marriage, [before the age of consent.] 5 Coke 80; 6 Coke 22.

CONSEQUENCE. The result following in natural sequence from an event which is adapted to produce, or to aid in producing, such result;—the correlative of "cause." Board of Trustees of Firemen's Relief and Pension Fund for City of Tulsa v. Miller, 186 Okl. 586, 99 P.2d 146, 147.

In Consequence of

This phrase has been used as equivalent to the words, "in the event of." In re Spalding's Estate, 84 Cal.App. 371, 258 P. 154, 155.

CONSEQUENTIÆ NON EST CONSEQUENTIA. Bac.Max. The consequence of a consequence exists not.

CONSEQUENTIAL CONTEMPT. The ancient name for what is now known as "constructive" contempt of court. Ex parte Wright, 65 Ind. 508. See Contempt.

CONSEQUENTIAL DAMAGES. See Damages.

CONSEQUENTS. In Scotch law. Implied powers or authorities. Things which follow, usually by implication of law. A commission being given to execute any work, every power necessary to carry it on is implied. 1 Kames, Eq. 242.

CONSERVATOR. A guardian; protector; preserver.

"When any person having property shall be found to be incapable of managing his affairs, by the court of probate in the district in which he resides, * * * it shall appoint some person to be his *conservator,* who, upon giving a probate bond, shall have the charge of the person and estate of such incapable person." Gen.St.Conn.1875, p. 346, § 1 (Gen.St.1930, § 4815); Hutchins v. Johnson, 12 Conn. 376, 30 Am.Dec. 622.

One whose business it is to attend to the enforcement of certain statutes. See Conservators of the Peace, *infra.*

One whose duty requires him to prevent and arrest for breaches of the peace in his presence, but not to arraign and try for them. Marcuchi v. Norfolk & W. Ry. Co., 81 W.Va. 548, 94 S.E. 979, 980.

A delegated umpire or standing arbitrator, chosen to compose and adjust difficulties arising between two parties. Cowell.

CONSERVATOR TRUCIS. Lat. An official appointed under an English act of 1414 passed to prevent breaches of truces made, or of safe conducts granted, by the king. 2 Holdsw.Hist.E.L. 392; 4 Bla.Comm. 69.

CONSERVATORS OF RIVERS. Commissioners or trustees in whom the control of a certain river is vested, in England, by act of parliament.

CONSERVATORS OF THE PEACE. Officers authorized to preserve and maintain the public peace. In England, these officers were locally elected by the people until the reign of Edward III, when their appointment was vested in the king. Their duties were to prevent and arrest for breaches of the peace, but they had no power to arraign and try the offender until about 1360, when this authority was given to them by act of parliament, and "then they acquired the more honorable appellation of justices of the peace." 1 Bl.Comm. 351.

Even after this time, however, many public officers were styled "conservators of the peace," not as a distinct office but by virtue of the duties and authorities pertaining to their offices. In this sense the term may include the king himself, the lord chancellor, justices of the king's bench, master of the rolls, coroners, sheriffs, constables, etc. 1 Bl.Comm. 350. See Smith v. Abbott, 17 N.J.L. 358. In Texas, the constitution provides that county judges shall be conservators of the peace. Const.Tex. art. 4, § 15; Jones v. State, Tex.Cr.App., 65 S.W. 92. The Constitution of Delaware (1831) provides that: "The members of the senate and house of representatives, the chancellor, the judges, and the attorney-general shall, by virtue of their offices, be conservators of the peace throughout the state; and the treasurer, secretary, and prothonotaries, registers, recorders, sheriffs, and coroners, shall, by virtue of their offices, be conservators thereof within the counties respectively in which they reside."

CONSERVE. To save from loss. U. S. v. Mammoth Oil Co., D.C.Wyo., 5 F.2d 330, 351.

CONSIDER. To fix the mind on, with a view to careful examination; to examine; to inspect. Eastman Kodak Co. v. Richards, 204 N.Y.S. 246, 248, 123 Misc. 83. To deliberate about and ponder over. People v. Tru-Sport Pub. Co., 291 N.Y.S. 449, 457, 160 Misc. 628. To entertain or give heed to. Rodolf v. Board of Com'rs of Tulsa County, 122 Okl. 120, 251 P. 740, 741. See, also, Considered.

CONSIDERABLE. Worthy of consideration; required to be observed. Gougar v. Buffalo Specialty Co., 26 Colo.App. 8, 141 P. 511, 514.

A "considerable" number, as of persons, does not necessarily mean a very great or any particular number of persons; the term "considerable" being merely relative. People v. Kings County Iron Foundry, 209 N.Y. 207, 102 N. E. 598, 599.

CONSIDERATIO CURIÆ. The judgment of the court.

CONSIDERATION. Practice. A technical term indicating that a tribunal has heard and judicially determined matters submitted to it. Meaney v. State Industrial Accident Commission, 113 Or. 371, 232 P. 789, 791.

Contracts

The inducement to a contract. The cause, motive, price, or impelling influence which induces a contracting party to enter into a contract. The reason or material cause of a contract. 2 Bla. Comm. 443; Cassinelli v. Stacy, 238 Ky. 827, 38 S.W.2d 980, 983.

Consideration is not to be confounded with motive. Consideration means something which is of value in the eye of the law, moving from the plaintiff, either of benefit to the plaintiff or of detriment to the defendant. Patteson, J., in Langd.Sel.Cas.Contr. 168; s. c. 2 Q.B. 851; Miller v. Bank of Holly Springs, 131 Miss. 55, 95 So. 129, 130, 31 A.L.R. 698. "Nothing is consideration that is not regarded as such by both parties." Schlecht v. Schlecht, 168 Minn. 168, 209 N.W. 883, 887. And "price" and "consideration," though sometimes the same, are not always identical. Oregon Home Builders v. Crowley, 87 Or. 517, 170 P. 718, 721.

The "inducement" for a contract is that which influences the act, while "consideration" means the parting with something by the one from whom it moves. E. F. Spears & Sons v. Winkle, 186 Ky. 585, 217 S.W. 691, 692.

An act or forbearance, or the promise thereof, which is offered by one party to an agreement, and accepted by the other as an inducement to that other's act or promise. Poll.Contr. 91.

Any benefit conferred, or agreed to be conferred, upon the promisor, by any other person, to which the promisor is not lawfully entitled, or any prejudice suffered, or agreed to be suffered, by such person, other than such as he is at the time of consent lawfully bound to suffer, as an inducement to the promisor. Hence doing only of what one is already under obligation to do is not "consideration" for a contract. Hogan v. Supreme Camp of the American Woodmen, 146 Fla. 413, 1 So.2d 256, 258.

Any act of the plaintiff (or the promisee) from which the defendant (the promisor) or a stranger derives a benefit or advantage, or any labor, detriment, or inconvenience sustained by the plaintiff, however small, if such act is performed or inconvenience suffered by the plaintiff by the consent, express or implied, of the defendant. 3 Scott, 250.

A benefit to the promisor, or a loss or detriment to the promisee. Harris v. Johnson, 75 Wash. 291, 134 P. 1048, 1050; Fowler v. Smith, 24 Ohio App. 324, 156 N.E. 913, 914. Or benefit to a third party. Wellshire Land Co. v. City and County of Denver, 103 Colo. 416, 87 P.2d 1. But nothing is "consideration" that is not regarded as such by both parties. Michael v. Holland, 111 Ind.App. 34, 40 N.E.2d 362, 365.

Some right, interest, gain, advantage, benefit, or profit to one party, usually the promisor, or some forbearance, detriment, prejudice, inconvenience, disadvantage, loss, or responsibility, act, or service given, suffered, or undertaken by the promisee. Exum v. Lynch, 125 S.E. 15, 17, 188 N.C. 392; Furman University v. Waller, 117 S.E. 356, 358, 124 S.C. 68, 33 A.L.R. 615; Robinson v. Oliver, 156 N.Y.S. 896, 898, 171 App.Div. 349; L.R. 10 Ex. 162; Train v. Gold, 5 Pick.(Mass.) 380; Bankers Trust Co. v. Economy Coal Co., 224 Iowa 36, 276 N.W. 16, 20.

Considerations are either *executed* or *executory; express* or *implied; good* or *valuable*. See definitions *infra*.

Adequate Consideration. See Adequate.

Concurrent Consideration. One which arises at the same time or where the promises are simultaneous.

Continuing Consideration. One consisting in acts or performances which must necessarily extend over a considerable period of time.

Equitable or Moral Considerations. Considerations which are devoid of efficacy in point of strict law, but are founded upon a moral duty, and may be made the basis of an express promise.

Executed or Executory Considerations. The former are acts done or values given before or at the time of making the contract; the latter are promises to give or do something in future.

Express or Implied Considerations. The former are those which are specifically stated in a deed, contract, or other instrument; the latter are those inferred or supposed by the law from the acts or situation of the parties.

Express consideration is a consideration which is distinctly and specifically named in the written contract or in the oral agreement of the parties.

Failure of Consideration. See Failure of Consideration.

Fair and Valuable Consideration. See Fair and Valuable Consideration.

Fair Consideration. See Fair Consideration.

Good Consideration. Such as is founded on natural duty and affection, or on a strong moral obligation. Chit.Cont. 7. A consideration for love and affection entertained by and for one within degree recognized by law. Gay v. Fricks, 211 Ala. 119, 99 So. 846, 847. See, also, Berry v. Berry, 83 W.Va. 763, 99 S.E. 79.

Motives of natural duty, generosity, and prudence come under this class. 2 Bla.Comm. 297; Doran v. McConlogue, 150 Pa. 98, 24 A. 357; Mascolo v. Montesanto, 61 Conn. 50, 23 A. 714, 29 Am.St.Rep. 170.

The term is sometimes used in the sense of a consideration valid in point of law; and it then includes a valuable or sufficient as well as a meritorious consideration. Hodgson v. Butts, 3 Cra. (U.S.) 140, 2 L.Ed. 391; Lang v. Johnson, 24 N.H. 302; Ambl. 598. Generally, however, *good* is used in antithesis to *valuable consideration (q. v.)*.

Gratuitous Consideration. One which is not founded upon any such loss, injury, or inconvenience to the party to whom it moves as to make it valid in law.

Illegal Consideration. An act which if done, or a promise which if enforced, would be prejudicial to the public interest. Harriman, Cont. 101.

Implied Considerations. See Express or Implied Considerations, supra.

Impossible Consideration. One which cannot be performed.

Inadequate Consideration. See that title.

Legal Consideration. One recognized or permitted by the law as valid and lawful; as distinguished from such as are illegal or immoral. The term is also sometimes used as equivalent to "good" or "sufficient" consideration. See Sampson v. Swift, 11 Vt. 315; Albert Lea College v. Brown, 88 Minn. 524, 93 N.W. 672, 60 L.R.A. 870.

Meritorious Consideration. See Good Consideration.

Moral Considerations. See Equitable or Moral Considerations, supra.

Nominal Consideration. One bearing no relation to the real value of the contract or article, as where a parcel of land is described in a deed as being sold for "one dollar," no actual consideration passing, or the real consideration being concealed. This term is also sometimes used as descriptive of an inflated or exaggerated value placed upon property for the purpose of an exchange. Boyd v. Watson, 101 Iowa 214, 70 N.W. 123; Emmi v. Patane, 220 N.Y.S. 495, 498, 128 Misc. 901.

Past Consideration. An act done before the contract is made, which is ordinarily by itself no consideration for a promise. Anson, Cont. 82; Witt v. Wilson, Tex.Civ.App., 160 S.W. 309, 310.

As to time, considerations may be of the past, present, or future. Those which are present or future will support a contract not void for other reasons. Story, Contr. 71.

Pecuniary Consideration. A consideration for an act or forbearance which consists either in money presently passing or in money to be paid in the future, including a promise to pay a debt in full which otherwise would be released or diminished by bankruptcy or insolvency proceedings. See Phelps v. Thomas, 6 Gray (Mass.) 328; In re Ekings, D.C.N.J., 6 F. 170.

Sufficient Consideration. One deemed by the law of sufficient value to support an ordinary contract between parties, or one sufficient to support the particular transaction. Golson v. Dunlap, 73 Cal. 157, 14 P. 576.

Valuable Consideration. See Consideration.

Want of Consideration. See Want of Consideration.

CONSIDERATUM EST PER CURIAM. (It is considered by the court.) The formal and ordinary commencement of a judgment. Baker v. State, 3 Ark. 491.

CONSIDERATUR. L. Lat. It is considered. Held to mean the same with *consideratum est.* 2 Strange, 874.

CONSIDERED. Deemed; determined; adjudged; reasonably regarded. State v. District Court of Eighth Judicial Dist. in and for Cascade County, 64 Mont. 181, 208 P. 952, 955. See Consider.

Evidence may be said to have been "considered" when it has been reviewed by a court to determine whether any probative force should be given it. Taylor v. Gossett, Tex. Civ.App., 269 S.W. 230, 233.

CONSIGN. In the civil law. To deposit in the custody of a third person a thing belonging to the debtor, for the benefit of the creditor, under the authority of a court of justice. Poth.Obl. pt. 3, c. 1, art. 8.

In Commercial Law. To deliver goods to a carrier to be transmitted to a designated factor or agent. Powell v. Wallace, 44 Kan. 656, 25 P. 42; Ide Mfg. Co. v. Sager Mfg. Co., 82 Ill.App. 685. To deliver or transfer as a charge or trust; to commit, intrust, give in trust; to transfer from oneself to the care of another; to send or transmit goods to a merchant, factor, or agent for sale; to deposit with another to be sold, disposed of, or called for. Edwards v. Baldwin Piano Co., 79 Fla. 143, 83 So. 915, 918.

CONSIGNATION. In Scotch law. The payment of money into the hands of a third party, when the creditor refuses to accept of it. The person to whom the money is given is termed the "consignatory." Bell.

In French law. A deposit which a debtor makes of the thing that he owes into the hands of a third person, and under the authority of a court of justice. 1 Poth.Obl. 536; Weld v. Hadley, 1 N. H. 304.

CONSIGNEE. In mercantile law. One to whom a consignment is made. The person to whom goods are shipped for sale. Lyon v. Alvord, 18 Conn. 80; Comm. v. Harris, 168 Pa. 619, 32 A. 92. One to whom goods are consigned, shipped, or otherwise transmitted. State v. Chadbourne, 132 Me. 5, 164 A. 630, 631. The one to whom the carrier may lawfully make delivery in accordance with its contract of carriage. Great Northern Pac. S. S. Co. v. Rainier Brewing Co., C.C.A.Wash., 255 F. 762, 764; One to whom merchandise has been delivered. International Trust Co. v. Webster Nat. Bank, 258 Mass. 17, 154 N.E. 330, 332, 49 A. L.R. 267; Under a statute, the person who, under circumstances in which he might be entitled to the delivery of the goods, represents that he is so entitled, tenders a bond in the statutory form, and requests delivery. St. Louis, I. M. & S. R. Co. v. Bankers' Surety Co., 115 Ark. 58, 172 S.W. 266, 268.

CONSIGNMENT. The act or process of consigning goods; the transportation of goods consigned; an article or collection of goods sent to a factor; goods or property sent, by the aid of a common carrier, from one person in one place to another person in another place; something consigned and shipped. See Consign. In re Taylor, D.C.Mich., 46 F.2d 326, 328.

Feature which distinguishes "conditional sale" from "consignment" is that in the former the purchaser undertakes an absolute obligation to pay for the goods, whereas the latter is nothing more than a bailment for sale. In re Sachs, D.C.Md., 31 F.2d 799, 800.

In stockyard parlance, all the livestock of one species delivered in the name of one person to one market agency to be offered for sale during the trading hours of one day. Acker v. U. S., D.C.Ill., 12 F.Supp. 776, 780. Mutual Transfer Corporation of Galax v. Commonwealth, 172 Va. 622, 1 S.E.2d 477, 479.

CONSIGNOR. One who sends or makes a consignment; a shipper of goods.

CONSILIA MULTORUM QUÆRUNTUR IN MAGNIS. 4 Inst. 1. The counsels of many are required in great things.

CONSILIARIUS. In the civil law. A counsellor, as distinguished from a pleader or advocate. An assistant judge. One who participates in the decisions. Du Cange.

CONSILIUM. A day appointed to hear the counsel of both parties. A case set down for argument.

It is commonly used for the day appointed for the argument of a demurrer, or errors assigned. 1 Tidd, Pr. 438; 2 Tidd, Pr. 684, 1122; 1 Sell.Pr. 336; 1 Archb.Pr. 191, 246.

CONSIMILI CASU. In practice. A writ of entry, framed under the provisions of the statute Westminster 2, (13 Edw. I.,) c. 24, which lay for the benefit of the reversioner, where a tenant by the curtesy aliened in fee or for life. 3 Bla.Comm., 4th Dublin ed. 183 n.; Bac.Abr. Court of Chancery (A).

Many other new writs were framed under the provisions of this statute; but this particular writ was known emphatically by the title here defined. The writ is now practically obsolete. See 3 Bla.Comm. 51.

CONSIST. To stand together, to be composed of or made up of. Hoskins Mfg. Co. v. General Electric Co., D.C.Ill., 212 F. 422; In re Clark's Estate, 100 Vt. 217, 136 A. 389, 393. See Consisting.

CONSISTENT. Having agreement with itself or something else; accordant; harmonious; congruous; compatible; compliable; not contradictory. Baldwin-Heckes Co. v. Kammerlohr, 123 Neb. 317, 242 N.W. 661, 663; Ryan v. Roach Drug Co., 113 Okl. 130, 239 P. 912, 914.

"Consistent with" means in harmony with. Shay v. Roth, 64 Cal.App. 314, 221 P. 967, 969.

CONSISTING. Being composed or made up of. This word is not synonymous with "including;" for the latter, when used in connection with a number of specified objects, always implies that there may be others which are not mentioned. In re Wright's Estate, 166 Misc. 52, 2 N.Y.S.2d 25, 28.

CONSISTOR. A magistrate. Jacob L. D.

CONSISTORIUM. The state council of the Roman emperors. Mackeld.Rom.Law, § 58.

CONSISTORY. An assembly of cardinals convoked by the pope.

A tribunal (*prœtorium*).

CONSISTORY COURTS. The courts of diocesan bishops held in their several cathedrals (before the bishop's chancellor, or commissary, who is the judge) for the trial of all ecclesiastical causes arising within their respective dioceses, and also for granting probates and administrations. Mozley & Whitley; 1 Holdsw.Hist.E.L. 369, citing L.R. 1902, 1 K.B. 816. From the sentence of these courts an appeal lies to the Provincial Court of the archbishop of each province respectively. 2 Steph. Comm. 230; 3 Steph.Comm. 430; 3 Bla.Comm. 64; 1 Woodd.Lect. 145; Halifax, An. b. 3, c. 10, n. 12.

CONSOBRINI. In the civil law. Cousins-german, in general; brothers' and sisters' children, considered in their relation to each other.

CONSOCIATIO. Lat. An association, fellowship, or partnership. Applied by some of the older writers to a corporation, and even to a nation considered as a body politic. Thomas v. Dakin, 22 Wend. (N.Y.) 104.

CONSOLATION. Comfort, contentment, ease, enjoyment, happiness, pleasure, satisfaction. National Surety Co. v. Jarrett, 95 W.Va. 420, 121 S.E. 291, 295.

CONSOLATO DEL MARE. The name of a code of sea-laws, said to have been compiled by order of the kings of Arragon (or, according to other authorities, at Pisa or Barcelona) in the fourteenth century, which comprised the maritime ordinances of the Roman emperors, of France and Spain, and of the Italian commercial powers. This compilation exercised a considerable influence in the formation of European maritime law.

CONSOLIDATE. In a general sense, to unite into one mass or body, as to consolidate the forces of an army, or various funds. In parliamentary usage, to consolidate two bills is to unite them into one. In law, to consolidate benefices is to combine them into one. The term means something more than to rearrange or redivide. Fairview v. Durland, 45 Iowa 56.

To make solid or firm; to unite, compress, or pack together and form into a more compact mass, body, or system. Marfield v. Cincinnati, D. & T. Traction Co., 111 Ohio St. 139, 144 N.E. 689, 696, 40 A.L.R. 357. To cause to become united and extinguished in a superior right or estate by both becoming vested in the same person. Swaim v. Smith, 174 Tenn. 688, 130 S.W.2d 116, 120.

CONSOLIDATED FUND. In England. (Usually abbreviated to *Consols.*) A fund for the payment of the public debt.

CONSOLIDATED LAWS OR STATUTES. A collection or compilation into one statute or one code or volume of all the laws of the state in general, or of those relating to a particular subject; nearly the same as "compiled laws" or "compiled statutes." See Compilation. And see Ellis v. Parsell, 100 Mich. 170, 58 N.W. 839.

CONSOLIDATED ORDERS. The orders regulating the practice of the English court of chancery, which were issued, in 1860, in substitution for the various orders which had previously been promulgated from time to time.

CONSOLIDATION. Act of consolidating, or the status of being consolidated. O'Malley v. Wilson, 182 Ga. 97, 185 S.E. 109, 114.

In the civil law. The union of the usufruct with the estate out of which it issues, in the same person; which happens when the usufructuary acquires the estate, or *vice versa.* In either case the usufruct is extinct. Lec.El.Dr.Rom. 424.

In ecclesiastical law. The union of two or more benefices in one. Cowell.

In practice. The union of two or more actions, as in the same declaration, or for the purpose of trial or appellate review. See Consolidation of Actions.

In Scotch law. The junction of the property and superiority of an estate, where they have been disjoined. Bell.

Consolidation of actions. The act or process of uniting several actions into one trial and judgment, by order of a court, where all the actions are between the same parties, pending in the same court, and involving substantially the same subject-matter, issues and defenses; or the court may order that one of the actions be tried, and the others decided without trial according to the judgment in the one selected. 249 N.Y.S. 33, 36, 139 Misc. 564; National Union Fire Ins. Co. v. Chesapeake and O. Ry. Co., D.C.Ky., 4 F.Supp. 25, 30.

It means the merging of two or more actions into one so that they lose their separate identity, while in trial of "several actions together" each retains its separate character and requires the entry of a separate judgment. Ramswick v. Messerer, 200 Minn. 299, 274 N.W. 179; Reeves v. Philadelphia Gas Works Co., 107 Pa.Super. 422, 164 A. 132, 134, 107.

CONSOLIDATION OF BENEFICES. The act or process of uniting two or more of them into one.

CONSOLIDATIONS OF CORPORATIONS. Takes place when two or more corporations are extinguished, and by the same process a new one is created, taking over the assets and assuming the liabilities of those passing out of existence. A unifying of two or more corporations into a single new corporation having the combined capital, franchises, and powers of all its constituents. Alabama Power Co. v. McNinch, 68 App.D.C. 132, 94 F.2d 601, 611, 612. Freeman v. Hiznay, 349 Pa. 89, 36 A.2d 509; Murphy v. Niehus, 50 Ohio App. 299, 198 N.E. 197, 200.

Merger distinguished. In a "merger," one corporation absorbs the other and remains in existence while the other is dissolved, and in a "consolidation" a new corporation is created and the consolidating corporations are extinguished. Von Weise v. Commissioner of Internal Revenue, C.C.A., 69 F.2d 439, 442; Alabama Power Co. v. McNinch, 94 F.2d 601, 610, 611, 612, 68 App.D.C. 132. See, also, Merger.

Consolidation rule. In practice. A rule or order of court requiring a plaintiff who has instituted separate suits upon several claims against the same defendant, to consolidate them in one action, where that can be done consistently with the rules of pleading. Brown v. Scott, 1 Dall. (Pa.) 147, 1 L.Ed. 74; Groff v. Musser, 3 Serg. & R. (Pa.) 264; 2 Archb.Pr. 180. The Federal courts are authorized to consolidate actions involving a common question of law or fact. Federal Rules of Civil Procedure, Rule 42, 28 U.S.C.A.

CONSOLS. An abbreviation of the expression "consolidated annuities," and used in modern times as a name of various funds united in one for the payment of the British national debt. Also, a name given to certain issues of bonds of the state of South Carolina. Whaley v. Gaillard, 21 S.C. 568. See Consolidated Fund.

CONSONANT STATEMENT. A prior declaration of a witness whose testimony has been attacked and whose credibility stands impeached, which the court will allow to be proved by the person to whom the declaration was made in order to support the credibility of the witness and which but for the existence of such impeachment would ordinarily be excluded as hearsay. Commonwealth v. White, 16 A.2d 407, 409, 340 Pa. 139.

CONSORTIO MALORUM ME QUOQUE MALUM FACIT. Moore, 817. The company of wicked men makes me also wicked.

CONSORTIUM. Conjugal fellowship of husband and wife, and the right of each to the company, co-operation, affection, and aid of the other in every conjugal relation. McMillan v. Smith, 47 Ga.App. 646, 171 S.E. 169, 170; Shedrick v. Lathrop, 106 Vt. 311, 172 A. 630, 632; Harris v. Kunkel, 227 Wis. 435, 278 N.W. 868, 869.

The term includes the exclusive right to the services of the spouse, and to his or her society, companionship, and conjugal affection. Smith v. Nicholas Bldg. Co., 93 Ohio St. 101, 112 N.E. 204.

In its original application the term was not confined to society, companionship, and conjugal affection, but included service as a prominent, if not the predominant, factor—not so much the service resulting in the performance of labor or the earning of wages as the service which contributed aid and assistance in all the relations of domestic life. Hinnant v. Tide Water Power Co., 189 N.C. 120, 126 S.E. 307, 309, 37 A.L.R. 889.

In the civil law. A union of fortunes; a lawful Roman marriage. The joining of several persons as parties to one action.

In old English law, the term signified company or society, and in the language of pleading, as in the phrase *per quod consortium amisit,* it has substantially the same meaning, viz., the companionship or society of a wife. 3 Bla.Comm. 140; Kelley v. Railroad Co., 168 Mass. 308, 46 N.E. 1063, 38 L.R.A. 631, 60 Am.St.Rep. 397.

CONSORTSHIP. In maritime law. An agreement or stipulation between the owners of different vessels that they shall keep in company, mutually aid, instead of interfering with each other, in wrecking and salvage, and share any money awarded as salvage, whether earned by one vessel or both. Andrews v. Wall, 3 How. 571, 11 L.Ed. 729.

CONSPICUOUS PLACE. Within the meaning of a statute relating to the posting of notices, a "conspicuous place" means one which is reasonably calculated to impart the information in question. Didier v. Webster Mines Corporation, 49 Nev. 5, 234 P. 520, 523.

CONSPIRACY. In criminal law. A combination or confederacy between two or more persons formed for the purpose of committing, by their joint efforts, some unlawful or criminal act, or some act which is innocent in itself, but becomes unlawful when done by the concerted action of the conspirators, or for the purpose of using criminal or unlawful means to the commission of an act not in itself unlawful. Pettibone v. U. S., 148 U.S. 197, 13 S.Ct. 542, 37 L.Ed. 419; Mitchell v. Hitchman Coal & Coke Co., C.C.A.W.Va., 214 F. 685, 708; Hamilton v. Cooley, 184 N.E. 568, 571,

99 Ind.App. 1; Browning v. Browning, 226 Mo. App. 322, 41 S.W.2d 860, 868.

A combination, or an agreement between two or more persons, for accomplishing an unlawful end or a lawful end by unlawful means. 4 B. & Ad. 345; Cumberland Telephone & Telegraph Co. v. Stevens, D.C.Miss., 274 F. 745, 746; Lauf v. E. G. Shinner & Co., C.C.A.Wis., 82 F.2d 68, 72; Morrison v. Goodspeed, 100 Colo. 470, 68 P.2d 458, 464.

A partnership in criminal purposes. Marino v. United States, C.C.A.Cal., 91 F.2d 691, 113 A.L.R. 975.

The essence of "conspiracy" is an agreement, together with an overt act, to do an unlawful act, or do a lawful act in an unlawful manner. Cooper v. O'Connor, 99 F.2d 135, 142, 69 App.D.C. 100, 118 A.L.R. 1440. Mere knowledge, acquiescence, approval, or attempt on part of one to perpetrate illegal act is insufficient. People v. Link, 365 Ill. 266, 6 N.E.2d 201.

A conspiracy may be a continuing one; actors may drop out, and others drop in; the details of operation may change from time to time; the members need not know each other or the part played by others; a member need not know all the details of the plan or the operations; he must, however, know the purpose of the conspiracy and agree to become a party to a plan to effectuate that purpose. Craig v. U. S., C.C.A.Cal., 81 F.2d 816, 822.

A consultation or agreement between two or more persons, either falsely to accuse another of a crime punishable by law; or wrongfully to injure or prejudice a third person, or any body of men, in any manner; or to commit any offense punishable by law; or to do any act with intent to prevent the course of justice; or to effect a legal purpose with a corrupt intent, or by improper means. Hawk. P.C. c. 72, § 2; Archb.Crim.Pl. 390, adding also combinations by journeymen to raise wages. State v. Murphy, 6 Ala. 765, 41 Am.Dec. 79.

Civil and Criminal Conspiracies

The term "civil" is used to designate a conspiracy which will furnish ground for a civil action, as where, in carrying out the design of the conspirators, overt acts are done causing legal damage, the person injured has a right of action. It is said that the gist of civil conspiracy is the injury or damage. While criminal conspiracy does not require such overt acts, yet, so far as the rights and remedies are concerned, all criminal conspiracies are embraced within the civil conspiracies. Martha Mills v. Moseley, 50 Ga.App. 536, 179 S.E. 159.

Accurately speaking, there is no such thing as a civil action for conspiracy. The better view is that the damage sustained, and not the conspiracy is the gist of the action. The combination may be of no consequence except as bearing upon rules of evidence or the persons liable. Dahlquist v. Mattson, 40 Idaho, 378, 233 P. 883, 885.

The essence of a "civil conspiracy" is a concert or combination to defraud or cause other injury to person or property, which results in damage to the person or property of plaintiff. Conner v. Bryce, Sup., 170 N.Y.S. 94, 95.

CONSPIRATIONE. An ancient writ that lay against conspirators. Reg.Orig. 134; Fitzh.Nat. Brev. 114.

CONSPIRATORS. Persons guilty of a conspiracy. State v. Collins, 88 Mont. 514, 294 P. 957, 961, 73 A.L.R. 861.

Where two or more persons enter on a common enterprise or adventure and criminal offense is contemplated each is a "conspirator". Kelly v. State, 31 Ala.App. 194, 13 So.2d 691, 692.

Those who bind themselves by oath, covenant, or other alliance that each of them shall aid the other falsely and maliciously to indict persons; or falsely to move and maintain pleas, etc. 33 Edw. I. St. 2. Besides these, there are conspirators in treasonable purposes; as for plotting against the government. Wharton.

CONSPIRE. To engage in conspiracy. Wright v. United States, C.C.A.La., 48 C.C.A. 37, 108 F. 805, 809.

It carries with it the idea of agreement, concurrence and combination, and hence is inapplicable to a single person or thing, and one cannot agree or conspire with another who does not agree or conspire with him. Horton v. Johnson, 192 Ga. 338, 15 S.E.2d 605, 615.

CONSTABLE. In American law. An officer of a municipal corporation (usually elected) whose duties are similar to those of the sheriff, though his powers are less and his jurisdiction smaller. He is to preserve the public peace, execute the process of magistrates' courts, and of some other tribunals, serve writs, attend the sessions of the criminal courts, have the custody of juries, and discharge other functions sometimes assigned to him by the local law or by statute. Allor v. Wayne County, 43 Mich. 76, 4 N.W. 492.

In English law. A public civil officer, whose proper and general duty is to keep the peace within his district, though he is frequently charged with additional duties. 1 Bl.Comm. 356. There are "high," "petty," and "special" constables. See the definitions, *infra*.

In Medieval law. A high functionary under the French and English kings, the dignity and importance of whose office was second only to that of the monarch. He was in general the leader of the royal armies, and had cognizance of all matters pertaining to war and arms, exercising both civil and military jurisdiction. He was also charged with the conservation of the peace of the nation. Thus there was a "Constable of France" and a "Lord High Constable of England." Rich v. Industrial Commission, 80 Utah 511, 15 P.2d 641, 644.

Constable of a castle. In English law. An officer having charge of a castle; a warden, or keeper; otherwise called a "castellain." Stat. Westm. 1, c. 7 (3 Edw. I.); Spelman, Gloss.

Constable of England. (Called, also, "Marshal.") His office consisted in the care of the common peace of the realm in deeds of arms and matters of war. Lamb. Const. 4; 3 Steph. Comm. 47; 4 Bla. Comm. 92.

Constable of Scotland. An officer who was formerly entitled to command all the king's armies in the absence of the king, and to take cognizance of all crimes committed within four miles of the king's person or of parliament, the privy council, or any general convention of the states of the kingdom. The office was hereditary in the family of Errol, and was abolished by the 20 Geo. III, c. 43. Bell; Ersk. Inst. 1, 3, 37.

Constable of the exchequer. An officer mentioned in Fleta, lib. 2, c. 31, and in 51 Hen. III, stat. 5, cited by Cowell.

High constables. In England, officers appointed in every hundred or franchise, whose proper duty seems to be to keep the king's peace within their respective hundreds. 1 Bl.Comm. 356; 3 Steph. Comm. 47; Coke, 4th Inst. 267.

High constable of England, lord. His office has been disused (except only upon great and solemn occasions, as the coronation, or the like) since the attainder of Stafford, Duke of Buckingham, in the reign of Henry VII.

Petty constables. Inferior officers in every town and parish, subordinate to the high constable of the hundred, whose principal duty is the preservation of the peace, though they also have other particular duties assigned to them by act of parliament, particularly the service of the summonses and the execution of the warrants of justices of the peace. 1 Bl.Comm. 356; 3 Steph. Comm. 47, 48.

Special constables. Persons appointed (with or without their consent) by the magistrates to execute warrants on particular occasions, as in the case of riots, etc.

CONSTABLEWICK. In English law. The territorial jurisdiction of a constable; as bailiwick is of a bailiff or sheriff. 5 Nev. & M. 261.

CONSTABULARIUS. An officer of horse; an officer having charge of foot or horse; a naval commander; an officer having charge of military affairs generally. Spelman.

In England his power was early diminished and restricted to those duties which related to the preservation of the king's peace. The office is now abolished in England, except as a matter of ceremony, and in France. Guyot, *Rép. Univ.;* Cowell.

CONSTANT. Fixed or invariable; uniform. Webster. Continually recurring, regular, steady. Pfisterer v. Key, 218 Ind. 521, 33 N.E.2d 330, 335.

CONSTANTLY. In a constant manner; uniformly; continuously. Pfisterer v. Key, 218 Ind. 521, 33 N.E.2d 330, 335.

An instruction that a train crew knew that a railroad right of way had been "constantly," frequently, and regularly used by a considerable number of persons at a particular hour of the day was not subject to the criticism that the word "constantly" imported an uninterrupted and continuous presence of such persons on the track, so that at no moment of time it would be vacant of pedestrians. Grauer v. Alabama Great Southern R. Co., 209 Ala. 568, 96 So. 915, 919.

CONSTAT. It is clear or evident; it appears; it is certain; there is no doubt. *Non constat,* it does not appear.

A certificate which the clerk of the pipe and auditors of the exchequer made, at the request of any person who intended to plead or move in that court, for the discharge of anything. The effect of it was the certifying what appears *(constat)* upon record, touching the matter in question. Wharton.

A certificate by an officer that certain matters therein stated appear of record. Wilcox v. Ray, 2 N.C. 410.

An exemplification under the great seal of the enrolment of letters patent. Co. Litt. 225.

CONSTAT D'HUISSIER. In French law. An affidavit made by a *huissier,* setting forth the appearance, form, quality, color, etc., of any article upon which a suit depends. Arg. Fr. Merc. Law, 554.

CONSTATE. To establish, constitute, or ordain.

"Constating instruments" of a corporation are its charter, organic law, or the grant of powers to it. See examples of the use of the term, Green's Brice, Ultra Vires, p. 39; Ackerman v. Halsey, 37 N.J.Eq. 363.

CONSTITUENT. He who gives authority to another to act for him.

The term is used as a correlative to "attorney," to denote one who constitutes another his agent or invests the other with authority to act for him. Kunz v. Lowden, C.C.A.Kan., 124 F.2d 911, 913.

It is also used in the language of politics, as a correlative to "representative," the constituents of a legislator being those whom he represents and whose interests he is to care for in public affairs; usually the electors of his district.

CONSTITUERE. Lat. To appoint, constitute, establish, ordain, or undertake. Used principally in ancient powers of attorney, and now supplanted by the English word "constitute."

CONSTITUIMUS. A Latin term, signifying *we constitute* or *appoint.*

CONSTITUTED AUTHORITIES. Officers properly appointed under the constitution for the government of the people.

CONSTITUTIO. In the Civil law. An imperial ordinance, decree, or constitution, distinguished from *Lex, Senatus-Consultum,* and other kinds of law and having its effect from the sole will of the emperor. Dig. 1, 4, 1, Cooper's notes. An establishment or settlement. Used of controversies settled by the parties without a trial. Calvin. A sum paid according to agreement. Du Cange.

In Old English Law

An ordinance or statute. A provision of a statute.

CONSTITUTIO DOTIS. Establishment of dower.

CONSTITUTION. The organic and fundamental law of a nation or state, which may be written or unwritten, establishing the character and conception of its government, laying the basic principles to which its internal life is to be conformed, organizing the government, and regulating, distributing, and limiting the functions of its different departments, and prescribing the extent and manner of the exercise of sovereign powers. A charter of government deriving its whole authority from the governed. Fairhope Single Tax Corporation v. Melville, 193 Ala. 289, 69 So. 466, 470. See, also, Browne v. City of New York, 213 App. Div. 206, 211 N.Y.S. 306.

In a more general sense, any fundamental or important law or edict; as the Novel Constitutions of Justinian; the Constitutions of Clarendon.

CONSTITUTION. In American law. The written instrument agreed upon by the people of the Union or of a particular state, as the absolute rule of action and decision for all departments and officers of the government in respect to all the points covered by it, which must control until it shall be changed by the authority which established it, and in opposition to which any act or ordinance of any such department or officer is null and void. Cooley, Const. Lim. 3.

CONSTITUTIONAL. Consistent with the constitution; authorized by the constitution; not conflicting with any provision of the constitution or fundamental law of the state. Dependent upon a constitution, or secured or regulated by a constitution; as "constitutional monarchy," "constitutional rights."

CONSTITUTIONAL ALCALDE. A person of official status under Mexican law corresponding in many respects in dignity and authority to a justice of the peace under the American system of government. Tietzel v. Southwestern Const. Co., 48 N.M. 567, 154 P.2d 238, 242.

CONSTITUTIONAL CONVENTION. A duly constituted assembly of delegates or representatives of the people of a state or nation for the purpose of framing, revising, or amending its constitution. Bass v. Albright, Tex.Civ.App., 59 S.W.2d 891, 894.

CONSTITUTIONAL COURT. A court named or described and expressly protected by Constitution, or recognized by name or definite description in Constitution but given no express protection thereby. Gorham v. Robinson, 57 R.I. 1, 186 A. 832.

CONSTITUTIONAL LAW. (1) That branch of the public law of a state which treats of the organization and frame of government, the organs and powers of sovereignty, the distribution of political and governmental authorities and functions, the fundamental principles which are to regulate the relations of government and subject, and which prescribes generally the plan and method according to which the public affairs of the state are to be administered. (2) That department of the science of law which treats of constitutions, their establishment, construction, and interpretation, and of the validity of legal enactments as tested by the criterion of conformity to the fundamental law. (3) A constitutional law is one which is consonant to, and agrees with, the constitution; one which is not in violation of any provision of the constitution of the particular state.

CONSTITUTIONAL LIBERTY OR FREEDOM. Such freedom as is enjoyed by the citizens of a country or state under the protection of its constitution; the aggregate of those personal, civil, and political rights of the individual which are guaranteed by the constitution and secured against invasion by the government or any of its agencies. People v. Hurlbut, 24 Mich. 106, 9 Am.Rep. 103.

CONSTITUTIONAL OFFICER. One whose tenure and term of office are fixed and defined by the constitution, as distinguished from the incumbents of offices created by the legislature. Foster v. Jones, 79 Va. 642, 52 Am.Rep. 637.

CONSTITUTIONAL PSYCHOPATHIC INFERIORITY. Individuals who show a lifelong and constitutional tendency not to conform to the customs of the group, and who habitually misbehave, and have no sense of responsibility to their fellowmen or to society as a whole. These individuals fail to learn by experience and are inadequate, incompatible, and inefficient. State ex rel. Pearson v. Probate Court of Ramsey County, 205 Minn. 545, 287 N.W. 297, 300; Wilson v. Walters, Cal.App., 112 P.2d 964.

CONSTITUTIONAL RIGHT. A right guaranteed to the citizens by the Constitution and so guaranteed as to prevent legislative interference therewith. Delaney v. Plunkett, 146 Ga. 547, 91 S.E. 561, 567, L.R.A.1917D, 926, Ann.Cas.1917E, 685.

CONSTITUTIONES. Laws promulgated, *i. e.*, enacted, by the Roman Emperor. They were of various kinds, namely, the following: (1) *Edicta*; (2) *decreta*; (3) *rescripta*, called also *"epistolæ."* Sometimes they were general, and intended to form a precedent for other like cases; at other times they were special, particular, or individual, *(personales,)* and not intended to form a precedent. The emperor had this power of irresponsible enactment by virtue of a certain *lex regia*, whereby he was made the fountain of justice and of mercy. Brown.

CONSTITUTIONES TEMPORE POSTERIORES POTIORES SUNT HIS QUÆ IPSAS PRÆCESSERUNT. Dig. 1, 4, 4. Later laws prevail over those which preceded them.

CONSTITUTIONS OF CLARENDON. See Clarendon.

CONSTITUTIONS OF THE FOREST. See Charta de Foresta.

CONSTITUTOR. In the civil law. One who, by a simple agreement, becomes responsible for the payment of another's debt. Inst. 4, 6, 9.

CONSTITUTUM. In the civil law. An agreement to pay a subsisting debt which exists without any stipulation, whether of the promisor or another party. It differs from a stipulation in that it must be for an existing debt. Du Cange.

A day appointed for any purpose. A form of appeal. Calvinus, Lex.

CONSTITUTUM ESSE EAM DOMUM UNICUIQUE NOSTRUM DEBERE EXISTIMARI, UBI QUISQUE SEDES ET TABULAS HABERET, SUARUMQUE RERUM CONSTITUTIONEM FECISSET. It is settled that that is to be considered the home of each one of us where he may have his habitation and account-books, and where he may have made an establishment of his business. Dig. 50, 16, 203.

CONSTRAINT. This term is held to be exactly equivalent with "restraint." Edmondson v. Harris, 2 Tenn.Ch. 427.

An abridgement of liberty or hindrance of the will, identical in meaning with the word "compulsion." Edmondson v. Harris, 2 Tenn.Ch. 427.

In Scotch law. Duress.

CONSTRUCT. To build; erect; put together; make ready for use. State v. Abele, 119 Ohio St. 210, 162 N.E. 807, 809. To adjust and join materials, or parts of, so as to form a permanent whole. Kinney v. Ehrensperger, 16 Ala.App. 289, 77 So. 439, 440. To put together constituent parts of something in their proper place and order. State ex rel. St. Louis County v. State Highway Commission, 315 Mo. 707, 286 S.W. 1, 2.

"Construct" is distinguishable from "maintain," which means to keep up, to keep from change, to preserve. State v. Olympia Light & Power Co., 91 Wash. 519, 158 P. 85, 89. Under a broad interpretation, however, "construct" may be synonymous with maintain, repair, or improve. Independent Highway Dist. No. 2 of Ada County v. Ada County, 24 Idaho 416, 134 P. 542, 545.

CONSTRUCTIO LEGIS NON FACIT INJURIAM. The construction of the law (a construction made by the law) works no injury. Co. Litt. 183; Broom, Max. 603. The law will make such a construction of an instrument as not to injure a party.

CONSTRUCTION. The process, or the art, of determining the sense, real meaning, or proper explanation of obscure or ambiguous terms or provisions in a statute, written instrument, or oral agreement, or the application of such subject to the case in question, by reasoning in the light derived from extraneous connected circumstances or laws or writings bearing upon the same or a connected matter, or by seeking and applying the probable aim and purpose of the provision. Koy v. Schneider, 110 Tex. 369, 221 S.W. 880, 884.

As applied to statutes, constitutions, contracts, etc., the term necessarily presupposes doubt, obscurity, or ambiguity. Cohn-Hall-Marx Co. v. Vanosdall, 25 Ohio App. 360, 157 N.E. 908, 909.

Drawing conclusions respecting subjects that lie beyond the direct expression of the term. Lieber, Leg. & Pol. Herm. 20; Roberts v. Portland Water Dist., 124 Me. 63, 126 A. 162, 163.

This term is properly distinguished from *interpretation,* although the two are often used synonymously. In strictness, interpretation is limited to exploring the written text, while construction goes beyond and may call in the aid of extrinsic considerations, as above indicated.

The process of bringing together and correlating a number of independent entities, so as to form a definite entity. The Dredge A, D.C.N.C., 217 F. 617, 631.

The creation of something new, as distinguished from the repair or improvement of something already existing. Cabell v. City of Portland, 153 Or. 528, 57 P.2d 1292, 1297. The act of fitting an object for use or occupation in the usual way, and for some distinct purpose. Paterson N. & R. R. Co. v. City of Paterson, 81 N.J.Eq. 124, 86 A. 68, 69. See Construct.

Construction, court of. A court of equity or of common law, as the case may be, is called the court of construction with regard to wills, as opposed to the court of probate, whose duty is to decide whether an instrument be a will at all. Now, the court of probate may decide that a given instrument is a will, and yet the court of construction may decide that it has no operation, by reason of perpetuities, illegality, uncertainty, etc. Wharton.

Equitable construction. A construction of a law, rule, or remedy which has regard more to the equities of the particular transaction or state of affairs involved than to the strict application of the rule or remedy; that is, a liberal and extensive construction, as opposed to a literal and restrictive. Smiley v. Sampson, 1 Neb. 91.

By "equity of a statute" is intended the rule of construction which admits within the operation of a statute a class of cases which are neither named nor excluded, but which, from their analogy to those that are named, are clearly and justly within the spirit and general meaning of the law; such cases are said to be "within the equity of the statute."

The modern doctrine is that to construe a statute liberally or according to its equity is nothing more than to give effect to it according to the intention of the lawmaker as indicated by its terms and purposes. Read v. Dingess, C. C.A.W.Va., 60 F. 21, 29, 8 C.C.A. 389.

Strict and liberal construction. Strict (or literal) construction is construction of a statute or other instrument according to its letter, which recognizes nothing that is not expressed, takes the language used in its exact and technical meaning, and admits no equitable considerations or implications. Warner v. King, 267 Ill. 82, 107 N.E. 837, 839.

Liberal (or equitable) construction, on the other hand, expands the meaning of the statute to meet cases which are clearly within the spirit or reason of the law, or within the evil which it was designed to remedy, provided such an interpretation is not inconsistent with the language used; it resolves all reasonable doubts in favor of the applicability of the statute to the particular case. Black, Interp.Laws, 282; Causey v. Guilford County, 192 N.C. 298, 135 S.E. 40, 46. It means, not that the words should be forced out of their natural meaning, but simply that they should receive a fair and reasonable interpretation with respect to the objects and purposes of the instrument. Lawrence v. McCalmont, 2 How. 426, 11 L.Ed. 326.

CONSTRUCTIVE. That which is established by the mind of the law in its act of *construing* facts, conduct, circumstances, or instruments; that which has not the character assigned to it in its own essential nature, but acquires such character in consequence of the way in which it is regarded by a rule or policy of law; hence, inferred, implied, made out by legal interpretation;—the word "legal" being sometimes used in lieu of "constructive." Middleton v. Parke, 3 App.D. C. 160.

As to constructive "Bailment," "Breaking," "Contempt," "Contracts," "Conversion," "Delivery," "Escape," "Fraud," "Larceny," "Malice," "Notice," "Possession," "Seisin," "Service of Process," "Total Loss," "Treason," and "Trusts," see those titles.

CONSTRUCTIVE ASSENT. An assent or consent imputed to a party from a construction or interpretation of his conduct; as distinguished from one which he actually expresses.

CONSTRUCTIVE AUTHORITY. Authority inferred or assumed to have been given because of the grant of some other antecedent authority. Middleton v. Parke, 3 App.D.C. 160.

CONSTRUCTIVE BREAKING INTO A HOUSE. A breaking made out by construction of law. As where a burglar gains an entry into a house by threats, fraud, or conspiracy. 2 Russ. Crimes, 9, 10; Hawkins v. Commonwealth, 284 Ky. 33, 143 S.W.2d 853, 854.

CONSTRUCTIVE CRIME. Where, by a strained construction of a penal statute, it is made to include an act not otherwise punishable, it is said to be a "constructive crime," that is, one built up by the court with the aid of inference and implication. Ex parte McNulty, 77 Cal. 164, 19 P. 237, 11 Am.St.Rep. 257.

CONSTRUCTIVE EVICTION. As the term is used with reference to breach of the covenants of warranty and of quiet enjoyment, it means the inability of the purchaser to obtain possession by reason of a paramount outstanding title. Fritz v. Pusey, 31 Minn. 368, 18 N.W. 94.

With reference to the relation of landlord and tenant, there is a "constructive eviction" when the former, without intent to oust the latter, does some act which deprives the tenant of the beneficial enjoyment of the demised premises or materially impairs such enjoyment. Santrizos v. Public Drug Co., 143 Minn. 222, 173 N.W. 563, 564. Any disturbance of the tenant's possession by the landlord whereby the premises are rendered unfit or unsuitable for occupancy in whole or in substantial part for the purposes for which they were leased amounts to a constructive eviction, if the tenant so elects and surrenders his possession. Murry v. Merchants' Southwest Transfer & Storage Co., 98 Okl. 270, 225 P. 547, 549. There must be injurious interference with tenant's possession, substantial deprivation of tenant's beneficial use of premises, and material impairment of tenant's beneficial enjoyment of premises, so that he is compelled to vacate. Ben Hur Holding Corporation v. Fox, 263 N.Y.S. 695, 147 Misc. 300.

CONSTRUCTIVE FORCE. This has been said to be an acquiescence to an act obtained through duress or fear of personal violence. Shepherd v. State, 135 Ala. 9, 12, 33 So. 266.

With regard to rape, the force necessary to constitute the offense need not be actual, but may be constructive or implied. 52 C.J. p. 1018.

As regards robbery, a taking by force is the gist of the crime, but the force may be either actual or constructive. 54 C.J. p. 1016. " 'Constructive force' is anything which produces fear sufficient to suspend the power of resistance and prevent the free exercise of the will." Montsdoca v. State, 84 Fla. 82, 93 So. 157, 159, 27 A.L.R. 1291. "Actual force is applied to the body, constructive is by threatening words or gestures and operates on the mind." Tones v. State, 48 Tex.Cr. 363, 88 S.W. 217, 122 Am.St.Rep. 759, 1 L.R.A.,N.S., 1024.

CONSTRUCTIVE LOSS. One resulting from such injuries to the property, without its destruction, as render it valueless to the assured or prevent its restoration to the original condition except at a cost exceeding its value.

CONSTRUCTIVE MORTGAGE. A deed absolute on its face but intended as a mortgage is sometimes referred to as a "constructive mortgage," or, more commonly perhaps, as an "equitable mortgage." See Mortgage.

CONSTRUCTIVE TAKING. A phrase used in the law to characterize an act not amounting to an actual appropriation of chattels, but which shows an intention to convert them to his use; as if a person intrusted with the possession of goods deals with them contrary to the orders of the owner.

CONSTRUCTIVE VACANCY IN PUBLIC OFFICE. When the incumbent has no legal right or claim to continue in office, but can be legally replaced by another functionary. State ex rel. Satterthwaite v. Stover, 5 W.W.Harr. 85, 159 A. 239, 241.

CONSTRUCTIVE WILLFULNESS. Intentional disregard of a known duty necessary to the safety of a person, and an entire absence of care for the life, the person, or the property of others, such as exhibits a conscious indifference to consequences. Collins v. Missouri-Illinois R. Co., 233 Ill. App. 545, 551; Hughes v. Medendorp, 294 Ill.App. 424, 13 N.E.2d 1015, 1018.

CONSTRUE. To put together; to arrange or marshal the words of an instrument. To ascertain the meaning of language by a process of arrangement and inference. See Construction.

CONSTUPRATE. To ravish, debauch, violate, rape. See Harper v. Delp, 3 Ind. 230; Koenig v. Nott, 2 Hilt. (N.Y.) 329.

CONSUETUDINARIUS. In ecclesiastical law. A ritual or book, containing the rites and forms of divine offices or the customs of abbeys and monasteries.

CONSUETUDINARY LAW. Customary law. Law derived by oral tradition from a remote antiquity. Bell.

CONSUETUDINES. In old English law. Customs. Thus, *consuetudines et assisa forestæ*, the customs and assise of the forest.

CONSUETUDINES FEUDORUM. (Lat. feudal customs.) A compilation of the law of feuds or fiefs in Lombardy, made A.D. 1170. It is of great authority.

CONSUETUDINIBUS ET SERVICIIS. In old English law. A writ of right close, which lay against a tenant who deforced his lord of the rent or service due to him. Reg. Orig. 159; Fitzh. Nat. Brev. 151.

CONSUETUDO. Lat. A custom; an established usage or practice. Co. Litt. 58, 58b; Tolls; duties; taxes.

CONSUETUDO ANGLICANA. The custom of England; the ancient common law, as distinguished from *lex*, the Roman or civil law.

CONSUETUDO CONTRA RATIONEM INTRODUCTA POTIUS USURPATIO QUAM CONSUETUDO APPELLARI DEBET. A custom introduced against reason ought rather to be called a "usurpation" than a "custom." Co.Litt. 113.

CONSUETUDO CURIÆ. The custom or practice of a court. Hardr. 141.

CONSUETUDO DEBET ESSE CERTA; NAM INCERTA PRO NULLÂ HABETUR. Dav. 33. A custom should be certain; for an uncertain custom is considered null.

CONSUETUDO EST ALTERA LEX. Custom is another law. 4 Coke, 21.

CONSUETUDO EST OPTIMUS INTERPRES LEGUM. 2 Inst. 18. Custom is the best expounder of the laws.

CONSUETUDO ET COMMUNIS ASSUETUDO VINCIT LEGEM NON SCRIPTAM, SI SIT SPECIALIS; ET INTERPRETATUR LEGEM SCRIPTAM, SI LEX SIT GENERALIS. Jenk. Cent. 273. Custom and common usage overcomes the unwritten law, if it be special; and interprets the written law, if the law be general.

CONSUETUDO EX CERTA CAUSA RATIONABILI USITATA PRIVAT COMMUNEM LEGEM. A custom, grounded on a certain and reasonable cause, supersedes the common law. Litt. § 169; Co. Litt. 113; Broom, Max. 919.

CONSUETUDO, LICET SIT MAGNÆ AUCTORITATIS, NUNQUAM TAMEN, PRÆJUDICAT MANIFESTÆ VERITATI. A custom, though it be of great authority, should never prejudice manifest truth. 4 Coke, 18.

CONSUETUDO LOCI OBSERVANDA EST. Litt. § 169. The custom of a place is to be observed.

CONSUETUDO MANERII ET LOCI OBSERVANDA EST. 6 Coke, 67. A custom of a manor and place is to be observed.

CONSUETUDO MERCATORUM. Lat. The custom of merchants, the same with *lex mercatoria.*

CONSUETUDO NEQUE INJURIÂ ORIRI NEQUE TOLLI POTEST. Lofft, 340. Custom can neither arise from nor be taken away by injury.

CONSUETUDO NON TRAHITUR IN CONSEQUENTIAM. 3 Keb. 499. Custom is not drawn into consequence. 4 Jur. (N.S.) Ex. 139.

CONSUETUDO PRÆSCRIPTA ET LEGITIMA VINCIT LEGEM. A prescriptive and lawful custom overcomes the law. Co. Litt. 113; 4 Coke, 21.

CONSUETUDO REGNI ANGLIÆ EST LEX ANGLIÆ. Jenk. Cent. 119. The custom of the kingdom of England is the law of England. See 2 Bl. Comm. 422.

CONSUETUDO SEMEL REPROBATA NON POTEST AMPLIUS INDUCI. A custom once disallowed cannot be again brought forward, [or relied on]. Dav. 33.

CONSUETUDO TOLLIT COMMUNEM LEGEM. Co. Litt. 33*b*. Custom takes away the common law.

CONSUETUDO VINCIT COMMUNEM LEGEM. Custom overrules common law. 1 Rop. H. & W. 351; Co. Litt. 33*b*.

CONSUETUDO VOLENTES DUCIT, LEX NOLENTES TRAHIT. Custom leads the willing, law compels [drags] the unwilling. Jenk. Cent. 274.

CONSUL.

International Law

An officer of a commercial character, appointed by the different states to watch over the mercantile interests of the appointing state and of its subjects in foreign countries. There are usually a number of consuls in every maritime country, and they are usually subject to a chief consul, who is called a "consul general." Schunior v. Russell, 18 S.W. 484, 83 Tex. 83.

Old English Law

An ancient title of an earl.

Roman Law

During the republic, the name "consul" was given to the chief executive magistrate, two of whom were chosen annually. The office was continued under the empire, but its powers and prerogatives were greatly reduced. The name is supposed to have been derived from *consulo*, to consult, because these officers consulted with the senate on administrative measures.

The word "consul" has two meanings: (1) It denotes an officer of a particular grade in the consular service; (2) It has a broader generic sense, embracing all consular officers. Dainese v. U. S., 15 Ct.Cl. 64.

See, also, Foreign Service Act of 1946, 22 U.S.C.A. § 801 et seq.

CONSULAR COURTS. Courts held by the consuls of one country, within the territory of another, under authority given by treaty, for the settlement of civil cases. In some instances they have also a criminal jurisdiction, but in this respect are subject to review by the courts of the home government. See Rev.St. U.S. § 4083 (22 U.S.C.A. § 141.)

CONSULTA ECCLESIA. In ecclesiastical law. A church full or provided for. Cowell.

CONSULTARY RESPONSE. The opinion of a court of law on a special case.

CONSULTATION. A writ whereby a cause which has been wrongfully removed by prohibition out of an ecclesiastical court to a temporal court is returned to the ecclesiastical court. Phillim. Ecc. Law, 1439. Deliberation of persons on some subject. State v. District Court of Third Judicial Dist. in and for Powell County, 85 Mont. 215, 278 P. 122, 125.

A conference between the counsel engaged in a case, to discuss its questions or arrange the method of conducting it.

In French law. The opinion of counsel upon a point of law submittted to them.

CONSULTO. Lat. In the civil law. Designedly; intentionally. Dig. 28, 41.

CONSUMER. One who uses economic goods and so diminishes or destroys their utilities; opposed to producer. Ex parte Mehlman, 127 Tex.Cr.R. 257, 75 S.W.2d 689, 690.

CONSUMMATE, *adj.* Completed; as distinguished from *initiate,* or that which is merely begun. The husband of a woman seised of an estate of inheritance becomes, by the birth of a child, tenant by the curtesy *initiate,* and may do many acts to charge the lands, but his estate is not *consummate* till the death of the wife. 2 Bl. Comm. 126, 128; Co. Litt. 30*a*.

CONSUMMATE. *v.* To finish by completing what was intended; bring or carry to utmost point or degree; carry or bring to completion; finish; perfect; fulfill; achieve. American Mercantile Corporation v. Spielberg, C.C.A.N.Y., 262 F. 492, 496; Purcell v. Firth, 175 Cal. 746, 167 P. 379, 380; Oregon Home Builders v. Montgomery Inv. Co., 94 Or. 349, 184 P. 487, 492; Dahlinger v. Commissioner of Internal Revenue, C.C.A., 51 F.2d 662, 663.

CONSUMMATE LIEN. A term which may be used to describe the lien of a judgment when a motion for a new trial has been denied (the lien having theretofore been merely inchoate). Sterling v. Parker-Washington Co., 185 Mo.App. 192, 170 S.W. 1156, 1159.

CONSUMMATION. The completion of a thing; the completion of a marriage between two affianced persons by cohabitation. Sharon v. Sharon, 79 Cal. 633, 22 P. 26.

CONSUMPTION. Act or process of consuming; waste; decay; destruction; and using up of anything, as food, heat, or time. Moore v. Pleasant Hasler Const. Co., 50 Ariz. 370, 72 P.2d 573, 578. Destruction by use. Revzan v. Nudelman, 370 Ill. 180, 18 N.E.2d 219, 222.

CONTAGIOUS ABORTION. A disease of cows generally contracted through the digestive tract from infected food which causes premature birth of calves. Gesme v. Potter, 118 Or. 621, 247 P. 765, 766.

CONTAGIOUS DISEASE. One capable of being transmitted by mediate or immediate contact. Ex parte Liang Buck Chew, D.C.Mass., 296 F. 183. See Infection.

CONTANGO. A double bargain, consisting of a sale for cash of stock previously bought which the broker does not wish to carry, and a repurchase for the re-settlement two weeks ahead of the same stock at the same price as at the sale plus interest accrued up to the date of that settlement. The rate of interest is called a "contango" and contango days are the two days during the settlement when these arrangements are in effect.

CONTEK. L. Fr. A contest, dispute, disturbance, opposition, Britt. c. 42; Kelham. *Conteckours;* brawlers; disturbers of the peace. Britt. c. 29.

CONTEMNER. One who has committed contempt of court. Wyatt v. People, 17 Colo. 252, 28 P. 961.

CONTEMPLATE. To view or consider with continued attention; to regard thoughtfully; to have in view as contingent or probable as an end or intention. Wright v. Fuel Oil Co., Mo., 342 Mo. 173, 114 S.W.2d 959, 962. To ponder, to study, to plan, to meditate, to reflect. In re Thompson's Estate, 72 Utah, 17, 269 P. 103, 115.

CONTEMPLATION. The act of the mind in considering with attention. Continued attention of the mind to a particular subject. Consideration of an act or series of acts with the intention of doing or adopting them. The consideration of an event or state of facts with the expectation that it will transpire.

CONTEMPLATION OF BANKRUPTCY. Contemplation of the breaking up of one's business or an inability to continue it; knowledge of, and action with reference to, a condition of bankruptcy or ascertained insolvency, coupled with an intention to commit what the law declares to be an "act of bankruptcy," or to make provision against the consequences of insolvency, or to defeat the general distribution of assets which would take place under a proceeding in bankruptcy. Buckingham v. McLean, 13 How. 167, 14 L.Ed. 90; In re Carmichael, D.C.Iowa, 96 F. 594.

CONTEMPLATION OF DEATH. The apprehension or expectation of approaching dissolution; not that general expectation which every mortal entertains, but the apprehension which arises from some presently existing sickness or physical condition or from some impending danger. As applied to transfers of property, the phrase "in contemplation of death" means that thought of death is the impelling cause of transfer and that motive which induces transfer is of sort which leads to testamentary disposition and is practically equivalent to "causa mortis." In re Cornell's Estate, 73 N.Y.S. 32, 66 App.Div. 162; Nicholas v. Martin, 128 N.J.Eq. 344, 15 A.2d 235, 243; Pate v. C. I. R., C.C.A.8, 149 F.2d 669, 670.

CONTEMPLATION OF INSOLVENCY. Knowledge of, and action with reference to, an existing or contemplated state of insolvency, with a design to make provision against its results or to defeat the operation of the insolvency laws. Flockhart Foundry Co. v. Cox Automatic Pipe Bending Co., 95 N.J.Eq. 382, 123 A. 151, 152.

CONTEMPORANEA EXPOSITIO. Lat. Contemporaneous exposition, or construction; a construction drawn from the *time* when, and the circumstances under which, the subject-matter to be construed, as a statute or custom, originated.

CONTEMPORANEA EXPOSITIO EST OPTIMA ET FORTISSIMA IN LEGE. Contemporaneous exposition is the best and strongest in the law. 2 Inst. 11. A statute is best explained by following the construction put upon it by judges who lived at the *time* it was made, or soon after. 10 Coke, 70; Broom, Max. 682.

CONTEMPT. A willful disregard or disobedience of a public authority.

CONTEMPT OF COURT. Any act which is calculated to embarrass, hinder, or obstruct court in administration of justice, or which is calculated to lessen its authority or its dignity. Ex parte Hobrook, 133 Me. 276, 177 A. 418, 420. Committed by a person who does any act in willful contravention of its authority or dignity, or tending to impede or frustrate the administration of justice, or by one who, being under the court's authority as a party to a proceeding therein, willfully disobeys its lawful orders or fails to comply with an undertaking which he has given. Snow v. Hawkes, 183 N.C. 365, 111 S.E. 621, 622, 23 A.L.R. 183.

Classification

Contempts are of two kinds, direct and constructive.

Direct contempts are those committed in the immediate view and presence of the court (such as insulting language or acts of violence) or so near the presence of the court as to obstruct or interrupt the due and orderly course of proceedings. These are punishable summarily. They are also called "criminal" contempts, but that term is better used in contrast with "civil" contempts. See *infra.* State v. McClaugherty, 33 W.Va. 250, 10 S.E. 407. Pelletier v. Glacier County, Mont., 107 Mont. 221, 82 P.2d 595, 597.

Constructive (or indirect) contempts are those which arise from matters not occurring in or near the presence of the court, but which tend to obstruct or defeat the administration of justice, and the term is chiefly used with reference to the failure or refusal of a party to obey a lawful order, injunction, or decree of the court laying upon him a duty of action or forbearance. Maryott v. Maryott, 124 Neb. 274, 246 N.W. 343.

Constructive contempts were formerly called "consequential," and this term is still in occasional use.

Contempts are also classed as civil or criminal. The former are those quasi contempts which consists in the failure to do something which the party is ordered by the court to do for the benefit or advantage of another party to the proceeding before the court, while criminal contempts are acts done in disrespect of the court or its process or which obstruct the administration of justice or tend to bring the court into disrespect. A civil contempt is not an offense against the dignity of the court, but against the party in whose behalf the mandate of the court was issued, and a fine is imposed for his indemnity. But criminal contempts are offenses or injuries offered to the court, and a fine or imprisonment is imposed upon the contemnor for the purpose of punishment. Staley v. South Jersey Realty Co., 90 A. 1042, 1043, 83 N.J.Eq. 300, L.R.A.1917B, 113, Ann.Cas.1916E, 955; Fenton v. Walling, C.C.A.Cal., 139 F.2d 608, 609.

CONTEMPT OF CONGRESS, LEGISLATURE, or PARLIAMENT. Whatever obstructs or tends to obstruct the due course of proceeding of either house, or grossly reflects on the character of a member of either house, or imputes to him what it would be a libel to impute to an ordinary person, is a contempt of the house, and thereby a breach of privilege. Sweet.

CONTEMPTIBILITER. Lat. Contemptuously.

In old English law. Contempt, contempts. Fleta, lib. 2, c. 60, § 35.

CONTENEMENTUM. See Wainagium; Contentment.

CONTENTIOUS. Contested; adversary; litigated between adverse or contending parties; a judicial proceeding not merely *ex parte* in its character, but comprising attack and defense as between opposing parties, is so called. The litigious proceedings in ecclesiastical courts are sometimes said to belong to its "contentious" jurisdiction, in contradistinction to what is called its "voluntary" jurisdiction, which is exercised in the granting of licenses, probates of wills, dispensations, faculties, etc.

CONTENTIOUS JURISDICTION. In English ecclesiastical law. That branch of the jurisdiction of the ecclesiastical courts which is exercised upon adversary or *contentious* (opposed, litigated) proceedings.

CONTENTIOUS POSSESSION. In stating the rule that the possession of land necessary to give rise to a title by prescription must be a "contentious" one, it is meant that it must be based on opposition to the title of the rival claimant (not in recognition thereof or subordination thereto) and that the opposition must be based on good grounds, or such as might be made the subject of litigation. Railroad Co. v. McFarlan, 43 N.J. L. 621.

CONTENTMENT, CONTENEMENT. A man's countenance or credit, which he has together with, and by reason of, his freehold; or that which is necessary for the support and maintenance of men, agreeably to their several qualities or states of life. Wharton; Cowell.

Comfort; consolation; ease; enjoyment; happiness; pleasure; satisfaction. National Surety Co. v. Jarrett, 95 W.Va. 420, 121 S.E. 291, 295.

CONTENTS. The contents of a promissory note or other commercial instrument or chose in action means the specific sum named therein and payable by the terms of the instrument. Trading Co. v. Morrison, 20 S.Ct. 869, 178 U.S. 262, 44 L. Ed. 1061.

CONTENTS AND NOT CONTENTS. In parliamentary law. The "contents" are those who, in the house of lords, express assent to a bill; the "not" or "non contents" dissent. May, Parl. Law, cc. 12, 357.

CONTENTS UNKNOWN. Words sometimes annexed to a bill of lading of goods in cases. Their meaning is that the master only means to acknowledge the shipment, in good order, of the cases, as to their external condition. Miller v. Railroad Co., 90 N.Y. 433, 43 Am.Rep. 179.

CONTERMINOUS. Adjacent; adjoining; having a common boundary; coterminous.

CONTEST, *v.* To make defense to an adverse claim in a court of law; to oppose, resist, or dispute the case made by a plaintiff. Pratt v. Breckinridge, 112 Ky. 1, 65 S.W. 136; Parks v. State, 100 Ala. 634, 13 So. 756. To strive, to win or hold; to controvert, litigate, call in question, challenge; to defend, as a suit or other proceeding. Equitable Life Assur. Soc. of the United States v. First Nat. Bank of Birmingham, C.C.A.Ala., 113 F.2d 272, 274.

CONTESTATIO LITIS. In Roman law. Contestation of suit; the framing an issue; joinder in issue. The formal act of both the parties with which the proceedings *in jure* were closed when they led to a judicial investigation, and by which the neighbors whom the parties brought with them were called to testify. Mackeld, Rom.Law, § 219.

In old English law. Coming to an issue; the issue so produced. Crabb, Eng.Law, 216.

CONTESTATIO LITIS EGET TERMINOS CONTRADICTARIOS. An issue requires terms of contradiction. Jenk. Cent. 117. To constitute an issue, there must be an affirmative on one side and a negative on the other.

CONTESTATION OF SUIT. In an ecclesiastical cause, that stage of the suit which is reached when the defendant has answered the libel by giving in an allegation.

CONTESTED ELECTION. This phrase has no technical or legally defined meaning. An election may be said to be contested whenever an objection is formally urged against it which, if found to be true in fact, would invalidate it. This is true both as to objections founded upon some constitutional provision and to such as are based on statutes. Robertson v. State, 109 Ind. 116, 10 N.E. 600.

CONTEXT. The context of a particular sentence or clause in a statute, contract, will, etc., comprises those parts of the text which immediately precede and follow it. The context may sometimes be scrutinized, to aid in the interpretation of an obscure passage.

CONTIGUOUS. In close proximity; near, though not in contact; neighboring; adjoining; near in succession; in actual close contact; touching; bounded or traversed by. The term is not synonymous with "vicinal." Ehle v. Tenney Trading Co., 56 Ariz. 241, 107 P.2d 210, 212.

CONTIGUOUS AND COMPACT. In respect of school district, territory so closely united and so nearly adjacent to the school building that all the children residing in the district, their ages considered, may conveniently travel from their homes to the school building and return in a reasonable time and with a reasonable degree of comfort. People v. Simpson, 308 Ill. 418, 139 N.E. 890, 893; People v. Dodds, 310 Ill. 607, 142 N.E. 241, 242.

CONTINENCIA. In Spanish law. Continency or unity of the proceedings in a cause. White, New Recop. b. 3, tit. 6, c. 1.

CONTINENS. In the Roman law. Continuing; holding together. Adjoining buildings were said to be *continentia.*

CONTINENTAL. Pertaining or relating to a continent; characteristic of a continent; as broad in scope or purpose as a continent. Continental Ins. Co. v. Continental Fire Ass'n, C.C.Tex., 96 F. 848.

CONTINENTAL CONGRESS. The first national legislative assembly in the United States, which met in 1774, in pursuance of a recommendation made by Massachusetts and adopted by the other colonies. In this congress all the colonies were represented except Georgia. The delegates were in some cases chosen by the legislative assemblies in the states; in others by the people directly. The powers of the congress were undefined, but it proceeded to take measures and pass resolutions which concerned the general welfare and had regard to the inauguration and prosecution of the war for independence. Black, Const.Law (3d Ed.) 40; 1 Story, Const. §§ 198–217.

CONTINENTAL CURRENCY. Paper money issued under the authority of the continental congress. Wharton v. Morris, 1 Dall. 125, 1 L.Ed. 65.

CONTINENTIA. In old English practice. Continuance or connection. Applied to the proceedings in a cause. Bract. fol. 362*b*.

CONTINGENCY. Quality of being contingent or casual; the possibility of coming to pass; an event which may occur; a possibility; a casualty. Vandegrift v. Riley, 30 P.2d 516, 523, 220 Cal. 340. A fortuitous event, which comes without design, foresight, or expectation. People v. Yonkers, 39 Barb. (N.Y.) 272; American Ins. Co. v. Black, 46 Ga.App. 471, 168 S.E. 85.

CONTINGENCY OF A PROCESS. In Scotch law. Where two or more processes are so connected that the circumstances of the one are likely to throw light on the others, the process first enrolled is considered as the leading process, and those subsequently brought into court, if not brought in the same division, may be remitted to it, *ob contingentiam,* on account of their nearness or proximity in character to it. The effect of remitting processes in this manner is merely to bring them before the same division of the court or same lord ordinary. In other respects they remain distinct. Bell.

CONTINGENCY WITH DOUBLE ASPECT. A remainder is said to be "in a contingency with double aspect," when there is another remainder limited on the same estate, not in derogation of the first, but as a substitute for it in case it should fail. Fearne, Rem. 373.

CONTINGENT. Possible, but not assured; doubtful or uncertain, conditioned upon the occurrence of some future event which is itself uncertain, or questionable. Verdier v. Roach, 96 Cal. 467, 31 P. 554, synonymous with provisional. Robinson v. Edler, C.C.A.Nev., 78 F.2d 817, 819.

This term, when applied to a use, remainder, devise, bequest, or other legal right or interest, implies that no present interest exists, and that whether such interest or right ever will exist depends upon a future uncertain event. Jemison v. Blowers, 5 Barb. (N.Y.) 692.

As to contingent "Damages," "Fee," "Legacy," "Limitation," "Remainder," "Trust," and "Use," see those titles.

CONTINGENT CLAIM. One which has not accrued and which is dependent on some future event that may never happen. Hospes v. Car Co., 48 Minn. 174, 50 N.W. 1117, 15 L.R.A. 470, 31 Am. St.Rep. 637; Hicks v. Wilbur, 38 R.I. 268, 94 A. 872, 874; Cotting v. Hooper, Lewis & Co., 220 Mass. 273, 107 N.E. 931; In re Lexington Surety & Indemnity Co., 272 N.Y. 210, 5 N.E.2d 204, 205.

CONTINGENT ESTATE, INTEREST or RIGHT. An estate, interest or right which depends for its effect upon an event which may or may not happen; as an estate limited to a person not *in esse,* or not yet born. 2 Crabb, Real Prop. p. 4, § 946; Avery v. Curtiss, 108 Okl. 154, 235 P. 195, 197; Kahn v. Rockhill, 132 N.J.Eq. 188, 28 A.2d 34, 36.

CONTINGENT FUND. One set up by a municipality to pay expense items which will necessarily arise during the year but cannot appropriately be classified under any of the specific purposes for which other taxes are levied. First Nat. Bank of Norman v. City of Norman, 182 Okl. 7, 75 P.2d 1109, 1110.

CONTINGENT INTEREST IN PERSONAL PROPERTY. A future interest not transmissible to the representatives of the party entitled thereto, in case he dies before it vests in possession. Mozley & Whitley.

Thus, if a testator leaves the income of a fund to his wife for life, and the capital of the fund to be distributed among such of his children as shall be living at her death, the interest of each child during the widow's life-time is *contingent,* and in case of his death is not transmissible to his representatives. Mozley & Whitley.

CONTINGENT LIABILITY. One which is not now fixed and absolute, but which will become so in case of the occurrence of some future and uncertain event. Warren Co. v. C. I. R., C.C.A. Ga., 135 F.2d 679, 684, 685.

CONTINUAL CLAIM. In old English law. A formal claim made by a party entitled to enter upon any lands or tenements, but deterred from such entry by menaces, or bodily fear, for the purpose of preserving or keeping alive his right. It was called "continual," because it was required to be repeated once in the space of every year and day. It had to be made as near to the land as the party could approach with safety, and, when made in due form, had the same effect with, and in all respects amounted to, a legal entry. Litt. §§ 419–423; Co.Litt. 250*a*; 3 Bl.Comm. 175.

CONTINUANCE. The adjournment or postponement of an action pending in a court, to a subsequent day of the same or another term. Com. v. Maloney, 145 Mass. 205, 13 N.E. 482. Ferber v. Brueckl, 332 Mo. 892, 17 S.W.2d 524, 527.

Also the entry of a continuance made upon the record of the court, for the purpose of formally evidencing the postponement, or of connecting the parts of the record so as to make one continuous whole.

CONTINUANDO. In pleading. A form of allegation in which the trespass, criminal offense, or other wrongful act complained of is charged to have been committed on a specified day and to have "continued" to the present time, or is averred to have been committed at divers days and times within a given period or on a specified day and on divers other days and times between that day and another. This is called "laying the time with a continuando." State v. Brown, 10 Okl.Cr. 52, 133 P. 1143, 1144.

CONTINUING. Enduring; not terminated by a single act or fact; subsisting for a definite period or intended to cover or apply to successive similar obligations or occurrences.

As to continuing "Breach," "Consideration," "Conspiracy," "Covenant," "Damages," "Guaranty," "Nuisance," and "Offense," see those titles.

CONTINUOUS. Uninterrupted; unbroken; not intermittent or occasional; so persistently repeated at short intervals as to constitute virtually an unbroken series. Ingraham v. Hough, 46 N.C. 43. Connected, extended, or prolonged without cessation or interruption of sequence. Sullivan v. John Hancock Mut. Life Ins. Co. of Boston, Mo. App., 110 S.W.2d 870, 877.

As to continuous "Crime" and "Easements," see those titles.

CONTINUOUS ADVERSE USE. Is interchangeable with the term "uninterrupted adverse use." Davidson v. Nicholson, 59 Ind. 411.

CONTINUOUS INJURY. One recurring at repeated intervals, so as to be of repeated occurrence; not necessarily an injury that never ceases. Wood v. Sutcliffe, 8 Eng.Law & Eq. 217.

CONTINUOUSLY. Uninterruptedly; in unbroken sequence; without intermission or cessation; without intervening time; with continuity or continuation. U. S. v. Wooten, C.C.A.N.M., 40 F.2d 882, 887.

CONTIONES. General meetings of the Roman people. Launspach, State and Family in Early Rome 69.

CONTRA. Against, confronting, opposite to; on the other hand; on the contrary.

The word is used in many Latin phrases, as appears by the following titles. In the books of reports, *contra*, appended to the name of a judge or counsel, indicates that he held a view of the matter in argument *contrary* to that next before advanced. Also, after citation of cases in support of a position, *contra* is often prefixed to citations of cases opposed to it.

CONTRA BONOS MORES. Against good morals. Contracts *contra bonos mores* are void.

CONTRA FORMAM COLLATIONIS. In old English law. A writ that issued where lands given in perpetual alms to lay houses of religion, or to an abbot and convent, or to the warden or master of a hospital and his convent, to find certain poor men with necessaries, and do divine service, etc., were alienated, to the disherison of the house and church. By means of this writ the donor or his heirs could recover the lands. Reg.Orig. 238; Fitz. Nat.Brev. 210.

CONTRA FORMAM DONI. Against the form of the grant. See Formedon.

CONTRA FORMAM FEOFFAMENTI. In old English law. A writ that lay for the heir of a tenant, enfeoffed of certain lands or tenements, by charter of feoffment from a lord to make certain services and suits to his court, who was afterwards distrained for more services than were mentioned in the charter. Reg.Orig. 176; Old Nat.Brev. 162.

CONTRA FORMAM STATUTI. In criminal pleading. (Contrary to the form of the statute in such case made and provided.) The usual conclusion of every indictment, etc., brought for an offense created by statute.

CONTRA JUS BELLI. Lat. Against the law of war. 1 Kent.Comm. 6.

CONTRA JUS COMMUNE. Against common right or law; contrary to the rule of the common law. Bract. fol. 48*b*.

CONTRA LEGEM FACIT QUI ID FACIT QUOD LEX PROHIBIT; IN FRAUDEM VERO QUI, SALVIS VERBIS LEGIS, SENTENTIAM EJUS CIRCUMVENIT. He does contrary to the law who does what the law prohibits; he acts in fraud of the law who, the letter of the law being inviolate, uses the law contrary to its intention. Dig. 1, 3, 29.

CONTRA LEGEM TERRÆ. Against the law of the land.

CONTRA NEGANTEM PRINCIPIA NON EST DISPUTANDUM. There is no disputing against one who denies first principles. Co.Litt. 343.

CONTRA NON VALENTEM AGERE NULLA CURRIT PRÆSCRIPTIO. No prescription runs against a person unable to bring an action. Broom, Max. 903.

CONTRA OMNES GENTES. Against all people. Formal words in old covenants of warranty. Fleta, lib. 3, c. 14, § 11.

CONTRA PACEM. Against the peace. A phrase used in the Latin forms of indictments, and also of actions for trespass, to signify that the offense alleged was committed against the public peace, *i. e.*, involved a breach of the peace. The full formula was *contra pacem domini regis*, against the peace of the lord the king. In modern pleading, in this country, the phrase "against the peace of the commonwealth" or "of the people" is used.

CONTRA PROFERENTEM. Against the party who proffers or puts forward a thing. J. Zimmern's Co. v. Granade, 212 Ala. 172, 102 So. 210, 211.

CONTRA TABULAS. In the civil law. Against the will, (testament.) Dig. 37, 4.

CONTRA VADIUM ET PLEGIUM. In old English law. Against gage and pledge. Bract. fol. 15*b*.

CONTRA VERITATEM LEX NUNQUAM ALIQUID PERMITTIT. The law never suffers anything contrary to truth. 2 Inst. 252.

CONTRABAND. Against law or treaty; prohibited. Goods exported from or imported into a country against its laws. Brande. Articles, the importation or exportation of which is prohibited by law. State v. Butler, 148 S.C. 495, 146 S.E. 418, 419.

CONTRABAND OF WAR. Certain classes of merchandise, such as arms and ammunition, which, by the rules of international law, cannot lawfully be furnished or carried by a neutral nation to either of two belligerents; if found in transit in neutral vessels, such goods may be seized and condemned for violation of neutrality. The Peterhoff, 5 Wall. 58, 18 L.Ed. 564; Richardson v. Insurance Co., 6 Mass. 114, 4 Am.Dec. 92.

A recent American author on international law says that, "by the term 'contraband of war,' we now understand a class of articles of commerce which *neutrals* are prohibited from furnishing to either one of the belligerents, for the reason that, by so doing, injury is done to the other belligerent;" and he treats of the subject, chiefly, in its relation to commerce upon the high seas. Hall, Int.Law, 570, 592; Elrod v. Alexander, 4 Heisk. (Tenn.) 345.

CONTRABAND OIL. Oil produced contrary to state laws. Panama Refining Co. v. Railroad Commission of Texas, D.C.Tex., 16 F.Supp. 289, 291.

CONTRACAUSATOR. A criminal; one prosecuted for a crime.

CONTRACT. A promissory agreement between two or more persons that creates, modifies, or destroys a legal relation. Buffalo Pressed Steel Co. v. Kirwan, 138 Md. 60, 113 A. 628, 630; Mexican Petroleum Corporation of Louisiana v. North German Lloyd, D.C.La., 17 F.2d 113, 114.

An agreement, upon sufficient consideration, to do or not to do a particular thing. 2 Bl.Comm. 442; 2 Kent, Comm. 449. Justice v. Lang, 42 N.Y. 496, 1 Am.Rep. 576; Rabon v. State Finance Corporation, 203 S.C. 183, 26 S.E.2d 501, 502.

An agreement between two or more parties, preliminary step in making of which is offer by one and acceptance by other, in which minds of parties meet and concur in understanding of terms. Lee v. Travelers' Ins. Co. of Hartford, Conn., 173 S.C. 185, 175 S.E. 429.

A deliberate engagement between competent parties, upon a legal consideration, to do, or abstain from doing, some act. Wharton; Smith v. Thornhill, Tex.Com.App. 25 S.W.2d 597, 599.

It is agreement creating obligation, in which there must be competent parties, subject-matter, legal consideration, mutuality of agreement, and mutuality of obligation, and agreement must not be so vague or uncertain that terms are not ascertainable. H. Liebes & Co. v. Klengenberg, C. C.A.Cal., 23 F.2d 611, 612.

A contract or agreement is either where a promise is made on one side and assented to on the other; or where two or more persons enter into engagement with each other by a promise on either side. 2 Steph.Comm. 54.

The writing which contains the agreement of parties, with the terms and conditions, and which serves as a proof of the obligation.

Certain and Hazardous

Certain contracts are those in which the thing to be done is supposed to depend on the will of the party, or when, in the usual course of events, it must happen in the manner stipulated. Hazardous contracts are those in which the performance of that which is one of its objects depends on an uncertain event. Civ.Code La. 1776.

Classification

Contracts may be classified on several different methods, according to the element in them which is brought into prominence. The usual classifications are as follows:

Commutative and Independent

Commutative contracts are those in which what is done, given, or promised by one party is considered as an equivalent to or in consideration of what is done, given, or promised by the other. Civ.Code La. 1768; Ridings v. Johnson, 9 Sup.Ct. 72, 128 U.S. 212, 32 L.Ed. 401. Independent contracts are those in which the mutual acts or promises have no relation to each other, either as equivalents or as considerations. Civ.Code La. 1769.

Conditional Contract

An executory contract the performance of which depends upon a condition. It is not simply an executory contract, since the latter may be an absolute agreement to do or not to do something, but it is a contract whose very existence and performance depend upon a contingency. Railroad Co. v. Jones, 2 Cold. (Tenn.) 584; French v. Osmer, 67 Vt. 427, 32 A. 254.

Consensual and Real

Consensual contracts are such as are founded upon and completed by the mere agreement of the contracting parties, without any external formality or symbolic act to fix the obligation. Real contracts are those in which it is necessary that there should be something more than mere consent, such as a loan of money, deposit or pledge, which, from their nature, require a delivery of the thing, (*res.*) Inst. 3, 14, 2; Id. 3, 15; Halifax, Civil Law, b. 2, c. 15, No. 1. In the common law a contract respecting real property (such as a lease of land for years) is called a "real" contract. 3 Coke, 22*a*.

Constructive Contract

Constructive contracts are such as arise when the law prescribes the rights and liabilities of persons who have not in reality entered into a contract at all, but between whom circumstances make it just that one should have a right, and the other be subject to a liability, similar to the rights and liabilities in cases of express contract. Donovan v. Kansas City, 352 Mo. 430, 175 S.W.2d 874, 884.

Divisible and Indivisible

The effect of the breach of a contract depends in a large degree upon whether it is to be regarded as indivisible or divisible; *i. e.* whether it forms a whole, the performance of every part of which is a condition precedent to bind the other party, or is composed of several independent parts, the performance of any one of which will bind the other party *pro tanto.* The only test is whether the whole quantity of the things concerned, or the sum of the acts to be done, is of the essence of the contract. It depends, therefore, in the last resort, simply upon the intention of the parties. Integrity Flooring v. Zandon Corporation, 130 N.J.L. 244, 32 A.2d 507, 509.

When a consideration is entire and indivisible, and it is against law, the contract is void *in toto.* Frazier v. Thompson, 2 Watts & S. (Pa.) 235. When the consideration is divisible, and part of it is illegal, the contract is void only *pro tanto.* Harr.Contr. 132; Gelpcke v. Dubuque, 1 Wall. 220, 17 L.Ed. 530.

Entire and Severable

An *entire* contract is one the consideration of which is entire on both sides. The entire fulfillment of the promise by either is a condition precedent to the fulfillment of any part of the promise by the other. Whenever, therefore, there is a contract to pay the gross sum for a certain and definite consideration, the contract is entire. A *severable* contract is one the consideration of which is, by its terms, susceptible of apportionment on either side, so as to correspond to the unascertained consideration on the other side, as a contract to pay a person the worth of his services so long as he will do certain work; or to give a certain price for every bushel of so much corn as corresponds to a sample. Orenstein v. Kahn, 13 Del.Ch. 376, 119 A. 444, 446; Integrity Flooring v. Zandon Corporation, 130 N.J.L. 244, 32 A.2d 507, 509; Ruby v. United Sugar Cos., 56 Ariz. 535, 109 P.2d 845, 848.

Where a contract consists of many parts, which may be considered as parts of one whole, the contract is entire. When the parts may be considered as so many distinct contracts, entered into at one time, and expressed in the same instrument, but not thereby made one contract, the contract is a separable contract. But, if the consideration of the contract is single and entire, the contract must be held to be entire, although the subject of the contract may consist of several distinct and wholly independent items. 2 Pars.Cont. 517.

Executed and Executory

Contracts are also distinguished into executed and executory; *executed,* where nothing remains to be done by either party, and where the transaction is completed at the moment that the arrangement is made, as where an article is sold and delivered, and payment therefor is made on the spot; *executory,* where some future act is to be done, as where an agreement is made to build a house in six months, or to do an act on or before some future day, or to lend money upon a certain interest, payable at a future time. Farrington v. Tennessee, 95 U.S. 683, 24 L.Ed. 558; Fox v. Kitton, 19 Ill. 532; Mather v. Mather, 25 Cal.2d 582, 154 P.2d 684, 686.

But executed contracts are not properly contracts at all, except reminiscently. The term denotes rights in property which have been acquired by means of contract; but the parties are no longer bound by a contractual tie. Mettel v. Gales, 12 S.D. 632, 82 N.W. 181.

Express and Implied

An express contract is an actual agreement of the parties, the terms of which are openly uttered or declared at the time of making it, being stated in distinct and explicit language, either orally or in writing. 2 Bl.Comm. 443; 2 Kent, Comm. 450; Linn v. Ross, 10 Ohio 414, 36 Am.Dec. 95; A. J. Yawger & Co. v. Joseph, 184 Ind. 228; 108 N.E. 774, 775; In re Pierce, Butler & Pierce Mfg. Co., D.C.N.Y., 231 F. 312, 318.

An implied contract is one not created or evidenced by the explicit agreement of the parties, but inferred by the law, as a matter of reason and justice from their acts or conduct, the circumstances surrounding the transaction making it a reasonable, or even a necessary, assumption that a contract existed between them by tacit understanding. Miller's Appeal, 100 Pa. 568, 45 Am.Rep. 394; Landon v. Kansas City Gas Co., C.C.A.Kan., 10 F.2d 263, 266; Caldwell v. Missouri State Life Ins. Co., 230 S.W. 566, 568, 148 Ark. 474; Cameron, to Use of Cameron, v. Eynon, 332 Pa. 529, 3 A.2d 423, 424; American La France Fire Engine Co., to Use of American La France & Foamite Industries, v. Borough of Shenandoah, C.C.A.Pa., 115 F.2d 866, 867.

Implied contracts are sometimes subdivided into those "implied in fact" and those "implied in law," the former being covered by the definition just given, while the latter are obligations imposed upon a person by the law, not in pursuance of his intention and agreement, either expressed or implied, but even against his will and design, because the circumstances between the parties are such as to render it just that the one should have a right, and the other a corresponding liability, similar to those which would arise from a contract between them. This kind of obligation therefore rests on the principle that whatsoever it is certain a man ought to do that the law will suppose him to have promised to do. And hence it is said that, while the liability of a party to an express contract arises directly from the contract, it is just the reverse in the case of a contract "implied in law," the contract there being implied or arising from the liability. Bliss v. Hoyt, 70 Vt. 534, 41 A. 1026; Kellum v. Browning's Adm'r, 231 Ky. 308, 21 S.W.2d 459, 465. But obligations of this kind are not properly contracts at all, and should not be so denominated. There can be no true contract without a mutual and concurrent intention of the parties. Such obligations are more properly described as "quasi contracts." Union Life Ins. Co. v. Glasscock, 270 Ky. 750, 110 S.W.2d 681, 686, 114 A.L.R. 373.

Fair and Reasonable Contract

See Fair and Reasonable Contract.

Gratuitous and Onerous

Gratuitous contracts are those of which the object is the benefit of the person with whom it is made, without any profit or advantage received or promised as a consideration for it. It is not, however, the less gratuitous if it proceed either from gratitude for a benefit before received or from the hope of receiving one thereafter, although such benefit be of a pecuniary nature. Onerous contracts are those in which something is given or promised as a consideration for the engagement or gift, or some service, interest, or condition is imposed on what is given or promised, although unequal to it in value. Civ.Code La.1773, 1774; Penitentiary Co. v. Nelms, 65 Ga. 505, 38 Am.Rep. 793. A gratuitous contract is sometimes called a contract of beneficence. Howe, Studies in the Civil Law 107.

Joint and Several

A joint contract is one made by two or more promisors, who are jointly bound to fulfill its obligations, or made to two or more promisees, who are jointly entitled to require performance of the same. A contract may be "several" as to any one of several promisors or promisees, if he has a legal right (either from the terms of the agreement or the nature of the undertaking) to enforce his individual interest separately from the other parties. Jens-Marie Oil Co. v. Rixse, 72 Okl. 93, 178 P. 658. Generally all contracts are joint where the interest of the parties for whose benefit they are created is joint, and separate where that interest is separate. Shurtleff v. Udall, 97 Vt. 156, 122 A. 465, 468.

Mutual Interest, Mixed, etc.

Contracts of "mutual interest" are such as are entered into for the reciprocal interest and utility of each of the parties; as sales, exchange, partnership, and the like. "Mixed" contracts are those by which one of the parties confers a benefit on the other, receiving something of inferior value in return, such as a donation subject to a charge. Contracts "of beneficence" are those by which only one of the contracting parties is benefited; as loans, deposit and mandate. Poth.Obl. 1, 1, 1, 2.

Parol

A contract not entirely in writing. Louisville, N. A. and C. Ry. Co. v. Reynolds, 118 Ind. 170, 173, 20 N.E. 711.

A written contract, which leaves some essential term thereof to be shown by parol, is only "parol contract" not enforceable under statute of fraud. Sheldmyer v. Bias, 112 Ind.App. 522, 45 N.E.2d 347, 349.

Personal Contract

A contract relating to personal property, or one which so far involves the element of personal knowledge or skill or personal confidence that it can be performed only by the person with whom made, and therefore is not binding on his executor. See Janin v. Browne, 59 Cal. 44; Lucas v. J. H. Gross Motor Car Co., 27 Ohio App. 183, 161 N.E. 362, 363.

Pre-contract

An obligation growing out of a contract or contractual relation, of such a nature that it debars the party from legally entering into a similar contract at a later time with any other person; particularly applied to marriage.

Principal and Accessory

A principal contract is one entered into by both parties on their own account or in the several qualities they assume. It is one which stands by itself, justifies its own existence, and is not subordinate or auxiliary to any other. Accessory contracts are those made for assuring the performance of a prior contract, either by the same parties or by others, such as suretyship, mortgage, and pledge. Civ.Code La. art. 1771.

Quasi Contracts

In the civil law. A contractual relation arising out of transactions between the parties which give them mutual rights and obligations, but do not involve a specific and express convention or agreement between them. Keener, Quasi Contr. 1; Elbert County v. Brown, 16 Ga.App. 834, 86 S.E. 651, 665. The lawful and purely voluntary acts of a man, from which there results any obligation whatever to a third person, and sometimes a reciprocal obligation between the parties. Civ. Code La. art. 2293.

Persons who have not contracted with each other are often regarded by the Roman law, under a certain state of facts, as if they had actually concluded a convention between themselves. The legal relation which then takes place between these persons, which has always a similarity to a contract obligation, is therefore termed "*obligatio quasi ex contractu.*" Such a relation arises from the conducting of affairs without authority, *(negotiorum gestio,)* from the payment of what was not due, *(solutio indebiti,)* from tutorship and curatorship, and from taking possession of an inheritance. Mackeld.Rom.Law § 491.

Legal fiction invented by **common law** courts to permit recovery by contractual remedy of assumpsit in cases where, in fact, there is no contract, but where circumstances are such that justice warrants a recovery as though there had been a promise. Clark v. Peoples Savings and Loan Ass'n of De Kalb County, 221 Ind. 168, 46 N.E.2d 681, 682, 144 A.L.R. 1495. It is not based on intention or consent of the parties, but is founded on considerations of justice and equity, and on doctrine of unjust enrichment. Bruggeman v. Independent School Dist., No. 4, Union Tp., Mitchell County, 227 Iowa 661, 289 N.W. 5, 8, 11.

It is not in fact a contract, but an obligation which the law creates in absence of any agreement, when and because the acts of the parties or others have placed in the possession of one person money, or its equivalent, under such circumstances that in equity and good conscience he ought not to retain it. Grossbier v. Chicago, St. P., M. & O. Ry. Co., 173 Wis. 503, 181 N.W. 746, 748; It is an implication of law. First Nat. Bank v. Matlock, 99 Okl. 150, 226 P. 328, 331, 36 A.L.R. 1088; Caldwell v. Missouri State Life Ins. Co., 148 Ark. 474, 230 S.W. 566, 568.

It is what was formerly known as the contract implied in law; it has no reference to the intentions or expressions of the parties. The obligation is imposed despite, and frequently in frustration of their intention. Town of Balkan v. Village of Buhl, 158 Minn. 271, 197 N.W. 266, 35 A.L.R. 470.

Record, Specialty, Simple

Contracts of record are such as are declared and adjudicated by courts of competent jurisdiction, or entered on their records, including judgments, recognizances, and statutes staple. Hardeman v. Downer, 39 Ga. 425. These are not properly speaking contracts at all, though they may be enforced by action like contracts. Specialties, or special contracts, are contracts under seal, such as deeds and bonds. Ludwig v. Bungart, 26 Misc. Rep. 247, 56 N.Y.S. 51. All others are included in the description "simple" contracts; that is, a simple contract is one that is not a contract of record and not under seal; it may be either written or oral, in either case, it is called a "parol" contract, the distinguishing feature being the lack of a seal. Stackpole v. Arnold, 11 Mass. 30, 6 Am. Dec. 150; 4 B. & Ald. 588; 2 Bla.Comm. 472.

Special Contract

A contract under seal; a specialty; as distinguished from one merely oral or in writing not sealed. But in common usage this term is often used to denote an express or explicit contract, one which clearly defines and settles the reciprocal rights and obligations of the parties, as distinguished from one which must be made out, and its terms ascertained, by the inference of the law from the nature and circumstances of the transaction.

A special contract may rest in parol, and does not mean a contract by specialty; it is defined as one with peculiar provisions not found in the ordinary contracts relating to the same subject-matter. Midland Roofing Mfg. Co. v. Pickens, 96 S.C. 286, 80 S.E. 484, 485.

Subcontract

A contract subordinate to another contract, made or intended to be made between the contracting parties, on one part, or some of them, and a stranger. 1 H.Bl. 37, 45. One made under a prior contract. Mobley v. Leeper Bros. Lumber Co., 89 Okl. 95, 214 P. 174, 175.

Where a person has contracted for the performance of certain work (*e. g.*, to build a house,) and he in turn engages a third party to perform the whole or a part of that which is included in the original contract, (*e. g.*, to do the carpenter work,) his agreement with such third person is called a "subcontract," and such person is called a "subcontractor." Central Trust Co. v. Railroad Co., C.C.Ky., 54 F. 723; Lester v. Houston, 101 N.C. 605, 8 S.E. 366. The term "subcontractor" means one who has contracted with the original contractor for the performance of all or a part of the work or services which such contractor has himself contracted to perform. Republic Supply Co. v. Allen, Tex.Civ.App., 262 S.W. 113, 114.

Unconscionable Contract

One which no sensible man not under delusion, duress, or in distress would make, and such as no honest and fair man would accept. Franklin Fire Ins. Co. v. Noll, 115 Ind.App. 289, 58 N.E.2d 947, 949, 950.

Unilateral and Bilateral

A unilateral contract is one in which one party makes an express engagement or undertakes a performance, without receiving in return any express engagement or promise of performance from the other. Bilateral (or reciprocal) contracts are those by which the parties expressly enter into mutual engagements, such as sale or hire. Civ. Code La. art. 1765; Poth. Obl. 1, 1, 1, 2; Kling Bros. Engineering Works v. Whiting Corporation, 320 Ill.App. 630, 51 N.E.2d 1004, 1007. When the party to whom an engagement is made makes no express agreement on his part, the contract is called unilateral, even in cases where the law attaches certain obligations to his acceptance. La. Civ. Code, art. 1765. A contract is also said to be "unilateral" when there is a promise on one side only, the consideration on the other side being executed. McMahan v. McMahon, 122 S.C. 336, 115 S.E. 293, 294, 26 A.L.R. 1295.

Usurious Contract

See that title.

Written Contract

A "written contract" is one which in all its terms is in writing. Fey v. Loose-Wiles Biscuit Co., 147 Kan. 31, 75 P.2d 810, 813; and instrument signed by one party is orally accepted by other, Reeves Furniture Co. v. Simms, Tex.Civ.App., 59 S.W.2d 262, 263.

CONTRACT, ESTOPPEL BY. There are two sorts of "estoppel by contract," estoppel to deny truth of facts agreed on and settled by force of entering into contract, and estoppel arising from acts done under or in performance of contract. In re Schofield's Estate, 101 Colo. 443, 73 P.2d 1381. Finch v. Smith, 177 Okl. 307, 58 P.2d 850, 851.

"Estoppel by contract" is intended to embrace all cases in which there is an actual or virtual undertaking to treat a fact as settled. Jackson v. United Gas Public Service Co., 198 So. 633, 640, 196 La. 1. It means party is bound by terms of own contract until set aside or annulled for fraud, accident, or mistake. United Fidelity Life Ins. Co. v. Fowler, Tex.Civ.App., 38 S.W.2d 128, 131.

CONTRACT OF BENEVOLENCE. A contract made for the benefit of one of the contracting parties only, as a mandate or deposit.

CONTRACT OF RECORD. A contract of record is one which has been declared and adjudicated by a court having jurisdiction, or which is entered of record in obedience to, or in carrying out, the judgments of a court.

CONTRACT OF SALE. A contract by which one of the contracting parties, called the "seller," enters into an obligation to the other to cause him to have freely, by a title of proprietor, a thing, for the price of a certain sum of money, which the other contracting party, called the "buyer," on his part obliges himself to pay. Topzant v. Koshe, 242 Wis. 585, 9 N.W.2d 136, 138.

CONTRACT SYSTEM. As applied to state prisons, this phrase signifies that the labor of the prisoners is utilized by private persons or contractors, who thus secure the profits of such labor. People v. Hawkins, 157 N.Y. 1, 51 N.E. 257, 260, 42 L.R.A. 490, 68 Am.St.Rep. 736.

CONTRACTION. Abbreviation; abridgment or shortening of a word by omitting a letter or letters or a syllable, with a mark over the place where the elision occurs. This was customary in records written in the ancient "court hand," and is frequently found in the books printed in black-letter.

CONTRACTOR. This term is strictly applicable to any person who enters into a contract (Kent v. Railroad Co., 12 N.Y. 628), but is commonly reserved to designate one who, for a fixed price, undertakes to procure the performance of works on a large scale, or the furnishing of goods in large quantities, whether for the public or a company or individual. McCarthy v. Second Parish, 71 Me. 318, 36 Am.Rep. 320.

One who in pursuit of independent business undertakes to perform a job or piece of work, retaining in himself control of means, method and manner of accomplishing the desired result. Marion Malleable Iron Works v. Baldwin, 82 Ind.App. 206, 145 N.E. 559, 560.

CONTRACTUAL OBLIGATION. The obligation which arises from a contract or agreement.

CONTRACTUS. Lat. Contract; a contract; contracts.

CONTRACTUS BONÆ FIDEI. In Roman law. Contracts of good faith. Those contracts which, when brought into litigation, were not determined by the rules of the strict law alone, but allowed the judge to examine into the *bona fides* of the transaction, and to hear equitable considerations against their enforcement. In this they were opposed to contracts *stricti juris*, against which equitable defenses could not be entertained.

CONTRACTUS CIVILES. In Roman law. Civil contracts. Those contracts which were recognized as actionable by the strict civil law of Rome, or as being founded upon a particular statute, as distinguished from those which could not be enforced in the courts except by the aid of the prætor, who, through his equitable powers, gave an action upon them. The latter were called *"contractus prætorii."*

CONTRACTUS EST QUASI ACTUS CONTRA ACTUM. 2 Coke, 15. A contract is, as it were, act against act.

CONTRACTUS EX TURPI CAUSA, VEL CONTRA BONOS MORES, NULLUS EST. A contract founded on a base consideration, or against good morals, is null. Hob. 167.

CONTRACTUS LEGEM EX CONBENTIONE ACCIPIUNT. Contracts receive legal sanction from the agreement of the parties. Dig. 16, 3, 1, 6.

CONTRADICT. In practice. To disprove. To prove a fact contrary to what has been asserted by a witness.

CONTRADICTION IN TERMS. A phrase of which the parts are expressly inconsistent, as *e. g.*, "an innocent murder;" "a fee-simple for life."

CONTRÆSCRITURA. In Spanish law. A counter-writing; counter-letter. A document executed at the same time with an act of sale or other instrument, and operating by way of defeasance or otherwise modifying the apparent effect and purport of the original instrument.

CONTRAETATIO REI ALIENÆ ANIMO FURANDI, EST FURTUM. The touching or removing of another's property, with an intention of stealing, is theft. Jenk. Cent. 132.

CONTRAFACTIO. Counterfeiting; as *contrafactio sigilli regis,* counterfeiting the king's seal. Cowell.

CONTRAINTE PAR CORPS. In French law. The civil process of arrest of the person, which is imposed upon vendors falsely representing their property to be unincumbered, or upon persons mortgaging property which they are aware does not belong to them, and in other cases of moral heinousness. Brown.

CONTRALIGATIO. In old English law. Counter-obligation. Literally, counter-binding. *Est enim obligatio quasi contraligatio.* Fleta, lib. 2, c. 56, § 1.

CONTRAMANDATIO. A countermanding. *Contramandatio placiti,* in old English law, was the respiting of a defendant, or giving him further time to answer, by countermanding the day fixed for him to plead, and appointing a new day; a sort of imparlance.

CONTRAMANDATUM. A lawful excuse, which a defendant in a suit by attorney alleges for himself to show that the plaintiff has no cause of complaint. Blount.

CONTRAPLACITUM. In old English law. A counter-plea. Townsh. Pl. 61.

CONTRAPOSITIO. In old English law. A plea or answer. Blount. A counter-position.

CONTRARIENTS. This word was used in the time of Edw. II. to signify those who were opposed to the government, but were neither rebels nor traitors. Jacob.

CONTRARIORUM CONTRARIA EST RATIO. Hob. 344. The reason of contrary things is contrary.

CONTRAROTULATOR. A controller. One whose business it was to observe the money which the collectors had gathered for the use of the king or the people. Cowell.

CONTRAROTULATOR PIPÆ. An officer of the exchequer that writeth out summons twice every year, to the sheriffs, to levy the rents and debts of the pipe. Blount.

CONTRARY. Against; opposed or in opposition to; in conflict with.

CONTRARY TO THE EVIDENCE. Against the evidence; against the weight of the evidence. Olson v. Elliott, 245 Wis. 279, 15 N.W. 37, 39.

CONTRARY TO LAW. Illegal; in violation of statute or legal regulations at a given time. Feathers of Wild Birds v. U. S., C.C.A.N.Y., 267 F. 964, 967; Goldberg v. U. S., C.C.A.Minn., 277 F. 211, 215. In respect of verdict. In conflict with the law contained in court's instructions. Chetopa Motor Co. v. Douglas, 132 Okl. 92, 269 P. 365, 366.

CONTRAT. In French law. Contracts are of the following varieties: (1) *Bilateral,* or *synallagmatique,* where each party is bound to the other to do what is just and proper; or (2) *unilateral,* where the one side only is bound; or (3) *commutatif,* where one does to the other something which is supposed to be an equivalent for what the other does to him; or (4) *aléatoire,* where the consideration for the act of the one is a mere chance; or (5) *contrat de bienfaisance,* where the one party procures to the other a purely gratuitous benefit; or (6) *contrat à titre onereux,* where each party is bound under some duty to the other. Brown.

CONTRATALLIA. In old English law. A counter-tally. A term used in the exchequer. Mem. in Scacc. M. 26 Edw. 1.

CONTRATENERE. To hold against; to withhold. Whishaw.

CONTRAVENING EQUITY. A right or equity, in another person, which is inconsistent with and opposed to the equity sought to be enforced or recognized.

CONTRAVENTION. In French Law. An act which violates the law, a treaty, or an agreement which the party has made. That infraction of the law punished by a fine which does not exceed fifteen francs and by an imprisonment not exceeding three days. Pen.Code, 1.

In Scotch law. The act of breaking through any restraint imposed by deed, by covenant, or by a court.

CONTRECTARE. Lat. In the civil law. To handle; to take hold of; to meddle with.

In old English law. To treat. *Vel malè contrectet;* or shall ill treat. Fleta, lib. 1, c. 17, § 4.

CONTRECTATIO. In the civil and old English law. Touching; handling; meddling. The act of removing a thing from its place in such a manner that, if the thing be not restored, it will amount to theft.

CONTRECTATIO REI ALIENÆ, ANIMO FURANDI, EST FURTUM. Jenk. Cent. 132. The touching or removing of another's property, with an intention of stealing, is theft.

CONTREFACON. In French law. The offense of printing or causing to be printed a book, the copyright of which is held by another, without authority from him. Merl. Repert.

CONTRE-MAITRE. In French marine law. The chief officer of a vessel, who, in case of the sickness or absence of the master, commanded in his place. Literally, the countermaster.

CONTRIBUTE. To lend assistance or aid, or give something, to a common purpose; to have a share in any act or effect; to discharge a joint obligation. Christman v. Reichholdt, Mo.App., 150 S.W.2d 527, 532; James McCord Co. v. Citizens Hotel Co., Tex.Civ.App., 287 S.W. 906; Park v. Missionary Soc., 62 Vt. 19, 20 A. 107.

As applied to negligence signifies causal connection between injury and negligence, which transcends and is distinguished from negligent acts or omissions which play so minor a part in producing injuries that law does not recognize them as legal causes. Connellan v. Coffey, 122 Conn. 136, 187 A. 901, 903.

CONTRIBUTION. In the civil law. A partition by which the creditors of an insolvent debtor divide among themselves the proceeds of his property proportionably to the amount of their respective credits. Code La. art. 3556, par. 9. Division which is made among the heirs of the succession of the debts with which the succession is charged, according to the proportion which each is bound to bear. Civ.Code La. art. 1420.

In common law. The sharing of a loss or payment among several. The act of any one or several of a number of co-debtors, co-sureties, etc., in reimbursing one of their number who has paid the whole debt or suffered the whole liability, each to the extent of his proportionate share. Canosia Tp. v. Grand Lake Tp., 80 Minn. 357, 83 N.W. 346; Ratte v. Ratte, 260 Mass. 165, 156 N.E. 870, 871. Right of one who has discharged a common liability to recover of another also liable, the aliquot portion which he ought to pay or bear. St. Lewis v. Morrison, D.C.Ky., 50 F.Supp. 570, 572, 573. Parten v. First Nat. Bank & Trust Co., 283 N.W. 408, 412, 204 Minn. 200, 120 A.L.R. 962; Chapman v. Lamar-Rankin Drug Co., 64 Ga.App. 493, 13 S.E.2d 734, 737. Fidelity & Casualty Ins. Co. of New York v. Sears, Roebuck & Co., 124 Conn. 227, 199 A. 93, 94.

In maritime law. Where the property of one of several parties interested in a vessel and cargo has been voluntarily sacrificed for the common safety, (as by throwing goods overboard to lighten the vessel,) such loss must be made good by the contribution of the others, which is termed "general average." 3 Kent, Comm. 232–244; 1 Story, Eq. Jur. § 490.

CONTRIBUTION TO CAPITAL. A fund or property contributed by shareowners as financial basis for prosecution of corporation's business, and signifies resources whose dedication to users of the corporation is made the foundation for issuance of capital stock and which became irrevocably devoted to satisfaction of all obligations of corporation. Detroit Edison Co. v. Commissioner of Internal Revenue, C.C.A.6, 131 F.2d 619, 623.

CONTRIBUTIONE FACIENDA. In old English law. A writ that lay where tenants in common were bound to do some act, and one of them was put to the whole burthen, to compel the rest to make contribution. Reg. Orig. 175; Fitzh. Nat. Brev. 162.

CONTRIBUTORY, *n.* A person liable to contribute to the assets of a company which is being wound up, as being a member or (in some cases) a past member thereof. Mozley & Whitley.

CONTRIBUTORY, *adj.* Joining in the promotion of a given purpose; lending assistance to the production of a given result. Armstrong v. Green, 113 Okl. 254, 241 P. 789, 791.

As to contributory "Infringement" and "Negligence," see those titles.

CONTROL, *v.* To exercise restraining or directing influence over; regulate; restrain; dominate; curb; to hold from action; overpower; counteract; govern. Owen v. Trail, 302 Mo. 292, 258 S.W. 699, 702; Hopkins v. Howard's Ex'x, 266 Ky. 685, 99 S.W.2d 810, 812.

To control a thing is to have the right to exercise a directing or governing influence over it. Trust Co. of New Jersey v. Greenwood Cemetery, 21 N.J.Misc. 169, 32 A.2d 519, 523.

CONTROL, *n.* Power or authority to manage, direct, superintend, restrict, regulate, direct, govern, administer, or oversee. State v. First State Bank of Jud, 52 N.D. 231, 202 N.W. 391, 402.

The "control" involved in determining whether "principal and agent relationship" or "master and servant relationship" is involved must be accompanied by power or right to order or direct. Mid-Continent Petroleum Corporation v. Vicars, 221 Ind. 387, 47 N.E.2d 972, 975.

Driver must at all times have automobile under control, means having it under such control that it can be stopped before doing injury to any person in any situation that is reasonably likely to arise under the circumstances. Kindt v. Reading Co., 352 Pa. 419, 43 A.2d 145, 147.

CONTROL OF CARBON. Such a chemical action upon the carbon in an alloy as will keep it largely in a combined graphitic state. Pittsburgh Iron, & Steel Foundries Co. v. Seaman-Sleeth Co., D.C. Pa., 236 F. 756, 760.

CONTROLLER. A comptroller, which see.

CONTROLMENT. In old English law. The controlling or checking of another officer's account; the keeping of a counter-roll.

CONTROVER. In old English law. An inventor or deviser of false news. 2 Inst. 227.

CONTROVERSIES ARISING IN BANKRUPTCY PROCEEDINGS. Within Bankruptcy Act § 24a, 11 U.S.C.A. § 47(a), investing Circuit Courts of Appeals with appellate jurisdiction, include those matters arising in the course of a bankruptcy proceeding, which are not mere steps in the ordinary administration of the bankrupt estate, but present distinct and separable issues, between the trustee and adverse claimants concerning the right and title to the bankrupt's estate. Handlan v. Bennett, C.C.A.W.Va., 51 F.2d 21, 23.

CONTROVERSY. A litigated question; adversary proceeding in a court of law; a civil action or suit, either at law or in equity; a justiciable dispute. Barber v. Kennedy, 18 Minn. 216 (Gil. 196); State v. Guinotte, 156 Mo. 513, 57 S.W. 281, 50 L. R.A. 787.

It differs from "case," which includes all suits, criminal as well as civil; whereas "controversy" is a civil and not a criminal proceeding. Chisholm v. Georgia, 2 Dall. 419, 431, 432, 1 L.Ed. 440.

CONTROVERT. To dispute; to deny; to oppose or contest; to take issue on. Reese v. Adamson, 297 Pa. 13, 146 A. 262, 263.

CONTUBERNIUM. In Roman law. The marriage of slaves; a permitted cohabitation.

CONTUMACE CAPIENDO. In English law. Excommunication in all cases of contempt in the spiritual courts is discontinued by 53 Geo. III, c. 127, § 2, and in lieu thereof, where a lawful citation or sentence has not been obeyed, the judge shall have power, after a certain period, to pronounce such person contumacious and in contempt, and to signify the same to the court of chancery, whereupon a writ *de contumace capiendo* shall issue from that court, which shall have the same force and effect as formerly belonged, in case of contempt, to a writ *de excommunicato capiendo.* (2 & 3 Wm. IV, c. 93; 3 & 4 Vict. c. 93.) Wharton; 1 Holdsw. Hist. Engl. Law App. XVIII. See Excommunication.

CONTUMACY. The refusal or intentional omission of a person who has been duly cited before a court to appear and defend the charge laid against him, or, if he is duly before the court, to obey some lawful order or direction made in the cause. In the former case it is called "presumed" contumacy; in the latter, "actual." The term is chiefly used in ecclesiastical law. See 3 Curt. Ecc. 1.

CONTUMAX. One accused of a crime who refuses to appear and answer to the charge. An outlaw.

CONTUMELY. Rudeness compounded of haughtiness and contempt; scornful insolence; despiteful treatment; disdain, contemptuousness in act or speech; disgrace. United States v. Strong, D. C.Wash., 263 F. 789, 796.

CONTUSE. To bruise; to injure or disorganize a part of without breaking the skin. Ansley v. Travelers Ins. Co., 27 Tenn.App. 720, 173 S.W.2d 702, 704.

CONTUSION. In medical jurisprudence. A bruise; an injury to any external part of the body by the impact of a fall or the blow of a blunt instrument, without laceration of the flesh, and either with or without a tearing of the skin, but in the former case it is more properly called a "contused wound." Gasperino v. Prudential Ins. Co. of America, Mo.App., 107 S.W. 819, 827.

CONTUTOR. Lat. In the civil law. A co-tutor, or co-guardian. Inst. 1, 24, 1.

CONUSANCE. In English law. Cognizance or jurisdiction. Conusance of pleas. Termes de la Ley.

CONUSANCE, CLAIM OF. See Cognizance.

CONUSANT. Cognizant; acquainted with; having actual knowledge; as, if a party knowing of an agreement in which he has an interest makes no objection to it, he is said to be conusant. Co. Litt. 157.

CONUSEE. See Cognizee.

CONUSOR. See Cognizor.

CONVALESCENCE. Gradual recovery of health or physical strength after illness. Romesburg v. Federal Life Ins. Co., 147 Kan. 378, 76 P.2d 829, 831.

CONVENABLE. In old English law. Suitable; agreeable; convenient; fitting. Litt. § 103.

CONVENE. In the civil law. To bring an action.

CONVENIENCE AND NECESSITY. If there is a reasonable need apparent for use of the service, and if a common carrier is not unduly interfered with, nor the public highways unduly burdened, a case of "convenience and necessity" exists with respect to an application for a license to operate as a contract motor carrier. Short Way Lines v. Black, 182 S.W.2d 17, 19, 298 Ky. 67.

CONVENIENT. Proper; just; suitable; fit; adapted; proper; becoming appropriate. Finlay v. Dickerson, 29 Ill. 20; Railway Co. v. Smith, 19 S.Ct. 565, 173 U.S. 684, 43 L.Ed. 858; Prina v. Board of Sup'rs of Graham County, 16 Ariz. 252, 143 P. 567, 568.

CONVENIT. Lat. In civil and old English law. It is agreed; it was agreed.

CONVENT. The fraternity of an abbey or priory, as *societas* is the number of fellows in a college. A religious house, now regarded as a merely voluntary association, not importing civil death. 33 Law J. Ch. 308.

An association or community of recluses devoted to a religious life under a superior; a body of monks, friars, or nuns, constituting one local community; now usually restricted to a convent of nuns; as, to go into a convent. Sacred Heart Academy of Galveston v. Karsch, 122 S.W.2d 416, 417, 173 Tenn. 618.

CONVENTICLE. A private assembly or meeting for the exercise of religion. The word was first an appellation of reproach to the religious assemblies of Wycliffe in the reigns of Edward III, and Richard II., and was afterwards applied to a meeting of dissenters from the established church. As this word in strict propriety denotes an unlawful assembly, it cannot be justly applied to the assembling of persons in places of worship licensed according to the requisitions of law. Wharton.

CONVENTIO. Canon Law. The act of summoning or calling together the parties by summoning the defendant.

The Civil Law. A compact, agreement, or convention. An agreement between two or more persons respecting a legal relation between them. Mackeld. Rom. Law, §§ 385, 386.

The term is one of very wide scope, and applies to all classes of subjects in which an engagement or business relation may be founded by agreement. It is to be distinguished from the negotiations or preliminary transactions on the object of the convention and fixing its extent, which are not binding so long as the convention is not concluded.

In contracts. An agreement; a covenant. Cowell.

CONVENTIO IN UNUM. In the civil law. The agreement between the two parties to a contract upon the sense of the contract proposed. It is an essential part of the contract, following the pollicitation or proposal emanating from the one, and followed by the consension or agreement of the other.

CONVENTIO PRIVATORUM NON POTEST PUBLICO JURI DEROGARE. The agreement of private persons cannot derogate from public right, *i. e.*, cannot prevent the application of general rules of law, or render valid any contravention of law. Co. Litt. 166*a*; Wing. Max. p. 746, max. 201.

CONVENTIO VINCIT LEGEM. The express agreement of parties overcomes [prevails against] the law. Story, Ag. § 368.

CONVENTION. In English law. An extraordinary assembly of the houses of lords and commons, without the assent or summons of the sovereign. It can only be justified *ex necessitate rei*, as the parliament which restored Charles II., and that which disposed of the crown and kingdom to William and Mary. Wharton. Also the name of an old writ that lay for the breach of a covenant.

In Roman law. An agreement between parties; a pact. A convention was a mutual engagement between two persons, possessing all the subjective requisites of a contract, but which did not give rise to an action, nor receive the sanction of the law, as bearing an "obligation," until the objective requisite of a solemn ceremonial, (such as *stipulatio*) was supplied. In other words, convention was the informal agreement of the parties, which formed the basis of a contract, and which became a contract when the external formalities were superimposed. See Maine, Anc. Law, 313.

"The division of conventions into contracts and pacts was important in the Roman law. The former were such conventions as already, by the older civil law, founded an obligation and action; all the other conventions were termed 'pacts.' These generally did not produce an actionable obligation. Actionability was subsequently given to several pacts, whereby they received the same power and efficacy that contracts received." Mackeld.Rom.Law, § 395.

In legislation. An assembly of delegates or representatives chosen by the people for special and extraordinary legislative purposes, such as the framing or revision of a state constitution. Also an assembly of delegates chosen by a political party, or by the party organization in a larger or smaller territory, to nominate candidates for an approaching election. In re Opinion of the Justices, 132 Me. 491, 167 A. 176, 179.

In public and international law. A pact or agreement between states or nations in the nature of a treaty; usually applied (a) to agreements or arrangements preliminary to a formal treaty or to serve as its basis, or (b) international agreements for the regulation of matters of common interest but not coming within the sphere of politics or commercial intercourse, such as international postage or the protection of submarine cables. U. S. v. Hunter, C.C.Mo., 21 F. 615.

Constitutional convention. See Constitution.

Judicial convention. See Judicial.

CONVENTIONAL. Depending on, or arising from, the mutual agreement of parties; as distinguished from *legal*, which means created by, or arising from, the act of the law. De Vita v. Pianisani, 217 N.Y.S. 438, 440, 127 Misc. 611.

As to conventional "Estates," "Interest," "Mortgage," "Subrogation," and "Trustees," see those titles.

CONVENTIONAL LIEN. A lien is conventional where the lien, general or particular (Cro. Car. 271; 6 Term. 14; 2 Kent 637) is raised by the express agreement and stipulation of the parties, in circumstances where the law alone would not create a lien from the mere relation of the parties or the details of their transaction.

CONVENTIONE. The name of a writ for the breach of any covenant in writing, whether real or personal. Reg.Orig. 115; Fitzh.Nat.Brev. 145.

CONVENTIONS. This name is sometimes given to compacts or treaties with foreign countries as to the apprehension and extradition of fugitive offenders. See Extradition.

CONVENTUAL CHURCH. In ecclesiastical law. That which consists of regular clerks, professing some order or religion; or of dean and chapter; or other societies of spiritual men.

CONVENTUALS. Religious men united in a convent or religious house. Cowell.

CONVENTUS. Lat. A coming together; a convention or assembly. *Conventus magnatum vel procerum* (the assembly of chief men or peers) was one of the names of the English parliament. 1 Bl. Comm. 148.

In the civil law. The term meant a gathering together of people; a crowd assembled for any purpose; also a convention, pact, or bargain.

CONVENTUS JURIDICUS. In the Roman law. A court of sessions held in the Roman provinces, by the president of the province, assisted by a certain number of counsellors and assessors, at fixed periods, to hear and determine suits, and to provide for the civil administration of the province. Schm. Civil Law, Introd. 17.

CONVERSANT. One who is in the habit of being in a particular place is said to be conversant there. Barnes, 162. Acquainted; familiar.

CONVERSANTES. In old English law. Conversant or dwelling; commorant.

CONVERSATION. Manner of living; habits of life; conduct; as in the phrase "chaste life and conversation." Bradshaw v. People, 153 Ill. 156, 38 N.E. 652. Criminal conversation means seduction of another man's wife, considered as an actionable injury to the husband. Prettyman v. Williamson, 1 Pennewill (Del.) 224, 39 A. 731; Crocker v. Crocker, C.C.Mass., 98 F. 702.

CONVERSE. The transposition of the subject and predicate in a proposition, as: "Everything is good in its place." *Converse,* "Nothing is good which is not in its place." Wharton.

CONVERSION. Equity. The exchange of property from real to personal or from personal to real, which takes place under some circumstances in the consideration of the law, such as, to give effect to directions in a will or settlement, or to stipulations in a contract, although no such change has actually taken place, 1 Bro.C.C. 497; 1 Lead.Cas.Eq. 619; 1 Lead. Cas.Eq. 872; Lawrence v. Elliott, 3 Redf.Sur. (N.Y.) 235; Dodge v. Williams, 46 Wis. 70, 1 N.W. 92, 50 N.W. 1103; Mattison v. Stone, 99 S.C. 151, 82 S.E. 1046, 1047; and by which exchange the property so dealt with becomes invested with the properties and attributes of that into which it is supposed to have been converted; Seymour v. Freer, 8 Wall. 214, 19 L.Ed. 306; Haward v. Peavey, 128 Ill. 430, 21 N.E. 503, 15 Am.St.Rep. 120.

Although it is sometimes necessary for certain purposes of devolution and transfer to regard the property in its changed condition as though the change has not absolutely taken place; Davidson v. Bright, 267 Pa. 580, 110 A. 301, 302.

A qualified conversion is one directed for some particular purpose; Harker v. Reilly, 4 Del.Ch. 72.

Law

An unauthorized assumption and exercise of the right of ownership over goods or personal chattels belonging to another, to the alteration of their condition or the exclusion of the owner's rights. Stickney v. Munroe, 44 Me. 197; Baldwin v. Cole, 6 Mod. 212; In re Di Crocco's Estate, 12 N.Y.S.2d 276, 278, 170 Misc. 826; Powell v. A. K. Brown Motor Co., 20 S.E.2d 636, 637, 200 S.C. 75. Any unauthorized act which deprives an owner of his property permanently or for an indefinite time. Forbush v. San Diego Fruit & Produce Co., 46 Idaho, 231, 266 P. 659, 663.

Also one who aids and abets another in keeping property from its rightful owner is guilty of "conversion". Edwards v. Max Thieme Chevrolet Co., La.App., 191 So. 569, 571, 572.

Constructive conversion. An implied or virtual conversion, which takes place where a person does such acts in reference to the goods of another as amount in law to the appropriation of the property to himself. Scruggs v. Scruggs, C.C. Mo., 105 F. 28; Laverty v. Snethen, 68 N.Y. 524, 23 Am.Rep. 184; Wade v. Ray, 67 Okl. 39, 168 P. 447, 449, L.R.A.1918B, 796.

Direct conversion. The act of actually appropriating the property of another to his own beneficial use and enjoyment, or to that of a third person, or destroying it, or altering its nature. Ross v. Lewis, 23 N.M. 524, 169 P. 468, 469; or wrongfully assuming title in himself; Cass v. Ocean Park Bath Co., 45 Cal.App. 656, 188 P. 616, 617; there must be a positive wrong or act of malfeasance; American Surety Co. of New York v. Hill County, Tex.Civ.App., 254 S.W. 241, 245.

CONVEY. To pass or transmit the title to property from one to another; to transfer property or the title to property by deed or instrument under seal. Used popularly in sense of "assign," "sale," or "transfer." Crookshanks v. Ransbarger, 80 W.Va. 21, 92 S.E. 78, 82; McQuiddy Printing Co. v. Hirsig, 23 Tenn.App. 434, 134 S.W.2d 197, 205.

Convey relates properly to the disposition of real property, not to personal. Dickerman v. Abrahams, 21 Barb., N.Y., 551, 561. To convey real estate is, by an appropriate instrument, to transfer the legal title to it from the present owner to another. Abendroth v. Greenwich, 29 Conn. 356.

CONVEYANCE. In pleading. Introduction or inducement.

In real property law. In the strict legal sense, a transfer of legal title to land. In the popular sense, and as generally used by lawyers, it denotes any transfer of title, legal or equitable. Chupco v. Chapman, 76 Okl. 201, 170 P. 259, 266. The transfer of the title of land from one person or class of persons to another. Klein v. McNamara, 54 Miss. 105; Alexander v. State, 28 Tex. App. 186, 12 S.W. 595; In re Loes' Will, 55 N.Y.S. 2d 723, 726. An instrument in writing under seal, (anciently termed an "assurance,") by which some estate or interest in lands is transferred from one person to another; such as a deed, mortgage, etc. 2 Bl. Comm. 293, 295, 309.

Conveyance includes every instrument in writing by which any estate or interest in real estate is created, aliened, mortgaged, or assigned, or by which the title to any real estate may be affected in law or equity, except last wills and testaments, leases for a term not exceeding three years, and executory contracts for the sale or purchase of lands. Stearns Lighting & Power Co. v. Central Trust Co., C.C.A.Mich., 223 F. 962, 966; Shraiberg v. Hanson, 138 Minn. 80, 163 N.W. 1032, 1033.

General

Absolute or conditional conveyance. An absolute conveyance is one by which the right or property in a thing is transferred, free of any condition or qualification, by which it might be defeated or changed; as an ordinary deed of lands, in contradistinction to a mortgage, which is a conditional conveyance. Burrill; Falconer v. Buffalo, etc., R. Co., 69 N.Y. 491; Brown v. United States, C.C.A.Pa., 95 Fed.2d 487, 489.

Fraudulent conveyance. See Fraudulent.

Mesne conveyance. An intermediate conveyance; one occupying an intermediate position in a chain of title between the first grantee and the present holder.

Primary conveyances. Those by means whereof the benefit or estate is created or first arises; as distinguished from those whereby it may be enlarged, restrained, transferred, or extinguished. The term includes feoffment, gift, grant, lease, exchange, and partition, and is opposed to *derivative* conveyances, such as release, surrender, confirmation, etc. 2 Bl. Comm. 309.

Secondary conveyances. The name given to that class of conveyances which presuppose some other conveyance precedent, and only serve to enlarge, confirm, alter, restrain, restore, or transfer the interest granted by such original conveyance. 2 Bl. Comm. 324. Otherwise termed "derivative conveyances" (*q. v.*).

Voluntary conveyance. A conveyance without valuable consideration; such as a deed or settlement in favor of a wife or children. Gentry v. Field, 143 Mo. 399, 45 S.W. 286; Shannon v. Duffield, 218 Ky. 770, 292 S.W. 322, 323; English v. Brown, D.C.N.J., 219 F. 248, 256.

CONVEYANCER. One whose business it is to draw deeds, bonds, mortgages, wills, writs, or other legal papers, or to examine titles to real estate. 14 St. at Large, 118.

He who draws conveyances; especially a barrister who confines himself to drawing conveyances, and other chamber practice. Mozley & Whitley.

CONVEYANCING. A term including both the science and art of transferring titles to real estate from one man to another.

Conveyancing is that part of the lawyer's business which relates to the alienation and transmission of property and other rights from one person to another, and to the framing of legal documents intended to create, define, transfer, or extinguish rights. It therefore includes the investigation of the title to land, and the preparation of agreements, wills, articles of association, private statutes operating as conveyances, and many other instruments in addition to conveyances properly so called. Sweet; Livermore v. Bagley, 3 Mass. 505.

CONVEYANCING COUNSEL TO THE COURT OF CHANCERY. Certain counsel, not fewer than six in number, appointed by the lord chancellor, for the purpose of assisting the court of chancery, or any judge thereof, with their opinion in matters of title and conveyancing. Mozley & Whitley.

CONVICIA SI IRASCARIS TUA DIVULGAS; SPRETA EXOLESCUNT. 3 Inst. 198. If you be moved to anger by insults, you publish them; if despised, they are forgotten.

CONVICIUM. In the civil law. The name of a species of slander or injury uttered in public, and which charged some one with some act *contra bonos mores*.

CONVICT, *v.* To condemn after judicial investigation; to find a man guilty of a criminal charge. The word was formerly used also in the sense of finding against the defendant in a civil case.

Formerly a man was said to be convict when he had been found guilty of treason or felony, but before judgment had been passed on him, after which he was said to be attaint, (*q. v.*). Co.Litt. 390*b*.

CONVICT, *n.* One who has been finally condemned by a court. One who has been adjudged guilty of a crime or misdemeanor. Usually spoken of condemned felons or the prisoners in penitentiaries. Molineux v. Collins, 177 N.Y. 395, 69 N.E. 727, 65 L.R.A. 104.

CONVICTED. Means that a judgment of final condemnation has been pronounced against the accused. Gallagher v. State, 10 Tex.App. 469; Neibling v. Terry, 177 S.W.2d 502, 504, 352 Mo. 396, 152 A.L.R. 249.

CONVICTION. In a general sense, the result of a criminal trial which ends in a judgment or sentence that the prisoner is guilty as charged.

The act of convicting a person, or state of being convicted, of a criminal offense. Hershey v. People, 91 Colo. 113, 12 P.2d 345, 347. Finding a person guilty by verdict of a jury. 1 Bish.Crim.Law, § 223; Emmertson v. State Tax Commission of Utah, 93 Utah 219, 72 P.2d 467, 470, 113 A.L.R. 1174.

A record of the summary proceedings upon any penal statute before one or more justices of the peace or other persons duly authorized, in a case where the offender has been *convicted* and sentenced. Holthouse. In respect of pardoning power, verdict of guilty. State v. Garrett, 135 Tenn. 617, 188 S.W. 58, L.R.A.1917B, 567. *Contra,* Ex parte White, 28 Okl.Cr. 180, 230 P. 522.

In ordinary phrase, the meaning of the word "conviction" is the finding by the jury of a verdict that the accused is guilty. But, in legal parlance, it often denotes the final judgment of the court. Blaufus v. People, 69 N.Y. 109, 25 Am.Rep. 148; Marino v. Hibbard, 243 Mass. 90, 137 N.E. 369; Commonwealth v. Minnich, 250 Pa. 363, 95 A. 565, 567, L.R.A.1916B, 950.

The ordinary legal meaning of "conviction," when used to designate a particular stage of a criminal prosecution triable by a jury, is the confession of the accused in open court or the verdict returned against him by the jury, which ascertains and publishes the fact of his guilt; while "judgment" or "sentence" is the appropriate word to denote the action of the court before which the trial is had, declaring the consequences to the convict of the fact thus ascertained. A pardon granted after verdict of guilty, but before sentence, and pending a hearing upon exceptions taken by the accused during the trial, is granted after conviction, within the meaning of a constitutional restriction upon granting pardon before conviction. When, indeed, the word "conviction" is used to describe the effect of the guilt of the accused as judicially proved in one case, when pleaded or given in evidence in another, it is sometimes used in a more comprehensive sense, including the judgment of the court upon the verdict or confession of guilt; as, for instance, in speaking of the plea of *autrefois convict,* or of the effect of guilt, judicially ascertained, as a disqualification of the convict. Com. v. Lockwood, 109 Mass. 323, 12 Am.Rep. 699; In re Anderson, 34 Cal.App.2d 48, 92 P.2d 1020, 1022. Attorney General ex rel. O'Hara v. Montgomery, 275 Mich. 504, 267 N.W. 550, 554.

Former Conviction. A previous trial and conviction of the same offense as that now charged; pleadable in bar of the prosecution. State v. Ellsworth, 131 N.C. 773, 42 S.E. 699, 92 Am.St.Rep. 790; Williams v. State, 13 Tex.App. 285, 46 Am. Rep. 237.

Summary Conviction. The conviction of a person, (usually for a minor misdemeanor,) as the result of his trial before a magistrate or court, without the intervention of a jury, which is authorized by statute in England and in many of the states. In these proceedings there is no intervention of a jury, but the party accused is acquitted or condemned by the suffrage of such person only as the statute has appointed to be his judge. A conviction reached on such a magistrate's trial is called a "summary conviction." Brown; Blair v. Com., 25 Grat. (Va.) 853.

CONVINCING PROOF. Such as is sufficient to establish the proposition in question, beyond hesitation, ambiguity, or reasonable doubt, in an unprejudiced mind. Evans v. Rugee, 57 Wis. 623, 16 N.W. 49; French v. Day, 89 Me. 441, 36 A. 909. See Clear.

CONVIVIUM. A tenure by which a tenant was bound to provide meat and drink for his lord at least once in the year. Cowell.

CONVOCATION. In ecclesiastical law. The general assembly of the clergy to consult upon ecclesiastical matters.

CONVOY. A naval force, under the command of an officer appointed by government, for the protection of merchant-ships and others, during the whole voyage, or such part of it as is known to require such protection. Marsh. Ins. b. 1, c. 9, § 5; Park, Ins. 388; Peake, Add. Cas. 143*n*; 2 H. Bl. 551.

CO-OBLIGOR. A joint obligor; one bound jointly with another or others in a bond or obligation.

COOL BLOOD. In the law of homicide. Calmness or tranquillity; the undisturbed possession of one's faculties and reason; the absence of violent passion, fury, or uncontrollable excitement.

COOLING TIME. Time to recover "cool blood" after severe excitement or provocation; time for the mind to become so calm and sedate as that it is supposed to contemplate, comprehend, and coolly act with reference to the consequences likely to ensue. May v. People, 8 Colo. 210, 6 P. 816; Keiser v. Smith, 71 Ala. 481, 46 Am.Rep. 342.

CO-OPERATE. To act jointly or concurrently toward a common end. Darnell v. Equity Life Ins. Co.'s Receivers, 179 Ky. 465, 200 S.W. 967, 970.

CO-OPERATION. In economics. The combined action of numbers. It is of two distinct kinds: (1) Such co-operation as takes place when several persons help each other in the same employment; (2) such co-operation as takes place when several persons help each other in different employments. These may be termed "simple co-operation" and "complex co-operation." Mill, Pol. Ec. 142.

In patent law. Unity of action to a common end or a common result, not merely joint or simultaneous action. Boynton Co. v. Morris Chute Co., C.C.N.J., 82 F. 444; Fastener Co. v. Webb, C. C.Ohio, 89 F. 987; Holmes Burglar Alarm Tel. Co. v. Domestic, etc., Tel. Co., C.C.N.J., 42 F. 227.

CO-OPERATIVE ASSOCIATION. A union of individuals commonly laborers, farmers, or small capitalists, formed for the prosecution in common of some productive enterprise, the profits being shared in accordance with the capital or labor contributed by each. Mooney v. Farmers' Mercantile & Elevator Co. of Madison, 138 Minn. 199, 164 N.W. 804, 805.

CO-OPERATIVE NEGLIGENCE. Contributory negligence. Otte v. Miller, 24 S.E.2d 90, 93, 125 W.Va. 317.

COOPERTIO. In old English law. The head or branches of a tree cut down; though *coopertio arborum* is rather the bark of timber trees felled, and the chumps and broken wood. Cowell.

COOPERTUM. In forest law. A covert; a thicket *(dumetum)* or shelter for wild beasts in a forest. Spelman.

COOPERTURA. In forest law. A thicket, or covert of wood.

COOPERTUS. Covert; covered.

CO-OPTATION. A concurring choice; the election, by the members of a close corporation, of a person to fill a vacancy.

CO-ORDINATE. Equal, of the same order, rank, degree or importance; not subordinate. Empire Ins. Co. of Texas v. Cooper, Tex.Civ.App., 138 S. W.2d 159, 164. Adjusted to, in harmony with. Æolian-Skinner Organ Co. v. Shepard Broadcasting Service, C.C.A.Mass., 81 F.2d 392, 395. As to courts of "co-ordinate jurisdiction," see Jurisdiction.

Co-ordinate and *Subordinate* are terms often applied as a test to ascertain the doubtful meaning of clauses in an act of parliament. If there be two, one of which is grammatically governed by the other, it is said to be "subordinate" to it; but, if both are equally governed by some third clause, the two are called "co-ordinate." Wharton.

CO-ORDINATE JURISDICTION. That which is possessed by courts of equal rank, degree, or authority, equally competent to deal with the matter in question, whether belonging to the same or different systems; concurrent jurisdiction.

COPARCENARY. A species of estate, or tenancy, which exists where lands of inheritance descend from the ancestor to two or more persons. It arises in England either by common law or particular custom. By common law, as where a person, seised in fee-simple or fee-tail, dies, and his next heirs are two or more females, his daughters, sisters, aunts, cousins, or their representatives; in this case they all inherit, and these coheirs, are then called "coparceners," or, for brevity, "parceners" only. Litt. §§ 241, 242; 2 Bl. Comm. 187. By particular custom, as where lands descend, as in gavelkind, to all the males in equal degree, as sons, brothers, uncles, etc. Litt. § 265; 1 Steph. Comm. 319. An estate which several persons hold as one heir, whether male or female. This estate has the three unities of time, title, and possession; but the interests of the coparceners may be unequal. 1 Washb. Real Prop. 414; 2 Bl. Comm. 188; 4 Kent 366; Flynn v. Herye, 4 Mo.App. 360.

While joint tenancies refer to persons, the idea of coparcenary refers to the estate. The title to it is always by descent. The respective shares may be unequal; as, for instance, one daughter and two granddaughters, children of a deceased daughter, may take by the same act of descent. As to strangers, the tenants' seisin is a joint one, but, as between themselves, each is seised of his or her own share, on whose death it goes to the heirs, and not by survivorship. The right of possession of coparceners is in common, and the possession of one is, in general, the possession of the others. 1 Washb.Real Prop. *414.

COPARCENERS. Persons to whom an estate of inheritance descends jointly, and by whom it is held as an entire estate. 2 Bl. Comm. 187.

COPARTICEPS. In old English law. A coparcener.

COPARTNER. One who is a partner with one or more other persons; a member of a partnership.

COPARTNERSHIP. A partnership.

COPARTNERY. In Scotch law. The contract of copartnership. A contract by which the several partners agree concerning the communication of loss or gain, arising from the subject of the contract. Bell.

COPE. A custom or tribute due to the crown or lord of the soil, out of the lead mines in Derbyshire; also a hill, or the roof and covering of a house; a church vestment.

COPEMAN, or COPESMAN. A chapman, (*q. v.*).

COPESMATE. A merchant; a partner in merchandise.

COPIA. Lat. In civil and old English law. Opportunity or means of access.

In old English law. A copy. *Copia libelli*, the copy of a libel. Reg. Orig. 58.

COPIA LIBELLI DELIBERANDA. The name of a writ that lay where a man could not get a copy of a libel at the hands of a spiritual judge, to have the same delivered to him. Reg. Orig. 51.

COPIA VERA. In Scotch practice. A true copy. Words written at the top of copies of instruments.

COPPA. In English law. A crop or cock of grass, hay, or corn, divided into titheable portions, that it may be more fairly and justly tithed.

COPPER AND SCALES. See Mancipatio.

COPPER MATTE. A product of smelting copper ore in a furnace consisting almost entirely of a mixture of iron sulphide and copper sulphide. It requires further treatment to break up and remove iron sulphide, and then convert remaining copper sulphide which is called white metal to metallic copper. United Verde Copper Co. v. Peirce-Smith Converter Co., C.C.A.Del., 7 F.2d 13. Also known as "regulus of copper." U. S. v. Consolidated Kansas City Smelting & Refining Co,. 8 Ct.Cust.App. 226, 227.

COPPICE, or COPSE. A small wood consisting of underwood, which may be cut at twelve or fifteen years' growth for fuel.

COPROLALIA. In medical jurisprudence. A disposition or habit of using obscene language, developing unexpectedly in the particular individual or contrary to his previous history and habits, recognized as a sign of insanity or of aphasia.

COPULA. The corporal consummation of marriage. *Copula,* (in logic,) the link between subject and predicate contained in the verb.

COPULATIO VERBORUM INDICAT ACCEPTATIONEM IN EODEM SENSU. Coupling of words together shows that they are to be understood in the same sense. 4 Bacon's Works, p. 26; Broom, Max. 588.

COPULATIVE TERM. One which is placed between two or more others to join them together.

COPY. The transcript or double of an original writing; as the copy of a patent, charter, deed, etc. Nations v. Lowenstern, 27 N.M. 613, 204 P. 60, 62; State Text-Book Commission v. Weathers, 184 Ky. 748, 213 S.W. 207, 210; In re Janes' Estate, 18 Cal.2d 512, 116 P.2d 438, 441.

Carbon copies. Carbon copies made at the same time and with the same device as the original are not "copies" but duplicate originals. Martin & Lanier Paint Co. v. Daniels, 27 Ga.App. 302, 108 S.E. 246, 247; Liberty Nat. Bank and Trust Co. v. Louisville Trust Co., 295 Ky. 825, 175 S.W.2d 524, 528.

Exemplifications are copies verified by the great seal or by the seal of a court. West Jersey Traction Co. v. Board of Public Works, 57 N.J.Law, 313, 30 A. 581.

Examined copies are those which have been compared with the original or with an official record thereof.

Office copies are those made by officers intrusted with the originals and authorized for that purpose. Id., Stamper v. Gay, 3 Wyo. 322, 23 P. 69. See, also, Office.

In the law of copyrights. A reproduction or duplication of a thing, or that which comes so near to the original as to give to every person seeing it the idea created by the original. McConnor v. Kaufman, D.C.N.Y., 49 F.Supp. 738, 744.

COPYHOLD. A species of estate at will, or customary estate in England, the only visible title to which consists of the copies of the court rolls, which are made out by the steward of the manor, on a tenant's being admitted to any parcel of land, or tenement belonging to the manor. It is an estate at the will of the lord, yet such a will as is agreeable to the custom of the manor, which customs are preserved and evidenced by the rolls of the several courts baron, in which they are entered. 2 Bl.Comm. 95. In a larger sense, copyhold is said to import every customary tenure, (that is, every tenure pending on the particular custom of a manor,) as opposed to free socage, or freehold, which may now (since the abolition of knight-service) be considered as the general or common-law tenure of the country. 1 Steph. Comm. 210.

Copyhold commissioners. Commissioners appointed to carry into effect various acts of parliament, having for their principal objects the compulsory commutation of manorial burdens and restrictions, (fines, heriots, rights to timber and minerals, etc.,) and the compulsory enfranchisement of copyhold lands. 1 Steph. Comm. 643; Elton, Copyh.

Copyholder. A tenant by copyhold tenure, (by copy of court-roll.) 2 Bl. Comm. 95.

Privileged copyholds. Those copyhold estates which are said to be held according to the custom of the manor, and not *at the will of the lord,* as common copyholds are. They include customary freeholds and ancient demesnes. 1 Crabb, Real Prop. p. 709, § 919.

COPYRIGHT. The right of literary property as recognized and sanctioned by positive law. An intangible, incorporeal right granted by statute to the author or originator of certain literary or artistic productions, whereby he is invested, for a limited period, with the sole and exclusive privilege of multiplying copies of the same and publishing and selling them. In re Rider, 16 R.I. 271, 15 A. 72; Mott Iron Works v. Clow, C.C.A.Ill., 82 F. 316, 27 C.C.A. 250; Palmer v. De Witt, 47 N.Y. 536, 7 Am.Rep. 480; Stuff v. La Budde Feed & Grain Co., D.C.Wis., 42 F.Supp. 493, 497; Schill v. Remington Putnam Book Co., 179 Md. 83, 17 A.2d 175.

International copyright is the right of a subject of one country to protection against the republication in another country of a work which he originally published in his own country. Sweet.

CORAAGIUM, or CORAAGE. Measures of corn. An unusual and extraordinary tribute, arising only on special occasions. They are thus distinguished from services. Mentioned in connection with *hidage* and *carvage.* Cowell.

CORAM. Lat. Before; in presence of. Applied to persons only. Townsh. Pl. 22.

CORAM DOMINO REGE. Before our lord the king. *Coram domino rege ubicumque tunc fuerit Angliæ,* before our lord the king wherever he shall then be in England.

CORAM IPSO REGE. Before the king himself. The old name of the court of king's bench, which was originally held before the king in person. 3 Bl.Comm. 41.

CORAM NOBIS. Before us ourselves, (the king, *i. e.,* in the king's or queen's bench.) Applied to writs of error directed to another branch of the same court, *e. g.,* from the full bench to the court at *nisi prius.* 1 Archb. Pr. K. B. 234. See Writ of Error.

CORAM NON JUDICE. In presence of a person not a judge. When a suit is brought and determined in a court which has no jurisdiction in the matter, then it is said to be *coram non judice,* and the judgment is void. Manufacturing Co. v. Holt, 51 W.Va. 352, 41 S.E. 351.

CORAM PARIBUS. Before the peers or freeholders. The attestation of deeds, like all other solemn transactions, was originally done only *coram paribus.* 2 Bl.Comm. 307. *Coram paribus de vicineto,* before the peers or freeholders of the neighborhood. Id. 315.

CORAM SECTATORIBUS. Before the suitors. Cro. Jac. 582.

CORAM VOBIS. Before you. A writ of error directed by a court of review to the court which tried the cause, to correct an error in fact. 3 Md. 325; 3 Steph.Comm. 642. See Writ of Error.

CORD. A measure of wood containing 128 cubic feet, otherwise expressed as a pile of wood 8 feet long, 4 feet high, and 4 feet wide. Sacks v. State, 83 Tex.Cr.R. 560, 204 S.W. 430.

CO-RESPONDENT. A person summoned to answer a bill, petition, or libel, together with another respondent. Now chiefly used to designate the person charged with adultery with the respondent in a suit for divorce for that cause, and joined as a defendant with such party. Lowe v. Bennett, 27 Misc. 356, 58 N.Y.S. 88. Mortensen v. Los Angeles Examiner, 112 Cal.App. 194, 296 P. 927, 930.

CORIUM FORISFACERE. To forfeit one's skin, applied to a person condemned to be whipped; anciently the punishment of a servant. *Corium perdere,* the same. *Corium redimere,* to compound for a whipping. Wharton.

CORN. In English law, a general term for any sort of grain; but in America it is properly applied only to maize. Sullins v. State, 53 Ala. 476; Kerrick v. Van Dusen, 32 Minn. 317, 20 N.W. 228; Com. v. Pine, 3 Pa.Law J. 412.

In the memorandum clause in policies of insurance it includes pease and beans, but not rice. Park, Ins. 112; Scott v. Bourdillion, 2 Bos. & P., N. R., 213.

CORN LAWS. A species of protective tariff formerly in existence in England, imposing import-duties on various kinds of grain. The corn laws were abolished in 1846.

CORN MEAL. An unmixed meal made from entire grains of corn. Miller Grain & Commission Co. v. International Sugar Feed No. 2 Co., 197 Ala. 100, 72 So. 368.

CORN RENT. A rent in wheat or malt paid on college leases by direction of St. 18 Eliz. c. 6. 2 Bl.Comm. 609.

CORN WHISKY. An intoxicating whisky or liquor made from corn or containing a corn product, otherwise known as "moonshine," "white mule," "hootch," "corn liquor," "moonshine corn whisky." State v. Bilyeu, Mo.Sup., 295 S.W. 104, 105; State v. Pinto, 312 Mo. 99, 279 S.W. 144, 148; Mullins v. Commonwealth, 115 Va. 945, 79 S.E. 324, 327.

CORNAGE. A species of tenure in England, by which the tenant was bound to blow a horn for the sake of alarming the country on the approach of an enemy. It was a species of grand serjeanty. Bac. Abr. "Tenure," N.

CORNER. A combination among the dealers in a specific commodity, or outside capitalists, for the purpose of buying up the greater portion of that commodity which is upon the market or may be brought to market, and holding the same back from sale, until the demand shall so far outrun the limited supply as to advance the price abnormally. Kirkpatrick v. Bonsall, 72 Pa. 158; Wright v. Cudahy, 168 Ill. 86, 48 N.E. 39; United States v. Patten, C.C.N.Y., 187 F. 664, 668.

A "corner" is a condition arising when a much greater quantity of any given commodity is sold for future delivery within a given period than can be purchased in the market. The buyers, who are called in the slang of the exchanges, the "longs," then insist on delivery, and thus succeed in running up the prices to a fictitious point, at which the deals are "rung out" between the dealers by the payment of differences, or, where the buyers insist, by actual delivery. Kent v. Miltenberger, 13 Mo.App. 503, 506.

Surveying. An angle made by two boundary lines; the common end of two boundary lines, which run at an angle with each other.

Lost corner. One whose location as established by the government surveyors cannot be found. The mere fact that evidence of the physical location cannot now be seen, or that no one who saw the marked corner is produced, does not necessarily make the corner a lost one. Goroski v. Tawney, 121 Minn. 189, 141 N.W. 102, 103; Cooper v. Quade, 191 Iowa, 461, 182 N.W. 798, 799; Fehrman v. Bissell Lumber Co., 188 Wis. 82, 204 N.W. 582.

Obliterated corner. One where no visible evidence remains of the work of the original surveyor in establishing it. Fellows v. Willett, 98 Okl. 248, 224 P. 298, 300; Fehrman v. Bissell Lumber Co., 188 Wis. 82, 204 N.W. 582.

CORNET. A commissioned officer of cavalry, abolished in England in 1871, and not existing in the United States army.

CORODIO HABENDO. The name of a writ to exact a corody of an abbey or religious house.

CORODIUM. In old English law. A corody.

CORODY. In old English law. A sum of money or allowance of meat, drink, and clothing due to the crown from the abbey or other religious house, whereof it was founder, towards the sustentation of such one of its servants as is thought fit to receive it. It differs from a pension, in that it was allowed towards the maintenance of any of the king's servants in an abbey; a pension being given to one of the king's chaplains, for his better maintenance, till he may be provided with a benefice. Fitzh. Nat. Brev. 250. See 1 Bl.Comm. 283.

COROLLARY. In logic. A collateral or secondary consequence, deduction, or inference.

CORONA. The crown. *Placita coronæ*; pleas of the crown; criminal actions or proceedings, in which the crown was the prosecutor.

CORONA MALA. In old English law. The clergy who abuse their character were so called. Blount.

CORONARE. In old records. To give the tonsure, which was done on the crown, or in the form of a crown; to make a man a priest. Cowell.

CORONARE FILIUM. To make one's son a priest. *Homo coronatus* was one who had received the first tonsure, as preparatory to superior orders, and the tonsure was in form of a corona, or crown of thorns. Cowell.

CORONATION. It "is but a royal ornament and solemnization of the royal descent, but no part of the title." By the laws of England there can be no interregnum; 7 Co.Rep. 10*b*.

CORONATION OATH. The oath administered to a sovereign at the ceremony of crowning or investing him with the insignia of royalty, in acknowledgment of his right to govern the kingdom, in which he swears to observe the laws, customs, and privileges of the kingdom, and to act and do all things conformably thereto. Wharton.

CORONATOR. A coroner, (*q. v.*) Spelman.

CORONATORE ELIGENDO. The name of a writ issued to the sheriff, commanding him to proceed to the election of a coroner.

CORONATORE EXONERANDO. In English law. The name of a writ for the removal of a coroner, for a cause which is to be therein assigned, as that he is engaged in other business, or incapacitated by years or sickness, or has not a sufficient estate in the county, or lives in an inconvenient part of it.

CORONER. The name of an ancient officer of the common law, whose office and functions are continued in modern English and American administration. The coroner is an officer belonging to each county, and is charged with duties both judicial and ministerial, but chiefly the former. It is his special province and duty to make inquiry into the causes and circumstances of any death happening within his territory which occurs through violence or suddenly and with marks of suspicion. This examination (called the "coroner's inquest") is held with a jury of proper persons upon view of the dead body. See Bract. fol. 121; 1 Bl.Comm. 346–348; 3 Steph.Comm. 33. In England, another branch of his judicial office is to inquire concerning shipwrecks, and certify whether wreck or not, and who is in possession of the goods; and also to inquire concerning treasure trove, who were the finders, and where it is, and whether any one be suspected of having found and concealed a treasure. 1 Bl.Comm. 349. It belongs to the ministerial office of the coroner to serve writs and other process, and generally to discharge the duties of the sheriff, in case of the incapacity of that officer or a vacancy in his office. On the office and functions of coroners, see, further, Cox v. Royal Tribe, 42 Or. 365, 71 Pac. 73, 60 L.R.A. 620; Lancaster County v. Holyoke, 37 Neb. 328, 55 N.W. 950, 21 L.R.A. 394.

CORONER'S COURT. In England. A tribunal of record, where a coroner holds his inquiries. Cox v. Royal Tribe, 42 Or. 365, 71 P. 73, 60 L.R.A. 620.

CORONER'S INQUEST. An inquisition or examination into the causes and circumstances of any death happening by violence or under suspicious conditions within his territory, held by the coroner with the assistance of a jury. Boisliniere v. County Com'rs, 32 Mo. 378; Ehlers v. Blood, 175 Misc. 72, 22 N.Y.S.2d 1001, 1005.

CORPORAL. Relating to the body; bodily. Should be distinguished from corporeal (*q. v.*)

CORPORAL IMBECILITY. Physical inability to perform completely the act of sexual intercourse; not necessarily congenital, and not invariably a permanent and incurable impotence. Griffeth v. Griffeth, 162 Ill. 368, 44 N.E. 820.

CORPORAL OATH. An oath, the external solemnity of which consists in laying one's hand upon the Gospels while the oath is administered to him. More generally, a solemn oath. Jackson v. State, 1 Ind. 185; State v. Norris, 9 N.H. 102; Com. v. Jarboe, 89 Ky. 143, 12 S.W. 138.

The terms "corporal oath" and "solemn oath" are, in Indiana, at least, used synonymously; and an oath taken with the uplifted hand may be properly described by either term.

CORPORAL PUNISHMENT. Physical punishment as distinguished from pecuniary punishment or a fine; any kind of punishment of or inflicted on the body, such as whipping or the pillory; the term may or may not include imprisonment, according to the context. Ritchey v. People, 22 Colo. 251, 43 P. 1026; Fowler v. American Mail Line, C.C.A.Cal., 69 F.2d 905, 907.

The use of rubber hose or other weapon to suppress a threatened riot or to prevent prisoner from doing bodily harm to an officer or another inmate is not corporal punishment. O'Brien v. Olson, 42 Cal.App.2d 449, 109 P.2d 8, 16.

CORPORAL TOUCH. Bodily touch; actual physical contact; manual apprehension.

CORPORALE SACRAMENTUM. In old English law. A corporal oath.

CORPORALIS INJURIA NON RECIPIT ÆSTIMATIONEM DE FUTURO. A personal injury does not receive satisfaction from a future course of proceeding, [is not left for its satisfaction to a future course of proceeding.] Bac. Max. reg. 6; Broom, Max. 278.

CORPORATE. Belonging to a corporation; as a corporate name. Incorporated; as a corporate body.

CORPORATE ACT OR MINISTERIAL ACT OF MUNICIPAL CORPORATION. For which it can be held liable is act which is done by virtue of powers exercised for municipality's own advantage or in negligent performance of duty specifically imposed by statute. Broome v. City of Charlotte, 208 N.C. 729, 182 S.E. 325, 326.

CORPORATE ALTER EGO, DOCTRINE OF. Means that courts ignoring forms and looking to substance will regard stockholders as owners of corporation's property, or as the real parties in interest whenever it is necessary to do so to prevent fraud which might otherwise be perpetrated, to redress a wrong which might otherwise go without redress, or to do justice which might otherwise fail. Geary v. Cain, 79 Utah 268, 9 P.2d 396, 398.

CORPORATE AUTHORITIES. The title given in statutes of several states to the aggregate body of officers of a municipal corporation, or to certain of those officers (excluding the others) who are vested with authority in regard to the particular matter spoken of in the statute, as, taxation, bonded debt, regulation of the sale of liquors, etc. See People v. Knopf, 171 Ill. 191, 49 N.E. 424; State v. Andrews, 11 Neb. 523, 10 N.W. 410; White v. Papillion Drainage Dist., 96 Neb. 241, 147 N.W. 218, 219; Schaeffer v. Bonham, 95 Ill. 382.

CORPORATE BODY. This term, or its equivalent "body corporate," is applied to private corporations aggregate; not including municipal corporations. Cedar County v. Johnson, 50 Mo. 225; East Oakland Tp. v. Skinner, 94 U.S. 256, 24 L.Ed. 125; County Board of Education for Houston County v. Hunt, 29 Ga.App. 665, 116 S.E. 900.

CORPORATE BONDS. A written promise by a corporation under seal to pay a fixed sum of money at some future time named, with stated interest payable at some fixed time or intervals, given in return for money or its equivalent received by the corporation, sometimes secured, and sometimes not. Hammond Lumber Co. v. Adams, 7 Cal.2d 24, 59 P.2d 1030, 1031.

CORPORATE FRANCHISE. The right to exist and do business as a corporation; the right or privilege granted by the state or government to the persons forming an aggregate private corporation, and their successors, to exist and do business as a corporation and to exercise the rights and powers incidental to that form of organization or necessarily implied in the grant. Bank of California v. San Francisco, 142 Cal. 276, 75 Pac. 832, 64 L.R.A. 918; State on inf. Wear v. Business Men's Athletic Club, 178 Mo.App. 548, 163 S.W. 901, 907.

CORPORATE LEGAL INDIVIDUAL. Municipal corporation possesses two kinds of power, governmental and public, and proprietary and private, and in exercise of former, corporation is a "municipal government," while as to latter, it is a "corporate legal individual." Herkimer County v. Village of Herkimer, 251 App.Div. 126, 295 N.Y.S. 629, 633.

CORPORATE NAME. When a corporation is erected, a name is always given to it, or, supposing none to be actually given, will attach to it by implication, and by that name alone it must sue and be sued, and do all legal acts, though a very minute variation therein is not material, and the name is capable of being changed (by competent authority) without affecting the identity or capacity of the corporation. Wharton.

CORPORATE PURPOSE. In reference to municipal corporations, and especially to their powers of taxation, a "corporate purpose" is one which shall promote the general prosperity and the welfare of the municipality. Dickinson v. Salt Lake City, 57 Utah 530, 195 P. 1110, 1111; City of Quitman v. Jelks & McLeod, 139 Ga. 238, 77 S.E. 76; People ex rel. Moshier v. City of Springfield, 370 Ill. 541, 19 N.E.2d 598, 602; or a purpose necessary or proper to carry into effect the object of the creation of the corporate body, People v. School Trustees, 78 Ill. 140; or one which is germane to the general scope of the objects for which the corporation was created or has a legitimate connection with those objects and a manifest relation thereto. Weightman v. Clark, 103 U.S. 256, 26 L. Ed. 392; Denman v. City of Tacoma, 170 Wash. 406, 16 P.2d 596, 597.

CORPORATION. An artificial person or legal entity created by or under the authority of the laws of a state or nation, composed, in some rare instances, of a single person and his successors, being the incumbents of a particular office, but ordinarily consisting of an association of numerous individuals, who subsist as a body politic under a special denomination, which is regarded in law as having a personality and existence distinct from that of its several members, and which is, by the same authority, vested with the capacity of continuous succession, irrespective of changes in its membership, either in perpetuity or for a limited term of years, and of acting as a unit or single individual in matters relating to the common purpose of the association, within the scope of the powers and authorities conferred upon such bodies by law. Dartmouth College v. Woodward, 4 Wheat. 518, 636, 657, 4 L.Ed. 629; U. S. v. Trinidad Coal Co., 137 U.S. 160, 11 S.Ct. 57, 34 L.Ed. 640; Andrews Bros. Co. v. Youngstown Coke Co., 86 F. 585, 30 C.C.A. 293; Porter v. Railroad Co., 76 Ill. 573; Nebraska Wheat Growers' Ass'n v. Smith, 115 Neb. 177, 212 N.W. 39, 44; State v. Thistle Down Jockey Club, 114 Ohio St. 582, 151 N.E. 709, 711; Congdon v. Congdon, 160 Minn. 343, 200 N.W. 76, 87; Forest City Mfg. Co. v. International Ladies' Garment Workers' Union, Local No. 104, 233 Mo.App. 935, 111 S.W.2d 934; In re Crown Heights Hospital, 183 Misc. 563, 49 N.Y.S.2d 658, 660; Froelich and Kuttner, of Manila, P. I., v. Sutherland, 57 App.D.C. 294, 22 F.2d 870, 872.

A franchise possessed by one or more individuals, who subsist as a body politic, under a special denomination, and are vested by the policy of the law with the capacity of perpetual succession, and of acting in several respects, however numerous the association may be, as a single individual. 2 Kent, Comm. 267.

An artificial person or being, endowed by law with the capacity of perpetual succession; consisting either of a single individual, (termed a "corporation sole,") or of a collection of several individuals, (which is termed a "corporation aggregate.") 3 Steph.Comm. 166; 1 Bl.Comm. 467, 469. An intellectual body, created by law, composed of individuals united under a common name, the members of which succeed each other, so that the body continues always the same, notwithstanding the change of the individuals who compose it, and which, for certain purposes, is considered a natural person. Civil Code La. art. 427.

A "corporation" is more nearly a method than a thing, and the law, in dealing with a corporation, need not define it as a person or entity, or even as an embodiment of functions, rights, and duties. Farmers' Loan & Trust Co. v. Pierson, 222 N.Y.S. 532, 543, 130 Misc. 110.

The statement that a "corporation" is an artificial person or entity, apart from its members, is merely a description, in figurative language, of a corporation viewed as a collective body. McIntosh v. Dakota Trust Co., 52 N.D. 752, 204 N.W. 818, 825, 40 A.L.R. 1021.

A corporation is a collection of natural persons, joined together by their voluntary action or by legal compulsion, by or under the authority of an act of the Legislature, consisting either of a special charter or of a general permissive statute, to accomplish some purpose, pecuniary, ideal, or governmental, authorized by the charter or governing statute. State v. Knights of Ku Klux Klan, 117 Kan. 564, 232 P. 254, 257, 37 A.L.R. 1267.

Classification

According to the accepted definitions and rules, corporations are classified as follows:

Public and private. A public corporation is one created by the state for political purposes and to act as an agency in the administration of civil government, generally within a particular territory or subdivision of the state, and usually invested, for that purpose, with subordinate and local powers of legislation; such as a county, city, town, or school district. These are also sometimes called "political corporations." Goodwin v. East Hartford, 70 Conn. 18, 38 A. 876; Dean v. Davis, 51 Cal. 409; Ten Eyck v. Canal Co., 18 N.J. Law, 200, 37 Am.Dec. 233; Murphy v. Mercer County, 57 N.J.Law, 245, 31 A. 229; Van Campen v. Olean General Hospital, 210 App.Div. 204, 205 N.Y.S. 554, 555; Providence Engineering Corporation v. Downey Shipbuilding Corporation, C.C.A. N.Y., 294 F. 641, 646; National Bank of Commerce in New Orleans v. Board of Sup'rs of La. State University and Agricultural and Mechanical College, 206 La. 913, 20 So.2d 264, 269.

Private corporations are those founded by and composed of private individuals, for private pur poses, as distinguished from governmental purposes, and having no political or governmental franchises or duties. Santa Clara County v. Southern Pac. R. Co., C.C.Cal., 18 F. 385, 402; People v. McAdams, 82 Ill. 361; Providence Engineering Corporation v. Downey Shipbuilding Corporation, C.C.A.N.Y., 294 F. 641, 648.

The true distinction between public and private corporations is that the former are organized for governmental purposes, the latter not. The term "public" has sometimes been applied to corporations of which the government owned the entire stock, as in the case of a state bank. But bearing in mind that "public" is here equivalent to "political," it will be apparent that this is a misnomer. Again the fact that the business or operations of a corporation may directly and very extensively affect the general public (as in the case of a railroad company or a bank or an insurance company) is no reason for calling it a public corporation. If organized by private persons for their own advantage,—or even if organized for the benefit of the public generally, as in the case of a free public hospital or other charitable institution,—it is none the less a private corporation, if it does not possess governmental powers or functions. The uses may in a sense be called "public," but the corporation is "private," as much so as if the franchises were vested in a single person. Dartmouth College v. Woodward, 4 Wheat. 562, 4 L.Ed. 629; Ten Eyck v. Canal Co., 18 N.J.Law, 204, 37 Am.Dec. 233. It is to be observed, however, that those corporations which serve the public or contribute to the comfort and convenience of the general public, though owned and managed by private interests, are now (and quite appropriately) denominated "public-service corporations." See *infra*. Another distinction between public and private corporations is that the former are not voluntary associations (as the latter are) and that there is no contractual relation between the government and a public corporation or between the individuals who compose it. Mor.Priv.Corp. § 3; Goodwin v. East Hartford, 70 Conn. 18, 38 A. 876.

The terms "public" and "municipal," as applied to corporations, are not convertible. All municipal corporations are public, but not vice versa. Brown v. Board of Education, 108 Ky. 783, 57 S.W. 612. But there may also be "public" corporations which are not "municipal" even in this wider sense of the latter term. Such, according to some of the authorities, are the "irrigation districts" now known in several of the western states. Irrigation Dist. v. Collins, 46 Neb. 411, 64 N.W. 1086. Compare Herring v. Modesta Irrigation Dist., C.C.Cal., 95 F. 705.

Ecclesiastical and lay. In the English law, all corporations private are divided into ecclesiastical and lay, the former being such corporations as are composed exclusively of ecclesiastics organized for spiritual purposes, or for administering property held for religious uses, such as bishops and certain other dignitaries of the church and (formerly) abbeys and monasteries. 1 Bl. Comm. 470. Lay corporations are those composed of laymen, and existing for secular or business purposes. This distinction is not recognized in American law. Corporations formed for the purpose of maintaining or propagating religion or of supporting public religious services, according to the rites of particular denominations, and incidentally owning and administering real and personal property for religious uses, are called "religious corporations," as distinguished from business corporations; but they are "lay" corporations, and not "ecclesiastical" in the sense of the English law. Robertson v. Bullions, 11 N.Y. 243.

Eleemosynary and civil. Lay corporations are classified as "eleemosynary" and "civil;" the former being such as are created for the distribution of alms or for the administration of charities or for purposes falling under the description of "charitable" in its widest sense, including hospitals, asylums, and colleges; the latter being organized for the facilitating of business transactions and the profit or advantage of the members. 1 Bl.Comm. 471; Dartmouth College v. Woodward, 4 Wheat. 660, 4 L.Ed. 629.

In the law of Louisiana, the term "civil" as applied to corporations, is used in a different sense, being contrasted with "religious." Civil corporations are those which relate to temporal police; such are the corporations of the cities, the companies for the advancement of commerce and agriculture, literary societies, colleges or universities founded for the instruction of youth, and the like. Religious corporations are those whose establishment relates only to religion; such are the congregations of the different religious persuasions. Civ.Code La. art. 431.

Aggregate and sole. A corporation sole is one consisting of one person only, and his successors in some particular station, who are incorporated by law in order to give them some legal capacities and advantages, particularly that of perpetuity, which in their natural persons they could not have had. In this sense, the sovereign in England is a sole corporation, so is a bishop, so are some deans distinct from their several chapters, and so is every parson and vicar. 3 Steph.Comm. 168, 169; First Parish v. Dunning, 7 Mass. 447; Reid v. Barry, 93 Fla. 849, 112 So. 846, 859.

A corporation aggregate is one composed of a number of individuals vested with corporate powers; and a "corporation," as the word is used in general popular and legal speech, and as defined at the head of this title, means a "corporation aggregate."

Domestic and foreign. With reference to the laws and the courts of any given state, a "domestic" corporation is one created by, or organized under, the laws of that state; a "foreign" corporation is one created by or under the laws of another state, government, or country. In re Grand Lodge, 110 Pa. 613, 1 A. 582; Fowler v. Chillingworth, 94 Fla. 1, 113 So. 667, 669; In re Ewles' Estate, 105 Utah 507, 143 P.2d 903, 905.

Close and open. A "close" corporation is one in which the directors and officers have the power to fill vacancies in their own number, without allowing to the general body of stockholders any choice or vote in their election. An "open" corporation is one in which all the members or corporators have a vote in the election of the directors and other officers. McKim v. Odom, 3 Bland, Md., 416.

A close corporation is one which fills its own vacancies or in which power of voting is held through manipulation under fixed and virtually perpetual proxies. Brooks v. Willcuts, C.C.A.Minn., 78 F.2d 270, 273.

Subsidiary and parent. Subsidiary corporation is one in which another corporation (called parent corporation) owns at least a majority of the shares, and thus has control. Wheeler v. New York, N. H. and H. R. Co., 112 Conn. 510, 153 A. 159, 160; International Order of Twelve Knights and Daughters of Tabor v. Fridia, Tex.Civ.App., 91 S.W.2d 404.

Other Compound and Descriptive Terms

A business corporation. One formed for the purpose of transacting business in the widest sense of that term, including not only trade and commerce, but manufacturing, mining, banking, insurance, transportation, and practically every form of commercial or industrial activity where the purpose of the organization is pecuniary profit; contrasted with religious, charitable, educational, and other like organizations, which are sometimes grouped in the statutory law of a state under the general designation of "corporations not for profit." Winter v. Railroad Co., 30 Fed.Cas. 329; McLeod v. College, 69 Neb. 550, 96 N.W. 265.

Corporation de facto. One existing under color of law and in pursuance of an effort made in good faith to organize a corporation under the statute; an association of men claiming to be a legally incorporated company, and exercising the powers and functions of a corporation, but without actual lawful authority to do so. Foster v. Hare, 26 Tex. Civ.App. 177, 62 S.W. 541; Cedar Rapids Water Co. v. Cedar Rapids, 118 Iowa, 234, 91 N.W. 1081; Tulare Irrig. Dist. v. Shepard, 185 U.S. 1, 22 S.Ct. 531, 46 L.Ed. 773; Evens v. Anderson, 132 Minn. 59, 155 N.W. 1040, 1041.

Its elements are a law or charter authorizing such a corporation, an attempt in good faith to comply with law authorizing its incorporation, and unintentional omission of essential requirements of the law or charter, and exercise in good faith of corporate functions under the law or charter. Richmond v. Town of Largo, 155 Fla. 226, 19 So.2d 791, 793.

Corporation de jure. That which exists by reason of full compliance by incorporators with requirements of an existing law permitting organization of such corporation; it is impregnable to assault in the courts from any source. Henderson v. School Dist. No. 44, 75 Mont. 154, 242 P. 979, 980.

Joint-stock corporation. This differs from a joint-stock *company* in being regularly incorporated, instead of being a mere partnership, but resembles it in having a capital divided into shares of stock. Most business corporations (as distinguished from eleemosynary corporations) are of this character.

A "joint-stock corporation" is one organized under a general statute authorizing the creation of such corporations and providing the procedure for creating it, and is distinguished from a "corporation" created by special resolution or act of the Legislature, which resolution or act is the charter of the corporation, when accepted, and the corporation organized thereunder, and the corporation is a chartered corporation, as distinguished from a joint-stock corporation. Barber v. Morgan, 89 Conn. 583, 94 A. 984, 986, Ann.Cas.1916E, 102.

Migratory corporation. A corporation, organized under laws of another state than that of incorporators' residence for purpose of doing all or greater part of their business in state of their residence or in other state than that of incorporation. Toklan Royalty Corporation v. Tiffany, 193 Okl. 120, 141 P.2d 571, 573.

Moneyed corporations are, properly speaking, those dealing in money or in the business of receiving deposits, loaning money, and exchange; but in a wider sense the term is applied to all business corporations having a money capital and employing it in the conduct of their business. Mutual Ins. Co. v. Erie County, 4 N.Y. 444; In re California Pac. R. Co., 4 Fed.Cas. 1,060; Hobbs v. National Bank, C.C.A.N.Y., 101 F. 75, 41 C.C.A. 205.

Municipal corporations. See that title.

Public-service corporations. Those whose operations serve the needs of the general public or conduce to the comfort and convenience of an entire community, such as railroads, gas, water, and electric light companies. The business of such companies is said to be "affected with a public interest," and for that reason they are subject to legislative regulation and control to a greater extent than corporations not of this character. Washington & C. Ry. Co. v. Mobile & O. R. Co., C.C.A.Ala., 255 F. 12, 14.

Quasi corporations. Organizations resembling corporations; municipal societies or similar bodies which, though not true corporations in all respects, are yet recognized, by statutes or immemorial usage, as persons or aggregate corporations, with precise duties which may be enforced, and privileges which may be maintained, by suits at law. They may be considered *quasi* corporations, with limited powers, co-extensive with the duties imposed upon them by statute or usage, but restrained from a general use of the authority which belongs to those metaphysical persons by the common law. Scates v. King, 110 Ill. 456; Barnes v. District of Columbia, 91 U.S. 552, 23 L.Ed. 440.

This term is lacking in definiteness and precision. It appears to be applied indiscriminately (a) to all kinds of municipal corporations, the word "quasi" being introduced because it is said that these are not voluntary organizations like private corporations, but created by the legislature for its own purposes and without reference to the wishes of the people of the territory affected; (b) to all municipal corporations except cities and incorporated towns, the latter being considered the only true municipal corporations because they exist and act under charters or statutes of incorporation while counties, school districts, and the like are merely created or set off under general laws; (c) to municipal corporations possessing only a low order of corporate existence or the most limited range of corporate powers, such as hundreds in England, and counties, villages, and school districts in America.

A term applied to those bodies, or municipal societies, which, though not vested with the general powers of corporations, are yet recognized, by statutes or immemorial usage, as persons, or aggregate corporations, with precise duties, which may be enforced, and privileges, which may be maintained, by suits at law. State v. Hagen, 136 La. 868, 67 So. 935, 936.

There is a well-defined and marked distinction between municipal corporations proper and political or quasi corporations. Cities, towns, and villages are municipal corporations proper, while counties, townships, school districts, road districts, and the like are quasi corporations. City of East Cleveland v. Board of Education of City School Dist. of East Cleveland, 112 Ohio St. 607, 148 N.E. 350, 351.

"Quasi corporation" is a phrase used to designate bodies which possess a limited number of corporate powers, and which are low down in the scale or grade of corporate existence, and is generally applied to a body which exercises certain functions of a corporate character, but which has not been created a corporation by any statute, general or special. Eakle v. Board of Education of Independent School Dist. of Henry, 97 W.Va. 434, 125 S.E. 165, 167.

Quasi public corporation. This term is sometimes applied to corporations which are not strictly public, in the sense of being organized for governmental purposes, but whose operations contribute to the comfort, convenience, or welfare of the general public, such as telegraph and telephone companies, gas, water, and electric light companies, and irrigation companies. More commonly and more correctly styled "public-service corporations." Wiemer v. Louisville Water Co., C.C.Ky., 130 F. 251; Campbell v. Watson, 62 N.J. Eq. 396, 50 A. 120; Burgess v. City of Brockton, 235 Mass. 95, 126 N.E. 456, 460; Van Valkenburgh v. Ford, Tex.Civ.App., 207 S.W. 405, 414; Borough of Mt. Union v. Kunz, 290 Pa. 356, 139 A. 118, 121.

There is a large class of private corporations which on account of special franchises conferred on them owe a duty to the public which they may be compelled to perform. This class of corporations is known as public service corporations, and in legal phraseology as "quasi public corporations," or corporations affected with a public interest. A "quasi public corporation" may be said to be a private corporation which has given to it certain powers of a public nature, such, for instance, as the power of eminent domain, in order to enable it to discharge its duties for the public benefit, in which respect it differs from an ordinary private corporation, the powers of which are given and exercised for the exclusive advantage of its stockholders. State ex rel. Coco v. Riverside Irr. Co., 142 La. 10, 76 So. 216, 218.

The term is also applied to corporations of that class sometimes called "quasi municipal corporations," such as school districts; Courtright v. Consolidated Independent School Dist. of Mapleton, 203 Iowa, 26, 212 N.W. 368, 369; road districts; Road Improvement Dist. No. 7 of Poinsett County, Ark., v. Guardian Savings & Trust Co., C.C.A. Ark., 298 F. 272, 274; Taylor Coal Co. v. Board of Drainage Com'rs of Ohio County, 189 Ky. 793, 225 S.W. 368, 369; irrigation districts; Bonneville Irr. Dist. v. Ririe, 57 Utah, 306, 195 P. 204, 205; and counties, townships, etc. Forbes Pioneer Boat Line v. Board of Com'rs of Everglades Drainage Dist., 77 Fla. 742, 82 So. 346, 350.

Spiritual corporations. Corporations, the members of which are entirely spiritual persons, and incorporated as such, for the furtherance of religion and perpetuating the rights of the church.

Trading corporations. A commercial corporation engaged in buying and selling. The word "trading," is much narrower in scope than "business," as applied to corporations, and though a trading corporation is a business corporation, there are many business corporations which are not trading companies. Dartmouth College v. Woodward, 4 Wheat. 669, 4 L.Ed. 629; Adams v. Railroad Co., 1 Fed.Cas. 92.

Tramp corporations. Companies chartered in one state without any intention of doing business therein, but which carry on their business and operations wholly in other states. State v. Georgia Co., 112 N.C. 34, 17 S.E. 10, 19 L.R.A. 485.

Synonyms

The words "company" and "corporation" are commonly used as interchangeable terms. In strictness, however, a company is an association of persons for business or other purposes, embracing a considerable number of individuals, which may or may not be incorporated. In the former case, it is legally a partnership or a joint-stock company; in the latter case, it is properly called a "corporation." Goddard v. Railroad Co., 202 Ill. 362, 66 N.E. 1066. For the particulars in which corporations differ from "Joint-Stock Companies" and "Partnerships," see those titles.

CORPORATION ACT. In English law. The statute 13 Car. II. St. 2, c. 1; by which it was provided that no person should thereafter be elected to office in any corporate town that should not, within one year previously, have taken the sacrament of the Lord's Supper, according to the rites of the Church of England; and every person so elected was also required to take the oaths of allegiance and supremacy. 3 Steph.Comm. 103, 104; 4 Bl.Comm. 58. This statute is now repealed. 4 Steph.Comm. 511.

CORPORATION COURTS. Certain courts in Virginia described as follows: "For each city of the state, there shall be a court called a 'corporation court,' to be held by a judge, with like qualifications and elected in the same manner as judges of the county court." Code Va.1887, § 3050, Code 1919, § 5905.

CORPORATOR. A member of a corporation aggregate. Grant, Corp. 48; Seaborn v. Wingfield, 56 Nev. 260, 48 P.2d 881, 883.

CORPORE ET ANIMO. Lat. By the body and by the mind; by the physical act and by the mental intent. Dig. 41, 2, 3.

CORPOREAL. A term descriptive of such things as have an objective, material existence; perceptible by the senses of sight and touch; possessing a real body. Opposed to incorporeal and spiritual. Sullivan v. Richardson, 33 Fla. 1, 14 So. 692; Bourland v. State, 133 Tex.Cr.R. 544, 112 S.W.2d 720, 721.

There is a distinction between "corporeal" and "corporal." The former term means "possessing a body," that is, tangible, physical, material; the latter means "relating to or affecting a body," that is, bodily, external. Corporeal denotes the nature or physical existence of a body; corporal denotes its exterior or the co-ordination of it with some other body. Hence we speak of "corporeal hereditaments," but of "corporal punishment," "corporal touch," "corporal oath," etc.

CORPOREAL HEREDITAMENTS. See Hereditaments.

CORPOREAL PROPERTY. Such as affects the senses, and may be seen and handled, as opposed to incorporeal property, which cannot be seen or handled, and exists only in contemplation. Mozley & Whitley.

Thus a house is corporeal, but the annual rent payable for its occupation is incorporeal. Corporeal property is, if movable, capable of manual transfer; if immovable, possession of it may be delivered up. But incorporeal property cannot be so transferred, but some other means must be adopted for its transfer, of which the most usual is an instrument in writing.

In Roman law, the distinction between things corporeal and incorporeal rested on the sense of touch; tangible objects only were considered corporeal. In modern law, all things which may be perceived by any of the bodily senses are termed corporeal, although a common definition of the word includes merely that which can be touched and seen. 14a C.J. 1424 (citing Abbott's Dict.). Marnett Oil & Gas Co. v. Munsey, Tex.Civ.App., 232 S.W. 867, 869; Sullivan v. Richardson, 33 Fla. 1, 116, 14 So. 692.

The term "property," however, is a generic term of extensive application. 32 Cyc. 647. In its strict legal sense, "property" is nothing but the right of dominion, possession, and disposition which may be acquired over physical things. Braceville Coal Co. v. People, 147 Ill. 66, 35 N.E. 62, 22 L.R.A. 340; Fears v. State, 102 Ga. 274, 29 S.E. 463; De Lauder v. Baltimore County, 94 Md. 1, 50 A. 427. It follows that from that point of view, there is no such thing as "tangible" property or "corporeal" property, and the only meaning which can in law be given to the expression "corporeal property" is the right to possess, use, occupy, and enjoy corporeal things and take the profits thereof. Transcontinental Oil Co. v. Emmerson, 298 Ill. 394, 131 N.E. 645, 648, 16 A.L.R. 507.

CORPS DIPLOMATIQUE. In international law. Ambassadors and diplomatic persons at any court or capital.

CORPSE. The dead body of a human being. 1 Russ. & R. 366, n.; 2 Term 733; 1 Leach 497; Com. v. Loring, 8 Pick., Mass., 370; Dig. 47. 12. 3. 7; 11. 7. 38; Code, 3. 44. 1; Co. 3d Inst. 203; 1 Russ.Cr. 629.

CORPUS. (Lat.) Body; an aggregate or mass, (of men, laws, or articles;) physical substance, as distinguished from intellectual conception; the principal sum or capital, as distinguished from interest or income. In re Barron's Will, 163 Wis. 275, 155 N.W. 1087, 1089; United States Trust Co. of New York v. Heye, 181 App.Div. 544, 168 N.Y.S. 1051, 1057; Macy v. Ladd, 128 Misc. 732, 219 N.Y.S. 449, 460; In re Schley, 181 App.Div. 931, 173 N.Y.S. 317, 319.

A substantial or positive fact, as distinguished from what is equivocal and ambiguous. The *corpus delicti* (body of an offense) is the fact of its having been actually committed. Best, Pres. 269–279.

A corporeal act of any kind, (as distinguished from *animus* or mere intention,) on the part of him who wishes to acquire a thing, whereby he obtains the physical ability to exercise his power over it whenever he pleases. The word occurs frequently in this sense in the civil law. Mackeld. Rom.Law, § 248.

Corpus comitatus. The body of a county. The whole county, as distinguished from a part of it, or any particular place in it. U. S. v. Grush, 5 Mason, 290, Fed.Cas.No.15,268.

Corpus corporatum. A corporation; a corporate body, other than municipal.

Corpus cum causa. (The body with the cause.) An English writ which issued out of chancery, to remove both the *body* and the record, touching the *cause* of any man lying in execution upon a judgment for debt, into the king's bench, there to remain until he satisfied the judgment. Cowell; Blount.

Corpus delicti. The body of a crime. The body (material substance) upon which a crime has been committed, *e. g.*, the corpse of a murdered man, the charred remains of a house burned down. In a derivative sense, the substance or foundation of a crime; the substantial fact that a crime has been committed. People v. Dick, 37 Cal. 281; White v. State, 49 Ala. 347; Goldman v. Com., 100 Va. 865, 42 S.E. 923; State v. Schyhart, Mo. Sup., 199 S.W. 205, 211; State v. Brown, 103 S.C. 437, 88 S.E. 21, 22, L.R.A.1916D, 1295; State v. Johnson, 95 Utah 572, 83 P.2d 1010, 1014. When applied to any particular offense, the actual commission by some one of particular offense charged. Gorum v. State, 60 Okl.Cr. 248, 63 P.2d 765, 766.

Corpus pro corpore. In old records. Body for body. A phrase expressing the liability of manucaptors. 3 How.State Tr. 110.

CORPUS CHRISTI DAY. In English law. A feast instituted in 1264, in honor of the sacrament. 32 Hen. VIII. c. 21.

CORPUS HUMANUM NON RECIPIT ÆSTIMATIONEM. The human body does not admit of valuation. Hob. 59.

CORPUS JURIS. A body of law. A term used to signify a book comprehending several collections of law. There are two principal collections to which this name is given; the *Corpus Juris Civilis*, and the *Corpus Juris Canonici.* Also name of an encyclopædic statement of the principles of Anglo-American law.

Corpus juris canonici. The body of the canon law. A compilation of the canon law, comprising the decrees and canons of the Roman Church, constituting the body of ecclesiastical law of that church.

Corpus juris civilis. The body of the civil law. The system of Roman jurisprudence compiled and codified under the direction of the emperor Justinian, in A.D. 528–534. This collection comprises the Institutes, Digest, (or Pandects,) Code, and Novels. The name is said to have been first applied to this collection early in the seventeenth century.

CORRECT ATTEST. These words, used before the signatures of bank directors to reports made to the commissioner of banking, mean not alone to bear witness, but to affirm to be true or genuine, and such words are appropriately used for the affirmation of persons in their official capacity to attest the truth of a writing. Eland State Bank v. Massachusetts Bonding & Ins. Co., 165 Wis. 493, 162 N.W. 662, 663.

CORRECTED POLICY. Policy issued after investigation of risk to correct misstatements in policy first issued. Sherri v. National Surety Co., of New York, 243 N.Y. 266, 153 N.E. 70, 71.

CORRECTION. Discipline; chastisement administered by a master or other person in authority to one who has committed an offense, for the purpose of curing his faults or bringing him into proper subjection.

CORRECTION, HOUSE OF. A prison for the reformation of petty or juvenile offenders.

CORRECTOR OF THE STAPLE. In old English law. A clerk belonging to the staple, to write and record the bargains of merchants there made.

CORREGIDOR. In Spanish law. A magistrate who took cognizance of various misdemeanors, and of civil matters. 2 White, New Recop. 53.

CORREI. Lat. In the civil law. Co-stipulators; joint stipulators.

CORREI CREDENDI. In the civil and Scotch law. Joint creditors; creditors *in solido.* Poth. Obl. pt. 2, c. 4, art. 3, § 11.

CORREI DEBENDI. In Scotch law. Two or more persons bound as principal debtors to another. Ersk.Inst. 3, 3, 74.

CORRELATIVE. Having a mutual or reciprocal relation, in such sense that the existence of one necessarily implies the existence of the other. *Father* and *son* are correlative terms. *Claim* and *duty* are correlative terms.

CORRESPONDENCE. Interchange of written communications. The letters written by a person and the answers written by the one to whom they are addressed.

CORROBORATE. To strengthen; to add weight or credibility to a thing by additional and confirming facts or evidence. Lassiteo v. Seaboard Air Line Ry. Co., 171 N.C. 283, 88 S.E. 335, 337; Bradley v. State, 19 Ala.App. 578, 99 So. 321, 322; Holmes v. State, 70 Tex.Cr.R. 423, 157 S.W. 487, 493; State v. Fullerton Lumber Co., 35 S.D. 410, 152 N.W. 708, 715; Kincaid v. State, 131 Tex.Cr. R. 101, 97 S.W.2d 175, 177.

The expression "corroborating circumstances" clearly does not mean facts which, independent of a confession, will warrant a conviction; for then the verdict would stand not on the confession, but upon those independent circumstances. To corroborate is to strengthen, to confirm by additional security, to add strength. The testimony of a witness is said to be corroborated when it is shown to correspond with the representation of some other witness, or to comport with some facts otherwise known or established. Corroborating circumstances, then, used in reference to a confession, are such as serve to strengthen it, to render it more probable; such, in short, as may serve to impress a jury with a belief in its truth. State v. Guild, 10 N.J.Law, 163, 18 Am.Dec. 404.

CORROBORATING EVIDENCE. Evidence supplementary to that already given and tending to strengthen or confirm it; additional evidence of a different character to the same point. In re Cardoner's Estate, 27 N.M. 105, 196 P. 327, 328; State v. Smith, 75 Mont. 22, 241 P. 522, 523; People v. Follette, 74 Cal.App. 178, 240 P. 502, 519; Radcliffe v. Chavez, 15 N.M. 258, 110 P. 699, 701.

CORROBORATIVE EVIDENCE. See Corroborating Evidence.

CORRUPT. Spoiled; tainted; vitiated; depraved; debased. Webster.

CORRUPT INTENT. A "corrupt intent," as an element of usury, consists in the charging or receiving of excessive interest with knowledge that it is prohibited by law and the purpose to violate the law. Ector v. Osborne, 179 N.C. 667, 103 S.E. 388, 389, 13 A.L.R. 1207; Teshner v. Roome, 106 Or. 382, 212 P. 473, 474. But see Dege v. Produce Exchange Bank of St. Paul, 212 Minn. 44, 2 N.W. 2d 423, 425, which only requires intent to receive more than the law permits for forbearance of money, but does not require that taker knows that he is violating usury law.

CORRUPT PRACTICES ACT. The Act of June 25, 1910, c. 392, 36 Stat. 822, which, like the English act of 1883 and supplements, dealt with "corrupt and illegal practices" in connection with elections, and which was repealed by the "Federal Corrupt Practices Act" of Feb. 28, 1925, c. 368, Title III, 2 U.S.C.A. § 241 et seq.

CORRUPTIO OPTIMI EST PESSIMA. Corruption of the best is worst. Jacobs v. Beecham, 221 U.S. 263, 31 S.Ct. 555, 55 L.Ed. 729.

CORRUPTION. Illegality; a vicious and fraudulent intention to evade the prohibitions of the law; something against or forbidden by law; moral turpitude or exactly opposite of honesty involving intentional disregard of law from improper motives. State v. Barnett, 60 Okl.Cr. 355, 69 P.2d 77, 87.

An act done with an intent to give some advantage inconsistent with official duty and the rights of others. Johnson v. U. S., C.C.A.Alaska, 260 F. 783, 786.

The act of an official or fiduciary person who unlawfully and wrongfully uses his station or character to procure some benefit for himself or for another person, contrary to duty and the rights of others. U. S. v. Johnson, C.C.Ga., 26 F. 682; Worsham v. Murchison, 66 Ga. 719; U. S. v. Edwards, C.C.Ala., 43 F. 67.

CORRUPTION OF BLOOD. In English law. The consequence of *attainder,* being that the attainted person could neither inherit lands or other hereditaments from his ancestor, nor retain those he already had, nor transmit them by descent to any heir, because his blood was considered in law to be corrupted. Avery v. Everett, 110 N.Y. 317, 18 N.E. 148, 1 L.R.A. 264; 1 Steph.Comm. 446. This was abolished by St. 3 & 4 Wm. IV. c. 106, and 33 & 34 Vict. c. 23, and is unknown in America. Const.U.S. art. 3, § 3.

CORRUPTLY. When used in a statute, this term generally imports a wrongful design to acquire some pecuniary or other advantage. Grebe v. State, 112 Neb. 715, 201 N.W. 143, 144; Bosselman v. U. S., C.C.A.N.Y., 239 F. 82, 86; State v. Shipman, 202 N.C. 518, 163 S.E. 657.

CORSELET. Ancient armor which covered the body.

CORSE-PRESENT. In old English law. A mortuary, thus termed because, when a mortuary became due on the death of a man, the best or second-best beast was, according to custom, offered or presented to the priest, and carried with the corpse. In Wales a corse-present was due upon the death of a clergyman to the bishop of the diocese, till abolished by 12 Anne St. 2, c. 6. 2 Bl. Comm. 426; Stat. 21 Hen. VIII. cap. 6; Cowell.

CORSNED. In Saxon law. The morsel of execration. A species of ordeal in use among the Saxons, performed by eating a piece of bread over which the priest had pronounced a certain imprecation. If the accused ate it freely, he was pronounced innocent; but, if it stuck in his throat, it was considered as a proof of his guilt. Crabb, Eng.Law, 30; 1 Reeve, Eng.Law, 21; 4 Bl.Comm. 345; Spelman, Gloss. 439.

CORTES. The name of the legislative assemblies, the parliament or congress, of Spain and Portugal.

CORTEX. The bark of a tree; the outer covering of anything.

CORTIS. A court or yard before a house. Blount.

CORTULARIUM, or CORTARIUM. In old records. A yard adjoining a country farm.

CORVÉE. In French law. Gratuitous labor exacted from the villages or communities, especially for repairing roads, constructing bridges, etc. State v. Covington, 125 N.C. 641, 34 S.E. 272.

CORVÉE SEIGNEURIALE. Services due the lord of the manor. Guyot, *Rép.Univ.*; 3 Low.C. 1.

COSA JUZGADA. In Spanish law. A cause or matter adjudged, (*res judicata.*) White, New Recop. b. 3, tit. 8, note.

COSAS COMUNES. In Spanish law. A term corresponding to the *res communes* of the Roman law, and descriptive of such things as are open to the equal and common enjoyment of all persons and not to be reduced to private ownership, such as the air, the sea, and the water of running streams. Hall, Mex.Law, 447; Lux v. Haggin, 69 Cal. 255, 10 P. 707.

COSBERING. See Coshering.

COSDUNA. In feudal law. A custom or tribute.

COSEN, COZEN. In old English law. To cheat. "A cosening knave." 3 Leon. 171.

COSENAGE. (Also spelled "Cosinage," "Cousinage.") In old English law. A writ that lay for the heir where the *tresail, i. e.,* the father of the *besail,* or great-grandfather, was seised of lands in fee at his death, and a stranger entered upon the land and abated. Fitzh.Nat.Brev. 221; 3 Bla. Comm. *186.

Kindred; cousinship; relationship; affinity. Stat. 4 Hen. III. cap. 8; 3 Bla.Comm. 186; Co. Litt. 160*a*.

COSENING. In old English law. An offense, mentioned in the old books, where anything was done deceitfully, whether belonging to contracts or not, which could not be properly termed by any special name. The same as the *stellionatus* of the civil law. Cowell; West.Symb. pt. 2, *Indictment,* § 68; Blount; 4 Bla.Comm. 158.

COSHERING. In old English law. A feudal prerogative or custom for lords to lie and feast themselves at their tenants' houses. Cowell.

COSMOPATHIC. Open to the access of supernormal knowledge or emotion supposedly from a preternatural world;—applied to methods of healing. Commonwealth v. Zimmerman, 221 Mass. 184, 108 N.E. 893, 895, Ann.Cas.1916A, 858.

COSMUS. Clean. Blount.

COSS. A term used by Europeans in India to denote a road-measure of about two miles, but differing in different parts. Wharton.

COST. Expense. Barton v. Bowlin, 111 Ark. 123, 163 S.W. 502, 504. The price paid, as for an article purchased for exportation, with all incidental charges paid at the place of exportation. Goodwin v. U. S., 2 Wash.C.C. 493, Fed.Cas.No.5,554. The amount originally expended in performing a particular act or operation, or for production or construction, as of a building. Kempf v. Ranger, 132 Minn. 64, 155 N.W. 1059, 1060; Hoggson Bros. v. Spiekerman, 161 N.Y.S. 930, 933, 175 App.Div. 144. Cost is sometimes used as equivalent to "value." Loughney v. Klein, C.C.A.Pa., 221 F. 197, 199.

Cost-book. In English law. A book in which a number of adventurers who have obtained permission to work a lode, and have agreed to share the enterprise in certain proportions, enter the agreement, and from time to time the receipts and expenditures of the mine, the names of the shareholders, their respective accounts with the mine, and transfers of shares. These associations are called "Cost-Book Mining Companies," and are governed by the general law of partnership. Lindl.Partn. *147.

Cost-plus contract. One which fixes the amount to be paid the contractor on a basis, generally, of the cost of the material and labor, plus an agreed percentage thereof. The Spica, C.C.A.N.Y., 289 F. 436, 445.

Cost price. That which is actually paid for goods. Buck v. Burk, 18 N.Y. 337; Esterman-Verkamp Co. v. Rouse, 211 Ky. 791, 278 S.W. 124, 127.

Costs of collection. Strictly, expenses involved in endeavoring to make collection, as of a promissory note; but as used in or with reference to such notes, the phrase is synonymous with attorney's fees. McClain v. Continental Supply Co., 66 Okl. 225, 168 P. 815, 818; Wood v. Ferguson, 71 Mont. 540, 230 P. 592, 594. It does not refer to costs of suit, which are recoverable by law. Cox v. Hagan, 125 Va. 656, 100 S.E. 666, 674.

CO-STIPULATOR. A joint promisor.

COSTS. A pecuniary allowance, made to the successful party, (and recoverable from the losing party,) for his expenses in prosecuting or defending a suit or a distinct proceeding within a suit. Stevens v. Bank, 168 N.Y. 560, 61 N.E. 904; Bennett v. Kroth, 37 Kan. 235, 15 P. 221, 1 Am.St.Rep. 248; Pezel v. Yerex, 56 Cal.App. 304, 205 P. 475, 478; In re Leary's Estate, 172 Misc. 286, 14 N.Y.S. 2d 960, 961.

Expenses pending suit as allowed or taxed by the court. Jones v. Adkins, 170 Ark. 298, 280 S.W. 389, 394.

Fees and charges required by law to be paid to the courts or some of their officers, the amount of which is fixed by law. Blair v. Brownstone Oil & Refining Co., 20 Cal.App. 316, 128 P. 1022.

Costs and fees were originally altogether different in their nature. The one is an allowance to a *party* for expenses incurred in prosecuting or defending a suit; the other, a compensation to an *officer* for services rendered in the progress of a cause. Therefore, while an executor or administrator was not personally liable to his adversary for costs, yet, if at his instance an officer performed services for him, he had a personal demand for his fees. Musser v. Good, 11 Serg. & R., Pa., 247. Moreover, costs are an incident to the judgment; fees are compensation to public officers for services rendered individuals not in the course of litigation. Tillman v. Wood, 58 Ala. 579.

In Georgia, however, it is held that "costs," include all charges fixed by statute as compensation for services rendered by officers of the court in the progress of the cause. Walton County v. Dean, 23 Ga.App. 97, 97 S.E. 561, 562.

There is no general or controlling provision or principle of law to the effect that attorney fees that may by statute be recovered by the winning party against the losing party in a suit or action are, or should be regarded as, costs in the case. "Costs" do not include attorney fees unless such fees are by a statute denominated costs or are by statute allowed to be recovered as costs in the case. State ex rel. Royal Ins. Co. v. Barrs, 87 Fla. 168, 99 So. 668, 669; McRostie v. City of Owatonna, 152 Minn. 63, 188 N.W. 52, 54; Littlefield v. Scott, Tex.Civ.App., 244 S.W. 824, 826; Calman v. Cox, Mo.App., 296 S.W. 845, 846; City of Los Angeles v. Abbott, 217 Cal. 184, 17 P.2d 993, 996.

But the word "costs" is frequently understood as including attorney fees. McClain v. Continental Supply Co., 66 Okl. 225, 168 P. 815, 817; Livesley v. Strauss, 104 Or. 356, 207 P. 1095; Lonoke County v. Reed, 122 Ark. 111, 182 S.W. 563, 564; J. I. Case Plow-Works v. J. I. Case Threshing Mach. Co., 162 Wis. 185, 155 N.W. 128, 138.

In England, the term "costs" is also used to designate the charges which an attorney or solicitor is entitled to make and recover from his client, as his remuneration for professional services, such as legal advice, attendances, drafting and copying documents, conducting legal proceedings, etc.

Bill of Costs. A certified, itemized statement of the amount of costs in an action or suit.

Certificate for Costs. In English practice, a certificate or memorandum drawn up and signed by the judge before whom a case was tried, setting out certain facts, the existence of which must be thus proved before the party is entitled, under the statutes, to recover costs.

Cost Bond, or Bond for Costs. A bond given by a party to an action to secure the eventual payment of such costs as may be awarded against him.

Costs de Incremento. Increased costs, costs of increase. Costs adjudged by the court in addition to those assessed by the jury. Day v. Woodworth, 13 How. 372, 14 L.Ed. 181.

Those extra expenses incurred which do not appear on the face of the proceedings, such as witnesses' expenses, fees to counsel, attendances, court fees, etc. Wharton.

Costs of the Day. Costs which are incurred in preparing for the trial of a cause on a specified *day*, consisting of witnesses' fees, and other fees of attendance. Archb.N.Prac. 281; Ad.Eq. 343.

Costs to Abide Event. When an order is made by an appellate court reversing a judgment, with "costs to abide the event," the costs intended by the order include those of the appeal, so that, if the appellee is finally successful, he is entitled to tax the costs of the appeal. First Nat. Bank v. Fourth Nat. Bank, 84 N.Y. 469; Casualty Co. of America v. A. L. Swett Electric Light & Power Co., 121 Misc. 268, 200 N.Y.S. 796, 801.

Double Costs. The ordinary single costs of suit, and one-half of that amount in addition. 2 Tidd, Pr. 987. "Double" is not used here in its ordinary sense of "twice" the amount. Van Aulen v. Decker, 2 N.J.Law, 108; Gilbert v. Kennedy, 22 Mich. 19. But see Moran v. Hudson, 34 N.J.Law, 531. These costs are now abolished in England by St. 5 & 6 Vict. c. 97. Wharton.

Final Costs. Such costs as are to be paid at the end of the suit; costs, the liability for which depends upon the final result of the litigation. Goodyear v. Sawyer, C.C.Tenn., 17 F. 8.

Interlocutory Costs. In practice. Costs accruing upon proceedings in the intermediate stages of a cause, as distinguished from final costs; such as the costs of motions. 3 Chit.Gen.Pr. 597; Goodyear v. Sawyer, C.C.Tenn., 17 F. 6.

Security for Costs. In practice. A security which a defendant in an action may require of a plaintiff who does not reside within the jurisdiction of the court, for the payment of such costs as may be awarded to the defendant. 1 Tidd, Pr. 534. Ex parte Louisville & N. R. Co., 124 Ala. 547, 27 So. 239.

Treble Costs. A rate of costs given in certain actions, consisting, according to its technical import, of the common costs, half of these, and half of the latter. 2 Tidd, Pr. 988. The word "treble," in this application, is not understood in its literal sense of thrice the amount of single costs, but signifies merely the addition together of the three sums fixed as above. Id. Treble costs have been abolished in England, by St. 5 & 6 Vict. c. 97. In American law. In Pennsylvania and New Jersey the rule is different. When an act of assembly gives treble costs, the party is allowed three times the usual costs, with the exception that the fees of the officers are not to be trebled when they are not regularly or usually payable by the defendant. Shoemaker v. Nesbit, 2 Rawle, Pa., 203; Welsh v. Anthony, 16 Pa. 256; Mairs v. Sparks, 5 N.J.Law, 516.

COSTUMBRE. In Spanish law. Custom; an unwritten law established by usage, during a long space of time. Las Partidas, pt. 1, tit. 2, l. 4.

CO-SURETIES. Joint sureties; two or more sureties to the same obligation. State of Arkansas v. Pufahl, C.C.A.Ark., 52 F.2d 116, 120; French v. Young, 292 Mich. 443, 290 N.W. 861, 862, 863.

COTA. A cot or hut. Blount.

COTAGIUM. In old English law. A cottage.

COTARIUS. In old English law. A cottager, who held in free socage, and paid a stated fine or rent in provisions or money, with some occasional personal services. See Coterellus.

COTENANCY. A tenancy by several distinct titles but by unity of possession, or any joint ownership or common interest with its grantor. Shepard v. Mt. Vernon Lumber Co., 192 Ala. 322, 68 So. 880, 881, 15 A.L.R. 23. The term is broad enough to comprise both tenancy in common and joint tenancy. Caldwell v. Farrier, Tex.Civ.App., 248 S.W. 425, 427.

COTERELLI. Anciently, a kind of peasantry who were outlaws; robbers. Blount.

COTERELLUS. In feudal law. A cottager; a servile tenant, who held in mere villenage; his person, issue, and goods were disposable at the lord's pleasure. A coterellus, therefore, occupied a less favorable position than a cotarius (*q. v.*), for the latter held by socage tenure. Cowell.

COTERIE. A fashionable association, or a knot of persons forming a particular circle. The origin of the term was purely commercial, signifying an association, in which each member furnished his part, and bore his share in the profit and loss. Wharton.

COTESWOLD. In old records. A place where there is no wood.

COTLAND. In old English law. Land held by a cottager, whether in socage or villenage. Cowell; Blount.

COTSETHLA. In old English law. The little seat or mansion belonging to a small farm.

COTSETHLAND. The seat of a cottage with the land belonging to it. Spelman.

COTSETUS. A cottager or cottage-holder who held by servile tenure and was bound to do the work of the lord. Cowell.

COTTAGE. In English law. A small dwelling-house that has no land belonging to it. Shep. Touch. 94; Emerton v. Selby, 2 Ld.Raym. 1015; Scholes v. Hargreaves, 5 Term, 46; Hubbard v. Hubbard, 15 Adol. & E. (N.S.) 240; Gibson v. Brockway, 8 N.H. 470, 31 Am.Dec. 200. It has been held that the term includes a two-family house, not being limited to a structure for the use of only one family. Jones v. Mulligan, N.J.Ch., 121 A. 608, 609.

COTTIER TENANCY. A species of tenancy in Ireland, constituted by an agreement in writing, and subject to the following terms: That the tenement consists of a dwelling-house with not more than half an acre of land; at a rental not exceeding £5 a year; the tenancy to be for not more than a month at a time; the landlord to keep the house in good repair. Landlord and Tenant Act, Ireland, 23 & 24 Vict. c. 154, § 81.

COTTOLENE. A registered trade-mark name for cooking fat. Imperial Cotto Sales Co. v. N. K. Fairbanks Co., 50 App.D.C. 250, 270 F. 686, 687.

COTTON. A term which is applicable to such substance in whatever state it exists after it has been gathered and before it is manufactured into some article of merchandise, whether the seed have been removed at the gin or whether it is lint cotton in the seed or in the bale. Freeman v. State, 156 Ark. 592, 247 S.W. 51.

COTTON GIN. A term sometimes used as synonymous with ginhouse. State v. Rodgers, 168 N.C. 112, 83 S.E. 161, 162.

COTTON LINTERS. Called also "linters." An inferior grade of cotton, obtained by reginning cotton seed. Commercial Union Assur. Co., Limited, of London, England, v. Creek Cotton Oil Co., 96 Okl. 189, 221 P. 499, 501.

COTTON MILL OF FACTORY. One which manufactures cotton from the raw state into a finished product. Dumas v. State, 17 Ala.App. 492, 86 So. 162, 163.

COTTON NOTES. Receipts given for each bale of cotton received on storage by a public warehouse. Fourth Nat. Bank v. St. Louis Cotton Compress Co., 11 Mo.App. 337.

COTTON SEASON. The season for buying and selling cotton between September 1 and the following May 1. Morris v. Hellums Co., 131 Ark. 585, 199 S.W. 927, 928.

COTUCA. Coat armor.

COTUCHANS. A term used in Domesday for peasants, boors, husbandmen.

COUCHANT. Lying down; squatting. *Couchant and levant* (lying down and rising up) is a term applied to animals trespassing on the land of one other than their owner, for one night or longer. 3 Bl.Comm. 9.

COUCHER, or COURCHER. A factor who continues abroad for traffic, (37 Edw. III. c. 16;) also the general book wherein any corporation, etc., register their acts, (3 & 4 Edw. VI. c. 10.)

COULISSE. The stockbrokers' curb market in Paris.

COUNCIL. An assembly of persons for the purpose of concerting measures of state or municipal policy; hence called "councillors."

In American Law. The legislative body in the government of cities or boroughs. An advisory body selected to aid the executive; particularly in the colonial period (and at present in some of the United States) a body appointed to advise and assist the governor in his executive or judicial capacities or both. Opinion of the Justices, 14 Mass. 470; Opinion of the Justices, 3 Pick., Mass., 517; In re Adams, 4 Pick., Mass., 25; Answers of the Justices, 70 Me. 570.

Common Council. In American law. The lower or more numerous branch of the legislative assembly of a city. In English law. The councillors of the city of London. The parliament, also, was anciently called the "common council of the realm." Fleta, 2, 13.

Privy Council. See that title.

Select Council. The name given, in some states, to the upper house or branch of the council of a city.

COUNCIL OF CONCILIATION. By the Act 30 & 31 Vict. c. 105, power is given for the crown to grant licenses for the formation of councils of conciliation and arbitration, consisting of a certain number of masters and workmen in any trade or employment, having power to hear and determine all questions between masters and workmen which may be submitted to them by both parties, arising out of or with respect to the particular trade or manufacture, and incapable of being otherwise settled. They have power to apply to a justice to enforce the performance of their award. The members are elected by persons engaged in the trade. Davis, Bldg.Soc. 232; Sweet.

COUNCIL OF JUDGES. Under the English judicature act, 1873, § 75, an annual council of the judges of the supreme court is to be held, for the purpose of considering the operation of the new practice, offices, etc., introduced by the act, and of reporting to a secretary of state as to any alterations which they consider should be made in the law for the administration of justice. An extraordinary council may also be convened at any time by the lord chancellor. Sweet.

COUNCIL OF THE BAR. A body composed of members of the English bar which governs the bar. It hears complaints against barristers and reports its findings with recommendations to the benchers of the Inn of Court of which the barrister is a member, who alone can act. Leaming, Phila. Lawy. in Lond. Courts 67.

COUNCIL OF THE NORTH. A court instituted by Henry VIII. in 1537, to administer justice in Yorkshire and the four other northern counties. Under the presidency of Stratford, the court showed great rigor, bordering, it is alleged, on harshness. It was abolished by 16 Car. I., the same act which abolished the Star Chamber. Brown.

COUNSEL. 1. In practice. An advocate, counsellor, or pleader. 3 Bl.Comm. 26; 1 Kent, Comm. 307. One who assists his client with advice, and pleads for him in open court. One who has been admitted as an attorney and counsellor at law. Baker v. State, 9 Okl.Cr. 62, 130 P. 820, 821. See Counsellor.

Counsellors who are associated with those regularly retained in a cause, either for the purpose of advising as to the points of law involved, or preparing the case on its legal side, or arguing questions of law to the court, or preparing or conducting the case on its appearance before an appellate tribunal, are said to be "of counsel."

2. Knowledge. A grand jury is sworn to keep secret "the commonwealth's *counsel*, their fellows', and their own."

3. Advice given by one person to another in regard to a proposed line of conduct, claim, or contention. State v. Russell, 83 Wis. 330, 53 N.W. 441.

The words "counsel" and "advise" may be, and frequently are, used in criminal law to describe the offense of a person who, not actually doing the felonious act, by his will contributed to it or procured it to be done. Omer v. Com., 95 Ky. 353, 25 S.W. 594.

Counsel's signature. This is required, in some jurisdictions, to be affixed to pleadings, etc., as affording the court a means of judging whether they are interposed in good faith and upon legal grounds. It has been held that the word "counsel" in this connection denotes a person capable of testifying, and that a certificate bearing only the firm signatures of partnerships of attorneys is insufficient. Benedict v. Seiberling, D.C., 17 F.2d 831, 838.

Junior counsel. The younger of the counsel employed on the same side of a case, or the one lower in standing or rank, or who is intrusted with the less important parts of the preparation or trial of the cause.

COUNSELLOR. An advocate or barrister. A member of the legal profession whose special function is to give counsel or advice as to the legal aspects of judicial controversies, or their preparation and management, and to appear in court for the conduct of trials, or the argument of causes, or presentation of motions, or any other legal business that takes him into the presence of the court.

In some of the states, the two words "counsellor" and "attorney" are used interchangeably to designate all lawyers. In others, the latter term alone is used, "counsellor" not being recognized as a technical name. In still others, the two are associated together as the full legal title of any person who has been admitted to practice in the courts; while in a few they denote different grades, it being prescribed that no one can become a counsellor until he has been an attorney for a specified time and has passed a second examination.

In the practice of the United States supreme court, the term denotes an officer who is employed by a party in a cause to conduct the same on its trial on his behalf. He differs from an attorney at law.

In the supreme court of the United States, the two degrees of attorney and counsel were at first kept separate, and no person was permitted to practice in both capacities, but the present practice is otherwise. Weeks, Attys. at Law, 54. It is the duty of the counsel to draft or review and correct the special pleadings, to manage the cause on trial, and, during the whole course of the suit, to apply established principles of law to the exigencies of the case. 1 Kent, Comm. 307.

COUNT, *v.* In pleading. To declare; to recite; to state a case; to narrate the facts constituting a plaintiff's cause of action. In a special sense, to set out the claim or count of the demandant in a real action.

To plead orally; to plead or argue a case in court; to recite or read in court; to recite a count in court.

Count upon a statute. To make express reference to it, as by the words "against the form of the statute" (or "by the force of the statute") "in such case made and provided." Richardson v. Fletcher, 74 Vt. 417, 52 A. 1064.

"Pleading the statute" is stating the facts which bring the case within it, and "counting" on it is making express reference to it by apt terms to show the source of right relied on. Atlantic Coast Line R. Co. v. State, 73 Fla. 609, 74 So. 595, 599.

COUNT, *n.* In pleading. The plaintiff's statement of his cause of action. The different parts of a declaration, each of which, if it stood alone, would constitute a ground for action. Used also to signify the several parts of an indictment, each charging a distinct offense. Boren v. State, 23 Tex.App. 28, 4 S.W. 463; Bailey v. Mosher, C. C.A.Neb., 63 F. 490, 11 C.C.A. 304; Ryan v. Riddle, 109 Mo.App. 115, 82 S.W. 1117.

"Count" and "charge" when used relative to allegations in an indictment or information are synonymous. State v. Thornton, 142 La. 797, 77 So. 634, 636; State v. Puckett, 39 N.M. 511, 50 P.2d 964, 965.

Count sur concessit solvere. A claim based upon a promise to pay;—a count in the mayor's court of London. Under it the plaintiff can sue for any liquidated demand, but not for money due under a covenant. Particulars defining more precisely the nature of the claim must be delivered with the declaration. Odger, C. L. 1029.

Common counts. Certain general counts or forms inserted in a declaration in an action to recover a money debt, not founded on the circumstances of the individual case, but intended to guard against a possible variance, and to enable the plaintiff to take advantage of any ground of liability which the proof may disclose, within the general scope of the action. Nugent v. Teauchot, 67 Mich. 571, 35 N.W. 254.

In the action of *assumpsit*, these counts are as follows: For goods sold and delivered, or bargained and sold; for work done; for money lent; for money paid; for money received to the use of the plaintiff; for interest; or for money due on an account stated.

General count. One stating in a general way the plaintiff's claim. Wertheim v. Casualty Co., 72 Vt. 326, 47 A. 1071.

Money counts. A species of common counts, so called from the subject-matter of them; embracing the *indebitatus assumpsit* count for money lent and advanced, for money paid and expended, and for money had and received, together with the *insimul computassent* count, or count for money due on an account stated. 1 Burrill, Pr. 132.

Omnibus count. A count which combines in one all the money counts with one for goods sold and delivered, work and labor, and an account stated. Webber v. Tivill, 2 Saund. 122; Griffin v. Murdock, 88 Me. 254, 34 A. 30.

Several counts. Where a plaintiff has several distinct causes of action, he is allowed to pursue them cumulatively in the same action, subject to certain rules which the law prescribes. Wharton.

Special count. As opposed to the common counts, in pleading, a special count is a statement of the actual facts of the particular case, or a count in which the plaintiff's claim is set forth with all needed particularity. Wertheim v. Casualty Co., 72 Vt. 326, 47 A. 1071.

COUNT. (Fr. *comte*; from the Latin *comes.*) An earl.

It gave way as a distinct title to the Saxon earl, but was retained in countess, viscount, and as the basis of county. *Termes de la ley;* 1 Bla.Comm. 398.

COUNT-OUT. In English parliamentary law. Forty members form a house of commons; and, though there be ever so many at the beginning of a debate, yet, if during the course of it the house should be deserted by the members, till reduced below the number of forty, any one member may have it adjourned upon its being counted; but a debate may be continued when only one member is left in the house, provided no one choose to move an adjournment. Wharton.

The words "count and count-out" refer to the count of the house of commons by the speaker. Forty members, including the speaker, are required to constitute a quorum. Each day after parliament is opened, the speaker counts the house. If forty members are not present he waits till four o'clock, and then counts the house again. If forty members are not then present, he at once adjourns it to the following meeting day. May, Parl.Prac. 219.

COUNTEE. In old English law. The most eminent dignity of a subject before the Conquest. He was *præfectus* or *præpositus comitatus*, and had the charge and custody of the county; but this authority is now vested in the sheriff. 9 Coke, 46.

COUNTENANCE. In old English law. Credit; estimation. Wharton. Also, encouragement; aiding and abetting. Cooper v. Johnson, 81 Mo. 487.

COUNTER, *n.* (Spelled, also, "Compter.") The name of two prisons formerly standing in London, but now demolished. They were the Poultry Counter and Wood Street Counter. Cowell; Whish.L.D.; Coke, 4th Inst. 248.

COUNTER, *adj.* Adverse; antagonistic; opposing or contradicting; contrary. Silliman v. Eddy, 8 How.Prac., N.Y., 122.

Counter-affidavit. An affidavit made and presented in contradiction or opposition to an affidavit which is made the basis or support of a motion or application.

Counter-bond. In old practice. A bond of indemnity. 2 Leon. 90.

Counterclaim. See that title.

Counter-deed. A secret writing, either before a notary or under a private seal, which destroys, invalidates, or alters a public one.

Counter-letter. A species of instrument of defeasance common in the civil law. It is executed by a party who has taken a deed of property, absolute on its face, but intended as security for a loan of money, and by it he agrees to reconvey the property on payment of a specified sum. The two instruments, taken together, constitute what is known in Louisiana as an "*antichresis*," (*q. v.*). Karcher v. Karcher, 138 La. 288, 70 So. 228, 229; Livingston v. Story, 11 Pet. 351, 9 L.Ed. 746.

Counter-mark. A sign put upon goods already marked; also the several marks put upon goods belonging to several persons, to show that they must not be opened, but in the presence of all the owners or their agents.

Counter-plea. See Plea.

Counter-security. A security given to one who has entered into a bond or become surety for another; a countervailing bond of indemnity.

COUNTERCLAIM. A claim presented by a defendant in opposition to or deduction from the claim of the plaintiff. A species of set-off or recoupment introduced by the codes of civil procedure in many of the states, of a broad and liberal character. Quoted in Wollan v. McKay, 24 Idaho, 691, 135 P. 832, 837.

It is an offensive as well as a defensive plea, which is not necessarily confined to the justice of plaintiff's claim, and it represents the right of the defendant to have the claims of the parties counterbalanced in whole or in part, with judgment to be entered for the excess, if any. Olsen v. McMaken & Pentzien, 139 Neb. 506, 297 N.W. 830, 833.

Its sole requisites are that it must tend to defeat or diminish plaintiff's demand, and that demands must be reciprocal. Bond v. Farmers & Merchants Nat. Bank, Los Angeles, 64 Cal.App.2d 842, 149 P.2d 722, 724; Dobbins v. Horsfall, 58 Cal. App.2d 23, 136 P.2d 35, 38.

It is in effect a new suit in which the party named as defendant under the bill is plaintiff and the party named as plaintiff under the bill is defendant. Roberts Min. & Mill. Co. v. Schrader, C.C.A.Nev., 95 F.2d 522, 524.

The term is broader in meaning than set-off or recoupment, and includes them both. Williams v. Williams, 192 N.C. 405, 135 S.E. 39, 40; Fricke v. W. E. Fuetterer Battery & Supplies Co., 220 Mo.App. 623, 288 S.W. 1000, 1002; Curtis-Warner Corporation v. Thirkettle, 99 N.J.Eq. 806, 134 A. 299, 302; Otto v. Lincoln Sav. Bank of Brooklyn, 51 N.Y.S.2d 561, 563, 268 App.Div. 400; Ætna Life Ins. Co. v. Griffin, 200 N.C. 251, 156 S.E. 515, 516.

The counterclaim is a substitute for the cross-bill in equity. McAnarney v. Lembeck, 97 N.J.Eq. 361, 127 A. 197, 198; Vidal v. South American Securities Co., C.C.A.N.Y., 276 F. 855. It is but another name for a cross-petition, and may be so styled, especially in actions prosecuted by equitable proceedings. Taylor v. Wilson, 182 Ky. 592, 206 S.W. 865, 866; Clark v. Duncanson, 79 Okl. 180, 192 P. 806, 809, 16 A.L.R. 450.

Under rule 30 of Federal rules in equity see Fed.Rules Civ.Proc. rules 8, 13, 28 U.S.C.A., "counterclaim" means any claim, not such as to constitute a set-off, which, in equity, a defendant might assert against the plaintiff in the same suit. Terry Steam Turbine Co. v. B. F. Sturtevant Co., D.C.Mass., 204 F. 103, 105.

A counterclaim may be any cause of action in favor of defendants or some of them against plaintiffs or some of them, a person whom a plaintiff represents or a plaintiff and another person or persons alleged to be liable. New York Civ.Prac.Act, § 266.

A "counterclaim" must be a cause of action, and seeks affirmative relief, while a defense merely defeats the plaintiff's cause of action by a denial or confession and avoidance, and does not admit of affirmative relief to the defendant. Lovett v. Lovett, 93 Fla. 611, 112 So. 768, 780; Secor v. Siver, 165 Iowa, 673, 146 N.W. 845, 847.

COUNTEREXTENSION. In surgery, in connection with "Buck's extension" process, which is some uniform, continuous force or pull applied to the leg or foot below a break, to overcome the natural contraction of the muscles of the thigh, which have a strong tendency to pull the broken ends together and cause them to slip by each other and overlap, especially when the break is oblique across bone, "counterextension" denotes the pull upwards holding the body against the extension downwards, effected by a splint appliance, on the upper end of which is a ring fitting around the thigh and against the patient's groin. Sweet v. Douge, 145 Wash. 142, 259 P. 25.

COUNTERFEIT. In criminal law. To forge; to copy or imitate, without authority or right, and with a view to deceive or defraud, by passing the copy or thing forged for that which is original or genuine. Most commonly applied to the fraudulent and criminal imitation of money. State v. McKenzie, 42 Me. 392; U. S. v. Barrett, D.C.N.D., 111 F. 369; DeRose v. People, 64 Colo. 332, 171 P. 359, L.R.A.1918C, 1193; Metropolitan Nat. Bank v. National Surety Co., D.C.Minn., 48 F. 2d 611, 612.

COUNTERFEIT COIN. Coin not genuine, but resembling or apparently intended to resemble or pass for genuine coin, including genuine coin prepared or altered so as to resemble or pass for coin of a higher denomination. U. S. v. Hopkins, D.C.N.C., 26 F. 443; U. S. v. Bogart, 24 Fed.Cas. 1185; U. S. v. Gellman, D.C.Minn., 44 F.Supp. 360, 363.

COUNTERFEITER. In criminal law. One who unlawfully makes base coin in imitation of the true metal, or forges false currency, or any instrument of writing, bearing a likeness and similitude to that which is lawful and genuine, with an intention of deceiving and imposing upon mankind. Thirman v. Matthews, 1 Stew., Ala., 384.

COUNTER-FESANCE. The act of forging.

COUNTER LETTER. An agreement to reconvey where property has been passed by absolute deed with the intention that it shall serve as security only. Standard Oil Co. of Louisiana v. Futral, 204 La. 215, 15 So.2d 65, 73.

COUNTERMAND. A change or revocation of orders, authority, or instructions previously issued. It may be either express or implied; the former where the order or instruction already given is explicitly annulled or recalled; the latter where the party's conduct is incompatible with the further continuance of the order or instruction, as where a new order is given inconsistent with the former order.

COUNTERPART. In conveyancing. The corresponding part of an instrument; a duplicate or copy. Where an instrument of conveyance, as a lease, is executed in parts, that is, by having several copies or duplicates made and interchangeably executed, that which is executed by the grantor is usually called the "original," and the rest are "counterparts"; although, where all the parties execute every part, this renders them all originals. 2 Bl. Comm. 296; Shep. Touch. 50. Roosevelt v. Smith, 17 Misc.Rep. 323, 40 N.Y.S. 381. See Duplicate.

In granting lots subject to a ground-rent reserved to the grantor, both parties execute the deeds, of which there are two copies; although both are original, one of them is sometimes called the counterpart. See 12 Vin.Abr. 104; Dane, Abr.Index; 7 Com.Dig. 443; Merlin, *Rép. Double Ecrit.*

COUNTERPART WRIT. A copy of the original writ, authorized to be issued to another county when the court has jurisdiction of the cause by reason of the fact that some of the defendants are residents of the county or found therein. White v. Lea, 9 Lea, Tenn., 450.

COUNTER-ROLLS. In English law. The rolls which sheriffs have with the coroners, containing particulars of their proceedings, as well of appeals as of inquests, etc. 3 Edw. I. c. 10.

COUNTERSIGN. As a noun, the signature of a secretary or other subordinate officer to any writing signed by the principal or superior to vouch for the authenticity of it. Fifth Ave. Bank v. Railroad Co., 137 N.Y. 231, 33 N.E. 378, 19 L.R.A. 331; Gurnee v. Chicago, 40 Ill. 167.

As a verb, to sign in addition to the signature of another in order to attest the authenticity. Winsor v. Hunt, 29 Ariz. 504, 243 P. 407, 411; Henning v. American Ins. Co., 108 Kan. 194, 194 P. 647, 648; Waldo Bros. Co. v. Downing, 131 Me. 410, 163 A. 787, 789.

COUNTERVAIL. To counterbalance; to avail against with equal force or virtue; to compensate for, or serve as an equivalent of or substitute for.

COUNTERVAIL LIVERY. At common law, a release was a form of transfer of real estate where some right to it existed in one person but the actual possession was in another; and the possession in such case was said to "countervail livery," that is, it supplied the place of and rendered unnecessary the open and notorious delivery of possession required in other cases. Miller v. Emans, 19 N.Y. 387.

COUNTERVAILING EQUITY. See Equity.

COUNTEUR. In the time of Edward I, a pleader; also called a *Nurrator*, and *Serjeant-Counteur.* See Countors.

COUNTEZ. L. Fr. Count, or reckon. In old practice. A direction formerly given by the clerk of a court to the crier, after a jury was sworn, to *number* them; and which Blackstone says was given in his time, in good English, "count these." 4 Bl. Comm. 340, note (*u.*).

COUNTING UPON A STATUTE. See Count Upon a Statute.

COUNTORS. Advocates, or serjeants at law, whom a man retains to defend his cause and speak for him in court, for their fees. 1 Inst. 17.

COUNTRY. The portion of the earth's surface occupied by an independent nation or people, or the inhabitants of such territory.

In its primary meaning "country" signifies "place;" and, in a larger sense, the territory or dominions occupied by a community; or even waste and unpeopled sections or regions of the earth. But its metaphorical meaning is no less definite and well understood; and in common parlance, in historical and geographical writings, in diplomacy, legislation, treaties, and international codes, the word is employed to denote the population, the nation, the state, or the government, having possession and dominion over a territory. Stairs v. Peaslee, 18 How. 521, 15 L.Ed. 474; U. S. v. Recorder, 1 Blatchf. 218, 225, 5 N.Y.Leg.Obs. 286, Fed.Cas.No.16,129.

The word "country" as used in treaties made by the United States government, in so far as it applies to the United States, means the states of such country. Pagano v. Cerri, 93 Ohio St. 345, 112 N.E. 1037, 1039, L.R.A.1917A, 486.

In pleading and practice. The inhabitants of a district from which a jury is to be summoned; pais; a jury. 3 Bl.Comm. 349; 4 Bl. Comm. 349; Steph. Pl. 73, 78, 230.

COUNTRY WHENCE HE CAME. Within statute providing for deportation of aliens means country of alien's nativity, where domicile has not been acquired elsewhere. Immigration Act 1924, § 13, 8 U.S.C.A. § 213; 8 U.S.C.A. § 156. Schenck ex rel. Capodilupo v. Ward, C.C.A.Mass., 80 F.2d 422, 426.

Term means the country territorially rather than governmentally from which the alien came. Immigration Act 1917, § 20, 8 U.S.C.A. § 156. Moraitis v. Delany, D.C.Md., 46 F.Supp. 425, 430.

But deportation to "country whence alien came" would be complied with if the alien was returned to political dominion in exile and control of country from whence he came. Delany v. Moraitis, C.C.A.Md., 136 F.2d 129, 130, 131, 132, 133.

COUNTY. One of the civil divisions of a country for judicial and political purposes. 1 Bla. Comm. 113.

Etymologically, it denotes that portion of the country under the immediate government of a count or earl. 1 Bla. Comm. 116.

One of the principal subdivisions of the kingdom of England and of most of the states of the American Union, denoting a distinct portion of territory organized by itself for political and judicial purposes. In modern use, the word may denote either the territory marked off to form a county, or the citizens resident within such territory, taken collectively and considered as invested with political rights, or the county regarded as a municipal corporation possessing subordinate governmental powers, or an organized jural society invested with specific rights and duties. Eagle v. Beard, 33 Ark. 501; Wooster v. Plymouth, 62 N.H. 208; In re Becker, 179 App.Div. 789, 167 N.Y.S. 118, 119; Greb v. King County, 187 Wash. 587, 60 P.2d 690, 692.

In the English law, this word signifies the same as *shire,*—county being derived from the French, and *shire* from the Saxon. Both these words signify a circuit or portion of the realm into which the whole land is divided, for the better government thereof and the more easy administration of justice. There is no part of England that is not within some county; and the shirereeve *(sheriff)* was the governor of the province, under the *comes,* earl, or count.

Counties are political subdivisions of the state, created to aid in the administration of state law for the purpose of local self-government. Hunt v. Mohave County, 18 Ariz. 480, 162 P. 600, 602; Board of Com'rs of Osborne County v. City of Osborne, 104 Kan. 671, 180 P. 233, 234; Divide County v. Baird, 55 N.D. 45, 212 N.W. 236, 243, 51 A.L.R. 296; Dolezal v. Bostick, 41 Okl. 743, 139 P. 964, 968; Middlesex County v. City of Waltham, 278 Mass. 514, 180 N.E. 318, 319, and hence not "municipal corporations." Housing Authority of Birmingham Dist. v. Morris, 244 Ala. 557, 14 So.2d 527, 535.

Counties are held in some jurisdictions to be municipal corporations. Mosier v. Cowan, 295 Mich. 27, 294 N.W. 85, 86; Pacific Fruit & Produce Co. v. Oregon Liquor Control Commission, D.C.Or., 41 F.Supp. 175, 179; and are sometimes said to be involuntary municipal corporations. Perkins v. Board of Com'rs of Cook County, 271 Ill. 449, 111 N.E. 580, 584, Ann.Cas.1917A, 27. Other cases, seeking to distinguish between the two, say that counties are agencies or political subdivisions of the state for governmental purposes, and not, like municipal corporations, incorporations of the inhabitants of specified regions for purposes of local government. Dillwood v. Riecks, 42 Cal.App. 602, 184 P. 35, 37; Bexar County v. Linden, 110 Tex. 339, 220 S.W. 761. Counties are also said to be merely quasi corporations. Breathitt County v. Hagins, 183 Ky. 294, 207 S.W. 713, 714; MacKenzie v. Douglas County, 91 Or. 375, 178 P. 350, 352; Jefferson County ex rel. Grauman v. Jefferson County Fiscal Court, 274 Ky. 91, 118 S.W.2d 181, 184.

"Vicinage," in its primary and literary meaning, denotes a neighborhood or vicinity; a "county," on the other hand, is a definitely designated territory. Commonwealth v. Collins, 268 Pa. 295, 110 A. 738, 739.

Body of the county. The county at large, as distinguished from any particular place within it; a county considered as a territorial whole. Fluke v. State, 27 Okl.Cr. 234, 226 P. 118, 120.

County affairs. Those relating to the county in its organic and corporate capacity and included within its governmental or corporate powers. Scarbrough v. Wooten, 23 N.M. 616, 170 P. 743, 744. Such as affect the people of the county in question. Bradford v. Cole, 95 Okl. 35, 217 P. 470, 471.

County attorney. The public prosecutor. Kytka v. Weber County, 48 Utah, 421, 160 P. 111, 113.

A constitutional officer, acting under oath, vested with authority, and it is his duty to inquire into alleged violations of law, to institute criminal proceedings, and to represent the state in matters and proceedings in his county, he signs all informations, and may make application for leave to file information before examination, commitment, or admission to bail. State ex rel. Juhl v. District Court of First Judicial Dist. in and for Jefferson County, Mont., 107 Mont. 309, 84 P.2d 979, 981, 120 A.L.R. 353.

County board of equalization. A body created for the purpose of equalizing values of property subject to taxation., Overland Co. v. Utter, 44 Idaho, 385, 257 P. 480, 482.

County board of supervisors. Is not the county, but a body of town and city officers acting for and on behalf of county in such matters as have been turned over to them by law. Cort v. Smith, 249 App.Div. 1, 291 N.Y.S. 54, 60.

County bonds. Broadly, any bonds issued by county officials to be paid for by a levy on a special taxing district, whether or not coextensive with the county. Forrey v. Board of Com'rs of Madison County, 189 Ind. 257, 126 N.E. 673.

County bridge. A bridge of the larger class, erected by the county, and which the county is liable to keep in repair. Boone County v. Mutchler, 137 Ind. 140, 36 N.E. 534.

County business. All business pertaining to the county as a corporate entity. City of Astoria v. Cornelius, 119 Or. 264, 240 P. 233, 235. All business of the county, and any other business of such county connected with or interrelated with the business of any other county properly within the jurisdiction of the county commissioners' court. Glenn v. Dallas County Bois d'Arc Island Levee Dist., Tex.Civ.App., 275 S.W. 137, 145.

County commissioners. Officers of a county, charged with a variety of administrative and executive duties, but principally with the management of the financial affairs of the county, its police regulations, and its corporate business. Sometimes the local laws give them limited judicial powers. In some states they are called "supervisors." Com. v. Krickbaum, 199 Pa. 351, 49 A. 68.

In Georgia, the term is used interchangeably with "commissioners of roads and revenue." Morris v. Smith, 153 Ga. 438(2), 112 S.E. 468; Rhodes v. Jernigan, 155 Ga. 523, 117 S.E. 432, 434.

County corporate. A city or town, with more or less territory annexed, having the privilege to be a county of itself, and not to be comprised in any other county; such as London, York, Bristol, Norwich, and other cities in England. 1 Bl. Comm. 120. See State v. Finn, 4 Mo.App. 347. They differ in no material points from other counties.

County court. A court of high antiquity in England, incident to the jurisdiction of the sheriff. It is not a court of record, but may hold pleas of debt or damages, under the value of forty shillings. The freeholders of the county (anciently termed the "suitors" of the court) are the real judges in this court, and the sheriff is the ministerial officer. See 3 Bl. Comm. 35, 36; 3 Steph. Comm. 395. But in modern English law the name is appropriated to a system of tribunals established by the statute 9 & 10 Vict. c. 95, having a limited jurisdiction, principally for the recovery of small debts. It is also the name of certain tribunals of limited jurisdiction in the county of Middlesex, established under the statute 22 Geo. II. c. 33. In American law. The name is used in many of the states to designate the ordinary courts of record having jurisdiction for trials at nisi prius. Their powers generally comprise ordinary civil jurisdiction, also the charge and care of persons and estates coming within legal guardianship, a limited criminal jurisdiction, appellate jurisdiction over justices of the peace, etc.

County farm bureaus. Governmental agencies intrusted with the duty of disseminating among farmers scientific knowledge of an educational nature for the improvement of agriculture. State v. Miller, 104 Neb. 838, 178 N.W. 846, 848.

County funds. This term may include township funds, the legal title of which is in the county, which holds them for disbursement in accordance for the purpose for which they are created. Fidelity & Deposit Co. of Maryland v. Wilkinson County, 109 Miss. 879, 69 So. 865, 868. See, also, State v. McGraw, 74 Mont. 152, 240 P. 812, 817. Compare Board of Education v. Wake County, 167 N.C. 114, 83 S.E. 257, 258.

County general fund. A fund raised to meet the expenses incident to county government. County Board of Education v. Austin, 169 Ark. 436, 276 S.W. 2, 5.

County jail. A place of incarceration for the punishment of minor offenses and the custody of transient prisoners, where the ignominy of confinement is devoid of the infamous character which an imprisonment in the state jail or penitentiary carries with it. U. S. v. Greenwald, D.C. Cal., 64 F. 8.

County line. This term, when used in a statute providing that the trial for an offense committed on a county line may be in either county divided by such line, is not to be given the geometrical definition of a "line" as having neither breadth nor thickness, but includes all of a fenced public highway dividing two counties, so that a prosecution for robbery committed upon the highway may be maintained in either county, regardless of the side of the center line of the highway upon which the offense was committed. Stone v. People, 71 Colo. 162, 204 P. 897, 898.

County line bridge. A bridge over a stream constituting the boundary line between two counties, one end of which bridge is in one county and the other end in another county. Newberry v. Hall County, 52 Ga.App. 472, 183 S.E. 664, 665.

County officers. Those whose general authority and jurisdiction are confined within the limits of the county in which they are appointed, who are appointed in and for a particular county, and whose duties apply only to that county, and through whom the county performs its usual political functions. State v. Burns, 38 Fla. 367, 21 So. 290; State v. Glenn, 7 Heisk., Tenn., 473; In re Carpenter, 7 Barb., N.Y., 34; Hamilton v. Monroe, Tex.Civ.App., 287 S.W. 304, 306; State ex rel. Osborn v. Eddington, 208 Ind. 160, 195 N.E. 92.

Public officers who fill a position usually provided for in the organization of counties and county governments, and are selected by the county to represent it continuously and as part of the regular and permanent administration of public power in carrying out certain acts with the performance of which it is charged in behalf of the public. Coulter v. Pool, 187 Cal. 181, 201 P. 120, 123.

County palatine. A term bestowed upon certain counties in England, the lords of which in former times enjoyed especial privileges. They might pardon treasons, murders, and felonies. All writs and indictments ran in their names, as in other counties in the king's; and all offenses were said to be done against their peace, and not, as in other places, *contra pacem domini regis*. But these privileges have in modern times nearly disappeared. 1 Holdsw. Hist. E. L. 49; 4 Inst. 205.

County powers. Such only as are expressly provided by law or which are necessarily implied from those expressed. Hersey v. Nelson, 47 Mont. 132, 131 P. 30, 32, Ann.Cas.1914C, 963.

County property. That which a county is authorized to acquire, hold, and sell. State v. Brown, 73 Mont. 371, 236 P. 548, 549; State v. Poland, 61 Mont. 600, 203 P. 352, 353.

County purposes. Those exercised by the county acting as a municipal corporation. Conrad v. Shearer, 197 Iowa 1078, 198 N.W. 633, 634.

As regards the rate of taxation, all purposes for which county taxation may be levied. Test whether a tax is levied for county purposes is whether it is for strictly county uses, for which county or its inhabitants alone would benefit, or is it for a purpose in which entire state is concerned and will profit. Public Utilities Commission v. Manley, 99 Colo. 153, 60 P.2d 913, 917. Seaboard Air Line Ry. Co. v. Wright, 34 Ga.App. 88, 128 S.E. 234, 235. With reference to budgets, all legitimate components of a county budget. Garrison v. Jersey City, 92 N.J.Law, 624, 105 A. 460, 462. The term has been held to apply only to the constantly recurring expenditures, such as salaries of county officers. Obenchain v. Daggett, 68 Or. 374, 137 P. 212, 214. But it has also been held not to be equivalent to "current expenses." Seaboard Air-Line Ry. Co. v. Wright, 157 Ga. 722, 122 S.E. 35, 36.

County rate. In English law. An imposition levied on the occupiers of lands, and applied to many miscellaneous purposes, among which the most important are those of defraying the expenses connected with prisons, reimbursing to private parties the costs they have incurred in prosecuting public offenders, and defraying the expenses of the county police. 15 & 16 Vict. c. 81.

County road. One which lies wholly within one county, and which is thereby distinguished from a state road, which is a road lying in two or more counties. State v. Wood County, 17 Ohio, 186.

County-seat. A county-seat or county-town is the chief town of a county, where the county buildings and courts are located and the county business transacted. Williams v. Reutzel, 60 Ark. 155, 29 S.W. 374; In re Allison, 13 Colo. 525, 22 P. 820, 10 L.R.A. 790; McGregor v. Cain, 177 Ark. 474, 7 S.W.2d 13, 14.

The county town as the seat of government. Dunne v. Rock Island County, 283 Ill. 628, 119 N.E. 591, 595. The place where the courthouse is situated, and the district and county courts are held. Turner v. Tucker, 113 Tex. 434, 258 S.W. 149, 150.

County sessions. In England, the court of general quarter sessions of the peace held in every county once in every quarter of a year. Mozley & Whitley.

County site. The seat of government of the county. Board of Revenue of Covington County v. Merrill, 193 Ala. 521, 68 So. 971, 977. The courthouse site. Board of Revenue of Jefferson County v. Huey, 195 Ala. 83, 70 So. 744, 746.

County tax. Tax exclusively for county purposes, in which state has no sovereign interest or responsibility, and which has no connection with duties of county in its relation to state. Amos v. Mathews, 99 Fla. 1, 126 So. 308, 323.

County-town. The county-seat; the town in which the seat of government of the county is located. State v. Cates, 105 Tenn. 441, 58 S.W. 649.

County treasury. Not the physical place of deposit, but the funds deposited to the credit of the county. State v. Kurtz, 110 Ohio St. 332, 144 N.E. 120, 123.

County warrant. An order or warrant drawn by some duly authorized officer of the county, directed to the county treasurer and directing him to pay out of the funds of the county a designated sum of money to a named individual, or to his order or to bearer. Savage v. Mathews, 98 Ala. 535, 13 So. 328; Crawford v. Noble County, 8 Okl. 450, 58 P. 616; Quinn v. Reed, 130 Ark. 116, 197

S.W. 15, 16; Tyler v. Shelby County, Tex., C.C.A. Tex., 47 F.2d 103, 105.

Foreign county. Any county having a judicial and municipal organization separate from that of the county where matters arising in the former county are called in question, though both may lie within the same state or country.

COUPLED WITH AN INTEREST. This phrase, in the law of agency, has reference to a writing creating, conveying to, or vesting in the agent an interest in the estate or property which is the subject of the agency, as distinguished from the proceeds or profits resulting from the exercise of the agency. George H. Rucker & Co. v. Glennan, 130 Va. 511, 107 S.E. 725, 728.

COUPONS. Interest and dividend certificates; also those parts of a commercial instrument which are to be *cut,* and which are evidence of something connected with the contract mentioned in the instrument. They are generally attached to certificates of loan, where the interest is payable at particular periods, and, when the interest is paid, they are cut off and delivered to the payer. Wharton. Toon v. Wapinitia Irr. Co., 117 Or. 374, 243 P. 554, 556.

In England, they are known as *warrants* or *dividend warrants,* and the securities to which they belong, debentures; 13 C. B. 372.

Coupons are written contracts for the payment of a definite sum of money on a given day, and being drawn and executed in a form and mode for the purpose, that they may be separated from the bonds and other instruments to which they are usually attached, it is held that they are negotiable and that a suit may be maintained on them without the necessity of producing the bonds. Each matured coupon upon a negotiable bond is a separable promise, distinct from the promises to pay the bonds or the other coupons, and gives rise to a separate cause of action. Aurora v. West, 7 Wall. 88, 19 L.Ed. 42. Haven v. Depot Co., 109 Mass. 88; Thompson v. Perrine, 106 U.S. 589, 1 S.Ct. 564, 27 L.Ed. 298.

Coupon bonds. Bonds to which are attached coupons for the several successive installments of interest to maturity. Benwell v. Newark, 55 N.J.Eq. 260, 36 A. 668; Tennessee Bond Cases, 114 U.S. 663, 5 S.Ct. 974, 29 L.Ed. 281.

Coupon notes. Promissory notes with coupons attached, the coupons being notes for interest written at the bottom of the principal note, and designed to be cut off severally and presented for payment as they mature. Williams v. Moody, 95 Ga. 8, 22 S.E. 30.

COUR DE CASSATION. The supreme judicial tribunal of France, having appellate jurisdiction only. For an account of its composition and powers, see Jones, French Bar, 22; Guyot. Repert. Univ.

COURSE. In surveying, the direction of a line with reference to a meridian.

COURSE OF BUSINESS. What is usually done in the management of trade or business. Idom v. Weeks & Russell, 135 Miss. 65, 99 So. 761, 764; In re Malschick, D.C.Pa., 217 F. 492, 494.

In Workmen's Compensation Acts, the usual course of business of the employer covers the normal operations which form part of the ordinary business carried on, and not including incidental and occasional operations having for their purpose the preservation of the premises or the appliances used in the business. Walker v. Industrial Accident Commission, 177 Cal. 737, 171 P. 954, 955, L.R.A. 1918F, 212.

Commercial paper is said to be transferred, or sales alleged to have been fraudulent may be shown to have been made, "in the course of business," or "in the usual and ordinary course of business," when the circumstances of the transaction are such as usually and ordinarily attend dealings of the same kind and do not exhibit any signs of haste, secrecy, or fraudulent intention. Walbrun v. Babbitt, 16 Wall. 581, 21 L.Ed. 489; Brooklyn, etc., R. Co. v. National Bank, 102 U.S. 14, 26 L.Ed. 61.

COURSE OF EMPLOYMENT. Those words as applied to compensation for injuries within the purview of Workmen's Compensation Acts, refer to the time, place, and circumstances under which the accident takes place. Fogg's Case, 125 Me. 168, 132 A. 129, 130; Brady v. Oregon Lumber Co., 117 Or. 188, 243 P. 96, 99, 45 A.L.R. 812; Walker v. Hyde, 43 Idaho, 625, 253 P. 1104, 1105; Wilson v. Town of Mooresville, 222 N.C. 283, 22 S.E.2d 907, 910. A workman is in course of employment when, within time covered by employment, he is doing something which he might reasonably do while so employed at proper place. Dambold v. Industrial Commission, 323 Ill. 377, 154 N.E. 128, 129; In re Employers' Liability Assur. Corporation, 215 Mass. 497, 102 N.E. 697, L.R.A.1916A, 306; Conrad v. Cook-Lewis Foundry Co., 198 N.C. 723, 153 S.E. 266, 269; In re McCrary, 109 Neb. 796, 192 N.W. 237, 239.

In order that an injury may arise out of and in the course of employment, it must be received while the workman is doing the duty he is employed to perform and also as a natural incident of the work flowing therefrom as a natural consequence and directly connected therewith. Di Salvio v. Menihan Co., 225 N.Y. 123, 121 N.E. 766, 767. "In course of employment," as used in Workmen's Compensation Act, means in service of master, and is not synonymous with "during the period covered by his actual employment." An injury, to be within course of employment, must occur during hours of employment, which includes hours of leisure set apart in working hours for rest, recreation, or refreshment, but not time when employee is off premises, not engaged in employer's business, or at home preparing for work, or coming to or leaving work. Shoffler v. Lehigh Valley Coal Co., 290 Pa. 480, 139 A. 192, 193. An employee, even after closing time, is in the "course of employment" until a suitable opportunity has been given for him to leave the place of work. Field v. Charmette Knitted Fabric Co., 245 N.Y. 139, 156 N.E. 642, 643; Munn v. Industrial Board, 274 Ill. 70, 113 N.E. 110, 112.

The expression "in the course of his employment," in the rule that a master is liable for the torts of his servant done in the course of his employment, means while engaged in the service of the master, while engaged generally in the master's work, as distinguished from acts done when the servant steps outside of his employment to do an act for himself, not connected with his master's business. Sina v. Carlson, 120 Minn. 283, 139 N.W. 601, 602. And see Birmingham Ledger Co. v. Buchanan, 10 Ala.App. 527, 65 So. 667, 670.

See, also, Arising Out of and in the Course of Employment.

COURSE OF RIVER. The course of a river is a line parallel with its banks; the term is not synonymous with the "current" of the river. Attorney General v. Railroad Co., 9 N.J.Eq. 550.

COURSE OF THE VOYAGE. By this term is understood the regular and customary track, if such there be, which a ship takes in going from one port to another, and the shortest way. Marsh. Ins. 185; Phill. Ins. 981.

COURSE OF TRADE. What is customarily or ordinarily done in the management of trade or business.

COURSE OF VEIN. In mining, the "course of the vein" appearing on the surface is the course of its apex, which is generally inclined and undulated and departs more or less materially from the strike. Stewart Mining Co. v. Bourne, C.C.A. Idaho, 218 F. 327, 329.

COURSE OF VESSEL. In navigation, the "course" of a vessel is her apparent course, and not her heading at any given moment. The Eastern Glade, C.C.A.N.Y., 101 F.2d 4, 6. It is her actual course. Liverpool, Brazil & River Plate Steam Nav. Co. v. U. S., D.C.N.Y., 12 F.2d 128, 129.

COURT. A space which is uncovered, but which may be partly or wholly inclosed by buildings or walls. Smith v. Martin, 95 Okl. 271, 219 P. 312, 313. When used in connection with a street, indicates a short street, blind alley, or open space like a short street inclosed by dwellings or other buildings facing thereon. City of Miami v. Saunders, 151 Fla. 699, 10 So.2d 326, 329.

Legislation

A legislative assembly. Parliament is called in the old books a court of the king, nobility, and commons assembled. Finch, Law, b. 4, c. 1, p. 233; Fleta, lib. 2, c. 2.

The application of the term—which originally denoted the place of assembling—to denote the assemblage, resembles the similar application of the Latin term *curia,* and is readily explained by the fact that the earlier courts were merely assemblages, in the court-yard of the baron or of the king himself, of those who were qualified and whose duty it was so to appear at stated times or upon summons. Traces of this usage and constitution of courts still remain in the courts baron, the various courts for the trial of impeachments in England and the United States, and in the control exercised by the parliament of England and the legislatures of the various states of the United States over the organization of courts of justice, as constituted in modern times. This meaning of the word has also been retained in the titles of some deliberative bodies, such as the "general court" of Massachusetts, *i. e.,* the legislature.

International Law

The person and suite of the sovereign; the place where the sovereign sojourns with his regal retinue, wherever that may be. The English government is spoken of in diplomacy as the court of St. James, because the palace of St. James is the official palace.

Practice

An organ of the government, belonging to the judicial department, whose function is the application of the laws to controversies brought before it and the public administration of justice. White County v. Gwin, 136 Ind. 562, 36 N.E. 237, 22 L.R.A. 402; Bradley v. Town of Bloomfield, 85 N.J. Law, 506, 89 A. 1009.

The presence of a sufficient number of the members of such a body regularly convened in an authorized place at an appointed time, engaged in the full and regular performance of its functions. Brumley v. State, 20 Ark. 77; Wightman v. Karsner, 20 Ala. 446.

A body in the government to which the administration of justice is delegated. A body organized to administer justice, and including both judge and jury. Houston Belt & Terminal Ry. Co. v. Lynch, Tex.Com.App., 221 S.W. 959, 960; People ex rel. Thaw v. Grifenhagen, Sup., 154 N.Y.S. 965, 970; Peterson v. Fargo-Moorhead St. Ry. Co., 37 N.D. 440, 164 N.W. 42, 49.

A tribunal officially assembled under authority of law at the appropriate time and place, for the administration of justice. In re Carter's Estate, 254 Pa. 518, 99 A. 58.

An agency of the sovereign created by it directly or indirectly under its authority, consisting of one or more officers, established and maintained for the purpose of hearing and determining issues of law and fact regarding legal rights and alleged violations thereof, and of applying the sanctions of the law, authorized to exercise its powers in due course of law at times and places previously determined by lawful authority. Isbill v. Stovall, Tex.Civ.App., 92 S.W.2d 1067, 1070.

An incorporeal, political being, composed of one or more judges, who sit at fixed times and places, attended by proper officers, pursuant to lawful authority, for the administration of justice. State v. Le Blond, 108 Ohio St. 126, 140 N.E. 510, 512. An organized body with defined powers, meeting at certain times and places for the hearing and decision of causes and other matters brought before it, and aided in this, its proper business, by its proper officers, viz., attorneys and counsel to present and manage the business, clerks to record and attest its acts and decisions, and ministerial officers to execute its commands, and secure due order in its proceedings. Ex parte Gardner, 22 Nev. 280, 39 P. 570; Hertzen v. Hertzen, 104 Or. 423, 208 P. 580, 582.

It is a passive forum for adjusting disputes and has no power to investigate facts or to initiate proceedings. Sale v. Railroad Commission, 15 Cal.2d 612, 104 P.2d 38, 41.

The place where justice is judicially administered. Co. Litt. 58*a*; 3 Bl. Comm. 23. Railroad Co. v. Harden, 113 Ga. 456, 38 S.E. 950; Croft v. Croft, 119 N.J.Eq. 468, 182 A. 853.

The judge, or the body of judges, presiding over a court.

The words "court" and "judge," or "judges," are frequently used in statutes as synonymous. When used with reference to orders made by the court or judges, they are to be so understood. State v. Caywood, 96 Iowa, 367, 65 N.W. 385; Sale v. Railroad Commission, 15 Cal.2d 612, 104 P.2d 38, 41.

The word "court" is often employed in statutes otherwise than in its strict technical sense, and is applied to various tribunals not judicial in their character, State v. Howat, 107 Kan. 423, 191 P. 585, 589; for example, in New Jersey, the "court of pardons"; In re Court of Pardons, 97 N.J.Eq. 555, 129 A. 624, 625.

Classification

Courts may be classified and divided according to several methods, the following being the more usual:

Courts of record and **courts not of record.** The former being those whose acts and judicial proceedings are enrolled, or recorded, for a perpetual memory and testimony, and which have power to fine or imprison for contempt. Error lies to their judgments, and they generally possess a seal. Courts not of record are those of inferior dignity, which have no power to fine or imprison, and in which the proceedings are not enrolled or recorded. 3 Bl. Comm. 24; 3 Steph. Comm. 383; The Thomas Fletcher, C.C.Ga., 24 F. 481; Ex parte Thistleton, 52 Cal. 225; Erwin v. U. S., D.C.Ga., 37 F. 488, 2 L.R.A. 229; Heininger v. Davis, 96 Ohio St. 205, 117 N.E. 229, 231.

A "court of record" is a judicial tribunal having attributes and exercising functions independently of the person of the magistrate designated generally to hold it, and proceeding according to the course of common law, its acts and proceedings being enrolled for a perpetual memorial. Jones v. Jones, 188 Mo.App. 220, 175 S.W. 227, 229; Ex parte Gladhill, 8 Metc., Mass., 171, per Shaw, C. J. See, also, Ledwith v. Rosalsky, 244 N.Y. 406, 155 N.E. 688, 689.

Courts may be at the same time of record for some purposes and not of record for others. Lester v. Redmond, 6 Hill, N.Y., 590; Ex parte Gladhill, 8 Metc., Mass., 168.

Superior and **inferior courts.** The former being courts of general original jurisdiction in the first instance, and which exercise a control or supervision over a system of lower courts, either by appeal, error, or *certiorari;* the latter being courts of small or restricted jurisdiction, and subject to the review or correction of higher courts. Sometimes the former term is used to denote a particular group or system of courts of high powers, and all others are called "inferior courts."

To constitute a court a superior court as to any class of actions, within the common-law meaning of that term, its jurisdiction of such actions must be unconditional, so that the only thing requisite to enable the court to take cognizance of them is the acquisition of jurisdiction of the persons of the parties. Simons v. De Bare, 4 Bosw., N.Y., 547.

An inferior court is a court whose judgments or decrees can be reviewed, on appeal or writ of error, by a higher tribunal, whether that tribunal be the circuit or supreme court. Nugent v. State, 18 Ala. 521.

Civil and **criminal courts.** The former being such as are established for the adjudication of controversies between subject and subject, or the ascertainment, enforcement, and redress of private rights; the latter, such as are charged with the administration of the criminal laws, and the punishment of wrongs to the public.

Equity courts and **law courts.** The former being such as possess the jurisdiction of a chancellor, apply the rules and principles of chancery law, and follow the procedure in equity; the latter, such as have no equitable powers, but administer justice according to the rules and practice of the common law.

As to the division of courts according to their *jurisdiction,* see Jurisdiction.

As to several names or kinds of courts not specifically described in the titles immediately following, see Arches Court, Appellate, Circuit Courts, Consistory Courts, County, Customary Court-Baron, Ecclesiastical Courts, Federal Courts, Forest Courts, High Commission Court, Instance Court, Justice Court, Justiciary Court, Legislative Courts, Maritime Court, Mayor's Court, Moot Court, Municipal Court, Orphans' Court, Police Court, Prerogative Court, Prize Court, Probate Court, Superior Courts, Supreme Court, and Surrogate's Court.

As to **court-hand, court-house, court-lands, court rolls, courtyard,** see those titles in their alphabetical order *infra.*

General

Court above, court below. In appellate practice, the "court above" is the one to which a cause is removed for review, whether by appeal, writ of error, or certiorari; while the "court below" is the one from which the case is removed. Going v. Schnell, 6 Ohio Dec. 933.

Court in bank. A meeting of all the judges of a court, usually for the purpose of hearing arguments on demurrers, points reserved, motions for new trial, etc., as distinguished from sessions of the same court presided over by a single judge or justice.

Court of competent jurisdiction. One having power and authority of law at the time of acting to do the particular act. Ex parte Plaistridge, 68 Okl. 256, 173 P. 646, 647.

One having jurisdiction under the state Constitution and laws to determine the question in controversy. Texas Employers' Ins. Ass'n v. Nunamaker, Tex.Civ.App., 267 S.W. 749, 751. A court for the administration of justice as established by the Constitution or statute. Bradley v. Town of Bloomfield, 85 N.J.Law, 506, 89 A. 1009.

Court of limited jurisdiction. When a court of general jurisdiction proceeds under a special statute, it is a "court of limited jurisdiction" for the purpose of that proceeding, and its jurisdiction must affirmatively appear. Osage Oil & Refining Co. v. Interstate Pipe Co., 124 Okl. 7, 253 P. 66, 71.

De facto court. One established, organized, and exercising its judicial functions under authority of a statute apparently valid, though such statute may be in fact unconstitutional and may be afterwards so adjudged; or a court established and acting under the authority of a *de facto* government. 1 Bl. Judgm. § 173; In re Manning, 139 U.S. 504, 11 S.Ct. 624, 35 L.Ed. 264; Gildemeister v. Lindsay, 212 Mich. 299, 180 N.W. 633, 635.

Full court. A session of a court, which is attended by all the judges or justices composing it.

Spiritual courts. In English law. The ecclesiastical courts, or courts Christian. See 3 Bl. Comm. 61.

COURT–BARON. In English law. A court which, although not one of record, is incident to every manor, and cannot be severed therefrom. It was ordained for the maintenance of the services and duties stipulated for by lords of manors, and for the purpose of determining actions of a personal nature, where the debt or damage was under forty shillings. Wharton; 1 Poll. & Maitl. Hist. E. L. 580.

Customary court-baron is one appertaining entirely to copyholders. 3 Bl.Comm. 33.

Freeholders' court-baron is one held before the freeholders who owe suit and service to the manor. It is the court-baron proper.

Coke (1st Inst. 58*a*) speaks of the Court Baron as being of the two natures just indicated. Blackstone, 3 Comm. 33, says that, though in their nature distinct, they are frequently confounded together. Later writers doubt if there were two courts; 1 Poll. & Maitl.Hist.E.L. 580.

COURT CHRISTIAN. The ecclesiastical courts in England are often so called, as distinguished from the civil courts. 1 Bl. Comm. 83; 3 Bl. Comm. 64; 3 Steph. Comm. 430.

COURT FOR CONSIDERATION OF CROWN CASES RESERVED. A court established by St. 11 & 12 Vict. c. 78, composed of such of the judges of the superior courts of Westminster as were able to attend, for the consideration of questions of law reserved by any judge in a court of oyer and terminer, gaol delivery, or quarter sessions, before which a prisoner had been found guilty by verdict. Such question is stated in the form of a special case. Mozley & Whiteley; 4 Steph. Comm. 442. The trial judge was empowered to "state a case" for the opinion of that court. He could not be compelled to do so, and only a question of law could be raised. If the court considered that the point had been wrongly decided at the trial, the conviction would be quashed. By Act of 1907, the Court of Criminal Appeal was created and the Court for Crown Cases Reserved was abolished.

COURT FOR DIVORCE AND MATRIMONIAL CAUSES. This court was established by St. 20 & 21 Vict. c. 85, which transferred to it all jurisdiction then exercisable by any ecclesiastical court in England, in matters matrimonial, and also gave it new powers. The court consisted of the lord chancellor, the three chiefs, and three senior puisne judges of the common-law courts, and the judge ordinary, who together constituted, and still constitute, the "full court." The judge ordinary heard almost all matters in the first instance. By the judicature act, 1873, § 3, the jurisdiction of the court was transferred to the supreme court of judicature. Sweet.

COURT FOR THE CORRECTION OF ERRORS. The style of a court having jurisdiction for review, by appeal or writ of error. The name was formerly used in New York and South Carolina.

COURT FOR THE RELIEF OF INSOLVENT DEBTORS. In English law. A local court which had its sittings in London only, which received the petitions of insolvent debtors, and decided upon the question of granting a discharge. See 3 Steph. Com. 426; 4 *id.* 287. Abolished by the Bankruptcy Act of 1861.

COURT FOR THE TRIAL OF IMPEACHMENTS. A tribunal empowered to try any officer of government or other person brought to its bar by the process of impeachment. In England, the house of lords constitutes such a court; in the United States, the senate; and in the several states, usually the upper house of the legislative assembly.

COURT-HAND. In old English practice. The peculiar hand in which the records of courts were written from the earliest period down to the reign of George II. Its characteristics were great strength, compactness, and undeviating uniformity; and its use undoubtedly gave to the ancient record its acknowledged superiority over the modern, in the important quality of durability.

The writing of this hand, with its peculiar abbreviations and contractions, constituted, while it was in use, an art of no little importance, being an indispensable part of the profession of "clerkship," as it was called. Two sizes of it were employed, a large and a small hand; the former, called "great court-hand," being used for initial words or clauses, the *placita* of records, etc. Burrill.

COURT-HOUSE. The building occupied for the public sessions of a court, with its various offices. The building occupied and appropriated according to law for the holding of courts. Board of Sup'rs of Stone County v. O'Neal, 130 Miss. 57, 93 So. 483, 484. Johnson City Buick Co. v. Johnson, 165 Tenn. 349, 54 S.W.2d 946.

The term may be used of a place temporarily occupied for the sessions of a court, though not the regular courthouse. Harris v. State, 72 Miss. 960, 18 So. 387, 33 L.R.A. 85; Vigo County v. Stout, 136 Ind. 53, 35 N.E. 683, 22 L.R.A. 398.

The word may be synonymous with "county site" and signify the seat of government. Board of Revenue of Jefferson County v. Huey, 195 Ala. 83, 70 So. 744, 746.

COURT, HUNDRED. See Hundred Court.

COURT-LANDS. Domains or lands kept in the lord's hands to serve his family.

COURT-LEET. The name of an English court of record held once in the year, and not oftener, within a particular hundred, lordship, or manor, before the steward of the leet; being the king's court granted by charter to the lords of those hundreds or manors. Its office was to view the frankpledges,—that is, the freemen within the liberty; to present by jury crimes happening within the jurisdiction; and to punish trivial misdemeanors. It has now, however, for the most part, fallen into total desuetude; though in some manors a court-leet is still periodically held for the transaction of the administrative business of the manor. Mozley & Whitley; Odgers, C. L. 965; Powell, Courts Leet; 1 Reeve, Hist. Eng. Law; Inderwick, King's Peace, 11; 1 Poll. & Maitl. 568; 4 Steph. Com. 306.

COURT-MARTIAL. A military court, convened under authority of government and the Uniform Code of Military Justice, 10 U.S.C.A. § 801 et seq., for trying and punishing offenses committed by members of the armed forces.

Such courts exist and have their jurisdiction by virtue of the military law, the court being constituted and empowered to act in each instance by authority from a commanding officer.

COURT OF ADMIRALTY. A court having jurisdiction of causes arising under the rules of admiralty law. See Admiralty.

High Court of Admiralty. In English law. This was a court which exercised jurisdiction in prize cases, and had general jurisdiction in maritime causes, on the instance side. Its proceedings were usually *in rem,* and its practice and principles derived in large measure from the civil law. The judicature acts of 1873 transferred all the powers and jurisdiction of this tribunal to the probate, divorce, and admiralty division of the high court of justice.

COURT OF ANCIENT DEMESNE. In English law. A court of peculiar constitution, held by a bailiff appointed by the king, in which alone the tenants of the king's demesne could be impleaded. 2 Burrows, 1046; 1 Spence, Eq.Jur. 100; 2 Bl. Comm. 99; 1 Steph. Comm. 224; 1 Poll. & Maitl. 367.

COURT OF APPEAL, HIS MAJESTY'S. The chief appellate tribunal of England. It was established by the judicature acts of 1873 and 1875, and is invested with the jurisdiction formerly exercised by the court of appeal in chancery, the exchequer chamber, the judicial committee of the privy council in admiralty and lunacy appeals, and with general appellate jurisdiction from the high court of justice.

COURT OF APPEALS. In American law. An appellate tribunal which, in Kentucky, Maryland, the District of Columbia, and New York, is the court of last resort. In Virginia and West Virginia, it is known as the "supreme court of appeals"; in Connecticut, the Supreme Court of Errors; in Massachusetts and Maine, the Supreme Judicial Court. In other states the court of last resort is known as the Supreme Court. In Texas the Courts of Civil Appeals are inferior to the supreme court.

The United States is divided into eleven judicial circuits in each of which there is established a court of appeals known as the United States Court of Appeals for the circuit. 28 U.S.C.A. §§ 41, 43.

COURT OF APPEALS IN CASES OF CAPTURE. A court erected by act of congress under the articles of confederation which preceded the adoption of the constitution. It had appellate jurisdiction in prize causes.

COURT OF ARBITRATION OF THE CHAMBER OF COMMERCE. A court of arbitrators, created for the convenience of merchants in the city of New York, by act of the legislature of New York. It decides disputes between members of the chamber of commerce, and between members and outside merchants who voluntarily submit themselves to the jurisdiction of the court.

COURT OF ARCHDEACON. The most inferior of the English ecclesiastical courts, from which an appeal generally lies to that of the bishop (i. e., to the Consistory Court). 3 Bl. Comm. 64; 1 Holdsw. Hist. E. L. 369.

COURT OF ASSISTANTS. A court in Massachusetts organized in 1630, consisting of the governor, deputy governor and assistants. It exercised the whole power both legislative and judicial of the colony and an extensive chancery jurisdiction as well. S. D. Wilson in 18 Am.L.Rev. 226.

COURT OF ATTACHMENTS. The lowest of the three courts held in the forests. It has fallen into total disuse.

It was held before the verderers of the forest once in every forty days, to view the attachments by the foresters for offences against the vert and the venison. It had cognizance only of small trespasses. Larger ones were enrolled and heard by the Justices in Eyre. 1 Holdsw. Hist.E.L. 343.

COURT OF AUDIENCE. An ecclesiastical court, in which the primates once exercised in person a considerable part of their jurisdiction. Such courts seem to be now obsolete, or at least to be only used on the rare occurrence of the trial of a bishop. Phillim. Ecc. Law, 1201, 1204; 1 Holdsw. Hist. E. L. 371.

COURT OF AUGMENTATION. An English court created in the time of Henry VIII (27 Hen. VIII, c. 27), with jurisdiction over the property and revenue of certain religious foundations, which had been made over to the king by act of parliament, and over suits relating to the same.

It was called "The Court of the Augmentations of the Revenues of the King's Crown" (from the *augmentation* of the revenues of the crown derived from the suppression of the monasteries), and was dissolved in the reign of Queen Mary, but the Office of Augmentation remained long after; the records of the court are now at the Public Record Office. Cowell.

COURT OF BANKRUPTCY. An English court of record, having original and appellate jurisdiction in matters of bankruptcy, and invested with both legal and equitable powers for that purpose. The Bankrupt Law Consolidation Act, 1849. By the judicature acts, 1873 and 1875, the court of bankruptcy was consolidated into the supreme court of judicature.

In the United States, the Bankruptcy Act, § 1 (10), 11 U.S.C.A. § 1(10), as amended, provides that " 'courts of bankruptcy' shall include the district courts of the United States and of the Territories and possessions to which this title is or may hereafter be applicable, and the District Court of the United States for the District of Columbia."

COURT OF BROTHERHOOD. An assembly of the mayors or other chief officers of the principal towns of the Cinque Ports in England, originally administering the chief powers of those ports, now almost extinct. Cent. Dict.

COURT OF CHANCERY. A court having the jurisdiction of a chancellor; a court administering equity and proceeding according to the forms and principles of equity. In England, prior to the judicature acts, the style of the court possessing the largest equitable powers and jurisdiction was the "high court of chancery." In some of the United States, the title "court of chancery" is applied to a court possessing general equity powers, distinct from the courts of common law. Parmeter v. Bourne, 8 Wash. 45, 35 P. 586; Bull v. International Power Co., 84 N.J.Eq. 209, 93 A. 86, 88.

The terms "equity" and "chancery," "court of equity" and "court of chancery," are constantly used as synonymous in the United States. It is presumed that this custom arises from the circumstance that the equity jurisdiction which is exercised by the courts of the various states is assimilated to that possessed by the English courts of chancery. Indeed, in some of the states it is made identical therewith by statute, so far as conformable to our institutions. Wagner v. Armstrong, 93 Ohio St. 443, 113 N.E. 397, 401.

COURT OF CHIVALRY. In English law. The name of a court anciently held as a court of honor merely, before the earl-marshal, and as a criminal court before the lord high constable, jointly with the earl-marshal. (But it is also said that this court was held by the constable, and after that office reverted to the crown in the time of Henry VIII., by the earl-marshal. Davis, Mil. Law 13.) 3 Bl.Comm. 68; 4 Broom & H. Comm. 360, note; 3 Bl. Comm. 103; 3 Steph. Comm. 335, note *l*; 7 Mod. 137.

It had jurisdiction as to contracts and other matters touching deeds of arms or war, as well as pleas of life or member. It also corrected encroachments in matters of coat-armor, precedency, and other distinctions of families. It is now grown entirely out of use, on account of the feebleness of its jurisdiction and want of power to enforce its judgments, as it could neither fine nor imprison, not being a court of record.

COURT OF CLAIMS. One of the courts of the United States, established in 1855. U. S. v. Klein, 13 Wall., U.S., 128, 144, 20 L.Ed. 519. It consists of a chief justice and four associates, and holds one annual session. It is located at Washington. Its jurisdiction extends to all claims against the United States arising out of any contract with the government or based on an act of congress or regulation of the executive, and all claims referred to it by either house of congress, as well as to claims for exoneration by a disbursing officer. Its judgments are, in certain cases, reviewable by the United States supreme court. It has no equity powers. Its decisions are reported and published.

This name is also given, in some of the states, either to a special court or to the ordinary county court sitting "as a court of claims," having the special duty of auditing and ascertaining the claims against the county and expenses incurred by it, and providing for their payment by appropriations out of the county levy or annual tax. Meriweather v. Muhlenburg County Court, 120 U.S. 354, 7 S.Ct. 563, 30 L.Ed. 653.

COURT OF COMMISSIONERS OF SEWERS. The name of certain English courts created by commission under the great seal pursuant to the statute of sewers (23 Hen. VIII. c. 5).

COURT OF COMMON PLEAS. In English law. One of the four superior courts at Westminster, which existed up to the passing of the judicature acts. It was also styled the "Common Bench." It was one of the courts derived from the breaking up of the *aula regis,* and had exclusive jurisdiction of all real actions and of *communia placita,* or common pleas, *i. e.,* between subject and subject. It was presided over by a chief justice with four puisne judges (later five, by virtue of 31 & 32 Vict. c. 125, § 11, subsec. 8). Appeals lay anciently to the king's bench, but afterwards to the exchequer chamber. See 3 Bl.Comm. 37, et seq. Its jurisdiction was altogether confined to civil matters, having no cognizance in criminal cases, and was concurrent with that of the queen's bench and exchequer in personal actions and ejectment. Wharton.

In American law. The name sometimes given to a court of original and general jurisdiction for the trial of issues of fact and law according to the principles of the common law. Moore v. Barry, 30 S.C. 530, 9 S.E. 589, 4 L.R.A. 294.

COURT OF COMMON PLEAS FOR THE CITY AND COUNTY OF NEW YORK. The oldest court in the state of New York, no longer in existence.

COURT OF CONCILIATION. A court which proposes terms of adjustment, so as to avoid litigation. Kashefsky v. Futernick, 153 Misc. 733, 276 N.Y.S. 253.

COURT OF CONSCIENCE. The same as courts of request, (*q. v.*). This name is also frequently applied to the courts of equity or of chancery, not as a name but as a description. Harper v. Clayton, 84 Md. 346, 35 A. 1083, 35 L.R.A. 211. And see Conscience.

COURT OF CONVOCATION. In English ecclesiastical law. A court, or assembly, comprising all the high officials of each province and representatives of the minor clergy. It is in the nature of an ecclesiastical parliament; and, so far as its judicial functions extend, it has jurisdiction of cases of heresy, schism, and other purely ecclesiastical matters. An appeal lies to the king in council. 2 & 3 Will. IV. c. 92; Cowell; Bac. Abr. *Ecclesiastical Courts,* A, 1; 1 Bla. Comm. 279; 2 Steph. Com. 525, 668; 2 Burn, Eccl. Law, 18. Convocation exercises no jurisdiction at the present day. 1 Holdsw. Hist. E. L. 373.

COURT OF COUNTY COMMISSIONERS. In some states, a court of record in each county. Thus, in Alabama, it is composed of the judge of probate, as principal judge, and four commissioners, who are elected at the times prescribed by law, and hold office for four years.

COURT OF CUSTOMS AND PATENT APPEALS. The title given by Act Mar. 2, 1929, c. 488, § 1, 45 Stat. 1475, to a court of the United States created by Act Aug. 5, 1909, c. 6, § 28, 36 Stat. 91, 105, and then known as the Court of Customs Appeals, consisting of a presiding judge and four associate judges. In patent and trade-mark cases it has the appellate jurisdiction which prior to April 1, 1929, was vested in the Court of Appeals of the District of Columbia. Act Mar. 2, 1929, c. 488, § 2 (*a, d*), 45 Stat. 1476. As to its jurisdiction over appeals from the "Customs Court," see that title.

COURT OF DELEGATES. An English tribunal composed of delegates appointed by royal commission, and formerly the great court of appeal in all ecclesiastical causes. The powers of the court were, by 2 & 3 Wm. IV. c. 92, transferred to the privy council. Brown; 3 Bl. Comm. 66; 1 Holdsw. Hist. E. L. 373.

A commission of review was formerly granted, in extraordinary cases, to revise a sentence of the court of delegates, when that court had apparently been led into material error.

COURT OF EQUITY. A court which has jurisdiction in equity, which administers justice and decides controversies in accordance with the rules, principles, and precedents of equity, and which follows the forms and procedure of chancery; as distinguished from a court having the jurisdiction, rules, principles, and practice of the common law. Thomas v. Phillips, 4 Smedes & M., Miss., 423.

COURT OF ERROR. An expression applied especially to the court of exchequer chamber and the house of lords, as taking cognizance of *error* brought. Mozley & Whitley; 3 Steph. Comm. 333. It is applied in some of the United States to the court of last resort in the state; and in its most general sense denotes any court having power to review the decisions of lower courts on appeal, error, *certiorari*, or other process. See Court of Appeals.

COURT OF ERRORS AND APPEALS. The court of last resort in the state of New Jersey is so named. Formerly, the same title was given to the highest court of appeal in New York.

COURT OF EXCHEQUER. In English law. A very ancient court of record, set up by William the Conqueror as a part of the *aula regis*, and afterwards one of the four superior courts at Westminster. It was, however, inferior in rank to both the king's bench and the common pleas. It was presided over by a chief baron and four puisne barons. It was originally the king's treasury, and was charged with keeping the king's accounts and collecting the royal revenues. But pleas between subject and subject were anciently heard there, until this was forbidden by the *Articula super Chartas*, (1290,) after which its jurisdiction as a court only extended to revenue cases arising out of the non-payment or withholding of debts to the crown. But the privilege of suing and being sued in this court was extended to the king's accountants, and later, by the use of a convenient fiction to the effect that the plaintiff was the king's debtor or accountant, the court was thrown open to all suitors in personal actions. The exchequer had formerly both an equity side and a common-law side, but its equity jurisdiction was taken away by the statute 5 Vict. c. 5, (1842,) and transferred to the court of chancery. The judicature act (1873) transferred the business and jurisdiction of this court to the "Exchequer Division" of the "High Court of Justice."

In Scotch law. A court which formerly had jurisdiction of matters of revenue, and a limited jurisdiction over cases between the crown and its vassals where no questions of title were involved.

COURT OF EXCHEQUER CHAMBER. The name of a former English court of appeal, intermediate between the superior courts of common law and the house of lords. When sitting as a court of appeal from any one of the three superior courts of common law, it was composed of judges of the other two courts. 3 Bl.Comm. 56, 57; 3 Steph.Comm. 333, 356. By the judicature act (1873) the jurisdiction of this court is transferred to the court of appeal.

COURT OF FACULTIES. A tribunal of the archbishop in England.

It does not hold pleas in any suits, but creates rights to pews, monuments, and other mortuary matters. It had also various other powers under 25 Hen. VIII. c. 21. Co. 4th Inst. 337; 2 Chit.Gen.Pr. 507.

COURT OF FIRST INSTANCE. A court of primary jurisdiction. Courts of this title may be found in the jurisprudence of the Philippine Islands. 15 C.J. 688.

COURT OF GENERAL QUARTER SESSIONS OF THE PEACE. In American law. A court of criminal jurisdiction in New Jersey.

In English law. A court of criminal jurisdiction, in England, held in each county once in every quarter of a year, but in the county of Middlesex twice a month. 4 Steph. Comm. 317–320. When held at other times than quarterly, the sessions are called "general sessions of the peace." See 2 Odgers, C.L. 966.

COURT OF GENERAL SESSIONS. The name given in some states to a court of general original jurisdiction in criminal cases.

COURT OF GREAT SESSIONS IN WALES. A court formerly held in Wales; abolished by 11 Geo. IV. and 1 Wm. IV. c. 70, and the Welsh judicature incorporated with that of England. 3 Steph. Comm. 317, note; 3 Bla. Comm. 77.

COURT OF GUESTLING. An assembly of the members of the Court of Brotherhood *(supra)* together with other representatives of the corporate members of the Cinque Ports, invited to sit with the mayors of the seven principal towns. Cent. Dict.

COURT OF HIGH COMMISSION. In English law. An ecclesiastical court of formidable jurisdiction, for the vindication of the peace and dignity of the church, by reforming, ordering, and correcting the ecclesiastical state and persons, and all manner of errors, heresies, schisms, abuses, offenses, contempts, and enormities. 3 Bl. Comm. 67. It was erected by St. 1 Eliz. c. 1, and abolished by 16 Car. I, c. 11. 1 Holdsw. Hist. E. L. 375.

COURT OF HONOR. A court having jurisdiction to hear and redress injuries or affronts to a man's honor or personal dignity, of a nature not cognizable by the ordinary courts of law, or encroachments upon his rights in respect to heraldry, coat-armor, right of precedence, and the like. It was one of the functions of the Court of Chivalry (*q. v.*) in England to sit and act as a court of honor. 3 Bl. Comm. 104.

The name is also given in some European countries to a tribunal of army officers (more or less distinctly recognized by law as a "court") convened for the purpose of inquiring into complaints affecting the honor of brother officers and punishing derelictions from the code of honor and deciding on the causes and occasions for fighting duels, in which officers are concerned, and the manner of conducting them.

COURT OF HUSTINGS. In English law. The county court of London, held before the mayor, recorder, and sheriff, but of which the recorder, is, in effect, the sole judge. No actions can be brought in this court that are merely personal. 3 Steph.Comm. 293, n.; 449, note *l*; 3 Bla.Comm. 80, n.; Madox, Hist. Exch. c. 20; Co. 2d Inst. 327. Since the abolition of all real and mixed actions except ejectment, the jurisdiction of this court has fallen into comparative desuetude. Pulling on Cust. Lond.

In American Law. A local court in some parts of Virginia. Smith v. Commonwealth, 6 Grat. 696.

COURT OF INQUIRY. In English law. A court sometimes appointed by the crown to ascertain whether it be proper to resort to extreme measures against a person charged before a court-martial. 2 Steph.Comm. 590; 1 Coler.Bla.Comm. 418, n.; 2 Brod. & B. 130. Also a court for hearing the complaints of private soldiers. Moz. & W. Dict.; Simmons, Cts.Mart. § 341.

In American law. Formerly, a court constituted by authority of the articles of war, invested with the power to examine into the nature of any transaction of, or accusation or imputation against, any officer or soldier, when demanded by him. Rev.St. § 1342, arts. 115, 116. Repealed by Act June 4, 1920, c. 227, § 4, 41 Stat. 812.

They were not strictly courts, having no power to try and determine guilt or innocence. They were rather agencies created by statute to investigate facts and report thereon. They could not compel the attendance of witnesses nor require them to testify. Davis, Mil.Law 220.

COURT OF JUSTICE SEAT. In English law. The principal of the forest courts. Called also Court of the Chief Justice in Eyre (*q. v.*).

COURT OF JUSTICIARY. A Scotch court of general criminal jurisdiction of all offenses committed in any part of Scotland, both to try causes and to review decisions of inferior criminal courts. It is composed of five lords of session with the lord president or justice-clerk as president. It also has appellate jurisdiction in civil causes involving small amounts. An appeal lies to the house of lords.

COURT OF KING'S BENCH. In English law. The supreme court of common law in the kingdom, now merged in the high court of justice under the judicature act of 1873, § 16.

It was one of the successors of the *curia regis* and received its name, it is said, because the king formerly sat in it in person. During the reign of a queen it was called the Queen's Bench, and during Cromwell's Protectorate it was called the Upper Bench.

COURT OF LAW. In a wide sense, any duly constituted tribunal administering the laws of the state or nation; in a narrower sense, a court proceeding according to the course of the common law and governed by its rules and principles, as contrasted with a "court of equity."

COURT OF LODEMANAGE. An ancient court of the Cinque Ports, having jurisdiction in maritime matters, and particularly over pilots (lodemen).

COURT OF MAGISTRATES AND FREEHOLDERS. In American law. The name of a court formerly established in South Carolina for the trial of slaves and free persons of color for criminal offenses.

COURT OF MARSHALSEA. In English law, the court or seat of the marshal. A court originally held before the steward and marshal of the king's house, instituted to administer justice between the king's domestic servants. It had jurisdiction of all trespasses committed within the verge of the king's court, where one of the parties was of the royal household; and of all debts and contracts, when both parties were of that establishment. It was abolished by 12 & 13 Vict. c. 101, § 13. Mozley & Whitley.

COURT OF NISI PRIUS. In American law. Though this term is frequently used as a general designation of any court exercising general, original jurisdiction in civil cases, (being used interchangeably with "trial-court,") it belonged as a legal title only to a court which formerly existed in the city and county of Philadelphia, and which was presided over by one of the judges of the supreme court of Pennsylvania. This court was abolished by the constitution of 1874. See Courts of Assize and Nisi Prius.

COURT OF ORDINARY. In some of the United States (*e. g.*, Georgia) the name given to the probate or surrogate's court, or the court having the usual jurisdiction in respect to the proving of wills and the administration of decedents' estates. Veach v. Rice, 131 U.S. 293, 9 S.Ct. 730, 33 L.Ed. 163. Such a court formerly existed in New Jersey, South Carolina, and Texas. 2 Kent 409.

COURT OF ORPHANS. In English law. The court of the lord mayor and aldermen of London, which has the care of those orphans whose parent died in London and was free of the city. It is now said to be fallen into disuse. 2 Steph. Comm. 313; Pull. Cust. Lond. 196, *Orphans' Court.*

In American law. In Pennsylvania (and perhaps some other states) the name "orphans' court" is applied to that species of tribunal which is elsewhere known as the "probate court" or "surrogate's court."

COURT OF OYER AND TERMINER. In English law. A court for the trial of cases of treason and felony. The commissioners of assise and *nisi prius* are judges selected by the king and appointed and authorized under the great seal, including usually two of the judges at Westminster, and sent out twice a year into most of the counties of England, for the trial (with a jury of the county) of causes then depending at Westminster, both civil and criminal. They sit by virtue of several commissions, each of which, in reality, constitutes them a separate and distinct court. The commission of *oyer and terminer* gives them authority for the trial of treasons and felonies; that of *general gaol delivery* empowers them to try every prisoner then in gaol for whatever offense; so that, altogether, they possess full criminal jurisdiction.

In American law. This name is generally used (sometimes, with additions) as the title, or part of the title, of a state court of criminal jurisdiction, or of the criminal branch of a court of general jurisdiction, being commonly applied to such courts as may try *felonies*, or the higher grades of crime. Such courts exist in Delaware and Pennsylvania. They were abolished in New York and New Jersey in 1895.

COURT OF OYER AND TERMINER AND GENERAL GAOL (or JAIL) DELIVERY. In American law. A court of criminal jurisdiction in the state of Pennsylvania. It is held at the same time with the court of quarter sessions, as a general rule, and by the same judges. Const.Pa. art. 5, § 1; 17 P.S. §§ 371, 391, 471.

In English law. A tribunal for the examination and trial of criminals. 3 Steph. Comm. 352.

COURT OF PALACE AT WESTMINSTER. This court had jurisdiction of personal actions arising within twelve miles of the palace at Whitehall. Abolished by 12 & 13 Vict. c. 101, 3 Steph. Comm. 317, note. See Court of the Steward and Marshal.

COURT OF PASSAGE. An inferior court, possessing a very ancient jurisdiction over causes of action arising within the borough of Liverpool. It appears to have been also called the "Borough Court of Liverpool." It has the same jurisdiction in admiralty matters as the Lancashire county court. Rosc. Adm. 75.

COURT OF PECULIARS. A spiritual court in England, being a branch of, and annexed to, the Court of Arches. It has a jurisdiction over all those parishes dispersed through the province of Canterbury, in the midst of other dioceses, which are exempt from the ordinary's jurisdiction, and subject to the metropolitan only. All ecclesiastical causes arising within these *peculiar* or exempt jurisdictions are originally cognizable by this court, from which an appeal lies to the Court of Arches. 3 Steph. Comm. 431; 4 Reeve, Eng. Law, 104. Most of such courts have been abolished by legislation. 1 Holdsw. Hist. Eng. Law 352. See, also, Arches Court.

COURT OF PIEPOUDRE. (Also spelled Pipowder, Pie Powder, Py-Powder, Piedpoudre, etc.) The lowest (and most expeditious) of the courts of justice known to the older law of England. It is supposed (by Cowell and Blount) to have been so called from the dusty feet of the suitors. For another conjecture as to the origin of the name, see Co. 4th Inst. 472. It was a court of record incident to every fair and market, was held by the steward, and had jurisdiction to administer justice for all commercial injuries and minor offenses done in that same fair or market, (not a preceding one.) Inderwick, King's Peace 105. An appeal lay to the courts at Westminster. This court long ago fell into disuse. 3 Bl. Comm. 32; Barrington, Stat. 337; 3 Steph. Comm. 317, n.; Skene, *de verb. sig. Pede pulverosus*; Bracton 334; 22 L.Q.R. 244; 1 Holdsw. Hist. E. L. 309. See, however, Odgers, C. L. 1021.

COURT OF PLEAS. A court of the county palatine of Durham, having a local common-law jurisdiction. It was abolished by the judicature act, which transferred its jurisdiction to the high court. Jud.Act 1873, § 16; 3 Bl.Comm. 79.

COURT OF POLICIES OF ASSURANCE. A court established by statute 43 Eliz. c. 12, to determine in a summary way all causes between merchants, concerning policies of insurance. Crabb, Eng. Law, 503. The court was formally abolished by stat. 26 & 27 Vict. c. 125. 3 Bl.Comm. 74; 3 Steph. Comm. 317, n.

COURT OF PRIVATE LAND CLAIMS. A federal court created by act of Congress in 1891 (26 Stat. 854), to hear and determine claims by private parties to lands within the public domain, where such claims originated under Spanish or Mexican grants, and had not already been confirmed by Congress or otherwise adjudicated. The existence and authority of this court were to cease and determine at the end of the year 1895.

COURT OF PROBATE. In English law. The name of a court established in 1857, under the probate act of that year, (20 & 21 Vict. c. 77,) to be held in London, to which court was transferred the testamentary jurisdiction of the ecclesiastical courts. 2 Steph. Comm. 192. By the judicature acts, this court is merged in the high court of justice.

In American law. A court having jurisdiction over the probate of wills, the grant of administration, and the supervision of the management and settlement of the estates of decedents, including the collection of assets, the allowance of claims, and the distribution of the estate. In some states the probate courts also have jurisdiction of the estates of minors, including the appointment of guardians and the settlement of their accounts, and of the estates of lunatics, habitual drunkards, and spendthrifts. Pons v. Pons, 132 La. 370, 61 So. 406, 407. And in some states these courts possess a limited jurisdiction in civil and criminal cases. They are also called in some jurisdictions "orphans' courts" and "surrogate's courts."

COURT OF PYPOWDER, PY-POWDER, or PY-POWDERS. See Court of Piepoudre.

COURT OF QUARTER SESSIONS OF THE PEACE. In American law. A court of criminal jurisdiction in the state of Pennsylvania, having power to try misdemeanors, and exercising certain functions of an administrative nature. There is one such court in each county of the state. Its sessions are, in general, held at the same time and by the same judges as the *court of oyer and terminer and general jail delivery*. Const.Pa. art. 5, § 1; 17 P.S. §§ 331, 361.

COURT OF QUEEN'S BENCH. See Court of King's Bench.

COURT OF RECORD. See Court, *supra*.

COURT OF REGARD. In English law. One of the forest courts, in England, held every third year, for the lawing or expeditation of dogs, to prevent them from running after deer. It is now obsolete. 3 Steph. Comm. 440; 3 Bl. Comm. 71, 72.

COURT OF SESSION. The name of the highest court of civil jurisdiction in Scotland. It was composed of fifteen judges, now of thirteen. It sits in two divisions. The lord president and three ordinary lords form the first division; the lord justice clerk and three other ordinary lords form the second division. There are five permanent lords ordinary attached equally to both divisions; the last appointed of whom officiates on the bills, *i. e.*, petitions preferred to the court during the session, and performs the other duties of junior lord ordinary. The chambers of the parliament house in which the first and second divisions hold their sittings are called the "inner house;" those in which the lords ordinary sit as single judges to hear motions and causes are collectively called the "outer house." The nomination and appointment of the judges is in the crown. Wharton.

COURT OF SESSIONS. Courts of criminal jurisdiction existing in California, New York, and one or two other of the United States.

COURT OF SHEPWAY. A court held before the lord warden of the Cinque Ports. A writ of error lay from the mayor and jurats of each port to the lord warden in this court, and thence to the queen's bench. The civil jurisdiction of the Cinque Ports is abolished by 18 & 19 Vict. c. 48.

COURT OF SPECIAL SESSIONS. A generic term, applicable to those courts which have no stated terms and are not continuous, but which are organized only for the trial of each particular case and become functus officio when judgment is rendered therein. People v. Wagner, 45 N.Y.S.2d 314, 316.

COURT OF STANNARIES. In English law. A court established in Devonshire and Cornwall, for the administration of justice among the miners and tinners, that they might not be drawn away from their business to attend suits in distant courts. The stannary court is a court of record, with a special jurisdiction. 3 Bl. Comm. 79.

COURT OF STAR CHAMBER. This was an English court of very ancient origin, but new-modeled by St. 3 Hen. VII. c. 1, and 21 Hen. VIII. c. 20, consisting of divers lords, spiritual and temporal, being privy councillors, together with two judges of the courts of common law, without the intervention of any jury. The jurisdiction extended legally over riots, perjury, misbehavior of sheriffs, and other misdemeanors contrary to the laws of the land; yet it was afterwards stretched to the asserting of all proclamations and orders of state, to the vindicating of illegal commissions and grants of monopolies; holding for honorable that which it pleased, and for just that which it profited, and becoming both a court of law to determine civil rights and a court of revenue to enrich the treasury. It was finally abolished by St. 16 Car. I, c. 10, to the general satisfaction of the whole nation. Brown.

COURT OF SURVEY. A court for the hearing of appeals by owners or masters of ships, from orders for the detention of unsafe ships, made by the English board of trade, under the merchant shipping act, 1876, § 6.

COURT OF SWEINMOTE (spelled, also, *Swainmote, Swain-gemote;* Saxon, *swang,* an attendant, a freeholder, and *mote* or *gemote,* a meeting). One of the old forest courts, held before the verderers, as judges, by the steward, thrice in every year,—the sweins or freeholders within the forest composing the jury. This court had jurisdiction to inquire into grievances and oppressions committed by the officers of the forest, and also to receive and try presentments certified from the court of attachments, certifying the cause, in turn, under the seals of the jury, in case of conviction, to the court of justice seat for the rendition of judgment. Cowell; 3 Bla. Com. 71, 72; 3 Steph. Com. 317, n. See Inderwick, King's Peace 150; Forest Laws.

COURT OF THE CHIEF JUSTICE IN EYRE. The highest of the courts of the forest, held every three years, by the chief justice, to inquire of purprestures or encroachments, assarts, or cultivation of forest land, claims to franchises, parks, warrens, and vineyards in the forest, as well as claims of the hundred, claims to the goods of felons found in the forest, and any other civil questions that might arise within the forest limits. But it had no criminal jurisdiction, except of offenses against the forest laws. It was called also the court of justice seat. Inderwick, King's Peace. Since the Restoration the forest laws have fallen into disuse. The office was abolished in 1817.

COURT OF THE CLERK OF THE MARKET. An English court of inferior jurisdiction held in every fair or market for the punishment of misdemeanors committed therein. The jurisdiction over weights and measures formerly exercised was taken away by stat. 5 & 6 Will. IV. c. 63; 9 M. & W. 747. 4 Steph. Comm. 323.

COURT OF THE CORONER. In English law. A court of record, to inquire, when any one dies in prison, or comes to a violent or sudden death, by what manner he came to his end. 4 Steph. Comm. 323; 4 Bl. Comm. 274. Now generally known as an inquest. See Coroner.

COURT OF THE COUNTIES PALATINE. In English law. A species of private court which formerly appertained to the counties palatine of Lancaster and Durham. 1 Holdsw. Hist. E. L. 47; 1 Steph. Hist. C. L. 138; Coke, 4 Inst. 239; 1 Harg. L. Tr. 378.

COURT OF THE DUCHY OF LANCASTER. A court of special jurisdiction, held before the chancellor of the duchy or his deputy, concerning all matters of equity relating to lands holden of the king in right of the duchy of Lancaster. 3 Bl. Comm. 78.

COURT OF THE EARL MARSHAL. In the reign of William the Conqueror the marshal was next in rank to the constable, in command of the army. When the constable's office ceased, his duties devolved upon the earl marshal. The military Court of the Constable came to be known as the Marshal's Court, or, in its modern form, Court-Martial. Aside from its criminal jurisdiction, it had much to do with questions relating to fiefs and military tenures, though not to property rights involved therein. Davis, Mil. Laws of U. S. 14. See Hale, Hist. C. L. 36; Grose, Mil. Antiq. See Court of Chivalry; Courts-Martial; Constable of England.

COURT OF THE LORD HIGH ADMIRAL. In the earlier part of the 14th century, the Admiral possessed a disciplinary jurisdiction over his fleet. After 1340 it is reasonable to suppose that the Admiral could hold an independent court and administer justice in piracy and other maritime cases. There were at first several admirals and several courts. From the early 15th century there was one Lord High Admiral and one Court of Admiralty. 1 Holdsw. Hist. E. L. 313.

COURT OF THE LORD HIGH STEWARD. In English law. A court instituted for the trial, during the recess of parliament, of peers indicted for treason or felony, or for misprision of either. This court is not a permanent body, but is created in modern times, when occasion requires, and for the time being, only; and the lord high steward, so constituted, with such of the temporal lords as may take the proper oath, and act, constitute the court.

All peers who have a right to sit and vote in Parliament must be summoned. They are the sole judges of fact, and the majority, which must consist of twelve at least, decides. The Lord High Steward has a vote, and is judge of all matters of law.

COURT OF THE LORD HIGH STEWARD OF THE UNIVERSITIES. In English law. A court constituted for the trial of scholars or privileged persons connected with the university at Oxford or Cambridge who are indicted for treason, felony, or mayhem. 3 Bla. Comm. 83; 4 *id.* 277; 1 Steph. Comm. 67; 3 *id.* 341; 4 *id.* 261.

COURT OF THE OFFICIAL PRINCIPAL. This court, the Court of the "Official Principal" of the Archbishop of Canterbury, is more commonly called the Arches Court, or Court of the Arches. See Arches Court.

COURT OF THE STEWARD AND MARSHAL. A high court, formerly held in England by the steward and marshal of the king's household, having jurisdiction of all actions against the king's peace within the bounds of the household for twelve miles, which circuit was called the "verge." Crabb, Eng. Law, 185. It had also jurisdiction of actions of debt and covenant, where both the parties were of the household. 2 Reeve, Eng.Law, 235, 247. This court was created by Charles I., and abolished in 1849. It was held in the borough of Southwark, and was called also the "palace court," having jurisdiction of all personal actions arising within twelve miles of the royal palace of Whitehall, exclusive of London.

COURT OF THE STEWARD OF THE KING'S HOUSEHOLD. In English law. A court which had jurisdiction of all cases of treason, misprision of treason, murder, manslaughter, bloodshed, and other malicious strikings whereby blood is shed, occurring in or within the limits of any of the palaces or houses of the king, or any other house where the royal person is abiding. It was created by statute 33 Hen. VIII. c. 12, but long ago fell into disuse. 4 Bl. Comm. 276, 277, and notes.

COURT OF WARDS AND LIVERIES. A court of record, established in England in the reign of Henry VIII. For the survey and management of the valuable fruits of tenure, a court of record was created by St. 32 Hen. VIII. c. 46, called the "Court of the King's Wards." To this was annexed, by St. 33 Hen. VIII. c. 22, the "Court of Liveries;" so that it then became the "Court of Wards and Liveries." 4 Reeve, Eng. Law, 258. This court was not only for the management of "wards," properly so called, but also of idiots and natural fools in the king's custody, and for licenses to be granted to the king's widows to marry, and fines to be made for marrying without his license. Id. 259. It was abolished by St. 12 Car. II. c. 24. Crabb, Eng. Law, 468; 4 Reeve, Hist. E. L. 259; Crabb, Hist. E. L. 468; 1 Steph. Com. 183; 4 id. 40; 2 Bla. Com. 68; 3 id. 258.

COURT ROLLS. The rolls of a manor, containing all acts relating thereto. While belonging to the lord of the manor, they are not in the nature of public books for the benefit of the tenant.

COURTS OF APPEALS. A system of courts of the United States (one in each circuit) created by act of congress, composed of three or more judges (provision being made also for the allotment of the justices of the supreme court among the circuits), and having appellate jurisdiction as defined by statute. 28 U.S.C.A. §§ 41–48, 1291–1294.

Court of Appeals of the District of Columbia was held to be Circuit Court of Appeals, Swift & Co. v. U. S., App.D.C., 276 U.S. 311, 48 S.Ct. 311, 313, 72 L.Ed. 587.

COURTS OF ASSIZE AND NISI PRIUS. Courts in England composed of two or more commissioners, called "judges of assize," (or of "assize and *nisi prius*,") who are twice in every year sent by the king's special commission, on circuits all round the kingdom, to try, by a jury of the respective counties, the truth of such matters of fact as are there under dispute in the courts of Westminster Hall. 3 Steph. Comm. 421, 422; 3 Bl. Comm. 57; 2 Odger, Com. Law, 985.

COURTS OF CINQUE PORTS. In English law. Courts of limited local jurisdiction formerly held before the mayor and jurats (aldermen) of the Cinque Ports. Their jurisdiction was not affected by the Judicature Act of 1873. 1 Holdsw. Hist. E. L. 305; 3 Bla. Comm. 79; 2 Steph. Comm. 499.

COURTS OF THE FOREST. Courts held for the enforcement of the forest laws. Inderwick, King's Peace. See Forest Courts.

COURTS OF THE FRANCHISES. Jurisdictions in the early Norman period which rested upon royal grants—often assumed. Edward I., in 1274, sent out commissioners to enquire by what warrant different landowners were exercising their *jura regalia.* There were many varieties of lesser franchises. Some of these franchises were recognized as existing by the County Courts Acts, 1846–1888. 1 Holdsw. Hist. E. L. 61.

COURTS OF PRINCIPALITY OF WALES. A species of private courts of a limited though extensive jurisdiction, which, upon the thorough reduction of that principality and the settling of its polity in the reign of Henry VIII, were erected all over the country. These courts, however, have been abolished by 1 Wm. IV. c. 70; the principality being now divided into two circuits, which the judges visit in the same manner as they do the circuits in England, for the purpose of disposing of those causes which are ready for trial. Brown.

COURTS OF REQUEST. Inferior courts, in England, having local jurisdiction in claims for small debts, established in various parts of the kingdom by special acts of parliament. They were abolished in 1846, and the modern county courts (*q. v.*) took their place. 3 Steph. Comm. 283, 449; 1 Holdsw. H. E. L. 208; Bac. Abridg.; Select Cases in the Court of Requests (Selden Society, Publ. vol. 12).

COURTS OF THE UNITED STATES comprise the following: The senate of the United States, sitting as a court of impeachment; the supreme court; the courts of appeals; the district courts; the court of claims; the court of customs and patent appeals; the customs court; the tax court of the United States; and provisional courts; courts of territories and outlying possessions.

COURTS OF THE UNIVERSITIES of Oxford and Cambridge have jurisdiction in all personal actions to which any member or servant of the respective university is a party, provided that the cause of action arose within the liberties of the university, and that the member or servant was resident in the university when it arose, and when the action was brought. 3 Steph.Comm. 299; St. 25 & 26 Vict. c. 26, § 12, St. 19 & 20 Vict. c. 17. Each university court also has a criminal jurisdiction in all offenses committed by its members. 4 Steph. Comm. 325.

COURTS OF WESTMINSTER HALL. The superior courts, both of law and equity, were for centuries fixed at Westminster, an ancient palace of the monarchs of England. Formerly, all the superior courts were held before the king's capital justiciary of England, in the *aula regis,* or such of his palaces wherein his royal person resided, and removed with his household from one end of the kingdom to another. This was found to occasion great inconvenience to the suitors to remedy which it was made an article of the great charter of liberties, both of King John and King Henry III., that "common pleas should no longer follow the king's court, but be held in some certain place," in consequence of which they have ever since been held (a few necessary removals in times of the plague excepted) in the palace of Westminster only. The courts of equity also sit at Westminster, nominally, during term time, although, actually, only during the first day of term, for they generally sit in courts provided for the purpose in, or in the neighborhood of, Lincoln's Inn. Brown.

COURTESY. See Curtesy.

COURTYARD. A corrupted form of "curtilage," signifying a space of land about a dwelling house, which not only might be inclosed, but within which appurtenant buildings and structures might be erected. In re Lafayette Ave. in City of New York, 118 Misc.Rep. 161, 193 N.Y.S. 802, 804.

COUSIN. Kindred in the fourth degree, being the issue (male or female) of the brother or sister of one's father or mother. Harris v. Harris, 97 N. J.Eq. 190, 127 A. 108, 109; In re Hering's Estate, 137 Misc. 867, 244 N.Y.S. 138.

Those who descend from the brother or sister of the father of the person spoken of are called "paternal cousins;" "maternal cousins" are those who are descended from the brothers or sisters of the mother. Cousins-german are first cousins. Sanderson v. Bayley, 4 Myl. & C. 59.

In English writs, commissions, and other formal instruments issued by the crown, the word signifies any peer of the degree of an earl. The appellation is as ancient as the reign of Henry IV., who, being related or allied to every earl then in the kingdom, acknowledged that connection in all his letters and public acts; from which the use has descended to his successors, though the reason has long ago failed. Mozley & Whitley.

First cousins. Cousins-german; the children of one's uncle or aunt. Sanderson v. Bayley, 4 Mylne & C. 59.

Second cousins. Persons who are related to each other by descending from the same great-grandfather or great-grandmother. The children of one's first cousins are his second cousins. These are sometimes called "first cousins once removed." Slade v. Fooks, 9 Sim. 387; Corporation of Bridgnorth v. Collins, 15 Sim. 541.

Quarter cousin. Properly, a cousin in the fourth degree; but the term has come to express any remote degree of relationship, and even to bear an ironical signification in which it denotes a very trifling degree of intimacy and regard. Often corrupted into "cater" cousin.

COUSINAGE. See Cosinage.

COUSTOM. (Fr. Coutum.) Custom; duty; toll; tribute. 1 Bl. Comm. 314.

COUSTOUMIER. (Otherwise spelled *"Coustumier"* or *"Coutumier."*) In old French law. A collection of customs, unwritten laws, and forms of procedure. Two such volumes are of especial importance in juridical history, viz., the *Grand Coustumier de Normandie,* and the *Coutumier de France* or *Grand Coutumier.*

COUTHUTLAUGH. A person who willingly and knowingly received an outlaw, and cherished or concealed him; for which offense he underwent the same punishment as the outlaw himself. Bract. 128*b*; Spelman.

COUVERTURE. In French law. The deposit ("margin") made by the client in the hands of the broker, either of a sum of money or of securities, in order to guaranty the broker for the payment of the securities which he purchases for the client. Arg.Fr.Merc.Law, 555.

COVENABLE. A French word signifying convenient or suitable; as covenably endowed. Anciently written "convenable." Termes de la Ley.

COVENANT.

Practice

The name of a common-law form of action *ex contractu,* which lies for the recovery of damages for breach of a covenant, or contract under seal. Stickney v. Stickney, 21 N.H. 68; Utilities Production Corporation v. Southwestern Natural Gas Co., Del., 1 Terry 401, 11 A.2d 275, 276.

Law of Contracts

An agreement, convention, or promise of two or more parties, *by deed* in writing, signed, sealed, and delivered, by which either of the parties pledges himself to the other that something is either done or shall be done, or stipulates for the truth of certain facts. Commonwealth v. Robinson, 1 Watts, Pa., 160; Kent v. Edmondston, 49 N.C. 529; Schram v. Coyne, C.C.A.Mich., 127 F.2d 205, 209; Sabin v. Hamilton, 2 Ark. 485, 490 (see, however, the later case of Dyer v. Gill, 32 Ark. 410, pointing out that by virtue of statute in Arkansas, the distinction between sealed and unsealed instruments, with reference to contracts between individuals, has been abolished).

An agreement between two or more parties, reduced to writing and executed by a sealing and delivery thereof, whereby some of the parties named therein engage, or one of them engages, with the other, or others, or some of them, therein also named, that some act hath or hath not already been done, or for the performance or non-performance of some specified duty. De Bolle v. Insurance Co., 4 Whart., Pa., 71, 33 Am.Dec. 38.

In common parlance, any agreement, whether under seal or not. 15 C.J. 1209; 7 R.C.L. 1084; Jenkins v. John Taylor Dry Goods Co., 352 Mo. 660, 179 S.W.2d 54, 58.

In effect, this has become the legal meaning in many states, in which private seals have been abolished by statute. For a number of these state statutes, see 66 L.R.A. 686, 687. In those states it is commonly held that the affixing of a seal, when unnecessary to the validity of the instrument, has no effect, and may be disregarded. 24 R.C.L. 689. "Seals are a relic of that period when men, as a rule, could not write," and a covenant may "be created in this state [Georgia] by a writing not under seal." Atlanta, K. & N. Ry. Co. v. McKinney, 124 Ga. 929, 53 S.E. 701, 703, 6 L.R.A.,N.S., 436.

Classification

Covenants may be classified according to several distinct principles of division. According as one or other of these is adopted, they are:

Express or implied. The former being those which are created by the express words of the parties to the deed declaratory of their intention, while implied covenants are those which are inferred by the law from certain words in a deed which imply (though they do not express) them. Express covenants are also called covenants "in deed," as distinguished from covenants "in law." McDonough v. Martin, 88 Ga. 675, 16 S.E. 59, 18 L.R.A. 343; Garstang v. Davenport, 90 Iowa 359, 57 N.W. 876.

Dependent, concurrent, and independent. Covenants are either dependent, concurrent, or mutual and independent. The first depends on the prior performance of some act or condition, and, until the condition is performed, the other party is not liable to an action on his covenant. In the second, mutual acts are to be performed at the same time; and if one party is ready, and offers to perform his part, and the other neglects or refuses to perform his, he who is ready and offers has fulfilled his engagement, and may maintain an action for the default of the other, though it is not certain that either is obliged to do the first act. The third sort is where either party may recover damages from the other for the injuries he may have received by a breach of the covenants in his favor; and it is no excuse for the defendant to allege a breach of the covenants on the part of the plaintiff. Bailey v. White, 3 Ala. 330; Gray v. Smith, C.C.Cal., 76 F. 534; Lowery v. May, 213 Ala. 66, 104 So. 5, 8; Roberts v. Steelman, C.C.A.N.J., 1 F.2d 180, 182.

Mutual and independent covenants are such as do not go to the whole consideration on both sides, but only to a part, and where separate actions lie for breaches on either side to recover damages for the injury sustained by breach. Lowery v. May, 213 Ala. 66, 104 So. 5, 8; Big Run Coal Co. v. Employers' Indemnity Co., 163 Ky. 596, 174 S.W. 25, 26.

Covenants are dependent where performance by one party is conditioned on and subject to performance by the other, and in such case the party who seeks performance must show performance or a tender or readiness to perform on his part; but covenants are independent when actual performance of one is not dependent on another, and where, in consequence, the remedy of both sides is by action. Roberts v. Steelman, C.C.A.N.J., 1 F.2d 180, 182.

Principal and auxiliary. The former being those which relate directly to the principal matter of the contract entered into between the parties; while auxiliary covenants are those which do not relate directly to the principal matter of contract between the parties, but to something connected with it.

Inherent and collateral. The former being such as immediately affect the particular property, while the latter affect some property collateral thereto or some matter collateral to the grant or lease. Shep.Touch. 161.

A covenant inherent is one which is conversant about the land, and knit to the estate in the land; as, that the thing demised shall be quietly enjoyed, shall be kept in repair, or shall not be aliened. A covenant collateral is one which is conversant about some collateral thing that doth nothing at all, or not so immediately, concern the thing granted; as to pay a sum of money in gross, etc.

Joint or several. The former bind both or all the covenantors together; the latter bind each of them separately. A covenant may be both joint and several at the same time, as regards the covenantors; but, as regards the covenantees, they cannot be joint and several for one and the same cause, (5 Coke, 19*a*,) but must be either joint or several only. Brown. See Capen v. Barrows, 1 Gray, Mass., 379; In re Slingsby, 5 Coke, 18b.

Covenants are usually joint or several according as the interests of the covenantees are such; but the words of the covenant, where they are unambiguous, will decide, although, where they are ambiguous the nature of the interests as being joint or several is left to decide.

General or specific. The former relate to land generally and place the covenantee in the position of a specialty creditor only; the latter relate to particular lands and give the covenantee a lien thereon. Brown.

Executed or executory. The former being such as relate to an act already performed; while the latter are those whose performance is to be future. Shep.Touch. 161.

Affirmative or negative. The former being those in which the party binds himself to the existence of a present state of facts as represented or to the future performance of some act; while the latter are those in which the covenantor obliges himself *not* to do or perform some act.

Declaratory or obligatory. The former being those which serve to limit or direct uses; while the latter are those which are binding on the party himself. 1 Sid. 27; 1 Keb. 337.

Real and personal. A real covenant is one which binds the heirs of the covenantor and passes to assignees or purchasers; a covenant the obligation of which is so connected with the realty that he who has the latter is either entitled to the benefit of it or is liable to perform it; a covenant which has for its object something annexed to, or inherent in, or connected with, land or other real property, and runs with the land, so that the grantee of the land is invested with it and may sue upon it for a breach happening in his time. 4 Kent, Comm. 470; 2 Bl.Comm. 304; Chapman v. Holmes, 10 N.J.Law, 20; Skinner v. Mitchell, 5 Kan.App. 366, 48 P. 450; Oil Co. v. Hinton, 159 Ind. 398, 64 N.E. 224; Davis v. Lyman, 6 Conn. 249.

In the old books, a covenant real is also defined to be a covenant by which a man binds himself to pass a thing real, as lands or tenements. Termes de la Ley; 3 Bl. Comm. 156; Shep.Touch. 161. A personal covenant, on the other hand, is one which, instead of being a charge upon real estate of the covenantor, only binds himself and his personal representatives in respect to assets. 4 Kent, Comm. 470; Carter v. Denman, 23 N.J.Law, 270; Hadley v. Bernero, 97 Mo.App. 314, 71 S.W. 451. The phrase may also mean a covenant which is personal to the covenantor, that is, one which he must perform in person, and cannot procure another person to perform for him. De Sanno v. Earle, 273 Pa. 265, 117 A. 200, 202; Pearson v. Richards, 106 Or. 78, 211 P. 167, 171. "Real covenants" relate to realty and have for their main object some benefit thereto, inuring to benefit of and becoming binding on subsequent grantees, while "personal covenants" do not run with land. Bank of Hoxie v. Meriwether, 166 Ark. 39, 265 S.W. 642, 645. Very considerable confusion exists among the authorities in the use of the term real covenants. The definition of Blackstone which determines the character of covenants from the insertion or noninsertion of the word "heir" by the covenantor, is pretty generally rejected.

Transitive or intransitive. The former being those personal covenants the duty of performing which passes over to the representatives of the covenantor; while the latter are those the duty of performing which is limited to the covenantee himself, and does not pass over to his representative. Bac.Abr.Cov.

Disjunctive covenants. Those which are for the performance of one or more of several things at the election of the covenantor or covenantee, as the case may be. Platt, Cov. 21.

Absolute or conditional. An absolute covenant is one which is not qualified or limited by any condition.

Other Compound and Descriptive Terms

Continuing covenant. One which indicates or necessarily implies the doing of stipulated acts successively or as often as the occasion may require; as, a covenant to pay rent by installments, to keep the premises in repair or insured, to cultivate land, etc. McGlynn v. Moore, 25 Cal. 395.

Full covenants. As this term is used in American law, it includes the following: The covenants for seisin, for right to convey, against incumbrances, for quiet enjoyment, sometimes for further assurance, and almost always of warranty, this last often taking the place of the covenant for quiet enjoyment, and indeed in many states being the only covenant in practical use. Rawle, Cov. for Title, § 21.

Mutual covenants. A mutual covenant is one where either party may recover damages from the other for the injury he may have received from a breach of the covenants in his favor. Bailey v. White, 3 Ala. 330.

Separate covenant. A several covenant; one which binds the several covenantors each for himself, but not jointly.

Usual covenants. An agreement on the part of a seller of real property to give the usual covenants binds him to insert in the grant covenants of "seisin," "quiet enjoyment," "further assurance," "general warranty," and "against incumbrances." Wilson v. Wood, 17 N.J.Eq. 216, 88 Am.Dec. 231; Drake v. Barton, 18 Minn. 467, Gil. 414.

The result of the authorities appears to be that in a case where the agreement is silent as to the particular covenants to be inserted in the lease, and provides merely for the lease containing "usual covenants," or, which is the same thing, in an open agreement without any reference to the covenants, and there are no special circumstances justifying the introduction of other covenants, the following are the only ones which either party can insist upon, namely: Covenants by the lessee (1) to pay rent; (2) to pay taxes, except such as are expressly payable by the landlord; (3) to keep and deliver up the premises in repair; and (4) to allow the lessor to enter and view the state of repair; and the usual qualified covenant by the lessor for quiet enjoyment by the lessee. 7 Ch.Div. 561.

Specific Covenants

Covenants against incumbrances. A covenant that there are no incumbrances on the land conveyed; a stipulation against all rights to or interests in the land which may subsist in third persons to the diminution of the value of the estate granted. Bank v. Parisette, 68 Ohio St. 450, 67 N.E. 896; Shearer v. Ranger, 22 Pick., Mass., 447; Matzger v. Arcade Building & Realty Co., 102 Wash. 423, 173 P. 47.

Covenant for further assurance. An undertaking, in the form of a covenant, on the part of the vendor of real estate to do such further acts for the purpose of perfecting the purchaser's title as the latter may reasonably require. This covenant is deemed of great importance, since it relates both to the vendor's title of and to the instrument of conveyance to the vendee, and operates as well to secure the performance of all acts necessary for supplying any defect in the former as to remove all objections to the sufficiency and security of the latter. Platt, Cov.; Rawle, Cov. §§ 98, 99. See Sugd.Vend. 500; Armstrong v. Darby, 26 Mo. 520.

Covenant for quiet enjoyment. An assurance against the consequences of a defective title, and of any disturbances thereupon. Platt, Cov. 312; Rawle, Cov. 125. Gulf Refining Co. v. Fetschan, C.C.A.Ohio, 130 F.2d 129, 132.

A covenant that the tenant or grantee of an estate shall enjoy the possession of the premises in peace and without disturbance by hostile claimants. Poposkey v. Munkwitz, 68 Wis. 322, 32 N.W. 35, 60 Am.Rep. 858; Stewart v. Drake, 9 N.J.Law, 141; Christy v. Bedell, 10 Kan.App. 435, 61 P. 1095.

Covenants for title. Covenants usually inserted in a conveyance of land, on the part of the grantor, and binding him for the completeness, security, and continuance of the title transferred to the grantee. They comprise "covenants for seisin, for right to convey, against incumbrances, or quiet enjoyment, sometimes for further assurance, and almost always of warranty." Rawle, Cov. § 21.

Covenants in gross. Such as do not run with the land.

Covenant not to sue. A covenant by one who had a right of action at the time of making it against another person, by which he agrees not to sue to enforce such right of action. Pacific States Lumber Co. v. Bargar, C.C.A.Or., 10 F.2d 335, 337; McDonald v. Goddard Grocery Co., 184 Mo.App. 432, 171 S.W. 650, 651.

Covenant of non-claim. A covenant sometimes employed, particularly in the New England states, and in deeds of extinguishment of ground rents in Pennsylvania, that neither the vendor, nor his heirs, nor any other person, etc., shall claim any title in the premises conveyed. Rawle, Cov. § 22.

Covenant of right to convey. An assurance by the covenantor that the grantor has sufficient capacity and title to convey the *estate* which he by his deed undertakes to convey.

Covenant of seisin. An assurance to the purchaser that the grantor has the very estate in quantity and quality which he purports to convey. 11 East, 641; Rawle, Cov. § 58; Burton v. Price, 105 Fla. 544, 141 So. 728, 729.

It is said that the covenant of seisin is not now in use in England, being embraced in that of a right to convey; but it is used in several of the United States. 2 Washb. Real Prop. *648.

Covenant of warranty. An assurance by the grantor of an estate that the grantee shall enjoy the same without interruption by virtue of paramount title. King v. Kilbride, 58 Conn. 109, 19 A. 519; Blair v. Morris, 212 Ala. 91, 101 So. 745, 746; Biwer v. Martin, 294 Ill. 488, 128 N.E. 518, 522.

Covenant running with land. A covenant which goes with the land, as being annexed to the estate, and which cannot be separated from the land, and transferred without it. 4 Kent, Comm. 472, note.

A covenant is said to run with the land, when not only the original parties or their representatives, but each successive owner of the land, will be entitled to its benefit, or be liable (as the case may be) to its obligation. 1 Steph. Comm. 455. Or, in other words, it is so called when either the liability to perform it or the right to take advantage of it passes to the assignee of the land. Tillotson v. Prichard, 60 Vt. 94, 14 A. 302, 6 Am.St.Rep. 95; Spencer's Case, 3 Coke, 31. One which touches and concerns the land itself, so that its benefit or obligation passes with the ownership. Local Federal Savings & Loan Ass'n of Oklahoma City v. Eckroat, 186 Okl. 660, 100 P.2d 261, 262.

Covenant running with title. A covenant which goes with the title. Stipulation in a lease granting to lessee the option of renewing it for another specified period was such a covenant. Magnolia Petroleum Co. v. Carter, La.App., 2 So.2d 680, 682.

Covenant to convey. A covenant by which the covenantor agrees to convey to the covenantee a certain estate, under certain circumstances.

Covenant to renew. An executory contract, giving lessee the right to renew on compliance with the terms specified in the renewal clause, if any, or, if none, on giving notice, prior to termination of the lease, of his desire to renew, whereupon the contract becomes executed as to him. Freiheit v. Broch, 98 Conn. 166, 118 A. 828, 830.

Covenant to stand seised. A conveyance adapted to the case where a person seised of land in possession, reversion, or vested remainder, proposes to convey it to his wife, child, or kinsman. In its terms it consists of a covenant by him, in consideration of his natural love and affection, to stand seised of the land to the use of the intended transferee. Before the statute of uses this would merely have raised a use in favor of the convenantee; but by that act this use is converted into the legal estate, and the covenant therefore operates as a conveyance of the land to the covenantee. It is now almost obsolete. 1 Steph.Comm. 532; Williams, Seis. 145; French v. French, 3 N.H. 261; Jackson v. Swart, 20 Johns., N.Y., 85.

COVENANTEE. The party to whom a covenant is made. Shep.Touch. 160.

COVENANTOR. The party who makes a covenant. Shep.Touch. 160.

COVENANTS PERFORMED. In Pennsylvania practice. This is the name of a plea to the action of covenant whereby the defendant, upon informal notice to the plaintiff, may give anything in evidence which he might have pleaded. With the addition of the words "absque hoc" it amounts to a denial of the allegations of the declaration; and the further addition of "with leave," etc., imports an equitable defense, arising out of special circumstances, which the defendant means to offer in evidence. Zents v. Legnard, 70 Pa. 192; Stewart v. Bedell, 79 Pa. 336.

COVENT. A contraction, in the old books, of the word "convent."

COVENTRY ACT. The name given to the statute 22 & 23 Car. II. c. 1, which provided for the punishment of assaults with intent to maim or disfigure a person. It was so named from its being occasioned by an assault on Sir John Coventry in the street as was supposed, for some obnoxious words uttered by him in parliament. 4 Bl.Comm. 207; State v. Cody, 18 Or. 506, 23 P. 891.

COVER, *v.* In insurance. To protect by means of insurance; sometimes orally pending issuance of policy. Barrette v. Casualty Co. of America, 79 N.H. 59, 104 A. 126, 127; Michigan Idaho Lumber Co. v. Northern Fire & Marine Ins. Co., 35 N.D. 244, 160 N.W. 130, 136; Muntz v. Travelers Mut. Casualty Co., 229 Iowa 1015, 295 N.W. 837, 841.

COVER INTO. The phrase "covered into the treasury," as used in acts of congress and the practice of the United States treasury department, means that money has actually been paid into the treasury in the regular manner, as distinguished from merely depositing it with the treasurer. U. S. v. Johnston, 124 U.S. 236, 8 S.Ct. 446, 31 L.Ed. 389.

COVERING DEED. A trust deed executed by a trading company to secure an issue of debentures. Simonson, Debentures, 38.

COVERT. Covered, protected, sheltered. A *pound covert* is one that is closed or covered over, as distinguished from *pound overt,* which is open overhead. Co.Litt. 47*b*; 3 Bl.Comm. 12. A *feme covert* is so called, as being under the wing, protection, or *cover* of her husband. 1 Bl.Comm. 442.

COVERT BARON, or COVERT DE BARON. Under the protection of a husband; married. 1 Bl. Comm. 442. *La feme que est covert de baron,* the woman which is covert of a husband. Litt. § 670.

COVERTURE. The condition or state of a married woman. Sometimes used elliptically to describe the legal disability arising from a state of coverture. Osborn v. Horine, 19 Ill. 124; Roberts v. Lund, 45 Vt. 86.

COVIN. A secret conspiracy or agreement between two or more persons to injure or defraud another. Mix v. Muzzy, 28 Conn. 191; Anderson v. Oscamp, Ind.App., 35 N.E. 707; Hyslop v. Clarke, 14 Johns., N.Y., 465; Co.Litt. 357*b*; Comyns, Dig. *Covin,* A; 1 Viner, Abr. 473.

COVINOUS. Deceitful; fraudulent; having the nature of, or tainted by covin.

COW. Female of bovine genus of animals. Strictly, one that has calved. Often loosely used to include heifer, or young female that has not calved. 2 East, Pl.Cr. 616; 1 Leach 105. See Taylor v. State, 6 Humph., Tenn., 285; Tombigbee Valley R. Co. v. Wilks, 6 Ala.App. 473, 60 So. 559; Mathis v. State, 70 Fla. 194, 69 So. 697, 698; Parsons v. Kimmel, 206 Mich. 676, 173 N.W. 539, 540.

COWARDICE. Pusillanimity; fear; misbehavior through fear in relation to some duty to be performed before an enemy. O'Brien Ct.M. 142; Coil v. State, 62 Neb. 15, 86 N.W. 925.

CRACKING. The conversion, by means of heat and usually pressure, of the complex hydrocarbon molecules of heavier oils into the molecular structure of the desired lighter oils. Universal Oil Products Co. v. Skelly Oil Co., D.C.Del., 20 F.2d 995.

CRAFT. A general term, now commonly applied to all kinds of sailing vessels, though formerly restricted to the smaller vessels. The Wenonah, 21 Grat., Va., 697; Reed v. Ingham, 3 El. & B. 898.

A trade or occupation of the sort requiring skill and training, particularly manual skill combined with a knowledge of the principles of the art; also the body of persons pursuing such a calling; a guild. Ganahl v. Shore, 24 Ga. 23, Cole v. Commonwealth, 169 Va. 868, 193 S.E. 517, 519.

Guile, artful cunning, trickiness. Not a legal term in this sense, though often used in connection with such terms as "fraud" and "artifice."

CRANAGE. A liberty to use a crane for drawing up goods and wares of burden from ships and vessels, at any creek of the sea, or wharf, unto the land, and to make a profit of doing so. It also signifies the money paid and taken for the service. Tomlins.

CRANK. A term vulgarly applied to a person of eccentric, ill-regulated, and unpractical mental habits; a person half-crazed; a monomaniac; not necessarily equivalent to "insane person," "lunatic," or any other term descriptive of complete mental derangement, and not carrying any implication of homicidal mania. Walker v. Tribune Co., C.C.Ill., 29 F. 827.

CRASSUS. Large; gross; excessive; extreme. *Crassa ignorantia,* gross ignorance. Fleta, lib. 5, c. 22, § 18.

Crassa negligentia. Gross neglect; absence of ordinary care and diligence. Hun v. Cary, 82 N.Y. 72, 37 Am.Rep. 546.

CRASTINO. Lat. On the morrow, the day after. The return-day of writs; because the first day of the term was always some saint's day, and writs were returnable on the day after. 2 Reeve, Eng. Law, 56.

CRATES. An iron gate before a prison. 1 Vent. 304.

CRAVE. To ask or demand; as to crave oyer. See Oyer.

CRAVEN. In old English law. A word of disgrace and obloquy, pronounced on either champion, in the ancient trial by battle, proving recreant, *i. e.,* yielding. Glanville calls it *"infestum et inverecundum verbum."* His condemnation was *amittere liberam legem, i. e.,* to become infamous, and not to be accounted *liber et legalis homo,* being supposed by the event to have been proved forsworn, and not fit to be put upon a jury or admitted as a witness. Wharton.

CRAZY. A broken, shattered, or deranged condition of the mind; insane. Bates v. Oden, 198 Ala. 569, 73 So. 921. Thompson v. State, 104 Tex. Cr.R. 637, 285 S.W. 826, 830.

CREAMER. A foreign merchant, but generally taken for one who has a stall in a fair or market. Blount.

CREAMUS. Lat. We create. One of the words by which a corporation in England was formerly created by the king. 1 Bl.Comm. 473.

CREANCE. In French law. A claim; a debt; also belief, credit, faith.

CREANCER. One who trusts or gives credit; a creditor. Britt. cc. 28, 78.

CREANSOR. A creditor. Cowell.

CREATE. To bring into being; to cause to exist; to produce; as, to create a trust in lands, to create a corporation. Edwards v. Bibb, 54 Ala. 481; McClellan v. McClellan, 65 Me. 500; Pickett v. Board of Com'rs of Fremont County, 24 Idaho 200, 133 P. 112, 114; People v. California Fish Co., 166 Cal. 576, 138 P. 79, 91.

To *create* a charter or a corporation is to make one which never existed before, while to *renew* one is to give vitality to one which has been forfeited or has expired; and to *extend* one is to give an existing charter more time than originally limited. Indianapolis v. Navin, 151 Ind. 139, 51 N.E. 80, 41 L.R.A. 344; State v. Powell, 109 Ohio St. 383, 142 N.E. 401, 403; Town of Westernport v. Green, 144 Md. 85, 124 A. 403.

CREDENTIALS. In international law. The instruments which authorize and establish a public minister in his character with the state or prince to whom they are addressed. If the state or prince receive the minister, he can be received only in the quality attributed to him in his credentials. They are, as it were, his letter of attorney, his mandate patent, *mandatum manifestum.* Vattel, liv. 4, c. 6, § 76.

CREDIBILITY. Worthiness of belief; that quality in a witness which renders his evidence worthy of belief. After the competence of a witness is allowed, the consideration of his *credibility* arises, and not before. 3 Bl.Comm. 369; 1 Burrows, 414, 417; Smith v. Jones, 68 Vt. 132, 34 A. 424; Loeb v. State, 133 Miss. 883, 98 So. 449, 451; Dewein v. State, 120 Ark. 302, 179 S.W. 346, 347. As to the distinction between *competency* and *credibility,* see Competency.

CREDIBLE. Worthy of belief; entitled to credit. See Competency.

Credible person. One who is trustworthy and entitled to be believed; in law and legal proceedings, one who is entitled to have his oath or affidavit accepted as reliable, not only on account of his good reputation for veracity, but also on account of his intelligence, knowledge of the circumstances, and disinterested relation to the matter in question. Also one who is competent to testify. Dunn v. State, 7 Tex.App. 605; Territory v. Leary, 8 N.M. 180, 43 P. 688; Loeb v. State, 133 Miss. 883, 98 So. 449, 451; Burleson v. State, 131 Tex.Cr.R. 576, 100 S.W.2d 1019, 1020.

Credible witness. One who is competent to give evidence; also one who is worthy of belief. Peck v. Chambers, 44 W.Va. 270, 28 S.E. 706; Savage v. Bulger, 77 S.W. 717, 25 Ky.Law.Rep. 1269; Appeal of Clark, 114 Me. 105, 95 A. 517, Ann.Cas. 1917A, 837; Hill v. Chicago Title & Trust Co., 322 Ill. 42, 152 N.E. 545, 546; Burleson v. State, 131 Tex.Cr.R. 576, 100 S.W.2d 1019, 1020.

CREDIBLY INFORMED. The statement in a pleading or affidavit, that one is "credibly informed and verily believes" such and such facts, means that, having no direct personal knowledge of the matter in question, he has derived his information in regard to it from authentic sources or from the statements of persons who are not only "credible," in the sense of being trustworthy, but also informed as to the particular matter or conversant with it.

CREDIT. The ability of a business man to borrow money, or obtain goods on time, in consequence of the favorable opinion held by the community, or by the particular lender, as to his solvency and reliability. People v. Wasservogle, 77 Cal. 173, 19 P. 270; In re Ford, D.C.Wash., 14 F.2d 848, 849; State ex rel. Globe-Democrat Pub. Co. v. Gehner, 316 Mo. 694, 294 S.W. 1017, 1018. That influence connected with certain social positions. 20 Toullier, n. 19. Time allowed to the buyer of goods by the seller, in which to make payment for them. The correlative of a *debt;*

that is, a debt considered from the creditor's standpoint, or that which is incoming or due *to* one. Mountain State Motor Car Co. v. Solof, 97 W.Va. 196, 124 S.E. 824, 825. That which is due to a person, as distinguished from debit, that which is due by him. Claim or cause of action for specific sum of money. Richard v. American Union Bank, 204 N.Y.S. 719, 722, 123 Misc.Rep. 92; Thaden v. Bagan, 139 Minn. 46, 165 N.W. 864, 865; Richard v. American Union Bank, 204 N.Y. S. 719, 722, 123 Misc.Rep. 92; New York Life Ins. Co. v. Edwards, C.C.A.N.Y., 8 F.2d 851, 856; Humphreys v. County Court, 90 W.Va. 315, 110 S.E. 701, 702, 703.

A sum credited on the books of a company to person who appears to be entitled to it. Coons v. Home Life Ins. Co. of New York, 291 Ill.App. 313, 9 N.E.2d 419, 421. The credit of an individual is the trust reposed in him by those who deal with him that he is of ability to meet his engagements; and he is trusted because through the tribunals of the country he may be made to pay. The credit of a government is founded on a belief of its ability to comply with its engagements, and a confidence in its honor, that it will do that voluntarily which it cannot be compelled to do. Owen v. Branch Bank, 3 Ala. 258.

Bill of Credit. See Bill.

Letter of Credit. An open or sealed letter, from a merchant in one place, directed to another, in another place or country, requiring him, if a person therein named, or the bearer of the letter, shall have occasion to buy commodities, or to want money to any particular or unlimited amount, either to procure the same or to pass his promise, bill, or bond for it, the writer of the letter undertaking to provide him the money for the goods, or to repay him by exchange, or to give him such satisfaction as he shall require, either for himself, or the bearer of the letter. 3 Chit.Com.Law, 336. Powerine Co. v. Russel Inc., 103 Utah 441, 135 P.2d 906, 909, 910, 912.

A written instrument, addressed by one person to another, requesting the latter to give credit to the person in whose favor it is drawn. Mechanics Bank v. New York & N. H. R. Co., 13 N.Y. 599; Lafargue v. Harrison, 70 Cal. 380, 9 P. 261, 59 Am.Rep. 416. A letter of credit is in the nature of a negotiable instrument, and is a letter whereby a person requests another to advance money or give credit to a third person, and promises to repay person making advancement. Second Nat. Bank of Toledo v. M. Samuel & Sons, C.C.A.N.Y., 12 F.2d 963, 966, 53 A.L.R. 49; Border Nat. Bank of Eagle Pass, Tex., v. American Nat. Bank of San Francisco, Cal., C.C.A.Tex., 282 F. 73, 77; Liggett v. Levy, 233 Mo. 590, 136 S.W.2d 299, 301, Ann.Cas.1912C, 70; *General and special.* A general letter of credit is one addressed to any and all persons, without naming any one in particular, while a special letter of credit is addressed to a particular individual, firm, or corporation by name. Birckhead v. Brown, 5 Hill, N.Y., 642; American Steel Co. v. Irving Nat. Bank, C.C.A.N.Y., 266 F. 41, 43. A "confirmed irrevocable letter of credit," an "irrevocable letter," or a "confirmed credit" is a contract to pay on compliance with its terms, and needs no formal acknowledgment or acceptance other than is therein stated. Lamborn v. National Park Bank of New York, 240 N.Y. 520, 148 N.E. 664, 665.

Line of Credit. See Line.

Personal Credit. Personal credit is that credit which a person possesses as an individual, and which is founded on the opinion entertained of his character and business standing.

CRÉDIT. Fr. Credit in the English sense of the term, or more particularly, the security for a loan or advancement.

CRÉDIT FONCIER. A company or corporation formed for the purpose of carrying out improvements, by means of loans and advances on real estate security.

CRÉDIT MOBILIER. A company or association formed for carrying on a banking business or for the construction of public works, building of railroads, operation of mines, or other such enterprises, by means of loans or advances on the security of personal property. Barrett v. Savings Inst., 64 N.J.Eq. 425, 54 A. 543.

CREDITED. The alternative to paid. Lynchburg Trust & Savings Bank v. Commissioner of Internal Revenue, C.C.A.4, 68 F.2d 356, 358.

CREDITOR. A person to whom a debt is owing by another person who is the "debtor." Woolverton v. Taylor Co., 43 Ill.App. 424; Insurance Co. v. Meeker, 37 N.J.Law. 300; Walsh v. Miller, 51 Ohio St. 462, 38 N.E. 381; Rooney v. Inheritance Tax Commission of Kansas, 143 Kan. 143, 53 P.2d 500, 501. One who has a right to require the fulfillment of an obligation or contract. Mohr v. Minnesota Elevator Co., 40 Minn. 343, 41 N.W. 1074; Murphy v. Jos. Hollander, Inc., 131 N.J.L. 165, 34 A.2d 780, 783; one to whom money is due, and, in ordinary acceptation, has reference to financial or business transactions. State v. Ord State Bank, 117 Neb. 189, 220 N.W. 265, 266; The antonym of "debtor." Erickson v. Grande Ronde Lumber Co., 162 Or. 556, 92 P.2d 170, 177; The word is susceptible of latitudinous construction. Commerce Trust Co. v. Farmers' Exchange Bank of Gallatin, 332 Mo. 979, 61 S.W.2d 928, 89 A.L.R. 373.

The foregoing is the strict legal sense of the term; but in a wider sense it means one who has a legal right to demand and recover from another a sum of money on any account whatever, and hence may include the owner of any right of action against another, whether arising on contract or for a tort, a penalty, or a forfeiture. Bongard v. Block, 81 Ill. 186, 25 Am.Rep. 276; one having a claim for tort, Chalmers v. Sheehy, 132 Cal. 459, 64 P. 709, 84 Am.St. Rep. 62; an antenuptial agreement as constituting wife a "creditor" of husband's estate. In re Wilson's Estate, 346 Pa. 562, 31 A.2d 106, 108; parties claiming as trust funds deposits in insolvent bank, Dewey v. Commercial State Bank, 141 Kan. 356, 41 P.2d 1006, 1007.

The term "creditor," within the common-law and statutes that conveyances with intent to defraud creditors shall be void, includes every one having right to require the performance of any legal obligation, contract, or guaranty, or a legal right to damages growing out of contract or tort, Hernton v. Short, 121 Ark. 383, 181 S.W. 142, 144; and includes not merely the holder of a fixed and certain present debt, but every one having a right to require the performance of any legal obligation, contract, or guaranty, or a legal right to damages growing out of contract or tort, and includes one entitled to damages for breach of contract to convey real estate, notwithstanding the abandonment of his action for specific performance, In re Littleton's Estate, 223 N.Y.S. 470, 479, 129 Misc.Rep. 845; Mackenzie Oil Co. v. Omar Oil & Gas Co., 14 Del.Ch. 36, 120 A. 852, 854; holders of judgment for conversion, Bays v. Brown, 160 Or. 594, 86 P.2d 951, 954; a "person having any claim, whether matured or unmatured, liquidated or unliquidated, absolute, fixed or contingent." Richards v. Jones, 16 Del.Ch. 227, 142 A. 832, 833. Those having a cause of action for damages for wrongful death. Evers v. Evers, 146 Neb. 104,

18 N.W.2d 673, 678; in its broad sense the word "creditor" means one who has any legal liability upon a contract, express or implied, or in tort; in its narrow sense, the term is limited to one who holds a demand which is certain and liquidated. Superior Plating Works v. Art Metal Crafts Co., 218 Ill.App. 148, 150.

Plaintiff, in action to recover damages for a tort committed against him, is a "creditor" of defendant, within meaning of that term as it is employed in Shannon's Code, § 3143, denouncing conveyances and transfers of property collusively made with intent to delay, hinder, or defraud creditors. Oliphant v. Moore, 155 Tenn. 359, 293 S.W. 541, 542.

In statutes the term has various special meanings, dependent upon context, purpose of statute, etc. Toof v. City Nat. Bank of Paducah, Ky., C.C.A.Ky., 206 F. 250, 252; a bank taking chattel mortgage for pre-existing debt. Lindig v. Johnson City State Bank, Tex.Com.App., 41 S.W.2d 222, 224. An assignee of conditional seller taking trucks as creditor of purchaser, John W. Snyder, Inc., v. Aker, 134 Misc. 721, 236 N.Y.S. 28, 30. One who had recovered verdict against principal on attachment bond, Amer Realty Co. v. Spack, 280 Mass. 96, 181 N.E. 753, 754; the receiver of an insolvent national bank suing to enforce statutory stockholder's liability for benefit of creditors as a "creditor", Coffey v. Fisher, C.C.A.Tenn., 100 F.2d 51, 53; person to whom letters of administration granted. State ex rel. Gentry v. O'Byrne, 221 Ind. 282, 46 N.E.2d 687, 690. One, seeking to recover from a special administrator for conversion, United States Fidelity & Guaranty Co. v. Krow, 184 Okl. 444, 87 P.2d 950, 954; holders of participation certificates in mortgage, In re R. A. Security Holdings, D.C.N.Y., 46 F.Supp. 254, 255; persons who seize property under a legal process. Neils v. Bohlsen, 181 Minn. 25, 231 N.W. 248; state and political subdivisions, to which the forfeit is payable, International Harvester Co. v. Gully, 188 Miss. 115, 194 So. 472, 473. The National Labor Relations Board, seeking enforcement of a back pay allowance, National Labor Relations Board v. Killoren, C.C.A.Mo., 122 F.2d 609, 612. The United States which filed for record, Underwood v. United States, D.C.Tex., 37 F.Supp. 824, 826. The Reconstruction Finance Corporation, which had purchased over 86 per cent. of outstanding bonds of insolvent irrigation district, pursuant to plan to refinance entire bond indebtedness of district, West Coast Life Ins. Co. v. Merced Irr. Dist., C.C.A.Cal., 114 F.2d 654, 668, 669.

Classification

A creditor is called a "simple contract creditor," a "specialty creditor," a "bond creditor," or otherwise, according to the nature of the obligation giving rise to the debt.

Attaching creditor

One who has caused an attachment to be issued and levied on property of his debtor.

Catholic creditor

In Scotch law, one whose debt is secured on all or on several distinct parts of the debtor's property. The contracted term (designating one who is not so secured) is "secondary creditor."

Certificate creditor

A creditor of a municipal corporation who receives a certificate of indebtedness for the amount of his claim, there being no funds on hand to pay him. Johnson v. New Orleans, 46 La.Ann. 714, 15 So. 100.

Confidential creditor

A term sometimes applied to creditors of a failing debtor who furnished him with the means of obtaining credit to which his real circumstances did not entitle him, thus involving loss to other creditors not in his confidence. Gay v. Strickland, 112 Ala. 567, 20 So. 921.

Creditor at large

One who has not established his debt by the recovery of a judgment or has not otherwise secured a lien on any of the debtor's property. U. S. v. Ingate, C.C.Ala., 48 F. 254; Wolcott v. Ashenfelter, 5 N.M. 442, 23 P. 780, 8 L.R.A. 691.

Domestic creditor

One who resides in the same state or country in which the debtor has his domicile or his property.

Double creditor

See Double Creditor.

Execution creditor

One who, having recovered a judgment against the debtor for his debt or claim, has also caused an execution to be issued thereon. Chalmers & Williams v. Surprise, 70 Ind.App. 646, 123 N.E. 841, 844.

Executor creditor

In Scotch law. A creditor of a decedent who obtains a grant of administration on the estate, at least to the extent of so much of it as will be sufficient to discharge his debt, when the executor named in the will has declined to serve, as also those other persons who would be preferentially entitled to administer.

Existing creditors

See Existing Creditors.

Foreign creditor

One who resides in a state or country foreign to that where the debtor has his domicile or his property.

General creditor

A creditor at large (*supra*), or one who has no lien or security for the payment of his debt or claim. Wolcott v. Ashenfelter, 5 N.M. 442, 23 P. 780, 8 L.R.A. 691.

Joint creditors

Persons jointly entitled to require satisfaction of the same debt or demand.

Judgment creditor

See Judgment Creditor.

Junior creditor

One whose claim or demand accrued at a date later than that of a claim or demand held by another creditor, who is called correlatively the "senior" creditor.

Petitioning creditors

As used in Bankruptcy Act, § 64b, 11 U.S.C.A. § 104, authorizing one reasonable attorney's fee.

All creditors petitioning for adjudication, or seeking relief consistent with original petition by supplemental or intervening petition, in view of section 59f, 11 U.S.C.A. § 95. In re Marcuse & Co., C.C.A.Ill., 11 F.2d 513, 516.

Principal creditor

One whose claim or demand very greatly exceeds the claims of all other creditors in amount is sometimes so called. See In re Sullivan's Estate, 25 Wash. 430, 65 P. 793.

Secured creditor

See Secured Creditor.

Single creditor

See Single Creditor.

Subsequent creditor

One whose claim or demand accrued or came into existence after a given fact or transaction, such as the recording of a deed or mortgage or the execution of a voluntary conveyance. McGhee v. Wells, 57 S.C. 280, 35 S.E. 529, 76 Am.St.Rep. 567.

Warrant creditor

A creditor of a municipal corporation to whom is given a municipal warrant for the amount of his claim, because there are no funds in hand to pay it. Johnson v. New Orleans, 46 La.Ann. 714, 15 So. 100.

CREDITOR BENEFICIARY. A third person to whom performance of promise comes in satisfaction of legal duty. Breaux v. Banker, Tex.Civ. App., 107 S.W.2d 382, 389; Vail v. Reuben H. Donnelley Corporation, 56 Ohio App. 219, 10 N.E.2d 239, 241.

Company transporting material for school building under contract with subcontractor. J. T. Jackson Lumber Co. v. Union Transfer & Storage Co., 246 Ky. 653, 55 S.W.2d 670. Person entitled to enforce contract under which he is entitled to benefit. Hartman Ranch Co. v. Associated Oil Co., 10 Cal.2d 232, 73 P.2d 1163, 1169. Situation in which relationship between promisee and beneficiary is that of debtor and creditor. McCulloch v. Canadian Pac. Ry. Co., D.C.Minn., 53 F.Supp. 534, 542.

The lessor has a right of action for breach of parent lease as a "creditor beneficiary" against a sublessee or an assignee of the lease who has agreed with the original lessee to assume the parent lease. Hartman Ranch Co. v. Associated Oil Co., 10 Cal.2d 232, 73 P.2d 1163.

CREDITORS' BILL OR SUIT.

A suit by judgment creditor in equity for purpose of reaching property which cannot be reached by execution at law. B. L. E. Realty Corporation v. Mary Williams Co., 101 Fla. 254, 134 So. 47, 49; Ex parte Roddey, 171 S.C. 489, 172 S.E. 866, 868, 92 A.L.R. 1430; Hamburger Apparel Co. v. Werner, 17 Wash.2d 310, 135 P.2d 311, 315; City of Newark v. Jos. Hollander, Inc., 136 N.J. Eq. 539, 42 A.2d 872, 875. A proceeding to enforce the security of a judgment creditor against the property or interests of his debtor. This action proceeds upon the theory that the judgment is in the nature of a lien, such as may be enforced in equity. Hudson v. Wood, C.C.Ky., 119 F. 775; Fink v. Patterson, C.C.Va., 21 F. 602; W. G. Press & Co. v. Fahy, 313 Ill. 262, 145 N.E. 103, 104; San Bernardino County Sav. Bank v. Denman, 186 Cal. 710, 200 P. 606, 609; Harkin v. Brundage, 276 U.S. 36, 48 S.Ct. 268, 72 L.Ed. 457.

Strictly, it is a bill by which a creditor seeks to satisfy his debt out of some equitable estate of the defendant, which is not liable to levy and sale under an execution at law. But there is another sort of a creditors' bill, very nearly allied to the former, by means of which a party seeks to remove a fraudulent conveyance out of the way of his execution. But a naked bill to set aside a fraudulent deed, which seeks no discovery of any property, chose in action, or other thing alleged to belong to the defendant, and which ought to be subjected to the payment of the judgment, is not a creditors' bill. Newman v. Willetts, 52 Ill. 98; Yates v. Council, 137 Miss. 381, 102 So. 176, 177.

A "class action" is one in which one or more members of a numerous class, having a common interest, may sue in behalf of themselves and all other members of the class and such actions are sometimes called "creditors' suits" and "stockholders' suits". Farmers Co-op. Oil Co. v. Socony-Vacuum Oil Co., D.C.Iowa, 43 F.Supp. 735, 737.

In English Practice, a bill in equity, filed by one or more creditors, for an account of the assets of a decedent, and a legal settlement and distribution of his estate among themselves and such other creditors as may come in under the decree.

CREDITORUM APPELLATIONE NON HI TANTUM ACCIPIUNTUR QUI PECUNIAM CREDIDERUNT, SED OMNES QUIBUS EX QUALIBET CAUSA DEBETUR. Under the head of "creditors" are included, not alone those who have lent money, but all to whom from any cause a debt is owing. Dig. 50, 16, 11.

CREDITRIX. A female creditor.

CREDITS. A term of universal application to obligations due and to become due. Colbert v. Superior Confection Co., 154 Okl. 28, 6 P.2d 791, 793.

A term used in taxation statutes to designate certain forms of personal property. It includes every claim and demand for money and every sum of money receivable at stated periods, due or to become due, but not unaccrued rents to issue out of land. State v. Royal Mineral Ass'n, 132 Minn. 232, 156 N.W. 128, 130, Ann.Cas.1918A, 145. Legacies matured by the lapse of one year from the date of testator's death were included in term "credits". City of Newark v. Lehman's Estate, Tax App., 18 N.J.Misc. 510, 14 A.2d 792, 794. Shares of corporate stock were included. Holmes v. Borgen, 200 Minn. 97, 273 N.W. 623, 626.

Mutual Credits

In bankrupt law. Credits which must, from their nature, terminate in debts; as where a debt is due from one party, and credit given by him to the other for a sum of money payable at a future day, and which will then become a debt; or where there is a debt on one side, and a delivery of property with directions to turn it into money on the other. 8 Taunt. 499; 2 Smith, Lead. Cas. 179. By this phrase, in the rule under which courts of equity allow set-off in cases of mutual credit, we are to understand a knowledge on both sides of an existing debt due to one party, and a credit by the other party, founded on and trusting to such debt, as a means of discharging it. King v. King, 9 N.J.Eq. 44. Credits given by two persons mutually; *i. e.*, each giving credit to the other. It is a more extensive phrase than "mutual debts." Thus, the sum credited by one may be due at once, that by the other payable *in futuro*; yet the credits are mutual, though the transaction would not come within the meaning of "mutual debts." 1 Atk. 230; Atkinson v. Elliott, 7 Term.R. 378.

CREED. The word "creed" has been defined as "confession or articles of faith," "formal declaration of religious belief," "any formula or confession of religious faith," and "a system of religious belief." Cummings v. Weinfeld, 177 Misc. 129, 30 N.Y.S.2d 36, 38.

CREEK. In maritime law. Such little inlets of the sea, whether within the precinct or extent of a port or without, as are narrow passages, and have shore on each side of them. Call.Sew. 56. A small stream less than a river. Baker v. City of Boston, 12 Pick. 184, 22 Am.Dec. 421. The term imports a recess, cove, bay, or inlet in the shore of a river, and not a separate or independent stream; though it is sometimes used in the latter meaning. Schermerhorn v. Railroad Co., 38 N.Y. 103.

CREMATION. The act or practice of reducing a corpse to ashes by means of fire. Act Pa. 1891, June 8; P.L. 212, 35 P.S. §§ 1121–1123; L.R. 12 Q.B.D. 247; L.R. 20 Ch.D. 659. See 43 Alb.L.J. 140. See Dead Body.

CREMENTUM COMITATÛS. The increase of a county. The sheriffs of counties anciently answered in their accounts for the improvement of the king's rents, above the *viscontiel* rents, under this title.

CREPARE OCULUM. In Saxon law. To put out an eye; which had a pecuniary punishment of fifty shillings annexed to it.

CREPUSCULUM. Twilight. In the law of burglary, this terms means the presence of sufficient light to discern the face of a man; such light as exists immediately before the rising of the sun or directly after its setting. 4 Bla.Com. 224; Co. 3d Inst. 63; 1 Russell, Cr. 820; 3 Greenl.Ev. § 75.

CRESCENTE MALITIÂ CRESCERE DEBET ET PŒNA. 2 Inst. 479. Vice increasing, punishment ought also to increase.

CREST. A term used in heraldry; it signifies the devices set over a coat of arms.

CRETINISM. In medical jurisprudence. A form of imperfect or arrested mental development, which may amount to idiocy, with physical degeneracy or deformity or lack of development; endemic in Switzerland and some other parts of Europe, but the term is applied to similar states occurring elsewhere.

CRETINUS. In old records. A sudden stream or torrent; a rising or inundation.

CRETIO. Lat. In the civil law. A certain number of days allowed an heir to deliberate whether he would take the inheritance or not. Calvin.

CREW. Usually referred to and is primarily thought of as those who are on board and aiding in the navigation. Gulf Oil Corporation v. McManigal, D.C.W.Va., 49 F.Supp. 75, 78; Norton v. Warner Co., Pa., 321 U.S. 565, 64 S.Ct. 747, 751, 88 L.Ed. 931; Berwind-White Coal Mining Co. v. Rothensies, C.C.A.Pa., 137 F.2d 60, 62. "Crew" does not have an absolutely unvarying legal significance or any well-defined factual significance. Schantz v. American Dredging Co., C.C.A.Pa., 138 F.2d 534, 537. The aggregate of seamen who man a ship or vessel, including the master and officers; or it may mean the ship's company, exclusive of the master, or exclusive of the master and all other officers. See U. S. v. Winn, 3 Sumn. 209, 28 Fed.Cas. 733; The Buena Ventura, D.C.N.Y., 243 F. 797, 799; The Herdis, D.C.Md., 22 F.2d 304, 306.

CREW LIST. In maritime law. A list of the crew of a vessel; one of a ship's papers. This instrument is required by act of congress, and sometimes by treaties. Rev.St.U.S. §§ 4374, 4375, 46 U.S.C.A. §§ 322, 323. It is necessary for the protection of the crews of every vessel, in the course of the voyage, during a war abroad. Jac. Sea Laws, 66, 69, note.

CRIER. An officer of a court, who makes proclamations. His principal duties are to announce the opening of the court and its adjournment and the fact that certain special matters are about to be transacted, to announce the admission of persons to the bar, to call the names of jurors, witnesses, and parties, to announce that a witness has been sworn, to proclaim silence when so directed, and generally to make such proclamations of a public nature as the judges order.

CRIEZ LA PEEZ. Rehearse the concord, or peace. A phrase used in the ancient proceedings for levying fines. It was the form of words by which the justice before whom the parties appeared directed the serjeant or countor in attendance to recite or *read aloud* the *concord* or agreement between the parties, as to the lands intended to be conveyed. 2 Reeve, Eng.Law, 224, 225.

CRIM. CON. An abbreviation for "criminal conversation," of very frequent use, denoting adultery. Rash v. Pratt, 111 A. 225, 228, 1 W.W.Harr., Del., 18; Hargraves v. Ballou, 47 R.I. 186, 131 A. 643, 645.

The term in its general and comprehensive sense, is synonymous with "adultery"; but in its more limited and technical signification it may be defined as adultery in the aspect of a tort. Turner v. Heavrin, 182 Ky. 65, 206 S.W. 23, 4 A.L.R. 562.

CRIME. A positive or negative act in violation of penal law; an offense against the State. Wilkins v. U. S., C.C.A.Pa., 96 F. 837, 37 C.C.A. 588; People v. Williams, 24 Mich. 163, 9 Am.Rep. 119.

"Crime" and "misdemeanor," properly speaking, are synonymous terms; though in common usage "crime" is made to denote such offenses as are of a deeper and more atrocious dye. 4 Bl.Comm. 5; People v. Schiaffino, 73 Cal.App. 357, 238 P. 725; Guetling v. State, 199 Ind. 630, 158 N.E. 593, 594; McIntyre v. Commonwealth, 154 Ky. 149, 156 S. W. 1058, 1059; Commonwealth v. Smith, 266 Pa. 511, 109 A. 786, 788, 9 A.L.R. 922; Ex parte Brady, 116 Ohio St. 512, 157 N.E. 69, 70; An act committed or omitted in violation of a public law. City of Mobile v. McCown Oil Co., 226 Ala. 688, 148 So. 402, 405. Crimes are those wrongs which the government notices as injurious to the public, and punishes in what is called a "criminal proceeding," in its own name. 1 Bish.Crim.Law, § 43; In re Jacoby, 74 Ohio App. 147, 57 N.E.2d 932, 934, 935. A crime may be defined to be any act done in violation of those duties which an individual owes to the community, and for the breach of which the law has provided that the offender shall make satisfaction to the public. Bell. A crime or public offense is an act committed or omitted in violation of a law forbidding or commanding it, and to which is annexed, upon conviction, either of the following punishments: (1) Death; (2) imprisonment; (3) fine; (4) removal from office; or (5) disqualification to hold and enjoy any office of honor, trust, or profit in this state. Pen.Code Cal. § 15. "Crime" is strictly a violation of law either human or divine; in present usage the term is commonly applied to grave offenses against the laws of the state. Van Riper v. Constitutional Government League, 1 Wash.2d 635, 96 P.2d 588, 591, 125 A.L.R. 1100. A crime or misdemeanor shall consist in a violation of a public law, in the commission of which there shall be a union or joint operation of act and intention, or criminal negligence. Code Ga. 1882, § 4292, Pen.Code 1910, § 31.

Synonyms

According to Blackstone, the word "crime" denotes such offenses as are of a deeper and more atrocious dye, while smaller faults and omissions of less consequence are called "misdemeanors." But the better use appears to be to make *crime* a term of broad and general import, including both felonies and misdemeanors, and hence covering all infractions of the criminal law. In this sense it is not a technical phrase, strictly speaking, (as "felony" and "misdemeanor" are,) but a convenient general term. In this sense, also, "offense" or "public offense" should be used as synonymous with it.

The distinction between a *crime* and a *tort* or civil injury is that the former is a breach and violation of the public right and of duties due to the whole community considered as such, and in its social and aggregate capacity; whereas the latter is an infringement or privation of the civil rights of individuals merely. Brown.

A crime, as opposed to a civil injury, is the violation of a right, considered in reference to the evil tendency of such violation, as regards the community at large. 4 Steph.Comm. 4.

Varieties of Crimes

Capital crime. See Capital, *adj.*

Common law crimes

Such crimes as are punishable by the force of the common law, as distinguished from crimes created by statute. Wilkins v. U. S., C.C.A.Pa., 96 F. 837, 37 C.C.A. 588; In re Greene, C.C.Ohio, 52 F. 111. These decisions (and many others) hold that there are no common-law crimes against the United States.

Constructive crime

See Constructive Crime.

Continuous crime

One consisting of a continuous series of acts, which endures after the period of consummation, as, the offense of carrying concealed weapons. In the case of instantaneous crimes, the statute of limitations begins to run with the consummation, while in the case of continuous crimes it only begins with the cessation of the criminal conduct or act. U. S. v. Owen, D.C.Or., 32 F. 537.

Crime against nature

The offense of buggery or sodomy. State v. Vicknair, 52 La.Ann. 1921, 28 So. 273; Ausman v. Veal, 10 Ind. 355, 71 Am.Dec. 331. The strict common-law meaning has been greatly enlarged by statute. Borden v. State, 3C Okl.Cr. 69, 252 P. 446, 447; State v. Murry, 136 La. 253, 66 So. 963, 964; State v. Long, 133 La. 580, 63 So. 180; Frazier v. Grob, 194 Mo.App. 405, 183 S.W. 1083, 1084; State v. Griffin, 175 N.C. 767, 94 S.E. 678, 679. See Bestiality; Sodomy.

At common law the term "crime against nature" embraced both sodomy and "bestiality", defined as a connection between a human being and a brute of the opposite sex. State v. Poole, 59 Ariz. 44, 122 P.2d 415, 416. Within the statute it is the perverted act of uniting the mouth of one participant with the sexual organ of the other, with a view of gratifying the sexual desire, and a mere kiss or lick of the private organ, even though lewdly done, is not a "copulation" within the statute. People v. Angier, 44 Cal.App.2d 417, 112 P.2d 659, 660.

Crime against the other (husband or wife)

As used in 22 Okl.St.Ann. 702, providing that neither husband nor wife shall be a witness against the other except in a prosecution for a "crime committed against the other," the phrase denotes a public offense by husband or wife that is a direct violation of the rights of the other. Hunter v. State, 10 Okl.Cr. 119, 134 P. 1134, 1136, L.R.A. 1915A, 564. It does not make the wife a competent witness in a prosecution against the husband for incest. Lacey v. State, 27 Okl.Cr. 42, 224 P. 994, 995.

Murder by wife of husband's child, O'Loughlin v. People, 90 Colo. 368, 10 P.2d 543, 546. Rape against stepdaughter. State v. Goff, 64 S.D. 80, 264 N.W. 665, 666.

Crimes mala in se

"Crimes mala in se" embrace acts immoral or wrong in themselves, such as burglary, larceny, arson, rape, murder, and breaches of peace. Coleman v. State ex rel. Carver, 119 Fla. 653, 161 So. 89, 90.

Crimes mala prohibita

"Crimes mala prohibita" embrace things prohibited by statute as infringing on others' rights, though no moral turpitude may attach, and constituting crimes only because they are so prohibited. Coleman v. State ex rel. Carver, 119 Fla. 653, 161 So. 89, 90.

High crimes

High crimes and misdemeanors are such immoral and unlawful acts as are nearly allied and equal in guilt to felony, yet, owing to some technical circumstance, do not fall within the definition of "felony." State v. Knapp, 6 Conn. 417, 16 Am.Dec. 68. They are the more serious or aggravated misdemeanors; those more nearly allied and equal in guilt to felony, but which do not fall within its definition. Firmara v. Gardner, 86 Conn. 434, 85 A. 670, 672.

Infamous crime

A crime which entails infamy upon one who has committed it. Butler v. Wentworth, 84 Me. 25, 24 A. 456, 17 L.R.A. 764. The term "infamous" —*i. e.*, without fame or good report—was applied at common law to certain crimes, upon the conviction of which a person became incompetent to testify as a witness, upon the theory that a person would not commit so heinous a crime unless he was so depraved as to be unworthy of credit. These crimes are treason, felony, and the *crimen falsi.* Abbott. A crime punishable by imprisonment in the state prison or penitentiary, with or without hard labor, is an infamous crime, within the provision of the fifth amendment of the constitution that "no person shall be held to answer for a capital or otherwise infamous crime unless on a presentment or indictment of a grand jury." Mackin v. U. S., 117 U.S. 348, 6 S.Ct. 777, 29 L.Ed. 909; Brede v. Powers, 263 U.S. 4, 44 S.Ct. 8, 68 L.Ed. 132. It is not the character of the crime but the nature of the punishment which renders the crime "infamous." Weeks v. United States, C.C.A.N.Y., 216 F. 292, 298, L.R.A. 1915B, 651. But see Drazen v. New Haven Taxicab Co., 95 Conn. 500, 111 A. 861, 864. Whether an offense is infamous depends on the punishment which may be imposed therefor, not on the punishment which was imposed. United States v. Moreland, 258 U.S. 433, 42 S.Ct. 368, 370, 66 L.Ed. 700; De Jianne v. U. S., C.C.A.N.J., 282 F. 737, 740; Le Clair v. White, 117 Me. 335, 104 A. 516, 517. Under the constitution of Rhode Island, a crime, to be "infamous," must come within the "crimen falsi," such as forgery, perjury, subornation of perjury, offenses affecting the public administration of justice, or such as would affect civil or political rights, disqualifying or rendering a person incompetent to be a witness or juror. State v. Bussay, 38 R.I. 454, 96 A. 337, 339. By the Revised Statutes of New York the term "infamous crime," when used in any statute, is directed to be construed as including every offense punishable with death or by imprisonment in a state prison, and no other.

Quasi crimes

This term embraces all offenses not crimes or misdemeanors, but that are in the nature of crimes,—a class of offenses against the public which have not been declared crimes, but wrongs against the general or local public which it is proper should be repressed or punished by forfeitures and penalties. This would embrace all *qui tam* actions and forfeitures imposed for the neglect or violation of a public duty. A *quasi* crime would not embrace an indictable offense, whatever might be its grade, but simply forfeitures for a wrong done to the public, whether voluntary or involuntary, where a penalty is given, whether recoverable by criminal or civil process. Wiggins v. Chicago, 68 Ill. 375. Also, offenses for which some person other than the actual perpetrator is responsible, the perpetrator being presumed to act by command of the responsible party. Sometimes, injuries which have been unintentionally caused. Torts. McCaleb v. Fox Film Corporation, C.C.A.La., 299 F. 48, 50.

Statutory crimes

Those created by statutes, as distinguished from such as are known to, or cognizable by, the common law.

CRIMEN. Lat. Crime. Also an accusation or charge of crime.

Crimen furti. The crime or offense of theft.

Crimen incendii. The crime of burning, which included not only the modern crime of arson, but also the burning of a man, a beast, or other chattel. Britt. c. 9; Crabb, Eng.Law, 308.

Crimen innominatum. The nameless crime; the crime against nature; sodomy or buggery.

Crimen raptus. The crime of rape.

Crimen roberiæ. The offense of robbery.

Flagrans crimen; Locus criminis; Particeps criminis. See those titles.

CRIMEN FALSI. The term involves the element of falsehood, and includes everything which has a tendency to injuriously affect the administration of justice by the introduction of falsehood and fraud. Commonwealth v. Schambers, 110 Pa. Super. 61, 167 A. 645, 646; Commonwealth v. Jones, 334 Pa. 321, 5 A.2d 804, 805. A crime less than felony that by its nature tends to cast doubt on the veracity of one who commits it. Commonwealth v. Gold, 155 Pa.Super. 364, 38 A.2d 486, 489. This phrase is also used as a general designation of a class of offenses, including all such as involve deceit or falsification; *e. g.*, forgery, counterfeiting, using false weights or measures, perjury, etc. Includes forgery, perjury, subornation of perjury, and offenses affecting the public administration of justice. Matzenbaugh v. People, 194 Ill. 108, 62 N.E. 546, 88 Am.St.Rep. 134; Johnston v. Riley, 13 Ga. 97.

At common law. Any crime which rendered the perpetrator incompetent to be a witness, such as forgery, perjury, subornation of perjury and other crimes affecting the administration of justice. Drazen v. New Haven Taxicab Co., 95 Conn. 500, 111 A. 861, 862; Maxey v. United States, C.C.A.Ark., 207 F. 327, 331; Webb v. State, 29 Ohio St. 351, 358.

In the civil law, the crime of falsifying; which might be committed either by writing, as by the forgery of a will or other instrument; by words, as by bearing false witness, or perjury; and by acts, as by counterfeiting or adulterating the public money, dealing with false weights and measures, counterfeiting seals, and other fraudulent and deceitful practices. Dig. 48, 10; Hallifax, Civil Law, b. 3, c. 12, nn. 56–59.

In Scotch law. It has been defined: "A fraudulent imitation or suppression of truth, to the prejudice of another." Ersk.Inst. 4, 4, 66.

CRIMEN FALSI DICITUR, CUM QUIS ILLICITUS, CUI NON FUERIT AD HÆC DATA AUCTORITAS, DE SIGILLO REGIS, RAPTO VEL INVENTO, BREVIA, CARTASVE CONSIGNAVERIT. Fleta, lib. 1, c. 23. The crime of forgery is when any one illicitly, to whom power has not been given for such purposes, has signed writs or charters with the king's seal, either stolen or found.

CRIMEN LÆSÆ MAJESTATIS. In criminal law. The crime of *lese-majesty*, or injuring majesty or royalty; high treason. The term was used by the older English law writers to denote any crime affecting the king's person or dignity.

It is borrowed from the civil law, in which it signified the undertaking of any enterprise against the emperor or the republic. Inst. 4, 18, 3.

CRIMEN LÆSÆ MAJESTATIS OMNIA ALIA CRIMINA EXCEDIT QUOAD PŒNAM. 3 Inst. 210. The crime of treason exceeds all other crimes in its punishment.

CRIMEN OMNIA EX SE NATA VITIAT. Crime vitiates everything which springs from it. Henry v. Bank of Salina, 5 Hill, N.Y., 523, 531.

CRIMEN TRAHIT PERSONAM. The crime carries the person, (*i. e.*, the commission of a crime gives the courts of the place where it is committed jurisdiction over the person of the offender.) People v. Adams, 3 Denio, N.Y. 190, 210, 45 Am.Dec. 468.

CRIMINA MORTE EXTINGUUNTUR. Crimes are extinguished by death.

CRIMINAL, *n.* One who has committed a criminal offense; one who has been legally convicted of a crime; one adjudged guilty of crime. Molineux v. Collins, 177 N.Y. 395, 69 N.E. 727, 65 L.R.A. 104. Synonymous with word "crook." Weiner v. Leviton, 230 App.Div. 312, 244 N.Y.S. 176, 178.

CRIMINAL, *adj.* That which pertains to or is connected with the law of crimes, or the administration of penal justice, or which relates to or has the character of crime. Charleston v. Beller, 45 W.Va. 44, 30 S.E. 152; Van Riper v. Constitutional Government League, 1 Wash.2d 635, 96 P.2d 588, 591, 125 A.L.R. 1100. The word is defined as of the nature of or involving a crime; more generally, of the nature of a grave offense; wicked. Van Riper v. Constitutional Government League, 1 Wash.2d 635, 96 P.2d 588, 591, 125 A.L.R. 1100.

Criminal abortion

See Abortion.

Criminal act

A term which is equivalent to crime; or is sometimes used with a slight softening or glossing of the meaning, or as importing a possible question of the legal guilt of the deed. The intentional violation of statute designed to protect human life is criminal act. State v. Agnew, 202 N.C. 755, 164 S.E. 578, 579.

Criminal action

The proceeding by which a party charged with a public offense is accused and brought to trial and punishment is known as a "criminal action." Pen.Code Cal. § 683. A criminal action is (1) an action prosecuted by the state as a party, against a person charged with a public offense, for the punishment thereof; (2) an action prosecuted by the state, at the instance of an individual, to prevent an apprehended crime, against his person or property. Code N.C. 1883, § 129, C.S. § 395.

Criminal assault and battery

An accused may be guilty of a "criminal assault and battery" if he intentionally does an act which by reason of its wanton and grossly negligent character exposes another to personal injury and in fact causes injury. State v. Linville, 150 Kan. 617, 95 P.2d 332, 334.

Criminal case

An action, suit, or cause instituted to punish an infraction of the criminal laws. State v. Smalls, 11 S.C. 279; People v. Iron Co., 201 Ill. 236, 66 N.E. 349; Wilburn v. State, 140 Ga. 138, 78 S.E. 819, 820; Hankamer v. Templin, 143 Tex. 572, 187 S.W.2d 549, 550. The phrase has various meanings according to context and purpose of constitutional provision or statute. Ex parte Tahbel, 46 Cal.App. 755, 189 P. 804, 806; Childs v. City of Birmingham, 19 Ala.App. 71, 94 So. 790; Barnett v. Atlanta, 109 Ga. 166, 34 S.E. 322.

Criminal charge

An accusation of crime, formulated in a written complaint, information, or indictment, and taking shape in a prosecution. U. S. v. Patterson, 150 U.S. 65, 14 S.Ct. 20, 37 L.Ed. 999; Eason v. State, 11 Ark. 482; People v. Ross, 235 Mich. 433, 209 N.W. 663, 666.

Criminal contempt proceeding

"Criminal contempt proceedings" are brought to preserve the power and vindicate the dignity and integrity of the court and to punish for disobedience of its orders. O'Malley v. United States, C.C.A.Mo., 128 F.2d 676, 683.

Criminal conversation

Defilement of the marriage bed, sexual intercourse of an outsider with husband or wife, or a breaking down of the covenant of fidelity. Young v. Young, 236 Ala. 627, 184 So. 187, 190, 191. Adultery, considered in its aspect of a civil injury to the husband entitling him to damages; the tort of debauching or seducing of a wife. Often abbreviated to *crim. con.*

Criminal court

One where criminal cases are tried and determined, not one where civil cases are tried, or persons charged with criminal offenses are held for action by proper authority. Hobart v. First Criminal Judicial Dist. of Court of Bergen County, 10 N.J.Misc. 723, 160 A. 674, 675.

Criminal gross negligence

"Gross negligence" is culpable or criminal when accompanied by acts of commission or omission of a wanton or willful nature, showing a reckless or indifferent disregard of the rights of others, under circumstances reasonably calculated to produce injury, or which make it not improbable that injury will be occasioned, and the offender knows or is charged with knowledge of the probable result of his acts; "culpable" meaning deserving of blame or censure. Bell v. Commonwealth, 170 Va. 597, 195 S.E. 675, 681.

Criminal information

A criminal suit brought, without interposition of a grand jury, by the proper officer of the king or state. Cole, Cr.Inf.; 4 Bla.Com. 398.

Criminal insanity

Want of mental capacity and moral freedom to do or abstain from doing particular act. State v. Schafer, 156 Wash. 240, 286 P. 833, 838.

Criminal instrumentality rule

Where the wrong is accomplished by a crime, the crime and not the negligent act of the party which made it possible is the "proximate cause". Foutch v. Alexandria Bank & Trust Co., 177 Tenn. 348, 149 S.W.2d 76, 85.

Criminal intent

The intent to commit a crime; malice, as evidenced by a criminal act; an intent to deprive or defraud the true owner of his property. People v. Borden's Condensed Milk Co., 165 App.Div. 711, 151 N.Y.S. 547, 549; State v. Howard, 162 La. 719, 111 So. 72, 76.

Criminal malversation

A broad category of corrupt official practices. Jimenez v. Aristeguieta, C.A.Fla., 311 F.2d 547, 562.

Criminal Motive

"Criminal motive" is the inducement, existing in the minds of persons, causing them to intend, and afterward to commit, crime. State v. Richardson, 197 Wash. 157, 84 P.2d 699, 703.

Criminal Procedure

The method pointed out by law for the apprehension, trial, or prosecution, and fixing the punishment, of those persons who have broken or violated, or are supposed to have broken or violated, the laws prescribed for the regulation of the conduct of the people of the community, and who have thereby laid themselves liable to fine or imprisonment or other punishment. 4 Amer. & Eng. Enc. Law, 730.

Criminal Proceeding

One instituted and conducted for the purpose either of preventing the commission of crime, or for fixing the guilt of a crime already committed and punishing the offender; as distinguished from a "civil" proceeding, which is for the redress of a private injury. Mossew v. United States, C.C.A. N.Y., 266 F. 18, 22, 11 A.L.R. 1261. Strictly, a "criminal proceeding" means some step taken before a court against some person or persons charged with some violation of the criminal law. McGoldrick v. Downs, 184 Misc. 168, 53 N.Y.S.2d 333, 336.

Criminal Process

Process which issues to compel a person to answer for a crime or misdemeanor. Mowlan v. State, 197 Ind. 517, 151 N.E. 416, 417. Also process issued to aid in the detection or suppression of crime, such as search warrants—the primary purpose of the search being to obtain evidence for use in a criminal prosecution. Sugar Valley Land Co. v. Johnson, 17 Ala.App. 409, 85 So. 871, 874.

Criminal Prosecution

An action or proceeding instituted in a proper court on behalf of the public, for the purpose of securing the conviction and punishment of one accused of crime. Harger v. Thomas, 44 Pa. 128, 84 Am.Dec. 422; Ex parte Pepper, 185 Ala. 284, 64 So. 112, 113; State v. District Court of Fifth Judicial Dist. in and for Madison County, 53 Mont. 350, 165 P. 294, 296; McGoldrick v. Downs, 184 Misc. 168, 53 N.Y.S.2d 333, 336. A prosecution in a court of justice, in name of the Government, against one or more individuals accused of crime. United States v. Safeway Stores, Tex., C.C.A.Kan., 140 F.2d 834, 839.

As to criminal "Conspiracy," "Contempt," "Information," "Jurisdiction," "Negligence," "Operation," see those titles.

CRIMINAL JURISDICTION. That which exists for the trial and punishment of criminal offenses; the authority by which judicial officers take cognizance of and decide criminal cases. Ellison v.

State, 125 Ind. 492, 24 N.E. 739; In re City of Buffalo, 139 N.Y. 422, 34 N.E. 1103.

Criminal law

That branch or division of law which treats of crimes and their punishments. In the plural—"criminal laws"—the term may denote the laws which define and prohibit the various species of crimes and establish their punishments. U. S. v. Reisinger, 128 U.S. 398, 9 S.Ct. 99, 32 L.Ed. 480; Washington v. Dowling, 92 Fla. 601, 109 So. 588, 591.

CRIMINAL LAW AMENDMENT ACT. This act was passed in 1871, 34 & 35 Vict. c. 32, to prevent and punish any violence, threats, or molestation, on the part either of master or workmen, in the various relations arising between them. 4 Steph. Comm. 241.

CRIMINAL LAW CONSOLIDATION ACT. The statutes 24 & 25 Vict. cc. 94–100, passed in 1861, for the consolidation of the criminal law of England and Ireland. 4 Steph. Comm. 297. These important statutes amount to a codification of the modern criminal law of England.

CRIMINAL LETTERS. In Scotch law. A process used as the commencement of a criminal proceeding, in the nature of a summons issued by the lord advocate or his deputy. It resembles a criminal information at common law.

CRIMINAL LIBEL. A libel which is punishable criminally; one which tends to excite a breach of the peace. 3 Greenl. Ev. § 164; Walker v. Wickens, 49 Kan. 42, 30 P. 181; Kennerly v. Hennessy, 68 Fla. 138, 66 So. 729, 19 A.L.R. 1468. The malicious defamation of a person made public by any printing or writing tending to provoke him to wrath and to deprive him of the benefits of public confidence and social intercourse.

CRIMINALIST. One versed in criminal law, one addicted to criminality, and, also, a psychiatrist dealing with criminality. People v. Taylor, 312 P.2d 731, 734, 152 C.A.2d 29; Douglas v. State, 163 So.2d 477, 486, 42 Ala.App. 314.

CRIMINALITER. Lat. Criminally. This term is used, in distinction or opposition to the word "*civiliter*," civilly, to distinguish a criminal liability or prosecution from a civil one.

CRIMINATE. To charge one with crime; to furnish ground for a criminal prosecution; to expose a person to a criminal charge. A witness cannot be compelled to answer any question which has a tendency to *criminate* him. Stewart v. Johnson, 18 N.J.Law, 87; Kendrick v. Comm., 78 Va. 490.

CRIMINOLOGY. The science which treats of crimes and their prevention and punishment.

CRIMP. One who decoys and plunders sailors under cover of harboring them. Wharton.

CRIPPLING. The word "crippling" is equivalent of words "physical disability" and is defined as to deprive of use of limbs, particularly of leg or foot, to deprive of strength, activity or capability for service or use and to disable. People v. Lockwood, 308 Mich. 618, 14 N.W.2d 517, 518; Baker v. Chicago, B. & Q. R. Co., 327 Mo. 986, 39 S.W.2d 535, 545.

CRITICISM. Permitted "criticism" as distinguished from "defamation" deals only with such things as invite public comment, and does not follow a public man into his private life, and pry into his domestic concerns. Devany v. Shulman, 184 Misc. 613, 53 N.Y.S.2d 401, 403.

CRO, CROO. In old Scotch law. A weregild. A composition, satisfaction, or assythment for the slaughter of a man.

CROCIA. The *crosier*, or pastoral staff.

CROCIARIUS. A cross-bearer, who went before the prelate. Wharton.

CROCKARDS, CROCARDS. A foreign coin of base metal, prohibited by statute 27 Edw. I. St. 3, from being brought into the realm. 4 Bl. Comm. 98; Crabb, Eng. Law, 176.

CROFT. A little close adjoining a dwelling-house, and inclosed for pasture and tillage or any particular use. Jacob. A small place fenced off in which to keep farm-cattle. Spelman. The word is now entirely obsolete.

CROISES. Pilgrims; so called as wearing the sign of the *cross* on their upper garments. Britt. c. 122. The knights of the order of St. John of Jerusalem, created for the defense of the pilgrims. Cowell; Blount.

CROITEIR. A crofter; one holding a croft.

CROOK. A person given to crooked or fraudulent practices, a swindler, sharper, thief, forger, or the like. Rubenstein v. Lee, 56 Ga.App. 49, 192 S.E. 85, 87; Sinclair Refining Co. v. Fuller, 190 Ark. 426, 79 S.W.2d 736, 739. Term "crook" has been defined as a professional rogue; a criminal; or one consorting with criminals; a person recognized by the authorities as belonging to the criminal class; swindler; sharp; cheat. Gaare v. Melbostad, 186 Minn. 96, 242 N.W. 466, 467.

CROOKED. Deviating from rectitude or uprightness; not straightforward; dishonest; wrong; perverse. A "crook" is a dishonest person; one who is crooked in conduct; a tricky or underhand schemer; a thief or swindler. Villemin v. Brown, 193 App.Div. 777, 184 N.Y.S. 570, 571; Pandolfo v. Bank of Benson, C.C.A.Ariz., 273 F. 48, 51.

CROP. The products of the harvest; emblements. Mutual Fire Insurance Co. v. Dehaven, Pa., 5 A. 65; Verbeck v. Peters, 170 Iowa, 610, 153 N.W. 215, 216. Such products of the soil as are annually planted, severed, and saved by manual labor, as cereals, vegetables, grass maturing for harvest or harvested, etc., but not grass on lands used for pasturage. Moore v. Hope Natural Gas

Co., 76 W.Va. 649, 86 S.E. 564, 567. In its more general signification, means all products of the soil that are grown and raised annually and gathered during a single season. In this sense the term includes fructus industriales and fructus naturales. The word is also used, however, in a more restricted sense, as synonymous with fructus industriales or emblements. Etymology of word "crop" appears to be from the Saxon "crop" or "cropp," which signified a cluster of ears of corn or grapes; another derivation is from the Welch "cropiad," which meant a fathering or taking hold of. It is from this derivation that the word has been held to mean only products after they have been severed from the soil. At times a distinction has been drawn between fructus industriales and fructus naturales. Kennedy v. Spalding, 143 Kan. 76, 53 P.2d 804, 806; Miethke v. Pierce County, 173 Wash. 381, 23 P.2d 405; Weddle v. Parrish, 135 Or. 345, 295 P. 454, 455.

In a broader sense, any product of the soil. Ellis, McKinnon & Brown v. Hopps, 30 Ga.App. 453, 118 S.E. 583; Buchanan v. Jencks, 38 R.I. 443, 96 A. 307, 309, 2 A.L.R. 986.

CROPPER. One who, having no interest in the land, works it in consideration of receiving a portion of the crop for his labor. Wood v. Garrison, 23 Ky.Law Rep. 295, 62 S.W. 728; Maltbie v. Olds, 88 Conn. 633, 92 A. 403, 405; Davis v. State, 84 Tex. Cr.R. 282, 206 S.W. 690; Empire Gas & Fuel Co. v. Denning, 128 Okl. 145, 261 P. 929, 930.

The difference between a tenant and a cropper is: A tenant has an estate in the land for the term, and, consequently, he has a right of property in the crops. Until division, the right of property and of possession in the whole is the tenant's. A cropper has no estate in the land; and, although he has in some sense the possession of the crop, it is the possession of a servant only, and is, in law, that of the landlord, who must divide off to the cropper his share. Harrison v. Ricks, 71 N.C. 7; O'Brien v. Webb, D.C.Cal., 279 F. 117, 120; Cook-Reynolds Co. v. Wilson, 67 Mont. 147, 214 P. 1104, 1105; Halsell v. First Nat. Bank, 109 Okl. 220, 235 P. 532, 533; Gibbons v. Huntsinger, 105 Mont. 562, 74 P.2d 443.

CROSS. A mark made by persons who are unable to write, to stand instead of a signature. A mark usually in the form of an X, by which voters are commonly required to express their selection. There are four principal forms of the cross: The St. Andrew's cross, which is made in the form of an X; the Latin cross, †, as used in the crucifixion; St. Anthony's cross, which is made in the form of a T; and the Greek cross, +, which is made by the intersection at right angles of lines at their center point. Hunt v. Campbell, 19 Ariz. 254, 169 P. 596, 610.

As an adjective, the word is applied to various demands and proceedings which are connected in subject-matter, but opposite or contradictory in purpose or object.

As a verb it means to pass or extend from one side to the other, as to cross a stream. People v. Hawkins, 51 Cal.App.2d Supp. 781, 124 P.2d 691, 692.

As to cross "Appeal," "Bill," "Complaint," "Remainder," "Rules," see those titles.

CROSS–ACTION. An action brought by one who is defendant in a suit against the party who is plaintiff in such suit, upon a cause of action growing out of the same transaction which is there in controversy, whether it be a contract or tort. An independent suit brought by defendant against plaintiff. National Stock Yards Nat. Bank v. Valentine, Tex.Civ.App., 39 S.W.2d 907, 908.

CROSS–CLAIM. A "cross-claim" is one brought by a defendant against a plaintiff in the same action or against a codefendant or both concerning matters in question in the original petition, and its purposes are to discover facts in aid of defense, to bring in new matter in aid of defense, to obtain some affirmative relief concerning matters in issue, to obtain full relief for all parties and a complete determination of all controversies arising out of matters alleged in original petition, and to have affirmative relief against either plaintiff or codefendant in the nature of an original petition. Farr v. Detroit Trust Co., C.C.A.Mich., 116 F.2d 807, 811.

CROSS–DEMAND. Where a person against whom a demand is made by another, in his turn makes a demand against that other, these mutual demands are called "cross-demands." A *set-off* is a familiar example. Musselman v. Galligher, 32 Iowa, 383.

CROSS–ERRORS. Errors being assigned by the respondent in a writ of error, the errors assigned on both sides are called "cross-errors."

CROSS–EXAMINATION. In practice. The examination of a witness upon a trial or hearing, or upon taking a deposition, by the party opposed to the one who produced him, upon his evidence given in chief, to test its truth, to further develop it, or for other purposes.

CROSS–LAY. The winding of the outer strands of a rope in a reverse direction to the inner strands, the "lay" of a strand of rope being the length of rope within which such strand makes one complete turn. Macomber & Whyte Rope Co. v. Hazard Mfg. Co., C.C.A.N.Y., 211 F. 976, 977.

CROSS–SALE. Where a floor broker, holding orders from different customers to buy and sell on the same terms, cries out the transaction and makes the sale and purchase to himself at the price shown by the last sale shown on the exchange, the transaction is called a "cross-sale or trade," and is illegal under rules of exchange, requiring two brokers to every purchase or sale. Cohen v. Rothschild, 182 App.Div. 408, 169 N.Y.S. 659, 664.

CROSSED CHECK. See Check.

CROSSING. A portion of a street over which pedestrians may lawfully cross from one side to the other. Under Laws N.J.1915, P.L. p. 285, § 1, defining crossings to be all duly indicated crossings, marked by pavement or otherwise, at intersection of streets, the most direct route across the street from curb to curb is a "crossing," where no paved crossing is there necessary. Ferris v. McArdle, 92 N.J.Law, 580, 106 A. 460, 461.

With reference to railroads, that portion of the right of way covered by intersection with a street or highway. International-Great Northern R. Co. v. Mallard, Tex.Civ.App., 262 S.W. 789, 791. In a broader sense, the term includes embankments constructed as necessary approaches to a railroad track, St. Louis, I. M. & S. Ry. Co. v. Smith, 118 Ark. 72, 175 S.W. 415, 416, and approaches or embankments reasonably necessary to enable crossings or bridges to be used, Payne v. Stockton, 147 Ark. 598, 229 S.W. 44, 47. For "Farm Crossing", see that title.

CROWD. "Crowd" is indefinite, since difference in time and place may shape its meaning, but there is always implied in the word numbers with reference to the hour and location. People, on Complaint of Liroff, v. Phillips, 245 N.Y. 401, 157 N.E. 508, 509.

CROWN. The sovereign power in a monarchy, especially in relation to the punishment of crimes. "Felony is an offense of the crown." Finch, Law, b. 1, c. 16.

An ornamental badge of regal power worn on the head by sovereign princes. The word is frequently used when speaking of the sovereign himself, or the rights, duties, and prerogatives belonging to him. Also a silver coin of the value of five shillings. Wharton.

The facings and backings made to be sold to dentists to be set by them with appropriate fastenings in the jaws of their patients, when so in place are commonly called "crowns" or "artificial crowns." S. S. White Dental Mfg. Co. v. Dental Co. of America, D.C.Pa., 263 F. 719, 720.

Ship's crown is convex arc of vessel's deck from side to side. The Indien, C.C.A.Cal., 71 F.2d 752, 757.

CROWN CASES. In English law. Criminal prosecutions on behalf of the crown, as representing the public; causes in the criminal courts.

CROWN CASES RESERVED. In English law. Questions of law arising in criminal trials at the assizes, (otherwise than by way of demurrer,) and not decided there, but reserved for the consideration of the court of criminal appeal.

CROWN COURT. In English law. The court in which the crown cases, or criminal business, of the assizes is transacted.

CROWN DEBTS. In English law. Debts due to the crown, which are put, by various statutes, upon a different footing from those due to a subject.

CROWN LANDS. The demesne lands of the crown. In England and Canada, lands belonging to the sovereign personally or to the government or nation, as distinguished from such as have passed into private ownership.

CROWN LAW. Criminal law in England is sometimes so termed, the crown being always the prosecutor in criminal proceedings. 4 Bl.Comm. 2.

CROWN OFFICE. The criminal side of the court of king's bench. The king's attorney in this court is called "master of the crown office." 4 Bl.Comm. 308.

CROWN OFFICE IN CHANCERY. One of the offices of the English high court of chancery, now transferred to the high court of justice. The principal official, the clerk of the crown, is an officer of parliament, and of the lord chancellor, in his non-judicial capacity, rather than an officer of the courts of law.

CROWN PAPER. A paper containing the list of criminal cases, which await the hearing or decision of the court, and particularly of the court of king's bench; and it then includes all cases arising from informations *quo warranto*, criminal informations, criminal cases brought up from inferior courts by writ of *certiorari*, and cases from the sessions. Brown.

CROWN SIDE. The criminal department of the court of king's bench; the civil department or branch being called the "plea side." 4 Bl.Comm. 265.

CROWN SOLICITOR. In England, the solicitor to the treasury acts, in state prosecutions, as solicitor for the crown in preparing the prosecution. In Ireland there are officers called "crown solicitors" attached to each circuit, whose duty it is to get up every case for the crown in criminal prosecutions. They are paid by salaries. There is no such system in England, where prosecutions are conducted by solicitors appointed by the parish, or other persons bound over to prosecute by the magistrates on each committal; but in Scotland the still better plan exists of a crown prosecutor (called the "procurator-fiscal," and being a subordinate of the lord-advocate) in every county, who prepares every criminal prosecution. Wharton.

CROWNER. In old Scotch law. Coroner; a coroner. "Crowner's quest," a coroner's inquest.

CROY. In old English law. Marsh land. Blount.

CRUCE SIGNATI. In old English law. Signed or marked with a cross. Pilgrims to the holy land, or crusaders; so called because they wore the sign of the cross upon their garments. Spelman.

CRUDE. A flexible term depending largely on context. In natural state; raw; unrefined; not artificially altered; unfinished. U. S. v. Richard & Co., 8 Ct.Cust.App. 304, 305; Nortmann-Duffke v. Federal Crushed Stone Co., 167 Minn. 333, 209 N.W. 17, 18; Ishimitsu Co. v. U. S., 12 Ct.Cust.App. 477, 479.

CRUEL AND UNUSUAL PUNISHMENT. See Punishment.

CRUELTY. The intentional and malicious infliction of physical suffering upon living creatures, particularly human beings; or, as applied to the latter, the wanton, malicious, and unnecessary infliction of pain upon the body, or the feelings and emotions; abusive treatment; inhumanity;

outrage. Jacobs v. Jacobs, 95 Conn. 57, 110 A. 455, 456.

Chiefly used in the law of divorce, in such phrases as "cruel and abusive treatment," "cruel and barbarous treatment," or "cruel and inhuman treatment," as to the meaning of which, and of "cruelty" in this sense, see Rudnick v. Rudnick, 288 Mass. 256, 192 N.E. 501; Martin v. Martin, 154 Pa.Super. 313, 35 A.2d 546, 548; Price v. Price, 181 Miss. 539, 179 So. 855, 857; Campbell v. Campbell, 129 Pa.Super. 106, 194 A. 760, 763; Avdoyan v. Avdoyan, 265 App.Div. 763, 40 N.Y.S.2d 665, 668; Lowry v. Lowry, 170 Ga. 349, 153 S.E. 11, 14, 70 A.L.R. 488.

For "Extreme and Repeated Cruelty," see that title.

As between husband and wife. Those acts which affect the life, the health, or even the comfort, of the party aggrieved and give a reasonable apprehension of bodily hurt, are called "cruelty." What merely wounds the feelings is seldom admitted to be cruelty, unless the act be accompanied with bodily injury, either actual or menaced. Mere austerity of temper, petulance of manners, rudeness of language, a want of civil attention and accommodation, even occasional sallies of passion, will not amount to legal cruelty; *a fortiori,* the denial of little indulgences and particular accommodations, which the delicacy of the world is apt to number among its necessaries, is not cruelty. The negative descriptions of cruelty are perhaps the best, under the infinite variety of cases that may occur, by showing what is not cruelty. Evans v. Evans, 1 Hagg.Const. 35; Westmeath v. Westmeath, 4 Eng.Ecc. 238, 311, 312.

Cruelty includes both willfulness and malicious temper of mind with which an act is done, as well as a high degree of pain inflicted. Acts merely accidental, though they inflict great pain, are not "cruel," in the sense of the word as used in statutes against cruelty. Comm. v. McClellan, 101 Mass. 34.

Cruelty to Animals

The infliction of physical pain, suffering, or death upon an animal, when not necessary for purposes of training or discipline or (in the case of death) to procure food or to release the animal from incurable suffering, but done wantonly, for mere sport, for the indulgence of a cruel and vindictive temper, or with reckless indifference to its pain. State v. Porter, 112 N.C. 887, 16 S.E. 915; State v. Bosworth, 54 Conn. 1, 4 A. 248; McKinne v. State, 81 Ga. 164, 9 S.E. 1091; Waters v. People, 23 Colo. 33, 46 P. 112, 33 L.R.A. 836.

Legal Cruelty

See Legal Cruelty.

CRUISE. A voyage undertaken for a given purpose; a voyage for the purpose of making captures *jure belli.* The Brutus, 2 Gall. 538, Fed. Cas.No.2,060.

A voyage or expedition in quest of vessels or fleets of the enemy which may be expected to sail in any particular track at a certain season of the year. The region in which these cruises are performed is usually termed the "rendezvous," or "cruising latitude." Bouvier.

A report of a timber surveyor showing the character and amount of timber in a stand. Jones v. United States, C.C.A.Or., 265 F. 235, 239.

CRUSH. To break by means of pressure. Yagunchok v. Rutledge, 219 Mich. 82, 188 N.W. 412, 413.

It has been defined to mean to compress or bruise between two hard bodies; to squeeze or force by pressure so as to destroy the natural condition, shape, or integrity of the parts, or to force together into a mass. Atlantic Oil Producing Co. v. Malone, 152 Okl. 68, 3 P.2d 874, 875.

CRY. To call out aloud; to proclaim; to publish; to sell at auction. "To cry a tract of land." Carr v. Gooch, 1 Wash., Va., 335 (260).

A clamor raised in the pursuit of an escaping felon. 4 Bl.Comm. 293. See Hue and Cry.

CRY DE PAIS, or CRI DE PAIS. The hue and cry raised by the people in ancient times, where a felony had been committed and the constable was absent.

CRYER. An auctioneer. Carr v. Gooch, 1 Wash., Va., 337, (262.) One who calls out aloud; one who publishes or proclaims. See Crier.

CRYPTA. A chapel or oratory underground, or under a church or cathedral. Du Cange.

CUCKING–STOOL. An engine of correction for common scolds, which in the Saxon language is said to signify the scolding-stool, though now it is frequently corrupted into *ducking-stool,* because the judgment was that, when the woman was placed therein, she should be plunged in the water for her punishment. It was also variously called a "trebucket," "tumbrel," or "castigatory." 3 Inst. 219; 4 Bl.Comm. 169; Brown. James v. Comm., 12 Serg. & R., Pa., 220.

CUCKOLD. A man whose wife is unfaithful; the husband of an adulteress. It is explained that the word alludes to the habit of the female cuckold, which lays her eggs in the nests of other birds to be hatched by them. To make a cuckold of a man is to seduce his wife. Hall v. Huffman, 159 Ky. 72, 166 S.W. 770.

CUEILLETTE. A term of French maritime law. See A Cueillette.

CUI ANTE DIVORTIUM (L. Lat. The full phrase was, *Cui ipsa ante divortium contradicere non potuit,* whom she before the divorce could not gainsay). A writ which anciently lay in favor of a woman who had been divorced from her husband, to recover lands and tenements which she had in fee-simple, fee-tail, or for life, from him to whom her husband had aliened them during marriage, when she could not gainsay it; Fitzh.N.B. 240; 3 Bla.Com. 183, n.; Stearns, Real Act. 143; Booth, Real Act. 188. Abolished in 1833.

CUI BONO. For whose good; for whose use or benefit. "*Cui bono* is ever of great weight in all agreements." Parker, C. J., 10 Mod. 135. Sometimes translated, for what good, for what useful purpose.

CUI IN VITA (L. Lat. The full phrase was, *Cui in vita sua ipsa contradicere non potuit,* whom in his lifetime she could not gainsay). A writ of entry which lay for a widow against a person to whom her husband had in his lifetime aliened her lands. Fitzh.N.B. 193. It was a method of establishing the fact of death, being a trial with witnesses, but without a jury. The object of the writ was to avoid a judgment obtained against the husband by confession or default. It is obsolete in England by force of 32 Hen. VIII, c. 28, § 6. See 6 Co. 8, 9. As to its use in Pennsylvania, see 3 Binn.Appx.; Rep.Comm. on Penn.Civ.Code, 1835, 90. Abolished in England, 1833. Blackstone is said to have shown little knowledge of its history; Thayer, Evidence.

CUI JURISDICTIO DATA EST, EA QUOQUE CONCESSA ESSE VIDENTUR, SINE QUIBUS JURISDICTIO EXPLICARI NON POTEST. To whomsoever a jurisdiction is given, those things also are supposed to be granted, without which the jurisdiction cannot be exercised. Dig. 2, 1, 2. The grant of jurisdiction implies the grant of all powers necessary to its exercise. 1 Kent, Comm. 339.

CUI JUS EST DONANDI, EIDEM ET VENDENDI ET CONCEDENDI JUS EST. He who has the right of giving has also the right of selling and granting. Dig. 50, 17, 163.

CUILIBET IN ARTE SUA PERITO EST CREDENDUM. Any person skilled in his peculiar art or profession is to be believed, [*i. e.*, when he speaks of matters connected with such art.] Co. Litt. 125*a*. Credence should be given to one skilled in his peculiar profession. Broom.Max. 932; 1 Bla.Com. 75; Phill.Ev.Cowen & H. notes, 759; 1 Hagg.Ecc. 727; 11 Cl. & F. 85.

CUILIBET LICET JURI PRO SE INTRODUCTO RENUNCIARE. Any one may waive or renounce the benefit of a principle or rule of law that exists only for his protection.

CUI LICET GUOD MAJUS, NON DEBET QUOD MINUS EST NON LICERE. He who is allowed to do the greater ought not to be prohibited from doing the less. He who has authority to do the more important act ought not to be debarred from doing what is of less importance. 4 Coke 23.

CUICUNQUE ALIQUIS QUID CONCEDIT CONCEDERE VIDETUR ET ID, SINE QUO RES IPSA ESSE NON POTUIT. Whoever grants anything to another is supposed to grant that also without which the thing itself would be of no effect. 11 Co. 52; Broom, Max. 479; Hob. 234; Vaugh. 109; 11 Exch. 775; Shep.Touch. 89; Co.Litt. 56 *a*.

CUI PATER EST POPULUS NON HABET ILLE PATREM. He to whom the people is father has not a father. Co.Litt. 123.

CUIQUE IN SUA ARTE CREDENDUM EST. Everyone is to be believed in his own art. Dickinson v. Barber, 9 Mass. 227, 6 Am.Dec. 58.

CUJUS EST COMMODUM EJUS DEBET ESSE INCOMMODUM. Whose is the advantage, his also should be the disadvantage.

CUJUS EST DARE, EJUS EST DISPONERE. Wing.Max. 53. Whose it is to give, his it is to dispose; or, as Broom says, "the bestower of a gift has a right to regulate its disposal." Broom, Max. 459, 461, 463, 464.

CUJUS EST DIVISIO, ALTERIUS EST ELECTIO. Whichever [of two parties] has the division, [of an estate,] the choice [of the shares] is the other's. Co.Litt. 166*b*. In partition between coparceners, where the division is made by the eldest, the rule in English law is that she shall choose her share last. Id.; 2 Bl.Comm. 189; 1 Steph. Comm. 323.

CUJUS EST DOMINIUM EJUS EST PERICULUM. The risk lies upon the owner of the subject. Tray.Lat.Max. 114.

CUJUS EST INSTITUERE, EJUS EST ABROGARE. Whose right it is to institute, his right it is to abrogate. Broom, Max. 878, note.

CUJUS EST SOLUM EJUS EST USQUE AD CŒLUM. Whose is the soil, his it is up to the sky. Co.Litt. 4*a*. He who owns the soil, or surface of the ground, owns, or has an exclusive right to, everything which is upon or above it to an indefinite height. 9 Coke 54; Shep.Touch. 90; 2 Bl. Comm. 18; 3 Bl.Comm. 217; Broom.Max. 395.

CUJUS EST SOLUM, EJUS EST USQUE AD CŒLUM ET AD INFEROS. To whomsoever the soil belongs, he owns also to the sky and to the depths. The owner of a piece of land owns everything above and below it to an indefinite extent. Co.Litt. 4; Shell Oil Co. v. Manley Oil Corporation, D.C.Ill., 37 F.Supp. 289, 292.

CUJUS JURIS (*i. e.*, JURISDICTIONIS) EST PRINCIPALE, EJUSDEM JURIS ERIT ACCESSORIUM. 2 Inst. 493. An accessory matter is subject to the same jurisdiction as its principal.

CUJUS PER ERROREM DATI REPETITIO EST, EJUS CONSULTO DATI DONATIO EST. He who gives a thing by mistake has a right to recover it back; but, if he gives designedly, it is a gift. Dig. 50, 17, 53.

CUJUSQUE REI POTISSIMA PARS EST PRINCIPIUM. The chiefest part of everything is the beginning. Dig. 1, 2, 1; 10 Coke, 49*a*.

CUL DE SAC. (Fr. the bottom of a sack.) A blind alley; a street which is open at one end only. Bartlett v. Bangor, 67 Me. 467; Talbott v. Railroad Co., 31 Grat., Va., 691; Hickok v. Plattsburg, 41 Barb., N.Y., 135; Beckham v. State, 64 Cal.App.2d 487, 149 P.2d 296, 300.

CULAGIUM. In old records. The laying up a ship in a dock, in order to be repaired. Cowell; Blount.

CULPA. Lat. A term of the civil law, meaning fault, neglect, or negligence. There are three degrees of *culpa,—lata culpa*, gross fault or neglect; *levis culpa*, ordinary fault or neglect; *levissima culpa*, slight fault or neglect,—and the definitions of these degrees are precisely the same as those in our law. Story, Bailm. § 18. This term is to be distinguished from *dolus,* which means fraud, guile, or deceit.

CULPA CARET QUI SCIT SED PROHIBERE NON POTEST. He is clear of blame who knows, but cannot prevent. Dig. 50, 17, 50.

CULPA EST IMMISCERE SE REL AD SE NON PERTINENTI. 2 Inst. 208. It is a fault for any one to meddle in a matter not pertaining to him.

CULPA LATA DOLO ÆQUIPARATUR. Gross negligence is held equivalent to intentional wrong.

CULPA TENET [TENEAT] SUOS AUCTORES. Misconduct binds [should bind] its own authors. It is a never-failing axiom that every one is accountable only for his own delicts. Ersk.Inst. 4, 1, 14.

CULPABILIS. Lat. In old English law. Guilty. *Culpabilis de intrusione,*—guilty of intrusion. Fleta, lib. 4, c. 30, § 11. *Non culpabilis,* (abbreviated to *non cul.*) In criminal procedure, the plea of "not guilty." See Culprit.

CULPABLE. Blamable; censurable; involving the breach of a legal duty or the commission of a fault. The term is not necessarily equivalent to "criminal," for, in present use, and notwithstanding its derivation, it implies that the act or conduct spoken of is reprehensible or wrong but not that it involves malice or a guilty purpose. "Culpable" in fact connotes fault rather than guilt. Railway Co. v. Clayberg, 107 Ill. 651; Cain v. State, 55 Ga. App. 376, 190 S.E. 371, 374.

As to culpable "Homicide," "Ignorance," "Neglect," and "Negligence," "Wantonness," see those titles.

It also means that which is deserving of moral blame. Mercury Motor Transport v. State ex rel. Motor Vehicle Com'r, 197 Miss. 387, 21 So.2d 25, 28.

CULPÆ PŒNA PAR ESTO. PŒNA AD MENSURAM DELICTI STATUENDA EST. Let the punishment be proportioned to the crime. Punishment is to be measured by the extent of the offense.

CULPRIT. A person who is indicted for a criminal offense, but not yet convicted. It is not, however, a technical term of the law; and in its vernacular usage it seems to imply only a light degree of censure or moral reprobation.

Blackstone believes it an abbreviation of the old forms of arraignment, whereby, on the prisoner's pleading not guilty, the clerk would respond, *"culpabilis, prit," i. e.,* he is guilty and the crown is ready. It was (he says) the *viva voce* replication, by the clerk, on behalf of the crown, to the prisoner's plea of *non culpabilis; prit* being a technical word, anciently in use in the formula of joining issue. 4 Bl.Comm. 339.

But a more plausible explanation is that given by Donaldson, (cited Whart.Lex.,) as follows: The clerk asks the prisoner, "Are you guilty, or not guilty?" Prisoner "Not guilty." Clerk, *"Qu'il paroit,* [may it prove so.] How will you be tried?" Prisoner, "By God and my country." These words being hurried over, came to sound, "culprit, how will you be tried?" The ordinary derivation is from *culpa.*

CULRACH. In old Scotch law. A species of pledge or cautioner, (Scottice *back borgh,*) used in cases of the replevin of persons from one man's court to another's. Skene.

CULTIVATE. The word "cultivate" means to till, prepare for crops, manure, plow, dress, sow and reap, manage and improve in husbandry. Miller v. Richey, Tex.Civ.App., 173 S.W.2d 490, 493.

CULTIVATED. A field on which a crop of wheat is growing is a cultivated field, although not a stroke of labor may have been done in it since the seed was put in the ground, and it is a cultivated field after the crop is removed. It is, strictly, a cultivated piece of ground. Combs v. Rockingham County Com'rs, 170 N.C. 87, 86 S.E. 963, 964; Angus Cattle Co. v. McLeod, 98 Neb. 108, 152 N.W. 322, 323.

CULTIVATOR. A cropper, which see. Pearson v. Lafferty, 197 Mo.App. 123, 193 S.W. 40, 41.

CULTURA. A parcel of arable land. Blount.

CULVERTAGE. In old English law. A base kind of slavery. The confiscation or forfeiture which takes place when a lord seizes his tenant's estate. Blount; Du Cange.

CUM ACTIO FUERIT MERE CRIMINALIS, INSTITUI POTERIT AB INITIO CRIMINALITER VEL CIVILITER. When an action is merely criminal, it can be instituted from the beginning either criminally or civilly. Bract. 102.

CUM ADSUNT TESTIMONIA RERUM, QUID OPUS EST VERBIS? When the proofs of facts are present, what need is there of words? 2 Bulst. 53.

CUM ALIQUIS RENUNCIAVERIT SOCIETATI, SOLVITUR SOCIETAS. When any partner renounces the partnership, the partnership is dissolved. Tray. Lat. Max. 118.

CUM CONFITENTE SPONTE MITIUS EST AGENDUM. 4 Inst. 66. One confessing willingly should be dealt with more leniently.

CUM COPULA. Lat. With copulation, *i. e.,* sexual intercourse. Used in speaking of the validity of a marriage contracted "per verba de futuro cum copula," that is, with words referring to the future (a future intention to have the marriage solemnized) and consummated by sexual connection.

CUM DE LUCRO DUORUM QUÆRITUR, MELIOR EST CAUSA POSSIDENTIS. When the question is as to the gain of two persons, the cause of him who is in possession is the better. Dig. 50, 17, 126.

CUM DUO INTER SE PUGNANTIA REPERIUNTUR IN TESTAMENTO, ULTIMUM RATUM EST. Where two things repugnant to each other are found in a will, the last shall stand. Co. Litt. 112*b*; Shep. Touch. 451; Broom, Max. 583.

CUM DUO JURA CONCURRUNT IN UNA PERSONA ÆQUUM EST AC SI ESSENT IN DUOBUS. When two rights meet in one person, it is the same as if they were in two persons.

CUM GRANO SALIS. (With a grain of salt.) With allowance for exaggeration.

CUM IN CORPORE DISSENTITUR, APPARET NULLAM ESSE ACCEPTIONEM. When there is a disagreement in the substance, it appears that there is no acceptance. Gardner v. Lane, 12 Allen, Mass., 44.

CUM IN TESTAMENTO AMBIGUE AUT ETIAM PERPERAM SCRIPTUM EST BENIGNE INTERPRETARI ET SECUNDUM ID QUOD CREDIBILE EST COGITATUM CREDENDUM EST. Dig. 34, 5, 24. Where an ambiguous, or even an erroneous, expression occurs in a will, it should be construed liberally, and in accordance with the testator's probable meaning. Broom, Max. 568.

CUM LEGITIMÆ NUPTIÆ FACTÆ SUNT, PATREM LIBERI SEQUUNTUR. Children born under a legitimate marriage follow the condition of the father.

CUM ONERE. With the burden; subject to an incumbrance or charge. What is taken *cum onere* is taken subject to an existing burden or charge.

CUM PAR DELICTUM EST DUORUM, SEMPER ONERATUR PETITOR ET MELIOR HABETUR POSSESSORIS CAUSA. Dig. 50, 17, 154. When both parties are in fault the plaintiff must always fail, and the cause of the person in possession be preferred.

CUM PERA ET LOCULO. With satchel and purse. A phrase in old Scotch law.

CUM PERTINENTIIS. With the appurtenances. Bract. fol. 73*b*.

CUM PRIVILEGIO. The expression of the monopoly of Oxford, Cambridge, and the royal printers to publish the Bible.

CUM QUOD AGO NON VALET UT AGO, VALEAT QUANTUM VALERE POTEST. 4 Kent, Comm. 493. When that which I do is of no effect as I do it, it shall have as much effect as it can; *i. e.,* in some other way.

CUM TESTAMENTO ANNEXO. L. Lat. With the will annexed. A term applied to administration granted where a testator makes an incomplete will, without naming any executors, or where he names incapable persons, or where the executors named refuse to act. If the executor has died, an administrator *de bonis non cum testamento annexo* (of the goods not [already] administered upon with the will annexed) is appointed. Often abbreviated d. b. n. c. t. a. 2 Bl. Comm. 503, 504.

CUMULATIVE. Additional; heaping up; increasing; forming an aggregate. The word signifies that two things are to be added together, instead of one being a repetition or in substitution of the other. People v. Superior Court, 10 Wend., N.Y., 285; Regina v. Eastern Archipelago, Co., 18 Eng. Law & Eq. 183.

As to cumulative "Dividend," "Legacy," "Punishment" and "Sentences," see those titles.

CUMULATIVE EVIDENCE. Additional or corroborative evidence to the same point. That which goes to prove what has already been established by other evidence. Glidden v. Dunlap, 28 Me. 383; Parker v. Hardy, 24 Pick., Mass., 248; Waller v. Graves, 20 Conn. 310; Roe v. Kalb, 37 Ga. 459; Purcell Envelope Co. v. United States, 48 Ct.Cl. 66, 73.

All evidence material to the issue, after any such evidence has been given, is in a certain sense cumulative; that is, is added to what has been given before. It tends to sustain the issue. But cumulative evidence, in legal phrase, means evidence from the same or a new witness, simply repeating, in substance and effect, or adding to, what has been before testified to. Parshall v. Klinck, 43 Barb., N.Y., 212. Evidence is not cumulative merely because it tends to establish the same ultimate or *principally controverted* fact. Cumulative evidence is additional evidence of the same kind to the same point. Able v. Frazier, 43 Iowa, 177; Harlan v. Texas Fuel & Supply Co., Tex.Civ.App., 160 S.W. 1142, 1146.

Cumulative Offense

One which can be committed only by a repetition of acts of the same kind but committed on different days. The offense of being a "common seller" of intoxicating liquors is an example. Wells v. Com., 12 Gray., Mass., 328.

Cumulative Remedy

A remedy created by statute in addition to one which still remains in force. Railway Co. v. Chicago, 148 Ill. 141, 35 N.E. 881; State v. Barboglio, 63 Utah, 432, 226 P. 904, 907; Phillip Levy & Co. v. Davis, 115 Va. 814, 80 S.E. 791, 794; Wulff-Hansen & Co. v. Silvers, Cal.App., 120 P.2d 677, 680.

Cumulative Voting

A system of voting, by which the elector, having a number of votes equal to the number of officers to be chosen, is allowed to concentrate the whole number of his votes upon one person, or to distribute them as he may see fit. For example, if ten directors of a corporation are to be elected, then, under this system, the voter may cast ten votes for one person, or five votes for each of two persons, etc. It is intended to secure representation of a minority. Bridgers v. Staton, 150 N.C. 216, 63 S.E. 892; Chicago Macaroni Mfg. Co. v. Boggiano, 202 Ill. 312, 67 N.E. 17; Attorney General v. McVichie, 138 Mich. 387, 101 N.W. 552.

CUNADES. In Spanish law. Affinity; alliance; relation by marriage. Las Partidas, pt. 4, tit. 6, 1, 5.

CUNEATOR. A coiner. Du Cange. *Cuneare,* to coin. *Cuneus,* the die with which to coin. *Cuneata,* coined. Du Cange; Spelman.

CUNNILINGUS. An act of sex perversion committed with the mouth and the female sexual organ. State v. Murry, 136 La. 253, 66 So. 963, 965.

CUNTEY-CUNTEY. In old English law. A kind of trial, as appears from Bract. lib. 4, tract 3, ca. 18, and tract 4, ca. 2, where it seems to mean, one by the ordinary jury.

CUR. A common abbreviation of *curia.*

CURA. Lat. Care; charge; oversight; guardianship.

In the civil law a species of guardianship which commenced at the age of puberty (when the guardianship called "tutela" expired,) and continued to the completion of the twenty-fifth year. Inst. 1, 23, pr.; Id. 1, 25, pr.; Hallifax, Civil Law, b. 1, c. 9.

CURAGULOS. One who takes care of a thing.

CURATE. In ecclesiastical law. Properly, an incumbent who has the *cure* of souls, but now generally restricted to signify the spiritual assistant of a rector or vicar in his *cure.* An officiating temporary minister in the English church, who represents the proper incumbent; being regularly employed either to serve in his absence or as his assistant, as the case may be. 1 Bl. Comm. 393; 3 Steph. Comm. 88; Brande.

Perpetual Curacy, the office of a curate in a parish where there is no spiritual rector or vicar, but where a clerk (curate) is appointed to officiate there by the impropriator. 2 Burn.Ecc.Law, 55. The church or benefice filled by a curate under these circumstances is also so called.

CURATEUR. In French law. A person charged with supervising the administration of the affairs of an emancipated minor, of giving him advice, and assisting him in the important acts of such administration. Duverger.

CURATIO. In the civil law. The power or duty of managing the property of him who, either on account of infancy or some defect of mind or body, cannot manage his own affairs. The duty of a curator or guardian. Calvin.

CURATIVE. Intended to cure (that is, to obviate the ordinary legal effects or consequences of) defects, errors, omissions or irregularities. Meigs v. Roberts, 162 N.Y. 371, 56 N.E. 838, 76 Am.St. Rep. 322.

The word is defined as relating to, or employed in, the cure of diseases; tending to cure; a remedy. State v. Stoddard, 215 Iowa, 534, 245 N.W. 273, 275, 86 A.L.R. 616.

Applied particularly to statutes, a "curative act" being a retrospective law passed in order to validate legal proceedings, the acts of public officers, or private deeds or contracts, which would otherwise be void for defects or irregularities or for want of conformity to existing legal requirements. Meigs v. Roberts, 162 N.Y. 371, 56 N.E. 838, 76 Am.St.Rep. 322; one intended to give legal effect to some past act or transaction which is ineffective because of neglect to comply with some requirement of law. Anderson v. Lehmkuhl, 119 Neb. 451, 229 N.W. 773, 777; Carle v. Gehl, 193 Ark. 1061, 104 S.W.2d 445, 447; also one enacted to cure past irregularities not jurisdictional. Dunkum v. Maceck Bldg. Corporation, 256 N.Y. 275, 176 N.E. 392, 396. Applied to evidence curative admissibility is the doctrine that an opponent may reply with similar evidence whenever it is needed for removing an unfair prejudice which might otherwise have ensued. Biener v. St. Louis Public Service Co., Mo.App., 160 S.W.2d 780, 786.

CURATOR. In the Civil Law. A person who is appointed to take care of anything for another. A guardian. One appointed to take care of the estate of a minor above a certain age, a lunatic, a spendthrift, or other person not regarded by the law as competent to administer it for himself. The title was also applied to a variety of public officers in Roman administrative law. Sproule v. Davies, 69 App.Div. 502, 75 N.Y.S. 229; Le Blanc v. Jackson, Tex.Civ.App., 161 S.W. 60, 66; Daniels v. Metropolitan Life Ins. Co., 135 Pa.Super. 450, 5 A.2d 608, 611.

In Scotch Law

The term means a guardian.

In Louisiana

A person appointed to take care of the estate of an absentee.

In Missouri

The term "curator" has been adopted from the civil law, and it is applied to the guardian of the estate of the ward as distinguished from the guardian of his person. Duncan v. Crook, 49 Mo. 117.

Curator ad hoc

In the civil law. A guardian for this purpose; a special guardian.

Curator ad litem

Guardian for the suit. In English law, the corresponding phrase is "guardian *ad litem.*"

Curator bonis

In the civil law. A guardian or trustee appointed to take care of *property* in certain cases; as for the benefit of creditors. Dig. 42, 7. In Scotch law. The term is applied to guardians for minors, lunatics, etc.

Curatores viarum

Surveyors of the highways.

CURATORSHIP. The office of a curator. Curatorship differs from tutorship, (*q. v.*) in this; that the latter is instituted for the protection of property in the first place, and, secondly, of the person; while the former is intended to protect, first, the person, and secondly, the property. 1 Lec. El. Dr. Civ. Rom. 241.

CURATRIX. A woman who has been appointed to the office of curator; a female guardian. Cross' Curatrix v. Cross' Legatees, 4 Grat., Va., 257.

CURATUS NON HABET TITULUM. A curate has no title, [to tithes.] 3 Bulst. 310.

CURE. The act of healing; restoration to health from disease, or to soundness after injury. State

v. Gibson, 199 Iowa 177, 201 N.W. 590; State v. Stoddard, 215 Iowa, 534, 245 N.W. 273, 275, 86 A. L.R. 616. Under rule that a vessel and her owner must provide maintenance, and cure for seaman injured or falling ill while in service, "cure" is care, including nursing and medical attention during such period as the duty continues. Calmar S. S. Corporation v. Taylor, Pa., 303 U.S. 525, 58 S. Ct. 651, 653, 82 L.Ed. 993.

CURE BY VERDICT. The rectification or rendering nugatory of a defect in the pleadings by the rendition of a verdict; the court will presume, after a verdict, that the particular thing omitted or defectively stated in the pleadings was duly proved at the trial. State v. Keena, 63 Conn. 329, 28 A. 522; Treanor v. Houghton, 103 Cal. 53, 36 P. 1081.

CURE OF SOULS. In ecclesiastical law. The ecclesiastical or spiritual charge of a parish, including the usual and regular duties of a minister in charge. State v. Bray, 35 N.C. 290.

CURFEW. An institution supposed to have been introduced into England by order of William the Conqueror, which consisted in the ringing of a bell or bells at eight o'clock at night, at which signal the people were required to extinguish all lights in their dwellings, and to put out or rake up their fires, and retire to rest, and all companies to disperse. The word is probably derived from the French *couvre feu*, to cover the fire. The curfew is spoken of in 1 Social England 373, as having been ordained by William I, in order to prevent nightly gatherings of the people of England. But the custom is evidently older than the Norman; for we find an order of King Alfred that the inhabitants of Oxford should at the ringing of that bell cover up their fires and go to bed. And there is evidence that the same practice prevailed at this period in France, Normandy, Spain, and probably in most of the other countries of Europe. Henry, Hist. of Britain, vol. 3, 567. It was doubtless intended as a precaution against fires, which were very frequent and destructive when most houses were built of wood. It appears to have met with so much opposition that in 1103 we find Henry I, repealing the enactment of his father on the subject; and Blackstone says that, though it is mentioned a century afterwards, it is rather spoken of as a time of night than as a still subsisting custom. Shakespeare frequently refers to it in the same sense.

CURIA. In old European law. A court. The palace, household, or retinue of a sovereign. A judicial tribunal or court held in the sovereign's palace. A court of justice. The civil power, as distinguished from the ecclesiastical. A manor; a nobleman's house; the hall of a manor. A piece of ground attached to a house; a yard or courtyard. Spelman. A lord's court held in his manor. The tenants who did suit and service at the lord's court. A manse. Cowell.

In Roman Law

A division of the Roman people, said to have been made by Romulus. They were divided into three tribes, and each tribe into ten *curiæ*, making thirty *curiæ* in all. Spelman. The place or building in which each *curia* assembled to offer sacred rites. The place of meeting of the Roman senate; the senate house. The senate house of a province; the place where the *decuriones* assembled. Cod. 10, 31, 2. See Decurio.

CURIA ADMIRALITATIS. The court of admiralty.

CURIA ADVISARI VULT. L. Lat. The court will advise; the court will consider. A phrase frequently found in the reports, signifying the resolution of the court to suspend judgment in a cause, after the argument, until they have deliberated upon the question, as where there is a new or difficult point involved. It is commonly abbreviated to *cur. adv. vult*, or *c. a. v.*

CURIA BARONIS, OR BARONUM. In old English law. A court-baron. Fleta, lib. 2, c. 53.

CURIA CANCELLARIÆ OFFICINA JUSTITIÆ. 2 Inst. 552. The court of chancery is the workshop of justice.

CURIA CHRISTIANITATIS. The ecclesiastical court.

CURIA CLAUDENDA. The name of a writ to compel another to make a fence or wall, which he was bound to make, between his land and the plaintiff's. Reg. Orig. 155. Now obsolete.

CURIA COMITATUS. The county court (*q. v.*)

CURIA CURSUS AQUÆ. A court held by the lord of the manor of Gravesend for the better management of barges and boats plying on the river Thames between Gravesend and Windsor, and also at Gravesend bridge, etc. 2 Geo. II, c. 26.

CURIA DOMINI. In old English law. The lord's court, house, or hall, where all the tenants met at the time of keeping court. Cowell.

CURIA LEGITIME AFFIRMATA. A phrase used in old Scotch records to show that the court was opened in due and lawful manner.

CURIA MAGNA. In old English law. The great court; one of the ancient names of parliament.

CURIA MAJORIS. In old English law. The mayor's court. Calth. 144.

CURIA MILITUM. A court so called, anciently held at Carisbrook Castle, in the Isle of Wight. Cowell.

CURIA PALATII. The palace court. It was abolished by 12 & 13 Vict. c. 101.

CURIA PARLIAMENTI SUIS PROPRIIS LEGIBUS SUBSISTIT. 4 Inst. 50. The court of parliament is governed by its own laws.

CURIA PEDIS PULVERIZATI. In old English law. The court of *piedpoudre* or *piepouders*. 3 Bl. Comm. 32. See Court of Piepoudre.

CURIA PENTICIARUM. A court held by the sheriff of Chester, in a place there called the *"Pendice"* or *"Pentice;"* probably it was so called from being originally held under a pent-house, or open shed covered with boards. Blount.

CURIA PERSONÆ. In old records. A parsonage-house, or manse. Cowell.

CURIA REGIS. The king's court. A term applied to the *aula regis,* the *bancus,* or *communis bancus,* and the *iter* or *eyre,* as being courts of the king, but especially to the *aula regis,* (which title see.)

CURIALITY. In Scotch law. Curtesy. Also the privileges, prerogatives, or, perhaps, retinue, of a court.

CURING TITLE. "Clearing", "curing", "straightening out", or "removing cloud from" title denotes acts or proceedings necessary to render title marketable. Johnston v. Cox, 114 Fla. 243, 154 So. 206.

CURIOSA ET CAPTIOSA INTERPRETATIO IN LEGE REPROBATUR. A curious [overnice or subtle] and captious interpretation is reprobated in law. 1 Balst. 6.

CURNOCK. In old English law. A measure containing four bushels or half a quarter of corn. Cowell; Blount.

CURRENCY. Coined money and such banknotes or other paper money as are authorized by law and do in fact circulate from hand to hand as the medium of exchange. Griswold v. Hepburn, 2 Duv., Ky., 33; Insurance Co. v. Kupfer, 28 Ill. 332, 81 Am.Dec. 284. Certificates of deposit are "Currency." State ex rel. Cole v. Trimble, 307 Mo. 57, 269 S.W. 959, 961; Millikan v. Security Trust Co., 187 Ind. 307, 118 N.E. 568, 570. Gold certificate held "currency". Nortz v. U. S., Ct.Cl., 294 U.S. 317, 55 S.Ct. 428, 79 L.Ed. 907, 907 A.L.R. 1346.

The term "money" is synonymous with "currency," and imports any currency, token, bank notes, or other circulating medium in general use as the representative of value. People v. Miller, 292 Ill.App. 643, 11 N.E.2d 827.

CURRENT. Running; now in transit; whatever is at present in course of passage; as "the current month." Wharton v. Morris, 1 Dall. 124, 1 L.Ed. 65; Miller v. White, Tex.Civ.App., 264 S.W. 176, 178; Richardson v. Board of Education of City of Ashland, 208 Ky. 464, 271 S.W. 549, 550; American Fruit Growers v. United States, C.C.A. Cal., 105 F.2d 722, 726.

A continuous movement in the same direction, as a fluid or stream. Buckeye Incubator Co. v. Blum, D.C.Ohio, 17 F.2d 456, 458.

Passing in time or belonging to the time actually passing, now passing, present in its course, as the current month, and as applied to current obligations it denotes the obligations then passing or present in its progress, the service rendered and the compensation therefor measured by the time of the occurrence of the event. Pecos Mercantile Co. v. Texlite, Inc., Tex.Civ.App., 65 S.W.2d 811, 812.

The word "current," when used as an adjective, has many meanings, and definition depends largely on word which it modifies, or subject-matter with which it is associated. Commissioner of Internal Revenue v. Keller, C.C.A., 59 F.2d 499, 501.

CURRENT ACCOUNT. An open, running, or unsettled account between two parties. Tucker v. Quimby, 37 Iowa 19; Franklin v. Camp, 1 N.J.Law, 196; Wilson v. Calvert, 18 Ala. 274; Leland v. Johnson, 227 Iowa 520, 288 N.W. 595, 597; Miller v. Boyce, 219 Iowa 534, 258 N.W. 764.

CURRENT CATALOGUES. Under contract to sell automobiles as shown in current catalogues, "current catalogues" means such catalogues as should from time to time be issued, and not merely the catalogues in existence on execution of the contract. Imperial Motorcar Co. v. Skinner, 16 Ala. App. 443, 78 So. 641, 642.

CURRENT DEBT FUND RULE. The "current debt fund rule" is that creditors who have supplied labor, materials, or equipment essential to operation of railroad before adjudication of insolvency will be entitled to lien on properties prior to lien of pre-existing mortgages, if current operating revenues have been diverted to payment of principal or interest on mortgages, or to enhancement of mortgage security before current operating expenses have been met. Village of Stillwater v. Hudson Valley Ry. Co., 255 N.Y. 144, 309, 174 N.E. 306.

CURRENT EXPENSES. Ordinary, regular, and continuing expenditures for the maintenance of property, the carrying on of an office, municipal government, etc. State v. Board of Education, 68 N.J.Law, 496, 53 A. 236; Babcock v. Goodrich, 47 Cal. 510; St. Louis-San Francisco Ry. Co. v. Forbess, 111 Okl. 48, 237 P. 596, 597.

In connection with municipal finances, the usual, ordinary, running, and incidental expenses of a municipality. Atchison, T. & S. F. Ry. Co. v. City of Topeka, 95 Kan. 747, 149 P. 697. The term is equivalent to "running expenses," meaning any continuing regular expenditures in connection with the business. Meridian Line Drainage Dist. v. Wiss, 258 Ill. 600, 101 N.E. 941, 942.

CURRENT FUNDS. This phrase means gold or silver, or something equivalent thereto, and convertible at pleasure into coined money. Bull v. Bank, 123 U.S. 105, 8 S.Ct. 62, 31 L.Ed. 97; Henderson v. Farmers' Sav. Bank of Harper, 199 Iowa 496, 202 N.W. 259, 261.

CURRENT LIABILITIES. The phrase "current liability" carries with it the idea of a liability that is presently enforceable. Warren Co. v. Commissioner of Internal Revenue, C.C.A.Ga., 135 F.2d 679, 684, 685.

CURRENT MAINTENANCE. "Current maintenance" is defined as the expense occasioned in keeping the physical property in the condition required for continued use during its service life. Lindheimer v. Illinois Bell Telephone Co., Ill., 292 U.S. 151, 54 S.Ct. 658, 78 L.Ed. 1182.

CURRENT MONEY. The currency of the country; whatever is intended to and does actually circulate as currency; every species of coin or currency. Miller v. McKinney, 5 Lea, Tenn., 96. In this phrase the adjective "current" is not synonymous with "convertible." It is employed to describe money which passes from hand to hand, from person to person, and circulates through the community, and is generally received. Money is current which is received as money in the common business transactions, and is the common medium in barter and trade. Ferrell v. State, 68 Tex.Cr.R. 487, 152 S.W. 901, 905; Kupfer v. Marc, 28 Ill. 388; Conwell v. Pumphrey, 9 Ind. 135, 68 Am.Dec. 611.

CURRENT OBLIGATIONS. The word "current" means passing in time or belonging to the time actually passing, now passing, present in its course, as the current month, and as applied to current obligations it denotes the obligations then passing or present in its progress, the service rendered and the compensation therefor measured by the time of the occurrence of the event. Pecos Mercantile Co. v. Texlite, Inc., Tex.Civ.App., 65 S.W.2d 811, 812.

CURRENT PRICE. This term means the same as "market value," "market price," "going price," the price that runs or flows with the market. Hoff v. Lodi Canning Co., 51 Cal.App. 299, 196 P. 779, 780; Ford v. Norton, 32 N.M. 518, 260 P. 411, 414, 55 A.L.R. 261; Cases of Champagne, 23 Fed. Cas. 1168.

CURRENT RATE OF WAGES. Minimum, maximum, and intermediate amounts, indeterminately varying from time to time and dependent on the class and kind of work done, the efficiency of the workman, etc. Connally v. General Const. Co., 269 U.S. 385, 46 S.Ct. 126, 128, 70 L.Ed. 322.

"CURRENT REVENUES". Defined as including taxes for ensuing year and all liquid assets, such as delinquent taxes, licenses, fines, and other revenues which, in judgment of authorities, are collectible. Athens Nat. Bank v. Ridgebury Tp., 303 Pa. 479, 154 A. 791, 792.

CURRENT VALUE. The current value of imported commodities is their common market price at the place of exportation, without reference to the price actually paid by the importer. Tappan v. U. S., 23 Fed.Cas. 690.

CURRENT WAGES. Such as are paid periodically, or from time to time as the services are rendered or the work is performed; more particularly, wages for the current period, hence not including such as are past-due. Sydnor v. Galveston, Tex.App., 15 S.W. 202; Bell v. Indian Live Stock Co., Tex., 11 S.W. 346, 3 L.R.A. 642; Bruton v. Tearle, 7 Cal.2d 48, 59 P.2d 953, 957, 106 A.L.R. 580.

CURRENT YEAR. The year now running. Doe v. Dobell, 1 Adol. & El. 806; Clark v. Lancaster County, 69 Neb. 717, 96 N.W. 593. Ordinarily, a calendar year in which the event under discussion took place; Buffalo County v. Bowker, 197 N.W. 620, 622, 111 Neb. 762; Clark v. Tennessee Chemical Company, 167 Ga. 248, 145 S.E. 73, 75; Empire Petroleum Co. v. Southern Pipe Line Co., 174 Ark. 33, 294 S.W. 5, 6; unless the context shows a different intention; Miller v. White, Tex.Civ.App., 264 S.W. 176, 178; People v. Central Illinois Public Service Co., 324 Ill. 85, 154 N.E. 438, 439.

CURRICULUM. The year; of the course of a year; the set of studies for a particular period, appointed by a university.

CURRIT QUATUOR PEDIBUS. L. Lat. It runs upon four feet; or, as sometimes expressed, it runs upon all fours. A phrase used in arguments to signify the entire and exact application of a case quoted. "It does not follow that they run *quatuor pedibus*." 1 W.Bl. 145.

CURRIT TEMPUS CONTRA DESIDES ET SUI JURIS CONTEMPTORES. Time runs against the slothful and those who neglect their rights. Bract. fols. 100*b*, 101.

CURSING. Malediction; imprecation; execration; profane words intended to convey hate and to invoke harm; swearing. Johnson v. State, 15 Ala.App. 194, 72 So. 766.

CURSITOR BARON. An officer of the court of exchequer, who is appointed by patent under the great seal to be one of the barons of the exchequer. The office was abolished by St. 19 & 20 Vict. c. 86.

CURSITORS. Clerks in the chancery office, whose duties consisted in drawing up those writs which were of course, *de cursu,* whence their name. They were abolished by St. 5 & 6 Wm. IV, c. 82. Spence, Eq.Jur. 238; 4 Inst. 82.

CURSO. In old records. A ridge. *Cursones terræ,* ridges of land. Cowell.

CURSOR. An inferior officer of the papal court.

CURSORY EXAMINATION. An inspection for defects visible or ascertainable by ordinary examination. Coll v. Lehigh Valley R. Co., 3 N.J.Misc. 869, 130 A. 225, 226.

CURSUS CURIÆ EST LEX CURIÆ. 3 Bulst. 53. The practice of the court is the law of the court.

CURTAIL. "Curtail" means to cut off the end or any part of; hence to shorten, abridge; diminish; lessen, reduce; and has no such meaning as abolish. State v. Edwards, 207 La. 506, 21 So.2d 624, 625.

CURTESY. The estate to which by common law a man is entitled, on the death of his wife, in the lands or tenements of which she was seised in possession in fee-simple or in tail during her coverture, provided they have had lawful issue born alive which might have been capable of inheriting the estate. It is a freehold estate for the term of his natural life. 1 Washb.Real Prop. 127; 2 Bl. Comm. 126; Co.Litt. 30*a*; Dozier v. Toalson, 180 Mo. 546, 79 S.W. 420, 103 Am.St.Rep. 586;

Templeton v. Twitty, 88 Tenn. 595, 14 S.W. 435; Decker v. Decker, 205 Ky. 69, 265 S.W. 483, 485.

Initiate and consummate

Curtesy initiate is the interest which a husband has in his wife's estate after the birth of issue capable of inheriting, and before the death of the wife; after her death, it becomes an estate "by the curtesy consummate." Wait v. Wait, 4 Barb., N.Y. 205; Churchill v. Hudson, C.C.Mo., 34 F. 14; Pattison v. Baker, 148 Tenn. 399, 255 S.W. 710, 29 A.L.R. 1334; Bucci v. Popovich, 93 N.J. Eq. 121, 115 A. 95, 96; Hopper v. Gurtman, 126 N.J. 263, 18 A.2d 245, 246, 250, 133 A.L.R. 621.

CURTEYN. The name of King Edward the Confessor's sword. It is said that the point of it was broken, as an emblem of mercy. (Mat. Par. in Hen. III.) Wharton.

CURTILAGE. The inclosed space of ground and buildings immediately surrounding a dwelling-house. 1 Chit.Gen.Pr. 175; United States v. Vlahos, D.C.Or., 19 F.Supp. 166, 169.

In its most comprehensive and proper legal signification, it includes all that space of ground and buildings thereon which is usually inclosed within the *general fence* immediately surrounding a principal messuage and outbuildings, and yard closely adjoining to a dwelling-house, but it may be large enough for cattle to be levant and couchant therein. 1 Chit.Gen.Pr. 175.

The curtilage of a dwelling-house is a space, necessary and convenient and habitually used for the family purposes, and the carrying on of domestic employments. It includes the garden, if there be one, and it need not be separated from other lands by fence. State v. Shaw, 31 Me. 523; Derrickson v. Edwards, 29 N.J.Law, 474, 80 Am. Dec. 220; Bare v. Commonwealth, 122 Va. 783, 94 S.E. 168, 172; State v. Lee, 120 Or. 643, 253 P. 533, 534.

A piece of ground commonly used with the dwelling house. Fugate v. Commonwealth, 294 Ky. 410, 171 S.W.2d 1020, 1021. A small piece of land, not necessarily inclosed, around the dwelling house, and generally includes the buildings used for domestic purposes in the conduct of family affairs. Bruner v. State, 47 Okl.Cr. 241, 288 P. 369, 370; a courtyard or the space of ground adjoining the dwelling house necessary and convenient and habitually used for family purposes and the carrying on of domestic employments. Jones v. Commonwealth, 239 Ky. 110, 38 S.W.2d 971, 973. A piece of ground within the common inclosure belonging to a dwelling house, and enjoyed with it, for its more convenient occupation. Italian-American Building & Loan Ass'n of Passaic County v. Russo, 132 N.J.Eq. 319, 28 A.2d 196, 198; People v. Gedney, 10 Hun., N.Y., 154. In Michigan it has been extended to include more than an inclosure near the house. People v. Taylor, 2 Mich. 250.

CURTILES TERRÆ. In old English law. Court lands. Cowell. See Court Lands.

CURTILLIUM. A curtilage; the area or space within the inclosure of a dwellinghouse. Spelman.

CURTIS. A garden; a space about a house; a house, or manor; a court, or palace; a court of justice; a nobleman's residence. Spelman.

CUSSEDNESS. "Wantonness" is a synonym for what is popularly known as "cussedness," and "cussedness" is a disposition to perversity. Universal Concrete Pipe Co. v. Bassett, 130 Ohio St. 567, 200 N.E. 843, 845.

CUSSORE. A term used in Hindostan for the discount or allowance made in the exchange of rupees, in contradistinction to *batta,* which is the sum deducted. Enc.Lond.

CUSTA, CUSTAGIUM, CUSTANTIA. Costs.

CUSTODE ADMITTENDO, CUSTODE AMOVENDO. Writs for the admitting and removing of guardians.

CUSTODES.

In Roman Law

Guardians; observers; inspectors. Persons who acted as inspectors of elections, and who counted the votes given. Tayl.Civil Law, 193.

In Old English Law

Keepers; guardians; conservators.

CUSTODES LIBERTATIS ANGLIÆ AUCTORITATE PARLIAMENTI. The style in which writs and all judicial processes were made out during the great revolution, from the execution of King Charles I. till Oliver Cromwell was declared protector.

CUSTODES PACIS. Guardians of the peace. 1 Bl.Comm. 349.

CUSTODIA LEGIS. In the custody of the law. Stockwell v. Robinson, 9 Houst., Del., 313, 32 A. 528; Troll v. City of St. Louis, 257 Mo. 626, 168 S.W. 167, 178; Hopping v. Hopping, 233 Iowa 993, 10 N.W.2d 87, 152 A.L.R. 436.

CUSTODIAM LEASE. In English law. A grant from the crown under the exchequer seal, by which the custody of lands, etc., seised in the king's hands, is demised or committed to some person as custodee or lessee thereof. Wharton.

CUSTODY. The care and keeping of anything; as when an article is said to be "in the custody of the court." People v. Burr, 41 How.Prac., N.Y., 296; Emmerson v. State, 33 Tex.Cr.R. 89, 25 S.W. 290; Roe v. Irwin, 32 Ga. 39. Also the detainer of a man's person by virtue of lawful process or authority; actual imprisonment. In a sentence that the defendant "be in custody until," etc., this term imports actual imprisonment. Smith v. Com., 59 Pa. 320; Turner v. Wilson, 49 Ind. 581; Ex parte Powers, D.C.Ky., 129 F. 985. Detention; charge; control; possession. The term is very elastic and may mean actual imprisonment or physical detention or mere power, legal or physical, of imprisoning or of taking manual possession. Jones v. State, 26 Ga.App. 635, 107 S.E. 166; J. O. Nessen Lumber Co. v. Ray H. Bennett Lumber Co., 223 Mich. 349, 193 N.W. 789, 790; State ex rel. Bricker v. Griffith, Ohio App., 36 N.E.2d 489, 491; Willoughby v. State, 87 Tex.Cr.R. 40, 219 S.W. 468, 470; Carpenter v. Lord, 88 Or. 128,

171 P. 577, 579, L.R.A.1918D, 674; Little v. State, 100 Tex.Cr.R. 167, 272 S.W. 456, 457; Randazzo v. U. S., C.C.A.Mo., 300 F. 794, 797.

The word is defined as the care and possession of a thing, and means the keeping, guarding, care, watch, inspection, preservation or security of a thing, and carries with it the idea of the thing being within the immediate personal care and control of the person to whose custody it is subjected; charge; immediate charge and control, and not the final, absolute control of ownership, implying responsibility for the protection and preservation of the thing in custody. Southern Carbon Co. v. State, 171 Misc. 566, 13 N.Y.S.2d 7, 9.

"Custody" of property means such a relation towards it as would constitute possession if the person having custody had it on his own account. State v. Columbus State Bank, 124 Neb. 231, 246 N.W. 235, 238. "Custody" means a keeping, guardianship, the state of being held in keeping or under guard, restraint of liberty, imprisonment, and "fetter" is a synonym. Browder v. Cook, D.C.Idaho, 59 F.Supp. 225, 231.

CUSTODY OF THE LAW. Property is in the custody of the law when it has been lawfully taken by authority of legal process, and remains in the possession of a public officer (as, a sheriff) or an officer of a court (as, a receiver) empowered by law to hold it. Gilman v. Williams, 7 Wis. 334, 76 Am.Dec. 219; McFarland Carriage Co. v. Solanes, C.C.La., 108 F. 532; Allan v. Hargadine-McKittrick Dry Goods Co., 325 Mo. 400, 28 S.W.2d 670, 673.

CUSTOM. A usage or practice of the people, which, by common adoption and acquiescence, and by long and unvarying habit, has become compulsory, and has acquired the force of a law with respect to the place or subject-matter to which it relates. Adams v. Insurance Co., 95 Pa. 355, 40 Am.Rep. 662; King v. Shelton, Tex.Civ. App., 252 S.W. 194, 195; Conahan v. Fisher, 233 Mass. 234, 124 N.E. 13, 15; Lawrence v. Portland Ry., Light & Power Co., 91 Or. 559, 179 P. 485, 486; U. S. Shipping Board Emergency Fleet Corporation v. Levensaler, 53 App.D.C. 322, 290 F. 297, 300.

A "custom" is a practice or course of acting. Goslin v. Kurn, 351 Mo. 395, 173 S.W.2d 79, 86.

Ordinary or usual way of doing a thing, habit; practice. Adelman v. Altman, 209 Mo.App. 583, 240 S.W. 272, 276; Kent v. Town of Patterson, 141 N.Y.S. 932, 933, 80 Misc. Rep. 560; Maeder Steel Products Co. v. Zanello, 109 Or. 562, 220 P. 155, 161; Carter v. Sioux City Service Co., 160 Iowa 78, 141 N.W. 26, 29.

It results from a long series of actions, constantly repeated, which have, by such repetition and by uninterrupted acquiescence, acquired the force of a tacit and common consent. Louisville & N. R. Co. v. Reverman, 243 Ky. 702, 49 S.W.2d 558, 560.

A law not written, established by long usage, and the consent of our ancestors. Termes de la Ley; Cowell; Bract.fol. 2. Portuguese Beneficial Ass'n v. Xavier, 59 R.I. 265, 195 A. 231, 233. If it be universal, it is common law; if particular to this or that place, it is then properly *custom.* 3 Salk. 112.

Customs result from a long series of actions constantly repeated, which have, by such repetition, and by uninterrupted acquiescence, acquired the force of a tacit and common consent. Civil Code La. art. 3.

It differs from prescription, which is personal and is annexed to the person of the owner of a particular estate; while the other is local, and relates to a particular district. An instance of the latter occurs where the question is upon the manner of conducting a particular branch of trade at a certain place; of the former, where a certain person and his ancestors, or those whose estates he has, have been entitled to a certain advantage or privilege, as to have common of pasture in a certain close, or the like. The distinction has been thus expressed: "While prescription is the making of a right, custom is the making of a law." Lawson, Usages & Cust. 15, note 2.

Classification

Customs are general, local or particular. *General* customs are such as prevail throughout a country and become the law of that country, and their existence is to be determined by the court. Bodfish v. Fox, 23 Me. 95, 39 Am.Dec. 611. Or as applied to usages of trade and business, a general custom is one that is followed in all cases by all persons in the same business in the same territory, and which has been so long established that persons sought to be charged thereby, and all others living in the vicinity, may be presumed to have known of it and to have acted upon it as they had occasion. Sturges v. Buckley, 32 Conn. 267; Railroad Co. v. Harrington, 192 Ill. 9, 61 N.E. 622. *Local* customs are such as prevail only in some particular district or locality, or in some city, county, or town. Clough v. Wing, 2 Ariz. 371, 17 P. 457. *Particular* customs are nearly the same, being such as affect only the inhabitants of some particular district. 1 Bl.Comm. 74.

Custom of Merchants

A system of customs or rules relative to bills of exchange, partnership, and other mercantile matters, and which, under the name of the *"lex mercatoria,"* or "law merchant," has been ingrafted into and made a part of, the common law. 1 Bl. Comm. 75; 1 Steph.Comm. 54; 2 Burrows, 1226, 1228.

Custom of York

A custom of intestacy in the province of York similar to that of London. Abolished by 19 & 20 Vict. c. 94.

Customs and Services

Annexed to the tenure of lands are those which the tenants thereof owe unto their lords, and which, if withheld, the lord might anciently have resorted to "a writ of customs and services" to compel them. Cowell. But at the present day he would merely proceed to eject the tenant as upon a forfeiture, or claim damages for the subtraction. Brown.

Customs of London

Certain particular customs, peculiar to that city, with regard to trade, apprentices, widows, orphans and a variety of other matters; contrary to the general law of the land, but confirmed by act of parliament. 1 Bl.Comm. 75.

Special Custom

A particular or local custom; one which, in respect to the sphere of its observance, does not extend throughout the entire state or country, but is confined to some particular district or locality. 1 Bl.Comm. 67; Bodfish v. Fox, 23 Me. 95, 39 Am. Dec. 611.

CUSTOM DUTIES. Taxes on the importation and exportation of commodities; the tariff or tax assessed upon merchandise, imported from, or exported to a foreign country. United States v. Sischo, D.C.Wash., 262 F. 1001, 1005.

CUSTOM-HOUSE. In administrative law. The house or office where commodities are entered for importation or exportation; where the duties, bounties, or drawbacks payable or receivable upon such importation or exportation are paid or received; and where ships are cleared out, etc.

CUSTOM-HOUSE BROKER. One whose occupation it is, as an agent, to arrange entries and other custom-house papers, or transact business, at any port of entry, relating to the importation or exportation of goods, wares, or merchandise. 14 St. at Large, 117. A person authorized by the commissioners of customs to act for parties, at their option, in the entry or clearance of ships and the transaction of general business. Wharton; State v. William J. Oberle, Inc., La.App., 140 So. 239, 240.

CUSTOMARILY. Means usually, habitually, according to the customs, general practice or usual order of things, regularly. Fuller Brush Co. v. Industrial Commission of Utah, 99 Utah 97, 104 P.2d 201, 203, 129 A.L.R. 511.

CUSTOMARY. According to custom or usage; founded on, or growing out of, or dependent on, a custom (*q. v.*); ordinary; usual; common. Kent v. Town of Patterson, 80 Misc.Rep. 560, 141 N.Y.S. 932, 933; Montgomery v. O'Donnell, 178 Iowa 588, 159 N.W. 1025, 1026; Woods v. Postal Telegraph-Cable Co., 205 Ala. 236, 87 So. 681, 686, 27 A.L.R. 834.

CUSTOMARY COURT-BARON. See Court-Baron.

CUSTOMARY DISPATCH. In charter party. Due diligence according to lawful, reasonable and well-known custom of port or ports involved. Context and conditions existing or contemplated will, of course, affect the meaning of the phrase. Wasson v. Stetson, Cutler & Co., D.C.Mass., 214 F. 329, 333; Taisho Kaiun Kabushiki Kaisha v. Gano Moore Co., D.C.Del., 14 F.2d 985, 986.

CUSTOMARY ESTATES. Estates which owe their origin and existence to the custom of the manor in which they are held. 2 Bl.Comm. 149.

CUSTOMARY FREEHOLD. In English law. A variety of copyhold estate, the evidences of the title to which are to be found upon the court rolls; the entries declaring the holding to be according to the custom of the manor, but it is not said to be at the will of the lord. The incidents are similar to those of common or pure copyhold. 1 Steph. Comm. 212, 213, and note.

CUSTOMARY INTERPRETATION. See Interpretation.

CUSTOMARY SERVICES. Such as are due by ancient custom or prescription only.

CUSTOMARY TENANTS. Tenants holding by custom of the manor.

CUSTOME SERRA PRISE STRICTE. Custom shall be taken [is to be construed] strictly. Jenk. Cent. 83.

CUSTOMER. One who regularly or repeatedly makes purchases of, or has business dealings with, a tradesman or business house. Aiken Mills v. United States, D.C.S.C., 53 F.Supp. 524, 526; Arkwright Corporation v. United States, D.C.Mass., 53 F.Supp. 359, 361. Ordinarily, one who has had repeated business dealings with another. Lyons v. Otter Tail Power Co., 70 N.D. 681, 297 N.W. 691, 693; Gallopin v. Continental Casualty Co., 290 Ill. App. 8, 7 N.E.2d 771, 774. A buyer, purchaser, or patron. Nichols v. Ocean Accident & Guarantee Corporation, 70 Ga.App. 169, 27 S.E.2d 764, 766.

CUSTOMERS' GOODS. The words "customers' goods," as used in statement of claim on fire policy referring to merchandise destroyed as "customers' goods," in their ordinary sense, mean goods belonging to insured's customers in his custody as a bailee for the purpose of his trade. Sagransky v. Tokio Marine & Fire Ins. Co., 92 Pa.Super. 500, 502.

CUSTOMER'S MAN. One who has duty to greet customers of broker, when they appear in office on business, to assist them in placing their orders, and generally to see that their wants are taken care of. Fenner & Beane v. Lincoln, Tex.Civ.App., 101 S.W.2d 305, 308; an employee of a brokerage house who solicits from the investing public orders for the purchase and sale of commodities and securities to be executed upon various commodities and securities exchanges in the United States. Gould v. Witter, 10 Wash.2d 553, 117 P. 2d 210, 211. The term includes all employees who are regularly engaged in the solicitation of marginal business or the handling of customers' accounts, or who advise with customers about the purchase and sale of securities. Clothier v. Beane, 187 Okl. 693, 105 P.2d 752, 756.

CUSTOMS. This term is usually applied to those taxes which are payable upon goods and merchandise imported or exported. Story, Const. § 949; Pollock v. Trust Co., 158 U.S. 601, 15 S.Ct. 912, 39 L.Ed. 1108; Marriott v. Brune, 9 How. 632, 13 L. Ed. 282.

The duties, toll, tribute, or tariff payable upon merchandise exported or imported. These are called "customs" from having been paid from time immemorial. Expressed in law Latin by *custuma*, as distinguished from *consuetudines*, which are usages merely. 1 Bl. Comm. 314.

CUSTOMS CONSOLIDATION ACT. The statute 16 & 17 Vict. c. 107, which has been frequently amended. See 2 Steph. Comm. 563.

CUSTOMS COURT. By virtue of Act May 28, 1926, c. 411, § 1, 44 Stat. 669, 19 U.S.C.A. § 405a, the "United States Customs Court" became the title of what had theretofore been known as the "Board of General Appraisers." Ex parte Bakelite Corporation, 279 U.S. 438, 49 S.Ct. 411, 73 L. Ed. 789. Its decisions are appealable to the "Court of Customs and Patent Appeals" (*q. v.*) in all cases as to the construction of the law and facts respecting the classification of merchandise and the rate of duty imposed thereon, and the fees and charges connected therewith, and all appealable questions as to the court's jurisdiction, and as to the laws and regulations governing the collection of the customs revenues.

CUSTOS. Lat. A custodian, guard, keeper, or warden; a magistrate.

CUSTOS BREVIUM. The keeper of the writs. A principal clerk belonging to the courts of queen's bench and common pleas, whose office it was to keep the writs returnable into those courts. The office was abolished by 1 Wm. IV, c. 5.

CUSTOS FERARUM. A gamekeeper. Townsh. Pl. 265.

CUSTOS HORREI REGII. Protector of the royal granary. 2 Bl. Comm. 394.

CUSTOS MARIS. In old English law. Warden of the sea. The title of a high naval officer among the Saxons and after the Conquest, corresponding with *admiral.*

CUSTOS MORUM. The guardian of morals. The court of queen's bench has been so styled. 4 Steph. Comm. 377.

CUSTOS PLACITORUM CORONÆ. In old English law. Keeper of the pleas of the crown. Bract. fol. 14*b*. Cowell supposes this office to have been the same with the *custos rotulorum.* But it seems rather to have been another name for "coroner." Crabb, Eng. Law, 150; Bract. fol. 136*b*.

CUSTOS ROTULORUM. Keeper of the rolls. An officer in England who has the custody of the rolls or records of the sessions of the peace, and also of the commission of the peace itself. He is always a justice of the quorum in the county where appointed and is the principal civil officer in the county. 1 Bl. Comm. 349; 4 Bl. Comm. 272.

CUSTOS SPIRITUALIUM. In English ecclesiastical law. Keeper of the spiritualities. He who exercises the spiritual jurisdiction of a diocese during the vacancy of the see. Cowell.

CUSTOS STATUM HÆREDIS IN CUSTODIA EXISTENTIS MELIOREM, NON DETERIOREM, FACERE POTEST. 7 Coke, 7. A guardian can make the estate of an existing heir under his guardianship better, not worse.

CUSTOS TEMPORALIUM. In English ecclesiastical law. The person to whom a vacant see or abbey was given by the king, as supreme lord. His office was, as steward of the goods and profits, to give an account to the escheator, who did the like to the exchequer.

CUSTOS TERRÆ. In old English law. Guardian, warden, or keeper of the land.

CUSTUMA ANTIQUA SIVE MAGNA. (Lat. Ancient or great duties.) The duties on wool, sheepskin, or wool-pelts and leather exported were so called, and were payable by every merchant, stranger as well as native, with the exception that merchant strangers paid one-half as much again as natives. 1 Bl. Comm. 314.

CUSTUMA PARVA ET NOVA. (Small and new customs.) Imposts of 3d. in the pound, due formerly in England from merchant strangers only, for all commodities, as well imported as exported. This was usually called the "aliens duty," and was first granted in 31 Edw. I. 1 Bl. Comm. 314; 4 Inst. 29.

CUT. A wound made with a sharp instrument. State v. Patza, 3 La.Ann. 512; State v. Cody, 18 Or. 506, 23 Pac. 891; State v. Mairs, 1 N.J.Law, 453; the term is not limited to severance by use of a sharp instrument, but also means to fell, and in industry, to reduce by or as by removing a part. Waselinko v. Volpe Coal Co., 152 Pa.Super. 156, 31 A.2d 444, 445.

In Mining

A surface opening in the ground intersecting a vein. McLaughlin v. Bardsen, 50 Mont. 177, 145 P. 954, 955.

CUT-OVER LAND. Land which has been logged; from which desired timber has been removed. Carlisle-Pennell Lumber Co. v. Joe Creek Shingle Co., 131 Wash. 501, 230 P. 425; Tennessee Mining & Mfg. Co. v. New River Lumber Co., C.C.A.Tenn., 5 F.2d 559, 560.

CUT SHELL. One in which the part containing the shot is nearly severed from the part containing powder, so as to be projected in a unit, and inflict a more dangerous wound than if the shot were scattered. White v. State, 195 Ala. 681, 71 So. 452, 454.

CUTCHERRY. In Hindu law. Corrupted from *Kachari.* A court; a hall; an office; the place where any public business is transacted.

CUTH, COUTH. Sax. Known, knowing. *Uncuth,* unknown. See Couthutlaugh; Uncuth.

CUTHRED. A knowing or skillful counsellor.

CUTLER. Either a man who makes edged tools or one who grinds them. American Stainless Steel Co. v. Ludlum Steel Co., C.C.A.N.Y., 290 F. 103, 106.

CUTPURSE. One who steals by the method of cutting purses; a common practice when men wore their purses at their girdles, as was once the custom. Wharton.

CUTTER OF THE TALLIES. In old English law. An officer in the exchequer, to whom it belonged to provide wood for the tallies, and to cut the sum paid upon them, etc.

CUTWAL, KATWAL. The chief officer of police or superintendent of markets in a large town or city in India.

CWT. A hundred-weight; one hundred and twelve pounds. Helm v. Bryant, 11 B. Mon. (Ky.) 64.

CY. In law French. Here. (*Cy-apres,* hereafter; *cy-devant,* heretofore.) Also as, so.

CYCLE. A measure of time; a space in which the same revolutions begin again; a periodical space of time. Enc. Lond. In electrical nomenclature is two successive reversals of directions of electromotive force or current or full period of alternative current. Chicago Pneumatic Tool Co. v. Black & Decker Mfg. Co., Cust. & Pat.App., 39 F. 2d 684, 685.

CYCLONE. "A violent storm, often of vast extent, characterized by high winds rotating about a calm center of low atmospheric pressure. Popularly, any violent and destructive windstorm." Tupper v. Massachusetts Bonding & Insurance Co., 156 Minn. 65, 194 N.W. 99, 100; Cedergren v. Massachusetts Bonding & Insurance Co., C.C.A. Minn., 292 F. 5, 6; the term includes the hurricane, typhoon, bagino, and other tropical storms. Federal Life Ins. Co. v. Hall, 90 Colo. 581, 11 P. 2d 215, 216.

CYNE-BOT, or CYNE-GILD. The portion belonging to the nation of the mulct for slaying the king, the other portion or *were* being due to his family. Blount.

CYNEBOTE. A mulct anciently paid by one who killed another, to the kindred of the deceased. Spelman.

CYPHONISM. That kind of punishment used by the ancients, and still used by the Chinese, called by Staunton the "wooden collar," by which the neck of the malefactor is bent or weighed down. Enc. Lond.

CY-PRES. As near as [possible]. The rule of *cy-pres* is a rule for the construction of instruments in equity, by which the intention of the party is carried out *as near as may be,* when it would be impossible or illegal to give it literal effect. Thus, where a testator attempts to create a perpetuity, the court will endeavor, instead of making the devise entirely void, to explain the will in such a way as to carry out the testator's general intention as far as the rule against perpetuities will allow. So in the case of bequests to charitable uses; and particularly where the language used is so vague or uncertain that the testator's design must be sought by construction. Beekman v. Bonsor, 23 N.Y. 308, 80 Am.Dec. 269; Doyle v. Whalen, 87 Me. 414, 32 A. 1022, 31 L. R.A. 118; Philadelphia v. Girard, 45 Pa. 28, 84 Am. Dec. 470; People v. Braucher, 258 Ill. 604, 101 N. E. 944, 946, 47 L.R.A., N.S., 1015; Tincher v. Arnold, C.C.A.Ill., 147 F. 665; Crane v. Morristown School Foundations, 120 N.J.Eq. 583, 187 A. 632, 635.

CYRCE. In Saxon law. A church.

CYRICBRYCE. A breaking into a church. Blount.

CYRICSCEAT. (From *cyric,* church, and *sceat,* a tribute). In Saxon law. A tribute or payment due to the church. Cowell.

CYROGRAPHARIUS. In old English law. A cyrographer; an officer of the *bancus,* or court of common bench. Fleta, lib. 2, c. 36.

CYROGRAPHUM. A chirograph, (which see.)

CZAR. (Also written *zar, tsar, tzar,* etc.) The title of the former emperors of Russia, derived from the old Slavonic *cesar,* king or emperor, which, although long held to be derived from the Roman title *Caesar,* is almost certainly of Tartar origin. 8 Encyc. Americana, 378. The Slavonic word ultimately represents the Latin *Caesar,* but came, according to Miklosich, through the medium of a Germanic language in which the word had the general sense "emperor." 2 New English Dict. (Oxford, 1893), page 1308.

In the beginning of the 10th century the Bulgarian prince Symeon assumed this title, which remained attached to the Bulgarian crown. In 1346 it was adopted by Stephen Duschan, king of Serbia. Among the Russians the Byzantine emperors were so called, as were also the khans of the Mongols that ruled in Russia. Ivan III, grand prince of Moscow, held the title, and Ivan IV, the Terrible, in 1547, caused himself to be crowned as czar. In 1721 the Senate and clergy conferred on Peter I, in the name of the nation, the title Emperor of Russia, for which in Russia the Latin word *imperator* is used. 8 Encyc.Americana, 378. Peter the Great introduced the title *imperator,* "emperor," and the official style then became "Emperor of all the Russias, Tsar of Poland, and Grand Duke of Finland"; but the Russian popular appellation continued to be *tsar* (the preferable modern spelling). 2 New English Dict. 1308. The last tsar was Nicholas II, who abdicated on March 15, 1917, and was later executed.

CZAREVITCH. (Also spelled *czarewich, tsarevitch,* and, after the Polish, *czarowitz, czarowitch,* etc. 2 New English Dict. 1308.) A son of the Russian czar and czarina. Originally a title. Webster, Dict. The word was used as a title during the time of Peter I and his son, Alexis, after whose death imperial princes were called grand dukes. 6 New Internatl. Encyc. 420.

CZAREVNA, TSAREVNA. A daughter of the Russian czar. Originally a title. Webster, Dict. As a title, however, the word has been superseded, since the time of Paul I (1754–1801), by that of grand duchess. 6 New Internatl. Encyc. 420; 2 New English Dict. 1308. See Czarevitch; Cesarevna.

CZARINA. The title of former empresses of Russia.

CZARITZA, TSARITSA. The Russian title for which *czarina* is in ordinary English use. 2 New English Dist. 1308.

D

The fourth letter of the English alphabet. It is used as an abbreviation for a number of words, the more important and usual of which are as follows:

1. *Digestum,* or *Digesta,* that is, the Digest or Pandects in the Justinian collections of the civil law. Citations to this work are sometimes indicated by this abbreviation, but more commonly by "Dig."

2. *Dictum.* A remark or observation, as in the phrase *"obiter dictum,"* (*q. v.*).

3. *Demissione.* "On the demise." An action of ejectment is entitled "Doe *d.* Stiles v. Roe;" that is, "Doe, on the demise of Stiles, against Roe."

4. *"Doctor."* As in the abbreviated forms of certain academical degrees. "M. D.," "doctor of medicine;" "LL.D.," "doctor of laws;" "D. C. L.," "doctor of civil law."

5. *"District."* Thus, "U. S. Cir. Ct. W. *D.* Pa." stands for United States Circuit Court for the Western *District* of Pennsylvania.

6. *"Dialogue."* Used only in citations to the work called "Doctor and Student."

In the Roman system of notation, this letter stands for five hundred; and, when a horizontal dash or stroke is placed above it, it denotes five thousand.

D. B. Defined as day book, double biased, double breasted and, if capitalized, it means Doomsday Book, though there is no authoritative definition of d/b or d/b/a as a symbol or abbreviation in a legal document. City of St. Louis v. Stubley, Mo.App., 154 S.W.2d 407, 410.

D. B. A. Abbreviation for "doing business as." Lieberman v. Atlantic Mut. Ins. Co., 385 P.2d 53, 55, 62 Wash.2d 922.

D. B. E. An abbreviation for *de bene esse, (q. v.).*

D. B. N. An abbreviation for *de bonis non;* descriptive of a species of administration.

D. C. An abbreviation standing either for "District Court," or "District of Columbia."

D. E. R. I. C. An abbreviation used for *De ea re ita censuere,* (concerning that matter have so decreed,) in recording the decrees of the Roman senate. Tayl. Civil Law, 564, 566.

D. J. An abbreviation for "District Judge."

D. P. An abbreviation for *Domus Procerum,* the house of lords.

D. S. An abbreviation for "Deputy Sheriff." Jones County Land Co. v. Fox, 120 Miss. 798, 83 So. 241, 242.

D. S. B. An abbreviation for *debitum sine brevi,* or *debit sans breve.*

D. W. I. In genealogical tables, a common abbreviation for "died without issue."

DA TUA DUM TUA SUNT, POST MORTEM TUNC TUA NON SUNT. 3 Bulst. 18. Give the things which are yours whilst they are yours; after death they are not yours.

DABIS? DABO. Lat. (Will you give? I will give.) In the Roman law. One of the forms of making a verbal stipulation. Inst. 3, 15, 1; Bract. fol. 15*b*.

DACION. In Spanish law. The real and effective delivery of an object in the execution of a contract.

DACTYLOGRAPHY. Dactylography is the scientific study of finger prints as a means of identification. State v. Steffen, 210 Iowa, 196, 230 N.W. 536, 537, 78 A.L.R. 748.

DAGGE. A kind of gun. 1 How. State Tr. 1124, 1125.

DAGGER. Any straight knife, worn on person and capable of inflicting death, except pocket knife. Dagger is a generic term covering dirk, stiletto, poniard, etc. People v. Syed Shah, 91 Cal. App. 716, 205 P.2d 1081, 1083.

DAGUS, or DAIS. The raised floor at the upper end of a hall.

DAILY. Every day; every day in the week; every day in the week except one. A newspaper which is published six days in each week is a "daily" newspaper. Richardson v. Tobin, 45 Cal. 30; Tribune Pub. Co. v. Duluth, 45 Minn. 27, 47 N.W. 309; City of Bellingham v. Bellingham Pub. Co., 116 Wash. 65, 198 P. 369; State ex rel. Item Co. v. Commissioner of Public Finances of City of New Orleans, 161 La. 915, 109 So. 675, 676.

DAILY BALANCES, AVERAGE DAILY BALANCE. In school depository law. "Daily balances" means the various balances for the different days in the period for which interest is to be paid, and the "average daily balance" for the interest period means the sum of these daily balances divided by the number of days in the interest period. Jones v. Marrs, 114 Tex. 62, 263 S.W. 570, 574.

DAILY OCCUPATION. The same as "usual occupation". International Brotherhood of Boiler Makers, Iron Shipbuilders & Helpers of America v. Huval, 133 Tex. 136, 126 S.W.2d 476, 478.

DAILY RATE OF PAY. As used in Workmen's Compensation Law. Means one-sixth of the average weekly earnings of the employee during a six-day week. Boyett v. Urania Lumber Co., 8 La. App. 132, 133.

DAILY WAGES. As used in statute authorizing compensation for loss of an eye, means amount which could be earned by working ordinary number of hours, irrespective of enforced idleness during working hours and overtime employment. Carlson v. Condon-Kiewit Co., 135 Neb. 587, 283 N.W. 220, 221.

DAIRY. An establishment for the sale or distribution of milk or milk products. State v. McCosh, 134 Neb. 780, 279 N.W. 775, 777.

DAKER, or DIKER. Ten hides. Blount.

DALE and SALE. Fictitious names of places, used in the English books, as examples "The manor of *Dale* and the manor of *Sale*, lying both in Vale."

DALUS, DAILUS, DAILIA. A certain measure of land; such narrow slips of pasture as are left between the plowed furrows in arable land. Cowell.

DAM. A construction of wood, stone, reinforced concrete or other materials, made across a stream for the purpose of penning back the waters. This word is used in two different senses. It properly means the work or structure, raised to obstruct the flow of the water in a river; but, by a well-settled usage, it is often applied to designate the pond of water created by this obstruction. Burnham v. Kempton, 44 N.H. 89; Colwell v. Water Power Co., 19 N.J.Eq. 248; Mining Co. v. Hancock, 101 Cal. 42, 31 P. 112; State ex rel. Priegel v. Northern States Power Co., 242 Wis. 345, 8 N.W. 2d 350, 352.

DAMAGE. Loss, injury, or deterioration, caused by the negligence, design, or accident of one person to another, in respect of the latter's person or property. The word is to be distinguished from its plural,—"damages,"—which means a compensation in money for a loss or damage. An injury produces a right in them who have suffered any damage by it to demand reparation of such damage from the authors of the injury. By damage, we understand every loss or diminution of what is a man's own, occasioned by the fault of another. 1 Ruth. Inst. 399.

The harm, detriment, or loss sustained by reason of an injury. Yazoo & M. V. R. Co. v. Fields, 188 Miss. 725, 195 So. 489, 490.

Synonymous with "condemnation money." State v. Hale, Tex.Civ.App., 96 S.W.2d 135, 139. "Injury". Dohring v. Kansas City, 228 Mo.App. 519, 71 S.W.2d 170, 171. "Loss." Glinz v. State, 70 N.D. 776, 298 N.W. 238, 239; Wells v. Thomas W. Garland, Inc., Mo., 39 S.W.2d 409, 411.

DAMAGE-CLEER. A fee assessed of the tenth part in the common pleas, and the twentieth part in the queen's bench and exchequer, out of all damages exceeding five marks recovered in those courts, in actions upon the case, covenant, trespass, etc., wherein the damages were uncertain; which the plaintiff was obliged to pay to the prothonotary or the officer of the court wherein he recovered, before he could have execution for the damages. This was originally a gratuity given to the prothonotaries and their clerks for drawing special writs and pleadings; but it was taken away by statute, since which, if any officer in these courts took any money in the name of damage-cleer, or anything in lieu thereof, he forfeited treble the value. Wharton.

DAMAGE FEASANT or FAISANT. Doing damage. A term applied to a person's cattle or beasts found upon another's land, doing damage by treading down the grass, grain, etc. 3 Bl. Comm. 7, 211; Tomlins. This phrase seems to have been introduced in the reign of Edward III, in place of the older expression *"en son damage," (in damno suo.)* Crabb, Eng. Law, 292.

DAMAGE TO PERSON. Bodily or physical injury directly resulting from wrongful act, whether lying in trespass or trespass on the case, and does not include torts directly affecting the person but affecting only the feelings and reputation. Young v. Aylesworth, 35 R.I. 259, 86 A. 555, 556; Texas Employers' Ins. Ass'n v. Jimenez, Tex.Civ. App., 267 S.W. 752, 758; Howard v. Lunaburg, 192 Wis. 507, 213 N.W. 301, 303; Wilson v. Grace, 273 Mass. 146, 173 N.E. 524, 528.

DAMAGE TO TWO PERSONS. In bond for payment of damages that limited amount payable for any one accident. Where widow sued to recover damages to deceased and his estate and also her pecunary loss, there was "damage to two persons" within the bond. Ehlers v. Gold, 169 Wis. 494, 173 N.W. 325, 327.

DAMAGED. Made less valuable, less useful, or less desirable. Cleveland, C., C. & St. L. Ry. Co. v. Mumford, 208 Ind. 655, 197 N.E. 826, 835.

Synonymous with term "injuriously affected" within eminent domain statutes. Alabama Power Co. v. City of Guntersville, 235 Ala. 136, 177 So. 332, 337, 114 A.L.R. 181; term "injuriously affected" as used in condemnation statutes, is synonymous. Hirt v. City of Casper, 56 Wyo. 57, 103 P.2d 394, 398.

DAMAGED GOODS. Goods, subject to duties, which have received some injury either in the voyage home or while bonded in warehouse.

DAMAGES. A pecuniary compensation or indemnity, which may be recovered in the courts by any person who has suffered loss, detriment, or injury, whether to his person, property, or rights, through the unlawful act or omission or negligence of another. Scott v. Donald, 165 U.S. 58, 17 S.Ct. 265, 41 L.Ed. 632; Wainscott v. Loan Ass'n, 98 Cal. 253, 33 P. 88; Strong v. Neidermeier, 230 Mich. 117, 202 N.W. 938, 940; Greer v. Board of Com'rs of Knox County, 33 Ohio App. 539, 169 N. E. 709, 710.

Compensation for the loss or injury suffered. Holmes Electric Protective Co. of Philadelphia v. Goldstein, 147 Pa. Super. 506, 24 A.2d 161, 165; In re Rushford's Estate, 111 Vt. 494, 18 A.2d 175, 176; Brown v. Cummins Distilleries Corporation, D.C.Ky., 56 F.Supp. 941, 942. A just compensation or reparation for a loss or injury sustained. McNaghten Loan Co. v. Sandifer, 137 Kan. 353, 20 P.2d 523, 526. All factors going to make up total amount which plaintiff may recover under correct principles of law. Binder v. Harris, 267 Mass. 162, 166 N.E. 707, 708. Reasonable compensation for legal injury. Sechrist v. Bowman, 307 Pa. 301, 161 A. 332, 335. The award made to a person because of a legal wrong done to him by another. Eklund v. Evans, 211 Minn. 164, 300 N.W. 617, 619. The estimated reparation in money for detriment or injury sustained, and as payment for or indemnity for injuries. Sycamore Preserve Works v. Chicago & N. W. R. Co., 284 Ill.App. 445, 1 N.E.2d 522, 526. The pecuniary compensation, recompense, or satisfaction for an injury sustained, Fogle v. Frazel, 201 La. 899, 10 So.2d 695, 698. A sum awarded as a fair measure of compensation to plaintiff, the amount being, as near as can be estimated, that by which he is the worse for the defendant's wrongdoing. Chafin v. Gay Coal & Coke Co., 113 W.Va. 823, 169 S.E. 485, 487. A sum of money assessed by a jury on finding for the plaintiff or successful party in an action, as a compensation for the injury done him by the opposite party. 2 Bl.Comm. 438; Co.Litt. 257*a;* 2 Tidd, Pr. 869, 870. In its early signification the term included "costs", the terms are now regarded as distinct, State ex rel. Marcri v. City of Bremerton, 8 Wash.2d 93, 111 P.2d 612, 616. Synonymous with: "compensation", Maryland Casualty Co. v. Pitman, 70 Ga.App. 670, 29 S.E.2d 102; "condemnation money", Eldridge v. Sutton, 171 Okl. 11, 41 P.2d 680, 682; "judgment", Stearns v. Ritchie, 128 Me. 368, 147 A. 703, 705. In the ancient usage, the word "damages" was employed in two significations. According to Coke, its proper and general sense included the costs of suit, while its strict or relative sense was exclusive of costs. 10 Coke, 116, 117; Co.Litt. 257*a*; 9 East, 299. The latter meaning has alone survived.

Actual damages

Real, substantial and just damages, or the amount awarded to a complainant in compensation for his actual and real loss or injury, as opposed on the one hand to "nominal" damages, and on the other to "exemplary" or "punitive" damages. Ross v. Leggett, 61 Mich. 445, 28 N.W. 695, 1 Am.St.Rep. 608; Gatzow v. Buening, 106 Wis. 1, 81 N.W. 1003, 49 L.R.A. 475; Osborn v. Leach, 135 N.C. 628, 47 S.E. 811, 66 L.R.A. 648; Winans v. Chapman, 104 Kan. 664, 180 P. 266, 267. Synonymous with "compensatory damages" and with "general damages." Ringgold v. Land, 212 N.C. 369, 193 S.E. 267, 268; News Leader Co. v. Kocen, 173 Va. 95, 3 S.E.2d 385, 391, 122 A.L.R. 842; Anderson v. Alcus, Tex.Civ.App., 42 S.W.2d 294, 296.

Affirmative damages

In admiralty law, the damages which a respondent in a libel for injuries to a vessel may recover, which may be in excess of any amount which the libellant would be entitled to claim. Ebert v. The Reuben Doud, D.C.Wis., 3 F. 520.

Civil damages

Those awarded against a liquor-seller to the relative, guardian, or employer of the person to whom the sales were made, on a showing that the plaintiff has been thereby injured in person, property, or means of support. Headington v. Smith, 113 Iowa 107, 84 N.W. 982.

Compensatory damages

Compensatory damages are such as will compensate the injured party for the injury sustained, and nothing more; such as will simply make good or replace the loss caused by the wrong or injury. McKnight v. Denny, 198 Pa. 323, 47 A. 970; Wade v. Power Co., 51 S.C. 296, 29 S.E. 233, 64 Am.St.Rep. 676; Gatzow v. Buening, 106 Wis. 1, 81 N.W. 1003, 49 L.R.A. 475.

Consequential damages

Such damage, loss, or injury as does not flow directly and immediately from the act of the party, but only from some of the consequences or results of such act. Swain v. Copper Co., 111 Tenn. 430, 78 S.W. 93; McKibbin v. Pierce, Tex.Civ.App., 190 S.W. 1149, 1151; Mawson v. Vess Beverage Co., Mo.App., 173 S.W.2d 606, 613; U. S. v. Chicago, B. & Q. R. Co., C.C.A.Minn., 82 F.2d 131, 136, 106 A.L.R. 942.

The term means sometimes damage which is so remote as not to be actionable; sometimes damage which, though somewhat remote, is actionable; or damage which, though actionable, does not follow immediately, in point of time, upon the doing of the act complained of. Eaton v. Railroad Co., 51 N.H. 504, 12 Am.Rep. 147.

Contingent damages

Where a demurrer has been filed to one or more counts in a declaration, and its consideration is postponed, and meanwhile other counts in the same declaration, not demurred to, are taken as issues, and tried, and damages awarded upon them, such damages are called "contingent damages."

Continuing damages

Are such as accrue from the same injury, or from the repetition of similar acts, between two specified periods of time.

Damages ultra

Additional damages claimed by a plaintiff not satisfied with those paid into court by the defendant.

Direct damages

Direct damages are such as follow immediately upon the act done; Eaton v. Railroad Co., 51 N.H. 504, 12 Am.Rep. 147; City of Dublin v. Ogburn, 142 Ga. 840, 83 S.E. 939; McKibbin v. Pierce, Tex. Civ.App., 190 S.W. 1149, 1151; Washington & O. D. Ry. v. Westinghouse Electric & Mfg. Co., 120 Va. 620, 89 S.E. 131, 133.

Double damages

Twice the amount of actual damages as found by the verdict of a jury allowed by statute in some cases of injuries by negligence, fraud, or trespass. Cross v. United States, 6 Fed.Cas. 892; Daniel v. Vaccaro, 41 Ark. 329.

Excessive damages

Damages awarded by a jury which are grossly in excess of the amount warranted by law on the facts and circumstances of the case; unreasonable or outrageous damages. Taylor v. Giger, Hardin, Ky., 587; Harvesting Mach. Co. v. Gray, 114 Ind. 340, 16 N.E. 787.

Exemplary damages

Exemplary damages are damages on an increased scale, awarded to the plaintiff over and above what will barely compensate him for his property loss, where the wrong done to him was aggravated by circumstances of violence, oppression, malice, fraud, or wanton and wicked conduct on the part of the defendant, and are intended to solace the plaintiff for mental anguish, laceration of his feelings, shame, degradation, or other aggravations of the original wrong, or else to punish the defendant for his evil behavior or to make an example of him, for which reason they are also called "punitive" or "punitory" damages or "vindictive" damages, and (vulgarly) "smart-money." Springer v. Fuel Co., 196 Pa.St. 156, 46 A. 370; Scott v. Donald, 165 U.S. 58, 17 S.Ct. 265, 41 L.Ed. 632; Gillingham v. Railroad Co., 35 W.Va. 588, 14 S.E. 243, 14 L.R.A. 798; Murphy v. Hobbs, 7 Colo. 541, 5 P. 119, 49 Am.Rep. 366. It is said that the idea of punishment does not enter into the definition; the term being employed to mean an increased award in view of supposed aggravation of the injury to the feelings of plaintiff by the wanton or reckless act of defendant. Brause v. Brause, 190 Iowa 329, 177 N.W. 65, 70.

Fair damages

See Fair Damages.

Fee damages

Damages sustained by and awarded to an abutting owner of real property occasioned by the construction and operation of an elevated railroad in a city street, are so called, because compensation is made to the owner for the injury to, or deprivation of, his easements of light, air, and access, and these are parts of the fee. Dode v. Railway Co., 70 Hun, 374, 24 N.Y.S. 422; People v. Barker, 165 N.Y. 305, 59 N.E. 151.

General damages

General damages are such as the law itself implies or presumes to have accrued from the wrong complained of, for the reason that they are its immediate, direct, and proximate result, or such as necessarily result from the injury, or such as did in fact result from the wrong, directly and proximately, and without reference to the special character, condition, or circumstances of the plaintiff. Mood v. Telegraph Co., 40 S.C. 524, 19 S.E. 67; Hopkins v. Veo, 98 Vt. 433, 129 A. 157, 158; United States Frumentum Co. v. Lauhoff, C.C.A.Mich., 216 F. 610, 617; Kane v. New Idea Realty Co., 104 Conn. 508, 133 A. 686, 687.

Imaginary damages

This term is sometimes used as equivalent to "exemplary," "vindictive," or "punitive" damages. Murphy v. Hobbs, 7 Colo. 541, 5 P. 119, 49 Am. Rep. 366.

Inadequate damages

Damages are called "inadequate," within the rule that an injunction will not be granted where adequate damages at law could be recovered for the injury sought to be prevented, when such a recovery at law would not compensate the parties and place them in the position in which they formerly stood. Insurance Co. v. Bonner, 7 Colo. App. 97, 42 P. 681.

Intervening damages

Such damages to an appellee as result from the delay caused by the appeal. McGregor v. Balch, 17 Vt. 568; Roberts v. Warner, 17 Vt. 46, 42 Am. Dec. 478.

Irreparable damages

In the law pertaining to injunctions, damages for which no certain pecuniary standard exists for measurement. Philadelphia Ball Club, Limited, v. Lajoie, 202 Pa. 210, 51 A. 973, 58 L.R.A. 227. Damages not easily ascertainable at law. Krich v. Zemel, 96 N.J.Eq. 208, 124 A. 449, 450. With reference to public nuisances which a private party may enjoin, the term includes wrongs of a repeated and continuing character, or which occasion damages estimable only by conjecture, and not by any accurate standard. Bernard v. Willamette Box & Lumber Co., 64 Or. 223, 129 P. 1039, 1042.

Land damages

A term sometimes applied to the amount of compensation to be paid for land taken under the power of eminent domain or for injury to, or depreciation of, land adjoining that taken. People v. Hilts, 27 Misc.Rep. 290, 58 N.Y.S. 434; In re Lent, 47 App.Div. 349, 62 N.Y.S. 227.

Liquidated damages and penalties

The term is applicable when the amount of the damages has been ascertained by the judgment in the action, or when a specific sum of money has been expressly stipulated by the parties to a bond or other contract as the amount of damages to be recovered by either party for a breach of the agreement by the other. Keeble v. Keeble, 85 Ala. 552, 5 So. 149; Eakin v. Scott, 70 Tex. 442, 7 S.W. 777; Cochrane v. Forbes, 267 Mass. 417, 166 N.E. 752, 753; Varno v. Tindall, 164 Tenn. 642, 51 S.W. 2d 502, 503; Norwood Morris Plan Co. v. McCarthy, 295 Mass. 597, 4 N.E.2d 450, 454, 107 A.L. R. 1215; Factory Realty Corporation v. Corbin-Holmes Shoe Co., 312 Mass. 325, 44 N.E.2d 671, 674. The purpose of a penalty is to secure performance, while the purpose of stipulating damages is to fix the amount to be paid in lieu of performance. Christianson v. Haugland, 163 Minn. 73, 203 N.W. 433, 434; Davidow v. Wadsworth Mfg. Co., 211 Mich. 90, 178 N.W. 776, 777, 12 A.L.R. 605; Forsyth v. Central Foundry Co., 240 Ala. 277, 198 So. 706, 710. The essence of a penalty is a stipulation as in terrorem while the essence of liquidated damages is a genuine covenanted pre-estimate of such damages. Shields v. Early, 132 Miss. 282, 95 So. 839, 840. For other cases pertaining to the distinction between a penalty and liquidated damages, see Fiscal Court of Franklin County v. Kentucky Public Service Co., 181 Ky. 245, 204 S.W. 77, 79; In re Liberty Doll Co., D.C. N.Y., 242 F. 695, 701; Miller v. Blockberger, 111 Ohio St. 798, 146 N.E. 206, 209; Armstrong v. Irwin, 26 Ariz. 1, 221 P. 222, 225, 32 A.L.R. 609.

Necessary damages

A term said to be of much wider scope in the law of damages than "pecuniary." It embraces all those consequences of an injury usually denominated "general" damages, as distinguished from special damages; whereas the phrase "pecuniary damages" covers a smaller class of damages within the larger class of "general" damages. Browning v. Wabash Western R. Co., Mo., 24 S. W. 746.

Nominal damages

Nominal damages are a trifling sum awarded to a plaintiff in an action, where there is no substantial loss or injury to be compensated, but still the law recognizes a technical invasion of his rights or a breach of the defendant's duty, or in cases where, although there has been a real injury, the plaintiff's evidence entirely fails to show its amount. Seeling v. Missouri, K. & T. Ry. Co., 287 Mo. 343, 230 S.W. 94, 102; City of Rainier v. Masters, 79 Or. 534, 155 P. 1197, 1198, L.R.A. 1916E, 1175; Springer v. Fuel Co., 196 Pa. 156, 46 A. 370.

Pecuniary damages

Such as can be estimated in and compensated by money; not merely the loss of money or salable property or rights, but all such loss, deprivation, or injury as can be made the subject of calculation and of recompense in money. Walker v. McNeill, 17 Wash. 582, 50 P. 518; Davidson Benedict Co. v. Severson, 109 Tenn. 572, 72 S.W. 967.

Permanent damages

Damages awarded on theory that cause of injury is fixed and that the property will always remain subject to it. Chambers v. Spruce Lighting Co., 81 W.Va. 714, 95 S.E. 192, 194.

Presumptive damages

A term occasionally used as the equivalent of "exemplary" or "punitive" damages. Murphy v. Hobbs, 7 Colo. 541, 5 P. 119, 49 Am.Rep. 366.

Prospective damages

Damages which are expected to follow from the act or state of facts made the basis of a plaintiff's suit; damages which have not yet accrued, at the time of the trial, but which, in the nature of things, must necessarily, or most probably, result from the acts or facts complained of.

Proximate damages

Proximate damages are the immediate and direct damages and natural results of the act complained of, and such as are usual and might have been expected. Remote damages are those attributable immediately to an intervening cause, though it forms a link in an unbroken chain of causation, so that the remote damage would not have occurred if its elements had not been set in motion by the original act or event. Pielke v. Railroad Co., 5 Dak. 444, 41 N.W. 669; Chambers v. Everding & Farrell, 71 Or. 521, 143 P. 616, 619.

Remote damages

The unusual and unexpected result, not reasonably to be anticipated from an accidental or unusual combination of circumstances—a result beyond which the negligent party has no control. Chambers v. Everding & Farrel, 71 Or. 521, 143 P. 616, 620.

Damage is said to be too remote to be actionable when it is not the legal and natural consequence of the act complained of.

The terms "remote damages" and "consequential damages" are not synonymous nor to be used interchangeably; all remote damage is consequential, but it is by no means true that all consequential damage is remote. Eaton v. Railroad Co., 51 N.H. 511, 12 Am.Rep. 147; Chambers v. Everding & Farrell, 71 Or. 521, 143 P. 616, 620.

Special damages

Those which are the actual, but not the necessary, result of the injury complained of, and which in fact follow it as a natural and proximate consequence in the particular case, that is, by reason of special circumstances or conditions. Wallace v. Ah Sam, 71 Cal. 197, 12 P. 46, 60 Am. Rep. 534; Lawrence v. Porter, C.C.A.Mich., 63 F. 62, 11 C.C.A. 27, 26 L.R.A. 167; Huyler's v. Ritz-Carlton Restaurant & Hotel Co. of Atlantic City, D.C.Del., 6 F.2d 404, 406. Those which are the natural, but not the necessary, result of the injury. Butte Floral Co. v. Reed, 65 Mont. 138, 211 P. 325, 330; Ralph N. Blakeslee Co. v. Rigo, 94 Conn. 481, 109 A. 173, 175; Erick Bowman Remedy Co. v. Jensen Salsbery Laboratories, C.C.A.Minn., 17 F.2d 255, 259, 52 A.L.R. 1187.

Speculative damages

Prospective or anticipated damages from the same acts or facts constituting the present cause of action, but which depend upon future developments which are contingent, conjectural, or improbable.

Substantial damages

A sum, assessed by way of damages, which is worth having; opposed to nominal damages, which are assessed to satisfy a bare legal right. Wharton. Considerable in amount and intended as a real compensation for a real injury.

Temporary damages

Damages allowed for intermittent and occasional wrongs, such as injuries to real estate, where cause thereof is removable or abatable. Chambers v. Spruce Lighting Co., 81 W.Va. 714, 95 S.E. 192, 194.

Unliquidated damages

Such as are not yet reduced to a certainty in respect of amount, nothing more being established than the plaintiff's right to recover; or such as cannot be fixed by a mere mathematical calculation from ascertained data in the case. Cox v. McLaughlin, 76 Cal. 60, 18 P. 100, 9 Am. St.Rep. 164; Cook Pottery Co. v. Parker, 86 W. Va. 580, 104 S.E. 51, 53; United Cigarette Mach. Co. v. Brown, 119 Va. 813, 89 S.E. 850, 855, L.R.A. 1917A, 1190; Simons v. Douglas Ex'r, 189 Ky. 644, 225 S.W. 721, 723.

DAMAIOUSE. In old English law. Causing damage or loss, as distinguished from *torcenouse*, wrongful. Britt. c. 61.

DAME. In English law. The legal designation of the wife of a knight or baronet.

DAMN, *v.* To invoke condemnation, curse, swear, condemn to eternal punishment, or consign to perdition. Orf v. State, 147 Miss. 160, 113 So. 202.

DAMNA. Damages, both inclusive and exclusive of costs.

DAMNATUS. In old English law. Condemned; prohibited by law; unlawful. *Damnatus coitus,* an unlawful sexual connection.

DAMNI INJURIÆ ACTIO. An action given by the civil law for the damage done by one who intentionally injured the slave or beast of another. Calvin.

DAMNIFICATION. That which causes damage or loss.

DAMNIFY. To cause damage or injurious loss to a person or put him in a position where he must sustain it. A surety is "damnified" when a judgment has been obtained against him. McLean v. Bank, 16 Fed.Cas. 278.

DAMNOSA HÆREDITAS. In the civil law. A losing inheritance; an inheritance that was a charge, instead of a benefit. Dig. 50, 16, 119.

The term has also been metaphorically applied to that species of property of a bankrupt which, so far from being valuable, would be a charge to the creditors; for example, a term of years where the rent would exceed the revenue. 7 East, 342; 3 Camp. 340; 1 Esp.N.P. 234; Provident L. & Trust Co. v. Fidelity, etc., Co., 203 Pa. 82, 52 A. 34.

DAMNUM. Lat.

In the Civil Law

Damage; the loss or diminution of what is a man's own, either by fraud, carelessness, or accident.

In Pleading and Old English Law

Damage; loss.

DAMNUM ABSQUE INJURIA. Loss, hurt, or harm without injury in the legal sense, that is, without such breach of duty as is redressible by an action. A loss which does not give rise to an action for damages against the person causing it. West Virginia Transp. Co. v. Standard Oil Co., 50 W.Va. 611, 40 S.E. 591, 56 L.R.A. 804; J. A. & C. E. Bennett v. Winston-Salem Southbound Ry. Co., 170 N.C. 389, 87 S.E. 133, 134, L.R.A.1916D, 1074; Wisconsin Telephone Co. v. Railroad Commission of Wisconsin, 162 Wis. 383, 156 N.W. 614, 619, L. R.A.1916E, 748; Cleveland, C., C. & St. L. Ry. Co. v. Mumford, 208 Ind. 655, 197 N.E. 826, 834; Alabama Power Co. v. Ickes, App.D.C., 302 U.S. 464, 58 S.Ct. 300, 303, 82 L.Ed. 374.

DAMNUM FATALE. Fatal damage; damage from fate; loss happening from a cause beyond human control, (*quod ex fato contingit,*) or an act of God, for which bailees are not liable; such as shipwreck, lightning, and the like. Dig. 4, 9, 3, 1; Story, Bailm. § 465. The civilians included in the phrase "*damnum fatale*" all those accidents which are summed up in the common-law expression, "Act of God or public enemies;" though, perhaps, it embraced some which would not now be admitted as occurring from an irresistible force. Thickstun v. Howard, 8 Blackf. Ind. 535.

DAMNUM INFECTUM. In Roman law. Damage not yet committed, but threatened or impending. A preventive interdict might be obtained to prevent such damage from happening; and it was treated as a *quasi-delict,* because of the imminence of the danger.

DAMNUM REI AMISSAE. In the civil law. A loss arising from a payment made by a party in consequence of an error of law. Mackeld. Rom. Law, § 178.

DAMNUM SINE INJURIÂ ESSE POTEST. Lofft, 112. There may be damage or injury inflicted without any act of injustice.

DAN. Anciently the better sort of men in England had this title; so the Spanish *Don.* The old term of honor for men, as we now say Master or Mister. Wharton.

DANCEHALL. A place maintained for promiscuous and public dancing, the rules for admission to which are not based upon personal selection or invitation. State v. Loomis, 75 Mont. 88, 242 P. 344, 347; People v. Dever, 237 Ill.App. 65, 69.

DANEGELT, DANEGELD. A tribute originally of 1s. and afterwards of 2s., which came to be imposed upon every hide of land through the realm, levied by the Anglo-Saxons, for maintaining (it is supposed) such a number of forces as were thought sufficient to clear the British seas of Danish pirates, who greatly annoyed their coasts, or to buy off the ravages of Danish invaders. It continued a tax until the time of Stephen, and was one of the rights of the crown. Wharton; Webster, Dict. The Danegeld was levied as a land-tax by the Norman kings; it disappears under that name after 1163, but in fact continued under the name of *tallage.* 3 New English Dict. 26.

DANELAGE. A system of laws, introduced by the Danes on their invasion and conquest of England, which was principally maintained in some of the midland counties, and also on the eastern coast. 1 Bl.Comm. 65; 4 Bl.Comm. 411; 1 Steph. Comm. 42.

DANGER. Jeopardy; exposure to loss or injury; peril. U. S. v. Mays, 1 Idaho, 770; State v. Londe, 345 Mo. 185, 132 S.W.2d 501, 506.

DANGER ZONE. The "danger zone" within contemplation of the humanitarian doctrine depends upon the facts in the particular case. Brown v. Alton R. Co., Mo.App., 132 S.W.2d 713, 727; Brown v. Alton R. Co., 236 Mo.App. 26, 151 S.W.2d 727, 742.

Dangers of Navigation

The same as "dangers of the sea" or "perils of the sea." See Dangers of the sea, *infra*.

Dangers of the River

This phrase, as used in bills of lading, means only the natural accidents incident to river navigation, and does not embrace such as may be avoided by the exercise of that skill, judgment, or foresight which are demanded from persons in a particular occupation. Hill v. Sturgeon, 35 Mo. 213, 86 Am.Dec. 149. It includes dangers arising from unknown reefs which have suddenly formed in the channel, and are not discoverable by care and skill. Hill v. Sturgeon, 35 Mo. 213, 86 Am. Dec. 149; Hibernia Ins. Co. v. Transp. Co., 120 U. S. 166, 7 S.Ct. 550, 30 L.Ed. 621; Johnson v. Friar, 4 Yerg. 48, 26 Am.Dec. 215.

Dangers of the Road

This phrase, in a bill of lading, when it refers to inland transportation, means such dangers as are immediately caused by roads, as the overturning of carriages in rough and precipitous places. 7 Exch. 743.

Dangers of the Sea

The expression "dangers of the sea" means those accidents peculiar to navigation that are of an extraordinary nature, or arise from irresistible force or overwhelming power, which cannot be guarded against by the ordinary exertions of human skill and prudence. The Portsmouth, 9 Wall. 682, 19 L.Ed. 754; Hibernia Ins. Co. v. Transp. Co., 120 U.S. 166, 7 S.Ct. 550, 30 L.Ed. 621; The Maumee, D.C.N.C., 260 F. 862, 870; equivalent to "dangers of navigation." Norris Grain Co. v. Great Lakes Transit Corporation, C.C.A.Ill., 70 F. 2d 32, 34.

DANGERIA. In old English law. A money payment made by forest-tenants, that they might have liberty to plow and sow in time of pannage, or mast feeding.

DANGEROUS. Attended with risk; perilous; hazardous; unsafe. Scales v. Lewellyn, 172 N.C. 494, 90 S.E. 521, 522; King v. Smythe, 140 Tenn. 217, 204 S.W. 296, 297, L.R.A.1918F, 293; Bentson v. Brown, 186 Wis. 629, 203 N.W. 380, 382, 38 A.L. R. 1417; Davis v. East Contra Costa Irr. Dist., Cal.App., 109 P.2d 986, 989.

DANGEROUS MACHINE. A machine is "dangerous" in such sense that the employer is required to guard it, if, in the ordinary course of human affairs, danger may be reasonably anticipated from the use of it without protection. Simon v. St. Louis Brass Mfg. Co., 298 Mo. 70, 250 S.W. 74, 76.

DANGEROUS PER SE. A thing that may inflict injury without the immediate application of human aid or instrumentality. Southern Cotton Oil Co. v. Anderson, 80 Fla. 441, 86 So. 629, 632, 16 A. L.R. 255.

DANGEROUS PLACE. One where there is considerable risk, or danger, or peril, one where accidents or injuries are very apt to occur. Henrie v. Rocky Mountain Packing Corp., Utah, 196 P.2d 487, 489.

DANGEROUS WEAPON. One dangerous to life; one by the use of which a fatal wound may probably or possibly be given. As the manner of use enters into the consideration as well as other circumstances, the question is often one of fact for the jury, but not infrequently one of law for the court. U. S. v. Reeves, C.C.Tex., 38 F. 404; Parman v. Lemmon, 119 Kan. 323, 244 P. 227, 229, 44 A.L.R. 1500; State v. Penton, 157 La. 68, 102 So. 14, 15; deadly weapon distinguished State v. Walden, 41 N.M. 418, 70 P.2d 149, 150; Crawford v. State, 174 Md. 175, 197 A. 866, 867.

DANISM. The act of lending money on usury.

DANO. In Spanish law. Damage; the deterioration, injury, or destruction which a man suffers with respect to his person or his property by the fault (*culpa*) of another. White, New Recop. b. 2, tit. 19, c. 3, § 1.

DANS ET RETINENS, NIHIL DAT. One who gives and yet retains does not give effectually. Tray. Lat. Max. 129. Or, one who gives, yet retains, [possession,] gives nothing.

DAPIFER. A steward either of a king or lord. Spelman.

DARE. Lat. In the civil law. To transfer property. When this transfer is made in order to discharge a debt, it is *datio solvendi animo;* when in order to receive an equivalent, to create an obligation, it is *datio contrahendi animo;* lastly, when made *donandi animo,* from mere liberality, it is a gift, *dono datio.*

DARE AD REMANENTIAM. To give away in fee, or forever.

DARRAIGN. To clear a legal account; to answer an accusation; to settle a controversy.

DARREIN. L. Fr. Last.

DARREIN CONTINUANCE. The last continuance.

DARREIN PRESENTMENT. In old English law. The last presentment. See Assise of darrein presentment.

DARREIN SEISIN. Last seisin. A plea which lay in some cases for the tenant in a writ of right. See 1 Rosc. Real Act. 206; Hunt v. Hunt, 3 Metc. Mass. 184; Jackson, Real Act. 285. See 1 Roscoe, Real Act. 206; 2 Prest. Abstr. 345.

DASH. The em dash (—) or the en dash (–) is often used to indicate the omission of the intermediate terms of a series which are to be supplied in reading, being thus often equivalent to * * * inclusive; thus Mark iv, 3–20 (that is, verses 3 to 20, inclusive); the years 1880–1888 (that is, 1880 to 1888). Booe v. Sims, 139 Ark. 595, 215 S.W. 659, 660.

DATA. In old practice and conveyancing. The date of a deed; the time when it was *given;* that is, executed. Grounds whereon to proceed; facts from which to draw a conclusion.

DATE. The specification or mention, in a written instrument, of the time (day, month and year) when it was made. Also the time so specified. Interior Linseed Co. v. Becker-Moore Paint Co., 273 Mo. 433, 202 S.W. 566, 569; In re Carpenter's Estate, 172 Cal. 268, 156 P. 464, 465, L.R.A.1916E, 498; State v. Beckley, 192 Wis. 367, 212 N.W. 792, 793; Heller v. Sweeney, 101 N.J.Eq. 150, 135 A. 264, 265.

The word is derived from the Latin word "datum" meaning given and is defined as the time given or specified—in some way ascertained and fixed. The time when an instrument was made, acknowledged, delivered or recorded; the clause or memorandum which specifies that fact; and the time from which its operation is to be reckoned. In re Irvine's Estate, 114 Mont. 577, 139 P.2d 489, 490, 491, 47 A.L.R. 882.

That part of a deed or writing which expresses the day of the month and year in which it was made or *given.* 2 Bl.Comm. 304; Tomlins.

The primary signification of *date* is not time in the abstract, nor time taken absolutely, but time given or specified; time in some way ascertained and fixed. When we speak of the date of a deed, date of issue of a bond or date of a policy, we do not mean the time when it was actually executed, but the time of its execution, as given or stated in the deed itself. The date of an item, or of a charge in a book-account, is not necessarily the time when the article charged was, in fact, furnished, but rather the time given or set down in the account, in connection with such charge. And so the expression "the date of the last work done, or materials furnished," in a mechanic's lien law, may be taken, in the absence of anything in the act indicating a different intention, to mean the time when such work was done or materials furnished, as specified in the plaintiff's written claim. Bement v. Manufacturing Co., 32 N.J.Law, 513; Mutual Life Ins. Co. of New York v. Hurni Packing Co., 263 U.S. 167, 44 S.Ct. 90, 68 L.Ed. 235, 31 A.L.R. 102; Mutual Life Ins. Co. of New York v. Hurni Packing Co., C.C.A.Iowa, 280 F. 18, 20; Turner v. Roseberry Irr. Dist., 33 Idaho, 746, 198 P. 465, 467.

The precise meaning of date, however, depends upon context, since there are numerous instances when it means actual as distinguished from conventional time. Buckhannon & N. R. Co. v. Great Scott Coal & Coke Co., 75 W. Va. 423, 83 S.E. 1031, 1033; London Guarantee & Accident Co. v. Empire Plow Co., 115 Ohio St. 684, 155 N.E. 382, 384; National Liberty Ins. Co. v. Norman, C.C.A.N.C., 11 F.2d 59, 61; Cantrell v. Prudential Ins. Co. of America, 189 Wash. 99, 63 P.2d 509, 510.

DATE CERTAINE. In French law. A deed is said to have a *date certaine* (fixed date) when it has been subjected to the formality of registration; after this formality has been complied with, the parties to the deed cannot by mutual consent change the date thereof. Arg. Fr. Merc. Law, 555.

DATE OF INJURY. Means inception date of the injury and is regarded as coincident with date of occurrence or happening of accident which caused such injury. Indemnity Ins. Co. of North America v. Williams, 129 Tex. 51, 99 S.W.2d 905, 907; Associated Indemnity Corporation v. State Industrial Accident Commission, 124 Cal.App. 378, 12 P.2d 1075, 1076; Larson v. Industrial Commission, 224 Wis. 294, 271 N.W. 835, 836. Date of the compensable injury and not date of accident or occurrence from which incapacity resulted. Rossi v. Thomas F. Jackson Co., 120 Conn. 456, 181 A. 539.

"DATE OF ISSUE." When applied to notes, bonds, etc., of series, usually means an arbitrary date fixed as beginning of term for which they run, without reference to precise time when convenience or state of market may permit their sale or delivery, date which bonds and stocks bear, and not date when they were actually issued in sense of being signed and delivered and put into circulation. Whetstone v. City of Stuttgart, 193 Ark. 88, 97 S.W.2d 641, 643.

The words in life policy were held not to mean the date of actual execution or the delivery date, but the date set forth in the policy itself. Potts v. Metropolitan Life Ins. Co., 133 Pa.Super. 397, 2 A.2d 870, 872.

DATIO. In the civil law. A giving, or act of giving. *Datio in solutum;* a giving in payment; a species of accord and satisfaction. Called, in modern law, "dation."

DATION. In the civil law. A gift; a giving of something. It is not exactly synonymous with "donation," for the latter implies generosity or liberality in making a gift, while dation may mean the giving of something to which the recipient is already entitled.

DATION EN PAIEMENT. In French law. A giving by the debtor and receipt by the creditor of something in payment of a debt, instead of a sum of money. It is somewhat like the accord and satisfaction of the common law. 16 Toullier, no. 45; Poth. Vente, no. 601.

DATIVE. A word derived from the Roman law, signifying "appointed by public authority." Thus, in Scotland, an executor-dative is an executor appointed by a court; corresponding or equivalent to an English *administrator* or "administrator with the will annexed." Mozley & Whitley. In old English law. In one's gift; that may be given and disposed of at will and pleasure.

DATUM. A first principle; a thing given; a date.

DATUR DIGNIORI. It is given to the more worthy. 2 Vent. 268.

DAUGHTER. An immediate female descendant. People v. Kaiser, 119 Cal. 456, 51 P. 702. May include the issue of a daughter. Buchanan v. Lloyd,

88 Md. 462, 41 A. 1075; Jamison v. Hay, 46 Mo. 546. May designate a natural or illegitimate female child, State v. Laurence, 95 N.C. 659, not an adopted daughter, a stepdaughter, or daughter-in-law. State v. Youst, 74 Ohio App. 381, 59 N.E.2d 167, 168.

The female offspring of a man or woman. State v. Lee, 196 Miss. 311, 17 So.2d 277, 278, 151 A.L.R. 1143.

DAUGHTER-IN-LAW. The wife of one's son.

DAUPHIN. In French law. The title of the eldest sons of the kings of France. Disused since 1830.

DAY. 1. A period of time consisting of twenty-four hours and including the solar day and the night. Co. Litt. 135*a*; Fox v. Abel, 2 Conn. 541.

2. The period of time during which the earth makes one revolution on its axis. Long v. City of Wichita Falls, 142 Tex. 202, 176 S.W.2d 936, 938, 939.

3. The space of time which elapses between two successive midnights. 2 Bl.Comm. 141; State v. Michel, 52 La.Ann. 936, 27 So. 565, 49 L.R.A. 218; Stevenson v. Donnelly, 221 Mass. 161, 108 N.E. 926, 927, Ann.Cas.1917E, 932; Long v. City of Wichita Falls, 142 Tex. 202, 176 S.W.2d 936, 938, 939.

4. The whole or any part of period of 24 hours from midnight to midnight. Talbott v. Caudill, 248 Ky. 146, 58 S.W.2d 385.

5. That portion of time during which the sun is above the horizon, and, in addition, that part of the morning and evening during which there is sufficient light for the features of a man to be reasonably discerned. 3 Inst. 63; Nicholls v. State, 68 Wis. 416, 32 N.W. 543, 60 Am.Rep. 870; State v. McKnight, 111 N.C. 690, 16 S.E. 319; U. S. v. Martin, D.C.Mass., 33 F.2d 639, 640.

6. An artificial period of time, computed from one fixed point to another twenty-four hours later, without any reference to the prevalence of light or darkness. Fuller v. Schroeder, 20 Neb. 631, 31 N.W. 109.

7. The period of time, within the limits of a natural day, set apart either by law or by common usage for the transaction of particular business or the performance of labor; as in banking, in laws regulating the hours of labor, in contracts for so many "days' work," and the like, the word "day" may signify six, eight, ten, or any number of hours. Fay v. Brown, 96 Wis. 434, 71 N.W. 895; McCulsky v. Klosterman, 20 Or. 108, 25 P. 366, 10 L.R.A. 785.

8. In practice and pleading. A particular time assigned or given for the appearance of parties in court, the return of writs, etc.

When considered in computing time, it is an indivisible point of time, Williams v. Williams, 325 Mo. 963, 30 S.W.2d 69, 71; Fiedler v. Eckfeldt, 335 Ill. 11, 166 N.E. 504, 507; Greulich v. Monnin, 142 Ohio St. 113, 50 N.E.2d 310, 312; but that it is not divisible is a mere fiction, only observed for the purposes of justice and never adhered to when it would work mischief. Greulich v. Monnin, Ohio App., 45 N.E.2d 212, 217. Durstin v. Dodge, 138 Me. 12, 20 A.2d 671, 672.

Regardless of the duration of the "day," the law often disregards fractions, where priority is not concerned. Franklin v. State, 9 Okl.Cr. 178, 131 P. 183, 184; Harris County v. Hammond, Tex.Civ.App., 203 S.W. 451, 453; State ex rel. Jones v. Board of Deputy State Supervisors & Inspectors of Elections of Montgomery County, 93 Ohio St. 14, 112 N.E. 136, 137; First National Bank v. Burkhardt, 100 U.S. 686, 25 L.Ed. 766.

Astronomical Day

The period of twenty-four hours beginning and ending at noon.

Artificial Day

The time between the rising and setting of the sun; that is, day or daytime as distinguished from night.

Calendar Days

See Calendar.

Civil Day

The solar day, measured by the diurnal revolution of the earth, and denoting the interval of time which elapses between the successive transits of the sun over the same hour circle, so that the "civil day" commences and ends at midnight. Pedersen v. Eugster, D.C.La., 14 F. 422.

Clear Days

See Clear.

Common Day

In old English practice. An ordinary day in court. Cowell; Termes de la Ley.

Judicial Day

A day on which the court is actually in session. Heffner v. Heffner, 48 La.Ann. 1088, 20 So. 281.

Juridical Day

A day proper for the transaction of business in court; one on which the court may lawfully sit, excluding Sundays and some holidays.

Law Day

The day prescribed in a bond, mortgage, or defeasible deed for payment of the debt secured thereby, or, in default of payment, the forfeiture of the property mortgaged. But this does not now occur until foreclosure. Ward v. Lord, 100 Ga. 407, 28 S.E. 446; Kortright v. Cady, 21 N.Y. 345, 78 Am.Rep. 145.

Legal Day

A juridical day. See *supra*. And see Heffner v. Heffner, 48 La.Ann. 1088, 20 So. 281.

Natural Day

Properly the period of twenty-four hours from midnight to midnight. Co.Litt. 135; Fox v. Abel, 2 Conn. 541; People v. Hatch, 33 Ill. 137. Though sometimes taken to mean the daytime or time between sunrise and sunset. In re Ten Hour Law, 24 R.I. 603, 54 A. 602, 61 L.R.A. 612.

Non-judicial Day

One on which process cannot ordinarily issue or be served or returned and on which the courts do not ordinarily sit. Whitney v. Blackburn, 17 Or. 564, 21 P. 874, 11 Am.St.Rep. 857. More properly "non-juridical day."

Solar Day

A term sometimes used as meaning that portion of the day when the sun is above the horizon, but properly it is the time between two complete (apparent) revolutions of the sun, or between two consecutive positions of the sun over any given terrestrial meridian, and hence, according to the usual method of reckoning, from noon to noon at any given place.

DAY-BOOK. A tradesman's account book; a book in which all the occurrences of the day are set down. It is usually a book of original entries.

DAY CERTAIN. A fixed or appointed day; a specified particular day; a day in term. Regina v. Conyers, 8 Q.B. 991.

DAY FIXED FOR TRIAL. Has been held to mean return day of summons or any later day to which trial is adjourned and on which it is actually held. Okin v. Shafman, N.J., 11 N.J.Misc. 462, 166 A. 730.

DAY IN COURT. The time appointed for one whose rights are called judicially in question, or liable to be affected by judicial action, to appear in court and be heard in his own behalf. This phrase, as generally used, means not so much the time appointed for a hearing as the opportunity to present one's claims or rights in a proper forensic hearing before a competent tribunal. See Ferry v. Car Wheel Co., 71 Vt. 457, 45 A. 1035, 76 Am.St.Rep. 782.

A litigant has his "day in court" when he has been duly cited to appear and has been afforded an opportunity to appear and to be heard. Cohen v. City of Houston, Tex.Civ.App., 185 S.W.2d 450, 452; In re Hampton's Estate, 55 Cal.App.2d 543, 131 P.2d 565, 573; State ex rel. Allstate Ins. Co. v. Bowen, 130 Ohio St. 347, 199 N.E. 355, 363.

DAY OF ATONEMENT. See Yom Kippur.

DAYERIA. A dairy. Cowell.

DAYLIGHT. That portion of time before sunrise, and after sunset, which is accounted part of the day, (as distinguished from *night*,) in defining the offense of burglary. 4 Bl.Comm. 224; Cro. Jac. 106.

DAY-RULE, or DAY-WRIT. In English law. A permission granted to a prisoner to go out of prison, for the purpose of transacting his business, as to hear a case in which he is concerned at the assizes, etc. Abolished by 5 & 6 Vict. c. 22, § 12.

DAYS IN BANK. (L. Lat. *dies in banco.*) In practice. Certain stated days in term appointed for the appearance of parties, the return of process, etc., originally peculiar to the court of common pleas, or bench, (bank,) as it was anciently called. 3 Bl.Comm. 277.

By the common law, the defendant is allowed three full days in which to make his appearance in court, exclusive of the day of appearance or return-day named in the writ; 3 Bl.Comm. 278. Upon his appearance, time is usually granted him for pleading; and this is called giving him day, or, as it is more familiarly expressed, a continuance. 3 Bl.Comm. 316. When the suit is ended by discontinuance or by judgment for the defendant, he is discharged from further attendance, and is said to go thereof *sine die*, without day. See Continuance.

DAYS OF GRACE. A number of days allowed, as a matter of favor or *grace*, to a person who has to perform some act, or make some payment, after the time originally limited for the purpose has elapsed. In old practice. Three days allowed to persons summoned in the English courts, beyond the day named in the writ, to make their appearance; the last day being called the *"quarto die post."* 3 Bl.Comm. 278. In mercantile law. A certain number of days (generally three) allowed to the maker or acceptor of a bill, draft, or note, in which to make payment, after the expiration of the time expressed in the paper itself. Originally these days were granted only as a matter of *grace* or favor, but the allowance of them became an established custom of merchants, and was sanctioned by the courts, (and in some cases prescribed by statute,) so that they are now demandable as of right. Bell v. Bank, 115 U.S. 373, 6 S.Ct. 105, 29 L.Ed. 409; Renner v. Bank, 9 Wheat. 581, 6 L.Ed. 166.

DAYSMAN. An arbitrator, umpire, or elected judge. Cowell.

DAYTIME. The time during which there is the light of day, as distinguished from night or nighttime. That portion of the twenty-four hours during which a man's person and countenance are distinguishable. Trull v. Wilson, 9 Mass. 154; Rex v. Tandy, 1 Car. & P. 297; Linnen v. Banfield, 114 Mich. 93, 72 N.W. 1; U. S. v. Syrek, D.C.Mass., 290 F. 820, 821; Deese v. City of Lodi, 21 Cal.App.2d 631, 69 P.2d 1005, 1008.

DAYWERE. In old English law. A term applied to land, and signifying as much arable ground as could be plowed up in one day's work. Cowell.

DE. A Latin preposition, signifying of; by; from; out of; affecting; concerning; respecting.

DE ACQUIRENDO RERUM DOMINIO. Of (about) acquiring the ownership of things. Dig. 41, 1; Bract. lib. 2, fol. 8*b*.

DE ADMENSURATIONE. Of admeasurement. Thus, *de admensuratione dotis* was a writ for the admeasurement of dower, and *de admensuratione pasturæ* was a writ for the admeasurement of pasture.

DE ADVISAMENTO CONSILII NOSTRI. L. Lat. With or by the advice of our council. A phrase used in the old writs of summons to parliament. Crabb, Eng.Law, 240.

DE ÆQUITATE. In equity. *De jure stricto, nihil possum vendicare, de æquitate tamen, nullo modo hoc obtinet;* in strict law. I can claim nothing, but in equity this by no means obtains. Fleta, lib. 3, c. 2, § 10.

DE ÆSTIMATO. In Roman law. One of the innominate contracts, and, in effect, a sale of land or goods at a price fixed, (*æstimato,*) and guarantied by some third party, who undertook to find a purchaser.

DE ÆTATE PROBANDA. For proving age. A writ which formerly lay to summon a jury in order to determine the age of the heir of a tenant *in capite* who claimed his estate as being of full age. Fitzh.Nat.Brev. 257; Reg.Orig. 294.

DE ALEATORIBUS. About gamesters. The name of a title in the Pandects. Dig. 11, 5.

DE ALLOCATIONE FACIENDA, *Breve.* Writ for making an allowance. An old writ directed to the lord treasurer and barons of the exchequer, for allowing certain officers (as collectors of customs) in their accounts certain payments made by them. Reg.Orig. 192.

DE ALTO ET BASSO. Of high and low. A phrase anciently used to denote the absolute submission of all differences to arbitration. Cowell.

DE AMBITU. Lat. Concerning bribery. A phrase descriptive of the subject-matter of several of the Roman laws; as the *Lex Aufidia,* the *Lex Pompeia,* the *Lex Tullia,* and others. See Ambitus.

DE AMPLIORI GRATIA. Of more abundant or especial grace. Townsh.Pl. 18.

DE ANNO BISSEXTILI. Of the bissextile or leap year. The title of a statute passed in the twenty-first year of Henry III., which in fact, however, is nothing more than a sort of writ or direction to the justices of the bench, instructing them how the extraordinary day in the leap year was to be reckoned in cases where persons had a day to appear at the distance of a year, as on the essoin *de malo lecti,* and the like. It was thereby directed that the additional day should, together with that which went before, be reckoned only as one, and so, of course, within the preceding year. 1 Reeve, Eng.Law, 266.

DE ANNUA PENSIONE, *Breve.* Writ of annual pension. An ancient writ by which the king, having a yearly pension due him out of an abbey or priory for any of his chaplains, demanded the same of the abbot or prior, for the person named in the writ. Reg.Orig. 265*b*, 307; Fitzh.Nat.Brev. 231 G.

DE ANNUO REDITU. For a yearly rent. A writ to recover an annuity, no matter how payable, in goods or money. 2 Reeve, Eng.Law, 258.

DE APOSTATA CAPIENDO, *Breve.* Writ for taking an apostate. A writ which anciently lay against one who, having entered and professed some order of religion, left it and wandered up and down the country, contrary to the rules of his order, commanding the sheriff to apprehend him and deliver him again to his abbot or prior. Reg.Orig. 71*b*, 267; Fitzh.Nat.Brev. 233, 234.

DE ARBITRATIONE FACTA. (Lat. Of arbitration had.) A writ formerly used when an action was brought for a cause which had been settled by arbitration. Wats.Arb. 256.

DE ARRESTANDIS BONIS NE DISSIPENTUR. And old writ which lay to seize goods in the hands of a party during the pendency of a suit, to prevent their being made away with. Reg.Orig. 126*b*.

DE ARRESTANDO IPSUM QUI PECUNIAM RECEPIT. A writ which lay for the arrest of one who had taken the king's money to serve in the war, and hid himself to escape going. Reg.Orig. 24*b*.

DE ARTE ET PARTE. Of art and part. A phrase in old Scotch law. See Art and Part.

DE ASPORTATIS RELIGIOSORUM. Concerning the property of religious persons carried away. The title of the statute 35 Edward I. passed to check the abuses of clerical possessions, one of which was the waste they suffered by being drained into foreign countries. 2 Reeve, Eng.Law, 157; 2 Inst. 580.

DE ASSISA PROROGANDA. (Lat. For proroguing assise.) A writ to put off an assise, issuing to the justices, where one of the parties is engaged in the service of the king.

DE ATTORNATO RECIPIENDO. A writ which lay to the judges of a court, requiring them to receive and admit an attorney for a party. Reg. Orig. 172; Fitzh.Nat.Brev. 156.

DE AUDIENDO ET TERMINANDO. For hearing and determining; to hear and determine. The name of a writ, or rather commission granted to certain justices to hear and determine cases of heinous misdemeanor, trespass, riotous breach of the peace, etc. Reg.Orig. 123, *et seq.*; Fitzh.Nat. Brev. 110 B. See Oyer and Terminer.

DE AVERIIS CAPTIS IN WITHERNAMIUM. Writ for taking cattle in withernam. A writ which lay where the sheriff returned to a *pluries* writ of replevin that the cattle or goods, etc., were eloined, etc.; by which he was commanded to take the cattle of the defendant in withernam, (or reprisal,) and detain them until he could replevy the other cattle. Reg.Orig. 82; Fitzh. Nat.Brev. 73, E. F. See Withernam.

DE AVERIIS REPLEGIANDIS. A writ to replevy beasts. 3 Bl.Comm. 149.

DE AVERIIS RETORNANDIS. For returning the cattle. A term applied to pledges given in the old action of replevin. 2 Reeve, Eng.Law, 177.

DE BANCO. Of the bench. A term formerly applied in England to the justices of the court of common pleas, or "bench," as it was originally styled.

DE BENE ESSE. Conditionally; provisionally; in anticipation of future need. A phrase applied to proceedings which are taken *ex parte* or provisionally, and are allowed to stand as *well done* for the present, but which may be subject to future exception or challenge, and must then stand or fall according to their intrinsic merit and regularity.

Thus, "in certain cases, the courts will allow evidence to be taken out of the regular course, in order to prevent the evidence being lost by the death or the absence of the witness. This is called 'taking evidence *de bene esse*,' and is looked upon as a temporary and conditional examination, to be used only in case the witness cannot afterwards be examined in the suit in the regular way." Hunt, Eq. 75; Haynes, Eq. 183; Mitf. Eq. Pl. 52, 149; Willis v. Bank of Hardinsburg & Trust Co., 160 Ky. 808, 170 S.W. 188, 189.

Examination de bene esse

A provisional examination of a witness; an examination of a witness whose testimony is important and might otherwise be lost, held out of court and before the trial, with the proviso that the deposition so taken may be used on the trial in case the witness is unable to attend in person at that time or cannot be produced.

DE BIEN ET DE MAL. L. Fr. For good and evil. A phrase by which a party accused of a crime anciently put himself upon a jury, indicating his entire submission to their verdict; also the name of the special writ of jail delivery formerly in use in England, which issued for each particular prisoner, of course. It was superseded by the general commission of jail delivery.

DE BIENS LE MORT. L. Fr. Of the goods of the deceased. Dyer, 32.

DE BIGAMIS. Concerning men twice married. The title of the statute 4 Edw. I. St. 3; so called from the initial words of the fifth chapter. 2 Inst. 272; 2 Reeve, Eng.Law, 142.

DE BONE MEMORIE. L. Fr. Of good memory; of sound mind. 2 Inst. 510.

DE BONIS ASPORTATIS. For goods taken away; for taking away goods. The action of trespass for taking personal property is technically called "trespass *de bonis asportatis.*" 1 Tidd, Pr. 5.

DE BONIS NON. An abbreviation of *De bonis non administratis, (q. v.).* 1 Strange, 34.

DE BONIS NON ADMINISTRATIS. Of the goods not administered. When an administrator is appointed to succeed another, who has left the estate partially unsettled, he is said to be granted "administration *de bonis non;*" that is, of the goods not already administered. McNair v. Howle, 123 S.C. 252, 116 S.E. 279, 285.

DE BONIS NON AMOVENDIS. Writ for not removing goods. A writ anciently directed to the sheriffs of London, commanding them, in cases where a writ of error was brought by a defendant against whom a judgment was recovered, to see that his *goods* and chattels were safely kept *without being removed,* while the error remained undetermined, so that execution might be had of them, etc. Reg.Orig. 131*b*; Termes de la Ley.

DE BONIS PROPRIIS. Of his own goods. The technical name of a judgment against an administrator or executor to be satisfied from his own property, and not from the estate of the deceased, as in cases where he has been guilty of a *devastavit* or of a false plea of *plene administravit.*

DE BONIS TESTATORIS, or INTESTATI. Of the goods of the testator, or intestate. A term applied to a judgment awarding execution against the property of a testator or intestate, as distinguished from the individual property of his executor or administrator. 2 Archb.Pr.K.B. 148, 149.

DE BONIS TESTATORIS AC SI. (Lat. From the goods of the testator, *if he has any,* and, if *not, from those of the executor.*) A judgment rendered where an executor falsely pleads any matter as a release, or, generally, in any case where he is to be charged in case his testator's estate is insufficient. 1 Williams' Saund. 336*b*; Bac. Abr. "Executor," B, 3; 2 Archb.Pr.K.B. 148.

DE BONO ET MALO. See De Bien et De Mal.

DE BONO GESTU. For good behavior; for good abearance.

DE CÆTERO. Henceforth.

DE CALCETO REPARANDO. Writ for repairing a causeway. An old writ by which the sheriff was commanded to distrain the inhabitants of a place to repair and maintain a causeway, etc. Reg. Orig. 154.

DE CAPITALIBUS DOMINIS FEODI. Of the chief lords of the fee.

DE CAPITE MINUTIS. Of those who have lost their *status,* or civil condition. Dig. 4, 5. The name of a title in the Pandects. See Capitis Deminutio.

DE CARTIS REDDENDIS. (For restoring charters.) A writ to secure the delivery of charters or deeds; a writ of detinue. Reg. Orig. 159*b*.

DE CATALLIS REDDENDIS. (For restoring chattels.) A writ to secure the return specifically of chattels detained from the owner. Cowell.

DE CAUTIONE ADMITTENDA. Writ to take caution or security. A writ which anciently lay against a bishop who held an excommunicated person in prison for his contempt, notwithstanding he had offered sufficient security (*idoneam cautionem*) to obey the commands of the church; commanding him to take such security and release the prisoner. Reg. Orig. 66; Fitzh. Nat. Brev. 63, C.

DE CERTIFICANDO. A writ requiring a thing to be certified. A kind of *certiorari*. Reg. Orig. 151, 152.

DE CERTIORANDO. A writ for certifying. A writ directed to the sheriff, requiring him to certify to a particular fact. Reg. Orig. 24.

DE CHAMPERTIA. Writ of champerty. A writ directed to the justices of the bench, commanding the enforcement of the statute of *champertors*. Reg. Orig. 183; Fitzh. Nat. Brev. 172.

DE CHAR ET DE SANK. L. Fr. Of flesh and blood. *Affaire rechat de char et de sank.* Words used in claiming a person to be a villein, in the time of Edward II. Y. B. P. 1 Edw. II. p. 4.

DE CHIMINO. A writ for the enforcement of a right of way. Reg. Orig. 155.

DE CIBARIIS UTENDIS. Of victuals to be used. The title of a sumptuary statute passed 10 Edw. III. St. 3, to restrain the expense of entertainments. Barring. Ob. St. 240.

DE CLAMEA ADMITTENDA IN ITINERE PER ATTORNATUM. See Clamea Admittenda, etc.

DE CLARO DIE. By daylight. Fleta, lib. 2, c. 76, § 8.

DE CLAUSO FRACTO. Of close broken; of breach of close. See Clausum Fregit.

DE CLERICO ADMITTENDO. See Admittendo Clerico.

DE CLERICO CAPTO PER STATUTUM MERCATORIUM DELIBERANDO. Writ for delivering a clerk arrested on a statute merchant. A writ for the delivery of a clerk out of prison, who had been taken and imprisoned upon the breach of a statute merchant. Reg. Orig. 147*b*.

DE CLERICO CONVICTO DELIBERANDO. See Clerico Convicto, etc.

DE CLERICO INFRA SACROS ORDINES CONSTITUTO NON ELIGENDO IN OFFICIUM. See Clerico Infra Sacros, etc.

DE CLERO. Concerning the clergy. The title of the statute 25 Edw. III. St. 3; containing a variety of provisions on the subject of presentations, indictments of spiritual persons, and the like. 2 Reeve, Eng. Law, 378.

DE COMBUSTIONE DOMORUM. Of house burning. One of the kinds of appeal formerly in use in England. Bract. fol. 146*b*; 2 Reeve, Eng. Law, 38.

DE COMMUNI DIVIDUNDO. For dividing a thing held in common. The name of an action given by the civil law. Mackeld. Rom. Law, § 499.

DE COMON DROIT. L. Fr. Of common right; that is, by the common law. Co. Litt. 142*a*.

DE COMPUTO. Writ of account. A writ commanding a defendant to render a reasonable account to the plaintiff, or show cause to the contrary. Reg. Orig. 135–138; Fitzh. Nat. Brev. 117, E. The foundation of the modern action of account.

DE CONCILIO CURIÆ. By the advice (or direction) of the court.

DE CONFLICTU LEGUM. Concerning the conflict of laws. The title of several works written on that subject. 2 Kent, Comm. 455.

DE CONJUNCTIM FEOFFATIS. Concerning persons jointly enfeoffed, or seised. The title of the statute 34 Edw. I., which was passed to prevent the delay occasioned by tenants in novel disseisin, and other writs, pleading that some one else was seised jointly with them. 2 Reeve, Eng. Law, 243.

DE CONSANGUINEO, and DE CONSANGUINITATE. Writs of cosinage, (*q. v.*).

DE CONSILIO. In old criminal law. Of counsel; concerning counsel or advice to commit a crime. Fleta, lib. 1, c. 31, § 8.

DE CONSILIO CURIÆ. By the advice or direction of the court. Bract. fol. 345*b*.

DE CONTINUANDO ASSISAM. Writ to continue an assise. Reg. Orig. 217*b*.

DE CONTUMACE CAPIENDO. Writ for taking a contumacious person. A writ which issues out of the English court of chancery, in cases where a person has been pronounced by an ecclesiastical court to be contumacious, and in contempt. Shelf. Mar. & Div. 494–496, and notes. It is a commitment for contempt. Id.

DE COPIA LIBELLI DELIBERANDA. Writ for delivering the copy of a libel. An ancient writ directed to the judge of a spiritual court, commanding him to *deliver* to a defendant a *copy* of the libel filed against him in such court. Reg. Orig. 58. The writ in the register is directed to the Dean of the Arches, and his commissary. Id.

DE CORONATORE ELIGENDO. Writ for electing a coroner. A writ issued to the sheriff in England, commanding him to proceed to the election of a coroner, which is done in full county court, the freeholders being the electors. Sewell, Sheriffs, 372.

DE CORONATORE EXONERANDO. Writ for discharging or removing a coroner. A writ by which a coroner in England may be removed from office for some cause therein assigned. Fitzh. Nat. Brev. 163, 164; 1 Bl.Comm. 348.

DE CORPORE COMITATUS. From the body of the county at large, as distinguished from a particular neighborhood, (*de vicineto.*) 3 Bl.Comm. 360. Used with reference to the composition of a jury. State v. Kemp, 34 Minn. 61, 24 N.W. 349.

DE CORRODIO HABENDO. Writ for having a corody. A writ to exact a corody from a religious house. Reg. Orig. 264, Fitzh. Nat. Brev. 230. See Corody.

DE CUJUS. Lat. From whom. A term used to designate the person by, through, from, or under whom another claims. Brant v. New Orleans, 41 La.Ann. 1098, 6 So. 793.

DE CURIA CLAUDENDA. An obsolete writ, to require a defendant to fence in his court or land about his house, where it was left open to the injury of his neighbor's freehold. 1 Crabb, Real Prop. 314; Rust v. Low, 6 Mass. 90.

DE CURSU. Of course. The usual, necessary, and formal proceedings in an action are said to be *de cursu;* as distinguished from *summary* proceedings, or such as are incidental and may be taken on summons or motion. Writs *de cursu* are such as are issued of course, as distinguished from prerogative writs.

DE CUSTODE ADMITTENDO. Writ for admitting a guardian. Reg. Orig. 93*b*, 198.

DE CUSTODE AMOVENDO. Writ for removing a guardian. Reg. Orig. 198.

DE CUSTODIA TERRÆ ET HÆREDIS, *Breve.* L. Lat. Writ of ward, or writ of right of ward. A writ which lay for a guardian in knight's service or in socage, to recover the possession and custody of the infant, or the *wardship of the land and heir.* Reg. Orig. 161*b*; Fitzh. Nat. Brev. 139, B; 3 Bl.Comm. 141.

DE DEBITO. A writ of debt. Reg. Orig. 139.

DE DEBITORE IN PARTES SECANDO. In Roman law. "Of cutting a debtor in pieces." This was the name of a law contained in the Twelve Tables, the meaning of which has occasioned much controversy. Some commentators have concluded that it was literally the privilege of the creditors of an insolvent debtor (all other means failing) to cut his body into pieces and distribute it among them. Others contend that the language of this law must be taken figuratively, denoting a cutting up and apportionment of the debtor's *estate.*

The latter view has been adopted by Montesquieu, Bynkershoek, Heineccius, and Taylor. (Esprit des Lois, liv. 29, c. 2; Bynk.Obs.Jur.Rom. l. 1, c. 1; Heinecc.Ant.Rom. lib. 3, tit. 30, § 4; Tayl.Comm. in Leg.Decemv.) The literal meaning, on the other hand, is advocated by Aulus Gellius and other writers of antiquity, and receives support from an expression *(semoto omni cruciatu)* in the Roman code itself. (Aul.Gel.Noctes Atticæ, lib. 20, c. 1; Code, 7, 7, 8.) This is also the opinion of Gibbon, Gravina, Pothier, Hugo, and Niebuhr. (3 Gib.Rom.Emp., Am.Ed., p. 183; Grav. de Jur.Nat.Gent. et XII. Tab. § 72; Poth.Introd.Pand.; Hugo, Hist. du Droit Rom. tom. i. p. 233, § 149; 2 Nieb. Hist.Rom. p. 597; 1 Kent, Comm. 523, note.) Burrill.

DE DECEPTIONE. A writ of deceit which lay against one who acted in the name of another whereby the latter was damnified and deceived. Reg. Orig. 112.

DE DEONERANDA PRO RATA PORTIONIS. A writ that lay where one was distrained for rent that ought to be paid by others proportionably with him. Fitzh. Nat. Brev. 234; Termes de la Ley.

DE DIE IN DIEM. From day to day. Bract. fol. 205*b*.

DE DIVERSIS REGULIS JURIS ANTIQUI. Of divers rules of the ancient law. A celebrated title of the Digests, and the last in that collection. It consists of two hundred and eleven rules or maxims. Dig. 50, 17.

DE DOLO MALO. Of or founded upon fraud. Dig. 4, 3. See Actio de Dolo Malo.

DE DOMO REPARANDA. A writ which lay for one tenant in common to compel his cotenant to contribute towards the repair of the common property.

DE DONIS. Concerning gifts, (or more fully, *de donis conditionalibus,* concerning conditional gifts.) The name of a celebrated English statute, passed in the thirteenth year of Edw. I., and constituting the first chapter of the statute of Westm. 2, by virtue of which estates in fee-simple conditional (formerly known as "*dona conditionalia*") were converted into estates in fee-tail and rendered inalienable, thereby strengthening the power of the nobles. See 2 Bl.Comm. 112.

DE DOTE ASSIGNANDA. Writ for assigning dower. A writ which lay for the widow of a tenant *in capite,* commanding the king's escheater to cause her dower to be assigned to her. Reg. Orig. 297; Fitzh. Nat. Brev. 263, C.

DE DOTE UNDE NIHIL HABET. A writ of dower which lay for a widow where no part of her dower had been assigned to her. It is not much used; but a form closely resembling it is sometimes used in the United States. 4 Kent, Comm. 63; Stearns, Real Act. 302; 1 Washb. Real Prop. 230.

DE EJECTIONE CUSTODIÆ. A writ which lay for a guardian who had been forcibly ejected from his wardship. Reg. Orig. 162.

DE EJECTIONE FIRMÆ. A writ which lay at the suit of the tenant for years against the lessor, reversioner, remainderman, or stranger who had himself deprived the tenant of the occupation of the land during his term. 3 Bl.Comm. 199. By a gradual extension of the scope of this form of action its object was made to include not only damages for the unlawful detainer, but also the possession for the remainder of the term, and eventually the possession of land generally. And, as it turned on the right of possession, this involved a determination of the right of property, or the title, and thus arose the modern action of ejectment.

DE ESCÆTA. Writ of escheat. A writ which a lord had, where his tenant died without heir, to recover the land. Reg. Orig. 164*b*; Fitzh. Nat. Brev. 143, 144, E.

DE ESCAMBIO MONETÆ. A writ of exchange of money. An ancient writ to authorize a merchant to make a bill of exchange, (*literas cambitorias facere.*) Reg. Orig. 194.

DE ESSE IN PEREGRINATIONE. Of being on a journey. A species of essoin. 1 Reeve, Eng. Law, 119.

DE ESSENDO QUIETUM DE TOLONIO. A writ which lay for those who were by privilege free from the payment of toll, on their being molested therein. Fitzh. Nat. Brev. 226; Reg. Orig. 258*b*.

DE ESSONIO DE MALO LECTI. A writ which issued upon an essoin of *malum lecti* being cast, to examine whether the party was in fact sick or not. Reg. Orig. 8*b*.

DE ESTOVERIIS HABENDIS. Writ for having estovers. A writ which lay for a wife divorced *a mensa et thoro,* to recover her alimony or estovers. 1 Bl.Comm. 441; 1 Lev. 6.

DE ESTREPAMENTO. A writ which lay to prevent or stay waste by a tenant, during the pendency of a suit against him to recover the lands. Reg. Orig. 76*b*. Fitzh. Nat. Brev. 60.

DE EU ET TRENE. L. Fr. Of water and whip of three cords. A term applied to a neife, that is, a bond woman or female villein, as employed in servile work, and subject to corporal punishment. Co. Litt. 25*b*.

DE EVE ET DE TREVE. A law French phrase, equivalent to the Latin *de avo et de tritavo,* descriptive of the ancestral rights of lords in their villeins. Literally, "from grandfather and from great-grandfather's great-grandfather." It occurs in the Year Books.

DE EXCOMMUNICATO CAPIENDO. A writ commanding the sheriff to arrest one who was excommunicated, and imprison him till he should become reconciled to the church. 3 Bl.Comm. 102. Smith v. Nelson, 18 Vt. 511.

DE EXCOMMUNICATO DELIBERANDO. A writ to deliver an excommunicated person, who has made satisfaction to the church, from prison. 3 Bl.Comm. 102.

DE EXCOMMUNICATO RECAPIENDO. Writ for retaking an excommunicated person, where he had been liberated from prison without making satisfaction to the church, or giving security for that purpose. Reg. Orig. 67.

DE EXCUSATIONIBUS. "Concerning excuses." This is the title of book 27 of the Pandects, (in the *Corpus Juris Civilis.*) It treats of the circumstances which excuse one from filling the office of tutor or curator. The bulk of the extracts are from Modestinus.

DE EXECUTIONE FACIENDA IN WITHERNAMIUM. Writ for making execution in withernam. Reg. Orig. 82*b*. A species of *capias in withernam.*

DE EXECUTIONE JUDICII. A writ directed to a sheriff or bailiff, commanding him to do execution upon a judgment. Reg. Orig. 18; Fitzh. Nat. Brev. 20.

DE EXEMPLIFICATIONE. Writ of exemplification. A writ granted for the exemplification of an original. Reg. Orig. 290*b*.

DE EXONERATIONE SECTÆ. Writ for exoneration of suit. A writ that lay for the king's ward to be discharged of all suit to the county court, hundred, leet, or court-baron, during the time of his wardship. Fitzh. Nat. Brev. 158; New Nat. Brev. 352.

DE EXPENSIS CIVIUM ET BURGENSIUM. An obsolete writ addressed to the sheriff to levy the expenses of every citizen and burgess of parliament. 4 Inst. 46.

DE EXPENSIS MILITUM LEVANDIS. Writ for levying the expenses of knights. A writ directed to the sheriff for levying the allowance for knights of the shire in parliament. Reg. Orig. 191*b*, 192.

DE FACTO. In fact, in deed, actually. This phrase is used to characterize an officer, a government, a past action, or a state of affairs which must be accepted for all practical purposes, but is illegal or illegitimate. In this sense it is the contrary of *de jure,* which means rightful, legitimate, just, or constitutional. Thus, an officer, king, or government *de facto* is one who is in actual possession of the office or supreme power, but by usurpation, or without lawful title; while an officer, king, or governor *de jure* is one who has just claim and rightful title to the office or power, but has never had plenary possession of it, or is not in actual possession. 4 Bl.Comm. 77, 78. MacLeod v. United States, 229 U.S. 416, 33 S.Ct. 955, 57 L.Ed. 1260; Wheatley v. Consolidated Lumber Co., 167 Cal. 441, 139 P. 1057, 1059. So a wife *de facto* is one whose marriage is voidable by decree, as distinguished from a wife *de jure,* or lawful wife. 4 Kent, Comm. 36. But the term is also frequently used independently of any distinction from *de jure;* thus a blockade *de facto* is a blockade which is actually maintained, as distinguished from a mere paper blockade. 1 Kent, 44. As to *de facto* "Corporation," "Court," "Domicile," "Government," and "Officer," see those titles.

In old English law it means respecting or concerning the principal act of a murder, which was technically denominated *factum.* See Fleta, lib. 1, c. 27, § 18.

DE FACTO CONTRACT. One which has purported to pass the property from the owner to another. Bank v. Logan, 74 N.Y. 575; Edmunds v. Transp. Co., 135 Mass. 283.

DE FAIRE ÉCHELLE. In French law. A clause commonly inserted in policies of marine insurance, equivalent to a license to touch and trade at intermediate ports. American Ins. Co. v. Griswold 14 Wend., N.Y. 491.

DE FALSO JUDICIO. Writ of false judgment. Reg.Orig. 15; Fitzh.Nat.Brev. 18. See False Judgment.

DE FALSO MONETA. Of false money. The title of the statute 27 Edw. I. ordaining that persons importing certain coins, called "pollards," and "crokards," should forfeit their lives and goods, and everything they could forfeit. 2 Reeve, Eng.Law, 228, 229.

DE FIDE ET OFFICIO JUDICIS NON RECIPITUR QUÆSTIO, SED DE SCIENTIA, SIVE SIT ERROR JURIS, SIVE FACTI. Concerning the fidelity and official conduct of a judge, no question is [will be] entertained; but [only] concerning his knowledge, whether the error [committed] be of law or of fact. Bac.Max. 68, reg. 17. The *bona fides* and honesty of purpose of a judge cannot be questioned, but his decision may be impugned for error either of law or fact. Broom, Max, 85. The law doth so much respect the certainty of judgments, and the credit and authority of judges, that it will not permit any error to be assigned which impeacheth them in their *trust* and *office,* and in willful abuse of the same; but only in ignorance and mistaking either of the law, or of the case and matter of fact. Bac.Max. ubi supra. Thus, it cannot be assigned for error that a judge did that which he ought not to do; as that he entered a verdict for the plaintiff, where the jury gave it for the defendant. Fitzh.Nat.Brev. 20, 21; Bac.Max. ubi supra; Hardr. 127, arg.

DE FIDEI LÆSIONE. Of breach of faith or fidelity. 4 Reeve, Eng.Law, 99.

DE FINE FORCE. L. Fr. Of necessity; of pure necessity. See Fine Force.

DE FINE NON CAPIENDO PRO PULCHRE PLACITANDO. A writ prohibiting the taking of fines for beau pleader. Reg.Orig. 179.

DE FINE PRO REDISSEISINA CAPIENDO. A writ which lay for the release of one imprisoned for a re-disseisin, on payment of a reasonable fine. Reg.Orig. 222*b*.

DE FINIBUS LEVATIS. Concerning fines levied. The title of the statute 27 Edw. I. requiring fines thereafter to be levied, to be read openly and solemnly in court. 2 Inst. 521.

DE FORISFACTURA MARITAGII. Writ of forfeiture of marriage. Reg.Orig. 163, 164.

DE FRANGENTIBUS PRISONAM. Concerning those that break prison. The title of the statute 1 Edw. II. ordaining that none from thenceforth who broke prison should have judgment of life or limb for breaking prison only, unless the cause for which he was taken and imprisoned required such a judgment if he was lawfully convicted thereof. 2 Reeve, Eng.Law, 290; 2 Inst. 589.

DE FURTO. Of theft. One of the kinds of criminal appeal formerly in use in England. 2 Reeve, Eng.Law, 40.

DE GESTU ET FAMA. Of behavior and reputation. An old writ which lay in cases where a person's conduct and reputation were impeached.

DE GRATIA. Of grace or favor, by favor. *De speciali gratia,* of special grace or favor.

DE GRATIA SPECIALI CERTA SCIENTIA ET MERO MOTU, TALIS CLAUSULA NON VALET IN HIS IN QUIBUS PRÆSUMITUR PRINCIPEM ESSE IGNORANTEM. 1 Coke, 53. The clause "of our special grace, certain knowledge, and mere motion," is of no avail in those things in which it is presumed that the prince was ignorant.

DE GROSSIS ARBORIBUS DECIMÆ NON DABUNTUR SED DE SYLVIA CÆDUA DECIMÆ DABUNTUR. 2 Rolle, 123. Of whole trees, tithes are not given; but of wood cut to be used, tithes are given.

DE HÆREDE DELIBERANDO ILLI QUI HABET CUSTODIAM TERRÆ. Writ for delivering an heir to him who has wardship of the land. A writ directed to the sheriff, to require one that had the body of him that was ward to another to deliver him to the person whose ward he was by reason of his land. Reg.Orig. 161.

DE HÆREDE RAPTO ET ABDUCTO. Writ concerning an heir ravished and carried away. A writ which anciently lay for a lord who, having by right the wardship of his tenant under age could not obtain his body, the same being carried away by another person. Reg.Orig. 163; Old Nat.Brev. 93.

DE HÆRETICO COMBURENDO. (Lat. For burning a heretic.) A writ which formerly issued from the secular courts for the execution, by burning, of a heretic, who had been convicted in the ecclesiastical courts of heresy, had abjured, and had relapsed into heresy. It is said to be very ancient. Fitzh.Nat.Brev. 269; 4 Bl.Comm. 46. See Hæretico Comburendo.

DE HOMAGIO RESPECTUANDO. A writ for respiting or postponing homage. Fitzh.Nat.Brev. 269, A.

DE HOMINE CAPTO IN WITHERNAM. (Lat. For taking a man in withernam.) A writ to take a man who had carried away a bondman or bondwoman into another country beyond the reach of a writ of replevin.

DE HOMINE REPLEGIANDO. (Lat. For replevying a man.) A writ which lies to replevy a man out of prison, or out of the custody of a private person, upon giving security to the sheriff that the man shall be forthcoming to answer any charge against him. Fitzh.Nat.Brev. 66; 3 Bl. Comm. 129. This writ has been superseded almost wholly, in modern practice, by that of *habeas corpus;* but it is still used, in some of the states, in an amended and altered form. See 1 Kent, Comm. 404*n*; 34 Me. 136.

DE IDENTITATE NOMINIS. A writ which lay for one arrested in a personal action and committed to prison under a mistake as to his identity, the proper defendant bearing the same name. Reg.Orig. 194.

DE IDIOTA INQUIRENDO. An old common-law writ, long obsolete, to inquire whether a man be an idiot or not. 2 Steph.Comm. 509.

DE IIS QUI PONENDI SUNT IN ASSISIS. Of those who are to be put on assises. The title of a statute passed 21 Edw. I. defining the qualifications of jurors. Crabb, Eng.Law, 167, 189; 2 Reeve, Eng.Law, 184.

DE INCREMENTO. Of increase; in addition. Costs *de incremento,* or costs of increase, are the costs adjudged by the court in civil actions, *in addition* to the damages and nominal costs found by the jury. Gilb.Com.Pl. 260.

DE INFIRMITATE. Of infirmity. The principal essoin in the time of Glanville; afterwards called *"de malo."* 1 Reeve, Eng.Law, 115. See De Malo; Essoin.

DE INGRESSU. A writ of entry. Reg.Orig. 227*b*, et seq.

DE INJURIA. Of [his own] wrong. In the technical language of pleading, a replication *de injuria* is one that may be made in an action of tort where the defendant has admitted the acts complained of, but alleges, in his plea, certain new matter by way of justification or excuse; by this replication the plaintiff avers that the defendant committed the grievances in question "of his own wrong, and without any such cause," or motive or excuse, as that alleged in the plea, (*de injuria sua propria absque tali causa;*) or, admitting part of the matter pleaded, "without the rest of the cause" alleged, (*absque residuo causæ.*) In form it is a species of traverse, and it is frequently used when the pleading of the defendant, in answer to which it is directed, consists merely of matter of excuse of the alleged trespass, grievance, breach of contract, or other cause of action. Its comprehensive character in putting in issue all the material facts of the defendant's plea has also obtained for it the title of the general replication. Holthouse.

DE INOFFICIOSO TESTAMENTO. Concerning an inofficious or undutiful will. A title of the civil law. Inst. 2, 18.

DE INTEGRO. Anew; a second time. As it was before.

DE INTRUSIONE. A writ of intrusion; where a stranger entered after the death of the tenant, to the injury of the reversioner. Reg.Orig. 233*b*.

DE JACTURA EVITANDA. For avoiding a loss. A phrase applied to a defendant, as *de lucro captando* is to a plaintiff. Jones v. Sevier, 1 Litt., Ky., 51, 13 Am.Dec. 218.

DE JUDAISMO, STATUTUM. The name of a statute passed in the reign of Edward I. which enacted severe and arbitrary penalties against the Jews.

DE JUDICATO SOLVENDO. For payment of the amount adjudged. A term applied in the Scotch law to bail to the action, or special bail.

DE JUDICIIS. Of judicial proceedings. The title of the second part of the Digests or Pandects, including the fifth, sixth, seventh, eighth, ninth, tenth, and eleventh books. See Dig. Proœm. § 3.

DE JUDICIO SISTI. For appearing in court. A term applied in the Scotch and admiralty law, to bail for a defendant's appearance.

DE JURE. Of right; legitimate; lawful; by right and just title. In this sense it is the contrary of *de facto,* (which see.) It may also be contrasted with *de gratia,* in which case it means "as a matter of right," as *de gratia* means "by grace or favor." Again it may be contrasted with *de æquitate;* here meaning "by law," as the latter means "by equity." See Government.

DE JURE DECIMARUM, ORIGINEM DUCENS DE JURE PATRONATUS, TUNC COGNITIO SPECTAT AT LEGEM CIVILEM, i. e., COMMUNEM. Godb. 63. With regard to the right of tithes, deducing its origin from the right of the patron, then the cognizance of them belongs to the civil law; that is, the common law.

DE JURE JUDICES, DE FACTO JURATORES, RESPONDENT. The judges find the law, the jury the facts. See Co.Litt. 295; Broom, Max. 99.

DE LA PLUIS BEALE, or BELLE. L. Fr. Of the most fair. A term applied to a species of dower, which was assigned out of the fairest of the husband's tenements. Litt. § 48. See Dower de la Plus Belle.

DE LATERE. From the side; on the side; collaterally; of collaterals. Cod. 5, 5, 6.

DE LEGATIS ET FIDEI COMMISSIS. Of legacies and trusts. The name of a title of the Pandects. Dig. 30.

DE LEPROSO AMOVENDO. Writ for removing a leper. A writ to remove a leper who thrust himself into the company of his neighbors in any parish, in public or private places, to their annoyance. Reg.Orig. 267; Fitzh.Nat.Brev. 234, E; New Nat.Brev. 521.

DE LIBERA FALDA. Writ of free fold. A species of *quod permittat.* Reg.Orig. 155.

DE LIBERA PISCARIA. Writ of free fishery. A species of *quod permittat.* Reg.Orig. 155.

DE LIBERO PASSAGIO. Writ of free passage. A species of *quod permittat.* Reg.Orig. 155.

DE LIBERTATE PROBANDA. Writ for proving liberty. A writ which lay for such as, being demanded for villeins or niefs, offered to prove themselves free. Reg.Orig. 87*b;* Fitzh.Nat.Brev. 77, F.

DE LIBERTATIBUS ALLOCANDIS. A writ of various forms, to enable a citizen to recover the liberties to which he was entitled. Fitzh.Nat. Brev. 229; Reg.Orig. 262.

DE LICENTIA TRANSFRETANDI. Writ of permission to cross the sea. And old writ directed to the wardens of the port of Dover, or other seaport in England, commanding them to permit the persons named in the writ to cross the sea from such port, on certain conditions. Reg.Orig. 193*b*.

DE LUNATICO INQUIRENDO. The name of a writ directed to the sheriff, directing him to inquire by good and lawful men whether the party charged is a lunatic or not. Den v. Clark, 10 N.J. L. 217, 18 Am.Dec. 417; Hart v. Deamer, 6 Wend., N.Y., 497; In re Lindsley, 44 N.J.Eq. 564, 15 A. 1, 6 Am.St.Rep. 913.

DE MAGNA ASSISA ELIGENDA. A writ by which the grand assise was chosen and summoned. Reg.Orig. 8; Fitzh.Nat.Brev. 4.

DE MAJORI ET MINORI NON VARIANT JURA. Concerning greater and less laws do not vary. 2 Vern. 552.

DE MALO. Of illness. This phrase was frequently used to designate several species of essoin, *(q. v.,)* such as *de malo lecti,* of illness in bed; *de malo veniendi,* of illness (or misfortune) in coming to the place where the court sat; *de malo villæ,* of illness in the town where the court sat.

DE MANUCAPTIONE. Writ of manucaption, or mainprise. A writ which lay for one who, being taken and imprisoned on a charge of felony, had offered bail, which had been refused; requiring the sheriff to discharge him on his finding sufficient mainpernors or bail. Reg.Orig. 268*b;* Fitzh. Nat.Brev. 249, G.

DE MANUTENENDO. Writ of maintenance. A writ which lay against a person for the offense of maintenance. Reg.Orig. 189, 182*b*.

DE MEDIETATE LINGUÆ. Of the half tongue; half of one tongue and half of another. This phrase describes that species of jury which, at common law, was allowed in both civil and criminal cases where one of the parties was an alien, not speaking or understanding English. It was composed of six English denizens or natives and six of the alien's own countrymen.

DE MEDIO. A writ in the nature of a writ of right, which lay where upon a subinfeudation the *mesne* (or middle) lord suffered his under-tenant or tenant *paravail* to be distrained upon by the lord paramount for the rent due him from the *mesne* lord. Booth, Real Act, 136.

DE MELIORIBUS DAMNIS. Of or for the better damages. A term used in practice to denote the election by a plaintiff against which of several defendants (where the damages have been assessed separately) he will take judgment. 1 Arch. Pr.K.B. 219; Knickerbacker v. Colver, 8 Cow., N.Y., 111.

Judgment *de melioribus damnis* (of, or for, the better damages). Where, in an action against several persons for a joint tort, the jury by mistake sever the damages by giving heavier damages against one defendant than against the others, the plaintiff may cure the defect by taking judgment for the greater damages *(de melioribus damnis)* against that defendant, and entering a *nolle prosequi (q. v.)* against the others. Sweet.

DE MERCATORIBUS. "Concerning merchants." The name of a statute passed in the eleventh year of Edw. I. (1233,) more commonly called the "Statute of Acton Burnel," authorizing the recognizance by statute merchant. See 2 Reeve, Eng.Law, 160–162; 2 Bl.Comm. 161.

DE MINIMIS NON CURAT LEX. The law does not care for, or take notice of, very small or trifling matters. The law does not concern itself about trifles. Cro.Eliz. 353. Thus, error in calculation of a fractional part of a penny will not be regarded. Hob. 88. So, the law will not, in general, notice the fraction of a day. Broom, Max. 142.

DE MINIS. Writ of threats. A writ which lay where a person was threatened with personal violence, or the destruction of his property, to compel the offender to keep the peace. Reg.Orig. 88*b*, 89; Fitzh.Nat.Brev. 79, G, 80.

DE MITTENDO TENOREM RECORDI. A writ to send the tenor of a record, or to exemplify it under the great seal. Reg.Orig. 220*b*.

DE MODERATA MISERICORDIA CAPIENDA. Writ for taking a moderate amercement. A writ, founded on *Magna Charta,* (c. 14,) which lay for one who was excessively amerced in a court not of record, directed to the lord of the court, or his bailiff, commanding him *to take a moderate amercement* of the party. Reg.Orig. 86*b;* Fitzh. Nat.Brev. 75, 76.

DE MODO DECIMANDI. Of a *modus* of tithing. A term applied in English ecclesiastical law to a prescription to have a special manner of tithing. 2 Bl.Comm. 29; 3 Steph.Comm. 130.

DE MOLENDINO DE NOVO ERECTO NON JACET PROHIBITIO. Cro.Jac. 429. A prohibition lies not against a newly-erected mill.

DE MORTE HOMINIS NULLA EST CUNCTATIO LONGA. Where the death of a human being is concerned, [in a matter of life and death,] no delay is [considered] long. Co.Litt. 134.

DE NATIVO HABENDO. A writ which lay for a lord directed to the sheriff, commanding him to apprehend a fugitive villein, and restore him, with all his chattels, to the lord. Reg.Orig. 87; Fitzh. Nat.Brev. 77.

DE NATURA BREVIUM. (Lat.) Concerning the nature of writs. The title of more than one textbook of English Mediæval law. Maitland, 2 Sel. Essays in Anglo-Amer. Leg. Hist. 549. See Register of Writs.

DE NOMINE PROPRIO NON EST CURANDUM CUM IN SUBSTANTIA NON ERRETUR; QUIA NOMINA MUTABILIA SUNT, RES AUTEM IMMOBILES. 6 Coke, 66. As to the proper name, it is not to be regarded where it errs not in substance, because names are changeable, but things immutable.

DE NON APPARENTIBUS, ET NON EXISTENTIBUS, EADEM EST RATIO. 5 Coke, 6. As to things not apparent, and those not existing, the rule is the same. Bennehan v. Webb, 28 N.C. 61; U. S. v. Wilkinson, 12 How., U.S., 253, 13 L.Ed. 974, Fed.Cas.No. 16,696; 5 Co. 6; 6 Bingh. N.C. 453; 7 Cl. & F. 872; 5 C.B. 53; 8 *Id.* 286; 1 Term 404; Quarles v. Quarles, 4 Mass. 685; 8 *Id.* 401; Broom, Max. 163, 166.

DE NON DECIMANDO. Of not paying tithes. A term applied in English ecclesiastical law to a prescription or claim to be entirely discharged of tithes, and to pay no compensation in lieu of them. 2 Bl. Comm. 31.

DE NON PROCEDENDO AD ASSISAM. A writ forbidding the justices from holding an assise in a particular case. Reg.Orig. 221.

DE NON RESIDENTIA CLERICI REGIS. An ancient writ where a parson was employed in the royal service, etc., to excuse and discharge him of non-residence. 2 Inst. 264.

DE NON SANE MEMORIE. L. Fr. Of unsound memory or mind; a phrase synonymous with *non compos mentis.*

DE NOVI OPERIS NUNCIATIONE. In the civil law. A form of interdict or injunction which lies in some cases where the defendant is about to erect a "new work" (*q. v.*) in derogation or injury of the plaintiff's rights.

DE NOVO. Anew; afresh; a second time. Archer v. High, 193 Miss. 361, 9 So.2d 647, 648; Duncan v. Mack, 59 Ariz. 36, 122 P.2d 215, 217. A *venire de novo* is a writ for summoning a jury for the second trial of a case which has been sent back from above for a new trial. Slaughter v. Martin, 9 Ala.App. 285, 63 So. 689, 690; Parker v. Lewis, 45 Okl. 807, 147 P. 310, 311.

DE NULLO, QUOD EST SUA NATURA INDIVISIBILE, ET DIVISIONEM NON PATITUR, NULLAM PARTEM HABEBIT VIDUA, SED SATISFACIAT EI AD VALENTIAM. Co. Litt. 32. A widow shall have no part of that which in its own nature is indivisible, and is not susceptible of division, but let the heir satisfy her with an equivalent.

DE NULLO TENEMENTO, QUOD TENETUR AD TERMINUM, FIT HOMAGII, FIT TAMEN INDE FIDELITATIS SACRAMENTUM. In no tenement which is held for a term of years is there an avail of homage; but there is the oath of fealty. Co. Litt. 67*b*.

DE ODIO ET ATIA. A writ anciently called "*breve de bono et malo,*" addressed to the sheriff to inquire whether a man committed to prison upon suspicion of murder were committed on just cause of suspicion, or only upon malice and ill will (*propter odium et atiam*); and if, upon the inquisition, due cause of suspicion did not appear, then there issued another writ for the sheriff to admit him to bail. 3 Bl.Comm. 128; Reg.Orig. 133.

DE OFFICE. L. Fr. Of office; in virtue of office; officially; in the discharge of ordinary duty.

DE ONERANDO PRO RATA PORTIONE. Writ for charging according to a rateable proportion. A writ which lay for a joint tenant, or tenant in common, who was distrained for more rent than his proportion of the land came to. Reg.Orig. 182; Fitzh.Nat.Brev. 234, H.

DE PACE ET LEGALITATE TENENDA. For keeping the peace, and for good behavior.

DE PACE ET PLAGIS. Of peace, (breach of peace,) and wounds. One of the kinds of criminal appeal formerly in use in England, and which lay in cases of assault, wounding, and breach of the peace. Bract. fol. 144; 2 Reeve, Eng.Law, 33.

DE PACE ET ROBERIA. Of peace [breach of peace] and robbery. One of the kinds of criminal appeal formerly in use in England, and which lay in cases of robbery and breach of the peace. Bract. fol. 146; 2 Reeve, Eng.Law, 37.

DE PALABRA. Span. By word; by parol. White, New Recop. b. 2, tit. 19, c. 3, § 2.

DE PARCO FRACTO. A writ or action for damages caused by a pound-breach (*q. v.*). It has long been obsolete. Co.Litt. 47*b*; 3 Bl.Comm. 146.

DE PARTITIONE FACIENDA. A writ which lay to make partition of lands or tenements held by several as coparceners, tenants in common, etc. Reg.Orig. 76; Fitzh.Nat.Brev. 61, R; Old Nat.Brev. 142.

DE PERAMBULATIONE FACIENDA. A writ which lay where there was a dispute as to the boundaries of two adjacent lordships or towns, directed to the sheriff, commanding him to take with him twelve discreet and lawful knights of his county and make the perambulation and set the bounds and limits in certainty. Fitzh.Nat. Brev. 309, D.

DE PIGNORE SURREPTO FURTI, ACTIO. In the civil law. An action to recover a pledge stolen. Inst. 4, 1, 14.

DE PIPA VINI CARIANDA. A writ of trespass for carrying a pipe of wine so carelessly that it was stove, and the contents lost. Reg.Orig. 110. Alluded to by Sir William Jones in his remarks on the case of Coggs v. Bernard, 2 Ld.Raym. 909. Jones, Bailm. 59.

DE PLACITO. Of a plea; of or in an action. Formal words used in declarations and other proceedings, as descriptive of the particular action brought.

DE PLAGIS ET MAHEMIO. Of wounds and mayhem. The name of a criminal appeal formerly in use in England, in cases of wounding and maiming. Bract. fol. 144*b*; 2 Reeve, Eng. Law, 34. See Appeal.

DE PLANO. Lat. On the ground; on a level. A term of the Roman law descriptive of the method of hearing causes, when the prætor stood on the ground with the suitors, instead of the more formal method when he occupied a bench or tribunal; hence informal, or summary.

DE PLEGIIS ACQUIETANDIS. Writ for acquitting or releasing pledges. A writ that lay for a surety, against him for whom he had become surety for the payment of a certain sum of money at a certain day, where the latter had not paid the money at the appointed day, and the surety was compelled to pay it. Reg.Orig. 158; Fitzh.Nat. Brev. 137, C; 3 Reeve, Eng.Law, 65.

DE PONENDO SIGILLUM AD EXCEPTIONEM. Writ for putting a seal to an exception. A writ by which justices were formerly commanded to put their seals to exceptions taken by a party in a suit. Reg.Orig. 182.

DE POST DISSEISINA. Writ of post disseisin. A writ which lay for him who, having recovered lands or tenements by *præcipe quod reddat*, on default, or reddition, was again disseised by the former disseisor. Reg.Orig. 208; Fitzh.Nat.Brev. 190.

DE PRÆROGATIVA REGIS. The statute 17 Edw. I., St. 1, c. 9, defining the prerogatives of the crown on certain subjects, but especially directing that the king shall have ward of the lands of idiots, taking the profits without waste, and finding them necessaries. 2 Steph.Comm. 529.

DE PRÆSENTI. Of the present; in the present tense. See Per Verba de Præsenti.

DE PROCEDENDO AD JUDICIUM. A writ proceeding out of chancery and ordering the judges of any court to proceed to judgment. 3 Bla.Com. 109.

DE PROPRIETATE PROBANDA. Writ for proving property. A writ directed to the sheriff, to inquire of the property or goods distrained, where the defendant in an action of replevin claims the property. 3 Bl.Comm. 148; Reg.Orig. 85*b*.

DE QUARANTINA HABENDA. At common law, a writ which a widow entitled to quarantine might sue out in case the heir or other persons ejected her. It seems to have been a summary process, and required the sheriff, if no just cause were shown against it, speedily to put her into possession. Aiken v. Aiken, 12 Or. 203, 6 P. 682.

DE QUIBUS SUR DISSEISIN. An ancient writ of entry.

DE QUO, and DE QUIBUS. Of which. Formal words in the simple writ of entry, from which it was called a writ of entry "in the *quo*," or "in the *quibus*." 3 Reeve, Eng.Law, 33.

DE QUOTA LITIS. In the civil law. A contract by which one who has a claim difficult to recover agrees with another to give a part, for the purpose of obtaining his services to recover the rest. 1 Duval, note 201.

DE RAPTU VIRGINUM. Of the ravishment of maids. The name of an appeal formerly in use in England in cases of rape. Bract. fol. 147; 2 Reeve, Eng.Law, 38.

DE RATIONABILI PARTE BONORUM. A writ which lay for the widow (and children) of a deceased person against his executors, to recover a third part of the deceased's personalty, after payment of his debts, or to recover their reasonable part or share of his goods. 2 Bl.Comm. 492; Fitzh.Nat.Brev. 122, L; Hopkins v. Wright, 17 Tex. 36.

DE RATIONABILIBUS DIVISIS. Writ for fixing reasonable boundaries. A writ which lay to settle the boundaries between the lands of persons in different towns, where one complained of encroachment. Reg.Orig. 157*b*; Fitzh.Nat.Brev. 128, M; Rosc.Real Act. 31; 3 Reeve, Eng.Law, 48.

DE REBUS. Of things. The title of the third part of the Digests or Pandects, comprising books 12–19, inclusive.

DE REBUS DUBIIS. Of doubtful things or matters. Dig. 34, 5.

DE RECORDO ET PROCESSU MITTENDIS. Writ to send the record and process of a cause to a superior court; a species of writ of error. Reg. Orig. 209.

DE RECTO. Writ of right. Reg.Orig. 1, 2; Bract. fol. 327*b*. See Writ of Right.

DE RECTO DE ADVOCATIONE. Writ of right of advowson. Reg.Orig. 29*b*. A writ which lay for one who had an estate in an advowson to him and his heirs in fee-simple, if he were disturbed to present. Fitzh.Nat.Brev. 30, B. Abolished by St. 3 & 4 Wm. IV. c. 27.

DE RECTO DE RATIONABILI PARTE. Writ of right, of reasonable part. A writ which lay between privies in blood, as between brothers in gavelkind, or between sisters or other coparceners for lands in fee-simple, where one was deprived of his or her share by another. Reg.Orig. 3*b*; Fitzh. Nat.Brev. 9, B. Abolished by St. 3 & 4 Wm. IV. c. 27.

DE RECTO PATENS. Writ of right patent. Reg. Orig. 1.

DE REDISSEISINA. Writ of redisseisin. A writ which lay where a man recovered by assise of novel disseisin land, rent, or common, and the like, and was put in possession thereof by verdict, and afterward was disseised of the same land, rent, or common, by him by whom he was disseised before. Reg. Orig. 206*b*; Fitzh. Nat. Brev. 188, B.

DE REPARATIONE FACIENDA. A writ by which one tenant in common seeks to compel another to aid in repairing the property held in common. 8 Barn. & C. 269.

DE RESCUSSU. Writ of rescue or rescous. A writ which lay where cattle distrained, or persons arrested, were rescued from those taking them. Reg. Orig. 117, 118; Fitzh. Nat. Brev. 101, C, G.

DE RETORNO HABENDO. For having a return; to have a return. A term applied to the judgment for the defendant in an action of replevin, awarding him a return of the goods replevied; and to the writ or execution issued thereon. 2 Tidd, Pr. 993, 1038; 3 Bl. Comm. 149. Applied also to the sureties given by the plaintiff on commencing the action. Id. 147.

DE RIEN CULPABLE. L. Fr. Guilty of nothing; not guilty.

DE SA VIE. L. Fr. Of his or her life; of his own life; as distinguished from *pur autre vie*, for another's life. Litt. §§ 35, 36.

DE SALVA GARDIA. A writ of safeguard allowed to strangers seeking their rights in English courts, and apprehending violence or injury to their persons or property. Reg. Orig. 26.

DE SALVO CONDUCTU. A writ of safe conduct. Reg. Orig. 25*b*, 26.

DE SCACCARIO. Of or concerning the exchequer. The title of a statute passed in the fifty-first year of Henry III. 2 Reeve, Eng. Law, 61.

DE SCUTAGIO HABENDO. Writ for having (or to have) escuage or scutage. A writ which anciently lay against tenants by knight-service, to compel them to serve in the king's wars or send substitutes or to pay escuage; that is a sum of money. Fitzh. Nat. Brev. 83, C. The same writ lay for one who had already served in the king's army, or paid a fine instead, against those who held of him by knight-service, to recover his escuage or scutage. Reg. Orig. 88; Fitzh. Nat. Brev. 83, D, F.

DE SE BENE GERENDO. For behaving himself well; for his good behavior. Yelv. 90, 154.

DE SECTA AD MOLENDINUM. Of suit to a mill. A writ which lay to compel one to continue his custom (of grinding) at a mill. 3 Bl. Comm. 235; Fitzh. Nat. Brev. 122, M.

DE SIMILIBUS AD SIMILIA EADEM RATIONE PROCEDENUM EST. From like things to like things we are to proceed by the same rule or reason, [*i. e.*, we are allowed to argue from the analogy of cases.] Branch, Princ.

DE SIMILIBUS IDEM EST JUDICANDUM. Of [respecting] like things, [in like cases,] the judgment is to be the same. 7 Coke, 18.

DE SON TORT. L. Fr. Of his own wrong. A stranger who takes upon him to act as an executor without any just authority is called an "executor of his own wrong," (*de son tort.*) 2 Bl. Comm. 507; 2 Steph. Comm. 244.

An *executor de son tort* is an executor of his own wrong. A person who assumes to act as executor of an estate out any lawful warrant or authority, but who, by his intermeddling, makes himself liable as an executor to a certain extent. If a stranger takes upon him to act as executor without any just authority, (as by intermeddling with the goods of the deceased, and many other transactions,) he is called in law an "executor of his own wrong," *de son tort*. 2 Bl.Comm. 507. Allen v. Hurst, 120 Ga. 763, 48 S.E. 341; In re Pedroli's Estate, 47 Nev. 313, 21 P. 241, 242, 31 A.L.R. 841; Walker v. Portland Savings Bank, 113 Me. 353, 93 A. 1025, L.R.A.1915E, 840; Lowery v. Lowery, 225 Ala. 376, 143 So. 556, 557.

DE SON TORT DEMESNE. Of his own wrong. The law French equivalent of the Latin phrase *dė injuria (q. v.)*.

DE STATUTO MERCATORIO. The writ of statute merchant. Reg. Orig. 146*b*.

DE STATUTO STAPULÆ. The writ of statute staple. Reg. Orig. 151.

DE SUPERONERATIONE PASTURÆ. Writ of surcharge of pasture. A judicial writ which lay for him who was impleaded in the county court, for surcharging a common with his cattle, in a case where he was formerly impleaded for it in the same court, and the cause was removed into one of the courts at Westminster. Reg. Jud. 36*b*.

DE TABULIS EXHIBENDIS. Of showing the tablets of a will. Dig. 43, 5.

DE TALLAGIO NON CONCEDENDO. Of not allowing talliage. The name given to the statutes 25 and 34 Edw. I., restricting the power of the king to grant talliage. 2 Inst. 532; 2 Reeve, Eng. Law, 104.

DE TEMPORE CUJUS CONTRARIUM MEMORIA HOMINUM NON EXISTIT. From time whereof the memory of man does not exist to the contrary. Litt. § 170.

DE TEMPORE IN TEMPUS ET AD OMNIA TEMPORA. From time to time, and at all times. Townsh. Pl. 17.

DE TEMPS DONT MEMORIE NE COURT. L. Fr. From time whereof memory runneth not; time out of memory of man. Litt. §§ 143, 145, 170.

DE TESTAMENTIS. Of testaments. The title of the fifth part of the Digests or Pandects; comprising the twenty-eighth to the thirty-sixth books, both inclusive.

DE THEOLONIO. A writ which lay for a person who was prevented from taking toll. Reg. Orig. 103.

DE TRANSGRESSIONE. A writ of trespass. Reg. Orig. 92.

DE TRANSGRESSIONE, AD AUDIENDUM ET TERMINANDUM. A writ or commission for the hearing and determining any outrage or misdemeanor.

DE UNA PARTE. A deed *de una parte* is one where only one party grants, gives, or binds himself to do a thing to another. It differs from a deed *inter partes*, (*q. v.*) 2 Bouv. Inst. no. 2001.

DE UXORE RAPTA ET ABDUCTA. A writ which lay where a man's wife had been ravished and carried away. A species of writ of trespass. Reg. Orig. 97; Fitzh. Nat. Brev. 89, O; 3 Bl. Comm. 139.

DE VASTO. Writ of waste. A writ which might be brought by him who had the immediate estate of inheritance in reversion or remainder, against the tenant for life, in dower, by curtesy, or for years, where the latter had committed *waste* in lands; calling upon the tenant to appear and show cause why he committed waste and destruction in the place named, to the disinherison (*ad exhœredationem*) of the plaintiff. Fitzh. Nat. Brev. 55, C; 3 Bl. Comm. 227, 228. Abolished by St. 3 & 4 Wm. IV, c. 27. 3 Steph. Comm. 506.

DE VENTRE INSPICIENDO. A writ to inspect the body, where a woman feigns to be pregnant, to see whether she is with child. It lies for the heir presumptive to examine a widow suspected to be feigning pregnancy in order to enable a supposititious heir to obtain the estate. 1 Bl. Comm. 456; 2 Steph. Comm. 287. It lay also where a woman sentenced to death pleaded pregnancy. 4 Bl. Comm. 395. This writ has been recognized in America. 2 Chand. Crim. Tr. 381.

DE VERBO IN VERBUM. Word for word. Bract. fol. 138*b*. Literally, from word to word.

DE VERBORUM SIGNIFICATIONE. Of the signification of words. An important title of the Digests or Pandects, (Dig. 50, 16,) consisting entirely of definitions of words and phrases used in the Roman law.

DE VI LAICA AMOVENDA. Writ of (or for) removing lay force. A writ which lay where two parsons contended for a church, and one of them entered into it with a great number of *laymen*, and held out the other *vi et armis;* then he that was holden out had this writ directed to the sheriff, that he remove the force. Reg. Orig. 59; Fitzh. Nat. Brev. 54, D.

DE VICINETO. From the neighborhood, or vicinage. 3 Bl.Comm. 360. A term applied to a jury.

DE WARRANTIA CHARTÆ. Writ of warranty of charter. A writ which lay for him who was enfeoffed, with clause of warranty, [in the charter of feoffment,] and was afterwards impleaded in an assise or other action, in which he could not *vouch* or call to warranty; in which case he might have this writ against the feoffor, or his heir, to compel him to warrant the land unto him. Reg. Orig. 157*b*; Fitzh. Nat. Brev. 134, D. Abolished by St. 3 & 4 Wm. IV, c. 27.

DE WARRANTIA DIEI. A writ that lay where a man had a day in any action to appear in proper person, and the king at that day, or before, employed him in some service, so that he could not appear at the day in court. It was directed to the justices, that they should not record him to be in default for his not appearing. Fitzh. Nat. Brev. 17, A; Termes de la Ley.

DEACON. In ecclesiastical law. A minister or servant in the church, whose office is to assist the priest in divine service and the distribution of the sacrament. It is the lowest degree of holy orders in the Church of England. 2 Steph. Comm. 660.

DEAD BODY. A corpse. The body of a human being, deprived of life, but not yet entirely disintegrated. Meads v. Dougherty County, 98 Ga. 697, 25 S.E. 915.

DEAD–BORN. A dead-born child is to be considered as if it had never been conceived or born; in other words, it is presumed it never had life, it being a maxim of the common law that *mortuus exitus non est exitus* (a dead birth is no birth). Co. Litt. 29 *b*. See Marsellis v. Thalhimer, 2 Paige, Ch., N.Y., 35, 21 Am.Dec. 66; 4 Ves. 334. This is also the doctrine of the civil law. Dig. 50. 16. 129; La.Civ.Code, art. 28; Domat, liv. prél. t. 2, s. 1, nn. 4, 6.

DEAD FREIGHT. The amount paid by a charterer for that part of the vessel's capacity which he does not occupy although he has contracted for it. Gray v. Carr, L. R. 6 Q. B. 528; Phillips v. Rodie, 15 East 547.

When the charterer of a vessel has shipped part of the goods on board, and is not ready to ship the remainder, the master, unless restrained by his special contract, may take other goods on board, and the amount which is not supplied, required to complete the cargo, is considered *dead freight*. The dead freight is to be calculated according to the actual capacity of the vessel. 3 Chit.Com.Law 399; 2 Stark. 450; McCull.Com.Dic.

"Dead freight" is the compensation payable to the shipowner when the charterer has failed to ship a full cargo, and "freight" is recompense the shipowner is to receive for carrying the cargo into its port of discharge. Kish v. Taylor (1912) A.C. 604, 613, citing Carver's Carriage By Sea, par. 666.

DEAD LETTER. A term sometimes applied to an act that has become obsolete by long disuse.

DEAD LETTERS. Letters which the postal department has not been able to deliver to the persons for whom they were intended. They are sent to the "dead-letter office," where they are opened, and returned to the writer if his address can be ascertained.

DEAD MAN'S PART. In English law, that portion of the effects of a deceased person which, by the custom of London and York, is allowed to the administrator; being, where the deceased leaves a widow and children, one-third; where he leaves only a widow or only children, one-half; and, where he leaves neither, the whole. This portion the administrator was wont to apply to his own use, till the statute 1 Jac. II, c. 17, declared that the same should be subject to the statute of distributions. 2 Bl. Comm. 518; 2 Steph. Comm. 254; 4 Reeve, Eng.Law, 83. A similar portion in Scotch law is called "dead's part," (*q. v.*)

DEAD-PLEDGE. A mortgage, *mortuum vadium.*

DEAD RENT. In English law. A rent payable on a mining lease in addition to a royalty, so called because it is payable although the mine may not be worked.

DEAD STORAGE. The storage, especially of automobiles in public garages, where automobiles not in use are to remain uninterruptedly for a time, sometimes for the season. Hogan v. O'Brien, 123 Misc. 865, 206 N.Y.S. 831.

DEAD USE. A future use.

DEAD WIRE. One which never carries electricity, or which, at some particular time, is not charged with an electric current. City of Shawnee v. Sears, 39 Okl. 789, 137 P. 107, 110, 50 L.R.A.,N.S., 885.

DEAD'S PART. In Scotch law. The part remaining over beyond the shares secured to the widow and children by law. Of this the testator had the unqualified disposal. Bell; Stair, Inst. lib. iii. tit. 4, § 24; Paterson, Comp. §§ 674, 848, 902.

DEADHEAD. A term applied to persons other than the officers, agents, or employees of a railroad company who are permitted by the company to travel on the road without paying any fare therefor. Gardner v. Hall, 61 N.C. 21.

DEADLY FEUD. In old European law. A profession of irreconcilable hatred till a person is revenged even by the death of his enemy.

DEADLY WEAPON. Such weapons or instruments as are made and designed for offensive or defensive purposes, or for the destruction of life or the infliction of injury. Commonwealth v. Branham, 8 Bush (Ky.) 387. One likely to produce death or great bodily harm. People v. Fuqua, 58 Cal. 245; State v. Hedrick, 99 W.Va. 529, 130 S.E. 295, 298.

One which, from the manner used, is calculated or likely to produce death or serious bodily injury. Harris v. State, 72 Tex.Cr.R. 491, 162 S.W. 1150, 1151; Burgess v. Commonwealth, 176 Ky. 326, 195 S.W. 445.

Any weapon dangerous to life, or with which death may be easily and readily produced. Parman v. Lemmon, 119 Kan. 323, 244 P. 227, 229, 44 A.L.R. 1500; People v. Dwyer, 324 Ill. 363, 155 N.E. 316, 317.

The term may denote any instrument so used as to be likely to produce death or great bodily harm, and hence may include an automobile, especially within the meaning of statutes pertaining to assault. Williamson v. State, 92 Fla. 980, 111 So. 124, 125, 53 A.L.R. 250. But an automobile, when used innocently or negligently so as to be likely to produce death or bodily injury, or to actually produce them without criminal liability, has been held not to be a deadly weapon within the meaning of the criminal law. People v. Cash, 326 Ill. 104, 157 N.E. 76, 79; State v. Clark, 196 Iowa, 1134, 196 N.W. 82, 84.

DEADLY WEAPON PER SE. A weapon which of itself is deadly or one which would ordinarily result in death by its use. Baylor v. State, 151 Tex. Cr.R. 365, 208 S.W.2d 558, 561.

DEADMAN. As applied to a lifting appliance, a piece of timber placed across an opening in the ground to which a snatch hook is attached. The Teddy, D.C.N.Y., 226 F. 498, 500.

DEAF AND DUMB. A man that is born deaf, dumb, and blind is looked upon by the law as in the same state with an idiot, he being supposed incapable of any understanding. 1 Bl. Comm. 304. See, however, Alexier v. Matzke, 151 Mich. 36, 115 N.W. 251, 123 Am.St.Rep. 255. Nevertheless, a deaf and dumb person may be tried for felony if the prisoner can be made to understand by means of signs. 1 Bish. Cr. L. § 395; Commonwealth v. Hill, 14 Mass. 207; State v. Harris, 53 N.C. 136, 78 Am.Dec. 272; 1 Houst.Cr.Rep. 291; Felts v. Murphy, 201 U.S. 123, 26 S.Ct. 366, 50 L. Ed. 689.

DEAFFOREST. See Disafforest.

DEAL, *n.* An arrangement to attain a desired result by a combination of interested parties; Gaut v. Dunlap, Tex.Civ.App., 188 S.W. 1020, 1021; Ball v. Davenport, 170 Iowa 33, 152 N.W. 69, 71; the prime object being usually the purchase, sale, or exchange of property for a profit; Chambers v. Johnston, 180 Ky. 73, 201 S.W. 488, 493. Also, an act of buying and selling; a bargain. Oregon Home Builders v. Montgomery Inv. Co., 94 Or. 349, 184 P. 487, 493.

A "deal" between two parties includes any transaction of any kind between them, and when applied to a transaction concerning a house or block, the term does not necessarily imply an agreement to sell or convey, for the agreement might be to rent or lease the property. Osborne v. Moore, 112 Tex. 361, 247 S.W. 498, 499.

DEAL, *v.* To traffic; to transact business; to trade. See Borg v. International Silver Co., C.C. A.N.Y., 11 F.2d 147, 150. Also, to act between two persons, to intervene, or to have to do with. State v. Morro, 313 Mo. 114, 280 S.W. 697, 699.

To "deal" in a commodity, however, such as automobiles, within the meaning of a privilege tax statute, means something more than the making of an occasional sale in a municipality where the seller has no place of business, and no stock of automobiles on hand. City of Pascagoula v. Carter, 136 Miss. 750, 101 So. 687, 688.

As to dealing in futures, see Futures.

DEALER. In the popular sense, one who buys to sell,—not one who buys to keep, or makes to sell. Commonwealth v. Lutz, 284 Pa. 184, 130 A. 410, 411; Moore v. State, 148 Ga. 457, 97 S.E. 76, 77; In re I. Rheinstrom & Sons Co., D.C.Ky., 207 F. 119, 136.

The term includes one who carries on the business of selling goods, wares, and merchandise, manufactured by him at a store or warehouse apart from his own shop, or manufactory. Atlantic Refining Co. v. Van Valkenburg, 265 Pa. 456, 109 A. 208, 209.

A "dealer," as in narcotics, is one who sells promiscuously,—one who is ready and willing to sell to anyone applying to purchase, if unaware that they are officers or undercover men. Taylor v. U. S., C.C.A.Mo., 19 F.2d 813, 815.

Under Blue Sky Laws, a "dealer" is one making successive sales as a business. People v. Clum, 213 Mich. 651, 182 N.W. 136, 138, 15 A.L.R. 253; State v. Barrett, 121 Or. 57, 254 P. 198, 200. Compare, also, Commonwealth v. Silverman, 220 Mass. 552, 108 N.E. 358, Ann.Cas.1917A, 948.

For various definitions under particular statutes, see State v. Perkins, 88 Vt. 121, 92 A. 1, 2 (dealer in evergreen trees); Texas Co. v. State, 31 Ariz. 485, 254 P. 1060, 1063, 53 A.L.R. 258 (dealer in gasoline); Pierce v. Hutchinson, 241 Mass. 557, 136 N.E. 261, 263 (dealer in motor vehicles).

Makers of an accommodation note are deemed dealers with whoever discounts it. Vernon v. Manhattan Co., 17 Wend., N.Y., 524.

Dealers' talk. That picturesque and laudatory style affected by nearly every trader in setting forth the attractive qualities of the goods he offers for sale. Prince v. Brackett, Shaw & Lunt Co., 125 Me. 31, 130 A. 509, 511. The puffing of goods to induce the sale thereof; not regarded in law as fraudulent unless accompanied by some artifice to deceive the purchaser and throw him off his guard or some concealment of intrinsic defects not easily discoverable. Kimball v. Bangs, 144 Mass. 321, 11 N.E. 113; Williams v. Fouche, 164 Ga. 311, 138 S.E. 580, 581.

Real estate dealer. One who, on his own account and as a business independent of that of another real estate agent, engages for a consideration to aid others, whether the owners of the property or their agents, in selling real estate which is offered for sale. Horsley v. Woodley, 12 Ga.App. 456, 78 S.E. 260, 261.

DEALINGS. Transactions in the course of trade or business;—held to include payments to a bankrupt. Moody & M. 137; 3 Car. & P. 85.

DEAN. In English ecclesiastical law. An ecclesiastical dignitary who presides over the chapter of a cathedral, and is next in rank to the bishop. So called from having been originally appointed to superintend *ten* canons or prebendaries. 1 Bl. Comm. 382; Co. Litt. 95; Spelman.

There are several kinds of deans, namely: Deans of chapters; deans of peculiars; rural deans; deans in the colleges; honorary deans; deans of provinces.

DEAN AND CHAPTER. In ecclesiastical law. The council of a bishop, to assist him with their advice in the religious and also in the temporal affairs of the see. 3 Co. 75; 1 Bla. Comm. 382; Co. Litt. 103, 300; *Termes de la Ley*; 2 Burn, Eccl. Law 120.

DEAN OF THE ARCHES. The presiding judge of the Court of Arches. He is also an assistant judge in the court of admiralty. 1 Kent, Comm. 371; 3 Steph. Comm. 727.

DEATH. The cessation of life; the ceasing to exist; defined by physicians as a total stoppage of the circulation of the blood, and a cessation of the animal and vital functions consequent thereon, such as respiration, pulsation, etc.

This is "natural death," in contradistinction to "civil death," and, also, to "violent death," See those titles, *infra.*

Civil death. The state of a person who, though possessing natural life, has lost all his civil rights, and as to them, is considered as dead. Quick v. Western Ry. of Alabama, 207 Ala. 376, 92 So. 608, 609. At common law, the extinction of civil rights and relations, so that the property of a person declared civilly dead passes to his heirs as if dead in fact. Holmes v. King, 216 Ala. 412, 113 So. 274, 276.

The "civil death" spoken of in the books, is of two kinds: (1) Where there is a total extinction of the civil rights and relations of the party, so that he can neither take nor hold property, and his heirs succeed to his estate in the same manner as if he were really dead, or the estate is forfeited to the crown. (2) Where there is an incapacity to hold property, or to sue in the king's courts, attended with forfeiture of the estate to the crown. Of the first kind, are the cases of monks professed, and abjuration of the realm; all the other cases are of the second kind. Strictly speaking, there but two cases of civil death; those of a monk professed, and an abjuration of the realm. In re Erskine, C.C.A.Ind., 1 F.2d 149, 152. See, generally, Chit.Crim.Law 723; Co.Litt. §§ 133, 199, note; Littleton § 200; 1 Bl.Comm. 132; Avery v. Everett, 110 N.Y. 317, 18 N.E. 148, 1 L.R.A. 264; In re Donnelly's Estate, 125 Cal. 417, 58 P. 61, 73 Am.St.Rep. 62.

In New York a person sentenced to imprisonment is thereafter deemed civilly dead under Penal Law § 511. See Platner v. Sherwood, 6 Johns.Ch., N.Y., 118; Troup v. Wood, 4 Johns.Ch., N.Y., 228, 260.

Death-bed. In Scotch law. A state of sickness which ends in death. Ersk. Inst. 3, 8, 95.

Death-bed deed. In Scotch law. A deed made by a person while laboring under a distemper of which he afterwards died. Ersk. Inst. 3, 8, 96. A deed is understood to be in death-bed, if, before signing and delivery thereof, the grantor was sick, and never convalesced thereafter. 1 Forbes, Inst. pt. 3, b. 2, c. 4, tit. 1, § 1. But it is not necessary that he should be actually confined to his bed at the time of making the deed. Bell.

Death duty. A charge or toll which the state makes upon the right to transmit or to receive property on the death of the owner. In re Heck's Estate, 120 Or. 80, 250 P. 735, 736. The usual name in England for an inheritance tax.

Death warrant. A warrant from the proper executive authority appointing the time and place for the execution of the sentence of death upon a convict judicially condemned to suffer that penalty.

Death watch. A special guard set to watch a prisoner condemned to death, for some days before the time for the execution, the special purpose being to prevent any escape or any attempt to anticipate the sentence.

Natural death. A death which occurs by the unassisted operation of natural causes, as distinguished not only from "civil death," but also from "violent death" (*q. v.*)

Presumptive death. That which is presumed from proof of a long continued absence unheard from and unexplained. The general rule, as now understood, is that the presumption of the duration of life ceases at the expiration of seven years from the time when the person was last known to be living; and after the lapse of that period there is a presumption of death. Smith v. Knowlton, 11 N.H. 197; Chamb. Best Ev. 304, note, collecting the cases; 4 U.C.Q.B. 510; 1 Greenl. Ev. § 41; 5 B. & Ad. 86; Maley v. Pennsylvania R. Co., 258 Pa. 73, 101 A. 911, L.R.A.1918A, 563. In most of the states the subject is regulated by statute.

The better opinion is that there is no presumption as to the time of death. Davie v. Briggs, 97 U.S. 628, 24 L.Ed. 1086; Chamb.Best Ev. 305; 2 Brett, Com. 941; 2 M. & W. 894. But it has been held that death is presumed to take place at the end of the seven years' absence; Brotherhood of Locomotive Firemen and Engineers v. Nash, 144 Md. 623, 125 A. 441; Apitz v. Supreme Lodge Knights and Ladies of Honor, 274 Ill. 196, 113 N.E. 63, L.R.A.1917A, 183; or at a time of peril, Conner v. New York Life Ins. Co., 166 N.Y.S. 985, 179 App.Div. 596.

Violent death. One caused or accelerated by the interference of human agency;—distinguished from "natural death."

DEATH'S PART. See Dead's Part; Dead Man's Part.

DEATHSMAN. The executioner; hangman; he that executes the extreme penalty of the law.

DEATH TRAP. A structure or situation involving imminent risk of death or a place apparently safe but actually very dangerous to life. Benson v. Missouri, K. & T. R. Co., Tex.Civ.App., 200 S.W. 2d 233, 240.

DEBASING. This word, in a statute making it slander to charge another with being guilty of some "debasing act which may exclude him from society," has reference to those repulsive acts which would cause him to be shunned or avoided, in the same way as would a contagious disease. Morris v. Evans, 22 Ga.App. 11, 95 S.E. 385, 386.

DEBAUCH. To corrupt one's manners; to make lewd; to mar or spoil; to entice; and, when used of a woman, to seduce, or corrupt with lewdness. Litton v. Woliver, 126 Va. 32, 100 S.E. 827, 828; State v. Howard, 264 Mo. 386, 175 S.W. 58, 59. Originally, the term had a limited signification, meaning to entice or draw one away from his work, employment, or duty; and from this sense its application has enlarged to include the corruption of manners and violation of the person. In its modern legal sense, the word carries with it the idea of "carnal knowledge," aggravated by assault, violent seduction, ravishment. Koenig v. Nott, 2 Hilt., N.Y., 323. And see State v. Curran, 51 Iowa, 112, 49 N.W. 1006. See, also, Debauchery.

DEBAUCHERY. In general, excessive indulgence in sensual pleasures; in a narrower sense, sexual immorality or excesses, or the unlawful indulgence of lust. Suslak v. United States, C.C.A. Mont., 213 F. 913, 917; Gillette v. United States, C.C.A.N.D., 236 F. 215, 217.

In the White Slave Act, Act June 25, 1910, c. 395, 36 Stat. 825, 18 U.S.C.A. § 2421 et seq., making it an offense to procure the interstate transportation of a girl for the purpose of prostitution and debauchery, "debauchery" is not limited to the meaning of seduction, but includes a purpose to expose her to such influence as will naturally and inevitably so corrupt her character as to lead her to acts of sexual immorality, or, if she is already a sexually corrupt woman, a purpose that she shall engage or continue more or less habitually in sexually immoral practices. Van Pelt v. United States, C.C.A.Va., 240 F. 346, 348, L.R. A.1917E, 1135.

DEBENTURE. A certificate given by the collector of a port, under the United States customs laws, to the effect that an importer of merchandise therein named is entitled to a drawback, (*q. v.*,) specifying the amount and time when payable. See Act Cong. March 2, 1799, § 80, 1 St. at Large 687.

An instrument in use in some government departments, particularly in England, by which the government is charged to pay to a creditor or his assigns the sum found due on auditing his accounts. Brande; Blount.

A security for a loan of money issued by a public company, usually creating a charge on the whole or a part of the company's stock and property, though not necessarily in the form of a mortgage. They are subject to certain regulations as to the mode of transfer, and ordinarily have coupons attached to facilitate the payment of interest. They are generally issued in a series, with provision that they shall rank *pari passu* in proportion to their amounts. See Bank v. Atkins, 72 Vt. 33, 47 A. 176; Cavanagh, Mon. Sec. 267; 56 L.J.R.Ch.D. 815; Brice, *Ultra Vires* (2d Ed.) 279.

A charge in writing on certain property, with the repayment at a time fixed, of money lent by a person therein named at a given interest.

Any instrument (other than a covering or trust deed) which either creates or agrees to create a debt in favor of one person or corporation, or several persons or corporations, or acknowledges such debt. Simonson, Debentures, 5.

A debenture is distinguished (1) from a mortgage which is an actual transfer of property, (2) from a bond which does not directly affect property, and (3) from a mere charge on property which is individualized and does not form part of a series of similar charges; Cav.Mon.Sec. 267, citing L.R. 10 Ch.D. 530, 681; 15 Ch.D. 465; 21 Ch.D. 762; L.R. 7 App.Cas. 673; Jones, Corp. B. & M. § 32; 10 H.L.C. 191; L.R. 2 Ch.D. 337.

DEBENTURE INDENTURE. An indenture containing obligations not secured by a mortgage or other collateral; a key instrument in the process of long term debt financing for general business corporations. Its effect is to put the debenture-holder in substantially the same practical position as a bondholder secured by a first mortgage. See "Business Lawyer" (April 1966, pp. 678, 679, 680).

DEBENTURE STOCK. A stock or fund representing money borrowed by a company or public body, in England, and charged on the whole or part of its property. An issue of stock usually irredeemable and transferable in any amount, not including a fraction of a pound.

The terminability and fixity in amount of debentures being inconvenient to lenders has led to their being in many cases superseded by debenture stock. Whart. Lex.

Debet esse finis litium. There ought to be an end of suits; there should be some period put to litigation. Jenk. Cent. 61.

DEBET ET DETINET. (Lat. He owes and detains.) Words anciently used in the original writ, (and now, in English, in the plaintiff's declaration,) in an action of debt, where it was brought by one of the original contracting parties who personally gave the credit, against the other who personally incurred the debt, or against his heirs, if they were bound to the payment; as by the obligee against the obligor, by the landlord against the tenant, etc. The declaration, in such cases, states that the defendant *"owes* to," as well as *"detains* from," the plaintiff the debt or thing in question; and hence the action is said to be "in the *debet et detinet."* Where the declaration merely states that the defendant *detains* the debt, (as in actions by and against an executor for a debt due to or from the testator,) the action is said to be "in the *detinet"* alone. Fitzh. Nat. Brev. 119, G.; 3 Bl. Comm. 155.

DEBET ET SOLET. (Lat. He owes and is used to.) Where a man sues in a writ of right or to recover any right of which he is for the first time disseised, as of a suit at a mill or in case of a writ of *quod permittat,* he brings his writ in the *debet et solet.* Reg. Orig. 144*a*; Fitzh. Nat. Brev. 122, M.

Debet quis juri subjacere ubi delinquit. One [every one] ought to be subject to the law [of the place] where he offends. 3 Inst. 34. This maxim is taken from Bracton. Bract. fol. 154*b*. Finch, Law, 14, 36; Wing. Max. 113; 3 Co. 231; 8 Scott N. R. 567.

DEBET SINE BREVE. (Lat. He owes without declaration filed.) Used in relation to a confession of judgment.

Debet sua cuique domus esse perfugium tutissimum. Every man's house should be a perfectly safe refuge. Clason v. Shotwell, 12 Johns., N.Y., 31, 54.

Debile fundamentum fallit opus. A weak foundation frustrates [or renders vain] the work [built upon it.] Shep. Touch. 60; Noy, Max. 5, max. 12; Finch, Law, b. 1, ch. 3. When the foundation fails, all goes to the ground; as, where the cause of action fails, the action itself must of necessity fail. Wing. Max. 113, 114, max. 40; Broom, Max. 180.

DEBIT. A sum charged as due or owing. The term is used in book-keeping to denote the left page of the ledger, or the charging of a person or an account with all that is supplied to or paid out for him or for the subject of the account. Also, the balance of an account where it is shown that something remains due to the party keeping the account.

In industrial insurance nomenclature, a certain identified territory in which a solicitor operates by soliciting new business and taking care, as through collection of the debit accounts, of the company's patrons for insurance theretofore written; such insurance being usually written in small amounts on the weekly payment plan. Jones v. Prudential Ins. Co. of America, 173 Mo.App. 1, 155 S.W. 1106, 1107.

DEBITA FUNDI. L. Lat. In Scotch law. Debts secured upon land. Ersk. Inst. 4, 1, 11.

DEBITA LAICORUM. L. Lat. In old English law. Debts of the laity, or of lay persons. Debts recoverable in the civil courts. Crabb. Eng. Law, 107.

Debita sequuntur personam debitoris. Debts follow the person of the debtor; that is, they have no locality, and may be collected wherever the debtor can be found. 2 Kent, Comm. 429; Story, Confl. Laws, § 362; Halkers, Max. 13.

DEBITOR. In the civil and old English law. A debtor.

Debitor non præsumitur donare. A debtor is not presumed to make a gift. Whatever disposition he makes of his property is supposed to be in satisfaction of his debts. 1 Kames, Eq. 212. Where a debtor gives money or goods, or grants land to his creditor, the natural presumption is that he means to get free from his obligation, and not to make a present, unless donation be expressed. Ersk. Inst. 3, 3, 93; Dig. 50, 16, 108; 1 P. Wms. 239; Wh. & Tud. L. Cas. Eq. 378.

Debitorum pactionibus creditorum petitio nec tolli nec minui potest. 1 Poth. Obl. 108; Broom, Max. 697, Bart. Max. 115. The rights of creditors can neither be taken away nor diminished by agreements among (or of) the debtors.

DEBITRIX. A female debtor.

DEBITUM. Something due, or owing, a debt.

Debitum et contractus sunt nullius loci. Debt and contract are of [belong to] no place; have no particular locality. 7 Co. 61. The obligation in these cases is purely personal, and actions to enforce it may be brought anywhere. 2 Inst. 231; Story, Confl. Laws, § 362; 1 Smith, Lead. Cas. 340, 363; 7 M. & G. 1019, n.

DEBITUM IN PRÆSENTI SOLVENDUM IN FUTURO. A debt or obligation complete when contracted, but of which the performance cannot be required till some future period.

DEBITUM SINE BREVI. L. Lat. Debt without writ; debt without a declaration. In old practice, this term denoted an action begun by original bill, instead of by writ. In modern usage, it is sometimes applies to a debt evidenced by confession of judgment without suit. The equivalent Norman-French phrase was *"debit sans breve."* Both are abbreviated to *d. s. b.*

DEBT. A sum of money due by certain and express agreement; as by bond for a determinate sum, a bill or note, a special bargain, or a rent reserved on a lease, where the amount is fixed and specific, and does not depend upon any subsequent valuation to settle it. 3 Bl.Comm. 154; Hagar v. Reclamation Dist., 111 U.S. 701, 4 S.Ct. 663, 28 L.Ed. 569; Neilson v. Title Guaranty & Surety Co., 101 Or. 262, 199 P. 948, 951; Shultz v. Ritterbusch, 38 Okl. 478, 134 P. 961, 968; W. S. Tyler Co. v. Deutsche Dampfschifffahrts Gesellschaft Hansa, Bremen, Germany, D.C.Ohio, 276 F. 134, 136.

An unconditional promise to pay a fixed sum at a specified time. Lowery v. Fuller, 221 Mo.App. 495, 281 S.W. 968, 972. A contractual obligation to pay in the future for considerations received in the present. Lesser v. Warren Borough, 237 Pa. 501, 85 A. 839, 841, 43 L.R.A.,N.S., 839. The word "debt" carries with it the requirement of certainty, the foundation of promise by express contract, and necessarily implies legality. Clinton Mining & Mineral Co. v. Beacon, C.C.A.Pa., 266 F. 621, 622, 14 A.L.R. 263.

The word "debt," in the definition of a mortgage as a hypothecation or pledge of property as security for a debt, means a duty or obligation to pay, for the enforcement of which an action lies. Stollenwerck v. Marks & Gayle, 188 Ala. 587, 65 So. 1024, 1027, Ann.Cas.1917C, 981; Gibson v. Hopkins, 80 W.Va. 756, 93 S.E. 826, 827.

Standing alone, the word "debt" is as applicable to a sum of money which has been promised at a future day, as to a sum of money now due and payable. To distinguish between the two, it may be said of the former that it is a debt owing, and of the latter that it is a debt due. A sum of money which is certainly and in all events payable is a debt, without regard to the fact whether it be payable now or at a future time. A sum payable upon a contingency, however, is not a debt, or does not become a debt until the contingency has happened. People v. Arguello, 37 Cal. 524.

A sum of money arising upon a contract, express or implied. Kimpton v. Bronson, 45 Barb. N.Y., 618; Johnson v. Garner, D.C.Nev., 233 F. 756, 767. Also, the obligation to pay a sum certain; Indian Refining Co. v. Taylor, 195 Ind. 223, 143 N.E. 682, 689; or a sum which may be ascertained by simple mathematical calculation from known facts; H. G. Kilbourne Co. v. Standard Stamp Affixer Co., 216 Mass. 118, 103 N.E. 469, 470; regardless of whether the liability arises by contract or is implied or imposed by law; State v. Latham, 136 Tenn. 30, 188 S.W. 534, 535; Lindstrom v. Spicher, 53 N.D. 195, 205 N.W. 231, 233, 41 A.L.R. 968.

A "debt" is a specified sum of money owing to one person from another, including not only the obligation of the debtor to pay, but the right of the creditor to receive and enforce payment. Angola Brick & Tile Co. v. Millgrove School Tp., Steuben County, 73 Ind.App. 557, 127 N.E. 855, 856; Dewey v. Denson, 31 Ga.App. 352, 120 S.E. 805, 807.

A fixed and certain obligation to pay money or some other valuable thing or things, either in the present or in the future. Burke v. Boulder Milling & Elevator Co., 77 Colo. 230, 235 P. 574, 575.

In a still more general sense, that which is due from one person to another, whether money, goods, or services. Holman v. Hollis, 94 Fla. 614, 114 So. 254, 255; State v. State Board of Examiners, 74 Mont. 1, 238 P. 316, 323.

A "debt" is an obligation arising otherwise than by sentence by a court for a breach of the public peace or for crime. Ruggles v. State, 120 Md. 553, 87 A. 1080, 1084.

In a broad sense, any duty to respond to another in money, labor, or service; it may even mean a moral or honorary obligation, unenforceable by legal action. U. S. Sugar Equalization Board v. P. De Ronde & Co., C.C.A.Del., 7 F.2d 981, 984.

Also, sometimes, an aggregate of separate debts, or the total sum of the existing claims against a person or company. Thus we speak of the "national debt," the "bonded debt" of a corporation, etc.

The word "debt" has no fixed legal meaning; Electric Reduction Co. v. Lewellyn, C.C.A.Pa., 11 F.2d 493, 494; but takes shades of meaning from the occasion of its use and color from accompanying words; Morrow v. Hayes, 226 Mich. 301, 197 N.W. 554, 555.

The word is of large import, including not only debts by specialty, and debts of record, or judgments (Liberty Mut. Ins. Co. v. Johnson Shipyards Corporation, C.C.A.N.Y., 6 F.2d 752, 755; Schooley v. Schooley, 184 Iowa 835, 169 N. W. 56, 57, 11 A.L.R. 110; Bronson v. Syverson, 88 Wash. 264, 152 P. 1039, 1040, L.R.A.1916B, 993; Rosenberg v. Rosenberg, 152 Md. 49, 135 A. 840), but also obligations arising under simple contract, to a very wide extent; and in its popular sense includes all that is due to a man under any form of obligation or promise. McCrea v. First Nat. Bank, 162 Minn. 455, 203 N.W. 220; Ætna Ins. Co. v. Robertson, 126 Miss. 387, 88 So. 883, 890.

Synonyms

The term "demand" is of much broader import than "debt," and embraces rights of action belonging to the debtor beyond those which could appropriately be called "debts." In this respect the term "demand" is one of very extensive import. In re Denny, 2 Hill, N.Y., 223.

Nevertheless, "debt" may be synonymous with "claim"; In re Littleton's Estate, 223 N.Y.S. 470, 479, 129 Misc. 845; and may include any kind of a just demand. Goldberg v. Parker, 87 Conn. 99, 87 A. 555, 557, 46 L.R.A.,N.S., 1097, Ann.Cas.1914C, 1059.

The word dues is equivalent to "debts," or that which is owing and has a contractual significance. State v. Mortgage Security Co., 154 Minn. 453, 192 N.W. 348, 350.

"Debt" is not exactly synonymous with "duty." A debt is a legal liability to pay a specific sum of money; a duty is a legal obligation to perform some act. Allen v. Dickson, Minor, Ala., 120.

"Obligation" is a broader term than "debt." Bovee v. Boyle, 25 Colo.App. 165, 136 P. 467, 469. Every obligation is not a debt, though every debt is an obligation. Lindstrom v. Spicher, 53 N.D. 195, 205 N.W. 231, 233, 41 A.L.R. 968; In re Moorehead's Estate, 289 Pa. 542, 137 A. 802, 806, 52 A.L.R. 1251.

The words "debt" and "liability" are not necessarily synonymous. As applied to the pecuniary relations of parties, liability is a term of broader significance than debt. Coulter Dry Goods Co. v. Wentworth, 171 Cal. 500, 153 P. 939, 940. Liability is responsibility; the state of one who is bound in law and justice to do something which may be enforced by action. This liability may arise from contracts either express or implied, or in consequence of torts committed. McElfresh v. Kirkendall, 36 Iowa 226. "Liability" ordinarily means an obligation which may or may not ripen into a debt. Irving Bank-Columbia Trust Co. v. New York Rys. Co., D.C.N.Y., 292 F. 429, 433. Yet "debt" may sometimes include various kinds of liabilities. See Allen v. Cosmopolitan Trust Co., 247 Mass. 334, 142 N. E. 100, 103; Carroll v. Bowling, 151 Md. 59, 133 A. 851, 854.

In General

Active debt. One due to a person. Used in the civil law.

Ancestral debt. One of an ancestor which the law compels the heir to pay. Watkins v. Holman, 16 Pet. 25, 10 L.Ed. 873; A. & E. Encyc.

Debt by simple contract. A debt or demand founded upon a verbal or implied contract, or upon any written agreement that is not under seal.

Debt by specialty or special contract. A debt due, or acknowledged to be due, by some deed or instrument under seal; as a deed of covenant or sale, a lease reserving rent, or a bond or obligation. 2 Bl.Comm. 465; In re Harris, 101 N.J.Eq. 5, 137 A. 215, 216; Kerr v. Lydecker, 51 Ohio St. 240. 37 N.E. 267, 23 L.R.A. 842; Marriott v. Thompson, Willes, 189.

Debt ex mutuo. A species of debt or obligation mentioned by Glanville and Bracton, and which arose *ex mutuo,* out of a certain kind of loan. Glan. lib. 10, c. 3; Bract. fol. 99. See Mutuum; Ex Mutuo.

Debt of record. A debt which appears to be due by the evidence of a court of record, as by a judgment or recognizance. 2 Bl.Comm. 465.

Doubtful debt. One of which the payment is uncertain. *Clef des Lois Romaines.*

In Practice

The name of a common-law action, which lies to recover a certain specific sum of money, or a sum that can readily be reduced to a certainty. 3 Bl.Comm. 154; 3 Steph.Comm. 461; 1 Tidd, Pr. 3; Drennen Motor Car Co. v. Evans, 192 Ala. 150, 68 So. 303; Bullard v. Bell, 1 Mass. 243, Fed.Cas.No. 2,121; U. S. v. Claflin, 97 U.S. 546, 24 L.Ed. 1082; Baum v. Tonkin, 110 Pa. 569, 1 A. 535.

It is thus distinguished from *assumpsit,* which lies as well where the sum due is uncertain as where it is certain, and from *covenant,* which lies only upon contracts evidenced in a certain manner.

It is said to lie in the *debet* and *detinet,* (when it is stated that the defendant owes and detains,) or in the *detinet,* (when it is stated merely that he detains.) Debt in the *detinet* for goods differs from detinue, because it is not essential in this action, as in detinue, that the specific property in the goods should have been vested in the plaintiff at the time the action is brought. Dyer, 24*b*.

Existing debt. See Existing Debt.

Fraudulent debt. A debt created by fraud. Such a debt implies confidence and deception. It implies that it arose out of a contract, express or implied, and that fraudulent practices were employed by the debtor, by which the creditor was defrauded. Howland v. Carson, 28 Ohio St. 628.

Hypothecary debt. One which is a lien upon an estate.

Judgment debt. See Judgment Debt.

Legal debts. Those that are recoverable in a court of common law, as debt on a bill of exchange, a bond, or a simple contract. Rogers v. Daniell, 8 Allen, Mass., 348; Guild v. Walter, 182 Mass. 225, 65 N.E. 68.

Liquid debt. One which is immediately and unconditionally due.

Mutual debts. Money due on both sides between two persons. Such debts must be due to and from same persons in same capacity. Dole v. Chattabriga, 82 N.H. 396, 134 A. 347, 348. Cross debts in the same capacity and right, and of the same kind and quality. Lippitt v. Thames Loan & Trust Co., 88 Conn. 185, 90 A. 369, 374.

Passive debt. A debt upon which, by agreement between the debtor and creditor, no interest is payable, as distinguished from *active* debt; *i. e.,* a debt upon which interest is payable. In this sense, the terms "active" and "passive" are applied to certain debts due from the Spanish government to Great Britain. Wharton. In another sense of the words, a debt is "active" or "passive" according as the person of the creditor or debtor is regarded; a passive debt being that which a man owes; an active debt that which is owing to him. In this meaning every debt is both active and passive,—active as regards the creditor, passive as regards the debtor.

Privileged debt. One which is to be paid before others in case a debtor is insolvent.

Public debt. That which is due or owing by the government of a state or nation. The terms "public debt" and "public securities," used in legislation, are terms generally applied to national or state obligations and dues, and would rarely, if ever, be construed to include town debts or obligations; nor would the term "public revenue" ordinarily be applied to funds arising from town taxes. Morgan v. Cree, 46 Vt. 773, 14 Am.Rep. 640.

Pure debt. In Scotch law. A debt due now and unconditionally is so called. It is thus distinguished from a *future* debt,—payable at a fixed day in the future,—and a *contingent* debt, which will only become due upon the happening of a certain contingency.

Simple contract debt. One where the contract upon which the obligation arises is neither ascertained by matter of record nor yet by deed or special instrument, but by mere oral evidence the most simple of any, or by notes unsealed, which are capable of a more easy proof, and therefore only better than a verbal promise. 2 Bl.Comm. 466.

Solvent debts. In Pennsylvania, the "solvent debts" which a city may deduct from its gross indebtedness pursuant to Act April 20, 1874, P.L. 65, in ascertaining its borrowing capacity, are debts due it directly, payment of which it can enforce as one of its quick assets for the liquidation of any of its obligations. McGuire v. City of Philadelphia, 245 Pa. 287, 91 A. 622, 623.

Specialty debt. See Debt by Specialty or Special Contract, *supra.*

DEBTEE. A person to whom a debt is due; a creditor. 3 Bl.Comm. 18; Plowd. 543. Not used.

DEBTOR. One who owes a debt; he who may be compelled to pay a claim or demand. Anyone liable on a claim, whether due or to become due. Cozart v. Barnes, C.C.A.S.C., 240 F. 935, 938.

The term may be used synonymously with "obligor," "mortgagor," and the like. McDuffie v. Faulk, 214 Ala. 221, 107 So. 61, 62.

Common Debtor

In Scotch law. A debtor whose effects have been arrested by several creditors. In regard to these creditors, he is their common debtor, and by this term is distinguished in the proceedings that take place in the competition. Bell

Debtor's Act 1869

The statute 32 & 33 Vict. c. 62, abolishing imprisonment for debt in England, and for the punishment of fraudulent debtors. 2 Steph.Comm. 159–164. Not to be confounded with the Bankruptcy Act of 1869. Mozley & Whitley.

Debtor's Summons

In English law. A summons issuing from a court having jurisdiction in bankruptcy, upon the creditor proving a liquidated debt of not less than £50, which he has failed to collect after reasonable effort, stating that if the debtor fail, within one week if a trader, and within three weeks if a non-trader, to pay or compound for the sum specified, a petition may be presented against him praying that he may be adjudged a bankrupt. Bankruptcy Act 1869, § 7; Robs.Bankr.; Mozley & Whitley.

DECALOGUE. The ten commandments which, according to Exodus XX, 1–18, were given by God to Moses. The Jews called them the "Ten Words," hence the name.

DECANATUS. A deanery. Spelman. A company of ten persons. Calvin.

Also (and in this sense sometimes spelled Decania, or Decana), a town or tithing, consisting originally of ten families of freeholders. Ten tithings compose a hundred. 1 Bla.Comm. 114; Medley, Orig.Illus.Eng.Const.Hist.

DECANIA. The office, jurisdiction, territory, or command of a *decanus,* or dean. Spelman.

DECANUS.

In Ecclesiastical and Old European Law

An officer having supervision over *ten*; a dean. A term applied not only to ecclesiastical, but to civil and military, officers. *Decanus monasticus;* a monastic dean, or dean of a monastery; an officer over ten monks. *Decanus in majori ecclesiæ;* dean of a cathedral church, presiding over ten prebendaries. *Decanus episcopi*; a bishop's or rural dean, presiding over ten clerks or parishes. *Decanus friborgi*; dean of a friborg. An officer among the Saxons who presided over a friborg, tithing, decennary, or association of ten inhabitants; otherwise called a "tithing man," or "borsholder," his duties being those of an inferior judicial officer. Du Cange; Spelman, Gloss.; Calvinus, Lex. *Decanus militaris*; a military officer having command of ten soldiers. Spelman.

In Roman Law

An officer having the command of a company or "mess" of ten soldiers. Also an officer at Constantinople having charge of the burial of the dead. Nov.Jus. 43, 59; Du Cange.

DECAPITATION. The act of beheading. A mode of capital punishment by cutting off the head.

DECEASE, *n.* Death; not including civil death, (see Death.) In re Zeph's Estate, 50 Hun, 523, 3 N.Y.S. 460.

DECEASE, *v.* To die; to depart life, or from life. This has always been a common term in Scotch law. "Gif ane man *deceasis.*" Skene.

DECEASED. A dead person. In re Kite's Estate, 194 Iowa, 129, 187 N.W. 585, 587, 24 A.L.R. 850.

DECEDENT. A deceased person, especially one who has lately died. Etymologically the word denotes a person who is *dying,* but it has come to be used in law as signifying any deceased person, testate or intestate. In re Zeph's Estate, 50 Hun, 523, 3 N.Y.S. 460.

DECEIT. A fraudulent and cheating misrepresentation, artifice, or device, used by one or more persons to deceive and trick another, who is ignorant of the true facts, to the prejudice and damage of the party imposed upon. People v. Chadwick, 143 Cal. 116, 76 P. 884; French v. Vining, 102 Mass. 132, 3 Am.Rep. 440; In re Post, 54 Hun, 634, 7 N.Y.S. 438.

A fraudulent misrepresentation or contrivance, by which one man deceives another, who has no means of detecting the fraud, to the injury and damage of the latter.

A subtle trick or device, whereunto may be referred all manner of craft and collusion used to deceive and defraud another by any means whatsoever, which hath no other or more proper name than *deceit* to distinguish the offense. [West Symb. § 68]; Jacob.

A "deceit" is either: (1) The suggestion, as a fact, of that which is not true, by one who does not believe it to be true; (2) the assertion, as a fact, of that which is not true, by one who has no reasonable ground for believing it to be true; (3) the suppression of a fact, by one who is bound to disclose it, or who gives information of other facts which are likely to mislead for want of communication of that fact; or (4) a promise, made without any intention of performing it. Civ.Code Cal. § 1710; Civ.Code S.D. § 1293 (Comp.Laws 1929, § 797).

To constitute "deceit," the statement must be untrue, made with knowledge of its falsity or with reckless and conscious ignorance thereof, especially if parties are not on equal terms, made with intent that plaintiff act thereon or in a manner apparently fitted to induce him to act thereon, and plaintiff must act in reliance on the statement in the manner contemplated, or manifestly probable, to his injury. Corley Co. v. Griggs, 192 N.C. 171, 134 S.E. 406, 407; Pain v. Kiel, C.C.A.Mo., 288 F. 527, 529. See, also, Crossman v. Bacon & Robinson Co., 119 Me. 105, 109 A. 487, 489; Alpine v. Friend Bros., 244 Mass. 164, 138 N.E. 553, 554; Hood v. Wood, 61 Okl. 294, 161 P. 210, 213.

The essential elements of "deceit" are representation, falsity, scienter, deception, and injury. Ochs v. Woods, 221 N.Y. 335, 117 N.E. 305, 306.

In Old English Law

The name of an original writ, and the action founded on it, which lay to recover damages for any injury committed *deceitfully,* either in the name of another, (as by bringing an action in another's name, and then suffering a nonsuit, whereby the plaintiff became liable to costs,) or by a fraudulent warranty of goods, or other personal injury committed contrary to good faith and honesty. Reg.Orig. 112–116; Fitzh.Nat.Brev. 95, E, 98.

Also the name of a judicial writ which formerly lay to recover lands which had been lost by default by the tenant in a real action, in consequence of his not having been summoned by the sheriff, or by the collusion of his attorney. Rosc.Real Act. 136; 3 Bl.Comm. 166.

In General

Deceitful plea. A sham plea; one alleging as facts things which are obviously false on the face of the plea. Gray v. Gidiere, 4 Strob., S.C., 443.

DECEM TALES. (Ten such; or ten tales, jurors.) In practice. The name of a writ which issues in England, where, on a trial at bar, *ten* jurors are necessary to make up a full panel, commanding the sheriff to summon the requisite number. 3 Bl.Comm. 364; Reg.Jud. 30*b*; 3 Steph.Comm. 602.

DECEMVIRI LITIBUS JUDICANDIS. Lat. In the Roman law. Ten persons (five senators and five *equites*) who acted as the council or assistants of the prætor, when he decided on matters of law. Hallifax, Civil Law, b. 3, c. 8. According to others, they were themselves judges, appointed by Augustus to act in certain cases. Calvinus, Lex.; Anthon, Rom.Ant.

DECENCY. Propriety of action, speech, dress, etc. Universal Film Mfg. Co. v. Bell, 100 Misc. 281, 167 N.Y.S. 124, 128.

DECENNA. In old English law. A tithing or decennary; the precinct of a frank-pledge; consisting of ten freeholders with their families. Spelman.

DECENNARIUS. Lat. One who held one-half a virgate of land. Du Cange. One of the ten freeholders in a *decennary*. Id.; Calvin. *Decennier*. One of the *decennarii*, or ten freeholders making up a tithing. Spelman; Du Cange, *Decenna;* 1 Bla.Comm. 114.

DECENNARY. A tithing, composed of ten neighboring families. 1 Reeve, Eng.Law, 13; 1 Bl. Comm. 114.

King Alfred, for the better preservation of the peace, divided England into counties, the counties into hundreds, and the hundreds into tithings or decennaries: the inhabitants whereof, living together, were sureties or pledges for each other's good behavior.

DECEPTION. The act of deceiving; intentional misleading by falsehood spoken or acted. Smith v. State, 13 Ala.App. 399, 69 So. 402, 403.

DECEPTIONE. A writ that lieth properly against him that deceitfully doth anything in the name of another, for one that receiveth damage or hurt thereby. It is either original or judicial. Fitzh. N.B.

Deceptis non decipientibus, jura subveniunt. The laws help persons who are deceived, not those deceiving. Tray. Lat. Max. 149.

DECERN. In Scotch law. To decree. "Decernit and ordainit." 1 How. State Tr. 927. "Decerns." Shaw, 16.

DECESSUS. In the civil and old English law. Death; departure.

Decet tamen principem servare leges quibus ipse servatus est. It behooves, indeed, the prince to keep the laws by which he himself is preserved.

DECIDE. To "decide" includes the power and right to deliberate, to weigh the reasons for and against, to see which preponderate, and to be governed by that preponderance. Darden v. Lines, 2 Fla. 571; In re Milford & M. R. Co., 68 N.H. 570, 36 A. 545.

DECIES TANTUM (Ten times as much). The name of an ancient writ that was used against a juror who had taken a bribe in money for his verdict. The injured party could thus recover ten times the amount of the bribe.

DECIMÆ. In ecclesiastical law. Tenths, or tithes. The tenth part of the annual profit of each living, payable formerly to the pope. There were several valuations made of these livings at different times. The *decimæ* (tenths) were appropriated to the crown, and a new valuation established, by 26 Hen. VIII., c. 3. 1 Bl.Comm. 284. See Tithes.

Decimæ debentur paroche. Tithes are due to the parish priest.

Decimæ de decimatis solvi non debent. Tithes are not to be paid from that which is given for tithes.

Decimæ de jure divino et canonica institutione pertinent ad personam. Dal. 50. Tithes belong to the parson by divine right and canonical institution.

Decimæ non debent solvi, ubi non est annua renovatio; et ex annuatis renovantibus simui semei. Cro. Jac. 42. Tithes ought not to be paid where there is not an annual renovation, and from annual renovations once only.

DECIMATION. The punishing of every tenth soldier by lot, for mutiny or other failure of duty. This was termed "*decimatio legionis*" by the Romans. Sometimes only the twentieth man was punished, (*vicesimatio,*) or the hundredth, (*centesimatio.*)

DECIME. A French coin of the value of the tenth part of a franc, or nearly two cents.

DECINERS. Those that had the oversight and check of ten friburgs for the maintenance of the king's peace. Cunningham.

Decipi quam fallere est tutius. It is safer to be deceived than to deceive. Lofft, 396.

DECISION. A popular rather than technical or legal word; a comprehensive term having no fixed, legal meaning. It may be employed as referring to ministerial acts as well as to those that are judicial or of a judicial character, Palmer Pub. Co. v. Smith, 130 Tex. 346, 109 S.W.2d 158, 159; such as decision of architects, Independent School Dist. No. 35, St. Louis County, v. A. Hedenberg & Co., 214 Minn. 82, 7 N.W.2d 511, 515; of county commissioners, Houser v. Olmstead, 57 S.D. 41,

230 N.W. 224, 225; or of industrial commission, Rosenquist v. O'Neil & Preston, 187 Minn. 375, 245 N.W. 621.

A judgment or decree pronounced by a court in settlement of a controversy submitted to it and by way of authoritative answer to the questions raised before it. Adams v. Railroad Co., 77 Miss. 194, 24 So. 317, 60 L.R.A. 33; Board of Education v. State, 7 Kan.App. 620, 52 P. 466.

A judgment given by a competent tribunal. Eastman Kodak Co. v. Richards, 123 Misc. 83, 204 N.Y.S. 246, 248.

The findings of fact and conclusions of law which must be in writing and filed with the clerk. Stewart Mining Co. v. Ontario Mining Co., 23 Idaho, 724, 132 P. 787, 791; Wilcox v. Sway, 69 Cal.App.2d 141, 160 P.2d 154, 156.

A finding, as by a court, upon either a question of law or fact arising in a case. Vermont Marble Co. v. Eastman, 91 Vt. 425, 101 A. 151, 160. The court's finding or findings. Volderauer v. State, 195 Ind. 415, 143 N.E. 674, 676; Chambers v. Farnham, 39 Cal.App. 17, 179 P. 423, 424.

A determination of a judicial or quasi judicial nature. Codington County v. Board of Com'rs of Codington County, 51 S.D. 131, 212 N.W. 626, 628.

Statement by trial justice after trial before court without jury does not constitute "decision." Shaul v. Fidelity & Deposit Co. of Maryland, 131 Misc. 401, 227 N.Y.S. 163, 168. A "decision" involves reaching a conclusion. Lambros v. Young, 145 F.2d 341, 343, 79 U.S.App.D.C. 247.

The term is broad enough to cover both final judgments and interlocutory orders. Stout v. Stout, 68 Ind.App. 278, 131 N.E. 245, 246. And though sometimes limited to the sense of judgment; Industrial Commission of Ohio v. Musselli, 102 Ohio St. 10, 130 N.E. 32, 33; the term is at other times understood as meaning simply the first step leading to a judgment; Dorney v. Ives, 36 R.I. 276, 90 A. 164, 165; or as an order for judgment; Collins v. Belland, 37 Cal. App. 139, 173 P. 601, 602. The word may also include various rulings, as well as orders. U. S. v. Thompson, 251 U. S. 407, 40 S.Ct. 289, 291, 64 L.Ed. 333; Marr v. Marr, 194 Cal. 332, 228 P. 534, 535.

The words "decision" and judgment" may be used interchangeably, but in the abstract there is a shade of difference between the two. Smith v. State, 196 Ga. 595, 27 S.E.2d 369, 373.

"Decision" is not necessarily synonymous with "opinion." A decision of the court is its judgment; the opinion is the reasons given for that judgment, or the expression of the views of the judge. Craig v. Bennett, 158 Ind. 9, 62 N.E. 273; But the two words are sometimes used interchangeably. Pierce v. State, 109 Ind. 535, 10 N.E. 302; Keller v. Summers, 262 Mo. 324, 171 S.W. 336, 337.

The French lawyers call the opinions which they give on questions propounded to them, decisions. See Inst. 1, 2, 8; Dig. 1, 2, 2.

DECISIVE, or DECISORY, OATH. See Oath.

DECISION ON MERITS. A decision determining the validity of a written instrument or passing on a controversy with respect to the interpretation thereof which bars subsequent suit on same cause of action. Eulenberg v. Torley's Inc., 56 Cal.App. 2d 653, 133 P.2d 15, 17.

DECLARANT. A person who makes a declaration.

DECLARATION.

In Pleading

The first of the pleadings on the part of the plaintiff in an action at law, being a formal and methodical specification of the facts and circumstances constituting his cause of action. It commonly comprises several sections or divisions, called "counts," and its formal parts follow each other in this order: Title, venue, commencement, cause of action, counts, conclusion. The declaration, at common law, answers to the "libel" in ecclesiastical and admiralty law, the "bill" in equity, the "petition" in civil law, the "complaint" in code pleading, and the "count" in real actions. U. S. v. Ambrose, 108 U.S. 336, 2 S.Ct. 682, 27 L.Ed. 746; Railway Co. v. Nugent, 86 Md. 349, 38 A. 779, 39 L.R.A. 161; Dixon v. Sturgeon, 6 Serg. & R. (Pa.) 28; 1 Chit.Pl. 248; Co.Litt. 17 *a*, 303 *a*; Bacon, Abr. *Pleas* (B); Comyns, Dig. *Pleader*, C, 7; Lawes, Pl. 35; Steph.Pl. 36; Leslie v. Mendelson, 302 Mich. 95, 4 N.W.2d 481, 484.

It may be *general* or *special:* for example, in debt on a bond, a declaration counting on the penal part only is *general;* one which sets out both the bond and the condition and assigns the breach is *special;* Gould, Pl. c. 4, § 50.

In Evidence

An unsworn statement or narration of facts made by a party to the transaction, or by one who has an interest in the existence of the facts recounted. Also, similar statements made by a person since deceased, which are admissible in evidence in some cases, contrary to the general rule, *e. g.*, "dying declarations" (see that subtitle, *infra*).

In Practice

The declaration or declaratory part of a judgment, decree, or order is that part which gives the decision or opinion of the court on the question of law in the case. Thus, in an action raising a question as to the construction of a will, the judgment or order declares that, according to the true construction of the will, the plaintiff has become entitled to the residue of the testator's estate, or the like. Sweet.

In Scotch Practice

The statement of a criminal or prisoner, taken before a magistrate. 2 Alis. Crim. Pr. 555; 2 Hume 328; Arkl. Just. 70; Paterson, Comp. §§ 952, 970.

In General

A "declaration" is a statement made out of court. Dawson v. Davis, 125 Conn. 330, 5 A.2d 703, 704.

Declaration against interest. Such declarations are evidence of the fact declared, and are therefore distinct from admissions, which amount to a waiver of proof. Jelser v. White, 183 N.C. 126, 110 S.E. 849, 850. They are statements which, when made, conflict with the pecuniary interest of the person making them, who need not have been a party, privy or witness to the suit in which they are offered. Elliotte v. Lavier, 299 Mich. 373, 300 N.W. 116, 118.

Declaration in chief. A declaration for the principal cause of action. 1 Tidd, Pr. 419.

Declaration of dividend. The act of a corporation in setting aside a portion of the net or surplus proceeds for distribution among the stockholders according to their respective interests. First Nat. Bank & Trust Co. v. Glenn, D.C.Ky., 36 F.Supp. 552, 554. See, also, Dividend.

Declaration of homestead. A creature of, and its validity depends upon, compliance with homestead statute. It is merely an act of the owner whereby he avails himself of, and secures, a right or privilege given him by statute; it is neither a conveyance nor a contract, and there is no transfer of, or change in, title, nor any agreement of transfer or change. U. S. Fidelity & Guaranty Co. v. Alloway, 173 Wash. 404, 23 P.2d 408. See, also, Homestead.

Declaration of independence. A formal declaration or announcement, promulgated July 4, 1776, by the congress of the United States of America, in the name and behalf of the people of the colonies, asserting and proclaiming their independence of the British crown, vindicating their pretensions to political autonomy, and anouncing themselves to the world as a free and independent nation.

Declaration of intention. A declaration made by an alien, as a preliminary to naturalization, before a court of record, to the effect that it is his intention in good faith to become a citizen of the United States, and to renounce forever all allegiance and fidelity to any foreign prince, potentate, state, or sovereignty whereof at the time he may be a citizen or subject. 8 U.S.C.A. § 731.

Declaration of right. See Bill of Rights.

Declaration of trust. The act by which the person who holds the legal title to property or an estate acknowledges and declares that he holds the same in trust to the use of another person or for certain specified purposes. The name is also used to designate the deed or other writing embodying such a declaration. Griffith v. Maxfield, 66 Ark. 513, 51 S.W. 832. See Baker v. Baker, 123 Md. 32, 90 A. 776, 779 (bank deposit); Del Giorgio v. Powers, 27 Cal.App.2d 668, 81 P.2d 1006, 1012 (mining claim); Bingen v. First Trust Co. of St. Paul, C.C.A.Minn., 103 F.2d 260, 264 (letter).

Declaration of war. A public and formal proclamation by a nation, through its executive or legislative department, that a state of war exists between itself and another nation, and forbidding all persons to aid or assist the enemy.

An act of Congress is necessary to the commencement of a foreign war and is in itself a "declaration" and fixes the date of the war. West v. Palmetto State Life Ins. Co., 202 S.C. 422, 25 S.E.2d 475, 477, 145 A.L.R. 1461; Rosenau v. Idaho Mut. Ben. Ass'n, 65 Idaho 408, 145 P.2d 227, 230.

Dying declarations. Statements made by a person who is lying at the point of death, and is conscious of his approaching dissolution, in reference to the manner in which he received the injuries of which he is dying, or other immediate cause of his death, and in reference to the person who inflicted such injuries or the connection with such injuries of a person who is charged or suspected of having committed them; which statements are admissible in evidence in a trial for homicide (and occasionally, at least in some jurisdictions, in other cases) where the killing of the declarant is the crime charged to the defendant. Shepard v. U. S., Kan., 290 U.S. 96, 54 S.Ct. 22, 78 L.Ed. 196; See generally Simons v. People, 150 Ill. 66, 36 N.E. 1019; Frier v. State, 92 Fla. 241, 109 So. 334, 335; Lucas v. Commonwealth, 153 Ky. 424, 155 S.W. 721, 722; Edwards v. State, 113 Neb. 698, 204 N.W. 780, 783; People v. Selknes, 309 Ill. 113, 140 N.E. 852, 854. Also Barsch v. Hammond, 110 Colo. 441, 135 P.2d 519, 521 (motorist); Waller v. Commonwealth, 178 Va. 294, 16 S.E.2d 808, 813 (shooting); State v. Brown, 209 Minn. 478, 296 N.W. 582, 586 (abortion).

Statements made by deceased while on operating table were inadmissible as "dying declarations" where there was no statement by deceased himself that he knew that death was approaching. People v. Hall, 260 App.Div. 421, 22 N.Y. S.2d 973, 976.

Self-serving declaration. One made by a party in his own interest at some time and place out of court;—not including testimony which he gives as witness at the trial. Brosnan v. Boggs, 101 Or. 472, 198 P. 890, 892.

DECLARATION OF LONDON. A declaration concerning the laws of naval war, agreed upon February 26, 1909, by the powers assembled at the London Naval Conference.

The preamble states that the Declaration was made in view of the desirability of an agreement upon the rules to be applied by the International Prize Court established by the Second Hague Conference. A preliminary provision states that it is agreed that the rules adopted "correspond in substance with the generally recognized principles of international law." The subjects dealt with by the Declaration include Blockade, Contraband, Unneutral Service, Destruction of Neutral Prizes, Transfer to Neutral Flag, Enemy Character, Convoy, Search, and Compensation. Higgins, 538–613.

DECLARATION OF PARIS. The name given to an agreement announcing four important rules of international law effected between the principal European powers at the Congress of Paris in 1856. These rules are: (1) Privateering is and remains abolished; (2) the neutral flag covers enemy's goods, except contraband of war; (3) neutral goods, except contraband of war, are not liable to confiscation under a hostile flag; (4) blockades, to be binding, must be effective.

DECLARATION OF ST. PETERSBURG. A declaration made at St. Petersburg in 1868 on behalf of certain of the powers in relation to the prohibition of the use of explosive bullets in time of war.

DECLARATOR. In Scotch law. An action whereby it is sought to have some right of property, or of *status*, or other right judicially ascertained and declared. Bell.

DECLARATOR OF TRUST. An action resorted to against a trustee who holds property upon titles *ex facie* for his own benefit. Bell.

DECLARATORY. Explanatory; designed to fix or elucidate what before was uncertain or doubtful.

DECLARATORY ACTION. In Scotch law. An action in which the right of the pursuer (or plaintiff) is craved to be *declared,* but nothing claimed to be done by the defender (defendant.) Ersk. Inst. 5, 1, 46. Otherwise called an "action of declarator."

DECLARATORY DECREE. In practice. A binding declaration of right in equity without consequential relief.

DECLARATORY JUDGMENT. One which simply declares the rights of the parties or expresses the opinion of the court on a question of law, without ordering anything to be done. Its distinctive characteristics are that no executory process follows as of course, nor is it necessary that an actual wrong, giving rise to action for damages, should have been done, or be immediately threatened. Great Lakes Dredge & Dock Co. v. Huffman, La., 319 U.S. 293, 63 S.Ct. 1070, 87 L.Ed. 1407; Petition of Kariher, 284 Pa. 455, 131 A. 265, 268; Village of Bay v. Gelvick, 58 Ohio App. 51, 15 N.E. 2d 786, 791. It must deal with real dispute of real fact. Rauh v. Fletcher Savings & Trust Co., 207 Ind. 638, 194 N.E. 334, 335. It is distinguished from other actions in that it does not seek execution or performance from the defendant or opposing party. Brindley v. Meara, Ind., 209 Ind. 144, 198 N.E. 301, 101 A.L.R. 682; Gutensohn v. Kansas City Southern Ry. Co., C.C.A.Mo., 140 F. 2d 950.

DECLARATORY PART OF A LAW. That which clearly defines rights to be observed and wrongs to be eschewed.

DECLARATORY STATUTE. One enacted for the purpose of removing doubts or putting an end to conflicting decisions in regard to what the law is in relation to a particular matter. It may either be expressive of the common law, 1 Bl. Comm. 86; Gray v. Bennett, 3 Metc., Mass., 527; In re Ungaro's Will, 88 N.J.Eq. 25, 102 A. 244, 246, or may declare what shall be taken to be the true meaning and intention of a previous statute, though in the latter case such enactments are more commonly called "expository statutes." McMahon v. Maddox, Tex.Civ.App., 297 S.W. 310, 312.

A statute enacted to put an end to a doubt as to what is the common law, or the meaning of another statute, and which declares what it is and ever has been. Nelson v. Sandkamp, 227 Minn. 177, 34 N.W.2d 640, 642, 5 A.L.R.2d 1136.

DECLARE. To make known, manifest, or clear. Lasier v. Wright, 304 Ill. 130, 136 N.E. 545, 552, 28 A.L.R. 674. To signify, to show in any manner either by words or acts. Edwardson v. Gerwien, 41 N.D. 506, 171 N.W. 101, 102. To publish; to utter; to announce clearly some opinion or resolution. Knecht v. Ins. Co., 90 Pa. 121, 35 Am. Rep. 641. As to "declare" a dividend. A. T. Jergins Trust v. Rogan, D.C.Cal., 40 F.Supp. 40, 42. To allege or affirm. State v. Hostetter, Mo.Sup., 222 S.W. 750, 754. To solemnly assert a fact before witnesses, *e. g.,* where a testator *declares* a paper signed by him to be his last will and testament. Lane v. Lane, 95 N.Y. 498.

This also is one of the words customarily used in the promise given by a person who is *affirmed* as a witness,—"sincerely and truly declare and affirm." Hence, to make a positive and solemn asseveration. Bassett v. Denn, 17 N. J.Law, 433.

With reference to pleadings, it means to draw up, serve, and file a declaration; *e. g.,* a "rule to declare." Also to allege in a declaration as a ground or cause of action; as "he declares upon a promissory note."

DECLINATION. In Scotch law. A plea to the jurisdiction, on the ground that the judge is interested in the suit.

DÉCLINATOIRES. In French law. Pleas to the jurisdiction of the court; also of *lis pendens,* and of *connexité,* (*q. v.*).

DECLINATORY EXCEPTIONS are such dilatory exceptions as merely decline the jurisdiction of the judge before whom the action is brought. Code Proc. La. 334. A plea to the jurisdiction rationae personae. Diamond T. Motor Trucks v. Heck, La.App., 13 So.2d 512, 514.

DECLINATORY PLEA. In English practice. The plea of sanctuary, or of benefit of clergy, before trial or conviction. 2 Hale, P.C. 236; 4 Bl. Comm. 333. Now abolished. 6 & 7 Geo. IV, c. 28, § 6; Mozl. & W. Dict.; 4 Steph. Comm. 400, note; Id. 436, note.

DECLINATURE. In Scotch practice. An objection to the jurisdiction of a judge. Bell.

DECLINE. A failing process, a tendency to a worse state; to become gradually impaired; a falling off or downward tendency. Exum v. Laub, C.C.A.Tex., 87 F.2d 73, 74; Buffalo County v. Phelps County, 129 Neb. 268, 261 N.W. 360.

DECOCTION. The act of boiling a substance in water, for extracting its virtues. The operation of boiling certain ingredients in a fluid for the purpose of extracting the parts soluble at that temperature. Also the liquor in which a substance has been boiled; water impregnated with the principles of any animal or vegetable substance boiled in it. Webster; Sykes v. Magone, C.C.N.Y., 38 F. 497.

In an indictment "decoction" and "infusion" are *ejusdem generis;* and if one is alleged to have been administered, instead of the other, the variance is immaterial. 3 Camp. 74.

DECOCTOR. In the Roman law. A bankrupt; a spendthrift; a squanderer of public funds. Calvin.

DECOLLATIO. In old English and Scotch law. Decollation; the punishment of beheading. Fleta, lib. 1, c. 21, § 6.

DECOMPOSED. A state of decomposition. United States v. 1851 Cartons, More or Less, etc., D.C.Colo., 55 F.Supp. 343, 346; A. O. Anderson & Co. v. U. S., C.C.A.Wash., 284 F. 542, 544. A separation into components; specifically, decay or dissolution. In re Vetter, Cust. & Pat.App., 96 F.2d 999, 1000.

DÉCONFES. In French law. A name formerly given to those persons who died without confession, whether they refused to confess or whether they were criminals to whom the sacrament was refused. *Droit de Canon,* per M. l'Abbé André; Dupin, Gloss. to Loisel's Institutes.

DECORATE. To beautify. To do something, as to a house as such, to improve the condition of the house, or of a room. Grasell v. Brodhead, 175 App.Div. 874, 162 N.Y.S. 421, 423. The addition of something becoming or beautiful. Upsal Street Realty Co. v. Rubin, 326 Pa. 327, 192 A. 481, 483.

DECORATOR. One whose business is the decoration of dwellings or public edifices. Grasell v. Brodhead, 175 App.Div. 874, 162 N.Y.S. 421, 423.

DECOY. To inveigle, entice, tempt, or lure; as, to decoy a person within the jurisdiction of a court so that he may be served with process, or to decoy a fugitive criminal to a place where he may be arrested without extradition papers, or to decoy one away from his place of residence for the purpose of kidnapping him and as a part of that act. In all these uses, the word implies enticement or luring by means of some fraud, trick, or temptation, but excludes the idea of force. Eberling v. State, 136 Ind. 117, 35 N.E. 1023; John v. State, 44 P. 51, 6 Wyo. 203.

Also, a "decoy pond." See that title, *infra.*

DECOY LETTER. A letter prepared and mailed for the purpose of detecting a criminal, particularly one who is perpetrating frauds upon the postal or revenue laws. U. S. v. Whittier, 5 Dill. 39, Fed. Cas. No. 16,688.

DECOY POND. A pond used for the breeding and maintenance of water-fowl. Keeble v. Hickeringshall, 3 Salk. 10; 11 Mod. 74, 130; Holt 14; 11 East 571.

DECREE.

In Practice

The judgment of a court of equity or admiralty, answering for most purposes to the judgment of a court of common law. A decree in equity is a sentence or order of the court, pronounced on hearing and understanding all the points in issue, and determining the rights of all the parties to the suit, according to equity and good conscience. 2 Daniell, Ch.Pr. 986; Wooster v. Handy, C.C.N.Y., 23 F. 49, 56; Motion Picture Patents Co. v. Universal Film Mfg. Co., D.C., N.Y., 232 F. 263, 265; Bull v. International Power Co., 84 N.J.Eq. 209, 93 A. 86, 88; Alford v. Leonard, 88 Fla. 532, 102 So. 885, 890. It is a declaration of the court announcing the legal consequences of the facts found. Robertson v. Talmadge, Tex.Civ.App., 174 S.W. 627, 629.

A decree, as distinguished from an order, is final, and is made at the hearing of the cause, whereas an order is interlocutory, and is made on motion or petition. Wherever an order may, in a certain event resulting from the direction contained in the order, lead to the termination of the suit in like manner as a decree made at the hearing, it is called a "decretal order." Brown.

A judgment at law, as distinguished from a decree in equity, was either simply for the plaintiff or for the defendant. There could be no qualifications or modifications. But such a judgment does not always touch the true justice of the cause or put the parties in the position they ought to occupy. This result was attained by the *decree* of a court of equity which could be so moulded, or the execution of which could be so controlled and suspended, that the relative duties and rights of the parties could be secured and enforced. Bisph.Eq. § 7.

The words "judgment" and "decree," however, are often used synonymously; Finnell v. Finnell, 113 Okl. 269, 230 P. 912, 913; especially now that the Codes have abolished the distinction between law and equity; Henderson v. Arkansas, 71 Okl. 253, 176 P. 751, 753. But of the two terms, "judgment" is the more comprehensive, and includes "decree." Coleman v. Los Angeles County, 180 Cal. 714, 182 P. 440, 441.

Decision of an administrative board though based on facts adduced on a hearing, Dal Maso v. Board of Com'rs of Prince George's County, 182 Md. 200, 34 A.2d 464, 466, or rescript from reviewing court are not decrees. City of Boston v. Santosuosso, 308 Mass. 189, 31 N.E.2d 564, 568.

Classification

Decrees in equity are either *final* or *interlocutory.* A final decree is one which fully and finally disposes of the whole litigation, determining all questions raised by the case, and leaving nothing that requires further judicial action. Sawyer v. White, 125 Me. 206, 132 A. 421, 422; Draper Corporation v. Stafford Co., C.C.A.Mass., 255 F. 554, 555; Burgin v. Sugg, 210 Ala. 142, 97 So. 216, 217. An interlocutory decree is a provisional or preliminary decree, which is not final and does not determine the suit, but directs some further proceedings preparatory to the final decree. It is a decree pronounced for the purpose of ascertaining matter of law or fact preparatory to a final decree. 1 Barb. Ch. Pr. 326, 327; Wooster v. Handy, C.C. N.Y., 23 F. 49, 56; Beebe v. Russell, 19 How. 283, 15 L.Ed. 668; Cornely v. Marckwald, 131 U.S. 159, 9 S.Ct. 744, 33 L.Ed. 117. Where something more than the ministerial execution of the decree as rendered is left to be done, the decree is interlocutory, and not final, even though it settles the equities of the bill. Lodge v. Twell, 135 U.S. 232, 10 S.Ct. 745, 34 L.Ed. 153. The difficulty of exact definition is mentioned in McGourkey v. Ry. Co., 146 U.S. 536, 13 S.Ct. 170, 36 L.Ed. 1079. See, also, Keystone Manganese & Iron Co. v. Martin, 132 U. S. 91, 10 S.Ct. 32, 33 L.Ed. 275; Leyhe v. McNamara, Tex.Com.App., 243 S.W. 1074, 1076.

In French Law

Certain acts of the Legislature or of the sovereign which have the force of law are called *"decrees"*; as the Berlin and Milan decrees.

In Scotch Law

A final judgment or sentence of court by which the question at issue between the parties is decided.

In General

Consent decree. One entered by consent of the parties; it is not properly a judicial sentence, but is in the nature of a solemn contract or agreement of the parties, made under the sanction of the court, and in effect an admission by them that the decree is a just determination of their rights upon the real facts of the case, if such facts had been proved. Allen v. Richardson, 9 Rich.Eq., S.C., 53; Schmidt v. Mining Co., 28 Or. 9, 40 P. 1014, 52 Am. St.Rep. 759; Hodgson v. Vroom, C.C.A.N.Y., 266 F. 267, 268; Barnes v. American Fertilizer Co., 144 Va. 692, 130 S.E. 902, 911. It binds only the consenting parties; Myllius v. Smith, 53 W.Va. 173, 44 S.E. 542; and is not binding upon the court; Ex parte Loung June, D.C.N.Y., 160 F. 251, 259. Parties thereto must be competent to contract. Consaer v. Wisniewski, 293 Ill.App. 529, 13 N.E.2d 93, 94.

Decree dative. In Scotch law. An order of a probate court appointing an administrator.

Decree nisi. A provisional decree, which will be made absolute on motion unless cause be shown against it. In English practice, it is the order made by the court for divorce, on satisfactory proof being given in support of a petition for dissolution of marriage; it remains imperfect for at least six months, (which period may be shortened by the court down to three,) and then, unless sufficient cause be shown, it is made absolute on motion, and the dissolution takes effect, subject to appeal. Wharton. It effects a conditional divorce, becoming absolute only upon the happening of a prescribed contingency. Grant v. Grant, 84 N.J.Eq. 81, 92 A. 791, 793.

Decree of constitution. In Scotch practice. A decree by which a debt is ascertained. Bell. In technical language, a decree which is requisite to found a title in the person of the creditor, whether that necessity arises from the death of the debtor or of the creditor. Id.

Decree of distribution. An instrument by which heirs receive property of a deceased; it is a final determination of the parties to a proceeding. Fischer v. Dolwig, 29 N.D. 561, 151 N.W. 431, 432; In re Bradford's Estate, 128 N.J.Eq. 372, 16 A.2d 268, 270.

Decree of forthcoming. In Scotch law. A decree made after an arrestment (*q. v.*) ordering the debt to be paid or the effects of the debtor to be delivered to the arresting creditor. Bell.

Decree of insolvency. One entered in a probate court, declaring the estate in question to be insolvent, that is, that the assets are not sufficient to pay the debts in full. Bush v. Coleman, 121 Ala. 548, 25 So. 569; Walker v. Newton, 85 Me. 458, 27 A. 347.

Decree of locality. In Scotch law. The decree of a teind court allocating stipend upon different heritors. It is equivalent to the apportionment of a tithe rent-charge.

Decree of modification. In Scotch law. A decree of the teind court modifying or fixing a stipend.

Decree of nullity. One entered in a suit for the annulment of a marriage, and adjudging the marriage to have been null and void *ab initio.* See Nullity.

Decree of registration. In Scotch law. A proceeding giving immediate execution to the creditor; similar to a warrant of attorney to confess judgment.

Decree pro confesso. One entered in a court of equity in favor of the complainant where the defendant has made no answer to the bill and its allegations are consequently taken "as confessed." Ohio Cent. R. Co. v. Central Trust Co., 133 U.S. 83, 10 S.Ct. 235, 33 L.Ed. 561; Equity Rules 16, 17, see Fed.Rules Civ.Proc. rules 6, 55, 28 U.S.C.A.; Freem. Judg. § 11; 1 Dan.Ch.Pr. 5th Am. ed. 517, n. It is merely an admission of the allegations of the bill well pleaded. Remington v. Barney, 35 R.I. 267, 86 A. 891, 892; Majure v. Johnson, 192 Miss. 810, 7 So.2d 545, 549.

Deficiency decree. In a mortgage foreclosure suit, a decree for the balance of the indebtedness after applying the proceeds of a sale of the mortgaged property to such indebtedness. Commercial Bank of Ocala v. First Nat. Bank, 80 Fla. 685, 87 So. 315, 316.

For "Execution of decree," see Execution of Judgment or Decree.

DECREET. In Scotch law. The final judgment or sentence of a court.

DECREET ABSOLVITOR. A decree dismissing a claim, or acquitting a defendant. 2 Kames, Eq. 367.

DECREET ARBITRAL. An award of arbitrators. 1 Kames, Eq. 312, 313; 2 Kames, Eq. 367.

DECREET COGNITIONIS CAUSÂ. When a creditor brings his action against the heir of his debtor in order to constitute the debt against him and attach the lands, and the heir appears and renounces the succession, the court then pronounces a decree *cognitionis causâ.* Bell.

DECREET CONDEMNATOR. One where the decision is in favor of the plaintiff. Ersk.Inst. 4, 3, 5.

DECREET OF VALUATION OF TEINDS. A sentence of the court of sessions, (who are now in the place of the commissioners for the valuation of teinds,) determining the extent and value of teinds. Bell.

DECREMENTUM MARIS. Lat. In old English law. Decrease of the sea; the receding of the sea from the land. Callis, Sewers, (53,) 65. See Reliction.

DECREPIT. This term designates a person who is disabled, incapable, or incompetent, either from physical or mental weakness or defects, whether produced by age or other causes, to such an extent as to render the individual comparatively helpless in a personal conflict with one possessed of ordinary health and strength. Hall v. State, 16 Tex.App. 11, 49 Am.Rep. 824; Lutz v. State, 147 Tex.Cr.R. 236, 179 S.W.2d 979, 980. The term includes a blind man. Lewing v. State, 135 Tex.Cr. R. 485, 121 S.W.2d 599, 600.

DECRETA. In the Roman law. Judicial sentences given by the emperor as supreme judge.

Decreta conciliorum non ligant reges nostros. Moore, 906. The decrees of councils bind not our kings.

DECRETAL. The granting or denying of remedy sought. State v. Reagan County Purchasing Co., Tex.Civ.App., 186 S.W.2d 128, 134.

DECRETAL ORDER. A preliminary order that determines no question upon the merits and establishes no right. Electrical Research Products v. Vitaphone Corporation, 20 Del.Ch. 417, 171 A. 738.

DECRETALES BONIFACII OCTAVI. A supplemental collection of the canon law, published by Boniface VIII. in 1298, called, also, "*Liber Sextus Decretalium,*" (Sixth Book of the Decretals.)

DECRETALES GREGORII NONI. The decretals of Gregory the Ninth. A collection of the laws of the church, published by order of Gregory IX. in 1227. It is composed of five books, subdivided into titles, and each title is divided into chapters. They are cited by using an X, (or *extra;*) thus "*Cap.* 8 X *de Regulis Juris,*" etc.

DECRETALS. In ecclesiastical law. Letters of the pope, written at the suit or instance of one or more persons, determining some point or question in ecclesiastical law, and possessing the force of law, within the Roman Catholic Church. The decretals form the second part of the body of canon law.

This is also the title of the second of the two great divisions of the canon law, the first being called the "*Decree,*" (decretum.)

DECRETO. In Spanish colonial law. An order emanating from some superior tribunal, promulgated in the name and by the authority of the sovereign, in relation to ecclesiastical matters. Schm.Civil Law, 93, note.

DECRETUM.

In the Civil Law

A species of imperial constitution, being a judgment or sentence given by the emperor upon hearing of a cause (*quod imperator cognoscens decrevit*). Inst. 1, 2, 6.

In Canon Law

An ecclesiastical law, in contradistinction to a secular law, (*lex.*) 1 Mackeld.Civil Law, p. 81, § 93, (Kaufmann's note.)

DECRETUM GRATIANI. Gratian's decree, or *decretum.* A collection of ecclesiastical law in three books or parts, made in the year 1151, by Gratian, a Benedictine monk of Bologna, being the oldest as well as the first in order of the collections which together form the body of the Roman canon law. 1 Bl.Comm. 82; 1 Reeve, Eng. Law, 67.

DECROWNING. The act of depriving of a crown.

DECRY. To cry down; to deprive of credit. "The king may at any time *decry* or cry down any coin of the kingdom, and make it no longer current." 1 Bl.Comm. 278.

DECURIO. Lat. A decurion. In the provincial administration of the Roman empire, the decurions were the chief men or official personages of the large towns. Taken as a body, the decurions of a city were charged with the entire control and administration of its internal affairs; having powers both magisterial and legislative. See 1 Spence, Eq.Jur. 54.

DEDBANA. In Saxon law. An actual homicide or manslaughter.

DEDI. (Lat. I have given.) A word used in deeds and other instruments of conveyance when such instruments were made in Latin, and anciently held to imply a warranty of title. Deakins v. Hollis, 7 Gill & J., Md., 315.

DEDI ET CONCESSI. I have given and granted. The operative words of conveyance in ancient charters of feoffment, and deeds of gift and grant; the English "*given and granted*" being still the most proper, though not the essential, words by which such conveyances are made. 2 Bl.Comm. 53, 316, 317; 1 Steph.Comm. 164, 177, 473, 474.

DEDICATE. To appropriate and set apart one's private property to some public use; as to make a private way public by acts evincing an intention to do so.

DEDICATION. In real property law. An appropriation of land to some public use, made by the owner, and accepted for such use by or on behalf of the public. Harris v. City of St. Helens, 72 Or. 377, 143 P. 941, 943, Ann.Cas.1916D, 1073. A deliberate appropriation of land by its owner for any general and public uses, reserving to himself no other rights than such as are compatible with the full exercise and enjoyment of the public uses to which the property has been devoted. Longley v. City of Worcester, 304 Mass. 580, 24 N.E.2d 533, 537; Consolidated Realty Co. v. Richmond Hotel & Building Co., 253 Ky. 463, 69 S.W.2d 985. See Alden Coal Co. v. Challis, 200 Ill. 222, 65 N.E. 665 (streets in company owned village); Du Pont v. Miller, 310 Ill. 140, 141 N.E. 423, 425 (artificial waterway); Western Union Telegraph Co. v. Georgia R. & Banking Co., D.C.Ga., 227 F. 276, 285 (right of way for telegraph lines); Manning v. House, 211 Ala. 570, 100 So. 772, 774; Mebane v. City of Wynne, 127 Ark. 364, 192 S.W. 221,

222. (Streets on platted land); Johnston v. Medina Improvement Club, 10 Wash.2d 44, 116 P.2d 272, 277, (park and recreation purposes).

By Adverse User

A dedication may arise from an adverse exclusive use by the public under a claim of right with the knowledge, actual or imputed, and acquiescence of the owner. Carpenter v. City of St. Joseph, 263 Mo. 705, 174 S.W. 53, 56; Dickinson v. Ruble, 211 Minn. 373, 1 N.W.2d 373, 374, 375; Clark v. State, 25 Ala.App. 467, 140 So. 178, 179.

Tax Revenues

Statute dedicating certain tax revenues to hospital to be remitted directly from Secretary of State made a "dedication" rather than an "appropriation." State ex rel. Porterie v. Charity Hospital of Louisiana at New Orleans, 182 La. 268, 161 So. 606.

Express Common-Law Dedication

An "express common-law dedication" is one where the intent is expressly manifested, such as by ordinary deeds, recorded plats not executed pursuant to statute or defectively certified so as not to constitute a statutory dedication. Board of Com'rs of Garfield County v. Anderson, 167 Okl. 253, 29 P.2d 75, 78.

Express or Implied

A dedication may be express, as where the intention to dedicate is expressly manifested by a deed or an explicit oral or written declaration of the owner, or some other explicit manifestation of his purpose to devote the land to the public use. An implied dedication may be shown by some act or course of conduct on the part of the owner from which a reasonable inference of intent may be drawn, or which is inconsistent with any other theory than that he intended a dedication. Hurley v. West St. Paul, 83 Minn. 401, 86 N.W. 427; Porter v. City of Stuttgart, 135 Ark. 48, 204 S.W. 607, 608; H. A. Hilmer Co. v. Behr, 264 Ill. 568, 106 N.E. 481, 486; Village of Benld v. Dorsey, 311 Ill. 192, 142 N.E. 563, 565; Illinois Cent. R. Co. v. Bennett, C.C.A.Miss., 296 F. 436, 437; City of Brownsville v. West, Tex.Civ.App., 149 S.W.2d 1034, 1037, 1038.

Common-Law or Statutory

A common-law dedication is one made as above described, and may be either express or implied. A statutory dedication is one made under and in conformity with the provisions of a statute regulating the subject, and is of course necessarily express. Poindexter v. Schaffner, Tex.Civ.App., 162 S.W. 22, 23; Kaufman v. City of Butte, 48 Mont. 400, 138 P. 770, 771; Neill v. City of Glendale, 106 Cal.App. 553, 289 P. 877, 879.

Where complete statutory dedication does not exist, sale of lots by reference to plat constitutes common-law "dedication." Byam v. Kansas City Public Service Co., 328 Mo. 813, 41 S.W.2d 945, 949.

In Copyright Law

The first publication of a work, without having secured a copyright, is a dedication of it to the public; that having been done, any one may republish it. Bartlett v. Crittenden, 5 McLean, 32, Fed.Cas.No.1,076; Deward & Rich v. Bristol Savings & Loan Corporation, C.C.A.Va., 120 F.2d 537, 540 (partial publication).

Where copyrighted lectures were not delivered to the general public, but only to paying audiences and classes, they were not abandoned or dedicated to the public. National Institute for Improvement of Memory v. Nutt, D.C. Conn., 28 F.2d 132, 134.

DEDICATION-DAY. The feast of dedication of churches, or rather the feast day of the saint and patron of a church, which was celebrated not only by the inhabitants of the place, but by those of all the neighboring villages, who usually came thither; and such assemblies were allowed as lawful. It was usual for the people to feast and to drink on those days. Cowell.

DEDIMUS ET CONCESSIMUS. (Lat. We have given and granted.) Words used by the king, or where there were more grantors than one, instead of *dedi et concessi.*

DEDIMUS POTESTATEM. (We have given power.) In English practice. A writ or commission issuing out of chancery, empowering the persons named therein to perform certain acts, as to administer oaths to defendants in chancery and take their answers, to administer oaths of office to justices of the peace, etc. 3 Bl.Comm. 447. It was anciently allowed for many purposes not now in use, as to make an attorney, to take the acknowledgment of a fine, etc.

In the United States, a commission to take testimony is sometimes termed a "*dedimus potestatem.*" Buddicum v. Kirk, 3 Cranch, 293, 2 L.Ed. 444; Sergeant's Lessee v. Biddle, 4 Wheat. 508, 4 L.Ed. 627.

DEDIMUS POTESTATEM DE ATTORNO FACIENDO. In old English practice. A writ, issued by royal authority, empowering an attorney to appear for a defendant. Prior to the statute of Westminster 2, a party could not appear in court by attorney without this writ.

DEDITION. The act of yielding up anything; surrender.

DEDITITII. In Roman law. Criminals who had been marked in the face or on the body with fire or an iron, so that the mark could not be erased, and subsequently manumitted. Calvin.

DEDUCTIBLE. That which may be taken away or subtracted; an item which may be subtracted from income for tax purposes, such as a deductible debt. In re Hermann's Estate, 349 Pa. 230, 36 A.2d 804, 806; a deductible expense. Pacific Southwest Realty Co. v. McColgan, 53 Cal.App. 2d 549, 128 P.2d 86, 87, or; a deductible loss. Helvering v. Gordon, C.C.A.4, 134 F.2d 685, 689; Bickerstaff v. Commissioner of Internal Revenue, C.C. A.Ga., 128 F.2d 366, 367.

DEDUCTION. That which is deducted; the part taken away; abatement; as a deduction from the yearly rent. Don Lee, Inc., v. United States, D.C. Cal., 42 F.Supp. 884, 885; Pittsburgh Brewing Co. v. Commissioner of Internal Revenue, C.C.A.3, 107 F.2d 155, 156.

In Probate Law

By "deduction" is understood a portion or thing which an heir has a right to take from the mass of the succession before any partition takes place. Civil Code La. art. 1358.

Taxation

As used in Internal Revenue Code, relating to tax on corporations, "deduction" refers to items which may be subtracted from a corporation's gross income in arriving at net income. McKesson & Robbins v. Walsh, 130 Conn. 460, 35 A.2d 865.

An amount refunded by corporation to federal government under Renegotiation Act as excess profits from war contracts is not a "deduction" from corporation's gross income subject to state taxation, but must be considered in determining corporation's true gross income. Southern Weaving Co. v. Query, 206 S.C. 307, 34 S.E.2d 51, 54.

Trial

Argument of counsel based on the evidence is not improper as unsworn testimony, but is warranted as a "deduction" from the testimony. Texas & P. R. Co. v. Smith, Tex.Civ.App., 115 S. W.2d 1238, 1242.

DEDUCTION FOR NEW. In marine insurance. An allowance or drawback credited to the insurers on the cost of repairing a vessel for damage arising from the perils of the sea insured against. This allowance is usually one-third, and is made on the theory that the parts restored with new materials are better, in that proportion than they were before the damage.

DEED. A conveyance of realty, a writing signed by grantor, whereby title to realty is transferred from one to another. National Fire Ins. Co. v. Patterson, 170 Okl. 593, 41 P.2d 645, 647; Mitchell v. Nicholson, 71 N.D. 521, 3 N.W.2d 83, 85, 139 A.L.R. 1175.

In order that an instrument may be operative as a "deed," it must pass a present interest, although it is not necessary that grantee take a present estate in property conveyed. Blair v. Blair, 111 Vt. 53, 10 A.2d 188, 189.

The term is also used as synonymous with "fact," "actuality," or "act of parties." Thus a thing "in deed" is one that has been really or expressly done; as opposed to "in law," which means that it is merely implied or presumed to have been done. Powell v. Powell, 196 Ga. 694, 27 S.E.2d 393, 396, 397.

At Common Law

At common law, a sealed instrument, containing a contract or covenant, delivered by the party to be bound thereby, and accepted by the party to whom the contract or covenant runs. Co. Litt. 171; 2 Bl.Comm. 295; Shepp. Touchst. 50. A writing containing a contract sealed and delivered. 3 Washb. Real Prop. 239; Sanders v. Riedinger, 30 App.Div. 277, 284, 51 N.Y.S. 937, 942. An instrument in writing, upon paper or parchment, between parties able to contract, subscribed, sealed, and delivered. 4 Kent, Comm. 452; Interstate R. Co. v. Roberts, 127 Va. 688, 105 S.E. 463, 464. There is authority, however, that signing is unnecessary to validity of deed. Bowling v. Wilkerson, D.C.Ky., 19 F.Supp. 584, 587.

A writing under seal by which lands, tenements, or hereditaments are conveyed for an estate not less than freehold. 2 Bl.Comm. 294.

A deed implies, at common law, a sealed instrument. 2 Bl.Comm. 295; Rondot v. Rogers Tp., 39 C.C.A. 462, 99 F. 202, 209; Strain v. Fitzgerald, 128 N.C. 396, 38 S.E. 929, 930; Williams v. State, 25 Fla. 734, 6 So. 831, 832, 6 L.R.A. 821; *e. g.*, a bond is a deed for the reason that it is sealed by the obligor. In re Contest of Election of Burns, 315 Pa. 23, 171 A. 888, 889. But the term is also applied to similar instruments, not under seal, executed in jurisdictions in which the use of seals is unknown (see Steigenberger v. Carr, 3 M. & G., 191, 199, 42 ECL 107, 133 Reprint. 1111), or in which seals have been rendered unnecessary by statute. See Henderson v. Howard, 147 Ga. 371, 94 S.E. 251; Gibbs v. McGuire, 70 Miss. 646, 12 So. 829.

Modern Rule

A written instrument, signed, sealed, and delivered, by which one person conveys land, tenements, or hereditaments to another. This is its ordinary modern meaning, at least in those jurisdictions which adhere to the common-law rule making a seal essential to the validity and operative effect of a deed of conveyance. McMee v Henry, 163 Ky. 729, 174 S.W. 746, 747; Dunham v. Marsh, 52 N.J.Eq. 256, 30 A. 473, 474; Hood v. Fletcher, 31 Ariz. 456, 254 P. 223, 224.

The term may include a mortgage of real estate. Lockridge v. McCommon, 90 Tex. 234, 38 S.W. 33, 35 (citing Hellman v. Howard, 44 Cal. 110); Daly v. Minnesota Loan & Investment Co., 43 Minn. 517, 45 N.W. 1100, 1101; Morgan v. Wickliffe, 115 Ky. 226, 72 S.W. 1122. But, contra, see Eaton v. White, 18 Wis. 517, 519; National Bank of Columbus v. Tennessee Coal, Iron & Railroad Co., 62 Ohio St. 564, 57 N.E. 450. Similarly a lease for years under seal may be a deed. Hutchinson v. Bramhall, 42 N.J.Eq. 372, 7 A. 873, 875. And a lease exceeding twenty-one years is held to be within the term. St. Vincent's Roman Catholic Congregation of Plymouth v. Kingston Coal Co., 221 Pa. 349, 70 A. 838, 839. But a stipulation for a deed prohibiting drilling for oil or gas was held not to include a lease. Test Oil Co. v. La Tourette, 19 Okl. 214, 91 P. 1025, 1029.

The essential difference between a "deed" and a "will" is that the former passes a present interest and the latter passes no interest until after the death of the maker. Willis v. Fiveash, Tex.Civ.App., 297 S.W. 509, 510; Harber v. Harber, 152 Ga. 98, 108 S.E. 526; Henderson v. Henderson, 210 Ala. 73, 97 So. 353, 372; Bowdoin College v. Merritt, C.C.Cal., 75 F. 480, 483. A will is "an instrument by which a person makes a disposition of his property to take effect after his decease, which is in its own nature ambulatory and revocable during his life. It is this ambulatory quality which forms the characteristic of wills; for, though a disposition by deed may postpone the possession or enjoyment, or even the vesting, until the death of the disposing party, yet the postponement is in such case produced by the express terms, and does not result from the nature of the instrument." In re Hall's Estate, 149 Cal. 143, 84 P. 839, 840; Robb v. Washington & Jefferson College, 185 N.Y. 485, 78 N.E. 359, 361 (quoting and adopting definition in Jarman, Wills, p. 17). The main test, however, whether a writing is a will or deed, is the animus testandi. Belgrade v. Carter, Tex.Civ.App., 146 S.W. 964, 965; McLain v. Garrison, 39 Tex.Civ.App. 431, 88 S.W. 484, 89 S.W. 284 (citing Gillham v. Mustin, 42 Ala. 366; Trawick v. Davis, 85 Ala. 345, 5 So. 83); Ecklar's Adm'r v. Robinson, 96 S.W. 845, 846, 29 Ky.Law Rep. 1038. Harber v. Harber, 152 Ga. 98, 108 S.E. 520. "Deeds" are irrevocable and take effect by delivery, while "wills" are always revocable during testamentary capacity and take effect only after testator's death. Self v. Self, 212 Ala. 512, 103 So. 591, 592. If a document cannot be revoked or impaired by the grantor, it is a "deed," but if the grantor recites an unqualified power of revocation, it is a "will." Craft v. Moon, 201 Ala. 11, 75 So. 302, 303. An instrument purporting to convey title to lands on its delivery is a deed and not a will, though possession be deferred until the grantor's death. Lovenskoild v. Casas, Tex.Civ.App., 196 S.W. 629, 631.

A deed is distinguished from a contract in that a deed is a mere transfer of title to realty, and is the act of but one of the parties, made pursuant to a previous contract either in parol or in writing. Collins v. Lyon, Inc., 181 Va. 230, 24 S.E.2d 572, 579. Accordingly; want of consideration of itself will not warrant setting aside a deed, though want of consideration would be good defense to an executory contract. Lawson v. Boo, 227 Iowa 100, 287 N.W. 282, 284. However, a deed is a contract, for the purpose of reformation in equity to make it truly speak the legally ascertained intention of the parties. Sawyer Coal & Ice Co. v. Kinnett-Odom Co., 192 Ga. 166, 14 S.E.2d 879, 883.

Deed for a nominal sum. In effect the same as a deed of gift. Bertelsen v. Bertelson, 49 Cal.App. 2d 479, 122 P.2d 130, 133.

Deed in fee. A deed conveying the title to land in fee simple with the usual covenants. Rudd v. Savelli, 44 Ark. 152; Moody v. Spokane & U. H. St. Ry. Co., 5 Wash. 699, 32 P. 751.

Deed indented, or indenture. In conveyancing. A deed executed or purporting to be executed in parts, between two or more parties, and distinguished by having the edge of the paper or parchment on which it is written indented or cut at the top in a particular manner. This was formerly done at the top or side, in a line resembling the teeth of a saw; a formality derived from the ancient practice of dividing chirographs; but the cutting is now made either in a waving line, or more commonly by notching or nicking the paper at the edge. 2 Bl.Comm. 295, 296; Litt. § 370; Smith, Cont. 12.

Deed of covenant. Covenants are sometimes entered into by a separate deed, for title, or for the indemnity of a purchaser or mortgagee, or for the production of title-deeds. A covenant with a penalty is sometimes taken for the payment of a debt, instead of a bond with a condition, but the legal remedy is the same in either case.

Deed of gift. A deed executed and delivered without consideration.

Thus a conveyance to church mission board for which board agreed to educate a relative of grantors for the ministry should grantors die before his education was completed, was not a strict "deed of gift". Forbes v. Board of Missions of M. E. Church, South, 17 Cal.2d 332, 110 P.2d 3, 7.

Deed of release. One releasing property from the incumbrance of a mortgage or similar pledge upon payment or performance of the conditions; more specifically, where a deed of trust to one or more trustees has been executed, pledging real property for the payment of a debt or the performance of other conditions, substantially as in the case of a mortgage, a deed of release is the conveyance executed by the trustees, after payment or performance, for the purpose of divesting themselves of the legal title and revesting it in the original owner. See Swain v. McMillan, 30 Mont. 433, 76 Pac. 943.

Deed of separation. An instrument by which, through the medium of some third person acting as trustee, provision is made by a husband for separation from his wife and for her separate maintenance. Whitney v. Whitney, 15 Misc. 72, 36 N.Y.S. 891, 892.

Deed of settlement. A deed formerly used in England for the formation of joint stock companies constituting certain persons trustees of the partnership property and containing regulations for the management of its private affairs. They are now regulated by articles of association.

Deed of trust. An instrument in use in many states, taking the place and serving the uses of a common-law mortgage, by which the legal title to real property is placed in one or more trustees, to secure the repayment of a sum of money or the performance of other conditions. Bank v. Pierce, 144 Cal. 434, 77 P. 1012; In re Sherman, D.C.Va., 12 F.Supp. 297, 298, 299. Though differing in form from mortgage, it is essentially a security. Bank of America Nat. Trust & Savings Ass'n v. Bank of Amador County, 135 Cal.App. 714, 28 P.2d 86, 88. In re Title Guaranty Trust Co., Mo.App., 113 S.W.2d 1053, 1057. See Trust Deed.

Deed poll. A deed which is made by one party only. See Hawkins v. Corbit, 83 Okl. 275, 201 P. 649, 653. A deed in which only the party making it executes it or binds himself by it as a deed. 3 Washb. R. P. 311. It was originally so called because the edge of the paper or parchment was *polled* or cut in a straight line, wherein it was distinguished from a deed indented or indenture. As to a special use of this term in Pennsylvania in colonial times, see Herron v. Dater, 120 U.S. 464, 7 S.Ct. 620, 624, 30 L.Ed. 748 (citing Evans v. Patterson, 71 U.S. 224, 4 Wall. 224, 18 L.Ed. 393).

Deed to lead uses. A deed made before a fine or common recovery, to show the object thereof.

As to "execution of deed," see Execution of Instrument.

Gratuitous deed. One made without consideration. 2 Steph.Com. 47. As to "Quitclaim" deed, "Tax" deed, "Trust" deed, and "Warranty" deed, see those titles.

DEED, ESTOPPEL BY. Such as arises from the provisions of a deed. Erickson v. Wiper, 33 N.D. 193, 157 N.W. 592, 598; Green v. Clark, 13 Vt. 158; Reinhard v. Virginia Lead Min. Co., 107 Mo. 616, 18 S.W. 17, 28 Am.St.Rep. 441.

A preclusion against the competent parties to a valid sealed contract and their privies to deny its force and effect by any evidence of inferior solemnity. Hart v. Anaconda Copper Mining Co., 69 Mont. 354, 222 P. 419, 421.

Such an estoppel occurs where a party has executed a deed, that is, a writing under seal (as a bond) reciting a certain fact, and is thereby precluded from afterwards denying, in any action brought upon that instrument, the fact so recited. Steph.Pl. 197. A man shall always be *estopped* by his own deed, or not permitted to aver or prove anything in contradiction to what he has once so solemnly and deliberately avowed. 2 Bl.Comm. 295; Plowd. 434; Hudson v. Winslow Tp., 35 N.J.Law, 441; Taggart v. Risley, 4 Or. 242; Appeal of Waters, 35 Pa. 526, 78 Am. Dec. 354.

A warranty deed by one having only a contingent remainder passes title, by way of "estoppel" to grantee, as soon as remainder vests by happening of contingency. Thames v. Goode, 217 N.C. 639, 9 S.E.2d 485, 488.

"Estoppel by deed" is a bar precluding party from denying truth of his deed. Talley v. Howsley, Tex.Civ.App., 170 S.W.2d 240, 243. It is limited to an action founded on the deed itself. Hughes v. Cobb, 195 Ga. 213, 23 S.E.2d 701, 715. It applies to the maker of the deed, and does not ordinarily apply to the grantee. Hughes v. Cobb, 195 Ga. 213, 23 S.E.2d 701, 715. It arises only when suit is on the deed or concerning a right arising out of the deed and between parties or privies to the deed. Robert v. O'Connell, 269 Mass. 532, 169 N.E. 487, 488. It arises only where there is express representation as to ownership, title, or interest in question, or where there are express warranties thereto. Petition of Testan, 156 Misc. 449, 281 N.Y.S. 96. It cannot be invoked by one through whose imposition a statement was inserted in the deed. Capitol Nat. Bank & Trust Co. v. David B. Roberts, Inc., 129 Conn. 194, 27 A.2d 116, 119, 141 A.L.R. 1179. It precludes a party thereto and his privies as against other party and his privies. Sammons v. Brunson, Tex.Civ.App., 25 S.W.2d 685, 688.

A distinct and precise assertion or admission of fact is necessary. Cook v. Farley, 195 Miss. 638, 15 So.2d 352, 357.

Inducement to change course to one's disadvantage is essential. Funderburk v. Magnolia Sugar Co-op., La.App., 8 So.2d 374, 377.

The effect of doctrine is same as if in deed itself, there had been inserted express provision that it conveyed not only all title then possessed but all that might thereafter be acquired. Meyers v. American Oil Co., 192 Miss. 180, 5 So.2d 218, 220.

DEEM. To hold; consider; adjudge; condemn; determine; treat as if; construe. Douglas v. Edwards, C.C.A.N.Y., 298 F. 229, 237; In re Schmidt's Estate, 134 Wash. 525, 236 P. 274, 275; In re Green's Estate, 99 Misc. 582, 164 N.Y.S. 1063, 1083; Harder v. Irwin, D.C.N.Y., 285 F. 402, 404; First Nat. Bank v. Dodd, 118 Or. 1, 245 P. 503, 504. But see Kleppe v. Odin Tp., McHenry County, 40 N.D. 595, 169 N.W. 313, 314, which gives "deemed" the force of only a "disputable presumption," or of prima facie evidence. When, by statute, certain acts are "deemed" to be a crime of a particular nature, they are such crime, and not a semblance of it, nor a mere fanciful approximation to or designation of the offense. Com. v. Pratt, 132 Mass. 247; Commonwealth v. Brue, 284 Pa. 294, 131 A. 367, 368.

DEEMSTERS. Judges in the Isle of Man, who decide all controversies without process, writings, or any charges. These judges are chosen by the people, and are said by Spelman to be two in number. Spelman.

DEER-FALD. A park or fold for deer.

DEER-HAYES. Engines or great nets made of cord to catch deer. 19 Hen. VIII, c. 11.

DEFACE. To mar or destroy the face (that is, the physical appearance of written or inscribed characters as expressive of a definite meaning) of a written instrument, signature, inscription, etc., by obliteration, erasure, cancellation, or superinscription, so as to render it illegible or unrecognizable. Linney v. State, 6 Tex. 1, 55 Am.Dec. 756. See Cancel. In re Parsons' Will, 195 N.Y.S. 742, 745, 119 Misc. 26. Also used in respect of injury to monument, buildings and other structures. Saffell v. State, 113 Ark. 97, 167 S.W. 483. So, to deface the flag carries the meaning of dishonor, which imputes a lively sense of shaming or an equivalent acquiescent callousness. State v. Schlueter, 127 N.J.L. 496, 23 A.2d 249, 251.

DE FACTO. In fact; actually; indeed; in reality. Ridout v. State, 161 Tenn. 248, 30 S.W.2d 255, 257, 71 A.L.R. 830. Thus, an office, position or status existing under a claim or color of right such as a deputy county clerk. Heron v. Gaylor, 49 N.M. 62, 157 P.2d 239, 241; deputy clerk of court. State v. Brandon, 186 S.C. 448, 197 S.E. 113, 115; corporate office. In re Hillmark Associates, D.C.N.Y., 47 F.Supp. 605, 606; corporation, Municipal Bond & Mortgage Corporation v. Bishop's Harbor Drainage Dist., 133 Fla. 430, 182 So. 794, 797; Ebeling v. Independent Rural Telephone Co., 187 Minn. 604, 246 N.W. 373; court, Marckel Co. v. Zitzow, 218 Minn. 305, 15 N.W.2d 777, 778; depositary, School Dist. No. 1, Itasco County, v. Aiton, 173 Minn. 428, 217 N.W. 496, 499; deputy sheriff, Malone v. Howell, 140 Fla. 693, 192 So. 224, 227; fire district commissioner, Petition of Board of Fire Com'rs of Columbia-Litchfield Fire Dist., Sup., 29 N.Y.S.2d 605, 619; grand jury, McDonald v. Colden, 181 Misc. 407, 41 N.Y.S.2d 323, 327; guardian, State ex rel. Symons v. East Chicago State Bank, 106 Ind.App. 4, 17 N.E.2d 491, 494; judge, Annoni v. Blas Nadal's Heirs, C.C.A.Puerto Rico, 94 F.2d 513, 515; officer, Eaker v. Common School Dist. No. 73 of Butler County, Mo.App., 62 S.W.2d 778, 783; police officer, People ex rel. Mitchell v. Armspach, 314 Ill.App. 573, 41 N.E.2d 781; trustee, In re Wohl's Estate, 36 N.Y.S.2d 926, 930.

DE FACTO GOVERNMENT. One that maintains itself by a display of force against the will of the rightful legal government and is successful, at least temporarily, in overturning the institutions of the rightful legal government by setting up its own in lieu thereof. Wortham v. Walker, 133 Tex. 255, 128 S.W.2d 1138, 1145.

DEFALCATION. The act of a defaulter; misappropriation of trust funds or money held in any fiduciary capacity; failure to properly account for such funds. Usually spoken of officers of corporations or public officials. In re Butts, D.C.N.Y., 120 F. 970; Crawford v. Burke, 201 Ill. 581, 66 N.E. 833.

Also set-off. The diminution of a debt or claim by deducting from it a smaller claim held by the debtor or payor. Iron Works v. Cuppey, 41 Iowa, 104; Houk v. Foley, 2 Pen. & W., Pa., 250; McDonald v. Lee, 12 La. 435.

Colloquially, perhaps, the word "defalcation" ordinarily implies some moral dereliction. As used in the Bankruptcy Act, it may demand some portion of misconduct, but it is not synonymous with "embezzlement." The act of a receiver in a mortgage foreclosure suit in withdrawing and spending an amount allowed him by an order passing his intermediate account without waiting for the time for appeal to expire or consulting plaintiff as to whether it intended to appeal, is a "defalcation". Central Hanover Bank & Trust Co. v. Herbst, C.C.A.N.Y., 93 F.2d 510, 511, 512, 114 A.L.R. 769.

DEFALK. To set off one claim against another; to deduct a debt due to one from a debt which one owes. Johnson v. Signal Co., 57 N.J.Eq. 79, 40 A. 193; Burris v. Boone, 4 Boyce, Del., 148, 86 A. 730. This verb corresponds only to the second meaning of "defalcation" as given above; a public officer or trustee who misappropriates or embezzles funds in his hands is not said to "defalk."

DEFAMACAST. Defamation by broadcast. American Broadcasting-Paramount Theatres, Inc. v. Simpson, 126 S.E.2d 873, 879, 106 Ga.App. 230.

DEFAMATION. The taking from one's reputation. The offense of injuring a person's character, fame, or reputation by false and malicious statements. The term seems to include both libel and slander. In general, see Shaw Cleaners & Dyers v. Des Moines Dress Club, 215 Iowa, 1130, 245 N.W. 231, 86 A.L.R. 839; Snavely v. Booth, 6 W. W.Harr. 378, 176 A. 649; Washer v. Bank of America Nat. Trust & Savings Ass'n, 128 P.2d 799. Libel. Seested v. Post Printing & Publishing Co., 326 Mo. 559, 31 S.W.2d 1045, 1052. Slander. Connelly v. McKay, 176 Misc. 685, 28 N.Y.S.2d 327, 329.

The distinction between "criticism" and "defamation" is that criticism deals only with such things as invite public attention or call for public comment, and does not follow a man into his private life, or pry into his domestic concerns, and it never attacks the individual, but only his work. Schwimmer v. Commercial Newspaper Co., 131 Misc. 552, 228 N.Y.S. 220, 221.

The fundamental difference between a right to "privacy" and a right to freedom from "defamation" is that the former directly concerns one's own peace of mind whereas the latter concerns primarily one's reputation. Themo v. New England Newspaper Pub. Co., 306 Mass. 54, 27 N.E.2d 753, 755.

DEFAMATORY. Calumnious; containing defamation; injurious to reputation; libelous; slanderous; words which produce any perceptible injury to the reputation of another. Sheridan v. Davies, 139 Kan. 256, 31 P.2d 51, 54.

DEFAMATORY PER QUOD. In respect of words: Those which require an allegation of facts, aside from the words contained in the article, by way of innuendo, to show wherein the words used libel the plaintiff, in order to state a cause of action in a complaint. Rowan v. Gazette Printing Co., 74 Mont. 326, 239 P. 1035, 1037.

DEFAMATORY PER SE. In respect of words: Those which by themselves, and as such, without reference to extrinsic proof, injure the reputation of the person to whom they are applied. Manley v. Harer, 73 Mont. 253, 235 P. 757, 758; Conrad v. Allis-Chalmers Mfg. Co., 228 Mo.App. 817, 73 S. W.2d 438, 446.

DEFAMES. L. Fr. Infamous. Britt. c. 15.

DEFAULT. By its derivation, a failure. Meadows v. Continental Assur. Co., C.C.A.Tex., 89 F. 2d 256. An omission of that which ought to be done. Town of Milton v. Bruso, 111 Vt. 82, 10 A. 2d 203, 205. Specifically, the omission or failure to perform a legal duty. Easterwood v. Willingham, Tex.Civ.App., 47 S.W.2d 393, 395; to observe a promise or discharge an obligation, Bradbury v. Thomas, 27 P.2d 402, 135 Cal.App. 435; or to perform an agreement, Eastman v. Morgan, D.C.N.Y., 43 F.Supp. 637, 641. The term also embraces the idea of dishonesty, In re State, 210 Wis. 9, 245 N. W. 844, 845, and of wrongful act, Greco v. S. S. Kresge Co., 277 N.Y. 26, 12 N.E.2d 557, 562, 115 A.L.R. 1020; or an act or omission discreditable to one's profession, Hilkert v. Canning, 58 Ariz. 290, 119 P.2d 233, 236.

In Practice

Omission; neglect or failure of any party to take step required of him in progress of cause. Indiana State Board of Medical Registration and Examination v. Pickard, 93 Ind.App. 171, 177 N.E. 870, 872. When a defendant in an action at law omits to plead within the time allowed him for that purpose, or fails to appear on the trial, he is said to *make default*, McCabe v. Tom, 35 Ohio App. 73, 171 N.E. 868, 869, and the judgment entered in the former case is technically called a "judgment by default." 3 Bl.Comm. 396; 1 Tidd, Pr. 562.

A "default" in an action at law is somewhat similar to the entry of a decree in equity that the bill be taken for confessed, neither being a final disposition. Felton v. Felton, 128 Conn. 564, 196 A. 791, 793.

In General

Default of issue. Failure to have living children or descendants at a given time or fixed point. George v. Morgan, 16 Pa. 106; In re Van Cleef, 92 Misc. 689, 157 N.Y.S. 549, 551.

Defaulter. One who makes default. One who misappropriates money held by him in an official or fiduciary character, or fails to account for such money.

Judgment by default. See Judgment.

DEFEASANCE. An instrument which defeats the force or operation of some other deed or estate. That which is in the same deed is called a "condition"; and that which is in another deed is a "defeasance." Com. Dig. "Defeasance." Beindorf v. Thorpe, 90 Okl. 191, 203 P. 475, 477; In re A. Roth Co., C.C.A.Ill., 118 F.2d 156, 158.

A "defeasance" is a collateral deed made at the same time as a feoffment or other conveyance, containing certain conditions upon the performance of which the estate then created may be defeated or totally undone. Bach v. First Nat. Bank, 99 Ind.App. 590, 193 N.E. 696, 697.

In Conveyancing

A collateral deed made at the same time with a feoffment or other conveyance, containing certain conditions, upon the performance of which the estate then created may be *defeated* or totally undone. 2 Bl.Comm. 327; Co. Litt. 236, 237.

An instrument accompanying a bond, recognizance, or judgment, containing a condition which, when performed, *defeats* or undoes it. 2 Bl. Comm. 342; Miller v. Quick, 158 Mo. 495, 59 S.W. 955.

DEFEASIBLE. Subject to be defeated, annulled, revoked, or undone upon the happening of a future event or the performance of a condition subsequent, or by a conditional limitation. Usually spoken of estates and interests in land. For instance, a mortgagee's estate is defeasible (liable to be defeated) by the mortgagor's equity of redemption. Penick v. Atkinson, 139 Ga. 649, 77 S.E. 1055, 1057, 46 L.R.A.,N.S., 284; Murphy v. Murphy, 182 Ky. 731, 207 S.W. 491, 493.

DEFEASIBLE FEE. An estate in fee that is liable to be defeated by some future contingency; *e. g.*, a vested remainder which might be defeated by the death of the remainderman before the time fixed for the taking effect of the devise. Giltner's Trustee v. Talbott, 253 Ky. 474, 69 S.W.2d 981; Daly v. Pate, 210 N.C. 222, 186 S.E. 348, 349.

DEFEASIBLE TITLE. One that is liable to be annulled or made void, but not one that is already void or an absolute nullity. Elder v. Schumacher, 18 Colo. 433, 33 P. 175.

DEFEASIVE. Describes counterclaim which, if it prevails, will defeat right of plaintiffs to recover. Hayden v. Collins, 90 Utah, 238, 63 P.2d 223, 225.

DEFEAT. To prevent, frustrate, or circumvent; as in the phrase "hinder, delay, or defeat creditors." Coleman v. Walker, 3 Metc., Ky., 65, 77 Am.Dec. 163; Reuff-Griffin Decorating Co. v. Wilkes, 191 S.W. 443, 446, 173 Ky. 566.

To overcome or prevail against in any contest; as in speaking of the "defeated party" in an action at law. Wood v. Bailey, 21 Wall. 642, 22 L.Ed. 689. Or "defeated candidate" in an election. Norcop v. Jordan, 216 Cal. 764, 17 P.2d 123, 124.

To annul, undo, or terminate; as, a title or estate. See Defeasible.

DEFECT. The want or absence of some legal requisite; deficiency; imperfection; insufficiency. Sappenfield v. National Zinc Co., 94 Kan. 22, 145 P. 862, 863; Galloway v. City of Winchester, 299 Ky. 87, 184 S.W.2d 890, 892, 893. The want or absence of something necessary for completeness or perfection; a lack or absence of something essential to completeness; a deficiency in something essential to the proper use for the purpose for which a thing is to be used. Roberts v. Rogers, 129 Neb. 298, 261 N.W. 354; Terrell v. City of Orangeburg, 176 S.C. 518, 180 S.E. 670.

Thus, a bamboo vaulting pole which was not straight and was unbalanced had a "defect." McCormick v. Lowe & Campbell Athletic Goods Co., 235 Mo.App. 612, 144 S.W. 2d 866, 876.

DEFECT IN HIGHWAY OR STREET. Ordinarily anything in the condition or state of highway or street that renders it unreasonably safe for travel. Payne v. State Highway Commission, 136 Kan. 561, 16 P.2d 509, 511. Thus courts have held as highway or street defects corrugations, Cheney v. State Highway Commission, 142 Kan. 149, 45 P.2d 864, 866; spike in cross walk, Fay v. City of Green Bay, 240 Wis. 36, 1 N.W.2d 767, 768, a hollow, Adams v. Town of Bolton, 297 Mass. 459, 9 N.E.2d 562, 111 A.L.R. 856, and anything that may reasonably be expected to interfere with safe use of sidewalk by pedestrian. City of Birmingham v. Wood, 240 Ala. 138, 197 So. 885, 887.

DEFECT IN MACHINERY. Under Code 1907, § 3910, subd. 1, making the master liable for injury from defects in the condition of works or machinery, it is essential that there be inherent condition of a permanent nature which unfits machine for its uses, some weakness of construction with reference to the proposed uses, some misplacement of parts, or the absence of some part, some innate abnormal quality rendering its use dangerous, or some obstacle to the use or the way of use which is part of the condition of the machinery itself. Caldwell-Watson Foundry & Machine Co. v. Watson, 183 Ala. 326, 62 So. 859, 862.

DEFECT OF FORM. An imperfection in the style, manner, arrangement, or non-essential parts of a legal instrument, plea, indictment, etc., as distinguished from a "defect of substance." See *infra*.

DEFECT OF PARTIES. In pleading and practice. Insufficiency of the parties before a court in any given proceeding to give it jurisdiction and authority to decide the controversy, arising from the omission or failure to join plaintiffs or defendants who should have been brought in; never applied to a superfluity of parties or the improper addition of plaintiffs or defendants. Porter Const. Co. v. Berry, 136 Or. 80, 298 P. 179, 182; Salisbury v. Berry Motor Co., 122 Neb. 605, 241 N.W. 86, 87; De Pass v. City of Spartanburg, 190 S.C. 22, 1 S.E.2d 904, 908. It is not synonymous with "misjoinder of parties". Okmulgee Supply Co. v. Rotman, 144 Okl. 293, 291 P. 1, 2.

DEFECT OF SUBSTANCE. An imperfection in the body or substantive part of a legal instrument, plea, indictment, etc., consisting in the omission of something which is essential to be set forth. Sweeney v. Greenwood Index-Journal Co., D.C.S.C., 37 F.Supp. 484, 487.

DEFECTIVE. Lacking in some particular which is essential to the completeness, legal sufficiency, or security of the object spoken of; as a "defective" highway or bridge (Mennito v. Town of Wayland, Sup., 56 N.Y.S.2d 654, 664; Warren County v. Battle, 48 Ga.App. 240, 172 S.E. 673, 674); car coupler (McAllister v. St. Louis Merchants' Bridge Terminal Ry. Co., 324 Mo. 1005, 25 S.W.2d 791, 795); machinery (Riccio v. Town of Plainville, 106 Conn. 61, 136 A. 872, 873; Chaney v. Village of Riverton, 104 Neb. 189, 177 N.W. 845, 846, 10 A.L.R. 244; Bryan v. City of West Palm Beach, 75 Fla. 19, 77 So. 627); writ or recognizance (State v. Lavalley, 9 Mo. 836; McArthur v. Boynton, 19 Colo.App. 234, 74 P. 542); or title (Copertini v. Oppermann, 76 Cal. 181, 18 P. 256); service of process or return of service (Tioga Coal

Corporation v. Silman, 125 W.Va. 58, 22 S.E.2d 873, 876; State ex rel. Briggs v. Barns, 121 Fla. 857, 164 So. 539, 542).

DEFECTIVE OR INSUFFICIENT SPECIFICATIONS BY PATENTEE. Any failure either to describe or to claim the complete invention upon which the application for patent is founded. Robert v. Krementz, C.C.A.N.J., 243 F. 877, 881.

DEFECTIVE TITLE. With respect to negotiable paper within Negotiable Instruments Law, the title of a person who obtains instrument or any signature thereto by fraud, duress, or force and fear, or other unlawful means, or for an illegal consideration, or when he negotiates it in breach of faith or under such circumstances as amount to fraud. Stevens v. Pierce, 79 Okl. 290, 193 P. 417, 18 A.L.R. 7; (fraud) German-American Nat. Bank v. Kelley, 183 Iowa, 269, 166 N.W. 1053; Commercial Security Co. v. Jack, 29 N.D. 67, 150 N.W. 460, 461.

DEFECTUS. Lat. Defect; default; want; imperfection; disqualification.

Challenge Propter Defectum

A challenge to a juror on account of some legal disqualification, such as infancy, etc. See Challenge.

Defectus Sanguinis

Failure of the blood, *i. e.*, failure or want of issue.

DEFEND. To prohibit or forbid. To deny. To contest and endeavor to defeat a claim or demand made against one in a court of justice. Boehmer v. Irrigation Dist., 117 Cal. 19, 48 P. 908. To oppose, repel, or resist.

To protect, to shield, to make a stand for, or uphold by force or argument, vindicate, to maintain or keep secure, to guaranty, to agree to indemnify. Powell v. U. S., D.C.Va., 60 F.Supp. 433, 439.

Although a contract between mortgagee and mortgagor's creditor who purchased mortgaged automobile that creditor will "defend" mortgagee against all suits, etc., was held to be contract to defend litigation, not to indemnify. Hall v. Cannon, 90 Colo. 465, 9 P.2d 1057.

DEFENDANT. The person defending or denying; the party against whom relief or recovery is sought in an action or suit. Graham Bros. Aktiebolag v. St. Paul Fire & Marine Ins. Co., 126 Misc. 32, 212 N.Y.S. 380, 381; Atlantic Mut. Insurance Co. v. Alexandre, D.C.N.Y., 16 F. 279, 281; Siekmann v. Kern, 136 La. 1068, 68 So. 128. See, also, Ferguson v. Montgomery, 148 Ark. 83, 229 S.W. 30, 36 (election contest); Boyd v. Lambert, 58 Okl. 497, 160 P. 586, 587 (injunction bond); Alexander v. United States, C.C.A.Mo., 95 F.2d 873, 879 (joinder); Welty v. Schmutte, 128 Neb. 415, 258 N.W. 873 (mortgage foreclosure); Loft, Inc. v. Corn Products Refining Co., C.C.A.Ind., 103 F.2d 1, 5 (anti-trust prosecution).

Thus, railroads, on appeal by city to state district court from order of Minnesota Railroad and Warehouse Commission requiring grade separation, were held defendants entitled to remove cause to federal court. In re Chicago, M. St. P. & P. R. Co., D.C.Minn., 50 F.2d 430, 434.

In common usage, this term is applied to the party put upon his defense, or summoned to answer a charge or complaint, in any species of action, civil or criminal, at law or in equity. Strictly, however, it does not apply to the person against whom a real action is brought, for in that proceeding the technical usage is to call the parties respectively the "demandant" and the "tenant."

Defendant in error. The distinctive term appropriate to the party against whom a writ of error is sued out.

Principal defendant. One who has an interest in the controversy presented by the bill, and whose presence is requisite to the complete and partial adjudication of the controversy. Bird v. Sleppy, 265 Pa. 295, 108 A. 618, 619.

DEFENDARE. To answer for; to be responsible for. Medley.

DEFENDEMUS. Lat. A word used in grants and donations, which binds the donor and his heirs to defend the donee, if any one go about to lay any incumbrance on the thing given other than what is contained in the deed of donation. Bract. 1. 2, c. 16.

DEFENDER. (Fr.) To deny; to defend; to conduct a suit for a defendant; to forbid; to prevent; to protect.

In Scotch and canon law. A defendant.

DEFENDER OF THE FAITH. A peculiar title belonging to the sovereign of England, as that of "Catholic" to the king of Spain, and that of "Most Christian" to the king of France. These titles were originally given by the popes of Rome; and that of *Defensor Fidei* was first conferred by Pope Leo X. on King Henry VIII., as a reward for writing against Martin Luther; and the bull for it bears date *quinto Idus Octob.*, 1521. Enc. Lond.

DEFENDERE SE PER CORPUS SUUM. To offer duel or combat as a legal trial and appeal. Abolished by 59 Geo. III. § 46. See Battel.

DEFENDERE UNICA MANU. To wage law; a denial of an accusation upon oath. See Wager of Law.

DEFENDIT VIM ET INJURIAM. He defends the force and injury. Fleta, lib. 5, c. 39, § 1.

DEFENDOUR. L. Fr. A defender or defendant; the party accused in an appeal. Britt. c. 22.

DEFENERATION. The act of lending money on usury.

DEFENSA. In old English law. A park or place fenced in for deer, and defended as a property and peculiar for that use and service. Cowell.

DEFENSE. That which is offered and alleged by the party proceeded against in an action or suit, as a reason in law or fact why the plaintiff should not recover or establish what he seeks; what is put forward to diminish plaintiff's cause of action or defeat recovery. Ætna Life Ins. Co. v. Braukman, C.C.A.Colo., 70 F.2d 647, 649; Lindsay v. State, Tex.Civ.App., 25 S.W.2d 1113, 1115. More properly what is *sufficient* when offered for this purpose. In either of these senses it may be either a denial, justification, or confession and avoidance of the facts averred as a ground of action, or an exception to their sufficiency in point of law. Whitfield v. Aetna Life Insurance Co., C.C.Mo., 125 F. 270; Eagle Savings & Loan Ass'n v. West, 71 Ohio App. 485, 50 N.E.2d 352, 356; Paillet v. Vroman, 52 Cal.App.2d 297, 126 P. 2d 419, 421; (challenge to jurisdiction) Tradesmens Nat. Bank & Trust Co. v. Charlton Steam Shipping Co., D.C.Pa., 3 F.R.D. 363, 364; (denial) Levine v. Behn, 282 N.Y. 120, 25 N.E.2d 871, 873; (legal insufficiency) Dysart v. Remington Rand, D.C.Conn., 31 F.Supp. 296, 297; (payment) Hoadley v. W. T. Rawleigh Co., 112 Ind.App. 563, 44 N. E.2d 231, 232; (statute of limitations) Waggoner v. Feeney, 220 Ind. 543, 44 N.E.2d 499, 502.

In a stricter sense, defense is used to denote the answer made by the defendant to the plaintiff's action, by demurrer or plea at law or answer in equity. This is the meaning of the term in Scotch law. Ersk. Inst. 4, 1, 66. However, it has been held that the filing of a demurrer is not the making of a defense within meaning of the statute providing that, if no defense be made, the plaintiff cannot have judgment for any relief not specifically demanded, but, if defense be made, he may have judgment for other relief, under a prayer therefor. Union Light, Heat & Power Co. v. City of Bellevue, 284 Ky. 405, 144 S.W.2d 1046, 1047.

Half defense was that which was made by the form "defends the force and injury, and says," *(defendit vim et injuriam, et dicit.)*

Full defense was that which was made by the form "defends the force and injury when and where it shall behoove him, and the damages, and whatever else he ought to defend," *(defendit vim et injuriam quando et ubi curia consideravit, et damna et quicquid quod ipse defendere debet, et dicit,)* commonly shortened into "defends the force and injury when," etc. Gilb.Com.Pl. 188; 8 Term, 632; 3 Bos. & P. 9, note; Co.Litt. 127*b*.

In matrimonial suits, in England, defenses are divided into *absolute, i. e.,* such as, being established to the satisfaction of the court, are a complete answer to the petition, so that the court can exercise no discretion, but is bound to dismiss the petition; and *discretionary,* or such as, being established, leave to the court a discretion whether it will pronounce a decree or dismiss the petition. Thus, in a suit for dissolution, condonation is an absolute, adultery by the petitioner a discretionary, defense. Browne, Div. 30.

Defense is not something by means of which party who interposes it can obtain relief for himself. Crisman v. Corbin, 169 Or. 332, 128 P.2d 959, 964.

Defense, as respects right to counsel to conduct defense of one charged with crime, includes every step in proceedings from time of arraignment until acquittal or conviction. State v. Hudson, 55 R.I. 141, 179 A. 130, 135, 100 A.L.R. 313.

Defense also means the forcible repelling of an attack made unlawfully with force and violence, such as the defense of the nation in time of war. United States v. 243.22 Acres of Land in Village of Farmingdale, Town of Babylon, Suffolk County, N. Y., D.C.N.Y., 43 F.Supp. 561, 567.

In old statutes and records, the term means prohibition; denial or refusal. *Enconter le defense et le commandement de roy;* against the prohibition and commandment of the king. St. Westm. 1, c. 1. Also a state of severalty, or of several or exclusive occupancy; a state of inclosure.

Affidavit of Defense

See Affidavit.

Affirmative Defense

See that title.

Equitable Defense

See that title.

Frivolous Defense

One which at first glance can be seen to be merely pretensive, setting up some ground which cannot be sustained by argument. Dominion Nat. Bank v. Olympia Cotton Mills, C.C.S.C., 128 F. 182.

Legal Defense

(1) A defense which is complete and adequate in point of law. (2) A defense which may be set up in a court of law; as distinguished from an "equitable defense," which is cognizable only in a court of equity or court possessing equitable powers.

Meritorious Defense

One going to the merits, substance, or essentials of the case, as distinguished from dilatory or technical objections. Cooper v. Lumber Co., 61 Ark. 36, 31 S.W. 981.

Partial Defense

One which goes only to a part of the cause of action, or which only tends to mitigate the damages to be awarded. Carter v. Bank, 33 Misc. 128, 67 N.Y.S. 300.

Peremptory Defense

A defense which insists that the plaintiff never had the right to institute the suit, or that, if he had, the original right is extinguished or determined. 4 Bouv. Inst. No. 4206.

Personal Defense

In negotiable instruments law. A defense which, though not good as against a holder in due course, is good against certain parties, because of their participation in or knowledge of certain transactions or facts from which such defense arises. Such defenses include all defenses that are not real or absolute defenses. Bauer and Simpson, Law of Business, 2d Ed., p. 329.

Pretermitted Defense

One which was available to a party and of which he might have had the benefit if he had pleaded it in due season, but which cannot afterwards be heard as a basis for affirmative relief. Swennes v. Sprain, 120 Wis. 68, 97 N.W. 511.

Real Defense

In negotiable instruments law. A defense inherent in the res and therefore good against anyone seeking to enforce the instrument, even a holder in due course. Real defenses include illegality, incapacity, forgery, material alteration, nondelivery of an incomplete instrument, and fraud in the inception. These defenses are good even against a holder in due course because, where they exist, no contract was formed. Bauer and Simpson, Law of Business, 2d Ed., p. 330.

Sham Defense

A false or fictitious defense, interposed in bad faith, and manifestly untrue, insufficient, or irrelevant on its face.

Self Defense

See that title.

DEFENSE ACTIVITY. The performance of war contracts by industry. The construction of implements of war. Any activity in aid of the war effort. Equitable Trust Co. v. Bowles, Em.App., 143 F.2d 735, 741.

DEFENSE AU FOND EN DROIT (called, also, *défense en droit*). A demurrer. 2 Low. C. 278. See, also, 1 Low. C. 216.

DÉFENSE AU FOND EN FAIT. The general issue. 3 Low. C. 421.

DEFENSIVA. In old English law. A lord or earl of the marches, who was the warden and defender of his country. Cowell.

DEFENSIVE ALLEGATION. In English ecclesiastical law. A species of pleading, where the defendant, instead of denying the plaintiff's charge upon oath, has any circumstances to offer in his defense. This entitles him, in his turn, to the plaintiff's answer upon oath, upon which he may proceed to proofs as well as his antagonist. 3 Bl. Comm. 100; 3 Steph. Comm. 720.

DEFENSIVE WAR. A war in defense of, or for the protection of, national rights. It may be *defensive* in its principles, though *offensive* in its operations. 1 Kent, Comm. 50, note.

DEFENSO. That part of any open field or place that was allotted for corn or hay, and upon which there was no common or feeding, was anciently said to be *in defenso;* so of any meadow ground that was laid in for hay only. The same term was applied to a wood where part was inclosed or fenced, to secure the growth of the underwood from the injury of cattle. Cowell.

In the Civil Law

A defender; one who assumed the defense of another's case in court. Also an advocate. A tutor or curator.

In Canon Law

The advocate or patron of a church. An officer who had charge of the temporalities of the church.

In Old English Law

A guardian, defender, or protector. The defendant in an action. A person vouched in to warranty.

In General

Defensor civitatis. Defender or protector of a city or municipality. An officer under the Roman empire, whose duty it was to protect the people against the injustice of the magistrates, the insolence of the subaltern officers, and the rapacity of the money-lenders. Schm. Civil Law, Introd. 16; Cod. 1, 55, 4. He had the powers of a judge, with jurisdiction of pecuniary causes to a limited amount, and the lighter species of offenses. Cod. 1, 55, 1; Nov. 15, c. 3, § 2; Id. c. 6, § 1: He had also the care of the public records, and powers similar to those of a notary in regard to the execution of wills and conveyances.

Defensor fidei. Defender of the faith. See Defender.

DEFENSUM. A prohibition. An inclosure of land; any fenced ground. Medley, Eng. Const. Hist. See Defenso.

DEFER. Delay; put off; remand; postpone to a future time. The term does not have, however, the meaning of abolish, Moore v. Sampson County, 220 N.C. 232, 17 S.E.2d 22, 23, or omit, United States v. Murine Co., C.C.A.Ill., 90 F.2d 549, 551.

DEFERRED LIFE ANNUITIES. In English law. Annuities for the life of the purchaser, but not commencing until a date subsequent to the date of buying them, so that, if the purchaser die before that date, the purchase money is lost. Granted by the commissioners for reduction of the national debt. See 16 & 17 Vict. c. 45, § 2. Wharton.

DEFERRED PAYMENTS. Payments of principal or interest postponed to a future time; installment payments; a method of paying insurance proceeds. (Life insurance) Holmes v. John Hancock Mut. Life Ins. Co., 41 N.E.2d 909, 911, 288 N.Y. 106; (notes) First Nat. Bank v. Bosler, 297 Pa. 353, 147 A. 74, 75; (highway contract) Central Tractor & Equipment Co. v. Betz, 63 S.D. 435, 260 N.W. 269; (will) In re Mitinger's Estate, 114 Pa. Super. 209, 173 A. 432, 433.

DEFERRED SENTENCE. A sentence, the pronouncement of which has been postponed. It does not operate as a suspension of sentence. State v. Powell, 153 Wash. 110, 279 P. 573, 574.

DEFERRED STOCK. See Stock.

DEFIANCE. A contemptuous opposition or disregard openly expressed in words or action. State v. Mohar, 168 Wash. 368, 13 P.2d 454, 455. A provoking to combat, a challenge, a declaration of hostilities. Anderson-Berney Bldg. Co. v. Lowry, Tex.Civ.App., 143 S.W.2d 401, 403.

DEFICIENCY. A lack, shortage or insufficiency. The amount by which the income tax imposed exceeds the amount shown as the tax by the taxpayer upon his return. American Woolen Co. v. United States, Ct.Cl., 21 F.Supp. 1021, 1022.

That part of a debt secured by mortgage not realized from sale of mortgaged property. Harrow v Metropolitan Life Ins. Co., 285 Mich. 349, 280 N.W. 785, 787. A judgment or decree for the amount of such deficiency is called a "deficiency judgment" or "decree." Phillips v. Union Central Life Ins. Co., C.C.A.Minn., 88 F.2d 188, 189 (judgment); Grace v. Hendricks, 103 Fla. 1158, 140 So. 790, 794 (decree).

Technically speaking, there is no such thing under our law as a "deficiency judgment" in the sense that a formal judgment of that description is rendered by the court, or entered by the clerk for the amount not made by the sale of the mortgaged property. There is only the original judgment for the full amount of the indebtedness, upon which a deficiency may exist after the issuance and return of the special execution, or even perhaps of one or more general executions in addition. It has nevertheless been customary in ordinary parlance to refer to the amount still due after the return of the special execution as a "deficiency judgment." Bank of Douglas v. Neel, 30 Ariz. 375, 247 P. 132, 134.

DEFICIENCY BILL. In parliamentary practice, an appropriation bill covering items of expense omitted from the general appropriation bill or bills, or for which insufficient appropriations were made. If intended to cover a variety of such items, it is commonly called a "general deficiency bill;" if intended to make provision for expenses which must be met immediately, or which cannot wait the ordinary course of the general appropriation bills, it is called an "urgent deficiency bill."

Deficiente uno sanguine non potest esse hæres. 3 Coke, 41. One blood being wanting, he cannot be heir. But see 3 & 4 Wm. IV. c. 106, § 9, and 33 & 34 Vict. c. 23, § 1.

DEFICIT. Something wanting, generally in the accounts of one intrusted with money, or in the money received by him. Mutual L. & B. Ass'n v. Price, 19 Fla. 135. The term is broad enough to cover defalcation, misappropriation, shrinkage, or costs, and, in its popular meaning, signifies deficiency from any cause. Clement v. Whisnant, 208 N.C. 167, 179 S.E. 430, 433, 101 A.L.R. 698.

DEFILE. To debauch, deflower, or corrupt the chastity of a woman. The term does not necessarily imply force or ravishment, nor does it connote previous immaculateness. State v. Fernald, 88 Iowa, 553, 55 N.W. 534; State v. Besares, 73 Utah 141, 283 P. 738, 739. The term, when used in a statute penalizing any person who shall publicly defile any flag of the United States, has the meaning of dishonor. State v. Schlueter, 127 N.J.L. 496, 23 A.2d 249, 251.

DEFILEMENT. Uncleanness; impurity; corruption of morals or conduct. Young v. State, 194 Ind. 221, 141 N.E. 309, 311.

DEFINE. To explain or state the exact meaning of words and phrases; to state explicitly; to limit; to determine essential qualities of; to determine the precise signification of; to settle; to establish or prescribe authoritatively; to make clear. U. S. v. Smith, 5 Wheat. 160, 5 L.Ed. 57; Walling v. Yeakley, C.C.A.Colo., 140 F.2d 830, 832; Walters v. Richardson, 93 Ky. 374, 20 S.W. 279. To declare that a certain act shall constitute an offense is defining that offense. U. S. v. Arjona, 120 U.S. 488, 7 S.Ct. 628, 30 L.Ed. 728.

To "define" with respect to space, means to set or establish its boundaries authoritatively; to mark the limits of; to determine with precision or to exhibit clearly the boundaries of; to determine the end or limit; to fix or establish the limits. It is the equivalent to declare, fix or establish. Seeking out what exists already is not "defining." Redlands Foothill Groves v. Jacobs, D.C. Cal., 30 F.Supp. 995, 1004.

DEFINITE. Fixed, determined, defined, bounded. Board of Sup'rs of Yavapai County v. Stephens, 20 Ariz. 115, 177 P. 261, 262; Kintner v. Atlantic Communication Co., C.C.A.N.Y., 240 F. 716, 721.

A definite failure of issue occurs when a precise time is fixed by a will for a failure of issue. An indefinite failure of issue is the period when the issue of the first taker shall become extinct and when there shall no longer be any issue of the grantee, but without reference to a particular time or event; Huxford v. Milligan, 50 Ind. 546; McWilliams v. Havely, 214 Ky. 320, 283 S.W. 103, 105.

DEFINITIO. Lat. Definition, or more strictly, limiting or bounding; as in the maxim of the civil law: *Omnis definitio periculosa est, parum est enim ut non subverti possit,* (Dig. 50, 17, 202;) *i. e.*, the attempt to bring the law within the boundaries of precise definitions is hazardous, as there are but few cases in which such a limitation cannot be subverted.

DEFINITION. A description of a thing by its properties; an explanation of the meaning of a word or term. Webster. The process of stating the exact meaning of a word by means of other words. Worcester. See Warner v. Beers, 23 Wend., N.Y., 103; Marvin v. State, 19 Ind. 181. Such a description of the thing defined, including all essential elements and excluding all nonessential, as to distinguish it from all other things and classes. Wilson v. Else, 204 Iowa 857, 216 N.W. 33, 37.

DEFINITIVE. That which finally and completely ends and settles a controversy. A definitive sentence or judgment is put in opposition to an interlocutory judgment. Thompson v. Graham, 246 Pa. 202, 92 A. 118, 119; Interstate Electric Co. v. Interstate Electric Co. of Shreveport, La.App., 6 So.2d 39, 40.

A distinction may be taken between a *final* and a *definitive* judgment. The former term is applicable when the judgment exhausts the powers of the particular court in which it is rendered; while the latter word designates a judgment that is above any review or contingency of reversal. U. S. v. The Peggy, 1 Cranch, 103, 2 L.Ed. 49.

DEFINITIVE SENTENCE. The final judgment, decree, or sentence of an ecclesiastical court. 3 Bl.Comm. 101.

DEFLECT. To turn aside, to deviate from a straight or horizontal line or from a proper position, to swerve, to deviate. Grip Nut Co. v. MacLean-Fogg Lock Nut Co., D.C.Ill., 34 F.2d 41, 42.

DEFLORATION. Seduction or debauching. The act by which a woman is deprived of her virginity.

DEFORCE.

In English Law

To withhold wrongfully; to withhold the possession of lands from one who is lawfully entitled to them. 3 Bl.Comm. 172; Phelps v. Baldwin, 17 Conn. 212.

In Scotch Law

To resist the execution of the law; to oppose by force a public officer in the execution of his duty. Bell.

DEFORCEMENT. Deforcement is where a man wrongfully holds lands to which another person is entitled. It therefore includes disseisin, abatement, discontinuance, and intrusion. Co. Litt. 277*b*, 331*b*; Hopper v. Hopper, 21 N.J.L. 543. But it is applied especially to cases, not falling under those heads, where the person entitled to the freehold has never had possession; thus, where a lord has a seignory, and lands escheat to him *propter defectum sanguinis,* but the seisin is withheld from him, this is a deforcement, and the person who withholds the seisin is called a "deforceor." 3 Bl.Comm. 172.

In Scotch Law

The opposition or resistance made to messengers or other public officers while they are actually engaged in the exercise of their offices. Ersk. Inst. 4, 4, 32.

DEFORCIANT. One who wrongfully keeps the owner of lands and tenements out of the possession of them. 2 Bl.Comm. 350.

DEFORCIARE. L. Lat. To withhold lands or tenements from the rightful owner. This is a word of art which cannot be supplied by any other word. Co. Litt. 331*b*.

DEFORCIATIO. L. Lat. In old English law. A distress, distraint, or seizure of goods for satisfaction of a lawful debt. Cowell.

DEFORMITY. A deformed or misshapen condition; an unnatural growth, or a distorted or misshapen part or member; disfigurement; as a bodily deformity. People v. Lehrman, 251 App.Div. 451, 296 N.Y.S. 580, 582.

In insurance. Representations in application for insurance that applicant never had any "infirmity" or "deformity" must be construed as meaning deformity or infirmity of substantial character apparently materially impairing applicant's health, which, if known, probably would have deterred company from issuing policy. (Life insurance) Eastern Dist. Piece Dye Works v. Travelers' Ins. Co., 234 N.Y. 441, 138 N.E. 401, 404, 405, 26 A.L.R. 1505; (accident insurance) Commercial Casualty Ins. Co. v. Mathews, 57 Ga.App. 446, 195 S.E. 887, 892.

DEFOSSION. The punishment of being buried alive.

DEFRAUD. To practice fraud; to cheat or trick. State v. Harroun, 199 Mo. 519, 98 S.W. 467, 470; James v. State, 43 Ga.App. 324, 158 S.E. 644, 645. To deprive a person of property or any interest, estate, or right by fraud, deceit, or artifice. State v. Vandenburg, 9 W.W.Harr. 498, 2 A.2d 916, 919. But not by force or intimidation. Hammerschmidt v. U. S., 265 U.S. 182, 44 S.Ct. 511, 68 L.Ed. 968; Norton v. U. S., C.C.A.Cal., 92 F.2d 753, 756.

DEFRAUDACION. In Spanish law. The crime committed by a person who fraudulently avoids the payment of some public tax.

DEFRAUDATION. Privation by fraud.

DEFUNCT. Deceased; a deceased person. A common term in Scotch law. A corporation which has ceased to function. Tozier v. Woodworth, 135 Me. 46, 188 A. 771, 773.

The term is synonymous with "dead." Farmers Union Co-op. Brokerage v. Palisade Farmers Union Local No. 714, 69 S.D. 126, 7 N.W.2d 293, 295.

DEFUNCTUS. Lat. Dead. "Defunctus sine prole," dead without (leaving) issue.

DEGASTER. L. Fr. To waste.

DEGRADATION. A deprivation of dignity; dismission from office. An ecclesiastical censure, whereby a clergyman is divested of his holy orders. There are two sorts by the canon law,—one *summary,* by word only; the other *solemn,* by stripping the party degraded of those ornaments and rights which are the ensigns of his degree. Degradation is otherwise called "deposition," but the canonists have distinguished between these two terms, deeming the former as the greater punishment of the two. There is likewise a degradation of a lord or knight at common law, and also by act of parliament. Wharton.

DEGRADATIONS. A term for waste in the French law.

DEGRADING. Reviling; holding one up to public obloquy; lowering a person in the estimation of the public.

DEGREE.

In General

The state or civil condition of a person, State v. Bishop, 15 Me. 122; An honorable state or condition to which a student is advanced in testimony of proficiency in arts and sciences. Commonwealth v. New England College of Chiropractic, 221 Mass. 190, 108 N.E. 895, 896; The grade or distance one thing may be removed from another. Superior Lloyds of America v. Foxworth, Tex. Civ.App., 178 S.W.2d 724, 725.

They are of pontifical origin. See 1 Schmidt, Thesaurus, 144; Vicat, *Doctores;* Minshew, Dict. *Bacheler;* Merlin *Répertoire Univ.;* Van Espen. pt. 1, tit. 10; Giannone, *Istoria di Napoli,* lib. xi. c. 2, for a full account of this matter.

In the Law of Descent and Family Relations

A step or grade, *i. e.*, the distance, or number of removes, which separates two persons who are related by consanguinity. Thus we speak of a brother as being in the second degree of kindred. Calvert v. Beck, 240 Ala. 442, 199 So. 846, 847.

In Criminal Law

The term "degree" denotes a division or classification of one specific crime into several grades or *stadia* of guilt, according to the circumstances attending its commission. Thus, in some states, there may be "murder in the second degree."

DEHORNER. A rubbing alcohol addict. Powell v. State, 179 Md. 399, 18 A.2d 587, 590.

DEHORS. L. Fr. Out of; without; beyond; foreign to; unconnected with. Blackford v. Anderson, 226 Iowa 1138, 286 N.W. 735, 746. *Dehors* the record; foreign to the record. 3 Bl.Comm. 387.

DEHYDRATE. To deprive or to be free of water or elements of water or to suffer loss of water. In re Benner, Cust. & Pat.App., 46 F.2d 383, 384.

DEI GRATIA. Lat. By the grace of God. A phrase used in the formal title of a king or queen, importing a claim of sovereignty by the favor or commission of God. In ancient times it was incorporated in the titles of inferior officers, (especially ecclesiastical,) but in later use was reserved as an assertion of "the divine right of kings."

DEI JUDICIUM. The judgment of God. The old Saxon trial by ordeal, so called because it was thought to be an appeal to God for the justice of a cause, and it was believed that the decision was according to the will and pleasure of Divine Providence. Wharton.

DEJACION. In Spanish law. Surrender; release; abandonment; *e. g.*, the act of an insolvent in surrendering his property for the benefit of his creditors, of an heir in renouncing the succession, the abandonment of insured property to the underwriters.

DEJERATION. A taking of a solemn oath.

DEL BIEN ESTRE. L. Fr. In old English practice. Of well being; of form. The same as *de bene esse.* Britt. c. 39.

DEL CREDERE. In mercantile law. A phrase borrowed from the Italians, equivalent to our word "guaranty" or "warranty," or the Scotch term "warrandice;" an agreement by which a factor, when he sells goods on credit, for an additional commission, (called a "*del credere* commission,") guaranties the solvency of the purchaser and his performance of the contract. Such a factor is called a "*del credere* agent." He is a mere surety, liable to his principal only in case the purchaser makes default. Story, Ag. 28; Lemnos Broad Silk Works v. Spiegelberg, 217 N.Y.S. 595, 597, 127 Misc. 855; Commercial Investment Trust v. Stewart, 235 Mich. 502, 209 N.W. 660, 661; Commonwealth v. Thorne, Neale & Co., 264 Pa. 408, 107 A. 814, 815; State v. Tuffs, 54 Mont. 20, 165 P. 1107, 1108.

DÉLAISSEMENT. In French marine law. Abandonment. Emerig. Tr. des Ass. ch. 17.

DELATE. In Scotch law. To accuse. Delated, accused. *Delatit off arte and parte,* accused of being accessary to. 3 How. St. Tr. 425, 440.

DELATIO. In the civil law. An accusation or information.

DELATOR. An accuser; an informer; a sycophant.

DELATURA. In old English law. The reward of an informer. Whishaw.

DELAY. To retard; obstruct; put off; postpone; defer; procrastinate; prolong the time of or before; hinder; interpose obstacles; as, when it is said that a conveyance was made to "hinder and delay creditors." Mercantile Co. v. Arnold, 108 Ga. 449, 34 S.E. 176; Ellis v. Valentine, 65 Tex. 532; Blair v. Blair, 122 Me. 500, 120 A. 902, 905. The term does not imply dishonesty or involve moral wrong. Citizens & Southern Nat. Bank v. Kontz, 185 Ga. 131, 194 S.E. 536, 544.

DELAY RENTAL. Rent, usually on oil and gas leases, paid for additional time in which to utilize land. It does not depend on oil or gas produced, does not exhaust substance of land, and resembles a bonus payment, which is an advance royalty. Commissioner of Internal Revenue v. Wilson, C. C.A.Tex., 76 F.2d 766, 769; State v. Magnolia Petroleum Co., Tex.Civ.App., 173 S.W.2d 186, 190.

DELECTUS PERSONÆ. Lat. Choice of the person. Johnston v. Winn, Tex.Civ.App., 105 S.W.2d 398, 400. By this term is understood the right of a partner to exercise his choice and preference as to the admission of any new members to the firm, and as to the persons to be so admitted, if any. People v. Herbert, 162 Misc. 817, 295 N.Y.S. 251, 253. The doctrine does not apply to corporations. Adams v. St. Clair, 185 Miss. 416, 188 So. 559, 560.

In Scotch Law

The personal preference which is supposed to have been exercised by a landlord in selecting his tenant, by the members of a firm in making choice of partners, in the appointment of persons to office, and other cases. Nearly equivalent to personal trust, as a doctrine in law. Bell.

Delegata potestas non potest delegari. 2 Inst. 597. A delegated power cannot be delegated.

DELEGATE. A person who is delegated or commissioned to act in the stead of another, Landro v. Pacific Atlantic S. S. Co., D.C.Wash., 30 F.Supp. 538, 539; a person to whom affairs are committed by another; an attorney.

A person elected or appointed to be a member of a representative assembly. Usually spoken of one sent to a special or occasional assembly or convention. Manston v. McIntosh, 58 Minn. 525, 60 N.W. 672, 28 L.R.A. 605.

The representative in congress of one of the organized territories of the United States. To send as an agent or representative; to commit to the care or management of another.

DELEGATES, THE HIGH COURT OF. In English law. Formerly the court of appeal from the ecclesiastical and admiralty courts. Abolished upon the judicial committee of the privy council being constituted the court of appeal in such cases.

DELEGATION. A sending away; a putting into commission; the assignment of a debt to another; the intrusting another with a general power to act for the good of those who depute him; a body of delegates.

At Common Law

The transfer of authority by one person to another; the act of making or commissioning a delegate.

The whole body of delegates or representatives sent to a convention or assembly from one district, place, or political unit are collectively spoken of as a "delegation."

In the Civil Law

A species of novation which consists in the change of one debtor for another, when he who is indebted substitutes a third person who obligates himself in his stead to the creditor, or to the person appointed by him so that the first debtor is acquitted and his obligation extinguished, and the creditor contents himself with the obligation of the second debtor. Delegation is essentially distinguished from any other species of novation, in this: that the former demands the consent of all three parties, but the latter that only of the two parties to the new debt. 1 Domat, § 2318; Adams v. Power, 48 Miss. 454.

Delegation is novation effected by the intervention of another person whom the debtor, in order to be liberated from his creditor, gives to such creditor, or to him whom the creditor appoints; and such person so given becomes obliged to the creditor in the place of the original debtor. Burge, Sur. 173.

Perfect delegation exists when the debtor who makes the obligation is discharged by the creditor.

Imperfect delegation exists when the creditor retains his rights against the original debtor. 2 Duvergnoy, n. 169.

Delegatus non potest delegare. A delegate cannot delegate; an agent cannot delegate his functions to a subagent without the knowledge or consent of the principal; the person to whom an office or duty is delegated cannot lawfully devolve the duty on another, unless he be expressly authorized so to do. 9 Coke, 77; Broom, Max. 840; 2 Kent, Comm. 633; 2 Steph.Comm. 119; Blake v. Allen, 221 N.C. 445, 20 S.E.2d 552, 554.

DÉLESTAGE. In French marine law. A discharging of ballast (*lest*) from a vessel.

DELETE. In Scotch law. To erase; to strike out.

DELETERIOUS. Hurtful, morally or physically; injurious, as influence; poisonous; unwholesome. State v. Crabtree Co., 218 Minn. 36, 15 N.W.2d 98.

Thus struvite crystals which developed in jar of wet shrimp after packing, O'Hare v. Petersen, 174 Misc. 481, 21 N.Y.S.2d 487, 491, and bones in fish and fragments of shell in oysters constitute "deleterious substances". United States v. 1232 Cases American Beauty Brand Oysters, D.C.Mo., 43 F.Supp. 749, 751.

DELF. A quarry or mine. 31 Eliz. c. 7.

Deliberandum est diu quod statuendum est semel. 12 Coke, 74. That which is to be resolved once for all should be long deliberated upon.

DELIBERATE, *v.* To weigh, ponder, discuss, regard upon, consider. Cole v. List & Weatherly Const. Co., La.App., 156 So. 88, 90. To examine, to consult, in order to form an opinion. McGregor v. State, 83 Tex.Cr.R. 35, 201 S.W. 184, 186. To weigh in the mind; to consider the reasons for and against; to consider maturely; reflect upon; as to deliberate a question; to weigh the arguments for and against a proposed course of action. People v. Thomas, 25 Cal.2d 880, 156 P.2d 7, 17, 18.

DELIBERATE, *adj.* Well advised; carefully considered; not sudden or rash; circumspect; slow in determining. McClendon v. Louisiana Cent. Lumber Co., 17 La.App. 246, 135 So. 754, 756. Willful rather than merely intentional. Cole v. List & Weatherly Const. Co., La.App., 156 So. 88, 90. Formed, arrived at, or determined upon as a result of careful thought and weighing of considerations, as a deliberate judgment or plan; carried on coolly and steadily, especially according to a preconceived design; given to weighing facts and arguments with a view to a choice or decision; careful in considering the consequences of a step; slow in action; unhurried; characterized by reflection; dispassionate; not rash. People v. Thomas, 25 Cal.2d 880, 156 P.2d 7, 17, 18. The word carries with it an implication of some obstinacy, headstrongness, foolish daring, or intentional wrongdoing. Brown v. Kansas City Bridge Co., La.App., 191 So. 755, 757.

By the use of this word, in describing a crime, the idea is conveyed that the perpetrator weighs the motives for the act and its consequences, the nature of the crime, or other things connected with his intentions, with a view to a decision thereon; that he carefully considers all these; and that the act is not suddenly committed. It implies that the perpetrator must be capable of the exercise of such mental powers as are called into use by deliberation and the consideration and weighing of motives and consequences. In re Nunns, 188 App.Div. 424, 176 N.Y.S. 858, 865; Jenkins v. Carman Mfg. Co., 79 Or. 448, 155 P. 703, 705.

"Deliberation" and "premeditation" are of the same character of mental operations, differing only in degree. Deliberation is but prolonged premeditation. In other words, in law, deliberation is premeditation in a cool state of the blood, or, where there has been heat of passion, it is premeditation continued beyond the period within which there has been time for the blood to cool, in the given case. Deliberation is not only to think of beforehand, which may be but for an instant, but the inclination to do the act is considered, weighed, pondered upon, for such a length of time after a provocation is given as the jury may find was sufficient for the blood to cool. One in a heat of passion may premeditate without deliberating. Deliberation is only exercised in a cool state of the blood, while premeditation may be either in that state of the blood or in the heat of passion. State v. Hall, 40 N.M. 128, 55 P.2d 740, 742; People v. Thomas, 25 Cal.2d 880, 156 P.2d 7, 17; State v. Payne, 213 N.C. 719, 197 S.E. 573, 579.

DELIBERATELY. Willfully; with premeditation; intentionally; purposely; in cold blood. Averheart v. State, 158 Ark. 639, 238 S.W. 620, 621; State v. Young, 314 Mo. 612, 286 S.W. 29, 34; Csanyi v. Csanyi, 93 N.J.Eq. 11, 115 A. 76, 78; State v. Johnson, 92 Kan. 441, 140 P. 839, 840.

DELIBERATION. The act or process of deliberating. The act of weighing and examining the reasons for and against a contemplated act or course of conduct or a choice of acts or means. See Deliberate.

DELICATESSEN. Prepared foods, such as cooked meats, relishes, preserves and the like. North Ave. Market v. Keys, 164 Md. 185, 164 A. 152, 154. Also, a store that sells such prepared foods. Parker v. Levin, 285 Mass. 125, 188 N.E. 502, 503, 90 A. L.R. 1446.

Delicatus debitor est odiosus in lege. A luxurious debtor is odious in law. 2 Bulst. 148. Imprisonment for debt has now, however, been generally abolished.

DELICT. In the Roman and civil law. A wrong or injury; an offense; a violation of public or private duty.

It will be observed that this word, taken in its most general sense, is wider in both directions than our English term "tort." On the one hand, it includes those wrongful acts which, while directly affecting some individual or his property, yet extend in their injurious consequences to the peace or security of the community at large, and hence rise to the grade of crimes or misdemeanors. These acts were termed in the Roman law "public delicts;" while those for which the only penalty exacted was compensation to the person primarily injured were denominated "private delicts." On the other hand, the term appears to have included injurious actions which transpired without any malicious intention on the part of the doer. Thus Pothier gives the name *"quasi delicts"* to the acts of a person who, without malignity, but by an inexcusable imprudence, causes an injury to another. Poth.Obl. 116. But the term is used in modern jurisprudence as a convenient synonym of "tort."

Quasi Delict

An act whereby a person, without malice, but by fault, negligence, or imprudence not legally excusable, causes injury to another. They were four in number, viz.: (1) *Qui judex litem suam fecit*, being the offense of partiality or excess in the *judex*, (juryman.) (2) *Dejectum effusumve aliquid*, being the tort committed by one's servant in emptying or throwing something out of an attic or upper story upon a person passing beneath. (3) *Damnum infectum*, being the offense of hanging dangerous articles over the heads of persons passing along the king's highway. (4) Torts committed by one's agents in the course of their employment. Brown.

DELICTUAL FAULT. An act, productive of obligations, which takes place between persons juridically strangers to each other; it supposes the absence of obligation and its result is the creation of one. Reserve Ins. Co. v. Fabre, 149 So.2d 413, 416, 243 La. 982.

DELICTUM. Lat. A delict, tort, wrong, injury, or offense. Actions *ex delicto* are such as are founded on a tort, as distinguished from actions on contract.

Culpability, blameworthiness, or legal delinquency. The word occurs in this sense in the maxim, *"In pari delicto melior est conditio defendentis"* (which see).

A challenge of a juror *propter delictum* is for some crime or misdemeanor that affects his credit and renders him infamous. 3 Bl.Comm. 363; 2 Kent, Comm. 241.

DELIMIT. To mark or lay out the limits or boundary line of a territory or country; to fix or to mark the limits of; to demarcate; bound. Walling v. Yeakley, C.C.A.Colo., 140 F.2d 830, 832.

DELIMITATION. The act of fixing, marking off, or describing the limits or boundary line of a territory, country, authority, right, statutory exception or the like. See Delimit.

DELINQUENCY. Failure, omission, violation of duty. State or condition of one who has failed to perform his duty. Travelers' Protective Ass'n of America v. Ziegler, Tex.Civ.App., 250 S.W. 1115, 1116; Robinson v. Miller, 317 Ill. 501, 148 N.E. 319, 322. Synonymous with misconduct and offense. Boynton Cab Co. v. Neubeck, 237 Wis. 249, 296 N.W. 636, 639.

Delinquens per iram provocatus puniri debet mitius. 3 Inst. 55. A delinquent provoked by anger ought to be punished more mildly.

DELINQUENT, *n.* In the civil law. He who has been guilty of some crime, offense, or failure of duty.

DELINQUENT, *adj.* As applied to a debt or claim, it means simply due and unpaid at the time appointed by law or fixed by contract; as, a delinquent tax. Chauncey v. Wass, 35 Minn. 1, 30 N.W. 826; Gallup v. Schmidt, 154 Ind. 196, 56 N. E. 450. As applied to a person, it commonly means that he is grossly negligent or in willful default in regard to his pecuniary obligations, or even that he is dishonest and unworthy of credit. Boyce v. Ewart, Rice S. C., 140; Ferguson v. Pittsburgh, 159 Pa. 435, 28 Atl. 118; Grocers' Ass'n v. Exton, 18 Ohio Cir.Ct.R. 321.

DELINQUENT CHILD. An infant of not more than specified age, Phillips v. State, Tex.Cr.App., 20 S.W.2d 790, 791, who has violated any law or who is incorrigible; (prostitute) Bolker v. State, 134 Neb. 255, 278 N.W. 377, 379; (thief) Rose v. State, 137 Tex.Cr.R. 316, 129 S.W.2d 639, 640; (felony) State v. Connally, 190 La. 175, 182 So. 318, 319.

Although the terms dependent child and delinquent child, as used in juvenile court law, are largely synonymous, State v. Clevenger, 161 Wash. 306, 296 P. 1054; a neglected and dependent child is not necessarily a delinquent child. In re Santillanes, 47 N.M. 140, 138 P.2d 503, 513.

DELINQUENT JUVENILE. See Delinquent Child.

DELINQUENT TAXES. Past due and unpaid taxes. Ryan v. Roach Drug Co., 113 Okl. 130, 239 P. 912, 918; Cornell v. Maverick Loan & Trust Co., 95 Neb. 9, 144 N.W. 1072, 1074.

DELIRIUM. In medical jurisprudence. Delirium is that state of the mind in which it acts without being directed by the power of volition, which is wholly or partially suspended. This happens most perfectly in dreams. But what is commonly called "delirium" is always preceded or attended by a feverish and highly diseased state of the body. The patient in delirium is wholly unconscious of surrounding objects, or conceives them to be different from what they really are. His thoughts seem to drift about, wildering and tossing amidst distracted dreams. And his observations, when he makes any, as often happens, are wild and incoherent; or, from excess of pain, he sinks into a low muttering, or silent and death-like stupor. The law contemplates this species of mental derangement as an intellectual eclipse; as a darkness occasioned by a cloud of disease passing over the mind; and which must soon terminate in health or in death. Supreme Lodge v. Lapp, 25 Ky.Law Rep. 74, 74 S.W. 656; Sommerville v. Greenhood, 65 Mont. 101, 210 P. 1048, 1054; Grand Lodge, A. O. U. W. of Arkansas, v. Mode, 157 Ark. 62, 247 S.W. 386, 388; (distinguished from insane delusion) Schoenhoff v. Haering, 327 Mo. 837, 38 S.W.2d 1011, 1015.

DELIRIUM FEBRILE. In medical jurisprudence. A form of mental aberration incident to fevers, and sometimes to the last stages of chronic diseases.

DELIRIUM TREMENS. A disorder of the nervous system, involving the brain and setting up an attack of temporary delusional insanity, sometimes attended with violent excitement or mania, caused by excessive and long continued indulgence in alcoholic liquors, or by the abrupt cessation of such use after a protracted debauch. Horn v. Commonwealth, 292 Ky. 587, 167 S.W.2d 58, 61; Hartin v. Hysee Inghram Tire Co., 153 Pa.Super. 121, 33 A.2d 471, 473. See Insanity.

DELITO. In Spanish law. Crime; a crime, offense, or delict. White, New Recop. b. 2, tit. 19, c. 1, § 4.

DELIVERANCE. In practice. The verdict rendered by a jury.

Second Deliverance

In practice. A writ allowed a plaintiff in replevin, where the defendant has obtained judgment for return of the goods, by default or nonsuit, in order to have the same distress again delivered to him, on giving the same security as before. 3 Bl.Comm. 150; 3 Steph.Comm. 668.

DELIVERY. The act by which the res or substance thereof is placed within the actual or constructive possession or control of another. Poor v. American Locomotive Co., C.C.A.Ill., 67 F.2d 626, 630.

What constitutes delivery depends largely on the intent of the parties. It is not necessary that delivery should be by manual transfer. Miller v. Kospelhorn, 176 Md. 356, 4 A.2d 728, 733.

"Delivery" required in conveyance of personal chattels as against all but vendor, is delivery in its natural sense; that is, a change of possession. Goodhue v. State St. Trust Co., 267 Mass. 28, 165 N.E. 701, 705.

In General

The transfer from one person to another of the res or a right or interest therein, which means more than physical transfer of possession, Murphy v. Smith, 291 Mass. 93, 195 N.E. 912; Pure Oil Co. v. Evans, 369 Ill. 416, 17 N.E.2d 23, 24. Although in the popular sense, in the case of a contract or lease or the like, it implies a transfer of the tangible contract. Lease, Roberts v. Cyr, 136 Me. 39, 1 A.2d 281, 282; release for injury, Pevesdorf v. Union Electric Light & Power Co., 333 Mo. 1155, 64 S.W.2d 939; check, Irving Trust Co. v. Leff, 253 N.Y. 359, 171 N.E. 569; bank passbook, Brooks v. Mitchell, 163 Md. 1, 161 A. 261, 266, 84 A.L.R. 547.

Absolute and conditional. An absolute delivery, as distinguished from conditional delivery or delivery in escrow, is one which is complete upon the actual transfer of the instrument from the possession of the grantor. Dyer v. Skadan, 128 Mich. 348, 87 N.W. 277, 278, 92 Am.St.Rep. 461. A conditional delivery is one which passes the thing subject to delivery from the possession of the grantor, but is not to be completed by possession of the grantee, or a third person as his agent, until the happening of a specified event. Silliman v. Dobner, 165 Minn. 87, 205 N.W. 696, 697.

Actual and constructive. Actual delivery consists in the giving real possession to the vendee or his servants or special agents who are identified with him in law and represent him. Carr v. St. Louis-San Francisco Ry. Co., Mo.App., 284 S.W. 184, 185. It is a formal immediate tradition of the property to the vendee. Bridgham v. Hinds, 120 Me. 444, 115 A. 197, 199, 21 A.L.R. 1024. It contemplates a manual transfer of the property. Callan v. Mutual Life Ins. Co., La.App., 147 So. 110, 111.

Constructive delivery is a general term, comprehending all those acts which, although not truly conferring a real possession of the thing sold on the vendee, have been held, by construction of law, equivalent to acts of real delivery.

Constructive delivery includes symbolic or substituted delivery and all those *traditiones fictæ* which have been admitted into the law as sufficient to vest the absolute property in the vendee and bar the rights of lien and stoppage *in transitu*, such as marking and setting apart the goods as belonging to the vendee, charging him with warehouse rent, etc. See In re Nesto, C.C.A.Pa., 270 F. 503. A constructive delivery of personalty takes place when the goods are set apart and notice given to the person to whom they are to be delivered. The Titania, C.C.A., 131 F. 229, 65 C.C.A. 215, or when, without actual transfer of the goods or their symbol, the conduct of the parties is such as to be inconsistent with any other supposition than that there has been a change in the nature of the holding. Swafford v. Spratt, 93 Mo.App. 631, 67 S.W. 701.

Delivery bond. A bond given upon the seizure of goods (as under the revenue laws) conditioned for their restoration to the defendant, or the payment of their value, if so adjudged.

Delivery order. An order addressed, in England, by the owner of goods to a person holding them on his behalf, requesting him to deliver them to a person named in the order. Delivery orders are chiefly used in the case of goods held by dock companies, wharfingers, etc. National Wholesale Grocery Co. v. Mann, 251 Mass. 238, 146 N.E. 791, 793.

Failure to make delivery, see Failure to Make Delivery.

Second delivery. The legal delivery by the depositary of a deed placed in escrow. Thornhill v. Olson, 31 N.D. 81, 153 N.W. 442, 445, L.R.A.1916A, 493, Ann.Cas.1917E, 427.

Symbolical delivery. The constructive delivery of the subject-matter of a sale, where it is cumbersome or inaccessible, by the actual delivery of some article which is conventionally accepted as the symbol or representative of it, or which renders access to it possible, or which is the evidence of the purchaser's title to it; as the key of a warehouse, or a bill of lading of goods on shipboard. Hall v. Kansas City Terra Cotta Co., 97 Kan. 103, 154 P. 210, 212, L.R.A.1916D, 361, Ann. Cas.1918D, 605.

In Conveyancing

The final and absolute transfer of a deed, properly executed, to the grantee, or to some person for his use, in such manner that it cannot be recalled by the grantor. Gatchell v. Gatchell, 127 Me. 328, 143 A. 169, 170; Arndt v. Lapel, 214 Iowa 594, 243 N.W. 605, 610; delivery to a stranger, Hall v. Hall, 292 Ky. 772, 168 S.W.2d 10, 14; or depositary, Stalting v. Stalting, 52 S.D. 309, 217 N.W. 386, 389.

In Law of Sales

The tradition or transfer of the possession of personal property from one person to another. Bowles v. Beucher, D.C.Mass., 53 F.Supp. 984, 987; delivery of a bill of sale or written evidence of title as sufficient delivery, Smith v. Acorn, D.C. Mun.App., 32 A.2d 252, 255; by carrier, Rice & Lockwood Lumber Co. v. Boston & M. R. R., 308 Mass. 101, 31 N.E.2d 219, 221, 222, 223.

"Delivery" occurs whenever, at time and place fixed by law or agreed on by parties, seller does everything necessary to put goods completely and unconditionally at buyer's disposal. Fox v. Young, Tex.Civ.App., 91 S.W.2d 857, 859.

In Medical Jurisprudence

The act of a woman giving birth to her offspring. Blake v.-Junkins, 35 Me. 433.

DELUSION. In medical jurisprudence. An insane delusion is an unreasoning and incorrigible belief in the existence of facts which are either impossible absolutely, or, at least, impossible under the circumstances of the individual. It is never the result of reasoning and reflection; it is not generated by them, and it cannot be dispelled by them; and hence it is not to be confounded with an *opinion*, however fantastic the latter may be. Guiteau's Case, D.C.D.C., 10 Fed. 161, 170; Davidson v. Piper, 221 Iowa 171, 265 N.W. 107, 109; McKinnon v. State, 51 Ga.App. 549, 181 S.E. 91; Hallucination as a delusion, Petroleum Casualty Co. v. Kincaid, Tex.Civ.App., 93 S.W.2d 499, 501; belief in the impossible, In re Leedom's Estate, 347 Pa. 180, 32 A.2d 3; as respects testamentary capacity, In re McDowell's Estate, 103 N.J.Eq. 346, 143 A. 325, 326.

Systematized Delusion

One based on a false premise, pursued by a logical process of reasoning to an insane conclusion; there being one central delusion around which other aberrations of the mind converge; Taylor v. McClintock, 87 Ark. 243, 112 S.W. 405. See Insanity.

DEM. An abbreviation for "demise;" *e. g., Doe dem. Smith,* Doe, on the demise of Smith.

DEMAIN. See Demesne.

DEMAND, *v.* In practice. To claim as one's due; to require; to ask relief. To summon; to call in court. "Although solemnly *demanded,* comes not, but makes default." Fossett v. State, 34 Okl.Cr. 106, 245 P. 668, 669.

DEMAND, *n.* A peremptory claim to thing of right, differing from claim, in that it presupposes that there is no defense or doubt upon question of right, Golden v. Golden, 155 Okl. 10, 8 P.2d 42, 45; Anderson v. Commercial Credit Co., 110 Mont. 333, 101 P.2d 367, 369; National Life & Accident Ins. Co. v. Dove, 141 Tex. 464, 174 S.W.2d 245, 247.

The assertion of a legal right; a legal obligation asserted in the courts; a word of art of an extent greater in its signification than any other word except "claim." Nunn v. Titche-Goettinger Co., Tex.Civ.App., 196 S.W. 890, 892. Demand for payment. Peterson v. Rodgers, 51 Ariz. 502, 78 P.2d 480, 482; assessment upon corporate stock of deceased. Smith v. Fechheimer, 124 Fla. 757, 169 So. 395, 398; presentment of statement, Davison v. Klaess, 280 N.Y. 252, 20 N.E.2d 744, 746. However, under some statutes "demand" has a more restricted meaning. Hillside Securities Co. v. Minter, 300 Mo. 380, 254 S.W. 188, 193.

A debt or amount due. Inhabitants of Town of Frankfort v. Waldo Lumber Co., 128 Me. 1, 145 A. 241, 243; Caldwell v. Morfa, D.C.Tex., 24 F.2d 106, 107.

An imperative request preferred by one person to another, under a claim of right, requiring the latter to do or yield something or to abstain from some act. Zimmerman v. Hicks, C.C.A., 7 F.2d 443, 445; Norwood Nat. Bank v. Piedmont Pub. Co., 106 S.C. 472, 91 S.E. 866, 867; school district's request that depositary honor checks for salaries. School District of City of Lansing v. Fidelity & Casualty Co. of New York, 266 Mich. 189, 253 N.W. 263; demand for extradition, Ex parte King, 139 Me. 203, 28 A.2d 562, 564.

The seeking after a commodity or service. It is not something static, but necessarily contains the idea of "competition" and a realization that markets are as much limited by sales efforts as by capacity to produce. Mendota Coal & Coke Co. v. Eastern Ry. & Lumber Co., C.C.A.Wash., 53 F.2d 77, 82.

—Compulsory demand. "Compulsory demand" by the true owner of an article, justifying surrender and recovery by the one who surrenders it as against his vendor, means when the true owner presents his claim and establishes his paramount title. Jordan v. Van Duzee, 139 Minn. 103, 165 N.W. 877, 879, L.R.A. 1918B, 1136.

—Cross-demand. A demand that is preferred by one party to an action in opposition to a demand already preferred against him by his adversary. Drovers' State Bank v. Elliott, 97 Kan. 64, 154 P. 255, 256.

—Demand in reconvention. A demand which the defendant institutes in consequence of that which the plaintiff has brought against him. Used in Louisiana. Equivalent to a "counterclaim" elsewhere. McLeod v. Bertschey, 33 Wis. 177, 14 Am. Rep. 755.

—Demand note. A note that is due at once; one on which suit may be brought without any formal demand. Wilson v. Stark, 146 Miss. 498, 112 So. 390, 392.

—Legal demand. A demand properly made, as to form, time, and place, by a person lawfully authorized. Foss v. Norris, 70 Me. 118.

—On demand. A promissory note payable "on demand" is a present debt, and is payable without any actual demand, or, if a demand is necessary, the bringing of a suit is enough. Appeal of Andress, 99 Pa. 424.

—Personal demand. A demand for payment of a bill or note, made upon the drawer, acceptor or maker, in person. See 1 Daniel, Neg. Inst. § 589.

—Reasonable public demand for a bank. Such a desire upon the part of the community for the bank as will make its coming welcome and insure an amount of business sufficient to promise it success. It may come from the natural desire of the community and upon its own initiative, or it may be the result of propaganda. State v. State Securities Commission, 145 Minn. 221, 176 N.W. 759, 760.

DEMAND NOTE. A note which expressly states that it is payable on demand, on presentation or at sight; a note in which no time for payment is expressed, Cassity v. Cassity, 147 Kan. 411, 76 P.2d 862, 866; Kent v. Lampman, 59 Cal.App.2d 407, 139 P.2d 57, 59; Tarlton v. Johnson, Mo.App., 138 S.W.2d 49, 52; a note issued, accepted or indorsed when overdue, as regards person so issuing, accepting or indorsing it. Nees v. Hagan, 22 Tenn.App. 28, 118 S.W.2d 566, 568; DeLoach v. Adams Loan & Investment Co., 62 Ga.App. 61, 7 S.E.2d 580, 581.

DEMANDA. In Spanish law. The petition of a plaintiff, setting forth his demand. Las Partidas, pt. 3, tit. 10, l. 3.

DEMANDANT. The plaintiff or party suing in a real action. Co. Litt. 127.

DEMANDRESS. A female demandent.

DEMEANOR. As respects a witness or other person, relates to physical appearance. People v. Vaughan, 131 Cal.App. 265, 21 P.2d 438. It embraces such facts as the tone of voice in which a witness' statement is made, the hesitation or readiness with which his answers are given, the look of the witness, his carriage, his evidences of surprise, his gestures, his zeal, his bearing, his expression, his yawns, the use of his eyes, his furtive or meaning glances, or his shrugs, the pitch of his voice, his self-possession or embarrassment, his air of candor or seeming levity. Rains v. Rains, 17 N.J.Misc. 310, 8 A.2d 715, 717.

DEMEASE. In old English law. Death.

DEMEMBRATION. In Scotch law. Maliciously cutting off or otherwise separating one limb from another. 1 Hume, 323; Bell.

DEMENS. One whose mental faculties are enfeebled; one who has lost his mind; distinguished from *amens,* one totally insane. 4 Coke, 128.

DEMENTED. Of unsound mind.

DEMENTENANT EN AVANT. L. Fr. From this time forward. Kelham.

DEMENTIA. See Insanity.

DEMENTIA PRAECOX. A term used to include a wide range of mental disorders which occur in early life. It is also called adolescent insanity and schizophrenia. Dementia praecox includes three types, namely, primary dementia, catatonia, and hebephrenia. Loftin v. Yancey, 182 Okl. 313, 77 P.2d 107, 108; Honrath v. New York Life Ins. Co., 65 S.D. 480, 275 N.W. 258, 259, 112 A.L.R. 1272; Lee v. United States, C.C.A.Ga., 91 F.2d 326, 330. Also, see Insanity.

DEMESNE. Domain; dominical; held in one's own right, and not of a superior; not allotted to tenants.

In the language of pleading, own; proper; original. Thus, *son assault demesne,* his own assault, his assault originally or in the first place.

Ancient Demesne

See Ancient.

Demesne as of Fee

A man is said to be seised *in his demesne as of fee* of a corporeal inheritance, because he has a property, *dominicum* or *demesne,* in the *thing* itself. But when he has no dominion in the thing itself, as in the case of an incorporeal hereditament, he is said to be *seised* as of fee, and not in his *demesne* as of fee. 2 Bl. Comm. 106; Littleton, § 10; Barnet v. Ihrie, 17 Serg. & R. (Pa.) 196.

Demesne Lands

In English law. Those lands of a manor not granted out in tenancy, but reserved by the lord for his own use and occupation. Lands set apart and appropriated by the lord for his own private use, as for the supply of his table, and the maintenance of his family; the opposite of *tenemental* lands. Tenancy and demesne, however, were not in every sense the opposites of each other; lands held for years or at will being included among demesne lands, as well as those in the lord's actual possession. Spelman; 2 Bl. Comm. 90.

Demesne Lands of the Crown

That share of lands reserved to the crown at the original distribution of landed property, or which came to it afterwards by forfeiture or otherwise. 1 Bl. Comm. 286; 2 Steph. Comm. 550.

Demesnial

Pertaining to a *demesne.*

DEMI. French. Half; the half. Used chiefly in composition.

As to demi "Mark," "Official," "Vill," see those titles.

DEMI-SANGUE, or DEMY-SANGUE. Half-blood.

DEMIDIETAS. In old records. A half or moiety.

DEMIES. In some universities and colleges this term is synonymous with "scholars."

DEMINUTIO. In the civil law. A taking away; loss or deprivation. See Capitis Deminutio.

DEMISE, *v.* In conveyancing. To convey or create an estate for years or life; to lease. The usual and operative word in leases: "Have granted, *demised,* and to farm let, and by these presents do grant, *demise,* and to farm let." 2 Bl. Comm. 317; 1 Steph. Comm. 476; Co. Litt. 45*a*; Carr v. King, 24 Cal.App. 713, 142 P. 131, 133.

DEMISE, *n.* In conveyancing. A conveyance of an estate to another for life, for years, or at will; most commonly for years; a lease. 1 Steph. Comm. 475. Priddy v. Green, Tex.Civ.App., 220 S.W. 243, 248. Originally a posthumous grant; commonly a lease or conveyance for a term of years; sometimes applied to any conveyance, in fee, for life, or for years. Pub. St. Mass. 1882, p. 1289.

"Demise" is synonymous with "lease" or "let." The use of the term in a lease imports a covenant for quiet enjoyment. Evans v. Williams, 291 Ky. 484, 165 S.W.2d 52, 55; Sixty-Third & Halsted Realty Co. v. Chicago City Bank & Trust Co., 299 Ill.App. 297, 20 N.E.2d 162, 167; and implies a covenant by lessor of good right and title to make the lease. Evans v. Williams, 291 Ky. 484, 165 S.W.2d 52, 55.

A charter of a barge without motive power accompanied by bargee paid by owner, The Nat. E. Sutton, D.C.N.Y., 42 F.2d 229, 232; Harbor Towboat Co. v. Lowe, D.C.N.Y., 47 F.Supp. 454, 456; or of a tug or other vessel under circumstances making charterer owner pro hac vice, Davison Chemical Corporation v. The Henry W. Card, D.C. N.Y., 51 F.Supp. 380, 382; Conners Marine Co. v. Wathen, D.C.N.Y., 43 F.Supp. 283, 284. Under a demise charter, there is but a hiring of the vessel, under which no title passes to the charterer but merely the right to possess and control it for a limited period. McGahern v. Koppers Coal Co., C.C.A.Pa., 108 F.2d 652, 653.

The word is also used as a synonym for "decease" or "death." In England it is especially employed to denote the death of the sovereign.

—Demise and redemise. In conveyancing. Mutual leases made from one party to another on each side, of the same land, or something out of it; as when A. grants a lease to B. at a nominal rent (as of a pepper corn), and B. redemises the same property to A. for a shorter time at a real, substantial rent. Jacob; Whishaw.

—Demise of the crown. The natural dissolution of the king is generally so called; an expression which signifies merely a transfer of property. By demise of the crown we mean only that, in consequence of the disunion of the king's natural body from his body politic, the kingdom is transferred or demised to his successor, and so the royal dignity remains perpetual. 1 Bl. Comm. 249; Plowd. 234.

—Several demises. In English practice. In the action of ejectment, it was formerly customary, in case there were any doubt as to the legal estate being in the plaintiff, to insert in the declaration several demises from as many different persons; but this was rendered unnecessary by the provisions of the common-law procedure acts.

—Single demise. A declaration in ejectment might contain either one demise or several. When it contained only one, it was called a "declaration with a single demise."

DEMISI. Lat. I have demised or leased. *Demisi, concessi, et ad firmam tradidi;* have demised, granted, and to farm let. The usual operative words in ancient leases, as the corresponding English words are in the modern forms. 2 Bl. Comm. 317, 318; Koch v. Hustis, 113 Wis. 599, 87 N.W. 834.

DEMISSIO. L. Lat. A demise or letting. Chiefly used in the phrase *ex demissione* (on the demise), which formed part of the title of the cause in the old actions of ejectment, where it signified that the nominal plaintiff (a fictitious person) held the estate "on the demise" of, that is, by a lease from, the real plaintiff.

DEMOBILIZATION. In military law. The dismissal of an army or body of troops from active service.

DEMOCRACY. That form of government in which the sovereign power resides in and is exercised by the whole body of free citizens, as distinguished from a monarchy, aristocracy, or oligarchy. According to the theory of a pure democracy, every citizen should participate directly in the business of governing, and the legislative assembly should comprise the whole people. But the ultimate lodgment of the sovereignty being the distinguishing feature, the introduction of the representative system does not remove a government from this type. However, a government of the latter kind is sometimes specifically described as a "representative democracy."

Town form of government constitutes pure democracy as distinguished from representative government. Commonwealth v. Town of Hudson, 315 Mass. 335, 52 N.E.2d 566, 572.

Democracy is loosely used of governments in which the sovereign powers are exercised by all the people or a large number of them, or specifically, in modern use, of a representative government where there is equality of rights without hereditary or arbitrary differences in rank or privilege; and is distinguished from *aristocracy*. * * * In modern representative democracies, as the United States and France, though the governing body, that is, the electorate, is a minority of the total population, the principle on which the government is based is popular sovereignty, which distinguishes them from *aristocracies*. Webster's New Int.Dict.

DEMOCRATIC. Of or pertaining to democracy, or to a political party called "democratic," particularly, in the United States, the Democratic party, which succeeded the Anti-federalist, or Republican, party.

DEMOLISH. To throw or pull down; to raze; to destroy the fabrication of; to pull to pieces; hence to ruin; destroy. Star Mfg. Co. v. Quarrles, 172 Okl. 550, 46 P.2d 497, 498. To destroy totally or to commence the work of total destruction with the purpose of completing the same. 50 L.J.M.C. 141. It is not synonymous with "remove." Durrett v. Woods, 155 La. 533, 99 So. 430, 431.

DEMONETIZATION. The disuse of a particular metal for purposes of coinage. The withdrawal of the value of a metal as money.

DEMONSTRATE. To teach by exhibition of samples; to derive from admitted premises by steps of reasoning which admit of no doubt; to prove indubitably. Espenhain v. Barker, 121 Or. 621, 256 P. 766, 768. To show or prove value or merits by operation. J. A. Fay & Egan Co. v. Mims, 151 S.C. 484, 149 S.E. 246, 248.

DEMONSTRATIO. Lat. Description; addition; denomination. Occurring often in the phrase, *"Falsa demonstratio non nocet,"* (a false description does not harm.) 2 Bla. Comm. 382, n.; 2 P. Wms. 140; 1 Greenl. Ev. § 291; Wigr. Wills 208, 233.

DEMONSTRATION. Description; pointing out. That which is said or written to designate a thing or person.

Evidence

Absolutely convincing proof. That proof which excludes all possibility of error. Treadwell v. Whittier, 80 Cal. 574, 22 P. 266, 5 L.R.A. 498, 13 Am.St.Rep. 175.

False Demonstration

See False Demonstration.

DEMONSTRATIVE EVIDENCE. That evidence addressed directly to the senses without intervention of testimony. Kabase v. State, 31 Ala.App. 77, 12 So.2d 758, 764.

Demonstrative evidence of negligence has been applied to that kind of negligence which is usually expressed by *res ipsa loquitur*.

DEMONSTRATIVE LEGACY. See Legacy.

DEMOTION. A reduction to lower rank or grade, or to lower type of position, though holder's salary remains the same. Reed v. City Council of City of Roseville, 60 Cal.App.2d 628, 141 P.2d 459, 463. Assistant fire chief reduced in rank, McCarthy v. Steinkellner, 223 Wis. 605, 270 N.W. 551; under Teachers' Tenure Act. Smith v. School Dist. of Philadelphia, 334 Pa. 197, 5 A.2d 535, 539; indefinite suspension without pay. City of Knoxville v. Smith, 176 Tenn. 73, 138 S.W.2d 422, 424.

DEMPSTER. In Scotch law. A doomsman. One who pronounced the sentence of court. 1 How. State Tr. 937.

DEMUR. To present a demurrer; to take an exception to the sufficiency in point of law of a pleading or state of facts alleged. See Demurrer.

DEMURRABLE. Subject to a demurrer. A pleading, petition, or the like, is said to be demurrable when it does not state such facts as support the claim, prayer, or defense put forward. 5 Ch. Div. 979.

DEMURRAGE. In maritime law. The sum which is fixed by the contract of carriage, or which is allowed, as remuneration to the owner of a ship for the detention of his vessel beyond the number of days allowed by the charter-party for loading and unloading or for sailing. Also the detention of the vessel by the freighter beyond such time. See 3 Kent, Comm. 203; 2 Steph. Comm. 185. Continental Grain Co. v. Armour Fertilizer Works, D.C.N.Y. 22 F.Supp. 49, 54; Yone Suzuki v. Central Argentine Ry., C.C.A.N.Y., 27 F.2d 795, 804. The term has been adopted in railroad practice. Central R. Co. of N. J. v. Gallena-Poole, Inc., 107 N.J.Eq. 267, 152 A. 251, 252; Sibley, L. B. & S. Ry. Co. v. Braswell Sand & Gravel Co., La.App., 199 So. 427, 428.

The sum agreed to be paid to the ship for delay caused without her fault, and which ordinarily does not begin to run until the lay days have been used up. Earn Line S. S. Co. v. Manati Sugar Co., C.C.A.N.Y., 269 F. 774, 776. The amount agreed upon or allowed by law for unreasonable detention. Clyde v. Wood, 179 N.Y.S. 252, 255, 189 App. Div. 737; W. R. Grace & Co. v. Hansen, C.C.A.Wash., 273 F. 486, 496.

"Demurrage" is only an extended freight or reward to the vessel, in compensation for the earnings she is improperly caused to lose. Every improper detention of a vessel may be considered a demurrage, and compensation under that name be obtained for it. Donaldson v. McDowell, Holmes, 290, Fed.Cas.No.3,985.

"Demurrage" is a claim for damages for failure of the consignee to accept delivery of the goods. Little v. One Cargo of Lumber, D.C.Fla., 2 F.2d 608, 609.

DEMURRANT. One who demurs; the party who, in pleading, interposes a demurrer.

DEMURRER.

In Equity

An allegation of a defendant, which, admitting the matters of fact alleged by the bill to be true, shows that as they are therein set forth they are insufficient for the plaintiff to proceed upon or to oblige the defendant to answer; or that, for some reason apparent on the face of the bill, or on account of the omission of some matter which ought to be contained therein, or for want of some circumstances which ought to be attendant thereon, the defendant ought not to be compelled to answer to the whole bill, or to some certain part thereof. Mitf. Eq. Pl. 107. See, also, Goldsmith v. Mead Johnson & Co., 176 Md. 682, 7 A.2d 176, 179.

A general demurrer in equity, as a separate entity from a demurrer on specific grounds, tests the equity of a bill in the same manner as a motion to dismiss for want of equity, and, in considering the bill on such a demurrer, amendable defects are taken as amended. Johnson v. Pugh, 193 So. 317, 239 Ala. 12.

By Federal Rules of Civil Procedure, demurrers, pleas and exceptions for insufficiency of a pleading are abolished; every defence in law shall be made by motion or by answer; motions going to jurisdiction, venue, process, or failure to state a claim are to be disposed of before trial, unless the court orders otherwise.

In Pleading

The formal mode of disputing the sufficiency in law of the pleading of the other side. In effect it is an allegation that, even if the facts as stated in the pleading to which objection is taken be true, yet their legal consequences are not such as to put the demurring party to the necessity of answering them or proceeding further with the cause. Green v. Carter, 28 Ohio App. 492, 162 N.E. 814, 815; State v. Broad River Power Co., 177 S.C. 240, 181 S.E. 41; Mountain Park Institute v. Lovill, 198 N.C. 642, 153 S.E. 114, 116; State v. California Packing Corporation, 105 Utah 191, 145 P.2d 784.

A "demurrer" is not an absolute admission of any fact but simply admits those facts that are well pleaded. Commonwealth ex rel. Duff v. Keenan, 347 Pa. 574, 33 A.2d 244, 248.

An objection made by one party to his opponent's pleading, alleging that he ought not to answer it, for some defect in law in the pleading. It admits the facts, and refers the law arising thereon to the court. R. L. Davies & Co. v. Blomberg, 185 N.C. 496, 117 S.E. 497.

It imports that the objecting party will not proceed, but will wait the judgment of the court whether he is bound so to do. Co.Litt. 71*b;* Steph.Pl. 61; Kramer v. Barth, 139 N.Y.S. 341, 344, 79 Misc. 80.

Classification and Varieties

A *general* demurrer is a demurrer framed in general terms, without showing specifically the nature of the objection, and which is usually resorted to where the objection is to matter of substance. Steph.Pl. 140–142; 1 Chit.Pl. 663. See Maryland Casualty Co. v. Arnold, 51 Ga.App. 562, 180 S.E. 906, 907.

Thus, a demurrer on the ground that the complaint sets forth no cause of action, is a general demurrer, Alabama Power Co. v. Curry, 228 Ala. 444, 153 So. 634; and a motion to dismiss a bill on ground that there is no equity apparent on the face thereof or that court has no jurisdiction is treated as a general demurrer. People v. Sterling, 357 Ill. 354, 192 N.E. 229, 231.

A general demurrer to an indictment challenges only matters of form and substance appearing on its face. It is one which raises an objection that averments are insufficient in law to support the action or defense without specifying any particular cause or defect, and is sufficient only to reach matters of substance. Mountain Park Institute v. Lovill, 198 N.C. 642, 153 S.E. 114, 116.

A motion to dismiss a complaint for failure to state a claim upon which relief can be granted is equivalent to a general demurrer. Louisiana Farmers' Protective Union v. Great Atlantic & Pacific Tea Co. of America, D.C.Ark., 40 F.Supp. 897, 908.

A *special* demurrer goes merely to structure or form of pleading which it attacks, and usually only to some portion thereof, and must distinctly specify wherein defect lies. Huff v. Palmer, 356 Ill. 563, 191 N.E. 199, 202; Cameron v. Evans Securities Corp., 119 Cal.App. 164, 6 P.2d 272, 274; It is one which excepts to the sufficiency of the pleadings on the opposite side, and shows specifically the nature of the objection, and the particular ground of the exception. 3 Bouv. Inst. no. 3022. Dairy Region Land Corporation v. Harding, Tex.Civ.App., 266 S.W. 181, 182; Johanson v. Cudahy Packing Co., 107 Utah 114, 152 P.2d 98, 105.

While general demurrer on specific grounds relating to different allegations of bill may be called "special demurrer," which attacks different parts of bill specifically, such demurrer fails, if bill is good as pleading and remaining allegations are sufficient to support relief prayed. Forcum v. Symmes, 106 Fla. 510, 143 So. 630, 631.

A *speaking* demurrer is one which, in order to sustain itself, requires the aid of a fact not appearing on the face of the pleading objected to, or, in other words, which alleges or assumes the existence of a fact not already pleaded, and which constitutes the ground of objection and is condemned both by the common law and the code system of pleading. Ellis v. Perley, 200 N.C. 403, 157 S.E. 29, 30. Ferris v. Union Sav. Bank, 45 Ga.App. 544, 165 S.E. 450; Preston A. Blair Co. v. Rose, 56 Idaho 114, 51 P.2d 209, 212; Metropolitan Life Ins. Co. v. Perrin, 184 Miss. 249, 183 So. 917, 920; Town of Randolph v. Lyon, 106 Vt. 495, 175 A. 1, 2; Whaley v. First Nat. Bank, 229 Ala. 153, 155 So. 574.

A speaking demurrer is one which alleges some new matter, not disclosed by the pleading against which the demurrer is aimed and not judicially known or legally presumed to be true. Blythe v. Enslen, 219 Ala. 638, 123 So. 71, 73; Kansas Life Ins. Co. v. First Bank of Truscott, Tex.Civ. App., 47 S.W.2d 675, 677; In re Ferris' Estate, Iowa, 14 N.W.2d 889, 894.

A *parol* demurrer (not properly a demurrer at all) was a staying of the pleadings; a suspension of the proceedings in an action during the nonage of an infant, especially in a real action. Now abolished. 3 Bl. Comm. 300.

Demurrer book. In practice. A record of the issue on a demurrer at law, containing a transcript of the pleadings, with proper entries; and intended for the use of the court and counsel on the argument. 3 Bl. Comm. 317; 3 Steph. Comm. 581.

Demurrer ore tenus. An objection to the introduction of any evidence on the ground that the complaint or petition fails to state a cause of action. Cleveland v. Bateman, 21 N.M. 675, 158 P. 648, 652, Ann.Cas.1918E, 1011; Peerless Fixture Co. v. Frick, Mo.App., 133 S.W.2d 1089, 1090. This name is sometimes given to a ruling on an objection to evidence, but is not properly a demurrer at all. Mandelert v. Land Co., 104 Wis. 423, 80 N.W. 726; It should be considered as a general demurrer only. Dawkins v. People's Bank & Trust Co., 117 Okl. 181, 245 P. 594, 596.

Demurrer to evidence. This proceeding is analogous to a demurrer to a pleading. It is an objection or exception by one of the parties in an action at law, to the effect that the evidence which his adversary produced is insufficient in point of law (whether true or not) to make out his case or sustain the issue. Upon joinder in demurrer, the jury is discharged, and the case is argued to the court *in banc*, who gives judgment upon the facts as shown in evidence. See 3 Bl. Comm. 372; State v. Moody, 150 N.C. 847, 64 S.E. 431, 432. The practice has been largely superseded by motions for nonsuit and directed verdict. Hopkins v. Nashville, C. & St. L. Ry., 96 Tenn. 409, 34 S.W. 1029, 1034, 32 L.R.A. 354. Thus, a motion to nonsuit, Herrick v. Barzee, 96 Or. 357, 190 P. 141, 145; Perkins v. Maiden, 57 Cal.App.2d 46, 134 P.2d 30, 34, a motion to dismiss at close of plaintiff's evidence for failure to prove essential facts, Mansfield v. Reserve Oil Co., 38 N.M. 187, 29 P.2d 491, 492; Fewkes v. Borah, 376 Ill. 596, 35 N.E.2d 69, 72, have been held to be, and a defendant's motion for a directed verdict, made at close of the evidence, is equivalent to, a "demurrer to the evidence" for insufficiency to sustain a verdict for plaintiff. Mills v. Richardson, 126 Me. 244, 137 A. 689, 690. A motion to exclude evidence has the effect of a demurrer to the evidence, the chief points of difference being the stage of the proceeding at which each is available and the consequences resulting from deferring the motion to exclude. Thornhill v. Thornhill, 172 Va. 553, 2 S.E.2d 318, 319. For a discussion of the subject see Hopkins v. Nashville, C. & St. L. R. R., 96 Tenn. 409, 34 S.W. 1029, 32 L.R.A. 354.

Demurrer to interrogatories. Where a witness objects to a question propounded (particularly on the taking of a deposition) and states his reason for objecting or refusing to answer, it is called a "demurrer to the interrogatory," though the term cannot here be understood as used in its technical sense. 2 Swanst. 194; Gresl. Eq. Ev. 61; 2 Atk. 524; 1 Y. & J. 132.

DEMY SANKE, DEMY SANGUE. Half-blood. A corruption of *demi-sang*.

DEN. A valley. Blount. A hollow place among woods. Cowell.

DEN AND STROND. In old English law. Liberty for ships or vessels to run aground, or come ashore (strand themselves). Cowell.

DENARIATE. In old English law. As much land as is worth one penny *per annum*.

DENARII. An ancient general term for any sort of *pecunia numerata*, or ready money. The French use the word "*denier*" in the same sense, —*payer de ses propres deniers*.

DENARII DE CARITATE. In English law. Customary oblations made to a cathedral church at Pentecost.

DENARII S. PETRI. (Commonly called "Peter's Pence.") An annual payment on St. Peter's feast of a penny from every family to the pope, during the time that the Roman Catholic religion was established in England.

DENARIUS. The chief silver coin among the Romans, worth 8d.; it was the seventh part of a Roman ounce. Also an English penny. The denarius was first coined five years before the first Punic war, B. C. 269. In later times a copper coin was called "*denarius.*" Smith, Dict. Antiq.

DENARIUS DEI. (Lat. "God's penny.") Earnest money; money given as a token of the completion of a bargain. It differs from *arrhæ* in this: that *arrhæ* is a part of the consideration, while the *denarius Dei* is no part of it. The latter was given away in charity; whence the name. 1 Duvergnoy, n. 132; 3 Duvergnoy, n. 49; *Répert. de Jur., Denier à Dieu.*

DENARIUS TERTIUS COMITATUS. In old English law. A third part or penny of the county paid to its earl, the other two parts being reserved to the crown.

DENIAL. A traverse in the pleading of one party of an allegation of fact set up by the other; a defense. See Flack v. O'Brien, 43 N.Y.S. 854, 19 Misc. 399; Mott v. Baxter, 29 Colo. 418, 68 P. 220. A deprivation, as the denial of a constitutional right, U. S. v. Carolene Products Co., Ill., 58 S.Ct. 778, 783, 304 U.S. 144, 82 L.Ed. 1234, or a denial of civil rights. State of New Jersey v. Weinberger, D.C.N.J., 38 F.2d 298, 302. A refusal or rejection, as the denial of a claim on a war risk policy by Veterans' Administration, U. S. v. Green, C.C.A.Tenn., 84 F.2d 449, 450; Morris v. U. S., C.C.A.Miss., 96 F.2d 731, 732, or of a claim for workmen's compensation. Commercial Casualty Ins. Co. v. Hilton, Tex.Civ.App., 55 S.W.2d 120, or of probation. People v. Lopez, 43 Cal. App.2d 854, 110 P.2d 140, 144. A disavowal. People v. Bell, 96 Cal.App. 503, 274 P. 393, 396; Massell v. Fourth Nat. Bank, 38 Ga.App. 601, 144 S.E. 806, 807.

General and Specific

In code pleading, a general denial is one which puts in issue all the material averments of the complaint or petition, and permits the defendant to prove any and all facts tending to negative those averments or any of them. Telford v. Iowa Guarantee Mortg. Corp., 58 S.D. 261, 235 N.W. 663, 665. A specific denial is a separate denial applicable to one particular allegation of the complaint. Gas Co. v. San Francisco, 9 Cal. 470; An answer by way of a general denial is the equivalent of, and substitute for, the general issue under the common-law system of pleading. It gives to the defendant the same right to require the plaintiff to establish by proof all the material facts necessary to show his right to a recovery as was given by that plea. Kline v. Harris, 30 N.D. 421, 152 N.W. 687, 688, Ann.Cas.1917D, 1176.

DENIER. L. Fr. In old English law. Denial; refusal. *Denier* is when the rent (being demanded upon the land) is not paid. Finch, Law, b. 3, c. 5.

DENIER A DIEU. In French law. Earnest money; a sum of money given in token of the completion of a bargain. The phrase is a translation of the Latin *Denarius Dei*, (*q. v.*).

DENIZATION. The act of making one a denizen; the conferring of the privileges of citizenship upon an alien born. Cro. Jac. 540. See Denizen.

DENIZE. To make a man a denizen or citizen.

DENIZEN. In English law. A person who, being an alien born, has obtained, *ex donatione regis*, letters patent to make him an English subject,—a high and incommunicable branch of the royal prerogative. A denizen is in a kind of middle state between an alien and a natural-born subject, and partakes of the *status* of both of these. 1 Bl. Comm. 374; 7 Coke 6; Ex parte Gilroy, D.C. N.Y., 257 F. 110, 128.

The term is used to signify a person who, being an alien by birth, has obtained letters patent making him an English subject. The king may denize, but not naturalize, a man; the latter requiring the consent of parliament, as under the naturalization act, 1870, 33 & 34 Vict. c. 14. A denizen holds a position midway between an alien and a natural-born or naturalized subject, being able to take lands by purchase or devise, (which an alien could not until 1870 do,) but not able to take lands by descent, (which a natural-born or naturalized subject may do.) Brown.

The denizen becomes a British subject from the date of the letters while a naturalized person is placed in a position equivalent to that of a natural-born subject; Dicey, Confl.Laws 164.

The word is also used in this sense in South Carolina. See McClenaghan v. McClenaghan, 1 Strob.Eq., S.C., 319, 47 Am.Dec. 532.

In American law. A dweller; a stranger admitted to certain rights in a foreign country or as one who lives habitually in a country but is not a native born citizen; one holding a middle state between an alien and a natural born subject. United States ex rel. Zdunic v. Uhl, D.C. N.Y., 46 F.Supp. 688, 691. One who has some relation to the enemy nation which is not lost by the alien's presence within the United States. United States ex rel. Zdunic v. Uhl, C.C.A.N.Y., 137 F.2d 858, 861; United States ex rel. D'Esquiva v. Uhl, C.C.A.N.Y., 137 F.2d 903, 905.

Thus, one who lived and worked in Austria in 1938 at time Germany obtained control of Austrian government, and continued to live there until leaving for the United States in 1939, at which time he was issued a German passport, was a "denizen" of Germany, within Enemy Alien Act. United States ex rel. Zdunic v. Uhl, D.C.N.Y., 47 F.Supp. 520.

A denizen, in the primary, but obsolete, sense of the word, is a natural-born subject of a country. Co. Litt. 129*a*; Levy v. McCartee, 6 Pet. 102, 116, 8 L.Ed. 334.

DENMAN'S (LORD) ACT. An English statute, for the amendment of the law of evidence, (6 & 7 Vict. c. 85,) which provides that no person offered as a witness shall thereafter be excluded by reason of incapacity, from crime or interest, from giving evidence.

DENMAN'S (MR.) ACT. An English statute, for the amendment of procedure in criminal trials, (28 & 29 Vict. c. 18,) allowing counsel to sum up the evidence in criminal as in civil trials, provided the prisoner be defended by counsel.

DENOMBREMENT. In French feudal law. A minute or act drawn up, on the creation of a fief, containing a description of the fief, and all the rights and incidents belonging to it. Guyot, Inst. Feud. c. 3.

DENOMINATIO FIERI DEBET A DIGNIORIBUS. Denomination should be made from the more worthy.

DENOMINATION. The act of naming. A society of individuals known by the same name, usually a religious society.

DENOMINATIONAL. *adj.* Of, or pertaining to, a denomination; sectarian. Wesley Foundation at Seattle v. King County, 185 Wash. 12, 52 P.2d 1247, 1250; Constitutional Defense League v. Waters, 308 Pa. 150, 162 A. 216, 217.

DENOUNCE. To declare (an act or thing) to be a crime and prescribe a punishment for it. State v. De Hart, 109 La. 570, 33 So. 605. The word is also used (not technically but popularly) as the equivalent of "accuse" or "inform against."

The term is frequently used in regard to treaties, indicating the act of one nation in giving notice to another nation of its intention to terminate an existing treaty between the two nations. The French *dénoncer* means to declare, to lodge an information against. Bellows, Fr. Dict.

DENOUNCEMENT.

In Mexican Mining Law

Denouncement is an application to the authorities for a grant of the right to work a mine, either on the ground of new discovery, or on the ground of forfeiture of the rights of a former owner, through abandonment or contravention of the mining law. Cent. Dict. See Castillero v. U. S., 2 Black, 109, 17 L.Ed. 360; Stewart v. King, 85 Or. 14, 166 P. 55, 56.

A "denouncement" is an application for the acquisition of land for mining purposes, under certain rules prescribed by Mexican laws. The application is called the "denouncement," and, when approved by the Mexican government, is called "concession" or "title," sometimes "patent." It is then a grant given by the government to use the land applied for, for the purpose of mining, and is called the "title." Winningham v. Dyo, Tex.Com.App., 48 S.W.2d 600, 603.

In Spanish and Mexican Law

A judicial proceeding for the forfeiture of land held by an alien.

Though real property might be acquired by an alien in fraud of the law,—that is, without observing its requirements,—he nevertheless retained his right and title to it, but was liable to be deprived of it by the proper proceeding of denouncement, which in its substantive characteristics was equivalent to the inquest of office found, at common law. De Merle v. Mathews, 26 Cal. 477.

The "denouncement of a new work" is a proceeding to obtain an order of court, in the nature of an injunction, against the construction of a new building or other work, which, if completed, would injuriously affect the plaintiff's property. Von Schmidt v. Huntington, 1 Cal. 55.

DENSHIRING OF LAND. (Otherwise called "burn-beating.") A method of improving land by casting parings of earth, turf, and stubble into heaps, which when dried are burned into ashes for a compost. Cowell.

DENTIFRICE. Any preparation used for cleansing the teeth. In re Edmand, Cust. & Pat.App., 39 F.2d 723.

DENTIST. One whose business it is to diagnose and treat imperfections or diseases of human teeth. People v. Hewson, 181 App.Div. 212, 168 N.Y.S. 104. Defined by the California Dental Act as any person who shall for remuneration perform an operation of any kind, or treat diseases of the human teeth. Jacobs v. Board of Dental Examiners of California, 189 Cal. 709, 209 P. 1006, 1007.

DENTISTRY. A special department of medical science, dealing with the treatment of the diseases, etc., of human teeth. Commonwealth v. Heller, 277 Pa. 539, 121 A. 558, 559. The term includes the supplying of dentures, bridges and other artificial substitutes to the user or prospective user thereof. Curtis v. State, 78 Okl.Cr. 282, 147 P.2d 465, 468. Winner v. Kadow, 373 Ill. 192, 25 N.E.2d 882, 883.

DENUMERATION. The act of present payment.

DENUNCIA DE OBRA NUEVA. In Spanish law. The denouncement of a new work; being a proceeding to restrain the erection of some new work, as, for instance, a building which may, if completed, injuriously affect the property of the complainant; it is of a character similar to the interdicts of possession. Escriche; Von Schmidt v. Huntington, 1 Cal. 63.

DENUNCIATION.

In the Civil Law

The act by which an individual informs a public officer, whose duty it is to prosecute offenders, that a crime has been committed. See 1 Bro.Civ. Law 447; Ayliffe, Parerg. 210; Pothier, Proc.Cr. sect. 2, § 2.

The giving of an information in the ecclesiastical courts by one who was not the accuser.

In Scotch Practice

The act by which a person is declared to be a rebel, who has disobeyed the charge given on letters of horning. Bell.

DENUNTIATIO. In old English law. A public notice or summons. Bract. 202*b*.

DENY. To traverse. Perry v. Tumlin, 161 Ga. 392, 131 S.E. 70, 73. To refuse to grant a petition or protest. Safeway Stores v. Brown, Em.App., 138 F.2d 278, 280.

DEODAND. (L. Lat. *Deo dandum*, a thing to be given to God.) In English law. Any personal chattel which was the immediate occasion of the death of any reasonable creature, and which was forfeited to the crown to be applied to *pious* uses, and distributed in alms by the high almoner. 1 Hale, P.C. 419; Fleta, lib. 1, c. 25; 1 Bl.Comm. 300; 2 Steph.Comm. 365. See Parker-Harris Co. v. Tate, 135 Tenn. 509, 188 S.W. 54, L.R.A.1916F, 935.

DEOR HEDGE. In old English law. The hedge inclosing a deer park.

DEPART. To divide or separate actively. The departers of gold and silver were no more than the dividers and refiners of those metals. Cowell.

To go away, especially with reference to permanent visits. Pezzoni v. Pezzoni, 38 Cal.App. 209, 175 P. 801, 802. To withdraw from. Pomeroy v. National City Co., 209 Minn. 155, 296 N.W. 513, 517, 133 A.L.R. 766; City Co. of New York v. Stern, C.C.A.Minn., 110 F.2d 601, 603. To depart, as from the state, is not necessarily synonymous with the phrase "leave the state," or the phrase "absent from the state." Williams v. Williams, 57 Cal.App. 36, 206 P. 650, 652; Aronow v. Bishop, 112 Mont. 611, 120 P.2d 423, 424.

In Maritime Law

To leave a port; to be out of a port. To *depart* imports more than to *sail*, or set sail. A warranty in a policy that a vessel shall *depart* on or before a particular day is a warranty not only that she shall sail, but that she shall be *out of the port* on or before that day. 3 Maule & S. 461; 3 Kent Comm. 307, note. "To depart" does not mean merely to break ground, but fairly to set forward upon the voyage. Moir v. Assur. Co., 6 Taunt. 241; Young v. The Orpheus, 119 Mass. 185; The Helen Brown (D.C.) 28 F. 111.

In Pleading

To forsake or abandon the ground assumed in a former pleading, and assume a new one. See Departure.

DEPARTMENT. One of the territorial divisions of a country. The term is chiefly used in this sense in France, where the division of the country into departments is somewhat analogous, both territorially and for governmental purposes, to the division of an American state into counties. The United States have been divided into military departments, including certain portions of the country. Parker v. U. S., 1 Pet. 293, 7 L.Ed. 150.

Generally, a branch or division of governmental administration. Glendinning v. Curry, 153 Fla. 398, 14 So.2d 794, 802.

One of the divisions of the executive branch of government. Used in this sense in the United States, where each department is charged with a specific class of duties, and comprises an organized staff of officials; *e. g.*, the department of state, department of war, etc.

With reference to state or municipal administration, a "bureau" is merely a division of a department. In re McLaughlin, 210 N.Y.S. 68, 72, 124 Misc. 766.

Also, a division of a business, or of something comparable thereto. See State v. Arkansas Lumber Co., 126 Ark. 107, 189 S.W. 671; U. S. v. Elgin, J. & E. Ry. Co., Ill., 56 S.Ct. 841, 298 U.S. 492, 80 L.Ed. 1300.

DEPARTMENT STORE. Generally, a store in which a variety of merchandise is arranged in or offered for sale from several departments or sections, but the term cannot be applied with any certainty to a particular business and is too indefinite to be used as a classification for the purpose of taxation. Barker Bros. v. City of Los Angeles, 10 Cal.2d 603, 76 P.2d 97.

DEPARTURE. A deviation or divergence, from a standard rule or measurement. Hamilton Mfg. Co. v. Tubbs Mfg. Co., D.C.Mich., 216 F. 401, 409. From a permitted use of vehicle or route, Reddy-Waldhauer-Maffett Co. v. Spivey, 53 Ga.App. 117, 185 S.E. 147, 148. Jeffries v. Jodawelky, 304 Mich. 421, 8 N.W.2d 121, 122. From employment or work, United Employers Casualty Co. v. Barker, Tex.Civ.App., 148 S.W.2d 260, 263; Hartford Accident & Indemnity Co. v. Cardillo, 112 F.2d 11, 15, 72 App.D.C. 52.

A variance between pleading and proof. Kintner v. U. S., C.C.A.Colo., 71 F.2d 961, 962.

In Maritime Law

A deviation from the course prescribed in the policy of insurance.

In Pleading

The statement of matter in a replication, rejoinder, or subsequent pleading, as a cause of action or defense, which is not pursuant to the previous pleading of the same party, and which does not support and fortify it. 2 Williams, Saund. 84*a*, note 1; 2 Wils. 98; Co.Litt. 304*a*; Hanna v. Royce, 119 Or. 450, 249 P. 173, 175.

A departure occurs when party departs from cause or defense first made and has recourse to another. Livingston v. Malever, 103 Fla. 200, 137 So. 113, 118; Clonts v. State, 19 Ala.App. 130, 95 So. 562; Northwestern Nat. Life Ins. Co. v. Ward, 56 Okl. 188, 155 P. 524, 525; Burrell v. Masters, 65 Colo. 310, 176 P. 316, 317. Or, in other words, when the second pleading contains matter not pursuant to the former, and which does not support and fortify it. Hence a departure obviously can never take place till the replication. Steph.Pl. 410. Each subsequent pleading must pursue or support the former one; *i. e.*, the replication must support the declaration, and the rejoinder the plea, without departing out of it. 3 Bl.Comm. 310. An amendment to a petition changing the cause of action is not, technically, a "departure." King v. Milner, 63 Colo. 407, 167 P. 957, 960; MacGerry v. Rodgers, 144 Wash. 375, 258 P. 314, 315.

DEPARTURE IN DESPITE OF COURT. In old English practice. The tenant in a real action, having once appeared, was considered as constructively present in court until again called upon. Hence if, upon being demanded, he failed to appear, he was said to have "departed in despite [*i. e.*, contempt] of the court." Co.Litt. 139*a*; 8 Co. 62*a*; 1 Rolle, Abr. 583; Metc.Yelv. 211.

DEPASTURE. In old English law. To pasture. "If a man *depastures* unprofitable cattle in his ground." Bunb. 1, case 1.

DEPECULATION. A robbing of the prince or commonwealth; an embezzling of the public treasure.

DEPENDABLE, *adj.* Trustworthy or reliable, Anderson v. Wyoming Development Co., 60 Wyo. 417, 154 P.2d 318, 340; Evidence, Taylor v. Latimer, D.C.Mo., 47 F.Supp. 236, 238.

DEPENDENCE. A state of looking to another for support, maintenance, food, clothing, comfort and protection of a home and care. Central Life Assur. Soc. (Mutual) v. Gray, Tex., 32 S.W.2d 259, 261; Soderstrom v. Missouri Pac. R. Co., Mo.App., 141 S.W.2d 73, 79.

DEPENDENCY. A territory distinct from the country in which the supreme sovereign power resides, but belonging rightfully to it, and subject to the laws and regulations which the sovereign may think proper to prescribe. U. S. v. The Nancy, 3 Wash.C.C. 286, Fed.Cas.No.15,854; Posadas v. National City Bank of N. Y., Phil.Islands, 56 S.Ct. 349, 350, 296 U.S. 497, 80 L.Ed. 351.

It differs from a *colony,* because it is not settled by the citizens of the sovereign or mother state; and from *possession,* because it is held by other title than that of mere conquest.

A relation between two persons, where one is sustained by another or looks to or relies on aid of another for support or for reasonable necessaries consistent with dependent's position in life. Peterson v. Industrial Commission, 331 Ill. 254, 162 N.E. 846, 847.

DEPENDENT, *n.* One who derives support from another; Milkovich v. Industrial Comm., 91 Utah, 498, 64 P.2d 1290, 1293; Texas Employers Ins. Ass'n v. Arnold, Tex.Civ.App., 62 S.W.2d 609, 611; not merely persons who derive a benefit from the earnings of the deceased; [1899] 1 Q.B. 1005; Havey v. Erie R. Co., 88 N.J.Law, 684, 96 A. 995, 996. One who depends on or is sustained by another, or who relies on another for support or favor. King v. Illinois Steel Corporation, 92 Ind. App. 456, 176 N.E. 161, 162.

DEPENDENT, *adj.* Deriving existence, support, or direction from another; conditioned, in respect to force or obligation, upon an extraneous act or fact.

Under a statute relating to dependent children, "dependent" is synonymous with "neglected," but not with "delinquent." People v. Ellis, 185 Ill.App. 417, 420; Dumes v. Deckard, 105 Ind.App. 674, 17 N.E.2d 481, 484.

Under a California juvenile act, a "dependent person" is one under the age of 21 years who is in danger of growing up to lead an idle, dissolute, or immoral life. People v. Cruse, 24 Cal.App. 497, 141 P. 936.

Dependent conditions. Mutual covenants which go to the whole consideration on both sides. Long v. Addix, 184 Ala. 236, 63 So. 982, 984; Palmer v. Fox, 274 Mich. 252, 264 N.W. 361, 104 A.L.R. 1057.

Dependent contract. One which depends or is conditional upon another. One which it is not the duty of the contractor to perform until some obligation contained in the same agreement has been performed by the other party. Ham. Parties, 17, 29, 30, 109.

Dependent covenant. See Covenant.

Dependent promise. One which it is not the duty of the promisor to perform until some obligation contained in the same agreement has been performed by the other party. Hamm.Partn. 17, 29, 30, 109; Harr.Const. 152.

DEPENDENT RELATIVE REVOCATION. The doctrine which regards as mutually dependent the acts of one destroying a will and thereupon substituting another instrument for distribution of estate, when both acts are result of one plan, so that, if second act, through incompleteness or other defect, fails to accomplish its intended purpose, and it thereby becomes evident that testator was misled when he destroyed his will, act of destruction is regarded as bereft of intent of revocation and way for probate of destroyed will is opened. Flanders v. White, 142 Or. 375, 18 P.2d 823, 827; In re Nelson's Estate, 183 Minn. 295, 236 N.W. 459, 461.

DEPENDING. In practice. Pending or undetermined; in progress. See 5 Coke, 47.

Under a statute, 28 U.S.C.A. § 1781, note, permitting the taking of testimony by deposition de bene esse, a cause is "depending" from the time of the issuance of the original writ. Oklahoma Gas & Electric Co. v. Bates Expanded Steel Truss Co., D.C.Del., 296 F. 281, 283.

In patent law. A convenient means of saying that the parts of a device were so attached as to have a right-angle relationship to each other, not a gravitational hanging of one part upon another. Alemite Mfg. Corporation v. Rogers Products Co., C.C.A.N.J., 42 F.2d 648, 651.

DEPESAS. In Spanish-American law. Spaces of ground in towns reserved for commons or public pasturage. 12 Pet. 443, note, 9 L.Ed. 1150.

DEPLETABLE ECONOMIC INTEREST. The interest in mineral land which is subject to depletion by the removal of the minerals by operation of an oil well, mine, or the like. 26 U.S.C.A.Int. Rev.Code § 114. Spalding v. U. S., C.C.A.Cal., 97 F.2d 697, 700; U. S. v. Spalding, C.C.A.Cal., 97 F.2d 701, 704.

DEPLETE. To reduce or lessen, as by use, exhaustion, or waste. McKnight v. U. S., C.C.A.Cal., 78 F.2d 931, 933.

DEPLETION. An emptying, exhausting or wasting of assets. Arkansas-Louisiana Gas Co. v. City of Texarkana, D.C.Ark., 17 F.Supp. 447, 460. For tax purposes, a return of capital, not a special bonus for enterprise. Untermyer v. Commissioner of Internal Revenue, C.C.A., 59 F.2d 1004. A reduction during taxable year of oil, gas or other mineral deposits or reserves as result of production. Darby-Lynde Co. v. Alexander, C.C.A.Okl., 51 F.2d 56.

DEPOLYMERIZATION. In connection with the devulcanizing of vulcanized rubber, the act of breaking into smaller aggregations the rubber molecules, which consist of hydrogen and carbon, thus rendering the waste rubber plastic. Philadelphia Rubber Works Co. v. United States Rubber Reclaiming Works, D.C.N.Y., 225 F. 789, 791.

DEPONE. In Scotch practice. To depose; to make oath in writing.

DEPONENT. In practice. One who *deposes* (that is, testifies or makes oath, now in *writing*) to the truth of certain facts; one who gives under oath testimony which is reduced to writing; one who makes oath to a written statement. The party making an affidavit is generally so called, though in the United States the term "affiant" is also commonly applied to such party, the terms, when used with reference to one making an affidavit, are synonymous. Walden v. Crego's Estate, 238 Mich. 564, 285 N.W. 457, 461.

The word "depone," from which is derived "deponent," has relation to the mode in which the oath is administered, (by the witness placing his hand upon the book of the holy evangelists,) and not as to whether the testimony is delivered orally or reduced to writing. "Deponent" is included in the term "witness," but "witness" is more general. Bliss v. Shuman, 47 Me. 248.

DEPONER. In old Scotch practice. A deponent. 3 How. State Tr. 695.

DEPOPULATIO AGRORUM. In old English law. The crime of destroying, ravaging, or laying waste a country. 2 Hale, P. C. 333; 4 Bl.Comm. 373.

DEPOPULATION. In old English law. A species of waste by which the population of the kingdom was diminished. Depopulation of houses was a public offense. 12 Coke, 30, 31.

DEPORTATIO. Lat. In the civil law. A kind of banishment, where a condemned person was sent or carried away to some foreign country, usually to an island, (*in insulam deportatur,*) and thus taken out of the number of Roman citizens.

DEPORTATION. Banishment to a foreign country, attended with confiscation of property and deprivation of civil rights. A punishment derived from the *deportatio* (*q. v.*) of the Roman law, and still in use in France.

In American Law

The removal or sending back of an alien to the country from which he came, the removal from the country of an alien considered inimical to public welfare; the removal of an alien out of the country simply because his presence is deemed inconsistent with the public welfare, and without any punishment being imposed or contemplated. Yonejiro Nakasuji v. Seager, D.C.Cal., 3 F.Supp. 410, 413.

"The removal of an alien out of the country, simply because his presence is deemed inconsistent with the public welfare, and without any punishment being imposed or contemplated, either under the laws of the country out of which he is sent, or under those of the country to which he is taken." It differs from *transportation*, which is by way of punishment of one convicted of an offence against the laws of the country; and from *extradition (q. v.)*, which is the surrender to another country of one accused of an offence against its laws, there to be tried, and, if found guilty, punished. Fong Yue Ting v. U. S., 149 U.S. 698, 13 S.Ct. 1016, 37 L.Ed. 905.

"Deportation," as distinguished from "exclusion," is depriving a person already in the United States of a privilege which he, at least at the time, is enjoying; whereas "exclusion" is the denial of entry, and does not deprive one of any liberties he had theretofore enjoyed. Ex parte Domingo Corypus, D.C., 6 F.2d 336.

In Roman Law

A perpetual banishment, depriving the banished of his rights as a citizen; it differed from relegation (*q. v.*) and exile, (*q. v.*) 1 Brown, Civil & Adm. Law, 125, note; Inst. 1, 12, 1, and 2; Dig. 48, 22, 14, 1.

DEPOSE. To deprive an individual of a public employment or office against his will. Wolffius, Inst. § 1063. The term is usually applied to the deprivation of all authority of a sovereign.

In Modern Usage

To make a deposition; to give evidence in the shape of a deposition; to make statements which are written down and sworn to; to give testimony which is reduced to writing by a duly-qualified officer and sworn to by the deponent. To say (in a deposition) under oath. Webb v. Iowa-Nebraska Coal Co., 198 Iowa 776, 200 N.W. 225, 226. To bear witness, to state of oath, or give testimony. Favello v. Bank of America Nat. T. & S. Ass'n, 24 Cal.App.2d 342, 74 P.2d 1057, 1059.

In Practice

In ancient usage, to testify as a witness; to give evidence under oath.

DEPOSIT, *v.* To commit to custody, or to lay down; to place; to put; to let fall (as sediment); Jefferson County ex rel. Grauman v. Jefferson County Fiscal Court, 273 Ky. 674, 117 S.W.2d 918, 924; to lodge for safe-keeping or as a pledge, to intrust to the care of another. White v. Greenlee, 330 Mo. 135, 49 S.W.2d 132, 134.

DEPOSIT, *n.* A naked bailment of goods to be kept for the depositor without reward, and to be returned when he shall require it. Jones, Bailm. 36, 117; Rozelle v. Rhodes, 116 Pa. 129, 9 Atl. 160, 2 Am.St.Rep. 591; Occidental Life Ins. Co. v. Rogan, C.C.A.Cal., 141 F.2d 1011, 1012.

A bailment of goods to be kept by the bailee without reward, and delivered according to the object or purpose of the original trust. Story, Bailm. § 41; Elbert Sales Co. v. Granite City Bank, 55 Ga.App. 835, 192 S.E. 66, 67.

In general, an act by which a person receives the property of another, binding himself to preserve it and return it in kind. Henry Rose Mercantile & Mfg. Co. v. Stearns, 159 La. 957, 106 So. 455, 458.

The delivery of chattels by one person to another to keep for the use of the bailor.

The giving of the possession of personal property by one person to another, with his consent, to keep for the use and benefit of the first or of a third person. Moumal v. Parkhurst, 89 Or. 248, 173 P. 669, 671.

Something intrusted to the care of another, either for a permanent or a temporary disposition. Davidson v. U. S., C.C.A.Pa., 292 F. 750, 751, aff. U. S. v. Davidson, D.C.Pa., 285 F. 661.

Also, money lodged with a person as an earnest or security for the performance of some contract, to be forfeited if the depositor fails in his undertaking. It may be deemed to be part payment, and to that extent may constitute the purchaser the actual owner of the estate. Larson v. Metcalf, 201 Iowa, 1208, 207 N.W. 382, 384, 45 A.L.R. 344.

Classification

According to the classification of the civil law, deposits are of the following several sorts: (1) *Necessary,* made upon some sudden emergency, and from some pressing necessity; as, for instance, in case of a fire, a shipwreck, or other overwhelming calamity, when property is confided to any person whom the depositor may meet without proper opportunity for reflection or choice, and thence it is called *"miserabile depositum."* (2) *Voluntary,* which arises from the mere consent and agreement of the parties. Dig. 16, 3, 2; Story, Bailm. § 44. The common law has made no such division.

There is another class of deposits called "involuntary," which may be without the assent or even knowledge of the depositor; as lumber, etc., left upon another's land by the subsidence of a flood. An "involuntary" deposit is one made by the accidental leaving or placing of personal property in the possession of any person without negligence on the part of the owner. Copelin v. Berlin Dyeworks & Laundry Co., 168 Cal. 715, 144 P. 961, 963, L.R.A.1915C, 712.

The civilians again divide deposits into "simple deposits," made by one or more persons having a common interest, and "sequestrations," made by one or more persons, each of whom has a different and adverse interest in controversy touching it; and these last are of two sorts,—"conventional," or such as are made by the mere agreement of the parties without any judicial act; and "judicial," or such as are made by order of a court in the course of some proceeding. Thus, under Louisiana statutes, it is said that the difference between "sequestration" and "deposit" is that the former may have for its object both movable and immovable property, while the latter is confined to movables. Raines v. Dunson, 145 La. 1011, 83 So. 224, 226.

There is another class of deposits called "irregular," as when a person, having a sum of money which he does not think safe in his own hands, confides it to another, who is to return to him, not the same money, but a like sum when he shall demand it. Poth. du Depot. 82, 83; Story, Bailm. § 84. A *regular* deposit is a strict or special deposit; a deposit which must be returned *in specie; i. e.,* the thing deposited must be returned. A *quasi* deposit is a kind of implied or involuntary deposit, which takes place where a party comes lawfully to the possession of another person's property, by finding it. Story, Bailm. § 85. Particularly with reference to money, deposits are also classed as *general* or *special.* A general deposit is where the money deposited is not itself to be returned, but an equivalent in money (that is, a like sum) is to be returned. It is equivalent to a loan, and the money deposited becomes the property of the depositary. City of Canby v. Bank of Canby, 192 Minn. 571, 257 N.W. 520.

A special deposit is a deposit in which the identical thing deposited is to be returned to the depositor. The particular object of this kind of deposit is safekeeping. Koetting v. State, 88 Wis. 502, 60 N.W. 822. Marine Bank v. Fulton Bank, 69 U.S. 252, 2 Wall. 252, 17 L.Ed. 785. In banking law, this kind of deposit is contrasted with a "general" deposit, as above; but in the civil law it is the antithesis of an "irregular" deposit. A *gratuitous* or *naked* deposit is a bailment of goods to be kept for the depositor without hire or reward on either side, or one for which the depositary receives no consideration beyond the mere possession of the thing deposited. Properly and originally, all deposits are of this description; for according to the Roman law, a bailment of goods for which hire or a price is to be paid, is not called "depositum" but "locatio." If the owner of the property pays for its custody or care, it is a "locatio custodiæ;" if, on the other hand, the bailee pays for the use of it, it is "locatio rei." (See Locatio.) But in the modern law of those states which have been influenced by the Roman jurisprudence, a gratuitous or naked deposit is distinguished from a "deposit for hire," in which the bailee is to be paid for his services in keeping the article. There is also a *specific* deposit, which exists where money or property is given to a bank for some specific and particular purpose, as a note for collection, money to pay a particular note, or property for some other specific purpose. Officer v. Officer, 120 Iowa 389, 94 N.W. 947, 98 Am.St.Rep. 365.

In Banking Law

The act of placing or lodging money in the custody of a bank or banker, for safety or convenience, to be withdrawn at the will of the depositor or under rules and regulations agreed on. Also, the money so deposited, or the credit which the depositor receives for it. State Banking Board v. James, Tex.Civ.App., 264 S.W. 145, 149.

"Deposit," according to its commonly accepted and generally understood meaning among bankers and by the public, includes not only deposits payable on demand and subject to check, but deposits not subject to check, for which certificates, whether interest-bearing or not, may be issued, payable on demand, or on certain notice, or at a fixed future time. Jones v. O'Brien, 58 S.D. 213, 235 N.W. 654, 659.

In Insurance Law

The delivery by a life insurance company of securities to state commissioner of insurance as required by statutes. Central Life Assur. Soc. v. Birmingham, D.C.Iowa, 48 F.Supp. 863, 865.

In Mining

A quantity of ore or mineral substances occurring naturally in the earth; as, a deposit of gold, oil, etc. See Colorado Gold Dredging Co. v. Stearns-Roger Mfg. Co., 60 Colo. 412, 153 P. 765.

In General

Deposit account. An account of sums lodged with a bank not to be drawn upon by checks, and usually not to be withdrawn except after a fixed notice.

Deposit company. A company whose business is the safe-keeping of securities or other valuables deposited in boxes or safes in its building which are leased to the depositors.

Deposit of title-deeds. A method of pledging real property as security for a loan, by placing the title-deeds of the land in the keeping of the lender as pledgee.

Deposit slip. An acknowledgment that the amount named therein has been received by the bank; it is a receipt intended to furnish evidence as between the depositor and depositary that on a given date there was deposited the sum named therein, the time of deposit, and amount deposited, being also shown. In re Ruskay, C.C.A.N.Y., 5 F.2d 143, 147.

DEPOSITARY. The party receiving a deposit; one with whom anything is lodged in trust, as "depository" is the place where it is put. A trustee; fiduciary; one to whom goods are bailed to be held without recompense. Stand. Dict. The obligation on the part of the depositary is that he keep the thing with reasonable care, and, upon request, restore it to the depositor, or otherwise deliver it, according to the original trust. Brunner v. Edwards, 337 Pa. 513, 12 A.2d 36, 37.

DEPOSITATION. In Scotch law. Deposit or *depositum*, the species of bailment so called. Bell.

DEPOSITION. The testimony of a witness taken upon interrogatories, not in open court, but in pursuance of a commission to take testimony issued by a court, or under a general law on the subject, and reduced to writing and duly authenticated, and intended to be used upon the trial of an action in court. It is sometimes used as synonymous with "affidavit" or "oath," but its technical meaning does not include such terms. State v. Lord, 42 N.M. 638, 84 P.2d 80, 94.

A written declaration under oath, made upon notice to the adverse party for the purpose of enabling him to attend and cross-examine; or upon written interrogatories. N. S. Sherman Machine & Iron Works v. R. D. Cole Mfg. Co., 51 Okl. 353, 151 P. 1181, 1182. It is the giving of notice to the adverse party which especially distinguishes a deposition from an affidavit. Zinner v. Louis Meyers & Son, 181 Misc. 344, 43 N.Y.S.2d 319, 320.

The term sometimes is used in a special sense to denote a statement made orally by a person on oath before an examiner, commissioner, or officer of the court, (but not in open court,) and taken down in writing by the examiner or under his direction. Sweet.

In Ecclesiastical law. The act of depriving a clergyman, by a competent tribunal, of his clerical orders, to punish him for some offense and to prevent his acting in future in his clerical character. Ayl. Par. 206.

DEPOSITION DE BENE ESSE. Testimony to be read at the trial, so far as relevant and competent, as though the witness were present in court. Milprint, Inc., v. Macleod Laboratories, 127 N.J.L. 333, 22 A.2d 566, 567.

DEPOSITO. In Spanish law. Deposit; the species of bailment so called. Schm. Civil Law, 193.

A real contract by which one person confides to the custody of another an object on the condition that it shall be returned to him whenever he shall require it.

DEPOSITOR. One who makes a deposit.

In banking law, one who delivers and leaves money with a bank on his order or subject to check. Lummus Cotton Gin Co. v. Walker, 195 Ala. 552, 70 So. 754, 756; Austin v. Avant, Tex. Civ.App., 277 S.W. 409, 410.

DEPOSITORY. The place where a deposit (*q. v.*) is placed and kept.

Sometimes, also, a depositary; one with whom something is deposited. Jones v. Marrs, 114 Tex. 62, 263 S.W. 570, 573.

United States depositories. Banks selected and designated to receive deposits of the public funds of the United States.

DEPOSITUM. Lat. In the civil law. One of the forms of the contract of bailment, being a naked bailment of goods to be kept for the use of the bailor without reward. Coe v. Ricker, 214 Mass. 212, 101 N.E. 76, 78, 45 L.R.A.,N.S., 30, Ann.Cas. 1914B, 1178. See Deposit.

One of the four real contracts specified by Justinian, and having the following characteristics: (1) The depositary or depositee is not liable for negligence, however extreme, but only for fraud, *dolus;* (2) the property remains in the depositor, the depositary having only the possession. *Precarium* and *sequestre* were two varieties of the *depositum.*

DEPOT. A railroad freight or passenger station; a place on the line of a railroad where passengers may enter and leave the trains and where freight is deposited for delivery; a place where the carrier is accustomed to receive merchandise, deposit it, and keep it ready for transportation or delivery. Missouri Pac. R. Co. v. Williamson, 195 Ark. 487, 112 S.W.2d 957, 958. Chesapeake & O. Ry. Co. v. Ricks, 146 Va. 10, 135 S.E. 685, 688.

A place for the deposit of goods; a warehouse, or a storehouse. Weyman v. City of Newport, 153 Ky. 487, 156 S.W. 109, 111.

A place where military supplies or stores are kept or troops assembled. U. S. v. Caldwell, 19 Wall. 264, 22 L.Ed. 114.

—Depot grounds. Station grounds. Atchison, T. & S. F. Ry. Co. v. McCall, 48 Okl. 602, 150 P. 173, 174. The place where passengers get off and on trains, where goods are loaded and unloaded, and all grounds necessary, convenient, and actually used for such purposes by the public and by the railway company, including the place where cars are switched and trains made up, also where tracks are used for storing cars, and where the public require open and free access to the railroad for the purpose of such business. Prince v. Chicago & N. W. Ry. Co., 165 Wis. 212, 161 N.W. 765, 766.

DÉPÔT. In French law. The *depositum* of the Roman and the deposit of the English law. It is of two kinds, being either (1) *dépôt* simply so called, and which may be either voluntary or necessary, and (2) *séquestre,* which is a deposit made either under an agreement of the parties, and to abide the event of pending litigation regarding it, or by virtue of the direction of the court or a judge, pending litigation regarding it. Brown; Civ.Code La. 2926.

DEPRAVE. To defame; vilify; exhibit contempt for. In England it is a criminal offense to "deprave" the Lord's Supper or the Book of Common Prayer. Steph.Crim.Dig. 99.

DEPRAVED MIND. An inherent deficiency of moral sense and rectitude, equivalent to statutory phrase "depravity of heart" defined as highest grade of malice. Ramsey v. State, 114 Fla. 766, 154 So. 855.

A mind which may become inflamed by liquor and passion to such a degree that it ceases to care for human life and safety is a "depraved mind." State v. Weltz, 155 Minn. 143, 193 N.W. 42, 44.

DEPRECIATION. A fall in value; reduction of worth. New York Life Ins. Co. v. Anderson, C.C.A. N.Y., 263 F. 527, 529. The deterioration, or the loss or lessening in value, arising from age, use, and improvements, due to better methods. Boston & A. R. Co. v. New York Cent. R. Co., 256 Mass. 600, 153 N.E. 19, 23; Miles v. People's Telephone Co., 166 Wis. 94, 163 N.W. 652, 655.

DEPRECIATION RESERVE. An account kept on the books, as of a public utility, to offset the depreciation of the property due to time and use. People ex rel. Adirondack Power & Light Corporation v. Public Service Commission, 193 N.Y.S. 186, 191, 200 App.Div. 268. It does not represent the actual depreciation of its properties which is to be deducted from the reproduction cost new to ascertain the present value for rate purposes; but only what observation and experience suggest as likely to happen, with a margin over. Southern Bell Telephone & Telegraph Co. v. Railroad Commission of South Carolina, D.C.S.C., 5 F.2d 77, 96.

DEPREDATION. The act of plundering, robbing, or pillaging. Deal v. U. S., 274 U.S. 277, 47 S.Ct. 613, 615, 71 L.Ed. 1045.

In French law. Pillage, waste, or spoliation of goods, particularly of the estate of a decedent.

DEPRESSION. A period of economic stress; deflation; panic. Trust Co. of N. J. v. Jefferson Trust Co., 14 N.J.Misc. 656, 186 A. 732; McCuiston v. Haggard, 21 Tenn.App. 277, 109 S.W.2d 413.

A hole or hollow. Rice v. Kansas City, Mo.App., 16 S.W.2d 659, 661.

DEPRIVATION. In English ecclesiastical law. The taking away from a clergyman of his benefice or other spiritual promotion or dignity, either by sentence declaratory in the proper court for fit and sufficient causes or in pursuance of divers penal statutes which declare the benefice void for some nonfeasance or neglect, or some malfeasance or crime. 3 Steph.Comm. 87, 88; Burn, Ecc.Law, tit. "Deprivation." See Ayliffe, Parerg. 206; 1 Bla. Comm. 393. See Degradation.

In American law. A taking away; confiscation; as the deprivation of a constitutional right. Thus a taking of property without due process of law; Sundlun v. Zoning Board of Review of City of Pawtucket, 50 R.I. 108, 145 A. 451, 454; or of liberty. Lynch v. City of Muskogee, D.C.Okl., 47 F.Supp. 589, 592.

DEPRIVE. To take. The term has this meaning in a constitutional provision that no person shall be "*deprived* of his property" without due process of law, and denotes a taking altogether, a seizure, a direct appropriation, dispossession of the owner. Brown v. City of Atlanta, 167 Ga. 416, 145 S.E. 855, 857. It connotes want of consent. Sandel v. State, 104 S.E. 567, 571, 115 S.C. 168, 13 A.L.R. 1268.

DEPUTIZE. To appoint a deputy; to appoint or commission one to act as deputy to an officer. In a general sense, the term is descriptive of empowering one person to act for another in any capacity or relation, but in law it is almost always restricted to the substitution of a person appointed to act for an officer of the law.

DEPUTY. A substitute; a person duly authorized by an officer to exercise some or all of the functions pertaining to the office, in the place and stead of the latter. Byrnes v. Windels, 265 N.Y. 403, 193 N.E. 248, 249. One appointed to substitute for another with power to act for him in his name or behalf. Saxby v. Sonnemann, 149 N.E. 526, 528, 318 Ill. 600; Waggoner v. State, 183 Miss. 510, 184 So. 633, 634.

A deputy differs from an assignee, in that an assignee has an interest in the office itself, and does all things in his own name, for whom his grantor shall not answer, except in special cases; but a deputy has not any interest in the office, and is only the shadow of the officer in whose name he acts. And there is a distinction in doing an act by an agent and by a deputy. An agent can only bind his principal when he does the act in the name of the principal. But a deputy may do the act and sign his own name, and it binds his principal; for a deputy has, in law, the whole power of his principal. Wharton.

Deputy consul. See Consul.

Deputy lieutenant. The deputy of a lord lieutenant of a county in England.

Deputy sheriff. One appointed to act in the place and stead of the sheriff in the official business of the latter's office. A *general* deputy (sometimes called "undersheriff"; see Shirran v. Dallas, 21 Cal.App. 405, 132 P. 454, 458; Delfelder v. Teton Land & Investment Co., 46 Wyo. 142, 24 P.2d 702, is one who, by virtue of his appointment, has authority to execute all the ordinary duties of the office of sheriff, and who executes process without any special authority from his principal. A *special* deputy, who is an officer *pro hac vice,* is one appointed for a special occasion or a special service, as, to serve a particular writ or to assist in keeping the peace when a riot or tumult is expected or in progress. He acts under a specific and not a general appointment and authority. Allen v. Smith, 12 N.J.Law, 162; Wilson v. Russell, 4 Dak. 376, 31 N.W. 645.

Deputy steward. A steward of a manor may depute or authorize another to hold a court; and the acts done in a court so holden will be as legal as if the court had been holden by the chief steward in person. So an under steward or deputy may authorize another as subdeputy, *pro hac vice,* to hold a court for him; such limited authority not being inconsistent with the rule *delegatus non potest delegare.* Wharton.

Special deputy. One appointed to exercise some special function or power of the official or person for whom he is appointed. Saxby v. Sonnemann, 318 Ill. 600, 149 N.E. 526, 528.

DERAIGN. Apparently, literally, to confound, and disorder, or to turn out of course, or displace; as deraignment or departure out of religion, in St. 31 Hen. VIII. c. 6. In the common law, the word is used generally in the sense of to prove; viz., to deraign a right, deraign the warranty, etc. Glanv. lib. 2, c. 6; Fitzh.Nat.Brev. 146. Perhaps this word "deraign," and the word "deraignment," derived from it, may be used in the sense of to prove and a proving, by disproving of what is asserted in opposition to truth and fact. Jacob. It is used as referring to a decree "which deraigns his title from a false source." Paxson v. Brown, 61 F. 874, 884, 10 C.C.A. 135.

DERAILER. A small but heavy iron device attached to a rail which opens and closes over the rail by a lever, so as to derail or turn off the track cars approaching the closed derailer from the expected direction. Brady v. Southern Ry. Co., 64 S.Ct. 232, 234, 320 U.S. 476, 88 L.Ed. 239.

DERAILMENT. The act of going off or the state of being off the rails of a railroad. Graham v. Insurance Co. of North America, 220 Mass. 230, 107 N.E. 915.

DERANGEMENT. See Insanity.

DERECHO. In Spanish law. Law or right. *Derecho comun,* common law. The civil law is so called. A right. *Derechos,* rights. Also, specifically, an impost laid upon goods or provisions, or upon persons or lands, by way of tax or contribution. Noe v. Card, 14 Cal. 576, 608.

DERELICT. Forsaken; abandoned; deserted; cast away.

Personal property abandoned or thrown away by the owner in such manner as to indicate that he intends to make no further claim thereto. 2 Bl.Comm. 9; 2 Reeve, Eng.Law, 9; Thompson v. One Anchor and Two Anchor Chains, D.C.Wis., 221 F. 770, 772.

Land left uncovered by the receding of water from its former bed. 2 Rolle, Abr. 170; 2 Bl. Comm. 262; 1 Crabb, Real Prop. 109.

In Maritime Law

A boat or vessel found entirely deserted or abandoned on the sea without hope or intention of recovery or return by the master or crew, whether resulting from wreck, accident, necessity, or voluntary abandonment. U. S. v. Stone, C.C.Tenn., 8 F. 232–243; Cromwell v. The Island City, 1 Black

121, 17 L.Ed. 70; The Hyderabad, D.C.Wis., 11 F. 749–754; The No. 105, Belcher Oil Co. v. Griffin, C.C.A.Fla., 97 F.2d 425, 426; Mengel Box Co. v. Joest, 127 Miss. 461, 90 So. 161, 163.

Quasi Derelict

When a vessel, without being abandoned, is no longer under the control or direction of those on board, (as where part of the crew are dead, and the remainder are physically and mentally incapable of providing for their own safety,) she is said to be *quasi derelict*. Sturtevant v. Nicholaus, 1 Newb.Adm. 449, Fed.Cas.No.13,578. When the crew have left their vessel temporarily, with the intention of returning to resume possession, she is not technically a derelict, but is what may be termed a "quasi derelict." The Alcazar, D.C. N.C., 227 F. 633, 650.

DERELICTION. The gaining of land from the water, in consequence of the sea shrinking back below the usual water mark; the opposite of *alluvion* (*q. v.*) Dyer, 326*b*; 2 Bl.Comm. 262; 1 Steph.Comm. 419; Linthicum v. Coan, 64 Md. 439, 2 A. 826, 54 Am.Rep. 775; Also, land left dry by running water retiring imperceptibly from one of its shores and encroaching on the other. Slattery v. Arkansas Natural Gas Co., 138 La. 793, 70 So. 806. See Reliction; Accretion.

In the Civil Law

The voluntary abandonment of goods by the owner, without the hope or the purpose of returning to the possession. Jones v. Nunn, 12 Ga. 473; Livermore v. White, 74 Me. 456, 43 Am.Rep. 600.

"Dereliction" or "renunciation" of property at sea as well as on land requires both the intention to abandon and external action. The No. 105, C.C.A.Fla., 97 F.2d 425, 426.

Derivativa potestas non potest esse major primitiva. Noy, Max.; Wing.Max. 66. The derivative power cannot be greater than the primitive. The power which is derived cannot be greater than that from which it is derived. Finch.Law, b. 1, c. 3, p. 11.

DERIVATIVE. Coming from another; taken from something preceding; secondary; that which has not its origin in itself, but owes its existence to something foregoing. Anything obtained or deduced from another. State v. Wong Fong, 75 Mont. 81, 241 P. 1072.

DERIVATIVE ACTION. A suit by a shareholder to enforce a corporate cause of action. The corporation is a necessary party, and the relief which is granted is a judgment against a third person in favor of the corporation. Price v. Gurney, Ohio, 65 S.Ct. 513, 516, 324 U.S. 100, 89 L.Ed. 776.

DERIVATIVE CONVEYANCES. Conveyances which presuppose some other conveyance precedent, and only serve to enlarge, confirm, alter, restrain, restore, or transfer the interest granted by such original conveyance. They are releases, confirmations, surrenders, assignments, and defeasances. 2 Bl.Comm. 324.

DERIVE. To receive, as from a source or origin. Crews v. Commissioner of Internal Revenue, C.C. A.10, 89 F.2d 412, 416. To proceed from property, sever from capital, however invested or employed, and to come in, receive or draw by taxpayer for his separate use, benefit, and disposal. Staples v. United States, D.C.Pa., 21 F.Supp. 737, 739.

DERIVED. Received. Langstaff v. Lucas, D.C., 9 F.2d 691, 693. See, also, Connell v. Harper, 202 Ky. 406, 259 S.W. 1017, 1019.

DEROGATION. The partial repeal or abolishing of a law, as by a subsequent act which limits its scope or impairs its utility and force. Distinguished from *abrogation*, which means the entire repeal and annulment of a law. Dig. 50, 17, 102.

DEROGATORY CLAUSE. In a will, this is a sentence or secret character inserted by the testator, of which he reserves the knowledge to himself, with a condition that no will he may make thereafter should be valid, unless this clause be inserted word for word. This is done as a precaution to guard against later wills being extorted by violence, or otherwise improperly obtained. By the law of England such a clause would be void, as tending to make the will irrevocable. Wharton.

Derogatur legi, cum pars detrahitur; abrogatur legi, cum prorsus tollitur. To derogate from a law is to take away part of it; to abrogate a law is to abolish it entirely. Dig. 50, 17, 102.

DESAFUERO. In Spanish law. An irregular action committed with violence against law, custom, or reason.

DESAMORTIZACION. In Mexican law. The *desamortizacion* of property is to take it out of mortmain, (dead hands;) that is, to unloose it from the grasp, as it were, of ecclesiastical or civil corporations. The term has no equivalent in English. Hall, Mex.Law, § 749.

DESCEND. To pass by succession; as when the estate vests by operation of law in the heirs immediately upon the death of the ancestor. Trahern v. Woolwine, 109 W.Va. 623, 155 S.E. 909, 910. The term, as used in some statutes, includes an acquisition by devise. Cordon v. Gregg, 164 Or. 306, 101 P.2d 414, 415.

To pass down from generation to generation. Weedin v. Chin Bow, C.C.A.Wash., 7 F.2d 369.

To go;—often used as a word of transfer. Gordon v. Cadwalader, 164 Cal. 509, 130 P. 18, 20.

As used in wills, the word "descend" is often regarded as a general expression equivalent to the words "go to" or "belong to," and as indicating a passing of title by the force of the will rather than of the statute. Klingman v. Gilbert, 90 Kan. 545, 135 P. 682, 684; Carter v. Reserve Gas Co., 84 W.Va. 741, 100 S.E. 738, 742.

DESCENDANT. One who is descended from another; a person who proceeds from the body of another, such as a child, grandchild, etc., to the remotest degree. The term is the opposite of "ascendant," (*q. v.*) Rasmusson v. Unknown Wife of Hoge, 293 Ill. 101, 127 N.E. 356, 359; State v. Yturria, 204 S.W. 315, 316, 109 Tex. 220, L.R.A.

1918F, 1079. In the plural, the term means offspring or posterity in general; Carter Oil Co. v. Scott, D.C.Okl., 12 F.2d 780, 783. Issue. Burkley v. Burkley, 266 Pa. 338, 109 A. 687, 688; In re Tinker's Estate, 91 Okl. 21, 215 P. 779, 781. Also, all those to whom an estate descends, whether it be in a direct or collateral line from the intestate. Oakley v. Davey, 49 Ohio App. 113, 195 N.E. 406.

One on whom the law has cast the property by descent. Smith v. Thom, 158 Ky. 655, 166 S.W. 182. An heir. Lee v. Roberson, 297 Ill. 321, 130 N.E. 774, 778. In this sense, the term is frequently held to include an adopted child. In re Cadwell's Estate, 26 Wyo. 412, 186 P. 499, 501. For "Family," see that title.

Descendants is a good term of description in a will, and includes all who proceed from the body of the person named; as grandchildren and great-grandchildren. Amb. 397; 2 Hil.Real Prop. 242.

Lineal Descendant

One who is in the line of descent from the ancestor. Green v. Hussey, 228 Mass. 537, 117 N.E. 798. Lawful issue. Bassier v. J. Connelly Const. Co., 227 Mich. 251, 198 N.W. 989, 991. The term may include an adopted child; Denton v. Miller, 110 Kan. 292, 203 P. 693, 694; who is as lawfully in the line of descent as if placed there by birth; Fisher v. Gardnier, 183 Mich. 660, 150 N.W. 358. Contra: State v. Yturria, 109 Tex. 220, 204 S.W. 315, 316, L.R.A.1918F, 1079.

DESCENDER. Descent; in the descent. See Formedon.

DESCENDIBLE. Capable of passing by descent, or of being inherited or transmitted by devise, (spoken of estates, titles, offices, and other property.) Collins v. Smith, 105 Ga. 525, 31 S.E. 449.

DESCENT. Hereditary succession. Succession to the ownership of an estate by inheritance, or by any act of law, as distinguished from "purchase." Title by descent is the title by which one person, upon the death of another, acquires the real estate of the latter as his heir at law. 2 Bl.Comm. 201; Adams v. Akerlund, 168 Ill. 632, 48 N.E. 454; In re Yahola's Heirship, 142 Okl. 79, 285 P. 946. The title by inheritance is in all cases called descent, although by statute law the title is sometimes made to ascend.

"Descent" in its broadest sense signifies an inheritance cast upon any one capable of receiving it, whether heir at common law or not. Kicey v. Kicey, 114 N.J.Eq. 116, 168 A. 424, 426.

The division among those legally entitled thereto of the real property of intestates.

Classification

Descents are of two sorts, *lineal* and *collateral*. Lineal descent is descent in a direct or right line, as from father or grandfather to son or grandson. In re Herrick's Estate, 273 N.Y.S. 803, 152 Misc. 9. Collateral descent is descent in a collateral or oblique line, that is, up to the common ancestor and then down from him, as from brother to brother, or between cousins. Levy v. McCartee, 6 Pet. 112, 8 L.Ed. 334. They are also distinguished into *mediate* and *immediate* descends. But these terms are used in different senses. A descent may be said to be a mediate or immediate descent of the estate or right; or it may be said to be mediate or immediate, in regard to the mediateness or immediateness of the pedigree or consanguinity. Thus, a descent from the grandfather, who dies in possession, to the grandchild, the father being then dead, or from the uncle to the nephew, the brother being dead, is, in the former sense, in law, immediate descent, although the one is collateral and the other lineal; for the heir is in the *per*, and not in the *per* and *cui*. On the other hand, with reference to the line of pedigree or consanguinity, a descent is often said to be immediate, when the ancestor from whom the party derives his blood is immediate, and without any intervening link or degrees; and mediate, when the kindred is derived from him *mediante altero,* another ancestor intervening between them. Thus a descent in lineals from father to son is in this sense immediate; but a descent from grandfather to grandson, the father being dead, or from uncle to nephew, the brother being dead, is deemed mediate; the father and the brother being, in these latter cases, the *medium deferens,* as it is called, of the descent or consanguinity. Furenes v. Mickelson, 86 Iowa, 508, 53 N.W. 416.

Descent was denoted, in the Roman law, by the term *"successio,"* which is also used by Bracton, from which has been derived the *succession* of the Scotch and French jurisprudence.

Line of Descent

The order or series of persons who have descended one from the other or all from a common ancestor, considered as placed in a line of succession in the order of their birth, the line showing the connection of all the blood-relatives.

Collateral line. A line of descent connecting persons who are not directly related to each other as ascendants or descendants, but whose relationship consists in common descent from the same ancestor.

Direct line. A line of descent traced through those persons only who are related to each other directly as ascendants or descendants. State ex rel. Walton v. Yturria, 109 Tex. 220, 204 S.W. 315, 316, L.R.A.1918F, 1079.

Maternal line. A line of descent or relationship between two persons which is traced through the mother of the younger.

Paternal line. A similar line of descent traced through the father.

For "Family," see that title.

DESCENT CAST. The devolving of realty upon the heir on the death of his ancestor intestate.

Another name for what the older writers called a "descent which tolls entry." When a person had acquired land by disseisin, abatement, or intrusion, and died seised of the land, the descent of it to his heir took away or tolled the real owner's right of entry, so that he could only recover the land by an action. Co.Litt. 237 *b*; Rap. & L. Dict.

DESCRIBE. To narrate, express, explain. Boynton Real Estate Co. v. Woodbridge Tp., 94 N.J. Law, 226, 109 A. 514, 515. Of land, to give the metes and bounds. Livingston v. Seaboard Air Line R. Co., 100 S.C. 18, 84 S.E. 303.

DESCRIPTIO PERSONÆ. Lat. Description of the person. By this is meant a word or phrase used merely for the purpose of identifying or pointing out the person intended, and not as an intimation that the language in connection with which it occurs is to apply to him only in the official or technical character which might appear to be indicated by the word. Forrester v. Cantley, 227 Mo.App. 325, 51 S.W.2d 550, 551.

In wills, it frequently happens that the word heir is used as a *descriptio personæ*. A legacy "to the eldest son" of A would be a designation of the person. See 1 Roper, Leg. c. 2.

DESCRIPTION. A delineation or account of a particular subject by the recital of its characteristic accidents and qualities. Ayliffe, Pand. 60.

A written enumeration of items composing an estate, or of its condition, or of titles or documents; like an inventory, but with more particularity, and without involving the idea of an appraisement.

An exact written account of an article, mechanical device, or process which is the subject of an application for a patent.

A method of pointing out a particular person by referring to his relationship to some other person or his character as an officer, trustee, executor, etc.

That part of a conveyance, advertisement of sale, etc., which identifies the land or premises intended to be affected. Argyle v. Bonneville Irr. Dist., 74 Utah, 480, 280 P. 722, 727.

A fair portrayal of the chief features of the proposed law in words of plain meaning, so that it can be understood by the persons entitled to vote. Sawyer Stores v. Mitchell, 103 Mont. 148, 62 P.2d 342, 348; In re Opinion of the Justices, Mass., 9 N.E.2d 189, 192.

That part of affidavit for search warrant describing the place to be searched. Turner v. State, 39 Okl.Cr. 74, 263 P. 476.

DESCRIPTIVE. Containing a description; serving or aiming to describe; having the quality of representing. Sawyer Stores v. Mitchell, 103 Mont. 148, 62 P.2d 342, 348.

Descriptive words are not susceptible of exclusive adoption by any one as part of a corporate name. Sterling Products Corporation v. Sterling Products, D.C.N.Y., 43 F.Supp. 548, 550; are not registerable under the Trade-Mark Act § 2; 15 U.S.C.A. § 1052. Judson Dunaway Corp. v. Hygienic Products Corp., 178 F.2d 461; and cannot ordinarily form the basis for an injunction against their use by another on ground of unfair competition. Merlino v. Schmetz, 66 R.I. 425, 20 A.2d 266, 268.

DESECRATE. To violate sanctity of, to profane, or to put to unworthy use. City of Shreveport v. Harris, 178 La. 685, 152 So. 330.

The calling on householders after 10 a. m. on Sunday by members of an organized religious order for purpose of propagandizing their religious views by spoken and printed words, however unwelcome to householders, did not, in itself, constitute a desecration of the Sabbath. State v. Mead, 230 Iowa 1217, 300 N.W. 523, 524.

DESERT. To leave or quit with an intention to cause a permanent separation; to forsake utterly; to abandon. It is essentially willful in nature. Stevens v. Stevens, 304 Ill. 297, 136 N.E. 785, 787; Stover v. Stover, 94 N.J.Eq. 703, 120 A. 788, 789.

DESERTER. As applied to seamen, one continually and intentionally absent from the ship, constituting a quitting of the service of the vessel. The Strathearn, D.C.Fla., 239 F. 583, 586. Compare Mystic S. S. Co. v. Stromland, C.C.A.Va., 20 F.2d 342, 344; The Ella Pierce Thurlow, D.C.Va., 18 F.2d 675, 676.

Under the regulations of the Navy Department, a "deserter" is one who is absent without leave and with a manifest intention not to return, while a "straggler" is one absent without leave, with the probability that he does not intend to desert, but, if his absence continues for 10 days, he becomes a deserter. Reed v. United States, C.C.A. N.Y., 252 F. 21, 22.

As applied to the matrimonial home, one who by his words, conduct, demeanor, and attitude produces an intolerable condition which forces the other spouse to withdraw from the joint habitation to a more peaceful one. West v. West, 264 Ky. 826, 95 S.W.2d 789, 790.

DESERTION. The act by which a person abandons and forsakes, without justification, or unauthorized, a station or condition of public or social life, renouncing its responsibilities and evading its duties.

A willful abandonment of an employment or duty in violation of a legal or moral obligation. Stoneburner v. Theodoratos, Cal.App., 30 P.2d 1001, 1003.

Constructive Desertion

That arising where an existing cohabitation is put an end to by misconduct of one of the parties, provided such misconduct is itself a ground for divorce a vinculo or a mensa. Succhierelli v. Succhierelli, 101 N.J.Eq. 30, 137 A. 839. See, also, Hoffhines v. Hoffhines, 146 Md. 350, 126 A. 112, 113, 38 A.L.R. 332.

Obstinate Desertion

See that title.

In Maritime Law

The act by which a seaman deserts and abandons a ship or vessel, in which he had engaged to perform a voyage, before the expiration of his time, and without leave. By desertion, in the maritime law, is meant, not a mere unauthorized absence from the ship without leave, but an unauthorized absence from the ship, with an intention not to return to her service, or, as it is often expressed, *animo non revertendi;* that is, with an intention to desert. The Cripple Creek, D.C.Pa., 52 F.Supp. 710, 712; (strike) The Youngstown, C. C.A.La., 110 F.2d 968, 970.

In Matrimonial and Divorce Law

An actual abandonment or breaking off of matrimonial cohabitation, by either of the parties, and a renouncing or refusal of the duties and obligations of the relation, with an intent to abandon or forsake entirely and not to return to or resume marital relations, occurring without legal justification either in the consent or the wrongful conduct of the other party. State v. Baker, 112 La. 801, 36 So. 703. Williams v. Williams, 29 N.E. 98, 130 N.Y. 193, 14 L.R.A. 220, 27 Am.St.Rep. 517.

The willful forsaking and desertion of duties of parenthood, and leaving child in a dependent condition. Bowling v. State, 62 Ga. 540, 8 S.E.2d 697.

In Military Law

An offense which consists in the abandonment of his post and duties by a person commissioned or enlisted in the army or navy, without leave and with the intention not to return. Hollingsworth v. Shaw, 19 Ohio St. 432, 2 Am.Rep. 411; In re Sutherland, D.C., 53 F. 551. There is a difference between desertion and simple "absence without leave;" in order to constitute the former, there must be an intention not to return to the service. Hanson v. South Scituate, 115 Mass. 336. See Deserter.

DESERVING. Worthy or meritorious, without regard to condition or circumstances. In no sense of the word is it limited to persons in need of assistance, or objects which come within the class of charitable uses. Nichols v. Allen, 130 Mass. 211, 39 Am.Rep. 445.

DESHONORA. In Spanish law. Dishonor; injury; slander. Las Partidas, pt. 7, tit. 9, l. 1, 6.

DESICCATE. To exhaust or remove moisture from; dry thoroughly; especially to free from moisture with view to preserving. In re Benner, Cust. & Pat. App., 46 F.2d 383, 384.

DESIGN. To form plan or scheme of, conceive and arrange in mind, originate mentally, plan out, contrive. Also, the plan or scheme conceived in mind and intended for subsequent execution, preliminary conception of idea to be carried into effect by action, contrivance in accordance with preconceived plan. State v. Pickus, 63 S.D. 209, 257 N.W. 284. A project, an idea. 3 H. & N. 301. See, also, Designed.

As a term of art, the giving of a visible form to the conceptions of the mind, or invention. Binns v. Woodruff, 4 Wash.C.C. 48, Fed. Cas. No. 1,424.

In Evidence

Purpose or intention, combined with plan, or implying a plan in the mind. Burrill, Circ.Ev. 331; State v. Grant, 86 Iowa 216, 53 N.W. 120.

In Patent Law

The drawing or depiction of an original plan or conception for a novel pattern, model, shape, or configuration, to be used in the manufacturing or textile arts or the fine arts, and chiefly of a decorative or ornamental character. "Design patents" are contrasted with "utility patents," but equally involve the exercise of the inventive or originative faculty. Gorham Co. v. White, 14 Wall. 524, 20 L.Ed. 731; Western Electric Manufacturing Co. v. Odell, D.C.Ill., 18 F. 321; Binns v. Woodruff, 3 Fed.Cas. 424; Henderson v. Tompkins, C.C.Mass., 60 F. 758.

"Design, in the view of the patent law, is that characteristic of a physical substance which, by means of lines, images, configuration, and the like, taken as a whole, makes an impression, through the eye, upon the mind of the observer. The essence of a design resides not in the elements individually, nor in their method of arrangement, but in the tout ensemble—in that indefinable whole that awakens some sensation in the observer's mind. Impressions thus imparted may be complex or simple; * * *. But whatever the impression, there is attached in the mind of the observer, to the object observed, a sense of uniqueness and character." Pelouze Scale & Mfg. Co. v. American Cutlery Co., 102 F. 916, 919, 43 C.C.A. 52; Bayley & Sons v. Braunstein Bros. Co., D.C.N.Y., 246 F. 314, 317.

DESIGNATE. To indicate or set apart for a purpose or duty—with, to or for—as, to designate an officer for a command. Mutual Discount Corporation v. Nagy, 111 N.J.L. 592, 169 A. 185, 186. To nominate. Sredzinski v. Schmieding, 283 N.Y.S. 332, 334, 245 App.Div. 398.

Designatio justiciariorum est a rege; jurisdictio vero ordinaria a lege. 4 Inst. 74. The appointment of justices is by the king, but their ordinary jurisdiction by the law.

DESIGNATING PETITION. Means used to designate a candidate for a party nomination at a primary election or for election to party position. Potash v. Molik, 230 N.Y.S.2d 544, 548, 35 Misc.2d 1.

DESIGNATIO PERSONÆ. The description of a person or a party to a deed or contract. See, also, Descriptio Personæ.

Designatio unius est exclusio alterius, et expressum facit cessare tacitum. Co. Litt. 210. The specifying of one is the exclusion of another, and that which is expressed makes that which is understood to cease. (The appointment or designation of one is the exclusion of the other; and that which is expressed prevails over that which is implied.)

DESIGNATION. An addition to a name, as of title, profession, trade, or occupation, to distinguish the person from others. Inglis v. Pontius, 102 Ohio St. 140, 131 N.E. 509, 511, 512.

A description or descriptive expression by which a person or thing is denoted in a will without using the name.

Also, an appointment or assignment, as to a particular office. Santa Barbara County v. Janssens, 177 Cal. 114, 169 P. 1025, 1027, L.R.A.1918C, 558; Cunio v. Franklin County, 315 Mo. 405, 285 S.W. 1007, 1008.

The act of pointing out, distinguishing by marks of description, or calling by a distinctive title. Thrailkill v. Smith, 106 Ohio St. 1, 138 N.E. 532, 534; West v. Edward Rutledge Timber Co., C.C.A.Idaho, 221 F. 30, 35; State v. Madison State Bank of Virginia City, 77 Mont. 498, 351 P. 548, 549; Carlyle v. State Highway Commission, 193 N.C. 36, 136 S.E. 612, 620.

DESIGNED. Contrived or taken to be employed for a particular purpose. People v. Dorrington,

221 Mich. 571, 191 N.W. 831, 832. Fit, adapted, prepared, suitable, appropriate. Thomas v. State, 34 Okl.Cr. 49, 244 P. 816. Intended, adapted, or designated. The term may be employed as indicating a bad purpose with evil intent. Bruce v. Sibeck, Cal.App., 78 P.2d 741, 743.

DESIGNEDLY. Sometimes equivalent to the words "wilfully," "knowingly," "unlawfully," and "feloniously." State v. Avery, 111 Kan. 588, 207 P. 838, 840, 23 A.L.R. 453.

DESIRE. To ask, to request. Fossett v. State, 34 Okl.Cr. 106, 245 P. 668, 669. Ordinarily, to wish for more or less earnestly. Woods v. Postal Telegraph-Cable Co., 205 Ala. 236, 87 So. 681, 684, 27 A.L.R. 834. Sometimes, to empower or authorize. Walters' Guardian v. Ransdell, 218 Ky. 267, 291 S.W. 399, 400. According to context or circumstances, the word may import a request or even a demand. Cleveland Clinic Foundation v. Humphrys, C.C.A.Ohio, 97 F.2d 849, 857, 121 A. L.R. 163.

This term, used in a will in relation to the management and distribution of property, has been interpreted by the courts with different shades of meaning, varying from the mere expression of a preference to a positive command. See In re Bearinger's Estate, 336 Pa. 253, 9 A.2d 342, 343; Beakey v. Knutson, 90 Or. 574, 174 P. 1149, 1150.

The word "desire" may be as effective as if the word "devise" or "bequeath" had been used. Drinkard v. Hughes, Tex.Civ.App., 32 S.W.2d 935, 936.

The word "desire," in a will, raises a trust, where the objects of that desire are specified; Vandyck v. Van Beuren, 1 Cai. (N.Y.) 84.

DESISTEMENT. The name of a doctrine under which the court, in construing a foreign will, applies the law of the forum on the theory that there is a hiatus. In re Tallmadge, 181 N.Y.S. 336, 341, 109 Misc. 696.

DESLINDE. A term used in the Spanish law, denoting the act by which the boundaries of an estate or portion of a country are determined.

DESMEMORIADOS. In Spanish law. Persons deprived of memory. White, New Recop. b. 1, tit. 2, c. 1, § 4.

DESPACHEURS. In maritime law. Persons appointed to settle cases of average.

DESPATCHES. Official communications of official persons on the affairs of government.

DESPERATE. Hopeless; worthless. This term is used in inventories and schedules of assets, particularly by executors, etc., to describe debts or claims which are considered impossible or hopeless of collection. See Schultz v. Pulver, 11 Wend. (N.Y.) 365; Darrow v. Rohrer, 71 Colo. 417, 207 P. 861; Toll. Ex. 248; 2 Wms. Ex. 644; 1 Chitt. Pr. 580.

DESPERATE DEBT. A hopeless debt; an irrecoverable obligation.

DESPITE. Contempt. *Despitz*, contempts. Kelham.

DESPITUS. Contempt. See Despite. A contemptible person. Fleta, lib. 4, c. 5.

DESPOIL. This word involves, in its signification, violence or clandestine means by which one is deprived of that which he possesses. Its Spanish equivalent, *despojar*, is a term used in Mexican law. Sunol v. Hepburn, 1 Cal. 268.

DESPOJAR. A possessory action of the Mexican law. It is brought to recover possession of immovable property, of which one has been despoiled (*despojado*) by another. See, also, Despoil.

DESPONSATION. The act of betrothing persons to each other.

DESPOSORIO. In Spanish law. Espousals; mutual promises of future marriage. White, New Recop. b. 1, tit. 6, c. 1, § 1.

DESPOT. This word, in its original and most simple acceptation, signifies *master and supreme lord;* it is synonymous with monarch; but taken in bad part, as it is usually employed, it signifies a tyrant. In some states, despot is the title given to the sovereign, as king is given in others. Enc. Lond.

DESPOTISM. That abuse of government where the sovereign power is not divided, but united in the hands of a single man, whatever may be his official title. It is not, properly, a form of government. Toullier, Dr.Civ.Fr. tit. prél. n. 32; Rutherf. Inst. b. 1, c. 20, § 1.

"Despotism" is not exactly synonymous with "autocracy," for the former involves the idea of tyranny or abuse of power, which is not necessarily implied by the latter. Every despotism is autocratic; but an autocracy is not necessarily despotic.

DESRENABLE. L. Fr. Unreasonable. Britt. c. 121.

DESSAISISSEMENT. In French law. When a person is declared bankrupt, he is immediately deprived of the enjoyment and administration of all his property; this deprivation, which extends to all his rights, is called "dessaisissement." Arg. Fr. Merc. Law, 556.

DESTINATION. The purpose to which it is intended an article or a fund shall be applied. A testator gives a destination to a legacy when he prescribes the specific use to which it shall be put.

The port at which a ship is to end her voyage is called her "port of destination." Pardessus, no. 600.

The phrases "port of destination" and "port of discharge" are not equivalent; U. S. v. Barker, 5 Mason 404, Fed.Cas.No.14,516. See Sheridan v. Ireland, 66 Me. 65.

DESTINATION DU PÈRE DE FAMILLE. A use which owner has intentionally established on one part of his property in favor of another part, and which is equal to a title with respect to perpetual and apparent servitudes thereon. Woodcock v. Baldwin, 51 La.Ann. 989, 26 So. 46.

DESTITUTE. Not possessing the necessaries of life and in a condition of extreme want. Moorman v. State, 129 Miss. 864, 93 So. 368. Necessitous. Ex parte Strong, 95 Tex.Cr.R. 250, 252 S.W. 767, 769. Having no money or other property available for one's maintenance or support. Norridgewock v. Solon, 49 Me. 385; Woods v. Perkins, 43 La.Ann. 347, 9 So. 48.

DESTITUTE OR NECESSITOUS CIRCUMSTANCES. Circumstances in which one needs the necessaries of life, which cover not only primitive physical needs, things absolutely indispensable to human existence and decency, but those things, also, which are in fact necessary to the particular person left without support. State v. Waller, 90 Kan. 829, 136 P. 215, 217, 49 L.R.A.,N.S., 588.

A wife may be in "destitute or necessitous circumstances" though she is being given shelter and food by a child or by sympathizing relatives, friends, or strangers, if she does not have property or money available for such necessities or ordinary comforts of life as her husband can reasonably furnish. State v. Sharp, 111 A. 909, 910, 1 W.W. Harr., Del., 148; Brandel v. State, 161 Wis. 532, 154 N.W. 997.

Young children, without property, are in "destitute or necessitous circumstances," within the Delaware Nonsupport Act (Rev.Code 1915, §§ 3033–3046), when the father can, but does not, and the mother cannot out of her independent means, provide for them, though the mother and children are supported by the maternal grandmother or grandfather. State v. Nelson, 114 A. 863, 864, 1 W.W. Harr. (Del.) 436; Donaghy v. State, 100 A. 696, 710, 6 Boyce (Del.) 467.

DESTROY. As used in policies of insurance, leases, and in maritime law, and under various statutes, this term is often applied to an act which renders the subject useless for its intended purpose, though it does not literally demolish or annihilate it. Davis v. Parker, 200 Ky. 847, 255 S.W. 836 (leased buildings); Louisville & N. R. Co. v. Commonwealth, 190 Ky. 78, 226 S.W. 113, 117 (railroad station); George v. McManus, 27 Cal.App. 414, 150 P. 73, 74 (automobile).

To "destroy" a vessel within the meaning of an act of congress means to unfit the vessel for service, beyond the hope of recovery by ordinary means. U. S. v. Johns, 1 Wash.C.C. 363, Fed.Cas.No.15,481; U. S. v. Johns, 4 Dall. 412, 1 L.Ed. 888.

The contents of a glass and bottle, emptied into a pail of water immediately when accused saw two uniformed police officers enter his building, are "destroyed" within the meaning of a statute making it unlawful to secrete or destroy any fluids on premises being searched for the purpose of preventing seizure. Pitkunas v. State, 183 Wis. 90, 197 N.W. 191, 192.

Land covered by spoil dirt from drainage channel is destroyed within constitutional provision that land destroyed for drainage purposes shall be paid for at a price not to exceed assessed value for preceding year. Scott v. Red River-Bayou Pierre Levee & Drainage Dist. of Louisiana, La.App., 7 So.2d 429, 433.

In relation to wills, contracts, and other documents, the term "destroy" does not import the annihilation of the instrument or its resolution into other forms of matter, but a destruction of its legal efficacy, which may be by cancellation, obliterating, tearing into fragments, etc. In re Kapp's Estate, 317 Pa. 253, 176 A. 501, 502.

DESTRUCTION. A term used in old English law, generally in connection with *waste,* and having, according to some, the same meaning. 1 Reeve, Eng. Law, 385; 3 Bl.Comm. 223. Britton, how ever, makes a distinction between waste of woods and destruction of houses. Britt. c. 66.

DESUBITO. To weary a person with continual barkings, and then to bite; spoken of dogs. Leg Alured, 26, cited in Cunningham's Dict.

DESUETUDE. Disuse; cessation, or discontinuance of use;—especially in the phrase, "to fall into desuetude." Applied to obsolete statutes. James v. Comm., 12 Serg. & R. (Pa.) 227.

DETACHIARE. To seize or take into custody another's goods or person by writ of attachment or course of law. Cunningham.

DETAIL, *v.* To enumerate minutely, particularize. In re California Land Buyers Syndicate, D.C. Cal., 22 F.Supp. 183, 186.

DETAIL, *n.* An individual part, an item, a particular. Board of Education of Prince George's County v. County Com'rs of Prince George's County, 131 Md. 658, 102 A. 1007, 1010.

One who belongs to the army, but is only detached, or set apart, for the time to some particular duty or service, and who is liable at any time to be recalled to his place in the ranks. In re Strawbridge, 39 Ala. 379.

DETAIN. To retain as the possession of personalty. First Nat. Bank v. Yocom, 96 Or. 438, 189 P. 220, 221. To arrest, to check, to delay, to hinder, to hold, or keep in custody, to retard, to restrain from proceeding, to stay, to stop. People v. Smith, 17 Cal.App.2d 468, 62 P.2d 436, 438.

DETAINER. The act (or the juridical fact) of withholding from a person lawfully entitled the possession of land or goods, or the restraint of a man's personal liberty against his will; detention.

The wrongful keeping of a person's goods is called an "unlawful detainer" although the original taking may have been lawful. As, if one distrains another's cattle, *damage feasant,* and before they are impounded the owner tenders sufficient amends; now, though the original taking was lawful, the subsequent detention of them after tender of amends is not lawful, and the owner has an action of replevin to recover them, in which he will recover damages for the *detention,* and not for the *caption,* because the original taking was lawful. 3 Steph.Comm. 548.

In Practice

A writ or instrument, issued or made by a competent officer, authorizing the keeper of a prison to keep in his custody a person therein named. A detainer may be lodged against one within the walls of a prison, on what account soever he is there. Com.Dig. "Process," E, (3 B.) This writ was superseded by 1 & 2 Vict. c. 110, §§ 1, 2.

Forcible Detainer

See that title.

DETAINMENT. This term is used in policies of marine insurance, in the clause relating to "arrests, restraints, and detainments." The last two words are construed as equivalents, each meaning the effect of superior force operating directly on the vessel. Schmidt v. Insurance Co., 1 Johns., N.Y., 262, 3 Am.Dec. 319.

DETECTION. A discovery or laying open of that which was hidden; investigation. Meunier v. Bernich, La.App., 170 So. 567, 572.

DETECTIVE. One whose business it is to watch, and furnish information concerning, alleged wrongdoers by investigating their haunts and habits. One whose business it is to detect criminals or discover matters of secret and pernicious import for the protection of the public. Smith v. S. H. Kress & Co., 210 Ala. 436, 98 So. 378, 380.

Private Detective

One engaged by individuals for private protection. Smith v. S. H. Kress & Co., 210 Ala. 436, 98 So. 378, 380.

DETECTOR. Any device, or piece of apparatus, which, when energized, actuated, or acted upon by or by means of the so-called Hertzian waves, enable men, through the senses of hearing or sight, to understand signals based upon the intentionally regulated emission or propagation of the waves aforesaid. Marconi Wireless Telegraph Co. of America v. De Forest Radio Telephone & Telegraph Co., C.C.A.N.Y., 243 F. 560, 561. In wireless telegraphy, the "detector" or "coherer" and "wave responsive device" is a device by which the electromagnetic waves cause the indicator to respond. National Electric Signaling Co. v. Telefunken Wireless Telegraph Co. of United States, C.C.A.N.Y., 221 F. 629, 631.

DETENTIO. In the civil law. That condition of fact under which one can exercise his power over a corporeal thing at his pleasure, to the exclusion of all others. It forms the substance of possession in all its varieties. Mackeld. Rom. Law, § 238.

DETENTION. The act of keeping back or withholding, either accidentally or by design, a person or thing. State v. Crappel, 181 La. 715, 160 So. 309. See Detainer.

DETENTION IN A REFORMATORY, as a punishment or measure of prevention, is where a juvenile offender is sentenced to be sent to a reformatory school, to be there detained for a certain period of time. 1 Russ. Crimes, 82.

DETER. To discourage or stop by fear, to stop or prevent from acting or proceeding by danger, difficulty, or other consideration which disheartens or countervails the motive for the act. Haynesworth v. Hall Const. Co., 44 Ga.App. 807, 163 S.E. 273, 277.

DETERIORATION. Of a commodity, a constitutional hurt or impairment, involving some degeneration in the substance of the thing, such as that arising from decay, corrosion, or disintegration. The mere soiling of a commodity with sea water or other foreign substance, resulting in a purely superficial hurt or impairment removable by the simple process of cleansing, cannot be said to be "deterioration" within the ordinary meaning of that term. Rosen-Reichardt Brokerage Co. v. London Assur. Corporation, 214 Mo.App. 672, 264 S.W. 433, 436.

Of values, a decline. Laxson v. Scarborough, Tex.Civ.App., 221 S.W. 1029.

DETERMINABLE. Liable to come to an end upon the happening of a certain contingency. 2 Bl. Comm. 121.

Susceptible of being determined, found out, definitely decided upon, or settled. Utah State Nat. Bank v. Smith, 180 Cal. 1, 179 P. 160, 161.

As to determinable "Fee" and "Freehold," see those titles.

DETERMINATE. That which is ascertained; what is particularly designated.

As used in Good Time Law covering prisoners confined for a determinate, the term, signifies a definite number of years fixed by the court. Hinkle v. Dowd, Ind., 58 N.E. 2d 342, 343.

DETERMINATE OBLIGATION. See Obligation.

DETERMINATION. The decision of a court of justice. It implies an ending or finality, the ending of a controversy or suit. People v. Jackson, 181 N.Y.S. 226, 191 App.Div. 269. The ending or expiration of an estate or interest in property, or of a right, power, or authority. The coming to an end in any way whatever. Hanchett Bond Co. v. Glore, 208 Mo.App. 169, 232 S.W. 159, 160.

Also, an estimate. Unton v. Liverpool, London & Globe Ins. Co., 166 Minn. 273, 207 N.W. 625, 626.

As respects an assessment, the term implies judgment and decision after weighing the facts; Appeal of Hoskins Mfg. Co., 270 Mich. 592, 259 N.W. 334, not mere arithmetical computation. Hanlon v. Rollins, 286 Mass. 404, 190 N.E. 606, 608.

DETERMINATION OF WILL. A phrase used of the putting an end to an estate at will. 2 Bl. Comm. 146.

DETERMINE. To come to an end. To bring to an end. 2 Bl.Comm. 121; 1 Washb. Real Prop. 380.

To bring to a conclusion, to settle by authoritative sentence, to decide. Eastman Kodak Co. v. Richards, 123 Misc. 83, 204 N.Y.S. 246, 248. To adjudicate on an issue presented. Glenn v. Mitchell, 71 Colo. 394, 207 P. 84, 85.

To estimate. Twin Falls Salmon River Land & Water Co. v. Caldwell, C.C.A.Idaho, 242 F. 177, 184.

To decide, and analogous to "adopt" or "accept." Goldberger v. City of Perth Amboy, 16 N.J.Misc. 84, 197 A. 267, 269.

DETESTATIO. Lat. In the civil law. A summoning made, or notice given, in the presence of witnesses, (*denuntiatio facta cum testatione.*) Dig. 50, 16, 40.

DETINET. Lat. He detains. In old English law. A species of action of debt, which lay for the specific recovery of goods, under a contract to deliver them. 1 Reeves, Eng. Law, 159.

In Pleading

An action of *debt* is said to be in the *detinet* when it is alleged merely that the defendant withholds or unjustly detains from the plaintiff the thing or amount demanded.

An action of *replevin* is said to be in the *detinet* when the defendant retains possession of the property until after judgment in the action. Bull, N.P. 52; Chit.Pl. 145.

DETINUE. In practice. A form of action which lies for the recovery, *in specie,* of personal chattels from one who acquired possession of them lawfully, but retains it without right, together with damages for the detention. 3 Bl.Comm. 152. Sinnott v. Feiock, 165 N.Y. 444, 59 N.E. 265, 53 L. R.A. 565, 80 Am.St.Rep. 736.

The action of *detinue* is defined in the old books as a remedy founded upon the delivery of goods by the owner to another to keep, who afterwards refuses to redeliver them to the bailor; and it is said that, to authorize the maintenance of the action, it is necessary that the defendant should have come lawfully into the possession of the chattel, either by delivery to him or by finding it. In fact, it was once understood to be the law that *detinue* does not lie where the property had been tortiously taken. But it is, upon principle, very unimportant in what manner the defendant's possession commenced, since the gist of the action is the wrongful detainer, and not the original taking.

It is only incumbent upon the plaintiff to prove property in himself, and possession in the defendant. At present, the action of *detinue* is proper in every case where the owner prefers recovering the specific property to damages for its conversion, and no regard is had to the manner in which the defendant acquired the possession. Tiefel Bros. & Winn v. Maxwell, Tex.Civ.App., 154 S.W. 319, 320.

DETINUE OF GOODS IN FRANK MARRIAGE. A writ formerly available to a wife after a divorce, for the recovery of the goods given with her in marriage. Mozley & Whitley.

DETINUIT. In pleading. An action of replevin is said to be in the *detinuit* when the plaintiff acquires possession of the property claimed by means of the writ. The right to retain is, of course, subject in such case to the judgment of the court upon his title to the property claimed. Bull, N.P. 521.

DETOUR. A temporary turning aside from usual or regular route, course or procedure or from a task or employment. Reddy-Waldhauer-Maffett Co. v. Spivey, 53 Ga.App. 117, 185 S.E. 147, 148.

A temporary road or a longer road in temporary use because of an obstruction on regularly used road.

DETOURNEMENT. The misappropriation by a servant of funds the property of his master; fraudulent abstraction of documents; or "abus de confiance" which is fraudulently misusing or spending to anybody's prejudice goods, cash, bills, documents, or contracts handed over for a special object. See Embezzlement. The Washington D.C.N.Y., 19 F.Supp. 719, 722.

DETRACTARI. To be torn in pieces by horses. Fleta, l. 1, c. 37.

DETRACTION. The removal of property from one state to another upon a transfer of the title to it by will or inheritance. Frederickson v. Louisiana, 23 How. 445, 16 L.Ed. 577.

DETRIMENT. Any loss or harm suffered in person or property; *e. g.*, the consideration for a contract may consist not only in a payment or other thing of value given, but also in loss or "detriment" suffered by the promisee. In that connection, "detriment" means that the promisee has, in return for the promise, forborne some legal right which he otherwise would have been entitled to exercise. Wallace v. Cook, 190 Ky. 262, 227 S.W. 279, 281; or that he has given up something which he had a right to keep, or done something which he had a right not to do. Irving v. Irwin, 133 Cal.App. 374, 24 P.2d 215.

DETUNICARI. To discover or lay open to the world. Matt. Westm. 1240.

DEUNX, pl. DEUNCES. Lat. In the Roman law. A division of the *as*, containing eleven *unciæ* or duodecimal parts; the proportion of eleven-twelfths. 2 Bl.Comm. 462, note. See As.

Deus solus hæredem facere potest, non homo. God alone, and not man, can make an heir. Co. Litt. 7*b*; Broom, Max. 516; 5 B. & C. 440, 454.

DEUTEROGAMY. The act, or condition, of one who marries after the death of a former wife or husband.

DEVADIATUS, or DIVADIATUS. An offender without sureties or pledges. Cowell.

DEVASTATION. Wasteful use of the property of a deceased person, as for extravagant funeral or other unnecessary expenses. 2 Bl.Comm. 508.

DEVASTAVERUNT. They have wasted. A term applied in old English law to waste by executors and administrators, and to the process issued against them therefor. Cowell. See Devastavit.

DEVASTAVIT. Lat. He has wasted. The act of an executor or administrator in wasting the goods of the deceased; mismanagement of the estate by which a loss occurs; Grigg v. Hanna, 283 Mich. 443, 478 N.W. 125; a breach of trust or misappropriation of assets held in a fiduciary character; any violation or neglect of duty by an executor or administrator, involving loss to the decedent's estate, which makes him personally responsible to heirs, creditors, or legatees. McGlaughlin v. McGlaughlin, 43 W.Va. 226, 27 S.E. 378.

Also, if plaintiff, in an action against an executor or administrator, has obtained judgment, the usual execution runs *de bonis testatoris;* but, if the sheriff returns such a writ *nulla bona testatoris nec propria,* the plaintiff may, forthwith, upon this return, sue out an execution against the property or person of the executor or administrator, in as full a manner as in an action against him, sued in his own right. Such a return is called a *"devastavit."* Brown.

DEVELOP. To progress to a more advanced state or condition, as an injury. Rabin v. Central Business Men's Ass'n, 116 Kan. 280, 226 P. 764, 766, 38 A.L.R. 26. To bring, or attempt to bring, to a state of fruition; to continue the work in hand, as in operating under an oil and gas lease, in a manner that would discover oil, if it existed, and promote its production. Lacer v. Sumpter, 198 Ky. 752, 249 S.W. 1026, 1027. To unfold more completely; to evolve the possibilities or power of; to make active; to perfect; advance; further; to make; to increase; to promote the growth of. Leingang v. Geller, Ward & Hasner Hardware Co., 335 Mo. 549, 73 S.W.2d 256, 261.

DEVELOPED WATER. Such subterranean or underground water as is discovered and brought to the surface by the exploitation of man, and which otherwise would run to waste. Rock Creek Ditch & Flume Co. v. Miller, 17 P.2d 1074, 1077, 93 Mont. 248, 89 A.L.R. 200; Jones v. Warmsprings Irr. Dist., 162 Or. 186, 91 P.2d 542.

DEVENERUNT. A writ, now obsolete, directed to the king's escheators when any of the king's tenants *in capite* dies, and when his son and heir dies within age and in the king's custody, commanding the escheators, that by the oaths of twelve good and lawful men they shall inquire what lands or tenements by the death of the tenant have come to the king. Dyer, 360; Termes de la Ley; Keilw. 199*a*; Blount; Cowell.

DEVEST. To deprive; to take away; to withdraw. Usually spoken of an authority, power, property, or title; as the estate is devested.

Devest is opposite to invest. As to invest signifies to deliver the possession of anything to another, so to devest signifies to take it away. Jacob.

It is sometimes written "d*i*vest" but "d*e*vest" has the support of the best authority. Burrill.

DEVIATION.

In General

A change made in the progress of a work from the original terms or design or method agreed upon. Ward v. City of Monrovia, 16 Cal.2d 815, 108 P.2d 425, 429.

A voluntary departure by railroad carrier, without necessity or reasonable cause, from the regular or usual route or from a stipulated or customary mode of carriage. Ward v. Gulf, M. & N. R. Co., 23 Tenn.App. 533, 134 S.W.2d 917, 924.

In Insurance

Varying from the risks insured against, as described in the policy, without necessity or just cause, after the risk has begun. 1 Phil.Ins. § 977, *et seq.*; 1 Arn.Ins. 415, *et seq.* Hostetter v. Park, 137 U.S. 30, 11 Sup.Ct. 1, 34 L.Ed. 568.

Any unnecessary or unexcused departure from the usual or general mode of carrying on the voyage insured. 15 Amer. Law Rev. 108; Shackman v. Cunard White Star, D.C.N.Y., 31 F.Supp. 948, 951.

A voluntary departure without reasonable cause from the course of the voyage insured, or an unreasonable delay in pursuing the voyage, or the commencement of an entirely different voyage. The Chester Valley, C.C.A.La., 110 F.2d 592, 594; The Willdomino v. Citro Chemical Co. of America, 272 U.S. 718, 47 S.Ct. 261, 262, 71 L.Ed. 491.

In the Law of Master and Servant

A departure on the part of a servant from his master's service, for some purpose of his own. Jeffries v. Jodawelky, 304 Mich. 421, 8 N.W.2d 121, 122. The liability of the master to third persons injured by the servant depends on the degree of deviation and all the attending circumstances. Johnson v. Maryland Cas. Co., C.C.A. Wis., 125 F.2d 337, 338. To exonerate the master, the deviation must be so substantial as to amount to an entire departure, and must be for purposes entirely personal to the servant. Thomas v. Lockwood Oil Co., 174 Wis. 486, 182 N.W. 841, 843. Contra, it is held that the test is whether master impliedly consented to route taken, and there can be no such thing as a slight deviation. Kalinowski v. Odlewany, 289 Mich. 684, 287 N.W. 344, 345. As to a distinction between "deviation," "temporary abandonment," and "complete abandonment," see Dockweiler v. American Piano Co., 94 Misc. 712, 160 N.Y.S. 270, 273.

DEVICE. An invention or contrivance; any result of design; as in the phrase "gambling device," which means a machine or contrivance of any kind for the playing of an unlawful game of chance or hazard. State v. Blackstone, 115 Mo. 424, 22 S.W. 370. Also, a plan or project; a scheme to trick or deceive; a stratagem or artifice; as in the laws relating to fraud and cheating. State v. Smith, 82 Minn. 342, 85 N.W. 12. Also an emblem, pictorial representation, or distinguishing mark or sign of any kind; as in the laws prohibiting the marking of ballots used in public elections with "any device." Baxter v. Ellis, 111 N.C. 124, 15 S.E. 938, 17 L.R.A. 382.

In a statute against gaming devices, this term is to be understood as meaning something formed by design, a contrivance, an invention. It is to be distinguished from "substitute," which means something put in the place of another thing, or used instead of something else. Henderson v. State, 59 Ala. 91.

In Patent Law

A plan or contrivance, or an application, adjustment, shaping, or combination of materials or members, for the purpose of accomplishing a particular result or serving a particular use, chiefly by mechanical means and usually simple in character or not highly complex, but involving the exercise of the inventive faculty.

DEVIL ON THE NECK. An instrument of torture, formerly used to extort confessions, etc. It was made of several irons, which were fastened to the neck and legs, and wrenched together so as to break the back. Cowell.

DEVILLING. A term used in London of a barrister recently admitted to the bar, who assists a junior barrister in his professional work, without compensation and without appearing in any way in the matter.

DEVISABLE. Capable of being devised. 1 Pow. Dev. 165; 2 Bl.Comm. 373.

DEVISAVIT VEL NON. In practice. The name of an issue sent out of a court of chancery, or one which exercises chancery jurisdiction, to a court of law, to try the validity of a paper asserted and denied to be a will, to ascertain whether or not the testator did devise, or whether or not that paper was his will. 7 Brown, Parl.Cas. 437; 2 Atk. 424; Asay v. Hoover, 5 Pa. 21, 45 Am.Dec. 713.

DEVISE. A testamentary disposition of land or realty; a gift of real property by the last will and testament of the donor. Scholle v. Scholle, 113 N.Y. 261, 21 N.E. 84; Murchison v. Wallace, 156 Va. 728, 159 S.E. 106, 108.

Classification

Devises are *contingent* or *vested;* that is, after the death of the testator. Contingent, when the vesting of any estate in the devisee is made to depend upon some future event, in which case, if the event never occur, or until it does occur, no estate vests under the devise. But, when the future event is referred to merely to determine the time at which the devisee shall come into the use of the estate, this does not hinder the vesting of the estate at the death of the testator. 1 Jarm.Wills, c. 26. Devises are also classed as *general* or *specific.* A general devise is one which passes lands of the testator without a particular enumeration or description of them; as, a devise of "all my lands" or "all my other lands." In a more restricted sense, a general devise is one which grants a parcel of land without the addition of any words to show how great an estate is meant to be given, or without words indicating either a grant in perpetuity or a grant for a limited term; in this case it is construed as granting a life estate. Hitch v. Patten, 8 Houst. (Del.) 334, 16 A. 558, 2 L.R.A. 724. Specific devises are devises of lands particularly specified in the terms of the devise, as opposed to general and residuary devises of land, in which the local or other particular descriptions are not expressed. For example, "I devise my Hendon Hall estate" is a specific devise; but "I devise all my lands," or, "all other my lands," is a *general* devise or a *residuary* devise. But all devises are (in effect) specific, even residuary devises being so. L.R. 3 Ch. 420; Id. 136. At common law, all devises of land were deemed to be "specific" whether the land was identified in the devise or passed under the residuary clause. In re Sutton's Estate, 11 Del.Ch. 460, 97 A. 624, 626. A *conditional* devise is one which depends upon the occurrence of some uncertain event, by which it is either to take effect or be defeated. An *executory* devise of lands is such a disposition of them by will that thereby no estate vests at the death of the devisor, but only on some future contingency. It differs from a remainder in three very material points: (1) That it needs not any particular estate to support it; (2) that by it a fee-simple or other less estate may be limited after a fee-simple; (3) that by this means a remainder may be limited of a chattel interest, after a particular estate for life created in the same. 2 Bl.Comm. 172. In a stricter sense, a limitation by will of a future contingent interest in lands, contrary to the rules of the common law. 4 Kent, Comm. 263; 1 Steph.Comm. 564; Dean v. Crews, 77 Fla. 319, 81 So. 479. A limitation by will of a future estate or interest in land, which cannot, consistently with the rules of law, take effect as a remainder. 2 Pow.Dev. (by Jarman,) 237; Bean v. Atkins, 87 Vt. 376, 89 A. 643, 646. See Poor v. Considine, 6 Wall. 474, 18 L.Ed. 869; Glover v. Condell, 163 Ill. 566, 45 N.E. 173, 35 L.R.A. 360. A future interest taking effect as a fee in derogation of a defeasible fee devised or conveyed to the first taker, when created by will, is an "executory devise," and, when created by deed, is a "conditional limitation," and in either event is given effect as a shifting or springing use. McWilliams v. Havely, 214 Ky. 320, 283 S.W. 103, 104.

The estates known as a contingent remainder and an "executory devise" are both interests or estates in land to take effect in the future and depend upon a future contingency; an "executory devise" being an interest which the rules of law do not permit to be created in conveyances, but allow in case of wills. It follows a fee estate created by a will. A contingent remainder may be created by will or other conveyance and must follow a particular or temporary estate created by the same instrument of conveyance. Wilkins v. Rowan, 107 Neb. 180, 185 N.W. 437, 439. *Lapsed* devise. A devise which fails, or takes no effect, in consequence of the death of the devisee before the testator; the subject-matter of it being considered as not disposed of by the will. 1 Steph.Comm. 559; 4 Kent, Comm. 541. Murphy v. McKeon, 53 N.J.Eq. 406, 32 A. 374. *Residuary* devise. A devise of all the residue of the testator's real property, that is, all that remains over and above the other devises.

Synonyms

The term "devise" is properly restricted to real property; testamentary dispositions of personal property being properly called "bequests" or "legacies." Borgner v. Brown, 133 Ind. 391, 33 N.E. 92.

To contrive; plan; scheme; invent; prepare. Stockton v. United States, C.C.A.Ill., 205 F. 462, 464, 46 L.R.A.,N.S., 936.

DEVISEE. The person to whom lands or other real property are devised or given by will. 1 Pow. Dev. c. 7. In re Lewis' Estate, 39 Nev. 445, 159 P. 961, 962, 4 A.L.R. 241.

Residuary Devisee

The person named in a will, who is to take all the real property remaining over and above the other devises.

DEVISOR. A giver of lands or real estate by will; the maker of a will of lands; a testator.

DEVOIR. Fr. Duty. It is used in the statute of 2 Rich. II. c. 3, in the sense of duties or customs.

DEVOLUTION. The transfer or transition from one person to another of a right, liability, title, estate, or office. Francisco v. Aguirre, 94 Cal. 180, 29 P. 495.

In Ecclesiastical Law

The forfeiture of a right or power (as the right of presentation to a living) in consequence of its non-user by the person holding it, or of some other act or omission on his part, and its resulting transfer to the person next entitled.

In Scotch Law

The transference of the right of purchase, from the highest bidder at an auction sale, to the next highest, when the former fails to pay his bid or furnish security for its payment within the time appointed. Also, the reference of a matter in controversy to a third person (called "oversman") by two arbitrators to whom it has been submitted and who are unable to agree.

DEVOLUTIVE APPEAL. In the law of Louisiana, one which does not suspend the execution of the judgment appealed from. Brock v. Police Jury of Rapides Parish, 198 La. 787, 4 So.2d 829, 832.

DEVOLVE. To pass or be transferred from one person to another; to fall on, or accrue to, one person as the successor of another; as a title, right, office, liability. The term is said to be peculiarly appropriate to the passing of an estate from a person dying to a person living. Babcock v. Maxwell, 29 Mont. 31, 74 P. 64; Fitzpatrick v. McAlister, 121 Okl. 83, 248 P. 569, 573; People ex rel. Robin v. Hayes, 149 N.Y.S. 250, 252, 163 App. Div. 725. See Devolution.

DEVULCANIZE. Of rubber. A more or less perfect restoration of vulcanized rubber to a state in which it might be used as crude rubber. Philadelphia Rubber Works Co. v. Portage Rubber Co., D.C.Ohio, 227 F. 623, 627.

DEVY. L. Fr. Dies; deceases. Bendloe, 5.

DEXTANS. Lat. In Roman law. A division of the *as*, consisting of ten *unciæ;* ten-twelfths, or five-sixths. 2 Bl.Comm. 462, note *m*.

DEXTRARIUS. One at the right hand of another.

DEXTRAS DARE. To shake hands in token of friendship; or to give up oneself to the power of another person.

DI COLONNA. In maritime law. The contract which takes place between the owner of a ship, the captain, and the mariners, who agree that the voyage shall be for the benefit of all. The term is used in the Italian law. Emerig. Mar. Loans, § 5.

DI. ET FI. L.Lat. In old writs. An abbreviation of *dilecto et fideli*, (to his beloved and faithful.)

DIACONATE. The office of a deacon.

DIACONUS. A deacon.

DIAGNOSIS. A medical term, meaning the discovery of the source of a patient's illness or the determination of the nature of his disease from a study of its symptoms. Said to be little more than a guess enlightened by experience. Swan v. Railroad Co., 29 N.Y.S. 337, 79 Hun 612; People v. Jordan, 172 Cal. 391, 156 P. 451, 454.

The art or act of recognizing the presence of disease from its symptoms, and deciding as to its character, also the decision reached, for determination of type or condition through case or specimen study or conclusion arrived at through critical perception or scrutiny. A "clinical diagnosis" is one made from a study of the symptoms only, and a "physical diagnosis" is one made by means of physical measure, such as palpation and inspection. Williams v. Elias, 140 Neb. 656, 1 N.W.2d 121, 123.

DIAGONAL, *n.* A right line drawn from the one angle to another not adjacent of a figure of four or more sides and dividing it into two parts. Semerad v. Dunn County, 35 N.D. 437, 160 N.W. 855, 858.

DIAGONAL, *adj.* Joining two not adjacent angles of a quadrilateral or multilateral figure running across from corner to corner; crossing at an angle with one of the sides. Semerad v. Dunn County, 35 N.D. 437, 160 N.W. 855, 858.

DIALECTICS. That branch of logic which teaches the rules and modes of reasoning.

DIALLAGE. A rhetorical figure in which arguments are placed in various points of view, and then turned to one point. Enc.Lond.

DIALOGUS DE SCACCARIO. Dialogue of or about the exchequer. An ancient treatise on the court of exchequer, attributed by some to Gervase of Tilbury, by others to Richard Fitz Nigel, bishop of London in the reign of Richard I. It is quoted by Lord Coke under the name of Ockham. Crabb, Eng. Law, 71.

DIANATIC. A logical reasoning in a progressive manner, proceeding from one subject to another. Enc. Lond.

DIARIUM. Daily food, or as much as will suffice for the day. Du Cange.

DIATHERMY. Heat treatment by electricity. Biener v. St. Louis Public Service Co., Mo.App., 160 S.W.2d 780, 788.

DIATIM. In old records. Daily; every day; from day to day. Spelman.

DICA. In old English law. A tally for accounts, by number of cuts, (*taillees*,) marks, or notches. Cowell. See Tallia; Tally.

DICAST. An officer in ancient Greece answering in some respects to our juryman, but combining, on trials had before them, the functions of both judge and jury. The dicasts sat together in numbers varying, according to the importance of the case, from one to five hundred.

DICE. Small cubes of bone or ivory, marked with figures or devices on their several sides, used in playing certain games of chance. See Wetmore v. State, 55 Ala. 198.

DICTA. Opinions of a judge which do not embody the resolution or determination of the court. Deer Island Fish & Oyster Co. v. First Nat. Bank, 166 Miss. 162, 146 So. 116, 119. See Dictum.

DICTATE. To order or instruct what is to be said or written. To pronounce, word by word, what is meant to be written by another. Hamilton v. Hamilton, 6 Mart., N.S., La., 143. See Dictation.

DICTATION. In Louisiana, this term is used in a technical sense, and means to pronounce orally what is destined to be written at the same time by another. It is used in reference to nuncupative wills. Prendergast v. Prendergast, 16 La.Ann. 220, 79 Am.Dec. 575. The dictation of a will refers to the substance, and not the style, and it is sufficient if the will, as written, conveys the identity of thought expressed by the testator, though not the identity of words used by him. Succession of Beattie, 163 La. 831, 112 So. 802, 803.

DICTATOR. A magistrate invested with unlimited power, and created in times of national distress and peril. Among the Romans, he continued in office for six months only, and had unlimited power and authority over both the property and lives of the citizens.

One in whom supreme authority in any line is invested, one who rules as dictator, and one who prescribes for others authoritatively. Houston Printing Co. v. Hunter, Tex.Civ.App., 105 S.W.2d 312, 317.

DICTATORSHIP OF PROLETARIAT. The class power of the revolutionary proletariat (unskilled laborers without property) arising upon destruction of the state. People v. Gitlow, 234 N.Y. 132, 136 N.E. 317, 322.

DICTORES. Arbitrators.

DICTUM.

In General

A statement, remark, or observation. *Gratis dictum;* a gratuitous or voluntary representation; one which a party is not bound to make. 2 Kent, Comm. 486. *Simplex dictum*; a mere assertion; an assertion without proof. Bract. fol. 320.

The word is generally used as an abbreviated form of *obiter dictum,* "a remark by the way;" that is, an observation or remark made by a judge in pronouncing an opinion upon a cause, concerning some rule, principle, or application of law, or the solution of a question suggested by the case at bar, but not necessarily involved in the case or essential to its determination; any statement of the law enunciated by the court merely by way of illustration, argument, analogy, or suggestion. See Railroad Co. v. Schutte, 103 U.S. 118, 143, 26 L.Ed. 327; City of Lincoln v. Steffensmeyer, 134 Neb. 613, 279 N.W. 272, 119 A.L.R. 914; Deer Island Fish & Oyster Co. v. First Nat. Bank, 166 Miss. 162, 146 So. 116, 119.

Statements and comments in an opinion concerning some rule of law or legal proposition not necessarily involved nor essential to determination of the case in hand are obiter dicta, and lack the force of an adjudication. Wheeler v. Wilkin, 98 Colo. 568; 58 P.2d 1223, 1226; Roquemore v. Sovereign Camp, W.O.W., 226 Ala. 279, 146 So. 619, 622.

Dicta are opinions of a judge which do not embody the resolution or determination of the court, and made without argument, or full consideration of the point, are not the professed deliberate determinations of the judge himself. *Obiter dicta* are such opinions uttered by the way, not upon the point or question pending, as if turning aside for the time from the main topic of the case to collateral subjects. Rohrbach v. Insurance Co., 62 N.Y. 47, 58, 20 Am. Rep. 451.

In Old English Law

Dictum meant an arbitrament, or the award of arbitrators.

In French Law

The report of a judgment made by one of the judges who has given it. Poth.Proc.Civil, pt. 1, c. 5, art. 2.

DICTUM DE KENILWORTH. The edict or declaration of Kenilworth. An edict or award between King Henry III. and all the barons and others who had been in arms against him; and so called because it was made at Kenilworth Castle in Warwickshire, in the fifty-first year of his reign, containing a composition of five years' rent for the lands and estates of those who had forfeited them in that rebellion. Blount; 2 Reeve, Eng.Law, 62.

DIE, *v.* To expire; cease to live; the equivalent to the phrase "lose his life." Hershey v. Agnew, 83 Colo. 89, 262 P. 526, 528.

DIE, *n.* A mold. Cole v. United States, C.C.A. Colo., 269 F. 250, 251.

DIE WITHOUT ISSUE. See Dying Without Issue.

DIEI DICTIO. Lat. In Roman law. This name was given to a notice promulgated by a magistrate of his intention to present an impeachment against a citizen before the people, specifying the day appointed, the name of the accused, and the crime charged.

DIEM CLAUSIT EXTREMUM. (Lat. He has closed his last day,—died.) A writ which formerly lay on the death of a tenant *in capite,* to ascertain the lands of which he died seised, and reclaim them into the king's hands. It was directed to the king's escheators. Fitzh.Nat.Brev. 251, K; 2 Reeve, Eng.Law, 327.

A writ awarded out of the exchequer after the death of a crown debtor, the sheriff being commanded by it to inquire by a jury when and where the crown debtor died, and what chattels, debts, and lands he had at the time of his decease, and to take and seize them into the crown's hands. 4 Steph.Comm. 47, 48.

DIES. Lat. A day; days. Days for appearance in court. Provisions or maintenance for a day. The king's rents were anciently reserved by so many days' provisions. Spelman; Cowell; Blount.

DIES A QUO. (The day from which.) In the civil law. The day from which a transaction begins; the commencement of it; the conclusion being the *dies ad quem.* Mackeld.Rom.Law, § 185.

DIES AMORIS. A day of favor. The name given to the appearance day of the term on the fourth day, or *quarto die post.* It was the day given by the favor and indulgence of the court to the defendant for his appearance, when all parties appeared in court, and had their appearance recorded by the proper officer. Wharton.

DIES CEDIT. The day begins; *dies venit,* the day has come. Two expressions in Roman law which signify the vesting or fixing of an interest, and the interest becoming a present one. Sandars' Just.Inst. (5th Ed.) 225, 232.

DIES COMMUNES IN BANCO. Regular days for appearance in court; called, also "common return-days." 2 Reeve, Eng.Law, 57.

DIES DATUS. A day given or allowed, (to a defendant in an action;) amounting to a continuance. But the name was appropriate only to a continuance before a declaration filed; if afterwards allowed, it was called an "imparlance."

DIES DATUS IN BANCO. A day given in the *bench,* (or court of common pleas.) Bract. fols. 257*b*, 361. A day given in bank, as distinguished from a day at *nisi prius*. Co.Litt. 135.

DIES DATUS PARTIBUS. A day given to the parties to an action; an adjournment or continuance. Crabb, Eng.Law, 217.

DIES DATUS PRECE PARTIUM. A day given on the prayer of the parties. Bract. fol. 358; Gilb. Comm.Pl. 41; 2 Reeve, Eng.Law, 60.

DIES DOMINICUS. The Lord's day; Sunday.

Dies dominicus non est juridicus. Sunday is not a court day, or day for judicial proceedings, or legal purposes. Co.Litt. 135*a*; Noy, Max. 2; Wing. Max. 7, max. 5; Broom, Max. 21.

DIES EXCRESCENS. In old English law. The added or increasing day in leap year. Bract. fols. 359, 359*b*.

DIES FASTI. In Roman law. Days on which the courts were open, and justice could be legally administered; days on which it was lawful for the prætor to pronounce (*fari*) the *three* words, "*do*," "*dico*," "*addico*." Mackeld.Rom.Law, § 39, and note; 3 Bl.Comm. 424, note; Calvin. Hence called "*triverbial* days," answering to the *dies juridici* of the English law.

DIES FERIATI. In the civil law. Holidays. Dig. 2, 12, 2, 9.

DIES GRATIÆ. In old English practice. A day of grace, courtesy, or favor. Co.Litt. 134*b*. The *quarto die post* was sometimes so called. Id. 135*a*.

Dies inceptus pro completo habetur. A day begun is held as complete.

Dies incertus pro conditione habetur. An uncertain day is held as a condition.

DIES INTERCISI. In Roman law. Divided days; days on which the courts were open for a part of the day. Calvin.

DIES JURIDICUS. A lawful day for the transaction of judicial or court business; a day on which the courts are or may be open for the transaction of business. Didsbury v. Van Tassell, 56 Hun, 423, 10 N.Y.Supp. 32.

DIES LEGITIMUS. In the civil and old English law. A lawful or law day; a term day; a day of appearance.

DIES MARCHIÆ. In old English law. The day of meeting of English and Scotch, which was annually held on the marches or borders to adjust their differences and preserve peace.

DIES NEFASTI. In Roman law. Days on which the courts were closed, and it was unlawful to administer justice; answering to the *dies non juridici* of the English law. Mackeld.Rom.Law, § 39, note.

DIES NON. An abbreviation of *Dies non juridicus, (q. v.).*

DIES NON JURIDICUS. In practice. A day not juridical; not a court day. A day on which courts are not open for business, such as Sundays and some holidays. Havens v. Stiles, 8 Idaho, 250, 67 P. 921, 56 L.R.A. 736, 101 Am.St.Rep. 195.

DIES PACIS. (Days of peace.) The year was formerly divided into the days of the peace of the church and the days of the peace of the king, including in the two divisions all the days of the year. Crabb, Eng.Law, 35.

DIES SOLARIS. In old English law. A solar day, as distinguished from what was called "*dies lunaris*," (a lunar day;) both composing an artificial day. Bract. fol. 264. See Day.

DIES SOLIS. In the civil and old English law. Sunday, (literally, the day of the sun.) See Cod. 3, 12, 7.

DIES UTILES. Juridical days; useful or available days. A term of the Roman law, used to designate those especial days occurring within the limits of a prescribed period of time upon which it was lawful, or possible, to do a specific act.

DIET. A general legislative assembly is sometimes so called on the continent of Europe.

In Scotch Practice

The sitting of a court. An appearance day. A day fixed for the trial of a criminal cause. A criminal cause as prepared for trial.

DIETA. A day's journey; a day's work; a day's expenses.

DIETS OF COMPEARANCE. In Scotch law. The days within which parties in civil and criminal prosecutions are cited to appear. Bell.

DIEU ET MON DROIT. Fr. God and my right. The motto of the royal arms of England, first assumed by Richard I.

DIEU SON ACTE. L. Fr. In old law. God his act; God's act. An event beyond human foresight or control. Termes de la Ley.

DIFFACERE. To destroy; to disfigure or deface.

DIFFERENCE. In an agreement for submission to arbitration, a disagreement or dispute. Fravert v. Fesler, 11 Colo.App. 387, 53 Pac. 288; Pioneer Mfg. Co. v. Phœnix Assur. Co., 106 N.C. 28, 10 S.E. 1057.

As respects contract specifications or material described therein, a state of being unlike. Mc-

Garry Contracting Co. v. Board of Education of City of New York, 284 N.Y. 218, 30 N.E.2d 482.

In mathematics, the magnitude or quantity by which one magnitude or quantity differs from another of the same kind; the remainder left after subtracting the one from the other. Riley Stoker Corporation v. Jeffrey Mfg. Co., 62 Ohio App. 199, 23 N.E.2d 519, 522.

Difficile est ut unus homo vicem duorum sustineat. 4 Coke, 118. It is difficult that one man should sustain the place of two.

DIFFICULT. For the meaning of the phrase "difficult and extraordinary case," as used in New York statutes and practice, see Standard Trust Co. v. New York, etc., R. Co., 178 N.Y. 407, 70 N.E. 925; Realty Associates v. Packard Motor Car Co. of New York, 119 Misc. 292, 196 N.Y.S. 198, 200; Cohen v. Texas Co., D.C.N.Y., 23 F.2d 128, 129.

DIFFORCIARE. In old English law. To deny, or keep from one. *Difforciare rectum,* to deny justice to any one, after having been required to do it.

DIFFUSE. To spread widely; scatter; disperse. Ex parte Hinkelman, 183 Cal. 392, 191 P. 682, 683, 11 A.L.R. 1222.

DIGAMA, or DIGAMY. Second marriage; marriage to a second wife after the death of the first, as "bigamy," in law, is having two wives at once. Originally, a man who married a widow, or married again after the death of his wife, was said to be guilty of bigamy. Co.Litt. 40*b*, note.

DIGEST. A collection or compilation, embodying the chief matter of numerous books in one, disposed under proper heads or titles, and usually by an alphabetical arrangement, for facility in reference.

As a legal term, "digest" is to be distinguished from "abridgment." The latter is a summary or epitome of the contents of a single work, in which, as a rule, the original order or sequence of parts is preserved, and in which the principal labor of the compiler is in the matter of consolidation. A digest is wider in its scope; is made up of quotations or paraphrased passages; and has its own system of classification and arrangement. An "index" merely points out the places where particular matters may be found, without purporting to give such matters *in extenso.* A "treatise" or "commentary" is not a compilation, but an original composition, though it may include quotations and excerpts.

A reference to the "Digest," or "Dig.," is always understood to designate the Digest (or Pandects) of the Justinian collection; that being the digest *par eminence,* and the authoritative compilation of the Roman law.

The American Digest System embraces the Century, First, Second, Third, Fourth Decennials, and General Digest. It covers the decisions of all American courts of last resort, State and Federal, from 1658 to date, under one uniform classification. The First Decennial, Second Decennial, Third Decennial, Fourth Decennial and General Digest, are Key-Numbered. There are also the United States Supreme Court Digest, covering all cases in that court, and the Federal Digest, covering the Federal Reporter, Federal Supplement and the Supreme Court Reporter.

DIGESTA. Digests. One of the titles of the Pandects of Justinian. Inst. *Prœm,* § 4. Bracton uses the singular, "*Digestum.*" Bract. fol. 19.

DIGESTS. The ordinary name of the Pandects of Justinian, which are now usually cited by the abbreviation "Dig." instead of "Ff.," as formerly. Sometimes called "Digest," in the singular.

DIGGING. Has been held as synonymous with "excavating," and not confined to the removal of earth. Sherman v. New York, 1 N.Y. 316.

DIGNITARY. In canon law. A person holding an ecclesiastical benefice or dignity, which gave him some pre-eminence above mere priests and canons. To this class exclusively belonged all bishops, deans, archdeacons, etc.; but it now includes all the prebendaries and canons of the church. Brande.

DIGNITY. In English law. An honor; a title, station, or distinction of honor. Dignities are a species of incorporeal hereditaments, in which a person may have a property or estate. 2 Bl.Comm. 37; 1 Bl.Comm. 396; 1 Crabb, Real Prop. 468, et seq.

DIJUDICATION. Judicial decision or determination.

DIKE. A bank, as of earth, thrown up to form a barrier, line of demarcation, or the like; especially an embankment to prevent inundation. Parker v. Department of Labor and Industries, 14 Wash.2d 481, 128 P.2d 497, 500.

DIKING. Leveling land in arid regions, particularly sagebrush land. An essential operation in the conversion of such land into farms or orchards. Craig v. Crystal Realty Co., 89 Or. 25, 173 P. 322, 325.

DILACION. In Spanish law. A space of time granted to a party to a suit in which to answer a demand or produce evidence of a disputed fact.

DILAPIDATION. A species of ecclesiastical waste which occurs whenever the incumbent suffers any edifices of his ecclesiastical living to go to ruin or decay. It is either voluntary, by pulling down, or permissive, by suffering the church, parsonage-houses, and other buildings thereunto belonging, to decay. And the remedy for either lies either in the spiritual court, where the canon law prevails, or in the courts of common law. It is also held to be good cause of deprivation if the bishop, parson, or other ecclesiastical person dilapidates buildings or cuts down timber growing on the patrimony of the church, unless for necessary repairs; and that a writ of prohibition will also lie against him in the common-law courts. 3 Bl. Comm. 91.

The term is also used, in the law of landlord and tenant, to signify the neglect of necessary repairs to a building, or suffering it to fall into a state of decay, or the pulling down of the building or any part of it. Wall Estate Co. v. Standard Box Co., 20 Cal.App. 311, 128 P. 1020, 1021.

Dilationes in lege sunt odiosæ. Delays in law are odious. Branch, Princ.

DILATORY. Tending or intended to cause delay or to gain time or to put off a decision.

DILATORY DEFENSE. In chancery practice. One the object of which is to dismiss, suspend, or obstruct the suit, without touching the merits, until the impediment or obstacle insisted on shall be removed. 3 Bl.Comm. 301, 302.

DILATORY EXCEPTIONS are such as do not tend to defeat the action, but only to retard its progress.

DILATORY PLEAS. A class of defenses at common law, founded on some matter of fact not connected with the merits of the case, but such as might exist without impeaching the right of action itself. They were either pleas to the *jurisdiction*, showing that, by reason of some matter therein stated, the case was not within the jurisdiction of the court; or pleas in *suspension*, showing some matter of temporary incapacity to proceed with the suit; or pleas in *abatement*, showing some matter for abatement or quashing the declaration. 3 Steph.Comm. 576. Parks v. McClellan, 44 N.J. Law, 513, 558; Shaw v. Southern Ry. Co., 17 Ga. App. 78, 86 S.E. 95.

DILIGENCE. Prudence; vigilant activity; attentiveness; or care, of which there are infinite shades, from the slightest momentary thought to the most vigilant anxiety. People v. Hewitt, 78 Cal.App. 426, 248 P. 1021, 1024. The law recognizes only three degrees of diligence: (1) Common or ordinary, which men, in general, exert in respect of their own concerns; the standard is necessarily variable with respect to the facts, although it may be uniform with respect to the principle. (2) High or great, which is extraordinary diligence, or that which very prudent persons take of their own concerns. (3) Low or slight, which is that which persons of less than common prudence, or indeed of no prudence at all, take of their own concerns. Brown & Flowers v. Central of Georgia Ry. Co., 197 Ala. 71, 72 So. 366, 367.

The civil law is in perfect conformity with the common law. It lays down three degrees of diligence,—ordinary, (*diligentia*;) extraordinary, (*exactissima diligentia*;) slight, (*levissima diligentia*.) Story, Bailm. 19.

There may be a high degree of diligence, a common degree of diligence, and a slight degree of diligence, with their corresponding degrees of negligence, and these can be clearly enough defined for all practical purposes, and, with a view to the business of life, seem to be all that are really necessary. Common or ordinary diligence is that degree of diligence which men in general exercise in respect to their own concerns; high or great diligence is of course extraordinary diligence, or that which very prudent persons take of their own concerns; and low or slight diligence is that which persons of less than common prudence, or indeed of any prudence at all, take of their own concerns.

Ordinary negligence is the want of ordinary diligence; slight, or less than ordinary, negligence is the want of great diligence; and gross or more than ordinary negligence is the want of slight diligence. Railroad Co. v. Rollins, 5 Kan. 180.

In Scotch Law and Practice

Process of law, by which persons, lands, or effects are seized in execution or in security for debt. Ersk. Inst. 2, 11, 1. Brande. Process for enforcing the attendance of witnesses, or the production of writings. Ersk. Inst. 4, 1, 71.

Other Classifications and Compound Terms

—Due diligence. Such a measure of prudence, activity, or assiduity, as is properly to be expected from, and ordinarily exercised by, a reasonable and prudent man under the particular circumstances; not measured by any absolute standard, but depending on the relative facts of the special case. Perry v. Cedar Falls, 87 Iowa, 315, 54 N.W. 225.

—Extraordinary diligence. That extreme measure of care and caution which persons of unusual prudence and circumspection use for securing and preserving their own property or rights. Railroad Co. v. Huggins, 89 Ga. 494, 15 S.E. 848; Railroad Co. v. White, 88 Ga. 805, 15 S.E. 802.

—Great diligence. Such a measure of care, prudence, and assiduity as persons of unusual prudence and discretion exercise in regard to any and all of their own affairs, or such as persons of ordinary prudence exercise in regard to very important affairs of their own. Litchfield v. White, 7 N.Y. 438, 57 Am.Dec. 534.

—High diligence. The same as great diligence.

—Low diligence. The same as slight diligence.

—Necessary diligence. That degree of diligence which a person placed in a particular situation must exercise in order to entitle him to the protection of the law in respect to rights or claims growing out of that situation, or to avoid being left without redress on account of his own culpable carelessness or negligence. Garahy v. Bayley, 25 Tex.Supp. 302; Sanderson v. Brown, 57 Me. 312.

—Ordinary diligence is that degree of care which men of common prudence generally exercise in their affairs, in the country and the age in which they live. Zell v. Dunkle, 156 Pa. 353, 27 A. 38.

—Reasonable diligence. A fair, proper and due degree of care and activity, measured with reference to the particular circumstances; such diligence, care, or attention as might be expected from a man of ordinary prudence and activity. Ford v. Engleman, 118 Va. 89, 86 S.E. 852, 855.

—Special diligence. The measure of diligence and skill exercised by a good business man in his particular specialty, which must be commensurate with the duty to be performed and the individual circumstances of the case; not merely the diligence of an ordinary person or non-specialist. Brady v. Jefferson, 5 Houst. (Del.) 79.

DILIGENT. Attentive and persistent in doing a thing; steadily applied; active; sedulous; laborious; unremitting; untiring. People v. Mancuso, 255 N.Y. 463, 175 N.E. 177, 179, 76 A.L.R. 514.

DILIGIATUS. (Fr. *De lege ejectus*, Lat.) Outlawed.

DILLIGROUT. In old English law. Pottage formerly made for the king's table on the coronation day. There was a tenure in serjeantry, by which lands were held of the king by the service of finding this pottage at that solemnity.

DIME. A copper-nickel clad (formerly silver) coin of the United States, of the value of ten cents, or one-tenth of the dollar.

DIMIDIA, DIMIDIUM, DIMIDIUS. Half; a half; the half.

DIMIDIETAS. The moiety or half of a thing.

DIMINISHED RESPONSIBILITY DOCTRINE. A misnomer for doctrine under which proof of mental derangement short of insanity is submitted as evidence of lack of deliberate or premeditated design. State v. Franco, 347 P.2d 312, 314, 66 N.M. 289, 78 A.L.R.2d 908.

DIMINUTIO. In the civil law. Diminution; a taking away; loss or deprivation. *Diminutio capitis*, loss of *status* or condition. See Capitis Diminutio.

DIMINUTION. Incompleteness. A word signifying that the record sent up from an inferior to a superior court for review is incomplete, or not fully certified. In such case the party may suggest a "diminution of the record," which may be rectified by a *certiorari*. 2 Tidd, Pr. 1109; Stepp v. Stepp, 195 Ga. 595, 25 S.E.2d 6, 8.

DIMISI. In old conveyancing. I have demised. *Dimisi, concessi, et ad firmam tradidi*, have demised, granted, and to farm let. The usual words of operation in a lease. 2 Bl.Comm. 317, 318.

DIMISIT. In old conveyancing. [He] has demised. See Dimisi.

DIMISSORIÆ LITTERÆ. In the civil law. Letters dimissory or dismissory, commonly called "apostles," (*quæ vulgo apostoli dicuntur.*) Dig. 50, 16, 106. See Apostoli, Apostles.

DIMISSORY LETTERS. Where a candidate for holy orders has a title of ordination in one diocese in England, and is to be ordained in another, the bishop of the former diocese gives letters dimissory to the bishop of the latter to enable him to ordain the candidate. Holthouse.

DINARCHY. A government of two persons.

DINERO.

In Roman Law

A civil division of the Roman empire embracing several provinces. Calvin.

In Spanish Law

Money. *Dinero contado*, money counted. White, New Recop. b. 2, tit. 13, c. 1, § 1.

DIOCESAN. Belonging to a diocese; a bishop, as he stands related to his own clergy or flock.

DIOCESAN COURTS. In English law. The consistorial courts of each diocese, exercising general jurisdiction of all matters arising locally within their respective limits, with the exception of places subject to *peculiar* jurisdiction; deciding all matters of spiritual discipline,—suspending or depriving clergymen,—and administering the other branches of the ecclesiastical law. 2 Steph.Com. 672.

DIOCESAN MISSION. A mission which does missionary work in single diocese. Domestic & Foreign Missionary Soc. v. Crippled Children's Hospital, 163 Va. 114, 176 S.E. 193.

DIOCESE. The territorial extent of a bishop's jurisdiction. The circuit of every bishop's jurisdiction. Co. Litt. 94; 1 Bl.Comm. 111.

DIOICHIA. The district over which a bishop exercised his spiritual functions.

DIP, *v.* To immerse for a short time in any liquid; to place in fluid and withdraw again; the act of dipping or immersing; a plunge; a brief bath, as the dip of the oars; a dip in the sea. Standard Dictionary, "dip." Covington County v. Pickering, 123 Miss. 20, 85 So. 114, 115.

DIP, *n.* In mining law. The line of declination of strata; the angle which measures the deviation of a mineralized vein or lode from the vertical plane; the slope or slant of a vein, away from the perpendicular, as it goes downward into the earth; distinguished from the "strike" of the vein, which is its extension in the horizontal plane, or its lengthwise trend or course with reference to the points of the compass. King v. Mining Co., 9 Mont. 543, 24 P. 200.

In Animal Husbandry

A liquid preparation into which infected animals may be plunged for eradication of fever ticks, or other sanitary or medical purposes. Ungles-Hoggette Mfg. Co. v. Farmers' Hog & Cattle Powder Co., C.C.A.Neb., 232 F. 116, 117.

DIPLOMA. In the civil law. A royal charter; letters patent granted by a prince or sovereign. Calvin.

An instrument given by colleges and societies on the conferring of any degrees. State v. Gregory, 83 Mo. 130, 53 Am.Rep. 565.

A license granted to a physician, etc., to practice his art or profession. See Brooks v. State, 88 Ala. 122, 6 So. 902.

DIPLOMACY. The science which treats of the relations and interests of nations with nations.

Negotiation or intercourse between nations through their representatives. The rules, customs, and privileges of representatives at foreign courts.

DIPLOMATIC AGENT. In international law. A general name for all classes of persons charged with the negotiation, transaction, or superintendence of the diplomatic business of one nation at the court of another. See Rev.St.U.S. § 1674 (22 USCA §§ 40, 51).

DIPLOMATICS. The science of diplomas, or of ancient writings and documents; the art of judging of ancient charters, public documents, diplomas, etc., and discriminating the true from the false. Webster.

DIPPING. The practice of taking snuff by rubbing teeth or gums with stick or brush dipped in snuff. Federal Trade Commission v. American Snuff Co., C.C.A., 38 F.2d 547, 550.

DIPSOMANIA. In medical jurisprudence. A mental disease characterized by an uncontrollable desire for intoxicating drinks. An irresistible impulse to indulge in intoxication, either by alcohol or other drugs. Ballard v. State, 19 Neb. 614, 28 N.W. 271; State v. Wallace, 170 Or. 60, 131 P.2d 222, 223.

DIPSOMANIAC. A person subject to dipsomania. One who has an irresistible desire for alcoholic liquors. Taylor v. Koenigstein, 128 Neb. 809, 260 N.W. 544. See Insanity.

DIPTYCHA. Diptychs; tablets of wood, metal, or other substance, used among the Romans for the purpose of writing, and folded like a book of two leaves. The diptychs of antiquity were especially employed for public registers. They were used in the Greek, and afterwards in the Roman, church, as registers of the names of those for whom supplication was to be made, and are ranked among the earliest monastic records. Burrill.

DIRECT, *v.* To point to; guide; order; command; instruct. In re Durkee's Estate, 47 N.Y.S. 2d 721, 725, 726, 183 Misc. 382.

To advise; suggest; request. Bowden v. Cumberland County, 123 Me. 359, 123 A. 166, 168.

To assume the role of a director, one whose directions are binding. Gentle v. Frederick, 234 Ala. 184, 174 So. 606, 607.

DIRECT, *adj.* Immediate; proximate; by the shortest course; without circuity; operating by an immediate connection or relation, instead of operating through a medium; the opposite of *indirect.* Trexler Lumber Co. v. Allemannia Fire Ins. Co. of Pittsburgh, 289 Pa. 13, 136 A. 856, 858; Western Assur. Co. v. Hann, 201 Ala. 376, 78 So. 232, 234; Carter v. Carter Coal Co., App.D.C., 298 U.S. 238, 56 S.Ct. 855, 80 L.Ed. 1160.

In the usual or natural course or line; immediately upwards or downwards; as distinguished from that which is out of the line, or on the side of it; the opposite of *collateral.*

In the usual or regular course or order, as distinguished from that which diverts, interrupts, or opposes; the opposite of *cross* or contrary.

Without any intervening medium, agency or influence; unconditional. General Finance Co. v. Powell, 118 P.2d 751, 753, 112 Mont. 535.

DIRECT ATTACK. A direct attack on a judgment or decree is an attempt, for sufficient cause, to have it annulled, reversed, vacated, corrected, declared void, or enjoined, in a proceeding instituted for that specific purpose, such as an appeal, writ of error, bill of review, or injunction to restrain its execution; distinguished from a collateral attack, which is an attempt to impeach the validity or binding force of the judgment or decree as a side issue or in a proceeding instituted for some other purpose. Morrill v. Morrill, 20 Or. 96, 25 P. 362; In re Melgaard's Will, 200 Minn. 493, 74 N.W. 641, 649. A direct attack on a judicial proceeding is an attempt to void or correct it in some manner provided by law.

DIRECT CAUSE. The active, efficient cause that sets in motion a train of events which brings about a result without the intervention of any force started and working actively from a new and independent source. Anderson v. Steinle, 289 Ill. App. 167, 6 N.E.2d 879. See, Cause.

DIRECT EVIDENCE. Is that means of proof which tends to show the existence of a fact in question, without the intervention of the proof of any other fact, and is distinguished from circumstantial evidence, which is often called "indirect." See Brown; State v. Calder, 23 Mont. 504, 59 P. 903.

Direct evidence means evidence which in the first instance applies directly to the factum probandum, or which immediately points to a question at issue, or is evidence of the precise fact in issue and on trial by witnesses who can testify that they saw the acts done or heard the words spoken which constituted the precise fact to be proved. Garner v. New Jersey Fidelity & Plate Glass Ins. Co., Mo. App., 200 S.W. 448, Greenl.Ev. § 13; 1 Stark, Ev. 19; Tayl, Ex. 84.

Proof of facts by witnesses who saw acts done or heard words spoken. Texas & N. O. R. Co. v. Warden, 125 Tex. 193, 78 S.W.2d 164, 167, 125 Tex. 193.

DIRECT EXAMINATION. In practice. The first interrogation or examination of a witness, on the merits, by the party on whose behalf he is called.

This is to be distinguished from an examination *in pais,* or on the *voir dire,* which is merely preliminary, and is had when the competency of the witness is challenged; from the cross-examination, which is conducted by the adverse party; and from the redirect examination which follows the cross-examination, and is had by the party who first examined the witness.

DIRECT INJURY. A wrong which directly results in the violation of a legal right and which must exist to permit a court to determine the constitutionality of an act of Congress. Wallace v. Ganley, 95 F.2d 364, 366, 68 App.D.C. 235.

DIRECT INTEREST. A direct interest, such as would render the interested party incompetent to testify in regard to the matter, is an interest which is certain, and not contingent or doubtful. Rine

v. Rine, 100 Neb. 225, 158 N.W. 941, 943. A matter which is dependent alone on the successful prosecution of an execution cannot be considered as uncertain, or otherwise than direct, in this sense. In re Van Alstine's Estate, 26 Utah, 193, 72 P. 942.

Direct line. See Descent.

DIRECT LOSS. One resulting immediately and proximately from the occurrence and not remotely from some of the consequences or effects thereof. Ermentrout v. Insurance Co., 63 Minn. 305, 65 N.W. 635, 30 L.R.A. 346, 56 Am.St.Rep. 481. See Loss.

DIRECT PAYMENT. One which is absolute and unconditional as to the time, amount, and the persons by whom and to whom it is to be made. People v. Boylan, C.C.Colo., 25 F. 595; Hurd v. McClellan, 14 Colo. 213, 23 P. 792.

As to direct "Consanguinity," "Contempt," "Damages," "Examination," "Interrogatories," "Tax," and "Trust," see those titles.

DIRECT TAX. One that is imposed directly upon property, according to its value. It is generally spoken of as a property tax or an ad valorem tax. City of De Land v. Florida Public Service Co., 161 So. 735, 739, 119 Fla. 804.

Under federal law. One that must be apportioned among the states according to population; a capitation tax, or a tax on real estate. Commonwealth of Pennsylvania ex rel. Schnader v. Fix, D.C.Pa., 9 F.Supp. 272, 276.

DIRECTION. The act of governing; management; superintendence. Denton v. Yazoo & M. V. R. Co., Miss., 284 U.S. 305, 52 S.Ct. 141, 142, 76 L.Ed. 310. Also the body of persons (called "directors") who are charged with the management and administration of a corporation or institution.

The charge or instruction given by the court to a jury upon a point of law arising or involved in the case, to be by them applied to the facts in evidence.

The clause of a bill in equity containing the address of the bill to the court.

That which is imposed by directing; a guiding or authoritative instruction; order; command. State ex rel. Johnson v. Tilley, 137 Neb. 173, 288 N. W. 521, 524; Hughes v. Van Bruggen, 44 N.M. 534, 105 P.2d 494, 496.

The line or course upon which anything is moving or aimed to move. Ruff v. Federal Tea Co., 129 Conn. 455, 29 A.2d 441, 442.

DIRECTLY. In a direct way without anything intervening; not by secondary, but by direct, means. Clark v. Warner, 85 Okl. 153, 204 P. 929, 934; Olsen v. Standard Oil Co., 188 Cal. 20, 204 P. 393, 396.

DIRECTOR OF THE MINT. An officer having the control, management, and superintendence of the United States mint and its branches. He is appointed by the president, by and with the advice and consent of the senate.

DIRECTOR. One who, or that which directs; as one who directs or regulates, guides or orders; a manager or superintendent, or a chief administrative official. State ex inf. McKittrick v. Bode, 342 Mo. 162, 113 S.W.2d 805, 808.

DIRECTORS. Persons appointed or elected according to law, authorized to manage and direct the affairs of a corporation or company. The whole of the directors collectively form the board of directors. Jones Min. Co. v. Cardiff Min. Co., 56 Utah, 449, 191 P. 426, 428.

DIRECTORY, *adj.* A provision in a statute, rule of procedure, or the like, which is a mere direction or instruction of no obligatory force, and involving no invalidating consequence for its disregard, as opposed to an imperative or mandatory provision, which must be followed. In re Opinion of the Justices, 124 Me. 453, 126 A. 354, 363. The general rule is that the prescriptions of a statute relating to the performance of a public duty are so far directory that, though neglect of them may be punishable, yet it does not affect the validity of the acts done under them, as in the case of a statute requiring an officer to prepare and deliver a document to another officer on or before a certain day. And see Pearse v. Morrice, 2 Adol. & El. 94; Nelms v. Vaughan, 84 Va. 696, 5 S.E. 704.

A "directory" provision in a statute is one, the observance of which is not necessary to the validity of the proceeding to which it relates; State v. Barnell, 109 Ohio St. 246, 142 N.E. 611, 613; one which leaves it optional with the department or officer to which it is addressed to obey or not as he may see fit; In re Thompson, 94 Neb. 658, 144 N.W. 243, 244.

Statutory requisitions are deemed "directory" only when they relate to some immaterial matter where a compliance is matter of convenience rather than of substance. This mode of getting rid of a statutory provision by calling it "directory" is not only unsatisfactory, on account of the vagueness of the rule itself, but it is the exercise of a dispensing power by the courts, which approaches so near legislative discretion that it ought to be resorted to with reluctance, only in extraordinary cases, where great public mischief would otherwise ensue, or important private interests demand the application of the rule. Ellis v. Tillman, 125 Miss. 678, 88 So. 281, 283.

Directory calls. Those which merely direct the neighborhood where the different calls may be found, whereas "locative calls" are those which serve to fix boundaries. Cates v. Reynolds, 143 Tenn. 667, 228 S.W. 695, 696.

Directory statute. Under a general classification, statutes are either "mandatory" or "directory," and, if mandatory, they prescribe, in addition to requiring the doing of the things specified, the result that will follow if they are not done, whereas, if directory, their terms are limited to what is required to be done. Hudgins v. Mooresville Consol. School Dist., 312 Mo. 1, 278 S.W. 769, 770. A statute is mandatory when the provision of the statute is the essence of the thing required to be done; otherwise, when it relates to form and manner, and where an act is incident, or after jurisdiction acquired, it is directory merely. State v. Kozer, 108 Or. 550, 217 P. 827, 832.

Directory trust. Where, by the terms of a trust, the fund is directed to be vested in a particular manner till the period arrives at which it is to be appropriated, this is called a "directory trust." It is distinguished from a discretionary trust, in which the trustee has a discretion as to the management of the fund. Deaderick v. Cantrell, 10 Yerg. (Tenn.) 272, 31 Am.Dec. 576.

DIRECTORY, *n.* Book containing names, addresses, and occupations of inhabitants of city. Also any list or compilation, usually in book or pamphlet form, of persons, firms or corporations forming some class separate and distinct from others, *e. g.*, telephone directory, hotel directory, etc. American Travel & Hotel Directory Co. v. Gehring Publishing Co., D.C., 4 F.2d 415.

DIRIBITORES. In Roman law. Officers who distributed ballots to the people, to be used in voting. Tayl. Civil Law, 192.

DIRIMENT IMPEDIMENTS. In canon law. Absolute bars to marriage, which would make it null *ab initio.*

DIRT. Filth or excrement; garden loam; earth or soil, especially when loose; dust; garden earth. Highley v. Phillips, 176 Md. 463, 5 A.2d 824, 827.

DISABILITY. The want of legal capability to perform an act. Berkin v. Marsh, 18 Mont. 152, 44 Pac. 528, 56 Am.St.Rep. 565.

A crippled condition. Kimbrough v. National Protective Ins. Ass'n, 225 Mo.App. 913, 35 S.W.2d 654, 657.

At the present day, disability is generally used to indicate an incapacity for the full enjoyment of ordinary legal rights; thus married women, persons under age, insane persons, and felons convict are said to be under disability. Sometimes the term is used in a more limited sense, as when it signifies an impediment to marriage, or the restraints placed upon clergymen by reason of their spiritual avocations. Mozley & Whitley.

Classification

Disability is either *general* or *special;* the former when it incapacitates the person for the performance of all legal acts of a general class, or giving to them their ordinary legal effect; the latter when it debars him from one specific act. State ex rel. Sathre v. Moodie, 258 N.W. 558, 567, 65 N.D. 340. Disability is also either *personal* or *absolute;* the former where it attaches to the particular person, and arises out of his *status*, his previous act, or his natural or juridical incapacity; State ex rel. Olson v. Langer, 65 N.D. 68, 256 N.W. 377; the latter where it originates with a particular person, but extends also to his descendants or successors. Lord de le Warre's Case, 6 Coke, 1*a*; Avegno v. Schmidt, 5 Sup.Ct. 487, 113 U.S. 293, 28 L.Ed. 976. Considered with special reference to the capacity to contract a marriage, disability is either *canonical* or *civil;* a disability of the former class makes the marriage voidable only, while the latter, in general, avoids it entirely. However, it has been held that, in the absence of statute, a court does not have jurisdiction to annul a marriage for a canonical disability. D. v. D., 2 Terry 263, 20 A.2d 139, 141. The term *civil* disability is also used as equivalent to *legal* disability, both these expressions meaning disabilities or disqualifications created by positive law, as distinguished from *physical* disabilities. Stieffel v. Valentine Sugars, 188 La. 1091, 179 So. 6, 15. A *physical* disability is a disability or incapacity caused by physical defect or infirmity, or bodily imperfection, or mental weakness or alienation; as distinguished from *civil* disability, which relates to the civil *status* or condition of the person, and is imposed by the law.

Absence of competent physical, intellectual, or moral powers; impairment of earning capacity; loss of physical function that reduces efficiency; inability to work. Rorabaugh v. Great Eastern Casualty Co., 117 Wash. 7, 200 P.2d 587, 590.

Temporary Disability

Temporary, as distinguished from permanent, disability is a condition that exists until the injured employee is as far restored as the permanent character of the injuries will permit. Consolidated Coal Co. of St. Louis v. Industrial Commission, 311 Ill. 61, 142 N.E. 498, 500.

Total Disability

Total disability to follow insured's usual occupation arises where he is incapacitated from performing any substantial part of his ordinary duties, though still able to perform a few minor duties and be present at his place of business. Fidelity & Casualty Co. of New York v. Bynum, 221 Ky. 450, 298 S.W. 1080, 1082. "Total disability" within an accident policy does not mean absolute physical disability to transact any business pertaining to insured's occupation, but disability from performing substantial and material duties connected with it. Jacobs v. Loyal Protective Ins. Co., 97 Vt. 516, 124 A. 848, 852; Brown v. Missouri State Life Ins. Co., 136 S.C. 90, 134 S.E. 224–225. The term may also apply to any impairment of mind or body rendering it impossible for insured to follow continuously a substantially gainful occupation without seriously impairing his health, the disability being permanent when of such nature as to render it reasonably certain to continue throughout the lifetime of insured. Starnes v. U. S., D.C.Tex., 13 F.2d 212, 213. See, also, Wholly Disabled.

DISABLE. Ordinarily, to take away the ability of, to render incapable of proper and effective action. Federal Union Life Ins. Co. of Cincinnati, Ohio v. Richey's Adm'x, 256 Ky. 262, 75 S.W.2d 767, 768.

In the old language of pleading, to disable is to take advantage of one's own or another's disability. Thus, it is "an express maxim of the common law that the party shall not disable himself;" but "this disability to disable himself * * * is personal." 4 Coke, 123*b*.

DISABLING STATUTES. These are acts of parliament, restraining and regulating the exercise of a right or the power of alienation; the term is specially applied to 1 Eliz. c. 19, and similar acts restraining the power of ecclesiastical corporations to make leases.

DISADVOCARE. To deny a thing.

DISAFFIRM. To repudiate; to revoke a consent once given; to recall an affirmance. To refuse one's subsequent sanction to a former act; to disclaim the intention of being bound by an antecedent transaction.

DISAFFIRMANCE. The repudiation of a former transaction. The refusal by one who has the legal power to refuse, (as in the case of a voidable contract,) to abide by his former acts, or accept the legal consequences of them. It may either be "express" (in words) or "implied" from acts inconsistent with a recognition of validity of former transaction. Ryan v. Morrison, 40 Okl. 49, 135 P. 1049, 1050.

DISAFFOREST. To restore to their former condition lands which have been turned into forests. To remove from the operation of the forest laws. 2 Bl.Comm. 416.

DISAGREEMENT. Difference of opinion or want of uniformity or concurrence of views; as, a disagreement among the members of a jury, among the judges of a court, or between arbitrators. Darnell v. Lyon, 85 Tex. 466, 22 S.W. 304.

In Real Property Law

The refusal by a grantee, lessee, etc., to accept an estate, lease, etc., made to him; the annulling of a thing that had essence before. No estate can be vested in a person against his will. Consequently no one can become a grantee, etc., without his *agreement*. The law implies such an agreement until the contrary is shown, but his disagreement renders the grant, etc., inoperative. Wharton.

DISALT. To disable a person.

DISALLOW. To refuse to allow, to deny the validity of, to disown or reject. Stewart v. Yellowtail, D.C.Mont., 35 F.Supp. 798, 799.

DISAPPROPRIATION. In ecclesiastical law. This is where the appropriation of a benefice is severed, either by the patron presenting a clerk or by the corporation which has the appropriation being dissolved. 1 Bl.Comm. 385.

DISAPPROVE. To pass unfavorable judgment upon; to refuse official approbation to; to disallow; to decline to sanction; to refuse to confirm, ratify or consent to. Stewart v. Yellowtail, D.C. Mont., 35 F.Supp. 798, 799.

DISASTER. A sudden and ruinous misfortune, hence, one who had been pronounced by eminent physicians to be afflicted with dementia praecox, who had nervous breakdown, and who was without funds or ability to earn them by either mental or physical exertion, was overtaken by disaster. Robison v. Elston Bank & Trust Co., 113 Ind.App. 633, 48 N.E.2d 181, 188.

DISAVOW. To repudiate the unauthorized acts of an agent; to deny the authority by which he assumed to act.

DISBAR. In England, to deprive a barrister permanently of the privileges of his position; it is analogous to striking an attorney off the rolls. In America, the word describes the act of a court in rescinding an attorney's license to practice at its bar. Gresham v. Superior Court of Los Angeles County, 44 Cal.App.2d 664, 112 P.2d 965, 967.

DISBOCATIO. In old English law. A conversion of wood grounds into arable or pasture; an assarting. Cowell. See Assart.

DISBURSEMENTS. Money paid out or expended for which one is entitled to a credit upon rendering an account of his doings. Tinkler v. Powell, 23 Wyo. 352, 151 P. 1097, 1098.

The term is also used under the codes of civil procedure, to designate the expenditures necessarily made by a party in the progress of an action, aside from the fees of officers and court costs, which are allowed, *eo nomine*, together with costs. Fertilizer Co. v. Glenn, 48 S.C. 494, 26 S.E. 796; Sasser v. Stuyvesant Ins. Co., 258 App.Div. 340, 16 N.Y.S.2d 401, 402, 403.

DISCARCARE. In old English law. To discharge, to unload; as a vessel. *Carcare et discarcare;* to charge and discharge; to load and unload. Cowell.

DISCARGARE. In old European law. To discharge or unload, as a wagon. Spelman.

DISCEPTIO CAUSÆ. In Roman law. The argument of a cause by the counsel on both sides. Calvin.

DISCHARGE. To release, Clark v. Sperry, 125 W.Va. 718, 25 S.E.2d 870, 872; liberate, People ex rel. La Velle v. Trophagen, 236 N.Y.S. 214, 216, 134 Misc. 604; annul, Glaser v. Haskin, 140 Or. 392, 13 P.2d 1071, 1074; unburden; disincumber; dismiss, The Losmar, D.C.Md., 20 F.Supp. 887, 891; extinguish an obligation, Mazur v. Stein, 314 Ill. App. 529, 41 N.E.2d 979, 981; remove from employment, Bourne v. Board of Education of City of Roswell, 46 N.M. 310, 128 P.2d 733, 735.

In the Law of Contracts

To cancel or unloose the obligation of a contract; to make an agreement or contract null and inoperative. As a noun, the word means the act or instrument by which the binding force of a contract is terminated, irrespective of whether the contract is carried out to the full extent contemplated (in which case the discharge is the result of *performance*) or is broken off before complete execution. Rivers v. Blom, 163 Mo. 442, 63 S.W. 812.

Discharge is a generic term; its principal species are rescission, release, accord and satisfaction, performance, judgment, composition, bankruptcy, merger (*q. v.*). Leake, Cont. 413.

As applied to demands, claims, rights of action, incumbrances, etc., to discharge the debt or claim is to extinguish it, to annul its obligatory force, to satisfy it. And here also the term is generic; thus a debt, a mortgage, a legacy, may be discharged by payment or performance, or by any act short of that, lawful in itself, which the creditor accepts as sufficient. Blackwood v. Brown, 29 Mich. 484; Rangely v. Spring, 28 Me. 151. To discharge a person is to liberate him from the binding force of an obligation, debt, or claim.

There is a distinction between a "debt discharged" and a "debt paid." When discharged the debt still exists though divested of its character as a legal obligation during the operation of the discharge. Something of the original vitality of the debt continues to exist which may be transferred, even though the transferee takes it subject to its disability incident to the discharge. The fact that it carries something which may be a consideration for a new promise to pay, so as to make an otherwise worthless promise a legal obligation, makes it the subject of transfer by assignment. Stanek v. White, 172 Minn. 390, 215 N.W. 784.

Discharge by operation of law is where the discharge takes place, whether it was intended by the parties or not; thus, if a creditor appoints his debtor his executor, the debt is discharged by operation of law, because the executor cannot have an action against himself. Co.Litt. 264*b*, note 1; Williams, Ex'rs, 1216; Chit.Cont. 714.

In Bankruptcy Practice

The discharge of the bankrupt is the step which regularly follows the adjudication of bankruptcy and the administration of his estate. By it he is released from the obligation of all his debts which were or might be proved in the proceedings, so that they are no longer a charge upon him, and so that he may thereafter engage in business and acquire property without its being liable for the satisfaction of such former debts. Pitcairn v. Scully, 252 Pa. 82, 97 A. 120, 121.

In Civil Practice

To discharge a rule, an order, an injunction, a certificate, process of execution, or in general any proceeding in a court, is to cancel or annul it, or to revoke it, or to refuse to confirm its original provisional force. Nichols v. Chittenden, 14 Colo. App. 49, 59 P. 954.

To discharge a jury is to relieve them from any further consideration of a cause. This is done when the continuance of the trial is, by any cause, rendered impossible; also when the jury, after deliberation, cannot agree on a verdict.

In Criminal Practice

The act by which a person in confinement, held on an accusation of some crime or misdemeanor, is set at liberty. The writing containing the order for his being so set at liberty is also called a "discharge." In re Eddinger, 236 Mich. 668, 211 N.W. 54.

In Equity Practice

In the process of accounting before a master in chancery, the *discharge* is a statement of expenses and counter-claims brought in and filed, by way of set-off, by the accounting defendant; which follows the *charge* in order.

In Maritime Law

The unlading or unlivery of a cargo from a vessel. The Bird of Paradise v. Heyneman, 5 Wall. 557, 18 L.Ed. 662.

In Military Law

The release or dismissal of a soldier, sailor, or marine, from further military service, either at the expiration of his term of enlistment, or previous thereto on special application therefor, or as a punishment. An "honorable" discharge is one granted at the end of an enlistment and accompanied by an official certificate of good conduct during the service. A "dishonorable" discharge is a dismissal from the service for bad conduct or as a punishment imposed by sentence of a court-martial for offenses against the military law. There is also in occasional use a form of "discharge without honor," which implies censure, but is not in itself a punishment. U. S. v. Sweet, 23 S.Ct. 638, 189 U.S. 471, 47 L.Ed. 907.

A *discharge from the army* is the discharge given one who was actually in military service, as distinguished from a mere discharge from draft. Patterson v. Lamb, App.D.C., 67 S.Ct. 448, 329 U.S. 539, 91 L.Ed. 485.

A *discharge from draft* is the discharge given selectees who reported for military service in World War I and were rejected at camp after induction for unfitness, dependency and the like. Thus a selectee who reported on November 11, 1918 but was told that draft call was cancelled because of the armistice was properly given a discharge from draft, rather than a discharge from the army and could not claim veterans' rights. Patterson v. Lamb, App.D.C., 67 S.Ct. 448, 329 U.S. 539, 91 L.Ed. 485.

DISCIPLINE. Instruction, comprehending the communication of knowledge and training to observe and act in accordance with rules and orders. In re Swenson, 183 Minn. 602, 237 N.W. 589.

Correction, chastisement, punishment, penalty. Rules and regulations. Reutkemeier v. Nolte, 179 Iowa, 342, 161 N.W. 290, 292, L.R.A.1917D, 273.

DISCLAIMER. The repudiation or renunciation of a claim or power vested in a person or which he had formerly alleged to be his. The refusal, or rejection of an estate or right offered to a person. The disavowal, denial, or renunciation of an interest, right, or property imputed to a person or alleged to be his. Also the declaration, or the instrument, by which such disclaimer is published. Moores v. Clackamas County, 40 Or. 536, 67 P. 662.

Of Estate

The act by which a party refuses to accept an estate which has been conveyed to him. Thus, a trustee who releases to his fellow-trustees his estate, and relieves himself of the trust, is said to disclaim. Kentucky Union Co. v. Cornett, 112 Ky. 677, 66 S.W. 728.

A renunciation or a denial by a tenant of his landlord's title, either by refusing to pay rent, denying any obligation to pay, or by setting up a title in himself or a third person, and this is a distinct ground of forfeiture of the lease or other tenancy, whether of land or tithe. See 16 Ch. Div. 730.

In Patent Law

When the title and specifications of a patent do not agree, or when part of that which it covers is not strictly patentable, because neither new nor useful, the patentee is empowered, with leave of the court, to enter a disclaimer of any part of either the title or the specification, and the disclaimer is then deemed to be part of the letters patent or specification, so as to render them valid for the future. Permutit Co. v. Wadham, C.C.A. Mich., 15 F.2d 20, 21.

In Pleading

A renunciation by the defendant of all claim to the subject of the demand made by the plaintiff's bill. Wilson v. McCoy, 93 W.Va. 667, 117 S.E. 473, 475.

DISCLAMATION. In Scotch law. Disavowal of tenure; denial that one holds lands of another. Bell.

DISCLOSE. To bring into view by uncovering, to lay bare, to reveal to knowledge, to free from secrecy or ignorance, or make known. State v. Krokston, 187 Mo.App. 67, 172 S.W. 1156, 1157.

DISCLOSURE. Revelation; the impartation of that which is secret. Commonwealth v. Chesapeake & O. Ry. Co., 137 Va. 526, 120 S.E. 506, 509.

That which is disclosed or revealed. Webster, Dict.

In patent law, the specification; the statement of the subject-matter of the invention, or the manner in which it operates. Westinghouse Electric & Mfg. Co. v. Metropolitan Electric Mfg. Co., C.C.A.N.Y., 290 F. 661, 664.

What any patentee has invented is theoretically what he discloses, and the "disclosure" is the specification while a "claim" is a definition of that which has been disclosed in the specification; the disclosure telling how to do that of which the claimant attempts definition. Westinghouse Electric & Mfg. Co. v. Metropolitan Electric Mfg. Co., C.C. A.N.Y., 290 F. 661, 664.

DISCOMMON. To deprive commonable lands of their commonable quality, by inclosing and appropriating or improving them.

DISCONTINUANCE.

In Pleading

That technical interruption of the proceedings in an action which follows where a defendant does not answer the whole of the plaintiff's declaration, and the plaintiff omits to take judgment for the part unanswered. Steph. Pl. 216, 217.

In Practice

The termination of an action, in consequence of the plaintiff's omitting to continue the process or proceedings by proper entries on the record. 3 Bl.Comm. 296; 1 Tidd, Pr. 678; 2 Arch.Pr.K.B. 233. Hadwin v. Railway Co., 67 S.C. 463, 45 S.E. 1019.

In practice, a discontinuance is a chasm or gap left by neglecting to enter a continuance. By our practice, a neglect to enter a continuance, even in a defaulted action, by no means puts an end to it, and such actions may always be brought forward. Taft v. Northern Transp. Co., 56 N.H. 416; Porter v. Watkins, 196 Ala. 333, 71 So. 687, 688.

The cessation of the proceedings in an action where the plaintiff voluntarily puts an end to it, either by giving notice in writing to the defendant before any step has been taken in the action subsequent to the answer, or at any other time by order of the court or a judge; a non-suit; dismissal. Payne v. Buena Vista Extract Co., 124 Va. 296, 98 S.E. 34, 39.

In practice, discontinuance and dismissal import the same thing, viz., that the cause is sent out of court. Thurman v. James, 48 Mo. 235.

In Public Works

Refers to the termination or abandonment of a project, structure, highway, or the like. Fulton County v. Board of Hudson River Regulating Dist., 248 N.Y.S. 8, 10, 231 App.Div. 408.

Ending, causing to cease, ceasing to use, giving up, leaving off. Keenan v. Broad River Power Co., 163 S.C. 133, 161 S.E. 330, 331.

In Zoning Ordinances

Synonymous with abandonment. State ex rel. Schaetz v. Manders, 206 Wis. 121, 238 N.W. 835, 837.

DISCONTINUANCE OF AN ESTATE. The termination or suspension of an estate-tail, in consequence of the act of the tenant in tail, in conveying a larger estate in the land than he was by law entitled to do. 2 Bl.Comm. 275; 3 Bl.Comm. 171. An alienation made or suffered by tenant in tail, or by any that is seised in *autre droit*, whereby the issue in tail, or the heir or successor, or those in reversion or remainder, are driven to their action, and cannot enter. Co. Litt. 325*a*. The cesser of a seisin under an estate, and the acquisition of a seisin under a new and necessarily a wrongful title. Prest. Merg. c. ii.

Discontinuare nihil aliud significat quam intermittere, desuescere, interrumpere. Co. Litt. 325. To discontinue signifies nothing else than to intermit, to disuse, to interrupt.

DISCONTINUANCE. Occasional; intermittent; characterized by separate repeated acts; as, discontinuous easements and servitudes. See Easement.

DISCONVENABLE. L. Fr. Improper; unfit. Kelham.

DISCOUNT. In a general sense, an allowance or deduction made from a gross sum on any account whatever. In a more limited and technical sense, the taking of interest in advance. Cooper v. National Bank of Savannah, 21 Ga.App. 356, 94 S. E. 611, 614.

By the language of the commercial world and the settled practice of banks, a discount by a bank means a drawback or deduction made upon its advances or loans of money, upon negotiable paper or other evidences of debt payable at a future day, which are transferred to the bank. See, also, Valley Mortg. Co. v. Patterson, 30 Ala.App. 492, 8 So.2d 213, 214.

Although the discounting of notes or bills, in its most comprehensive sense, may mean lending money and taking notes in payment, yet, in its more ordinary sense, the discounting of notes or bills means advancing a consideration for a bill or note, deducting or discounting the interest which will accrue for the time the note has to run. In re Worth Lighting & Fixture Co., D.C.N.Y., 292 F. 769, 772.

Discounting by a bank means lending money upon a note, and deducting the interest or premium in advance. Meserole Securities Co. v. Cosman, 253 N.Y. 130, 170 N.E. 519, 521.

Discount, as we have seen, is the difference between the price and the amount of the debt, the evidence of which is transferred. That difference represents interest charged, being at the same rate, according to which the price paid, if invested until the maturity of the debt, will just produce its amount. Napier v. John V. Farwell Co., 60 Colo. 319, 153 P. 694, 695.

Commission Equivalent

Where agreement provides for underwriting shares at "discount" of certain per cent., word "discount" is equivalent to commission. Stewart v. G. L. Miller & Co., 161 Ga. 919, 132 S.E. 535, 538, 45 A.L.R. 559.

Discounting a note and buying it are not identical in meaning, the latter expression being used to denote the transaction when the seller does not indorse the note, and is not accountable for it. Bank v. Baldwin, 23 Minn. 206, 23 Am.Rep. 683.

In Practice

A set-off or defalcation in an action. Vin. Abr. "Discount." But see Trabue's Ex'r v. Harris, 1 Metc. (Ky.) 597.

DISCOUNT BROKER. A bill broker; one who discounts bills of exchange and promissory notes, and advances money on securities.

DISCOVER. To uncover that which was hidden, concealed, or unknown from every one. Stanolind Oil & Gas Co. v. State, Tex.Civ.App., 114 S.W.2d 699, 706.

To get first sight or knowledge of; to get knowledge of what has existed but has not theretofore been known to the discoverer. Shellmar Products Co. v. Allen-Qualley Co., C.C.A.Ill., 87 F.2d 104, 108.

DISCOVERED PERIL, DOCTRINE OF. A name for the doctrine otherwise known as that of the "last clear chance." See that title.

DISCOVERT. Not married; not subject to the disabilities of a coverture. It applies equally to a maid and a widow.

DISCOVERY. In a general sense, the ascertainment of that which was previously unknown; the disclosure or coming to light of what was previously hidden; the acquisition of notice or knowledge of given acts or facts; as, in regard to the "discovery" of fraud affecting the running of the statute of limitations, or the granting of a new trial for newly "discovered" evidence. Parker v. Kuhn, 21 Neb. 413, 32 N.W. 74, 59 Am.Rep. 852. Howton v. Roberts, 49 S.W. 340, 20 Ky.Law Rep. 1331.

In International Law

As the foundation for a claim of national ownership or sovereignty, discovery is the finding of a country, continent, or island previously unknown, or previously known only to its uncivilized inhabitants. Martin v. Waddell, 16 Pet. 409, 10 L.Ed. 997.

In Mining Law

As the basis of the right to locate a mining claim upon the public domain, discovery means the finding of mineralized rock in place. U. S. v. Safe Investment Gold Mining Co., C.C.A.S.D., 258 F. 872, 877; Dalton v. Clark, 129 Cal.App. 136, 18 P.2d 752.

In Patent Law

The finding out some substance, mechanical device, improvement, or application, not previously known. Dunbar v. Meyers, 94 U.S. 197, 24 L.Ed. 34. It is something less than invention, and may be the result of industry, application, or be perhaps merely fortuitous. A. O. Smith Corporation v. Petroleum Iron Works Co. of Ohio, C.C.A.Ohio, 73 F.2d 531, 538.

In Practice

The disclosure by the defendant of facts, titles, documents, or other things which are in his exclusive knowledge or possession, and which are necessary to the party seeking the discovery as a part of a cause or action pending or to be brought in another court, or as evidence of his rights or title in such proceeding. Tucker v. U. S., 151 U.S. 164, 14 S.Ct. 299, 38 L.Ed. 112; Kelley v. Boettcher, 85 F. 55, 29 C.C.A. 14.

Also used of the disclosure by a bankrupt of his property for the benefit of creditors.

A favored equitable remedy to secure evidence in the other party's possession. C. F. Simonin's Sons v. American Can Co., D.C.Pa., 22 F.Supp. 784, 786.

DISCOVERY, BILL OF. In equity pleading. A bill for the discovery of facts resting in the knowledge of the defendant, or of deeds or writings, or other things in his custody or power; but seeking no relief in consequence of the discovery, though it may pray for a stay of proceedings at law till the discovery is made. Story, Eq. Pl. §§ 311, 312, and notes; Mitf. Eq. Pl. 53.

DISCOVERY VEIN. See Vein.

DISCREDIT. To destroy or impair the credibility of a person; to impeach; to lessen the degree of credit to be accorded to a witness or document, as by impugning the veracity of the one or the genuineness of the other; to disparage or weaken the reliance upon the testimony of a witness, or upon documentary evidence, by any means whatever.

DISCREETLY. Prudently; judiciously; with discernment. Parks v. City of Des Moines, 195 Iowa, 972, 191 N.W. 728, 731.

DISCREPANCY. A difference between two things which ought to be identical, as between one writing and another; a variance, (*q. v.*) Also discord, discordance, dissonance, dissidence, unconformity, disagreement, difference. State v. Superior Court of King County, 138 Wash. 488, 244 P. 702, 703.

DISCRETELY. Separately; disjunctively. Parks v. City of Des Moines, 195 Iowa, 972, 191 N.W. 728, 731.

Discretio est discernere per legem quid sit justum. 10 Coke, 140. Discretion is to know through law what is just.

Discretio est scire per legem quid sit justum. Discretion consists in knowing what is just in law. Le Roy v. New York, 4 Johns. Ch. (N. Y.) 352, 356.

DISCRETION. Power or privilege of the court to act unhampered by legal rule. Osborn v. United States Bank, 9 Wheat. 866, 6 L.Ed. 204; Murray v. Buell, 74 Wis. 14, 41 N.W. 1010, 11 L.R.A. 446.

When applied to public functionaries, discretion means a power or right conferred upon them by law of acting officially in certain circumstances, according to the dictates of their own judgment and conscience, uncontrolled by the judgment or conscience of others. This discretion undoubtedly is to some extent regulated by usage, or, if the term is preferred, by fixed principles. But by this is to be understood nothing more than that the same court cannot, consistently with its own dignity, and with its character and duty of administering impartial justice, decide in different ways two cases in every respect exactly alike. The question of fact whether the two cases are alike in every color, circumstance, and feature is of necessity to be submitted to the judgment of some tribunal. State v. Tindell, 112 Kan. 256, 210 P. 619, 622. Board of Permanent Road Com'rs of Hunt County v. Johnson, Tex.Civ.App., 231 S.W. 859, 860.

Judicial Discretion, Legal Discretion

These terms are applied to the discretionary action of a judge or court, and mean discretion as above defined, that is, discretion bounded by the rules and principles of law, and not arbitrary, capricious, or unrestrained. "Judicial discretion" is substantially synonymous with judicial power. Griffin v. State, 12 Ga.App. 615, 77 S.E. 1080, 1083. It is not the indulgence of a judicial whim, but the exercise of judicial judgment, based on facts and guided by law, Smith v. Hill, C.C.A., 5 F.2d 188, or the equitable decision of what is just and proper under the circumstances, People v. Pfanschmidt, 262 Ill. 411, 104 N.E. 804, 816, Ann.Cas.1915A, 1171. It is simply the technical name of the decision of certain questions of fact by the court. Nawn v. Boston & M. R. R., 77 N.H. 299, 91 A. 181, 182.

Lord Coke defines judicial discretion to be *"discernere per legem quid sit justum,"* to see what would be just according to the laws in the premises. It does not mean a wild self-willfulness, which may prompt to any and every act; but this judicial discretion is guided by the law, (see what the law declares upon a certain statement of facts, and then decide in accordance with the law,) so as to do substantial equity and justice. Faber v. Bruner, 13 Mo. 543. It is a legal discretion to be exercised in discerning the course prescribed by law and is not to give effect to the will of the judge, but to that of the law. McGurty v. Delaware, L. & W. R. Co., 158 N.Y.S. 285, 286, 172 App. Div. 46.

True, it is a matter of discretion; but then the discretion is not willful or arbitrary, but legal. And, although its exercise be not purely a matter of law, yet it *"involves* a matter of law or legal inference," in the language of the Code, and an appeal will lie. Lovinier v. Pearce, 70 N. C. 171.

Legal discretion, is the exercise of discretion where there are two alternative provisions of law applicable, under either of which court could proceed. Shannon v. Hendrixson, Ohio App., 32 N.E.2d 431, 432.

In criminal law and the law of torts, it means the capacity to distinguish between what is right and wrong, lawful or unlawful, wise or foolish, sufficiently to render one amenable and responsible for his acts. Towle v. State, 3 Fla. 214.

Wise conduct and management; cautious discernment, especially as to matters of propriety and self-control; prudence; circumspection; wariness. Arkansas Valley Town & Land Co. v. Atchison, T. & S. F. Ry. Co., 49 Okl. 282, 151 P. 1028, 1031.

DISCRETIONARY DAMAGES. Those which are measureable by enlightened conscience of impartial jurors. Southern Ry. Co. v. Groover, 41 Ga. App. 746, 154 S.E. 706, 707.

DISCRETIONARY POWER. One which is not imperative or, if imperative, the time, manner, or extent of execution of which is left to donee's discretion; the power to do or to refrain from doing a certain thing. City of San Antonio v. Zogheib, Tex.Civ.App., 70 S.W.2d 333, 334.

DISCRETIONARY TRUSTS. Such as are not marked out on fixed lines, but allow a certain amount of discretion in their exercise. Those which cannot be duly administered without the application of a certain degree of prudence and judgment. Greenwich Trust Co. v. Tyson, 129 Conn. 211, 27 A.2d 166, 172.

DISCRIMINATION. With reference to common carriers (especially railroads), a breach of the carrier's duty to treat all shippers alike, and afford them equal opportunities to market their product. Cox v. Pennsylvania R. Co., 240 Pa. 27, 87 A. 581, 583. A carrier's failure to treat all alike under substantially similar conditions. Kentucky Traction & Terminal Co. v. Murray, 176 Ky. 593, 195 S.W. 1119, 1120.

"Discrimination" is a term well understood in the nomenclature of transportation over railroads. It implies to charge shippers of freight, as compensation for carrying the same over railroads, unequal sums of money for the same quantity of freight for equal distances; more for a shorter than a longer distance, more in proportion of distance for a shorter than a longer distance; more for freights called local freights than those designated otherwise; more for the former in proportion to distance such freights may be carried than the latter. Atchison, T. & S. F. Ry. Co. v. State, 85 Okl. 223, 206 P. 236, 239.

In constitutional law, the effect of a statute which confers particular privileges on a class arbitrarily selected from a large number of persons, all of whom stand in the same relation to the privileges granted and between whom and those not favored no reasonable distinction can be found. Franchise Motor Freight Ass'n v. Seavey, 196 Cal. 77, 235 P. 1000, 1002.

In general, a failure to treat all equally; favoritism. Employment, Mische v. Kaminski, 127 Pa.Super. 66, 193 A. 410, 416; Board of Com'rs of Huron County v. State ex rel. Clarke, 127 Ohio St. 341, 188 N.E. 551, 552; Selective service, United States ex rel. Lynn v. Downer, C.C.A.N.Y., 140 F.2d 397, 401; marriages between negroes or mulattoes and white persons, Jackson v. City and County of Denver, 109 Colo. 196, 124 P.2d 240, 241; differential in teachers' salaries based solely on the ground of race and color, Thomas v. Hibbitts, D.C.Tenn., 46 F.Supp. 368, 371; taxation, Atlantic Pipe Line Co. v. Brown County, D.C.Tex., 12 F. Supp. 642, 647.

DISCUSSION.

In the Civil Law

A proceeding, at the instance of a surety, by which the creditor is obliged to exhaust the property of the principal debtor, towards the satisfaction of the debt, before having recourse to the surety; and this right of the surety is termed the "benefit of discussion."

In Scotch Law

The ranking of the proper order in which heirs are liable to satisfy the debts of the deceased. Bell.

DISEASE. Deviation from the healthy or normal condition of any of the functions or tissues of the body; an alteration in the state of the body or of some of its organs, interrupting or disturbing the performance of the vital functions, and causing or threatening pain and weakness; illness; sickness; disorder; malady; bodily infirmity. Order of United Commercial Travelers of America v. Nicholson, C.C.A.N.Y., 9 F.2d 7, 14; Merriam v. Hamilton, 64 Or. 476, 130 P. 406, 407.

In construing a policy of life insurance, it is generally true that, before any temporary ailment can be called a "disease," it must be such as to indicate a vice in the constitution, or be so serious as to have some bearing upon general health and the continuance of life, or such as, according to common understanding, would be called a "disease." Delaney v. Modern Acc. Club, 121 Iowa 528, 97 N.W. 91, 63 L.R.A. 603; Metropolitan Casualty Ins. Co. v. Cato, 113 Miss. 303, 74 So. 118, 119.

An ulcer is a "disease" or "infection," within Workmen's Compensation Law, § 3, subd. 7, declaring that "injury," or "personal injury," as used in the act, means only accidental injuries arising out of and in the course of employment and such disease or infection as may naturally and unavoidably result therefrom. Pinto v. Chelsea Fibre Mills, 186 N.Y.S. 748, 750, 196 App.Div. 221; For "Existing Disease" see that title.

DISEASE COMMON TO BOTH SEXES. Malady, sickness, or illness that both males and females have. National Life & Accident Ins. Co. v. Weaver, Tex.Civ.App., 226 S.W. 754, 757.

DISENTAILING DEED. In English law. An enrolled assurance barring an entail, pursuant to 3 & 4 Wm. IV. c. 74.

DISFIGUREMENT. That which impairs or injures the beauty, symmetry, or appearance of a person or thing; that which renders unsightly, misshapen, or imperfect, or deforms in some manner. Vukelich v. Industrial Commission of Utah, 62 Utah, 486, 220 P. 1073, 1075; Lee v. Commonwealth, 135 Va. 572, 115 S.E. 671, 673.

DISFRANCHISE. To deprive of the rights and privileges of a free citizen; to deprive of chartered rights and immunities; to deprive of any franchise, as of the right of voting in elections, etc. Webster.

In any election where the party system furnishes the means by which the citizen's right of suffrage is made effective, denial of his party's right to participate in the election accomplishes the "disfranchisement of voters" or compels them, if they vote, to vote for representatives of political parties other than that to which they belong, and the deprivation of the right of selection is a deprivation of the right of franchise. Communist Party of United States of America v. Peek, 20 Cal.2d 536, 127 P.2d 889, 894.

DISFRANCHISEMENT. The act of disfranchising. The act of depriving a member of a corporation of his right as such, by expulsion. 1 Bouv. Inst. no. 192. In re Koch, 257 N.Y. 318, 178 N.E. 545, 546.

It differs from amotion (*q. v.*) which is applicable to the removal of an officer from office, leaving him his rights as a member. Ang. & A. Corp. 237.

In a more popular sense, the taking away of the elective franchise (that is, the right of voting in public elections) from any citizen or class of citizens.

DISGAVEL. In English law. To deprive lands of that principal quality of gavelkind tenure by which they descend equally among all the sons of the tenant. 2 Wood. Lect. 76; 2 Bl. Comm. 85.

DISGRACE. Ignominy; shame; dishonor. No witness is required to disgrace himself. 13 How. State Tr. 17, 334; Bander v. Metropolitan Life Ins. Co., 313 Mass. 337, 47 N.E.2d 595, 600.

DISGRADING. In old English law. The depriving of an order or dignity.

DISGUISE, *v.* To change the guise or appearance of, especially to conceal by unusual dress; to hide by a counterfeit appearance; to affect or change by liquor; to intoxicate. Darneal v. State, 14 Okl.Cr. 540, 174 P. 290, 292, 1 A.L.R. 638.

DISGUISE, *n.* A counterfeit habit; a dress intended to conceal the person who wears it. Webster. Also slight intoxication. Darneal v. State, 14 Okl.Cr. 540, 174 P. 290, 292, 1 A.L.R. 638.

Anything worn upon the person with the intention of so altering the wearer's appearance that he shall not be recognized by those familiar with him, or that he shall be taken for another person.

A person lying in ambush, or concealed behind bushes, is not in "disguise," within the meaning of a statute declaring the county liable in damages to the next of kin of any one murdered by persons in disguise. Dale County v. Gunter, 46 Ala. 118, 142.

DISHERISON. Disinheritance; depriving one of an inheritance. Obsolete. See Abernethy v. Orton, 42 Or. 437, 71 P. 327, 95 Am.St.Rep. 774.

DISHERITOR. One who disinherits, or puts another out of his freehold. Obsolete.

DISHONESTY. Disposition to lie, cheat or defraud; untrustworthiness; lack of integrity. Alsup v. State, 91 Tex.Cr.R. 224, 238 S.W. 667, 669.

DISHONOR. In mercantile law and usage. To refuse or decline to accept a bill of exchange, or to refuse or neglect to pay a bill or note at maturity. Shelton v. Braithwaite, 7 Mees. & W. 436; Brewster v. Arnold, 1 Wis. 276.

Notice of Dishonor

A notice given by the holder to the drawer of a bill, or to an indorser of a bill or note, that it has been dishonored by nonacceptance on presentment for acceptance, or by nonpayment at its maturity. 2 Daniel, Neg. Inst. § 970.

As respects the flag, to deface or defile, imputing a lively sense of shaming or an equivalent acquiescent callousness. State v. Schlueter, 127 N.J.L. 496, 23 A.2d 249, 251.

DISINCARCERATE. To set at liberty, to free from prison.

DISINFECTED. Made free from injurious or contagious diseases. Clampitt v. St. Louis Southwestern Ry. Co. of Texas, Tex.Civ.App., 185 S.W. 342, 344.

DISINHERISON. In the civil law. The act of depriving a forced heir of the inheritance which the law gives him.

Disinherison is a testamentary disposition and not a mere penalty for lack of filial respect, but such a testamentary disposition is not self-operative and something more than its mere appearance in a will is required to give it effect. Successions of Lissa, 198 La. 129, 3 So.2d 534, 542.

DISINHERITANCE. The act by which the owner of an estate deprives a person, who would otherwise be his heir, of the right to inherit it. Copeland v. Johnson, 101 Okl. 228, 224 P. 986, 988.

DISINTER. To exhume, unbury, take out of the grave. People v. Baumgartner, 135 Cal. 72, 66 P. 974.

DISINTERESTED. Not concerned, in respect to possible gain or loss, in the result of the pending proceedings; impartial, not biased or prejudiced. McGilvery v. Staples, 16 A. 404, 81 Me. 101; Kraft v. Tenningkeit, 204 Iowa, 15, 214 N.W. 562, 563.

DISINTERESTED WITNESS. One who has no interest in the cause or matter in issue, and who is lawfully competent to testify. Fitzhugh v. Nirschl, 77 Or. 514, 151 P. 735, 736. In re Palethorp's Estate, 249 Pa. 389, 94 A. 1060, 1065.

DISJUNCTIM. Lat. In the civil law. Separately; severally. The opposite of *conjunctim, (q. v.)* Inst. 2, 20, 8.

DISJUNCTIVE ALLEGATION. A statement in a pleading or indictment which expresses or charges a thing alternatively, with the conjunction "or;" for instance, an averment that defendant "murdered or caused to be murdered," etc., would be of this character. Hand v. Hand, 23 N.J.Misc. 118, 41 A.2d 270, 271.

DISJUNCTIVE TERM. One which is placed between two contraries, by the affirming of one of which the other is taken away; it is usually expressed by the word "or."

DISLOCATION. To put out of proper place. Gallagher v. Monroe, 222 Mich. 202, 192 N.W. 609.

DISLOYAL. Not true to; unfaithful; United States v. Krafft, C.C.A.N.J., 249 F. 919, 925, L.R.A. 1918F, 402; uncooperative, Sullivan v. Warner Bros. Theatres, 42 Cal.App.2d 660, 109 P.2d 760, 762.

DISMES. Tenths; tithes, *(q. v.)*. The original form of "dime," the name of the American coin.

DISMISS. To send away; to discharge; to cause to be removed temporarily or permanently; to relieve from duty. To dismiss an action or suit is to send it out of court without any further consideration or hearing. School District No. 1 of Jefferson County v. Parker, 82 Colo. 385, 260 P. 521, 522; People ex rel. Tims v. Bingham, Sup., 166 N.Y.S. 28, 29; Nichols v. Sunderland, 77 Cal. App. 627, 247 P. 614, 618.

DISMISSAL. An order or judgment finally disposing of an action, suit, motion, etc., by sending it out of court, though without a trial of the issues involved. Brackenridge v. State, 27 Tex. App. 513, 11 S.W. 630, 4 L.R.A. 360. The term is often used to indicate an adjudication on the merits. Knox v. Crump, 15 Ga.App. 697, 84 S.E. 169, 173; Butler v. McSweeney, 222 Mass. 5, 109 N.E. 653, 655. Although use of the term frequently signifies that it is not decision on merits. Wight v. Wight, 272 Mass. 154, 172 N.E. 335, 336.

A release or discharge from employment. Taggart v. School Dist. No. 52, Carroll County, Mo. App., 88 S.W.2d 447, 449; Gentner v. Board of Education of Los Angeles City High School Dist., 219 Cal. 135, 25 P.2d 824.

DISMISSAL AGREED. A dismissal entered in accordance with the agreement of the parties, amounting to an adjudication of the matters in dispute between them or to a renunciation by the complainant of the claims asserted in his pleadings. Root v. Water Supply Co., 46 Kan. 183, 26 P. 398; Lindsay v. Allen, 112 Tenn. 637, 82 S.W. 171.

Dismissal agreed made in Supreme Court of Appeals upon a writ of error to a judgment of the Circuit Court has no reference to the controversy between the parties, but leaves the judgment standing and purges error, releases error, and bars another writ of error. Fletcher v. Parker, 53 W. Va. 422, 44 S.E. 422.

DISMISSAL COMPENSATION. The payment of a specific sum, made by employer to employee for permanently terminating employment relationship primarily for reasons beyond employee's control. Gayner v. The New Orleans, D.C.Cal., 54 F.Supp. 25, 28.

DISMISSAL WITH PREJUDICE. An adjudication on the merits, and final disposition, barring the right to bring or maintain an action on the same claim or cause. Pulley v. Chicago, R. I. & P. Ry. Co., 122 Kan. 269, 251 P. 1100, 1101. It is res judicata as to every matter litigated. Roden v. Roden, 29 Ariz. 549, 243 P. 413, 415. A judgment of dismissal and a judgment of nonsuit have the same legal effect. Suess v. Motz, 220 Mo.App. 32, 285 S.W. 775, 776.

Temporary or permanent removal from office; termination of a servant's employment. Nichols v. Sunderland, 77 Cal.App. 627, 247 P. 614, 618.

DISMISSAL WITHOUT PREJUDICE. Dismissal, as of a bill in equity, without prejudice to the right of the complainant to sue again on the same cause of action. The effect of the words "without prejudice" is to prevent the decree of dismissal from operating as a bar to a subsequent suit. Northrup v. Jay, 262 Mich. 463, 247 N.W. 717, 718.

DISMISSED. A judgment of "Dismissed," without qualifying words indicating a right to take further proceedings, is presumed to be dismissed on the merits; Durant v. Essex Co., 7 Wall. 107, 19 L.Ed. 154. But a bill "dismissed" on motion of complainant does not bar a second suit; Ex parte Loung June, D.C.N.Y., 160 F. 251, 259.

DISMISSED FOR WANT OF EQUITY. A phrase used to indicate a decision on the merits, as distinguished from one based upon some formal defect. The dismissal may be because the averments of complainant's bill have been found untrue in fact, or because they are insufficient to entitle complainant to the relief sought. Reinman v. Little Rock, 35 S.Ct. 511, 513, 237 U.S. 171, 59 L.Ed. 900.

DISMORTGAGE. To redeem from mortgage.

DISORDER. Turbulent or riotous behavior; immoral or indecent conduct. The breach of the public decorum and morality.

Usually, a slight, partial, and temporary physical ailment. Pacific Mut. Life Ins. Co. v. McCombs, 188 Ark. 52, 64 S.W.2d 333.

DISORDERLY. Contrary to the rules of good order and behavior; violative of the public peace or good order; turbulent, riotous, or indecent.

DISORDERLY CONDUCT. A term of loose and indefinite meaning (except as occasionally defined in statutes), but signifying generally any behavior that is contrary to law, and more particularly such as tends to disturb the public peace or decorum, scandalize the community, or shock the public sense of morality. People v. Keeper of State Reformatory, 176 N.Y. 465, 68 N.E. 884; City of Mt. Sterling v. Holly, 108 Ky. 621, 57 S.W. 491.

DISORDERLY HOUSE. In criminal law. A house the inmates of which behave so badly as to become a nuisance to the neighborhood. It has a wide meaning, and includes bawdy houses, common gaming houses, and places of a like character. 1 Bish. Crim.Law, § 1106. State v. Everhardt, 203 N.C. 610, 166 S.E. 738, 741; gaming, Martin v. State, 62 Ga.App. 902, 10 S.E.2d 254, 255; prostitution, State v. Berman, 120 N.J.L. 381, 199 A. 776, 777.

DISORDERLY PERSONS. Such as are dangerous or hurtful to the public peace and welfare by reason of their misconduct or vicious habits, and are therefore amenable to police regulation. The phrase is chiefly used in statutes, and the scope of the term depends on local regulations. See 4 Bl. Comm. 169. One who violates peace and good order of society, State v. Harlowe, 174 Wash. 227, 24 P.2d 601; one who abandons a child, People v. Gross, 291 N.Y.S. 597, 602, 604, 161 Misc. 514; giving false fire alarm, Piliszek v. Burlington County Court of Special Sessions, 129 N.J.L. 604, 30 A.2d 578; spiritualist pastor telling fortune, People v. Plaskett, 13 N.Y.S.2d 682, 683, 171 Misc. 563; vagrant, People v. Marciano, Mag.Ct., 17 N.Y.S.2d 722, 723.

DISPARAGARE. In old English law. To bring together those that are unequal, (*dispares conferre;*) to connect in an indecorous and unworthy manner; to connect in marriage those that are unequal in blood and parentage.

DISPARAGATIO. In old English law. Disparagement. *Hœredes maritentur absque disparagatione,* heirs shall be married without disparagement. *Magna Charta* (9 Hen. III.) c. 6.

DISPARAGATION. L. Fr. Disparagement; the matching an heir, etc., in marriage, under his or her degree or condition, or against the rules of decency. Kelham.

DISPARAGE. To connect unequally; to match unsuitably.

DISPARAGEMENT. In old English law. An injury by union or comparison with some person or thing of inferior rank or excellence.

Marriage without *disparagement* was marriage to one of suitable rank and character. 2 Bl.Comm. 70; Co. Litt. 82*b*. Shutt v. Carloss, 36 N.C. 232.

Matter which is intended by its publisher to be understood or which is reasonably understood to cast doubt upon the existence or extent of another's property in land, chattels or intangible things, or upon their quality. Restatement, Torts, § 629.

Of Goods

A statement about a competitor's goods which is untrue or misleading and is made to influence or tends to influence the public not to buy. Edwin L. Wiegand Co. v. Harold E. Trent Co., C.C.A. Pa., 122 F.2d 920, 924.

DISPARAGIUM. In old Scotch law. Inequality in blood, honor, dignity, or otherwise. Skene de Verb. Sign.

Disparata non debent jungi. Things unlike ought not to be joined. Jenk. Cent. 24, Marg.

DISPARK. To dissolve a park. Cro. Car. 59. To convert it into ordinary ground.

DISPATCH, or DESPATCH. A message, letter, or order sent with speed on affairs of state; a telegraphic message.

Celerity; expedition; speed. Stockman v. Boston & M. R. R., 117 Me. 35, 102 A. 560, 562.

In Maritime Law

Diligence, due activity, or proper speed in the discharge of a cargo; the opposite of delay. Sleeper v. Puig, 22 Fed.Cas. 321.

Customary Dispatch

Such as accords with the rules, customs, and usages of the port where the discharge is made.

Dispatch Money

Dispatch money, which arises purely from contract, is a premium paid charterer by vessel for days saved that may be used in completing voyage. The Driebergen, C.C. A.Fla., 60 F.2d 367, 371.

Quick Dispatch

Speedy discharge of cargo without allowance for the customs or rules of the port or for delay from the crowded state of the harbor or wharf. Mott v. Frost, D.C.S.C., 47 F. 82; Bjorkquist v. Certain Steel Rail Crop Ends, D.C. Md., 3 F. 717; Davis v. Wallace, 7 Fed.Cas. 182.

DISPAUPER. When a person, by reason of his poverty, is admitted to sue *in formâ pauperis,* and afterwards, before the suit be ended, acquires any lands, or personal estate, or is guilty of anything whereby he is liable to have this privilege taken from him, then he loses the right to sue *in formâ pauperis,* and is said to be dispaupered. Wharton.

DISPEL. To drive away by scattering, to clear away, to banish, to dissipate. Karle v. Cincinnati St. Ry. Co., 69 Ohio App. 327, 43 N.E.2d 762, 767.

DISPENSARY. A "dispensary" is a place where a drug is prepared or distributed. People v. Cohen, 94 Misc. 355, 157 N.Y.S. 591, 593.

Dispensatio est mali prohibiti provida relaxatio, utilitate seu necessitate pensata; et est de jure domino regi concessa, propter impossibilitatem prævidendi de omnibus particularibus. A dispensation is the provident relaxation of a *malum prohibitum* weighed from utility or necessity; and it is conceded by law to the king on account of the impossibility of foreknowledge concerning all particulars. 10 Coke, 88.

Dispensatio est vulnus, quod vulnerat jus commune. A dispensation is a wound, which wounds common law. Dav. Ir. K. B. 69.

DISPENSATION. An exemption from some laws; a permission to do something forbidden; an allowance to omit something commanded; the canonistic name for a license. Sweeney v. Independent Order of Foresters, 190 App.Div. 787, 181 N.Y.S. 4, 5.

A relaxation of law for the benefit or advantage of an individual. In the United States, no power exists, except in the legislature, to dispense with law; and then it is not so much a dispensation as a change of the law.

DISPENSE. Etymologically, "dispense" means to weigh out, pay out, distribute, regulate, manage, control, etc., but when used with "with," it has, among other meanings, that of "doing without," and "doing away with," being synonymous with "abolish." United States v. Reynolds, D.C. Mont., 244 F. 991.

DISPERSONARE. To scandalize or disparage. Blount.

DISPLACE. To crowd out; to take the place of. Ford v. Department of Water and Power of City of Los Angeles, 4 Cal.App.2d 526, 41 P.2d 188, 189.

This term, as used in shipping articles, means "disrate," and does not import authority of the master to discharge a second mate, notwithstanding a usage in the whaling trade never to disrate an officer to a seaman. Potter v. Smith, 103 Mass. 68.

DISPLAY. An opening or unfolding, exhibition, manifestation, ostentatious show, exhibition for effect, parade. 20th Century Lites v. Goodman, 64 Cal.App.2d Supp., 938, 149 P.2d 88, 91.

As applied to printing, means a varying arrangement of lines, as by the use of unequal lengths or different styles or sizes of type faces; also matter thus printed. Display advertising means advertising not under specific headings in newspapers, magazines and trade papers. Rust v. Missouri Dental Board, 348 Mo. 616, 155 S.W.2d 80, 85.

DISPONE. In Scotch law. To grant or convey. A technical word essential to the conveyance of heritable property, and for which no equivalent is accepted, however clear may be the meaning of the party. Paters. Comp.

DISPONO. Lat. To dispose of, grant, or convey. *Disponet,* he grants or alienates. *Jus disponendi,* the right of disposition, *i. e.,* of transferring the title to property.

DISPOSABLE PORTION. That portion of a man's property which he is free to dispose of by will to beneficiaries other than his wife and children. By the ancient common law, this amounted to one-third of his estate if he was survived by both wife and children. 2 Bl. Comm. 492; Hopkins v. Wright, 17 Tex. 36. In the civil law (by the *Lex Falcidia*) it amounted to three-fourths. Mackeld. Rom. Law, §§ 708, 771.

DISPOSAL. Sale, pledge, giving away, use, consumption or any other disposition of a thing. C. B. Norton Jewelry Co. v. Maddock, 115 Kan. 108, 222 P. 113, 114. To exercise control over; to direct or assign for a use; to pass over into the control of some one else; to alienate, bestow, or part with. Popp v. Munger, 131 Okl. 282, 268 P. 1100, 1102.

DISPOSE OF. To alienate or direct the ownership of property, as disposition by will. Used also of the determination of suits. Carnagio v. State, 106 Fla. 209, 143 So. 162. Called a word of large extent.

To exercise finally, in any manner, one's power of control over; to pass into the control of someone else; to alienate, relinquish, part with, or get rid of; to put out of the way; to finish with; to bargain away. Carpenter v. Lothringer, 224 Iowa 439, 275 N.W. 98, 103; Roe v. Burt, 66 Okl. 193, 168 P. 405, 406.

Often used in restricted sense of "sale" only, or so restricted by context. Roby v. Herr, 194 Ky. 622, 240 S.W. 49, 51; Merchants' Nat. Bank of Mandan v. First Nat. Bank, C.C.A.N.D., 238 F. 502, 507.

DISPOSING CAPACITY OR MIND. These are alternative or synonymous phrases in the law of wills for "sound mind," and "testamentary capacity" *(q. v.)*. Lockhart v. Ferguson, 243 Mass. 226, 137 N.E. 355, 356.

DISPOSITION. In Scotch law. A deed of alienation by which a right to property is conveyed. Bell.

An attitude; a willingness. In re Schaefer's Estate, 207 Wis. 404, 241 N.W. 382, 386.

The parting with, alienation of, or giving up property. Long v. Commissioner of Internal Revenue, C.C.A., 96 F.2d 270, 271; Ashwander v. Tennessee Valley Authority, Ala., 56 S.Ct. 466, 479, 297 U.S. 288, 80 L.Ed. 688. A destruction of property. Pioneer Cooperage Co. v. Commissioner of Internal Revenue, C.C.A., 53 F.2d 43, 44.

DISPOSITIVE FACTS. Jural facts, or those acts or events that create, modify or extinguish jural relations. Kocourek, Jural Relations (2d Ed.) p. 17.

DISPOSSESS. To oust from land by legal process; to eject, to exclude from realty. Matthews v. Deason, Tex.Civ.App., 200 S.W. 855, 856.

DISPOSSESS PROCEEDINGS. Summary process by a landlord to oust the tenant and regain possession of the premises for nonpayment of rent or other breach of the conditions of the lease. Of local origin and colloquial use in New York.

DISPOSSESSION. Ouster; a wrong that carries with it the amotion of possession. An act whereby the wrongdoer gets the actual occupation of the land or hereditament. It includes abatement, intrusion, disseisin, discontinuance, deforcement. 3 Bl. Comm. 167.

DISPROVE. To refute; to prove to be false or erroneous; not necessarily by mere denial, but by affirmative evidence to the contrary. Irsch v. Irsch, 12 N.Y.Civ.Proc.R. 182.

DISPUNISHABLE. In old English law. Not answerable. Co. Litt. 27*b*, 53. 1 Steph. Comm. 245. Not punishable. "This murder is dispunishable." 1 Leon. 270.

DISPUTATIO FORI. In the civil law. Discussion or argument before a court. Mackeld. Rom. Law, § 38; Dig. 1, 2, 2, 5.

DISPUTABLE PRESUMPTION. A species of evidence that may be accepted and acted upon when there is no other evidence to uphold contention for which it stands; and when evidence is introduced supporting such contention, evidence takes place of presumption, and there is no necessity for indulging in any presumption. Noble v. Key System, 10 Cal.App.2d 132, 51 P.2d 887, 889.

A rule of law to be laid down by the court, which shifts to the party against whom it operates the burden of evidence merely. City of Montpelier v. Town of Calais, 114 Vt. 5, 39 A.2d 350, 356. See Presumptions.

DISPUTE. A conflict or controversy; a conflict of claims or rights; an assertion of a right, claim, or demand on one side, met by contrary claims or allegations on the other. Keith v. Levi, C.C.Mo., 2 F. 745; Ft. Pitt Gas Co. v. Borough of Sewickley, 198 Pa. 201, 47 A. 957.

Matter in Dispute

The subject of litigation; the matter for which a suit is brought and upon which issue is joined, and in relation to which jurors are called and witnesses examined. Lee v. Watson, 1 Wall. 339, 17 L.Ed. 557; Smith v. Adams, 130 U. S. 167, 9 S.Ct. 566, 32 L.Ed. 985.

DISQUALIFY. To divest or deprive of qualifications; to incapacitate; to render ineligible or unfit; as, in speaking of the "disqualification" of a judge by reason of his interest in the case, of a juror by reason of his holding a fixed preconceived opinion, or of a candidate for public office by reason of non-residence, lack of statutory age, previous commission of crime, etc. Carroll v. Green, 148 Ind. 362, 47 N.E. 223; Coats v. Benton, 80 Okla. 93, 194 P. 198, 200, 19 A.L.R. 1038.

DISRATE. In maritime law. To deprive a seaman or petty officer of his "rating" or rank; to reduce to a lower rate or rank.

DISRATIONARE, or DIRATIONARE. To justify; to clear one's self of a fault; to traverse an indictment; to disprove. Enc. Lond.

DISREGARD. To treat as unworthy of regard or notice; to take no notice of; to leave out of consideration; to ignore; to overlook; to fail to observe. Cunningham v. Fredericks, 106 Conn. 665, 138 A. 790, 793.

DISREPAIR. The state of being in need of repair or restoration after decay or injury. Wyoming Coal Mining Co. v. Stanko, 22 Wyo. 110, 138 P. 182, 183.

DISREPUTE. Loss or want of reputation; ill character; disesteem; discredit. U. S. v. Ault, D. C.Wash., 263 F. 800, 810; U. S. v. Strong, D.C. Wash., 263 F. 789, 796.

DISSASINA. In old Scotch law. Disseisin; dispossession. Skene.

DISSECTION. The act of cutting into pieces an animal or vegetable for the purpose of ascertaining the structure and use of its parts. The anatomical examination of a dead body by cutting into pieces or exscinding one or more parts or organs. Wehle v. Accident Ass'n, 31 N.Y.S. 865, 11 Misc. 36; Rhodes v. Brandt, 21 Hun (N.Y.) 3. Anatomy; the act of separating into constituent parts for the purpose of critical examination.

DISSEISE. To dispossess; to deprive.

DISSEISEE. One who is wrongfully put out of possession of his lands; one who is disseised.

DISSEISIN. Dispossession; a deprivation of possession; a privation of seisin; a usurpation of the right of seisin and possession, and an exercise of such powers and privileges of ownership as to keep out or displace him to whom these rightfully belong. 3 Washb. Real Prop. 125; Sweeney v. Dahl, 140 Me. 133, 34 A.2d 673, 675, 151 A.L.R. 356.

It is a wrongful putting out of him that is seised of the freehold, not, as in *abatement* or *intrusion,* a wrongful entry, where the possession was vacant, but an attack upon him who is in actual possession, and turning him out. It is an ouster from a freehold in deed, as abatement and intrusion are ousters in law. 3 Steph.Comm. 386.

When one man invades the possession of another, and by force or surprise turns him out of the occupation of his lands, this is termed a "disseisin," being a deprivation of that actual seisin or corporal possession of the freehold which the tenant before enjoyed. In other words, a disseisin is said to be when one enters intending to usurp the possession, and to oust another from the freehold. To constitute an entry a disseisin, there must be an ouster of the freehold, either by taking the profits or by claiming the inheritance. Brown.

According to the modern authorities, there seems to be no legal difference between the words "seisin" and "possession," although there is a difference between the words "disseisin" and "dispossession;" the former meaning an estate gained by wrong and injury, whereas the latter may be by right or by wrong; the former denoting an ouster of the disseisee, or some act equivalent to it, whereas by the latter no such act is implied. Slater v. Rawson, 6 Metc. (Mass.) 439.

Equitable disseisin is where a person is wrongfully deprived of the equitable seisin of land, *e. g.,* of the rents and profits. 2 Meriv. 171; 2 Jac. & W. 166.

Disseisin by election is where a person alleges or admits himself to be disseised when he has not really been so.

Disseisinam satis facit, qui uti non permittit possessorem, vel minus commode, licet omnino non expellat. Co. Litt. 331. He makes disseisin enough who does not permit the possessor to enjoy, or makes his enjoyment less beneficial, although he does not expel him altogether.

DISSEISITRIX. A female disseisor; a disseisoress. Fleta, lib. 4, c. 12, § 4.

DISSEISITUS. One who has been disseised.

DISSEISOR. One who puts another out of the possession of his lands wrongfully. A settled trespasser on the land of another. Flinn v. Blakeman, 254 Ky. 416, 71 S.W.2d 961, 968.

DISSEISORESS. A woman who unlawfully puts another out of his land.

DISSEMBLE. To conceal by assuming some false appearance. Darneal v. State, 14 Okl.Cr. 540, 174 P. 290, 292, 1 A.L.R. 638.

DISSENSUS. Lat. In the civil law. The mutual agreement of the parties to a simple contract obligation that it shall be dissolved or annulled; technically, an undoing of the *consensus* which created the obligation. Mackeld. Rom. Law, § 541.

DISSENT. Contrariety of opinion; refusal to agree with something already stated or adjudged or to an act previously performed.

The term is most commonly used in American law to denote the explicit disagreement of one or more judges of a court with the decision passed by the majority upon a case before them. In such event, the non-concurring judge is reported as "dissenting." Mere failure of a justice to vote is not a dissent. Charles W. Sommer & Bro. v. Albert Lorsch & Co., 254 N.Y. 146, 172 N.E. 271, 272. A dissent may or may not be accompanied by an opinion.

Dissenting Opinion

The opinion in which a judge announces his dissent from the conclusions held by the majority of the court, and expounds his own views.

In Ecclesiastical Law

A refusal to conform to the rites and ceremonies of the established church. 2 Burn, Eccl. Law 165.

DISSENTER. One who refuses to conform to the rites and ceremonies of the established church; a non-conformist. 2 Burn, Eccl. Law 165.

DISSENTERS. Protestant seceders from the established church of England. They are of many denominations, principally Presbyterians, Independents, Methodists, and Baptists; but, as to church government, the Baptists are Independents.

DISSENTIENTE. (Lat. dissenting.) Used with the name or names of one or more judges, it indicates a dissenting opinion in a case. *Nemine dissentiente.* No one dissenting; unanimous.

DISSIGNARE. In old law. To break open a seal. Whishaw.

Dissimilium dissimilis est ratio. Co. Litt. 191. Of dissimilars the rule is dissimilar.

Dissimulatione tollitur injuria. An injury is extinguished by the forgiveness or reconcilement of the party injured. Ersk. Inst. 4, 4, 108.

DISSOLUTE. Loosed from restraint, unashamed, lawless, loose in morals and conduct, recklessly abandoned to sensual pleasures, profligate, wanton, lewd, debauched, thus, evidence that defendants danced in nude at a smoker authorized their conviction as dissolute persons. People v. Scott, 113 Cal.App. 778, 296 P. 601, 603.

DISSOLUTION.

In Contracts

The dissolution of a contract is the cancellation or abrogation of it by the parties themselves, with the effect of annulling the binding force of the agreement, and restoring each party to his original rights. In this sense it is frequently used in the phrase "dissolution of a partnership." Williston v. Camp, 9 Mont. 88, 22 P. 501.

In Practice

The act of rendering a legal proceeding null, abrogating or revoking it; unloosing its constraining force; as when an injunction is dissolved by the court. Jones v. Hill, 6 N.C. 131.

Of Corporations

The dissolution of a corporation is the termination of its existence as a body politic. This may take place in several ways; as by act of the legislature, where that is constitutional; by surrender or forfeiture of its charter; by expiration of its charter by lapse of time; by proceedings for winding it up under the law; by loss of all its members or their reduction below the statutory limit. New York Title & Mortgage Co. v. Friedman, 276 N.Y.S. 72, 153 Misc. 697; Bruun v. Katz Drug Co., 351 Mo. 731, 173 S.W.2d 906, 909.

De Facto Dissolution

That which takes place when corporation, by reason of insolvency or for other reason, suspends all operations and goes into liquidation. Hidden v. Edwards, 313 Mo. 642, 285 S.W. 462, 468.

Of Marriage

The act of terminating a marriage; divorce; but the term does not include annulment. Deihl v. Jones, 170 Tenn. 217, 94 S.W.2d 47, 48.

DISSOLUTION OF PARLIAMENT. The crown may dissolve parliament either in person or by proclamation; the dissolution is usually by proclamation, after a prorogation. No parliament may last for a longer period than seven years. Septennial Act, 1 Geo. I. c. 38. Under 6 Anne, c. 37, upon a demise of the crown, parliament became *ipso facto* dissolved six months afterwards, but under the Reform Act, 1867, its continuance is now nowise affected by such demise. May, Parl. Pr. (6th Ed.) 48. Brown.

DISSOLVE. To terminate; abrogate; cancel; annul; disintegrate. To release or unloose the binding force of anything. As to "dissolve a corporation," to "dissolve an injunction." See Dissolution.

DISSOLVING BOND. A bond given to obtain the dissolution of a legal writ or process, particularly an attachment or an injunction, and conditioned to indemnify the opposite party or to abide the judgment to be given. See Sanger v. Hibbard, 2 Ind. T. 547, 53 S.W. 330.

DISSUADE. In criminal law. To advise and procure a person not to do an act.

To dissuade a witness from giving evidence against a person indicted is an indictable offense at common law. Hawk. P. C. b. 1, c. 21, § 15. People v. Hamm, 250 N.Y.S. 603, 605, 140 Misc. 335.

DISTANCE. A straight line along a horizontal plane from point to point and is measured from the nearest point of one place to the nearest point of another. Evans v. U. S., C.C.A.N.Y., 261 F. 902, 904.

It may however be a broken line and represented by country roads or a railroad track. State v. Mostad, 34 N.D. 330, 158 N.W. 349, 350.

DISTILL. To subject to a process of distillation, *i. e.*, vaporizing the more volatile parts of a substance and then condensing the vapor so formed. In law, the term is chiefly used in connection with the manufacture of intoxicating liquors. Williams v. State, 161 Ark. 383, 256 S.W. 354.

DISTILLED LIQUOR or DISTILLED SPIRITS. A term which includes all potable alcoholic liquors obtained by the process of distillation (such as whisky, brandy, rum, and gin) but excludes fermented and malt liquors, such as wine and beer. Sarlls v. U. S., 14 S.Ct. 720, 152 U.S. 570, 38 L.Ed. 556; Commonwealth v. Nickerson, 236 Mass. 281, 128 N.E. 273, 283, 10 A.L.R. 1568; Maresca v. U. S., C.C.A.N.Y., 277 F. 727, 740.

DISTILLER. One who produces distilled spirits, or who brews or makes mash, wort, or wash, fit for distillation or for the production of spirits, or who, by any process of evaporization, separates alcoholic spirit from any fermented substance, or who, making or keeping mash, wort, or wash, has also in his possession or use a still. U. S. v. Ridenour, D.C.Va., 119 F. 411; Motlow v. U. S., C.C.A.Mo., 35 F.2d 90, 91.

DISTILLERY. The strict meaning of "distillery" is a place or building where alcoholic liquors are distilled or manufactured; not every building where the process of distillation is used. U. S. v. Blaisdell, 24 Fed.Cas. 1162; Atlantic Dock Co. v. Leavitt, 54 N.Y. 35, 13 Am.Rep. 556.

DISTILLING APPARATUS. Under National Prohibition Act, tit. 2, § 25 (27 USCA § 39) "distilling apparatus" is not limited to a completed still fully equipped and ready for operation, but may cover a 15-gallon pot and coil of copper tubing or worm, which, when connected by gooseneck, would produce a completed still. Rossman v. U. S., C.C.A.Ohio, 280 F. 950, 952.

DISTINCT. Clear to the senses or mind; easily perceived or understood; plain; unmistakable. Hill v. Norton, 74 W.Va. 428, 82 S.E. 363, 367, Ann. Cas.1917D, 489.

Evidently not identical; observably or decidedly different. Bayne v. Kansas City, Mo.App., 263 S.W. 450, 451.

Distinguished by nature or station; not the same; different in the place or the like; separate; individual; that which is capable of being distinguished; actually divided or apart from other things. Gavin v. Webb, Tex.Civ.App., 99 S.W.2d 372, 379.

DISTINCTE ET APERTE. In old English practice. Distinctly and openly. Formal words in writs of error, referring to the return required to be made to them. Reg. Orig. 17.

DISTINCTIVELY. Characteristically, or peculiarly, but not necessarily exclusively. Western Union Telegraph Co. v. Green, 153 Tenn. 522, 284 S.W. 898, 899, 48 A.L.R. 313.

Distinguenda sunt tempora. The time is to be considered. 1 Coke, 16*a;* Bloss v. Tobey, 2 Pick. (Mass.) 327; Owens v. Missionary Society, 14 N.Y. 380, 393, 67 Am.Dec. 160.

Distinguenda sunt tempora; aliud est facere, aliud perficere. Times must be distinguished; it is one thing to do, another to perfect. 3 Leon. 243; Branch. Princ.

Distinguenda sunt tempora; distingue tempora et concordabis leges. Times are to be distinguished; distinguish times, and you will harmonize laws. 1 Coke, 24. A maxim applied to the construction of statutes.

DISTINGUISH. To point out an essential difference; to prove a case cited as applicable, inapplicable.

DISTINGUISHING MARK. Any deliberate marking of ballot by voter that is not made in attempt to indicate his choice of candidates and which is also effective as mark by which his ballot may be distinguished. Hanson v. Emanuel, 210 Minn. 271, 297 N.W. 749, 752, 753, 754.

DISTORT. To twist out of natural or regular shape, to twist aside physically, to force or put out of true posture, to twist, wrest, or deform. Grip Nut Co. v. MacLean-Fogg Lock Nut Co., D.C.Ill., 34 F.2d 41, 42.

DISTRACTED PERSON. A term used in the statutes of Illinois and New Hampshire to express a state of insanity. Snyder v. Snyder, 142 Ill. 60, 31 N.E. 303.

DISTRACTIO. Lat. In the civil law. A separation or division into parts; also an alienation or sale. Sometimes applied to the act of a guardian in appropriating the property of his ward.

DISTRACTIO BONORUM. The sale at retail of the property of an insolvent estate, under the management of a curator appointed in the interest of the creditors, and for the purpose of realizing as much as possible for the satisfaction of their claim. Mackeld. Rom. Law, § 524.

DISTRACTIO PIGNORIS. The sale of a thing pledged or hypothecated, by the creditor or pledgee, to obtain satisfaction of his claim on the debtor's failure to pay or redeem. Mackeld. Rom. Law, § 348.

DISTRACTION RULE. If plaintiff's attention is diverted from known danger by a sufficient cause, under this rule the question of contributory negligence is for jury. Deane v. Johnston, Fla., 104 So.2d 3, 9.

DISTRAHERE. To sell; to draw apart; to dissolve a contract; to divorce. Calvin.

DISTRAIN. To take as a pledge property of another, and keep it until he performs his obligation or until the property is replevied by the sheriff. It was used to secure an appearance in court, payment of rent, performance of services, etc. 3 Bl. Comm. 231; Also, any detention of personal property, whether lawful or unlawful, for any purpose. Wolfe v. Montgomery, 41 S.D. 267, 170 N.W. 158.

Distress is now generally used.

DISTRAINER, or DISTRAINOR. He who seizes a distress.

DISTRAINT. Seizure; the act of distraining or making a distress. Regional Agr. Credit Corp. v. Griggs County, 73 N.D. 1, 10 N.W.2d 861, 866.

DISTRESS. The taking a personal chattel out of the possession of a wrong-doer into the custody of the party injured, to procure a satisfaction for a wrong committed; as for non-payment of rent, or injury done by cattle. 3 Bl.Comm. 6, 7; Co. Litt. 47. The taking of beasts or other personal property by way of pledge, to enforce the performance of something due from the party distrained upon. 3 Bl.Comm. 231. Hall v. Marshall, 145 Or. 221, 27 P.2d 193. The taking of a defendant's goods, in order to compel an appearance in court. 3 Bl.Comm. 280; 3 Steph.Comm. 361, 363.

The seizure of personal property to enforce payment of taxes, to be followed by its public sale if the taxes are not voluntarily paid. Marshall v. Wadsworth, 64 N.H. 386, 10 A. 685; also the thing taken by distraining, that which is seized to procure satisfaction. And in old Scotch law, a pledge taken by the sheriff from those attending fairs or markets, to secure their good behavior, and returnable to them at the close of the fair or market if they had been guilty of no wrong.

Distress infinite. One that has no bounds with regard to its quantity, and may be repeated from time to time, until the stubbornness of the party is conquered. Such are distresses for fealty or suit of court, and for compelling jurors to attend. 3 Bl.Comm. 231.

A power of attorney by which landlord delegates exercise of his right to his duly authorized agent. In re Koizim, D.C.N.J., 52 F.Supp. 357, 358.

Distress warrant. A writ authorizing an officer to make a distraint; particularly, a writ authorizing the levy of a distress on the chattels of a tenant for non-payment of rent. Commercial Credit Co. of Baltimore v. Vineis, 98 N.J.Law, 376, 120 A. 417, 418.

Grand distress, writ of. A writ formerly issued in the real action of *quare impedit,* when no appearance had been entered after the attachment; it commanded the sheriff to distrain the defendant's lands and chattels in order to compel appearance. It is no longer used, 23 & 24 Vict. c. 126, § 26, having abolished the action of *quare impedit,* and substituted for it the procedure in an ordinary action. Wharton.

Second distress. A supplementary distress for rent in arrear, allowed by law in some cases, where the goods seized under the first distress are not of sufficient value to satisfy the claim.

DISTRESS AND DANGER. The "distress" and "danger" to which a ship needs to be exposed to entitle its rescuer to salvage need not be actual or immediate, or the danger imminent and absolute. It is sufficient if at the time the assistance is rendered, the ship has encountered any damage or misfortune which might possibly expose her to destruction if the services were not rendered, or if a vessel is in a situation of actual apprehension though not of actual danger. The Urko Mendi, D.C., 216 F. 427, 429.

DISTRIBUTE. To deal or divide out in proportion or in shares. Buchan v. Buchan, 177 N.Y.S. 176, 177, 108 Misc. 31; Foreman v. United States, C.C.A., 255 F. 621, 623.

DISTRIBUTEE. An heir; a person entitled to share in the distribution of an estate. This term is admissible to denote one of the persons who are entitled, under the statute of distributions, to the personal estate of one who is dead intestate. Allen v. Foth, 210 Ky. 343, 275 S.W. 804, 805.

DISTRIBUTION. In probate practice. The apportionment and division, under authority of a court, of the remainder of the estate of an intestate, after payment of the debts and charges, among those who are legally entitled to share in the same. Rogers v. Gillett, 56 Iowa, 266, 9 N.W. 204.

Statute of Distributions

A law prescribing the manner of the distribution of the estate of an intestate among his heirs or relatives. Such statutes exist in all the states.

In general. The giving out or division among a number, sharing or parceling out, allotting, dispensing, apportioning. People v. Dime Sav. Bank, 350 Ill. 503, 183 N.E. 604, 608.

DISTRIBUTIVE. That which exercises or accomplishes distribution; apportions, divides, and assigns in separate items or shares.

DISTRIBUTIVE FINDING OF THE ISSUE. The jury are bound to give their verdict for that party who, upon the evidence, appears to them to have succeeded in establishing his side of the issue. But there are cases in which an issue may be found distributively, *i. e.*, in part for plaintiff, and in part for defendant. Thus, in an action for goods sold and work done, if the defendant pleaded that he never was indebted, on which issue was joined, a verdict might be found for the plaintiff as to the goods, and for the defendant as to the work. Steph. Pl. (7th Ed.) 77*d*.

DISTRIBUTIVE JUSTICE. See Justice.

DISTRIBUTIVE SHARE. The share or portion which a given heir receives on the legal distribution of an intestate estate; Van Buren v. Plainfield Trust Co., 130 N.J.Eq. 244, 22 A.2d 189, 191, or from a dissolved partnership. Helvering v. Enright's Estate, 61 S.Ct. 777, 781, 312 U.S. 636, 85 L.Ed. 1093. Sometimes, by an extension of meaning, the share or portion assigned to a given person on the distribution of any estate or fund, as, under an assignment for creditors or under insolvency proceedings.

DISTRICT. One of the portions into which an entire state or country, county, municipality or other political subdivision or geographical territory is divided, for judicial, political, or administrative purposes. Briggs v. Stevens, 119 Or. 138, 248 P. 169; State ex rel. Schur v. Payne, 57 Nev. 286, 63 P.2d 921, 925.

The United States are divided into judicial districts, in each of which is established a district court. They are also divided into election districts, collection districts, etc.

The circuit or territory within which a person may be compelled to appear. Cowell. Circuit of authority; province. Enc. Lond.

District attorney. The prosecuting officer of the United States government in each of the federal judicial districts. Also, under the state governments, the prosecuting officer who represents the state in each of its judicial districts. In some states, where the territory is divided, for judicial purposes, into sections called by some other name than "districts," the same officer is denominated "county attorney" or "state's attorney." Hill County v. Sheppard, 142 Tex. 358, 178 S.W.2d 261, 263; State v. Henry, 196 La. 217, 198 So. 910, 914.

District clerk. The clerk of a district court of either a state or the United States.

District courts. Courts of the United States, each having territorial jurisdiction over a *district*, which may include a whole state or only part of it. Each of these courts is presided over by one judge, who must reside within the district. These courts have original jurisdiction over all admiralty and maritime causes and all proceedings in bankruptcy, and over all penal and criminal matters cognizable under the laws of the United States, exclusive jurisdiction over which is not vested either in the supreme or circuit courts. Also inferior courts in Colorado, Idaho, Iowa, Kansas, Louisiana, Minnnesota, Montana, Nebraska, Nevada, New Jersey, New Mexico, North Dakota, Ohio, Oklahoma, Texas, Utah, and Wyoming, are also called "district courts." Their jurisdiction is for the most part similar to that of county courts (*q. v.*).

District judge. The judge of a United States district court; also, in some states, the judge of a district court of the state.

District parishes. Ecclesiastical divisions of parishes in England, for all purposes of worship, and for the celebration of marriages, christenings, churchings, and burials, formed at the instance of the queen's commissioners for building new churches. See 3 Steph.Comm. 744.

District registry. By the English judicature act, 1873, § 60, it is provided that to facilitate proceedings in country districts the crown may, from time to time, by order in council, create district registries, and appoint district registrars for the purpose of issuing writs of summons, and for other purposes. Documents sealed in any such district registry shall be received in evidence without further proof, (section 61;) and the district registrars may administer oaths or do other things as provided by rules or a special order of the court, (section 62.) Power, however, is given to a judge to remove proceedings from a district registry to the office of the high court. Section 65. By order in council of 12th of August, 1875, a number of district registries have been established in the places mentioned in that order; and the prothonotaries in Liverpool, Manchester, and Preston, the district registrar of the court of admiralty at Liverpool, and the county court registrars in the other places named, have been appointed district registrars. Wharton.

As to "Fire," "Judicial," "Land," "Levee," "Mineral," "Mining," "Road," "School," and "Taxing," districts, see those titles.

DISTRICT MESSENGER SERVICE. The service is not that of a common carrier, but the furnishing of messengers to be used by the employer in any way in which they could be properly employed, in the course of which the messenger becomes for the time the servant of the employer and the company is not liable for his dishonesty in the ordinary course of his employment unless there was failure to use proper care in his selection; Haskell v. Messenger Co., 190 Mass. 189, 76 N.E. 215, 2 L.R.A.,N.S., 1091, 112 Am.St.Rep. 324, 5 Ann.Cas. 796.

DISTRICT OF COLUMBIA. A territory situated on the Potomac river, and being the seat of government of the United States. It was originally ten miles square, and was composed of portions of Maryland and Virginia ceded by those states to the United States; but in 1846 the tract coming from Virginia was retroceded. Legally it is neither a state nor a territory, but is made subject, by the constitution, to the exclusive jurisdiction of congress.

DISTRICTIO. Lat. A distress; a distraint. Cowell.

DISTRINGAS. In English practice. A writ directed to the sheriff of the county in which a defendant resides, or has any goods or chattels, commanding him to *distrain* upon the goods and chattels of the defendant for forty shillings, in order to compel his appearance. 3 Steph.Comm. 567. This writ issues in cases where it is found impracticable to get at the defendant personally, so as to serve a summons upon him. Id.

A *distringas* is also used in equity, as the first process to compel the appearance of a corporation aggregate. St. 11 Geo. IV. and 1 Wm. IV. c. 36.

A form of execution in the actions of detinue and assise of nuisance. Brooke, Abr. pl. 26; Barnet v. Ihrie, 1 Rawle (Pa.) 44.

DISTRINGAS JURATORES. A writ commanding the sheriff to have the bodies of the jurors, or to *distrain* them by their lands and goods, that they may appear upon the day appointed. 3 Bl.Comm. 354. It issues at the same time with the *venire,* though in theory afterwards, founded on the supposed neglect of the juror to attend. 3 Steph. Comm. 590.

DISTRINGAS NUPER VICE COMITEM. A writ to distrain the goods of one who lately filled the office of sheriff, to compel him to do some act which he ought to have done before leaving the office; as to bring in the body of a defendant, or to sell goods attached under a *fi. fa.*

DISTRINGAS VICE COMITEM. A writ of *distringas,* directed to the coroner, may be issued against a sheriff if he neglects to execute a writ of *venditioni exponas.* Arch. Pr. 584.

DISTRINGERE. In feudal and old English law. To distrain; to coerce or compel. Spelman; Calvin.

DISTURB. To throw into disorder; to move from a state of rest or regular order; to interrupt a settled state of, to throw out of course or order. Stinchcomb v. Oklahoma City, 81 Okl. 250, 198 P. 508, 510.

DISTURBANCE. Any act causing annoyance, disquiet, agitation, or derangement to another, or interrupting his peace, or interfering with him in the pursuit of a lawful and appropriate occupation or contrary to the usages of a sort of meeting and class of persons assembled that interferes with its due progress or irritates the assembly in whole or in part. State v. Mancini, 91 Vt. 507, 101 A. 581, 583.

A wrong done to an incorporeal hereditament by hindering or disquieting the owner in the enjoyment of it. Finch, 187; 3 Bl. Comm. 235.

DISTURBANCE OF COMMON. The doing any act by which the right of another to his common is incommoded or diminished; as where one who has no right of common puts his cattle into the land, or where one who has a right of common puts in cattle which are not commonable, or surcharges the common; or where the owner of the land, or other person, incloses or otherwise obstructs it. 3 Bl. Comm. 237–241; 3 Steph. Comm. 511, 512.

DISTURBANCE OF FRANCHISE. The disturbing or incommoding a man in the lawful exercise of his franchise, whereby the profits arising from it are diminished. 3 Bl. Comm. 236; 3 Steph. Comm. 510; 2 Crabb, Real Prop. § 2472*a*.

DISTURBANCE OF PATRONAGE. The hindrance or obstruction of a patron from presenting his clerk to a benefice. 3 Bl. Comm. 242; 3 Steph. Comm. 514.

DISTURBANCE OF PUBLIC OR RELIGIOUS WORSHIP. Any acts or conduct which interfere with the peace and good order of an assembly of persons lawfully met together for religious exercises. Minter v. State, 104 Ga. 743, 30 S.E. 989, 991; Stafford v. State, 154 Ala. 71, 45 So. 673, 674.

DISTURBANCE OF PEACE. Interruption of the peace, quiet, and good order of a neighborhood or community, particularly by unnecessary and distracting noises. Platt v. Greenwood, 69 P.2d 1032, 1034, 50 Ariz. 158; Levert v. Katz & Besthoff, 164 La. 1094, 115 So. 281, 283.

DISTURBANCE OF TENURE. In the law of tenure, disturbance is where a stranger, by menaces, force, persuasion, or otherwise, causes a tenant to leave his tenancy; this disturbance of tenure is an injury to the lord for which an action will lie. 3 Steph. Comm. 414.

DISTURBANCE OF WAYS. This happens where a person who has a right of way over another's ground by grant or prescription is obstructed by inclosures or other obstacles, or by plowing across it, by which means he cannot enjoy his right of way, or at least in so commodious a manner as he might have done. 3 Bl. Comm. 241.

DISTURBER. If a bishop refuse or neglect to examine or admit a patron's clerk, without reason assigned or notice given, he is styled a "disturber" by the law, and shall not have any title to present by lapse; for no man shall take advantage of his own wrong. 2 Bl. Comm. 278.

DITCH. The words "ditch" and "drain" have no technical or exact meaning. They both may mean a hollow space in the ground, natural or artificial, where water is collected or passes off; also, entire irrigation project. Dickey v. Bullock, 28 Wyo. 265, 202 P. 1104, 1105.

DITCHING, DIKING, or TILING. Every kind of work necessary to convert parts of arid lands, particularly sagebrush lands, into farms and orchards,—the word "diking" as applied to arid regions implying a leveling of the land, and the term "clearing land" as applied to arid regions covered with sagebrush meaning not only the removal or the destruction of the brush but the plowing or breaking up of the roots as well. Craig v. Crystal Realty Co., 89 Or. 25, 173 P. 322, 324.

DITES OUSTER. L. Fr. Say over. The form of awarding a *respondeas ouster,* in the Year Books, M. 6 Edw. III. 49.

DITTAY. In Scotch law. A technical term in civil law, signifying the matter of charge or ground of indictment against a person accused of crime. *Taking up dittay* is obtaining informations and presentments of crime in order to trial. Skene, de Verb. Sign.; Bell.

DIVERGE. To extend from a common point in different directions. Daylight Inv. Co. v. St. Louis Merchants' Bridge Terminal Ry. Co., Mo.Sup., 176 S.W. 7, 8.

DIVERS. Various, several, sundry; a collective term grouping a number of unspecified persons, objects, or acts. Harris v. Zanone, 93 Cal. 59, 28 P. 845; Hilton Bridge Const. Co. v. Foster, 57 N.Y.S. 140, 141, 26 Misc. 338.

DIVERSION. A turning aside or altering the natural course of a thing. The term is chiefly applied to the unauthorized changing the course of a water course to the prejudice of a lower proprietor, Archer v. City of Los Angeles, 19 Cal.2d 19, 119 P.2d 1, 5; Syret v. Tropic & East Fork Irr. Co., 97 Utah 56, 89 P.2d 474, 475; or to unauthorized or illegal use of corporate funds; Farracy v. Security Nat. Bank of Dallas, Tex., 4 S.W.2d 331, 335; Hornstein v. Paramount Pictures, 37 N.Y.S. 2d 404, 407; of estate or trust funds; Bray Bros. v. Marine Trust Co. of Buffalo, 35 N.Y.S.2d 356; or of alcohol. U. S. v. Hartford Acc. & Indem. Co., D.C.Md., 15 F.Supp. 791, 801.

DIVERSITÉ DES COURTS. A treatise on courts and their jurisdiction, written in French in the reign of Edward III. as is supposed, and by some attributed to Fitzherbert. It was first printed in 1525, and again in 1534. Crabb, Eng. Law, 330, 483.

DIVERSITY. In criminal pleading. A plea by the prisoner in bar of execution, alleging that he is not the same who was attainted, upon which a jury is immediately impaneled to try the collateral issue thus raised, viz., the identity of the person, and not whether he is guilty or innocent, for that has been already decided. 4 Bl. Comm. 396.

DIVERSITY OF CITIZENSHIP. A phrase used with reference to the jurisdiction of the federal courts, which, under U.S.Const. art. 3, § 2, extends to cases between citizens of different states, designating the condition existing when the party on one side of a lawsuit is a citizen of one state, and the party on the other side is a citizen of another state. When this is the basis of jurisdiction, all the persons on one side of the controversy must be citizens of different states from all the persons on the other side. Albert Pick & Co. v. Cass-Putnam Hotel Co., D.C.Mich., 41 F.2d 74; Soptich v. St. Joseph Nat. Croation Beneficiary Ass'n, D. C.Kan., 34 F.2d 566.

DIVERSO INTUITU. Lat. With a different view, purpose, or design; in a different view or point of view; by a different course or process. 1 W. Bl. 89; 4 Kent Comm. 211, note.

DIVERSORIUM. In old English law. A lodging or inn. Townsh. Pl. 38.

DIVERT. To turn aside; to turn out of the way; to alter the course of things. Usually applied to water-courses. Ang. Water-Courses, § 97 et seq. Sometimes to roads. 8 East, 394.

DIVES. In the practice of the English chancery division, "dives costs" are costs on the ordinary scale, as opposed to the costs formerly allowed to a successful pauper suing or defending *in formâ pauperis,* which consisted only of his costs out of pocket. Daniell, Ch. Pr. 43.

DIVEST. Equivalent to devest, (*q. v.*).

DIVESTITIVE FACT. Any act or event that extinguishes or modifies a jural relation. Kocourek, Jural Relations (2d ed.) 17.

DIVIDE. To cut into parts, disunite, separate, keep apart. The term is synonymous with distribute. Watters v. First Nat. Bank, 233 Ala. 227, 171 So. 280, 288.

Divide et impera, cum radix et vertex imperii in obedientium consensu rata sunt. 4 Inst. 35. Divide and govern, since the foundation and crown of empire are established in the consent of the obedient.

DIVIDEND. A fund to be divided. The share allotted to each of several persons entitled to share in a division of profits or property. Thus, dividend may denote a fund set apart by a corporation out of its profits, to be apportioned among the shareholders, or the proportional amount falling to each. Hadley v. Commissioner of Internal Revenue, 36 F.2d 543, 544, 59 App.D.C. 139; Penington v. Commonwealth Hotel Const. Corp., 17 Del.Ch. 394, 155 A. 514, 517, 75 A.L.R. 1136; Lewis v. O'Malley, D.C.Neb., 49 F.Supp. 173, 179. In bankruptcy or insolvency practice, a dividend is a proportional payment to the creditors out of the insolvent estate. United States Fidelity & Guarantee Co. v. Sweeney, C.C.A.Mo., 80 F.2d 235, 241.

So-called dividend paid by life insurer is not in fact a "dividend" but is the excess payment of premiums over actual cost. Scholem v. Prudential Ins. Co. of America, 15 N.Y.S.2d 947, 948, 172 Misc. 664.

"Dividends," common or preferred, are what shareholder earns from property without liability in case dividends are not paid. Commonwealth v. Philadelphia Rapid Transit Co., 287 Pa. 190, 134 A. 455, 458.

Cumulative Dividend

A dividend, usually preferred, which if not earned or paid, pursuant to agreement must be paid at some subsequent date. Lockwood v. General Abrasive Co., 205 N.Y.S. 511, 513, 210 App.Div. 141.

Dividend Addition

Something added to the policy in the form of paid-up insurance, and does not mean unapportioned assets or surplus. State Life Ins. Co. of Indianapolis v. McNeese, 106 Ind.App. 378, 19 N.E.2d 854, 857. The term does not refer to dividends added directly to the loan value. Anderson v. Liberty Life Ins. Co. of Topeka, 149 Kan. 447, 87 P.2d 499, 502.

Ex Dividend

A phrase used by stock brokers, meaning that a sale of corporate stock does not carry with it the seller's right to receive his proportionate share of a dividend already declared and shortly payable.

Extraordinary Dividends

See Extraordinary Dividends.

Liquidation Dividend

See Liquidation Dividend.

Preferred Dividend

One paid on the preferred stock of a corporation; a dividend paid to one class of shareholders in priority to that paid to another. Jefferson Banking Co. v. Trustees of Martin Institute, 146 Ga. 383, 91 S.E. 463, 468.

Scrip Dividend

One paid in scrip, or in certificates of the ownership of a corresponding amount of capital stock of the company thereafter to be issued. Bailey v. Railroad Co., 22 Wall. 604, 22 L.Ed. 840.

Stock Dividend

One paid in stock, that is, not in money, but in a proportional number of shares of the capital stock of the company, which is ordinarily increased for this purpose to a corresponding extent. Thomas v. Gregg, 78 Md. 545, 28 A. 565, 44 Am.St.Rep. 310. A stock dividend is not in the ordinary sense a dividend, which is a cash distribution to stockholders of profits on their investments, but rather it is an increase in the number of shares declared out of profits, the increased number representing exactly the same property as was represented by the smaller number of shares. Booth v. Gross, Kelley & Co., 30 N.M. 465, 238 P. 829, 831, 41 A.L.R. 868. It is really nothing more than a process in corporation bookkeeping. Hayes v. St. Louis Union Trust Co., Mo.Sup., 298 S.W. 91, 98.

In Old English Law

The term denotes one part of an indenture, (*q. v.*).

DIVIDENDA. In old records. An indenture; one counterpart of an indenture.

DIVINARE. Lat. To divine; to conjecture or guess; to foretell. *Divinatio,* a conjecturing or guessing.

Divinatio, non interpretatio est, quæ omnino recedit a litera. That is guessing, not interpretation, which altogether departs from the letter. Bac. Max. 18, (in reg. 3,) citing Yearb. 3 Hen. VI. 20.

DIVINE LAWS. Those ascribed to God. Borden v. State, 11 Ark. 527, 44 Am.Dec. 217.

DIVINE RIGHT OF KINGS. The right of a king to rule as posited by the patriarchal theory of government, especially under the doctrine that no misconduct and no dispossession can forfeit the right of a monarch or his heirs to the throne, and to the obedience of the people. Webster, Dict. This theory "was in its origin directed, not against popular liberty, but against papal and ecclesiastical claims to supremacy in temporal as well as spiritual affairs." Figgis, "The Theory of the Divine Right of Kings."

DIVINE SERVICE. Divine service was the name of a feudal tenure, by which the tenants were obliged to do some special divine services in certain; as to sing so many masses, to distribute such a sum in alms, and the like. (2 Bl. Comm. 102; 1 Steph. Comm. 227.) It differed from tenure in *frankalmoign,* in this: that, in case of the tenure by divine service, the lord of whom the lands were holden might distrain for its nonperformance, whereas, in case of *frankalmoign,* the lord has no remedy by distraint for neglect of the service, but merely a right of complaint to the visitor to correct it. Mozley & Whitley.

DIVINITY STUDENT. A student in a seminary in preparation for ministry, priesthood or rabbinate. United States ex rel. Rubin v. Magruder, D.C.R.I., 55 F.Supp. 947, 955.

DIVISA. In old English law. A device, award, or decree; also a devise; also bounds or limits of division of a parish or farm, etc. Cowell. Also a court held on the boundary, in order to settle disputes of the tenants.

Divisibilis est semper divisibilis. A thing divisible may be forever divided.

DIVISIBLE. That which is susceptible of being divided.

DIVISIBLE CONTRACT. One which is in its nature and purposes susceptible of division and apportionment, having two or more parts in respect to matters and things contemplated and embraced by it, not necessarily dependent on each other nor intended by the parties so to be. Horseman v. Horseman, 43 Or. 83, 72 P. 698; Stavisky v. General Footwear Co., City Ct.N.Y., 185 N.Y.S. 760, 761.

DIVISIBLE OBLIGATION. See Obligation.

DIVISIBLE OFFENSE. One that includes one or more offenses of lower grade, e. g., murder includes assault, battery, assault with intent to kill, and other offenses. Williams v. State, 20 Ala.App. 604, 104 So. 280, 281.

DIVISIM. In old English law. Severally; separately. Bract. fol. 47.

DIVISION. In English law. One of the smaller subdivisions of a county. Used in Lincolnshire as synonymous with "riding" in Yorkshire.

The separation of members of a legislative body to take a vote. An operating section of a railroad. Burton v. Oregon-Washington R. & Nav. Co., 148 Or. 648, 38 P.2d 72. A separation of an administrative body or court for the conducting of the business thereof. Foss v. Commissioner of Internal Revenue, C.C.A. 1, 75 F.2d 326, 329.

DIVISION OF OPINION. In the practice of appellate courts, this term denotes such a disagreement among the judges that there is not a majority in favor of any one view, and hence no decision can be rendered on the case. But it sometimes also denotes a division into two classes, one of which may comprise a majority of the judges; as when we speak of a decision having proceeded from a "divided court."

DIVISIONAL COURTS. Courts in England, consisting of two or (in special cases) more judges of the high court of justice, sitting to transact certain kinds of business which cannot be disposed of by one judge.

DIVISUM IMPERIUM. Lat. A divided jurisdiction. Applied, *e. g.*, to the jurisdiction of courts of common law and equity over the same subject. 1 Kent, Comm. 366; 4 Steph. Comm. 9.

DIVORCE. The legal separation of man and wife, effected, for cause, by the judgment, of a court, and either totally dissolving the marriage relation, or suspending its effects so far as concerns the cohabitation of the parties. Atherton v. Atherton, 181 U.S. 155, 21 S.Ct. 544, 45 L.Ed. 794. Sometimes it includes "annulment." Millar v. Millar, 175 Cal. 797, 167 P. 394, 398, L.R.A. 1918B, 415, Ann.Cas.1918E, 184.

The dissolution is termed "divorce from the bond of matrimony," or, in the Latin form of the expression, *"a vinculo matrimonii;"* the suspension, "divorce from bed and board," *"a mensa et thoro."* The former divorce puts an end to the marriage; the latter leaves it in full force. 2 Bish.Mar. & Div. § 225.

The term "divorce" is now applied, in England, both to decrees of nullity and decrees of dissolution of marriage, while in America it is ordinarily used only in cases of divorce *a mensa* or *a vinculo,* a decree of nullity of marriage being granted for the causes for which a divorce *a vinculo* was formerly obtainable in England.

Divorce a mensa et thoro. A divorce from table and bed, or from bed and board. A partial or qualified divorce, by which the parties are separated and forbidden to live or cohabit together, without affecting the marriage itself. 1 Bl. Comm. 440; 3 Bl. Comm. 94; 2 Steph. Comm. 311; 2 Bish. Mar. & Div. § 225; Fisher v. Harrison, 165 Va. 323, 182 S.E. 543, 544, 104 A.L.R. 102.

Divorce a vinculo matrimonii. A divorce from the bond of marriage. A total divorce of husband and wife, dissolving the marriage tie, and releasing the parties wholly from their matrimonial obligations. 1 Bl. Comm. 440; 2 Steph. Comm. 310, 311; 2 Bish. Mar. & Div. § 225; De Roche v. De Roche, 12 N.D. 17, 94 N.W. 770.

Divorce suit. A "divorce suit" is a civil proceeding founded on a matrimonial wrong, wherein the married parties are plaintiff and defendant, and the government, or public, occupies, without being mentioned in the pleadings, the position of a third party, resulting in a triangle and otherwise sui generis action of tort. Gallemore v. Gallemore, 94 Fla. 516, 114 So. 371, 372.

Foreign divorce. A divorce obtained out of the state or country where the marriage was solemnized. 2 Kent, Comm. 106, et seq.

Limited divorce. A divorce from bed and board; or a judicial separation of husband and wife not dissolving the marriage tie. Yost v. Yost, 143 Neb. 80, 8 N.W.2d 686.

DIVORTIUM DICITUR A DIVERTENDO, QUIA vir divertitur ab uxore. Co. Litt. 235. Divorce is called from *divertendo*, because a man is diverted from his wife.

DIVULGE. To disclose or make known, as to divulge a telephone message. United States v. Gruber, C.C.A.N.Y., 123 F.2d 307, 309.

DIXIÈME. Fr. Tenth; the tenth part. Ord.Mar. liv. 1, tit. 1, art. 9.

In Old French Law

An income tax payable to the crown. Steph. Lect. 359.

DO. Lat. I give. The ancient and aptest word of feoffment and of gift. 2 Bl. Comm. 310, 316; Co. Litt. 9.

DO, DICO, ADDICO. Lat. I give, I say, I adjudge. Three words used in the Roman law, to express the extent of the civil jurisdiction of the prætor. *Do* denoted that he *gave* or granted actions, exceptions, and judices; *dico,* that he pronounced judgment; *addico,* that he adjudged the controverted property, or the goods of the debtor, etc., to the plaintiff. Mackeld. Rom. Law, § 39.

DO, LEGO. Lat. I give, I bequeath; or I give and bequeath. The formal words of making a bequest or legacy, in the Roman law. *Titio et Seio hominem Stichum do, lego,* I give and bequeath to Titius and Seius my man Stichus. Inst. 2, 20, 8, 30, 31. The expression is literally retained in modern wills.

DO UT DES. Lat. I give that you may give; I give [you] that you may give [me.] A formula in the civil law, constituting a general division under which those contracts (termed "innominate") were classed in which something was *given* by one party as a consideration for something *given* by the other. Dig. 19, 4; Id. 19, 5, 5; 2 Bl. Comm. 444.

DO UT FACIAS. Lat. I give that you may do; I give [you] that you may do or make [for me.] A formula in the civil law, under which those contracts were classed in which one party *gave* or agreed to give money, in consideration the other party *did* or performed certain work. Dig. 19, 5, 5; 2 Bl. Comm. 444.

In this and the foregoing phrase, the conjunction *"ut"* is not to be taken as the technical means of expressing a consideration. In the Roman usage, this word imported a *modus,* that is, a qualification; while a consideration *(causa)* was more aptly expressed by the word *"quia."*

DOCIMASIA PULMONUM. In medical jurisprudence. The hydrostatic test used chiefly in cases of alleged infanticide to determine whether the child was born alive or dead. See Hydrostatic Test.

DOCK, *v.* To curtail or diminish, as to dock an entail.

DOCK, *n.* The cage or inclosed space in a criminal court where prisoners stand when brought in for trial.

The space, in a river or harbor, inclosed between two wharves. City of Boston v. Lecraw, 17 How. 434, 15 L.Ed. 118.

A slip or waterway extending between two piers or projecting wharfs for the reception of ships, sometimes including the piers themselves. Wescott v. American Creosoting Co., 97 A. 493, 494, 86 N.J.Eq. 104.

"A dock is an artificial basin in connection with a harbor, used for the reception of vessels in the taking on or discharging of their cargoes, and provided with gates for preventing the rise and fall of the waters occasioned by the tides, and keeping a uniform level within the docks." Perry v. Haines, 24 S.Ct. 8, 191 U.S. 17, 48 L.Ed. 73.

DOCK–MASTER. An officer invested with powers within the docks, and a certain distance therefrom, to direct the mooring and removing of ships, so as to prevent obstruction to the dock entrances. Mozley & Whiteley.

DOCK WARRANT. In English law. A warrant given by dock-owners to the owner of merchandise imported and warehoused on the dock, upon the faith of the bills of lading, as a recognition of his title to the goods. It is a negotiable instrument. Pull. Port of London, p. 375.

DOCKAGE. A charge against vessels for the privilege of mooring to the wharves or in the slips. People v. Roberts, 92 Cal. 659, 28 Pac. 689. A pecuniary compensation for the use of a dock while a vessel is undergoing repairs. Ives v. The Buckeye State, 13 Fed.Cas. 184; The Indomable, C.C.A.N.Y., 279 F. 827, 831; Wilkens v. Trafikaktiebolaget Grangesberg Okelosund, C.C. A.Tex., 10 F.2d 129, 131.

DOCKET, *v.* To abstract and enter in a book. 3 Bl. Comm. 397, 398. To make a brief entry of any proceeding in a court of justice in the docket.

DOCKET, *n.* A minute, abstract, or brief entry; or the book containing such entries. A small piece of paper or parchment having the effect of a larger. Blount. A file. Touchstone Live Stock Co. v. Easters, 172 Ga. 454, 157 S.E. 683, 684.

In Practice

A formal record, entered in brief, of the proceedings in a court of justice. Brinn v. Wooding, 298 N.Y.S. 971, 975, 164 Misc. 850.

A book containing an entry in brief of all the important acts done in court in the conduct of each case, from its inception to its conclusion.

The name of "docket" or "trial docket" is sometimes given to the list or calendar of causes set to be tried at a specified term, prepared by the clerks for the use of the court and bar.

Kinds of Dockets

An *appearance* docket is one in which the appearances in actions are entered, containing also a brief abstract of the successive steps in each action. A *bar* docket is an unofficial paper consisting of a transcript of the docket for a term of court, printed for distribution to members of the bar. Gifford v. Cole, 57 Iowa, 272, 10 N.W. 672. An *execution* docket is a list of the executions sued out or pending in the sheriff's office. A *judgment* docket is a list or docket of the judgments entered in a given court, methodically kept by the clerk or other proper officer, open to public inspection, and intended to afford official notice to interested parties of the existence or lien of judgments.

In General

Docket fee. An attorney's fee, of a fixed sum, chargeable with or as a part of the costs of the action, for the attorney of the successful party; so called because chargeable on the docket, not as a fee for making docket entries. Bank v. Neill, 13 Mont. 377, 34 Pac. 180; Goodyear v. Sawyer, C.C., 17 Fed. 2.

Docket, striking a. A phrase formerly used in English bankruptcy practice. It referred to the entry of certain papers at the bankruptcy office, preliminary to the prosecution of the fiat against a trader who had become bankrupt. These papers consisted of the affidavit, the bond, and the petition of the creditor, and their object was to obtain from the lord chancellor his fiat, authorizing the petitioner to prosecute his complaint against the bankrupt in the bankruptcy courts. Brown.

DOCTOR, *v.* To prescribe or treat medically or to treat as a doctor or physician. Haines v. Indiana Trust Co., 95 Ind.App. 651, 131 N.E. 89, 91.

DOCTOR, *n.* A learned man; one qualified to give instruction of the higher order in a science or art; particularly, one who has received the highest academical degree in his art or faculty, as, a doctor of laws, medicine, or theology. In colloquial language, however, the term is practically restricted to practitioners of medicine. Harrison v. State, 102 Ala. 170, 15 So. 563; State v. McKnight, 131 N.C. 717, 42 S.E. 580, 59 L.R.A. 187. But it is not synonymous with surgeon. State v. Miller, 59 N.D. 286, 229 N.W. 569, 574.

DOCTOR AND STUDENT. The title of a work written by St. Germain in the reign of Henry VIII, in which many principles of the common law are discussed in a popular manner. It is in the form of a dialogue between a doctor of divinity and a student in law, and has always been considered a book of merit and authority. 1 Kent, Comm. 504; Crabb, Eng. Law, 482.

DOCTORS' COMMONS. An institution near St. Paul's Churchyard, in London, where, for a long time previous to 1857, the ecclesiastical and admiralty courts used to be held.

DOCTRINAL INTERPRETATION. See Interpretation.

DOCTRINE. A rule, principle, theory, or tenet of the law; as, the doctrine of merger, the doctrine of relation, etc.

DOCUMENT. An instrument on which is recorded, by means of letters, figures, or marks, matter which may be evidentially used. In this sense the term "document" applies to writings; to words printed, lithographed, or photographed; to seals, plates, or stones on which inscriptions are cut or engraved; to photographs and pictures: to maps or plans. The inscription may be of stone or gems, or on wood, as well as on paper or parchment. 1 Whart. Ev. § 614; Johnson Steel Street-Rail Co. v. North Branch Steel Co., C.C.Pa., 48 F. 194; Arnold v. Water Co., 18 R.I. 189, 26 A. 55, 19 L.R.A. 602. It has various statutory meanings. Hays v. Hinkle, Tex.Civ.App., 193 S.W. 153, 155; Cohn v. U. S., C.C.A.N.Y., 258 F. 355, 361; Smith v. Lingelbach, 177 Wis. 170, 187 N.W. 1007, 1008.

In the plural, the deeds, agreements, title-papers, letters, receipts, and other written instruments used to prove a fact.

In the Civil Law

Evidence delivered in the forms established by law, of whatever nature such evidence may be. The term is, however, applied principally to the testimony of witnesses. Sav. Dr. Rom. § 165.

In General

Ancient documents. Deeds, wills, and other writings more than thirty years old are so called; they are presumed to be genuine without express proof, when coming from the proper custody.

Foreign document. One which was prepared or executed in, or which comes from, a foreign state or country.

Judicial documents. Proceedings relating to litigation. They are divided into (1) judgments, decrees, and verdicts; (2) depositions, examinations, and inquisitions taken in the course of a legal process; (3) writs, warrants, pleadings, etc., which are incident to any judicial proceedings. See 1 Starkie, Ev. 252.

Public document. A state paper, or other instrument of public importance or interest, issued or published by authority of congress or a state legislature. Also any document or record, evidencing or connected with the public business or the administration of public affairs, preserved in or issued by any department of the government. See Hammatt v. Emerson, 27 Me. 335, 46 Am. Dec. 598. One of the publications printed by order of congress or either house thereof. McCall v. U. S., 1 Dak. 328, 46 N.W. 608. Broadly, any document open to public inspection. Flint v. Stone Tracy Co., 220 U.S. 107, 31 S.Ct. 342, 55 L.Ed. 389, Ann.Cas.1912B, 1312.

DOCUMENTARY EVIDENCE. Evidence supplied by writings and documents of every kind in the widest sense of the term; evidence derived from conventional symbols (such as letters) by which ideas are represented on material substances. Such evidence as is furnished by written instruments, inscriptions, documents of all kinds, and also any inanimate objects admissible for the purpose, as distinguished from "oral" evidence, or that delivered by human beings viva voce. People v. Purcell, 22 Cal.App.2d 126, 70 P.2d 706, 709.

DODRANS. Lat. In Roman law. A subdivision of the *as*, containing nine *unciæ;* the proportion of nine-twelfths, or three-fourths. 2 Bl.Comm. 462, note.

DOE, JOHN. The name of the fictitious plaintiff in the action of ejectment. 3 Steph. Comm. 618.

DOED–BANA. In Saxon law. The actual perpetrator of a homicide.

DOER. In Scotch law. An agent or attorney. 1 Kames, Eq. 325.

DOG–DRAW. In old forest law. The manifest deprehension of an offender against venison in a forest, when he was found drawing after a deer by the scent of a hound led in his hand; or where a person had wounded a deer or wild beast, by shooting at him, or otherwise, and was caught with a dog drawing after him to receive the same. Manwood, Forest Law, 2, c. 8.

DOG–LATIN. The Latin of illiterate persons; Latin words put together on the English grammatical system.

DOGGER. In maritime law. A light ship or vessel. Cowell.

Dogger-fish, fish brought in ships.

Dogger-men, fishermen that belong to doggerships.

DOGMA. In the civil law. A word occasionally used as descriptive of an ordinance of the senate. See Nov. 2, 1, 1; Dig. 27, 1, 6.

DOGS. Steel rods with clamps or tongs thereon, for carrying heavy steel rails. Jefferson v. Denkmann Lumber Co., 148 So. 237, 239, 167 Miss. 246.

DOING. The formal word by which *services* were reserved and expressed in old conveyances; as "rendering" *(reddendo)* was expressive of *rent.* Perk. c. 10, §§ 625, 635, 638. As used in La.Civ. Code, art. 1931, the word signifies activity. Noel Estate v. Louisiana Oil Refining Corporation, 188 La. 45, 175 So. 744, 746.

DOING BUSINESS. Within statutes on service of process on foreign corporations, equivalent to conducting or managing business. Wichita Film & Supply Co. v. Yale, 194 Mo.App. 60, 184 S.W. 119. A foreign corporation is "doing business", making it amenable to process within state, if it does business therein in such a manner as to warrant the inference that it is present there. Cannon Mfg. Co. v. Cudahy Packing Co., D.C.N.C., 292 F. 169, 171. Or that it has subjected itself to the jurisdiction and laws in which the service is made. W. J. Armstrong Co. v. New York Cent. & H. R. R. Co., 129 Minn. 104, 151 N.W. 917, 919, L.R.A.1916E, 232, Ann.Cas.1916E, 335; The doing of business is the exercise in the state of some of the ordinary functions for which the corporation was organized. Davis & Worrell v. General Motors Acceptance Corporation, 153 Ark. 626, 241 S.W. 44, 46. What constitutes "doing business" depends on the facts in each particular case. Walton N. Moore Dry Goods Co. v. Commercial Industrial Co., C.C.A.,Cal., 282 F. 21, 25. The activities of the corporation, however, must represent a more or less continuous effort; Knapp v. Bullock Tractor Co., D.C.Cal., 242 F. 543, 550; Johnson v. Cass & Emerson, 91 Vt. 103, 99 A. 633, 635; or be of a systematic and regular nature; Home Lumber Co. v. Hopkins, 107 Kan. 153, 190 P. 601, 605, 10 A.L.R. 879.

The transaction of single piece of business is not enough. Wood & Selick v. American Grocery Co., 96 N.J.Law, 218, 114 A. 756, 757; Anderson v. Morris & E. R. Co., C.C.A.N.Y., 216 F. 83, 87. To the contrary. Tripp State Bank of Tripp v. Jerke, 45 S.D. 448, 188 N.W. 314, 315.

No general definition can be made of phrase "doing business" in statutes relating to foreign corporations. Each case must be determined on its own facts, by considering objective of statute in which phrase is found, its purpose and orientation to the carrying on of business, nature of activities, their magnitude, multiplicity of contracts, and possibility that incidents may occur and liabilities be created, especially where entrance into state is in ordinary prosecution of corporation's business. State Highway and Public Works Commission v. Diamond S. S. Transp. Corp., 225 N.C. 198, 34 S.E.2d 78, 80, 81.

Ordinarily the phrase means engaging in activities in pursuit of gain. Welch Holding Co. v. Galloway, 161 Or. 515, 89 P.2d 559; People v. Jones, 16 N.Y.S.2d 558, 559, 172 Misc. 368.

The following transactions and businesses illustrate, what constitutes or does not constitute "doing business": advertising, Society Milion Athena v. National Bank of Greece, 1 N.Y.S.2d 155, 2 N.Y.S.2d 155; Deighan v. Beverage Retailer Weekly & Trade Newspaper Corporation, 18 N.J.Misc. 705, 16 A.2d 612, 613; bringing of actions, R. L. Witters Associates v. Ebsary Gypsum Co., D.C.Fla., 19 F. Supp. 646, 648; Schneider v. Greater M. & S. Circuit, 259 N.Y.S. 319, 144 Misc. 534; broadcasting system, Hoffman v. Carter, 118 N.J.L. 379, 192 A. 825; State ex rel. Columbia Broadcasting Co. v. Superior Court for King County, 1 Wash.2d 379, 96 P.2d 248, 250; consignment, Oyler v. J. P. Seeburg Corporation, D.C.Tex., 29 F.Supp. 927; Thew Shovel Co. v. Superior Court in and for City and County of San Francisco, 35 Cal.App.2d 183, 95 P.2d 149, 151, 152; holding companies, Wilhelm v. Consolidated Oil Corporation, D.C.Okl., 11 F.Supp. 444, 447; Cliffs Corporation v. Evatt, 138 Ohio St. 336, 35 N.E.2d 144, 151; insurance, Sasnett v. Iowa State Traveling Men's Ass'n, C.C.A.Iowa, 90 F.2d 514; Hoopeston Canning Co. v. Pink, 288 N.Y. 291, 43 N.E.2d 49, 53; newspapers, Layne v. Tribune Co., 71 F.2d 223, 224, 63 App.D.C. 213; Neely v. Philadelphia Inquirer Co., 62 F.2d 873, 874, 61 App.D.C. 334; railroads, Klabzuba v. Southern Pac. Co., D.C.Wash., 33 F.2d 359, 360; Gadboury v. Central Vermont Ry. Co., 231 N.Y.S. 630, 632, 225 App.Div. 145; solicitation, Mandel Bros. v. Henry A. O'Neil, Inc., C.C.A.S.D., 69 F.2d 452, 455; Bank v. Charles Meyers & Co., 182 Md. 556, 35 A.2d 110, 113.

Illustrations of what constitutes "doing business" within various taxing statutes follow: Capital stock tax, Goodyear Inv. Corporation v. Campbell, C.C.A.Ohio, 139 F.2d 188, 190, 191; Refrigeration Discount Corporation v. Metzger, D.C.Pa., 10 F.Supp. 748, 749; excise tax, Harmar Coal Co. v. Heiner, D.C.Pa., 26 F.2d 729, 730; Queens Run Refractories Co. v. Commonwealth, 270 Mass. 19, 169 N.E. 515, 516; franchise tax, Stone v. Interstate Natural Gas Co., C.C.A.Miss., 103 F.2d 544, 548; Cliffs Corporation v. Evatt, 138 Ohio St. 336, 35 N.E.2d 144, 151; income tax, Blair v. Wilson Syndicate Trust, C.C.A., 39 F.2d 43, 45; Welch Holding Co. v. Galloway, 161 Or. 515, 89 P.2d 559, 564.

DOITKIN, or DOIT. A base coin of small value, prohibited by St. 3 Hen. V. c. 1. We still retain the phrase, in the common saying, when we would undervalue a man, that he is not worth a doit. Jacob.

DOLE. A part, share, or portion, as of a meadow. To "dole out" anything is to deal or distribute in small portions. Holthouse. In Scotch law, criminal intent; evil design. Bell, Dict. voc. "Crime."

DOLÉANCE. A peculiar appeal in the Channel Islands. It is a personal charge against a judicial officer, either of misconduct or of negligence. L. R. 6 P. C. 155. It still exists in a modified form. L. R. 5 A. C. 348. See 48 L. Jour. 281.

DOLES, or DOOLS. Slips of pasture left between the furrows of plowed land.

DOLG. Sax. A wound. Spelman.

DOLG–BOTE. A recompense for a scar or wound. Cowell.

DOLI. Lat. See Dolus.

DOLI CAPAX. Capable of malice or criminal intention; having sufficient discretion and intelligence to distinguish between right and wrong, and so to become amenable to the criminal laws.

DOLI INCAPAX. Incapable of criminal intention or malice; not of the age of discretion; not possessed of sufficient discretion and intelligence to distinguish between right and wrong to the extent of being criminally responsible for his actions.

DOLLAR. The unit employed in the United States in calculating money values. It is of the value of one hundred cents. People v. Alba, 46 Cal.App.2d 859, 117 P.2d 63. Money or currency issued by lawful authority and intended to pass and circulate as such. Neufield v. United States, 118 F.2d 375, 387, 73 App.D.C. 174.

DOLLY. A kind of handbarrow or handcart, consisting essentially of a strong, braced frame terminating in a pair of handles at one end and supported on a pair of small heavy wheels with broad rim. A small heavy rectangular frame supported on four small wheels used instead of rollers for moving heavy objects as on a floor. McGillivary v. Montgomery Ward & Co., 19 Wash. 2d 582, 143 P.2d 550, 552. See, Box Dolly.

DOLO. In Spanish law. Bad or mischievous design. White, New Recop. b. 1, tit. 1, c. 1, § 3.

DOLO FACIT QUI PETIT QUOD REDDITURUS EST. He acts with guile who demands that which he will have to return. Broom, Max. 346.

DOLO MALO PACTUMSE NON SERVATURUM. Dig. 2, 14, 7, § 9. An agreement induced by fraud cannot stand.

DOLORIMETER. An instrument used by a physician to measure a patient's pain threshold. The instrument emits a ray of light which is shined into one's eye at various degrees of brightness. Dolorimetry is the science of measuring pain.

DOLOSUS VERSATUR IN GENERALIBUS. A person intending to deceive deals in general terms. Wing. Max. 636; 2 Coke, 34*a;* 6 Clark & F. 699; Broom, Max. 289.

DOLUM EX INDICIIS PERSPICUIS PROBARI CONVENIT. Fraud should be proved by clear tokens. Code, 2, 21, 6; 1 Story, Cont. § 625.

DOLUS. In the civil law. Guile; deceitfulness; malicious fraud. A fraudulent address or trick used to deceive some one; a fraud. Dig. 4, 3, 1. Any subtle contrivance by words or acts with a design to circumvent. 2 Kent, Comm. 560; Code, 2, 21.

Such acts or omissions as operate as a deception upon the other party, or violate the just confidence reposed by him, whether there be a deceitful intent (*malus animus*) or not. Poth. Traité de Dépôt, nn. 23, 27; Story, Bailm. § 20*a;* 2 Kent, Comm. 506, note.

Fraud, willfulness, or intentionality. In that use it is opposed to *culpa,* which is negligence merely, in greater or less degree. The policy of the law may sometimes treat extreme *culpa* as if it were *dolus,* upon the maxim *culpa dolo comparatur*. A person is always liable for *dolus* producing damage, but not always for *culpa* producing damage, even though extreme. Brown.

DOLUS AUCTORIS NON NOCET SUCCESSORI. The fraud of a predecessor prejudices not his successor.

DOLUS BONUS, DOLUS MALUS. In a wide sense, the Roman law distinguishes between "good," or rather "permissible" *dolus* and "bad" or fraudulent *dolus.* The former is justifiable or allowable deceit; it is that which a man may employ in self-defense against an unlawful attack, or for another permissible purpose, as when one dissembles the truth to prevent a lunatic from injuring himself or others. The latter exists where one intentionally misleads another or takes advantage of another's error wrongfully, by any form of deception, fraud, or cheating. Mackeld. Rom. Law, § 179; Broom, Max. 349; 2 Kent, Comm. 560, note.

DOLUS CIRCUITU NON PURGATUR. Fraud is not purged by circuity. Bac. Max. 4; Broom, Max. 228.

DOLUS DANS LOCUM CONTRACTUI. Fraud (or deceit) giving rise to the contract; that is, a fraudulent misrepresentation made by one of the parties to the contract, and relied upon by the other, and which was actually instrumental in inducing the latter to enter into the contract.

DOLUS EST MACHINATIO, CUM ALIUD DISSIMULAT ALIUD AGIT. Lane, 47. Deceit is an artifice, since it pretends one thing and does another.

DOLUS ET FRAUS NEMINI PATROCINENTUR, (PATROCINARI DEBENT.) Deceit and fraud shall excuse or benefit no man. Yearb. 14 Hen. VIII. 8; Best, Ev. p. 469, § 428; 1 Story, Eq. Jur. § 395.

DOLUS LATET IN GENERALIBUS. Fraud lurks in generalities. Tray. Lat. Max. 162.

DOLUS VERSATUR IN GENERALIBUS. Fraud deals in generalities. 2 Coke, 34*a;* 3 Coke, 81*a.*

DOM. PROC. An abbreviation of *Domus Procerum* or *Domo Procerum;* the house of lords in England. Sometimes expressed by the letters D. P.

DOMAIN. The complete and absolute ownership of land; a paramount and individual right of property in land. People v. Shearer, 30 Cal. 658. Also the real estate so owned. The inherent sovereign power claimed by the legislature of a state, of controlling private property for public uses, is termed the "right of eminent domain." 2 Kent, Comm. 339. See Eminent Domain.

A distinction has been made between "property" and "domain." The former is said to be that quality which is conceived to be in the thing itself, considered as belonging to such or such person, exclusively of all others. By the latter is understood that right which the owner has of disposing of the thing. Hence "domain" and "property" are said to be correlative terms. The one is the active right to dispose of; the other a passive quality which follows the thing and places it at the disposition of the owner. 3 Toullier, no. 83.

National domain is sometimes applied to the aggregate of the property owned directly by a nation. Civ. Code La. art. 486. Public domain embraces all lands, the title to which is in the United States, including as well land occupied for the purposes of federal buildings, arsenals, dock-yards, etc., as land of an agricultural or mineral character not yet granted to private owners. Day Land & Cattle Co. v. State, 68 Tex. 526, 4 S.W. 865.

DOMBEC, DOMBOC. (Sax. From *dom,* judgment, and *bec, boc,* a book.) Dome-book or doom-book. A name given among the Saxons to a code of laws. Several of the Saxon kings published *dombocs,* but the most important one was that attributed to Alfred. Crabb, Com. Law, 7. This is sometimes confounded with the celebrated *Domesday-Book.* See Dome-Book; Domesday.

DOME. (Sax.) Doom; sentence; judgment. An oath. The homager's oath in the black book of Hereford. Blount.

DOME-BOOK. A book or code said to have been compiled under the direction of Alfred, for the general use of the whole kingdom of England; containing, as is supposed, the principal maxims of the common law, the penalties for misdemeanors, and the forms of judicial proceedings. It is said to have been extant so late as the reign of Edward IV., but is now lost. 1 Bl.Comm. 64, 65.

DOMESDAY, DOMESDAY-BOOK. (Sax.) An ancient record made in the time of William the Conqueror, and now remaining in the English exchequer, consisting of two volumes of unequal size, containing minute and accurate surveys of the lands in England. 2 Bl.Comm. 49, 50. The work was begun by five justices in each county in 1081, and finished in 1086.

DOMESMEN. (Sax.) An inferior kind of judges. Men appointed to doom (judge) in matters in controversy. Cowell. Suitors in a court of a manor in ancient demesne, who are judges there. Blount; Whishaw; Termes de la Ley.

DOMESTIC, *n.* A domestic, or, in full, domestic servant, is a servant who resides in the same house with the master. The term does not extend to workmen or laborers employed out of doors. Ex parte Meason, 5 Bin. (Pa.) 167; Richardson v. State, 43 Tex. 456; Anderson v. Ueland, 197 Minn. 518, 267 N.W. 517, 518.

The Louisiana Civil Code enumerates as domestics those who receive wages and stay in the house of the person paying and employing them, for his own service or that of his family; such as valets, footmen, cooks, butlers, and others who reside in the house. Persons employed in public houses are not included. Cook v. Dodge, 6 La.Ann. 276.

The term is sometimes extended, however, to include servants who do not reside in the same house as the master. Catto v. Plant, 106 Conn. 236, 137 A. 764, 766 (gardner); Douglas v. State, 88 Tex.Cr.R. 295, 225 S.W. 536, 538 (house porter).

DOMESTIC, *adj.* Pertaining, belonging, or relating to a home, a domicile, or to the place of birth, origin, creation, or transaction. Catto v. Plant, 106 Conn. 236, 137 A. 764, 765; In re Savin's Estate, 131 N.J.Eq. 563, 26 A.2d 270, 273.

As to domestic "Administrators," "Attachment," "Bill of Exchange," "Commerce," "Corporations," "Creditors," "Factors," "Fixtures," "Judgment," and "Manufactures," see those titles.

DOMESTIC ANIMALS. Such as are habituated to live in or about the habitations of men, or such as contribute to the support of a family or the wealth of the community. This term includes horses, (State v. Gould, 26 W.Va. 264; Osborn v. Lenox, 2 Allen [Mass.] 207,) male goat, (Young v. Blaum, La.App., 146 So. 168, 169); cattle (Yazoo & Mississippi R. Co. v. Gordon, 184 Miss. 885, 186 So. 631, 632; parrot (K. G. O. Construction Co. v. King, N.J.Dist.Ct., 12 N.J.Misc. 291, 171 A. 164, 165.

DOMESTIC COURTS. Those existing and having jurisdiction at the place of the party's residence or domicile. Dickinson v. Railroad Co., 7 W.Va. 417.

DOMESTIC PURPOSES. As regards rights of riparian owner, extends to culinary purposes and to purposes of cleansing, washing, feeding, and supplying an ordinary quantity of cattle. Cowell v. Armstrong, 290 P. 1036, 1038, 210 Cal.App. 218. It includes consumption and sustenance of human being and does not necessarily exclude occupants of hotels, apartments, boarding houses, etc. Prather v. Hoberg, 24 Cal.2d 549, 150 P.2d 405, 412.

DOMESTIC SERVANT. See Domestic.

DOMESTICATED. Made domestic or converted to domestic use. Commonwealth v. Flynn, 285 Mass. 136, 188 N.E. 627, 628, 92 A.L.R. 206.

DOMESTICUS. In old European law. A *seneschal,* steward, or *major domo;* a judge's assistant; an assessor, (*q. v.*). Spelman.

DOMICELLA. In old English law. A damsel. Fleta, lib. 1, c. 20, § 80.

DOMICELLUS. In old English law. A better sort of servant in monasteries; also an appellation of a king's bastard.

DOMICILE. That place where a man has his true, fixed, and permanent home and principal establishment, and to which whenever he is absent he has the intention of returning. Kurilla v. Roth, 132 N.J.L. 213, 38 A.2d 862, 864; In re Stabile, 348 Pa. 587, 36 A.2d 451, 458; Shreveport Long Leaf Lumber Co. v. Wilson, D.C.La., 38 F.Supp. 629, 631, 632. Not for a mere special or temporary purpose, but with the present intention of making a permanent home, for an unlimited or indefinite period. In re Garneau, 127 F. 677, 62 C.C.A. 403; In re Gilbert's Estate, 15 A.2d 111, 117, 118, 18 N.J. Misc. 540; In re Schultz' Estate, 316 Ill.App. 540, 45 N.E.2d 577, 582. Davis v. Davis, Ohio App., 57 N.E.2d 703, 704.

In international law, a residence at a particular place, accompanied with positive or presumptive proof of an intention to continue there for an unlimited time. State v. Collector of Bordentown, 32 N.J.Law, 192; Graham v. Graham, 81 N. W. 44, 9 N.D. 88; Phillimore, Int. Law 49.

The word "domicile" is derived from latin "domus", meaning home or dwelling house, and domicile is legal conception of "home". In re Schultz' Estate, 316 Ill.App. 540, 45 N.E.2d 577, 582, 316 Ill.App. 540.

The established, fixed, permanent, or ordinary dwelling-place or place of residence of a person, as distinguished from his temporary and transient, though actual, place of residence. It is his legal residence, as distinguished from his temporary place of abode; or his home, as distinguished from a place to which business or pleasure may temporarily call him. Towson v. Towson, 126 Va. 640, 102 S.E. 48, 52.

"Citizenship," "habitancy," and "residence" are severally words which in the particular case may mean precisely the same as domicile. Baker v. Keck, D.C.Ill., 13 F.Supp. 487. Earley v. Hershey Transit Co., D.C.Pa., 55 F.Supp. 981, 982; Dodd v. Lorenz, 210 Iowa 513, 231 N.W. 422, 424; Commonwealth ex rel. Fortney v. Bobrofskie, 329 Pa. 44, 196 A. 489, 490; Perkins v. Guaranty Trust Co., of New York, 274 N.Y. 250, 8 N.E.2d 849, 852.

"Domicile" and "residence," however, are frequently distinguished, in that domicile is the home, the fixed place of habitation; while residence is a transient place of dwelling. Fisher v. Jordan, C.C.A.Tex., 116 F.2d 183, 186; Minick v. Minick, 111 Fla. 469, 149 So. 483, 488; Hartzler v. Radeka, 265 Mich. 451, 251 N.W. 554.

Domicile may be deemed to be of three sorts,—domicile by birth, domicile by choice, and domicile by operation of law. The first is the common case of the place of birth, *domicilium originis;* the second is that which is voluntarily acquired by a party, *proprio motu;* the last is consequential, as that of the wife arising from marriage. Story, Confl. Laws, § 46. And see Railroad Co. v. Kimbrough, 115 Ky. 512, 74 S.W. 229; Johnson v. Harvey, 261 Ky. 522, 88 S.W.2d 42, 46, 47.

Abandonment of domicile, see Abandonment.

Commercial Domicile

A domicile acquired by the maintenance of a commercial establishment; a domicile which a citizen of a foreign country may acquire by conducting business in another country. 1 Kent, 82. See Dicey, Dom. 341; The Dos Hermanos, 2 Wheat. 76, 4 L.Ed. 189.

De Facto Domicile

In French law, permanent and fixed residence in France of an alien who has not acquired French citizenship nor taken steps to do so, but who intends to make his home permanently or indefinitely in that country; called domicile "de facto" because domicile in the full sense of that term, as used in France, can only be acquired by an act equivalent to naturalization. In re Cruger's Will, 36 Misc. 477, 73 N.Y.S. 812.

Domestic Domicile

A name sometimes used for "municipal domicile" (*q. v.*). Hayward v. Hayward, 65 Ind.App. 440, 115 N.E. 966, 970.

Domicile of Choice

The essentials of "domicile" of choice are the fact of physical presence at a dwelling place and the intention to make that place home. New York Trust Co. v. Riley, Del., 16 A.2d 772, 776, 783, 785; In re Eisenberg's Estate, 31 N.Y.S.2d 380, 384, 385, 386, 177 Misc. 655; Prince v. New York Life Ins. Co., D.C.Mass., 24 F.Supp. 41, 42.

Domicile of Corporation

Place considered by law as center of corporate affairs and place where its functions are discharged. Fisher & Van Gilder v. First Trust Joint-Stock Land Bank, 210 Iowa 531, 231 N.W. 671, 672, 69 A.L.R. 1340.

Domicile of Origin

The home of the parents. Phillim. Dom. 25, 101. That which arises from a man's birth and connections. 5 Ves. 750. The domicile of the parents at the time of birth, or what is termed the "domicile of origin," constitutes the domicile of an infant, and continues until abandoned, or until the acquisition of a new domicile in a different place. Struble v. Struble, Tex.Civ.App., 177 S.W.2d 279, 283.

Domicile of Succession

As distinguished from a commercial, political, or forensic domicile, the actual residence of a person within some jurisdiction, of such a character as shall, according to the well-established principles of public law, give direction to the succession of his personal estate. Smith v. Croom, 7 Fla. 81.

Elected Domicile

The domicile of parties fixed in a contract between them for the purposes of such contract. Woodworth v. Bank of America, 19 Johns., N.Y., 417, 10 Am.Dec. 239.

Foreign Domicile

A domicile established by a citizen or subject of one sovereignty within the territory of another.

Matrimonial Domicile

The place where a husband and wife have established a home, in which they reside in the relation of husband and wife, and where the matrimonial contract is being performed. Gould v. Gould, 201 App.Div. 670, 194 N.Y.S. 745, 747.

Municipal Domicile

One which as distinguished from "national domicile" and "quasi national domicile" (see those titles, *infra*), has reference to residence in a county, township, or municipality. Hayward v. Hayward, 65 Ind.App. 440, 115 N.E. 966, 970.

National Domicile

The domicile of a person, considered as being within the territory of a particular nation, and not with reference to a particular locality or subdivision of a nation.

Natural Domicile

The same as domicile of origin or domicile by birth. Johnson v. Twenty-One Bales, 13 Fed.Cas. 863.

Necessary Domicile

That kind of domicile which exists by operation of law, as distinguished from voluntary domicile or domicile of choice. Phillim. Dom. 27–97.

Quasi National Domicile

One involving residence in a state. Hayward v. Hayward, 65 Ind.App. 440, 115 N.E. 966, 970. See National Domicile, *supra*.

DOMICILED. Established in a given domicile; belonging to a given state or jurisdiction by right of domicile.

DOMICILIARY. Pertaining to domicile; relating to one's domicile. Existing or created at, or connected with, the domicile of a suitor or of a decedent.

DOMICILIARY ADMINISTRATION. Administration in state where person was domiciled at time of death is deemed principal or primary administration and is ordinarily termed "domiciliary administration." First Nat. Bank v. Blessing, 231 Mo.App. 288, 98 S.W.2d 149, 151, 231 Mo.App. 288.

DOMICILIATE. To establish one's domicile; to take up one's fixed residence in a given place. To establish the domicile of another person whose legal residence follows one's own.

DOMICILIATION. In Spanish law. The acquisition of domiciliary rights and status, nearly equivalent to naturalization, which may be accomplished by being born in the kingdom, by conversion to the Catholic faith there, by taking up a permanent residence in some settlement and marrying a native woman, and by attaching oneself to the soil, purchasing or acquiring real property and possessions. Yates v. Iams, 10 Tex. 168.

DOMICILIUM. Lat. Domicile (*q. v.*).

DOMIGERIUM. In old English law. Power over another; also danger. Bract. l. 4, t. 1, c. 10.

DOMINA (DAME). A title given to honorable women, who anciently, in their own right of inheritance, held a barony. Cowell.

DOMINANT ESTATE OR TENEMENT. That to which a servitude or easement is due, or for the benefit of which it exists. A term used in the civil and Scotch law, and thence in ours, relating to servitudes, meaning the tenement or subject in favor of which the service is constituted; as the tenement over which the servitude extends is called the "servient tenement." Union Falls Power Co. v. Marinette County, 238 Wis. 134, 298 N.W. 598, 600, 601, 134 A.L.R. 958.

DOMINATE. To master, to rule, or to control. Humble Oil & Refining Co. v. National Labor Relations Board, C.C.A.5, 113 F.2d 85, 88, 90.

DOMINATIO. In old English law. Lordship.

DOMINICA PALMARUM. (*Dominica in ramis palmarum.*) L. Lat. Palm Sunday. Townsh. Pl. 131; Cowell; Blount.

DOMINICAL. That which denotes the Lord's day, or Sunday.

DOMINICAN NUNS. An order of nuns founded by St. Dominic under a modified form of St. Augustine's rule, chiefly employed in teaching girls. Sacred Heart Academy of Galveston v. Karsch, 173 Tenn. 618, 122 S.W.2d 416, 417.

DOMINICIDE. The act of killing one's lord or master.

DOMINICUM. Lat. Domain; demain; demesne. A lordship. That of which one has the lordship or ownership. That which remains under the lord's immediate charge and control. Spelman; Blount.

In Domesday Book it meant the home farm as distinguished from the holdings of the tenants. Vinogradoff, Engl.Soc. in Eleventh Century 253.

Property; domain; anything pertaining to a lord. Cowell. In Ecclesiastical law. A church, or any other building consecrated to God. Du Cange.

DOMINICUM ANTIQUUM. In old English law. Ancient demesne. Bract. fol. 369*b*.

DOMINIO. Sp. In Spanish law. A term corresponding to and derived from the Latin *dominium* (*q. v.*). *Dominio alto*, eminent domain; *dominio directo*, immediate ownership; *dominio utile*, beneficial ownership. Hart v. Burnett, 15 Cal. 556.

DOMINION. Ownership, or right to property or perfect or complete property or ownership. Whelan v. Henderson, Tex.Civ.App., 137 S.W 2d 150, 153. Title to an article of property which arises from the power of disposition and the right of claiming it. Baker v. Westcott, 73 Tex. 129, 11 S.W. 157, 8 East, 579. See, also, State v. Johnson, 34 S.D. 601, 149 N.W. 730, 734.

Sovereignty or lordship; as the dominion of the seas. Moll. de Jure Mar. 91, 92.

In the civil law, with reference to the title to property which is transferred by a sale of it, dominion is said to be either "proximate" or "remote," the former being the kind of title vesting in the purchaser when he has acquired both the ownership and the possession of the article, the latter describing the nature of his title when he has legitimately acquired the ownership of the property but there has been no delivery. Coles v. Perry, 7 Tex. 109.

DOMINIUM. In the civil and old English law. Ownership; property in the largest sense, including both the right of property and the right of possession or use.

The mere right of property, as distinguished from the possession or usufruct. Dig. 41, 2, 17, 1; Calvin. The right which a lord had in the fee of his tenant. In this sense the word is very clearly distinguished by Bracton from *dominicum*.

The estate of a feoffee to uses. "The feoffees to use shall have the *dominium*, and the *cestui que use* the disposition." Latch. 137.

Sovereignty or dominion. *Dominium maris*, the sovereignty of the sea.

DOMINIUM DIRECTUM.

In the civil law. Strict ownership; that which was founded on strict law, as distinguished from equity. In later law. Property without use; the right of a landlord. Tayl. Civil Law 478. In feudal law. Right or proper ownership;—the right of a superior or lord, as distinguished from that of his vassal or tenant. The title or property which the sovereign in England is considered as possessing in all the lands of the kingdom, they being holden either immediately or mediately of him as lord paramount.

DOMINIUM DIRECTUM ET UTILE. The complete and absolute dominion in property; the union of the title and the exclusive use. Fairfax v. Hunter, 7 Cranch, 603, 3 L.Ed. 453.

DOMINIUM EMINENS. Eminent domain.

DOMINIUM NON POTEST ESSE IN PENDENTI. Lordship cannot be in suspense, *i. e.*, property cannot remain in abeyance. Halk. Law Max. 39.

DOMINIUM PLENUM. Full ownership; the union of the *dominium directum* with the *dominium utile*. Tayl. Civil Law, 478.

DOMINIUM UTILE. In the civil law. Equitable or prætorian ownership; that which was founded on equity. Mackeld. Rom. Law, § 327, note. In later law. Use without property; the right of a tenant. Tayl. Civil Law, 478. In feudal law. Useful or beneficial ownership; the usufruct, or right to the use and profits of the soil, as distinguished from the *dominium directum* (*q. v.*) or ownership of the soil itself; the right of a vassal or tenant. 2 Bl.Comm. 105.

DOMINO VOLENTE. Lat. The owner being willing; with the consent of the owner.

DOMINUS.

In feudal and ecclesiastical law. A lord, or feudal superior. *Dominus rex*, the lord the king; the king's title as lord paramount. 1 Bl.Comm. 367. *Dominus capitalis*, a chief lord. *Dominus medius*, a mesne or intermediate lord. *Dominus ligius*, liege lord or sovereign. Id.

Lord or sir; a title of distinction. It usually denoted a knight or clergyman; and, according to Cowell, was sometimes given to a gentleman of quality, though not a knight, especially if he were lord of a manor.

The owner or proprietor of a thing, as distinguished from him who uses it merely. Calvin. A master or principal, as distinguished from an agent or attorney. Story, Ag. § 3.

In the civil law. A husband. A family. Vicat.

DOMINUS CAPITALIS LOCO HÆREDIS HABETUR, QUOTIES PER DEFECTUM VEL DELICTUM EXTINGUITUR SANGUIS SUI TENENTIS. Co. Litt. 18. The supreme lord takes the place of the heir, as often as the blood of the tenant is extinct through deficiency or crime.

DOMINUS LITIS. Lat. The master of the suit; *i. e.*, the person who was really and directly interested in the suit as a party, as distinguished from his attorney or advocate. But the term is also applied to one who, though not originally a party, has made himself such, by intervention or otherwise, and has assumed entire control and responsibility for one side, and is treated by the court as liable for costs. Virginia Electric & Power Co. v. Bowers, 181 Va. 542, 25 S.E.2d 361, 363.

It is also said that the attorney himself, when the cause has been tried, becomes the *dominus litis*. Vicat.

DOMINUS NAVIS. In the civil law. The owner of a vessel. Dig. 39, 4, 11, 2; Wharton.

DOMINUS NON MARITABIT PUPILLUM NISI SEMEL. Co. Litt. 9. A lord cannot give a ward in marriage but once.

DOMINUS REX NULLUM HABERE POTEST PAREM, MULTO MINUS SUPERIOREM. The king cannot have an equal, much less a superior. 1 Reeve, Eng. Law, 115.

DOMITÆ. Lat. Tame; domesticated; not wild. Applied to domestic animals, in which a man may have an absolute property. 2 Bl.Comm. 391.

DOMMAGES INTÉRÊTS. In French law. Damages.

DOMO REPARANDA. A writ that lay for one against his neighbor, by the anticipated fall of whose house he feared a damage and injury to his own. Reg. Orig. 153.

DOMUS. Lat. In the civil and old English law. A house or dwelling; a habitation. Inst. 4, 4, 8; Townsh.Pl. 183–185. Shreveport Long Leaf Lumber Co. v. Wilson, D.C.La., 38 F.Supp. 629, 631. See Domicile.

DOMUS CAPITULARIS. In old records. A chapter-house; the chapter-house. Dyer, 26*b*.

DOMUS CONVERSORUM. An ancient house built or appointed by King Henry III. for such Jews as were converted to the Christian faith; but King Edward III., who expelled the Jews from the kingdom, deputed the place for the custody of the rolls and records of the chancery. Jacob.

DOMUS DEI. The house of God; a name applied to many hospitals and religious houses.

DOMUS MANSIONALIS. A mansion house. 1 Hale, P.C. 558; State v. Brooks, 4 Conn. 446; State v. Sutcliffe, 4 Strob. (S.C.) 376.

DOMUS PROCERUM. The house of lords, abbreviated into *Dom. Proc.*, or *D. P.*

DOMUS SUA CUIQUE EST TUTISSIMUM REFUGIUM. To every man his own house is his safest refuge. 5 Coke, 91*b*; 11 Coke, 82; 3 Inst. 162. The house of every one is to him as his castle and fortress, as well for his defense against injury and violence as for his repose. 5 Coke, 91*b*; Say. 227; Broom, Max. 432. A man's dwelling-house is his castle, not for his own personal protection merely, but also for the protection of his family and his property therein. 19 How.St. Tr. 1030.

DOMUS TUTISSIMUM CUIQUE REFUGIUM ATQUE RECEPTACULUM SIT. A man's house should be his safest refuge and shelter. The habitation of each one is an inviolable asylum for him. A maxim of the Roman law. Dig. 2, 4, 18.

DONA CLANDESTINA SUNT SEMPER SUSPICIOSA. 3 Coke, 81. Clandestine gifts are always suspicious. Noy, Max., 9th Ed. 152; 4 B. & C. 652; 1 M. & S. 253; Broom, Max. 289, 290.

DONARI VIDETUR, QUOD NULLO JURE COGENTE CONCEDITUR. Dig. 50, 17, 82. A thing is said to be given when it is yielded otherwise than by virtue of right (that is considered to be given which is granted when no law compels).

DONATARIUS. A donee; one to whom something is given. See Donee.

DONATIO. Lat. A gift. A transfer of the title to property to one who receives it without paying for it. Vicat. The act by which the owner of a thing voluntarily transfers the title and possession of the same from himself to another person, without any consideration. See Indiana N. & S. R. W. Co. v. City of Attica, 56 Ind. 476.

Its literal translation, "gift," has acquired in real law a more limited meaning, being applied to the conveyance of estates tail. 2 Bl.Comm. 316; Littleton, § 59; West, Symb. § 254; 4 Cruise, Dig. 51.

By the civil law (adopted into the English and American law) donations are either *inter vivos* (between living persons) or *mortis causa* (in anticipation of death.) As to these forms, see *infra*. A *donatio* or gift as between living persons is called *donatio mera* or *pura* when it is a simple gift without compulsion or consideration, that is, resting solely on the generosity of the donor, as in the case of most charitable gifts. It is called *donatio remuneratoria* when given as a reward for past services, but still not under any legal compulsion, as in the case of pensions and land-grants. It is called *donatio sub modo (*or *modalis)* when given for the attainment of some special object or on condition that the donee shall do something not specially for the benefit of the donor, as in the case of the endowment of hospitals, colleges, etc., coupled with the condition that they shall be established and maintained. Mackeld. Rom.Law, § 466; Fisk v. Flores, 43 Tex. 340; Noe v. Card, 14 Cal. 576. The following terms are also used: *Donatio conditionalis*, a conditional gift; *donatio relata*, a gift made with reference to some service already done, (Fisk v. Flores, 43 Tex. 340;) *donatio stricta et coarctura*, a restricted gift, as an estate tail.

DONATIO INOFFICIOSA. An inofficious (undutiful) gift; a gift of so great a part of the donor's property that the birthright portion of his heirs is diminished. Mackeld.Rom.Law, § 469.

DONATIO INTER VIVOS. A gift between the living. The ordinary kind of gift by one person to another. 2 Kent, Comm. 438; 2 Steph.Comm. 102. A term derived from the civil law. Inst. 2, 7, 2. A donation *inter vivos* (between living persons) is an act by which the donor divests himself at present and irrevocably of the thing given in favor of the donee who accepts it. Succession of Brand, 162 La. 880, 111 So. 267, 268.

There are three kinds of "donations inter vivos", namely, "gratuitous donations", "onerous donations", and "remunerative donations", the first being based on mere liberality, the second being burdened with charges imposed by the donee, and the third being recompense for services rendered. White v. White, La.App., 7 So.2d 255, 257.

DONATIO MORTIS CAUSA. A gift made by a person in sickness, who, apprehending his dissolution near, delivers, or causes to be delivered, to another the possession of any personal goods, to keep as his own in case of the donor's decease. 2 Bl.Comm. 514. The civil law defines it to be a gift under apprehension of death; as when anything is given upon condition that, if the donor dies, the donee shall possess it absolutely, or return it if the donor should survive or should repent of having made the gift, or if the donee should die before the donor. Adams v. Nicholas, 1 Miles (Pa.) 109-117. A gift in view of death is one which is made in contemplation, fear, or peril of death, and with intent that it shall take effect only in case of the death of the giver. Prendergast v. Drew, 103 Conn. 88, 130 A. 75, 76. A donation *mortis causa* (in prospect of death) is an act to take effect when the donor shall no longer exist, by which he disposes of the whole or a part of his property, and which is revocable.

DONATIO NON PRÆSUMITUR. A gift is not presumed. Jenk.Cent. 109.

DONATIO PERFICITUR POSSESSIONE ACCIPIENTIS. A gift is perfected [made complete] by the possession of the receiver. Jenk.Cent. 109, case 9. A gift is incomplete until possession is delivered. 2 Kent, Comm. 438; Ewing v. Ewing, 2 Leigh (Va.) 337.

DONATIO PRINCIPIS INTELLIGITUR SINE PRÆJUDICIO TERTII. Dav.Ir.K.B. 75. A gift of the prince is understood without prejudice to a third party.

DONATIO PROPTER NUPTIAS. A gift on account of marriage. In Roman law, the bridegroom's gift to the bride in anticipation of marriage and to secure her *dos* was called "*donatio* *ante nuptias;*" but by an ordinance of Justinian such gift might be made after as well as before marriage, and in that case it was called "*donatio propter nuptias.*" Mackeld.Rom.Law, § 572.

DONATION. A gift. Mills v. Stewart, 76 Mont. 429, 247 P. 332, 334, 47 A.L.R. 424; Darnell v. Equity Life Ins. Co.'s Receiver, 179 Ky. 465, 200 S. W. 967, 972; Fairfield v. Huntington, 23 Ariz. 528, 205 P. 814, 815, 22 A.L.R. 1438. United Brotherhood of Carpenters and Joiners of America v. Rogers, 165 Okl. 131, 25 P.2d 57. See Donatio.

As sometimes used, however, the term does not necessarily mean an absolute gift without any condition or consideration whatever. International & G. N. Ry. Co. v. Anderson County, Tex.Civ.App., 174 S.W. 305, 315.

A donation of real estate is certainly not a mortgage or privilege, but is a transfer of property of a peculiar kind, subject to revocation, sometimes without cause, and always subject to reduction at the suit of the forced heirs of the donor. Bank of Delphi v. Lea, 139 La. 730, 72 So. 187, 188.

In ecclesiastical law. A mode of acquiring a benefice by deed of gift alone, without presentation, institution, or induction. 3 Steph.Comm. 81.

DONATION LANDS. Lands granted from the public domain to an individual as a bounty, gift, or donation; particularly, in early Pennsylvania history, lands thus granted to soldiers of the revolutionary war.

DONATIONUM ALIA PERFECTA, ALIA INCEPTA ET NON PERFECTA, UT SI DONATIO LECTA FUIT ET CONCESSA, AO TRADITIO NONDUM FUERIT SUBSECUTA. Some gifts are perfect, others incipient and not perfect as if a gift were read and agreed to, but delivery had not then followed. Co.Litt. 56.

DONATIVE ADVOWSON. In ecclesiastical law. A species of advowson, where the benefice is conferred on the clerk by the patron's deed of donation, without presentation, institution, or induction. 2 Bl.Comm. 23; Termes de la Ley.

DONATIVE TRUST. May be created by transfer of property in trust as gift for benefit of another person or by proper declaration of legal owner of property that he will hold it in trust for another's benefit and does not require payment of any consideration by the beneficiary. Elbert v. Waples-Platter Co., Tex.Civ.App., 156 S.W.2d 146, 150, 151.

DONATOR. A donor; one who makes a gift, (*donatio.*)

DONATOR NUNQUAM DESINIT POSSIDERE, ANTEQUAM DONATORIUS INCIPIAT POSSIDERE. The donor never ceases to possess, until the donee begins to possess. Bract. fol. 41*b*; Dyer 281.

DONATORIUS. A donee; a person to whom a gift is made; a purchaser. Bract. fol. 13, et seq.

DONATORY. The person on whom the king bestows his right to any forfeiture that has fallen to the crown.

DONE. Distinguished from "made." "A 'deed made' may no doubt mean an 'instrument made;' but a 'deed done' is not an 'instrument done,'—it is an 'act done;' and therefore these words, 'made and done,' apply to acts, as well as deeds." Lord Brougham, 4 Bell, App.Cas. 38.

DONEC. Lat. As long as; while; until; within a certain time.

DONEC PROBETUR IN CONTRARIUM. [Given] until proof to the contrary. 19 C.J. p. 445.

DONEE. One who is invested with a power of appointment; the party executing a power; otherwise called the "appointer." 4 Kent, Comm. 316. One to whom a gift is made or a bequest given. He to whom lands or tenements are given in tail. Litt. § 57. In old English law. He to whom lands were given; the party to whom a *donatio* was made.

DONIS, STATUTE DE. See De Donis, the Statute.

DONNEUR D'AVAL. In French law. Guarantor of negotiable paper other than by indorsement.

DONOR. The party conferring a power. 4 Kent, Comm. 316. One who makes a gift. One who creates a trust. Ulmer v. Fulton, 129 Ohio St. 323, 195 N.E. 557, 97 A.L.R. 1170. He who gives lands or tenements to another in tail. Litt. § 57; Termes de la Ley. In old English law. He by whom lands were given to another; the party making a *donatio.*

DONUM. Lat. In the civil law. A gift; a free gift. Calvin.

The difference between *donum* and *munus* is said to be that *donum* is more general, while *munus* is specific. Vicat, Voc.Jur.; Calvin.

DOOM. In Scotch law. Judicial sentence, or judgment. The decision or sentence of a court orally pronounced by an officer called a "dempster" or "deemster." In modern usage, criminal sentences still end with the words "which is pronounced for doom."

DOOMSDAY-BOOK. See Domesday-Book.

DOOR. The place of usual entrance in a house, or into a room in the house. State v. McBeth, 49 Kan. 584, 31 P. 145.

DOPE. Any thick liquid or pasty preparation, as of opium for medicinal purposes, of grease for a lubricant, etc., and in popular meaning signifies opium derivative, ranging from harmless concoction to most powerful narcotics containing opium as ingredient. Abbott v. Vinson, 230 Ky. 786, 20 S.W.2d 995, 996.

DORMANT. Literally, sleeping; hence inactive; in abeyance; unknown; concealed; silent.

DORMANT CLAIM. One which is in abeyance.

DORMANT EXECUTION. One which a creditor delivers to the sheriff with directions to levy only, and not to sell, until further orders, or until a junior execution is received. See Storm v. Woods, 11 Johns. (N.Y.) 110; Kimball v. Munger, 2 Hill (N.Y.) 364.

DORMANT JUDGMENT. One which has not been satisfied, nor extinguished by lapse of time, but which has remained so long unexecuted that execution cannot now be issued upon it without first reviving the judgment, or one which has lost its lien on land from the failure to issue execution on it or take other steps to enforce it within the time limited by statute. 1 Black, Judgm., 2d Ed., § 462; Draper v. Nixon, 93 Ala. 436, 8 So. 489; General Electric Co. v. Hurd, C.C., 171 F. 984; Burlington State Bank v. Marlin Nat. Bank, Tex.Civ.App., 207 S.W. 954, 956.

DORMANT PARTNER. See Partners.

DORMITORY. A sleeping room or building containing a series of sleeping rooms, a sleeping apartment capable of containing many beds, especially one connected with a college or boarding school. Russell v. Trustees of Purdue University, 201 Ind. 367, 168 N.E. 529, 534, 65 A.L.R. 1384.

DORMIUNT ALIQUANDO LEGES, NUNQUAM MORIUNTUR. 2 Inst. 161. The laws sometimes sleep, never die.

DORSUM. Lat. The back. *In dorso recordi*, on the back of the record. 5 Coke, 44*b*.

DORTURE. (Contracted from *dormiture*.) A dormitory of a convent; a place to sleep in.

DOS. In Roman law. Dowry; a wife's marriage portion; all that property which on marriage is transferred by the wife herself or by another to the husband with a view of diminishing the burden which the marriage will entail upon him. It is of three kinds. *Profectitia dos* is that which is derived from the property of the wife's father or paternal grandfather. That *dos* is termed *adventitia* which is not *profectitia* in respect to its source, whether it is given by the wife from her own estate or by the wife's mother or a third person. It is termed *receptitia dos* when accompanied by a stipulation for its reclamation by the constitutor on the termination of the marriage. See Mackeld.Rom.Law, §§ 561, 563; Vicat; Calvinus, Lex.; Du Cange; 1 Washb.R.P. 147.

In old English law. The portion given to the wife by the husband at the church door, in consideration of the marriage; dower; the wife's portion out of her deceased husband's estate in case he had not endowed her. 1 Washb.R.P. 147; 1 Cruise, Dig. 152; Park, Dower.

DOS DE DOTE PETI NON DEBET. Dower ought not to be demanded of dower. Co.Litt. 31; 4 Coke, 122*b*. A widow is not dowable of lands assigned to another woman in dower. 1 Hill.Real Prop. 135; 4 Dane, Abr. 671; 1 Washb.R.P. 209; Brooks v. Everett, 13 Allen (Mass.) 459.

DOS RATIONABILIS. A reasonable marriage portion. A reasonable part of her husband's estate, to which every widow is entitled, of lands of which her husband may have endowed her on the day of marriage. Co.Litt. 336. Dower, at common law. 2 Bl.Comm. 134.

DOS RATIONABILIS VEL LEGITIMA EST CUJUSLIBET MULIERIS DE QUOCUNQUE TENEMENTO TERTIA PARS OMNIUM TERRARUM ET TENEMENTORUM, QUÆ VIR SUUS TENUIT IN DOMINIO SUO UT DE FEODO, ETC. Co.Litt. 336. Reasonable or legitimate dower belongs to every woman of a third part of all the lands and tenements of which her husband was seised in his demesne, as of fee, etc.

DOSSIER. Fr. A brief; a bundle of papers.

DOT. (A French word, adopted in Louisiana.) The fortune, portion, or dowry which a woman brings to her husband by the marriage. Buisson v. Thompson, 7 Mart.La., N.S., 460.

DOTAGE. That feebleness of the mental faculties which proceeds from old age. It is a diminution or decay of that intellectual power which was once possessed. It is the slow approach of death; of that irrevocable cessation, without hurt or disease, of all the functions which once belonged to the living animal. The external functions gradually cease; the senses waste away by degrees; and the mind is imperceptibly visited by decay. Owing's Case, 1 Bland (Md.) 389, 17 Am. Dec. 311.

DOTAL. Relating to the *dos* or portion of a woman; constituting her portion; comprised in her portion.

DOTAL PROPERTY. In the civil law, in Louisiana. Property which the wife brings to the husband to assist him in bearing the expenses of the marriage establishment. Extradotal property, otherwise called "paraphernal property," is that which forms no part of the dowry. Fleitas v. Richardson, 13 Sup.Ct. 495, 147 U.S. 550, 37 L.Ed. 276. See, also, Community.

DOTALITIUM. In canon and feudal law. Dower. Spelman, voc. "Doarium"; Calvin.; 2 Bl.Comm. 129. Used as early as A.D. 841.

DOTATION. The act of giving a dowry or portion; endowment in general, including the endowment of a hospital or other charitable institution.

DOTE, *n.* In Spanish law. The marriage portion of a wife. White, New Recop. b. 1, tit. 6, c. 1. The property which the wife gives to the husband on account of marriage, or for the purpose of supporting the matrimonial expenses. Id. b. 1, tit. 7, c. 1, § 1; Schm.Civil Law, 75; Cutter v. Waddingham, 22 Mo. 254; Hart v. Burnett, 15 Cal. 566; Las Partidas, 4. 11. 1; Escriche, Dic. Raz. *Dote*.

DOTE, *v.* To be besotted, delirious, silly, or insane. Gates v. Meredith, 7 Ind. 441.

DOTE ASSIGNANDA. A writ which lay for a widow, when it was judicially ascertained that a tenant to the king was seised of tenements in fee or fee-tail at the day of his death, and that he held of the king in chief. In such case the widow might come into chancery, and then make oath that she would not marry without the king's leave, and then she might have this writ. These widows were called the "king's widows." Jacob; Holthouse.

DOTE UNDE NIHIL HABET. A writ which lies for a widow to whom no dower has been assigned. 3 Bl.Comm. 182. By 23 & 24 Vict. c. 126, an ordinary action commenced by writ of summons has taken its place; but it remains in force in the United States, and under the designation of "dower *unde nihil habet*" (see that title), is the form in common use for the recovery of dower at law. 1 Washb.R.P. 290; 4 Kent 63.

DOTI LEX FAVET; PRÆMIUM PUDORIS EST; IDEO PARCATUR. Co.Litt. 31; Branch, Princ. The law favors dower; it is the reward of chastity; therefore let it be preserved.

DOTIS ADMINISTRATIO. Admeasurement of dower, where the widow holds more than her share, etc.

DOTISSA. A dowager.

DOUBLE. Twofold; acting in two capacities or having two aspects; multiplied by two. This term has ordinarily the same meaning in law as in popular speech. The principal compound terms into which it enters are noted below.

DOUBLE ASSESSMENT. The imposition of same tax, by same taxing power, upon same subject matter. Aragon v. Empire Gold Mining & Milling Co., 47 N.M. 299, 142 P.2d 539, 541.

DOUBLE ADULTERY. Adultery committed by two persons each of whom is married to another as distinguished from "single" adultery, where one of the participants is unmarried. Hunter v. U. S., 1 Pin. (Wis.) 91, 39 Am.Dec. 277.

DOUBLE AVAIL OF MARRIAGE. In Scotch law. Double the ordinary or single value of a marriage. Bell. See Duplex Valor Maritagii.

DOUBLE BOND. In Scotch law. A bond with a penalty, as distinguished from a single bond. 2 Kames, Eq. 359.

DOUBLE COMPLAINT, DOUBLE QUARREL, or DUPLEX QUERELA. A grievance made known by a clerk or other person, to the archbishop of the province, against the ordinary, for delaying or refusing to do justice in some cause ecclesiastical, as to give sentence, institute a clerk, etc. It is termed a "double complaint," because it is most commonly made against both the judge and him at whose suit justice is denied or delayed; the effect whereof is that the archbishop, taking notice of the delay, directs his letters, under his authentical seal, to all clerks of his province, commanding them to admonish the ordinary, within a certain number of days, to do the justice required, or otherwise to appear before him or his official, and there allege the cause of his delay; and to signify to the ordinary that if he neither perform the thing enjoined, nor appear nor show cause against it, he himself, in his court of audience, will forthwith proceed to do the justice that is due. Cowell.

DOUBLE COSTS. See Costs.

DOUBLE CREDITOR. One who has a lien on two funds. Newby v. Fox, 90 Kan. 317, 133 P. 890, 47 L.R.A.(N.S.) 302.

DOUBLE DAMAGES. See Damages.

DOUBLE EAGLE. A gold coin of the United States of the value of twenty dollars.

DOUBLE ENTRY. A system of mercantile bookkeeping, in which the entries in the day-book, etc., are posted twice into the ledger. First, to a personal account, that is, to the account of the person with whom the dealing to which any given entry refers has taken place; secondly, to an impersonal account, as "goods." Mozley & Whitley.

DOUBLE FINE. In old English law. A fine *sur done grant et render* was called a "double fine," because it comprehended the fine *sur cognizance de droit come ceo*, etc., and the fine *sur concessit*. 2 Bl.Comm. 353.

DOUBLE FLEMISH BOND. An arrangement whereby two stretchers are followed by a header throughout the entire course, while on the succeeding course the header is centered over the vertical joint between the two stretchers of the course below. Seglin Const. Co. v. State, Ct.Cl., 22 N.Y.S. 2d 94, 96.

DOUBLE GLAZING. That by which two panes of glass are set in each section of the window sash instead of one. Johnson v. Olsen, 134 Minn. 53, 158 N.W. 805, 806.

DOUBLE HOUSE. A building having accommodations for two families, divided vertically instead of horizontally. Donnelly v. Spitza, 246 Mich. 284, 224 N.W. 396. Schwarzer v. Calcasieu Lumber Co., Tex.Civ.App., 176 S.W.2d 597, 599.

DOUBLE INSURANCE. Double insurance is where divers insurances are made upon the same interest in the same subject against the same risks in favor of the same assured, in proportions exceeding the value. 1 Phill.Ins. §§ 359, 366. A double insurance exists where the same person is insured by several insurers separately in respect to the same subject and interest. Insurance Co. v. Gwathmey, 1 S.E. 209, 82 Va. 923; Lowell Mfg. Co. v. Safeguard F. Ins. Co., 88 N.Y. 597; Chereway v. Grangers Mut. Fire Ins. Co., 181 Md. 149, 28 A.2d 824, 825; Broune v. Franklin Fire Ins. Co., 225 Mo.App. 665, 37 S.W.2d 977, 981.

DOUBLE JEOPARDY. Common-law and constitutional prohibition against "double jeopardy" refers not to the same offense eo nomine but to the same crime, transaction or omission. Driggers v. State, 137 Fla. 182, 188 So. 118, 120. A second prosecution after a first trial for the same offense. People ex rel. Rozea v. Warden of Queens County Jail, 43 N.Y.S.2d 211, 213.

DOUBLE PATENTING. The test respecting "double patenting" is whether the claims of both patents, when properly construed in the light of the descriptions given, define essentially the same things. Waterbury Buckle Co. v. G. E. Prentice Mfg. Co., D.C.Conn., 294 F. 930, 937. Occurs only when claims of two patents issued to one applicant are the same. Scharf v. Weinfeld & Kahn, D.C. N.Y., 31 F.Supp. 689, 692.

The imposition of the same tax, by the same taxing power, upon the same subject matter. City of Philadelphia v. Heinel Motors, 16 A.2d 761, 764, 142 Pa.Super. 493. People ex rel. Toman v. Advance Heating Co., 376 Ill. 158, 33 N.E.2d 206, 209, 210.

DOUBLE PLEA, DOUBLE PLEADING. See Duplicity; Plea; Pleading.

DOUBLE POSSIBILITY. A possibility upon a possibility. 2 Bl.Comm. 170.

DOUBLE RECOVERY. Recovery which represents more than the total maximum loss which all parties have sustained. Hindmarsh v. Sulpho Saline Bath Co., 108 Neb. 168, 187 N.W. 806, 808.

DOUBLE RENT. In English law. Rent payable by a tenant who continues in possession after the time for which he has given notice to quit, until the time of his quitting possession. St. 11 Geo. II. c. 19.

DOUBLE TAX RULE. Collections made in taxable year on sales made in prior years, and which had already been taxed in prior years. Hoover-Bond Co. v. Denman, C.C.A.Ohio, 59 F.2d 909, 910.

DOUBLE TAXATION. The taxing of the same item or piece of property twice to the same person, or taxing it as the property of one person and again as the property of another; but this does not include the imposition of different taxes concurrently on the same property (*e. g.*, a city tax and a school tax), nor the taxation of the same piece of property to different persons when they hold different interests in it or when it represents different values in their hands, as when both the mortgagor and mortgagee of property are taxed in respect to their interests in it, or when a tax is laid upon the capital or property of a corporation and also upon the value of its shares of stock in the hands of the separate stockholders. Cook v. Burlington, 59 Iowa, 251, 13 N. W. 113, 44 Am.Rep. 679. "Double taxation" means taxing twice for the same purpose in the same year some of the property in the territory in which the tax is laid without taxing all of it. Diefendorf v. Gallet, 51 Idaho 619, 10 P.2d 307, 315; Amarillo-Pecos Valley Truck Lines v. Gallegos, 44 N.M. 120, 99 P.2d 447, 451.

DOUBLE USE. In patent law. An application of a principle or process, previously known and applied, to some new use, but which does not lead to a new result or the production of a new article. De Lamar v. De Lamar Min. Co., C.C.Idaho, 110 F. 542.

DOUBLE VALUE. In English law. This is a penalty on a tenant holding over after his landlord's notice to quit. By 4 Geo. II. c. 28, § 1, it is enacted that if any tenant for life or years hold over any lands, etc., after the determination of his estate, after demand made, and notice in writing given, for delivering the possession thereof, by the landlord, or the person having the reversion or remainder therein, or his agent thereunto lawfully authorized, such tenant so holding over shall pay to the person so kept out of possession at the rate of *double* the yearly value of the lands, etc., so detained, for so long a time as the same are detained. See Woodf. Landl. & Ten. (12th Ed.) 717, *et seq.*

DOUBLE VOUCHER. This was when a common recovery was had, and an estate of freehold was first conveyed to any indifferent person against whom the *præcipe* was brought, and then he vouched the tenant in tail, who vouched over the common vouchee. For, if a recovery were had immediately against a tenant in tail, it barred only the estate in the premises of which he was then actually seised, whereas, if the recovery were had against another person, and the tenant in tail were vouchee, it barred every latent right and interest which he might have in the lands recovered. 2 Bl.Comm. 359.

DOUBLE WASTE. When a tenant bound to repair suffers a house to be wasted, and then unlawfully fells timber to repair it, he is said to commit double waste. Co. Litt. 53.

DOUBLE WILL. A will in which two persons join, each leaving his property and estate to the other, so that the survivor takes the whole. Evans v. Smith, 28 Ga. 98, 73 Am.Dec. 751.

DOUBLES. Letters-patent. Cowell.

DOUBT, *v.* To question or hold questionable. Claussen v. State, 21 Wyo. 505, 133 P. 1055, 1056.

DOUBT, *n.* Uncertainty of mind; the absence of a settled opinion or conviction; the attitude of mind towards the acceptance of or belief in a proposition, theory, or statement, in which the judgment is not at rest but inclines alternately to either side. Rowe v. Baber, 93 Ala. 422, 8 So. 865; Smith v. Railway Co., 143 Mo. 33, 44 S.W. 718; West Jersey Traction Co. v. Camden Horse R. Co., 52 N.J.Eq. 452, 29 A. 333. An equipoise of the mind arising from an equality of contrary reasons. Ayliffe, Pand. 121.

Reasonable Doubt

This is a term often used, probably pretty well understood, but not easily defined. It does not mean a mere possible doubt, because everything relating to human affairs, and depending on moral evidence, is open to some possible or imaginary doubt. It is that state of the case which, after the entire comparison and consideration of all the evidence, leaves the minds of jurors in that condition that they cannot say they feel an abiding conviction to a moral certainty of the truth of the charge. If upon proof there is reasonable doubt remaining, the accused is entitled to the benefit of it by an acquittal; for it is not sufficient to establish a probability, though a strong one, arising from the doctrine of chances, that the fact charged is more likely to be true than the contrary, but the evidence must establish the truth of the fact to a reasonable and moral certainty,—a certainty that convinces and directs the understanding and satisfies the reason and judgment of those who are bound to act conscientiously upon it. This is proof beyond reasonable doubt; because if the law, which mostly depends upon considerations of a moral nature, should go further than this, and require absolute certainty, it would exclude circumstantial evidence altogether. Egan v. U. S., 52 App.D.C. 384, 287 F. 958.

Proof "beyond a reasonable doubt" is not beyond all possible or imaginary doubt, but such proof as precludes every reasonable hypothesis except that which it tends to support. It is proof "to a moral certainty,"—such proof as satisfies the judgment and consciences of the jury, as reasonable men, and applying their reason to the evidence before them, that the crime charged has been committed by the defendant, and so satisfies them as to leave no other reasonable conclusion possible. State v. Koski, 100 W.Va. 98, 130 S.E. 100, 101.

The difficulty of a satisfactory definition is discussed in 57 Am.L.Reg. 419, where C. J. Shaw's definition is criticized and that in Com. v. Costley, 118 Mass. 1, *supra,* is suggested as better. And in Hopt v. Utah, 120 U.S. 430, 7 S.Ct. 614, 30 L.Ed. 708, it was approved as contrasted with C. J. Shaw's definition.

A "reasonable doubt" is such a doubt as would cause a reasonable and prudent man in the graver and more important affairs of life to pause and hesitate to act upon the truth of the matter charged. But a reasonable doubt is not a mere possibility of innocence, nor a caprice, shadow, or speculation as to innocence not arising out of the evidence or the want of it. State v. Perkins, 21 N.M. 135, 153 P. 258, 259.

A "reasonable doubt" is such a doubt as an upright man might entertain in an honest investigation after truth. Peterson v. State, 47 Ga. 524(5); Lochamy v. State, 152 Ga. 235, 109 S.E. 497.

A "reasonable doubt" is one for which a reason can be given. State v. Jefferson, 43 La.Ann. 995, 10 So. 199. *Contra:* Abbott v. Territory, 20 Okl. 119, 94 P. 179, 16 L. R.A.,N.S., 260, 129 Am.St.Rep. 818.

The term needs no definition. People v. Rogers, 324 Ill. 224, 154 N.E. 909, 913.

DOUBTFUL PAPER. "Slow" paper and "doubtful paper" are not synonymous. American Nat. Bank of Portsmouth v. Ames, 169 Va. 711, 194 S.E. 784, 793.

DOUBTFUL TITLE. One as to the validity of which there exists some doubt, either as to matter of fact or of law; one which invites or exposes the party holding it to litigation. Barrett v. McMannis, 153 Kan. 420, 110 P.2d 774, 778; Black v. American International Corporation, 264 Pa. 260, 107 A. 737, 739. Distinguished from a "marketable" title, which is of such a character that the courts will compel its acceptance by a purchaser who has agreed to buy the property or has bid it in at public sale. Herman v. Somers, 158 Pa. 424, 27 A. 1050, 38 Am.St.Rep. 851.

DOUN. L. Fr. A gift. Otherwise written *"don"* and *"done."* The thirty-fourth chapter of Britton is entitled *"De Douns."*

DOVE. Doves are animals *feræ naturæ,* and not the subject of larceny unless they are in the owner's custody. Com. v. Chace, 9 Pick., Mass. 15, 19 Am.Dec. 348; Ruckman v. Outwater, 28 N.J.Law 581.

DOVETAIL. A structure in the form of a tenon having oppositely-flared edges similar in shape to the tail of a bird. Cheney Co. v. Cunningham, D.C.Pa., 37 F.Supp. 224, 226.

DOWABLE. Subject to be charged with dower; as dowable lands.

Entitled or entitling to dower. Thus, a dowable interest in lands is such as entitles the owner to have such lands charged with dower.

DOWAGER. A widow who is endowed, or who has a jointure in lieu of dower. In England, this is a title or addition given to the widows of princes, dukes, earls, and other noblemen, to distinguish them from the wives of the heirs, who have right to bear the title. 1 Bl.Comm. 224.

DOWAGER–QUEEN. The widow of the king. As such she enjoys most of the privileges belonging to her as queen consort. It is not treason to conspire her death or violate her chastity, because the succession to the crown is not thereby endangered. No man, however, can marry her without a special license from the sovereign, on pain of forfeiting his lands or goods. 1 Bl.Comm. 233.

DOWER. The provision which the law makes for a widow out of the lands or tenements of her husband, for her support and the nurture of her children. Co. Litt. 30*a*; 2 Bl.Comm. 130; In re Miller's Estate, 44 N.M. 214, 100 P.2d 908, 911. A species of life-estate which a woman is, by law, entitled to claim on the death of her husband, in the lands and tenements of which he was seised in fee during the marriage, and which her issue, if any, might by possibility have inherited. 1 Steph.Comm. 249; 2 Bl.Comm. 129; Cruise, Dig. tit. 6; 2 Crabb, Real Prop. p. 124, § 1117; 4 Kent, Comm. 35. See Inchoate Dower.

"Dower" is the life estate to which every married woman is entitled on death of her husband, intestate, or, in case she dissents from his will, one-third in value of all lands of which husband was beneficially seized in law or in fact, at any time during coverture. McGehee v. McGehee, 189 N. C. 558, 127 S.E. 684, 687. McLawhorn v. Smith, 211 N.C. 513, 191 S.E. 35, 38, 110 A.L.R. 980.

The term, both technically and in popular acceptation, has reference to real estate exclusively. Shackelford v. Shackelford, 181 Va. 869, 27 S.E.2d 354, 359.

"Dower," in modern use, is distinguished from "dowry." The former is a provision for a widow on her husband's death; the latter is a bride's portion on her marriage. Wendler v. Lambeth, 163 Mo. 428, 63 S.W. 684.

DOWER AD OSTIUM ECCLESIÆ. Dower at the church door or porch. An ancient kind of dower in England, where a man, (being tenant in fee-simple, of full age,) openly *at the church door,* where all marriages were formerly celebrated, after affiance made and troth plighted between them, *endowed* his wife with the whole of his lands, or such quantity as he pleased, at the same time specifying and ascertaining the same. Litt. § 39; 2 Bl.Comm. 133.

DOWER BY COMMON LAW. The ordinary kind of dower in English and American law, consisting of a life interest in one-third of the lands of which the husband was seised in fee at any time during the coverture. Litt. § 36; 2 Bl.Comm. 132; 2 Steph.Comm. 302; 4 Kent, Comm. 35.

DOWER BY CUSTOM. A kind of dower in England, regulated by custom, where the quantity allowed the wife differed from the proportion of the common law; as that the wife should have half the husband's lands; or, in some places, the whole; and, in some, only a quarter. 2 Bl.Comm. 132; Litt. § 37.

DOWER DE LA PLUS BELLE (DE LA PLUIS BEALE). L. Fr. Dower of the fairest [part.] A species of ancient English dower, incident to the old tenures, where there was a guardian in chivalry, and the wife occupied lands of the heir as guardian in socage. If the wife brought a writ of dower against such guardian in chivalry, he might show this matter, and pray that the wife might be endowed *de la plus belle* of the tenement in socage. Litt. § 48. This kind of dower was abolished with the military tenures. 2 Bl.Comm. 132.

DOWER EX ASSENSU PATRIS. Dower by the father's assent. A species of dower *ad ostium ecclesiœ,* made when the husband's father was alive, and the son, by his consent expressly given, endowed his wife with parcel of his father's lands. Litt. § 40; 2 Bl.Comm. 133; Grogan v. Garrison, 27 Ohio St. 61.

DOWER UNDE NIHIL HABET. A writ of right which lay for a widow to whom no dower had been assigned.

DOWLE STONES. Stones dividing lands, etc. Cowell.

DOWMENT. In old English law. Endowment; dower. Grogan v. Garrison, 27 Ohio St. 61.

DOWNWARD COURSE. Term "dip" is miners' word synonymous with expression "downward course" in mining act, and means direction of ore vein or lode in its descent into earth at right angles to its strike or course. 30 U.S.C.A. § 26. Brugger v. Lee Yim, 12 Cal.App.2d 38, 55 P.2d 564, 570.

DOWRESS. A woman entitled to dower; a tenant in dower. 2 P.Wms. 707.

DOWRY. The property which a woman brings to her husband in marriage; now more commonly called a "portion."

This word expresses the proper meaning of the *"dos"* of the Roman, the *"dot"* of the French, and the *"dote"* of the Spanish, law, but is a very different thing from "dower," with which it has sometimes been confounded. See Co.Litt. 31; Dig. 23, 3, 76; Code 5, 12, 20; Buard v. De Russy, 6 Rob., La., 111; Gates v. Legendre, 10 Rob., La., 74; Cutter v. Waddingham, 22 Mo. 254.

By dowry, in the Louisiana Civil Code (see article 2337), is meant the effects which the wife brings to the husband to support the expenses of marriage. It is given to the husband, to be enjoyed by him so long as the marriage shall last, and the income of it belongs to him. He alone has the administration of it during marriage, and his wife cannot deprive him of it. The real estate settled as dowry is inalienable during marriage, unless the marriage contract contains a stipulation to the contrary. De Young v. De Young, 6 La.Ann. 786.

DOYLE RULE. A formula for computing the board measure from the dimensions of a log. Peter v. Owl Bayou Cypress Co., 137 La. 1067, 69 So. 840, 841. The rule is to deduct four inches from the diameter of the log, as an allowance for slab, square one-quarter of the remainder, and multiply the result by the length of the log in feet. Morrison v. Pickrell Walnut Co., 199 Ill. App. 175, 176.

DOZE. To slumber or sleep lightly. St. Paul Fire & Marine Ins. Co. of St. Paul, Minn., v. Kendle, 163 Ky. 146, 173 S.W. 373, 374.

DOZEIN. L. Fr. Twelve; a person twelve years of age. St. 18 Edw. II.; Barring. Ob. St. 208.

DOZEN PEERS. Twelve peers assembled at the instance of the barons, in the reign of Henry III., to be privy counselors, or rather conservators of the kingdom.

DR. An abbreviation for "doctor;" also, in commercial usage, for "debtor," indicating the items or particulars in a bill or in an account-book chargeable against the person to whom the bill is rendered or in whose name the account stands, as opposed to "Cr." ("Credit" or "creditor"), which indicates the items for which he is given credit. Jaqua v. Shewalter, 10 Ind.App. 234, 37 N.E. 1072.

DRACHMA. A term employed in old pleadings and records, to denote a groat. Townsh. P. 180.

An Athenian silver coin, of the value of about fifteen cents.

DRACO REGIS. The standard, ensign, or military colors borne in war by the ancient kings of England, having the figure of a dragon painted thereon.

DRACONIAN LAWS. A code of laws prepared by Draco, the celebrated lawgiver of Athens. These laws were exceedingly severe, and the term is now sometimes applied to any laws of unusual harshness.

DRAFF. Waste matter, sweepings, refuse, lees, or dregs. In weighing commodities the term signifies dust and dirt, and not what is generally meant by "draught" or "draft" (*q. v.*). 28 C.J.S. p. 227.

DRAFT. The common term for a bill of exchange; as being *drawn* by one person on another. Hinnemann v. Rosenback, 39 N.Y. 100; Ennis v. Coshocton Nat. Bank, 27 Ga.App. 479, 108 S.E. 811.

An order for the payment of money drawn by one person on another. It is said to be a *nomen generalissimum,* and to include all such orders. Wilson v. Buchenau, D.C.Cal., 43 F.Supp. 272, 275.

The term includes a cashier's check, People v. Miller, 278 Ill. 490, 116 N.E. 131, 138 L.R.A.1917E, 797; Advance-Rumely Thresher Co. v. Hess, 85 Mont. 293, 279 P. 236, 237; but a draft is distinguishable from a cashier's check in that a draft is a bill of exchange payable on demand purporting to be drawn on deposit while a cashier's check is a primary obligation of a bank which issues it and constitutes its written promise to pay it on demand. In re Bank of U. S., 277 N.Y.S. 96, 243 App.Div. 287. It is distinguished from "check" by the fact that in a draft the drawer is a bank, while in the ordinary check the drawer is an individual. Leach v. Mechanics' Sav. Bank, 202 Iowa, 899, 211 N.W. 506, 508, 50 A.L.R. 388.

A tentative, provisional, or preparatory writing out of any document (as a will, contract, lease, etc.) for purposes of discussion and correction, which is afterwards to be copied out in its final shape.

Also, a small arbitrary deduction or allowance made to a merchant or importer, in the case of goods sold by weight or taxable by weight, to cover possible loss of weight in handling or from differences in scales. Marriott v. Brune, 9 How. 633, 13 L.Ed. 282; Seeberger v. Mfg. Co., 15 S. Ct. 583, 157 U.S. 183, 39 L.Ed. 665; Napier v. Barney, 17 Fed.Cas. 1149.

A draft in stockyard parlance is all those animals in one consignment weighed as a single sales or purchase classification. Acker v. U. S., D. C.Ill., 12 F.Supp. 776, 780.

DRAFTSMAN. Any one who draws or frames a legal document, *e. g.,* a will, conveyance, pleading, etc.

In the marine engineering profession, any of various men who design the several parts of vessels and other machinery in the different departments. Ex parte Aird, D.C.Pa., 276 F. 954, 956.

DRAG. In a technical sense, the lower part of the mold for casting iron pipe. Casey-Hedges Co. v. Gates, 139 Tenn. 282, 201 S.W. 760, 761.

DRAGO DOCTRINE. The principle asserted by Luis Drago, Minister of Foreign Affairs of the Argentine Republic, in a letter to the Argentine Minister at Washington, December 29, 1902, that the forcible intervention of states to secure the payment of public debts due to their citizens from foreign states is unjustifiable and dangerous to the security and peace of the nations of South America. The subject was brought before the Conference by the United States and a Convention was adopted in which the contracting powers agreed, with some restrictive conditions, not to have recourse to armed force for the recovery of contract debts claimed by their nationals against a foreign state. Higgins, 184–197. See Calvo Doctrine.

DRAGOMAN. An interpreter employed in the east, and particularly at the Turkish court.

DRAIN, *v.* To conduct water from one place to another, for the purpose of drying the former. To make dry; to draw off water; to rid land of its superfluous moisture by adapting or improving natural water courses and supplementing them, when necessary, by artificial ditches. People v. Parks, 58 Cal. 639.

To "drain," in its larger sense, includes not only the supplying of outlets and channels to relieve the land from water, but also the provision of ditches, drains, and embankments to prevent water from accumulating. Holt v. State, Tex.Civ.App., 176 S.W. 743, 746; In re Mississippi and Fox River Drainage Dist., 270 Mo. 157, 192 S.W. 727, 731; Pioneer Real Estate Co. v. City of Portland, 119 Or. 1, 247 P. 319, 323.

DRAIN, *n.* A trench or ditch to convey water from wet land; a channel through which water may flow off.

The word has no technical legal meaning. Any hollow space in the ground, natural or artificial, where water is collected and passes off, is a ditch or drain. Sherrod v. Battle, 154 N.C. 345, 70 S.E. 834, 836.

The term may be synonymous with "water course." Green v. County Com'rs of Harbine, 74 Ohio St. 318, 78 N.E. 521, 522.

"Sewers" differ from "drains" only in that the former are in cities, and generally covered over, while the latter are in rural communities, and open. Barton v. Drainage Dist. No. 30, 174 Ark. 173, 294 S.W. 418, 419. But "drains" may sometimes include sewers. City of Charlestown, 170 Ill. 336, 48 N.E. 985, 986. See, generally, Mound City Land & Stock Co. v. Miller, 170 Mo. 240, 70 S.W. 721, 724, 6 L.R.A. 190, 94 Am.St.Rep. 727.

Also, sometimes, the easement or servitude (acquired by grant or prescription) which consists in the right to drain water through another's land. See 3 Kent, Comm. 436; 7 M. & G. 354.

DRAINAGE DISTRICT. A political subdivision of the state, created for the purpose of draining and reclaiming wet and overflowed land, as well as to preserve the public health and convenience. Commander v. Board of Com'rs of Buras Levee Dist., 202 La. 325, 11 So.2d 605, 607.

DRAM. In common parlance, a drink of some substance containing alcohol; something which can produce intoxication. Lacy v. State, 32 Tex. 228. See Wright v. People, 101 Ill. 134.

DRAM-SHOP. A drinking saloon, where liquors are sold to be drunk on the premises. Com. v. Marzynski, 21 N.E. 228, 149 Mass. 68. A place where spirituous liquors are sold by the dram or the drink; a barroom. McCormick v. Brennan, 224 Ill.App. 251, 254.

DRAM SHOP ACT. A civil damage statute directed at the operators of dram shops and at owners of buildings and premises wherein the operators are tenants. It permits an action to be brought by a person injured by an intoxicated person against one who contributed to the intoxication. See 1958 Univ. of Ill.Law Forum, No. 2 "Actions under the Illinois Dram Shop Act," and John A. Appleman, "Civil liability under the Illinois Dram Shop Act," 34 Ill.L.Rev. 30 (1939), Wanna v. Miller (N.Dak.) 136 N.W.2d 563 (1965).

DRAMA. A term descriptive of any representation in which a story is told, a moral conveyed, or the passions portrayed, whether by words and actions combined, or by mere actions alone. Asa G. Candler, Inc., v. Georgia Theater Co., 148 Ga. 188, 96 S.E. 226, 227, L.R.A.1918F, 389. A story put in action. Zucarro v. State, 82 Tex.Cr.R. 1, 197 S.W. 982, 985, L.R.A.1918B, 354.

DRAMATIC COMPOSITION. In copyright law. A literary work setting forth a story, incident, or scene from life, in which, however, the narrative is not related, but is represented by a dialogue and action; may include a descriptive poem set to music, or a pantomime, but not a composition for musical instruments alone, nor a mere spectacular exhibition or stage dance. Martinetti v. McGuire, 16 Fed.Cas. 920; Fuller v. Bemis, C. C.N.Y., 50 Fed. 926.

DRAMATIC WORK. Photoplay is "dramatic work" within Copyright Law. Metro-Goldwyn-Mayer Distributing Corporation v. Bijou Theatre of Holyoke, D.C.Mass., 3 F.Supp. 66, 73; contra. Metro-Goldwyn-Mayer Distributing Corporation v. Bijou Theatre, D.C.Mass., 50 F.2d 908, 909.

DRAUGHT. Act of drawing, or the thing drawn; act of moving loads by drawing as by beasts of burden, and the like; and the term may be used in the sense of pull. Jackson Floor Covering v. Maryland Casualty Co. of Baltimore, 117 N.J.L. 401, 189 A. 84, 85.

DRAW, *n.* A movable section of a bridge, which may be raised up or turned to one side, so as to admit the passage of vessels. Gildersleeve v. Railroad Co., D.C.N.Y., 82 Fed. 766; A depression in the surface of the earth, in the nature of a shallow ravine or gulch, sometimes many miles in length, forming a channel for the escape of rain and melting snow draining into it from either side. Railroad Co. v. Sutherland, 44 Neb. 526. 62 N.W. 859.

DRAW, *v.* To draw a firearm or deadly weapon is to point it intentionally. State v. Boyles, 24 N. M. 464, 174 P. 423. To draw a bead on; to bring into line with the bead or fore sight of a rifle and the hind sight; to aim at. Hatfield v. Commonwealth, 200 Ky. 243, 254 S.W. 748, 749.

To prepare a draft; to compose and write out in due form, as, a deed, complaint, petition, memorial, etc. Winnebago County State Bank v. Hustel, 119 Iowa 115, 93 N.W. 70.

To draw a jury is to select the persons who are to compose it, either by taking their names successively, but at hazard, from the jury box, or by summoning them individually to attend the court. Smith v. State, 34 So. 168, 136 Ala. 1.

In old criminal practice. To drag (on a hurdle) to the place of execution. Anciently no hurdle was allowed, but the criminal was actually dragged along the road to the place of execution. A part of the ancient punishment of traitors was to be thus drawn. 4 Bl.Comm. 92, 377.

In mercantile law. To draw a bill of exchange is to write (or cause it to be written) and sign it; to make, as a note. Knox v. Rivers Bros., 17 Ala.App. 630, 88 So. 33, 34.

In fiscal law and administration. To take out money from a bank, treasury, or other depository in the exercise of a lawful right and in a lawful manner. But to "draw a warrant" is not to draw the money; it is to make or execute the instrument which authorizes the drawing of the money. Brown v. Fleischner, 4 Or. 149.

DRAWBACK. In the customs laws, an allowance made by the government upon the duties due on imported merchandise when the importer, instead of selling it here, re-exports it; or the refunding of such duties if already paid. This allowance amounts, in some cases, to the whole of the original duties; in others, to a part only. See 19 U.S.C.A. § 1313.

DRAWEE. A person to whom a bill of exchange is addressed, and who is requested to pay the amount of money therein mentioned.

DRAWER. The person drawing a bill of exchange and addressing it to the drawee. Boatenreiter v. Williams, 58 Ga.App. 635, 199 S.E. 558, 559.

DRAWING. In patent law. A representation of the appearance of material objects by means of lines and marks upon paper, cardboard, or other substance. Ampt v. Cincinnati, 8 Ohio Dec. 628; 35 U.S.C.A. § 34.

DRAWLATCHES. Thieves; robbers. Cowell.

DRAYAGE. A charge for the transportation of property in wheeled vehicles, such as drays, wagons, and carts. Soule v. San Francisco Gaslight Co., 54 Cal. 242.

DREDGE. Formerly applied to a net or drag for taking oysters; now a machine for cleansing canals and rivers. To "dredge" is to gather or take with a dredge, to remove sand, mud, and filth from the beds of rivers, harbors, and canals, with a dredging machine. 15 Can.L.T. 268.

DREIT-DREIT. Droit-droit. (Also written without the hyphen.) Double right. A union of the right of possession and the right of property. 2 Bl.Comm. 199.

DRENCHES, or DRENGES. In Saxon law. Tenants *in capite*. They are said to be such as, at the coming of William the Conqueror, being put out of their estates, were afterwards restored to them, on their making it appear that they were the true owners thereof, and neither *in auxilio* or *consilio* against him. Spelman.

DRENGAGE. The tenure by which the drenches, or drenges, held their lands. A variety of feudal tenure by *serjeanty* (*q. v.*), often occurring in the northern counties of England, involving a kind of general service. Vinogradoff, Engl.Soc. in Eleventh Cent. 62. Little is known of it; 3 Holdsw.Hist.E.L. 132.

DRESSING. In the meat packing industry. The freeing of the carcass of hair, scurf, toenails, evisceration of the carcass, the cleaning and separation of the warm fancy meats, and the placing of these in the coolers. Likewise, all the operations performed upon the carcasses after slaughtering and until they go to the coolers, are included. The cleaning of casings is considered as "dressing", as is the grading of casings, if the grading takes place prior to salting. The removal of hides, pelts, bones, fats, blood and other materials from the dressing floor is also considered as "dressing" in the meat packing industry. Fleming v. Swift & Co., D.C.Ill., 41 F.Supp. 825, 828. Freeing of body from feathers and matters not suitable for consumption. Shain v. Armour & Co., D.C.Ky., 50 F.Supp. 907, 911.

DRIER. In the paper-making trade, a hot drum. Tompkins-Hawley-Fuller Co. v. Holden, C.C.A.N.Y., 273 F. 424, 430.

DRIFT, *v.* To float or be driven along by or as a current of water or air; to accumulate in heaps by the force of the wind; to be driven into heaps, as snow or sand drifts. State ex rel. Perkins v. Hardwick, 144 Kan. 3, 57 P.2d 1231, 1234.

DRIFT, *n.* In mining law. An underground passage driven horizontally along the course of a mineralized vein or approximately so. Distinguished from "shaft," which is an opening made at the surface and extending downward into the earth vertically, or nearly so, upon the vein or intended to reach it; and from "tunnel," which is a lateral or horizontal passage underground intended to reach the vein or mineral deposit, where drifting may begin. Jurgenson v. Diller, 114 Cal. 491, 46 P. 610, 55 Am.St.Rep. 83; Empire Star Mines Co. v. Butler, 62 Cal.App.2d 49, 145 P.2d 49, 63.

In old English law. A driving, especially of cattle.

DRIFT NET. A net with both ends free to drift with the current;—distinguished from a "set net," which is one fastened at one or both ends, so the whole net cannot drift with the current. State v. Blanchard, 96 Or. 79, 189 P. 421, 427.

DRIFT-STUFF. This term signifies, not goods which are the subject of salvage, but matters floating at random, without any known or discoverable ownership, which, if cast ashore, will probably never be reclaimed, but will, as a matter of course, accrue to the riparian proprietor. Watson v. Knowles, 13 R.I. 641.

DRIFTS OF THE FOREST. A view or examination of what cattle are in a forest, chase, etc., that it may be known whether it be surcharged or not; and whose the beasts are, and whether they are commonable. These drifts are made at certain times in the year by the officers of the forest, when all cattle are driven into some pound or place inclosed, for the before-mentioned purposes, and also to discover whether any cattle of strangers be there, which ought not to common. Manwood, p. 2, c. 15.

DRIFTING. The natural tendency of wells drilled in search of oil or gas to deflect from vertical. Gliptis v. Fifteen Oil Co., 204 La. 896, 16 So.2d 471, 476.

DRIFTLAND, DROFLAND, or DRYFLAND. A Saxon word, signifying a tribute or yearly payment made by some tenants to the king, or their landlords, for driving their cattle through a manor to fairs or markets. Cowell.

DRIFTWAY. A road or way over which cattle are driven. Selw.N.P. 1037; Woolr.Ways 1; 2 Hilliard, Abr.Prop. 33; Smith v. Ladd, 41 Me. 314; Swensen v. Marino, 306 Mass. 582, 29 N.E.2d 15, 18, 130 A.L.R. 763.

DRILL AND COMPLETE A WELL. Term "drill and complete a well" to known oil sand for purpose of testing and operating for oil production means cleaning out of well, so that sand reached may give flow of production. Arnold v. Adams, 147 Okl. 57, 294 P. 142, 147.

DRILLED. Completed;—said of oil wells and the like. Texas Pac. Coal & Oil Co. v. Harris, Tex. Civ.App., 230 S.W. 237, 238. The term implies progress in the work, and not mere use of the drill. Texas Const. Co. v. Dearing, Tex.Civ.App., 296 S.W. 1112, 1115.

DRILLING IN. Drilling, as an oil well, after the casing has been set. Smith & Hayslip v. Wilcox Oil Co., Tex.Civ.App., 253 S.W. 641, 642.

DRINCLEAN. Sax. A contribution of tenants, in the time of the Saxons, towards a potation, or ale, provided to entertain the lord, or his steward. Cowell. See Cervisarii.

DRINK. To use liquid as a beverage to slake thirst. State v. Woodward, 41 Idaho 353, 238 P. 525, 527. See, also, Merle v. Beifeld, 194 Ill.App. 364, 385. Specifically, to use intoxicating liquors.

DRINKABLE. Capable of being drunk; fit to drink. McChristy v. State, 138 Tex.Cr.R. 26, 133 S.W.2d 976, 977.

DRINKING MAN. One who takes a drink of liquor when he chooses, even though it may be so infrequent as to produce no harmful effect on his health. Tuepker v. Sovereign Camp, W. O. W., Mo.App., 226 S.W. 1002, 1003.

DRINKING-SHOP. A place where intoxicating liquors are sold, bartered, or delivered to be drunk on the premises. Portland v. Schmidt, 13 Or. 17, 6 Pac. 221.

DRIP. A species of easement or servitude obligating one man to permit the water falling from another man's house to fall upon his own land. 3 Kent, Comm. 436; 1 Rolle, Abr. 107. A mechanism which hastens the condensation of moisture and collects the liquid in a reservoir from which it is drained into a storage tank. Slater v. United Fuel Gas Co., 126 W.Va. 127, 27 S.E.2d 436, 437.

DRIVE, *n.* An underground process. Diller v. St. Louis, S. & P. R. R., 304 Ill. 373, 136 N.E. 703, 704.

DRIVE, *v.* To impel motion and quicken. Bosse v. Marye, 80 Cal.App. 109, 250 P. 693, 696. To compel, urge, or move in some manner or direction. Howell v. J. Mandelbaum & Sons, 160 Iowa 119, 140 N.W. 397, 398, Ann.Cas.1915D, 349. To control the motive power, as of a motor vehicle. Grant v. Chicago, M. & St. P. Ry. Co., 78 Mont. 97, 252 P. 382, 385. To go by, or pass in, a carriage whose course is wholly or partly under one's direction. Federal Life Ins. Co. v. McAleer, 161 Okl. 251, 17 P.2d 681, 683.

DRIVE-IT-YOURSELF CARS. A term used to describe automobiles which their owners, as a regular business, rent out for hire without furnishing drivers. City of Rockford v. Nolan, 316 Ill. 60, 146 N.E. 564. See, also, Welch v. Hartnett, 127 Misc. 221, 215 N.Y.S. 540; White v. Holmes, 89 Fla. 251, 103 So. 623; Blashfield's Cyclopedia of Automobile Law, p. 2802.

DRIVER. One employed in conducting or operating a coach, carriage, wagon, or other vehicle, with horses, mules, or other animals, or a bicycle, tricycle, or motor car, though not a street railroad car. A person actually doing driving, whether employed by owner to drive or driving his own vevehicle. Wallace v. Woods, 340 Mo. 452, 102 S.W.2d 91, 97.

DRIVING. To urge forward under guidance, compel to go in a particular direction, urge onward, and direct the course of. Mould v. Travelers' Mut. Casualty Co., 219 Iowa 16, 257 N.W. 349.

DROFDEN, or DROFDENNE. A grove or woody place where cattle are kept. Jacob.

DROFLAND. Sax. A quit rent, or yearly payment, formerly made by some tenants to the king, or their landlords, for *driving* their cattle through a manor to fairs or markets. Cowell; Blount.

DROIT. In French law. Right, justice, equity, law, the whole body of law; also a right. Toullier, n. 96; Pothier, *Droit.*

This term exhibits the same ambiguity which is discoverable in the German equivalent, *"recht"* and the English word *"right."* On the one hand, these terms answer to the Roman *"jus,"* and thus indicate law in the abstract, considered as the foundation of all rights, or the complex of underlying moral principles which impart the character of justice to all positive law, or give it an ethical content. Taken in this abstract sense, the terms may be adjectives, in which case they are equivalent to "just," or nouns, in which case they may be paraphrased by the expressions "justice," "morality," or "equity." On the other hand, they serve to point out *a* right; that is, a power, privilege, faculty, or demand, inherent in one person, and incident upon another. In the latter signification, *droit* (or *recht* or *right*) is the correlative of "duty" or "obligation." In the former sense, it may be considered as opposed to wrong, injustice, or the absence of law. *Droit* has the further ambiguity that it is sometimes used to denote the existing body of law considered as one whole, or the sum total of a number of individual laws taken together. See Jus; Recht; Right.

In old English law. Law; right; a writ of right. Co.Litt. 158*b*.

A person was said to have *droit droit, plurimum juris,* and *plurimum possessionis,* when he had the freehold, the fee, and the property in him. Crabb, Hist.E.L. 406.

—Autre droit. The right of another.

DROITS CIVILS. This phrase in French law denotes private rights, the exercise of which is independent of the *status* (*qualité*) of citizen. Foreigners enjoy them; and the extent of that enjoyment is determined by the principle of reciprocity. Conversely, foreigners may be sued on contracts made by them in France. Brown.

DROIT-CLOSE. An ancient writ, directed to the lord of ancient demesne on behalf of those of his tenants who held their lands and tenements by charter in fee-simple, in fee-tail, for life, or in dower. Fitzh.Nat.Brev. 23.

DROIT COMMON. The common law. Litt. § 213; Co.Litt. 142*a*.

DROIT COUTUMIER. Common law.

DROIT D'ACCESSION. That property which is acquired by making a new species out of the material of another. It is equivalent to the Roman *"specificatio."* This subject is treated of in the *Code Civil de Napoléon*, arts. 565, 577; Merlin, *Répert. Accession;* Malleville's Discussion, art. 565.

DROIT D'ACCROISSEMENT. The right which an heir or legatee has of combining with his own interest in a succession the interest of a coheir or colegatee who either refuses to or cannot accept his interest. Houghton v. Brantingham, 86 Conn. 630, 86 A. 664, 667.

DROIT D'AUBAINE. A rule by which all the property of a deceased foreigner, whether movable or immovable, was confiscated to the use of the state, to the exclusion of his heirs, whether claiming *ab intestato* or under a will of the deceased. Finally abolished in 1819. Opel v. Shoup, 100 Iowa 407, 69 N.W. 560, 37 L.R.A. 583.

DROIT D'EXÉCUTION. The right of a stockbroker to sell the securities bought by him for account of a client, if the latter does not accept delivery thereof. The same expression is also applied to the sale by a stockbroker of securities deposited with him by his client, in order to guaranty the payment of operations for which the latter has given instructions. Arg.Fr.Merc.Law, 557.

DROIT DE BRIS. A right formerly claimed by the lords of the coasts of certain parts of France, to shipwrecks, by which not only the property, but the persons of those who were cast away, were confiscated for the prince who was lord of the coast. Otherwise called *"droit de bris sur le naufrage."* This right prevailed chiefly in Bretagne, and was solemnly abrogated by Henry III. as duke of Normandy, Aquitaine, and Guienne, in a charter granted A. D. 1226, preserved among the rolls at Bordeaux.

DROIT DE DÉTRACTION. A tax upon the removal from one state or country to another of property acquired by succession or testamentary disposition; it does not cover a tax upon the succession to or transfer of property. Moody v. Hagen, 162 N.W. 704, 708, 36 N.D. 471, L.R.A.1918F, 947, Ann.Cas.1918A, 933. Cf. Duties of Detraction.

DROIT DE GARDE. In French feudal law. Right of ward. The guardianship of the estate and person of a noble vassal, to which the king, during his minority, was entitled. Steph.Lect. 250.

DROIT DE GÎTE. In French feudal law. The duty incumbent on a *roturier*, holding lands within the royal domain, of supplying board and lodging to the king and to his suite while on a royal progress. Steph.Lect. 351.

DROIT DE GREFFE. In old French law. The right of selling various offices connected with the custody of judicial records or notarial acts. Steph. Lect. 354. A privilege of the French kings.

DROIT DE MAÎTRISE. In old French law. A charge payable to the crown by any one who, after having served his apprenticeship in any commercial guild or brotherhood, sought to become a master workman in it on his own account. Steph. Lect. 354.

DROIT DE NAUFRAGE. The right of a seigneur, who owns the seashore, or the king, when a vessel is wrecked, to take possession of the wreckage and to kill the crew or sell them as slaves. 14 Yale L.Jour. 129.

DROIT DE PRISE. In French feudal law. The duty (incumbent on a *roturier*) of supplying to the king on credit, during a certain period, such articles of domestic consumption as might be required for the royal household. Steph.Lect. 351.

DROIT DE QUINT. In French feudal law. A relief payable by a noble vassal to the king as his *seigneur*, on every change in the ownership of his fief. Steph.Lect. 350.

DROIT DE SUITE. The right of a creditor to pursue the debtor's property into the hands of third persons for the enforcement of his claim.

DROIT-DROIT. A double right; that is, the right of possession and the right of property. These two rights were, by the theory of our ancient law, distinct; and the above phrase was used to indicate the concurrence of both in one person, which concurrence was necessary to constitute a complete title to land. Mozley & Whitley.

DROIT ÉCRIT. In French law. (The written law.) The Roman civil law, or *Corpus Juris Civilis*. Steph.Lect. 130.

DROIT INTERNATIONAL. International law.

DROIT MARITIME. Maritime law.

DROIT NATUREL. Fr. The law of nature.

DROIT NE POET PAS MORIER. Right cannot die. Jenk.Cent. 100, case 95.

DROIT NE DONE PLUIS QUE SOIT DEMAUNDE. The law gives not more than is demanded. 2 Inst. 286.

DROITS OF ADMIRALTY. Rights or perquisites of the admiralty. A term applied to goods found derelict at sea. Applied also to property captured in time of war by non-commissioned vessels of a belligerent nation. 1 Kent, Comm. 96; 2 Sel.Essays in Anglo-Amer.Leg.Hist. 318; 15 L.Q.R. 359; Marsden, Admiralty, Droits and Salvage; 1 W. Rob. 423. In England, it has been usual in maritime wars for the government to seize and condemn, as droits of admiralty, the property of an enemy found in her ports at the breaking out of hostilities. 1 C.Rob. 196; 13 Ves. 71; 1 Edw. 60; 3 Bos. & P. 191. The power to exercise such a right has not been delegated to, nor has it ever been claimed by, the United States government. Benedict, Adm. § 33; Brown v. U. S., 8 Cranch, 110, 3 L.Ed. 504.

DROITURAL. What belongs of right; relating to right; as real actions are either droitural or possessory,—*droitural* when the plaintiff seeks to recover the property. Finch, Law, 257.

DROMONES, DROMOS, DROMUNDA. These were at first high ships of great burden, but afterwards those which we now call "men-of-war." Jacob.

DROP. In English practice. When the members of a court are equally divided on the argument showing cause against a rule *nisi*, no order is made, *i. e.*, the rule is neither discharged nor made absolute, and the rule is said to *drop*. In practice, there being a right to appeal, it has been usual to make an order in one way, the junior judge withdrawing his judgment. Wharton.

DROP-LETTER. A letter addressed for delivery in the same city or district in which it is posted.

DROP SHIPMENT DELIVERY. In mercantile usage, this phrase refers to ordinary freight unloaded from railroad cars;—distinguished from carload shipments, known as "track delivery shipments." Boshell v. Receivers of St. Louis & S. F. R. Co., 200 Ala. 366, 76 So. 282, 284.

DROPPING GROUND. In the logging industry, a place on the bank of a stream to store sawlogs, railroad ties, staves, and the products of the forest, while waiting for a rise of the stream that will enable the owner to float his timbered products down the river to a market. Lexington & E. Ry. Co. v. Grigsby, 176 Ky. 727, 197 S.W. 408.

DROVE. A number of animals collected and driven together in a body; a flock or herd of cattle in process of being driven; indefinite as to number, but including at least several. McConvill v. Jersey City, 39 N.J.Law, 43.

DROVE-ROAD. In Scotch law. A road for driving cattle. 7 Bell, App.Cas. 43, 53, 57. A drift-road. Lord Brougham, Id.

DROVE-STANCE. In Scotch law. A place adjoining a drove-road, for resting and refreshing sheep and cattle on their journey. 7 Bell, App.Cas. 53, 57.

DROVER'S PASS. A free pass given by a railroad company, accepting a drove of cattle for transportation, to the drover who accompanies and cares for the cattle on the train. Railway Co. v. Ivy, 71 Tex. 409, 9 S.W. 346, 1 L.R.A. 500, 10 Am.St.Rep. 758.

DROWN. To merge or sink. "In some cases a right of freehold shall *drown* in a chattel." Co. Litt. 266*a*, 321*a*.

DRU. A thicket of wood in a valley. Domesday.

DRUG. The general name of substances used in medicine; any substance, vegetable, animal, or mineral, used in the composition or preparation of medicines; any substance used as a medicine. Carroll Perfumers v. State, Ind., 7 N.E.2d 970, 972; Hammond v. State, 173 Ark. 674, 293 S.W. 714, 717. The term is also applied to materials used in dyeing and in chemistry. See, generally, Collins v. Banking Co., 79 N.C. 281, 28 Am.Rep. 322; Insurance Co. v. Flemming, 65 Ark. 54, 44 S.W. 464, 39 L.R.A. 789, 67 Am.St.Rep. 900.

DRUG STORE. A place where drugs are sold. Department of State v. Kroger Grocery & Baking Co., Ind.App., 40 N.E.2d 375, 378; Carroll Perfumers v. State, 212 Ind. 455, 7 N.E.2d 970, 972.

DRUGGIST. A dealer in drugs; one whose business is to sell drugs and medicines. In strict usage, this term is to be distinguished from "apothecary." A druggist deals in the uncompounded medicinal substances; the business of an apothecary is to mix and compound them. But in America the two words are used interchangeably, as the same persons usually discharge both functions. State v. Donaldson, 41 Minn. 74, 42 N.W. 781.

DRUGLESS PRACTITIONER. Any person who practises or holds himself out in any way as practising the treatment of any ailment, disease, defect, or disability of the human body by manipulation, adjustment, manual or electrotherapy, or by any similar method. State v. Houck, Wash., 203 P.2d 693, 699.

DRUMMER. A term applied to commercial agents who travel for wholesale merchants and supply the retail trade with goods or take orders for goods to be shipped to the retail dealer. Thomas v. Hot Springs, 34 Ark. 557, 36 Am.Rep. 24.

DRUNGARIUS. In old European law. The commander of a *drungus,* or band of soldiers. Applied also to a naval commander. Spelman.

DRUNGUS. In old European law. A band of soldiers, (*globus militum.*) Spelman.

DRUNK. A person is "drunk" when he is so far under the influence of liquor that his passions are visibly excited or his judgment impaired, or when his brain is so far affected by potations of liquor that his intelligence, sense-perceptions, judgment, continuity of thought or of ideas, speech, and coordination of volition with muscular action (or some of these faculties or processes) are impaired or not under normal control. Wilson v. Inter-Ocean Casualty Co., 210 N.C. 585, 188 S.E. 102, 106. It is a synonym of intoxicated. Gault v. State, 42 Okl.Cr. 89, 274 P. 687, 688.

DRUNKARD. He is a drunkard whose habit it is to get drunk; whose ebriety has become habitual. The terms "drunkard" and "habitual drunkard" mean the same thing. Gourlay v. Gourlay, 16 R.I. 705, 19 A. 142. Pollon v. State, 218 Wis. 466, 261 N.W. 224, 225.

A "common" drunkard is defined by statute in some states as a person who has been convicted of drunkenness (or proved to have been drunk) a certain number of times within a limited period. State v. Flynn, 16 R.I. 10, 11 A. 170. Elsewhere the word "common" in this connection is understood as being equivalent to "habitual," Com. v. McNamee, 112 Mass. 286; or perhaps as synonymous with "public," Com. v. Whitney, 5 Gray, Mass., 86.

DRUNKENNESS. In medical jurisprudence. The condition of a man whose mind is affected by the immediate use of intoxicating drinks; the state of one who is "drunk." Mutual Life Ins. Co. v. Johnson, 64 Okl. 222, 166 P. 1074, 1076. The effect produced upon the mind or body by drinking intoxicating liquors to such an extent that the normal condition of the subject is changed and his capacity for rational action and conduct is substantially lessened. Lecates v. Lecates, Del.Super., 190 A. 294, 296. See Drunk.

DRY, *adj.* In the vernacular, this term means desiccated or free from moisture; but, in legal use, it signifies formal or nominal, without imposing any duty or responsibility, or unfruitful, without bringing any profit or advantage.

DRY, *n.* Term used to designate a person who is opposed to allowing the sale of intoxicating liquors; a prohibitionist; in contradistinction to a "wet," or antiprohibitionist. State v. Shumaker, 200 Ind. 623, 157 N.E. 769, 778, 58 A.L.R. 954.

DRY CHECK. Synonymous with "cold check", and "hot check". Elder v. Evatt, Tex.Civ.App., 154 S.W.2d 684, 685.

DRY-CRÆFT. Witchcraft; magic. Anc. Inst. Eng.

DRY DOCK. Watertight basin, which allows examination and work on bottom of vessel after pumping out. Maryland Casualty Co. v. Lawson,

C.C.A.Fla., 101 F.2d 732, 733. Whatever may have been the definition of a "dry dock" in the past, the definition must be enlarged to include modern facilities for repairing boats out of the water, as the meaning of the term, used in its common, ordinary sense, is a dry place to work in. Continental Casualty Co. v. Lawson, D.C.Fla., 2 F. Supp. 459, 460.

DRY EXCHANGE. In English law. A term formerly in use, said to have been invented for the purpose of disguising and covering usury; something being pretended to pass on both sides, whereas, in truth, nothing passed but on one side, in which respect it was called "dry." Cowell; Blount.

DRY ICE. Solid carbon dioxide. Carbo-Frost v. Pure Carbonic, C.C.A.Mo., 103 F.2d 210, 213; New York Eskimo Pie Corporation v. Rataj, C.C.A.Pa., 73 F.2d 184, 186.

DRY MORTGAGE. One which creates a lien on land for the payment of money, but does not impose any personal liability upon the mortgagor, collateral to or over and above the value of the premises. Frowenfeld v. Hastings, 134 Cal. 128, 66 P. 178.

DRY-MULTURES. In Scotch law. Corn paid to the owner of a mill, whether the payers grind or not.

DRY NATURAL GAS. Natural gas that does not contain an appreciable amount of readily condensible gasoline. When natural gas contains readily condensible gasoline it is called "wet natural gas." Mussellem v. Magnolia Petroleum Co., 107 Okl. 183, 231 P. 526, 530.

DRY OIL. A petroleum liquid carrying in cohesion with it less than 3 per cent. by volume of water and sediment. Alamitos Land Co. v. Shell Oil Co., 3 Cal.2d 396, 44 P.2d 573, 575.

DRY RECEIVERSHIP. Receivership wherein there is no equity to be administered for general creditors, even if action is in statutory form. Maxwell Lumber Co. v. Connelly, 34 N.M. 562, 287 P. 64, 67.

DRY RENT. Rent seck; a rent reserved without a clause of distress.

DRY TRUST. A passive trust; one which requires no action on the part of the trustee beyond turning over money or property to the *cestui que trust.* Trautz v. Lemp, 329 Mo. 580, 46 S.W.2d 135, 142.

DRY WEIGHT. In tariff laws, this term does not mean the weight of an article after desiccation in a kiln, but its air-dry weight as understood in commerce. U. S. v. Perkins, 66 F. 50, 13 C.C.A. 324.

DUAL BUSINESS. Must show units of substantial separateness and completeness, such as might be maintained as an independent business and capable of producing profit in and of themselves. Maxwell v. Kent-Coffey Mfg. Co., 204 N.C. 365, 168 S.E. 397, 399, 90 A.L.R. 476.

DUAL NATIONALITY. Fact that two states make equal claim to the allegiance of an individual at the same time. Perkins v. Elg, App.D.C., 59 S.Ct. 884, 894, 307 U.S. 325, 83 L.Ed. 1320.

DUARCHY. A form of government where two reign jointly.

DUAS UXORES EODEM TEMPORE HABERE NON LICET. It is not lawful to have two wives at the same time. Inst. 1, 10, 6; 1 Bl.Comm. 436.

DUBITANS. Doubting. Dobbin, J., *dubitans.* 1 Show. 364.

DUBITANTE. Doubting. Is affixed to the name of a judge, in the reports, to signify that he doubted the decision rendered.

DUBITATUR. It is doubted. A word frequently used in the reports to indicate that a point is considered doubtful.

DUBITAVIT. Doubted. Vaughan, C. J., *dubitavit.* Freem. 150.

DUCAT. A foreign coin, varying in value in different countries, but usually worth about $2.26 of our money.

DUCATUS. In feudal and old English law. A duchy, the dignity or territory of a duke.

DUCES TECUM. (Lat. Bring with you.) The name of certain species of writs, of which the *subpœna duces tecum* is the most usual, requiring a party who is summoned to appear in court to bring with him some document, piece of evidence, or other thing to be used or inspected by the court.

DUCES TECUM LICET LANGUIDUS. (Bring with you, although sick.) In practice. An ancient writ, now obsolete, directed to the sheriff, upon a return that he could not bring his prisoner without danger of death, he being *adeo languidus,* (so sick;) whereupon the court granted a *habeas corpus* in the nature of a *duces tecum licet languidus.* Cowell; Blount.

DUCHY OF LANCASTER. Those lands which formerly belonged to the dukes of Lancaster, and now belong to the crown in right of the duchy. The duchy is distinct from the county palatine of Lancaster, and includes not only the county, but also much territory at a distance from it, especially the Savoy in London and some land near Westminster. 3 Bl.Comm. 78.

DUCHY COURT OF LANCASTER. A tribunal of special jurisdiction, held before the chancellor of the duchy, or his deputy, concerning all matters of equity relating to lands holden of the crown in right of the duchy of Lancaster; which is a thing very distinct from the county palatine, (which has also its separate chancery, for sealing of writs, and the like,) and comprises much territory which lies at a vast distance from it; as particularly a very large district surrounded by the city of Westminster. The proceedings in this court are the same as were those on the equity side of the court of chancery, so that it seems not to be a court of record; and, indeed, it has been holden that the court of chancery has a concurrent jurisdiction with the duchy court, and may take cognizance of the same causes. Jud.Act 1873, § 18; 3 Bl.Comm. 78.

DUCKING-STOOL. See Castigatory.

DUCROIRE. In French law. Guaranty; equivalent to *del credere,* (which see.)

DUE. Just; proper; regular; lawful; sufficient; remaining unpaid; reasonable; as in the phrases "due care," "due process of law," "due notice."

Owing; payable; justly owed. That which one contracts to pay or perform to another; that which law or justice requires to be paid or done.

Owed, or owing, as distinguished from payable. A debt is often said to be *due* from a person where he is the party owing it, or primarily bound to pay, whether the time for payment has or has not arrived. The same thing is true of the phrase "due and owing."

Payable. A bill or note is commonly said to be *due* when the time for payment of it has arrived.

Final is not synonymous with due. Twine v. Locke, D.C.N.Y., 3 F.Supp. 1012, 1013.

The word "due" always imports a fixed and settled obligation or liability, but with reference to the time for its payment there is considerable ambiguity in the use of the term, as will appear from the foregoing definitions, the precise signification being determined in each case from the context. It may mean that the debt or claim in question is now (presently or immediately) matured and enforceable, or that it matured at some time in the past and yet remains unsatisfied, or that it is fixed and certain but the day appointed for its payment has not yet arrived. But commonly, and in the absence of any qualifying expressions, the word "due" is restricted to the first of these meanings, the second being expressed by the term "overdue," and the third by the word "payable." See Feeser v. Feeser, 93 Md. 716, 50 A. 406.

DUE AND PROPER CARE. That degree of care which is required of one for prevention of the accident. Odgers v. Clark, Del.Super., 19 A.2d 724, 726, 2 Terry 232.

DUE AND REASONABLE CARE. Care which reasonably prudent man would exercise under circumstances. Southern Ry. Co. v. Whetzel, 159 Va. 796, 167 S.E. 427, 431.

DUE CARE. Just, proper, and sufficient care, so far as the circumstances demand it; the absence of negligence. That care which an ordinarily prudent person would have exercised under the circumstances. "Due care" is care proportioned to any given situation, its surroundings, peculiarities, and hazards. It may and often does require extraordinary care. Tower v. Camp, 103 Conn. 41, 130 A. 86, 89. "Due care," "reasonable care," and "ordinary care" are convertible terms. Corthell v. Great Atlantic & Pacific Tea Co., 291 Mass. 242, 196 N.E. 850, 851; Sweeney v. Blue Anchor Beverage Co., 325 Pa. 216, 189 A. 231, 234.

This term, as usually understood in cases where the gist of the action is the defendant's negligence, implies not only that a party has not been negligent or careless, but that he has been guilty of no violation of law in relation to the subject-matter or transaction which constitutes the cause of action.

DUE CONSIDERATION. To give such weight or significance to a particular factor as under the circumstances it seems to merit, and this involves discretion. United States ex rel. Maine Potato Growers & Shippers Ass'n v. Interstate Commerce Commission, 88 F.2d 780, 783, 66 App.D.C. 398.

DUE COMPENSATION. For condemned land is the value of land taken and the damages, if any, which result to him as a consequence of the taking without considering either general benefits or injuries. Mississippi State Highway Commission v. Hillman, 189 Misc. 850, 198 So. 565, 569.

DUE COURSE HOLDER. See "Holder in Due Course."

DUE COURSE OF LAW. This phrase is synonymous with "due process of law," or "the law of the land," and the general definition thereof is "law in its regular course of administration through courts of justice;" and, while not always necessarily confined to judicial proceedings, yet these words have such a signification, when used to designate the kind of an eviction, or ouster, from real estate by which a party is dispossessed, as to preclude thereunder proof of a constructive eviction resulting from the purchase of a paramount title when hostilely asserted by the party holding it. Direct Plumbing Supply Co. v. City of Dayton, 138 Ohio St. 540, 38 N.E.2d 70, 72, 137 A.L.R. 1058.

DUE DATE. Time appointed or required for filing a tax return and, in the event of an extension of time to file return, is the date to which period for filing is extended. Langer v. Gray, N.D., 15 N.W.2d 732, 735. Under federal Revenue Act, "due date," is the date fixed for payment of tax, or several installments thereof. American Exchange Irving Trust Co. v. U. S., Ct.Cl., 52 F.2d 1027, 1028.

Within Texas inheritance tax law due date is not date of assessment, but last day on which taxes could be paid without incurring penalty. Halff v. U. S., Ct.Cl., 5 F.Supp. 132, 135.

DUE DILIGENCE. See Diligence.

DUE INFLUENCE. Influence obtained by persuasion and argument or by appeals to the affections. In re Chamberlain's Estate, Cal.App., 109 P.2d 449, 452.

DUE NOTICE. No fixed rule can be established as to what shall constitute "due notice." "Due" is a relative term, and must be applied to each case in the exercise of the discretion of the court in view of the particular circumstances. Slattery v. Doyle, 61 N.E. 264, 180 Mass. 27; Shellenberger v. Warburton, 124 A. 189, 190, 279 Pa. 577; Carson v. Kalisch, 99 A. 199, 202, 89 N.J.Law, 458; Franklin Brass Foundry Co. v. Shapiro & Aronson, C.C.A.Pa., 278 F. 435, 436; City of Sebree v. Powell, 298 S.W. 1103, 1104, 221 Ky. 478.

DUE POSTING. Includes stamping and placing letter in United States mail. Tharp v. Loeb Hardware Co., 135 So. 412, 413, 24 Ala.App. 344.

DUE PROCESS OF LAW. Law in its regular course of administration through courts of justice. 3 Story, Const. 264, 661. "Due process of law in each particular case means such an exercise of the powers of the government as the settled maxims of law permit and sanction, and under such safeguards for the protection of individual rights as those maxims prescribe for the class of cases to which the one in question belongs." Cooley, Const. Lim. 441. Whatever difficulty may be experienced in giving to those terms a definition which will embrace every permissible exertion of power affecting private rights, and exclude such as is forbidden, there can be no doubt of their meaning when applied to judicial proceedings. They then mean a course of legal proceedings according to those rules and principles which have been established in our systems of jurisprudence for the enforcement and protection of private rights. To give such proceedings any validity, there must be a tribunal competent by its constitution—that is, by the law of its creation—to pass upon the subject-matter of the suit; and, if that involves merely a determination of the personal liability of the defendant, he must be brought within its jurisdiction by service of process within the state, or his voluntary appearance. Pennoyer v. Neff, 95 U.S. 733, 24 L.Ed. 565. Due process of law implies the right of the person affected thereby to be present before the tribunal which pronounces judgment upon the question of life, liberty, or property, in its most comprehensive sense; to be heard, by testimony or otherwise, and to have the right of controverting, by proof, every material fact which bears on the question of right in the matter involved. If any question of fact or liability be conclusively presumed against him, this is not due process of law. Zeigler v. Railroad Co., 58 Ala. 599. These phrases in the constitution do not mean the general body of the law, common and statute, as it was at the time the constitution took effect; for that would seem to deny the right of the legislature to amend or repeal the law. They refer to certain fundamental rights, which that system of jurisprudence, of which ours is a derivative, has always recognized. Brown v. Levee Com'rs, 50 Miss. 468. "Due process of law," as used in the constitution, cannot mean less than a prosecution or suit instituted and conducted according to the prescribed forms and solemnities for ascertaining guilt, or determining the title to property. Embury v. Conner, 3 N.Y. 511, 517, 53 Am.Dec. 325. And see, generally, Davidson v. New Orleans, 96 U.S. 104, 24 L.Ed. 616.

"Law of the land," "due course of law," and "due process of law" are synonymous. People v. Skinner, Cal., 110 P.2d 41, 45; State v. Rossi, 71 R.I. 284, 43 A.2d 323, 326; Direct Plumbing Supply Co. v. City of Dayton, 138 Ohio St. 540, 38 N.E.2d 70, 72, 137 A.L.R. 1058; Stoner v. Higginson, 316 Pa. 481, 175 A. 527, 531. But "judicial process" and "judicial proceedings" are not necessarily synonymous with "due process." Pennsylvania Publications v. Pennsylvania Public Utility Commission, 152 Pa.Super. 279, 32 A.2d 40, 49; Barry v. Hall, 98 F.2d 222, 68 App.D.C. 350. The essential elements of "due process of law" are notice and opportunity to be heard and to defend in orderly proceeding adapted to nature of case, and the guarantee of due process requires that every man have protection of day in court and benefit of general law. Dimke v. Finke, 209 Minn. 29, 295 N.W. 75, 79; Di Maio v. Reid, 13 N.J.L. 17, 37 A.2d 829, 830. Daniel Webster defined this phrase to mean a law which hears before it condemns, which proceeds on inquiry and renders judgment only after trial. Wichita Council No. 120 of Security Ben. Ass'n v. Security Ben. Assn., 138 Kan. 841, 28 P.2d 976, 980, 94 A.L.R. 629; J. B. Barnes Drilling Co. v. Phillips, 166 Okla. 154, 26 P.2d 766. This constitutional guaranty demands only that law shall not be unreasonable, arbitrary, or capricious, and that means selected shall have real and substantial relation to object. Nebbia v. People of State of New York, N.Y., 54 S.Ct. 505, 291 U.S. 502, 78 L.Ed. 940, 89 A.L.R. 1469; North American Co. v. Securities and Exchange Commission, C.C.A., 133 F.2d 148, 154.

DUE PROOF. Within policies requirements mean such a statement of facts, reasonably verified, as, if established in court, would prima facie require payment of the claim, and does not mean some particular form of proof which the insurer arbitrarily demands. Misskelley v. Home Life Ins. Co., 205 N.C. 496, 171 S.E. 862, 868; National Life Ins. Co. v. White, D.C.Mun.App., 38 A.2d 663, 666. Sufficient evidence to support or produce a conclusion; adequate evidence. Lando v. Equitable Life Assur. Soc. of U. S., D.C.Cal., 11 F.Supp. 729, 732.

DUE REGARD. Consideration in a degree appropriate to demands of the particular case. Willis v. Jonson, 279 Ky. 416, 130 S.W.2d 828, 832.

DUE TO. Expressions "sustained by," "due to," "resulting from," "sustained by means of," "sustained in consequence of," and "sustained through" have been held to be synonymous. Federal Life Ins. Co. v. White, Tex., 23 S.W.2d 832, 834. Also, synonymous with "caused by." American Stores Co. v. Herman, 166 Md. 312, 171 A. 54, 58.

DUE-BILL. A brief written acknowledgment of a debt. It is not made payable to order, like a promissory note. See Feeser v. Feeser, 93 Md. 716, 50 Atl. 406; Lee v. Balcom, 9 Colo. 216, 11 Pac. 74. See I. O. U.

DUEL. A duel is any combat with deadly weapons, fought between two or more persons, by previous agreement or upon a previous quarrel. Baker v. Supreme Lodge K. P., 103 Miss. 374, 60 So. 333, Ann.Cas.1915B, 547.

DUELLING. The fighting of two persons, one against the other, at an appointed time and place, upon a precedent quarrel. It differs from an affray in this, that the latter occurs on a sudden quarrel, while the former is always the result of design.

DUELLUM. The trial by battel or judicial combat. See Battel.

DUES. Certain payments; rates or taxes. See Ward v. Joslin, 105 Fed. 227, 44 C.C.A. 456; Whitman v. National Bank, 176 U.S. 559, 20 Sup.Ct. 477, 44 L.Ed. 587. As applied to club and other membership corporations, word refers to sums paid toward support of society and to retain membership therein. Jefferson County Farm Bureau

v. Sherman, 208 Iowa 614, 226 N.W. 182, 185. And covers only fixed and definite charges applicable to all club members. Hardt v. McLaughlin, D.C.Pa., 25 F.Supp. 684, 685.

DUKE, in English law, is a title of nobility, ranking immediately next to the Prince of Wales. It is only a title of dignity. Conferring it does not give any domain, territory, or jurisdiction over the place whence the title is taken. *Duchess,* the consort of a duke. Wharton.

DUKE OF EXETER'S DAUGHTER. The name of a rack in the Tower, so called after a minister of Henry VI, who sought to introduce it into England.

DUKE OF YORK'S LAWS. A body of laws compiled in 1665 for the government of the colony of New York.

DULOCRACY. A government where servants and slaves have so much license and privilege that they domineer. Wharton.

DULY. In due or proper form or manner; according to legal requirements.

Regularly; properly; suitable; upon a proper foundation, as distinguished from mere form; according to law in both form and substance. Welborn v. Whitney, 190 Okl. 630, 126 P.2d 263, 266; Cromwell v. Slaney, C.C.A.Mass., 65 F.2d 940, 941; Zechiel v. Firemen's Fund Ins. Co., C.C.A.Ind., 61 F.2d 27, 28.

DULY ORDAINED MINISTER OF RELIGION. Person who has been ordained in accordance with the ceremonial, ritual, or discipline of a recognized church, religious sect, or religious organization, to teach and preach its doctrines and to administer its rites and ceremonies and public worship, and who customarily performs those duties. In re Rogers, D.C.Tex., 47 F.Supp. 265, 266.

DULY QUALIFIED. Being "duly qualified" to fill an office, in the constitutional sense and in the ordinary acceptation of the words, means that the officer shall possess every qualification; that he shall in all respects comply with every requisite before entering on duties of the office; that, in addition to being elected by the qualified electors, he shall be commissioned by the governor, give bond as required by law; and that he shall be bound by oath or affirmation to support the Constitution of the commonwealth, and to perform the duties of the office with fidelity. Commonwealth v. Lomas, 302 Pa. 97, 153 A. 124, 126, 74 A.L.R. 481; State ex rel. Landis v. Bird, 120 Fla. 780, 163 So. 248.

DUM. Lat. While; as long as; until; upon condition that; provided that.

DUM BENE SE GESSERIT. While he shall conduct himself well; during good behavior. Expressive of a tenure of office not dependent upon the pleasure of the appointing power, nor for a limited period, but terminable only upon the death or misconduct of the incumbent.

DUM FERVET OPUS. While the work glows; in the heat of action. 1 Kent, Comm. 120.

DUM FUIT IN PRISONA. In English law. A writ which lay for a man who had aliened lands under duress by imprisonment, to restore to him his proper estates. 2 Inst. 482. Abolished by St. 3 & 4 Wm. IV. c. 27.

DUM FUIT INFRA ÆTATEM. (While he was within age.) In old English practice. A writ of entry which formerly lay for an infant after he had attained his full age, to recover lands which he had aliened in fee, in tail, or for life, during his infancy; and, after his death, his heir had the same remedy. Reg.Orig. 228*b*; Fitzh. Nat. Brev. 192, G; Litt. § 406; Co.Litt. 247*b*.

DUM NON FUIT COMPOS MENTIS. The name of a writ which the heirs of a person who was *non compos mentis,* and who aliened his lands, might have sued out to restore him to his rights. Abolished by 3 & 4 Wm. IV. c. 27.

DUM RECENS FUIT MALEFICIUM. While the offense was fresh. A term employed in the old law of appeal of rape. Bract. fol. 147.

DUM SOLA. While sole, or single. *Dum sola fuerit,* while she shall remain sole. *Dum sola et casta vixerit,* while she lives single and chaste. Words of limitation in old conveyances. Co.Litt. 235*a*. Also applied generally to an unmarried woman in connection with something that was or might be done during that condition.

DUMB. One who cannot speak; a person who is mute.

DUMB-BIDDING. In sales at auction, when the minimum amount which the owner will take for the article is written on a piece of paper, and placed by the owner under a candlestick, or other thing, and it is agreed that no bidding shall avail unless equal to that, this is called "dumb-bidding." Bab. Auct. 44.

DUMMODO. Provided; provided that. A word of limitation in the Latin forms of conveyances, of frequent use in introducing a reservation; as in reserving a rent.

DUMMY, *n.* One who holds legal title for another; a straw man. Hegstad v. Wysiecki, 178 App.Div. 733, 165 N.Y.S. 898, 900. Space 6⅓ feet in width between street railroad tracks. Schroeder v. Pittsburgh Rys. Co., 311 Pa. 398, 165 A. 733.

DUMMY, *adj.* Sham; make-believe; pretended; imitation. U. S. v. Warn, D.C.Idaho, 295 F. 328, 330. As respects basis for predicating liability on parent corporation for acts of subsidiary, "agency," "adjunct," "branch," "instrumentality," "dummy," "buffer," and "tool" all mean very much the same thing. Lowendahl v. Baltimore & O. R. Co., 287 N.Y.S. 62, 74, 247 App.Div. 144.

DUMMY DIRECTOR. One to whom (usually) a single share of stock in a corporation is transferred for the purpose of qualifying him as a director of the corporation, in which he has no real or active interest. Ashby v. Peters, 128 Neb. 338, 258 N.W. 639, 99 A.L.R. 843. One who is a mere figurehead and in effect discharges no duties. Golden Rod Mining Co. v. Bukvich, 108 Mont. 569, 92 P. 2d 316, 319.

DUMP. To put or throw down with more or less of violence; to unload. Baney v. Chicago, B. & Q. R. Co., 116 Neb. 615, 218 N.W. 424, 428. To drop down; to deposit something in a heap or unshaped mass. Lambert v. City of Port Arthur, Tex., 22 S.W.2d 320, 321.

DUMP CARS. A cart or car having a body that can be tilted or a bottom opening downwards for emptying. Baney v. Chicago, B. & Q. R. Co., 116 Neb. 615, 218 N.W. 424, 428.

DUMPING. In commercial usage, the act of selling in quantity at a very low price or practically regardless of the price; also, selling (surplus goods) abroad at less than the market price at home. Webster, Dict. The act of forcing a product such as cotton on the market during the short gathering season. Arkansas Cotton Growers' Co-op. Ass'n v. Brown, 270 S.W. 946, 953, 168 Ark. 504.

DUMPING BOARD. An elevated structure of timber, which in part overhangs the water, to enable a scow to go under it for the purpose of taking on a load. Healey v. Moran Towing & Transportation Co., C.C.A.N.Y., 253 F. 334, 337.

DUN. One who duns or urges for payment; a troublesome creditor. A demand for payment whether oral or written. Stand. Dict.

A mountain or high open place. The names of places ending in *dun* or *don* were either built on hills or near them in open places.

DUNA. In old records. A bank of earth cast up; the side of a ditch. Cowell.

DUNGEON. Such an underground prison or cell as was formerly placed in the strongest part of a fortress; a dark or subterraneous prison.

DUNIO. A double; a kind of base coin less than a farthing.

DUNNAGE. Pieces of wood placed against the sides and bottom of the hold of a vessel, to preserve the cargo from the effect of leakage, according to its nature and quality. Abb.Shipp. 227.

There is considerable resemblance between dunnage and ballast. The latter is used for trimming the ship, and bringing it down to a draft of water proper and safe for sailing. Dunnage is placed under the cargo to keep it from being wetted by water getting into the hold, or between the different parcels to keep them from bruising and injuring each other. Great Western Ins. Co. v. Thwing, 13 Wall. 674, 20 L.Ed. 607; Richards v. Hansen, C.C.Mass., 1 F. 56.

"Dunnage" belongs to the category of crating and boxing employed to protect more valuable articles in shipment, the weight of which, unless some provision to the contrary appears in a tariff classification, naturally takes the rate applicable to the contents. "Dunnage" used in blocking and securing automobiles was held subject to the automobile rate and not to the lumber rate, under tariff classification providing charges shall be computed on gross weights. Butler Motor Co. v. Atchison, T. & S. F. Ry. Co., C.C.A.Mo., 272 F. 683, 684.

DUNSETS. People that dwell on hilly places or mountains. Jacob.

DUO NON POSSUNT IN SOLIDO UNAM REM POSSIDERE. Two cannot possess one thing in entirety. Co.Litt. 368.

DUO SUNT INSTRUMENTA AD OMNES RES AUT CONFIRMANDAS AUT IMPUGNANDAS, RATIO ET AUTHORITAS. There are two instruments for confirming or impugning all things,—reason and authority. 8 Coke, 16.

DUODECEMVIRALE JUDICIUM. The trial by twelve men, or by jury. Applied to juries *de medietate linguæ.* Mol. de Jure Mar. 448.

DUODECIMA MANUS. Twelve hands. The oaths of twelve men, including himself, by whom the defendant was allowed to make his law. 3 Bl. Comm. 343.

DUODENA. In old records. A jury of twelve men. Cowell.

DUODENA MANU. A dozen hands, *i. e.,* twelve witnesses to purge a criminal of an offense.

DUODENUM. The intestine that joins onto the lower portion of the stomach and that goes out of the stomach. Metropolitan Life Ins. Co. v. Crowder, 71 Ga.App. 612, 31 S.E.2d 618, 620.

DUORUM IN SOLIDUM DOMINIUM VEL POSSESSIO ESSE NON POTEST. Ownership or possession in entirety cannot be in two persons of the same thing. Dig. 13, 6, 5, 15; Mackeld. Rom. Law, § 245. Bract. fol. 28*b*.

DUPLA. In the civil law. Double the price of a thing. Dig. 21, 2, 2.

DUPLEX HOUSE. A house which has accommodations for two families on two or more floors, without regard to whether such accommodations are identical or not. Donnelly v. Spitza, 246 Mich. 284, 224 N.W. 396, 397.

DUPLEX QUERELA. A double complaint. An ecclesiastical proceeding, which is in the nature of an appeal. Phillim.Ecc.Law, 440. See Double Complaint.

DULPEX VALOR MARITAGII. In old English law. Double the value of the marriage. While an infant was in ward, the guardian had the power of tendering him or her a suitable match, without disparagement, which if the infants refused, they forfeited the value of the marriage to their guardian, that is, so much as a jury would assess or any one would give to the guardian for such an alliance; and, if the infants married themselves without the guardian's consent, they forfeited double the value of the marriage. 2 Bl.Comm. 70; Litt. § 110; Co.Litt. 82*b*.

DUPLICATE, *v.* To double, repeat, make, or add a thing exactly like a preceding one; reproduce exactly. State v. Ogden, 20 N.M. 636, 151 P. 758, 760.

DUPLICATE, *n.* When two written documents are substantially alike, so that each might be a copy or transcript from the other, while both stand on the same footing as original instruments, they are called "duplicates." Agreements, deeds, and other documents are frequently executed in duplicate, in order that each party may have an original in his possession. Lorch v. Page, 97 Conn. 66, 115 A. 681, 682, 24 A.L.R. 1204.

A duplicate is sometimes defined to be the "copy" of a thing; but, though generally a copy, a duplicate differs from a mere copy, in having all the validity of an original. Nor, it seems need it be an exact copy. Defined also to be the "counterpart" of an instrument; but in indentures there is a distinction between *counterparts* executed by the several parties respectively, each party affixing his or her seal to only one counterpart, and *duplicate originals,* each executed by all the parties. Maston v. Glen Lumber Co., 65 Okl. 80, 163 P. 128, 129. The old indentures, charters, or chirographs seem to have had the character of duplicates. Burrill.

That which exactly resembles or corresponds to something else; another, correspondent to the first; hence, a copy; transcript; counterpart; an original instrument repeated; a document the same as another in essential particulars; differing from a copy as being valid as an original. Baker v. Sovereign Camp, W. O. W., Mo.App., 116 S.W.2d 513, 517.

The term is also frequently used to signify a new original, made to take the place of an instrument that has been lost or destroyed, and to have the same force and effect. Benton v. Martin, 40 N.Y. 347.

In English law. The certificate of discharge given to an insolvent debtor who takes the benefit of the act for the relief of insolvent debtors.

The ticket given by a pawnbroker to the pawner of a chattel.

DUPLICATE TAXATION. The same as "double taxation." See that title.

DUPLICATE WILL. A term used in England, where a testator executes two copies of his will, one to keep himself, and the other to be deposited with another person. Upon application for probate of a duplicate will, both copies must be deposited in the registry of the court of probate.

DUPLICATIO. In the civil law. The defendant's answer to the plaintiff's replication; corresponding to the rejoinder of the common law.

DUPLICATIONEM POSSIBILITATIS LEX NON PATITUR. The law does not allow the doubling of a possibility. 1 Rolle, 321.

DUPLICATUM JUS. Double right. Bract. fol. 283*b*. See Droit-Droit.

DUPLICITOUS. A pleading which joins in one and the same count different grounds of action of different nature, or of the same nature, to enforce a single right to recovery, or which is based on different theories of the defendant's liability. Peck v. Woomack, Nev., 192 P.2d 874, 884. In an information the joinder of separate and distinct offenses in one and the same count. State v. Seward, 163 Kan. 136, 181 P.2d 478, 480.

DUPLICITOUS APPEAL. Appeal from two separate judgments or from judgment and order or from two independent orders, both of which are appealable. City of Duncan v. Abrams, 171 Okl. 619, 43 P.2d 720, 723.

DUPLICITY. The technical fault, in pleading, of uniting two or more causes of action in one count in a writ, or two or more grounds of defense in one plea, or two or more breaches in a replication, or two or more offenses in the same count of an indictment, or two or more incongruous subjects in one legislative act, or two or more controverted ultimate issues submitted in a single special issue. Empire Oil & Gas Corporation v. U. S., C.C.A.Cal., 136 F.2d 868, 872; People v. Link, 365 Ill. 266, 6 N.E.2d 201, 207; Clay Drilling Co. v. Furman, Tex.Civ.App., 150 S.W.2d 869, 871; Hartley v. Hartley, 198 Ga. 294, 31 S.E.2d 655.

DUPLY, *n.* (From Lat. *duplicatio, q. v.*) In Scotch pleading. The defendant's answer to the plaintiff's replication.

DUPLY, *v.* In Scotch pleading. To rejoin. "It is *duplyed* by the panel." 3 State Trials, 471.

DUPUYTREN'S CONTRACTION. A pathological condition involving the palmar fascia of the hands. American Maize Products Co. v. Nichiporchik, 108 Ind.App. 502, 29 N.E.2d 801, 802.

DURABLE LEASES. Leases reserving a rent payable annually, with right of re-entry for nonpayment of the same, and for the term "as long as grass grows or water runs," or equivalent terms. University of Vermont and State Agr. College v. Ward, Vt., 158 A. 773, 778.

DURALUMIN. A light weight aluminum alloy. Reed Propeller Co. v. United States, Ct.Cl., 42 F. Supp. 545, 567.

DURANTE. Lat. During. A word of limitation in old conveyances. Co.Litt. 234*b*.

DURANTE ABSENTIA. During absence. In some jurisdictions, administration of a decedent's estate is said to be granted *durante absentia* in cases where the absence of the proper proponents of the will, or of an executor, delays or imperils the settlement of the estate.

DURANTE BENE PLACITO. During good pleasure. The ancient tenure of English judges was *durante bene placito.* 1 Bl.Comm. 267, 342.

DURANTE MINORE ÆTATE. During minority. 2 Bl.Comm. 503; 5 Coke, 29, 30. Words taken from the old form of letters of administration. 5 Coke, *ubi supra.*

DURANTE VIDUITATE. During widowhood. 2 Bl.Comm. 124. *Durante casta viduitate,* during chaste widowhood. 10 East, 520.

DURANTE VIRGINITATE. During virginity, (so long as she remains unmarried.)

DURANTE VITA. During life.

DURATION. Extent, limit or time. People v. Hill, 7 Cal. 102. The portion of time during which anything exists. Morrison v. Farmers' & Traders' State Bank, 70 Mont. 146, 225 P. 123, 125.

DURBAR. In India. A court, audience, or levee. Mozley & Whitley.

DURESS, *v.* To subject to duress. A word used by Lord Bacon. "If the party *duressed* do make any motion," etc. Bac. Max. 89, reg. 22.

DURESS, *n.* Unlawful constraint exercised upon a man whereby he is forced to do some act that he otherwise would not have done. It may be either "duress of imprisonment," where the person is deprived of his liberty in order to force him to compliance, or by violence, beating, or other actual injury, or duress *per minas,* consisting in threats of imprisonment or great physical injury or death. Duress may also include the same injuries, threats, or restraint exercised upon the man's wife, child, or parent. Coughlin v. City of Milwaukee, 227 Wis. 357, 279 N.W. 62, 67, 119 A.L.R. 990; Radich v. Hutchins, 95 U.S. 213, 24 L. Ed. 409.

Duress consists in any illegal imprisonment, or legal imprisonment used for an illegal purpose, or threats of bodily or other harm, or other means amounting to or tending to coerce the will of another, and actually inducing him to do an act contrary to his free will. Heider v. Unicume, 142 Or. 410, 20 P.2d 384, 385; Shlensky v. Shlensky, 369 Ill. 179, 15 N.E.2d 694, 698. And it is never "duress" to threaten to do that which a party has a legal right to do. Doernbecher v. Mutual Life Ins. Co. of New York, 16 Wash.2d 64, 132 P.2d 751, 755, 756; Miller v. Walden, 53 Cal.App.2d 353, 127 P.2d 952, 956, 957. Such as, instituting or threatening to institute civil actions. Standard Radio Corporation v. Triangle Radio Tubes, 125 N.J.L. 131, 14 A.2d 763, 765; Shipman v. Moseley, 319 Ill.App. 443, 49 N.E.2d 662, 666.

DURESS OF GOODS. Where the act consists of a tortious seizure or detention of property from the person entitled to it, and requires some act as a condition for its surrender, the act is "duress of goods". Sistrom v. Anderson, 51 Cal.App.2d 213, 124 P.2d 372, 376.

DURESS OF IMPRISONMENT. The wrongful imprisonment of a person, or the illegal restraint of his liberty, in order to compel him to do some act. 1 Bl.Comm. 130, 131, 136, 137; 1 Steph.Comm. 137; 2 Kent, Comm. 453.

DURESS PER MINAS. Duress by threats. The use of threats and menaces to compel a person, by the fear of death, or grievous bodily harm, as mayhem or loss of limb, to do some lawful act, or to commit a misdemeanor. 1 Bl.Comm. 130; 4 Bl.Comm. 30; 4 Steph.Comm. 83; In re Nightingale's Estate, 182 S.C. 527, 189 S.E. 890, 898. See Metus.

DURESSOR. One who subjects another to duress; one who compels another to do a thing, as by menace. Bac.Max. 90, reg. 22.

DURHAM. A county palatine in England, the jurisdiction of which was vested in the Bishop of Durham until the statute 6 & 7 Wm. IV. c. 19, vested it as a separate franchise and royalty in the crown. The jurisdiction of the Durham court of pleas was transferred to the supreme court of judicature by the judicature act of 1873.

DURHAM RULE. The irresistible impulse test of criminal responsibility. The rule states that when there is some evidence that the accused suffered from a diseased or defective mental condition at the time the unlawful act was committed the accused is not criminally responsible if it is found beyond a reasonable doubt that the act was the product of such mental abnormality. Durham v. United States, C.A.D.C., 214 F.2d 862, 875.

DURING. Throughout the course of; throughout the continuance of; in the time of; after the commencement and before the expiration of. Continental Bank & Trust Co. of N. Y. v. Chemical Bank & Trust Co., 51 N.Y.S.2d 903, 909.

DURING GOOD BEHAVIOR. While defendant whose sentence had been suspended, was obedient to the state law. State v. Hardin, 183 N.C. 815, 112 S.E. 593, 595.

DURING THE HOURS OF SERVICE. Working-hours plus reasonable periods for ingress and egress. Lienau v. Northwestern Telephone Exch. Co., 151 Minn. 258, 186 N.W. 945, 946.

DURING THE TRIAL. Period beginning with swearing of jury and ending with rendition of verdict. Kokas v. Commonwealth, 237 S.W. 1090, 1091, 194 Ky. 44. Period commencing with presentation of indictment by grand jury to court and terminating with final judgment. State v. Hudson, 55 R.I. 141, 179 A. 130, 133, 100 A.L.R. 313.

DURSLEY. In old English law. Blows without wounding or bloodshed; dry blows. Blount.

DUST EXPLOSION. Almost instantaneous combustion of myriads of small particles of solid matter held in suspension by air. Cornec v. Baltimore & O. R. Co., C.C.A.Md., 48 F.2d 497, 500.

DUSTUCK. A term used in Hindostan for a passport, permit, or order from the English East Indian Company. It generally meant a permit under their seal exempting goods from the payment of duties. Enc.Lond.

DUTCH AUCTION. See Auction.

DUTCH LOTTERY. Also known as the "class lottery." As distinguished from the "Genoese lottery" (*q. v.*), it is a scheme in which the number and value of the prizes are regularly estimated, all the ticket holders are interested at once in the play, and chance determines whether a prize or a blank falls to a given number. Fleming v. Bills, 3 Or. 286.

DUTCH NET. A kind of fishing net commonly known as a "pound net" (*q. v.*).

DUTIES. In its most usual signification this word is the synonym of imposts or customs; but it is sometimes used in a broader sense, as including all manner of taxes, charges, or governmental impositions. Cooley v. Board of Wardens, 12 How. 299, 13 L.Ed. 996.

DUTIES OF DETRACTION. Taxes levied upon the removal from one state to another of property acquired by succession or testamentary disposition. Frederickson v. Louisiana, 23 How. 445, 16 L.Ed. 577; In re Strobel's Estate, 5 App.Div. 621, 39 N.Y.S. 169. Cf. Droit de détraction.

DUTIES ON IMPORTS. This term signifies not merely a duty on the act of importation, but a duty on the thing imported. It is not confined to a duty levied while the article is entering the country, but extends to a duty levied after it has entered the country. Brown v. Maryland, 12 Wheat. 437, 6 L.Ed. 678.

DUTY. A human action which is exactly conformable to the laws which require us to obey them. Chicago, etc., R. Co. v. Filson, 35 Okl. 89, 91, 128 P. 298.

The words, "it shall be the duty," in ordinary legislation, imply the assertion of the power to command and to coerce obedience. Kentucky v. Dennison, 24 How. 66, 107, 16 L.Ed. 717.

In its use in jurisprudence, this word is the correlative of *right*. Thus, wherever there exists a right in any person, there also rests a corresponding duty upon some other person or upon all persons generally. But it is also used, in a wider sense, to designate that class of moral obligations which lie outside the jural sphere; such, namely, as rest upon an imperative ethical basis, but have not been recognized by the law as within its proper province for purposes of enforcement or redress. Thus, gratitude towards a benefactor is a *duty*, but its refusal will not ground an action. In this meaning "duty" is the equivalent of "moral obligation," as distinguished from a "legal obligation." Harrison v. Bush, 5 El. & Bl. 349.

Duty is considered by some modern ethicists to be the fundamental conception of ethics and to be subject to intuitive knowledge; by others it is conceived as that which is ethically valid because sanctioned by law, society, or religion. Webster, Dict.

As a technical term of the law, "duty" signifies a thing due; that which is due from a person; that which a person owes to another. An obligation to do a thing. A word of more extensive signification than "debt," although both are expressed by the same Latin word "*debitum.*" Bankers' Deposit Guaranty & Surety Co. v. Barnes, 81 Kan. 422, 105 P. 697, 698. Sometimes, however, the term is used synonymously with debt. Fox v. Hills, 1 Conn. 295, 303.

But in practice it is commonly reserved as the designation of those obligations of performance, care, or observance which rest upon a person in an official or fiduciary capacity; as the *duty* of an executor, trustee, manager, etc. Goodwine v. Vermilion County, 271 Ill. 126, 110 N.E. 890, 892.

It also denotes a tax or impost due to the government upon the importation or exportation of goods.

Judicial Duty. See Judicial.

Legal Duty. See Legal Duty.

DUTY OF TONNAGE. A charge upon a vessel as an instrument of commerce for entering, lying in or leaving a port, and includes all taxes and duties, regardless of name or form. In re Los Angeles Lumber Products Co., D.C.Cal., 45 F.Supp. 77, 81; Marine Lighterage Corporation v. Luckenbach S. S. Co., 139 Misc. 612, 248 N.Y.S. 71, 72.

DUTY OF WATER. Such a quantity of water necessary when economically conducted and applied to land without unnecessary loss as will result in the successful growing of crops. Enterprise Irr. Dist. v. Willis, 135 Neb. 827, 284 N.W. 326, 329.

DUUMVIRI. (From *duo*, two, and *viri*, men.) A general appellation among the ancient Romans, given to any magistrates elected in pairs to fill any office, or perform any function. Brande.

Duumviri municipales were two annual magistrates in the towns and colonies, having judicial powers. Calvin.

Duumviri navales were officers appointed to man, equip, and refit the navy. Calvin.

DUX. A military governor of a province. See Cod. 1, 27, 2. A military officer having charge of the borders or frontiers of the empire, called "*dux limitis.*" Cod. 1, 49, 1, pr. At this period, the word began to be used as a title of honor or dignity.

In Roman law. A leader or military commander. The commander of an army. Dig. 3, 2, 2, pr.

In feudal and old European law. Duke; a title of honor, or order of nobility. 1 Bl.Comm. 397; Crabb, Eng.Law, 236.

DWELL. To have an abode; to inhabit; to live in a place. Gardener v. Wagner, 9 Fed.Cas. 1,154; Putnam v. Johnson, 10 Mass. 502; Eatontown v. Shrewsbury, 49 N.J.Law, 188, 6 A. 319. More than mere physical presence is sometimes required. It must be in conformity with law. Kaplan v. Tod, 45 S.Ct. 257, 267 U.S. 228, 69 L.Ed. 585; U. S. v. Tod, D.C., 292 F. 243, 245.

To delay, to pause or linger, to abide as a permanent residence or for a time; to live in a place, to have one's residence or domicile, to reside. It is synonymous with inhabit, live, sojourn, stay, rest. MacLeod v. Stelle, 43 Idaho, 64, 249 P. 254, 256.

DWELLING HOUSE. The house in which a man lives with his family; a residence; abode; habitation; the apartment or building, or group of buildings, occupied by a family as a place of residence.

"Dwelling house" is a very flexible term. Its meaning depends not only on context, but on the determination of the courts not to permit public policy or justice to be defeated by a word. "Dwelling house" often means any building within the curtilage. Daniels v. Commonwealth, 172 Va. 583, 1 S.E.2d 333, 335. It may mean a single house used by one family exclusively as a home. It may include an apartment building, or any structure used by human beings, partly for business and partly for residential purposes, or a building regardless of habitation. Gerstell v. Knight, 345 Pa. 83, 26 A.2d 329, 330.

In conveyancing. Includes all buildings attached to or connected with the house. 2 Hil.Real Prop. 338, and note. In the law of burglary. A house in which the occupier and his family usually reside, or, in other words, dwell and lie in. Whart. Crim.Law, 357. Temporary absence will not destroy character as "dwelling house." Haynes v. State, 180 Miss. 291, 177 So. 360; State v. Bair, 112 W.Va. 655, 166 S.E. 369, 370, 85 A.L.R. 424.

Private Dwelling

Within a restrictive covenant, a place or house in which a person or family lives in an individual or private state, the covenant being violated by the conversion of a house theretofore used as a residence for a single family into a residence for two families, even though the outward appearance of the house was not materially affected. Paine v. Bergrose Development Corp., 198 N.Y.S. 311, 312, 119 Misc. 796. The distinction between a boarding house and a "private dwelling house" is whether the house is occupied as a home for the occupant and his wife and child, or whether he occupied it as a place for carrying on the business of keeping boarders, although while prosecuting the business and as a means of prosecuting it, he and his wife and children live in the house also. Trainor v. Le Beck, 101 N.J.Eq. 823, 139 A. 16, 17.

DWELLING-PLACE, or home, is some permanent abode or residence, in which one has the intention of remaining; it is not synonymous with "domicile," as used in international law, but has a more limited and restricted meaning. Nor is it synonymous with a "place of pauper settlement." Lisbon v. Lyman, 49 N.H. 553.

DYED HANGING PAPER. See Hanging Paper.

DYING DECLARATION. See Declaration.

DYING WITHOUT ISSUE. At common law this phrase imports an indefinite failure of issue, and not a dying without issue surviving at the time of the death of the first taker. But this rule has been changed in some of the states, by statute or decisions, and in England by St. 7 Wm. IV, and 1 Vict. c. 26, § 29.

The words "die without issue," and "die without leaving issue," in a devise of real estate, import an indefinite failure of issue, and not the failure of issue at the death of the first taker. And no distinction is to be made between the words "without issue" and "without leaving issue." Harwell v. Harwell, 151 Tenn. 587, 271 S.W. 353, 355.

In Connecticut and other states it has been repeatedly held that the expression "dying without issue," and like expressions, have reference to the time of the death of the party, and not to an indefinite failure of issue. Phelps v. Phelps, 55 Conn. 359, 11 A. 596; Briggs v. Hopkins, 103 Ohio St. 321, 132 N.E. 843.

Dying without children imports not a failure of issue at any indefinite future period, but a leaving no children at the death of the legatee. Condict v. King, 13 N.J.Eq. 375. The law favors vesting of estates, and limitation such as "dying without issue," refers to a definite period, fixed in will, rather than to an indefinite failure of issue. Howard v. Howard's Trustee, 212 Ky. 847, 280 S.W. 156, 157. Where context is such as to show clearly that testator intended the phrase "die without issue" to mean that, if first taker die without issue during life of testator, the second taker shall stand in his place and prevent a lapse, the words "die without issue" are taken to mean death during life of testator. Martin v. Raff, 114 Ind.App. 507, 52 N.E.2d 839, 845.

DYKE-REED, or DYKE-REEVE. An officer who has the care and oversight of the *dykes* and *drains* in fenny counties.

DYNASTY. A succession of kings in the same line or family.

DYSNOMY. Bad legislation; the enactment of bad laws.

DYSPAREUNIA. In medical jurisprudence. Incapacity of a woman to sustain the act of sexual intercourse except with great difficulty and pain; anaphrodisia (which see).

DYSPEPSIA. A state of the stomach in which its functions are disturbed, without the presence of other diseases, or when, if other diseases are present, they are of minor importance. Dungl.Med. Dict.

DYVOUR. In Scotch law. A bankrupt.

DYVOUR'S HABIT. In Scotch law. A habit which debtors who are set free on a *cessio bonorum* are obliged to wear, unless in the summons and process of *cessio* it be libeled, sustained, and proved that the bankruptcy proceeds from misfortune. And bankrupts are condemned to submit to the habit, even where no suspicion of fraud lies against them, if they have been dealers in an illicit trade. Ersk.Prin. 4, 3, 13.

E

E. As an abbreviation, this letter may stand for "Exchequer," "English," "Edward," "Equity," "East," "Eastern," "Easter," or "Ecclesiastical." A Latin preposition, meaning from, out of, after, or according. It occurs in many Latin phrases; but (in this form) only before a consonant.

E. E. O. C. Equal Employment Opportunity Commission.

E. G. An abbreviation of *exempli gratia.* For the sake of an example.

E. O. E. Errors and omissions excepted. Vernon Metal & Produce Co. v. Joseph Joseph & Bros. Co., 212 App.Div. 358, 209 N.Y.S. 6, 11.

E CONTRA. From the opposite; on the contrary.

E CONVERSO. Conversely. On the other hand; on the contrary. Equivalent to *e contra.*

E MERA GRATIA. Out of mere grace or favor.

E PILI ANA. Hawaiian. Adjoining.

E PLURIBUS UNUM. One out of many. The motto of the United States of America.

EA. Sax. The water or river; also the mouth of a river on the shore between high and low water-mark.

EA EST ACCIPIENDA INTERPRETATIO, QUÆ VITIO CARET. That interpretation is to be received [or adopted] which is free from fault [or wrong.] The law will not intend a wrong. Bac. Max. 17, (in reg. 3.)

EA INTENTIONE. With that intent. Held not to make a condition, but a confidence and trust. Dyer, 138*b*.

EA QUÆ, COMMENDANDI CAUSA, IN VENDITIONIBUS DICUNTUR, SI PALAM APPAREANT, VENDITOREM NON OBLIGANT. Those things which are said on sales, in the way of commendation, if [the qualities of the thing sold] appear openly, do not bind the seller. Dig. 18, 1, 43, pr.

EA QUÆ DARI IMPOSSIBILIA SUNT, VEL QUÆ IN RERUM NATURA NON SUNT, PRO NON ADJECTIS HABENTUR. Those things which are impossible to be given, or which are not in the nature of things, are regarded as not added, [as no part of an agreement.] Dig. 50, 17, 135.

EA QUÆ IN CURIA NOSTRA RITE ACTA SUNT DEBITÆ EXECUTIONI DEMANDARI DEBENT. Co.Litt. 289. Those things which are properly transacted in our court ought to be committed to a due execution.

EA QUÆ RARO ACCIDUNT NON TEMERE IN AGENDIS NEGOTIIS COMPUTANTUR. Those things which rarely happen are not to be taken into account in the transaction of business without sufficient reason. Dig. 50, 17, 64.

EACH. A distributive adjective pronoun, which denotes or refers to every one of the persons or things mentioned; every one of two or more persons or things, composing the whole, separately considered. The effect of this word, used in the covenants of a bond, is to create a several obligation. Seiler v. State, 160 Ind. 605, 67 N.E. 448; Knickerbocker v. People, 102 Ill. 233; Costigan v. Lunt, 104 Mass. 219; State v. Monfred, 183 Md. 303, 37 A.2d 912, 914. The word "any" is equivalent to "each." Conerty v. Richtsteig, 308 Ill.App. 321, 31 N.E.2d 351.

EADEM CAUSA DIVERSIS RATIONIBUS CORAM JUDICIBUS ECCLESIASTICIS ET SECULARIBUS VENTILATUR. 2 Inst. 622. The same cause is argued upon different principles before ecclesiastical and secular judges.

EADEM EST RATIO, EADEM EST LEX. The same reason, the same law. Charles River Bridge v. Warren Bridge, 7 Pick. (Mass.) 493.

EADEM MENS PRÆSUMITUR REGIS QUÆ EST JURIS ET QUÆ ESSE DEBET, PRÆSERTIM IN DUBIIS. Hob. 154. The mind of the sovereign is presumed to be coincident with that of the law, and with that which it ought to be, especially in ambiguous matters.

EAGLE. A gold coin of the United States of the value of ten dollars.

EALDER, or EALDING. In old Saxon law. An elder or chief.

EALDERMAN, or EALDORMAN. The name of a Saxon magistrate; alderman; analogous to *earl* among the Danes, and *senator* among the Romans. See Alderman.

The name of *Ealdorman* is one of a large class; among a primitive people age implies command and command implies age; hence, in a somewhat later stage of language, the elders are simply the rulers. 1 Freeman, Norman Conquest, 51, quoted in Cent.Dict.

EALDOR-BISCOP. An archbishop.

EALDORBURG. Sax. The metropolis; the chief city. Obsolete.

EALEHUS. (Fr. *eale*, Sax., ale, and *hus*, house.) An ale-house.

EALHORDA. Sax. The privilege of assising and selling beer. Obsolete.

EAR GRASS. In English law. Such grass which is upon the land after the mowing, until the feast of the Annunciation after. 3 Leon. 213.

EAR-MARK. A mark put upon a thing to distinguish it from another. Originally and literally, a mark upon the ear; a mode of marking sheep and other animals.

Property is said to be *ear-marked* when it can be identified or distinguished from other property of the same nature.

Money has no ear-mark, but it is an ordinary term for a privy mark made by any one on a coin.

EAR-MARK RULE. Rule that through the process of commingling money or deposit with the funds of a bank it loses its identity, with the resultant effect of defeating the right of preference over general creditors. Hitt Fireworks Co. v. Scandinavian American Bank of Tacoma, 121 Wash. 261, 209 P. 680, 682.

EAR-WITNESS. In the law of evidence. One who attests or can attest anything as heard by himself.

EARL. A title of nobility, formerly the highest in England, now the third, ranking between a marquis and a viscount, and corresponding with the French *"comte"* and the German *"graf."* The title originated with the Saxons, and is the most ancient of the English peerage. William the Conqueror first made this title hereditary, giving it in fee to his nobles; and allotting them for the support of their state the third penny out of the sheriff's court, issuing out of all pleas of the shire, whence they had their ancient title "shiremen." At present the title is accompanied by no territory, private or judicial rights, but merely confers nobility and an hereditary seat in the house of lords. Wharton.

EARL MARSHAL OF ENGLAND. A great officer of state who had anciently several courts under his jurisdiction, as the court of chivalry and the court of honor. Under him is the herald's office, or college of arms. He was also a judge of the Marshalsea court, now abolished. This office is of great antiquity, and has been for several ages hereditary in the family of the Howards. 3 Bl.Comm. 68, 103; 3 Steph.Comm. 335, note.

EARLDOM. The dignity or jurisdiction of an earl. The dignity only remains now, as the jurisdiction has been given over to the sheriff. 1 Bl.Comm. 339.

EARLES-PENNY, or EARL'S PENNY. Money given in part payment. See Earnest; Arles.

EARLIER MATURITY RULE. The rule under which bonds first maturing are entitled to priority when sale of security is not sufficient to satisfy all obligations. Scherk v. Newton, C.C.A.Colo., 152 F.2d 747, 749.

EARN. To acquire by labor, service or performance. Hartford Electric Light Co. v. McLaughlin, 37 A.2d 361, 363, 131 Conn. 1.

EARNED INCOME. Implies some labor, management or supervision in production thereof, not income derived merely from ownership of property. Pennsylvania Co. for Insurances on Lives & Granting Annuities v. City of Philadelphia, 346 Pa. 406, 31 A.2d 137, 141.

EARNER. One whose personal efforts produces income, or who owns property which produces it, or combination of both. Van Meter v. Commissioner of Internal Revenue, C.C.A., 61 F.2d 817, 818; Wells v. Commissioner of Internal Revenue, C.C.A., 63 F.2d 425, 430.

EARNEST. The payment of a part of the price of goods sold, or the delivery of part of such goods, for the purpose of binding the contract. Weidner v. Hyland, 216 Wis. 12, 255 N.W. 134.

A token or pledge passing between the parties, by way of evidence, or ratification of the sale. 2 Kent, Comm. 495, note.

EARNING CAPACITY. "Earning capacity" does not necessarily mean the actual earnings that one who suffers an injury was making at the time the injuries were sustained, but refers to that which, by virtue of the training, the experience, and the business acumen possessed, an individual is capable of earning. Texas Electric Ry. v. Worthy, Tex.Civ.App., 250 S.W. 710, 711. Not saving ability, but capacity to acquire money, less the necessary expense of his own living. Pitman v. Merriman, 80 N.H. 295, 117 A. 18, 19, 26 A.L.R. 589. Fitness, readiness and willingness to work, considered in connection with opportunity to work. Hartford Accident & Indemnity Co. v. Hoage, 85 F.2d 411, 416, 66 App.D.C. 154.

EARNING POWER. Power of an individual to create property. Reward for labor performed. Ransom v. Matson Nav. Co., D.C.Wash., 1 F.Supp. 244, 246. Not synonymous with wages. Micek v. Omaha Steel Works, 136 Neb. 843, 287 N.W. 645, 648.

EARNINGS. That which is earned; money earned; the price of services performed; reward; the reward of labor or the price of personal service performed, the reward for personal services, whether in money or chattels, the fruit or reward of labor; the fruits of the proper skill, experience, and industry; the gains of a person derived from his services or labor without the aid of capital; money or property gained or merited by labor, service, or the performance of something; that which is gained or merited by labor, services, or performances. Saltzman v. City of Council Bluffs, 214 Iowa 1033, 243 N.W. 161, 162. "Income" is synonymous with "earnings." State ex rel. Froedtert Grain and Malting Co. v. Tax Commission of Wisconsin, 221 Wis. 225, 265 N.W. 672, 673, 104 A.L.R. 1478.

This term is used to denote a larger class of credits than would be included in the term "wages." Somers v. Keliher, 115 Mass. 165; Jenks v. Dyer, 102 Mass. 235.

The gains of the person derived from his services or labor without the aid of capital. Brown v. Hebard, 20 Wis. 330, 91 Am.Dec. 408; United Benefit Life Ins. Co. of Omaha v. Zwan, Tex.Civ. App., 143 S.W.2d 977, 980. Either gross or net earnings. Springfield Coal Mining Co. v. Industrial Commission, 291 Ill. 408, 126 N.E. 133, 22 A. L.R. 859.

Gross Earnings and Net Earnings

The gross earnings of a business or company are the total receipts before deducting expenditures. Net earnings are the excess of the gross earnings over the expenditures defrayed in producing them, and aside from and exclusive of capital laid out in constructing and equipping the works or plant. State v. Railroad Co., 30 Minn. 311, 15 N.W. 307. "Gross earnings" means all receipts from the employment of capital, without deduction for expenses incurred. People ex rel. Genesee Light & Power Co. v. Saxe, 165 N.Y.S. 938, 939, 179 App.Div. 486.

Net Earnings Rule

The net earnings rule for assessing a special franchise for taxation starts with the gross earnings for the year ending with the commencement of the year for which the valuation is made from which is deducted operating expenses and a fair and reasonable return on that portion of the corporation's capital invested in tangible property, the balance being deemed to give the net earnings attributable to the special franchise, the value of which is then found by capitalizing such balance at a rate 1 per cent. higher than that found as a matter of fact to be a fair and reasonable return on the tangible property. People ex rel. Third Ave. R. Co. v. State Board of Tax Com'rs, 142 N.Y.S. 986, 997, 157 App.Div. 731.

Surplus Earnings

Amount owned by company over and above its capital and actual liabilities. People v. Com'rs of Taxes, 76 N.Y. 74.

EARNINGS OF PROSTITUTE. Income derived from practice of prostitution. State v. Crane, 88 Wash. 210, 152 P. 989.

EARTH. Soil of all kinds, including gravel, clay, loam, and the like, in distinction from the firm rock. Dickinson v. Poughkeepsie, 75 N.Y. 76; Davis v. Commissioners of Sewerage of City of Louisville, D.C.Ky., 13 F.Supp. 672, 680.

EASE. Comfort, consolation, contentment, enjoyment, happiness, pleasure, satisfaction. National Surety Co. v. Jarrett, 95 W.Va. 420, 121 S.E. 291, 295.

EASEMENT. A right in the owner of one parcel of land, by reason of such ownership, to use the land of another for a special purpose not inconsistent with a general property in the owner. Hollomon v. Board of Education of Stewart County, 168 Ga. 359, 147 S.E. 882, 884; Frye v. Sebbitt, 145 Neb. 600, 17 N.W.2d 617, 621.

A privilege which the owner of one adjacent tenement hath of another, existing in respect of their several tenements, by which that owner against whose tenement the privilege exists is obliged to suffer or not to do something on or in regard to his own land for the advantage of him in whose land the privilege exists. Termes de la Ley, *Easements.*

A privilege, service, or convenience which one neighbor has of another, by prescription, grant, or necessary implication, and without profit; as a way over his land, a gate-way, water-course, and the like. Kitch. 105; 3 Cruise, Dig. 484. And see Harrison v. Boring, 44 Tex. 267.

A liberty, privilege, or advantage without profit, which the owner of one parcel of land may have in the lands of another. Magnolia Petroleum Co. v. Caswell, Tex., 1 S.W.2d 597, 600; Hasselbring v. Koepke, 263 Mich. 466, 248 N.W. 869, 873, 93 A. L.R. 1170.

The land against which the easement or privilege exists is called the "servient" tenement, and the estate to which it is annexed the "dominant" tenement; and their owners are called respectively the "servient" and "dominant" owner. These terms are taken from the civil law. Saratoga State Waters Corporation v. Pratt, 227 N.Y. 429, 125 N.E. 834, 838; Joachim v. Belfus, 108 N.J.Eq. 622, 156 A. 121, 122; Brasengton v. Williams, 143 S.C. 223, 141 S.E. 375, 382.

Distinguished from "servitude", Stephenson v. St. Louis Southwestern Ry. Co. of Texas, Tex.Civ.App., 181 S.W. 568, 572; "profit à prendre", Richfield Oil Co. of California v. Hercules Gasoline Co., 112 Cal.App. 437, 297 P. 73, 75; "covenant", Lingle Water Users' Ass'n v. Occidental Building & Loan Ass'n, 43 Wyo. 41, 297 P. 385, 387; "franchise", City of Fort Worth v. Southwestern Bell Telephone Co., C.C.A.Tex., 80 F.2d 972, 974; "restriction", Kutschinski v. Thompson, 101 N.J.Eq. 649, 138 A. 569, 573; Stanolind Pipe Line Co. v. Ellis, 142 Kan. 102, 45 P.2d 846, 848; Morrison v. Fellman, 271 N.Y.S. 436, 150 Misc. 772; "prescription", Black v. Whitacre, 206 Iowa 1084, 221 N.W. 825.

Affirmative Easement

One where the servient estate must permit something to be done thereon, as to pass over it, or to discharge water on it. Miller v. Babb, Tex. Com.App., 263 S.W. 253, 254.

Apparent Easement

One the existence of which appears from the construction or condition of one of the tenements, so as to be capable of being seen or known on inspection. Miller v. Skaggs, 79 W.Va. 645, 91 S.E. 536, 537, Ann.Cas.1918D, 929.

Appurtenant Easement

An "incorporeal right" which is attached to and belongs with some greater and superior right or something annexed to another thing more worthy and which passes as incident to it and is incapable of existence separate and apart from the particular land to which it is annexed. Union Falls Power Co. v. Marinette County, 238 Wis. 134, 298 N.W. 598, 600, 601, 134 A.L.R. 958. One which is attached to and passes with the dominant tenement as an appurtenance thereof. Cadwalader v. Bailey, 17 R.I. 495, 23 A. 20, 14 L.R.A. 300; Waller v. Hildebrecht, 295 Ill. 116, 128 N.E. 807, 809. Safety Building & Loan v. Lyles, 131 S.C. 540, 128 S.E. 724, 725.

Continuing Easement

One that is self-perpetuating, independent of human intervention, as, the flow of a stream, or one which may be enjoyed without any act on the part of the person entitled thereto, such as a spout which discharges the water whenever it rains, a drain by which surface water is carried off, windows which admit light and air, and the like. Starrett v. Baudler, 181 Iowa, 965, 165 N.W. 216, 219, L.R.A.1918B, 528. Also, it is sometimes termed an "apparent" easement, and defined as one depending on some artificial structure upon, or natural conformation of, the servient tenement, obvious and permanent, which constitutes the easement or is the means of enjoying it. Fetters v. Humphreys, 18 N.J.Eq. 260; Larsen v. Peterson, 53 N.J.Eq. 88, 30 A. 1094. See, also, Apparent Easement.

Discontinuing Easement

Discontinuous, non-continuous, or non-apparent easements are those the enjoyment of which can be had only by the interference of man, as, a right of way or a right to draw water. Outerbridge v. Phelps, 45 N.Y.Super.Ct. 570.

Easement by Prescription

A mode of acquiring title to property by immemorial or long-continued enjoyment, and refers to personal usage restricted to claimant and his ancestors or grantors. J. C. Vereen & Sons, Inc. v. Houser, 123 Fla. 641, 167 So. 45.

Easement in Gross

Easement in gross is not appurtenant to any estate in land (or not belonging to any person by virtue of his ownership of an estate in land) but a mere personal interest in, or right to use, the land of another. Weigold v. Bates, 258 N.Y.S. 695, 144 Misc. 395; Joachim v. Belfus, 108 N.J.Eq. 622, 156 A. 121, 122.

Easement of Access

Right of ingress and egress to and from the premises of a lot owner to a street appurtenant to the land of the lot owner. Lang v. Smith, 113 Pa. Super. 559, 173 A. 682, 683.

Easement of Convenience

One which increases the facility, comfort, or convenience of the enjoyment of the dominant estate, or of some right connected with it.

Easement of Necessity

One in which the easement is indispensable to the enjoyment of the dominant estate. Richards v. Trezvant, 185 S.C. 489, 194 S.E. 326, 329.

Equitable Easements

The special easements created by derivation of ownership of adjacent proprietors from a common source, with specific intentions as to buildings for certain purposes, or with implied privileges in regard to certain uses, are sometimes so called. A name frequently applied to building restrictions in a deed. Werner v. Graham, 181 Cal. 174, 183 P. 945, 947.

Implied Easement

An easement resting upon the principle that, where the owner of two or more adjacent lots sells a part thereof, he grants by implication to the grantee all those apparent and visible easements which are necessary for the reasonable use of the property granted, which at the time of the grant are used by the owner of the entirety for the benefit of the part granted. Farley v. Howard, 68 N.Y.S. 159, 33 Misc. 57.

Intermittent Easement

One which is usable or used only at times, and not continuously. Eaton v. Railroad Co., 51 N.H. 504, 12 Am.Rep. 147.

Negative Easement

Those where the owner of the servient estate is prohibited from doing something otherwise lawful upon his estate, because it will affect the dominant estate, (as interrupting the light and air from the latter by building on the former.) South Buffalo Stores v. W. T. Grant Co., 274 N.Y.S. 549, 153 Misc. 76; Pierce v. Keator, 70 N.Y. 447, 26 Am. Rep. 612; Miller v. Babb, Tex.Com.App., 263 S.W. 253, 254. As to "reciprocal negative easement," see that title, infra.

Private or Public Easements

A private easement is one in which the enjoyment is restricted to one or a few individuals, while a public easement is one the right to the enjoyment of which is vested in the public generally or in an entire community; such as an easement of passage on the public streets and highways or of navigation on a stream. Kennelly v. Jersey City, 57 N.J.Law, 293, 30 A. 531, 26 L.R.A. 281.

Quasi Easement

An "easement," in the proper sense of the word, can only exist in respect of two adjoining pieces of land occupied by different persons, and can only impose a negative duty on the owner of the servient tenement. Hence an obligation on the owner of land to repair the fence between his and his neighbor's land is not a true easement, but is sometimes called a "*quasi* easement." Gale, Easem. 516; Sweet.

Reciprocal Negative Easement

If the owner of two or more lots, so situated as to bear the relation, sells one with restrictions of benefit to the land retained, the servitude becomes mutual, and, during the period of restraint, the owner of the lot or lots retained can do nothing forbidden to the owner of the lot sold; this being known as the doctrine of "reciprocal negative easement." Sanborn v. McLean, 233 Mich. 227, 206 N.W. 496, 497.

Secondary Easement

One which is appurtenant to the primary or actual easement; every easement includes such "secondary easements," that is, the right to do such things as are necessary for the full enjoyment of the easement itself. Toothe v. Bryce, 50 N.J.Eq. 589, 25 A. 182.

EAST. In the absence of other words qualifying its meaning, the word "east" describing boundaries means due east. Anaheim Sugar Co. v. Orange County, 181 Cal. 212, 183 P. 809, 813; Livingston Oil & Gas Co. v. Shasta Oil Co., Tex.Civ.App., 114 S.W.2d 378, 381. See, also, Easterly.

In the customs laws of the United States, the words "countries *east* of the Cape of Good Hope" mean countries with which, formerly, the United States ordinarily carried on commercial intercourse by passing around that cape. Powers v. Conley, 101 U.S. 790, 25 L.Ed. 805.

EAST GREENWICH. The name of a royal manor in the county of Kent, England; mentioned in royal grants or patents, as descriptive of the tenure of free socage.

EAST INDIA COMPANY. Originally established for prosecuting the trade between England and India, which they acquired a right to carry on exclusively. Since the middle of the last century, however, the company's political affairs had become of more importance than their commerce. In 1858, by 21 & 22 Vict. c. 106, the government of the territories of the company was transferred to the crown. Wharton.

EASTER. A feast of the Christian church held in memory of the Saviour's resurrection. The Greeks and Latins call it "pascha," (passover,) to which Jewish feast our Easter answers. This feast has been annually celebrated since the time of the apostles, and is one of the most important festivals in the Christian calendar, being that which regulates and determines the times of all the other movable feasts. Enc. Lond.

EASTER-OFFERINGS, or EASTER-DUES. In English law. Small sums of money paid to the parochial clergy by the parishioners at Easter as a compensation for personal tithes, or the tithe for personal labor; recoverable under 7 & 8 Wm. III. c. 6, before justices of the peace.

EASTER TERM. In English law. Formerly one of the four movable terms of the courts, but afterwards a fixed term, beginning on the 15th of April and ending on the 8th of May in every year, though sometimes prolonged so late as the 13th of May, under St. 11 Geo. IV. and 1 Wm. IV. c. 70. From November 2, 1875, the division of the legal year into terms is abolished so far as concerns the administration of justice. 3 Steph.Comm. 482–486; Mozley & Whiteley.

EASTERLING. A coin struck by Richard II. which is supposed by some to have given rise to the name of "sterling," as applied to English money.

EASTERLY. This word, when used alone, will be construed to mean "due east." But that is a rule of necessity growing out of the indefiniteness of the term, and has no application where other words are used for the purpose of qualifying its meaning. Where such is the case, it means precisely what the qualifying word makes it mean. Walker v. City of Los Angeles, 23 Cal.App. 634, 139 P. 89, 90. See East.

EASTINUS. An easterly coast or country.

EASTMAN FORMULA. In determining fixed charges under railroad reorganization plan, the "Eastman Formula" is that such charges should not exceed 80 per cent. of the net available for interest in the three worst years of the last ten. In re Denver & R. G. W. R. Co., D.C.Colo., 38 F. Supp. 106, 110.

EAT INDE SINE DIE. In criminal practice. Words used on the acquittal of a defendant, or when a prisoner is to be discharged, *that he may go thence without a day, i. e.,* be dismissed without any further continuance or adjournment. Dane, Abr. Index.

EATING-HOUSE. Any place where food or refreshments of any kind, not including spirits, wines, ale, beer, or other malt liquors, are provided for casual visitors, and sold for consumption therein. Act Cong. July 13, 1866, § 9 (14 St. at Large, 118). And see Carpenter v. Taylor, 1 Hilt. (N.Y.) 195; State v. Hall, 73 N.C. 253. A place where the public may go and be served with meals. Babb v. Elsinger, Sup., 147 N.Y.S. 98, 99.

EAVES. The edge of a roof, built so as to project over the walls of a house, in order that the rain may drop therefrom to the ground instead of running down the wall. Center St. Church v. Machias Hotel Co., 51 Me. 413.

EAVES-DRIP. The drip or dropping of water from the eaves of a house on the land of an adjacent owner; the easement of having the water so drip, or the servitude of submitting to such drip; the same as the *stillicidium* of the Roman law. See Stillicidium.

EAVESDROPPING. In English criminal law. The offense of listening under walls or windows, or the *eaves* of a house, to hearken after discourse, and thereupon to frame slanderous and mischievous tales. 4 Bl.Comm. 168. It is a misdemeanor at common law, indictable at sessions, and punishable by fine and finding sureties for good behavior. Id.; Steph.Crim.Law, 109. Selden v. State, 74 Wis. 271, 42 N.W. 218, 17 Am.St. Rep. 144.

EBB AND FLOW. An expression used formerly in this country to denote the limits of admiralty jurisdiction. See United States v. Aborn, 3 Mason, 127, Fed.Cas.No.14,418.

EBBA. In old English law. Ebb. *Ebba et fluctus;* ebb and flow of tide; ebb and flood. Bract. fols. 255, 338. The time occupied by one ebb and flood was anciently granted to persons essoined as being beyond sea, in addition to the period of forty days. See Fleta, lib. 6, c. 8, § 2.

EBDOMADARIUS. In ecclesiastical law. An officer in cathedral churches who supervised the regular performance of divine service, and prescribed the particular duties of each person in the choir.

EBEREMORTH, EBEREMORS, EBEREMURDER. See Aberemurder.

EBRIETY. In criminal law and medical jurisprudence. Drunkenness; alcoholic intoxication. Com. v. Whitney, 11 Cush. (Mass.) 479.

ECCE MODO MIRUM, QUOD FŒMINA FERT BREVE REGIS, NON NOMINANDO VIRUM, CONJUNCTUM ROBORE LEGIS. Co.Litt. 132*b*. Behold, indeed, a wonder! that a woman has the king's writ without naming her husband, who by law is united to her.

ECCENTRICITY. In criminal law and medical jurisprudence. Personal or individual perculiarities of mind and disposition which markedly distinguish the subject from the ordinary, normal, or average types of men, but do not amount to mental unsoundness or insanity. Ekin v. McCracken, 11 Phila. (Pa.) 535.

ECCHYMOSIS. In medical jurisprudence. Localized discoloration in and under the skin; a livid or black and blue spot; blackness. An extravasation of blood by rupture of capillary vessels, and hence it follows contusion; but it may exist, as in cases of scurvy, asphyxiation, and other morbid conditions, without the latter. Ryan Med.Jur. 172. Ecchymoses produced by blows upon a body but a few hours dead cannot be distinguished from those produced during life. 1 Witth. & Beck.Med.Jur. 485; 2 Beck, Med.Jur. 22. It is generally attended by swelling. People v. Mummert, 50 N.Y.S.2d 699, 703, 183 Misc. 243.

ECCLESIA. Lat. An assembly. A Christian assembly; a church. A place of religious worship. In the law, generally, the word is used to denote a place of religious worship, and sometimes a parsonage. Spelman.

ECCLESIA ECCLESIÆ DECIMAS SOLVERE NON DEBET. Cro.Eliz. 479. A church ought not to pay tithes to a church.

ECCLESIA EST DOMUS MANSIONALIS OMNIPOTENTIS DEI. 2 Inst. 164. The church is the mansionhouse of the Omnipotent God.

ECCLESIA EST INFRA ÆTATEM ET IN CUSTODIA DOMINI REGIS, QUI TENETUR JURA ET HÆREDITATES EJUSDEM MANU TENERE ET DEFENDERE. 11 Coke, 49. The church is under age, and in the custody of the king, who is bound to uphold and defend its rights and inheritances.

ECCLESIA FUNGITUR VICE MINORIS; MELIOREM CONDITIONEM SUAM FACERE POTEST, DETERIOREM NEQUAQUAM. Co.Litt. 341. The church enjoys the privilege of a minor; it can make its own condition better, but not worse.

ECCLESIA NON MORITUR. 2 Inst. 3. The church does not die.

ECCLESIÆ MAGIS FAVENDUM EST QUAM PERSONÆ. Godol. Ecc. Law, 172. The church is to be more favored than the parson (or an individual).

ECCLESIÆ SCULPTURA. The image or sculpture of a church in ancient times was often cut out or cast in plate or other metal, and preserved as a religious treasure or relic, and to perpetuate the memory of some famous churches. Jacob.

ECCLESIARCH. The ruler of a church.

ECCLESIASTIC. A clergyman; a priest; a man consecrated to the service of the church; as, a bishop, a priest, a deacon.

ECCLESIASTICAL. Pertaining to anything belonging to or set apart for the church, as distinguished from "civil" or "secular," with regard to the world. Wharton.

ECCLESIASTICAL AUTHORITIES. In England, the clergy, under the sovereign, as temporal head of the church, set apart from the rest of the people or laity, in order to superintend the public worship of God and the other ceremonies of religion, and to administer spiritual counsel and instruction. The several orders of the clergy are: (1) Archbishops and bishops; (2) deans and chapters; (3) archdeacons; (4) rural deans; (5) parsons (under whom are included appropriators) and vicars; (6) curates. Church-wardens or sidesmen, and parish clerks and sextons, inasmuch as their duties are connected with the church, may be considered to be a species of ecclesiastical authorities. Wharton.

ECCLESIASTICAL COMMISSIONERS. In English law. A body corporate, erected by St. 6 & 7 Wm. IV, c. 77, empowered to suggest measures conducive to the efficiency of the established church, to be ratified by orders in council. Wharton. See 3 Steph.Comm. 156, 157.

ECCLESIASTICAL CORPORATION. See Corporation.

ECCLESIASTICAL COUNCIL. In New England. A church court or tribunal, having functions partly judicial and partly advisory, appointed to determine questions relating to church discipline, orthodoxy, standing of ministers, controversies between ministers and their churches, differences and divisions in churches, and the like. Stearns v. First Parish, 21 Pick., Mass., 124; Sheldon v. Congregational Parish, 24 Pick., Mass., 281.

ECCLESIASTICAL COURTS (called, also, "Courts Christian"). A generic name for certain courts having cognizance mainly of spiritual matters. D. v. D., Del.Super., 20 A.2d 139, 140. A system of courts in England, held by authority of the sovereign, and having jurisdiction over matters pertaining to the religion and ritual of the established church, and the rights, duties, and discipline of ecclesiastical persons as such. They are as follows: The archdeacon's court, arches court, consistory court, court of archdeacon, court of peculiars, prerogative court, court of delegates, court of convocation, court of audience, and court of faculties. 3 Bl.Comm. 64–68. Equitable Life Assur. Soc. v. Paterson, 41 Ga. 364, 5 Am.Rep. 535.

ECCLESIASTICAL DIVISION OF ENGLAND. This is a division into provinces, dioceses, archdeaconries, rural deaneries, and parishes.

ECCLESIASTICAL JURISDICTION. Jurisdiction over ecclesiastical cases and controversies; such as appertains to the ecclesiastical courts. Short v. Stotts, 58 Ind. 35.

ECCLESIASTICAL LAW. The body of jurisprudence administered by the ecclesiastical courts of England; derived, in large measure, from the canon and civil law. As now restricted, it applies mainly to the affairs, and the doctrine, discipline, and worship, of the established church. De Witt v. De Witt, 67 Ohio St. 340, 66 N.E. 136.

ECCLESIASTICAL MATTER. One that concerns doctrine, creed, or form of worship of the church, or the adoption and enforcement within a religious association of needful laws and regulations for the government of the membership, and the power of excluding from such associations those deemed unworthy of membership. Olear v. Haniak, 235 Mo. App. 249, 131 S.W.2d 375, 380.

ECCLESIASTICAL THINGS. This term, as used in the canon law, includes church buildings, church property, cemeteries, and property given to the church for the support of the poor or for any other pious use. Smith v. Bonhoof, 2 Mich. 115.

ECDICUS. The attorney, proctor, or advocate of a corporation. 1 Reeve, Eng.Law, 65.

ECHANTILLON. In French law. One of the two parts or pieces of a wooden tally. That in possession of the debtor is properly called the "tally," the other "*échantillon*." Poth.Obl. pt. 4, c. 1, art. 2, § 8.

ECHEVIN. In French law. A municipal officer corresponding with alderman or burgess, and having in some instances a civil jurisdiction in certain causes of trifling importance.

ECHOLALIA. In medical jurisprudence. The constant and senseless repetition of particular words or phrases, recognized as a sign or symptom of insanity or of aphasia.

ECHOUEMENT. In French marine law. Stranding. Emerig.Tr. des Ass. c. 12, s. 13, no. 1.

ECLAMPSIA PARTURIENTIUM. In medical jurisprudence. Puerperal convulsions; a convulsive seizure which sometimes suddenly attacks a woman in labor or directly after, generally attended by unconsciousness and occasionally by mental aberration, which may be permanent. The attack closely resembles the convulsions of epilepsy, and is often fatal.

ECLECTIC PRACTICE. In medicine. That system followed by physicians who select their modes of practice and medicines from various schools. Webster.

"Without professing to understand much of medical phraseology, we suppose that the terms 'allopathic practice' and 'legitimate business' mean the ordinary method commonly adopted by the great body of learned and eminent physicians, which is taught in their institutions, established by their highest authorities, and accepted by the larger and more respectable portion of the community. By 'eclectic practice,' without imputing to it, as the counsel for the plaintiff seem inclined to, an odor of illegality, we presume is intended another and different system, unusual and eccentric, not countenanced by the classes before referred to, but characterized by them as spurious and denounced as dangerous. It is sufficient to say that the two modes of treating human maladies are essentially distinct, and based upon different views of the nature and causes of diseases, their appropriate remedies, and the modes of applying them." Bradbury v. Bardin, 34 Conn. 453.

ECONOMIZER. As applied to boiler construction, a contrivance or device in which water is heated preliminary to entering the boiler proper. Ithaca Traction Corporation v. Travelers' Indemnity Co., Sup., 177 N.Y.S. 753, 754.

ECONOMY. Frugality; prudent economy. Not synonymous with "parsimony." Includes that which pertains to the satisfaction of man's needs. D'Arcy v. Snell, 162 Or. 351, 91 P.2d 537, 540, 122 A.L.R. 928.

ÉCRIVAIN. In French marine law. The clerk of a ship. Emerig.Tr. des Ass. c. 11, s. 3, no. 2.

ECUMENICAL. General; universal; as an ecumenical council. Groesbeeck v. Dunscomb, 41 How.Prac. (N.Y.) 344.

EDDERBRECHE. In Saxon law. The offense of hedge-breaking. Obsolete.

EDESTIA. In old records. Buildings.

EDGE. A line where two surfaces meet. I. T. S. Rubber Co. v. Essex Rubber Co., D.C., 270 F. 593, 605.

EDGE LEASE. One located on the edge of an oil bearing structure. Carter Oil Co. v. Mitchell, C. C.A.Okl., 100 F.2d 945, 947.

EDICT. A positive law promulgated by the sovereign of a country, and having reference either to the whole land or some of its divisions, but usually relating to affairs of state. It differs from a "public proclamation," in that it enacts a new statute, and carries with it the authority of law, whereas the latter is, at most, a declaration of a law before enacted. In Roman law. Sometimes, a citation to appear before a judge. A "special edict" was a judgment in a case; a "general edict" was in effect a statute. See Edictum.

EDICTAL CITATION. In Scotch law. A citation published at the market-cross of Edinburgh, and pier and shore of Leith. Used against foreigners not within the kingdom, but having a landed estate there, and against natives out of the kingdom. Bell.

EDICTS OF JUSTINIAN. Thirteen constitutions or laws of this prince, found in most editions of the *Corpus Juris Civilis,* after the Novels. Being confined to matters of police in the provinces of the empire, they are of little use.

EDICTUM. In the Roman law. An edict; a mandate, or ordinance. An ordinance, or law, enacted by the emperor without the senate; belonging to the class of *constitutiones principis.* Inst. 1, 2, 6. An edict was a mere voluntary constitution of the emperor; differing from a rescript, in not being returned in the way of answer; and from a decree, in not being given in judgment; and from both, in not being founded upon solicitation. Tayl. Civil Law, 233.

A general order published by the prætor, on entering upon his office, containing the system of rules by which he would administer justice during the year of his office. Dig. 1, 2, 2, 10; Mackeld. Rom.Law, § 35; Tayl.Civil Law, 214. See Calvin.

EDICTUM ANNUUM. The annual edict or system of rules promulgated by a Roman prætor immediately upon assuming his office, setting forth the principles by which he would be guided in determining causes during his term of office. Mackeld. Rom.Law, § 36.

EDICTUM PERPETUUM. The perpetual edict. A compilation or system of law in fifty books, digested by Julian, from the prætor's edicts and other parts of the *Jus Honorarium.* All the remains of it which have come down to us are the extracts of it in the Digests. Butl.Hor.Jur. 52.

EDICTUM PROVINCIALE. An edict or system of rules for the administration of justice, similar to the edict of the prætor, put forth by the proconsuls and proprætors in the provinces of the Roman Empire. Mackeld.Rom.Law, § 36.

EDICTUM THEODORICI. This is the first collection of law that was made after the downfall of the Roman power in Italy. It was promulgated by Theodoric, king of the Ostrogoths, at Rome in A.D. 500. It consists of 154 chapters, in which we recognize parts taken from the Code and Novellæ of Theodosius, from the Codices Gregorianus and Hermogenianus, and the Sententiæ of Paulus. The edict was doubtless drawn up by Roman writers, but the original sources are more disfigured and altered than in any other compilation. This collection of law was intended to apply both to the Goths and the Romans, so far as its provisions went; but, when it made no alteration in the Gothic law, that law was still to be in force. Savigny, Geschichte des R. R.

EDICTUM TRALATITIUM. Where a Roman prætor, upon assuming office, did not publish a wholly new edict, but retained the whole or a principal part of the edict of his predecessor (as was usually the case) only adding to it such rules as appeared to be necessary to adapt it to changing social conditions or juristic ideas, it was called "edictum tralatitium." Mackeld.Rom.Law, § 36.

EDITION. Any quantity of books put forth to the bookselling trade at one time by the publisher. 4 K. & J. 656. A new edition is published whenever, having in his warehouse a certain number of copies, the publisher issues a fresh batch of them to the public.

EDITOR. One who directs or supervises the policies and contributions of a newspaper, magazine, work of reference, or the like. Brokaw v. Cottrell, 211 N.W. 184, 187, 114 Neb. 858. The term is held to include not only the person who writès or selects the articles for publication, but he who publishes a paper and puts it in circulation. Pennoyer v. Neff, 95 U.S. 721, 24 L.Ed. 565.

EDITUS. In old English law. Put forth or promulgated, when speaking of the passage of a statute; and brought forth, or born, when speaking of the birth of a child.

EDMUNDS ACT. An act of congress of March 22, 1882, punishing polygamy. See 22 Stat. 31.

EDUCATE. To give proper moral, as well as intellectual and physical, instruction. See Williams v. MacDougall, 39 Cal. 80; Peck v. Claflin, 105 Mass. 420. To prepare and fit oneself for any calling or business, or for activity and usefulness in life. In re Wolfe's Estate, 299 N.Y.S. 99, 102, 164 Misc. 504.

EDUCATION. Comprehends not merely the instruction received at school or college, but the whole course of training, moral, intellectual, and physical. Education may be particularly directed to either the mental, moral, or physical powers and faculties, but in its broadest and best sense it relates to them all. Barbers' Commission of Mobile County v. Hardeman, 21 So.2d 118, 120, 31 Ala.App. 626. Acquisition of all knowledge tending to train and develop the individual. Mitchell v. Reeves, 123 Conn. 549, 196 A. 785, 788, 15 A.L.R. 1114.

"Education" is not confined to the improvement and cultivation of the mind, but may consist of the cultivation of one's religious or moral sentiments, and likewise may consist in the development of one's physical faculties. Commissioners of District of Columbia v. Shannon & Luchs Const. Co., 57 App.D.C. 67, 17 F.2d 219, 220; Jones v. Better Business Bureau of Oklahoma City, C.C.A.Okla., 123 F.2d 767, 769.

EDUCATIONAL INSTITUTION. A school, seminary, college, or educational establishment, not necessarily a chartered institution. Ward Seminary for Young Ladies v. City of Nashville, 129 Tenn. 412, 167 S.W. 113. As used in a zoning ordinance, the term may include not only buildings, but also all grounds necessary for the accomplishment of the full scope of educational instruction, including those things essential to mental, moral, and physical development. Commissioners of District of Columbia v. Shannon & Luchs Const. Co., 57 App.D.C. 67, 17 F.2d 219, 220.

EDUCATIONAL PURPOSES. Synonymous with an educational undertaking, and whatever educates is within the meaning of an "educational undertaking." Ancient and Accepted Scottish Rite of Freemasonry v. Board of County Com'rs, 122 Neb. 586, 241 N.W. 93, 95.

EDUCATIONAL TRAINING. Acquisition of information or inspirational suggestions which cause the individual to think and act along proper lines. Jones v. Better Business Bureau of Oklahoma City, C.C.A.Okl., 123 F.2d 767, 769.

EFFECT, *v.* To do; to produce; to make; to bring to pass; to execute; enforce; accomplish. Vailsburg Motor Corporation v. Fidelity & Casualty Co., 110 N.J.L. 209, 164 A. 408, 409. A belief that a mortgage would "effect" a preference under the bankruptcy act is equivalent to a belief that it would "operate as" a preference. Ogden v. Reddish, D.C.Ky., 200 F. 977, 979.

EFFECT, *n.* Result. Western Indemnity Co. v. MacKechnie, Tex.Civ.App., 214 S.W. 456, 460; Beeler v. People, 58 Colo. 451, 146 P. 762, 764. The result which an instrument between parties will produce in their relative rights, or which a statute will produce upon the existing law, as discovered from the language used, the forms employed, or other materials for construing it. The operation of a law, of an agreement, or an act. Maize v. State, 4 Ind. 342.

The phrases "take effect," "be in force," "go into operation," etc., are used interchangeably. Maize v. State, 4 Ind. 342.

With Effect

With success; as, to prosecute an action with effect. Schutze v. Dabney, Tex.Civ.App., 204 S.W. 342, 347.

EFFECTING LOAN. Renewal of original note without lending of new money held not "effecting of loan," within statute prohibiting officers or employees of banking department from effecting loans from state bank. To effect a loan within such statute means to bring about a loan, to accomplish, fulfill, or produce or make a loan. It means the result or consequence, the bringing into operation of a loan; while "renewal" is not a loan, but an extension of the time of payment. State v. Love, 150 So. 196, 199, 170 Miss. 666, 90 A.L.R. 506.

EFFECTIVE PROCURING CAUSE. The "effective procuring cause," of sale of realty is ordinarily the broker who first secures the serious attention of the customer and is instrumental in bringing the parties together. In re Cowan's Estate, 13 N.Y.S.2d 374, 377.

EFFECTS. Personal estate or property. See Johnson v. Olson, 92 Kan. 819, 142 P. 256, 258, L.R.A.1915E, 327. Movable or chattel property of any kind. Ettlinger v. Importers' & Exporters' Ins. Co. of New York, 247 N.Y.S. 260, 262, 138 Misc. 743.

In this sense, the term is more comprehensive than the word "goods," as including fixtures and choses in action, which "goods" will not include. Bank v. Byram, 131 Ill. 92, 22 N.E. 842.

Also, every kind of property, real and personal. Child v. Orton, 119 N.J.Eq. 438, 183 A. 709, 710; Adams v. Akerlund, 48 N.E. 454, 168 Ill. 632; Castle v. Castle, C.C.A.Hawaii, 267 F. 521, 523; Erickson v. Carlson, 145 N.W. 352, 95 Neb. 182; Peterson's Estate, 151 N.W. 66, 68, 168 Iowa 511, L.R.A. 1916A, 469.

In Wills

Personal property; goods; worldly substance. If the term is used *simpliciter,* as in a gift of "all my effects," it will carry the whole personal estate, unless an intention appears to the contrary. Schouler, Wills, § 509. In re Mitchell's Will, 38 N.Y.S.2d 673, 674, 675. The meaning of the term is determined by the context and surrounding circumstances; Coffman's Adm'r v. Coffman, 131 Va. 456, 109 S.E. 454, 459; and is broad enough to include property of any kind. In re Lafferty's Estate, 311 Pa. 469, 167 A. 49, 50.

The words "real and personal effects" will embrace the whole estate. Hogan v. Jackson, Cowp. 304; The Alpena, D.C., 7 F. 361; 15 M. & W. 450; Foxall v. McKenney, 3 Cranch C.C. 206, Fed.Cas. No.5,016.

EFFECTUS SEQUITUR CAUSAM. Wing. 226. The effect follows the cause.

EFFENDI. Turkish. Master; a title of respect.

EFFET. In France an "effet" is a bill of exchange; "effets" means goods, movables, chattels. In re Steimes' Estate, 270 N.Y.S. 339, 150 Misc. 279.

EFFETS MOBILIERS. Funds or stocks. In re Steimes' Estate, 270 N.Y.S. 339, 150 Misc. 279.

EFFICIENT. Causing an effect;—particularly the result or results contemplated. Tate-Jones & Co. v. Union Electric Steel Co., 281 Pa. 448, 126 A. 813, 816. The term is not an antonym of "defective." Adequate in performance or producing properly a desired effect. Spotts v. Baltimore & O. R. Co., C.C.A.Ind., 102 F.2d 160, 162.

EFFICIENT CAUSE. The working cause; that cause which produces effects or results; an intervening cause, which produces results which would not have come to pass except for its interposition, and for which, therefore, the person who set in motion the original chain of causes is not responsible. Southland-Greyhound Lines v. Cotten, Tex. Civ.App., 55 S.W.2d 1066, 1069; The cause which originates and sets in motion the dominating agency that necessarily proceeds through other causes as mere instruments or vehicles in a natural line of causation to the result. That cause of an injury to which legal liability attaches. Bole v. Pittsburgh Athletic Club, C.C.A., 205 F. 468, 471, 46 L.R.A.,N.S., 602. The "proximate cause." Munger v. Hancock, Tex.Civ.App., 271 S.W. 228, 231. Hilles v. Home Owners' Loan Corporation, 348 Mo. 601, 154 S.W.2d 761, 764. The phrase is practically synonymous with "procuring cause." Buhrmester v. Independent Plumbing & Heating Supply Co., Mo.App., 151 S.W.2d 509, 513.

EFFICIENT INTERVENING CAUSE. One not produced by a wrongful act or omission but independent of it, and adequate to bring the injurious results. State v. Des Champs, 126 S.C. 416, 120 S. E. 491, 493. A new and independent force which breaks casual connection between original wrong and injury. Anderson v. Byrd, 133 Neb. 483, 275 N.W. 825, 826; Bennett v. Robertson, 107 Vt. 202, 177 A. 625, 628, 98 A.L.R. 152.

EFFIGY. The figure or corporeal representation of a person.

EFFLUX. The running, as of a prescribed period of time to its end; expiration by lapse of time. Particularly applied to the termination of a lease by the expiration of the term for which it was made.

EFFLUXION OF TIME. When this phrase is used in leases, conveyances, and other like deeds, or in agreements expressed in simple writing, it indicates the conclusion or expiration of an agreed term of years specified in the deed or writing, such conclusion or expiration arising in the natural course of events, in contradistinction to the determination of the term by the acts of the parties or by some unexpected or unusual incident or other sudden event. Brown.

EFFORCIALITER. Forcibly; applied to military force.

EFFORT. An attempt; an endeavor; a struggle directed to the accomplishment of an object. Dulaney v. Burns, 218 Ala. 493, 119 So. 21, 24.

EFFRACTION. A breach made by the use of force.

EFFRACTOR. One who breaks through; one who commits a burglary.

EFFUSIO SANGUINIS. In old English law. The shedding of blood; the mulct, fine, *wite,* or penalty imposed for the shedding of blood, which the king granted to many lords of manors. Cowell; Tomlins. See Bloodwit.

EFTERS. In Saxon law. Ways, walks, or hedges. Blount.

EGALITY. Owelty, (*q. v.*) Co. Litt. 169*a*.

EGG ALBUMEN. The white of egg. For commercial purposes, dried, uncoagulated egg. International Cork Co. v. New Process Cork Co., C.C.A.N.Y., 6 F.2d 420, 421.

EGLISE. A church.

EGO. I; myself. This term is used in forming genealogical tables, to represent the person who is the object of inquiry.

EGO, TALIS. I, such a one. Words used in describing the forms of old deeds. Fleta, lib. 3, c. 14, § 5.

EGREDIENS ET EXEUNS. In old pleading. Going forth and issuing out of (land.) Townsh. Pl. 17.

EGRESS. Often used interchangeably with the word "access." C. Hacker Co. v. City of Joliet, 196 Ill.App. 415, 423.

EGYPTIANS, commonly called "Gypsies" (in old English statutes,) are counterfeit rogues, Welsh or English, that disguise themselves in speech and apparel, and wander up and down the country, pretending to have skill in telling fortunes, and to deceive the common people, but live chiefly by filching or stealing, and, therefore, the statutes of 1 & 2 Mar. c. 4, and 5 Eliz. c. 20, were made to punish such as felons if they departed not the realm or continued to a month. Termes de la Ley.

EI INCUMBIT PROBATIO, QUI DICIT, NON QUI NEGAT; CUM PER RERUM NATURAM FACTUM NEGANTIS PROBATIO NULLA SIT. The proof lies upon him who affirms, not upon him who denies; since, by the nature of things, he who denies a fact cannot produce any proof. Dig. 22, 3, 2; 1 Phill. Ev. 194; 1 Greenl. Ev. § 74; Dranguet v. Prudhomme, 3 La. 83; 2 Dan.Ch.Pr. 408.

EI NIHIL TURPE, CUI NIHIL SATIS. To him to whom nothing is enough, nothing is base. 4 Inst. 53.

EIA, or EY. An island. Cowell.

EIGNE. L. Fr. Eldest; eldest-born. The term is of common occurrence in the old books. Thus, *bastard eigne* means an illegitimate son whose parents afterwards marry and have a second son for lawful issue, the latter being called *mulier puisne,* (after-born.) *Eigne* is probably a corrupt form of the French "*aîné.*" 2 Bl.Comm. 248; Litt. § 399.

EIGNESSE. See Esnecy.

EIK. In Scotch law. An addition; as, *eik* to a reversion, *eik* to a confirmation. Bell.

EINECIA. Eldership. See Esnecy.

EINETIUS. In English law. The oldest; the first-born. Spelman.

EIRE, or EYRE. In old English law. A journey, route, or circuit. Justices *in eire* were judges who were sent by commission, every seven years, into various counties to hold the assizes and hear pleas of the crown. 3 Bl.Comm. 58.

EIRENARCHA. A name formerly given to a justice of the peace. In the Digests, the word is written "*irenarcha.*"

EISDEM MODIS DISSOLVITUR OBLIGATIO QUÆ NASCITUR EX CONTRACTU, VEL QUASI, QUIBUS CONTRAHITUR. An obligation which arises from contract, or *quasi* contract, is dissolved in the same ways in which it is contracted. Fleta, lib. 2, c. 60, § 19.

EISNE. The senior; the oldest son. Spelled, also, "*eigne,*" "*einsne,*" "*aisne,*" "*eign.*" Termes de la Ley; Kelham.

EISNETIA, EINETIA. The share of the oldest son. The portion acquired by primogeniture. Termes de la Ley; Co.Litt. 166*b*; Cowell.

EITHER. Each of two; the one and the other; one or the other of two alternatives; one of two. Dallas Ry. & Terminal Co. v. Allen, Tex., 43 S.W. 2d 165, 170; Alswager v. Dwelle, 70 N.D. 118, 292 N.W. 223, 224, 128 A.L.R. 1150. Often used, however, with reference to more than two, in which case it may mean "each" or "any." In re Broun's Estate, 343 Pa. 19, 21 A.2d 898, 901. Carr-Lowry Lumber Co. v. Martin, 144 Miss. 106, 109 So. 849, 850; Southern Ry. Co. v. Gaston County, 200 N. C. 780, 158 S.E. 481, 483. Watson v. Watson, 223 Mass. 425, 111 N.E. 904, 906.

EJECT. To cast, or throw out; to oust, or dispossess; to put or turn out of possession. 3 Bl. Comm. 198, 199, 200. See Bohannon v. Southern Ry. Co., 112 Ky. 106, 65 S.W. 169. To expel or thrust forcibly, as passengers from a train. Louisville & N. R. Co. v. Ogles, 142 Ga. 720, 83 S.E. 681, 683.

EJECTA. In old English law. A woman ravished or deflowered, or cast forth from the virtuous. Blount.

EJECTION. A turning out of possession. 3 Bl. Comm. 199.

EJECTIONE CUSTODIÆ. In old English law. Ejectment of ward. This phrase, which is the Latin equivalent for the French *"ejectment de garde,"* was the title of a writ which lay for a guardian when turned out of any land of his ward during the minority of the latter. Brown. It lay to recover the land or person of his ward, or both. Fitzh. N.B. 139, L.; Co.Litt. 199.

EJECTIONE FIRMÆ. Ejection, or ejectment of farm. The name of a writ or action of trespass, which lay at common law where lands or tenements were let for a term of years, and afterwards the lessor, reversioner, remainder-man, or any stranger *ejected* or ousted the lessee of his term, *ferme,* or *farm, (ipsum a firma ejecit.)* In this case the latter might have his writ of *ejection,* by which he recovered at first damages for the trespass only, but it was afterwards made a remedy to recover back the term itself, or the remainder of it, with damages. Reg.Orig. 227*b*; Fitzh. Nat. Brev. 220, F, G; 3 Bl.Comm. 199; Litt. § 322; Crabb, Eng.Law, 290, 448. It is the foundation of the modern action of ejectment.

EJECTMENT. At common law, this was the name of a mixed action (springing from the earlier personal action of *ejectione firmæ*) which lay for the recovery of the possession of land, and for damages for the unlawful detention of its possession. The action was highly fictitious, being in theory only for the recovery of a term for years, and brought by a purely fictitious person, as lessee in a supposed lease from the real party in interest. The latter's title, however, must be established in order to warrant a recovery, and the establishment of such title, though nominally a mere incident, is in reality the object of the action. Hence this convenient form of suit came to be adopted as the usual method of trying titles to land. See 3 Bl.Comm. 199. French v. Robb, 67 N.J.Law, 260, 51 A. 509, 57 L.R.A. 956, 91 Am.St. Rep. 433. In England, since the Judicature Act, ejectment has given place to a new action for the recovery of land. Ejectment has been materially modified in many of the states, though still retaining the name. For the history of ejectment, see 3 Sel.Essays in Anglo-Amer. L. Hist. 611.

It was the only mixed action at common law, the whole method of proceeding in which was anomalous, and depended on fictions invented and upheld by the court for the convenience of justice, in order to escape from the inconveniences which were found to attend the ancient forms of real and mixed actions.

It is also a form of action by which possessory titles to corporeal hereditaments may be tried and possession obtained.

Ejectment Bill

A bill in equity brought merely for the recovery of real property, together with an account of the rents and profits, without setting out any distinct ground of equity jurisdiction; hence demurrable. Crane v. Conklin, 1 N.J.Eq. 353, 22 Am.Dec. 519.

Equitable Ejectment

A proceeding in use in Pennsylvania, brought to enforce specific performance of a contract for the sale of land, and for some other purposes, which is in form an action of ejectment, but is in reality a substitute for a bill in equity. Riel v. Gannon, 161 Pa. 289, 29 A. 55.

Justice Ejectment

A statutory proceeding in Vermont, for the eviction of a tenant holding over after termination of the lease or breach of its conditions. Foss v. Stanton, 76 Vt. 365, 57 A. 942.

EJECTOR. One who ejects, puts out, or dispossesses another.

Casual Ejector

The nominal defendant in an action of ejectment; so called because, by a fiction of law peculiar to that action, he is supposed to come casually or by accident upon the premises and to eject the lawful possessor. 3 Bl.Comm. 203.

EJECTUM. That which is thrown up by the sea. Also jetsam, wreck, etc. Warder v. La Belle Creole, 1 Pet.Adm.Dec. 43, Fed.Cas.No.17,165.

EJECTUS. In old English law. A whore-monger. Blount.

EJERCITORIA. In Spanish law. The name of an action lying against a ship's owner, upon the contracts or obligations made by the master for repairs or supplies. It corresponds to the *actio exercitoria* of the Roman law. Mackeld. Rom. Law, § 512.

EJIDOS. In Spanish law. Commons; lands used in common by the inhabitants of a city, pueblo, or town, for pasture, wood, threshing-ground, etc. Hart v. Burnett, 15 Cal. 554.

EJURATION. Renouncing or resigning one's place.

EJUS EST INTERPRETARI CUJUS EST CONDERE. It is his to interpret whose it is to enact. Tayl. Civil Law, 96.

EJUS EST NOLLE, QUI POTEST VELLE. He who can will, [exercise volition,] has a right to refuse to will, [to withhold consent.] Dig. 50, 7, 3. This maxim is sometimes written, *Ejus est non nolle qui potest velle,* and is translated, "He may consent tacitly who may consent expressly."

EJUS EST PERICULUM CUJUS EST DOMINIUM AUT COMMODUM. He who has the dominion or advantage has the risk. Bart.Max. 33.

EJUS NULLA CULPA EST, CUI PARERE NECESSE SIT. No guilt attaches to him who is compelled to obey. Dig. 50, 17, 169, pr. Obedience to existing laws is a sufficient extenuation of guilt before a civil tribunal. Broom, Max. 12, note.

EJUSDEM GENERIS. Of the same kind, class, or nature.

In the construction of laws, wills, and other instruments, the "ejusdem generis rule" is, that where general words follow an enumeration of persons or things, by words of a particular and specific meaning, such general words are not to be construed in their widest extent, but are to be held as applying only to persons or things of the same general kind or class as those specifically mentioned. Black, Interp. of Laws, 141; Goldsmith v. U. S., C.C.A.N.Y., 42 F.2d 133, 137; Aleksich v. Industrial Accident Fund, 116 Mont. 69, 151 P.2d 1016, 1021. The rule, however, does not necessarily require that the general provision be limited in its scope to the identical things specifically named. Nor does it apply when the context manifests a contrary intention.

The maxim "ejusdem generis," is only an illustration of the broader maxim, "noscitur a sociis." State v. Western Union Telegraph Co., 196 Ala. 570, 72 So. 99, 100.

ELABORARE. In old European law. To gain, acquire, or purchase, as by labor and industry.

ELABORATUS. Property which is the acquisition of labor. Spelman.

ELASTIC. Pertaining to a substance having the property of returning or springing back to its original form after being disarranged by pressure or applied force;—to be distinguished from "plastic," which applies to a substance capable of being molded and pressed into form. Diamond Patent Co. v. Webster Bros., C.C.A.Cal., 249 F. 155, 157; Kitson Co. v. Lattimer-Stevens Co., C.C.A.Pa., 37 F.2d 562, 563.

ELDER BRETHREN. A distinguished body of men, elected as masters of Trinity House, an institution incorporated in the reign of Henry VIII., charged with numerous important duties relating to the marine, such as the superintendence of light-houses. Mozley & Whitley; 2 Steph.Comm. 502. The full title of the corporation is Elder Brethren of the Holy and Undivided Trinity.

ELDER TITLE. A title of earlier date, but coming simultaneously into operation with a title of younger origin, is called the "elder title," and prevails.

ELDEST. He or she who has the greatest age. The eldest son is the first-born, the *primo-genitus;* L.R. 2 App.Cas. 698; L.R. 12 Ch.Div. 171; Anderson v. Anderson, C.C.A.S.C., 221 F. 871, 874. If there is only one son, he may still be described as the "eldest." L.R. 7 H.L. 644.

ELECTA UNA VIA, NON DATUR RECURSUS AD ALTERAM. He who has chosen one way cannot have recourse to another. 10 Toull. no. 170.

ELECTED. The word "elected," in its ordinary signification, carries with it the idea of a vote, generally popular, sometimes more restricted, and cannot be held the synonym of any other mode of filling a position. Kimberlin v. State, 130 Ind. 120, 29 N.E. 773, 14 L.R.A. 858, 30 Am.St.Rep. 208.

ELECTIO EST INTERNA LIBERA ET SPONTANEA SEPARATIO UNIUS REI AB ALIA, SINE COMPULSIONE, CONSISTENS IN ANIMO ET VOLUNTATE. Dyer, 281. Election is an internal, free, and spontaneous separation of one thing from another, without compulsion, consisting in intention and will.

ELECTIO SEMEL FACTA, ET PLACITUM TESTATUM NON PATITUR REGRESSUM. Co.Litt. 146. Election once made, and plea witnessed (or intent shown), suffers not a recall.

ELECTION. The act of choosing or selecting one or more from a greater number of persons, things, courses, or rights. The choice of an alternative. State v. Tucker, 54 Ala. 210.

The internal, free, and spontaneous separation of one thing from another, without compulsion, consisting in intention and will. Dyer, 281.

The selection of one person from a specified class to discharge certain duties in a state, corporation, or society. Smith v. McQueen, 232 Ala. 90, 166 So. 788, 791.

With respect to the choice of persons to fill public office or the decision of a particular public question or public policy the term means in ordinary usage the expression by vote of the will of the people or of a somewhat numerous body of electors. State v. State Board of Canvassers, 78 S.C. 461, 59 S.E. 145. But this is not necessarily so, for the term may apply to the selection by a city council of one of their number as mayor.

"Election" ordinarily has reference to a choice or selection by electors, while "appointment" refers to a choice or selection by an individual, as the Governor, or an official body. Board of Education of Boyle County v. McChesney, 235 Ky. 692, 32 S.W.2d 26, 27. But the terms are sometimes used interchangeably. Van Cleve v. Wallace, 216 Minn. 500, 13 N.W.2d 467, 469.

A primary election is an "election" within the constitutional provision. United States v. Classic, 61 S.Ct. 1031, 1039, 313 U.S. 299, 85 L.Ed. 1368; Ex parte Hawthorne, 116 Fla. 608, 156 So. 619, 622, 96 A.L.R. 572. But the contrary view has been expressed, Mathes v. State, 173 Tenn. 511, 121 S.W.2d 548, 549; People ex rel. Lindstrand v. Emmerson, 333 Ill. 606, 165 N.E. 217, 223, 62 A.L.R. 912. Referendum elections are "elections". Masters v. Duval County, 114 Fla. 205, 154 So. 172, 176. To the contrary, Vulcan Last Co. v. State, 194 Wis. 636, 217 N.W. 412, 414.

The choice which is open to a debtor who is bound in an alternative obligation to select either one of the alternatives.

Equitable Election

See Equitable Election.

General Election

One at which the officers to be elected are such as belong to the *general* government,—that is, the general and central political organization of the whole state; as distinguished from an election of officers for a particular locality only. Also, one held for the selection of an officer after the expiration of the full term of the former officer; thus distinguished from a *special* election, which is one held to supply a vacancy in office occurring before the expiration of the full term for which the incumbent was elected. Downs v. State, 78 Md. 128, 26 A. 1005. One that regularly recurs in each election precinct of the state on a day designated by law for the selection of officers, or is held in such entire territory pursuant to an enactment specifying a single day for the ratification or rejection of one or more measures submitted to the people by the Legislative Assembly, and not for the election of any officer. Bethune v. Funk, 166 P. 931, 932, 85 Or. 246. One that is held throughout the entire state or territory. Territory v. Ricordati, 18 N.M. 10, 132 P. 1139, 1140. An election for the choice of a national, state, judicial, district, municipal, county, or township official, required by law to be held regularly at a designated time, to fill a new office or a vacancy in an office at the expiration of the full term thereof. Eakle v. Board of Education of Independent School Dist. of Henry, 97 W.Va. 434, 125 S.E. 165, 168. In statutes, the term may include a primary election. Kelso v. Cook, 184 Ind. 173, 110 N.E. 987, 993, Ann.Cas.1918E, 68. *Contra*, under a municipal charter, City Council of San Jose v. Goodwin, 196 Cal. 274, 237 P. 548, 549. In Vermont, the term is used throughout the Public Statutes to designate what before had commonly been known as "freeman's meeting." Martin v. Fullam, 97 A. 442, 445, 90 Vt. 163.

In Criminal Law

The choice, by the prosecution, upon which of several counts in an indictment (charging distinct offenses of the same degree, but not parts of a continuous series of acts) it will proceed. Jackson v. State, 95 Ala. 17, 10 So. 657.

In Practice

The liberty of choosing (or the act of choosing) one out of several means afforded by law for the redress of an injury, or one out of several available forms of action.

An "election of remedies" arises when one having two coexistent but inconsistent remedies chooses to exercise one, in which event he loses the right to thereafter exercise the other. Mosher Mfg. Co. v. Eastland W. F. & G. R. Co., Tex.Civ.App., 259 S.W. 253, 255.

An "election of remedies" is choosing between two or more different and coexisting modes of procedure and relief allowed by law on the same state of facts. Pacific Mut. Life Ins. Co. of California v. Rhame, D.C.S.C., 32 F.Supp. 59, 63; Doggett Lumber Co. v. Perry, 212 N.C. 713, 194 S.E. 475, 478.

"Election of remedies" is a species of estoppel in pais. Mansfield v. Pickwick Stages, Northern Division, 191 Cal. 129, 215 P. 389, 390.

In the Law of Wills

A widow's election is her choice whether she will take under the will or under the statute; that is, whether she will accept the provision made for her in the will, and acquiesce in her husband's disposition of his property, or disregard it and claim what the law allows her. Logan v. Logan, Tex.Civ.App., 112 S.W.2d 515, 518; Schlimme v. Schlimme, 364 Ill. 303, 4 N.E.2d 369, 370.

An "election under the will" means that a legatee or devisee under a will is put to the choice of accepting the beneficial interest offered by the donor in lieu of some estate which he is entitled to, but which is taken from him by the terms of the will. McDermid v. Bourhill, 101 Or. 305, 199 P. 610, 612, 22 A.L.R. 428.

Primary Election

An election by the voters of a ward, precinct, or other small district, belonging to a particular party, of representatives or delegates to a convention which is to meet and nominate the candidates of their party to stand at an approaching municipal or general election. State v. Woodruff, 68 N.J.Law, 89, 52 A. 294. Also, an election to select candidates for office by a political organization, the voters being restricted to the members or supporters of such organization. Kelso v. Cook, 184 Ind. 173, 110 N.E. 987, Ann.Cas.1918E, 68. They are not in reality elections but are merely nominating devices. Van Dyke v. Thompson, 136 Tenn. 136, 189 S.W. 62, 66.

Regular Election

One recurring at stated times fixed by law. State v. Andresen, 110 Or. 1, 222 P. 585, 587. A general, usual, or stated election. When applied to elections, the terms "regular" and "general" are used interchangeably and synonymously. The word "regular" is used in reference to a general election occurring throughout the state. State v. Conrades, 45 Mo. 47; Ward v. Clark, 35 Kan. 315, 10 P. 827.

Result of Election

Usually, the expression of the will of the voters as determined by a count of the ballots. Cipowski v. Calumet City, 322 Ill. 575, 153 N.E. 613, 614.

Special Election

An election for a particular emergency; out of the regular course; as one held to fill a vacancy arising by death of the incumbent of the office. State v. Andresen, 110 Or. 1, 222 P. 585, 587. In a statute, any election at which officers are not chosen. Hutchins v. City of Des Moines, 176 Iowa 189, 157 N.W. 881, 883. In determining whether an election is special or general, regard must be had to the subject-matter as well as date of the election, and, if an election occurs throughout state uniformly by direct operation of law, it is a "general election," but, if it depends on employment of special preliminary proceeding peculiar to process which may or may not occur, and the election is applicable only to a restricted area less than whole state, it is a "special election." Hill v. Hartzell, 121 Or. 4, 252 P. 552, 555.

ELECTION AUDITORS. In English law. Officers annually appointed, to whom was committed the duty of taking and publishing the account of all expenses incurred at parliamentary elections. See 17 & 18 Vict. c. 102, §§ 18, 26–28. But these sections have been repealed by 26 Vict. c. 29, which throws the duty of preparing the accounts on the declared agent of the candidate, and the duty of publishing an abstract of it on the returning officer. Wharton.

ELECTION CONTEST. A contest in behalf of one who has failed of success in election against right of one who has been declared or determined by proper authority to have been successful. State ex rel. Ingles v. Circuit Court of Spink County, 63 S.D. 313, 258 N.W. 278.

ELECTION DISTRICT. A subdivision of territory, whether of state, county, or city, the boundaries of which are fixed by law, for convenience in local or general elections. Lane v. Otis, 68 N.J. Law, 656, 54 A. 442.

The term has been held not to refer to senatorial district. Appeal of Phillips, 262 Pa. 396, 105 A. 547, 548.

ELECTION DOWER. A name sometimes given to the provision which a law or statute makes for a widow in case she "elects" to reject the provision made for her in the will and take what the statute accords. Stanton v. Leonard, 344 Mo. 998, 130 S.W.2d 487, 489.

ELECTION, ESTOPPEL BY. An estoppel which arises by a choice between inconsistent remedies. Aladdin Temple Ben. Ass'n, D. O. K. K. v. American Standard Life Ins. Co., 235 Ala. 431, 179 So. 243, 245.

An estoppel predicated on a voluntary and intelligent action or choice of one of several things which is inconsistent with another, the effect of the estoppel being to prevent the party so choosing from afterwards reversing his election or disputing the state of affairs or rights of others resulting from his original choice. Yates v. Hurd, 8 Colo. 343, 8 Pac. 575.

The doctrine of "estoppel by election" against beneficiary who has elected to take favorable provisions of will from objecting to other provisions of will applies only where will undertakes to bestow a gift and also deprive donee of a prior existing right, thus confronting devisee with alternative of accepting devise and renouncing prior right or of retaining latter and renouncing devise. Mason & Mason v. Brown, Tex.Civ.App., 182 S.W.2d 729, 733.

ELECTION JUDGES. In English law. Judges of the high court selected in pursuance of 31 & 32 Vict. c. 125, § 11, and Jud. Act 1873, § 38, for the trial of election petitions.

ELECTION PETITIONS. Petitions for inquiry into the validity of elections of members of parliament when it is alleged that the return of a member is invalid for bribery or any other reason.

ELECTION RETURNS. The report made to the board of canvassers of the number of votes cast for each candidate, or proposition voted upon by those charged by law with the duty of counting or tallying the votes for or against the respective candidates or propositions. Spear v. Marshall, 95 Utah 62, 79 P.2d 15, 16.

ELECTIONES FIANT RITE ET LIBERE SINE INTERRUPTIONE ALIQUA. Elections should be made in due form, and freely, without any interruption. 2 Inst. 169.

ELECTIVE. Dependent upon choice; bestowed or passing by election. Also pertaining or relating to elections; conferring the right or power to vote at elections.

ELECTIVE FRANCHISE. The right of voting at public elections; the privilege of qualified voters to cast their ballots for the candidates they favor at elections authorized by law. People v. Barber, 48 Hun, N.Y. 198; State v. Staten, 6 Cold. Tenn. 255; Xippas v. Commonwealth, 141 Va. 497, 126 S.E. 207, 209.

ELECTIVE OFFICE. One which is to be filled by popular election. One filled by the direct exercise of the voters' franchise. In re Opinion of the Justices, 83 N.H. 589, 139 A. 180, 183.

ELECTOR. A duly qualified voter; one who has a vote in the choice of any officer; a constituent. DeBauche v. City of Green Bay, 227 Wis. 148, 277 N.W. 147, 148. One who elects or has the right of choice, or who has the right to vote for any functionary, or for the adoption of any measure. Aczel v. United States, C.C.A.Ind., 232 F. 652, 657. In a narrower sense, one who has the general right to vote, and the right to vote for public officers. One authorized to exercise the elective franchise. McEvoy v. Christensen, 178 Iowa, 1180, 159 N.W. 179, 181. But a woman citizen, though having such general right and authority to vote, may nevertheless not be an "elector" entitled to have her name put on a jury list, in view of a state constitution and statute. People v. Barnett, 319 Ill. 403, 150 N.E. 290, 291.

While the terms "electors" and "voters" are sometimes used interchangeably, their meaning is not precisely the same, "electors" being properly applied to all those entitled to vote, whereas "voters" appropriately designates only those actually voting. State ex rel. Chaney v. Grinstead, 314 Mo. 55, 282 S.W. 715, 719. A fortiori, "electors" is a broader term than "registered voters." City of Dayton, Ohio, v. City Ry. Co., C.C.A.Ohio, 16 F.2d 401, 405.

One of the persons chosen to comprise the "electoral college" (*q. v.*).

Also, the title of certain German princes who had a voice in the election of the Holy Roman Emperors. The office of elector in some instances became hereditary and was connected with territorial possessions.

Sometimes, one who exercises the right of election in equity. Brett, L. Cas. Mod. Eq. 257.

Registered Qualified Elector

One possessing the constitutional qualifications, and registered under the registration statute. Minges v. Board of Trustees of City of Merced, 27 Cal.App. 15, 148 P. 816, 817.

ELECTORAL. Pertaining to electors or elections; composed or consisting of electors.

ELECTORAL COLLEGE. A name sometimes given, in the United States, to the college or body of electors of a state chosen to elect the president and vice-president; also, the whole body of such electors, composed of the electoral colleges of the several states. Webster; Cent. Dict.; 2 Sto. Const. § 1463; 1 Hare, Am.Const.L. 219; Stevens, Sources of the Constitution of the U. S. 153, note; Black, Const.L. 86; 1 Calhoun's Works, 175.

ELECTORAL COMMISSION. A commission created by an act of congress of January 29, 1877, to decide certain questions arising out of the presidential election of November, 1876, in which Hayes and Wheeler had been candidates of the Republican party and Tilden and Hendricks of the Democratic party.

ELECTRIC CONDENSER. A device by which excesses of current are stored and released, acting as a sort of elastic cushion for its variations. It is made up of two electrodes, anode and cathode, separated by a nonconductor, the dielectric. The capacity of the condenser depends upon the dielectric, and varies inversely with its thickness. Aerovox Corporation v. Concourse Electric Co., C.C.A.N.Y., 65 F.2d 386, 387. A reservoir of electrical energy. Aurynger v. R C A Mfg. Co., D.C. Md., 35 F.Supp. 69.

ELECTRICITY. A highly subtle imponderable fluid, whose presence or influence is only known by its effect. Myers v. Portland Ry., Light & Power Co., 68 Or. 599, 138 P. 213. An imponderable and invisible agent producing light, heat, chemical decomposition, and other physical phenomena. United States v. City and County of San Francisco, D.C.Cal., 23 F.Supp. 40, 52.

ELECTROCARDIOGRAPHY. The recording in the form of a graph of certain minute electric currents produced by the human heart in the course of its action. Nichols v. Sanborn Co., D.C. Mass., 35 F.Supp. 707, 708.

ELECTROCUTE. To put (a criminal) to death by passing through the body a current of electricity of high power; also, by extension, to kill by an electric current. Ferguson v. State, 90 Fla. 105, 105 So. 840.

The word is a hybrid, and has met with the disapproval of some for that reason. "This barbarism jars the unhappy latinist's nerves much more cruelly than the operation denoted jars those of its victim." Fowler, Dict. of Mod. English Usage (1926), p. 130. "To one having even an elementary knowledge of Latin grammar this word is no less than disgusting, and the thing meant by it is felt to be altogether too good for the word's inventor." Bierce, Write it Right (1909), p. 24. It is not included in the New English Dict. (Oxford, 1897), but is listed without comment in the New Cent. Dict. (1927) and also in Funk & Wagnalls' New Standard Dict. (1925), which spells it "electricute." "It is considered by many to be inelegant, but is widely used and has no accepted equivalent." Webster, New Internatl. Dict. (1927). The word is "now in established use, though formerly much criticized from the learned point of view because of the manner of its formation." Krapp, Comprehensive Guide to Good English (1927), p. 218.

ELECTROCUTION. A method of punishment of death inflicted by causing to pass through the body of the convicted person a current of electricity. See 1 Witth. & Beck. Med. Jur. 663; People v. Durston, 119 N.Y. 569. See Electrocute.

ELECTROLYSIS. The decomposition of a metal solution in water, liquid ammonia, etc., accompanied by decomposition of the water into oxygen and hydrogen or of a mass of molten metal by having an electric current passed through it, Peoria Waterworks Co. v. Peoria Ry. Co., C.C.Ill., 181 F. 990.

As applied to water pipes electrolysis is the stripping off of small particles of the iron when a suitable electrolytic solution is present leaving the carbon of which the pipe is partly composed intact. Peoria Waterworks Co. v. Peoria R. Co., C.C.Ill., 181 F. 990.

The term covers a wide variety of acts, ranging from the removal of superfluous hair by electricity to the electrocution of a human being. People v. Lehrman, 296 N.Y.S. 580, 581, 251 App.Div. 451.

ELECTROLYTE. A substance which when dissolved in liquid is capable of conducting an electric current. Lee v. Congress Beauty Equipment Co., D.C.Mass., 48 F.Supp. 827, 829; Ruben v. Ariston Laboratories, D.C.Ill., 40 F.Supp. 551, 563.

ELEEMOSYNA REGIS, and ELEEMOSYNA ARATRI, or CARUCARUM. A penny which King Ethelred ordered to be paid for every plow in England towards the support of the poor. Leg. Ethel. c. 1.

ELEEMOSYNÆ. Possessions belonging to the church. Blount.

ELEEMOSYNARIA. The place in a religious house where the common alms were deposited, and thence by the almoner distributed to the poor. In old English law, the *aumerie, aumbry,* or *ambry;* words still used in common speech in the north of England, to denote a pantry or cupboard. Cowell. The office of almoner. Cowell.

ELEEMOSYNARIUS. In old English law. An almoner, or chief officer, who received the eleemosynary rents and gifts, and in due method distributed them to pious and charitable uses. Cowell; Wharton.

The name of an officer (lord almoner) of the English kings, in former times, who distributed the royal alms or bounty. Fleta, lib. 2, c. 23.

ELEEMOSYNARY. Relating to the distribution of alms, bounty, or charity; charitable. In re Bailey's Estate, 19 Cal.App.2d 135, 65 P.2d 102, 103.

ELEEMOSYNARY CORPORATION. A private corporation created for charitable and benevolent purposes. Society for Propagation of Gospel v. New Haven, 8 Wheat. 464, 5 L.Ed. 662; 1 Bl. Comm. 471. See Corporations.

ELEGANTER. In the civil law. Accurately; with discrimination. Veazie v. Williams, 3 Story, 611, 636, Fed.Cas.No.16,907.

ELEGIT. (Lat. He has chosen.) This is the name, in English practice, of a writ of execution first given by the statute of Westm. 2 (13 Edw. I. c. 18) either upon a judgment for a debt or damages or upon the forfeiture of a recognizance taken in the king's court. It is so called because it is in the choice or election of the plaintiff whether he will sue out this writ or a fi. fa. By it the defendant's goods and chattels are appraised and all of them (except oxen and beasts of the plow) are delivered to the plaintiff, at such reasonable appraisement and price, in part satisfaction of his debt. If the goods are not sufficient, then the moiety of his freehold lands, which he had at the time of the judgment given, are also to be delivered to the plaintiff, to hold till out of the rents and profits thereof the debt be levied, or till the defendant's interest be expired. During this period the plaintiff is called "tenant by *elegit*," and his estate, an "estate by *elegit*." This writ, or its analogue, is in use in some of the United States, as Virginia and Kentucky. See 3 Bl. Comm. 418; North American F. Ins. Co. v. Graham, 5 Sandf. (N.Y.) 197.

ELEMENT. Material; substance. Hoskins Mfg. Co. v. General Electric Co., D.C.Ill., 212 F. 422, 427.

Also, one of the simple substances or principles of which, according to early natural philosophers, the physical universe is composed, the four elements pointed out by Empedocles being air, water, earth, and fire. Webster. See Elements.

ELEMENTS. The forces of nature. The ultimate undecomposable parts which unite to form anything. Leahy v. Wenonah Theater Co., 251 Mich. 594, 232 N.W. 184, 185. Popularly, fire, air, earth, and water, anciently supposed to be the four simple bodies of which the world was composed. Encyc. Dict. Often applied in a particular sense to wind and water, as "the fury of the elements." Cent. Dict. Fire is one of the elements included in the expression "damages by the elements" as used in a lease of a building. O'Neal v. Bainbridge, 94 Kan. 518, 146 P. 1165, 1167, Ann. Cas.1917B, 293. The same is true of water. Mills v. United States, 52 Ct.Cl. 452, 458. It has also been said that "damages by the elements" means the same thing as "damages by the act of God." Van Wormer v. Crane, 51 Mich. 363, 16 N.W. 686, 47 Am.Rep. 582.

ELEVATOR. A building containing one or more mechanical elevators, especially a warehouse for the storage of grain; a hoisting apparatus; a lift; a car or cage for lifting and lowering passengers or freight in a hoistway. Cent. Dict.

In Insurance Law

The term has been held not to be limited to the car, or platform, but to include the elevator shaft. London Guarantee & Accident Co. v. Ladd, C.C.A.Mich., 299 F. 562, 565; Boles v. Royal Union Life Ins. Co., 219 Iowa 178, 257 N.W. 386, 96 A.L. R. 1400. It has also been held to include the machinery to which the car is attached, and by which it is operated; and the fixed equipment necessary to operate the elevator. The term has been interpreted as meaning only a passenger elevator. Jahns & Knuth Co. v. American Indemnity Co., 182 Wis. 556, 196 N.W. 569, 571.

Passenger Elevator

Any elevator ordinarily or customarily used for conveying passengers, though also used for conveying freight, and though not of any particular form laid in any particular way or with any particular kind of gates or safety contrivances. Wilmarth v. Pacific Mut. Life Ins. Co. of California, 168 Cal. 536, 143 P. 780, 782, Ann.Cas.1915B, 1120.

ELIGIBILITY. Proper to be chosen; qualified to be elected; legally qualified. Rainey v. Taylor, 166 Ga. 476, 143 S.E. 383; State ex rel. Evans v. Wheatley, 197 Ark. 997, 125 S.W.2d 101, 103. A word which, when used in connection with an office, where there are no explanatory words indicating that it is used with reference to the time of election, may be deemed to refer to the qualification to hold the office rather than to be elected. Bradfield v. Avery, 16 Idaho, 769, 102 P. 687, 23 L. R.A.,N.S., 1228. See Eligible.

ELIGIBLE. Fit to be chosen. State ex rel. Sundfor v. Thorson, 72 N.D. 246, 6 N.W.2d 89, 92, 143 A.L.R. 599. Capable of serving, legally qualified to serve. State v. Johnson, 123 S.C. 50, 115 S.E. 748, 749. Capable of being chosen, as a candidate for office. Board of Com'rs of Guadalupe County v. District Court of Fourth Judicial Dist., 29 N. M. 244, 223 P. 516, 522. Also, capable of holding office. State v. Wait, 95 Neb. 806, 146 N.W. 1048, 1049.

ELIMINATION. In old English law. The act of banishing or turning out of doors; rejection.

ELINGUATION. The punishment of cutting out the tongue.

ELISORS. In practice. Electors or choosers. Persons appointed by the court to execute writs of *venire*, in cases where both the sheriff and coroner are disqualified from acting, and whose duty is to *choose*—that is, name and return—the jury. 3 Bl.Comm. 355; Doherty v. Kalmbach, 87 F.2d 539, 541, 66 App.D.C. 322.

Persons appointed to execute *any* writ, in default of the sheriff and coroner, are also called "elisors." See Bruner v. Superior Court, 92 Cal. 239, 28 Pac. 341. An elisor may be appointed to take charge of a jury retiring to deliberate upon a verdict, when both sheriff and coroner are disqualified or unable to act. People v. Fellows, 122 Cal. 233, 54 Pac. 830.

ELL. A measure of length, answering to the modern yard. 1 Bl.Comm. 275.

ELLENBOROUGH'S ACT. An English statute (43 Geo. III. c. 58) punishing offenses against the person.

ELLIPSIS. Omission of words or clauses necessary to complete the construction, but not necessary to convey the meaning. State v. Staub, 182 La. 1040, 162 So. 766.

ELOGIUM. In the civil law. A will or testament.

ELOIGNE. (Fr. *éloigner,* to remove to a distance; to remove afar off.) In practice. A return to a writ of replevin, when the chattels have been removed out of the way of the sheriff.

ELOIGNMENT. The getting a thing or person out of the way; or removing it to a distance, so as to be out of reach. Garneau v. Mill Co., 8 Wash. 467, 36 P. 463.

ELONGATA. In practice. Eloigned; carried away to a distance. The old form of the return made by a sheriff to a writ of replevin, stating that the goods or beasts had been *eloigned;* that is, carried to a distance, to places to him unknown. 3 Bl.Comm. 148; 3 Steph.Comm. 522; Fitzh. Nat. Brev. 73, 74; Archb. N. Pract. 552. The word *eloigne* is sometimes used as synonymous with *elongata.*

ELONGATUS. Eloigned. A return made by a sheriff to a writ *de homine replegiando,* stating that the party to be replevied has been eloigned, or conveyed out of his jurisdiction. 3 Bl.Comm. 129.

ELONGAVIT. In England, where in a proceeding by foreign attachment the plaintiff has obtained judgment of appraisement, but by reason of some act of the garnishee the goods cannot be appraised, (as where he has removed them from the city, or has sold them, etc.,) the serjeant-at-mace returns that the garnishee has eloigned them, *i. e.,* removed them out of the jurisdiction, and on this return (called an "elongavit") judgment is given for the plaintiff that an inquiry be made of the goods eloigned. This inquiry is set down for trial, and the assessment is made by a jury after the manner of ordinary issues. Sweet.

ELOPEMENT. The act of a wife who voluntarily deserts her husband to go away with and cohabit with another man. 2 Bl.Comm. 130; State v. O'Higgins, 178 N.C. 708, 100 S.E. 438. The departure of a married woman from her husband and dwelling with an adulterer. Cowell; Tomlin. Also, the act of a man in going away with a woman who has voluntarily left her husband, to indulge in sexual intercourse with her. State v. Hopp, 186 N.C. 405, 119 S.E. 769, 773.

To constitute an elopement, the wife must not only leave the husband, but go beyond his actual control; for if she abandons the husband, and goes and lives in adultery in a house belonging to him, it is said not to be an elopement. Cogswell v. Tibbetts, 3 N.H. 42.

In a popular sense, also, the act of an unmarried woman in secretly leaving her home with a man, especially with a view to marriage without her parents' consent.

ELSEWHERE. In another place; in any other place. See 1 Vern. 4, and note; 3 P.Wms. 56; Azbill v. State, 19 Ariz. 499, 172 P. 658, 659; Supreme Ruling of Fraternal Mystic Circle v. Hoskins, Tex.Civ.App., 171 S.W. 812, 815. The term does not always mean literally any other place whatever, but may be more or less limited by the context. See Commonwealth v. Bowser, 61 Pa. Super.Ct. 107, 108, 114, 214; State v. Sanders, 136 La. 1059, 68 So. 125, Ann.Cas.1916E, 105.

In shipping articles, this term, following the designation of the port of destination, must be construed either as void for uncertainty or as subordinate to the principal voyage stated in the preceding words. Brown v. Jones, 2 Gall. 477, Fed. Cas. No. 2,017.

ELUVIONES. In old pleading. Spring tides. Townsh. Pl. 197.

EMANCIPATION. The act by which one who was unfree, or under the power and control of another, is rendered free, or set at liberty and made his own master. Town of Plainville v. Town of Milford, 119 Conn. 380, 177 A. 138, 140.

The term is principally used with reference to the emancipation of a minor child by its parents, which involves an entire surrender of the right to the care, custody, and earnings of such child as well as a renunciation of parental duties. Delaware L. & W. R. Co. v. Petrowsky, C.C.A., 250 F. 554, 559; Public Service Co. of Indiana v. Tackett, 113 Ind.App. 307, 47 N.E.2d 851, 853. The emancipation may be express, as by voluntary agreement of parent and child, or implied from such acts and conduct as import consent, and it may be conditional or absolute, complete or partial. Wallace v. Cox, 136 Tenn. 69, 188 S.W. 611, 612, L.R.A.1917B, 690.

Complete emancipation is entire surrender of care, custody, and earnings of child, as well as renunciation of parental duties. Beebe v. Kansas City, 223 Mo.App. 642, 17 S.W.2d 608, 612. And a "partial emancipation" frees a child for only a part of the period of minority, or from only a part of the parent's rights, or for some purposes, and not for others. Memphis Steel Const. Co. v. Lister, 138 Tenn. 307, 197 S.W. 902, 903, L.R.A.1918B, 406.

Express Emancipation

That which results when parent and child voluntarily agree that the child, able to take care of himself, may go out from his home and make his own living, receive his own wages, and spend them as he pleases. Nichols v. Harvey & Hancock, 206 Ky. 112, 266 S.W. 870, 871.

In England

The term "emancipation" has been borrowed from the Roman law, and is constantly used in the law of parochial settlements. 7 Adol. & E., N.S., 574, note.

In Roman Law

The enfranchisement of a son by his father, which was anciently done by the formality of an imaginary sale. This was abolished by Justinian, who substituted the simpler proceeding of a manumission before a magistrate. Inst. 1, 12, 6.

EMANCIPATION PROCLAMATION. An executive proclamation, issued January 1, 1863, by Abraham Lincoln, declaring that all persons held in slavery in certain designated states and districts were and should remain free.

EMBARGO. A proclamation or order of state, usually issued in time of war or threatened hostilities, prohibiting the departure of ships or goods from some or all the ports of such state until further order. The William King, 2 Wheat. 148, 4 L.Ed. 206. For the use of the term as applied in a loose sense to the government's control of coal exports during a strike, see Ernesto Foglino & Co. v. Webster, 216 N.Y.S. 225, 237, 217 App.Div. 282.

Embargo is the hindering or detention by any government of ships of commerce in its ports. If the embargo is laid upon ships belonging to citizens of the state imposing it, it is called a "civil embargo;" if, as more commonly happens, it is laid upon ships belonging to the enemy, it is called a "hostile embargo." The effect of this latter embargo is that the vessels detained are restored to the rightful owners if no war follows, but are forfeited to the embargoing government if war does follow, the declaration of war being held to relate back to the original seizure and detention. Brown.

The temporary or permanent sequestration of the property of individuals for the purposes of a government, *e. g.*, to obtain vessels for the transport of troops, the owners being reimbursed for this forced service. Man. Int. Law, 143.

EMBASSADOR. See Ambassador.

EMBASSAGE, or EMBASSY. The message or commission given by a sovereign or state to a minister, called an "ambassador," empowered to treat or communicate with another sovereign or state; also the establishment of an ambassador.

EMBER DAYS. In ecclesiastical law. Those days which the ancient fathers called *"quatuor tempora jejunii"* are of great antiquity in the church. They are observed on Wednesday, Friday, and Saturday next after Quadragesima Sunday, or the first Sunday in Lent, after Whitsuntide, Holyrood Day, in September, and St. Lucy's Day, about the middle of December. Brit. c. 53. Our almanacs call the weeks in which they fall the "Ember Weeks," and they are now chiefly noticed on account of the ordination of priests and deacons; because the canon appoints the Sundays next after the Ember weeks for the solemn times of ordination, though the bishops, if they please, may ordain on any Sunday or holiday. Enc. Lond.

EMBEZZLEMENT. The fraudulent appropriation to his own use or benefit of property or money intrusted to him by another, by a clerk, agent, trustee, public officer, or other person acting in a fiduciary character. See 4 Bl.Comm. 230, 231.

The fraudulent appropriation of property by a person to whom it has been intrusted, or to whose hands it has lawfully come. American Life Ins. Co. v. U. S. Fidelity & Guaranty Co., 261 Mich. 221, 246 N.W. 71.

Embezzlement is not an offense at common law, but was created by statute. "Embezzle" includes in its meaning appropriation to one's own use, and therefore the use of the single word "embezzle," in the indictment or information, contains within itself the charge that the defendant appropriated the money or property to his own use. State v. Wolff, 34 La.Ann. 1153; State v. Hudson, 93 W.Va. 435, 117 S.E. 122, 125.

Embezzlement is common-law larceny extended by statute to cover cases where the stolen property comes originally into the possession of the defendant without a trespass. Moody v. People, 65 Colo. 339, 176 P. 476.

Embezzlement is a species of larceny, and the term is applicable to cases of furtive and fraudulent appropriation by clerks, servants, or carriers of property coming into their possession by virtue of their employment. It is distinguished from "larceny," properly so called, as being committed in respect of property which is not at the time in the actual or legal possession of the owner. That is to say, that in embezzlement the original taking of the property was lawful or with the consent of the owner, while in larceny the felonious intent must have existed at the time of the taking. Tredwell v. U. S., C.C.A.Va., 266 F. 350, 352. Both words, however, may be used, as in a bond, as generic terms to indicate the dishonest and fraudulent breach of any duty or obligation upon the part of an employee to pay over to his employer, or account to him for any money, securities, or other personal property, title to which is in the employer, but which may come into the possession of the employee. National Surety Co. v. Williams, 74 Fla. 446, 77 So. 212, 222. Under statute declaring guilty of a felony an officer or clerk of a state bank who "embezzles, abstracts, or willfully misapplies" its funds, "embezzle" refers to acts done for the benefit of the actor as against the bank, "misapply" covers acts having no relation to pecuniary profit or advantage to the doer, while "abstract" means only to take and withdraw from the possession and control of the bank; and while "embezzlement" may include the offenses of abstraction and willful misapplication, either of those offenses may be committed without embezzlement. Ferguson v. State, 80 Tex.Cr.R. 383, 189 S.W. 271, 273. See, however, Winkelmann v. State, 114 Neb. 1, 205 N.W. 565, 566.

EMBLEMATA TRIBONIANI. In the Roman law. Alterations, modifications, and additions to the writings of the older jurists, selected to make up the body of the Pandects, introduced by Tribonian and his associates who constituted the commission appointed for that purpose, with a view to harmonize contradictions, exscind obsolete matter, and make the whole conform to the law as understood in Justinian's time, were called by this name. Mackeld. Rom. Law, § 71.

EMBLEMENTS. The vegetable chattels called "emblements" are the corn and other growth of the earth which are produced annually, not spontaneously, but by labor and industry, and thence are called *"fructus industriales."* Reiff v. Reiff, 64 Pa. 137. See Crop.

The growing crops of those vegetable productions of the soil which are annually produced by the labor of the cultivator. They are deemed personal property, and pass as such to the executor or administrator of the occupier, whether he were the owner in fee, or for life, or for years, if he die before he has actually cut, reaped, or gathered the same; and this, although, being affixed to the soil, they might for some purposes be considered, while growing, as part of the realty. Wharton.

The term also denotes the right of a tenant to take and carry away, after his tenancy has ended, such annual products of the land as have resulted from his own care and labor.

Emblements are the away-going crop; in other words, the crop which is upon the ground and unreaped when the tenant goes away, his lease having determined; and the right to emblements is the right in the tenant to take away the away-going crop, and for that purpose to come upon the land, and do all other necessary things thereon. Miller v. Gray, Tex.Civ.App., 108 S.W.2d 265, 267, 268.

Where a life tenant, having leased the premises, died, and the remainderman did not recognize the lease, the lessee of the life tenant was entitled to the emblements, which are the crops of grain growing yearly, but requiring an outlay of labor or industry, without payment of any compensation for use of the land in harvesting the emblements. Turner v. Turner, 132 Tenn. 592, 179 S.W. 132, 133.

EMBLERS DE GENTZ. L. Fr. A stealing from the people. The phrase occurs in the old rolls of parliament: "Whereas divers murders, *emblers de gentz,* and robberies are committed," etc.

EMBOLISM. In medical jurisprudence. The mechanical obstruction of an artery or capillary by some body traveling in the blood current, as, a blood-clot (embolus), a globule of fat or an air-bubble.

Embolism is to be distinguished from "thrombosis," a thrombus being a clot of blood formed in the heart or a blood vessel in consequence of some impediment of the circulation from pathological causes, as distinguished from mechanical causes, for example, an alteration of the blood or walls of the blood vessels. When embolism occurs in the brain (called "cerebral embolism") there is more or less coagulation of the blood in the surrounding parts, and there may be apoplectic shock or paralysis of the brain, and its functional activity may be so far disturbed as to cause entire or partial insanity. See Cundall v. Haswell, 23 R.I. 508, 51 A. 426.

EMBOLUS. In case of wounds is a product of coagulation of the blood or blood clot. Berryhill v. Nichols, 171 Miss. 769, 158 So. 470. A plug which floats along until it becomes lodged so as to obstruct the passage of the blood. It consists usually of a clot or fibrin, a shred from a morbid growth, a globule of fat, air bubbles, or a micro-organism. An embolus or floating particle by attaching itself or becoming wedged may form a thrombosis or occlusion. Norris v. Industrial Commission, 90 Utah 256, 61 P.2d 413, 414.

EMBRACEOR. A person guilty of the offense of embracery (*q. v.*). See Co. Litt. 369.

EMBRACERY. In criminal law. This offense consists in the attempt to influence a jury corruptly to one side or the other, by promises, persuasions, entreaties, entertainments, *douceurs,* and the like. The person guilty of it is called an "embraceor." Moss v. Arnold, 63 Okla.Cr. 343, 75 P.2d 491, 503; Commonwealth v. Fahey, 113 Pa.Super. 598, 173 A. 854, 856.

Embracery being but an attempt corruptly to influence juror, there is no such crime as attempt to commit embracery. Wiseman v. Commonwealth, 143 Va. 631, 130 S.E. 249, 251.

EMENDA. Amends; something given in reparation for a trespass; or, in old Saxon times, in compensation for an injury or crime. Spelman.

EMENDALS. An old word still made use of in the accounts of the society of the Inner Temple, where so much in *emendals* at the foot of an account on the balance thereof signifies so much money in the bank or stock of the houses, for reparation of losses, or other emergent occasions. Spelman.

EMENDARE. In Saxon law. To make amends or satisfaction for any crime or trespass committed; to pay a fine; to be fined. Spelman. *Emendare se,* to redeem, or ransom one's life, by payment of a weregild.

EMENDATIO. In old English law. Amendment, or correction. The power of amending and correcting abuses, according to certain rules and measures. Cowell.

In Saxon law. A pecuniary satisfaction for an injury; the same as *emenda* (*q. v.*). Spelman.

EMENDATIO PANIS ET CEREVISIÆ. In old English law. The power of supervising and correcting the weights and measures of bread and ale, (assising bread and beer.) Cowell.

EMERGE. To arise; to come to light. "Unless a matter happen to *emerge* after issue joined." Hale, Anal. § 1.

EMERGENCY. A sudden unexpected happening; an unforeseen occurrence or condition; specifically, perplexing contingency or complication of circumstances; a sudden or unexpected occasion for action; exigency; pressing necessity.

A relatively permanent condition of insufficiency of service or of facilities resulting in social disturbance or distress. Kardasinksi v. Koford, 88 N.H. 444, 190 A. 702, 703, 111 A.L.R. 1017; Contract Cartage Co. v. Morris, D.C.Ill., 59 F.2d 437, 446; Los Angeles Dredging Co. v. City of Long Beach, 210 Cal. 348, 291 P. 839, 843, 71 A.L.R. 161.

"Emergency" in sense of constitutional provision respecting referendum does not mean expediency, convenience, or best interest. State v. Hinkle, 161 Wash. 652, 297 P. 1071, 1072.

EMERGENCY EMPLOYMENT DOCTRINE. A regularly employed servant possesses implied authority to engage an assistant to aid in performing a task, within scope of servant's duties in case of emergency rendering it absolutely necessary to obtain such assistance, and without which emergency conditions could not be overcome by servant or any of his coemployees in regular service of their common master. Hall v. O. C. Whitaker Co., 143 Tex. 397, 185 S.W.2d 720, 722, 723.

EMERGENCY LANDING AREA. Any area that a plane could possibly be landed into with or without motor. It should be from five hundred to a thousand feet in length, depending on obstructions around it, and width is not so important, although it should be at least two or three times that of plane. Shaw v. Carson, 218 Iowa 1251, 257 N.W. 194.

EMERGENT YEAR. The epoch or date whence any people begin to compute their time.

EMIGRANT. One who quits his country for any lawful reason, with a design to settle elsewhere, and takes his family and property, if he has any, with him. Vattel, b. 1, c. 19, § 224. Benson v. State, 36 Ga.App. 87, 135 S.E. 514.

EMIGRANT AGENT. One engaged in the business of hiring laborers for work outside the state. Gleaton v. State, 55 Ga.App. 875, 191 S.E. 926.

EMIGRATION. The act of removing from one country or state to another.

It is to be distinguished from "expatriation." The latter means the abandonment of one's country and renunciation of one's citizenship in it, while emigration denotes merely the removal of person and property to another country. The former is usually the consequence of the latter. Emigration is also used of the removal from one section to another of the same country.

EMINENCE. An honorary title given to cardinals. They were called *"illustrissimi"* and *"reverendissimi"* until the pontificate of Urban VIII.

EMINENT DOMAIN. The power to take private property for public use. MacVeagh v. Multonomah County, 126 Or. 417, 270 P. 502, 507.

The right of eminent domain is the right of the state, through its regular organization, to reassert, either temporarily or permanently, its dominion over any portion of the soil of the state on account of public exigency and for the public good. Thus, in time of war or insurrection, the proper authorities may possess and hold any part of the territory of the state for the common safety; and in time of peace the legislature may authorize the appropriation of the same to public purposes, such as the opening of roads, construction of defenses, or providing channels for trade or travel.

The right of society, or of the sovereign, to dispose, in case of necessity, and for the public safety, of all the wealth contained in the state, is called "eminent domain." Jones v. Walker, 2 Paine, 688, Fed.Cas.No.7,507.

Eminent domain is the highest and most exact idea of property remaining in the government, or in the aggregate body of the people in their sovereign capacity. It gives a right to resume the possession of the property in the manner directed by the constitution and the laws of the state, whenever the public interest requires it. Beekman v. Saratoga & S. R. Co., 3 Paige, N.Y., 45, 73, 22 Am.Dec. 679.

"The exaction of money from individuals under the right of taxation, and the appropriation of private property for public use by virtue of the power of eminent domain, must not be confused. In paying taxes the citizen contributes his just and ascertained share to the expenses of the government under which he lives. But when his property is taken under the power of eminent domain, he is compelled to surrender to the public something above and beyond his due proportion for the public benefit. The matter is special. It is in the nature of a compulsory sale to the state." Black, Tax-Titles, § 3; Beeland Wholesale Co. v. Kaufman, 234 Ala. 249, 174 So. 516, 520.

The term "eminent domain" is sometimes (but inaccurately) applied to the land, buildings, etc., owned directly by the government, and which have not yet passed into any private ownership. This species of property is much better designated as the "public domain," or "national domain."

EMISSARY. A person sent upon a mission as the agent of another; also a secret agent sent to ascertain the sentiments and designs of others, and to propagate opinions favorable to his employer.

EMISSION. In medical jurisprudence. The ejection or throwing out of any secretion or other matter from the body; the expulsion of urine, semen, etc.

EMIT. To put forth or send out; to issue. "No state shall *emit* bills of credit." Const. U. S. art. 1, § 10.

To issue; to give forth with authority; to put into circulation. See Bill of Credit.

The word "emit" is never employed in describing those contracts by which a state binds itself to pay money at a future day for services actually received, or for money borrowed for present use. Nor are instruments executed for such purposes, in common language, denominated "bills of credit." "To emit bills of credit" conveys to the mind the idea of issuing paper intended to circulate through the community, for its ordinary purposes, as money, which paper is redeemable at a future day. Briscoe v. Bank of Kentucky, 11 Pet. 316, 9 L.Ed. 709.

To throw off; give out; discharge. Alabama Great Southern R. Co. v. Stewart, 15 Ala.App. 466, 73 So. 827, 828.

In Scotch practice. To speak out; to state in words. A prisoner is said to *emit* a declaration. 2 Alis.Crim.Pr. 560.

EMMENAGOGUES. In medical jurisprudence. The name of a class of medicines supposed to have the property of promoting the menstrual discharge, and sometimes used for the purpose of procuring abortion.

EMOLUMENT. The profit arising from office or employment; that which is received as a compensation for services, or which is annexed to the possession of office as salary, fees, and perquisites; advantage; gain, public or private. Webster. Any perquisite, advantage, profit, or gain arising from the possession of an office. Apple v. Crawford County, 105 Pa. 303, 51 Am.Rep. 205; United States v. MacMillan, D.C.Ill., 209 F. 266, 272; McLean v. United States, 38 S.Ct. 122, 124, 226 U.S. 374, 57 L.Ed. 260; State ex rel. Todd v. Reeves, 196 Wash. 145, 82 P.2d 173, 175, 118 A.L.R. 177.

EMOTIONAL INSANITY. The species of mental aberration produced by a violent excitement of the emotions or passions, though the reasoning faculties may remain unimpaired. A passion, effecting for a space of time complete derangement of accused's intellect, or an impulse, which his mind is not able to resist, to do the act. Fannon v. Commonwealth, 295 Ky. 817, 175 S.W.2d 531, 533. See Insanity.

EMPALEMENT. In ancient law. A mode of inflicting punishment, by thrusting a sharp pole up the fundament. Enc. Lond.

EMPANNEL. See Impanel.

EMPARLANCE. See Imparlance.

EMPARNOURS. L. Fr. Undertakers of suits. Kelham.

EMPEROR. The title of the sovereign ruler of an empire. This designation was adopted by the rulers of the Roman world after the decay of the republic, and was assumed by those who claimed to be their successors in the "Holy Roman Empire," as also by Napoleon. "The sovereigns of Japan and Morocco are often, though with little propriety, called emperors." 10 Encyc. Amer. (1929), p. 300. In western speech the former sovereigns of Turkey and China were called emperors. Cent. Dict.

The title "emperor" seems to denote a power and dignity superior to that of a "king." It appears to be the appropriate style of the executive head of a federal government, constructed on the monarchial principle, and comprising in its organization several distinct kingdoms or other *quasi* sovereign states; as was the case with the German empire from 1871 to 1918. "The proper meaning of *emperor* is the chief of a confederation of states of which kings are members." Cent. Dict., quoting Encyc. Brit. "In general, an *emperor* is the holder of a sovereignty extending over conquered or confederated peoples, a *king* is ruler of a single people. Thus * * * the 'King of England' is 'Emperor of India.'" Webster's New Int. Dict. Before the dissolution of the Austro-Hungarian empire in November, 1918, its monarch was known as the Emperor of Austria and King of Hungary.

EMPHASIZING FACTS. An instruction is said to emphasis facts which may contain sufficient facts to authorize a verdict, but nevertheless some fact or facts are selected from the evidence and mentioned in such a way as to indicate to the jury that they have especial potency when that is not justified. Robinson v. Ross, Mo., 47 S.W.2d 122, 125.

EMPHYTEUSIS. In the Roman and civil law. A contract by which a landed estate was leased to a tenant, either in perpetuity or for a long term of years, upon the reservation of an annual rent or *canon,* and upon the condition that the lessee should improve the property, by building, cultivating, or otherwise, and with a right in the lessee to alien the estate at pleasure or pass it to his heirs by descent, and free from any revocation, re-entry, or claim of forfeiture on the part of the grantor, except for non-payment of the rent. Inst. 3, 25, 3; 3 Bl.Comm. 232; Maine, Anc. Law, 289.

The right granted by such a contract, (*jus emphyteuticum,* or *emphyteuticarium.*) The real right by which a person is entitled to enjoy another's estate as if it were his own, and to dispose of its substance, as far as can be done without deteriorating it. Mackeld. Rom. Law, § 326.

EMPHYTEUTA. In the civil law. The person to whom an *emphyteusis* is granted; the lessee or tenant under a contract of *emphyteusis.*

EMPHYTEUTICUS. In the civil law. Founded on, growing out of, or having the character of, an *emphyteusis;* held under an *emphyteusis.* 3 Bl. Comm. 232.

EMPIRE. The dominion or jurisdiction of an emperor; the region over which the dominion of an emperor extends; imperial power; supreme dominion; sovereign command.

EMPIRIC. A practitioner in medicine or surgery, who proceeds on experience only, without science or legal qualification; a quack. Parks v. State, 159 Ind. 211, 64 N.E. 862, 59 L.R.A. 190.

EMPLAZAMIENTO. In Spanish law. A summons or citation, issued by authority of a judge, requiring the person to whom it is addressed to appear before the tribunal at a designated day and hour.

EMPLEAD. To indict; to prefer a charge against; to accuse.

EMPLOI. In French law. Equitable conversion. When property covered by the *régime dotal* is sold, the proceeds of the sale must be reinvested for the benefit of the wife. It is the duty of the purchaser to see that the price is so reinvested. Arg. Fr. Merc. Law, 557.

EMPLOY. To engage in one's service; to use as an agent or substitute in transacting business; to commission and intrust with the management of one's affairs; and, when used in respect to a servant or hired laborer, the term is equivalent to hiring, which implies a request and a contract for a compensation, and has but this one meaning when used in the ordinary affairs and business of life. Tennessee Coal, Iron & R. Co. v. Muscoda Local No. 123, Ala., 64 S.Ct. 698, 703, 705, 321 U.S. 590, 88 L.Ed. 949; Slocum Straw Works v. Industrial Commission, 232 Wis. 71, 286 N.W. 593, 598; It is a synonym of "appoint". Morris v. Parks, 145 Or. 481, 28 P.2d 215, 216; Board of Com'rs of Colfax County v. Department of Public Health, 44 N.M. 189, 100 P.2d 222, 223, It is also synonymous with "hire." Nat. Wooden Box Ass'n v. U. S., Ct.Cl., 103 Ct.Cl. 595, 59 F.Supp. 118, 119.

EMPLOYED. This signifies both the act of doing a thing and the being under contract or orders to do it. To give employment to; to have employment. State v. Birmingham Beauty Shop, Ala., 198 So. 435, 436.

EMPLOYEE. This word "is from the French, but has become somewhat naturalized in our language. Strictly and etymologically, it means 'a person employed,' but, in practice in the French language, it ordinarily is used to signify a person in some official employment, and as generally used with us, though perhaps not confined to any official employment, it is understood to mean some permanent employment or position." The word may be more extensive than "clerk" or "officer," and may signify any one in place, or having charge or using a function, as well as one in office. Hopkins v. Cromwell, 89 App.Div. 481, 85 N.Y.S. 839.

One who works for an employer; a person working for salary or wages; applied to anyone so working, but usually only to clerks, workmen, laborers, etc., and but rarely to the higher officers of a corporation or government or to domestic servants. Keefe v. City of Monroe, 120 So. 106, 9 La.App. 545; State ex rel. Gorczyca v. City of Minneapolis, 174 Minn. 594, 219 N.W. 924.

Generally, when person for whom services are performed has right to control and direct individual who performs services not only as to result to be accomplished by work but also as to details and means by which result is accomplished, individual subject to direction is an "employee". Young v. Demos, 70 Ga.App. 577, 28 S.E. 2d 891, 893.

"Servant" is synonymous with "employee". Gooden v. Mitchell, Del.Super., 21 A.2d 197, 200, 201, 203, 2 Terry 301; Gibson v. Gillette Motor Transport, Tex.Civ.App., 138 S.W.2d 293, 294. Tennessee Valley Appliances v. Rowden, 24 Tenn. App. 487 146 S.W.2d 845, 848.

"Employee" must be distinguished from "independent contractor," "officer," "vice-principal," "agent," etc. The term is often specially defined by statutes; and whether one is an employee or not within a particular statute will depend upon facts and circumstances. For examples: Fair Labor Standards Act, Fleming v. Demeritt Co., D.C.Vt., 56 F.Supp. 376, 378, 390; Schroepfer v. A. S. Abell Co., D.C.Md., 48 F.Supp. 88, 94, 95, 98. Motor Carriers' Act, United States v. American Trucking Ass'n, App.D.C., 60 S.Ct. 1059, 1065, 310 U.S. 534, 84 L.Ed. 1345; West v. Smoky Mountain Stages, D.C.Ga., 40 F.Supp. 296, 298, 299. National Labor Relations Act. Standard Lime & Stone Co. v. National Labor Relations Board, C.C.A.4, 97 F.2d 531, 534, 535, 537; Eagle-Picher Mining Co. v. National Labor Relations Board, C.C.A.8, 119 F.2d 903, 911. Social Security Act, Kentucky Cottage Industries v. Glenn, D.C.Ky., 39 F.Supp. 642, 644, 645; Yearwood v. United States, D.C.La., 55 F.Supp. 295, 299, 300. State Labor Relations Law, In re New York State Labor Relations Board, 37 N.Y.S.2d 304, 308, 309; New York State Labor Relations Board v. Union Club of City of N. Y., 52 N.Y.S.2d 74, 83, 268 App.Div. 516. Unemployment Compensation Act. In re General Electric Co., 66 Idaho 91, 156 P.2d 190, 191. In re Keith, 30 N.Y.S.2d 206, 262 App.Div. 984. Workmen's Compensation Act, Stiles v. Des Moines Council of Boy Scouts of America, 209 Iowa 1235, 229 N.W. 841, 844; Essex County Country Club v. Chapman, 113 N.J.L. 182, 173 A. 591, 592.

For "Executive Employee", see that title.

EMPLOYER. One who employs the services of others; one for whom employees work and who pays their wages or salaries. The correlative of employee." Angell v. White Eagle Oil & Refining Co., 169 Minn. 183, 210 N.W. 1004, 1005. "Master" is a synonymous term. Tennessee Valley Appliances v. Rowden, 24 Tenn.App. 487, 146 S.W. 2d 845, 846; Gooden v. Mitchell, 2 Terry 301, 21 A. 2d 197, 200.

The following are examples of persons who have been or have not been classified as "employers" within various statutes. Carriers' Taxing Act. Interstate Transit Lines v. U. S., D.C.Neb., 56 F.Supp. 332; Walling v. Baltimore Steam Packet Co., C.C.A.Md., 144 F.2d 130, 132. Fair Labor Standards Act. Bowe v. Judson C. Burns, Inc., D.C.Pa., 46 F.Supp. 745, 748; Barrow v. Adams & Co. Real Estate, 46 N.Y.S.2d 357, 359, 182 Misc. 641. National Labor Relations Act. National Labor Relations Board v. Condenser Corporation of America, C.C.A.3, 128 F.2d 67, 71; N. L. R. B. v. Hofmann, C.C.A.3, 147 F.2d 679, 681, 157 A.L.R. 1149. Social Security Act. Matcovich v. Anglem, C.C.A.Cal., 134 F.2d 834, 837; Florida Industrial Commission v. Peninsular Life Ins. Co., 152 Fla. 55, 10 So.2d 793, 794. Unemployment Compensation Act, Smith v. Brooklyn Bar Ass'n, 44 N.Y.S.2d 620, 621, 266 App.Div. 1038; State ex rel. Merion v. Unemployment Compensation Board of Review, 142 Ohio St. 628, 53 N.E.2d 818, 820.

EMPLOYERS' LIABILITY ACTS. Statutes defining or limiting the occasions and the extent to which employers shall be liable in damages for injuries to their employees occurring in the course of the employment, and particularly (in recent times) abolishing the common-law rule that the employer is not liable if the injury is caused by the fault or negligence of a fellow servant.

EMPLOYMENT. The act of hiring (People v. Hyde, 89 N.Y. 11, 16), implying a request and a contract for compensation. State v. Deck, 108 Mo. App. 292, 83 S.W. 314, 315, (quoting and adopting definition in State v. Foster, 37 Iowa, 404; McCluskey v. Cromwell, 11 N.Y. 593).

It does not necessarily import an engagement or rendering services for another. A person may as well be "employed" about his own business as in the transaction of the same for a principal. State v. Canton, 43 Mo. 51.

Act of employing or state of being employed; that which engages or occupies; that which consumes time or attention; also an occupation, profession, trade, post or business. Hinton v. Columbia River Packers' Ass'n, C.C.A.Or., 117 F.2d 310; Davis v. Lincoln County, 117 Neb. 148, 219 N.W. 899, 900.

Includes the doing of the work and a reasonable margin of time and space required in passing to and from the place where the work is to be done. California Casualty Indemnity Exchange v. Industrial Accident Commission, 21 Cal. 2d 751, 135 P.2d 158, 161; Park Utah Consol. Mines Co. v. Industrial Commission, 103 Utah 64, 133 P.2d 314, 317.

The term "office" implies a delegation of a portion of the sovereign power to, and the possession of it by, the person filling the office, while an "employment" does not comprehend a delegation of any part of the sovereign authority. Dade County v. State, 95 Fla. 465, 116 So. 72, 76.

EMPLOYMENT AGENCY. Business operated by a person, firm or corporation engaged in procuring, for a fee, employment for others and employees for employers. McMillan v. City of Knoxville, 139 Tenn. 319, 202 S.W. 65, 66.

EMPORIUM. A place for wholesale trade in commodities carried by sea. The name is sometimes applied to a seaport town, but it properly signifies only a particular place in such a town. Smith, Dict. Antiq.

EMPOWER. A grant of authority rather than a command of its exercise. In re Whiteman's Will, 52 N.Y.S.2d 723, 725, 268 App.Div. 591.

EMPRESARIOS. In Mexican law. Undertakers or promoters of extensive enterprises, aided by concessions or monopolistic grants from government; particularly, persons receiving extensive land grants in consideration of their bringing emigrants into the country and settling them on the lands, with a view of increasing the population and developing the resources of the country. U. S. v. Maxwell Land-Grant Co., 7 S.Ct. 1015, 121 U.S. 325, 30 L.Ed. 949.

EMPRESTIDO. In Spanish law. A loan. Something lent to the borrower at his request. Las Partidas, pt. 3, tit. 18, l. 70.

EMPTIO. In the Roman and civil law. The act of buying; a purchase.

EMPTIO BONORUM. A species of forced assignment for the benefit of creditors; being a public sale of an insolvent debtor's estate whereby the purchaser succeeded to all his property, rights, and claims, and became responsible for his debts and liabilities to the extent of a quota fixed before the transfer. See Mackeld. Rom. Law, § 521.

EMPTIO ET VENDITIO. Purchase and sale; sometimes translated "emption and vendition." The name of the contract of sale in the Roman law. Inst. 3, 23; Bract. fol. 61*b*. Sometimes made a compound word, *emptio-venditio*.

EMPTIO REI SPERATÆ. A purchase in the hope of an uncertain future profit; the purchase of a thing not yet in existence or not yet in the possession of the seller, as, the cast of a net or a crop to be grown, and the price of which is to depend on the actual gain. On the other hand, if the price is fixed and not subject to fluctuation, but is to be paid whether the gain be greater or less, it is called *emptio spei*. Mackeld. Rom. Law, § 400.

EMPTOR. Lat. A buyer or purchaser. Used in the maxim *"caveat emptor,"* let the buyer beware; *i. e.*, the buyer of an article must be on his guard and take the risks of his purchase.

EMPTOR EMIT QUAM MINIMO POTEST, VENDITOR VENDIT QUAM MAXIMO POTEST. The buyer purchases for the lowest price he can; the seller sells for the highest price he can. 2 Kent, Comm. 486.

EMTIO. In the civil law. Purchase. This form of the word is used in the Digests and Code. Dig. 18, 1; Cod. 4, 49. See Emptio.

EMTOR. In the civil law. A buyer or purchaser; the buyer. Dig. 18, 1; Cod. 4, 49.

EMTRIX. In the civil law. A female purchaser; the purchaser. Cod. 4, 54, 1.

EN ARERE. L. Fr. In time past. 2 Inst. 506.

EN AUTRE DROIT. In the right of another. See Autre Droit.

EN BANC. L. Fr. In the bench. 1 Anders. 51.

EN BREVET. In French law. An *acte* is said to be *en brevet* when a copy of it has not been recorded by the notary who drew it.

EN DÉCLARATION DE SIMULATION. A form of action used in Louisiana. Its object is to have a contract declared judicially a simulation and a nullity, to remove a cloud from the title, and to bring back, for any legal purpose, the thing sold to the estate of the true owner. Edwards v. Ballard, 20 La.Ann. 169.

EN DEMEURE. In default. Used in Louisiana of a debtor who fails to pay on demand according to the terms of his obligation. See Bryan v. Cox, 3 Mart. (La. N. S.) 574.

EN ESCHANGE IL COVIENT QUE LES ESTATES SOIENT EGALES. Co. Litt. 50. In an exchange it is desirable that the estates be equal.

EN FAIT. Fr. In fact; in deed; actually.

EN GROS. Fr. In gross. Total; by wholesale.

EN JUICIO. Span. Judicially; in a court of law; in a suit at law. White, New Recop. b. 2, tit. 8, c. 1.

EN MASSE. Fr. In a mass; in a lump; at wholesale.

EN MORT MAYNE. L. Fr. In a dead hand; in mortmain. Britt. c. 43.

EN OWEL MAIN. L. Fr. In equal hand. The word *"owel"* occurs also in the phrase *"owelty* of partition."

EN RECOUVREMENT. Fr. In French law. An expression employed to denote that an indorsement made in favor of a person does not transfer to him the property in the bill of exchange, but merely constitutes an authority to such person to recover the amount of the bill. Arg. Fr. Merc. Law, 558.

EN ROUTE. Fr. On the way; in the course of a voyage or journey; in course of transportation. McLean v. U. S., 17 Ct.Cl. 90.

EN VENTRE SA MERE. L. Fr. In its mother's womb. A term descriptive of an unborn child. For some purposes the law regards an infant *en ventre* as in being. It may take a legacy; have a guardian; an estate may be limited to its use, etc. 1 Bl. Comm. 130.

EN VIE. L. Fr. In life; alive. Britt. c. 50.

ENABLE. To give power to do something. In the case of a person under disability as to dealing with another, "enable" has the primary meaning of removing that disability; not of conferring a compulsory power as against that other; 66 L. J. Ch. 208; [1897] A. C. 647. To make able. Summers v. Chicago Title & Trust Co., 335 Ill. 564, 167 N.E. 777, 779.

ENABLING POWER. When the donor of a power, who is the owner of the estate, confers upon persons not seised of the fee the right of creating interests to take effect out of it, which could not be done by the donee of the power unless by such authority, this is called an "enabling power." 2 Bouv. Inst. no. 1928.

ENABLING STATUTE. The act of 32 Henry VIII. c. 28, by which tenants in tail, husbands seised in right of their wives, and others were empowered to make leases for their lives or for twenty-one years, which they could not do before. 2 Bl. Comm. 319; Co. Litt. 44*a*. The phrase is also applied to any statute enabling persons or corporations to do what before they could not. It is applied to statutes which confer new powers.

ENACH. In Saxon law. The satisfaction for a crime; the recompense for a fault. Skene.

ENACT. To establish by law; to perform or effect; to decree. The usual introductory formula in making laws is, *"Be it enacted."* In re Senate File, 25 Neb. 864, 41 N.W. 981.

ENACTING CLAUSE. That part of a statute which declares its enactment and serves to identify it as an act of legislation proceeding from the proper legislative authority. Various formulas are used for this clause, such as "Be it enacted by the people of the state of Illinois represented in general assembly," "Be it enacted by the senate and house of representatives of the United States of America in congress assembled," "The general assembly do enact," etc. A section of a statute denouncing an offense is sometimes spoken of as the "enacting clause." City of Astoria v. Malone, 169 P. 749, 750, 87 Or. 88. See United States v. Mendelsohn, D.C.N.J., 32 F.Supp. 622, 623, questioning this definition.

ENAJENACION. In Spanish and Mexican law. Alienation; transfer of property. The act by which the property in a thing, by lucrative title, is transferred, as a donation; or by onerous title, as by sale or barter. In a more extended sense, the term comprises also the contracts of emphyteusis, pledge, and mortgage, and even the creation of a servitude upon an estate. Escriche; Mulford v. Le Franc, 26 Cal. 88.

ENBREVER. L. Fr. To write down in short; to abbreviate, or, in old language, *imbreviate;* to put into a schedule. Britt. c. 1.

ENCAUSTUM. In the civil law. A kind of ink or writing fluid appropriate to the use of the emperor. Cod. 1, 23, 6.

ENCEINTE. Pregnant. See Pregnancy.

ENCHESON. The occasion, cause, or reason for which anything is done. Termes de la Ley.

ENCLOSE. See Inclose.

ENCLOSURE. See Inclosure.

ENCOMIENDA. In Spanish law. A grant from the crown to a private person of a certain portion of territory in the Spanish colonies, together with the concession of a certain number of the native inhabitants, on the feudal principle of commendation. 2 Wools. Pol. Science, 161, 162. Also a royal grant of privileges to the military orders of Spain.

ENCOURAGE. In criminal law. To instigate; to incite to action; to give courage to; to inspirit; to embolden; to raise confidence; to make confident; to help; to forward; to advise. Comitez v. Parkerson, C.C.La., 50 F. 170.

ENCROACH. To enter by gradual steps or stealth into the possessions or rights of another; to trespass; intrude. Miami Corporation v. State, 186 La. 784, 173 So. 315, 318. To gain unlawfully upon the lands, property, or authority of another; as if one man presses upon the grounds of another too far, or if a tenant owe two shillings rent-service, and the lord exact three. So, too, the Spencers were said to encroach the king's authority. Blount; Plowd. 94*a*.

ENCROACHMENT. An encroachment upon a street or highway is a fixture, such as a wall or fence, which illegally intrudes into or invades the highway or incloses a portion of it, diminishing its width or area, but without closing it to public travel. State v. Scott, 82 N.H. 278, 132 A. 685, 686.

In the law of easements. Where the owner of an easement alters the dominant tenement, so as to impose an additional restriction or burden on the servient tenement, he is said to commit an encroachment. Sweet.

ENCUMBER. See Incumber.

ENCUMBRANCE. See Incumbrance.

END. Object; intent. Things are construed according to the end. Finch, Law, b. 1, c. 3, no. 10.

END LINES. In mining law, the end lines of a claim, as platted or laid down on the ground, are those which mark its boundaries on the shorter dimension, where it crosses the vein, while the "side lines" are those which mark its longer dimension, where it follows the course of the vein. But with reference to extra-lateral rights, if the claim as a whole crosses the vein, instead of following its course, the end lines will become side lines and vice versa. Consolidated Wyoming Gold Min. Co. v. Champion Min. Co., C.C.Cal., 63 F. 549.

END OF WILL. Point in will at which despositive provisions terminate. In re Levanti's Will, 252 N.Y.S. 497, 498, 141 Misc. 248. In re Coyne's Estate, 349 Pa. 331, 37 A.2d 509, 510.

END ON OR NEARLY SO. Approaching vessels whose courses diverge not more than one or two points are meeting "end on or nearly so," within article 18 of the Inland Rules (33 USCA § 203), and are required to pass port to port. The Amolco, C.C.A.Mass., 283 F. 890, 893.

END SILLS. The sill of a car is one of the main longitudinal timbers which are connected transversely by the end sills, bolsters, and cross-ties. Sills are divided into side sills, intermediate sills, and center sills. The end sill is the transverse member of the under frame of a car framed across the ends of all the longitudinal sills. In passenger cars the end sill comes directly under the end door; the platform with its various parts usually being a separate construction. The platform end sill is the transverse end piece of the platform frame, and is also called the "end timber" and buffer beam on passenger equipment cars. Hill v. Minneapolis, St. P. & S. S. M. Ry. Co., 160 Minn. 484, 200 N.W. 485, 486.

END TO END. The expression "end to end," used in a patent claim in describing the relative position of rollers, does not necessarily require that there shall be no longitudinal space between the ends of the rollers, nor impose a limitation which will enable another to avoid infringement by leaving a space between them, where it does not change their function or mode of operation. Stebler v. Riverside Heights Orange Growers' Ass'n, C.C.A.Cal., 205 F. 735, 740.

ENDEAVOR. To exert physical and intellectual strength toward the attainment of an object; a systematic or continuous effort. Thompson v. Corbin, Tex.Civ.App., 137 S.W.2d 157, 159.

ENDENZIE, or ENDENIZEN. To make free; to enfranchise.

ENDOCARDITIS. In medical jurisprudence. An inflammation of the living membrane of the heart.

ENDORSE. See Indorse.

ENDOW. To give a dower; to bestow upon; to make pecuniary provision for. Fish v. Fish, 184 Ky. 700, 212 S.W. 586, 587.

ENDOWED SCHOOLS. In England, certain schools having endowments are distinctively known as "endowed schools;" and a series of acts of parliament regulating them are known as the "endowed schools acts." Mozley & Whitley.

ENDOWMENT. The assignment of dower; the setting off a woman's dower. 2 Bl. Comm. 135.

In appropriations of churches (in English law,) the setting off a sufficient maintenance for the vicar in perpetuity. 1 Bl. Comm. 387.

The act of settling a fund, or permanent pecuniary provision, for the maintenance of a public institution, charity, college, etc.

A fund settled upon a public institution, etc., for its maintenance or use.

The words "endowment" and "fund," in a statute exempting from taxation the real estate, the furniture and personal property, and the "endowment or fund" of religious and educational corporations, are *ejusdem generis*, and intended to comprehend a class of property different from the other two, not real estate or chattels. The difference between the words is that "fund" is a general term, including the endowment, while "endowment" means that particular fund, or part of the fund, of the institution, bestowed for its more permanent uses, and usually kept sacred for the purposes intended. The word "endowment" does not, in such an enactment, include real estate. See First Reformed Dutch Church v. Lyon, 32 N.J.Law, 360; Appeal of Wagner Institute, 116 Pa. 555, 11 A. 402.

ENDOWMENT POLICY. In life insurance. A policy which is payable when the insured reaches a given age, or upon his decease, if that occurs earlier. Central States Life Ins. Co. v. Morris, 202 Ark. 969, 155 S.W.2d 333, 336, 202 Ark. 969.

ENDURANCE. State or capability of lasting; continuance; or act or instance of bearing or suffering; a continuing or the power of continuing under pain, hardship, or distress without being overcome; sufferance; as beyond endurance. State ex rel. Adams v. Crowder, 46 N.M. 20, 120 P.2d 428, 431.

ENEMY, in public law, signifies either the state which is at war with another, or a citizen or subject of such state, or a person, partnership, or corporation doing business within the territory of an enemy state or an ally thereof. United States v. Fricke, D.C.N.Y., 259 F. 673, 675; Rossie v. Garvan, D.C.Conn., 274 F. 447, 453.

Alien Enemy

An alien, that is, a citizen or subject of a foreign state or power, residing within a given country, is called an "alien ami" if the country where he lives is at peace with the country of which he is a citizen or subject; but if a state of war exists between the two countries, he is called an "alien enemy," and in that character is denied access to the courts or aid from any of the departments of government.

Enemy Belligerent

Citizens who associate themselves with the military arm of an enemy government and enter the United States bent on hostile acts. Ex parte Quirin, App.D.C., 63 S.Ct. 2, 15, 317 U.S. 1, 87 L.Ed. 3.

Enemy's Property

In international law, and particularly in the usage of prize courts, this term designates any property which is engaged or used in illegal intercourse with the public enemy, whether belonging to an ally or a citizen, as the illegal traffic stamps it with the hostile character and attaches to it all the penal consequences. Prize Cases, 2 Black, 674, 17 L.Ed. 459.

Public Enemy

A nation at war with the United States; also every citizen or subject of such nation. Not including robbers, thieves, private depredators, or riotous mobs. State v. Moore, 74 Mo. 417, 41 Am. Rep. 322.

The term has latterly acquired, in the vocabulary of journalism and civic indignation, a more extended meaning, denoting a particularly notorious offender against the criminal laws, especially one who seems more or less immune from successful prosecution.

ENFEOFF. To invest with an estate by feoffment. To make a gift of any corporeal hereditaments to another. See Feoffment.

ENFEOFFMENT. The act of investing with any dignity or possession; also the instrument or deed by which a person is invested with possessions.

ENFITEUSIS. In Spanish law. Emphyteusis, (*q. v.*). See Mulford v. Le Franc, 26 Cal. 103.

ENFORCE. To put into execution; to cause to take effect; to make effective; as, to enforce a writ, a judgment, or the collection of a debt or fine; to compel obedience to. Dozier v. City of Gatesville, Tex.Civ.App., 51 S.W.2d 1091.

ENFORCEABLE. Word "enforceable," standing alone, does not mean "perform" or "performable," but, when employed in contract for performance of obligation relating to venue, it is synonymous with word "execute," and must be given meaning of "perform," "performable," and "to perform." It does not necessarily imply actual force or coercion, but may mean to be executed; to put into execution; to cause to take effect. Glover v. American Mortgage Corporation, Tex.Civ.App., 94 S.W.2d 1235, 1236.

ENFRANCHISE. To make free; to incorporate a man in a society or body politic.

ENFRANCHISEMENT. The act of making free; giving a franchise or freedom to; investiture with privileges or capacities of freedom, or municipal or political liberty. Admission to the freedom of a city; admission to political rights, and particularly the right of suffrage. Anciently, the acquisition of freedom by a villein from his lord.

The word is now used principally either of the manumission of slaves, (*q. v.*,) of giving to a borough or other constituency a right to return a member or members to parliament, or of the conversion of copyhold into freehold. Mozley & Whiteley.

ENFRANCHISEMENT OF COPYHOLDS. In English law. The conversion of copyhold into freehold tenure, by a conveyance of the fee-simple of the property from the lord of the manor to the copyholder, or by a release from the lord of all seigniorial rights, etc., which destroys the customary descent, and also all rights and privileges annexed to the copyholder's estate. 1 Watk. Copyh. 362; 2 Steph. Comm. 51.

ENGAGE. To employ or involve one's self; to take part in; to embark on. State ex rel. Kusie v. Weber, 72 N.D. 705, 10 N.W.2d 741, 745. It imports more than a single act or transaction or an occasional participation. Head v. New York Life Ins. Co., C.C.A.Okl., 43 F.2d 517, 519; Lee v. Guardian Life Ins. of America, 46 N.Y.S.2d 241, 246, 187 Misc. 221.

"Engage" means to take part in or be employed in and denotes more than a single act or single transaction while "participate" means simply to take or have a part or share in, and may apply equally to a single act or many acts. Lawyers Lloyds of Texas v. Webb, Tex.Civ.App., 150 S.W.2d 181, 184.

ENGAGED IN AVIATION. See Aviation.

ENGAGED IN COMMERCE. To be "engaged in commerce" an employee must be actually engaged in the movement of commerce or the services he performs must be so closely related thereto as to be for all practical purposes an essential part thereof; McLeod v. Threlkeld, Tex., 63 S.Ct. 1248, 1251, 1252, 319 U.S. 491, 87 L.Ed. 1538; Boutell v. Walling, C.C.A.Mich., 148 F.2d 329, 331.

ENGAGED IN EMPLOYMENT. To be rendering service for employer under terms of employment, and is more than being merely hired to commence work. Walling v. Consumers Co., C.C.A.Ill., 149 F.2d 626, 629.

ENGAGEMENT. In French law. A contract. The obligation arising from a *quasi* contract. The terms "obligation" and "engagement" are said to be synonymous, (17 Toullier, no. 1;) but the Code seems specially to apply the term "engagement" to those obligations which the law imposes on a man without the intervention of any contract, either on the part of the obligor or the obligee, (article 1370.) An engagement to do or omit to do something amounts to a promise. Rue v. Rue, 21 N.J.Law, 369.

In English practice. The term has been appropriated to denote a contract entered into by a married woman with the intention of binding or charging her separate estate, or, with stricter accuracy, a promise which in the case of a person *sui juris* would be a contract, but in the case of a married woman is not a contract, because she cannot bind herself personally, even in equity. Her engagements, therefor, merely operate as dispositions or appointments *pro tanto* of her separate estate. Sweet.

Under statute rendering national bank stockholders liable to assessment in order to discharge an "engagement" of the bank, the quoted word includes all pecuniary liabilities and obligations of the bank. Oppenheimer v. Harriman Nat. Bank & Trust Co. of City of New York, N.Y., 57 S.Ct. 719, 723, 301 U.S. 206, 81 L.Ed. 1042.

ENGENDER. To cause, to bring about, to excite, to occasion, to call forth. Lacy v. State, 30 Okl. Cr. 273, 236 P. 53, 54.

ENGINE. This is said to be a word of very general signification; and, when used in an act, its meaning must be sought out from the act itself, and the language which surrounds it, and also from other acts *in pari materia,* in which it occurs. Abbott, J., 6 Maule & S. 192. In a large sense, it applies to all utensils and tools which afford the means of carrying on a trade. But in a more limited sense it means a thing of considerable dimensions, of a fixed or permanent nature, analogous to an erection or building. Id. 182. And see Lefler v. Forsberg, 1 App.D.C. 41; Brown v. Benson, 101 Ga. 753, 29 S.E. 215.

Within Employers' Liability Law, § 1, par. 2, subd. (a), an "engine" is an ingenious or skillful contrivance used to effect a purpose, and is often synonymous with the word "machine"; machinery being any combination of mechanical means designed to work together so as to effect a given end. Haddad v. Commercial Motor Truck Co., 146 La. 897, 84 So. 197, 198, 9 A.L.R. 1380.

Machine by which power is applied to the doing of work, particularly one that converts some motive energy, especially heat, into mechanical power. Chrysler Corporation v. Trott, Cust. & Pat.App., 83 F.2d 302, 310.

Compound Compressed Air Engine

An engine in which the compressed air is first used in a high pressure cylinder, that is, in a cylinder of relatively small diameter, and after driving the piston connected therewith, instead of being permitted to escape, is conveyed to a low pressure cylinder, that is, to a cylinder of larger diameter, where it still has sufficient expansive force to drive another piston. This operation may again be repeated in a third cylinder or the air be permitted to escape to the atmosphere. H. K. Porter Co. v. Baldwin Locomotive Works, D.C.Pa., 219 F. 226, 229.

ENGINEER. One who is versed in or follows as a calling or profession any branch of engineering. Employers' Liability Assur. Corporation v. Accident & Casualty Ins. Co. of Winterthur, Switzerland, C.C.A.Ohio, 134 F.2d 566, 569. One who manages or runs any stationary or locomotive engine; an engine driver. Baggaley v. Aetna Ins. Co., C. C.A.Ill., 111 F.2d 134, 135.

ENGINEERING. The art and science by which mechanical properties of matter are made useful to man in structures and machines. Employers' Liability Assur. Corporation v. Accident & Casualty Ins. Co. of Winterthur, Switzerland, C.C.A. Ohio, 134 F.2d 566, 569, 146 A.L.R. 1186.

ENGLESHIRE. A law was made by Canute, for the preservation of his Danes, that, when a man was killed, the hundred or town should be liable to be amerced, unless it could be proved that the person killed was an Englishman. This proof was called *"Engleshire."* 1 Hale, P. C. 447; 4 Bl. Comm. 195; Spelman.

ENGLETERRE. L. Fr. England.

ENGLISH INFORMATION. In English law. A proceeding in the court of exchequer in matters of revenue.

ENGLISH MARRIAGE. This phrase may refer to the place where the marriage is solemnized, or it may refer to the nationality and domicile of the parties between whom it is solemnized, the place where the union so created is to be enjoyed. 6 Prob. Div. 51.

ENGRAVING. The art of producing on hard material incised or raised patterns, lines, and the like, from which an impression or print is taken. The term may apply to a text or script, but is generally restricted to pictorial illustrations or works connected with the fine arts, not including the reproduction of pictures by means of photography. American Historical Co. v. Clark, 316 Ill.App. 309, 44 N.E.2d 761.

ENGROSS. To copy the rude draft of an instrument in a fair, large hand. To write out, in a large, fair hand, on parchment.

In old criminal law. To buy up so much of a commodity on the market as to obtain a monopoly and sell again at a forced price.

ENGROSSER. One who engrosses or writes on parchment in a large, fair hand.

One who purchases large quantities of any commodity in order to acquire a monopoly, and to sell them again at high prices.

ENGROSSING. In English law. The getting into one's possession, or buying up, large quantities of corn, or other dead victuals, with intent to sell them again. The total engrossing of any other commodity, with intent to sell it at an unreasonable price. 4 Bl.Comm. 158, 159. This was a misdemeanor, punishable by fine and imprisonment. Steph.Crim.Law, 95. Now repealed by 7 & 8 Vict. c. 24. 4 Steph.Comm. 291, note.

ENHANCED. This word, taken in an unqualified sense, is synonymous with "increased," and comprehends any increase of value, however caused or arising. Thornburn v. Doscher, C.C.Or., 32 Fed. 812.

ENHERITANCE. L. Fr. Inheritance.

ENITIA PARS. The share of the eldest. A term of the English law descriptive of the lot or share chosen by the eldest of coparceners when they make a voluntary partition. The first choice (*primer election*) belongs to the eldest. Co.Litt. 166.

ENITIA PARS SEMPER PRÆFERENDA EST PROPTER PRIVILEGIUM ÆTATIS. Co.Litt. 166. The part of the elder sister is always to be preferred on account of the privilege of age.

ENJOIN. To require; command; positively direct. To require a person, by writ of injunction from a court of equity, to perform, or to abstain or desist from, some act. Clifford v. Stewart, 95 Me. 38, 49 A. 52; Lawrence v. Cooke, 32 Hun, 126; Brimberg v. Hartenfeld Bag Co., 89 N.J.Eq. 425, 105 A. 68, 69.

ENJOY. To have, possess, and use with satisfaction; to occupy or have benefit of. Salway v. Multnomah Lumber & Box Co., 134 Or. 428, 293 P. 420, 422.

ENJOYMENT. The exercise of a right; the possession and fruition of a right, privilege or incorporeal hereditament.

Comfort, consolation, contentment, ease, happiness, pleasure and satisfaction. National Surety Co. v. Jarrett, 95 W.Va. 420, 121 S.E. 291, 295.

Adverse Enjoyment

The possession or exercise of an easement, under a claim of right against the owner of the land out of which such easement is derived. 2 Washb. Real Prop. 42; Cox v. Forrest, 60 Md. 79.

Quiet Enjoyment

Covenant for. See Covenant.

ENLARGE. To make larger; to increase; to extend a time limit; to grant further time. Also to set at liberty one who has been imprisoned or in custody.

ENLARGER L'ESTATE. A species of release which inures by way of enlarging an estate, and consists of a conveyance of the ulterior interest to the particular tenant; as if there be tenant for life or years, remainder to another in fee, and he in remainder releases all his right to the particular tenant and his heirs, this gives him the estate in fee. 1 Steph.Comm. 518.

ENLARGING. Extending, or making more comprehensive; as an enlarging statute, which is a remedial statute enlarging or extending the common law. 1 Bl.Comm. 86, 87.

ENLISTMENT. The act of one who voluntarily enters the military or naval service of the government, contracting to serve in a subordinate capacity. Morrissey v. Perry, 137 U.S. 157, 11 Sup. Ct. 57, 34 L.Ed. 644; Babbitt v. U. S., 16 Ct.Cl. 213.

The words "enlist" and "enlistment," in law, as in common usage, may signify either the complete fact of entering into the military service, or the first step taken by the recruit towards that end. When used in the former sense, as in statutes conferring a right to compel the military service of enlisted men, the enlistment is not deemed completed until the man has been mustered into the service. Tyler v. Pomeroy, 8 Allen, Mass., 480.

Enlistment does not include the entry of a person into the military service under a commission as an officer. Hilliard v. Stewartstown, 48 N.H. 280.

Enlisted applies to a drafted man as well as a volunteer, whose name is duly entered on the military rolls. Sheffield v. Otis, 107 Mass. 282.

ENORMIA. In old practice and pleading. Unlawful or wrongful acts; wrongs. *Et alia enormia,* and other wrongs. This phrase constantly occurs in the old writs and declarations of trespass.

ENORMOUS. Aggravated. "So enormous a trespass." Vaughan, 115. Written "enormious," in some of the old books. *Enormious* is where a thing is made without a rule or against law. Brownl. pt. 2, p. 19.

ENPLEET. Anciently used for implead. Cowell.

ENQUÊTE, or ENQUEST. In canon law. An examination of witnesses, taken down in writing, by or before an authorized judge, for the purpose of gathering testimony to be used on a trial.

ENRÉGISTREMENT. In French law. Registration. A formality which consists in inscribing on a register, specially kept for the purpose by the government, a summary analysis of certain deeds and documents. At the same time that such analysis is inscribed upon the register, the clerk places upon the deed a memorandum indicating the date upon which it was registered, and at the side of such memorandum an impression is made with a stamp. Arg.Fr.Merc.Law, 558.

ENROLL. To register; to make a record; to enter on the rolls of a court; to transcribe. Ream v. Com., 3 Serg. & R. (Pa.) 209; Anderson v. Commonwealth, 275 Ky. 232, 121 S.W.2d 46, 47.

ENROLLED BILL. In legislative practice, a bill which has been duly introduced, finally passed by both houses, signed by the proper officers of each, approved by the governor (or president) and filed by the secretary of state. Sedgwick County Com'rs v. Bailey, 13 Kan. 608.

ENROLLMENT. The act of putting upon a roll. A record made. Anderson v. Commonwealth, 275 Ky. 232, 121 S.W.2d 46, 47.

In English law. The registering or entering on the rolls of chancery, king's bench, common pleas, or exchequer, or by the clerk of the peace in the records of the quarter sessions, of any lawful act; as a recognizance, a deed of bargain and sale, and the like. Jacob.

ENROLLMENT OF VESSELS. In the laws of the United States on the subject of merchant shipping, the recording and certification of vessels employed in coastwise or inland navigation; as distinguished from the "registration" of vessels employed in foreign commerce. U. S. v. Leetzel, 3 Wall. 566, 18 L.Ed. 67.

ENROLLMENT RECORDS. All the testimony and exhibits tending to establish age that were in evidence before the Commission to the Five Civilized Tribes and the conclusions of the Commission based thereon from the date of the application for enrollment of any particular individual up to the date of the ascertainment by the Commission as to whether the name of such person was intended to be included upon the final roll of the nation in which he claimed citizenship. Duncan v. Byars, 44 Okl. 538, 144 P. 1053, 1054.

ENS LEGIS. L. Lat. A creature of the law; an artificial being, as contrasted with a natural person. Applied to corporations, considered as deriving their existence entirely from the law.

ENSCHEDULE. To insert in a list, account, or writing.

ENSEAL. To seal. *Ensealing* is still used as a formal word in conveyancing.

ENSERVER. L. Fr. To make subject to a service or servitude. Britt. c. 54.

ENSUE. To follow after; to follow in order or train of events. Agricultural Publishers' Ass'n v. Homestead Co., 197 Iowa, 380, 197 N.W. 314.

ENTAIL, *v.* To settle or limit the succession to real property; to create an estate tail.

ENTAIL, *n.* A fee abridged or limited to the issue, or certain classes of issue, instead of descending to all the heirs. 1 Washb. Real Prop. 66; Cowell; 2 Bl.Comm. 112, note.

Entail, in legal treatises, is used to signify an estate tail, especially with reference to the restraint which such an estate imposes upon its owner, or, in other words, the points wherein such an estate differs from an estate in fee-simple. And this is often its popular sense; but sometimes it is, in popular language, used differently, so as to signify a succession of life-estates, as when it is said that "an entail ends with A.," meaning that A. is the first person who is entitled to bar or cut off the entail, being in law the first tenant in tail. Mozley & Whiteley.

Break or Bar an Entail

To free an estate from the limitations imposed by an entail and permit its free disposition, anciently by means of a fine or common recovery, but now by deed in which the tenant and next heir join.

Quasi Entail

An estate *pur autre vie* may be granted, not only to a man and his heirs, but to a man and the heirs of his body, which is termed a *"quasi* entail;" the interest so granted not being properly an estate-tail, (for the statute *De Donis* applies only where the subject of the entail is an estate of inheritance,) but yet so far in the nature of an estate-tail that it will go to the heir of the body as special occupant during the life of the *cestui que vie,* in the same manner as an estate of inheritance would descend, if limited to the grantee and the heirs of his body. Wharton.

ENTAILED. Settled or limited to specified heirs, or in tail.

ENTAILED MONEY. Money directed to be invested in realty to be entailed. 3 & 4 Wm. IV, c. 74, §§ 70, 71, 72.

ENTAILMENT. An interference with and curtailment of the ordinary rules pertaining to devolution by inheritance; a limitation and direction by which property is to descend different from the course which it would take if the creator of the entailment, grantor or testator, had been content that the estate should devolve in regular and general succession to heirs at law in the statutory order of precedence and sequence. Gardner v. Anderson, 114 Kan. 778, 227 P. 743, 748.

ENTENCION. In old English law. The plaintiff's count or declaration.

ENTENDMENT. The old form of *intendment (q. v.)* derived directly from the French, and used to denote the true meaning or signification of a word or sentence; that is, the understanding or construction of law. Cowell.

ENTER. To form a constituent part, to become a part or partaker; to impenetrate; share; with into; as, tin enters into the composition of pewter. Bedford v. Colorado Fuel & Iron Corporation, 102 Colo. 538, 81 P.2d 752, 755.

In the law of real property. To go upon land for the purpose of taking possession of it. In strict usage, the entering is preliminary to the taking possession but in common parlance the entry is now merged in the taking possession. See Entry.

In practice. To place anything before a court, or upon or among the records, in a formal and regular manner, and usually in writing; as to "enter an appearance," to "enter a judgment." In this sense the word is nearly equivalent to setting down formally in writing, in either a full or abridged form.

ENTERCEUR. L. Fr. A party challenging (claiming) goods; he who has placed them in the hands of a third person. Kelham.

ENTERING. Generally synonymous with "recording". In re Labb, D.C.N.Y., 42 F.Supp. 542, 544.

ENTERING JUDGMENTS. The formal entry of the judgment on the rolls of the court, which is necessary before bringing an appeal or an action on the judgment. Blatchford v. Newberry, 100 Ill. 491. The entering of judgment is a ministerial act performed by the clerk of court by means of which permanent evidence of judicial act in rendering judgment is made a record of the court. Jones v. Sun Oil Co., Tex.Civ.App., 145 S.W.2d 615, 619. Under some statutes, the entering consists merely in the filing of a judgment with the clerk; Mathison v. Anderson, 107 Wash. 617, 182 P. 622. But under other acts, the entry of a judgment consists in the recording of it in the judgment book. Wilson v. Durkee, 20 Cal.App. 492, 129 P. 617, 618.

Entry of judgment differs from rendition of judgment. "Rendition" of a judgment is the judicial act of the court in pronouncing the sentence of the law upon the facts in controversy. The "entry" is a ministerial act, which consists in spreading upon the record a statement of the final conclusion reached by the court in the matter, thus furnishing external and incontestable evidence of the sentence given, and designed to stand as a perpetual memorial of its action. Jaqua v. Harkens, 40 Ind.App. 639, 82 N.E. 920, 922; Beetchenow v. Bartholet, 162 Wash. 119, 298 P. 335, 336.

ENTERING SHORT. When bills not due are paid into a bank by a customer, it is the custom of some bankers not to carry the amount of the bills directly to his credit, but to "enter them short," as it is called, *i. e.,* to note down the receipt of the bills, their amounts, and the times when they become due in a previous column of the page, and the amounts when received are carried forward into the usual cash column. Sometimes, instead of entering such bills short, bankers credit the customer directly with the amount of the bills as cash, charging interest on any advances they may make on their account, and allow him at once to draw upon them to that amount. If the banker becomes bankrupt, the property in bills entered short does not pass to his assignees, but the customer is entitled to them if they remain in his hands, or to their proceeds, if received, subject to any lien the banker may have upon them. Wharton.

ENTERPRISE. A project or undertaking. Sizemore v. Hall, 148 Kan. 233, 80 P.2d 1092, 1095. In Workmen's Compensation Law. A hazardous undertaking or project. Hahnemann Hospital v. Industrial Board of Illinois, 282 Ill. 316, 118 N.E. 767, 770.

ENTERTAINMENT. This word is synonymous with "board," and includes the ordinary necessaries of life. See Lasar v. Johnson, 125 Cal. 549, 58 P. 161. Hospitable provision for the wants of a guest, especially a provision for the table. That which serves as amusement. Young v. Board of Trustees of Broadwater County High School, 90 Mont. 576, 4 P.2d 725, 726.

ENTHUSIASTS. Those who believe far more than they can prove and can prove far more than any one else can believe. Peskind v. State, 115 Ohio St. 279, 152 N.E. 670.

ENTICE. To wrongfully solicit, persuade, procure, allure, attract, draw by blandishment, coax or seduce. Nash v. Douglass, 12 Abb.Prac.N.S., N.Y., 190. To lure, induce, tempt, incite, or persuade a person to do a thing. Berger v. Levy, 5 Cal.App.2d 544, 43 P.2d 610, 611.

ENTIRE. Whole; without division, separation, or diminution; unmingled; complete in all its parts; not participated in by others. 15 Cyc. 1054; 11 Amer. & Eng. Enc. Law, 48; People v. Tahaures Purchase, 26 N.Y.S.2d 795, 813.

ENTIRE ACT. The words "entire Act" as used in the rule of statutory construction that it is the duty of the court to examine the entire act means the caption, the body of the act, and the emergency clause. Anderson v. Penix, 138 Tex. 596, 161 S.W.2d 455, 459.

ENTIRE BALANCE OF MY ESTATE. The residue. In re Taylor's Estate, 86 A. 708, 711, 239 Pa. 153; In re Brothers' Estate, 156 Pa.Super. 292, 40 A.2d 156, 157.

ENTIRE BLOOD. Relations of the "entire blood" are those derived not only from the same ancestor, but from the same couple of ancestors. In re Skidmore's Estate, 266 N.Y.S. 312, 148 Misc. 569.

ENTIRE CONTRACT. See Contract.

ENTIRE DAY. This phrase signifies an undivided day, not parts of two days. An entire day must have a legal, fixed, precise time to begin, and a fixed, precise time to end. A day, in contemplation of law, comprises all the twenty-four hours, beginning and ending at twelve o'clock at night. Robertson v. State, 43 Ala. 325. In a statute requiring the closing of all liquor saloons during "the entire day of any election," etc., this phrase means the natural day of twenty-four hours, commencing and terminating at midnight. Haines v. State, 7 Tex.App. 30.

ENTIRE INTEREST. The whole interest or right, without diminution. Where a person in selling his tract of land sells also his entire interest in all improvements upon public land adjacent thereto, this vests in the purchaser only a quitclaim of his interest in the improvements. McLeroy v. Duckworth, 13 La.Ann. 410.

ENTIRE LOSS OF SIGHT. In respect of one eye, or both. Substantial blindness, not necessarily absolute. International Travelers' Ass'n v. Rogers, Tex.Civ.App., 163 S.W. 421, 422. There was "entire loss of sight" of eye within accident policy, where insured could not distinguish one object from another in the strongest light, though he could distinguish between light and darkness. Tracey v. Standard Acc. Ins. Co., 119 Me. 131, 109 A. 490, 494, 9 A.L.R. 521. Locomotive Engineers' Mut. Life Accident Ins. Co. v. Meeks, 157 Miss. 57, 127 So. 699, 702. See Blind; Complete and Permanent Loss of Sight of Both Eyes.

ENTIRE STRUCTURE. Under lien statute. Not a completed, as distinguished from an uncompleted, building, but a new structure, not before existing, as distinguished from betterments and repairs on previously constructed improvements. Atkinson v. Colorado Title & Trust Co., 59 Colo. 528, 151 P. 457, 461.

ENTIRE TENANCY. A sole possession by one person, called "severalty," which is contrary to several tenancy, where a joint or common possession is in one or more.

ENTIRE USE, BENEFIT, etc. These words in the *habendum* of a trust-deed for the benefit of a married woman are equivalent to the words "sole use," or "sole and separate use," and consequently her husband takes nothing under such deed. Heathman v. Hall, 38 N.C. 414.

ENTIRELY WITHOUT UNDERSTANDING. Inability to comprehend nature and effect of transaction involved, not necessarily absolute imbecility, idiocy or mental incapacity. Barlow v. Strange, 120 Ga. 1015, 1018, 48 S.E. 344.

ENTIRETY. The whole, in contradistinction to a moiety or part only. When land is conveyed to husband and wife, they do not take by moieties, but both are seised of the *entirety.* 2 Kent, Comm. 132; 4 Kent, Comm. 362. Parceners, on the other hand, have not an *entirety* of interest, but each is properly entitled to the whole of a distinct moiety. 2 Bl.Comm. 188. See Estate by the Entirety.

The word is also used to designate that which the law considers as one whole, and not capable of being divided into parts. Thus, a judgment, it is held, is an *entirety,* and, if void as to one of the two defendants, cannot be valid as to the other. So, if a contract is an *entirety,* no part of the consideration is due until the whole has been performed.

ENTITLE. In its usual sense, to entitle is to give a right or title. Felter v. McClure, 135 Wash. 410, 237 P. 1010, 1011. To qualify for; to furnish with proper grounds for seeking or claiming. Fitts v. Terminal Warehousing Corporation, 170 Tenn. 198, 93 S.W.2d 1265, 1267. In re Graves, 325 Mo. 888, 30 S.W.2d 149, 151. In ecclesiastical law. To entitle is to give a title or ordination as a minister.

ENTITY. A real being; existence. Department of Banking v. Hedges, 136 Neb. 382, 286 N.W. 277, 281.

ENTRAILS. Intestines. "Entrails" of a calf do not include pluck and sweetbread. Commonwealth v. Cohen, 250 Mass. 570, 146 N.E. 228, 230.

ENTRANCE. A door or gate for entering; a gate; an opening, and perhaps a passage. Weatherby v. Travelers Indemnity Co., Tex.Civ.App., 171 S.W.2d 540, 541.

ENTRAP. To catch, to entrap, to ensnare; hence, to catch by artifice; to involve in difficulties or distresses; to catch or involve in contradictions. Roane v. State, 55 Okl.Cr. 332, 29 P.2d 990, 992.

ENTRAPMENT. The act of officers or agents of the government in inducing a person to commit a crime not contemplated by him, for the purpose of instituting a criminal prosecution against him. Falden v. Commonwealth, 167 Va. 549, 189 S.E. 329, 332. Lee v. State, 66 Okl.Cr. 399, 92 P.2d 621, 623. But the mere act of an officer in furnishing the accused an opportunity to commit the crime, where the criminal intent was already present in the accused's mind, is not ordinarily entrapment. State v. Cowling, 161 Wash. 519, 297 P. 172, 174.

ENTREATY. Beseeching, or suppliant, or prayerful in nature. In re Sloan's Estate, 7 Cal.App.2d 319, 46 P.2d 1007, 1018.

ENTREBAT. L. Fr. An intruder or interloper. Britt. c. 114.

ENTREGA. Span. Delivery. Las Partidas, pt. 6, tit. 14, l. 1.

ENTREPÔT. A warehouse or magazine for the deposit of goods. In France, a building or place where goods from abroad may be deposited, and from whence they may be withdrawn for exportation to another country, without paying a duty. Brande; Webster.

ENTRY. The act of making or entering a record; a setting down in writing of particulars; or that which is entered; an item. United States v. Darby, D.C.Md., 2 F.Supp. 378, 379. Generally synonymous with "recording." In re Labb, D.C.N.Y., 42 F.Supp. 542, 544.

Passage leading into a house or other building or to a room; a vestibule. Weatherby v. Travelers Indemnity Co., Tex.Civ.App., 171 S.W.2d 540, 541.

In commercial law. Entry denotes the act of a merchant, trader, or other business man in recording in his account-books the facts and circumstances of a sale, loan, or other transaction. Also the note or record so made. Bissell v. Beckwith, 32 Conn. 517; U. S. v. Crecelius, D.C.Mo., 34 F. 30. The books in which such memoranda are first (or originally) inscribed are called "books of original entry," and are *prima facie* evidence for certain purposes.

In copyright law. Depositing with the register of copyrights the printed title of a book, pamphlet, etc., for the purpose of securing copyright on the same. The old formula for giving notice of copyright was, "Entered according to act of congress," etc.

In criminal law. Entry is the unlawful making one's way into a dwelling or other house, for the purpose of committing a crime therein.

In cases of burglary, the least entry with the whole or any part of the body, hand, or foot, or with any instrument or weapon, introduced for the purpose of committing a felony, is sufficient to complete the offense. 3 Inst. 64. And see Walker v. State, 63 Ala. 49, 35 Am.Rep. 1. State v. Chappell, 185 S.C. 111, 193 S.E. 924, 925.

In customs law. The entry of imported goods at the custom house consists in submitting them to the inspection of the revenue officers, together with a statement or description of such goods, and the original invoices of the same, for the purpose of estimating the duties to be paid thereon. U. S. v. Legg, 105 F. 930, 45 C.C.A. 134.

In mining law. A place in coal mines used by the miners and other workmen generally in going to and from their work, through which coal is hauled from the necks of the rooms to the foot of the shaft; a "room" being the place in which a miner works and from which he mines coal. Ricardo v. Central Coal & Coke Co., 100 Kan. 95, 163 P. 641, 643.

In parliamentary law. The "entry" of a proposed constitutional amendment or of any other document or transaction in the journal of a house of the legislature consists in recording it in writing in such journal, and (according to most of the authorities) at length. See Koehler v. Hill, 60 Iowa, 543, 15 N.W. 609.

In practice. Entry denotes the formal inscription upon the rolls or records of a court of a note or minute of any of the proceedings in an action; and it is frequently applied to the filing of a proceeding in writing, such as a notice of appearance by a defendant, and, very generally, to the filing of the judgment roll as a record in the office of the court. Thomason v. Ruggles, 69 Cal. 465, 11 P. 20.

In public land laws. Under the provisions of the land laws of the United States, the term "entry" denotes the filing at the land-office, or inscription upon its records, of the documents required to found a claim for a homestead or preemption right, and as preliminary to the issuing of a patent for the land. Chotard v. Pope, 12 Wheat. 588, 6 L.Ed. 737; Stephens v. Terry, 178 Ky. 129, 198 S.W. 768, 771.

The word "entry," as used in the public land laws, covers all methods by which a right to acquire title to public lands may be initiated. United States v. Northern Pac. Ry. Co., C.C.Mont., 204 F. 485, 487.

Homestead Entry

An entry under the United States land laws for the purpose of acquiring title to a portion of the public domain under the homestead laws, consisting of an affidavit of the claimant's right to enter, a formal application for the land, and payment of the money required. Whitmire v. Spears, 212 Ala. 583, 103 So. 668, 669.

Mineral Land Entry

Filing a claim to hold or purchase lands belonging to the public domain and valuable for the minerals they contain, implying a prior discovery of ore and the opening of a mine. U. S. v. Four Bottles Sour Mash Whisky, D.C.Wash., 90 F. 720.

Pre-emption Entry

An entry of public lands for purchase under the pre-emption laws, giving the entryman a preferred right to acquire the land by virtue of his occupation and improvement of it. Hartman v. Warren, 76 F. 161, 22 C.C.A. 30.

Timber Culture Entry

An entry of public lands under the various acts of congress opening portions of the public domain to settlement and to the acquisition of title by the settlers on condition of the planting and cultivation of timber trees. Hartman v. Warren, 76 F. 160, 22 C.C.A. 30.

In real property law. Entry is the act of going peaceably upon a piece of land which is claimed as one's own, but is held by another person, with the intention and for the purpose of taking possession of it.

Entry is a remedy which the law affords to an injured party ousted of his lands by another person who has taken possession thereof without right. This remedy (which must in all cases be pursued peaceably) takes place in three only out of the five species of ouster, viz., abatement, intrusion, and disseisin; for, as in these three cases the original entry of the wrong-doer is unlawful, so the wrong may be remedied by the mere entry of the former possessor. But it is otherwise upon a discontinuance or deforcement, for in these latter two cases the former possessor cannot remedy the wrong by entry, but must do so by action, inasmuch as the original entry being in these cases lawful, and therefore conferring an apparent right of possession, the law will not suffer such apparent right to be overthrown by the mere act or entry of the claimant. Brown. Johnson v. Cobb, 29 S.C. 372, 7 S.E. 601.

Forcible Entry

See that title.

Open Entry

An entry upon real estate, for the purpose of taking possession, which is not clandestine nor effected by secret artifice or stratagem, and (in some states by statute) one which is accomplished in the presence of two witnesses. Thompson v. Kenyon, 100 Mass. 108.

Re-Entry

The resumption of the possession of leased premises by the landlord on the tenant's failure to pay the stipulated rent or otherwise to keep the conditions of the lease.

In Scotch law. The term refers to the acknowledgment of the title of the heir, etc., to be admitted by the superior.

ENTRY AD COMMUNEM LEGEM. Entry at common law. The name of a writ of entry which lay for a reversioner after the alienation and death of the particular tenant for life, against him who was in possession of the land. Brown.

ENTRY AD TERMINUM QUI PRÆTERIIT. The writ of entry *ad terminum qui prœteriit* lies where a man leases land to another for a term of years, and the tenant holds over his term. And if lands be leased to a man for the term of another's life, and he for whose life the lands are leased dies, and the lessee holds over, then the lessor shall have this writ. Termes de la Ley.

ENTRY BY COURT. Acts 1923, c. 6, amending Acts 1921, c. 112, § 138, provides that county court may enter upon lands and build roads and within 60 days after such entry shall petition for assessment of compensation. An "entry" within statute means the establishing of the road on, and appropriation of, the land, by a proper order of the county court. To effect an entry under the statute it is not necessary that the county court go upon the lands and begin the work of construction. McGibson v. Roane County Court, 95 W.Va. 338, 121 S.E. 99, 104.

ENTRY FOR MARRIAGE IN SPEECH. A writ of entry *causa matrimonii prœloquuti* lies where lands or tenements are given to a man upon condition that he shall take the donor to be his wife within a certain time, and he does not espouse her within the said term, or espouses another woman, or makes himself priest. Termes de la Ley.

ENTRY IN CASU CONSIMILI. A writ of entry *in casu consimili* lies where a tenant for life or by the curtesy aliens in fee. Termes de la Ley.

ENTRY IN REGULAR COURSE OF BUSINESS. A record setting forth a fact or transaction made by one in the ordinary and usual course of one's business, employment, office or profession, which it was the duty of the enterer in such manner to make, or which was commonly and regularly made, or which it was convenient to make, in the conduct of the business to which such entry pertains. Leonard v. State, 100 Ohio St. 456, 127 N.E. 464, 468.

ENTRY IN THE CASE PROVIDED. A writ of entry *in casu proviso* lies if a tenant in dower alien in fee, or for life, or for another's life, living the tenant in dower. Termes de la Ley.

ENTRY OF CAUSE FOR TRIAL. In English practice. The proceeding by a plaintiff in an action who had given notice of trial, depositing with the proper officer of the court the *nisi prius* record, with the panel of jurors annexed, and thus bringing the issue before the court for trial.

ENTRY OF JUDGMENT. See Entering Judgment.

ENTRY ON THE ROLL. In former times, the parties to an action, personally or by their counsel, used to appear in open court and make their mutual statements *vivâ voce,* instead of as at the present day delivering their mutual pleadings, until they arrived at the issue or precise point in dispute between them. During the progress of this oral statement, a minute of the various proceedings was made on parchment by an officer of the court appointed for that purpose. The parchment then became the record; in other words, the official history of the suit. Long after the practice of oral pleading had fallen into disuse, it continued necessary to enter the proceedings in like manner upon the parchment roll, and this was called "entry on the roll," or making up the "issue roll." But by a rule of H. T. 4 Wm. IV. the practice of making up the issue roll was abolished; and it was only necessary to make up the issue in the form prescribed for the purpose by a rule of H. T. 1853, and to deliver the same to the court and to the opposite party. The issue which was delivered to the court was called the *"nisi prius record;"* and that was regarded as the official history of the suit, in like manner as the issue roll formerly was. Under the present practice, the issue roll or *nisi prius record* consists of the papers delivered to the court, to facilitate the trial of the action, these papers consisting of the pleadings simply, with the notice of trial. Brown.

ENTRY WITHOUT ASSENT OF THE CHAPTER. A writ of entry *sine assensu capituli* lies where an abbot, prior, or such as hath covent or common seal, aliens lands or tenements of the right of his church, without the assent of the covent or chapter, and dies. Termes de la Ley.

ENTRY, WRIT OF. In old English practice. This was a writ made use of in a form of real action brought to recover the possession of lands from one who wrongfully withheld the same from the demandant.

Its object was to regain the *possession* of lands of which the demandant, or his ancestors, had been unjustly deprived by the tenant of the freehold, or those under whom he claimed, and hence it belonged to the *possessory* division of real actions. It decided nothing with respect to the *right of property,* but only restored the demandant to that situation in which he was (or by law ought to have been) before the dispossession committed. 3 Bl.Comm. 180.

It was usual to specify in such writs the degree or degrees within which the writ was brought, and it was said to be "in the *per*" or "in the *per and cui,*" according as there had been one or two descents or alienations from the original wrongdoer. If more than two such transfers had intervened, the writ was said to be "in the *post.*" See 3 Bl.Comm. 181. See, further, Writ of Entry.

ENTRYMAN. One who makes an entry of land under the public land laws of the United States. Indian Cove Irr. Dist. v. Prideaux, 25 Idaho 112, 136 P. 618, 620, Ann.Cas.1916A, 1218.

ENUMERATED. This term is often used in law as equivalent to "mentioned specifically," "designated," or "expressly named or granted"; as in speaking of "enumerated" governmental powers, items of property, or articles in a tariff schedule. See Bloomer v. Todd, 3 Wash.T. 599, 19 P. 135, 1 L.R.A. 111.

ENUMERATIO INFIRMAT REGULAM IN CASIBUS NON ENUMERATIS. Enumeration disaffirms the rule in cases not enumerated. Bac.Aph. 17.

ENUMERATIO UNIUS EST EXCLUSIO ALTERIUS. The specification of one thing is the exclusion of a different thing. A maxim more generally expressed in the form *"expressio unius est exclusio alterius,"* (*q. v.*).

ENUMERATORS. Persons appointed to collect census papers or schedules. 33 & 34 Vict. c. 108, § 4.

ENURE. To operate or take effect. To serve to the use, benefit, or advantage of a person. A release to the tenant for life *enures* to him in reversion; that is, it has the same effect for him as for the tenant for life. Often written "inure."

ENVELOPE. That which envelops; a wrapper; an inclosing cover; especially, the cover or wrapper of a document, as of a letter. In re Eastman Kodak Co., Cust. & Pat.App., 80 F.2d 270, 271, 272.

ENVOY. In international law. A public minister of the second class, ranking next after an ambassador.

Envoys are either ordinary or extraordinary; by custom the latter is held in greater consideration.

ENZYME. Any one of a series of catalytic agents, animal or vegetable, produced by living cells, effecting chemical change in absorbed or surrounding substances so as to render them fit for the requirements of the cells. In re Reese, Cust. & Pat.App., 143 F.2d 1021.

EO DIE. Lat. On that day; on the same day.

EO INSTANTI. Lat. At that instant; at the very or same instant; immediately. 1 Bl.Comm. 196, 249; 2 Bl.Comm. 168; Co.Litt. 298*a*; 1 Coke 138. Also written *eo instante.*

EO INTUITU. Lat. With or in that view; with that intent or object. Hale, Anal. § 2.

EO LOCI. Lat. In the civil law. In that state or condition; in that place, (*eo loco.*) Calvin.

EO NOMINE. Lat. Under that name; by that appellation. *Perinde ac si eo nomine tibi tradita fuisset,* just as if it had been delivered to you by that name. Inst. 2, 1, 43. A common phrase in the books.

EODEM LIGAMINE QUO LIGATUM EST DISSOLVITUR. A bond is released by the same formalities with which it is contracted. Co.Litt. 212*b*; Broom, Max. 891.

EODEM MODO QUO QUID CONSTITUITUR, DISSOLVITUR. In the manner in which [by the same means by which] a thing is constituted, is it dissolved. 6 Coke, 53*b*.

EORLE. In Saxon law. An earl.

EOTH. In Saxon law. An oath.

EPICYCLOIDAL CURVE. A curve generated by the motion of a point on the circumference of a circle which rolls upon the convex side of a fixed circle. Hill v. Hill, Cust. & Pat.App., 54 F.2d 950, 952.

EPIDEMIC. This term, in its ordinary and popular meaning, applies to *any* disease which is widely spread or generally prevailing at a given place and time. Bethlehem Steel Co. v. Industrial Accident Commission, 21 Cal.2d 742, 135 P.2d 153, 157; Martin v. Springfield City Water Co., Mo.App., 128 S.W.2d 674, 679.

EPILEPSY. In medical jurisprudence. A disease of the brain, which occurs in paroxysms with uncertain intervals between them. Vulgarly called "fits." Westphall v. Metropolitan Life Ins. Co., 27 Cal.App. 734, 151 P. 159, 162; Morse v. Caldwell, 55 Ga.App. 804, 191 S.E. 479, 485.

The disease is generally organic, though it may be functional and symptomatic of irritation in other parts of the body. The attack is characterized by loss of consciousness, sudden falling down, distortion of the eyes and face, grinding or gnashing of the teeth, stertorous respiration, and more or less severe muscular spasms or convulsions. Epilepsy, though a disease of the brain, is not to be regarded as a form of insanity, in the sense that a person thus afflicted can be said to be permanently insane, for there may be little or no mental aberration in the intervals between the attacks. But the paroxysm is frequently followed by a temporary insanity, varying in particular instances from slight alienation to the most violent mania. In the latter form the affection is known as "epileptic fury." But this generally passes off within a few days. But the course of the principal disease is generally one of deterioration, the brain being gradually more and more deranged in its functions in the intervals of attack, and the memory and intellectual powers in general becoming enfeebled, leading to a greatly impaired state of mental efficiency, or to dementia, or a condition bordering on imbecility. See Aurentz v. Anderson, 3 Pittsb.R., Pa., 310; Lawton v. Sun Mutual Ins. Co., 2 Cush., Mass., 517.

Hystero-epilepsy. A condition initiated by an apparently mild attack of convulsive hysteria, followed by an epileptiform convulsion, and succeeded by a period of "clownism" (Osler) in which the patient assumes a remarkable series of droll contortions or cataleptic poses, sometimes simulating attitudes expressive of various passions, as, fear, joy, erotism, etc. The final stage is one of delirium with unusual hallucinations. The attack differs from true epilepsy in that the convulsions may continue without serious result for several successive days, while true epilepsy, if persistent, is always serious, associated with fever, and frequently fatal.

EPIMENIA. Expenses or gifts. Blount.

EPIPHANY. A Christian festival, otherwise called the "Manifestation of Christ to the Gentiles," observed on the 6th of January, in honor of the appearance of the star to the three *magi*, or wise men, who came to adore the Messiah, and bring him presents. It is commonly called "Twelfth Day." Enc.Lond.

EPIPHYSEITIS. Inflammation of an epiphysis—a process of bone attached for a time to another bone by cartilage. Eckenroad v. Rochester & Pittsburgh Coal Co., 149 Pa.Super. 257, 27 A.2d 759, 761.

EPIPHYSEAL SEPARATION. Not a bone fracture in true sense, but a separation of the fibers and cartilaginous tissues which attach the epiphysis to the femur. Elsen v. State Farmers Mut. Ins. Co., 219 Minn. 315, 17 N.W.2d 652, 655.

EPIPHYSIS. Part or process of a bone which ossifies separately and subsequently becomes ankylosed (to grow together into one) into the main part of the bone. Elsen v. State Farmers Mut. Ins. Co., 219 Minn. 315, 17 N.W.2d 652, 655.

EPIQUEYA. In Spanish law. A term synonymous with "equity" in one of its senses, and defined as "the benignant and prudent interpretation of the law according to the circumstances of the time, place, and person."

EPISCOPACY. The office of overlooking or overseeing; the office of a bishop, who is to overlook and oversee the concerns of the church. A form of church government by diocesan bishops. Trustees of Diocese of Central New York v. Colgrove, 4 Hun (N.Y.) 366.

EPISCOPALIA. In ecclesiastical law. Synodals, pentecostals, and other customary payments from the clergy to their diocesan bishop, formerly collected by the rural deans. Cowell.

EPISCOPALIAN. Of or pertaining to episcopacy, or to the Episcopal Church.

EPISCOPATE. A bishopric. The dignity or office of a bishop.

EPISCOPORUM ECDICUS. Bishop's proctors; church lawyers. 1 Reeve, Eng.Law, 65.

EPISCOPUS. In the civil law. An overseer; an inspector. A municipal officer who had the charge and oversight of the bread and other provisions which served the citizens for their daily food. Vicat. In medieval history. A bishop; a bishop of the Christian church.

EPISCOPUS ALTERIUS MANDATO QUAM REGIS NON TENETUR OBTEMPERARE. Co.Litt. 134. A bishop needs not obey any mandate save the king's.

EPISCOPUS PUERORUM. It was an old custom that upon certain feasts some lay person should plait his hair, and put on the garments of a bishop, and in them pretend to exercise episcopal jurisdiction, and do several ludicrous actions, for which reason he was called "bishop of the boys;" and this custom obtained in England long after several constitutions were made to abolish it. Blount.

EPISCOPUS TENEAT PLACITUM, IN CURIA CHRISTIANITATIS, DE IIS QUÆ MERE SUNT SPIRITUALIA. 12 Coke, 44. A bishop may hold plea in a Court Christian of things merely spiritual.

EPISTOLA. A letter; a charter; an instrument in writing for conveyance of lands or assurance of contracts. Calvin.; Spelman.

EPISTOLÆ. In the civil law. Rescripts; opinions given by the emperors in cases submitted to them for decision.

Answers of the emperors to petitions.

The answers of counsellors, (*juris-consulti*,) as Ulpian and others, to questions of law proposed to them, were also called "*epistolœ*."

Opinions written out. The term originally signified the same as *literœ*. Vicat.

EPOCH. The time at which a new computation is begun; the time whence dates are numbered. Enc. Lond.

EQUAL. Alike; uniform; on the same plane or level with respect to efficiency, worth, value, amount, or rights. People v. Hoffman, 116 Ill. 587, 5 N.E. 600, 56 Am.Rep. 793.

EQUAL AND UNIFORM TAXATION. Taxes are said to be "equal and uniform" when no person or class of persons in the taxing district, whether it be a state, county, or city, is taxed at a different rate than are other persons in the same district upon the same value or the same thing, and where the objects of taxation are the same, by whomsoever owned or whatsoever they may be. Weatherly Independent School Dist. v. Hughes, Tex.Civ. App., 41 S.W.2d 445, 447.

EQUAL DEGREE. Persons are said to be related to a decedent "in equal degree" when they are all removed by an equal number of steps or degrees from the common ancestor. Fidler v. Higgins, 21 N.J.Eq. 162; Helmes v. Elliott, 14 S.W. 930, 89 Tenn. 446, 10 L.R.A. 535.

EQUAL ELECTION. Elections are "equal," when vote of each voter is equal in its influence upon result to vote of every other elector. Blue v. State ex rel. Brown, 206 Ind. 98, 188 N.E. 583, 589, 91 A.L.R. 334.

EQUAL PROTECTION OF THE LAWS. The equal protection of the laws of a state is extended to persons within its jurisdiction, within the meaning of the constitutional requirement, when its courts are open to them on the same conditions as to others, with like rules of evidence and modes of procedure, for the security of their persons and property, the prevention and redress of wrongs, and the enforcement of contracts; when they are subjected to no restrictions in the acquisition of property, the enjoyment of personal liberty, and the pursuit of happiness, which do not generally affect others; when they are liable to no other or greater burdens and charges than such as are laid upon others; and when no different or greater punishment is enforced against them for a violation of the laws. State v. Montgomery, 94 Me. 192, 47 A. 165.

"Equal protection of the law" means that equal protection and security shall be given to all under like circumstances in his life, his liberty, and his property, and in the pursuit of happiness, and in the exemption from any greater burdens and charges than are equally imposed upon all others under like circumstances. Sovereign Camp, W. O. W., v. Casados, D.C.N.M., 21 F.Supp. 989, 994.

EQUAL WATCHES. Under statute requiring division of sailors at sea into equal watches, "equal watches" means successive and continuous watches to be constituted in numbers as nearly equal as the sum of the whole number will permit. New York & Cuba Mail S. S. Co. v. Continental Ins. Co. of City of New York, C.C.A.N.Y., 117 F.2d 404, 409.

EQUALITY. The condition of possessing substantially the same rights, privileges, and immunities, and being liable to substantially the same duties. Louisville & N. R. Co. v. Commonwealth, 160 Ky. 769, 170 S.W. 162, Ann.Cas.1916A, 405.

EQUALIZATION. The act or process of making equal or bringing about conformity to a common standard. The process of equalizing assessments or taxes, as performed by "boards of equalization" in various states, consists in comparing the assessments made by the local officers of the various counties or other taxing districts within the jurisdiction of the board and reducing them to a common and uniform basis, increasing or diminishing by such percentage as may be necessary, so as to bring about, within the entire territory affected, a uniform and equal ratio between the assessed value and the actual cash value of property. The term is also applied to a similar process of leveling or adjusting the assessments of individual taxpayers, so that the property of one shall not be assessed at a higher (or lower) percentage of its market value than the property of another. See Harney v. Mitchell County, 44 Iowa 203.

EQUALIZE. To make equal, to cause to correspond, or be like in amount or degree, as compared with something. Los Angeles County v. Ransohoff, 24 Cal.App.2d 238, 74 P.2d 828, 830; De Mille v. Los Angeles County, Cal.App., 77 P.2d 905, 906.

EQUALLY DIVIDED. Provision in will that property shall be "equally divided," or divided "share and share alike" means that the property shall be divided per capita and not per stirpes. However, these phrases may be so modified by other parts of the will as to require distribution per stirpes. In re Mays' Estate, 197 Mo.App. 555, 196 S.W. 1039, 1040.

EQUERRY. An officer of state under the master of the horse.

EQUES. Lat. In Roman and old English law. A knight.

EQUILIBRIUM. As applied in chemistry, the balanced state reached when the action apparently stops in a chemical reaction, that is, the concentration between reaction products and the original reacting substances has become such that decomposition and recombination proceeds with equal speed. In re Sussman, 141 F.2d 267, 271, 31 C.C. P.A.(Patents) 921.

EQUILOCUS. An equal. It is mentioned in Simeon Dunelm, A.D. 882. Jacob.

EQUINOXES. The two periods of the year (vernal equinox about March 21st, and autumnal equinox about September 22d) when the time from the rising of the sun to its setting is equal to the time from its setting to its rising. See Dig. 43, 13, 1, 8.

EQUIP. To furnish for service or against a need or exigency; to fit out; to supply with whatever is necessary to efficient action in any way. Synonymous with furnish. State ex rel. Davis v. Barber, 139 Fla. 706, 190 So. 809.

EQUIPMENT. Furnishings, or outfit for the required purposes. An exceedingly elastic term, the meaning of which depends on context. Elliott v. Payne, 293 Mo. 581, 239 S.W. 851, 852, 23 A.L.R. 706; Midland Special School Dist. of Sebastian

County, Ark., v. Central Trust Co. of Illinois, C.C.A.Ark., 1 F.2d 124, 126.

Whatever is needed in equipping; the articles comprised in an outfit; equippage. Department of Treasury, Gross Income Tax Division, v. Ranger-Cook, Inc., Ind.App., 49 N.E.2d 548, 550. Farm & Home Saving & Loan Ass'n of Missouri v. Empire Furniture Co., Tex.Civ.App., 87 S.W.2d 1111, 1112. Nearly synonymous with "instrumentality." Nekoosa-Edwards Paper Co. v. Minneapolis St. P. & S. S. M. Ry. Co., 217 Wis. 426, 259 N.W. 618, but not synonymous with "maintenance". Neal v. City of Morrilton, 192 Ark. 450, 92 S.W.2d 208, 209.

EQUITABLE. Just; conformable to the principles of justice and right.

Just, fair, and right, in consideration of the facts and circumstances of the individual case.

Existing in equity; available or sustainable only in equity, or only upon the rules and principles of equity.

As to "Fair and Equitable Value," see that title. As to equitable "Assets," "Construction," "Conversion," "Easement," "Ejectment," "Estate," "Garnishment," "Levy," "Mortgage," "Title," and "Waste." see those titles.

EQUITABLE ACTION. One founded on an equity or cognizable in a court of equity; or, more specifically, an action arising, not immediately from the contract in suit, but from an equity in favor of a third person, not a party to it, but for whose benefit certain stipulations or promises were made. Wenzel & Henoch Const. Co. v. Metropolitan Water Dist. of Southern California, D.C.Cal., 18 F.Supp. 616, 620.

EQUITABLE ASSIGNMENT. An assignment which, though invalid at law, will be recognized and enforced in equity; *e. g.*, an assignment of a chose in action, or of future acquisitions of the assignor. Lewis v. Braun, 356 Ill. 467, 191 N.E. 56, 60; Stewart v. Kane, Mo.App., 111 S.W.2d 971, 974.

In order to work an "equitable assignment", there must be an absolute appropriation by the assignor of the debt or fund sought to be assigned. Blount v. Metropolitan Life Ins. Co., 192 Ga. 325, 15 S.E.2d 413, 415; Sneesby v. Livington, 182 Wash. 229, 46 P.2d 733, 735.

EQUITABLE CONVERSION. A fiction which results in treating land as personalty and personalty as land under certain circumstances. It takes place when a contract for sale of realty becomes binding on parties. Shay v. Penrose, 185 N.E.2d 218, 219, 25 Ill.2d 447; Panushka v. Panushka, 349 P.2d 450, 452, 221 Or. 145; Parr-Richmond Indus. Corp. v. Boyd, 272 P.2d 16, 22, 43 C.2d 157.

EQUITABLE DEFENSE. A defense to an action on grounds which, prior to the passing of the Common Law Procedure Act (17 and 18 Vict. c. 125), would have been cognizable only in a court of equity. Moz. & W. In American practice, a defense which is cognizable in a court of equity, but which is available there only, and not in an action at law, except under the reformed codes of practice. Kelly v. Hurt, 74 Mo. 561–570; City of New York v. Holzderber, 90 N.Y.S. 63, 44 Misc. 509. The codes of procedure and the practice in some of the states likewise permit both a legal and equitable defense to the same action. Susquehanna S. S. Co. v. A. O. Andersen & Co., 239 N.Y. 285, 146 N.E. 381, 383. It has also been construed to mean a defense which a court of equity would recognize, or one founded on some distinct ground of equitable jurisdiction. City of New York v. Holzderber, 44 Misc. 509, 90 N.Y.S. 63, 64.

EQUITABLE DOCTRINE OF APPROXIMATION. This doctrine differs from "Cy pres doctrine" in purpose and application. The last mentioned doctrine applies where an apparent charitable intention has failed, whether by an incomplete disposition at the outset or by subsequent inadequacy of the original object, and its purpose is to give a cy pres or proximate application to testator's intention, whereas the "equitable doctrine of approximation" merely authorizes a court of chancery to vary the details of administration, in order to preserve the trust, and carry out the general purpose of the donor. National Bank of Greece v. Savarika, 167 Miss. 571, 148 So. 649, 654.

EQUITABLE ELECTION. The choice to be made by a person who may, under a will or other instrument, have either one of two alternative rights or benefits, but not both. Peters v. Bain, 133 U.S. 670, 10 S.Ct. 354, 33 L.Ed. 696.

The obligation imposed upon a party to choose between two inconsistent or alternative rights or claims, in cases where there is clear intention of the person from whom he derives one that he should not enjoy both. 2 Story, Eq.Jur. § 1075; Dakan v. Dakan, 83 S.W.2d 620, 624, 125 Tex. 305.

A choice shown by an overt act between two inconsistent rights, either of which may be asserted at the will of the chooser alone. Bierce v. Hutchins, 205 U.S. 346, 27 S.Ct. 524, 51 L.Ed. 828; Macbeth-Evans Glass Co. v. General Electric Co., C.C.A.Ohio, 246 F. 695, 701; Jenkins v. U. S., D.C.R.I., 22 F.2d 568, 571.

EQUITABLE ESTOPPEL is that condition in which justice forbids one to gainsay his own acts or assertions. Goodwin Tile & Brick Co. v. DeVries, Iowa, 13 N.W.2d 310, 312, 155 A.L.R. 346. The preclusion of person by his act or conduct or silence from asserting rights which might otherwise have existed. Marshall v. Wilson, Or., 154 P.2d 547, 551. The species of estoppel which equity puts upon a person who has made a false representation or a concealment of material facts, with knowledge of the facts, to a party ignorant of the truth of the matter, with the intention that the other party should act upon it, and with the result that such party is actually induced to act upon it, to his damage. Bigelow, Estop. 484.

See, also, In Pais, Estoppel In.

Elements or essentials of such estoppel include change of position for the worse by party asserting estoppel, Malone v. Republic Nat. Bank & Trust Co., Tex.Civ.App., 70 S.W.2d 809, 812; Clover v. Peterson, 203 Minn. 337, 281 N.W. 275, 278; conduct by party estopped such that it would be contrary to equity and good conscience for him to allege and prove the truth, Rody v. Doyle, 181 Md. 195, 29 A.2d 290, 293; false representation or concealment of facts, Clark v. National Aid Life Ass'n, 177 Okl. 137, 57 P.2d 832, 833; Antrim Lumber Co. v. Wagner, 175 Okl. 564, 54 P.2d 173, 176; ignorance of party asserting estoppel of facts and absence of opportunity to ascertain them, Trenton Banking Co. v. Howard, N.J.Ch., 187 A. 569, 574; Fipps v. Stidham, 174 Okl. 473, 50 P.2d 680, 684; injury from declarations, acts, or omissions of party were he permitted to gainsay their truth, Fleishbein v. Western Auto Supply Agency, 19 Cal.App.2d 424, 65 P.2d 928; Roberts v. Friedell, 218 Minn. 88, 15 N.W.2d 496, 500; intention that representation should be acted on, Stookesberry v. Burgher, 220 Iowa 916, 262 N.W. 820; Consolidated Cut Stone Co. v. Seidenbach, 181 Okl. 578, 75 P.2d 442, 452; knowledge, actual or constructive, of facts by party estopped, Antrim Lumber Co. v. Wagner, 175 Okl. 564, 54 P.2d 173, 176; Lillywhite v. Coleman, 46 Ariz. 523, 52 P.2d 1157, 1160; misleading person to his prejudice, United States, for Use and Benefit of Noland Co., v. Wood, C.C.A.Va., 99 F.2d 80, 82; omission, misconduct or misrepresentation misleading another, Security Savings & Trust Co. v. Portland Flour Mills Co., 124 Or. 276, 261 P. 432, 437; reliance upon representation or conduct of person sought to be estopped, Wilkinson v. Lieberman, 327 Mo. 420, 37 S.W.2d 533, 536, George W. Armbruster, Jr., Inc., v. City of Wildwood, D.C.N.J., 41 F.2d 823, 829.

Estoppel in pais and equitable estoppel are convertible terms. Brown v. Corn Exchange Nat. Bank & Trust Co., 42 A.2d 474, 480, 136 N.J.Eq. 430; State ex rel. Squire v. Murfey, Blossom & Co., 131 Ohio St. 289, 2 N.E.2d 866, 870.

"Legal estoppel" excludes evidence of the truth and the equity of the particular case to support a strict rule of law on grounds of public policy whereas "equitable estoppel" is admitted on exactly the opposite ground of promoting the equity and justice of the individual case by preventing a party from asserting his rights under a general technical rule of law, when he has so conducted himself that it would be contrary to equity and good conscience for him to allege and prove the truth. First Nat. Bank v. Boles, 231 Ala. 473, 165 So. 586, 592.

Such estoppel may be based on acts, omission to act, representations, admissions, concealment or silence, Carter v. Curlew Creamery Co., 16 Wash.2d 476, 134 P.2d 66; West v. Cleveland Ry. Co., Ohio App., 58 N.E.2d 799, 801; Mahoney v. Mahoney, Tex.Civ.App., 103 S.W.2d 459, 462.

EQUITABLE EXECUTION. This term is sometimes applied to the appointment of a receiver with power of sale. Hatch v. Van Dervoort, 54 N.J. Eq. 511, 34 A. 938.

Though a garnishment is not an "execution," garnishment after execution is practically an equitable "execution" brought for purpose of reaching nonleviable assets, issuing on judgment in somewhat same manner as an "execution" and in immediate aid or in lieu thereof. First Nat. Bank v. City Guaranty Bank of Hobart, 174 Okl. 545, 51 P.2d 573, 576.

EQUITABLE LIENS are such as exist in equity.

An equitable lien arises either from a written contract which shows an intention to charge some particular property with a debt or obligation or is implied and declared by a court of equity out of general considerations of right and justice as applied to relations of the parties and circumstances of their dealings, Owensboro Banking Co. v. Lewis, 269 Ky. 277, 106 S.W.2d 1000, 1004; Clark v. Armstrong & Murphy, 180 Okl. 514, 72 P.2d 362, 365, 366; It is a mere floating and ineffective equity until such time as judgment or decree is rendered actually subjecting property to the payment of the debt or claim, Langford v. Fanning, Mo., 7 S.W.2d 726, 728; Nelson v. Nelson Neal Lumber Co., 171 Wash. 55, 17 P.2d 626, 628, 92 A.L.R. 554. It is founded upon an agreement indicating intention that some specific property is to be held, given, or transferred as security, In re Friedlander's Estate, 32 N.Y.S.2d 991, 994, 995, 178 Misc. 65. It is neither a jus in re nor jus ad rem, Folsom v. Farmers' Bank of Vero Beach, 136 So. 524, 527, 102 Fla. 899; Clements v. Holmes, 22 Tenn.App. 230, 120 S.W.2d 988, 993; It is not an estate or property in the thing itself or a right to recover the same. Foster v. Thornton, 179 So. 882, 892; Jamison Coal & Coke Co. v. Goltra, C.C.A.Mo., 143 F.2d 889, 893, 154 A.L.R. 1191; it more properly constitutes a charge upon the thing. Equitable liens most commonly grow out of constructive trusts. Story, Eq.Jur. § 1215; Jones v. Carpenter, 90 Fla. 407, 106 So. 127, 129, 43 A.L.R. 1409; Aldrich v. R. J. Ederer Co., 302 Ill. 391, 134 N.E. 726, 728.

It is right by which a creditor is entitled to obtain satisfaction of his debt by resort to specified property belonging to debtor, Pincus v. Collins, 198 Miss. 283, 22 So.2d 361, 362; right of a special nature over property constituting a charge or incumbrance thereon. Miller v. Heisler, Mo.App., 187 S.W.2d 485, 491; Gables Racing Assoc. v. Persky, 148 Fla. 627, 6 So.2d 257, 262, 263; right, not recognized at law, to have a fund or specific property, or the proceeds, applied in whole or in part to payment of a particular debt or class of debts or obligation, Bank of Aurora v. Aurora Co-Op. Fruit Growing & Marketing Ass'n, Mo.App., 91 S.W.2d 177; Jamison Coal & Coke Co. v. Goltra, C.C.A.Mo., 143 F.2d 889, 893, 154 A.L.R. 1191; Shipley v. Metropolitan Life Ins. Co., 25 Tenn.App. 452, 158 S.W.2d 739, 741; right over subject-matter of contract, whereby obligee is enabled to follow identical thing to which lien attaches and enforce obligation by remedy operating directly thereon, Bassett v. City Bank & Trust Co., 116 Conn. 617, 165 A. 557; right to have property subjected in court of equity to payment of a claim, Theatre Realty Co. v. Aronberg-Fried Co., C.C.A.Mo., 85 F.2d 383, 388; right to proceed in an equitable action against the subject-matter of the lien and have it sold or sequestered and its proceeds or rents and profits applied to the demand of the owner of the lien, Oppenheimer v. Szulerecki, 297 Ill. 81, 130 N.E. 325, 328, 28 A.L.R. 1439.

The equitable lien differs essentially from a common-law lien, in that in the equitable lien, possession remains with the debtor or person who holds the proprietary interest. Jones v. Carpenter, 90 Fla. 407, 106 So. 127, 129, 43 A.L.R. 1409.

Every express executory agreement in writing, whereby the contracting party sufficiently indicates an intention to make some particular property, real or personal, or fund therein identified, a security for a debt or other obligation, or whereby the party promises to convey, assign, or transfer the property as security, creates an equitable lien upon the property so indicated, which is enforceable against the property. Knott v. Mfg. Co., 30 W.Va. 790, 5 S.E. 266; Geddes v. Reeves Coal & Dock Co., C.C.A.Minn., 20 F.2d 48, 50, 54 A.L.R. 282; Root Mfg. Co. v. Johnson, C.C.A.Ind., 219 F. 397, 406.

EQUITABLE RATE OF INTEREST. In England, the interest, generally at a lower rate than legal, charged against a trustee or executor improperly or unnecessarily keeping balances or portion of trust moneys in his hands. In re Ricker's Estate, 14 Mont. 153, 35 P. 960, 968, 29 L.R.A. 622.

EQUITABLE RECOUPMENT. Rule of the law which diminishes the right of a party invoking legal process to recover a debt, to the extent that he holds money or property of his debtor, to which he has no moral right, and it is ordinarily a defensive remedy going only to mitigation of damages. Electric Storage Battery Co. v. Rothensies, D.C.Pa., 57 F.Supp. 731, 735.

EQUITABLE RESCISSION. Rescission decreed by court of equity, as distinguished from "legal rescission" which is effected by restoration or offer to restore. Mueller v. Michels, 184 Wis. 324, 199 N.W. 380, 382.

EQUITABLE RULE. In broad sense in which term is sometimes used, signifies natural justice. In re New Jersey State Bar Ass'n, 111 N.J. Eq. 234, 162 A. 99, 101.

EQUITAS SEQUITUR LEGEM. Equity follows the law. Tallman v. Varick, 5 Barb. (N.Y.) 277, 282. Cas *temp.* Talb. 52; 1 Sto.Eq.Jur. § 64.

In respect of this maxim it has been said: "Operative only within a very narrow range." 1 Pom.Eq.Jur. § 427. The reverse is quite as sound a maxim; 9 Harv.L.Rev. 18. "The main business of equity is avowedly to correct and supplement the law." Phelps, Jurid.Eq. § 237. The English Judicature Act, 1873, provides that when law and equity conflict equity shall prevail. See Equity Follows the Law.

EQUITATURA. In old English law. Traveling furniture, or riding equipments, including horses, horse harness, etc. Reg.Orig. 100*b*; St.Westm. 2, c. 39.

EQUITY. In its broadest and most general signification, this term denotes the spirit and the habit of fairness, justness, and right dealing which would regulate the intercourse of men with men, —the rule of doing to all others as we desire them to do to us; or, as it is expressed by Justinian, "to live honestly, to harm nobody, to render to every man his due." Inst. 1, 1, 3. It is therefore the synonym of natural right or justice. But in this sense its obligation is ethical rather than jural, and its discussion belongs to the sphere of morals. It is grounded in the precepts of the conscience, not in any sanction of positive law.

In a restricted sense, the word denotes equal and impartial justice as between two persons whose rights or claims are in conflict; justice, that is, as ascertained by natural reason or ethical insight, but independent of the formulated body of law. This is not a technical meaning of the term, except in so far as courts which administer equity seek to discover it by the agencies above mentioned, or apply it beyond the strict lines of positive law. See Miller v. Kenniston, 86 Me. 550, 30 A. 114.

In a still more restricted sense, it is a system of jurisprudence, or branch of remedial justice, administered by certain tribunals, distinct from the common-law courts and empowered to decree "equity" in the sense last above given. Here it becomes a complex of well-settled and well-understood rules, principles, and precedents. Isabelle Properties v. Edelman, 297 N.Y.S. 572, 574, 164 Misc. 192.

"The meaning of the word 'equity,' as used in its technical sense in English jurisprudence, comes back to this: that it is simply a term descriptive of a certain field of jurisdiction exercised, in the English system, by certain courts, and of which the extent and boundaries are not marked by lines founded upon principle so much as by the features of the original constitution of the English scheme of remedial law, and the accidents of its development." Bisp.Eq. § 11.

A system of jurisprudence collateral to, and in some respects independent of, "law," properly so called; the object of which is to render the administration of justice more complete, by affording relief where the courts of law are incompetent to give it, or to give it with effect, or by exercising certain branches of jurisdiction independently of them. This is equity in its proper modern sense; an elaborate system of rules and process, administered in many cases by distinct tribunals, (termed "courts of chancery,") and with exclusive jurisdiction over certain subjects. It is "still distinguished by its original and animating principle that no right should be without an adequate remedy," and its doctrines are founded upon the same basis of natural justice; but its action has become systematized, deprived of any loose and arbitrary character which might once have belonged to it, and as carefully regulated by fixed rules and precedents as the law itself. Burrill.

Equity, in its technical and scientific legal use, means neither natural justice nor even all that portion of natural justice which is susceptible of being judicially enforced. It has a precise, limited, and definite signification, and is used to denote a system of justice which was administered in a particular court,—the English high court of chancery,— which system can only be understood and explained by studying the history of that court, and how it came to exercise what is known as its extraordinary jurisdiction. Bisp.Eq. § 1.

That part of the law which, having power to enforce discovery, (1) administers trusts, mortgages, and other fiduciary obligations; (2) administers and adjusts common-law rights where the courts of common law have no machinery; (3) supplies a specific and preventive remedy for common-law wrongs where courts of common law only give subsequent damages. Chute, Eq. 4.

Equity is a body of jurisprudence, or field of jurisdiction, differing in its origin, theory, and methods from the common law. Laird v. Union Traction Co., 208 Pa. 574, 57 A. 987.

It is a body of rules existing by the side of the original civil law, founded on distinct principles, and claiming incidentally to supersede the civil law in virtue of a superior sanctity inherent in those principles. Maine, Anc. Law, 27.

"As old rules become too narrow, or are felt to be out of harmony with advancing civilization, a machinery is needed for their gradual enlargement and adaption to new views of society. One mode of accomplishing this object on a large scale, without appearing to disregard existing law, is the introduction, by the prerogative of some high functionary, of a more perfect body of rules, discoverable in his judicial conscience, which is to stand side by side with the law of the land, overriding it in case of conflict, as on some title of inherent superiority, but not purporting to repeal it. Such a body of rules has been called 'Equity.' " Holl.Jur. 59.

"Equity," in its technical sense, contradistinguished from natural and universal equity or justice, may well be described as a "portion of justice" or natural equity, not embodied in legislative enactments, or in the rules of common law, yet modified by a due regard thereto and to the complex relations and conveniences of an artificial state of society, and administered in regard to cases where the particular rights, in respect of which relief is sought come within some general class of rights enforced at law, or may be enforced without detriment or inconvenience to the community; but where, as to such particular rights, the ordinary courts of law cannot, or originally did not, clearly afford relief. Rob.Eq.

The remaining interest belonging to one who has pledged or mortgaged his property, or the surplus of value which may remain after the property has been disposed of for the satisfaction of liens. The amount or value of a property above the total liens or charges. Des Moines Joint Stock Land Bank of Des Moines v. Allen, 220 Iowa 448, 261 N.W. 912.

"Chancery" is synonymous and interchangeable with "equity." Const. art. 4, § 6. Ireland v. Cheney, 129 Ohio St. 527, 196 N.E. 267, 270.

Equitable Right

Equity also signifies an equitable right, *i. e.*, a right enforceable in a court of equity; hence, a bill of complaint which did not show that the plaintiff had a right entitling him to relief was said to be demurrable for want of equity; and certain rights now recognized in all the courts are still known as "equities," from having been originally recognized only in the court of chancery. Sweet.

Better Equity

The right which, in a court of equity, a second incumbrancer has who has taken securities against subsequent dealings to his prejudice, which a prior incumbrancer neglected to take although he had an opportunity. 1 Ch.Prec. 470, note. See 3 Bouv.Inst. note 2462.

Countervailing Equity

A contrary and balancing equity; an equity or right opposed to that which is sought to be enforced or recognized, and which ought not to be sacrificed or subordinated to the latter, because it is of equal strength and justice, and equally deserving of consideration.

Existing Equity

See Existing Equity.

Latent or Secret Equity

An equitable claim or right, the knowledge of which has been confined to the parties for and against whom it exists, or which has been concealed from one or several persons interested in the subject-matter.

Natural Equity

A term sometimes employed in works on jurisprudence, possessing no very precise meaning, but used as equivalent to justice, honesty, or morality in business relations, or man's innate sense of right dealing and fair play. Inasmuch as equity, as now administered, is a complex system of rules, doctrines, and precedents, and possesses, within the range of its own fixed principles, but little more elasticity than the law, the term "natural equity" may be understood to denote, in a general way, that which strikes the ordinary conscience and sense of justice as being fair, right, and equitable, in advance of the question whether the technical jurisprudence of the chancery courts would so regard it.

Perfect Equity

An equitable title or right which lacks nothing to its completeness as a legal title or right except the formal conveyance or other investiture which would make it cognizable at law; particularly, the equity or interest of a purchaser of real estate who has paid the purchase price in full and fulfilled all conditions resting on him, but has not yet received a deed or patent. See Shaw v. Lindsey, 60 Ala. 344; Smith v. Cockrell, 66 Ala. 75.

EQUITY, COURTS OF. Courts which administer justice according to the system of equity, and according to a peculiar course of procedure or practice. Frequently termed "courts of chancery." See 1 Bl.Comm. 92; Dowell v. Goodwin, 22 R.I. 287, 27 A. 693, 695, 51 L.R.A. 873, 84 Am.St.Rep. 842.

EQUITY DELIGHTS TO DO JUSTICE, AND THAT NOT BY HALVES. Tallman v. Varick, 5 Barb. (N.Y.) 277, 280; Story, Eq.Pl. § 72.

EQUITY FOLLOWS THE LAW. Talb. 52. Equity adopts and follows the rules of law in all cases to which those rules may, in terms, be applicable. Equity, in dealing with cases of an equitable nature, adopts and follows the analogies furnished by the rules of law. A leading maxim of equity jurisprudence, which, however, is not of universal application, but liable to many exceptions. Frink v. Commercial Bank of Emmettsburg, 195 Iowa, 1011, 191 N.W. 513.

EQUITY JURISDICTION. In a general sense, the jurisdiction belonging to a court of equity, but more particularly the aggregate of those cases, controversies, and occasions which form proper subjects for the exercise of the powers of a chancery court. See Wadham Oil Co. v. Tracy, 141 Wis. 150, 123 N.W. 785, 787, 18 Ann.Cas. 779; Venner v. Great Northern R. Co., C.C.N.Y., 153 F. 408, 413, 414.

"Equity jurisdiction," in its ordinary acceptation, as distinguished on the one side from the general power to decide matters at all, and on the other from the jurisdiction "at law" or "common-law jurisdiction," is the power to hear certain kinds and classes of civil causes according to the principles of the method and procedure adopted by the court of chancery, and to decide them in accordance with the doctrines and rules of equity jurisprudence, which decision may involve either the determination of the equitable rights, estates, and interests of the parties to such causes, or the granting of equitable remedies. In order that a cause may come within the scope of the equity jurisdiction, one of two alternatives is essential; either the primary right, estate, or interest to be maintained, or the violation of which furnishes the cause of action, must be equitable rather than legal; or the remedy granted must be in its nature purely equitable, or if it be a remedy which may also be given by a court of law, it must be one which, under the facts and circumstances of the case, can only be made complete and adequate through the equitable modes of procedure. Norback v. Board of Directors of Church Extension Soc., 84 Utah 506, 37 P.2d 339.

EQUITY JURISPRUDENCE. That portion of remedial justice which is exclusively administered by courts of equity as distinguished from courts of common law. Jackson v. Nimmo, 3 Lea (Tenn.) 609. More generally speaking, the science which treats of the rules, principles, and maxims which govern the decisions of a court of equity, the cases and controversies which are considered proper subjects for its cognizance, and the nature and form of the remedies which it grants.

EQUITY LOOKS UPON THAT AS DONE WHICH OUGHT TO HAVE BEEN DONE. 1 Story, Eq.Jur. § 64*g*. Equity will treat the subject-matter, as to collateral consequences and incidents, in the same manner as if the final acts contemplated by the parties had been executed exactly as they ought to have been; not as the parties might have executed them. Rankin v. Rankin, 36 Ill. 293, 87 Am.Dec. 205.

EQUITY OF A STATUTE. By this phrase is intended the rule of statutory construction which admits within the operation of a statute a class of cases which are neither expressly named nor excluded, but which, from their analogy to the cases that are named, are clearly and justly within the spirit and general meaning of the law; such cases are said to be "within the equity of the statute."

EQUITY OF PARTNERS. A term used to designate the right of each of them to have the firm's property applied to the payment of the firm's debts. Colwell v. Bank, 16 R.I. 288, 17 A. 913.

EQUITY OF REDEMPTION. The right of the mortgagor of an estate to redeem the same after it has been forfeited, at law, by a breach of the condition of the mortgage, upon paying the amount of debt, interest and costs. Riddick v. Davis, 220 N.C. 120, 16 S.E.2d 662, 666; Broun v. United States, C.C.A.Pa., 95 F.2d 487, 489.

The right of redemption after sale is distinct from the equity of redemption after breach of condition and before the sale. The former commences only when the latter ends. One rests on the principles of equity, the other on the terms of the statute. Hummel v. Citizens' Building & Loan Ass'n, Ariz., 296 P. 1014, 1015.

EQUITY SUFFERS NOT A RIGHT WITHOUT A REMEDY. 4 Bouv.Inst. No. 3726. Graselli Chemical Company v. Ætna Explosives Co., 252 F. 456, 164 C.C.A. 380.

EQUITY TERM. An equity term of court is one devoted exclusively to equity business, that is, in which no criminal cases are tried nor any cases requiring the impaneling of a jury. Hesselgrave v. State, 63 Neb. 807, 89 N.W. 295.

EQUITY TO A SETTLEMENT. The equitable right of a wife, when her husband sues in equity for the reduction of her equitable estate to his own possession, to have the whole or a portion of such estate settled upon herself and her children. Also a similar right now recognized by the equity courts as directly to be asserted against the husband. Also called the "wife's equity." Poindexter v. Jeffries, Clarke v. McCleary, 12 Smedes & M. (Miss.) 354.

EQUIVALENT, *adj.* Equal in value, force, measure, volume, power, and effect or having equal or corresponding import, meaning or significance; alike, identical. Salt Lake County v. Utah Copper Co., C.C.A.Utah, 93 F.2d 127, 132; Nahas v. Nahas, 59 Nev. 220, 90 P.2d 223, 224; Kelley v. Clark, 23 Idaho, 1, 129 P. 921, 925, Ann.Cas.1914C, 665.

EQUIVALENT, *n.* In patent law. Any act or substance which is known in the arts as a proper substitute for some other act or substance employed as an element in the invention, whose substitution for that other act or substance does not in any manner vary the idea of means. It possesses three characteristics: It must be capable of performing the same office in the invention as the act or substance whose place it supplies; it must relate to the form or embodiment alone and not affect in any degree the idea of means; and it must have been known to the arts at the date of the patent as endowed with this capability. Duff Mfg. Co. v. Forgie, 59 F. 772, 8 C.C.A. 261; For "Fair Equivalent," see that title.

For one device to be the equivalent of another, it must perform the same function in substantially the same way. Chicago Forging & Mfg. Co. v. Bade-Cummins Mfg. Co., C.C.A.Ky., 63 F.2d 928, 931; Donner v. Sheer Pharmacal Corporation, C.C.A.Mo., 64 F.2d 217, 223; Corcoran v. Riness, D.C.Cal., 19 F.Supp. 344, 347.

"Equivalents" in an art or process are such acts as, in accordance with preceding rules, are interchangeable with those which the inventor has himself employed. Superior Skylight Co. v. August Kuhnla, D.C.N.Y., 265 F. 282, 284.

An "equivalent," in patent law, is not the same as a "substitute." McCaskey Register Co. v. Mantz, D.C.N.Y., 217 F. 415, 419.

EQUIVOCAL. Having a double or several meanings or senses. Synonymous with "ambiguous". Fleck v. Baldwin, 141 Tex. 340, 172 S.W.2d 975, 979. See Ambiguity.

EQUULEUS. A kind of rack for extorting confessions.

EQUUS COOPERTUS. A horse equipped with saddle and furniture.

ERABILIS. A maple tree. Not to be confounded with *arabilis*, (arable land.)

ERASTIANS. The followers of Erastus. The sect obtained much influence in England, particularly among common lawyers in the time of Selden. They held that offenses against religion and morality should be punished by the civil power, and not by the censures of the church or by excommunication. Wharton.

ERASURE. The obliteration of words or marks from a written instrument by rubbing, scraping, or scratching them out. Also the place in a document where a word or words have been so removed. The term is sometimes used for the removal of parts of a writing by any means whatever, as by cancellation; but this is not an accurate use. Cloud v. Hewitt, 5 Fed.Cas. 1,085; In re Fergeson, 126 Misc. 286, 213 N.Y.S. 656, 658; Murray v. Floyd, 216 Minn. 69, 11 N.W.2d 780, 783.

ERCISCUNDUS. In the civil law. To be divided. *Judicium familiæ erciscundæ*, a suit for the partition of an inheritance. Inst. 4, 17, 4. An ancient phrase derived from the Twelve Tables. Calvin.

ERECT. One of the formal words of incorporation in royal charters. "We do, incorporate, *erect*, ordain, name, constitute, and establish." "Construct" is synonymous with "erect". State ex rel. Davis v. Barber, 139 Fla. 706, 190 So. 809.

ERECTION. Raising up; building; a completed building; to build; construct; set up. In a statute on the "erection" of wooden buildings, this term does not include repairing, alteration, enlarging, or removal. See Shaw v. Hitchcock, 119 Mass. 256; Escambia County v. Blount Const. Co., 66 Fla. 129, 62 So. 650, 651; Flynn v. New York, W. & B. Ry. Co., 218 N.Y. 140, 112 N.E. 913, 914, Ann. Cas.1918B, 588; Watson v. Greely, 69 Cal.App.

643, 232 P. 475, 479. There is a distinction between "erection" and maintenance. Turturro v. Calder, 307 Mass. 159, 29 N.E.2d 744, 746.

ERECTOR SPINÆ MUSCLES. A group of muscles on each side of the spine running all the way up from the sacrum to the skull. Biener v. St. Louis Public Service Co., Mo.App., 160 S.W.2d 780, 788.

ERGO. Lat. Therefore; hence; because.

ERGOLABI. In the civil law. Undertakers of work; contractors. Cod. 4, 59.

ERGOT. A medicinal used as a uterine contractor to contract the muscles so as to expel certain material from the uterus. People v. Chester, 179 Misc. 864, 42 N.Y.S.2d 293, 295.

ERIACH. A term of the Irish Brehon law, denoting a pecuniary mulct or recompense which a murderer was judicially condemned to pay to the family or relatives of his victim. It corresponded to the Saxon "weregild." See 4 Bl.Comm. 313.

ERIGIMUS. We erect. One of the words by which a corporation may be created in England by the king's charter. 1 Bl.Comm. 473.

ERMINE. By metonymy, this term is used to describe the office or functions of a judge, whose state robe, lined with ermine, is emblematical of purity and honor without stain. Webster.

ERNES. In old English law. The loose scattered ears of corn that are left on the ground after the binding.

EROSION. The gradual eating away of the soil by the operation of currents or tides. Distinguished from *submergence,* which is the disappearance of the soil under the water and the formation of a navigable body over it. Mulry v. Norton, 100 N.Y. 433, 3 N.E. 584, 53 Am.Rep. 206; State of Arkansas v. State of Tennessee, 246 U.S. 158, 38 S. Ct. 301, 304, 62 L.Ed. 638, L.R.A.1918D, 258.

EROTOMANIA. See Insanity.

ERRANT. Wandering; itinerant; applied to justices on circuit, and bailiffs at large, etc.

ERRANT WATER. Stream water, which does not have channel of navigable river or which returns to stream after overflowing its banks, is not "errant water" in which riparian owner can acquire no vested rights. Tallassee Power Co. v. Clark, C.C.A.Tenn., 77 F.2d 601, 603.

ERRATICUM. In old law. A waif or stray; a wandering beast. Cowell.

ERRATUM. Lat. Error. Used in the Latin formula for assigning errors, and in the reply thereto, "in nullo est erratum," *i. e.,* there was no error, no error was committed.

ERRONEOUS. Involving error; deviating from the law. This term is never used by courts or law-writers as designating a corrupt or evil act. Thompson v. Doty, 72 Ind. 338; U. S. v. Sakharam Ganesh Pandit, C.C.A.Cal., 15 F.2d 285, 286. "False" as a constituent of a fraud action may at times be said to be synonymous with "erroneous." Abel v. Paterno, 153 Misc. 248, 274 N.Y.S. 749.

ERRONEOUS ASSESSMENT. Refers to an assessment that deviates from the law and is therefore invalid, and is a defect that is jurisdictional in its nature, and does not refer to the judgment of the assessing officer in fixing the amount of valuation of the property. In re Blatt, 41 N.M. 269, 67 P.2d 293, 301, 110 A.L.R. 656; Ritchie Grocer Co. v. City of Texarkana, 182 Ark. 137, 30 S.W. 2d 213, 214; Flourney v. First Nat. Bank of Shreveport, 197 La. 1067, 3 So.2d 244, 252.

ERRONEOUS JUDGMENT. One rendered according to course and practice of court, but contrary to law, upon mistaken view of law, or upon erroneous application of legal principles. Herbert B. Newton & Co. v. Wilson Furniture Mfg. Co., 206 N.C. 533, 174 S.E. 449, 450.

ERRONEOUS OR ILLEGAL TAX. One levied without statutory authority, or upon property not subject to taxation, or by some officer having no authority to levy the tax, or one which in some other similar respect is illegal. Jewett Realty Co. v. Board of Sup'rs of Polk County, 239 Iowa 988, 33 N.W.2d 377.

ERRONICE. Lat. Erroneously; through error or mistake.

ERROR. A mistaken judgment or incorrect belief as to the existence or effect of matters of fact, or a false or mistaken conception or application of the law.

Such a mistaken or false conception or application of the law to the facts of a cause as will furnish ground for a review of the proceedings upon a writ of error; a mistake of law, or false or irregular application of it, such as vitiates the proceedings and warrants the reversal of the judgment.

Error is also used as an elliptical expression for "writ of error;" as in saying that *error* lies; that a judgment may be reversed *on error.*

An act involving a departure from truth or accuracy. Gronseth v. Mohn, 57 S.D. 604, 234 N.W. 603, 604.

Assignment of Errors

In practice. The statement of the plaintiff's case on a writ of error, setting forth the errors complained of; corresponding with the declaration in an ordinary action. 2 Tidd, Pr. 1168; 3 Steph.Comm. 644. Armour v. Pennsylvania R. Co., 353 Ill. 575, 187 N.E. 532, 534; Fahrenbrink v. Moore, 51 Ariz. 176, 75 P.2d 360, 361. A specification of the errors upon which the appellant will rely, with such fullness as to give aid to the court in the examination of the transcript. Squires v. Foorman, 10 Cal. 298; Streeter v. State, 89 Fla. 400, 104 So. 858, 859; Largent v. Etheridge, Tex. Civ.App., 13 S.W.2d 974, 976; Helms v. Cook, 62

Ind.App. 629, 111 N.E. 632, 633; Wine v. Jones, 183 Iowa, 1166, 168 N.W. 318, 320.

The office of an assignment of error, which is in the nature of a pleading by the plaintiff in error or appellant, is not only to inform the appellate court of the exact complaint against rulings, whereby, if the complaint be sustained, a judgment or decree may be changed or reversed, but is to inform the defendant in error or appellee of the precise errors relied upon, in order that such defendant in error or appellee may take proper steps, or give proper directions in his own behalf, for making up a sufficient transcript of the record to exhibit to the court what might otherwise be insufficiently shown. Davidson v. Bezant, 101 Fla. 1296, 132 So. 488, 489.

"Assignment of error" is formal complaint of some action of trial court, as distinguished from "proposition," which merely sets forth reasons why such action is erroneous. Standard v. Texas Pacific Coal & Oil Co., Tex.Civ.App., 47 S.W.2d 443, 449.

Clerical Error

See Clerical.

Common Error

(Lat. *communis error, q. v.*) An error for which there are many precedents. "Common error goeth for a law." Finch, Law, b. 1, c. 3, no. 54. "Common errors" are that the declaration is insufficient in law to maintain the action, and that judgment was given for plaintiff instead of defendant, or vice versa. Margolics v. Goldberg, 101 N.J.L. 75, 127 A. 271, 272.

Cross-Errors

Errors assigned by the respondent in a writ of error, or appellee.

Error Apparent of Record

Plain, fundamental error that goes to the foundation of the action irrespective of the evidence; an obvious misapprehension of the applicable law. Kenedy Mercantile Co. v. Ainsworth, Tex.Civ.App., 281 S.W. 637; Provident Life & Accident Ins. Co. v. Johnson, Tex.Civ.App., 235 S.W. 650, 652; Parks v. Parks, 68 App.D.C. 363, 98 F.2d 235, 236.

Fundamental Error

In appellate practice. Error which goes to the merits of the plaintiff's cause of action, and which will be considered on review, whether assigned as error or not, where the justice of the case seems to require it. Hollywood v. Wellhausen, 28 Tex.Civ. App. 541, 68 S.W. 329; Goodhue v. Fuller, Tex.Civ. App., 193 S.W. 170, 172. Error in law apparent on the face of the record. St. Louis Southwestern Ry. Co. of Texas v. Anderson, Tex.Civ.App., 206 S.W. 696, 698.

Harmful Error

Error which more probably than improbably affected the verdict or judgment prejudicially to the party complaining. Ashby v. Virginia Ry. & Power Co., 138 Va. 310, 122 S.E. 104, 110.

Harmless Error

In appellate practice. An error committed in the progress of the trial below, but which was not prejudicial to the rights of the party assigning it, and for which, therefore, the court will not reverse the judgment, as, where the error was neutralized or corrected by subsequent proceedings in the case, or where, notwithstanding the error, the particular issue was found in that party's favor, or where, even if the error had not been committed, he could not have been legally entitled to prevail.

Invited Error

In appellate practice. The principle of "invited error" is that if, during the progress of a cause, a party requests or moves the court to make a ruling which is actually erroneous, and the court does so, that party cannot take advantage of the error on appeal or review. Gresham v. Harcourt, 93 Tex. 149, 53 S.W. 1019.

Judicial Errors

Errors into which the court itself falls. State v. District Court of Second Judicial District in and for Silver Bow County, 55 Mont. 324, 176 P. 608, 609.

Reversible Error

In appellate practice. Such an error as warrants the appellate court in reversing the judgment before it; substantial error, that which reasonably might have prejudiced the party complaining. Shinn v. United Rys. Co. of St. Louis, 248 Mo. 173, 154 S.W. 103, 105; New Mexican R. Co. v. Hendricks, 6 N.M. 611, 30 Pac. 901.

Technical Error

In appellate practice. A merely abstract or theoretical error, which is practically not injurious to the party assigning it. Epps v. State, 102 Ind. 539, 1 N.E. 491.

ERROR CASE. An appeal on questions of law. In re Green's Estate, Ohio App., 41 N.E.2d 586.

ERROR CORAM NOBIS. Error committed in the proceedings "before us;" i. e., error assigned as a ground for reviewing, modifying, or vacating a judgment in the same court in which it was rendered. A writ to bring before the court that pronounced judgment errors in matters of fact which had not been put in issue or passed on and were material to validity and regularity of legal proceeding itself. Hiawassee Lumber Co. v. United States, C.C.A.N.C., 64 F.2d 417, 418.

ERROR CORAM VOBIS. Error in the proceedings "before you;" words used in a writ of error directed by a court of review to the court which tried the cause.

ERROR FUCATUS NUDA VERITATE IN MULTIS.EST PROBABILIOR; ET SÆPENUMERO RATIONIBUS VINCIT VERITATEM ERROR. Error artfully disguised [or colored] is, in many instances, more probable than naked truth; and frequently error overwhelms truth by [its show of] reasons. 2 Coke, 73.

ERROR IN EXERCISE OF JURISDICTION. Error in determination of questions of law or fact on which the court's jurisdiction in particular case depends. Burgess v. Nail, C.C.A.Okl., 103 F.2d 37, 43.

ERROR IN FACT. In judicial proceedings, error in fact occurs when, by reason of some fact which is unknown to the court and not apparent on the record (e. g., the coverture, infancy, or death of one of the parties), it renders a judgment which is void or voidable. Cruger v. McCracken, 87 Tex. 584, 30 S.W. 537; Kihlholz v. Wolff, 8 Ill. App. 371.

ERROR IN LAW. An error of the court in applying the law to the case on trial, e. g., in ruling on the admission of evidence, or in charging the jury. McKenzie v. Bismarck Water Co., 6 N.D. 361, 71 N.W. 608; Scherrer v. Hale, 9 Mont. 63, 22 Pac. 151.

ERROR IN VACUO. Error in adverse ruling without adverse effect is "error in vacuo" which may subject the erring judge to criticism but not the case to re-trial. United States v. A Certain Tract or Parcel of Land in Chatham County, Ga., D.C.Ga., 47 F.Supp. 30, 36.

ERROR JURIS NOCET. Error of law injures. A mistake of the law has an injurious effect; that is, the party committing it must suffer the consequences. Mackeld.Rom.Law, § 178; 1 Story, Eq. Jur. § 139, note.

ERROR NOMINIS. Error of name. A mistake of detail in the name of a person; used in contradistinction to error *de personâ,* a mistake as to identity.

ERROR NOMINIS NUNQUAM NOCET, SI DE IDENTITATE REI CONSTAT. A mistake in the name of a thing is never prejudicial, if it be clear as to the identity of the thing itself, [where the thing intended is certainly known.] 1 Duer, Ins. 171. This maxim is applicable only where the means of correcting the mistake are apparent on the face of the instrument to be construed. Id.

ERROR OF FACT. That is called "error of fact" which proceeds either from ignorance of that which really exists or from a mistaken belief in the existence of that which has none. See Norton v. Marden, 15 Me. 45, 32 Am.Dec. 132. Finding of fact contrary to the weight of the evidence is an error of fact. Wear v. Imperial Window Glass Co., C.C.A.Mo., 224 F. 60, 62. Cf. Error in Fact, *supra.*

ERROR OF LAW. He is under an error of law who is truly informed of the existence of facts, but who draws from them erroneous conclusions of law. Civ.Code La. art. 1822. Mowatt v. Wright, 1 Wend., N.Y., 360, 19 Am.Dec. 508.

ERROR QUI NON RESISTITUR APPROBATUR. An error which is not resisted or opposed is approved. Doct. & Stud. c. 40.

ERROR, WRIT OF. See Writ of Error.

ERRORES AD SUA PRINCIPIA REFERRE, EST REFELLERE. To refer errors to their sources is to refute them. 3 Inst. 15. To bring errors to their beginning is to see their last.

ERRORES SCRIBENTIS NOCERE NON DEBENT. The mistakes of the writer ought not to harm. Jenk.Cent. 324.

ERRORS EXCEPTED. A phrase appended to an account stated, in order to excuse slight mistakes or oversights.

ERTHMIOTUM. In old English law. A meeting of the neighborhood to compromise differences among themselves; a court held on the boundary of two lands.

ERUBESCIT LEX FILIOS CASTIGARE PARENTES. 8 Coke, 116. The law blushes when children correct their parents.

ESBRANCATURA. In old law. A cutting off the branches or boughs of trees. Cowell; Spelman.

ESCALATOR CLAUSE. A clause usually found in leases or contracts executed subject to price control regulations. Under this clause, in the case of a lease, the landlord is authorized to collect the maximum rent permissible under rent regulations in force at time of execution of the lease. The escalator part of the clause of the lease consists in the provision that in the event that the rent regulations are modified during the term of the lease, the tenant will pay the increased rental following the allowance thereof. Wasservogel v. Meyerowitz, 191 Misc. 594, 79 N.Y.S.2d 256; and 89 N.Y.S. 2d 290, 275 App.Div. 387. In the case of a sales contract, the escalator clause usually provides in effect that should the maximum prices promulgated be increased or decreased during the life of the contract, payment will be made by the purchaser at a rate of increase or decrease not to exceed the same ratio that the prices quoted bear to the maximum prices authorized. Simpson Bros. v. District of Columbia, D.C.D.C., 73 F.Supp. 858, and 179 F.2d 430. Pfotzer et al. v. United States, 176 F.2d 675; Record & Tribune Co. v. Brandtjen & Kluge, Inc., Iowa, 39 N.W.2d 288. Escalator clauses authorizing the contractor to increase the contract price should the prices of labor or material advance also appear in other contracts, such as a contract to furnish steam. Lincoln Rug Co. v. East Newark Realty Corp., 142 N.J.Eq. 743, 61 A.2d 448.

ESCALDARE. To scald. It is said that to *scald hogs* was one of the ancient tenures in serjeanty. Wharton.

ESCAMBIO. In old English law. A writ of exchange. A license in the shape of a writ, formerly granted to an English merchant to draw a bill of exchange on another in foreign parts. Reg. Orig. 194.

ESCAMBIUM. An old English law term, signifying exchange.

ESCAPE. The departure or deliverance out of custody of a person who was lawfully imprisoned, before he is entitled to his liberty by the process of law.

The voluntarily or negligently allowing any person lawfully in confinement to leave the place. 2 Bish.Crim.Law, § 917.

Escapes are either *voluntary* or *negligent*. The former is the case when the keeper voluntarily concedes to the prisoner any liberty not authorized by law. The latter is the case when the prisoner contrives to leave his prison by forcing his way out, or any other means, without the knowledge or against the will of the keeper, but through the latter's carelessness or the insecurity of the building. Cortis v. Dailey, 21 App.Div. 1, 47 N.Y.S. 454; U. S. v. Hoffman, D.C.Ill., 13 F.2d 269, 270; Whitaker v. Commonwealth, 188 Ky. 95, 221 S.W. 215, 216, 10 A.L.R. 145; State v. Pace, 192 N.C. 780, 136 S.E. 11, 12.

To flee from; to a void; to get out of the way, as to flee to avoid arrest. Life & Casualty Ins. Co. v. Hargraves, 169 Tenn. 388, 88 S.W.2d 451, 452; State v. Dreiling, 136 Kan. 78, 12 P.2d 735, 736.

—Constructive escape. This takes place when a prisoner obtains more liberty than the law allows, although he still remains in custody. 21 C.J. p. 827. An example is the unauthorized production of a prisoner in court by his custodian. In re Rigg, 123 A. 243, 95 N.J.Eq. 341.

ESCAPE FROM PRISON. A prisoner serving a sentence of imprisonment in a state prison is, in contemplation of law, a prisoner therein, as well when at work outside under the surveillance of prison guards as when confined within its walls, so that if he escapes when outside he escapes from a prison within Pen.Code, §§ 106, 787. People v. Vanderburg, 67 Cal.App. 217, 227 P. 621.

ESCAPE WARRANT. In English practice. This was a warrant granted to retake a prisoner committed to the custody of the king's prison who had escaped therefrom. It was obtained on affidavit from the judge of the court in which the action had been brought, and was directed to all the sheriffs throughout England, commanding them to retake the prisoner and commit him to gaol when and where taken, there to remain until the debt was satisfied. Jacob; Brown.

ESCAPE WAY. Passageway leading from the inside to the outside of the mine. Roberts v. Tennessee Coal, Iron & R. Co., C.C.A.Ala., 255 F. 469, 471; Robinson v. Maryland Coal & Coke Co., 196 Ala. 604, 72 So. 161, 162.

ESCAPIO QUIETUS. In old English law. Delivered from that punishment which by the laws of the forest lay upon those whose beasts were found upon forbidden land. Jacob.

ESCAPIUM. That which comes by chance or accident. Cowell

ESCEPPA. A measure of corn. Cowell.

ESCHÆTA DERIVATUR A VERBO GALLICO ESCHOIR, QUOD EST ACCIDERE, QUIA ACCIDIT DOMINO EX EVENTU ET EX INSPERATO. Co.Litt. 93. Escheat is derived from the French word "*eschoir*," which signifies to happen, because it falls to the lord from an event and from an unforeseen circumstance.

ESCHÆTÆ VULGO DICUNTUR QUÆ DECIDENTIBUS IIS QUÆ DE REGE TENENT, CUM NON EXISTIT RATIONE SANGUINIS HÆRES, AD FISCUM RELABUNTUR. Those things are commonly called "escheats" which revert to the exchequer from a failure of issue in those who hold of the king, when there does not exist any heir by consanguinity.

ESCHEAT. In feudal law. Escheat is an obstruction of the course of descent, and consequent determination of the tenure, by some unforeseen contingency, in which case the land naturally results back, by a kind of reversion, to the original grantor, or lord of the fee. 2 Bl.Comm. 15; Wallace v. Harmstad, 44 Pa. 501; Marshall v. Lovelass, 1 N.C. 445; Kavanaugh v. Cohoes Power & Light Corporation, 114 Misc. 590, 187 N.Y.S. 216, 231; State v. Phoenix Sav. Bank & Trust Co., 60 Ariz. 138, 132 P.2d 637, 638.

It is the casual descent, in the nature of forfeiture, of lands and tenements within his manor, to a lord, either on failure of issue of the tenant dying seised or on account of the felony of such tenant. Jacob.

Also the land or fee itself, which thus fell back to the lord. Such lands were called "*excadentiæ*," or "*terræ excadentiales*." Fleta, lib. 6, c. 1; Co. Litt. 13*a*.

In American law. Escheat signifies a reversion of property to the state in consequence of a want of any individual competent to inherit. The state is deemed to occupy the place and hold the rights of the feudal lord. See 4 Kent, Comm. 423, 424. Center v. Kramer, 112 Ohio St. 269, 147 N.E. 602, 604; In re O'Connor's Estate, 126 Neb. 182, 252 N.W. 826; Braun v. McPherson, 277 Mich. 396, 269 N.W. 211, 212.

"Escheat at feudal law was the right of the lord of a fee to re-enter upon the same when it became vacant by the extinction of the blood of the tenant. This extinction might either be *per defectum sanguinis* or else *per delictum tenentis*, where the course of descent was broken by the corruption of the blood of the tenant. As a fee might be holden either of the crown or from some inferior lord, the escheat was not always to the crown. The word 'escheat,' in this country, at the present time, merely indicates the preferable right of the state to an estate left vacant, and without there being any one in existence able to make claim thereto." 29 Am.Dec. 232, note.

Single Escheat

When all a person's movables fall to the crown, as a casualty, because of his being declared rebel. Wharton.

ESCHEAT, WRIT OF. A writ which anciently lay for a lord, to recover possession of lands that had escheated to him. Reg.Orig. 164*b*; Fitzh. Nat.Brev. 143.

ESCHEATOR. In English law. The name of an officer who was appointed in every county to look after the escheats which fell due to the king in that particular county, and to certify the same into the exchequer. An escheator could continue in office for one year only, and was not re-eligible until three years. There does not appear to exist any such officer at the present day. Brown. See 10 Vin.Abr. 158; Co.Litt. 13*b*.

ESCHECCUM. In old English law. A jury or inquisition.

ESCHIPARE. To build or equip. Du Cange.

ESCOBEDO RULE. Where police investigation begins to focus on a particular suspect, the suspect is in custody, the suspect requests and is denied counsel, and the police have not warned him of his right to remain silent, the accused has been denied assistance of counsel and no statement elicited during such interrogation may be used in a criminal trial. Escobedo v. State of Illinois, 378 U.S. 478, 490, 491, 84 S.Ct. 1758, 12 L.Ed.2d 977.

ESCOT. A tax formerly paid in boroughs and corporations towards the support of the community, which is called "scot and lot."

ESCRIBANO. In Spanish law. An officer, resembling a notary in French law, who has authority to set down in writing, and verify by his attestation, transactions and contracts between private persons, and also judicial acts and proceedings.

ESCRITURA. In Spanish law. A written instrument. Every deed that is made by the hand of a public *escribano,* or notary of a corporation or council (*concejo,*) or sealed with the seal of the king or other authorized persons. White, New Recop. b. 3, tit. 7, c. 5.

ESCROQUERIE. Fr. Fraud, swindling, cheating.

ESCROW. A scroll, writing, or deed, delivered by the grantor, promisor or obligor into the hands of a third person, to be held by the latter until the happening of a contingency or performance of a condition, and then by him delivered to the grantee, promisee or obligee. Minnesota & Oregon Land & Timber Co. v. Hewitt Inv. Co., D.C.Or., 201 F. 752, 759.

The state or condition of a deed which is conditionally held by a third person, or the possession and retention of a deed by a third person pending a condition; as when an instrument is said to be delivered "in escrow." This use of the term, however, is a perversion of its meaning.

ESCROWL. In old English law. An escrow; a scroll. "And deliver the deed to a stranger, as an escrowl." Perk. c. 1, § 9; Id. c. 2, §§ 137, 138.

ESCUAGE. Service of the shield. One of the varieties of tenure in knight's service, the duty imposed being that of accompanying the king to the wars for forty days, at the tenant's own charge, or sending a substitute. In later times, this service was commuted for a certain payment in money, which was then called "escuage certain." See 2 Bl.Comm. 74, 75.

ESCURARE. To scour or cleanse. Cowell.

ESGLISE, or EGLISE. A church. Jacob.

ESKETORES. Robbers, or destroyers of other men's lands and fortunes. Cowell.

ESKIPPAMENTUM. Tackle or furniture; outfit. Certain towns in England were bound to furnish certain ships at their own expense and with double *skippage* or tackle. Cowell.

ESKIPPER, ESKIPPARE. To ship.

ESKIPPESON. Shippage, or passage by sea. Spelled, also, "*skippeson.*" Cowell.

ESLISORS. See Elisors.

ESNE. In old law. A hireling of servile condition.

ESNECY. Seniority; the condition or right of the eldest; the privilege of the eldest-born. Particularly used of the privilege of the eldest among coparceners to make a first choice of purparts upon a voluntary partition.

ESPEDIENT. In Spanish law. A junction of all the separate papers made in the course of any one proceeding and which remains in the office at the close of it. Castillero v. U. S., 2 Black 109, 17 L. Ed. 360.

ESPERA. A period of time fixed by law or by a court within which certain acts are to be performed, *e. g.*, the production of papers, payment of debts, etc.

ESPERONS. L. Fr. Spurs.

ESPLEES. An old term for the products which the ground or land yields; as the hay of the meadows, the herbage of the pasture, corn of arable fields, rent and services, etc. The word has been anciently applied to the land itself. Jacob; Fosgate v. Hydraulic Co., 9 Barb., N.Y., 293.

ESPOUSALS. A mutual promise between a man and a woman to marry each other at some other time. It differs from a marriage, because then the contract is completed. Wood, Inst. 57.

ESPURIO. Span. In Spanish law. A spurious child; one begotten on a woman who has promiscuous intercourse with many men. White, New Recop. b. 1, tit. 5, c. 2, § 1.

ESQUIRE. In English law. A title of dignity next above gentleman, and below knight. Also a title of office given to sheriffs, serjeants, and barristers at law, justices of the peace, and others. 1 Bl.Comm. 406; 3 Steph.Comm. 15, note; Tomlins. On the use of this term in American law, particularly as applied to justices of the peace and other inferior judicial officers, see Christian v. Ashley County, 24 Ark. 151; Com. v. Vance, 15 Serg. & R., Pa., 37.

ESSARTER. L. Fr. To cut down woods; to clear land of trees and underwood; properly to thin woods, by cutting trees, etc., at intervals. Spelman. See Assart.

ESSARTUM. Woodlands turned into tillage by uprooting the trees and removing the underwood.

ESSENCE. That which is indispensable. Pittsburgh Iron & Steel Foundries Co. v. Seaman-Sleeth Co., D.C.Pa., 236 F. 756, 757. The gist or substance of any act; the vital constituent of a thing; that without which a thing cannot be itself. Norman v. Department of Labor and Industries, 10 Wash.2d 180, 116 P.2d 360, 362.

ESSENCE OF THE CONTRACT. Any condition or stipulation in a contract which is mutually understood and agreed by the parties to be of such vital importance that a sufficient performance of the contract cannot be had without exact compliance with it is said to be "of the essence of the contract." Flatow, Riley & Co. v. Roy Campbell Co., Tex.Com.App., 280 S.W. 517, 520; Dayvault & Newsome v. Townsend, Tex.Civ.App., 244 S.W. 1108, 1110.

ESSENDI QUIETUM DE TOLONIO. A writ to be quit of toll; it lies for citizens and burgesses of any city or town who, by charter or prescription, ought to be exempted from toll, where the same is exacted of them. Reg.Orig. 258.

ESSENTIAL. Indispensably necessary; important in the highest degree; requisite. Solter v. Macmillan, 147 Md. 580, 128 A. 356, 358; City of Kalamazoo v. Balkema, 252 Mich. 308, 233 N.W. 325, 326.

ESSENTIAL GOVERNMENTAL DUTIES. Those duties which framers of Constitution intended each member of union would assume in functioning under form of government guaranteed by Constitution. Commissioner of Internal Revenue v. Stilwell, C.C.A.7, 101 F.2d 588, 591.

ESSENTIAL OIL. A group of volatile oils having marked characteristic odors, occurring in fruits, flowers, leaves, stems, etc. In re Johnston, Cust. & Pat.App., 132 F.2d 136, 139.

ESSENTIALLY. "Substantially" is not necessarily synonymous. Robins v. Wettlaufer, Cust. & Pat.App., 81 F.2d 882, 893.

ESSOIN, *v.* In old English practice. To present or offer an excuse for not appearing in court on an appointed day in obedience to a summons; to cast an essoin. Spelman. This was anciently done by a person whom the party sent for that purpose, called an "essoiner."

ESSOIN, *n.* In old English law. An excuse for not appearing in court at the return of the process. Presentation of such excuse. Spelman; 1 Sel.Pr. 4; Com.Dig. "Exoine," B 1. Essoin is not now allowed at all in personal actions. 2 Term, 16; 16 East, 7*a*; 3 Bl.Comm. 278, note.

ESSOIN DAY. Formerly the first general return-day of the term, on which the courts sat to receive essoins, *i. e.*, excuses for parties who did not appear in court, according to the summons of writs. 3 Bl.Comm. 278; Boote, Suit at Law, 130; Gilb. Com.Pl. 13; 1 Tidd, Pr. 107. But, by St. 11 Geo. IV. and 1 Wm. IV. c. 70, § 6, these days were done away with, as a part of the term.

ESSOIN DE MALO VILLÆ. When the defendant is in court the first day; but gone without pleading, and being afterwards surprised by sickness, etc., cannot attend, but sends two essoiners, who openly protest in court that he is detained by sickness in such a village, that he cannot come *pro lucrari* and *pro perdere*; and this will be admitted, for it lieth on the plaintiff to prove whether the essoin is true or not. Jacob.

ESSOIN ROLL. A roll upon which essoins were formerly entered, together with the day to which they were adjourned. Boote, Suit at Law, 130; Rosc.Real Act. 162, 163; Gilb.Com.Pl. 13.

ESSOINIATOR. A person who made an essoin.

EST ALIQUID QUOD NON OPORTET ETIAM SI LICET; QUICQUID VERO NON LICET CERTE NON OPORTET. Hob. 159. There is that which is not proper, even though permitted; but whatever is not permitted is certainly not proper.

EST ASCAVOIR. It is to be understood or known; "it is to-wit." Litt. §§ 9, 45, 46, 57, 59. A very common expression in Littleton, especially at the commencement of a section; and, according to Lord Coke, "it ever teacheth us some rule of law, or general or sure leading point." Co.Litt. 16.

EST AUTEM JUS PUBLICUM ET PRIVATUM, QUOD EX NATURALIBUS PRÆCEPTIS AUT GENTIUM, AUT CIVILIBUS EST COLLECTUM; ET QUOD IN JURE SCRIPTO JUS APPELLATUR, ID IN LEGE ANGLIÆ RECTUM ESSE DICITUR. Public and private law is that which is collected from natural precepts, on the one hand of nations, on the other of citizens; and that which in the civil law is called "*jus*," that, in the law of England, is said to be right. Co.Litt. 558.

EST AUTEM VIS LEGEM SIMULANS. Violence may also put on the mask of law.

EST IPSORUM LEGISLATORUM TANQUAM VIVA VOX. The voice of the legislators themselves is like the living voice; that is, the language of a statute is to be understood and interpreted like ordinary spoken language. 10 Coke, 101*b*.

EST QUIDDAM PERFECTIUS IN REBUS LICITIS. There is something more perfect in things allowed.

ESTABLISH. This word occurs frequently in the constitution of the United States, and it is there used in different meanings: (1) To settle firmly, to fix unalterably; as to establish justice, which is the avowed object of the constitution. (2) To make or form; as to establish a uniform rule of naturalization, and uniform laws on the subject of bankruptcies, which evidently does not mean that these laws shall be unalterably established as justice. (3) To found, to create, to regulate; as: "Congress shall have power to establish post-roads and post-offices." (4) To found, recognize, confirm, or admit; as: "Congress shall make no law respecting an establishment of religion." (5) To create, to ratify, or confirm; as: "We, the people," etc., "do ordain and establish this constitution." 1 Story, Const. § 454. And see Ware v. U. S., 4 Wall. 632, 18 L.Ed. 389; U. S. v. Smith, 4 N.J. L. 33.

To settle or fix firmly; place on a permanent footing; found; create; put beyond doubt or dispute; prove; convince. Smith v. Forrest, 49 N.H. 230; Rowley v. Braly, Tex.Civ.App., 286 S.W. 241, 245; Village of Villa Park v. Wanderer's Rest Cemetery Co., 316 Ill. 226, 147 N.E. 104, 106; Thompson v. U. S., C.C.A.N.J, 283 F. 895, 899; Wells Lamont Corp. v. Bowles, Emp.App, 149 F.2d 364, 366.

To bring into being; to build; to constitute; to create; to erect; to form, to found; to found and regulate, to institute, to locate; to make; to model; to organize; to originate; to prepare; to set up. Georgia Public Service Commission v. Georgia Power Co., 182 Ga. 706, 186 S.E. 839, 844; Muscatine Lighting Co. v. City of Muscatine, 205 Iowa 82, 217 N.W. 468, 470; Ronnow v. City of Las Vegas, 57 Nev. 332, 65 P.2d 133, 140.

ESTABLISHMENT, ETABLISSEMENT. An ordinance or statute. Especially used of those ordinances or statutes passed in the reign of Edw. I. 2 Inst. 156; Britt. c. 21.

Etablissement is also used to denote the settlement of dower by the husband upon his wife. Britt. c. 102.

Institution, place where conducted and equipment; industrial plant and appurtenances; place of business and fixtures; residence with grounds, furniture, equipage, etc. State v. Scullin-Gallagher Iron & Steel Co., 268 Mo. 178, 186 S.W. 1007, 1008, Ann.Cas.1918E, 620; Benjamin Rose Institute v. Myers, 92 Ohio St. 252, 110 N.E. 924, 927, L.R.A. 1916D, 1170; Walling v. American Stores Co., C.C.A.Pa., 133 F.2d 840, 844; Continental Baking Co. v. Campbell, 176 Okl. 218, 55 P.2d 114, 116. In a narrow sense, "to bring into being, create, build, set up, etc." Gunnar v. Town of Montezuma, 229 Iowa 734, 294 N.W. 895, 897.

ESTABLISHMENT OF DOWER. The assurance of dower made by the husband, or his friends, before or at the time of the marriage. Britt. cc. 102, 103.

ESTACHE. A bridge or stank of stone or timber. Cowell.

ESTADAL. In Spanish law. In Spanish America, a measure of land of sixteen square varas, or yards. 2 White, Recop. 139.

ESTADIA (or Sobrestadia). In Spanish law. Delay in a voyage, or in the delivery of cargo, caused by the charterer or consignee, for which demurrage is payable. The time for which the party who has chartered a vessel, or is bound to receive the cargo, has to pay demurrage on account of his delay in the execution of the contract.

ESTANDARD. L. Fr. A standard (of weights and measures.) So called because it stands constant and immovable, and hath all other measures coming towards it for their conformity. Termes de la Ley.

ESTANQUES. Wears (weirs) or kiddles in rivers.

ESTATE. The interest which any one has in lands, or in any other subject of property. 1 Prest.Est. 20. And see Mulford v. Le Franc, 26 Cal. 103; Robertson v. VanCleave, 129 Ind. 217, 29 N.E. 781, 15 L.R.A. 68; Ball v. Chadwick, 46 Ill. 31. An estate in lands, tenements, and hereditaments signifies such interest as the tenant has therein. 2 Bl.Comm. 103. The condition or circumstance in which the owner *stands* with regard to his property. 2 Crabb, Real Prop. p. 2, § 942; Boyd v. Sibold, 7 Wash.2d 279, 109 P.2d 535, 539. In this sense, "estate" is constantly used in conveyances in connection with the words "right," "title," and "interest," and is, in a great degree, synonymous with all of them. See Co.Litt. 345.

The degree, quantity, nature, and extent of interest which a person has in real property is usually referred to as an estate, and it varies from absolute ownership down to naked possession. Nicholson Corporation v. Ferguson, 114 Okl. 10, 243 P. 195, 200; Washington Ins. Co. v. Pass, for Use of Nalley, 64 Ga.App. 221, 12 S.E.2d 460, 461; Gibbs v. Lester, Tex.Com.App., 41 S.W.2d 28, 29, 80 A.L.R. 431.

In another sense, "estate" designates the property (real or personal) in which one has a right or interest; the subject-matter of ownership; the *corpus* of property. Thus, we speak of a "valuable estate," "all my estate," "separate estate," "trust estate," etc. This, also, is its meaning in the classification of property into "real estate" and "personal estate." Connertin v. Concannon, 122 Or. 387, 259 P. 290, 292; Bates v. Sparrell, 10 Mass. 323; Archer v. Deneale, 1 Pet. 585, 7 L.Ed. 272; Den v. Snitcher, 14 N.J.L. 53.

There is no such legal entity as an "estate." Hansen v. Stanton, 177 Wash. 257, 31 P.2d 903, 904, 92 A.L.R. 1037. It is a convenient phrase, to identify the subject of litigation in the orphans' court, and in proceedings in rem it may be treated as harmless superfluity, but as a designation of a party to be served with a writ it is unknown to the law. It cannot be made the plaintiff in an action, as it is not a person and cannot sue or be sued. In re Harrisburg Trust Co., 80 Pa.Super.Ct. 585.

The word "estate" is a word of the greatest extension, and comprehends every species of property, real and personal. It describes both the *corpus* and the extent of interest. Deering v. Tucker, 55 Me. 284; Frazer v. First Nat. Bank of Mobile, 235 Ala. 252, 178 So. 441, 444. When used in some connections, it signifies everything of which riches or fortune may consist. Williams v. Chicago, B. & Q. R. Co., 155 S.W. 64, 66, 169 Mo.App. 468.

"Estate" comprehends everything a man owns, real and personal, and ought not to be limited in its construction, unless connected with some other word which must necessarily have that effect. Weber v. Bardon, 92 N.J.Eq. 190, 111 A. 649, 650; Black v. Sylvania Producing Co., 105 Ohio St. 346, 137 N.E. 904, 905.

It means, ordinarily, the whole of the property owned by anyone, the realty as well as the personalty. Hunter v. Husted, 45 N.C. 141; Wingard v. Harrison, 337 Ill. 387, 169 N.E. 232, 233; Miller v. Miller, 200 Iowa, 1070, 205 N.W. 870, 874, 43 A.L.R. 567; In re Quackenbush's Will, 127 Misc. 731, 217 N.Y.S. 493, 496; Jennings v. Jennings, 299 Ky. 779, 187 S.W.2d 459, 463.

A man's "estate" is that which he can sell or dispose of at his pleasure or what he can pass on to another. Howard v. Mitchell, 268 Ky. 429, 105 S.W.2d 128, 133.

Estates may be either *absolute* or *conditional.* An absolute estate is a full and complete estate, Cooper v. Cooper, 56 N.J.Eq. 48, 38 A. 198, or an estate in lands not subject to be defeated upon any condition. In this phrase the word "absolute" is not used legally to distinguish a fee from a life-estate, but a qualified or conditional fee from a fee simple. Greenawalt v. Greenawalt, 71 Pa. 483. A conditional estate is one, the existence of which depends upon the happening or not happening of some uncertain event, whereby the estate may be either originally created, or enlarged, or finally defeated. 2 Bl.Comm. 151. Estates are also classed as *executed* or *executory.* The former is an estate whereby a present interest passes to and resides in the tenant, not dependent upon any subsequent circumstance or contingency. They are more commonly called "estates in possession." 2 Bl.Comm. 162. An estate where there is vested in the grantee a present and immediate right of present or future enjoyment. An executory estate is an estate or interest in lands, the vesting or enjoyment of which depends upon some future contingency. Such estate may be an *executory devise,* or an *executory remainder,* which is the same as a contingent remainder, because no present interest passes. Further, estates may be *legal* or *equitable.* The former is that kind of estate which is properly cognizable in the courts of common law, though noticed, also, in the courts of equity. 1 Steph.Comm. 217. And see Sayre v. Mohney, 30 Or. 238, 47 P. 197; In re Qualifications of Electors, 19 R.I. 387, 35 A. 213. An equitable estate is an estate an interest in which can only be enforced in a court of chancery. Avery v. Dufrees, 9 Ohio 145. That is properly an equitable estate or interest for which a court of equity affords the only remedy; and of this nature, especially, is the benefit of every trust, express or implied, which is not converted into a legal estate by the statute of uses. The rest are equities of redemption, constructive trusts, and all equitable charges. Burt. Comp. c. 8. Brown v. Freed, 43 Ind. 253; In re Qualifications of Electors, 19 R.I. 387, 35 A. 213. "Equitable estates" are in equity what legal estates are in law; the ownership of the equitable estate is regarded by equity as the real ownership, and the legal estate is, as has been said, no more than the shadow always following the "equitable estate," which is the substance. Town of Cascade v. Cascade County, 75 Mont. 304, 243 P. 806, 808.

A *contingent* estate is one which depends for its effect upon an event which may or may not happen, as, where an estate is limited to a person not yet born. *Conventional* estates are those freeholds not of inheritance or estates for life, which are created by the express acts of the parties, in contradistinction to those which are legal and arise from the operation of law. A *dominant* estate, in the law of easements, is the estate for the benefit of which the easement exists, or the tenement whose owner, as such, enjoys an easement over an adjoining estate. An *expectant* estate is one which is not yet in possession, but the enjoyment of which is to begin at a future time; a present or vested contingent right of future enjoyment. Examples are remainders and reversions. A *future* estate is an estate which is not now vested in the grantee, but is to commence in possession at some future time. It includes remainders, reversions, and estates limited to commence *in futuro* without a particular estate to support them, which last are not good at common law, except in the case of chattel interests. See 2 Bl. Comm. 165. An estate limited to commence in possession at a future day, either without the intervention of a precedent estate, or on the determination by lapse of time, or otherwise, of a precedent estate created at the same time. Griffin v. Shepard, 124 N.Y. 70, 26 N.E. 339; Sabledowsky v. Arbuckle, 50 Minn. 475, 52 N.W. 920; A *particular* estate is a limited estate which is taken out of the fee, and which precedes a remainder; as an estate for years to A., remainder to B. for life; or an estate for life to A., remainder to B. in tail. This precedent estate is called the "particular estate," and the tenant of such estate is called the "particular tenant." 2 Bl.Comm. 165; Bunting v. Speek, 41 Kan. 424, 21 P. 288, 3 L.R.A. 690. A *servient* estate, in the law of easements, is the estate upon which the easement is imposed or against which it is enjoyed; an estate subjected to a burden or servitude for the benefit of another estate. Walker v. Clifford, 128 Ala. 67, 29 So. 588, 86 Am.St.Rep. 74; Dillman v. Hoffman, 38 Wis. 572. A *settled* estate, in English law, is one created or limited under a settlement; that is, one in which the powers of alienation, devising, and transmission according to the ordinary rules of descent are restrained by the limitations of the settlement. Micklethwait v. Micklethwait, 4 C.B., N.S., 858. A *vested* estate is one in which there is an immediate right of present enjoyment or a present fixed right of future enjoyment; an estate as to which there is a person in being who would have an immediate right to the possession upon the ceasing of some intermediate or precedent estate. Flanner v. Fellows, 206 Ill. 136, 68 N.E. 1057.

Original and *derivative* estates. An original is the first of several estates, bearing to each other the relation of a particular estate and a reversion. An original estate is contrasted with a derivative estate; and a derivative estate is a particular interest carved out of another estate of larger extent. Prest.Est. 125.

For the names and definitions of the various kinds of estates in land, see the different titles below.

"Estate" and "heirs" are not equivalent terms, Martin v. Hale, 167 Tenn. 438, 71 S.W.2d 211, 214; Abraham v. Abraham, 245 App.Div. 302, 280 N.Y.S. 825.

"Estate" and "property" may be used synonymously, McVicar v. McVicar, 128 Kan. 394, 278 P. 36, 38; Ponsonby v. Sacramento Suburban Fruit Lands Co., 210 Cal. 229, 291 P. 167, 168.

Fast Estate

Real property. A term sometimes used in wills. Lewis v. Smith, 9 N.Y. 502, 61 Am.Dec. 706.

Landed Estate or Property

See Landed Estate or Property.

Qualified Estate

Interests in real property which are not absolute and unconditional including fee tail, estates on condition, estates on limitation, and estates on conditional limitation. Carpender v. City of New Brunswick, 135 N.J.Eq. 397, 39 A.2d 40, 43.

Real Estate

Landed property, including all estates and interests in lands which are held for life or for some greater estate, and whether such lands be of freehold or copyhold tenure. Wharton.

As to "Homestead," "Movable," "Residuary," "Separate," and "Trust" estate, see those titles.

Financial or Personal Status

In a wider sense, a man's whole financial *status* or condition,—the aggregate of his interests and concerns, so far as regards his situation with reference to wealth or its objects, including debts and obligations, as well as possessions and rights. Thus, we speak of "debts due the estate," or say that "A.'s estate is a stockholder in the bank." In this sense it is a fictitious or juridical person, the idea being that a man's business *status* continues his existence, for its special purposes, until its final settlement and dissolution. See Morgannelli's Estate v. City of Derby, 105 Conn. 545, 135 A. 911; In re Watson, 86 Misc. 588, 148 N.Y.S. 902, 908.

In its broadest sense, the social, civic, or political condition or standing of a person; or a class of persons considered as grouped for social, civic, or political purposes; as in the phrases, "the third estate," "the estates of the realm." See 1 Bl.Comm. 153.

"Estate" and "degree," when used in the sense of an individual's personal *status*, are synonymous, and indicate the individual's rank in life. State v. Bishop, 15 Me. 122.

ESTATE AD REMANENTIAM. An estate in fee-simple. Glan. l. 7, c. 1.

ESTATE AT SUFFERANCE. The interest of a tenant who has come rightfully into possession of lands by permission of the owner, and continues to occupy the same after the period for which he is entitled to hold by such permission. 1 Washb. Real Prop. 392; 2 Bl.Comm. 150; Co.Litt. 57*b*. The estate arises where one comes into possession of land by lawful title, but keeps it afterwards without any title at all, and the original entry need not have been under lease or as a tenant of the dispossessing landlord. Malone v. Floyd, 50 Ga.App. 701, 179 S.E. 176.

ESTATE AT WILL. A species of estate less than freehold, where lands and tenements are let by one man to another, to have and to hold at the will of the lessor; and the tenant by force of this lease obtains possession. 2 Bl.Comm. 145; 4 Kent, Comm. 110; Litt. § 68; Co.Litt. 55*a;* Tud.L.Cas.R. P. 10, 14. Or it is where lands are let without limiting any certain and determinate estate. 2 Crabb, Real Prop. p. 403, § 1543.

The estate arises where lands or tenements are expressly demised by one person to another to be held during the joint wills of both parties, or it may arise by implication of law wherever one person is put in possession of another's land with the owner's consent, but under an agreement which does not suffice to create in the tenant an estate of freehold or for years. Eason v. Rose, 183 Va. 359, 32 S.E.2d 66, 68.

ESTATE BY ELEGIT. See Elegit.

ESTATE BY ENTIRETY. A form of co-ownership of realty or personalty held by husband and wife in which there is unity of estate, unity of possession and unity of control of entire property, and on death of one, survivor takes estate under original conveyance. In re Cochran's Real Estate, Sel. Orph., 66 A.2d 497, 499; In re Gallagher's Estate, 352 Pa. 476, 43 A.2d 132, 133.

ESTATE BY PURCHASE. One acquired in any other method than descent. In re Field, 182 App. Div. 226, 169 N.Y.S. 677, 679. See, also, Purchase.

ESTATE BY STATUTE MERCHANT. An estate whereby the creditor, under the custom of London, retained the possession of all his debtor's lands until his debts were paid. 1 Greenl. Cruise, Dig. 515. See Statute Merchant.

ESTATE BY STATUTE STAPLE. See Staple.

ESTATE BY THE CURTESY. See Curtesy.

ESTATE BY THE ENTIRETY. Called also estate in entirety, or estate by the entireties. An estate in joint tenancy, plus the unity of the marital relation. Hoyt v. Winstanley, 221 Mich. 515, 191 N.W. 213, 214. A common-law estate, based on the doctrine that husband and wife are one, and that a conveyance of real property to husband and wife creates but one estate. Klorfine v. Cole, 121 Or. 76, 252 P. 708, 709. An estate held by husband and wife together so long as both live, and, after the death of either, by the survivor. It is an estate held by husband and wife by virtue of a title acquired by them jointly after marriage. Bailey v. Smith, 89 Fla. 303, 103 So. 833, 834. A creature of the common law created by legal fiction based wholly on the common-law doctrine that husband and wife are one, and hence a conveyance to husband and wife created only one estate, and each was owner of the whole estate, and neither could dispose of it without the consent of the other, and on the death of one survivor was the owner in fee simple. Wimbush v. Danford, 292 Mo. 588, 238 S.W. 460, 466; In re Flynn, D.C.Pa., 1 F.2d 566, 567; Alexander v. Alexander, 154 Or. 317, 58 P.2d 1265, 1270, 1271.

An "estate by entireties" resembles a "joint tenancy" in that there is a right of survivorship in both, but such an estate is distinguishable from a joint tenancy in that the latter may be invested in any number of natural persons each of whom is seized of an undivided moiety of the whole, whereas a "tenancy by entirety" is vested in two persons only, who in law are regarded as only one, and each of whom becomes seized of the estate as a whole. Heffner v. White, 113 Ind.App. 296, 45 N.E.2d 342, 346; Carlisle v. Parker, 8 W.W.Harr. 83, 188 A. 67.

ESTATE DUTY. A duty imposed in England (act of 1894) superseding probate duty, taxing not the interest to which some person succeeds on a death, but the interest which ceased by reason of the death. Hansen, Death Duties 63. It is leviable on property which was left untouched by probate duty, such as real estate, yet it is in substance of the same nature as the old probate duty.

ESTATE FOR LIFE. See Life Estate.

ESTATE FOR YEARS. A species of estate less than freehold, where a man has an interest in lands and tenements, and a possession thereof, by virtue of such interest, for some fixed and determinate period of time; as in the case where lands are let for the term of a certain number of years, agreed upon between the lessor and the lessee, and the lessee enters thereon. 1 Steph.Comm. 263, 264. Blackstone calls this estate a "contract" for the possession of lands or tenements for some determinate period. 2 Bl.Comm. 140. See Hutcheson v. Hodnett, 115 Ga. 990, 42 S.E. 422; Harbottle v. Central Coal & Coke Co., 134 Ark. 254, 203 S.W. 1044, 1046; 2 Crabb, R.P. § 1267; Bac.Abr. *Leases;* Wms.R.P. 195. Such estates are frequently called terms.

"Estates for years" embrace all terms limited to endure for a definite and ascertained period, however short or long the period may be; they embrace terms for a fixed number of weeks or months or for a single year, as well as for any definite number of years, however great. Guy v. Brennan, 60 Cal.App. 452, 213 P. 265, 267. Compare Metcalf Auto Co. v. Norton, 119 Me. 103, 109 A. 384.

ESTATE FROM PERIOD TO PERIOD. An estate continuing for successive periods of a year, or successive periods of a fraction of a year, unless it is terminated. Pitney-Bowes Postage Meter Co. v. United States, D.C.Conn., 57 F.Supp. 365, 366.

ESTATE FROM YEAR TO YEAR. An example of an estate for years. It is of later origin and is not found in Littleton (see § 381). It exists in cases where the parties stipulate for it, and also where the parties by their conduct have placed themselves in the relation of landlord and tenant without adopting any other term. If a tenant has been allowed to hold over after the expiration of his term in such a way as to preclude the possibility of his becoming a tenant on sufferance, it is a tenancy from year to year. Jenks, Mod.Land Law 88. See, also, Odger, C.L. 869; 7 Q.B. 958. It was originally a development of a tenancy at will, by which the tenancy was terminable only at the time of the year at which it began, and on notice.

ESTATE IN COMMON. An estate in lands held by two or more persons, with interests accruing under different titles; or accruing under the same title, but at different periods; or conferred by words of limitation importing that the grantees are to take in distinct shares. 1 Steph.Comm. 323. See Tenancy in Common. An estate held in joint possession by two or more persons at the same time by several and distinct titles. 1 Washb.R.P. 415; 2 Bla.Comm. 191; 1 Pres.Est. 139.

ESTATE IN COPARCENARY. See Coparcenary.

ESTATE IN DOWER. See Dower.

ESTATE IN EXPECTANCY. One which is not yet in possession, but the enjoyment of which is to begin at a future time; an estate giving a present or vested contingent right of future enjoyment. One in which the right to pernancy of the profits is postponed to some future period. Such are estates in remainder and reversion. Underhill v. R. Co., 20 Barb. 455; Fenton v. Miller, 108 Mich. 246, 65 N.W. 966; Ayers v. Trust Co., 187 Ill. 42, 58 N.E. 318.

ESTATE IN FEE SIMPLE. See Fee Simple.

ESTATE IN FEE-TAIL. See Tail, Estate in.

ESTATE IN JOINT TENANCY. See Tenancy.

ESTATE IN LANDS. Property one has in lands, tenements or hereditaments, or conditions or circumstances in which tenant stands as to his property. Tallman v. Eastern Illinois & Peoria R. Co., 379 Ill. 441, 41 N.E.2d 537, 540.

ESTATE IN REMAINDER. See Remainder.

ESTATE IN REVERSION. See Reversion.

ESTATE IN SEVERALTY. An estate held by a person in his own right only, without any other person being joined or connected with him in point of interest, during his estate. This is the most common and usual way of holding an estate. 2 Bl. Comm. 179; Cruise, Dig. tit. 18, c. 1, § 1.

ESTATE IN VADIO. An estate in gage or pledge. 2 Bl.Comm. 157; 1 Steph.Comm. 282. See Mortgage.

ESTATE LESS THAN FREEHOLD. An estate for years, estate at will, or estate at sufferance. Fowler v. Marion & Pittsburg Coal Co., 315 Ill. 312, 146 N.E. 318, 319. See Estate of Freehold.

ESTATE OF FREEHOLD. See Freehold.

ESTATE OF INHERITANCE. An estate which may descend to heirs. 1 Washb.R.P. 51; Administration & Trust Co. v. Catron, 171 Tenn. 268, 102 S.W.2d 59, 60. A species of freehold estate in lands, otherwise called a "fee," where the tenant is not only entitled to enjoy the land for his own life, but where, after his death, it is cast by the law upon the persons who successively represent him *in perpetuum,* in right of blood, according to a certain established order of descent. 1 Steph. Comm. 218; Litt. § 1; Nellis v. Munson, 108 N.Y. 453, 15 N.E. 739; Roulston v. Hall, 66 Ark. 305, 50 S.W. 690, 74 Am.St.Rep. 97; George v. George, 51 Ohio App. 169, 200 N.E. 142, 143.

Estates of freehold are divided into those of inheritance and those not of inheritance. All estates of inheritance in tenements are freehold; but, since freeholds embrace estates for life and those of indefinite duration which may endure for life, all freeholds are not "estates of inheritance." Beirl v. Columbia County, 73 Or. 107, 144 P. 457, 460; Crabb, R.P. § 945.

ESTATE ON CONDITIONAL LIMITATION. An estate conveyed to one person so that, upon occurrence or failure of occurrence of some contingent event, whether conditional or limitative, the estate shall depart from original grantee and pass to another. Carpender v. City of New Brunswick, 135 N.J.Eq. 397, 39 A.2d 40, 43.

ESTATE ON LIMITATION. An estate originated by the use of words denoting duration of time, such as while, during, so long as, and the like and when designated limitative event happens, such estate ends naturally without any re-entry and property reverts to grantor. Carpender v. City of New Brunswick, 135 N.J.Eq. 397, 39 A.2d 40, 43. Sometimes referred to as "base fee", "qualified fee", "determinable fee", or "fee simple defeasible". Lehigh Valley R. Co. v. Chapman, 171 A.2d 653, 657, 35 N.J. 177.

ESTATE PUR AUTRE VIE. See Pur Autre Vie.

ESTATE SUBJECT TO A CONDITIONAL LIMITATION. The distinction between an estate upon condition subsequent and an "estate subject to a conditional limitation" is that in former words creating condition do not originally limit term, but merely permit its termination upon happening of contingency, while in latter words creating it limit continuation of estate to time preceding happening of contingency. Johnson v. Lane, 199 Ark. 740, 135 S.W.2d 853, 866.

ESTATE TAIL. See Tail, Estate in.

ESTATE TAIL, QUASI. When a tenant for life grants his estate to a man and his heirs, as these words, though apt and proper to create an estate tail, cannot do so, because the grantor, being only tenant for life, cannot grant *in perpetuum*, therefore they are said to create an estate tail *quasi*, or improper. Brown.

ESTATE TAX. An excise tax upon privilege of transferring or transmitting property by reason of death and is not tax on property itself. Friend v. Commissioner of Internal Revenue, C.C.A.7, 119 F.2d 959, 960; In re Vanderbilt's Estate, 281 N.Y. 297, 22 N.E.2d 379, 390. An "estate tax" taxes, not the interest to which some person succeeds on a death, but the interest which ceases by reason of the death; while the "inheritance tax" is based on the interest to which the living person succeeds. In re Ogden's Estate, 209 Wis. 162, 244 N.W. 571, 573.

It is an "estate tax" when the tax is required to be paid on the entire net estate before it is divided into its several parts to be distributed. State Tax Commission v. Backman, 88 Utah 424, 55 P.2d 171, 174.

ESTATE UPON CONDITION. An estate in lands, the existence of which depends upon the happening or not happening of some uncertain event, whereby the estate may be either originally created, or enlarged, or finally defeated. 2 Bl.Comm. 151; 1 Steph.Comm. 276; Co. Litt. 201*a*. An estate having a qualification annexed to it, by which it may, upon the happening of a particular event, be created, or enlarged, or destroyed. 4 Kent, Comm. 121. United States v. 1,010.8 Acres, More or Less, Situate in Sussex County, Del., D.C.Del., 56 F.Supp. 120, 127.

ESTATE UPON CONDITION EXPRESSED. An estate granted, either in fee-simple or otherwise, with an express qualification annexed, whereby the estate granted shall either commence, be enlarged, or be defeated upon performance or breach of such qualification or condition. 2 Bl.Comm. 154. An estate which is so expressly defined and limited by the words of its creation that it cannot endure for any longer time than till the contingency happens upon which the estate is to fail. 1 Steph.Comm. 278.

ESTATE UPON CONDITION IMPLIED. An estate having a condition annexed to it inseparably from its essence and constitution, although no condition be expressed in words. 2 Bl.Comm. 152; 4 Kent, Comm. 121.

ESTATES OF THE REALM. The lords spiritual, the lords temporal, and the commons of Great Britain. 1 Bl.Comm. 153. Sometimes called the "three estates." Inasmuch as the lords spiritual have no separate assembly or negative in their political capacity, some authorities reduce the estates in Great Britain to two, the lords and commons. Webster, Dict.

Generally in feudal Europe there were three estates, the clergy, nobles, and commons. In England (until about the 14th century) the three estates of the realm were the clergy, barons, and knights. In legal practice the lords spiritual and lords temporal are usually collectively designated under the one name *lords*. Webster, Dict.

ESTENDARD, ESTENDART, or STANDARD. An ensign for horsemen in war.

ESTER. A compound ether derived from oxygenated acid. E. I. Du Pont De Nemours & Co. v. Byrnes, D.C.N.Y., 1 F.R.D. 34, 36.

ESTER IN JUDGMENT. L. Fr. To appear before a tribunal either as plaintiff or defendant. Kelham.

ESTIMATE. A valuing or rating by the mind, without actually measuring, weighing, or the like. City of Tulsa v. Weston, 102 Okl. 222, 229 P. 108, 122. A rough or approximate calculation only. Bair v. Montrose, 58 Utah 398, 199 P. 667, 669; United States v. Foster, C.C.A.Iowa, 131 F.2d 3, 7; P. M. Hennessy Const. Co. v. Hart, 141 Minn. 449, 170 N.W. 579, 598. Thus, a census is a finding of the population, not an "estimate." State ex rel. Reynolds v. Jost, 265 Mo. 51, 175 S.W. 591, 597, Ann.Cas.1917D, 1102.

This word is used to express the mind or judgment of the speaker or writer on the particular subject under consideration. It implies a calculation or computation, as to *estimate* the gain or loss of an enterprise. People v. Clark, 37 Hun, N.Y., 203; New Orleans Terminal Co. v. Dixie Rendering, La.App., 179 So. 98, 100.

As used in a contract for the sale of an estimated quantity of goods, "estimated" may mean practically the same as "more or less." Robbins v. Hill, Tex.Civ.App., 259 S.W.

1112, 1115. Generally, the word "estimated" indicates that a statement of quantity is a matter of description, and not of the essence of the contract. Biglione v. Bronge, 192 Cal. 167, 219 P. 69, 70.

ESTIMATED COST. The "estimated cost" of a building means the reasonable cost of a building erected in accordance with the plans and specifications referred to, and not necessarily the amount of some actual estimate made by a builder, nor an estimate agreed upon by the parties, nor yet an estimate or bid accepted by the defendant. New Orleans Terminal Co. v. Dixie Rendering, La. App., 179 So. 98, 100.

ESTOP. To stop, bar, or impede; to prevent; to preclude. Co.Litt 352*a*; Olsgard v. Lemke, 32 N. D. 551, 156 N.W. 102, 103. See Estoppel.

ESTOPPEL. A man's own act or acceptance stops or closes his mouth to allege or plead the truth. Caulfield v. Noonan, 229 Iowa 955, 295 N. W. 466, 471; Williams v. Edwards, 163 Okl. 246, 22 P.2d 1026.

An estoppel arises when one is concluded and forbidden by law to speak against his own act or deed. Gural v. Engle, 128 N.J.L. 252, 25 A.2d 257, 261; an inconsistent position, attitude or course of conduct may not be adopted to loss or injury of another. Brand v. Farmers Mut. Protective Ass'n of Texas, Tex.Civ.App., 95 S.W.2d 994, 997.

Estoppel is a bar or impediment which precludes allegation or denial of a certain fact or state of facts, in consequence of previous allegation or denial or conduct or admission, or in consequence of a final adjudication of the matter in a court of law, Lewis v. King, 157 La. 718, 103 So. 19, 22; Agoodash Achim of Ithaca v. Temple Beth-El, 147 Misc. 405, 263 N.Y.S. 81; Chernick v. National Surety Co., 50 R.I. 419, 148 A. 418, 419; an equitable doctrine to accomplish justice, Sisson v. Swift, 243 Ala. 289, 9 So.2d 891, 903; Elowe v. Superior Fire Ins. Co., 307 Ill. App. 569, 30 N.E.2d 953, 958; preclusion by act or conduct from asserting right which might otherwise have existed. Reynolds v. Travelers' Ins. Co., 176 Wash. 36, 28 P.2d 310, 314; Tucker v. Brown, 20 Wash.2d 740, 150 P.2d 604, 652; Preclusion from alleging or denying fact because of previous action, inaction, allegation, or denial. Steph.Pl. 239; Spear v. Farwell, 5 Cal.App.2d 111, 42 P.2d 391, 392; Scholl v. Scholl, 123 Ohio St. 1, 173 N.E. 305, 306; preclusion from denying truth of fact which has in contemplation of law become settled by acts and proceedings of judicial or legislative officers, or by act of party himself, either by conventional writing or by representations, express or implied in pais, May v. City of Kearney, 145 Neb. 475, 17 N.W.2d 448, 458; shield for defense but not a weapon of attack, United States, to Use of Noland Co. v. Maryland Casualty Co., D.C.Md., 38 F.Supp. 479, 484. It is available only for protection, and cannot be used as a weapon of assault. Stanio v. Berner Lohne Co., 127 Conn. 431, 17 A.2d 502, 504; It operates to put party entitled to its benefits in same position as if thing represented were true. May v. City of Kearney, 145 Neb. 475, 17 N.W.2d 448, 458.

Under law of "estoppel" where one of two innocent persons must suffer, he whose act occasioned loss must bear it. Buxbaum v. Assicurazioni Generali, 175 Misc. 785, 25 N.Y.S.2d 357, 360; Sackenreuther v. Winston, Tex.Civ. App., 137 S.W.2d 93, 96.

Elements or essentials of estoppel include change of position of parties so that party against whom estoppel is invoked has received a profit or benefit or party invoking estoppel has changed his position to his detriment, Wertz v. Shane, 216 Iowa 768, 249 N.W. 661; Lebold v. Inland Steel Co., C.C.A.Ill., 125 F.2d 369, 375; Garmon v. Fitzgerald, 168 Miss. 532, 151 So. 726, 728; circumstances such that a knowledge of truth is necessarily imputed to party estopped, Froslee v. Sonju, 209 Minn. 522, 297 N.W. 1, 3, 4; conduct intended to deceive or of such nature that reasonably prudent person would have been deceived, Cellized Floors v. Glens Falls Indemnity Co. of New York, 9 N.J. Misc. 1111, 156 A. 845, 846; Agnew v. Mullenix, La.App., 11 So.2d 106, 107; direct or immediate influence on party claiming benefit of estoppel, Stanolind Oil & Gas Co. v. Midas Oil Co., Tex.Civ.App., 173 S.W.2d 342, 345; false representation or wrongful silence or concealment, Noxon v. Cockburn, Tex.Civ.App., 147 S.W.2d 872, 875; Weber v. Fohl, 111 Ind.App. 388, 41 N.E.2d 648, 650, 651; Van Antwerp v. United States, C.C.A.Cal., 92 F.2d 871, 875; inducing another to alter his position or to do that which he would not otherwise have done, Babcock v. McKee, S.D., 18 N.W.2d 750, 754; Wellsville East Field Irr. Co. v. Lindsay Land & Livestock Co., 104 Utah 448, 137 P.2d 634, 647; Albermarle County v. Massey, 183 Va. 310, 32 S.E.2d 228, 230; intent or reasonable expectation of party estopped that other would act, Bank of Sutton v. Skidmore, 113 W.Va. 25, 167 S.E. 144, 146; Mercer Casualty Co. v. Lewis, 41 Cal.App.2d 918, 108 P.2d 65, 67; knowledge of facts by party to be estopped, Caveney v. Caveney, 234 Wis. 637, 291 N.W. 818, 824; In re Dimon's Estate, Sur., 32 N.Y.S.2d 239, 243; lack of knowledge and means of knowledge by party claiming estoppel, Ainscow v. Alexander, Del.Super., 39 A.2d 54, 60; Froslee v. Sonju, 209 Minn. 522, 297 N.W. 1, 3, 4; misleading of one party by another party, Williams v. Middle-West Roads Co., 295 Ky. 648, 175 S.W.2d 136, 138; United States, to Use of Noland Co. v. Marfand Casualty Co., D.C.Md., 38 F.Supp. 479, 484; prejudice or loss or injury to party invoking estoppel, Vinton v. Atlas Assur. Co., 107 Vt. 272, 178 A. 909, 912; Commission v. Shell Oil Co., Tex.Civ.App., 170 S.W.2d 568, 570; Hooper v. Ball, 133 Me. 412, 179 A. 404, 406; reliance by one party on act, word or conduct of other party, Gosney v. Metropolitan Life Ins. Co., C.C.A.Mo., 114 F.2d 649, 652; In re Sarvey's Estate, 206 Iowa 527, 219 N.W. 318, 321; right of party asserting estoppel to believe party estopped intended that his conduct should be acted upon, Lusitanian-American Development Co. v. Seaboard Dairy Credit Corporation, 1 Cal.2d 121, 34 P.2d 139, 142; wrongdoing on part of person sought to be estopped, Sovereign Camp, W. O. W., v. Johnson, Tex.Civ.App., 64 S.W.2d 1084, 1087. Nor on mere delay in asserting a claim, Peyrefitte v. Union Homestead Ass'n, La. App., 185 So. 693, *695*.

Nor on errors of judgment, Northwestern Nat. Bank v. Commonwealth, 345 Pa. 192, 27 A.2d 20, 23; nor on error of law, United States v. Du Pont, D.C.Del., 47 F.Supp. 894, 897.

Estoppel is or may be based on acceptance of benefits, Rhodus v. Geatley, 347 Mo. 397, 147 S.W.2d 631, 637, 638, 639; Harjo v. Johnston, 187 Okl. 561, 104 P.2d 985, 992, 998; acknowledgments of matters of fact but not acknowledgments or statements of propositions of law, McDonald v. Richard, 203 La. 155, 13 So.2d 712, 718; acquiescence, In re Kennedy's Estate, 321 Pa. 225, 183 A. 798, 801; acts done under or in performance of contract, Jackson v. United Gas Public Service Co., 196 La. 1, 198 So. 633, 640; Finch v. Smith, 177 Okl. 307, 58 P.2d 850, 851; actual or constructive fraudulent conduct, Peterson v. Hudson Ins. Co., 41 Ariz. 31, 15 P.2d 249, 252; adjudication, Kunkel v. Eastern Iowa Light & Power Co-op., 232 Iowa 649, 5 N.W.2d 899, 903; Citizens' Loan & Trust Co. of Washington, Ind. v. Sanders, 99 Ind.App. 77, 187 N.E. 396, 398; admissions or denials by which another is induced to act to his injury, New York Life Ins. Co. v. Oates, 122 Fla. 540, 166 So. 269, 276; Wabash Drilling Co. v. Ellis, 230 Ky. 769, 20 S.W.2d 1002, 1004; agreement on and settlement of facts by force of entering into contract, Masterson v. Bouldin, Tex.Civ. App., 151 S.W.2d 301, 307; In re Schofield's Estate, 101 Colo. 443, 73 P.2d 1381; assertion of facts on which another relies, Fedas v. Insurance Co. of State of Pennsylvania, 300 Pa. 555, 151 A. 285, 287; assumption of position which, if not maintained, would result in injustice to another, Harvey v. J. P. Morgan & Co., 166 Misc. 455, 2 N.Y. S.2d 520; concealment of facts, Greer v. Franklin Life Ins. Co., Tex.Civ.App., 109 S.W.2d 305, 315; Rosser v. Texas Co., 173 Okl. 309, 48 P.2d 327, 330; conduct or acts amounting to a representation or a concealment, Spradling v. Spradling, 118 W.Va. 308, 190 S.E. 537, 540; consent to copyright infringement, whether express or implied from long acquiescence with knowledge of the infringement, Edwin L. Wiegand Co. v. Harold E. Trent Co., C.C.A.Pa., 122 F.2d 920, 925; election between rights or remedies, Hartley v. Hartley, 173 Ga. 710, 161 S.E. 358, 360; Mason & Mason v. Brown, Tex.Civ.App., 182 S.W.2d 729, 733; fault of party estopped, Conner v. Caldwell, 208 Minn. 502, 294 N.W. 650, 653; inaction, Utah State Building Commission, for Use and Benefit of Mountain States Supply Co., v. Great American Indemnity Co., 105 Utah 11, 140 P.2d 763,

771, 772; Hankins v. Waddell, 26 Tenn.App. 71, 167 S.W. 2d 694, 696; injury resulting from parties' conduct, In re Bastanchury Corporation, C.C.A.Cal., 66 F.2d 653, 657; innocent misrepresentation, Countway v. Commissioner of Internal Revenue, C.C.A.1, 127 F.2d 69, 76; laches, Oak Lawn Cemetery of Baltimore County v. Baltimore County Com'rs, 174 Md. 356, 198 A. 600, 605, 115 A.L.R. 1478; language or conduct which has induced another to act, French Market Ice Mfg. Co. of New Orleans v. Dalton, 15 La.App. 115, 130 So. 122, 123; Brown v. Federal Land Bank of Houston, Tex.Civ.App., 180 S.W.2d 647, 652; matter of record, Coral Realty Co. v. Peacock Holding Co., 103 Fla. 916, 138 So. 622, 624; misrepresentation, Cushing v. United States, D.C.Mass., 18 F.Supp. 83, 85; Rhoads v. Rhoads, 342 Mo. 934, 119 S.W.2d 247, 252; negligence, Postal v. Home State Bank for Savings, 284 Mich. 220, 279 N.W. 488, 491; Fisher v. Beckwith, 30 Wis. 55, 11 Am. Rep. 546; omission to act, West v. Cleveland Ry. Co., Ohio App., 58 N.E.2d 799, 801; prejudice, Alderman v. Town of West Haven, 124 Conn. 391, 200 A. 330, 333; prior judgment, Morrell v. Towle, 141 Neb. 370, 3 N.W.2d 655, 664; Kelliher v. Stone & Webster, C.C.A.Fla., 75 F.2d 331, 332; Promise of future performance, Albachten v. Bradley, 212 Minn. 359, 3 N.W.2d 783, 785; provisions of a deed, Carson v. Cochran, 52 Minn. 67, 53 N.W. 1130; Robert v. O'Connell, 269 Mass. 532, 169 N.E. 487, 488; public policy, Ervin v. City of Pittsburgh, 339 Pa. 241, 14 A.2d 297, 300; Bloomfield Village Drain Dist. v. Keefe, C.C.A.Mich., 119 F.2d 157, 163, 165; representation or concealment of facts, Kerestury v. Elkhart Packing Co., 108 Ind.App. 148, 27 N. E.2d 383, 385; Albermarle County v. Massey, 183 Va. 310, 32 S.E.2d 228, 230; silence, Rone v. Sawrey, 197 Ark. 472, 123 S.W.2d 524, 526, 527; Brown v. Brown, 347 Mo. 45, 146 S.W.2d 553, 555.

Estoppels are sometimes said to be of three kinds: (1) by deed; (2) by matter of record; (3) by matter *in pais*. The first two are also called legal estoppels, as distinguished from the last kind, known as equitable estoppels.

Acts and Declarations

An "estoppel by acts and declarations" is such as arises from the acts and declarations of a person by which he designedly induces another to alter his position injuriously to himself. Brauch v. Freking, 219 Iowa 556, 258 N.W. 892.

Adjudication Distinguished

"Adjudication" and an "estoppel" from relitigating things are different in that there is an adjudication when a suit is repeated, but that there may be an estoppel because some fact which is controlling in both actions was litigated and set at rest in first action. Kunkel v. Eastern Iowa Light & Power Co-Op., 232 Iowa 649, 5 N.W.2d 899, 903.

Common Law

"Estoppel at common law" includes estoppel by record, estoppel by deed, and certain cases of estoppel in pais which are recognized in courts of law. Thomas v. Conyers, 198 N.C. 229, 151 S.E. 270, 273.

Election Distinguished

"Election" differs from an "estoppel in pais" in that in order to be effective it need not be acted upon by the other party by way of a detrimental change of his position, provided the election is a decisive one. Phillips v. Rooker, 134 Tenn. 457, 184 S.W. 12, 14.

Estoppel Against Estoppel

Doctrine that two estoppels may destroy each other, or that one estoppel may set another at large. Shean v. United States Fidelity & Guaranty Co., 263 Mich. 535, 248 N.W. 892, 893.

In wife's divorce suit, evidence showed that wife in procuring void Nevada divorce decree was under husband's duress, domination, and compulsion, and hence there arose an "estoppel against estoppel" destroying each other, and wife was not barred from setting up invalidity of Nevada decree. Lippincott v. Lippincott, 141 Neb. 186, 3 N.W.2d 207, 215, 140 A.L.R. 901.

Fraud

Estoppel is a penalty paid by perpetrator of wrong by affirmative act which, though without fraudulent intent, may result in legal fraud on another. Harris v. Prince, Tex.Civ.App., 98 S.W. 2d 1022, 1026.

A judgment procured by fraud may not be used as the basis of an "estoppel". Seubert v. Seubert, 68 S.D. 195, 299 N.W. 873, 875; Actual or intended fraud is not an essential element of estoppel, but estoppel arises when omission to speak is an actual or constructive fraud. Kelley-Springfield Tire Co. v. Stein, 163 Misc. 393, 297 N.Y.S. 22, 26. An act done which cannot be contravened without fraud may be basis of estoppel, Tradesmens Nat. Bank of New Haven v. Minor, 122 Conn. 419, 190 A. 270, 272, An essential element of "equitable estoppel" is fraudulent intent. Fleishbein v. Western Auto Supply Agency, 19 Cal. App.2d 424, 65 P.2d 928; An estoppel does not require a showing of fraudulent intent. New Jersey Suburban Water Co. v. Town of Harrison, 122 N.J.L. 189, 3 A.2d 623, 625, 626, 627; An estoppel may arise although there is no designed fraud. Laraway v. First Nat. Bank of La Verne, 39 Cal.App.2d 718, 104 P.2d 95, 101; Estoppel is an equitable principle dependent on fraud. Volk v. City of New York, 259 App.Div. 247, 19 N.Y.S.2d 53, 60.

Intent

"Estoppel" in its broadest sense is penalty paid by one perpetrating wrong by known fraud or by affirmative act which, though without fraudulent intent, may result in legal fraud on another. Harris v. Prince, Tex.Civ.App., 98 S.W.2d 1022, 1026.

Actual or intended fraud is not an essential element of estoppel but estoppel arises when omission to speak is an actual or constructive fraud. Kelley-Springfield Tire Co. v. Stein, 163 Misc. 393, 297 N.Y.S. 22, 26. Elements of equitable estoppel are representations intentionally made under such circumstances as show that party making them intended, or might reasonably have anticipated, that party to whom they are made, or to whom they are communicated, will rely and act on them as true, Crane Co. of Minnesota v. Advance Plumbing & Heating Co., 177 Minn. 132, 224 N.W. 847, 848. An essential element of equitable estoppel is fraudulent intent but careless and culpable conduct is equivalent to intent to deceive. Fleishbein v. Western Auto Supply Agency, 19 Cal.App.2d 424, 65 P.2d 928. An estoppel arises when one by acts, representations, admissions or silence intentionally induces another to change his position for the worse. Smith v. Vara, 136 Misc. 500, 241 N.Y.S. 202, 209; American Exchange Nat. Bank v. Winder, 198 N.C. 18, 150 S.E. 489, 491. An estoppel does not require a showing of fraudulent intent. New Jersey Suburban Water Co. v. Town of Harrison, 122 N.J. L. 189, 3 A.2d 623, 625, 626, 627. An estoppel may arise where there is no intent to mislead. Mancini v. Thomas, 113 Vt. 322, 34 A.2d 105, 109.

Legal Title to Land

Estoppel affecting legal title to land requires conduct amounting to knowing representation or concealment relied on by other party changing his position for the worse. Crane v. Esmond, 214 Wis. 571, 253 N.W. 780.

It requires conduct amounting to representation or concealment of material facts known to party estopped at time of conduct, or at least under circumstances necessarily imputing knowledge thereof, and truth concerning such facts must be unknown to other party claiming benefit of estoppel, with further requirement that conduct was done with intention or expectation that it would be acted on, and other party led to act thereon in reliance on conduct so as to change his position for the worse. Jacksonville Public Service Corporation v. Calhoun Water Co., 219 Ala. 616, 123 So. 79, 81, 64 A.L.R. 1550.

Misrepresentation

See Representation, Estoppel By.

Pleading

Pleader must allege and prove not only that person sought to be estopped made misleading statements and representations but that pleader actually believed and relied on them and was misled to his injury thereby. Stanolind Oil & Gas Co. v. Midas Oil Co., Tex.Civ.App., 173 S.W.2d 342, 345.

A plea, replication, or other pleading, which, without confessing or denying the matter of fact adversely alleged, relies merely on some matter of estoppel as a ground for excluding the opposite party from the allegation of the fact. Steph.Pl. 219; 3 Bl.Comm. 308.

A plea which neither admits nor denies the facts alleged by the plaintiff, but denies his right to allege them. Gould, Pl. c. 2, § 39.

A special plea in bar, which happens where a man has done some act or executed some deed which precludes him from averring anything to the contrary. 3 Bl.Comm. 308.

A pleader is not "estopped" by judicial allegations which have neither deceived nor damaged anyone. Thomas v. Leonard Truck Lines, La.App., 7 So.2d 753, 756; Hearon v. Davis, La.App., 8 So.2d 787, 791.

Person pleading estoppel must have been misled to his injury by acts of omission or commission of him who is sought to be estopped. Selber Bros. v. Newstadt's Shoe Stores, 203 La. 316, 14 So.2d 10, 13.

Plea of estoppel lacks merit unless it appears that opposing litigant has been misled, deceived or has suffered damage from the allegations of pleader. Mounger v. Ferrell, La.App., 11 So.2d 56, 60.

Plea of "estoppel" was fatally defective where there was no statement that defendant relied on course alleged to have been taken by plaintiff. Sertic v. Roberts, 171 Or. 121, 136 P.2d 248, 251.

Statements in pleading in former action which are merely assertions of conclusion of law do not constitute "estoppel by pleading." Smith v. Saulsberry, 157 Wash. 270, 288 P. 927, 930.

Ratification Distinguished

The substance of "estoppel" is the inducement of another to act to his prejudice. The substance of "ratification" is confirmation after conduct. Citizens State Bank of Thedford v. United States Fidelity & Guaranty Co. of Baltimore, Md., 130 Neb. 603, 266 N.W. 81, 84, 103 A.L.R. 1401; Cudahy Bros. Co. v. West Michigan Dock & Market Corporation, 285 Mich. 18, 280 N.W. 93, 95; Gillihan v. Morguelan, 299 Ky. 671, 186 S.W.2d 807, 809.

By ratification party is bound because he intended to be, while under "estoppel" he is bound because other party will be prejudiced unless the law treats him as legally bound. Carlile v. Harris, Tex.Civ.App., 38 S.W.2d 622, 624; doctrine of ratification is based on fact of intention to carry out terms of certain agreement, while doctrine of estoppel is based on right of party to deny existence of agreement by reason of misleading acts. B. F. C. Morris Co. v. Mason, 171 Okl. 589, 39 P.2d 1, 3; Ratification requires no change of position or prejudice. Texas & Pacific Coal & Oil Co. v. Kirtley, Tex.Civ.App., 288 S.W. 619, 622. Ratification is retroactive and validates all of the act involved, while estoppel extends only to so much of the act as is affected by the conduct working the estoppel. Woodworth v. School Dist. No. 2, Stevens County, 92 Wash. 456, 159 P. 757, 760. Generally speaking, "ratification" applies to a formal declaration of the approval of another's act, whereas "estoppel" is where the party is bound by his own act, but the legal effect is the same. Zenos v. Britten-Cook Land & Live Stock Co., 75 Cal.App. 299, 242 P. 914, 917; Marion Sav. Bank v. Leahy, 200 Iowa 220, 204 N.W. 456, 458.

Recital

The theory of "estoppel by recital" is that holder of instrument is entitled to rely upon facts recited therein. Bloomfield Village Drain Dist. v. Keefe, C.C.A.Mich., 119 F.2d 157, 163, 165.

Res Judicata Distinguished

A prior judgment between same parties, which is not strictly res judicata because based upon different cause of action, operates as an "estoppel" only as to matters actually in issue or points controverted. Ætna Life Ins. Co. of Hartford, Conn., v. Martin, C.C.A.Ark., 108 F.2d 824, 827; Cunningham v. Oklahoma City, 188 Okl. 466, 110 P.2d 1102, 1104.

Doctrine that issues decided may not be drawn in question in any future action between same parties or their privies, whether cause of action in the two actions be identical or different, is based on "estoppel" rather than upon "res judicata". Norwood v. McDonald, 142 Ohio St. 299, 52 N.E.2d 67, 71, 74; In a later action upon a different cause of action a judgment operates as an "estoppel" only as to such issues in second action as were actually determined in the first action. Lorber v. Vista Irr. Dist., C. C.A.Cal., 127 F.2d 628, 634. The doctrine of "res judicata" is a branch of law of "estoppel". Krisher v. McAllister, 71 Ohio App. 58, 47 N.E.2d 817, 819; The plea of "res judicata" is in its nature an "estoppel" against the losing party from again litigating matters involved in previous action, but the plea does not have that effect as to matters transpiring subsequently. Fort Worth Stockyards Co. v. Brown, Tex.Civ.App., 161 S.W.2d 549, 555. Where a second action between same parties involves different cause of action, under doctrine of "res judicata", judgment in first action operates as an "estoppel" only as to those matters which were in issue and actually litigated. International Brotherhood of Electrical Workers v. Bridgeman, 179 Va. 533, 19 S.E.2d 667, 670.

Stare Decisis

The doctrine of "stare decisis" is but an application of the doctrine of "estoppel." Brown v. Rosenbaum, 175 Misc. 295, 23 N.Y.S.2d 161, 171; The doctrine of "stare decisis" involves no element of "estoppel". Joslin v. State, Tex.Civ.App., 146 S.W.2d 208, 212.

Suppression

The doctrine of "estoppel by concealment and suppression" applies only where there has been reduction to practice of invention. Bogoslowsky v. Huse, 142 F.2d 75, 76, 31 C.C.P.A. (Patents) 1034.

Waiver Distinguished

Waiver is intentional relinquishment of a known right. Globe Indemnity Co. v. Cohen, C.C.A.Pa., 106 F.2d 687, 691; Beatty v. Employers' Liability Assur. Corporation, 106 Vt. 25, 168 A. 919, 922; but may be more narrowly and accurately defined as intended giving up of known privilege or power. John Alt Furniture Co. v. Maryland Casualty Co., C.C.A.Mo., 88 F.2d 36, 41. Waiver is voluntary and intentional. Insurance Co. of North America v. Williams, 42 Ariz. 331, 26 P.2d 117, 119; Sentinel Fire Ins. Co. v. McRoberts, 50 Ga.App. 732, 179 S.E. 256. Waiver is voluntary surrender or relinquishment of some known right, benefit or advantage; estoppel is the inhibition to assert it. Benson v. Borden, 174 Md. 202, 198 A. 419, 427, 428; Johnston v. Columbian Nat. Life Ins. Co., 130 Me. 143, 154 A. 79, 80.

Acts, conduct or declarations insufficient to create a technical estoppel may create a waiver. Benson v. Borden, 174 Md. 202, 198 A. 419, 427, 428. Acts or conduct of only one of the parties is involved in waiver while an estoppel may arise where there is no intent to mislead. Beatty v. Employers' Liability Assur. Corporation, 106 Vt. 25, 168 A. 919, 922; Benson v. Borden, 174 Md. 202, 198 A. 419, 427, 428. Actual intent to abandon or surrender right is essential in waiver and immaterial in estoppel. Equitable Life Assur. Soc. of U. S. v. Pettid, 40 Ariz. 239, 11 P.2d 833, 838; Boyce v. Toke Point Oyster Co., Consol., 145 Or. 114, 25 P.2d 930; Actual or constructive fraudulent conduct is essential to estoppel but not to waiver. Insurance Co. of North America v. Williams, 42 Ariz. 331, 26 P.2d 117, 119; An act which operates to injury of other party is essential to estoppel whereas there may be a waiver, although the opposite party is beneficially affected. Sentinel Fire Ins. Co. v. McRoberts, 50 Ga.App. 732, 179 S.E. 256; Conduct or dealings with another by which other is induced to act or to forbear to act is basis of estoppel whereas waiver is intentional relinquishment of a known right. De Pasquale v. Union Indemnity Co., 50 R.I. 509, 149 A. 795; Reynolds v. Travelers' Ins. Co., 176 Wash. 36, 28 P.2d 310, 314. Estoppel results from an act which operates to the injury of the other party, while waiver may even affect him beneficially. City of Glendale v. Coquat, 46 Ariz. 478, 52 P.2d 1178, 1180, 102 A.L.R. 837. Fraud may be implied in estoppel but never in waiver. City of Glendale v. Coquat, 46 Ariz. 478, 52 P.2d 1178, 1180, 102 A.L.R. 837; Benson v. Borden, 174 Md. 202, 198 A. 419, 427, 428. Ignorance of party who invokes estoppel, representations or conduct of party estopped which misled, and an innocent and deleterious change of position in reliance upon such representations or conduct are essential to estoppel whereas waiver is an intentional relinquishment. Ellis v. Metropolitan Casualty Ins. Co. of New York, 187 S.C. 162, 197 S. E. 510; Knowledge and intention are both involved in waiver while an estoppel may arise where there is no intent to mislead. Benson v. Borden, 174 Md. 202, 198 A. 419, 427, 428; Beatty v. Employers' Liability Assur. Corporation, 106 Vt. 25, 168 A. 919, 922. Misleading of party to his injury or prejudice or into altered position is essential to estoppel but not to waiver. A-1 Cleaners & Dyers v. American Mut. Liability Ins. Co. of Boston, 307 Ill.App. 64, 30 N. E.2d 87, 88; Beatty v. Employers' Liability Assur. Corporation, 106 Vt. 25, 168 A. 919, 922. Waiver consists merely in renouncing some right or in ratifying what one might repudiate. Williams v. Anaconda Copper Mining Co., 96 Mont. 204, 29 P.2d 649, 651. Waiver depends on what one party intends to do, rather than upon what he induces his adversary to do, as in "estoppel". Nathan Miller, Inc., v. Northern Ins. Co. of New York, 3 Terry 523, 39 A.2d 23, 25; Wisdom v. Board of Sup'rs of Polk County, 236 Iowa 669, 19 N.W.2d 602, 610.

Implied waiver is kin to estoppel and rests on course of conduct evidencing intention not to insist on some performance due. Kansas City Life Ins. Co. v. Davis, C.C.A.Cal., 95 F.2d 952, 957. It does not necessarily include all elements of estoppel. Smith v. Coutant, 232 Iowa 887, 6 N.W. 2d 421, 425.

Legal effect of waiver and estoppel is the same. Woodmen of the World Life Ins. Soc. v. Greathouse, 242 Ala. 532, 7 So.2d 89, 91.

Technically, a distinction exists between "waiver" and "estoppel" but under insurance law, terms are used interchangeably. Boyle Road & Bridge Co. v. American Employers' Ins. Co. of Boston, Mass., 195 S.C. 397, 11 S.E.2d 438, 440, 441; The doctrine of waiver, as asserted against insurance companies to avoid the strict enforcement of conditions contained in their policies, is only another name for the doctrine of estoppel. Rushville Nat. Bank of Rushville v. State Life Ins. Co., 210 Ind. 492, 1 N.E.2d 445, 448. While there are distinguishing features between "waiver" and "estoppel," waiver belongs to family of estoppel and the terms are frequently used as meaning the same thing in law of insurance contracts. Ellis v. Metropolitan Casualty Ins. Co. of New York, 187 S.C. 162, 197 S.E. 510, 512.

Warranty

An estoppel based on principle of giving effect to manifest intent of grantor and of preventing grantor from derogating or destroying his own grant by subsequent act. Lewis v. King, 157 La. 718, 103 So. 19, 22; Jordan v. Marks, D.C.La., 55 F.Supp. 204, 209. See, also, Deed, Estoppel By.

For "Acquiescence, Estoppel By", "Admissions, Estoppel By", "Collateral Attack", "Concealment, Estoppel By," "Conduct, Estoppel By", "Contract, Estoppel By", "Deed, Estoppel By", "Election, Estoppel By", "Equitable Estoppel", "In Pais, Estoppel In", "Judgment, Estoppel By", "Judicial Estoppel," "Laches, Estoppel By," "Legal Estoppel," "Negligence, Estoppel By," "Promissory Estoppel," "Quasi Estoppel," "Record, Estoppel By," "Representation, Estoppel By," "Silence, Estoppel By" and "Verdict, Estoppel By," see those titles.

ESTOVERIA SUNT ARDENDI, ARANDI, CONSTRUENDI ET CLAUDENDI. 13 Coke, 68. Estovers are of fire-bote, plow-bote, house-bote, and hedge-bote.

ESTOVERIIS HABENDIS. A writ for a wife judicially separated to recover her alimony or estovers. Obsolete.

ESTOVERS. The right to use, during lease, whatever timber there may be on leased premises necessary to promote good husbandry. Hood v. Foster, 194 Miss. 812, 13 So.2d 652, 653.

An allowance made to a person out of an estate or other thing for his or her support, as for food and raiment.

An allowance (more commonly called "alimony") granted to a woman divorced *a mensa et thoro*, for her support out of her husband's estate. 1 Bl.Comm. 441.

The right or privilege which a tenant has to furnish himself with so much wood from the demised premises as may be sufficient or necessary for his fuel, fences, and other agricultural operations. 2 Bl.Comm. 35; Woodf.Landl. & Ten. 232; Zimmerman v. Shreeve, 59 Md. 363; Van Rensselaer v. Radcliff, 10 Wend. (N.Y.) 639, 25 Am.Dec. 582.

There is much learning in the old books relative to the creation, apportionment, suspension, and extinguishment of these rights, very little of which, however, is applicable to the condition of things in this country, except perhaps in New York, where the grants of the manor-lands have led to some litigation on the subject. Tayl.Landl. & T. § 220. See 4 Wash.R.P. 99; 7 Bing. 640; Richardson v. York, 14 Me. 221; Dalton v. Dalton, 42 N.C. 197; Loomis v. Wilbur, 5 Mas. 13, Fed.Cas.No.8,498.

Common of estovers, see Common.

ESTRAY. Cattle whose owner is unknown. 2 Kent, Comm. 359; Spelman. Any beast, not wild, found within any lordship, and not owned by any man. Cowell; 1 Bl.Comm. 297. These belonged to the lord of the soil. Britt. c. 17. An animal that has strayed away and lost itself; a wandering beast which no one seeks, follows, or claims. Campbell v. Hamilton, 42 N.D. 216, 172 N.W. 810.

Estray must be understood as denoting a wandering beast whose owner is unknown to the person who takes it up. An estray is an animal that has escaped from its owner, and wanders or strays about; usually defined, at common law, as a wandering animal whose owner is unknown. An animal cannot be an estray when on the range where it was raised, and permitted by its owner to run, and especially when the owner is known to the party who takes it up. The fact of its being breachy or vicious does not make it an estray. Kinney v. Roe, 70 Iowa, 509, 30 N.W. 776; Shepherd v. Hawley, 4 Or. 208; Lyman v.

Gipson, 18 Pick., Mass., 426; but see Worthington v. Brent, 69 Mo. 205; State v. Apel, 14 Tex. 431.

Heifers trespassing unattended upon adjoining ranch when taken up held "estrays" within Estray Act even if heifers' owners were known, since act covers animals belonging to known as well as to unknown owners. Soares v. Ghisletta, 1 Cal.App.2d 402, 36 P.2d 668, 669.

The term is used of flotsam at sea. 15 L.Q.R. 357.

ESTREAT, *v*. To take out a forfeited recognizance from the records of a court, and return it to the court of exchequer, to be prosecuted. See Estreat, *n*.

A forfeited recognizance taken out from among the other records for the purpose of being sent up to the exchequer, that the parties might be sued thereon, was said to be estreated. 4 Bl.Comm. 253. And see Louisiana Society v. Cage, 45 La.Ann. 1394, 14 So. 422.

There is no "estreat" or taking a judgment of forfeiture of a bail recognizance from the records and sending it up to the exchequer for suit thereon in Louisiana, since the same court which renders a judgment executes it, and the same officers who are charged with procuring it to be rendered are also charged with procuring it to be executed. State v. Johnson, 132 La. 11, 60 So. 702, 703.

ESTREAT, *n*. (From Lat. *extractum*.) In English law. A copy or extract from the book of estreats, that is, the rolls of any court, in which the amercements or fines, recognizances, etc., imposed or taken by that court upon or from the accused, are set down, and which are to be levied by the bailiff or other officer of the court. Cowell; Brown. A true copy or note of some original writing or record, and especially of fines and amercements imposed by a court, *extracted* from the record, and certified to a proper officer or officers authorized and required to collect them. Fitzh. N.B. 57, 76.

ESTRECIATUS. Straightened, as applied to roads. Cowell.

ESTREPE. To strip; to despoil; to lay waste; to comit waste upon an estate, as by cutting down trees, removing buildings, etc. To injure the value of a reversionary interest by stripping or spoiling the estate.

ESTREPEMENT. A species of aggravated waste, by stripping or devastating the land, to the injury of the reversioner, and especially pending a suit for possession.

ESTREPEMENT, WRIT OF. This was a common-law writ of waste, which lay in particular for the reversioner against the tenant for life, in respect of damage or injury to the land committed by the latter.

As it was only auxiliary to a real action for recovery of the land, and as equity afforded the same relief by injunction, the writ fell into disuse in England, and was abolished by 3 & 4 Will. IV. c. 27. In Pennsylvania, by statute, the remedy by estrepement is extended for the benefit of specified persons. See 10 Viner, Abr. 497; Woodf.Landl. & T. 447; Arch.Civ.Pl. 17; 7 Com.Dig. 659; Byrne v. Boyle, 37 Pa. 260.

ESTUARY, is that part of the mouth or lower course of a river flowing into the sea which is subject to tide; especially, an enlargement of a river channel toward its mouth in which the movement of the tide is very prominent. Alameda County v. Garrison, 108 Cal.App. 122, 291 P. 464, 466.

ET. And. The introductory word of several Latin and law French phrases formerly in common use.

ET ADJOURNATUR. And it is adjourned.

A phrase used in the old reports, where the argument of a cause was adjourned to another day, or where a second argument was had. 1 Keb. 692, 754, 773.

ET AL. An abbreviation for *et alii*, "and others." Mitchell v. Mason, 90 Fla. 192, 105 So. 404, 405. The singular is "et alius" (*q. v.*). It may also mean "and another" in the singular. Babb v. Dowdy, 229 Ky. 767, 17 S.W.2d 1014, 1016; Glen Falls Indemnity Co. v. Manning, La.App., 168 So. 787, 788.

Where the words "et al." are used in a judgment against defendants, the quoted words include all defendants. Williams v. Williams, 25 Tenn.App. 290, 156 S.W.2d 363, 369.

ET ALII È CONTRA. And others on the other side.

A phrase constantly used in the Year Books, in describing a joinder in issue. P. 1 Edw. II. *Prist; et alii è contra, et sic ad patriam:* ready; and others, *è contra,* and so to the country. T. 3 Edw. III. 4.

ET ALIUS. And another.

The abbreviation et al. (sometimes in the plural written *et als.*) is often affixed to the name of the person first mentioned, where there are several plaintiffs, grantors, persons addressed, etc. See In re McGovern's Estate, 77 Mont. 182, 250 P. 812, 815; Anderson v. Haas, 160 Ga. 420, 128 S.E. 178, 179; Conery v. Webb, 12 La.Ann. 282; Lyman v. Milton, 44 Cal. 630.

ET ALLOCATUR. And it is allowed.

ET CETERA (or ET CÆTERA). And others; and other things; and others of like character; and others of the like kind; and the rest; and so on; and so forth. Muir v. Kay, 66 Utah, 550, 244 P. 901, 904; Osterberg v. Section 30 Development Co., 160 Minn. 497, 200 N.W. 738, 739; State on Inf. Haw v. Three States Lumber Co., 274 Mo. 361, 202 S.W. 1083, 1084; Wagner v. Brady, 130 Tenn. 554, 171 S.W. 1179; Fleck v. Harmstad, 304 Pa. 302, 155 A. 875, 877, 77 A.L.R. 874. In its abbreviated form (*etc.*) this phrase is frequently affixed to one of a series of articles or names to show that others are intended to follow or understood to be included. So, after reciting the initiatory words of a set formula, or a clause already given in full, *etc.* is added, as an abbreviation, for the sake of convenience. And other things of like kind or purpose as compared with those immediately theretofore mentioned. Hisaw v. Ellison Ridge Consolidated School Dist., 189 Miss. 664, 198 So. 557, 558.

In its abbreviated form (etc.) this phrase means and other like purposes. Anderson & Kerr Drilling Co. v. Bruhlme er, Tex.Civ.App., 115 S.W.2d 1212, 1214; other things of like character. Lewis v. Ladner, 177 Miss. 473, 168 So. 281, 282; other things or the rest; and so forth; used to indicate others of a kind specified, Potter v. Borough of Metuchen, 108 N.J.L. 447, 155 A. 369, 370; others of the like kind; and the rest; and so on; and so forth, Forman v. Columbia Theater Co., 20 Wash.2d 685, 148 P.2d 951, 953. In such form it is frequently affixed to one of a series of articles or names to show that others are intended to follow or understood to be included so, after reciting the initiatory words of a set formula, or a clause already given in full, etc. is added, as an abbreviation, for the sake of convenience. See Lathers v. Keogh, 39 Hun, N.Y., 579; Morton v. Young, 173 Ky. 301, 190 S.W. 1090; Becker v. Hopper, 22 Wyo. 237, 138 P. 179, 180, Ann.Cas. 1916D, 1041.

ET DE CEO SE METTENT EN LE PAYS. L. Fr. And of this they put themselves upon the country.

ET DE HOC PONIT SE SUPER PATRIAM. And of this he puts himself upon the country. The formal conclusion of a common-law plea in bar by way of traverse. See 3 Bl.Comm. 313. The literal translation is retained in the modern form.

ET EI LEGITUR IN HÆC VERBA. L. Lat. And it is read to him in these words. Words formerly used in entering the prayer of oyer on record.

ET HABEAS IBI TUNC HOC BREVE. And have you then there this writ. The formal words directing the return of a writ. The literal translation is retained in the modern form of a considerable number of writs.

ET HABUIT. And he had it.

A common phrase in the Year Books, expressive of the allowance of an application or demand by a party. Parn. *demanda la view. Et habuit,* etc. M. 6 Edw. III. 49.

ET HOC PARATUS EST VERIFICARE. And this he is prepared to verify.

The Latin form of concluding a plea in confession and avoidance; that is, where the defendant has confessed all that the plaintiff has set forth, and has pleaded new matter in avoidance. 1 Salk. 2.

These words were used, when the pleadings were in Latin, at the conclusion of any pleading which contained new affirmative matter. They expressed the willingness or readiness of the party so pleading to establish by proof the matter alleged in his pleading. A pleading which concluded in that manner was technically said to "conclude with a verification," in contradistinction to a pleading which simply denied matter alleged by the opposite party, and which for that reason was said to "conclude to the country," because the party merely put himself upon the country, or left the matter to the jury. Brown.

ET HOC PETIT QUOD INQUIRATUR PER PATRIAM. And this he prays may be inquired of by the country. The conclusion of a plaintiff's pleading, tendering an issue to the country. 1 Salk. 6. Literally translated in the modern forms.

ET INDE PETIT JUDICIUM. And thereupon [or thereof] he prays judgment. A clause at the end of pleadings, praying the judgment of the court in favor of the party pleading. It occurs as early as the time of Bracton, and is literally translated in the modern forms. Bract. fol. 57*b*; Crabb, Eng. Law, 217.

ET INDE PRODUCIT SECTAM. And thereupon he brings suit. The Latin conclusion of a declaration, except against attorneys and other officers of the court. 3 Bl.Comm. 295.

ET MODO AD HUNC DIEM. Lat. And now at this day. This phrase was the formal beginning of an entry of appearance or of a continuance. The equivalent English words are still used in this connection.

ET NON. Lat. And not. A technical phrase in pleading, which introduces the negative averments of a special traverse. It has the same force and effect as the words *absque hoc,* "without this," and is occasionally used instead of the latter.

ET SEQ. An abbreviation for *et sequentes* (masculine and feminine plural) or *et sequentia* (neuter), "and the following." Thus a reference to "p. 1, et seq." means "page first and the following pages." Also abbreviated "et sqq.," which is preferred by some authorities for a reference to more than one following page.

ET SIC. And so. In the Latin forms of pleading these were the introductory words of a special conclusion to a plea in bar, the object being to render it positive and not argumentative; as *et sic nil debet.*

ET SIC AD JUDICIUM. And so to judgment. Yearb. T. 1 Edw. II. 10.

ET SIC AD PATRIAM. And so to the country. A phrase used in the Year Books, to record an issue to the country.

ET SIC FECIT. And he did so. Yearb. P. 9 Hen. VI. 17.

ET SIC PENDET. And so it hangs. A term used in the old reports to signify that a point was left undetermined. T. Raym. 168.

ET SIC ULTERIUS. And so on; and so further; and so forth. Fleta, lib. 2, c. 50, § 27.

ET UX. An abbreviation for *et uxor,*—"and wife." Where a grantor's wife joins him in the conveyance, it is sometimes expressed (in abstracts, etc.) to be by "A. B. *et ux.*"

ETCHING. Strictly, the art of using acid to bite a design on metal; in a broader sense, the word includes the sand-blast process, which uses no acid, but relies on abrasion by sand, emery, or a like substance. Graphic Arts Co. v. Photo-Chromotype Engraving Co., C.C.A.Pa., 231 F. 146, 148.

ETERNAL SECURITY. The doctrine of "eternal security" means that once one becomes a Christian or has been "regenerated" his future conduct, no matter what it may be, will not jeopardize his salvation. Ashman v. Studebaker, 115 Ind.App. 73, 56 N.E.2d 674, 678.

ETHICAL. "Of or relating to moral action, motive or character; as, ethical emotion; also, treating of moral feelings, duties or conduct; containing precepts of morality; moral"; and secondarily as "professionally right or befitting; conforming to professional standards of conduct." Kraushaar v. La Vin, 181 Misc. 508, 42 N.Y.S.2d 857, 859.

ETHICS. What is generally called the "ethics" of the profession is but consensus of expert opinion as to necessity of professional standards. Cherry v. Board of Regents of University of State of New York, 289 N.Y. 148, 44 N.E.2d 405, 412.

ETHICS, LEGAL. See Legal Ethics.

ETIQUETTE OF THE PROFESSION. The code of honor agreed on by mutual understanding and tacitly accepted by members of the legal profession, especially by the bar. Wharton.

EUM QUI NOCENTEM INFAMAT, NON EST ÆQUUM ET BONUM OB EAM REM CONDEMNARI; DELICTA ENIM NOCENTIUM NOTA ESSE OPORTET ET EXPEDIT. It is not just and proper that he who speaks ill of a bad man should be condemned on that account; for it is fitting and expedient that the crimes of bad men should be known. Dig. 47, 10, 17; 1 Bl.Comm. 125.

EUNDO, MORANDO, ET REDEUNDO. Lat. Going, remaining, and returning.

A person who is privileged from arrest (as a witness, legislator, etc.) is generally so privileged *eundo, morando, et redeundo;* that is, on his way to the place where his duties are to be performed, while he remains there, and on his return journey.

EUNDO ET REDEUNDO. Lat. In going and returning. Applied to vessels. 3 C.Rob.Adm. 141.

EUNOMY. Equal laws and a well-adjusted constitution of government.

EUNUCH. A male of the human species who has been castrated. See Domat. liv. prél. tit. 2, § 1, n. 10. Eckert v. Van Pelt, 69 Kan. 357, 76 P. 909, 66 L.R.A. 266.

EUTHANASIA. The act or practice of painlessly putting to death persons suffering from incurable and distressing disease. An easy or agreeable death.

EVASIO. Lat. In old practice. An escape from prison or custody. Reg. Orig. 312.

EVASION. An act of eluding or avoiding, or avoidance by artifice. City of Wink v. Griffith Amusement Co., 129 Tex. 40, 100 S.W.2d 695, 701.

A subtle endeavoring to set aside truth or to escape the punishment of the law.

Thus, if one person says to another that he will not strike him, but will give him a pot of ale to strike first, and, accordingly, the latter strikes, the returning the blow is punishable; and, if the person first striking is killed, it it is murder, for no man shall evade the justice of the law by such a pretense. 1 Hawk.P.C. 81; Bac.Abr. *Fraud,* A. So no one may plead ignorance of the law to evade it. Jacob.

Artifice or cunning is implicit in the term as applied to contest between citizen and government over taxation. Clapp v. Heiner, C.C.A.Pa., 51 F.2d 224, 225.

In a general way the words "suppression," "evasion," and "concealment" mean to avoid by some device or strategy or the concealment or intentional withholding some fact which ought in good faith to be communicated. Murray v. Brotherhood of American Yeomen, 180 Iowa, 626, 163 N.W. 421, 428.

When an act is condemned as an "evasion," what is meant is that it is on the wrong side of the line indicated by the policy if not by the mere letter of the law. Wyndmoor Building & Loan Ass'n v. Power Building & Loan Ass'n, Pa.Super., 121 Pa.Super. 236, 183 A. 367, 369; Bullen v. State of Wisconsin, Wis., 240 U.S. 625, 36 S.Ct. 473, 474, 60 L.Ed. 830.

EVASIVE. Tending or seeking to evade; elusive; shifting; as an *evasive* argument or plea.

Deprivation of lessee of free enjoyment of premises, and, if it does so, deprivation need not be permanent. Title & Trust Co. v. Durkheimer Inv. Co., 155 Or. 427, 63 P.2d 909.

EVASIVE ANSWER. One which consists in refusing either to admit or to deny a matter as to which the defendant is necessarily presumed to have knowledge.

Hence, where a defendant is alleged to be a corporation, an answer declining, for want of sufficient information, either to admit or to deny such an averment would be evasive. Raleigh & Gaston Ry. Co. v. Pullman Co., 122 Ga. 700, 50 S.E. 1008. But an answer distinctly denying an allegation that the defendant is a corporation, although it may be false, is not evasive. Gaynor v. Travelers' Ins. Co., 12 Ga.App. 601, 77 S.E. 1072, 1073.

EVE. The period immediately preceding an important event. Jarvis v. Jarvis, 286 Ill. 478, 122 N.E. 121, 123.

EVEN. Although; if. May v. Missouri Pac. R. Co., 143 Ark. 75, 219 S.W. 756, 757.

EVENING. The closing part of the day and beginning of the night; in a strict sense, from sunset till dark; in common speech, the latter part of the day and the earlier part of the night, until bedtime. Golay v. Stoddard, 60 Idaho 168, 89 P. 2d 1002, 1005. The period between sunset or the evening meal and ordinary bedtime. City of Albany v. Black, 216 Ala. 4, 112 So. 433; State v. Foley, 89 Vt. 193, 94 A. 841, 842.

EVENINGS. In old English law. The delivery at even or night of a certain portion of grass, or corn, etc., to a customary tenant, who performs the service of cutting, mowing, or reaping for his lord, given him as a gratuity or encouragement. Kennett, Gloss.

EVENT. The consequence of anything, the issue, conclusion, end; that in which an action, operation, or series of operations, terminates. Geis v. Geis, 125 Neb. 394, 250 N.W. 252; Brewer v. Ash Grove Lime & Portland Cement Co., 223 Mo.App. 983, 25 S.W.2d 1086, 1088.

Anything that happens or comes to pass as distinguished from a thing that exists, Quinn v. Streeter, Sup., 175 Misc. 932, 24 N.Y.S.2d 916, 920. That which comes, arrives, or happens, especially an incident which is important or remarkable, Schulz v. Great Atlantic & Pacific Tea Co., 331 Mo. 616, 56 S.W.2d 126; the consequence, outcome, sequel, or end effected by prior operation of medium or contributing force or agency referred to as the "means" or "cause", Toups v. Penn Mut. Life Ins. Co., D.C.La., 49 F.Supp. 348, 349; the culmination or end that means may have produced or brought about. Whatcott v. Continental Casualty Co., 85 Utah 406, 39 P.2d 733, 736; Sentinel Life Ins. Co. v. Blackmer, C.C.A.Colo., 77 F.2d 347, 350.

An event may be injury itself rather than means producing it. Juhl v. Hussman-Ligonier Co., Mo.App., 146 S.W.2d 106, 108. An event need not necessarily be a cause, but may be and generally is a result. Guillod v. Kansas City Power & Light Co., 224 Mo.App. 382, 18 S.W.2d 97, 100.

The word includes all of steps or connected incidents from first cause to final result, and may include both cause and effect. Rinehart v. F. M. Stamper Co., 227 Mo.App. 653, 55 S.W.2d 729. The word is broad enough to include an omission. Texas Cities Gas Co. v. Dickens, Tex.Civ. App., 156 S.W.2d 1010, 1016.

The "making of a contract" is an "event". Brown v. Oneida Knitting Mills, 226 Wis. 662, 277 N.W. 653, 655.

In reference to judicial and quasi judicial proceedings, "event" means the conclusion, end, or final outcome or result of a litigation; as, in the phrase "abide the event," speaking of costs or of an agreement that one suit shall be governed by the determination in another. Reeves v. McGregor, 9 Adol. & El. 576; Benjamin v. Ver Nooy, 168 N.Y. 578, 61 N.E. 971; Gordon v. Krellman, 217 App.Div. 477, 216 N.Y.S. 778, 779.

Where costs are awarded to an appellant to abide the event, the "event" which determines whether the appellant is entitled to an award of costs of appeal is his success in obtaining a judgment on the merits on the retrial. Commercial Sealeaf Co. v. Purepac Corporation, 169 Misc. 133, 7 N.Y.S.2d 146, 148.

EVENT OF ANY SUIT. Means legal event of any suit. Drainage Dist. No. 1 of Lincoln County v. Kirkpatrick-Pettis Co., 140 Neb. 530, 300 N.W. 582, 587; Geis v. Geis, 125 Neb. 394, 250 N.W. 252.

EVENTUS EST QUI EX CAUSÂ SEQUITUR; ET DICITUR EVENTUS QUIA EX CAUSIS EVENIT. 9 Coke, 81. An event is that which follows from the cause, and is called an "event" because it eventuates from causes.

EVENTUS VARIOS RES NOVA SEMPER HABET. Co. Litt. 379. A new matter always produces various events.

EVERY. Each one of all; all the separate individuals who constitute the whole, regarded one by one. Smith v. Hall, 217 Ky. 615, 290 S.W. 480, 482; Salo v. Pacific Coast Casualty Co., 95 Wash. 109, 163 P. 384, 385, L.R.A.1917D, 613. The term is sometimes equivalent to "all"; Erskine v. Pyle, 51 S.D. 262, 213 N.W. 500, 502; and sometimes to "each"; Miller v. Rodd, 285 Pa. 16, 131 A. 482, 483.

EVERY CONTRACT OF HIRING, VERBAL, WRITTEN OR IMPLIED. Means wherever and by whomsoever made. De Gray v. Miller Bros. Const. Co., 106 Vt. 259, 173 A. 556, 562.

EVERY CORPORATION. Statute providing that books of "every corporation" shall be open to inspection of shareholders, held applicable to foreign corporation doing business within state. Getridge v. State Capital Co., 129 Cal.App. 86, 18 P. 2d 375, 376.

EVERY MAN MUST BE TAKEN TO CONTEMPLATE THE PROBABLE CONSEQUENCES OF THE ACT HE DOES. Lord Ellenborough, 9 East, 277. A fundamental maxim in the law of evidence. Best, Pres. § 16; 1 Phil.Ev. 444. (Every man is presumed to intend the natural and probable consequences of his own voluntary acts. 1 Greenl.Evid. § 18; 9 B. & C. 643; 3 Maule & S. 11; Webb, Poll.Torts 35.)

EVERY OTHER THING. This phrase, as used in requiring employer to furnish safe place of employment and to do "every other thing" reasonably necessary to protect employees, relates to things of same kind that employer must necessarily do in making place safe. Northwestern Casualty & Surety Co. v. Industrial Commission, 194 Wis. 337, 216 N.W. 485, 486.

EVERY OWNER. As used in law making "every owner" of a motor vehicle liable for personal injuries in certain circumstances include a municipality. Kelly v. City of Niagara Falls, 131 Misc. 934, 229 N.Y.S. 328, 331.

EVERY PART. As used in charge on caveat to probate of will, the signature is included in "every part" of will. Dulin v. Dulin, 197 N.C. 215, 148 S.E. 175, 178.

EVERY PERSON. Statute making it misdemeanor for "every person" to sell appointments to public office applies to all persons whether public officials or not. Smalley v. State, 75 Okl.Cr. 10, 127 P.2d 869, 870.

Statute making it duty of "every person" to pay taxes without demand includes receivers. Hood v. Bond, 42 N.M. 295, 77 P.2d 180, 188.

Statute providing for arrest of every person in city engaged in violating law or ordinance includes female offenders. City of Janesville v. Tweedell, 217 Wis. 395, 258 N.W. 437.

Where a law specifically excludes any person engaged in certain transportation from definition of "contract hauler" and defines "for hire carrier" to include "every person," except "certified operator" and "contract hauler," "every person" includes those engaged in such transportation. State ex rel. Scott v. Superior Court for Thurston County, 173 Wash. 547, 24 P.2d 87.

EVERY PERSON, FIRM OR CORPORATION. City ordinance providing "every person, firm or corporation" should pay gasoline tax held to include receivers. Kansas City, Mo. v. Johnson, C. C.A.Mo., 70 F.2d 360, 361.

EVERY RESIDENT OF THIS STATE. As used in constitutional provision partially exempting from taxation those honorably discharged from military service applies to every person who fulfills requirements of provision regardless of sex. Lockhart v. Wolden, 17 Cal.2d 628, 111 P.2d 319, 320.

EVERY RIGHT, TITLE, INTEREST OR THING. Tender of "every right, title, interest or thing" received is tender of everything received in action to rescind land contract. Mathews v. Tannenbaum, 139 Cal.App. 500, 34 P.2d 233, 235.

EVERY STOCK CORPORATION. Statute making stockholders of "every stock corporation" liable for employees' services refers to domestic stock corporations only. Bogardus v. Fitzpatrick, 139 Misc. 533, 247 N.Y.S. 692, 693.

EVERY SUCH PROVISION. In statute providing that devise for jointure of wife shall bar her dower and that every such provision by will shall be taken as intended in lieu of dower, "every such provision" means devise for jointure of wife. Shackelford v. Shackelford, 181 Va. 869, 27 S.E.2d 354, 359.

EVES-DROPPERS. See Eaves-Droppers.

EVICT. Civil law. To recover anything from a person by virtue of the judgment of a court or judicial sentence.

Common law. To dispossess, or turn out of the possession of lands by process of law. Also to recover land by judgment at law. "If the land is *evicted,* no rent shall be paid." 10 Coke, 128*a*.

The term "evicted," means deprivation by one of office, or of salary attached thereto, to which another is, or may be, entitled. The term "evicted" properly applies only to realty and has been used to describe inability to get promised possession, and also, as deprivation of the possession of lands and tenements. Hawkins v. Voisine, 292 Mich. 357, 290 N.W. 827, 828.

To "evict" a tenant is to deprive him of possession of the leased premises or disturb him in their beneficial enjoyment so as to cause tenant to abandon the premises. Estes v. Gatliff, 291 Ky. 93, 163 S.W.2d 273, 276.

EVICTION. Dispossession by process of law; the act of depriving a person of the possession of lands which he has held, in pursuance of the judgment of a court. Reasoner v. Edmundson, 5 Ind. 395; Cowdrey v. Coit, 44 N.Y. 392, 4 Am.Rep. 690; Home Life Ins. Co. v. Sherman, 46 N.Y. 372.

Originally and technically, the dispossession must be by judgment of law; if otherwise, it was an *ouster*; Webb v. Alexander, 7 Wend.N.Y. 285; but the necessity of legal process was long ago abandoned in England; 4 Term 617; and in this country also it is settled that there need not be legal process; Green v. Irving, 54 Miss. 450, 28 Am.Rep. 360; Thomas v. Becker, 190 Iowa 237, 180 N.W. 285, 286. Any actual entry and dispossession, adversely and lawfully made under paramount title, will be an eviction. Rawle, Cov. § 133; Gallison v. Downing, 244 Mass. 33, 138 N.E. 315, 318.

In a more popular sense, the term denotes turning a tenant of land out of possession, either by re-entry or by legal proceedings, such as an action of ejectment. Sweet.

By a loose extension, the term is sometimes applied to the ousting of a person from the possession of chattels; but, properly, it applies only to realty.

A wrongful act upon the part of the landlord is involved in eviction. Cerruti v. Burdick, 130 Conn. 284, 33 A.2d 333, 335.

An entry under paramount title, so as to interfere with the rights of the grantee, is implied in eviction. The object of the party making the entry is immaterial, whether it be to take all or a part of the land itself or merely an incorporeal right. Phrases equivalent in meaning are "ouster by paramount title," "entry and disturbance," "possession under an elder title," and the like. Mitchell v. Warner, 5 Conn. 497.

An "eviction by title paramount" arises when a third person establishes title to demised premises superior to that of landlord, and by virtue of that title gains possession. John R. Thompson Co. v. Northwestern Mut. Life Ins. Co., D.C.Ohio, 31 F.Supp. 399, 400.

Any act of landlord which deprives tenant of beneficial enjoyment of premises. Adler v. Sklaroff, 154 Pa.Super. 444, 36 A.2d 231, 233.

Any wrong of lessor which results in substantial interference with lessee's rights. Harrison v. Fregger, 88 Mont. 448, 294 P. 372, 373.

Deprivation of lessee of possession of premises or disturbance of lessee in beneficial enjoyment so as to cause tenant to abandon the premises. Estes v. Gatliff, 291 Ky. 93, 163 S.W.2d 273, 276.

Dispossession of tenant by landlord. Lesher v. Louisville Gas & Electric Co., D.C.Ky., 49 F.Supp. 88, 89, 90.

Dispossession under judgment, though it need not be by force of process under judgment. Edgemont Coal Co. v. Asher, D.C.Ky., 298 F. 1000; Walker v. Robinson, 163 Ky. 618, 174 S.W. 503, 505.

Entry on and taking possession of any part of demised premises by landlord during continuance of lease and exclusion of tenant. Landon v. Hill, 136 Cal.App. 560, 29 P.2d 281, 282.

Formerly the word was used to denote an expulsion by the assertion of a paramount title or by process of law. Port Utilities Commission of Charleston v. Marine Oil Co., 173 S.C. 345, 175 S.E. 818.

Intentional exclusion of lessee from some part of leased premises. Gorfinkle v. Abrams, 263 Mass. 569, 161 N.E. 795.

Interference with tenant's beneficial enjoyment of premises. Peale v. Tvete, 172 Wash. 296, 20 P.2d 12, 13; Kahn v. Bancamerica-Blair Corporation, 327 Pa. 209, 193 A. 905, 906.

Manual or physical explusion or exclusion from demised premises, or any part thereof is unnecessary to constitute eviction. Kennerly v. B. F. Avery & Sons Plow Co., Tex. Civ.App., 300 S.W. 159, 161.

Originally an eviction was understood to be a dispossession of the tenant by some act of his landlord or the failure of his title. Of later years it has come to include any wrongful act of the landlord which may result in an interference with the tenant's possession in whole or in part. The act may be one of omission as well as one of commission. Holden v. Tidwell, 37 Okl. 553, 133 P. 54, 56, 49 L.R.A.,N.S., 369.

Something of a grave and permanent character by landlord or those acting under his authority with intent and effect to deprive tenant of use, occupation, and enjoyment of premises or part thereof, or the establishment or assertion against tenant of a title paramount to the landlord. Blomberg v. Evans, 194 N.C. 113, 138 S.E. 593, 594, 53 A.L.R. 686; Aguglia v. Cavicchia, 229 Mass. 263, 118 N.E. 283, 284, L.R.A.1918C, 59; Waldorf System v. Dawson, 49 R.I. 57, 139 A. 789, 790; Automobile Supply Co. v. Scene-in-Action Corporation, 340 Ill. 196, 172 N.E. 35, 37, 69 A.L.R. 1085.

When it would be useless for covenantee to attempt to maintain his title, as where holder of superior title has taken actual possession or threatens suit, an eviction occurs in legal contemplation. Love v. Minerva Petroleum Corporation, Tex.Civ.App., 105 S.W.2d 892, 894.

When tenant's possession or enjoyment of premises is interfered with by a third person not acting by landlord's authority, or consent, there is no "eviction". Smith v. Nortz Lumber Co., N.D., 72 N.D. 353, 7 N.W.2d 435, 437; Prospect Point Land Improvement Co. v. Jackson, 109 N.J.L. 385, 162 A. 576, 577.

Civil Law

The abandonment which one is obliged to make of a thing, in pursuance of a sentence by which he is condemned to do so. Poth.Contr.Sale, pt. 2, c. 1, § 2, art. 1, no. 83. The abandonment which a buyer is compelled to make of a thing purchased, in pursuance of a judicial sentence.

Eviction is the loss suffered by the buyer of the totality of the thing sold, or of a part thereof, occasioned by the right or claims of a third person. Civil Code La. art. 2500.

For "Actual Eviction," "Constructive Eviction," "Partial Eviction," and "Total Eviction," see those titles.

EVIDENCE. Any species of proof, or probative matter, legally presented at the trial of an issue, by the act of the parties and through the medium of witnesses, records, documents, concrete objects, etc., for the purpose of inducing belief in the minds of the court or jury as to their contention. Hotchkiss v. Newton, 10 Ga. 567; O'Brien v. State, 69 Neb. 691, 96 N.W. 650; Hubbell v. U. S., 15 Ct.Cl. 606; McWilliams v. Rodgers, 56 Ala. 93.

All circumstances in case, including opportunity of witnesses for observation, interest in case, demeanor on stand, and other circumstances. Auschwitz v. Wabash Ry. Co., 346 Ill. 190, 178 N.E. 403, 410; all kinds of proof, Kneezle v. Scott County Milling Co., Mo.App., 113 S.W.2d 817, 822.

All the means by which any alleged matter of fact, the truth of which is submitted to investigation, is established or disproved. 1 Greenl.Ev. c. 1, § 1; Bednarik v. Bednarik, 18 N.J.Misc. 633, 16 A.2d 80, 89; Latikos v. State, 17 Ala.App. 592, 88 So. 45, 47.

Any matter of fact, the effect, tendency, or design of which is to produce in the mind a persuasion of the existence or nonexistence of some matter of fact. State v. Heavener, 146 S.C. 138, 143 S.E. 674, 676.

Anything perceptible to the five senses constituting "evidence," when submitted to court or jury, if competent. In re Fisher's Estate, 47 Idaho 668, 279 P. 291, 293.

As a part of procedure "evidence" signifies those rules of law whereby it is determined what testimony should be admitted and what should be rejected in each case, and what is the weight to be given to the testimony admitted. Kellman v. Stoltz, D.C.Iowa, 1 F.R.D. 726, 728.

Competent evidence is meant by statute requiring trial court to hear evidence on controverted applications for change of venue. State ex rel. Kansas City Public Service Co. v. Waltner, 350 Mo. 1021, 169 S.W.2d 697, 703.

Documents and other exhibits which may properly be submitted to jury are evidence. Madison v. State, 138 Fla. 467, 189 So. 832, 835.

Evidence legally and properly introduced is meant by "evidence". Young v. Industrial Accident Commission, 38 Cal.App.2d 250, 100 P.2d 1062, 1066.

Exhibits are evidence, Worland v. McGill, 26 Ohio App. 442, 160 N.E. 478, 480.

Facts admitted upon trial of cause become "evidence". American Extension School of Law v. Ragland, 232 Mo.App. 763, 112 S.W.2d 110, 113.

Facts judicially noticed are equivalent to "evidence". Zickefoose v. Thompson, 347 Mo. 579, 148 S.W.2d 784, 792.

Inference arising under doctrine of "res ipsa loquitur" is "evidence". Druzanich v. Criley, 19 Cal.2d 439, 122 P.2d 53, 56.

Medical testimony is "evidence". Farmer Motor Co. v. Smith, 253 Ky. 151, 69 S.W.2d 1.

Opinion of expert is evidence which is to be weighed and considered like any other evidence. Southern California Edison Co. v. Gemmill, 30 Cal.App.2d 23, 85 P.2d 500, 502.

Reasonable inferences drawn from affirmative facts proven are "evidence". Hepp v. Quickel Auto & Supply Co., 37 N.M. 525, 25 P.2d 197.

Something of substance and relevant consequence. Broadway & Fourth Ave. Realty Co. v. Metcalfe, 230 Ky. 800, 20 S.W.2d 988, 990.

Substantial evidence is meant by word "evidence", Indianapolis Power & Light Co. v. National Labor Relations Board, C.C.A.7, 122 F.2d 757, 761; Gelb v. Federal Trade Commission, C.C.A.2, 144 F.2d 580, 582.

Such kinds of proof as may be legally presented at a trial, by the act of the parties, and through the aid of such concrete facts as witnesses, records or other documents.

That which demonstrates, makes clear, or ascertains the truth of the very fact or point in issue, either on the one side or on the other. Leonard v. State, 100 Ohio St. 456, 127 N.E. 464, 466; Lynch v. Rosenberger, 121 Kan. 601, 249 P. 682, 683, 60 A.L.R. 376.

That which furnishes or tends to furnish proof. It is that which brings to the mind a just conviction of the truth or falsehood of any substantive proposition which is asserted or denied. Wong Yee Toon v. Stump, C.C.A.Md., 233 F. 194, 198; Ex parte Lam Pui, D.C.N.C., 217 F. 456, 467.

That which is legally submitted to a jury, to enable them to decide upon the questions in dispute or issue, as pointed out by the pleadings, and distinguished from all comment and argument. 1 Starkie, Ev. pt. 1, § 3.

That which tends to produce conviction in the mind as to existence of a fact. Magazine v. Shull, 116 Ind.App. 79, 60 N.E.2d 611, 613.

That which tends to prove or disprove any matter in question, or to influence the belief respecting it. Belief is produced by the consideration of something presented to the mind. The matter thus presented, in whatever shape it may come, and through whatever material organ it is derived, is evidence. Parker, Lectures on Medical Jurisprudence, in Dartmouth College.

The means sanctioned by law of ascertaining in a judicial proceeding the truth respecting a question of fact. Cal.Code Civ.Proc. § 1823.

The word signifies, in its original sense, the state of being evident, i. e., plain, apparent or notorious. But by an almost peculiar inflection of our language, it is applied to that which tends to render evident or to generate proof. Best, Ev. §§ 10, 11; Dupont v. Pelletier, 120 Me. 114, 113 A. 11, 12.

What transpires in jury's presence and what is necessarily obvious to them is "evidence" if relevant and unprejudicial. Williamson v. Derry Electric Co., 89 N.H. 216, 196 A. 265 266.

Whatever is received to establish or disprove an alleged fact. In re Seigle's Estate, 26 N.Y.S.2d 410, 413, 176 Misc. 15.

Whatever may be given to the jury as tending to prove a case; includes testimony of witnesses, documents, admissions of parties, etc. Harris v. Tomlinson, 130 Ind. 426, 30 N.E. 214; Carroll v. Bancker, 43 La.Ann. 1078, 10 So. 192.

Whatever may properly be submitted to a court or jury to elucidate an issue or prove a case. Superior Meat Products v. Holloway, 113 Ind.App. 320, 48 N.E.2d 83, 86.

Within prohibition against requiring an accused to give evidence against himself, "evidence" means evidence by accused out of court as well as in court. State v. Bates, 187 Miss. 172, 192 So. 832, 835.

Evidence may be false and of no probative value and so it differs from proof. State v. Howard, 162 La. 719, 111 So. 72, 75.

To "evidence" means to attest, prove, show clearly, make plain. Indiana Harbor Belt R. Co. v. Jacob Stern & Sons, D.C.Ill., 37 F.Supp. 690, 691.

For Presumption as evidence, see Presumption; Proof and evidence distinguished, see Proof; Testimony as synonymous or distinguishable, see Testimony; View as evidence, see View.

For "Adminicular Evidence", "Aliunde", "Best Evidence", "Beyond Reasonable Doubt", "Circumstantial Evidence", "Competent Evidence", "Corroborating Evidence", "Cumulative Evidence", "Demonstrative Evidence", "Direct Evidence", "Documentary Evidence," "Expert Evidence", "Extrajudicial Evidence", "Extraneous Evidence," "Extrinsic Evidence", "Fact", "Fair Preponderance", "Hearsay", "Incompetent Evidence", "Inculpatory", "Indirect Evidence", "Indispensable Evidence", "Inference", "Intrinsic Evidence", "Legal Evidence", "Material Evidence", "Mathematical Evidence", "Moral Evidence," "Newly-Discovered Evidence", "Opinion Evidence", "Oral Evidence", "Original Evidence", "Parol Evidence", "Partial Evidence," "Preponderance," "Presumptive Evidence," "Prima Facie Evidence," "Primary Evidence," "Probable Evidence," "Probative," "Probative Facts," "Proof," "Proper Evidence," "Real Evidence," "Rebutting Evidence," "Relevancy," "Satisfactory Evidence," "Scintilla of Evidence," "Second-Hand Evidence," "Secondary Evidence," "State's Evidence," "Substantive Evidence," "Substitutionary Evidence," "Traditionary Evidence," and "Weight of Evidence," see those titles.

EVIDENCE BY INSPECTION is such evidence as is addressed directly to the senses without intervention of testimony. Kabase v. State, 31 Ala. App. 77, 12 So.2d 758, 764.

EVIDENCE COMPLETED. Means that both sides have offered testimony and rested, or that plaintiff has rested and defendant has made motion for finding on plaintiff's case and stands on motion and declines to offer evidence. Merriam v. Sugrue, D.C.Mun.App., 41 A.2d 166, 167.

EVIDENCE, LAW OF. The aggregate of rules and principles regulating the admissibility, relevancy, and weight and sufficiency of evidence in legal proceedings. See Ballinger's Ann.Codes & St.Or.1901, § 678, Code 1930, § 9-102.

EVIDENCE OF DEBT. A term applied to written instruments or securities for the payment of money, importing on their face the existence of a debt. 1 Rev.St.N.Y. p. 599, § 55.

EVIDENCE OF INSURABILITY SATISFACTORY TO COMPANY. Means evidence which would satisfy a reasonable person experienced in the life insurance business that insured was in an insurable condition. Bowie v. Bankers Life Co., C.C.A.Colo., 105 F.2d 806, 808.

EVIDENCE OF TITLE. A deed or other document establishing the title to property, especially real estate.

EVIDENCE PROPER is something capable of being weighed in scales of reason and compared and estimated with other matter of the probative sort. Neely v. Provident Life & Accident Ins. Co. of Chattanooga, Tenn., 322 Pa. 417, 185 A. 784, 788.

EVIDENCE REASONABLY TENDING TO SUPPORT VERDICT. Means evidence that is competent, relevant, and material, and which to rational and impartial mind naturally leads, or involuntarily tends to lead, to conclusion for which there is valid, just, and substantial reason. Kelly v. Oliver Farm Equipment Sales Co., 169 Okl. 269, 36 P.2d 888, 891.

EVIDENCE SUFFICIENT IN LAW. Substantial evidence. Almon v. Morgan County, 245 Ala. 241, 16 So.2d 511, 516.

EVIDENCE TO SUPPORT FINDINGS. In action to review an order of the Unemployment Compensation Commission "evidence" to support findings meant substantial evidence or such relevant evidence as a reasonable mind might accept as adequate to support a conclusion and enough to justify, if the trial were to a jury, a refusal to direct a verdict when the conclusion sought to be drawn from it is one of fact for jury. Jordan v. Craighead, 114 Mont. 337, 136 P.2d 526, 528.

EVIDENCE TO SUPPORT THE VERDICT. Means some legal evidence tending to prove every material fact in issue as to which the party in whose favor the verdict was rendered had the burden of proof. Nicolai-Neppach Co. v. Smith, 154 Or. 450, 58 P.2d 1016, 1024, 107 A.L.R. 1124.

EVIDENT. Clear to the understanding and satisfactory to the judgment; manifest; plain; obvious; conclusive. Russell v. State, 71 Fla. 236, 71 So. 27, 28. Noticeable; apparent to observation. Hamill v. Joseph Schlitz Brewing Co., 165 Iowa 266, 143 N.W. 99, 107. That is "evident" that suggests more than a mental process, but no difficulty in seeing that the thing is true. Bremner v. Marc Eidlitz & Son, 118 Conn. 666, 174 A. 172, 174.

A constitutional provision forbidding bail in capital cases when the proof is "evident," means that, if the evidence is such as to lead a dispassionate mind to the conclusion that the accused is guilty, and that if the law is properly administered a conviction would be had of a capital offense, bail should be denied. Ex parte Vermillion, 102 Tex.Cr.R. 590, 280 S.W. 771; Ex parte Bates, 90 Tex.Cr.R. 406, 235 S.W. 879, 880; Ex parte Dumas, 110 Tex.Cr.R. 1, 7 S.W.2d 90, 91.

Under constitutional provision that all prisoners shall be bailable unless for capital offenses when the proof is evident, the word "evident" means that the accused, with a cool and deliberate mind and formed design, did maliciously kill another, and that a dispassionate jury would not only convict him, but would also assess the death penalty. Ex parte Redding, 147 Tex.Cr.R. 434, 180 S.W.2d 951, 952; Ex parte Shults, 127 Tex.Cr.R. 484, 77 S.W.2d 877.

—Proof Evident. See Proof.

EVIDENTIA. L. Evidence. See Preuve.

EVIDENTIARY. Having the quality of evidence; constituting evidence; evidencing. A term introduced by Bentham, and, from its convenience, adopted by other writers.

EVIDENTIARY FACTS. Facts necessary to prove the essential or ultimate fact. People ex rel. Hudson & M. R. Co. v. Sexton, Sup., 44 N.Y. S.2d 884, 885. Facts which furnish evidence of existence of some other fact. General Tire & Rubber Co. v. Cooper, 176 Miss. 491, 165 So. 420, 421; proofs and testimony. In re Britton's Will, 167 Misc. 747, 4 N.Y.S.2d 715, 719; such facts must be found from testimony and other evidence. Texas Employers Ins. Ass'n v. Reed, Tex.Civ.App., 150 S.W.2d 858, 862.

Those which have a legitimate bearing on the matter or question in issue and which are directly (not inferentially) established by the evidence in the case. Woodfill v. Patton, 76 Ind. 579, 40 Am.Rep. 269. Facts which can be directly established by testimony or evidence;—distinguished from "ultimate facts." Real Estate Title, Ins. & Trust Co. v. Lederer, D.C.Pa., 229 F. 799, 804.

EVIDENTLY. Means in an evident manner, perceptibly, clearly, obviously, plainly. It is employed to express the idea of full-proof conviction. Tennes v. Tennes, 320 Ill.App. 19, 50 N.E.2d 132, 139.

EVIL. It is an "evil" within rule that either means or end of conspiracy must be evil, to frustrate or impede a government function, whether that function is performed under a constitutional or an unconstitutional law. U. S. v. Rhoads, D.C. D.C., 48 F.Supp. 175, 176.

EVIL REPUTATION. Character imputed to person in community is generally bad. People v. Pieri, 269 N.Y. 315, 199 N.E. 495, 497.

EVOCATION. In French law. The withdrawal of a cause from the cognizance of an inferior court, and bringing it before another court or judge. In some respects this process resembles the proceedings upon *certiorari.*

EVOLUTION. Every useful art has its technique which is practiced by those who are skilled in it, and which is broadened in its usefulness thereto from precedent to precedent. This is the process of "evolution"—a phenomenon in which the expectable follows the expectable. Less Car Load Lots Co. v. Pennsylvania R. Co., D.C.N.Y., 10 F. Supp. 642, 648.

EVOLVED. Means "developed" and may apply to any person attaining highly developed mental training and experience in arts and sciences and profession of teaching, medicine, or law. In re Carpenter's Estate, 163 Misc. 474, 297 N.Y.S. 649, 654.

EWAGE. (L. Fr. *Ewe,* water.) In old English law. Toll paid for water passage. Cowell. The same as *aquage* or *aquagium.* Tomlins.

EWBRICE. Adultery; spouse-breach; marriage-breach. Cowell; Tomlins.

EWRY. An office in the royal household where the table linen, etc., is taken care of. Wharton.

EX. A latin preposition meaning from, out of, by, on, on account of, or according to.

A prefix, denoting removal, cessation or former. Prefixed to the name of an office, relation, *status,* etc., it denotes that the person spoken of once occupied that office or relation, but does so no longer, or that he is now *out* of it. Thus, *ex*-mayor, *ex*-partner, *ex*-judge.

A prefix which is equivalent to "without," "reserving," or "excepting." In this use, probably an abbreviation of "except." Thus, *ex*-interest, *ex*-coupons.

"A sale of bonds 'ex. July coupons' means a sale reserving the coupons; that is, a sale in which the seller receives, in addition to the purchase price, the benefit of the coupons, which benefit he may realize either by detaching them or receiving from the buyer an equivalent consideration." Porter v. Wormser, 94 N.Y. 445.

Also used as an abbreviation for "exhibit." See Dugan v. Trisler, 69 Ind. 555.

EX ABUNDANTI. Out of abundance; abundantly; superfluously; more than sufficient. Calvin.

EX ABUNDANTI CAUTELA. Lat. Out of abundant caution. "The practice has arisen *abundanti cautela.*" 8 East, 326; Lord Ellenborough, 4 Maule & S. 544.

EX ADVERSO. On the other side. 2 Show. 461. Applied to counsel.

EX ÆQUITATE. According to equity; in equity. Fleta, lib. 3, c. 10, § 3.

EX ÆQUO ET BONO. A phrase derived from the civil law, meaning, in justice and fairness; according to what is just and good; according to equity and conscience. 3 Bl. Comm. 163.

EX ALTERA PARTE. Of the other part.

EX ANTECEDENTIBUS ET CONSEQUENTIBUS FIT OPTIMA INTERPRETATIO. A passage in a statute is best interpreted by reference to what precedes and what follows it. Behrens v. State, 140 Neb. 671, 1 N.W.2d 289, 292; The best interpretation [of a part of an instrument] is made from the antecedents and the consequents, [from the preceding and following parts.] 2 Inst. 317.

The law will judge of a deed or other instrument, consisting of divers parts or clauses, by looking at the whole; and will give to each part its proper office, so as to ascertain and carry out the intention of the parties. Broom, Max. *577. The whole instrument is to be viewed and compared in all its parts, so that every part of it may be made consistent and effectual. 2 Kent, Comm. 555.

EX ARBITRIO JUDICIS. At, in, or upon the discretion of the judge. 4 Bl. Comm. 394. A term of the civil law. Inst. 4, 6, 31.

EX ASSENSU CURIÆ. By or with the consent of the court.

EX ASSENSU PATRIS. By or with the consent of the father.

A species of dower *ad ostium ecclesiæ,* during the life of the father of the husband; the son, by the father's consent expressly given, endowing his wife with parcel of his father's lands. Abolished by 3 & 4 Wm. IV, c. 105, § 13.

EX ASSENSU SUO. With his assent. Formal words in judgments for damages by default. Comb. 220.

EX BONIS. Of the goods or property. A term of the civil law; distinguished from *in bonis,* as being descriptive of or applicable to property not in actual possession. Calvin.

EX CATHEDRA. From the chair. Originally applied to the decisions of the popes from their *cathedra,* or chair. Hence, authoritative; having the weight of authority.

EX CAUSA. L. Lat. By title.

EX CERTA SCIENTIA. Of certain or sure knowledge. These words were anciently used in patents, and imported full knowledge of the subject-matter on the part of the king. See 1 Coke, 40*b*.

EX COLORE. By color; under color of; under pretense, show, or protection of. Thus, *ex colore officii,* under color of office.

EX COMITATE. Out of comity or courtesy.

EX COMMODATO. From or out of loan. A term applied in the old law of England to a right of action arising out of a loan, (*commodatum.*) Glanv. lib. 10, c. 13; 1 Reeve, Eng. Law, 166.

EX COMPARATIONE SCRIPTORUM. By a comparison of writings or handwritings. A term in the law of evidence. Best, Pres. 218.

EX CONCESSIS. From the premises granted. According to what has been already allowed.

EX CONSULTO. With consultation or deliberation.

EX CONTINENTI. Immediately; without any interval or delay; incontinently. A term of the civil law. Calvin.

EX CONTRACTU. From or out of a contract.

In both the civil and the common law, rights and causes of action are divided into two classes,—those arising *ex contractu*, (from a contract,) and those arising *ex delicto*, (from a delict or tort.) See 3 Bl.Comm. 117; Mackeld. Rom.Law, § 384. See Scharf v. People, 134 Ill. 240, 24 N.E. 761; Federal Life Ins. Co. v. Maxam, 70 Ind.App. 266, 117 N.E. 801, 807.

If cause of action declared in pleading arises from breach of promise, the action is "ex contractu". Chambers v. Birmingham Trust & Savings Co., 232 Ala. 609, 168 So. 893.

EX CURIA. Out of court; away from the court.

EX DEBITO JUSTITIÆ. From or as a debt of justice; in accordance with the requirement of justice; of right; as a matter of right. The opposite of *ex gratia, (q. v.)*. 3 Bl. Comm. 48, 67.

EX DEFECTU SANGUINIS. From failure of blood; for want of issue.

EX DELICTO. From a delict, tort, fault, crime, or malfeasance.

In both the civil and the common law, obligations and causes of action are divided into two great classes,—those arising *ex contractu*, (out of a contract,) and those *ex delicto*. The latter are such as grow out of or are founded upon a wrong or tort, *e. g.*, trespass, trover, replevin. These terms were known in English law at a very early period. See Inst. 4, 1, pr.; Mackeld.Rom.Law, § 384; 3 Bl.Comm. 117; Bract. fol. 101*b*; King v. New Orleans Ry. & Light Co., 140 La. 843, 74 So. 168, 169; Lamb v. McHan, 17 Ga.App. 5, 86 S.E. 252, 253; Seney v. Knight, 292 Ill. 206, 126 N.E. 761, 763.

An action "ex delicto" is an action of tort; an action arising out of fault, misconduct, or malfeasance. Sayers & Muir Service Station v. Indian Refining Co., 266 Ky. 779, 100 S.W.2d 687, 689. If cause of action declared in pleading arises from breach of duty growing out of contract, it is in form "ex delicto" and case. Chambers v. Birmingham Trust & Savings Co., 232 Ala. 609, 168 So. 893.

EX DELICTO NON EX SUPPLICIO EMERGIT INFAMIA. Infamy arises from the crime, not from the punishment.

EX DEMISSIONE (commonly abbreviated *ex dem.*) Upon the demise. A phrase forming part of the title of the old action of ejectment.

EX DIRECTO. Directly; immediately. Story, Bills, § 199.

EX DIUTURNITATE TEMPORIS, OMNIA PRÆSUMUNTUR SOLEMNITER ESSE ACTA. From length of time [after lapse of time] all things are presumed to have been done in due form. Co. Litt. 6*b*; Best, Ev. Introd. § 43; 1 Greenl. Ev. § 20.

EX DOLO MALO. Out of fraud; out of deceitful or tortious conduct. A phrase applied to obligations and causes of action vitiated by fraud or deceit.

EX DOLO MALO NON ORITUR ACTIO. Out of fraud no action arises; fraud never gives a right of action. No court will lend its aid to a man who founds his cause of action upon an immoral or illegal act. Cowp. 343; Broom, Max. 729.

EX DONATIONIBUS AUTEM FEODA MILITARIA VEL MAGNUM SERJEANTIUM NON CONTINENTIBUS ORITUR NOBIS QUODDAM NOMEN GENERALE, QUOD EST SOCAGIUM. Co. Litt. 86. From grants not containing military fees or grand serjeanty, a kind of general name is used by us, which is "socage."

EX EMPTO. Out of purchase; founded on purchase. A term of the civil law, adopted by Bracton. Inst. 4, 6, 28; Bract. fol. 102. See Actio ex Empto.

EX FACIE. From the face; apparently; evidently. A term applied to what appears on the face of a writing.

EX FACTO. From or in consequence of a fact or action; actually. Usually applied to an unlawful or tortious act as the foundation of a title, etc. Sometimes used as equivalent to *"de facto."* Bract. fol. 172.

EX FACTO JUS ORITUR. The law arises out of the fact. Broom, Max. 102. A rule of law continues in abstraction and theory, until an act is done on which it can attach and assume as it were a body and shape. Best, Ev. Introd. § 1.

EX FICTIONE JURIS. By a fiction of law.

EX FREQUENTI DELICTO AUGETUR PŒNA. 2 Inst. 479. Punishment increases with increasing crime.

EX GRATIA. Out of grace; as a matter of grace, favor, or indulgence; gratuitous. A term applied to anything accorded as a favor; as distinguished from that which may be demanded *ex debito*, as a matter of right.

EX GRAVI QUERELA. (From or on the grievous complaint.) In old English practice. The name of a writ (so called from its initial words) which lay for a person to whom any lands or tenements in fee were devised by will, (within any city, town, or borough wherein lands were devisable by custom,) and the heir of the devisor entered and detained them from him. Fitzh. Nat. Brev. 198, L, et seq.; 3 Reeve, Eng. Law, 49. Abolished by St. 3 & 4 Wm. IV. c. 27, § 36.

EX HYPOTHESI. By the hypothesis; upon the supposition; upon the theory or facts assumed.

EX INDUSTRIA. With contrivance or deliberation; designedly; on purpose. See 1 Kent, Comm. 318; Martin v. Hunter, 1 Wheat. 334, 4 L.Ed. 97.

EX INTEGRO. Anew; afresh.

EX JUSTA CAUSA. From a just or lawful cause; by a just or legal title.

EX LEGE. By the law; by force of law; as a matter of law.

EX LEGIBUS. According to the laws. A phrase of the civil law, which means according to the intent or spirit of the law, as well as according to the words or letter. Dig. 50, 16, 6. See Calvin.

EX LICENTIA REGIS. By the king's license. 1 Bl. Comm. 168, note.

EX LOCATO. From or out of lease or letting. A term of the civil law, applied to actions or rights of action arising out of the contract of *locatum, (q. v.)* Inst. 4, 6, 28. Adopted at an early period in the law of England. Bract. fol. 102; 1 Reeve, Eng. Law, 168.

EX MALEFICIO. Has been defined variously as from or growing out of wrongdoing; tortious; tortiously; growing out of, or founded on, misdoing or tort; on account of misconduct; by virtue of or out of an illegal act. "Ex maleficio" is probably synonymous with "malfeasance". Lucas v. Central Missouri Trust Co., 350 Mo. 593, 166 S.W.2d 1053, 1056.

This term is frequently used in the civil law as the synonym of *"ex delicto," (q. v.,)* and is thus contrasted with *"ex contractu,"* In this sense it is of more rare occurrence in the common law, though found in Bracton (fols. 99, 101, 102.)

EX MALEFICIO NON ORITUR CONTRACTUS. A contract cannot arise out of an act radically vicious and illegal. 1 Term, 734; 3 Term, 422; Broom, Max. 734.

EX MALIS MORIBUS BONÆ LEGES NATÆ SUNT. 2 Inst. 161. Good laws arise from evil morals, *i. e.*, are necessitated by the evil behavior of men.

EX MALITIA. From malice; maliciously. In the law of libel and slander, this term imports a publication that is false and without legal excuse. Dixon v. Allen, 69 Cal. 527, 11 P. 179.

EX MERO MOTU. Of his own mere motion; of his own accord; voluntarily and without prompting or request.

Royal letters patent which are granted at the crown's own instance, and without request made, are said to be granted *ex mero motu.* When a court interferes, of its own motion, to object to an irregularity, or to do something which the parties are not strictly entitled to, but which will prevent injustice, it is said to act *ex mero motu,* or *ex proprio motu,* or *sua sponte,* all these terms being here equivalent.

EX MORA. From or in consequence of delay. Interest is allowed *ex mora;* that is, where there has been delay in returning a sum borrowed. A term of the civil law. Story, Bailm. § 84.

EX MORE. According to custom. Calvin.

EX MULTITUDINE SIGNORUM, COLLIGITUR IDENTITAS VERA. From a great number of signs or marks, true identity is gathered or made up. Bac. Max. 103, in *regula* 25. A thing described by a great number of marks is easily identified, though, as to some, the description may not be strictly correct. Id.

EX MUTUO. From or out of loan. In the old law of England, a debt was said to arise *ex mutuo* when one lent another anything which consisted in number, weight, or measure. 1 Reeve, Eng. Law, 159; Bract. fol. 99.

EX NECESSITATE. Of necessity. 3 Rep. Ch. 123.

EX NECESSITATE LEGIS. From or by necessity of law. 4 Bl. Comm. 394.

EX NECESSITATE REI. From the necessity or urgency of the thing or case. 2 Pow. Dev. (by Jarman,) 308.

EX NIHILO NIHIL FIT. From nothing nothing comes. Jackson v. Waldron, 13 Wend. N.Y. 178, 221; Root v. Stuyvesant, 18 Wend. N.Y. 257, 301.

EX NUDO PACTO NON ORITUR [NASCITUR] ACTIO. Out of a nude or naked pact [that is, a bare parol agreement without consideration] no action arises. Bract. fol. 99; Fleta, lib. 2, c. 56, § 3; Plowd. 305. Out of a promise neither attended with particular solemnity (such as belongs to a specialty) nor with any consideration no legal liability can arise. 2 Steph. Comm. 113. A parol agreement, without a valid consideration, cannot be made the foundation of an action. A leading maxim both of the civil and common law. Cod. 2, 3, 10; Id. 5, 14, 1; 2 Bl. Comm. 445; Smith, Cont. 85, 86.

EX OFFICIO. From office; by virtue of the office; without any other warrant or appointment than that resulting from the holding of a particular office.

Powers may be exercised by an officer which are not specifically conferred uopn him, but are necessarily implied in his office; these are *ex officio.* Thus, a judge has *ex officio* the powers of a conservator of the peace. Courts are bound to notice public statutes judicially and *ex officio.* King v. Physicians' Casualty Ass'n of America, 97 Neb. 637, 150 N.W. 1010, 1011; Lobrano v. Police Jury of Parish of Plaquemines, 150 La. 14, 90 So. 423, 424; Allin v. Mercer County, 174 Ky. 566, 192 S.W. 638, 640.

EX OFFICIO INFORMATION. In English law. A criminal information filed by the attorney general *ex officio* on behalf of the crown, in the court of king's bench, for offenses more immediately affecting the government, and to be distinguished from informations in which the crown is the nominal prosecutor. Mozley & Whitley; 4 Steph. Comm. 372–378.

EX OFFICIO OATH. An oath taken by offending priests; abolished by 13 Car. II. St. 1, c. 12.

EX OFFICIO SERVICES. Services which the law annexes to a particular office and requires the incumbent to perform. City of Birmingham v. Hawkins, 208 Ala. 79, 94 So. 62, 64; Nichols v. Galveston County, 111 Tex. 50, 228 S.W. 547, 548.

"Ex officio services," which deputy attorney general may perform in place of Attorney General, are services imposed by law on public officer by virtue of his office and relating to public interests or business of county or state. Chemical Bank & Trust Co. v. Oakland County, 264 Mich. 673, 251 N.W. 395.

EX PACTO ILLICITO NON ORITUR ACTIO. From an illegal contract an action does not arise. Broom, Max. 742. See 7 Clark & F. 729.

EX PARTE. On one side only; by or for one party; done for, in behalf of, or on the application of, one party only.

A judicial proceeding, order, injunction, etc., is said to be *ex parte* when it is taken or granted at the instance and for the benefit of one party only, and without notice to, or contestation by, any person adversely interested. Janin v. Logan, 209 Ky. 811, 273 S.W. 531, 532; Van Alen v. Superior Court in and for Los Angeles County, 37 Cal.App. 696, 174 P. 672; Stella v. Mosele, 299 Ill.App. 53, 19 N.E.2d 433, 435.

In its primary sense, *ex parte*, as applied to an application in a judicial proceeding, means that it is made by a person who is not a party to the proceeding, but who has an interest in the matter which entitles him to make the application. Thus, in a bankruptcy proceeding or an administration action, an application by A. B., a creditor, or the like, would be described as made *"ex parte* A. B.," *i. e.*, on the part of A. B.

In its more usual sense, *ex parte* means that an application is made by one party to a proceeding in the absence of the other. Thus, an *ex parte* injunction is one granted without the opposite party having had notice of the application. It would not be called *"ex parte"* if he had proper notice of it, and chose not to appear to oppose it. Sweet.

"Ex parte," in the heading of a reported case, signifies that the name following is that of the party upon whose application the case is heard.

EX PARTE MATERNA. On the mother's side; of the maternal line.

EX PARTE PATERNA. On the father's side; of the paternal line.

The phrases *"ex parte materna"* and *"ex parte paterna"* denote the line or blood of the mother or father, and have no such restricted or limited sense as from the mother or father exclusively. Banta v. Demarest, 24 N.J.L. 431.

EX PARTE TALIS. A writ that lay for a bailiff or receiver, who, having auditors appointed to take his accounts, cannot obtain of them reasonable allowance, but is cast into prison. Fitzh. Nat. Brev. 129.

EX PAUCIS DICTIS INTENDERE PLURIMA POSSIS. Litt. § 384. You can imply many things from few expressions.

EX PAUCIS PLURIMA CONCIPIT INGENIUM. Litt. § 550. From a few words or hints the understanding conceives many things.

EX POST FACTO. After the fact; by an act or fact occurring after some previous act or fact, and relating thereto; by subsequent matter; the opposite of *ab initio*. Thus, a deed may be good *ab initio*, or, if invalid at its inception, may be confirmed by matter *ex post facto*.

EX POST FACTO LAW. A law passed after the occurrence of a fact or commission of an act, which retrospectively changes the legal consequences or relations of such fact or deed. By Const. U. S. art. 1, § 10, the states are forbidden to pass "any *ex post facto* law." In this connection the phrase has a much narrower meaning than its literal translation would justify, as will appear from the extracts given below.

A statute which changes punishment which may be imposed for a crime theretofore committed is "ex post facto" only if it prescribes or permits imposition of a greater sentence. People ex rel. Pincus v. Adams, 274 N.Y. 447, 9 N.E.2d 46, 110 A.L.R. 1303.

An "ex post facto law" has been defined as (1) Every law that makes an action, done before the passing of the law, and which was innocent when done, criminal, and punishes such action. (2) Every law that aggravates a crime, or makes it greater than it was when committed. (3) Every law that changes the punishment, and inflicts a greater punishment than the law annexed to the crime when committed. (4) Every law that alters the legal rules of evidence, and receives less or different testimony than the law required at the time of the commission of the offense, in order to convict the offender. All these, and similar laws, are prohibited by the constitution. But a law may be *ex post facto*, and still not amenable to this constitutional inhibition; that is, provided it mollifies, instead of aggravating, the rigor of the criminal law. Cummings v. Missouri, 4 Wall. 277, 18 L.Ed. 356; 3 Story, Const. 212; State v. Malloy, 95 S.C. 441, 78 S.E. 995, 997, Ann.Cas.1915C, 1053; In re Jamestown Caucus Law, 43 R.I. 421, 112 A. 900, 902; State v. Teasley, 194 Ala. 574, 69 So. 723, 725, Ann.Cas. 1918E, 347; Beazell v. State of Ohio, 269 U.S. 167, 46 S.Ct. 68, 70 L.Ed. 216; Hernandez v. State, 43 Ariz. 424, 32 P. 2d 18, 24.

An "ex post facto law" includes every law that creates and punishes a criminal offense which, when done before the passing of the law, was innocent, and every law that aggravates a crime or makes it greater than it was when committed, and every law that inflicts a greater punishment than was attached to the crime when committed. State v. Pleason, 56 N.D. 499, 218 N.W. 154, 155.

An "ex post facto law" is defined as a law which provides for the infliction of punishment upon a person for an act done which, when it was committed, was innocent; a law which aggravates a crime or makes it greater than when it was committed; a law that changes the punishment or inflicts a greater punishment than the law annexed to the crime when it was committed; a law that changes the rules of evidence and receives less or different testimony than was required at the time of the commission of the offense in order to convict the offender; a law which, assuming to regulate civil rights and remedies only, in effect imposes a penalty or the deprivation of a right which, when done, was lawful; a law which deprives persons accused of crime of some lawful protection to which they have become entitled, such as the protection of a former conviction or acquittal, or of the proclamation of amnesty; every law which, in relation to the offense or its consequences, alters the situation of a person to his disadvantage. State v. Rowe, 116 N.J.L. 48, 181 A. 706.

An "ex post facto law" is one which makes an act punishable in a manner in which it was not punishable when it was committed. Statler v. U. S. Savings & Trust Co., 122 Pa.Super. 189, 186 A. 290, 292; Southern Kraft Corporation v. Hardin, 205 Ark. 512, 169 S.W.2d 637, 643.

An "ex post facto law" is one which makes a crime of an act which when committed was not a crime or a law which increases the punishment for an act already committed. Commonwealth ex rel. Wall v. Smith, 345 Pa. 512, 29 A.2d 912, 913.

An "ex post facto law" is one which renders an act punishable in manner in which it was not punishable when it was committed, or which deprives accused of any substantial right or immunity possessed by him before its passage as to prior offenses. People of U. S. ex rel. Umbenhowar v. McDonnell, D.C.Ill., 11 F.Supp. 1014, 1015.

An *ex post facto* law is one which renders an act punishable in manner in which it was not punishable when committed. Such a law may inflict penalties on the person, or pecuniary penalties which swell the public treasury. The legislature is therefore prohibited from passing a law by which a man's estate, or any part of it, shall be seized for a crime, which was not declared, by some previous law, to render him liable to such punishment. Fletcher v. Peck, 6 Cranch, 87, 138, 3 L.Ed. 162.

An increase in possible penalty is "ex post facto" regardless of length of sentence actually imposed. Ex parte Flora, Ohio App., 31 N.E.2d 482, 485.

The plain and obvious meaning of prohibition is that the legislature shall not pass any law, after a fact done by any citizen, which shall have relation to that fact, so as to punish that which was innocent when done; or to add to the punishment of that which was criminal; or to increase the malignity of a crime; or to retrench the rules of evidence, so as to make conviction more easy. This definition of an *ex post facto law* is sanctioned by long usage. Strong v. State, 1 Black., Ind., 196.

The term "*ex post facto* law," in the United States constitution, cannot be construed to include and to prohibit the enacting any law after a fact, nor even to prohibit the depriving a citizen of a vested right to property. Calder v. Bull, 3 Dall. 386, 1 L.Ed. 648.

Any law passed after commission of offense for which the defendant is tried which inflicts greater punishment or which alters situation of accused is "ex post facto". United States v. Platt, D.C.Tex., 31 F.Supp. 788, 793.

Statute which punishes as a crime an act previously committed, which was innocent when done, which makes more burdensome punishment for a crime after its commission, or which deprives one charged with crime of any defense available according to law at time act was committed, is "ex post facto". People ex rel. Luciano v. Murphy, 290 N.Y.S. 1011, 1014, 160 Misc. 573.

The operation of a statute to repeal, extend the period of, or provide for the tolling of a statute of limitations under which a complete defense has already accrued, would be "ex post facto". Hill v. State, 146 Tex.Cr.R. 333, 171 S.W.2d 880, 882, 883, 884.

The prohibition of "ex post facto" laws applies only to criminal or penal matters. Bannister v. Bannister, 181 Md. 177, 29 A.2d 287, 289; Garrett Freight Lines v. State Tax Commission, 103 Utah 390, 135 P.2d 523, 527, 146 A.L.R. 1003; Southern Kraft Corporation v. Hardin, 205 Ark. 512, 169 S.W.2d 637, 643.

To render a statute "ex post facto," it must be one which imposes punishment for an act which was not punishable when it was committed, or imposes additional punishment or alters the situation of the accused to his disadvantage. Andrus v. McCauley, D.C.Wash., 21 F.Supp. 70.

Trial procedure may be changed by Legislature, and new procedure may be made applicable to offenses previously committed, without violation of constitutional provision. People ex rel. Pincus v. Adams, 274 N.Y. 447, 9 N.E.2d 46, 49, 50, 110 A.L.R. 1303.

"Ex post facto" and "retrospective" are not convertible terms. The latter is a term of wider signification than the former and includes it. All *ex post facto* laws are necessarily retrospective, but not *e converso*. A curative or confirmatory statute is retrospective, but not *ex post facto*. Constitutions of nearly all the states contain prohibitions against *ex post facto* laws, but only a few forbid retrospective legislation in specific terms. Black, Const.Prohib. §§ 170, 172, 222.

Retrospective laws divesting vested rights are impolitic and unjust; but they are not *"ex post facto* laws," within the meaning of the constitution of the United States, nor repugnant to any other of its provisions; and, if not repugnant to the state constitution, a court cannot pronounce them to be void, merely because in their judgment they are contrary to the principles of natural justice. Albee v. May, 2 Paine, 74 Fed.Cas.No.134.

Every retrospective act is not necessarily an *ex post facto* law. That phrase embraces only such laws as impose or affect penalties or forfeitures. Locke v. New Orleans, 4 Wall. 172, 18 L.Ed. 334.

Retrospective laws which do not impair the obligation of contracts, or affect vested rights, or partake of the character of *ex post facto* laws, are not prohibited by the constitution. Bay v. Gage, 36 Barb., N.Y., 447.

The act providing that every sentence of death imposed shall be by electrocution is not an "ex post facto law" because of its retrospective effect. State ex rel. Pierre v. Jones, 200 La. 808, 9 So.2d 42, 45, 47.

EX PRÆCEDENTIBUS ET CONSEQUENTIBUS OPTIMA FIT INTERPRETATIO. 1 Roll. 374. The best interpretation is made from the context.

EX PROPRIO MOTU. Of his own accord. See Ex Mero Motu.

EX PROPRIO VIGORE. By their or its own force. 2 Kent, Comm. 457.

EX PROVISIONE HOMINIS. By the provision of man. By the limitation of the party, as distinguished from the disposition of the law. 11 Coke, 80*b*.

EX PROVISIONE MARITI. From the provision of the husband.

EX QUASI CONTRACTU. From *quasi* contract. Fleta, lib. 2, c. 60.

EX RELATIONE. Upon relation or information.

Legal proceedings which are instituted by the attorney general (or other proper person) in the name and behalf of the state, but on the information and at the instigation of an individual who has a private interest in the matter, are said to be taken "on the relation" *(ex relatione)* of such person, who is called the "relator." Such a cause is usually entitled thus: "State *ex rel.* Doe *v.* Roe."

In the books of reports, when a case is said to be reported *ex relatione*, it is meant that the reporter derives his account of it, not from personal knowledge, but from the relation or narrative of some person who was present at the argument.

EX RIGORE JURIS. According to the rigor or strictness of law; in strictness of law. Fleta, lib. 3, c. 10, § 3.

EX SCRIPTIS OLIM VISIS. From writings formerly seen.

A term used as descriptive of that kind of proof of handwriting where the knowledge has been acquired by the witness having seen letters or other documents professing to be the handwriting of the party, and having afterwards communicated personally with the party upon the contents of those letters or documents, or having otherwise acted upon them by written answers, producing further correspondence or acquiescence by the party in some matter to which they relate, or by the witness transacting with the party some business to which they relate, or by any other mode of communication between the party and the witness which, in the ordinary course of the transactions of life, induces a reasonable presumption that the letters or documents were the handwriting of the party. 5 Adol. & E. 730.

EX SHIP. See Ship.

EX STATUTO. According to the statute. Fleta. lib. 5, c. 11, § 1.

EX STIPULATU ACTIO. In the civil law. An action of stipulation. An action given to recover marriage portions. Inst. 4, 6, 29.

EX TEMPORE. From or in consequence of time; by lapse of time. Bract. fols. 51, 52. *Ex diuturno tempore*, from length of time. Id. fol. 51*b*.

Without preparation or premeditation.

EX TESTAMENTO. From, by, or under a will. The opposite of *ab intestato (q. v.)*.

EX TOTA MATERIA EMERGAT RESOLUTIO. The explanation should arise out of the whole subject-matter; the exposition of a statute should be made from all its parts together. Wing. Max. 238.

EX TURPI CAUSA NON ORITUR ACTIO. Out of a base [illegal, or immoral] consideration, an action does [can] not arise. 1 Selw. N. P. 63; Broom, Max. 730, 732; Story, Ag. § 195.

No disgraceful matter can ground an action. Eldson v. Maddox, 195 Ga. 641, 24 S.E.2d 895, 897.

EX TURPI CONTRACTU ACTIO NON ORITUR. From an immoral or iniquitous contract an action does not arise. A contract founded upon an illegal or immoral consideration cannot be enforced by action. 2 Kent, Comm. 466; Dig. 2, 14, 27, 4.

EX UNA PARTE. Of one part or side; on one side.

EX UNO DISCES OMNES. From one thing you can discern all.

EX UTRAQUE PARTE. On both sides. Dyer, 126*b*.

EX UTRISQUE PARENTIBUS CONJUNCTI. Related on the side of both parents; of the whole blood. Hale, Com. Law, c. 11.

EX VI TERMINI. From or by the force of the term. From the very meaning of the expression used. 2 Bl. Comm. 109, 115.

EX VISCERIBUS. From the bowels. From the vital part, the very essence of the thing. 10 Coke, 24*b;* Homer v. Shelton, 2 Metc. Mass. 213. *Ex visceribus verborum,* from the mere words and nothing else. 1 Story, Eq. Jur. § 980; Fisher v. Fields, 10 Johns. N.Y. 495.

EX VISITATIONE DEI. By the dispensation of God; by reason of physical incapacity. Anciently, when a prisoner, being arraigned, stood silent instead of pleading, a jury was impaneled to inquire whether he obstinately stood mute or was dumb *ex visitatione Dei.* 4 Steph. Comm. 394.

Also by natural, as distinguished from violent, causes. When a coroner's inquest finds that the death was due to disease or other natural cause, it is frequently phrased *"ex visitatione Dei."*

EX VISU SCRIPTIONIS. From sight of the writing; from having seen a person write. A term employed to describe one of the modes of proof of handwriting. Best, Pres. 218.

EX VOLUNTATE. Voluntarily; from freewill or choice.

EXACTION. The wrongful act of an officer or other person in compelling payment of a fee or reward for his services, under color of his official authority, where no payment is due.

Between "extortion" and "exaction" there is this difference: that in the former case the officer extorts more than his due, when something is due to him; in the latter, he exacts what is not his due, when there is nothing due to him. Co.Litt. 368.

EXACTLY ALIKE. Representation that the living apartment on the first floor was exactly like the living apartment on the second floor is specific and definite; exactly alike meaning not absolutely identical, but substantially so in size, design, finish, and fixtures. Lipsher v. Resnikoff, 99 Conn. 13, 120 A. 859.

EXACTOR.
Civil law. A gatherer or receiver of money; a collector of taxes. Cod. 10, 19.

Old English law. A collector of the public moneys; a tax gatherer. Thus, *exactor regis* was the name of the king's tax collector, who took up the taxes and other debts due the treasury.

EXALTARE. In old English law. To raise; to elevate. Frequently spoken of water, *i. e.,* to raise the surface of a pond or pool.

EXAMEN. L. Lat. A trial. *Examen computi,* the balance of an account. Townsh. Pl. 223.

EXAMINATION. An investigation; search; interrogating.

Criminal Practice

An investigation by a magistrate of a person who has been charged with crime and arrested, or of the facts and circumstances which are alleged to have attended the crime and to fasten suspicion upon the party so charged, in order to ascertain whether there is sufficient ground to hold him to bail for his trial by the proper court. U. S. v. Stanton, C.C.A.Conn., 17 C.C.A. 475, 70 F. 890; State v. Conrad, 95 N.C. 669. The preliminary hearing to determine whether person charged with having committed a crime should be held for trial. Commonwealth v. Cohen, 102 Pa.Super. 397, 157 A. 32, 33.

Trial Practice

The examination of a witness consists of the series of questions put to him by a party to the action, or his counsel, for the purpose of bringing before the court and jury in legal form the knowledge which the witness has of the facts and matters in dispute, or of probing and sifting his evidence previously given.

Of a long account. This phrase does not mean examination of the account to ascertain the result or effect of it, but proof by testimony of correctness of items composing it. Magown v. Sinclair, 5 Daly N.Y. 63; State ex rel. Hustisford Light, Power & Mfg. Co. v. Grimm, 208 Wis. 366, 243 N.W. 763.

Of bankrupt. This is the interrogation of a bankrupt, in the course of proceedings in bankruptcy, or prior to the adjudication (Cameron v. United States, 231 U.S. 710, 34 S.Ct. 244, 58 L.Ed. 448; In re Fleischer, D.C.N.Y., 151 F. 81), concerning the conduct of his business, the cause of his bankruptcy, his dealings with his creditors and other persons, the amount, kind, and whereabouts of his property, and all matters which may affect the administration and settlement of his estate. This is authorized by Bankruptcy Act, § 7, 30 Stat. 548, 11 U.S.C.A. § 25. The bankrupt's wife or any other person may also be examined concerning the bankrupt's acts, conduct, or property. Bankruptcy Act, § 21, 30 Stat. 551, as amended by Act Feb. 5, 1903, c. 487, § 7, 32 Stat. 798, 11 U.S.C.A. § 44. In re Horgan, C.C.A.N.Y., 39 C.C.A. 118, 98 F. 414.

Of invention. An inquiry made at the patent-office, upon application for a patent, into the novelty and utility of the alleged invention, and as to its interfering with any other patented invention. Rev.St. U. S. § 4893, 35 U.S.C.A. § 36.

Of title. An investigation made by or for a person who intends to purchase real estate, in the offices where the public records are kept, to ascertain the history and present condition of the title to such land, and its *status* with reference to liens, incumbrances, clouds, etc.

Of wife. See Private Examination.

On his own behalf. For executor or devisee to be "examined on his own behalf", such executor or devisee must be a party to the action. In re Custer's Estate, 229 Iowa 1061, 295 N.W. 848, 852.

For "Cross-Examination," "De Bene Esse", "Direct Examination," "Preliminary Examination," "Pro Interesse Suo," "Reexamination," and "Separate Examination," see those titles.

EXAMINED COPY. A copy of a record, public book, or register, and which has been compared with the original. 1 Campb. 469.

EXAMINER. English law. A person appointed by a court to take the examination of witnesses in an action, *i. e.*, to take down the result of their interrogation by the parties or their counsel, either by written interrogatories or *vivâ voce*. An examiner is generally appointed where a witness is in a foreign country, or is too ill or infirm to attend before the court, and is either an officer of the court, or a person specially appointed for the purpose. Sweet.

New Jersey. An examiner is an officer appointed by the court of chancery to take testimony in causes depending in that court. His powers are similar to those of the English examiner in chancery.

Patent Office. An officer in the patent-office charged with the duty of examining the patentability of inventions for which patents are asked.

For "Special Examiner," see that title.

EXAMINER IN CHANCERY. An officer of the court of chancery, before whom witnesses are examined, and their testimony reduced to writing, for the purpose of being read on the hearing of the cause. Cowell.

EXAMINERS. Persons appointed to question students of law in order to ascertain their qualifications before they are admitted to practice.

EXANNUAL ROLL. In old English practice. A roll into which (in the old way of exhibiting sheriffs' accounts) the illeviable fines and desperate debts were transcribed, and which was *annually* read to the sheriff upon his accounting, to see what might be gotten. Cowell.

EXCAMB. In Scotch law. To exchange. 6 Bell, App. Cas. 19, 22.

EXCAMBIATOR. An exchanger of lands; a broker. Obsolete.

EXCAMBION. In Scotch law. Exchange. 1 Forb. Inst. pt. 2, p. 173.

EXCAMBIUM. An exchange; a place where merchants meet to transact their business; also an equivalent in recompense; a recompense in lieu of dower *ad ostium ecclesiæ*.

EXCELLENCY.

America. The title is sometimes given to the chief executive of a state or of the nation.

English law. The title of a viceroy, governor general, ambassador, or commander in chief.

EXCEPT. But. In re Naftzger's Estate, 24 Cal. 2d 595, 150 P.2d 873, 875; Not including. In re Kelly's Estate, 153 Misc. 445, 274 N.Y.S. 488. Other than, In re Nelson's Estate, 152 Misc. 245, 273 N.Y.S. 268; Ingram v. State, 241 Ala. 166, 3 So.2d 431, 432; Otherwise than, State v. White, 195 La. 1028, 197 So. 745, 747; Reserve. Adams v. Osage Tribe of Indians, C.C.A.Okl., 59 F.2d 653, 655; Brown v. Weare, 348 Mo. 135, 152 S.W.2d 649, 656, 136 A.L.R. 286. To exclude from an enumeration, the scope of statement or enactment, a privilege, etc.; to leave out of account or consideration. In re Garvin's Estate, 335 Pa. 542, 6 A.2d 796, 800; Rickman v. Commonwealth, 195 Ky. 715, 243 S.W. 929.

The expression "except for" is synonymous in many cases with "but for" and "only for." Rickman v. Commonwealth, 195 Ky. 715, 243 S.W. 929.

EXCEPT AS PROVIDED BY LAW. As used in statute held to refer to statutory and not general law of state, Pace v. Pace Bros. Co., 91 Utah 132, 59 P.2d 1, 8.

EXCEPT FOR THE INTESTATE SHARE OF THE SURVIVING SPOUSE, IF ANY, OF SUCH RELICT. Phrase as used in statute relating to disposition of property coming from a deceased spouse to relict dying intestate and without issue, refers to share a surviving spouse would take under section covering generally distribution of an intestate's property. Russell v. Roberts, 54 Ohio App. 441, 7 N.E.2d 811, 813.

EXCEPT IN TIME OF WAR. In statute providing for delivery to civil authorities of persons accused of crime but subject to military law, "except in time of war", quoted words merely relieve military authorities in time of war of duty to deliver accused persons to civil authorities. Articles of War, art. 74, 10 U.S.C.A. § 1546. People v. Williams, 184 Misc. 510, 55 N.Y.S.2d 181, 182.

EXCEPT RIGHT OF WAY. Recitals "less the right of way" and "except right of way" in granting clause of deed have well-defined accepted certain and unambiguous meaning by which grantor conveys entire interest in servient estate and at same time expressly recognizes and acknowledges dominant estate. Jennings v. Amerada Petroleum Corporation, 179 Okl. 561, 66 P.2d 1069, 1071.

EXCEPTING. As used in a deed, the terms "reserving" and "excepting" are used interchangeably, and their technical meaning will give way to the manifest intent. Porter v. Warner-Caldwell Oil Co., 183 Okl. 1, 80 P.2d 252, 253.

The words "reserving" and "excepting," although strictly distinguishable, may be used interchangeably or indiscriminately. Stephan v. Kentucky Valley Distilling Co., 275 Ky. 705, 122 S.W.2d 493, 496.

EXCEPTIO.

Modern civil law. A plea by which the defendant admits the cause of action, but alleges new facts which, provided they be true, totally or partially answer the allegations put forward on the other side; thus distinguished from a mere traverse of the plaintiff's averments. Tomkins & J. Mod. Rom. Law, 90. In this use, the term corresponds to the common-law plea in confession and avoidance.

Roman law. An exception. In a general sense, a judicial allegation opposed by a defendant to the plaintiff's action. Calvin. A stop or stay to an action opposed by the defendant. Cowell.

Answering to the "defense" or "plea" of the common law. An allegation and defense of a defendant by which the plaintiff's claim or complaint is defeated, either according to strict law or upon grounds of equity.

In a stricter sense, the exclusion of an action that lay in strict law, on grounds of equity, *(actionis jure stricto competentis ob æquitatem exclusio.)* Heinecc. A kind of limitation of an action, by which it was shown that the action, though otherwise just, did not lie in the particular case. Calvin. A species of defense allowed in cases where, though the action as brought by the plaintiff was in itself just, yet it was unjust as against the particular party sued. Inst. 4, 13, pr.

EXCEPTIO DILATORIA. A dilatory exception; called also *"temporalis,"* (temporary;) one which defeated the action for a time, *(quæ ad tempus nocet,)* and created delay, *(et temporis dilationem tribuit;)* such as an agreement not to sue within a certain time, as five years. Inst. 4, 13, 10. See Dig. 44, 1, 3.

EXCEPTIO DOLI MALI. An exception or plea of fraud. Inst. 4, 13, 1, 9; Bract. fol. 100*b*.

EXCEPTIO DOMMINII. A claim of ownership set up in an action for the recovery of property not in the possession of the plaintiff. Mackeld. Rom. Law, § 299.

EXCEPTIO DOTIS CAUTÆ NON NUMERATÆ. A defense to an action for the restitution of a dowry that it was never paid, though promised, available upon the dissolution of the marriage within a limited time. Mackeld. Rom. Law, § 458.

EXCEPTIO EJUS REI CUJUS PETITUR DISSOLUTIO NULLA EST. A plea of that matter the dissolution of which is sought [by the action] is null, [or of no effect.] Jenk. Cent. 37, case 71.

EXCEPTIO FALSI OMNIUM ULTIMA. A plea denying a fact is the last of all.

EXCEPTIO FIRMAT REGULAM IN CASIBUS NON EXCEPTIS. An exception affirms the rule in cases not excepted. Bacon, Aph. 17.

EXCEPTIO FIRMAT REGULAM IN CONTRARIUM. An exception proves an opposite rule. See *exceptio probat regulam.* Bacon, Aph. 17.

EXCEPTIO IN FACTUM. An exception on the fact. An exception or plea founded on the peculiar circumstances of the case. Inst. 4, 13, 1.

EXCEPTIO IN PERSONAM. A plea or defense of a personal nature, which may be alleged only by the person himself to whom it is granted by the law. Mackeld. Rom. Law, § 217.

EXCEPTIO IN REM. A plea or defense not of a personal nature, but connected with the legal circumstances on which the suit is founded, and which may therefore be alleged by any party in interest, including the heirs and sureties of the proper or original debtor. Mackeld. Rom. Law, § 217.

EXCEPTIO JURISJURANDI. An exception of oath; an exception or plea that the matter had been sworn to. Inst. 4, 13, 4. This kind of exception was allowed where a debtor, at the instance of his creditor, *(creditore deferente,)* had sworn that nothing was due the latter, and had notwithstanding been sued by him.

EXCEPTIO METUS. An exception or plea of fear or compulsion. Inst. 4, 13, 1, 9; Bract. fol. 100*b*. Answering to the modern plea of duress.

EXCEPTIO NON ADIMPLETI CONTRACTUS. An exception in an action founded on a contract involving mutual duties or obligations, to the effect that the plaintiff is not entitled to sue because he has not performed his own part of the agreement. Mackeld. Rom. Law, § 394.

EXCEPTIO NON SOLUTÆ PECUNIÆ. A plea that the debt in suit was not discharged by payment (as alleged by the adverse party) notwithstanding an acquittance or receipt given by the person to whom the payment is stated to have been made. Mackeld. Rom. Law, § 534.

EXCEPTIO NULLA EST VERSUS ACTIONEM QUÆ EXCEPTIONEM PERIMIT. There is [can be] no plea against an action which destroys [the matter of] the plea. Jenk. Cent. 106, case 2.

EXCEPTIO PACTI CONVENTI. An exception of compact; an exception or plea that the plaintiff had agreed not to sue. Inst. 4, 13, 3.

EXCEPTIO PECUNIÆ NON NUMERATÆ. An exception or plea of money not paid; a defense which might be set up by a party who was sued on a promise to repay money which he had never received. Inst. 4, 13, 2.

EXCEPTIO PEREMPTORIA. A peremptory exception; called also *"perpetua,"* (perpetual;) one which forever destroyed the subject-matter or ground of the action, *(quæ semper rem de qua agitur perimit;)* such as the *exceptio doli mali,* the *exceptio metus,* etc. Inst. 4, 13, 9. See Dig. 44, 1, 3.

EXCEPTIO PROBAT REGULAM. The exception proves the rule. 11 Coke, 41; 3 Term, 722. Sometimes quoted with the addition *"de rebus non exceptis,"* ("so far as concerns the matters not excepted.")

EXCEPTIO QUÆ FIRMAT LEGEM, EXPONIT LEGEM. An exception which confirms the law explains the law. 2 Bulst. 189.

EXCEPTIO QUOQUE REGULAM DECLARAT. The exception also declares the rule. Bacon, Aph. 17.

EXCEPTIO REI JUDICATÆ. An exception or plea of matter adjudged; a plea that the subject-matter of the action had been determined in a previous action. Inst. 4, 13, 5.

This term is adopted by Bracton, and is constantly used in modern law to denote a defense founded upon a previous adjudication of the same matter. Bract. fols. 100*b*, 177; 2 Kent, Comm. 120. A plea of a former recovery or judgment.

EXCEPTIO REI VENDITÆ ET TRADITÆ. An exception or plea of the sale and delivery of the thing.

This exception presumes that there was a valid sale and a proper tradition; but though, in consequence of the rule that no one can transfer to another a greater right than he himself has, no property was transferred, yet because of some particular circumstance the real owner is estopped from contesting it. Mackeld. Rom.Law, § 299.

EXCEPTIO SEMPER ULTIMO PONENDA EST. An exception should always be put last. 9 Coke, 53.

EXCEPTIO SENATUSCONSULTI MACEDONIANI. A defense to an action for the recovery of money loaned, on the ground that the loan was made to a minor or person under the paternal power of another; so named from the decree of the senate which forbade the recovery of such loans. Mackeld. Rom. Law, § 432.

EXCEPTIO SENATUSCONSULTI VELLEIANI. A defense to an action on a contract of suretyship, on the ground that the surety was a woman and therefore incapable of becoming bound for another; so named from the decree of the senate forbidding it. Mackeld. Rom. Law, § 455.

EXCEPTIO TEMPORIS. An exception or plea analogous to that of the statute of limitations in our law; viz., that the time prescribed by law for bringing such actions has expired. Mackeld. Rom. Law, § 213.

EXCEPTION. Act of excepting or excluding from a number designated or from a description; that which is excepted or separated from others in a general rule or description; a person, thing, or case specified as distinct or not included; an act of excepting, omitting from mention or leaving out of consideration; and "except" means not including. In re Kelly's Estate, 153 Misc. 445, 274 N.Y.S. 488.

For "General Exception" and "Special Exception," see those titles.

Admiralty and Equity Practice

An exception is a formal allegation tendered by a party that some previous pleading or proceeding taken by the adverse party is insufficient. Peck v. Osteen, 37 Fla. 427, 20 So. 549; Arnold v. Slaughter, 36 W.Va. 589, 15 S.E. 250.

In admiralty, an "exception" serves the function of a demurrer in common law or equity pleading. The Nea Hellis, C.C.A.N.Y., 116 F.2d 803, 805.

Bail

An exception to bail is an objection to the special bail put in by the defendant to an action at law made by the plaintiff on grounds of the insufficiency of the bail. 1 Tidd, Pr. 255.

Bequests

Bequests of sums made to same persons by different paragraphs in same codicil held accumulative, where second paragraph stated that bequest was "exception" to other bequests made; term as used meaning in addition to person's bequests. In re Kelly's Estate, 153 Misc. 445, 274 N.Y.S. 488.

Civil Law

An *exceptio* or plea. Used in this sense in Louisiana. For "Declaratory Exceptions," "Dilatory Exceptions" and "Peremptory Exceptions," see those titles.

Constitution

Provision granting Legislature discretionary power to tax merchants, peddlers, and privileges is "exception" to constitutional requirement of equality. A "proviso" and an "exception" are substantially the same thing. Evans v. McCabe, 164 Tenn. 672, 52 S.W.2d 159, 160.

Contracts

An exception is something taken out of instrument and of kind dealt with in contract. Reliance Ins. Co. v. Naman, 118 Tex. 21, 6 S.W.2d 743, 745.

Deeds or Conveyances

A clause by which grantor excepts something out of that which he granted before by the deed. Winston v. Johnson, 42 Minn. 398, 45 N.W. 958; Cox v. Colossal Cavern Co., 210 Ky. 612, 276 S.W. 540, 542; Worcester v. Smith, 117 Me. 168, 103 A. 65; De Moss v. Sample, 143 La. 243, 78 So. 482, 485; Beardslee v. New Berlin Light & Power Co., 207 N.Y. 34, 100 N.E. 434, 437, Ann.Cas.1914B, 1287.

An exception withdraws from operation of deed part of thing granted which would otherwise pass to grantee. Powell v. Big Horn Low Line Ditch Co., 81 Mont. 430, 263 P. 692, 693; Johnson v. Peck, 90 Utah, 544, 63 P.2d 251, 254; Slone v. Kentucky West Virginia Gas Co., 289 Ky. 623, 159 S.W.2d 993, 994, 995.

Insurance Contract or Policy

An exclusion of one or more risks. Kirkby v. Federal Life Ins. Co., C.C.A.Mich., 35 F.2d 126, 128; Mancini v. Thomas, 113 Vt. 322, 34 A.2d 105, 109. Provision of life and accident policy specifying that indemnity should be paid only when death occurred within thirty days after accident. Mowery v. Washington Nat. Ins. Co., 289 Ill.App. 443, 7 N.E.2d 334, 336. Things taken out. Raymond v. Great American Indemnity Co., 86 N.H. 93, 163 A. 713, 716.

The object of an exception is to exclude that which otherwise would be included, Estabrook v. Eastern Commercial Travelers Accident Ass'n, 308 Mass. 439, 32 N.E.2d 250, 252; to take special cases out of a general class or to guard against misinterpretation. Landau v. Equitable Life Assur. Soc. of United States, 1 N.Y.S.2d 891, 895, 166 Misc. 42.

Under liability policy, excluded uses of automobile held not "exceptions" since they were not in first instance included within any statement of insurance. Raymond v. Great American Indemnity Co., 86 N.H. 93, 163 A. 713, 716.

Practice

A formal objection to the action of the court, during the trial of a cause, in refusing a request or overruling an objection; implying that the party excepting does not acquiesce in the decision of the court, but will seek to procure its reversal, and that he means to save the benefit of his request or objection in some future proceeding. United States v. United States Fidelity & Guaranty Co., 236 U.S. 512, 35 S.Ct. 298, 303, 59 L.Ed. 696; Liquid Carbonic Co. v. Rodman, 52 Okl. 211, 152 P. 439; State v. Laundy, 103 Or. 443, 206 P. 290. It is also somewhat used to signify other objections in the course of a suit; for example, exception to bail is a formal objection that special bail offered by defendant is insufficient. 1 Tidd, Pr. 255.

An exception is, an objection formally taken to a decision of the court on a matter of law. State v. Wolzenski, 340 Mo. 1181, 105 S.W.2d 905, 907; an objection on a matter of law to a decision made, either before or after judgment, by a court, tribunal, judge, or other judicial officer in an action or proceeding. Hearn v. Gunther, 57 Cal. App.2d 82, 134 P.2d 3, 5; an objection, oral or written, taken, in course of an action or proceeding, as to bail, to the decision or a ruling of a judge, or to something in his charge to a jury. In re Pardue's Estate, 57 Cal.App.2d 918, 135 P.2d 394, 395.

An objection to a pleading or any part thereof for want of substance is a general exception; an objection to the form in which a cause of action is stated is a special exception. Cochran v. People's Nat. Bank, Tex.Civ.App., 271 S.W. 433, 434.

Objections to report of master on bill for injunction held "exceptions". Respro, Inc., v. Worcester Backing Co., 291 Mass. 467, 197 N.E. 198, 200.

To authorize review of alleged error in admitting evidence in compensation case, there must be an "exception", that known to equity practice, and defined as act of appealing from rulings appearing of record, and nothing more. Indrisano's Case, 307 Mass. 520, 30 N.E.2d 538, 539.

Proviso and Exception Distinguished

A "proviso" and an "exception" are substantially the same thing. Evans v. McCabe, 164 Tenn. 672, 52 S.W.2d 159, 160.

A proviso differs from an exception. 1 Barn. & Ald. 99. An exception *exempts,* absolutely, from the operation of an engagement or an enactment; a proviso, properly speaking, defeats their operation, *conditionally.* An exception takes out of an engagement or enactment something which would otherwise be part of the subject-matter of it; a proviso avoids them by way of defeasance or excuse. 8 Am.Jur. 242; Board of Com'rs of Noble County v. Whitney, 73 Okl. 160, 175 P. 112, 113; Philadelphia Life Ins. Co. v. Farnsley's Adm'r, 162 Ky. 27, 171 S.W. 1004, 1005; New Jersey State Board of Optometrists v. S. S. Kresge Co., Sup., 113 N.J.L. 287, 174 A. 353, 357; Sowers Plan Crop Ins. Mut. Co. v. Hobbs, 146 Kan. 166, 68 P.2d 1110, 1111.

The ordinary office of an "exception" or "proviso" in a policy is to take special cases out of a general class or to guard against misinterpretation. Landau v. Equitable Life Assur. Soc. of United States, 1 N.Y.S.2d 891, 895, 166 Misc. 42.

Reservation and Exception as Synonymous or Distinguishable

A reservation is always of a thing not in esse, but newly created or reserved out of the land or tenement demised; an exception is always of a part of the thing granted, and of a thing in esse. Co.Litt. 47*a;* 4 Kent, Comm. 468.

A "reservation" creates some new right in grantor while an "exception" withholds from grant title to some part of property which would otherwise pass. Clark v. Pauley, 291 Ky. 637, 165 S.W.2d 161, 162; Federal Land Bank of New Orleans v. Cooper, 190 Miss. 490, 200 So. 729, 730, 731; Goss v. Congdon, 114 Vt. 155, 40 A.2d 429, 430.

A reservation does not affect the description of the property conveyed, but retains to the grantor some right upon the property, as an easement, whereas an exception operates upon the description and withdraws from the description the excepted property. Moore v. Davis, 273 Ky. 838, 117 S.W.2d 1033, 1035.

A "reservation" is always of something taken back out of that which is clearly granted, while an "exception" is of some part of the estate not granted at all. Houghtaling v. Stoothoff, 170 Misc. 773, 12 N.Y.S.2d 207, 210; Lewis v. Standard Oil Co. of California, C.C.A.Cal., 88 F.2d 512, 514.

A reservation provides for return of rent or service, regarded as issuing out of land granted. An exception withholds particular portion of land granted. Cook v. Farley, 195 Miss. 638, 15 So.2d 352, 355; Marias River Syndicate v. Big West Oil Co., 98 Mont. 254, 38 P.2d 599, 601.

Reservation means something issuing or arising out of thing granted while an exception means some part of the estate not granted, or withdrawn from the effect of the grant, although the terms are often used indiscriminately and given effect according to the obvious intent of the parties. Vance v. Pritchard, 213 N.C. 552, 197 S.E. 182, 185.

Reservation must always be in favor of and for benefit of grantor, whereas exception is mere exclusion from grant, of some interest which may be vested in grantor or outstanding in another; reservation reserves to grantor some new thing, either issuing out of or incident to thing granted, while exception in deed is clause exempting from operation thereof and retaining in grantor title to some part of the thing granted or excepting some part of thing granted, title to which is at the time in another. Klein v. Humble Oil & Refining Co., Tex.Civ.App., 67 S.W.2d 911, 915.

Reservation reserves to grantor some new interest out of thing granted, while exception excludes from operation of grant some existing part of estate. Petty v. Griffith, Mo., 165 S.W.2d 412, 414; U. S. v. 1,010.8 Acres, More or Less, Situate in Sussex County, Del., D.C.Del., 56 F.Supp. 120, 128.

The terms "reservation" and "exception" are frequently used as interchangeable for synonymous terms. Nelson v. Bacon, 113 Vt. 161, 32 A.2d 140, 145; Murphy v. Sunset Hills Ass'n, 243 Wis. 139, 9 N.W.2d 613, 615; Meaning intended must be determined by reference to subject matter and surrounding circumstances. Federal Land Bank of New Orleans v. Cooper, 190 Miss. 490, 200 So. 729, 730, 731; Duus v. Town of Ephrata, 14 Wash.2d 426, 128 P.2d 510, 511; Parties' intention, not language used, is dominating factor in determining whether provision is reservation or exception. Goss v. Congdon, 114 Vt. 155, 40 A.2d 429, 430; Technical meaning will yield to the manifest intent. Jensen v. Sheker, 231 Iowa 240, 1 N.W.2d 262, 267; Technical misnomer does not operate to defeat attempted reservation or exception. Clark v. Pauley, 291 Ky. 637, 165 S.W. 2d 161, 162; It has been also said that there is a diversity between an exception and a saving, for an exception exempts clearly, but a saving goes to the matters touched, and does not exempt. Plowd. 361. Ogden v. Straus Bldg. Corporation, 187 Wis. 232, 202 N.W. 34, 44; Haymaker v. Windsor Reservoir & Canal Co., 81 Colo. 168, 254 P. 768, 770; Central Bank & Trust Co. v. Wyatt, 189 N.C. 107, 126 S.E. 93, 94; Greenspan v. Yaple, 194 N.Y.S. 658, 659, 201 App.Div. 575.

Statutory Law

An exception in a statute is a clause designed to reserve or exempt some individuals from the general class of persons or things to which the language of the act in general attaches. People v. Bailey, 103 Misc. 366, 171 N.Y.S. 394, 397.

An exception differs from an explanation, which, by the use of a *videlicet, proviso,* etc., is allowed only to explain doubtful clauses precedent, or to separate and distribute generals into particulars. Cutler v. Tufts, 3 Pick., Mass., 272.

An "exception" exempts absolutely from the operation of the statute, while a "proviso" generally defeats operation of statute conditionally. Oregon Liquor Control Commission v. Coe, 163 Or. 646, 99 P.2d 29, 31; People v. Thursam, City Ct., 23 N.Y.S.2d 706, 710, 713.

The office of an "exception" in a statute is to except something from the operative effect of a statute or to qualify or restrain the generality of the substantive enactment to which it is attached, and it is not necessarily limited to the section of the statute immediately following or preceding. Gatliff Coal Co. v. Cox, C.C.A.Ky., 142 F.2d 876, 882.

Two statutes relating to same subject must be read together, and provisions of one having special application to particular subject will be deemed an "exception" to other statute general in its terms. Eagleton v. Murphy, 348 Mo. 949, 156 S.W.2d 683, 685, 138 A.L.R. 749.

Zoning

An "exception" in zoning ordinance is one allowable where conditions detailed therein as those on which exception may be permitted exist. Application of Devereux Foundation, 351 Pa. 478, 41 A.2d 744, 746.

Exceptions may be treated as a legislative process, conditions for which must be found in the zoning ordinance and may not be varied, and variances may be treated as judicial function through appeals from administrative orders, whereby literal enforcement of ordinance may be disregarded. Stone v. Cray, 89 N.H. 483, 200 A. 517, 521.

EXCEPTION EN MASSE. An assignment in defendant's amended motion for new trial that "court erred in giving Instructions Nos. 1 to 10, inclusive", is "exception en masse". Tugg v. State, 206 Ark. 161, 174 S.W.2d 374, 376.

EXCEPTION OF LACK OF CAPACITY TO STAND IN JUDGMENT. Challenges authority of plaintiff to institute and prosecute suit regardless of whether plaintiff owns or has an interest in the claim. It is usually resorted to where plaintiff is alleged to be under some disability or where he sues through a representative who, it is alleged, has no authority. Riche v. Ascension Parish School Board, La.App., 200 So. 681, 685.

EXCEPTION OF MISJOINDER seeks to restrain plaintiff's pursuit of the cause when there is present another party whose liabilities or rights are not connected with the exceptor. Henrichs v. New Orleans Public Service, La.App., 179 So. 610.

EXCEPTION OF NO CAUSE OF ACTION addresses itself to sufficiency in law of the petition and exhibits attached. Bartholomew v. Impastato, La.App., 12 So.2d 700, 702.

EXCEPTION OF NO RIGHT OF ACTION challenges plaintiff's interest or right to assert cause of action. McCain v. Le Blanc Bros., La.App., 10 So.2d 116, 118.

EXCEPTION OF WANT OF INTEREST or of "no right of action" is afforded as means of challenging preliminarily either interest or right of plaintiff to assert cause of action and is not limited to want of capacity in plaintiff as such to bring suit. McCain v. Le Blanc Bros., La.App., 10 So.2d 116, 118.

EXCEPTIONAL CIRCUMSTANCES. Peculiar urgency, existed where death sentence was imposed, or defendant had not been given a reasonable opportunity to prepare for trial, or the commonwealth conceded belatedly, though not too late, that its material evidence is perjured. Sharpe v. Commonwealth of Kentucky, C.C.A.Ky., 135 F.2d 974, 977.

EXCEPTIS EXCIPIENDIS. Lat. With all necessary exceptions.

EXCEPTOR. In old English law. A party who entered an exception or plea.

EXCERPTA, or EXCERPTS. Extracts.

EXCESS. When a defendant pleaded to an action of assault that the plaintiff trespassed on his land, and he would not depart when ordered, whereupon he, *molliter manus imposuit*, gently laid hands on him, the replication of *excess* was to the effect that the defendant used more force than necessary. Wharton.

Degree or amount by which one thing or number exceeds another, and the remainder or the difference between two numbers is the excess of one over the other. In re Bunce's Estate, 100 Misc. 385, 165 N.Y.S. 426.

Statute providing that, if capital used or invested in business of corporations includes borrowed capital in "excess" of capital stock, surplus and undivided profits, such excess of borrowed capital shall be added to capital stock, surplus and undivided profits as basis for computing franchise tax, means that, if corporation uses any borrowed or additional capital, such borrowed or additional capital must be added to the other capital in order to form basis for computing the tax. State v. Union Bldg. Corporation, 185 La. 598, 170 So. 7, 12.

EXCESS FEES of tax collector consist of sum remaining in collector's hands after deducting from total of all lawful fees collected, his maximum annual fees, his deputy hire, his official expenses and one-fourth of remainder until such one-fourth amounts to specified sum. American Indemnity Co. v. Red River Nat. Bank in Clarksville, Tex. Civ.App., 132 S.W.2d 473, 480.

EXCESS INSURANCE. No recovery for loss of cotton which was insured under another policy could be had except that recoverable as "excess insurance," although the other policy also provided for its avoidance by other insurance, for, as to such other policy, the litigated policy was not "other" but merely "excess insurance." St. Paul Fire & Marine Ins. Co. v. Garza County Warehouse & Marketing Ass'n, C.C.A.Tex., 93 F.2d 590, 592; Travelers Indemnity Co. v. State Automobile Ins. Co., 67 Ohio App. 457, 37 N.E.2d 198, 200.

Where fire and theft policy issued to conditional seller of truck contained indorsement against accidental collision occurring after insured had repossessed truck, and policy provided that such insurance was excess insurance where any specific insurance existed for benefit of insured, when seller later repossessed truck, insurance taken by seller became "excess insurance." Fageol Truck & Coach Co. v. Pacific Indemnity Co., 18 Cal.2d 731, 117 P.2d 661, 669.

Where materials which belonged to owners who carried fire insurance covering merchandise while in possession of contractors, were sent to contractors to be made into finished garments, fire policies of contractors covering merchandise held in trust but excluding property otherwise specifically insured, provided only "excess insurance" in accordance with terms thereof, as to goods in possession of contractors who had insured themselves as bailees. Gordon v. Franklin Fire Ins. Co. of Philadelphia, 262 App.Div. 328, 28 N.Y.S.2d 480, 482.

EXCESS OF JURISDICTION. A case in which court has initially proceeded properly within its jurisdiction but steps out of jurisdiction in making of some order or in the doing of some judicial act. Olson v. District Court of Salt Lake County, 93 Utah, 145, 71 P.2d 529, 534, 112 A.L.R. 438. Act within judge's general power is unauthorized in particular case. Beckwith v. McAlister, 165 S.C. 1, 162 S.E. 623, 628; Carter v. Mitchell, 225 Ala. 287, 142 So. 514, 517; In re Knox' Estate, 52 Cal.App.2d 338, 126 P.2d 108, 112. Acts which exceed defined power of court in any instance. Abelleira v. District Court of Appeal, Third Dist., 17 Cal.2d 280, 109 P.2d 942, 948, 132 A.L.R. 715.

A departure by a court from those recognized and established requirements of law, however close apparent adherence to mere form in method of procedure, which has the effect of depriving one of a constitutional right, is an "excess of jurisdiction." Wuest v. Wuest, 53 Cal.App.2d 339, 127 P.2d 934, 937.

EXCESS OR SURPLUS WATER. Mean simply water which is flowing in stream in addition to what may be termed adjudicated waters. Quigley v. McIntosh, 88 Mont. 103, 290 P. 266, 268; Any water not needed for reasonable beneficial uses of those having prior rights is "excess or surplus water". City of Pasadena v. City of Alhambra, Cal., 207 P.2d 17, 28.

EXCESSES. Spouse's gambling habits or extravagances when carried to excess, constitute "excesses" authorizing separation from bed and board. Moore v. Moore, 192 La. 289, 187 So. 670, 672.

EXCESSIVE. Greater than what is usual or proper; overmuch; a general term for what goes beyond just measure or amount. Austin St. Ry. Co. v. Oldham, Tex.Civ.App., 109 S.W.2d 235, 237. Tending to or marked by excess, which is the quality or state of exceeding the proper or reasonable limit or measure. Railway Co. v. Johnston, 106 Ga. 130, 32 S.E. 78; Morrow v. Missouri Gas & Electric Service Co., 315 Mo. 367, 286 S.W. 106, 111.

EXCESSIVE ASSESSMENT. A tax assessment grossly disproportionate as compared with other assessments. Southern California Telephone Co. v. Los Angeles County, 45 Cal.App.2d 111, 113 P.2d 773, 776.

EXCESSIVE BAIL. Bail in a sum more than will be reasonably sufficient to prevent evasion of the law by flight or concealment; bail which is per se unreasonably great and clearly disproportionate to the offense involved, or shown to be so by the special circumstances of the particular case. In re Losasso, 15 Colo. 163, 24 P. 1080, 10 L.R.A. 847; Ex parte Ryan, 44 Cal. 558.

The denial of bail is not necessarily "excessive bail", although such denial may be in a particular case the equivalent of excessive bail. People ex rel. Shapiro v. Keeper of City Prison, Tombs, New York County, 265 App.Div. 474, 39 N.Y.S.2d 526, 531.

EXCESSIVE DAMAGES. See Damages.

EXCESSIVE DRUNKENNESS. Drunkenness is excessive where a party is so far deprived of his reason and understanding as to render him incapable of understanding character and consequences of his act. Taylor v. Koenigstein, 128 Neb. 809, 260 N.W. 544.

EXCESSIVE FINE OR PENALTY. Any fine or penalty which seriously impairs the capacity of gaining a business livelihood. C. F. Smith Co. v. Fitzgerald, 270 Mich. 659, 259 N.W. 352.

EXCESSIVE OR INTEMPERATE USE OF INTOXICANTS. In benefit certificate. Habitual indulgence in intoxicating liquors to such extent as to impair health or otherwise render insurance risk more hazardous. Wising v. Brotherhood of American Yeomen, 132 Minn. 303, 156 N.W. 247, 248, Ann.Cas.1918A, 621.

EXCESSIVE OXIDATION. As used in product patent for improvement in bleached and dyed furs and the like, relate to what would occur if it was attempted to effect oxidation, bleaching of a dark skin with an ordinary bleach, such as strong hydrogen peroxide, without a protecting agent. Steinfur Patents Corporation v. J. Meyerson, Inc., D.C.N.Y., 56 F.2d 372, 382.

EXCESSIVE SENTENCE. No sentence is excessive which is within limits fixed by law. Bryant v. State, 39 Ga.App. 26, 145 S.E. 911; State v. Brackett, 218 N.C. 369, 11 S.E.2d 146, 149.

EXCESSIVE SPEED. Automobile's speed is "excessive" whenever it places car beyond driver's control. Esponette v. Wiseman, 130 Me. 297, 155 A. 650, 653.

EXCESSIVE TAX. One that exceeds what the tax would be if correctly calculated at the legal rate on the valuation as finally fixed by the county authorities. Pocomoke Guano Co. v. City of New Bern, 172 N.C. 258, 90 S.E. 202, 203.

EXCESSIVE VERDICT. A verdict which is result of passion or prejudice. Babb v. Murray, 26 Cal.App.2d 153, 79 P.2d 159, 160.

The test of whether a verdict is "excessive" is whether the amount thereof is such as to shock the conscience of the court. Scheidegger v. Thompson, Mo.App., 174 S.W.2d 216, 222.

EXCESSIVELY. To excess. Penn Mut. Life Ins. Co. v. Nunnery, 176 Miss. 197, 167 So. 416, 419.

EXCESSIVELY INTOXICATED. Where one is so intoxicated as to be so far deprived of his reason and understanding as to render him incapable of knowing the character and consequences of his act. Keedick v. Brogan, 116 Neb. 339, 217 N.W. 583, 585.

EXCESSIVUM IN JURE REPROBATUR. EXCESSUS IN RE QUALIBET JURE REPROBATUR COMMUNI. Co. Litt. 44. Excess in law is reprehended. Excess in anything is reprehended at common law.

EXCHANGE. To barter; to swap. Dairymen's League Co-op. Ass'n v. Metropolitan Casualty Ins. Co. of New York, Sup., 8 N.Y.S.2d 403, 412. To part with, give or transfer for an equivalent. Kessler v. United States, C.C.A.Pa., 124 F.2d 152, 154; Dairymen's League Co-op. Ass'n v. Metropolitan Casualty Ins. Co. of New York, Sup., 8 N.Y.S. 2d 403, 412.

Act of giving or taking one thing for another. United States v. Paine, D.C.Mass., 31 F.Supp. 898, 900; Kessler v. United States, C.C.A.Pa., 124 F.2d 152, 154; contract by terms of which specific property is given in consideration of the receipt of property other than money. Capps v. Mines Service, 175 Or. 248, 152 P.2d 414, 416; Mutual grant of equal interests, the one in consideration of the other, Hale v. Helvering, 66 App.D.C. 242, 85 F.2d 819, 821, 822; mutual transfer of property other than for money although one of parties may pay a sum of money in addition to property, Law v. McLaughlin, D.C.Cal., 2 F.Supp. 601, 603; transaction in which one piece of property, usually something other than money or its equivalent, is given in return for another piece of property, Hadley Falls Trust Co. v. United States, C.C.A.Mass., 110 F.2d 887, 891; transfer of property for other property, Helvering v. Nebraska Bridge Supply & Lumber Co., C.C.A.8, 115 F.2d 288, 290; transfer of property for property or some value other than money, Burger-Phillips Co. v. Commissioner of Internal Revenue, C.C.A.Ala., 126 F.2d 934, 936; transfers of enduring interests and not such as must immediately be reconveyed in fulfillment of preconceived plan, Morgan v. Helvering, C.C.A.2, 117 F.2d 334, 336.

An exchange is two sales. Robbins v. Pacific Eastern Corporation, 8 Cal.2d 241, 65 P.2d 42, 56.

The criterion in determining whether a transaction is a sale or an exchange is whether there is a determination of value of things exchanged, and if no price is set for either property it is an "exchange". Gruver v. Commissioner of Internal Revenue, C.C.A.4, 142 F.2d 363, 366.

The mutual transfers must be in kind, and any transaction into which money enters, either as the consideration or as a basis of measure is excluded. Hoovel v. State, 125 Tex.Cr.R. 545, 69 S.W.2d 104, 108; Trenton Cotton Oil Co. v. C. I. R., C.C.A.6, 147 F.2d 33, 36.

Capital Assets

Reciprocal transfers. Helvering v. William Flaccus Oak Leather Co., 313 U.S. 247, 61 S.Ct. 878, 880, 85 L.Ed. 1310; Harwick v. Commissioner of Internal Revenue, C.C.A.8, 133 F.2d 732, 737.

Conveyance of mortgaged realty by mortgagor in consideration of payment of past-due taxes thereon. Philips v. Commissioner of Internal Revenue, C.C.A.3, 112 F.2d 721, 722.

Mortgagor's transfers of equity of redemption in property which constituted a capital asset of mortgagor to mortgagee in return for release of liability on accompanying bond given to evidence or further secure the mortgage debt. Stamler v. C. I. R., C.C.A.3, 145 F.2d 37, 39.

Commercial Law

A negotiation by which one person transfers to another funds which he has in a certain place, either at a price agreed upon or which is fixed by commercial usage. Nicely v. Bank, 15 Ind.App. 563, 44 N.E. 572, 57 Am.St.Rep. 245; Iowa State Sav. Bank of Fairfield v. City Nat. Bank, 183 Iowa, 1347, 168 N.W. 148, 149, L.R.A.1918F, 169.

The process of settling accounts or debts between parties residing at a distance from each other, without the intervention of money, by exchanging orders or drafts, called bills of exchange; the payment of debts in different places by an exchange or transfer of credits. Webster, Dict.

The profit which arises from a maritime loan, when such profit is a percentage on the money lent, considering it in the light of money lent in one place to be returned in another, with a difference in amount in the sum borrowed and that paid, arising from the difference of time and place. The term is commonly used in this sense by French writers. Hall, Emerig, Mar.Loans, 56*n*.

A public place where merchants, brokers, factors, etc., meet to transact their business.

Conveyancing

A mutual grant of equal interests, (in lands or tenements,) the one in consideration of the other. 2 Bl.Comm. 323; Windsor v. Collinson, 32 Or. 297, 52 P. 26; Herring Motor Co. v. Ætna Trust & Savings Co., 87 Ind.App. 83, 154 N.E. 29, 31; Baltimore & O. R. Co. v. Western Union Telegraph Co., D.C.N.Y., 241 F. 162, 169; Finke v. Boyer, 331 Mo. 1242, 56 S.W.2d 372.

Nontaxable Exchange

Elements are that property be transferred to a corporation solely in exchange for stock or securities in corporation and that transferors immediately after exchange be in control of corporation, through ownership of 80 per cent. of all voting stock and at least 80 per cent. of all other classes of stock of corporation. Commissioner of Internal Revenue v. Cement Investors, C.C.A.10, 122 F.2d 380, 383.

Personal Property Law

Exchange of goods is a commutation, transmutation, or transfer of goods for other goods, as distinguished from *sale*, which is a transfer of goods for money. 2 Bl.Comm. 446; 2 Steph. Comm. 120; Elwell v. Chamberlin, 31 N.Y. 624; Cooper v. State, 37 Ark. 418; Preston v. Keene, 14 Pet. 137, 10 L.Ed. 387.

Exchange is a contract by which the parties mutually give, or agree to give, one thing for another, neither thing, or both things, being money only.

The distinction between a sale and exchange of property is rather one of shadow than of substance. In both cases the title to property is absolutely transferred; and the same rules of law are applicable to the transaction, whether the consideration of the contract is money or by way of barter. It can make no essential difference in the rights and obligations of parties that goods and merchandise are transferred and paid for by other goods and merchandise instead of by money, which is but the representative of value or property. Com. v. Clark, 14 Gray, Mass., 367.

Stock and Securities

To exchange one security for a different security of some kind or for other property or rights. Mertz v. H. D. Hudson Mfg. Co., 194 Minn. 636, 261 N.W. 472.

Plan whereby preferred stock was issued in exchange for half of common stock held by voting trustees and other half was split up on basis of two for one constituted a genuine "exchange" of common stock for preferred stock in pursuance of a plan of "recapitalization". Bass v. Commissioner of Internal Revenue, C.C.A.1, 129 F.2d 300, 307.

Where holder of nearly all of a corporation's stock delivered securities to corporation, gave corporation his check in payment of preferred stock, and received from corporation its check in payment of his securities, and checks, which were simultaneously deposited, cancelled each other almost entirely, transaction was exchange. Louis W. Gunby, Inc., v. Helvering, 74 App.D.C. 185, 122 F.2d 203, 206.

For "Arbitration of Exchange," "Bill of Exchange," "Dry Exchange," "First of Exchange," and "Owelty of Exchange," see those titles.

EXCHANGE BROKER. One who negotiates bills of exchange drawn on foreign countries or on other places in the same country; one who makes and concludes bargains for others in matters of money or merchandise. Little Rock v. Barton, 33 Ark. 444; Portland v. O'Neill, 1 Or. 219.

EXCHANGE OF LIVINGS. In ecclesiastical law. This is effected by resigning them into the bishop's hands, and each party being inducted into the other's benefice. If either die before both are inducted, the exchange is void.

EXCHANGED means a complete divestment of property. Lord v. Smith, 293 Mass. 555, 200 N.E. 547, 550.

EXCHEQUER. That department of the English government which has charge of the collection of the national revenue; the treasury department.

It is said to have been so named from the chequered cloth, resembling a chess-board, which anciently covered the table there, and on which, when certain of the king's accounts were made up, the sums were marked and scored with counters. 3 Bl.Comm. 44.

For "Court of Exchequer" and "Court of Exchequer Chamber," see those titles.

EXCHEQUER BILLS. Bills of credit issued in England by authority of parliament. Brande.

Instruments issued at the exchequer, under the authority, for the most part, of acts of parliament passed for the purpose, and containing an engagement on the part of the government for repayment of the principal sums advanced with interest. 2 Steph.Comm. 586. See Briscoe v. Bank of Kentucky, 11 Pet. 328, 9 L.Ed. 709.

EXCHEQUER DIVISION. A division of the English high court of justice, to which the special business of the court of exchequer was specially assigned by section 34 of the judicature act of 1873. Merged in the queen's bench division from and after 1881, by order in council under section 31 of that act. Wharton.

EXCISE. An inland imposition, paid sometimes upon the consumption of the commodity, and frequently upon the retail sale. 1 Bl.Comm. 318; Patton v. Brady, 184 U.S. 608, 22 S.Ct. 493, 46 L. Ed. 713; Portland Bank v. Apthorp, 12 Mass. 256.

An excise has been defined as meaning tribute, custom, tax, tollage, or assessment, a fixed absolute and direct charge laid on merchandise, products, or commodities without any regard to amount of property belonging to those on whom it may fall, or to any supposed relation between money expended for a public object and a special benefit occasioned to those by whom the charge is to be paid. In re Opinion of the Justices, 282 Mass. 619, 186 N. E. 490, 491.

An excise is an impost for a license to pursue certain callings or to deal in special commodities or to exercise particular franchises. East Ohio Gas Co. v. Tax Commission of Ohio, D.C.Ohio, 43 F.2d 170, 172; any tax not falling within classification of poll or property tax, Diefendorf v. Gallet, 51 Idaho 619, 10 P.2d 307, 312; any tax which is not directly on property or the rents or incomes from real estate, Anne Arundel County Com'rs v. English, 182 Md. 514, 35 A.2d 135, 141; duties laid on manufacture, sale, or consumption of commodities, or upon certain callings or occupations, In re City of Enid, 195 Okl. 365, 158 P.2d 348, 350, 159 A.L.R. 358; every form of charge imposed by public authority on performance of act, enjoyment of privilege, or engagement in occupation, Idaho Gold Dredging Co. v. Balderston, 258 Idaho 692, 78 P.2d 105, 112; every form of taxation which is not laid directly on persons or property. Gila Meat Co. v. State, 35 Ariz. 194, 276 P. 1, 2; Lutz v. Arnold, 208 Ind. 480, 193 N.E. 840; public charges on subjects other than manufacture and sale of commodities, such as licenses to pursue particular callings, franchises of corporations and particularly the franchise of corporate existence, and inheritance or succession of estates. Pollock v. Farmers' L. & T. Co., 158 U.S. 601, 15 S.Ct. 912, 39 L.Ed. 1108; Albert Pick & Co. v. Jordan, 169 Cal. 1, 145 P. 506, 513, Ann.Cas.1916C, 1237; Des Moines Union Ry. Co. v. Chicago Great Western Ry. Co., 188 Iowa, 1019, 177 N.W. 90, 9 A.L.R. 1557; Northern Cent. Ry. Co. v. Fidelity Trust Co., 152 Md. 94, 136 A. 66, 68, 60 A.L.R. 558; Hattiesburg Grocery Co. v. Robertson, 126 Miss. 34, 88 So. 4, 5, 25 A.L.R. 748; something cut off from price paid on sale of goods as contribution to government, City of Louisville v. Churchill Downs, 267 Ky. 339, 102 S. W.2d 10, 13; tax imposed on performance of act, engagement in occupation, or enjoyment of privilege, State v. Fields, Ohio App., 35 N.E.2d 744, 747; tax laid on manufacture, sale, or consumption of commodities or upon licenses to pursue certain occupations or upon corporate privileges. Alexander Theatre Ticket Office v. U. S., C.C.A. N.Y., 23 F.2d 44, 46; City of De Land v. Florida Public Service Co., 119 Fla. 804, 161 So. 735, 738.

An "excise tax" is often used as synonymous with "privilege" or "license tax". Shannon v. Streckfus Steamers, 279 Ky. 649, 131 S.W.2d 833, 838.

The terms excise tax and privilege tax are synonymous. American Airways v. Wallace, D.C.Tenn., 57 F.2d 877, 880.

English Law

The name given to the duties or taxes laid on certain articles produced and consumed at home, among which spirits have always been the most important; but, exclusive of these, the duties on the licenses of auctioneers, brewers, etc., and on the licenses to keep dogs, kill game, etc., are included in the excise duties. Wharton.

Tax and Excise Distinguished

A tax imposed directly by Legislature without assessment and measured by amount of business done, income previously received, or by extent to which privilege may have been enjoyed or exercised by the taxpayer, irrespective of nature or value of his assets or his investments in business, is excise tax while assessed tax on valuation of property is property tax. City of De Land v. Florida Public Service Co., 119 Fla. 804, 161 So. 735, 738.

A "property tax" is a visitational tax and is the taking of part of taxpayer's wealth, represented by property he owns for needs of government, and is not an "excise tax" for privilege of owning property for period of fiscal year. Bemis Hardwood Lumber Co. v. Graham County, N. C., 214 N.C. 167, 198 S.E. 843, 845.

A tax directly on property is a property tax; but a tax is an excise tax where it is not a tax on property as such, but on certain kinds of property, having reference to their origin and their intended use. State ex rel. Porterie v. H. L. Hunt, Inc., 182 La. 1073, 162 So. 777, 103 A.L.R. 9.

An excise tax is an inland impost on articles of manufacture or sale, and also upon licenses to pursue certain trades, or to deal in certain commodities, and property tax is a tax which is not a capitation tax or a direct tax on land or personalty. Flynn, Welch & Yates v. State Tax Commission, 38 N.M. 131, 28 P.2d 889, 891.

As usually used, "franchise tax" is tax on intangible values inhering to business and added value given to tangible property, being "ad valorem" as distinguished from "excise" or "privilege" tax. State Tax Commission v. Petroleum Exploration, 253 Ky. 119, 68 S.W.2d 777.

If a mortgage registration tax is in effect upon the instrument itself, the tax is a "property tax", but if the tax is imposed solely upon the privilege of registration, and validity or use of the instrument is not affected by failure to pay the tax, the tax is an "excise tax". Community Public Service Co. v. James, Tex.Civ.App., 167 S.W.2d 588, 595.

Income tax is a "property tax" and not an "excise tax." Jensen v. Henneford, 185 Wash. 209, 53 P.2d 607, 610.

The words "tax" and "excise," although often used as synonymous, are to be considered as having entirely distinct and separate significations, under Const.Mass. c. 1, § 1, art. 4. The former is a charge apportioned either among the whole people of the state or those residing within certain districts, municipalities, or sections. It is required to be imposed, so that, if levied for the public charges of government, it shall be shared according to the estate, real and personal, which each person may possess; or, if raised to defray the cost of some local improvement of a public nature, it shall be borne by those who will receive some special and peculiar benefit or advantage which an expenditure of money for a public object may cause to those on whom the tax is assessed. An excise, on the other hand, is of a different character. It is based on no rule of apportionment or equality whatever. It is a fixed, absolute, and direct charge laid on merchandise, products, or commodities, without any regard to the amount of property belonging to those on whom it may fall, or to any supposed relation between money expended for a public object and a special benefit occasioned to those by whom the charge is to be paid. Oliver v. Washington Mills, 11 Allen, Mass., 268.

EXCISE LAW. A law imposing excise duties on specified commodities, and providing for the collection of revenue therefrom. In a more restricted and more popular sense, a law regulating, restricting, or taxing the manufacture or sale of intoxicating liquors.

A statute requiring payment of license fee for operating motor vehicle on state highway for hire is an "excise tax measure" rather than a "police measure." Comp.Laws Nev. § 4437. Ziemer v. Babcock & Wilcox Co., D.C.Nev., 22 F.Supp. 384, 385.

EXCISE LIEU PROPERTY TAX. Tax on gross premiums received and collected by designated classes of insurance companies held "excise lieu property tax." United Pacific Ins. Co. v. Bakes, 57 Idaho 537, 67 P.2d 1024, 1029.

EXCLUSA. In old English law. A sluice to carry off water; the payment to the lord for the benefit of such a sluice. Cowell.

EXCLUSION. Denial of entry. Ex parte Domingo Corypus, D.C.Wash., 6 F.2d 336.

"Exclusions" are things barred and not admitted. Raymond v. Great American Indemnity Co., 86 N.H. 93, 163 A. 713, 716.

EXCLUSION, RULE OF. A witness, whether a party to the cause or not, may not testify as to his uncommunicated intent, purpose or motive. Occidental Life Ins. Co. of Cal. v. Nichols, 97 So.2d 879, 885, 266 Ala. 521. This rule applies even though witness' intent or state of mind is material to the issue. McCain v. City of Montgomery, 92 So.2d 678, 681, 38 Ala.App. 568.

EXCLUSIVE. Appertaining to the subject alone, not including, admitting, or pertaining to any others. Fellows v. Seymour, 171 Misc. 833, 13 N.Y.S.2d 803, 805. Sole. State v. Bridges, 246 Ala. 486, 21 So.2d 316, 319. Shutting out; debarring from interference or participation; vested in one person alone.

The term "exclusive" as used to define quantity of control of offending agency for res ipsa loquitur to apply means that control must be exclusive as against all who do not have a concurrent joint control. Frenkil v. Johnson National Retailers Mut. Ins. Co., 175 Md. 592, 3 A.2d 479, 485.

EXCLUSIVE AGENCY. A contract to give an "exclusive agency" to deal with property is ordinarily interpreted as not precluding competition by the principal generally, but only as precluding him from appointing another agent to accomplish the result. Navy Gas & Supply Co. v. Schoech, 105 Colo. 374, 98 P.2d 860, 861, 863, 126 A.L.R. 1225.

The grant of an "exclusive agency to sell," that is, the exclusive right to sell the products of a wholesaler in a specified territory, ordinarily is interpreted as precluding competition in any form within designated area. Navy Gas & Supply Co. v. Schoech, 105 Colo. 374, 98 P.2d 860, 861, 126 A.L.R. 1225.

Relationship such as that created by contract between manufacturer and sole distributors within specified territory for outright sales to distributors who established retail prices. Stratton & Terstegge Co. v. Stiglitz Furnace Co., 258 Ky. 678, 81 S.W.2d 1, 3.

EXCLUSIVE AGENCY CONTRACT means that owner will not sell property through any other agency. Torrey & Dean v. Coyle, 138 Or. 509, 7 P.2d 561, 562.

EXCLUSIVE CONTROL. The "exclusive control" of thing causing accident, applies to right of control of instrumentality causing injury. Gerhart v. Southern California Gas Co., 56 Cal.App.2d 425, 132 P.2d 874, 877.

As used in statute giving city exclusive control of school system, means control to exclusion of control exercised by county or state over other types of independent school districts authorized by school laws. Temple Independent School Dist. v. Proctor, Tex.Civ.App., 97 S.W.2d 1047, 1054.

EXCLUSIVE JURISDICTION. These words preclude idea of co-existence, and mean possessed to exclusion of others. Dunn Const. Co. v. Craig, 191 Miss. 682, 2 So.2d 166, 171.

The words "exclusive jurisdiction" when used in statutes with respect to inferior criminal courts were only intended to define jurisdiction of inferior criminal courts established thereby as between themselves. People ex rel. Kawiecki v. Carhart, 170 Misc. 894, 13 N.Y.S.2d 293, 294.

Under statute giving United States District Courts "exclusive jurisdiction" of violations of Securities Exchange Act, all criminal or civil proceedings for violations of the act must be brought in such courts. Wright v. Securities and Exchange Commission, C.C.A.2, 112 F.2d 89, 95.

EXCLUSIVE LICENSE is permission to do thing and contract not to give leave to any one else to do same thing. Overman Cushion Tire Co. v. Goodyear Tire & Rubber Co., C.C.A.N.Y., 59 F.2d 998, 999.

A license which binds licensor not to enlarge thereafter the scope of other licenses already granted, or increase the number of licenses, is an "exclusive license", Mechanical Ice Tray Corporation v. General Motors Corporation, C.C.A.N.Y., 144 F.2d 720, 725.

EXCLUSIVE LICENSEE. One granted exclusive right and license to use, manufacture, and sell patented article. Deitel v. Chisholm, C.C.A.N.Y., 42 F.2d 172, 173. One having exclusive right to use patented method and apparatus in designated territory. Paul E. Hawkinson Co. v. Carnell, C. C.A.Pa., 112 F.2d 396, 398.

EXCLUSIVE MOVING PICTURE RIGHTS. Granted by author in book held to include technical improvements in motion pictures developed during license. L. C. Page & Co. v. Fox Film Corporation, C.C.A.N.Y., 83 F.2d 196, 199.

EXCLUSIVE OF ANY OUT BUILDINGS as used in covenant that within restricted area, no residence should be erected, "actual bona fide cost" of which "exclusive of any outbuildings" should be less than $10,000, meant that no buildings other than the residence could or should be considered. Dillingham v. Kahn, 188 Ark. 759, 67 S.W.2d 735.

EXCLUSIVE OF INTEREST AND COSTS as used in statute defining court's pecuniary jurisdiction, refers to interest accrued before filing of complaint, not that accruing after suit was brought. Athan v. Hartford Fire Ins. Co., C.C.A.N.Y., 73 F. 2d 66, 67.

EXCLUSIVE ORIGINAL JURISDICTION IN ALL CASES. Constitutional provision, giving circuit court "exclusive original jurisdiction in all cases in equity", established in circuit court exclusive jurisdiction in all cases in equity involving matters which were of exclusive equity jurisdiction under the common law. In re Niernsee's Estate, 147 Fla. 388, 2 So.2d 737, 739.

EXCLUSIVE OWNERSHIP. Ownership free from any kind of legal or equitable interest in any one else. U. S. Casualty Co. v. Timmerman, 118 N.J. Eq. 563, 180 A. 629.

EXCLUSIVE POSSESSION. Possession may be "exclusive" so as to entitle possessor to title by adverse possession, notwithstanding that the land is subject to exercise of easement by private party. Young v. City of Lubbock, Tex.Civ.App., 130 S.W.2d 418, 420.

Defendant, if in actual adverse open and notorious possession of land, had exclusive possession, visible to another accepting mortgage on premises sought to be foreclosed. Whittaker v. Farmers' Nat. Bank of Somerset, 237 Ky. 596, 36 S.W.2d 18, 19.

Exclusive possession by adverse possessor means that adverse possessor must show an exclusive dominion over the land and an appropriation of it to his own use and benefit. Vernon's Ann.Civ.St. art. 5510. W. T. Carter & Bro. v. Holmes, 131 Tex. 365, 113 S.W.2d 1225, 1226.

Under lease providing that lessor should give exclusive possession which was defined to include consent agreements signed by lienholder satisfactory to lessee, lessor whose mortgage was in default did not comply with lease requirement by tendering a consent agreement from a company which agreed to refinance the mortgage. Fox Realty Co. v. Montgomery Ward & Co., C.C.A.Ind., 124 F.2d 710, 712, 713.

EXCLUSIVE POWER. If special power permits donee to bar one or more members of class from receiving portion of property it is "exclusive". Moore v. Emery, 137 Me. 259, 18 A.2d 781, 788, 792.

Power upon specified condition to appoint by will such full-blood relations of donor to take estate as donee might designate held exclusive power. In re Skidmore's Estate, 148 Misc. 569, 266 N.Y.S. 312.

Under will giving testator's daughters power to dispose of principal of trusts created in their favor, provided it be bequeathed to testator's descendants, where testator's general intent was that property should be kept in the family, but that his children should share equally, power of appointment was exclusive. Moore v. Emery, 137 Me. 259, 18 A.2d 781, 788, 792.

EXCLUSIVE PRIVILEGE or FRANCHISE. A statute does not grant an "exclusive" privilege or franchise, unless it shuts out or excludes others from enjoying a similar privilege or franchise. Sunnyside Land & Investment Co. v. Bernier, 119 Wash. 386, 205 P. 1041, 1042, 20 A.L.R. 1261; Toten v. Stuart, 143 Va. 201, 129 S.E. 217, 218.

EXCLUSIVE REMEDY. Where a statute creates a new right or imposes a new duty or liability, unknown to the common law, and gives a remedy for its enforcement, the remedy prescribed is "exclusive". Kosicki v. S. A. Healy Co., 312 Ill.App. 307, 38 N.E.2d 525, 528; Kosicki v. S. A. Healy Co., 380 Ill. 298, 44 N.E.2d 27, 29.

Statute declaring right to compensation under Compensation Law exclusive remedy of employee injured by fellow employee means that injured employee suing fellow employee without having elected to take compensation under such law loses remedy against employer. Hall v. Hill, 158 Misc. 341, 285 N.Y.S. 815.

Statute providing method of recovery does not furnish exclusive remedy unless its terms indicate an intent to make statutory remedy exclusive. Kosicki v. S. A. Healy Co., 312 Ill.App. 307, 38 N.E.2d 525, 528.

EXCLUSIVE RIGHT. An exclusive right is one which only the grantee thereof can exercise, and from which all others are prohibited or shut out.

By "exclusive right" essential to a right of way by prescription, the law means that the right should not depend for its enjoyment upon a similar right in others; it must be exclusive as against the right of the community at large. Downie v. City of Renton, 162 Wash. 181, 298 P. 454, 457.

The word "exclusive," as used in deed granting exclusive right to erect and maintain poles with wires meant that the right was exclusive of grantor, not exclusive in grantee. American Telephone & Telegraph Co. of Massachusetts v. McDonald, 273 Mass. 324, 173 N.E. 502, 503.

EXCLUSIVE USE. As used in law authorizing registration of trade-marks, means exclusive use not only of specific mark but also any other confusingly similar mark or term. McKesson & Robbins v. Charles H. Phillips Chemical Co., C.C.A. Conn., 53 F.2d 1011.

Exclusive use does not mean that no one may or does not use way except claimant of easement, but means only that claimant's right to do so does not depend on like right in others. Rush v. Collins, 366 Ill. 307, 8 N.E.2d 659, 662.

Seminary property is fairly to be regarded as in "exclusive use" for educational purposes. Trustees of Phillips Exeter Academy v. Exeter, 90 N.H. 472, 27 A.2d 569, 591.

EXCLUSIVELY. Apart from all others. Lee v. Gulf Oil Corporation, 148 Fla. 612, 4 So.2d 868, 870, 871; People ex rel. Divico v. Adams, 264 App.Div. 315, 35 N.Y.S.2d 453, 455; Only, Lee v. Gulf Oil Corporation, 148 Fla. 612, 4 So.2d 868, 870, 871; Standard Oil Co. of Texas v. State, Tex.Civ.App., 142 S.W.2d 519, 521, 522, 523. Purely. Baptist Memorial Hospital v. Couillens, 176 Tenn. 300, 140 S.W.2d 1088, 1092. Solely. Provident Life & Accident Ins. Co. v. Campbell, 18 Tenn.App. 452, 79 S.W.2d 292, 296; Stuart v. Occidental Life Ins. Co., 156 Or. 522, 68 P.2d 1037, 1044. Substantially all or for the greater part. Anoka County v. City of St. Paul, 194 Minn. 554, 261 N.W. 588, 99 A.L.R. 1137. To the exclusion of all others; without admission of others to participation; in a manner to exclude. Standard Oil Co. of Texas v. State, Tex. Civ.App., 142 S.W.2d 519, 521, 522, 523. Wholly. People ex rel. Divico v. Adams, 264 App.Div. 315, 35 N.Y.S.2d 453, 455; Baptist Memorial Hospital v. Couillens, 176 Tenn. 300, 140 S.W.2d 1088, 1092.

EXCLUSIVELY FOR PUBLIC PURPOSES. It is not essential to exemption from taxation under provisions exempting from taxation public property used "exclusively for any public purpose" that all the property that is part of the utility unit be used for public purposes. City of Toledo v. Jenkins, 143 Ohio St. 141, 54 N.E.2d 656, 664, 665.

EXCLUSIVELY INTERSTATE. Transportation of passengers by motor vehicles between points within state over route lying partly outside state held exclusively interstate. Conlin Bus Lines v. Old Colony Coach Lines, 282 Mass. 498, 185 N.E. 350, 352.

EXCLUSIVELY OF ALL OTHER CAUSES. Mean that, if accident is shown to be cause of injury for which action is brought, insured can recover. Williams v. General Accident Fire & Life Assur. Corporation, Limited, of Perth, Scotland, 144 Kan. 755, 62 P.2d 856, 857.

EXCLUSIVELY USED. The phrase in provision exempting from taxation properties exclusively used for religious worship, for schools or for purposes purely charitable, has reference to primary and inherent as over against a mere secondary and incidental use. Salvation Army v. Hoehn, Mo., 354 Mo. 107, 188 S.W.2d 826, 830.

EXCOMMENGEMENT. Excommunication (*q. v.*). Co. Litt. 134*a*.

EXCOMMUNICATION. A sentence of censure pronounced by one of the spiritual courts for offenses falling under ecclesiastical cognizance.

It is described in the books as two-fold: (1) The lesser excommunication, which is an ecclesiastical censure, excluding the party from the sacraments; (2) the greater, which excludes him from the company of all Christians. Formerly, too, an excommunicated man was under various civil disabilities. He could not serve upon juries, or be a witness in any court; neither could he bring an action to recover lands or money due to him. These penalties are abolished by St. 53 Geo. III. c. 127. 3 Steph.Comm. 721.

EXCOMMUNICATO CAPIENDO. In ecclesiastical law. A writ issuing out of chancery, founded on a bishop's certificate that the defendant had been excommunicated, and requiring the sheriff to arrest and imprison him, returnable to the king's bench. 4 Bl.Comm. 415; Bac. Abr. "Excommunication," E.

EXCOMMUNICATO DELIBERANDO. A writ to the sheriff for delivery of an excommunicated person out of prison, upon certificate from the ordinary of his conformity to the ecclesiastical jurisdiction. Fitzh. Nat. Brev. 63.

EXCOMMUNICATO INTERDICITUR OMNIS ACTUS LEGITIMUS, ITA QUOD AGERE NON POTEST, NEC ALIQUEM CONVENIRE, LICET IPSE AB ALIIS POSSIT CONVENIRI. Co. Litt. 133. Every legal act is forbidden an excommunicated person, so that he cannot act, nor sue any person, but he may be sued by others.

EXCOMMUNICATO RECAPIENDO. A writ commanding that persons excommunicated, who for their obstinacy had been committed to prison, but were unlawfully set free before they had given caution to obey the authority of the church, should be sought after, retaken, and imprisoned again. Reg. Orig. 67.

EXCULPATE is employed in sense of excuse of justification. State v. Langdon, 46 N.M. 277, 127 P.2d 875, 876.

EXCULPATION. In Scotland the law allows of an "exculpation", by which the prisoner is suffered before his trial to prove the thing to be impossible. State v. Langdon, 46 N.M. 277, 127 P.2d 875, 876.

EXCULPATION, LETTERS OF. In Scotch law. A warrant granted at the suit of a prisoner for citing witnesses in his own defense.

EXCULPATORY. Clearing or tending to clear from alleged fault or guilt; excusing. Moore v. State, 124 Tex.Cr.R. 97, 60 S.W.2d 453.

EXCULPATORY CLAUSE. Such clause in favor of a trustee in will implies that trustee has power which he purports to execute, and it exculpates him where this power is exercised in good faith. In re Wacht's Estate, Sur., 32 N.Y.S.2d 871, 897.

EXCUSABLE. Admitting of excuse or palliation.

As used in the law, this word implies that the act or omission spoken of is on its face unlawful, wrong, or liable to entail loss or disadvantage on the person chargeable, but that the circumstances attending it were such as to constitute a legal "excuse" for it, that is, a legal reason for withholding or foregoing the punishment, liability, or disadvantage which otherwise would follow.

EXCUSABLE ASSAULT. One committed by accident or misfortune in doing any lawful act by lawful means, with ordinary caution and without any unlawful intent. People v. O'Connor, 82 App. Div. 55, 81 N.Y.S. 555.

EXCUSABLE HOMICIDE. See Homicide.

EXCUSABLE NEGLECT. In practice, and particularly with reference to the setting aside of a judgment taken against a party through his "excusable neglect," this means a failure to take the proper steps at the proper time, not in consequence of the party's own carelessness, inattention, or willful disregard of the process of the court, but in consequence of some unexpected or unavoidable hindrance or accident, or reliance on the care and vigilance of his counsel or on promises made by the adverse party. See 1 Bl. Judgm. § 340; Brothers v. Brothers, 71 Mont. 378, 230 P. 60, 61; Westbrook v. Rice, 28 N.D. 324, 148 N.W.

827, 828; Boise Valley Traction Co. v. Boise City, 37 Idaho, 20, 214 P. 1037, 1038; Haas v. Scott, 115 Or. 580, 239 P. 202, 204.

EXCUSAT AUT EXTENUAT DELICTUM IN CAPITALIBUS QUOD NON OPERATUR IDEM IN CIVILIBUS. Bac. Max. r. 15. That may excuse or palliate a wrongful act in capital cases which would not have the same effect in civil injuries. See Broom, Max. 324.

EXCUSATIO. In the civil law. An excuse or reason which exempts from some duty or obligation.

EXCUSATOR.

English law. An excuser.

Old German law. A defendant; he who utterly denies the plaintiff's claim. Du Cange.

EXCUSATUR QUIS QUOD CLAMEUM NON OPPOSUERIT, UT SI TOTO TEMPORE LITIGII FUIT ULTRA MARE QUACUNQUE OCCASIONE. Co. Litt. 260. He is excused who does not bring his claim, if, during the whole period in which it ought to have been brought, he has been beyond sea for any reason.

EXCUSE. A reason alleged for doing or not doing a thing. Worcester; State v. Weagley, 286 Mo. 677, 228 S.W. 817, 820; State v. Saffron, 143 Wash. 34, 254 P. 463. A matter alleged as a reason for relief or exemption from some duty or obligation.

That which is offered as a reason for being excused, or a plea offered in extenuation of a fault or irregular deportment; it is that plea or statement made by the accused which arises out of the state of facts constituting and relied on as the cause. State v. Craig, 161 S.C. 232, 159 S.E. 559, 560.

EXCUSS. To seize and detain by law.

EXCUSSIO.

Civil law. A diligent prosecution of a remedy against a debtor; the exhausting of a remedy against a principal debtor, before resorting to his sureties. Translated "discussion" (*q. v.*).

Old English law. Rescue or rescous. Spelman.

EXEAT. A permission which a bishop grants to a priest to go out of his diocese; also leave to go out generally. For "Ne Exeat", see that title.

EXECUTE. To complete; to make; to perform; to do; to follow out. Glover v. American Mortgage Corporation, Tex.Civ.App., 94 S.W.2d 1235, 1236.

To finish, accomplish, make complete, fulfill. To perform; obey the injunctions of.

To make; as to execute a deed, which includes signing, sealing, and delivery; performance of all necessary formalities. Heinbach v. Heinbach, 274 Mo. 301, 202 S.W. 1123, 1130; White v. Hendley, 35 Cal.App. 267, 169 P. 710, 713; Hathaway v. Cook, 258 Ill. 92, 101 N.E. 227, 228; Williams v. Kidd, 170 Cal. 631, 151 P. 1, 8, Ann.Cas.1916E, 703. The "execution" of a note involves not only the signing but the delivery of the note. Kennedy & Parsons Co. v. Lander Dairy & Produce Co., 36 Wyo. 58, 252 P. 1036, 1038, 51 A. L.R. 315; Lynch v. Figge, 192 N.Y.S. 873, 876, 200 App. Div. 92; Perko v. Rock Springs Commercial Co., 37 Wyo. 98, 259 P. 520, 522; The execution of a contract includes performance of all acts necessary to render it complete as an instrument. Hofgesang v. Silver, 223 Ky. 101, 3 S.W.2d 185, 186; To make and sign contract, Glick v. Daniel, 184 Ark. 576, 42 S.W.2d 1007, 1008.

To perform; carry out according to its terms; as to execute a contract, or a writ. State v. Miller, 104 W.Va. 226, 139 S.E. 711, 712; Harrity v. Steers, 185 N.Y.S. 704, 195 App.Div. 11.

To fulfill the purpose of; to obey; to perform the commands of; as to execute a writ.

A statute is said to *execute* a use where it transmutes the equitable interest of the *cestui que use* into a legal estate of the same nature, and makes him tenant of the land accordingly, in lieu of the feoffee to uses or trustee, whose estate, on the other hand, is at the same moment annihilated. 1 Steph.Comm. 339.

Word "sign" as used in trial court's general oral charge and in special written charge given at request of defendant was synonymous with word "execute". Kinney v. Glenn, 29 Ala.App. 478, 198 So. 250, 253.

EXECUTED. Completed; carried into full effect; already done or performed; taking effect immediately; now in existence or in possession; conveying an immediate right or possession. The opposite of *executory.*

A contract is "executed" by being signed. Mastin Realty & Mining Co. v. Commissioner of Internal Revenue, C.C.A. 8, 130 F.2d 1003, 1005. A trust does not become fully "executed" until subject matter of it has been properly paid over to beneficiaries. Harlan v. Gleason, 180 Md. 24, 22 A. 2d 579, 581. Act or course of conduct carried to completion. Northwest Steel Rolling Mills v. Commissioner of Internal Revenue, C.C.A.9, 110 F.2d 286, 290. Term imports idea that nothing remains to be done. Pacific Finance Corporation v. Hendley, 119 Cal.App. 697, 7 P.2d 391, 393. Term when applied to contract includes delivery and implies complete contract. Smith v. School Dist. No. 1, Marshall County, 187 Okl. 184, 102 P.2d 131, 134, 135. Term when applied to deed includes the signing thereof. National Fire Ins. Co. v. Patterson, 170 Okl. 593, 41 P.2d 645, 647.

Generally a jail sentence is "executed" only when the convict has actually suffered the imprisonment. State ex rel. Libtz v. Coleman, 149 Fla. 28, 5 So.2d 60, 61.

EXECUTED CONSIDERATION. A consideration which is wholly past. 1 Pars. Cont. 391. An act done or value given before the making of the agreement.

EXECUTED CONTRACT. See Contract.

EXECUTED ESTATE. See Estate.

EXECUTED FINE. The fine *sur cognizance de droit, come ceo que il ad de son done;* or a fine upon acknowledgment of the right of the cognizee, as that which he has of the gift of the cognizor. Abolished by 3 & 4 Wm. IV. c. 74.

EXECUTED NOTE. Under Small Loan Act note was not "executed" until it was both signed and delivered. Trustees System Co. of Newark v. Stoll, 13 N.J.Misc. 490, 179 A. 372, 373.

EXECUTED ORAL AGREEMENT. An oral agreement is not "executed" unless it has been fully performed by both parties. Walther v. Occidental Life Ins. Co., 40 Cal.App.2d 160, 104 P.2d 551, 554.

EXECUTED REMAINDER. See Remainder.

EXECUTED SALE. See Sale.

EXECUTED TRUST. See Trust.

EXECUTED USE. See Use.

EXECUTED WRIT. In practice. A writ carried into effect by the officer to whom it is directed The term "executed," applied to a writ, has been held to mean "used." Amb. 61.

EXECUTIO. Lat. The doing or following up of a thing; the doing a thing completely or thoroughly; management or administration.

In old practice. Execution; the final process in an action.

EXECUTIO BONORUM. In old English law. Management or administration of goods. *Ad ecclesiam et ad amicos pertinebit executio bonorum,* the execution of the goods shall belong to the church and to the friends of the deceased. Bract. fol. 60*b*.

EXECUTIO EST EXECUTIO JURIS SECUNDUM JUDICIUM. 3 Inst. 212. Execution is the execution of the law according to the judgment.

EXECUTIO EST FINIS ET FRUCTUS LEGIS. Co. Litt. 289. Execution is the end and fruit of the law.

EXECUTIO JURIS NON HABET INJURIAM. 2 Roll. 301. The execution of law does no injury.

EXECUTION. Carrying out some act or course of conduct to its completion. Northwest Steel Rolling Mills v. Commissioner of Internal Revenue, C.C.A.9, 110 F.2d 286, 290. Completion of an act. Domestic Finance Corporation v. Williams, 174 Misc. 227, 20 N.Y.S.2d 467, 469. Putting into force, Greene v. Wheeler, C.C.A.Wis., 29 F.2d 468, 469. The completion, fulfillment, or perfecting of anything, or carrying it into operation and effect.

At common law, executions are said to be either *final* or *quousque;* the former, where complete satisfaction of the debt is intended to be procured by this process; the latter, where the execution is only a means to an end, as where the defendant is arrested on *ca. sa.*

The word cannot be stretched to include prescription; the natural meaning of "execution" is "performance," including excuses for performance. Wood & Selick v. Compagnie Generale Transatlantique, C.C.A.N.Y., 43 F.2d 941, 942.

Where testatrix left residue of her estate to be divided equally among named individuals, but provided that, if any of those beneficiaries should be deceased at time of "execution" of the will, their share "is" to revert to testatrix' estate, the word "execution" had reference to time when will should take effect and not to time when will was signed. Central Nat. Bank v. Stevenson, 25 Del.Ch. 215, 16 A.2d 114, 115.

Writ of assistance is in the nature of an "execution." Davis v. Federal Land Bank of Columbia, 217 N.C. 145, 7 S.E.2d 373, 376.

Attachment distinguished

Term "executions" as used in Code section dealing with commissions which sheriff may charge in cases where sheriff has collected a judgment on execution without making a sale of the judgment debtor's property is sufficiently broad to include attachment, Jones-Noland Drilling Co. v. Bixby, 34 N.M. 413, 282 P. 382, 384.

Under an attachment, property of defendant is placed in custody of law to await final determination of suit, and the attachment is really a preliminary execution dependent for its ultimate efficacy upon the rendering of a judgment in plaintiff's favor; on the other hand, an "execution" is a remedy afforded by law for the enforcement of a judgment of the court. J. M. Radford Grocery Co. v. Owenby, Tex.Civ.App., 34 S.W.2d 385, 387.

Criminal Law

The carrying into effect of the sentence of the law by the infliction of capital punishment. 4 Bl.Comm. 403; 4 Steph. Comm. 470.

French Law

A method of obtaining satisfaction of a debt or claim by sale of the debtor's property privately, *i. e.*, without judicial process, authorized by the deed or agreement of the parties or by custom; as, in the case of a stockbroker, who may sell securities of his customer, bought under his instructions or deposited by him, to indemnify himself or make good a debt. Arg.Fr.Merc.Law, 557.

Garnishment

Execution includes writ of garnishment. Buckley v. F. L. Riley Mercantile Co., 155 Miss. 150, 124 So. 267.

Garnishee execution is an execution against property. In re Howard Hotel Corporation, 150 Misc. 782, 270 N.Y.S. 259.

Garnishment after judgment "is execution" within statute providing that execution shall only be issued from court in which judgment is rendered. Though a garnishment is not an execution, garnishment after execution is practically an equitable execution. First Nat. Bank of Cordell v. City Guaranty Bank of Hobart, 174 Okl. 545, 51 P.2d 573, 576.

Order of Sale

"Execution" in statute includes an order of sale. Bartlett Mortg. Co. v. Morrison, 183 Okl. 214, 81 P.2d 318, 322; Blanscet v. Palo Duro Furniture Co., Tex.Civ.App., 68 S.W.2d 527, 528.

Practice

The name of a writ issued to a sheriff, constable, or marshal, authorizing and requiring him to execute the judgment of the court. Raulerson v. Peeples, 81 Fla. 206, 87 So. 629, 630.

For "Attachment execution," see Attachment.

For "Body Execution," "Dormant Execution," "Equitable Execution," "General Execution," "Junior Execution" and "Special Execution," see those titles.

For "Execution of Judgment or Decree," see that title.

For "Testatum execution," see Testatum.

EXECUTION CREDITOR. See Creditor.

EXECUTION LIEN. An "execution lien" may be created by service of execution, levy upon real estate, and filing of a certificate of levy in the proper office of county in which real estate is located. Reconstruction Finance Corporation v. Maley, C.C.A.Ill., 125 F.2d 131, 135.

EXECUTION OF INSTRUMENT. Execution includes signing, sealing, and delivering. Erie R. Co. v. S. J. Groves & Sons Co., 111 N.J.L. 100, 166 A. 205, 207. Completion of instrument. Domestic Finance Corporation v. Williams, 174 Misc. 227, 20 N.Y.S.2d 467, 469. Subscribing and delivery of instrument. Miller v. Jansen, Cal. App., 128 P.2d 97, 98.

Delivery is essential to complete execution of deed. Barnes v. Aycock, 219 N.C. 360, 13 S.E.2d 611, 612.

Execution imports, includes or involves delivery. Miller v. Jansen, 21 Cal.2d 473, 132 P.2d 801, 802; McCarthy Co.

v. Commissioner of Internal Revenue, C.C.A.9, 80 F.2d 618, 620; Stocks v. Inzer, 232 Ala. 482, 168 So. 877, 878.

Execution includes performance of all acts necessary to render instrument complete and of every act required to give instrument validity or to carry it into effect. Northwest Steel Rolling Mills v. Commissioner of Internal Revenue, C.C.A.9, 110 F.2d 286, 290.

Execution of deed means making thereof, Turlington v. Neighbors, 222 N.C. 694, 24 S.E.2d 648, 650.

Execution of instruments means making thereof, and when spoken of deeds, it includes all acts such as signing, sealing, and delivering, which are necessary to give effect thereto. United States v. Peppa, D.C.Cal., 13 F.Supp. 669, 670.

Execution of prescription means preparation and delivery by authorized person. U. S. v. Peppa, D.C.Cal., 13 F.Supp. 669.

"Execution" of written contract includes signing, unconditional delivery by promisor, and acceptance by promisee. Coen v. American Surety Co. of New York, C.C.A. Mo., 120 F.2d 393, 397.

Performance and completion of all of those formal acts essential for mortgage's effectiveness. Southern Enterprises v. Foster, La.App., 12 So.2d 842, 844.

Signing, acknowledging, delivering and acceptance of mortgage are essential to "execution" of mortgage. Illinois Nat. Bank & Trust Co. v. Holmes, 311 Ill.App. 286, 35 N.E.2d 823, 825.

Term "execution" as employed in respect to promissory note means both signing and delivery of bill or note, and mere signing is insufficient. In re Tynan's Estate, 142 Neb. 671, 7 N.W.2d 628, 630.

The signing and publication of a will.

The signing, sealing, and delivery of deeds. Turlington v. Neighbors, 222 N.C. 694, 24 S.E.2d 648, 650.

Words "issuing" and "execution," used in statutes in relation to passing of title by tax deed, are interchangeable terms. Lance v. Smith, 123 Fla. 461, 167 So. 366, 369.

EXECUTION OF JUDGMENT OR DECREE. "Execution" is putting into effect of final judgment of court. Tice v. Tice, 208 Iowa 145, 224 N. W. 571, 572.

As used in Code provision regarding right to demand that nullity of judgment be declared unless defendant suffered judgment to be executed, means the seizure of property. Frank v. Currie, La.App., 172 So. 843, 848.

Execution embraces all appropriate means to execution of judgment, Buckley v. F. L. Riley Mercantile Co., 155 Miss. 150, 124 So. 267.

Process to carry into effect decree or judgment is execution. Painter v. Berglund, 31 Cal.App.2d 63, 87 P.2d 360, 363; Miller v. London, 294 Mass. 300, 1 N.E.2d 198, 200.

Sometimes from the neglect of parties, or some other cause, it became impossible to carry a decree into execution without the further decree of the court upon a bill filed for that purpose. This happened generally in cases where, parties having neglected to proceed upon the decree, their rights under it became so embarrassed by a variety of subsequent events that it was necessary to have the decree of the court to settle and ascertain them. Such a bill might also be brought to carry into execution the judgment of an inferior court of equity, if the jurisdiction of that court was not equal to the purpose; as in the case of a decree in Wales, which the defendant avoided by fleeing into England. This species of bill was generally partly an original bill, and partly a bill in the nature of an original bill, though not strictly original. Story, Eq.Pl. 342; Daniell, Ch.Pr. 1429.

Statutory means provided for enforcement of judgment requiring the payment of money is execution. Lupton v. Edmundson, 220 N.C. 188, 16 S.E.2d 840, 841.

The last stage of a suit, whereby possession is obtained of anything recovered. It is styled "final process," and consists in putting the sentence of the law in force. 3 Bl. Comm. 412. The carrying into effect of the sentence or judgment of a court. U. S. v. Nourse, 9 Pet. 28, 9 L.Ed. 31; Griffith v. Fowler, 18 Vt. 394; Hurlbutt v. Currier, 68 N.H. 94, 38 A. 502.

Within statute providing for execution of judgment after five years from its entry, "execution" is used in broad sense of execution or carrying into effect by such means as are provided by law for enforcement of various classes of judgments. Bank of America N. T. & S. A. v. Katz, 45 Cal.App.2d 138, 113 P.2d 759, 760.

Writ of execution is a civil proceeding for enforcement of a judgment against property. Lash v. Mann, 141 Ohio St. 577, 49 N.E.2d 689, 691.

EXÉCUTION PARÉE. In French law. A right founded on an act passed before a notary, by which the creditor may immediately, without citation or summons, seize and cause to be sold the property of his debtor, out of the proceeds of which to receive his payment. It imports a confession of judgment, and is not unlike a warrant of attorney. Code Proc. La. art. 732; 6 Toullier, no. 208; 7 Toullier, no. 99.

EXECUTION SALE. A sale by a sheriff or other ministerial officer under the authority of a writ of execution which he has levied on property of the debtor. Noland v. Barrett, 122 Mo. 181, 26 S.W. 692, 43 Am.St.Rep. 572; Norton v. Reardon, 67 Kan. 302, 72 P. 861, 100 Am.St.Rep. 459.

Sale under order in mortgage foreclosure proceeding is sale on execution. Goslen v. Waddell Inv. Co., 145 Okl. 269, 292 P. 362, 364.

Execution sales relate to sales under a writ of execution. Peebler v. Olds, 56 Cal.App.2d 13, 132 P.2d 236, 237.

EXECUTION THEREOF. In ordinance providing that contractor should not have claim under city contract unless controller certified that at date of "execution thereof" sufficient amount stood to credit of appropriation for contract, words "execution thereof" mean date of certification. Edwin E. Hallenbeck, Inc., v. Hadley, 312 Pa. 176, 167 A. 574, 575.

EXECUTIONE FACIENDA. A writ commanding execution of a judgment. Obsolete. Cowell.

EXECUTIONE FACIENDÂ IN WITHERNAMIUM. A writ that lay for taking cattle of one who has conveyed the cattle of another out of the county, so that the sheriff cannot replevy them. Reg. Orig. 82.

EXECUTIONE JUDICII. A writ directed to the judge of an inferior court to do execution upon a judgment therein, or to return some reasonable cause wherefore he delays the execution. Fitzh. Nat. Brev. 20.

EXECUTIONER. The name given to him who puts criminals to death, according to their sentence; a hangman.

EXECUTIVE. As distinguished from the legislative and judicial departments of government, the executive department is that which is charged with the detail of carrying the laws into effect and securing their due observance. The word "executive" is also used as an impersonal designation of the chief executive officer of a state or nation. In re Railroad Com'rs, 15 Neb. 679, 50

N.W. 276; In re Davies, 168 N.Y. 89, 61 N.E. 118, 56 L.R.A. 855; State v. Denny, 118 Ind. 382, 21 N.E. 252, 4 L.R.A. 79.

Under constitutional provision dividing powers of government into the legislative, the executive, including the administrative, and the judicial departments, the word "administrative" is not used as synonymous with "executive". Tucker v. State, 218 Ind. 614, 35 N.E.2d 270, 290.

Words "executive" and "administrative" may be used as synonymous or interchangeable terms. Saint v. Allen, 169 La. 1046, 126 So. 548, 555.

EXECUTIVE ACT. "Executive" and "administrative" duties are such as concern the execution of existing laws. People ex rel. Holvey v. Kapp, 355 Ill. 596, 189 N.E. 920, 923.

EXECUTIVE ADMINISTRATION, or MINISTRY. A political term in England, applicable to the higher and responsible class of public officials by whom the chief departments of the government of the kingdom are administered.

The number of these amounts to fifty or sixty persons. Their tenure of office depends on the confidence of a majority of the house of commons, and they are supposed to be agreed on all matters of general policy except such as are specifically left open questions. Cab.Lawy.

EXECUTIVE AGENCY. These words include collector and Secretary of Treasury. U. S. v. Paramount Publix Corporation, Cust. & Pat. App., 73 F.2d 103, 105; Selective Training and Service Act boards. United States ex rel. Beers v. Selective Training and Service Local Board No. 1, Rock County, Wis., D.C.Wis., 50 F.Supp. 39, 40. Works Projects Administration. Thomason v. Works Projects Administration, C.C.A.Idaho, 138 F.2d 342, 343.

EXECUTIVE AGENT. President of a bank is but the "executive agent" of board of directors. Ex parte Lamberth, 242 Ala. 165, 5 So.2d 622, 623.

EXECUTIVE AUTHORITY. Petition for referendum filed with clerk is filed with executive authority of municipality. State ex rel. Tietje v. Collett, 138 Ohio St. 425, 35 N.E.2d 568, 570. State ex rel. City of Middletown v. City Commission of City of Middletown, 140 Ohio St. 368, 44 N.E.2d 459, 463.

EXECUTIVE CAPACITY. Duties in such capacity relate to active participation in control, supervision, and management of business. Arkansas Amusement Corporation v. Kempner, C.C.A.Ark., 57 F.2d 466, 473; Wilkinson v. Noland Co., D.C. Va., 40 F.Supp. 1009, 1012.

EXECUTIVE EMPLOYEES. Persons whose duties include some form of managerial authority, actually directing the work of other persons. Stanger v. Glenn L. Martin Co., D.C.Md., 56 F. Supp. 163, 166; persons whose duties relate to active participation in control, supervision and management of business, or who administer affairs, or who direct, manage, execute or dispense. Steiner v. Pleasantville Constructors, 181 Misc. 798, 46 N.Y.S.2d 120, 123.

The term executive employee carries the idea of supervision of or control over ordinary employees. Ralph Knight, Inc., v. Mantel, C.C.A.Mo., 135 F.2d 514, 517.

EXECUTIVE FUNCTIONS have relation to management of all or some part of a business and imply activity. Arkansas Amusement Corporation v. Kempner, 182 Ark. 897, 33 S.W.2d 42, 43.

General charge, control, and conduct of taxation is "executive function." In re Opinion of the Justices, 87 N.H. 492, 179 A. 357, 110 A.L.R. 819.

EXECUTIVE OFFICER. An officer of the executive department of government; one in whom resides the power to execute the laws; one whose duties are to cause the laws to be executed and obeyed. People v. Salsbury, 134 Mich. 537, 96 N. W. 939; Petterson v. State, Tex.Cr.App., 58 S.W. 100; Mekota v. State Board of Equalization and Assessment, Neb., 19 N.W.2d 633, 640. An administrative officer. Sheely v. People, 54 Colo. 136, 129 P. 201, 203.

Officers who are neither judicial nor legislative are executive officers. Spivey v. State, 69 Okl.Cr. 397, 104 P.2d 263, 277; State v. Emory, 55 Idaho 649, 46 P.2d 67, 68.

One vested with power to carry out obligations intrusted to him and charged with administrative duties relative to executing, performing, and carrying into effect purposes of his employment. State Automobile Mutual Ins. Ass'n of Columbus v. Friedman, 122 Ohio St. 334, 171 N.E. 591, 592.

One who assumes command or control and directs course of business, or some part thereof, and who outlines duties and directs work of subordinate employees. Arkansas Amusement Corporation v. Kempner, 182 Ark. 897, 33 S.W. 2d 42, 43.

Cashier of bank is executive officer. Mays v. Board of Com'rs of Creek County, 164 Okl. 231, 23 P.2d 664.

President and vice president of corporation are executive officers. Emmerglick v. Philip Wolf, Inc., C.C.A.N.Y., 138 F.2d 661, 662.

EXECUTIVE ORDER INDIAN RESERVATION is reservation created by order of Chief Executive withdrawing land within its boundaries from settlement or making other disposition of it under public land laws of United States. Santa Rita Oil & Gas Co. v. Board of Equalization, 101 Mont. 268, 54 P.2d 117, 122.

EXECUTIVE PARDON is an executive act of grace exempting an individual from punishment for a crime he has committed. People ex rel. Prisament v. Brophy, 287 N.Y. 132, 38 N.E.2d 468, 470, 139 A.L.R. 667. See Pardon.

EXECUTIVE POWERS AND DUTIES on which Supreme Court may advise Governor, means a duty appertaining to the execution of the laws as they exist. In re Advisory Opinion to Governor, 154 Fla. 866, 19 So.2d 370, 371.

The "executive power" vested in the Governor by the Constitution is the power to "execute" the laws, that is, to carry them into effect, as distinguished from the power to make the laws and the power to judge them. Tucker v. State, 218 Ind. 614, 35 N.E.2d 270, 291.

EXECUTIVE SALARIES. Means salaries of officers only. Leonard v. S. G. Frantz Co., 268 App. Div. 144, 49 N.Y.S.2d 329, 332.

EXECUTIVE WARRANT of Governor of asylum state is but license or privilege to move within state, and may be revoked before border is crossed. Downey v. Schmidt, D.C.Tex., 4 F.Supp. 1, 3.

EXECUTOR. A person appointed by a testator to carry out the directions and requests in his will, and to dispose of the property according to his testamentary provisions after his decease. In re Lamb's Estate, 122 Mich. 239, 80 N.W. 1081; In re Sipchen's Estate, 180 Wis. 504, 193 N.W. 385, 387; Ricks v. Johnson, 134 Miss. 676, 99 So. 142, 146.

A person to whom a testator by his will commits the execution, or putting in force, of that instrument and its codicils. Fonbl. 307.

Appointment as executor of person on whom will casts affirmative duty to collect debts, adjust claims and make distribution of assets, is validated. In re Hazen's Estate, 175 Misc. 851, 25 N.Y.S.2d 293, 295, 296.

One named in will as executor is an "executor" even before probate of will. McKibban v. Scott, 131 Tex. 182, 114 S.W.2d 213, 215, 115 A.L.R. 1421.

One to whom another man commits by his last will the execution of that will and testament. 2 Bl.Comm. 503.

Person appointed under will appointing person as "administrator of my estate after my death," held testamentary "executor". Succession of Rassat, La.App., 157 So. 412, 414.

Person nominated as executor becomes "executor" only when will is admitted to probate and when he takes oath. Robertson v. National Spiritualists' Ass'n, Tex., 25 S.W.2d 889, 894.

Person or corporation empowered to discharge duties of a fiduciary, appointed as such by testator in his will. In re Watkins' Estate, 113 Vt. 126, 30 A.2d 305, 310.

Term "executor" as employed in statute providing that county judge shall receive commission on actual cash receipts of each executor, refers to executor administering estate of testator under control of probate court. Willis v. Harvey, Tex., 26 S.W.2d 288, 289.

Words "custodian and administrator" in will directing appointment of named person mean "executor." Frazier v. Frazier, 83 Colo. 188, 263 P. 413, 414.

Civil Law

A ministerial officer who executed or carried into effect the judgment or sentence in a cause.

Ecclesiastical Law

Executor à lege constitutus, an executor appointed by law; the ordinary of the diocese.

Executor ab episcopo constitutus, or *executor dativus,* an executor appointed by the bishop; an administrator to an intestate.

Executor à testatore constitutus, an executor appointed by a testator. Otherwise termed *"executor testamentarius;"* a testamentary executor.

An *executor to the tenor* is one who, though not directly constituted executor by the will, is therein charged with duties in relation to the estate which can only be performed by the executor.

For "Coexecutor," "General Executor," "Instituted Executor," "Joint Executors," "Limited Executor," "Special Executor" and "Substituted Executor," see those titles.

EXECUTOR BY SUBSTITUTION. A successor executor appointed by testator entitled to succeed to administration of estate following resignation of first executor who had partially administered upon such estate. In re Stahl's Estate, 113 Ind. App. 29, 44 N.E.2d 529, 532.

EXECUTOR CREDITOR. See Creditor.

EXECUTOR DATIVE. See Dative.

EXECUTOR DE SON TORT. See De Son Tort.

EXECUTOR LUCRATUS. An executor who has assets of his testator who in his life-time made himself liable by a wrongful interference with the property of another. 6 Jur., N.S., 543.

EXECUTOR NAMED IN WILL. Where will requested that executor named designate some person to act as executor in case of his own disability and requested that a bank be named as executor in event of failure of executor named to designate another to act in his place, and executor named executed formal instrument requesting that the bank be appointed in his stead, such bank was "executor named in the will." In re Crosby's Estate, 218 Minn. 149, 15 N.W.2d 501, 505.

EXECUTOR OR ADMINISTRATOR OF A DECEASED EXECUTOR. Under statute relating to right to require an accounting from "executor or administrator, of a deceased executor," representative of deceased representative of deceased representative of an estate cannot be compelled to file an account. In re Griffin's Estate, 170 Misc. 496, 1066, 10 N.Y.S.2d 161.

EXECUTOR–TRUSTEE. An executor whose duties of holding and managing assets were extended by the will beyond the period usually permissible for their administration. In re Putnam's Will, 173 Misc. 151, 17 N.Y.S.2d 238, 239.

EXECUTORIAL DUTIES are what any layman could perform or was capable of performing. In re Owen's Estate, 144 Misc. 688, 259 N.Y.S. 892.

For the most part, "executorial duties" consist in ascertaining proper net amount of various parts of testator's property after payment of debts and expenses, and distributing them among persons entitled. Keel v. First Nat. Bank of Pikeville, 271 Ky. 745, 113 S.W.2d 33, 36, 116 A.L.R. 151.

Generally, a power of sale given an executor which is of an imperative nature, and the exercise of which is not left to executor's discretion, creates an "executorial duty" rather than a "trust". Esser v. Chimel, Del.Ch., 30 A.2d 685, 687.

EXECUTORY. That which is yet to be executed or performed; that which remains to be carried into operation or effect; incomplete; depending upon a future performance or event. The opposite of *executed.*

Right which is not vested but lies in action and which requires resort to court of equity to invest plaintiff with right claimed is "executory." Parks v. Classen Co., 156 Okl. 43, 9 P.2d 432, 435.

As to executory "Bequests," "Contracts," "Devises," "Estates," "Remainders," "Trusts," and "Uses," see those titles.

EXECUTORY CONSIDERATION. A consideration which is to be performed after the contract for which it is a consideration is made.

EXECUTORY CONTRACT TO SELL. Under which something remains to be done by either party before delivery and passing of title. Martin v. John Clay & Co., Mo.App., 167 S.W.2d 407, 411.

EXECUTORY FINES. These are the fines *sur cognizance de droit tantum; sur concessit;* and *sur done, grant et render.* Abolished by 3 & 4 Wm. IV. c. 74.

EXECUTORY INTERESTS. A general term, comprising all future estates and interests in land or personalty, other than reversions and remainders.

A right which is not vested in possession but lies in action, and which it is necessary to obtain the peculiar relief afforded by courts of equity in order to invest plaintiff with the right claimed, is an "executory interest". Lang v. Shell Petroleum Corporation, Tex.Civ.App., 141 S.W.2d 667, 671.

EXECUTORY LIMITATION. A limitation of a future interest by deed or will; if by will, it is also called an "executory devise."

EXECUTORY PROCESS. A process which can be resorted to in the following cases, namely: (1) When the right of the creditor arises from an act importing confession of judgment, and which contains a privilege or mortgage in his favor; (2) when the creditor demands the execution of a judgment which has been rendered by a tribunal different from that within whose jurisdiction the execution is sought. Code Prac. La. art. 732; Marin v. Lalley, 17 Wall. 14, 21 L.Ed. 596.

EXECUTORY SALE. See Sale.

EXECUTORY UNILATERAL ACCORD. Nothing more than an offer to enter a contract. Boyd v. Christiansen, 229 Iowa 1, 293 N.W. 826, 828.

EXECUTORY WARRANTIES. Arise where insured undertakes to perform some executory stipulation, as that certain acts will be done, or that certain facts will continue to exist. Procacci v. United States Fire Ins. Co., 118 N.J.L. 423, 193 A. 180, 182.

EXECUTRESS. A female executor. Hardr. 165, 473.

EXECUTRIX. A woman who has been appointed by will to execute such will or testament.

EXECUTRY. In Scotch law. The movable estate of a person dying, which goes to his nearest of kin. So called as falling under the distribution of an executor. Bell.

EXEDOS. See Ejidos.

EXIDOS. See Ejidos.

EXEMPLA ILLUSTRANT NON RESTRINGUNT LEGEM. Co. Litt. 240. Examples illustrate, but do not restrain, the law.

EXEMPLAR. A specimen which is capable of supporting both deduction and inference. In re Fisher's Estate, 47 Idaho 668, 279 P. 291, 293.

EXEMPLARY DAMAGES. See Damages.

EXEMPLI GRATIÂ. For the purpose of example, or for instance. Often abbreviated *"ex. gr."* or *"e. g."*

EXEMPLIFICATION. An official transcript of a document from public records, made in form to be used as evidence, and authenticated as a true copy.

EXEMPLIFICATIONE. A writ granted for the exemplification or transcript of an original record. Reg. Orig. 290.

EXEMPLUM. In the civil law. Copy; a written authorized copy. This word is also used in the modern sense of "example,"—*ad exemplum constituti singulares non trahi,* exceptional things must not be taken for examples. Calvin.

EXEMPT, *v.* To release, discharge, waive, relieve from liability. Davidow v. Jenks, Sup., 48 N.Y.S. 2d 586, 588.

To relieve, excuse, or set free from a duty or service imposed upon the general class to which the individual exempted belongs; as to exempt from militia service. Jones v. Wells Fargo Co. Express, 83 Misc. 508, 145 N.Y.S. 601, 602. See 1 St. at Large, 272.

To relieve certain classes of property from liability to sale on execution.

EXEMPT, *n.* One who is free from liability to military service; as distinguished from a *detail,* who is one belonging to the army, but detached or set apart for the time to some particular duty or service, and liable, at any time, to be recalled to his place in the ranks. In re Strawbridge, 39 Ala. 379. Relieved. In re Miller's Estate, 330 Pa. 477, 199 A. 148, 149. See Exempts.

EXEMPT FROM ALL TAXATION. In proposed constitutional amendment, exempting specified homesteads from taxation, mean exempt when not restrained by Federal Constitution. Gray v. Winthrop, 115 Fla. 721, 156 So. 270, 94 A.L.R. 804.

EXEMPTION. Freedom from a general duty or service; immunity from a general burden, tax, or charge. Green v. State, 59 Md. 128, 43 Am.Rep. 542; Koenig v. Railroad Co., 3 Neb. 380; Long v. Converse, 91 U.S. 113, 23 L.Ed. 233; Poore v. Bowlin, 150 Tenn. 412, 265 S.W. 671.

A privilege allowed by law to a judgment debtor, by which he may hold property to a certain amount, or certain classes of property, free from all liability to levy and sale on execution or attachment. Turrill v. McCarthy, 114 Iowa, 681, 87 N.W. 667; Williams v. Smith, 117 Wis. 142, 93 N.W. 464; In re Trammell, D.C.Ga., 5 F.2d 326, 327.

A right given by law to a debtor to retain portion of his property free from claims of creditors. Pickens v. Pickens, 125 Tex. 410, 83 S.W.2d 951, 954.

An "exemption" contemplated by constitutional provision forbidding exemption of property from taxation is an exemption from all taxation in any form. Turco Paint & Varnish Co. v. Kalodner, 320 Pa. 421, 184 A. 37, 43.

An "exemption" from inheritance tax is a deduction. In re Maxson's Estate, 30 Cal.App.2d 566, 86 P.2d 922, 924.

As applied to taxation "exemption" is freedom from burden of enforced contributions to expenses and maintenance of government. Washington Chocolate Co. v. King County, 21 Wash.2d 630, 152 P.2d 981, 984.

Credit against income tax for income tax paid to other state or country is an "exemption". Miller v. McColgan, 17 Cal.2d 432, 110 P.2d 419, 424, 134 A.L.R. 1424; Keasbey & Mattison Co. v. Rothensies, C.C.A.3, 133 F.2d 894, 898.

Deduction made in determining taxable income is an "exemption," Tupelo Garment Co. of Tupelo, Miss. v. State Tax Commission, 178 Miss. 730, 173 So. 656, 660.

The words "exemption from seizure" in statute providing that a pension or other reward granted by the United States for military service is exempt from seizure in legal proceeding meant "not subject to debts." In re McCormick's Estate, 169 Misc. 672, 8 N.Y.S.2d 179, 188.

EXEMPTION LAWS. Laws which provide that a certain amount or proportion of a debtor's property shall be exempt from execution.

EXEMPTION, WORDS OF. It is a maxim of law that words of exemption are not to be construed to import any liability; the maxim *expressio unius exclusio alterius,* or its converse, *exclusio unius inclusio alterius,* not applying to such a case. For example, an exemption of the crown from the bankruptcy act 1869, in one specified particular, would not inferentially subject the crown to that act in any other particular. Brown.

EXEMPTS. Persons who are not bound by law, but excused from the performance of duties imposed upon others.

EXENNIUM. In old English law. A gift; a new year's gift. Cowell.

EXEQUATUR. Lat. Let it be executed.

In French practice, this term is subscribed by judicial authority upon a transcript of a judgment from a foreign country, or from another part of France, and authorizes the execution of the judgment within the jurisdiction where it is so indorsed.

International Law

A certificate issued by the foreign department of a state to a consul or commercial agent of another state, recognizing his official character, and authorizing him to fulfill his duties.

EXERCISE. To make use of. Thus, to exercise a right or power is to do something which it enables the holder to do. U. S. v. Souders, 27 Fed. Cas. 1267; Cleaver v. Comm., 34 Pa. 284; Snead v. Wood, 24 Ga.App. 210, 100 S.E. 714, 715.

To put in action or practice, to carry on something, to transact. Salway v. Multnomah Lumber & Box Co., 134 Or. 428, 293 P. 420, 421.

The "exercise" of an option to purchase is merely the election of optionee to purchase. Floyd v. Morgan, 60 Ga. App. 496, 4 S.E.2d 91, 97.

EXERCISE OF JUDGMENT. Exercise of sound discretion, that is, discretion exercised, not arbitrarily or willfully, but with regard to what is right and equitable. United States v. Beckman, C.C.A.Pa., 104 F.2d 260, 262.

EXERCISE OF JUDICIAL DISCRETION. In practical effect, "exercise of judicial discretion" by trial judge means doing as he pleases, unguided by law. Borger v. Mineral Wells Clay Products Co., Tex.Civ.App., 80 S.W.2d 333, 334.

EXERCISED DOMINION. Open acts and conduct relative to land as evidence claim of the right of absolute possession, use, and ownership. Whelan v. Henderson, Tex.Civ.App., 137 S.W.2d 150, 153.

EXERCISING AN OPTION. Elements are decision of optionee to purchase property under terms of option and communication of decision to optionor within life of option. Floyd v. Morgan, 60 Ga.App. 496, 4 S.E.2d 91, 95.

EXERCITALIS. A soldier; a vassal. Spelman.

EXERCITOR NAVIS. Lat. The temporary owner or charterer of a ship. Mackeld. Rom. Law, § 512; The Phebe, 19 Fed.Cas. 418.

EXERCITORIA ACTIO. In the civil law. An action which lay against the employer of a vessel *(exercitor navis)* for the contracts made by the master. Inst. 4, 7, 2; 3 Kent, Comm. 161; Mackeld. Rom. Law, § 512.

EXERCITORIAL POWER. The trust given to a ship-master.

EXERCITUAL. In old English law. A heriot paid only in arms, horses, or military accouterments.

EXERCITUS. In old European law. An army; an armed force. The term was absolutely indefinite as to number. It was applied, on various occasions, to a gathering of forty-two armed men, of thirty-five, or even of four. Spelman.

EXETER DOMESDAY. The name given to a record preserved among the muniments and charters belonging to the dean and chapter of Exeter Cathedral, which contains a description of the western parts of the kingdom, comprising the counties of Wilts, Dorset, Somerset, Devon, and Cornwall. The Exeter Domesday was published with several other surveys nearly contemporary, by order of the commissioners of the public records, under the direction of Sir Henry Ellis, in a volume supplementary to the Great Domesday, folio, London, 1816. Wharton.

EXFESTUCARE. To abdicate or resign; to resign or surrender an estate, office, or dignity, by the symbolical delivery of a staff or rod to the alienee.

EXFREDIARE. To break the peace; to commit open violence. Jacob.

EXHÆREDATIO. In the civil law. Disinheriting; disherison. The formal method of excluding an indefeasible (or forced) heir from the entire inheritance, by the testator's express declaration in the will that such person shall be *exhæres.* Mackeld. Rom. Law, § 711.

EXHÆRES. In the civil law. One disinherited. Vicat; Du Cange.

EXHAUSTION OF ADMINISTRATIVE REMEDIES. The doctrine is that, where an administrative remedy is provided by statute, relief must be sought from administrative body and such remedy exhausted before courts will act. Abelleira v. District Court of Appeal, Third Dist., 17 Cal.2d 280, 109 P.2d 942, 949, 132 A.L.R. 715; Hill v. Brisbane, 66 Cal.App.2d 15, 151 P.2d 578, 582.

EXHEREDATE. In Scotch law. To disinherit; to exclude from an inheritance.

EXHIBERE. To present a thing corporeally, so that it may be handled. Vicat. To appear personally to conduct the defense of an action at law.

EXHIBIT, *v.* To show or display; to offer or present for inspection. To produce anything in public, so that it may be taken into possession. Dig. 10, 4, 2.

To present; to offer publicly or officially; to file of record. Thus we speak of *exhibiting* a charge of treason, *exhibiting* a bill against an officer of the king's bench by way of proceeding against him in that court. In re Wiltse, 5 Misc. 105, 25 N.Y.Supp. 737; Newell v. State, 2 Conn. 40.

To administer; to cause to be taken; as medicines.

To submit to a court or officer in course of proceedings. In re Edwards' Estate, 138 Neb. 671, 294 N.W. 422, 425.

The word implies some affirmative act or at least some conduct on part of person charged with duty of exhibiting a thing or who exhibits it. Pecht v. Colby Management Corporation, 131 Cal.App. 2, 20 P.2d 768, 769.

EXHIBIT, *n.* A paper or document produced and exhibited to a court during a trial or hearing, or to a commissioner taking depositions, or to auditors, arbitrators, etc., as a voucher, or in proof of facts, or as otherwise connected with the subject-matter, and which, on being accepted, is marked for identification and annexed to the deposition, report, or other principal document, or filed of record, or otherwise made a part of the case.

A paper referred to in and filed with the bill, answer, or petition in a suit in equity, or with a deposition. Brown v. Redwyne, 16 Ga. 68.

EXHIBITANT. A complainant in articles of the peace. 12 Adol. & E. 599.

EXHIBITED. Displayed. Callison v. State, Tex. Civ.App., 146 S.W.2d 468, 469.

EXHIBITIO BILLÆ. Lat. Exhibition of a bill. In old English practice, actions were instituted by presenting or exhibiting a bill to the court, in cases where the proceedings were by bill; hence this phrase is equivalent to "commencement of the suit."

EXHIBITION. Something that one views, or at which one looks, and at the same time hears. Longwell v. Kansas City, 199 Mo.App. 480, 203 S.W. 657, 659.

As used in consignment of art objects, indicates a special showing, Lion v. Lilienfeld, Sup., 30 N.Y.S.2d 866, 869.

Motion pictures are "exhibitions" subject to regulation. Thayer Amusement Corporation v. Moulton, 63 R.I. 182, 7 A.2d 682, 686, 124 A.L.R. 236.

Ecclesiastical law. An allowance for meat and drink, usually made by religious appropriators of churches to the vicar. Also the benefaction settled for the maintaining of scholars in the universities, not depending on the foundation. Paroch. Antiq. 304.

Scotch law. An action for compelling the production of writings.

EXHIBITION VALUE. "Minimum sale" or "exhibition value" is interchangeably used with term "price expectancy" in moving picture industry, denoting minimum receipts which distributors expect to realize from exhibition of pictures. Export & Import Film Co. v. B. P. Schulberg Productions, 125 Misc. 756, 211 N.Y.S. 838, 839.

EXHUMATION. Disinterment; the removal from the earth of anything previously buried therein, particularly a human corpse.

EXIGENCE, or EXIGENCY. Demand, want, need, imperativeness; emergency, something arising suddenly out of the current of events; any event or occasional combination of circumstances, calling for immediate action or remedy; a pressing necessity; a sudden and unexpected happening or an unforeseen occurrence or condition. United States v. Atlantic Coast Line Co., D.C.N.C., 224 F. 160, 162; Los Angeles County v. Payne, 8 Cal.2d 563, 66 P.2d 658, 663. Something arising suddenly out of circumstances calling for immediate action or remedy, or where something helpful needs to be done at once, yet not so pressing as an emergency. State ex rel. Odenwald v. District Court of Tenth Judicial Dist. in and for Fergus County, 98 Mont. 1, 38 P.2d 269, 271.

EXIGENCY OF A BOND. That which the bond demands or exacts, *i. e.,* the act, performance, or event upon which it is conditioned.

EXIGENCY OF A WRIT. The command or imperativeness of a writ; the directing part of a writ; the act or performance which it commands.

EXIGENDARY. In English law. An officer who makes out exigents. See Exigenter.

EXIGENT, or EXIGI FACIAS. L. Lat. In English practice. A judicial writ made use of in the process of outlawry, commanding the sheriff to *demand* the defendant, (or *cause him to be demanded, exigi faciat,*) from county court to county court, until he be outlawed; or, if he appear, then to take and have him before the court on a day certain in term, to answer to the plaintiff's action. 1 Tidd Pr. 132; 3 Bl. Comm. 283, 284; Archb. N. Pr. 485. Outlawry has long been obsolete. See Allocato Comitatu; Allocatur Exigent.

EXIGENT LIST. A phrase used to indicate a list of cases set down for hearing upon various incidental and ancillary motions and rules.

EXIGENTER. An officer of the English court of common pleas, whose duty it was to make out the *exigents* and proclamations in the process of outlawry. Cowell. Abolished by St. 7 Wm. IV. and 1 Vict. c. 30. Holthouse.

EXIGI FACIAS. That you cause to be demanded. The emphatic words of the Latin form of the writ of *exigent.* They are sometimes used as the name of that writ.

EXIGIBLE. Demandable; requirable.

EXIGIBLE DEBT. A liquidated and demandable or matured claim. Gulf Refining Co. of Louisiana v. Glassell, 186 La. 190, 171 So. 846, 853.

EXILE. Banishment; the person banished.

EXILIUM. Lat. In old English law. (1) Exile; banishment from one's country. (2) Driving away; despoiling. The name of a species of waste, which consisted in driving away tenants or vassals from the estate; as by demolishing buildings, and so compelling the tenants to leave, or by enfranchising the bond-servants, and unlawfully turning them out of their tenements. Fleta, l. 1, c. 9.

EXILIUM EST PATRIÆ PRIVATIO, NATALIS SOLI MUTATIO, LEGUM NATIVARUM AMISSIO. 7 Coke, 20. Exile is a privation of country, a change of natal soil, a loss of native laws.

EXIST. To live; to have life or animation; to be in present force, activity, or effect at a given time; as in speaking of "existing" contracts, creditors, debts, laws, rights, or liens. Wing v. Slater, 19 R.I. 597, 35 Atl. 302, 33 L.R.A. 566; Poe v. Poe, 125 Ark. 391, 188 S.W. 1190; In re Havel's Estate, 156 Minn. 253, 194 N.W. 633, 34 A.L.R. 1300. To be or continue to be. State v. Sawtooth Men's Club, 59 Idaho 616, 85 P.2d 695, 698.

See, also, Existing.

EXISTENCE. As applied to will means physical existence. In re Kerckhof's Estate, 13 Wash.2d 469, 125 P.2d 284, 287, 290; unrevoked. In re Flood's Estate, 47 Cal.App.2d 809, 119 P.2d 168, 169.

EXISTIMATIO. In the civil law. The civil reputation which belonged to the Roman citizen, as such. Mackeld. Rom. Law, § 135. Called a state or condition of unimpeached dignity or character, (*dignitatis inlœsœ status*;) the highest standing of a Roman citizen. Dig. 50, 13, 5, 1.

Also the decision or award of an arbiter.

EXISTING. The force of this word is not necessarily confined to the present.

EXISTING CLAIM. Claim which has arisen. Great Western Oil Co. v. Bailey, 35 N.M. 277, 295 P. 298, 299.

EXISTING CREDITORS. As used in statute regarding validity of chattel mortgage against existing creditors, means general creditors who have acquired a lien thereon. In re Lewis' Estate, 230 Iowa 694, 298 N.W. 842.

Persons having subsisting obligations against debtor at time fraudulent alienation was made or secret trust created, although claims may not have matured or been reduced to judgment until after such conveyance. First Nat. Bank v. Merrick, 103 N.J.Eq. 63, 142 A. 243; First State Bank of Mobeetie v. Goodner, Tex.Civ.App., 168 S.W. 2d 941, 944.

To determine whether person is such an "existing creditor" as can invoke protection of statute of Elizabeth, inception of debt is time which controls. Matthews v. Montgomery, 193 S.C. 118, 7 S.E.2d 841, 848.

EXISTING DEBT. To have an "existing debt" it is sufficient if there is an absolute debt owing though the period for its payment may not yet have arrived. Helms v. State, 137 Okl. 55, 280 P. 416, 417.

A tax may be a "debt" within meaning of agreement to assume "existing debts". Shepard v. Commissioner of Internal Revenue, C.C.A.7, 101 F.2d 595, 598.

EXISTING DISEASE. A chronic or definite affliction such as would be embraced in the common understanding and meaning of the term "diseased" or "sick." Browning v. Equitable Life Assur. Soc. of United States, 94 Utah 532, 72 P.2d 1060, 1074.

EXISTING EQUITY implies an existing right to future payment, and including a contingent liability, as distinguished from an "existing debt," implying a present, enforceable liability. Barkley v. Kerfoot, 77 Wash. 556, 137 P. 1046, 1047; State v. Smith, 107 Ohio St. 1, 140 N.E. 737, 738.

EXISTING INDEBTEDNESS ON THE POLICY. Reference in statute to any "existing indebtedness on the policy," to be deducted from reserve value in computing extended term insurance, means indebtedness created by "proper assignment of policy". Occidental Life Ins. Co. v. Jamora, Tex.Civ. App., 44 S.W.2d 808, 812.

EXISTING LAW. As used in appropriation act for street improvements requiring refund from street railways under "existing law" refer to statute law. District of Columbia v. Georgetown & T. Ry. Co., 59 App.D.C. 335, 41 F.2d 424, 425.

As used in federal statute rendering initial carrier liable for negligence of connecting carrier and providing that nothing in statute should deprive holder of bill of lading of any remedy or right of action which he has under existing law mean existing federal law and not state law. Fort Worth & Denver City Ry. Co. v. Motley, Tex.Civ.App., 87 S.W.2d 551, 554.

EXISTING LIABILITIES embrace conditional or contingent obligations, which may or may not in the future result in indebtedness. Daniels v. Goff, 192 Ky. 15, 232 S.W. 66, 67.

A tax may be a "liability" within meaning of agreement to assume "existing liabilities." Shepard v. Commissioner of Internal Revenue, C.C.A. 7, 101 F.2d 595, 598.

EXISTING PERSON. A child conceived, but not born, is to be deemed an "existing person" so far as may be necessary for its interests in the event of its subsequent birth. Comp.Laws N.D.1913, § 4337; 1 Bl.Comm. 130.

EXISTING PUBLIC SCHOOL. Mean not only the building, but the school grounds. State ex rel. Fronton Exhibition Co. v. Stein, 144 Fla. 387, 198 So. 82, 87.

EXISTING RAILROAD CORPORATIONS. Extends to such as are incorporated after as well as before its passage, unless exception is provided in their charters. Indianapolis & St. L. R. Co. v. Blackman, 63 Ill. 117; Lawrie v. State, 5 Ind. 525; Fox v. Edwards, 38 Iowa, 215.

EXISTING RIGHT. Rights as exist under general laws. Funk v. Inland Power & Light Co., 164 Wash. 110, 1 P.2d 872, 874.

EXISTING USE. Construction or adaptability of a building or room for purpose, and employment of building or room or land within the purpose. Appeal of Yocom, 142 Pa.Super. 165, 15 A.2d 687, 690.

Utilization of premises so that they may be known in neighborhood as being employed for given purpose. De Felice v. Zoning Board of Appeals of Town of East Haven, 130 Conn. 156, 32 A. 2d 635, 637, 638; Landay v. MacWilliams, 173 Md. 460, 196 A. 293, 297, 114 A.L.R. 984.

EXISTS OR IS KEPT OR MAINTAINED. An actual being; something in fact in existence; something continuing and not failing. McCarron v. Commonwealth, 169 Va. 387, 193 S.E. 509, 512.

EXIT. Lat. It goes forth. This word is used in docket entries as a brief mention of the issue of process. Thus, "*exit fi. fa.*" denotes that a writ of *fieri facias* has been issued in the particular case. The "*exit* of a writ" is the fact of its issuance.

EXIT WOUND. A term used in medical jurisprudence to denote the wound made by a weapon on the side where it emerges, after it has passed completely through the body, or through any part of it.

EXITUS. Children; offspring. The rents, issues, and profits of lands and tenements. An export duty. The conclusion of the pleadings.

EXLEGALITAS. In old English law. Outlawry. Spelman.

EXLEGALITUS. He who is prosecuted as an outlaw. Jacob.

EXLEGARE. In old English law. To outlaw; to deprive one of the benefit and protection of the law, (*exuere aliquem beneficio legis.*) Spelman.

EXLEX. In old English law. An outlaw; *qui est extra legem,* one who is *out* of the *law's* protection. Bract. fol. 125. *Qui beneficio legis privatur.* Spelman.

EXOINE. In French law. An act or instrument in writing which contains the reasons why a party in a civil suit, or a person accused, who has been summoned, agreeably to the requisitions of a decree, does not appear. Poth. Proc. Crim. § 3, art. 3. The same as "Essoin" (*q. v.*).

EXONERATE. To relieve, to exculpate. Standard Oil Co. of New York v. Stevens, 103 Vt. 1, 151 A. 507, 508.

EXONERATION. The removal of a burden, charge, or duty. Particularly, the act of relieving a person or estate from a charge or liability by casting the same upon another person or estate. Louisville & N. R. Co. v. Comm., 114 Ky. 787, 71 S.W. 916; Bannon v. Burnes, C.C.Mo., 39 Fed. 898.

A right or equity which exists between those who are successively liable for the same debt. "A surety who discharges an obligation is entitled to look to the principal for reimbursement, and to invoke the aid of a court of equity for this purpose, and a subsequent surety who, by the terms of the contract, is responsible only in case of the default of the principal and a prior surety, may claim *exoneration* at the hands of either." Bisp.Eq. § 331.

A right to have a fund applied to payment of guaranteed claims. Stulz-Sickles Co. v. Fredburn Const. Corporation, 114 N.J.Eq. 475, 169 A. 27, 28.

The right which a person has who has been compelled to pay what another should be forced to pay in full. Fidelity & Casualty Ins. Co. of New York v. Sears, Roebuck & Co., 124 Conn. 227, 199 A. 93, 94.

Scotch Law

A discharge; or the act of being legally disburdened of, or liberated from, the performance of a duty or obligation. Bell.

EXONERATIONE SECTÆ. A writ that lay for the crown's ward, to be free from all suit to the county court, hundred court, leet, etc., during wardship. Fitzh. Nat. Brev. 158.

EXONERATIONE SECTÆ AD CURIAM BARON. A writ of the same nature as that last above described, issued by the guardian of the crown's ward, and addressed to the sheriffs or stewards of the court, forbidding them to distrain him, etc., for not doing suit of court, etc. New Nat. Brev. 352.

EXONERETUR. Lat. Let him be relieved or discharged. An entry made on a bailpiece, whereby the surety is relieved or discharged from further obligation, when the condition is fulfilled by the surrender of the principal or otherwise.

EXORBITANT. Deviating from the normal or customary course, or going beyond the rule of established limits of right or propriety. U. S. v. Oglesby Grocery Co., D.C.Ga., 264 F. 691, 695.

EXORDIUM. The beginning or introductory part of a speech.

EXPATRIATION. The voluntary act of abandoning one's country, and becoming the citizen or subject of another. Ludlam v. Ludlam, 31 Barb. (N. Y.) 489. See Emigration; Reynolds v. Haskins, C.C.A.Kan., 8 F.2d 473, 475, 45 A.L.R. 759; United States ex rel. Wrona v. Karnuth, D.C.N.Y., 14 F. Supp. 770, 771; 1 Barton, Conv. 31, note; Vaugh. 227, 281; 7 Co. 16; Dy. 2, 224, 298*b*, 300*b*; 2 P. Wms. 124; 1 Hale, Pl.Cr. 68; 1 Wood, Conv. 382; Westl.Priv.Int.Law; Story, Confl. Laws; Cockburn, Nationality. The voluntary renunciation or abandonment of nationality and allegiance. Schaufus v. Attorney General of United States, D.C.Md., 45 F.Supp. 61, 66; Perkins v. Elg, D.C., 307 U.S. 325, 59 S.Ct. 884, 889, 83 L.Ed. 1320.

EXPECT. To await; to look forward to something intended, promised, or likely to happen. Atchison, etc., R. Co. v. Hamlin, 67 Kan. 476, 73 P. 58; Kronenberg v. Whale, 21 Ohio App. 322, 153

N.E. 302, 308; to look for mentally, to look forward to, as to something about to happen or come, to have a previous apprehension of whether good or evil, to look for with some confidence, and once meant to demand, to require. Holcomb v. Holcomb, 173 Miss. 192, 159 So. 564, 566.

The word has also a secondary meaning, in which it implies a demand rather than anticipation, as where a person, in negotiating a contract, says he will "expect" to write half the fire insurance. Sillman v. Spokane Savings & Loan Soc., 103 Wash. 619, 175 P. 296, 297.

Where testator gave life estate provided that after life tenant's death he "expected" his realty to be sold the word "expect" was almost equivalent of word "direct". Wattjes v. Faeth, 379 Ill. 290, 40 N.E.2d 521, 524.

EXPECTABLE RISK. Risk which is indefinite and uncertain. Martin v. Hodson, 93 N.H. 66, 35 A.2d 402, 404.

EXPECTANCY. That which is expected or hoped for. The condition of being deferred to a future time, or of dependence upon an expected event; contingency as to possession or enjoyment. With respect to the time of their enjoyment, estates may either be in possession or in expectancy; and of expectancies there are two sorts,—one created by the act of the parties, called a "remainder;" the other by act of law, called a "reversion." 2 Bl.Comm. 163.

" 'Expectancy' as applied to property, is contingency as to possession, that which is expected or hoped for. At most it is a mere hope or expectation, contingent upon the will and pleasure of the landowner, and hardly reaches the height of a property right, much less a vested right, because where there is no obligation, there is no right. It is a possibility for which a party may under certain circumstances properly hope." Robinson v. Eagle-Picher Lead Co., 132 Kan. 860, 297 P. 697, 698, 75 A.L.R. 840.

EXPECTANCY OF LIFE. In the doctrine of life annuities, the share or number of years of life which a person of a given age may, upon an equality of chance, expect to enjoy. Wharton.

EXPECTANT. Contingent as to enjoyment. Having relation to, or dependent upon, a contingency.

EXPECTANT ESTATES. See Estate in Expectancy.

EXPECTANT HEIR. A person who has the expectation of inheriting property or an estate, but small present means.

The term is chiefly used in equity, where relief is afforded to such persons against the enforcement of "catching bargains," (*q. v.*) Jeffers v. Lampson, 10 Ohio St. 106; In re Robbins' Estate, 199 Pa. 500, 49 A. 233. "The phrase is used not in its literal meaning, but as including every one who has either a vested remainder, or a contingent remainder in a family property, including a remainder in a portion, as well as a remainder in an estate, and every one who has the hope of succession to the property of an ancestor, either by reason of his being the heir-apparent or presumptive, or by reason, merely, of the expectation of a devise or bequest on account of the supposed or presumed affection of his ancestor or relation. More than this, the doctrine as to expectant heirs has been extended to all reversioners and remaindermen. So that the doctrine not only included the class mentioned, who in some popular sense might be called 'expectant heirs,' but also all remaindermen and reversioners." Jessel, M. R.

EXPECTANT RIGHT. A contingent right, not vested; one which depends on the continued existence of the present condition of things until the happening of some future event. Pearsall v. Great Northern R. Co., 161 U.S. 646, 16 S.Ct. 705, 40 L. Ed. 838; Pollack v. Meyer Bros. Drug Co., C.C.A. Mo., 233 F. 861, 868; Adams v. Ernst, 1 Wash.2d 254, 95 P.2d 799, 804. A right is contingent, not vested, when it comes into existence only on an event or condition which may not happen. Wirtz v. Nestos, 51 N.D. 603, 200 N.W. 524, 530.

EXPECTATION OF LIFE. See Expectancy of Life.

EXPECTED. A shipping agent's letter that a ship was "expected" to be ready to be loaded at a port on a stated date constituted a representation of a belief or expectation. L. N. Jackson & Co. v. Seas Shipping Co., 185 Misc. 94, 56 N.Y.S.2d 501, 503.

EXPECTED SERVICE. Incidental to employment is that service which an employee has no absolute duty to perform but is of the type of duty which has the approval of the employer. Severson v. Industrial Commission, 221 Wis. 169, 266 N.W. 235, 236.

EXPEDIENCY. Involves utility. Woolf v. Fuller, 87 N.H. 64, 174 A. 193, 196, 94 A.L.R. 1067.

EXPEDIENT. Apt and suitable to end in view. Werner v. Biederman, 64 Ohio App. 423, 28 N.E.2d 957, 959. Whatever is suitable and appropriate in reason for the accomplishment of a specified object. Eustace v. Dickey, 240 Mass. 55, 132 N.E. 852, 862.

EXPEDIENTE. An historical record of proceedings in connection with grant of land by the sovereign. State v. Balli, Tex.Civ.App., 173 S.W.2d 522, 526. In Mexican law, a term including all the papers or documents constituting a grant or title to land from government. Vanderslice v. Hanks, 3 Cal. 27, 38.

EXPEDIMENT. The whole of a person's goods and chattels, bag and baggage. Wharton.

EXPEDIT REIPUBLICÆ NE SUA RE QUIS MALE UTATUR. It is for the interest of the state that a man should not enjoy his own property improperly (to the injury of others). Inst. 1, 8, 2.

EXPEDIT REIPUBLICÆ UT SIT FINIS LITIUM. It is for the advantage of the state that there be an end of suits; it is for the public good that actions be brought to a close. Co.Litt. 303*b*; Broom, Max. 365–6; Belcher v. Farrar, 8 Allen, Mass. 329. This maxim belongs to the law of all countries: 1 Phill. Int. L. 553; French v. Shotwell, 5 Johns. Ch., N.Y., 555, 568.

EXPEDITATÆ ARBORES. Trees rooted up or cut down to the roots. Fleta, l. 2, c. 41.

EXPEDITATION. In old forest law. A cutting off the claws or ball of the forefeet of mastiffs or other dogs, to prevent their running after deer;—a practice for the preservation of the royal forests. Cart. de For. c. 17; Spelman; Cowell.

EXPEDITE. To hasten; to make haste; to speed. Atchison, T. & S. F. Ry. Co. v. Ridley, 119 Okl. 138, 249 P. 289, 290.

EXPEDITER. An employee whose duty is to see that shortage in material at one point in a plant is remedied by delivery of the needed material from another part of the plant where it is stacked or stored. American Mut. Liability Ins. Co. v. Louisville & N. R. Co., 250 Ala. 354, 34 So. 2d 474, 476.

EXPEDITIO. An expedition; an irregular kind of army. Spelman.

EXPEDITIO BREVIS. In old practice. The service of a writ. Townsh. Pl. 43.

EXPEDITION. A sending forth or setting forth for the execution of some object of consequence. Progress. An important journey or excursion for a specific purpose; as, a military or exploring expedition; also, the body of persons making such an excursion. Equitable Life Assur. Soc. of United States v. Dyess, 194 Ark. 1023, 109 S.W.2d 1263, 1265.

An important journey or excursion for specific purpose; a journey, march, or voyage generally of several or many persons for definite purpose, such as a military or exploring expedition or a trading expedition to the African coast; the word carries an implication of a military exploit or of an exploration into remote regions or over new routes. Day v. Equitable Life Assur. Soc. of U. S., C.C.A.Colo., 83 F.2d 147, 149.

EXPEDITIOUS. Possessed of, or characterized by, expedition or efficiency and rapidity in action; performed with, or acting with, expedition; quick; speedy. Atchison, T. & S. F. Ry. Co. v. Ridley, 119 Okl. 138, 249 P. 289, 290.

EXPEL. In regard to trespass and other torts, this term means to eject, to put out, to drive out, and generally with an implication of the use of force. Perry v. Fitzhowe, 8 Q.B. 779; Smith v. Leo, 92 Hun, 242, 36 N.Y.S. 949.

EXPEND. To pay out, use up, consume. Adams v. Prather, 176 Cal. 33, 167 P. 534, 538, 3 A.L.R. 928; School Dist. No. 24 of Marion County v. Smith, 82 Or. 443, 161 P. 706, 708. To pay out, lay out, use up, and implies receiving something in return. In re Holmes' Estate, 233 Wis. 274, 289 N.W. 638, 641.

EXPENDERE. The word "expense" had its origin in the Latin word "expendere"; "ex" meaning "out," and "pendere" meaning "to weigh." State v. DeWitt C. Jones Co., 108 Fla. 613, 147 So. 230, 233.

EXPENDITORS. Paymasters. Those who expend or disburse certain taxes. Especially the sworn officer who supervised the repairs of the banks of the canals in Romney Marsh. Cowell.

EXPENDITURE. An expending, a laying out of money; disbursement;—it is not the same as an "appropriation," the setting apart or assignment to a particular person or use, in exclusion of all others. Grout v. Gates, 97 Vt. 434, 124 A. 76, 80.

As used in constitutional provision relating to allowable increase over preceding fiscal year, includes all expenditures legally made by county rather than expenditures in enforcement of law only. Crow v. Board of Sup'rs of Stanislaus County, 135 Cal.App. 451, 27 P.2d 655.

The word "expenditure" has been defined as the spending of money; the act of expending; disbursement expense; money expended; a laying out of money; payment; expenditure. Crow v. Board of Sup'rs of Stanislaus County, 135 Cal.App. 451, 27 P.2d 655.

EXPENSÆ LITIS. Costs or expenses of the suit, which are generally allowed to the successful party.

EXPENSE. That which is expended, laid out or consumed; an outlay; charge; cost; price. Rowley v. Clarke, 162 Iowa 732, 144 N.W. 908, 911.

Actual outlay or actual obligation to make outlay, U. S. v. Block & Kohner Mercantile Co., D.C.Mo., 33 F.2d 196, 197; an actual and honest disbursement, H. B. Humphrey Co. v. Pollack Roller Runner Sled Co., 278 Mass. 350, 180 N. E. 164, 166; an outlay of money; the expenditure of time, labor, and thought; the employment and consumption of time and labor; act of expending, disbursement, expenditure, etc., State v. De Witt C. Jones Co., 108 Fla. 613, 147 So. 230, 233; expenditures, outlays, or disbursements of money, In re McMurray, 131 Misc. 182, 227 N.Y.S. 115, 117; laying out or expending of money or other resources, as time or strength; expenditure; hence drain on resources; detriment; loss; as, at the expense of health; the habit of expending; money expended; outlay; charge; as, expenses for the journey, In re Bates' Will, 152 Misc. 627, 274 N.Y.S. 93; laying out or spending of money or other resources, In re Bond & Mortgage Guarantee Co., Sup., 39 N.Y.S.2d 760, 767.

For "Current Expenses," see that title.

EXPENSE IN CARRYING ON BUSINESS. Usual or customary expenditure in course of business during the year. Whitney v. Commissioner of Internal Revenue, C.C.A.3, 73 F.2d 589, 591.

EXPENSES OF ADMINISTRATION. As used in Revenue Act means obligations incurred after decedent's death by his representatives in administering his estate. Mayer v. Reinecke, D.C.Ill., 28 F.Supp. 334, 339.

EXPENSES OF FAMILY. Medical and funeral expenses are "expenses of the family" within meaning of statute making expenses of family chargeable upon property of both husband and wife. Hansen v. Hayes, 175 Or. 358, 154 P.2d 202, 205.

Under such a statute the term includes not only merchandise used by family as a whole, but also expenses, such as medical aid, hospital services and burial attendance, incurred or supplied for one of the spouses. In re De Nisson's Guardianship, 197 Wash. 265, 84 P.2d 1024, 1026.

EXPENSES OF RECEIVERSHIP. Comprehend allowances to receivers' counsel, master's fees, appraisers' fees, auditors' fees, and rent and expenses incurred by receivers in conducting business. Philadelphia Dairy Products Co. v. Summit Sweets Shoppe, Ch., 113 N.J.Eq. 458, 167 A. 667.

EXPENSES OF THE STATE. Within constitutional provision for raising revenue has reference to general operating expenses of state government for fiscal year. State ex rel. Conrad v. Langer, 68 N.D. 167, 277 N.W. 504, 509.

EXPENSIS MILITUM NON LEVANDIS. An ancient writ to prohibit the sheriff from levying any allowance for knights of the shire upon those who held lands in ancient demesne. Reg.Orig. 261.

EXPERIENCE. A state, extent, or duration of being engaged in a particular study or work; the real life as contrasted with the ideal or imaginary. Arthur v. City of Pittsburgh, 330 Pa. 202, 198 A. 637, 638. A word implying skill, facility, or practical wisdom gained by personal knowledge, feeling, and action, and also the course or process by which one attains knowledge or wisdom. Chicago, I. & L. Ry. Co. v. Gorman, 58 Ind.App. 381, 106 N.E. 897, 898.

EXPERIENCE RATE. Under compensation policy "experience rate," which is payable or applicable rate, is made up by taking the basic rate and considering the business conducted by the insured. Metropolitan Casualty Ins. Co. of New York v. Rochester Fruit & Vegetable Co., 232 App.Div. 321, 249 N.Y.S. 572, 575.

EXPERIENTIA PER VARIOS ACTUS LEGEM FACIT. MAGISTRA RERUM EXPERIENTIA. Co.Litt. 60; Branch, Princ. Experience by various acts makes law. Experience is the mistress of things.

EXPERIMENT. A trial or special test or observation made to confirm or disprove something doubtful. Stone v. City of Florence, 203 S.C. 527, 28 S.E.2d 409, 410, 150 A.L.R. 953; Bragg v. Ohio Chemical & Manufacturing Co., 349 Mo. 577, 162 S.W.2d 832, 837.

In patent law, either a trial of an uncompleted mechanical structure to ascertain what changes or additions may be necessary to make it accomplish the design of the projector, or a trial of a completed machine to test or illustrate its practical efficiency. In the former case, the inventor's efforts, being incomplete, if they are then abandoned, will have no effect upon the right of a subsequent inventor; but if the experiment proves the capacity of the machine to effect what its inventor proposed, the law assigns to him the merit of having produced a complete invention. Northwestern Fire Extinguisher Co. v. Philadelphia Fire Extinguisher Co., 10 Phila. 227, 18 Fed.Cas. 394.

EXPERIMENTAL TESTIMONY. That of some witness who, after the commission of the crime, makes experiments for the purpose of ascertaining the effect of a certain act under certain conditions, and swears to such experiments. State v. Harlan, Mo.Sup., 240 S.W. 197, 201.

EXPERT EVIDENCE. Testimony given in relation to some scientific, technical, or professional matter by experts, *i. e.*, persons qualified to speak authoritatively by reason of their special training, skill, or familiarity with the subject.

Evidence of persons who are skilled in some art, science, profession, or business, which skill or knowledge is not common to their fellow men, and which has come to such experts by reason of special study and experience in such art, science, profession, or business. Culver v. Prudential Ins. Co. of America, 6 W.W.Harr. 582, 179 A. 400.

Opinion by qualified person on facts already proved involving scientific or technical knowledge, and not evidence of thing done or measurement taken which any one is competent to prove. Crichton v. Krouse, La.App., 150 So. 443, 445; Allen v. Tex. & N. O. R. Co., Tex.Civ.App., 70 S.W.2d 758, 763.

Opinion of witness possessing peculiar knowledge, wisdom, skill or information regarding subject matter under consideration, acquired by study, investigation, observation, practice or experience and not likely to be possessed by ordinary layman or inexperienced person. Baker v. Kansas City Public Service Co., 353 Mo. 625, 183 S.W.2d 873, 875; Ambruster v. Levitt Realty & Investment Co., 341 Mo. 364, 107 S.W.2d 74, 79.

Such as is given on questions of science, skill, or trade by persons learned or experienced therein. Langford v. State, 124 Tex.Cr.R. 473, 63 S.W.2d 1027.

EXPERT WITNESSES may be men of science educated in the art, or persons possessing special or peculiar knowledge acquired from practical experience. Empire Oil & Refining Co. v. Hoyt, C. C.A.Mich., 112 F.2d 356, 360.

One who gives result of process of reasoning which can be mastered only by special scientists. Phillips v. Tidwell, 26 Tenn.App. 543, 174 S.W.2d 472, 477; one who has skilled experience or extensive knowledge in his calling, or in any branch of learning, King v. State, 109 Tex.Cr.R. 173, 3 S. W.2d 802, 804, 57 A.L.R. 407; one who has special knowledge of subject, Pennsylvania Threshermen & Farmers' Mut. Casualty Ins. Co. v. Messenger, 181 Md. 295, 29 A.2d 653, 655; Hutchens v. Humble Oil & Refining Co., Tex.Civ.App., 161 S.W.2d 571, 573; Greenstreet v. Greenstreet, 65 Idaho 36, 139 P.2d 239, 242; one who is skilled in some art, science, trade, profession, or other human activity, and possesses peculiar knowledge concerning it, Tri-State Broadcasting Co. v. Federal Communications Commission, 68 App.D.C. 292, 96 F.2d 564, 568; person competent to give expert testimony, Ambruster v. Levitt Realty & Investment Co., 341 Mo. 364, 107 S.W.2d 74, 79.

Witnesses who have acquired ability to deduce correct inferences from hypothetically stated facts, or from facts involving scientific or technical knowledge. City of Chicago v. Lehmann, 262 Ill. 468, 104 N.E. 829, 830.

Witnesses who have had special opportunity for observation, or special training or special skill in obtaining the facts in a case. Mills v. Richardson, 126 Me. 244, 137 A. 689, 690.

Experts. An expert is a skillful or experienced person; a person having skill or experience, or peculiar knowledge on certain subjects, or in certain professions; a scientific witness. See Congress & E. Spring Co. v. Edgar, 99 U.S. 657, 25 L.Ed. 487; Koccis v. State, 56 N.J.Law, 44, 27 A. 800; Ellingwood v. Bragg, 52 N.H. 489; United States Fidelity & Guaranty Co. v. Rochester, Tex.Civ.App., 281 S.W. 306, 311.

One possessing, with reference to particular subject, knowledge not acquired by ordinary persons, Oklahoma Natural Gas Corporation v. Schwartz, 146 Okl. 250, 293 P. 1087, 1090; one skilled in any particular art, trade, or profession, being possessed of peculiar knowledge concerning the same, and one who has given subject in question particular study, practice, or observation. Hardy v. Dahl, 210 N.C. 530, 187 S.E. 788, 790; one who by habits of life and business has peculiar skill in forming opinion on subject in dispute, Robertson v. Ætna Life Ins. Co., 37 Ga.App. 703, 141 S.E. 504, 505; Sims v. State, 40 Ga.App. 10, 148 S.E. 769, 771; one who can see all sides of a subject, Kentucky & West Virginia Power Co. v. Howes, 246 Ky. 843, 56 S.W.2d 539.

Persons professionally acquainted with the science or practice in question. Strickl.Ev. 408. Persons conversant with the subject-matter on questions of science, skill, trade, and others of like kind. Best, Ev. § 346; Crosby v. City of East Orange, 84 N.J.Law, 708, 87 A. 341, 342; Pridgen v. Gibson, 194 N.C. 289, 139 S.E. 443, 445, 54 A.L.R. 885.

Persons selected by the court or parties in a cause, on account of their knowledge or skill, to examine, estimate, and ascertain things and make a report of their opinions. Merlin, *Répert.*

Persons who are professionally acquainted with some science or are skilled in some art or trade, or who have experience or knowledge in relation to matters which are not generally known to the people. Miller v. State, 9 Okl.Cr. 255, 131 P. 717, 718, L.R.A.1915A, 1088.

EXPILARE. In the civil law. To spoil; to rob or plunder. Applied to inheritances. Dig. 47, 19; Cod. 9, 32.

EXPILATIO. In the civil law. The offense of unlawfully appropriating goods belonging to a succession. It is not technically theft (*furtum*) because such property no longer belongs to the decedent, nor to the heir, since the latter has not yet taken possession.

In the common law, the grant of letters testamentary, or letters of administration, relates back to the time of the death of the testator or intestate; so that the property of the estate is vested in the executor or administrator from that period.

EXPILATOR. In the civil law. A robber; a spoiler or plunderer. *Expilatores sunt atrociores fures.* Dig. 47, 18, 1, 1.

EXPIRATION. Cessation; termination from mere lapse of time; as the expiration of a lease, statute, and the like. Marshall v. Rugg, 6 Wyo. 270, 45 Pac. 486, 33 L.R.A. 679; Harris v. Goldberg, 111 Misc.Rep. 600, 182 N.Y.S. 262, 263. Coming to a close. Clevenger v. Kern, 100 Ind.App. 581, 197 N.E. 731, 737. Termination or end. Petition of Prime, 335 Pa. 218, 6 A.2d 530, 532.

The record known in insurance circles as "expirations" is in effect a copy of policy issued to insured which contains the date of issuance, name of insured, expiration, amount, premiums, property covered and terms of insurance. Woodruff v. Auto Owners Ins. Co., 300 Mich. 54, 1 N.W.2d 450, 453; Kerr & Elliott v. Green Mountain Mut. Fire Ins. Co., 111 Vt. 502, 18 A.2d 164, 168.

The term "expiration," as in an insurance policy, refers to termination of the policy by lapse of time covering the policy period, while "cancellation" refers to termination of the policy by act of either or both parties prior to ending of the policy period. Beha v. Breger, 223 N.Y.S. 726, 731, 130 Misc.Rep. 235; Hanson v. Royal Ins. Co., C.C.A.Tenn., 257 F. 715, 716.

EXPIRATION OF CREDIT. As used in statute, refers to expiration of additional period of grace or credit extension accorded the debtor. Fleshman v. Whiteside, 148 Or. 73, 34 P.2d 648, 650, 93 A.L.R. 1456.

EXPIRATION OF PERIOD FOR REDEMPTION. As used in statute concerning conveyance of title by tax deed, it means time of application for tax deed. Hartman v. Mimmack, 116 Mont. 392, 154 P.2d 279, 281.

EXPIRE. Where term of lease has ended, either by lapse of time or by limitation, it has expired. Burnee Corporation v. Uneeda Pure Orange Drink Co., 132 Misc. 435, 230 N.Y.S. 239, 246.

EXPIRY OF THE LEGAL. In Scotch law and practice. Expiration of the period within which an adjudication may be redeemed, by paying the debt in the decree of adjudication. Bell; 3 Jurid. Styles, 3d ed. 1107.

EXPLEES. See Esplees.

EXPLETA, EXPLETIA, or EXPLECIA. In old records. The rents and profits of an estate.

EXPLICATIO. In the civil law. The fourth pleading; equivalent to the surrejoinder of the common law. Calvin.

EXPLICIT. Not obscure or ambiguous, having no disguised meaning or reservation. Eclipse Lumber Co. v. Bitler, 213 Iowa 1313, 241 N.W. 696, 698.

EXPLOITATION. Act or process of exploiting, making use of, or working up; utilization by application of industry, argument, or other means of turning to account, as the exploitation of a mine or a forest. State Finance Co. v. Hamacher, 171 Wash. 15, 17 P.2d 610, 613.

EXPLORATION. In mining law. The examination and investigation of land supposed to contain valuable minerals, by drilling, boring, sinking shafts, driving tunnels, and other means, for the purpose of discovering the presence of ore and its extent. Colvin v. Weimer, 64 Minn. 37, 65 N.W. 1079.

EXPLORATOR. A scout, huntsman, or chaser.

EXPLOSION. A sudden expansion of a liquid substance with result that gas generated by the expansion escapes with violence, usually causing a loud noise. Standard Accident Ins. Co. v. Harrison-Wright Co., 207 N.C. 661, 178 S.E. 235.

A sudden and rapid combustion, causing violent expansion of the air, and accompanied by a report. United Life, Fire & Marine Ins. Co. v. Foote, 22 Ohio St. 348, 10 Am. Rep. 735; Hartford Fire Ins. Co. v. Empire Coal Mining Co., C.C.A.Colo., 30 F.2d 794, 798. In the common acceptance of the term, it includes the sudden bursting or breaking up from an internal or other force, and is not limited to cases caused by combustion or fire. American Paper Products Co. v. Continental Ins. Co., 208 Mo.App. 87, 225 S.W. 1029, 1030. The ordinary idea is that the explosion is the cause, while the rupture is the effect. Mitchell v. Ins. Co., 183 U.S. 42, 22 S.Ct. 22, 46 L.Ed. 74.

A violent bursting or expansion with noise following the sudden production of great pressure or a sudden release of pressure. Lever Bros. Co. v. Atlas Assur. Co., C.C.A.Ind., 131 F.2d 770, 775, 776.

A violent expansion of some force, accompanied by noise. Sweeney v. Blue Anchor Beverage Co., 325 Pa. 216, 189 A. 331, 335.

Bursting of something with great noise and violence. Lever Bros. Co. v. Atlas Assur. Co., C.C.A.Ind., 131 F.2d 770, 775, 776.

Bursting with a loud noise or detonation. Bower v. Aetna Ins. Co., D.C.Tex., 54 F.Supp. 897, 898.

Sudden release of pressure such as disruption of steam boiler, Travellers' Indemnity Co. v. B. & B. Ice & Coal Co., 248 Ky. 443, 58 S.W.2d 640.

The word "explosion" is variously used in ordinary speech, and is not one that admits of exact definition. Every combustion of an explosive substance, whereby other property is ignited and consumed, would not be an "explosion," within the ordinary meaning of the term. It is not used as a synonym of "combustion." An explosion may be described generally as a sudden and rapid combustion, causing violent expansion of the air, and accompanied by a report. But the rapidity of the combustion, the violence of the expansion, and the vehemence of the report vary in intensity as often as the occurrences multiply. Hence an explosion is an idea of degrees; and the true meaning of the word, in each particular case, must be settled, not by any fixed standard or accurate measurement, but by the common experience and notions of men in matters of that sort. Insurance Co. v. Foote, 22 Ohio St. 348, 10 Am.Rep. 735. And see Insurance Co. v. Dorsey, 56 Md. 81, 40 Am.Rep. 403; Louisville Underwriters v. Durland, 123 Ind. 544, 24 N.E. 221, 7 L.R.A. 399.

The word "explosion," when used in a fire policy, is that which ordinary men, not scientists, understand an explosion to be. Roma Wine Co. v. Hardware Mut. Fire Ins. Co. of Minnesota, 31 Cal.App.2d 455, 88 P.2d 260, 262.

EXPLOSION OF ANY KIND. Under fire policy exempting insurer from liability, phrase refers not to agency producing explosion, but to kinds of material which explode. McDonald v. Royal Ins. Co., 98 Mont. 572, 40 P.2d 1005, 1006.

EXPLOSIVE. Any substance by whose decomposition or combustion gas is generated with such rapidity that it can be used for blasting or in firearms. Schwartz v. Northern Life Ins. Co., C.C.A.Cal., 25 F.2d 555, 559.

"Explosive" is compound or mixture susceptible of explosive chemical reaction, as gunpowder or nitroglycerine, and has been construed not to cover specific things which do explode or contain explosive material. Henderson v. Massachusetts Bonding & Ins. Co., 337 Mo. 1, 84 S.W.2d 922, 925.

EXPORT, *v.* To carry or to send abroad. Tennessee Oil Co. v. McCanless, 178 Tenn. 683, 157 S.W. 2d 267, 271, 272. To send, take, or carry an article of trade or commerce out of the country. To transport merchandise from one country to another in the course of trade. To carry out or convey goods by sea. State v. Turner, 5 Har., Del., 501.

Transportation of goods from United States to foreign country. West India Oil Co. v. Sancho, C.C.A.Puerto Rico, 108 F.2d 144, 147.

"Export," in its primary sense, means to carry or send out of a place, and in secondary sense means to carry from one state or country. McKesson & Robbins v. Collins, 18 Cal.App.2d 648, 64 P.2d 469, 470.

While the word *export* technically includes the landing in as well as the shipment to a foreign country, it is often used as meaning only the shipment from this country. U. S. v. Chavez, 228 U.S. 525, 33 S.Ct. 595, 57 L.Ed. 950.

EXPORT, *n.* A thing or commodity exported. More commonly used in the plural.

In American law, this term is only used of goods carried to foreign countries, not of goods transported from one state to another. Swan v. U. S., 190 U.S. 143, 23 S.Ct. 702, 47 L.Ed. 984; Rothermel v. Meyerle, 136 Pa. 250, 20 A. 583, 9 L.R.A. 366.

EXPORT TAX. A tax on goods going out and which actually leave the country. Krauter v. Menchacatorre, 202 App.Div. 200, 195 N.Y.S. 361, 363.

EXPORTATION. A severance of goods from mass of things belonging to United States with intention of uniting them to mass of things belonging to some foreign country. U. S. v. Hill, C.C.A.N.Y., 34 F.2d 133, 135. The act of sending or carrying goods and merchandise from one country to another.

EXPOSE, *v.* To show publicly; to display; to offer to the public view; as, to "expose" goods to sale, to "expose" a tariff or schedule of rates, to "expose" the person. Comm. v. Byrnes, 158 Mass. 172, 33 N.E. 343; Adams Exp. Co. v. Schlessinger, 75 Pa. 246. To "expose for sale" means to keep and show for the purpose of selling. State v. Hogan, 212 Mo.App. 473, 252 S.W. 90; to have in stock. People ex rel. Goldstein v. Glass, 154 Misc. 569, 278 N.Y.S. 764.

To place in a position where the object spoken of is open to danger, on where it is near or accessible to anything which may affect it detrimentally; as, to "expose" a child, or to expose oneself or another to a contagious disease or to danger or hazard of any kind. In re Smith, 146 N.Y. 68, 40 N.E. 497, 28 L.R.A. 820; Davis v. Insurance Co., 81 Iowa, 496, 46 N.W. 1073, 10 L.R.A. 359; Eau Claire Sand & Gravel Co. v. Industrial Commission of Wisconsin, 173 Wis. 561, 181 N.W. 718. To cast out to chance, to place abroad, or in a situation unprotected. Shannon v. People, 5 Mich. 90.

Word "exposed" as used in pedestrian's complaint against city meant that city negligently permitted hole to remain in street open and unguarded. City of Birmingham v. Chambless, 222 Ala. 249, 132 So. 313.

EXPOSÉ. Fr. A statement; account; recital; explanation. The term is used in diplomatic language as descriptive of a written explanation of the reasons for a certain act or course of conduct.

EXPOSITIO. Lat. Explanation; exposition; interpretation.

EXPOSITIO QUÆ EX VISCERIBUS CAUSÆ NASCITUR, EST APTISSIMA ET FORTISSIMA IN LEGE. That kind of interpretation which is born [or drawn] from the bowels [or vitals] of a cause is the aptest and most forcible in the law. 10 Coke, 24*b*.

EXPOSITION. Explanation; interpretation.

EXPOSITION DE PART. In French law. The abandonment of a child, unable to take care of itself, either in a public or private place.

EXPOSITORY STATUTE. One the office of which is to declare what shall be taken to be the true meaning and intent of a statute previously enacted. Black, Const.Law (3d ed.) 89. And see Lindsay v. United States Sav. & Loan Co., 120 Ala. 156, 24 So. 171, 42 L.R.A. 783; People v. Board of Sup'rs, 16 N.Y. 424.

They are often expressed thus: "The true intent and meaning of an act passed * * * be and is hereby declared to be;" "the provisions of the act shall not hereafter extend"; or "are hereby declared and enacted not to apply," and the like. This is a common mode of legislation.

EXPOSURE. The act or state of exposing or being exposed. See Expose.

Words "exposure to unnecessary danger" and the words "unnecessary exposure to danger", include all cases of exposure to unnecessary danger attributable to insured's negligence. Oakley v. National Casualty Co., 217 N.C. 150, 7 S.E.2d 495, 496; Micca v. Wisconsin Nat. Life Ins. Co., C.C.A.Ill., 75 F.2d 710, 712.

For "Indecent exposure", see Indecent.

EXPOSURE OF CHILD. Placing it (with the intention of wholly abandoning it) in such a place or position as to leave it unprotected against danger and jeopard its health or life or subject it to the peril of severe suffering or serious bodily harm. Shannon v. People, 5 Mich. 90.

EXPOSURE OF PERSON. In criminal law. Such an intentional exposure, in a public place, of the naked body or the private parts as is calculated to shock the feelings of chastity or to corrupt the morals of the community. Gilmore v. State, 118 Ga. 299, 45 S.E. 226.

EXPRESS. Clear; definite; explicit; unmistakable; not dubious or ambiguous. In re Moon's Will, 107 Vt. 92, 176 A. 410, 412. Clear, definite, plain, direct. State ex rel. Andrews v. Zangerle, 101 Ohio St. 235, 128 N.E. 165, 167. Declared in terms; set forth in words. Directly and distinctly stated. State ex rel. Ashauer v. Hostetter, 344 Mo. 665, 127 S.W.2d 697, 699. Explicit. Elliott v. Hudson, 117 W.Va. 345, 185 S.E. 465, 467; made known distinctly and explicitly, and not left to inference. Minneapolis Steel & Machinery Co. v. Federal Surety Co., C.C.A.Minn., 34 F.2d 270, 274. Manifested by direct and appropriate language, as distinguished from that which is inferred from conduct. The word is usually contrasted with "implied." State v. Denny, 118 Ind. 449, 21 N.E. 274, 4 L.R.A. 65.

"Express" necessarily implies previous knowledge of intended personal use. Burford v. Huesby, 35 Cal.App.2d 643, 96 P.2d 380, 381.

To force out by pressure; to press or squeeze out, as the juice of a fruit; to empty by pressure or squeezing. Strommen v. Prudential Ins. Co., 187 Minn. 381, 245 N.W. 632, 634.

As to express "Conditions," "Consent," "Consideration," "Contracts," "Covenants," "Dedication," "Emancipation," "Invitation," "Malice," "Notice," "Obligation," "Trust," "Waiver," and "Warranty," see those titles.

EXPRESS ABROGATION. Abrogation by express provision or enactment; the repeal of a law or provision by a subsequent one, referring directly to it.

Express abrogation is that literally pronounced by the new law either in general terms, as when a final clause abrogates or repeals all laws contrary to the provisions of the new one, or in particular terms, as when it abrogates certain preceding laws which are named.

EXPRESS ACTIVE TRUST. See Trust.

EXPRESS ASSUMPSIT. An undertaking to do some act, or to pay a sum of money to another, manifested by express terms.

An assumpsit is "express" if promisor puts his engagement in distinct and definite language. Dukes v. Rogers, 67 Ga.App. 661, 21 S.E.2d 295, 297.

An undertaking made orally, by writing not under seal, or by matter of record, to perform act or to pay sum of money to another. Holcomb v. Kentucky Union Co., 262 Ky. 192, 90 S.W.2d 25, 27; Anderson v. Biesman & Carrick Co., 287 Ill. App. 507, 4 N.E.2d 639, 640, 641.

EXPRESS AUTHORITY. Authority delegated to agent by words which expressly authorize him to do a delegable act. Greep v. Bruns, 160 Kan. 48, 159 P.2d 803, 808. Authority distinctly, plainly expressed, orally or in writing. Ulen v. Knecttle, 50 Wyo. 94, 58 P.2d 446, 449, 111 A.L.R. 565. Authority which is directly granted to or conferred upon agent in express terms. Stevens v. Frost, 140 Me. 1, 32 A.2d 164, 168; Riefsnyder v. Dougherty, 301 Pa. 328, 152 A. 98, 100.

That which confers power to do a particular identical thing set forth and declared exactly, plainly, and directly with well-defined limits; an authority given in direct terms, definitely and explicitly, and not left to inference or implication, as distinguished from authority which is general, implied, or not directly stated or given. Fergus v. Brady, 277 Ill. 272, 115 N.E. 393, 396, Ann.Cas.1918B, 220.

EXPRESS COLOR. An evasive form of special pleading in a case where the defendant ought to plead the general issue. Abolished by the common-law procedure act, 1852, 15 & 16 Vict. c. 76, § 64.

EXPRESS COMMON-LAW DEDICATION. See Dedication.

EXPRESS COMPANY. A firm or corporation engaged in the business of transporting parcels or other movable property, in the capacity of common carriers, and especially undertaking the safe carriage and speedy delivery of small but valuable packages of goods and money. Alsop v. Southern Exp. Co., 104 N.C. 278, 10 S.E. 297, 6 L.R.A. 271; Pfister v. Central Pac. Ry. Co., 70 Cal. 169, 11 P. 686, 59 Am.Rep. 404.

A common carrier that carries at regular and stated times, over fixed and regular routes, money and other valuable packages, which cannot be conveniently or safely carried as common freight; and also other articles and packages of any description which the shipper desires or the nature of the article requires should have safe and rapid transit and quick delivery, transporting the same in the immediate charge of its own messenger on passenger steamers and express and passenger railway trains, which it does not own or operate, but with the owners of which it contracts for the carriage of its messengers and freights. Pacific Exp. Co. v. Seibert, C.C.Mo., 44 F. 310.

EXPRESS DISSATISFACTION. Where will declares that any one expressing dissatisfaction with its provisions should forfeit his interest, "dissatisfaction" is legally "expressed" when beneficiary contests or objects in legal proceeding to enforcement of any provision of will. In re Hickman's Estate, 308 Pa. 230, 162 A. 168, 169.

EXPRESS PERMISSION within statute respecting automobile owner's liability includes prior knowledge of intended use and affirmative and active consent thereto. Bradford v. Sargent, 136 Cal.App. 324, 27 P.2d 93.

EXPRESS PRIVATE TRUST. See Trust.

EXPRESS REPEAL. Abrogation or annulment of previously existing law by enactment of subsequent statute declaring that former law shall be revoked or abrogated. Brockman v. Board of Directors of Jefferson County Bridge Dist., 188 Ark. 396, 66 S.W.2d 619. A repeal of statute is "express" when it is literally declared by a subsequent statute. Stoker v. Police Jury of Sabine Parish, La.App., 190 So. 192, 194.

EXPRESS REPUBLICATION of will occurs where testator repeats ceremonies essential to valid execution, with avowed intention of republishing will. In re Simeone's Estate, 141 Misc. 737, 253 N.Y.S. 683, 689.

EXPRESS REQUEST. That which occurs when one person commands or asks another to do or give something, or answers affirmatively when asked whether another shall do a certain thing. Zeidler v. Goelzer, 191 Wis. 378, 211 N.W. 140, 144.

EXPRESS TERMS. Within provision that qualified acceptance, in "express terms," varies effect of draft, "express terms" means clear, unambiguous, definite, certain, and unequivocal terms. International Finance Corp. v. Philadelphia Wholesale Drug Co., 312 Pa. 280, 167 A. 790, 792.

EXPRESSA NOCENT, NON EXPRESSA NON NOCENT. Things expressed are [may be] prejudicial; things not expressed are not. Express words are sometimes prejudicial, which, if omitted, had done no harm. Dig. 35, 1, 52; Id. 50, 17, 195. See Calvin.

EXPRESSA NON PROSUNT QUÆ NON EXPRESSA PRODERUNT. 4 Coke, 73. The expression of things of which, if unexpressed, one would have the benefit, is useless. Thing expressed may be prejudicial which when not expressed will profit.

EXPRESSED. Means stated or declared in direct terms, set forth in words; not left to inference or implication. Anderson v. Board of Ed. of School Dist. No. 91, 390 Ill. 412, 61 N.E.2d 562, 567.

EXPRESSIO EORUM QUÆ TACITE INSUNT NIHIL OPERATUR. The expression or express mention of those things which are tacitly implied avails nothing. 2 Inst. 365.

A man's own words are void, when the law speaketh as much. Finch, Law, b. 1, c. 3, no. 26. Words used to express what the law will imply without them are mere words of abundance. 5 Coke, 11; Broom, Max. 669, 753; 2 Pars.Contr. 28; 4 Co. 73; Andr.Steph.Pl. 366; Hob. 170; 3 Atk. 138; 11 M. & W. 569; 7 Exch. 28.

EXPRESSIO UNIUS EST EXCLUSIO ALTERIUS. Expression of one thing is the exclusion of another. Co.Litt. 210*a*; Burgin v. Forbes, 293 Ky. 456, 169 S.W.2d 321, 325; Newblock v. Bowles, 170 Okl. 487, 40 P.2d 1097, 1100. Mention of one thing implies exclusion of another. Fazio v. Pittsburgh Rys. Co., 321 Pa. 7, 182 A. 696, 698; Saslaw v. Weiss, 133 Ohio St. 496, 14 N.E.2d 930, 932. When certain persons or things are specified in a law, contract, or will, an intention to exclude all others from its operation may be inferred. Little v. Town of Conway, 171 S.C. 27, 170 S.E. 447, 448.

Under this maxim, if statute specifies one exception to a general rule or assumes to specify the effects of a certain provision, other exceptions or effects are excluded. People v. One 1941 Ford 8 Stake Truck, Engine No. 99T370053, License No. P.8410, Cal., 159 P.2d 641, 642.

EXPRESSIO UNIUS PERSONÆ EST EXCLUSIO ALTERIUS. Co.Litt. 210. The mention of one person is the exclusion of another. See Broom, Max. 651.

EXPRESSLY. In an express manner; in direct or unmistakable terms; explicitly; definitely; directly. Le Ballister v. Redwood Theatres, 1 Cal. App.2d 447, 36 P.2d 827; St. Louis Union Trust Co. v. Hill, 336 Mo. 17, 76 S.W.2d 685, 689. In an express manner; in direct terms; with distinct purpose; particularly. Hawkins v. Mattes, 171 Okl. 186, 41 P.2d 880, 891; the opposite of impliedly. Bolles v. Toledo Trust Co., 144 Ohio St. 195, 58 N.E.2d 381, 396.

EXPRESSUM FACIT CESSARE TACITUM. That which is expressed makes that which is implied to cease, [that is, supersedes it, or controls its effect.] Thus, an implied covenant in a deed is in all cases controlled by an express covenant. 4 Coke, 80; Broom, Max. 651; 5 Bingh.N.C. 185; 6 B. & C. 609; 2 C. & M. 459; 2 E. & B. 856; Andover & Medford Turnpike Corp. v. Hay, 7 Mass. 106; Galloway v. Holmes, 1 Doug., Mich., 330.

Where a law sets down plainly its whole meaning the court is prevented from making it mean what the court pleases. Munro v. City of Albuquerque, 48 N.M. 306, 150 P.2d 733, 743.

EXPRESSUM SERVITIUM REGAT VEL DECLARET TACITUM. Let service expressed rule or declare what is silent.

EXPROMISSIO. In the civil law. The species of novation by which a creditor accepts a new debtor, who becomes bound instead of the old, the latter being released. 1 Bouv.Inst. no. 802.

EXPROMISSOR. In the civil law. A person who assumes the debt of another, and becomes solely liable for it, by a stipulation with the creditor. He differs from a surety, inasmuch as this contract is one of novation, while a surety is jointly liable with his principal. Mackeld.Rom.Law, § 538; Dig. 12, 4, 4; 16, 1, 13; 24, 3, 64, 4; 38, 1, 37, 8.

EXPROMITTERE. In the civil law. To undertake for another with the view of becoming liable in his place. Calvin.

EXPROPRIATION. This word primarily denotes a voluntary surrender of rights or claims; the act of divesting oneself of that which was previously claimed as one's own, or renouncing it. In this sense it is the opposite of "appropriation."

A meaning has been attached to the term, imported from its use in foreign jurisprudence, which makes it synonymous with the exercise of the power of eminent domain, *i. e.*, the compulsory taking from a person, on compensation made, of his private property for the use of a railroad, canal, or other public work. Brownsville v. Pavazos, 2 Woods 293, Fed.Cas.No.2,043. In Louisiana expropriation is used as is taking under eminent domain in most of the other states. In England "compulsory purchase" is used; Halsbury, Laws of England.

French Law

Expropriation is the compulsory realization of a debt by the creditor out of the lands of his debtor, or the usufruct thereof. When the debtor is cotenant with others, it is necessary that a partition should first be made. It is confined, in the first place, to the lands (if any) that are in *hypothèque*, but afterwards extends to the lands not in *hypothèque*. Moreover, the debt must be of a liquidated amount. Brown.

EXPULSION. A putting or driving out. Ejectment; banishment; a cutting off from the privileges of an institution or society permanently. John B. Stetson University v. Hunt, 88 Fla. 510, 102 So. 637, 639. The act of depriving a member of a corporation, legislative body, assembly, society, commercial organization, etc., of his membership in the same, by a legal vote of the body itself, for breach of duty, improper conduct, or other sufficient cause. New York Protective Ass'n v. McGrath, Super.Ct., 5 N.Y.S. 10; Palmetto Lodge v. Hubbell, 2 Strob., S.C., 462, 49 Am. Dec. 604. Also, in the law of torts and of landlord and tenant, an eviction or forcible putting out. See Expel.

"Separation" from a church by reason of a schism is not like "expulsion" or "excommunication," which terms necessarily involve involuntary and compulsory separation of members. Lindstrom v. Tell, 131 Minn. 203, 154 N.W. 969, 971.

EXPUNGE. Means to destroy or obliterate; it implies not a legal act, but a physical annihilation. Andrews v. Police Court of City of Stockton, Cal. App., 123 P.2d 128, 129. To blot out; to efface designedly; to obliterate; to strike out wholly. Webster. See Cancel.

EXPURGATION. The act of purging or cleansing, as where a book is published without its obscene passages.

EXPURGATOR. One who corrects by expurging.

EXQUÆSTOR. In Roman law. One who had filled the office of *quæstor*. A title given to Tribonian. Inst. prœm. § 3. Used only in the ablative case, (*exquæstore*.)

EXROGARE. (From *ex*, from, and *rogare*, to pass a law.) In Roman law. To take something from an old law by a new law. Tayl. Civil Law, 155.

EXTEND. Lends itself to great variety of meanings, which must in each case be gathered from context. Blouch v. Stevens, 106 N.J.L. 488, 150 A. 581, 583.

It may mean to broaden the application or action of, Meyering v. Miller, 30 Mo. 885, 51 S.W.2d 65, 66; to carry forward, Loeffler v. Federal Supply Co., 187 Okl. 373, 102 P.2d 862, 864; to cause to reach or continue as from point to point, Henderson Development Co. v. United Fuel Gas Co., 121 W.Va. 284, 3 S.E.2d 217, 219; to expand, enlarge, prolong, lengthen, widen, carry out, further than the original limit; as, to extend the time for filing an answer, to extend a lease, term of office, charter, railroad track, etc., State v. Armstrong, 31 N.M. 220, 243 P. 333, 345; Lesser-Goldman Cotton Co. v. Cache River Drainage Dist., 174 Ark. 160, 294 S.W. 711, 713; State v. Scott, 113 Mo. 559, 20 S.W. 1076; Moers v. Reading, 21 Pa. 201; Keetch v. Cordner, 90 Utah 423, 62 P.2d 273, 277, 108 A.L.R. 52; to give as a privilege, Tantum v. Keller, 95 N.J.Eq. 466, 123 A. 299, 300, 301, 302; to give wider range, State ex rel. Berthot v. Gallatin County High School Dist., 102 Mont. 356, 58 P.2d 264, 266; to make more comprehensive or capricious, Meyering v. Miller, 33 Mo. 885, 51 S.W.2d 65, 66; Keetch v. Cordner, 90 Utah 423, 62 P.2d 273, 277, 108 A.L.R. 52; to stretch out or to draw out, Crane Enamelware Co. v. Smith, 168 Tenn. 203, 76 S.W.2d 644; Loeffler v. Federal Supply Co., 187 Okl. 373, 102 P.2d 862, 864.

Statute authorizing Interstate Commerce Commission to require carriers to "extend" lines is confined to extensions within undertaking of carriers to serve, and does not embrace new lines reaching new territory. Interstate Commerce Commission v. Oregon-Washington R. & Nav. Co., Or., 288 U.S. 14, 53 S.Ct. 266, 77 L.Ed. 588.

To extend a charter is to give one which now exists greater or longer time to operate in than that to which it was originally limited. Fidelity & Columbia Trust Co. v. Louisville Ry. Co., 258 Ky. 817, 81 S.W.2d 896, 900.

To "extend" a lease or contract is not necessarily the same as "renew," for a stipulation to renew requires the making of a new lease, while one to extend does not. Sanders v. Wender, 205 Ky. 422, 265 S.W. 939, 941. See, also, Nenzel v. Rochester Silver Corporation, 48 Nev. 41, 226 P. 1102, 1105; Livingston Waterworks v. City of Livingston, 53 Mont. 1, 162 P. 381, 383, L.R.A.1917D, 1074; Buckland v. Tarble, 95 Vt. 87, 112 A. 217, 218. But whether a clause in a lease is a covenant of renewal or an agreement for an extension depends on the parties' intention and the use of the word "renewal"; Freiheit v. Broch, 98 Conn. 166, 118 A. 828, 829; and the two terms may be used practically synonymously; American Press v. City of St. Louis, 314 Mo. 288, 284 S.W. 482, 486; Orr v. Doubleday, Page & Co., 157 N.Y.S. 1009, 1012, 172 App.Div. 96. The word "extend" as used in a lease does not necessarily mean the same, as "renew," but context may show intent that the words be given a similar meaning. Candler v. Smyth, 168 Ga. 276, 147 S.E. 552, 554.

To extend a street means to prolong and continue it in the direction in which it already points, but does not include deflecting it from the course of the existing portion. In re Charlotte St., 23 Pa. 288; Seattle & M. Ry. Co. v. State, 7 Wash. 150, 34 P. 551, 22 L.R.A. 217.

English Practice

To value the lands or tenements of a person bound by a statute or recognizance which has become forfeited, to their full *extended* value. 3 Bl.Comm. 420; Fitzh.Nat.Brev. 131. To execute the writ of *extent* or *extendi facias* (*q. v.*). 2 Tidd, Pr. 1043, 1044.

Taxation

Extending a tax consists in adding to the assessment roll the precise amount due from each person whose name appears thereon. "The subjects for taxation having been properly listed, and a basis for apportionment established, nothing will remain to fix a definite liability but to *extend* upon the list or roll the several proportionate amounts, as a charge against the several taxables." Cooley, Tax'n, 2d Ed., 423.

EXTENDED. A lengthening out of time previously fixed and not the arbitrary setting of a new date. In re Parent, D.C.N.H., 30 F.Supp. 943, 945. Stretched, spread, or drawn out. Rathbone v. State Board of Land Com'rs of Montana, 100 Mont. 109, 47 P.2d 47, 49.

As used in constitutional inhibition against extending provisions of statute by reference to its title only, has reference to an attempt to add something to text of pre-existing law. Hollis & Co. v. McCarroll, 200 Ark. 523, 140 S.W.2d 420, 422.

EXTENDED INSURANCE. An option to use dividend to procure extended insurance is one to procure extension of term of insurance from date to which premiums have been paid, without further payment. Williams v. Union Central Life Ins. Co., Tex., 291 U.S. 170, 54 S.Ct. 348, 78 L.Ed. 711, 92 A.L.R. 693.

EXTENDED LEASE. An "extended lease" is merely enlarged upon all the terms and conditions of the instrument, while a "renewed lease" is a new lease. Rathbone v. State Board of Land Com'rs of Montana, 100 Mont. 109, 47 P.2d 47, 49.

EXTENDI FACIAS. Lat. You cause to be extended. In English practice. The name of a writ of execution, (derived from its two emphatic words;) more commonly called an "extent." 2 Tidd, Pr. 1043; 4 Steph.Comm. 43.

EXTENDING as used in agreement to extend railroad siding at point of termination signified making connection with. Blouch v. Stevens, 106 N.J.L. 488, 150 A. 581, 582.

EXTENSION. A part constituting an addition or enlargement, as an annex, as to build on an extension to a house. Northwestern Light & Power Co. v. Town of Grundy Center, 220 Iowa 108, 261 N.W. 604. Addition of existing facilities. People ex rel. Anderson v. Baltimore & O. S. W. R. Co., 359 Ill. 301, 194 N.E. 568, 569. Enlargement of main body; addition of something smaller than that to which it is attached; to cause to reach or continue as from point to point; to lengthen or prolong. City of Lancaster v. Public Service Commission, 120 Pa.Super. 597, 182 A. 781, 783. That property of a body by which it occupies a portion of space. Newark Stove Co. v. Gray & Dudley Co., D.C.Tenn., 39 F.Supp. 992, 993.

Renewal of paper is not a loan but an extension of time for payment. McRoberts v. Spaulding, D.C.Iowa, 32 F.2d 315, 318.

The word "extension" ordinarily implies the existence of something to be extended. State v. Graves, 352 Mo. 1102, 182 S.W.2d 46, 51.

Bankruptcy

An extension proposal is an agreement on part of creditors that they will extend time within which their claims are probably to be paid, in full as to secured creditors, on terms proposed by debtor and approved by court. Heldstab v. Equitable Life Assur. Soc. of United States, C.C.A. Kan., 91 F.2d 655, 658.

"Extension" under Bankruptcy Act is proceeding wherein debtor merely obtains extension of time within which to pay in full. In re Thompson, D.C.Va., 51 F.Supp. 12, 14.

Proposal under which debts which were not settled in full but were merely extended in time for ultimate payment in full was an "extension proposal". Mullican v. Texas Land & Mortgage Co., C.C.A.Tex., 117 F.2d 576, 578.

Carrier's Lines

Tracks over which there are to be train movements in the sense that such movements are a part of the actual transportation haul from shipper to the consignee. Missouri Pac. R. Co. v. Chicago Great Western R. Co., 137 Kan. 217, 19 P.2d 484, 489.

Lease

An option for renewal implies giving of new lease on same terms as old lease, while an option for extension contemplates a continuance of old lease for a further period. Mutual Paper Co. v. Hoague-Sprague Corporation, 297 Mass. 294, 8 N.E.2d 802, 806.

"Renewal" and "extension," as used in leases with reference to options for renewal or for extension, are synonymous. Economy Stores v. Moran, 178 Miss. 62, 172 So. 865, 867.

The distinction between "extension" and "renewal" of lease is chiefly that, in the case of renewal, a new lease is requisite, while, in the case of extension, the same lease continues in force during additional period upon performance of stipulated act. Carrano v. Shoor, 118 Conn. 86, 171 A. 17, 20.

The word "extension," when used in its proper and usual sense in connection with a lease, means a prolongation of the previous leasehold estate. Talbot v. Rednalloh Co., 283 Mass. 225, 186 N.E. 273, 275.

Mercantile Law

An allowance of additional time for the payment of debts. An agreement between a debtor and his creditors, by which they allow him further time for the payment of his liabilities. A creditor's indulgence by giving a debtor further time to pay an existing debt. State v. Mestayer, 144 La. 601, 80 So. 891, 892. Among the French, a similar agreement is known by the name of attermoiement. Merlin, *Répert.* mot *Attermoiement.*

Patent Law

An extension of the life of a patent for an additional period of seven years, formerly allowed by law in the United States, upon proof being made that the inventor had not succeeded in obtaining a reasonable remuneration from his patent-right. This is no longer allowed, except as to designs. See Rev.St.U.S. § 4924.

EXTENSION OF PAYMENT. To constitute "extension of payment" of obligation which would release sureties, there must be agreement between obligor and obligee supported by consideration by which obligee has precluded himself from taking action against obligor during period of extension. O'Banion v. Willis, 14 La.App. 638, 129 So. 440, 441.

EXTENSION OR RENEWAL OF NOTE. Takes place when parties agree upon valuable consideration for maturity of debt on day subsequent to that provided in original contract. Elk Horn Bank & Trust Co. v. Spraggins, 182 Ark. 27, 30 S.W.2d 858, 859.

EXTENSIVE. Widely extended in space, time, or scope; great or wide or capable of being extended. American Cannel Coal Co. v. Indiana Cotton Mills, 78 Ind.App. 115, 134 N.E. 891, 893.

EXTENSIVE RAINFALL is not same as "extraordinary rainfall," for which damages could not be recovered; word "extensive" being applicable to area embraced in circumference of particular rainfall, but not implying necessarily rainfall out of ordinary. Johnson v. Ratliff, 233 Ky. 187, 25 S.W.2d 355, 356. See Extraordinary Rainfall.

EXTENSORES. In old English law. Extenders or appraisers.

The name of certain officers appointed to appraise and divide or apportion lands. It was their duty to make a survey, schedule, or inventory of the lands, to lay them out under certain heads, and then to ascertain the value of each, as preparatory to the division or partition. Bract. fols. 72*b*, 75; Britt. c. 71.

EXTENT. Amount. Cox v. State Industrial Accident Commission, 121 P.2d 919, 921, 168 Or. 508, 23 P.2d 800, 159 A.L.R. 899.

English Practice

A writ of execution issuing from the exchequer upon a debt due the crown, or upon a debt due a private person, if upon recognizance or statute merchant or staple, by which the sheriff is directed to appraise the debtor's lands, and, instead of selling them, to set them off to the creditor for a term during which the rental will satisfy the judgment. Hackett v. Amsden, 56 Vt. 201; Nason v. Fowler, 70 N.H. 291, 47 A. 263. It is so called because the sheriff is to cause the lands to be appraised at their full extended value before he delivers them to the plaintiff. Fitzh.N.B. 131. The term is sometimes used in the various states of the United States to denote writs which give the creditor possession of the debtor's lands for a limited time till the debt be paid. Roberts v. Whiting, 16 Mass. 186.

Scotch Practice

The value or valuation of lands. Bell.

The rents, profits, and issues of lands. Skene.

For "Manorial Extent," see that title.

EXTENT IN AID. That kind of extent which issues at the instance and for the benefit of a debtor to the crown, for the recovery of a debt due to himself. 2 Tidd, Pr. 1045; 4 Steph.Comm. 47. This writ was much abused, owing to some peculiar privileges possessed by crown-debtors, and its use was regulated by Stat. 57 Geo. III. c. 117. See 3 Bla.Comm. 419. The writ used by a debtor of the king against his debtor to enforce the right of preference given to him because of his indebtedness to the king. United States Fidelity & Guaranty Co. v. Carter, 161 Va. 381, 170 S.E. 764, 768, 90 A.L.R. 191.

EXTENT IN CHIEF. A summary process by which the king's action was commenced against his debtor and his body, personal property (tangible and intangible), and lands at once seized for the satisfaction of the king's debt. United States Fidelity & Guaranty Co. v. Carter, 161 Va. 381, 170 S.E. 764, 768, 90 A.L.R. 191. The principal kind of extent, issuing at the suit of the crown, for the recovery of the crown's debt. 4 Steph.Comm. 47. An adverse proceeding by the king, for the recovery of his own debt. 2 Tidd, Pr. 1045.

EXTENT OF SUCH PAYMENT. Under statute extending right of subrogation to Federal Deposit Insurance Corporation, phrase "to the extent of such payment" is equivalent to term "pro tanto" or words "as to the portion of the deposit paid". Federal Deposit Ins. Corporation v. Citizens State Bank of Niangua, C.C.A.Mo., 130 F.2d 102, 103.

EXTENTA MANERII. (The extent or survey of a manor.) The title of a statute passed 4 Edw. I. St. 1; being a sort of direction for making a *survey* or terrier of a *manor*, and all its appendages. 2 Reeve, Eng.Law, 140.

EXTENUATE. To lessen; to palliate; to mitigate. Connell v. State, 46 Tex.Cr.R. 259, 81 S.W. 748.

EXTENUATING CIRCUMSTANCES. Such as render a delict or crime less aggravated, heinous, or reprehensible than it would otherwise be, or tend to palliate or lessen its guilt. Such circumstances may ordinarily be shown in order to reduce the punishment or damages.

EXTENUATION. That which renders a crime or tort less heinous than it would be without it. It is opposed to aggravation.

EXTERIOR. As used in policy means on the outside, external, pertaining to the outside part, Northwestern Casualty & Surety Co. v. Barzune, Tex.Civ.App., 42 S.W.2d 100, 103; the surface outside, Jackson Steam Laundry v. Ætna Casualty & Surety Co., 156 Miss. 649, 126 So. 478, 480.

The phrase "exterior of the building" as used in a lease of a building adjacent to another building, each having its own wall, the two against each other forming a solid double wall, means coextensive with its external parts and including the four walls. B. Siegel Co. v. Codd, 183 Mich. 145, 149 N.W. 1015, 1017.

EXTERNAL. Apparent, outward, visible from the outside, capable of being perceived. Toliver v. Massachusetts Bonding & Insurance Co., Mo. App., 47 S.W.2d 140, 141. Outward; exterior; relating to the outside, as of the body; really being without; acting from without, as the external surface of a body; and outwardly; perceptible, visible; physical or corporeal; as distinguished from mental or moral. Provident Life & Accident Ins. Co. v. Campbell, 18 Tenn.App. 452, 79 S.W.2d 292, 296.

In double indemnity clause of life policy, the term "external" applies to the force or means and not to the injury. Hanna v. Rio Grande Nat. Life Ins. Co., Tex.Civ. App., 181 S.W.2d 908, 911.

EXTERNAL, VIOLENT AND ACCIDENTAL MEANS. Death through "external, violent and accidental means" necessarily implies that death did not result indirectly from disease or bodily infirmity. Mutual Life Ins. Co. of New York v. Hassing, C.C.A.10, 134 F.2d 714, 716.

EXTERRITORIALITY. The privilege of those persons (such as foreign ministers) who, though temporarily resident within a state, are not subject to the operation of its laws. The exemption from the operation of the ordinary laws of the state accorded to foreign monarchs temporarily within the state and their retinue, to diplomatic agents and the members of their household, to consuls in non-Christian states, and to foreign men of war in port. 1 Opp. 460–469. See Capitulation; Extraterritoriality.

EXTERUS. Lat. A foreigner or alien; one born abroad. The opposite of *civis*.

EXTERUS NON HABET TERRAS. An alien holds no lands. Tray.Lat.Max. 203.

EXTINCT. Extinguished. A rent is said to be extinguished when it is destroyed and put out. Co.Litt. 147*b*. See Extinguishment.

EXTINCTO SUBJECTO, TOLLITUR ADJUNCTUM. When the subject [or substance] is extinguished, the incident [or adjunct] ceases. Thus, when the business for which a partnership has been formed is completed, or brought to an end, the partnership itself ceases. Inst. 3, 26, 6; 3 Kent, Comm. 52, note; Griswold v. Waddington, 16 Johns., N.Y., 438, 492.

EXTINGUISH. To put an end to. Onondaga Water Service Corporation v. Crown Mills, Inc., 132 Misc. 848, 230 N.Y.S. 691, 698. To put out, quench, stifle, as to extinguish a fire or flame. Gally v. Wynne, 96 Cal.App. 145, 273 P. 825, 826.

EXTINGUISHMENT. The destruction or cancellation of a right, power, contract, or estate. The annihilation of a collateral thing or subject in the subject itself out of which it is derived. Prest. Merg. 9. For the distinction between an extinguishment and passing a right, see 2 Shars.Bl. Comm. 325, note.

"Extinguishment" is sometimes confounded with "merger," though there is a clear distinction between them. "Merger" is only a mode of extinguishment, and applies to estates only under particular circumstances; but "extinguishment" is a term of general application to rights, as well as estates. 2 Crabb, Real Prop. p. 367, § 1487. "Extinguishment" connotes the end of a thing, precluding the existence of future life therein; in "mergers" there is a carrying on of the substance of the thing, except that it is merged into and becomes a part of a separate thing with a new identity. McRoberts v. McRoberts, 177 Okl. 156, 57 P.2d 1175, 1177.

EXTINGUISHMENT OF COMMON. Loss of the right to have common. This may happen from various causes. 2 Steph.Com. 41; Co.Litt. 280; 1 Bacon, Abr. 628; Cro.Eliz. 594.

EXTINGUISHMENT OF COPYHOLD. In English law. A copyhold is said to be extinguished when the freehold and copyhold interests unite in the same person and in the same right, which may be either by the copyhold interest coming to the freehold or by the freehold interest coming to the copyhold. 1 Crabb, Real Prop. p. 670, § 864; Hutt. 81; Cro.Eliz. 21; Wms.R.P. 287.

EXTINGUISHMENT OF DEBTS. This takes place by payment; by accord and satisfaction; by novation, or the substitution of a new debtor; by merger, when the creditor recovers a judgment or accepts a security of a higher nature than the original obligation; by a release; by the marriage of a *feme sole* creditor with the debtor, or of an obligee with one of two joint obligors; and where one of the parties, debtor or creditor, makes the other his executor.

EXTINGUISHMENT OF LEGACY. This occurs in case the identical thing bequeathed is not in existence, or has been disposed of so that it does not form part of the testator's estate, at the time of his death. Welch v. Welch, 147 Miss. 728, 113 So. 197, 198. See Ademption.

EXTINGUISHMENT OF LIEN. Discharge by operation of law. Schreiber v. Cook County, 388 Ill. 297, 58 N.E.2d 40, 44, 155 A.L.R. 1162.

EXTINGUISHMENT OF RENT. If a person have a yearly rent of lands, and afterwards purchase those lands, so that he has as good an estate in the land as in the rent, the rent is extinguished. Termes de la Ley; Cowell; Co.Litt. 147. Rent may also be extinguished by conjunction of estates, by confirmation, by grant, by release, and by surrender. 1 Crabb, Real Prop. pp. 210–213, § 209.

EXTINGUISHMENT OF WAYS. This is usually effected by unity of possession. As if a man have a way over the close of another, and he purchase that close, the way is extinguished. 1 Crabb, Real Prop. p. 341, § 384; 2 Washb.Real Prop.

EXTIRPATION. In English law. A species of destruction or waste, analogous to estrepement. See Estrepement.

EXTIRPATIONE. A judicial writ, either before or after judgment, that lay against a person who, when a verdict was found against him for land, etc., maliciously overthrew any house or extirpated any trees upon it. Reg.Jud. 13, 56.

EXTOCARE. In old records. To grub woodland, and reduce it to arable or meadow; "to stock up." Cowell.

EXTORSIVELY. A technical word used in indictments for extortion.

It is a sufficient averment of a corrupt intent, in an indictment for extortion, to allege that the defendant "extorsively" took the unlawful fee. Leeman v. State, 35 Ark. 438, 37 Am.Rep. 44. When a person is charged with extorsively taking, the very import of the word shows that he is not acquiring possession of his own, 4 Cox, Cr.Cas. 387. In North Carolina the crime may be charged without using this word, State v. Dickens, 2 N.C. 406.

EXTORT. To compel or coerce, as a confession or information by any means serving to overcome one's power of resistance, or making the confession or admission involuntary. Sutton v. Commonwealth, 207 Ky. 597, 269 S.W. 754, 757.

To gain by wrongful methods, to obtain in an unlawful manner, to compel payments by means of threats of injury to person, property, or reputation. McKenzie v. State, 113 Neb. 576, 204 N.W. 60, 61; State v. Richards, 97 Wash. 587, 167 P. 47, 48. To take from unlawfully; to exact something wrongfully by threats or putting in fear. State v. Adams, Del., 106 A. 287, 288, 7 Boyce, 335. See Extortion.

To wrest from, to exact, to take under a claim of protection. Commonwealth v. Neubauer, 142 Pa.Super. 528, 16 A.2d 450, 452.

The natural meaning of the word "extort" is to obtain money or other valuable thing either by compulsion, by actual force, or by the force of motives applied to the will, and often more overpowering and irresistible than physical force. Com. v. O'Brien, 12 Cush., Mass., 90.

EXTORTIO EST CRIMEN QUANDO QUIS COLORE OFFICII EXTORQUET QUOD NON EST DEBITUM, VEL SUPRA DEBITUM, VEL ANTE TEMPUS QUOD EST DEBITUM. 10 Coke, 102. Extortion is a crime when, by color of office, any person extorts that which is not due, or more than is due, or before the time when it is due.

EXTORTION. Unlawful obtaining of money from another. People v. Parkinson, 181 Misc. 603, 41 N.Y.S.2d 331, 334.

It has also been defined as corrupt demanding or receiving by a person in office of a fee for services which should be performed gratuitously; or, where compensation is permissible, of a larger fee than the law justifies, or a fee not due, 2 Bish.Crim.Law, § 390; exaction of money by reason of oppressive conditions or circumstances, People v. Weller, 237 N.Y. 316, 143 N.E. 205, 208, 38 A.L.R. 613; obtaining of property from another, with his consent, induced by wrongful use of force or fear, or under color of official right. And see State v. Logan, 104 La. 760, 29 So. 336; In re Rempfer, 51 S.D. 393, 216 N.W. 355, 359, 55 A.L.R. 1346; Lee v. State, 16 Ariz. 291, 145 P. 244, 246, Ann.Cas.1917B, 131. Obtaining of property of another by threats to injure him and to destroy his property, State v. Phillips, 62 Idaho 656, 115 P.2d 418, 420. Taking or obtaining of anything from another by means of illegal compulsion or oppressive exaction, Daniels v. U. S., C.C.A.Cal., 17 F.2d 339, 342; whether by an officer or otherwise, United States v. Dunkley, D.C.Cal., 235 F. 1000, 1001. Unlawful taking by any officer, by color of his office, of any money or thing of value that is not due to him, or more than is due, or before it is due, 4 Bla.Comm. 141; Com. v. Saulsbury, 152 Pa. 554, 25 A. 610; 1 Russ.Cr.* 144; 2 Bish.Cr.L. 390; U. S. v. Deaver, D.C.N.C., 14 F. 595; Bush v. State, 19 Ariz. 195, 168 P. 508, 509. Wrongful exaction of money or other valuable thing, either by compulsion, actual force, or by force of motives applied at will, Commonwealth v. Donoghue, 250 Ky. 343, 63 S.W.2d 3, 89 A.L.R. 819.

A taking under color of office is of essence of offense. La Tour v. Stone, 139 Fla. 681, 190 So. 704, 709, 710.

At common law, any oppression by color or pretense of right, and particularly and technically the exaction or unlawful taking by an officer of money or thing of value, by color of his office, either when none at all is due, or not so much is due, or when it is not yet due. Preston v. Bacon, 4 Conn. 480. See People v. Barondess, 16 N.Y.S. 436, 61 Hun, 571; Murray v. State, 125 Tex.Cr.R. 252, 67 S.W.2d 274, 275; State v. Anderson, 66 N.D. 522, 267 N.W. 121, 123; Whart.Cr.L. 833.

Term applies to persons who exact money either for the performance of a duty, the prevention of injury, or the exercise of influence, and covers the obtaining of money or other property by operating on fear or credulity, or by promise to conceal the crimes of others. Commonwealth v. Mann, 111 Pa.Super. 371, 170 A. 381, 382.

Term in comprehensive or general sense signifies any oppression under color of right, and in strict or technical sense signifies unlawful taking by any officer, under color of office, of any money or thing of value not due him, more than is due, or before it is due. State v. Barts, 132 N.J.L. 74, 38 A.2d 838, 843, 844, 848; State v. Vallee, 136 Me. 432, 12 A.2d 421.

To constitute "extortion," money or other thing of value must have been wilfully and corruptly received. La Tour v. Stone, 139 Fla. 681, 190 So. 709, 710.

To constitute "extortion," the wrongful use of fear must be the operating cause producing consent. People v. Biggs, 178 Cal. 79, 172 P. 152, 153.

The distinction between "bribery" and "extortion" seems to be this: the former offense consists in the offering a present, or receiving one, if offered; the latter, in demanding a fee or present, by color of office. Jacob.

For the distinction between "extortion" and "exaction," see Exaction.

EXTRA. A Latin preposition, occurring in many legal phrases, and meaning beyond, except, without, out of, outside.

Work outside contract, performed by subcontractor was properly claimed as an "extra." United States ex rel. Park L. Davis Co. v. Matthew Cummings Co., D.C.Mass., 27 F.Supp. 405, 407, 408.

EXTRA ALLOWANCE. In New York practice. A sum in addition to costs, which may, in the discretion of the court, be allowed to the successful party in cases of unusual difficulty. See Hascall v. King, 54 App.Div. 441, 66 N.Y.S. 1112.

EXTRA COMMERCIA. Property once dedicated to public use is "extra commercia". J. B. McCrary Co. v. Town of Winnfield, D.C.La., 40 F.Supp. 427, 435.

EXTRA COMPENSATION. Within constitutional provision prohibiting Legislature from granting extra compensation to contractor, is compensation over and above that fixed by contract for agreed work, and is in nature of gratuity. Weston v. State, 262 N.Y. 46, 186 N.E. 197, 200, 88 A.L.R. 1219.

Under statutes providing for extra compensation to customs inspectors payment made by licensees to Collector at rates fixed by Secretary of the Treasury constitute "extra compensation" over and above the annual salary, and not a payment from licensees. United States v. Myers, Ct.Cl., 320 U.S. 561, 64 S.Ct. 337, 341, 88 L.Ed. 312.

EXTRA COSTS. In English practice. Those charges which do not appear upon the face of the proceedings, such as witnesses' expenses, fees to counsel, attendances, court fees, etc., an affidavit of which must be made, to warrant the master in allowing them upon taxation of costs. Wharton.

EXTRA-DOTAL PROPERTY. In Louisiana this term is used to designate that property which forms no part of the dowry of a woman, and which is also called "paraphernal property." Civ. Code La. art. 2335. Fleitas v. Richardson, 147 U.S. 550, 13 S.Ct. 495, 37 L.Ed. 276.

EXTRA FEODUM. Out of his fee; out of the seigniory, or not holden of him that claims it. Co.Litt. 1*b*; Reg.Orig. 97*b*.

EXTRA JUDICIUM. Extrajudicial; out of the proper cause; out of court; beyond the jurisdiction. See Extrajudicial.

EXTRA JUS. Beyond the law; more than the law requires. *In jure, vel extra jus.* Bract. fol. 169*b*.

EXTRA LEGEM. Out of the law; out of the protection of the law.

EXTRA LEGEM POSITUS EST CIVILITER MORTUUS. Co. Litt. 130. He who is placed out of the law is civilly dead. A bankrupt is, as it were, civilly dead. International Bank v. Sherman, 101 U.S. 406, 25 L.Ed. 866.

EXTRA PRÆSENTIAM MARITI. Out of her husband's presence.

EXTRA QUATUOR MARIA. Beyond the four seas; out of the kingdom of England. 1 Bl. Comm. 457.

EXTRA REGNUM. Out of the realm. 7 Coke, 16*a*; 2 Kent, Comm. 42, note.

EXTRA SERVICES, when used with reference to officers, means services incident to the office in question, but for which compensation has not been provided by law. Miami County v. Blake, 21 Ind. 32.

EXTRA TERRITORIUM. Beyond or without the territory. 6 Bin. 353; 2 Kent, Comm. 407. Outside the territorial limits of a state. Milne v. Moreton, 6 Binn., Pa., 353, 6 Am.Dec. 466.

EXTRA TERRITORIUM JUS DICENTI IMPUNE NON PARETUR. One who exercises jurisdiction out of his territory is not obeyed with impunity. Dig. 2, 1, 20; Branch, Princ.; 10 Coke, 77; Story, Confl.Laws, § 539. He who exercises judicial authority beyond his proper limits cannot be obeyed with safety.

EXTRA VIAM. Outside the way. Where the defendant in trespass pleaded a right of way in justification, and the replication alleged that the trespass was committed outside the limits of the way claimed, these were the technical words to be used. 16 East, 343, 349.

EXTRA VIRES. Beyond powers. See Ultra Vires.

EXTRA WORK. As used in connection with construction contract, means work done not required in performance of the contract, something done or furnished in addition to or in excess of the requirement of the contract. Kansas City Bridge Co. v. State, 61 S.D. 580, 250 N.W. 343; work entirely outside and independent of contract—something not required or contemplated in its performance. Bradshaw v. Wolfe City, Tex.Civ.App., 3 S.W.2d 527, 530; while additional work on the other hand, is usually work which results from a change or alteration in plans concerning work which has to be done under a contract. De Martini v. Elade Realty Corp., Co.Ct., 52 N.Y.S.2d 487, 489; or such work as may fairly be presumed to arise in the construction, and is within the contract, although not included in the plans and specifications. Wilson v. Salt Lake City, 52 Utah, 506, 174 P. 847, 850.

But in a sewer construction contract providing that the city engineer might make such changes in the lines, grades, and dimensions which do not entail any extra expense to the contractor, the word "extra" was deemed equivalent to additional work which was required in the performance of the contract, and not necessary to such performance in the sense that the contract could not have been carried out without it, but necessary in the sense that by means of it the contract could be more conveniently and beneficially performed in the interest of both parties thereto, and did not include work arising out of and entirely independent of the contract, something not required in its performance. City of Richmond v. Burton, 115 Va. 206, 78 S.E. 560, 563. See, also, Fetterolf v. S. & L. Const. Co., 161 N.Y.S. 549, 550, 175 App.Div. 177; McHugh v. City of Tacoma, 76 Wash. 127, 135 P. 1011, 1015.

Materials and labor not contemplated by the contract, but which are required by changes in the plans and specifications made after the contract had been entered into, are "extra work". Collins v. Hall, Tex.Civ.App., 161 S.W.2d 311, 314.

EXTRACT, *v.* To draw out or forth; to pull out from a fixed position. Webster.

To "extract" ore within the meaning of a royalty provision in a mining lease contemplates not only the removal of the ore from the mine and throwing it on a dump, but also the separation of the ore from the dirt and refuse in which it was found on the dump. Giersa v. Creech, Mo.App., 181 S.W. 588, 589.

EXTRACT, *n.* A portion or fragment of a writing. In Scotch law, the certified copy, by a clerk of a court, of the proceedings in an action carried on before the court, and of the judgment pronounced; containing also an order for execution or proceedings thereupon. Jacob; Whishaw.

EXTRACTA CURIÆ. In old English law. The issues or profits of holding a court, arising from the customary fees, etc.

EXTRADITION. The surrender by one state to another of an individual accused or convicted of an offense outside its own territory and within the territorial jurisdiction of the other, which, being competent to try and punish him, demands the surrender. Waller v. Jordan, 58 Ariz. 169, 118 P. 2d 450, 451.

The surrender of a criminal by a foreign state to which he has fled for refuge from prosecution to the state within whose jurisdiction the crime was committed, upon the demand of the latter state, in order that he may be dealt with according to its laws. Extradition may be accorded as a mere matter of comity, or may take place under treaty stipulations between the two nations. It also obtains as between the different states of the American Union. Terlinden v. Ames, 184 U.S. 270, 22 S.Ct. 484, 46 L.Ed. 534; Fong Yue Ting v. U. S., 149 U.S. 698, 13 S.Ct. 1016, 37 L.Ed. 905.

Extradition between the states must be considered and defined to be a political duty of imperfect obligation, founded upon compact, and requiring each state to surrender one who, having violated the criminal laws of another state, has fled from its justice, and is found in the state from which he is demanded, on demand of the executive authority of the state from which he fled. Abbott.

—Extradition warrant. See Executive Warrant.

EXTRAHAZARDOUS. In the law of insurance. Characterized or attended by circumstances or conditions of special and unusual danger. Reynolds v. Insurance Co., 47 N.Y. 597; Russell v. Insurance Co., 71 Iowa 69, 32 N.W. 95.

EXTRAHURA. In old English law. An animal wandering or straying about, without an owner; an estray. Spelman.

EXTRAJUDICIAL. That which is done, given, or effected outside the course of regular judicial proceedings; not founded upon, or unconnected with, the action of a court of law; as extrajudicial evidence, an extrajudicial oath.

That which, though done in the course of regular judicial proceedings, is unnecessary to such proceedings, or interpolated, or beyond their scope; as an extrajudicial opinion, (*dictum.*)

That which does not belong to the judge or his jurisdiction, notwithstanding which he takes cognizance of it.

EXTRAJUDICIAL CONFESSION. See Confession.

EXTRAJUDICIAL EVIDENCE is that which is used to satisfy private persons as to facts requiring proof.

EXTRAJUDICIAL OATH. One taken not in the course of judicial proceedings, or taken without any authority of law, though taken formally before a proper person. State v. Scatena, 84 Minn. 281, 87 N.W. 764.

EXTRAJUDICIALLY. The testimony of an expert witness based upon information obtained "extrajudicially", which means in any other manner than from evidence given in court, is objectionable. State v. David, 222 N.C. 242, 22 S.E.2d 633, 640.

EXTRALATERAL RIGHT. In mining law. The right of the owner of a mining claim duly located on the public domain to follow, and mine, any vein or lode the apex of which lies within the boundaries of his location on the surface, notwithstanding the course of the vein on its dip or downward direction may so far depart from the perpendicular as to extend beyond the planes which would be formed by the vertical extension downwards of the side lines of his location. See Rev.Stat. U.S. § 2322, 30 U.S.C.A. § 26.

EXTRAMURAL. As applied to the powers of a municipal corporation, its "extramural" powers are those exercised outside the corporate limits, as distinguished from "intramural" powers. State v. Port of Astoria, 79 Or. 1, 154 P. 399, 404.

EXTRANEOUS EVIDENCE. With reference to a contract, deed, will, or any writing, extraneous evidence is such as is not furnished by the document itself, but is derived from outside sources; the same as evidence *aliunde*. See, also, Aliunde.

EXTRANEOUS OFFENSE. Is one that is extra, beyond, or foreign to the offense for which the party is on trial. Ridinger v. State, 146 Tex. Cr.R. 286, 174 S.W.2d 319, 320.

EXTRANEUS.

Old English law. One foreign born; a foreigner. 7 Coke, 16.

Roman law. An heir not born in the family of the testator. Those of a foreign state. The same as *alienus*. Vicat; Du Cange.

EXTRANEUS EST SUBDITUS QUI EXTRA TERRAM, i. e., POTESTATEM REGIS NATUS EST. 7 Coke, 16. A foreigner is a subject who is born out of the territory, *i. e.*, government of the king.

EXTRAORDINARY. Out of the ordinary; exceeding the usual, average, or normal measure or degree; beyond or out of the common order or rule; not usual, regular, or of a customary kind; remarkable; uncommon; rare. Puget Sound Traction, Light & Power Co. v. Reynolds, D.C. Wash., 223 F. 371, 378; Courtney v. Ocean Accident & Guaranty Corporation, 346 Mo. 703, 142 S. W.2d 858, 861, 130 A.L.R. 234. The word is both comprehensive and flexible in meaning. Zollman v. Baltimore & O. S. W. R. Co., 121 N.E. 135, 140, 70 Ind.App. 395.

Beyond or out of the common order or method; exceeding the ordinary degree; not ordinary; unusual; employed for an exceptional purpose or on a special occasion; as a noun it is defined as, something extraordinary; especially, an extraordinary expense or allowance; specifically (Eng.) any allowance made to troops beyond the customary gross paid. State v. Rogers, 142 Kan. 841, 52 P.2d 1185, 1195.

EXTRAORDINARY AVERAGE. A contribution by all the parties concerned in a mercantile voyage, either as to the vessel or cargo, toward a loss sustained by some of the parties in interest for the benefit of all. Wilson v. Cross, 33 Cal. 69.

EXTRAORDINARY CARE. Synonymous with greatest care, utmost care, highest degree of care. Railroad Co. v. Baddeley, 54 Ill. 24, 5 Am.Rep. 71; Railway Co. v. Causler, 97 Ala. 235, 12 So. 439; Sorey v. Yazoo & M. V. R. Co., 17 La.App. 538, 136 So. 155, 158. See Care; Diligence; Negligence.

EXTRAORDINARY CASE. "The extraordinary motions or cases contemplated by the statute are such as do not ordinarily occur in the transaction of human affairs; as, when a man has been convicted of murder, and it afterwards appears that the supposed deceased is still alive, or where one is convicted on the testimony of a witness who is subsequently found guilty of perjury in giving that testimony, or where there has been some providential cause, and cases of like character." Herrington v. State, 32 Ga.App. 83, 123 S.E. 147, 148; Farmers' Union Warehouse of Metter v. Boyd, 31 Ga.App. 104, 119 S.E. 542.

The presence of an unexplored point of law determinative of litigation makes litigation an "extraordinary case" within statute authorizing additional allowance. National Bank of Far Rockaway v. City of New York, Sup., 46 N.Y.S.2d 153, 154.

EXTRAORDINARY DANGER. In the law of master and servant, one not ordinarily incident to the service. Piorkowski v. A. Leschen & Sons Rope Co., 190 Mo.App. 597, 176 S.W. 258, 260.

EXTRAORDINARY DIVIDENDS. Cash disbursements by "wasting asset" companies are apportioned as "extraordinary dividends" where they represent, in part at least, distribution of proceeds of capital assets. In re Nirdlinger's Estate, 327 Pa. 160, 193 A. 33.

"Extraordinary dividends" may assume unusual form and amount, paid at irregular intervals from accumulated surplus or earnings. In re Nirdlinger's Estate, 327 Pa. 160, 193 A. 33.

EXTRAORDINARY EXPENSES. This term in a constitutional provision that the state may incur indebtedness for extraordinary expenses, means other than ordinary expenses and such as are incurred by the state for the promotion of the general welfare, compelled by some unforeseen condition which is not regularly provided for by law, such as flood, famine, fire, earthquake, pestilence, war, or any other condition that will compel the state to put forward its highest endeavors to protect the people, their property, liberty, or lives. State v. Davis, 113 Kan. 4, 213 P. 171, 172.

EXTRAORDINARY FLOOD. One of those unexplained visitations whose comings are not foreshadowed by the usual course of nature, Jensen v. Buffalo Drainage Dist. of Cloud County, 148 Kan. 712, 84 P.2d 961, 965; and whose magnitude and destructiveness could not have been anticipated or provided against by the exercise of ordinary foresight. Eikland v. Casey, C.C.A.Alaska, 266 F. 821, 823, 12 A.L.R. 179; Clements v. Phœnix Utility Co., 119 Kan. 190, 237 P. 1062, 1065.

One of such unusual occurrence that it could not have been foreseen by men of ordinary experience and prudence.

Soules v. Northern Pac. R. Co., 34 N.D. 7, 157 N.W. 823, 830, L.R.A.1917A, 501. A flood is not extraordinary which is such as residents of the neighborhood might expect from their observation. City of Richmond v. Cheatwood, 130 Va. 76, 107 S.E. 830, 833.

EXTRAORDINARY GRAND JURY is limited in scope of its investigation which may not go beyond terms of executive proclamation, and examination of witness must be confined within those terms, and must not be used as means of disclosing or intermeddling with extraneous matters. People v. Doe, 247 App.Div. 324, 286 N.Y.S. 343.

EXTRAORDINARY HAZARD. If hazards are increased by what other servants do, and injured servant has no part in increasing them, they are "extraordinary". Stone v. Howe, 92 N.H. 425, 32 A.2d 484, 487.

EXTRAORDINARY MOTIONS FOR NEW TRIAL are such as do not ordinarily occur. King v. State, 174 Ga. 432, 163 S.E. 168, 171.

EXTRAORDINARY OBSOLESCENCE. An extensive supersession of property used for transmission or generation of power or instrumentalities used for the transportation of passengers. State ex rel. City of St. Louis v. Public Service Commission, 341 Mo. 920, 110 S.W.2d 749, 775.

EXTRAORDINARY RAINFALL. Not such a downpour of rain as may not have been known to occur, but only such rainfall that is so unusual and extraordinary that men of ordinary prudence would not have anticipated and provided for. City of Portsmouth v. Weiss, 145 Va. 94, 133 S.E. 781, 787. Cf. Extensive Rainfall.

EXTRAORDINARY REMEDIES. The writs of *mandamus, quo warranto, habeas corpus,* and some others are sometimes called "extraordinary remedies," in contradistinction to the ordinary remedy by action. Receivership is also said to be an "extraordinary remedy." Prudential Securities Co. v. Three Forks, H. & M. V. R. Co., 49 Mont. 567, 144 P. 158, 159.

EXTRAORDINARY REPAIRS. Within the meaning of a lease, such as are made necessary by some unusual or unforeseen occurrence which does not destroy the building but merely renders it less suited to the use for which it was intended. Nixon v. Gammon, 191 Ky. 175, 229 S.W. 75, 77; Courtney v. Ocean Accident & Guaranty Corporation, 346 Mo. 703, 142 S.W.2d 858, 861, 130 A.L.R. 234.

EXTRAORDINARY RISK. The expression is generally used to describe risks arising from the negligence of the master. Tenney v. Baird Machine Co., 87 Conn. 119, 87 A. 352, 354; Royal Collieries Co. v. Wells, 210 Ky. 600, 276 S.W. 515, 518. An "extraordinary risk" is one lying outside of the sphere of the normal, arising out of conditions not usual in the master's business. Brazeale v. Piedmont Mfg. Co., 184 S.C. 471, 193 S.E. 39, 43. It is one which is not normally and necessarily incident to the employment. Pollard v. Weeks, 60 Ga.App. 664, 4 S.E.2d 722, 727. It is one which is not naturally incident to occupation and grows out of future of employer to furnish safe place to work and proper and safe appliances and tools for work. Snow v. Texas & P. Ry. Co., La.App., 166 So. 200, 203. It is one which may be obviated by the exercise of reasonable care by the employer. Wheeler v. Chicago & W. I. R. Co., 267 Ill. 306, 108 N.E. 330, 336; Louisiana Ry. & Nav. Co. of Texas v. Disheroon, Tex.Civ.App., 295 S.W. 250, 252. It is a risk which is only indirectly connected with the employment. Emerick v. Slavonian Roman Greek Catholic Union, 93 N.J.L. 282, 108 A. 223.

As respects assumption of risks, an "extraordinary risk" is not one which is uncommon or unusual in the sense that it is rare, but is one which arises out of unusual conditions not resulting in the ordinary course of business, as by reason of the master's negligence, Leyba v. Albuquerque & Cerrillos Coal Co., 22 N.M. 455, 164 P. 823, 825; Houston Lighting & Power Co., 1905 v. Conley, Tex.Civ.App., 171 S.W. 561, 563; it is a risk arising from the master's negligence, Simowitz v. Register, 60 Ga.App. 180, 3 S.E.2d 231, 233; it is a risk which may be obviated by exercise of reasonable care on master's part. Tyner v. Atlantic Coast Line R. Co., 149 S.C. 89, 146 S.E. 663, 670. A servant does not assume "extraordinary risks" unless they are known to and appreciated by him, or are so obvious that ordinarily prudent person under circumstances would have observed and appreciated them, Brazeale v. Piedmont Mfg. Co., 184 S.C. 471, 193 S.E. 39, 43; unless they are known or obvious. Pollard v. Weeks, 60 Ga.App. 664, 4 S.E.2d 722, 727. If injury results from master's breach of duty of due care the risk is "extraordinary" and is assumed only if servant knew or ought to have known of dangerous condition and comprehended it or must be taken to have known of and comprehended it. Stone v. Howe, 92 N.H. 425, 32 A.2d 484, 486.

Under Federal Employers' Liability Act, "extraordinary risks" are risks not normally and necessarily incident to employment, Southern Ry. Co. v. Blanton, 63 Ga.App. 93, 10 S.E.2d 430, 434; an employee is not treated as assuming extraordinary risks arising from defects due to negligence of employer unless he has knowledge of them or danger is so obvious that it would be appreciated by ordinarily prudent person, Snow v. Texas & P. Ry. Co., La.App., 166 So. 200, 203.

EXTRAORDINARY SERVICES. As applied to the care and attention of an old and infirm person, such services as are unusual, extra, or above those generally required or to be anticipated in usual course of things, not such services as are rendered to an old and feeble person, even though sick, which are not different from those usually required by such persons in similar circumstances. Allen v. Smith, 208 Ky. 207, 270 S.W. 782, 783.

As used in statute authorizing allowance of additional compensation to guardian, means services in addition to guardian's usual or regular services. In re Gislason's Estate, 73 N.D. 731, 19 N.W.2d 447, 451, 452.

EXTRAORDINARY STORM is not necessarily an unprecedented one, but one that happens so rarely that it is unusual and not ordinarily to be expected. Spitzer v. City of Waterbury, 113 Conn. 84, 154 A. 157, 160; Oklahoma City v. Evans, 173 Okl. 586, 50 P.2d 234, 238.

EXTRAPAROCHIAL. Out of a parish; not within the bounds or limits of any parish. 1 Bl. Comm. 113, 284.

EXTRATERRITORIALITY. The extraterritorial operation of laws; that is, their operation upon persons, rights, or jural relations, existing beyond the limits of the enacting state, but still amendable to its laws. A term used, especially formerly, to express, in lieu of the word *exterritoriality* (*q. v.*), the exemption from the obligation of the laws of a state granted to foreign diplomatic agents, warships, etc. Wheaton, § 224. The term is used to indicate jurisdiction exercised by a nation in other countries, by treaty, as, by the United States in China or Egypt; or by its own ministers or consuls in foreign lands. Crime is said to be extraterritorial when committed in a country other than that of the forum in which the party is tried. See 2 Moore, Int.L.Dig.; U. S. v. Lucas, D.C.Wash., 6 F.2d 327, 328.

EXTRAVAGANTES. In canon law. Those decretal epistles which were published after the Clementines.

They were so called because at first they were not digested or arranged with the other papal constitutions, but seemed to be, as it were, detached from the canon law. They continued to be called by the same name when they were afterwards inserted in the body of the canon law. The first extravagantes are those of Pope John XXII., successor of Clement V. The last collection was brought down to the year 1483, and was called the "Common Extravagantes," notwithstanding that they were likewise incorporated with the rest of the canon law. Enc.Lond.

EXTREME. At the utmost point, edge, or border; most remote. Last; conclusive. Greatest, highest, strongest, or the like. Immoderate; violent. Webster.

EXTREME AND REPEATED CRUELTY. Acts of physical violence producing bodily harm. Holmstedt v. Holmstedt, 383 Ill. 290, 49 N.E.2d 25, 29; physical acts of violence, bodily harm or suffering, or such acts as endanger life or limb, or raise a reasonable apprehension of great bodily harm, but does not include bad temper, petulance, rude language, want of civil attentions, or angry and abusive words. Moore v. Moore, 362 Ill. 177, 199 N.E. 98, 99.

EXTREME CARE. Such care as prudent man would exercise in place of danger. Schlossstein v. Bernstein, 293 Pa. 245, 142 A. 324, 327.

EXTREME CASE. An extreme case, in which an injunction granted inadvertently or improvidently may be dissolved ex parte, means one in which the injunction was manifestly granted improperly, and its continuation until hearing in due course might cause great injury. Teacle v. Hughes, 146 La. 195, 83 So. 457, 458.

EXTREME CRUELTY is condition of extreme discomfort and wretchedness incapacitating spouse to discharge duties or seriously endangering health. McKee v. McKee, 107 N.J.Eq. 1, 151 A. 620, 622. It is grave and serious misconduct which defeats marriage relation. Kennedy v. Kennedy, 101 Fla. 239, 134 So. 201, 203.

Any habitual indulgence by one spouse, that causes mental torture, undermines the health, or tends to dethrone reason of other, is sufficient to constitute "extreme cruelty". Bergman v. Bergman, 145 Fla. 10, 199 So. 920, 922.

As respects constructive abandonment, "extreme cruelty" per se by husband is conduct which law presumes to be malicious, intended to force separation, and dangerous to life or health of wife, or incapacitates her from performing her duties. Fallon v. Fallon, 111 N.J.Eq. 512, 162 A. 406, 409.

Extreme cruelty is conduct or treatment which: causes reasonable apprehension of bodily hurt, Chisholm v. Chisholm, 98 Fla. 1196, 125 So. 694, 702; constitutes aggravated or inhuman ill treatment, having regard to the physical and temperamental constitution of the parties and all the surrounding circumstances, Donald v. Donald, 21 Fla. 573; Blain v. Blain, 45 Vt. 544; Poor v. Poor, 8 N.H. 315, 29 Am.Dec. 664; damages health, Chisholm v. Chisholm, 98 Fla. 1196, 125 So. 694, 703; destroys concord, harmony, happiness, or affection, Hassell v. Hassell, 185 Okl. 154, 90 P.2d 885; destroys happiness and health and defeats the very purposes of matrimony, Hassell v. Hassell, 185 Okl. 154, 90 P.2d 885; destroys legitimate ends and objects of matrimony, Dier v. Dier, 141 Neb. 685, 4 N.W.2d 731, 734; McCarty v. McCarty, 193 Okl. 18, 141 P.2d 103, 104; destroys peace of mind, Dier v. Dier, 141 Neb. 685, 4 N.W.2d 731, 734; destroys peace of mind as to seriously impair health or endanger life, Smith v. Smith, 61 Ariz. 373, 149 P.2d 683, 684; McCarty v. McCarty, 193 Okl. 18, 141 P.2d 103, 104; Hornor v. Hornor, 151 Okl. 292, 3 P.2d 670, 671; endangers health and prevents proper discharge of matrimonial duties, Brinkerhoff v. Brinkerhoff, 106 N.J.Eq. 331, 150 A. 679, 680; endangers health or safety, MacArthur v. MacArthur, 135 N.J.Eq. 215, 37 A.2d 76; whether actually inflicted or reasonably apprehended, Rosengren v. Rosengren, 115 N.J.Eq. 283, 170 A. 660, 661; Bamberg v. Bamberg, 123 N.J.Eq. 570, 199 A. 54, 55; endangers life or health, Fallon v. Fallon, 111 N.J.Eq. 512, 162 A. 406, 408; Chisholm v. Chisholm, 98 Fla. 1196, 125 So. 694, 702; impairs bodily health, Dier v. Dier, 141 Neb. 685, 4 N.W.2d 731, 734; incapacitates one from performing marital duties, Fallon v. Fallon, 111 N.J.Eq. 512, 162 A. 406, 408; inflicts grievous bodily injury or grievous mental suffering. Civ. Code Cal. § 94, McFall v. McFall, 58 Cal.App.2d 208, 136 P.2d 580, 583; produces bodily hurt to physical system or reasonable apprehension thereof, Morris v. Morris, 132 Okl. 291, 133 Okl. 176, 270 P. 833, 835; produces continuous, intense mental pain and suffering, danger to health, or a forced abnegation of the marital relation, Currie v. Currie, 120 Fla. 28, 162 So. 152; wounds, feelings, Nelson v. Nelson, 89 Okl. 318, 117 P.2d 110, 111; Smith v. Smith, 61 Ariz. 373, 149 P.2d 683, 684; renders cohabitation intolerable, Stocker v. Stocker, 173 Okl. 64, 47 P.2d 107, 108; renders cohabitation intolerable and unsafe, Chisholm v. Chisholm, 98 Fla. 1196, 125 So. 694, 703.

Physical violence is extreme cruelty. Baker v. Baker, 94 Fla. 1001, 114 So. 661, 663. But "extreme cruelty" is not confined to physical violence. Henderson v. Henderson, 137 Fla. 770, 189 So. 24, 25; Bastien v. Bastien, 57 R.I. 176, 189 A. 37, 38.

To constitute "extreme cruelty" within divorce statute, the acts must be directed toward the other party and must be committed with a malevolent motive. Nason v. Nason, 48 Cal.App.2d 500, 120 P.2d 37, 39, 40.

Voluntary or intentional extreme cruelty is the "extreme cruelty," which is ground for divorce, Heim v. Heim, 35 Ohio App. 408, 172 N.E. 451.

EXTREME HAZARD. To constitute extreme hazard, the situation of a vessel must be such that there is imminent danger of her being lost, notwithstanding all the means that can be applied to get her off. King v. Hartford Ins. Co., 1 Conn. 421.

EXTREME LOW TIDE are tides which are lower than lower low. State v. Edwards, 188 Wash. 467, 62 P.2d 1094, 1095.

EXTREMIS. When a person is sick, beyond the hope of recovery, and near death, he is said to be *in extremis*.

EXTREMIS PROBATIS, PRÆSUMUNTUR MEDIA. Extremes being proved, intermediate things are presumed. Tray, Lat. Max. 207.

EXTREMITY. The furthest point. Roberts v. Hart, Tex.Civ.App., 165 S.W. 473, 476.

EXTRINSIC. Foreign; from outside sources; *dehors*. As to "Extrinsic Fraud", see "Fraud."

Grounds for quashing of indictment may be matters "intrinsic" to the pleading, as defects apparent upon its face, United States v. Frankfeld, D.C.D.C., 38 F.Supp. 1018, 1019.

EXTRINSIC AMBIGUITY. In a written contract is an uncertainty which does not arise by the terms of the instrument itself, but is created by some collateral matter not appearing in the instrument. Pacific Indemnity Co. v. California Electric Works, 29 Cal.App.2d 260, 84 P.2d 313, 320.

EXTRINSIC EVIDENCE is external evidence, or that which is not contained in the body of an agreement, contract, and the like. Extrinsic evidence is also said to be evidence not legitimately before the tribunal in which the determination is made. Baldwin v. City of Buffalo, 35 N.Y. 375, 382.

EXTUMÆ. In old records. Relics. Cowell.

EXUERE PATRIAM. To throw off or renounce one's country or native allegiance; to expatriate one's self. Phillim. Dom. 18.

EXULARE. In old English law. To exile or banish. *Nullus liber homo, exuletur, nisi,* etc., no freeman shall be exiled, unless, etc. Magna Charta, c. 29; 2 Inst. 47.

EXUPERARE. To overcome; to apprehend or take. Leg. Edm. c. 2.

EY. A watery place; water. Co.Litt. 6.

EYDE. Aid; assistance; relief. A subsidy.

EYEWITNESS. A person who could testify as to what he had seen. Wigginton v. Order of United Commercial Travelers of America, C.C.A.Ind., 126 F.2d 659, 662, 665, 666, 667. One who saw the act, fact, or transaction to which he testifies. Distinguished from an ear-witness, (*auritus.*) Bankers' Health & Accident Ass'n v. Wilkes, Tex.Civ.App., 209 S.W. 230, 233; Pannell v. Sovereign Camp, W. O.W., 171 Tenn. 245, 102 S.W.2d 50, 52. Persons able to testify from their observation. Hayes v. Stunkard, 233 Iowa 582, 10 N.W.2d 19.

"Eye-witness" does not necessarily mean one who obtains knowledge of an act through the sense of sight alone, and may include one who is able to identify a person by his voice and who could not recognize the person on account of absence of sight. Anderson v. Commonwealth, 291 Ky. 727, 166 S.W.2d 30, 36.

EYEWITNESS RULE is that, in absence of eyewitness, or of any obtainable direct evidence as to what deceased did or failed to do by way of precaution, at and immediately before injury, presumption is that he, prompted by natural instinct, was in exercise of care for his own safety, obtains. Edwards v. Perley, 223 Iowa 1119, 274 N.W. 910, 915.

EYGNE. The same as "eigne" (*q. v.*).

EYOTT. A small island arising in a river. Fleta, 1. 3, c. 2, § b; Bract. 1. 2, c. 2.

EYRE. A journey; a court of itinerant justices.

Justices in eyre were judges commissioned in Anglo-Norman times in England to travel systematically through the kingdom, once in seven years, holding courts in specified places for the trial of certain descriptions of causes.

EYRER. L. Fr. To travel or journey; to go about or itinerate. Britt. c. 2. See Eyre.

EZARDAR. In Hindu law. A farmer or renter of land in the districts of Hindoostan.

F

F. The sixth letter of the alphabet.

Under the old English criminal law, this letter was branded upon felons upon their being admitted to clergy; as also upon those convicted of fights or frays, or falsity. Jacob; Cowell; 2 Reeve, Eng.Law, 392; 4 Reeve, Eng.Law, 485.

F. A. A. Federal Aviation Agency.

F. A. A. In marine insurance. "Free of all average," denoting that the insurance is against total loss only. Wharton.

F. A. S. Free alongside ship. Larkin v. Geisenheimer, 201 App.Div. 741, 195 N.Y.S. 577, 578; Iwai & Co. v. Hercules Powder Co., 162 Ga. 795, 134 S.E. 763. The term implies delivery at dock for ship named. Christenson v. Gorton-Pew Fisheries Co., C.C.A.N.Y., 8 F.2d 689, 691.

A lumber contract providing that prices were f. o. b, f. a. s. is too indefinite for enforcement; the expression "f. o. b." designating that the seller should bear the expense of loading onto the vessel, while the expression "f. a. s." denotes that the lumber should merely be placed within reach of the vessel's tackle. McGowin Lumber & Export Co. v. R. J. & B. F. Lumber Co., 192 Ala. 35, 68 So. 263, 264.

The delivery of goods under contract "F. A. S." which means free aside ship, is complete and relieves consignor of liability after the goods have been delivered in good order to dock where ship is to sail. Tex-O-Kan Flour Mills Co. v. Nord, La.App., 18 So.2d 50, 54.

F. C. A. Farm Credit Administration.

F. C. C. Federal Communications Commission.

F. C. L. means Femme Couleur Libre. Sunseri v. Cassagne, 191 La. 209, 185 So. 1, 4.

F. D. A. Food and Drug Administration.

F. D. I. C. Federal Deposit Insurance Corporation.

F. G. A. In marine insurance. "Free from general average"; also, sometimes, "foreign general average." The precise meaning of this abbreviation must be gathered from the context. Wharton.

F. H. A. Federal Housing Administration; Farmers Home Administration.

F. H. L. B. B. Federal Home Loan Bank Board.

F. M. C. S. Federal Mediation and Conciliation Service.

F. N. M. A. Federal National Mortgage Association.

F. O. B. Term "f. o. b." is an abbreviation for "free on board," and means that seller or consignor of goods will deliver them on car, vessel, or other conveyance by which they are to be transported without expense to buyer or consignee. Hatcher v. Ferguson, 33 Idaho, 639, 198 P. 680, 681, 16 A.L.R. 590; Swerdfeger v. United Acceptance Corporation, 9 Cal.App.2d 590, 50 P.2d 818, 820; Olsen v. McMaken & Pentzien, 139 Neb. 506, 297 N.W. 830, 832; Fernholtz Machinery Co. v. Wilson, 118 Cal.App. 573, 5 P.2d 679, 682.

Contract provision for shipment of goods by seller "f. o. b." place of manufacture means that they are to be delivered to carrier by seller without expense to buyer. State ex rel. Day Pulverizer Co. v. Fitts, 166 Tenn. 156, 60 S.W.2d 167; Humphries v. Frick Co., 56 Ga.App. 124, 192 S.E. 247, 248.

The term "F. O. B." as used in contract for purchase of scrap iron from railroad for overseas shipment, might reasonably be construed as meaning merely that purchase price of scrap iron was fixed on basis that railroad would transport it free of charge and not as indicating the point of passage of title. Expression "F. O. B." signifies generally an intention to pass title. Southern Pac. Co. v. Hyman-Michaels Co., 63 Cal.App.2d 757, 147 P.2d 692, 696.

"F. o. b. factory" means "f. o. b. railroad cars at factory," obligating seller to deliver to carrier without cost to buyer, who takes risk thereafter. Richter v. Zoccoli, 8 N.J.Misc. 289, 150 A. 1, 2.

Generally, place "f. o. b." where goods are sold is regarded as place of delivery, but effect of term "f. o. b." depends on connection in which used. Craig Brokerage Co. v. Joseph A. Goddard Co., 92 Ind.App. 234, 175 N.E. 19, 22.

The initials "f. o. b." are generally construed as an intention that the price is to be paid when the property is delivered to carrier. Rudy-Patrick Seed Co. v. Roseman, 247 Iowa 597, 13 N.W.2d 347, 349, 350.

Under contract to sell sage leaves providing for shipment "f. o. b." Greek port, buyer and not seller had the duty of supplying ship at Greek port. Carvel v. John Kellys (London), Limited, Sup., 53 N.Y.S.2d 640, 641.

When used in connection with the price of goods, the term is commonly construed as fixing only the price, and not as relating to the time, place, or mode of delivery. Lee v. Northway Motor Sales Co., R.I., 121 A. 425; Pond Creek Mill & Elevator Co. v. Clark, C.C.A.Ill., 270 F. 482, 486; Bott v. N. Snellenburg & Co., 177 Va. 331, 14 S.E.2d 372, 374.

F. P. A. In marine insurance. "Free from particular average." Wharton. See Average.

F. R. S. Federal Reserve System.

F. T. C. Federal Trade Commission.

FABRIC. With reference to the reinforcement of concrete, a union of drawn wires made up in rows. Soule v. Northern Construction Co., 33 Cal.App. 300, 165 P. 21, 22.

A woven, felted, or knitted material for wear or ornament, as cloth, felt, hosiery, or lace; also the material used in its making; something that has been fabricated, constructed, or put together; any complex construction; a system built up of correlated parts; structure or edifice. Guaranty Trust Co. of New York v. Johns-Manville Corporation, D.C.N.Y., 14 F.Supp. 792, 797.

Something that has been fabricated, constructed, or put together; the structure of anything or anything manufactured, and in a broad sense includes a flexible sheet metal. Johns-Manville Corporation v. National Tank Seal Co., C.C.A.Okl., 49 F.2d 142, 145.

FABRIC LANDS. In English law. Lands given towards the maintenance, rebuilding, or repairing of cathedral and other churches. Cowell; Blount. Called by the Saxons *timber-lands*. Spelman.

It was the custom, says Cowell, for almost every one to give by will more or less to the *fabric* of the cathedral or parish church where he lived. These lands so given were called fabric lands, because given *ad fabricam ecclesiœ reparandam* (for repairing the fabric of the church).

FABRICA. In old English law. The making or coining of money.

FABRICARE. Lat. To make. Used in old English law of a lawful coining, and also of an unlawful making or counterfeiting of coin. Used in an indictment for forging a bill of lading; 1 Salk. 341.

FABRICATE. To invent; to devise falsely. Invent is sometimes used in a bad sense, but fabricate never in any other.

To fabricate a story implies that it is so contrary to probability as to require the skill of a workman to induce belief in it. Crabbe, Syn. The word implies fraud or falsehood; a false or fraudulent concoction, knowing it to be wrong. L.R. 10 Q.B. 162.

To fabricate evidence is to arrange or manufacture circumstances or *indicia,* after the fact committed, with the purpose of using them as evidence, and of deceitfully making them appear as if accidental or undesigned; to devise falsely or contrive by artifice with the intention to deceive. Such evidence may be wholly forged and artificial, or it may consist in so warping and distorting real facts as to create an erroneous impression in the minds of those who observe them and then presenting such impression as true and genuine.

FABRICATED EVIDENCE. Evidence manufactured or arranged after the fact, and either wholly false or else warped and discolored by artifice and contrivance with a deceitful intent. See *supra.*

FABRICATED FACT. In the law of evidence. A fact existing only in statement, without any foundation in truth. An actual or genuine fact to which a false appearance has been designedly given; a physical object placed in a false connection with another, or with a person on whom it is designed to cast suspicion.

FABRICATING. The word "fabricating," in its context, does not mean "manufacturing," but means cutting, carving, dressing, shaping and working over stone. Commonwealth v. Paul W. Bounds Co., 316 Pa. 29, 173 A. 633.

FABRICATION. "Manufacture" and "fabrication," are often, in broadest sense, interchangeable in meaning; definition in particular instance depending on environment of particular use of either. Union Wire Rope Corporation v. Atchison, T. & S. F. Ry. Co., C.C.A.Mo., 66 F.2d 965, 970.

The word "fabrication," meaning "making," although not generally synonymous with "reworking," meaning a working over, was expressly so used in railroad tariff in question, as distinguished from "manufacture." Atchison, T. & S. F. R. Co. v. Union Wire Rope Corporation, D.C.Mo., 1 F.Supp. 399.

FABULA. In old European law. A contract or formal agreement; particularly used in the Lombardic and Visigothic laws to denote a marriage contract or a will. Burrill.

FACE. That which is shown by the mere language employed without any explanation, modification, or addition from extrinsic facts or evidence, the principal sum which it expresses to be due or payable, without any additions in the way of interest and costs. Cunningham v. Great Southern Life Ins. Co., Tex.Civ.App., 66 S.W.2d 765, 773. The outward appearance or aspect of a thing.

For "Regular on its face," see that title.

The surface of anything; especially the front, upper, or outer part or surface; that which particularly offers itself to the view of a spectator. The words of a written paper in their apparent or obvious meaning, as, the face of a note, bill, bond, check, draft, judgment record, or contract; the face of a judgment for which it was rendered exclusive of interest. Cunningham v. Great Southern Life Ins. Co., Tex.Civ.App., 66 S.W.2d 765, 773.

FACE AMOUNT. The "face amount" of an instrument is that shown by the mere language employed, and excludes any accrued interest. Burns v. Corn Exch. Nat. Bank of Omaha, Neb., 33 Wyo. 474, 240 P. 683, 687. See Face of instrument.

The face amount of a policy means the amount which is, in all events, payable under the policy as straight life insurance without regard to any additional features, such as accident or disability insurance, Smith v. Equitable Life Assur. Soc. of United States, 232 Mo.App. 935, 107 S.W.2d 191, 195; face values specified in policies plus dividend additions postdating lapse, and exclusive of accidental death benefits, Valenti v. Prudential Ins. Co. of America, C.C.A.Mo., 71 F.2d 229, 233.

FACE AMOUNT INSURED BY THE POLICY. Within statute relating to extended life insurance, means the amount which is, in all events, payable under the policy as straight life insurance without regard to additional features such as accident or disability insurance. Wilkins v. Metropolitan Life Ins. Co., 350 Mo. 185, 165 S.W.2d 858, 861, 862; Wilkins v. Metropolitan Life Ins. Co., 236 Mo.App. 586, 159 S.W.2d 354, 356.

FACE OF BOOK. Under an act providing that a public or private statute or the proceedings of any legislative body purporting on the face of the book to be printed by authority of the government of the state are evidence without further proof, the "face of the book" and the "title page" need not coincide, as "face" is used in contradistinction to "cover." Pensacola, St. A. & G. S. S. Co. v. Brooks, 14 Ala.App. 364, 70 So. 968, 970.

FACE OF INSTRUMENT. That which is shown by the language employed, without any explanation, modification, or addition from extrinsic facts or evidence. Adopted in Re Stoneman, Sur., 146 N.Y.S. 172, 175; Investors' Syndicate v. Willcuts, D.C.Minn., 45 F.2d 900, 902. Thus, if the express terms of the paper disclose a fatal legal defect, it is said to be "void on its face." Regarded as an evidence of debt, the face of an instrument is the principal sum which it expresses to be due or payable, without any additions in the way of interest or costs. Osgood v. Bringolf, 32 Iowa, 265. See, also, State v. Newby, 169 Wis. 208, 171 N.W. 953, 954.

FACE OF JUDGMENT. The sum for which it was rendered, exclusive of interest. Osgood v. Bringolf, 32 Iowa, 265. See, also, Face of instrument.

FACE OF POLICY. A phrase which, as used in a statute forbidding life insurance policies to contain provision for any mode of settlement at maturity of less value than the amount insured on the "face of the policy," does not mean merely the first page, but denotes the entire insurance contract contained in the policy, including a rider attached and referred to on the first page. Julius v. Metropolitan Life Ins. Co., 299 Ill. 343, 132 N.E. 435, 437, 17 A.L.R. 956.

FACE OF RECORD. The entire record in a case, not merely what the judgment recites. Carson v. Taylor, Tex.Civ.App., 261 S.W. 824; San Bernardo Townsite Co. v. Hocker, Tex.Civ.App., 176 S.W. 644, 646.

The "face of the record" means, in a criminal case, the indictment and the verdict. Jones v. State, 58 Ga.App. 374, 198 S.E. 566.

The phrases "judgment roll," "judgment record," and "face of the record" are synonymous. Every part of trial proceedings reserved in courts of record under direction of court for purpose of its records constitutes the "judgment roll." Permian Oil Co. v. Smith, 129 Tex. 413, 107 S.W.2d 564, 566, 111 A.L.R. 1152.

FACE VALUE. This term, in a statute taxing transfers of corporate stock, means par value. Goodyear Tire & Rubber Co. v. U. S., 273 U.S. 100, 47 S.Ct. 263, 71 L.Ed. 558. See, also In re Stoneman, Sur., 146 N.Y.S. 172, 174.

As used in statute concerning acceptance of bonds as bail means that value, written or printed on face of instrument and the unmatured coupons attached thereto, without reference to the actual or market value of bonds. Wilson v. Justice's Court of Township of San Diego, 22 Cal.App.2d 278, 70 P.2d 695, 696.

The "face value" of an interest bearing note, is the principal plus accrued interest. American Nat. Bank of Portsmouth v. Ames, 169 Va. 711, 194 S.E. 784, 798.

The value which can be ascertained from the language of the instrument without aid from extrinsic facts or evidence. Investors' Syndicate v. Willcuts, D.C.Minn., 45 F.2d 900, 902.

FACERE. Lat. To do; to make. Thus, *facere defaltam,* to make default; *facere duellum,* to make the duel, or make or do battle; *facere finem,* to make or pay a fine; *facere legem,* to make one's law; *facere sacramentum,* to make oath.

FACIAL DISFIGUREMENT. That which impairs or injures the beauty, symmetry, or appearance of a person, that which renders unsightly, misshapen or imperfect or deforms in some manner. Ferguson v. State Highway Department, 197 S.C. 520, 15 S.E.2d 775, 778; Poole v. Saxon Mills, 192 S.C. 339, 6 S.E.2d 761, 764.

FACIAS. That you cause.

Occurring in the phrases *"scire facias,"* (that you cause to know,) *"fieri facias,"* (that you cause to be made,) etc. Used also in the phrases *Do ut facias* (I give that you may do), *Facio ut facias* (I do that you may do), two of the four divisions of considerations made by Blackstone, 2 Comm. 444. See Facio ut des; Facio ut facias.

FACIENDO. In doing or paying; in some activity.

FACIES. Lat. The face or countenance; the exterior appearance or view; hence, contemplation or study of a thing on its external or apparent side.

Thus, *prima facie* means at the first inspection, on a preliminary or exterior scrutiny. When we speak of a *"prima facie* case," we mean one which, on its own showing, on a first examination, or without investigating any alleged defenses, is apparently good and maintainable.

FACILE. In Scotch law. Easily persuaded; easily imposed upon. Bell.

FACILITATE. To make easy or less difficult, or to free from difficulty or impediment. Pon Wing Quong v. United States, C.C.A.Cal., 111 F.2d 751, 756. To make more easy or less difficult; free more or less completely from obstruction or hindrance; lessen the labor of. United States v. One Dodge Coupe, Motor No. D14–105424, Serial No. 30284066, D.C.N.Y., 43 F.Supp. 60, 61.

FACILITIES. That which promotes the ease of any action, operation, transaction, or course of conduct. Webster. The term denotes inanimate means rather than human agencies. Sloss-Sheffield Steel & Iron Co. v. Smith, 185 Ala. 607, 64 So. 337, 338.

Also, a name formerly given to certain notes of some of the banks in the state of Connecticut, which were made payable in two years after the close of the war of 1812. Springfield Bank v. Merrick, 14 Mass. 322.

As applied to carriers, means everything necessary for the convenience of passengers and the safety and prompt transportation of freight; everything incident to the general, prompt, safe, and impartial performance of the duties to the public at large imposed by the state, in the proper exercise of its police power, upon transportation or transmission companies. As applied to a ferry franchise, everything incident to the general, prompt, and safe carriage of passengers, boats in good repair, appliances answering the purpose, and readiness and willingness to perform the services incident to the grant. Fraters v. Keeling, 20 Cal. App.2d 490, 67 P.2d 118, 119.

As used in phrase "special facilities within the place of amusement," in statute creating amusement tax, referred to personal accommodations furnished for comfort of patron to enable him to obtain a better view of what he paid for when he entered the ground or to more conveniently do so. Martin v. F. H. Bee Shows, 271 Ky. 822, 113 S.W.2d 448, 452.

As used in statute giving Public Service Commission control over service and facilities of public service companies, means something owned by or under the control of a public utility. Borough of Swarthmore v. Public Service Commission, 277 Pa. 472, 121 A. 488, 489.

Electric company which transmitted electricity from generating plant through a line to another company which transmitted such electricity in interstate commerce, operated "facilities" subject to jurisdiction of Federal Power Commission. Jersey Central Power & Light Co. v. Federal Power Commission, C.C.A.3, 129 F.2d 183, 195.

Electric company's corporate organization, contracts, accounts, memorandum, papers, and other records constituted "facilities" within Federal Power Act. The word "facilities" embraces anything which aids or makes easier the performance of the activities involved in the business of a person or corporation. Hartford Electric Light Co. v. Federal Power Commission, C.C.A.2, 131 F.2d 953, 960, 961, 962.

Freight cars are "facilities" of transportation as defined by Interstate Commerce Act. General American Tank Car Corporation v. El Dorado Terminal Co., Cal., 308 U.S. 422, 60 S.Ct. 325, 329, 84 L.Ed. 361.

Sidetracks constituting part of a transportation system are "facilities" of the railroad, even though privately owned. Lehigh Nav. Coal Co. v. Pennsylvania Public Utility Commission, 133 Pa.Super. 67, 1 A.2d 540, 544.

Street railroad's "facilities" include tracks and land reasonably necessary for operation of railroad and accommodation of patrons. Munoz v. Porto Rico Ry., Light & Power Co., C.C.A.Puerto Rico, 74 F.2d 816, 821.

FACILITY. In Scotch law. Pliancy of disposition. Bell.

A switch engine and crew is a "facility" within statute authorizing rental thereof by railroad. Nekoosa-Edwards Paper Co. v. Minneapolis, St. P. & S. S. M. Ry. Co., 217 Wis. 426, 259 N.W. 618.

As ordinarily used, is not as narrow a term as "instrumentality." Nekoosa-Edwards Paper Co. v. Minneapolis, St. P. & S. S. M. Ry. Co., 217 Wis. 426, 259 N.W. 618.

Convenient means. Briggs Mfg. Co. v. U. S., D.C.Conn., 30 F.2d 962, 964.

Where electric company transmitted electricity to another company which transmitted it in interstate commerce, the former company's line was a "facility" subject to jurisdiction of Federal Power Commission. Jersey Central Power & Light Co. v. Federal Power Commission, 319 U.S. 61, 63 S.Ct. 953, 959, 87 L.Ed. 1258.

FACILITY OF PAYMENT CLAUSE, is appointment by assured and beneficiary of persons authorized to receive payment. French v. Lanham, App.D.C., 57 F.2d 422; Fulcher v. Parker, 169 Va. 479, 194 S.E. 714, 716. It confers on insurer an option as to whom it will make payment, Metropolitan Life Ins. Co. v. Brown for Use and Benefit of Fleming, 25 Tenn.App. 514, 160 S.W.2d 434, 438; Rohde v. Metropolitan Life Ins. Co., 233 Mo.App. 865, 111 S.W.2d 1006.

Such clause in group policy giving employer under certain contingencies power to designate beneficiary controls only where no other beneficiary is named. Potter v. Young, 193 Ark. 957, 104 S.W.2d 802, 804.

FACING. In deed containing building restrictions applicable to lots "facing" and "having a frontage" on named street, quoted words as applied to oblong lots referred to the street which buildings to be erected on the lots were intended to face. Aller v. Berkeley Hall School Foundation, 40 Cal.App.2d 31, 103 P.2d 1052, 1054.

FACINUS QUOS INQUINAT ÆQUAT. Guilt makes equal those whom it stains.

FACIO UT DES. (Lat. I do that you may give.)

A species of contract in the civil law (being one of the *innominate* contracts) which occurs when a man agrees to perform anything for a price either specifically mentioned or left to the determination of the law to set a value on it; as when a servant hires himself to his master for certain wages or an agreed sum of money. 2 Bl.Comm. 445. Also, the consideration of that species of contract.

FACIO UT FACIAS. (Lat. I do that you may do.)

The consideration of that species of contract in the civil law, or the contract itself (being one of the *innominate* contracts), which occurs when I agree with a man to do his work for him if he will do mine for me; or if two persons agree to marry together, or to do any other positive acts on both sides; or it may be to forbear on one side in consideration of something done on the other. 2 Bl.Comm. 444.

FACSIMILE. An exact copy, preserving all the marks of the original.

FACSIMILE PROBATE. In England, where the construction of a will may be affected by the appearance of the original paper, the court will order the probate to pass in *facsimile,* as it may possibly help to show the meaning of the testator. 1 Williams, Ex'rs, 7th Ed., 331, 386, 566.

FACT. A thing done; an action performed or an incident transpiring; an event or circumstance; an actual occurrence. An actual happening in time or space or an event mental or physical. Fowler-Curtis Co. v. Dean, 203 App.Div. 317, 196 N.Y.S. 750, 754; German-American Ins. Co. v. Huntley, 62 Okl. 39, 161 P. 815, 817; Rost v. Kessler, 267 App.Div. 686, 49 N.Y.S.2d 97, 99. That which has taken place, not what might or might not have taken place. Churchill v. Meade, 92 Or. 626, 182 P. 368, 371.

A fact is either a state of things, that is, an existence, or a motion, that is, an event. 1 Benth.Jud.Ev. 48.

Fact *(factum, fait)* stands in lawbooks for: 1. An act; 2. For a completed and operative transaction brought about by sealing and executing a certain sort of writing, and so for the instrument itself, a deed *(factum);* 3. As designating what exists, in contradistinction to what should exist *(de facto* as contrasted with *de jure);* 4. As indicating things, events, actions, conditions, as happening, existing, really taking place. Thayer, Evid. 190.

"Fact" was formerly used almost exclusively in the sense of "action" or "deed." This usage survives in phrases such as "accessory before the fact."

As used in statute providing that malice shall be presumed from publication of matter not privileged, unless the "fact" and the testimony rebut such presumption, means the act, the thing done, the circumstance, the publication itself. Reininger v. Prickett, 192 Okl. 486, 137 P.2d 595, 597.

As used in statute requiring statement of facts constituting cause of action, "facts" mean narrative of events, acts, and things done which show legal liability of defendant to plaintiff. Rhoads v. Columbia Fire Underwriters' Agency, 128 Neb. 710, 260 N.W. 174.

"Facts" to which Supreme Court is limited on certiorari to quash Court of Appeals' decision for conflict comprise record before Court of Appeals, evidence, documentary and oral, and instructions and pleadings. State ex rel. Horspool v. Haid, 328 Mo. 327, 40 S.W.2d 611, 613.

Good reputation of an accused when proved is a "fact". State v. Fenimore, 3 Terry 183, 29 A.2d 170, 171. Intent is a "fact". Majestic Securities Corporation v. Commissioner of Internal Revenue, C.C.A.8, 120 F.2d 12, 14. "Knowledge" is a "fact", and an "assertion of knowledge", when knowledge does not exist, is an assertion not in accordance with the facts. Eastern States Petroleum Co. v. Universal Oil Products Co., 24 Del.Ch. 11, 3 A.2d 768, 775. Representations as to boundaries of land are representations of "fact". Algee v. Hillman Inv. Co., 12 Wash.2d 672, 123 P.2d 332, 334. Where knowledge is possible, one who represents a mere belief as knowledge misrepresents a "fact". Sovereign Pocohontas Co. v. Bond, 74 App.D.C. 175, 120 F.2d 39, 40.

Law and Fact as Distinguishable

"Fact" is very frequently used in opposition or contrast to "law."

Thus, questions of *fact* are for the jury; questions of *law* for the court. So an attorney *at law* is an officer of the courts of justice; an attorney *in fact* is appointed by the written authorization of a principal to manage business affairs usually not professional. Fraud *in fact* consists in an actual intention to defraud, carried into effect; while fraud imputed by *law* arises from the man's conduct in its necessary relations and consequences.

A "fact", as distinguished from the "law", may be taken as that out of which the point of law arises, that which is asserted to be or not to be, and is to be presumed or proved to be or not to be for the purpose of applying or refusing to apply a rule of law. Hinckley v. Town of Barnstable, 311 Mass. 600, 42 N.E.2d 581, 584.

Law is a principle; fact is an event. Law is conceived; fact is actual. Law is a rule of duty; fact is that which has been according to or in contravention of the rule. The distinction is well illustrated in the rule that the existence of foreign laws is matter of fact. Within the territory of its jurisdiction, law operates as an obligatory rule which judges must recognize and enforce; but, in a tribunal outside that jurisdiction, it loses its obligatory force and its claim to judicial notice. The fact that it exists, if important to the rights of parties, must be alleged and proved the same as the actual existence of any other institution. Abbott.

Law of Evidence

A circumstance, event or occurrence as it actually takes or took place; a physical object or appearance, as it actually exists or existed. An actual and absolute reality, as distinguished from mere supposition or opinion; a truth, as distinguished from fiction or error. Burrill, Circ.Ev. 218.

"Circumstances" are but minor facts, Scott v. State, 57 Ga.App. 489, 195 S.E. 923, 924. Facts admitted upon trial of cause become "evidence". American Extension School of Law v. Ragland, 232 Mo.App. 763, 112 S.W.2d 110, 113. Facts judicially noticed are equivalent to evidence. Zickefoose v. Thompson, 347 Mo. 579, 148 S.W.2d 784, 792.

"Facts" and "evidence" are sometimes used interchangeably. Mackey v. First Nat. Bank, Mo.App., 293 S.W. 66, 71. But the terms are not really synonymous; evidence, broadly defined, being means from which an inference may logically be drawn as to existence of a fact. Tjernstrom v. Ford Motor Co., 285 Mich. 450, 280 N.W. 823, 825. Yet, although "facts" and the "evidence" are quite different, it sometimes may happen that they constitute one and the same thing. Gates v. Haw, 150 Ind. 370, 50 N.E. 299.

Hypothetical question propounded to plaintiff's witness in which an assumed fact was that a test made by another expert had a specified result referred to a "fact" and not an "opinion" of the expert. Cody v. Toller Drug Co., 232 Iowa 475, 5 N.W.2d 824, 828.

In rule 41(b), providing for motion for dismissal at close of plaintiff's evidence in nonjury case on ground that upon the facts and the law plaintiff has shown no right to relief, the "facts" referred to are the prima facie facts shown by plaintiff's evidence viewed in light most favorable to him. Schad v. Twentieth Century-Fox Film Corporation, C.C.A. Pa., 136 F.2d 991, 993.

Ownership of property is, generally, a "fact" to which a witness may testify. Diamond v. Grath, 46 Cal.App.2d 443, 116 P.2d 114, 116.

Statement that cause of death was a gunshot wound was a statement of "fact" but further statements that such wound was self-inflicted and that death was suicide were mere expressions of "opinion". Kentucky Home Mut. Life Ins. Co. v. Watts, 298 Ky. 471, 183 S.W.2d 499, 502.

Where person states matter which might otherwise be only an "opinion" as an existing fact material to the transaction, the statement clearly becomes a statement of "fact". Fidelity & Casualty Co. of New York v. J. D. Pittman Tractor Co., 244 Ala. 354, 13 So.2d 669, 672.

Words "facts" and "circumstances" are used interchangeably in the phrase circumstantial evidence. Pulliam v. State, 196 Ga. 782, 28 S.E.2d 139, 147.

Workmen's compensation claimant's testimony that he was well related to a "fact" and not to an "opinion". Texas Employers Ins. Ass'n v. Griffis, Tex.Civ.App., 141 S.W.2d 687, 690.

Truth and Fact Distinguished

The terms "fact" and "truth" are often used in common parlance as synonymous, but, as employed in reference to pleading, they are widely different. A fact in pleading is a circumstance, act, event, or incident; a truth is the legal principle which declares or governs the facts and their operative effect. Admitting the facts stated in a complaint, the truth may be that the plaintiff is not entitled, upon the face of his complaint, to what he claims. The mode in which a defendant sets up that truth for his protection is a demurrer. Drake v. Cockroft, 4 E. D. Smith, N.Y., 37.

For "Collateral Facts," "Dispositive Facts," "Evidentiary Facts," "Finding of Fact," "Immaterial Facts," "Jurisdictional Facts," "Material Fact," "Principal Fact," and "Ultimate Facts," see those heads.

FACT MATERIAL TO RISK. See Material Fact.

FACTA. In old English law. Deeds. *Facta armorum,* deeds or feats of arms; that is, jousts or tournaments. Cowell.

Facts. *Facta et casus,* facts and cases. Bract. fol. 1*b*.

FACTA SUNT POTENTIORA VERBIS. Deeds [or facts] are more powerful than words.

FACTA TENENT MULTA QUÆ FIERI PROHIBENTUR. 12 Coke, 124. Deeds contain many things which are prohibited to be done.

FACTIO TESTAMENTI. In the civil law. The right, power, or capacity of making a will; called *"factio activa."* Inst. 2, 10, 6.

The right or capacity of taking by will; called *"factio passiva."* Inst. 2, 10, 6; Vicat, Voc.Jur.

FACTO. In fact; by an act; by the act or fact. *Ipso facto,* by the act itself; by the mere effect of a fact, without anything superadded, or any proceeding upon it to give it effect. 3 Kent, Comm. 55, 58.

FACTO ET ANIMO. In fact and intent. Northwestern Mortgage & Security Co. v. Noel Const. Co., 71 N.D. 256, 300 N.W. 28, 31.

FACTOR. A commercial agent, employed by a principal to sell merchandise consigned to him for that purpose, for and in behalf of the principal, but usually in his own name, being intrusted with the possession and control of the goods, and being remunerated by a commission, commonly called "factorage." Howland v. Woodruff, 60 N.Y. 80; In re Rabenau, D.C.Mo., 118 F. 474; Graham v. Duckwall, 8 Bush, Ky., 17; Pal.Ag. 13; Sto.Ag. § 33; Com.Dig. *Merchant,* B; Malynes, Lex Merc. 81; Beawes, Lex Merc. 44; 3 Chit.Com.L. 193; 2 Kent 622; 1 Bell, Comm. 385, § 408; 2 B. & Ald. 143.

In Scotch law, a person appointed to transact business or manage affairs for another, but more particularly an estate-agent or one intrusted with the management of a landed estate, who finds tenants, makes leases, collects the rents, etc.

In some of the states, the person who is elsewhere called "garnishee" or "trustee." See Factorizing Process.

A commercial agent to whom the possession of personalty is entrusted by or for the owner, to be sold, for a compensation, in pursuance of the agent's usual trade or business, with title to goods remaining in principal and the "factor" being merely a bailee for the purposes of the agency. Neild v. District of Columbia, 71 App.D.C. 306, 110 F.2d 246, 259.

Although a "factor" is in the last analysis an agent, the agency is a limited one. Falls Rubber Co. v. La Fon, Tex. Civ.App., 256 S.W. 577, 579.

An agent employed to sell goods for principal, The Robin Gray, D.C.N.Y., 53 F.2d 1037, 1041. An agent employed to sell goods for his principal which are in his possession for a commission and ordinary consignment contract create relation of factor and principal. Robertson v. State, 207 Ind. 374, 192 N.E. 887, 888.

An agent employed to sell goods or merchandise consigned or delivered to him, by or for his principal, for a compensation, commonly called factorage or commission, and an agent for the sale of goods in his possession or consigned to him. Hughes v. Young, 17 Tenn.App. 24, 65 S.W.2d 858.

An agent, who, in pursuance of his usual trade or business, and for compensation, sells goods or merchandise consigned or intrusted to his possession for that purpose by or for the owner. Sams v. Arthur, 135 S.C. 123, 133 S.E. 205, 207; M. H. Thomas & Co. v. Hawthorne, Tex.Civ.App., 245 S.W. 966, 971; Lemnos Broad Silk Works v. Spiegelberg, 127 Misc.Rep. 855, 217 N.Y.S. 595, 597.

An agent who, in the pursuit of an independent calling, is employed by another to sell property for him, and is vested by the latter with the possession or control of the property, or authorized to receive payment therefor from the purchaser. Civ.Code Cal. § 2026; Comp.Laws N.D.1913, § 6145; Comp.Laws S.D.1929, § 1288; Leland v. Oliver, 82 Cal.App. 474, 255 P. 775, 777.

One who, in pursuance of business, receives goods from principal and sells them for compensation called factorage or commission. Holleman v. Taylor, 200 N.C. 618, 158 S.E. 88, 89.

One whose business is to receive and sell goods for a commission, being intrusted with the possession of the goods to be sold, and usually selling in his own name. City of Atlanta v. York Mfg. Co., 155 Ga. 33, 116 S.E. 195, 199; Tyson v. Jennings Produce Co., 16 Ala.App. 374, 77 So. 986, 987; G. H. Hammond Co. v. Joseph Mercantile Co., 144 Ark. 108, 222 S.W. 27, 28.

In the old law, one to whom goods are consigned to sell by a merchant at a distance from the place of sale. Eames v. H. B. Claflin Co., C.C.A.N.Y., 239 F. 631, 635.

Broker and Factor Distinguished

A factor differs from a "broker" in that he is intrusted with the possession, management, and control of the goods, (which gives him a special property in them,); while a broker acts as a mere intermediary without control or possession of the property. A factor may buy and sell in his own name, as well as in that of the principal, while a broker, as such, cannot ordinarily buy or sell in his own name. Commercial Inv. Trust v. Stewart, 235 Mich. 502, 209 N.W. 660, 661; Sutton & Cummins v. Kiel Cheese & Butter Co., 155 Ky. 465, 159 S.W. 950, 951; Hughes v. Young, 17 Tenn.App. 24, 65 S.W.2d 858; Gadsden County Tobacco Co. v. Corry, 103 Fla. 217, 137 So. 255, 257. A factor or commission merchant has a lien upon the goods for his charges, advances, and commissions, while the broker has no control of the property and is responsible only for bad faith. McCornick & Co., Bankers v. Tolmie Bros., 42 Idaho 1, 243 P. 355, 358.

A factor or commission merchant is one who has the actual or technical possession of goods or wares of another for sale. A "merchandise broker" is one who negotiates the sale of merchandise without having it in his possession or control. He is simply an agent with very limited powers, J. M. Robinson, Norton & Co. v. Cotton Factory, 124 Ky. 435, 99 S.W. 305, 102 S.W. 869, 8 L.R.A.,N.S., 474.

Commission Merchants and Factors as Synonymous

Factors are also frequently called "commission merchants;" and it is said that there is no difference in the meaning of these terms, the latter being perhaps more commonly used in America. Thompson v. Woodruff, 7 Cold. 410; Duguid v. Edwards, 50 Barb., N.Y., 288; Lyon v. Alvord, 18 Conn. 80. See, also, Commission Merchant.

Domestic and Foreign Factors

Factors are called "domestic" or "foreign" according as they reside and do business in the same state or country with the principal or in a different state or country.

A domestic factor is sometimes called a "home" factor. Ruffner v. Hewitt, 7 W.Va. 585; 1 Term 112; 4 Maule & S. 576.

A "foreign factor," as understood in marine matters, was a person who had charge of the cargo to handle it, dispose of it, convert it into money, or exchange it for other property, but who had nothing to do with the management of the boat when he sailed thereon, at which time he was called a "supercargo." Gilchrist Transp. Co. v. Worthington & Sill, 193 App.Div. 250, 184 N.Y.S. 81, 83; Beawes, Lex Merc. 44; Liverm.Ag. 69; 1 Domat, b. 1, t. 16, § 3, art. 2.

Judicial Factor

In Scotch law. A factor appointed by the courts in certain cases where it becomes necessary to intrust the management of property to another than the owner, as, where the latter is insane or imbecile or the infant heir of a decedent.

Supercargo as a Factor

Where an owner of goods to be shipped by sea consigns them to the care of an agent, who sails on the same vessel, has charge of the cargo on board, sells it abroad, and buys a return cargo out of the proceeds, such agent is strictly and properly a "factor," though in maritime law and usage he is commonly called a "supercargo." Beawes, Lex Merc. 44, 47; Liverm.Ag. 69, 70.

FACTORAGE. The wages, allowance, or commission paid to a factor for his services. Winne v. Hammond, 37 Ill. 103; State v. Thompson, 25 S.W. 346, 120 Mo. 12.

FACTORING is a system involving notice to the trade debtors, and is confined principally to the textile industry. Corn Exchange Nat. Bank & Trust Co., Philadelphia, v. Klauder, Pa., 318 U.S. 434, 63 S.Ct. 679, 682, 87 L.Ed. 884, 144 A.L.R. 1189.

FACTORIZING PROCESS. In American law. A process by which the effects of a debtor are attached in the hands of a third person. A term peculiar to the practice in Vermont and Connecticut. Otherwise termed "trustee process," "garnishment," and process by "foreign attachment." Cross v. Brown, 19 R.I. 220, 33 A. 147; Drake, Attach. § 451.

FACTORS' ACTS. The name given to several English statutes (6 Geo. IV. c. 94; 5 & 6 Vict. c. 39; 40 & 41 Vict. c. 39) by which a factor is enabled to make a valid pledge of the goods, or of any part thereof, to one who believes him to be the *bona fide* owner of the goods. Similar legislation is not uncommon in the United States.

FACTORY.

American Law

A building or group of buildings appropriated to the manufacture of goods, including the machinery necessary to produce the goods, and the engine or other power by which the machinery is propelled; the place where workers are employed in fabricating goods, wares, or utensils. Cent. Dict.; Mayhew v. Hardesty, 8 Md. 479. A structure where something is made or manufactured. People v. R. F. Stevens Co., 178 App.Div. 306, 165 N.Y.S. 39.

An undertaking in which the business of working at commodities is carried on with power-driven machinery. Gowey v. Seattle Lighting Co., 108 Wash. 479, 184 P. 339.

Any mill, workshop, or any manufacturing or business establishment, and all buildings, sheds, structures, or other places used for or in connection therewith where one or more persons are employed at labor. Under such statute, the term includes a machine shop, People v. Transit Development Co., 165 N.Y.S. 114, 115, 178 App.Div. 288; and a theatrical company; Ursprung v. Winter Garden Co., 169 N.Y.S. 738, 745, 183 App.Div. 718; but not a butcher shop; O'Connor v. Webber, 219 N.Y. 439, 114 N.E. 799.

Any premises where steam, water, or other mechanical power is used in the aid of any manufacturing process without reference to whether it is inclosed in a building. Casey v. Barber Asphalt Paving Co., C.C.A.Wash., 202 F. 1, 5.

Any premises wherein power is used in manufacturing, making, altering, adapting, ornamenting, finishing, repairing, or renovating articles for purpose of trade or gain, or of business carried on therein. Bradley v. Blakley, La.App., 147 So. 709, 710; Menke v. Hauber, 99 Kan. 171, 160 P. 1017, 1018.

The word does not necessarily mean a single building or edifice, but may apply to several, where they are used in connection with each other, for a common purpose, and stand together in the same inclosure. Liebenstein v. Insurance Co., 45 Ill. 303. And see Hernischel v. Texas Drug Co., 26 Tex.Civ.App. 1, 61 S.W. 419; Schott v. Harvey, 105 Pa. 227, 51 Am.Rep. 201; Amberg v. Kinley, 214 N.Y. 531, 108 N.E. 830, 833, L.R.A.1915E, 519.

To bring acts within statutory definition of "factory" as used in statute relating to employees' rest each week, the acts must be manufacturing ones. People v. Middletown & U. R. Co., 169 Misc. 773, 8 N.Y.S.2d 193, 195, 196.

English Law and Statutes

The term includes all buildings and premises wherein, or within the close or curtilage of which, steam, water, or any mechanical power is used to move or work any machinery employed in preparing, manufacturing, or finishing cotton, wool, hair, silk, flax, hemp, jute, or tow. So defined by the statute 7 Vict. c. 15, § 73.

By later acts this definition has been extended to various other manufacturing places. Mozley & Whitley.

Also a place where a considerable number of factors reside, in order to negotiate for their masters or employers. Enc.Brit.

Scotch Law

A species of contract or employment which falls under the general designation of "agency," but which partakes both of the nature of a mandate and of a bailment of the kind called *"locatio ad operandum."* 1 Bell, Comm. 259.

FACTORY ACTS. Laws enacted for the purpose of regulating the hours of work, and the sanitary condition, and preserving the health and morals, of the employés, and promoting the education of young persons employed at such labor.

FACTORY PRICES. The prices at which goods may be bought at the factories, as distinguished from the prices of goods bought in the market after they have passed into the hands of third persons or shop-keepers. Whipple v. Levett, 2 Mason, 90, Fed.Cas.No.17,518.

FACTORY RATING. Of carrying capacity of motortrucks as used in statute imposing license fee means customary public announcement of manufacturer in placing motortrucks on market. Memphis Steam Laundry Co. v. Crenshaw, 166 Tenn. 168, 61 S.W.2d 669.

FACTS. See Fact.

FACTS CANNOT LIE. 18 How.State Tr. 1187; 17 How.State Tr. 1430; but see Best, Ev. 587.

FACTS IN ISSUE. Those matters of fact on which the plaintiff proceeds by his action, and which the defendant controverts in his pleadings. Maeder Steel Products Co. v. Zanello, 109 Or. 562, 220 P. 155, 158; King v. Chase, 15 N.H. 9, 41 Am. Dec. 675; Caperton v. Schmidt, 26 Cal. 494, 85 Am.Dec. 187.

FACTS INCOMPLETE. A certificate of trial judge to bill of exceptions not certifying to correctness of any recital therein and only certifying that the bill "is facts incomplete", that is, not finished, not perfect, defective, verifies nothing and brings nothing before the Court of Appeals for review. Loving v. Kamm, 34 N.E.2d 591.

FACTS OF THE CASE. With which Supreme Court will deal in case brought from Court of Appeal by writ of review, are facts that were proved or admitted, not deductions or conclusions as to duty of parties or negligence. Llorens v. McCann, 187 La. 642, 175 So. 442, 444.

FACTS WELL PLEADED are those of a substantive nature necessary to the framing of the issue submitted. Bushman v. Barlow, 321 Mo. 1052, 15 S.W.2d 329, 331.

FACTUM. Lat. With respect to change of domicile, "factum" is person's physical presence in new domicile. Guilfoil v. Hayes, 169 Va. 548, 194 S.E. 804, 807.

Civil Law. Fact; a fact; a matter of fact, as distinguished from a matter of law. Dig. 41, 2, 1, 3.

French Law. A memoir which contains concisely set down the fact on which a contest has happened, the means on which a party founds his pretensions, with the refutation of the means of the adverse party. Vicat.

Old English Law. A deed; a person's act and deed. A culpable or criminal act; an act not founded in law. Anything stated or made certain; a deed of conveyance; a written instrument under seal: called, also, *charta*. Spelman; 2 Bla. Comm. 295. A fact; a circumstance; particularly a fact in evidence. Bract. fol. 1*b*. *Factum probandum* (the fact to be proved). 1 Greenl. Ev. § 13.

Old European Law. A portion or allotment of land; otherwise called a hide, *bovata*, etc. Spelman.

Testamentary Law. The execution or due execution of a will. The *factum* of an instrument means not barely the signing of it, and the formal publication or delivery, but proof that the party well knew and understood the contents thereof, and did give, will, dispose, and do, in all things, as in the said will is contained. Weatherhead v. Baskerville, 11 How. 354, 13 L.Ed. 717.

FACTUM A JUDICE QUOD AD EJUS OFFICIUM NON SPECTAT NON RATUM EST. An action of a judge which relates not to his office is of no force. Dig. 50, 17, 170; 10 Coke, 76; Broom, Max. 93, n.

FACTUM CUIQUE SUUM NON ADVERSARIO, NOCERE DEBET. Dig. 50, 17, 155. A party's own act should prejudice himself, not his adversary.

FACTUM INFECTUM FIERI NEQUIT. A thing done cannot be undone. 1 Kames, Eq. 96, 259.

FACTUM JURIDICUM. A juridical fact. Denotes one of the factors or elements constituting an obligation.

FACTUM NEGANTIS NULLA PROBATIO SIT. Cod. 4, 19, 23. There is no proof incumbent upon him who denies a fact.

"FACTUM" NON DICITUR QUOD NON PERSEVERAT. That is not called a "deed" which does not continue operative. That is not said to be done which does not last. 5 Coke, 96; Shep. Touch., Preston ed. 391.

FACTUM PROBANDUM. Lat. In the law of evidence. The fact to be proved; a fact which is in issue, and to which evidence is to be directed. 1 Greenl. Ev. § 13.

FACTUM PROBANS. A probative or evidentiary fact; a subsidiary or connected fact tending to prove the principal fact in issue; a piece of circumstantial evidence.

FACTUM UNIUS ALTERI NOCERI NON DEBET. Co. Litt. 152. The deed of one should not hurt another.

FACULTAS PROBATIONUM NON EST ANGUSTANDA. The power of proofs [right of offering or giving testimony] is not to be narrowed. 4 Inst. 279.

FACULTATIVE COMPENSATION is that which operates by the will of the parties, when one of them removes an obstacle preventing compensation, resulting from the dispositions of the law. In re Interstate Trust & Banking Co., La.App., 194 So. 35, 40, 42.

FACULTATIVE REINSURANCE. Under type designated "facultative", the reinsurer has the option of accepting the tendered part of the original insurer's risk. Lincoln Nat. Life Ins. Co. v. State Tax Commission, 196 Miss. 82, 16 So.2d 369.

FACULTIES. In the law of divorce. The capability of the husband to render a support to the wife in the form of alimony, whether temporary or permanent, including not only his tangible property, but also his income and his ability to earn money. 2 Bish. Mar. & Div. § 446; Lovett v. Lovett, 11 Ala. 763; Wright v. Wright, 3 Tex. 168; Fowler v. Fowler, 61 Okl. 280, 161 P. 227, 230, L.R.A.1917C, 89. See Allegation of Faculties.

FACULTIES, COURT OF. In English ecclesiastical law. A jurisdiction or tribunal belonging to the archbishop.

It does not hold pleas in any suits, but creates rights to pews, monuments, and particular places, and modes of burial. It has also various powers under 25 Hen. VIII. c. 21, in granting licenses of different descriptions, as a license to marry, a faculty to erect an organ in a parish church, to level a church-yard, to remove bodies previously buried. 4 Inst. 337.

FACULTIES, MASTER OF THE. An official in the archdiocese of Canterbury who granted dispensations. 4 Inst. 337. See Arches Court.

FACULTY.

Ecclesiastical Law. A license or authority; a privilege granted by the ordinary to a man by favor and indulgence to do that which by law he may not do; *e. g.*, to marry without banns, to erect a monument in a church, etc. Termes de la Ley.

Faculties are of two kinds: first, when the grant is to a man and his heirs in gross; second, when it is to a person and his heirs as appurtenant to a house which he holds in the parish; 1 Term 429, 432; 12 Co. 106.

Scotch Law. A power founded on consent, as distinguished from a power founded on property. 2 Kames, Eq. 265.

FACULTY OF A COLLEGE OR UNIVERSITY. The corps of professors, instructors, tutors, and lecturers. To be distinguished from the board of trustees, who constitute the corporation.

The teaching body. West v. Board of Trustees of Miami University and Miami Normal School, 41 Ohio App. 367, 181 N.E. 144, 150.

FACULTY OF ADVOCATES. The college or society of advocates in Scotland.

FADE THE GAME. Means that spectators of a game of "craps" bet on the success of actual participants. Sullivan v. State, 146 Tex.Cr.R. 79, 171 S.W.2d 353.

FADERFIUM. In old English law. A marriage gift coming from the father or brother of the bride. Spelman.

FÆDER-FEOH. In old English law. The portion brought by a wife to her husband, and which reverted to a widow, in case the heir of her deceased husband refused his consent to her second marriage; *i. e.*, it reverted to her family in case she returned to them. Wharton.

FÆSTING-MEN. Approved men who were strong-armed; *habentes homines* or rich men, men of substance; pledges or bondsmen, who, by Saxon custom, were bound to answer for each other's good behavior. Cowell; Du Cange.

FAGGOT. A badge worn in popish times by persons who had recanted and abjured what was then adjudged to be heresy, as an emblem of what they had merited. Cowell.

FAGGOT VOTE. A term applied to votes manufactured by nominally transferring land to persons otherwise disqualified from voting for members of parliament.

A faggot vote occurs where a man is formally possessed of a right to vote for members of parliament, without possessing the substance which the vote should represent; as if he is enabled to buy a property, and at the same moment mortgage it to its full value, for the mere sake of the vote. See 7 & 8 Wm. III. c. 25, § 7. Wharton.

FAIDA. In Saxon law. Malice; open and deadly hostility; deadly feud.

The word designated the enmity between the family of a murdered man and that of his murderer, which was recognized, among the Teutonic peoples, as justification for vengeance taken by any one of the former upon any one of the latter. Du Cange; Spelman.

FAIL. Fault, negligence, or refusal. Walker v. Sheffield Steel Corporation, 224 Mo.App. 849, 27 S.W.2d 44, 48; Anderson v. Commercial Credit Co., 110 Mont. 333, 101 P.2d 367, 369.

It also means:

Involuntarily to fall short of success or the attainment of one's purpose. See Cobb v. Morrison, 197 Ala. 550, 73 So. 42; Pennsylvania Co. v. Good, 56 Ind.App. 562, 103 N.E. 672, 673; lapse, Gredig v. Sterling, C.C.A.Tex., 47 F.2d 832, 834; Wilmington Trust Co. v. Wilmington Trust Co., 25 Del.Ch. 204, 15 A.2d 830, 834; to become insolvent and unable to meet one's obligations as they mature. Davis v. Campbell, 3 Stew., Ala., 321; Mayer v. Hermann, 16 Fed. Cas. 1,242; to come short of; lack; to prove ineffective or inoperative; to become or be found deficient or wanting, In re Merritt's Will, 14 N.Y.S.2d 103, 107, 171 Misc. 812; to decline, Buffalo County v. Phelps County, 129 Neb. 268, 261 N.W. 360; to keep or cease from an appointed, proper, expected, or required action, Romero v. Department of Public Works, 17 Cal.2d 189, 109 P.2d 662, 665; to lapse, as a legacy which has never vested or taken effect, Sherman v. Richmond Hose Co., No. 2, 230 N.Y. 462, 130 N.E. 613; to leave unperformed; to omit; to neglect; to be wanting in action, Buffalo County v. Phelps County, 129 Neb. 268, 261 N.W. 360; A. Widemann Co. v. Digges, 21 Cal.App. 342, 131 P. 882, 883; Ginnochio v. Hydraulic Press Brick Co., D.C.Ohio, 266 F. 564, 569.

The difference between "fail" and "refuse" is that the latter involves an act of the will, while the former may be an act of inevitable necessity. Taylor v. Mason, 9 Wheat. 344, 6 L.Ed. 101. See Stallings v. Thomas, 55 Ark. 326, 18 S.W. 184; Persons v. Hight, 4 Ga. 497; Maestas v. American Metal Co. of New Mexico, 37 N.M. 203, 20 P.2d 924, 928.

The words "fail to comply," however, have in general the same operation in law as the words "refuse to comply." Ginnochio v. Hydraulic Press Brick Co., D.C.Ohio, 266 F. 564, 569. And an allegation in an indictment that defendant "failed and refused" to comply with a statute should not be expanded to carry the implication that there was a deliberate, intentional, and inexcusable refusal, especially where the indictment is not good without such expansion. Mackey v. U. S., C.C.A.Tenn., 290 F. 18, 21.

The term may imply an inopportunity to act. Worthington Pump & Machinery Corporation v. City of Cudahy, 182 Wis. 8, 195 N.W. 717.

FAILING CIRCUMSTANCES. Insolvency, that is, the lack of sufficient assets to pay one's debts. Brown v. State, 71 Tex.Cr.R. 353, 162 S.W. 339, 346. A person (or a corporation or institution) is said to be in failing circumstances when he is about to fail, that is, when he is actually insolvent and is acting in contemplation of giving up his business because he is unable to carry it on. Appeal of Millard, 62 Conn. 184, 25 A. 658; Utley v. Smith, 24 Conn. 310, 63 Am.Dec. 163.

A bank is in "failing circumstances" when, from any cause, it is unable to pay its debts in the ordinary or usual course of business, Sanders v. Owens, Mo.App., 47 S.W.2d 132, 134; when in state of uncertainty as to whether it will be able to sustain itself, depending on favorable or unfavorable contingencies, over which its officers have no control. Graf v. Allen, 230 Mo.App. 721, 74 S.W.2d 61, 66.

FAILING OF RECORD. When an action is brought against a person who alleges in his plea matter of record in bar of the action, and avers to prove it by the record, but the plaintiff saith *nul tiel record*, viz., denies there is any such record, upon which the defendant has a day given him by the court to bring it in, if he fail to do it, then he is said to fail of his record, and the plaintiff is entitled to sign judgment. Termes de la Ley.

FAILLITE. In French law. Bankruptcy; failure; the situation of a debtor who finds himself unable to fulfill his engagements. Code de Com. arts. 442, 580; Civil Code La. art. 3556, No. 11; 3 Massè, *Droit Comm.* 171; Guyot, *Répert.*

FAILS TO ATTEND AT THE TRIAL. Must be such a prolonged absence and failure to attend as to hinder and delay the orderly business of the court. Smith v. State, 42 Okl.Cr. 308, 275 P. 1071, 1072.

FAILURE. Abandonment or defeat, State v. Summers, 320 Mo. 189, 6 S.W.2d 883, 885. Deficiency, want, or lack; ineffectualness; inefficiency as measured by some legal standard; an unsuccessful attempt. State v. Butler, 81 Minn. 103, 83 N.W. 483; In re Moore, 79 Ind.App. 470, 138 N.E. 783. Lapse. Wilmington Trust Co. v. Wilmington Trust Co., 25 Del.Ch. 204, 15 A.2d 830, 834. See, also, Fail.

As used in municipal charter concerning "failure" to fill certain office by certain methods, the term presupposes efforts that had proved fruitless, and demands a bona fide and seasonable attempt to select by such methods. Scott v. Suitor, 103 Vt. 175, 152 A. 801, 802.

Discontinuance of business from insolvency, bankruptcy, or the like. State v. Thompson, 333 Mo. 1069, 64 S.W.2d 277.

"Failure" of appeal tax court to reduce assessment giving right of appeal means failure to reduce after application by owner asking that assessment be reduced. Aejis Co. v. Ray, 156 Md. 590, 144 A. 842, 844.

Insolvency. Goess v. A. D. H. Holding Corporation, C.C.A.N.Y., 85 F.2d 72, 74.

"Failure" is not always synonymous with "insolvency." State v. Tunnicliffe, 98 Fla. 731, 124 So. 279, 281.

Suspension or abandonment of business by a merchant, manufacturer, bank, etc., in consequence of insolvency, American Credit Indemnity Co. v. Carrolton Furniture Mfg. Co., C.C.A.N.Y., 95 F. 115, 36 C.C.A. 671; Terry v. Calman, 13 S.C. 220; State v. Lewis, 42 La.Ann. 847, 8 So. 602.

The failure to note action for trial is a "neglect" or "failure" within practice rule relating to dismissal of action without prejudice for want of prosecution. State ex rel. Woodworth & Cornell v. Superior Court for King County, 9 Wash.2d 37, 113 P.2d 527, 530.

The neglect of any duty may be a "failure." See Christhilf v. City of Baltimore, 152 Md. 204, 136 A. 527, 528; Washington v. State, 22 Okl.Cr. 69, 209 P. 967, 968. Compare, however, In re Green, 192 Cal. 714, 221 P. 903, 905. But to constitute a statutory offense, such as the failure to work on public roads, the term may imply willfulness and the absence of sufficient excuse. Jones v. State, 7 Ala. App. 180, 62 So. 306, 307.

FAILURE OF CONSIDERATION. As applied to notes, contracts, conveyances, etc., this term does not mean a want of consideration, but implies that a consideration, originally existing and good, has since become worthless or has ceased to exist or been extinguished, partially or entirely. Shirk v. Neible, 156 Ind. 66, 59 N.E. 281, 83 Am.St.Rep. 150; Williamson v. Cline, 40 W.Va. 194, 20 S.E. 920.

It means that sufficient consideration was contemplated by the parties at time contract was entered into, but either on account of some innate defect in the thing to be given or nonperformance in whole or in part of that which the promisee agreed to do or forbear nothing of value can be or is received by the promisee. Holcomb v. Long Beach Inv. Co., 129 Cal.App. 285, 19 P.2d 31, 36.

It occurs where the thing expected to be received by one party and given by the other party cannot be or has not been given without fault of the party contracting to give it. Edmund D. Cook, Inc. v. Commercial Casualty Ins. Co., 15 N.J.Misc. 256, 190 A. 99, 101.

"Fraud" cannot be pleaded as defense to note on ground that it amounts to "failure of consideration." Fraud is in its essence a tort, while "failure of consideration" ordinarily involves no actionable wrong, but occurs by reason of accident or mistake. Kothmann v. Southwest Co., Tex. Civ.App., 92 S.W.2d 272, 276.

Want of consideration as synonymous or distinguishable

"Failure of consideration" is in fact simply a want of consideration. Farrell v. Third Nat. Bank, 20 Tenn.App. 540, 101 S.W.2d 158, 163.

"Want of consideration" embraces transactions or instances where no consideration was intended to pass while "failure of consideration" implies that a valuable consideration moving from obligee to obligor was contemplated. In re Conrad's Estate, 333 Pa. 561, 3 A.2d 697, 699; Rauschenbach v. McDaniel's Estate, 122 W.Va. 632, 11 S.E.2d 852, 854.

There is "want of consideration" when nothing of value has ever been received, and "failure of consideration" where something of value was originally received which has since lost its value. Columbia Restaurant v. Sadnovick, La.App., 157 So. 280, 282.

FAILURE OF EVIDENCE. Judicially speaking, a total "failure of evidence" means not only the utter absence of all evidence, but it also means a failure to offer proof, either positive or inferential, to establish one or more of the many facts, the establishment of *all* of which is indispensable to the finding of the issue for the plaintiff. Cole v. Hebb, 7 Gill & J., Md., 28.

FAILURE OF GOOD BEHAVIOR. Enumerated in statute as ground for removal of a civil service employee means behavior contrary to recognized standards of propriety and morality, misconduct or wrong conduct. State ex rel. Ashbaugh v. Bahr, 68 Ohio App. 308, 40 N.E.2d 677, 680, 682.

FAILURE OF ISSUE. The failure at a fixed time, or the total extinction, of issue to take an estate limited over by an executory devise. A definite failure of issue is when a precise time is fixed by the will for the failure of issue, as in the case where there is a devise to one, but if he dies without issue or lawful issue living at the time of his death, etc. An indefinite failure of issue is the period when the issue or descendants of the first taker shall become extinct, and when there is no longer any issue of the issue of the grantee, without reference to any particular time or any particular event. 4 Kent, Comm. 275; Huxford v. Milligan, 50 Ind. 546; Parkhurst v. Harrower, 142 Pa. 432, 21 A. 826, 24 Am.St.Rep. 507; Woodlief v. Duckwall, 19 Ohio Cir.Ct.R. 564.

FAILURE OF JUSTICE. The defeat of a particular right, or the failure of reparation for a particular wrong, from the lack or inadequacy of a legal remedy for the enforcement of the one or the redress of the other. The term is also colloquially applied to the miscarriage of justice which occurs when the result of a trial is so palpably wrong as to shock the moral sense.

FAILURE OF PROOF. In this phrase, the word "failure" is of broader significance than either "want" or "lack." State v. Davis, 154 La. 295, 97 So. 449, 456.

A "failure of proof" consists in failure to prove the cause of action or defense in its entire scope and meaning. Breslin-Griffitt Carpet Co. v. Asadorian, Mo.App., 145 S.W.2d 494, 496.

An omission of a material fact from special finding is deemed a "failure of proof". Kelley, Glover & Vale v. Heitman, 220 Ind. 625, 44 N.E.2d 981, 984.

As used in a statute authorizing dismissal of suit without prejudice on account of failure of proof, the term does not mean failure to convince the court by preponderance of evidence, but failure to make prima facie case. Crim v. Thompson, 112 Or. 399, 229 P. 916, 920; Wolke v. Schmidt, 112 Or. 99, 228 P. 921, 923.

Under a statute pertaining to variance, a "failure of proof" results when the evidence offered so far departs from the cause of action pleaded that it may be said fairly that the allegations of the pleading in their general scope and meaning are unproved. Chealey v. Purdy, 54 Mont. 489, 171 P. 926, 927; Nelson v. Dowgiallo, 73 Or. 342, 143 P. 924, 925.

Where evidence is such as would support either of two contradictory inferences, or presumptions, respecting the ultimate facts, there is a "failure of proof". Muesenfechter v. St. Louis Car Co., Mo.App., 139 S.W.2d 1102, 1106.

Where time is not of essence of offense, showing that crime, which information alleged was committed "on or about" certain day, was committed on next day, was not a failure of proof, even had words "on or about" been omitted. State v. Woodall, Mo., 300 S.W. 712, 713.

FAILURE OF RECORD. Failure of the defendant to produce a record which he has alleged and relied on in his plea.

See Failing of Record.

FAILURE OF TITLE. The inability or failure of a vendor to make good title to the whole or a part of the property which he has contracted to sell. See Alger-Sullivan Lumber Co. v. Union Trust Co., 207 Ala. 138, 92 So. 254, 257.

FAILURE OF TRUST. The lapsing or nonefficiency of a proposed trust, by reason of the defect or insufficiency of the deed or instrument creating it, or on account of illegality, indefiniteness, or other legal impediment.

FAILURE OTHERWISE THAN UPON MERITS. Imports some action by court by which plaintiff is defeated without a trial upon the merits. Kimberlin v. Stoley, 49 Ohio App. 1, 194 N.E. 885.

FAILURE TO ACT. Under statute setting up system of classification of offices and giving incumbent right to an administrative appeal in case of any failure to act by officers in charge of the classification plan, the words "failure to act" referred to duties in connection with classification of offices. Dolan v. Suffolk County, 310 Mass. 318, 37 N.E.2d 998, 1000.

FAILURE TO BARGAIN COLLECTIVELY. An employer's refusal to discuss with union, as employees' bargaining agency, questions involving conditions of employment and interpretation of contract constituted a "failure to bargain collectively" with union. Rapid Roller Co. v. National Labor Relations Board, C.C.A.7, 126 F.2d 452, 459.

FAILURE TO COOPERATE. Material or intentional, or fraudulent variations of statements, of assured's driver as given at trial and before trial would constitute failure to co-operate with automobile insurance company. Brooks Transp. Co. v. Merchants' Mut. Casualty Co., 6 W.W.Harr. 40, 171 A. 207.

FAILURE TO LOOK. A failure to see an object within range of vision is equivalent. Brooks v. City of Ste. Genevieve, Mo.App., 164 S.W.2d 164, 168.

FAILURE TO MAKE DELIVERY. Misdelivery is "failure to make delivery". Coos Bay Amusement Co. v. American Ry. Express Co., 129 Or. 216, 277 P. 107, 109. Nondelivery is "failure to make delivery". Mt. Arbor Nurseries v. American Ry. Express Co., 221 Mo.App. 241, 300 S.W. 1051, 1053. This phrase is fully adequate to cover all cases where delivery has not been made as required. Kahn v. American Railway Express Co., 88 W.Va. 17, 106 S.E. 126, 128; Watts v. Southern Ry. Co., 139 S.C. 516, 138 S.E. 290, 293; Georgia, F. & A. Ry. Co. v. Blish Milling Co., 241 U.S. 190, 36 S.Ct. 541, 543, 60 L.Ed. 948.

FAILURE TO MEET OBLIGATIONS. Bank's failure to pay depositors on demand constitutes "failure to meet obligations" in most cases. State of Ohio ex rel. Squire v. Union Trust Co. of Pittsburgh, 137 Pa.Super. 75, 8 A.2d 476, 480.

Where bank closed its doors and ceased to transact business or make transfers of capital stock, and thereafter ordinary deposits could not be drawn out and checks in process of collection were dishonored, returned unpaid, was "failure to meet obligations". State of Ohio ex rel. Squire v. Union Trust Co. of Pittsburgh, 137 Pa.Super. 75, 8 A.2d 476, 480.

FAILURE TO PERFORM. As regards reciprocal promises, allegation of defendant's "failure to perform" when demanded is equivalent to allegation of "refusal to perform," unless performance by plaintiff is condition precedent to cause of action. Brooks v. Scoville, 81 Utah 163, 17 P.2d 218, 220.

FAILURES IN REVENUE. Terms "casual deficits" and "failures in revenue," within provision authorizing Legislature to contract debt to meet such deficits, are synonymous. State Budget Commission v. Lebus, 244 Ky. 700, 51 S.W.2d 965.

FAINT (or FEIGNED) ACTION. In old English practice. An action was so called where the party bringing it had no title to recover, although the words of the writ were true; a *false* action was properly where the words of the writ were false. Litt. § 689; Co. Litt. 361.

FAINT PLEADER. A fraudulent, false, or collusive manner of pleading to the deception of a third person.

FAIR, *n.* In English law. A greater species of market; a privileged market. Cowell; Cunningham, Law Dict. It is an incorporeal hereditament, granted by royal patent, or established by prescription presupposing a grant from the crown. A public mart or place of buying or selling. 1 Bla.Comm. 274.

Though etymologically signifying a market for buying and selling exhibited articles, it includes a place for the exhibition of agricultural and mechanical products. State v. Long, 48 Ohio St. 509, 28 N.E. 1038.

A fair is usually attended by a greater concourse of people than a market, for the amusement of whom various exhibitions are gotten up. McCulloch, Comm.Dict.; Wharton, Dict.

A fair is a franchise which is obtained by a grant from the crown. 2d Inst. 220; 3 Mod. 123; 1 Ld.Raym. 341; 2 Saund. 172; 1 Rolle, Abr. 106; Tomlin; Cunningham, Law Dict.

In the earlier English law, the franchise to hold a fair conferred certain important privileges; and fairs, as legally recognized institutions, possessed distinctive legal characteristics. Most of these privileges and characteristics, however, are now obsolete. In America, fairs, in the ancient technical sense, are unknown, and, in the modern and popular sense, they are entirely voluntary and nonlegal, and transactions arising in or in connection with them are subject to the ordinary rules governing sales, etc.

FAIR, *adj.* Equitable as a basis for exchange; reasonable; a fair value. Utah Assets Corporation v. Dooley Bros. Ass'n, 92 Utah 577, 70 P.2d 738, 741. Honest. East Bay Municipal Utility Dist. v. Kieffer, 99 Cal.App. 240, 278 P. 476, 482. Impartial, free from suspicion, bias, etc. Looney v. Elliott, Tex.Civ.App., 52 S.W.2d 949, 952. Just; equitable; even-handed; equal, as between conflicting interests.

FAIR ABRIDGMENT. In copyright law. An abridgment consisting not merely in the arrangement of excerpts, but one involving real and substantial condensation of the materials by the exercise of intellectual labor and judgment. Folsom v. Marsh, 9 Fed.Cas. 345.

FAIR AND EQUITABLE. A proposed plan to dissolve parent public utility holding company and to reclassify its preferred and voting common stock is "fair and equitable", if preferred stockholders' rights are transmuted into their equitable equivalents. In re Securities and Exchange Commission, C.C.A.Del., 142 F.2d 411, 419.

As condition of confirmation under provisions of Bankruptcy Act relating to corporate reorganization, signify that the final arrangement must conform to principle that unsecured creditors are entitled to priority over stockholders to full extent of their debts and that any scaling down of claims of creditors without fair compensating advantage to them which is prior to rights of stockholders is inadmissible. Securities and Exchange Commission v. United States Realty & Improvement Co., 310 U.S. 434, 60 S.Ct. 1044, 1051, 84 L.Ed. 1293; In re Janson Steel & Iron Co., D.C.Pa., 47 F.Supp. 652, 655, 656.

Statutory requirements of "fair and equitable" railroad reorganization are satisfied so long as creditors receive full compensatory treatment and each group shares in securities of the whole enterprise on an equitable basis. Ecker v. Western Pac. R. R. Corporation, 318 U.S. 448, 63 S.Ct. 692, 713, 87 L.Ed. 892.

FAIR AND EQUITABLE VALUE. In a contract to purchase a waterworks plant at fair and equitable value, the amount is to be determined not by capitalization of the earnings nor limited to the cost of reproducing the plant, but allowance should be made for the additional value created by connection with and supply of buildings, although the company did not own the connections. National Waterworks Co. v. Kansas City, Mo., 62 F. 863.

FAIR AND FEASIBLE. As test in determining whether corporate reorganization plan should be approved means economically expedient, without discrimination or destruction of vested rights. In re Stanley Drug Co., D.C.Pa., 22 F.Supp. 664, 665.

FAIR AND FULL EQUIVALENT FOR LOSS. The same as a full and perfect equivalent. Fonticello Mineral Springs Co. v. City of Richmond, 147 Va. 355, 137 S.E. 458, 460.

FAIR AND IMPARTIAL JURY means that every member of the jury must be a fair and impartial juror. City of San Antonio v. McKenzie Const. Co., 136 Tex. 315, 150 S.W.2d 989, 993.

FAIR AND IMPARTIAL SYSTEM OF SEPARATION FROM SERVICE. Of employees of department of state involves specific reasons for removal and reasonable hearing before some designated and proper authority. Welch v. State Board of Social Security and Welfare, 53 Ariz. 167, 87 P.2d 109, 112.

FAIR AND IMPARTIAL TRIAL. One where accused's legal rights are safeguarded and respected. Floyd v. State, 166 Miss. 15, 148 So. 226, 232; Raney v. Commonwealth, 287 Ky. 492, 153 S.W. 2d 935, 937, 938.

A fair and impartial trial by a jury of one's peers contemplates counsel to look after one's defense, compulsory attendance of witnesses, if need be, and a reasonable time in the light of all prevailing circumstances to investigate, properly prepare, and present the defense. Christie v. State, 94 Fla. 469, 114 So. 450, 451.

One wherein defendant is permitted to be represented by counsel and neither witnesses nor counsel are intimidated. George v. Kanape, 284 Ill.App. 648, 3 N.E.2d 149. One wherein no undue advantage is taken by the district attorney or any one else. People v. Nationwide News Service, 16 N.Y.S.2d 277, 279, 172 Misc. 752. One wherein witnesses of litigants are permitted to testify under rules of court within proper bounds of judicial discretion, and under law governing testimony of witnesses with right in parties to testify, if qualified, and of counsel to be heard. Fessenden v. Fessenden, 32 Ohio App. 16, 165 N.E. 746, 748.

Defendant has a "fair and impartial trial" when opportunity is given him to object and except to what is done to his prejudice upon the trial. State v. Burns, 181 Iowa 1098, 165 N.W. 346, 347.

Such a trial contemplates a trial before a jury of 12 impartial and unbiased men, neither more nor less, in the presence and under the superintendence of a judge having the power to instruct them as to the law and advise them in respect to the facts, and the establishment of guilt by a unanimous verdict of such jury. Baker v. Hudspeth, C.C.A. Kan., 129 F.2d 779, 782, 783. It contemplates counsel, compulsory attendance of witnesses, and time in which to prepare for trial. Wood v. State, 155 Fla. 256, 19 So.2d 872, 875. It excludes jurors who have an opinion on the merits of the case, based on such testimony as may reasonably be expected to be presented on the trial, or an opinion founded on personal ill will towards the accused. Murphy v. State, 72 Okl.Cr. 1, 112 P.2d 438, 453, 454. It includes a reasonable opportunity to prepare for trial. Cruthirds v. State, 190 Miss. 892, 2 So.2d 145, 146.

It requires that the jury of 12 men chosen to sit in judgment shall have no fixed opinion concerning the guilt or innocence of one on trial. Baker v. Hudspeth, C.C.A.Kan., 129 F.2d 779, 782, 783. There must not only be fair and impartial jury, and learned and upright judge, but there should be atmosphere of calm in which witnesses can deliver their testimony without fear and intimidation, in which attorneys can assert accused's rights freely and fully, and in which the truth may be received and given credence without fear of violence. Raney v. Commonwealth, 287 Ky. 492, 153 S.W.2d 935, 937, 938.

FAIR AND PROPER LEGAL ASSESSMENT. Such as places the value of property on a fair, equal, and uniform basis with other property of like character and value throughout the county and state. Edward Hines Yellow Pine Trustees v. Knox, 144 Miss. 560, 108 So. 907, 911.

FAIR AND REASONABLE COMPENSATION. Full compensation. Pfeiffer v. Schee, Mo.App., 107 S.W.2d 170, 175.

FAIR AND REASONABLE CONTRACT. One which, when made with an infant, must not be one wasting the infant's estate, but must be a provident one, advantageous to the minor. Berglund v. American Multigraph Sales Co., 135 Minn. 67, 160 N.W. 191, 193.

FAIR AND REASONABLE MARKET VALUE. Under statute requiring determination of fair and reasonable market value of mortgaged premises in connection with deficiency judgment, means market value and should be determined by those market conditions prevailing where willing buyers meet willing sellers and deal on that basis. Berkshire Life Ins. Co. of Pittsfield, Mass. v. Van Voorhis, 245 App.Div. 592, 283 N.Y.S. 95, 97, 98.

FAIR AND REASONABLE TOLLS. The term is broad enough to include such fair and reasonable charges as may be deemed "fair and reasonable" for value of privilege the toll payer obtains for his money in use of bridge. In re Tolls on St. Johns River Bridge, 108 Fla. 172, 146 So. 99, 100.

FAIR AND REASONABLE VALUE. This phrase in a statute imposing a tax on property means the best price obtainable at a voluntary sale, to be paid at once in money, and excluding any additional amount that might be had were credit or terms allowed. State v. Woodward, 208 Ala. 31, 93 So. 826.

Provision of statute for appraisal of farm debtor's property at "fair and reasonable value, not necessarily market value," for purpose of discharging debtor from his obligations, means that market value is minimum value to be found, beyond which other circumstances may be considered to arrive at "fair and reasonable value". Louisville Joint Stock Land Bank v. Radford, C.C.A.Ky., 74 F.2d 576, 582.

FAIR AND VALUABLE CONSIDERATION. One which is a substantial compensation for the property conveyed, or which is reasonable, in view of the surrounding circumstances and conditions, in contradistinction to an adequate consideration. Jones v. Wey, 124 Okl. 1, 253 P. 291, 292; Lucas v. Coker, 189 Okl. 95, 113 P.2d 589, 590.

FAIR CASH MARKET VALUE. Terms "cash market value", "fair market value", "reasonable market value" or "fair cash market value" are substantially synonymous. Housing Authority of Birmingham Dist. v. Title Guarantee Loan & Trust Co., 243 Ala. 157, 8 So.2d 835, 837. Terms "market value," "fair market value," "cash market value," and "fair cash market value" are synonymous. Fort Worth & D. N. Ry. Co. v. Sugg, Tex.Civ.App., 68 S.W.2d 570, 572.

FAIR CASH VALUE. The phrase is practically synonymous with "reasonable value," and "actual cash value," meaning the fair or reasonable cash price for which the property can be sold on the market. Montesano Lumber & Mfg. Co. v. Portland Iron Works, 94 Or. 677, 186 P. 428, 432; State v. Woodward, 208 Ala. 31, 93 So. 826, 827.

The words "fair cash value" and the words "fair market value" are frequently treated as synonymous. Commissioner of Corporations and Taxation v. Boston Edison Co., 310 Mass. 674, 39 N.E.2d 584, 593.

"Fair cash value" of dissenting stockholder's stock is the intrinsic worth of the stock and not necessarily its market price. Miller v. Canton Motor Coach, 58 Ohio App. 94, 16 N.E.2d 486, 488; Adams v. U. S. Distributing Corp., 184 Va. 134, 34 S.E.2d 244, 250, 162 A.L.R. 1227.

For tax purposes "fair cash value", means the highest price the property would bring free of incumbrances, at a fair and voluntary private sale for cash. Commonwealth v. Sutcliffe, 287 Ky. 809, 155 S.W.2d 243, 245. The price that an owner willing but not compelled to sell ought to receive from one willing but not compelled to buy. Assessors of Quincy v. Boston Consolidated Gas Co., 309 Mass. 60, 34 N.E.2d 623, 626. The price that the property would bring at a voluntary sale where the owner is ready, willing and able to sell but not compelled to do so. In re 168 Adams Bldg. Corporation, C.C.A.Ill., 105 F.2d 704, 708; People ex rel. McGaughey v. Wilson, 367 Ill. 494, 12 N.E.2d 5, 6; the price which some one will pay for it in open market. Donovan v. City of Haverhill, 141 N.E. 564, 565, 247 Mass. 69, 30 A.L.R. 358.

It is ascertained by a consideration of all elements making it attractive for valuable use to one under no compulsion to purchase, but yet willing to buy for a fair price, attributing to each element of value the amount it adds to the price likely to be offered by such a buyer. Massachusetts General Hospital v. Inhabitants of Belmont, 233 Mass. 190, 124 N.E. 21, 26.

Taxable "fair cash value", of annuity contract was to be determined according to mortality tables. Evans v. Boyle County Board of Sup'rs, 296 Ky. 353, 177 S.W.2d 137, 139.

Under corporate franchise tax statute, the term "fair cash value" meant exchange value, Commissioner of Corporations and Taxation v. Boston Edison Co., 310 Mass. 674, 39 N.E.2d 584, 592, 593.

FAIR COMMENT. A term used in the law of libel, applying to statements made by a writer in an honest belief of their truth, relating to official acts, even though the statements are not true in fact. People v. Hebbard, 96 Misc. 617, 162 N.Y.S. 80, 92. In a privileged communication the words used, if defamatory and libelous, are excused, while in "fair comment" the words are not a defamation and not libelous. Van Lonkhuyzen v. Daily News Co., 203 Mich. 570, 170 N.W. 93, 99.

Defense of "fair comment" is not destroyed by circumstance that jury may believe that the comment is logically unsound, but it suffices that a reasonable man may honestly entertain such opinion, on facts found. Cohalan v. New York Tribune, 172 Misc. 20, 15 N.Y.S.2d 58, 60, 61.

"Fair comment" must be based on facts truly stated, must not contain imputations of corrupt or dishonorable motives except as warranted by the facts, and must be honest expression of writer's real opinion. Cohalan v. New York World-Telegram Corporation, 16 N.Y.S.2d 706, 712, 172 Misc. 1061; Hall v. Binghamton Press Co., 33 N.Y.S.2d 840, 848, 263 App.Div. 403.

Imputation to official of corrupt or dishonorable motives is justified as "fair comment" if it is inference which fair-minded man might reasonably draw from facts. Tanzer v. Crowley Pub. Corporation, 240 App.Div. 203, 268 N.Y.S. 620.

Mere exaggeration, slight irony, or wit, or all those delightful touches of style going to make article readable, do not push beyond limitations of fair comment. Briarcliff Lodge Hotel v. Westchester Newspapers, 260 N.Y. 106, 183 N.E. 193, 197.

FAIR COMPETITION. Open, equitable, just competition, which is fair as between competitors and as between any of them and his customers. U. S. v. Sutherland, D.C.Mo., 9 F.Supp. 204, 205; U. S. v. National Garment Co., D.C.Mo., 10 F. Supp. 104, 107. Opposite of "unfair competition." Wilentz v. Crown Laundry Service, 116 N.J.Eq. 40, 172 A. 331, 333; State on Complaint of Lief v. Packard-Bamberger & Co., 123 N.J.L. 180, 8 A.2d 291, 293.

The words "fair competition" in National Industrial Recovery Act do not include price fixing, since price regulation is the antithesis of competition, fair or otherwise. Mississippi Valley Hardwood Co. v. McClanahan, D.C. Tenn., 8 F.Supp. 388.

FAIR CONSIDERATION. A fair equivalent. Farmers' Exchange Bank v. Oneida Motor Truck Co., 202 Wis. 266, 232 N.W. 536, 538; Drury v. State Capitol Bank of Eastern Shore Trust Co., 163 Md. 84, 161 A. 176, 179. One which, under all the circumstances, is honest, reasonable, and free from suspicion, whether or not strictly "adequate" or "full." Ferguson v. Dickson, C.C.A.N.J., 300 F. 961, 963. Payment of an antecedent debt. McDougal v. Central Union Conference Ass'n of Seventh Day Adventists, C.C.A.Colo., 110 F.2d 939, 942. Pre-existing debt. In re Seim Const. Co., D.C.Md., 37 F.Supp. 855, 858. Reasonable in contractual sense, and free from suspicion of intent to evade inheritance tax, though not fraudulent. Phillips v. Gnichtel, C.C.A.N.J., 27 F.2d 662, 665.

In bankruptcy law, one which is honest or free from suspicion, or one actually valuable, but not necessarily adequate or a full equivalent. Myers v. Fultz, 124 Iowa, 437, 100 N.W. 351.

Under Fraudulent Conveyance Law. An antecedent debt, Klaseus v. Meester, 173 Minn. 468, 217 N.W. 593, 594; Barishefsky v. Cohen, 299 Mass. 360, 12 N.E.2d 832, 833; Holander v. Gautier, 114 N.J.Eq. 485, 168 A. 860, 862; an enforceable promise by grantee at time of transfer, Holander v. Gautier, 114 N.J.Eq. 485, 168 A. 860, 861; full and adequate consideration, Klaseus v. Meester, 173 Minn. 468, 217 N.W. 593, 594; good-faith satisfaction of an antecedent debt, Bennett v. Rodman & English, D.C.N.Y., 2 F.Supp. 355, 358; one which fairly represents the value of the property transferred, Bianco v. Lay, 313 Mass. 444, 48 N.E.2d 36, 40; one which is not disproportionate to the value of the property conveyed. Buhl v. McDowell, 51 S.D. 603, 216 N.W. 346, 347; Klaseus v. Meester, 173 Minn. 468, 217 N.W. 593, 594; the test of "fair consideration", is whether conveyance, by debtor, which includes every payment of money, renders the debtor execution proof. McCaslin v. Schouten, 294 Mich. 180, 292 N.W. 696, 699.

FAIR DAMAGES are something more than nominal damages; and are even more than such damages as would compensate for injury suffered. Gurfein v. Howell, 142 Va. 197, 128 S.E. 644, 646.

FAIR EQUIVALENT. As used in statute providing that fair consideration is given for property exchanged at fair equivalent means value at time of conveyance; "equivalent" means equal in worth or value; "fair" means equitable as a basis for exchange; reasonable; a fair value. Utah

Assets Corporation v. Dooley Bros. Ass'n, 92 Utah 577, 70 P.2d 738, 741.

As used in Uniform Fraudulent Conveyance Law does not mean that adequacy of consideration is to be determined by weighing value of goods sold and price received in very precise scales. Bianco v. Lay, 313 Mass. 444, 48 N.E.2d 36, 40.

The test to be used in determining what constitutes a "fair equivalent" under Fraudulent Conveyance Act, for conveyance by debtor, is whether the conveyance, which includes every payment of money, renders the debtor execution proof. McCaslin v. Schouten, 294 Mich. 180, 292 N.W. 696, 699.

FAIR HEARING. One in which authority is fairly exercised; that is, consistently with the fundamental principles of justice embraced within the conception of due process of law. U. S. ex rel. Dean, for and on behalf of Mahfood, v. Reynolds, D.C.Ind., 2 F.Supp. 290, 291.

A hearing before the immigration authorities is "fair" if conducted with due regard to those rights of the alien that are embraced in the phrase "due process of law". United States ex rel. Eng Fon Sing v. Reimer, D.C.N.Y., 30 F.Supp. 602, 604.

Although rules of evidence and of procedure have not been strictly followed a hearing may be "fair." Ex parte Bridges, D.C.Cal., 49 F.Supp. 292, 306; U. S. ex rel. Shaw v. Van De Mark, D.C.N.Y., 3 F.Supp. 101, 102.

Fair hearing of an alien's right to enter the United States means a hearing before the immigration officers in accordance with the fundamental principles that inhere in due process of law, and implies that alien shall not only have a fair opportunity to present evidence in his favor, but shall be apprised of the evidence against him, so that at the conclusion of the hearing he may be in a position to know all of the evidence on which the matter is to be decided; it being not enough that the immigration officials meant to be fair. Ex parte Petkos, D.C.Mass., 212 F. 275, 277. See, also, Ex parte Keisuki Sata, D.C.Cal., 215 F. 173, 176.

The obligation of a local draft board to grant a registrant a "fair hearing" on matter of classification does not mean a trial by court or a trial in strict or formal sense. Rase v. United States, C.C.A.Mich., 129 F.2d 204, 210; Seele v. U. S., C.C.A.Mo., 133 F.2d 1015, 1022.

The test of a "fair hearing" before the National Labor Relations Board is whether the issues were clearly defined, so that the employer could address itself to the charges made against it. National Labor Relations Board v. Air Associates, C.C.A.2, 121 F.2d 586, 591.

Where students were charged with sale of examination papers and expelled, a "fair hearing" did not contemplate a trial as in a chancery court or court of law. State ex rel. Sherman v. Hyman, 180 Tenn. 99, 171 S.W.2d 822, 826.

FAIR KNOWLEDGE OR SKILL. A reasonable degree of knowledge or measure of skill. Jones v. Angell, 95 Ind. 382.

FAIR MARKET PRICE means not only that the price be ascertained by sales, but that the sales so made and the subject-matter of the sales are to be considered. In re Spitly's Estate, 124 Cal. App. 642, 13 P.2d 385, 386.

For inheritance tax purposes, "clear market price" is synonymous with "fair market price." In re Spitly's Estate, 124 Cal.App. 642, 13 P.2d 385, 386.

For tax purposes, means price fixed by manufacturer for sale of its products where there is no market price other than price so fixed. Bourjois, Inc., v. McGowan, D.C.N. Y., 12 F.Supp. 787, 792.

Within statute governing valuation of property for assessment of income tax, resultant of two opposing views of willing seller and willing buyer where seller is not compelled to sell and buyer is not required to buy. Vale v. du Pont, Del., 7 W.W.Harr. 254, 182 A. 668, 673, 674, 103 A. L.R. 946.

Ordinarily, "actual cash value," "fair market price," and "market value" are synonymous terms. Butler v. Ætna Ins. Co. of Hartford, Conn., 64 N.D. 764, 256 N.W. 214.

FAIR MARKET VALUE. Price at which a willing seller and a willing buyer will trade. Montrose Cemetery Co. v. Commissioner of Internal Revenue, C.C.A.7, 105 F.2d 238, 242; Utah Assets Corporation v. Dooley Bros. Ass'n, 92 Utah 577, 70 P.2d 738, 741.

It has also been defined to mean: Amount that would in all probability have been arrived at between owner willing to sell and purchaser desiring to buy, Karlson v. U. S., C.C.A.Minn., 82 F.2d 330, 337; Whitlow v. Commissioner of Internal Revenue, C.C.A.8, 82 F.2d 569, 572; exchangeable value, Walls v. Commissioner of Internal Revenue, C. C.A.Wyo., 60 F.2d 347, 350; price at which a willing seller under no compulsion and a willing buyer under no compulsion will trade, Rheinstrom v. Willcuts, D.C.Minn., 26 F. Supp. 306, 310; State ex rel. Farmers & Merchants State Bank v. Schanke, 247 Wis. 182, 19 N.W.2d 264, 267; Talbot v. City of Norfolk, 158 Va. 387, 163 S.E. 100, 101; price at which specified quantity of a given economic good is actually sold, or general or future power in exchange, Jenkins v. Smith, D.C.Conn., 21 F.Supp. 251, 253; price such as a capable and diligent business man could presently obtain from the property after conferring with those accustomed to buy such property, Appeal of Hickey, 124 Pa. Super. 213, 188 A. 95, 96; price which a willing purchaser would pay a willing seller, Ozette Ry. Co. v. Grays Harbor County, 16 Wash.2d 459, 133 P.2d 983, 988; Baetjer v. United States, C.C.A.Puerto Rico, 143 F.2d 391, 396; price which property would bring at a fair sale between parties dealing on equal terms, Union Nat. Bank of Pittsburgh v. Crump, 349 Pa. 339, 37 A.2d 733, 735; sum a purchaser willing but not obliged to buy would pay an owner willing but not obliged to sell, Appeal of Hickey, 124 Pa.Super. 213, 188 A. 95, 96; City of Tampa v. Colgan, 121 Fla. 218, 163 So. 577, 582; City of Tulsa v. Creekmore, 167 Okl. 298, 29 P.2d 101, 103; value in money as between one who wishes to purchase and one who wishes to sell, Wood v. United States, Ct.Cl., 29 F.Supp. 853, 859, 860; Stiles v. Commissioner of Internal Revenue, C.C.A.Fla., 69 F.2d 951, 952.

"Fair market value" assumes agreement between owner willing but not obliged to sell for cash and buyer desirous but not compelled to purchase. Lewis v. Beall, 162 Md. 18, 158 A. 354, 356. It implies not only a willing buyer, but a willing seller. Syracuse Engineering Co. v. Haight, C.C.A.N.Y., 110 F.2d 468, 471. It means neither panic value, auction value, speculative value, nor a value fixed by depressed or inflated prices. In re Board of Water Supply of City of New York, 277 N.Y. 452, 14 N.E.2d 789, 792. It resides in estimate and determination of what is fair, economic, just and equitable value under normal conditions. State ex rel. Buck v. Rapp, Sup., 36 N.Y.S.2d 790, 794.

As of a certain date. Fair market value of a given date means amount stock is fairly worth as marketable security or equity to be bought and sold in course of business, Robertson v. Routzahn, D.C.Ohio, 1 F.Supp. 355, 356; price that could actually have been realized on that date, Jenkins v. Smith, D.C.Conn., 21 F.Supp. 251; price that probably would have resulted had goods been exchanged between willing, informed, and normal buyer and similar seller, Jenkins v. Smith, D.C.Conn., 21 F.Supp. 251; price that property would bring at voluntary sale to willing buyer; both seller and buyer having adequate knowledge of material facts affecting value, Robertson v. Routzahn, C.C.A. Ohio, 75 F.2d 537, 539; price which intelligent and reasonable buyers and sellers, having due regard for their mercenary interests, would have most likely agreed upon. Vale v. State School Tax Department, 6 W.W.Harr. 252, 173 A. 795.

It resides in an estimate and a determination of what is the fair, economic, just, and equitable value under normal conditions. In re Board of Water Supply of City of New York, 277 N.Y. 452, 14 N.E.2d 789, 792.

"Fair market value" of stock received by taxpayer in payment of bonuses was value of stock received in extinguishment of bonus claims and not amount credited for bonuses. Commissioner of Internal Revenue v. Vandeveer, C.C.A.6, 114 F.2d 719, 722.

Primary evidence of "fair market value" of stock is what willing purchasers pay to willing sellers on open market. Hazeltine Corporation v. Commissioner of Internal Revenue, C.C.A.3, 89 F.2d 513, 518.

Synonymous or identical terms are:

Actual cash value. Stiles v. Commissioner of Internal Revenue, C.C.A.Fla., 69 F.2d 951, 952; actual value, Appeals of Matson, 152 Pa.Super. 424, 33 A.2d 464, 465; cash market value, West Texas Hotel Co. v. City of El Paso, Tex.Civ.App., 83 S.W.2d 772, 775; Housing Authority of Birmingham Dist. v. Title Guarantee Loan & Trust Co., 243 Ala. 157, 8 So.2d 835, 837; cash value, Thomison v. Hillcrest Athletic Ass'n, 9 W.W.Harr. 590, 5 A.2d 236, 238; In re Ryerson's Estate, 239 Wis. 120, 300 N.W. 782, 784, 785; clear market value, In re Ryerson's Estate, 239 Wis. 120, 300 N.W. 782, 784, 785; fair cash market value, Housing Authority of Birmingham Dist. v. Title Guarantee Loan & Trust Co., 243 Ala. 157, 8 So.2d 835, 837; fair cash value, Commissioner of Corporations and Taxation v. Boston Edison Co., 310 Mass. 674, 39 N.E.2d 584, 593; market value, Fort Worth & D. N. Ry. Co. v. Sugg, Tex.Civ.App., 68 S.W.2d 570, 572; United States v. 3969.59 Acres of Land, D.C.Idaho, 56 F.Supp. 831, 837; reasonable market value, Housing Authority of Birmingham Dist. v. Title Guarantee Loan & Trust Co., 243 Ala. 157, 8 So.2d 835, 837; true cash value, Appeals of Matson, 152 Pa.Super. 424, 33 A.2d 464, 465; value, United States v. 3969.59 Acres of Land, D.C. Idaho, 56 F.Supp. 831, 837.

Value of ıeal property for railroad purposes approximated by capitalizing net income considered with other factors, may be accepted as indicative of "fair market value". Appeal of Pitney, 20 N.J.Misc. 448, 28 A.2d 660, 664.

FAIR ON ITS FACE. A tax deed "fair on its face," is one which cannot be shown to be illegal without extraneous evidence. Denny v. Stevens, 52 Wyo. 253, 73 P.2d 308, 310, 113 A.L.R. 1337.

A process fair on its face does not mean that it must appear to be perfectly regular or in all respects in accord with proper practice and after the most approved form, but that it shall apparently be process lawfully issued and such as the officer may lawfully serve, and a process is fair on its face which proceeds from a court, magistrate, or body having authority of law to issue process of that nature and which is legal in form and on its face contains nothing to notify or fairly apprise the officer that it is issued without authority. Brown v. Hadwin, 182 Mich. 491, 148 N.W. 693, L.R.A.1915B, 505.

FAIR PERSUASION means argument, exhortation, or entreaty addressed to a person without threat of physical harm or economic loss, or persistent molestation or harassment or material and fraudulent misrepresentations. City of Reno v. Second Judicial District Court in and for Washoe County, 59 Nev. 416, 95 P.2d 994, 998, 125 A.L.R. 948.

FAIR-PLAY MEN. A local irregular tribunal which existed in Pennsylvania about the year 1769, as to which see Serg. Land Laws Pa. 77; 2 Smith, Laws Pa. 195.

FAIR PLEADER. See Beau-pleader.

FAIR PREPONDERANCE. In the law of evidence. A "clear" preponderance. M. E. Smith & Co. v. Kimble, 38 S.D. 511, 162 N.W. 162, 163. Evidence sufficient to create in the minds of the triers of fact the conviction that the party upon whom is the burden has established its case. Jackson Furniture Co. v. Lieberman, 65 R.I 224, 14 A.2d 27, 32. The greater and weightier evidence, the more convincing evidence. Barbero v. Pellegrino, 108 N.J.L. 156, 156 A. 765. The greater weight of the evidence. Belmont Hotel v. New Jersey Title Guaranty & Trust Co., 22 N.J. Misc. 261, 37 A.2d 681, 682. Weight, credit, and value. Chenery v. Russell, 132 Me. 130, 167 A. 857, 858.

If evidence on any material allegation is equally balanced, verdict should be for defendant. Funk v. Bonham, 204 Ind. 170, 183 N.E. 312, 317.

Such a superiority of evidence on one side that the fact of its outweighing the evidence on the other side can be perceived if the whole evidence is fairly considered. Bryan v. Railroad Co., 63 Iowa, 464, 19 N.W. 295; City Bank's Appeal, 54 Conn. 274, 7 A. 548. Such evidence as when weighed with that which is offered to oppose it, has more convincing power in the minds of the jury. Neely v. Detroit Sugar Co., 138 Mich. 469, 101 N.W. 665, 666.

The probability of truth; In re Oliver's Will, 126 Misc. 511, 214 N.Y.S. 154, 166; not necessarily the largest number of witnesses; Verdi v. Donahue, 91 Conn. 448, 99 A. 1041, 1043; Chenery v. Russell, 132 Me. 130, 167 A. 857, 858.

The term conveys the idea of something more than a preponderance. Bryan v. Chicago, R. I. & P. Ry. Co., 63 Iowa, 464, 19 N.W. 295, 296; De St. Aubin v. Marshall Field & Co., 27 Colo. 414, 62 P. 199, 201; The term is not a technical term, but simply means that evidence which outweighs that which is offered to oppose it, and does not necessarily mean the greater number of witnesses. Devencenzi v. Cassinelli, 28 Nev. 222, 81 P. 41, 42 (quoting and adopting definition in Strand v. Chicago & N. M. Ry. Co., 67 Mich. 380, 34 N.W. 712); Hynes v. Metropolitan St. Ry. Co., 31 Misc. 825, 64 N.Y.S. 382, 383.

FAIR PRICE. The words "fair price" have been held to be of an ascertainable valuation. McCormick v. Tissier, 222 Ala. 422, 133 So. 22, 24. For "Fair Market Price," see that title.

FAIR RENT. A reasonable rent. Shapiro v. Goldstein, 113 Misc. 258, 185 N.Y.S. 234.

FAIR RETURN. A net return upon fair value of property. State ex rel. City of St. Louis v. Public Service Commission, 341 Mo. 920, 110 S.W. 2d 749, 778.

A "fair return" is to be largely measured by usual returns in like investments in the same vicinity over the same period of time. Natural Gas Pipeline Co. of America v. Federal Power Commission, C.C.A.7, 120 F.2d 625, 633, 634.

FAIR RETURN ON INVESTMENT. A fair return on value of property used and useful in carrying on the enterprise, performing the service or supplying the thing for which the rates are paid. Lubin v. Finkelstein, 82 N.Y.S.2d 329, 335.

FAIR SALE. In foreclosure and other judicial proceedings, this means a sale conducted with fairness and impartiality as respects the rights and interests of the parties affected. Lalor v. McCarthy, 24 Minn. 419. A sale at a price sufficient to warrant confirmation o: approval when it is required.

FAIR TRIAL. A hearing by an impartial and disinterested tribunal; a proceeding which hears before it condemns, which proceeds upon inquiry, and renders judgment only after trial. Johnson v. City of Wildwood, 116 N.J.L. 462, 184 A. 616, 617.

A legal trial or one conducted in all material things in substantial conformity to law. Stacey v. State, 79 Okl.Cr. 417, 155 P.2d 736, 739; A trial which insures substantial justice, Capone v. Union County Park Commission, 9 N.J. Misc.R. 1105, 156 A. 782, 783; A trial without prejudice to the accused, State v. Smith, 119 W.Va. 347, 193 S.E. 573, 574; an orderly trial before an impartial jury, and judge whose neutrality is indifferent to every factor in trial but that of administering justice. State ex rel. Brown v. Dewell, 131 Fla. 566, 179 So. 695, 698, 115 A.L.R. 857. One conducted according to due course of law; a trial before a competent and impartial jury. Railroad Co. v. Cook, 37 Neb. 435, 55 N.W. 943; Railroad Co. v. Gardner, 19 Minn. 136, Gil. 99, 18 Am.Rep. 334. One conducted according to rules of common law except in so far as it has been changed by statute. Di Maio v. Reid, 132 N.J.L. 17, 37 A.2d 829, 830. One conducted in substantial conformity to law. Sunderland v. U. S., C.C.A.Neb., 19 F.2d 202, 216; People v. Ephraim, 77 Cal.App. 29, 245 P. 769, 774. One where accused's legal rights are safeguarded and respected. Levinson v. Mooney, 128 N.J.L. 569, 27 A.2d 9, 10; Garrett v. State, 187 Miss. 441, 193 So. 452, 458; Johnson v. City of Wildwood, 116 N.J.L. 462, 184 A. 616.

A full and fair trial, required in order that a foreign judgment against a citizen be accorded credit in the courts of the United States, means not a summary proceeding, though sanctioned by the law of the forum, but an opportunity to be heard on the proof, where it is apparent that the cause involves questions of fact, and to have it considered by an unprejudiced court. Banco Minero v. Ross, 106 Tex. 522, 172 S.W. 711, 714.

Essential factors are a fair and impartial jury and a learned and upright judge to instruct jury and pass upon legal questions, and an atmosphere of calm in which witnesses can deliver their testimony without fear and intimidation, in which attorneys can assert defendant's rights freely and fully, and in which truth may be received and given credence without fear of violence, Floyd v. State, 166 Miss. 15, 148 So. 226, 232. A trial before an impartial judge, an impartial jury, and in an atmosphere of judicial calm; that, while the judge may and should direct and control the proceedings, and may exercise his right to comment on the evidence, yet he may not extend his activities so far as to become in effect either an assisting prosecutor or a thirteenth juror, Goldstein v. U. S., C.C.A.Mo., 63 F.2d 609, 613; an adequate hearing and an impartial tribunal, free from any interest, bias, or prejudice. The Reno, C.C. A.N.Y., 61 F.2d 966, 968.

FAIR USAGE. The doctrine of "fair usage" means that the matter which was under copyright was neither copied nor adopted, but that the uncopyrightable underlying idea was used, since a theme or idea is not copyrightable. Towle v. Ross, D.C.Or., 32 F.Supp. 125, 127.

FAIR VALUATION. Present market value; such sum as the property will sell for to a purchaser desiring to buy, the owner wishing to sell; such a price as a capable and diligent business man could presently obtain from the property after conferring with those accustomed to buy such property; the amount the property would bring at a sale on execution shown to have been in all respects fair and reasonable; the fair market value of the property as between one who wants to purchase and one who wants to sell the property. Market St. Nat. Bank v. Huff, 319 Pa. 286, 179 A. 582, 583.

As used in Bankruptcy Act the term means fair cash value or fair market value of property as between one who wants to purchase and one who wants to sell, Harman v. Defatta, 182 La. 463, 162 So. 44; Trenton Trust Co. v. Carlisle Tire Corporation, 110 Conn. 125, 147 A. 366, 367; fair market value, or value that can be made promptly effective by owner of property for payment of debts, Nicolai-Neppach Co. v. Smith, 154 Or. 450, 58 P.2d 1016, 1019, 107 A.L.R. 1124; In re Sedalia Farmers' Coop. Packing & Produce Co., D.C.Mo., 268 F. 898, 900; present market value of property and the value that the debtor might realize thereon if permitted to continue in business, Arnold v. Knapp, 75 W.Va. 804, 84 S.E. 895, 899; value of property taken in relation to business of debtor as a going concern, In re Gibson Hotels, D.C.W.Va., 24 F.Supp. 859, 863. It is not the value that would or did prevail at sacrified or forced sale. Bank of Forest v. Capital Nat. Bank, 176 Miss. 163, 169 So. 193, 198. Where no definite market value can be established and expert testimony must be relied on, fair valuation is the amount which the property ought to give to a going concern as a fair return, if sold to some one who is willing to purchase under ordinary selling conditions. In re Kobre, D.C.N.Y., 224 F. 106, 117. The term is not synonymous with "salable value." In re Crystal Ice & Fuel Co., D.C.Mont., 283 F. 1007, 1009.

In determining "fair valuation" of property, court should consider all elements entering into the intrinsic value, as well as the selling value, and also the earning power of the property. In re Gibson Hotels, D.C.W.Va., 24 F.Supp. 859, 863; the "fair valuation" of accounts is what with reasonable diligence can be realized from their collection within a reasonable time, Matthews v. Concrete Engineering Co., 228 Iowa 493, 292 N.W. 64, 65, 133 A.L.R. 1270.

FAIR VALUE. Present market value; such sum as the property will sell for to a purchaser desiring to buy, the owner wishing to sell; such a price as a capable and diligent business man could presently obtain from the property after conferring with those accustomed to buy such property; the amount the property would bring at a sale on execution shown to have been in all respects fair and reasonable; fair market value of the property as between one who wants to purchase and one who wants to sell the property. Market St. Nat. Bank v. Huff, 319 Pa. 286, 179 A. 582, 583.

"Actual value," "market value," "fair value," and the like, may be used as convertible terms. Kerr v. Clinchfield Coal Corporation, 169 Va. 149, 192 S.E. 741, 744.

In determining depreciation, "fair value" implies consideration of all factors material in negotiating sale and purchase of property, such as wear, decay, deterioration, obsolescence, inadequacy, and redundancy. Idaho Power Co. v. Thompson, D.C.Idaho, 19 F.2d 547, 566.

Price which a seller, willing but not compelled to sell, would take, and a purchaser, willing but not compelled to buy, would pay, Masonite Corporation v. Robinson-Slagle Lumber Co., D.C.La., 3 F.Supp. 754, 755; U. S. v. Crary, D.C.Va., 2 F.Supp. 870, 879. Price which buyers of the class which would be interested in buying property would be justified in paying for it. In re Crane's Estate, 344 Pa. 141, 23 A.2d 851, 855. Value which willing purchaser and seller would likely agree on. In re Aranoff & Son, D.C.Ga., 1 F.Supp. 708, 710.

As affecting stockholder's right to participate in reorganization plan, "fair value" of corporate debtor's property, connotes fair market value in dealing with certain kinds of property, and in certain cases stock exchange quotations are the best index of value, but bonds of Republic of Cuba, secured by apparently adequate pledges of revenues, should be valued at par rather than market price in absence of specific showing that Cuba might default. In re Warren Bros. Co., D.C.Mass., 39 F.Supp. 381, 384, 385.

Dissenting stockholder is entitled on combination or merger of corporations to "fair value" of stock determined by an ascertainment of all assets and liabilities of corporation, intrinsic value of stock, and not merely its market value, when traded in by the public. American General Corporation v. Camp, 171 Md. 629, 190 A. 225, 228.

For purpose of credit upon a deficiency claim arising out of a mortgage foreclosure proceeding, that sum which the mortgagee purchaser ought, under all circumstances, reasonably expect to realize from the acquired premises either by way of sale in the future or upon the basis of a permanent investment. Fidelity Union Trust Co. v. Ritz Holding Co., 126 N.J.Eq. 148, 8 A.2d 235, 245.

Reproduction cost of a public utility's property is an essential element in ascertainment of its "fair value". Peoples Natural Gas Co. v. Pennsylvania Public Utility Commission, 153 Pa.Super. 475, 34 A.2d 375, 380.

Under Deficiency Judgment Act, fair market value at time of execution sale as based on testimony of qualified witnesses. Market St. Nat. Bank v. Huff, 319 Pa. 286, 179 A. 582, 583.

Within a Revenue Act levying an excise tax on corporations measured by the fair value of their capital stock, "fair value" is the exact equivalent of "actual value." Central Union Trust Co. of New York v. Edwards, C.C.A. N.Y., 287 F. 324, 327.

Within statute requiring fair value of mortgaged premises to be credited on mortgage debt, interest, and costs before confirmation of foreclosure sale or rendition of deficiency judgment, that amount which under all circumstances of case will not shock conscience of court. Northwestern Loan & Trust Co. v. Bidinger, 226 Wis. 239, 276 N.W. 645, 648.

Rate Purposes

"Fair value" rule requires that consideration be given to original cost of construction, amount expended in permanent improvements, amount and market value of bonds and stock, present cost of construction, probable earning capacity under rates prescribed, operating expenses, accrued depreciation, market value of land, working capital, going concern value, and future costs of construction. State ex rel. and to Use of City of St. Louis v. Public Service Commission, 326 Mo. 751, 34 S.W.2d 507, 510.

A "fair value" for rate making is not the value for exchange, but such a value found after considering all relevant facts as will give the public utility a reasonable return and the public a reasonable rate. It is one which will enable the public utility to realize the expense of operating and keeping up its road and meeting its financial obligations for investments with a reasonable excess for dividends and ordinary contingencies. City of Rochester v. New York State Rys., 127 Misc. 766, 217 N.Y.S. 452, 458.

"Fair value" must include increase in value over original cost. Northern States Power Co. v. Public Service Commission, 73 N.D. 211, 13 N.W.2d 779, 786, 787.

"Fair value of the property" is not necessarily synonymous with "reconstruction cost depreciated." State ex rel. Oregon-Washington Water Service Co. v. Department of Public Works of Washington, 184 Wash. 45, 51 P.2d 610, 612.

Historical cost, provided consideration is given to changes in price level, reproduction cost at time of inquiry, less accrued depreciation, provided reproduction cost of components can be found with reasonable certainty, financial history of utility, and other relevant facts, may be considered in determining "fair value" of a utility's property. State v. Tri-State Telephone & Telegraph Co., 204 Minn. 516, 284 N.W. 294, 306.

Reproduction cost of a utility is an element in ascertainment of "fair value". Solar Electric Co. v. Pennsylvania Public Utility Commission, 137 Pa.Super. 325, 9 A.2d 447, 456, 460, 463, 464, 466.

Reproduction cost of telephone company's property, less actual depreciation, is not the legal equivalent of "fair value" but is merely evidence of value. New York Telephone Co. v. Prendergast, D.C.N.Y., 36 F.2d 54, 59.

The book cost of a telephone company's exchange plant and the "reproduction cost new" basis are recognized methods of ascertaining "fair value" of the company's property. Application of Northwestern Bell Tel. Co., 69 S.D. 36, 6 N.W.2d 165, 169.

The "fair value" as a rate base and the "value" in money for purposes of taxation of a public utility are not necessarily the same. State ex rel. Public Service Commission v. Southern Pac. Co., 95 Utah 84, 79 P.2d 25, 34.

The "fair value" of a utility's property is the cost of reproduction, less depreciation at time in question, whether more or less than original cost. Citizens' Gas Co. of Hannibal v. Public Service Commission of Missouri, D.C.Mo., 8 F.2d 632, 633. It is the reasonable value of property, used and useful, for the service of the public at the time the property is being so used. Northern States Power Co. v. Board of Railroad Com'rs, 71 N.D. 1, 298 N.W. 423, 431.

Value of additions completed and in use by a utility should be allowed in rate case in determining "fair value". Northern States Power Co. v. Board of Railroad Com'rs, 71 N.D. 1, 298 N.W. 423, 431.

FAIRLY. Equitably, honestly, impartially. Looney v. Elliott, Tex.Civ.App., 52 S.W.2d 949, 952. In good faith, People v. Mancuso, 255 N.Y. 463, 175 N.E. 177, 179. Justly; rightly. With substantial correctness. Reasonably. Conway v. Robinson, 216 Ala. 495, 113 So. 531, 533. Equitably. Satcher v. Satcher's Adm'r, 41 Ala. 40, 91 Am.Dec. 498. "Fairly merchantable" conveys the idea of mediocrity in quality, or something just above it. Warner v. Ice Co., 74 Me. 479.

"Fairly" is not synonymous with "truly," and "truly" should not be substituted for it in a commissioner's oath to take testimony fairly. Language may be truly, yet unfairly, reported; that is, an answer may be truly written down, yet in a manner conveying a different meaning from that intended and conveyed. And language may be fairly reported, yet not in accordance with strict truth. Lawrence v. Finch, 17 N.J.Eq. 234.

FAIRWAY. A strip of land, where the grass is kept mowed, and at the opposite ends of which are a green and a tee. Page v. Unterreiner, Mo. App., 106 S.W.2d 528, 532.

The middle and deepest or most navigable channel. Water on which vessels of commerce habitually move; Horst v. Columbia Contract Co., 89 Or. 344, 174 P. 161, 163.

The word "thalweg" (*q.v.*), from which it is apparently derived, has reference more particularly to navigable channels as boundaries. Johnnsson v. American Tugboat Co., 147 P. 1147, 85 Wash. 212.

FAIT. L. Fr. Anything done. A deed; act; fact.

A deed lawfully executed. Com. Dig.

Feme (or *Femme*) *de fait.* A wife *de facto.*

FAIT ENROLLE. A deed enrolled, as a bargain and sale of freeholds. 1 Keb. 568.

FAIT JURIDIQUE. In French law. A juridical fact. One of the factors or elements constitutive of an obligation.

FAITH. Confidence; credit; reliance. Thus, an act may be said to be done "on the faith" of certain representations.

Belief; credence; trust. Thus, the constitution provides that "full faith and credit" shall be given to the judgments of each state in the courts of the others.

Purpose; intent; sincerity; state of knowledge or design. This is the meaning of the word in the phrases "good faith" and "bad faith."

Scotch Law. A solemn pledge; an oath. "To make faith" is to swear, with the right hand uplifted, that one will declare the truth. 1 Forb. Inst. pt. 4, p. 235.

FAITHFUL. Trusty, honest, trustworthy. Wright v. Fidelity & Deposit Co. of Maryland, 176 Okl. 274, 54 P.2d 1084, 1087.

As used in the rule that executors must be "faithful," means that they must act in good faith. In re McCafferty's Will, 147 Misc. 179, 264 N.Y.S. 38.

The guaranty required by statute and bond of "faithful" discharge of school district treasurer's duties is a guaranty not only of treasurer's personal honesty but also of his competency, skill and diligence in discharge of his duties. Thurston County, to Use of Vesely, v. Chmelka, 138 Neb. 696, 294 N.W. 857, 863, 132 A.L.R. 1077.

Where a public officer gives a bond for the "faithful" discharge of his duties, "faithful" implies that he has assumed that measure of responsibility laid on him by law had no bond been given. Thurston County, to Use of Vesely, v. Chmelka, 138 Neb. 696, 294 N.W. 857, 863, 132 A.L.R. 1077; London & Lancashire Indemnity Co. of America v. Community Savings & Loan Ass'n, 102 Ind.App. 665, 4 N.E. 2d 688, 693.

FAITHFULLY. Conscientious diligence or faithfulness, adequate to due execution of object of bailment, or just regard of adherence to duty, or due observance of undertaking of contract. Commonwealth v. Polk, 256 Ky. 100, 75 S.W.2d 761, 765. Diligently, and without unnecessary delay;—not synonymous with "fairly" or "impartially." Den v. Thompson, 16 N.J.L. 72, 73. Truthfully, sincerely, accurately. Kansas City, M. & O. R. Co., of Texas v. Whittington & Sweeney, Tex.Civ.App., 153 S.W. 689, 690.

As used in bonds of public and private officers, this term imports not only honesty, but also a punctilious discharge of all the duties of the office, requiring competence, diligence, and attention, without any malfeasance or nonfeasance, aside from mere mistakes. State v. Chadwick, 10 Or. 468; Hoboken v. Evans, 31 N.J.L. 343; Harris v. Hanson, 11 Me. 245.

FAITOURS. Idle persons; idle livers; vagabonds. *Termes de la Ley;* Cowell; Blount; Cunningham, Law Dict.

FAKE. To make or construct. A "faked alibi" is a made, manufactured, or false alibi. U. S. v. Heitler, D.C.Ill., 274 F. 401, 409.

FAKER. A petty swindler. National Automobile Ass'n v. Strunk, 122 Neb. 890, 240 N.W. 294.

FAKIR. A term applied among the Mohammedans to a kind of religious ascetic or beggar, whose claim is that he "is in need of mercy, and poor in the sight of God, rather than in need of worldly assistance." Hughes, Dict. of Islam.

Sometimes spelled *Faqueer* or *Fakeer.* It is commonly used in English to designate a person engaged in some useless or dishonest business. Fake is also so used and also to designate the quality of such business.

A street peddler who disposes of worthless wares, or of any goods above their value, by means of any false representation, trick, device, lottery, or game of chance. Mills' Ann.St.Colo. § 1400, '35 C.S.A. c. 48, § 227.

FALANG. In old English law. A jacket or close coat. Blount.

FALCARE. In old English law. To mow. For "Jus Folcandi", see that title.

Falcare prata, to mow or cut grass in meadows laid in for hay. A customary service to the lord by his inferior tenants. Kennett, Gloss.

Falcata, grass fresh mown, and laid in swaths. That which was mowed. Kennett, Gloss.; Cowell; Jacobs.

Falcatio, a mowing. Bract. fols. 35*b*, 230.

Falcator, a mower; a servile tenant who performed the labor of mowing.

Falcatura, a day's mowing. *Falcatura una.* Once mowing the grass.

FALCARIOUS. See Falsarius.

FALCIDIA. In Spanish law. The Falcidian portion; the portion of an inheritance which could not be legally bequeathed away from the heir, viz., one-fourth.

FALCIDIAN LAW. In Roman law. A law on the subject of testamentary disposition.

It was enacted by the people during the reign of Augustus, in the year of Rome 714, on the proposition of the tribune Falcidius. By this law, the testator's right to burden his estate with legacies was subjected to an important restriction. It prescribed that no one could bequeath more than three-fourths of his property in legacies, and that the heir should have at least one-fourth of the estate, and that, should the testator violate this prescript, the heir may have the right to make a proportional deduction from each legatee, so far as necessary. Mackeld.Rom.Law, § 771; Inst. 2, 22; Heinecc.Elem. lib. 2, tit. 22.

A similar principle exists in Louisiana. See Legitime. In some of the states the statutes authorizing bequests and devises to charitable corporations limit the amount which a testator may give, to a certain fraction of his estate.

FALCIDIAN PORTION. That portion of a testator's estate which, by the Falcidian law, was required to be left to the heir, amounting to at least one-fourth.

FALD, or FALDA. A sheep-fold. Cowell.

FALDA. Span. In Spanish law. The slope or skirt of a hill. Fossat v. United States, 2 Wall. 673, 17 L.Ed. 739.

FALDÆ CURSUS. In old English law. A fold-course; the course (going or taking about) of a fold. Spelman. A sheep walk, or feed for sheep. 2 Vent. 139.

FALDAGE. The privilege which anciently several lords reserved to themselves of setting up folds for sheep in any fields within their manors, the better to manure them, and this not only with their own but their tenants' sheep. Called, variously, "*secta faldare,*" "fold-course," "free-hold," "*faldagii.*" Cowell; Spelman; Cunningham, Law Dict.

FALDATA. In old English law. A flock or fold of sheep. Cowell.

FALDFEY. Sax. A fee or rent paid by a tenant to his lord for leave to fold his sheep on his own ground. Blount; Cunningham, Law Dict.

FALDISDORY. In ecclesiastical law. The bishop's seat or throne within the chancel.

FALDSOCA. Sax. The liberty or privilege of foldage.

FALDSTOOL. A place at the south side of the altar at which the sovereign kneels at his coronation. Wharton.

A folding seat similar to a camp stool, made either of wood or metal, sometimes covered with silk or other material. It was used by a bishop when officiating in other than his own cathedral church. Encyc.Dic.

FALDWORTH. In Saxon law. A person reckoned old enough to become a member of the decennary, and so subject to the law of frank-pledge. Spelman; Du Fresne.

FALERÆ. In old English law. The tackle and furniture of a cart or wain. Blount.

FALESIA. In old English law. A hill or down by the sea-side. Co. Litt. 5*b;* Domesday.

FALK-LAND. See Folc-Land.

FALL, *n.* One of the four seasons of the year, embracing the three months commencing with the 1st of September and terminating with the last day of November. Rosenau v. Lansing, 113 Or. 638, 232 P. 648; Horn v. State, 19 Ala.App. 572, 99 So. 58. But a finding that certain persons occupied a house until the fall of each year has been held ambiguous, since "fall" covers a period of time of upward of three months. Clegg v. Bishop, 105 Conn. 564, 136 A. 102, 104.

FALL, *v.* In Scotch law. To lose or loose. To fall from a right is to lose or forfeit it. 1 Kames, Eq. 228.

As used in fire policy provision that if building or any part thereof "fall," except as result of fire, all insurance on contents of building should immediately cease, includes any situation where building once erect lies prostrate. Nalley v. Hanover Fire Ins. Co., 56 Ga.App. 555, 193 S.E. 619, 622.

The statute provision concerning holding of courts which fall between January and June, both inclusive, includes any term which begins in June, the word "fall" meaning to come, become, occur, or arise. West v. F. W. Woolworth Co., 214 N.C. 214, 198 S.E. 659, 660.

FALL OF LAND. In English law. A quantity of land six ells square superficial measure.

FALLING. When the one object descends upon the other, we do not speak of it as colliding with the second, but as "falling" upon it. Atlas Assur. Co. v. Lies, 70 Ga.App. 162, 27 S.E.2d 791, 794.

FALLO. In Spanish law. The final decree or judgment given in a controversy at law.

FALLOPIAN TUBE. An essential part of the female reproductive system, consisting of a narrow conduit, some four inches in length, that extends on each side of a woman's body from the base of the womb to the ovary upon that side. Smith v. Board of Examiners of Feeble-Minded, 85 N.J.L. 46, 88 A. 936, 965.

FALLOW. Barren or unproductive. May v. American Trust Co., 153 Cal.App. 385, 27 P.2d 101.

FALLOW-LAND. Land plowed, but not sown, and left uncultivated for a time after successive crops; land left untilled for a year or more.

FALLUM. In old English law. An unexplained term for some particular kind of land. Cowell; Jacob, L. Dic.

FALSA DEMONSTRATIO. In the civil law. False designation; erroneous description of a person or thing in a written instrument. Inst. 2, 20, 30.

FALSA DEMONSTRATIO NON NOCET, CUM DE CORPORE (PERSONA) CONSTAT. False description does not injure or vitiate, provided the thing or person intended has once been sufficiently described. Mere false description does not make an instrument inoperative. Broom, Max. 629; 6 Term, 676; 11 Mees. & W. 189; Cleaveland v. Smith, 2 Story, 291, Fed.Cas.No.2,874. See 1 Greenleaf, Evidence, § 301; 2 Pars. Contr. 62, n.; 4 C. B. 328; 14 C. B. 122; Sargent v. Adams, 3 Gray (Mass.) 78, 63 Am.Dec. 718.

FALSA DEMONSTRATIONE LEGATUM NON PERIMI. A bequest is not rendered void by an erroneous description. Inst. 2, 20, 30; Broom, Max. 645; Roman Catholic Orphan Asylum v. Emmons, 3 Bradf. Sur., N.Y., 144, 149.

FALSA GRAMMATICA NON VITIAT CONCESSIONEM. False or bad grammar does not vitiate a grant. Shep. Touch. 55; 9 Coke, 48*a*. Neither false Latin nor false English will make a deed void when the intent of the parties doth plainly appear. Shep. Touch. 87.

FALSA MONETA. In the civil law. False or counterfeit money. Cod. 9, 24.

FALSA ORTHOGRAPHIA NON VITIAT CHARTAM, CONCESSIONEM. False spelling does not vitiate a deed. Shep. Touch. 55, 87; 9 Coke, 48*a;* Wing. Max. 19; Bart. Max. 164.

FALSARE. In old English law. To counterfeit. *Quia falsavit sigillum,* because he counterfeited the seal. Bract. fol. 276*b*.

FALSARIUS (or FALCARIOUS). A counterfeiter. Townsh. Pl. 260.

FALSE. Not true. State v. Arnett, 338 Mo. 907, 92 S.W.2d 897, 900; Sentinel Life Ins. Co. v. Blackmer, C.C.A.Colo., 77 F.2d 347, 352.

It also means:

Artificial. U. S. v. Darby, D.C.Md., 2 F.Supp. 378, 379; Sentinel Life Ins. Co. v. Blackmer, C.C.A.Colo., 77 F.2d 347, 352; assumed or designed to deceive. Sentinel Life Ins. Co. v. Blackmer, C.C.A.Colo., 77 F.2d 347, 352; North American Accident Ins. Co. v. Tebbs, C.C.A.Utah, 107 F.2d 853, 855; contrary to fact. In re Davis, 349 Pa. 651, 37 A. 2d 498, 499; counterfeit, Sentinel Life Ins. Co. v. Blackmer, C.C.A.Colo., 77 F.2d 347, 352; North American Accident Ins. Co. v. Tebbs, C.C.A.Utah, 107 F.2d 853, 855; deceitful; deliberately and knowingly false, People v. Mangan, 140 Misc. 783, 252 N.Y.S. 44, 52; designedly untrue, W. T. Rawleigh Co. v. Brantley, 97 Miss. 244, 19 So.2d 808, 811, 157 A.L.R. 188; erroneous, Abel v. Paterno, 153 Misc. 248, 274 N.Y.S. 749; Gilbert v. Inter-Ocean Casualty Co. of Cincinnati, Ohio, 41 N.M. 463, 71 P.2d 56, 59; hypocritical; sham; feigned, Sentinel Life Ins. Co. v. Blackmer, C.C.A. Colo., 77 F.2d 347, 352; North American Accident Ins. Co. v. Tebbs, C.C.A.Utah, 107 F.2d 853, 855; incorrect, State v. Arnett, 338 Mo. 907, 92 S.W.2d 897, 900; intentionally untrue. In re Venturella, D.C.Conn., 25 F.Supp. 332, 333; In re Cleveland, D.C.Mich., 40 F.Supp. 343; not according to truth or reality. State v. Arnett, 338 Mo. 907, 92 S.W. 2d 897, 900; North American Accident Ins. Co. v. Tebbs, C.C.A.Utah, 107 F.2d 853, 855; not genuine or real; U. S. v. Darby, D.C.Md., 2 F.Supp. 378, 379; North American Accident Ins. Co. v. Tebbs, C.C.A.Utah, 107 F.2d 853, 855; uttering falsehood; unveracious; given to deceit; dishonest, Wilensky v. Goodyear Tire & Rubber Co., C.C.A. Mass., 67 F.2d 389, 390; wilfully and intentionally untrue. In re Brown, D.C.N.Y., 37 F.Supp. 526, 527; North American Accident Ins. Co. v. Tebbs, C.C.A.Utah, 107 F.2d 853, 855.

Court's substitution in charge of term "fraudulent" in place of term "false" held not misleading. Wood v. Williams, Tex.Civ.App., 46 S.W.2d 332, 334.

In law, this word usually means something more than untrue; it means something designedly untrue and deceitful, and implies an intention to perpetrate some treachery or fraud. Hatcher v. Dunn, 102 Iowa, 411, 71 N.W. 343, 36 L.R.A. 689; Mason v. Association, 18 U.C.C.P. 19; State v. Leonard, 73 Or. 451, 144 P. 113, 118; State v. Smith, 63 Vt. 201, 22 A. 604. It implies either conscious wrong or culpable negligence, and signifies knowingly or negligently untrue. United States v. Ninety-Nine Diamonds, C.C.A. Minn., 139 F. 961, 72 C.C.A. 9, 2 L.R.A.,N.S., 185.

The word "false" has two distinct and well-recognized meanings: (1) intentionally or knowingly or negligently untrue; (2) untrue by mistake or accident, or honestly after the exercise of reasonable care. Metropolitan Life Ins. Co. v. Adams, D.C.Mun.App., 37 A.2d 345, 350. In jurisprudence, "false" and "falsely" are oftenest used to characterize a wrongful or criminal act, such as involves an error or untruth, intentionally or knowingly put forward. A thing is called "false" when it is done, or made, with knowledge, actual or constructive, that it is untrue or illegal, or is said to be done falsely when the meaning is that the party is in fault for its error. Fouts v. State, 113 Ohio St. 450, 149 N.E. 551, 554; Monahan v. Mutual Life Ins. Co. of New York, 192 Wis. 102, 212 N.W. 269, 271.

The word "false" in its juristic use implies something more than a mere untruth, Dombroski v. Metropolitan Life Ins. Co., 126 N.J.L. 545, 19 A.2d 678, 680.

The word "false" sometimes connotes an intent to deceive, People v. Wahl, 39 Cal.App.2d Supp. 771, 100 P.2d 550, 551; Salt's Textile Mfg. Co. v. Ghent, 107 Conn. 211, 139 A. 694, 695.

FALSE ACTION. See Feigned Action.

FALSE AND FRAUDULENT. The phrase "false and fraudulent" in Food and Drugs Act of 1906 means that the statement must have been made with actual intent to deceive. United States v. Dr. David Roberts Veterinary Co., C.C.A.Wis., 104 F.2d 785, 788.

To amount to actionable "false and fraudulent representations", they must have been as to existing fact or known by one making them, from his superior knowledge, to have been untrue when made. Burlison v. Weis, Mo. App., 152 S.W.2d 201, 203.

FALSE AND MISLEADING STATEMENT. Failure to state material fact made letter a "false and misleading statement" within rule of Securities and Exchange Commission. Securities and Exchange Commission v. Okin, C.C.A.N.Y., 132 F.2d 784, 787.

FALSE ANSWER. In pleading. A sham answer; one which is false in the sense of being a mere pretense set up in bad faith and without color of fact. Howe v. Elwell, 57 App.Div. 357, 67 N.Y. Supp. 1108; Farnsworth v. Halstead, Sup., 10 N.Y. S. 763.

FALSE ARREST. Any unlawful physical restraint by one of another's liberty, whether in prison or elsewhere. Gariety v. Fleming, 121 Kan. 42, 245 P. 1054, 1055; Russell v. Levinsohn, 5 N.J. Misc. 765, 138 A. 205; Great Atlantic & Pacific Tea Co. v. Phillips, 253 Ky. 126, 69 S.W.2d 5.

FALSE CHARACTER. Personating the master or mistress of a servant, or any representative of such master or mistress, and giving a false character to the servant is an offense punishable in England with a fine of £20. St. 32 Geo. III. c. 56.

FALSE CHECKS. Obtaining money by means and use of a check upon a bank, in which the drawer at the time had no funds or credit with which to meet the same, and which he had no reason to believe would honor such check upon presentation at said bank for payment, is obtaining money by use of a false check. Gunther v. State, 42 Okl.Cr. 129, 276 P. 237, 238.

FALSE CLAIM, in the forest law, was where a man claimed more than his due, and was amerced and punished for the same. Manw. c. 25; Tomlins.

As used in a statute making it a felony to present to any state, county, or city board or officer a false or fraudulent claim, a "false claim" is something more than a merely excessive claim. Burke v. Knox, 59 Utah, 596, 206 P. 711, 714. The act of knowingly making untruthful statements of material facts in "reasons for refund" of excise taxes, supported by fictitious copies of letters and cards attached thereto, constitutes "false claim" against government, within Criminal Code, § 35 (18 USCA §§ 80, 82–86). Evans v. U. S., C.C.A.S.C., 11 F.2d 37, 39.

FALSE DECRETALS. A collection of canon law, dated about the middle of the 9th century, probably by a Frankish ecclesiastic who called himself Isadon. It continued to be the chief repertory of the canon law till the 15th century when its untrustworthy nature was demonstrated.

FALSE DEMONSTRATION. Where description of person or thing in will is partly true and partly false, if part which is true describes subject or object of gift with sufficient certainty, untrue part may be rejected and gift sustained, under doctrine of "false demonstration." In re Heins' Estate, 132 Cal.App. 131, 22 P.2d 549.

FALSE ENTRY. An entry in books of a bank or trust company which is intentionally made to represent what is not true or does not exist, with intent either to deceive its officers or a bank examiner or to defraud the bank or trust company. Agnew v. U. S., 165 U.S. 36, 17 S.Ct. 235, 41 L.Ed. 624; Fricke v. State, 112 Neb. 767, 201 N.W. 667, 670; Commonwealth v. Bardolph, 111 Pa.Super. 85, 169 A. 574, 575; U. S. v. Mulloney, D.C.Mass., 5 F.Supp. 77, 79.

An untrue statement of items of account by written words, figures, or marks. United States v. Herrig, D.C. Mont., 204 F. 124, 125. One making an original false entry makes a false entry in every book which is made up in regular course from the entry or entries from the original book of entry. State v. Davidson, 46 N.D. 564, 180 N.W. 31, 32.

Where entry upon books of bank of matter contained in deposit slip is not true it is a "false entry," Adams v. State, 179 Ark. 1047, 20 S.W.2d 130, 133.

Entries made by cashier of balance in insurance company's account after deducting unauthorized withdrawals made by cashier as agent of insurance company held "false entries" within statute. 18 U.S.C.A. § 1005. Laws v. U. S., C.C.A.Okl., 66 F.2d 870, 873.

FALSE FACT. In the law of evidence. A feigned, simulated, or fabricated fact; a fact not founded in truth, but existing only in assertion; the deceitful semblance of a fact.

FALSE IMPERSONATION. To impersonate another falsely, and in such assumed character to do any act whereby any benefit might accrue to the offender or to another person. People v. Horkans, 109 Colo. 177, 123 P.2d 824.

FALSE IMPRISONMENT. See Imprisonment.

FALSE INSTRUMENT. A counterfeit; one made in the similitude of a genuine instrument and purporting on its face to be such. U. S. v. Howell, 11 Wall. 435, 20 L.Ed. 195; U. S. v. Owens, C.C.Tenn., 37 Fed. 115; State v. Willson, 28 Minn. 52, 9 N.W. 28.

FALSE JUDGMENT. In old English law. A writ which lay when a false judgment had been pronounced in a court not of record, as a county court, court baron, etc. Fitzh. Nat. Brev. 17, 18. In old French law. The defeated party in a suit had the privilege of accusing the judges of pronouncing a false or corrupt judgment, whereupon the issue was determined by his challenging them to the combat or *duellum*. This was called the "appeal of false judgment." Montesq. Esprit des Lois, liv. 28, c. 27.

FALSE LATIN. When law proceedings were written in Latin, if a word were significant though not good Latin, yet an indictment, declaration, or fine should not be made void by it; but if the word were not Latin, nor allowed by the law, and it were in a material point, it made the whole vicious. (5 Coke, 121; 2 Nels. 830.) Wharton.

FALSE LIGHTS AND SIGNALS. Lights and signals falsely and maliciously displayed for the purpose of bringing a vessel into danger. See stat. 24 & 25 Vict. c. 97, § 47; 18 U.S.C.A. § 488.

FALSE MAKING. An essential element of forgery, where material alteration is not involved. Term has reference to manner in which writing is made or executed rather than to its substance or effect. A falsely made instrument is one that is fictitious, not genuine, or in some material particular something other than it purports to be and without regard to truth or falsity of facts stated therein. Wright v. U. S., C.A.Ariz., 172 F.2d 310, 311.

FALSE NEWS. Spreading false news, whereby discord may grow between the queen of England and her people, or the great men of the realm, or which may produce other mischiefs, still seems to be a misdemeanor, under St. 3 Edw. I. c. 34. Steph. Cr. Dig. § 95.

FALSE OATH. To defeat discharge in bankruptcy "false oath" must contain all the elements involved in "perjury" at common law, namely, an intentional untruth in matter material to a material issue, In re Bergman, D.C.N.Y., 6 F.Supp. 898, 901, it must have been knowingly and fraudulently made. In re Stone, D.C.N.H., 52 F.2d 639, 641. See, also, Perjury.

FALSE OR FRAUDULENT CLAIM. A "false or fraudulent claim" within meaning of statute providing for punishment of any one receiving proceeds of fraudulent audit or payment, since to be "false or fraudulent," must be a claim for services or materials not actually rendered or furnished. People v. Dally, 175 Misc. 680, 24 N.Y.S.2d 692, 695.

FALSE PAPER. In a statute defining an offense of willfully and knowingly subscribing to "false papers" to deceive bank examiners, the term refers not to one which is forged or spurious, but to a paper duly subscribed by the person purporting to sign it, and containing an untrue statement in the body of the instrument. State v. Pierson, 101 Wash. 318, 172 P. 236, 238.

FALSE PERSONATION. The criminal offense of falsely representing some other person and acting in the character thus unlawfully assumed, in order to deceive others, and thereby gain some profit or advantage, or enjoy some right or privilege belonging to the one so personated, or subject him to some expense, charge, or liability. See 4 Steph. Comm. 181, 290.

FALSE PLEA. See Sham Plea.

FALSE PRETENSES. Designed misrepresentation of existing fact or condition whereby person obtains another's money or goods. People v. Gould, 363 Ill. 348, 2 N.E.2d 324.

Elements of offense include actual fraud, State v. Nuser, 199 Minn. 315, 271 N.W. 811, 812; State v. Mayer, 196 N.C. 454, 146 S.E. 64, 65; assertion of a present or past fact, Slaughter v. Commonwealth, 222 Ky. 225, 300 S.W. 619, 621, 56 A.L.R. 1209; State v. Nuser, 199 Minn. 315, 271 N.W. 811, 812, falsity of representation, State v. Mayer, 196 N.C. 454, 146 S.E. 64, 65; People v. Leaverton, 107 Cal. App. 51, 289 P. 890, 892; intent to cheat and defraud. Commonwealth v. Campbell, 116 Pa.Super. 180, 176 A. 246, 250; State v. Johnson, 195 N.C. 506, 142 S.E. 775, 776; knowledge of the falsity, fraud. Couch v. State, 31 Ala.App. 586, 20 So.2d 57, 58; Dennis v. Thomson, 240 Ky. 727, 43 S.W.2d 18, 25; obtaining of property or something of value. State v. Johnson, 195 N.C. 506, 142 S.E. 775, 776; Couch v. State, 31 Ala.App. 586, 20 So.2d 57, 58; perpetration of fraud by means of such false pretenses, State v. Hintz, 200 Wis. 636, 229 N.W. 54, 55; reliance on representation, State v. Howley, 220 N.C. 113, 16 S.E.2d 705, 708, 709; use of pretenses or false representations, Dennis v. Thomson, 240 Ky. 727, 43 S.W.2d 18, 25; State v. Mayer, 196 N.C. 454, 146 S.E. 64, 65.

Other definitions of "false pretenses" include:

False representation of existing fact or condition by which a party obtains property of another, People ex rel. Courtney v. Sullivan, 363 Ill. 34, 1 N.E.2d 206, 208; false representation of existing fact, whether by oral or written words or conduct, calculated to deceive, intended to deceive, and does in fact deceive, whereby one person obtains value from another without compensation, Commonwealth v. Johnson, 312 Pa. 140, 167 A. 344, 345, 89 A.L.R. 333; State v. Alick, 62 S.D. 220, 252 N.W. 644; false representation of existing or past fact calculated to induce confidence on part of one to whom representation is made, and accompanied by or blended with a promise to do something in future, State v. Parkinson, 181 Wash. 69, 41 P.2d 1095, 1097; false representation of existing fact, made with knowledge of falsity, with intent that party to whom it is made should act upon it, and acted upon by such party to his detriment. Griffith v. State, 93 Ohio St. 294, 112 N.E. 1017, 1018; State v. Hathaway, 168 Wis. 518, 170 N.W. 654, 656; State v. Whitney, 43 Idaho, 745, 254 P. 525, 526; Smith v. State, 74 Fla. 594, 77 So. 274, 276; false representation of past or existing fact, made with knowledge of falsity, with intent to deceive and defraud, and which is adapted to deceive person to whom made, State v. Allck, 62 S.D. 220, 252 N.W. 644; false representations and statements, made with a fraudulent design to obtain money, goods, wares, or merchandise, with intent to cheat, 2 Bouv. Inst. no. 2308; false statement made with knowledge of its falsity, which is intended to deceive, and which in fact does deceive, and injury results, Morris Plan Bank of Richmond v. Henderson, D.C.N.C., 57 F.2d 326, 327; fraudulent representation of fact by one who knows it not to be true as is adapted to induce person to whom made to part with something of value, Fisher v. State, 161 Ark. 586, 256 S.W. 858, 860; State v. Tanner, 22 N.M. 493, 164 P. 821, 822, L.R.A.1917E, 849; State v. Luff, 1 Boyce (Del.) 152, 74 A. 1079, 1080; State v. Barr, 63 Idaho 59, 117 P.2d 282, 286; misrepresentation of past fact, knowingly made to induce another to part with his property, People v. Martin, 372 Ill. 484, 24 N.E.2d 380, 381, 382; misstatement of fact, Carr v. State, 60 Ga.App. 590, 4 S.E.2d 500, 501; representation of some fact or circumstance, calculated to mislead or deceive, which is not true, State v. Grant, 86 Iowa 216, 53 N.W. 120; Commonwealth v. McKnight, 289 Mass. 530, 195 N.E. 499, 506.

A "false pretense" must be as to an existing or past fact. State v. Neal, 350 Mo. 1002, 169 S.W.2d 686, 689; Commonwealth v. Becker, 151 Pa.Super. 169, 30 A.2d 195, 197.

A pretense is the holding out or offering to others something false and feigned. This may be done either by words or actions, which amount to false representations. In fact, false representations are inseparable from the idea of a pretense. Without a representation which is false there can be no pretense. State v. Joaquin, 43 Iowa, 132.

Gist of offense of "obtaining money by false pretenses" is the fraud and deception by the perpetrator, his motive, and the result—the fact that a person was deceived and defrauded. Frazier v. Commonwealth, 291 Ky. 467, 165 S.W.2d 33, 34.

Giving of worthless check is, in itself, "false pretense". State v. Augustine, 114 W.Va. 143, 171 S.E. 111, 113; Laird v. Employers Liability Assur. Corporation, Limited, of London, England, 2 Terry 216, 18 A.2d 861, 862.

In "false pretenses" owner intends to part with his property in money or chattel but it is obtained from him by fraud. People v. Santora, 51 Cal.App.2d 707, 125 P.2d 606, 608.

One distinction between "embezzlement" and "false pretenses" is that in the former case the defendant does not have title to the property, while in the latter, he has. State v. Serkau, 128 Conn. 153, 20 A.2d 725, 727.

Confidence game distinguished

A "confidence game" is any swindling operation in which advantage is taken of the confidence reposed by the victim in the swindler. It consists of gaining the possession of money or property by means of some trick, device, or swindling operation in which advantage is taken of the confidence of the victim reposed in the swindler. In obtaining money by "false pretenses," the false pretenses used must have been believed and relied on by the defrauded party and been the means of inducing the victim to part with his property. People v. Blume, 345 Ill. 524, 178 N.E. 48, 52.

"Confidence game" is not established by mere proof that property has been obtained by false pretense. Clark v. State, 53 Ariz. 416, 89 P.2d 1077, 1080.

Larceny and false pretenses distinguished

In larceny owner has no intention to part with his property, although he may intend to part with possession, while in false pretenses the owner does intend to part with the property but it is obtained from him by fraud. People v. Shwartz, 43 Cal.App. 696, 185 P. 686, 687. Roberts v. State, 181 Ind. 520, 104 N.E. 970, 971.

In larceny owner has no intention to part with title to and possession of property taken, while in false pretenses he does so intend, but it is obtained from him by fraud. Simmons v. State, 165 Md. 155, 167 A. 60, 64.

Only a very narrow distinction exists between "larceny" and "false pretense"; the character of the crime depending on the intention of the parties. Riley v. State, 64 Okl. Cr. 183, 78 P.2d 712, 716.

The intention of owner of property not to part with title when relinquishing possession of property is vital point to be determined in distinguishing between "larceny by fraud" and obtaining property by "false pretenses". Dobson v. State, 74 Okl.Cr. 341, 126 P.2d 95, 101.

Obtaining money or property by false pretenses

Elements are intent to defraud, actual fraud, false pretense, and fraud resulting therefrom, Simmons v. State, 165 Md. 155, 167 A. 60, 64; false pretenses, that property was obtained thereby, that false pretenses were made with intent to cheat and defraud, and that money was paid in reliance upon and under inducement of false pretenses, People v. Sloane, 165 Misc. 444, 300 N.Y.S. 1032, 1035.

It is sufficient if false pretenses are a part of the moving cause, and, without them, the defrauded party would not have parted with the property. State v. Faulkner, 139 Kan. 665, 33 P.2d 175, 177.

The distinction between "obtaining money by false pretenses" and forgery is that in the former, the acquisition of the money is the principal thing, while in forgery the making, altering, uttering, or publishing of the written instrument is the principal part, and money need not necessarily be obtained. State v. Hobl, 108 Kan. 261, 194 P. 921, 924.

The false representations may be made by implication. Johnson v. People, 110 Colo. 283, 133 P.2d 789, 792.

The "false pretense" may be the failure to speak when it was necessary to do so. People v. Etzler, 292 Mich. 489, 290 N.W. 879, 880.

The "false pretense" must relate to existing fact, or to fact which has theretofore occurred. Jones v. State, 236 Ala. 30, 182 So. 404, 405.

FALSE RECORD. The Fair Labor Standards Act prohibiting the making of "false records" refers to falsification of payroll records customarily made available to a wage and hour inspector. United States v. Selman-Reinstein, Inc., D.C. Minn., 52 F.Supp. 208, 209, 210.

FALSE REPRESENTATION. A representation which is untrue, willfully made to deceive another to his injury. See, also, Deceit and Fraud.

A deceitful representation, or one contrary to the fact, made knowingly and with the design and effect of inducing the other party to enter into the contract to which it relates; a declaration of present intention, false when made, to perform act in future, Pease & Elliman v. Wegeman, 223 App.Div. 682, 229 N.Y.S. 398, 400; a representation known to be false by person making it, or made without knowledge as a positive statement of known fact upon which another relied and acted, Platte Valley Bank v. Lemke, 141 Neb. 218, 3 N.W.2d 396, 399; a representation of what is true, which nevertheless creates an impression which is false. Newark Trust Co. v. Lackawanna Inv. Co., 88 N.J.Eq. 541, 103 A. 168, 169; McClellan v. Tobin, Ind., 219 Ind. 563, 39 N.E.2d 772, 774; an assertion of knowledge which in fact one does not have, Tone v. Halsey, Stuart & Co., 286 Ill.App. 169, 3 N.E.2d 142, 147; an assertion of something as true which one does not know to be true, Hargrove v. Henderson, 108 Cal.App. 667, 292 P. 148; such representations as will deceive persons of ordinary prudence. Union Central Life Ins. Co. v. Kerron, 128 Or. 70, 264 P. 453, 455; Holmberg v. Prudential Savings & Loan Ass'n, 130 Or. 1, 278 P. 943, 945.

A "false representation" may arise from any conduct capable of being turned into a statement of fact. Bundesen v. Lewis, 291 Ill.App. 83, 9 N.E.2d 327, 334.

A "false representation" may be made scienter, so as to afford a right of action in damages, in any of the following ways: (1) With actual knowledge of its falsity; (2) without knowledge either of its truth or falsity; or (3) under circumstances in which the person making it ought to have known if he did not know of its falsity. Horton v. Tyree,

104 W.Va. 238, 139 S.E. 737, 738; Sebastian County Bank v. Gann, 121 Ark. 145, 180 S.W. 754, 755.

A false representation, within Bankruptcy Act not affected by discharge, must involve moral turpitude or intentional wrong. Hisey v. Lewis-Gale Hospital, D.C.Va., 27 F.Supp. 20, 23.

False statements although future in form may be "false representations" of existing facts and conditions. National Theatre Supply Co. v. Rigney, Mo.App., 130 S.W.2d 258, 263.

To maintain an action for damages for "false representation," the plaintiff, in substance, must allege and must prove by a preponderance of the evidence the following elements: (1) What representation was made; (2) that it was false; (3) that the defendant knew it was false, or else made it without knowledge as a positive statement of known fact; (4) that the plaintiff believed the representation to be true; (5) that the plaintiff relied on and acted upon the representation; (6) that the plaintiff was thereby injured; and (7) the amount of the damages. Peterson v. Schaberg, 116 Neb. 346, 217 N.W. 586, 587.

FALSE RETURN. See Return.

FALSE STATEMENT. Under statutory provision, making it unlawful for officer or director of corporation to make any false statement in regard to corporation's financial condition, the phrase means something more than merely untrue or erroneous, but implies that statement is designedly untrue and deceitful, and made with intention to deceive person to whom false statement is made or exhibited. State v. Johnston, 149 S.C. 138, 146 S.E. 657, 660.

As used in bankruptcy statute provision concerning discharge, these words denote or connote guilty scienter on part of bankrupt, In re Krulewitch, D.C.N.J., 60 F.2d 1039, 1041; Wilensky v. Goodyear Tire & Rubber Co., C.C.A. Mass., 67 F.2d 389, 390. They mean an incorrect statement made or acquiesced in with knowledge of incorrectness or with reckless indifference to actual facts and with no reasonable ground to believe it correct. International Shoe Co. v. Lewine, C.C.A.Miss., 68 F.2d 517, 518; statement false to bankrupt's knowledge and made with fraudulent intent, In re Johnson, D.C.Conn., 1 F.Supp. 649, 651; statement knowingly false, or made recklessly without honest belief in its truth, and with purpose to mislead or deceive, Third Nat. Bank v. Schatten, C.C.A.Tenn., 81 F.2d 538, 540; In re Venturella, D.C.Conn., 25 F.Supp. 332. They mean more than erroneous or untrue and import intention to deceive, Schapiro v. Tweede Footwear Corporation, C.C.A.Pa., 131 F.2d 876, 878.

Bank's statement which gives result showing bank substantially stronger than it is in fact, constitutes "false statement" within statute defining offense of making or publishing false statement. Rosenberg v. State, 212 Wis. 434, 249 N.W. 541.

FALSE SWEARING. The essential elements of "false swearing" consist in willfully, knowingly, absolutely and falsely swearing under oath or affirmation on a matter concerning which a party could legally be sworn and on oath administered by one legally authorized to administer it. Smith v. State, 66 Ga.App. 669, 19 S.E.2d 168, 169.

To constitute "false swearing", it must appear that matter sworn to was judicially pending or was being investigated by grand jury, or was a subject on which accused could legally have been sworn, or on which he was required to be sworn. Capps v. Commonwealth, 294 Ky. 743, 172 S.W.2d 610, 611. The oath need not be taken in a matter judicially pending or any matter material to any point in question. Capps v. Commonwealth, 294 Ky. 743, 172 S.W.2d 610, 611. See, also, Perjury.

As used in provision concerning denial of liability under policy, means false statement willfully made with respect to a material matter with intention of thereby deceiving insurer, Sands v. Bankers' Fire Ins. Co., 168 Va. 645, 192 S.E. 617; false statements made knowingly and willfully, with intent to deceive insurer concerning matter material to insurance, Buccola v. National Fire Ins. Co. of Hartford, Conn., 18 La.App. 353, 137 So. 346, 350; knowingly and intentionally stating upon oath what is not true, or statement of a fact as true, which the party does not know to be true, Harwood v. United States Fire Ins. Co., 136 Me. 223, 7 A.2d 899, 902; knowingly and willfully false swearing to deceive or mislead insurers, Young v. California Ins. Co., 55 Idaho 682, 46 P.2d 718, 722; misstatement in proofs of loss willfully made, Palace Cafe v. Hartford Fire Ins. Co., C.C.A.Ind., 97 F.2d 766, 769; statements which are not only untrue but knowingly and intentionally made with knowledge of their untruthfulness or those statements which are made as the truth when party did not know them to be true and had no reasonable grounds for believing them to be true, and statements must be made for purpose of defrauding insurer, United States Fire Ins. Co. v. Merrick, 171 Md. 476, 190 A. 335, 342; swearing knowingly and intentionally false and not through mere mistake. Knight v. Boston Ins. Co., 113 N.J.L. 132, 172 A. 594, 595.

"Perjury" and "false swearing" may be interchangeable. Ray v. Times Pub. Co., Tex.Com.App., 12 S.W.2d 165, 166.

The misdemeanor committed in English law by a person who swears falsely before any person authorized to administer an oath upon a matter of public concern, under such circumstances that the false swearing would have amounted to perjury if committed in a judicial proceeding; as where a person makes a false affidavit under the bills of sale acts. Steph.Cr.Dig. p. 84. And see O'Bryan v. State, 27 Tex.App. 339, 11 S.W. 443. In Texas, it is not necessary, to complete the offense, that the affidavit be used for the purpose for which it was intended. Welch v. State, 71 Tex. Cr.R. 17, 157 S.W. 946. Under the Texas and Kentucky statutes, however, "false swearing" is distinct from the common-law crime of perjury; Commonwealth v. Hinkle, 177 Ky. 22, 197 S.W. 455, 456; Shipp v. State, 81 Tex.Cr.R. 328, 196 S.W. 840, 842; inasmuch as "false swearing" consists in making a false oath on a subject about which the party could legally be sworn, and before a person legally authorized to administer the oath; Commonwealth v. Bradshaw, 210 Ky. 405, 276 S.W. 124, 125; it not being necessary, as in perjury, that the testimony be material; Sullivan v. Commonwealth, 158 Ky. 536, 165 S.W. 696, 697.

FALSE TOKEN. In criminal law. A false document or sign of the existence of a fact,—in general used for the purpose of fraud. See 3 Term, 98; 2 Starkie, Ev. 563; 1 Bish. Cr. L. 585; People v. Haynes, 14 Wend., N.Y., 570, 28 Am.Dec. 530; Smith v. State, 74 Fla. 594, 77 So. 274, 276; State v. Renick, 33 Or. 584, 56 P. 275, 44 L.R.A. 266.

A written release of fictitious claim was a "false token" People v. Beilfuss, 59 Cal.App.2d 83, 138 P.2d 332, 339.

FALSE VERDICT. See Verdict.

FALSE WEIGHTS. False weights and measures are such as do not comply with the standard prescribed by the state or government, or with the custom prevailing in the place and business in which they are used.

FALSE WITNESS. One who is intentionally rather than merely mistakenly false. State v. Weston, 109 Or. 19, 219 P. 180, 189.

FALSE WORDS, which may be eliminated from descriptions in wills, deeds, etc., are misdescriptions of property that are not applicable to any property owned or intended to be devised or conveyed. Brown v. Ray, 314 Ill. 570, 145 N.E. 676, 679; Armstrong v. Armstrong, 327 Ill. 85, 158 N.E. 356, 358.

FALSEDAD. In Spanish law. Falsity; an alteration of the truth. Las Partidas, pt. 3, tit. 26, l. 1.

Deception; fraud. Id. pt. 3, tit. 32, l. 21.

FALSEHOOD. A statement or assertion known to be untrue, and intended to deceive. A willful act or declaration contrary to the truth. Putnam v. Osgood, 51 N.H. 207.

The term is perhaps generally used in the second sense here given. It is committed either by the wilful act of the party, or by dissimulation, or by words.

Crabbe thus distinguishes between falsehood and untruth: "The latter is an untrue saying, and may be unintentional, in which case it reflects no disgrace on the agent. A falsehood and a lie are intentional false sayings, differing only in degree of the guilt of the offender; falsehood being not always for the express purpose of deceiving, but a lie always for the worst of purposes." See Rosc.Cr.Ev. 362; Deceit; Fraud; Misrepresentation.

A fabrication. Werner v. Southern Cal. Associated Newspapers, Cal.App., 206 P.2d 952, 961.

Scotch Law

A fraudulent imitation or suppression of truth, to the prejudice of another. Bell. "Something used and published falsely." An old Scottish *nomen juris.* "Falsehood is undoubtedly a nominate crime, so much so that Sir George Mackenzie and our older lawyers used no other term for the falsification of writs, and the name 'forgery' has been of modern introduction." "If there is any distinction to be made between 'forgery' and 'falsehood,' I would consider the latter to be more comprehensive than the former." 2 Broun, 77, 78.

FALSELY. In a false manner, erroneously, not truly, perfidiously or treacherously. Dombroski v. Metropolitan Life Ins. Co., 126 N.J.L. 545, 19 A. 2d 678, 680. Knowingly affirming without probable cause. Hicks v. State, 67 Ga.App. 475, 21 S.E. 2d 113, 118. See, also, False.

As applied to making or altering a writting in order to make it forgery, implies that the paper or writing is not genuine; that in itself it is false or counterfeit. People v. Kramer, 352 Ill. 304, 185 N.E. 590, 591.

The use of the word falsely in a statute (against counterfeiting) implies that there must be a fraudulent or criminal intent in the act; U. S. v. King, 5 McLean 208, Fed. Cas.No.15,535. See, also, 4 B. & C. 329; 6 Com.Dig. 58; Stark, Cr.Pl. 86.

The word "falsely", particularly in a criminal statute, suggests something more than a mere untruth and includes perfidiously or treacherously or with intent to defraud. United States v. Achtner, C.C.A.N.Y., 144 F.2d 49, 52.

Usually used in the sense of designedly untrue and deceitful, and as implying an intention to perpetrate some treachery or fraud. Fouts v. State, 113 Ohio St. 450, 149 N.E. 551, 554; State v. Merlo, 92 Or. 678, 173 P. 317, 319; McDonald v. McNeil, 92 Vt. 356, 104 A. 337, 339; Cro.Eliz. 201; 7 D. & R. 665. But see 1 Den.C.C. 157.

FALSELY IMPERSONATE. To "falsely impersonate" may mean to pretend to be a particular person without lawful authority. People v. Horkans, 109 Colo. 177, 123 P.2d 824, 826.

FALSELY MAKE, means to make an instrument which has no original as such and no genuine maker whose work is copied, although in form it may resemble a type of recognized security. Pines v. United States, C.C.A.Iowa, 123 F.2d 825, 828.

FALSI CRIMEN. Fraudulent subornation or concealment, with design to darken or hide the truth, and make things appear otherwise than they are. It is committed (1) by words, as when a witness swears falsely; (2) by writing, as when a person antedates a contract; (3) by deed, as selling by false weights and measures. Wharton. See Crimen Falsi.

FALSIFICATION. In equity practice. The showing an item in the debit of an account to be either wholly false or in some part erroneous. 1 Story, Eq. Jur. § 525. And see Phillips v. Belden, 2 Edw. Ch. 23; Pit v. Cholmondeley, 2 Ves. Sr. 565; Tate v. Gairdner, 119 Ga. 133, 46 S.E. 73; Armstrong v. Toler, 11 Wheat., U.S., 237, 6 L.Ed. 468.

FALSIFY. To disprove; to prove to be false or erroneous; to avoid or defeat; spoken of verdicts, appeals, etc. Co. Litt. 104*b*.

To counterfeit or forge; to make something false; to give a false appearance to anything. To make false by mutilation or addition; to tamper with; as, to falsify a record or document. Pou v. Ellis, 66 Fla. 358, 63 So. 721, 722.

To show, as in an accounting before a master in chancery, that a charge has been inserted which is wrong; that is, either wholly false or in some part erroneous. Pull. Accts. 162; 1 Story, Eq.Jur. § 525. See Shores-Mueller Co. v. Bell, 21 Ga.App. 194, 94 S.E. 83, 84; Falsification.

The word "falsify" may be used to convey two distinct meanings—either that of being intentionally or knowingly untrue, made with intent to defraud, or mistakenly and accidentally untrue. Washer v. Bank of America Nat. Trust & Savings Ass'n, 21 Cal.2d 822, 136 P.2d 297, 301.

FALSIFYING A JUDGMENT. A term sometimes used for reversing a judgment. See 4 Steph. Com. 553.

FALSIFYING A RECORD. A high offense against public justice, punishable in England by 24 & 25 Vict. c. 98, §§ 27, 28, and in the United States, generally, by statute. See U. S. Rev.Stat. § 5394, 18 U.S.C.A. § 1506.

FALSING. In Scotch law. False making; forgery. "Falsing of *evidentis.*" 1 Pitc. Crim. Tr. pt. 1, p. 85.

Making or proving false.

FALSING OF DOOMS. In Scotch law. The proving the injustice, *falsity,* or error of the *doom* or sentence of a court. Tomlins; Jacob. The reversal of a sentence or judgment; an action to set aside a decree. Skene. Protesting against a sentence and taking an appeal to a higher tribunal. Bell, Dict.

FALSITY implies more than erroneous or untrue; it indicates knowledge of untruth. Abercrombie v. Hair, 185 Ga. 728, 196 S.E. 447, 451.

FALSO RETORNO BREVIUM. In old English law. A writ which formerly lay against the sheriff who had execution of process for false returning of writs. Reg. Jud. 43*b;* Cunningham, Law Dict.

FALSONARIUS. A forger; a counterfeiter. Hov. 424.

FALSUM. Lat. In the civil law. A false or forged thing; a fraudulent simulation; a fraudulent counterfeit or imitation, such as a forged signature or instrument. Also falsification, which may be either by falsehood, concealment of the truth, or fraudulent alteration, as by cutting out or erasing part of a writing.

FALSUS. Lat. False; fraudulent; erroneous. Deceitful; mistaken.

In the sense of "deceiving" or "fraudulent," it is applied to persons in respect to their acts and conduct, as well as to things; and in the sense of "erroneous," it is applied to persons on the question of personal identity.

FALSUS IN UNO, FALSUS IN OMNIBUS. False in one thing, false in everything. Commonwealth v. Billings, 97 Mass. 406; Mercer v. Wright, 3 Wis. 645; State v. Williams, 47 N.C. 257; Dawson v. Bertolini, 70 R.I. 325, 38 A.2d 765, 768.

The doctrine means that, if testimony of a witness on a material issue is willfully false and given with an intention to deceive, jury may disregard all the witness' testimony. Hargrave v. Stockloss, 127 N.J.L. 262, 21 A.2d 820, 823.

The maxim deals only with weight of evidence, Metropolitan Life Ins. Co. v. Wright, 190 Miss. 53, 199 So. 289, 290. It does not relieve jury from passing on credibility of the whole testimony of a false swearing witness or excuse jury from weighing the whole testimony. State v. Willard, 346 Mo. 773, 142 S.W.2d 1046, 1052. It is a mere rule of evidence affirming a rebuttable presumption of fact, under which the jury must consider all the evidence of the witness, other than that which is found to be false, and it is their duty to give effect to so much of it, if any, as is relieved from the presumption against it and found to be true. Levine Bros. v. Mantell, 90 W.Va. 166, 111 S.E. 501, 504; Shecil v. United States, C.C.A.Wis., 226 F. 184, 187. It is not a rule of law and false statement, State v. Sturchio, 127 N.J.L. 366, 22 A.2d 235, 237. It is not a rule of the law of evidence, but is merely an aid in weighing and sifting of evidence. Dawson v. Bertolini, 70 R.I. 325, 38 A.2d 765, 768. It is particularly applied to the testimony of a witness who, if he is shown to have sworn falsely in one detail, may be considered unworthy of belief as to all the rest of his evidence. Grimes v. State, 63 Ala. 168; Wilson v. Coulter, 51 N.Y.S. 804, 29 App.Div. 85; White v. Disher, 67 Cal. 402, 7 P. 826.

The rule is merely permissive and not mandatory. Bankers' Health & Life Ins. Co. v. Nichols, 44 Ga.App. 536, 162 S.E. 161.

Where a party is clearly shown to have embezzled one article of property, it is a ground of presumption that he may have embezzled others also. The Boston, 1 Sumn. 328, 356, Fed.Cas.No.1,673; The Santissima Trinidad, 7 Wheat. 339, 5 L.Ed. 454.

FAMA. Lat. Fame; character, reputation; report of common opinion.

FAMA, FIDES ET OCULUS NON PATIUNTUR LUDUM. 3 Bulst. 226. Fame, faith, and eyesight do not suffer a cheat.

FAMA QUÆ SUSPICIONEM INDUCIT, ORIRI DEBET APUD BONOS ET GRAVES, NON QUIDEM MALEVOLOS ET MALEDICOS, SED PROVIDAS ET FIDE DIGNAS PERSONAS, NON SEMEL SED SÆPIUS, QUIA CLAMOR MINUIT ET DEFAMATIO MANIFESTAT. 2 Inst. 52. Report, which induces suspicion, ought to arise from good and grave men; not, indeed, from malevolent and malicious men, but from cautious and credible persons; not only once, but frequently; for clamor diminishes, and defamation manifests.

FAMACIDE. A killer of reputation; a slanderer.

FAMILIA.

Old English Law. A household; the body of household servants; a quantity of land, otherwise called "*mansa,*" sufficient to maintain one family. Du Cange; Cowell; Cunningham, Law Dict.; Creasy, Church Hist.

Roman Law. A household; a family. On the composition of the Roman family, see Agnati; Cognati; and see Mackeld. Rom. Law, § 144.

Family right; the right or *status* of being the head of a family, or of exercising the *patria potestas* over others. This could belong only to a Roman citizen who was a "man in his own right," *(homo sui juris.)* Mackeld.Rom.Law, §§ 133, 144.

Spanish Law. A family, which might consist of domestics or servants. It seems that a single person owning negroes was the "head of a family," within the meaning of the colonization laws of Coahuila and Texas. State v. Sullivan, 9 Tex. 156.

FAMILIÆ EMPTOR. In Roman law. An intermediate person who purchased the aggregate inheritance when sold *per œs et libram,* in the process of making a will under the Twelve Tables. This purchaser was merely a man of straw, transmitting the inheritance to the *hœres* proper. Brown.

FAMILIÆ ERCISCUNDÆ. In Roman law. An action for the partition of the aggregate succession of a *familia,* where that devolved upon *cohœredes.* It was also applicable to enforce a contribution towards the necessary expenses incurred on the *familia.* See Mackeld. Rom. Law, § 499; Stair, Inst. l. 1, tit. 7, § 15.

FAMILIAR. The word is equivalent to the word "know." Smiley v. Lenane, 363 Ill. 66, 1 N.E.2d 213, 216.

FAMILIARES REGIS. Persons of the king's household. The ancient title of the "six clerks" of chancery in England. Crabb, Com. Law, 184; 2 Reeve, Eng. Law, 249, 251.

FAMILIARITY. Acquaintance expresses less than "familiarity"; familiarity less than intimacy. Acquaintance springs from occasional intercourse, familiarity from daily intercourse, intimacy from unreserved intercourse; acquaintance, having some knowledge, familiarity, from long habit, intimacy, by close connection. Atkins Corporation v. Tourny, 6 Cal.2d 206, 57 P.2d 480, 483.

FAMILY. The word is used to designate many relationships. Collins v. Northwest Casualty Co., 180 Wash. 347, 39 P.2d 986, 989, 97 A.L.R. 1235; State ex rel. Kemp v. Arnold, 234 Mo. 154, 113 S.W.2d 143, 146.

In broad or primary sense "family" means: a collective body of any two persons living together in one house as their common home for the time; In re Barnes' Estate, 149 Misc. 149, 267 N.Y.S. 634; a collective body of persons, living together in one home, in a permanent and domestic character, under one head or management,

State ex rel. Kemp v. Arnold, 234 Mo. 154, 113 S.W.2d 143, 146; a collective body of persons who live in one house and under one head or management, Fratellanza Italiana v. Nugnes, 114 N.J.Eq. 185, 168 A. 589, 590; a group of blood-relatives; all the relations who descend from a common ancestor, or who spring from a common root, Civil Code La. art. 3556, no. 12; 9 Ves. 323; a group of kindred persons, Hartley v. Bohrer, 52 Idaho 72, 11 P.2d 616, 618; husband and wife and their children. Franklin Fire Ins. Co. v. Shadid, Tex. Com.App., 68 S.W.2d 1030, 1032.

In most common use, the word implies father, mother and children, immediate blood relatives. Collins v. Northwest Casualty Co., 180 Wash. 347, 39 P.2d 986, 989, 97 A.L.R. 1235.

In narrow or restricted sense "family" means: a father, mother, and children, whether living together or not, Higgins v. Safe Deposit & Trust Co. of Baltimore, 127 Md. 171, 96 A. 322, 323; group of parents and children founded on principle of monogamy, In re Schmidt's Estate, 159 Misc. 373, 289 N.Y.S. 247, 250; husband and wife and their children, State ex rel. Kemp v. Arnold, 234 Mo.App. 154, 113 S.W.2d 143, 146.

In ordinary conversation, the word is descriptive of a person's wife and children. Adams v. Carrie F. Wright Hospital, 82 N.H. 260, 132 A. 525, 526.

In restricted sense, the word "family" may be used interchangeably with household. Collins v. Northwest Casualty Co., 180 Wash. 347, 39 P.2d 986, 989, 97 A.L.R. 1235.

In secondary meaning, "family" means those who are of the same lineage, or descend from one common progenitor. Fratellanza Italiana v. Nugnes, 114 N.J.Eq. 185, 168 A. 589, 590.

The word conveys the notion of some relationship, blood or otherwise. Collins v. Northwest Casualty Co., 180 Wash. 347, 39 P.2d 986, 989, 97 A.L.R. 1235.

The word may mean: a body of persons who live in one house and under one head or manager, Lumbermens Mut. Casualty Co. v. Pulsifer, D.C.Me., 41 F.Supp. 249, 252; Collins v. Northwest Casualty Co., 180 Wash. 347, 39 P.2d 986, 989, 97 A.L.R. 1235. A collection of persons living under a common roof, or constituting a domestic circle, In re Keegan's Estate, Sur., 37 N.Y.S.2d 368, 370, 371. A collective body of any two persons living together in one house as their common home for the time, In re Barnes' Estate, 267 N.Y.S. 634, 149 Misc. 149; a collective body of persons, consisting of parents or children, or other relatives, domestics, or servants, residing together in one house or on the same premises, Sullivan v. Walburn, 9 N.J.Misc. 280, 154 A. 617, 619. A collective body of persons living together in one house or within the curtilage. Sullivan v. Walburn, 9 N.J.Misc. 280, 154 A. 617, 619. A collective body of persons who form one household under one head and one domestic government. Sullivan v. Walburn, 9 N.J.Misc. 280, 154 A. 617, 619. A collective body of persons who form one household under one head and one domestic government and who have reciprocal natural and moral duties to support and care for one another, Krug v. Mills, 159 Md. 670, 152 A. 493, 495; Hartley v. Bohrer, 52 Idaho 72, 11 P.2d 616, 618. A collective body of persons who live in one home under one head or management. Dalton v. Poinsett, Mo.App., 164 S.W.2d 124, 128; Vaughn v. American Alliance Ins. Co. of New York, 138 Kan. 731, 27 P.2d 212; a collective body of persons who live in one house or within the same curtilage and under one head or management (thereby including domestic servants, lodgers, boarders, guests, etc.). Jarboe v. Jarboe, 106 Mo.App. 459, 79 S.W. 1162; Wilson v. Else, 204 Iowa 857, 216 N.W. 33, 37; City of Mexico v. Gray, 203 Mo.App. 547, 219 S.W. 707, 709; Wilson v. Cochran, 31 Tex. 680, 98 Am.Dec. 553; a group, comprising immediate kindred, consisting of the parents and their children, whether actually living together or not, Uden v. B. F. Goodrich Co., 58 Ohio App. 151, 16 N.E.2d 277, 279; a group of blood relatives; a group of kindred persons, Hartley v. Bohrer, 52 Idaho 72, 11 P.2d 616, 618; a household. Sullivan v. Walburn, 9 N.J.Misc. 280, 154 A. 617, 619; a household composed of parents or children, or other relatives or domestics and servants, Sullivan v. Walburn, 9 N.J.Misc. 280, 154 A. 617, 619; a small select corps attached to an army chief, Boston-Edison Protective Ass'n v. Paulist Fathers, 306 Mich. 253, 10 N.W.2d 847, 849, 148 A.L.R. 364; a whole sect, such as Shakers, Boston-Edison Protective Ass'n v. Paulist Fathers, 306 Mich. 253, 10 N.W.2d 847, 849, 148 A.L.R. 364; all members of the household living under the authority of the head thereof, Sullivan v. Walburn, 9 N.J.Misc. 280, 154 A. 617, 619; all persons of the blood of a common ancestor, Collins v. Northwest Casualty Co., 180 Wash. 347, 39 P.2d 986, 989, 97 A.L.R. 1235; all the relations who descend from a common ancestor or who spring from a common root; all who are descended from a not too distant common progenitor, In re Lund's Estate, 26 Cal.2d 472, 159 P.2d 643, 655; an entire household. Sullivan v. Walburn, 9 N.J.Misc. 280, 154 A. 617, 619; any group of persons closely related by blood, In re Schmidt's Estate, 289 N.Y.S. 247, 250, 159 Misc. 373; any group of persons constituting a distinct domestic body, Sullivan v. Walburn, 9 N.J.Misc. 280, 154 A. 617, 619; or social body, Boston-Edison Protective Ass'n v. Paulist Fathers, 306 Mich. 253, 10 N.W.2d 847, 849, 148 A.L.R. 364; group of parents and children founded on principles of monogamy, In re Schmidt's Estate, 289 N.Y.S. 247, 250, 159 Misc. 373; immediate domestic circle of a particular person, Collins v. Northwest Casualty Co., 180 Wash. 347, 39 P.2d 986, 989, 97 A.L.R. 1235; immediate members of one's household, Niemes v. Niemes, 97 Ohio St. 145, 119 N.E. 503, 506; members of the domestic circle, Sullivan v. Walburn, 9 N.J.Misc. 280, 154 A. 617, 619; one or more persons living together in same house who are supported by one in whole or in part and are dependent on him therefore, where he is under natural or moral obligation to render such support, Umbarger v. State Farm Mut. Automobile Ins. Co., 218 Iowa 203, 254 N.W. 87; the genealogical stock from which a man and those related to him by blood have sprung, Albright v. Albright, 116 Ohio St. 668, 157 N.E. 760, 764; the personnel of the home. Sullivan v. Walburn, 9 N.J.Misc. 280, 154 A. 617, 619; those members of the household who are dependent on the householder to whom he owes some duty, Cheshire v. Burlington, 31 Conn. 326; those who are of the same lineage, or descend from one common progenitor, Fratellanza Italiana v. Nugnes, 114 N.J.Eq. 185, 168 A. 589, 590; those who live in one house, In re Lund's Estate, 26 Cal.2d 472, 159 P.2d 643, 655; those who live in same household subject to general management and control of the head thereof, McGee v. Crawford, 205 N.C. 318, 171 S.E. 326, 327; those who live with the pater familias, Vaughn v. American Alliance Ins. Co. of New York, 138 Kan. 731, 27 P.2d 212; Indemnity Ins. Co. of North America v. Sanders, 169 Okl. 378, 36 P.2d 271, 273; those whom it is the natural or moral duty of one to support, or who are dependent on him for support, Finn v. Eminent Household of Columbia Woodmen, 163 Ky. 187, 173 S.W. 349, 350.

The word may mean, include or embrace an adult child, Watson v. Burley, 105 W.Va. 416, 143 S.E. 95, 96, 64 A.L.R. 839; Yadon v. Yadon, 202 Ark. 634, 151 S.W.2d 969, 970; aunts, In re Schmidt's Estate, 289 N.Y.S. 247, 250, 159 Misc. 373; blood relatives, Boston-Edison Protective Ass'n v. Paulist Fathers, 306 Mich. 253, 10 N.W.2d 847, 849; In re Keegan's Estate, Sur., 37 N.Y.S.2d 368, 370, 371; children, In re Dooling's Will, 285 N.Y.S. 603, 609, 158 Misc. 333; In re Schmidt's Estate, 289 N.Y.S. 247, 250, 159 Misc. 373; cousins, In re Schmidt's Estate, 289 N.Y.S. 247, 250, 159 Misc. 373; father and child, Hinds v. Buck, 177 Tenn. 444, 150 S.W.2d 1071, 1072; father, mother, and all children, wherever they may reside, Barrett v. Commercial Standard Ins. Co., Tex.Civ.App., 145 S.W.2d 315, 318; group of parents and children founded on principle of monogamy, In re Schmidt's Estate, 289 N.Y.S. 247, 250, 159 Misc. 373; husband and wife, In re De Nisson's Guardianship, 197 Wash. 265, 84 P.2d 1024, 1027, 1028; Boston-Edison Protective Ass'n v. Paulist Fathers, 306 Mich. 253, 10 N.W.2d 847, 849; Hinds v. Buck, 177 Tenn. 444, 150 S.W.2d 1071, 1072; husband and wife and their children, Franklin Fire Ins. Co.

v. Shadid, Tex.Com.App., 68 S.W.2d 1030, 1032; State ex rel. Kemp v. Arnold, 234 Mo.App. 154, 113 S.W.2d 143, 146; husband or wife and children. In re Keegan's Estate, Sur., 37 N.Y.S.2d 368, 370, 371; parents, In re Schmidt's Estate, 289 N.Y.S. 247, 250, 159 Misc. 373; parents and children, In re Schmidt's Estate, 289 N.Y.S. 247, 250, 159 Misc. 373; Uden v. B. F. Goodrich Co., 58 Ohio App. 151, 16 N.E.2d 277, 279; parents, children, and servants, and, as the case may be, lodgers or boarders, Cleaves v. Funk, D.C.Okl., 3 F.Supp. 804, 805; In re Schmidt's Estate, 289 N.Y.S. 247, 250, 159 Misc. 373; parents or children, or other relatives, or domestics and servants, Sullivan v. Walburn, 9 N.J.Misc. 280, 154 A. 617, 619; parents with their children whether they dwell together or not, In re Schmidt's Estate, 289 N.Y.S. 247, 250, 159 Misc. 373; Higgins v. Safe Deposit & Trust Co. of Baltimore, 127 Md. 171, 96 A. 322, 323; spouse and the issue of designated person, and no other persons, Restatement, Property, § 293; uncles, In re Schmidt's Estate, 289 N.Y.S. 247, 250, 159 Misc. 373.

Sisters of a religious order who were employed in hospital and lived together in a community as members of a "family". Goss v. Klipfel, 112 Colo. 87, 146 P.2d 217, 218.

Son-in-law is not a member of father-in-law's family, nor is his daughter, after she becomes son-in-law's wife. Bryant v. Keen, 43 Ga.App. 251, 158 S.E. 445, 446.

Widow who lived with her children in her father-in-law's house and received board for herself and children for keeping house was member of father-in-law's "family". Hollibaugh v. School Dist. No. 89, 131 Neb. 727, 269 N.W. 819, 820.

Allowances

Where marriage between decedent and his widow occurred years before decedent's death, parties lived together for about three weeks and never resumed their relationship as husband and wife, widow was not entitled to statutory allowance for the benefit of decedent's family. In re Feciuch's Estate, Sur., 26 N.Y.S.2d 390, 391.

Widow constitutes "family" within statute providing for allowance for maintenance from husband's estate. In re Hilleware's Estate, 159 Wash. 580, 294 P. 230, 231.

Word "family" in code provision authorizing family allowance where property set apart is insufficient for support of widow and children, does not include husband, Hills v. Superior Court in and for Los Angeles County, 207 Cal. 666, 279 P. 805, 806, 65 A.L.R. 266.

Beneficial and fraternal associations

As used in beneficial association's by-law providing that death benefit should be payable to member's family, the word means next of kin, including widow. Fratellanza Italiana v. Nugnes, 114 N.J.Eq. 185, 168 A. 589, 590.

As used in statutes or charters relating to who may become beneficiaries in fraternal associations, the word is not to receive a restrictive construction, and it may include stepchildren. Brotherhood of Locomotive Firemen and Enginemen v. Hogan, D.C.Minn., 5 F.Supp. 598, 603.

When used in constitution of benefit society, declaring its purpose among others as that of aiding the families of members, the word means such persons as habitually reside under one roof and form one domestic circle, or such persons as are dependent on each other for support or among whom there is legal or equitable obligation to furnish support and in its widest scope it would include all descendants of a common progenitor, Logan v. St. Louis Police Relief Ass'n, Mo.App., 133 S.W.2d 1048, 1049, 1050.

Compensation Law

A collective body of persons who live in one house and under one head or management is the significance ordinarily attributed to the word "family". Roney's Case, 316 Mass. 732, 56 N.E.2d 859, 864, 866.

Deceased adult son was a member of his parents' "family" though at time of his death he lived apart from his parents but contributed to support of parents. Baker v. Western Power & Light Co., 147 Kan. 571, 78 P.2d 36, 40.

Persons related by kinship or marriage, though not living in same household, may be members of "family". Moore's Case, 294 Mass. 557, 3 N.E.2d 5.

Descent and descendants

As used in act changing descent as between relatives of half blood, "family" comprehends only the descendants of ancestor, those who have his blood running in their veins; in that sense is nearly if not quite of same import as the word "issue." Ryder v. Myers, 113 N.J.Eq. 360, 167 A. 22, 24.

The word "family" may mean: all descendants of a common progenitor, Logan v. St. Louis Police Relief Ass'n, Mo.App., 133 S.W.2d 1048, 1049, 1050; In re Lund's Estate, 26 Cal.2d 472, 159 P.2d 643, 645; those who are of the same lineage, or descend from one common progenitor. Fratellanza Italiana v. Nugnes, 114 N.J.Eq. 185, 168 A. 589, 590.

Homestead and exemption laws

A "family" is a collection of persons living together under one head, Holsomback v. Slaughter, 177 Miss. 553, 171 So. 542, 543; a collection of persons living together, where there is an obligation, legal or moral, on head of the house to support the others or some of them, Logue v. Von Almen, 379 Ill. 208, 40 N.E.2d 73, 80, 140 A.L.R. 251; a collective body of persons, consisting of parents or children, or other relatives, domestics, or servants, residing together in one house or upon the same premises, and person to be member of family must be member in good faith, Lobban v. Vander Vries Realty & Mortgage Co., 48 Ariz. 180, 60 P.2d 933, 935; a collective body of persons who live in one house and under one head or manager, Hurt v. Perryman, 173 Tenn. 646, 122 S.W.2d 426, 427; a group of two or more persons dwelling together under one head, and which cannot consist of but one person, Zuniga v. Evans, 87 Utah, 198, 48 P.2d 513, 524, 101 A.L.R. 532.

A husband dying leaving a wife from whom he was not judicially separated left a "family". In re Zalewski's Estate, 30 N.Y.S.2d 658, 664, 177 Misc. 384.

An unmarried adult daughter who remains continuously with the "family" is member. Reconstruction Finance Corporation v. Burgess, Tex.Civ.App., 155 S.W.2d 977, 980.

Constitution and statute exempting homestead in each "head of a family" include not only a father, or husband, in his lifetime, but a widow, and after death of both, any minor children. Whitfield v. People's Union Bank & Trust Co., 168 Tenn. 24, 73 S.W.2d 690, 691.

"Family", continues to exist so long as widow lives and remains widow. Miers v. Miers, 160 Miss. 746, 133 So. 133, 134.

Husband who, after wife had abandoned him and remarried without obtaining divorce, purchased release of wife's right in his estate and abandoned her held not entitled to exemption provided on death of person leaving family. In re Schmidt's Estate, 287 N.Y.S. 44, 47, 247 App.Div. 505.

Husband, who had lived apart from wife prior to her death and had not contributed to her support held entitled to exemption provided on death of person having family. In re Gluer's Will, 278 N.Y.S. 994, 155 Misc. 41.

Persons who may constitute a family include: husband and wife. Bigelow v. Dunphe, 144 Fla. 330, 198 So. 13; husband and wife living together, Miller v. Finegan, 26 Fla. 29, 7 So. 140, 6 L.R.A. 813; Oppenheim v. Myers, 99 Va. 582, 39 S.E. 218; Dye v. Cooke, 88 Tenn. 275, 12 S.W. 631, 17 Am.St.Rep. 882; husband and wife so long as marriage continues in existence, In re Brown's Will, 274 N.Y.S. 924, 153 Misc. 282; mother and children living under father's authority, Washington Bank & Trust Co. v. Carrier, 178 La. 902, 152 So. 560, 561; school teacher on whom moral obligation rested to support and care for her sister. Standard Paving Co. v. Tolson, Tex.Civ.App., 86 S.W.2d 789, 791. Sister, owning property, and semi-invalid brother, who was cared for and supported by sister, and younger sister, who contributed to household expenses. Real Estate Land Title & Trust Co. v. Street, Tex.Civ.App., 85 S.W.2d 341, 342; stepchildren and stepfather living together after stepfather's divorce from children's mother, Smith Bros. v. Lucas, Tex.Com.App., 26 S.W.2d 1055, 1056. With particular reference to homestead laws, one parent and his or her children; Carle v. Bamberger, 53 Okl. 777, 158 P. 599, 600; Solnar v. Solnar, 205 Iowa, 701, 216 N.W. 288, 290; and even a widow or widower, though without children; Coleman v. Bosworth, 180 Iowa, 975, 164 N.W. 238, 240; may constitute a "family." See, also, In re Hooper's Estate, 117 Wash. 463, 201 P. 740, 742.

FAMILY

Test of whether husband has a "family" within statute providing for exemptions to widow if husband dies having a family cannot be measured by number of years husband and wife lived apart nor by distance of miles separating them. In re Brown's Will, 274 N.Y.S. 924, 153 Misc. 282.

To constitute family, status must be social and head of family must be legally or morally obligated to support other members, who must be dependent on such support. United Fidelity Life Ins. Co. v. Plainview Building & Loan Ass'n, Tex.Civ.App., 81 S.W.2d 1092, 1093; Lobban v. Vander Vries Realty & Mortgage Co., 48 Ariz. 180, 60 P.2d 933, 935.

To constitute family there must be one whom law designates or recognizes as head of family who by natural ties or by legal or moral obligation is under duty to support others of the household. Owens v. Altsheller & Co., 263 Ky. 727, 93 S.W.2d 844, 846.

To constitute persons living with another in same house a "family", it must appear that they are being supported by that other in whole or in part, and are dependent on him therefor, and that he is under a natural or moral obligation to render such support. Poffinbarger v. Administrator of Poffinbarger's Estate, 206 Iowa 961, 221 N.W. 550.

Where relatives live together because such arrangement is more convenient or economical, or for reasons of friendship or affection, such relation does not constitute them "family". Rock Island Bank & Trust Co. v. Lamont, 361 Ill. 432, 198 N.E. 430.

Household

A "family" is a collective body of persons who form one household under one head and one domestic government, Sullivan v. Walburn, 9 N.J.Misc. 280, 154 A. 617, 619; a collective body of persons forming one household under one head and domestic government, having reciprocal, natural and moral duties to care for one another. Hartley v. Bohrer, 52 Idaho 72, 11 P.2d 616, 618; Krug v. Mills, 159 Md. 670, 152 A. 493, 495; a household, Sullivan v. Walburn, 9 N.J.Misc. 280, 154 A. 617, 619; a household composed of parents or children or other relatives, or domestics and servants, Sullivan v. Walburn, 9 N.J.Misc. 280, 154 A. 617, 619; all members of the household living together under the authority of the head thereof, Sullivan v. Walburn, 9 N.J.Misc. 280, 154 A. 617, 619; all persons who dwell together under a common head as a household, Hoff v. Hoff, 132 Pa.Super. 431, 1 A.2d 506, 508; an entire household, Sullivan v. Walburn, 9 N.J.Misc. 280, 154 A. 617, 619; the immediate members of one's household, as wife, children, brothers, and sisters or father and mother. Niemes v. Niemes, 97 Ohio St. 145, 119 N.E. 503, 506; those who live in same household subject to general management and control of the head thereof, McGee v. Crawford, 205 N.C. 318, 171 S.E. 326, 327.

Family and household are substantially synonymous, Umbarger v. State Farm Mut. Automobile Ins. Co., 218 Iowa 203, 254 N.W. 87; the words are often used interchangeably, Indemnity Ins. Co. of North America v. Sanders, 169 Okl. 378, 36 P.2d 271, 273; Brovdy v. Jones & Laughlin Steel Corporation, 145 Pa.Super. 602, 21 A.2d 437, 438; while in a restricted sense the word "family" may be used interchangeably with "household," there is a difference in the ideas suggested by the two words, Collins v. Northwest Casualty Co., 180 Wash. 347, 39 P.2d 986, 989, 97 A.L.R. 1235.

Insane Persons

Under statute providing for support of family of insane person out of his estate, "family" includes those whom insane person under normal circumstances would be under legal duty to support, such as wife and children, and under some circumstances may include others. Woman who had become insane person's stepmother when he was infant and had cared for him during his infancy and to whose support he had contributed during his minority and until he joined Army held member of his "family" so as to be entitled to support. In re Freeman's Estate, 171 Miss. 147, 157 So. 253.

Insurance

Accident policy condition that insurer should have opportunity to be present at autopsy performed with consent of insured's "family" held to apply to person who, as surviving wife or husband, or next of kin, had right of possession of body. If insured left no wife, and sister was nearest kin, sister held "family" within such condition. Sheehan v. Commercial Travelers' Mut. Acc. Ass'n, 283 Mass. 543, 186 N.E. 627, 631, 88 A.L.R. 975.

Pauper

Duty of town to support "family" of pauper includes only those persons whom head of family is bound by law to support. Town of St. Johnsbury v. Town of Sutton, 102 Vt. 451, 150 A. 133, 135.

Reservation lands

Words "family" and "heirs," within statute providing for holding of reservation lands by Seneca Indians, mean family and heirs which Indians themselves recognize. Woodin v. Seeley, 141 Misc. 207, 252 N.Y.S. 818, 826.

Servants

A family is a body of persons who live in one household under one head or management; a household including parents, children and servants, and, as the case may be, lodgers or boarders. Cleaves v. Funk, D.C.Okl., 3 F.Supp. 804, 805.

Domestic servants, when living in establishment, are included in term "family" for purposes of serving summons. Sullivan v. Walburn, 9 N.J.Misc. 280, 154 A. 617, 619.

Service of Process

A domestic servant may be included in term "family." Sullivan v. Walburn, 9 N.J.Misc. 280, 154 A. 617, 619.

Defendant's mother, who maintained permanent home, but who usually visited in defendant's home during winter months, held not a member of defendant's "family." Cleaves v. Funk, C.C.A.Okl., 76 F.2d 828, 829.

The word "family", as used in acts regulating service of process, is given its restricted meaning and held to include only a father, a mother, and their children, but the relationship between the person receiving a copy of the summons and the person on whom service is attempted must be more confidential and intimate than in most employer and employee or master and servant relationships in order that the receipt by the former may be deemed valid service on the latter. Moore v. Kasishke, 189 Okl. 336, 117 P.2d 113, 115, 136 A.L.R. 1502.

Support of persons

A "family" is a collection of persons living together under one head, under such circumstances or conditions that the head is under a legal or moral obligation to support the other members, and the other members are dependent upon him for support, Hurt v. Perryman, 173 Tenn. 646, 122 S.W.2d 426, 427; those entitled by law to look to person for support and protection, In re Fulton's Estate, 15 Cal. App.2d 202, 59 P.2d 508, 510; those members of the household who are dependent on the householder to whom he owes some duty, Brokaw v. Ogle, 170 Ill. 115, 48 N.E. 394; those whom it is the natural or moral duty of one to support, or who are dependent on him for support, Finn v. Eminent Household of Columbia Woodmen, 163 Ky. 187, 173 S.W. 349, 350.

Bankrupt whose minor children were living separately from him in custody of his divorced wife held person having "family dependent on him for support". In re McFarland, D.C.Wash., 49 F.2d 342, 343.

"Family," within statute imposing liability for articles going to support of "family," held to include wife as well as children. Baledes v. Greenbaum, 112 Conn. 64, 151 A. 333, 334.

He upon whom law imposes duty to support growing out of status and not out of contract, and persons to whom he owes this duty if dwelling together in a domestic establishment constitute a "family" of which he is the head. Owens v. Altsheller & Co., 263 Ky. 727, 93 S.W.2d 844, 846.

Householder's sister and her husband living with householder and dependent upon him may constitute "family". Rock Island Bank & Trust Co. v. Lamont, 361 Ill. 432, 198 N.E. 430.

Moral duty to support arising from ties of blood or possibly other similar relations will be sufficient to support claim that one is head of a family. Owens v. Altsheller & Co., 263 Ky. 727, 93 S.W.2d 844, 846.

Sister on whom moral obligation rested to support her sister and such sister constituted "family." Standard Paving Co. v. Tolson, Tex.Civ.App., 86 S.W.2d 789, 791.

To constitute "family" within homestead or exemption provision there must be legal or moral or natural obligation of one to support other members and corresponding dependence of others. L. E. Whitham & Co. v. Briggs' Estate, Tex.Com.App., 58 S.W.2d 49; Lobban v. Vander Vries Realty & Mortgage Co., 48 Ariz. 180, 60 P.2d 933, 935; Wineblood v. Payne, 129 Okl. 103, 263 P. 669, 671.

Town of residence of head of "family" held not liable to reimburse another town for support furnished stepchildren. Town of St. Johnsbury v. Town of Sutton, 102 Vt. 451, 150 A. 133, 135.

Wills

As respects construction of will, the word "family" denotes a group of persons related to each other by marriage or blood living together under a single roof and comprising a household whose head is usually the father or husband, but the word is not one of inflexible meaning and its significance to a large extent depends upon the context and the purpose for which it is employed. The word "family" includes those who have left father's home and have married and established their own homes when context and purpose indicate such significance should be attributed to the word. Magill v. Magill, 317 Mass. 89, 56 N.E.2d 892, 894, 896, 154 A.L.R. 1406.

Testamentary precatory trust created in favor of any of testatrix' "family" held to comprehend those who would take under statute of distribution. Ryder v. Myers, 113 N.J.Eq. 360, 167 A. 22, 24.

Testatrix in creating trust for benefit of granddaughter during her life and providing that upon granddaughter's death without issue principal should go to then living members of granddaughter's father's "family" did not use word family to designate those who comprised her son's household, where testatrix knew when she executed will that son was dead and that his widow and daughter made their homes with testatrix and his other children lived separate from each other. Magill v. Magill, 317 Mass. 89, 56 N.E.2d 892, 894, 896, 154 A.L.R. 1406.

The use of the word "family" disclosed a testamentary intent to make a gift to a class including those who would have been distributees of the deceased brothers of testatrix had such brothers died as of the date of death of testatrix and included therein the widows of such brothers. In re Keegan's Estate, Sur., 37 N.Y.S.2d 368, 370, 371.

Under will of widow, providing that "I wish my husband's family to share and share alike the remainder of my property," the word "family" is equivalent to "heirs," In re McCrum's Estate, 97 Cal.App. 576, 275 P. 971, 972.

When the word "family" is used to designate those entitled to receive a legacy, the intended meaning of the word depends upon the context of the will and upon a showing as to whom were the objects of the testator's bounty by reason of kinship or friendship. Where a legacy was to a class, consisting of family of testatrix' deceased brother who was survived by widow and three children, each of which children maintained separate households, "family" included widow and three children. In re Keegan's Estate, Sur., 37 N.Y.S.2d 368, 370, 371.

Where testatrix created trust for benefit of granddaughter during her life and, knowing that one of granddaughter's brothers was already dead, provided that any issue granddaughter might leave should share equally with then living members of granddaughter's father's "family" in division of principal of trust and thereafter upon death of another grandson leaving a widow and two infant children executed a codicil giving grandson's legacy under another provision of will to his widow, word "family" was used to designate lineal descendants of granddaughter's father where such construction was consistent with provisions of the will and carried out intention of testatrix. Magill v. Magill, 317 Mass. 89, 56 N.E.2d 892, 894, 896, 154 A.L.R. 1406.

FAMILY ARRANGEMENT. A term denoting an agreement between a father and his children, or between the heirs of a deceased father, to dispose of property, or to partition it in a different manner than that which would result if the law alone directed it, or to divide up property without administration. In these cases, frequently, the mere relation of the parties will give effect to bargains otherwise without adequate consideration. 1 Chit. Pr. 67; 1 Turn. & R. 13; Boyd v. Robinson, 93 Tenn. 1, 23 S.W. 72; De Hatre v. De Hatre, 50 Mo. App. 1.

FAMILY AUTOMOBILE DOCTRINE. The doctrine is that one who owns and maintains an automobile for the general use of his household makes use of automobile for such purposes a part of his business so that any member using automobile for those purposes under general authority to do so becomes his representative, for whose negligence he is responsible. Durso v. A. D. Cozzolino, Inc., 128 Conn. 24, 20 A.2d 392, 394.

It is an extension of the principle of respondeat superior to the relation created by operation of family use automobile. Buss v. Wachsmith, 190 Wash. 673, 70 P.2d 417, 421. See, also, Family Car Doctrine and Family Purpose Doctrine.

It is based on theory that members of family were engaged in a joint enterprise or that child was agent of parents. Paulson v. McMillan, 8 Wash.2d 295, 111 P.2d 983, 989.

If an automobile is owned and maintained by a family corporation for general use of a family, such as that of corporation's manager and one of its principal stockholders, corporation may be held liable under the "family automobile doctrine" to third parties. Durso v. A. D. Cozzolino, Inc., 128 Conn. 24, 20 A.2d 392, 394.

FAMILY BIBLE. A Bible containing a record of the births, marriages, and deaths of the members of a family. As to its admissibility in evidence, see Whart. Ev. § 219; Tayl. Ev. 572; 1 Greenl. Ev. § 104; L. R. 1 Ex. 255; Greenleaf v. R. Co., 30 Iowa, 301; Southern Life Ins. Co. v. Wilkinson, 53 Ga. 535; Weaver v. Leiman, 52 Md. 709.

FAMILY CAR. Automobile used to send owner's children to school was "family car." Coleman v. Rollo, Tex.Civ.App., 50 S.W.2d 391, 392.

FAMILY CAR DOCTRINE. The doctrine rests upon the basis that the automobile is furnished by the husband in his individual capacity and as common-law head of the family for the use of the family, and not as the agent of the community. Donn v. Kunz, 52 Ariz. 219, 79 P.2d 965. It rests on theory that operator is husband's agent and runs automobile in husband's "business," Hart v. Hogan, 173 Wash. 598, 24 P.2d 99; that wife is husband's agent in carrying out one of the purposes for which the automobile is purchased and owned, Moffitt v. Krueger, 11 Wash.2d 658, 120 P.2d 512, 513.

Under the doctrine, a father furnishing automobile for pleasure and convenience of family makes the use of automobile by family his business and any member of family driving automobile with father's express or implied consent is the father's agent and the father is liable for the member's negligence. Donn v. Kunz, 52 Ariz. 219, 79 P.2d 965, 966, 967.

See, also, Family Automobile Doctrine and Family Purpose Doctrine.

The person upon whom it is sought to fasten liability under the doctrine must own, provide, or maintain an automobile for the general use, pleasure, and convenience of the family. Liability under the doctrine is not confined to owner or driver. It depends upon control and use. A widow, wife, or mother may be liable as well as a husband or father. Hart v. Hogan, 173 Wash. 598, 24 P.2d 99. To bring a case within doctrine, it must be shown that automobile was in fact a family pleasure automobile, but automobile purchased and used for business purposes may come within the doctrine, where it is also used for family pleasure. Dillon v. Burnett, 197 Wash. 371, 85 P.2d 656, 658.

FAMILY COUNCIL. See Family Arrangement; Family Meeting; Conseil de Famille.

FAMILY DEPENDENT UPON HIM FOR SUPPORT. Bankrupt whose minor children were living separately from him in custody of his divorced wife held to have "family dependent on him for support." In re McFarland, D.C.Wash., 49 F.2d 342, 343.

FAMILY EXPENSES. Obligations incurred for something intended for the use or comfort of the collection spoken of as the family, as distinguished from individual or personal expenses. Vose v. Myott, 141 Iowa, 506, 120 N.W. 58, 21 L.R.A.,N.S., 277.

Purchase price of team of horses used on farm was a "family expense". Wall v. Crawford, 103 Colo. 66, 82 P.2d 749, 750.

Tuition for education of children of taxpayer held "family expense". Channing v. U. S., D.C.Mass., 4 F.Supp. 33, 34.

FAMILY GROUP, within purview of the family car doctrine, is not confined to persons related to the owner, but includes members of the collective body of persons living in his household for whose convenience the car is maintained and who have authority to use it. Smart v. Bissonette, 106 Conn. 447, 138 A. 365, 366; Hart v. Hogan, 173 Wash. 598, 24 P.2d 99. See Family Purpose Doctrine, *infra.*

The children of trust settlor including an adult son are members of the settlor's "family group" for income tax purposes. Commissioner of Internal Revenue v. Wilson, C. C.A.7, 125 F.2d 307, 310.

FAMILY HOTEL. A "family hotel", as distinguished from an ordinary "public hotel", in construction of covenant, is designed primarily for the accommodation of permanent guests. Kew Gardens Corporation v. Ciro's Plaza, 175 Misc. 475, 23 N.Y.S.2d 957, 959.

FAMILY LIBRARY. Which one spouse cannot mortgage without consent of other may be composed of such books as family or head of family chooses to select. Lupton v. Merchants' Nat. Bank of Topeka, 140 Kan. 615, 38 P.2d 125, 127.

FAMILY MEETING. An institution of the laws of Louisiana, being a council of the relatives (or, if there are no relatives, of the friends) of a minor, for the purpose of advising as to his affairs and the administration of his property.

The family meeting is called by order of a judge, and presided over by a justice or notary, and must consist of at least five persons, who are put under oath. In re Bothick, 44 La.Ann. 1037, 11 So. 712; Civ. Code La. art. 305. It corresponds to the "conseil de famille" of French law, *q. v.* See Lemoine v. Ducote, 45 La.Ann. 857, 12 So. 939; Commaux v. Barbin, 6 Mart.La. N.S. 455.

FAMILY PHYSICIAN. A physician who regularly attends and is consulted by the members of the family as their medical adviser; but he need not attend in all cases or be consulted by all the members of the family. Price v. Ins. Co., 17 Minn. 519, Gil. 473, 10 Am.Rep. 166; Reid v. Ins. Co., 58 Mo. 424; Cromeens v. Sovereign Camp, W. O. W., Mo.App., 247 S.W. 1033, 1034.

FAMILY POOL. A species of contract that must have something to stand on besides wishful thinking, and the parties to it must be conscious that they are in it and contributing to it to be bound by it. Sherman v. Florida Tar & Creosote Corp., 160 Fla. 696, 36 So.2d 267, 269.

FAMILY PURPOSE DOCTRINE. A doctrine that the owner of a car, who gives it over to the use of his family and permits it to be operated by the members thereof, is liable for the injuries inflicted while being operated by a member of the family. Turoff v. Burch, 60 App.D.C. 221, 50 F.2d 986, 987; McNamara v. Prother, 277 Ky. 754, 127 S.W.2d 160, 161; Schwartz v. Johnson, 152 Tenn. 586, 280 S.W. 32, 33, 47 A.L.R. 323. The doctrine, that the owner of an automobile purchased or maintained for the pleasure of his family is liable for injuries inflicted by the machine while being used by the members of the family for their own pleasure. Doss v. Monticello Electric Light & Power Co., 193 Ky. 499, 236 S.W. 1046, 1047; Thompson v. Kansas City Rys. Co., 113 Kan. 74, 213 P. 633.

See, also, Family Automobile Doctrine; Family Car Doctrine; Family Group.

The doctrine imputes relationship of principal and agent where one maintains an automobile for pleasure or other use of member of his family. United States Fidelity & Guaranty Co. v. Brann, 297 Ky. 381, 180 S.W.2d 102, 104; it is based on theory that each family member in using such car for own pleasure is carrying out the purpose for which it is furnished, and is the owner's agent or servant, Behseleck v. Andrus, 60 S.D. 204, 244 N.W. 268, 269, 88 A.L.R. 596; Hackley v. Robey, 170 Va. 55, 195 S.E. 689, 692; Ener v. Gandy, Tex.Civ.App., 141 S.W.2d 772, 775. It is founded upon principles of agency or of master and servant. Kalil v. Spivey, 70 Ga.App. 84, 27 S.E.2d 475, 479; Baptist v. Slate, 162 Va. 1, 173 S.E. 512, 515; It is restricted to automobiles maintained by owner for comfort, pleasure, and convenience of members of his family. Mitchell v. Mullen, 45 Ga.App. 285, 164 S.E. 278, 280; Commonwealth of Kentucky, for Use and Benefit of Kern, v. Maryland Casualty Co. of Baltimore, Md., C.C.A.Ky., 112 F.2d 352, 356.

A father is not liable merely because he is head of family, but the one who owns or provides the automobile is liable. McNamara v. Prather, 277 Ky. 754, 127 S.W.2d 160, 161, 162. A wife may be held liable for the torts of her husband under the doctrine. Goldstein v. Johnson, 64 Ga. App. 31, 12 S.E.2d 92, 94. Agency is the very genesis of the doctrine, Vaughn v. Booker, 217 N.C. 479, 8 S.E.2d 603, 604, 605; Grandmother standing in loco parentis to grandson was liable under the doctrine for grandson's negligent operation of her automobile. Rutherford v. Smith, 284 Ky. 592, 145 S.W.2d 533, 536; Where wife owned automobile, husband was not liable under "family purpose doctrine," for minor son's negligent operation of the automobile, notwithstanding husband paid part of gasoline and garage bills. McNamara v. Prather, 277 Ky. 754, 127 S.W.2d 160, 161, 162.

It has been said that the family purpose doctrine has been accepted by the courts of about half of the states. Jacobsen v. Dailey, 36 N.W.2d 711, 228 Minn. 201. Among those states are Georgia, Nebraska, North Carolina, and Oregon.

On the other hand, the doctrine has been specifically rejected, or not adopted, by fully one-half of the states, including California, Illinois, Mississippi, New York, Pennsylvania, Virginia, and Wisconsin. In Minnesota it has been held that the doctrine has been superseded by a financial responsibility statute (M.S.A. § 170.54). Ellingboe v. Guerin, 36 N.W.2d 598, 228 Minn. 211. For a full discussion of the subject, see Blashfield, Cyc. of Automobile Law and Prac., Perm.Ed., § 3111 et seq.

FAMILY RELATION. A relationship which may exist between one taken into the family by the head of the family, notwithstanding the absence of blood relationship or of legal adoption. Nelson v. Poorman's Estate, Mo.App., 215 S.W. 753, 754.

Such relation exists: between two sisters when there is moral obligation on part of one to support and care for the other and when necessity for such care and support exists, Standard Paving Co. v. Tolson, Tex.Civ.App., 86 S.W.2d 789, 791; when child receives from parent services, maintenance, or gifts reasonably frequent to lead to expectation of future enjoyment thereof. Gaydos v. Dombyl, 301 Pa. 523, 152 A. 549, 551; Where brother owes moral obligation to support sister and necessity for such support exists, Central Life Assur. Soc. (Mutual) v. Gray, Tex.Civ.App., 32 S.W.2d 259, 260. Where father lives on homestead after mother's death with two adult sons, his only heirs, one of whom marries and remains on with father until father's death, Cumberland & Liberty Mills v. Keggin, 139 Fla. 133, 190 So. 492, 493. Where there is legal or moral obligation on head of family to support the other members, and there is dependence upon such members for support, Standard Paving Co. v. Tolson, Tex.Civ.App., 86 S.W.2d 789, 791.

FAMILY SERVICE RULE. Under "family-purpose doctrine" or "family-service rule" or "family-automobile doctrine" or "family-car rule", family head maintaining automobile for use of family is liable for injury resulting from negligence of minor son who is member of family while operating automobile with knowledge and consent of family head for comfort or pleasure of family. Cohen v. Whiteman, 75 Ga.App. 286, 43 S.E.2d 184, 186.

FAMILY SETTLEMENT. An agreement between members of a family settling the distribution of family property among them. Fitzgerald v. Nelson, 159 Or. 264, 79 P.2d 254, 255.

An arrangement or an agreement, between heirs of a deceased person, by which they agree on distribution or management of estate without administration by court having jurisdiction of such administration proceedings. Wright v. Saltmarsh, 174 Okl. 226, 50 P.2d 694, 703.

An agreement made between a father and his son or children or between brothers to dispose of property in a different manner from that which would otherwise take place. Peterson v. Hegna, 158 Minn. 289, 197 N.W. 484, 487. A term of practically the same signification as "family arrangement," *q. v. supra.* See Willey v. Hodge, 104 Wis. 81, 80 N.W. 75, 76 Am.St.Rep. 852.

Where decedent's widow and son were only parties concerned in distribution of decedent's estate, an agreement between the widow and son for division of the estate was a "family settlement". Stark v. Stark, 201 Ark. 133, 143 S.W.2d 875, 878.

FAMILY USE. That use ordinarily made by and suitable for the members of a household whether as individuals or collectively. Spring Valley Water Works v. San Francisco, 52 Cal. 120. The supply of water in a municipal corporation for family use includes the supply of jails, hospitals, almhouses, schools, and other municipal institutions; *id.*

FAMOSUS. In the civil and old English law. Relating to or affecting injuriously the character or reputation; defamatory; slanderous; scandalous.

FAMOSUS LIBELLUS. A libelous writing. A term of the civil law denoting that species of *injuria* which corresponds nearly to libel or slander.

FANAL. Fr. In French marine law. A large lantern, fixed upon the highest part of a vessel's stern.

FANATIC. A religious enthusiast; a bigot; a person entertaining wild and extravagant notions, or affected by zeal or enthusiasm, especially upon religious subjects.

Also, a person pretending to be inspired;—formerly applied to Quakers, Anabaptists, and all other sectaries, and factious dissenters from the Church of England. St. 13 Car. II. c. 6. Jacob.

FANCIFUL TRADE-NAME. Trade-names are "fanciful" when they do not, by their usual and ordinary meaning, denote or describe products to which they are applied, but indicate their purpose by application and association. Skinner Mfg. Co. v. General Foods Sales Co., D.C.Neb., 52 F.Supp. 432, 445.

FANEGA. In Spanish law. A measure of land varying in different provinces, but in the Spanish settlements in America consisting of 6,400 square varas or yards. *Diccionario de la Acad.;* 2 White Recop. 49; 138.

FAQUEER. See Fakir.

FARANDMAN. In Scotch law. A traveler or merchant stranger. Skene.

FARDEL OF LAND. In old English law. The fourth part of a yard-land. Spelman. Noy says an eighth only, because, according to him, two fardels make a nook, and four nooks a yard-land. Wharton. See Noy, Complete Lawyer 57; Cowell; Cunningham, Law Dict.

FARDELLA. In old English law. A bundle or pack; a fardel. Fleta, lib. 1, c. 22, § 10.

FARDING-DEAL. The fourth part of an acre of land. Spelman.

FARE. A voyage or passage by water; also the money paid for a passage either by land or by water. Cowell.

The sum paid or to be paid for carrying a passenger. Chase v. New York Cent. R. Co., 26 N.Y. 526; Clark v. Southern Ry. Co., 69 Ind.App. 697, 119 N.E. 539, 543.

As used in connection with interstate transportation, means a rate of charge for the carriage of passengers, as approved by the proper governmental agency. Krause v. Pacific Mut. Life Ins. Co. of California, 141 Neb. 844, 5 N.W.2d 229, 232.

In case of a water company it means the tax or compensation which the company may charge for furnishing a supply of water. McNeal Pipe & Foundry Co. v. Howland, 111 N.C. 615, 16 S.E. 857, 20 L.R.A. 743.

FARE PAYING PASSENGER is a passenger who pays the legal fare. Krause v. Pacific Mut. Life Ins. Co. of California, 141 Neb. 844, 5 N.W. 2d 229, 232.

FARINAGIUM. A mill; a toll of meal or flour. Jacob; Spelman.

FARLEU (or FARLEY). Money paid by tenants in lieu of a heriot. It was often applied to the best chattel, as distinguished from *heriot,* the best beast. Cowell.

FARLINGARII. Whoremongers; adulterers.

FARM, *n.* A body of land under one ownership, devoted to agriculture, either to raising crops, or pasture, or both. Dorsett v. Watkins, 59 Okl. 198, 158 P. 608, 9 A.L.R. 278. With the development particularly of the western states, a large part of whose wealth consists of cattle, the word "farm" has acquired a somewhat broader meaning, and in its generic sense is as applicable to a stock farm as to one where grain is raised. Porter v. Yakima County, 77 Wash. 299, 137 P. 466, 467. A certain amount of provision reserved as the rent of a messuage. Spelman. A considerable tract of land cultivated or used in some one of the usually recognized ways of farming. Mattison v. Dunlap, 191 Okl. 168, 127 P.2d 140, 141. A term, a lease of lands; a leasehold interest. 2 Bl.Comm. 17; 1 Reeve, Eng. Law, 301, note. The land itself, let to farm or rent. 2 Bl.Comm. 368. Rent generally which is reserved on a lease; when it was to be paid in money, it was called *"blanche firme."* Spelman; 2 Bl.Comm. 42.

Old English Law. A lease of other things than land, as of imposts. There were several of these, such as "the sugar farm," "the silk farm," and farms of wines and currants, called "petty farms." See 2 How. State Tr. 1197–1206.

The word has been defined to mean: a considerable tract of land, or a number of small tracts, devoted wholly or partially to agricultural purposes or pasturage of cattle but may also include woodland, Jones v. Holloway, 183 Md. 40, 36 A.2d 551, 554, 152 A.L.R. 933; A large tract or portion of land taken by a lease under a yearly rent payable by the tenant, Tomlin, Law Dict.; a parcel or group of parcels of land cultivated as a unit, Supervisors of Manheim Tp., Lancaster County, v. Workman, 154 Pa.Super. 146, 35 A.2d 747, 749; a piece of land held under lease for cultivation; Supervisors of Manheim Tp., Lancaster County, v. Workman, 154 Pa.Super. 146, 35 A.2d 747, 749; a piece of land used wholly or principally for agricultural purposes. State Industrial Accident Commission v. Eggiman, 172 Or. 19, 139 P.2d 565, 567; a plot or tract of land devoted to the raising of domestic or other animals; as a chicken farm; a fox farm; Hagenburger v. City of Los Angeles, 51 Cal.App.2d 161, 124 P.2d 345, 347; a portion of land used for agricultural purposes, either wholly or in part; a tract of land devoted in part, at least, to cultivation, for agricultural purposes, without reference to its extent, or to the tenure by which it is held. People ex rel. Rogers v. Caldwell, 142 Ill. 434, 32 N.E. 691; Fleckles v. Hille, 83 Ind.App. 715, 149 N.E. 915.

A tract of land devoted to agricultural purposes. Hagenburger v. City of Los Angeles, 51 Cal.App.2d 161, 124 P.2d 345, 347; a tract of land devoted to agriculture, stock raising, or some allied industry, Winship v. Inspector of Buildings of Town of Wakefield, 274 Mass. 380, 174 N.E. 476, 477; a tract of land devoted to general or special cultivation under single control. Supervisors of Manheim Tp., Lancaster County, v. Workman, 154 Pa.Super. 146, 35 A.2d 747, 749; a tract of land used for raising crops or rearing animals. Gordon v. Buster, 113 Tex. 382, 257 S.W. 220; a wheat, fruit, dairy or market farm, Township of Marple v. Lynam, 151 Pa.Super. 288, 30 A.2d 208, 210.

Both grazing and cultivated lands, sold on mortgage foreclosure, constituted "farm," State ex rel. Wahluke Inv. Co. v. Superior Court for Walla Walla County, 168 Wash. 142, 10 P.2d 986, 987.

The original meaning of the word was "rent," and by a natural transition it came to mean the land out of which the rent issued.

The term does not necessarily include only the land under cultivation and within a fence. It may include all the land which forms part of the tract, and may also include several connected parcels under one control. Succession of Williams, 132 La. 865, 61 So. 852, 853.

The word "farm" within town zoning by-law, means land used for production of crops, livestock grazing, raising of hay for cows to produce milk and other dairy products, raising of poultry and sale of chickens and eggs, or growing of fruit. Town of Lincoln v. Murphy, 314 Mass. 16, 49 N.E.2d 453, 455, 146 A.L.R. 1196.

Usually the chief messuage in a village or town whereto belongs a great demesne of all sorts. Cowell; Cunningham, Law Dict.; *Termes de la Ley.*

FARM, *v.* To lease or let; to demise or grant for a limited term and at a stated rental.

FARM CROSSING. A roadway over a railroad track at grade for the purpose of reaching tillage land cut off by the track. True v. Maine Cent. R. Co., 113 Me. 375, 94 A. 183, 184. See, also, In re Colvin Street in City of Buffalo, 155 App.Div. 808, 140 N.Y.S. 882, 883.

A conveyance of strip of land across farm to railroad as right of way, which reserved to grantor right to maintain two "farm crossings" over right of way, is broad enough to permit installation of an underground conduit for purpose of supplying electricity to farm of grantor for domestic and farm purposes. New York Cent. R. Co. v. Yarian, 719 Ind. 477, 39 N.E.2d 604, 607, 139 A.L.R. 455.

A farm crossing is a crossing used in connection with a farm and not property within city limits. Chicago, M., St. P. & P. R. Co. v. Cross, 212 Iowa 218, 234 N.W. 569, 572.

FARM LABOR. Agricultural employment and farm labor are used as practically synonymous and include all farm work and work incidental thereto. Smythe v. Phoenix, 63 Idaho 585, 123 P. 2d 1010, 1012.

Ordinarily, the term "farm labor" connotes the tilling of the soil, its products and the raising and caring for such domestic animals as are usually found in those surroundings. Tucker v. Newman, 217 Minn. 473, 14 N.W.2d 767, 771, 772.

Under Unemployment Insurance Law an employee employed on a farm devoted to the raising of fur-bearing animals was engaged in "farm labor". In re Bridges, 262 App.Div. 19, 28 N.Y.S.2d 312, 314.

FARM LABORER. Generally, a man hired to go on a farm. Klein v. McCleary, 154 Minn. 498, 192 N.W. 106, 107. The term "farm laborer" is ordinarily synonymous with the term "hired man." Lowe v. North Dakota Workmen's Compensation Bureau, 66 N.D. 246, 264 N.W. 837, 107 A.L.R. 973.

One employed as a laborer on a farm, especially one who does all kinds of farm work, In re Keaney, 217 Mass. 5, 104 N.E. 438; one employed in or about business of farming. Pridgen v. Murphy, 44 Ga.App. 147, 160 S.E. 701, 702; one employed on a farm in customary types of farm work or employed and paid directly by a farmer in transporting his raw produce. Cedarburg Fox Farms v. Industrial Commission, 241 Wis. 604, 6 N.W.2d 687, 689, 690; one who devotes his time to ordinary farm labor as gainful occupation with some reasonable degree of regularity and continuity, Adams v. Ross, 230 App.Div. 216, 243 N.Y.S.

464, 466; Makeever v. Marlin, 92 Ind.App. 158, 174 N.E. 517, 518; one who labors on a farm in raising crops, or in doing general farm work. H. Duys & Co. v. Tone, 125 Conn. 300, 5 A.2d 23, 28; Wayland v. Kleck, 57 Ariz. 135, 112 P.2d 207, 208. .

On question whether the term as used in Workmen's Compensation Acts includes an employee on a corn husking or a grain threshing outfit, or the like, which goes from one farm to another for compensation, the decisions are conflicting. See Slyoord v. Horn, 179 Iowa, 936, 162 N.W. 249, 252, 7 A.L.R. 1285. For cases *contra*, holding that such an employee is not a farm laborer, see In re Boyer, 65 Ind. App. 408, 117 N.E. 507, 508; Industrial Commission of State of Colorado v. Shadowen, 68 Colo. 69, 187 P. 926, 927, 13 A.L.R. 952.

The term includes a compensation claimant hired to feed and water poultry and clean poultry bins and houses and collect eggs, Bennett v. Stoneleigh Farms, 254 App.Div. 790, 4 N.Y.S.2d 255, 256; a ranch laborer, Gordon v. Buster, 113 Tex. 382, 257 S.W. 220; a sheep herder, Davis v. Industrial Commission, 59 Utah, 607, 206 P. 267, 268; Finger v. Northwest Properties, 63 S.D. 176, 257 N.W. 121; employee injured while carting firewood for domestic use from a farm that employer was operating on shares, Butterfield v. Brown, 261 App.Div. 1022, 25 N.Y.S.2d 803, 804; employee of independent contractor engaged in business of spraying trees for owners of citrus orchards, Maryland Casualty Co. v. Dobbs, 128 Tex. 547, 100 S.W.2d 349, 350. Employee of owner of farm land employed solely to dig ditch, Culpepper v. White, 52 Ga.App. 740, 184 S.E. 349; farm hand injured while cranking tractor furnishing power for buzz saw used to saw wood of employer's neighbor, McAllister v. Cobb, 237 App.Div. 674, 263 N.Y.S. 349; nurseryman's helper or employee, held "farm laborer", Georgia Casualty Co. v. Hill, Tex.Civ.App., 30 S.W.2d 1055, 1057; In re Bronxville Nurseries, 258 App.Div. 1019, 17 N.Y.S.2d 95.

FARM LAND. A term applicable to all the land contained in a farm, and not necessarily merely to land which has been plowed. De Woffe v. Kupers, 106 Or. 176, 211 P. 927, 930.

FARM LEASE. A contract upon a printed lease form, containing all provisions of standard Nebraska farm leases, was a "farm lease," notwithstanding inserted provision that first party employed second party to farm the premises and would pay second party half the corn and hay. In re Mulligan, D.C.Neb., 45 F.Supp. 763, 766.

FARM LET. Technical words in a lease creating a term for years. Co. Litt. 45 *b;* 1 Washb. R. Pr. Index, *Lease.* Operative words in a lease, which strictly mean to let upon payment of a certain rent in farm; *i. e.,* in agricultural produce.

FARM OUT. To let for a term at a stated rental.

Among the Romans the collection of revenue was farmed out, and the same system existed in France before the revolution of 1789; in England the excise taxes were farmed out, and thereby their evils were greatly aggravated. The farming of the excise was abolished in Scotland by the union, having been before that time abandoned in England. In all these cases the custom gave rise to great abuse and oppression of the people, and in France most of the farmers-general, as they were called, perished on the scaffold.

FARM PRODUCTS. Include swine, horses, meat cattle, sheep, manure, cordwood, hay, as well as vegetables, fruit, eggs, milk, butter, lard, and other provisions for the mouth. Keeney v. Beasman, 169 Md. 582, 182 A. 566, 569, 103 A.L.R. 1515.

FARM-TO-MARKET ROADS. Within act designating purposes for which road funds were allotted to counties, held to mean county public highways leading directly to, or intersecting, state highways leading to markets. Hastings v. Pfeifer, 184 Ark. 952, 43 S.W.2d 1073, 1074.

FARM UTENSILS. A term which, in an insurance policy, is broader than the term garden tools, and includes any instrumentalities within the meaning of the word utensils made use of on a farm, including a stock scale or a new windmill not erected. Murphy v. Continental Ins. Co., 178 Iowa 375, 157 N.W. 855, L.R.A.1917B, 934.

FARM WAGON. This term in an exemption statute includes a farm wagon moved by mechanical as well as by animal power. People v. Corder, 82 Colo. 318, 259 P. 613.

FARMER. A cultivator; a husbandman; an agriculturist. Kaslovitz v. Reid, C.C.A.Utah, 128 F.2d 1017, 1018. One who assumes the collection of the public revenues, taxes, excise, etc., for a certain commission or percentage; as a *farmer* of the revenues. The lessee of a farm. It is said that every lessee for life or years, although it be but of a small house and land, is called "farmer." This word implies no mystery, except it be that of husbandman. Cunningham; Cowell; 3 Sharsw. Bla.Comm. 318. There may also be a farmer of other personal property as well as of revenue and of lands. Plowd. 195; Cunn. Law Dict.

The word "farmer" also includes: an individual primarily, bona fide, personally engaged in producing products of the soil, in dairy farming, the production of poultry or live stock, the production of poultry or live stock products, or the principal part of whose income is derived from any one or more of the foregoing operations, In re Davis, D.C.Iowa, 22 F.Supp. 12, 13; employer cutting valuable timber off land incidental to his occupation of agriculture, Robinson v. Stockley, 166 Tenn. 380, 61 S.W.2d 677. One continuously and profitably engaged in farming, though much of his efforts were devoted to unprofitable seed business, Stoller v. Cleveland Trust Co., C.C.A.Ohio, 133 F.2d 180, 181; one engaged exclusively in raising tomato plants to sell to others who actually grow the tomatoes for market, In re Horner, C.C.A.Ill., 104 F.2d 600, 602; one engaged in agricultural pursuits as a livelihood or business, Skinner v. Dingwell, C.C.A.Iowa, 134 F.2d 391, 393; one engaged in dairy farming and in production of poultry or livestock, Leonard v. Bennett, C.C.A.Or., 116 F.2d 128, 131, 132, 134; one engaged in the business of cultivating land or employing it for the purpose of husbandry, Kaslovitz v. Reid, C.C.A.Utah, 128 F.2d 1017, 1018; one living on his farm from revenue thereof and personally operating it on large scale as his primary activity, In re Lindsay, D.C. Tex., 41 F.Supp. 948, 950, 951; one personally engaged in farming. Shyvers v. Security-First Nat. Bank of Los Angeles, C.C.A.Cal., 108 F.2d 611, 612, 613, 126 A.L.R. 674; In re Davis, D.C.Iowa, 22 F.Supp. 12, 13; one primarily engaged in agricultural pursuits. Leonard v. Bennett, C.C.A. Or., 116 F.2d 128, 131, 132, 134; one who cultivates a considerable tract of land in some one of the usual recognized ways of farming, Kaslovitz v. Reid, C.C.A.Utah, 128 F.2d 1017, 1018; Matteson v. Dunlap, 191 Okl. 168, 127 P.2d 140, 141; one who cultivates a farm either as owner or lessee. Kaslovitz v. Reid, C.C.A.Utah, 128 F.2d 1017, 1018; one who cultivates a farm, whether the land be his own or another's; one who directs the business of a farm and works at farm labor. Kaslovitz v. Reid, C.C.A.Utah, 128 F.2d 1017, 1018; Stoner v. New York Life Ins. Co., Mo.App., 90 S.W.2d 784, 795; one who expends his energies and production efforts in tilling the soil, raising crops and marketing them, thereby promoting his financial interest and advancement, Kaslovitz v. Reid, C.C.A.Utah, 128 F.2d 1017, 1018; one who is devoted to the tillage of the soil, Kaslovitz v. Reid, C.C.A.Utah, 128 F.2d 1017, 1018; one who is primarily, personally, and bona fide engaged in farming although he does not spend all of his time therein, work farm without assistance, or refrain from engaging in secondary activities, In re Lindsay, D.C.Tex., 41 F.Supp. 948, 950, 951; one who owns and resides on a farm, Kaslovitz v. Reid, C.C.A.Utah, 128 F.2d 1017, 1018; one who resides on a farm with his family, cultivating such farm, and mainly deriving his support from it, Kaslovitz v. Reid, C.C.A.Utah, 128 F.2d 1017, 1018; one who resides on and cultivates a farm, mainly deriving his support therefrom, State v. Hines, 94 Or. 607, 186 P. 420, 422.

The term "farmer" in Bankruptcy Act includes an administrator, Harris v. Zion Sav. Bank & Trust Co., 317 U. S. 447, 63 S.Ct. 354, 357, 87 L.Ed. 390; personal representative of a deceased farmer. In re Stoner, C.C.A.Pa., 133 F. 2d 696, 697.

FARMER GENERAL. See Farm Out.

FARMING. Tillage of the soil. In re Brown, D.C.Mo., 284 F. 899, 900; Hart-Parr Co. v. Barkley, C.C.A.Okl., 231 F. 913, 914.

Other definitions include:

Act or business of cultivating the land, Hagenburger v. City of Los Angeles, 51 Cal.App.2d 161, 124 P.2d 345, 347; business of cultivating land or employing it for the purposes of husbandry, Kaslovitz v. Reid, C.C.A.Utah, 128 F. 2d 1017, 1018; business of tilling the soil, Hagenburger v. City of Los Angeles, 51 Cal.App.2d 161, 124 P.2d 345, 347; commercial production of any plant, even horticultural or annual which has economic value, Township of Marple v. Lynam, 151 Pa.Super. 288, 30 A.2d 208, 210; conduct of a farm, State Industrial Accident Commission v. Eggiman, 172 Or. 19, 139 P.2d 565, 567, 569; cultivation and fertilization of the soil as well as caring for and harvesting the crops, Kaslovitz v. Reid, C.C.A.Utah, 128 F.2d 1017, 1018; cultivation of land for production of agricultural crops with incidental enterprises, Collins v. Mills, 198 Ga. 18, 30 S.E. 2d 866, 870; cultivation of the soil for the production of crops, Chudnov v. Board of Appeals of Town of Bloomfield, 113 Conn. 49, 154 A. 161, 162; operation of a farm, In re McMurray, D.C.Iowa, 8 F.Supp. 449, 454; operation of a nursery from which no sales were made on lots within zoning district, Hagenburger v. City of Los Angeles, 51 Cal.App.2d 161, 124 P.2d 345, 347, 348; stock raising and dairying if in connection with and incidental to tillage of the soil, In re Brown, D.C.Wash., 251 F. 365, 370; to produce crops or animals on a farm. Hagenburger v. City of Los Angeles, 51 Cal.App.2d 161, 124 P.2d 345, 347.

Cultivation of an indefinite quantity of land, and including gardening or horticulture, fruit growing, raising of vegetables, trees, shrubs, plants and similar products is farming within zoning ordinance. Hagenburger v. City of Los Angeles, 51 Cal.App.2d 161, 124 P.2d 345, 347, 348. Pasturing sheep is "farming or agriculture". Weddle v. Parrish, 135 Or. 345, 295 P. 454, 455.

"Farming" implies that the operator is dealing with the natural products of the soil in a natural manner, Dye v. McIntyre Floral Co., 176 Tenn. 527, 144 S.W.2d 752, 753.

To be engaged in "farming" within Bankruptcy Act, debtor need not be actually engaged in manual farm work, but may operate farm himself, or may operate many farms through overseers and wage hands. Florida Nat. Bank v. Evans, D.C.Ga., 28 F.2d 67, 68.

FARMING BUSINESS. A farmer's employee engaged in delivering a farm product to market or to buyer is employed in the "farming business". Hayes v. Barras, La.App., 6 So.2d 66, 68; Robichaux v. Realty Operators, 195 La. 70, 196 So. 23, 26.

FARMING OPERATIONS within statute providing for relief to farm debtors, means production of raw food or other material by natural processes of growth, and includes production of poultry and eggs. In re Knight, D.C.Conn., 9 F.Supp. 502.

Clearing wood land, if a mere incident to farming operations, is itself a "farming operation," Stahl v. Patrick, 206 Minn. 413, 288 N.W. 854, 855.

Persons employed to pack tobacco in warehouses by corporation which grew its own tobacco were engaged in "farming operations" where there was no market for tobacco at time it was brought to warehouses. American Sumatra Tobacco Corporation v. Tone, 127 Conn. 132, 15 A.2d 80, 82.

FARMING PRODUCTS. All things are considered as "farming products" or "agricultural products" which have a situs of their production upon the farm and which are brought into condition for uses of society by labor of those engaged in agricultural pursuits as contradistinguished from manufacturing or other industrial pursuits. In re Rodgers, 134 Neb. 832, 279 N.W. 800, 803.

FARMING PURPOSES. These words are not limited in meaning to mere cultivation of soil and maintenance of improvements thereon for such purposes, but include raising of live stock, as well as production of farm crops directly from soil. State v. Superior Court for Walla Walla County, 168 Wash. 142, 10 P.2d 986, 987.

FARO. An unlawful game of cards, in which all the other players play against the banker or dealer, staking their money upon the order in which the cards will lie and be dealt from the pack. Webster; Ward v. State, 22 Ala. 19; U. S. v. Smith, 27 Fed.Cas. 1149; Patterson v. State, 12 Tex.App. 224.

FARO LAY-OUT. A board commonly covered with green cloth to which the entire spade suit is affixed in a certain order. State v. Williams, 157 P. 957, 52 Mont. 369.

FARRAGO LIBELLI. Lat. An ill-composed book containing a collection of miscellaneous subjects not properly associated nor scientifically arranged. Wharton.

FARRIER. One who takes upon himself the public employment of shoeing horses. See 1 Bl.Comm. 431; 2 Salk. 440; Hanover, Horses 215.

FARTHING. The fourth part of an English penny.

FARTHING OF GOLD. An ancient English coin, containing in value the fourth part of a noble. 9 Hen. V. c. 7.

FARTHING OF LAND. A great quantity of land, differing much from farding-deal, *q. v.*

FARVAND. Standing by itself, this word signifies "passage by sea or water." In charter-parties, it means voyage or passage by water. 18 C.B. 880.

FARYNDON INN. The ancient designation of Serjeants' Inn, Chancery Lane, London.

FAS. Lat. Right; justice; the divine law. 3 Bl. Comm. 2; Calvin.

In primitive times it was the will of the gods, embodied in rules regulating not only ceremonials but the conduct of all men. Taylor, Science of Jurispr. 65.

FASCISM. Is defined as the principles and organization of the patriotic and anti-communist movement in Italy started during the great war, culminating in the virtual dictatorship of Signor

Mussolini and imitated by fascist or blackshirt organizations in other countries. Luotto v. Field, Sup., 49 N.Y.S.2d 785, 788.

FASCIST. A member of the Fascisti, pertaining to, sponsored by or embodying the principles of the Fascisti, which principles are described as nationalist and conservative and embodying principles of syndicalism, whether applied to an Italian party or to a similar party in other countries. Luotto v. Field, Sup., 49 N.Y.S.2d 785, 788.

A totalitarian; a believer in the corporate state; one opposed to the exercise of democratic methods or of civil liberties; high handed. A name of opprobium sometimes given to those who oppose proposed reforms or who are conservative in their political views.

FASIUS. In old English law. A faggot of wood.

FAST BILL OF EXCEPTIONS. One which may be taken in Georgia in injunction suits and similar cases, at such time and in such manner as to bring the case up for review with great expedition. It must be certified within twenty days from the rendering of the decision. Sewell v. Edmonston, 66 Ga. 353.

FAST-DAY. A day of fasting and penitence, or of mortification by religious abstinence. As to counting it in legal proceedings, see 1 Chit. Archb. Pr., 12th Ed., 160, et seq.

FAST ESTATE. See Estate.

FASTERMANS, FASTERMANNES, or FASTING-MEN. Men in repute and substance; pledges, sureties, or bondsmen, who, according to the Saxon polity, were *fast* bound to answer for each other's peaceable behavior. Spelman; Enc. Lond.

FASTI. In Roman law. Lawful. *Dies fasti,* lawful days; days on which justice could lawfully be administered by the prætor. See Dies Fasti.

FAT SPOT. A "fat spot" is a spot where there is an excessive amount of bituminous material on the surface of the pavement. Karl v. State, 279 N.Y. 555, 18 N.E.2d 852, 853.

FATAL ERRORS. Are such only as may reasonably be held to have worked injury to complaining party. Willard v. Stauffer, 91 Ind.App. 119, 170 N.E. 332, 334.

FATAL INJURY. A term embracing injuries resulting in death, which, as used in accident and disability insurance policies is distinguished from "disability," which embraces injuries preventing the insured from performing the work in which he is usually employed, but not resulting in death. Provident Life & Accident Ins. Co. v. Johnson, Tex.Civ.App., 235 S.W. 650, 652.

FATAL VARIANCE. A variance tending to mislead defendant in making defense or one preventing plea of former jeopardy. Burke v. U. S., C.C. A.Cal., 58 F.2d 739, 741.

A variance in order to be "fatal" must be material. Whittier v. Leifert, 72 N.D. 528, 9 N.W.2d 402, 405; People v. Mizer, 37 Cal.App.2d 148, 99 P.2d 333, 335, 336; it must be misleading or serve to mislead the adverse party, Lorenz v. Santa Monica City High School Dist., 51 Cal.App.2d 393, 124 P.2d 846, 851; it must be substantial and material, Miller v. Arliskas, 324 Ill.App. 588, 58 N.E. 2d 743.

Attempt to introduce evidence of special damages from breach of tort or breach of contract, under general averment of damage is a "fatal variance". W. C. Hardesty Co. v. Schaefer, Mo.App., 139 S.W.2d 1031, 1035.

The general rule with respect to proof of time when an offense is committed is that there is no "fatal variance" from the allegation that it was committed on a particular date, to show that it was actually committed on or about or near that date unless the variance results in misleading defendant so as to prevent him from making his defense to the charge or to deprive him of the benefit of a plea of former jeopardy in event of another trial for the same offense. People v. Tracy, 50 Cal.App.2d 460, 123 P.2d 138, 140, 141.

FATETUR FACINUS QUI JUDICIUM FUGIT. He who flees judgment confesses his guilt. 3 Inst. 14; 5 Co. 109*b*. But see Best, Pres. § 248.

FATHER. A male parent. In re Clark's Estate, 228 Iowa 75, 290 N.W. 13, 32. He by whom a child is begotten. Natural father; procreator of a child. In re Dexheimer's Estate, 197 Wis. 145, 221 N.W. 737. For "Putative Father," see that title.

As used in law, this term may (according to the context and the nature of the instrument) include a putative as well as a legal father, also a stepfather, an adoptive father, or a grandfather, but is not as wide as the word "parent," and cannot be so construed as to include a female. Thornburg v. American Strawboard Co., 141 Ind. 443, 40 N.E. 1062, 50 Am.St.Rep. 334; McGaughey v. Grand Lodge, A. O. U. W. of State of Minnesota, 148 Minn. 136, 180 N.W. 1001; Fienup v. Stamer, Mo.App., 28 S.W.2d 437, 439. The term may, however, be so limited as to mean only the father of a legitimate child. People v. Wolf, 216 App.Div. 771, 215 N.Y.S. 95, 96; Howard v. U. S., D.C.Ky., 2 F.2d 170, 173.

As used in law, this term may mean natural father and not adoptive parent. McKinney v. Minkler, Tex.Civ.App., 102 S.W.2d 273, 279; Jackson's Adm'x v. Alexiou, 223 Ky. 95, 3 S.W.2d 177, 178, 56 A.L.R. 1345.

As used in statute providing that father may inherit from his illegitimate children, includes heirs of the father. State v. Chavez, 42 N.M. 569, 82 P.2d 900, 906.

As used in statutes relating to duty of a father and other relatives to support adult children likely to become public charges, refers to foster father after adoption, Betz v. Horr, 276 N.Y. 83, 11 N.E.2d 548, 550, 114 A.L.R. 491.

The appellation "Father" indicates that the one to whom it is applied is a priest of the Catholic Church, Sweeney v. Newspaper Printing Corporation, 177 Tenn. 196, 147 S.W.2d 406, 407.

The word may be used in will as equivalent of "parent," which is defined as meaning father and mother. In re Frist's Estate, 18 Del.Ch. 409, 161 A. 918.

FATHER-IN-LAW. The father of one's wife or husband.

FATHOM. A nautical measure of six feet in length. Occasionally used as a superficial measure of land and in mining, and in that case it means a square fathom or thirty-six square feet. Nahaolelua v. Kaaahu, 9 Hawaii, 601.

FATUA MULIER. A whore. Du Fresne.

FATUITAS. In old English law. Fatuity; idiocy. Reg. Orig. 266.

FATUM. Lat. Fate; a superhuman power; an event or cause of loss, beyond human foresight or means of prevention.

FATUOUS PERSON. In Scotch law. One entirely destitute of reason; *is qui omnino desipit.* Ersk. Inst. 1, 7, 48. An idiot. Jacob. One who is incapable of managing his affairs, by reason of a total defect of reason. He is described as having uniform stupidity and inattention of manner and childishness of speech. Bell's Law Dict.

FATUUM JUDICIUM. A foolish judgment or verdict. As applied to the latter it is one rather false by reason of folly than criminally so, or as amounting to perjury. Bract. fol. 289.

FATUUS. An idiot or fool. Bract. fol. 420*b*. Foolish; silly; absurd; indiscreet; or ill considered. See *Fatuum judicium.*

FATUUS, APUD JURISCONSULTOS NOSTROS, ACCIPITUR PRO NON COMPOS MENTIS; ET FATUUS DICITUR, QUI OMNINO DESIPIT. 4 Coke, 128. Fatuous, among our jurisconsults, is understood for a man not of right mind; and he is called *"fatuus"* who is altogether foolish.

FATUUS PRÆSUMITUR QUI IN PROPRIO NOMINE ERRAT. A man is presumed to be simple who makes a mistake in his own name. Code, 6, 24, 14; Van Alst v. Hunter, 5 Johns. Ch., N.Y. 148, 161.

FAUBOURG. In French law, and in Louisiana. A district or part of a town adjoining the principal city; a suburb. See City Council of Lafayette v. Holland, 18 La. 286.

FAUCES TERRÆ. (Jaws of the land.) Narrow headlands and promontories, inclosing a portion or arm of the sea within them. 1 Kent, Comm. 367, and note; Hale, De Jure Mar. 10; The Harriet, 1 Story, 251, 259, Fed. Cas. No. 6,099; 16 Yale L.J. 471.

FAULT.

American Law. Negligence; an error or defect of judgment or of conduct; any deviation from prudence, duty, or rectitude; any shortcoming, or neglect of care or performance resulting from inattention, incapacity, or perversity; a wrong tendency, course, or act; bad faith or mismanagement; neglect of duty. School Dist. v. Boston, H. & E. R. Co., 102 Mass. 553, 3 Am.Rep. 502; Dorr v. Harkness, 49 N.J.Law, 571, 10 A. 400, 60 Am. Rep. 656; Cochrane v. Forbes, 257 Mass. 135, 153 N.E. 566, 570; Continental Oil Co. v. Horsey, 175 Md. 609, 3 A.2d 476, 478; Continental Ins. Co. v. Sabine Towing Co., C.C.A.Tex., 117 F.2d 694, 697.

As respects wife's fault as ground for divorce, it means more than a deviation from the rules of propriety and also means a blemish or impairment of excellence. Barnett v. Barnett, 292 Ky. 672, 167 S.W.2d 845, 847.

As used in statute respecting suits for separate maintenance, means voluntary separation, or failure of duty or misconduct materially contributing to disruption of marital relation. Amberson v. Amberson, 349 Ill. 214, 181 N.E 825, 826.

As used in Unemployment Compensation Act protecting persons unemployed through no fault of their own, means failure or volition, White v. Review Board of Indiana Employment Security Division, 114 Ind.App. 383, 52 N.E.2d 500, 502.

The word "fault," the primary lexical meaning of which is defect or failing, in the language of the law and in the interpretation of statutes signifies a failure of duty, and is the equivalent of negligence. Milliken v. Fenderson, 110 Me. 306, 86 A. 174, 175; Marston v. Pickwick Stages, 78 Cal.App. 526, 248 P. 930, 933. But see Liberty Highway Co. v. Callahan, 24 Ohio App. 374, 157 N.E. 708, 714.

Civil Law. Negligence; want of care. An improper act or omission, injurious to another, and transpiring through negligence, rashness, or ignorance.

There are in law three degrees of faults,—the gross, the slight, and the very slight fault. The *gross* fault is that which proceeds from inexcusable negligence or ignorance; it is considered as nearly equal to fraud. The *slight* fault is that want of care which a prudent man usually takes of his business. The *very slight* fault is that which is excusable, and for which no responsibility is incurred. Civil Code La. art. 3556, par. 13.

Commercial Law. Defect; imperfection; blemish. See With All Faults.

Mining Law. A dislocation of strata; particularly, a severance of the continuity of a vein or lode by the dislocation of a portion of it.

FAUTOR. Old English law. A favorer or supporter of others; an abettor. Cowell; Jacob. A partisan. One who encouraged resistance to the execution of process.

Spanish Law. Accomplice; the person who aids or assists another in the commission of a crime.

FAUX.

Civil Law. The fraudulent alteration of the truth. The same with the Latin *falsum* or *crimen falsi.*

French Law. A falsification or fraudulent alteration or suppression of a thing by words, by writings, or by acts without either. Biret.

"*Faux* may be understood in three ways. In its most extended sense it is the alteration of truth, with or without intention; it is nearly synonymous with 'lying.' In a less extended sense, it is the alteration of truth, accompanied with fraud, *mutatio veritatis cum dolo facta.* And lastly, in a narrow, or rather the legal, sense of the word, when it is a question to know if the *faux* be a crime, it is the fraudulent alteration of the truth in those cases ascertained and punished by the law." Touillier, t. 9, n. 188.

Old English Law. False; counterfeit. *Faux action*, a false action. Litt. § 688. *Faux money*, counterfeit money. St. Westm. 1, c. 15. *Faux peys*, false weights. Britt. c. 20. *Faux serement*, a false oath. St. Westm. 1, c. 38.

FAVOR, *n.* An act of kindness or generosity, as distinguished from one that is inspired by regard for justice, duty, or right. Ross v. Davis, 138 Misc. 863, 248 N.Y.S. 441, 443. Bias; partiality; lenity; prejudice. See Challenge.

FAVOR, *v.* To regard with favor; to aid or to have the disposition to aid; to show partiality or unfair bias towards;—practically synonymous with "support." United States v. Schulze, D.C.

Cal., 253 F. 377, 379. The word implies a mental attitude or intent. Schulze v. United States, C.C.A.Cal., 259 F. 189, 190.

FAVORABILIA IN LEGE SUNT FISCUS, DOS, VITA, LIBERTAS. Jenk. Cent. 94. Things favorably considered in law are the treasury, dower, life, liberty.

FAVORABILIORES REI, POTIUS QUAM ACTORES, HABENTUR. The condition of the defendant must be favored, rather than that of the plaintiff. In other words, *melior est conditio defendentis*. Dig. 50, 17, 125; Broom, Max. 715. See Hunt v. Rousmanier's Adm'r, 8 Wheat. U.S. 195, 196, 5 L.Ed. 589.

FAVORABILIORES SUNT EXECUTIONES ALIIS PROCESSIBUS QUIBUSCUNQUE. Co. Litt. 289. Executions are preferred to all other processes whatever.

FAVORED BENEFICIARY. Within rule that confidential relations and activity by favored beneficiary in the execution of the will raises a prima facie presumption of undue influence, is one who in the circumstances has been favored over others having equal claims to testator's bounty. Mindler v. Crocker, 245 Ala. 578, 18 So.2d 278, 281.

FAVORES AMPLIANDI SUNT; ODIA RESTRINGENDA. Jenk. Cent. 186. Favors are to be enlarged; things hateful restrained.

FEAL. Faithful; truthful; true. Tenants by knight service swore to their lords to be *feal* and *leal; i. e.*, faithful and loyal. *Feal homager*, faithful subject.

FEAL AND DIVOT. A right in Scotland, similar to the right of turbary in England, for fuel, etc. Wharton; Ersk. ii. tit. ix. s. 17.

FEALTY. In feudal law. Fidelity; allegiance to the feudal lord of the manor; the feudal obligation resting upon the tenant or vassal by which he was bound to be faithful and true to his lord, and render him obedience and service. See De Peyster v. Michael, 6 N.Y. 497, 57 Am.Dec. 470; Littleton §§ 117, 131; Wright, Ten. 35; *Termes de la Ley;* 1 Washb. R. P. 19; 1 Poll. & Maitl. 277–287; Stubbs, Const. Hist. § 462 n; Co. Lit. 67*b;* 3 Kent 510.

This fealty was of two sorts: that which is general, and is due from every subject to his prince; the other special, and required of such only as in respect of their fee are tied by this oath to their landlords; 1 Bla.Comm. 367; Cowell.

Fealty signifies fidelity, the phrase "feal and leal" meaning simply "faithful and loyal." Tenants by knights' service and also tenants in socage were required to take an oath of fealty to the king or others, their immediate lords; and fealty was one of the conditions of their tenure, the breach of which operated a forfeiture of their estates. Brown.

Although foreign jurists considered fealty and homage as convertible terms, because in some continental countries they are blended so as to form one engagement, yet they are not to be confounded in our country, for they do not imply the same thing, *homage* being the acknowledgment of tenure, and *fealty,* the vassal oath of fidelity, being the essential feudal bond, and the animating principle of a feud, without which it could not subsist. Wharton.

FEAR. Apprehension of harm; dread; consciousness of approaching danger.

Apprehension of harm or punishment, as exhibited by outward and visible marks of emotion. An evidence of guilt in certain cases. See Burrill, Circ. Ev. 476.

The "fear" which renders evidence of female's utmost resistance unnecessary to support conviction of "rape" is a fear of death or great bodily harm, or a fear that so overpowers female that she dares not resist, or a fear and terror so extreme as to preclude resistance, or a fear which renders female's mind well nigh incapable of continuing her resistance. State v. Hoffman, 228 Wis. 235, 280 N.W. 357, 359, 361.

Statutes defining crime of extortion and providing punishment therefor must be read together, and "fear," within statute defining term as obtaining of property from another with his consent induced by "fear," must be induced by threats, and hence threat is necessary ingredient of crime. State v. Anderson, 66 N.D. 522, 267 N.W. 121, 124.

FEASANCE. A doing; the doing of an act; a performing or performance. See Malfeasance; Misfeasance; Nonfeasance.

A making; the making of an indenture, release, or obligation. Litt. § 371; Dyer, (Fr. Ed.) 56*b*. The making of a statute. Keilw. 1*b*.

FEASANT. Doing, or making, as, in the term "damage feasant," (doing damage or injury,) spoken of cattle straying upon another's land.

FEASIBLE. Capable of being done, executed, or affected. Lowe v. Chicago Lumber Co. of Omaha, 135 Neb. 735, 283 N.W. 841, 844.

It also means: capable of being successfully done or accomplished. Gilmartin v. D. & N. Transp. Co., 123 Conn. 127, 193 A. 726, 729, 113 A.L.R. 1322; fit to be dealt with successfully, Hinchman v. City Water Co., 179 Tenn. 545, 167 S.W.2d 986, 990; practically possible or capable of being managed, utilized, or dealt with successfully, In re Washakie Needles Irr. Dist., 52 Wyo. 518, 76 P.2d 617, 621.

A "feasible method of liquidation", as used in section of Bankruptcy Act setting out conditions precedent to confirmation of agricultural extension proposal, means that court must be convinced before confirming proposal that proposal to creditors is one that probably can be carried out by debtor and result in liquidation to secured creditors and rehabilitation for farmer, and that it is to best interests of all creditors. Heldstab v. Equitable Life Assur. Soc. of United States, C.C.A.Kan., 91 F.2d 655, 659.

The word "feasible", within meaning of rule that a plan of corporate reorganization must be feasible, does not connote absolute insurance of success but only reasonable assurance of success. In re Waern Bldg. Corporation, C.C.A. Ill., 145 F.2d 584, 588.

FEASOR. Doer; maker. *Feasors del estatute,* makers of the statute. Dyer, 3*b*. Also used in the compound term, "tort-feasor," one who commits or is guilty of a tort.

FEASTS. Certain established festivals or holidays in the ecclesiastical calendar. These days were anciently used as the dates of legal instruments, and in England the quarter-days, for paying rent, are four feast-days. The terms of the courts, in England, before 1875, were fixed to begin on certain days determined with reference to the occurrence of four of the chief feasts.

FECIAL LAW. The nearest approach to a system of international law known to the ancient world. It was a branch of Roman jurisprudence, concerned with embassies, declarations of war, and treaties of peace. It received this name from the *feciales*, (*q. v.*,) who were charged with its administration.

FECIALES. Among the ancient Romans, that order of priests who discharged the duties of ambassadors. Subsequently their duties appear to have related more particularly to the declaring war and peace. Calvin.; 1 Kent, Comm. 6.

FEDERAL.

American Law. Belonging to the general government or union of the states. Founded on or organized under the constitution or laws of the United States.

The United States has been generally styled, in American political and judicial writings, a "federal government." The term has not been imposed by any specific constitutional authority, but only expresses the general sense and opinion upon the nature of the form of government. In recent years, there is observable a disposition to employ the term "national" in speaking of the government of the Union. Neither word settles anything as to the nature or powers of the government. "Federal" is somewhat more appropriate if the government is considered a union of the states; "national" is preferable if the view is adopted that the state governments and the Union are two distinct systems, each established by the people directly, one for local and the other for national purposes. See United States v. Cruikshank, 92 U.S. 542, 23 L.Ed. 588; Abbott; Mills, Representative Government 301; Freeman, Fed. Gov't.

Constitutional Law. A term commonly used to express a league or compact between two or more states, to become united under one central government. Montana Auto Finance Corporation v. British & Federal Underwriters of Norwich Union Fire Ins. Soc., 72 Mont. 69, 232 P. 198, 199, 36 A.L.R. 1495.

FEDERAL CENSUS. A census of each state or territory or of a certain state or of any subdivision or portion of any state, provided it is taken by and under the direction and supervision of the Census Bureau of the United States, and approved and certified by it as the census of that state or subdivision. In re Cleveland's Claim, 72 Okl. 279, 180 P. 852, 885.

FEDERAL COMMON LAW is a body of decisional law developed by the federal courts untrammeled by state court decisions. O'Brien v. Western Union Telegraph Co., C.C.A.Mass., 113 F.2d 539, 541.

FEDERAL COURTS. The courts of the United States. See Courts of the United States.

FEDERAL GOVERNMENT. The system of government administered in a state formed by the union or confederation of several independent or *quasi* independent states; also the composite state so formed.

In strict usage, there is a distinction between a *confederation* and a *federal government*. The former term denotes a league or permanent alliance between several states, each of which is fully sovereign and independent, and each of which retains its full dignity, organization, and sovereignty, though yielding to the central authority a controlling power for a few limited purposes, such as external and diplomatic relations. In this case, the component states are the units, with respect to the confederation, and the central government acts upon them, not upon the individual citizens. In a *federal government*, on the other hand, the allied states form a union,—not, indeed, to such an extent as to destroy their separate organization or deprive them of *quasi* sovereignty with respect to the administration of their purely local concerns, but so that the central power is erected into a true state or nation, possessing sovereignty both external and internal,—while the administration of national affairs is directed, and its effects felt, not by the separate states deliberating as units, but by the people of all, in their collective capacity, as citizens of the nation. The distinction is expressed, by the German writers, by the use of the two words *"Staatenbund"* and *"Bundesstaat;"* the former denoting a league or confederation of states, and the latter a federal government, or state formed by means of a league or confederation.

FEDERAL INSTRUMENTALITY. A means or agency used by the federal government. Capitol Building & Loan Ass'n v. Kansas Commission of Labor and Industry, 148 Kan. 446, 83 P.2d 106, 107, 118 A.L.R. 1212. A government agency immune from state control. Waterbury Sav. Bank v. Danaher, 128 Conn. 78, 20 A.2d 455, 458.

FEDERAL PROHIBITION OFFICER. An officer of the federal government charged with the enforcement of the national prohibition statute. De Marco v. U. S., C.C.A.Va., 296 F. 667, 668.

FEDERAL QUESTION. Cases arising under Constitution of United States, Acts of Congress, or treaties, and involving their interpretation and application, and of which jurisdiction is given to federal courts, are commonly described as involving a "federal question." McAllister v. St. Louis Merchants' Bridge Terminal Ry. Co., 324 Mo. 1005, 25 S.W.2d 791, 792.

FEDERAL TRADE COMMISSION. An administrative body created by statute, with only the duties and powers granted expressly or by fair implication. Chamber of Commerce of Minneapolis v. Federal Trade Commission, C.C.A.8, 13 F.2d 673, 683. See 15 U.S.C.A. §§ 41–51.

FEDERALIST, THE. A series of 85 essays by Alexander Hamilton, James Madison, and John Jay, expounding and advocating the adoption of the Constitution of the United States. All but six of the essays were first published in the "Independent Journal" of New York City from October, 1787, to April, 1788. Webster, New Int. Dict. "The opinion of the Federalist has always [been] considered as of great authority." Cohens v. Virginia, 6 Wheat. 264, 418, 5 L.Ed. 257.

FEDERATED STATE. An independent central organism, having its own machinery absorbing, in view of international law, all the individual states associated together. Molina v. Comision Reguladora Del Mercado De Henequen, 91 N.J.L. 382, 103 A. 397, 400.

FEDERATION. Ordinarily, an unincorporated association of persons for a common purpose. Hughes v. State, 109 Ark. 403, 160 S.W. 209.

FEE. A charge fixed by law for services of public officers or for use of a privilege under control of government. Fort Smith Gas Co. v. Wiseman, 189 Ark. 675, 74 S.W.2d 789, 790. A recompense for an official or professional service or a charge or emolument or compensation for a particular act or service. Craig v. Shelton, 201 Ky. 790, 258 S.W. 694. A fixed charge or perquisite charged as recompense for labor and trouble, a reward, compensation, or wage given to a person for performance of professional services or something done or to be done. People v. Goulding, 275 Mich. 353, 266 N.W. 378, 379.

A contingent fee is a fee stipulated to be paid to an attorney for his services in conducting a suit or other forensic proceeding only in case he wins it; it may be a percentage of the amount recovered. Adopted in Gray v. Stern, 85 Wash. 645, 149 P. 26, 28.

For docket fee, see Docket.

Estates

Ordinarily, word "fee" or "fee simple" is applied to an estate in land, but term is applicable to any kind of hereditament, corporeal or incorporeal, and is all the property in thing referred to or largest estate therein which person may have. In re Forsstrom, 44 Ariz. 472, 38 P.2d 878, 888.

A freehold estate in lands, held of a superior lord, as a reward for services, and on condition of rendering some service in return for it. The true meaning of the word "fee" is the same as that of "feud" or "fief," and in its original sense it is taken in contradistinction to "allodium," which latter is defined as a man's own land, which he possesses merely in his own right, without owing any rent or service to any superior. 2 Bl.Comm. 105. See Wendell v. Crandall, 1 N.Y. 491.

In modern English tenures, "fee" signifies an estate of inheritance, being the highest and most extensive interest which a man can have in a feud; and when the term is used simply, without any adjunct, or in the form "fee-simple," it imports an absolute inheritance clear of any condition, limitation, or restriction to particular heirs, but descendible to the heirs general, male or female, lineal or collateral. 2 Bl.Comm. 106; Cowell; *Termes de la Ley;* 1 Washb.R.P. 51; Co.Litt. 1 *b;* 1 Prest.Est. 420; 3 Kent 514.

Base fee. A determinable or qualified fee; an estate having the nature of a fee, but not a fee simple absolute. In re Douglass' Estate, 94 Neb. 280, 143 N.W. 299, 302.

Conditional fee. An estate restrained to some particular heirs, exclusive of others, Blume v. Pearcy, 204 S.C. 409, 29 S.E.2d 673, 674, as to the heirs of a man's body, by which only his lineal descendants were admitted, in exclusion of collateral; or to the heirs male of his body, in exclusion of heirs female, whether lineal or collateral. It was called a "conditional fee," by reason of the condition expressed or implied in the donation of it that, if the donee died without such particular heirs, the land should revert to the donor. 2 Bl.Comm. 110. The term includes a fee that is either to commence or determine on some condition, 10 Co. 95*b;* Prest.Est. 476; Fearne, Cont.Rem. 9; and is sometimes used interchangeably with "base fee," that is, one to determine or be defeated on the happening of some contingent event or act. Citizens' Electric Co. v. Susquehanna Boom Co., 270 Pa. 517, 113 A. 559, 561; Glass v. Johnson, 297 Ill. 149, 130 N.E. 473, 474.

Determinable fee. Also called a "base" or "qualified" fee. Stubbs v. Abel, 114 Or. 610, 233 P. 852, 859. One which has a qualification subjoined to it, and which must be determined whenever the qualification annexed to it is at an end. Littleton § 254; Co.Litt. 27*a,* 220; 1 Prest.Est. 449; 2 Bla.Comm. 109; Cruise, Dig. tit. 1, § 82. An estate in fee which is liable to be determined by some act or event expressed on its limitation to circumscribe its continuance, or inferred by law as bounding its extent. 1 Washb. Real Prop. 62; McLane v. Bovee, 35 Wis. 36. An estate which may last forever is a "fee," but if it may end on the happening of a merely possible event, it is a "determinable," or "qualified fee." Reichard v. Chicago, B. & Q. R. Co., 231 Iowa 563, 1 N.W.2d 721, 727.

Determinable fee or fee simple. Estate created with special limitation which delimits duration of estate in land. P C K Properties, Inc., v. City of Cuyahoga Falls, 176 N.E.2d 441, 444, 112 Ohio App. 492.

Fee damages. See Damages.

Fee expectant. A name sometimes applied to an estate created where lands are given to a man and his wife and the heirs of their bodies. See also Frank-Marriage.

Fee simple defeasible. Title created in trustees where legal title in fee simple to active trust estate is by will placed in trustees who are required to distribute property in fee simple upon happening of event. Also called a "determinable fee", "base fee", or "qualified fee". Kanawha Val. Bank v. Hornbeck, W.Va., 151 S.E.2d 694, 700.

Great fee. In feudal law, the designation of a fee held directly from the crown.

Knight's fee. See Knight's Fee.

Limited fee. An estate of inheritance in lands, which is clogged or confined with some sort of condition or qualification. Such estates are base or qualified fees, conditional fees, and fees-tail. The term is opposed to "fee-simple." 2 Bl.Comm. 109; Lott v. Wyckoff, 1 Barb., N.Y., 575; Paterson v. Ellis, 11 Wend., N.Y., 259.

Plowman's fee. In old English law, was a species of tenure peculiar to peasants or small farmers, somewhat like gavelkind, by which the lands descended in equal shares to all the sons of the tenant.

Qualified fee. In English law. A fee having a qualification subjoined thereto, and which must be determined whenever the qualification annexed to it is at an end; otherwise termed a "base fee." 2 Bl.Comm. 109; 1 Steph. Comm. 225. An interest which may continue forever, but is liable to be determined, without the aid of a conveyance, by some act or event, circumscribing its continuance or extent. 4 Kent, Comm. 9; Moody v. Walker, 3 Ark. 190; U. S. v. Reese, 27 Fed.Cas. 744. An interest given to a man *and certain of his heirs* at the time of its limitation. See Kelso v. Stigar, 75 Md. 397, 24 A. 18.

Quasi fee. An estate gained by wrong. Wharton.

Also, the land which is held in fee.

American Law

An estate of inheritance without condition, belonging to the owner, and alienable by him or transmissible to his heirs absolutely and simply, and is an absolute estate in perpetuity and the largest possible estate a man can have, being, in fact, allodial in its nature. Stanton v. Sullivan, 63 R.I. 216, 7 A.2d 696, 698, 699.

Every estate which is not for life, for years or at will. Chance v. Weston, 96 Or. 390, 190 P. 155, 157.

Terms "fee," "fee simple," and "fee simple absolute," are equivalent. Boon v. Boon, 348 Ill. 120, 180 N.E. 792, 794.

FEE AND LIFE-RENT. In Scotch law, two estates in land—the first of which is the full right of proprietorship, the second the limited right of usufruct during life—may be held together, or may co-exist in different persons at the same time. See Bell, Prin. § 1712; Ersk. Prin. 420; Fiar.

FEE-FARM. A species of tenure, where land is held of another in perpetuity at a yearly rent, without fealty, homage, or other services than such as are specially comprised in the feoffment. It corresponds very nearly to the *"emphyteusis"* of the Roman law. Cowell. Fealty, however, was incident to a holding in fee-farm, according to some authors. Spelman; Termes de la Ley.

Fee-farm is where an estate in fee is granted subject to a rent in fee of at least one-fourth of the value of the lands at the time of its reservation. Such rent appears to be called "fee-farm" because a grant of lands reserving so considerable a rent is indeed only letting lands to farm in fee-simple, instead of the usual method of life or years. 2 Bl.Comm. 43; 1 Steph.Comm. 676.

Fee-farms are lands held in fee to render for them annually the true value, or more or less; so called because a farm rent is reserved upon a grant in fee. Such estates are estates of inheritance. They are classed among estates in fee-simple. No reversionary interest remains in the lessor, and they are therefore subject to the operation of the legal principles which forbid restraints upon alienation in all cases where no feudal relation exists between grantor and grantee. De Peyster v. Michael, 6 N.Y. 497, 57 Am.Dec. 470.

FEE–FARM RENT. The rent reserved on granting a fee-farm. It might be one-fourth the value of the land, according to Cowell; one-third, according to other authors. Spelman; Termes de la Ley; 2 Bl. Comm. 43. Fee-farm rent is a rent-charge issuing out of an estate in fee; a perpetual rent reserved on a conveyance in fee-simple. De Peyster v. Michael, 6 N.Y. 467, 495, 57 Am.Dec. 470.

FEE SIMPLE.

Absolute

A fee simple absolute is an estate limited absolutely to a man and his heirs and assigns forever without limitation or condition. Rathbun v. State, 284 Mich. 521, 280 N.W. 35, 40.

Conditional

At the common law, an estate in fee simple conditional was a fee limited or restrained to some particular heirs, exclusive of others. But the statute "De Donis" converted all such estates into estates tail. 2 Bl. Comm. 110.

American Law

An absolute or fee-simple estate is one in which the owner is entitled to the entire property, with unconditional power of disposition during his life, and descending to his heirs and legal representatives upon his death intestate. Code Ga. 1882, § 2246 (Civ.Code 1910, § 3657). Friedman v. Steiner, 107 Ill. 131; Woodberry v. Matherson, 19 Fla. 785; Lyle v. Richards, 9 Serg. & R., Pa. 374. Unlimited as to duration, disposition, and descendibility. Slayden v. Hardin, 257 Ky. 685, 79 S.W. 2d 11, 12.

The estate which a man has where lands are given to him and to his heirs absolutely without any end or limit put to his estate. 2 Bl. Comm. 106; Plowd. 557; 1 Prest. Est. 425; Litt. § 1. The word "fee," used alone, is a sufficient designation of this species of estate, and hence "simple" is not a necessary part of the title, but it is added as a means of clearly distinguishing this estate from a fee-tail or from any variety of conditional estates.

Fee-simple signifies a pure fee; an absolute estate of inheritance clear of any condition or restriction to particular heirs, being descendible to the heirs general, whether male or female, lineal or collateral. It is the largest estate and most extensive interest that can be enjoyed in land. Haynes v. Bourn, 42 Vt. 686; Powers v. Trustees of Caledonia County Grammar School, 93 Vt. 220, 106 A. 836, 841; Smith v. Smith's Ex'r, 122 Va. 341, 94 S.E. 777, 779. When a person owns in common with another, he does not own the entire fee,—a fee-simple; it is a fee divided or shared with another. Brackett v. Ridlon, 54 Me. 426.

Terms "fee," "fee simple," and "fee simple absolute," are equivalent. Boon v. Boon, 348 Ill. 120, 180 N.E. 792, 794.

English Law

A freehold estate of inheritance, absolute and unqualified. It stands at the head of estates as the highest in dignity and the most ample in extent; since every other kind of estate is derivable thereout, and mergeable therein. It may be enjoyed not only in land, but also in advowsons, commons, estovers, and other hereditaments, as well as in personalty, as an annuity or dignity, and also in an upper chamber, though the lower buildings and soil belong to another. Wharton; Co.Litt. 1 *b;* 2 Bla. Comm. 106.

FEE TAIL. A freehold estate in which there is a fixed line of inheritable succession limited to the issue of the body of the grantee or devisee, and in which the regular and general succession of heirs at law is cut off. Coleman v. Shoemaker, 147 Kan. 689, 78 P.2d 905, 907.

An estate tail; an estate of inheritance given to a man and the heirs of his body, or limited to certain classes of particular heirs. It corresponds to the *feudum talliatum* of the feudal law, and the idea is believed to have been borrowed from the Roman law, where, by way of *fidei commissa,* lands might be entailed upon children and freedmen and their descendants, with restrictions as to alienation. 1 Washb.Real Prop. *66. For the varieties and special characteristics of this kind of estate, see Tail, Estate in.

FEED. To lend additional support; to strengthen *ex post facto.* "The interest when it accrues *feeds* the estoppel." Christmas v. Oliver, 5 Mood. & R. 202. Similarly, a subsequent title acquired by the mortgagor is said "to feed the mortgage."

The word is used in its ordinary sense with reference to cattle and hogs which are said to be made marketable by feeding. Brockway v. Rowley, 66 Ill. 102.

It is also used in the phrase *feeding of a cow by and on the land* to signify from the land while there is food on it, and with hay by the owner of the land at other times; 2 Q.B.Div. 49.

FEGANGI. In old English law, a thief caught while escaping with the stolen goods in his possession. Spelman.

FEHMGERICHTE. The name given to certain secret tribunals which flourished in Germany from the end of the twelfth century to the middle of the sixteenth, usurping many of the functions of the governments which were too weak to maintain law and order, and inspiring dread in all who came within their jurisdiction. Enc. Brit. Such a court existed in Westphalia (though with greatly diminished powers) until finally suppressed by Jerome Bonaparte in 1811. See Bork, *Geschichte der Westphaelischen Vehmgerichte;* Paul Wigand, Das Fehmgericht Westphaleus.

FEIGNED. Fictitious; pretended; supposititious; simulated.

FEIGNED ACCOMPLICE. One who pretends to consult and act with others in the planning or commission of a crime, but only for the purpose of discovering their plans and confederates and securing evidence against them. State v. Verganadis, 50 Nev. 1, 248 P. 900, 903; People v. Bolanger, 71 Cal. 17, 11 P. 800.

FEIGNED ACTION. In practice, an action brought on a pretended right, when the plaintiff has no true cause of action, for some illegal purpose. In a feigned action the words of the writ are true. It differs from *false action,* in which case the words of the writ are false. Co. Litt. 361.

FEIGNED DISEASES. Simulated maladies. Diseases are generally feigned from one of three causes,—fear, shame, or the hope of gain.

FEIGNED ISSUE. An issue framed to try questions of fact. Miles v. Layton, 8 W.W.Harr. 411, 193 A. 567, 574, 112 A.L.R. 786.

An issue made up by the direction of a court of equity, (or by consent of parties,) and sent to a common-law court, for the purpose of obtaining the verdict of a jury on some disputed matter of fact which the court has not jurisdiction, or is unwilling, to decide. It rests upon a supposititious wager between the parties. See 3 Bl.Comm. 452. Under the reformed codes of some states issues may be framed in certain exceptional cases. In England, the practice has been disused since the passing of the stat. 8 and 9 Vict. c. 109, s. 19, permitting any court to refer any question of fact to a jury in a direct form. The act 21 and 22 Vict. c. 27, provided for trial by jury in the court of chancery.

FELAGUS. In Saxon law, one bound for another by oath; a sworn brother. A friend bound in the decennary for the good behavior of another. One who took the place of the deceased. Thus, if a person was murdered, the recompense due from the murderer went to the *felagus* of the slain, in default of parents or lord. Cunningham; Cowell; Du Cange.

FELD. A field; in composition, wild. Blount.

FELE, FEAL. L. Fr. Faithful. See Feal.

FELLATIO, or FELLATION. The offense committed with the male sexual organ and the mouth. State v. Murry, 136 La. 253, 66 So. 963. See Sodomy.

FELLOW. A co-worker; a partaker or sharer of; a companion; one with whom we consort; one joined with another in some legal *status* or relation; a member of a college or corporate body.

FELLOW-HEIR. A co-heir; partner of the same inheritance.

FELLOW SERVANT. One who serves and is controlled by the same master. Walsh v. Eubanks, 183 Ark. 34, 34 S.W.2d 762, 764.

Those engaged in the same common pursuit, under the same general control. Cooley, Torts 541. Those who derive authority and compensation from the same common source, and are engaged in the same general business, though it may be in different grades or departments of it. 2 Thomp. Neg. p. 1026, § 31; Southern Ry. Co. v. Taylor, 57 App.D.C. 21, 16 F.2d 517, 519; Brush Electric Light Co. v. Wells, 110 Ga. 192, 35 S.E. 365. When servants are employed and paid by the same master, and their duties are such as to bring them into such relation that negligence of one in doing his work may injure other in performance of his, then they are engaged in the same common business, and are "fellow servants." Hercules Powder Co. v. Hammack, 145 Miss. 304, 110 So. 676, 677. But it has been held that an inferior employee is not a "fellow servant" of a superior employee. McDonald v. Louisville & N. R. Co., 232 Ky. 734, 24 S.W.2d 585, 587.

Convicts in involuntary servitude, having no power to refuse to enter upon the service to which they have been hired out by the state, or to quit it, are not "fellow servants." Sloss-Sheffield Steel & Iron Co. v. Weir, 179 Ala. 227, 60 So. 851, 853.

FELLOW-SERVANT RULE. The rule that the master is not liable for injuries to a servant, caused by the negligence of a fellow servant engaged in the same general business, where the master has exercised due care in selection of servants. Setzkorn v. City of Buffalo, 219 App.Div. 416, 219 N.Y.S. 351, 352.

FELO DE SE. A felon of himself; a suicide or murderer of himself.

Where a man of the age of discretion (14 years at common law) and compos mentis voluntarily kills himself. Southern Life & Health Ins. Co. v. Wynn, 29 Ala.App. 207, 194 So. 421, 422. One who commits some unlawful or malicious act which results in his own death. Hale, P.C. 411; 4 Bl.Comm. 189; Life Ass'n v. Waller, 57 Ga. 536.

FELON. A person who commits a felony. In re La Grange, 153 Misc. 236, 274 N.Y.S. 702. One convicted of felony.

But a person who has committed a felony, been convicted, served his sentence, and been discharged, may be deemed, at least for some purposes, to be no longer a felon; 3 Exch.Div. 352.

FELONIA. Felony. The act or offense by which a vassal forfeited his fee. Spelman; Calvin. *Per feloniam,* with a criminal intention. Co. Litt. 391.

FELONIA, EX VI TERMINI SIGNIFICAT QUODLIBET CAPITALE CRIMEN FELLEO ANIMO PERPETRATUM. Co. Litt. 391. Felony, by force of the term, signifies any capital crime perpetrated with a malignant mind.

FELONIA IMPLICATUR IN QUALIBET PRODITIONE. 3 Inst. 15. Felony is implied in every treason.

FELONICE. Feloniously. Cunningham, Law Dict.

Anciently an indispensable word in indictments for felony, and classed by Lord Coke among those *voces artis* (words of art) which cannot be expressed by any periphrasis or circumlocution. 4 Coke, 39; Co.Litt. 391*a;* 4 Bl.Comm. 307.

FELONIOUS. A technical word of law which means done with intent to commit crime; of the grade or quality of a felony; such an assault on the person as, if consummated, would subject party making it, on conviction, to punishment of a felony. Martin v. State, 163 Miss. 454, 142 So. 15, 16. Malicious; villainous; traitorous. People v. Knapp, 152 Misc. 368, 274 N.Y.S. 85. Malignant. People v. Moore, 37 Hun, N.Y., 93. Wrongful. State v. Uhler, 32 N.D. 483, 156 N.W. 220, 226. Proceeding from an evil heart or purpose. Gatewood v. Commonwealth, 215 Ky. 360, 285 S.W. 193, 194. Wickedly and against the admonition of the law; unlawfully. State v. Allister, 317 Mo.

348, 295 S.W. 754, 757. In the law of larceny, "felonious" is synonymous with fraudulent; State v. Albert, 117 Or. 179, 242 P. 1116, 1117; and means done "animo furandi," that is, with intent to steal. Fountain v. State, 92 Fla. 262, 109 So. 463, 464.

FELONIOUS ASSAULT. Such an assault upon the person as, if consummated, would subject the party making it, upon conviction, to the punishment of a felony, that is, to imprisonment in the penitentiary. Hinkle v. State, 94 Ga. 595, 21 S.E. 595.

FELONIOUS HOMICIDE. Killing of human being without justification or excuse. State v. Plumlee, 177 La. 687, 149 So. 425, 431. There are two degrees: manslaughter and murder. It may include killing oneself. 4 Bl. Comm. 188, 190; 4 Steph. Comm. 108, 111; State v. Symmes, 40 S.C. 383, 19 S.E. 16.

FELONIOUSLY. Of, pertaining to, or having, the quality of felony. People v. Thomas, 58 Cal. App. 308, 208 P. 343, 344.

Means proceeding from an evil heart or purpose done with a deliberate intention of committing a crime. Golden v. Commonwealth, 245 Ky. 19, 53 S.W.2d 185, 186. Without color of right or excuse. State v. Enanno, 96 Conn. 420, 114 A. 386, 387. Malignantly; maliciously. State v. Horne, 62 Utah, 376, 220 P. 378, 381. Wickedly and against the admonition of the law. State v. Young, 314 Mo. 612, 286 S.W. 29, 34. With a felonious intent.

An indispensable word at common law in indictments for felony, as *felonice* was in the Latin forms. 4 Bl.Comm. 307; State v. Jesse, 19 N.C. 300; Com.Dig. *Indictment* (G 6); Bac.Abr. *Indictment* (G 1); 2 Hale, Pl.Cr. 172, 184; 1 Ben. & H. Lead. Cr.Cas. 154. It is still necessary in describing a common-law felony, or where its use is prescribed by statute; Whart.Cr.Pl. § 260; Bowler v. State, 41 Miss. 570; Cain v. State, 18 Tex. 387.

FELONY. A crime of a graver or more atrocious nature than those designated as misdemeanors. Ex parte Ramirez, 49 Cal.App.2d 709, 122 P. 2d 361, 362. Generally an offense punishable by death or imprisonment in penitentiary. People v. Pointer, 348 Ill. 277, 180 N.E. 796, 797, or state prison. State v. Harwood, 206 N.C. 87, 173 S.E. 24, 25. And at common law, an offense occasioning total forfeiture of either land or goods to which capital or other punishment might be superadded according to degree of guilt. Bell v. Commonwealth, 167 Va. 526, 189 S.E. 441, 443.

Felony, compounding of. See Compounding Felony.

Misprision of felony. See Misprision.

Reducible felony. A felony upon conviction of which the offender may be punished as for a misdemeanor, upon recommendation of the jury. Atkins v. State, 154 Ga. 540, 114 S.E. 878.

American Law

The term has no very definite or precise meaning, except in some cases where it is defined by statute. In general, what is felony under the English common law is such under ours, 1 Bish.Cr.L. § 617; Clark, Cr.L. 33. A crime is not a felony unless so declared by statute, or it was such at the common law; State v. Murphy, 17 R.I. 698, 24 A. 473, 16 L.R.A. 550.

Whether an offense is a "felony" depends on whether the offense may be punished by confinement in the penitentiary and not on whether such punishment of necessity follows conviction of that offense. Lashley v. State, 236 Ala. 1. 180 So. 717, 718, 719. Sentence actually given determines nature of offense. People v. Brown, 52 Cal.App.2d 428, 126 P.2d 406, 408.

Under U. S. Cr. Code, § 335, 18 U.S.C.A. § 1, offenses punishable by death or imprisonment for a term exceeding one year are felonies. Joplin Mercantile Co. v. United States, C.C.A.Mo., 213 F. 926, 935, Ann.Cas.1916C, 470.

English Law

This term meant originally the state of having forfeited lands and goods to the crown upon conviction for certain offenses, and then, by transition, any offense upon conviction for which such forfeiture followed, in addition to capital or any other punishment prescribed by law; as distinguished from a "misdemeanor," upon conviction for which no forfeiture followed. All indictable offenses are either felonies or misdemeanors, but a material part of the distinction is taken away by St. 33 & 34 Vict. c. 23, which abolishes forfeiture for felony. Wharton; 4 Bla.Comm. 94; 1 Russ.Cr. 78; Co.Litt. 391; 1 Hawk Pl.Cr. c. 37; U. S. v. Smith, 5 Wheat., U. S., 153, 5 L.Ed. 57; 1 Bish. New Cr.L. § 616.

At early common law the term was applied to describe the more serious offenses cognizable in the royal courts, conviction for which entailed forfeiture of life, limb and chattels and escheat of lands to the felon's lord after a year and a day in the king's hands. Subsequently, however, the classification was so greatly enlarged that many offenses not involving moral turpitude were included therein. In re Donegan, 282 N.Y. 285, 26 N.E.2d 260, 261.

Feudal Law

An act or offense on the part of the vassal, which cost him his fee, or in consequence of which his fee fell into the hands of his lord; that is, became forfeited. (See Felonia.) Perfidy, ingratitude, or disloyalty to a lord.

FELONY ACT. The statute 33 & 34 Vict. c. 23, abolishing forfeitures for felony, and sanctioning the appointment of *interim* curators and administrators of the property of felons. Mozley & Whiteley; 4 Steph. Comm. 10, 459.

FELONY-MURDER RULE. Any homicide committed while perpetrating or attempting felony is first-degree murder. Payne v. State, 406 P.2d 922, 924, 81 Nev. 503; Element of legal malice is supplied from the commission of the felony. Com. v. Cater, 152 A.2d 259, 261, 396 Pa. 172.

FELTING. In the process of "felting," as applied to the manufacture of fur felt hats, the fur fibers become interlocked with the wool fibers, or with other fibers of fur, for their whole length. Matteawan Mfg. Co. v. Emmons Bros. Co., C.C.A. Mass., 253 F. 372, 375. See, also, Werk v. Parker, C.C.A.Pa., 231 F. 121, 123.

FEMALE. The sex which conceives and gives birth to young. Also a member of such sex. The term is generic, but may have the specific meaning of "woman," if so indicated by the context. State v. Hemm, 82 Iowa, 609, 48 N.W. 971; State v. Phillips, 26 N.D. 206, 144 N.W. 94, 95, 49 L.R.A., N.S., 470, Ann.Cas.1916A, 320.

Unmarried female, is a term descriptive not only of those who have never married, but also of widows and divorced women. People v. Weinstock, 27 N.Y.Cr.R. 53, 140 N.Y.S. 453, 458.

FEME, FEMME. L. Fr. A woman. Ducre v. Milner, La.App., 146 So. 734, 736. Also, a wife, as in the phrase *"baron et feme"* (*q. v.*).

FEME COVERT. A married woman. Generally used in reference to the legal disabilities of a married woman, as compared with the condition of a *feme sole.* Hoker v. Boggs, 63 Ill. 161.

FEME SOLE. A single woman, including those who have been married, but whose marriage has been dissolved by death or divorce, and, for most purposes, those women who are judicially separated from their husbands. Mozley & Whiteley; 2 Steph. Comm. 250. Kirkley v. Lacey, 7 Houst. Del. 213, 30 A. 994.

FEME SOLE TRADER. In English law, a married woman, who, by the custom of London, trades on her own account, independently of her husband; so called because, with respect to her trading, she is the same as a *feme sole.* Jacob; Cro. Car. 68. The term is applied also to women deserted by their husbands, who do business as *femes sole.* Rhea v. Rhenner, 1 Pet. 105, 7 L.Ed. 72.

The custom was recognized as common law in South Carolina, but did not extend beyond trading in merchandise; McDaniel v. Cornwell, 1 Hill, S.C., 429; Newbiggin v. Pillans, 2 Bay, S.C., 164. By statute in several states a similar custom is recognized, as in Pennsylvania, by act of Feb. 22, 1718, 48 P.S. § 41. Black v. Tricker, 59 Pa. 13; People's Sav. Bank v. Denig, 131 Pa. 241, 18 A. 1083.

FEMICIDE. The killing of a woman. Wharton. One who kills a woman.

FEMININE. Of or belonging to females.

FEMME COULEUR LIBRE. Up to the time of Civil War, term applied to all persons not of the white race, including Indians. Sunseri v. Cassagne, 191 La. 209, 185 So. 1, 4.

FENATIO (or FEONATIC). In forest law, the fawning of deer; the fawning season. Spelman.

FENCE, *v.* In old Scotch law, to defend or protect by formalities.

To "fence a court" was to open it in due form, and interdict all manner of persons from disturbing their proceedings. This was called "fencing," *q. d.*, defending or protecting the court. Pitcairn, Cr.Law, pt. 1, p. 75.

FENCE, *n.* A hedge, structure, or partition, erected for the purpose of inclosing a piece of land, or to divide a piece of land into distinct portions, or to separate two contiguous estates. Kimball v. Carter, 95 Va. 77, 27 S.E. 823, 38 L.R.A. 570; Estes v. Railroad Co., 63 Me. 309.

An enclosure about a field or other space, or about any object; especially an enclosing structure of wood, iron or other materials, intended to prevent intrusion from without or straying from within. Mutual Lumber Co. v. Sheppard, Tex.Civ.App., 173 S.W.2d 494, 499.

A colloquial characterization of a receiver of stolen property. People v. Fishel, 270 Mich. 82, 258 N.W. 217.

FENCE COUNTY. A county where the stock law has not been adopted. McKenzie v. Powell, 68 Ga.App. 285, 22 S.E.2d 735, 736.

FENCE-MONTH, or DEFENSE-MONTH. In old English law, a period of time, occurring in the middle of summer, during which it was unlawful to hunt deer in the forest, that being their fawning season. Probably so called because the deer were then *defended* from pursuit or hunting. Manwood; Cowell; Spelman.

FENCING PATENTS. Patents procured in an effort to broaden the scope of the invention beyond the article or process which is actually intended to be manufactured or licensed. Special Equipment Co. v. Coe, 79 U.S.App.D.C. 133, 144 F. 2d 497, 499.

FENDER. A guard or protection against danger. Cape May, D. B. & S. P. R. Co. v. Cape May, 59 N.J.L. 396, 36 A. 696, 36 L.R.A. 653. A safety device sometimes called life guard, on street cars. Tampa Electric Co. v. Bazemore, 85 Fla. 164, 96 So. 297, 298; Galveston Electric Co. v. Swank, Tex.Civ.App., 188 S.W. 704, 706.

FENERATION. Usury; the gain of interest; the practice of increasing money by lending. Sometimes applied to interest on money lent. See Colebrook, Dig. Hindu Law, I. 7.

FENGELD. In Saxon law, a tax or imposition, exacted for the repelling of enemies. Spelman.

FENIAN. A champion, hero, giant. This word, in the plural, is generally used to signify invaders or foreign spoilers. The modern meaning of "Fenian" is a member of an organization of persons of Irish birth, resident in the United States, Canada, and elsewhere, having for its aim the overthrow of English rule in Ireland. Webster.

FEOD. The same as *feud* or *fief.* 2 Bla. Comm. 45; Spelman.

FEODAL. Belonging to a fee or feud; feudal. More commonly used by the old writers than *feudal.*

FEODAL ACTIONS. Real actions. 3 Bla. Comm. 117.

FEODAL SYSTEM. See Feudal System.

FEODALITY. Fidelity or fealty. Cowell. See Fealty.

FEODARUM (or FEUDARAM) CONSUETUDINES. The customs of feuds. The name of a compilation of feudal laws and customs made at Milan in the twelfth century. It is the most ancient work on the subject, and was always regarded, on the continent of Europe, as possessing the highest authority.

FEODARY. An officer of the court of wards, appointed by the master of that court, under 32 Hen. VIII. c. 26, whose business it was to be present with the escheator in every county at the finding of offices of lands, and to give evidence for the king, as well concerning the value as the tenure; and his office was also to survey the land of the ward, after the office found, and to rate it

He also assigned the king's widows their dower; and received all the rents, etc. Abolished by 12 Car. II. c. 24. Wharton; Kennett, Gloss.; Cowell.

FEODATORY, or FEUDATORY. In feudal law, the grantee of a *feod, feud,* or fee; the vassal or tenant who held his estate by feudal service. Termes de la Ley. Blackstone uses *"feudatory."* 2 Bl. Comm. 46.

FEODI FIRMA. In old English law, fee-farm *(q. v.).*

FEODI FIRMARIUS. The lessee of a fee-farm.

FEODUM. This word (meaning a feud or fee) is the one most commonly used by the older English law-writers, though its equivalent, *"feudum" (q. v.),* is used generally by the more modern writers and by the *feudal* law-writers. Litt. § 1; Spelman.

There were various classes of *feoda,* among which may be enumerated the following: *Feodum laicum,* a lay fee. *Feodum militare,* a knight's fee. *Feodum improprium,* an improper or derivative fee. *Feodum proprium,* a proper and original fee, regulated by the strict rules of feudal succession and tenure. *Feodum simplex,* a simple or pure fee; fee-simple. *Feodum talliatum,* a fee-tail. See 2 Bl.Comm. 58, 62; Litt. §§ 1, 13; Bract. fol. 175; Glan. 13, 23.

In old English law, a seigniory or jurisdiction. Fleta, lib. 2, c. 63, § 4. A fee, a perquisite or compensation for a service. Fleta, lib. 2, c. 7.

FEODUM ANTIQUUM. A feud which devolved upon a vassal from his intestate ancestor.

FEODUM EST QUOD QUIS TENET EX QUACUNQUE CAUSA SIVE SIT TENEMENTUM SIVE REDDITUS. Co. Litt. 1. A fee is that which any one holds from whatever cause, whether tenement or rent.

FEODUM NOBILE. A fief for which the tenant did guard and owed homage. Spelman.

FEODUM NOVUM. A feud acquired by a vassal himself.

FEODUM SIMPLEX QUIA FEODUM IDEM EST QUOD HÆREDITAS, ET SIMPLEX IDEM EST QUOD LEGITIMUM VEL PURUM; ET SIC FEODUM SIMPLEX IDEM EST QUOD HÆREDITAS LEGITIMA VEL HÆREDITAS PURA. Litt. § 1. A fee-simple, so called because fee is the same as inheritance, and simple is the same as lawful or pure; and thus fee-simple is the same as a lawful inheritance, or pure inheritance.

FEODUM TALLIATUM, i. e., HÆREDITAS IN QUANDAM CERTITUDINEM LIMITATA. Litt. § 13. Fee-tail, *i. e.,* an inheritance limited in a definite descent.

FEOFFAMENTUM. A feoffment. 2 Bl. Comm. 310.

FEOFFARE. To enfeoff; to bestow a fee. The bestower was called *"feoffator,"* and the grantee or feoffee, *"feoffatus."* 1 Reeve, Hist. Eng. Law, 91.

FEOFFATOR. In old English law, a feoffer or feoffor; one who gives or bestows a fee; one who makes a feoffment. Bract. fols. 12*b*, 81.

FEOFFATUS. In old English law, a feoffee; one to whom a fee is given, or a feoffment made. Bract. fols. 17*b*, 44*b*.

FEOFFEE. He to whom a fee is conveyed. Litt. § 1; 2 Bl. Comm. 20.

FEOFFEE TO USES. A person to whom land was conveyed for the use of a third party. (The latter was called *"cestui que use."*) One holding the same position with reference to a use that a trustee does to a trust. 1 Greenl. Cruise, Dig. 333. He answers to the *hæres fiduciarius* of the Roman law.

FEOFFMENT. The gift of any corporeal hereditament to another (2 Bl. Comm. 310), operating by transmutation of possession, and requiring, as essential to its completion, that the seisin be passed (Watk. Conv. 183), which might be accomplished either by investiture or by livery of seisin. 1 Washb. Real Prop. 33. Thatcher v. Omans, 3 Pick., Mass., 532; French v. French, 3 N.H. 260. A gift of a freehold interest in land accompanied by livery of seisin. The essential part is the livery of seisin. 3 Holdsw. Hist. E. L. 187.

Also the deed or conveyance by which such corporeal hereditament is passed.

A feoffment originally meant the grant of a *feud* or *fee;* that is, a barony or knight's fee, for which certain services were due from the feoffee to the feoffor. By custom it came afterwards to signify also a grant (with livery of seisin) of a free inheritance to a man and his heirs, referring rather to the perpetuity of the estate than to the feudal tenure. 1 Reeve, Eng.Law, 90, 91. It was for ages the only method (in ordinary use) for conveying the freehold of land in possession, but has now fallen in great measure into disuse, even in England, having been almost entirely supplanted by some of that class of conveyances founded on the statute law of the realm. 1 Steph.Comm. 467, 468; Dane, Abr. c. 104; Stearn, Real Act. 2; Green v. Liter, 8 Cranch, U.S., 229, 3 L.Ed. 545.

FEOFFMENT TO USES. A feoffment of lands to one person to the use of another.

In such case the feoffee was bound in conscience to hold the lands according to the use, and could himself derive no benefit. Sometimes such feoffments were made to the use of the feoffer. The effect of such conveyance was entirely changed by the statute of uses. See Wms.R.P., 6th Ed., 155; 2 Sand.Us. 13; Watk.Conv. 288.

FEOFFOR. The person making a feoffment, or enfeoffing another in fee. 2 Bl. Comm. 310; Litt. §§ 1, 57.

FEOH. This Saxon word meant originally cattle, and thence property or money, and, by a second transition, wages, reward, or fee. It was probably the original form from which the words "feod," "feudum," "fief," "feu," and "fee" (all meaning a feudal grant of land) have been derived. Spelman, Feuds.

FEONATIO. In forest law, the fawning season of deer.

FEORME. A certain portion of the produce of the land due by the grantee to the lord according to the terms of the charter. Spel. Feuds, c. 7.

FERÆ BESTIÆ. Wild beasts.

FERÆ NATURÆ. Lat. Of a wild nature or disposition.

Animals which are by nature wild are so designated, by way of distinction from such as are naturally tame, the latter being called *"domitæ naturæ."* Fleet v. Hegeman, 14 Wend., N.Y., 43; State v. Taylor, 27 N.J.L. 119, 72 Am. Dec. 347; Gillet v. Mason, 7 Johns., N.Y., 17.

FERCOSTA. Ital. A kind of small vessel or boat. Mentioned in old Scotch law, and called *"fercost."* Skene.

FERDELLA TERRÆ. A fardel-land; ten acres; or perhaps a yard-land. Cowell.

FERDFARE. Sax. A summons to serve in the army. An acquittance from going into the army. Fleta, lib. 1, c. 47, § 23.

FERDINGUS. A term denoting, apparently, a freeman of the lowest class, being named after the *cotseti.* Anc. Inst. Eng.

FERDWITE. In Saxon law, an acquittance of manslaughter committed in the army; also a fine imposed on persons for not going forth on a military expedition. Cowell.

FERIA. In old English law, a weekday; a holiday; a day on which process could not be served; a fair; a ferry. Cowell; Du Cange; Spelman; 4 Reeve, Hist. Eng. Law 17.

FERIÆ. In Roman law, holidays; generally speaking, days or seasons during which free-born Romans suspended their political transactions and their lawsuits, and during which slaves enjoyed a cessation from labor.

All *feriæ* were thus *dies nefasti.* All *feriæ* were divided into two classes,—*"feriæ publicæ"* and *"feriæ privatæ."* The latter were only observed by single families or individuals, in commemoration of some particular event which had been of importance to them or their ancestors. Smith, Dict.Antiq.

Numerous festivals were called by this name in the early Roman empire. In the later Roman empire the single days occurring at intervals of a week apart, commencing with the seventh day of the ecclesiastical year, were so called. Du Cange.

FERIAL DAYS. Originally and properly, days free from labor and pleading; holidays. In statute 27 Hen. VI. c. 5, working-days; weekdays, as distinguished from Sunday. Cowell.

FERITA. In old European law, a wound; a stroke. Spelman.

FERLING. In old records, the fourth part of a penny; also the quarter of a ward in a borough.

FERLINGATA. A fourth part of a yard-land.

FERLINGUS, or FERLINGUM. A furlong. Co. Litt. 5 *b.*

FERM, or FEARM. A house or land, or both, let by lease. Cowell.

FERME. A farm; a rent; a lease; a house or land, or both, taken by indenture or lease. Plowd. 195; Vicat; Cowell. See Farm.

FERMENTATION. A decomposition produced in an organic substance by the physiological action of a living organism, or by certain unorganized agents. U. S. v. Dodson, D.C.Cal., 268 F. 397, 403.

FERMENTED LIQUORS. Beverages produced by, or which have undergone, a process of alcoholic fermentation, to which they owe their intoxicating properties, including beer, wine, hard cider, and the like, but not spirituous or distilled liquors. State v. Lemp, 16 Mo. 391; State v. Biddle, 54 N. H. 383; People v. Foster, 64 Mich. 715, 31 N.W. 596; Hill v. State, 174 Md. 137, 197 A. 795, 799.

FERMER, FERMOR. A lessee; a farmer. One who holds a term, whether of lands or an incorporeal right, such as customs or revenue.

FERMIER. In French law, one who farms any public revenue.

FERMISONA. In old English law, the winter season for killing deer.

FERMORY. In old records, a place in monasteries, where they received the poor, (*hospicio excipiebant,*) and gave them provisions (*ferm, firma.*) Spelman. Hence the modern *infirmary,* used in the sense of a hospital.

FERNIGO. In old English law, a waste ground, or place where fern grows. Cowell.

FERRATOR. A farrier (*q. v.*).

FERRI. In the civil law, to be borne; that is on or about the person. This was distinguished from *portari,* (to be carried,) which signified to be carried on an animal. Dig. 50, 16, 235.

FERRIAGE. The toll or fare paid for the transportation of persons and property across a ferry.

Literally speaking, it is the price or fare fixed by law for the transportation of the traveling public, with such goods and chattels as they may have with them, across a river, bay, or lake. People v. San Francisco & A. R. Co., 35 Cal. 606.

FERRIFODINA. In old pleading, an iron mine. Townsh.Pl. 273.

FERRUERE, or FERRURA. The shoeing of horses. Kelham. See Ferrum.

FERRUM. Iron. In old English law, a horseshoe. *Ferrura,* shoeing of horses.

FERRY. A place of transit across a river or arm of the sea. Woolr.Ways 217. In law it is treated as a franchise, and defined as the exclusive right to carry passengers across a river, or arm of the sea, from one vill to another, or to connect a continuous line of road leading from township or vill to another. Canadian Pac. Ry. Co. v. U. S., C.C.A. Wash., 73 F.2d 831, 832.

A continuation of the highway from one side of the water over which it passes to the other, for transportation of passengers or of travelers with their teams and vehicles and such other property as they may carry or have with them. U. S. v. Puget Sound Nav. Co., D.C.Wash., 24 F.Supp. 431, 432.

A liberty to have a boat on a stream, river, arm of the sea, lake, or other body of water for the transportation of men, horses, and vehicles with their contents, for a reasonable toll. Sometimes limited to the landing place. State Highway Commission v. Smith, 250 Ky. 269, 62 S.W.2d 1044.

It may be said to be necessary service by specially constructed boat to carry passengers and property across rivers or bodies of water from place on one shore to point conveniently opposite on other shore and continuation of highway making connection with thoroughfare at each terminus. U. S. v. Canadian Pac. Ry. Co., D.C.Wash., 4 F.Supp. 851, 853. It comprises not merely the exclusive privilege of transportation, but also the use for that purpose of the respective landings, with the outlets therefrom. Hale v. Record, 74 Okl. 77, 176 P. 756, 757.

A public ferry is one to which all the public have the right to resort, for which a regular fare is established, and the ferryman is a common carrier, bound to take over all who apply, and bound to keep his ferry in operation and good repair. Hudspeth v. Hall, 111 Ga. 510, 36 S.E. 770; Broadnax v. Baker, 94 N.C. 681, 55 Am.Rep. 633.

A private ferry is one mainly for the use of the owner, and though he may take pay for ferriage, he does not follow it as a business. His ferry is not open to the public at its demand, and he may or may not keep it in operation. Hudspeth v. Hall, supra; St. Paul Fire & Marine Ins. Co. v. Harrison, 140 Ark. 158, 215 S.W. 698.

FERRY FRANCHISE. The public grant of a right to maintain a ferry at a particular place; a right conferred to land at a particular point and secure toll for the transportation of persons and property from that point across the stream. Mills v. St. Clair County, 7 Ill. 208. A grant to a named person empowering him to continue an interrupted land highway over the interrupting waters. U. S. v. Puget Sound Nav. Co., D.C.Wash., 24 F. Supp. 431, 432.

FERRYBOAT. A vessel traversing any of the waters of the state between two constant points regularly employed for the transfer of passengers and freight, authorized by law so to do, and also any boat employed as a part of the system of a railroad for the transfer of passengers and freight plying at regular and stated periods between two points. Pol.Code Cal. § 3643; Lake Tahoe Ry. & Transp. Co. v. Roberts, 168 Cal. 551, 143 P. 786, 789, Ann.Cas.1916E, 1196.

FERRYMAN. One employed in taking persons across a river or other stream, in boats or other contrivances, at a ferry. Covington Ferry Co. v. Moore, 8 Dana, Ky., 158; State v. Clarke, 2 McCord, S.C., 48, 13 Am.Dec. 701.

FESTA IN CAPPIS. In old English law, grand holidays, on which choirs wore caps. Jacob.

FESTINATIO JUSTITIÆ EST NOVERCA INFORTUNII. Hob. 97. Hasty justice is the stepmother of misfortune.

FESTING-MAN. In old English law, a bondsman; a surety; a frank-pledge, or one who was surety for the good behavior of another. Monasteries enjoyed the privilege of being "free from festing-men," which means that they were "not bound for any man's forthcoming who should transgress the law." Cowell. See Frank-Pledge.

FESTING-PENNY. Earnest given to servants when hired or retained. The same as *arles-penny.* Cowell.

FESTINUM REMEDIUM. Lat. A speedy remedy.

A term applied to those cases where the remedy for the redress of an injury is given without any unnecessary delay. Bacon, Abr. *Assise,* A. The action of dower is *festinum remedium.* The writ of assise was also thus characterized (in comparison with the less expeditious remedies previously available) by the statute of Westminster 2 (13 Edw. I. c. 24.)

FESTUCA. In Frankish law, a rod or staff or (as described by other writers) a stick, on which imprecatory runs were cut, which was used as a gage or pledge of good faith by a party to a contract, or for symbolic delivery in the conveyance or quit-claim of land, before a court of law, anterior to the introduction of written documents by the Romans. 2 Poll. & Maitl. 86, 184, 190; Maitl. Domesday Book and Beyond 323.

FESTUM. A feast, holiday, or festival. *Festum stultorum,* the feast of fools.

FETICIDE. In medical jurisprudence, destruction of the *fetus;* the act by which criminal abortion is produced. 1 Beck, Med.Jur. 288; Guy, Med. Jur. 133. See, also, Prolicide.

FETTERS. Chains or shackles for the feet; irons used to secure the legs of convicts, unruly prisoners, etc. Similar chains securing the wrists are called "handcuffs."

FEU. In Scotch law, a holding or tenure where the vassal, in place of military service, makes his return in grain or money. Distinguished from "wardholding," which is the military tenure of the country. Bell; Erskine, Inst. lib. ii. tit. 3, § 7.

FEU ANNUALS. In Scotch law, the *reddendo,* or annual return from the vassal to a superior in a feu holding. Wharton, Dict., 2d Lond.Ed.

FEU ET LIEU. Fr. In old French and Canadian law, hearth and home. A term importing actual settlement upon land by a tenant.

FEU HOLDING. A holding by tenure of rendering grain or money in place of military service. Bell.

FEUAR. In Scotch law, the tenant or vassal of a feu; a feu-vassal. Bell.

FEUD. Feudal law. An estate in land held of a superior on condition of rendering him services. 2 Bl.Comm. 105. An inheritable right to the use and occupation of lands, held on condition of rendering services to the lord or proprietor, who himself retains the property in the lands. See Spel. Feuds, c. 1.

In this sense the word is the same as "feod," "feodum," "feudum," "fief," or "fee." 1 Sullivan

Lect. 128; 1 Spence, Eq.Jur. 34; Dalrymple, Feud. Pr. 99; 1 Washb.R.P. 18; Mitch.R.P. 80.

Saxon and Old German Law

An enmity, or species of private war, existing between the family of a murdered man and the family of his slayer. In Scotland and the north of England, a combination of all the kin to revenge the death of any of the blood upon the slayer and all his race. *Termes de la Ley;* Whishaw. See Deadly Feud; Faida.

Military Feuds

The genuine or original feuds which were in the hands of military men, who performed military duty for their tenures.

FEUDA. Feuds or fees.

FEUDAL. Pertaining to feuds or fees; relating to or growing out of the feudal system or feudal law; having the quality of a feud, as distinguished from "allodial."

FEUDAL ACTIONS. An ancient name for real actions, or such as concern real property only. 3 Bl.Comm. 117.

FEUDAL COURTS. In the 12th century a lord *qua* lord had the right to hold a court for his tenants.

In the 13th century, they became of less importance and for three reasons: The feudal principle would have led to a series of courts one above the other, and the dominions of the large landowners were usually scattered, so that great feudal courts became impossible. The growth of the jurisdiction of the king's court removed the necessity for feudal courts. All the incidents of the feudal system came to be regarded in a commercial spirit—as property. Its jurisdiction became merely appendant to landowning. 1 Holdsw.Hist.E.L. 64.

FEUDAL LAW. The body of jurisprudence relating to feuds; the real-property law of the feudal system; the law anciently regulating the property relations of lord and vassal, and the creation, incidents, and transmission of feudal estates.

The body of laws and usages constituting the "feudal law" was originally customary and unwritten, but a compilation was made in the twelfth century, called "Feodarum Consuetudines," which has formed the basis of later digests. The feudal law prevailed over Europe from the twelfth to the fourteenth century, and was introduced into England at the Norman Conquest, where it formed the entire basis of the law of real property until comparatively modern times. Survivals of the feudal law, to the present day, so affect and color that branch of jurisprudence as to require a certain knowledge of the feudal law in order to the perfect comprehension of modern tenures and rules of real-property law.

FEUDAL POSSESSION. The equivalent of "seisin" under the feudal system.

FEUDAL SYSTEM. The system of feuds. A political and social system which prevailed throughout Europe during the eleventh, twelfth, and thirteenth centuries, and is supposed to have grown out of the peculiar usages and policy of the Teutonic nations who overran the continent after the fall of the Western Roman Empire, as developed by the exigencies of their military domination, and possibly furthered by notions taken from the Roman jurisprudence.

It was introduced into England, in its completeness, by William I., A. D. 1085, though it may have existed in a rudimentary form among the Saxons before the Conquest. It formed the entire basis of the real-property law of England in medieval times; and survivals of the system, in modern days, so modify and color that branch of jurisprudence, both in England and America, that many of its principles require for their complete understanding a knowledge of the feudal system. The feudal system originated in the relations of a military chieftain and his followers, or king and nobles, or lord and vassals, and especially their relations as determined by the bond established by a grant of *land* from the former to the latter. From this it grew into a complete and intricate complex of rules for the tenure and transmission of real estate, and of correlated duties and services; while, by tying men to the land and to those holding above and below them, it created a close-knit hierarchy of persons, and developed an aggregate of social and political institutions. For an account of the feudal system in its juristic relations, see 2 Bl.Comm. 44; 1 Steph.Comm. 160; 3 Kent, Comm. 487; Spel.Feuds; Litt.Ten.; Sull.Lect.; Spence, Eq.Jur.; 1 Washb.Real Prop. 15; Dalr.Feu.Prop. For its political and social relations, see Hall, Middle Ages; Maine, Anc.Law; Rob. Car. V.; Montesq. Esprit des Lois, bk. 30; Guizot, Hist.Civilization.

FEUDAL TENURES. The tenures of real estate under the feudal system, such as knight-service, socage, villenage, etc.

FEUDALISM. The feudal system; the aggregate of feudal principles and usages.

It is a vague term to describe a congeries of customs and legal relations by no means uniform throughout Europe and never static. But feudalism had one basic characteristic traceable through all its variations: It rested on relations to land, the primary factor in a relatively primitive agrarian civilization. United States v. Forness, C.C.A. N.Y., 125 F.2d 928, 933.

FEUDALIZE. To reduce to a feudal tenure; to conform to feudalism. Webster.

FEUDARY. A tenant who holds by feudal tenure, (also spelled "feodatory" and "feudatory.") Held by feudal service. Relating to feuds or feudal tenures.

FEUDBOTE. A recompense for engaging in a feud, and the damages consequent, it having been the custom in ancient times for all the kindred to engage in their kinsman's quarrel. Jacob.

FEUDE. An occasional early form of "feud" in the sense of private war or vengeance. Termes de la Ley. See Feud.

FEUDIST. A writer on feuds, as Cujacius, Spelman, etc.

FEUDO. In Spanish law, feud or fee. White, New Recop. b. 2, tit. 2, c. 2.

FEUDORUM LIBER. The book of feuds.

This was a compilation of feudal law, prepared by order of the emperor Frederick I., and published at Milan in 1170. It comprised five books, of which only the first two are now extant with fragmentary portions of the others, printed at the end of modern editions of the Corpus Juris Civilis. Giannone, b. 13, c. 3; Cruise, Dig. prel. diss. c. 1, § 31.

FEUDORUM LIBRI. The Books of Feuds published during the reign of Henry III., about the year 1152.

The particular customs of Lombardy as to feuds began about the year 1152, to be the standard of authority to other nations, by reason of the greater refinement with which that branch of learning had been there cultivated. This compilation was probably known in England, but does not appear to have had any other effect than to influence English lawyers to the more critical study of their own tenures, and to induce them to extend the learning of real property so as to embrace more curious matter of similar kind. 2 Reeves, Hist.Eng.Law, 55.

FEUDUM. L. Lat. A feud, fief, or fee. A right of using and enjoying forever the lands of another, which the lord grants on condition that the tenant shall render fealty, military duty, and other services. Spelman. It is not properly the land, but a right in the land.

This form of the word is used by the feudal writers. The earlier English writers generally prefer the form *feodum*. There was an older word *feum*.

Its use by the Normans is exceedingly obscure. "Feudal" was not in their vocabulary. Usually it denoted a stretch of land, rarely a tenure or mass of rights. It came to be applied to every person who had heritable rights in land. Maitl.Domesday Book and Beyond 152.

FEUDUM ANTIQUUM. An ancient feud or fief; a fief descended to the vassal from his ancestors. 2 Bl.Comm. 212, 221. A fief which ancestors had possessed for more than four generations. Spelman; Priest v. Cummings, 20 Wend. N.Y. 349.

FEUDUM APERTUM. An open feud or fief; a fief resulting back to the lord, where the blood of the person last seised was utterly extinct and gone or where the tenant committed a crime, or gave other legal cause. Spelman; 2 Bl.Comm. 245.

FEUDUM FRANCUM. A free feud. One which was noble and free from talliage and other subsidies to which the *plebeia feuda* (vulgar feuds) were subject. Spelman.

FEUDUM HAUBERTICUM. A fee held on the military service of appearing fully armed at the *ban* and *arriere ban*. Spelman.

FEUDUM IMPROPRIUM. An improper or derivative feud or fief. 2 Bl.Comm. 58.

FEUDUM INDIVIDUUM. An indivisible or impartible feud or fief; descendible to the eldest son alone. 2 Bl.Comm. 215.

FEUDUM LAICUM. A lay fee.

FEUDUM LIGIUM. A liege feud or fief; a fief held immediately of the sovereign; one for which the vassal owed fealty to his lord against all persons. 1 Bl.Comm. 367; Spelman.

FEUDUM MATERNUM. A maternal fief; a fief descended to the feudatory from his mother. 2 Bl.Comm. 212.

FEUDUM MILITARE. A knight's fee, held by knight service and esteemed the most honorable species of tenure. 2 Bla.Comm. 62.

FEUDUM NOBILE. A fee for which the tenant did guard and owed fealty and homage. Spelman.

FEUDUM NOVUM. A new feud or fief; a fief which began in the person of the feudatory, and did not come to him by succession. Spelman; 2 Bl.Comm. 212; Priest v. Cummings, 20 Wend. N.Y. 349.

FEUDUM NOVUM UT ANTIQUUM. A new fee held with the qualities and incidents of an ancient one. 2 Bl.Comm. 212.

FEUDUM PATERNUM. A fee which the paternal ancestors had held for four generations. Calvin.; Spelman. One descendible to heirs on the paternal side only. 2 Bl.Comm. 223. One which might be held by males only. Du Cange.

FEUDUM PROPRIUM. A proper, genuine, and original feud or fief; being of a purely military character, and held by military service. 2 Bl. Comm. 57, 58.

FEUDUM TALLIATUM. A restricted fee. One limited to descend to certain classes of heirs. 2 Bl.Comm. 112, note; 1 Washb. Real Prop. 66; Spelman.

FEUM. An older form of *feudum*. Maitl. Domesday Book and Beyond 152.

FEW. Not many; of small number. U. S. v. Margolis, C.C.A.N.J., 138 F.2d 1002, 1003. An indefinite expression for a small or limited number. Pittsburgh, C., C. & St. L. Ry. Co. v. Broderick, 56 Ind.App. 58, 102 N.E. 887, 893. Indicating a small number of units or individuals which constitute a whole. Provident Loan Bank v. Parham, 137 Tenn. 483, 194 S.W. 570. A relative term of great elasticity of meaning. Klann v. Minn, 161 Wis. 517, 154 N.W. 996.

FF. A Latin abbreviation for "Fragmenta," designating the Digest or Pandects in the *Corpus Juris Civilis* of Justinian; so called because that work is made up of fragments or extracts from the writings of numerous jurists. Mackeld. Rom. Law, § 74.

FI. FA. An abbreviation for *fieri facias,* (which see.)

FIANCER. L. Fr. To pledge one's faith. Kelham.

FIANZA. Sp. In Spanish law, trust, confidence, and correlatively a legal duty or obligation arising therefrom.

The term is sufficiently broad in meaning to include both a general obligation and a restricted liability under a single instrument. Martinez v. Runkle, 57 N.J.L. 111, 30 A. 593. But in a special sense, it designates a surety or guarantor, or the contract or engagement of suretyship; the contract by which one person engages to pay the debt or fulfil the obligations of another if the latter should fail to do so.

FIAR. In Scotch law, he that has the fee or *feu*. The proprietor is termed "fiar," in contradistinction to the life renter. 1 Kames, Eq. Pref. One whose property is charged with a life-rent. Where a right is taken to a husband and wife in conjunct fee and life-rent, the husband, as the *persona dignior,* is the only fiar. Ersk. Prin. 421.

FIARS PRICES. The value of grain in the different counties of Scotland, fixed yearly by the respective sheriffs, in the month of February, with the assistance of juries. These regulate the prices of grain stipulated to be sold at the fiar prices, or when no price has been stipulated. Ersk. 1, 4, 6.

FIAT. (Lat. "Let it be done.") In English practice, a short order or warrant of a judge or magistrate directing some act to be done; an authority issuing from some competent source for the doing of some legal act. See 1 Tidd Pr. 100.

One of the proceedings in the English bankrupt practice, being a power, signed by the lord chancellor, addressed to the court of bankruptcy, authorizing the petitioning creditor to prosecute his complaint before it. 2 Steph.Comm. 199. By the statute 12 & 13 Vict. c. 116, fiats were abolished.

Joint fiat. In English law, a fiat in bankruptcy, issued against two or more trading partners.

FIAT JUSTITIA. Let justice be done. On a petition to the king for his warrant to bring a writ of error in parliament, he writes on the top of the petition, "*Fiat justitia,*" and then the writ of error is made out, etc. Jacob.

FIAT JUSTITIA, RUAT CŒLUM. Let right be done, though the heavens should fall. Branch, Princ. 161.

FIAT PROUT FIERI CONSUEVIT, (NIL TEMERE NOVANDUM.) Let it be done as it hath used to be done, (nothing must be rashly innovated.) Jenk. Cent. 116, case 39; Branch, Princ.

FIAT UT PETITUR. Let it be done as it is asked. A form of granting a petition.

FIAUNT. An order; command. See Fiat.

FICTIO. In Roman law, a fiction; an assumption or supposition of the law.

"*Fictio*" in the old Roman law was properly a term of pleading, and signified a false averment on the part of the plaintiff which the defendant was not allowed to traverse; as that the plaintiff was a Roman citizen, when in truth he was a foreigner. The object of the fiction was to give the court jurisdiction. Maine, Anc.Law, 25.

FICTIO CEDIT VERITATI. FICTIO JURIS NON EST UBI VERITAS. Fiction yields to truth. Where there is truth, fiction of law exists not. 11 Co. 51.

FICTIO EST CONTRA VERITATEM, SED PRO VERITATE HABETUR. Fiction is against the truth, but it is to be esteemed truth.

FICTIO JURIS NON EST UBI VERITAS. Where truth is, fiction of law does not exist.

FICTIO LEGIS INIQUE OPERATUR ALICUI DAMNUM VEL INJURIAM. A legal fiction does not properly work loss or injury. 2 Coke, 35; 3 Coke, 36; Broom, Max. 129; Gilb. 223. Fiction of law is wrongful if it works loss or injury to anyone.

FICTIO LEGIS NEMINEM LÆDIT. A fiction of law injures no one. 2 Rolle, 502; 3 Bl.Comm. 43; Low v. Little, 17 Johns. N.Y. 348.

FICTION. An assumption or supposition of law that something which is or may be false is true, or that a state of facts exists which has never really taken place. New Hampshire Strafford Bank v. Cornell, 2 N.H. 324; Hibberd v. Smith, 67 Cal. 547, 4 P. 473, 56 Am.Rep. 726; Murphy v. Murphy, 190 Iowa 874, 179 N.W. 530, 533. An assumption, for purposes of justice, of a fact that does not or may not exist. Dodo v. Stocker, 74 Colo. 95, 219 P. 222, 223.

A rule of law which assumes as true, and will not allow to be disproved, something which is false, but not impossible. Best, Ev. 419.

These assumptions are of an innocent or even beneficial character, and are made for the advancement of the ends of justice. They secure this end chiefly by the extension of procedure from cases to which it is applicable to other cases to which it is not strictly applicable, the ground of inapplicability being some difference of an immaterial character. Brown.

Fictions are to be distinguished from presumptions of law. By the former, something known to be false or unreal is assumed as true; by the latter, an inference is set up, which may be and probably is true, but which, at any rate, the law will not permit to be controverted. It may also be said that a presumption is a rule of law prescribed for the purpose of getting at a certain conclusion, though arbitrary, where the subject is intrinsically liable to doubt from the remoteness, discrepancy, or actual defect of proofs.

Fictions are also to be distinguished from estoppels; an estoppel being the rule by which a person is precluded from asserting a fact by previous conduct inconsistent therewith on his own part or the part of those under whom he claims, or by an adjudication upon his rights which he cannot be allowed to question.

Best distinguishes legal fictions from presumptions *juris et de jure,* and divides them into three kinds,—affirmative or positive fictions, negative fictions, and fictions by relation. Best, Pres. p. 27, § 24.

FICTION OF LAW. Something known to be false is assumed to be true. Ryan v. Motor Credit Co., 130 N.J.Eq. 531, 23 A.2d 607, 621.

FICTITIOUS. Founded on a fiction; having the character of a fiction; pretended; counterfeit. People v. Carmona, 79 Cal.App. 159, 251 P. 315, 317; State v. Tinnin, 64 Utah 587, 232 P. 543, 545, 43 A.L.R. 46. Feigned, imaginary, not real, false, not genuine, nonexistent. Bill alleging that amount of mortgage sought to be canceled was "fictitious" held to allege that mortgage was without consideration. Kinney v. Kinney, 230 Ala. 558, 161 So. 798, 800. Arbitrarily invented and set up, to accomplish an ulterior object. West Virginia Mortgage & Discount Corporation v. Newcomer, 101 W.Va. 292, 132 S.E. 748, 749.

FICTITIOUS ACTION. An action brought for the sole purpose of obtaining the opinion of the court on a point of law, not for the settlement of any actual controversy between the parties. Smith v. Junction Ry. Co., 29 Ind. 551.

FICTITIOUS NAME. A counterfeit, feigned, or pretended name taken by a person, differing in some essential particular from his true name, (consisting of Christian name and patronymic,) with the implication that it is meant to deceive or mislead. Pollard v. Fidelity F. Ins. Co., 1 S.D. 570, 47 N.W. 1060; Carlock v. Cagnacci, 88 Cal. 600, 26 P. 597; Mangan v. Schuylkill County, 273 Pa. 310, 116 A. 920, 921.

FICTITIOUS PAYEE. Negotiable instrument is drawn to fictitious payee whenever payee named in it has no right to it, and its maker does not intend that such payee shall take anything by it; whether name of payee used by maker is that of person living or dead or one who never existed is immaterial. Goodyear Tire & Rubber Co. of California v. Wells Fargo Bank & Union Trust Co., 1 Cal.App.2d 694, 37 P.2d 483.

"Fictitiousness" depends on the intention to pay, rather than on the payee's existence. Norton v. City Bank & Trust Co., C.C.A.Va., 294 F. 839, 844; Mueller & Martin v. Liberty Ins. Bank, 187 Ky. 44, 218 S.W. 465, 466.

FICTITIOUS PERSON. A person, who, though named as payee in a check has no right to it or its proceeds because the drawer of it so intended. Johnston v. Exchange Nat. Bank of Tampa, 152 Fla. 228, 9 So.2d 810, 811, 812.

FICTITIOUS PLAINTIFF. A person appearing in the writ or record as the plaintiff in a suit, but who in reality does not exist, or who is ignorant of the suit and of the use of his name in it. It is a contempt of court to sue in the name of a fictitious party. See 4 Bl.Comm. 134.

FICTITIOUS PROMISE. See Promise.

FIDE-COMMISSARY. A term derived from the Latin "*fidei-commissarius*," and occasionally used by writers on equity jurisprudence as a substitute for the law French term "*cestui que trust*," as being more elegant and euphonious. See Brown v. Brown, 83 Hun, 160, 31 N.Y.S. 650.

FIDEI-COMMISSARIUS. In the civil law, this term corresponds nearly to our "*cestui que trust*." It designates a person who has the real or beneficial interest in an estate or fund, the title or administration of which is temporarily confided to another. See Story, Eq.Jur. § 966; 1 Greenl.Cruise, Dig. 295.

According to Du Cange, the term was sometimes used to denote the executor of a will.

FIDEI-COMMISSUM. In the civil law, a species of trust; being a gift of property (usually by will) to a person, accompanied by a request or direction of the donor that the recipient will transfer the property to another, the latter being a person not capable of taking directly under the will or gift. In re Courtin, 144 La. 971, 81 So. 457, 459; Succession of Reilly, 136 La. 347, 67 So. 27, 33; Gortario v. Cantu, 7 Tex. 44.

FIDE-JUBERE. In the civil law, to order a thing upon one's faith; to pledge one's self; to become surety for another. *Fide-jubes? Fide-jubeo:* Do you pledge yourself? I do pledge myself. Inst. 3, 16, 1. One of the forms of stipulation.

FIDE-JUSSIO. An act by which any one binds himself as an additional security for another. This giving security does not destroy the liability of the principal, but adds to the security of the surety. Vicat, Voc.Jur.; Hallifax, Annals, b. 2, c. 16, n. 10.

FIDE-JUSSOR. In Roman law, a guarantor; one who becomes responsible for the payment of another's debt, by a stipulation which binds him to discharge it if the principal debtor fails to do so. Mackeld.Rom.Law, § 452; 3 Bl.Comm. 108. He differs from a co-obligor in this, that the latter is equally bound to a debtor, with his principal, while the former is not liable till the principal has failed to fulfil his engagement; Dig. 12, 4, 4; 16, 1, 13; 24, 3, 64; 38, 1, 37; 50, 17, 110; 6, 14, 20; Hall, Pr. 33; Dunl.Adm.Pr. 300; Clerke, Prax. tit. 63.

The obligation of the fide-jussor was an accessory contract; for, if the principal obligation was not previously contracted, his engagement then took the name of mandate. *Lec. Elém.* § 872; *Code Nap.* 2012.

The sureties taken on the arrest of a defendant, in the court of admiralty, were formerly denominated "*fide jussors.*" 3 Bl.Comm. 108.

FIDE-PROMISSOR. See Fide-Jussor.

FIDELITAS. Fealty; fidelity. See Fealty.

FIDELITAS. DE NULLO TENEMENTO, QUOD TENETUR AD TERMINUM, FIT HOMAGII; FIT TAMEN INDE FIDELITATIS SACRAMENTUM. Co.Litt. 676. Fealty. For no tenement which is held for a term is there the oath of homage, but there is the oath of fealty.

FIDELITY BOND. Contract of fidelity insurance. Runcie v. Corn Exchange Bank Trust Co., Sup., 6 N.Y.S.2d 616, 620. A guaranty of personal honesty of officer furnishing indemnity against his defalcation or negligence. Phillips v. Board of Education of Pineville, 283 Ky. 173, 140 S.W.2d 819, 822.

FIDELITY INSURANCE. See Insurance.

FIDEM MENTIRI. Lat. To betray faith or fealty. A term used in feudal and old English law of a feudatory or feudal tenant who does not keep that fealty which he has sworn to the lord. Leg. Hen. I. c. 53.

FIDES. Lat. Faith; honesty; confidence; trust; veracity; honor. Occurring in the phrases "*bona fides*" (good faith), "*mala fides*" (bad faith), and "*uberrima fides*," (the utmost or most abundant good faith.)

FIDES EST OBLIGATIO CONSCIENTIÆ ALICUJUS AD INTENTIONEM ALTERIUS. Bacon. A trust is an obligation of conscience of one to the will of another.

FIDES FACTA. Among the Franks and Lombards undertakings were guaranteed by "making one's faith"—*fides facta*. This was symbolized by such formal acts as the giving of a rod; in suretyship giving the "festuca" or "vadium." 2 Holdsw.Hist.E.L. 73.

FIDES SERVANDA EST. Faith must be observed. An agent must not violate the confidence reposed in him. Story, Ag. § 192; Coolidge v. Brigham, 1 Metc., Mass., 551.

FIDES SERVANDA EST; SIMPLICITAS JURIS GENTIUM PRÆVALEAT. Faith must be kept; the simplicity of the law of nations must prevail. A rule applied to bills of exchange as a sort of sacred instruments. 3 Burrows, 1672; Story, Bills, § 15.

FIDUCIA. In Roman law, an early form of mortgage or pledge, in which both the title and possession of the property were passed to the creditor by a formal act of sale, (properly with the solemnities of the transaction known as *mancipatio,*) there being at the same time an express or implied agreement on the part of the creditor to reconvey the property by a similar act of sale provided the debt was duly paid; but on default of payment, the property became absolutely vested in the creditor without foreclosure and without any right of redemption.

In course of time, this form of security gave place to that known as *hypotheca,* while the contemporary contract of *pignus* or pawn underwent a corresponding development. See Mackeld.Rom.Law, § 334; Tomk. & J. Mod.Rom.Law, 182; Hadley, Rom.Law, 201–203; Pothier, Pand. tit. *"Fiducia."*

FIDUCIAL. An adjective having the same meaning as "fiduciary;" as, in the phrase "public or fiducial office." Ky.St. § 3752; Moss v. Rowlett, 112 Ky. 121, 65 S.W. 153.

FIDUCIARIUS HÆRES. See Fiduciary Heir.

FIDUCIARIUS TUTOR. In Roman law, the elder brother of an emancipated *pupillus,* whose father had died leaving him still under fourteen years of age.

FIDUCIARY. The term is derived from the Roman law, and means (as a noun) a person holding the character of a trustee, or a character analogous to that of a trustee, in respect to the trust and confidence involved in it and the scrupulous good faith and candor which it requires. Svanoe v. Jurgens, 144 Ill. 507, 33 N.E. 955; Stoll v. King, 8 How.Prac.,N.Y., 299. A person having duty, created by his undertaking, to act primarily for another's benefit in matters connected with such undertaking. Haluka v. Baker, 66 Ohio App. 308, 34 N.E.2d 68, 70. As an adjective it means of the nature of a trust; having the characteristics of a trust; analogous to a trust; relating to or founded upon a trust or confidence.

FIDUCIARY CAPACITY. One is said to act in a "fiduciary capacity" or to receive money or contract a debt in a "fiduciary capacity," when the business which he transacts, or the money or property which he handles, is not his own or for his own benefit, but for the benefit of another person, as to whom he stands in a relation implying and necessitating great confidence and trust on the one part and a high degree of good faith on the other part. The term is not restricted to technical or express trusts, but includes also such offices or relations as those of an attorney at law, a guardian, executor, or broker, a director of a corporation, and a public officer. Templeton v. Bockler, 73 Or. 494, 144 P. 405, 409; Madison Tp. v. Dunkle, 114 Ind. 262, 16 N.E. 593. As used in the Bankruptcy Act, § 17, subd. 4, 11 U.S.C.A. § 35, however, the term imports a technical trust, actually and expressly constituted, and not such merely as the law implies, and has no application to debts or obligations merely because they were created under circumstances in which trust or confidence in the popular sense of those terms was reposed in debtor. Culp v. Robey, Tex.Civ.App., 294 S.W. 647, 651; American Agricultural Chemical Co. v. Berry, 110 Me. 528, 87 A. 218, 45 L.R.A., N.S., 1106, Ann.Cas.1915A, 1293.

FIDUCIARY CONTRACT. An agreement by which a person delivers a thing to another on the condition that he will restore it to him. Cicero, *de Offic,* lib. 3, cap. 17; *Lec. du Dr.Civ.Rom.* § 237. See Chapman v. Forsyth, 2 How., U.S., 202, 11 L. Ed. 236; Fisk v. Sarber, 6 W. & S., Pa., 18; McGinn v. Shaeffer, 7 Watts, Pa., 415.

FIDUCIARY DEBT. A debt founded on or arising from some confidence or trust as distinguished from a "debt" founded simply on contract. Montgomery v. Phillips Petroleum Co., Tex.Civ.App., 49 S.W.2d 967, 973.

FIDUCIARY DEBTORS. Only public officers and trustees, not agents, factors, commission men, and the like, within the meaning of Bankruptcy Act, § 14, subd. 4, 11 U.S.C.A. § 32. Keefauver v. Hevenor, 163 App.Div. 531, 148 N.Y.S. 434, 435.

FIDUCIARY HEIR. The Roman laws called a fiduciary heir the person who was instituted heir, and who was charged to deliver the succession to a person designated by the testament. Merlin, *Répert.* But Pothier, Pand. vol. 22, says that *fiduciarius hæres* properly signifies the person to whom a testator has sold his inheritance under the condition that he should sell it to another.

FIDUCIARY OR CONFIDENTIAL RELATION. A very broad term embracing both technical fiduciary relations and those informal relations which exist wherever one man trusts in or relies upon another. State v. Gautier, 108 Fla. 390, 147 So. 240, 242. One founded on trust or confidence reposed by one person in the integrity and fidelity of another. Kerrigan v. O'Meara, 71 Mont. 1, 227 P. 819, 821.

The origin of the confidence and the source of the influence are immaterial. Quinn v. Phipps, 93 Fla. 805, 113 So. 419, 420, 54 A.L.R. 1173. The relations and duties involved need not be legal but may be moral, social, domestic, or merely personal. Trustees of Jesse Parker Williams Hospital v. Nisbet, 191 Ga. 821, 14 S.E.2d 64, 76. See also, Fiduciary Relation.

FIDUCIARY RELATION. An expression including both technical fiduciary relations and those informal relations which exist whenever one man trusts and relies upon another. Peckham v. Johnson, Tex.Civ.App., 98 S.W.2d 408, 416. It exists where there is special confidence reposed in one who in equity and good conscience is bound to act in good faith and with due regard to interests of one reposing the confidence. Neagle v. McMullen, 334 Ill. 168, 165 N.E. 605, 608. A relation subsisting between two persons in regard to a business, contract, or piece of property, or in regard to the general business or estate of one of them, of such a character that each must repose trust and confidence in the other and must exercise a corresponding degree of fairness and good faith.

Out of such a relation, the law raises the rule that neither party may exert influence or pressure upon the other, take selfish advantage of his trust, or deal with the subject-matter of the trust in such a way as to benefit himself or prejudice the other except in the exercise of the utmost good faith and with the full knowledge and consent of that other, business shrewdness, hard bargaining, and astuteness to take advantage of the forgetfulness or negligence of another being totally prohibited as between persons standing in such a relation to each other. Examples of fiduciary relations are those existing between attorney and client, guardian and ward, principal and agent, executor and heir, trustee and *cestui que trust,* landlord and tenant, etc. Robins v. Hope, 57 Cal. 497; Thomas v. Whitney, 186 Ill. 225, 57 N.E. 808; Central Nat. Bank v. Connecticut Mut. L. Ins. Co., 104 U.S. 68, 26 L.Ed. 693. The relation need not be legal, but may be moral, social, domestic, or merely personal. Miranovitz v. Gee, 163 Wis. 246, 157 N.W. 790, 792; Higgins v. Chicago Title & Trust Co., 312 Ill. 11, 143 N.E. 482, 484. It is one in which, if a wrong arise, the same remedy exists against the wrongdoer on behalf of the principal as would exist against a trustee on behalf of a cestui que trust. Smith v. Smith, 222 Mass. 102, 109 N.E. 830, 832. Sometimes confidential and fiduciary relations are regarded as synonymous; In re Cover's Estate, 188 Cal. 133, 204 P. 583, 588; but on the other hand, a technical distinction may be taken between a "fiducial relation" which is more correctly applicable to legal relationships between parties, such as guardian and ward, administrator and heirs, and other similar relationships, and a "confidential relation" which includes the legal relationships, and also every other relationship wherein confidence is rightfully reposed and is exercised. Roberts v. Parsons, 195 Ky. 274, 242 S.W. 594, 596.

FIEF. A fee, feod, or feud.

FIEF D'HAUBERT (or D'HAUBERK). Fr. In Norman feudal law, a fief or fee held by the tenure of knight-service; a knight's fee. 2 Bl.Comm. 62. A fee held on the military tenure of appearing fully armed on the *ban* and *arrière-ban. Feudum hauberticum.* Spelman; Calvinus, Lex.; Du Cange.

FIEF-TENANT. In old English law, the holder of a fief or fee; a feeholder or freeholder.

FIEL. In Spanish law, a sequestrator; a person in whose hands a thing in dispute is judicially deposited; a receiver. Las Partidas, pt. 3, tit. 9, l. 1.

FIELD. A cultivated tract of land; State v. Mack, 92 Vt. 103, 102 A. 58, 59; but not a one-acre lot used for cultivating vegetables; Simons v. Lovell, 7 Heisk., Tenn., 510. This term might well be considered as definite and certain a description as "close," and might be used in law; but it is not a usual description in legal proceedings. 1 Chit.Gen.Pr. 160.

Armies away from the home base on an operational, hostile mission are in the "field". In re Di Bartolo, D.C.N.Y., 50 F.Supp. 929, 933.

FIELD-ALE, or FILKDALE. An ancient custom in England, by which officers of the forest and bailiffs of hundreds had the right to compel the hundred to furnish them with ale. Tomlins.

FIELD BOOK. A description of the courses and distances of the lines, and of the corners of the lots of the town as they were surveyed, and as they appear by number and division on the town plan. Neill v. Ward, 103 Vt. 117, 153 A. 219, 225.

FIELD HOSPITAL. See Hospital.

FIELD NOTES. A description of a survey. Outlaw v. Gulf Oil Corporation, Tex.Civ.App., 137 S.W.2d 787, 794.

FIELD REEVE. An officer elected, in England, by the owners of a regulated pasture to keep in order the fences, ditches, etc., on the land, to regulate the times during which animals are to be admitted to the pasture, and generally to maintain and manage the pasture subject to the instructions of the owners. (General Inclosure Act, 1845, § 118.) Sweet.

FIELD VISION. The general vision used in catching in sight, following and locating objects; —distinguished from "binocular vision" (*q. v.*). Turpin v. St. Regis Paper Co., 199 App.Div. 64, 192 N.Y.S. 85, 87.

FIELD WORK. Work in the field, specifically the task of gathering scientific data from the field. Includes the sphere of practical operation, as of an organization or enterprise; also, the place or territory where direct contacts, as with a clientele may be made or first-hand knowledge may be gained; sphere of action or place of contest, either literally or figuratively; hence, any scene of operations or opportunity for activity. State ex rel. McPherson v. Snell, 168 Or. 153, 121 P.2d 930, 937.

FIELDAD. In Spanish law, sequestration. This is allowed in six cases by the Spanish law where the title to property is in dispute. Las Partidas, pt. 3, tit. 3, l. 1.

FIERDING COURTS. Ancient Gothic courts of an inferior jurisdiction, so called because *four* were instituted within every inferior district or hundred. 3 Bl.Comm. 34; 3 Steph.Com. 393; Stiernhook, *De Jure Goth.* i. 1, c. 2.

FIERI. Lat. To be made; to be done. See In Fieri.

FIERI FACIAS. Means that you cause to be made. In practice, a writ of execution commanding the sheriff to levy and make the amount of a judgment from the goods and chattels of the judgment debtor.

FIERI FACIAS DE BONIS ECCLESIASTICIS. When a sheriff to a common *fi. fa.* returns *nulla bona,* and that the defendant is a beneficed clerk, not having any lay fee, a plaintiff may issue a *fi. fa. de bonis ecclesiasticis,* addressed to the bishop of the diocese or to the archbishop, (during the vacancy of the bishop's see,) commanding him to make of the ecclesiastical goods and chattels belonging to the defendant within his diocese the sum therein mentioned. 2 Chit.Archb.Pr. (12th Ed.) 1062.

FIERI FACIAS DE BONIS TESTATORIS. The writ issued on an ordinary judgment against an executor when sued for a debt due by his testator. If the sheriff returns to this writ *nulla bona*, and a *devastavit*, (*q. v.*,) the plaintiff may sue out a *fieri facias de bonis propriis*, under which the goods of the executor himself are seized. Sweet.

FIERI FECI. Means I have caused to be made. In practice, the return made by a sheriff or other officer to a writ of *fieri facias*, where he has collected the whole, or a part, of the sum directed to be levied. 2 Tidd, Pr. 1018. The return, as actually made, is expressed by the word "Satisfied" indorsed on the writ.

FIERI NON DEBET, (DEBUIT,) SED FACTUM VALET. It ought not to be done, but [if] done, it is valid. Shep. Touch. 6; 5 Coke, 39; T.Raym. 58; 1 Strange, 526. A maxim frequently applied in practice. Nichols v. Ketcham, 19 Johns., N.Y., 84, 92.

FIFTEENTHS. In English law, this was originally a tax or tribute, levied at intervals by act of parliament, consisting of one-fifteenth of all the movable property of the subject or personalty in every city, township, and borough.

Under Edward III., the taxable property was assessed, and the value of its fifteenth part (then about £29,000) was recorded in the exchequer, whence the tax, levied on that valuation, continued to be called a "fifteenth," although as the wealth of the kingdom increased, the name ceased to be an accurate designation of the proportion of the tax to the value taxed. See 1 Bl.Comm. 309; Co. 2d Inst. 77; 1 Poll. & Maitl. 604; Cowell.

FIFTH DEGREE OF KINSHIP. The degree of kinship between a deceased intestate and the children of decedent's first cousin, sometimes designated as "first cousins once removed", was in the "fifth degree". Simonton v. Edmunds, 202 S.C. 397, 25 S.E.2d 284, 285.

FIFTY DECISIONS. Ordinances of Justinian (529–532) upon the authority of which all moot points were settled in the preparation of the second edition of the Code. Taylor, Science of Jurispr. 144.

FIGHT. "Fight" means combat or battle, as hostile encounter or engagement between opposing forces, suggesting primarily the notion of a brawl or unpremeditated encounter, or that of a pugilistic combat. Gitlow v. Kiely, D.C.N.Y., 44 F.2d 227, 232.

An encounter, with blows or other personal violence, between two persons. Carpenter v. People, 31 Colo. 284, 72 P. 1072; Coles v. New York Casualty Co., 87 App.Div. 41, 83 N.Y.S. 1063. The term does not necessarily imply that both parties should give and take blows. It is sufficient that they voluntarily put their bodies in position with that intent; State v. Gladden, 73 N.C. 155; Tate v. State, 46 Ga. 148.

FIGHTWITE. Sax. A mulct or fine for making a quarrel to the disturbance of the peace. Called also by Cowell *"forisfactura pugnæ."* The amount was one hundred and twenty shillings. Cowell.

A payment to a lord possessing soc over a place where a wrong was done. 2 Holdsw. Hist.E.L. 35.

FIGURES. Artificial representations of a form, as in sculpture, drawing, or painting, especially the human body represented by art of any kind. People v. Eastman, 89 Misc. 596, 152 N.Y.S. 314, 317.

Numerals. They are either Roman, made with letters of the alphabet: for example, MDCCLXXVI; or they are Arabic, as follows: 1776.

FILACER. An officer of the superior courts at Westminster, whose duty it was to file the writs on which he made process. There were fourteen filacers, and it was their duty to make out all original process. Cowell; Blount; Jacob L.Dict. It is used in 8 Mod. 284. The office was abolished in 1837.

FILARE. In old English practice, to file. Townsh.Pl. 67.

FILCHING. "Filching" means to steal money, commonly of little value, secretly or underhandedly. Peck v. Bez, W.Va., 40 S.E.2d 1, 10.

FILE, *n.* A record of the court. Milton v. United States, C.C.A.La., 105 F.2d 253, 255. A thread, string, or wire upon which writs and other exhibits in courts and offices are fastened or filed for the more safe-keeping and ready turning to the same. Spelman; Cowell; Tomlins. Papers put together and tied in bundles. A paper is said also to be filed when it is delivered to the proper officer, and by him received to be kept on file. 13 Vin.Abr. 211; 1 Litt. 113; 1 Hawk.P.C. 7, 207; Beebe v. Morrell, 76 Mich. 114, 42 N.W. 1119, 15 Am.St.Rep. 288. But, in general, "file," or "the files," is used loosely to denote the official custody of the court or the place in the offices of a court where the records and papers are kept. The "file" in a cause includes original subpœnas and all papers belonging thereto. Jackson v. Mobley, 157 Ala. 408, 47 So. 590.

FILE, *v.* To lay away papers for presentation and reference. Murphy v. Burlington Overall Co., 225 Mo.App. 866, 34 S.W.2d 1035, 1037. In practice, to put upon the *files*, or deposit in the custody or among the records of a court. To deliver an instrument or other paper to the proper officer for the purpose of being kept on file by him in the proper place. Gallagher v. Linwood, 30 N.M. 211, 231 P. 627, 629, 37 A.L.R. 664; Dillon v. Superior Court of Nevada County, 24 Cal.App. 760, 142 P. 503, 505; Pendrey v. Brennan, 31 Idaho, 54, 169 P. 174, 175. It carries the idea of permanent preservation as a public record. In re Gubelman, C.C.A., 10 F.2d 926, 929.

The term "filed" is used to denote the paper placed with the clerk, and assigned by law to his official keeping. Ex parte Leifeste, 127 Tex.Cr.R. 445, 77 S.W.2d 675, 676.

"To file" a paper, on the part of a party, is to place it in the official custody of the clerk. "To file," on the part of the clerk, is to indorse upon the paper the date of its reception, and retain it in his office, subject to inspection by whomsoever it may concern. Holman v. Chevaillier, 14 Tex. 339.

"Filing a bill" in equity is an equivalent expression to "commencing a suit."

FILE WRAPPER ESTOPPEL. The doctrine depends upon the fact that, when an applicant has accepted the rejection of a broad claim he may not later assert that another claim, deliberately restricted to secure its allowance, is its equivalent. Tampax, Inc. v. Personal Products Corporation, C.C.A.N.Y., 123 F.2d 722, 723.

FILED FOR RECORD. Left with recorder or registrar for recording. In re Grodzins, D.C.Cal., 27 F.Supp. 521, 523, 524.

FILEINJAID. Brit. A name given to villeins in the laws of Hoel Dda. Barring. Obs.St. 302.

FILIATE. To fix a bastard child on some one, as its father. To declare whose child it is. 2 W.Bl. 1017.

FILIATIO NON POTEST PROBARI. Co.Litt. 126. Filiation cannot be proved; that is, the husband is presumed to be the father of a child born during coverture. But see 7 & 8 Vict. c. 101.

FILIATION. The relation of parent and child, but does not import legitimacy, although often a step to that end. Rodrigues v. Rodrigues, 286 Mass. 77, 190 N.E. 20, 22. Correlative to "paternity."

The judicial assignment of an illegitimate child to a designated man as its father.

In the civil law, the descent of son or daughter, with regard to his or her father, mother, and their ancestors.

FILIATION PROCEEDING. A special statutory proceeding, criminal in form, but in the nature of a civil action to enforce a civil obligation or duty specifically for the purpose of establishing parentage and the putative father's duty to support his illegitimate child. State v. Morrow, 158 Or. 412, 75 P.2d 737, 738, 739, 744.

FILICETUM. In old English law, a ferny or bracky ground; a place where fern grows. Co. Lit. 4*b*; Shep.Touch. 95.

FILIOLUS (or FILIOUS). In old records, a godson. Spelman.

FILIUS. Lat. A son; a child.

As distinguished from heir *filius* is a term of nature, *hæres* a term of law. 1 Powell, Dev. 311. In the civil law the term was used to denote a child generally. Calvinus, Lex.; Vicat, Voc.Jur.

A distinction was sometimes made, in the civil law, between *"filii"* and *"liberi;"* the latter word including grandchildren, *(nepotes,)* the former not. Inst. 1, 14, 5. But, according to Paulus and Julianus, they were of equally extensive import. Dig. 50, 16, 84; Id. 50, 16, 201.

FILIUS EST NOMEN NATURÆ, SED HÆRES NOMEN JURIS. 1 Sid. 193. 1 Pow.Dev. 311. Son is a name of nature, but heir is a name of law.

FILIUS FAMILIAS. In the civil law, the son of a family; an unemancipated son. Inst. 2, 12, pr.; Id. 4, 5, 2; Story, Confl.Laws, § 61.

FILIUS IN UTERO MATRIS EST PARS VISCERUM MATRIS. 7 Coke, 8. A son in the mother's womb is part of the mother's vitals.

FILIUS MULIERATUS. In old English law, the eldest legitimate son of a woman, who previously had an illegitimate son by his father. Glanv. lib. 7, c. 1. Otherwise called *"mulier."* 2 Bl.Comm. 248.

FILIUS NULLIUS. An illegitimate child; son of nobody. In re Ellis' Estate, 225 Iowa 1279, 282 N.W. 758, 762, 120 A.L.R. 975.

FILIUS POPULI. A son of the people. In re Clark's Estate, 228 Iowa 75, 290 N.W. 13, 29. Natural child.

FILL. To make full; to complete; to satisfy or fulfill; to possess and perform the duties of; to occupy the whole capacity or extent of, so as to leave no space vacant.

Word "fill" in agreement to "take and *fill*" a certain number of shares, amounts to a promise to pay assessments. Bangor Bridge Co. v. McMahon, 10 Me. 478.

To *fill* a prescription is to furnish, prepare, and combine the requisite materials in due proportion as prescribed. Ray v. Burbank, 61 Ga. 505, 34 Am.Rep. 103.

To "fill" embroidery is to stuff out the figure, which is the ornamentation, by covering the stuffing with the silk, cotton, or other threads used by the embroiderer. G. Reis & Bro. v. Reform Initial Co., C.C.A.N.Y., 266 F. 219.

The term "fill," used in relation to shipments of live stock, means feeding and watering stock just prior to sale so as to increase their weight and thus enhance their value. Texas & P. Ry. Co. v. West Bros., Tex.Com.App., 207 S.W. 918, 922.

FILLED MILK. Milk to which has been added fat or oil other than milk fat so that the resulting product is in imitation or semblance of milk, cream, or skim milk. State v. Hershman, 346 Mo. 892, 143 S.W.2d 1025, 1026.

FILLING CHAMBER. A place in which a bottle mouth is held so as to cut off communication with open air while the bottle is being filled with gaseous liquids to be sealed in it under pressure. Crown Cork & Seal Co. of Baltimore City v. Carper Automatic Bottling Mach. Co. of Baltimore City, D.C.Md., 229 F. 748, 750.

FILLING STATION. A building or structure where motor vehicle fuel is stored for sale to the public. Hanes v. Carolina Cadillac Co., 176 N.C. 350, 97 S.E. 162.

FILLY. A young mare; a female colt. An indictment charging the theft of a "filly" is not sustained by proof of the larceny of a "mare." Lunsford v. State, 1 Tex.App. 448, 28 Am.Rep. 414.

FILTHY. Under Cr.Code, § 211, 18 U.S.C.A. § 1461, an unmailable filthy letter is morally foul, polluted, nasty. United States v. Davidson, D.C. N.Y., 244 F. 523, 526. Dirty, vulgar, indecent, offensive to the moral sense, morally depraving, debasing. Tyomies Pub. Co. v. United States, C.C.A. Mich., 211 F. 385, 390.

In Federal Food, Drug, and Cosmetic Act, § 402(a) (3), 21 U.S.C.A. § 342(a) (3), word "filthy" is used in its usual and ordinary meaning, and is not to be confined to any scientific or medical definition. U. S. v. Lazere, D.C.Iowa, 56 F.Supp. 730, 732.

FILUM. Lat. In old practice, a file, *i. e.*, a thread or wire on which papers were strung, that being the ancient method of filing.

An imaginary thread or line passing through the middle of a stream or road, as in the titles following.

FILUM AQUÆ. A thread of water; a line of water; the middle line of a stream of water, supposed to divide it into two equal parts, and constituting in many cases the boundary between the riparian proprietors on each side. Ingraham v. Wilkinson, 4 Pick., Mass., 273, 16 Am.Dec. 342. *Medium filum* is sometimes used with no additional meaning. Cf. Thalweg.

FILUM FORESTÆ. The border of the forest. 2 Bla.Comm. 419; 4 Inst. 303; Manw. *Purlieu.*

FILUM VIÆ. The thread or middle line of a road. The boundary between the owners of the land on each side of a road. 2 Smith, Lead.Cas. Am.Ed., 98, note. City of Chicago v. Rumsey, 87 Ill. 348; Cox v. Freedley, 33 Pa. 124, 75 Am.Dec. 584.

FIN. Fr. An end, or limit; a limitation, or period of limitation.

FIN DE NON RECEVOIR. In French law, an exception or plea founded on law, which, without entering into the merits of the action, shows that the plaintiff has no right to bring it, either because the time during which it ought to have been brought has elapsed, which is called "prescription," or that there has been a compromise, accord and satisfaction, or any other cause which has destroyed the right of action which once subsisted. Poth.Proc. Civile, pt. 1, c. 2, § 2, art. 2; Story, Confl.Laws, § 580.

FINAL. Last; conclusive. Standard Oil Co. (New Jersey) v. U. S., Ct.Cl., 10 F.Supp. 550, 560. Decisive; definitive. State ex rel. Grodin v. Barns, 119 Fla. 405, 161 So. 568, 574. Terminating; completed. In its use in jurisprudence, this word is generally contrasted with "interlocutory." Johnson v. New York, 48 Hun, 620, 1 N.Y.S. 254; Garrison v. Dougherty, 18 S.C. 488; U. S. v. Broude, D.C.Minn., 299 F. 332, 333.

As to final "Costs," "Decree," "Judgment," "Injunction," "Order," "Process," "Recovery," "Sentence," and "Settlement," see those titles.

FINAL ARCHITECT'S CERTIFICATE. One which is issued after a job is done and which finally determines the rights of the parties as to money and disputes. Johnson v. Hogg, 202 Ill. App. 253, 255; Hunt v. Owen Bldg. & Inv. Co., Mo.App., 219 S.W. 138, 140.

FINAL DECISION. One which leaves nothing open to further dispute and which sets at rest cause of action between parties. Hammond v. Boston Terminal Co., 295 Mass. 566, 4 N.E.2d 328. One which settles rights of parties respecting the subject-matter of the suit and which concludes them until it is reversed or set aside. Orwig v. Conley, 322 Ill. 291, 153 N.E. 371, 372; Pawtucket Cabinet & Builders' Finish Co. v. People's Excursion Line, 45 R.I. 426, 123 A. 354. See, however, Wyman v. Hageman, 318 Ill. 64, 148 N.E. 852, 855. The filing of signed findings and conclusions and order for judgment. Crane v. First Nat. Bank, 26 N.D. 268, 144 N.W. 96, 97. Synonymous with final judgment or decree. In re Tiffany, 252 U.S. 32, 40 S.Ct. 239, 240, 64 L.Ed. 443. Also, a decision from which no appeal or writ of error can be taken. Moore v. Mayfield, 47 Ill. 167; 6 El. & Bl. 408; U. S. v. Tod, C.C.A.N.Y., 1 F.2d 246, 251; Blanding v. Sayles, 23 R.I. 226, 49 A. 992.

FINAL DETERMINATION. Final judgment is synonymous. The final settling of the rights of the parties to the action beyond all appeal. Quarture .v. Allegheny County, 141 Pa.Super. 356, 14 A.2d 575, 578. See Judgment.

FINAL DISPOSITION. Such a conclusive determination of the subject-matter embraced in a submission to arbitrators, that after the award is made nothing further remains to fix the rights and obligations of the parties, and no further controversy or litigation can arise thereon. Quarture v. Allegheny County, 141 Pa.Super. 356, 14 A.2d 575, 578. It is such an award that the party against whom it is made can perform or pay it without any further ascertainment of rights or duties. Colcord v. Fletcher, 50 Me. 401.

FINAL HEARING. Describes that stage of proceedings relating to the determination of a suit upon its merits as distinguished from those of preliminary questions. Menard v. Bowman Dairy Co., 296 Ill.App. 323, 15 N.E.2d 1014, 1015. It may also be used with reference to a dismissal on the motion of plaintiff. Christensen v. General Electric Co., D.C.N.Y., 248 F. 284, 286.

FINAL PASSAGE. The vote on a passage of a bill or resolution in either house of the legislature after it has received the prescribed number of readings and has been subjected to such action as is required by the fundamental law governing the body or its own rule. State v. Buckley, 54 Ala. 613. The actual final vote necessary to a bill becoming a law, regardless of parliamentary fictions. Roane Iron Co. v. Francis, 130 Tenn. 694, 172 S. W. 816.

FINAL RECEIVER'S RECEIPT. An acknowledgment by the government that it has received full payment for public land, that it holds the legal title in trust for the entryman, and will in due course issue to him a patent. Bovey-Shute Lumber Co. v. Erickson, 41 N.D. 365, 170 N.W. 628, 630.

FINAL SETTLEMENT. In probate proceeding, a direct adjudication that the estate is fully administered; that the administrator has completely executed his trust and has accounted for all moneys received as the law requires. In re Braun's Estate, 140 Kan. 188, 34 P.2d 94, 95.

The final determination of amount due contractor by proper governmental authority. Consolidated Indemnity & Insurance Co. v. W. A. Smoot & Co., C.C.A.Va., 57 F.2d 995, 996.

A formal determination by commissioners' court, in cases involving contract with county, of amount finally due under contract. Austin Bros. Bridge Co. v. Love, Tex.Com.App., 34 S.W.2d 574, 577.

FINAL SUBMISSION. Exists when nothing remains to be done to render submission complete. Thompson v. Schalk, 228 Iowa 705, 292 N.W. 851, 852.

Where the whole case, both requested instructions and evidence, is submitted to the court for its ruling and the court takes the case under advisement, there is a "final submission" of the entire case. Platt v. Heim & Overly Realty Co., 342 Mo. 772, 117 S.W.2d 327, 329.

FINAL TRIAL. Under a statute such trial in the court having original trial jurisdiction as is the basis of entry of judgment finally disposing of action in that court; the term does not apply to proceedings in the appellate court. Wynne v. Smith, 23 Ga.App. 330, 98 S.E. 271, 272.

FINALIS CONCORDIA. A final or conclusive agreement.

In the process of "levying a fine," this was a final agreement entered by the litigating parties upon the record, by permission of court, settling the title to the land, and which was binding upon them like any judgment of the court. 1 Washb.Real Prop. *70.

FINANCE CHARGE. The consideration for privilege of deferring payment of purchase price. Cowart v. Lang, 252 App.Div. 720, 298 N.Y.S. 875.

FINANCES. Money resources generally. The state of the finances of an individual or corporation, being his condition in a monetary point of view. The cash he has on hand, and that which he expects to receive, as compared with the engagements he has made to pay.

The public wealth of a state or government, considered either statically (as the property or money which a state now owns) or dynamically, (as its income, revenue, or public resources.) Monetary affairs, funds in a treasury or accruing to it, etc. City of Newburgh v. Dickey, 150 N.Y.S. 175, 177, 164 App.Div. 791.

FINANCIAL. Fiscal. Armstrong v. State Bank of Mayville, 177 App.Div. 265, 165 N.Y.S. 5, 8. Dealing in money. Crown Finance Corporation v. McColgan, 23 Cal.2d 280, 144 P.2d 331, 333.

FINANCIAL RESPONSIBILITY. Obligation to pay to a third party. Christensen v. Hennepin Transp. Co., 215 Minn. 394, 10 N.W.2d 406, 415, 147 A.L.R. 945.

FINANCIAL WORTH. The value of one's property less what he owes, or the value of his resources less his liabilities. Boney v. Central Mut. Ins. Co. of Chicago, 213 N.C. 470, 196 S.E. 837, 841.

FINANCIALLY ABLE. Means purchaser must be able to command the necessary funds to close the deal within the required time. Hersh v. Garau, 218 Cal. 460, 23 P.2d 1022.

FINANCIER. A person employed in the economical management and application of public money; one skilled in matters appertaining to the judicious management of money affairs.

FIND. To come upon by seeking or by effort. Shields v. Shields, 115 Mont. 146, 139 P.2d 528, 530. To discover; to determine; to ascertain and declare.

To announce a conclusion, as the result of judicial investigation, upon a disputed fact or state of facts; as a jury are said to "find a will." To determine a controversy in favor of one of the parties; as a jury "find for the plaintiff." State v. Bulkeley, 61 Conn. 287, 23 A. 186, 14 L.R.A. 657. The term usually means to ascertain by judicial inquiry, State ex inf. of Barker v. Crandall, 269 Mo. 44, 190 S.W. 889, 893; in contradistinction to acts by a clerk of court, State v. Halaby, 148 La. 1, 86 So. 561, 563; or by administrative boards, Union Pac. R. Co. v. Board of Com'rs of Weld County, Colo., C.C.A.Colo., 217 F. 540, 541. But the term does not always require a judicial or official finding. City of Chicago v. Atwood, 269 Ill. 624, 110 N.E. 127, 128.

FINDER. One who discovers and takes possession of another's personal property, which was then lost. Kincaid v. Eaton, 98 Mass. 139, 93 Am. Dec. 142.

A searcher employed to discover goods imported or exported without paying custom. Jacob.

FINDER'S FEE. A sum of money paid by a banker to one who brings to him a deal out of which he makes money. Cray, McFawn & Co. v. Hegarty, Conroy & Co., D.C.N.Y., 27 F.Supp. 93, 97, 98, 100, 101.

FINDING. The result of the deliberations of a jury or a court. Denslow v. Moore, 2 Day (Conn.) 12; U. S. v. Moller, 16 Blatchf. 65, Fed.Cas.No. 15,794. A decision upon a question of fact reached as the result of a judicial examination or investigation by a court, jury, referee, coroner, etc. Benton v. Roberts, 53 Ga.App. 121, 185 S.E. 292, 294. A recital of the facts as found. Crighton v. Jacobs, 100 Conn. 281, 123 A. 437, 438. The word commonly applies to the result reached by a judge, Maeder Steel Products Co. v. Zanello, 109 Or. 562, 220 P. 155, 158; it being sometimes, however, as a matter of interpretation, treated as a ruling of law, Garden Cemetery Corporation v. Baker, 218 Mass. 339, 105 N.E. 1070, 1072, Ann.Cas.1916B, 75.

FINDING OF FACT. A determination of a fact by the court, averred by one party and denied by the other, and founded on evidence in case. C.I.T. Corp. v. Elliott, 66 Idaho 384, 159 P.2d 891, 897. A conclusion by way of reasonable inference from the evidence. Barker v. Narragansett Racing Ass'n, 65 R.I. 489, 16 A.2d 495, 497. Also the answer of the jury to a specific interrogatory propounded to them as to the existence or non-existence of a fact in issue. Miles v. McCallan, 1 Ariz. 491, 3 P. 610; Murphy v. Bennett, 68 Cal. 528, 9 P. 738.

The term is not applicable, with special reference to review on appeal, to a mere conclusion that the evidence is insufficient to authorize relief, Monetaire Mining Co. v. Columbus Rexall Consol. Mines Co., 53 Utah, 413, 174 P.

172, 174; nor to the opinion of the trial court, delivered in announcing judgment, Rogers v. Harris, 76 Okl. 215, 184 P. 459, 462; nor to a memorandum of the decision of the trial judge, Preston v. Preston, 102 Conn. 96, 128 A. 292, 296; nor to a transcript of the evidence, State v. Chin Lung, 106 Conn. 701, 139 A. 91, 97.

A general finding by a court is a general statement that the facts are in favor of a party or entitle him to judgment. It is a complete determination of all matters, and is a finding of every special thing necessary to be found to sustain the general finding. Miller v. Thompson, 80 Okl. 70, 194 P. 103, 105.

A special finding is a specific setting forth of the ultimate facts established by the evidence and which are determinative of the judgment which must be given. Rhodes v. United States Nat. Bank, Ill., 66 F. 514, 13 C.C.A. 612, 34 L.R.A. 742; Humphreys v. Third Nat. Bank, Ohio, 75 F. 856, 21 C.C.A. 538. It is only a determination of the ultimate facts on which the law must be determined, Societe Nouvelle d'Armement v. Barnaby, C.C.A.Wash., 246 F. 68, 70. A special finding may also be said to be one limited to the fact issue submitted. Ex parte Woodward Iron Co., 212 Ala. 220, 102 So. 103, 106.

The term "fact" in the phrase "finding of fact" denotes the inferences drawn by the trior from ascertained facts. Porter v. Industrial Commission of Wisconsin, 173 Wis. 267, 181 N.W. 317, 318.

FINE, *v.* To impose a pecuniary punishment or mulct.

To sentence a person convicted of an offense to pay a penalty in money. Goodman v. Durant B. & L. Ass'n, 71 Miss. 310, 14 So. 146; State v. Belle, 92 Iowa 258, 60 N.W. 525.

FINE, *n.* A sum of money paid at the *end,* to make an end of a transaction, suit, or prosecution; mulct; penalty. Railroad Co. v. State, 22 Kan. 15; Sunderland Bros. Co. v. Chicago, B. & I. R. Co., 104 Neb. 319, 177 N.W. 156, 157. A forfeit or forfeiture. Keinath, Schuster & Hudson v. Reed, 18 N.M. 358, 137 P. 841, 844; Bryant v. Rich's Grill, 216 Mass. 344, 103 N.E. 925, 927, Ann.Cas.1915B, 869.

Conveyancing

An amicable composition or agreement of a suit, either actual or fictitious, by leave of the court, by which the lands in question become, or are acknowledged to be, the right of one of the parties. 2 Bl.Comm. 349; Christy v. Burch, 25 Fla. 942, 2 So. 258; Hitz v. Jenks, 123 U.S. 297, 8 S.Ct. 143, 31 L.Ed. 156. Fines were abolished in England by St. 3 & 4 Wm. IV. c. 74, substituting a disentailing deed. (*q. v.*).

A fine is so called because it puts an *end* not only to the suit thus commenced, but also to all other suits and controversies concerning the same matter. The party who parted with the land, by acknowledging the right of the other, was said to *levy* the fine, and was called the "cognizor" or "conusor," while the party who recovered or received the estate was termed the "cognizee" or "conusee," and the fine was said to be levied to him.

Criminal Law

A pecuniary punishment imposed by lawful tribunal upon person convicted of crime or misdemeanor. In re Chester School District's Audit, 301 Pa. 203, 151 A. 801, 808. A pecuniary penalty. Hanks v. Shreveport Yellow Cabs, La.App., 187 So. 817, 819. It may include a forfeiture or penalty recoverable in a civil action. Vitelli v. Mayor and Council of Wilmington, 9 W.W.Harr. 336, 199 A. 283, 287.

The word "penalty" is broader than word "fine", which is always a penalty; whereas, a penalty may be a fine or it may designate some other form of punishment. McHugh v. Placid Oil Co., 206 La. 511, 19 So.2d 221.

Executed Fine

See Executed.

Joint Fine

In old English law. "If a whole vill is to be fined, a joint fine may be laid, and it will be good for the necessity of it; but, in other cases, fines for offenses are to be severally imposed on each particular offender, and not jointly upon all of them." Jacob.

Law of Tenure

A money payment made by a feudal tenant to his lord.

The most usual fine is that payable on the admittance of a new tenant, but there are also due in some manors fines upon alienation, on a license to demise the lands, or on the death of the lord, or other events. Elton, Copyh. 159; De Peyster v. Michael, 6 N.Y. 495, 57 Am.Dec. 470.

FINE AND RECOVERY ACT. The English statutes 3 & 4 Wm. IV. c. 74, for abolishing fines and recoveries. 1 Steph.Comm. 514, et seq.

FINE ANULLANDO LEVATO DE TENEMENTO QUOD FUIT DE ANTIQUO DOMINICO. An abolished writ for disannulling a fine levied of lands in ancient demesne to the prejudice of the lord. Reg.Orig. 15.

FINE CAPIENDO PRO TERRIS. An obsolete writ which lay for a person who, upon conviction by jury, had his lands and goods taken, and his body imprisoned, to be remitted his imprisonment, and have his lands and goods redelivered to him, on obtaining favor of a sum of money, etc. Reg. Orig. 142.

FINE FOR ALIENATION. A fine anciently payable upon the alienation of a feudal estate and substitution of a new tenant. It was payable to the lord by all tenants holding by knight's service or tenants *in capite* by socage tenure. Abolished by 12 Car. II. c. 24. See 2 Bl.Comm. 71, 89; De Peyster v. Michael, 6 N.Y. 467, 495, 57 Am.Dec. 470.

FINE FOR ENDOWMENT. A fine anciently payable to the lord by the widow of a tenant, without which she could not be endowed of her husband's lands. Abolished under Henry I., and by *Magna Charta.* 2 Bl.Comm. 135; Mozley & Whitley.

FINE NON CAPIENDO PRO PULCHRE PLACITANDO. An obsolete writ to inhibit officers of courts to take fines for fair pleading.

FINE PRO REDISSEISINÂ CAPIENDO. An old writ that lay for the release of one imprisoned for a redisseisin, on payment of a reasonable fine. Reg.Orig. 222.

FINE ROLLS. See Oblate Rolls.

FINE SUR COGNIZANCE DE DROIT, CUM CEO QUE IL AD DE SON DONE. A fine upon acknowledgment of the right of the cognizee as that which he hath of the gift of the cognizor. By this the deforciant acknowledged in court a former feoffment or gift in possession to have been made by him to the plaintiff. 2 Bl.Comm. 352.

FINE SUR COGNIZANCE DE DROIT TANTUM. A fine upon acknowledgment of the right merely, and not with the circumstance of a *preceding gift* from the cognizor.

This was commonly used to pass a *reversionary* interest which was in the cognizor, of which there could be no feoffment supposed. 2 Bl.Comm. 353; 1 Steph.Comm. 519; Jacob, Law Dict.; Com., Dig.

FINE SUR CONCESSIT. A fine upon *concessit* (he hath granted). A species of fine, where the cognizor, in order to make an end of disputes, though he acknowledged no precedent right, yet *granted* to the cognizee an estate *de novo,* usually for life or years, by way of supposed composition. 2 Bl.Comm. 353; 1 Steph.Comm. 519.

FINE SUR DONE GRANT ET RENDER. A double fine, comprehending the fine *sur cognizance de droit come ceo* and the fine *sur concessit.*

It might be used to convey particular limitations of estates, whereas the fine *sur cognizance de droit come ceo,* etc., conveyed nothing but an absolute estate, either of inheritance, or at least freehold. In this last species of fines, the cognizee, after the right was acknowledged to be in him, granted back again or rendered to the cognizor, or perhaps to a stranger, some other estate in the premises. 2 Bl.Comm. 353; Viner, Abr. *Fine;* Comyns, Dig. *Fine.*

FINE-FORCE. An absolute necessity or inevitable constraint. Plowd. 94; 6 Coke, 11; Cowell; Old N.B. 78.

FINEM FACERE. To make or pay a fine. Bract. 106; Skene.

FINES LE ROY. In old English law, the king's fines. Fines formerly payable to the king for any contempt or offense, as where one committed any trespass, or falsely denied his own deed, or did anything in contempt of law. Termes de la Ley.

FINGER. The loss of the use of a thumb cannot be considered the loss of a finger within Workmen's Compensation Law. Doris v. James Butler, Inc., 199 App.Div. 116, 192 N.Y.S. 515.

FINGER PRINTS. See Anthropometry.

FINIRE. In old English law, to fine, or pay a fine. Cowell. To end or finish a matter.

FINIS. Lat. An end; a fine; a boundary or treminus; a limit. Also in L. Lat., a fine (*q. v.*).

FINIS EST AMICABILIS COMPOSITIO ET FINALIS CONCORDIA EX CONCENSU ET CONCORDIA DOMINI REGIS VEL JUSTICIARUM. Glan. lib. 8, c. 1. A fine is an amicable settlement and decisive agreement by consent and agreement of our lord, the king, or his justices.

FINIS FINEM LITIBUS IMPONIT. A fine puts an end to litigation. 3 Inst. 78.

FINIS REI ATTENDENDUS EST. 3 Inst. 51. The end of a thing is to be attended to.

FINIS UNIUS DIEI EST PRINCIPIUM ALTERIUS. 2 Bulst. 305. The end of one day is the beginning of another.

FINITIO. An ending; death, as the end of life. Blount; Cowell.

FINIUM REGUNDORUM ACTIO. In the civil law, action for regulating boundaries. The name of an action which lay between those who had lands bordering on each other, to settle disputed boundaries. Mackeld.Rom.Law, § 499.

FINORS. Those that purify gold and silver, and part them by fire and water from coarser metals; and therefore, in the statute of 4 Hen. VII. c. 2, they are also called "parters." Termes de la Ley.

FIRDFARE. Sax. In old English law, a summoning forth to a military expedition, (*indictio ad profectionem militarem.*) Spelman.

FIRDIRINGA. Sax. A preparation to go into the army. Leg. Hen. I.

FIRDSOCNE. Sax. In old English law, exemption from military service. Spelman.

FIRDWITE. In old English law, a fine for refusing military service (*mulcta detrectantis militiam.*) Spelman. A mulct or penalty imposed on military tenants for their default in not appearing in arms or coming to an expedition. Cowell.

A fine imposed for murder committed in the army; an acquittance of such fine. Fleta, lib. 1, c. 47.

FIRE. The effect of combustion. The juridical meaning of the word does not differ from the vernacular. 1 Pars.Mar.Law, 231, et seq.

The word "fire," as used in insurance policies, does not have the technical meaning developed from analysis of its nature, but more nearly the popular meaning, being an effect rather than an elementary principle, and is the effect of combustion, being equivalent to ignition or burning, but heat is not fire, though fire may proximately cause loss from heat. Lavitt v. Hartford County Mut. Fire Ins. Co., 105 Conn. 729, 136 A. 572.

The ordinary meaning of the word as used in an insurance policy includes the idea of visible heat or light. Security Ins. Co. of New Haven, Conn., v. Choctaw Cotton Oil Co., 149 Okl. 140, 299 P. 882, 884. Damage to wool by spontaneous combustion with smoke and great heat, but without any visible flame or glow, is held not to be fire. The "fire is always caused by combustion, but combustion does not always cause fire." Western Woolen Mill Co. v. Assurance Co., Kan., 139 F. 637, 72 C.C.A. 1.

Under a fire policy it must be a "hostile fire," that is one which becomes uncontrollable or breaks out from where it was intended to be and becomes a hostile element. Mode, Limited, v. Fireman's Fund Ins. Co., 62 Idaho 270, 110 P.2d 840, 842, 133 A.L.R. 791.

FIRE AND SWORD, LETTERS OF. In old Scotch law, letters issued from the privy council in Scotland, addressed to the sheriff of the county, authorizing him to call for the assistance of the county to dispossess a tenant retaining possession, contrary to the order of a judge or the sentence of a court. Wharton; Bell, Dict.

FIREARM. An instrument used in the propulsion of shot, shell, or bullets by the action of gunpowder exploded within it. A weapon which acts by force of gunpowder. People v. Simons, 124 Misc. 28, 207 N.Y.S. 56, 57. This word comprises all sorts of guns, fowling-pieces, blunderbusses, pistols, etc.; Harris v. Cameron, 81 Wis. 239, 51 N.W. 437, 29 Am.St.Rep. 891; Atwood v. State, 53 Ala. 509; Whitney Arms Co. v. Barlow, 38 N.Y.Super.Ct. 563; fountain pen primarily intended for discharge of tear gas, People v. Anderson, 236 App.Div. 586, 260 N.Y.S. 329; but not an air pistol. People v. Schmidt, 221 App.Div. 77, 222 N.Y.S. 647, 650.

FIREBARE. A beacon or high tower by the seaside, wherein are continual lights, either to direct sailors in the night, or to give warning of the approach of an enemy. Cowell.

FIREBOTE. Allowance of wood or *estovers* to maintain competent firing for the tenant. A sufficient allowance of wood to burn in a house. 1 Washb.Real Prop. 99.

FIREBUG. A popular phrase referring to persons guilty of the crime of arson; commonly understood to mean an incendiary or pyromaniac. Blechner v. Kraser, Co.Ct., 157 N.Y.S. 256.

FIRE DAMP. "Fire damp" consists of light carburated hydrogen, and is so called from its tendency to explode when mixed with atmospheric air and brought into contact with flame. Wells' Adm'r v. Sutherland Coal & Coke Co., 116 Va. 1003, 83 S.E. 384, 385.

FIRE DISTRICT. One of the districts into which a city may be (and commonly is) divided for the purpose of more efficient service by the fire department in the extinction of fires. Des Moines v. Gilchrist, 67 Iowa 210, 25 N.W. 136. Under a statute, a territorial subdivision of the state, established to provide protection against fire within its limits, maintain street lights, etc., and, although composed of one or more towns, it is in substance a quasi municipal corporation of definitely restricted powers, and as such it may raise money by taxation for its legitimate uses. President, etc., of Williams College v. Inhabitants of Town of Williamstown, 219 Mass. 46, 106 N.E. 687, 688.

FIRE DOOR. A fireproof barrier for closing openings to prevent the spread of fire. People v. One Hundred and Thirty-One Boerum St. Co., 233 N.Y. 268, 135 N.E. 327, 328.

FIRE ESCAPE. An apparatus constructed to afford a safe and convenient method of escape from a burning building. The term includes fire ladders of such sort and location as to permit safe descent of persons caught in a building on fire, but not a balcony or an interior staircase in a hotel. West v. Spratling, 204 Ala. 478, 86 So. 32, 36.

FIRE EXIT. A reasonable, practicable, safe exit. Keefe v. Annpaul Realty Co., 215 App.Div. 301, 213 N.Y.S. 637, 642.

FIRE FIGHTING MACHINE. An instrument of public utility designed and used exclusively for putting out fires; the average or normal fire-fighting machine is in all its parts essentially designed for that purpose. American-La France Fire Engine Co. v. Riordan, C.C.A.N.Y., 6 F.2d 964, 966.

FIRE INSURANCE. See Insurance.

FIREMAN. A person engaged in the fighting and extinguishment of fires. City of Galveston v. Fredrickson, Tex.Civ.App., 174 S.W.2d 994, 995.

FIRE ORDEAL. See Ordeal.

FIRE POLICY. A contract for payment of indemnity to insured in case of loss. Converse v. Boston Safe Deposit & Trust Co., 315 Mass. 544, 53 N.E.2d 841, 843. See Insurance.

FIRE-PROOF. Incombustible; not in danger from the action of fire.

To say of a building that it is fire-proof excludes the idea that it is of wood, and necessarily implies that it is of some substance fitted for the erection of fire-proof buildings. To say of a certain portion of a building that it is fire-proof warrants conclusion that it is of a different material. Hickey v. Morrell, 102 N.Y. 459, 7 N.E. 321, 55 Am.Rep. 824. A "fire-proof safe" within an insurance policy is one which, in the judgment of prudent men in locality of property insured, is sufficient, National Liberty Ins. Co. of America v. Spharler, 172 Ark. 715, 290 S.W. 594, 596; or one which is of the kind commonly regarded as fire-proof; Knoxville Fire Ins. Co. v. Hird, 4 Tex.Civ.App. 82, 23 S.W. 393.

FIRE RAISING. In Scotch law, the wilfully setting on fire buildings, growing or stored cereals, growing wood, or coalheughs. Ersk.Pr. 577. See Arson.

FIRE WALL. This term, as used in a municipal building code, has been held to refer to a wall that is noncombustible, and to require that such quality adhere to the openings in the wall as well as the solid wall itself. Robenson v. Turner, 199 Ky. 642, 251 S.W. 857, 860.

FIRE-WOOD. Wood suitable for fuel, not including standing or felled timber which is suitable and valuable for other purposes. Hogan v. Hogan, 102 Mich. 641, 61 N.W. 73.

FIREWORKS. Contrivances of inflammable and explosive materials combined of various proportions for purpose of producing in combustion beautiful or amusing scenic effects, or to be used as night signal on land or sea or for various purposes in war. Henderson v. Massachusetts Bonding & Ins. Co., 337 Mo. 1, 84 S.W.2d 922, 925.

FIRKIN. A measure of capacity, equal to nine gallons. The word is also used to designate a weight, used for butter and cheese, of fifty-six pounds avoirdupois.

FIRLOT. A Scotch measure of capacity, containing two gallons and a pint. Spelman.

FIRM. The word "firm" is conventional term, applicable only to persons who are members of firm on particular occasion when name is used, and means name, title, or style under which a company transacts business, a partnership of two or more persons, or a commercial house, and is synonymous with "company", "house", "partnership", and "concern". Firestone Tire & Rubber Co. v. Webb, 207 Ark. 820, 182 S.W.2d 941, 943; 1 Chitty, Bailm. 49.

FIRM NAME. The name or title of a firm in business.

FIRMA. In old English law, the contract of lease or letting; also the rent (or farm) reserved upon a lease of lands, which was frequently payable in provisions, but sometimes in money, in which latter case it was called *"alba firma,"* white rent. Spelman, Gloss.; Cunningham, Law Dict.

A messuage with the house, garden, or lands, etc., connected therewith. Co.Litt. 5 *a*; Shepp. Touchst. 93.

A banquet; supper; provisions for the table. Du Cange.

A tribute or custom paid towards entertaining the king for one night. Domesday; Cowell.

FIRMA BURGI. The right, in medieval days, to take the profits of a borough, paying for them a fixed sum to the crown or other lord of the borough. 2 Holdsw.Hist.E.L. 276.

FIRMA FEODI. In old English law, a farm or lease of a fee; a fee-farm.

FIRMAN. A Turkish word denoting a decree or grant of privileges, or passport to a traveler. A passport granted by the Great Mogul to captains of foreign vessels to trade within the territories over which he has jurisdiction; a permit.

FIRMARATIO. The right of a tenant to his lands and tenements. Cowell.

FIRMARIUM. In old records, a place in monasteries, and elsewhere, where the poor were received and supplied with food. Spelman. Hence the word "infirmary."

FIRMARIUS. L. Lat. A fermor. A lessee of a term. *Firmarii* comprehend all such as hold by lease for life or lives or for year, by deed or without deed. 2 Inst. 144, 145; 1 Washb.Real Prop. 107; Sackett v. Sackett, 8 Pick. (Mass.) 312; 7 Ad. & E. 637.

FIRMATIO. The doe season. Also a supplying with food. Cowell.

FIRME. In old records, a farm.

FIRMIOR ET POTENTIOR EST OPERATIO LEGIS QUAM DISPOSITIO HOMINIS. The operation of the law is firmer and more powerful [or efficacious] than the disposition [or will] of man. Co.Litt. 102*a*.

FIRMITAS. In old English law, an assurance of some privilege, by deed or charter.

FIRMLY. A statement that an affiant "firmly believes" the contents of the affidavit imports a strong or high degree of belief, and is equivalent to saying that he "verily" believes it. Bradley v. Eccles, 1 Browne, Pa., 258; Thompson v. White, 4 Serg. & R., Pa., 137. The operative words in a bond or recognizance, that the obligor is held and "firmly bound," are equivalent to an acknowledgment of indebtedness and promise to pay. Shattuck v. People, 5 Ill. 477.

FIRMURA. In old English law, liberty to scour and repair a mill-dam, and carry away the soil, etc. Blount.

FIRST. Preceding all others; foremost; used as an ordinal of one, as earliest in time or succession or foremost in position; in front of or in advance of all others. Colgate-Palmolive-Peet Co. v. U. S., C.C.A.Del., 130 F.2d 913, 915. Initial; leading; chief; entitled to priority or preference above others. Redman v. Railroad Co., 33 N.J.Eq. 165; Thompson v. Grand Gulf R. & B. Co., 3 How. Miss. 247, 34 Am.Dec. 81; Hapgood v. Brown, 102 Mass. 452.

The word commonly, but not necessarily, connotes precedence. Hill v. Prior, 79 N.H. 188, 106 A. 641; Beckley v. Alling, 91 Conn. 362, 99 A. 1034, 1035. Thus, under a contract that, if the purchaser should "first" make payment, the vendor would convey, payment was to precede the execution of the conveyance. Walker v. Hewitt, 109 Or. 366, 220 P. 147, 151, 35 A.L.R. 100. But in a will the word "first" may not import precedence of one bequest over another. Everett v. Carr, 59 Me. 330; Swasey v. American Bible Society, 57 Me. 523.

As to first "Cousin," "Distress," and "Mortgage," see those titles.

FIRST BLUSH. By the phrase "first blush," within the rule that damages, to justify reversal, must be so great as to strike the mind at first blush as having been superinduced by passion or prejudice on the part of the jury, is meant that immediately the judicial mind is shocked and surprised at the great disproportion of the size of the verdict to what the facts of the case would authorize. Cole & Crane v. May, 185 Ky. 135, 214 S.W. 885, 887.

FIRST-CLASS. Of the most superior or excellent grade or kind; belonging to the head or chief or numerically precedent of several classes into which the general subject is divided. See Pacific Feed Co. v. Kennel, 63 Cal.App. 108, 218 P. 274, 275.

FIRST-CLASS MAIL-MATTER. In the postal laws, all mailable matter containing writing and all else that is sealed against inspection.

FIRST-CLASS MISDEMEANANT. In English law. Under the prisons act (28 & 29 Vict. c. 126, § 67) prisoners in the county, city, and borough prisons convicted of misdemeanor, and not sentenced to hard labor, are divided into two classes, one of which is called the "first division;" and it is in the discretion of the court to order that such a prisoner be treated as a misdemeanant of the first division, usually called "first-class misdemeanant," and as such not to be deemed a criminal prisoner, *i. e.*, a prisoner convicted of a crime.

FIRST-CLASS TITLE. A marketable title, shown by a clean record, or at least not depending on presumptions that must be overcome or facts that are uncertain. Vought v. Williams, 120 N.Y. 253, 24 N.E. 195, 8 L.R.A. 591, 17 Am.St.Rep. 634.

FIRST DEGREE BURN. One which produces an inflammation of the outer layer of the skin, like a sunburn. Smith v. Beard, 56 Wyo. 375, 110 P. 2d 260, 261, 262.

FIRST DEVISEE. The person to whom the estate is first given by the will, term "next devisee" referring to the person to whom the remainder is given. Young v. Robinson, 5 N.J.L. 689; Wilcox v. Heywood, 12 R.I. 198.

FIRST DOMESTIC PROCESSING. Refining or saponification of coconut oil is a "processing" or use thereof, and if the refining or saponification is the first processing or use of the oil in the United States, and occurs in the course of the manufacture or production of any article intended for sale, it is the "first domestic processing" within the statute taxing the first domestic processing. Revenue Act of 1934, § 602½(a), 26 U.S.C.A. § 2470(a). Cincinnati Soap Co. v. U. S., D.C.Ohio, 22 F.Supp. 141.

FIRST FRUITS. In English ecclesiastical law, the first year's whole profits of every benefice or spiritual living, anciently paid by the incumbent to the pope, but afterwards transferred to the fund called "Queen Anne's Bounty," for increasing the revenue from poor livings.

In feudal law, one year's profits of land which belonged to the king on the death of a tenant *in capite;* otherwise called *"primer seisin."* One of the incidents to the old feudal tenures. 2 Bl. Comm. 66, 67.

FIRST HEIR. The person who will be first entitled to succeed to the title to an estate after the termination of a life estate or estate for years. Winter v. Perratt, 5 Barn. & C. 48.

FIRST IMPRESSION. First examination. First presentation to a court for examination or decision. A case is said to be "of the first impression" when it presents an entirely novel question of law for the decision of the court, and cannot be governed by any existing precedent.

FIRST IN, FIRST OUT RULE. It is not a rule of law nor of logic, but a rule of thumb. It is a presumption of fact and really a regulation of the burden of proof. What is first sold is presumed to be what was first bought. Ninth Bank & Trust Co. v. U. S., D.C.Pa., 15 F.Supp. 951, 952.

FIRST INVENTOR. Within the meaning of that phrase as used in the fourth paragraph of Rev.St. § 4920 (35 U.S.C.A. § 69), providing that it shall be a defense to a suit for infringement that the patentee was not the original or first inventor, a person who perfects his invention, the only evidence of such perfected invention ordinarily derivable from any patent being a union of disclosure and claim. Davis-Bournonville Co. v. Alexander Milburn Co., C.C.A.N.Y., 1 F.2d 227, 232.

FIRST LIEN. One which takes priority or precedence over all other charges or incumbrances upon the same piece of property, and which must be satisfied before such other charges are entitled to participate in the proceeds of its sale.

FIRST MEETING. As used in a statute providing that, for insulting words or conduct to reduce homicide to manslaughter, killing must occur immediately or at "first meeting" after slayer is informed thereof, quoted words mean first time parties are in proximity under such circumstances as would enable slayer to act in the premises. Smith v. State, 288 S.W. 458, 462, 105 Tex.Cr.R. 327.

FIRST OF EXCHANGE. Where a set of bills of exchange is drawn in duplicate or triplicate, for greater safety in their transmission, all being of the same tenor, and the intention being that the exceptance and payment of any one of them (the first to arrive safely) shall cancel the others of the set, they are called individually the "first of exchange," "second of exchange," etc. See Bank of Pittsburgh v. Neal, 22 How. 96, 110, 16 L.Ed. 323.

FIRST POLICY YEAR. This phrase in a statute eliminating suicide of insured after such year as defense, means year for which policy, annually renewed, was first issued. Carter v. Standard Acc. Ins. Co., 65 Utah, 465, 238 P. 259, 267, 41 A.L.R. 1495. The year beginning with the issuance of the policy. American Nat. Ins. Co. v. Thompson, Tex.Civ.App., 186 S.W. 254, 255.

FIRST PROCESSING. The processing that first results in a marketable product. Hendricks v. Di Giorgio Fruit Corporation, D.C.Cal., 49 F.Supp. 573, 575, 576.

FIRST PURCHASER. In the law of descent, this term signifies the ancestor who first acquired (in any other manner than by inheritance) the estate which still remains in his family or descendants. Blair v. Adams, C.C.Tex., 59 F. 247.

FIRST RETURN. The "first return", within statute as to depletion deduction is a first return listing items of gross income and deductions arising out of the property. Commissioner of Internal Revenue v. Alta Mines, C.C.A.10, 139 F.2d 580, 582.

FIRST TRIAL. Under a statute providing when a case at law is tried by a jury, and the successful party excepts to the granting of a new trial for insufficiency of the evidence, and the evidence is certified, the appellate court, if there have been two trials below, shall first look to the evidence and proceedings on the first trial, and, if the setting aside of the first verdict was error, all proceedings subsequent thereto shall be annulled, and judgment rendered thereon, the "first trial" means the first at which exceptions to the granting of a new trial were taken. Chesapeake & O. Ry. Co. v. Parker's Adm'r, 116 Va. 368, 82 S.E. 183, 187.

FISC. A treasury of a kingdom or state; a money chest. Daly v. Beery, 45 N.D. 287, 178 N.W. 104, 109. An Anglicized form of the Latin "*fiscus*," (which see.)

FISCAL. Of or pertaining to the public treasury or revenue, of or pertaining to financial matters generally. Wall v. Close, 203 La. 345, 14 So. 2d 19, 26. Belonging to the fisc, or public treasury. Relating to accounts or the management of revenue. Of or pertaining to the public finances of a government. Daly v. Beery, 45 N.D. 287, 178 N.W. 104, 109. Financial. Armstrong v. State Bank of Mayville, 177 App.Div. 265, 165 N.Y.S. 5, 8.

FISCAL AGENT. This term does not necessarily imply a depositary of the public funds, so as, by the simple use of it in a statute, without any directions in this respect, to make it the duty of the state treasurer to deposit with him any moneys in the treasury. State v. Dubuclet, 27 La.Ann. 29.

FISCAL COURT. A ministerial and executive body in some states. Stone v. Winn, 165 Ky. 9, 176 S.W. 933, 941.

FISCAL JUDGE. A public officer named in the laws of the Ripuarians and some other Germanic peoples, apparently the same as the "*Graf*," "*reeve*," "*comes*," or "*count*," and so called because charged with the collection of public revenues, either directly or by the imposition of fines. See Spelman, voc. "Grafio."

FISCAL OFFICERS. Those charged with the collection and distribution of public money, as, the money of a state, county, or municipal corporation.

FISCAL YEAR. The year by or for which accounts are reckoned, or the year between one annual time of settlement or balancing of accounts and another. People ex rel. Pollastrini v. Whealan, 353 Ill. 500, 187 N.E. 491, 494. An accounting period of 12 months. U. S. v. Mabel Elevator Co. D.C.Minn., 17 F.2d 109, 110; U. S. v. Carroll Chain Co., D.C.Ohio, 8 F.2d 529, 530. A period of twelve months (not necessarily concurrent with the calendar year) with reference to which appropriations are made and expenditures authorized, and at the end of which accounts are made up and the books balanced. Shaffner v. Lipinsky, 194 N.C. 1, 138 S.E. 418, 419.

FISCUS. Roman law. The treasury of the prince or emperor, as distinguished from "*ærarium*," which was the treasury of the state. Spelman; Paillet, *Droit Public*, 21, n. This distinction was not observed in France. In course of time the *fiscus* absorbed the *ærarium* and became the treasury of the state. Gray, Nature and Sources of Law 58. See Law 10, ff. *De jure Fisci.*

The treasury or property of the state, as distinguished from the private property of the sovereign.

English law. The king's treasury, as the repository of forfeited property.

The treasury of a noble, or of any private person. Spelman.

FISH. An animal which inhabits the water, breathes by means of gills, swims by the aid of fins, and is oviparous. The term includes crabs, State v. Savage, 96 Or. 53, 184 P. 567, 570; escallops, State v. Dudley, 182 N.C. 822, 109 S.E. 63, 65; and mussels and other shellfish, Gratz v. McKee, C.C.A.Mo., 258 F. 335, 336.

The object to be removed from oil well is known as a "fish." Raymond v. Wickersham, Cust. & Pat.App., 110 F.2d 863, 864.

FISH COMMISSIONER. A public officer of the United States, created by act of congress of February 9, 1871, R.S. § 4395, whose duties principally concerned the preservation and increase throughout the country of fish suitable for food. Office of Commissioner of Fisheries was abolished and functions were transferred to the U. S. Fish and Wildlife Service, 16 U.S.C.A. § 241 notes.

FISH POTS. Contrivances in the nature of screens and traps, placed at the junction of low dams or walls extending out from each shore and somewhat down stream, in such a way as to collect the water and send it through the pot, so that fish may be screened out there. Middlekauff v. Le Compte, 149 Md. 621, 132 A. 48.

Cf. Pound Net.

FISH ROYAL. These were the whale and the sturgeon, which, when thrown ashore or caught near the coast of England, became the property of the king by virtue of his prerogative and in recompense for his protecting the shore from pirates and robbers. Brown; 1 Bl.Comm. 290. Arnold v. Mundy, 6 N.J.L. 86, 10 Am.Dec. 356. Some authorities include the porpoise. Hale, *De Jure Mar.* pt. 1, c. 7; Plowd. 305; Bracton, l. 3, c. 3.

FISHERY. A place prepared for catching fish with nets or hooks. This is commonly applied to the place of drawing a seine or net. Hart v. Hill, 1 Whart., Pa., 131, 132.

A right or liberty of taking fish; a species of incorporeal hereditament, anciently termed "piscary," of which there are several kinds. 2 Bl. Comm. 34, 39; 3 Kent, Comm. 409–418; Arnold v. Mundy, 6 N.J.L. 22, 10 Am.Dec. 356; Gould v. James, 6 Cow., N.Y., 376; Hart v. Hill, 1 Whart., Pa., 124.

Common fishery. A fishing ground where all persons have a right to take fish. Bennett v. Costar, 8 Taunt. 183; Albright v. Park Com'n, 68 N.J.L. 523, 53 A. 612. Not to be confounded with "common of fishery," as to which see Common, *n.*

Free fishery. A franchise in the hands of a subject, existing by grant or prescription, distinct from an ownership in the soil. It is an exclusive right, and applies to a public navigable river, without any right in the soil. 3 Kent, Comm. 410. Arnold v. Mundy, 6 N.J.L. 87, 10 Am. Dec. 356.

Right of fishery. The general and common right of the citizens to take fish from public waters, such as the sea, great lakes, etc. Shively v. Bowlby, 152 U.S. 1, 14 S.Ct. 548, 38 L.Ed. 331.

Several fishery. A fishery of which the owner is also the owner of the soil, or derives his right from the owner of the soil. 2 Bl.Com. 39, 40; 1 Steph.Comm. 671, note. One by which the party claiming it has the right of fishing, independently of all other, so that no person can have a coextensive right with him in the object claimed; but a partial and independent right in another, or a limited liberty, does not derogate from the right of the owner. 5 Burr. 2814.

FISHERY LAWS. A series of statutes passed in England for the regulation of fishing, especially to prevent the destruction of fish during the breeding season, and of small fish, spawn, etc., and the employment of improper modes of taking fish. 3 Steph.Comm. 165.

FISHGARTH. A dam or weir in a river for taking fish. Cowell.

FISHING BANKS. A fishing ground of comparative shoal water in the sea. Parker v. Thomson, 21 Or. 523, 28 P. 502.

FISHING BILL. A bill showing no cause of action and endeavoring to compel defendants to disclose one in plaintiff's favor. White v. National Paving Co., Tex.Civ.App., 101 S.W.2d 588, 590. Or seeking disclosure by adversary of facts supporting suit. Puget Sound Nav. Co. v. Associated Oil Co., D.C.Wash., 56 F.2d 605, 606. A discovery sought on general, loose, and vague allegations. Story, Eq.Pl. § 325; In re Pacific Ry. Com'n, C.C.Cal., 32 F. 263; or on suspicion, surmise, or vague guesses. Marietta Mfg. Co. v. Hedges-Walsh-Weidner Co., 9 W.W.Harr. 511, 2 A.2d 922, 926.

Where purpose of proposed examination of witness was to examine books and records to determine status of an account on which petitioner expected to sue, the proceeding was a "fishing expedition". State ex rel. Pitcher v. District Court of Fifth Judicial Dist. in and for Madison County, 114 Mont. 128, 133 P.2d 350, 353.

FISK. In Scotch law, the *fiscus* or fisc. The revenue of the crown. Generally used of the personal estate of a rebel which has been forfeited to the crown. Bell.

FISSURE VEIN. In mining law, a vein or lode of mineralized matter filling a pre-existing fissure or crack in the earth's crust extending across the *strata* and generally extending indefinitely downward. See Crocker v. Manley, 164 Ill. 282, 45 N.E. 577, 56 Am.St.Rep. 196.

FISTUCA, or FESTUCA. In old English law, the rod or wand, by the delivery of which the property in land was formerly transferred in making a feoffment. Called, also, *"baculum," "virga,"* and *"fustis."* Spelman. See Festuca.

FISTULA. In the civil law, a pipe for conveying water. Dig. 8, 2, 18.

FIT. Suitable or appropriate. Whisnant v. State, 39 Okl.Cr. 214, 264 P. 837, 839. Conformable to a duty. Adapted to, designed, prepared. Thomas v. State, 34 Okl.Cr. 49, 244 P. 816. Proper. Hanes v. Southern Public Utilities Co., 191 N.C. 13, 131 S.E. 402, 406.

FIT, *n.* In medical jurisprudence, an attack or spasm of muscular convulsions, generally attended with loss of self-control and of consciousness; particularly, such attacks occurring in epilepsy. In a more general sense, the period of an acute attack of any disease, physical or mental, as, a fit of insanity. See Gunter v. State, 83 Ala. 96, 3 So. 600. Also used in the plural, in which sense it is a layman's term for epilepsy. Westphall v. Metropolitan Life Ins. Co., 27 Cal.App. 734, 151 P. 159, 162.

FITZ. A Norman word, meaning "son." It is used in law and genealogy; as *Fitzherbert,* the son of Herbert; *Fitzjames,* the son of James; *Fitzroy,* the son of the king. It was originally applied to illegitimate children.

FIVE-MILE ACT. An act of parliament, passed in 1665, against non-conformists, whereby ministers of that body who refused to take the oath of non-resistance were prohibited from coming within five miles of any corporate town, or place where they had preached or lectured since the passing of the act of oblivion in 1660, nullified by act of 1689. Brown.

FIX. Adjust or regulate. McKann v. Town of Irvington, 133 N.J.L. 63, 42 A.2d 391, 393. Determine; settle. Bunn v. Kingsbury County, 3 S.D. 87, 52 N.W. 673; In re McLure's Estate, 68 Mont. 556, 220 P. 527, 530. Make permanent. Kendall v. Stafford, 178 N.C. 461, 101 S.E. 15, 17. It imports finality and stability. MacNeill v. Bazemore, 194 Ga. 406, 21 S.E.2d 414, 416. Certainty and definiteness. Commercial Casualty Ins. Co. v. State Board of Tax Appeals, 119 N.J.L. 94, 194 A. 390, 391.

To liquidate or render certain. To fasten a liability upon one. To transform a possible or contingent liability into a present and definite liability. Zimmerman v. Canfield, 42 Ohio St. 468; Polk v. Minnehaha County, 5 Dak. 129, 37 N.W. 93; Logansport & W. V. Gas Co. v. Peru, C.C.Ind., 89 F. 187.

FIX UP. A promise by a debtor to visit his creditor and "fix it up" with him was not a sufficient promise to pay to toll the statute of limitations, as the expression "fix it" would ordinarily be understood as meaning "make some kind of agreement or adjustment that may dispose of it." Shaw v. Bubier, 119 Me. 83, 109 A. 373, 374.

FIXED. In a charter entered into by the captain of a ship, containing the condition, "Provided ship not fixed previously," "fixed" was equivalent to "tied up," "closed," "not free." Richichi v. James B. Drake & Sons, D.C.Me., 280 F. 421, 424.

Prices are "fixed" when they are agreed upon. United States v. Masonite Corporation, N.Y., 316 U.S. 265, 62 S.Ct. 1070, 1076, 86 L.Ed. 1461.

FIXED ASSET. An asset essential to continuance of undertaking and proper operation of business. Ruden v. City of Platte, 62 S.D. 175, 252 N.W. 32.

FIXED CAPITAL. Cost of total plant and general equipment. Lindheimer v. Illinois Bell Telephone Co., Ill., 292 U.S. 151, 54 S.Ct. 658, 78 L.Ed. 1182.

FIXED INDEBTEDNESS. An established or settled indebtedness; not contingent. State ex rel. Hawkins v. State Board of Examiners, 97 Mont. 441, 35 P.2d 116, 120.

FIXED LIABILITIES. Those certain and definite as to both obligation and amount. National Commercial Title & Mortgage Guaranty Co. v. City of Newark, 18 N.J.Misc. 186, 11 A.2d 759, 763.

FIXED OPINION. A conviction, prejudgment, disqualifying juror to impartially consider whole evidence and apply free from bias law as given in charge by court. Peterson v. State, 227 Ala. 361, 150 So. 156, 159.

FIXED PRICES. Agreed prices. United States v. Food and Grocery Bureau of Southern California, D.C.Cal., 43 F.Supp. 966, 972.

FIXED SALARY. One which is definitely ascertained and prescribed as to amount and time of payment, and does not depend upon the receipt of fees or other contingent emoluments; not necessarily a salary which cannot be changed by competent authority. Sharpe v. Robertson, 5 Grat., Va., 518; Hedrick v. U. S., 16 Ct.Cl. 101. Established or settled, to remain for a time. Board of Sup'rs of Yavapai County v. Stephens, 177 P. 261, 262, 20 Ariz. 115.

FIXING BAIL. In practice, rendering absolute the liability of special bail.

FIXTURE. A chattel attached to realty, In re Triborough Bridge Approach, City of New York, 159 Misc. 617, 288 N.Y.S. 697, 707. Becoming accessory to it and part and parcel of it. Farmers & Merchants Bank v. Sawyer, 26 Ala.App. 520, 163 So. 657. And ordinarily the property of the owner of the land. Hill.; Atlantic Refining Co. v. Feinberg, 1 W.W.Harr., Del., 183, 112 A. 685, 687; Red Diamond Clothing Co. v. Steidemann, 169 Mo. App. 306, 152 S.W. 609, 617.

A thing is deemed to be affixed to land when it is attached to it by roots, imbedded in it, permanently resting upon it, or permanently attached to what is thus permanent, as by means of cement, plaster, nails, bolts, or screws. Civ.Code Cal. § 660; Big Sespe Oil Co. v. Cochran, C.C.A.Cal., 276 F. 216, 225.

Ordinarily, requisites are actual annexation to realty, or something appurtenant thereto, appropriation to use or purpose of realty, and intention to make article permanent accession to freehold as gathered from nature of articles affixed, relation and situation of person making annexation, structure and mode of annexation, and purpose or use for which it has been made. Bankers Life Ins. Co. v. Ohrt, 131 Neb. 858, 270 N.W. 497, 502.

It has been said, however, that a "fixture" formerly meant any chattel which on becoming affixed to the soil became a part of the realty; but it now means those things which formed an exception to that rule and can be removed by the person who affixed them to the soil, L.R. 4 Ex. 328; if they can be taken away without material injury to the realty. Boise Ass'n of Credit Men v. Ellis, 26 Idaho, 438, 144 P. 6, 9, L.R.A.1915E, 917.

It has also been said that it is generally understood to comprehend any article which a tenant has the power to remove. Sheen v. Rickie, 5 Mees. & W. 174; Rogers v. Gilinger, 30 Pa. 185, 189, 72 Am.Dec. 694.

The general result seems to be that three views have been taken. One is that "fixture" means something which has been affixed to the realty, so as to become a part of it; it is fixed, irremovable. An opposite view is that "fixture" means something which appears to be a part of the realty, but is not fully so; it is only a chattel fixed to it, but removable. An intermediate view is that "fixture" means a chattel annexed, affixed, to the realty, but imports nothing as to whether it is removable; that is to be determined by considering its circumstances and the relation of the parties. Abbott; New Castle Theater Co. v. Ward, 57 Ind.App. 473, 104 N.E. 526, 527; Review Printing Co. v. Hartford Fire Ins. Co., 133 Minn. 213, 158 N.W. 39, 40.

Things fixed or affixed to other things. The rule of law regarding them is that which is expressed in the maxim, *"accessio cedit principali,"* "the accessory goes with, and as part of, the principal subject-matter." Brown.

That which is fixed or attached to something permanently as an appendage, and not removable. Webster. Something fixed or immovable. Worcester.

A piece of metal having the same function as a jig, except that the operation upon the casting, which it is designed to facilitate, is an operation of grooving and planing, instead of drilling holes. Commonwealth Trust Co. of Pittsburgh v. Harkins, 312 Pa. 402, 167 A. 278, 280.

Agricultural fixtures. Those annexed for the purpose of farming. In re Shelar, D.C.Pa., 21 F.2d 136, 138.

Domestic fixtures. All such articles as a tenant attaches to a dwelling house in order to render his occupation more comfortable or convenient, and which may be separated from it without doing substantial injury, such as furnaces, stoves, cupboards, shelves, bells, gas fixtures, or things merely ornamental, as painted wainscots, pier and chimney glasses, although attached to the walls with screws, marble chimney pieces, grates, beds nailed to the walls, window blinds and curtains. Wright v. Du Bignon, 40 S.E. 747, 114 Ga. 765, 57 L.R.A. 669.

Trade fixtures. Articles placed in or attached to rented buildings by the tenant, to prosecute the trade or business for which he occupies the premises, or to be used in connection with such business, or promote convenience and efficiency in conducting it. Herkimer County L. & P. Co. v. Johnson, 37 App.Div. 257, 55 N.Y.Supp. 924; Brown v. Reno Electric L. & P. Co., C.C.Nev., 55 F. 231; Northwestern Lumber & Wrecking Co. v. Parker, 125 Minn. 107, 145 N.W. 964, 965. Such chattels as merchants usually possess and annex to the premises occupied by them to enable them to store, handle, and display their goods, which are generally removable without material injury to the premises. Lovett v. Bermingham-Seaman-Patrick Co., 192 Mich. 372, 158 N.W. 881, 883.

FLACO. A place covered with standing water.

FLAG. A national standard on which are certain emblems; an ensign; a banner.

It is carried by soldiers, ships, etc., and commonly displayed at forts and many other suitable places.

In common parlance, the word "flag," when used as denoting a signal, does not necessarily mean the actual use of a flag, but by figure of speech the word is used in the secondary sense and signifies a signal given as with a flag, that is to say, as by a waiving of the hand for the purpose of communicating information. Bergfeld v. Kansas City Rys. Co., 285 Mo. 654, 227 S.W. 106, 110.

FLAG, DUTY OF THE. This was an ancient ceremony in acknowledgment of British sovereignty over the British seas, by which a foreign vessel struck her flag and lowered her top-sail on meeting the British flag.

FLAG, LAW OF. In maritime law. The law of that nation or country whose flag is flown by a particular vessel.

A shipowner who sends his vessel into a foreign port gives notice by his flag to all who enter into contracts with the master that he intends the law of that flag to regulate such contracts, and that they must either submit to its operation or not contract with him. Ruhstrat v. People, 185 Ill. 133, 57 N.E. 41, 49 L.R.A. 181, 76 Am.St.Rep. 30.

FLAG OF THE UNITED STATES. By the act entitled "An act to establish the flag of the United States," (Rev.St. §§ 1791, 1792), it was provided "that, from and after the fourth day of July next, the flag of the United States be thirteen horizontal stripes, alternate red and white; that the union be twenty stars, white in a blue field; that, on the admission of every new state into the Union, one star be added to the union of the flag; and that such addition shall take effect on the fourth day of July then next succeeding such admission." See Act July 30, 1947, c. 389, §§ 1, 2, 61 Stat. 641; 4 U.S.C.A. §§ 1, 2.

FLAG OF TRUCE. A white flag displayed by one of two belligerent parties to notify the other party that communication and a cessation of hostilities are desired.

FLAGELLAT. Whipped; scourged. An entry on old Scotch records. 1 Pitc.Crim.Tr. pt. 1, p. 7.

FLAGRANS. Lat. Burning; raging; in actual perpetration.

FLAGRANS BELLUM. A war actually going on.

FLAGRANS CRIMEN. In Roman law, a fresh or recent crime. This term designated a crime in the very act of its commission, or while it was of recent occurrence.

FLAGRANT DELIT. In French law, a crime which is in actual process of perpetration or which has just been committed. Code d'Instr. Crim. art. 41.

FLAGRANT NECESSITY. A case of urgency rendering lawful an otherwise illegal act, as an assault to remove a man from impending danger.

FLAGRANTE BELLO. During an actual state of war.

FLAGRANTE DELICTO. In the very act of committing the crime. 4 Bl.Comm. 307.

FLAGRANTLY AGAINST EVIDENCE. Without any substantial support in evidence. Williams v. Commonwealth, 276 Ky. 754, 125 S.W.2d 221, 223. So much against weight of evidence as to shock conscience and clearly indicate passion and prejudice of jury. Smith v. Commonwealth, 216 Ky. 813, 288 S.W. 752, 754.

FLASH CHECK. A check drawn upon a banker by a person who has no funds at the banker's and knows that such is the case.

FLAT. A place covered with water too shallow for navigation with vessels ordinarily used for commercial purposes. The space between high and low water mark along the edge of an arm of the sea, bay, tidal river, etc. Thomas v. Hatch, 23 F.Cas. 946; Church v. Meeker, 34 Conn. 424; Jones v. Janney, 8 Watts & S., Pa., 443, 42 Am.Dec. 309.

A floor or separate division of a floor, fitted for housekeeping and designed to be occupied by a single family. Cent.Dict. A building, the various floors of which are fitted up as flats, either residential or business.

A contrivance upon which lumber is piled and is not movable by wheels affixed thereto but must be moved by the use of jacks. Mengel Co. v. Parker, 192 Miss. 634, 7 So.2d 521, 522.

FLATTERY. False or excessive praise, insincere complimentary language or conduct. Smith v. State, 13 Ala.App. 399, 69 So. 402, 404.

FLAVIANUM JUS. In Roman law, the title of a book containing the forms of actions, published by Cneius Flavius, A. U. C. 449. Mackeld.Rom.Law, § 39. Calvin.

FLECTA. A feathered or fleet arrow. Cowell.

FLEDWITE. A discharge or freedom from amercements where one, having been an outlawed fugitive, cometh to the place of our lord of his own accord. Termes de la Ley.

The liberty to hold court and take up the amercements for beating and striking. Cowell.

The fine set on a fugitive as the price of obtaining the king's freedom. Spelman.

FLEE FROM JUSTICE. Removing one's self from or secreting one's self within jurisdiction wherein offense was committed, Renner v. Renner, 13 N.J.Misc. 749, 181 A. 191, or leaving one's home, residence, or known place of abode, or concealing one's self therein, with intent, in either case, to avoid detection or punishment for some public offense. Streep v. U. S., 160 U.S. 128, 16 S.Ct. 244, 40 L.Ed. 365; Lay v. State, 42 Ark. 110; U. S. v. O'Brian, 3 Dill. 381, F.Cas.No.15,908.

FLEE TO THE WALL. A metaphorical expression, used in connection with homicide done in self-defense, signifying the exhaustion of every possible means of escape, or of averting the assault, before killing the assailant.

FLEET. A place where the tide flows; a creek, or inlet of water; a company of ships or navy; a prison in London (so called from a river or ditch formerly in its vicinity,) now abolished by 5 & 6 Vict. c. 22. See Fleta.

FLEM. In Saxon and old English law, a fugitive bondman or villein. Spelman.

The privilege of having the goods and fines of fugitives.

FLEMENE FRIT, FLEMENES FRINTHE, OR FLYMENA FRYNTHE. (A corrupt pseudo-archaic form is *flemens-firth,* representing the old law Latin form, *flemenaferth,* of the Anglo-Saxon *flyman fyrmth* or *flymena fyrmth.* Cent. Dict.) The reception or relief of a fugitive or outlaw. Jacob.

FLEMESWITE. The possession of the goods of fugitives. Fleta, lib. 1, c. 147.

FLET. In Saxon law, land; a house; home.

FLETA. The name given to an ancient treatise on the laws of England, founded mainly upon the writings of Bracton and Glanville, and supposed to have been written in the time of Edw. I. The author is unknown, but it is surmised that he was a judge or learned lawyer who was at that time confined in the Fleet prison, whence the name of the book.

FLEXIBLE PARTICIPATION BANK NIGHT. A scheme whereby some method is employed by means of which some persons obtain chances to win without purchasing theater tickets. Commonwealth v. Lund, 142 Pa.Super. 208, 15 A.2d 839, 842.

FLEXIBLE PARTICIPATION SCHEME. A scheme whereby sum of money is given to member of audience holding registered number drawn from a hopper at theater. The scheme is one form of a lottery. Commonwealth v. Lund, 142 Pa.Super. 208, 15 A.2d 839, 846.

FLICHWITE. In Saxon law, a fine on account of brawls and quarrels. Spelman.

FLIGHT. The evading of the course of justice by voluntarily withdrawing one's self in order to avoid arrest or detention, or the institution or continuance of criminal proceedings, regardless of whether one leaves jurisdiction. Commonwealth v. Myers, 131 Pa.Super. 258, 200 A. 143, 146. Also comprehends continued concealment. Commonwealth v. Fusci, 153 Pa.Super. 617, 35 A.2d 93, 95.

FLIM-FLAM. "Flim-flam" is a form of bunco or confidence game. Commonwealth v. Townsend, 149 Pa.Super. 337, 27 A.2d 462, 463.

FLOAT. Checks in process of collection. Lewis v. West Side Trust & Savings Bank, 376 Ill. 23, 32 N.E.2d 907, 914; Hillmer v. Chicago Bank of Commerce, 375 Ill. 266, 31 N.E.2d 309, 316.

In American land law, especially in the western states, a certificate authorizing the entry, by the holder, of a certain quantity of land not yet specifically selected or located. U. S. v. Central Pac. R. Co., C.C.Cal., 26 F. 480; Hays v. Steiger, 76 Cal. 555, 18 P. 670; Wisconsin Cent. R. Co. v. Price County, 133 U.S. 496, 10 S.Ct. 341, 33 L.Ed. 687.

FLOATABLE. Used for floating. A floatable stream is a stream used for floating logs, rafts, etc. Gerrish v. Brown, 51 Me. 260, 81 Am.Dec. 569; Gaston v. Mace, 33 W.Va. 14, 10 S.E. 60, 5 L.R.A. 392, 25 Am.St.Rep. 848; Fortson Shingle Co. v. Skagland, 77 Wash. 8, 137 P. 304, 305.

FLOATING BOG. A mass of grass reeds or other acquatic vegetation growing and floating on the water. Attorney General v. Bay Boom Wild Rice & Fur Farm, 172 Wis. 363, 178 N.W. 569, 572.

FLOATING CAPITAL (or circulating capital). Capital retained for the purpose of meeting current expenditure.

The capital which is consumed at each operation of production and reappears transformed into new products.

At each sale of these products the capital is represented in cash, and it is from its transformations that profit is derived. Floating capital includes raw materials destined for fabrication, such as wool and flax, products in the warehouses of manufacturers or merchants, such as cloth and linen, and money for wages, and stores. De Laveleye, Pol.Ec.

FLOATING CHARGE. A continuing charge on the assets of the company creating it, but permitting the company to deal freely with the property in the usual course of business until the security holder shall intervene to enforce his claim. Pennsylvania Co. for Insurance on Lives and Granting Annuities v. United Railways of Havana & Regla Warehouses, D.C.Me., 26 F.Supp. 379, 387, 388.

FLOATING DEBT. Loans for which no permanent provision was required to be made, which have been obtained for temporary purposes, with intention of paying them off within a brief period. State Budget Commission v. Lebus, 244 Ky. 700, 51 S.W.2d 965.

Lawful and valid claims against the corporation for the payment of which there is no money in the corporate treasury specifically designed, nor any taxation nor other means of providing money to pay particularly provided. People v. Wood, 71 N. Y. 374; City of Huron v. Second Ward Sav. Bank, S.D., 30 C.C.A. 38, 86 F. 276, 49 L.R.A. 534.

Debt not in the form of bonds or stocks bearing regular interest. Pub.St.Mass.1882, p. 1290. State v. Faran, 24 Ohio St. 541; People v. Carpenter, 31 App.Div. 603, 52 N.Y.S. 781.

FLOATING POLICY. A policy intended to supplement specific insurance on property and attaches only when the latter ceases to cover the risk, and the purpose of such policy is to provide indemnity for property which cannot, because of its frequent change in location and quantity, be covered by specific insurance. Davis Yarn Co. v. Brooklyn Yarn Dye Co., 293 N.Y. 236, 56 N.E.2d 564, 570.

FLOATING SECURITY. An equitable charge on the assets for the time being of a going concern. Lord Macnaghten in Government Stock Inv. Co. v. Manila Ry. Co., [1897] A.C. 81. Pennsylvania Co. for Insurance on Lives and Granting Annuities v. United Railways of Havana & Regla Warehouses, D.C.Me., 26 F.Supp. 379, 387.

FLODE-MARK. Flood-mark, high-water mark. The mark which the sea, at flowing water and highest tide, makes on the shore. Blount.

FLOGGING. Thrashing or beating with a whip or lash.

FLOOD. An inundation of water over land not usually covered by it. Such an accident is an Act of God. McHenry v. R. Co., 4 Harr. (Del.) 449. See Act of God. Of variable meaning. City of Tulsa v. Grier, 114 Okl. 93, 243 P. 753, 757.

Ordinary and extraordinary floods. Extraordinary or unprecedented floods are floods which are of such unusual occurrence that they could not have been foreseen by men of ordinary experience and prudence. Ordinary floods are those, the occurrence of which may be reasonably anticipated from the general experience of men residing in the region where such floods happen. Soules v. Northern Pac. Ry. Co., 34 N.D. 7, 157 N.W. 823, 830, L.R.A.1917A, 501; Elkland v. Casey, C.C.A.Alaska, 12 A.L.R. 179, 266 F. 821, 823; Clements v. Phœnix Utility Co., 119 Kan. 190, 237 P. 1062, 1065.

FLOOD WATERS. Waters which escape from stream or other body of water and overflow adjacent territory, Poole v. Sun Underwriters Ins. Co. of New York, 65 S.D. 422, 274 N.W. 658, 660; under conditions which do not usually occur. Thomson v. Public Service Commission, 241 Wis. 243, 5 N.W.2d 769, 771; Everett v. Davis, 18 Cal. 2d 389, 115 P.2d 821, 823, 824.

Where a stream coming out of the mouth of a canyon has left a cone of detritus and flows down one side thereof, but in a time of high water it breaks out of its channel to flow down the other slope of the cone, such waters are "flood waters", it being immaterial that the escaping waters have made for themselves a channel or follow some natural channel, gulley, or depression. Horton v. Goodenough, 184 Cal. 451, 194 P. 34, 35; Motl v. Boyd, 116 Tex. 82, 286 S.W. 458, 468; Herminghaus v. Southern California Edison Co., 200 Cal. 81, 252 P. 607, 610.

FLOOR. A section of a building between horizontal planes. Lowell v. Strahan, 145 Mass. 1, 12 N.E. 401, 1 Am.St.Rep. 422. A story, including outer walls. Leominster Fuel Co. v. Scanlon, 243 Mass. 126, 137 N.E. 271, 24 A.L.R. 1459.

The word "floor" may mean the mere bottom plane of an inclosure or artificial structure, the surface on which we walk, ride, or travel, or it may mean such surface or plane, together with the timbers, framework, and materials which enter into and form part of its construction. So of the word "flooring." If used without reference to a structure in its completed form, it would ordinarily convey the idea of materials suitable for use in constructing a floor, or in a narrower sense the boards or planks for covering the framework of a floor. When used with reference to a completed structure, it may mean either the materials of which the floor is composed, or the completed floor structure. When not attempting to speak with technical exactness, the words "floor" and "flooring" may be, and often are, used as synonymous or interchangeable terms. Cedar Rapids & M. C. R. Co. v. City of Cedar Rapids, 173 Iowa 386, 155 N.W. 842; Missouri Pac. R. Co. v. Holt, C.C.A. Ark. 293 F. 155, 157.

A term used metaphorically, in parliamentary practice, to denote the exclusive right to address the body in session.

A member who has been recognized by the chairman, and who is in order, is said to "have the floor," until his remarks are concluded. Similarly, the "floor of the house" means the main part of the hall where the members sit, as distinguished from the galleries, or from the corridors or lobbies.

In England, the floor of a court is that part between the judge's bench and the front row of counsel. Litigants appearing in person, in the high court or court of appeal, are supposed to address the court from the floor.

FLOOR BROKER. Broker's sub-agent. Helfhat v. Whitehouse, 258 N.Y. 274, 179 N.E. 493, 496.

FLOOR PLAN. A horizontal section drawing showing the thickness of walls and partitions, arrangement of passages, apartments, and openings at any floor of a building. Webster.

FLOOR PLAN RULE. Rule by which an owner who has placed an automobile on the floor of a retail dealer's showroom for sale is estopped to deny the title of an innocent purchaser from such dealer in the ordinary retail dealing, without knowledge of any conflicting claim. National Guarantee & Finance Co. v. Russell, Ohio App., 36 N.E.2d 1015, 1018.

FLOOR PLAN SERVICE. The buying and financing of automobiles by finance company and placing them on the floor of the dealer, so that dealer may resell automobiles to his retail trade. Associates Discount Corporation v. Haynes Garage, 304 Mass. 526, 24 N.E.2d 685, 687.

FLOOR PLANNING. Financing automobiles for dealers. Associates Discount Corporation v. Haynes Garage, 304 Mass. 526, 24 N.E.2d 685, 687.

FLOORED. In automobile law. An automobile is *floored* when it is financed under a trust receipt or similar title retention document, whereby retail dealer obtains possession of automobile from distributor for exhibition and sale through payment to distributor by finance company. Commercial Credit Co. v. Barney Motor Co., 10 Cal.2d 718, 76 P.2d 1181, 1183; Blashfield, Cyc. of Automobile Law and Prac., Perm. Ed., § 4755.

FLORENTINE PANDECTS. A copy of the Pandects discovered accidentally about the year 1137, at Amalphi, a town in Italy, near Salerno.

FLORIN. A coin originally made at Florence, now of the value of about two English shillings.

FLOTAGES. Such things as by accident float on the top of great rivers or the sea. Blount.

A commission paid to water bailiffs. Cun.Dict.

FLOTERIAL DISTRICT. A legislative district which includes within its boundaries several separate districts or political subdivisions which independently would not be entitled to additional representation but whose conglomerate population entitles the entire area to another seat in the particular legislative body being apportioned. Kilgarlin v. Martin, D.C.Tex., 252 F.Supp. 404, 419; Davis v. Mann, Va., 84 S.Ct. 1441, 1446, 377 U.S. 678, 12 L.Ed.2d 609.

FLOTSAM, FLOTSAN. A name for the goods which float upon the sea when cast overboard for the safety of the ship, or when a ship is sunk. Distinguished from "jetsam" and "ligan." Bract. lib. 2, c. 5; 5 Coke, 106; 1 Bl.Comm. 292.

FLOUD-MARKE. In old English law, high-water mark; flood-mark. 1 And. 88, 89.

FLOURISH. The act of brandishing or waving; a swinging or whirling movement as flourish of a whip or sword; to fling or whirl about while holding in the hand, brandish, flaunt, as, he flourished his whip. State v. Boyles, 24 N.M. 464, 174 P. 423.

FLOWAGE. The natural flow or movement of water from an upper estate to a lower one is a servitude which the owner of the latter must bear, though the flowage be not in a natural water course with well defined banks. Leidlein v. Meyer, 95 Mich. 586, 55 N.W. 367; Ogburn v. Connor, 46 Cal. 346, 13 Am.Rep. 213; Gray v. McWilliams, 98 Cal. 157, 32 P. 976, 21 L.R.A. 593, 35 Am.St.Rep. 163.

FLOWING. Movement, as if in a current or stream. Homer Brooke Glass Co. v. Hartford-Fairmont Co., C.C.A.Conn., 262 F. 427, 431.

FLOWING LANDS. Imports raising and setting back water on another's land, by a dam placed across a stream or water course which is the natural drain and outlet for surplus water on such land. Call v. Middlesex County Com'rs, 2 Gray, Mass., 235.

FLUCTUS. Flood; flood-tide. Bract. fol. 255.

FLUME. Primarily, a stream or river, but usually used to designate an artificial channel applied to some definite use, and may mean either an open or a covered aqueduct. Talbot v. Joseph, 79 Or. 308, 155 P. 184, 186.

FLUMEN.

In Roman law, a servitude which consists in the right to conduct the rain-water, collected from the roof and carried off by the gutters, onto the house or ground of one's neighbor. Mackeld.Rom. Law, § 317; Ersk.Inst. 2, 9, 9. Also a river or stream.

In old English law, flood; flood-tide.

FLUMINA ET PORTUS PUBLICA SUNT, IDEOQUE JUS PISCANDI OMNIBUS COMMUNE EST. Rivers and ports are public. Therefore the right of fishing there is common to all. Day. Ir. K. B. 55; Branch, Princ.

FLUMINÆ VOLUCRES. Wild fowl; waterfowl. 11 East, 571, note.

FLUVIUS. Lat. A river; a public river; flood; flood-tide.

FLUXUS. In old English law, flow. *Per fluxum et refluxum maris,* by the flow and reflow of the sea. Dal. pl. 10.

FLY FOR IT. Anciently, it was the custom in a criminal trial to inquire after a verdict, "Did he fly for it?" After the verdict, even if not guilty, forfeiture of goods followed conviction upon such inquiry. Abolished by 7 & 8 Geo. IV. c. 28. Wharton.

FLYING MACHINE. A heavier-than-air machine capable of soaring in the air and susceptible to being guided by a pilot into different altitudes when aloft. Myers v. United States, Ct.Cl., 25 F. Supp. 500, 501.

FLYING SWITCH. In railroading, a flying switch is made by uncoupling the cars from the engine while in motion, and throwing the cars onto the side track, by turning the switch, after the engine has passed it upon the main track. Greenleaf v. Illinois Cent. R. Co., 29 Iowa 39, 4 Am.Rep. 181; Hanson v. Chicago, M. & St. P. R. Co., 157 Wis. 455, 146 N.W. 524, 525.

FLYMA. In old English law, a runaway; fugitive; one escaped from justice, or who has no "hlaford."

FLYMAN-FRYMTH. See Flemene Frit.

FLY-POWER. A written assignment in blank, whereby, on being attached to a stock certificate, the stock may be transferred. Carlisle v. Norris, 215 N.Y. 400, 109 N.E. 564, 565, Ann.Cas.1917A, 429; Carlisle v. Norris, 157 App.Div. 313, 142 N. Y.S. 393, 396.

FOAL, *v.* To bring forth young; said of animals of the horse family. O'Rear v. Richardson, 17 Ala.App. 87, 81 So. 865, 866.

FOCAGE. House-bote; fire-bote. Cowell.

FOCALE. In old English law, firewood. The right of taking wood for the fire. Fire-bote. Cunningham.

FODDER. Food for horses or cattle. In feudal law, the term also denoted a prerogative of the prince to be provided with corn, etc., for his horses by his subjects in his wars.

FODERTORIUM. Provisions to be paid by custom to the royal purveyors. Cowell.

FODERUM. See Fodder.

FODINA. A mine. Co.Litt. 6*a*.

FŒDUS. In international law, a treaty; a league; a compact.

FŒMINA VIRO CO-OPERTA. A married woman; a *feme covert.*

FŒMINÆ AB OMNIBUS OFFICIIS CIVILIBUS VEL PUBLICIS REMOTÆ SUNT. Women are excluded from all civil and public charges or offices. Dig. 50, 17, 2; 1 Exch. 645; 6 Mees. & W. 216.

FŒMINÆ NON SUNT CAPACES DE PUBLICIS OFFICIIS. Jenk.Cent. 237. Women are not admissible to public offices.

FŒNERATION. Lending money at interest; the act of putting out money to usury.

FŒNUS. Lat. In the civil law, interest on money; the lending of money on interest.

FŒNUS NAUTICUM. Nautical or maritime interest.

FŒNUS UNCIARIUM. Interest of one-twelfth, that is, interest amounting annually to one-twelfth of the principal, hence at the rate of eight and one-third per cent. per annum. This was the highest legal rate of interest in the early times of the Roman republic. See Mackeld.Rom.Law, § 382.

An extraordinary rate of interest agreed to be paid for the loan of money on the hazard of a voyage; sometimes called *"usura maritima."* Dig. 22, 2; Code, 4, 33; 2 Bl. Comm. 458. The extraordinary rate of interest, proportioned to the risk, demanded by a person, lending money on a ship, or on "bottomry," as it is termed. The agreement for such a rate of interest is also called *"fœnus nauticum."* (2 Bl.Comm. 458; 2 Steph.Comm. 93.) Mozley & Whitley.

FŒSA. In old records, grass; herbage. 2 Mon. Angl. 906*b*; Cowell.

FŒTICIDE. See Feticide.

FŒTURA. In the civil law, the produce of animals, and the fruit of other property, which are acquired to the owner of such animals and property by virtue of his right. Bowyer, Mod.Civil Law, c. 14, p. 81

FŒTUS. In medical jurisprudence, an unborn child. An infant *in ventre sa mère.*

FOG. In maritime law, any atmospheric condition (including not only fog properly so called, but also mist or falling snow) which thickens the air, obstructs the view, and so increases the perils of navigation. Flint & P. M. R. Co. v. Marine Ins. Co., C.C.Mich., 71 F. 210; Dolner v. The Monticello, 7 F.Cas. 859.

FOGAGIUM. In old English law, foggage or fog; a kind of rank grass of late growth, and not eaten in summer. Spelman; Cowell.

FOI. In French feudal law, faith; fealty. Guyot, Inst.Feod. c. 2.

FOINESUN. In old English law, the fawning of deer. Spelman.

FOIRFAULT. In old Scotch law, to forfeit. 1 How.State Tr. 927.

FOIRTHOCHT. In old Scotch law, forethought; premeditated. 1 Pitc.Crim.Tr. pt. 1, p. 90.

FOITERERS. Vagabonds. Blount.

FOLC-GEMOTE (spelled, also, *folkmote, folcmote, folkgemote*; from *folc*, people, and *gemote*, an assembly). In Saxon law, a general assembly of the people in a town or shire.

It appears to have had judicial functions of a limited nature, and also to have discharged political offices, such as deliberating upon the affairs of the commonwealth or complaining of misgovernment, and probably possessed considerable powers of local self-government. The name was also given to any sort of a popular assembly. See Spelman; Manwood; Cunningham.

FOLC-LAND. In Saxon law, land of the folk or people. Land belonging to the people or the public.

Folc-land was the property of the community. It might be occupied in common, or possessed in severalty; and, in the latter case, it was probably parceled out to individuals in the folc-gemote or court of the district, and the grant sanctioned by the freemen who were there present. But, while it continued to be folc-land, it could not be alienated in perpetuity; and therefore, on the expiration of the term for which it had been granted, it reverted to the community, and was again distributed by the same authority. It was subject to many burdens and exactions from which boc-land was exempt. Wharton.

FOLC-MOTE. A general assembly of the people, under the Saxons. See Folc-Gemote.

FOLC-RIGHT. The common right of all the people. 1 Bl.Comm. 65, 67.

The *jus commune*, or common law, mentioned in the laws of King Edward the Elder, declaring the same equal right, law, or justice to be due to persons of all degrees. Wharton.

FOLD-COURSE. In English law, land to which the sole right of folding the cattle of others is appurtenant. Sometimes it means merely such right of folding. The right of folding on another's land, which is called "common foldage." Co.Litt. 6*a*, note 1.

FOLD-SOKE. A feudal service which consisted in the obligation of the tenant not to have a fold of his own but to have his sheep lie in the lord's fold.

He was said to be *consuetus ad foldam*, tried to his lord's fold. The basis of his service is thus expressed by a recent writer: "It is manure that the lord wants; the demand for manure has played a large part in the history of the human race." Maitland, Domesday Book 76. In East Anglia the peasants had sheep enough to make this an important social institution; *id.* 442.

FOLDAGE. A privilege possessed in some places by the lord of a manor, which consists in the right of having his tenant's sheep to feed on his fields, so as to manure the land. The name of foldage is also given in parts of Norfolk to the customary fee paid to the lord for exemption at certain times from this duty. Elton, Com. 45, 46.

FOLGARII. Menial servants; followers. Bract.

FOLGERE. In old English law, a freeman, who has no house or dwelling of his own, but is the follower or retainer of another, (*heorthfœst,*) for whom he performs certain predial services.

FOLGERS. Menial servants or followers. Cowell.

FOLGOTH. Official dignity.

FOLIE BRIGHTIQUE. See Insanity.

FOLIE CIRCULAIRE. See Insanity.

FOLIO. A leaf. In the ancient lawbooks it was the custom to number the leaves, instead of the pages; hence a folio would include both sides of the leaf, or two pages. The references to these books are made by the number of the folio, the letters "*a*" and "*b*" being added to show which of the two pages is intended; thus "Bracton, fol. 100*a*."

A large size of book, the page being obtained by folding the sheet of paper once only in the binding. Many of the ancient lawbooks are folios.

When used in connection with legal documents, it means a certain number of words varying from 72 to 100, but generally in the United States consisting of 100. Reed v. Sackett, 135 Okl. 69, 273 P. 1002, 1004.

In pleading denying allegations of a specified folio, it refers to a division in a document for purpose of measurement or reference. Mahin v. Mahin, 131 Fla. 546, 179 So. 651.

FOLK-LAND; FOLK-MOTE. See Folc-Land; Folc-Gemote.

FOLLOW. To conform to, comply with, or be fixed or determined by; as in the expressions "costs follow the event of the suit," "the *situs* of personal property follows that of the owner," "the offspring follows the mother," (*partus sequitur ventrem*).

To walk in, to attend upon closely, as a profession or calling. Spears v. Ford, 247 S.W. 713, 197 Ky. 575.

FOLLOWS THE PROPERTY. Synonymous with "adheres to the property." Tonopah Mining Co. of Nevada v. Commissioner of Internal Revenue, C.C.A.3, 127 F.2d 239, 244.

FONDS ET BIENS. Fr. In French law, goods and effects. Adams v. Akerlund, 168 Ill. 632, 48 N.E. 454.

Including realty. Erickson v. Carlson, 95 Neb. 182, 145 N.W. 352, approved and followed. Engen v. Union State Bank of Harvard, 118 Neb. 105, 223 N.W. 664, 666.

FONDS PERDUS. In French law, a capital is said to be invested *à fonds perdus* when it is stipulated that in consideration of the payment of an amount as interest, higher than the normal rate, the lender shall be repaid his capital in this manner. The borrower, after paying the interest during the period determined, is free as regards the capital itself. Arg.Fr.Merc.Law, 560.

FONSADERA. In Spanish law, any tribute or loan granted to the king for the purpose of enabling him to defray the expenses of a war.

FONTANA. A fountain or spring. Bract. fol. 233.

FOOT. A measure of length containing twelve inches or one-third of a yard. Spicer v. Hartford Fire Ins. Co. of Hartford, Conn., 171 Va. 428, 199 S.E. 499, 501.

The base, bottom, or foundation of anything; and, by metonomy, the end or termination; as the foot of a fine.

The terminal part of the leg. Reno v. Holmes, 238 Mich. 572, 214 N.W. 174, 175. That part of leg at or below ankle joint. Mills v. Mills & Connelly, 214 Ky. 675, 283 S.W. 1010, 1011. Embraces the arch. Trustees for Arch Preserver Shoe Patents v. James McCreery & Co., Cust. & Pat.App., 49 F.2d 1068, 1071.

FOOT ACRE. One acre of coal one foot thick. In re Hudson Coal Co., 327 Pa. 247, 193 A. 8, 10.

FOOT DROP. A loss of ability to turn the foot inward, a loss of ability to extend the toes and to raise them, and a loss of sensation in the lower frontal portions of the leg below the knee, and the greater portion of the top of the foot. Engelking v. Carlson, Cal.App., 80 P.2d 96, 97.

FOOT-FRONTAGE RULE. Under rule, assessment is confined to actual frontage on line of improvement, and depth of lot, number or character of improvements, or value thereof, is immaterial. Borough of Berwick v. Smethers, 105 Pa.Super. 40, 160 A. 148.

FOOTGELD. In the forest law, an amercement for not cutting out the ball or cutting off the claws of a dog's feet, (expeditating, him.) To be quit of *footgeld* is to have the privilege of keeping dogs in the forest *unlawed* without punishment or control. Manwood.

FOOT OF THE FINE. The fifth part of the conclusion of a fine. It includes the whole matter, reciting the names of the parties, day, year, and place, and before whom it was acknowledged or levied. 2 Bl.Comm. 351.

FOOT POUND. A unit of energy, or work, equal to work done in raising one pound avoirdupois against the force of gravity to the height of one foot. Webster, Dict. Healey v. Moran Towing & Transportation Co., C.C.A.N.Y., 253 F. 334, 337.

FOOTPRINTS. In the law of evidence, impressions made upon earth, snow, or other surface by the feet of persons, or by the shoes, boots, or other covering of the feet. Burrill, Circ.Ev. 264.

FOR. Fr. In French law, a tribunal. *Le for interieur,* the interior forum; the tribunal of conscience. Poth.Obl. pt. 1, c. 1, § 1, art. 3, § 4.

FOR. In behalf of, in place of, in lieu of, instead of, representing, as being which, or equivalent to which, and sometimes imports agency. Medler v. Henry, 44 N.M. 63, 97 P.2d 661, 662.

During; throughout; for the period of; as, where a notice is required to be published "for" a certain number of weeks or months. Wilson v. Northwestern Mut. L. Ins. Co., C.C.A.Kan., 65 F. 39, 12 C.C.A. 505; Northrop v. Cooper, 23 Kan. 432; Burdine v. Sewell, 92 Fla. 375, 109 So. 648, 653. Duration, when put in connection with time. Progressive Building & Loan Ass'n v. McIntyre, 169 Tenn. 491, 89 S.W.2d 336, 337.

In consideration for; as an equivalent for; in exchange for; in place of; as where property is agreed to be given "for" other property or "for" services. Norton v. Woodruff, 2 N.Y. 153; Duncan v. Franklin Tp., 10 A. 546, 43 N.J.Eq. 143; Mudge v. Black, Sheridan & Wilson, C.C.A.Mo., 224 F. 919, 921.

Belonging to, exercising authority or functions within; as, where one describes himself as "a notary public in and for the said county."

By reason of; with respect to; for benefit of; for use of; in consideration of. Basler v. Sacramento Electric, Gas & Ry. Co., 166 Cal. 33, 134 P. 993, 994; Elmore-Schultz Grain Co. v. Stonebraker, 202 Mo.App. 81, 214 S.W. 216, 221; Work v. U. S., ex rel. Rives, 54 App.D.C. 84, 295 F. 225, 226. The cause, motive or occasion of an act, state or condition. American Ins. Co. v. Naylor, 103 Colo. 461, 87 P.2d 260, 265. Used in sense of "because of," "on account of," or "in consequence of." Kelly v. State Personnel Board of California, 31 Cal.App.2d 443, 88 P.2d 264, 266. By means of, or growing out of. Cormier v. Hudson, 284 Mass. 231, 187 N.E. 625, 626.

It connotes the end with reference to which anything is, acts, serves, or is done. Bates v. Schillinger, 128 Me. 14, 145 A. 395, 399. In consideration of which, in view of which, or with reference to which, anything is done or takes place.

Fleming v. Atlantic Co., D.C.Ga., 40 F.Supp. 654, 660. In direction of; with view of reaching; with reference to needs, purposes or uses of; appropriate or adapted to; suitable to purpose, requirement, character or state of. Robert v. Clapp Co. v. Fox, 124 Ohio St. 331, 178 N.E. 586, 588.

FOR ACCOUNT OF. Introduces name of person entitled to receive proceeds of indorsed note or draft. Freiberg v. Stoddard, 161 Pa. 259, 28 A. 1111; White v. Miners' Nat. Bank, 102 U.S. 658, 26 L.Ed. 250; Equitable Trust Co. of New York v. Rochling, 275 U.S. 248, 48 S.Ct. 58, 59, 72 L.Ed. 264.

FOR AND DURING SUCH TIME, FOR SO LONG AS. Temporarily. Burdine v. Sewell, 92 Fla. 375, 109 So. 648, 653.

FOR AT LEAST. As applied to a number of days required for notice this phrase includes either the first or last day, but not both. Stroud v. Water Co., 56 N.J.L. 422, 28 A. 578.

FOR CAUSE. Means for reasons which law and public policy recognize as sufficient warrant for removal and such cause is "legal cause" and not merely a cause which the appointing power in the exercise of discretion may deem sufficient. State ex rel. Nagle v. Sullivan, 98 Mont. 425, 40 P.2d 995, 998, 99 A.L.R. 321.

FOR COLLECTION. A form of indorsement on a note or check where it is not intended to transfer title to it or to give it credit or currency, but merely to authorize the transferee to collect the amount of it. Central R. Co. v. Bank, 73 Ga. 383; Sweeny v. Easter, 1 Wall. 166, 17 L.Ed. 681. But see In re Ziegenhein, Mo.App., 187 S.W. 893, 895.

FOR HIRE OR REWARD. To transport passengers or property of other persons than owner or operator of the vehicle for a reward or stipend, to be paid by such passengers, or persons for whom such property is transported, to owner or operator. Michigan Consol. Gas Co. v. Sohio Petroleum Co., 32 N.W.2d 353, 356, 321 Mich. 102.

FOR PURPOSE OF. With the intention of. State v. Derrickson, 1 W.W.Harr., Del., 342, 114 A. 286, 288.

FOR THAT. In pleading, words used to introduce the allegations of a declaration. "For that" is a positive allegation; "For that whereas" is a recital. Ham. N.P. 9.

FOR THAT WHEREAS. In pleading, formal words introducing the statement of the plaintiff's case, by way of recital, in his declaration, in all actions except trespass. 1 Instr.Cler. 170; 1 Burrill, Pr. 127. In trespass, where there was no recital, the expression used was, "For that." Id.; 1 Inst.Cler. 202.

FOR USE. (1) For the benefit or advantage of another. Thus, where an assignee is obliged to sue in the name of his assignor, the suit is entitled "A. *for use* of B. v. C." (2) For enjoyment or employment without destruction.

A loan "for use" is one in which the bailee has the right to use and enjoy the article, but without consuming or destroying it, in which respect it differs from a loan "for consumption." In re Houk's Estate, 186 Cal. 643, 200 P. 417, 418.

FOR VALUE. See Holder.

FOR VALUE RECEIVED. See Value Received.

FOR WHOM IT MAY CONCERN. Phrase creates presumption of intention on part of named insured to cover any persons who may have an insurable interest in the property. Allemannia Fire Ins. Co. v. Winding Gulf Collieries, D.C.W. Va., 60 F.Supp. 65, 68.

FORAGE. Hay and straw for horses, particularly in the army. Jacob.

FORAGIUM. Straw when the corn is threshed out. Cowell.

FORAKER ACT. A name usually given to the act of congress of April 12, 1900, 31 Stat.L. 77, c. 191 (48 U.S.C.A. § 731 et seq.), which provided civil government for Porto Rico. See a synopsis of it by Harlan, J., in Downes v. Bidwell, 182 U.S. 244, 390, 21 S.Ct. 770, 45 L.Ed. 1088.

FORANEUS. One from without; a foreigner; a stranger. Calvin.

FORATHE. In forest law, one who could make oath, *i. e.*, bear witness for another. Cowell; Spelman.

FORBALCA. In old records, a forebalk; a balk (that is, an unplowed piece of land) lying forward or next the highway. Cowell.

FORBANNITUS. A pirate; an outlaw; one banished.

FORBARRER. L.Fr. To bar out; to preclude; hence, to estop.

FORBATUDUS. In old English law, the aggressor slain in combat. Jacob.

FORBEARANCE. Act by which creditor waits for payment of debt due him by debtor after it becomes due. Upton v. Gould, 64 Cal.App.2d 814, 149 P.2d 731, 733. A delay in enforcing rights. Shaw v. Philbrick, 129 Me. 259, 151 A. 423, 74 A. L.R. 290. Indulgence granted to a debtor. Dry Dock Bank v. American Life Ins., etc., Co., 3 N. Y. 354.

Refraining from action. The term is used in this sense in general jurisprudence, in contradistinction to "act."

Within usury law, term signifies contractual obligation of lender or creditor to refrain, during given period of time, from requiring borrower or debtor to repay loan or debt then due and payable. Hafer v. Spaeth, 22 Wash.2d 378, 156 P.2d 408, 411.

FORCE. Power dynamically considered, that is, in motion or in action; constraining power, compulsion; strength directed to an end. Usually the word occurs in such connections as to show that unlawful or wrongful action is meant. Watson v. Railway Co., 7 Misc.Rep. 562, 28 N.Y.S. 84; Plank

Road Co. v. Robbins, 22 Barb., N.Y., 667; Temple Lumber Co. v. Living, Tex.Civ.App., 289 S.W. 746, 749; Hafner Mfg. Co. v. City of St. Louis, 262 Mo. 621, 172 S.W. 28, 34.

Unlawful violence. It is either *simple,* as entering upon another's possession, without doing any other unlawful act; *compound,* when some other violence is committed, which of itself alone is criminal; or *implied,* as in every trespass, rescous, or disseisin. Lambert v. Helena Adjustment Co., 69 Mont. 510, 222 P. 1057, 1058.

It may mean either exact pressure times exact area to which the pressure is applied, or it may mean simply an operative physical power without taking account of the exact quantity applied. Hydraulic Press Corporation v. Coe, 77 U.S.App.D.C. 251, 134 F.2d 49, 56.

Such display of physical power as is reasonably calculated to inspire fear of physical harm to those opposing possession of premises by trespasser. Smith v. Sinclair Refining Co., Tex.Civ.App., 77 S.W.2d 894, 895.

Terms "violence" and "force" are synonymous when used in relation to assault. People v. James, 9 Cal.App.2d 162, 48 P.2d 1011, 1012.

Power statically considered; that is at rest, or latent, but capable of being called into activity upon occasion for its exercise. Efficacy; legal validity. This is the meaning when we say that a statute or a contract is "in force."

As used in divorce statute, "force" or "coercion" are synonymous. Santer v. Santer, 115 Pa.Super. 1, 174 A. 651, 652.

In old English law, a technical term applied to a species of accessary before the fact.

In Scotch law, coercion; duress. Bell.

—Of force. See that title.

FORCE AND ARMS. A phrase used in declarations of trespass and in indictments, but now unnecessary in declarations, to denote that the act complained of was done with violence. 2 Chit.Pl. 846, 850.

FORCE AND FEAR, called also *"vi metuque,"* means that any contract or act extorted under the pressure of force (*vis*) or under the influence of fear (*metus*) is voidable on that ground, provided, of course, that the force or the fear was such as influenced the party. Brown.

FORCE MAJESTURE. Includes lightnings, earthquakes, storms, flood, sunstrokes, freezing, etc., wherein latter two can be considered hazards in contemplation of employer within Compensation Act. Fogg v. Van Saun Coal Co., N.J.Dept. Labor, 12 N.J.Misc. 680, 174 A. 419, 420.

FORCE MAJEURE. Fr. In the law of insurance, superior or irresistible force. Emerig. Tr. des Ass. c. 12

FORCED HEIRS. Those persons whom the testator or donor cannot deprive of the portion of his estate reserved for them by law, except in cases where he has a just cause to disinherit them. Civil Code La. art. 1495. And see Crain v. Crain, 17 Tex. 90; Hagerty v. Hagerty, 12 Tex. 456; Miller v. Miller, 105 La. 257, 29 So. 802.

FORCED SALE. In practice, a sale made at the time and in the manner prescribed by law, in virtue of execution issued on a judgment already rendered by a court of competent jurisdiction; a sale made under the process of the court, and in the mode prescribed by law. Sampson v. Williamson, 6 Tex. 110, 55 Am.Dec. 762.

A sale against the consent of the owner. The term should not be deemed to embrace a sale under a power in a mortgage. Patterson v. Taylor, 15 Fla. 336.

FORCES. The military and naval power of the country.

FORCHEAPUM. Pre-emption; forestalling the market. Jacob.

FORCIBLE DETAINER. Exists where one originally in rightful possession of realty refuses to surrender it at termination of his possessory right. Sayers & Muir Service Station v. Indian Refining Co., 266 Ky. 779, 100 S.W.2d 687, 689.

The offense of violently keeping possession of lands and tenements, with menaces, force, and arms, and without the authority of law. 4 Bl.Comm. 148; 4 Steph.Comm. 280.

Forcible detainer may ensue upon a peaceable entry, as well as upon a forcible entry; but it is most commonly spoken of in the phrase "forcible entry and detainer."

FORCIBLE ENTRY. Violently taking possession of lands and tenements with menaces, force, and arms, against the will of those entitled to the possession, and without the authority of law. 4 Bl. Comm. 148; 4 Steph. Comm. 280; Code Ga. 1882, § 4524 (Pen. Code, 1910, § 344). Accompanied with circumstances tending to excite terror in the occupant, and to prevent him from maintaining his rights. Barbee v. Winnsboro Granite Corporation, 190 S.C. 245, 2 S.E.2d 737, 739. Angry words and threats of force may be sufficient. Calidino Hotel Co. of San Bernardino v. Bank of America Nat. Trust & Savings Ass'n, 31 Cal.App. 2d 295, 87 P.2d 923, 931.

Every person is guilty of forcible entry who either (1) by breaking open doors, windows, or other parts of a house, or by any kind of violence or circumstance of terror, enters upon or into any real property; or (2) who, after entering peaceably upon real property, turns out by force, threats, or menacing conduct the party in possession. Code Civil Proc.Cal. § 1159.

In many states, an entry effected without consent of rightful owner, or against his remonstrance, or under circumstances which amount to no more than a mere trespass, is now technically considered "forcible," while a detainer of the property consisting merely in the refusal to surrender possession after a lawful demand, is treated as a "forcible" detainer, the "force" required at common law being now supplied by a mere fiction. See Vernon's Tex. Ann.Civ.St. art. 3975; Goldsberry v. Bishop, 2 Duv., Ky., 144; Wells v. Darby, 13 Mont. 504, 34 P. 1092; Willard v. Warren, 17 Wend., N.Y. 261; California Products v. Mitchell, 52 Cal.App. 312, 198 P. 646.

FORCIBLE ENTRY AND DETAINER. A summary proceeding for restoring to possession of land one who is wrongfully kept out or has been wrongfully deprived of the possession. Wein v. Albany Park Motor Sales Co., 312 Ill.App. 357, 38 N.E.2d 556, 559.

The title cannot be inquired into for any purpose. Davis v. Robinson, 374 Ill. 553, 30 N.E.2d 52, 54. The inquiry is confined to the actual and peaceable possession of the plaintiff and the unlawful or forcible ouster or detention by defendant; the object of the law being to prevent the disturbance of the public peace by the forcible assertion of a private right. Gore v. Altice, 33 Wash. 335, 74 P. 556; Eveleth v. Gill, 97 Me. 315, 54 A. 757; Harris v. Harris, 190 Ala. 619, 67 So. 465, 466; Long v. Bagwell, 38 Okl. 312, 133 P. 50, 51.

FORCIBLE TRESPASS. In North Carolina, this is an invasion of the rights of another with respect to his personal property, of the same character, or under the same circumstances, which would constitute a "forcible entry and detainer" of real property at common law. It consists in taking or seizing the personal property of another by force, violence, or intimidation or in forcibly injuring it. State v. Lawson, 123 N.C. 740, 31 S.E. 667, 68 Am.St.Rep. 844; State v. Holder, 188 N.C. 561, 125 S.E. 113, 114.

There must be actual violence used, or such demonstration of force as is calculated to intimidate or tend to a breach of the peace. It is not necessary that the person be actually put in fear. State v. Stinnett, 167 S.E. 63, 64, 203 N.C. 829.

FORDA. In old records, a ford or shallow, made by damming or penning up the water. Cowell.

FORDAL. A butt or headland, jutting out upon other land. Cowell.

FORDANNO. In old European law, he who first assaulted another. Spelman.

FORDIKA. In old records, grass or herbage growing on the edge or bank of dykes or ditches. Cowell.

FORE. Sax. Before. Fr. Out. Kelham.

FORE-MATRON. In a jury of women this word corresponds to the foreman of a jury. She was sworn in separately; 8 Carr. & P. 264.

FORE-OATH. Before the Norman Conquest, an oath required of the complainant in the first instance (in the absence of manifest facts) as a security against frivolous suits. Pollock, 1 Sel. Essays Anglo-Amer. Leg. Hist. 93.

FOREBALK. See Headland.

FORECLOSE. To shut out; to bar; to terminate. State v. Darling, 39 S.D. 558, 165 N.W. 536, 537.

Method of terminating mortgagor's right of redemption. Hibernia Savings & Loan Soc. v. Lauffer, 41 Cal.App.2d 725, 107 P.2d 494, 497.

FORECLOSURE. To shut out, to bar, to destroy an equity of redemption. Anderson v. Barr, 178 Okl. 508, 62 P.2d 1242, 1246. A termination of all rights of the mortgagor or his grantee in the property covered by the mortgage. Levin v. Century Indemnity Co., 279 Mass. 256, 181 N.E. 223, 225.

A process in chancery by which all further right existing in a mortgagor to redeem the estate is defeated and lost to him, and the estate becomes the absolute property of the mortgagee; being applicable when the mortgagor has forfeited his estate by non-payment of the money due on the mortgage at the time appointed, but still retains the equity of redemption. 2 Washb. Real Prop. 237. Goodman v. White, 26 Conn. 322; Trustees of Schools v. St. Paul Fire & Marine Ins. Co., 296 Ill. 99, 129 N.E. 567, 568.

The term is also loosely applied to any of the various methods, statutory or otherwise, known in different jurisdictions, of enforcing payment of the debt secured by a mortgage, by taking and selling the mortgaged estate. Dikeman v. Jewel Gold Mining Co., C.C.A.Alaska, 13 F.2d 118; Realty Mortgage Co. v. Moore, 80 Fla. 2, 85 So. 155, 156.

Foreclosure is also applied to proceedings founded upon some other liens; thus there are proceedings to foreclose a mechanic's lien. Insurance Co. of North America v. Cheathem, 221 Ky. 668, 299 S.W. 545, 547. It is a proceeding in court or out of court, when provided for by a valid contract, to subject property or part thereof covered by a lien to payment of debt secured by the lien, and it has effect of extinguishing all right, title, or interest, if any, of defendants in the property. Southwestern Peanut Growers Ass'n v. Womack, Tex.Civ.App., 179 S.W.2d 371, 373.

Statutory foreclosure. The term is sometimes applied to foreclosure by execution of a power of sale contained in the mortgage, without recourse to the courts, as it must conform to the provisions of the statute regulating such sales. See Mowry v. Sanborn, 11 Hun, N.Y., 548.

Strict foreclosure. A decree of strict foreclosure of a mortgage finds the amount due under the mortgage, orders its payment within a certain limited time, and provides that, in default of such payment, the debtor's right and equity of redemption shall be forever barred and foreclosed; its effect is to vest the title of the property absolutely in the mortgagee, on default in payment, without any sale of the property. Champion v. Hinkle, 45 N.J.Eq. 162, 16 A. 701; Lightcap v. Bradley, 186 Ill. 510, 58 N.E. 221; Warner Bros. Co. v. Freud, 138 Cal. 651, 72 P. 345.

FORECLOSURE DECREE. Properly speaking, a decree ordering the strict foreclosure of a mortgage; but the term is also loosely and conventionally applied to a decree ordering the sale of the mortgaged premises and the satisfaction of the mortgage out of the proceeds. Hanover F. Ins. Co. v. Brown, 77 Md. 64, 25 A. 989, 39 Am.St. Rep. 386.

FORECLOSURE SALE. A sale of mortgaged property to obtain satisfaction of the mortgage out of the proceeds, whether authorized by a decree of the court or by a power of sale contained in the mortgage. Johnson v. Cook, 96 Mo.App. 442, 70 S.W. 526.

FORECLOSURE SUIT. A proceeding for legal determination of existence of lien, ascertainment of its extent, and subjection to sale of estate pledged for its satisfaction, and to settle conflicting claims by selling equity of redemption. Reichert v. McCool, 92 Ind.App. 406, 169 N.E. 86, 88.

FOREFAULT. In Scotch law, to forfeit; to lose.

FOREGIFT. A premium for a lease.

FOREGOERS. Royal purveyors. 26 Edw. III. c. 5.

FOREHAND RENT. In English law, rent payable in advance; or, more properly, a species of premium or bonus paid by the tenant on the making of the lease, and particularly on the renewal of leases by ecclesiastical corporations.

FOREIGN. Belonging to another nation or country; belonging or attached to another jurisdiction; made, done, or rendered in another state or jurisdiction; subject to another jurisdiction; operating or solvable in another territory; extrinsic; outside; extraordinary. Nonresident.

Blanchette v. New England Telephone & Telegraph Co., 90 N.H. 207, 6 A.2d 161, 162.

As to foreign "Administrator," "Assignment," "Attachment," "Bill of Exchange," "Charity," "Commerce," "Corporation," "County," "Creditor," "Divorce," "Document," "Domicile," "Factor," "Judgment," "Jury," "Minister," "Plea," "Port," "State," "Vessel," and "Voyage," see those titles.

FOREIGN ANSWER. In old English practice, an answer which was not triable in the county where it was made. (St. 15 Hen. VI. c. 5.) Blount.

FOREIGN APPOSER. An officer in the exchequer who examines the sheriff's *estreats*, comparing them with the records, and apposeth (interrogates) the sheriff what he says to each particular sum therein. 4 Inst. 107; Blount; Cowell.

FOREIGN BOUGHT AND SOLD. A custom in London which, being found prejudicial to sellers of cattle in Smithfield, was abolished. Wharton.

FOREIGN COINS. Coins issued as money under the authority of a foreign government. As to their valuation in the United States, see 46 Stat. 739, 31 U.S.C.A. § 372.

FOREIGN COURTS. The courts of a foreign state or nation. In the United States, this term is frequently applied to the courts of one of the states when their judgments or records are introduced in the courts of another.

FOREIGN DOMINION. In English law this means a country which at one time formed part of the dominions of a foreign state or potentate, but which by conquest or cession has become a part of the dominions of the British crown. 5 Best & S. 290.

FOREIGN ENLISTMENT ACT. The statute 59 Geo. III. c. 69, prohibiting the enlistment, as a soldier or sailor, in any foreign service. 4 Steph. Comm. 226. A later and more stringent act is that of 33 & 34 Vict. c. 90.

FOREIGN EXCHANGE. Drafts drawn on a foreign state or country.

FOREIGN–GOING SHIP. By the English merchant shipping act, 1854, (17 & 18 Vict. c. 104,) § 2, any ship employed in trading, going between some place or places in the United Kingdom and some place or places situate beyond the following limits, that is to say: The coasts of the United Kingdom, the islands of Guernsey, Jersey, Sark, Alderney, and Man, and the continent of Europe, between the river Elbe and Brest, inclusive. Home-trade ship includes every ship employed in trading and going between places within the last-mentioned limits.

FOREIGN JUDGMENT. See Judgment.

FOREIGN JURISDICTION. Any jurisdiction foreign to that of the forum. Also the exercise by a state or nation of jurisdiction beyond its own territory, the right being acquired by treaty or otherwise.

FOREIGN LAWS. The laws of a foreign country, or of a sister state. People v. Martin, 38 Misc. Rep. 67, 76 N.Y.S. 953; Bank of Chillicothe v. Dodge, 8 Barb., N.Y., 233. Foreign laws are often the suggesting occasions of changes in, or additions to, our own laws, and in that respect are called "*jus receptum.*" Brown.

FOREIGN MATTER. In old practice, matter triable or done in another county. Cowell.

FOREIGN OFFICE. The department of state through which the English sovereign communicates with foreign powers. A secretary of state is at its head. Till the middle of the last century, the functions of a secretary of state as to foreign and home questions were not disunited.

FOREIGN SERVICE, in feudal law, was that whereby a mesne lord held of another, without the compass of his own fee, or that which the tenant performed either to his own lord or to the lord paramount out of the fee. (Kitch. 299.) Foreign service seems also to be used for knight's service, or escuage uncertain. (Perk. 650.) Jacob.

FOREIGN TRADE. Commercial interchange of commodities from different countries; export and import trade. Standard Oil Co. of New Jersey v. United States, 29 Cust. & Pat.App. 82, 120 F.2d 340, 342.

FOREIGN WILL. Will of person not domiciled within state at time of death. De Tray v. Hardgrove, Tex.Com.App., 52 S.W.2d 239, 240.

FOREIGNER. In old English law, this term, when used with reference to a particular city, designated any person who was not an inhabitant of that city. According to later usage, it denotes a person who is not a citizen or subject of the state or country of which mention is made, or any one owing allegience to a foreign state or sovereign.

For the distinctions, in Spanish law, between "domiciliated" and "transient" foreigners, see Yates v. Iams, 10 Tex. 168.

FOREIN. An old form of *foreign* (*q. v.*). Blount.

FOREJUDGE. In old English law and practice, to expel from court for some offense or misconduct. When an officer or attorney of a court was expelled for any offense, or for not appearing to an action by bill filed against him, he was said to be *forejudged the court.* Cowell.

To deprive or put out of a thing by the judgment of a court. To condemn to lose a thing.

To expel or banish.

FOREJUDGER. In English practice, a judgment by which a man is deprived or *put out* of a thing; a judgment of expulsion or banishment.

FOREMAN. The presiding member of a grand or petit jury, who speaks or answers for the jury.

Person designated by master to direct work of employees; superintendent, overseer. White v. Kansas City Stockyards Co., 104 Kan. 90, 177 P. 522; Browning v. Smiley-Lampert Lumber Co., 68 Or. 502, 137 P. 777, 780; Brokaw v. Cottrell, 114 Neb. 858, 211 N.W. 184, 187.

FORENSIC. Belonging to courts of justice.

FORENSIC MEDICINE, or medical jurisprudence, as it is also called, is "that science which teaches the application of every branch of medical knowledge to the purposes of the law; hence its limits are, on the one hand, the requirements of the law, and, on the other, the whole range of medicine. Anatomy, physiology, medicine, surgery, chemistry, physics, and botany lend their aid as necessity arises; and in some cases all these branches of science are required to enable a court of law to arrive at a proper conclusion on a contested question affecting life or property." Tayl. Med. Jur. 1.

FORENSIS.

In Civil law, belonging to or connected with a court; forensic. *Forensis homo,* an advocate; a pleader of causes; one who practices in court. Calvin.

In old Scotch law, a strange man or stranger; an out-dwelling man; an "unfreeman," who dwells not within burgh.

FORESAID. Used in Scotch law as *aforesaid* is in English, and sometimes, in a plural form, foresaids. 2 How. State Tr. 715. *Forsaidis* occurs in old Scotch records. "The Loirdis assesouris forsaidis." 1 Pitc. Crim. Tr. pt. 1, p. 107.

FORESCHOKE. Foresaken; disavowed. 10 Edw. II. c. 1.

FORESEEABILITY. The ability to see or know in advance, hence, the reasonable anticipation that harm or injury is a likely result of acts or omissions. Emery v. Thompson, 347 Mo. 494, 148 S.W.2d 479, 480.

FORESHORE. The strip of land that lies between the high and low water marks and that is alternately wet and dry according to the flow of the tide. Tenenbaum v. Sea Gate Ass'n, 253 App. Div. 166, 1 N.Y.S.2d 224, 227. According to the medium line between the greatest and least range of tide (spring tides and neap tides). Sweet. See, also, Shore.

FORESIGHT. Heedful thought for the future; reasonable anticipation of result of certain acts or omissions. Emery v. Thompson, 347 Mo. 494, 148 S.W.2d 479.

FOREST. A tract of land covered with trees and one usually of considerable extent. Forest Preserve Dist. of Cook County v. Jirsa, 336 Ill. 624, 168 N.E. 690, 691.

In old English law, a certain territory of wooded ground and fruitful pastures, privileged for wild beasts and fowls of forest, chase, and warren, to rest and abide in the safe protection of the prince for his princely delight and pleasure, having a peculiar court and officers. Manw. For. Laws, c. 1, no. 1; Termes de la Ley; 1 Bl.Comm. 289.

A royal hunting-ground which lost its peculiar character with the extinction of its courts, or when the franchise passed into the hands of a subject. Spelman; Cowell.

The word is also used to signify a franchise or right, being the right of keeping, for the purpose of hunting, the wild beasts and fowls of forest, chase, park, and warren, in a territory or precinct of woody ground or pasture set apart for the purpose. 1 Steph.Comm. 665.

FOREST COURTS. In English law. Courts instituted for the government of the king's forest in different parts of the kingdom, and for the punishment of all injuries done to the king's deer or *venison,* to the *vert* or greensward, and to the *covert* in which such deer were lodged. They consisted of the courts of attachments, of regard, of sweinmote, and of justice-seat; but in later times these courts are no longer held. 3 Bl. Comm. 71.

FOREST LAW. The system or body of old law relating to the royal forests.

FORESTAGE. A duty or tribute payable to the king's foresters. Cowell.

FORESTAGIUM. A duty or tribute payable to the king's foresters. Cowell.

FORESTALL. To intercept or obstruct a passenger on the king's highway. Cowell. To beset the way of a tenant so as to prevent his coming on the premises. 3 Bl. Comm. 170. To intercept a deer on his way to the forest before he can regain it. Cowell.

FORESTALLER. In old English law, obstruction; hindrance; the offense of stopping the highway; the hindering a tenant from coming to his land; intercepting a deer before it can regain the forest. Also one who forestalls; one who commits the offense of forestalling. 3 Bl. Comm. 170; Cowell.

FORESTALLING. Obstructing the highway. Intercepting a person on the highway.

FORESTALLING THE MARKET. Securing control of commodities on way to market. Raney v. Montgomery County Com'rs, 170 Md. 183, 183 A. 548, 551.

The act of the buying or contracting for any merchandise or provision on its way to the market, with the intention of selling it again at a higher price; or the dissuading persons from bringing their goods or provisions there; or persuading them to enhance the price when there. 4 Bl. Comm. 158. Barton v. Morris, 10 Phila., Pa., 361. This was formerly an indictable offense in England, but is now abolished by St. 7 & 8 Vict. c. 24. 4 Steph.Comm. 291, note.

FORESTARIUS.

In English law, a forester. An officer who takes care of the woods and forests. *De forestario apponendo,* a writ which lay to appoint a forester to prevent further commission of waste when a tenant in dower had committed waste. Bract. 316; Du Cange.

In Scotch law, a forester or keeper of woods, to whom, by reason of his office, pertains the bark and the hewn branches. And, when he rides through the forest, he may take a tree as high as his own head. Skene de Verb. Sign.

FORESTER. A sworn officer of the *forest,* appointed by the king's letters patent to walk the forest, watching both the vert and the venison, attaching and presenting all trespassers against them within their own bailiwick or walk. These letters patent were generally granted during good behavior; but sometimes they held the office in fee. Blount.

FORETHOUGHT FELONY. In Scotch law, murder committed in consequence of a previous design. Ersk. Inst. 4, 4, 50; Bell.

FORFANG. In old English law, the taking of provisions from any person in fairs or markets before the royal purveyors were served with necessaries for the sovereign. Cowell. Also the seizing and rescuing of stolen or strayed cattle from the hands of a thief, or of those having illegal possession of them; also the reward fixed for such rescue.

FORFEIT. To lose, or lose the right to, by some error, fault, offense, or crime, or to subject, as property, to forfeiture or confiscation. State v. Cowen, 231 Iowa 1117, 3 N.W.2d 176, 180. To lose, in consequence of breach of contract, neglect of duty, or offense, some right, privilege, or property to another or to the State. United States v. Chavez, C.C.A.N.M., 87 F.2d 16, 19.

To incur a penalty; to become liable to the payment of a sum of money, as the consequence of a certain act. Sands v. Holbert, 93 W.Va. 574, 117 S.E. 896, 899; Ford v. Ellison, 287 Mo. 683, 230 S.W. 637, 640.

To lose an estate, a franchise, or other property belonging to one, by the act of the law, and as a consequence of some misfeasance, negligence, or omission. Cassell v. Crothers, 193 Pa. 359, 44 A. 446; State v. De Gress, 72 Tex. 242, 11 S.W. 1029; State v. Baltimore & O. R. Co., 12 Gill & J., Md., 432, 38 Am.Dec. 319. The further ideas connoted by this term are that it is a deprivation, (that is, against the will of the losing party,) and that the property is either transferred to another or resumed by the original grantor.

FORFEITABLE. Liable to be forfeited; subject to forfeiture for non-user, neglect, crime, etc.

FORFEITURE. Something to which the right is lost by the commission of a crime or fault or the losing of something by way of penalty. Ridgeway v. City of Akron, Ohio App., 42 N.E.2d 724, 726. A deprivation or destruction of a right in consequence of the nonperformance of some obligation or condition. Connellan v. Federal Life & Casualty Co., 134 Me. 104, 182 A. 13, 14.

1. A punishment annexed by law to some illegal act or negligence in the owner of land, tenements, or hereditaments whereby he loses all interest therein. Hammond v. Johnson, 94 Utah 20, 66 P.2d 894, 900. And which go to the party injured as a recompense for the wrong which he alone, or the public together with himself, hath sustained. 2 Bl.Comm. 267. Wiseman v. McNulty, 25 Cal. 237; Stephenson v. Calliham, Tex.Civ.App., 289 S.W. 158, 159; Fratt v. Daniels-Jones Co., 47 Mont. 487, 133 P. 700, 701.

2. The loss of land by a tenant to his lord, as the consequence of some breach of fidelity. 1 Steph.Comm. 166.

3. The loss of lands and goods to the state, as the consequence of crime. 4 Bl.Comm. 381, 387; 4 Steph.Comm. 447, 452; 2 Kent, Comm. 385; 4 Kent, Comm. 426; Avery v. Everett, 110 N.Y. 317, 18 N.E. 148, 1 L.R.A. 264, 6 Am. St.Rep. 368.

4. The loss of goods or chattels, as a punishment for some crime or misdemeanor in the party forfeiting, and as a compensation for the offense and injury committed against him to whom they are forfeited. 2 Bl.Comm. 420.

5. The loss of office by abuser, non-user, or refusal to exercise it. City of Williamsburg v. Weesner, 164 Ky. 769, 176 S.W. 224, 225.

6. The loss of a corporate franchise or charter in consequence of some illegal act, or of malfeasance or nonfeasance. Murphy v. Missouri & Kansas Land & Loan Co., 28 N.D. 519, 149 N.W. 957, 959; Village of Fredonia v. Fredonia Natural Gas Light Co., 87 Misc. 592, 149 N.Y.S. 964, 965.

7. The loss of the right to life, as the consequence of the commission of some crime to which the law has affixed a capital penalty. In re New Jersey Court of Pardons, 97 N.J.Eq. 555, 129 A. 624, 630.

8. The incurring a liability to pay a definite sum of money as the consequence of violating the provisions of some statute, or refusal to comply with some requirement of law. State v. Marion County Com'rs, 85 Ind. 493.

9. A thing or sum of money forfeited. Something imposed as a punishment for an offense or delinquency. The word in this sense is frequently associated with the word "penalty." Van Buren v. Digges, 11 How. 477, 13 L.Ed. 771; Bryant v. Rich's Grill, 216 Mass. 344, 103 N.E. 925, 927, Ann.Cas.1915B, 869; Miller v. Bopp, 136 La. 788, 67 So. 831; Missouri, K & T. Ry. Co. v. Dewey Portland Cement Co., 113 Okl. 142, 242 P. 257, 259.

10. In mining law, the loss of a mining claim held by location on the public domain (unpatented) in consequence of the failure of the holder to make the required annual expenditure upon it within the time allowed. McKay v. McDougall, 25 Mont. 258, 64 P. 669, 87 Am.St.Rep. 395; St. John v. Kidd, 26 Cal. 271.

FORFEITURE OF BOND. A failure to perform the condition upon which obligor was to be excused from the penalty in the bond. Hall v. Browning, 71 Ga.App. 835, 32 S.E.2d 424, 427.

FORFEITURE OF MARRIAGE. A penalty incurred by a ward in chivalry who married without the consent or against the will of the guardian. See Duplex Valor Maritagii.

FORFEITURE OF SILK, supposed to lie in the docks, used, in times when its importation was prohibited, to be proclaimed each term in the exchequer.

FORFEITURES ABOLITION ACT. Another name for the felony act of 1870, abolishing forfeitures for felony in England.

FORGABULUM, or FORGAVEL. A quit-rent; a small reserved rent in money. Jacob.

FORGE. To fabricate by false imitation. Carter v. State, 135 Tex.Cr.R. 457, 116 S.W.2d 371, 377. To fabricate, construct, or prepare one thing in imitation of another thing, with the intention of substituting the false for the genuine, or otherwise deceiving and defrauding by the use of the spurious article. To counterfeit or make falsely. Especially, to make a spurious written instrument with the intention of fraudulently substituting it for another, or of passing it off as genuine; or to fraudulently alter a genuine instrument to another's prejudice; or to sign another person's name to a document, with a deceitful and fraudulent intent. In re Cross, D.C.N.C., 43 F. 520; U. S. v. Watkins, 28 Fed.Cas. 445; Johnson v. State, 9 Tex.App. 251; Longwell v. Day, 1 Mich. N.P. 290.

To forge (a metaphorical expression, borrowed from the occupation of the smith) means, properly speaking, no more than *to make* or *form*, but in our law it is always taken in an evil sense. 2 East, P. C. p. 852, c. 19, § 1.

To forge is to make in the likeness of something else; to counterfeit is to make in imitation of something else, with a view to defraud by passing the false copy for genuine or original. Both words, "forged" and "counterfeited," convey the idea of similitude. State v. McKenzie, 42 Me. 392.

In common usage, however, *forgery* is almost always predicated of some private instrument or writing, as a deed, note, will, or a signature; and *counterfeiting* denotes the fraudulent imitation of coined or paper money or some substitute therefor.

FORGERY.

Criminal Law

The false making or material altering, with intent to defraud, of any writing which, if genuine, might apparently be of legal efficacy or the foundation of a legal liability. People v. Routson, 354 Ill. 573, 188 N.E. 883, 885; 2 Bish. Crim. Law, § 523; McCornack v. Central State Bank, 203 Iowa 833, 211 N.W. 542, 545, 52 A.L.R. 1297. A fraudulent making and alteration of writing to prejudice of another man's right, or a false making, a making malo animo of any instrument, for the purpose of fraud or deceit. Iberville Trust & Saving Bank v. City Café, La.App., 143 So. 73. See Forge.

The thing itself, so falsely made, imitated or forged; especially a forged writing. A forged signature is frequently said to be "a *forgery*."

Evidence

The fabrication or counterfeiting of evidence. The artful and fraudulent manipulation of physical objects, or the deceitful arrangement of genuine facts or things, in such a manner as to create an erroneous impression or a false inference in the minds of those who may observe them. See Burrill, Circ. Ev. 131, 420.

FORGERY ACT, 1870. The statute 33 & 34 Vict. c. 58, was passed for the punishment of forgers of stock certificates, and for extending to Scotland certain provisions of the forgery act of 1861. Mozley & Whitley.

FORHERDA. In old records, a herdland, headland, or foreland. Cowell.

FORI DISPUTATIONES. In the civil law, discussions or arguments before a court. 1 Kent, Comm. 530.

FORINSECUS. Lat. Foreign; exterior; outside; extraordinary.

Servitium forinsecum, the payment of aid, scutage, and other extraordinary military services. *Forinsecum manerium,* the manor, or that part of it which lies outside the bars or town, and is not included within the liberties of it. Cowell; Blount; Jacob; 1 Reeve, Eng.Law, 273.

FORINSIC. In old English law, exterior; foreign; extraordinary.

In feudal law, the term "forinsic services" comprehended the payment of extraordinary aids or the rendition of extraordinary military services, and in this sense was opposed to "intrinsic services." 1 Reeve, Eng. Law, 273.

FORIS. Lat. Abroad; out of doors; on the outside of a place; without; extrinsic.

FORISBANITUS. In old English law, banished.

FORISFACERE. Lat. To forfeit; to lose an estate or other property on account of some criminal or illegal act. To confiscate.

To act beyond the law, *i. e.*, to transgress or infringe the law; to commit an offense or wrong; to do any act against or beyond the law. See Co. Litt. 59*a;* Du Cange; Spelman.

FORISFACERE, i. e., EXTRA LEGEM SEU CONSUETUDINEM FACERE. Co. Litt. 59. *Forisfacere, i. e.,* to do something beyond law or custom.

FORISFACTUM. Forfeited. *Bona forisfacta,* forfeited goods. 1 Bl. Comm. 299. A crime. Du Cange; Spelman.

FORISFACTURA. A crime or offense through which property is forfeited.

A fine or punishment in money.

Forfeiture. The loss of property or life in consequence of crime.

FORISFACTURA PLENA. A forfeiture of all a man's property. Things which were forfeited. Du Cange. Spelman.

FORISFACTUS. A criminal. One who has forfeited his life by commission of a capital offense. Spelman.

FORISFACTUS SERVUS. A slave who has been a free man, but has forfeited his freedom by crime. Du Cange.

FORISFAMILIARE. In old English and Scotch law, literally, to put out of a family (*foris familiam ponere*). To portion off a son, so that he could have no further claim upon his father. Glanv. lib. 7, c. 3.

To emancipate, or free from paternal authority.

FORISFAMILIATED. In old English law, portioned off.

A son was said to be forisfamiliated *(forisfamiliari)* if his father assigned him part of his land, and gave him seisin thereof, and did this at the request or with the free consent of the son himself, who expressed himself satisfied with such portion. 1 Reeve, Eng. Law, 42, 110.

FORISFAMILIATUS. In old English law, put out of a family; portioned off; emancipated; forisfamiliated. Bract. fol. 64.

FORISJUDICATIO. In old English law, forejudger. A forejudgment. A judgment of court whereby a man is put out of possession of a thing. Co. Litt. 100*b*.

FORISJUDICATUS. Forejudged; sent from court; banished. Deprived of a thing by judgment of court. Bract. fol. 250*b;* Co. Litt. 100*b;* Du Cange.

FORISJURARE. To forswear; to abjure; to abandon.

Provinciam forisjurare. To forswear the country. Spelman.

FORISJURARE PARENTILAM. To remove oneself from parental authority. The person who did this lost his rights as heir. Du Cange.

FORJUDGE. See Forejudge.

FORJURER. L. Fr. In old English law, to forswear; to abjure.

FORJURER ROYALME. To abjure the realm. Britt. cc. 1, 16.

FORLER-LAND. Land in the diocese of Hereford, which had a peculiar custom attached to it, but which has been long since disused, although the name is retained. But. Surv. 56.

FORM. A model or skeleton of an instrument to be used in a judicial proceeding, containing the principal necessary matters, the proper technical terms or phrases, and whatever else is necessary to make it formally correct, arranged in proper and methodical order, and capable of being adapted to the circumstances of the specific case.

In contradistinction to "substance," "form" means the legal or technical manner or order to be observed in legal instruments or juridical proceedings, or in the construction of legal documents or processes.

Antithesis of "substance." Phœnix Building & Homestead Ass'n v. Meraux, 189 La. 819, 180 So. 648, 649.

Common Form, Solemn Form. See Probate.

Forms of Action. This term is the general designation of the various species or kinds of personal actions known to the common law, such as trover, trespass, debt, *assumpsit,* etc. These differ in their pleadings and evidence, as well as in the circumstances to which they are respectively applicable. Truax v. Parvis, 7 Houst. (Del.) 330, 32 A. 227.

Matter of Form. In pleadings, in indictments, in affidavits, conveyances, etc., matter of form (as distinguished from matter of substance) is all that relates to the mode, form, or style of expressing the facts involved, the choice or arrangement of words, and other such particulars, without affecting the substantial validity or sufficiency of the instrument, or without going to the merits. Railway Co. v. Kurtz, 10 Ind.App. 60, 37 N.E. 303; Meath v. Mississippi Levee Com'rs, 109 U.S. 268, 3 S.Ct. 284, 27 L.Ed. 930; State v. Amidon, 58 Vt. 524, 2 A. 154.

Form of the Statute. This expression means the words, language, or frame of a statute, and hence the inhibition or command which it may contain; used in the phrase (in criminal pleading) "against the form of the statute in that case made and provided."

FORMA. Lat. Form; the prescribed form of judicial proceedings.

FORMA DAT ESSE. Form gives being. Called "the old physical maxim." Lord Henley, Ch., 2 Eden, 99.

FORMA ET FIGURA JUDICII. The form and shape of judgment or judicial action. 3 Bl. Comm. 271.

FORMA LEGALIS FORMA ESSENTIALIS. Legal form is essential form. 10 Coke, 100.

FORMA NON OBSERVATA, INFERTUR ADNULLATIO ACTUS. Where form is not observed, a nullity of the act is inferred. 12 Coke, 7. Where the law prescribes a form, the nonobservance of it is fatal to the proceeding, and the whole becomes a nullity. Best, Ev. Introd. § 59.

FORMA PAUPERIS. See In Forma Pauperis.

FORMAL. Relating to matters of form; as, "formal defects"; inserted, added, or joined *pro forma.* See Parties.

FORMALITIES. In England, robes worn by the magistrates of a city or corporation, etc., on solemn occasions. Enc. Lond.

FORMALITY. The conditions, in regard to method, order, arrangement, use of technical expressions, performance of specific acts, etc., which are required by the law in the making of contracts or conveyances, or in the taking of legal proceedings, to insure their validity and regularity. Succession of Seymour, 48 La.Ann. 993, 20 So. 217.

FORMATA. In canon law, canonical letters. Spelman.

FORMATA BREVIA. Formed writs; writs of form. See Brevia Formata.

FORMED ACTION. An action for which a set form of words is prescribed, which must be strictly adhered to. 10 Mod. 140, 141.

FORMED DESIGN. In criminal law, and particularly with reference to homicide, this term means a deliberate and fixed intention to kill, whether directed against a particular person or not. Mitchell v. State, 60 Ala. 33; Wilson v. State, 128 Ala. 17, 29 So. 569; Ake v. State, 30 Tex. 473.

FORMEDON. An ancient writ in English law which was available for one who had a right to lands or tenements by virtue of a gift in tail.

It was in the nature of a writ of right, and was the highest action that a tenant in tail could have; for he could not have an absolute writ of right, that being confined to such as claimed in fee-simple, and for that reason this writ of formedon was granted to him by the statute *de donis,* (Westm. 2, 13 Edw. I. c. 1,) and was emphatically called "his" writ of right. The writ was distinguished into three species, viz.: Formedon in the descender, in the remainder, and in the reverter. It was abolished in England by St. 3 & 4 Wm. IV. c. 27. See 3 Bl.Comm. 191; Co. Litt. 316; Fitzh.Nat.Brev. 255.

FORMEDON IN THE DESCENDER. A writ of formedon which lay where a gift was made in tail, and the tenant in tail aliened the lands or was disseised of them and died, for the heir in tail to recover them, against the actual tenant of the freehold. 3 Bl. Comm. 192.

FORMEDON IN THE REMAINDER. A writ of formedon which lay where a man gave lands to another for life or in tail, with remainder to a third person in tail or in fee, and he who had the particular estate died without issue inheritable, and a stranger intruded upon him in remainder, and kept him out of possession. In this case he in *remainder,* or his heir, was entitled to this writ. 3 Bl. Comm. 192.

FORMEDON IN THE REVERTER. A writ of formedon which lay where there was a gift in tail, and afterwards, by the death of the donee or his heirs without issue of his body, the reversion fell in upon the donor, his heirs or assigns. In such case, the *reversioner* had this writ to recover the lands. 3 Bl. Comm. 192.

FORMELLA. A certain weight of above 70 lbs., mentioned in 51 Hen. III. Cowell.

FORMER ACQUITTAL. See Autrefois.

FORMER ADJUDICATION. An adjudication in a former action. See Res Judicata.

Either a final determination of the rights of the parties or an adjudication of certain questions of fact. Johnson v. Fontana County Fire Protection Dist., 101 P.2d 1092, 1097, 15 Cal.2d 380; Johnson v. Fontana County Fire Protection Dist., Cal.App., 87 P.2d 426, 430.

FORMER JEOPARDY. Plea of "former jeopardy," that a man cannot be brought into danger of his life or limb for the same offense more than once, is fundamental common law and constitutional right of defendant, affording protection against his being again tried for the same offense, and not against the peril of second punishment. State v. Fredlund, 200 Minn. 44, 273 N.W. 353, 355, 113 A.L.R. 215.

FORMER RECOVERY. Recovery in a former action. See Res Judicata.

FORMIDO PERICULI. Lat. Fear of danger. 1 Kent, Comm. 23.

FORMS OF ACTION. This term comprehends the various classes of personal action at common law, viz.: trespass, case, trover, detinue, replevin, covenant, debt, assumpsit, *scire facias,* and revivor, as well as the nearly obsolete actions of account and annuity, and the modern action of mandamus.

They are now abolished in England by the Judicature Acts of 1873 and 1875, and in many of the states of the United States, where a uniform course of proceeding under codes of procedure has taken their place. But the principles regulating the distinctions between the common-law actions are still found applicable even where the technical forms are abolished.

FORMULA. In common-law practice, a set form of words used in judicial proceedings.

In the civil law, an action. Calvin.

FORMULA DEAL. An agreement between motion picture distributors and independent or affiliated circuits to exhibit a feature in all theatres at specified percentage of national gross receipts realized from such feature by all theatres in the United States. U. S. v. Paramount Pictures, D.C. N.Y., 66 F.Supp. 323, 333, 347.

FORMULA INSTRUCTION. An instruction intended to be complete statement of law upon which jury may base verdict. Harvey v. Aceves, 115 Cal.App. 333, 1 P.2d 1043, 1045.

FORMULÆ. In Roman law, when the *legis actiones* were proved to be inconvenient, a mode of procedure called *"per formulas," (i. e.,* by means of *formulæ,)* was gradually introduced, and eventually the *legis actiones* were abolished by the *Lex Æbutia,* B. C. 164, excepting in a very few exceptional matters.

The *formulæ* were four in number, namely: (1) The *Demonstratio,* wherein the plaintiff stated, *i. e.,* showed, the facts out of which his claim arose; (2) the *Intentio,* where he made his claim against the defendant; (3) the *Adjudicatio,* wherein the judex was directed to assign or adjudicate the property or any portion or portions thereof according to the rights of the parties; and (4) the *Condemnatio,* in which the judex was authorized and directed to condemn or to acquit according as the facts were or were not proved. These *formulæ* were obtained from the magistrate, *(in jure,)* and were thereafter proceeded with before the judex, *(in judicio).* Brown. See Mackeld.Rom. Law, § 204.

FORMULARIES. Collections of *formulæ,* or forms of forensic proceedings and instruments used among the Franks, and other early continental nations of Europe. Among these the formulary of Marculphus may be mentioned as of considerable interest. Butl. Co. Litt. note 77, lib. 3.

FORNAGIUM. The fee taken by a lord of his tenant, who was bound to bake in the lord's common oven *(in furno domini),* or for a commission to use his own.

FORNICATION. Unlawful sexual intercourse between two unmarried persons. Further, if one of the persons be married and the other not, it is fornication on the part of the latter, though adultery for the former. In some jurisdictions, however, by statute, it is adultery on the part of both persons if the woman is married, whether the man is married or not. Banks v. State, 96 Ala. 78, 11 So. 404; Hood v. State, 56 Ind. 263, 26 Am. Rep. 21; State v. Phillips, 26 N.D. 206, 144 N.W. 94, 95, 49 L.R.A.,N.S., 470, Ann.Cas.1916A, 320; State v. Ling, 91 Kan. 647, 138 P. 582, Ann.Cas. 1915D, 374.

FORNIX. Lat. A brothel; fornication.

FORNO. In Spanish law, an oven. Las Partidas, pt. 3, tit. 32, l. 18.

FORO. In Spanish law, the place where tribunals hear and determine causes,—*exercendarum litium locus.*

FOROS. In Spanish law, emphyteutic rents. Schm. Civil Law, 309.

FORPRISE. An exception; reservation; excepted; reserved. Anciently, a term of frequent use in leases and conveyances. Cowell; Blount.

In another sense, the word is taken for any exaction.

FORSCHEL. A strip of land lying next to the highway.

FORSES. Waterfalls. Camden, Brit.

FORSPEAKER. An attorney or advocate in a cause. Blount; Whishaw.

FORSPECA. In old English law, prolocutor; paranymphus.

FORSTAL. See Forestall.

FORSTELLARIUS EST PAUPERUM DEPRESSOR ET TOTIUS COMMUNITATIS ET PATRIÆ PUBLICUS INIMICUS. 3 Inst. 196. A forestaller is an oppressor of the poor, and a public enemy of the whole community and country.

FORSWEAR. In criminal law, to make oath to that which the deponent knows to be untrue.

This term is wider in its scope than "perjury," for the latter, as a technical term, includes the idea of the oath being taken before a competent court or officer, and relating to a material issue, which is not implied by the word "forswear." Fowle v. Robbins, 12 Mass. 501; Tomlinson v. Brittlebank, 4 Barn. & A. 632; Railway Co. v. McCurdy, 114 Pa. 554, 8 A. 230, 60 Am.Rep. 363.

FORT. This term means "something more than a mere military camp, post, or station. The term implies a fortification, or a place protected from attack by some such means as a moat, wall, or parapet." U. S. v. Tichenor, C.C.Or., 12 F. 424.

FORTALICE, or FORTELACE. A fortress or place of strength, which anciently did not pass without a special grant. 11 Hen. VII. c. 18.

FORTALITIUM. In old Scotch law, a fortalice; a castle. Properly a house or tower which has a battlement or a ditch or moat about it.

FORTAXED. Wrongly or extortionately taxed.

FORTHCOMING. In Scotch law, the action by which an arrestment (garnishment) is made effectual. It is a decree or process by which the creditor is given the right to demand that the sum arrested be applied for payment of his claim. 2 Kames, Eq. 288, 289; Bell.

FORTHCOMING BOND. A bond conditioned on the forthcoming of property to answer such judgment as may be entered. If the property be forthcoming, no liability ensues. U. S. Fidelity & Guaranty Co. v. Sabath, 286 Ill.App. 320, 3 N.E.2d 330, 335.

A bond given to a sheriff who has levied on property, conditioned that the property shall be forthcoming, *i. e.*, produced, when required. On the giving of such bond, the goods are allowed to remain in the possession of the debtor. Hill v. Manser, 11 Grat., Va., 522; Nichols v. Chittenden, 14 Colo.App. 49, 59 P. 954; Burnham-Munger-Root Dry Goods Co. v. Strahl, 102 Neb. 142, 166 N.W. 266.

FORTHWITH. Immediately; without delay, directly, hence within a reasonable time under the circumstances of the case; promptly and with reasonable dispatch. State ex rel. Board of Education of City of Tulsa v. Morley, 168 Okl. 259, 34 P.2d 258, 261; 1 Chit. Archb. Pr. (12th Ed.) 164. Within such time as to permit that which is to be done, to be done lawfully and according to the practical and ordinary course of things to be performed or accomplished. Harris v. Stewart, 187 Miss. 489, 193 So. 339, 342. The first opportunity offered. Abbott v. State, 117 Neb. 350, 220 N.W. 578, 579.

FORTIA. Force. In old English law. Force used by an accessory, to enable the principal to commit a crime, as by binding or holding a person while another killed him, or by aiding or counseling in any way, or commanding the act to be done. Bract. fols. 138, 138*b*.

According to Lord Coke, *fortia* was a word of art, and properly signified the furnishing of a weapon of force to do the fact, and by force whereof the fact was committed, and he that furnished it was not present when the fact was done. 2 Inst. 182.

FORTIA FRISCA. Fresh force (*q. v.*).

FORTILITY. In old English law, a fortified place; a castle; a bulwark. Cowell; 11 Hen. VII. c. 18.

FORTIOR. Lat. Stronger. A term applied, in the law of evidence, to that species of presumption, arising from facts shown in evidence, which is strong enough to shift the burden of proof to the opposite party. Burrill, Circ.Ev. 64, 66.

FORTIOR EST CUSTODIA LEGIS QUAM HOMINIS. 2 Rolle, 325. The custody of the law is stronger than that of man.

FORTIOR ET POTENTIOR EST DISPOSITIO LEGIS QUAM HOMINIS. The disposition of the law is of greater force and effect than that of man. Co.Litt. 234*a*; Shep.Touch. 302; 15 East, 178. The law in some cases overrides the will of the individual, and renders ineffective or futile his expressed intention or contract. Broom, Max. 697.

FORTIORI. See A Fortiori.

FORTIS. Lat. Strong. *Fortis et sana*, strong and sound; staunch and strong; as a vessel. Townsh.Pl. 227.

FORTLETT. A place or port of some strength; a little fort. Old Nat. Brev. 45.

FORTUIT. In French law, accidental; fortuitous. *Cas fortuit*, a fortuitous event. *Fortuitement*, accidentally; by chance; casually.

FORTUITOUS. Happening by chance or accident. Kermani v. Insurance Co. of North America, 142 Misc. 542, 255 N.Y.S. 687, 689. Occurring unexpectedly, or without known cause. Stanton v. Minneapolis St. Ry. Co., 195 Minn. 457, 263 N.W. 433, 434. Accidental; undesigned; adventitious. Resulting from unavoidable physical causes. Zappala v. Industrial Ins. Commission, 82 Wash. 314, 144 P. 54, L.R.A.1916A, 295.

FORTUITOUS COLLISION. In maritime law, the accidental running foul of vessels. Peters v. Warren Ins. Co., 14 Pet. 112, 10 L.Ed. 371.

FORTUITOUS EVENT. In the civil law, that which happens by a cause which cannot be resisted. An unforeseen occurrence, not caused by either of the parties, nor such as they could prevent.

In French it is called *"cas fortuit."* Civ. Code La. art. 3556, no. 15.

There is a difference between a fortuitous event, or inevitable accident, and irresistible force. By the former, commonly called the "act of God," is meant any accident produced by physical causes which are irresistible; such as a loss by lightning or storms, by the perils of the seas, by inundations and earthquakes, or by sudden death or illness. By the latter is meant such an interposition of human agency as is, from its nature and power, absolutely uncontrollable. Of this nature are losses occasioned by the inroads of a hostile army, or by public enemies. Story, Bailm. § 25. In Workmen's Compensation Acts fortuitous event is accidental happening, or accident that takes place without design or expectation, or thing that happens from irresistible cause. The term is expressly defined in several acts. Stolp v. Department of Labor and Industries, 138 Wash. 685, 245 P. 20, 21; Stertz v. Industrial Insurance Commission of Washington, 91 Wash. 588, 158 P. 256, 259, Ann.Cas.1918B, 354; Zappala v. Industrial Ins. Commission, 82 Wash. 314, 144 P. 54, L.R.A.1916A, 295.

FORTUNA. Lat. Fortune; also treasure-trove. Jacob.

FORTUNAM FACIUNT JUDICEM. They make fortune the judge. Co. Litt. 167. Spoken of the process of making partition among coparceners by drawing lots for the several purparts.

FORTUNE TELLER. One who professes to tell future events in the life of another. People v. Plaskett, 171 Misc. 563, 13 N.Y.S.2d 682, 684.

In English law, persons pretending or professing to tell fortunes, and punishable as rogues and vagabonds or disorderly persons. 4 Bl.Comm. 62.

FORTUNIUM. In old English law, a tournament or fighting with spears, and an appeal to fortune therein.

FORTY. In land laws and conveyancing, in those regions where grants, transfers, and deeds are made with reference to the subdivisions of the government survey, this term means forty acres of land in the form of a square, being the tract obtained by quartering a section of land (640 acres) and again quartering one of the quarters. Lente v. Clarke, 22 Fla. 515, 1 So. 149.

FORTY-DAYS COURT. In old English forest law, the court of attachment in forests, or woodmote court.

FORUM. Lat. A court of justice, or judicial tribunal; a place of jurisdiction; a place of litigation. 3 Story, 347. Place where remedy is pursued. Rubin v. Gallagher, 294 Mich. 124, 292 N.W. 584, 586.

In Roman law, the market place, or public paved court, in the city of Rome, where such public business was transacted as the assemblies of the people and the judicial trial of causes, and where also elections, markets, and the public exchange were held.

FORUM ACTUS. The forum of the act. The forum of the place where the act was done which is now called in question.

FORUM BOVARIUM. See Bovarius.

FORUM CONSCIENTIÆ. The forum or tribunal of conscience.

FORUM CONTENTIOSUM. A contentious forum or court; a place of litigation; the ordinary court of justice, as distinguished from the tribunal of conscience. 3 Bl.Comm. 211.

FORUM CONTRACTUS. The forum of the contract; the court of the place where a contract is made; the place where a contract is made, considered as a place of jurisdiction. 2 Kent, Comm. 463.

FORUM CONVENIENS. Place where testamentary trustee may be reached by process. In re Knox' Estate, 52 Cal.App.2d 338, 126 P.2d 108, 113.

FORUM DOMESTICUM. A domestic forum or tribunal. The visitatorial power is called a *"forum domesticum,"* calculated to determine, *sine strepitu*, all disputes that arise within themselves. 1 W.Bl. 82.

FORUM DOMICILII. The forum or court of the domicile; the domicile of a defendant, considered as a place of jurisdiction. 2 Kent, Comm. 463.

FORUM ECCLESIASTICUM. An ecclesiastical court. The spiritual jurisdiction, as distinguished from the secular.

FORUM LIGEANTIÆ REI. The forum of defendant's allegiance. The court or jurisdiction of the country to which he owes allegiance.

FORUM NON CONVENIENS. The doctrine is patterned upon the right of the court in the exercise of its equitable powers to refuse the imposition upon its jurisdiction of the trial of cases even though the venue is properly laid if it appears that for the convenience of litigants and witnesses and in the interest of justice the action should be instituted in another forum where the action might have been brought. Hayes v. Chicago, R. I. & P. R. Co., D.C.Minn., 79 F.Supp. 821, 824. The doctrine presupposes at least two forums in which the defendant is amenable to process and furnishes criteria for choice between such forums. Wilson v. Seas Shipping Co., D.C.Pa., 78 F.Supp. 464, 465; Neal v. Pennsylvania R. Co., D.C.N.Y., 77 F.Supp. 423, 424. The application of the doctrine rests in the sound discretion of the court and the factors to be considered in the doctrine are the private interests of the litigant and the interest of the public. Cullinan v. New York Cent. R. Co., D. C.N.Y., 83 F.Supp. 870, 871. And a court, either state or federal, will generally decline to interfere with or control by injunction or otherwise the management of internal affairs of a corporation organized under the laws of another state, leaving controversies as to such matters to courts of state of domicile. Garrett v. Phillips Petroleum Co., Tex.Civ.App., 218 S.W.2d 238, 240; Murray v. Union Pac. R. Co., D.C.Ill., 77 F.Supp. 219; Kelley v. American Sugar Refining Co., C.C.A.Mass., 139 F. 2d 76; Tiuoli Realty v. Interstate Circuit, C.C.A. Tex., 167 F.2d 155; Rogers v. Guaranty Trust Co., 288 U.S. 123, 53 S.Ct. 295, 77 L.Ed. 652, 89 A.L.R. 720.

The rule is an equitable one embracing the discretionary power of a court to decline to exercise jurisdiction which it has over a transitory cause of action when it believes that the action may be more appropriately and justly tried elsewhere. Leet v. Union Pac. R. Co., 155 P.2d 42, 44, 25 Cal.2d 605.

In determining whether doctrine should be applied, court should consider relative ease of access to sources of proof, availability of compulsory process for attendance of unwilling witnesses, cost of obtaining attendance of willing witnesses, possibility of view of premises, and all other practical problems that make trial easy, expeditious and inexpensive. Di Lella v. Lehigh Val. R. Co., D.C.N.Y., 7 F.R. D. 192, 193.

FORUM ORIGINIS. The court of one's nativity. The place of a person's birth, considered as a place of jurisdiction.

FORUM REGIUM. The king's court. St. Westm. 2, c. 43.

FORUM REI. This term may mean either (1) the forum of the defendant, that is, of his residence or domicile; or (2) the forum of the *res* or thing in controversy, that is, of the place where the property is situated. The ambiguity springs from the fact that *rei* may be the genitive of either *reus* or *res*.

FORUM REI GESTÆ. The forum or court of a *res gesta* (thing done;) the place where an act is done, considered as a place of jurisdiction and remedy. 2 Kent, Comm. 463.

FORUM REI SITÆ. The court where the thing in controversy is situated. The place where the subject-matter in controversy is situated, considered as a place of jurisdiction. 2 Kent, Comm. 463.

FORUM SECULARE. A secular, as distinguished from an ecclesiastical or spiritual, court.

FORURTH. In old records, a long slip of ground. Cowell.

FORWARD. To send forward; to send toward the place of destination; to transmit. Nicoletti v. Bank of Los Banos, 190 Cal. 637, 214 P. 51, 52, 27 A.L.R. 1479; Katcher v. American Express Co., 94 N.J.L. 165, 109 A. 741, 742.

FORWARDING MERCHANT, or FORWARDER. One who receives and forwards goods, taking upon himself the expenses of transportation, for which he receives a compensation from the owners, having no concern in the vessels or wagons by which they are transported, and no interest in the freight, and not being deemed a common carrier, but a mere warehouseman and agent. Story, Bailm. §§ 502, 509. Schloss v. Wood, 11 Colo. 287, 17 P. 910; Bush v. Miller, 13 Barb. N.Y. 488.

FOSSA. In the Civil law, a ditch; a receptacle of water, made by hand. Dig. 43, 14, 1, 5.

In Old English law, a ditch. A pit full of water, in which women committing felony were drowned. A grave or sepulcher. Spelman.

FOSSAGIUM. In old English law, the duty levied on the inhabitants for repairing the moat or ditch round a fortified town.

FOSSATORUM OPERATIO. In old English law, fosse-work; or the service of laboring, done by inhabitants and adjoining tenants, for the repair and maintenance of the ditches round a city or town, for which some paid a contribution, called *"fossagium."* Cowell.

FOSSATUM. A dyke, ditch, or trench; a place inclosed by a ditch; a moat; a canal.

FOSSE-WAY, or FOSSE. One of the four ancient Roman ways through England. Spelman.

FOSSELLUM. A small ditch. Cowell.

FOSTER PARENT. One who has performed the duties of a parent to the child of another by rearing the child as his own child; "foster child." In re Norman's Estate, 209 Minn. 19, 295 N.W. 63, 66.

FOSTERAGE. Care of a foster child, brother, sister, parent, etc.—one considered as holding the relationship indicated in consequence of nursing and rearing, though not related by blood. In re Norman's Estate, 295 N.W. 63, 66, 209 Minn. 19.

FOSTERING. A ancient custom in Ireland, in which persons put away their children to fosterers. Fostering was held to be a stronger alliance than blood, and the foster children participated in the fortunes of their foster fathers. Mozley & Whitley.

FOSTERLAND. Land given, assigned, or allotted to the finding of food or victuals for any person or persons; as in monasteries for the monks, etc. Cowell; Blount.

FOSTERLEAN. The remuneration fixed for the rearing of a foster child; also the jointure of a wife. Jacob.

FOUJDAR. In Hindu law, under the Mogul government a magistrate of the police over a large district, who took cognizance of all criminal matters within his jurisdiction, and sometimes was employed as receiver general of the revenues. Wharton.

FOUJDARRY COURT. In Hindu law, a tribunal for administering criminal law.

FOUND. A person is said to be found within a state when actually present therein. Patient removed to a sanitarium in county was "found" in county. In re Cash, 383 Ill. 409, 50 N.E.2d 487, 490. But only if a person is in a place voluntarily and not by reason of plaintiff's fraud, artifice, or trick for purpose of obtaining service. Shields v. Shields, 115 Mont. 140, 139 P.2d 528, 530, 531. It does not necessarily mean physical presence: defendant who, after removal of action for breach of contract to federal court, entered general appearance, defended on the merits, and filed counterclaim, was "found" in the district. Freeman v. Bee Mach. Co., Mass., 319 U.S. 448, 63 S.Ct. 1146, 1149, 87 L.Ed. 1509.

As applied to a corporation it is necessary that it be doing business in such state through an officer or agent or by statutory authority in such manner as to render it liable then to suit and to constructive or substituted service of process. Romaine v. Ins. Co., C.C.Tenn., 55 F. 751; Venner v. Pennsylvania Steel Co. of New Jersey, D.C.N.J., 250 F. 292, 295; Haskell v. Aluminum Co. of America, D.C.Mass., 14 F.2d 864, 867. And to such an extent that actual presence is established. Westor Theatres v. Warner Bros. Pictures, D.C.N.J., 41 F.Supp. 757, 760.

FOUNDATION. The founding or building of a college or hospital. The incorporation or endowment of a college or hospital is the foundation; and he who endows it with land or other property is the founder. Dartmouth College v. Woodward, 4 Wheat. 667, 4 L.Ed. 629; Seagrave's Appeal, 125 Pa. 362, 17 A. 412; Union Baptist Ass'n v. Hunn, 7 Tex.Civ.App. 249, 26 S.W. 755.

FOUNDED. Based upon; arising from, growing out of, or resting upon; as in the expressions "founded in fraud," "founded on a consideration," "founded on contract," and the like. In re Grant Shoe Co., C.C.A.N.Y., 130 F. 881, 66 C.C.A. 78; Palmer v. Preston, 45 Vt. 158, 12 Am.Rep. 191; Steele v. Hoe, 14 Adol. & El. 431; In re Morales, D.C.Fla., 105 F. 761.

FOUNDED ON. To serve as a base or basis for. Keen v. Mid-Continent Petroleum Corp., D.C.Iowa, 58 F.Supp. 915, 922.

FOUNDER. The person who endows an eleemosynary corporation or institution, or supplies the funds for its establishment. See Foundation.

FOUNDERS' SHARES. In English Company Law, shares issued to the founders of (or vendors to) a public company as a part of the consideration for the business, or concession, etc., taken over, and not forming a part of, the ordinary capital. As a rule, such shares only participate in profits after the payment of a fixed minimum dividend on paid-up capital. Encyc. Dict.

FOUNDEROSA. Founderous; out of repair, as a road. Cro. Car. 366.

FOUNDLING. A deserted or exposed infant; a child found without a parent or guardian, its relatives being unknown. It has a settlement in the district where found. State ex rel. Wilson v. Pierre, 155 La. 510, 99 So. 421.

FOUNDLING HOSPITALS. Charitable institutions which exist in most countries for taking care of infants forsaken by their parents, such being generally the offspring of illegal connections. The foundling hospital act in England is the 13 Geo. II. c. 29.

FOUR. Fr. In old French law, an oven or bakehouse. *Four banal,* an oven, owned by the seignior of the estate, to which the tenants were obliged to bring their bread for baking. Also the proprietary right to maintain such an oven.

FOUR CORNERS. The face of a written instrument.

That which is contained on the face of a deed (without any aid from the knowledge of the circumstances under which it is made) is said to be within its four corners, because every deed is still supposed to be written on one entire skin, and so to have but four corners.

To look at the *four corners* of an instrument is to examine the whole of it, so as to construe it as a whole, without reference to any one part more than another. 2 Smith, Lead.Cas. 295.

FOUR SEAS. The seas surrounding England. These were divided into the Western, including the Scotch and Irish; the Northern, or North sea; the Eastern, being the German ocean; the Southern, being the British channel.

FOURCHER. Fr. To fork. This was a method of delaying an action anciently resorted to by defendants when two of them were joined in the suit. Instead of appearing together, each would appear in turn and cast an essoin for the other, thus postponing the trial.

FOURIERISM. A form of socialism. See 1 Mill, Pol. Ec. 260.

FOURTEENTH AMENDMENT. The Fourteenth Amendment of the constitution of the United States.

It became a part of the organic law July 28, 1868, and its importance entitles it to special mention. It creates or at least recognizes for the first time a citizenship of the United States, as distinct from that of the states; forbids the making or enforcement by any state of any law abridging the privileges and immunities of citizens of the United States; and secures all "persons" against any state action which is either deprivation of life, liberty, or property without due process of law or denial of the equal protection of the laws.

FOWLS OF WARREN. Such fowls as are preserved under the game laws in warrens. According to Manwood, these are partridges and pheasants. According to Coke, they are partridges, rails, quails, woodcocks, pheasants, mallards, and herons. Co. Litt. 233.

FOX'S LIBEL ACT. In English law, this was the statute 52 Geo. III. c. 60, which secured to juries, upon the trial of indictments for libel, the right of pronouncing a general verdict of guilty or not guilty upon the whole matter in issue, and no longer bound them to find a verdict of guilty on proof of the publication of the paper charged to be a libel, and of the sense ascribed to it in the indictment. Wharton.

FOY. L. Fr. Faith; allegiance; fidelity.

FR. A Latin abbreviation for "fragmentum," a fragment, used in citations to the Digest or Pandects in the *Corpus Juris Civilis* of Justinian, the several extracts from juristic writings of which it is composed being so called.

FRACTIO. Lat. A breaking; division; fraction; a portion of a thing less than the whole.

FRACTION. A breaking, or breaking up; a fragment or broken part; a portion of a thing, less than the whole. Jory v. Palace Dry Goods Co., 30 Or. 196, 46 P. 786.

FRACTION OF A DAY. A portion of a day. The dividing a day. Generally, the law does not allow the fraction of a day. 2 Bl.Comm. 141.

FRACTIONAL. As applied to tracts of land, particularly townships, sections, quarter sections, and other divisions according to the government survey, and also mining claims, this term means that the exterior boundary lines are laid down to include the whole of such a division or such a claim, but that the tract in question does not measure up to the full extent or include the whole acreage, because a portion of it is cut off by an overlapping survey, a river or lake, or some other external interference. Tolleston Club v. State, 38 N.E. 214, 141 Ind. 197; Parke v. Meyer, 28 Ark. 287; Goltermann v. Schiermeyer, 111 Mo. 404, 19 S.W. 487. Any irregular division whether containing more or less than conventional amount of acreage. Graysonia-Nashville Lumber Co. v. Wright, 117 Ark. 151, 175 S.W. 405; South Florida Farms Co. v. Goodno, 84 Fla. 532, 94 So. 672, 675.

FRACTIONEM DIEI NON RECIPIT LEX. Lofft, 572. The law does not take notice of a portion of a day.

FRACTITIUM. Arable land. Mon. Angl.

FRACTURA NAVIUM. Lat. The breaking or wreck of ships; the same as *naufragium*, (*q. v.*)

FRAGMENTA. Lat. Fragments. A name sometimes applied (especially in citations) to the Digest or Pandects in the *Corpus Juris Civilis* of Justinian, as being made up of numerous extracts or "fragments" from the writings of various jurists. Mackeld. Rom. Law, § 74.

FRAIS. Fr. Expense; charges; costs. *Frais d'un procès*, costs of a suit.

FRAIS DE JUSTICE. In French and Canadian law, costs incurred incidentally to the action.

FRAIS JUSQU'À BORD. Fr. In French commercial law, expenses to the board; expenses incurred on a shipment of goods, in packing, cartage, commissions, etc., up to the point where they are actually put on board the vessel. Bartels v. Redfield, C.C.N.Y., 16 F. 336.

FRAME-UP. Conspiracy or plot, especially for evil purpose, as to incriminate person on false evidence. State v. Bissell, 106 Vt. 80, 170 A. 102, 108.

FRAMED. When used to describe evidence, word is generally accepted as implying that willful perjurers, suborned by and conspiring with parties in interest to litigation, are swearing or have sworn to matters without any basis in fact. Tri-State Transit Co. of Louisiana v. Westbrook, 207 Ark. 270, 180 S.W.2d 121, 125.

FRANC. A French coin of the value of a little over eighteen cents. Levy v. Cleveland, C., C. & St. L. Ry. Co., 210 App.Div. 422, 206 N.Y.S. 261, 262.

FRANC ALEU. In French feudal law, an allod; a free inheritance; or an estate held free of any services except such as were due to the sovereign.

FRANC TENANCIER. In French law, a freeholder.

FRANCHILANUS. A freeman. Chart. Hen. IV. A free tenant. Spelman.

FRANCHISE. A special privilege conferred by government on individual or corporation, and which does not belong to citizens of country generally of common right. Elliott v. City of Eugene, 135 Or. 108, 294 P. 358, 360. In England it is defined to be a royal privilege in the hands of a subject.

A "franchise," as used by Blackstone in defining quo warranto, (3 Com. 262 [4th Am. Ed.] 322), had reference to a royal privilege or branch of the king's prerogative subsisting in the hands of the subject, and must arise from the king's grant, or be held by prescription, but today we understand a franchise to be some special privilege conferred by government on an individual, natural or artificial, which is not enjoyed by its citizens in general. State v. Fernandez, 106 Fla. 779, 143 So. 638, 639, 86 A.L.R. 240.

In this country a franchise is a privilege or immunity of a public nature, which cannot be legally exercised without legislative grant. To be a corporation is a franchise. The various powers conferred on corporations are franchises. The execution of a policy of insurance by an insurance company, and the issuing a bank-note by an incorporated bank, are franchises. People v. Utica Ins. Co., 15 Johns., N.Y., 387, 8 Am.Dec. 243. But it does not embrace the property acquired by the exercise of the franchise. Bridgeport v. New York & N. H. R. Co., 36 Conn. 255, 4 Am.Rep. 63. Nor involve interest in land acquired by grantee. Whitbeck v. Funk, 140 Or. 70, 12 P.2d 1019, 1020. In a popular sense, the political rights of subjects and citizens are franchises, such as the right of suffrage, etc. Pierce v. Emery, 32 N.H. 484; State v. Black Diamond Co., 97 Ohio St. 24, 119 N.E. 195, 199, L.R.A.1918E, 352.

Elective Franchise. The right of suffrage; the right or privilege of voting in public elections.

Exclusive Franchise. See Exclusive Privilege or Franchise.

General and Special. The charter of a corporation is its "general" franchise, while a "special" franchise consists in any rights granted by the public to use property for a public use but with private profit. Lord v. Equitable Life Assur. Soc., 194 N.Y. 212, 87 N.E. 443, 22 L.R.A.,N.S., 420.

Personal Franchise. A franchise of corporate existence, or one which authorizes the formation and existence of a corporation, is sometimes called a "personal" franchise, as distinguished from a "property" franchise, which authorizes a corporation so formed to apply its property to some particular enterprise or exercise some special privilege in its employment, as, for example, to construct and operate a railroad. See Sandham v. Nye, 9 Misc.Rep. 541, 30 N.Y.S. 552.

Secondary Franchises. The franchise of corporate existence being sometimes called the "primary" franchise of a corporation, its "secondary" franchises are the special and peculiar rights, privileges, or grants which it may receive under its charter or from a municipal corporation, such as the right to use the public streets, exact tolls, collect fares, etc. State v. Topeka Water Co., 61 Kan. 547, 60 P. 337; Virginia Canon Toll Road Co. v. People, 22 Colo. 429, 45 P. 398, 37 L.R.A. 711. The franchises of a corporation are divisible into (1) corporate or general franchises; and (2) "special or secondary franchises." The former is the franchise to exist as a corporation, while the latter are certain rights and privileges conferred upon existing corporations. Gulf Refining Co. v. Cleveland Trust Co., 166 Miss. 759, 108 So. 158, 160.

Special Franchises. See Secondary Franchises, *supra.*

FRANCHISE TAX. A tax on the franchise of a corporation, that is, on the right and privilege of carrying on business in the character of a corporation, for the purposes for which it was created, and in the conditions which surround it. In re Commercial Safe Deposit Co. of Buffalo, 148 Misc. 527, 266 N.Y.S. 626.

Though the value of the franchise, for purposes of taxation, may be measured by the amount of business done, or the amount of earnings or dividends, or by the total value of the capital or stock of the corporation in excess of its tangible assets, a franchise tax is not a tax on either property, capital, stock, earnings, or dividends. Home Ins. Co. v. New York, 134 U.S. 594, 10 S.Ct. 593, 33 L.Ed. 1025; Worth v. Petersburg R. Co., 89 N.C. 305; People v. Knight, 174 N.Y. 475, 67 N.E. 65, 63 L.R.A. 87; Greene v. Louisville & I. R. Co., 244 U.S. 499, 37 S.Ct. 673, 678, 61 L.Ed. 1280, Ann.Cas.1917E, 88; American Refining Co. v. Staples, Tex.Com.App., 269 S.W. 420, 421. Nor a tax on franchise in technical sense, but on all intangible property of such a corporation, not otherwise taxed, used in state as component part of corporation's entire system. Western Union Telegraph Co. v. Weaver, D.C.Neb., 5 F.Supp. 493, 497.

It is tax on intangible values inhering to business and added value given to tangible property, being "ad valorem" as distinguished from "excise" or "privilege" tax. State Tax Commission v. Petroleum Exploration, 253 Ky. 119, 68 S.W.2d 777.

FRANCIA. France. Bract. fol. 427*b*.

FRANCIGENA. A man born in France. A designation formerly given to aliens in England.

See Frenchman.

FRANCUS. L. Lat. Free; a freeman; a Frank. Spelman.

FRANCUS BANCUS. Free bench (*q. v.*).

FRANCUS HOMO. In old European law. A free man. Domesday.

FRANCUS PLEGIUS. In old English law, a frank pledge, or free pledge. See Frank-Pledge.

FRANCUS TENENS. A freeholder. See Frank-Tenement.

FRANK, *v.* To send matter through the public mails free of postage, by a personal or official privilege.

FRANK, *adj.* In old English law, free. Occurring in several compounds.

FRANK-ALMOIGNE. In English law, free alms. A spiritual tenure whereby religious corporations, aggregate or sole, held lands of the donor to them and their successors forever.

They were discharged of all other except religious services, and the *trinoda necessitas.* It differs from tenure by divine service, in that the latter required the performance of certain divine services, whereas the former, as its name imports, is free. This tenure is expressly excepted in the 12 Car. II. c. 24, § 7, and therefore still subsists in some few instances. 2 Broom & H. Comm. 203.

FRANK BANK. In old English law, free bench. Litt. § 166; Co. Litt. 110*b*. See Free-Bench.

FRANK-CHASE. A liberty of free chase enjoyed by any one, whereby all other persons having ground within that compass are forbidden to cut down wood, etc., even in their own demesnes, to the prejudice of the owner of the liberty. Cowell. See Chase.

FRANK-FEE. Freehold lands exempted from all services, but not from homage; lands held otherwise than in ancient demesne. That which a man holds to himself and his heirs, and not by such service as is required in ancient demesne, according to the custom of the manor. Cowell.

FRANK FERM. In English law, a species of estate held in socage, said by Britton to be "lands and tenements whereof the nature of the fee is changed by feoffment out of chivalry for certain yearly services, and in respect whereof neither homage, ward, marriage, nor relief can be demanded." Britt. c. 66; 2 Bl.Comm. 80.

FRANK-FOLD. In old English law, free-fold; a privilege for the lord to have all the sheep of his tenants and the inhabitants within his seigniory, in his fold, in his demesnes, to manure his land. Keilw. 198.

FRANK-LAW. An obsolete expression signifying the rights and privileges of a citizen, or the liberties and civic rights of a freeman.

FRANK-MARRIAGE. A species of entailed estates, in English law, now grown out of use, but still capable of subsisting.

When tenements are given by one to another, together with a wife, who is a daughter or cousin of the donor, to hold in frank-marriage, the donees shall have the tenements to them and the heirs of their two bodies begotten, *i. e.,* in special tail. For the word "frank-marriage," *ex vi termini,* both creates and limits an inheritance, not only supplying words of descent, but also terms of procreation. The donees are liable to no service except fealty, and a reserved rent would be void, until the fourth degree of consanguinity be passed between the issues of the donor and donee, when they were capable by the law of the church of intermarrying. Litt. § 19; 2 Bl.Comm. 115.

FRANK-PLEDGE. In old English law, a pledge or surety for freemen; that is, the pledge, or corporate responsibility, of all the inhabitants of a tithing for the general good behavior of each free-born citizen above the age of fourteen, and for his being forthcoming to answer any infraction of the law. Termes de la Ley; Cowell.

FRANK-TENANT. A freeholder. Litt. § 91.

FRANK-TENEMENT. In English law, a free tenement, freeholding, or freehold. 2 Bl.Comm. 61, 62, 104; 1 Steph.Comm. 217; Bract. fol. 207. Used to denote both the tenure and the estate.

FRANKING PRIVILEGE. The privilege of sending certain matter through the public mails without payment of postage, in pursuance of a personal or official privilege.

FRANKLEYN (spelled, also, "Francling" and "Franklin"). A freeman; a freeholder; a gentleman. Blount; Cowell.

FRASSETUM. In old English law, a wood or wood-ground where ash-trees grow. Co. Litt. 4*b*.

FRATER. In the civil law, a brother. *Frater consanguineus,* a brother having the same father, but born of a different mother. *Frater uterinus,* a brother born of the same mother, but by a different father. *Frater nutricius,* a bastard brother.

FRATER FRATRI UTERINO NON SUCCEDET IN HÆREDITATE PATERNA. A brother shall not succeed a uterine brother in the paternal inheritance. 2 Bl.Comm. 223; Fortes. de Laud. c. 5. A maxim of the common law of England, now superseded by the statute 3 & 4 Wm. IV. c. 106, § 9. See Broom, Max. 530.

FRATERIA. In old records, a fraternity, brotherhood, or society of religious persons, who were mutually bound to pray for the good health and life, etc., of their living brethren, and the souls of those that were dead. Cowell.

FRATERNAL. Brotherly; relating or belonging to a fraternity or an association of persons formed for mutual aid and benefit, but not for profit. In re Mason Tire & Rubber Co., 56 App.D.C. 170, 11 F. 2d 556, 557.

FRATERNAL BENEFIT ASSOCIATION. One whose members have adopted the same, or a very similar, calling, avocation, or profession, or who are working in unison to accomplish some worthy object, and who for that reason have banded themselves together as an association or society to aid and assist one another, and to promote the common cause. Alpha Rho Alumni Ass'n v. City of New Brunswick, 126 N.J.L. 233, 18 A.2d 68, 70. An association having a representative form of government and a lodge system with a ritualistic form of work for the meeting of its chapters, or other subordinate bodies. Fain v. Feldman, 191 Ga. 519, 13 S.E.2d 179, 181. A society or voluntary association organized and carried on for the mutual aid and benefit of its members, not for profit; which ordinarily has a lodge system, a ritualistic form of work, and a representative government, makes provision for the payment of death benefits, and (sometimes) for benefits in case of accident, sickness, or old age, the funds therefor being derived from dues paid or assessments levied on the members. National Union v. Marlow, Mo., 74 F. 778, 21 C.C.A. 89; Walker v. Giddings, 103 Mich. 344, 61 N.W. 512.

FRATERNAL INSURANCE. The form of life (or accident) insurance furnished by a fraternal beneficial association, consisting in the payment to a member, or his heirs in case of death, of a stipulated sum of money, out of funds raised for that purpose by the payment of dues or assessments by all the members of the association.

FRATERNIA. A fraternity or brotherhood.

FRATERNITY. A body of men associated for their common interest, business or pleasure. Woman's Club of Little Falls v. Township of Little Falls, 20 N.J.Misc. 278, 26 A.2d 739, 741; Alpha Rho Alumni Ass'n v. City of New Brunswick, 126 N.J.L. 233, 18 A.2d 68, 71. Organizations composed of either or both sexes. State v. Allen, 189 Ind. 369, 127 N.E. 145, 146. Brotherly regard and sympathy for others. Donnelly v. Sovereign Camp W. O. W., 111 Neb. 499, 197 N.W. 125, 127.

In American colleges, a student organization, either a nationally chartered society comprising many affiliated chapters or a single chapter in one institution formed chiefly to promote friendship and welfare among the members, and usually having secret rites and a name consisting of Greek letters. Woman's Club of Little Falls v. Township of Little Falls, 20 N.J.Misc. 278, 26 A.2d 739, 741; Alpha Rho Alumni Ass'n v. City of New Brunswick, 126 N.J.L. 233, 18 A.2d 68, 71.

In old English law, "some people of a place united together in respect to a mystery or business into a company, and their laws and ordinances cannot bind strangers." Cuddon v. Eastwick, 1 Salk. 192.

FRATRES CONJURATI. Sworn brothers or companions for the defense of their sovereign, or for other purposes. Hoved. 445.

FRATRES PYES. In old English law, certain friars who wore white and black garments. Walsingham, 124.

FRATRIAGE. A younger brother's inheritance.

FRATRICIDE. One who has killed a brother or sister; also the killing of a brother or sister.

FRAUD. An intentional perversion of truth for the purpose of inducing another in reliance upon it to part with some valuable thing belonging to him or to surrender a legal right; a false representation of a matter of fact, whether by words or by conduct, by false or misleading allegations, or by concealment of that which should have been disclosed, which deceives and is intended to deceive another so that he shall act upon it to his legal injury. Brainerd Dispatch Newspaper Co. v. Crow Wing County, 196 Minn. 194, 264 N.W. 779, 780. Any kind of artifice employed by one person to deceive another. Goldstein v. Equitable Life Assur. Soc. of U. S., 160 Misc. 364, 289 N.Y.S. 1064, 1067. A generic term, embracing all multifarious means which human ingenuity can devise, and which are resorted to by one individual to get advantage over another by false suggestions or by suppression of truth, and includes all surprise, trick, cunning, dissembling, and any unfair way by which another is cheated. Johnson v. McDonald, 170 Okl. 117, 39 P.2d 150. "Bad faith" and "fraud" are synonymous, and also synonyms of dishonesty, infidelity, faithlessness, perfidy, unfairness, etc. Joiner v. Joiner, Tex.Civ.App., 87 S.W. 2d 903, 914, 915.

It consists of some deceitful practice or willful device, resorted to with intent to deprive another of his right, or in some manner to do him an injury. As distinguished from negligence, it is always positive, intentional. Maher v. Hibernia Ins. Co., 67 N.Y. 292; Alexander v. Church, 53 Conn. 561, 4 A. 103; Studer v. Bleistein, 115 N.Y. 316, 22 N.E. 243, 7 L.R.A. 702; McNair v. Southern States Finance Co., 191 N.C. 710, 133 S.E. 85, 88. It comprises all acts, omissions, and concealments involving a breach of a legal or equitable duty and resulting in damage to another. Coppo v. Coppo, 163 Misc. 249, 297 N.Y.S. 744, 750. And includes anything calculated to deceive, whether it be a single act or combination of circumstances, whether the suppression of truth or the suggestion of what is false, whether it be by direct falsehood or by innuendo, by speech or by silence, by word of mouth, or by look or gesture. People v. Gilmore, 345 Ill. 28, 177 N.E. 710, 717. Fraud, as applied to contracts, is the cause of an error bearing on a material part of the contract, created or continued by artifice, with design to obtain some unjust advantage to the one party, or to cause an inconvenience or loss to the other. Civil Code La. art. 1847. Strauss v. Insurance Co. of North America, 157 La. 661, 102 So. 861, 865; Jesse French Piano & Organ Co. v. Gibbon, Tex.Civ.App., 180 S. W. 1185, 1187.

Fraud, in the sense of a court of equity, properly includes all acts, omissions, and concealments which involve a breach of legal or equitable duty, trust, or confidence justly reposed, and are injurious to another, or by which an undue and unconscientious advantage is taken of another. 1 Story, Eq.Jur. § 187; Howard v. West Jersey & S. S. R. Co., 102 N.J.Eq. 517, 141 A. 755, 757.

Fraud is either *actual* or *constructive*. Actual fraud consists in deceit, artifice, trick, design, some direct and active operation of the mind; it includes cases of the intentional and successful employment of any cunning, deception, or artifice used to circumvent or cheat another; it is something said, done, or omitted by a person with the design of perpetrating what he knows to be a cheat or deception. Constructive fraud consists in any act of commission or omission contrary to legal or equitable duty, trust, or confidence justly reposed, which is contrary to good conscience and operates to the injury of another. Or, as otherwise defined, it is an act, statement or omission which operates as a virtual fraud on an individual, or which, if generally permitted, would be prejudicial to the public welfare, and yet may have been unconnected with any selfish or evil design. Or, according to Story, constructive frauds are such acts or contracts as, though not originating in any actual evil design or contrivance to perpetrate a positive fraud or injury upon other persons, are yet, by their tendency to deceive or mislead other persons, or to violate private or public confidence, or to impair or injure the public interests, deemed equally reprehensible with actual fraud. 1 Story, Eq.Jur. § 258. Code Ga.1882, § 3173 (Civ.Code 1910, § 4622); People v. Kelly, 35 Barb., N.Y., 457; Jackson v. Jackson, 47 Ga. 99; Massachusetts Ben. L. Ass'n v. Robinson, 104 Ga. 256, 30 S.E. 918, 42 L.R. A. 261; Allen v. United States Fidelity & Guaranty Co., 269 Ill. 234, 109 N.E. 1035, 1038.

Fraud is also classified as *fraud in fact* and *fraud in law*. The former is actual, positive, intentional fraud. Fraud disclosed by matters of fact, as distinguished from constructive fraud or fraud in law. McKibbin v. Martin, 64 Pa. 356, 3 Am.Rep. 588; Cook v. Burnham, 3 Kan.App. 27, 44 P. 447. Fraud in law is fraud in contemplation of law; fraud implied or inferred by law; fraud made out by construction of law, as distinguished from fraud found by a jury from matter of fact; constructive fraud *(q. v.)*. See 2 Kent, Comm. 512–532; Delaney v. Valentine, 154 N.Y. 692, 49 N.E. 65; Lovato v. Catron, 20 N.M. 168, 148 P. 490, 492, L.R.A.1915E, 451; Furst & Thomas v. Merritt, 190 N.C. 397, 130 S.E. 40, 43.

Fraud is also said to be *legal* or *positive*. The former is fraud made out by legal construction or inference, or the same thing as constructive fraud. Newell v. Wagness, 1 N. D. 62, 44 N.W. 1014. Positive fraud is the same thing as actual fraud. Douthitt v. Applegate, 33 Kan. 395, 6 P. 575, 52 Am.Rep. 533; Nocatee Fruit Co. v. Fosgate, C.C.A. Fla., 12 F.2d 250, 252.

Actionable fraud. See Actionable.

Extrinsic or *collateral fraud* justifying equitable relief against a judgment or decree means some intentional act or conduct by which the prevailing party has prevented the unsuccessful party from having a fair submission of the controversy. Farley v. Davis, 10 Wash.2d 62, 116 P.2d 263, 268.

Pious fraud is a subterfuge or evasion considered morally justifiable on account of the ends sought to be promoted; particularly applied to an evasion or disregard of the laws in the interests of religion or religious institutions, such as circumventing the statutes of mortmain.

Statute of Frauds. This is the common designation of a very celebrated English statute, (29 Car. II. c. 3,) passed in 1677, and which has been adopted, in a more or less modified form, in nearly all of the United States. Its chief characteristic is the provision that no suit or action shall be maintained on certain classes of contracts or engagements unless there shall be a note or memorandum thereof in writing signed by the party to be charged or by his authorized agent. Its object was to close the door to the numerous frauds and perjuries. It is more fully named as the "statute of frauds and perjuries." Smith v. Morton, 70 Okl. 157, 173 P. 520, 521; Housley v. Strawn Merchandise Co., Tex.Com.App., 291 S.W. 864, 867; Norman v. Bullock County Bank, 187 Ala. 33, 65 So. 371, 372; Garber v. Goldstein, 92 Conn. 226, 102 A. 605, 606.

FRAUD IN TREATY. Arises where a person is induced by some fraudulent representation or pretense to execute the very instrument intended to be executed but under a misrepresentation as to the contents thereof. Meyers v. Murphy, 181 Md. 98, 28 A.2d 861, 862.

FRAUD ORDER. A name given to orders issued by the postmaster general, under Rev.St. §§ 3929, 4041, 39 U.S.C.A. §§ 259, 732, for preventing the use of the mails as an agency for conducting schemes for obtaining money or property by means of false or fraudulent pretences, etc.

They are not restricted to schemes which lack all the elements of legitimate business, but the statute applies "when a business, even if otherwise legitimate, is systematically and designedly conducted upon the plan of inducing its patrons by means of false representations to part with their money in the belief that they are purchasing something different from, superior to, and worth more than, what is actually sold;" Harris v. Rosenberger, Mo., 145 F. 449, 16 C.C.A. 225, 13 L.R.A.,N.S., 762.

The fraud order is issued to the postmaster of the office through which the person affected by it receives his mail. It forbids the post-master to pay any postal money order to the specified person, and instructs the postmaster to return all letters to the senders if practicable, or if not, to the dead letter office, stamped in either case with the word "fraudulent." The method of testing the validity of the fraud order is to apply to the federal court for an injunction to restrain the postmaster from executing it. The decision of the postmaster-general is not the exercise of a judicial function; if he exceeds his jurisdiction, the party injured may have relief in equity; Degge v. Hitchcock, 229 U.S. 162, 33 S.Ct. 639, 57 L.Ed. 1135.

FRAUDARE. Lat. In the civil law, to deceive, cheat, or impose upon; to defraud.

FRAUDULENT. Based on fraud; proceeding from or characterized by fraud; tainted by fraud; done, made, or effected with a purpose or design to carry out a fraud. For "False and Fraudulent" and "False or Fraudulent Claim," see those titles.

FRAUDULENT ALIENATION. In a general sense, the transfer of property with an intent to defraud creditors, lienors, or others. In a particular sense, the act of an administrator who wastes the assets of the estate by giving them away or selling at a gross undervalue. Rhame v. Lewis, 13 Rich.Eq., S.C., 269.

FRAUDULENT ALIENEE. One who knowingly receives from an administrator assets of the estate under circumstances which make it a fraudulent alienation on the part of the administrator. Rhame v. Lewis, 13 Rich.Eq., S.C., 269.

FRAUDULENT CONCEALMENT. The hiding or suppression of a material fact or circumstance which the party is legally or morally bound to disclose. Magee v. Insurance Co., 92 U.S. 93, 23 L.Ed. 699; Small v. Graves, 7 Barb., N.Y., 578.

The test of whether failure to disclose material facts constitutes fraud is the existence of a duty, legal or equitable, arising from the relation of the parties; failure to disclose a material fact with intent to mislead or defraud under such circumstances being equivalent to an actual "fraudulent concealment." Newell Bros. v. Hanson, 97 Vt. 297, 123 A. 208, 210.

Fraudulent concealment justifying a rescission of a contract is the intentional concealment of some fact known to the party charged, which is material for the party injured to know to prevent being defrauded; the concealment of a fact which one is bound to disclose being the equivalent of an indirect representation that such fact does not exist. Long v. Martin, Tex.Civ.App., 234 S.W. 91, 94.

To suspend running of limitations, it means employment of artifice, planned to prevent inquiry or escape investigation and mislead or hinder acquirement of information disclosing a right of action, and acts relied on must be of an affirmative character and fraudulent. McNaughton v. Rockford State Bank, 261 Mich. 265, 246 N.W. 84, 86.

FRAUDULENT CONVERSION. Receiving into possession money or property of another and fraudulently withholding, converting, or applying the same to or for one's own use and benefit, or to use and benefit of any person other than the one to whom the money or property belongs. Commonwealth v. Mitchneck, 130 Pa.Super. 433, 198 A. 463, 464.

FRAUDULENT CONVEYANCE. A conveyance or transfer of property, the object of which is to defraud a creditor, or hinder or delay him, or to put such property beyond his reach. Seymour v. Wilson, 14 N.Y. 569; Lockyer v. De Hart, 6 N.J.L. 458; Surratt v. Eskridge, 131 Va. 325, 108 S.E. 677, 679; Dean v. Davis, 242 U.S. 438, 37 S.Ct. 130, 61 L.Ed. 419. Conveyance made with intent to avoid some duty or debt due by or incumbent on person making transfer. Farmers Elevator Co. v. Peck, 134 Neb. 305, 278 N.W. 499, 501.

FRAUDULENT CONVEYANCES, STATUTES OF, OR AGAINST. The name given to two celebrated English statutes,—the statute 13 Eliz. c. 5, made perpetual by 29 Eliz. c. 5; and the statute 27 Eliz. c. 4, made perpetual by 29 Eliz. c. 18.

FRAUDULENT OR DISHONEST ACT. One which involves bad faith, a breach of honesty, a want of integrity, or moral turpitude. Hartford Acc. & Indem. Co. v. Singer, 185 Va. 620, 39 S.E. 2d 505, 507, 508.

FRAUDULENT PREFERENCES. In English law, every conveyance or transfer of property or charge thereon made, every judgment made, every obligation incurred, and every judicial proceeding taken or suffered by any person unable to pay his debts as they become due from his own moneys, in favor of any creditor, with a view of giving such creditor a preference over other creditors, shall be deemed fraudulent and void if the debtor become bankrupt within three months. 32 & 33 Vict. c. 71, § 92.

FRAUDULENT REPRESENTATION. A false statement as to material fact, made with intent that another rely thereon, which is believed by other party and on which he relies and by which he is induced to act and does act to his injury, and statement is fraudulent if speaker knows statement to be false or if it is made with utter disregard of its truth or falsity. Osborne v. Simmons, Mo.App., 23 S.W.2d 1102, 1104.

As basis for law action, establishment of representation, falsity, scienter, deception, and injury, is required. Gray v. Shell Petroleum Corporation, 212 Iowa, 825, 237 N.W. 460, 463.

But a promise made without intent to perform constitutes "fraudulent representation," which generally affords ground for rescission. Mitchell v. Mitchell, 206 N.C. 546, 174 S.E. 447, 448.

FRAUNC, FRAUNCHE, FRAUNKE. See Frank.

FRAUNCHISE. L. Fr. A franchise.

FRAUS. Lat. Fraud. More commonly called, in the civil law, "*dolus*," and "*dolus malus*" (*q. v.*). A distinction, however, was sometimes made between "*fraus*" and "*dolus;*" the former being held to be of the most extensive import. Calvin.

FRAUS DANS LOCUM CONTRACTUI. A misrepresentation or concealment of some fact that is material to the contract, and had the truth regarding which been known the contract would not have been made as made, is called a "fraud *dans locum contractui;*" *i. e.*, a fraud occasioning the contract, or giving place or occasion for the contract.

FRAUS EST CELARE FRAUDEM. It is a fraud to conceal a fraud. 1 Vern. 240; 1 Story, Eq. Jur. §§ 389, 390.

FRAUS EST ODIOSA ET NON PRÆSUMENDA. Fraud is odious, and not to be presumed. Cro. Car. 550.

FRAUS ET DOLUS NEMINI PATROCINARI DEBENT. Fraud and deceit should defend or excuse no man. 3 Coke, 78; Fleta, lib. 1, c. 13, § 15; Id. lib. 6, c. 6, § 5.

FRAUS ET JUS NUNQUAM COHABITANT. Wing. 680. Fraud and justice never dwell together.

FRAUS LATET IN GENERALIBUS. Fraud lies hid in general expressions.

FRAUS LEGIS. Lat. In the civil law, fraud of law; fraud upon law. See In Fraudem Legis.

FRAUS MERETUR FRAUDEM. Plowd. 100. Fraud merits fraud.

FRAXINETUM. In old English law, a wood of ashes; a place where ashes grow. Co. Litt. 4*b;* Shep. Touch. 95.

FRAY. See Affray.

FRECTUM. In old English law, freight. *Quoad frectum navium suarum,* as to the freight of his vessels. Blount.

FREDNITE. In old English law, a liberty to hold courts and take up the fines for beating and wounding. To be free from fines. Cowell.

FREDSTOLE. Sanctuaries; seats of peace.

FREDUM. A fine paid for obtaining pardon when the peace had been broken. Spelman; Blount. A sum paid the magistrate for protection against the right of revenge.

FREDWIT, or FREDWITE. A liberty to hold courts and take up the fines for beating and wounding. Jacob, Law Dict.

FREE. Not subject to legal constraint of another.

Unconstrained; having power to follow the dictates of his own will. Not subject to the dominion of another. Not compelled to involuntary servitude. Used in this sense as opposed to "slave."

Not bound to service for a fixed term of years; in distinction to being bound as an apprentice.

Enjoying full civic rights.

Available to all citizens alike without charge; as a free school.

Available for public use without charge or toll; as a free bridge.

Not despotic; assuring liberty; defending individual rights against encroachment by any person or class; instituted by a free people; said of governments, institutions, etc. Webster.

Certain, and also consistent with an honorable degree in life; as free services, in the feudal law.

Confined to the person possessing, instead of being shared with others; as a free fishery.

Not engaged in a war as belligerent or ally; neutral; as in the maxim, "Free ships make free goods."

FREE ALMS. The name of a species of tenure. See Frank-almoigne.

FREE AND CLEAR (and like phrases). The title to property is said to be "free and clear" when it is not incumbered by any liens; but it is said that an agreement to convey land "free and clear" is satisfied by a conveyance passing a good title. Meyer v. Madreperla, 68 N.J.L. 258, 53 A. 477, 96 Am.St.Rep. 536; Smith v. Toth, 61 Ind.App. 42, 111 N.E. 442, 444; Grisso v. Milsey, 104 Okl. 173, 230 P. 883, 889.

FREE AND EQUAL. As used in a constitutional provision that election shall be free and equal, the word "free" means that every one entitled to vote should have a reasonable opportunity to do so, a reasonable manner of doing so, etc., and the word "equal" means that every vote cast should have its decisive effect in the selection or choice to be made at the election. McKinney v. Barker, 180 Ky. 526, 203 S.W. 303, 304, L.R.A.1918E, 581. The term means that the voter shall not be physically restrained in the exercise of his right of franchise, by either civil or military authority, and that every voter shall have the same right as every other voter. Asher v. Arnett, 280 Ky. 347, 132 S.W.2d 772, 775.

A "free and equal" election is one at which every person entitled to vote may do so if he desires, although it can hardly be said that, if only a few are prevented from voting, the election is not free and equal in the constitutional sense. Wallbrecht v. Ingram, 164 Ky. 463, 175 S.W. 1022, 1026.

It is the essence of free elections that the right of suffrage be untrammeled and unfettered, and that the ballot represent and express the electors' own intelligent judgment and conscience, and there can be no "free election" unless there is freedom of opinion. An election to be free must be without coercion of any description or any deterrent from the elector's exercise of his free will by means of any intimidation or influence whatever, although there is no violence or physical coercion. Neelley v. Farr, 61 Colo. 485, 158 P. 458, 467, Ann.Cas.1918A, 23.

FREE-BENCH. A widow's dower out of copyholds to which she is entitled by the custom of some manors. It is regarded as an excrescence growing out of the husband's interest, and is indeed a continuance of his estate. Wharton.

FREE-BORD. In old records, an allowance of land over and above a certain limit or boundary, as so much beyond or without a fence. Cowell; Blount. The right of claiming that quantity. Termes de la Ley.

FREE BOROUGH MEN. Such great men as did not engage, like the frank-pledge men, for their decennier. Jacob.

FREE CHAPEL. In English ecclesiastical law, a place of worship, so called because not liable to the visitation of the ordinary. It is always of royal foundation, or founded at least by private persons to whom the crown has granted the privilege. 1 Burn, Ecc. Law, 298.

FREE COURSE. In admiralty law, a vessel having the wind from a favorable quarter is said to sail on a "free course," or said to be "going free" when she has a fair (following) wind and her yards braced in. The Queen Elizabeth, D.C.N.Y., 100 F. 876.

FREE ELECTION. Where each voter is allowed to cast his ballot as his own conscience dictates. Moran v. Bowley, 347 Ill. 148, 179 N.E. 526, 531.

See Free and Equal, *supra.*

FREE ENTERPRISE. The right to conduct a legitimate business for profit. Lafayette Dramatic Productions v. Ferentz, 305 Mich. 193, 9 N.W.2d 57, 62, 145 A.L.R. 1158.

FREE ENTRY, EGRESS, AND REGRESS. An expression used to denote that a person has the right to go on land again and again as often as may be reasonably necessary. Thus, in the case of a tenant entitled to emblements.

FREE FISHERY. See Fishery.

FREE ICE. All ice in navigable streams not included within that authorized to be appropriated is sometimes called "free" ice, and does not belong to the adjacent riparian owners, but to the person who first appropriates it. Hudson River Ice Co. v. Brady, 158 App.Div. 142, 142 N.Y.S. 819, 821.

FREE LAW. A term formerly used in England to designate the freedom of civil rights enjoyed by freemen. It was liable to forfeiture on conviction of treason or an infamous crime. McCafferty v. Guyer, 59 Pa. 116.

FREE LOVE. Consorting with opposite sex at pleasure without marriage. Robinson v. Casey, Tex.Civ.App., 272 S.W. 536, 538.

FREE MEN. Before the Norman Conquest, a free man might be a man of small estate dependent on a lord. Every man, not himself a lord, was bound to have a lord or be treated as unworthy of a free man's right. Among free men there was a difference in their estimation for *Wergild.* See Liber Homo.

FREE ON BOARD. Means that the subject of sale is to be loaded for shipment without expense to the buyer. Olsen v. McMaken & Pentzien, 139 Neb. 506, 297 N.W. 830, 832.

FREE PASS. The power of riding over a railroad without payment of the customary fare. Coco v. Oden, 143 La. 718, 79 So. 287, 288, 8 A.L.R. 679; Tripp v. Michigan Cent. R. Co., C.C.A.Mich., 238 F. 449, 458, L.R.A.1918A, 758.

FREE SCHOOL. Where no charge is made for tuition. Vincent v. County Board of Education of Talladega County, 222 Ala. 216, 131 So. 893, 894.

FREE SERVICES. In feudal and old English law, such feudal services as were not unbecoming the character of a soldier or a freeman to perform; as to serve under his lord in the wars, to pay a sum of money, and the like. 2 Bl.Comm. 60, 61.

FREE SHAREHOLDERS. The free shareholders of a building and loan association are subscribers to its capital stock who are not borrowers from the association. Steinberger v. Independent B. & S. Ass'n, 84 Md. 625, 36 A. 439.

FREE SHIPS. In international law, ships of a neutral nation. The phrase "free ships shall make free goods" is often inserted in treaties, meaning that goods, even though belonging to an enemy, shall not be seized or confiscated, if found in neutral ships. Wheat. Int. Law, 507, et seq.

FREE SOCAGE. See Socage.

FREE TENURE. Tenure by free services; freehold tenure.

FREE TIME. Period that railroad car may remain unloaded before demurrage charges begin to accrue. Lehigh Valley R. Co. v. Maas & Waldstein Co., 102 N.J.L. 332, 131 A. 884; Central of Georgia Ry. Co. v. Leverette, 34 Ga.App. 304, 129 S.E. 292, 293.

FREE WARREN. See Warren.

FREE WHITE PERSONS. "Free white persons" referred to in Naturalization Act, as amended by Act July 14, 1870, has meaning naturally given to it when first used in 1 Stat. 103, c. 3, meaning all persons belonging to the European races then commonly counted as white, and their descendants, including such descendants in other countries to which they have emigrated.

It includes all European Jews, more or less intermixed with peoples of Celtic, Scandinavian, Teutonic, Iberian, Latin, Greek, and Slavic descent. It includes Magyars, Lapps, and Finns, and the Basques and Albanians. It includes the mixed Latin, Celtic-Iberian, and Moorish inhabitants of Spain and Portugal, the mixed Greek, Latin, Phoenician, and North African inhabitants of Sicily, and the mixed Slav and Tarter inhabitants of South Russia. It does not mean Caucasian race, Aryan race, or Indo-European races, nor the mixed Indo-European, Dravidian, Semitic and Mongolian peoples who inhabit Persia. A Syrian of Asiatic birth and descent will not be entitled to become a naturalized citizen of the United States as being a free white person. Ex parte Shahid, D.C.S.C., 205 F. 812, 813; United States v. Cartozian, D.C.Or., 6 F.2d 919, 921; Ex parte Dow, D.C.S.C., 211 F. 486, 487; In re En Sk Song, D.C.Cal., 271 F. 23. Nor a native-born Filipino. U. S. v. Javier, 22 F.2d 879, 880, 57 App.D.C. 303. Nor a native of India who belonged to Hindu race. Kharaiti Ram Samras v. United States, C.C.A.Cal., 125 F.2d 879, 881.

FREE WOMAN OF COLOR. Term, up to the time of the Civil War, applied to all persons not of the white race, including Indians. Sunseri v. Cassagne, 191 La. 209, 185 So. 1, 4.

FREEDMAN. In Roman law, one who was set free from a state of bondage; an emancipated slave. The word is used in the same sense in the United States, respecting negroes who were formerly slaves. Fairfield v. Lawson, 50 Conn. 513, 47 Am.Rep. 669; Davenport v. Caldwell, 10 S.C. 333.

FREEDOM. The state of being free; liberty; self-determination; absence of restraint; the opposite of slavery.

The power of acting, in the character of a moral personality, according to the dictates of the will, without other check, hindrance, or prohibition than such as may be imposed by just and necessary laws and the duties of social life.

The prevalence, in the government and constitution of a country, of such a system of laws and institutions as secure civil liberty to the individual citizen.

FREEDOM OF RELIGION. Embraces the concept of freedom to believe and freedom to act, the first of which is absolute, but the second of which remains subject to regulation for protection of society. Oney v. Oklahoma City, C.C.A.Okl., 120 F. 2d 861, 865.

FREEDOM OF SPEECH AND OF THE PRESS. See Liberty.

FREEDOM OF THE CITY. In English law, this phrase signifies immunity from county jurisdiction, and the privilege of corporate taxation and self-government held under a charter from the crown. This freedom is enjoyed of right, subject to the provision of the charter, and is often conferred as an honor on princes and other distinguished individuals. The freedom of a city carries the parliamentary franchise. Encyc. Dict. The rights and privileges possessed by the burgesses or freemen of a municipal corporation under the old English law; now of little importance, and conferred chiefly as a mark of honor. See 11 Chic. L. J. 357.

The phrase has no place in American law, and as frequently used in addresses of welcome made to organizations visiting an American city, particularly by mayors, has no meaning whatever except as an expression of good will.

The form of the grant made by the city of New York to Andrew Hamilton of Philadelphia as quoted at large in 13 Law Notes 150.

FREEHOLD. An estate for life or in fee. Intermountain Realty Co. v. Allen, 60 Idaho 228, 90 P. 2d 704, 706, 122 A.L.R. 647.

A "freehold estate" is a right of title to land Cohn v. Litwin, 311 Ill.App. 55, 35 N.E.2d 410, 413.

An estate in land or other real property, of uncertain duration; that is, either of inheritance or which may possibly last for the life of the tenant at the least, (as distinguished from a leasehold;) and held by a free tenure, (as distinguished from copyhold or villeinage.) Nevitt v. Woodburn, 175 Ill. 376, 51 N.E. 593; Railroad Co. v. Hemphill, 35 Miss. 22; Ralston Steel Car Co. v. Ralston, 112 Ohio St. 306, 147 N.E. 513, 516, 39 A.L.R. 334; Lakeside Irr. Co. v. Markham Irr. Co., 116 Tex. 65, 285 S.W. 593, 596.

An oil and gas lease. Cravens v. Hubble, 375 Ill. 51, 30 N.E.2d 622, 623.

A 99-year lease renewable forever is a "freehold estate". Baltimore & O. R. Co. v. Carman, 71 Ohio App. 508, 50 N.E.2d 358, 359.

Such an interest in lands of frank-tenement as may endure not only during the owner's life, but which is cast after his death upon the persons who successively represent him, according to certain rules elsewhere explained. Such persons are called "heirs," and he whom they thus represent, the "ancestor." When the interest extends beyond the ancestor's life, it is called a "freehold of inheritance," and, when it only endures for the ancestor's life, it is a freehold not of inheritance.

An estate to be a freehold must possess these two qualities: (1) Immobility, that is, the property must be either land or some interest issuing out of or annexed to land; and (2) indeterminate duration, for, if the utmost period of time to which an estate can endure be fixed and determined, it cannot be a freehold. Wharton.

Freehold *in deed* is the real possession of land or tenements in fee, fee-tail, or for life. Freehold *in law* is the right to such tenements before entry. The term has also been applied to those offices which a man holds in fee or for life. Mozl. & W. Dict.; 1 Washb. R. P. 71, 637. See Gage v. Scales, 100 Ill. 221; State v. Ragland, 75 N.C. 12, L.R. 11 Eq. 454; Liberum Tenementum.

Determinable freeholds are estates for life, which may determine upon future contingencies before the life for which they are created expires, as if an estate be granted to a woman during her widowhood, or to a man until he be promoted to a benefice. In these and similar cases, whenever the contingency happens,—when the widow marries, or when the grantee obtains the benefice,—the respective estates are absolutely determined and gone. Yet, while they subsist, they are reckoned estates for life; because they may by possibility last for life, if the contingencies upon which they are to determine do not sooner happen. 2 Bl. Comm. 121.

Freehold in law is a freehold which has descended to a man, upon which he may enter at pleasure, but which he has not entered on. Termes de la Ley.

FREEHOLD LAND SOCIETIES. Societies in England designed for the purpose of enabling mechanics, artisans, and other workingmen to purchase at the least possible price a piece of freehold land of a sufficient yearly value to entitle the owner to the elective franchise for the county in which the land is situated. Wharton.

FREEHOLDER. One having title to realty. State ex rel. Peterson v. City of Fraser, 191 Minn. 427, 254 N.W. 776. Either of inheritance or for life. Warren v. Chouteau County, 82 Mont. 115, 265 P. 676, 680. Either legal or equitable title. Daniels v. Fossas, 152 Wash. 516, 278 P. 412, 413.

A person who possesses a freehold estate. Shively v. Lankford, 174 Mo. 535, 74 S.W. 835. Statutory meaning not infrequently differs from common law meaning of the term. Payne v. Fiscal Court of Carlisle County, 200 Ky. 41, 252 S.W. 127, 129; In re Consolidation of School Dists. in Blue Earth County, 140 Minn. 475, 168 N.W. 552; Gordon v. White, 33 S.D. 234, 145 N.W. 439.

FREEMAN. A person in the possession and enjoyment of all the civil and political rights accorded to the people under a free government.

In the Roman law, it denoted one who was either born free or emancipated, and was the opposite of "slave." In feudal law, it designated an allodial proprietor, as distinguished from a vassal or feudal tenant. (And so in Pennsylvania colonial law. Fry's Election Case, 71 Pa. 308, 10 Am.Rep. 698.) In old English law, the word described a freeholder or tenant by free services; one who was not a villein. In modern legal phraseology, it is the appellation of a member of a city or borough having the right of suffrage, or a member of any municipal corporation invested with full civic rights.

FREEMAN'S ROLL. A list of persons admitted as burgesses or freemen for the purposes of the rights reserved by the municipal corporation act, (5 & 6 Wm. IV. c. 76.) Distinguished from the Burgess Roll. 3 Steph.Comm. 197. The term was used, in early colonial history, in some of the American colonies.

FREIGHT. Freight is properly the price or compensation paid for the transportation of goods by a carrier, at sea, from port to port. The Bill, D. C.Md., 55 F.Supp. 780, 783. But the term is also used to denote the hire paid for the carriage of goods on land from place to place, (usually by a railroad company, not an express company,) or on inland streams or lakes. The name is also applied to the goods or merchandise transported by any of the above means. Brittan v. Barnaby, 21 How. 533, 16 L.Ed. 177; Christie v. Davis Coal Co., D.C.N.Y., 95 F. 837, 838; Paradise v. Sun Mut. Ins. Co., 6 La.Ann. 596.

The sum agreed on for the hire of a ship, entirely or in part, for the carriage of goods from one port to another. 13 East, 300. All rewards or compensation paid for the use of ships. Giles v. Cynthia, 1 Pet.Adm. 206, Fed.Cas.No. 5,424.

The reward, if any, to be paid for its carriage is called "freightage;" the person who delivers the freight to the carrier is called the "consignor;" and the person to whom it is to be delivered is called the "consignee." Civil Code Cal. § 2110; Comp.Laws N.D.1913, § 6197; Comp.Laws S.D. 1929, § 1119.

Property carried is called "freight." Lyman-Richey Sand & Gravel Co. v. State, 123 Neb. 674, 243 N.W. 891, 893, 83 A.L.R. 1301.

"Dead freight" is money payable by a person who has chartered a ship and only partly loaded her, in respect of the loss of freight caused to the ship-owner by the deficiency of cargo. L.R. 2 H.L. Sc. 128; The Rosemary, C. C.A.Miss., 277 F. 674, 678.

FREIGHT BOOKING. The making of specific arrangements for the transportation of goods by particular vessel in advance of its sailing day. Iwai & Co., Limited, v. Hercules Powder Co., 162 Ga. 795, 134 S.E. 763, 765.

FREIGHT CAR. A railroad car adapted to the transportation from one point to another of movable articles of every kind, character, and description, and a box car while so used is at least temporarily a car carrying freight. State v. Jones, 84 W.Va. 85, 99 S.E. 271, 274.

FREIGHT IS THE MOTHER OF WAGES. 2 Show. 283; 3 Kent, Comm. 196. Where a voyage is broken up by *vis major,* and no freight earned, no wages, *eo nomine,* are due.

FREIGHT THEN PENDING. Earnings of the voyage. The C. F. Coughlin, D.C.N.Y., 25 F.Supp. 649, 650.

FREIGHT TRAIN. A train that carries freight alone, having a caboose attached for use of crew. Arizona Eastern R. Co. v. State, 29 Ariz. 446, 242 P. 870, 871; Mammoth Cave R. Co. v. Commonwealth, 176 Ky. 747, 197 S.W. 406, 407.

FREIGHTER. In maritime law, the party by whom a vessel is engaged or chartered; otherwise called the "charterer." 2 Steph. Comm. 148. In French law, the owner of a vessel is called the "freighter" (*fréteur*); the merchant who hires it is called the "affreighter" (*affréteur*). Emerig. Tr. des Ass. ch. 11, § 3.

FRENCH POOL. A system of gambling, especially on horse races, now generally known as "pari mutuel" (*q. v.*).

FRENCHMAN. In early times, in English law, this term was applied to every stranger or "outlandish" man. Bract. lib. 3, tr. 2, c. 15.

FRENDLESMAN. Sax. An outlaw. So called because on his outlawry he was denied all help of friends after certain days. Cowell; Blount.

FRENDWITE. In old English law, a mulct or fine exacted from him who harbored an outlawed friend. Cowell; Tomlins.

FRENETICUS. In old English law, a madman, or person in a frenzy. Fleta, lib. 1, c. 36.

FREOBORGH. A free-surety, or free-pledge. Spelman. See Frank-Pledge.

FREOLING. (Sax. *freoh,* free, plus *ling,* progeny.) A freeman born. Wharton. See Frilingi.

FREQUENT, *v.* To visit often; to resort to often or habitually. Green v. State, 109 Ind. 175, 9 N.E. 781; Ex parte Werner, 46 R.I. 1, 124 A. 195, 196.

FREQUENTER. Any person not an employee who may go in or be in place of employment or public building under circumstances which render him other than trespasser. Tomlin v. Chicago, M., St. P. & P. Ry. Co., 220 Wis. 325, 265 N.W. 72.

FREQUENTIA ACTUS MULTUM OPERATUR. The frequency of an act effects much. 4 Coke, 78; Wing. Max. p. 719, max. 192. A continual usage is of great effect to establish a right.

FRÈRE. Fr. A brother. *Frère eyne,* elder brother. *Frère puisne,* younger brother. Britt. c. 75.

FRESCA. In old records, fresh water, or rain and land flood.

FRESH. Immediate; recent; following without any material interval.

FRESH DISSEISIN. By the ancient common law, where a man had been disseised, he was allowed to right himself by force, by ejecting the disseisor from the premises, without resort to law, provided this was done forthwith, while the disseisin was *fresh, (flagrante disseisina.)* Bract. fol. 162*b*. No particular time was limited for doing this, but Bracton suggested it should be fifteen days. Id. fol. 163. See Britt. cc. 32, 43, 44, 65.

FRESH FINE. In old English law, a fine that had been levied within a year past. St. Westm. 2, c. 45; Cowell.

FRESH FORCE. Force done within forty days. Fitzh. Nat. Brev. 7; Old Nat. Brev. 4. The heir or reversioner in a case of disseisin by *fresh force* was allowed a remedy in chancery by bill before the mayor. Cowell.

FRESH PURSUIT. A pursuit instituted immediately and with intent to reclaim or recapture, after an animal escaped, a thief flying with stolen goods, etc. People v. Pool, 27 Cal. 578; White v. State, 70 Miss. 253, 11 So. 632.

FRESH SUIT. In old English law, immediate and unremitting pursuit of an escaping thief. "Such a present and earnest following of a robber as never ceases from the time of the robbery until apprehension." Staundef, P. C. lib. 3, cc. 10, 12; 1 Bl. Comm. 297.

FRESHET. A flood, or overflowing of a river, by means of rains or melted snow; an inundation. Stover v. Insurance Co., 3 Phila., Pa., 42; Harris v. Social Mfg. Co., 9 R.I. 99, 11 Am.Rep. 224.

FRET. Fr. In French marine law, freight. Ord. Mar. liv. 3, tit. 3.

FRÉTER. Fr. In French marine law, to freight a ship; to let it. Emerig. Tr. des Ass. c. 11, § 3.

FRÉTEUR. Fr. In French marine law, freighter. The owner of a ship, who lets it to the merchant. Emerig. Tr. des Ass. c. 11, § 3.

FRETTUM, FRECTUM. In old English law, the freight of a ship; freight money. Cowell.

FRETUM. Lat. A strait.

FRETUM BRITANNICUM. The strait between Dover and Calais.

FRIARS. An order of religious persons, of whom there were four principal branches, viz.: (1) Minors, Grey Friars, or Franciscans; (2) Augustines; (3) Dominicans, or Black Friars; (4) White Friars, or Carmelites, from whom the rest descend. Wharton.

FRIBURGH. (Also, Frithborg, Frithborgh, Friborg, Froborg, and Freoburgh.) (Sax.) A kind of frank-pledge whereby the principal men were bound for themselves and servants. Fleta, lib. 1, cap. 47. Cowell says it is the same as frank-pledge.

FRIBUSCULUM. In the civil law, a temporary separation between husband and wife, caused by a quarrel or estrangement, but not amounting to a divorce, because not accompanied with an intention to dissolve the marriage.

FRIDBORG, FRITHBORG. Frank-pledge. Cowell. Security for the peace. Spelman.

FRIDHBURGUS. In old English law, a kind of frank-pledge, by which the lords or principal men were made responsible for their dependents or servants. Bract. fol. 124*b*.

FRIEND. One favorably disposed. Ned v. Robinson, 181 Okl. 507, 74 P.2d 1156. Varying in degree from greatest intimacy to acquaintance more or less casual. United States Trust Co. of Newark v. Montclair Trust Co., 133 N.J.Eq. 579, 33 A.2d 901, 903.

FRIEND OF THE COURT. See Amicus Curiæ.

FRIENDLESS MAN. In old English law, an outlaw; so called because he was denied all help of friends. Bract. lib. 3, tr. 2, c. 12.

FRIENDLY FIRE. Fire burning in place where it was intended to burn, although damages may result. Progress Laundry & Cleaning Co. v. Reciprocal Exchange, Tex.Civ.App., 109 S.W.2d 226, 227.

FRIENDLY SOCIETIES. In English law, associations supported by subscription, for the relief and maintenance of the members, or their wives, children, relatives, and nominees, in sickness, infancy, advanced age, widowhood, etc. The statutes regulating these societies were consolidated and amended by St. 38 & 39 Vict. c. 60. Wharton.

FRIENDLY SUIT. A suit brought by a creditor in chancery against an executor or administrator, being really a suit by the executor or administrator, in the name of a creditor, against himself, in order to compel the creditors to take an equal distribution of the assets. 2 Williams, Ex'rs, 1915.

Also any suit instituted by agreement between the parties to obtain the opinion of the court upon some doubtful question in which they are interested.

FRIGIDITY. Impotence. Johnson. The term in this sense is obsolete. Webster's New Int. Dict.

FRILINGI. Persons of free descent, or freemen born; the middle class of persons among the Saxons. Spelman. See Freoling.

FRISCUS. Fresh uncultivated ground. Mon. Angl. t. 2, p. 56. Fresh; not salt. Reg. Orig. 97. Recent or new. See Fresh, and subtitles thereunder.

FRISK, *v.* The running of hands rapidly over another's person, as distinguished from "search," which is to strip and examine contents more particularly. Kalwin Business Men's Ass'n v. McLaughlin, 126 Misc. 698, 214 N.Y.S. 99, 102.

FRITH. Sax. Peace, security, or protection. This word occurs in many compound terms used in Anglo-Saxon law.

FRITHBORG. Frank-pledge. Cowell.

FRITHBOTE. A satisfaction or fine, for a breach of the peace.

FRITHBREACH. The breaking of the peace.

FRITHGAR. The year of jubilee, or of meeting for peace and friendship.

FRITHGILDA. Guildhall; a company or fraternity for the maintenance of peace and security; also a fine for breach of the peace. Jacob.

FRITHMAN. A member of a company or fraternity.

FRITHSOCNE. Surety of defense. Jurisdiction of the peace. The franchise of preserving the peace. Also spelled *"frithsoken."*

FRITHSPLOT. A spot or plot of land, encircling some stone, tree, or well, considered sacred, and therefore affording sanctuary to criminals.

FRITHSTOOL. The stool of peace. A stool or chair placed in a church or cathedral, and which was the symbol and place of sanctuary to those who fled to it and reached it.

FRIVOLOUS. An answer is "frivolous" where it appears from bare inspection to be lacking in legal sufficiency, and, where in any view of the facts pleaded, it does not present a defense. Neefus v. Neefus, 209 Minn. 495, 296 N.W. 579, 581. Any pleading is called "frivolous" when it is clearly insufficient on its face, and does not controvert the material points of the opposite pleading, and is presumably interposed for mere purposes of delay or to embarrass the opponent. Erwin v. Lowery, 64 N.C. 321; Strong v. Sproul, 53 N.Y. 499; Gray v. Gidiere, 4 Strob., S.C., 442; In re Beam, 93 N.J.Eq. 593, 117 A. 613, 614; Milberg v. Keuthe, 98 N.J.L. 779, 121 A. 713, 714.

"Frivolous pleas" are those which are so clearly and palpably bad as to require no argument to convince the court thereof, and which would be pronounced by the court indicative of bad faith in the pleader on a mere inspection. U. S. v. Delaney, D.C.N.J., 8 F.Supp. 224, 227.

A frivolous demurrer has been defined to be one which is so clearly untenable, or its insufficiency so manifest upon a bare inspection of the pleadings, that its character may be determined without argument or research. Cottrill v. Cramer, 40 Wis. 558.

A "frivolous appeal" is one presenting no justiciable question and so readily recognizable as devoid of merit on face of record that there is little prospect that it can ever succeed. Treat v. State ex rel. Mitton, 121 Fla. 509, 163 So. 883.

A sham plea is good on its face, but false in fact; it may, to all appearances, constitute a perfect defense, but is a pretense because false and because not pleaded in good faith. A frivolous plea may be perfectly true in its allegations, but yet is liable to be stricken out because totally insufficient in substance. Andreæ v. Bandler, Sup., 56 N.Y. S. 614; Brown v. Jenison, 1 Code R.N.S., N.Y., 157; Sheets v. Ramer, 125 Minn. 98, 145 N.W. 787. See, further, Answer.

FRODMORTEL, or FREOMORTEL. An immunity for committing manslaughter. Mon. Angl. t. 1, p. 173.

FROM. Implies a starting point, whether it be of time, place, or condition; and meaning: Having a starting point of motion; noting the point of departure, origin, withdrawal, etc.; out of, starting at, as, he traveled "from" New York to Chicago. Silva v. MacAuley, 135 Cal.App. 249, 26 P.2d 887. Word "from" or "after" an event or day does not have an absolute and invariable meaning, but each should receive an inclusion or exclusion construction according to intention with which such word is used. Acme Life Ins. Co. v. White, Tex.Civ.App., 99 S.W.2d 1059, 1060. Words "from" and "to," used in contract, may be given meaning to which reason and sense entitles them, under circumstances of case. Woodruff v. Adams, 134 Cal.App. 490, 25 P.2d 529.

As to whether the word was to be treated as inclusive or exclusive of a *terminus a quo,* whether of time or place, a critical writer formulated a rule that when referring to a certain point as a *terminus a quo,* though in vulgar acceptation it were capable of being taken indifferently, either inclusively or exclusively, yet in law it has obtained a certain fixed import and is always taken as exclusive of the *terminus a quo.* Powell, Powers 449. It generally excludes the day to which it relates, but the general rule will yield to the intent of parties; Kendall v. Kingsley, 120 Mass. 94. The views of Lord Mansfield, in Cowp. 714 (overruling his own decision of three years before, *id.* 189), was that it is either exclusive or inclusive according to context and subject-matter, and the court will construe it to effectuate the intent of parties and not to destroy it. Lowman v. Shotkoski, 106 Neb. 540, 184 N.W. 107, 108; Allen v. Effler, 144 Tenn. 685, 235 S.W. 67, 68; Martin v. Travelers' Ins. Co., 310 Mo. 411, 276 S.W. 380, 382, 41 A.L.R. 1372; Platt v. Flaherty, 96 Kan. 42, 149 P. 734.

As to time, after an examination of authorities, Washington, J., laid down what he considered the settled principles to be deduced from them: (1) When time is computed *from* an act done, the day of its performance is included; (2) when the words are from the date, if a present interest is to commence, the day is included, if it is a terminus from which to impute time the day is excluded; Pearpoint v. Graham, 4 Wash.C.C. 240, Fed.Cas.No.10,877; where the latter principle was applied to a lease, as it was also in Lord Raym. 84; and to a bond; Lysle v. Williams, 15 S. & R., Pa., 135; and the first proposition has been laid down with reference to the words "from and after the passage of this act;" Arnold v. U. S., 9 Cra., U.S., 104, 3 L.Ed. 671; U. S. v. Williams, 1 Paine 261, Fed.Cas.No. 16,723; *contra,* Lorent v. Ins. Co., 1 Nott. & McC., S.C., 505. See U. S. v. Heth, 3 Cra., U.S., 399, 2 L.Ed. 479. From is generally held a word of exclusion; Wilcox v. Wood, 9 Wend., N.Y., 346; Ordway v. Remington, 12 R.I. 319, 34 Am.Rep. 646. But a promise made November 1st, 1811, and sued November 1st, 1817, was held barred by statute of limitation; Presbrey v. Williams, 15 Mass. 193. Where an act was to be done in a given number of days *from the time of the contract,* the day on which the contract was made was included; Brown v. Buzan, 24 Ind. 194; but if the contract merely says in so may days it means so many days from the day of date, and that is excluded; Blake v. Crowninshield, 9 N.H. 304. A fire policy *from one given date to another* includes the last day; whether the first is included was not decided; L.R. 5 Exch. 296. In most cases when something is required to be done in a given time from the day on which an event has happened, that day is excluded, as in case of proving claims against the estate of a decedent or insolvent; Weeks v. Hull, 19 Conn. 376, 50 Am.Dec. 249; enrolling deeds, after execution; Seawell v. Williams, 5 Hayw., Tenn., 283; appeal from arbitrators, afterward; Browne v. Browne, 3 S. & R., Pa., 496; issuing a *scire facias* to revive a judgment, after entry; Appeal of Green, 6 W. & S., Pa., 327; the time an execution runs, after its date; Homan v. Liswell, 6 Cow., N.Y., 659; redemption from execution sale; *id.* 518; allowing appeal from a justice; Ex parte Dean, 2 Cow., N.Y., 605, 14 Am.Dec. 521. The principle is thus well expressed. When time is to be computed from a particular day or a particular event, as when an act is to be performed within a specified period from or after a day named, that day is excluded and the last day included; Sheets v. Selden, 2 Wall., U.S., 177, 17 L.Ed. 822. But it was held that in considering the question of barring a writ of error, the day of the decree is included; Chiles v. Smith's Heirs, 13 B.Monr., Ky., 460. Six months *from testator's death* allowed a legatee to give security not to marry, are exclusive of that day; 15 Ves. 248.

Whenever they are used with respect to places it is said that "from," "to," and "at" are taken inclusively according to the subject-matter; Union Pac. R. Co. v. Hall, 91 U.S. 343, 23 L.Ed. 428 (fixing the terminus of a railroad under an act of congress). *From an object to an object* in a deed excludes the terminus referred to; Bonney v. Morrill, 52 Me. 252; State v. Bushey, 84 Me. 459, 24 A. 940. *From place to place* means from one place in a town to another in the same town; Com. v. Inhabitants of Cambridge, 7 Mass. 158; Com. v. Waters, 11 Gray, Mass., 81. *From a street* means from any part of it according to circumstances; City of Pittsburg v. Cluley, 74 Pa. 259. *From a town* is not always and indeed is seldom exclusive of the place named; it generally means from some indefinite place within the town; Chesapeake & O. Canal Co. v. Key, 3 Cra.C.C. 599, 606, Fed.Cas.No.2,649. Authority in a railroad charter to construct a railroad *from a city* to another point gives power to construct the road from any point within the city; Hazlehurst v. Freeman, 52 Ga. 244; *contra* North-Eastern R. Co. v. Payne, 8 Rich.L., S.C., 177. But *from a town* to another in an indictment for transportation of liquor does not charge it as done within the town; State v. Bushey, 84 Me. 459, 24 A. 940. To construe reasonably the expression a road *from a village* to a creek within the same village, in a statute, requires that it be taken inclusively; Smith v. Helmer, 7 Barb., N.Y., 416. Sailing *from a port* means out of it; U. S. v. La Coste, 2 Mass. 129, Fed.Cas.No.15,548.

Descent *from a parent* cannot be construed to mean through a parent, it must be immediate, from the person designated; Gardner v. Collins, 2 Pet., U.S., 58, 86, 7 L.Ed. 347; but the words *from the part of the father* include a descent, either immediately from the father or from any person in the line of the father; Shippen v. Izard, 1 S. & R., Pa., 222.

From the loading in a marine policy ordinarily means that the risk is covered after the goods are on board, but this meaning may be qualified by any words in the policy indicating a different intention, 16 East 240; L.R. 7 Q.B. 580, 702.

From day to day, in reference to adjournments, usually means to the next day but, under a statute authorizing the adjournment of a sale from day to day, a sale is good if made by adjournment to a day, certain, which did not immediately succeed the first, Burns v. Lyon, 4 Watts, Pa., 363. *From henceforth* in a lease means from the delivery; 5 Co. 1; so also does one from March 25th last past (the execution being March 25th); 4 B. & C. 272; or one from an impossible date (as February 30th), or no date, but if it has a sensible date, the word date in other parts of it means date, not delivery; 4 B. & C. 908.

FROM ONE PLACE TO ANOTHER. From premises owned by one person to premises owned by another person in some legal subdivision or from one legal subdivision to another. Liquor Transportation Cases, 140 Tenn. 582, 205 S.W. 423, 426; Ready v. State, 155 Tenn. 15, 290 S.W. 28, 29; State v. White, 111 Kan. 196, 206 P. 903, 904.

FROM PERSON. Includes taking from presence of person assaulted as well as taking of property in actual contact with person of one robbed. People v. Kubish, 357 Ill. 531, 192 N.E. 543, 545.

FROM, THROUGH, OR UNDER. The term refers to origin or devolution of property, and unless some title to or interest therein has been derived by assignment or otherwise from party adverse to decedent's estate, statute barring testimony is inapplicable. In re Iwers' Estate, 225 Iowa 389, 280 N.W. 579, 582.

FROM TIME TO TIME. Occasionally, at intervals, now and then. Spade v. Hawkins, 60 Ind. App. 388, 110 N.E. 1010, 1012. See From.

FRONT. Forepart, as opposed to the back or rear. State v. Read, 162 Iowa, 572, 144 N.W. 310, 311; Howland v. Andrus, 81 N.J.Eq. 175, 86 A. 391, 393.

Any side or face of a building is a front, although the word is more commonly used to denote the entrance side. In re McInerney, 47 Wyo. 258, 34 P.2d 35, 43. As applied to a bare lot, it is that side of lot towards which, in ordinary circumstances, house, when built, will most likely face, and very general usage of building houses with their main entrance toward shorter street line results in common understanding that this is side intended when front of lot is referred to. Rhinehart v. Leitch, 107 Conn. 400, 140 A. 763.

FRONT FOOT. As respects assessment, synonymous with "abutting foot." Moberly v. Hogan, 131 Mo. 19, 32 S.W. 1014.

The rate of assessment is obtained by having the total cost of the work divided by the total number of square feet of paving done under the contract; and the quotient multiplied by one-half of the number of linear feet in the width of the pavement opposite the property lines. City of Crowley v. Police Jury of Acadia Parish, 138 La. 488, 70 So. 487, 488.

FRONT-FOOT RULE. One by which cost of improvement is to be apportioned among several properties in proportion to their frontage on improvement and without regard to benefits conferred. Davy v. McNeill, 31 N.M. 7, 240 P. 482, 488.

FRONTAGE, FRONTAGER. Frontage denotes line of property on street. Smidt v. McKee, 262 N.Y. 373, 186 N.E. 869, 870. Extent of front along road or street. Tzeses v. Barbahenn, 125 N.J.L. 643, 17 A.2d 539, 540. Space available for erection of buildings, and does not include cross streets or space occupied by sidewalk or any ornamental spaces in plat between sidewalks and curb. Wallace v. Kramer, 296 Mich. 680, 296 N.W. 838, 842.

In English law a frontager is a person owning or occupying land which abuts on a highway, river, seashore, or the like. The term is generally used with reference to the liability of frontagers on streets to contribute towards the expense of paving, draining, or other works on the highway carried out by a local authority, in proportion to the frontage of their respective tenements. Sweet.

The term is also in a similar sense in American law, the expense of local improvements made by municipal corporations (such as paving, curbing, and sewering) being generally assessed on abutting property owners in proportion to the "frontage" of their lots on the street or highway, and an assessment so levied being called a "frontage assessment." Neenan v. Smith, 50 Mo. 531; Lyon v. Tonawanda, C.C.N.Y., 98 F. 366; City of Youngstown v. Fishel, 89 Ohio St. 247, 104 N.E. 141, 143, 50 L.R.A.,N.S., 921, Ann.Cas. 1915D, 1073; Standard Oil Co. of Indiana v. Kamradt, 319 Ill. 51, 149 N.E. 538, 539.

FRONTING AND ABUTTING. Very often, "fronting" signifies abutting, adjoining, or bordering on, depending largely on the context. Rombauer v. Compton Heights Christian Church, 328 Mo. 1, 40 S.W.2d 545, 551. As used in statutes relating to assessment for improvements, property between which and the improvement there is no intervening land. Oklahoma Ry. Co. v. Severns Paving Co., 67 Okl. 206, 170 P. 216–218, 10 A.L.R. 157; Flynn v. Chiappari, 191 Cal. 139, 215 P. 682, 686.

FRONTIER. In international law, that portion of the territory of any country which lies close along the border line of another country, and so "fronts" or faces it. The term means something more than the boundary line itself, and includes a tract or strip of country, of indefinite extent, contiguous to the line. Stoughton v. Mott, 15 Vt. 169.

FROZEN SNAKE. A term used to impute ingratitude and held libelous, the court taking judicial notice of its meaning without an innuendo. 12 Ad. & El. 624.

FRUCTUARIUS. Lat. In the civil law, one who had the usufruct of a thing; *i. e.,* the use of the fruits, profits, or increase, as of land or animals. Inst. 2, 1, 36, 38. Bracton applies it to a lessee, fermor, or farmer of land, or one who held lands *ad firmam,* for a farm or term. Bract. fol. 261.

FRUCTUS. Lat. In the civil law, fruit, fruits; produce; profit or increase; the organic productions of a thing.

The right to the fruits of a thing belonging to another.

The compensation which a man receives from another for the use or enjoyment of a thing, such as interest or rent. See Mackeld. Rom. Law, § 167; Inst. 2, 1, 35, 37; Dig. 7, 1, 33; Id. 5, 3, 29; Id. 22, 1, 34.

FRUCTUS AUGENT HÆREDITATEM. The yearly increase goes to enhance the inheritance. Dig. 5, 3, 20, 3.

FRUCTUS CIVILES. All revenues and recompenses which, though not *fruits,* properly speaking, are recognized as such by the law. The term includes such things as the rents and income of real property, interest on money loaned, and annuities. Civ.Code La. 1900, art. 545.

FRUCTUS FUNDI. The fruits (produce or yield) of land.

FRUCTUS INDUSTRIALES. Industrial fruits, or fruits of industry. Those fruits of a thing, as of land, which are produced by the labor and industry of the occupant, as crops of grain; as distinguished from such as are produced solely by the powers of nature. Emblements are so called in the common law. 2 Steph. Comm. 258; 1 Chit. Gen. Pr. 92. Sparrow v. Pond, 49 Minn. 412, 52 N.W. 36, 16 L.R.A. 103, 32 Am.St.Rep. 571; Twin Falls Bank & Trust Co. v. Weinberg, 44 Idaho 332, 257 P. 31, 33, 54 A.L.R. 1527. Annual crops obtained by yearly labor and cultivation. Koerner v. Wilson, 85 Colo. 140, 274 P. 737, 738, 63 A.L.R. 227.

FRUCTUS LEGIS. The fruit of the law, *i. e.* execution.

FRUCTUS NATURALES. Those products which are produced by the powers of nature alone; as wool, metals, milk, the young of animals. Sparrow v. Pond, 49 Minn. 412, 52 N.W. 36, 16 L.R.A. 103, 32 Am.St.Rep. 571; Clark v. Strohbeen, 190 Iowa 989, 181 N.W. 430, 433, 13 A.L.R. 1419.

FRUCTUS PECUDUM. The produce or increase of flocks or herds.

FRUCTUS PENDENTES. Hanging fruits; those not severed. The fruits united with the thing which produces them. These form a part of the principal thing.

FRUCTUS PENDENTES PARS FUNDI VIDENTUR. Hanging fruits make part of the land. Dig. 6, 1, 44; 2 Bouv. Inst. no. 1578.

FRUCTUS PERCEPTOS VILLÆ NON ESSE CONSTAT. Gathered fruits do not make a part of the farm. Dig. 19, 1, 17, 1; 2 Bouv. Inst. no. 1578.

FRUCTUS REI ALIENÆ. The fruits of another's property; fruits taken from another's estate.

FRUCTUS SEPARATI. Separate fruits; the fruits of a thing when they are separated from it. Dig. 7, 4, 13.

FRUCTUS STANTES. Standing fruits; those not yet severed from the stalk or stem.

FRUGES. In the civil law, anything produced from vines, underwood, chalk-pits, stone-quarries. Dig. 50, 16, 77.

Grains and leguminous vegetables. In a more restricted sense, any esculent growing in pods. Vicat, Voc. Jur.; Calvin.

FRUIT. The produce of a tree or plant which contains the seed or is used for food. Klas v. Kuehl, 159 Wis. 561, 150 N.W. 973, 975.

This term, in legal acceptation, is not confined to the produce of those trees which in popular language are called "fruit trees," but applies also to the produce of oak, elm, and walnut trees. Bullen v. Denning, 5 Barn. & C. 847.

Fruit fallen. The produce of any possession detached therefrom, and capable of being enjoyed by itself. Thus, a next presentation, when a vacancy has occurred, is a fruit fallen from the advowson. Wharton.

FRUITS, FRUITS OF THE LAND. In replevy bond, "fruits" includes natural accession to livestock. Southern Surety Co. v. Adams, Tex.Civ. App., 278 S.W. 943, 946. Includes the increase and the clip of replevied goats and sheep; "offspring" and "that which is produced." Southern Surety Co. v. Adams, 119 Tex. 489, 34 S.W.2d 789, 798. The right of a possessor to "fruits of the land" does not permit possessor to extract mineral oil and gas from land. Elder v. Ellerbe, 135 La. 990, 66 So. 337.

Civil fruits, in the civil law, (*fructus civiles*) are such things as the rents and income of real property, the interest on money loaned, and annuities. Civ.Code La. art. 545. Rents and revenues of an immovable. Posey v. Fargo. 187 La. 122, 174 So. 175, 179.

Natural fruits. The produce of the soil, or of fruit-trees, bushes, vines, etc., which are edible or otherwise useful or serve for the reproduction of their species. The term is used in contradistinction to "artificial fruits," *i. e.,* such as by metaphor or analogy are likened to the fruits of the earth. Of the latter, interest on money is an example. See Civ.Code La. art. 545.

FRUITS OF CRIME. In the law of evidence, material objects acquired by means and in consequence of the commission of crime, and sometimes constituting the subject-matter of the crime. Burrill, Circ. Ev. 445; 3 Benth. Jud. Ev. 31.

FRUMENTA QUÆ SATA SUNT SOLO CEDERE INTELLIGUNTUR. Grain which is sown is understood to form a part of the soil. Inst. 2, 1, 32.

FRUMENTUM. In the civil law, grain. That which grows in an ear. Dig. 50, 16, 77.

FRUMGYLD. Sax. The first payment made to the kindred of a slain person in recompense for his murder. Blount.

FRUMSTOLL. Sax. In Saxon law, a chief seat, or mansion house. Cowell.

FRUSCA TERRA. In old records, uncultivated and desert ground. 2 Mon. Angl. 327; Cowell.

FRUSSURA. A breaking; plowing. Cowell.

FRUSTRA. Lat. Without effect, in vain, to no purpose, uselessly; without reason or cause, groundlessly; in error. Harpers' Lat. Dict.

FRUSTRA AGIT QUI JUDICIUM PROSEQUI NEQUIT CUM EFFECTU. He sues to no purpose who cannot prosecute his judgment with effect, [who cannot have the fruits of his judgment.] Fleta, lib. 6, c. 37, § 9.

FRUSTRA [VANA] EST POTENTIA QUÆ NUNQUAM VENIT IN ACTUM. That power is to no purpose which never comes into act, or which is never exercised. 2 Coke, 51.

FRUSTRA EXPECTATUR EVENTUS CUJUS EFFECTUS NULLUS SEQUITUR. An event is vainly expected from which no effect follows.

FRUSTRA FERUNTUR LEGES NISI SUBDITIS ET OBEDIENTIBUS. Laws are made to no purpose, except for those that are subject and obedient. Branch, Princ.

FRUSTRA FIT PER PLURA, QUOD FIERI POTEST PER PAUCIORA. That is done to no purpose by many things which can be done by fewer. Jenk.Cent. p. 68, case 28. The employment of more means or instruments for effecting a thing than are necessary is to no purpose.

FRUSTRA LEGIS AUXILIUM INVOCAT [QUÆRIT] QUI IN LEGEM COMMITTIT. He vainly invokes the aid of the law who transgresses the law. Fleta, lib. 4, c. 2, § 3; 2 Hale, P.C. 386; Broom, Max. 279, 297.

FRUSTRA PETIS QUOD MOX ES RESTITURUS. In vain you ask that which you will have immediately to restore. 2 Kames, Eq. 104; 5 Man. & G. 757.

FRUSTRA PETIS QUOD STATIM ALTERI REDDERE COGERIS. Jenk.Cent. 256. You ask in vain that which you might immediately be compelled to restore to another.

FRUSTRA PROBATUR QUOD PROBATUM NON RELEVAT. That is proved to no purpose which, when proved, does not help. Halk.Lat.Max. 50.

FRUSTRATION. Where, from nature of contract and surrounding circumstances, parties from beginning must have known it could not be fulfilled unless, when time thereof arrived, some particular condition continued to exist, under doctrine of "frustration", in absence of warranty that such condition of things shall exist, contract is to be construed as subject to implied condition that parties shall be excused in case, before breach, performance becomes impossible or purpose frustrated from such condition ceasing to exist without default of either. Johnson v. Atkins, 53 Cal. App.2d 430, 127 P.2d 1027, 1028, 1029, 1030.

FRUSTRUM TERRÆ. A piece or parcel of land lying by itself. Co.Litt. 5*b*.

FRUTECTUM. In old records, a place overgrown with shrubs and bushes. Spelman; Blount.

FRUTOS. In Spanish law, fruits; products; produce; grains; profits. White, New Recop. b. 1, tit. 7, c. 5, § 2.

FRYMITH. In old English law, the affording harbor and entertainment to any one.

FRYTHE. Sax. In old English law, a plain between woods. Co.Litt. 5*b*.

An arm of the sea, or a strait between two lands. Cowell.

FUAGE, FOUAGE, or FEUAGE. Hearth money. A tax laid upon each fire-place or hearth. An imposition of a shilling for every hearth, levied by Edward III. in the dukedom of Aquitaine. Spelman; 1 Bl.Comm. 324.

FUER. In old English law, flight. It is of two kinds: (1) *Fuer in fait,* or *in facto,* where a person does apparently and corporally flee; (2) *fuer in ley,* or *in lege,* when, being called in the county court, he does not appear, which legal interpretation makes flight. Wharton.

FUERO. In Spanish law, a law; a code.

A general usage or custom of a province, having the force of law. Strother v. Lucas, 12 Pet. 446, 9 L.Ed. 1137. *Ir contra fuero,* to violate a received custom.

A grant of privileges and immunities. *Conceder fueros,* to grant exemptions.

A charter granted to a city or town. Also designated as "*cartas pueblas.*"

An act of donation made to an individual, a church, or convent, on certain conditions.

A declaration of a magistrate, in relation to taxation, fines, etc.

A charter granted by the sovereign, or those having authority from him, establishing the franchises of towns, cities, etc.

A place where justice is administered.

A peculiar *forum,* before which a party is amenable.

The jurisdiction of a tribunal, which is entitled to take cognizance of a cause; as *fuero ecclesiastico, fuero militar.* See Schm.Civil Law, Introd. 64.

FUERO DE CASTILLA. The body of laws and customs which formerly governed the Castilians.

FUERO DE CORREOS Y CAMINOS. A special tribunal taking cognizance of all matters relating to the post-office and roads.

FUERO DE GUERRA. A special tribunal taking cognizance of all matters in relation to persons serving in the army.

FUERO DE MARINA. A special tribunal taking cognizance of all matters relating to the navy and to the persons employed therein.

FUERO JUZGO. The *Forum Judicium;* a code of laws established in the seventh century for the Visigothic kingdom in Spain. Some of its principles and rules are found surviving in the modern jurisprudence of that country. Schm.Civil Law, Introd. 28.

FUERO MUNICIPAL. The body of laws granted to a city or town for its government and the administration of justice.

FUERO REAL. The title of a code of Spanish law promulgated by Alphonso the Learned, (*el Sabio,*) A.D. 1255. It was the precursor of the Partidas. Schm.Civil Law, Introd. 67.

FUERO VIEJO. The title of a compilation of Spanish law, published about A.D. 992. Schm. Civil Law, Introd. 65.

FUGA CATALLORUM. In old English law. A drove of cattle. Blount.

FUGACIA. A chase. Blount.

FUGAM FECIT. Lat. He has made flight; he fled. A clause inserted in an inquisition, in old English law, meaning that a person indicted for treason or felony had fled. The effect of this is to make the party forfeit his goods absolutely, and the profits of his lands until he has been pardoned or acquitted.

FUGATOR. In old English law, a privilege to hunt. Blount.

A driver. *Fugatores carrucarum,* drivers of wagons. Fleta, lib. 2, c. 78.

FUGITATE. In Scotch practice, to outlaw by the sentence of a court; to outlaw for non-appearance in a criminal case. 2 Alis. Crim. Pr. 350.

FUGITATION. When a criminal does not obey the citation to answer, the court pronounces sentence of fugitation against him, which induces a forfeiture of goods and chattels to the crown.

FUGITIVE. One who flees; always used in law with the implication of a flight, evasion, or escape from some duty or penalty or from the consequences of a misdeed.

FUGITIVE FROM JUSTICE. A person who, having committed a crime, flees from jurisdiction of court where crime was committed or departs from his usual place of abode and conceals himself within the district. United States ex rel. Demarois v. Farrell, C.C.A.Minn., 87 F.2d 957, 960. State v. Clough, 71 N.H. 594, 53 A. 1086, 67 L.R.A. 946; People v. Hyatt, 172 N.Y. 176, 64 N.E. 825, 60 L.R. A. 774, 92 Am.St.Rep. 706.

To be regarded as a "fugitive from justice," it is not necessary that one shall have left the state for the very purpose of avoiding prosecution; it being sufficient that, having committed there an act constituting a crime, he afterwards has departed from its jurisdiction, and when sought to be prosecuted is found in another state. Hogan v. O'Neill, 255 U.S. 52, 41 S.Ct. 222, 65 L.Ed. 497; People ex rel. Gottschalk v. Brown, 237 N.Y. 483, 143 N.E. 653, 654, 32 A.L.R. 1164; State v. Hayes, 162 La. 917, 111 So. 327, 329 (one who did not flee).

No matter for what purpose or with what motive or under what belief he leaves state, and even though at time of leaving he had no belief he had violated criminal laws and did not contemplate fleeing from justice to avoid prosecution for crime with which he is charged. Ex parte Morris, 131 Tex.Cr.R. 596, 101 S.W.2d 259.

FUGITIVE OFFENDERS. In English law, where a person accused of any offense punishable by imprisonment, with hard labor for twelve months or more, has left that part of his majesty's dominions where the offense is alleged to have been committed, he is liable, if found in any other part of his majesty's dominions, to be apprehended and returned in manner provided by the fugitive offenders' act, 1881, to the part from which he is a fugitive. Wharton.

FUGITIVE OIL. Oil escaping from well which was out of control and flowing down creek to point 10 or 12 miles below the well where it was picked up was "fugitive" or "waste oil" and belonged to the first taker who might reduce it to his possession. Linkenhoger v. Brown, Tex.Civ. App., 128 S.W.2d 163, 164.

FUGITIVE SLAVE. One who, held in bondage, flees from his master's power.

FUGITIVE SLAVE LAW. An act of congress passed in 1793 (and also one enacted in 1850) providing for the surrender and deportation of slaves who escaped from their masters and fled into the territory of another state, generally a "free" state.

FUGITIVE'S GOODS. Under the old English Law, where a man fled for felony, and escaped, his own goods were not forfeited as *bona fugitivorum* until it was found by proceedings of record (*e. g.* before the coroner in the case of death) that he fled for the felony. Foxley's Case, 5 Co. 109 *a.*

FUGITIVUS. In the civil law, a fugitive; a runaway slave. Dig. 11, 4; Cod. 6, 1. See the various definitions of this word in Dig. 21, 1, 17.

FUGUES. Fr. In medical jurisprudence. Ambulatory automatism. See Automatism.

FULL. Abundantly provided, sufficient in quantity or degree, complete, entire, and detailed. City of Orlando v. Evans, 132 Fla. 609, 182 So. 264, 268. Having no open space. In re California Land Buyers Syndicate, D.C.Cal., 22 F.Supp. 183, 186. Ample; perfect; mature; not wanting in any essential quality. Mobile School Com'rs v. Putnam, 44 Ala. 537; McCrary v. McCrary, Tex.Civ.App., 230 S.W. 187, 207.

FULL AGE. The age of legal majority, twenty-one years at common law, twenty-five in the civil law. 1 Bl.Comm. 463; Inst. 1, 23, pr.

FULL ANSWER. In pleading, a complete and meritorious answer, not wanting in any essential requisite. Frizell v. Northern Trust Co. of Chicago, Ill., 144 Kan. 481, 61 P.2d 1344, 1345, 1346.

FULL BLOOD. Relations of the "full blood," "whole blood," or "entire blood" are those derived not only from the same ancestor, but from the same couple of ancestors. In re Skidmore's Estate, 148 Misc. 569, 266 N.Y.S. 312.

Brothers and sisters of *full blood* are those who are born of the same father and mother, or, as Justinian calls them, *"ex utroque parente conjuncti."* Nov. 118, cc. 2, 3; Mackeld.Rom.Law, § 145. The more usual term in modern law is "whole blood" *(q. v.)*.

FULL COPY. In equity practice, a complete and unabbreviated transcript of a bill or other pleading, with all indorsements, and including a copy of all exhibits. Finley v. Hunter, 2 Strob. Eq., S. C., 210, note.

FULL COURT. In practice, a court *in banc.* A court duly organized with all the judges present.

Court containing permissible complement of judges, as distinguished from a quorum of two. Textile Mills Securities Corporation v. Commissioner of Internal Revenue, 314 U.S. 326, 62 S.Ct. 272, 277, 86 L.Ed. 249.

FULL COUSIN. Son or daughter of one's uncle or aunt. Culver v. Union & New Haven Trust Co., 120 Conn. 97, 179 A. 487, 489, 99 A.L.R. 663.

FULL COVENANTS. See Covenant.

FULL DEFENSE. In pleading, the formula of defense in a plea, stated at length and without abbreviation, thus: "And the said C. D., by E. F., his attorney, comes and defends the force (or wrong) and injury when and where it shall behoove him, and the damages, and whatsoever else he ought to defend, and says," etc. Steph. Pl. p. 481.

FULL FAITH AND CREDIT. "Full faith and credit" clause of Const. U. S. art. 4, § 1, requires that foreign judgment be given such faith and credit as it had by law or usage of state of its origin. First Nat. Bank v. Terry, 103 Cal.App. 501, 285 P. 336, 337. That foreign statutes are to have force and effect to which they are entitled in home state. Flahive v. Missouri, K. & T. R. Co., 131 Misc. 586, 227 N.Y.S. 587, 588. And that a judgment or record shall have the same faith, credit, conclusive effect, and obligatory force in other states as it has by law or usage in the state from whence taken. Christmas v. Russell, 5 Wall. 302, 18 L.Ed. 475; McElmoyle v. Cohen, 13 Pet. 326, 10 L.Ed. 177; Pennsylvania Fire Ins. Co. of Philadephia v. Gold Issue Min. & Mill. Co., 243 U.S. 93, 37 S.Ct. 344, 61 L.Ed. 610.

FULL HEARING. Embraces not only the right to present evidence, but also a reasonable opportunity to know the claims of the opposing party, and to meet them. Morgan v. U. S., 304 U.S. 1, 58 S.Ct. 773, 776, 777, 82 L.Ed. 1129.

One in which ample opportunity is afforded to all parties to make, by evidence and argument, a showing fairly adequate to establish the propriety or impropriety from the standpoint of justice and law of the step asked to be taken. Akron, C. & Y. Ry. Co. v. U. S., 261 U.S. 184, 43 S.Ct. 270, 67 L.Ed. 605; State v. Hunt, 137 Tenn. 243, 192 S.W. 931, 932.

FULL INDORSEMENT. See Indorsement.

FULL JURISDICTION. Complete jurisdiction over a given subject-matter or class of actions (as, in equity) without any exceptions or reservations. Bank of Mississippi v. Duncan, 52 Miss. 740.

FULL LIFE. Life in fact and in law. See In Full Life.

FULL-PAID STOCK. Stock on which no further payments can be demanded by the issuing company. Middleton v. Wooster, 184 App.Div. 165, 171 N.Y.S. 593, 595.

FULL PARTICULARS. Where contract of insurance requires giving "full particulars" of an accident as a condition precedent to liability, unnecessary details are not required, but only such as enables insurer to determine, whether a claim was likely to be made, and the insured was not required to make an exhaustive investigation of all the attendant circumstances or decide what the facts were on conflicting evidence. Silberstein v. Vellerman, 241 Mass. 80, 134 N.E. 395, 397.

FULL POWERS. A document issued by the government of a state empowering its diplomatic agent to conduct special business with a foreign government.

FULL PROOF. In the civil law, proof by two witnesses, or a public instrument. Hallifax, Civil Law, b. 3, c. 9, nn. 25, 30; 3 Bl.Comm. 370. Evidence which satisfies the minds of the jury of the truth of the fact in dispute, to the entire exclusion of every reasonable doubt. Kane v. Hibernia Mut. F. Ins. Co., 38 N.J.L. 450, 20 Am.Rep. 409.

FULL RIGHT. The union of a good title with actual possession.

FULL SETTLEMENT. Implies an adjustment of all pending matters, the mutual release of all prior obligations existing between the parties. Hickox v. Hickox, Tex.Civ.App., 151 S.W.2d 913, 918.

FULLUM AQUÆ. A fleam, or stream of water. Blount.

FULLY ADMINISTERED. The English equivalent of the Latin phrase *"plene administravit;"* being a plea by an executor or administrator that he has completely and legally disposed of all the assets of the estate, and has nothing left out of which a new claim could be satisfied. See Ryans v. Boogher, 169 Mo. 673, 69 S.W. 1048.

FUMAGE. In old English law, the same as *fuage,* or smoke farthings. 1 Bl.Comm. 324. See Fuage.

FUNCTION. Derived from Latin "functus," the past participle of the verb "fungor" which means to perform, execute, administer. McNamara v. Powell, Sup., 52 N.Y.S.2d 515, 551.

The nature and proper action of anything; activity appropriate to any business or profession. Rosenblum v. Anglim, D.C.Cal., 43 F.Supp. 889, 892.

Office; duty; fulfillment of a definite end or set of ends by the correct adjustment of means. The occupation of an office. By the performance of its duties, the officer is said to fill his function.

Dig. 32, 65, 1. State v. Hyde, 121 Ind. 20, 22 N.E. 644. The proper activities or duties of municipality. Bean v. City of Knoxville, 180 Tenn. 448, 175 S.W.2d 954, 955.

FUNCTIONAL CLAIM. One which claims function. In re Tucker, Cust. & Pat. App., 46 F.2d 214, 216. See Claim.

FUNCTIONAL DEPRECIATION. Results from necessary replacement of equipment before it is worn out, by reason of invention and improved appliances which render more efficient and satisfactory service. Guaranty Trust Co. of New York v. Grand Rapids, G. H. & M. Ry. Co., D.C.Mich., 7 F.Supp. 511, 521.

FUNCTIONAL DISEASE. In medical jurisprudence, one which prevents, obstructs, or interferes with the due performance of its special functions by any organ of the body, without anatomical defect or abnormality in the organ itself. See Higbee v. Guardian Mut. L. Ins. Co., 66 Barb., N.Y. 472. Distinguished from "organic" disease, which is due to some injury to, or lesion or malformation in, the organ in question.

FUNCTIONARY. A public officer or employee. An officer of a private corporation is also sometimes so called.

Functus officio. Lat. A task performed. Board of School Trustees of Washington City Administrative Unit v. Benner, 222 N.C. 566, 24 S.E.2d 259, 263.

Having fulfilled the function, discharged the office, or accomplished the purpose, and therefore of no further force or authority. Applied to an officer whose term has expired, and who has consequently no further official authority; and also to an instrument, power, agency, etc., which has fulfilled the purpose of its creation, and is therefore of no further virtue or effect. Blanton Banking Co. v. Taliaferro, Tex.Civ.App., 262 S.W. 196.

FUND, *v.* To capitalize with a view to the production of interest. Stephen v. Milnor, 24 N.J. Eq. 376. Also, to put into the form of bonds, stocks, or other securities, bearing regular interest, and to provide or appropriate a fund or permanent revenue for the payment thereof. Merrill v. Monticello, C.C.Ind., 22 F. 596. City of Long Beach v. Lisenby, 180 Cal. 52, 179 P. 198, 201.

To fund a debt is to pledge a specific fund to keep down the interest and reduce the principal.

Funded debt. As applied to states or municipal corporations, a funded debt is one for the payment of which (interest and principal) some fund is appropriated, either specifically, or by provision made for future taxation and the *quasi* pledging in advance of the public revenue. Ketchum v. Buffalo, 14 N.Y. 356; People v. Carpenter, 52 N.Y.S. 781, 31 App.Div. 603. As applied to the financial management of corporations (and sometimes of estates in course of administration or properties under receivership) funding means the borrowing of a sufficient sum of money to discharge a variety of floating or unsecured debts, or debts evidenced by notes or secured by bonds but maturing within a short time, and creating a new debt in lieu thereof, secured by a general mortgage, a series of bonds, or an issue of stock, generally maturing at a more remote period, and often at a lower rate of interest. The new debt thus substituted for the pre-existing debts is called the "funded debt." Ketchum v. Buffalo, 14 N.Y. 356; Lawrey v. Sterling, 41 Or. 518, 69 P. 460. This term is very seldom applied to the debts of a private individual; but when so used it must be understood as referring to a debt embodied in securities of a permanent character and to the payment of which certain property has been applied or pledged. Wells v. Wells, Super.N.Y., 24 N.Y.S. 874.

Funding system. The practice of borrowing money to defray the expenses of government, and creating a "sinking fund," designed to keep down interest, and to effect the gradual reduction of the principal debt. Merrill v. Monticello, C.C.Ind., 22 F. 596.

FUND, *n.* A generic term and all-embracing as compared with term "money," etc., which is specific. Bivins v. State, 47 Ga.App. 391, 170 S.E. 513, 516.

A sum of money set apart for a specific purpose, or available for the payment of debts or claims. State v. Finney, 141 Kan. 12, 40 P.2d 411, 421.

In its narrower and more usual sense, "fund" signifies "capital," as opposed to "interest" or "income;" as where we speak of a corporation funding the arrears of interest due on its bonds, or the like, meaning that the interest is capitalized and made to bear interest in its turn until it is repaid. Sweet.

In the plural, this word has a variety of slightly different meanings, as follows:

Moneys and much more, such as notes, bills, checks, drafts, stocks and bonds, and in broader meaning may include property of every kind. State v. Finney, 141 Kan. 12, 40 P.2d 411, 421.

Money in hand; assets; cash; money available for the payment of a debt, legacy, etc. Galena Ins. Co. v. Kupfer, 28 Ill. 335, 81 Am.Dec. 284; U. S. v. Jenks, D.C.Pa., 264 F. 697, 698; Johnson v. State, 37 Ga.App. 129, 139 S.E. 118, 119.

The proceeds of sales of real and personal estate, or the proceeds of any other assets converted into money. Doane v. Insurance Co., 43 N.J. Eq. 533, 11 A. 739; Illinois Christian Missionary Soc. v. American Christian Missionary Soc., 277 Ill. 193, 115 N.E. 118, 120.

Corporate stocks or government securities; in this sense usually spoken of as the "funds."

Assets, securities, bonds, or revenue of a state or government appropriated for the discharge of its debts. State v. Hudson, 93 W.Va. 435, 117 S.E. 122, 126; Broadway Bank of St. Louis, Mo., v. McGee Creek Levee & Drainage Dist., 292 Ill. 560, 127 N.E. 165, 166; State v. Board of Education of Sharples Village School Dist., 114 Ohio St. 602, 151 N.E. 669, 670.

Current funds. Current money, whatever is receivable and current by law as money. Henderson v. Farmers' Sav. Bank of Harper, 199 Iowa 496, 202 N.W. 259, 261; Feder v. Elliott, 198 Iowa 447, 199 N.W. 288, 289, 36 A.L.R. 1353.

General fund. This phrase, in New York, is a collective designation of all the assets of the state which furnish the means for the support of government and for defraying the discretionary appropriations of the legislature. People v. Orange County Sup'rs, 27 Barb., N.Y., 575, 588. It has also been used in Delaware in the messages of the governor and other state papers to distinguish such funds as are available in the hands of the state treasurer for general purposes from assets of a special character, such as the school fund.

General revenue fund. As used in connection with municipal finances, the usual, ordinary, running, and incidental expenses of a municipality. Atchison, T. & S. F. Ry. Co. v. City of Topeka, 95 Kan. 747, 149 P. 697.

No funds. This term denotes a lack of assets or money for a specific use. It is the return made by a bank to a check drawn upon it by a person who has no deposit to his credit there; also by an executor, trustee, etc., who has no assets for the specific purpose.

Public funds. An untechnical name for (1) the revenue or money of a government, state, or municipal corporation; (2) the bonds, stocks, or other securities of a national or state government. Money, warrants, or bonds, or other paper having a money value, and belonging to the state, or to any county, city, incorporated town or school district. Crawford & Moses' Dig. (Ark.) § 2835; Bank of Blytheville v. State, 148 Ark. 504, 230 S.W. 550, 553. The term applies to funds of every political subdivision of state wherein taxes are levied for public purposes. Ætna Casualty & Surety Co. v. Bramwell, D.C.Or., 12 F.2d 307, 309.

Revolving fund. Usually, a renewable credit over a defined period. In simple parlance it relates usually to a situation where a banker or merchant extends credit for a certain amount which can be paid off from time to time and then credit is again given not to exceed the same amount. It may also mean a fund, which, when reduced, is replenished by new funds from specified sources. U. S. v. Butterworth-Judson Corporation, C.C.A.N.Y., 297 F. 971, 979.

Sinking fund. The aggregate of sums of money (as those arising from particular taxes or sources of revenue) set apart and invested, usually at fixed intervals, for the extinguishment of the debt of a government or corporation, by the accumulation of interest. Elser v. Ft. Worth, Tex.Civ. App., 27 S.W. 740; Brooke v. Philadelphia, 162 Pa. 123, 29 A. 387, 24 L.R.A. 781. A fund arising from particular taxes, imposts, or duties, which is appropriated towards the payment of the interest due on a public loan and for the gradual payment of the principal. Union Pac. R. Co. v. Buffalo Co., 9 Neb. 453, 4 N.W. 53; Sidney Spitzer & Co. v. Commissioners of Franklin County, 188 N.C. 30, 123 S.E. 636, 639. A fund created for extinguishing or paying a funded debt. Ketchum v. Buffalo, 14 N.Y. 379, cited in Chicago & I. R. Co. v. Pyne, C.C.N.Y., 30 F. 89.

Sinking fund tax. A tax raised to be applied to the payment of interest on, and principal of public loan. Sidney Spitzer & Co. v. Commissioners of Franklin County, 188 N.C. 30, 123 S.E. 636, 639; Union Pac. R. Co. v. York County, 10 Neb. 612, 7 N.W. 270.

FUNDAMENTAL ERROR. See Error.

FUNDAMENTAL LAW. The law which determines the constitution of government in a state, and prescribes and regulates the manner of its exercise; the organic law of a state; the constitution.

FUNDAMUS. We found. One of the words by which a corporation may be created in England. 1 Bl.Comm. 473; 3 Steph.Comm. 173.

FUNDATIO. Lat. A founding or foundation. Particularly applied to the creation and endowment of corporations.

As applied to eleemosynary corporations such as colleges and hospitals, it is said that *"fundatio incipiens"* is the incorporation or grant of corporate powers, while "fundatio perficiens" is the endowment or grant or gift of funds or revenues. Dartmouth College v. Woodward, 4 Wheat. 667, 4 L.Ed. 629.

FUNDATOR. A founder (*q. v.*).

FUNDI PATRIMONIALES. Lands of inheritance.

FUNDI PUBLICI. Public lands.

FUNDITORES. Pioneers. Jacob.

FUNDUS. In the civil and old English law, land; land or ground generally; land, without considering its specific use; land, including buildings generally; a farm.

FUNERAL EXPENSES. Money expended in procuring the interment, cremation, or other disposition of a corpse, including suitable monument, perpetual care of burial lot and entertainment of those participating in wake. Gooch v. Beasley, 137 Tenn. 407, 193 S.W. 132, 133; Nelson v. Schoonover, 89 Kan. 388, 131 P. 147, 149; In re Borchardt's Will, 184 Wis. 561, 200 N.W. 461, 464; Oster's Ex'r v. Ohlman, 187 Ky. 341, 219 S.W. 187, 190; In re Gilchrist's Estate, 110 N.J.Eq. 666, 128 A. 876.

FUNGIBLE THINGS. Movable goods which may be estimated and replaced according to weight, measure, and number. Things belonging to a class, which do not have to be dealt with *in specie.* Standard Bank of Canada v. Lowman, D.C.Wash., 1 F.2d 935, 940; Edwards v. Cleveland Mill & Power Co., 193 N.C. 780, 138 S.E. 131, 134, 53 A.L.R. 1404.

Those things one specimen of which is as good as another, as is the case with half-crowns, or pounds of rice of the same quality. Horses, slaves, and so forth, are non-fungible things, because they differ individually in value, and cannot be exchanged indifferently one for another. Holl.Jur. 88.

Where a thing which is the subject of an obligation (which one man is bound to deliver to another) must be delivered *in specie,* the thing is not fungible; that very individual thing, and not another thing of the same or another class, in lieu of it, must be delivered. Where the subject of the obligation is a thing of a given class, the thing is said to be fungible; *i. e.,* the delivery of any object which answers to the generic description will satisfy the terms of the obligation. Aust.Jur. 483, 484.

FUNGIBILES RES. Lat. In the civil law, fungible things. See that title.

FUR. Lat. A thief. One who stole secretly or without force or weapons, as opposed to robber.

FUR MANIFESTUS. In the civil law, a manifest thief. A thief who is taken in the very act of stealing.

FURANDI ANIMUS. Lat. An intention of stealing.

FURCA. In old English law, a fork. A gallows or gibbet. Bract. fol. 56.

FURCA ET FLAGELLUM. Gallows and whip. *Tenure ad furcam et flagellum,* tenure by gallows and whip. The meanest of servile tenures, where the bondman was at the disposal of his lord for life and limb. Cowell.

FURCA ET FOSSA. Gallows and pit, or pit and gallows. A term used in ancient charters to signify a jurisdiction of punishing thieves, viz., men by hanging, women by drowning. Spelman; Cowell.

FURIAN LAW. See Lex Furia Caninia.

FURIGELDUM. A fine or mulct paid for theft.

FURIOSI NULLA VOLUNTAS EST. A madman has no will. Dig. 50, 17, 40; Broom, Max. 314.

FURIOSITY. In Scotch law, madness, as distinguished from fatuity or idiocy.

FURIOSUS. Lat. An insane man; a madman; a lunatic.

FURIOSUS ABSENTIS LOCO EST. A madman is the same with an absent person, [that is, his presence is of no effect.] Dig. 50, 17, 24, 1.

FURIOSUS NULLUM NEGOTIUM CONTRAHERE POTEST. A madman can contract nothing, [can make no contract]. Dig. 50, 17, 5.

FURIOSUS SOLO FURORE PUNITUR. A madman is punished by his madness alone; that is, he is not answerable or punishable for his actions. Co.Litt. 247*b*; 4 Bl.Comm. 24, 396; Broom, Max. 15.

FURIOSUS STIPULARE NON POTEST NEC ALIQUID NEGOTIUM AGERE, QUI NON INTELLIGIT QUID AGIT. 4 Coke, 126. A madman who knows not what he does cannot make a bargain, nor transact any business.

FURLINGUS. A furlong, or a furrow one-eighth part of a mile long. Co.Litt. 5*b*.

FURLONG. A measure of length, being forty poles, or one-eighth of a mile.

FURLOUGH. A leave of absence. Smith v. Sovereign Camp, W. O. W., 204 S.C. 193, 28 S.E.2d 808, 811. A temporary leave of absence to one in the armed service of the country, or to a government official or an employee, indicating some voluntary act on part of employee as contrasted with the phrase "lay-off" which contemplates action by employer. Jones v. Metropolitan Life Ins. Co., 156 Pa.Super. 156, 39 A.2d 721, 725. Also the document granting leave of absence.

In United States army furloughs are given only to enlisted men, officers being given leaves of absence. In United States navy furlough is an extended leave of absence, or a suspension from duty by an executive order, on half leave-of-absence pay, given only to an officer. A permit or passport. As a transitive verb, it means "to grant a furlough to; broadly, to allow leave of absence to." Ex parte Roach, D.C.Ala., 244 F. 625, 628.

FURNAGE. See Fornagium; Four.

FURNISH. To supply or provide. Talbott v. Caudill, 58 S.W.2d 385, 248 Ky. 146. For use in the accomplishment of a particular purpose. William M. Graham Oil & Gas Co. v. Oil Well Supply Co., 128 Okl. 201, 264 P. 591, 599. Implying some degree of active effort to accomplish the designated end. In re Opinion of the Justices, Mass., 304 Mass. 172, 14 N.E.2d 392, 393, 115 A.L.R. 1158. To provide for, to provide what is necessary for, to give, or afford. Juno v. Northland Elevator Co., 56 N.D. 223, 216 N.W. 562, 563. Equip synonymous. State ex rel. Davis v. Barber, 139 Fla. 706, 190 So. 809. To deliver, whether gratuitously or otherwise. Delp v. Brewing Co., 123 Pa. 42, 15 A. 871; Wyatt v. Larimer & W. Irr. Co., 1 Colo. App. 480, 29 P. 906. As used in the liquor laws, "furnish" means to provide in any way, and includes giving as well as selling. State v. Freeman, 27 Vt. 520; State v. Tague, 76 Vt. 118, 56 A. 535; Creel v. U. S., C.C.A.Okl., 21 F.2d 690; In re American Lime Co., D.C.Tenn., 201 F. 433, 434. To supply or provide in any way other than by sale. State v. McDermott, 108 Vt. 58, 182 A. 191, 192.

FURNITURE. This term includes that which furnishes, or with which anything is furnished or supplied; whatever must be supplied to a house, a room, place of business, or public building or the like, to make it habitable, convenient, or agreeable; goods, vessels, utensils, and other appendages necessary or convenient for housekeeping; whatever is added to the interior of a house or apartment, for use or convenience. Bell v. Golding, 27 Ind. 173; C. Ludwig Baumann & Co., Brooklyn, v. Manwit Corporation, 213 App.Div. 300, 207 N.Y.S. 437, 439; Fire Ass'n of Philadelphia v. Powell, Tex.Civ.App., 188 S.W. 47, 49; Smalley v. Dent County, Mo.Sup., 177 S.W. 620, 623.

The word comprehends only such furniture as is intended for use and ornament of apartments, but not libraries which happen to be there, nor plate. Civ.Code La. art. 477.

The term embraces everything about the house that has been usually enjoyed therewith, including plate, linen, china, and pictures, rugs, draperies and furnishings. Endicott v. Endicott, 41 N.J.Eq. 96, 3 A. 157; In re Kathan's Estate, 153 N.Y.S. 366, 368, 90 Misc.Rep. 540; Peckham v. Peckham, 97 N.J.Eq. 174, 127 A. 93. Readily movable articles which would be serviceable generally as household furniture. Farm & Home Savings & Loan Ass'n of Missouri v. Empire Furniture Co., Tex.Civ.App., 87 S.W.2d 1111, 1112.

Household furniture includes all personal chattels that may contribute to the use or convenience of the householder, or the ornament of the house; as plate, linen, china, both useful and ornamental, and pictures. But goods in trade, books, and wines will not pass by a bequest of household furniture. 1 Rop.Leg. 203.

FURNITURE OF A SHIP. This term includes everything with which a ship requires to be furnished or equipped to make her seaworthy; it comprehends all articles furnished by ship chandlers, which are almost innumerable. Weaver v. The S. G. Owens, 1 Wall.Jr. 369, Fed.Cas.No.17,310.

FURNIVAL'S INN. Formerly an inn of chancery. See Inns of Chancery.

FUROR BREVIS. A sudden transport of passion. Mosby v. Commonwealth, 168 Va. 688, 190 S.E. 152, 155.

FUROR CONTRAHI MATRIMONIUM NON SINIT, QUIA CONSENSU OPUS EST. Insanity prevents marriage from being contracted, because consent is needed. Dig. 23, 2, 16, 2; 1 Ves. & B. 140; 1 Bl.Comm. 439; Wightman v. Wightman, 4 Johns.Ch., N.Y., 343, 345.

FURST AND FONDUNG. In old English law, time to advise or take counsel. Jacob.

FURTA. A right derived from the king as supreme lord of a state to try, condemn, and execute *thieves* and felons within certain bounds or districts of an honour, manor, etc. Cowell seems to be doubtful whether this word should not read *furca*, which means directly a gallows. Cowell; Holthouse, L.Dict.

FURTHER. Not word of strict legal or technical import, and may be used to introduce negation or qualification of some precedent matter, but generally when used as an adverb it is word of comparison, and means "additional," and is equivalent to "moreover, or furthermore, something beyond what has been said or likewise, or also." Hollman v. Hollman, 88 Cal.App. 748, 264 P. 289, 290. Wider, or fuller, or something new. In re Andrus' Will, 156 Misc. 268, 281 N.Y.S. 831. Occasionally it may mean any, future, or other. London & S. F. Bank v. Parrott, 125 Cal. 472, 58 P. 164, 73 Am.St.Rep. 64; Galpin v. City of Chicago, 269 Ill. 27, 109 N.E. 713, 717, L.R.A.1917B, 176; Smith v. Craig, 211 N.Y. 456, 105 N.E. 798, 800, Ann.Cas.1915B, 937.

FURTHER ADVANCE. A second or subsequent loan of money to a mortgagor by a mortgagee, either upon the same security as the original loan was advanced upon, or an additional security. Equity considers the arrears of interest on a mortgage security converted into principal, by agreement between the parties, as a further advance. Wharton.

FURTHER ASSURANCE, COVENANT FOR. See Covenant.

FURTHER CONSIDERATION. In English practice, upon a motion for judgment or application for a new trial, the court may, if it shall be of opinion that it has not sufficient materials before it to enable it to give judgment, direct the motion to stand over for *further consideration,* and direct such issues or questions to be tried or determined, and such accounts and inquiries to be taken and made, as it may think fit. Rules Sup. Ct. xl, 10.

FURTHER DIRECTIONS. Where a master made a separate report, or one not in pursuance of a decree or decretal order, a petition for consequential directions had to be presented, since the cause could not be set down for further directions under such circumstances. See 2 Daniell, Ch.Pr. (5th Ed.) 1233, note.

FURTHER HEARING, or FURTHER PROCEEDINGS. In practice, hearing at another time; new trial; or other proceedings directed by appellate court. C. W. Hunt Co. v. Boston Elevated Ry. Co., 217 Mass. 319, 104 N.E. 728, 729; Morgan Esgineering Co. v. Cache River Drainage Dist., 122 Ark. 491, 184 S.W. 57, 59. Not a new proceeding but rather a continuation of an existing proceeding. In re Mills' Estate, 171 Misc. 42, 11 N.Y.S.2d 929, 932.

FURTHER INSTRUCTIONS. Additional instructions given to jury after they have once been instructed and have retired. White v. Sharpe, 219 Mass. 393, 107 N.E. 56.

FURTHER MAINTENANCE OF ACTION, PLEA TO. A plea grounded upon some fact or facts which have arisen since the commencement of the suit, and which the defendant puts forward for the purpose of showing that the plaintiff should not further maintain his action. Brown.

FURTHERANCE. Act of furthering, helping forward, promotion, advancement, or progress. Maryland Casualty Co. v. Smith, Tex.Civ.App., 40 S.W.2d 913, 914.

FURTHERANCE OF BUSINESS OF EMPLOYER. Discharge of duties of employment, as respects employer's liability for employees' torts. West v. F. W. Woolworth Co., 215 N.C. 211, 1 S.E. 2d 546, 548.

FURTIVE. In old English law, stealthily; by stealth. Fleta, lib. 1, c. 38, § 3.

FURTUM. Lat. Theft. The fraudulent appropriation to one's self of the property of another, with an intention to commit theft without the consent of the owner. Fleta, l. 1, c. 36; Bract. fol. 150; 3 Inst. 107.

The thing which has been stolen. Bract. fol. 151.

FURTUM CONCEPTUM. In Roman law, the theft which was disclosed where, upon searching any one in the presence of witnesses in due form, the thing stolen was discovered in his possession.

FURTUM EST CONTRECTATIO REI ALIENÆ FRAUDULENTA, CUM ANIMO FURANDI, INVITO ILLO DOMINO CUJUS RES ILLA FUERAT. 3 Inst. 107. Theft is the fraudulent handling of another's property, with an intention of stealing, against the will of the proprietor, whose property it was.

FURTUM GRAVE. In Scotch law, an aggravated degree of theft, anciently punished with death. It still remains an open point what amount of value raises the theft to this serious denomination. 1 Broun, 352, note. See 1 Swint. 467.

FURTUM MANIFESTUM. Open theft. Theft where a thief is caught with the property in his possession. Bract. fol. 150*b*.

FURTUM NON EST UBI INITIUM HABET DETENTIONIS PER DOMINIUM REI. 3 Inst. 107. There is no theft where the foundation of the detention is based upon ownership of the thing.

FURTUM OBLATUM. In the civil law, offered theft. *Oblatum furtum dicitur cum res furtiva ab aliquo tibi oblata sit, eaque apud te concepta sit.* Theft is called "*oblatum*" when a thing stolen is offered to you by any one, and found upon you. Inst. 4, 1, 4.

FUSE PLUG LEVEES. Under Mississippi Flood Control Act lower points for possible flood spillways were designated "fuse plug levees." U. S. v. Sponenbarger, Ark., 308 U.S. 256, 60 S.Ct. 225, 227, 84 L.Ed. 230.

FUSEL OIL. A volatile oily liquid obtained in the rectification of spirituous liquors made from the fermentation of grain, potatoes, the marc of grapes, and other material; its chief constituent being amyl alcohol, a direct nerve poison. Calkins v. National Travelers' Ben. Ass'n of Des Moines, 200 Iowa 60, 204 N.W. 406, 407, 41 A.L.R. 363.

FUST. See Fuz.

FUSTIGATIO. In old English law, a beating with sticks or clubs; one of the ancient kinds of punishment of malefactors. Bract. fol. 104*b*, lib. 3, tr. 1, c. 6.

FUSTIS. In old English law, a staff, used in making livery of seisin. Bract. fol. 40.

A baton, club, or cudgel.

FUTHWITE, or FITHWITE. A fine for fighting or breaking the peace. Cowell; Cun.L.Dict.

FUTURE ACQUIRED PROPERTY. Mortgages, especially of railroad companies are frequently made in terms to cover after-acquired property; such as rolling stock, etc. Philadelphia, W. & B. R. Co. v. Woelpper, 64 Pa. 366, 3 Am.Rep. 596; Shaw v. Bill, 95 U.S. 10, 24 L.Ed. 333; L.R. 16 Eq. 383. This may include future net earnings; Dunham v. Isett, 15 Iowa 284; the proceeds to be received from the sale of surplus lands; L.R. 2 Ch. 201; a ditch or flume in process of construction, which was held to cover all improvements and fixtures thereafter to be put on the line thereof; De Arguello v. Greer, 26 Cal. 620; rolling stock etc.; Philadelphia, W. & B. R. Co. v. Woelpper, 64 Pa. 366, 3 Am.Rep. 596; Benjamin v. R. Co., 49 Barb., N.Y., 441. Future calls of assessments on stock cannot be mortgaged; L.R. 10 Eq. 681; but calls already made can be; *id.*

A will speaks as of the death of the testator and ordinarily passes property acquired after its date.

FUTURE DEBT. In Scotch law, a debt which is created, but which will not become due till a future day. 1 Bell, Comm. 315.

FUTURE EARNINGS. A convenient way of designating earnings which, if it had not been for injury, could have been made in future, but which were lost as result of injury. Nowlin v. Kansas City Public Service Co., Mo.App., 58 S.W.2d 324.

FUTURE ESTATE. See Estate.

FUTURE INTERESTS. Interests in land or other things in which the privilege of possession or of enjoyment is future and not present. Commissioner of Internal Revenue v. Wells, C.C.A.6, 132 F.2d 405, 407.

FUTURES. This term has grown out of those purely speculative transactions, in which there is a nominal contract of sale for future delivery, but where in fact none is ever intended or executed.

The nominal seller does not have or expect to have the stock or merchandise he purports to sell, nor does the nominal buyer expect to receive it or to pay the price. Instead of that, a percentage or margin is paid, which is increased or diminished as the market rates go up or down, and accounted for to the buyer. King v. Quidnick Co., 14 R.I. 138; Lemonius v. Mayer, 71 Miss. 514, 14 So. 33; Plank v. Jackson, 128 Ind. 424, 26 N.E. 568; S. M. Weld & Co. v. Austin, 107 Miss. 279, 65 So. 247, 248.

FUTURI. Lat. Those who are to be. Part of the commencement of old deeds. "*Sciant præsentes et futuri, quod ego talis, dedi et concessi,*" etc., (Let all men now living and to come know that I, A. B., have, etc.) Bract. fol. 34*b*.

FUZ, or FUST. A Celtic word, meaning a wood or forest.

F. W. C. Free Woman of Color, up to the time of Civil War, applied to all persons not of the white race, including Indians. Sunseri v. Cassagne, 191 La. 209, 185 So. 1, 4.

FYHTWITE. One of the fines incurred for homicide.

FYKE. A fish-trap consisting of several successive conical nets with widestretched mouths. Mitchell v. Curtis, 135 Or. 595, 296 P. 1078. A bownet for catching fish. Pub.St.Mass.1882, p. 1291. Cf. Pound Net.

FYLE. In old Scotch law, to defile; to declare foul or defiled. Hence, to find a prisoner guilty.

FYLIT. In old Scotch practice, fyled; found guilty. See Fyle.

FYNDERINGA. (Sax.) An offense or trespass for which the fine or compensation was reserved to the king's pleasure. Leges Hen. I. c. 10. Its nature is not known. Spelman reads *fynderinga,* and interprets it *treasure trove;* but Cowell reads *fyrderinga,* and interprets it a joining of the king's *fird* or host, a neglect to do which was punished by a fine called *firdwite.* See Spelman, Gloss. Du Cange agrees with Cowell.

FYRD. Sax. In Anglo-Saxon law, the military array or land force of the whole country. Contribution to the fyrd was one of the imposts forming the *trinoda necessitas.* (Also spelled "ferd" and "fird.")

FYRDFARE. A summoning forth to join a military expedition; a summons to join the *fyrd* or army.

FYRDSOCNE, (or *fyrdsoken.*) Exemption from military duty; exemption from service in the *fyrd.*

FYRDWITE. A fine imposed for neglecting to join the *fyrd* when summoned. Also a fine imposed for murder committed in the army; also an acquittance of such fine.

G

G. In the Law French orthography, this letter is often substituted for the English W, particularly as an initial. Thus, "gage" for "wage," "garranty" for "warranty," "gast" for "waste."

G. A. O. General Accounting Office.

G. S. A. General Services Administration.

GABEL. An excise; a tax on movables; a rent, custom, or service. Co.Litt. 142a, 213.

A tax, impost, or excise duty, especially in continental Europe; formerly, in France, specifically the tax on salt, but also applied to taxes on other industrial products. "The gabels of Naples are very high on oil, wine, tobacco * * *." Cent. Dict.

—Land Gabel. See Land Gabel.

GABELLA. The Law Latin form of *"gabel,"* (*q. v.*).

Also, in Teutonic and early English history, the peasantry constituting a village or hamlet; the holdings of such a group of freemen and serfs, or of either. The original significance of the word seems to be in its indication of a small rent-paying community, the rents being rendered in kind or in labor. Cent. Dict. "So that *Gabella* meant all the member of a family having an interest in a certain holding, and sometimes meant the holding itself." W. K. Sullivan.

GABLATORES. Persons who paid *gabel*, rent, or tribute. Domesday; Cowell.

GABLUM. A rent; a tax. Domesday; Du Cange. The gable-end of a house. Cowell.

GABULUS DENARIORUM. Rent paid in money. Seld.Tit.Hon. 321.

GADSDEN PURCHASE. A term commonly applied to the territory acquired by the United States from Mexico by treaty of December 30, 1853, known as the Gadsden Treaty.

GAFFOLDGILD. The payment of custom or tribute. Scott.

GAFFOLDLAND. Property subject to the gaffoldgild, or liable to be taxed. Scott.

GAFOL. The same word as "gabel" or "gavel." Rent; tax; interest of money.

GAGE, *v.* In old English law, to pawn or pledge; to give as security for a payment or performance; to wage or wager.

GAGE, *n.*

In old English law, a pawn or pledge; something deposited as security for the performance of some act or the payment of money, and to be forfeited on failure or non-performance. Glanv. lib. 10, c. 6; Britt. c. 27.

A mortgage is a *dead-gage* or pledge; for, whatsoever profit it yields, it redeems not itself, unless the whole amount secured is paid at the appointed time. Cowell.

In French law, the contract of pledge or pawn; also the article pawned.

Gage, estates in. Those held *in vadio*, or pledge. They are of two kinds: (1) *Vivum vadium*, or living pledge, or vifgage; (2) *mortuum vadium*, or dead pledge, better known as "mortgage."

GAGER DE DELIVERANCE. In old English law, when he who has distrained, being sued, has not delivered the cattle distrained, then he shall not only avow the distress, but *gager deliverance, i. e.*, put in surety or pledge that he will deliver them. Fitzh.Nat.Brev.

GAGER DEL LEY. Wager of law (*q. v.*).

GAIN. Profits; winnings; increment of value. Gray v. Darlington, 15 Wall. 65, 21 L.Ed. 45; Thorn v. De Breteuil, 86 App.Div. 405, 83 N.Y.S. 849. Difference between receipts and expenditures; pecuniary gain. Stanton v. Zercher, 101 Wash. 383, 172 P. 559, 562; Rooney v. City of Omaha, 105 Neb. 447, 181 N.W. 143, 145. Difference between cost and sale price. Weil v. State, 237 Ala. 293, 186 So. 467, 469.

"Gain derived from capital," is a gain, profit, or something of exchangeable value proceeding from the property, severed from the capital however invested, and received or drawn by claimant for his separate use, benefit, and disposal. Commissioner of Internal Revenue v. Simmons Gin Co., C.C.A.10, 43 F.2d 327, 328.

GAINAGE. The gain or profit of tilled or planted land, raised by cultivating it; and the draught, plow, and furniture for carrying on the work of tillage by the baser kind of *sokemen* or *villeins*. Bract. l. i. c. 9.

GAINERY. Tillage, or the profit arising from it, or from the beasts employed therein.

GAINFUL. Profitable, advantageous, or lucrative. Smith v. Mutual Life Ins. Co. of New York, La. App., 165 So. 498, 500.

GAINFUL OCCUPATION. Within disability clause of policy, term means ordinary employment of particular insured, or such other employment, if any, as insured may fairly be expected to follow. Mutual Life Ins. Co. of New York v. Barron, 198 Ga. 1, 30 S.E.2d 879, 882.

GAINOR. In old English law, a sokeman; one who occupied or cultivated arable land. Old Nat. Brev. fol. 12.

GAIUS, INSTITUTES OF. See Institutes.

GAJUM. A thick wood. Spelman.

GALE. The payment of a rent, tax, duty, or annuity.

A gale is the right to open and work a mine within the Hundred of St. Briavel's, or a stone quarry within the open lands of the Forest of Dean.

The right is a license or interest in the nature of real estate, conditional on the due payment of rent and observance of the obligations imposed on the galee. It follows the ordinary rules as to the devolution and conveyance of real estate. The galee pays the crown a rent known as a "galeage rent," "royalty," or some similar name, proportionate to the quantity of minerals got from the mine or quarry. Sweet.

GALEA. In old records, a piratical vessel; a galley.

GALENES. In old Scotch law, amends or compensation for slaughter. Bell.

GALLI-HALFPENCE. A kind of coin which, with suskins and doitkins, was forbidden by St. 3 Hen. V. c. 1.

GALLIVOLATIUM. A cock-shoot, or cock-glade.

GALLON. A liquid measure containing 231 cubic inches, or four quarts; the standard gallon of the United States. State v. Standard Oil Co. of Louisiana, 188 La. 978, 178 So. 601, 607. The imperial gallon contains about 277, and the ale gallon 282, cubic inches. Hollender v. Magone, C.C.N.Y., 38 F. 914; Nichols v. Beard, C.C.Mass., 15 F. 437.

GALLOWS. A scaffold; a beam laid over either one or two posts, from which malefactors are hanged.

GAMACTA. In old European law, a stroke or blow. Spelman.

GAMALIS. A child born in lawful wedlock; also one born to betrothed but unmarried parents. Spelman.

GAMBLE. To play, or game, for money or other stake; hence to stake money or other thing of value on an uncertain event. It involves, not only chance, but a hope of gaining something beyond the amount played. State v. Mint Vending Machine No. 195084, 85 N.H. 22, 154 A. 224, 226.

The word "gamble" is perhaps the most apt and substantial to convey the idea of unlawful play that our language affords. It is inclusive of hazarding and betting as well as playing. Bennett v. State, 2 Yerg., Tenn., 474. Allen v. Commonwealth, 178 Ky. 250, 198 S.W. 896, 897.

It is not necessary that the player shall hazard what he plays, but it is equally "gambling" if he may win by chance more than the value expended by him. Nelson v. State, 37 Okl.Cr. 90, 256 P. 939, 940; City of Moberly v. Deskin, 169 Mo.App. 672, 155 S.W. 842, 843.

To constitute "gambling," winner must either pay consideration for his chance to win, or without paying anything in advance stand chance to lose or win. R. J. Williams Furniture Co. v. McComb Chamber of Commerce, 147 Miss. 649, 112 So. 579, 580, 57 A.L.R. 421; Almy Mfg. Co. v. City of Chicago, 202 Ill.App. 240.

Commercialized gambling is such gambling as is a source of sure and steady profit. State v. Gardner, 151 La. 874, 92 So. 368, 371.

A common gambler is one who furnishes facilities for gambling, or keeps or exhibits a gambling table, establishment, device, or apparatus. People v. Sponsler, 1 Dak. 291, 46 N.W. 459, citing cases.

GAMBLER. One who follows or practices games of chance or skill, with the expectation and purpose of thereby winning money or other property. Buckley v. O'Niel, 113 Mass. 193, 18 Am.Rep. 466; Brannon v. State, 16 Ala.App. 259, 76 So. 991, 993.

GAMBLING DEVICE. Such device, apparatus, and the like, as is used and employed for gambling, in the sense that in using it, money or the like is staked, wagered, won, or lost as a direct result of its employment or operation. Commonwealth v. Mihalow, 142 Pa.Super. 433, 16 A.2d 656, 659. A machine, implement, or contrivance of any kind for the playing of an unlawful game of chance or hazard. In re Lee Tong, D.C.Or., 18 F. 257; State v. McTeer, 129 Tenn. 535, 167 S.W. 121, 122.

GAMBLING POLICY. In life insurance, one issued to a person, as beneficiary, who has no pecuniary interest in the life insured. Otherwise called a "wager policy." Gambs v. Covenant Mut. L. Ins. Co., 50 Mo. 47.

GAME. Wild birds and beasts. The word includes all game birds, game fowl, and game animals. State ex rel. Sofeico v. Heffernan, 41 N.M. 219, 67 P.2d 240, 246.

Birds and beasts of a wild nature, obtained by fowling and hunting. Bacon, Abr. Coolidge v. Choate, 11 Metc., Mass., 79. The term is said to include (in England) hares, pheasants, partridges, grouse, heath, or moor game, black game, and bustards. Brown. 1 & 2 Wm. IV. c. 32. Graves v. Dunlap, 87 Wash. 648, 152 P. 532, 533, L.R.A.1916C, 338, Ann.Cas.1917B, 944.

A sport, pastime or contest. Lasseter v. O'Neill, 162 Ga. 826, 135 S.E. 78, 80, 49 A.L.R. 1076; Everhart v. People, 54 Colo. 272, 130 P. 1076, 1077. A contrivance which has for its object to furnish sport, recreation, or amusement. Ex parte Williams, 127 Cal.App. 424, 16 P.2d 172, 173. See Gaming.

GAME-KEEPER. One who has the care of keeping and preserving the game on an estate, being appointed thereto by a lord of a manor.

GAME LAWS. Laws passed for the preservation of game, usually forbidding the killing of specified game during certain seasons, Poulos v. State, 49 Ga.App. 20, 174 S.E. 253, or by certain described means. As to English game-laws, see 2 Steph. Comm. 82; 1 & 2 Wm. IV. c. 32.

GAME OF CHANCE. One in which result as to success or failure depends less on skill and experience of player than on purely fortuitous or accidental circumstances incidental to game or manner of playing it or device or apparatus with which it is played, but not under control of player. People v. Cohen, 160 Misc. 10, 289 N.Y.S. 397, 400.

GAMING. An agreement between two or more persons to play together at a game of chance for a stake or wager which is to become the property of the winner, and to which all contribute. In re Stewart, D.C.N.J., 21 F. 398; People v. Todd, 51 Hun, 446, 4 N.Y.S. 25; Carpenter v. Beal-McDonnell & Co., D.C.Ark., 222 F. 453, 460.

"Gaming" and "gambling," in statutes, are similar in meaning, and either one comprehends the idea that, by a bet, by chance, by some exercise of skill, or by the transpiring of some event unknown until it occurs, something of value is, as the conclusion of premises agreed, to be transferred from a loser to a winner. Bish.St.Crimes, § 858. Town of Eros v. Powell, 137 La. 342, 68 So. 632, 634; Reinmiller v. State, 93 Fla. 462, 111 So. 633, 635.

"Gaming" is properly the act or engagement of the players. If by-standers or other third persons put up a stake or wager among themselves, to go to one or the other according to the result of the game, this is more correctly termed "betting."

GAMING CONTRACTS. See Wager.

GAMING HOUSE. A building, place, or room kept for use as a place to gamble, or to keep or exhibit for the purpose of gaming, any bank, table, alley, machine, wheel, or device, Davis v. State, Tex.Civ. App., 165 S.W.2d 757, 758; as the business of the occupants. 1 Russ.Crimes, 299; Rosc.Crim.Ev. 663; People v. Jackson, 3 Denio, N.Y., 101, 45 Am. Dec. 449.

GAMING TABLE. Any table that may be used for playing games of chance for money or property. State v. Leaver, 171 Mo.App. 371, 157 S.W. 821, 822; Everhart v. People, 54 Colo. 272, 130 P. 1076, 1080.

GANANCIAL PROPERTY. In Spanish law, a species of community in property enjoyed by husband and wife, the property being divisible between them equally on a dissolution of the marriage. 1 Burge, Confl.Law, 418. Cartwright v. Cartwright, 18 Tex. 634; Cutter v. Waddingham, 22 Mo. 254. See Community.

GANANCIALES. A Spanish term, used as either a noun or adjective, and applied to property acquired during marriage. Discussed in Sanchez v. Bowers, C.C.A.N.Y., 70 F.2d 715, 716. See Ganancial Property, *supra*.

GANANCIAS. In Spanish law, gains or profits.

GANG. Any company of persons who go about together or act in concert, in modern use mainly for criminal purposes. State v. Gaynor, 119 N.J.L. 582, 197 A. 360, 362.

GANG-WEEK. The time when the bounds of the parish are lustrated or gone over by the parish officers,—rogation week. Enc.Lond.

GANGIATORI. Officers in ancient times whose business it was to examine weights and measures. Skene.

GANGSTER. A member of a gang of roughs, hireling criminals, thieves, or the like. State v. Gaynor, 119 N.J.L. 582, 197 A. 360, 362.

GANSER SYNDROME. A state in which questions are given nonsensical answers from which a hidden relevancy may be inferred. This is observed in prisoners who wish to gain leniency by simulating mental clouding.

GANTELOPE (pronounced "gauntlett.") A military punishment, in which the criminal running between the ranks receives a lash from each man. Enc.Lond. This was called "running the gauntlett."

GAOL. A prison for temporary confinement; a jail; a place for the confinement of offenders against the law.

As distinguished from "prison," it is said to be a place for temporary or provisional confinement, or for the punishment of the lighter offenses and misdemeanors. See, also, Jail.

GAOL DELIVERY. In criminal law, the delivery or clearing of a gaol of the prisoners confined therein, by trying them.

In popular speech, the clearing of a gaol by the escape of the prisoners.

General Gaol Delivery. In English law, at the assizes (*q. v.*) the judges sit by virtue of five several authorities, one of which is the commission of "general gaol delivery." This empowers them to try and deliverance make of every prisoner who shall be in the gaol when the judges arrive at the circuit town, whether an indictment has been preferred at any previous assize or not. 4 Bl.Comm. 270. This is also a part of the title of some American criminal courts, as, in Pennsylvania, the "court of oyer and terminer and general jail delivery."

GAOL LIBERTIES, GAOL LIMITS. A district around a gaol, defined by limits, within which prisoners are allowed to go at large on giving security to return. It is considered a part of the gaol. Singer v. Knott, 237 N.Y. 110, 142 N.E. 435, 436.

GAOLER. A variant of "jailer" (*q. v.*).

GARAGE. A place in which motor vehicles are stored and cared for. Legum v. Carlin, 168 Md. 191, 177 A. 287, 290, 99 A.L.R. 536.

GARANDIA, or GARANTIA. A warranty. Spelman.

GARANTIE. In French law, this word corresponds to warranty or covenants for title in English law. In the case of a sale this *garantie* extends to two things: (1) Peaceful possession of the thing sold; and (2) absence of undisclosed defects, (*défauts cachés.*) Brown.

GARATHINX. In old Lombardic law, a gift; a free or absolute gift; a gift of the whole of a thing. Spelman.

GARAUNTOR. L. Fr. In old English law, a warrantor of land; a vouchee; one bound by a warranty to defend the title and seisin of his alienee, or, on default thereof, and on eviction of the tenant, to give him other lands of equal value. Britt. c. 75.

GARBA. In old English law, a bundle or sheaf. *Blada in garbis,* corn or grain in sheaves. Reg. Orig. 96; Bract. fol. 209.

GARBA SAGITTARUM. A sheaf of arrows, containing twenty-four. Otherwise called *"schaffa sagittarum."* Skene.

GARBALES DECIMÆ. In Scotch law, tithes of corn, (grain.) Bell.

GARBLE. In English statutes, to sort or cull out the good from the bad in spices, drugs, etc. Cowell.

GARBLER OF SPICES. An ancient officer in the city of London, who might enter into any shop, warehouse, etc., to view and search drugs and spices, and garble and make clean the same, or see that it be done. Mozley & Whiteley.

GARCIO STOLÆ. "Groom of the stole" (*q. v.*).

GARCIONES. Servants who follow a camp. Wals. 242.

GARD, or GARDE. L. Fr. Wardship; care; custody; also the ward of a city.

GARDEIN. A keeper; a guardian.

GARDEN. A small piece of land, appropriated to the cultivation of herbs, fruits, flowers, or vegetables. People v. Greenburgh, 57 N.Y. 550; Ferry v. Livingston, 115 U.S. 542, 6 S.Ct. 175, 29 L.Ed. 489; Hubel v. McAdon, 190 Iowa 677, 180 N.W. 994, 995.

GARDEN SEEDS. Seeds for kitchen gardens. Ross & Co. v. U. S., 9 Ct.Cust.App. 235.

GARDEN TOOLS. Instruments or devices movable in character and operated by hand, or possibly by other motive power in the performance of work in the garden or on the farm. Murphy v. Continental Ins. Co., 178 Iowa 375, 157 N.W. 855, 857, L.R.A.1917B, 934.

GARDIA. L. Fr. Custody; wardship.

GARDIANUS. In old English law, a guardian, defender, or protector. In feudal law, *gardio*. Spelman.

A warden. *Gardianus ecclesiæ*, a churchwarden. *Gardianus quinque portuum*, warden of the Cinque Ports. Spelman.

GARDINUM. In old English law, a garden. Reg. Orig. 1*b*, 2.

GARENE. L. Fr. A warren; a privileged place for keeping animals.

GARNESTURA. In old English law, victuals, arms, and other implements of war, necessary for the defense of a town or castle. Mat.Par. 1250.

GARNISH, *n*. In English law, money paid by a prisoner to his fellow-prisoners on his entrance into prison.

GARNISH, *v*. To warn or summon.

To issue process of garnishment against a person.

GARNISHEE. One garnished; a person against whom process of garnishment is issued; one who has money or property in his possession belonging to a defendant, or who owes the defendant a debt, which money, property, or debt is attached in his hands, with notice to him not to deliver or pay it over until the result of the suit be ascertained. Welsh v. Blackwell, 14 N.J.L. 348; Smith v. Miln, 22 Fed.Cas. 606; Edwards v. Stein, 94 N.J.Eq. 251, 119 A. 504, 505.

GARNISHMENT. A warning to a person in whose hands the effects of another are attached, not to pay the money or deliver the property of the defendant in his hands to him, but to appear and answer the plaintiff's suit. Drake, Attachm. § 451; National Bank of Wilmington v. Furtick, 2 Marv., Del., 35, 42 A. 479, 44 L.R.A. 115, 69 Am.St.Rep. 99; Jeary v. American Exch. Bank, 2 Neb. (Unof.) 657, 89 N.W. 772.

A statutory proceeding whereby person's property, money, or credits in possession or under control of, or owing by, another are applied to payment of former's debt to third person by proper statutory process against debtor and garnishee. Beggs v. Fite, 130 Tex. 46, 106 S.W.2d 1039, 1042.

It is an incident to or an auxiliary of judgment rendered in principal action, and is resorted to as a means of obtaining satisfaction of judgment by reaching credits or property of judgment debtor in hands of garnishee. Graber v. Ft. Dearborn Casualty Underwriters of Chicago, Ill., Mo. App., 35 S.W.2d 933, 934. Or by reaching goods, moneys, or effects of debtor in possession of another, or by applying on a judgment, debts or credits due to debtor by another. Nacy v. Le Page, 341 Mo. 1039, 111 S.W.2d 25, 114 A.L.R. 259.

Also a warning to any one for his appearance, in a cause in which he is not a party, for the information of the court and explaining a cause. Cowell; Crawford State Bank of Crawford v. Murphy, 142 Neb. 795, 7 N.W.2d 762, 763.

Equitable garnishment, is sometimes applied to the statutory proceedings authorized in some states, upon the return of an execution unsatisfied, whereby an action something like a bill of discovery may be maintained against the judgment debtor and any third person, to compel the disclosure of any money or property or chose in action belonging to the debtor or held in trust for him by such third person, and to procure satisfaction of the judgment out of such property. Geist v. St. Louis, 156 Mo. 643, 57 S.W. 766, 79 Am.St.Rep. 545. See St. Louis v. O'Neil Lumber Co., 114 Mo. 74, 21 S.W. 484.

Execution. See Execution.

GARNISTURA. In old English law, garniture; whatever is necessary for the fortification of a city or camp, or for the ornament of a thing. 8 Rymer, 328; Du Cange; Cowell; Blount.

GARRISON. The permanent home of the army in time of peace, where soldiers are given proper training with a view of having them prepared for the intelligent performance of duty in event of conflict. Hines v. Mikell, C.C.A.S.C., 259 F. 28, 31.

GARROTING. A method of inflicting the death penalty on convicted criminals practiced in Spain, Portugal, and some Spanish-American countries, consisting in strangulation by means of an iron collar which is mechanically tightened about the neck of the sufferer, sometimes with the variation that a sharpened screw is made to advance from the back of the apparatus and pierce the base of the brain. Also, popularly, any form of strangling resorted to to overcome resistance or induce unconsciousness, especially as a concomitant to highway robbery.

GARSUMME. In old English law, an amerciament or fine. Cowell.

GARTER. A string or ribbon by which the stocking is held upon the leg.

The mark of the highest order of English knighthood, ranking next after the nobility.

This military order of knighthood is said to have been first instituted by Richard I., at the siege of Acre, where he caused twenty-six knights who firmly stood by him to wear thongs of blue leather about their legs. It is also said to have been perfected by Edward III. and to have received some alterations, which were afterwards laid aside, from Edward VI. The badge of the order is the image of St. George, called the "George," and the motto is "*Honi soit qui mal y pense.*" Wharton.

This order called "Knights of the Garter" is otherwise called "Knights of the Order of St. George." They form the highest order of knights.

GARTH. In English law, a yard; a little close or homestead in the north of England. Cowell; Blount.

A dam or wear in a river, for the catching of fish.

GARYTOUR. In old Scotch law, warder. 1 Pitc. Crim. Tr. pt. 1, p. 8.

GAS. An aeriform fluid. Lamar v. Iowa State Traveling Men's Ass'n, 216 Iowa 371, 249 N.W. 149, 92 A.L.R. 159. That gas used for illuminating purposes and for fuel. Birss v. Order of United Commercial Travelers of America, 109 Neb. 226, 190 N.W. 486, 487.

Casing-head gas is gas which flows from oil wells, coming between casing and tubing. Humble Oil & Refining Co. v. Poe, Tex.Com.App., 29 S.W.2d 1019, 1020.

Natural gas is the gas obtained from wells in coal and oil regions, and used for lighting and heating. Dry natural gas is natural gas which does not contain an appreciable amount of readily condensible gasoline; it is usually not intimately associated with petroleum. Wet natural gas is natural gas from which a gasoline can be extracted in sufficient quantities to warrant the installation of a plant, or natural gas which contains readily condensible gasoline. Mussellem v. Magnolia Petroleum Co., 107 Okl. 183, 231 P. 526, 530.

It is a colorless inflammable fluid, the first and highest distillant of crude petroleum. Being the most volatile component of petroleum, it readily separates from it, and, in the process of distillation, is the oil drawn off at the lowest temperature. Locke v. Russell, 75 W.Va. 602, 84 S.E. 948, 949; Hammett Oil Co. v. Gypsy Oil Co., 95 Okl. 235, 218 P. 501, 504, 34 A.L.R. 275.

GASOLINE. A volatile, inflammable hydrocarbon mixture used as a fuel, especially for internal combustion engines. Coleman v. United States, Ct.Cl., 37 F.Supp. 273, 277.

GAST. L. Fr. Waste. See the letter "G," *supra.*

GASTALDUS. A temporary governor of the country. Blount. A bailiff or steward. Spelman.

GASTEL. L. Fr. Wastel; wastel bread; the finest sort of wheat bread. Britt. c. 30: Kelham.

GASTINE. L. Fr. Waste or uncultivated ground. Britt. c. 57.

GATE (Sax. *geat*), at the end of names of places, signifies way or path. Cunningham, Law Dict.

In the words *beast-gate* and *cattle-gate*, it means a right of pasture.

In modern railroad practice, movable barriers which close entrance through which public is permitted to enter upon, pass over, and leave property of railway company inclosed within its right of way fences. Jeffery v. Kewaunee, G. B. & W. Ry. Co., 189 Wis. 207, 207 N.W. 283, 284.

These rights are local to Suffolk and Yorkshire respectively; they are considered as corporeal hereditaments, for which ejectment will lie; 2 Stra. 1084, 1 Term 137; and are entirely distinct from right of common. The right is sometimes connected with the duty of repairing the *gates* of the pasture; and perhaps the name comes from this.

GAUDIES. A term used in the English universities to denote double commons.

GAUGE. The measure of width of a railway, fixed, with some exceptions, at 4 feet 8½ inches in Great Britain and America, and 5 feet 3 inches in Ireland.

GAUGEATOR. A gauger. Lowell.

GAUGER. A surveying officer under the customs, excise, and internal revenue laws, appointed to examine all tuns, pipes, hogsheads, barrels and tierces of wine, oil, and other liquids, and to give them a mark of allowance, as containing lawful measure. There are also private gaugers in large seaport towns, who are licensed by government to perform the same duties. Rapal. & L.

GAUGETUM. A gauge or gauging; a measure of the contents of any vessel.

GAVEL. In English law, custom; tribute; toll; yearly rent; payment of revenue; of which there were anciently several sorts; as *gavel-corn, gavel-malt, oat-gavel, gavel-fodder,* etc. Termes de la Ley; Cowell; Co.Litt. 142*a*.

GAVEL-MAN. A tenant liable to the payment of gavel or tribute. Somn. Gavelkind, 23.

GAVELBRED. Rent reserved in bread, corn, or provision; rent payable in kind. Cowell.

GAVELCESTER. A certain measure of rent-ale. Cowell.

GAVELET. An obsolete writ. An ancient and special kind of *cessavit,* used in Kent and London for the recovery of rent. The statute of gavelet is 10 Edw. II. 2 Reeve, Eng.Law, c. 12, p. 298. See Emig v. Cunningham, 62 Md. 460.

GAVELGELD. That which yields annual profit or toll. The tribute or toll itself. Cowell; Du Cange.

GAVELHERTE. A service of plowing performed by a customary tenant. Cowell; Du Cange.

GAVELING MEN. Tenants who paid a reserved rent, besides some customary duties to be done by them. Cowell.

GAVELKIND. A species of socage tenure common in Kent, in England, where the lands descend to all the sons, or heirs of the nearest degree, together; may be disposed of by will; do not escheat for felony; may be aliened by the heir at the age of fifteen; and dower and curtesy is given of half the land. Stim.Law Gloss.

GAVELLA. See Gabella.

GAVELLER. An officer of the English crown having the general management of the mines, pits, and quarries in the Forest of Dean and Hundred of St. Briavel's, subject, in some respects, to the control of the commissioners of woods and forests. He grants gales to free miners in their proper order, accepts surrenders of gales, and keeps the registers required by the acts. There is a deputy-gaveller, who appears to exercise most of the gaveller's functions. Sweet.

GAVELMED. A customary service of mowing meadow-land or cutting grass (*consuetudo falcandi*). Blount.

GAVELREP. Bedreap or bidreap; the duty of reaping at the bid or command of the lord. Somn. Gavelkind, 19, 21; Cowell.

GAVELWERK. A customary service, either *manuopera,* by the person of the tenant, or *carropera,* by his carts or carriages. Blount; Somn. Gavelkind, 24; Du Cange.

GAZETTE. The official publication of the English government, also called the "London Gazette."

It is evidence of acts of state, and of everything done by the king in his political capacity. Orders of adjudication in bankruptcy are required to be published therein; and the production of a copy of the "Gazette," containing a copy of the order of adjudication, is evidence of the fact. Mozley & Whitley.

GDN. Equivalent to guardian. National Surety Co. v. McNeill's Guardian, 251 Ky. 509, 65 S.W.2d 721.

GEBOCCED. An Anglo-Saxon term, meaning "conveyed."

GEBOCIAN. In Saxon law, to convey; to transfer *boc* land, (book-land or land held by charter.) The grantor was said to *gebocian* the alienee. See 1 Reeve, Eng.Law, 10.

GEBRAUCHSMUSTER. Issued in accordance with law of Germany, it is a patent. Permutit Co. v. Graver Corporation, D.C.Ill., 37 F.2d 385, 390.

GEBUR (Sax.). A boor.

His services varied in different places—to work for his lord two or more days a week; to pay gafols in money, barley, etc.; to pay hearth money, etc. He was a tenant with a house and a yard land or virgate or two oxen. Maitl. Domesday and Beyond 37.

GEBURSCRIPT. In old English law, neighborhood or adjoining district. Cowell.

GEBURUS. In old English law, a country neighbor; an inhabitant of the same *geburscript,* or village. Cowell.

GELD. In Saxon law, money or tribute. A mulct, compensation, value, price.

Angeld was the single value of a thing; *twigeld,* double value, etc. So, *weregeld* was the value of a man slain; *orfgeld,* that of a beast. Brown. A land tax of so much per hide or carucate. Maitl. Domesday Book 120. The compensation for a crime.

GELDABILIS. In old English law, taxable; geldable.

GELDABLE. Liable to pay geld; liable to be taxed. Kelham.

GELDING. A horse that has been castrated, and which is thus distinguished from the horse in his natural and unaltered condition. A "ridgling" (a half-castrated horse) is not a gelding, but a horse, within the denomination of animals in the statutes. Brisco v. State, 4 Tex.App. 219, 30 Am.Rep. 162.

GELT. As a verb, an alternative form of the past tense of "geld," commonly "gelded." See Gelding.

As a noun, used incorrectly for *geld* (*q. v.*). Webster, New Int. Dict.

GEMMA. Lat. In the civil law, a gem; a precious stone. Gems were distinguished by their transparency; such as emeralds, chrysolites, amethysts. Dig. 34, 2, 19, 17.

GEMOT. In Saxon law, a meeting or moot; a convention; a public assemblage.

These were of several sorts, such as the *witena-gemot,* or meeting of the wise men; the *folc-gemot,* or general assembly of the people; the *shire-gemot,* or county court; the *burg-gemot,* or borough court; the *hundred-gemot,* or hundred court; the *hali-gemot,* or court-baron; the *hal-mote,* a convention of citizens in their public hall; the *holy-mote,* or holy court; the *swein-gemote,* or forest court; the *ward-mote,* or ward court. Wharton; Cunningham.

GENEALOGY. The summary history or table of a family, showing how the persons there named are connected together.

GENEARCH. The head of a family.

GENEATH. In Saxon law, a villein, or agricultural tenant, (*villanus villicus;*) a hind or farmer, (*firmarius rusticus.*) Spelman.

GENER. Lat. In the civil law, a son-in-law; a daughter's husband. (*Filiæ vir.*) Dig. 38, 10, 4, 6.

GENERAL. From Latin word genus. It relates to the whole kind, class, or order. Leuthold v. Brandjord, 100 Mont. 96, 47 P.2d 41, 45. Pertaining to or designating the genus or class, as distinguished from that which characterizes the species or individual; universal, not particularized, as opposed to special; principal or central, as opposed to local; open or available to all, as opposed to select; obtaining commonly, or recognized universally, as opposed to particular; universal or unbounded, as opposed to limited; comprehending the whole or directed to the whole, as distinguished from anything applying to or designed for a portion only. Board of Sup'rs of Attala County v. Illinois Cent. R. Co., 186 Miss. 294, 190 So. 241. Extensive or common to many. Record v. Ellis, 97 Kan. 754, 156 P. 712, 713, L.R.A.1916E, 654, Ann. Cas.1917C, 822; McNeill v. McNeill, 166 Iowa, 680, 148 N.W. 643, 651.

As a noun, the word is the title of a principal officer in the army, usually one who commands a whole army, division, corps, or brigade. In the United States army, the rank of "general" is one of the highest, next to the commander in chief, and is only occasionally created. The officers next in rank are lieutenant general, major general, and brigadier general.

As to general "Acceptance," "Administration of Estates," "Agent," "Appearance," "Assignment," "Average," "Benefit," "Challenge," "Character," "Charge," "Covenant," "Creditor," "Custom," "Damages," "Demurrer," "Denial," "Deposit," "Device," "Election," "Finding," "Franchise," "Fund," "Gaol Delivery," "Guardian," "Guaranty," "Imparlance," "Insurance," "Intent," "Issue," "Legacy," "Letter of Credit," "Malice," "Meeting," "Monition," "Mortgage," "Occupant," "Orders," "Owner," "Partnership," "Power," "Property," "Replication," "Restraint of Trade," "Retainer," "Return Day," "Rules," "Sessions," "Ship," "Statute," "Tail," "Tenancy," "Term," "Traverse," "Usage," "Verdict," "Warrant," and "Warranty," see those titles.

GENERAL AGENCY BUSINESS. One engaged in such general agency business is one not engaged as agent for single firm or person, but holding himself out to public as being engaged in business of being agent. Comer v. State Tax Commission of New Mexico, 41 N.M. 403, 69 P.2d 936, 939.

GENERAL ASSEMBLY. State Senate and House of Representatives. Pirtle v. Brown, C.C.A.Tenn., 118 F.2d 218, 220.

The policy making body of the United Nations. It is composed of from one to five delegates from each member nation, although each member nation has but one vote.

The highest "judicatory" of the Presbyterian church, representing in one body all of the particular churches of the denomination. Trustees of Pencader Presbyterian Church in Pencader Hundred v. Gibson, 26 Del.Ch. 375, 22 A.2d 782, 788.

GENERAL ASSIGNMENT FOR BENEFIT OF CREDITORS. A transfer of legal and equitable title to all debtor's property to trustee, with authority to liquidate debtor's affairs and distribute proceeds equitably to creditors. Central Fibre Products Co. v. Hardin, C.C.A.Tex., 82 F.2d 692, 694.

GENERAL ASSUMPSIT. An action of assumpsit brought upon the promise or contract implied by law in certain cases. Holcomb v. Kentucky Union Co., 262 Ky. 192, 90 S.W.2d 25, 28.

GENERAL AVERAGE CONTRIBUTION. A contribution by all parties in a sea adventure to make good loss sustained by one of their number on account of sacrifices voluntarily made of part of ship or cargo to save residue and lives of those on board from an impending peril or for extraordinary expenses necessarily incurred by one or more of the parties for the general benefit of all the interests embarked in the enterprise. Pacific Freighters Co. v. St. Paul Fire & Marine Ins. Co., C.C.A.Cal., 109 F.2d 310, 312.

GENERAL AVERAGE STATEMENT. Statement of account and admission on shipowner's part as to amount due cargo owner. Kohler & Chase v. United American Lines, D.C.N.Y., 60 F. 2d 530, 533.

GENERAL BEQUEST. One not segregated or withdrawn from estate under terms of will but to be paid in money or property as latter directs. In re McDougald's Estate, 149 Fla. 468, 6 So.2d 274.

GENERAL BOARD OF THE NAVY. A general advisory board to the Secretary of the Navy as to the preparation, maintenance and distribution of the fleet, plans of campaign, number and types of vessels, etc., number and ranks of officers and number and ratings of enlisted men, etc.

GENERAL BUILDING SCHEME. One under which owner of large tract of land divides it into building lots, to be sold to different persons for separate occupancy by deeds which contain uniform covenants restricting the use which the several grantees may make of their premises. Besch v. Hyman, 221 App.Div. 455, 223 N.Y.S. 231, 233.

GENERAL CIRCULATION. That of a general newspaper only, as distinguished from one of a special or limited character; 1 Lack.Leg.N., Pa., 114. It is not determined by number of subscribers but by the diversity of subscribers. Eisenberg v. Wabash, 355 Ill. 495, 189 N.E. 301, 302.

GENERAL COUNCIL. (1) A council consisting of members of the Roman Catholic Church from most parts of the world, but not from every part, as an ecumenical council. (2) One of the names of the English parliament.

GENERAL COURT. The name given to the legislature of Massachusetts and of New Hampshire, in colonial times, and subsequently by their constitutions; so called because the colonial legislature of Massachusetts grew out of the general court or meeting of the Massachusetts Company. Cent.Dict. See Citizens' Sav. & Loan Ass'n v. Topeka, 20 Wall. 666, 22 L.Ed. 455.

GENERAL CREDIT. The character of a witness as one generally worthy of credit. A distinction is sometimes insisted upon between this and "particular credit," which may be affected by proof of particular facts relating to the particular action. See Bemis v. Kyle, 5 Abb.Prac.,N.S., N.Y., 233.

GENERAL ESTATE. Customarily, the entire estate held by a person in his individual capacity. In re Shipley's Estate, 337 Pa. 580, 12 A.2d 347, 348.

In will requiring estate taxes to be paid out of general estate, "general estate" referred to "residuary estate" remaining after gift of personalty and use of realty to testator's wife, and hence gift to wife was exempt from contribution to estate taxes and interest thereon. In re Chambers' Estate, Sur., 54 N.Y.S.2d 88, 90.

GENERAL EXCEPTION. General exception is an objection to a pleading, or any part thereof, for want of substance, while a special exception is an objection to the form in which a cause of action is stated. Cochran v. People's Nat. Bank, Tex.Civ.App., 271 S.W. 433, 434.

GENERAL EXECUTION. A writ commanding an officer to satisfy a judgment out of any personal property of the defendant. If authorizing him to levy only on certain specified property, the writ is sometimes called a "special" execution. Pracht v. Pister, 30 Kan. 568, 1 P. 638.

GENERAL EXECUTOR. One whose power is not limited either territorially or as to the duration or subject of his trust. One who is to have charge of the whole estate, wherever found, and administer it to a final settlement.

GENERAL FEE CONDITIONAL. A grant to a person and heirs of his body. Blume v. Pearcy, 204 S.C. 409, 29 S.E.2d 673, 674.

GENERAL FIELD. Several distinct lots or pieces of land inclosed and fenced in as one common field. Mansfield v. Hawkes, 14 Mass. 440.

GENERAL IMPROVEMENT. Where primary purpose and effect of improvement is to benefit public generally, though it may incidentally benefit property owners in particular locality. Hinman v. Temple, 133 Neb. 268, 274 N.W. 605, 608, 111 A.L.R. 1217.

GENERAL INCLOSURE ACT. The statute 41 Geo. III, c. 109, which consolidates a number of regulations as to the inclosure of common fields and waste lands.

GENERAL INSTRUCTION. An explanation of legal terms specifically provided for by statute. Humble Oil & Refining Co. v. Owings, Tex.Civ. App., 128 S.W.2d 67, 76.

GENERAL INTEREST. In regard to admissibility of hearsay evidence, a distinction has been taken between "public" and "general" interest, the term "public" being strictly applied to that which concerns every member of the state, and the term "general" being confined to a lesser, though still a considerable, portion of the community. Tayl. Ev. § 609.

GENERAL JURISDICTION. Such as extends to all controversies that may be brought before a court within the legal bounds of rights and remedies; as opposed to *special* or *limited* jurisdiction, which covers only a particular class of cases, or cases where the amount in controversy is below a prescribed sum, or which is subject to specific exceptions. The terms "general" and "special," applied to jurisdiction, indicate the difference between a legal authority extending to the whole of a particular subject and one limited to a part; and, when applied to the terms of court, the occasion upon which these powers can be respectively exercised. Gracie v. Freeland, 1 N.Y. 232.

GENERAL LAND OFFICE. Formerly an office of the United States government, being a division of the Department of the Interior, having charge of all executive action relating to the public lands, including their survey, sale or other disposition, and patenting; originally constituted by Act of Congress in 1812. The General Land Office and the U. S. Grazing Service were consolidated into the Bureau of Land Management under the Department of the Interior by 1946 Reorganization Plan No. 3, § 403. See notes to 43 U.S.C.A. § 1.

GENERAL LAW. A law that affects the community at large. A general law as contradistinguished from one that is special or local, is a law that embraces a class of subjects or places, and does not omit any subject or place naturally belonging to such class. Van Riper v. Parsons, 40 N.J.Law, 1; Mathis v. Jones, 84 Ga. 804, 11 S.E. 1018; Brooks v. Hyde, 37 Cal. 376; Arms v. Ayer, 192 Ill. 601, 61 N.E. 851, 58 L.R.A. 277, 85 Am.St. Rep. 357.

A law, framed in general terms, restricted to no locality, and operating equally upon all of a group of objects, which, having regard to the purposes of the legislation, are distinguished by characteristics sufficiently marked and important to make them a class by themselves, is not a special or local law, but a general law. Jones v. Power County, 27 Idaho, 656, 150 P. 35, 37; Scarbrough v. Wooten, 23 N.M. 616, 170 P. 743; Toombs v. Sharkey, 140 Miss. 676, 106 So. 273, 275; Van Riper v. Parsons, 40 N.J.L. 123, 29 Am.Rep. 210.

GENERAL LIEN. A general lien is a right to detain a chattel, etc., until payment be made, not only of any debt due in respect of the particular chattel, but of any balance that may be due on general account in the same line of business. A general lien, being against the ordinary rule of law, depends entirely upon contract, express or implied, from the special usage of dealing between the parties. Wharton. Crommelin v. Railroad Co., 10 Bosw., N.Y., 80; McKenzie v. Nevius, 22 Me. 150, 38 Am.Dec. 291; Brooks v. Bryce, 21 Wend., N.Y., 16; 3 B. & P. 494.

GENERAL MANAGER. One having general direction and control of corporation's affairs, and who may do everything which corporation could do in transaction of its business. Continental Supply Co. v. Forrest E. Gilmore Co. of Texas, Tex. Civ.App., 55 S.W.2d 622. A manager for all general purposes of the corporation. Phœnix Finance Corporation v. Iowa-Wisconsin Bridge Co., 2 Terry 130, 16 A.2d 789, 793.

GENERAL POWER OF APPOINTMENT. One exercisable in favor of any person the donee may select. Johnstone v. Commissioner of Internal Revenue, C.C.A.9, 76 F.2d 55, 57.

GENERAL TAXES. Those imposed by and paid to state as a state which return taxpayer no special benefit other than the protection afforded him and his property by government, and promotion of schemes which have for their benefit the welfare of all. Pacific Gas & Electric Co. v. Sacramento Municipal Utility Dist., D.C.Cal., 17 F.Supp. 685, 686. A tax, imposed solely or primarily for purpose of raising revenue and merely granting person taxed right to conduct business or profession. American Can Co. v. City of Tampa, 152 Fla. 798, 14 So.2d 203, 210.

GENERAL WORDS. Such words of a descriptive character as are used in conveyances in order to convey, not only the specific property described, but also all kinds of easements, privileges, and appurtenances which may possibly belong to the property conveyed.

Such words are in general unnecessary; but are properly used when there are any easements or privileges reputed to belong to the property not legally appurtenant to it.

Such words are rendered unnecessary by the English conveyancing act of 1881, under which they are presumed to be included.

See, as to the effect of such words in deeds, 4 M. & S. 423; in a will; 1 P.Wms. 302; in a lease; 2 Moo. 592; in a release; 3 Mod. 277; in a covenant; 3 Moo. 703; in a statute; 1 Bla.Com. 88; 2 Co. 46.

GENERALE. The usual commons in a religious house, distinguished from *pietantiæ*, which on extraordinary occasions were allowed beyond the commons. Cowell.

GENERALE DICTUM GENERALITER EST INTERPRETANDUM. A general expression is to be interpreted generally. 8 Coke, 116*a*.

GENERALE NIHIL CERTUM IMPLICAT. A general expression implies nothing certain. 2 Coke, 34*b*. A general recital in a deed has not the effect of an estoppel. Best, Ev. p. 408, § 370.

GENERALE TANTUM VALET IN GENERALIBUS, QUANTUM SINGULARE IN SINGULIS. What is general is of as much force among general things as what is particular is among things particular. 11 Coke, 59*b*.

GENERALIA PRÆCEDUNT, SPECIALIA SEQUUNTUR. Things general precede, things special follow. Reg.Brev.; Branch, Princ.

GENERALIA SPECIALIBUS NON DEROGANT. Jenk.Cent. 120, cited L.R. 4 Exch. 226. General words do not derogate from special.

GENERALIA SUNT PRÆPONENDA SINGULARIBUS. Branch, Princ. General things are to precede particular things.

GENERALIA VERBA SUNT GENERALITER INTELLIGENDA. General words are to be understood generally, or in a general sense. 3 Inst. 76; Broom, Max. 647.

GENERALIBUS SPECIALIA DEROGANT. Special things take from generals. Halk.Lat.Max. 51.

GENERALIS CLAUSULA NON PORRIGITUR AD EA QUÆANTEA SPECIALITER SUNT COMPREHENSA. A general clause does not extend to those things which are previously provided for specially. 8 Coke, 154*b*. Therefore, where a deed at the first contains special words, and afterwards concludes in general words, both words, as well general as special, shall stand.

GENERALIS REGULA GENERALITER EST INTELLIGENDA. A general rule is to be understood generally. 6 Coke, 65.

GENERALS OF ORDERS. Chiefs of the several orders of monks, friars, and other religious societies.

GENERATIO. The issue or offspring of a mother-monastery. Cowell.

GENERATION. May mean either a degree of removal in computing descents, or a single succession of living beings in natural descent. McMillan v. School Committee, 107 N.C. 609, 12 S.E. 330, 10 L.R.A. 823.

GENEROSA. Gentlewoman. Cowell; 2 Inst. 668.

GENEROSI FILIUS. The son of a gentleman. Generally abbreviated "*gen. fil.*"

GENEROSUS. Lat. Gentleman; a gentleman. Spelman.

GENICULUM. A degree of consanguinity. Spelman.

GENOESE LOTTERY. Also known as the "numerical" lottery. As distinguished from the "class" lottery (see the title Dutch Lottery), it is a scheme by which, out of 90 consecutive numbers, five are to be selected or drawn by lot. The players have fixed on certain numbers, wagering that one, two, or more of them will be drawn among the five, or that they will appear in a certain order. Fleming v. Bills, 3 Or. 286.

GENS. Lat. In Roman law, a tribe or clan; a group of families, connected by common descent and bearing the same name, being all free-born and of free ancestors, and in possession of full civic rights.

GENS DE JUSTICE. In French law, officers of a court.

GENTES. Lat. People. *Contra omnes gentes*, against all people. Bract. fol. 37b. Words used in the clause of warranty in old deed.

GENTILES. In Roman law, the members of a *gens* or common tribe.

GENTLEMAN. Refers to a man of birth, but not noble; a man raised above the vulgar by his character or past. Bramblett v. Trust Co. of Georgia, 182 Ga. 87, 185 S.E. 72, 76. In English law. A person of superior birth.

Under the denomination of "gentlemen" are comprised all above yeoman; whereby noblemen are truly called "gentlemen." Smith de Rep. Ang. lib. 1, cc. 20, 21.

A "gentleman" is defined to be one who, without any title, bears a coat of arms, or whose ancestors have been freemen; and, by the coat that a gentleman giveth, he is known to be, or not to be, descended from those of his name that lived many hundred years since. Jacob. See Cresson v. Cresson, 6 Fed.Cas. 809.

GENTLEMAN USHER. One who holds a post at court to usher others to the presence, etc.

GENTLEWOMAN. The word is a relative one without any legal significance. It refers to a woman of the same rank or status as that of a "gentleman." Bramblett v. Trust Co. of Georgia, 182 Ga. 87, 185 S.E. 72, 76. A woman of birth above the common, or equal to that of a gentleman; an addition of a woman's state or degree.

GENTOO LAW. See Hindu Law.

GENUINE. As applied to notes, bonds, and other written instruments, this term means that they are truly what they purport to be, and that they are not false, forged, fictitious, simulated, spurious, or counterfeit. Baldwin v. Van Deusen, 37 N.Y. 492; Smeltzer v. White, 92 U.S. 392, 23 L.Ed. 508; Krug v. Sinclaire, 57 Cal.App. 563, 207 P. 696, 697. A will that has been revoked by later instrument and not revived by republication is not "genuine," within Surrogate's Court Act, § 144. In re Kiltz's Will, 125 Misc. 475, 211 N.Y.S. 450, 461.

GENUS. In the civil law, a general class or division, comprising several species. *In toto jure generi per speciem derogatur, et illud potissimum habetur quod ad speciem directum est,* throughout the law, the species takes from the genus, and that is most particularly regarded which refers to the species. Dig. 50, 17, 80.

A man's lineage, or direct descendants.

In logic, it is the first of the universal ideas, and is when the idea is so common that it extends to other ideas which are also universal; *e. g.*, incorporeal hereditament is *genus* with respect to a *rent,* which is *species.* Woolley, Introd. Log. 45; 1 Mill, Log. 133.

GEORGE-NOBLE. An English gold coin, value 6s. 8d.

GERECHTSBODE. In old New York law, a court messenger or constable. O'Callaghan, New Neth. 322.

GEREFA. In Saxon law, greve, reve, or reeve; a ministerial officer of high antiquity in England; answering to the *grave* or *graf* (*grafio*) of the early continental nations. The term was applied to various grades of officers, from the *scyre-gerefa, shire-grefe,* or *shire-reve,* who had charge of the county, (and, whose title and office have been perpetuated in the modern "sheriff,") down to the *tungerefa,* or town-reeve, and lower. Burrill.

GERENS. Bearing. *Gerens datum,* bearing date. 1 Ld. Raym. 336; Hob. 19.

GERMAN. Whole, full, or own, in respect to relationship or descent. Brothers-german, as opposed to half-brothers, are those who have both the same father and mother. Cousins-german are "first" cousins; that is, children of brothers or sisters.

GERMANE. In close relationship, appropriate, relative, pertinent. State ex rel. Riley v. District Court of Second Judicial Dist. in and for Silver Bow County, 103 Mont. 576, 64 P.2d 115, 119.

GERMANUS. Lat. Descended of the same stock, or from the same couple of ancestors; of the whole or full blood. Mackeld.Rom.Law, § 145.

GERMEN TERRÆ. Lat. A sprout of the earth. A young tree, so called.

GERONTOCOMI. In the civil law, officers appointed to manage hospitals for the aged poor.

GERONTOCOMIUM. In the civil law, an institution or hospital for taking care of the old. Cod. 1, 3, 46, 1; Calvin.

GERRYMANDER. A name given to the process of dividing a state or other territory into the authorized civil or political divisions, but with such a geographical arrangement as to accomplish a sinister or unlawful purpose, as, for instance, to secure a majority for a given political party in districts where the result would be otherwise if they were divided according to obvious natural lines, or to arrange school districts so that children of certain religions or nationalities shall be brought within the district and those of a different religion or nationality in another district. State v. Whitford, 54 Wis. 150, 11 N.W. 424.

GERSUMARIUS. In old English law, finable; liable to be amerced at the discretion of the lord of a manor. Cowell.

GERSUME. In old English law, expense; reward; compensation; wealth. It is also used for a fine or compensation for an offense. 2 Mon.Angl. 973.

GEST. In Saxon law, a guest. A name given to a stranger on the *second night* of his entertainment in another's house. *Twanight gest.*

GESTATION. The time during which a woman carries a fetus in her womb, from conception to birth. But, as used in all medical authorities, this phrase does not mean the actual number of days from conception to birth. Dazey v. Dazey, 50 Cal. App.2d 15, 122 P.2d 308, 309.

GESTIO. In the civil law, behavior or conduct.

Management or transaction. *Negotiorum gestio,* the doing of another's business; an interference in the affairs of another in his absence, from benevolence or friendship, and without authority. Dig. 3, 5, 45; Id. 46, 3, 12, 4; 2 Kent, Comm. 616, note.

GESTIO PRO HÆREDE. Behavior as heir.

This expression was used in the Roman law, and adopted in the civil law and Scotch law, to denote conduct on the part of a person appointed heir to a deceased person, or otherwise entitled to succeed as heir, which indicates an intention to enter upon the inheritance, and to hold himself out as heir to creditors of the deceased; as by receiving the rents due to the deceased, or by taking possession of his title-deeds, etc. Such acts will render the heir liable to the debts of his ancestor. Mozley & Whitley.

GESTOR. In the civil law, one who acts for another, or transacts another's business. Calvin.

GESTU ET FAMA. An ancient and obsolete writ resorted to when a person's good behavior was impeached. Lamb.Eir. l. 4, c. 14.

GESTUM. Lat. In Roman law, a deed or act; a thing done. Some writers affected to make a distinction between "*gestum*" and "*factum.*" But the best authorities pronounced this subtile and indefensible. Dig. 50, 16, 58.

GET, *n.* Under Hebraic law, evidence of the granting of a divorce. Kopit v. Zilberszmidt, Sup., 35 N.Y.S.2d 558, 560. A bill of divorce among the

Jews which is drawn in the Aramaic language, uniformly worded and carefully written by a proper scribe, and after proper ceremonies and questionings by the rabbi, especially as to whether both parties agree to the divorce, the husband hands to the wife in the presence of ten witnesses. Shilman v. Shilman, 105 Misc. 461, 174 N.Y.S. 385, 386.

GEVILLOURIS. In old Scotch law. Gaolers. 1 Pitc.Crim.Tr. pt. 2, p. 234.

GEWINEDA. In Saxon law, the ancient convention of the people to decide a cause.

GEWITNESSA. In Saxon and old English law, the giving of evidence.

GEWRITE. In Saxon law, deeds or charters; writings. 1 Reeve, Eng.Law 10.

GIBBET. A gallows; the post on which malefactors are hanged, or on which their bodies are exposed. It differs from a common gallows, in that it consists of one perpendicular post, from the top of which proceeds one arm, except it be a double gibbet, which is formed in the shape of the Roman capital T. Enc.Lond.

GIBBET LAW. Lynch law; in particular a custom anciently prevailing in the parish of Halifax, England, by which the free burghers held a summary trial of any one accused of petit larceny, and, if they found him guilty, ordered him to be decapitated.

GIFT. A voluntary transfer of personal property without consideration. Gordon v. Barr, Cal.App., 82 P.2d 955, 956, 957. A parting by owner with property without pecuniary consideration. Hays' Adm'rs v. Patrick, 266 Ky. 713, 99 S.W.2d 805, 809. A voluntary conveyance of land, or transfer of goods, from one person to another, made gratuitously, and not upon any consideration of blood or money. 2 Bl.Comm. 440; 2 Steph.Comm. 102; 2 Kent, Comm. 437. Ingram v. Colgan, 106 Cal. 113, 38 P. 315, 28 L.R.A. 187, 46 Am.St.Rep. 221; Gray v. Barton, 55 N.Y. 72, 14 Am.Rep. 181; Hynes v. White, 47 Cal.App. 549, 190 P. 836, 838; In re Van Alstyne, 207 N.Y. 298, 100 N.E. 802, 804.

Essential requisites of "gift" are capacity of donor, intention of donor to make gift, completed delivery to or for donee, and acceptance of gift by donee. In re Greenberg's Will, 286 N.Y.S. 56, 58, 158 Misc. 446.

In popular language, a voluntary conveyance or assignment is called a "deed of gift."

An "advancement" is a gift made with the intention that it shall be charged to the donee in the distribution of the donor's estate, while a "gift" is made without any purpose that it shall be thereafter accounted for. Hon v. Connelly, 253 Ky. 181, 69 S.W.2d 23.

An absolute gift, or gift inter vivos, as distinguished from a testamentary gift, or one made in contemplation of death, is one by which the donee becomes in the lifetime of the donor the absolute owner of the thing given, whereas a *donatio mortis causa* leaves the whole title in the donor, unless the event occurs (the death of the donor) which is to divest him. Buecker v. Carr, 60 N.J.Eq. 300, 47 A. 34; Goodan v. Goodan, 184 Ky. 79, 211 S.W. 423, 424; Baker v. Baker, 123 Md. 32, 90 A. 776, 779; McCoy v. Shawnee Building & Loan Ass'n, 122 Kan. 38, 251 P. 194, 195, 49 A.L.R. 1441; First Nat. Bank v. Liberty Trust Co., 151 Md. 241, 134 A. 210, 213, 47 A.L.R. 730; Starks v. Lincoln, 316 Mo. 483, 291 S.W. 132, 134.

As distinguished from a gift in trust, it is one where not only the legal title but the beneficial ownership as well is vested in the donee. Watkins v. Bigelow, 93 Minn. 210, 100 N.W. 1104; Allen v. Hendrick, 104 Or. 202, 206 P. 733, 740.

The only important difference between a "gift" and a "voluntary trust" is that in the case of a gift the thing itself passes to the donee, while in the case of a trust the actual, beneficial, or equitable title passes to the cestui que trust, while the legal title is transferred to a third person, or retained by the person creating it. In re Alberts' Estate, 38 Cal.App.2d 42, 100 P.2d 538, 540.

In English law, a conveyance of lands in tail; a conveyance of an estate tail in which the operative words are "I give," or "I have given." 2 Bl.Comm. 316; 1 Steph.Comm. 473.

—Gift in Default of Appointment. One implied on failure of donee to exercise a power of appointment where it was his duty to do so or where donor expresses an intention to make a legal gift to members of class in default of appointment. Restatement, Real Property, vol. 3, Topic 9, § 367.

GIFT CAUSA MORTIS. A gift of personalty made in expectation of death, then imminent, on an essential condition that property shall belong fully to donee in case donor dies as anticipated, leaving donee surviving him, and gift is not in meantime revoked. Flint v. Varney, 220 Iowa 1241, 264 N.W. 277, 278, 279.

GIFT DEED. A deed for a nominal sum. Bertelsen v. Bertelson, 49 Cal.App.2d 479, 122 P.2d 130, 133.

GIFT ENTERPRISE. A scheme for the division or distribution of articles to be determined by chance amongst those who have taken shares in the scheme. City of Oxford v. Ritz Theatre, Miss., 180 So. 88, 89; State v. Shugart, 138 Ala. 86, 35 So. 28, 100 Am.St.Rep. 17; Winston v. Beeson, 135 N.C. 271, 47 S.E. 457, 65 L.R.A. 167.

A sporting artifice by which, for example, a merchant or tradesman sells his wares for their market value, but, by way of inducement, gives to such purchaser a ticket which entitles him to a chance to win certain prizes to be determined after the manner of a lottery. Code 1933, § 26-6501. Barker v. State, 56 Ga.App. 705, 193 S.E. 605, 607, 609.

GIFTS INTER VIVOS. Gifts between the living, which are perfected and become absolute during lifetime of donor and donee. Neal v. Neal, 194 Ark. 226, 106 S.W.2d 595, 600.

GIFT OVER. A gift to one for life, and from and after his deceased to another, created a "gift over." In re Feeney's Estate, 293 Pa. 273, 142 A. 284, 289.

GIFT TO A CLASS. A gift of aggregate sum to body of persons uncertain in number at time of gift, to be ascertained at future time, who are all to take in equal shares, or some other definite proportion; share of each being dependent for its amount upon ultimate number taking. In re Murphy's Estate, 99 Mont. 114, 43 P.2d 233, 236; Wessborg v. Merrill, 195 Mich. 556, 162 N.W. 102, 106, L.R.A.1918E, 1074; Blackstone v. Althouse, 278 Ill. 481, 116 N.E. 154, 157, L.R.A.1918B, 230.

GIFTA AQUÆ. The stream of water to a mill. Mon.Angl. tom. 3.

GIFTOMAN. In Swedish law, the right to dispose of a woman in marriage, or the person possessing such right,—her father, if living, or, if he be dead, the mother.

GILD. In Saxon law, a tax or tribute. Spelman.

A fine, mulct, or amerciament; a satisfaction or compensation for an injury.

A fraternity, society, or company of persons combined together, under certain regulations, and with the king's license, and so called because its expenses were defrayed by the *contributions* (*geld, gild*) of its members. Spelman. In other words, a corporation; called, in Latin, *"societas," "collegium," "fratria," "fraternitas," "sodalitium," "adunatio;"* and, in foreign law, *"gildonia."* Spelman. There were various kinds of these *gilds,* as merchant or commercial *gilds,* religious *gilds,* and others. 3 Turn.Anglo Sax. 98; 3 Steph.Comm. 173, note *u.* See Gilda Mercatoria.

A friborg, or decennary; called, by the Saxons, *"gyldscipes,"* and its members, *"gildones"* and *"congildones."* Spelman.

GILD-HALL. See Guildhall.

GILD-RENT. Certain payments to the crown from any gild or fraternity.

GILDA MERCATORIA. A gild merchant, or merchant gild; a gild, corporation, or company of merchants. 10 Coke, 30.

GILDABLE. In old English law, taxable, tributary, or contributory; liable to pay tax or tribute. Cowell; Blount.

GILDO. In Saxon law, members of a *gild* or decennary. Oftener spelled *"congildo."* Du Cange; Spelman.

GILL. A measure of capacity, equal to one-fourth of a pint.

GILOUR. L. Fr. A cheat or deceiver. Applied in Britton to those who sold false or spurious things for good, as pewter for silver or laten for gold. Britt. c. 15.

GILT EDGE. As applied to commercial paper, a colloquialism, meaning of the best quality or highest price, first class, and not implying that a note which is not gilt edge is not collectible, or that the maker is irresponsible. Martin v. Moreland, 93 Or. 61, 180 P. 933, 934.

GIN MEN. In mining. Men employed in coal mines who have no specific work to do, but are hired to do general work, or any kind of work they are directed to do. The word "gin" in this expression is apparently a contraction of the word "general." Smith v. North Jellico Coal Co., 114 S.W. 785, 786, 131 Ky. 196, 28 L.R.A.N.S. 1266.

GINNING ADVANCES. Include cost to grower of picking crop, wages of weigher, rent of sleeping tents for pickers, and cost of trucking cotton from field to gin and other such expenses. Schumann v. California Cotton Credit Corporation, 105 Cal. App. 136, 286 P. 1068, 1070.

GIRANTE. An Italian word, which signifies the drawer of a bill. It is derived from *"girare,"* to draw.

GIRDLE, *v.* To "girdle" a tree for the purpose of obtaining crude turpentine is to cut off a ring of bark around the trunk. Howard v. State, 17 Ala.App. 9, 81 So. 345, 346.

GIRTH. In Saxon and old English law, a measure of length, equal to one yard, derived from the girth or circumference of a man's body.

GIRTH AND SANCTUARY. In old Scotch law, an asylum given to murderers, where the murder was committed without any previous design, and in *chaude mella,* or heat of passion. Bell.

GISEMENT. L. Fr. Agistment; cattle taken in to graze at a certain price; also the money received for grazing cattle.

GISER. L. Fr. To lie. *Gist en le bouche,* it lies in the mouth. *Le action bien gist,* the action well lies. *Gisant,* lying.

GISETAKER. An agister; a person who takes cattle to graze.

GISLE. In Saxon law, a pledge. *Fredgisle,* a pledge of peace. *Gislebert,* an illustrious pledge.

GIST. In pleading, the essential ground or object of the action in point of law, without which there would be no cause of action. Gould, Pl. c. 4, § 12.

The cause for which an action will lie, the ground or foundation of a suit, without which it would not be maintainable, the essential ground or object of the suit without which there is no cause of action. Casavalo v. D'Auria, 12 N.J. Misc. 81, 169 A. 520.

GIVE. To transfer ownership or possession without compensation. University of Vermont v. Wilbur's Estate, 105 Vt. 147, 163 A. 572, 575. To bestow upon another gratuitously or without consideration. Neblett v. Smith, 142 Va. 840, 128 S.E. 247, 251.

To transfer or yield to, or bestow upon, another. One of the operative words in deeds of conveyance of real property, importing at common law, a warranty or covenant for quiet enjoyment during the lifetime of the grantor. Mack v. Patchin, 29 How.Prac., N.Y., 23; Young v. Hargrave, 7 Ohio, 69, pt. 2; Dow v. Lewis, 4 Gray, Mass., 473.

GIVE AND BEQUEATH. These words, in a will, import a benefit in point of right, to take effect upon the decease of the testator and proof of the will, unless it is made in terms to depend upon some contingency or condition precedent. Eldridge v. Eldridge, 9 Cush., Mass., 519.

GIVE BAIL. To furnish or put in bail or security for one's appearance.

GIVE COLOR. To admit an apparent or colorable right in the opposite party.

Under the ancient system a plea of confession and avoidance must give color to the affirmative averments of the complaint, or it would be fatally defective. The "giving color" was simply the absence of any denials, and the express or silent admission that the declaration, as far as it went, told the truth. Smith v. Marley, 39 Idaho, 779, 230 P. 769, 770. See Color.

GIVE JUDGMENT. To render, pronounce, or declare the judgment of the court in an action at law; not spoken of a judgment obtained by confession. Schuster v. Rader, 13 Colo. 329, 22 P. 505.

GIVE NOTICE. To communicate to another, in any proper or permissible legal manner, information or warning of an existing fact or state of facts or (more usually) of some intended future action. O'Neil v. Dickson, 11 Ind. 254; In re Devlin, 7 Fed.Cas. 564; St. Louis, B. & M. Ry. Co. v. Hicks, Tex.Civ.App., 158 S.W. 192, 194.

GIVE TIME. Extending the period at which, by the contract between them, the principal debtor was originally liable to pay the creditor. Buffalo Forge Co. v. Fidelity & Casualty Co. of New York, 142 Misc. 647, 256 N.Y.S. 329, 334.

GIVE WAY. In the rules of navigation, one vessel is said to "give way" to another when she deviates from her course in such a manner and to such an extent as to allow the other to pass without altering her course. See Lockwood v. Lashell, 19 Pa. 350.

GIVER. A donor; he who makes a gift.

GIVING IN PAYMENT. In Louisiana law, a phrase (translating the Fr. "*dation en paiement*") which signifies the delivery and acceptance of real or personal property in satisfaction of a debt, instead of a payment in money. See Civil Code La. art. 265.

GIVING RINGS. A ceremony anciently performed in England by serjeants at law at the time of their appointment. The rings were inscribed with a motto, generally in Latin.

GLADIOLUS. A little sword or dagger; a kind of sedge. Mat. Paris.

GLADIUS. Lat. A sword. An ancient emblem of defense. Hence the ancient earls or *comites* (the king's attendants, advisers, and associates in his government) were made by being girt with swords, (*gladio succincti.*)

The emblem of the executory power of the law in punishing crimes. 4 Bl.Comm. 177.

In old Latin authors, and in the Norman laws, this word was used to signify supreme jurisdiction, (*jus gladii.*)

GLAIVE. A sword, lance, or horseman's staff. One of the weapons allowed in a trial by combat.

GLANS. In the civil law, acorns or nuts of the oak or other trees. In a larger sense, all fruits of trees.

GLASS-MEN. A term used in St. 1 Jac. I, c. 7, for wandering rogues or vagrants.

GLAVEA. A hand dart. Cowell.

GLEANING. The gathering of grain after reapers, or of grain left ungathered by reapers. Held not to be a right at common law. 1 H.Bl. 51.

GLEBA. A turf, sod, or clod of earth. The soil or ground; cultivated land in general. Church land (*solum et dos ecclesiæ*). Spelman. See Glebe.

GLEBÆ ASCRIPTITII. Villein-socmen, who could not be removed from the land while they did the service due. Bract. c. 7; 1 Reeve, Eng. Law, 269.

GLEBARIÆ. Turfs dug out of the ground. Cowell.

GLEBE. In Ecclesiastical law, the land possessed as part of the endowment or revenue of a church or ecclesiastical benefice.

In Roman law, a clod; turf; soil. Hence, the soil of an inheritance; an agrarian estate. *Servi addicti glebæ* were serfs attached to and passing with the estate. Cod. 11, 47, 7, 21; Nov. 54, 1.

GLIDER. A form of aircraft similar to an airplane but without any engine. Spychala v. Metropolitan Life Ins. Co., 339 Pa. 237, 13 A.2d 32, 33.

GLIDING. Art of flying a glider. Spychala v. Metropolitan Life Ins. Co., 339 Pa. 237, 13 A.2d 32, 33.

GLISCYWA. In Saxon law, a fraternity.

GLOBE DOCTRINE. That where the National Labor Relations Board could conclude that either a craft or a plant unit would be appropriate for collective bargaining purposes and where either contention if unopposed would be adopted by the Board, it normally gives paramount weight to the wishes of the employees within the craft unit. International Ass'n of Machinists, Tool and Die Makers' Lodge No. 35 v. National Labor Relations Board, 71 App.D.C. 175, 110 F.2d 29, 45.

GLOMERELLS. Commissioners appointed to determine differences between scholars in a school or university and the townsmen of the place. Jacob.

GLOS. Lat. In the civil law, a husband's sister. Dig. 38, 10, 4, 6.

GLOSS. An interpretation, consisting of one or more words, interlinear or marginal; an annotation, explanation, or comment on any passage in the text of a work, for purposes of elucidation or amplification. Particularly applied to the comments on the *Corpus Juris*.

GLOSSA. Lat. A gloss, explanation, or interpretation.

The *glossæ* of the Roman law are brief illustrative comments or annotations on the text of Justinian's collections, made by the professors who taught or lectured on them about the twelfth century, (especially at the law school of Bologna,) and were hence called "*glossators.*" These glosses were at first inserted in the text with the words to which they referred, and were called "*glossæ interline-*

ares;" but afterwards they were placed in the margin, partly at the side, and partly under the text, and called *"glossæ marginales."* A selection of them was made by Accursius, between A. D. 1220 and 1260, under the title of *"glossa Ordinaria,"* which is of the greatest authority. Mackeld.Rom.Law, § 90.

GLOSSA VIPERINA EST QUÆ CORRODIT VISCERA TEXTUS. 11 Coke, 34. It is a poisonous gloss which corrupts the essence of the text.

GLOSSATOR. In the civil law, a commentator or annotator. A term applied to the professors and teachers of the Roman law in the twelfth century, at the head of whom was Irnerius. Mackeld. Rom. Law, § 90.

GLOUCESTER, STATUTE OF. The statute is the 6 Edw. I, c. 1, A.D. 1278. It takes its name from the place of its enactment, and was the first statute giving costs in actions.

GLOVE SILVER. Extraordinary rewards formerly given to officers of courts, etc.; money formerly given by the sheriff of a county in which no offenders are left for execution to the clerk of assize and judges' officers. Jacob.

GLOVES. It was an ancient custom on a maiden assize, when there was no offender to be tried, for the sheriff to present the judge with a pair of white gloves. It is an immemorial custom to remove the glove from the right hand on taking oath. Wharton.

GLYN. A hollow between two mountains; a valley or glen. Co.Litt. 5*b*.

GO. To be dismissed from a court. To issue from a court. "The court said a *mandamus* must *go*." 1 W.Bl. 50. "Let a *supersedeas go*." 5 Mod. 421. "The writ may *go*." 18 C.B. 35.

GO BAIL. To assume the responsibility of a surety on a bail-bond.

GO FIFTY–FIFTY. Division into halves of something under discussion by the parties at the time. Boyer v. Bowles, 310 Mass. 134, 37 N.E.2d 489, 493.

GO HENCE. To depart from the court; with the further implication that a suitor who is directed to "go hence" is dismissed from further attendance upon the court in respect to the suit or proceeding which brought him there, and that he is finally denied the relief which he sought, or, as the case may be, absolved from the liability sought to be imposed upon him. See Hiatt v. Kinkaid, 40 Neb. 178, 58 N.W. 700.

GO TO. In a statute, will, or other instrument, a direction that property shall "go to" a designated person means that it shall pass or proceed to such person, vest in and belong to him. In re Hitchins' Estate, 43 Misc. 485, 89 N.Y.S. 472; Plass v. Plass, 121 Cal. 131, 53 P. 448.

GO TO PROTEST. Commercial paper is said to "go to protest" when it is dishonored by nonpayment or non-acceptance and is handed to a notary for protest.

GO WITHOUT DAY. Words used to denote that a party is dismissed the court. He is said to go without day, because there is no day appointed for him to appear again.

GOAF. In coal mining a space from which material has been removed or the waste left in old work. Harlan Ridgeway Mining Co. v. Jackson, 278 Ky. 767, 129 S.W.2d 585, 586.

GOAT, GOTE. In old English law, a contrivance or structure for draining waters out of the land into the sea. Callis describes *goats* as "usual engines erected and built with portcullises and doors of timber and stone or brick, invented first in Lower Germany." Callis, Sewers, (91), 112, 113. Cowell defines "gote," a ditch, sewer, or gutter.

GOB. In coal mining a space from which material has been removed or the waste left in old work. Harlan Ridgeway Mining Co. v. Jackson, 278 Ky. 767, 129 S.W.2d 585, 586. Space between face of coal and where props had been set by machine operators on previous trip. New Union Coal Co. v. Sult, 172 Ark. 753, 290 S.W. 580, 581.

GOD AND MY COUNTRY. The answer made by a prisoner, when arraigned, in answer to the question, "How will you be tried?"

In the ancient practice he had the choice (as appears by the question) whether to submit to the trial by ordeal (by God) or to be tried by a jury, (by the country;) and it is probable that the original form of the answer was, "By God *or* my country," whereby the prisoner averred his innocence by declining neither of the modes of trial.

GOD–BOTE. An ecclesiastical or church fine paid for crimes and offenses committed against God. Cowell.

GOD–GILD. That which is offered to God or his service. Jacob.

GOD'S PENNY. In old English law, earnest-money; money given as evidence of the completion of a bargain. This name is probably derived from the fact that such money was given to the church or distributed in alms.

GOGING–STOLE. An old form of the word "cucking-stool" (*q. v.*). Cowell.

GOING. In various compound phrases (as those which follow) this term implies either motion, progress, active operation, or present and continuous validity and efficacy.

GOING AND COMING RULE. Declares that employees while going to or returning from their places of employment are not within the scope of their employment. Robinson v. George, 16 Cal. 2d 238, 105 P.2d 914, 917, 918.

GOING BEFORE THE WIND. In the language of mariners and in the rules of navigation, a vessel is said to be going "before the wind" when the wind is free as respects her course, that is, comes from behind the vessel or over the stern, so that her yards may be braced square across. She is said to be "going off large" when she has the wind free on either tack, that is, when it blows from some point abaft the beam or from the quarter. Hall v. The Buffalo, 11 Fed.Cas. 216; Ward v. The Fashion, 29 Fed.Cas. 188.

GOING CONCERN. An enterprise which is being carried on as a whole, and with some particular object in view. The term refers to an existing solvent business, which is being conducted in the usual and ordinary way for which it was organized. When applied to a corporation, it means that it continues to transact its ordinary business. State ex rel. Sorensen v. Lincoln Hail Ins. Co., 133 Neb. 496, 276 N.W. 169, 174. A firm or corporation which, though embarrassed or even insolvent, continues to transact its ordinary business. White, etc., Mfg. Co. v. Pettes Importing Co., C.C.Mo., 30 F. 865; Corey v. Wadsworth, 99 Ala. 68, 11 So. 350, 23 L.R.A. 618, 42 Am.St.Rep. 55; Pioneer Telephone & Telegraph Co. v. State, 64 Okl. 304, 167 P. 995, 1000, L.R.A.1918C, 138; City and County of Denver v. Denver Union Water Co., 246 U.S. 178, 38 S.Ct. 278, 62 L.Ed. 649.

GOING CONCERN VALUE. The value which inheres in a plant where its business is established, as distinguished from one which has yet to establish its business. East Bay Water Co. v. McLaughlin, D.C.Cal., 24 F.Supp. 222, 226.

GOING INTO EFFECT OF ACT. Becoming operative as a law. State ex rel. Bishop v. Board of Education of Mt. Orab Village School Dist., Brown County, 139 Ohio St. 427, 40 N.E.2d 913, 919.

GOING OFF LARGE. See "Going Before the Wind," *supra*.

GOING PRICE. The prevalent price; the current market value of the article in question at the time and place of sale. Kelsea v. Haines, 41 N.H. 254; Hoff v. Lodi Canning Co., 51 Cal.App. 299, 196 P. 779, 780.

GOING THROUGH THE BAR. The act of the chief of an English common-law court in demanding of every member of the bar, in order of seniority, if he has anything to move.

This was done at the sitting of the court each day in term, except special paper days, crown paper days in the queen's bench, and revenue paper days in the exchequer. On the last day of term this order is reversed, the first and second time round. In the exchequer the postman and tubman are first called on. Wharton.

GOING TO THE COUNTRY. When a party, under the common-law system of pleading, finished his pleading by the words "and of this he puts himself upon the country," this was called "going to the country." It was the essential termination of a pleading which took issue upon a material fact in the preceding pleading. Wharton.

GOING VALUE. A value or asset which arises from having an established or going business. Southern Bell Telephone & Telegraph Co. v. Louisiana Public Service Commission, 187 La. 137, 174 So. 180, 195. Oshkosh Waterworks Co. v. Railroad Commission of Wisconsin, 161 Wis. 122, 152 N.W. 859, 861, L.R.A.1916F, 592; Public Service Gas Co. v. Board of Public Utility Com'rs, 84 N.J.L. 463, 87 A. 651, 657, L.R.A.1918A, 421.

GOING WITNESS. One who is about to take his departure from the jurisdiction of the court, although only into a state or country under the general sovereignty; as from one to another of the United States, or from England to Scotland.

GOLD BOND. One payable in gold coin or its equivalent, which means any money acceptable to United States government in payment of debts due it. Huron Lodge No. 444, B. P. O. E. v. McNamara, 53 S.D. 153, 220 N.W. 468, 470.

GOLDA. A mine. Blount. A sink or passage for water. Cowell.

GOLDSMITHS' NOTES. Bankers' cash notes (*i. e.*, promissory notes given by a banker to his customers as acknowledgments of the receipt of money) were originally called in London "goldsmiths' notes," from the circumstance that all the banking business in England was originally transacted by goldsmiths. Wharton.

GOLDWIT. A mulct or fine in gold.

GOLIARDUS. L. Lat. A jester, buffoon, or juggler. Spelman, voc. "Goliardensis."

GOMASHTAH. In Hindu law, an agent; a steward; a confidential factor; a representative.

GONORRHŒA. In medical jurisprudence, a venereal disease, characterized by a purulent inflammation of the urethra in the male and the vagina in the female. Vulgarly called "clap." Sally v. Brown, 220 Ky. 576, 295 S.W. 890, 891.

GOOD. Valid; sufficient in law; effectual; unobjectionable; sound. Morrison v. Farmers' & Traders' State Bank, 70 Mont. 146, 225 P. 123, 125; McNabb v. Juergens (Iowa) 180 N.W. 758, 761; Raney & Hamon v. Hamilton & White, Tex.Civ. App., 234 S.W. 229, 230.

Responsible; solvent; able to pay an amount specified.

Of a value corresponding with its terms; collectible. A note is said to be "good" when the payment of it at maturity may be relied on. Curtis v. Smallman, 14 Wend., N.Y., 232; Cooke v. Nathan, 16 Barb., N.Y., 344; In re Parker Bros. & Johnson, D.C.N.C., 279 F. 425, 428.

Writing the word "Good" across the face of a check is the customary mode in which bankers at the present day certify that the drawer has funds to meet it, and that it will be paid on presentation for that purpose. Merchants' Nat. Bank v. State Nat. Bank, 10 Wall. 645, 19 L.Ed. 1008; Irving Bank v. Wetherald, 36 N.Y. 335.

Public good. Under a statute providing that the Public Service Commission shall make an order permitting a transfer of the property of a public utility, when it is for the public good, such transfer is for the public good whenever it is not contrary to law and is reasonable, since it is not for the public good that such utilities be unreasonably restrained of their liberties. Grafton County Electric Light & Power Co. v. State, 77 N.H. 539, 94 A. 193, 194.

GOOD ABEARING. See Abearance.

GOOD AND CLEAR RECORD TITLE, FREE FROM ALL INCUMBRANCES. A title which on the record itself can be again sold as free from obvious defects and substantial doubts, and differs from a "good, marketable title," which is an actual title, but which may be established by evidence independently of the record. O'Meara v. Gleason, 246 Mass. 136, 140 N.E. 426, 427.

GOOD AND LAWFUL MEN. Those qualified for service on juries. Bonds v. State, Mart. & Y., Tenn. 146, 17 Am.Dec. 795; Turner v. State, 128 Tenn. 27, 157 S.W. 67, 68, Ann.Cas.1914D, 693.

GOOD AND SUBSTANTIAL DEPOT. A depot suitable to take care of both passenger and freight business. Louisville & N. R. Co. v. Letcher County Coal & Improvement Co., 195 Ky. 29, 243 S.W. 45, 48.

GOOD AND SUFFICIENT BRAKES. Brakes adequate to promptly check and slacken speed of motor vehicle and bring it to complete stop (Comp. St.1922, § 8395). Ziskovsky v. Miller, 120 Neb. 255, 231 N.W. 809, 811.

GOOD AND VALID. Reliable, sufficient, and unimpeachable in law; adequate; responsible.

GOOD AND WORKMANLIKE MANNER. In a manner generally considered skillful by those capable of judging such work in the community of the performance. Burnett & Bean v. Miller, 205 Ala. 606, 88 So. 871, 872; Morris v. Fox, 79 Ind. App. 389, 135 N.E. 663, 664.

GOOD BEHAVIOR. Orderly and lawful conduct; behavior such as is proper for a peaceable and law-abiding citizen. Huyser v. Com., 25 Ky.L. Rep. 608, 76 S.W. 175; In re Spenser, 22 Fed.Cas. 921. "Good behavior," as used in an order suspending sentence upon a defendant during good behavior, means merely conduct conformable to law, or to the particular law theretofore breached. Ex parte Hamm, 24 N.M. 33, 172 P. 190, 191, L.R. A.1918D, 694; Baker v. Commonwealth, 181 Ky. 437, 205 S.W. 399, 401.

GOOD CAUSE. Substantial reason, one that affords a legal excuse. Pines v. District Court in and for Woodbury County, 233 Iowa 1284, 10 N. W.2d 574, 580, 583. Legally sufficient ground or reason. Jackson v. U. S., C.C.A.Ariz., 295 F. 620, 622; Lockwood v. Lockwood, 19 Ariz. 215, 168 P. 501, 502.

As respects discharging employees in classified service, "good cause" includes any ground which is put forward by authorities in good faith and which is not arbitrary, irrational, unreasonable or irrelevant to the duties with which such authorities are charged, and is not limited to some form of inefficiency or of misconduct on the part of the person dismissed. Nephew v. Wills, 298 Mich. 187, 298 N.W. 376, 377, 135 A.L.R. 1340.

As respects Industrial Accident Commission's rescinding its decision, "good cause" included a mistake of law, unless the award had been sustained on appeal. Stearns Coal & Lumber Co. v. Vanover, 262 Ky. 808, 91 S.W.2d 518.

"Good cause" for extension of time in which to serve bill of exceptions exists if delay was for good reason, or that there was justification or excuse for the delay. Kisten v. Kisten, 229 Wis. 479, 282 N.W. 629, 632.

GOOD CONSIDERATION. "Good consideration" and "valuable consideration" are synonymous terms, although technically "good consideration" was defined as consideration of blood, or natural love and affection; that founded on motives of generosity, prudence, and natural duty. Belknap v. Northwestern Mut. Life Ins. Co., 108 Vt. 421, 188 A. 897, 899.

GOOD COUNTRY. In Scotch law, good men of the country. A name given to a jury.

GOOD FAITH. Honesty of intention, and freedom from knowledge of circumstances which ought to put the holder upon inquiry. Siano v. Helvering, D.C.N.J., 13 F.Supp. 776, 780. An honest intention to abstain from taking any unconscientious advantage of another, even through technicalities of law, together with absence of all information, notice, or benefit or belief of facts which render transaction unconscientious. Warfield Natural Gas Co. v. Allen, 248 Ky. 646, 59 S. W.2d 534, 91 A.L.R. 890; Crouch v. First Nat. Bank, 156 Ill. 342, 40 N.E. 974; Waugh v. Prince, 121 Me. 67, 115 A. 612, 614.

GOOD HEALTH. "Good health," as employed in insurance contract, ordinarily means a reasonably good state of health. Kroon v. Travelers' Ins. Co., 290 Ill.App. 35, 7 N.E.2d 935, 937. It means that the applicant has no grave, important, or serious disease, and is free from any ailment that seriously affects the general soundness and healthfulness of the system. Mincy v. Washington Nat. Ins. Co., 130 Pa.Super. 285, 196 A. 893, 897. Not mere temporary indisposition not tending to weaken or undermine constitution. Zogg v. Bankers' Life Co. of Des Moines, Iowa, C.C.A.W.Va., 62 F. 2d 575, 578. It does not mean a condition of perfect health. White v. Sovereign Camp, W. O. W., 184 S.C. 215, 192 S.E. 161, 165.

GOOD JURY. A jury of which the members are selected from the list of special jurors. See L.R. 5 C.P. 155.

GOOD, MERCHANTABLE ABSTRACT OF TITLE. An abstract showing a good title, clear from incumbrances, and not merely an abstract of matters of record affecting the title, made by one engaged in the business of making abstracts in such form as is customary, as passing current among persons buying and selling real estate and examining titles. Geithman v. Eichler, 265 Ill. 579, 107 N.E. 180, 182.

GOOD OF SERVICE. Discharge of a civil service employee for "good of the service" or "for cause" implies some personal misconduct, or fact, rendering incumbent's further tenure harmful to the public interest. State ex rel. Eckles v. Kansas City, Mo.App., 257 S.W. 197, 200.

GOOD RECORD TITLE. A "good record title," without words of limitation, means that the proper records shall show an unincumbered, fee-simple title, the legal estate in fee, free and clear of all valid claims, liens, and incumbrances. Riggins v. Post, Tex.Civ.App., 172 S.W. 210, 211.

GOOD REPUTE. An expression, synonymous with and meaning only "of good reputation." State v. Wheeler, 108 Mo. 658, 665, 18 S.W. 924.

GOOD SAMARITAN DOCTRINE. One who sees a person in imminent and serious peril through negligence of another cannot be charged with contributory negligence, as a matter of law, in risking his own life or serious injury in attempting to effect a rescue, provided the attempt is not recklessly or rashly made. Jobst v. Butler Well Servicing, Inc., 372 P.2d 55, 59, 190 Kan. 86. Under doctrine, negligence of a volunteer rescuer must worsen position of person in distress before liability will be imposed. U. S. v. DeVane, C.A. Fla., 306 F.2d 182, 186.

GOOD TITLE. One free from reasonable doubt, that is, not only a valid title in fact, but one that can again be sold to a reasonable purchaser or mortgaged to a person of reasonable prudence. Langford v. Berry, 68 Ga.App. 193, 22 S.E.2d 349, 351, a title free from litigation, palpable defects and grave doubts. Collins v. Martin, Tex.Civ. App., 6 S.W.2d 126, 128; Williams v. Hefner, 89 Mont. 361, 297 P. 492, 496.

GOOD WILL. The favor which the management of a business wins from the public. Seneca Hotel Co. v. U. S., Ct.Cl., 42 F.2d 343, 344. The fixed and favorable consideration of customers arising from established and well-conducted business. Colton v. Duvall, 254 Mich. 346, 237 S.W.2d 48, 49. The favorable consideration shown by the purchasing public to goods known to emanate from a particular source. White Tower System v. White Castle System of Eating Houses Corporation, C.C.A.Mich., 90 F.2d 67, 69. Something in business which gives reasonable expectancy of preference in race of competition. In re Witkind's Estate, 167 Misc. 885, 4 N.Y.S.2d 933, 947. The custom or patronage of any established trade or business; the benefit or advantage of having established a business and secured its patronage by the public. The advantage or benefit which is acquired by an establishment, beyond the mere value of the capital, stocks, funds, or property employed therein, in consequence of the general public patronage and encouragement which it receives from constant or habitual customers, on account of its local position, or common celebrity, or reputation for skill or affluence or punctuality, or from other accidental circumstances or necessities, or even from ancient partialities or prejudices. Story, Partn. § 99; Haverly v. Elliott, 39 Neb. 201, 57 N.W. 1010. And as property incident to business sold, favor vendor has won from public, and probability that all customers will continue their patronage. Nye Odorless Incinerator Corporation v. Felton, 5 W.W.Harr. 236, 162 A. 504, 511. It means every advantage, every positive advantage, that has been acquired by a proprietor in carrying on his business, whether connected with the premises in which the business is conducted, or with the name under which it is managed, or with any other matter carrying with it the benefit of the business. Glen & Hall Mfg. Co. v. Hall, 61 N.Y. 226, 19 Am.Rep. 278; In re Ball's Estate, 161 App.Div. 79, 146 N.Y.S. 499, 501; Whittle v. Davie, 116 Va. 575, 82 S.E. 724. 726; Acme, Palmers & De Mooy Foundry Co. v. Weiss, D.C.Ohio, 21 F.2d 492, 493.

GOODRIGHT, GOODTITLE. The fictitious plaintiff in the old action of ejectment, most frequently called "John Doe," was sometimes called "Goodright" or "Goodtitle."

GOODS. A term of variable content. It may include every species of personal property or it may be given a very restricted meaning. Cate v. Merrill, 116 Me. 235, 102 A. 235, 236, 237; Canales v. Earl, Mun.Ct.N.Y., 168 N.Y.S. 726, 727.

In contracts, the term "goods" is not so wide as "chattels," for it applies to inanimate objects, and does not include animals or chattels real, as a lease for years of house or land, which "chattels" does include. Co. Litt. 118; St. Joseph Hydraulic Co. v. Wilson, 133 Ind. 465, 33 N.E. 113; Putnam v. Westcott, 19 Johns, N.Y., 76.

In wills, "goods" is *nomen generalissimum,* and, if there is nothing to limit it, will comprehend all the personal estate of the testator, as stocks, bonds, notes, money, plate, furniture, etc. Kendall v. Kendall, 4 Russ. 370; Chamberlain v. Western Transp. Co., 44 N.Y. 310, 4 Am.Rep. 681; Keyser v. School Dist., 35 N.H. 483.

GOODS AND CHATTELS. This phrase is a general denomination of personal property, as distinguished from real property; the term "chattels" having the effect of extending its scope to any objects of that nature which would not properly be included by the term "goods" alone, *e. g.,* living animals, emblements, and fruits, and terms under leases for years. Larson v. Judd, 200 Ill. App. 420. The general phrase also embraces choses in action, as well as personalty in possession. In wills. The term "goods and chattels" will, unless restrained by the context, pass all the personal estate, including leases for years, cattle, corn, debts, and the like. Ward, Leg. 208, 211.

GOODS SOLD AND DELIVERED. A phrase frequently used in the action of *assumpsit,* when the sale and delivery of goods furnish the cause.

GOODS, WARES, AND MERCHANDISE. A general and comprehensive designation of such chattels as are ordinarily the subject of traffic and sale. The phrase is used in the statute of frauds, and is frequently found in pleadings and other instruments. As to its scope, see State v. Brooks, 4 Conn. 449; French v. Schoonmaker, 69 N.J.L. 6, 54 A. 225; Sewall v. Allen, 6 Wend., N.Y., 355; Smith v. Wilcox, 24 N.Y. 358, 82 Am.Dec. 302; Banta v. Chicago, 172 Ill. 204, 50 N.E. 233, 40 L. R.A. 611; Basset v. City of Boston, 226 Mass. 64, 114 N.E. 1035; Culp v. Holbrook, 76 Ind.App. 272, 129 N.E. 278, 280.

GOOLE. In old English law, a breach in a bank or sea wall, or a passage worn by the flux and reflux of the sea. St. 16 & 17 Car. II. c. 11.

GOPHER HOLING. The " 'gopher hole' method of blasting" consists in boring holes, horizontally into the bank of earth and inserting therein charges of powder, the explosion of which dislodges the bank. Bartnes v. Pittsburg Iron Ore Co., 123 Minn. 131, 143 N.W. 117.

GORCE, or GORS. A wear, pool, or pit of water. Termes de la Ley.

GORE. In old English law, a small, narrow slip of ground. Cowell. In modern land law, a small triangular piece of land, such as may be left between surveys which do not close. In some of the New England states (as Maine and Vermont) the term is applied to a subdivision of a county, having a scanty population and for that reason not organized as a town.

GORGE. A defile between hills or mountains, that is a narrow throat or outlet from a region of country. Gibbs v. Williams, 25 Kan. 214, 37 Am.Rep. 241.

GOSSIPRED. In canon law, compaternity; spiritual affinity.

GOUT. In medical jurisprudence, an inflammation of the fibrous and ligamentous parts of the joints, characterized or caused by an excess of uric acid in the blood; usually, but not invariably, occurring in the joints of the feet, and then specifically called "podagra."

GOVERN. To direct and control the actions or conduct of, either by established laws or by arbitrary will; to direct and control, rule, or regulate, by authority. Tucker v. State, 218 Ind. 614, 35 N.E.2d 270, 291. To be a rule, precedent, law or deciding principle for. Asnon v. Foley, 105 Cal.App. 624, 288 P. 792, 795.

GOVERNMENT. From the Latin *gubernaculum.* Signifies the instrument, the helm, whereby the ship to which the state was compared, was guided on its course by the "gubernator" or helmsman, and in that view, the government is but an agency of the state, distinguished as it must be in accurate thought from its scheme and machinery of government. State v. Chase, 175 Minn. 259, 220 N.W. 951, 953.

The system of polity in a state; that form of fundamental rules and principles by which a nation or state is governed, or by which individual members of a body politic are to regulate their social actions; a constitution, either written or unwritten, by which the rights and duties of citizens and public officers are prescribed and defined, as a monarchical government, a republican government, etc. Webster.

An empire, kingdom, state or independent political community; as in the phrase, "Compacts between independent governments."

The sovereign or supreme power in a state or nation.

The machinery by which the sovereign power in a state expresses its will and exercises its functions; or the framework of political institutions, departments, and offices, by means of which the executive, judicial, legislative, and administrative business of the state is carried on.

The whole class or body of office-holders or functionaries considered in the aggregate, upon whom devolves the executive, judicial, legislative, and administrative business of the state. Stokes v. United States, C.C.A.Mo., 264 F. 18, 22.

In a colloquial sense, the United States or its representatives, considered as the prosecutor in a criminal action; as in the phrase, "the government objects to the witness."

The regulation, restraint, supervision, or control which is exercised upon the individual members of an organized jural society by those invested with authority; or the *act* of exercising supreme political power or control. Chicago, B. & Q. R. Co. v. School Dist. No. 1 in Yuma County, 63 Colo. 159, 165 P. 260, 263.

Federal government. The government of the United States of America, as distinguished from the governments of the several states.

Local government. The government or administration of a particular locality; especially, the governmental authority of a municipal corporation, as a city or county, over its local and individual affairs, exercised in virtue of power delegated to it for that purpose by the general government of the state or nation.

Mixed government. A form of government combining some of the features of two or all of the three primary forms, viz., monarchy, aristocracy, and democracy.

Republican government. One in which the powers of sovereignty are vested in the people and are exercised by the people, either directly, or through representatives chosen by the people, to whom those powers are specially delegated. Black, Const. Law (3d Ed.) 309; In re Duncan, 139 U.S. 449, 11 S.Ct. 573, 35 L.Ed. 219; Minor v. Happersett, 21 Wall. 175, 22 L.Ed. 627.

GOVERNMENT ANNUITIES SOCIETIES. Societies formed in England under 3 & 4 Wm. IV. c. 14, 7 & 8 Vict. c. 83, 16 & 17 Vict. c. 45, and 27 & 28 Vict. c. 43, to enable the industrious classes to make provisions for themselves by purchasing, on advantageous terms, a government annuity for life or term of years. Wharton.

GOVERNMENT DE FACTO. A government of fact. A government actually exercising power and control in the state, as opposed to the true and lawful government; a government not established according to the constitution of the state, or not lawfully entitled to recognition or supremacy, but which has nevertheless supplanted or displaced the government *de jure.* A government deemed unlawful, or deemed wrongful or unjust, which, nevertheless, receives presently habitual obedience from the bulk of the community. Aust. Jur. 324.

There are several degrees of what is called *"de facto* government." Such a government, in its highest degree, assumes a character very closely resembling that of a lawful government. This is when the usurping government expels the regular authorities from their customary seats and functions, and establishes itself in their place, and so becomes the actual government of a country. The distinguishing characteristic of such a government is that adherents to it in war against the government *de jure* do not incur the penalties of treason; and, under certain limitations, obligations assumed by it in behalf of the country or otherwise will, in general, be respected by the government *de jure* when restored.

Such a government might be more aptly denominated a "government of paramount force," being maintained by active military power against the rightful authority of an established and lawful government; and obeyed in civil matters by private citizens. They are usually administered directly by military authority, but they may be administered, also, by civil authority, supported more or less by military force. Thorington v. Smith, 8 Wall. 8, 9, 19 L.Ed. 361.

GOVERNMENT DE JURE. A government of right; the true and lawful government; a government established according to the constitution of the state, and lawfully entitled to recognition and supremacy and the administration of the state, but which is actually cut off from power or control. A government deemed lawful, or deemed rightful or just, which, nevertheless, has been supplanted or displaced; that is to say, which receives not presently (although it received formerly) habitual obedience from the bulk of the community. Aust. Jur. 324.

GOVERNMENT INSTRUMENTALITY DOCTRINE. The doctrine that government instrumentalities are tax exempt.

The dominion exercised over the estate of deceased full-blood restricted Creek Indian, would not vest in the government a control sufficient to exempt the estate from estate taxes under the "government instrumentality doctrine". Landman v. Commissioner of Internal Revenue, C.C.A.10, 123 F.2d 787, 789.

One owning and operating trucks under contract with federal government for transportation of mail held not entitled to have trucks exempted from state motor vehicle registration tax, on ground that trucks were immune from state taxation as agencies and instrumentalities of United States government. Moody v. Louwein, Tex.Civ.App., 300 S.W. 957, 958.

GOVERNMENTAL. Of, pertaining to, or proceeding from government.

Generally, what are purely governmental duties of a city can be settled only by the particular facts. City of Waco v. Thompson, Tex.Civ.App., 127 S.W.2d 223, 225.

GOVERNMENTAL ACT. An act in exercise of police power or in exercise of legislative, discretionary, or judicial powers conferred on municipality for benefit of public. Broome v. City of Charlotte, 208 N.C. 729, 182 S.E. 325. Any act a state may lawfully perform or authorize and, as applied to the federal government, it is its every action within its constitutional power. Orme v. Atlas Gas & Oil Co., 217 Minn. 27, 13 N.W.2d 757, 762. A step physically taken by persons capable of exercising the sovereign authority of the foreign nation. Banco de Espana v. Federal Reserve Bank of New York, C.C.A.N.Y., 114 F.2d 438, 444.

GOVERNMENTAL ACTION. Any action of the federal government within its constitutional power. Graves v. People of State of New York ex rel. O'Keefe, N.Y., 306 U.S. 466, 59 S.Ct. 595, 596, 83 L.Ed. 927, 120 A.L.R. 1466; Chapman v. State, 179 Miss. 507, 176 So. 391, 392.

GOVERNMENTAL ACTIVITY. A function of government in providing for its own support or in providing services to the public. For example taxation and the collection of taxes, Goble v. Zolot, 144 Neb. 70, 12 N.W.2d 311, 312; maintenance of firehouse property, Haynes v. City of New York, 259 App.Div. 837, 19 N.Y.S.2d 164, 165.

Generally when a municipality's activity is for advantage of state as a whole, or is in performance of a duty imposed by sovereign power, activity is "public" and "governmental." Department of Treasury v. City of Evansville, Ind., 223 Ind. 435, 60 N.E.2d 952, 955.

GOVERNMENTAL AGENCY. A subordinate creature of the sovereign created to carry out a governmental function. Frequently, a political subdivision or corporation. Hence a charitable hospital which cared for free patients sent to it by city, Jewish Hospital of Brooklyn v. Doe, 252 App.Div. 581, 300 N.Y.S. 1111, 1117; city fire department, Ring v. Minneapolis St. Ry. Co., 173 Minn. 265, 217 N.W. 130, 131; county, Jefferson County ex rel. Grauman v. Jefferson County Fiscal Court, 274 Ky. 91, 118 S.W.2d 181, 184; county water district, Laguna Beach County Water Dist. v. Orange County, 30 Cal.App.2d 740, 87 P.2d 46, 48; irrigation district, Outlook Irr. Dist. v. Fels, 176 Wash. 211, 28 P.2d 996, 998; municipal corporation, Town of Falls Church v. Arlington County Board, 166 Va. 192, 184 S.E. 459, 463; Millar v. Town of Wilson, 222 N.C. 340, 23 S.E.2d 42, 44; National Guard, Lind v. Nebraska National Guard, 144 Neb. 122, 12 N.W.2d 652, 656, 150 A.L.R. 1449; poor district, Managers for Relief and Employment of Poor of Germantown Tp. v. Witkin, 329 Pa. 410, 196 A. 837, 840; school district, State ex rel. Klimek v. School Dist. No. 70, Otter Tail County, 204 Minn. 279, 283 N.W. 397, 399; Tennessee Valley Authority, Posey v. Tennessee Valley Authority, C.C.A.Ala., 93 F.2d 726, 727; and every agency which Congress can constitutionally create. Graves v. People of State of New York ex rel. O'Keefe, N.Y., 306 U.S. 466, 59 S.Ct. 595, 597, 83 L.Ed. 927, 120 A.L.R. 1466.

GOVERNMENTAL AGENTS. Those performing duties of a public character for benefit of all citizens of community. The term includes firemen and policemen. Miller v. City of Albany, 158 Misc. 720, 287 N.Y.S. 889, 891.

GOVERNMENTAL BODY. See Governmental Agency.

GOVERNMENTAL CAPACITY. In its "governmental capacity," a municipality acts mainly as an arm of the state for convenient administration of government in incorporated territory, for public good on behalf of the state rather than for itself. Public Service Co. of Oklahoma v. City of Tulsa, 174 Okl. 58, 50 P.2d 166, 168; Oklahoma Natural Gas Corporation v. City of Enid, 179 Okl. 283, 65 P.2d 440, 442.

GOVERNMENTAL CHARACTER. See Governmental Capacity.

GOVERNMENTAL DUTIES. Those duties of a municipality have reference to some part or element of the state's sovereignty granted it to be exercised for the benefit of the public, and all other duties are "proprietary". City of Miami v. Oates, 152 Fla. 21, 10 So.2d 721, 723.

Those duties that the framers of the Constitution intended each member of the union of states would assume in order adequately to function under the form of government guaranteed by the Constitution. First State Bank of Gainesville v. Thomas, D.C.Tex., 38 F.Supp. 849, 851.

GOVERNMENTAL ENTERPRISE. A project or undertaking by the government of a more or less permanent nature, such as a drainage district. Rorick v. United States Sugar Corporation, C.C.A. Fla., 120 F.2d 418, 421.

GOVERNMENTAL EXPENDITURE OR EXPENSE. One made in preserving health, good order, and peace of community (Const. art. 8, § 10). Town of Amherst v. Erie County, 236 App. Div. 58, 258 N.Y.S. 76, 81; keeping and dieting of prisoners and taking care of jail, Breathitt County v. Cockrell, 250 Ky. 743, 63 S.W.2d 920, 92 A.L.R. 626.

GOVERNMENTAL FACILITY. A building or institution provided by the government to care for a specified need, such as a court house or county jail. Haney v. Town of Rainelle, 125 W.Va. 397, 25 S.E.2d 207, 211.

GOVERNMENTAL FUNCTION. Duties imposed by state on municipal corporation, which latter must perform at peril. Seafeldt v. Port of Astoria, 141 Or. 418, 16 P.2d 943, 945. Where duty involves general public benefit not in nature of corporate or business undertaking for corporate benefit and interest of municipality, function is "governmental," whether duty be directly imposed or voluntarily assumed. Gebhardt v. Village of La Grange Park, 354 Ill. 234, 188 N.E. 372, 374. Those conferred upon municipality as local agency of prescribed and limited jurisdiction to be employed in administering the affairs of the state and promoting the public welfare generally. State ex rel. Gebhardt v. City Council of Helena, 102 Mont. 27, 55 P.2d 671, 673, 675.

GOVERNMENTAL IMMUNITY. A doctrine of implied limitation of the power of the federal government to tax a state or any of its instrumentalities, and of power of state to tax federal government or any of its instrumentalities, and is applicable only to taxing relations of federal and state governments, and does not apply to state and municipalities therein. Marson v. City of Philadelphia, 342 Pa. 369, 21 A.2d 228, 229, 230. See, also, Sovereign Immunity of State from Liability.

GOVERNMENTAL INSTRUMENTALITY. Any agency constitutionally created by Congress. Unemployment Compensation Commission of North Carolina v. Wachovia Bank & Trust Co., 215 N.C. 491, 2 S.E.2d 592, 595, 596; Home Owners' Loan Corporation v. Hardie & Caudle, 171 Tenn. 43, 100 S.W.2d 238, 239, 108 A.L.R. 702; Indian oil lease, Barnsdall Refineries v. Oklahoma Tax Commission, 171 Okl. 140, 41 P.2d 918; liquor control commission, Pacific Fruit & Produce Co. v. Oregon Liquor Control Commission, D.C.Or., 41 F.Supp. 175, 179.

GOVERNMENTAL POWERS. Those pertaining to making and enforcing by a city of police regulations to prevent crime, preserve public health, prevent fires, care for the poor, and educate the young. Huffman v. City of Columbus, Ohio App., 51 N.E.2d 410, 412.

Powers exercised by city as agency of state. State ex rel. Gebhardt v. City Council of Helena, 102 Mont. 27, 55 P.2d 671, 673.

GOVERNMENTAL PURPOSE. One which has for its objective the promotion of the public health, safety, morals, general welfare, security, prosperity and contentment of the inhabitants of a given political division. Green v. Frazier, 44 N.D. 395, 176 N.W. 11, 17.

It has been held that, if an electric plant is used by a city for furnishing light and power for its own use and the use of its inhabitants, it is a "governmental purpose". Chadwick v. City of Crawfordsville, 216 Ind. 399, 24 N.E.2d 937, 941, 129 A.L.R. 469; State v. Lincoln County Power Dist. No. 1, 60 Nev. 401, 111 P.2d 528, 531.

A lot purchased for jail but actually used to store cordwood used in county buildings and to store county road machinery, was prima facie used for "governmental purposes". Security State Bank v. Dent County, 345 Mo. 1050, 137 S.W.2d 960, 964.

Some courts distinguish between public purpose and governmental purpose. Spalding v. United States, D.C.Cal., 17 F.Supp. 957, 961.

GOVERNMENTAL SUBDIVISION. An agency created to carry out a governmental purpose or function. It has been held to include a public corporation authorized to use waters of natural stream for irrigation and for development of electric power, Platte Valley Public Power and Irrigation Dist. v. Lincoln County, 144 Neb. 584, 14 N.W.2d 202, 206, 155 A.L.R. 412; and a housing authority, Lennox v. Housing Authority of City of Omaha, 137 Neb. 582, 290 N.W. 451, 459; but not to include the Mortgage Commission Service Corporation, In re Batter, 257 App.Div. 546, 14 N.Y.S. 2d 42, 44; or a receiver operating for the account of the United States. The Southern Cross, C.C.A. N.Y., 120 F.2d 466, 468.

GOVERNOR. The chief executive official of a state in the United States, State ex rel. Martin v. Heil, 242 Wis. 41, 7 N.W.2d 375, 380; and territories of the United States; and also of the chief magistrate of some colonies, provinces, and dependencies of other nations.

GRABBOTS. Oilmill motes, composed of small particles of refuse cotton, detached from, but left with, the seed in the first ginning process and generally separated and recovered by a process of reginning. Chicago, R. I. & P. Ry. Co. v. Cleveland, 61 Okl. 64, 160 P. 328, 330.

GRACE. A favor or indulgence as distinguished from a right. State v. Boston, Iowa, 234 Iowa 1047, 14 N.W.2d 676, 679. Thus, in St. 22 Edw. III., the lord chancellor was instructed to take cognizance of matters of grace, being such subjects of equity jurisdiction as were exclusively matters of equity. Brown.

A faculty, license, or dispensation; also general and free pardon by act of parliament. See Act of Grace.

For Of Grace, see that title.

GRACE, DAYS OF. Time of indulgence granted to an acceptor or maker for the payment of his bill of exchange or note. It was originally a gratuitous favor, (hence the name,) but custom has rendered it a legal right.

GRACE PERIOD. In Insurance Law. A period beyond the due date of premium during which insurance is continued in force and during which payment may be made to keep policy in good standing. The grace period for payment of premium does not contemplate free insurance or operate to continue the policy in force after it expires by agreement of the parties. Miller v. Travelers Ins. Co., 143 Pa.Super. 270, 17 A.2d 907, 909.

GRADATIM. In old English law, by degrees or steps; step by step; from one degree to another. Bract. fol. 64.

GRADE, *v.* To establish a level by mathematical points and lines, and then to bring the surface of the street or highway to the level by the elevation or depression of the natural surface to the line fixed. Gas & Electric Securities Co. v. Manhattan & Queens Traction Corporation, C.C.A.N.Y., 266 F. 625, 639; Louisville & N. R. Co. v. State, 137 Tenn. 341, 193 S.W. 113; Giles v. City of Olympia, 115 Wash. 428, 197 P. 631, 633, 16 A.L.R. 493. To bring property to the level of an abutting highway. Nassau County v. O'Connell, Sup., 37 N.Y.S. 2d 1009, 1012.

GRADE, *n.* Used in reference to streets: (1) The line of the street's inclination from the horizontal; (2) a part of a street inclined from the horizontal. Cent. Dict. The hypothetical line to which the work is to be constructed. Musto-Keenan Co. v. City of Los Angeles, 139 Cal.App. 506, 34 P.2d 506, 509. The street wrought to the line; Little Rock v. Ry. Co., 56 Ark. 28, 19 S.W. 17; Austin v. Tillamook City, 121 Or. 385, 254 P. 819, 824.

"Grades of crime" in legal parlance are understood as higher or lower in grade or degree, according to the measure of punishment attached and meted out on conviction and the consequences resulting to the party convicted. State v. Doucet, 202 La. 1074, 13 So.2d 353, 361.

Quality, value, relative position, rank, status, or standing. Mossman v. Chicago & Southern Air Lines, 236 Mo.App. 282, 153 S.W.2d 799, 801, 802.

GRADE CROSSING. A place where a railroad is crossed at grade by a public or private road, or by another railroad, or where one highway crosses another. Armour & Co. v. New York, N. H. & H. R. Co., 41 R.I. 361, 103 A. 1031, 1033.

GRADED OFFENSE. One for which offender is subject to a more severe penalty for a higher grade than for a lower grade of offense according to terms of statute. State v. Doucet, 202 La. 1074, 13 So.2d 353, 361.

GRADUATE. One who has taken a degree in a college or university. State v. Ins. Co., 40 La. Ann. 463, 4 So. 504; Valentine v. Independent School District of Casey, 191 Iowa 1100, 183 N.W. 434, 437.

GRADUS. In the civil and old English law, a measure of space. A degree of relationship.

A step or degree generally; *e. g., gradus honorum,* degrees of honor. Vicat. A pulpit; a year; a generation. Du Cange.

A port; any place where a vessel can be brought to land. Du Cange.

GRADUS PARENTELÆ. A pedigree; a table of relationship.

GRAFFARIUS. In old English law, a graffer, notary, or scrivener. St. 5 Hen. VIII. c. 1.

GRAFFER. A notary or scrivener. See St. 5 Hen. VIII, c. 1. The word is a corruption of the French *"greffier,"* (*q. v.*)

GRAFFIUM. A writing-book, register, or cartulary of deeds and evidences. Cowell.

GRAFIO. A baron, inferior to a count. A fiscal judge. An advocate. Spelman; Cowell.

GRAFT. The popular meaning is the fraudulent obtaining of public money unlawfully by the corruption of public officers. Smith v. Pure Oil Co., 278 Ky. 430, 128 S.W.2d 931, 933.

A term used in equity to denote the confirmation, by relation back, of the right of a mortgagee in premises to which, at the making of the mortgage, the mortgagor had only an imperfect title, but to which the latter has since acquired a good title.

Advantage or personal gain received because of peculiar position or superior influence of one holding position of trust and confidence without rendering compensatory services, or dishonest transaction in relation to public or official acts, and sometimes implies theft, corruption, dishonesty, fraud, or swindle, and always want of integrity. Mount v. Welsh, 118 Or. 568, 247 P. 815, 822; Cooper v. Romney, 49 Mont. 119, 141 P. 289, 291; Gill v. Ruggles, 95 S.C. 90, 78 S.E. 536, 540.

GRAIN. In Troy weight, the twenty-fourth part of a pennyweight. Any kind of corn sown in the ground.

GRAIN RENT. A payment for the use of land in grain or other crops; the return to the landlord paid by croppers or persons working the land on shares. Railroad Co. v. Bates, 40 Neb. 381, 58 N.W. 963.

GRAINAGE. An ancient duty in London under which the twentieth part of salt imported by aliens was taken.

GRAMMAR SCHOOL. In England, this term designates a school in which such instruction is given as will prepare the student to enter a college or university, and in this sense the phrase was used in the Massachusetts colonial act of 1647, requiring every town containing a hundred householders to set up a "grammar school." Jenkins v. Andover, 103 Mass. 97. But in modern American usage the term denotes a school, intermediate between the primary school and the high school, in which English grammar and other studies of that grade are taught.

GRAMMATICA FALSA NON VITIAT CHARTAM. 9 Coke, 48. False grammar does not vitiate a deed.

GRAMMATOPHYLACIUM. (Græco-Lat.) In the civil law, a place for keeping writings or records. Dig. 48, 19, 9, 6.

GRAMME. The unit of weight in the metric system. The gramme is the weight of a cubic centimeter of distilled water at the temperature of 4° C. It is equal to 15.4341 grains troy, or 5.6481 drachms avoirdupois.

GRANATARIUS. In old English law, an officer having charge of a granary. Fleta, lib. 2, c. 82, § 1; Id. c. 84.

GRAND, *n.* In cant of gangsters, thieves, and underworld, one thousand dollars.

As to grand "Assize," "Bill of Sale," "Cape," "Distress," "Jury," "Larceny," and "Serjeanty," see those titles.

GRAND COUTUMIER. A collection of customs, laws, and forms of procedure in use in early times in France. See Coutumier.

GRAND DAYS. In English practice, certain days in the terms, which are solemnly kept in the inns of court and chancery, viz., Candlemas day in Hilary term, Ascension day in Easter, St. John the Baptist day in Trinity, and All Saints in Michaelmas; which are *dies non juridici.* Termes de la Ley; Cowell; Blount. They are days set apart for peculiar festivity; the members of the respective inns being on such occasions regaled at their dinner in the hall, with more than usual sumptuousness. Holthouse.

GRAND REMONSTRANCE. A constitutional document passed by the British House of Commons in November, 1641.

It was in the nature of an appeal to the country, setting forth political grievances. It consisted of a preamble of 20 clauses and the body of the remonstrance with 206 clauses, each of which was voted separately. Its first remedial measure was against papists; its second demanded that all illegal grievances and exactions should be presented and punished at the sessions and assizes and that judges and justices should be sworn to the due execution of the Petition of Rights and other laws. The third was a series of precautions to prevent the employment of evil councillors. See Taswell-Langmead, Engl.Const.Hist. 464; Forsher, Grand Remonstrance. The text will be found in History for Ready Reference, II, 833.

GRAND-STAND PLAY. In baseball, etc., a play made more showily than necessary in order to draw the applause of those in the grand stand; hence, figuratively, an act done to draw applause. Webster, Dict.

GRANDCHILD. Generally, child of one's child. Rieck v. Richards, 40 Ohio App. 201, 178 N.E. 276, 278. Descendant of second degree. Spencer v. Title Guarantee Loan & Trust Co., 222 Ala. 221, 132 So. 32, 34. The word may, however, be enlarged by context. Ball v. Weightman, 273 Pa. 120, 116 A. 653, 654; Davidson v. Blackwell, 152 Ga. 48, 108 S.E. 469, 471; Splitdorf Electrical Co. v. King, 90 N.J.Law, 421, 103 A. 674.

GRANDFATHER. The father of either of one's parents.

GRANDFATHER CLAUSE. A clause introduced into several of the constitutions of the southern states, limiting the right to vote to those who can read and write any article of the constitution of the United States, and have worked or been regularly employed in some lawful employment for the greater part of the year next preceding the time they offer to register unless prevented from labor or ability to read or write by physical disability, or who own property assessed at three hundred dollars upon which the taxes have been paid; but excepting those who have served in the army or navy of the United States or in the Confederate States in time of war, their lawful descendants in every degree, and persons of good character who understand the duties and obligations of citizenship under a republican form of government.

One of the original purposes of the "grandfather" clause of the Motor Carrier Act was to permit the operation of carrier businesses already established. Transamerican Freight Lines v. United States, D.C.Del., 51 F.Supp. 405, 409.

GRANDMOTHER. The mother of either of one's parents.

GRANGE. A farm furnished with barns, granaries, stables, and all conveniences for husbandry. Co. Litt. 5*a*.

GRANGEARIUS. A keeper of a grange or farm.

GRANGER CASES. A name applied to six cases decided by the supreme court of the United States in 1876, which are reported in Munn v. Illinois, 94 U.S. 113, 24 L.Ed. 77; Chicago, B. & Q. R. Co. v. Iowa, 94 U.S. 155, 24 L.Ed. 94; Peik v. Ry. Co., 94 U.S. 165, 24 L.Ed. 97; Chicago, M. & St. P. R. Co. v. Ackley, 94 U.S. 179, 24 L.Ed. 99; Winona & St. Peter R. Co. v. Blake, 94 U.S. 180, 24 L.Ed. 99; those most frequently cited being Munn v. Illinois, and C., B. & Q. R. Co. v. Iowa. They are so called because they arose out of an agitation commenced by the grangers which resulted in the enactment of statutes for the regulation of the tolls and charges of common carriers, warehousemen, and the proprietors of elevators.

The enforcement of these acts was resisted and their constitutionality questioned. The supreme court affirmed the common-law doctrine that private property appropriated by the owner to a public use is thereby subjected to public regulation. They also held that the right of regulation was not restrained by the prohibition of the fourteenth amendment of the federal constitution against the taking by the states of private property without due process of law. A text writer, who was at that time a member of the court, says of these cases: "But these decisions left undecided the question how far this legislative power of regulation belonged to the States, and how far it was in the congress of the United States"; Miller, Const.U.S. 397.

GRANGIA. A grange. Co. Litt. 5*a*.

GRANT. To bestow; to confer, Traylor v. State, 117 Tex.Cr.R. 323, 36 S.W.2d 506, 507; upon some one other than the person or entity which makes the grant. Porto Rico Ry., Light & Power Co. v. Colom, C.C.A.Puerto Rico, 106 F.2d 345, 354.

Deed. Walker v. Deppe, 346 Mo. 354, 141 S.W. 2d 783, 785. A conveyance. Dearing v. Brush Creek Coal Co., 182 Tenn. 302, 186 S.W.2d 329, 331. Transfer of property real or personal by deed or writing. Commissioner of Internal Revenue v. Plestcheeff, C.C.A.9, 100 F.2d 62, 64, 65.

A generic term applicable to all transfers of real property, 3 Washb. Real Prop. 181, 353; including transfers by operation of law as well as voluntary transfers. White v. Rosenthal, 140 Cal. App. 184, 35 P.2d 154, 155.

A transfer by deed of that which cannot be passed by livery. Williams, Real Prop. 147, 149; Jordan v. Indianapolis Water Co., 159 Ind. 337, 64 N.E. 680.

An act evidenced by letters patent under the great seal, granting something from the king to a subject. Cruise, Dig. tit. 33, 34; Downs v. United States, C.C.A.Md., 113 F. 147, 51 C.C.A. 100.

A technical term made use of in deeds of conveyance of lands to import a transfer. 3 Washb. Real Prop. 378–380.

As distinguished from a mere license, a grant passes some estate or interest, corporeal or incorporeal, in the lands which it embraces. Jamieson v. Millemann, 3 Duer, N.Y., 255, 258.

The term "grant," in Scotland, is used in reference (1) to original dispositions of land, as when a lord makes grants of land among tenants; (2) to gratuitous deeds. Paterson. In such case, the superior or donor is said to grant the deed; an expression totally unknown in English law. Mozley & Whitley.

By the word "grant," in a treaty, is meant not only a formal grant, but any concession, warrant, order, or permission to survey, possess, or settle, whether written or parol, express, or presumed from possession. Such a grant may be made by law, as well as by a patent pursuant to a law. Strother v. Lucas, 12 Pet. 436, 9 L.Ed. 1137; Bryan v. Kennett, 113 U.S. 179, 5 S.Ct. 413, 28 L.Ed. 908; Hastings v. Turnpike Co., 9 Pick., Mass., 80; Dudley v. Sumner, 5 Mass. 470.

For *office grant,* see Office.

Private land grant. A grant by a public authority vesting title to public land in a private (natural) person. United Land Ass'n v. Knight, 85 Cal. 448, 24 P. 818.

Public grant. A grant from the public; a grant of a power, license, privilege, or property, from the state or government to one or more individuals, contained in or shown by a record, conveyance, patent, charter, etc.

GRANT AND DEMISE. In a lease for years these words create an implied warranty of title and a covenant for quiet enjoyment; Stott v. Rutherford, 92 U.S. 107, 23 L.Ed. 486.

GRANT AND TO FREIGHT LET. Operative words in a charter party, implying the placing of the vessel at the disposition of the charterer for the purposes of the intended voyage, and generally, transferring the possession. See Christie v. Lewis, 2 Brod. & B. 441.

GRANT, BARGAIN, AND SELL. Operative words in conveyances of real estate. Muller v. Boggs, 25 Cal. 187; Hawk v. McCullough, 21 Ill. 221.

GRANT OF PERSONAL PROPERTY. A method of transferring personal property, distinguished from a gift by being always founded on some consideration or equivalent. 2 Bl. Comm. 440, 441. Its proper legal designation is an "assignment," or "bargain and sale." 2 Steph. Comm. 102.

GRANT TO USES. The common grant with uses superadded, which has become the favorite mode of transferring realty in England. Wharton.

GRANTEE. One to whom a grant is made. Commissioner of Internal Revenue v. Plestcheeff, C.C. A.9, 100 F.2d 62, 65.

GRANTOR. The person by whom a grant is made.

GRANTOR'S LIEN. Lien which exists for payment of purchase money when title is transferred. Kosters v. Hoover, 69 App.D.C. 66, 98 F.2d 595, 596.

GRANTZ. In old English law, noblemen or grandees. Jacob.

GRASS HEARTH. In old records, the grazing or turning up the earth with a plow. The name of a customary service for inferior tenants to bring their plows, and do one day's work for their lords. Cowell.

GRASS WEEK. Rogation week, so called anciently in the inns of court and chancery.

GRASS WIDOW. A slang term for a woman separated from her husband by abandonment or prolonged absence; a woman living apart from her husband. Webster. A divorcee.

GRASSON, or GRASSUM. A fine paid upon the transfer of a copyhold estate. See Gressume.

GRATIFICATION. A gratuity; a recompense or reward for services or benefits, given voluntarily, without solicitation or promise.

GRATIS. Without reward or consideration. Highway Department of Georgia v. Bass, 197 Ga. 356, 29 S.E.2d 161, 169. Freely; gratuitously.

GRATIS DICTUM. A voluntary assertion; a statement which a party is not legally bound to make, or in which he is not held to precise accuracy. 2 Kent, Comm. 486; Medbury v. Watson, 6 Metc., Mass., 260, 39 Am.Dec. 726.

GRATUITOUS. Without valuable or legal consideration. A term applied to deeds of conveyance and to bailments and other contracts.

In old English law, voluntary; without force, fear, or favor. Bract. fols. 11, 17.

As to gratuitous "Bailment," "Contract," and "Deposit," see those titles.

GRATUITOUS ALLOWANCE. A pension. Moran v. Firemen's and Policemen's Pension Fund Commission of Jersey City, 20 N.J.Misc. 479, 28 A. 2d 885, 887. State ex rel. Parker v. Board of Education of City of Topeka, 155 Kan. 754, 129 P.2d 265, 267.

GRATUITOUS GUEST. In automobile law. A person riding at invitation of owner or authorized agent without payment of a consideration or fare. McLain v. Atlantic Ice & Coal Corporation, 54 Ga. App. 103, 187 S.E. 153; Hart v. Hogan, 173 Wash. 598, 24 P.2d 99; Blashfield, Cyc. of Automobile Law and Prac., Perm. Ed., § 2292.

GRATUITOUS LICENSEE. Any licensee other than a business visitor. Smith v. Southwest Missouri R. Co., 333 Mo. 314, 62 S.W.2d 761.

GRATUITOUS PASSENGER. See Gratuitous Guest.

GRATUITY. Something acquired without bargain or inducement. State ex rel. Stafford v. Fox-Great Falls Theatre Corporation, 114 Mont. 52, 132 P.2d 689, 697. Something given freely or without recompense; a gift; something voluntarily given in return for a favor or especially a service, hence, a bounty; a tip; a bribe. McCook v. Long, 193 Ga. 299, 18 S.E.2d 488, 490.

GRAVA. In old English law, a grove; a small wood; a coppice or thicket. Co. Litt. 4*b*.

A thick wood of high trees. Blount.

GRAVAMEN. The material part of a grievance, charge, etc. Williamson v. Pacific Greyhound Lines, 67 Cal.App.2d 250, 153 P.2d 990, 991. The burden or gist of a charge; the grievance or injury specially complained of.

In English Ecclesiastical law, a grievance complained of by the clergy before the bishops in convocation.

GRAVATIO. In old English law, an accusation or impeachment. Leg. Ethel. c. 19.

GRAVE. An excavation in earth in which a dead body is or is to be buried, or place for interment of a corpse, such as a tomb, or a sepulcher. Leaphart v. Harmon, 186 S.C. 362, 195 S.E. 628, 629.

GRAVEL. Small stones, or fragments of stone often intermixed with particles of sand. Fellows v. Dorsey, 171 Mo.App. 289, 157 S.W. 995, 1000.

GRAVEL PIT. An excavation from which gravel is removed. Walker v. Dwelle, 187 Iowa 1384, 175 N.W. 957, 964.

GRAVEN DOCK. A "graven dock" is distinguished from a "floating dock," in that it is permanently attached to, and in that manner is, a part of land. Butler v. Robins Dry Dock & Repair Co., 240 N.Y. 23, 147 N.E. 235; Manufacturers' Liability Ins. Co. v. Hamilton, 129 Misc. 665, 222 N.Y.S. 394.

GRAVEYARD. A cemetery; a place for the interment of dead bodies; sometimes defined in statutes as a place where a minimum number of persons (as "six or more") are buried. See Stockton v. Weber, 98 Cal. 433, 33 P. 332; Gray v. Craig, 103 Kan. 100, 172 P. 1004, 1005.

GRAVEYARD INSURANCE. A term applied to insurances fraudulently obtained (as, by false personation or other means) on the lives of infants, very aged persons, or those in the last stages of disease. Also occasionally applied to an insurance company which writes wager policies, takes extra-hazardous risks, or otherwise exceeds the limits of prudent and legitimate business. See McCarty's Appeal, 110 Pa. 379, 4 A. 925.

GRAVIS. Grievous; great. *Ad grave damnum,* to the grievous damage. 11 Coke, 40.

GRAVIUS. A graf; a chief magistrate or officer. A term derived from the more ancient *"grafio,"* and used in combination with various other words, as an official title in Germany; as *Margravius, Rheingravius, Landgravius,* etc. Spelman.

GRAVIUS EST DIVINAM QUAM TEMPORALEM LÆDERE MAJESTATEM. It is more serious to hurt divine than temporal majesty. 11 Coke, 29.

GRAY'S INN. An inn of court. See Inns of Court.

GREAT. Considerable in magnitude, power, intensity or degree. Thompson v. Anderson, 107 Utah 331, 153 P.2d 665, 666. As used in various compound legal terms, this word generally means extraordinary, that is, exceeding the common or ordinary measure or standard, in respect to physical size, or importance, dignity, etc. Gulf, etc., R. Co. v. Smith, 87 Tex. 348, 28 S.W. 520; San Christina Inv. Co. v. City and County of San Francisco, 167 Cal. 762, 141 P. 384, 388, 52 L.R.A.,N.S., 676; American Express Co. v. Terry, 126 Md. 254, 94 A. 1026, 1030, Ann.Cas.1917C, 650.

For *presumption great,* see Proof.

As to great "Care," "Ponds," "Seal," "Tithes," see those titles.

GREAT CATTLE. All manner of beasts except sheep and yearlings. 2 Rolle, 173.

GREAT CHARTER. *Magna Charta (q. v.).*

GREAT–GRANDCHILDREN. Children of one's grandchildren. Jenkins v. Harris, 135 Miss. 457, 100 So. 280.

GREAT LAW, THE, or "The Body of Laws of the Province of Pennsylvania and Territories thereunto belonging, Past at an Assembly held at Chester *alias* Upland, the 7th day of the tenth month, called 'December,' 1682." This was the first code of laws established in Pennsylvania, and is justly celebrated for the provision in its first chapter for liberty of conscience.

GREAT TITHES. In ecclesiastical law, the more valuable tithes: as, corn, hay, and wood. 3 Burn, Eccl. Law, 680, 681; 3 Steph. Comm. 127. See Tithes.

GREAT WRIT OF LIBERTY. The writ of "habeas corpus and subjiciendum", issuing at common law out of courts of Chancery, King's Bench, Common Pleas, and Exchequer. Ex parte Kelly, 123 N.J.Eq. 489, 198 A. 203, 207.

GREE. Satisfaction for an offense committed or injury done. Cowell.

GREEK CROSS. See Cross.

GREEK KALENDS. A colloquial expression to signify a time indefinitely remote, there being no such division of time known to the Greeks.

GREEN CLOTH. In English law, a board or court of justice held in the countinghouse of the king's (or queen's) household, and composed of the lord steward and inferior officers. It takes its name from the green cloth spread over the board at which it is held. Wharton; Cowell.

GREEN SILVER. A feudal custom in the manor of Writtel, in Essex, where every tenant whose front door opens to Greenbury shall pay a halfpenny yearly to the lord, by the name of "green silver" or "rent." Cowell.

GREEN WAX. In English law, the name of the estreats in the exchequer, delivered to the sheriff under the seal of that court which was impressed upon green wax.

GREENBACK. The popular and almost exclusive name applied to all United States treasury issues. Hickey v. State, 23 Ind. 23; U. S. v. Howell, D.C. Cal., 64 F. 114.

GREENHEW. In forest law, the same as *vert (q. v.)*. Termes de la Ley.

GREFFIERS. In French law, registrars, or clerks of the courts.

They are officials attached to the courts to assist the judges in their duties. They keep the minutes, write out the judgments, orders, and other decisions given by the tribunals, and deliver copies thereof to applicants.

GREGORIAN CODE. The code or collection of constitutions made by the Roman jurist Gregorius. See Codex Gregorianus.

GREGORIAN EPOCH. The time from which the Gregorian calendar or computation dates; *i. e.,* from the year 1582.

GREMIO. In Spanish law, a guild; an association of workmen, artificers, or merchants following the same trade or business; designed to protect and further the interests of their craft.

GREMIUM. Lat. The bosom or breast; hence, derivatively, safeguard or protection. In English law, an estate which is in abeyance is said to be *in gremio legis;* that is, in the protection or keeping of the law.

GRENVILLE ACT. The statute 10 Geo. III. c. 16, by which the jurisdiction over parliamentary election petitions was transferred from the whole house of commons to select committees. Repealed by 9 Geo. IV. c. 22, § 1.

GRESSUME. In English law, a customary fine due from a copyhold tenant on the death of the lord. 1 Strange, 654; 1 Crabb, Real Prop. p. 615, § 778. Spelled also *"grassum," "grossome,"* and *"gressame."*

In Scotland *grassum* is a fine paid for the making or renewing of a lease. Paterson.

GRETNA GREEN MARRIAGE. A marriage celebrated at Gretna, in Dumfries, (bordering on the county of Cumberland,) in Scotland.

By the law of Scotland a valid marriage may be contracted by consent alone, without any other formality. When the marriage act (26 Geo. II. c. 33) rendered the publication of banns, or a license, necessary in England, it became usual for persons who wished to marry clandestinely to go to Gretna Green, the nearest part of Scotland, and marry according to the Scotch law; so a sort of chapel was built at Gretna Green, in which the English marriage service was performed by the village blacksmith. Wharton.

GREVA. In old records, the sea shore, sand, or beach. 2 Mon. Angl. 625; Cowell.

GREVE. A word of power or authority. Cowell.

GRIEVANCE. An injury, injustice or wrong which gives ground for complaint because it is unjust and oppressive. In re Borough of North Braddock, 126 Pa.Super. 53, 190 A. 357, 361.

GRIEVED. Aggrieved. 3 East, 22.

GRIEVOUS. Causing grief or sorrow, painful, afflictive, hard to bear, offensive, harmful. State v. Bowers, 178 Minn. 589, 228 N.W. 164, 165.

GRIFF. A word said to have a definite meaning in Louisiana, indicating the offspring of a Negro and a mulatto; a person too black to be a mulatto and too pale in color to be readily identified as a Negro. State v. Treadaway, 52 So. 500, 508, 126 La. 300, 139 Am.St.Rep. 514, 20 Ann.Cas. 1297. Also spelled *griffe*, and applied to a person of mixed Negro and American Indian blood. Webster, New Int. Dict.

GRITH. In Saxon law, peace; protection.

GRITHBRECH, or GRITHBRECHE. Breach of the peace. Cowell.

GRITHSTOLE. A place of sanctuary. Cowell.

GROAT. An English silver coin (value four pence) issued from the fourteenth to the seventeenth century. See Reg. v. Connell, 1 Car. & K. 191.

GROCER. In old English law, a merchant or trader who *engrossed* all vendible merchandise; an engrosser. St. 37 Edw. III. c. 5. See Engrosser.

GROG-SHOP. A liquor saloon, barroom, or dram-shop; a place where intoxicating liquor is sold to be drunk on the premises. See Leesburg v. Putnam, 103 Ga. 110, 29 S.E. 602.

GRONNA. In old records, a deep hollow or pit; a bog or miry place. Cowell.

GROOM OF THE STOLE. In England, an officer of the royal household, who has charge of the king's wardrobe.

GROOM PORTER. Formerly an officer belonging to the royal household. Jacob.

GROSS. Great; culpable. General. Absolute. A thing *in gross* exists in its own right, and not as an appendage to another thing. Before or without diminution or deduction. Standard Chemical Co. v. Curtis, 77 Colo. 10, 233 P. 1112, 1113; Smith v. Toth, 61 Ind.App. 42, 111 N.E. 442, 444; Klafter v. State Board of Examiners of Architects, 259 Ill. 15, 102 N.E. 193, 195, 46 L.R.A.,N.S., 532, Ann.Cas.1914B, 1221. Whole; entire; total; as the gross sum, amount, weight—opposed to net. State v. Hallenberg-Wagner Motor Co., 341 Mo. 771, 108 S.W.2d 398, 401.

Out of all measure; beyond allowance; not to be excused; flagrant; shameful; as a gross dereliction of duty; a gross injustice; gross carelessness. State Board of Dental Examiners v. Savelle, 90 Colo. 177, 8 P.2d 693, 697.

As to gross "Adventure," "Average," "Earnings," "Fault," "Negligence," and "Weight," see those titles.

GROSS INADEQUACY. In compensation cases. Compensation so unreasonably small as to shock sense of justice and evince lack of fair and intelligent consideration. Albertsen v. Swift & Co., 117 Kan. 337, 230 P. 1057, 1058.

GROSS INCOME. The term may mean the "gross receipts" of a business before deduction or expenditures for any purpose being equivalent to "gross proceeds" or "gross receipts" as distinguished from "net income," which is that portion of the receipts which remain after paying wages and paying for materials, or, in the narrower sense, profits over and above interest on capital invested. First Trust Co. of St. Paul v. Commonwealth Co., C.C.A.S.D., 98 F.2d 27, 31, 32.

GROSS PREMIUM. Net premium plus loading for expenses and contingencies; i. e., the net premium represents the cost of insurance. Fox v. Mutual Ben. Life Ins. Co., C.C.A.Mo., 107 F.2d 715, 719.

GROSS PROFIT. Excess of price received over price paid for goods before deductions are made for cost of operation. Hill v. City of Richmond, 181 Va. 744, 26 S.E.2d 48, 54.

GROSS WEIGHT. The total weight of goods or merchandise, with the chests, bags, and the like, from which are to be deducted tare and tret.

GROSSE AVENTURE. Fr. In French marine law, the contract of bottomry. Ord. Mar. liv. 3, tit. 5.

GROSSE BOIS. Timber. Cowell.

GROSSEMENT. L. Fr. Largely, greatly. *Grossement enseint,* big with child. Plowd. 76.

GROSSOME. In old English law, a fine, or sum of money paid for a lease. Plowd. 270, 271. Supposed to be a corruption of *gersuma (q. v.).* See Gressume.

GROUND. Soil; earth; the earth's surface appropriated to private use and under cultivation or susceptible of cultivation.

Though this term is sometimes used as equivalent to "land," it is properly of a more limited signification, because it applies strictly only to the surface, and always means dry land. See Wood v. Carter, 70 Ill App. 218; State v. Jersey City, 25 N.J.L. 529; Com. v. Roxbury, 9 Gray, Mass., 491.

A foundation or basis; points relied on. People v. Wilkins, 67 Cal.App. 758, 228 P. 367; People v. Preciado, 31 Cal.App. 519, 160 P. 1090, 1091; In re Egan, 36 S.D. 228, 154 N.W. 521, 522.

GROUND ANNUAL. In Scotch law, an annual rent of two kinds: *First,* the feu duties payable to the lords of erection and their successors; *second,* the rents reserved for building lots in a city, where *sub-feus* are prohibited. This rent is in the nature of a perpetual annuity. Bell; Ersk. Inst. 11, 3, 52.

GROUND LANDLORD. The grantor of an estate on which a ground-rent is reserved.

GROUND OF ACTION. The basis of a suit; the foundation or fundamental state of facts on which an action rests; the real object of the plaintiff in bringing his suit. Nash v. Adams, 24 Conn. 39; Appeal of Huntington, 73 Conn. 582, 48 A. 766.

GROUND RENT. A perpetual rent reserved to himself and his heirs, by the grantor of land in fee-simple, out of the land conveyed. It is in the nature of an emphyteutic rent. Also, in English law, rent paid on a building lease. Hart v. Anderson, 48 A. 636, 198 Pa. 558; Sturgeon v. Ely, 6 Pa. 406; Franciscus v. Reigart, 4 Watts., Pa., 116.

GROUND WRIT. Prior to the English common-law procedure act, 1852, c. 121 a *ca. sa.* or *fi. fa.* could not be issued into a county different from that in which the venue in the action was laid, without first issuing a writ, called a "ground writ," into the latter county, and then another writ, which was called a *"testatum* writ," into the former. Wharton.

GROUNDAGE. A custom or tribute paid for the standing of shipping in port. Jacob.

GROUP INSURANCE. A contract of "group insurance" is one between insurer and employer for benefit of employees. Crawford v. Metropolitan Life Ins. Co., Mo.App., 167 S.W.2d 915, 924. In its nature group insurance is similar, if not identical with that form of insurance known as term insurance. Watkins v. Metropolitan Life Ins. Co., La.App., 174 So. 885, 888.

GROWING CROP. A crop must be considered and treated as a *growing* crop from the time the seed is deposited in the ground, as at that time the seed loses the qualities of a chattel, and becomes a part of the freehold, and passes with a sale of it. Wilkinson v. Ketler, 69 Ala. 435. Things commonly planted, cultivated, and harvested for use or profit of husbandman. Pelham v. State, 20 Ala.App. 359, 102 So. 462, 463.

GROWTH HALF-PENNY. A rate paid in some places for the tithe of every fat beast, ox, or other unfruitful cattle. Clayt. 92.

GRUARII. The principal officers of a forest.

GRUB STAKE. In mining law, a contract between two parties by which one undertakes to furnish the necessary provisions, tools, and other supplies, and the other to prospect for and locate mineral lands and stake out mining claims thereon, the interest in the property thus acquired inuring to the benefit of both parties, either equally or in such proportion as their agreement may fix. Berry v. Woodburn, 107 Cal. 512, 40 P. 804; Hartney v. Gosling, 10 Wyo. 346, 68 P. 1118, 98 Am.St. Rep. 1005; Mattocks v. Gibbons, 94 Wash. 44, 162 P. 19, 22.

GUADALUPE HIDALGO, TREATY OF. A treaty between the United States and Mexico, terminating the Mexican War, dated February 2, 1848. See Gadsden Purchase.

GUADIA. In old European law, a pledge. Spelman; Calvin. A custom. Spelman. Spelled also "wadia."

GUARANTEE. One to whom a guaranty is made. Dallas v. Wagner, 204 N.C. 517, 168 S.E. 838, 839. This word is also used, as a noun, to denote the contract of guaranty or the obligation of a guarantor, and, as a verb, to denote the action of assuming the responsibilities of a guarantor.

GUARANTEE STOCK. "Guarantee stock" of a building and loan association is a fixed non-withdrawal investment which guarantees to all other investors in the association a fixed rate of dividend or interest. Stumph v. Wheat Belt Building & Loan Ass'n of Pratt, 148 Kan. 25, 79 P.2d 896, 899.

GUARANTIED STOCK. See Stock.

GUARANTOR. He who makes a guaranty. In re Ford, D.C.Wash., 14 F.2d 848, 849.

GUARANTY, *v.* To undertake collaterally to answer for the payment of another's debt or the performance of another's duty, liability, or obligation; to assume the responsibility of a guarantor; to warrant. See Guaranty, *n.*

GUARANTY, *n.* A collateral agreement for performance of another's undertaking. Kelly-Springfield Tire Co. v. Hamilton, 230 Mo.App. 430, 91 S.W.2d 193. A promise to answer for payment of debt or performance of obligation if person liable in first instance fails to make payment or perform obligation. McGee v. F. W. Poe Mfg. Co., 176 S.C. 288, 180 S.E. 48, 51, 99 A.L.R. 1468. An undertaking by one person to be answerable for the payment of some debt, or the due performance of some contract or duty, by another person, who himself remains liable to pay or perform the same. Story, Prom. Notes, § 457. A promise to answer for the debt, default, or miscarriage of another person. Civil Code Cal. § 2787.

A guaranty is a contract that some particular thing shall be done exactly as it is agreed to be done, whether it is to be done by one person or another, and whether there be a prior or principal contractor or not. Redfield v. Haight, 27 Conn. 31.

The definition of a "guaranty," by text-writers, is an undertaking by one person that another shall perform his contract or fulfill his obligation, or that, if he does not, the guarantor will do it for him. A guarantor of a bill or note is said to be one who engages that the note shall be paid, but is not an indorser or surety. Gridley v. Capen, 72 Ill. 13.

Synonyms

The terms *guaranty* and *suretyship* are sometimes used interchangeably; but they should not be confounded. The contract of a guarantor is his own separate contract. It is in the nature of a warranty by him that the thing guarantied to be done by the principal shall be done, not merely an engagement jointly with the principal to do the thing. The original contract of the principal is not his contract, and he is not bound to take notice of its non-performance. Durham v. Manrow, 2 N.Y. 548; Nading v. McGregor, 121 Ind. 465, 23 N.E. 283, 6 L.R.A. 686; Hoosier Brick Co. v. Floyd County Bank, 64 Ind.App. 445, 116 N.E. 87, 90; W. T. Rawleigh Co. v. Salter, 31 Ga.App. 329, 120 S.E. 679, 681.

Guaranty and *warranty* are derived from the same root, and are in fact etymologically the same word, the "g" of the Norman French being interchangeable with the English "w." They are often used colloquially and in commercial transactions as having the same signification, as where a piece of machinery or the produce of an estate is "guarantied" for a term of years, "warranted" being the more appropriate term in such a case. Accumulator Co. v. Dubuque St. R. Co., Iowa, 64 F. 70, 12 C.C.A. 37; Martinez v. Earnshaw, 36 Wkly.Notes Cas., Pa., 502. A distinction is also sometimes made in commercial usage, by which the term "guaranty" is understood as a collateral warranty (often a conditional one) against some default or event in the future, while the term "warranty" is taken as meaning an absolute undertaking *in præsenti*, against the defect, or for the quantity or quality contemplated by the parties in the subject-matter of the contract. Sturges v. Bank of Circleville, 11 Ohio St. 169, 78 Am.Dec. 296. But in strict legal usage the two terms are widely distinguished in this, that a warranty is an absolute undertaking or liability on the part of the warrantor, and the contract is void unless it is strictly and literally performed, while a guaranty is a promise, entirely collateral to the original contract, and not imposing any primary liability on the guarantor, but binding him to be answerable for the failure or default of another. Masons' Union L. Ins. Ass'n v. Brockman, 20 Ind. App. 206, 50 N.E. 493.

Absolute guaranty. An unconditional undertaking by a guarantor that debtor will pay debt or perform the obligation. An unconditional promise of payment or performance of principal contract on default of principal debtor or obligor. Robey v. Walton Lumber Co., 17 Wash.2d 242, 135 P.2d 95, 102, 145 A.L.R. 924.

Collateral guaranty. A contract by which the guarantor undertakes, in case the principal fails to do what he has promised or undertaken to do, to pay damages for such failure; distinguished from an engagement of suretyship in this respect, that a surety undertakes to do the very thing which the principal has promised to do, in case the latter defaults. Woody v. Haworth, 24 Ind.App. 634, 57 N.E. 272; Nading v. McGregor, 121 Ind. 470, 23 N.E. 283, 6 L.R.A. 686.

Conditional guaranty. One which depends upon some extraneous event, beyond the mere default of the principal, and generally upon notice of the guaranty, notice of the principal's default, and reasonable diligence in exhausting proper remedies against the principal. Yager v. Title Co., 112 Ky. 932, 66 S.W. 1027; Tobacco Co. v. Heid, D.C. Alaska, 62 F. 962; Wall v. Eccles, 61 Utah, 247, 211 P. 702, 703.

Continuing guaranty. One relating to a future liability of the principal, under successive transactions, which either continue his liability or from time to time renew it after it has been satisfied. Sewing Mach. Co. v. Courtney, 141 Cal. 674, 75 P. 296; Buck v. Burk, 18 N.Y. 340; German Sav. Bank v. Drake, Iowa, 79 N.W. 121; Glaser, Kohn & Co. v. U. S., C.C.A.Ill., 224 F. 84, 86; Hirning v. Jacobsen, 51 S.D. 270, 213 N.W. 505, 507.

Special guaranty. A guaranty which is available only to the particular person to whom it is offered or addressed; as distinguished from a *general* guaranty, which will operate in favor of any person who may accept it. Everson v. Gere, 40 Hun, N.Y., 250; Tidioute Sav. Bank v. Libbey, 101 Wis. 193, 77 N.W. 182, 70 Am.St.Rep. 907; Jobes v. Miller, 201 Mo.App. 45, 209 S.W. 549, 550.

Guaranty company. A corporation authorized to transact the business of entering into contracts of guaranty and suretyship; as, one which, for fixed premiums, becomes surety on judicial bonds, fidelity bonds, and the like. See Ætna L. Ins. Co. v. Coulter, 25 Ky.L.Rep. 193, 74 S.W. 1050.

GUARANTY FUND. Statutes have made provision for depositors' guaranty funds to be raised, in whole or in part, by assessments on banks and to be used to pay the depositors of an insolvent bank. Noble State Bank v. Haskell, 219 U.S. 104, 31 S.Ct. 186, 55 L.Ed. 112, 32 L.R.A.,N.S., 1062, Ann. Cas.1912A, 487; Shallenberger v. Bank, 219 U.S. 114, 31 S.Ct. 189, 55 L.Ed. 117; Assaria State Bank v. Dolley, 219 U.S. 121, 31 S.Ct. 189, 55 L.Ed. 123; Abilene Nat. Bank v. Dolley, 228 U.S. 1, 33 S.Ct. 409, 57 L.Ed. 707.

GUARANTY INSURANCE. See Insurance.

GUARDAGE. A state of wardship.

GUARDIAN. A guardian is a person lawfully invested with the power, and charged with the duty, of taking care of the person and managing the property and rights of another person, who, for some peculiarity of *status,* or defect of age, understanding, or self-control, is considered incapable of administering his own affairs. Bass v. Cook, 4 Port., Ala., 392; Sparhawk v. Allen, 21 N.H. 27; Burger v. Frakes, 67 Iowa, 460, 23 N.W. 746; Fleming v. Leibe, 95 N.J.Eq. 129, 122 A. 616.

One who legally has the care and management of the person, or the estate, or both, of a child during its minority. Reeve, Dom. Rel. 311.

This term might be appropriately used to designate the person charged with the care and control of idiots, lunatics, habitual drunkards, spendthrifts, and the like; but such person is, under many of the statutory systems authorizing the appointment, styled "committee," and in common usage the name "guardian" is applied only to one having the care and management of a minor.

Classification

A *testamentary* guardian is one appointed by the deed or last will of the child's father; while a guardian *by election* is one chosen by the infant himself in a case where he would otherwise be without one.

A *general* guardian is one who has the general care and control of the person and estate of his ward; while a *special* guardian is one who has special or limited powers and duties with respect to his ward, *e. g.,* a guardian who has the custody of the estate but not of the person, or vice versa, or a guardian *ad litem.*

A *domestic* guardian is one appointed at the place where the ward is legally domiciled; while a *foreign* guardian derives his authority from appointment by the courts of another state, and generally has charge only of such property as may be located within the jurisdiction of the power appointing him.

A *guardian ad litem* is a guardian appointed by a court of justice to prosecute or defend for an infant in any suit to which he may be a party, 2 Steph.Comm. 342; Crawford v. Amusement Syndicate Co., Mo., 37 S.W.2d 581, 584. Most commonly appointed for infant *defendants,* infant plaintiffs generally suing by *next friend.* This kind of guardian has no right to interfere with the infant's person or property. 2 Steph.Comm. 343; Richter v. Leiby, 107 Wis. 404, 83 N.W. 694; Morris v. Standard Oil Co., 192 Cal. 343, 219 P. 998, 1000, 30 A.L.R. 1103.

A *guardian by appointment of court* has custody of the infant until the attainment of full age. 2 Steph.Comm. 341; 2 Kent, Comm. 226.

A *guardian by nature* is the father, and, on his death, the mother, of a child. 1 Bl.Comm. 461; 2 Kent, Comm. 219; Daniels v. Metropolitan Life Ins. Co., 135 Pa.Super. 450, 5 A.2d 608, 611. This guardianship extends only to the custody of the person of the child to the age of twenty-one years. Sometimes called "natural guardian," but this is rather a popular than a technical mode of expression. 2 Steph.Comm. 337; Kline v. Beebe, 6 Conn. 500; Mauro v. Ritchie, 16 Fed.Cas. 1171.

A *guardian by statute* is a guardian appointed for a child by the deed or last will of the father, and who has the custody both of his person and estate until the attainment of full age. This kind of guardianship is founded on the statute of 12 Car. II. c. 24, and has been pretty extensively adopted in this country. 1 Bl.Comm. 462; 2 Steph. Comm. 339, 340; 2 Kent, Comm. 224–226; Huson v. Green, 88 Ga. 722, 16 S.E. 255.

A *guardian for nurture* is the father, or, at his decease, the mother, of a child. This kind of guardianship extends only to the person, and determines when the infant arrives at the age of fourteen. 2 Kent, Comm. 221; 1 Bl.Comm. 461; 2 Steph.Comm. 338; Mauro v. Ritchie, 16 Fed.Cas. 1171; Arthurs' Appeal, 1 Grant Cas., Pa., 56.

Guardian in chivalry. In the tenure by knight's service, in the feudal law, if the heir of the feud was under the age of twenty-one, being a male, or fourteen, being a female, the lord was entitled to the wardship (and marriage) of the heir, and was called the "guardian in chivalry." This wardship consisted in having the custody of the body and lands of such heir, without any account of the profits. 2 Bl.Comm. 67.

Guardian in socage. At the common law, this was a species of guardian who had the custody of lands coming to the infant by descent, as also of the infant's person, until the latter reached the age of fourteen. Such guardian was always "the next of kin to whom the inheritance cannot possibly descend." 1 Bl.Comm. 461; 2 Steph.Comm. 338; Byrne v. Van Hoesen, 5 Johns., N.Y., 67; Combs v. Jackson, 2 Wend., N.Y., 157, 19 Am.Dec. 568.

Natural guardian. The father of a child, or the mother if the father be dead.

"Guardian de son tort," sometimes described as "quasi guardian" or "guardian by estoppel," is one who assumes to act as guardian without valid authority. Rear v. Olson, 219 Wis. 322, 263 N.W. 357.

GUARDIAN DE L'EGLISE. A church-warden.

GUARDIAN DE L'ESTEMARY. The warden of the stannaries or mines in Cornwall, etc.

GUARDIAN OF THE PEACE. A warden or conservator of the peace.

GUARDIAN OF THE POOR. In English law, a person elected by the ratepayers of a parish to have the charge and management of the parish work-house or union. See 3 Steph. Comm. 203, 215.

GUARDIAN OF THE SPIRITUALITIES. The person to whom the spiritual jurisdiction of any diocese is committed during the vacancy of the see.

GUARDIAN OF THE TEMPORALITIES. The person to whose custody a vacant see or abbey was committed by the crown.

GUARDIAN OR WARDEN, OF THE CINQUE PORTS. A magistrate who has the jurisdiction of the ports or havens which are called the "Cinque Ports," *(q. v.)*. This office was first created in England, in imitation of the Roman policy, to strengthen the sea-coasts against enemies, etc.

GUARDIANSHIP. The office, duty, or authority of a guardian. Also the relation subsisting between guardian and ward.

GUARDIANUS. A guardian, warden, or keeper. Spelman.

GUARENTIGIO. In Spanish law, a written authorization to a court to enforce the performance of an agreement in the same manner as if it had been decreed upon regular legal proceedings.

GUARNIMENTUM. In old European law, a provision of necessary things. Spelman. A furnishing or garnishment.

GUASTALD. One who had the custody of the royal mansions.

GUBERNATOR. Lat. In Roman law, the pilot or steersman of a ship.

GUERILLA PARTY. In military law, an independent body of marauders or armed men, not regularly or organically connected with the armies of either belligerent, who carry on a species of irregular war, chiefly by depredation and massacre.

GUERPI, GUERPY. L. Fr. Abandoned; left; deserted. Britt. c. 33.

GUERRA, GUERRE. War. Spelman.

GUEST. A person entertained for pay at inn, tavern, or hotel on general undertaking of keeper thereof. Murray v. Hagens, La.App., 143 So. 505, 506, 507. A traveler who lodges at an inn or tavern with the consent of the keeper. Bac. Abr. "Inns," C, 5; 8 Coke, 32; McDaniels v. Robinson, 26 Vt. 316, 62 Am.Dec. 574.

A guest, as distinguished from a boarder, is bound for no stipulated time. He stops at the inn for a short or as long time as he pleases, paying, while he remains, the customary charge. Stewart v. McCready, 24 How.Prac. N.Y. 62; McIntosh v. Schops, 92 Or. 307, 180 P. 593, 595; Goodyear Tire & Rubber Co. v. Altamont Springs Hotel Co., 206 Ky. 494, 267 S.W. 555, 557.

A "guest" in an automobile is one who takes ride in automobile driven by another person, merely for his own pleasure or on his own business, and without making any return or conferring any benefit on automobile driver. Elliott v. Camper, 8 W.W.Harr. 504, 194 A. 130, 133; Blashfield, Cyc. of Automobile Law and Prac., Perm. Ed., § 2291.

GUEST-TAKER. An agister; one who took cattle in to feed in the royal forests. Cowell.

GUET. In old French law, watch. Ord. Mar. liv. 4, tit. 6.

GUIA. In Spanish law, a right of way for narrow carts. White, New Recop. l. 2, c. 6, § 1.

GUIDAGE. In old English law, that which was given for safe conduct through a strange territory, or another's territory. Cowell.

The office of guiding of travelers through dangerous and unknown ways. 2 Inst. 526.

GUIDE-PLATE. An iron or steel plate to be attached to a rail for the purpose of guiding to their place on the rail wheels thrown off the track. Pub. St. Mass. 1882, p. 1291.

GUIDON DE LA MER. The name of a treatise on maritime law, by an unknown author, supposed to have been written about 1671 at Rouen, and considered, in continental Europe, as a work of high authority.

GUILD. A voluntary association of persons pursuing the same trade, art, profession, or business, such as printers, goldsmiths, wool merchants, etc., united under a distinct organization of their own, analogous to that of a corporation, regulating the affairs of their trade or business by their own laws and rules, and aiming, by co-operation and organization, to protect and promote the interests of their common vocation.

In medieval history these fraternities or guilds played an important part in the government of some states; as at Florence, in the thirteenth and following centuries, where they chose the council of government of the city. The word is said to be derived from the Anglo-Saxon *"gild"* or *"geld,"* a tax or tribute, because each member of the society was required to pay a tax towards its support.

GUILD RENTS. Rents payable to the crown by any guild, or such as formerly belonged to religious guilds, and came to the crown at the general dissolution of the monasteries. Tomlins.

GUILDHALL. The hall or place of meeting of a guild, or gild.

The place of meeting of a municipal corporation. 3 Steph. Comm. 173, note. The mercantile or commercial gilds of the Saxons are supposed to have given rise to the present municipal corporations of England, whose place of meeting is still called the "Guildhall."

GUILDHALL SITTINGS. The sittings held in the Guildhall of the city of London for city of London causes.

GUILLOTINE. An instrument for decapitation, used in France for the infliction of the death penalty on convicted criminals, consisting, essentially, of a heavy and weighted knife-blade moving perpendicularly between grooved posts, which is made to fall from a considerable height upon the neck of the sufferer, immovably fixed in position to receive the impact.

GUILT. In criminal law, that quality which imparts criminality to a motive or act, and renders the person amenable to punishment by the law.

That disposition to violate the law which has manifested itself by some act already done. The opposite of innocence. See Ruth. Inst. b. 1, c. 18, § 10.

GUILTY. Having committed a crime or tort; the word used by a prisoner in pleading to an indictment when he confesses the crime of which he is charged, and by the jury in convicting. Com. v. Walter, 83 Pa. 108, 24 Am.Rep. 154; Jessie v. State, 28 Miss. 103; State v. White, 25 Wis. 359. Responsible for a delinquency, crime, or sin, and the connotation of such word is "evil", "wrongdoing", or "culpability". Hilkert v. Canning, 58 Ariz. 290, 119 P.2d 233, 236.

GUINEA. A coin formerly issued by the English mint, but all these coins were called in the time of Wm. IV. The word now means only the sum of £1 1*s*., in which denomination the fees of counsel are always given.

GULA-THING. A collection of Scandinavian customs in force in the southern part of Norway. The *Frosta-thing* was in force in the more northerly division of Dronheim. They are said to help to an understanding of the law prevailing in the northern part of England, where the Danish influence was strongest. 2 Holdsw. Hist. E. L. 23.

GULE OF AUGUST. The first of August, being the day of *St. Peter ad Vincula.*

GULES. The heraldic name of the color usually called "red." The word is derived from the Arabic word *"gule,"* a rose, and was probably introduced by the Crusaders. Gules is denoted in engravings by numerous perpendicular lines. Heralds who blazoned by planets and jewels called it "Mars," and "ruby." Wharton.

GUN. A firearm for throwing a projectile with gunpowder. Highsaw v. Creech, 17 Tenn.App. 573, 69 S.W.2d 249. A portable firearm such as a rifle, shotgun, carbine, etc. Henderson v. State, 75 Fla. 464, 78 So. 427, 428. A pistol or revolver. State v. Christ, 189 Iowa, 474, 177 N.W. 54, 57.

GURGES. Lat. Properly a whirlpool, but in old English law and conveyancing, a deep pit filled with water, distinguished from "stagnum," which was a shallow pool or pond. Co. Litt. 5; Johnson v. Rayner, 6 Gray, Mass., 107.

GURGITES. Wears. Jacob.

GUST. See Gest.

GUTI. Jutes; one of the three nations who migrated from Germany to Britain at an early period. According to Spelman, they established themselves chiefly in Kent and the Isle of Wight.

GUTTER. The diminutive of a sewer. Callis, Sew. (80,) 100. In modern law, an open ditch or conduit designed to allow the passage of water from one point to another in a certain direction, whether for purposes of drainage, irrigation, or otherwise. Warren v. Henly, 31 Iowa 31; Willis v. State, 27 Neb. 98, 42 N.W. 920.

GWABR MERCHED. Maid's fee. A British word signifying a customary fine payable to lords of some manors on marriage of the tenant's daughters, or otherwise on their committing incontinence. Cowell.

GWALSTOW. A place of execution. Jacob.

GWAYF. Waif, or waived; that which has been stolen and afterwards dropped in the highway for fear of a discovery. Cowell.

GYLPUT. The name of a court which was held every three weeks in the liberty or hundred of Pathbew in Warwick. Jacob.

GYLTWITE, or GUILTWIT. Sax. Compensation for fraud or trespass. Cowell.

GYNARCHY, or GYNÆCOCRACY. Government by a woman; a state in which women are legally capable of the supreme command; *e. g.*, in Great Britain.

GYNECOLOGIST. A physician specializing in diseases of the female organs. Simonet v. Frank F. Pellissier & Sons, 61 Cal.App.2d 41, 141 P.2d 922, 924.

GYNECOLOGY. The science which treats of the structure and diseases of women. Zerr v. Zerr, 188 Ky. 233, 221 S.W. 550, 551.

GYRATION. Movement about a fixed point. Great Western Mfg. Co. v. Lowe, D.C.Mich., 13 F.2d 880, 881.

GYRATORY STONE-CRUSHER. A machine with a shaft or crushing means which, instead of rotating, gyrates or moves in a circular course under the control of an eccentric. Traylor Engineering & Mfg. Co. v. Worthington Pump & Machinery Co., C.C.A.Pa., 1 F.2d 833.

GYROVAGI. Wandering monks.

GYVES. Fetters or shackles for the legs.

H

H. This letter, as an abbreviation, stands for Henry (a king of that name) in the citation of English statutes. In the Year Books, it is used as an abbreviation for Hilary term. In tax assessments and other such official records, "h" may be used as an abbreviation for "house," and the courts will so understand it. Alden v. Newark, 36 N.J.L. 288; Parker v. Elizabeth, 39 N.J.L. 693.

H. A. An abbreviation for *hoc anno,* this year, in this year.

H. B. An abbreviation for house bill, *i. e.,* a bill in the house of representatives, as distinguished from a senate bill.

H. B. M. An abbreviation for His (or Her) Britannic Majesty.

H. C. An abbreviation for house of commons, or for *habeas corpus.*

H. H. F. A. Housing and Home Finance Agency.

H. I. H. His (or Her) Imperial Highness.

H. L. An abbreviation for house of lords.

H. R. An abbreviation for house of representatives.

H. T. An abbreviation for *hoc titulo,* this title, under this title; used in references to books.

H. V. An abbreviation for *hoc verbo* or *hac voce,* this word, under this word; used in references to dictionaries and other works alphabetically arranged.

HABE, or HAVE. Lat. A form of the salutatory expression *"Ave"* (hail) in the titles of the constitutions of the Theodosian and Justinian Codes. Calvin; Spelman.

HABEAS CORPORA JURATORUM. A writ commanding the sheriff to bring up the persons of jurors, and, if need were, to distrain them of their lands and goods, in order to insure or compel their attendance in court on the day of trial of a cause. It issued from the Common Pleas, and served the same purpose as a *distringas juratores* in the King's Bench. It was abolished by the C. L. P. Act, 1852, § 104. Brown.

HABEAS CORPUS. Lat. (You have the body.) The name given to a variety of writs, (of which these were anciently the emphatic words,) having for their object to bring a party before a court or judge. In common usage, and whenever these words are used alone, they are understood to mean the *habeas corpus ad subjiciendum,* (see *infra.*) Dancy v. Owens, 126 Okl. 37, 258 P. 879, 884; In re McDevitt, 101 Misc. 588, 168 N.Y.S. 433; U. S. v. Tod, 263 U.S. 149, 44 S.Ct. 54, 57, 68 L.Ed. 221; Payne v. Graham, 20 Ala.App. 439, 102 So. 729, 731.

The sole function of the writ is to release from unlawful imprisonment. People ex rel. Luciano v. Murphy, 160 Misc. 573, 290 N.Y.S. 1011. The office of the writ is not to determine prisoner's guilt or innocence, and only issue which it presents is whether prisoner is restrained of his liberty by due process. Ex parte Presnell, 58 Okl.Cr. 50, 49 P.2d 232.

HABEAS CORPUS ACT. The English statute of 31 Car. II. c. 2, is the original and prominent *habeas corpus* act. It was amended and supplemented by St. 56 Geo. III. c. 100. And similar statutes have been enacted in all the United States. This act is justly regarded as the great constitutional guaranty of personal liberty.

HABEAS CORPUS AD DELIBERANDUM ET RECIPIENDUM. A writ which is issued to remove, for trial, a person confined in one county to the county or place where the offense of which he is accused was committed. Bac. Abr. *"Habeas Corpus,"* A; 1 Chit. Crim. Law, 132. Ex parte Bollman, 4 Cranch, 97, 2 L.Ed. 554. Thus, it has been granted to remove a person in custody for contempt to take his trial for perjury in another county. 1 Tyrw. 185.

HABEAS CORPUS AD FACIENDUM ET RECIPIENDUM. A writ issuing in civil cases to remove the cause, as also the body of the defendant, from an inferior court to a superior court having jurisdiction, there to be disposed of. It is also called *"habeas corpus cum causa."* Ex parte Bollman, 4 Cranch, 97, 2 L.Ed. 554.

HABEAS CORPUS AD PROSEQUENDUM. A writ which issues when it is necessary to remove a prisoner in order to *prosecute* in the proper jurisdiction wherein the fact was committed. 3 Bl. Comm. 130; State ex rel. Deeb v. Fabisinski, 111 Fla. 454, 152 So. 207, 210.

HABEAS CORPUS AD RESPONDENDUM. A writ which is usually employed in civil cases to remove a person out of the custody of one court into that of another, in order that he may be sued and answer the action in the latter. 2 Sell. Pr. 259; 2 Mod. 198; 3 Bl. Comm. 129; 1 Tidd, Pr. 300.

HABEAS CORPUS AD SATISFACIENDUM. In English practice. A writ which issues when a prisoner has had judgment against him in an action, and the plaintiff is desirous to bring him up to some superior court, to charge him with process of execution. 3 Bl. Comm. 129, 130; 3 Steph. Comm. 693; 1 Tidd, Pr. 350.

HABEAS CORPUS AD SUBJICIENDUM. A writ directed to the person detaining another, and commanding him to produce the body of the prisoner, (or person detained,) with the day and cause of his caption and detention, *ad faciendum, subjiciendum et recipiendum,* to do, submit to, and receive whatsoever the judge or court awarding the writ shall consider in that behalf. 3 Bl. Comm. 131; 3 Steph. Comm. 695.

This is the well-known remedy for deliverance from illegal confinement, called by Sir William Blackstone the most celebrated writ in the English law, and the great and efficacious writ in all manner of illegal confinement. 3 Bl. Comm. 129. The "great writ of liberty," issuing at common law out of courts of Chancery, King's Bench, Common Pleas, and Exchequer. Ex parte Kelly, 123 N.J.Eq. 489, 198 A. 203, 207.

HABEAS CORPUS AD TESTIFICANDUM. At common law, the writ, meaning "you have the body to testify", used to bring up a prisoner detained in a jail or prison to give evidence before the court. Hottle v. District Court in and for Clinton County, 233 Iowa 904, 11 N.W.2d 30, 34; 3 Bl. Comm. 130; 2 Tidd, Pr. 809. Ex parte Marmaduke, 91 Mo. 250, 4 S.W. 91, 60 Am.Rep. 250.

HABEAS CORPUS CUM CAUSA. (You have the body, with the cause.) Another name for the writ of *habeas corpus ad faciendum et recipiendum,* (*q. v.*) 1 Tidd, Pr. 348, 349.

HABEMUS OPTIMUM TESTEM, CONFITENTEM REUM. 1 Phil. Ev. 397. We have the best witness,—a confessing defendant. "What is taken *pro confesso* is taken as indubitable truth. The plea of guilty by the party accused shuts out all further inquiry. *Habemus confitentem reum* is demonstration, unless indirect motives can be assigned to it." 2 Hagg. Eccl. 315.

HABENDUM. Lat. Portion of deed beginning with the words "To have and to hold". Bannin v. Peck, 266 App.Div. 209, 41 N.Y.S.2d 668, 670. The clause usually following the granting part of the premises of a deed, which defines the extent of the ownership in the thing granted to be held and enjoyed by the grantee. 3 Washb. Real Prop. 437; New York Indians v. U. S., 170 U.S. 1, 18 S.Ct. 531, 42 L.Ed. 927; Freudenberger Oil Co. v. Simmons, 75 W.Va. 337, 83 S.E. 995, 997, Ann.Cas.1918A, 873; In re Tamargo, 220 N.Y. 225, 115 N.E. 462, 464.

The office of the "habendum" is properly to determine what estate or interest is granted by the deed, though office may be performed by the premises, in which case the habendum may lessen, enlarge, explain, or qualify, but not totally contradict or be repugnant to, estate granted in the premises. Claridge v. Phelps, Ind.App., 105 Ind. App. 344, 11 N.E.2d 503, 504.

HABENDUM ET TENENDUM. In old conveyancing, to have and to hold. Formal words in deeds of land from a very early period. Bract. fol. 17*b*.

HABENTES HOMINES. In old English law, rich men; literally, having men. The same with *fæsting-men,* (*q. v.*) Cowell.

HABENTIA. Riches. Mon. Angl. t. 1, 100.

HABERE. Lat. In the civil law, to have. Sometimes distinguished from *tenere,* (to hold,) and *possidere,* (to possess;) *habere* referring to the right, *tenere* to the fact, and *possidere* to both. Calvin.

HABERE FACIAS POSSESSIONEM. Lat. That you cause to have possession. The name of the process commonly resorted to by the successful party in an action of ejectment, for the purpose of being placed by the sheriff in the actual possession of the land recovered. It is commonly termed simply "*habere facias,*" or "*hab. fa.*"

HABERE FACIAS SEISINAM. L. Lat. That you cause to have seisin. The writ of execution in real actions, directing the sheriff to cause the demandant to have seisin of the lands recovered. It was the proper process for giving seisin of a freehold, as distinguished from a chattel interest in lands.

HABERE FACIAS VISUM. Lat. That you cause to have a view. A writ to cause the sheriff to take a view of lands or tenements.

HABERE LICERE. Lat. In Roman law, to allow [one] to have [possession.] This phrase denoted the duty of the seller of property to allow the purchaser to have the possession and enjoyment. For a breach of this duty, an *actio ex empto* might be maintained.

HABERGEON. A diminutive of *hauberk* (*q. v.*), denoting a short coat of mail without sleeves. Blount.

HABERJECTS. A cloth of a mixed color. Magna Charta, c. 26.

HABETO TIBI RES TUAS. Lat. Have or take your effects to yourself. One of the old Roman forms of divorcing a wife. Calvin.

HABILIS. Lat. Fit; suitable; active; useful, (of a servant.) Proved; authentic, (of Book of Saints.) Fixed; stable, (of authority of the king.) Du Cange.

HABIT. A disposition or condition of the body or mind acquired by custom or a usual repetition of the same act or function. Conner v. Citizens' St. R. Co., 146 Ind. 430, 45 N.E. 662; State v. Skillicorn, 104 Iowa, 97, 73 N.W. 503; Com. v. Whitney, 5 Gray, Mass., 85. The customary conduct, to pursue which one has acquired a tendency, from frequent repetition of the same acts. Knickerbocker Life Ins. Co. v. Foley, 105 U.S. 350, 26 L.Ed. 1055; National Council of Knights and Ladies of Security v. Fowler, 66 Okl. 294, 168 P. 914, 915, 6 A.L.R. 591; Woodmen of the World Life Ins. Soc. v. Reese, 206 Ark. 530, 176 S.W.2d 708, 714.

HABIT AND REPUTE. Applied in Scotch law to a general understanding and belief of something's having happened: thus, by the law of Scotland, marriage may be established by "habit and repute" where the parties cohabit and are at the same time held and reputed as man and wife. See Bell. The same rule obtains in some of the United States.

HABITABLE REPAIR. A covenant by a lessee to "put the premises into habitable repair" binds him to put them into such a state that they may be occupied, not only with safety, but with reasonable comfort, for the purposes for which they are taken. Miller v. McCardell, 19 R.I. 304, 33 A. 445, 30 L.R.A. 682; 2 Mood. & R. 186.

HABITANCY. That fixed place of abode to which a person intends to return habitually when absent.

Owens v. Huntling, C.C.A.Or., 115 F.2d 160, 162. Settled dwelling in a given place; fixed and permanent residence there.

This term is more comprehensive than "domicile," for one may be domiciled in a given place though he does not spend the greater portion of his time there, or though he may be absent for long periods. It is also more comprehensive than "residence," for one may reside in a given place only temporarily or for short periods on the occasion of repeated visits. But in neither case could he properly be called an "inhabitant" of that place or be said to have his "habitancy" there. Atkinson v. Washington & Jefferson College, 54 W.Va. 32, 46 S.E. 253; Hairston v. Hairston, 27 Miss. 711, 61 Am.Dec. 530; Abington v. North Bridgewater, 23 Pick., Mass., 170. And see Domicile; Residence.

It is difficult to give an exact definition of "habitancy." In general terms, one may be designated as an "inhabitant" of that place which constitutes the principal seat of his residence, of his business, pursuits, connections, attachments, and of his political and municipal relations. The term, therefore, embraces the fact of residence at a place, together with the intent to regard it and make it a home. The act and intent must concur. Lyman v. Fiske, 17 Pick., Mass., 231, 28 Am.Dec. 293.

HABITANT. Fr. In French and Canadian law, a resident tenant; a settler; a tenant who kept hearth and home on the seigniory. A native of Canada of French descent, particularly of the peasant or farming class.

HABITATIO. Lat. In the civil law, the right of dwelling; the right of free residence in another's house. Inst. 2, 5; Dig. 7, 8.

HABITATION.

In the civil law. The right of a person to live in the house of another without prejudice to the property. It differed from a usufruct, in this: that the usufructuary might apply the house to any purpose, as of a store or manufactory; whereas the party having the right of habitation could only use it for the residence of himself and family. 1 Browne, Civil Law, 184.

In Estates. A dwelling-house; a homestall. 2 Bl.Comm. 4; 4 Bl.Comm. 220; Holmes v. Oregon & C. R. Co., D.C.Or., 5 F. 527; Nowlin v. Scott, 10 Grat., Va., 65; Harvard College v. Gore, 5 Pick., Mass., 372.

In its generic sense, the term denotes a place of abode, but as used in a restrictive building covenant it may be synonymous simply with "dwelling." Goodhue v. Pennell, 164 App.Div. 821, 150 N.Y.S. 435, 436.

HABITUAL. Customary, usual, of the nature of a habit; its synonyms are customary, common, regular; while its antonyms are unusual, unwonted, extraordinary, rare. Illinois Bankers Life Ass'n v. Theodore, 47 Ariz. 314, 55 P.2d 806, 811. Formed or acquired by or resulting from habit; frequent use or custom. Moore v. State, 111 Tex.Cr.R. 461, 14 S.W.2d 1041. The "habitual" indulgence in violent and ungovernable temper as a ground for divorce is not synonymous with "frequent." Kellogg v. Kellogg, 93 Fla. 261, 111 So. 637, 638.

HABITUAL CRIMINAL. By statute in several states, one who is convicted of a felony, having been previously convicted of any crime (or twice so convicted), or who is convicted of a misdemeanor and has previously (in New York) been five times convicted of a misdemeanor. Crim.Code N.Y. § 510; Rev.St.Utah, 1898, § 4067 (Comp.Laws 1917, § 7907). In a more general sense, one made subject to police surveillance and arrest on suspicion, on account of his previous criminal record and absence of honest employment.

HABITUAL CRIMINALS ACT. The statute 32 & 33 Vict. c. 99. By this act power was given to apprehend on suspicion convicted persons holding license under the penal servitude acts, 1853, 1857, and 1864. The act was repealed and replaced by the prevention of crimes act, 1871, (34 & 35 Vict. c. 112.)

HABITUAL DRUNKARD. One who has a fixed habit of frequently getting drunk, though not oftener drunk than sober, and though sober for weeks at a time. Patton v. Commonwealth, 273 Ky. 307, 116 S.W.2d 652, 653.

One who frequently and repeatedly becomes intoxicated by excessive indulgence in intoxicating liquor so as to acquire a fixed habit and an involuntary tendency to become intoxicated as often as the temptation is presented, even though he remains sober for days or even weeks at a time. Leonard v. Leonard, 221 Iowa 722, 266 N.W. 537, 538.

A person given to inebriety or the excessive use of intoxicating drink, who has lost the power or the will, by frequent indulgence, to control his appetite for it. Ludwick v. Com., 18 Pa. 174; Gourlay v. Gourlay, 16 R.I. 705, 19 A. 142; McBee v. McBee, 22 Or. 329, 29 P. 887, 29 Am.St. Rep. 613.

It is not necessary that the person shall have lost his will power so that he cannot resist stimulants, Lester v. Sampson, Mo.App., 180 S.W. 419, 421; or that he be intoxicated so often as to incapacitate him from attending to his business for a considerable portion of time. Runkle v. Southern Pac. Milling Co., 184 Cal. 714, 195 P. 398, 400, 16 A.L.R. 275.

In England, defined by the habitual drunkards act, 1879, (42 & 43 Vict. c. 19,) which authorizes confinement in a retreat, upon the party's own application, as "a person who, not being amenable to any jurisdiction in lunacy, is, notwithstanding, by reason of habitual intemperate drinking of intoxicating liquor, at times dangerous to himself, or herself, or others, or incapable of managing himself or herself, or his or her affairs."

HABITUAL DRUNKENNESS, INTOXICATION, or INTEMPERANCE. The custom or habit of getting drunk; the constant indulgence in stimulants, whereby intoxication is produced; not the ordinary use, but the habitual use of them; the habit should be actual and confirmed, but need not be continuous, or even of daily occurrence. Williams v. Goss, 43 La.Ann. 868, 9 So. 750; Short v. Morrison, 159 La. 193, 105 So. 286, 288. As a cause for divorce, the fixed habit of frequently getting drunk; it does not necessarily imply continual drunkenness. Moor v. Moor, 211 Ala. 56, 99 So. 316, 318; Holm v. Holm, 44 Utah, 242, 139 P. 937, 938. That degree of intemperance from the use of intoxicating drinks which disqualifies the person a great portion of the time from properly attending to business, or which would reasonably inflict a course of great mental anguish upon the innocent party. Rev.Codes Idaho, § 2652 (Code 1932, § 31-608). It has no reference to the excessive or habitual use of drugs. Hayes v. Hayes, 86 Fla. 350, 98 So. 66, 67; Smith v. Smith, 7 Boyce, Del., 283, 105 A. 833.

HABITUALLY. Customarily; by frequent practice or use. It does not mean entirely or exclusively. Stanton v. French, 91 Cal. 274, 27 P. 657, 25 Am.St.Rep. 174.

HABITUM ET TONSURAM CLERICALEM. Clerical attire and tonsure. 4 Bl.Comm. 367.

HABLE. L. Fr. In old English law, a port or harbor; a station for ships. St. 27 Hen. VI. c. 3.

HACIENDA. In Spanish law, the public domain; the royal estate; the aggregate wealth of the state. The science of administering the national wealth; public economy.

Also an estate or farm belonging to a private person.

A royal estate. Newman & B. Dict.

HACK STAND. A private hack stand is a station where taxicabs or other vehicles are kept standing to solicit trade from the public indiscriminately at all hours. Borland v. Curto, 121 Misc. 336, 201 N.Y.S. 236, 237.

HACKNEY. Let out for hire, or devoted to common use; as, "hackney coaches," "hackney carriages." State v. Jarvis, 89 Vt. 239, 95 A. 541, 543.

HACKNEY CARRIAGES. Carriages plying for hire in the street. 2 C. 13, 877; Masterson v. Short, 33 How.Pr., N.Y., 481; 17 & 18 Vict. c. 86; Com. v. Matthews, 122 Mass. 60.

HAD. As used in a statute providing that no suit, action or proceeding to foreclose a mortgage or trust deed shall be had or maintained, "had" means commenced or begun. Friel v. Alewel, 318 Mo. 1, 298 S.W. 762, 764.

HADBOTE. In Saxon law, a recompense or satisfaction for the violation of holy orders, or violence offered to persons in holy orders. Cowell; Blount.

HADD. In Hindu law, a boundary or limit. A statutory punishment defined by law, and not arbitrary. Mozley & Whitley.

HADERUNGA. In old English law, hatred; ill will; prejudice, or partiality. Spelman; Cowell.

Respect or distinction of persons. Jacob.

HADGONEL. In old English law, a tax or mulct. Jacob.

HÆC EST CONVENTIO. Lat. This is an agreement. Words with which agreements anciently commenced. Yearb. H. 6 Edw. II. 191.

HÆC EST FINALIS CONCORDIA. L. Lat. This is the final agreement. The words with which the foot of a fine commenced. 2 Bl.Comm. 351.

HÆREDA. In Gothic law, a tribunal answering to the English court-leet or hundred court.

HÆREDE ABDUCTO. An ancient writ that lay for the lord, who, having by right the wardship of his tenant under age, could not obtain his person, the same being carried away by another person. Old Nat. Brev. 93.

HÆREDE DELIBERANDO ALTERI QUI HABET CUSTODIUM TERRÆ. An ancient writ, directed to the sheriff, to require one that had the body of an heir, being in ward, to deliver him to the person whose ward he was by reason of his land. Reg. Orig. 161.

HÆREDE RAPTO. An ancient writ that lay for the ravishment of the lord's ward. Reg. Orig. 163.

HÆREDEM DEUS FACIT, NON HOMO. God makes the heir, not man. Co. Litt. 7*b;* Bract. 62*b*.

HÆREDES. Lat. In the civil law, heirs. The plural of *hæres* (*q. v.*).

HÆREDES PROXIMI. Nearest or next heirs. The children or descendants of the deceased.

HÆREDES REMOTIORES. More remote heirs. The kinsmen other than children or descendants.

HÆREDES SUI ET NECESSARII. In Roman law, own and necessary heirs; *i. e.*, the lineal descendants of the estate-leaver. They were called "necessary" heirs, because it was the law that made them heirs, and not the choice of either the decedent or themselves. But since this was also true of slaves (when named "heirs" in the will) the former class were designated *"sui et necessarii,"* by way of distinction, the word *"sui"* denoting that the necessity arose from their relationship to the decedent. Mackeld. Rom. Law, § 733.

HÆREDIPETA. Lat. In old English law, a seeker of an inheritance; hence, the next heir to lands. Du Cange.

HÆREDIPETÆ SUO PROPINQUO VEL EXTRANEO PERICULOSO SANE CUSTODI NULLUS COMMITTATUR. To the next heir, whether a relation or a stranger certainly a dangerous guardian, let no one be committed. Co. Litt. 88*b*.

HÆREDITAS.

In Roman law. The *hæreditas* was a universal succession by law to any deceased person, whether such person had died testate or intestate, and whether in trust (*ex fideicommisso*) for another or not. The like succession according to Prætorian law was *bonorum possessio*.

The *hæreditas* was called *"jacens,"* until the *hæres* took it up, *i. e.*, made his *aditio hæreditatis;* and such *hæres,* if a *suus hæres,* had the right to abstain, *(potestas abstinendi,)* and, if an *extraneus hæres,* had the right to consider whether he would accept or decline, *(potestas deliberandi,)* the reason for this precaution being that (prior to Justinian's enactment to the contrary) a *hæres* after his *aditio* was liable to the full extent of the debts of the deceased person, and could have no relief therefrom, except in the case of a *damnum emergens* or *damnosa hæreditas, i. e.*, an *hæreditus* which disclosed (after the *aditio*) some enormous unsuspected liability. Brown. The theory was that, though the physical person of the deceased had perished, his legal personality survived and descended unimpaired on his heirs in whom his legal identity was continued.

In Old English Law. An estate transmissible by descent; an inheritance. Co. Litt. 9.

HÆREDITAS, ALIA CORPORALIS, ALIA INCORPORALIS; CORPORALIS EST, QUÆ TANGI POTEST ET VIDERI; INCORPORALIS QUÆ TANGI NON POTEST NEC VIDERI. Co. Litt. 9. An inheritance is either corporeal or incorporeal. Corporeal is that which can be touched and seen; incorporeal, that which can neither be touched nor seen.

HÆREDITAS DAMNOSA. A burdensome inheritance; one which would be a burden instead of a benefit, that is, the debts to be paid by the heir would exceed the assets.

HÆREDITAS EST SUCCESSIO IN UNIVERSUM JUS QUOD DEFUNCTUS HABUERIT. Co. Litt. 237. Inheritance is the succession to every right which the deceased had.

HÆREDITAS JACENS. In civil law, a prostrate or vacant inheritance. The inheritance left to a voluntary heir was so called so long as he had not manifested, either expressly or by silence, his acceptance or refusal of the inheritance. So long as no one had acquired the inheritance, it was termed *"hæreditas jacens;"* and this, by a legal fiction, represented the person of the decedent. Mackeld. Rom. Law, § 737. The estate of a person deceased, where the owner left no heirs or legatee to take it, called also *"caduca;"* an escheated estate. Cod. 10, 10, 1; 4 Kent, Comm. 425. The term has also been used in English law to signify an estate in abeyance; that is, after the ancestor's death, and before assumption of heir. Co. Litt. 342*b*. An inheritance without legal owner, and therefore open to the first occupant. 2 Bl.Comm. 259.

HÆREDITAS LEGITIMA. A succession or inheritance devolving by operation of law (intestate succession) rather than by the will of the decedent. Mackeld. Rom. Law, § 654.

HÆREDITAS LUCTUOSA. A sad or mournful inheritance or succession; as that of a parent to the estate of a child, which was regarded as disturbing the natural order of mortality *(turbato ordine mortalitatis.)* Cod. 6, 25, 9; 4 Kent, Comm. 397. It was sometimes termed *tristis successio.*

HÆREDITAS NIHIL ALIUD EST, QUAM SUCCESSIO IN UNIVERSUM JUS, QUOD DEFUNCTUS HABUERIT. The right of inheritance is nothing else than the faculty of succeeding to all the rights of the deceased. Dig. 50, 17, 62.

HÆREDITAS NUNQUAM ASCENDIT. An inheritance never ascends. Glanv. lib. 7, c. 1; 2 Bl. Comm. 211. A maxim of feudal origin, and which invariably prevailed in the law of England down to the passage of the statute 3 & 4 Wm. IV. c. 106, § 6, by which it was abrogated. 1 Steph.Comm. 378. See Broom, Max. 527, 528.

HÆREDITAS TESTAMENTARIA. Testamentary inheritance, that is, succession to an estate under and according to the last will and testament of the decedent. Mackeld. Rom. Law, § 654.

HÆREDUM APPELLATIONE VENIUNT HÆREDES HÆREDUM IN INFINITUM. By the title of heirs, come the heirs of heirs to infinity. Co. Litt. 9.

HÆRES.

In Roman Law. The heir, or universal successor in the event of death. The heir is he who actively or passively succeeds to the entire property of the estate-leaver. He is not only the successor to the rights and claims, but also to the estate-leaver's debts, and in relation to his estate is to be regarded as the identical person of the estate-leaver, inasmuch as he represents him in all his active and passive relations to his estate. Mackeld. Rom. Law, § 651.

The institution of the *hæres* was the essential characteristic of a *testament:* if this was not done, the instrument was called a *codicillus.* Mack.C.L. §§ 632, 650.

It should be remarked that the office, powers, and duties of the *hæres,* in Roman law, were much more closely assimilated to those of a modern *executor* than to those of an heir at law. Hence "heir" is not at all an accurate translation of *"hæres,"* unless it be understood in a special, technical sense.

In Common Law. An heir; he to whom lands, tenements, or hereditaments by the act of God and right of blood to descend, of some estate of inheritance. Co. Litt. 7*b*.

HÆRES ASTRARIUS. In old English law, an heir in actual possession of the house of his ancestor. Bract. 85, 267*b*.

HÆRES DE FACTO. In old English law, heir from fact; that is, from the disseisin or other act of his ancestor, without or against right. An heir in fact, as distinguished from an heir *de jure,* or by law.

HÆRES EST ALTER IPSE, ET FILIUS EST PARS PATRIS. An heir is another self, and a son is part of the father. 3 Coke, 12*b*.

HÆRES EST AUT JURE PROPRIETATIS AUT JURE REPRESENTATIONIS. An heir is either by right of property, or right of representation. 3 Coke, 40*b*.

HÆRES EST EADEM PERSONA CUM ANTECESSORE. An heir is the same person with his ancestor. Co. Litt. 22; Branch, Princ. See Nov. 48, c. 1, § 1.

HÆRES EST NOMEN COLLECTIVUM. "Heir" is a collective name or noun. 1 Vent. 215.

HÆRES EST NOMEN JURIS; FILIUS EST NOMEN NATURÆ. "Heir" is a name or term of law; "son" is a name of nature. Bac. Max. 52, in reg. 11.

HÆRES EST PARS ANTECESSORIS. An heir is a part of the ancestor. So said because the ancestor, during his life, bears in his body (in judgment of law) all his heirs. Co. Litt. 22*b;* Schoonmaker v. Sheely, 3 Hill, N.Y., 165, 167.

HÆRES EX ASSE. In the civil law, an heir to the whole estate; a sole heir. Inst. 2, 23, 9.

HÆRES EXTRANEUS. In the civil law, a strange or foreign heir; one who was not subject to the power of the testator, or person who made him heir. *Qui testatoris juri subjecti non sunt, extranei hœredes appellantur.* Inst. 2, 19, 3.

HÆRES FACTUS. In the civil law, an heir made by will; a testamentary heir; the person created universal successor by will. Story, Confl. Laws, § 507; 3 Bl.Comm. 224. Otherwise called *"hœres ex testamento,"* and *"hœres institutus."* Inst. 2, 9, 7; Id. 2, 14.

HÆRES FIDEICOMMISSARIUS. In the civil law, the person for whose benefit an estate was given to another (termed *"hœres fiduciarius," q. v.*) by will. Inst. 2, 23, 6, 7, 9. Answering nearly to the *cestui que trust* of the English law.

HÆRES FIDUCIARIUS. A fiduciary heir, or heir in trust; a person constituted heir by will, in trust for the benefit of another, called the *"fideicommissarius."*

HÆRES HÆREDIS NEI EST MEUS HÆRES. The heir of my heir is my heir. Wharton, Law Dict.

HÆRES INSTITUTUS. A testamentary heir; one appointed by the will of the decedent.

HÆRES LEGITIMUS. A lawful heir; one pointed out as such by the marriage of his parents.

HÆRES LEGITIMUS EST QUEM NUPTIÆ DEMONSTRANT. He is a lawful heir whom marriage points out as such; who is born in wedlock. Co. Litt. 7*b*; Bract. fol. 88; Fleta, lib. 6, c. 1; Broom, Max. 515; Mirror of Just. 70; Dig. 2, 4, 5. (As to the application of the principle when the marriage is subsequent to the birth of the child, see 2 Cl. & F. 571; 6 Bingh. N. C. 385; 5 Wheat. 226, 262, n., 5 L.Ed. 70.)

HÆRES MINOR UNO ET VIGINTI ANNIS NON RESPONDEBIT, NISI IN CASU DOTIS. Moore, 348. An heir under twenty-one years of age is not answerable, except in the matter of dower.

HÆRES NATUS. In the civil law, an heir born; one born heir, as distinguished from one made heir, (*hœres factus, q. v.*;) an heir at law, or by intestacy, (*ab intestato*;) the next of kin by blood, in cases of intestacy. Story, Confl. Laws, § 507; 3 Bl.Comm. 224. This is the only form of heirship recognized in the English law. Wms. R. P., 6th Am. ed. 96.

HÆRES NECESSARIUS. In the civil law, a necessary or compulsory heir. This name was given to the heir when, being a slave, he was named "heir" in the testament, because on the death of the testator, whether he would or not, he at once became free, and was compelled to assume the heirship. Inst. 2, 19, 1.

HÆRES NON TENETUR IN ANGLIA AD DEBITA ANTECESSORIS REDDENDA, NISI PER ANTECESSOREM AD HOC FUERIT OBLIGATUS, PRÆTERQUAM DEBITA REGIS TANTUM. Co. Litt. 386. In England, the heir is not bound to pay his ancestor's debts, unless he be bound to it by the ancestor, except debts due to the king. But now, by 3 & 4 Wm. IV. c. 104, he is liable.

HÆRES RECTUS. In old English law, a right heir. Fleta, lib. 6, c. 1, § 11.

HÆRES SUUS. In the civil law, a man's *own* heir; a decedent's proper or natural heir. This name was given to the lineal descendants of the deceased. Persons who were in the power of the testator but became *sui juris* at his death. Inst. 2, 13; 3, 1, 4, 5. Those descendants who were under the power of the deceased at the time of his death, and who are most nearly related to him. Calvin.

HÆRETARE. In old English law, to give a right of inheritance, or make the donation hereditary to the grantee and his heirs. Cowell.

HÆRETICO COMBURENDO. The statute 2 Hen. IV. c. 15, *de hœretico comburendo,* was the first penal law enacted against heresy, and imposed the penalty of death by burning against all heretics who relapsed or who refused to abjure their opinions. It was repealed by the statute 29 Car. II. c. 9. Brown. This was also the name of a writ for the purpose indicated. See, also, De Hæretico Comburendo.

HAFNE. A haven or port. Cowell.

HAFNE COURTS. Haven courts; courts anciently held in certain ports in England. Spelman.

HAG. A division of a coppice or wood on which timber was cut annually by the proprietor. Ersk. Pr. 222.

HAGA. A house in a city or borough. Scott.

HAGIA. A hedge. Mon. Angl. tom. 2, p. 273.

HAGNE. A little hand-gun. St. 33 Hen. VIII. c. 6.

HAGNEBUT. A hand-gun of a larger description than the hagne. St. 2 & 3 Edw. VI. c. 14; 4 & 5 P. & M. c. 2.

HAGUE TRIBUNAL. The Court of Arbitration established by the Hague Peace Conference of 1899.

The object of the establishment was to facilitate the immediate recourse to arbitration for the settlement of international differences by providing a permanent court, "accessible at all times, and acting, in default of agreement to the contrary between the parties, in accordance with the rules of procedure inserted in the present convention." The court is given jurisdiction over all arbitration cases, provided the parties do not agree to institute a special tribunal. An international Bureau was likewise established to serve as a registry for the court and to be the channel of communications relative to the meetings of the court. The court, although called "permanent," is really so only in the fact that there is a permanent list of members from among whom the arbitrators in a given case are selected. At the Second Hague Conference of 1907, apart from minor changes made in the court, it was provided that, of the two arbitrators appointed by each of the parties, only one should be a national of the appointing state. 1 Scott, 274–318, 423–464.

HAIA. In old English law, a park inclosed. A hedge. Cowell.

HAIEBOTE. In old English law, a permission or liberty to take thorns, etc., to make or repair hedges. Blount.

HAILL. In Scotch law, whole; the whole. "All and haill" are common words in conveyances. 1 Bell, App.Cas. 499.

HAILWORKFOLK (*i. e.*, holyworkfolk.) Those who formerly held lands by the service of defending or repairing a church or monument. See, also, Halywercfolk.

HAIMHALDARE. In old Scotch law, to seek restitution of one's own goods and gear, and bring the same *home* again. Skene de Verb. Sign.

HAIMSUCKEN. In Scotch law, the crime of assaulting a person in his own house. Bell. See Hamesecken.

HAIR. A capillary outgrowth from the skin. It has been held not to include the bristles of animals. Von Stade v. Arthur, 13 Blatchf. 251, Fed. Cas. No. 16,998.

HAKH. Truth; the true God; a just or legal prescriptive right or claim; a perquisite claimable under established usage by village officers. Wilson, Gloss. Ind.

HAKHDAR. The holder of a right. Moz. & W. See Hakh.

HALAKAR. The realization of the revenue. Wilson, Gloss. Ind.; Moz. & W.

HALF. One of two equal parts into which anything may be divided. Hoyne v. Schneider, 138 Kan. 545, 27 P.2d 558.

A moiety. Prentiss v. Brewer, 17 Wis. 644, 86 Am.Dec. 730.

HALF BLOOD. See Blood.

HALF BROTHER, HALF SISTER. Persons who have the same father, but different mothers; or the same mother, but different fathers. Wood v. Mitcham, 92 N.Y. 379; In re Weiss' Estate, 1 Montg. Co. Law Rep'r, Pa., 210.

HALF CENT. A copper coin of the United States, of the value of five mills, and of the weight of ninety-four grains. The coinage of these was discontinued in 1857.

HALF CHEST. In connection with tea, a "half chest" is a chest containing 75 to 80 pounds, but the weight varies according to the kind of tea. Japan Tea Co. v. Franklin MacVeagh & Co., 142 Minn. 152, 171 N.W. 305, 307.

HALF DEFENSE. See Defense.

HALF DIME. A copper-nickel clad (formerly silver) (now nickel) coin of the United States, of the value of five cents.

HALF DOLLAR. A silver coin of the United States, of the value of fifty cents, or one-half the value of a dollar.

HALF EAGLE. A gold coin of the United States, of the value of five dollars.

HALF ENDEAL OR HALFEN-DEAL. A moiety or half of a thing.

HALF-KINEG. In Saxon law, half-king, (*semi-rex.*) A title given to the aldermen of all England. Crabb, Eng. Law, 28; Spelman.

HALF-MARK. A noble, or six shillings and eight pence in English money.

HALF NEPHEW OR HALF NIECE. Son or daughter of a half brother or half sister. Pierson v. National Fire Proofing Corporation, 117 N.J.L. 600, 190 A. 73, 74.

HALF PILOTAGE. Compensation for services which a pilot has put himself in readiness to perform, by labor, risk, and cost, and has offered to perform, at half the rate he would have received if the services had actually been performed. Gloucester Ferry Co. v. Pennsylvania, 114 U.S. 196, 5 S.Ct. 826, 29 L.Ed. 158.

HALF-PROOF. In the civil law, proof by one witness, or a private instrument. Hallifax, Civil Law, b. 3, c. 9, no. 25; 3 Bl.Comm. 370. Or *prima facie* proof, which yet was not sufficient to found a sentence or decree.

HALF-SEAL. That which was formerly used in the English chancery for sealing of commissions to delegates, upon any appeal to the court of delegates, either in ecclesiastical or marine causes. 8 Eliz. c. 3.

HALF SECTION. In American land law, the half of a section of land according to the divisions of the government survey, laid off either by a north-and-south or by an east-and-west line, and containing 320 acres. See Brown v. Hardin, 21 Ark. 324.

HALF-TIMER. A child who, by the operation of the English factory and education acts, is employed for less than the full time in a factory or workshop, in order that he may attend some "recognized efficient school." See factory and workshop act, 1878, § 23; elementary education act, 1876, § 11.

HALF-TONGUE. A jury half of one *tongue* or nationality and half of another. See De Medietate Linguæ.

HALF YEAR. In legal computation, the period of one hundred and eighty-two days; the odd hours being rejected. Co. Litt. 135*b*; Cro. Jac. 166; Yel. 100; 1 Steph.Comm. 265; Pol. Code Cal. 1903, § 3257.

HALI. A man employed in ploughing. Wilson, Gloss. Ind.; Moz. & W.

HALIFAX LAW. A synonym for lynch law, or the summary (and unauthorized) trial of a person accused of crime and the infliction of death upon him; from the name of the parish of Halifax, in England, where anciently this form of private justice was practised by the free burghers in the case of persons accused of stealing; also called "gibbet law."

HALIGEMOT, or HALIMOTE. In Saxon law, the meeting of a hall, (*conventus aulæ,*) that is, a lord's court; a court of a manor, or court-baron. Spelman. So called from the *hall,* where the tenants or freemen met, and justice was administered. Crabb, Eng. Law, 26.

It was sometimes used to designate a convention of citizens in their public hall and was also called folkmote and hallmote. The word *halimote* rather signifies the lord's court or a court baron held in a manor in which the differences between the tenants were determined. Cunn. L.Dict.; Cowell.

"Furthermore, it seems to have been a common practice for a wealthy abbey to keep a court, known as a *halimote,* on each of its manors, while in addition to these manorial courts it kept a central court, a *libera curia* for all its greater freehold tenants. And we may now and again meet with courts which are distinctly called courts of honors. The rule then was not merely this, that the lord of a manor may hold a court for the manor; but rather this, that a lord may hold a court for his tenants." 1 Poll. & Maitl. 573.

HALIMAS. In English law, the feast of All Saints, on the 1st of November; one of the cross-quarters of the year, was computed from Halimas to Candlemas. Wharton.

HALIWORKFOLK. See Halywercfolk.

HALL. A building or room of considerable size, used as a place for the meeting of public assemblies, conventions, courts, etc.; as, the city hall, the town hall.

In English law, a name given to many manor-houses because the magistrate's court was held in the hall of his mansion; a chief mansion-house. Cowell.

Hence, *hall day,* a court day.

HALL-MARK. An official stamp affixed by the goldsmiths upon articles made of gold or silver as an evidence of genuineness, and hence used to signify any mark of genuineness. "The power of free alienation is the 'hall-mark' of a fee-simple absolute." Rand. Em. Dom. § 206.

HALLAGE. In old English law, a fee or toll due for goods or merchandise vended in a hall. Jacob; 6 Co. 62.

A toll due to the lord of a fair or market, for such commodities as were vended in the common hall of the place. Cowell; Blount.

HALLAZCO. In Spanish law, the finding and taking possession of something which previously had no owner, and which thus becomes the property of the first occupant. Las Partidas, 3, 5, 28; 5, 48, 49; 5, 20, 50.

HALLE-GEMOTE. In Saxon law, haligemot (*q. v.*).

HALLMOOT. See Haligemot.

HALLUCINATION. In medical jurisprudence, a trick or deceit of the senses; a morbid error either of the sense of sight or that of hearing, or possibly of the other senses; a psychological state, such as would be produced naturally by an act of sense-perception, attributed confidently, but mistakenly, to something which has no objective existence; as, when the patient imagines that he sees an object when there is none, or hears a voice or other sound when nothing strikes his ear. See Staples v. Wellington, 58 Me. 459; McNett v. Cooper, C.C.Mich., 13 F. 590; People v. Krist, 168 N.Y. 19, 60 N.E. 1057.

An error, a blunder, a mistake, a fallacy; and when used in describing the condition of a person, does not necessarily carry an imputation of insanity. Foster's Ex'rs v. Dickerson, 64 Vt. 233, 24 A. 253.

The perception by any of the senses of an object which has no existence. The conscious recognition of a sensation of sight, hearing, feeling, taste, or smell which is not due to any impulse received by the perceptive apparatus from without, but arises within the perceptive apparatus itself. A false *perception* in contradistinction to a *delusion* or false belief. Wood, Am. Text-Book of Med.

Hallucinations are tricks of the senses, differing from delusions in that hallucinations pass away while delusions remain. Bensberg v. Washington University, 251 Mo. 641, 158 S.W. 330, 333.

HALMOTE. See Haligemot.

HALYMOTE. A holy or ecclesiastical court.

A court held in London before the lord mayor and sheriffs, for regulating the bakers.

It was anciently held on Sunday next before St. Thomas' day, and therefore called the "*holymote,*" or holy court. Cowell.

HALYWERCFOLK. Sax. In old English law, tenants who held land by the service of repairing or defending a church or monument, whereby they were exempted from feudal and military services. Especially in the county of Durham, those who held by service of defending the corpse of St. Cuthbert. Jacob, Law Dict.

HAM. A place of dwelling; a homeclose; a little narrow meadow. Blount. A house or little village. Cowell.

HAMA. In old English law, a hook; an engine with which a house on fire is pulled down. Yel. 60.

A piece of land.

HAMBLING, or HAMELING. In forest law, the hoxing or hock-sinewing of dogs; an old mode of laming or disabling dogs. Termes de la Ley. Expeditation (*q. v.*).

HAMEL, HAMELETA, or HAMLETA. A hamlet.

HAMESECKEN. In Scotch law, the violent entering into a man's house without license or against the peace, and the seeking and assaulting him there. Skene de Verb. Sign.; 2 Forb. Inst. 139.

The crime of housebreaking or burglary. 4 Bl. Comm. 223. Spelled, also, "hamesucken."

The common genus of offences that comes under the name of *hamesucken* is that which is usually called house-breaking; which sometimes comes under the common appellation of *burglary,* whether committed in the day or night to the intent to commit felony; so that house-breaking of this kind is of two natures. 1 Hale, Pl.Cr. 547; Com. v. Hope, 22 Pick., Mass., 4.

See also, Hamsocne.

HAMFARE. (Sax. From *ham,* a house.) In Saxon law, an assault made in a house; a breach of the peace in a private house. Cowell. This word by some is said to signify the freedom of a man's house. Holthouse. See, also, Hamsocne.

HAMLET. A small village; a part or member of a vill. It is the diminutive of *"ham,"* a village. Cowell. See Rex v. Morris, 4 Term, 552.

A "village" or "hamlet" in a rural community may be no more than a store, a school, a church, and two or three residences. Rantoul Rural High School Dist. No. 2, Franklin County, v. Davis, 99 Kan. 185, 160 P. 1008, 1009.

HAMMA. A close joining to a house; a croft; a little meadow. Cowell.

HAMMER. Metaphorically, a forced sale or sale at public auction. "To bring to the hammer," to put up for sale at auction. "Sold under the hammer," sold by an officer of the law or by an auctioneer.

HAMSOCNE. In Saxon law, the word is variously spelled *hamsoca, hamsocna, haimsuken, hamesaken, hamsocn.* The right of security and privacy in a man's house. Du Cange. The breach of this privilege by a forcible entry of a house is breach of the peace. Anc. Laws & Inst. of Eng. Gloss.; Du Cange; Bracton, lib. 3, tr. 2, c. 2, § 3. The right to entertain jurisdiction of the offence. Spelman; Du Cange. Immunity from punishment for such offence. Du Cange; Fleta, lib. 1, c. 47, § 18. An insult offered in one's own house (*insultus factus in domo*). Brompton, p. 957; Du Cange.

Among the Anglo-Saxons it was breaking into a house; perhaps the time of the day was not an element. See 3 Holdsw. Hist. E. L. 293; 2 Poll. & Maitl. 492. See, also, Hamesecken.

HANAPER. A hamper or basket in which were kept the writs of the court of chancery relating to the business of a subject, and their returns; 5 & 6 Vict. c. 113; 10 Ric. II. c. 1; 3 Bl.Comm. 49; equivalent to the Roman *fiscus.* According to others, the fees accruing on writs, etc., were there kept. Spelman; Du Cange.

HANAPER-OFFICE. An office belonging to the common-law jurisdiction of the court of chancery, so called because all writs relating to the business of a subject, and their returns, were formerly kept in a hamper, *in hanaperio.* 5 & 6 Vict. c. 103. See Yates v. People, 6 Johns., N.Y., 363.

HAND. A measure of length equal to four inches, used in measuring the height of horses.

A person's signature. Salazar v. Taylor, 18 Colo. 538, 33 P. 369; 10 Mod. 103.

In anatomical usage the hand, or manus, includes the phalanges, or fingers and thumb; the metacarpus, or hand proper; and the carpus, or wrist; but in popular usage the wrist is often excluded. Champlin Refining Co. v. State Industrial Commission, 153 Okl. 45, 4 P.2d 751, 752. The arm up to but not including the elbow. Gondak v. Wilson Gas Coal Co., 148 Pa.Super. 566, 25 A.2d 854, 855.

In the plural, the term may be synonymous with "possession"; as, the "hands" of an executor, garnishee, etc. Brownwood Gas Co. v. Belser, Tex. Civ.App., 257 S.W. 605, 607.

In old English law, an oath. For the meaning of the terms "strong hand" and "clean hands," see those titles.

HAND DOWN. To announce or file an opinion in a cause. Used originally and properly of the opinions of appellate courts transmitted to the court below; but in later usage the term is employed more generally with reference to any decision by a court upon a case or point reserved for consideration.

HAND-FASTING. In old English law, betrothment.

HAND-GRITH. Peace or protection given by the king with his own hand; used in the laws of Henry I. Tomlin; Cowell; Moz. & W.; Stat. Hen. I. c. 13.

HAND MONEY. Money paid in hand to bind a bargain; earnest money, when it is in cash.

HANDBILL. A written or printed notice displayed to inform those concerned of something to be done. Kelly v. Board of Trustees of Evarts Common Graded School Dist., 162 Ky. 612, 172 S.W. 1047, 1048; People v. McLaughlin, 33 Misc. 691, 68 N.Y.S. 1108.

HANDBOROW. In Saxon law, a hand pledge; a name given to the nine pledges in a decennary or friborg; the tenth or chief, being called *"headborow,"* (*q. v.*). So called as being an inferior pledge to the chief. Spelman.

HANDCUFFS. See Fetters.

HANDLE. To control, direct, to deal with, to act upon, to perform some function with regard to or to have passed through one's hands, to buy and sell, or to deal or trade in. State ex rel. Bell v. Phillips Petroleum Co., 349 Mo. 360, 160 S.W.2d 764, 769. To manage or operate. The term includes the act of placing a truck on a depot platform for the purpose of loading. Wells Fargo & Co. v. Lowery, Tex.Civ.App., 197 S.W. 605, 608.

HANDHABEND, or HAND-HABENDE. In Saxon law, one having a thing in his hand; that is, a thief found having the stolen goods in his possession. Jurisdiction to try such thief. See Laws of Hen. I. c. 59; Laws of Athelstane § 6; Fleta, lib. 1, c. 38, § 1; Britton p. 72; Du Cange, *Handhabenda.* See, also, Backberend.

HANDSALE. Anciently, among all the northern nations, shaking of hands was held necessary to bind a bargain,—a custom still retained in verbal contracts. A sale thus made was called "handsale," (*venditio per mutuam manum complexionem.*) In process of time the same word was used to signify the price or earnest which was given immediately after the shaking of hands, or instead thereof. 2 Bl.Comm. 448.

HANDSEL. Handsale, or earnest money.

HANDWRITING. The chirography of a person; the cast or form of writing peculiar to a person, including the size, shape, and style of letters, tricks of penmanship, and whatever gives individuality to his writing, distinguishing it from that of other persons. In re Hyland's Will, 1 Gib. 41, 58 St.R. 798, 27 N.Y.S. 961, 963.

Anything written by hand; an instrument written by the hand of a person, or a specimen of his writing.

Handwriting, considered under the law of evidence, includes not only the ordinary writing of one able to write, but also writing done in a disguised hand, or in cipher, and a mark made by one able or unable to write. 9 Amer. & Eng.Enc.Law, 264. See Com. v. Webster, 5 Cush., Mass., 301, 52 Am.Dec. 711.

Typewriting is not "handwriting" within a statute allowing experts' opinions as to who executed a writing. Wolf v. Gall, 176 Cal. 787, 169 P. 1017, 1019.

HANDY MAN. A man of all work. Sovereign Camp, W. O. W., v. Craft, 208 Ala. 467, 94 So. 831, 834.

HANG. In old practice, to remain undetermined. "It has *hung* long enough; it is time it were made an end of." Holt, C. J., 1 Show. 77.

Thus, the present participle means pending; during the pendency. "If the tenant alien, *hanging* the *præcipe*." Co.Litt. 266*a*. Remaining undetermined. 1 Show. 77.

HANGED, DRAWN AND QUARTERED. A method of executing traitors in England, said to have been introduced in 1241. The traitor was carried on a sled, or hurdle to the gallows (formerly dragged there tied to the tail of a horse); hanged till half dead and then cut down; his entrails cut out and burnt; his head cut off and his body to be divided into quarters, which, with his head, were hung in some public place. In practice the executioner usually cut out the heart and held it up to view. See Andrews, Old Time Punishments; 1 Eng.Rep. 87.

HANGING. In criminal law, suspension by the neck; the mode of capital punishment used in England from time immemorial, and generally adopted in the United States. 4 Bl.Comm. 403.

HANGING IN CHAINS. In atrocious cases it was at one time usual, in England, for the court to direct a murderer, after execution, to be hanged upon a gibbet in chains near the place where the murder was committed, a practice quite contrary to the Mosaic law. (Deut. xxi. 23.) Its legality was declared by acts in 1751 and 1828. Abolished by 4 & 5 Wm. IV, c. 26. Wharton.

HANGING PAPER. Ordinarily, paper for hanging or hangings, or paper which hangs. Within the meaning of the Tariff Act (19 U.S.C.A. § 121), paper used for covering walls, ceiling, etc., whether such paper is tinted or decorative or not;—a more inclusive term than "paper hangings," meaning tinted or decorative paper used for the purpose mentioned. Downing & Co. v. U. S., 12 Ct. Cust.App. 451, 454.

Merchandise known as grass cloth, made by pasting a fabric of weed bark sewed with cotton thread on a paper backing and dyeing the surface, imported to be used as wall hangings, is dutiable as dyed hanging paper. Downing & Co. v. U. S., 12 Ct.Cust.App. 451.

HANGMAN. An executioner. One who executes condemned criminals by hanging.

HANGWITE. In Saxon law, a fine for illegal hanging of a thief, or for allowing him to escape. Immunity from such fine. Du Cange.

HANIG. Some customary labor to be performed. Holthouse.

HANSE. An alliance or confederation among merchants or cities, for the good ordering and protection of the commerce of its members. An imposition upon merchandise. Du Cange.

HANSE TOWNS. The collective name of certain German cities, including Lübeck, Hamburg, and Bremen, which formed an alliance for the mutual protection and furtherance of their commercial interests, in the twelfth century. The powerful confederacy thus formed was called the "Hanseatic League." The league framed and promulgated a code of maritime law, which was known as the "Laws of the Hanse Towns," or *Jus Hanseaticum Maritimum*.

The years 1356 to 1377 marked the zenith of the league's power. The league gradually declined till, in 1669, the last general assembly was held and Lübeck, Hamburg and Bremen were left alone to preserve the name and small inheritance of the "Hansa."

HANSE TOWNS, LAWS OF THE. The maritime ordinances of the Hanseatic towns, first published in German at Lübeck, in 1597, and in May, 1614, revised and enlarged.

HANSEATIC. Pertaining to a hance or commercial alliance; but, generally, the union of the Hanse towns is the one referred to, as in the expression the "Hanseatic League."

HANSGRAVE. The chief of a company; the head man of a corporation.

HAOLE. White foreign. Refers to rank rather than to race. International Longshoremen's & Warehousemen's Union v. Ackerman, D.C.Hawaii, 82 F.Supp. 65, 76.

HANTELOD, or HANTELODE. In old European law, an arrest, or attachment. Spelman; Du Cange; Toml.; Holthouse.

HAP. To catch. Thus, "hap the rent," "hap the deed-poll," were formerly used.

HAPPINESS. Comfort, consolation, contentment, ease, enjoyment, pleasure, satisfaction. National Surety Co. v. Jarrett, 121 S.E. 291, 295, 95 W.Va. 420.

The constitutional right of men to pursue their "happiness" means the right to pursue any lawful business or vocation, in any manner not inconsistent with the equal rights of others, which may increase their prosperity, or develop their faculties, so as to give to them their highest enjoyment. Butchers' Union Co. v. Crescent City Co., 111 U.S. 757, 4 S.Ct. 652, 28 L.Ed. 585; 1 Bl.Comm. 41. English v. English, 32 N.J.Eq. 750.

HAQUE. In old statutes, a hand-gun, about three-quarters of a yard long.

HARACIUM. In old English law, a race of horses and mares kept for breed; a stud. Spelman.

HARBINGER. In England, an officer of the royal household.

HARBOR, *n.* A haven, or a space of deep water so sheltered by the adjacent land as to afford a safe anchorage for ships. Rowe v. Smith, 51 Conn. 271, 50 Am.Rep. 16; The Aurania, D.C.N.Y., 29 F. 103; People v. Kirsch, 67 Mich. 539, 35 N.W. 157; The Cuzco, D.C.Wash., 225 F. 169, 176. A port or haven for ships; a sheltered place, natural or artificial, on the coast of a sea, lake, or other body of water. State v. Savidge, 95 Wash. 240, 163 P. 738, 740.

"Port" is a word of larger import than "harbor," since it implies the presence of wharves, or at any rate the means and opportunity of receiving and discharging cargo. See 7 M. & G. 870; Martin v. Hilton, 9 Metc., Mass., 371; 2 B. & Ald. 460. Thus, we have the "said *harbor,* basin, and docks of the *port* of Hull." 2 B. & Ald. 60. But they are generally used as synonymous. Webster, Dict.

HARBOR, *v.* To afford lodging to, to shelter, or to give a refuge to. Hancock v. Finch, 126 Conn. 121, 9 A.2d 811. To clandestinely shelter, succor, and protect improperly admitted aliens. Susnjar v. U. S., C.C.A.Ohio, 27 F.2d 223, 224. To receive clandestinely and without lawful authority a person for the purpose of so concealing him that another having a right to the lawful custody of such person shall be deprived of the same. Jones v. Van Zandt, 5 How. 215, 227, 12 L.Ed. 122. Or, in a less technical sense, it is the reception of persons improperly. Poll.Torts 275; Wood v. Gale, 10 N.H. 247, 34 Am.Dec. 150; Eells v. People, 4 Scam., Ill., 498. It may be aptly used to describe the furnishing of shelter, lodging, or food clandestinely or with concealment, and under certain circumstances, may be equally applicable to those acts divested of any accompanying secrecy. U. S. v. Grant, C.C.Or., 55 F. 415.

As used in U. S. Criminal Code, § 42, 18 U.S.C.A. § 1381, the word "harbor" means to lodge, to care for, after secreting the deserter. Firpo v. U. S., C.C.A.N.Y., 261 F. 850, 853.

To "harbor" a dog involves the idea of protection, and of treating it as living at one's house, and undertaking to control its actions. Hagenau v. Millard, 182 Wis. 544, 195 N.W. 718, 719. See, also, Markwood v. McBroom, 110 Wash. 208, 188 P. 521, 522.

HARBOR AUTHORITY. In England a harbor authority is a body of persons, corporate or unincorporate, being proprietors of, or intrusted with the duty of constructing, improving, managing, or lighting, any harbor. St. 24 & 25 Vict. c. 47.

HARBOR LINE. A line marking the boundary of a certain part of a public water which is reserved for a harbor. Engs v. Peckham, 11 R.I. 224. The line beyond which wharves and other structures cannot be extended. Garrison v. Greenleaf Johnson Lumber Co., C.C.A.Va., 215 F. 576, 579.

HARD. As applied to liquors, rough; acid; sour. In re Stiller, 161 N.Y.S. 594, 597, 175 App.Div. 211.

HARD CASES. A phrase used to indicate decisions which, to meet a case of hardship to a party, are not entirely consonant with the true principle of the law. It is said of such: Hard cases make bad law. Hard cases must not make bad equity any more than bad law; Moore v. Pierson, 6 Iowa 279, 71 Am.Dec. 409. Hard cases are the quicksands of the law. Metropolitan Nat. Bank of Kansas City, Mo. v. Campbell Commission Co., C.C.Mo., 77 F. 705.

HARD CIDER. Cider which has lost its sweetness from fermentation—fermented cider possessing a stimulating and intoxicating effect, due to its acquisition of a substantial and potent alcoholic content, through fermentation. People v. Emmons, 178 Mich. 126, 144 N.W. 479, 481, Ann.Cas. 1915D, 425.

HARD LABOR. A punishment, additional to mere imprisonment, sometimes imposed upon convicts sentenced to a penitentiary. But the labor is not, as a rule, any harder than ordinary mechanical labor. Thompson v. State, 19 Ala.App. 328, 97 So. 258, 260. Compulsory labor. In re Danton, 108 Kan. 451, 195 P. 981, 983.

HARD MONEY. Lawful coined money. Henry v. Bank of Salina, 5 Hill (N.Y.) 523, 536.

HARD OF HEARING. A relative term, applied to one that cannot hear as well as one possessing normal faculties of hearing or does not hear as well as the average person. Sharps v. Jones, 100 W.Va. 662, 131 S.E. 463, 464.

HARDHEIDIS. In old Scotch law, lions; coins formerly of the value of three half-pence. 1 Pitc. Crim.Tr. pt. 1, p. 64, note.

HARDPAN. Any earth not popularly recognized as rock through which it is hard to dig or to make excavation of any sort. It may be: (1) Semiindurated clay, with or without admixture of stony matter; (2) cemented gravel; or (3) clay, with or without admixture of stony matter, which is very tough because of its strong cohesion. Baker v. Multnomah County, 118 Or. 143, 246 P. 352, 355.

HARDSHIP. The severity with which a proposed construction of the law would bear upon a particular case, founding, sometimes, an argument against such construction, which is otherwise termed the "argument *ab inconvenienti.*" See Hard Cases.

HARIOT. The same as heriot (*q. v.*) Cowell; *Termes de la Ley.* Sometimes spelled Harriott. Wms. Seis. 203.

HARMFUL or HARMLESS ERROR. See Error.

HARMONIC PLANE. The zero adopted by the United States Coast and Geodetic Survey of the Department of Commerce upon which its tidal tables, charts, and maps are based. It is an arbitrary plane, and, in Puget Sound, is the lowest plane of the tide recognized by that department. State v. Scott, 89 Wash. 63, 154 P. 165, 168.

HARMONIZE. Though not strictly synonymous with the word "reconcile," it is not improperly used by a court in instructing the jury that it is their duty to "harmonize" conflicting evidence if possible. Holdridge v. Lee, 3 S.D. 134, 52 N.W. 265.

HARMONY. The phrase "in harmony with" is synonymous with "in agreement, conformity, or accordance with." Brown Real Estate Co. v. Lancaster County, 110 Neb. 665, 194 N.W. 897, 898.

HARNASCA. In old European law, the defensive armor of a man; harness. Spelman.

HARNESS. The defensive armor of a soldier or knight. All warlike instruments. In modern poetical sense, a suit of armor. Sometimes, the trappings of a war-horse.

The tackle or furniture of a ship.

HARO, HARRON. Fr. In Norman and early English law, an outcry, or hue and cry after felons and malefactors. Cowell. The original of the *clamour de haro* comes from the Normans. Moz. & W.

HARRIOTT. The old form of "heriot," (*q. v.*) Williams, Seis. 203.

HART. A stag or male deer of the forest, generally over five years old.

HARTER ACT. A name commonly applied to the act of congress of February 13, 1893, c. 105, providing: (§ 1) that agreements in a bill of lading relieving the owner, etc., of a vessel sailing between the United States and foreign ports, from liability for negligence or fault in proper loading, storage, custody, care, or delivery of merchandise, are void (46 U.S.C.A. § 190); (§ 2) that no bill of lading shall contain any agreement whereby the obligations of the owner to exercise due diligence, properly equip, man, provision and outfit a vessel and make it seaworthy, and whereby the obligations of the master, etc., carefully to handle, store, care for and deliver the cargo, are in any way lessened, weakened or avoided (46 U.S.C.A. § 191); (§ 3) that if the owner shall exercise due diligence to make such vessel in all respects seaworthy and properly manned, equipped and supplied, neither the vessel nor her owners, etc., shall be liable for loss resulting from faults or errors in navigation or management, nor for losses arising from dangers of the sea, acts of God, or public enemies, or the inherent defect of the thing carried, or insufficiency of package, or seizure under legal process, or any act or omission of the shipper of the goods, or from saving or attempting to save life at sea, or deviation in rendering such service (46 U.S.C.A. § 192).

HARVESTING. The gathering of crops of any kind. Cook v. Massey, 38 Idaho 264, 220 P. 1088, 1091.

HARVESTING EXPENSES. Includes expenses for repairs of machinery used in harvesting the crop, the rent of live stock, implements, and the cost of labor. Betts v. Orton, 34 Cal.App. 397, 167 P. 1147, 1148.

HASP AND STAPLE. In old Scotch law, the form of entering an heir in a subject situated within a royal borough. It consisted of the heir's taking hold of the hasp and staple of the door (which was the symbol of possession,) with other formalities. Bell; Burrill. A mode of entry in Scotland by which a bailee declared a person heir on evidence brought before himself, at the same time delivering the property over to him by the hasp and staple of the door. Bell; Ersk.Pr. 433.

HASPA. In old English law, the hasp of a door; by which livery of seisin might anciently be made, where there was a house on the premises.

HASTA. Lat. A spear. In the Roman law, a spear was the sign of a public sale of goods or sale by auction. Hence the phrase "*hastæ subjicere*" (to put under the spear) meant to put up at auction. Calvin.

In feudal law, a spear, the symbol used in making investiture of a fief. Feud. lib. 2, tit. 2.

HAT MONEY. In maritime law, primage; a small duty paid to the captain and mariners of a ship.

HATCH. A nautical term, generally signifying an opening in the deck of a ship. State v. Armstrong, 97 Neb. 343, 149 N.W. 786, 788, Ann.Cas. 1917A, 554.

HATCHWAY. Specifically, an opening in the deck of a boat; hence any similar opening, as in a floor or sidewalk; a trapdoor. Kelly v. Theo. Hamm Brewing Co., 140 Minn. 371, 168 N.W. 131, 132. The term is inapplicable to the head of a stairway; Peterson v. Shapiro, 171 Minn. 408, 214 N.W. 269, 270; or to basement ways; State v. Armstrong, 97 Neb. 343, 149 N.W. 786, 788, Ann. Cas.1917A, 554.

HAUBER. O. Fr. A high lord; a great baron. Spelman.

HAUBERK. A long coat or tunic of ring or chain mail. Sometimes applied loosely to a *habergeon* (*q. v.*).

HAUGH, HOUGH, or HOWGH. Low-lying rich lands, lands which are occasionally overflowed. Encyc.Dict. A green plot in a valley.

HAUL. To pull or draw with force; to drag; to transport by hauling. Denius v. North Dakota Workmen's Compensation Bureau, 68 N.D. 506, 281 N.W. 361, 363.

HAULA. See Aula.

HAULAGE ROYALTY. Damages at a certain amount per ton for coal from adjacent lands hauled through subterranean passageways of lessor's land. Quality Excelsior Coal Co. v. Reeves, 206 Ark. 713, 177 S.W.2d 728, 732.

HAULM. See Helm.

HAUR. In old English law, hatred. Used in the laws of William the Conqueror. Toml.; Leg.Wm. I. c. 16; Blount.

HAUSTUS. Lat. In the civil law, a species of servitude, consisting in the right to draw water from another's well or spring, in which the *iter*, (right of way to the well or spring,) so far as it is necessary, is tacitly included. Dig. 8, 3, 1; Mackeld.Rom.Law, § 318; Fleta, 1. 4, c. 27, § 9.

HAUT CHEMIN. L. Fr. Highway. Yearb. M. 4 Hen. VI. 4.

HAUT ESTRET. L. Fr. High street; highway. Yearb. P. 11 Hen. VI. 2.

HAUTHONER. In old English law, a man armed with a coat of mail. Jacob.

HAVE. Lat. A form of the salutatory expression "*Ave*," used in the titles of some of the constitutions of the Theodosian and Justinian Codes. See Cod. 7, 62, 9; Id. 9, 2, 11.

HAVE. Imports ownership, and has been defined to mean "to keep," "to hold in possession," "to own." Busteed v. Cambridge Sav. Bank, 306 Mass. 9, 26 N.E.2d 983, 986. To bear (children). Nickerson v. Hoover, 70 Ind.App. 343, 115 N.E. 588, 593. To possess corporally. Walker v. Trollinger, 192 N.C. 744, 135 S.E. 871, 873.

"No one, at common law, was said to *have* or to be in possession of land, unless it were conveyed to him by the livery of seisin, which gave him the corporal investiture and bodily occupation thereof." Bl.Law Tracts, 113.

HAVE AND HOLD. A common phrase in conveyancing, derived from the *habendum et tenendum* of the old common law. See Habendum et Tenendum.

HAVEN. A place of a large receipt and safe riding of ships, so situate and secured by the land circumjacent that the vessels thereby ride and anchor safely, and are protected by the adjacent land from dangerous or violent winds; as Milford Haven, Plymouth Haven, and the like. Hale de Jure Mar. par. 2, c. 2; The Cuzco, D.C.Wash., 225 F. 169, 176; 15 East 304, 305. Lowndes v. Board of Trustees, 14 S.Ct. 758, 153 U.S. 1, 38 L.Ed. 615; De Lovio v. Boit, 7 Fed.Cas. 429.

HAW. A small parcel of land so called in Kent; houses. Co.Litt. 5; Cowell.

HAWBERK, or HAWBERT. A coat or shirt of mail; hence, derivatively (in feudal law) one who held a fief on the duty or service of providing himself with such armor and standing ready, thus equipped, for military service when called on. Wharton. See Fief d'Haubert.

HAWGH, HOWGH. In old English law, a valley. Co.Litt. 5*b*. See Haugh.

HAWKER. An itinerant or traveling trader, who carries goods about, in order to sell them, and who actually sells them to purchasers, in contradistinction to a trader who has goods for sale and sells them in a fixed place of business. Commonwealth v. Bergeron, 296 Mass. 60, 5 N.E.2d 31, 32. A peddler who uses beast of burden to carry wares and who cries out merits of wares in street. City of Washington v. Reed, 229 Mo.App. 1195, 70 S.W. 2d 121, 122. See Hawking.

It is perhaps not essential to the idea, but is generally understood from the word, that a hawker is to be one who not only carries goods for sale, but seeks for purchasers, either by outcry, which some lexicographers conceive as intimated by the derivation of the word, or by attracting notice and attention to them, as goods for sale, by an actual exhibition or exposure of them, by placards or labels, or by a conventional signal, like the sound of a horn for the sale of fish. Graffty v. Rushville, 107 Ind. 502, 8 N.E. 609, 57 Am.Rep. 128.

One who goes about a village carrying samples and taking orders for a non-resident firm is not a hawker or peddler. Village of Cerro Gordo v. Rawlings, 135 Ill. 36, 25 N.E. 1006.

HAWKING. The act of offering goods for sale on the streets by outcry or by attracting the attention of persons by exposing goods in a public place, or by placards, labels, or signals. Pastorino v. City of Detroit, 182 Mich. 5, 148 N.W. 231, 235, Ann. Cas.1916D, 768.

The business of peddling is distinct from that of a manufacturer selling his own products, and those who raise or produce what they sell, such as farmers and butchers, are not peddlers. Ex parte Hogg, 70 Tex.Cr.R. 161, 156 S.W. 931, 932. The occupation of a dairyman, going about delivering the milk from his farm to his regular customers according to their previous orders, is not, within the ordinary meaning of the term, peddling or hawking. State ex rel. Brittain v. Hayes, 143 La. 39, 78 So. 143, 144.

HAY. Commonly means grasses or seeds which have been harvested. Sandall v. Hoskins, 104 Utah 50, 137 P.2d 819, 823. In statute, term does not apply to the stalks, stems, and other residue, left after bean plants have been threshed and the bean kernel or seeds removed. State v. Choate, 41 Idaho 251, 238 P. 538, 540.

HAY IN STACK. A stack of hay, grain, straw, or the like is a large quantity thereof collected and usually built up in layers in conical, oblong, or rectangular form to a point or ridge at the top so that it will be preserved against the inclemencies of the weather. A policy covering "hay in stack" does not cover hay in the mow of a barn. Murphy v. Continental Ins. Co., 178 Iowa 375, 157 N.W. 855, 856, L.R.A.1917B, 934.

HAY-BOTE. Another name for "hedge-bote," being one of the estovers allowed to a tenant for life or years, namely, material for repairing the necessary hedges or fences of his grounds, or for making necessary farming utensils. 2 Bl.Comm. 35; 1 Washb.Real Prop. 129.

HAYWARD. In old English law, an officer appointed in the lord's court to keep a common herd of cattle of a town; so called because he was to see that they did not break or injure the hedges of inclosed grounds. His duty was also to impound trespassing cattle, and to guard against pound-breaches. Kitch. 46; Cowell. Adams v. Nichols, 1 Aikens (Vt.) 319.

HAZAR-ZAMIN. A bail or surety for the personal attendance of another. Moz. & W.

HAZARD. In old English law, an unlawful game at dice, those who play at it being called "hazardors." Jacob.

In modern law, any game of chance or wagering. Cheek v. Com., 100 Ky. 1, 37 S.W. 152; Somers v. State, 5 Sneed (Tenn.) 438.

A risk or peril, assumed or involved, whether in connection with contract relation, personal relation, or golf or gambling. State v. Hagan, 44 N.D. 306, 175 N.W. 372, 377. A danger or risk lurking in a situation which by change or fortuity develops into an active agency of harm. Hough v. Contributory Retirement Appeal Board, 309 Mass. 534, 36 N.E.2d 415, 417, 418. Exposure to the chance of loss or injury. Caminetti v. Guaranty Union Life Ins. Co., 52 Cal.App.2d 330, 126 P.2d 159, 163.

A stationary unlighted freight train upon a railroad crossing at night. Plante v. Canadian Nat. Rys., 138 Me. 215, 23 A.2d 814, 817. An accident incidental to or result of an act done while in the course of one's employment. Tipple v. High Street Hotel Co., 70 Ohio App. 397, 41 N.E.2d 879, 885.

In insurance law, the risk, danger, or probability that the event insured against may happen, varying with the circumstances of the particular case. See State Ins. Co. v. Taylor, 14 Colo. 499, 24 P. 333, 20 Am.St.Rep. 281.

Moral hazard. In fire insurance, the risk or danger of the destruction of the insured property by fire, as measured by the character and interest of the insured owner, his habits as a prudent and careful man or the reverse, his known integrity or his bad reputation, and the amount of loss he would suffer by the destruction of the property or the gain he would make by suffering it to burn and collecting the insurance. Davenport v. Firemen's Ins. Co. of Newark, N. J., 47 S.D. 426, 199 N.W. 203, 205.

HAZARDOR. In old English law, one who played at a hazard, *i. e.*, an unlawful game of dice. Jacob.

HAZARDOUS. Exposed to or involving danger; perilous; risky.

Involving risk of loss. Caminetti v. Guaranty Union Life Ins. Co., 52 Cal.App.2d 330, 126 P.2d 159, 162, 163.

The terms "hazardous," "extra-hazardous," "specially hazardous," and "not hazardous" are well-understood technical terms in the business of insurance, having distinct and separate meanings. Although what goods are included in each designation may not be so known as to dispense with actual proof, the terms themselves are distinct and known to be so. Russell v. Insurance Co., 50 Minn. 409, 52 N.W. 906.

HAZARDOUS CONTRACT. See Contract.

HAZARDOUS INSURANCE. Insurance effected on property which is in unusual or peculiar danger of destruction by fire, or on the life of a man whose occupation exposes him to special or unusual perils.

HAZARDOUS NEGLIGENCE. See Negligence.

HE. Properly a pronoun of the masculine gender, but commonly construed in statutes to include both sexes as well as corporations. Dickson v. Strickland, 114 Tex. 176, 265 S.W. 1012, 1021; City of Janesville v. Tweedell, 217 Wis. 395, 258 N.W. 437. May be read "they". Buono v. Yankee Maid Dress Corporation, C.C.A.N.Y., 77 F.2d 274, 278.

HE WHO COMES INTO A COURT OF EQUITY MUST COME WITH CLEAN HANDS.

HE WHO HAS COMMITTED INIQUITY SHALL NOT HAVE EQUITY. Francis, Max.

HE WHO IS SILENT WHEN CONSCIENCE REQUIRES HIM TO SPEAK SHALL BE DEBARRED FROM SPEAKING WHEN CONSCIENCE REQUIRES HIM TO BE SILENT.

HE WHO SEEKS EQUITY MUST DO EQUITY. This expression means that the party asking the aid of an equity court must stand in a conscientious relation toward his adversary and the transaction from which his claim arises must be fair and just and the relief must not be harsh and oppressive upon defendant. Jacklich v. Baer, 57 Cal. App.2d 684, 135 P.2d 179, 184. And that court will not confer equitable relief on party seeking its aid, unless he has acknowledged and conceded or will admit and provide for all equitable rights, claims, and demands justly belonging to adverse party and growing out of or necessarily involved in subject matter of controversy. Bates v. Dana, 345 Mo. 311, 133 S.W.2d 326, 329. It is in pursuance of this maxim that equity enforces the right of the wife's equity to a settlement. Snell, Eq. (5th Ed.) 374. Drake v. Sherman, 67 Ill.App. 440.

HE WHO WILL HAVE EQUITY DONE TO HIM MUST DO EQUITY TO THE SAME PERSON. 4 Bouv.Inst. 3723.

HEAD. Chief; leading; principal; the upper part or principal source of a stream.

The principal person or chief of any organization, corporation, or firm.

HEAD MONEY. A sum of money reckoned at a fixed amount for each head (person) in a designated class.

Particularly (1) a capitation or poll tax. (2) A bounty offered by the laws of the United States for each person on board an enemy's ship or vessel, at the commencement of a naval engagement, which shall be sunk or destroyed by a ship or vessel of the United States of equal or inferior force, the same to be divided among the officers and crew in the same manner as prize money. In re Farragut, 7 D.C. 97. A similar reward is offered by the British statutes. (3) The tax or duty imposed by act of congress of Aug. 3, 1882, on owners of steamships and sailing vessels for every immigrant brought into the United States. Head Money Cases, 112 U.S. 580, 5 Sup.Ct. 247, 28 L.Ed. 798. (4) A bounty or reward paid to one who pursues and kills a bandit or outlaw and produces his head as evidence; the offer of such a reward being popularly called "putting a price on his head."

HEAD OF A FAMILY. An individual who actually supports and maintains in one household one or more individuals who are closely connected with him by blood relationship, relationship by marriage, or by adoption, and whose right to exercise family control and provide for the dependent individuals is based upon some moral or legal obligation. Miller v. Glenn, D.C.Ky., 47 F.Supp. 794, 796, 797.

A term used in homestead and exemption laws to designate a person who maintains a family; a householder. Not necessarily a husband or father, but any person who has charge of, supervises, and manages the affairs of the household or the collective body of persons residing together and constituting the family. Armstrong-McClenahan Co. v. Rhoads, 180 Iowa, 710, 163 N.W. 356, 357; The term may thus include an abandoned wife maintaining minor children, Mennell v. Wells, 51 Mont. 141, 149 P. 954, 955; and also a widow, Wilkey v. Wilkey, 130 Tenn. 430, 171 S.W. 78; Burrell Tp. v. Pittsburg Guardians of Poor, 62 Pa. 475, 1 Am.Rep. 441.

There must be at least two persons who live together in relation of one family. Whidden v. Abbott, 124 Fla. 293, 168 So. 253, 254.

To be the head of a family, one must either have a responsibility (i. e., at least a natural or moral obligation) to support, or have parental authority over, another member of the family. Whyte v. Grant, 142 La. 822, 77 So. 643. "Head of family," within exemption laws, must be under some obligation to support other members, and the other members must be dependent on the head. Lena v. Clinkenbeard, 172 Okl. 6, 44 P.2d 2, 4, (but see In re Taylor, D.C., 282 F. 315, 316).

HEAD OF CREEK. This term means the source of the longest branch, unless general reputation has given the appellation to another. Davis v. Bryant, 2 Bibb. (Ky.) 110.

HEAD OF DEPARTMENT. One of the members of the president's cabinet, and not a mere bureau head. Brooks v. United States, D.C.N.Y., 33 F. Supp. 68, 69.

The expression "head of any department of the state government" is one of varied and therefore of equivocal meaning, construed in one statute as having been employed in a narrow, restricted sense, and in another to have been used in its general popular sense, depending on effectuation of the legislative objective as the controlling element. Rainey v. Malone, Tex.Civ.App., 141 S.W.2d 713, 715.

HEAD OF STREAM. The highest point on the stream which furnishes a continuous stream of water, not necessarily the longest fork or prong. Uhl v. Reynolds, 64 S.W. 498, 23 Ky.Law Rep. 759; State v. Coleman, 13 N.J.Law, 104.

HEAD OF WATER. In hydraulic engineering, mining, etc., the effective force of a body or volume of water, expressed in terms of the vertical distance from the level of the water in the pond, reservoir, dam, or other source of supply, to the point where it is to be mechanically applied, or expressed in terms of the pressure of the water per square inch at the latter point. Shearer v. Middleton, 88 Mich. 621, 50 N.W. 737.

HEADBOROUGH. In Saxon law, the head or chief officer of a borough; chief of the frankpledge tithing or decennary. This office was afterwards, when the petty constableship was created, united with that office.

HEAD-COURTS. Certain tribunals in Scotland, abolished by 20 Geo. II. c. 50. Ersk. 1, 4, 5.

HEADERS. In mining, a "cap" is a square piece of plank or block wedged between the top of posts and the roof to better hold the roof, and "headers" are longer pieces of plank supported by a prop at each end and supporting a larger area of the roof with fewer posts. Big Branch Coal Co. v. Wrenchie, 160 Ky. 668, 170 S.W. 14, 16.

HEADLAND. In old English law, a narrow piece of unplowed land left at the end of a plowed field for the turning of the plow. Called, also, "Butt." 2 Leon. 70, case 93; 1 Litt. 13.

HEAD-NOTE. A syllabus to a reported case; a summary of the points decided in the case, which is placed at the head or beginning of the report.

HEAD-PENCE. An exaction of 40*d.* or more, collected by the sheriff of Northumberland from the people of that county twice in every seven years, without account to the king. Abolished by 23 Hen. VI. c. 6, in 1444. Cowell.

HEADRIGHT. Under the Allotment Act (Act Cong. June 28, 1906 [34 Stat. 539]), creating a trust fund from all tribal funds which included funds from sale of tribal lands, funds allowed on claims against the United States and received from tribal oil, gas, and mineral rights, each allottee owned his pro rata share of the trust fund, and this pro rata beneficial interest is commonly called a "headright." Cook v. First Nat. Bank, 145 Okl. 5, 291 P. 43, 46.

HEADRIGHT CERTIFICATE. In the laws of the republic of Texas, a certificate issued under authority of an act of 1839, which provided that every person immigrating to the republic between October 1, 1837, and January 1, 1840, who was the head of a family and actually resided within the government with his or her family should be entitled to a grant of 640 acres of land, to be held under such a certificate for three years, and then conveyed by absolute deed to the settler, if in the meantime he had resided permanently within the republic and performed all the duties required of citizens. Cannon v. Vaughan, 12 Tex. 401.

HEAD-SILVER. A name sometimes given to a Common Fine (*q. v.*). By a payment of a certain sum of money to the lord, litigants might try their suits nearer home. Blount.

HEAFODWEARD. In old English law, one of the services to be rendered by a thane, or a geneath or villein, the precise nature of which is unknown. Anc.Eng.Inst.

HEALER. One who heals or cures; specifically, one who professes to cure bodily diseases without medicine or any material means, according to the tenets and practices of so-called "Christian Science," whose beliefs and practices, being founded on their religious convictions, are not per se proof of insanity. In re Brush's Will, 72 N.Y.S. 425, 35 Misc. 689.

HEALGEMOTE. In Saxon law, a court-baron; an ecclesiastical court; Haligemot (*q. v.*).

HEALING ACT. Another name for a curative act or statute. See Lockhart v. Troy, 48 Ala. 584.

HEALSFANG. In Saxon law, a sort of pillory, by which the head of the culprit was caught between two boards, as feet are caught in a pair of stocks. Cowell. It was very early disused, no mention of it occurring in the laws of the Saxon kings. Anc.Laws & Inst. of Eng. Gloss.; Spelman, Gloss.

HEALTH. State of being hale, sound, or whole in body, mind or soul, well being. Venable v. Gulf Taxi Line, 105 W.Va. 156, 141 S.E. 622, 624. Freedom from pain or sickness; the most perfect state of animal life. Not synonymous with "sanitation." Black v. Lambert, Tex.Civ.App., 235 S.W. 704, 706. The right to the enjoyment of health is a subdivision of the right of personal security, one of the absolute rights of persons. 1 Bl.Comm. 129, 134. As to injuries affecting health, see 3 Bl. Comm. 122.

Bill of health. See Bill.

Board of health. See Board.

Health laws. Laws prescribing sanitary measures, and designed to promote or preserve the health of the community.

Health officer. The officer charged with the execution and enforcement of health laws. The powers and duties of health officers are regulated by local laws.

Public health. As one of the objects of the police power of the state, the "public health" means the prevailingly healthful or sanitary condition of the general body of people or the community in mass, and the absence of any general or widespread disease or cause of mortality. The wholesome sanitary condition of the community at large. State ex rel. Pollock v. Becker, 289 Mo. 660, 233 S.W. 641, 649.

Sound Health. See "Sound."

HEALTHY. Free from disease or bodily ailment, or any state of the system peculiarly susceptible or liable to disease or bodily ailment. Bell v. Jeffreys, 35 N.C. 356.

HEARING. Proceeding of relative formality, generally public, with definite issues of fact or of law to be tried, in which parties proceeded against have right to be heard, and is much the same as a trial and may terminate in final order. In re Securities and Exchange Commission, D.C.N.Y., 14 F.Supp. 417, 419. Synonymous with trial, and includes reception of evidence and arguments thereon. Grant v. Michaels, 94 Mont. 452, 23 P.2d 266. It is frequently used in a broader and more popular significance to describe whatever takes place before magistrates clothed with judicial functions and sitting without jury at any stage of the proceedings subsequent to its inception, and may include proceedings before an auditor. Menard v. Bowman Dairy Co., 296 Ill.App. 323, 15 N.E.2d 1014, 1015.

In equity practice. The trial of the case, including introduction of evidence, argument of counsel, and decree of court. Wolfe v. Wolfe, 144 Neb. 55, 12 N.W.2d 368, 369.

The words "final hearing" have long been used to designate the trial of an equity case upon the merits, as distinguished from the hearing of any preliminary questions arising in the cause, which are termed "interlocutory." Akerly v. Vilas, 24 Wis. 171, 1 Am.Rep. 166.

The term is broad enough to include judicial examination of issue between the parties whether of law or of fact. Keown v. Keown, 231 Mass. 404, 121 N.E. 153, 154.

In criminal law. The examination of a prisoner charged with a crime or misdemeanor, and of the witnesses for the accused.

Fair hearing. See Fair Hearing.

Final hearing. See Final.

Preliminary examination. The examination of a person charged with crime, before a magistrate. Van Buren v. State, 65 Neb. 223, 91 N.W. 201.

Preliminary hearing. In criminal law. Synonymous with "preliminary examination." State v. Rogers, 31 N.M. 485, 247 P. 828, 833.

The hearing given to a person accused of crime, by a magistrate or judge, exercising the functions of a committing magistrate, to ascertain whether there is evidence to warrant and require the commitment and holding to bail of the person accused. See Bish. New Cr.L. §§ 32, 225.

It is in no sense a trial for the determination of accused's guilt or innocence, but simply a course of procedure whereby a possible abuse of power may be prevented, and accused discharged or held to answer, as the facts warrant. State v. Langford, 293 Mo. 436, 240 S.W. 167, 168.

Unfair hearing. See that title.

HEARING DE NOVO. Generally, a new hearing or a hearing for the second time, contemplating an entire trial in same manner in which matter was originally heard and a review of previous hearing. On hearing "de novo" court hears matter as court of original and not appellate jurisdiction. Collier & Wallis v. Astor, 9 Cal.2d 202, 70 P.2d 171, 173.

HEARSAY. Evidence not proceeding from the personal knowledge of the witness, but from the mere repetition of what he has heard others say. That which does not derive its value solely from the credit of the witness, but rests mainly on the veracity and competency of other persons. The very nature of the evidence shows its weakness, and it is admitted only in specified cases from necessity. State v. Ah Lee, 18 Or. 540, 23 P. 424, 425. Young v. Stewart, 191 N.C. 297, 131 S.E. 735, 737.

It is second-hand evidence, as distinguished from original evidence; it is the repetition at second-hand of what would be original evidence if given by the person who originally made the statement. Literally, it is what the witness says he heard another person say. Stockton v. Williams, 1 Doug., Mich., 546, 570 (citing 1 Starkie, Ev. 229). Evidence, oral or written, is hearsay when its probative force depends in whole or in part on the competency and credibility of a person other than the witness. State v. Kluttz, 206 N.C. 726, 804, 175 S.E. 81. Hearsay is a statement made by a person not called as a witness, received in evidence on the trial. People v. Kraft, 36 N.Y.S. 1034, 1035, 91 Hun, 474. The term is sometimes used synonymously with "report", State v. Vettere, 76 Mont. 574, 248 P. 179, 183; and with "rumor".

HEARTH MONEY. A tax levied in England by St. 14 Car. II. c. 10, consisting of two shillings on every hearth or stove in the kingdom. It was extremely unpopular, and was abolished by 1 W. &

M. St. 1, c. 10. This tax was otherwise called "chimney money."

HEARTH SILVER. In English law, a species of *modus* or composition for tithes; Anstr. 323, 326; viz.: a prescription for cutting down and using for fuel the tithe of wood. 2 Burn, Eccl.Law 304.

HEAT OF PASSION. In criminal law, a state of violent and uncontrollable rage engendered by a blow or certain other provocation given, which will reduce a homicide from the grade of murder to that of manslaughter. Disney v. State, 72 Fla. 492, 73 So. 598, 601.

Passion or anger suddenly aroused at the time by some immediate and reasonable provocation, by words or acts of one at the time. State v. Seaton, 106 Mo. 198, 17 S.W. 169.

HEAT PROSTRATION. Sunstroke. U. S. Fidelity & Guaranty Co. v. Hoflinger, Ark., 45 S.W.2d 866, 867.

HEAT STROKE. Sunstroke. A sudden prostration resulting from exposure to excessive heat regardless of the source from which the heat emanates. Herbert v. State, 124 Neb. 312, 246 N.W. 454. A depression of the vital powers; due to exposure to excessive heat, and manifesting itself as prostration with syncope, etc. (heat exhaustion), as prostration with insensibility, fever, etc. (true sunstroke), or rarely as acute meningitis; sunstroke or insolation (in the wider sense). Smith v. Standard Sanitary Mfg. Co., 211 Ky. 454, 277 S. W. 806, 807.

HEAVE TO. In maritime parlance and admiralty law, to stop a sailing vessel's headway by bringing her head "into the wind," that is, in the direction from which the wind blows. A steamer is said to be "hove to" when held in such a position that she takes the heaviest seas upon her quarter. The Hugo, D.C.N.Y., 57 Fed. 411.

HEBBERMAN. An unlawful fisher in the Thames below London bridge; so called because they generally fished at *ebbing* tide or water. 4 Hen. VII, c. 15; Jacob.

HEBBERTHEF. In Saxon law, the privilege of having the goods of a thief, and the trial of him, within a certain liberty. Cowell.

HEBBING-WEARS. A device for catching fish in ebbing water. St. 23 Hen. VIII, c. 5.

HEBDOMAD. A week; a space of seven days.

HEBDOMADIUS. A week's man; the canon or prebendary in a cathedral church, who had the peculiar care of the choir and the offices of it for his own week. Cowell.

HEBOTE. The king's edict commanding his subjects into the field.

HEBREW. Not the same as Yiddish. U. S. ex rel. Engel v. Tod, C.C.A.N.Y., 294 F. 820, 822. See Yiddish.

HECCAGIUM. In feudal law, rent paid to a lord of the fee for a liberty to use the engines called "hecks."

HECK. An engine to take fish in the river Ouse. 23 Hen. VIII. c. 18.

HECK DAY. See Hoke Day.

HEDA. A small haven, wharf, or landing place.

HEDAGIUM. Toll or customary dues at the hithe or wharf, for landing goods, etc., from which exemption was granted by the crown to some particular persons and societies. Wharton; Cowell.

HEDGE. A purchase of grain to protect against loss due to fluctuations in price. Aberdeen Farmers' Equity Exchange v. Sand, 53 S.D. 574, 221 N. W. 597. See Hedging.

To safeguard one's self from loss on a bet or speculation by making compensatory arrangements on the other side. Whorley v. Patton-Kjose Co., 90 Mont. 461, 5 P.2d 210, 214.

HEDGE-BOTE. An allowance of wood for repairing hedges or fences, which a tenant or lessee has a right to take off the land let or demised to him. 2 Bl.Comm. 35; Livingston v. Ten Broeck, 16 Johns. (N.Y.) 15, 8 Am.Dec. 287.

HEDGE-PRIEST. A vagabond priest in olden time.

A hedge-parson; specifically, in Ireland, formerly, a priest who has been admitted to orders directly from a hedge-school, without preparation in theological studies at a regular college. Cent. Dict.

HEDGING. A means by which collectors and exporters of grain or other products, and manufacturers, who make contracts in advance for the sale of their goods, secure themselves against the fluctuations of the market by counter contracts for the purchase or sale of an equal quantity of the product or of the material of manufacture. Whorley v. Patton-Kjose Co., 90 Mont. 461, 5 P.2d 210, 214. The action of one who buys commodities in selling an equal amount of such commodities on exchange for the purpose of insurance against fluctuations in price. Fraser v. Farmers' Co-op. Co., 167 Minn. 369, 209 N.W. 33, 36.

The term "hedge," as used in the milling business, means when the miller enters into a contract for the delivery of flour at a future date, he buys wheat on the stock exchange for future delivery, and when he purchases wheat for actual delivery from the grain elevator to fulfill the contract which he had previously made to furnish flour, he sells the wheat which he has bought on the stock exchange. Bluefield Milling Co. v. Western Union Telegraph Co., 104 W.Va. 150, 139 S.E. 638, 55 A.L.R. 636.

HEEDLESS. It is almost as strong as word "reckless" and includes the element of disregard of the rights of others. State v. Sullivan, 58 N.D. 732, 227 N.W. 230, 232. Careless. Bordonaro v. Senk, 109 Conn. 428, 147 A. 136, 137.

HEEL BLANK. Several heel lifts cemented together, forming the height of the heel minus the rand and a bottom or finishing lift. Brockton Heel Co. v. International Shoe Co., D.C.N.H., 19 F.2d 145.

HEEL LOG. Succession of heel lifts coated with an adhesive, piled one upon the other, to which pressure has been applied, making a log of some indeterminate length. Brockton Heel Co. v. International Shoe Co., D.C.N.H., 19 F.2d 145.

HEEL LOG SECTION. A portion of a heel log of any convenient length. Brockton Heel Co. v. International Shoe Co., D.C.N.H., 19 F.2d 145.

HEELER. An opprobrious term, meaning in common acceptation a person who is the lackey or hangeron of another, and in a political sense an unscrupulous and disreputable person. Winnsboro Cotton Oil Co. v. Carson, Tex.Civ.App., 185 S.W. 1002, 1008.

HEGEMONY. The leadership of one among several independent confederate states.

HEGIRA. The epoch or account of time used by the Arabians and the Turks, who begin the Mohammedan era and computation from the day that Mohammed was compelled to escape from Mecca to Medina which happened on the night of Thursday, July 15, A.D. 622, under the reign of the Emperor Heraclius. Townsend, Dict. Dates; Wilson, Gloss. The era begins July 16. The word is sometimes spelled hejira but the former is the ordinary usage. It is derived from *hijrah,* in one form or another, an oriental term denoting flight, departure.

The flight of Mohammed from Mecca. Webster, Dict.

HEGUMENOS. The leader of the monks in the Greek Church.

HEIFER. A young cow; a cow that has not had a calf. Fletcher v. State, 198 Ark. 376, 128 S.W. 2d 997, 999.

HEIR. At common law. The person appointed by law to succeed to the estate in case of intestacy. 2 Bla.Comm. 201; Dukes v. Faulk, 37 S.C. 255, 16 S.E. 122, 34 Am.St.Rep. 745.

One who inherits property, whether real or personal. Hartford-Connecticut Trust Co. v. Lawrence, 106 Conn. 178, 138 A. 159, 160.

A person who succeeds, by the rules of law, to an estate in lands, tenements, or hereditaments, upon the death of his ancestor, by descent and right of relationship. Hoover v. Smith, 96 Md. 393, 54 A. 102. Sewall v. Roberts, 115 Mass. 268. He who is born or begotten in lawful wedlock, and upon whom the law casts the inheritance immediately upon the death of his ancestor. Moffett v. Conley, 63 Okl. 3, 163 P. 118, 120.

One who would receive his estate under statute of descent and distribution. Faulkner's Guardian v. Faulkner, 237 Ky. 147, 35 S.W.2d 6, 7.

Moreover, the term is frequently used in a popular sense to designate a successor to property either by will or by law. Wallace v. Privett, 198 Cal. 746, 247 P. 906, 907.

According to many authorities, heir may be *nomen collectivum,* as well in a deed as in a will, and operate in both in the same manner as the word heirs. 1 Rolle, Abr. 253; Ambl. 453; Cro. Eliz. 313; 1 Burr. 38. But see 2 Prest.Est. 9, 10.

The word must be construed according to testator's intention as gathered from whole will. Fadler v. Gabbert, 333 Mo. 851, 63 S.W.2d 121.

See, also, Heirs.

In the civil law. A universal successor in the event of death. He who actively or passively succeeds to the entire property or estate, rights and obligations, of a decedent, and occupies his place.

The term is indiscriminately applied to all persons who are called to the succession, whether by the act of the party or by operation of law. The person who is created universal successor by a will is called the "testamentary heir;" and the next of kin by blood is, in cases of intestacy, called the "heir at law," or "heir by intestacy." The executor of the common law in many respects corresponds to the testamentary heir of the civil law. Again, the administrator in many respects corresponds with the heir by intestacy. By the common law, executors and administrators have no right except to the personal estate of the deceased; whereas the heir by the civil law is authorized to administer both the personal and real estate. Story, Confl.Laws, §§ 57, 508; 1 Brown, Civ.Law, 344.

The term "heir" has several significations. Sometimes it refers to one who has formally accepted a succession and taken possession thereof; sometimes to one who is called to succeed, but still retains the faculty of accepting or renouncing, and it is frequently used as applied to one who has formally renounced. Mumford v. Bowman, 26 La.Ann. 417.

In Scotch law. The person who succeeds to the heritage or heritable rights of one deceased. 1 Forb.Inst. pt. 3, p. 75. The word has a more extended signification than in English law, comprehending not only those who succeed to lands, but successors to personal property also. Wharton.

Right heir. This term was formerly used, in the case of estates tail, to distinguish the preferred heir, to whom the estate was limited, from the heirs in general, to whom, on the failure of the preferred heir and his line, the remainder over was usually finally limited. With the abolition of estates tail, the term has fallen into desuetude, but when still used, in modern law, it has no other meaning than "heir at law." Brown v. Wadsworth, 168 N.Y. 225, 61 N.E. 250.

HEIR APPARENT. An heir whose right of inheritance is indefeasible, provided he outlive the ancestor; as in England the eldest son, or his issue, who must, by the course of the common law, be heir to the father whenever he happens to die. 2 Bl.Comm. 208; 1 Steph.Comm. 358; Jones v. Fleming, 37 Hun. (N.Y.) 230. One who, before the death of the ancestor, is next in the line of succession, provided he be heir to the ancestor whenever he happens to die. Reese v. Stires, 87 N.J.Eq. 32, 103 A. 679. See, also, Apparent Heir.

HEIR AT LAW. He who, after his ancestor dies intestate, has a right to all lands, tenements, and hereditaments which belonged to him or of which he was seised. The same as "heir general." Forrest v. Porch, 100 Tenn. 391, 45 S.W. 676.

The heir at common law is that person who succeeds to the real estate in case of intestacy. Walker v. Walker, 283 Ill. 11, 118 N.E. 1014, 1019. In its strict sense and technical import, the person or persons appointed by law to succeed to the estate in case of intestacy. Albright v. Albright, 116 Ohio St. 668, 157 N.E. 760, 762. In a comprehensive and popular sense, one who inherits either real or personal property; Gross v. Hartford-Connecticut Trust Co., 100 Conn. 332, 123 A. 907, 908. Next of kin, Meeker v. Forbes, 84 N.J.Eq. 271, 93 A. 887, 888.

In the term "heir at law," as used in will, suffix "at law" adds merely expectant feature of one's statutory position toward an ancestor or source of title who is considered as still living, whereas word "heir" alone denotes that ancestor has already died. In re Ward's Estate, 297 N.Y.S. 16, 19, 162 Misc. 855.

A deceased person's "heirs at law" are those who succeed to his estate of inheritance under statutes of descent and distribution, in absence of testamentary disposition, and not necessarily his heirs at common law, who are persons succeeding to deceased's realty in case of his intestacy. In re Towndrow's Will, 47 N.M. 173, 138 P.2d 1001, 1003.

HEIRS AT LAW SHALL NOT BE DISINHERITED BY CONJECTURE, BUT ONLY BY EXPRESS WORDS OR NECESSARY IMPLICATION. Schoul. Wills § 479.

HEIR BENEFICIARY. In the civil law, one who has accepted the succession under the benefit of an inventory regularly made.

Heirs are divided into two classes, according to the manner in which they accept the successions left to them, to-wit, unconditional and beneficiary heirs. Unconditional heirs are those who inherit without any reservation, or without making an inventory, whether their acceptance be express or tacit. Beneficiary heirs are those who have accepted the succession under the benefit of an inventory regularly made. Civ.Code La. art. 883. If the heir apprehend that the succession will be burdened with debts beyond its value, he accepts with benefit of inventory, and in that case he is responsible only for the value of the succession.

HEIR BY ADOPTION. An adopted child, "who is in a limited sense made an heir, not by the law, but by the contract evidenced by the deed of adoption." In re Sessions' Estate, 70 Mich. 297, 38 N.W. 249, 14 Am.St.Rep. 500.

HEIR BY CUSTOM. In English law, one whose right of inheritance depends upon a particular and local custom, such as gavelkind, or borough English. Co.Litt. 140.

HEIR BY DEVISE. One to whom lands are devised by will; a devisee of lands. Answering to the *hæres factus* (*q. v.*) of the civil law.

HEIR COLLATERAL. One who is not lineally related to the decedent, but is of collateral kin; *e. g.*, his uncle, cousin, brother, nephew.

HEIR CONVENTIONAL. In the civil law, one who takes a succession by virtue of a contract or settlement entitling him thereto.

HEIR EXPECTANT. One whose parents were living, as respects lots to which parents had title. Adams v. Adams, 348 Mo. 1041, 156 S.W.2d 610, 616.

HEIR, FORCED. One who cannot be disinherited. See Forced Heirs.

HEIR GENERAL. An heir at law. The ordinary heir by blood, succeeding to all the lands. Forrest v. Porch, 100 Tenn. 391, 45 S.W. 676.

HEIR INSTITUTE. In Scotch law, one to whom the right of succession is ascertained by disposition or express deed of the deceased. 1 Forb.Inst. pt. 3, p. 75.

HEIR, IRREGULAR. In Louisiana, irregular heirs are those who are neither testamentary nor legal, and who have been established by law to take the succession. See Civ.Code La. art. 878. When there are no direct or collateral relatives surviving the decedent, and the succession consequently devolves upon the surviving husband or wife, or illegitimate children, or the state, it is called an "irregular succession."

HEIR, LEGAL. In the civil law, a legal heir is one who takes the succession by relationship to the decedent and by force of law.

This is different from a testamentary or conventional heir, who takes the succession in virtue of the disposition of man. See Civ.Code La. arts. 877, 879. The term is also used in Anglo-American law in substantially the same sense, that is, the person to whom the law would give the decedent's property, real and personal, if he should die intestate. Waller v. Martin, 106 Tenn. 341, 61 S.W. 73, 82 Am.St.Rep. 882. In legal strictness, the term signifies one who would inherit real estate, but it is also used to indicate one who would take under the statute of distribution. Morse v. Ward, 92 Conn. 408, 103 A. 119, 120.

HEIR, MALE. In Scotch law, an heir institute, who, though not next in blood to the deceased, is his nearest male relation that can succeed to him. 1 Forb.Inst. pt. 3, p. 76. In English law, the nearest male blood-relation of the decedent, unless further limited by the words "of his body," which restrict the inheritance to sons, grandsons, and other male descendants in the right line. Jordan v. Adams, 6 C.B.,N.S., 764; Goodtitle v. Herring, 1 East, 275; Ewan v. Cox, 9 N.J.Law, 14.

HEIR OF CONQUEST. In Scotch law, one who succeeds to the deceased in *conquest*, *i. e.*, lands or other heritable rights to which the deceased neither did nor could succeed as heir to his predecessor.

HEIR OF LINE. In Scotch law, one who succeeds lineally by right of blood; one who succeeds to the deceased in his heritage; *i. e.*, lands and other heritable rights derived to him by succession as heir to his predecessor. 1 Forb.Inst. pt. 3, p. 77.

HEIR OF PROVISION. In Scotch law, one who succeeds as heir by virtue of a particular provision in a deed or instrument.

HEIR OF TAILZIE. In Scotch law, he on whom an estate is settled that would not have fallen to him by legal succession. 1 Forb.Inst. pt. 3, p. 75.

HEIR OF THE BLOOD. An inheritor who succeeds to the estate by virtue of consanguinity with the decedent, either in the ascending or descending line, including illegitimate children, but excluding husbands, wives, and adopted children. Hayden v. Barrett, 172 Mass. 472, 52 N.E. 530, 70 Am.St.Rep. 295.

HEIR OF THE BODY. An heir begotten or borne by the person referred to, or a child of such heir; any lineal descendant of the decedent, excluding a surviving husband or wife, adopted children, and collateral relations; bodily heir. Ratliffe v. Ratliffe, 182 Ky. 230, 206 S.W. 478, 479. Clarkson v. Hatton, 143 Mo. 47, 44 S.W. 761, 39 L.R.A. 748, 65 Am.St.Rep. 635.

May be used in either of two senses: In their unrestricted sense, as meaning the persons who from generation to generation become entitled by descent under the entail; and in the sense of heirs at law, or those persons who are descendants of him whom the statute of descent appoints to take intestate estate. Bunn v. Butler, 300 Ill. 269, 133 N.E. 246, 247. Unless the will discloses an intention to the contrary, the term "heirs of the body" is not synonymous with children. Clark v. Cammack, 216 Ala. 346, 113 So. 270, 271. And ordinarily, such words are words of limitation and not of purchase. Kirby v. Hulette, 174 Ky. 257, 192 S.W. 63, 65; *contra:* Owen v. Trail, 302 Mo. 292, 258 S.W. 699, 701. The words are sometimes deemed equivalent to "issue" or "descendants"; Rhode Island Hospital Trust Co. v. Bridgham, 42 R.I. 161, 106 A. 149, 152, 5 A.L.R. 185; and sometimes not; In re English's Estate, 270 Pa. 1, 112 A. 913, 914.

HEIR PRESUMPTIVE. The person who, if the ancestor should die immediately, would, in the present circumstances of things, be his heir, but whose right of inheritance may be defeated by the contingency of some nearer heir being born; as a brother or nephew, whose presumptive succession may be destroyed by the birth of a child. 2 Bl.Comm. 208; 1 Steph.Comm. 358; Jones v. Fleming, 37 Hun., N.Y., 230.

In Louisiana, the presumptive heir is he who is the nearest relation of the deceased capable of inheriting. This quality is given to him before the decease of the person from whom he is to inherit, as well as after the opening of the succession, until he has accepted or renounced it. La. Civ.Code, art. 880.

HEIR SPECIAL. In English law, the issue in tail, who claims *per formam doni*; by the form of the gift.

HEIR SUBSTITUTE, IN A BOND. In Scotch law, he to whom a bond is payable expressly in case of the creditor's decease, or after his death. 1 Forb.Inst. pt. 3, p. 76.

HEIR TESTAMENTARY. In the civil law, one who is named and appointed heir in the testament of the decedent. This name distinguishes him from a *legal* heir, (one upon whom the law casts the succession,) and from a *conventional* heir, (one who takes it by virtue of a previous contract or settlement.)

HEIR UNCONDITIONAL. In the civil law and in Louisiana, one who inherits without any reservation, or without making an inventory, whether his acceptance be express or tacit. Distinguished from *heir beneficiary.* La.Civ.Code, art. 882.

HEIRDOM. Succession by inheritance.

HEIRESS. A female heir to a person having an estate of inheritance. When there are more than one, they are called "co-heiresses," or "co-heirs."

HEIRLOOMS. Such goods and chattels as, contrary to the nature of chattels, shall go by special custom to the heir along with the inheritance, and not to the executor. The termination *"loom"* (Sax.) signifies a limb or member; so that an heirloom is nothing else but a limb or member of the inheritance. They are generally such things as cannot be taken away without damaging or dismembering the freehold; such as deer in a park, doves in a cote, deeds and charters, etc. 2 Bl. Comm. 427.

This word seems to be compounded of *heir,* and *loom,* that is, a frame, viz. to weave in. Some derive the word loom from the Saxon *loma,* or *geloma,* which signifies utensils or vessels generally. However, this may be, the word *loom,* by time, is drawn to a more general signification than it bore at the first, comprehending all implements of household, as tables, presses, cupboards, bedsteads, wainscots, and which, by the custom of some countries, having belonged to a house are never inventoried after the decease of the owner as chattels, but accrue to the heir with the house itself. Minshew; 2 Poll. & Maitl. 361.

HEIRS. Technically, those persons designated by law to succeed to the estate in case of intestacy. Potter v. Potter, 306 Ill. 37, 137 N.E. 425, 426. See, also, Heir.

A word used in deeds of conveyance, (either solely, or in connection with others,) where it is intended to pass a fee.

It is generally a word of limitation, and is not to be construed as a word of purchase unless there are other controlling words showing such intention by the person using it. McKnight v. Black, 240 Ky. 818, 43 S.W.2d 53, 54.

In the word is comprehended heirs of heirs *in infinitum.* Co.Litt. *7b, 9a;* Larew v. Larew, 146 Va. 134, 135 S.E. 819, 820.

It may have different meanings, just as under the English law the singular form, "heir," might have different meanings, but, if there is no context, the word "heirs" must be held to indicate the indefinite succession by inheritance. Ætna Life Ins. Co. v. Hoppin, C.C.A., 214 F. 928, 932. Under the terms of particular wills, however, or under statutes abolishing the rule in Shelley's Case, Menard v. Campbell, 180 Mich. 583, 147 N.W. 556, 558, Ann.Cas. 1916A, 802; it may be a word of purchase, and is frequently deemed synonymous with "children," Cultice v. Mills, 97 Ohio St. 112, 119 N.E. 200, 201; Williams v. J. C. Armiger & Bro., 129 Md. 222, 98 A. 542, 544.

A devise or bequest to "heirs" primarily means those who are heirs at the testator's death, and it is only when a contrary intention appears that this presumption fails. In re Bump's Will, 234 N.Y. 60, 136 N.E. 295, 296.

Bodily heirs. In a technical sense, the same as "heirs of the body." Hartman v. Flynn, 189 N.C. 452, 127 S.E. 517, 519.

Normally, words of limitation, not of purchase. Stamey v. McGinnis, 145 Ga. 226, 88 S.E. 935, 936. But they may be used synonymously with "children." Scott v. Scott, 172 Ky. 658, 190 S.W. 143.

Joint heirs. Co-heirs. The term is also applied to those who are or will be heirs to both of two designated persons at the death of the survivor of them, the word "joint" being here applied to the ancestors rather than the heirs. See Gardiner v. Fay, 182 Mass. 492, 65 N.E. 825.

Lawful heirs. The same as "heirs." In re Irish's Estate, 89 Vt. 56, 94 A. 173, 174, Ann.Cas. 1917C, 1154. In a general sense, those whom the law recognizes as the heirs of a decedent, but in a special and technical sense, lineal descendants only. Abbott v. Essex Co., 18 How. 215, 15 L.Ed. 352.

Legitimate heirs. Children born in lawful wedlock and their descendants, not including collateral heirs or issue in indefinite succession. Lytle v.

Beveridge, 58 N.Y. 605; Prindle v. Beveridge, 7 Lans., N.Y., 231. Sometimes synonymous with "lawful" heir. Corison v. Williams, 58 Cal.App. 282, 208 P. 331, 334.

Lineal heir. See Lineal Heir.

Living heirs. Technically words of description instead of purchase. Johnson v. Coler, 187 Iowa, 734, 174 N.W. 654, 655.

Under a will giving the testator's wife an estate for life, at her death all the property to be equally divided between "our living children or to their living heirs," the words "living heirs" should be given their technical meaning as including all the legal heirs of the deceased children of testator that died after the death of testator. Potter v. Potter, 306 Ill. 37, 137 N.E. 425, 427.

Natural heirs. Heirs by consanguinity as distinguished from heirs by adoption, and also as distinguished from collateral heirs. Smith v. Pendell, 19 Conn. 112, 48 Am.Dec. 146; children; heirs of the body, Maynard v. Henderson, 117 Ark. 24, 173 S.W. 831, 832, Ann.Cas.1917A, 1157. Yarrington v. Freeman, 201 Ky. 135, 255 S.W. 1034, 1035.

HEIRS AND ASSIGNS. Ordinarily words of limitation and not of purchase. In re Knapp's Will, 6 N.Y.S.2d 100, 168 Misc. 487. At common law, the words were essential to conveyance granting title in fee simple, and though they are unnecessary for that or any purpose under statute when used in wills or deeds, words still have that meaning. In re Denari's Will, 300 N.Y.S. 1279, 165 Misc. 450.

HEIRSHIP. The quality or condition of being heir, or the relation between the heir and his ancestor. It is a legal right, regulated by law, to be enjoyed subject to the provisions of the statute. Winke v. Olson, 164 Wis. 427, 160 N.W. 164, 166.

HEIRSHIP MOVABLES. In Scotch law. The movables which go to the heir, and not to the executor, that the land may not go to the heir completely dismantled, such as the best of furniture, horses, cows, etc., but not fungibles. Erskine, Inst. 3. 8. 13–17.

HELD. In reference to the decision of a court, decided. See, also, Hold.

HELL. The name formerly given to a place under the exchequer chamber, where the king's debtors were confined. Rich.Dict.

HELM. Thatch or straw; a covering for the head in war; a coat of arms bearing a crest; the tiller or handle of the rudder of a ship.

HELOWE-WALL. The end-wall covering and defending the rest of the building. Paroch. Antiq. 573.

HELSING. A Saxon brass coin, of the value of a half-penny.

HEMIPLEGIA. In medical jurisprudence. Unilateral paralysis; paralysis of one side of the body, commonly due to a lesion in the brain, but sometimes originating from the spinal cord, as in "Brown-Sequard's paralysis," unilateral paralysis with crossed *anæsthesia.* In the cerebral form, the *hemiplegia* is sometimes "alternate" or crossed, that is, occurring on the opposite side of the body from the initial lesion.

Paralysis of half of the body, as of both legs or of both arms, or an arm and leg. Gray v. United States, C.C.A. Ark., 109 F.2d 728. 729. If the disease comes on rapidly or suddenly, it is called "quick" *hemiplegia;* if slowly or gradually, "chronic." The former variety is more apt to affect the mental faculties than the latter; but, where *hemiplegia* is complete, the operations of the mind are generally much impaired. Baughman v. Baughman, 32 Kan. 538, 4 P. 1003.

HEMOLDBORH, or HELMELBORCH. A title to possession. The admission of this old Norse term into the laws of the Conqueror is difficult to be accounted for; it is not found in any Anglo-Saxon law extant. Wharton.

HENCEFORTH. A word of futurity, which, as employed in legal documents, statutes, and the like, always imports a continuity of action or condition from the present time forward, but excludes all the past. Thomson v. American Surety Co., 170 N.Y. 109, 62 N.E. 1073.

HENCHMAN. A page; an attendant; servant; a herald. See Barnes v. State, 88 Md. 347, 41 A. 781. A footman; one who holds himself at the bidding of another. It has come to mean here a political follower; used in a rather bad sense. Gates v. State, 140 Tex.Cr.R. 228, 143 S.W.2d 780, 783, 784.

HENEDPENNY. A customary payment of money instead of hens at Christmas; a composition for eggs. Cowell.

HENFARE. A fine for flight on account of murder. Domesday Book.

HENGHEN. In Saxon law. A prison, a goal, or house of correction.

HENGWYTE. Sax. In old English law. An acquittance from a fine for hanging a thief. Fleta, lib. 1, c. 47, § 17.

HENRICUS VETUS. Henry the Old, or Elder. King Henry I. is so called in ancient English chronicles and charters, to distinguish him from the subsequent kings of that name. Spelman.

HEORDFÆTE, or HUDEFÆST. In Saxon law. A master of a family, keeping house, distinguished from a lower class of freemen, viz., *folgeras,* (*folgarii,*) who had no habitations of their own, but were house-retainers of their lords.

HEORDPENNY. Peter-pence (*q. v.*).

HEORDWERCH. In Saxon law. The service of herdsmen, done at the will of their lord.

HEPBURN ACT. The name commonly given to an act of Congress, June 29, 1906, amending §§ 1, 6, 14, 15, 16 and 20 of the Interstate Commerce Act, Feb. 4, 1887. (49 U.S.C.A. §§ 1, 6, 11, 14, 15, 16, 18, 20).

HEPTARCHY. A government exercised by seven persons, or a nation divided into seven governments. In the year 560, seven different monarchies had been formed in England by the German tribes, namely, that of Kent by the Jutes; those of Sussex, Wessex, and Essex by the Saxons; and those of East Anglia, Bernicia, and Deira by the Angles. To these were added, about the year 586, an eighth, called the "Kingdom of Mercia," also founded by the Angles, and comprehending nearly the whole of the heart of the kingdom. These states formed what has been designated the "Anglo-Saxon Octarchy," or more commonly, though not so correctly, the "Anglo-Saxon Heptarchy," from the custom of speaking of Deira and Bernicia under the single appellation of the "Kingdom of Northumberland." Wharton.

HERALD. In ancient law, a herald was a diplomatic messenger who carried messages between kings or states, and especially proclamations of war, peace, or truce. In English law, a herald is an officer whose duty is to keep genealogical lists and tables, adjust armorial bearings, and regulate the ceremonies at royal coronations and funerals.

HERALDRY. The art, office, or science of heralds. Also an old and obsolete abuse of buying and selling precedence in the paper of causes for hearing.

HERALDS' COLLEGE. In England. An ancient royal corporation, first instituted by Richard III. in 1483. It comprises three kings of arms, six heralds, and four marshals or pursuivants of arms, together with the earl marshal and a secretary. The heralds' books, compiled when progresses were solemnly and regularly made into every part of the kingdom, to inquire into the state of families, and to register such marriages and descents as were verified to them upon oath, are allowed to be good evidence of pedigrees. The heralds' office is still allowed to make grants of arms and to permit change of names. 3 Starkie, Ev. 843; Wharton.

HERBAGE. In English law. An easement or liberty, which consists in the right to pasture cattle on another's ground.

Feed for cattle in fields and pastures. Bract. fol. 222; Co.Litt. 46; Steph.Touch. 97. A right to herbage does not include a right to cut grass, or dig potatoes, or pick apples. Simpson v. Coe, 4 N.H. 303.

HERBAGIUM ANTERIUS. The first crop of grass or hay, in opposition to aftermath or second cutting. Paroch.Antiq. 459.

HERBENGER, or HARBINGER. An officer in the royal house, who goes before and allots the noblemen and those of the household their lodgings; also an innkeeper.

HERBERGAGIUM. Lodgings to receive guests in the way of hospitality. Cowell.

HERBERGARE. To harbor; to entertain.

HERBERGATUS. Harbored or entertained in an inn. Cowell.

HERBERY, or HERBURY. An inn. Cowell.

HERCIA. A harrow. Fleta, lib. 2, c. 77.

HERCIARE. To harrow. 4 Inst. 270.

HERCIATURA. In old English law. Harrowing; work with a harrow. Fleta, lib. 2, c. 82, § 2.

HERCISCUNDA. In the civil law. To be divided. *Familia herciscunda,* an inheritance to be divided. *Actio familiœ herciscundœ,* an action for dividing an inheritance. *Erciscunda* is more commonly used in the civil law. Dig. 10, 2; Inst. 3, 28, 4; Id. 4, 6, 20.

HERD, *n.* An indefinite number, more than a few, of cattle, sheep, horses, or other animals of the larger sorts, assembled and kept together as one drove and under one care and management. Boland v. Cecil, 65 Cal.App.2d Supp. 832, 150 P.2d 819, 822.

HERD, *v.* To tend, take care of, manage, and control a herd of cattle or other animals, implying something more than merely driving them from place to place. Phipps v. Grover, 9 Idaho 415, 75 P. 65.

HERDER. One who herds or has charge of a herd of cattle, in the senses above defined. Hooker v. McAllister, 12 Wash. 46, 40 P. 617.

HERDEWICH. A grange or place for cattle or husbandry. Mon.Angl. pt. 3.

HERDWERCH, HEORDWERCH. Herdsmen's work, or customary labor, done by shepherds and inferior tenants, at the will of the lord. Cowell.

HEREAFTER. A word of futurity, always used in statutes and legal documents as indicative of future time, excluding both the present and the past. Tremont & S. Mills v. Lowell, 165 Mass. 265, 42 N.E. 1134.

HEREBANNUM. In old English law. A proclamation summoning the army into the field. A mulct or fine for not joining the army when summoned. Spelman. A tax or tribute for the support of the army. Du Cange.

HEREBOTE. The royal edict summoning the people to the field. Cowell.

HEREDAD. In Spanish law. A piece of land under cultivation; a cultivated farm, real estate; an inheritance or heirship.

HEREDAD YACENTE. From Lat. "*Hœreditas jacens,*" (*q. v.*) In Spanish law. An inheritance not yet entered upon or appropriated. White, New Recop. b. 2, tit. 19, c. 2, § 8.

HEREDERO. In Spanish law. Heir; he who, by legal or testamentary disposition, succeeds to the property of a deceased person. "*Hœres censeatur cum defuncto una eademque persona.*" Las Partidas, 7, 9, 13. Emeric v. Alvarado, 64 Cal. 529, 2 P. 433.

HEREDITAGIUM. In Sicilian and Neapolitan law. That which is held by hereditary right; the same with *hereditamentum (hereditament)* in English law. Spelman.

HEREDITAMENTS. Things capable of being inherited, be it corporeal or incorporeal, real, personal, or mixed, and including not only lands and everything thereon, but also heirlooms, and certain furniture which, by custom, may descend to the heir together with the land. Co.Litt. 5*b*; 2 Bl. Comm. 17; Nellis v. Munson, 108 N.Y. 453, 15 N.E. 739. Sox v. Miracle, 35 N.D. 458, 160 N.W. 716, 719.

Things which may be directly inherited, as contrasted with things which go to the personal representative of a deceased. Denver Joint Stock Land Bank of Denver v. Dixon, 57 Wyo. 523, 122 P.2d 842, 846, 140 A.L.R. 1270.

At common law corporeal hereditaments were physical objects, comprehended under the term land, and were said to lie in livery, while incorporeal hereditaments existed only in contemplation of law, were said to lie in grant and were affiliated with chattel interests. National Supply Co. v. McLeod, 116 Kan. 477, 227 P. 350.

The term includes a few rights unconnected with land, but it is generally used as the widest expression for real property of all kinds, and is therefore employed in conveyances after the words "lands" and "tenements," to include everything of the nature of realty which they do not cover. Sweet.

Corporeal Hereditaments. Substantial permanent objects which may be inherited. The term "land" will include all such. 2 Bl.Comm. 17; Sox v. Miracle, 35 N.D. 458, 160 N.W. 716, 719.

Incorporeal Hereditaments. Anything, the subject of property, which is inheritable and not tangible or visible. 2 Woodd.Lect. 4.

A right issuing out of a thing corporate (whether real or personal) or concerning or annexed to or exercisable within the same. 2 Bl.Comm. 20; 1 Washb.Real Prop. 10. A right growing out of, or concerning, or annexed to, a corporeal thing, but not the substance of the thing itself. Huston v. Cox, 103 Kan. 73, 172 P. 992.

HEREDITARY. That which is the subject of inheritance.

HEREDITARY DISEASE. Physical ailment transmitted or transmissible from parent to child in consequence of the infection of the former or the presence of the disease in his system, and without exposure of the latter to any fresh source of infection or contagion. South Atlantic Life Ins. Co. v. Hurt's Adm'x, 115 Va. 398, 79 S.E. 401, 404.

HEREDITARY RIGHT TO THE CROWN. The crown of England, by the positive constitution of the kingdom, has ever been descendible, and so continues, in a course peculiar to itself, yet subject to limitation by parliament; but, notwithstanding such limitation, the crown retains its descendible quality, and becomes hereditary in the prince to whom it is limited. 1 Bl.Comm. 191.

HEREDITARY SUCCESSION. Inheritance by law; title by descent; the title whereby a person, on the death of his ancestor, acquires his estate by right of representation as his heir at law. In re Yahola's Heirship, 142 Okl. 79, 285 P. 946.

HEREDITY. That biological law by which all living beings tend to repeat themselves in their descendants. Prewitt v. State, 106 Miss. 82, 63 So. 330, 331, 6 A.L.R. 1476.

HEREFARE. Sax. A going into or with an army; a going out to war, (*profectio militaris;*) an expedition. Spelman.

HEREGEAT. A heriot, (*q. v.*)

HEREGELD. Sax. In old English law. A tribute or tax levied for the maintenance of an army. Spelman.

HEREMITORIUM. A place of retirement for hermits. Mon.Angl. tom. 3, p. 18.

HEREMONES. Followers of an army.

HERENACH. An archdeacon. Cowell.

HERES. Heir; an heir. A form of *hæres,* very common in the civil law. See Hæres.

HERESCHIP. In old Scotch law. Theft or robbery. 1 Pitc.Crim.Tr. pt. 2, pp. 26, 89.

HERESLITA, HERESSA, HERESSIZ. A hired soldier who departs without license. 4 Inst. 128.

HERESY. In English law. An offense against religion, consisting not in a total denial of Christianity, but of some of its essential doctrines, publicly and obstinately avowed. 4 Bl.Comm. 44, 45. An opinion on divine subjects devised by human reason, openly taught, and obstinately maintained. 1 Hale, P.C. 384.

This offense is now subject only to ecclesiastical correction, and is no longer punishable by the secular law. 4 Steph.Comm. 233.

HERETOCH. A general, leader, or commander; also a baron of the realm. Du Fresne.

HERETOFORE. This word simply denotes time past, in distinction from time present or time future, and has no definite and precise signification beyond this. Andrews v. Thayer, 40 Conn. 157; Millers' Mut. Fire Ins. Co. v. City of Austin, Tex. Civ.App., 210 S.W. 825, 827.

HERETUM. In old records. A court or yard for drawing up guards or military retinue. Cowell.

HEREZELD. In Scotch law. A gift or present made or left by a tenant to his lord as a token of reverence. Skene.

HERGE. In Saxon law. Offenders who joined in a body of more than thirty-five to commit depredations.

HERIGALDS. In old English law. A sort of garment. Cowell.

HERIOT. In English law. A customary tribute of goods and chattels, payable to the lord of the fee on the decease of the owner of the land.

Heriots are divided into heriot *service* and heriot *custom.* The former expression denotes such as are due upon a special reservation in a grant or lease of lands, and therefore amount to little more than a mere rent; the latter arise upon no special reservation whatever, but depend solely upon immemorial usage and custom. 2 Bl.Comm. 422. See Adams v. Morse, 51 Me. 501.

HERISCHILD. In old English law. A species of military service, or knight's fee. Cowell.

HERISCHULDA. In old Scotch law. A fine or penalty for not obeying the proclamation made for warfare. Skene.

HERISCINDIUM. A division of household goods. Blount.

HERISLIT. Laying down of arms. Blount. Desertion from the army. Spelman.

HERISTAL. The station of an army; the place where a camp is pitched. Spelman.

HERITABLE. Capable of being taken by descent. A term chiefly used in Scotch law, where it enters into several phrases.

HERITABLE BOND. A bond for a sum of money to which is added, for further security of the creditor, a conveyance of land or heritage to be held by the creditor as pledge. 1 Ross, Conv. 76; 2 Ross, Conv. 324.

HERITABLE JURISDICTIONS. Grants of criminal jurisdiction formerly bestowed on great families in Scotland, to facilitate the administration of justice. Whishaw. Abolished in effect by St. 20 Geo. II. c. 50. Tomlins.

HERITABLE OBLIGATION. In Louisiana. An obligation is heritable when the heirs and assigns of one party may enforce the performance against the heirs of the other. Civ.Code La. art. 1997.

HERITABLE RIGHTS. In Scotch law. Rights of the heir; all rights to land or whatever is connected with land, as mills, fishings, tithes, etc.

HERITABLE SECURITY. Security constituted by heritable property. Encyc. Dict.

HERITAGE. In the civil law. Every species of immovable which can be the subject of property; such as lands, houses, orchards, woods, marshes, ponds, etc., in whatever mode they may have been acquired, either by descent or purchase. 3 Toullier, No. 472.

In Scotch law. Land, and all property connected with land; real estate, as distinguished from movables, or personal estate. Bell.

HERITOR. In Scotch law. A proprietor of land. 1 Kames, Eq.Pref.

HERMANDAD. In Spanish law. A fraternity formed among different towns and villages to prevent the commission of crimes, and to prevent the abuses and vexations to which they were subjected by men in power. Bouvier.

HERMAPHRODITE. In medical jurisprudence. A person of doubtful or double sex; one possessing, really or apparently, and in more or less developed form, some or all of the genital organs of both sexes.

HERMAPHRODITUS TAM MASCULO QUAM FŒMINÆ COMPARATUR, SECUNDUM PRÆVALENTIAM SEXUS INCALESCENTIS. An hermaphrodite is to be considered male or female according to the predominance of the exciting sex. Co.Litt. 8; Bract. fol. 5.

HERMENEUTICS. The science or art of construction and interpretation. By the phrase "legal hermeneutics" is understood the systematic body of rules which are recognized as applicable to the construction and interpretation of legal writings.

HERMER. A great lord. Jacob.

HERMOGENIAN CODE. See Codex Hermogenianus.

HERNESCUS. A heron. Cowell.

HERNESIUM, or HERNASIUM. Household goods; implements of trade or husbandry; the rigging or tackle of a ship. Cowell.

HERNIA. A protrusion of any organ through an abnormal opening in wall of the containing cavity; rupture. In re Frihauf, 135 P.2d 427, 430, 58 Wyo. 479; Stoddard v. Mason's Blue Link Stores, 55 Idaho 609, 45 P.2d 597, 600.

HEROUD, HERAUD. L. Fr. A herald.

HERPEX. A harrow. Spelman.

HERPICATIO. In old English law. A day's work with a harrow. Spelman.

HERRING SILVER. This was a composition in money for the custom of supplying herrings for the provision of a religious house. Wharton.

HERSHIP. The crime, in Scotland, of carrying off cattle by force; it is described as "the masterful driving off of cattle from a proprietor's grounds." Bell.

HERUS. Lat. A master. *Servus facit ut herus det,* the servant does [the work] in order that the master may give [him the wages agreed on.] *Herus dat ut servus facit,* the master gives [or agrees to give, the wages,] in consideration of, or with a view to, the servant's doing [the work.] 2 Bl.Comm. 445.

HESIA. An easement. Du Cange.

HEST CORN. In old records. Corn or grain given or devoted to religious persons or purposes. 2 Mon.Angl. 367*b*; Cowell.

HESTA, or HESTHA. A little loaf of bread. A capon or young cockerel.

HETÆRARCHA. The head of a religious house; the head of a college; the warden of a corporation.

HETÆRIA. In Roman law. A company, society, or college.

HEUVELBORH. Sax. In old English law. A surety, (*warrantus.*)

HEYLODE. In old records. A customary burden upon inferior tenants, for mending or repairing hays or hedges.

HEYMECTUS. A hay-net; a net for catching conies. Cowell.

HIBERNAGIUM. The season for sowing winter corn. Cowell.

HIDAGE. An extraordinary tax formerly payable to the crown for every hide of land. This taxation was levied, not in money, but provision of armor, etc. Cowell.

HIDALGO. In Spanish law. A noble; a person entitled to the rights of nobility. By *hidalgos* are understood men chosen from good situations in life, (*de buenos lugures,*) and possessed of property, (*algo.*) White, New Recop. b. 1, tit. 5, c. 1.

HIDALGUIA. In Spanish law. Nobility by descent or lineage. White, New Recop. b. 1, tit. 5, c. 3, § 4.

HIDE. In old English law. A measure of land, being as much as could be worked with one plow. It is variously estimated at from 60 to 100 acres, but was probably determined by local usage. Another meaning was as much land as would support one family or the dwellers in a mansion-house. Also a house; a dwelling-house. A hide was anciently employed as a unit of taxation. 1 Poll. & Maitl. 347, such tax being called *hidegild.*

HIDE AND GAIN. In English law. A term anciently applied to arable land. Co.Litt. 85*b*.

HIDE LANDS. In Saxon law. Lands belonging to a hide; that is, a house or mansion. Spelman.

HIDEL. In old English law. A place of protection; a sanctuary. St. 1 Hen. VII. cc. 5, 6; Cowell.

HIDGILD. A sum of money paid by a villein or servant to save himself from a whipping. Fleta, l. 1, c. 47, § 20.

HIERARCHY. Originally, government by a body of priests. Now, the body of officers in any church or ecclesiastical institution, considered as forming an ascending series of ranks or degrees of power and authority, with the correlative subjection, each to the one next above. Derivatively, any body of men, taken in their public capacity, and considered as forming a chain of power, as above described.

HIGH. This term, as used in various compound legal phrases, is sometimes merely an addition of dignity, not importing a comparison; but more generally it means exalted, either in rank or location, or occupying a position of superiority, and in a few instances it implies superiority in respect to importance, size, or frequency or publicity of use, *e. g.*, "high seas," "highway."

As to high "Bailiff," "Constable," "Crimes," "Justice," "Justiciar," "License," "Prerogative writ," "Probability rule," "School," "Sea," "Sheriff," "Tide," "Treason," and "Water-Mark," see those titles.

HIGH COMMISSION COURT. See Court of High Commission.

HIGH COURT OF ADMIRALTY. See Court of Admiralty.

HIGH COURT OF DELEGATES. See Court of Delegates.

HIGH COURT OF ERRORS AND APPEALS. See Court of Errors and Appeals.

HIGH COURT OF JUSTICE. See Supreme Court of Judicature.

HIGH COURT OF PARLIAMENT. See Parliament.

HIGH DEGREE OF CARE AND DILIGENCE. See Care.

HIGHBINDER. A rough, one of a Chinese secret society composed of blackmailers. People v. Ho Kim You, 24 Cal.App. 451, 141 P. 950, 956.

HIGHER AND LOWER SCALE. In the practice of the English supreme court of judicature there are two scales regulating the fees of the court and the fees which solicitors are entitled to charge. The lower scale applies (unless the court otherwise orders) to the following cases: All causes and matters assigned by the judicature acts to the king's bench, or the probate, divorce, and admiralty divisions; all actions of debt, contract, or tort; and in almost all causes and matters assigned by the acts to the chancery division in which the amount in litigation is under £1,000. The higher scale applies in all other causes and matters, and also in actions falling under one of the above classes, but in which the principal relief sought to be obtained is an injunction. Sweet.

HIGHEST DEGREE OF CARE. A standard of care exacted in some jurisdictions of common carriers of passengers. The standard is relative, not absolute, and is sometimes regarded as no more than reasonable care measured by the circumstances. See Blashfield, Cyc. of Automobile Law and Prac., Perm. Ed., § 2151.

HIGHEST PROVED VALUE. In an action of trover the amount which the jury from a consideration of all the evidence, may find to be the highest value of the property during the period between the conversion and the trial. Durden v. Durden, 58 Ga.App. 46, 197 S.E. 493, 494.

HIGHGRADING. The practice of stealing ore, in mining vernacular. People v. Siderius, 29 Cal. App.2d 361, 84 P.2d 545, 547.

HIGH-JACKER. Hi-jacker. Another name for robber. State v. One Certain Buick Sedan, 209 Iowa, 791, 229 N.W. 173, 176.

HIGHNESS. A title of honor given to princes. The kings of England, before the time of James I, were not usually saluted with the title of "Majesty," but with that of "Highness." The children of crowned heads generally receive the style of "Highness." Wharton.

HIGHWAY. An easement acquired by the public in the use of a road or way for thoroughfare. Bolender v. Southern Michigan Telephone Co., 182 Mich. 646, 148 N.W. 697, 700.

A free and public roadway, or street; one which every person has the right to use. Abbott v. Duluth, C.C.Minn., 104 F. 837. Illinois Cent. R. Co. v. Bennett, C.C.A.Miss., 296 F. 436, 437. Its prime essentials are the right of common enjoyment on the one hand and the duty of public maintenance on the other. Hildebrand v. Southern Bell Telephone & Telegraph Co., 219 N.C. 402, 14 S.E.2d 252, 254, 255.

The generic name for all kinds of public ways, whether carriage-ways, bridle-ways, foot-ways, bridges, turnpike roads, railroads, canals, ferries or navigable rivers; 6 Mod. 255; Ang.Highw. c. 1; 3 Kent 432; City of St. Louis v. Bell Place Realty Co., 259 Mo. 126, 168 S.W. 721, 722. As to streets and alleys, Iowa Telephone Co. v. City of Keokuk, D.C., 226 F. 82, 87; Burns v. Kendall, 96 S.C. 385, 80 S.E. 621, 622. Every public thoroughfare. Oregon Short Line R. Co. v. Pfost, 53 Idaho 559, 27 P.2d 877. It refers to roadway or street which can be used for travel, as distinguished from way upon which road can be or is being constructed. Allen v. Jones, 47 S.D. 603, 201 N.W. 353.

There is a difference in the shade of meaning conveyed by two uses of the word. Sometimes it signifies right of free passage, in the abstract, not importing anything about the character or construction of the way. Thus, a river is called a "highway;" and it has been not unusual for congress, in granting a privilege of building a bridge, to declare that it shall be a public highway. Again, it has reference to some system of law authorizing the taking a strip of land, and preparing and devoting it to the use of travelers. In this use it imports a roadway upon the soil, constructed under the authority of these laws. Abbott.

Commissioners of Highways. Public officers appointed in the several counties and municipalities, in many states, to take charge of the opening, altering, repair, and vacating of highways within their respective jurisdictions.

Common highway. A road to be used by the community at large for any purpose of transit or traffic. Ham. N. P. 239; Railway Co. v. State, 23 Fla. 546, 3 So. 158, 11 Am.St.Rep. 395.

Highway Acts, or Laws. The body or system of laws governing the laying out, repair, and use of highways.

Highway Crossing. A place where the track of a railroad crosses the line of a highway.

Highway-rate. In English law. A tax for the maintenance and repair of highways, chargeable upon the same property that is liable to the poor-rate.

Highway Robbery. See Robbery.

Highway Tax. A tax for and applicable to the making and repair of highways. Stone v. Bean, 15 Gray (Mass.) 44.

Public Highway. One under the control of and kept by the public, established by regular proceedings for the purpose, or generally used by the public for twenty years, or dedicated by the owner of the soil and accepted by the proper authorities and for the maintenance of which they are responsible. State v. Gross, 119 N.C. 868, 26 S.E. 91.

It includes roads, streets, alleys, lanes, courts, places, trails, and bridges, laid out or erected as such by the public, or, if laid out and erected by others, dedicated or abandoned to the public, or made such in actions for the partition of real property. Patterson v. Munyan, 93 Cal. 128, 29 P. 250.

It has been said that if the word "highway" is given its customary meaning, the phrase "public highway" is an example of tautology—the needless or useless repetition of the same idea, of which the law seems to furnish so many illustrations. See Galloway v. Wyatt Metal & Boiler Works, 181 So. 187, 189 La. 837; Blashfield, Cyc. of Automobile Law and Prac., Perm. Ed., § 3.

Royal Highways. There were four royal highways in Yorkshire, three by land and one by water, where the king claimed all forfeitures. Maitl. Domesd. Book and Beyond 87.

HIGHWAYMAN. A bandit; one who robs travelers upon the highway. Anderson v. Hartford Accident & Indemnity Co., 77 Cal.App. 641, 247 P. 507, 510.

HIGLER. In English law. A hawker or peddler. A person who carries from door to door, and sells by retail, small articles of provisions, and the like.

HIGUELA. In Spanish law. A receipt given by an heir of a decedent, setting forth what property he has received from the estate.

HIIS TESTIBUS. Words formerly used in deeds, signifying *these being witness.* They have been disused since Henry VIII. Co.Litt.; Cowell.

HI-JACKER. High-Jacker. See that title.

HIKENILD STREET. One of the four great Roman roads of Britain. More commonly called "Ikenild Street."

HILARY RULES. A collection of orders and forms extensively modifying the pleading and practice in the English superior courts of common law, established in Hilary term, 1834. Stimson.

HILARY TERM. In English law. A term of court, beginning on the 11th and ending on the 31st of January in each year. Superseded (1875) by Hilary sittings, which begin January 11th, and end on the Wednesday before Easter.

HINDENI HOMINES. A society of men. The Saxons ranked men into three classes, and valued them, as to satisfaction for injuries, etc., according to their class. The highest class were valued at 1,200s., and were called "*twelf hindmen;*" the middle class at 600s., and called "*sexhindmen;*" the lowest at 200s., called "*twyhindmen.*" Their wives were termed "hindas." Brompt. Leg. Alfred. c. 12.

HINDER AND DELAY. A phrase used to signify an act amounting to an attempt to defraud, rather than a successful fraud; to put some obstacle in the path of, or interpose some time, unjustifiably, before a creditor can realize what is owed out of his debtor's property. Walker v. Sayers, 5 Bush., Ky., 582.

HINDU LAW. The system of native law prevailing among the Gentoos, and administered by the government of British India. It is not the law of India or of any defined region. It is the law of castes, class, orders and even families which the Hindus carry about with them. 17 L.Q.R. 209. Bryce, Extension of Law in 1 Sel. Essays in Anglo-Amer. Leg. Hist. 597.

HINE, or HIND. In old English law. A husbandry servant.

HINEFARE. In old English law. The loss or departure of a servant from his master. Domesday.

HINEGELD. A ransom for an offense committed by a servant. Cowell.

HIPOTECA. In Spanish law. A mortgage of real property.

HIRCISCUNDA. See Herciscunda.

HIRE, *v.* To purchase the temporary use of a thing, or to stipulate for the labor or services of another. See Hiring.

For definitions of the various species of this class of contracts, under their Latin names, see Locatio and following titles.

To engage in service for a stipulated reward, as to hire a servant for a year, or laborers by the day or month; to engage a man to temporary service for wages. To "employ" is a word of more enlarged signification. A man hired to labor is employed, but a man may be employed in a work who is not hired. Ozark Minerals Co. v. Murphy, 384 Ill. 94, 51 N.E.2d 197, 201.

HIRE, *n.* Compensation for the use of a thing, or for labor or services. State v. Kenyon, Inc., Tex.Civ.App., 153 S.W.2d 195, 197.

A bailment in which compensation is to be given for the use of a thing, or for labor and services about it. 2 Kent 456; Story, Bailm. § 359. The divisions of this species of contract are denoted by Latin names.

HIREMAN. A subject. Du Cange.

HIRER. One who hires a thing, or the labor or services of another person. Turner v. Cross, 83 Tex. 218, 18 S.W. 578, 15 L.R.A. 262.

HIRING. A contract by which one person grants to another either the enjoyment of a thing or the use of the labor and industry, either of himself or his servant, during a certain time, for a stipulated compensation, or by which one contracts for the labor or services of another about a thing bailed to him for a specified purpose.

A contract by which one gives to another the temporary possession and use of property, other than money, for reward, and the latter agrees to return the same to the former at a future time.

Synonyms

"Hiring" and "borrowing" are both contracts by which a qualified property may be transferred to the hirer or borrower, and they differ only in this, that hiring is always for a price, stipend, or recompense, while borrowing is merely gratuitous. 2 Bl.Comm. 453; Neel v. State, 33 Tex. Cr.R. 408, 26 S.W. 726.

HIRING AT WILL. A general or indefinite hiring. Long v. Forbes, 58 Wyo. 533, 136 P.2d 242, 246.

HIRST, HURST. In old English law. A wood. Co.Litt. 4*b*.

HIS. This pronoun, generically used, may refer to a person of either sex. Danforth v. Emmons, 124 Me. 156, 126 A. 821, 823; Wilmette v. Brachle, 110 Ill.App. 356.

Its use in a written instrument, in referring to a person whose Christian name is designated therein by a mere initial, is not conclusive that the person referred to is a male; it may be shown by parol that the person intended is a female. Berniaud v. Beecher, 71 Cal. 38, 11 P. 802.

HIS EXCELLENCY. In English law. The title of a viceroy, governor general, ambassador, or commander in chief.

In American law. This title is given to the governor of Massachusetts by the constitution of that state; and it is commonly given, as a title of honor and courtesy, to the governors of the other states and to the president of the United States. It is also customarily used by foreign ministers in addressing the secretary of state in written communications.

HIS HONOR. A title given by the constitution of Massachusetts to the lieutenant governor of that commonwealth. Mass. Const. part 2, c. 2, § 2, art. 1. It is also customarily given to some inferior magistrates, as the mayor of a city.

HIS TESTIBUS. Lat. These being witnesses. The attestation clause in old deeds and charters. See Hiis Testibus.

HISSA. A lot or portion; a share of revenue or rent. Wilson's Gloss. Ind.

HITHERTO. In legal use, this term always restricts the matter in connection with which it is employed to a period of time already passed. Mason v. Jones, 13 Barb. (N.Y.) 479.

HIWISC. In old English law. A hide of land. According to Maitland (Domesday Book 359), a household.

HLAF ÆTA. Sax. A servant fed at his master's cost.

HLAFORD. Sax. A lord. 1 Spence, Ch. 36.

HLAFORDSOCNA. Sax. A lord's protection. Du Cange.

HLAFORDSWICE. Sax. In Saxon law. The crime of betraying one's lord, (*proditio domini;*) treason. Crabb, Eng.Law, 59, 301.

HLASOCNA. Sax. The benefit of the law. Du Cange.

HLOTHBOTE. In Saxon law. A fine for being present at an unlawful assembly. Spelman.

HLOTHE. In Saxon law. An unlawful assembly from eight to thirty-five, inclusive. Cowell.

HOASTMEN. In English law. An ancient gild or fraternity at Newcastle-upon-Tyne, who dealt in sea coal. St. 21 Jac. I. c. 3.

HOBBIT. A measure of weight in use in Wales, equal to 168 pounds, being made up of four Welsh pecks of 42 pounds each. Hughes v. Humphreys, 26 Eng. L. & Eq. 132.

HOBBLERS. In old English law. Light horsemen or bowmen; also certain tenants, bound by their tenure to maintain a little light horse for giving notice of any invasion, or such like peril, towards the seaside. Camden, Brit.

HOC. Lat. This. *Hoc intuitu,* with this expectation. *Hoc loco,* in this place. *Hoc nomine,* in this name. *Hoc titulo,* under this title. *Hoc voce,* under this word.

HOC PARATUS EST VERIFICARE. Lat. This he is ready to verify.

HOC QUIDEM PERQUAM DURUM EST, SED ITA LEX SCRIPTA EST. Lat. This indeed is exceedingly hard, but so the law is written; such is the written or positive law. An observation quoted by Blackstone as used by Ulpian in the civil law; and applied to cases where courts of equity have no power to abate the rigor of the law. Dig. 40, 9, 12, 1; 3 Bl. Comm. 430.

HOC SERVABITUR QUOD INITIO CONVENIT. This shall be preserved which is useful in the beginning. Dig. 50, 17, 23; Bract. 73*b*.

HOCCUS SALTIS. A hoke, hole, or lesser pit of salt. Cowell.

HOCK DAY. See Hock–Tuesday Money, *infra.*

HOCK–TUESDAY MONEY. This was a duty given to the landlord that his tenants and bondmen might solemnize the day on which the English conquered the Danes, being the second Tuesday after Easter week. Cowell. See Hoke Day, *infra.*

HOCKETTOR, or HOCQUETEUR. A knight of the post; a decayed man; a basket carrier. Cowell.

HODGE–PODGE ACT. A name applied to a statute which comprises a medley of incongruous subjects.

HOG. This word may include a sow; Shubrick v. State, 2 S.C. 21; a pig; Lavender v. State, 60 Ala. 60; Washington v. State, 58 Ala. 355; and may refer to dead as well as a living animal; Whitson v. Culbertson, 7 Ind. 195; Hunt v. State, 55 Ala. 140; Reed v. State, 16 Fla. 564; *contra,* State v. Hedrick, 272 Mo. 502, 199 S.W. 192, L.R.A. 1918C, 574; and it is synonymous with swine; Rivers v. State, 10 Tex.App. 177.

HOGA. In old English law. A hill or mountain. In old English, a *how. Grene hoga,* Grenehow. Domesday; Spelman.

HOGASTER. In old English law. A sheep of the second year. Fleta, lib. 2, c. 79, §§ 4, 12. A young hog. Cowell.

HOGGUS, or HOGIETUS. A hog or swine. Cowell.

HOGHENHYNE. In Saxon law. A house-servant. Any stranger who lodged three nights or more at a man's house in a decennary was called "*hoghenhyne,*" and his host became responsible for his acts as for those of his servant.

HOGSHEAD. A measure of a capacity containing the fourth part of a tun, or sixty-three gallons. Cowell. A large cast, of indefinite contents, but usually containing from one hundred to one hundred and forty gallons. Webster.

HOKE DAY (Heck Day). A day of feasting or mirth kept formerly in England on the second or third Tuesday after Easter; Cent. Dict.; or, as a recent writer concludes, the first Sunday after Easter; 28 L.Q.Rev. 283, where it is suggested that it was originally the great spring festival of the pre-Roman British. See Hock–Tuesday Money, *supra.*

HOLD, *v.* 1. To possess in virtue of a lawful title; as in the expression, common in grants, "to have and to hold," or in that applied to notes, "the owner and holder." Chicago Home for Girls v. Carr, 300 Ill. 478, 133 N.E. 344, 346.

2. To be the grantee or tenant of another; to take or have an estate from another. Properly, to have an estate on condition of paying rent, or performing service.

3. To adjudge or decide, spoken of a court, particularly to declare the conclusion of law reached by the court as to the legal effect of the facts disclosed.

4. To maintain or sustain; to be under the necessity or duty of sustaining or proving; as when it is said that a party "holds the affirmative" or negative of an issue in a cause.

5. To bind or obligate; to restrain or constrain; to keep in custody or under an obligation; as in the phrases "hold to bail," "hold for court," "held and firmly bound," etc.

6. To administer; to conduct or preside at; to convoke, open, and direct the operations of; as to hold a court, hold pleas, etc. Smith v. People, 47 N.Y. 334.

7. To prosecute; to direct and bring about officially; to conduct according to law; as to hold an election.

8. To possess; to occupy; to be in possession and administration of; as to hold office.

9. To keep; to retain; to maintain possession of or authority over. Dimock State Bank v. Boehnen, 46 S.D. 50, 190 N.W. 485.

Hold over. To retain possession as tenant of property leased, after the end of the term. To continue in possession of an office and continue to exercise its functions, after the end of the officer's lawful term. State v. Simon, 20 Or. 365, 26 P. 174.

Hold pleas. To hear or try causes. 3 Bl.Comm. 35, 298.

HOLD, *n.* In old law. Tenure. A word constantly occurring in conjunction with others, as *freehold, leasehold, copyhold,* etc., but rarely met with in the separate form.

HOLDER. The holder of a bill of exchange, promissory note, or check is the person who has legally acquired possession of the same, by indorsement or delivery, and who is entitled to receive payment of the instrument. Crocker-Woolworth Nat. Bank v. Nevada Bank, 139 Cal. 564, 73 P. 456, 63 L.R.A. 245, 96 Am.St.Rep. 169.

HOLDER IN DUE COURSE. A holder who has taken a bill of exchange (check or note) complete and regular on the face of it, under the following conditions, namely: (*a*) That he became the holder of it before it was overdue, and without notice that it had been previously dishonored, if such was the fact. (*b*) That he took the bill (check or note) in good faith and for value, and that at the time it was negotiated to him he had no notice of any defect in the title of the person who negotiated it. Uniform Negotiable Instrument Act, § 52; Peoples Loan & Finance Co. v. Ledbetter, 69 Ga.App. 729, 26 S.E.2d 671, 674.

HOLDES. Sax. In Saxon law. A military commander. Spelman.

HOLDING. In English law. A piece of land held under a lease or similar tenancy for agricultural, pastoral, or similar purposes.

In Scotch law. The tenure or nature of the right given by the superior to the vassal. Bell.

General

Holding over. See Hold, *v.*

Holding up the hand. In criminal practice. A formality observed in the arraignment of prisoners. Held to be not absolutely necessary. 1 W. Bl. 3, 4.

HOLDING COMPANY. A super-corporation which owns or at least controls such a dominant interest in one or more other corporations that it is enabled to dictate their policies through voting power; a corporation organized to hold the stock of other corporations; any company, incorporated or unincorporated, which is in a position to control or materially influence the management of one or more other companies by virtue, in part at least, of its ownership or securities in the other company or companies. Cities Service Co. v. Koeneke, 137 Kan. 7, 20 P.2d 460, 469, 87 A.L.R. 16; Kelley, Glover & Vale v. Heitman, 220 Ind. 625, 44 N.E.2d 981, 985.

HOLIDAY. A religious festival; a day set apart for commemorating some important event in history; a day of exemption from labor. Webster; Lamberti v. City of Stamford, 131 Conn. 396, 40 A.2d 190, 192. A day upon which the usual operations of business are suspended and the courts closed, and, generally, no legal process is served. United Cigar Stores Co. v. Worth-Gyles Grain Co., 212 Ill.App. 26.

Legal holiday. See Legal Holiday.

Public holiday. A legal holiday.

HOLM. An island in a river or the sea. Spelman. Plain grassy ground upon water sides or in the water. Blount. Low ground intersected with streams. Spelman.

HOLOGRAFO. In Spanish law. A holograph. An instrument (particularly a will) wholly in the handwriting of the person executing it; or which, to be valid, must be so written by his own hand.

HOLOGRAPH. A will or deed written entirely by the testator or grantor with his own hand. Estate of Billings, 64 Cal. 427, 1 P. 701; In re Irvine's Estate, 114 Mont. 577, 139 P.2d 489, 147 A.L.R. 882.

HOLT. Sax. In old English law. A wood or grove. Spelman; Cowell; Co. Litt. 4*b*.

HOLY ORDERS. In ecclesiastical law. The orders of bishops, (including archbishops,) priests, and deacons in the Church of England. The Roman canonists had the orders of bishop, (in which the pope and archbishops were included,) priest, deacon, subdeacon, psalmist, acolyte, exorcist, reader, ostiarius. 3 Steph.Comm. 55, and note *a*.

HOMAGE. In feudal law. A service (or the ceremony of rendering it) which a tenant was bound to perform to his lord on receiving investiture of a fee, or succeeding to it as heir, in acknowledgment of the tenure. It is described by Littleton as the most honorable service of reverence that a free tenant might do to his lord. The ceremony was as follows: The tenant, being ungirt and with bare head, knelt before the lord, the latter sitting, and held his hands extended and joined between the hands of the lord, and said: "I become your man [*homo*] from this day forward, of life and limb and earthly honor, and to you will be faithful and loyal, and bear you faith, for the tenements that I claim to hold of you, saving the faith that I owe unto our sovereign lord the king, so help me God." The tenant then received a kiss from the lord. Homage could be done only to the lord himself. Litt. § 85; Glanv. lib. 9, c. 1; Bract. fols. 77*b*, 78–80; Wharton.

"Homage" is to be distinguished from "fealty," another incident of feudalism, and which consisted in the solemn oath of fidelity made by the vassal to the lord, whereas homage was merely an acknowledgment of tenure. If the homage was intended to include fealty, it was called "liege homage;" but otherwise it was called "simple homage." Brown.

HOMAGE ANCESTRAL. In feudal law. Homage was called by this name where a man and his ancestors had immemorially held of another and his ancestors by the service of homage, which bound the lord to warrant the title, and also to hold the tenant clear of all services to superior lords. If the tenant aliened in fee, his alienee was a tenant by homage, but not by homage ancestral. Litt. § 143; 2 Bl.Comm. 300.

HOMAGE JURY. A jury in a court-baron, consisting of tenants that do homage, who are to inquire and make presentments of the death of tenants, surrenders, admittances, and the like.

HOMAGE LIEGE. That kind of homage which was due to the sovereign alone as supreme lord, and which was done without any saving or exception of the rights of other lords. Spelman.

HOMAGER. One who does or is bound to do homage. Cowell.

HOMAGIO RESPECTUANDO. A writ to the escheator commanding him to deliver seisin of lands to the heir of the king's tenant, notwithstanding his homage not done. Fitzh. Nat. Brev. 269.

HOMAGIUM. L. Lat. Homage (*q. v.*).

HOMAGIUM LIGIUM. Liege homage; that kind of homage which was due to the sovereign alone as supreme lord, and which was done without any saving or exception of the rights of other lords. Spelman. So called from *ligando,* (binding,) because it could not be renounced like other kinds of homage.

HOMAGIUM, NON PER PROCURATORES NEC PER LITERAS FIERI POTUIT, SED IN PROPRIA PERSONA TAM DOMINI QUAM TENENTIS CAPI DEBET ET FIERI. Co. Litt. 68. Homage cannot be done by proxy, nor by letters, but must be paid and received in the proper person, as well of the lord as the tenant.

HOMAGIUM PLANUM. In feudal law. Plain homage; a species of homage which bound him who did it to nothing more than fidelity, without any obligation either of military service or attendance in the courts of his superior. 1 Robertson's Car. V., Appendix, note 8.

HOMAGIUM REDDERE. To renounce homage. This was when a vassal made a solemn declaration of disowning and defying his lord; for which there was a set form and method prescribed by the feudal laws. Bract. l. 2, c. 35, § 35.

HOMAGIUM SIMPLEX. In feudal law. Simple homage; that kind of homage which was merely an acknowledgment of tenure, with a saving of the rights of other lords. Harg. Co. Litt. note 18, lib. 2.

HOMBRE BUENO. In Spanish law. The judge of a district. Also an arbitrator chosen by the parties to a suit. Also a man in good standing; one who is competent to testify in a suit.

HOME. One's own dwelling place; the house in which one lives; especially the house in which one lives with his family; the habitual abode of one's family; a dwelling house. Mann v. Haines, 146 Kan. 988, 73 P.2d 1066, 1072. That place in which one in fact resides with the intention of residence, or in which he has so resided, and with regard to which he retains residence or to which he intends to return. Dicey, Confl. L. 81; Langhammer v. Munter, 80 Md. 518, 31 A. 300, 27 L.R.A. 330.

Home is not synonymous with domicil, as used in international law, but has a more restricted meaning, Inhabitants of Jefferson v. Washington, 19 Me. 293.

Home includes place where one eats, bathes, reads, visits and rests, as well as sleeping place, Jakeway v. John V. Bauer Co., 218 N.Y.S. 193, 195, 218 App.Div. 302; and, as used in deed or will may include care or right of maintenance, Gwinn v. Hobbs, 83 Ind.App. 263, 141 N.E. 812, 818; In re Burr's Estate, 144 N.Y.S. 926, 927, 83 Misc. 240.

HOME BREW. An intoxicating home made beer. Jones v. State, 31 Ala.App. 378, 17 So.2d 545.

HOME OFFICE. The department of state through which the English sovereign administers most of the internal affairs of the kingdom, especially the police, and communicates with the judicial functionaries. As applied to a corporation, its principal office within the state or country where it was incorporated or formed.

HOME PORT. In maritime law, the home port of a vessel is either the port where she is registered or enrolled, or the port at or nearest to which her owner usually resides, or, if there be more than one owner, the port at or nearest to which the husband, or acting and managing owner resides. Com. v. Ayer & Lord Tie Co., 77 S.W. 688, 25 Ky.Law Rep. 1068. But for some purposes any port where the owner happens at the time to be with his vessel is its home port. Lever Transp. Co. v. Ollinger, 205 Ala. 22, 87 So. 597, 598.

HOME RULE. In constitutional and statutory law, local self-government, or the right thereof. Attorney General v. Lowrey, 131 Mich. 639, 92 N.W. 289. In British politics, a programme or plan (or a more or less definitely formulated demand) for the right of local self-government for Ireland under the lead of an Irish national parliament. Lemaire v. Crockett, 116 Me. 263, 101 A. 302, 303.

HOME, or HOMME. L. Fr. Man; a man.

HOME NE SERA PUNY PUR SUER DES BRIEFES EN COURT LE ROY, SOIT IL A DROIT OU A TORT. A man shall not be punished for suing out writs in the king's court, whether he be right or wrong. 2 Inst. 228.

HOMESOKEN, HOMSOKEN. See Hamesecken.

HOMESTALL. A mansion-house. Dickinson v. Mayer, 11 Heisk. (Tenn.) 521.

HOMESTEAD. The home, the house and the adjoining land where the head of the family dwells; the home farm. The fixed residence of the head of a family, with the land and buildings surrounding the main house. Oliver v. Snowden, 18 Fla. 825, 43 Am.Rep. 338.

Technically, and under the modern homestead laws, an artificial estate in land, devised to protect the possession and enjoyment of the owner against the claims of his creditors, by withdrawing the property from execution and forced sale, so long as the land is occupied as a home. Buckingham v. Buckingham, 81 Mich. 89, 45 N.W. 504. For "Family," see that title.

Business Homestead. In Texas, a place or property (distinct from the home of a family) used and occupied by the head of a family as a place to exercise his calling or business, which is exempt by law. Spence v. State Nat. Bank of El Paso, Tex.Civ.App., 294 S.W. 618, 623. A curious misnomer, the word "homestead" in this phrase having lost entirely its original meaning, and being retained apparently only for the sake of its remote and derivative association with the idea of an exemption.

Homestead Corporations. Corporations organized for the purpose of acquiring lands in large tracts, paying off incumbrances thereon, improving and subdividing them into homestead lots or parcels, and distributing them among the shareholders, and for the accumulation of a fund for such purposes. Civ. Code Cal. § 557.

Homestead Entry. See Entry.

Homestead Exemption Laws. Laws passed in most of the states allowing a householder or head of a family to designate a house and land as his homestead, and exempting the same homestead from execution for his general debts.

Homestead Right. The personal right to the beneficial, peaceful and uninterrupted use of the home property free from claims of creditors. Hill v. First Nat. Bank, 79 Fla. 391, 84 So. 190, 192, 20 A.L.R. 270.

Probate Homestead. A homestead set apart by the court for the use of a surviving husband or wife and the minor children out of the common property, or out of the real estate belonging to the deceased. In re Noah's Estate, 73 Cal. 590, 15 P. 290, 2 Am.St.Rep. 834.

Rural Homestead. See Urban Homestead, *infra.*

Urban Homestead. The residence or dwelling place of a family in a city, claimed or set apart as a homestead, including the principal house and lot, and such lots as are used in connection therewith, contributing to its enjoyment, comfort, and convenience. Harris v. Matthews, 36 Tex. 424, 81 S.W. 1204. Nevertheless, property may be located within the corporate limits of a town or city, and still constitute a "rural homestead," or it may be without the corporate limits, and constitute an "urban homestead." Boerner v. Cicero Smith Lumber Co., Tex.Civ.App., 293 S.W. 632, 636.

HOMICIDAL. Pertaining to homicide; relating to homicide, impelling to homicide; as a homicidal mania. (See Insanity.)

HOMICIDE. The killing of any human creature. 4 Bl.Comm. 177. The killing of one human being by the act, procurement, or omission of another. Pen. Code N. Y. § 179. The act of a human being in taking away the life of another human being. Sanders v. State, 113 Ga. 267, 38 S.E. 842. Hogan v. State, 127 Tex.Cr.R. 182, 74 S.W.2d 988, 994.

Homicide is not necessarily a crime. It is a necessary ingredient of the crimes of murder and manslaughter, but there are other cases in which homicide may be committed without criminal intent and without criminal consequences, as, where it is done in the lawful execution of a judicial sentence, in self-defense, or as the only possible means of arresting an escaping felon. The term "homicide" is neutral; while it describes the act, it pronounces no judgment on its moral or legal quality. People v. Connors, 35 N.Y.S. 475, 13 Misc. 582.

Classification

Homicide is ordinarily classified as "justifiable," "excusable," and "felonious." For the definitions of these terms, and of some other compound terms, see *infra.*

Culpable homicide

Described as a crime varying from the very lowest culpability, up to the very verge of murder. Lord Moncrieff, Arkley, 72.

Excusable homicide

The killing of a human being, either by misadventure or in self-defense. U. S. v. King, C.C.N.Y., 34 F. 306. The name itself imports some fault, error, or omission, so trivial, however, that the law excuses it from guilt of felony, though in strictness it judges it deserving of some little degree of punishment. 4 Bl.Comm. 182. It is of two sorts,—either *per infortunium,* by misadventure, or *se defendendo,* upon a sudden affray. Homicide *per infortunium* is where a man, doing a lawful act, without any intention of hurt, unfortunately kills another; but, if death ensue from any unlawful act, the offense is manslaughter, and not misadventure. Homicide *se defendendo* is where a man kills another upon a sudden affray, merely in his own defense, or in defense of his wife, child, parent, or servant, and not from any vindictive feeling. 4 Bl.Comm. 182.

Felonious homicide

The wrongful killing of a human being, of any age or either sex, without justification or excuse in law; of which offense there are two degrees, manslaughter and murder. 4 Bl.Comm. 190; 4 Steph.Comm. 111.

Homicide by misadventure

The accidental killing of another, where the slayer is doing a lawful act, unaccompanied by any criminally careless or reckless conduct. Commonwealth v. Flax, 331 Pa. 145, 200 A. 632, 637. The same as "homicide *per infortunium.*" State v. Disalvo, Del., 2 W.W.Harr. 232, 121 A. 661, 663.

Homicide by necessity

A species of justifiable homicide, because it arises from some unavoidable necessity, without any will, intention, or desire, and without any inadvertence or negligence in the party killing, and therefore without any shadow of blame. As, for instance, by virtue of such an office as obliges one, in the execution of public justice, to put a malefactor to death who has forfeited his life to the laws of his country. But the law must require it, otherwise it is not justifiable. 4 Bl.Comm. 178.

Homicide per infortunium

Homicide by misfortune, or accidental homicide; as where a man doing a lawful act, without any intention of hurt, unfortunately kills another; a species of excusable homicide. 4 Bl.Comm. 182; 4 Steph.Comm. 101.

Homicide se defendendo

Homicide in self-defense; the killing of a person in self-defense upon a sudden affray, where the slayer had no other possible (or, at least, probable) means of escaping from his assailant. 4 Bl.Comm. 183–186; 4 Steph.Comm. 103–105. A species of excusable homicide. Id.; 1 Russ. Crimes, 660.

Justifiable homicide

Such as is committed intentionally, but without any evil design, and under such circumstances of necessity or duty as render the act proper, and relieve the party from any shadow of blame; as where a sheriff lawfully executes a sentence of death upon a malefactor, or where the killing takes place in the endeavor to prevent the commission of felony which could not be otherwise avoided. Moran v. People, 163 Ill. 382, 45 N.E. 230. "Justifiable homicide" is the taking of a human life under circumstances of justification, as a matter of right, such as self-defense or other causes set out in the statute. Gaunce v. State, 22 Okl.Cr.

361, 211 P. 517, 518. "Justifiable homicide" is the killing of a human being by commandment of the law in execution of public justice; by permission of the law in advancement of public justice; in self-defense; or in defense of habitation, property or person, against one who manifestly intends or endeavors, by violence or surprise, to commit a felony on either. Paramore v. State, 161 Ga. 166, 129 S.E. 772, 778.

Negligent homicide

In Texas, the act of causing the death of another by negligence and carelessness in the performance of a lawful act. Anderson v. State, 27 Tex.App. 177, 11 S.W. 33, 3 L.R.A. 644, 11 Am.St.Rep. 189.

HOMICIDIUM. Lat. Homicide (*q. v.*).

Homicidium ex casu, homicide by accident.

Homicidium ex justitia, homicide in the administration of justice, or in the execution of the sentence of the law.

Homicidium ex necessitate, homicide from inevitable necessity, as for the protection of one's person or property.

Homicidium ex voluntate, voluntary or willful homicide. Bract. fols. 120*b*, 121.

HOMINATIO. The mustering of men; the doing of homage.

HOMINE CAPTO IN WITHERNAMIUM. A writ to take him that had taken any bond man or woman, and led him or her out of the country, so that he or she could not be replevied according to law. Reg. Orig. 79.

HOMINE ELIGENDO. In old English law. A writ directed to a corporation, requiring the members to make choice of a man to keep one part of the seal appointed for statutes merchant, when a former is dead, according to the statute of Acton Burnell. Reg. Orig. 178; Wharton.

HOMINE REPLEGIANDO. In English law. A writ which lay to replevy a man out of prison, or out of the custody of any private person, in the same manner that chattels taken in distress may be replevied. Brown.

HOMINES. Lat. In feudal law. Men; feudatory tenants who claimed a privilege of having their causes, etc., tried only in their lord's court. Paroch. Antiq. 15.

HOMINES LIGII. Liege men; feudal tenants or vassals, especially those who held immediately of the sovereign. 1 Bl.Comm. 367.

HOMINUM CAUSA JUS CONSTITUTUM EST. Law is established for the benefit of man.

HOMIPLAGIUM. In old English law. The maiming of a man. Blount.

HOMME. Fr. Man; a man. The term "man" as sometimes used may include a woman or women. This is expressly stated in Civ. Code La. art. 3556, No. 1.

HOMMES DE FIEF. Fr. In feudal law. Men of the fief; feudal tenants; the peers in the lords' courts. Montesq., Esprit des Lois, liv. 28, c. 27.

HOMMES FEODAUX. Fr. In feudal law. Feudal tenants; the same with *hommes de fief* (*q. v.*). Montesq., Esprit des Lois, liv. 28, c. 36.

HOMO. Lat. A man; a human being, male or female; a vassal, or feudal tenant; a retainer, dependent, or servant.

HOMO CHARTULARIUS. A slave manumitted by charter.

HOMO COMMENDATUS. In feudal law. One who surrendered himself into the power of another for the sake of protection or support. See Commendation.

HOMO ECCLESIASTICUS. A church vassal; one who was bound to serve a church, especially to do service of an agricultural character. Spelman.

HOMO EXERCITALIS. A man of the army, (*exercitus*;) a soldier.

HOMO FEODALIS. A vassal or tenant; one who held a fee, (*feodum*,) or part of a fee. Spelman.

HOMO FISCALIS, or FISCALINUS. A servant or vassal belonging to the treasury or *fiscus*.

HOMO FRANCUS. In old English law. A freeman. A Frenchman.

HOMO INGENUUS. A freeman. A free and lawful man. A yeoman.

HOMO LIBER. A free man; a freeman lawfully competent to act as juror. Ld. Raym. 417; Kebl. 563. An allodial proprietor, as distinguished from a vassal or feudatory. This was the sense of the term in the laws of the barbarous nations of Europe. Calvinus, Lex. *Alode*.

HOMO LIGIUS. A liege man; a subject; a king's vassal. The vassal of a subject.

HOMO NOVUS. In feudal law. A new tenant or vassal; one who was invested with a new fee. Spelman. Also one who, after conviction of a crime, had been pardoned, thus "making a new man of him."

HOMO PERTINENS. In feudal law. A feudal bondman or vassal; one who *belonged* to the soil, (*qui glebæ adscribitur.*)

HOMO POTEST ESSE HABILIS ET INHABILIS DIVERSIS TEMPORIBUS. 5 Coke, 98. A man may be capable and incapable at different times.

HOMO REGIUS. A king's vassal.

HOMO ROMANUS. A Roman. An appellation given to the old inhabitants of Gaul and other Roman provinces, and retained in the laws of the barbarous nations. Spelman.

HOMO TRIUM LITTERARUM. A man of the three letters; that is, the three letters, "f," "u," "r;" the Latin word *fur* meaning "thief."

HOMO VOCABULUM EST NATURÆ; PERSONA JURIS CIVILIS. Man (*homo*) is a term of nature; person (*persona*) of civil law. Calvin.

HOMOLOGACION. In Spanish law. The tacit consent and approval inferred by law from the omission of the parties, for the space of ten days, to complain of the sentences of arbitrators, appointment of syndics, or assignees of insolvents, settlements of successions, etc. Also the approval given by the judge of certain acts and agreements for the purpose of rendering them more binding and executory. Escriche.

HOMOLOGARE. In the civil law. To confirm or approve; to consent or assent; to confess. Calvin.

HOMOLOGATE. In modern civil law. To approve; to confirm; as a court *homologates* a proceeding. See Homologation. Literally, to use the *same words* with another; to say the like. Viales v. Gardenier, 9 Mart. O. S. (La.) 324. To assent to what another says or writes.

HOMOLOGATION. In the Civil law. Approbation; confirmation by a court of justice; a judgment which orders the execution of some act. Merl. Répert. The term is also used in Louisiana. Hecker v. Brown, 104 La. 524, 29 So. 232.

In English law. An estoppel *in pais.* L.R. 3 App.Cas. 1026.

In Scotch law. An act by which a person approves of a deed. The effect of which is to render that deed, though in itself defective, binding upon the person by whom it is homologated. Bell. Confirmation of a voidable deed.

HOMONYMIÆ. A term applied in the civil law to cases where a law was repeated, or laid down in the same terms or to the same effect, more than once. Cases of iteration and repetition. 2 Kent, Comm. 489, note.

HONDHABEND. Sax. Having in hand. See Handhabend.

HONESTE VIVERE. Lat. To live honorably, creditably, or virtuously. One of the three general precepts to which Justinian reduced the whole doctrine of the law, (Inst. 1, 1, 3; Bract. fols. 3, 3*b*,) the others being *alterum non lædere,* (not to injure others,) and *suum cuique tribuere,* (to render to every man his due.)

HONESTUS. Lat. Of good character or standing. *Coram duobus vel pluribus viris legalibus et honestis,* before two or more lawful and good men. Bract. fol. 61.

HONI. See Hony.

HONOR, *v.* To accept a bill of exchange, or to pay a note, check, or accepted bill, at maturity and according to its tenor. Peterson v. Hubbard, 28 Mich. 199; Clarke v. Cock, 4 East, 72; Lucas v. Groning, 7 Taunt. 168.

HONOR, *n.* In English law, a seigniory of several manors held under one baron or lord paramount. Also those dignities or privileges, degrees of nobility, knighthood, and other titles, which flow from the crown as the fountain of honor. Wharton.

In American law. The customary title of courtesy given to judges of the higher courts, and occasionally to some other officers; as "his honor," "your honor."

Act of honor. When a bill has been protested, and a third person wishes to take it up, or accept it, for the "honor" (credit) of one or more of the parties, the notary draws up an instrument, evidencing the transaction, which is called by this name.

Honor courts. Tribunals held within honors or seigniories.

Office of honor. As used in constitutional and statutory provisions, this term denotes a public office of considerable dignity and importance, to which important public trusts or interests are confided, but which is not compensated by any salary or fees, being thus contrasted with an "office of profit." See Dickson v. People, 17 Ill. 193.

HONORABLE. A title of courtesy given in England to the younger children of earls, and the children of viscounts and barons; and, collectively, to the house of commons. In America, the word is used as a title of courtesy for various classes of officials, but without any clear lines of distinction.

HONORABLE DISCHARGE. A formal final judgment passed by the government upon the entire military record of a soldier, and an authoritative declaration by the government that he has left the service in a status of honor. Parker v. Anderson, 112 Vt. 371, 25 A.2d 41, 44, Zearing v. Johnson, 10 Cal.App.2d 654, 52 P.2d 1019, 1020.

HONORARIUM. In the civil law. An honorary or free gift; a gratuitous payment, as distinguished from hire or compensation for service; a lawyer's or counsellor's fee. Dig. 50, 13, 1, 10–12.

A voluntary reward for that for which no remuneration could be collected by law. Cunningham v. Commissioner of Internal Revenue, C.C.A., 67 F.2d 205. A voluntary donation, in consideration of services which admit of no compensation in money; in particular, to advocates at law, deemed to practice for honor or influence, and not for fees. McDonald v. Napier, 14 Ga. 89.

HONORARIUM JUS. Lat. In Roman law. The law of the prætors and the edicts of the ædiles.

HONORARY. As applied to public offices and other positions of responsibility or trust, this term means either that the office or title is bestowed upon the incumbent as a mark of honor or compliment, without intending to charge him with the active discharge of the duties of the place, or else that he is to receive no salary or other compensation in money, the honor conferred by the incumbency of the office being his only reward. Haswell v. New York, 81 N.Y. 258. In other connections, it means attached to or growing out of some honor or dignity or honorable office, or else it imports an obligation or duty growing out of honor or trust only, as distinguished from legal accountability.

HONORARY CANONS. Those without emolument. 3 & 4 Vict. c. 113, § 23.

HONORARY FEUDS. Titles of nobility, descendible to the eldest son, in exclusion of all the rest. 2 Bl. Comm. 56.

HONORARY SERVICES. In feudal law. Special services to be rendered to the king in person, characteristic of the tenure by grand serjeanty; such as to carry his banner, his sword, or the like or to be his butler, champion, or other officer, at his coronation. Litt. § 153; 2 Bl. Comm. 73.

HONORARY TRUSTEES. Trustees to preserve contingent remainders, so called because they are bound, in honor only, to decide on the most proper and prudential course. Lewin, Trusts, 408.

HONORIS RESPECTUM. By reason of honor or privilege. See Challenge.

HONTFONGENETHEF. In Saxon law. A thief taken with *hondhabend; i. e.,* having the thing stolen in his hand. Cowell.

HONY. L. Fr. Shame; evil; disgrace. *Hony soit qui mal y pense,* evil be to him who evil thinks. Preferably written *honi.* See Garter.

HOO. In old English law. A hill. Co. Litt. 5*b*.

HOOKLAND. Land plowed and sown every year.

HOOTCH. Intoxicating liquor illicitly distilled for beverage purposes. State v. Cook, 318 Mo. 1233, 3 S.W.2d 365, 369.

HOPCON. In old English law. A valley. Cowell.

HOPE, *n.* In old English law. A valley. Co. Litt. 4*b*.

HOPE, *v.* As used in a will, this term is a precatory word, rather than mandatory or dispositive, but it is sufficient, in proper cases, to create a trust in or in respect to the property spoken of. Curd v. Field, 103 Ky. 293, 45 S.W. 92.

HOPPO. A Chinese term for a collector; an overseer of commerce.

HORA. Lat. An hour; the hour.

HORA AURORÆ. In old English law. The morning bell, as *ignitegium* or *coverfeu* (curfew) was the evening bell.

HORA NON EST MULTUM DE SUBSTANTIA NEGOTII, LICET IN APPELLO DE EA ALIQUANDO FIAT MENTIO. The hour is not of much consequence as to the substance of business, although in appeal it is sometimes mentioned. 1 Bulst. 82.

HORÆ JURIDICÆ or JUDICIÆ. Hours during which the judges sat in court to attend to judicial business.

HORCA. In Spanish law. A gallows; the punishment of hanging. White, New Recop. b. 2, tit. 19, c. 4, § 1.

HORDA. In old records. A cow in calf.

HORDERA. In old English law. A treasurer. Du Cange.

HORDERIUM. In old English law. A hoard; a treasure, or repository. Cowell.

HORDEUM. In old records. Barley. *Hordeum palmale,* beer barley, as distinguished from common barley, which was called *"hordeum quadragesimale."* Blount.

HORIZONTAL PRICE-FIXING CONTRACTS. Contracts between producers or between wholesalers or between retailers as to sale or resale prices. Seagram-Distillers Corporation v. Old Dearborn Distributing Co., 363 Ill. 610, 2 N.E.2d 940, 942.

HORN. In old Scotch practice. A kind of trumpet used in denouncing contumacious persons rebels and outlaws, which was done with three blasts of the horn by the king's sergeant. This was called "putting to the horn;" and the party so denounced was said to be "at the horn." Bell. See Horning.

HORN-BOOK. A primer; a book explaining the rudiments of any science or branch of knowledge. The phrase "horn-book law" is a colloquial designation of the rudiments or most familiar principles of law.

HORN TENURE. In old English law. Tenure by cornage; that is, by the service of winding a horn when the Scots or other enemies entered the land, in order to warn the king's subjects. This was a species of grand serjeanty. Litt. § 156; 2 Bl. Comm. 74.

HORN WITH HORN, or HORN UNDER HORN. The promiscuous feeding of bulls and cows or all horned beasts that are allowed to run together upon the same common. Spelman.

HORNER. A narcotic addict who inhales or snuffs heroin rather than one who takes it by injection. People v. Carner, 255 P.2d 835, 836, 117 C.A.2d 362.

HORNGELD. Sax. In old English law. A tax within a forest, paid for horned beasts. Cowell; Blount.

HORNING. In Scotch law. "Letters of horning" is the name given to a judicial process issuing on the decree of a court, by which the debtor is summoned to perform his obligation in terms of the decree, the consequence of his failure to do so being liability to arrest and imprisonment. It was anciently the custom to proclaim a debtor who had failed to obey such process a rebel or outlaw, which was done by three blasts of the horn by the king's sergeant in a public place. This was called "putting to the horn," whence the name.

HORNSWOGGLE. To triumph over; overcome; beat; bedevil. U. S. Fidelity & Guaranty Co. v. Rochester, Tex.Civ.App., 281 S.W. 306, 314.

HORREUM. Lat. A place for keeping grain; a granary. A place for keeping fruits, wines, and goods generally; a store-house. Calvin.; Bract. fol. 48.

HORS. L. Fr. Out; out of; without.

HORS DE SON FEE. Out of his fee. In old pleading, this was the name of a plea in an action for rent or services, by which the defendant alleged that the land in question was out of the compass of the plaintiff's fee. Mather v. Wood, 12 Pa. Co. Ct. R. 4.

HORS PRIS. Except. Literally translated by the Scotch "out taken."

HORS WEALH. In old English law. The wealh, or Briton who had care of the king's horses.

HORS WEARD. In old English law. A service or *corvée,* consisting in watching the horses of the lord. Anc. Inst. Eng.

HORSE. An animal of the genus *equus* and species *caballus.* In a narrow and strict sense, the term is applied only to the male, and only to males of four years old or thereabouts, younger horses being called "colts." But even in this sense the term includes both stallions and geldings. In a wider sense, and as generally used in statutes, the word is taken as *nomen generalissimum,* and includes not only horses strictly so called, but also colts, mares and fillies, and mules and asses. Pullen v. State, 11 Tex.App. 91; Ex parte Hancock, 61 Okl.Cr. 167, 66 P.2d 954, 955.

HORSE GUARDS. The directing power of the military forces of the kingdom of Great Britain. The commander in chief, or general commanding the forces, is at the head of this department. It is subordinate to the war office, but the relations between them are complicated. Wharton.

HORSE POWER. A unit of power capable of lifting 33,000 pounds a foot a minute. Foltz Grocery & Baking Co. v. Brown, 111 Ohio St. 646; 146 N.E. 97, 99.

Net Horse Power

Actually available horse power as distinguished from theoretical horse power. Kimberly-Clark Co. v. Patten Paper Co., 153 Wis. 69, 140 N.W. 1066, 1073.

HORTUS. Lat. In the civil law. A garden. Dig. 32, 91, 5.

HOSPES. Lat. A guest. 8 Coke, 32.

HOSPES GENERALIS. A great chamberlain.

HOSPITAL. An institution for the reception and care of sick, wounded, infirm, or aged persons; generally incorporated, and then of the class of corporations called "eleemosynary" or "charitable." Also the building used for such purpose. In re Curtiss (Sur.) 7 N.Y.S. 207; Noble v. First Nat. Bank of Anniston, 241 Ala. 85, 1 So.2d 289, 290.

Base Hospital

One established at a definite military or naval base of operations.

Field Hospital

One set up near the field of operations. It is generally equipped to care for emergency cases and can be moved readily.

Public Hospitals

Hospitals which appeal to the public for voluntary contributions, or those which are supported by compulsory contributions in the form of a rate.

HOSPITALIZATION. Placing a sick person in a hospital. Edwards v. West Texas Hospital, Tex. Civ.App., 89 S.W.2d 801, 815.

HOSPITALLERS. The knights of a religious order, so called because they built a hospital at Jerusalem, wherein pilgrims were received. All their lands and goods in England were given to the sovereign by 32 Hen. VIII. c. 24.

HOSPITATOR. A host or entertainer.

Hospitator communis. An innkeeper. 8 Coke, 32.

Hospitator magnus. The marshal of a camp.

HOSPITIA. Inns. *Hospitia communia,* common inns. Reg. Orig. 105. *Hospitia curiæ,* inns of court. *Hospitia cancellariæ,* inns of chancery. Crabb, Eng. Law, 428, 429; 4 Reeve, Eng. Law, 120.

HOSPITICIDE. One that kills his guest or host.

HOSPITIUM. An inn; a household. Cromwell v. Stephens, 2 Daly (N.Y.) 17.

HOSPODAR. A Turkish governor in Moldavia or Wallachia.

HOST. L. Fr. An army. Britt. c. 22. A military expedition; war. Kelham.

HOSTAGE. A person who is given into the possession of the enemy, in a public war, his freedom (or life) to stand as security for the performance of some contract or promise made by the belligerent power giving the hostage with the other.

HOSTELAGIUM. In old records. A right to receive lodging and entertainment, anciently reserved by lords in the houses of their tenants. Cowell.

HOSTELER. See Hostler.

HOSTES. Lat. Enemies. *Hostes humani generis,* enemies of the human race; *i. e.,* pirates.

HOSTES SUNT QUI NOBIS VEL QUIBUS NOS BELLUM DECERNIMUS; CÆTERI PRODITORES VEL PRÆDONES SUNT. 7 Coke, 24. Enemies are those with whom we declare war, or who declare it against us; all others are traitors or pirates.

HOSTIA. In old records. The hostbread, or consecrated wafer, in the eucharist. Cowell.

HOSTICIDE. One who kills an enemy.

HOSTILARIA, HOSPITALARIA. A place or room in religious houses used for the reception of guests and strangers.

HOSTILE. Having the character of an enemy; standing in the relation of an enemy. 1 Kent, Comm. c. 4.

HOSTILE EMBARGO. One laid upon the vessels of an actual or prospective enemy.

HOSTILE FIRE. One which becomes uncontrollable or breaks out from where it was intended to be and becomes hostile element. Swerling v. Connecticut Fire Ins. Co., 55 R.I. 252, 180 A. 343. Reliance Ins. Co. v. Naman, 6 S.W.2d 743, 744, 118 Tex. 21.

HOSTILE POSSESSION. See Possession.

HOSTILE WITNESS. A witness who manifests so much hostility or prejudice under examination in chief that the party who has called him, or his representative, is allowed to cross-examine him, *i. e.*, to treat him as though he had been called by the opposite party. Wharton.

HOSTILITY. In the law of nations. A state of open war. "At the breaking out of hostility." An act of open war. "When *hostilities* have commenced." 1 Kent, Comm. 56, 60.

A hostile character. "Hostility may attach only to the person." 1 Kent, Comm. 56.

HOSTLER. In Norman and old English law, this was the title of the officer in a monastery charged with the entertainment of guests. It was also applied (until about the time of Queen Elizabeth) to an innkeeper, and afterwards, when the keeping of horses at livery became a distinct occupation, to the keeper of a livery stable, and then (under the modern form "ostler") to the groom in charge of the stables of an inn. Cromwell v. Stephens, 2 Daly (N.Y.) 20.

In the language of railroading, an "ostler" or "hostler" at a roundhouse is one whose duty it is to receive locomotives as they come in from the road, care for them in the roundhouse, and have them cleaned and ready for departure when wanted. Louisville and N. R. Co. v. McCoy, 270 Ky. 603, 110 S.W.2d 433, 435.

HOTCHPOT. The blending and mixing property belonging to different persons, in order to divide it equally. 2 Bl. Comm. 190.

Anciently applied to the mixing and blending of lands given to one daughter in frank marriage, with those descending to her and her sisters in fee-simple, for the purpose of dividing the whole equally among them; without which the daughter who held in frank marriage could have no share in the lands in fee-simple. Litt. §§ 267, 268; Co.Litt. 177*a;* 2 Bl.Comm. 190.

Hotchpot, or the *putting in hotchpot,* is applied in modern law to the throwing the amount of an advancement made to a particular child, in real or personal estate, into the common stock, for the purpose of a more equal division, or of equalizing the shares of all the children. 2 Kent, Comm. 421, 422; In re Howlett's Estate, 275 Mich. 596, 267 N.W. 743, 744. This answers to or resembles the *collatio bonorum,* or *collation* of the civil law. Law v. Smith, 2 R.I. 249; In re Farmers' Loan & Trust Co., 168 N.Y.S. 952, 959, 181 App.Div. 642.

HOTEL. An inn; a public house or tavern; a house which is held out to well-behaved members of the traveling public, who are willing to pay reasonable rates for accommodations, as a place where they will be received and entertained as guests for compensation, and will be furnished with food, drink, and lodging, and everything which they have occasion for while on their way. City of St. Louis v. Siegrist, 46 Mo. 593; People v. Gold, Sp.Sess., 6 N.Y.S.2d 264, 267. For "Family Hotel", see that title.

Synonyms

In law, there is no difference whatever between the terms "hotel," "inn," and "tavern," except that in some states a statutory definition has been given to the word "hotel," especially with reference to the grant of licenses to sell liquor, as, that it shall contain a certain number of separate rooms for the entertainment of guests, or the like. But none of the three terms mentioned will include a boarding house (because that is a place kept for the entertainment of permanent boarders, while a hotel or inn is for travelers and transient guests), nor a lodging house (because the keeper thereof does not furnish food for guests, which is one of the requisites of a hotel or inn), nor a restaurant or eating-house, which furnishes food only and not lodging. Martin v. State Ins. Co., 44 N.J.Law, 485, 43 Am.Rep. 397; Debenham v. Short, Tex.Civ.App., 199 S.W. 1147.

HOT–WATER ORDEAL. In old English law. This was a test, in cases of accusation, by hot water; the party accused and suspected being appointed by the judge to put his arms up to the elbows in seething hot water, which, after sundry prayers and invocations, he did, and was, by the effect which followed, judged guilty or innocent. Wharton.

HOUGH. A valley. Co. Litt. 5*b*. See Haugh.

HOUR. The twenty-fourth part of a natural day; sixty minutes of time.

Hour of cause. In Scotch practice. The hour when a court is met. 3 How. State Tr. 603.

Office hours. See Office.

HOUSE. A dwelling; a building designed for the habitation and residence of men. Satterthwait v. Gibbs, 288 Pa. 428, 135 A. 862, 863.

"House" means, presumptively, a dwelling house; a building divided into floors and apartments, with four walls, a roof, and doors and chimneys; but it does not necessarily mean precisely this. Surman v. Darley, 14 Mees. & W. 183. It may mean any sort of structure or part thereof, whether used for human habitation or not. Dennis v. State, 71 Tex.Cr.R. 162, 158 S.W. 1008; Walker v. Terrell, Tex.Civ.App., 189 S.W. 75, 78.

"House" is not synonymous with "dwelling house." While the former is used in a broader and more comprehensive sense than the latter, it has a narrower and more restricted meaning than the word "building." State v. Garity, 46 N.H. 61.

A legislative assembly, or (where the bicameral system obtains) one of the two branches of the legislature; as the "house of lords," "house of representatives." Also a quorum of a legislative body. State of Ohio v. Cox, D.C. Ohio, 257 F. 334, 346.

The name "house" is also given to some collections of men other than legislative bodies, to some public institutions, and (colloquially) to mercantile firms or joint-stock companies.

Ancient House. One which has stood long enough to acquire an easement of support against the adjoining land or building. 3 Kent Comm. 437.

Bawdy House. A brothel; a house maintained for purposes of prostitution.

Beer House. See Beer.

Boarding House. See that title.

Duplex House. A double house. Kenwood Land Co. v. Hancock Inv. Co., 169 Mo.App. 715, 155 S.W. 861, 864.

Dwelling House. See that title.

House-bote. A species of estovers, belonging to a tenant for life or years, consisting in the right to take from the woods of the lessor or owner such timber as may be necessary for making repairs upon the house. Co.Litt. 41*b*.

House-burning. See Arson.

House-duty. A tax on inhabited houses imposed by 14 & 15 Vict. c. 36, in lieu of window-duty, which was abolished.

House of Commons. One of the constituent houses of the British parliament, composed of representatives of the counties, cities, and boroughs. The lower house, so called because the commons of the realm, that is, the knights, citizens, and burgesses returned to parliament, representing the whole body of the commons, sit there.

House of Correction. A reformatory. A place for the imprisonment of juvenile offenders, or those who have committed crimes of lesser magnitude. Ex parte Moon Fook, 72 Cal. 10, 12 P. 804.

House of Delegates. The official title of the lower branch of the legislative assembly of several of the American states, *e. g.,* Maryland and Virginia.

House of Ill Fame. A bawdy house; a brothel; a dwelling allowed by its chief occupant to be used as a resort of persons desiring unlawful sexual intercourse. People v. Lee, 307 Mich. 743, 12 N.W.2d 418, 421.

The authorities are conflicting as to whether and in what circumstances a house used solely by one woman for illicit intercourse is a house of ill fame. Fisher v. City of Paragould, 127 Ark. 268, 192 S.W. 219, 220.

House of Keys. The name of the lower branch of the legislative assembly or parliament of the Isle of Man, consisting of twenty-four representatives chosen by popular election.

House of Lords. The upper chamber of the British parliament. It comprises the archbishops and bishops, (called "Lords Spiritual,") the English peers sitting by virtue of hereditary right, sixteen Scotch peers elected to represent the Scotch peerage under the act of union, and twenty-eight Irish peers elected under similar provisions. The house of lords, as a judicial body, has ultimate appellate jurisdiction, and may sit as a court for the trial of impeachments.

House of Refuge. A prison for juvenile delinquents. A house of correction or reformatory.

House of Representatives. The name of the body forming the more popular and numerous branch of the congress of the United States; also of the similar branch in many of the state legislatures.

House of Worship. A building or place set apart for and devoted to the holding of religious services or exercises or public worship; a church or chapel or place similarly used. Old South Soc. v. Boston, 127 Mass. 379.

Inner House, Outer House. See those titles.

Mansion House. See Mansion.

Public House. An inn or tavern; a house for the entertainment of the public, or for the entertainment of all who come lawfully and pay regularly. Whatley v. State, 68 So. 491, 492, 12 Ala.App. 201. A place of public resort, particularly for purposes of drinking or gaming. In a more general sense, any house made public by the occupation carried on in it and the implied invitation to the public to enter, such as inns, taverns, drinking saloons, gambling houses, and perhaps also shops and stores. Cole v. State, 28 Tex.App. 536, 13 S.W. 859, 19 Am.St.Rep. 856.

Tippling House. A place where intoxicating liquors are sold in drams or small quantities to be drunk on the premises, and where men resort for drinking purposes.

HOUSEAGE. A fee paid for housing goods by a carrier, or at a wharf, etc.

HOUSEBREAKING. In criminal law. Breaking and entering a dwelling-house with intent to commit any felony therein. If done by night, it comes under the definition of "burglary."

Under statute housebreaking may consist in "breaking out" of a house after access had been gained without breaking. Lawson v. Commonwealth, 160 Ky. 180, 169 S.W. 587, 588, L.R.A. 1915 D, 972.

HOUSEHOLD, *adj.* Belonging to the house and family; domestic. Webster.

HOUSEHOLD, *n.* A family living together. Schurler v. Industrial Commission, 86 Utah, 284, 43 P.2d 696, 699, 100 A.L.R. 1085. Those who dwell under the same roof and compose a family. Webster. A man's family living together constitutes his household, though he may have gone to another state.

For "Family," see that title.

Synonymous with "family," but broader, in that it includes servants or attendants; all who are under one domestic head. Engebretson v. Austvold, 199 Minn. 399, 271 N.W. 809, 810.

HOUSEHOLD FURNITURE. See Furniture.

HOUSEHOLD SERVANTS AND HOUSEHOLD EMPLOYEES. Those employed in the mansion house, and do not embrace those who work out of doors upon the home place, and not regularly employed to do work within the curtilage. Raines v. Osborne, 184 N.C. 599, 114 S.E. 849.

HOUSEHOLD STUFF. This phrase, in a will, includes everything which may be used for the convenience of the house, as tables, chairs, bedding, and the like. But apparel, books, weapons, tools for artificers, cattle, victuals, and choses in action will not pass by those words, unless the context of the will clearly show a contrary intention. 1 Rop. Leg. 206. See Appeal of Hoopes, 60 Pa. 227, 100 Am.Dec. 562.

HOUSEHOLDER. The occupier of a house. Brande. More correctly, one who keeps house with his family; the head or master of a family. Webster; 18 Johns. 302. Berghean v. Berghean, 113 Ind.App. 412, 48 N.E.2d 1001, 1003. One who has a household; the head of a household. Gomez v. State, 75 Tex.Cr.R. 239, 170 S.W. 711, 713.

HOUSEKEEPER. One who is in actual possession of and who occupies a house, as distinguished from a "boarder," "lodger," or "guest." See Bell v. Keach, 80 Ky. 45. Head of a family. January v. Marler, 274 Mo. 543, 203 S.W. 817.

HOUSE LAW. A peculiar type of regulatory code, now largely obsolete, promulgated by the head of a royal or noble family, or of a prominent private family, governing intra-family relationships and acts with respect to policies of marriage, disposition of property, inheritance and the like. Usually these codes had no legal authority but were enforced within the family by sufficient personal and economic sanctions.

HOVEL. A place used by husbandmen to set their plows, carts, and other farming utensils out of the rain and sun. A shed; a cottage; a mean house.

HOWE. In old English law. A hill. Co. Litt. 5*b*.

HOWGH. See Haugh.

HOY. A small coasting vessel, usually sloop-rigged, used in conveying passengers and goods from place to place, or as a tender to larger vessels in port. Webster.

HOYMAN. The master or captain of a hoy.

HUCKSTER. A petty dealer and retailer of small articles of provisions, particularly farm and garden produce; a hawker; peddler. Hughes v. City of Detroit, 217 Mich. 567, 187 N.W. 530, 531.

HUCUSQUE. In old pleading. Hitherto. 2 Mod. 24.

HUDE–GELD. In old English law. An acquittance for an assault upon a trespassing servant. Supposed to be a mistake or misprint in Fleta for *"hinegeld."* Fleta, lib. 1, c. 47, § 20. Also the price of one's skin, or the money paid by a servant to save himself from a whipping. Du Cange.

HUE AND CRY. In old English law. A loud outcry with which felons (such as robbers, burglars, and murderers) were anciently pursued, and which all who heard it were bound to take up, and join in the pursuit, until the malefactor was taken. Bract. fols. 115*b*, 124; 4 Bl. Comm. 293. A written proclamation issued on the escape of a felon from prison, requiring all officers and people to assist in retaking him. 3 How. State Tr. 386.

HUEBRAS. In Spanish law. A measure of land equal to as much as a yoke of oxen can plow in one day. 2 White, Recop. (38), 49; Strother v. Lucas, 12 Pet. 443, 9 L.Ed. 1137.

HUI. Under the law of Hawaii. An association of persons in the ownership of land, members of which ordinarily hold the property as tenants in common. De Fries v. Scott, C.C.A.Hawaii, 268 F. 952, 959.

HUIS. L. Fr. A door. *"Al huis del esglise,"* at the door of the church. Bendloe, 133.

HUISSERIUM. A ship used to transport horses. Also termed *"uffer."*

HUISSIERS. In French law. Marshals; ushers; process-servers; sheriff's officers. Ministerial officers attached to the courts, to effect legal service of process required by law in actions, to issue executions, etc., and to maintain order during the sitting of the courts.

HULKA. In old records. A hulk or small vessel. Cowell.

HULKS. A place of punishment for convicts in England, abandoned with the reform in the punishment of convicts which began in England about 1840.

HULL. In a statute, 33 U.S.C.A. § 319, requiring ships of a certain size to carry lights, etc., it includes the forecastle deck. The Europe, 190 Fed. 475, 111 C.C.A. 307.

HULLUS. In old records. A hill. 2 Mon. Angl. 292; Cowell.

HUMAGIUM. A moist place. Mon. Angl.

HUMANITARIAN DOCTRINE. Another name for the doctrine of the last clear chance. See Last.

HUNDRED. Under the Saxon organization of England, each county or shire comprised an indefinite number of *hundreds*, each hundred containing ten *tithings*, or groups of ten families of freeholders or frankpledges. The hundred was governed by a high constable, and had its own court; but its most remarkable feature was the corporate responsibility of the whole for the crimes or defaults of the individual members. The introduction of this plan of organization into England is commonly ascribed to Alfred, but the idea, as well of the collective liability as of the division, was probably known to the ancient German peoples, as we find the same thing established in the Frankish kingdom under Clothaire, and in Denmark. See 1 Bl. Comm. 115; 4 Bl. Comm. 411.

HUNDRED COURT. In English law. A larger court-baron, being held for all the inhabitants of a particular *hundred*, instead of a manor. The free suitors are the judges, and the steward the registrar, as in the case of a court-baron. It is not a court of record, and resembles a court-baron in all respects except that in point of territory it is of greater jurisdiction. These courts have long since fallen into desuetude. 3 Bl. Comm. 34, 35; 3 Steph. Comm. 394, 395.

HUNDRED GEMOTE. Among the Saxons, a meeting or court of the freeholders of a hundred, which assembled, originally, twelve times a year, and possessed civil and criminal jurisdiction and ecclesiastical powers. 1 Reeve, Eng. Law, 7.

HUNDRED LAGH. The law of the hundred, or hundred court; liability to attend the hundred court. Spelman.

HUNDRED PENNY. In old English law. A tax collected from the hundred, by the sheriff or lord of the hundred.

HUNDRED ROLLS. Rolls embodying the result of investigations made by the commissioners in 1274 as to usurpations of the royal rights. 1 Holdsw. Hist. E. L. 48.

HUNDRED SECTA. The performance of suit and service at the hundred court.

HUNDRED SETENA. In Saxon law. The dwellers or inhabitants of a hundred. Cowell; Blount. Spelman suggests the reading of *sceatena* from Sax. *"sceat,"* a tax.

HUNDRED–FECTA. The performance of suit and service at the hundred court. Wharton.

HUNDREDARIUS. In old English law. A hundredary or hundredor. A name given to the chief officer of a hundred, as well as to the freeholders who composed it. Spel. voc. *"Hundredus."*

HUNDREDARY. The chief or presiding officer of a hundred.

HUNDREDES EARLDOR, or HUNDREDES MAN. The presiding officer in the hundred court. Anc. Inst. Eng.

HUNDREDORS. In English law. The inhabitants or freeholders of a hundred, anciently the suitors or judges of the hundred court. Persons impaneled or fit to be impaneled upon juries, dwelling within the hundred where the cause of action arose. Cromp. Jur. 217. It was formerly necessary to have some of these upon every panel of jurors. 3 Bl. Comm. 359, 360; 4 Steph. Comm. 370. The term "hundredor" was also used to signify the officer who had the jurisdiction of a hundred, and held the hundred court, and sometimes the bailiff of a hundred. Termes de la Ley; Cowell.

HUNDREDWEIGHT. A denomination of weight containing, according to the English system, 112 pounds; but in this country, generally, it consists of 100 pounds avoirdupois.

HUNG JURY. A jury so irreconcilably divided in opinion that they cannot agree upon any verdict.

HUNGER. The desire to eat. Hunger is no excuse for larceny; 1 Hale, Pl. Cr. 54; 4 Bla. Comm. 31. As to death from hunger, see Death.

HUNTING. The act of pursuing and taking wild animals; the chase. Commonwealth v. Bailey, 97 S.E. 774, 124 Va. 800. Robinson v. State, 76 S.E. 1061, 11 Ga.App. 847.

HURDEREFERST. A domestic; one of a family.

HURDLE. In English criminal law. A kind of sledge, on which convicted felons were drawn to the place of execution. See Draw, *v.*

HURRICANE. A storm of great violence or intensity, of which the particular characteristic is the high velocity of the wind. There is naturally no exact measure to distinguish between an ordinary storm and a hurricane, but the wind should reach a velocity of at least 50 or 60 miles an hour to be called by the latter name, or, as expressed in some of the cases, it should be sufficient to "throw down buildings." A hurricane is properly a circular storm in the nature of a cyclone. Pelican Ins. Co. v. Troy Co-op. Ass'n, 13 S.W. 980, 77 Tex. 225; Queen Ins. Co. v. Hudnut Co., 8 Ind.App. 22, 35 N.E. 397; George A. Hoagland and Co. v. Insurance Co. of North America, 131 Neb. 105, 267 N.W. 239, 241.

HURST, HYRST, HERST, or HIRST. A wood or grove of trees. Co. Litt. 4*b*.

HURT. In such phrases as "to the hurt or annoyance of another," or "hurt, molested, or restrained in his person or estate," this word is not restricted to physical injuries, but includes also mental pain, as well as discomfort or annoyance. Thurston v. Whitney, 2 Cush., Mass., 110.

HURTARDUS, or HURTUS. A ram or wether.

HURTO. In Spanish law. Theft. White, New Recop. b. 2, tit. 20.

HUSBAND. A married man; one who has a lawful wife living. The correlative of "wife." People v. Snyder, 353 Ill. 184, 187 N.E. 158, 160, 88 A.L.R. 1012.

Etymologically, the word signified the "house bond;" the man who, according to Saxon ideas and institutions, held around him the family, for whom he was in law responsible.

HUSBAND AND WIFE. One of the great domestic relationships; being that of a man and woman lawfully joined in marriage, by which, at common law, the legal existence of a wife is incorporated with that of her husband.

HUSBAND LAND. In old Scotch law. A quantity of land containing commonly six acres. Skene.

HUSBAND OF A SHIP. See Ship's Husband.

HUSBANDMAN. A farmer; a cultivator or tiller of the ground. The word "farmer" is colloquially used as synonymous with "husbandman," but originally meant a tenant who cultivates *leased* ground.

HUSBANDRIA. In old English law. Husbandry. Dyer, (Fr. Ed.) 35*b*.

HUSBANDRY. Agriculture; cultivation of the soil for food; farming, in the sense of operating land to raise provisions. Simons v. Lovell, 7 Heisk. (Tenn.) 516; State ex rel. Boynton v. Wheat Farming Co., 137 Kan. 697, 22 P.2d 1093.

HUSBREC. In Saxon law. The crime of housebreaking or burglary. Crabb, Eng. Law, 59, 308.

HUSCARLE. In old English law. A house servant or domestic; a man of the household. Spelman. A king's vassal, thane, or baron; an earl's man or vassal. A term of frequent occurrence in Domesday Book.

HUSFASTNE. He who holds house and land. Bract. l. 3, t. 2, c. 10.

HUSGABLUM. In old records. House rent; or a tax or tribute laid upon a house. Cowell; Blount.

HUSH-MONEY. A colloquial expression to designate a bribe to hinder information; pay to secure silence.

HUSTINGS. Council; court; tribunal. Apparently so called from being held within a building, at a time when other courts were held in the open air. It was a local court. The county court in the city of London bore this name. There were hustings at York, Winchester, Lincoln, and in other places similar to the London hustings. Also the raised place from which candidates for seats in parliament address the constituency, on the occasion of their nomination. Wharton.

In Virginia, some of the local courts are called "hustings," as in the city of Richmond. Smith v. Com., 6 Grat. Va., 696. The municipal courts established (in Virginia) in any city of over 5,000 inhabitants were at one time called *hustings* courts. Cent. Dict.

HUTESIUM ET CLAMOR. Hue and cry. See Hue and Cry.

HUTILAN. Taxes. Mon. Angl. i. 586.

HWATA, HWATUNG. In old English law. Augury; divination.

HYBERNAGIUM. In old English law. The season for sowing winter grain, between Michaelmas and Christmas. The land on which such grain was sown. The grain itself; winter grain or winter corn. Cowell.

HYBRID. A mongrel; an animal formed of the union of different species, or different genera; also (metaphorically) a human being born of the union of persons of different races.

HYD. In old English law. Hide; skin. A measure of land, containing according to some, a hundred acres, which quantity is also assigned to it in the *Dialogus de Scaccario.* It seems, however, that the hide varied in different parts of the kingdom.

HYDAGE. See Hidage.

HYDROMETER. An instrument for measuring the density of fluids. Being immersed in fluids, as in water, brine, beer, brandy, etc., it determines the proportion of their density, or their specific gravity, and thence their quality. See Rev. St. U. S. § 2918 (19 U.S.C.A. § 390).

HYDROSTATIC TEST. A method of determining whether or not a deceased infant was born alive, involving the removal of the lungs and the placing of them in a vessel of water; if the infant had breathed, the air in the lungs will cause them to float, though they may also float if decomposition has set in and gas has formed in the body. Morgan v. State, 256 S.W. 433, 148 Tenn. 417. Called, also, "docimasia pulmonum."

HYEMS, HIEMS. Lat. In the civil law. Winter. Dig. 43, 20, 4, 34. Written, in some of the old books, "*uems.*" Fleta, lib. 2, c. 73, §§ 16, 18.

HYGIENE. A system of principles or rules designed for the promotion of health. Lunn v. City of Auburn, 110 Me. 241, 85 A. 893, 894.

HYPNOTIC OR SOMNIFACIENT DRUGS. Drugs that produce sleep. State v. Jordan, 171 So.2d 650, 653, 247 La. 367.

HYPNOTISM. A condition, artificially produced, in which the person hypnotized, apparently asleep, acts in obedience to will of operator. Louis v. State, 24 Ala.App. 120, 130 So. 904, 905.

HYPOBOLUM. In the civil law. The name of the bequest or legacy given by the husband to his wife, at his death, above her dowry.

HYPOCHONDRIA; HYPOMANIA. See Insanity.

HYPOSTASIS. In medical jurisprudence. (1) The morbid deposition of a sediment of any kind in the body. (2) A congestion or flushing of the blood vessels, as in varicose veins. *Post-mortem hypostasis,* a peculiar lividity of the cadaver.

HYPOTHEC. In Scotland, the term *"hypothec"* is used to signify the landlord's right which, independently of any stipulation, he has over the crop and stocking of his tenant. It gives a security to the landlord over the crop of each year for the rent of that year, and over the cattle and stocking on the farm for the current year's rent, which last continues for three months after the last conventional term for the payment of the rent. Bell.

HYPOTHECA. "Hypotheca" was a term of the Roman law, and denoted a pledge or mortgage. As distinguished from the term *"pignus,"* in the same law, it denoted a mortgage, whether of lands or of goods, in which the subject in pledge remained in the possession of the mortgagor or debtor; whereas in the *pignus* the mortgagee or creditor was in the possession. Such an hypotheca might be either express or implied; express, where the parties upon the occasion of a loan entered into express agreement to that effect; or implied, as, *e. g.*, in the case of the stock and utensils of a farmer, which were subject to the landlord's right as a creditor for rent; whence the Scotch law of hypothec.

The word has suggested the term "hypothecate," as used in the mercantile and maritime law of England. Thus, under the factor's act, goods are frequently said to be "hypothecated;" and a captain is said to have a right to hypothecate his vessel for necessary repairs. Brown. See Mackeld. Rom. Law, §§ 334–359.

HYPOTHECARIA ACTIO. Lat. In the civil law. An hypothecary action; an action for the enforcement of an *hypotheca*, or right of mortgage; or to obtain the surrender of the thing mortgaged. Inst. 4, 6, 7; Mackeld. Rom. Law, § 356. Adopted in the Civil Code of Louisiana, under the name of *"l'action hypothècarie,"* (translated, "action of mortgage.") Civ. Code La. arts. 1433–1443; Code Prac. La. art. 61.

HYPOTHECARII CREDITORES. Lat. In the civil law. Hypothecary creditors; those who loaned money on the security of an *hypotheca*, (*q. v.*) Calvin.

HYPOTHECARY ACTION. The name of an action allowed under the civil law for the enforcement of the claims of a creditor by the contract of hypotheca. Lovell v. Cragin, 136 U.S. 130, 10 Sup.Ct. 1024, 34 L.Ed. 372.

An hypothecary action is a real action, which the creditor brings against the property which has been hypothecated to him by his debtor, in order to have it seized and sold for the payment of his debt. Code Prac.La. art. 61. In the hypothecary action proper, there is no pursuit of the person; the thing mortgaged is the debtor, and the action is directed against it. In this sense, the action is real. Wisdom v. Parker, 31 La.Ann. 52.

HYPOTHECATE. To pledge a thing without delivering the possession of it to the pledgee. "The master, when abroad, and in the absence of the owner, may *hypothecate* the ship, freight, and cargo, to raise money requisite for the completion of the voyage." 3 Kent, Comm. 171. Ogden v. Lathrop, 31 N.Y.Super.Ct. 651.

HYPOTHECATION. The term borrowed from the civil law. In so far as it is naturalized in English and American law, it means a contract of mortgage or pledge in which the subject-matter is not delivered into the possession of the pledgee or pawnee; or, conversely, a conventional right existing in one person over specific property of another, which consists in the power to cause a sale of the same, though it be not in his possession, in order that a specific claim of the creditor may be satisfied out of the proceeds. Whitney v. Peay, 24 Ark. 27.

The term is frequently used in our textbooks and reports, particularly upon the law of bottomry and maritime liens; thus a vessel is said to be hypothecated for the demand of one who has advanced money for supplies.

In the common law, there are but few, if any, cases of hypothecation, in the strict sense of the civil law; that is, a pledge without possession by the pledgee. The nearest approaches, perhaps, are cases of bottomry bonds and claims of materialmen, and of seamen for wages; but these are liens and privileges, rather than hypothecations. Story, Ballm. § 288.

HYPOTHECATION BOND. A bond given in the contract of bottomry or *respondentia*.

HYPOTHÈQUE. In French law. Hypothecation; a mortgage on real property; the right vested in a creditor by the assignment to him of real estate as security for the payment of his debt, whether or not it be accompanied by possession. See Civ. Code La. art. 3397.

It corresponds to the mortgage of real property in English law, and is a real charge, following the property into whosesoever hands it comes. It may be *légale*, as in the case of the charge which the state has over the lands of its accountants, or which a married woman has over those of her husband; *judiciaire*, when it is the result of a judgment of a court of justice; and *conventionelle*, when it is the result of an agreement of the parties. Brown.

HYPOTHESIS. A supposition, assumption, or theory; a theory set up by the prosecution, on a criminal trial, or by the defense, as an explanation of the facts in evidence, and a ground for inferring guilt or innocence, as the case may be, or as indicating a probable or possible motive for the crime.

HYPOTHETICAL QUESTION. A combination of assumed or proved facts and circumstances, stated in such form as to constitute a coherent and specific situation or state of facts, upon which the opinion of an expert is asked, by way of evidence on a trial. Howard v. People, 185 Ill. 552, 57 N.E. 441; State v. Smoak, 213 N.C. 79, 195 S.E. 72, 81.

It should be so framed as to recite all the facts in evidence which are relevant to the formation of an opinion and then, assuming the facts recited to be true, the witness should be asked whether he is able to form an opinion therefrom and if so to state his opinion. McMurrey v. State, 145 Tex.Cr.R. 439, 168 S.W.2d 858, 860.

HYPOTHETICAL YEARLY TENANCY. The basis, in England, of rating lands and hereditaments to the poor-rate, and to other rates and taxes that are expressed to be leviable or assessable in like manner as the poor-rate.

HYRNES. In old English law. A parish.

HYSTERIA. A paroxysmal disease or disorder of the nervous system, more common in females than males, not originating in any anatomical lesion, due to psychic rather than physical causes, and attended, in the acute or convulsive form, by extraordinary manifestations of secondary effects of extreme nervousness.

Hysteria is a state in which ideas control the body and produce morbid changes in its functions. Mœbius. A special psychic state, characterized by symptoms which can also be produced or reproduced by suggestion, and which can be treated by psychotherapy or persuasion, hysteric and hypnotic states being practically equivalent to each other. Babinski. A purely psychic or mental disorder due to hereditary predisposition. Charcot. A state resulting from a psychic lesion or nervous shock, leading to repression or aberration of the sexual instinct. Freud. Hysteria is much more common in women than in men, and was formerly thought to be due to some disorder of the uterus or sexual system; but it is now known that it may occur in men, in children, and in very aged persons of either sex.

In the convulsive form of hysteria, commonly called "hysterics" or "a fit of hysterics," there is nervestorm characterized by loss or abandonment of self-control in the expression of the emotions, particularly grief, by paroxysms of tears or laughter or both together, sensations of constriction as of a ball rising in the throat *(globus hystericus)*, convulsive movements in the chest, pelvis, and abdomen, sometimes leading to a fall with apparent unconsciousness, followed by a relapse into semiunconsciousness or catalepsy. In the non-convulsive forms, all kinds of organic paralyses may be simulated, as well as muscular contractions and spasms, tremor, loss of sensation *(anæsthesia)* or exaggerated sensation *(hyperæsthesia)*, disturbances of respiration, disordered appetite, accelerated pulse, hemorrhages in the skin *(stigmata)*, pain, swelling, or even dislocation of the joints, and great amenability to suggestion.

HYSTERO-EPILEPSY. See Epilepsy.

HYSTEROPOTMOI. Those who, having been thought dead, had, after a long absence in foreign countries, returned safely home; or those who, having been thought dead in battle, had afterwards unexpectedly escaped from their enemies and returned home. These, among the Romans, were not permitted to enter their own houses at the door, but were received at a passage opened in the roof. Enc. Lond.

HYSTEROTOMY. The Cæsarean operation. See Cæsarean Section.

HYTHE. In English law. A port, wharf, or small haven to embark or land merchandise at. Cowell; Blount.

I

I. The initial letter of the word *"Instituta,"* used by some civilians in citing the Institutes of Justinian. Tayl. Civil Law, 24.

I. C. C. Interstate Commerce Commission; Indian Claims Commission.

I—CTUS. An abbreviation for *"jurisconsultus,"* one learned in the law; a jurisconsult.

I. E. An abbreviation for *"id est,"* that is; that is to say.

I O U. A memorandum of debt, consisting of these letters, ("I owe you,") a sum of money, and the debtor's signature, is termed an "I O U." Kinney v. Flynn, 2 R.I. 329.

I. R. S. Internal Revenue Service.

IBERNAGIUM. In old English law. The season for sowing winter corn. Also spelled "hibernagium" and "hybernagium" (*q. v.*).

IBI SEMPER DEBET FIERI TRIATIO UBI JURATORES MELIOREM POSSUNT HABERE NOTITIAM. 7 Coke, 1*b*. A trial should always be had where the jurors can be the best informed.

IBIDEM. Lat. In the same place; in the same book; on the same page, etc. Abbreviated to *"ibid."* or *"ib."*

ICENI. The ancient name for the people of Suffolk, Norfolk, Cambridgeshire, and Huntingdonshire, in England.

ICONA. An image, figure, or representation of a thing. Du Cange.

ICTUS. In old English law. A stroke or blow from a club or stone; a bruise, contusion, or swelling produced by a blow from a club or stone, as distinguished from *"plaga,"* (a wound.) Fleta, lib. 1, c. 41, § 3.

ICTUS ORBIS. In medical jurisprudence. A maim, a bruise, or swelling; any hurt without cutting the skin. When the skin is cut, the injury is called a "wound." Bract. lib. 2, tr. 2, cc. 5, 24.

ID CERTUM EST QUOD CERTUM REDDI POTEST. That is certain which can be made certain. 2 Bl.Comm. 143; 1 Bl.Comm. 78; 4 Kent, Comm. 462; Broom, Max. 624.

ID CERTUM EST QUOD CERTUM REDDI POTEST, SED ID MAGIS CERTUM EST QUOD DE SEMETIPSO EST CERTUM. That is certain which can be made certain, but that is more certain which is certain of itself. 9 Coke, 47*a*.

ID EST. Lat. That is. Commonly abbreviated *"i. e."*

ID PERFECTUM EST QUOD EX OMNIBUS SUIS PARTIBUS CONSTAT. That is perfect which consists of all its parts. 9 Coke 9.

ID POSSUMUS QUOD DE JURE POSSUMUS. Lane, 116. We may do only that which by law we are allowed to do.

ID QUOD EST MAGIS REMOTUM, NON TRAHIT AD SE QUOD EST MAGIS JUNCTUM, SED E CONTRARIO IN OMNI CASU. That which is more remote does not draw to itself that which is nearer, but the contrary in every case. Co. Litt. 164.

ID QUOD NOSTRUM EST SINE FACTO NOSTRO AD ALIUM TRANSFERRI NON POTEST. That which is ours cannot be transferred to another without our act. Dig. 50, 17, 11.

ID SOLUM NOSTRUM QUOD DEBITIS DEDUCTIS NOSTRUM EST. That only is ours which remains to us after deduction of debts. Tray. Lat. Max. 227.

IDEM. Lat. The same. According to Lord Coke, *"idem"* has two significations, *sc., idem syllabis seu verbis,* (the same in syllabus or words,) and *idem re et sensu,* (the same in substance and in sense.) 10 Coke, 124*a*.

In Old Practice. The said, or aforesaid; said, aforesaid. Distinguished from *"prædictus"* in old entries, though having the same general signification. Townsh. Pl. 15, 16.

IDEM AGENS ET PATIENS ESSE NON POTEST. Jenk. Cent. 40. The same person cannot be both agent and patient; *i. e.,* the doer and person to whom the thing is done.

IDEM EST FACERE, ET NON PROHIBERE CUM POSSIS; ET QUI NON PROHIBIT, CUM PROHIBERE POSSIT, IN CULPÂ EST, (AUT JUBET.) 3 Inst. 158. To commit, and not to prohibit when in your power, is the same thing; and he who does not prohibit when he can prohibit is in fault, or does the same as ordering it to be done.

IDEM EST NIHIL DICERE, ET INSUFFICIENTER DICERE. It is the same thing to say nothing, and to say a thing insufficiently. To say a thing in an insufficient manner is the same as not to say it at all. Applied to the plea of a prisoner. 2 Inst. 178.

IDEM EST NON ESSE, ET NON APPARERE. It is the same thing not to be as not to appear. Jenk. Cent. 207. Not to appear is the same thing as not to be. Broom, Max. 165.

IDEM EST NON PROBARI ET NON ESSE; NON DEFICIT JUS, SED PROBATIO. What is not proved and what does not exist are the same; it is not a defect of the law, but of proof.

IDEM EST SCIRE AUT SCIRE DEBERE AUT POTUISSE. To be bound to know or to be able to know is the same as to know.

IDEM PER IDEM. The same for the same. An illustration of a kind that really adds no additional element to the consideration of the question.

IDEM SEMPER ANTECEDENTI PROXIMO REFERTUR. Co. Litt. 685. "The same" is always referred to its next antecedent.

IDEM SONANS. Sounding the same or alike; having the same sound. A term applied to names which are substantially the same, though slightly varied in the spelling, as "Lawrence" and "Lawrance," and the like. 1 Cromp. & M. 806; 3 Chit. Gen. Pr. 171; Golson v. State, 15 Ala.App. 420, 73 So. 753.

Two names are said to be *"idem sonantes"* if the attentive ear finds difficulty in distinguishing them when pronounced, or if common and long-continued usage has by corruption or abbreviation made them identical in pronunciation. State v. Griffie, 118 Mo. 188, 23 S.W. 878. The rule of *"idem sonans"* is that absolute accuracy in spelling names is not required in a legal document or proceedings either civil or criminal; that if the name, as spelled in the document, though different from the correct spelling thereof, conveys to the ear, when pronounced according to the commonly accepted methods, a sound practically identical with the correct name as commonly pronounced, the name thus given is a sufficient identification of the individual referred to, and no advantage can be taken of the clerical error. State v. Hattaway, 180 La. 12, 156 So. 159. But the doctrine of *"idem sonans"* has been much enlarged by modern decisions, to conform to the growing rule that a variance, to be material, must be such as has misled the opposite party to his prejudice.

IDENTICAL. Exactly the same for all practical purposes. Carn v. Moore, 74 Fla. 77, 76 So. 337, 340.

IDENTIFICATION. Proof of identity; the proving that a person, subject, or article before the court is the very same that he or it is alleged, charged, or reputed to be; as where a witness recognizes the prisoner at the bar as the same person whom he saw committing the crime; or where handwriting, stolen goods, counterfeit coin, etc., are recognized as the same which once passed under the observation of the person identifying them. Hall v. Cotton, 167 Ky. 464, 180 S.W. 779, 781, L.R.A.1916C, 1124.

IDENTITAS VERA COLLIGITUR EX MULTITUDINE SIGNORUM. True identity is collected from a multitude of signs. Bac. Max.

IDENTITATE NOMINIS. In English law. An ancient writ (now obsolete) which lay for one taken and arrested in any personal action, and committed to prison, by mistake for another man of the same name. Fitzh. Nat. Brev. 267.

IDENTITY. In the Law of Evidence. Sameness; the fact that a subject, person, or thing before a court is *the same* as it is represented, claimed, or charged to be. Burrill, Circ. Ev. 382, 453, 631, 644.

In Patent Law. Such sameness between two designs, inventions, combinations, etc., as will constitute the one an infringement of the patent granted for the other.

To constitute "identity of invention," and therefore infringement, not only must the result obtained be the same, but, in case the means used for its attainment is a combination of known elements, the elements combined in both cases must be the same, and combined in the same way, so that each element shall perform the same function: provided that the differences alleged are not merely colorable according to the rule forbidding the use of known equivalents. Electric Railroad Signal Co. v. Hall Railroad Signal Co., 114 U.S. 87, 5 Sup.Ct. 1069, 29 L.Ed. 96; Latta v. Shawk, 14 Fed.Cas. 1188. "Identity of design" means sameness of appearance, or, in other words, sameness of effect upon the eye,—not the eye of an expert, but of an ordinary intelligent observer. Smith v. Whitman Saddle Co., 148 U.S. 674, 13 Sup.Ct. 768, 37 L.Ed. 606.

IDEO. Lat. Therefore. Calvin.

IDEO CONSIDERATUM EST. Lat. Therefore it is considered. These were the words used at the beginning of the entry of judgment in an action, when the forms were in Latin. They are also used as a name for that portion of the record.

IDEOT. An old form for idiot (*q. v.*).

IDES. A division of time among the Romans. In March, May, July, and October, the Ides were on the 15th of the month; in the remaining months, on the 13th. This method of reckoning is still retained in the chancery of Rome, and in the calendar of the breviary. Wharton.

Under the word "Ides" in Bouvier's Law Dict., Rawle's 3d Rev., p. 1486, will be found a complete table of the calends, nones, and ides.

IDIOCHIRA. Græco-Lat. In the civil law. An instrument privately executed, as distinguished from such as were executed before a public officer. Cod. 8, 18, 11; Calvin.

IDIOCY, IDIOPATHIC INSANITY. See Insanity.

IDIOPATHIC DISEASE. A morbid state or condition not preceded or occasioned by any other disease. Christ v. Pacific Mutual Life Ins. Co., 231 Ill.App. 439.

IDIOT. A person who has been without understanding from his nativity, and whom the law, therefore, presumes never likely to attain any. Shelf. Lun. 2. See Insanity. State v. Haner, 186 Iowa, 1259, 173 N.W. 225; Jones v. Commonwealth, 154 Ky. 752, 159 S.W. 568, 569.

IDIOTA. In the Civil Law. An unlearned, illiterate, or simple person. Calvin. A private man; one not in office.

In Common Law. An idiot or fool.

IDIOTA INQUIRENDO, WRIT DE. This is the name of an old writ which directs the sheriff to inquire whether a man be an idiot or not. The inquisition is to be made by a jury of twelve men. Fitzh. Nat. Brev. 232. And, if the man were found an idiot, the profits of his lands and the custody of his person might be granted by the king to any subject who had interest enough to obtain them. 1 Bl.Comm. 303.

IDONEUM SE FACERE; IDONEARE SE. To purge one's self by oath of a crime of which one is accused.

IDONEUS. Lat. In the civil and common law. Sufficient; competent; fit or proper; responsible; unimpeachable. *Idoneus homo,* a responsible or solvent person; a good and lawful man. Sufficient; adequate; satisfactory. *Idonea cautio,* sufficient security.

IDONIETAS. In old English law. Ability or fitness (of a parson). Artic. Cleri, c. 13.

IF. In deeds and wills, this word, as a rule, implies a condition precedent, unless it be controlled by other words. 2 Crabb, Real Prop. p. 809, § 2152; Sutton v. West, 77 N.C. 431. Hughes v. John Hancock Mut. Life Ins. Co., 297 N.Y.S. 116, 122, 163 Misc. 31.

IFUNGIA. In old English law. The finest white bread, formerly called "cocked bread." Blount.

IGLISE. L. Fr. A church. Kelham. Another form of *"eglise."*

IGNIS JUDICIUM. Lat. The old judicial trial by fire. Blount.

IGNITEGIUM. In old English law. The curfew, or evening bell. Cowell. See Curfew.

IGNOMINY. Public disgrace; infamy; reproach; dishonor. Ignominy is the opposite of esteem. Wolff, § 145. See Brown v. Kingsley, 38 Iowa 220.

IGNORAMUS. Lat. "We are ignorant;" "We ignore it." Formerly the grand jury used to write this word on bills of indictment when, after having heard the evidence, they thought the accusation against the prisoner was groundless, intimating that, though the facts might possibly be true, the truth did not appear to them; but now they usually write in English the words "Not a true bill," or "Not found," if that is their verdict; but they are still said to *ignore* the bill. Brown.

IGNORANCE. The want or absence of knowledge.

Ignorance *of law* is want of knowledge or acquaintance with the laws of the land in so far as they apply to the act, relation, duty, or matter under consideration. Ignorance *of fact* is want of knowledge of some fact or facts constituting or relating to the subject-matter in hand. Marshall v. Coleman, 187 Ill. 556, 58 N.E. 628.

Ignorance is not a state of the mind in the sense in which sanity and insanity are. When the mind is ignorant of a fact, its condition still remains sound; the power of thinking, of judging, of willing, is just as complete before communication of the fact as after; the essence or texture, so to speak, of the mind, is not, as in the case of insanity, affected or impaired. Ignorance of a particular fact consists in this: that the mind, although sound and capable of healthy action, has never acted upon the fact in question, because the subject has never been brought to the notice of the perceptive faculties. Meeker v. Boylan, 28 N.J.Law, 274.

Synonyms

"Ignorance" and "error" or "mistake" are not convertible terms. The former is a lack of information or absence of knowledge; the latter, a misapprehension or confusion of information, or a mistaken supposition of the possession of knowledge. Error as to a fact may imply ignorance of the truth; but ignorance does not necessarily imply error. Culbreath v. Culbreath, 7 Ga. 70, 50 Am.Dec. 375.

General

Culpable ignorance is that which results from a failure to exercise ordinary care to acquire knowledge, and knowledge which could be acquired by the exercise of ordinary care is by law imputed to the person and he is held to have constructive knowledge. Luck v. Buffalo Lakes, Tex. Civ.App., 144 S.W.2d 672, 676.

Essential ignorance is ignorance in relation to some essential circumstance so intimately connected with the matter in question, and which so influences the parties, that it induces them to act in the business. Poth. Vente, nn. 3, 4; 2 Kent, Comm. 367.

Nonessential or *accidental ignorance* is that which has not of itself any necessary connection with the business in question, and which is not the true consideration for entering into the contract.

Involuntary ignorance is that which does not proceed from choice, and which cannot be overcome by the use of any means of knowledge known to a person and within his power; as the ignorance of a law which has not yet been promulgated.

Voluntary ignorance exists when a party might, by taking reasonable pains, have acquired the necessary knowledge. For example, every man might acquire a knowledge of the laws which have been promulgated. Doct. & Stud. 1, 46; Plowd. 343.

IGNORANTIA. Lat. Ignorance; want of knowledge. Distinguished from mistake, (error,) or wrong conception. Mackeld. Rom. Law, § 178; Dig. 22, 6. Divided by Lord Coke into *ignorantia facti* (ignorance of fact) and *ignorantia juris* (ignorance of law). And the former, he adds, is twofold—*lectionis et linquæ* (ignorance of reading and ignorance of language). 2 Coke, 3*b*.

IGNORANTIA EORUM QUÆ QUIS SCIRE TENETUR NON EXCUSAT. Ignorance of those things which one is bound to know excuses not. Hale, P. C. 42; Broom, Max. 267.

IGNORANTIA FACTI EXCUSAT. Ignorance of fact excuses or is a ground of relief. 2 Coke, 3*b*. Acts done and contracts made under mistake or ignorance of a material fact are voidable and relievable in law and equity. 2 Kent, Comm. 491, and notes.

IGNORANTIA FACTI EXCUSAT, IGNORANTIA JURIS NON EXCUSAT. Ignorance of the fact excuses; ignorance of the law excuses not. Every man must be taken to be cognizant of the law; otherwise there is no saying to what extent the excuse of ignorance may not be carried. 1 Coke, 177; Broom, Max. 253.

IGNORANTIA JURIS QUOD QUISQUE TENETUR SCIRE, NEMINEM EXCUSAT. Ignorance of the [or a] law, which every one is bound to know, excuses no man. A mistake in point of law is, in criminal cases, no sort of defense. 4 Bl. Comm. 27; 4 Steph.Comm. 81; Broom, Max. 253; 7 Car. & P. 456. And, in civil cases, ignorance of the law, with a full knowledge of the facts, furnishes no ground, either in law or equity, to rescind agreements, or reclaim money paid, or set aside solemn acts of the parties. 2 Kent, Comm. 491, and note.

IGNORANTIA JURIS SUI NON PRÆJUDICAT JURI. Ignorance of one's right does not prejudice the right. Lofft, 552.

IGNORANTIA LEGIS NEMINEM EXCUSAT. Ignorance of law excuses no one. 4 Bouv. Inst. no. 3828; 1 Story, Eq. Jur. § 111; 7 Watts, 374.

IGNORANTIA PRÆSUMITUR UBI SCIENTIA NON PROBATUR. Ignorance is presumed where knowledge is not proved. Bouvier.

IGNORARE LEGIS EST LATA CULPA. To be ignorant of the law is gross neglect. Bouvier.

IGNORATIO ELENCHI. Lat. A term of logic, sometimes applied to pleadings and to arguments on appeal, which signifies a mistake of the question, that is, the mistake of one who, failing to discern the real question which he is to meet and answer, addresses his allegations or arguments to a collateral matter or something beside the point. Case upon the Statute for Distribution, Wythe Va. 309.

IGNORATIS TERMINIS ARTIS, IGNORATUR ET ARS. Where the terms of an art are unknown, the art itself is unknown also. Co. Litt. 2*a*.

IGNORE. To be ignorant of, or unacquainted with. To disregard willfully; to refuse to recognize; to decline to take notice of. Cleburne County v. Morton, 69 Ark. 48, 60 S.W. 307.

To reject as groundless, false or unsupported by evidence; as when a grand jury *ignores* a bill of indictment.

IGNOSCITUR EI QUI SANGUINEM SUUM QUALITER REDEMPTUM VOLUIT. The law holds him excused from obligation who chose to redeem his blood (or life) upon any terms. Whatever a man may do under the fear of losing his life or limbs will not be held binding upon him in law. 1 Bl.Comm. 131.

IKBAL. Acceptance (of a bond, etc.). Wilson's Gloss. Ind.

IKBAL DAWA. Confession of judgment. Wilson's Gloss. Ind.

IKENILD STREET. One of the four great Roman roads in Britain; supposed to be so called from the *Iceni*.

IKRAH. Compulsion; especially constraint exercised by one person over another to do an illegal act, or to act contrary to his inclination. Wilson's Gloss. Ind.

IKRAR. Agreement, assent, or ratification. Wilson's Gloss. Ind.

IKRAR NAMA. A deed of assent and acknowledgment. Wilson's Gloss. Ind.

ILL. In old pleading. Bad; defective in law; null; naught; the opposite of good or valid.

ILL FAME. Evil repute; notorious bad character. Houses of prostitution, gaming houses, and other such disorderly places are called "houses of ill fame," and a person who frequents them is a person of ill fame. See Boles v. State, 46 Ala. 206.

ILLATA ET INVECTA. Lat. Things brought into the house for use by the tenant were so called, and were liable to the *jus hypothecæ* of Roman law, just as they are to the landlord's right of distress at common law.

ILLEGAL. Not authorized by law; illicit; unlawful; contrary to law; Protest of Downing, 164 Okl. 181, 23 P.2d 173.

Sometimes this term means merely that which lacks authority of or support from law; but more frequently it imports a violation. Etymologically, the word seems to convey the negative meaning only. But in ordinary use it has a severer, stronger signification; the idea of censure or condemnation for breaking law is usually presented. But the law implied in illegal is not necessarily an express statute. Things are called "illegal" for a violation of common-law principles. And the term does not imply that the act spoken of is immoral or wicked; it implies only a breach of the law. Tiedt v. Carstensen, 61 Iowa, 334, 16 N.W. 214.

ILLEGAL CONDITIONS. All those that are impossible, or contrary to law, immoral, or repugnant to the nature of the transaction.

ILLEGAL CONTRACT. An agreement with unlawful object and not merely lacking in valid subject-matter, but made for positively invalid purpose. American-LaFrance & Foamite Industries v. Arlington County, 169 Va. 1, 192 S.E. 758, 761.

ILLEGAL INTEREST. Usury; interest at a higher rate than the law allows. Parsons v. Babcock, 40 Neb. 119, 58 N.W. 726.

ILLEGAL TRADE. Such traffic or commerce as is carried on in violation of the municipal law, or contrary to the law of nations. See Illicit.

ILLEGALITY. That which is contrary to the principles of law, as contradistinguished from mere rules of procedure. It denotes a complete defect in the proceedings. Ex parte Davis, 118 Or. 693, 247 P. 809, 811.

ILLEGITIMACY. The condition before the law, or the social *status*, of a bastard; the state or condition of one whose parents were not intermarried at the time of his birth.

ILLEGITIMATE. That which is contrary to law; it is usually applied to bastards, or children born out of lawful wedlock.

The Louisiana Code divided illegitimate children into two classes: (1) Those born from two persons who, at the moment when such children were conceived, could have lawfully intermarried; and (2) those who are born from persons to whose marriage there existed at the time some legal impediment. Both classes, however, could be acknowledged and take by devise. Compton v. Prescott, 12 Rob., La., 56.

ILLEVIABLE. Not leviable; that cannot or ought not to be levied. Cowell.

ILLICENCIATUS. In old English law. Without license. Fleta, lib. 3, c. 5, § 12.

ILLICIT. Not permitted or allowed; prohibited; unlawful; as an *illicit* trade; *illicit* intercourse. State v. Miller, 60 Vt. 90, 12 A. 526.

ILLICIT CONNECTION. Unlawful sexual intercourse. State v. King, 9 S.D. 628, 70 N.W. 1046.

ILLICIT COHABITATION. The living together as man and wife of two persons who are not lawfully married, with the implication that they habitually practice fornication. Thomas v. United States, D.C.Mass., 14 F.2d 228, 229.

ILLICIT DISTILLERY. One carried on without a compliance with the provisions of the laws of the United States relating to the taxation of spirituous liquor. U. S. v. Johnson, C.C.Ga., 26 F. 684.

ILLICIT TRADE. Policies of marine insurance usually contain a covenant of warranty against "illicit trade," meaning thereby trade which is forbidden, or declared unlawful, by the laws of the country where the cargo is to be delivered. 1 Pars. Mar. Ins. 614.

"It is not the same with 'contraband trade,' although the words are sometimes used as synonymous. Illicit or prohibited trade is one which cannot be carried on without a distinct violation of some positive law of the country where the transaction is to take place."

ILLICITE. Lat. Unlawfully. This word has a technical meaning, and is requisite in an indictment where the act charged is unlawful; as in the case of a riot. 2 Hawk. P. C. c. 25, § 96.

ILLICITUM COLLEGIUM. Lat. An illegal corporation.

ILLITERATE. Unlettered; ignorant; unlearned. Generally used of one who cannot read and write. In re Succession of Carroll, 28 La.Ann. 388.

ILLNESS. In insurance law. A disease or ailment of such a character as to affect the general soundness and healthfulness of the system seriously, and not a mere temporary indisposition which does not tend to undermine or weaken the constitution of the insured. Prudential Ins. Co. of America v. Sellers, 54 Ind.App. 326, 102 N.E. 894, 897. Zogg v. Bankers' Life Co. of Des Moines, Iowa, C.C.A.W.Va., 62 F.2d 575, 578.

ILLOCABLE. Incapable of being placed out or hired.

ILLUD. Lat. That.

ILLUD, QUOD ALIAS LICITUM NON EST, NECESSITAS FACIT LICITUM; ET NECESSITAS INDUCIT PRIVILEGIUM QUOAD JURA PRIVATA. Bac. Max. That which is otherwise not permitted, necessity permits; and necessity makes a privilege as to private rights.

ILLUD, QUOD ALTERI UNITUR, EXTINGUITUR, NEQUE AMPLIUS PER SE VACARE LICET. Godol. Ecc. Law, 169. That which is united to another is extinguished, nor can it be any more independent.

ILLUSION. In medical jurisprudence. An image or impression in the mind, excited by some external object addressing itself to one or more of the senses, but which, instead of corresponding with the reality, is perverted, distorted, or wholly mistaken, the error being attributable to the imagination of the observer, not to any defect in the organs of sense. See Hallucination, and see *"Delusion,"* under Insanity.

ILLUSORY. Deceiving by false appearances; nominal, as distinguished from substantial; fallacious; illusive. Bolles v. Toledo Trust Co., 144 Ohio St. 195, 58 N.E.2d 381, 390.

ILLUSORY APPOINTMENT. Formerly the appointment of a merely nominal share of the property to one of the objects of a power, in order to escape the rule that an exclusive appointment could not be made unless it was authorized by the instrument creating the power, was considered illusory and void in equity. But this rule has been abolished in England. (1 Wm. IV. c. 46; 37 & 38 Vict. c. 37.) Sweet. Brown v. Fidelity Union Trust Co., 126 N.J.Eq. 406, 9 A.2d 322.

ILLUSORY APPOINTMENT ACT. The statute 1 Wm. IV. c. 46. This statute enacts that no appointment made after its passing, (July 16, 1830,) in exercise of a power to appoint property, real or personal, among several objects, shall be invalid, or impeached in equity, on the ground that an unsubstantial, illusory, or nominal share only was thereby appointed, or left unappointed, to devolve upon any one or more of the objects of such power; but that the appointment shall be valid in equity, as at law. See, too, 37 & 38 Vict. c. 37. Wharton.

ILLUSTRIOUS. The prefix to the title of a prince of the blood in England.

IMAGINE. In English law. In cases of treason the law makes it a crime to imagine the death of the king. But, in order to complete the crime, this act of the mind must be demonstrated by some overt act. The terms "imagining" and "compassing" are in this connection synonymous. 4 Bl. Comm. 78.

IMAN, IMAM, or IMAUM. A Mohammedan prince having supreme spiritual as well as temporal power; a regular priest of the mosque.

IMBARGO. An old form of "embargo," (*q. v.*) St. 18 Car. II. c. 5.

IMBASING OF MONEY. The act of mixing the specie with an alloy below the standard of sterling. 1 Hale, P. C. 102.

IMBECILITY. See Insanity.

IMBEZZLE. An occasional or obsolete form of "embezzle" (*q. v.*).

IMBLADARE. In old English law. To plant or sow grain. Bract. fol. 176*b*.

IMBRACERY. See Embracery.

IMBROCUS. A brook, gutter, or water-passage. Cowell.

IMITATION. The making of one thing in the similitude or likeness of another; as, counterfeit coin is said to be made "in imitation" of the genuine. Wagner v. Daly, 67 Hun. 477, 22 N.Y.S. 493.

An imitation of a trade-mark is that which so far resembles the genuine trade-mark as to be likely to induce the belief that it is genuine, whether by the use of words or letters similar in appearance or in sound, or by any sign, device, or other means.

The test of "colorable imitation" is, not whether a difference may be recognized between the names of two competing articles when placed side by side, but whether the difference will be recognized by the purchaser with no opportunity for comparison. The Best Foods v. Hemphill Packing Co., D.C.Del., 5 F.2d 355, 357.

IMMATERIAL. Not material, essential, or necessary; not important or pertinent; not decisive; of no substantial consequence; without weight; of no significance. State v. Cordaro, 211 Iowa 224, 233 N.W. 51, 53.

IMMATERIAL AVERMENT. An averment alleging with needless particularity or unnecessary circumstances what is material and necessary, and which might properly have been stated more generally, and without such circumstances and particulars; or, in other words, a statement of unnecessary particulars in connection with and as descriptive of what is material. Dunlap v. Kelly, 105 Mo.App. 1, 78 S.W. 664; Bulova v. E. L. Barnett, Inc., 111 Misc. 150, 181 N.Y.S. 247, 250.

IMMATERIAL FACTS. Those which are not essential to the right of action or defense.

IMMATERIAL ISSUE. In pleading. An issue taken on an immaterial point; that is, a point not proper to decide the action. Steph. Pl. 99, 130; 2 Tidd, Pr. 921.

IMMATERIAL VARIANCE. Discrepancy between the pleading and proof of a character so slight that the adverse party cannot say that he was misled thereby. E. B. Ryan Co. v. Russell, 52 Mont. 596, 161 P. 307, 308.

IMMEDIATE. Present; at once; without delay; not deferred by any interval of time. In this sense, the word, without any very precise signification, denotes that action is or must be taken either instantly or without any considerable loss of time. A reasonable time in view of particular facts and circumstances of case under consideration. Mullins v. Masonic Protective Ass'n, 181 Mo. App. 394, 168 S.W. 843, 844. George v. Aetna Casualty and Surety Co., 121 Neb. 647, 238 N.W. 36, 38. Next in line or relation; directly connected; not secondary or remote. Bunner v. Patti, 343 Mo. 274, 121 S.W.2d 153, 155. Not separated in respect to place; not separated by the intervention of any intermediate object, cause, relation, or right. Thus we speak of an action as prosecuted for the "immediate benefit" of A., of a devise as made to the "immediate issue" of B., etc.

IMMEDIATE CAUSE. The last of a series or chain of causes tending to a given result, and which, of itself, and without the intervention of any further cause, directly produces the result or event. Deisenrieter v. Kraus-Merkel Malting Co., 72 N.W. 735, 97 Wis. 279; Longabaugh v. Railroad Co., 9 Nev. 271. See, also, Proximate.

A cause may be immediate in this sense, and yet not "proximate;" and conversely, the proximate cause (that which directly and efficiently brings about the result) may not be immediate. The familiar illustration is that of a drunken man falling into the water and drowning. His intoxication is the proximate cause of his death, if it can be said that he would not have fallen into the water when sober; but the immediate cause of death is suffocation by drowning.

IMMEDIATE CONTROL (of motor vehicle upon approaching or traversing railroad crossing). Such constant control as would enable driver to instantly govern vehicle's movements, including the power to stop within a distance in which such a vehicle, in good mechanical condition, driven by a reasonably skillful driver, and traveling at a lawful rate of speed, could be stopped. Central of Georgia Ry. Co. v. Burton, 125 S.E. 868, 33 Ga. App. 199.

IMMEDIATE DESCENT. See Descent.

IMMEDIATE NOTICE. As required by policy as for proof of loss means within a reasonable time. Lydon v. New York Life Ins. Co., C.C.A.Mo., 89 F.2d 78, 82.

IMMEDIATELY. Without interval of time, without delay, straightway, or without any delay or lapse of time. Drumbar v. Jeddo-Highland Coal Co., 155 Pa.Super. 57, 37 A.2d 25, 27.

The words, "immediately" and "forthwith" have the same meaning. They are stronger than the expression "within a reasonable time" and imply prompt, vigorous action without any delay. Alsam Holding Co. v. Consolidated Taxpayers' Mut. Ins. Co., 4 N.Y.S.2d 498, 505, 167 Misc. 732.

IMMEMORIAL. Beyond human memory; time out of mind.

IMMEMORIAL POSSESSION. In Louisiana. Possession of which no man living has seen the beginning, and the existence of which he has learned from his elders. Civ.Code La. art. 766.

IMMEMORIAL USAGE. A practice which has existed time out of mind; custom; prescription. Miller v. Garlock, 8 Barb. (N.Y.) 154.

IMMEUBLES. Fr. These are, in French law, the immovables of English law. Things are *immeubles* from any one of three causes: (1) From their own nature, *e. g.*, lands and houses; (2) from their destination, *e. g.*, animals and instruments of agriculture when supplied by the landlord; or (3) by the object to which they are annexed, *e. g.*, easements. Brown.

IMMIGRATION. The coming into a country of foreigners for purposes of permanent residence. The correlative term "emigration" denotes the act of such persons in leaving their former country.

IMMINENT. Near at hand; mediate rather than immediate; close rather than touching; impending; on the point of happening; threatening; menacing; perilous. Furlow v. State, 72 Fla. 464, 73 So. 362; Jaroniec v. C. O. Hasselbarth, Inc., 228 N.Y.S. 302, 304, 223 App.Div. 182.

IMMINENT DANGER. In relation to homicide in self-defense, this term means immediate danger, such as must be instantly met, such as cannot be guarded against by calling for the assistance of others or the protection of the law. State v. Smith, 43 Or. 109, 71 P. 973. Or, as otherwise defined, such an appearance of threatened and impending injury as would put a reasonable and prudent man to his instant defense. State v. Fontenot, 50 La.Ann. 537, 23 So. 634, 69 Am.St.Rep. 455.

IMMINENTLY DANGEROUS ARTICLE. One that is reasonably certain to place life or limb in peril. Employers' Liability Assur. Corporation v. Columbus McKinnon Chain Co., D.C.N.Y., 13 F.2d 128.

IMMISCERE. Lat. In the civil law. To mix or mingle with; to meddle with; to join with. Calvin.

IMMITTERE. Lat. In the Civil Law. To put or let into, as a beam into a wall. Calvin.; Dig. 50, 17, 242, 1.

In old English law, to put cattle on a common. Fleta, lib. 4, c. 20, § 7.

IMMOBILIA SITUM SEQUUNTUR. Immovable things follow their site or position; are governed by the law of the place where they are fixed. 2 Kent, Comm. 67. Cf. Mobilia Sequuntur Personam.

IMMOBILIS. Lat. Immovable. *Immobilia* or *res immobiles,* immovable things, such as lands and buildings. Mackeld. Rom. Law, § 160.

IMMODERATE. Exceeding just, usual, or suitable bounds; not within reasonable limits. United States v. Oglesby Grocery Co., D.C.Ga., 264 F. 691, 695; People v. McMurchy, 249 Mich. 147, 228 N.W. 723, 726.

IMMORAL. Contrary to good morals; inconsistent with the rules and principles of morality; inimical to public welfare according to the standards of a given community, as expressed in law or otherwise. Exchange Nat. Bank of Fitzgerald v. Henderson, 139 Ga. 260, 77 S.E. 36, 37, 51 L.R.A. (N.S.) 549. Morally evil; impure; unprincipled; vicious; or dissolute. U. S. v. One Book, Entitled "Contraception," by Marie C. Stopes, D.C.N.Y., 51 F.2d 525, 527.

IMMORAL CONDUCT. Within rules authorizing disbarment of attorney is that conduct which is willful, flagrant, or shameless, and which shows a moral indifference to the opinions of the good and respectable members of the community. Warkentin v. Kleinwachter, 166 Okl. 218, 27 P.2d 160.

IMMORAL CONSIDERATION. One contrary to good morals, and therefore invalid. Contracts based upon an immoral consideration are generally void.

IMMORAL CONTRACTS. Contracts founded upon considerations *contra bonos mores* are void.

IMMORALITY. That which is *contra bonos mores.* See Immoral.

IMMOVABLES. In the civil law. Property which, from its nature, destination, or the object to which it is applied, cannot move itself, or be removed. Breaux v. Ganucheau, 3 La.App. 481, 482; Scott v. Brennan, 3 La.App. 452, 453.

Immovable things are, in general, such as cannot either move themselves or be removed from one place to another. But this definition, strictly speaking, is applicable only to such things as are immovable by their own nature, and not to such as are so only by the disposition of the law.

IMMUNITY. Exemption, as from serving in an office, or performing duties which the law generally requires other citizens to perform. Ex parte Levy, 43 Ark. 54, 51 Am.Rep. 550. Freedom from duty or penalty. Leatherwood v. Hill, 10 Ariz. 243, 89 P. 521, 523. The term aptly describes an exemption from taxation. Buchanan v. Knoxville & O. R. Co., C.C.A.Tenn., 71 F. 324, 334, 18 C.C.A. 122. A particular privilege. Webster, Dict.; Sacramento Orphanage, etc., Home v. Chambers, 25 Cal.App. 536, 144 P. 317, 319.

IMPAIR. To weaken, to make worse, to lessen in power, diminish, or relax, or otherwise affect in an injurious manner. Davey v. Ætna L. Ins. Co., C.C.N.J., 20 F. 482; State ex rel. Woman's Ben. Ass'n v. Port of Palm Beach Dist., 121 Fla. 746, 164 So. 851, 856.

IMPAIRING THE OBLIGATION OF CONTRACTS. A law which impairs the obligation of a contract is one which renders the contract in itself less valuable or less enforceable, whether by changing its terms and stipulations, its legal qualities and conditions, or by regulating the remedy for its enforcement. City of Indianapolis v. Robison, 186 Ind. 660, 117 N.E. 861.

To "impair the obligation of a contract" within Const. U.S. art. 1, § 10, is to weaken it, lessen its value, or make it worse in any respect or in any degree, and any law which changes the intention and legal effect of the parties, giving to one a greater and to the other a less interest or benefit, or which imposes conditions not included in the contract or dispenses with the performance of those included, impairs the obligation of the contract. O'Connor v. Hartford Accident & Indemnity Co., 97 Conn. 8, 115 A. 484, 486.

A statute "impairs the obligation of a contract" when by its terms it nullifies or materially changes existing contract obligations. Oil Fork Development Co. v. Huddleston, 202 Ky. 261, 259 S.W. 334, 335; McNee v. Wall, D.C.Fla., 4 F.Supp. 496, 498.

The word "impair" means, according to the standard writers in our language, simply "to diminish; to injure; to make worse," etc. It is remarkable that in framing the provision of the federal Constitution providing that no law should be passed, "impairing the obligation of any contract," the convention did not use the term "lessen" or "decrease" or "destroy," but one more comprehensive, which prohibited making worse in any respect a contract legitimate in its creation. The object, then, of its provision, may have been to establish an important principle, and that was the entire inviolability of contracts. Blair v. Williams, 14 Ky. (4 Litt.) 34, 35; Lapsley v. Brashears, 14 Ky. (4 Litt.) 47, 69.

See 2 Story, Const. §§ 1374–1399; 1 Kent, Comm. 413–422; Pom. Const. Law; Black, Const. Law (3d Ed.) p. 720 *et seq.*

IMPALARE. To impound. Du Cange.

IMPANEL. In English practice. To impanel a jury signifies the entering by the sheriff upon a piece of parchment, termed a "panel," the names of the jurors who have been summoned to appear in court on a certain day to form a jury of the country to hear such matters as may be brought before them. Brown.

In American practice. Besides the meaning above given, "impanel" signifies the act of the clerk of the court in making up a list of the jurors who have been selected for the trial of a particular cause. All the steps of ascertaining who shall be the proper jurors to sit in the trial of a particular case up to the final formation. People v. Poole, 284 Ill. 39, 119 N.E. 916.

Impaneling has nothing to do with drawing, selecting, or swearing jurors, but means simply making the list of those who have been selected. Porter v. People, 7 How.Prac. (N.Y.) 441; State ex rel. Green v. Pearson, 153 Fla. 314, 14 So.2d 565, 567.

IMPARCARE. In old English law. To impound. Reg. Orig. 92*b*. To shut up, or confine in prison. *Inducti sunt in carcerem et imparcati,* they were carried to prison and shut up. Bract. fol. 124.

IMPARGAMENTUM. The right of impounding cattle.

IMPARL. To have license to settle a litigation amicably; to obtain delay for adjustment.

IMPARLANCE. In early practice, imparlance meant time given to either of the parties to an action to answer the pleading of the other. It thus amounted to a continuance of the action to a further day. Literally the term signified leave given to the parties to *talk together; i. e.,* with a view to settling their differences amicably. But in modern practice it denotes a time given to the defendant to plead.

A general imparlance is the entry of a general prayer and allowance of time to plead till the next term, without reserving to the defendant the benefit of any exception; so that after such an imparlance the defendant cannot object to the jurisdiction of the court, or plead any matter in abatement. This kind of imparlance is always from one term to another. Colby v. Knapp, 13 N.H. 175; Mack v. Lewis, 67 Vt. 383, 31 Atl. 888.

A general special imparlance contains a saving of all exceptions whatsoever, so that the defendant after this may plead not only in abatement, but he may also plead a plea which affects the jurisdiction of the court, as privilege. He cannot, however, plead a tender, and that he was always ready to pay, because by craving time, he admits that he is not ready, and so falsifies his plea.

A special imparlance reserves to the defendant all exceptions to the writ, bill, or count; and therefore after it the defendant may plead in abatement, though not to the jurisdiction of the court. 1 Tidd, Pr. 462, 463.

IMPARSONEE. L. Fr. In ecclesiastical law. One who is inducted and in possession of a benefice. Parson imparsonee (*persona impersonata*). Cowell; Dyer, 40.

IMPARTIAL. Favoring neither; disinterested; treating all alike; unbiased; equitable, fair, and just. Evans v. Superior Court in and for Los Angeles County, 107 Cal.App. 372, 290 P. 662, 666.

The provision of the Bill of Rights requiring that the accused shall have a fair trial by an impartial jury, means that the jury must be not partial, not favoring one party more than another, unprejudiced, distinterested, equitable, and just, and that the merits of the case shall not be prejudged. Duncan v. State, 79 Tex.Cr.R. 206, 184 S.W. 195, 196.

IMPARTIAL JURY. Within constitutional provision is one which is of impartial frame of mind at beginning of trial, is influenced only by legal and competent evidence produced during trial, and bases its verdict upon evidence connecting defendant with the commission of the crime charged. Const.U.S. Amend. 6. Durham v. State, 182 Tenn. 577, 188 S.W.2d 555, 558, 160 A.L.R. 746.

For "Fair and Impartial Jury," and "Fair and Impartial Trial," see those titles.

IMPARTIBLE FEUD. See Feudum Individuum.

IMPATRONIZATION. In ecclesiastical law. The act of putting into full possession of a benefice.

IMPEACH. To accuse; to charge a liability upon; to sue. To dispute, disparage, deny, or contradict; as, to impeach a judgment or decree; or as used in the rule that a jury cannot "impeach their verdict." Wolfgram v. Schoepke, 123 Wis. 19, 100 N. W. 1056. To proceed against a public officer for crime or misfeasance, before a proper court, by the presentation of a written accusation called "articles of impeachment."

In the Law of Evidence. To call in question the veracity of a witness, by means of evidence adduced for that purpose, or the adducing of proof that a witness is unworthy of belief. Johnston v. Belk-McKnight Co. of Newberry, 188 S.C. 149, 198 S.E. 395, 399.

IMPEACHMENT. A criminal proceeding against a public officer, before a *quasi* political court, instituted by a written accusation called "articles of impeachment;" for example, a written accusation by the house of representatives of the United States to the senate of the United States against an officer.

"Impeachment" of the Governor, within the meaning of section 16, art. 6, of the Constitution, is the adoption of articles of impeachment by the House of Representatives, and the presentation thereof to the Senate, and the indication by that body that the same are accepted for the purpose of permitting prosecution thereof, and the impeachment of the Governor operates to suspend him; the duties and emoluments of the office automatically devolving upon the Lieutenant Governor for the remainder of the term or until the disability is removed by the acquittal of the Governor of the charges preferred against him. State v. Chambers, 96 Okl. 78, 220 P. 890, 891, 30 A.L.R. 1144; People ex rel. Robin v. Hayes, 143 N.Y.S. 325, 329, 82 Misc. 165.

In England, a prosecution by the house of commons before the house of lords of a commoner for treason, or other high crimes and misdemeanors, or of a peer for any crime.

Evidence

The adducing of proof that a witness is unworthy of belief. State v. Roybal, 33 N.M. 540, 273 P. 919, 922.

General

Articles of impeachment. The formal written allegation of the causes for an impeachment, answering the same purpose as an indictment in an ordinary criminal proceeding.

Collateral impeachment. See Collateral attack.

Impeachment of annuity. A term sometimes used in English law to denote anything that operates as a hindrance, impediment or obstruction of the making of the profits out of which the annuity is to arise. Pitt v. Williams, 4 Adol. & El. 885.

Impeachment of waste. Liability for waste committed; or a demand or suit for compensation for waste committed upon lands or tenements by a tenant thereof who, having only a leasehold or particular estate, had no right to commit waste. 2 Bl. Comm. 283; Sanderson v. Jones, 6 Fla. 480, 63 Am.Dec. 217.

Impeachment of witness. Adducing proof that a witness who has testified in a cause is unworthy of credit. White v. Railroad Co., 142 Ind. 648, 42 N.E. 456.

IMPECHIARE. To impeach, to accuse, or prosecute for felony or treason.

IMPEDE. To obstruct; hinder; check; delay. Erie R. Co. v. Board of Public Utility Com'rs, 98 A. 13, 19, 89 N.J.L. 57.

IMPEDIATUS. Disabled from mischief by expeditation (*q. v.*). Cowell.

IMPEDIENS. In old practice. One who hinders; an impedient. The defendant or deforciant in a fine was sometimes so called. Cowell; Blount.

IMPEDIMENTO. In Spanish law. A prohibition to contract marriage, established by law between certain persons.

IMPEDIMENTS. Disabilities, or hindrances to the making of contracts, such as coverture, infancy, want of reason, etc.

In the Civil Law. Bars to marriage.

Absolute impediments are those which prevent the person subject to them from marrying at all, without either the nullity of marriage or its being punishable. *Dirimant impediments* are those which render a marriage void; as where one of the contracting parties is unable to marry by reason of a prior undissolved marriage. *Prohibitive impediments* are those which do not render the marriage null, but subject the parties to a punishment. *Relative impediments* are those which regard only certain persons with respect to each other; as between two particular persons who are related within the prohibited degrees. Bowyer, Mod. Civil Law, 44, 45.

IMPEDITOR. In old English law. A disturber in the action of *quare impedit*. St. Marlb. c. 12.

IMPENSÆ. Lat. In the civil law. Expenses; outlays. Mackeld. Rom. Law, § 168; Calvin. Divided into necessary, (*necessariœ,*) useful, (*utiles,*) and tasteful or ornamental, (*voluptuariœ.*) Dig. 50, 16, 79. See Id. 25, 1.

IMPERATIVE. Mandatory. See Directory.

IMPERATOR. Emperor. The title of the Roman emperors, and also of the Kings of England before the Norman conquest. Cod. 1, 14, 12; 1 Bl. Comm. 242. See Emperor.

IMPERFECT. As used in various legal compound terms, this word means defective or incomplete; wanting in some legal or formal requisite; wanting in legal sanction or effectiveness; as in speaking of imperfect "obligations," "ownership," "rights," "title," "usufruct," or "war." See those nouns.

IMPERII MAJESTAS EST TUTELÆ SALUS. Co. Litt. 64. The majesty of the empire is the safety of its protection.

IMPERITIA. Lat. Unskillfulness; want of skill.

IMPERITIA CULPÆ ADNUMERATUR. Want of skill is reckoned as *culpa;* that is, as blamable conduct or neglect. Dig. 50, 17, 132.

IMPERITIA EST MAXIMA MECHANICORUM PŒNA. Unskillfulness is the greatest punishment of mechanics; [that is, from its effect in making them liable to those by whom they are employed.] 11 Coke, 54*a*. The word *"pœna"* in some translations is erroneously rendered "fault."

IMPERIUM. The right to command, which includes the right to employ the force of the state to enforce the laws. This is one of the principal attributes of the power of the executive. 1 Toullier, no. 58.

IMPERSONALITAS. Lat. Impersonality. A mode of expression where no reference is made to any person, such as the expression *"ut dicitur,"* (as is said.) Co. Litt. 352*b*.

IMPERSONALITAS NON CONCLUDIT NEC LIGAT. Co. Litt. 352 *b*. Impersonality neither concludes nor binds.

IMPERTINENCE. Irrelevancy; the fault of not properly pertaining to the issue or proceeding. The introduction of any matters into a bill, answer, or other pleading or proceeding in a suit, which are not properly before the court for decision, at any particular stage of the suit. Story, Eq. Pl. § 266; Harrison v. Perea, 18 S.Ct. 129, 168 U.S. 311, 42 L.Ed. 478.

In Practice. A question propounded to a witness, or evidence offered or sought to be elicited, is called "impertinent" when it has no logical bearing upon the issue, is not necessarily connected with it, or does not belong to the matter in hand. 1 Whart. Ev. § 20.

On the distinction between pertinency and relevancy, we may quote the following remark of Dr. Wharton: *"Relevancy* is that which conduces to the proof of a *pertinent* hypothesis; a pertinent hypothesis being one which, if sustained, would logically influence the issue."

IMPERTINENT. In Equity Pleading. That which does not belong to a pleading, interrogatory, or other proceeding; out of place; superfluous; irrelevant. Chew v. Eagan, 87 N.J.Eq. 80, 99 A. 611; Bean v. Central Maine Power Co., 133 Me. 9, 173 A. 498, 501.

At Law. A term applied to matter not necessary to constitute the cause of action or ground of defense. Cowp. 683; 5 East, 275; Tucker v. Randall, 2 Mass. 283. It constitutes surplusage, (which see.)

IMPESCARE. In old records. To impeach or accuse. *Impescatus,* impeached. Blount.

IMPETITIO VASTI. Impeachment of waste, (*q. v.*)

IMPETRARE. In old English practice. To obtain by request, as a writ or privilege. Bract. fols. 57, 172*b*. This application of the word seems to be derived from the civil law. Calvin.

IMPETRATION. In old English law. The obtaining anything by petition or entreaty. Particularly, the obtaining of a benefice from Rome by solicitation, which benefice belonged to the disposal of the king or other lay patron. Webster; Cowell.

IMPIER. Umpire (*q. v.*).

IMPIERMENT. Impairing or prejudicing. Jacob.

IMPIGNORATA. Pledged; given in pledge, (*pignori data;*) mortgaged. A term applied in Bracton to land. Bract. fol. 20.

IMPIGNORATION. The act of pawning or putting to pledge.

IMPIUS ET CRUDELIS JUDICANDUS EST QUI LIBERTATI NON FAVET. He is to be judged impious and cruel who does not favor liberty. Co. Litt. 124.

IMPLACITARE. Lat. To implead; to sue.

IMPLEAD. In practice. To sue or prosecute by due course of law. People v. Clarke, 9 N.Y. 368.

IMPLEADED. Sued or prosecuted; used particularly in the titles of causes where there are several defendants; as "A. B., impleaded with C. D."

IMPLEMENTS. Such things as are used or employed for a trade, or furniture of a house. Whatever may supply wants; particularly applied to tools, utensils, vessels, instruments of labor; as, the implements of trade or of husbandry. Goddard v. Chaffee, 2 Allen (Mass.) 395, 79 Am.Dec. 796. Mississippi Road Supply Co. v. Hester, 185 Miss. 839, 188 So. 281, 287, 124 A.L.R. 574.

IMPLICATA. A term used in mercantile law, derived from the Italian. In order to avoid the risk of making fruitless voyages, merchants have been in the habit of receiving small adventures, on freight, at so much per cent, to which they are entitled at all events, even if the adventure be lost; and this is called "*implicata.*" Wharton.

IMPLICATION. Intendment or inference, as distinguished from the actual expression of a thing in words. In a will, an estate may pass by mere *implication,* without any express words to direct its course. 2 Bl. Comm. 381.

An inference of something not directly declared, but arising from what is admitted or expressed.

In construing a will conjecture must not be taken for implication; but necessary implication means, not natural necessity, but so strong a probability of intention that an intention contrary to that which is imputed to the testator cannot be supposed. 1 Ves. & B. 466.

"Implication" is also used in the sense of "inference;" *i. e.,* where the existence of an intention is inferred from acts not done for the sole purpose of communicating it, but for some other purpose. Sweet.

Necessary implication

In construing a will, necessary implication means not natural necessity, but so strong a probability of intention that an intention contrary to that which is imputed to the testator cannot be supposed. Wilkinson v. Adam, 1 Ves. & B. 466; Gilbert v. Craddock, 67 Kan. 346, 72 P. 869.

IMPLIED. This word is used in law as contrasted with "express;" *i. e.,* where the intention in regard to the subject-matter is not manifested by explicit and direct words, but is gathered by implication or necessary deduction from the circumstances, the general language, or the conduct of the parties.

As to implied "Abrogation," "Agreement," "Assumpsit," "Condition," "Confession," "Consent," "Consideration," "Contract," "Covenant," "Dedication," "Easement," "Invitation," "Malice," "Notice," "Obligation," "Powers," "Trust," "Use," "Waiver," and "Warranty," see those titles.

IMPORTATION. The act of bringing goods and merchandise into a country from a foreign country. Cunard Steamship Co. v. Mellon, 43 S.Ct. 504, 262 U.S. 100, 67 L.Ed. 894, 27 A.L.R. 1306.

IMPORTED. This word, in general, has the same meaning in the tariff laws that its etymology shows, *in porto,* to carry in. To "import" is to bear or carry into. An "imported" article is one brought or carried into a country from abroad. The Conqueror, 49 Fed. 99. See Imports.

IMPORTS. Importations; goods or other property imported or brought into the country from a foreign country.

IMPORTUNITY. Pressing solicitation; urgent request; application for a claim or favor which is urged with troublesome frequency or pertinacity. Webster.

IMPOSE. To levy or exact as by authority; to lay as a burden, tax, duty or charge. State v. Nickerson, 97 Neb. 837, 151 N.W. 981, 982.

IMPOSITION. An impost; tax; contribution. Paterson v. Society, 24 N.J.L. 400; Singer Mfg. Co. v. Heppenheimer, 58 N.J.L. 633, 34 A. 1061, 32 L. R.A. 643; Town of Brandon v. Harvey, 105 Vt. 435, 168 A. 708, 710.

IMPOSSIBILITY. That which, in the constitution and course of nature or the law, no man can do or perform. Klauber v. San Diego Street-Car Co., 95 Cal. 353, 30 P. 555.

Impossibility of performance of contract, absolving party from liability for nonperformance, means not only strict impossibility, but impracticability because of extreme and unreasonable difficulty, expense, injury or loss involved.

Fisher v. United States Fidelity & Guaranty Co., 313 Ill. App. 66, 39 N.E.2d 67, 70; Transbay Const. Co. v. City and County of San Francisco, D.C.Cal., 35 F.Supp. 433, 436.

Impossible contract. One which the law will not hold binding upon the parties, because of the natural or legal impossibility of the performance by one party of that which is the consideration for the promise of the other. 7 Wait, Act. & Def. 124.

Impossible contracts, which will be deemed void in the eye of the law, or of which the performance will be excused, are such contracts as cannot be performed, either because of the nature of the obligation undertaken, or because of some supervening event which renders the performance of the obligation either physically or legally impossible. 10 Amer. & Eng.Enc.Law, 176.

Impossibility is of the following several sorts:

An act is *physically* impossible when it is contrary to the course of nature. Such an impossibility may be either *absolute, i. e.*, impossible in any case, (*e. g.*, to stop earth rotation) or *relative*, (sometimes called "impossibility in fact,") *i. e.*, arising from the circumstances of the case, (*e. g.*, for A. to make a payment to B., he being a deceased person.) To the latter class belongs what is sometimes called "*practical* impossibility," which exists when the act *can* be done, but only at an excessive or unreasonable cost. An act is *legally* or juridically impossible when a rule of law makes it impossible to do it; *e. g.*, for A. to make a valid will before his majority. This class of acts must not be confounded with those which are possible, although forbidden by law, as to commit a theft. An act is *logically* impossible when it is contrary to the nature of the transaction, as where A. gives property to B. expressly for his own benefit, on condition that he transfers it to C. Sweet.

IMPOSSIBILIUM NULLA OBLIGATIO EST. There is no obligation to do impossible things. Dig. 50, 17, 185; Broom, Max. 249.

IMPOSTS. Taxes, duties, or impositions levied for divers reasons. Crew Levick Co. v. Commonwealth of Pennsylvania, 38 S.Ct. 126, 245 U.S. 292, 62 L.Ed. 295.

Impost is a tax received by the prince for such merchandises as are brought into any haven within his dominions from foreign nations. It may in some sort be distinguished from customs, because customs are rather that profit the prince maketh of wares shipped out; yet they are frequently confounded. Cowell.

IMPOTENCE. In medical jurisprudence. Inability to copulate. Properly used of the male; but it has also been used synonymously with "sterility." Smith v. Smith, 206 Mo.App. 646, 229 S.W. 398; Heinemann v. Heinemann, 118 Or. 178, 245 P. 1082, 1083.

Impotency as a ground for divorce means want of potentia copulandi or incapacity to consummate the marriage, and not merely incapacity for procreation. Reed v. Reed, 26 Tenn.App. 690, 177 S.W.2d 26, 27.

IMPOTENTIA EXCUSAT LEGEM. Co.Litt. 29. The impossibility of doing what is required by the law excuses from the performance.

IMPOTENTIAM, PROPERTY PROPTER. A qualified property, which may subsist in animals *feræ naturæ* on account of their inability, as where hawks, herons, or other birds build in a person's trees, or conies, etc., make their nests or burrows in a person's land, and have young there, such person has a qualified property in them till they can fly or run away, and then such property expires. 2 Steph.Comm. (7th Ed.) 8.

IMPOUND. To shut up stray animals or distrained goods in a pound. Chenango County Humane Soc. v. Polmatier, 177 N.Y.S. 101, 103, 188 App.Div. 419. To take into the custody of the law or of a court. Thus, a court will sometimes *impound* a suspicious document produced at a trial.

IMPRESCRIPTIBILITY. The state or quality of being incapable of prescription; not of such a character that a right to it can be gained by prescription.

IMPRESCRIPTIBLE RIGHTS. Such rights as a person may use or not, at pleasure, since they cannot be lost to him by the claims of another founded on prescription.

IMPRESSION, CASE OF FIRST. One without a precedent; one presenting a wholly new state of facts; one involving a question never before determined.

IMPRESSMENT. A power possessed by the English crown of taking persons or property to aid in the defense of the country, with or without the consent of the persons concerned. It is usually exercised to obtain hands for the royal ships in time of war, by taking seamen engaged in merchant vessels, (1 Bl.Comm. 420; Maud & P. Shipp. 123;) but in former times impressment of merchant ships was also practiced. The admiralty issues protections against impressment in certain cases, either under statutes passed in favor of certain callings (*e. g.*, persons employed in the Greenland fisheries) or voluntarily. Sweet.

IMPREST MONEY. Money paid on enlisting or impressing soldiers or sailors.

IMPRETIABILIS. Lat. Beyond price; invaluable.

IMPRIMATUR. Lat. Let it be printed. A license or allowance, granted by the constituted authorities, giving permission to print and publish a book. This allowance was formerly necessary, in England, before any book could lawfully be printed, and in some other countries is still required.

IMPRIMERE. To press upon; to impress or press; to imprint or print.

IMPRIMERY. In some of the ancient English statutes this word is used to signify a printing-office, the art of printing, a print or impression.

IMPRIMIS. Lat. In the first place; first of all.

IMPRISON. To put in a prison; to put in a place of confinement. To confine a person, or restrain his liberty, in any way.

IMPRISONMENT. The act of putting or confining a man in prison; the restraint of a man's personal liberty; coercion exercised upon a person to prevent the free exercise of his powers of locomotion. State v. Shaw, 73 Vt. 149, 50 A. 863.

It is not a necessary part of the definition that the confinement should be in a place usually appropriated to that purpose; it may be in a locality used only for the specific occasion; or it may take place without the actual application of any physical agencies of restraint, (such as locks or bars,) but by verbal compulsion and the display of available force. Pike v. Hanson, 9 N.H. 491. Every confinement of the person is an "imprisonment," whether it be in a common prison, or in a private house, or in the stocks, or even by forcibly detaining one in the public streets. Norton v. Mathers, 222 Iowa 1170, 271 N.W. 321, 324.

False imprisonment

The unlawful arrest or detention of a person without warrant, or by an illegal warrant, or a warrant illegally executed, and either in a prison or a place used temporarily for that purpose, or by force and constraint without confinement. Eberling v. State, 136 Ind. 117, 35 N.E. 1023. False imprisonment consists in the unlawful detention of the person of another, for any length of time, whereby he is deprived of his personal liberty. Mahan v. Adam, 144 Md. 355, 124 A. 901, 904. The unlawful detention of the occupant of an automobile may be accomplished by driving so rapidly that he cannot alight. Blashfield, Cyc. of Automobile Law and Prac., Perm.Ed., § 5528.26.

The term is also used as the name of the action which lies for this species of injury. 3 Bl.Comm. 138; Buttrey v. Wilhite, 208 Ala. 573, 94 So. 585; Christ v. McDonald, 152 Or. 494, 52 P.2d 655, 658.

IMPRISTI. Adherents; followers. Those who side with or take the part of another, either in his defense or otherwise.

IMPROBABLE. Unlikely to be true, or to occur, not to be readily believed. Johnson v. Tregle, La. App., 8 So.2d 755, 758.

IMPROBATION. In Scotch law. An action brought for the purpose of having some instrument declared false and forged. 1 Forb.Inst. pt. 4, p. 161. The verb "improve" (*q. v.*) was used in the same sense.

IMPROPER. Not suitable; unfit; not suited to the character, time, and place. Godbey v. Godbey, 70 Ohio App. 455, 44 N.E.2d 810, 813.

IMPROPER CUMULATION OF ACTIONS. An attempt to join in one proceeding inconsistent causes of action. Toms v. Nugent, La.App., 12 So.2d 713, 715.

IMPROPER FEUDS. These were derivative feuds; as, for instance, those that were originally bartered and sold to the feudatory for a price, or were held upon base or less honorable services, or upon a rent in lieu of military service, or were themselves alienable, without mutual license, or descended indifferently to males or females. Wharton.

IMPROPER INFLUENCE. Undue influence (*q. v.*) Millican v. Millican, 24 Tex. 446.

IMPROPER NAVIGATION. Anything improperly done with the ship or part of the ship in the course of the voyage. L.R. 6 C.P. 563. See, also, 53 Law J.P.D. 65.

IMPROPRIATION. In ecclesiastical law. The annexing an ecclesiastical benefice to the use of a lay person, whether individual or corporate, in the same way as *appropriation* is the annexing of any such benefice to the proper and perpetual use of some spiritual corporation, whether sole or aggregate, to enjoy forever. Brown.

IMPROPRIATE RECTOR. In ecclesiastical law. Commonly signifies a lay rector as opposed to a spiritual rector; just as impropriate tithes are tithes in the hands of a lay owner, as opposed to appropriate tithes, which are tithes in the hands of a spiritual owner. Brown.

IMPROVE. In Scotch law. To disprove; to invalidate or impeach; to prove false or forged. 1 Forb. Inst. pt. 4, p. 162.

To improve a lease means to grant a lease of unusual duration to encourage a tenant, when the soil is exhausted, etc. Bell; Stair, Inst. p. 676, § 23.

To meliorate, make better, to increase the value or good qualities of, mend, repair, as to "improve" a street by grading, parking, curbing, paving, etc. State ex rel. County of Ramsey v. Babcock, 186 Minn. 132, 242 N.W. 474, 476.

IMPROVED. Improved land is such as has been reclaimed, is used for the purpose of husbandry, and is cultivated as such, whether the appropriation is for tillage, meadow, or pasture. "Improve" is synonymous with "cultivate." Clark v. Phelps, 4 Cow. (N.Y.) 190.

IMPROVEMENT. A valuable addition made to property (usually real estate) or an amelioration in its condition, amounting to more than mere repairs or replacement of waste, costing labor or capital, and intended to enhance its value, beauty or utility or to adapt it for new or further purposes. Spencer v. Tobey, 22 Barb., N.Y., 269; Allen v. McKay, 120 Cal. 332, 52 P. 828.

In American land law. An act by which a locator or settler expresses his intention to cultivate or clear certain land; an act expressive of the actual possession of land; as by erecting a cabin, planting a corn-field, deadening trees in a forest; or by merely marking trees, or even by piling up a brush-heap. Burrill. In re Leet Tp. Road, 159 Pa. 72, 28 A. 238.

An "improvement," under our land system, does not mean a general enhancement of the value of the tract from the occupant's operations. It has a more limited meaning, which has in view the population of our forests, and the increase of agricultural products. All works which are directed to the creation of homes for families, or are substantial steps towards bringing lands into cultivation, have in their results the special character of "improvements," and, under the land laws of the United States and of the several states, are encouraged. Sometimes their minimum extent is defined as requisite to convey rights. In other cases not. But the test which runs through all the cases is always this: Are they real, and made *bona fide,* in accordance with the policy of the law, or are they only colorable, and made for the purpose of fraud and speculation? Simpson v. Robinson, 37 Ark. 137.

In the law of patents. An addition to, or modification of, a previous invention or discovery, intended or claimed to increase its utility or value. 2 Kent, Comm. 366–372. Steiner Sales Co. v. Schwartz Sales Co., C.C.A.Utah, 98 F.2d 999, 1010.

It includes two necessary ideas: the idea of a complete and practical operative art or instrument and the idea of some change in such art or instrument not affecting its essential character but enabling it to produce its appropriate results in a more perfect or economical manner. Rob. Pat. § 210.

Local improvement. See Local Improvement.

IMPROVEMENTS. A term used in leases, of doubtful meaning. It would seem to apply principally to buildings, though generally it extends to the amelioration of every description of property, whether real or personal; but, when contained in any document, its meaning is generally explained by other words. 1 Chit. Gen. Pr. 174.

IMPROVIDENCE. As used in a statute excluding one found incompetent to execute the duties of an administrator by reason of improvidence, means that want of care and foresight in the management of property which would be likely to render the estate and effects of the intestate unsafe, and liable to be lost or diminished in value, in case the administration should be committed to the improvident person. In re Fulper's Estate, 99 N. J.Eq. 293, 132 A. 834, 843.

IMPROVIDENTLY. A judgment, decree, rule, injunction, etc., when given or rendered without adequate consideration by the court, or without proper information as to all the circumstances affecting it, or based upon a mistaken assumption or misleading information or advice, is sometimes said to have been "improvidently" given or issued.

IMPRUIARE. In old records. To improve land. *Impruiamentum*, the improvement so made of it. Cowell.

IMPUBES. Lat. In the civil law. A minor under the age of puberty; a male under fourteen years of age; a female under twelve. Calvin.; Mackeld.Rom.Law, § 138.

IMPULSE. As to "irresistible" or "uncontrollable" impulse, see Insanity.

IMPUNITAS CONTINUUM AFFECTUM TRIBUIT DELINQUENDI. 4 Coke, 45. Impunity confirms the disposition to commit crime.

IMPUNITIES SEMPER AD DETERIORA INVITAT. 5 Coke, 109. Impunity always invites to greater crimes.

IMPUNITY. Exemption or protection from penalty or punishment. Dillon v. Rogers, 36 Tex. 153.

IMPUTATIO. Lat. In the civil law. Legal liability.

IMPUTATION OF PAYMENT. In the civil law. The application of a payment made by a debtor to his creditor.

IMPUTED. As used in legal phrases, this word means attributed vicariously; that is, an act, fact, or quality is said to be "imputed" to a person when it is ascribed or charged to him, not because he is personally cognizant of it or responsible for it, but because another person is, over whom he has control or for whose acts or knowledge he is responsible.

IMPUTED KNOWLEDGE. This phrase is sometimes used as equivalent to "implied notice," *i. e.*, knowledge attributed or charged to a person (often contrary to the fact) because the facts in question were open to his discovery and it was his duty to inform himself as to them. Roche v. Llewellyn Iron Works Co., 140 Cal. 563, 74 P. 147.

IMPUTED NEGLIGENCE. Negligence which is not directly attributable to the person himself, but which is the negligence of a person who is in privity with him, and with whose fault he is chargeable. Smith v. Railroad Co., 38 N.Y.S. 666, 4 App. Div. 493.

IMPUTED NOTICE. Information as to a given fact or circumstance charged or attributed to a person, and affecting his rights or conduct on the ground that actual notice was given to some person whose duty was to report it to the person to be affected, as, his agent or his attorney of record.

IN. In the law of real estate, this preposition has always been used to denote the fact of seisin, title, or possession, and apparently serves as an elliptical expression for some such phrase as "in possession," or as an abbreviation for "*in*titled" or "*in*vested with title." Thus, in the old books, a tenant is said to be "*in* by lease of his lessor." Litt. § 82.

An elastic preposition in other cases, expressing relation of presence, existence, situation, inclusion, action, etc.; inclosed or surrounded by limits, as in a room; also meaning for, in and about, on, within, etc., according to context. Ex parte Perry, 71 Fla. 250, 71 So. 174, 176. Rester v. Moody & Stewart, 172 La. 510, 134 So. 690, 692.

IN ACTION. Attainable or recoverable by action; not in possession. A term applied to property of which a party has not the possession, but only a right to recover it by action. Things in action are rights of personal things, which nevertheless are not in possession. See Chose in Action.

IN ADVERSUM. Against an adverse, unwilling, or resisting party. "A decree not by consent, but *in adversum*." 3 Story, 318.

IN ÆDIFICIIS LAPIS MALE POSITUS NON EST REMOVENDUS. 11 Coke, 69. A stone badly placed in buildings is not to be removed.

IN ÆQUA MANU. In equal hand. Fleta, lib. 3, c. 14, § 2.

IN ÆQUALI JURE. In equal right; on an equality in point of right.

IN ÆQUALI JURE MELIOR EST CONDITIO POSSIDENTIS. In [a case of] equal right the condition of the party in possession is the better Plowd. 296; Broom, Max. 713.

IN ÆQUALI MANU. In equal hand; held equally or indifferently between two parties. Where an instrument was deposited by the parties to it in the hands of a third person, to keep on certain conditions, it was said to be held *in æquali manu.* Reg. Orig. 28.

IN ALIENO SOLO. In another's land. 2 Steph. Comm. 20.

IN ALIO LOCO. In another place.

IN ALTA PRODITIONE NULLUS POTEST ESSE ACCESSORIUS SED PRINCIPALIS SOLUMMODO. 3 Inst. 138. In high treason no one can be an accessary but only principal.

IN ALTERNATIVIS ELECTIO EST DEBITORIS. In alternatives the debtor has the election.

IN AMBIGUA VOCE LEGIS EA POTIUS ACCIPIENDA EST SIGNIFICATIO QUÆ VITIO CARET, PRÆSERTIM CUM ETIAM VOLUNTAS LEGIS EX HOC COLLIGI POSSIT. In an ambiguous expression of law, that signification is to be preferred which is consonant with equity, especially when the spirit of the law can be collected from that. Dig. 1, 3, 19; Broom, Max. 576.

IN AMBIGUIS CASIBUS SEMPER PRÆSUMITUR PRO REGE. In doubtful cases the presumption is always in favor of the king.

IN AMBIGUIS ORATIONIBUS MAXIME SENTENTIA SPECTANDA EST EJUS QUI EAS PROTULISSET. In ambiguous expressions, the intention of the person using them is chiefly to be regarded. Dig. 50, 17, 96; Broom, Max. 567.

IN AMBIGUO. In doubt.

IN AMBIGUO SERMONE NON UTRUMQUE DICIMUS SED ID DUNTAXAT QUOD VOLUMUS. When the language we use is ambiguous, we do not use it in a double sense, but in the sense in which we mean it. Dig. 34. 5. 3; 2 De G. M. & G. 313.

IN ANGLIA NON EST INTERREGNUM. In England there is no interregnum. Jenk. Cent. 205; Broom, Max. 50.

IN APERTA LUCE. In open daylight; in the day-time. 9 Coke, 65*b*.

IN APICIBUS JURIS. Among the subtleties or extreme doctrines of the law. 1 Kames, Eq. 190. See Apex Juris.

IN ARBITRIUM JUDICIS. At the pleasure of the judge.

IN ARCTA ET SALVA CUSTODIA. In close and safe custody. 3 Bl.Comm. 415.

IN ARTICULO. In a moment; immediately. Cod. 1, 34, 2.

IN ARTICULO MORTIS. In the article of death; at the point of death. Jackson v. Vredenbergh, 1 Johns. (N.Y.) 159.

IN ATROCIORIBUS DELICTIS PUNITUR AFFECTUS LICET NON SEQUATUR EFFECTUS. 2 Rolle R. 82. In more atrocious crimes the intent is punished, though an effect does not follow.

IN AUTRE DROIT. L. Fr. In another's right. As representing another. An executor, administrator, or trustee sues *in autre droit.*

IN BANCO. In bank; in the bench. A term applied to proceedings in the court in bank, as distinguished from the proceedings at *nisi prius.* Also, in the English court of common bench.

IN BEING. In existence or life at a given moment of time, as, in the phrase "life or lives in being" in the rule against perpetuities. An unborn child may, in some circumstances be considered as "in being." Phillips v. Herron, 55 Ohio St. 478, 45 N.E. 720.

IN BLANK. A term applied to the indorsement of a bill or note where it consists merely of the indorser's name, without restriction to any particular indorsee. 2 Steph.Comm. 164.

IN BONIS. Among the goods or property; in actual possession. Inst. 4, 2, 2. *In bonis defuncti,* among the goods of the deceased.

IN BULK. As a whole; as an entirety, without division into items or physical separation in packages or parcels. Standard Oil Co. v. Com., 119 Ky. 75, 82 S.W. 1022.

IN CAHOOTS. Jointly interested in property, or common participants in enterprise. Clark v. State, 154 Miss. 457, 122 So. 534.

IN CAMERA. In chambers; in private. A cause is said to be heard *in camera* either when the hearing is had before the judge in his private room or when all spectators are excluded from the courtroom.

IN CAPITA. To the heads; by heads or polls. Persons succeed to an inheritance *in capita* when they individually take equal shares. So challenges to individual jurors are challenges *in capita,* as distinguished from challenges to the array.

IN CAPITE. In chief. 2 Bl.Comm. 60. Tenure *in capite* was a holding directly from the king.

IN CASE. If, in the event. Barmore v. Darragh, Tex.Civ.App., 231 S.W. 472, 478.

IN CASU EXTREMÆ NECESSITATIS OMNIA SUNT COMMUNIA. Hale, P. C. 54. In cases of extreme necessity, everything is in common.

IN CASU PROVISO. In a (or the) case provided. *In tali casu editum et provisum,* in such case made and provided. Townsh. Pl. 164, 165.

IN CAUSA. In the cause, as distinguished from *in initialibus* (*q. v.*) A term in Scotch practice. 1 Brown, Ch. 252.

IN CHARGE OF. Means in the care or custody of, or intrusted to the management or direction of. Sky v. Keystone Mut. Casualty Co., 150 Pa. Super. 613, 29 A.2d 230, 232.

IN CHIEF. Principal; primary; directly obtained. A term applied to the evidence obtained from a witness upon his examination in court by the party producing him.

Tenure in chief, or *in capite,* is a holding directly of the king or chief lord.

IN CIVILIBUS MINISTERIUM EXCUSAT, IN CRIMINALIBUS NON ITEM. In civil matters agency (or service) excuses, but not so in criminal matters. Lofft, 228; Tray. Lat. Max. 243.

IN CLARIS NON EST LOCUS CONJECTURIS. In things obvious there is no room for conjecture.

IN COMMENDAM. In commendation; as a commended living. 1 Bl.Comm. 393. See Commenda.

A term applied in Louisiana to a limited partnership, answering to the French *"en commandite."* Civil Code La. art. 2810.

IN COMMODATO HÆC PACTIO, NE DOLUS PRÆSTETUR, RATA NON EST. In the contract of loan, a stipulation not to be liable for fraud is not valid. Dig. 13, 7, 17, pr.

IN COMMON. Shared in respect to title, use, or enjoyment, without apportionment or division into individual parts; held by several for the equal advantage, use, or enjoyment of all. Hewit v. Jewell, 59 Iowa 37, 12 N.W. 738.

IN COMMUNI. In common. Fleta, lib. 3, c. 4, § 2.

IN CONJUNCTION WITH. In association with. Blaisdell v. Inhabitants of Town of York, 110 Me. 500, 87 A. 361, 370.

IN CONJUNCTIVIS, OPORTET UTRAMQUE PARTEM ESSE VERAM. In conjunctives it is necessary that each part be true. Wing, Max. 13, max. 9. In a condition consisting of divers parts in the copulative, both parts must be performed.

IN CONSIDERATIONE INDE. In consideration thereof. 3 Salk. 64, pl. 5.

IN CONSIDERATIONE LEGIS. In consideration or contemplation of law; in abeyance. Dyer, 102*b*.

IN CONSIDERATIONE PRÆMISSORUM. In consideration of the premises. 1 Strange, 535.

IN CONSIMILI CASU. See Consimili Casu.

IN CONSIMILI CASU, CONSIMILE DEBET ESSE REMEDIUM. Hardr. 65. In a similar case the remedy should be similar.

IN CONSPECTU EJUS. In his sight or view. 12 Mod. 95.

IN CONSUETUDINIBUS, NON DIUTURNITAS TEMPORIS SED SOLIDITAS RATIONIS EST CONSIDERANDA. In customs, not length of time, but solidity of reason, is to be considered. Co. Litt. 141*a*. The antiquity of a custom is to be less regarded than its reasonableness.

IN CONTINENTI. Immediately; without any interval or intermission. Calvin. Sometimes written as one word *"incontinenti."*

IN CONTRACTIBUS, BENIGNA; IN TESTAMENTIS, BENIGNIOR; IN RESTITUTIONIBUS, BENIGNISSIMA INTERPRETATIO FACIENDA EST. Co. Litt. 112. In contracts, the interpretation is to be liberal; in wills, more liberal; in restitutions, most liberal.

IN CONTRACTIBUS, REI VERITAS POTIUS QUAM SCRIPTURA PERSPICI DEBET. In contracts, the truth of the matter ought to be regarded rather than the writing. Cod. 4, 22, 1.

IN CONTRACTIBUS, TACITE INSUNT [VENIUNT] QUÆ SUNT MORIS ET CONSUETUDINIS. In contracts, matters of custom and usage are tacitly implied. A contract is understood to contain the customary clauses, although they are not expressed. Story, Bills, § 143; 3 Kent, Comm. 260, note; Broom, Max. 842.

IN CONTRAHENDA VENDITIONE, AMBIGUUM PACTUM CONTRA VENDITOREM INTERPRETANDUM EST. In the contract of sale, an ambiguous agreement is to be interpreted against the seller. Dig. 50, 17, 172. See Id. 18, 1, 21.

IN CONVENTIONIBUS, CONTRAHENTIUM VOLUNTAS POTIUS QUAM VERBA SPECTARI PLACUIT. In agreements, the intention of the contracting parties, rather than the words used, should be regarded. Broom, Max. 551; Jackson v. Wilkinson, 17 Johns. (N.Y.) 150.

IN CORPORE. In body or substance; in a material thing or object.

IN CRASTINO. On the morrow. *In crastino Animarum,* on the morrow of All Souls. 1 Bl.Comm. 342.

IN CRIMINALIBUS, PROBATIONES DEBENT ESSE LUCE CLARIORES. In criminal cases, the proofs ought to be clearer than light. 3 Inst. 210.

IN CRIMINALIBUS, SUFFICIT GENERALIS MALITIA INTENTIONIS, CUM FACTO PARIS GRADUS. In criminal matters or cases, a general malice of intention is sufficient, [if united] with an act of equal or corresponding degree. Bac. Max. p. 65, reg. 15; Broom, Max. 323.

IN CRIMINALIBUS, VOLUNTAS REPUTABITUR PRO FACTO. In criminal acts, the will will be taken for the deed. 3 Inst. 106.

IN CUJUS REI TESTIMONIUM. In testimony whereof. The initial words of the concluding clause of ancient deeds in Latin, literally translated in the English forms.

IN CUSTODIA LEGIS. In the custody or keeping of the law. 2 Steph.Comm. 74.

IN DELICTO. In fault. See In Pari Delicto, etc.

IN DIEM. For a day; for the space of a day. Calvin.

IN DISJUNCTIVIS SUFFICIT ALTERAM PARTEM ESSE VERAM. In disjunctives it is sufficient that either part be true. Where a condition is in the disjunctive, it is sufficient if either part be performed. Wing. Max. 13, max. 9; Broom, Max. 592; 7 East, 272.

IN DOMINICO. In demesne. *In dominico suo ut de feodo,* in his demesne as of fee.

IN DORSO. On the back. 2 Bl.Comm. 468; 2 Steph.Comm. 164. *In dorso recordi,* on the back of the record. 5 Coke, 45. Hence the English *indorse, indorsement,* etc.

IN DUBIIS, BENIGNIORA PRÆFERENDA SUNT. In doubtful cases, the more favorable views are to be preferred; the more liberal interpretation is to be followed. Dig. 50, 17, 56; 2 Kent, Comm. 557.

IN DUBIIS, MAGIS DIGNUM EST ACCIPIENDUM. Branch, Princ. In doubtful cases, the more worthy is to be accepted.

IN DUBIIS, NON PRÆSUMITUR PRO TESTAMENTO. In cases of doubt, the presumption is not in favor of a will. Branch, Princ. But see Cro. Car. 51.

IN DUBIO. In doubt; in a state of uncertainty, or in a doubtful case.

IN DUBIO, HÆC LEGIS CONSTRUCTIO QUAM VERBA OSTENDUNT. In a case of doubt, that is the construction of the law which the words indicate. Branch, Princ.

IN DUBIO, PARS MITIOR EST SEQUENDA. In doubt, the milder course is to be followed.

IN DUBIO, PRO LEGE FORI. In a doubtful case, the law of the forum is to be preferred. "A false maxim." Meili, Int. L. 151.

IN DUBIO, SEQUENDUM QUOD TUTIUS EST. In doubt, the safer course is to be adopted.

IN DUPLO. In double. *Damna in duplo,* double damages. Fleta, lib. 4, c. 10, § 1.

IN EADEM CAUSA. In the same state or condition. Calvin.

IN EMULATIONEM VICINI. In envy or hatred of a neighbor. Where an act is done, or action brought, solely to hurt or distress another, it is said to be *in emulationem vicini.* 1 Kames, Eq. 56.

IN EO QUOD PLUS SIT, SEMPER INEST ET MINUS. In the greater is always included the less also. Dig. 50, 17, 110.

IN EQUITY. In a court of equity, as distinguished from a court of law; in the purview, consideration, or contemplation of equity; according to the doctrines of equity.

IN ESSE. In being. Actually existing. Distinguished from *in posse,* which means "that which is not, but may be." A child before birth is *in posse;* after birth, *in esse.*

IN EST DE JURE. (Lat.) It is implied of right or by law.

IN EVIDENCE. Included in the evidence already adduced. The "facts in evidence" are such as have already been proved in the cause.

IN EXCAMBIO. In exchange. Formal words in old deeds of exchange.

IN EXECUTION AND PURSUANCE OF. Words used to express the fact that the instrument is intended to carry into effect some other instrument, as in case of a deed in execution of a power. They are said to be synonymous with "to effect the object of;" U. S. v. Nunnemacher, 7 Biss. 129, Fed. Cas. No. 15,903.

IN EXITU. In issue. *De materia in exitu,* of the matter in issue. 12 Mod. 372.

IN EXPOSITIONE INSTRUMENTORUM, MALA GRAMMATICA, QUOD FIERI POTEST, VITANDA EST. In the construction of instruments, bad grammar is to be avoided as much as possible. 6 Coke, 39; 2 Pars. Cont. 26.

IN EXTENSO. In extension; at full length; from beginning to end, leaving out nothing.

IN EXTREMIS. In extremity; in the last extremity; in the last illness. 2 Bl.Comm. 375, 500; Prince v. Hazleton, 20 Johns. (N.Y.) 502, 11 Am. Dec. 307. *Agens in extremis,* being in extremity. Bract. fol. 373*b*. Declarations *in extremis,* dying declarations. 1 Greenl. Ev. § 156; State v. Burton, 111 S.C. 526, 98 S.E. 856, 863. In extremis does not always mean in articulo mortis. In re Mallery's Will, 127 Misc. 784, 217 N.Y.S. 489, 492.

IN FACIE CURIÆ. In the face of the court. Dyer, 28.

IN FACIE ECCLESIÆ. In the face of the church. A term applied in the law of England to marriages, which are required to be solemnized in a parish church or public chapel, unless by dispensation or license. 1 Bl.Comm. 439; 2 Steph.Comm. 288, 289. Applied in Bracton to the old mode of conferring dower. Bract. fol. 92; 2 Bl.Comm. 133.

IN FACIENDO. In doing; in feasance; in the performance of an act. 2 Story, Eq. Jur. § 1308.

IN FACT. Actual, real; as distinguished from implied or inferred. Resulting from the acts of parties, instead of from the act or intendment of law.

IN FACTO. In fact; in deed. *In facto dicit,* in fact says. 1 Salk. 22, pl. 1.

IN FACTO QUOD SE HABET AD BONUM ET MALUM, MAGIS DE BONO QUAM DE MALO LEX INTENDIT. In an act or deed which admits of being considered as both good and bad, the law intends more from the good than from the bad; the law makes the more favorable construction. Co. Litt. 78*b*.

IN FAVORABILIBUS MAGIS ATTENDITUR QUOD PRODEST QUAM QUOD NOCET. In things favored, what profits is more regarded than what prejudices. Bac. Max. p. 57, in reg. 12.

IN FAVOREM LIBERTATIS. In favor of liberty.

IN FAVOREM VITÆ. In favor of life.

IN FAVOREM VITÆ, LIBERTATIS, ET INNOCENTIÆ, OMNIA PRÆSUMUNTUR. In favor of life, liberty, and innocence, every presumption is made. Lofft, 125.

IN FEODO. In fee. Bract. fol. 207; Fleta, lib. 2, c. 64, § 15. *Seisitus in feodo,* seised in fee. Fleta, lib. 3, c. 7, § 1.

IN FICTIONE JURIS SEMPER ÆQUITAS EXISTIT. In the fiction of law there is always equity; a legal fiction is always consistent with equity. 11 Coke 51*a;* Broom, Max. 127, 130.

IN FIERI. In being made; in process of formation or development; hence, incomplete or inchoate. Legal proceedings are described as *in fieri* until judgment is entered.

IN FINE. Lat. At the end. Used, in references, to indicate that the passage cited is at the *end* of a book, chapter, section, etc.

IN FORMA PAUPERIS. In the character or manner of a pauper. Describes permission given to a poor person to sue without liability for costs.

IN FORO. In a (or the) forum, court, or tribunal.

IN FORO CONSCIENTIÆ. In the tribunal of conscience; conscientiously; considered from a moral, rather than a legal, point of view.

IN FORO CONTENTIOSO. In the forum of contention or litigation.

IN FORO ECCLESIASTICO. In an ecclesiastical forum; in the ecclesiastical court. Fleta, lib. 2, c. 57, § 13.

IN FORO SÆCULARI. In a secular forum or court. Fleta, lib. 2, c. 57, § 14; 1 Bl.Comm. 20.

IN FRAUDEM CREDITORUM. In fraud of creditors; with intent to defraud creditors. Inst. 1, 6, pr. 3.

IN FRAUDEM LEGIS. In fraud of the law. 3 Bl.Comm. 94. With the intent or view of evading the law. Jackson v. Jackson, 1 Johns. (N. Y.) 424, 432.

IN FULL. Relating to the whole or *full* amount; as a receipt in full. Complete; giving all details. Bard v. Wood, 3 Metc. (Mass.) 75.

IN FULL LIFE. Continuing in both physical and civil existence; that is, neither actually dead nor *civiliter mortuus.*

IN FUTURO. In future; at a future time; the opposite of *in præsenti.* 2 Bl.Comm. 166, 175.

IN GENERALI PASSAGIO. In the general passage; that is, on the journey to Palestine with the general company or body of Crusaders. This term was of frequent occurrence in the old law of essoins, as a means of accounting for the absence of the party, and was distinguished from *simplex passagium,* which meant that he was performing a pilgrimage to the Holy Land alone.

IN GENERALIBUS VERSATUR ERROR. Error dwells in general expressions. Pitman v. Hooper, 3 Sumn. 290, Fed. Cas. No. 11,186; Underwood v. Carney, 1 Cush. (Mass.) 292.

IN GENERE. In kind; in the same *genus* or class; the same in quantity and quality, but not individually the same. In the Roman law, things which may be given or restored *in genere* are distinguished from such as must be given or restored *in specie;* that is, identically. Mackeld. Rom. Law, § 161.

IN GREMIO LEGIS. In the bosom of the law; in the protection of the law; in abeyance. 1 Coke, 131*a*; T. Raym. 319; Hooper v. Farmers' Union Warehouse Co., 21 Ala.App. 91, 105 So. 725, 726.

IN GROSS. In a large quantity or sum; without division or particulars; by wholesale. Green v. Taylor, 10 Fed.Cas.No.1,126. At large; not annexed to or dependent upon another thing. Common in gross is such as is neither appendant nor appurtenant to land, but is annexed to a man's person. 2 Bl.Comm. 34.

IN HAC PARTE. In this behalf; on this side.

IN HÆC VERBA. In these words; in the same words.

IN HÆREDES NON SOLENT TRANSIRE ACTIONES QUÆ PŒNALES EX MALEFICIO SUNT. 2 Inst. 442. Penal actions arising from anything of a criminal nature do not pass to heirs.

IN HIS ENIM QUÆ SUNT FAVORABILIA ANIMÆ, QUAMVIS SUNT DAMNOSA REBUS, FIAT ALIQUANDO EXTENTIO STATUTI. In things that are favorable to the spirit, though injurious to property, an extension of the statute should sometimes be made. 10 Coke, 101.

IN HIS QUÆ DE JURE COMMUNI OMNIBUS CONCEDUNTUR, CONSUETUDO ALICUJUS PATRIÆ VEL LOCI NON EST ALLEGENDA. 11 Coke, 85. In those things which by common right are conceded to all, the custom of a particular district or place is not to be alleged.

IN HOC. In this; in respect to this.

IN IIS QUÆ SUNT MERÆ FACULTATIS NUNQUAM PRÆSCRIBITUR. Prescription does not run against a mere power or faculty to act. Tray. Leg. Max.

IN IISDEM TERMINIS. In the same terms. 9 East, 487.

IN INDIVIDUO. In the distinct, identical, or individual form; *in specie.* Story, Bailm. § 97.

IN INFINITUM. Infinitely; indefinitely. Imports indefinite succession or continuance.

IN INITIALIBUS. In the preliminaries. A term in Scotch practice, applied to the preliminary examination of a witness as to the following points: Whether he knows the parties, or bears ill will to either of them, or has received any reward or promise of reward for what he may say, or can lose or gain by the cause, or has been told by any person what to say. If the witness answer these questions satisfactorily, he is then examined *in causa,* in the cause. Bell, Dict. "Evidence."

IN INITIO. In or at the beginning. *In initio litis,* at the beginning, or in the first stage of the suit. Bract. fol. 400.

IN INTEGRUM. To the original or former state. Calvin.

IN INVIDIAM. To excite a prejudice.

IN INVITUM. Against an unwilling party; against one not assenting. A term applied to proceedings against an adverse party, to which he does not consent.

IN IPSIS FAUCIBUS. In the very throat or entrance. *In ipsis faucibus* of a port, actually entering a port. 1 C.Rob.Adm. 233, 234.

IN ITINERE. In eyre; on a journey or circuit. In old English law, the justices *in itinere* (or in eyre) were those who made a circuit through the kingdom once in seven years for the purposes of trying causes. 3 Bl.Comm. 58. In course of transportation; on the way; not delivered to the vendee. In this sense the phrase is equivalent to "*in transitu.*"

IN JUDGMENT. In a court of justice; in a seat of judgment. Lord Hale is called "one of the greatest and best men who ever sat in judgment." 1 East, 306.

IN JUDICIIS, MINORI ÆTATI SUCCURRITUR. In courts or judicial proceedings, infancy is aided or favored. Jenk.Cent. 46, case 89.

IN JUDICIO. In Roman law. In the course of an actual trial; before a judge, (*judex.*) A cause, during its preparatory stages, conducted before the prætor, was said to be *in jure;* in its second stage, after it had been sent to a *judex* for trial, it was said to be *in judicio.*

IN JUDICIO NON CREDITUR NISI JURATIS. Cro.Car. 64. In a trial, credence is given only to those who are sworn.

IN JURE. In law; according to law.

In the Roman practice, the procedure in an action was divided into two stages. The first was said to be *in jure;* it took place before the prætor, and included the formal and introductory part and the settlement of questions of law. The second stage was committed to the *judex,* and comprised the investigation and trial of the facts; this was said to be *in judicio.*

IN JURE ALTERIUS. In another's right. Hale, Anal. § 26.

IN JURE, NON REMOTA CAUSA SED PROXIMA SPECTATUR. Bac.Max. reg. 1. In law, the proximate, and not the remote, cause is regarded.

IN JURE PROPRIO. In one's own right. Hale, Anal. § 26.

IN JUS VOCARE. To call, cite, or summon to court. Inst. 4, 16, 3; Calvin. *In jus vocando,* summoning to court. 3 Bl.Comm. 279.

IN KIND. In the same kind, class, or genus. A loan is returned "in kind" when not the identical article, but one corresponding and equivalent to it, is given to the lender. See In Genere.

The agreement that a collector of taxes was to receive his commission "in kind" means the same kind of funds in which the tax is collected; Wilson v. State, 51 Ark. 213, 10 S.W. 491.

IN LAW. In the intendment, contemplation, or inference of the law; implied or inferred by law; existing in law or by force of law. See In Fact.

IN LECTO MORTALI. On the deathbed. Fleta, lib. 5, c. 28, § 12.

IN LIBERAM ELEMOSINAM. In free alms. Land given for a charitable motive was said to be so given. See Frankalmoin.

IN LIEU OF. Instead of; in place of; in substitution of. State v. Escalade, 91 So. 135, 136, 150 La. 638; Joiner v. Joiner, 117 Miss. 507, 78 So. 369, 370.

IN LIMINE. On or at the threshold; at the very beginning; preliminarily.

IN LITEM. For a suit; to the suit. Greenl.Ev. § 348.

IN LOCO. In place; in lieu; instead; in the place or stead. Townsh.Pl. 38.

IN LOCO PARENTIS. In the place of a parent; instead of a parent; charged, factitiously, with a parent's rights, duties, and responsibilities. Wetherby v. Dixon, 19 Ves. 412; Brinkerhoff v. Merselis, 24 N.J.L. 683; Howard v. United States, D.C.Ky., 2 F.2d 170, 174; Meisner v. United States, D.C.Mo., 295 F. 866, 868.

IN MAJORE SUMMA CONTINETUR MINOR. 5 Coke, 115. In the greater sum is contained the less.

IN MAJOREM CAUTELAM. For greater security. 1 Strange, 105, arg.

IN MALAM PARTEM. In a bad sense, so as to wear an evil appearance.

IN MALEFICIIS VOLUNTAS SPECTATUR, NON EXITUS. In evil deeds regard must be had to the intention, and not to the result. Dig. 48, 8, 14; Broom, Max. 324.

IN MALEFICIO, RATIHABITIO MANDATO COMPARATUR. In a case of malfeasance, ratification is equivalent to command. Dig. 50, 17, 152, 2.

IN MAXIMA POTENTIA MINIMA LICENTIA. In the greatest power there is the least freedom. Hob. 159.

IN MEDIAS RES. Into the heart of the subject, without preface or introduction.

IN MEDIO. Intermediate. A term applied, in Scotch practice, to a fund held between parties litigant.

IN MERCIBUS ILLICITIS NON SIT COMMERCIUM. There should be no commerce in illicit or prohibited goods. 3 Kent, Comm. 262, note.

IN MERCY. To be in mercy is to be at the discretion of the king, lord, or judge in respect to the imposition of a fine or other punishment.

IN MISERICORDIA. The entry on the record where a party was in mercy was, *"Ideo in misericordia,"* etc. Sometimes *"misericordia"* means the being quit of all amercements.

IN MITIORI SENSU. In the milder sense; in the less aggravated acceptation.

In actions of slander, it was formerly the rule that, if the words alleged would admit of two constructions, they should be taken in the less injurious and defamatory sense, or *in mitiori sensu.*

IN MODUM ASSISÆ. In the manner or form of an assize. Bract. fol. 183*b*. *In modum juratæ,* in manner of a jury. Id. fol. 181*b*.

IN MORA. In default; literally, in delay. In the civil law, a borrower who omits or refuses to return the thing loaned at the proper time is said to be *in mora.* Story, Bailm. §§ 254, 259.

In Scotch law. A creditor who has begun without completing diligence necessary for attaching the property of his debtor is said to be *in mora.* Bell.

IN MORTUA MANU. Property owned by religious societies was said to be held *in mortua manu,* or in mortmain, since religious men were *civiliter mortui.* 1 Bl.Comm. 479; Tayl.Gloss.

IN NOMINE DEI, AMEN. In the name of God, Amen. A solemn introduction, anciently used in wills and many other instruments. The translation is often used in wills at the present day.

IN NOTIS. In the notes.

IN NOVO CASU, NOVUM REMEDIUM APPONENDUM EST. 2 Inst. 3. A new remedy is to be applied to a new case.

IN NUBIBUS. In the clouds; in abeyance; in custody of law. *In nubibus, in mare, in terrâ, vel in custodiâ legis,* in the air, sea, or earth, or in the custody of the law. Tayl.Gloss. In case of abeyance, the inheritance is figuratively said to rest *in nubibus,* or *in gremio legis.*

IN NULLIUS BONIS. Among the goods or property of no person; belonging to no person, as treasure-trove and wreck were anciently considered.

IN NULLO EST ERRATUM. In nothing is there error. The name of the common plea or joinder in error, denying the existence of error in the record or proceedings; which is in the nature of a demurrer, and at once refers the matter of law arising thereon to the judgment of the court. 2 Tidd, Pr. 1173; Booth v. Com., 7 Metc. (Mass.) 285, 287.

IN OBSCURA VOLUNTATE MANUMITTENTIS, FAVENDUM EST LIBERTATI. Where the expression of the will of one who seeks to manumit a slave is ambiguous, liberty is to be favored. Dig. 50, 17, 179.

IN OBSCURIS, INSPICI SOLERE QUOD VERISIMILIUS EST, AUT QUOD PLERUMQUE FIERI SOLET. In obscure cases, we usually look at what is most probable, or what most commonly happens. Dig. 50, 17, 114.

IN OBSCURIS, QUOD MINIMUM EST SEQUIMUR. In obscure or doubtful cases, we follow that which is the least. Dig. 50, 17, 9; 2 Kent, Comm. 557.

IN ODIUM SPOLIATORIS. In hatred of a despoiler, robber, or wrong-doer. The Saratoga, 1 Gall. 174, Fed.Cas.No.12,355; Arthur v. The Cassius, 2 Story, 99, Fed.Cas.No.564. 1 Greenl.Ev. § 348.

IN ODIUM SPOLIATORIS OMNIA PRÆSUMUNTUR. To the prejudice (in condemnation) of a despoiler all things are presumed; every presumption is made against a wrongdoer. 1 Vern. 452.

IN OMNI ACTIONE UBI DUÆ CONCURRUNT DISTRICTIONES, VIDELICET, IN REM ET IN PERSONAM, ILLA DISTRICTIO TENENDA EST QUÆ MAGIS TIMETUR ET MAGIS LIGAT. In every action where two distresses concur, that is, *in rem* and *in personam,* that is to be chosen which is most dreaded, and which binds most firmly. Bract. fol. 372; Fleta, 1. 6, c. 14, § 28.

IN OMNI RE NASCITUR RES QUÆ IPSAM REM EXTERMINAT. In everything there arises a thing which destroys the thing itself. Everything contains the element of its own destruction. 2 Inst. 15.

IN OMNIBUS. In all things; on all points. "A case parallel *in omnibus.*" 10 Mod. 104.

IN OMNIBUS CONTRACTIBUS, SIVE NOMINATIS SIVE INNOMINATIS, PERMUTATIO CONTINETUR. In all contracts, whether nominate or innominate, an exchange [of value, *i. e.*, a consideration] is implied. Gravin. lib. 2, § 12; 2 Bl. Comm. 444, note.

IN OMNIBUS OBLIGATIONIBUS IN QUIBUS DIES NON PONITUR, PRÆSENTI DIE DEBETUR. In all obligations in which a date is not put, the debt is due on the present day; the liability accrues immediately. Dig. 50, 17, 14.

IN OMNIBUS [FERE] PŒNALIBUS JUDICIIS, ET ÆTATI ET IMPRUDENTIÆ SUCCURRITUR. In nearly all penal judgments, immaturity of age and imbecility of mind are favored. Dig. 50, 17, 108; Broom, Max. 314.

IN OMNIBUS QUIDEM, MAXIME TAMEN IN JURE, ÆQUITAS SPECTANDA SIT. In all things, but especially in law, equity is to be regarded. Dig. 50, 17, 90; Story, Bailm. § 257.

IN PACATO SOLO. In a country which is at peace.

IN PACE DEI ET REGIS. In the peace of God and the king. Fleta, lib. 1, c. 31, § 6. Formal words in old appeals of murder.

IN PAIS. This phrase, as applied to a legal transaction, primarily means that it has taken place without legal proceedings. Thus a widow was said to make a request *in pais* for her dower when she simply applied to the heir without issuing a writ. (Co. Litt. 32*b*.) So conveyances are divided into those by matter of record and those by matter *in pais*. In some cases, however, "matters *in pais*" are opposed not only to "matters of record," but also to "matters in writing," *i. e.*, deeds, as where estoppel by deed is distinguished from estoppel by matter *in pais*. Id. 352*a*.) Sweet. See, also, Pais.

IN PAIS, ESTOPPEL IN. An estoppel not arising from deed or record or written contract. Steph.Pl. 197; Duke v. Griffith, 9 Utah 476, 35 P. 512. The doctrine is that a person may be precluded by his act or conduct or silence, when it is his duty to speak, from asserting a right which he otherwise would have had. Marshall v. Wilson, 175 Or. 506, 154 P.2d 547, 551. The effect of a party's voluntary conduct whereby he is precluded from asserting rights as against another person who has in good faith relied upon such conduct and has been led thereby to change his condition for the worse and who acquires some corresponding right of property or contract. Oswego Falls Corporation v. City of Fulton, 265 N.Y.S. 436, 148 Misc. 170.

Elements or fundamentals of "estoppel in pais" include admission, statement, or act inconsistent with claim afterwards asserted, National Match Co. v. Empire Storage & Ice Co., 227 Mo.App. 1115, 58 S.W.2d 797; Peyrefitte v. Union Homestead Ass'n, La.App., 185 So. 693, 697; change of position to loss or injury of party claiming estoppel, Personal Finance Co. of Providence v. Henley-Kimball Co., 61 R.I. 402, 1 A.2d 121, 125, 117 A.L.R. 1476; Malloy v. City of Chicago, 369 Ill. 97, 15 N.E.2d 861, 865; circumstances such that party estopped knew or should have known facts to be otherwise or pretended to know facts which he did not know, Briscoe v. O'Connor, 119 N.J.Eq. 378, 182 A. 855; false representation or concealment of material facts, Pickens v. Maryland Casualty Co., 141 Neb. 105, 2 N.W.2d 593, 596; inducement to alter position, Haschenberger v. Dennis, 118 Neb. 411, 225 N.W. 25, 26, 63 A.L.R. 493; Wollenberger v. Hoover, 346 Ill. 511, 179 N.E. 42, 67; intention that false representation or concealment be acted on, Malloy v. City of Chicago, 369 Ill. 97, 15 N.E.2d 861, 865; Peterson v. City of Parsons, 139 Kan. 701, 33 P.2d 715, 720; knowledge of facts, by party to be estopped, Darling Stores v. Fidelity-Bankers Trust Co., 178 Tenn. 165, 156 S.W.2d 419, 424; Peterson v. City of Parsons, 139 Kan. 701, 33 P.2d 715, 720; lack of knowledge or means of knowledge of party claiming estoppel, Triplex Shoe Co. v. Rice & Hutchins, 17 Del.Ch. 356, 152 A. 342, 350, 72 A.L.R. 932; Sinclair Refining Co. v. Jenkins Petroleum Process Co., C.C.A.Me., 99 F.2d 9, 13, 14; misleading of one person by another person to his prejudice or injury, Garmon v. Davis, 63 Ga.App. 815, 12 S.E.2d 209, 211; Current News Features v. Pulitzer Pub. Co., C.C.A.Mo., 81 F.2d 288, 292; prejudice or loss or injury to party claiming estoppel, City of St. Louis v. Mississippi River Fuel Corporation, D.C.Mo., 57 F.Supp. 549, 554; In re Bremer's Estate, 141 Neb. 251, 3 N.W.2d 411, 413, 414; reliance by one party on belief induced by other party, Clover v. Peterson, 203 Minn. 337, 281 N.W. 275, 278; Strand v. State, 16 Wash.2d 107, 132 P.2d 1011, 1016.

Ratification is distinguishable in that the substance of "ratification" is confirmation of the unauthorized act or contract after it has been done or made, whereas substance of "estoppel" is the principal's inducement to another to act to his prejudice. Harvey v. J. P. Morgan & Co., Mun.Ct., 2 N.Y.S.2d 520, 531, 166 Misc. 455.

Silence when one should speak may be the basis of estoppel, Thomas v. Conyers, 198 N.C. 229, 151 S.E. 270, 273; waiver is distinguishable in that it is not essential to waiver that the opposite party do anything on the strength of the statement relied upon, Langley v. Norris, Tex.Civ.App., 167 S.W.2d 603, 613; waiver designates act or consequence of act of one person only; it is voluntary act and implies abandonment of right or privilege. McDanels v. General Ins. Co. of America, 1 Cal.App.2d 454, 36 P.2d 829, 832.

See, also, Equitable Estoppel.

IN PAPER. A term formerly applied to the proceedings in a cause before the record was made up. 3 Bl.Comm. 406; 2 Burrows, 1098. Probably from the circumstance of the record being always on parchment. The opposite of "on record." 1 Burrows, 322.

IN PARI CAUSA. In an equal cause. In a cause where the parties on each side have equal rights.

IN PARI CAUSA POSSESSOR POTIOR HABERI DEBET. In an equal cause he who has the possession should be preferred. Dig. 50, 17, 128, 1.

IN PARI DELICTO. In equal fault; equally culpable or criminal; in a case of equal fault or guilt. Rozell v. Vansyckle, 11 Wash. 79, 39 Pac. 270.

A person who is *in pari delicto* with another differs from a *particeps criminis* in this, that the former term always includes the latter, but the latter does not always include the former. 8 East, 381.

IN PARI DELICTO POTIOR EST CONDITIO POSSIDENTIS, [DEFENDENTIS.] In a case of equal or mutual fault [between two parties] the condition of the party in possession [or defending] is the better one. 2 Burrows, 926.

Where each party is equally in fault, the law favors him who is actually in possession. Broom, Max. 290, 729. Where the fault is mutual, the law will leave the case as it finds it. Story, Ag. § 195; Reaves Lumber Co. v. Cain-Hurley Lumber Co., 152 Tenn. 339, 279 S.W. 257, 258.

IN PARI MATERIA. Upon the same matter or subject. Statutes *in pari materia* are to be construed together. State v. Gerhardt, 145 Ind. 439, 44 N.E. 469, 33 L.R.A. 313.

IN PATIENDO. In suffering, permitting, or allowing.

IN PECTORE JUDICIS. In the breast of the judge. Latch, 180. A phrase applied to a judgment.

IN PEJOREM PARTEM. In the worst part; on the worst side. Latch, 159, 160.

IN PERPETUAM REI MEMORIAM. In perpetual memory of a matter; for preserving a record of a matter. Applied to depositions taken in order to preserve the testimony of the deponent.

IN PERPETUITY. Endless duration; forever. Central R. Co. of New Jersey v. New York Telephone Co., 101 N.J.L. 353, 128 A. 160, 161.

IN PERPETUUM REI TESTIMONIUM. In perpetual testimony of a matter; for the purpose of declaring and settling a thing forever. 1 Bl. Comm. 86.

IN PERSON. A party, plaintiff or defendant, who sues out a writ or other process, or appears to conduct his case in court himself, instead of through a solicitor or counsel, is said to act and appear *in person.*

IN PERSONAM, IN REM. In the Roman law, from which they are taken, the expressions "*in rem*" and "*in personam*" were always opposed to one another, an act or proceeding *in personam* being one done or directed against or with reference to a specific person, while an act or proceeding *in rem* was one done or directed with reference to no specific person, and consequently against or with reference to all whom it might concern, or "all the world." The phrases were especially applied to actions; an *actio in personam* being the remedy where a claim against a specific person arose out of an obligation, whether *ex contractu* or *ex maleficio,* while an *actio in rem* was one brought for the assertion of a right of property, easement, *status,* etc., against one who denied or infringed it. See Inst. 4, 6, 1; Gaius, 4, 1, 1–10.

From this use of the terms, they have come to be applied to signify the antithesis of "available against a particular person," and "available against the world at large." Thus, *jura in personam* are rights primarily available against specific persons; *jura in rem,* rights only available against the world at large. Hook v. Hoffman, 147 P. 722, 727, 16 Ariz. 540; Beck v. Natalie Oil Co., 143 La. 153, 78 So. 430.

So a judgment or decree is said to be *in rem* when it binds third persons. Such is the sentence of a court of admiralty on a question of prize, or a decree of nullity or dissolution of marriage, or a decree of a court in a foreign country as to the *status* of a person domiciled there.

Lastly, the terms are sometimes used to signify that a judicial proceeding operates on a thing or a person. Thus, it is said of the court of chancery that it acts *in personam,* and not *in rem,* meaning that its decrees operate by compelling defendants to do what they are ordered to do, and not by producing the effect directly. Sweet. See Cross v. Armstrong, 44 Ohio St. 613, 10 N.E. 160.

Judgment in Personam

See that title.

IN PERSONAM ACTIO EST, QUA CUM EO AGIMUS QUI OBLIGATUS EST NOBIS AD FACIENDUM ALIQUID VEL DANDUM. The action *in personam* is that by which we sue him who is under obligation to us to do something or give something. Dig. 44, 7, 25; Bract. 101*b*.

IN PIOS USUS. For pious uses; for religious purposes. 2 Bl.Comm. 505.

IN PLACE. In mining law, rock or mineralized matter is "in place" when remaining as nature placed it, that is, unsevered from the circumjacent rock, or which is fixed solid and immovable in the form of a vein or lode. Williams v. Gibson, 84 Ala. 228, 4 So. 350, 5 Am.St.Rep. 368.

IN PLENA VITA. In full life. Yearb. P. 18 Hen. VI. 2.

IN PLENO COMITATU. In full county court. 3 Bl.Comm. 36.

IN PLENO LUMINE. In public; in common knowledge; in the light of day.

IN PŒNALIBUS CAUSIS BENIGNIUS INTERPRETANDUM EST. In penal causes or cases, the more favorable interpretation should be adopted. Dig. 50, 17, (197), 155, 2; Plowd. 86*b*, 124; 2 Hale, P.C. 365.

IN POSSE. In possibility; not in actual existence. See In Esse.

IN POTESTATE PARENTIS. In the power of a parent. Inst. 1, 8, pr.; Id. 1, 9; 2 Bl.Comm. 498.

IN PRÆMISSORUM FIDEM. In confirmation or attestation of the premises. A notarial phrase.

IN PRÆPARATORIIS AD JUDICIUM FAVETUR ACTORI. 2 Inst. 57. In things preceding judgment the plaintiff is favored.

IN PRÆSENTI. At the present time. 2 Bl. Comm. 166. Used in opposition to *in futuro.* Van Wyck v. Knevals, 1 S.Ct. 336, 106 U.S. 360, 27 L. Ed. 201.

IN PRÆSENTIA MAJORIS POTESTATIS, MINOR POTESTAS CESSAT. In the presence of the superior power, the inferior power ceases. Jenk. Cent. 214, c. 53. The less authority is merged in the greater. Broom, Max. 111.

IN PRENDER. L. Fr. In taking. A term applied to such incorporeal hereditaments as a party entitled to them was to *take* for himself; such as common. 2 Steph.Comm. 23; 3 Bl.Comm. 15. See In Render.

IN PRETIO EMPTIONIS ET VENDITIONIS, NATURALITER LICET CONTRAHENTIBUS SE CIRCUMVENIRE. In the price of buying and selling, it is naturally allowed to the contracting parties to overreach each other. 1 Story, Cont. 606.

IN PRIMIS. In the first place. A phrase used in argument.

IN PRINCIPIO. At the beginning.

IN PROMPTU. In readiness; at hand. Usually written impromptu.

IN PROPRIA CAUSA NEMO JUDEX. No one can be judge in his own cause. 12 Code, 13.

IN PROPRIA PERSONA. In one's own proper person.

It is a rule in pleading that pleas to the jurisdiction of the court must be plead *in propria persona,* because if pleaded by attorney they admit the jurisdiction, as an attorney is an officer of the court, and he is presumed to plead after having obtained leave, which admits the jurisdiction. Lawes, Pl. 91.

In some jurisdictions, however, this rule is no longer recognized. 1 C.J. 255.

IN QUO QUIS DELINQUIT, IN EO DE JURE EST PUNIENDUS. In whatever thing one offends, in that is he rightfully to be punished. Co. Litt. 233*b*; Wing. Max. 204, max. 58. The punishment shall have relation to the nature of the offense.

IN RE. In the affair; in the matter of; concerning; re. This is the usual method of entitling a judicial proceeding in which there are not adversary parties, but merely some *res* concerning which judicial action is to be taken, such as a bankrupt's estate, an estate in the probate court, a proposed public highway, etc. It is also sometimes used as a designation of a proceeding where one party makes an application on his own behalf, but such proceedings are more usually entitled "*Ex parte* ———."

IN RE COMMUNI MELIOR EST CONDITIO PROHIBENTIS. In common property the condition of the one prohibiting is the better. In other words, either co-owner has a right of veto against the acts of the other. Gulf Refining Co. of Louisiana v. Carroll, 145 La. 299, 82 So. 277, 279.

IN RE COMMUNI NEMINEM DOMINORUM JURE FACERE QUICQUAM, INVITO ALTERO, POSSE. One co-proprietor can exercise no authority over the common property against the will of the other. Dig. 10, 3, 28. In other words, either co-owner has a right of veto against the acts of the other. Gulf Refining Co. of Louisiana v. Carroll, 145 La. 299, 82 So. 277, 279.

IN RE COMMUNI POTIOR EST CONDITIO PROHIBENTIS. In a partnership the condition of one who forbids is the more favorable.

IN RE DUBIA, BENIGNIOREM INTERPRETATIONEM SEQUI, NON MINUS JUSTIUS EST QUAM TUTIUS. In a doubtful matter, to follow the more liberal interpretation is not less the juster than the safer course. Dig. 50, 17, 192, 1.

IN RE DUBIA, MAGIS INFICIATIO QUAM AFFIRMATIO INTELLIGENDA. In a doubtful matter, the denial or negative is to be understood, [or regarded,] rather than the affirmative. Godb. 37.

IN RE LUPANARI, TESTES LUPANARES ADMITTENTUR. In a matter concerning a brothel, prostitutes are admitted as witnesses. Van Epps v. Van Epps, 6 Barb. (N.Y.) 320, 324.

IN RE PARI POTIOREM CAUSAM ESSE PROHIBENTIS CONSTAT. In a thing equally shared [by several] it is clear that the party refusing [to permit the use of it] has the better cause. Dig. 10, 3, 28. A maxim applied to partnerships, where one partner has a right to withhold his assent to the acts of his copartner. 3 Kent.Comm. 45.

IN RE PROPRIA INIQUUM ADMODUM EST ALICUI LICENTIAM TRIBUERE SENTENTIÆ. It is extremely unjust that any one should be judge in his own cause.

IN REBUS (Lat.) In things, cases, or matters.

IN REBUS MANIFESTIS, ERRAT QUI AUCTORITATES LEGUM ALLEGAT; QUIA PERSPICUA VERA NON SUNT PROBANDA. In clear cases, he mistakes who cites legal authorities; for obvious truths are not to be proved. 5 Coke, 67*a*. Applied to cases too plain to require the support of authority; "because," says the report, "he who endeavors to prove them obscures them."

IN REBUS QUÆ SUNT FAVORABILIA ANIMÆ, QUAMVIS SUNT DAMNOSA REBUS, FIAT ALIQUANDO EXTENSIO STATUTI. 10 Coke, 101. In things that are favorable to the spirit, though injurious to things, an extension of a statute should sometimes be made.

IN REGARD TO. Concerning; relating to; in respect of; with respect to; about. Hart v. Hart, 181 Iowa 527, 164 N.W. 849, 850.

IN REM. A technical term used to designate proceedings or actions instituted *against the thing,* in contradistinction to personal actions, which are said to be *in personam.* See In Personam.

It is true that, in a strict sense, a proceeding *in rem* is one taken directly against property, and has for its object the disposition of property, without reference to the title of individual claimants; but, in a larger and more general sense, the terms are applied to actions between parties, where the direct object is to reach and dispose of property owned by them, or of some interest therein. Such are cases commenced by attachment against the property of debtors, or instituted to partition real estate, foreclose a mortgage, or enforce a lien. So far as they affect property in this state, they are substantially proceedings *in rem* in the broader sense which we have mentioned. Pennoyer v. Neff, 95 U.S. 734, 24 L.Ed. 565; Continental Gin Co. v. Arnold, 66 Okl. 132, 167 P. 613, 617, L.R.A.1918B, 511.

In the strict sense of the term, a proceeding "in rem" is one which is taken directly against property or one which is brought to enforce a right in the thing itself. Austin v. Royal League, 316 Ill. 188, 147 N.E. 106, 109.

A divorce suit is a "suit in rem," the essential characteristic of which is found in the power of the state through the decree or judgment of its court to dispose of the subject-matter of the suit, the res, in accordance with the object of the suit, whether that subject-matter be physical property or the status of one or both of the parties litigant, which decree operates immediately and absolutely upon the status of the suitor which is the res in the suit without the necessity of execution, attachment, or contempt proceedings to enforce it. Lister v. Lister, 86 N.J.Eq. 30, 97 A. 170, 173.

A proceeding "in rem" is in effect a proceeding against the owner, as well as a proceeding against the goods, for it is his breach of the law which has to be proven to establish the forfeiture, and it is his property which is sought to be forfeited. Mack v. Westbrook, 148 Ga. 690, 98 S.E. 339, 343.

Judgment in rem. See that title.

Quasi in rem. A term applied to proceedings which are not strictly and purely *in rem,* but are brought against the defendant personally, though the real object is to deal with particular property or subject property to the discharge of claims asserted; for example, foreign attachment, or proceedings to foreclose a mortgage, remove a cloud from title, or effect a partition. Freeman v. Alderson, 7 S.Ct. 165, 119 U.S. 187, 30 L.Ed. 372; Hill v. Henry, 66 N.J.Eq. 150, 57 A. 555.

IN REM ACTIO EST PER QUAM REM NOSTRAM QUÆ AB ALIO POSSIDETUR PETIMUS, ET SEMPER ADVERSUS EUM EST QUI REM POSSIDET. The action *in rem* is that by which we seek our property which is possessed by another, and is always against him who possesses the property. Dig. 44, 7, 25; Bract. fol. 102.

IN RENDER. A thing is said to lie *in render* when it must be rendered or given by the tenant; as rent. It is said to lie *in prender* when it consists in the right in the lord or other person to *take* something. See In Prender.

IN REPUBLICA MAXIME CONSERVANDA SUNT JURA BELLI. In a state the laws of war are to be especially upheld. 2 Inst. 58.

IN RERUM NATURA. In the nature of things; in the realm of actuality; in existence. In a dilatory plea, an allegation that the plaintiff is not *in rerum natura* is equivalent to averring that the person named is fictitious. 3 Bl.Comm. 301.

In civil law, this phrase is applied to things. Inst. 2, 20, 7. It is a broader term than *in rebus humanis: e. g.* before quickening, an infant is *in rerum natura,* but not *in rebus humanis;* after quickening, he is *in rebus humanis* as well as *in rerum natura.* Calvinus, Lex.

IN RESTITUTIONEM, NON IN PŒNAM HÆRES SUCCEDIT. The heir succeeds to the restitution, not to the penalty. An heir may be compelled to make restitution of a sum unlawfully appropriated by the ancestor, but is not answerable criminally, as for a penalty. 2 Inst. 198.

IN RESTITUTIONIBUS BENIGNISSIMA INTERPRETATIO FACIENDA EST. Co.Litt. 112. The most benignant interpretation is to be made in restitutions.

IN SATISFACTIONIBUS NON PERMITTITUR AMPLIUS FIERI QUAM SEMEL FACTUM EST. In payments, more must not be received than has been received once for all. 9 Coke, 53.

IN SCRINIO JUDICIS. In the writing-case of the judge; among the judge's papers. "That is a thing that rests *in scrinio judicis,* and does not appear in the body of the decree." Hardr. 51.

IN SEPARALI. In several; in severalty. Fleta, lib. 2, c. 54, § 20.

IN SIMILI MATERIA. Dealing with the same or a kindred subject-matter.

IN SIMPLICI PEREGRINATIONE. In simple pilgrimage. Bract. fol. 338. A phrase in the old law of essoins. See In Generali Passagio.

IN SOLIDO. In the civil law. For the whole; as a whole. An obligation *in solido* is one where each of the several obligors is liable for the whole; that is, it is joint and several. Henderson v. Wadsworth, 6 S.Ct. 140, 115 U.S. 264, 29 L.Ed. 377. Possession *in solidum* is exclusive possession.

When several persons obligate themselves to the obligee by the terms *"in solido,"* or use any other expressions which clearly show that they intend that each one shall be separately bound to perform the whole of the obligation, it is called an "obligation *in solido*" on the part of the obligors. Civ.Code La. art. 2082.

IN SOLIDUM. For the whole. *Si plures sint fidejussores, quotquot erunt numero, singuli in solidum tenentur,* if there be several sureties, however numerous they may be, they are individually bound for the whole debt. Inst. 3, 21, 4. *In parte sive in solidum,* for a part or for the whole. Id. 4, 1, 16. See Id. 4, 6, 20; Id. 4, 7, 2.

IN SOLO. In the soil or ground. *In solo alieno,* in another's ground. *In solo proprio,* in one's own ground. 2 Steph.Comm. 20.

IN SPECIE. Specific; specifically. Thus, to decree performance *in specie* is to decree specific performance. In kind; in the same or like form. A thing is said to exist *in specie* when it retains its existence as a distinct individual of a particular class.

IN STATU QUO. In the condition in which it was. See Status Quo. McReynolds v. Harrigfeld, 26 Idaho 26, 140 P. 1096, 1098.

IN STIPULATIONIBUS CUM QUÆRITUR QUID ACTUM SIT VERBA CONTRA STIPULATOREM INTERPRETANDA SUNT. In the construction of agreements words are interpreted against the person using them. Thus, the construction of the *stipulatio* is against the stipulator, and the construction of the *promissio* against the promissor. Dig. 45, 1, 38, 18; Broom, Max. 599.

IN STIPULATIONIBUS, ID TEMPUS SPECTATUR QUO CONTRAHIMUS. In stipulations, the time when we contract is regarded. Dig. 50, 17, 144, 1.

IN STIRPES. In the law of intestate succession. According to the roots or stocks; by representation; as distinguished from succession *per capita.* See Per Stirpes; Per Capita.

IN SUBSIDIUM. In aid.

IN SUO QUISQUE NEGOTIO HEBETIOR EST QUAM IN ALIENO. Every one is more dull in his own business than in another's.

IN TALI CASU EDITUM ET PROVISUM. See In Casu Proviso.

IN TANTUM. In so much; so much; so far; so greatly. Reg. Orig. 97, 106.

IN TERMINIS TERMINANTIBUS. In terms of determination; exactly in point. 11 Coke, 40*b*. In express or determinate terms. 1 Leon. 93.

IN TERROREM. In terror or warning; by way of threat. Applied to legacies given upon condition that the recipient shall not dispute the validity or the dispositions of the will; such a condition being usually regarded as a mere threat.

IN TERROREM POPULI. Lat. To the terror of the people. A technical phrase necessary in indictments for riots. 4 Car. & P. 373.

IN TESTAMENTIS PLENIUS TESTATORIS INTENTIONEM SCRUTAMUR. In wills we more especially seek out the intention of the testator. 3 Bulst. 103; Broom, Max. 555.

IN TESTAMENTIS PLENIUS VOLUNTATES TESTANTIUM INTERPRETANTUR. Dig. 50, 17, 12. In wills the intention of testators is more especially regarded. "That is to say," says Mr. Broom, (Max., 568,) "a will will receive a more liberal construction than its strict meaning, if alone considered, would permit."

IN TESTAMENTIS RATIO TACITA NON DEBET CONSIDERARI, SED VERBA SOLUM SPECTARI DEBENT; ADEO PER DIVINATIONEM MENTIS A VERBIS RECEDERE DURUM EST. In wills an unexpressed meaning ought not to be considered, but the words alone ought to be looked to; so hard is it to recede from the words by guessing at the intention.

IN TESTIMONIUM. Lat. In witness; in evidence whereof.

IN THE FIELD. Any place, on land or water, apart from permanent cantonments or fortifications where military operations are being conducted. Hines v. Mikell, C.C.A., 259 F. 28, 30.

IN THE PEACE OF THE STATE. In definition of murder as unlawful and felonious killing of human being "in the peace of the state," the quoted phrase means the same as "in the king's peace" under the English common law, and negatives the idea that deceased was actually engaged in waging war against the state. State v. Corneille, 153 La. 929, 96 So. 813, 817.

IN TOTIDEM VERBIS. In so many words; in precisely the same words; word for word.

IN TOTO. In the whole; wholly; completely; as the award is void *in toto*.

IN TOTO ET PARS CONTINETUR. In the whole the part also is contained. Dig. 50, 17, 113.

IN TRADITIONIBUS SCRIPTORUM, NON QUOD DICTUM EST, SED QUOD GESTUM EST, INSPICITUR. In the delivery of writings, not what is said, but what is done, is looked to. 9 Coke, 137*a*.

IN TRAJECTU. In the passage over; on the voyage over. Sir William Scott, 3 C.Rob.Adm. 141.

IN TRANSITU. In transit; on the way or passage; while passing from one person or place to another. 2 Kent.Comm. 540–552. Amory Mfg. Co. v. Gulf, etc., R. Co., 89 Tex. 419, 37 S.W. 856, 59 Am.St.Rep. 65. On the voyage. 1 C.Rob.Adm. 338.

IN UTROQUE JURE. In both laws; *i. e.*, the civil and canon law.

IN VACUO. Without object; without concomitants or coherence.

IN VADIO. In gage or pledge. 2 Bl.Comm. 157.

IN VENTRE SA MERE. L. Fr. In his mother's womb; spoken of an unborn child.

IN VERAM QUANTITATEM FIDEJUSSOR TENEATUR, NISI PRO CERTA QUANTITATE ACCESSIT. Let the surety be holden for the true quantity, unless he agree for a certain quantity, Bean v. Parker, 17 Mass. 597.

IN VERBIS, NON VERBA, SED RES ET RATIO, QUÆRENDA EST. Jenk. Cent. 132. In the construction of words, not the mere words, but the thing and the meaning, are to be inquired after.

IN VINCULIS. In chains; in actual custody. Gilb. Forum Rom. 97.

Applied also, figuratively, to the condition of a person who is compelled to submit to terms which oppression and his necessities impose on him. 1 Story, Eq.Jur. § 302.

IN VIRIDI OBSERVANTIA. Present to the minds of men, and in full force and operation.

IN VOCIBUS VIDENDUM NON A QUO SED AD QUID SUMATUR. In discourses, it is to be considered not from what, but to what, it is advanced. Ellesmere, Postn. 62.

IN WITNESS WHEREOF. The initial words of the concluding clause in deeds: "In witness whereof the said parties have hereunto set their hands," etc. A translation of the Latin phrase *"in cujus rei testimonium."*

INADEQUATE. Insufficient; disproportionate; lacking in effectiveness or in conformity to a prescribed standard or measure.

INADEQUATE CONSIDERATION. One not adequate or equal in value to the thing conveyed. Farrell v. Third Nat. Bank, 20 Tenn.App. 540, 101 S.W.2d 158, 163.

INADEQUATE DAMAGES. See Damages.

INADEQUATE PRICE. A term applied to indicate the want of a sufficient consideration for a thing sold, or such a price as would ordinarily be entirely incommensurate with its intrinsic value. State v. Purcell, 131 Mo. 312, 33 S.W. 13.

INADEQUATE REMEDY AT LAW. Within the meaning of the rule that equity will not entertain a suit if there is an adequate remedy at law, this does not mean that there must be a failure to collect money or damages at law, but the remedy is considered inadequate if it is, in its nature and character, unfitted or not adapted to the end in view, as, for instance, when the relief sought is preventive rather than compensatory. Cruickshank v. Bidwell, 20 S.Ct. 280, 176 U.S. 73, 44 L. Ed. 377.

INADMISSIBLE. That which, under the established rules of law, cannot be admitted or received; *e. g.*, parol evidence to contradict a written contract.

INADVERTENCE. Heedlessness; lack of attention; want of care; carelessness; failure of a person to pay careful and prudent attention to the progress of a negotiation or a proceeding in court by which his rights may be affected. Used chiefly in statutory enumerations of the grounds on which a judgment or decree may be vacated or set aside; as, "mistake, inadvertence, surprise, or excusable neglect." Skinner v. Terry, 107 N.C. 103, 12 S.E. 118. State ex rel. Regis v. District Court of Second Judicial Dist. in and for Silver Bow County, 102 Mont. 74, 55 P.2d 1295, 1298.

INÆDIFICATIO. Lat. In the civil law. Building on another's land with one's own materials, or on one's own land with another's materials.

INALIENABLE. Not subject to alienation; the characteristic of those things which cannot be bought or sold or transferred from one person to another, such as rivers and public highways, and certain personal rights; *e. g.*, liberty.

INAUGURATION. The act of installing or inducting into office with formal ceremonies, as the coronation of a sovereign, the inauguration of a president or governor, or the consecration of a prelate. A word applied by the Romans to the ceremony of dedicating a temple, or raising a man to the priesthood, after the *augurs* had been consulted.

INBLAURA. In old records. Profit or product of ground. Cowell.

INBOARD. In maritime law, and particularly with reference to the stowage of cargo, this term is contrasted with "outboard." It does not necessarily mean under deck, but is applied to a cargo so piled or stowed that it does not project over the "board" (side or rail) of the vessel. Allen v. St. Louis Ins. Co., 46 N.Y.Super.Ct. 181.

INBORH. In Saxon law. A security, pledge, or *hypotheca*, consisting of the chattels of a person unable to obtain a personal "borg," or surety.

INBOROW. A forecourt or gate-house. A certain barony was inborow and outborow between England and Scotland. Cowell.

INBOUND COMMON. An uninclosed common, marked out, however, by boundaries.

INC. Incorporated. Goldberg, Bowen & Co. v. Dimick, 169 Cal. 187, 146 P. 672, 673; Norwood Bldg. v. Jackson, Tex.Civ.App., 175 S.W.2d 262, 265.

INCAPACITY. Want of capacity; want of power or ability to take or dispose; want of legal ability to act. Ellicott v. Ellicott, 90 Md. 321, 45 A. 183, 48 L.R.A. 58. Inefficiency; incompetency; lack of adequate power. Travelers' Ins. Co. v. Richmond, Tex.Com.App., 291 S.W. 1085, 1087.

Legal incapacity

This expression implies that the person in view has the right vested in him, but is prevented by some impediment from exercising it; as in the case of minors, *femes covert*, lunatics, etc. An administrator has no right until letters are issued to him. Therefore he cannot benefit (as respects the time before obtaining letters) by a saving clause in a statute of limitations in favor of persons under a legal incapacity to sue. Cates v. Brattle, 1 Root (Conn.) 187.

Total incapacity

In Workmen's Compensation Acts, such disqualification from performing the usual tasks of a workman that he cannot procure and retain employment. Western Indemnity Co. v. Corder, Tex.Civ.App., 249 S.W. 316, 317; Georgia Casualty Co. v. Ginn, Tex.Civ.App., 272 S.W. 601, 603; Moore v. Peet Bros. Mfg. Co., 99 Kan. 443, 162 P. 295, 296. Incapacity for work is total not only so long as the injured employee is unable to do any work of any character, but also while he remains unable, as a result of his injury, either to resume his former occupation or to procure remunerative employment at a different occupation suitable to his impaired capacity. Such period of total incapacity may be followed by a period of partial incapacity, during which the injured employee is able both to procure and to perform work at some occupation suitable to his then-existing capacity, but less remunerative than the work in which he was engaged at the time of his injury. That situation constitutes "partial incapacity." Austin Bros. Bridge Co. v. Whitmire, 121 S.E. 345, 346, 31 Ga.App. 560. Synonymous with "total disability." Consolidation Coal Co. v. Crislip, 289 S.W. 270, 273, 217 Ky. 371. See Disability.

INCARCERATION. Imprisonment; confinement in a jail or penitentiary. See Imprisonment.

This term is seldom used in law, though found occasionally in statutes. When so used, it appears always to mean confinement by competent public authority or under due legal process, whereas "imprisonment" may be effected by a private person without warrant of law, and if unjustifiable is called "false imprisonment." No occurrence of such a phrase as "false incarceration" has been noted.

INCASTELLARE. To make a building serve as a castle. Jacob.

INCAUSTUM, or ENCAUSTUM. Ink. Fleta, 1, 2, c. 27, § 5.

INCAUTE FACTUM PRO NON FACTO HABETUR. A thing done unwarily (or unadvisedly) will be taken as not done. Dig. 28, 4, 1.

INCENDIARY. A house-burner; one guilty of arson; one who maliciously and willfully sets another person's building on fire.

INCENDIUM ÆRE ALIENO NON EXUIT DEBITOREM. Cod. 4, 2, 11. A fire does not release a debtor from his debt.

INCEPTION. Commencement; opening; initiation. The beginning of the operation of a contract or will, or of a note, mortgage, lien, etc.; the beginning of a cause or suit in court. Oriental Hotel Co. v. Griffiths, 88 Tex. 574, 33 S.W. 652, 30 L.R.A. 765, 53 Am.St.Rep. 790.

INCERTA PRO NULLIS HABENTUR. Uncertain things are held for nothing. Dav.Ir.K.B. 33.

INCERTA QUANTITAS VITIAT ACTUM. 1 Rolle R. 465. An uncertain quantity vitiates the act.

INCERTÆ PERSONÆ. Uncertain persons, as posthumous heirs, a corporation, the poor, a juristic person, or persons who cannot be ascertained until after the execution of a will. Sohm.Inst. Rom.L.104, 458.

INCEST. The crime of sexual intercourse or cohabitation between a man and woman who are related to each other within the degrees wherein marriage is prohibited by law. People v. Stratton, 141 Cal. 604, 75 P. 166. Signs v. State, 35 Okl. Cr. 340, 250 P. 938, 940.

INCESTUOSI. Those offspring incestuously begotten. Mack.Rom.L. § 143.

INCESTUOUS ADULTERY. The elements of this offense are that defendant, being married to one person, has had sexual intercourse with another related to the defendant within the prohibited degrees. Cook v. State, 11 Ga. 53, 56 Am.Dec. 410.

INCESTUOUS BASTARDS. Incestuous bastards are those who are produced by the illegal connection of two persons who are relations within the degrees prohibited by law. Civ.Code La. art. 183.

INCH. A measure of length, containing one-twelfth part of a foot; originally supposed equal to three barleycorns.

Inch of candle. A mode of sale at one time in use among merchants. A notice is first given upon the exchange, or other public place, as to the time of sale. The goods to be sold are divided into lots, printed papers of which, and the conditions of sale, are published. When the sale takes place, a small piece of candle, about an inch long is kept burning, and the last bidder, when the candle goes out, is entitled to the lot or parcel for which he bids. Wharton.

Inch of water. The unit for the measurement of a volume of water or of hydraulic power, being the quantity of water which, under a given constant head or pressure, will escape through an orifice one inch square (or a circular orifice having a diameter of one inch) in a vertical plane. Jackson Milling Co. v. Chandos, 82 Wis. 437, 52 N.W. 759.

Miner's inch. The quantity of water which will escape from a ditch or reservoir through an orifice in its side one inch square, the center of the orifice being six inches below the constant level of the water, equivalent to about 1.6 cubic feet of water per minute. Defined by statute in Colorado as "an inch-square orifice under a five-inch pressure, a five-inch pressure being from the top of the orifice of the box put into the banks of the ditch to the surface of water." Mills' Ann.St.Colo. § 4643 (Comp.Laws 1921, § 4111). See Longmire v. Smith, 26 Wash. 439, 67 P. 246, 58 L.R.A. 308. The standard miner's inch of water, as fixed by St.Cal.1901, p. 660, is the equivalent of 1½ cubic feet of water per minute measured through any aperture or orifice, making it equivalent to one-fortieth of a second foot. Lillis v. Silver Creek & Panoche Land & Water Co., 32 Cal.App. 668, 163 P. 1040, 1043.

INCHARTARE. To give, or grant, and assure anything by a written instrument.

INCHOATE. Imperfect; partial; unfinished; begun, but not completed; as a contract not executed by all the parties. Good v. Crist, 23 Ohio App. 484, 156 N.E. 146, 148. Pacific Freight Lines v. Pioneer Express Co., 39 Cal.App.2d 609, 103 P.2d 1056, 1058.

INCHOATE DOWER. A wife's interest in the lands of her husband during his life, which may become a right of dower upon his death. Smith v. Shaw, 150 Mass. 297, 22 N.E. 924.

A contingent claim or possibility of acquiring dower by outliving husband and arises, not out of contract, but as an institution of law constituting a mere chose in action incapable of transfer by separate grant but susceptible of extinguishment, which is effected by wife joining with husband in deed, which operates as release or satisfaction of interest and not as conveyance. Auerbach v. Chase Nat. Bank of City of New York, 296 N.Y.S. 487, 489, 251 App. Div. 543.

INCHOATE INSTRUMENT. Instruments which the law requires to be registered or recorded are said to be "inchoate" prior to registration, in that they are then good only between the parties and privies and as to persons having notice. Wilkins v. McCorkle, 112 Tenn. 688, 80 S.W. 834.

INCHOATE INTEREST. An interest in real estate which is not a present interest, but which may ripen into a vested estate, if not barred, extinguished, or divested. Rupe v. Hadley, 113 Ind. 416, 16 N.E. 391.

INCHOATE LIEN. The lien of a judgment, from the day of its entry, subject to be defeated by its vacation, becoming a consummate lien if the motion for a new trial is thereafter overruled; such lien then relating back to the original entry of the judgment. Sterling v. Parker-Washington Co., 185 Mo.App. 192, 170 S.W. 1156, 1159.

INCHOATE RIGHT. In patent law. The right of an inventor to his invention while his application is pending which matures as "property" when the patent issues. Mullins Mfg. Co. v. Booth, C.C.A.Mich., 125 F.2d 660, 664.

INCIDENT. Used both substantively and adjectively of a thing which, either usually or naturally and inseparably, depends upon, appertains to, or follows another that is more worthy. Watts v. Copeland, 170 S.C. 449, 170 S.E. 780, 783. Used as a noun, it denotes anything which inseparably belongs to, or is connected with, or inherent in, another thing, called the "principal." In this sense, a court-baron is incident to a manor. Also, less strictly, it denotes anything which is usually connected with another, or connected for some purposes, though not inseparably. Thus, the right of alienation is incident to an estate in fee-simple, though separable in equity. Cromwell v. Phipps, Sur., 1 N.Y.S. 278; Mount Carmel Fruit Co. v. Webster, 140 Cal. 183, 73 P. 826.

INCIDENTAL. Depending upon or appertaining to something else as primary; something necessary, appertaining to, or depending upon another which is termed the principal; something incidental to the main purpose. The Robin Goodfellow, D.C.Wash., 20 F.2d 924, 925.

The term "incidental powers," within the rule that a corporation possesses only those powers which its charter confers upon it, either expressly or as incidental to its existence, means such powers as are directly and immediately appropriate to the execution of the powers expressly granted and exist only to enable the corporation to carry out the purpose of its creation. State ex inf. Harvey v. Missouri Athletic Club, 261 Mo. 576, 170 S.W. 904, 909, L.R.A. 1915C, 876, Ann.Cas.1916D, 931; State ex rel. Barrett v. First Nat. Bank, 297 Mo. 397, 249 S.W. 619, 622, 30 A.L.R. 918.

INCIDENTAL TO EMPLOYMENT. A risk is "incidental to employment" within Workmen's Compensation Act, when it belongs to or is connected with what a workman has to do in fulfilling his contract of service. Barresse v. Standard Silk Dyeing Co., 10 N.J.Misc. 892, 161 A. 653, 654.

INCIDERE. Lat. In the civil and old English law. To fall into; to fall out; to happen; to come to pass. Calvin. To fall upon or under; to become subject or liable to. *Incidere in legem,* to incur the penalty of a law. Brissonius.

INCILE. Lat. In the civil law. A trench. A place sunk by the side of a stream, so called because it is *cut* (*incidatur*) into or through the stone or earth. Dig. 43, 21, 1, 5. The term seems to have included ditches (*fossæ*) and wells, (*putei.*)

INCINERATION. Burning to ashes; destruction of a substance by fire, as, the corpse of a murdered person.

INCIPITUR. Lat. It is begun; it begins. In old practice, when the pleadings in an action at law, instead of being recited at large on the issue-roll, were set out merely by their commencements, this was described as entering the *incipitur*; *i. e.*, the beginning.

INCISED WOUND. In medical jurisprudence. A cut or incision on a human body; a wound made by a cutting instrument, such as a razor. Burrill, Circ.Ev. 693; Whart. & S. Med. Jur. § 808.

INCITE. To arouse; urge; provoke; encourage; spur on; goad; stir up; instigate; set in motion; as, to "incite" a riot. Also, generally, in criminal law to instigate, persuade, or move another to commit a crime; in this sense nearly synonymous with "abet." Long v. State, 23 Neb. 33, 36 N.W. 310; United States v. Ault, D.C.Wash., 263 F. 800, 810; Commonwealth v. Egan, 113 Pa.Super. 375, 173 A. 764, 766.

INCIVILE. Lat. Irregular; improper; out of the due course of law.

INCIVILE EST, NISI TOTA LEGE PERSPECTA, UNA ALIQUA PARTICULA EJUS PROPOSITA, JUDICARE, VEL RESPONDERE. It is improper, without looking at the whole of a law, to give judgment or advice, upon a view of any one clause of it. Dig. 1, 3, 24.

INCIVILE EST, NISI TOTA SENTENTIA INSPECTA, DE ALIQUA PARTE JUDICARE. It is irregular, or legally improper, to pass an opinion upon any part of a sentence, without examining the whole. Hob. 171*a*.

INCIVISM. Unfriendliness to the state or government of which one is a citizen.

INCLAUSA. In old records. A home close or inclosure near the house. Paroch. Antiq. 31; Cowell.

INCLOSE. To surround; to encompass; to bound; fence, or hem in, on all sides. White Chapel Memorial Ass'n v. Willson, 260 Mich. 238, 244 N.W. 460. To shut up. "To inclose a jury," in Scotch practice, is to shut them up in a room by themselves. Bell. Union Pac. Ry. Co. v. Harris, 28 Kan. 210; Campbell v. Gilbert, 57 Ala. 569.

INCLOSED LANDS. Lands which are actually inclosed and surrounded with fences. Kimball v. Carter, 95 Va. 77, 27 S.E. 823, 38 L.R.A. 570.

INCLOSURE. In English law. Act of freeing land from rights of common, commonable rights, and generally all rights which obstruct cultivation and the productive employment of labor on the soil.

Land surrounded by some visible obstruction. Whittet v. Bertsch, 39 R.I. 31, 97 A. 18, 19, L.R.A. 1916E, 710. An artificial fence around one's estate. See Close.

INCLOSURE ACTS. English statutes regulating the subject of inclosure. The most notable was that of 1801.

INCLOSURE COMMISSION ACT, 1845. The statute 8 and 9 Vict. c. 118, establishing a board of commissioners for England and Wales and empowering them, on the application of persons interested to the amount of one-third of the value of the land, and provided the consent of persons interested to the amount of two-thirds of the land and of the lord of the manor (in case the land be waste of a manor) be ultimately obtained, to inquire into the case and to report to parliament as to the expediency of making the inclosure. 1 Steph.Com. 655.

INCLUDE. (Lat. *inclaudere,* to shut in, keep within). To confine within, hold as in an inclosure, take in, attain, shut up, contain, inclose, comprise, comprehend, embrace, involve. *Including* may, according to context, express an enlargement and have the meaning of *and* or *in addition to,* or merely specify a particular thing already included within general words theretofore used. Miller v. Johnston, 173 N.C. 62, 91 S.E. 593. Prairie Oil and Gas Co. v. Motter, D.C.Kan., 1 F.Supp. 464, 468; Decorated Metal Mfg. Co. v. U. S., 12 Ct.Cust.App. 140; In re Sheppard's Estate, 179 N.Y.S. 409, 412, 189 App.Div. 370; Rose v. State, 184 S.W. 60, 61, 122 Ark. 509; United States ex rel. Lyons v. Hines, 103 F.2d 737, 740, 70 App.D.C. 36, 122 A.L.R. 674.

INCLUSIO UNIUS EST EXCLUSIO ALTERIUS. The inclusion of one is the exclusion of another. The certain designation of one person is an absolute exclusion of all others. 11 Coke, 58*b*; Burgin v. Forbes, 293 Ky. 456, 169 S.W.2d 321, 325.

INCLUSIVE. Embraced; comprehended; comprehending the stated limits or extremes. Opposed to "exclusive."

INCLUSIVE SURVEY. In land law, one which includes within its boundaries prior claims excepted from the computation of the area within such boundaries and excepted in the grant. Stockton v. Morris, 19 S.E. 531, 39 W.Va. 432.

INCOLA. Lat. In the civil law. An inhabitant; a dweller or resident. Properly, one who has transferred his domicile to any country.

INCOLAS DOMICILIUM FACIT. Residence creates domicile. Arnold v. United Ins. Co., 1 Johns. Cas., N.Y., 363, 366.

INCOME. The return in money from one's business, labor, or capital invested; gains, profits, or private revenue. In re Slocum, 169 N.Y. 153, 62 N.E. 130.

The gain derived from capital, from labor or effort, or both combined, including profit or gain through sale or conversion of capital; income is not a gain accruing to capital or a growth in the value of the investment, but is a gain, a profit, something of exchangeable value, proceeding from the property, severed from the capital, however invested or employed, and coming in, being derived, that is, received or drawn by the recipient for his separate use, benefit, and disposal. Goodrich v. Edwards, 41 S.Ct. 390, 255 U.S. 527, 65 L.Ed. 758. The true increase in amount of wealth which comes to a person during a stated period of time. Commissioner of Corporations and Taxation v. Filoon, 310 Mass. 374, 38 N.E.2d 693, 700.

INCOME TAX. A tax relating to the product or income from property or from business pursuits; a tax on the yearly profits arising from property, professions, trades, or offices; a tax on a person's income, emoluments, profits, and the like, or the excess thereof over a certain amount. Interstate Bond Co. v. State Revenue Commission of Georgia, 50 Ga.App. 744, 179 S.E. 559.

An income tax is not levied upon property, funds, or profits, but upon the right of an individual or corporation to receive income or profits. Paine v. City of Oshkosh, 190 Wis. 69, 208 N.W. 790, 791. Under various constitutional and statutory provisions, a tax on incomes is sometimes said to be an excise tax and not a tax on property, Hattiesburg Grocery Co. v. Robertson, 126 Miss. 34, 88 So. 4, 5, 25 A.L.R. 748; nor on business, but a tax on the proceeds arising therefrom, Young v. Illinois Athletic Club, 310 Ill. 75, 141 N.E. 369, 371, 30 A.L.R. 985. But in other cases an income tax is said to be a property and not a personal or excise tax: Commonwealth v. P. Horillard Co., 129 Va. 74, 105 S.E. 683, 684; Kennedy v. Commissioner of Corporations & Taxation, 256 Mass. 426, 152 N.E. 747, 748.

An "excise tax" is an indirect charge for the privilege of following an occupation or trade, or carrying on a business; while an "income tax" is a direct tax imposed upon income, and is as directly imposed as is a tax on land. United States v. Philadelphia, B. & W. R. Co., D.C.Pa., 262 F. 188, 190.

INCOME TAX DEFICIENCY. Exists whenever taxpayer has failed to make adequate return of income, notwithstanding lack of determination by commissioner or his agents. Moore v. Cleveland Ry. Co., C.C.A.Ohio, 108 F.2d 656, 659.

INCOMMODUM NON SOLVIT ARGUMENTUM. An inconvenience does not destroy an argument.

INCOMMUNICATION. In Spanish law. The condition of a prisoner who is not permitted to see or to speak with any person visiting him during his confinement. A person accused cannot be subjected to this treatment unless it be expressly ordered by the judge, for some grave offense, and it cannot be continued for a longer period than is absolutely necessary. This precaution is resorted to for the purpose of preventing the accused from knowing beforehand the testimony of the witnesses, or from attempting to corrupt them and concert such measures as will efface the traces of his guilt. As soon, therefore, as the danger of his doing so has ceased, the interdiction ceases likewise. Escriche.

INCOMMUTABLE. Not capable of or entitled to be commuted. See Commutation.

INCOMPATIBILITY. Incapability of existing or being exercised together.

Thus the relations of landlord and of tenant cannot exist in one man at the same time in reference to the same land. "Incompatibility" which at common law operates to vacate one office by reason of incumbency of another exists when the character and nature of offices or relation to each other are such that one person should not hold both because of the contrariety and antagonism which would result toward incumbent of one office in attempt to discharge duties of other office faithfully and impartially. It is apparent when the holder of one office is subordinate to or has supervision over the other, or has the power of appointment, removal, or punishment of that other, or the audit of his accounts, or the regulation of his compensation. State ex rel. Schenck v. Barrett, 121 Conn. 237, 184 A. 379, 381.

INCOMPATIBLE. Not compatible, incapable of harmonizing or agreeing, mutually repelling, incongruous. And two or more relations, offices, functions, or rights which cannot naturally, or may not legally, exist in or be exercised by the same person at the same time, are said to be incompatible. People v. Green, 46 How.Prac., N.Y., 170; Com. v. Sheriff, 4 Serg. & R. (Pa.) 276; State v. Johnson, 37 N.M. 280, 21 P.2d 813, 89 A.L.R. 1368. See, also, Incompatibility.

INCOMPETENCY. Lack of ability, legal qualification, or fitness to discharge the required duty. In re Leonard's Estate, 95 Mich. 295, 54 N.W. 1082.

In New York, the word "incompetency" is used to designate the condition or legal status of a person who is unable or unfitted to manage his own affairs by reason of insanity, imbecility, or feeble-mindedness, and for whom, therefore, a committee may be appointed; and such a person is designated and "incompetent." In re Palestine's Estate, 270 N.Y.S. 844, 151 Misc. 100.

In French law. Inability or insufficiency of a judge to try a cause brought before him, proceeding from lack of jurisdiction.

INCOMPETENT EVIDENCE. Evidence which is not admissible under the established rules of evidence; evidence which the law does not permit to be presented at all, or in relation to the particular matter, on account of lack of originality or of some defect in the witness, the document, or the nature of the evidence itself. Texas Brewing Co. v. Dickey, Tex.Civ.App., 43 S.W. 578; Bell v. Bumstead, 14 N.Y.S. 697, 60 Hun. 580.

As applied to evidence, the word "incompetent" means not proper to be received; inadmissible, as distinguished from that which the court should admit for the consideration of the jury, though they may not find it worthy of credence.

INCONCLUSIVE. That which may be disproved or rebutted; not shutting out further proof or consideration. Applied to evidence and presumptions.

INCONSISTENT. Mutually repugnant or contradictory; contrary, the one to the other, so that both cannot stand, but the acceptance or establishment of the one implies the abrogation or abandonment of the other; as, in speaking of "inconsistent defenses," or the repeal by a statute of "all laws inconsistent herewith." Borough of Oakland v. Board of Conservation and Development, 98 N.J.L. 99, 118 A. 787, 788. Berry v. City of Fort Worth, Tex.Civ.App., 110 S.W.2d 95, 103.

INCONSULTO. Lat. In the civil law. Unadvisedly; unintentionally. Dig. 28, 4, 1.

INCONTESTABILITY CLAUSE. In life policy means that within the limits of the coverage, the policy shall stand unaffected by any defense that it was invalid in its inception or thereafter became invalid by reason of a condition broken by insured. Berkshire Life Ins. Co. v. Weinig, 290 N.Y. 6, 47 N.E.2d 418, 421. Jolley v. Jefferson Standard Life Ins. Co., 199 N.C. 269, 154 S.E. 400, 402.

INCONTINENCE. Want of chastity; indulgence in unlawful carnal connection. State v. Hewlin, 128 N.C. 571, 37 S.E. 952.

INCONTINENTI. See In Continenti.

INCONVENIENCE. In the rule that statutes should be so construed as to avoid "inconvenience," this means, as applied to the public, the sacrifice or jeoparding of important public interests or hampering the legitimate activities of government or the transaction of public business, and, as applied to individuals, serious hardship or injustice. Black, Interp.Laws, 102; Betts v. U. S., C.C.A.Mass., 132 F. 237, 65 C.C.A. 452.

INCOPOLITUS. A proctor or vicar.

INCORPORALIA BELLO NON ADQUIRUNTUR. Incorporeal things are not acquired by war. 6 Maule & S. 104.

INCORPORAMUS. We incorporate. One of the words by which a corporation may be created in England. 1 Bl.Comm. 473; 3 Steph.Comm. 173.

INCORPORATE. To create a corporation; to confer a corporate franchise upon determinate persons.

To declare that another document shall be taken as part of the document in which the declaration is made as much as if it were set out at length therein. Railroad Co. v. Cupp, 8 Ind.App. 388, 35 N.E. 703.

INCORPORATED LAW SOCIETY. A society of attorneys and solicitors whose function it is to carry out the acts of parliament and orders of court with reference to articled clerks; to keep an alphabetical roll of solicitors; to issue certificates to persons duly admitted and enrolled, and to exercise a general control over the conduct of solicitors in practice, and to bring cases of misconduct before the judges. 3 Steph. Com. 217.

INCORPORATION. The act or process of forming or creating a corporation; the formation of a legal or political body, with the quality of perpetual existence and succession, unless limited by the act of incorporation. Abbott v. Limited Mut. Compensation Ins. Co., 30 Cal.App.2d 157, 85 P.2d 961, 964.

The method of making one document of any kind become a part of another separate document by referring to the former in the latter, and declaring that the former shall be taken and considered as a part of the latter the same as if it were fully set out therein. This is more fully described as "incorporation by reference." If the one document is copied at length in the other, it is called "actual incorporation."

In the civil law. The union of one domain to another.

INCORPOREAL. Without body; not of material nature; the opposite of "corporeal," (*q. v.*).

INCORPOREAL CHATTELS. A class of incorporeal rights growing out of or incident to things *personal;* such as patent-rights and copyrights. 2 Steph.Comm. 72. See Boreel v. New York, 2 Sandf. (N.Y.) 559.

INCORPOREAL HEREDITAMENTS. See Hereditaments.

INCORPOREAL PROPERTY. In the civil law. That which consists in legal right merely. The same as choses in action at common law.

INCORPOREAL THINGS. In the civil law. Things which can neither be seen nor touched, such as consist in rights only, such as the mind alone can perceive. Inst. 2, 2; Civ. Code La. art. 460; Sullivan v. Richardson, 33 Fla. 1, 14 So. 692.

INCORRIGIBLE. Incapable of being corrected, amended, or improved; with respect to juvenile offenders, unmanageable by parents or guardians. People v. Purcell, 70 Colo. 399, 201 P. 881. Shinn v. Barrow, Tex.Civ.App., 121 S.W.2d 450, 451.

INCORRIGIBLE ROGUE. A species of rogue or offender, described in the statutes 5 Geo. IV. c. 83, and 1 & 2 Vict. c. 38. 4 Steph.Comm. 309.

INCORRUPTIBLE. That which cannot be affected by immoral or debasing influences, such as bribery or the hope of gain or advancement.

INCREASE. Enlargement, growth, development, increment, addition, accession, extension, production, profit, interest, issue. Heitzig v. Goetten, 347 Ill. 619, 180 N.E. 428, 433. The produce of land; the offspring of animals. Sorrells v. Sigel-Campion Live Stock Commission Co., 27 Colo.App. 154, 148 P. 279, 280.

INCREASE, AFFIDAVIT OF. Affidavit of payment of increased costs, produced on taxation.

INCREASE, COSTS OF. In English law. It was formerly a practice with the jury to award to the successful party in an action the nominal sum of 40s. only for his costs; and the court assessed by their own officer the actual amount of the successful party's costs; and the amount so assessed, over and above the nominal sum awarded by the jury, was thence called "costs of increase." Lush, Com. Law Pr. 775. The practice has now wholly ceased. Rapal. & Law.

INCREMENT. An increasing, growth in bulk, quantity, number, value, etc.; enlargement, increase. That which is gained or added; the act or process of increasing, augmenting, or growing; enlargement, that which is added; increase; opposed to decrement. In re Corning's Will, 289 N.Y.S. 1101, 1103, 160 Misc. 434.

INCREMENTUM. Lat. Increase or improvement, opposed to *decrementum* or abatement.

INCRIMINATE. To charge with crime; to expose to an accusation or charge of crime; to involve oneself or another in a criminal prosecution or the danger thereof; as, in the rule that a witness is not bound to give testimony which would tend to incriminate him. In re Dendy, Tex. Civ.App., 175 S.W.2d 297, 302.

INCRIMINATING ADMISSION. An acknowledgment of facts tending to establish guilt. People v. Gibbs, 349 Ill. 83, 181 N.E. 628, 630.

INCRIMINATING CIRCUMSTANCE. A fact or circumstance, collateral to the fact of the commission of a crime, which tends to show either that such a crime has been committed or that some particular person committed it. Davis v. State, 51 Neb. 301, 70 N.W. 984.

INCRIMINATORY STATEMENT. A statement which tends to establish guilt of the accused or from which, with other facts, his guilt may be inferred, or which tends to disprove some defense. Shellman v. State, 157 Ga. 788, 122 S.E. 205, 207.

INCROACHMENT. An unlawful gaining upon the right or possession of another. See Encroachment.

INCULPATE. To impute blame or guilt; to accuse; to involve in guilt or crime.

INCULPATORY. In the law of evidence. Going or tending to establish guilt; intended to establish guilt; criminative. Burrill, Circ. Ev. 251, 252; People v. White, 35 Cal.App.2d 61, 94 P.2d 617, 621.

INCUMBENT. A person who is in present possession of an office; one who is legally authorized to discharge the duties of an office. State v. Blakemore, 15 S.W. 960, 104 Mo. 340.

In ecclesiastical law, the term signifies a clergyman who is in possession of a benefice.

INCUMBER. To incumber land is to make it subject to a charge or liability; *e. g.*, by mortgaging it. Incumbrances include not only mortgages and other voluntary charges, but also liens, *lites pendentes*, registered judgments, and writs of execution, etc. Sweet; Newhall v. Insurance Co., 52 Me. 181.

INCUMBRANCE. Any right to, or interest in, land which may subsist in another to the diminution of its value, but consistent with the passing of the fee. Huyck v. Andrews, 113 N.Y. 81, 20 N.E. 581, 3 L.R.A. 789, 10 Am.St.Rep. 432; Miller v. Schwinn, Inc., 113 F.2d 748, 751, 752, 753, 72 App. D.C. 282.

A claim, lien, charge, or liability attached to and binding real property. Harrison v. Railroad Co., 91 Iowa, 114, 58 N.W. 1081; Johnson v. Bridge, 60 Cal.App. 629, 213 P. 512, 513. An incumbrance may be a mortgage, Funk v. Voneida, 11 Serg. & R. (Pa.) 112, 14 Am.Dec. 617; a judgment lien, Bowman v. Franklin Ins. Co., 40 Md. 631; an attachment, Kelsey v. Remer, 43 Conn. 129, 21 Am. Rep. 638; an inchoate right of dower, Bigelow v. Hubbard, 97 Mass. 195; a mechanic's lien, Redmon v. Insurance Co., 51 Wis. 293, 8 N.W. 226, 37 Am. Rep. 830; a lease, Shunk v. Fuller, 118 Kan. 682, 236 P. 449, 451; Estep v. Bailey, 94 Or. 59, 185 P. 227, 229; restriction in deed, Hyman v. Boyle, 239 Mich. 357, 214 N.W. 163, 164; encroachment of a building, Gamorsil Realty Corporation v. Graef, 220 N.Y.S. 221, 222, 128 Misc. 596; an easement or right of way, Krotzer v. Clark, 178 Cal. 736, 174 P. 657, 658; Thackeray v. Knight, 57 Utah, 21, 192 P. 263, 265; accrued and unpaid taxes, Ex parte Helm, 209 Ala. 1, 95 So. 546; the statutory right of redemption, Roy v. F. M. Martin & Son, 16 Ala.App. 650, 81 So. 142, 143.

The term "incumbrance" is sometimes used to denote a burden or charge on personal property as *e. g.* a chattel mortgage on a stock of goods. Hartford Fire Ins. Co. v. Jones, 31 Ariz. 8, 250 P. 248, 251.

INCUMBRANCER. The holder of an incumbrance, *e. g.*, a mortgage, on the estate of another. De Voe v. Rundle, 33 Wash. 604, 74 P. 836.

INCUMBRANCES, COVENANT AGAINST. See Covenant.

INCUR. To have liabilities cast upon one by act or operation of law, as distinguished from contract, where the party acts affirmatively. Beekman v. Van Dolsen, 70 Hun, 288, 24 N.Y.S. 414. Boise Development Co. v. City of Boise, 26 Idaho 347, 143 P. 531, 534.

INCURABLE DISEASE. Any disease which has reached an incurable stage in the patient afflicted therewith, according to general state of knowledge of the medical profession. Freeman v. State Board of Medical Examiners, 54 Okl. 531, 154 P. 56, 57, L.R.A.1916D, 436; State Board of Medical Examiners v. Jordan, 92 Wash. 234, 158 P. 982, 985.

INCURRAMENTUM. L. Lat. The liability to a fine, penalty, or amercement. Cowell.

INDE. Lat. Thence; thenceforth; thereof; thereupon; for that cause.

INDE DATÆ LEGES NE FORTIOR OMNIA POSSET. Laws are made to prevent the stronger from having the power to do everything. Dav. Ir. K. B. 36.

INDEBITATUS. Lat. Indebted. *Nunquam indebitatus,* never indebted. The title of the plea substituted in England for *nil debet.*

INDEBITATUS ASSUMPSIT. Lat. Being indebted, he promised or undertook. That form of the action of *assumpsit* in which the declaration alleges a debt or obligation to be due from the defendant, and then avers that, in consideration thereof, he promised to pay or discharge the same.

This form of action is brought to recover in damages the amount of the debt or demand and upon the trial the jury will, according to evidence, give verdict for whole or part of that sum; 3 Bla.Com. 155; Selw.N.P. 68; whereas *debt* and *covenant* proceed directly for the debt, and damages are given only for the detention of the debt.

INDEBITI SOLUTIO. Lat. In the civil and Scotch law. A payment of what is not due. When made through ignorance or by mistake, the amount paid might be recovered back by an action termed *"conditio indebiti."* (Dig. 12, 6.) Bell.

INDEBITUM. In the civil law. Not due or owing. (Dig. 12, 6.) Calvin.

INDEBTEDNESS. The state of being in debt, without regard to the ability or inability of the party to pay the same. 1 Story, Eq. Jur. 343; Jewell v. Nuhn, 173 Iowa 112, 155 N.W. 174, 177, Ann.Cas.1918D, 356. The owing of a sum of money upon a certain and express agreement. City of Perry v. Johnson, 233 P. 679, 680, 106 Okl. 32.

Strictly the word implies an absolute or complete liability. McCrea v. First Nat. Bank, 162 Minn. 455, 203 N.W. 220; West Florida Grocery Co. v. Teutonia Fire Ins. Co., 74 Fla. 220, 77 So. 209, 211, L.R.A.1918B, 968. A contingent liability, such as that of a surety before the principal has made default, does not constitute indebtedness. On the other hand, the money need not be immediately payable. Obligations yet to become due constitute indebtedness, as well as those already due. St. Louis Perpetual Ins. Co. v. Goodfellow, 9 Mo. 149. And in a broad sense and in common understanding the word may mean anything that is due and owing. Jones v. Heinzle, 75 Ind.App. 431, 130 N.E. 815, 816.

Involuntary indebtedness. Of a county, a liability imposed by law, which the county is not privileged to evade or postpone. Dexter Horton Trust & Savings Bank v. Clearwater County, D.C. Idaho, 235 F. 743, 756; Wingate v. Clatsop County, 71 Or. 94, 142 P. 561, 562.

Voluntary indebtedness. One which a county is at liberty to evade or postpone until means are provided for the payment of the expenses incident thereto; opposed to involuntary indebtedness. Wingate v. Clatsop County, 71 Or. 94, 142 P. 561, 562.

INDECENCY. An act against good behavior and a just delicacy. Timmons v. U. S., C.C.A.Ohio, 85 F. 205, 30 C.C.A. 74.

This is scarcely a technical term of the law, and is not susceptible of exact definition or description in its juridical uses. The question whether or not a given act, publication, etc., is indecent is for the court and jury in the particular case.

INDECENT. Offensive to common propriety; offending against modesty or delicacy; grossly vulgar; obscene; lewd; unseemly; unbecoming; indecorous; unfit to be seen or heard. Hutcheson v. State, 24 Ga.App. 54, 99 S.E. 715; Wood v. State, 45 Ga.App. 783, 165 S.E. 908.

Indecent assault. The act of a male person taking indecent liberties with the person of a female. Martin v. Jansen, 113 Wash. 290, 193 P. 674, 675; Commonwealth v. Gregory, 132 Pa.Super. 507, 1 A.2d 501, without her consent and against her will, but with no intent to commit the crime of rape.

Indecent exhibition. Any exhibition *contra bonos mores,* as the taking a dead body for the purpose of dissection or public exhibition. 2 T.R. 734.

Indecent exposure. Exposure to sight of the private parts of the body in a lewd or indecent manner in a public place. It is an indictable offense at common law, and by statute in many of the states. Commonwealth v. Broadland, 315 Mass. 20, 51 N.E.2d 961, 962. See, further, Exposure of Person.

Indecent liberties. In the statutory offense of "taking indecent liberties with the person of a female child," this phrase means such liberties as the common sense of society would regard as indecent and improper. According to some authorities, it involves an assault or attempt at sexual intercourse, (State v. Kunz, 90 Minn. 526, 97 N. W. 131,) but according to others, it is not necessary that the liberties or familiarities should have related to the private parts of the child, (People v. Hicks, 98 Mich. 86, 56 N.W. 1102.)

Indecent publications. Such as are offensive to modesty and delicacy; obscene; lewd; tending to the corruption of morals. Dunlop v. U. S., 17 S. Ct. 375, 165 U.S. 486, 41 L.Ed. 799.

Public indecency. This phrase has no fixed legal meaning, is vague and indefinite, and cannot, in itself, imply a definite offense. The courts, by a kind of judicial legislation, in England and the United States, have usually limited the operation of the term to public displays of the naked person, the publication, sale, or exhibition of obscene books and prints, or the exhibition of a monster,—acts which have a direct bearing on public morals, and affect the body of society. Irven v. State, 138 Tex.Cr.R. 368, 136 S.W.2d 608, 609.

INDECIMABLE. In old English law. That which is not titheable, or liable to pay tithe. 2 Inst. 490.

INDEFEASIBLE. That which cannot be defeated, revoked, or made void. This term is usually applied to an estate or right which cannot be defeated.

INDEFENSUS. Lat. In old English practice. Undefended; undenied by pleading. A defendant who makes no defense or plea. Blount.

INDEFINITE. Without fixed boundaries or distinguishing characteristics; not definite, determinate, or precise. In re Knoll's Estate, 262 N.Y.S. 619, 146 Misc. 613.

INDEFINITE FAILURE OF ISSUE. A failure of issue not merely at the death of the party whose issue are referred to, but at any subsequent period, however remote. 1 Steph.Comm. 562. A failure of issue whenever it shall happen, sooner or later, without any fixed, certain, or definite period within which it must happen. 4 Kent.Comm. 274. Anderson v. Jackson, 16 Johns. (N.Y.) 399, 8 Am.Dec. 330.

INDEFINITE LEGACY. See Legacy.

INDEFINITE NUMBER. A number which may be increased or diminished at pleasure.

INDEFINITE PAYMENT. In Scotch law. Payment without specification. Indefinite payment is where a debtor, owing several debts to one creditor, makes a payment to the creditor, without specifying to which of the debts he means the payment to be applied. See Bell.

INDEFINITUM AEQUIPOLLET UNIVERSALI. The undefined is equivalent to the whole. 1 Vent. 368.

INDEFINITUM SUPPLET LOCUM UNIVERSALIS. The undefined or general supplies the place of the whole. Branch. Princ. 4 Co. 77.

INDEMNIFICATUS. Lat. Indemnified. See Indemnify.

INDEMNIFY. To save harmless; to secure against loss or damage; to give security for the reimbursement of a person in case of an anticipated loss falling upon him. Hasbrouck v. Carr, 19 N.M. 586, 145 P. 133, 136.

To make good; to compensate; to make reimbursement to one of a loss already incurred by him. Cousins v. Paxton & Gallagher Co., 98 N.W. 277, 122 Iowa 465; U. S. Fidelity & Guaranty Co. v. Williams, 148 Md. 289, 129 A. 660, 664.

INDEMNIS. Lat. Without hurt, harm, or damage; harmless.

INDEMNITEE. The person who, in a contract of indemnity, is to be indemnified or protected by the other. Hasbrouck v. Carr, 19 N.M. 586, 145 P. 133, 136.

INDEMNITOR. The person who is bound, by an indemnity contract, to indemnify or protect the other. Hasbrouck v. Carr, 19 N.M. 586, 145 P. 133, 136.

INDEMNITY. A collateral contract or assurance, by which one person engages to secure another against an anticipated loss or to prevent him from being damnified by the legal consequences of an act or forbearance on the part of one of the parties or of some third person. National Bank of Tifton v. Smith, 142 Ga. 663, 83 S.E. 526, 528, L.R.A.1915B, 1116.

The term is also used to denote a compensation given to make the person whole from a loss already sustained; as where the government gives indemnity for private property taken by it for public use. Proctor v. Dillon, 235 Mass. 538, 129 N.E. 265, 269. It means, also, restitution or reimbursement. Travelers Ins. Co. v. Georgia Power Co., 51 Ga.App. 579, 181 S.E. 111.

A legislative act, assuring a general dispensation from punishment or exemption from prosecution to persons involved in offenses, omissions of official duty, or acts in excess of authority, is called an indemnity; strictly it is an act of indemnity. Loss. See Loss.

Thus, insurance is a contract of indemnity. So an indemnifying bond is given to a sheriff who fears to proceed under an execution where the property is claimed by a stranger.

INDEMNITY AGAINST LIABILITY. A contract to indemnify when liability of person indemnified arises, irrespective of whether person indemnified has suffered actual loss. Indemnity against loss, on the other hand, does not render indemnitor liable until person indemnified makes payment or sustains loss. City of Topeka v. Ritchie, 102 Kan. 384, 170 P. 1003, 1004.

INDEMNITY BOND. A bond for the payment of a penal sum conditioned to be void if the obligor shall indemnify and save harmless the obligee against some anticipated loss.

INDEMNITY CONTRACT. A contract between two parties whereby the one undertakes and agrees to indemnify the other against loss or damage arising from some contemplated act on the part of the indemnitor, or from some responsibility assumed by the indemnitee, or from the claim or demand of a third person, that is, to make good to him such pecuniary damage as he may suffer. See Wicker v. Hoppock, 6 Wall. 99, 18 L.Ed. 752.

INDEMNITY LANDS. Lands granted to railroads, in aid of their construction, being portions of the public domain, to be selected in lieu of other parcels embraced within the original grant, but which were lost to the railroad by previous disposition or by reservation for other purposes. Altschul v. Clark, 39 Or. 315, 65 P. 991.

INDEMNITY POLICY. As distinguished from general liability policy, a policy on which no action can be maintained except to indemnify for money actually paid. Most v. Massachusetts Bonding & Ins. Co., Mo.App., 196 S.W. 1064, 1065.

See *Indemnity insurance* and *Liability insurance* under Insurance.

INDEMPNIS. The old form of writing *indemnis*. Townsh. Pl. 19. So, *indempnificatus* for *indemnificatus*.

INDENIZATION. The act of making a denizen, or of naturalizing.

INDENT, *n.* In American law. A certificate or indented certificate issued by the government of the United States at the close of the Revolution, for the principal or interest of the public debt. Webster; U. S. v. Irwin, 26 Fed.Cas. 546.

INDENT, *v.* To cut in a serrated or waiving line. In old conveyancing, if a deed was made by more parties than one, it was usual to make as many copies of it as there were parties, and each was cut or indented (either in acute angles, like the teeth of a saw, or in a waving line) at the top or side, to tally or correspond with the others, and the deed so made was called an "indenture." Anciently, both parts were written on the same piece of parchment, with some word or letters written between them through which the parchment was cut, but afterwards, the word or letters being omitted, indenting came into use, the idea of which was that the genuineness of each part might be proved by its fitting into the angles cut in the other. But at length even this was discontinued, and at present the term serves only to give name to the species of deed executed by two or more parties, as opposed to a deed-poll (*q. v.*) 2 Bl. Comm. 295.

To bind by indentures; to apprentice; as to indent a young man to a shoe-maker. Webster.

INDENTURE. A deed to which two or more persons are parties, and in which these enter into reciprocal and corresponding grants or obligations towards each other; whereas a deed-poll is properly one in which only the party making it executes it, or binds himself by it as a deed, though the grantors or grantees therein may be several in number. 3 Washb. Real Prop. 311. See Indent, *v.*

INDENTURE OF A FINE. Indentures made and engrossed at the chirographer's office and delivered to the cognizor and the cognizee, usually beginning with the words: *"Hœc est finalis concordia."* And then reciting the whole proceedings at length. 2 Bla. Com. 351.

INDENTURE OF APPRENTICESHIP. A contract in two parts, by which a person, generally a minor, is bound to serve another in his trade, art, or occupation for a stated time, on condition of being instructed in the same.

INDEPENDENCE. The state or condition of being free from dependence, subjection, or control. A state of perfect irresponsibility. Political independence is the attribute of a nation or state which is entirely autonomous, and not subject to the government, control, or dictation of any exterior power.

INDEPENDENT. Not dependent; not subject to control, restriction, modification, or limitation from a given outside source.

INDEPENDENT ADJUSTER. A person, firm or corporation who holds himself or itself out for employment to more than one insurance company, is not a regular employee of the company, does not work exclusively for one company and is paid in each case assigned for time consumed and expenses incurred. Cole v. State, 37 N.Y.S.2d 1002, 1006, 179 Misc. 172.

INDEPENDENT ADVICE. Concerning a trust deed or will which must be shown where a fiduciary relationship exists, means that the donor had the preliminary benefit of conferring fully and privately upon the subject of his intended gift with a person who was not only competent to inform him correctly as to its legal effect, but who was, furthermore, so disassociated from the interests of the donee as to be in a position to advise with the donor impartially and confidentially as to the consequences to himself of his proposed benefaction. Madden v. Glathart, 125 Kan. 466, 265 P. 42, 45.

INDEPENDENT CONTRACT. See Contract.

INDEPENDENT CONTRACTOR. One who, exercising an independent employment, contracts to do a piece of work according to his own methods and without being subject to the control of his employer except as to the result of the work. People v. Orange County Road Const. Co., 175 N.Y. 84, 67 N.E. 129, 65 L.R.A. 33. Fox v. Dunning, 124 Okl. 228, 255 P. 582, 584; Bell v. State, 153 Md. 333, 138 A. 227, 228, 58 A.L.R. 1051.

One who exercises an independent employment and contracts to do a piece of work according to his own judgment and methods, and without being subject to his employer except as to the results of the work, and who has the right to employ and direct the action of the workmen, independently of such employer and freed from any superior authority in him to say how the specified work shall be done, or what the laborers shall do as it progresses. Johnson v. Asheville Hosiery Co., 199 N.C. 38, 153 S.E. 591, 593. It is very generally held that the right of control as to the mode of doing the work contracted for is the principal consideration in determining whether one employed is an "independent contractor" or servant. Thompson v. Twiss, 90 Conn. 444, 97 A. 328, 330, L.R.A.1916E, 506. If the employee is merely subject to the control or direction of the employer as to the result to be obtained, he is an independent contractor; if he is subject to the control of the employer as to the means to be employed, he is not an independent contractor. Gulf Refining Co. v. Wilkinson, 94 Fla. 664, 114 So. 503. Nettleship v. Shipman, 161 Wash. 292, 296 P. 1056, 1057.

INDEPENDENT COVENANT. See Covenant.

INDEPENDENTER SE HABET ASSECURATIO A VIAGGIO NAVIS. The voyage insured is an independent or distinct thing from the voyage of the ship. 3 Kent, Comm. 318, note.

INDETERMINATE. That which is uncertain, or not particularly designated; as if I sell you one hundred bushels of wheat, without stating what wheat. 1 Bouv. Inst. no. 950.

INDETERMINATE OBLIGATION. See Obligation.

INDETERMINATE SENTENCE. A sentence to imprisonment for the maximum period defined by law, subject to termination by the parole board or other agency at any time after service of the minimum period. Such a sentence is invalid unless specifically authorized by statute. 24 C.J.S. p. 1217.

INDEX. A book containing references, alphabetically arranged, to the contents of a series or collection of volumes; or an addition to a single volume or set of volumes containing such references to its contents.

INDEX ANIMI SERMO. Language is the exponent of the intention. The language of a statute or instrument is the best guide to the intention. Broom, Max. 622.

INDIAN COUNTRY. As the term is used in the federal statutes, is a country to which the Indians retained the right of use and occupancy, involving under certain restrictions freedom of action and of enjoyment in their capacity as a distinct people, and ceases to be such when their title is extinguished, unless by virtue of some reservation expressed at the time and clearly appearing. Schaap v. United States, C.C.A.Ark., 210 F. 853, 855; Royal Brewing Co. v. Missouri, K. & T. Ry. Co., D.C.Kan., 217 F. 146, 148. This term does not necessarily import territory owned and occupied by Indians, but it means all those portions of the United States designated by this name in the legislation of congress. Waters v. Campbell, 4 Sawy. 121, Fed.Cas. No.17,264.

INDIAN DEPREDATIONS ACTS. As early as May 19, 1796, an act was passed by congress, providing an eventual indemnification to citizens of the United States for depredations committed by Indians in taking or destroying their property; 1 St.L. 472. Other acts of a similar character were passed from time to time. By the act of March 3, 1891, congress conferred on the court of claims jurisdiction of claims for property taken and destroyed by Indians.

INDIAN RESERVATION. A part of public domain set aside by proper authority for use and occupation of tribe or tribes of Indians. Peters v. Pauma School Dist. of San Diego County, 91 Cal. App. 792, 267 P. 576, 577; United States v. Parton, D.C.N.C., 46 F.Supp. 843, 844.

INDIAN TITLE. Claim of Indian tribes of right, because of immemorial occupancy, to roam certain territory to exclusion of any other Indians. Northwestern Bands of Shoshone Indians v. U. S., Ct. Cl., 65 S.Ct. 690, 692, 324 U.S. 335, 89 L.Ed. 985.

INDIAN TRIBE. A separate and distinct community or body of the aboriginal Indian race of men found in the United States. Montoya v. U. S., 21 S.Ct. 358, 180 U.S. 261, 45 L.Ed. 521.

INDIANS. The aboriginal inhabitants of North America. Frazee v. Spokane County, 29 Wash. 278, 69 P. 782.

INDICARE. Lat. In the civil law. To show or discover. To fix or tell the price of a thing. Calvin. To inform against; to accuse.

INDICATIF. An abolished writ by which a prosecution was in some cases removed from a court-christian to the queen's bench. Enc. Lond.

INDICATION. In the law of evidence. A sign or token; a fact pointing to some inference or conclusion. Burrill, Circ. Ev. 251, 252, 263, 275.

INDICATIVE EVIDENCE. This is not evidence properly so called, but the mere suggestion of evidence proper, which may possibly be procured if the suggestion is followed up. Brown.

INDICAVIT. In English practice. A writ of prohibition that lies for a patron of a church, whose clerk is sued in the spiritual court by the clerk of another patron, for tithes amounting to a fourth part of the value of the living. 3 Bl.Comm. 91; 3 Steph.Comm. 711. So termed from the emphatic word of the Latin form. Reg.Orig. 35*b*, 36.

INDICIA. Signs; indications. Circumstances which point to the existence of a given fact as probable, but not certain. For example, "*indicia* of partnership" are any circumstances which would induce the belief that a given person was in reality, though not ostensibly, a member of a given firm.

The term is much used in the civil law in a sense nearly or entirely synonymous with circumstantial evidence. It denotes facts which give rise to inferences, rather than the inferences themselves. Graham Ice Cream Co. v. Petros, 127 Neb. 172, 254 N.W. 869.

INDICIUM. In the civil law. A sign or mark. A species of proof, answering very nearly to the circumstantial evidence of the common law. Best, Pres. p. 13, § 11, note; Wills, Circ. Ev. 34.

INDICT. See Indictment.

INDICTABLE. Proper or necessary to be prosecuted by process of indictment. Indictable offenses embrace common-law offenses or statutory offenses the punishments for which are infamous. Lakes v. Goodloe, 195 Ky. 240, 242 S.W. 632, 639.

INDICTED. Charged in an indictment with a criminal offense. See Indictment.

INDICTEE. A person indicted.

INDICTIO. In old public law. A declaration; a proclamation. *Indictio belli,* a declaration or indiction of war. An indictment.

INDICTION, CYCLE OF. A mode of computing time by the space of fifteen years, instituted by Constantine the Great; originally the period for the payment of certain taxes. Some of the charters of King Edgar and Henry III. are dated by indictions. Wharton.

INDICTMENT. An accusation in writing found and presented by a grand jury, legally convoked and sworn, to the court in which it is impaneled, charging that a person therein named has done some act, or been guilty of some omission, which, by law, is a public offense, punishable on indictment. Kennedy v. State, 86 Tex.Cr.R. 450, 216 S.W. 1086; State v. Engler, 217 Iowa 138, 251 N.W. 88.

A presentment differs from an indictment in that it is an accusation made by a grand jury of their own motion, either upon their own observation and knowledge, or upon evidence before them; while an indictment is preferred at the suit of the government, and is usually framed in the first instance by the prosecuting officer of the government, and by him laid before the grand jury, to be found or ignored. An information resembles in its form and substance an indictment, but is filed at the mere discretion of the proper law officer of the government, without the intervention or approval of a grand jury, and an affidavit is a charge made and preferred by an individual. 2 Story,

Const. §§ 1784, 1786; People v. Foster, 198 Cal. 112, 243 P. 667, 670.

In Scotch law. The form of process by which a criminal is brought to trial at the instance of the lord advocate. Where a private party is a principal prosecutor, he brings his charge in what is termed the "form of criminal letters."

Joint Indictment

When several offenders are joined in the same indictment, as when principals in the first and second degree, and accessaries before and after the fact, are all joined in the same indictment. 2 Hale, P.C. 173; Brown.

INDICTMENT DE FELONY EST CONTRA PACEM DOMINI REGIS, CORONAM ET DIGNITATEM SUAM, IN GENERE ET NON IN INDIVIDUO; QUIA IN ANGLIÅ NON EST INTERREGNUM. Jenk. Cent. 205. Indictment for felony is against the peace of our lord the king, his crown and dignity in general, and not against his individual person; because in England there is no interregnum.

INDICTOR. He who causes another to be indicted. The latter is sometimes called the "indictee."

INDIFFERENT. Impartial; unbiased; disinterested. People v. Vermilyea, 7 Cow. (N.Y.) 122; Fox v. Hills, 1 Conn. 307.

INDIGENA. In old English law. A subject born; one born within the realm, or naturalized by act of parliament. Co.Litt. 8*a*. The opposite of "*alienigena*," (*q. v.*).

INDIGENT. In a general sense, one who is needy and poor, or one who has not sufficient property to furnish him a living nor anyone able to support him to whom he is entitled to look for support. Storrs Agricultural School v. Whitney, 54 Conn. 342, 8 A. 141.

INDIGENT INSANE PERSON. An insane person with insufficient estate to pay for his maintenance in the hospital, after providing for those who could claim his support. Massachusetts General Hospital v. Inhabitants of Belmont, 233 Mass. 190, 124 N.E. 21, 23.

INDIGNITY. In the law of divorce, a species of cruelty addressed to the mind, sensibilities, self-respect, or personal honor of the subject, rather than to the body, and defined as "unmerited contemptuous conduct towards another; any action towards another which manifests contempt for him; contumely, incivility, or injury accompanied with insult." Goodman v. Goodman, 80 Mo.App. 281; 1 Bish. Mar. & Div. § 826; O'Hern v. O'Hern, 206 Mo.App. 651, 228 S.W. 533, 536.

The phrase "indignities to the person," as used in statutes, has reference to bodily indignities, as distinguished from such as may be offered to the mind, sensibilities, or reputation. Kurtz v. Kurtz, 38 Ark. 123. But compare Miller v. Miller, 78 N.C. 105.

INDIRECT. Not direct in relation or connection; not having an immediate bearing or application; not related in the natural way. Runyon v. Western & Southern Life Ins. Co., 48 Ohio App. 251, 192 N.E. 882, 883. Almost always used in law in opposition to "direct," though not the only antithesis of the latter word, as the terms "collateral" and "cross" are sometimes used in contrast with "direct."

As to indirect "Attack," "Confession," "Contempt," and "Tax," see those titles.

INDIRECT EVIDENCE. Is that which only tends to establish the issue by proof of various facts sustaining by their consistency the hypothesis claimed. It consists of both inferences and presumptions. Lake County v. Neilon, 44 Or. 14, 74 P. 212, 214.

See, also, Circumstantial Evidence; Inference; Presumption.

INDIRECT TAX. A tax upon some right or privilege or corporate franchise. Madison Suburban Utility Dist. of Davidson County v. Carson, 232 S.W.2d 277, 280, 191 Tenn. 300; a tax laid upon the happening of an event as distinguished from its tangible fruits. Chickering v. Commissioner of Internal Revenue, C.C.A.1, 118 F.2d 254, 258.

INDISPENSABLE. That which cannot be spared, omitted, or dispensed with.

INDISPENSABLE EVIDENCE. That without which a particular fact cannot be proved. Ballinger's Ann. Codes & St. Or. 1901, § 689 (Code 1930, § 9—113).

INDISPENSABLE PARTIES. In a suit in equity, those who not only have an interest in the subject-matter of the controversy, but an interest of such a nature that a final decree cannot be made without either affecting their interests or leaving the controversy in such a condition that its final determination may be wholly inconsistent with equity and good conscience. Kendig v. Dean, 97 U.S. 425, 24 L.Ed. 1061. State of Washington v. United States, C.C.A.Or. & Wash., 87 F.2d 421, 426, 427, 429, 431.

INDISTANTER. Forthwith; without delay.

INDITEE. L. Fr. In old English law. A person indicted. Mirr. c. 1, § 3; 9 Coke, pref.

INDIVIDUAL. As a noun, this term denotes a single person as distinguished from a group or class, and also, very commonly, a private or natural person as distinguished from a partnership, corporation, or association; but it is said that this restrictive signification is not necessarily inherent in the word, and that it may, in proper cases, include artificial persons. State v. Bell Telephone Co., 36 Ohio St. 310, 38 Am.Rep. 583.

As an adjective, "individual" means pertaining or belonging to, or characteristic of, one single person, either in opposition to a firm, association, or corporation, or considered in his relation thereto.

INDIVIDUAL ASSETS. In the law of partnership, property belonging to a member of a partnership as his separate and private fortune, apart from the assets or property belonging to the firm as such or the partner's interest therein.

INDIVIDUAL DEBTS. Such as are due from a member of a partnership in his private or personal capacity, as distinguished from those due from the firm or partnership. Goddard v. Hapgood, 25 Vt. 360, 60 Am.Dec. 272.

INDIVIDUAL SYSTEM OF LOCATION. A term formerly used in Pennsylvania to designate the location of public lands by surveys, in which the land called for by each warrant was separately surveyed. Ferguson v. Bloom, 144 Pa. 549, 23 A. 49.

INDIVIDUALLY. Separately and personally, as distinguished from jointly or officially, and as opposed to collective or associate action or common interest. Southern Distributing Co. v. Carraway, 189 N.C. 420, 127 S.E. 427, 428.

INDIVIDUUM. Lat. In the civil law. That cannot be divided. Calvin.

INDIVISIBLE. Not susceptible of division or apportionment; inseparable; entire. Thus, a contract, covenant, consideration, etc., may be divisible or indivisible; *i. e.*, separable or entire. Garon v. Credit Foncier Canadien, 37 R.I. 273, 92 A. 561, 564. See, also, Contract.

INDIVISUM. Lat. That which two or more persons hold in common without partition; undivided.

INDORSAT. In old Scotch law. Indorsed. 2 Pitc. Crim. Tr. 41.

INDORSE. To write a name on the back of a paper or document. Bills of exchange and promissory notes are indorsed by a party's writing his name on the back. Hartwell v. Hemmenway, 7 Pick. (Mass.) 117.

"Indorse" is a technical term, having sufficient legal certainty without words of more particular description. Brooks v. Edson, 7 Vt. 351.

See In Dorso.

INDORSEE. The person to whom a bill of exchange, promissory note, bill of lading, etc., is assigned by indorsement.

INDORSEE IN DUE COURSE. An indorsee in due course is one who, in good faith, in the ordinary course of business, and for value, before its apparent maturity or presumptive dishonor, and without knowledge of its actual dishonor, acquires a negotiable instrument duly indorsed to him, or indorsed generally, or payable to the bearer. More v. Finger, 128 Cal. 313, 60 P. 933.

INDORSEMENT. The act of a payee, drawee, accommodation indorser, or holder of a bill, note, check, or other negotiable instrument, in writing his name upon the back of the same, with or without further or qualifying words, whereby the property in the same is assigned and transferred to another.

That which is so written upon the back of a negotiable instrument. State v. Hearn, 115 Ohio St. 340, 154 N.E. 244, 245.

In the law of negotiable instruments, a new and substantive contract by which title to the instrument is transferred and by which indorser becomes a party to the instrument and is liable, on certain conditions for its payment. Johnson v. Beickey, 64 Utah, 43, 228 P. 189, 191. In this respect indorsement differs from a common-law assignment. Jones County Trust & Savings Bank v. Kurt, 192 Iowa, 965, 182 N.W. 409, 413.

One who writes his name upon a negotiable instrument, otherwise than as a maker or acceptor, and delivers it, with his name thereon, to another person, is called an "indorser," and his act is called "indorsement."

The word "indorsement" is also used with reference to writs, insurance policies, certificates of stock, etc. The term as used in the Uniform Stock Transfer Act contemplates a writing passing or attempting to pass title or an interest. Stoltz v. Carroll, 99 Ohio St. 289, 124 N.E. 226, 231. As applied to a writ or warrant "indorsement" is an entry made on the back thereof. Gondas v. Gondas, 99 N.J.Eq. 473, 134 A. 615, 617.

Accommodation indorsement

In the law of negotiable instruments, one made by a third person without any consideration, but merely for the benefit of the holder of the instrument, or to enable the maker to obtain money or credit on it. Unless otherwise explained, it is understood to be a loan of the indorser's credit without restriction. Young v. Exchange Bank of Kentucky, 152 Ky. 293, 153 S.W. 444, 445, Ann.Cas.1915B, 148.

Blank indorsement

One made by the mere writing of the indorser's name on the back of the note or bill, without mention of the name of any person in whose favor the indorsement is made, but with the implied understanding that any lawful holder may fill in his own name above the indorsement if he so chooses. Northern Trading Co. v. Drexel State Bank of Chicago, 37 N.D. 521, 164 N.W. 151, 154; Aufderheide v. Moeller, 221 Mo.App. 442, 281 S.W. 965, 967.

Conditional indorsement

One by which the indorser annexes some condition (other than the failure of prior parties to pay) to his liability. The condition may be either precedent or subsequent. 1 Daniel, Neg.Inst. § 697.

Full indorsement

One by which the indorser orders the money to be paid to some particular person by name; it differs from a blank indorsement, which consists merely in the name of the indorser written on the back of the instrument. Kilpatrick v. Heaton, 3 Brev., S.C., 92; Lee v. Chillicothe Branch of State Bank, 15 Fed.Cas. 153.

Irregular indorsement

One made by a third person before delivery of the note to the payee; an indorsement in blank by a third person above the name of the payee, or when the payee does not indorse at all. Bank of Bellows Falls v. Dorset Marble Co., 61 Vt. 106, 17 Atl. 43; Metropolitan Bank v. Muller, 50 La.Ann. 1278, 24 South. 295, 69 Am.St.Rep. 475.

Proper indorsement

Such indorsement as the law merchant requires to authorize payment to the holder of the instrument. Security State Bank v. State Bank of Brantford, N. D., 31 N.D. 454, 154 N.W. 282, 283.

Qualified indorsement

One which restrains or limits, or qualifies or enlarges, the liability of the indorser, in any manner different from what the law generally imports as his true liability, deducible from the nature of the instrument. Chitty, Bills, 261; Stover Bank v. Welpman, Mo.App., 284 S.W. 177, 180. A transfer of a bill of exchange or promissory note to an indorsee, without any liability to the indorser. The words usually employed for this purpose are *"sans recours,"* without recourse. 1 Bouv.Inst. No. 1138.

Regular indorsement

An indorsement in blank by a third person under the name of the payee or after delivery of the note to him. Bank of Bellows Falls v. Dorset Marble Co., 61 Vt. 106, 17 Atl. 42.

Restrictive indorsement

One which stops the negotiability of the instrument, or which contains such a definite direction as to the payment as to preclude the indorsee from making any further transfer of the instrument. People's Bank v. Jefferson County Sav. Bank, 106 Ala. 524, 17 So. 728, 54 Am.St.Rep. 59. Defined by statute in some states as an indorsement which either prohibits the further negotiation of the instrument, or constitutes the indorsee the agent of the indorser, or vests the title in the indorsee in trust for or to the use of some other person. Negotiable Instruments Law N. D. § 36 (Comp.Laws 1913, § 6921); Bates' Ann.St.Ohio 1904, § 3172*h* (Gen.Code, § 8141).

Special indorsement

An indorsement *in full,* which specifically names the indorsee. Carolina Sav. Bank v. Florence Tobacco Co., 45 S.C. 373, 23 S.E. 139.

Special indorsement of writ

In English practice. The writ of summons in an action may, under Order iii. 6, be indorsed with the particulars of the amount sought to be recovered in the action, after giving credit for any payment or set-off; and this special indorsement (as it is called) of the writ is applicable in all actions where the plaintiff seeks merely to recover a debt or liquidated demand in money payable by the defendant, with or without interest, arising upon a contract, express or implied, as, for instance, on a bill of exchange, promissory note, check, or other simple contract debt, or on a bond or contract under seal for payment of a liquidated amount of money, or on a statute where the sum sought to be recovered is a fixed sum of money or in the nature of a debt, or on a guaranty, whether under seal or not. Brown.

INDORSER. He who indorses; *i. e.,* being the payee or holder, writes his name on the back of a bill of exchange, etc.

INDUBITABLE PROOF. Evidence which is not only found credible, but is of such weight and directness as to make out the facts alleged beyond a doubt. Jermyn v. McClure, 195 Pa. 245, 45 A. 938.

INDUCE. To bring on or about, to affect, cause, to influence to an act or course of conduct, lead by persuasion or reasoning, incite by motives, prevail on. State v. Stratford, 55 Idaho 65, 37 P.2d 681, 682.

INDUCEMENT. In Contracts. The benefit or advantage which the promisor is to receive from a contract is the inducement for making it. Collins v. Harris, 130 Wash. 394, 227 P. 508, 509.

In Criminal Evidence. Motive; that which leads or tempts to the commission of crime. Burrill, Circ. Ev. 283.

In Pleading. That portion of a declaration or of any subsequent pleading in an action which is brought forward by way of explanatory introduction to the main allegations. Brown. Houston v. Tyler, 140 Mo. 252, 36 S.W. 654.

INDUCIÆ. In International Law. A truce; a suspension of hostilities; an agreement during war to abstain for a time from warlike acts.

In Old Maritime Law. A period of twenty days after the safe arrival of a vessel under bottomry, to dispose of the cargo, and raise the money to pay the creditor, with interest.

In Old English Practice. Delay or indulgence allowed a party to an action; further time to appear in a cause. Bract. fol. 352*b;* Fleta, lib. 4, c. 5, § 8.

In Scotch Practice. Time allowed for the performance of an act. Time to appear to a citation. Time to collect evidence or prepare a defense.

Induciæ legales. In Scotch law. The days between the citation of the defendant and the day of appearance; the days between the test day and day of return of the writ.

INDUCT. To put in enjoyment or possession, especially to introduce into possession of an office or benefice, with customary ceremonies, to bring in, initiate, to be put formally in possession, inaugurate or install. State ex rel. Slattery v. Raupp, 303 Mo. 684, 263 S.W. 834, 835.

INDUCTI SUNT IN CARCEREM ET IMPARCATI. See Imparcare.

INDUCTIO. Lat. In the civil law. Obliteration, by drawing the pen or *stylus* over the writing. Dig. 28, 4; Calvin.

INDUCTION. In ecclesiastical law. The ceremony by which an incumbent who has been instituted to a benefice is vested with full possession of all the profits belonging to the church, so that he becomes seised of the temporalities of the church, and is then complete incumbent. It is performed by virtue of a mandate of induction directed by the bishop to the arch-deacon, who either performs it in person, or directs his precept to one or more other clergymen to do it. Phillim. Ecc. Law, 477.

In military law. Induction is complete where a man successfully passes the physical examination and is accepted by the army for training and service, and all the steps prescribed by statute and regulations having the force of law have been taken, whether he takes the oath administered to him or not. United States ex rel. Diamond v. Smith, D.C.Mass., 47 F.Supp. 607, 609.

INDULGENCE. In the Roman Catholic Church. A remission of the punishment due to sins, granted by the pope or church, and supposed to save the sinner from purgatory. Its abuse led to the Reformation in Germany. Wharton. Forbearance, (*q. v.*)

INDULTO. In Ecclesiastical law. A dispensation granted by the pope to do or obtain something contrary to the common law.

In Spanish Law. The condonation or remission of the punishment imposed on a criminal for his offense. This power is exclusively vested in the king.

INDUMENT. Endowment, (*q. v.*)

INDUSTRIAL AND PROVIDENT SOCIETIES. Societies formed in England for carrying on any labor, trade, or handicraft, whether wholesale or retail, including the buying and selling of land and also (but subject to certain restrictions) the business of banking.

INDUSTRIAL SCHOOLS. Schools (established by voluntary contribution) in which industrial training is provided, and in which children are lodged, clothed, and fed, as well as taught.

INDUSTRIAL TRACK. One connecting with main line track and used and equipped for moving freight in carloads to or from one or more industries thereby reached and served, in incidental services such as loading, reloading, or storing, and in incidental switching or yard movements. Gulf, C. & S. F. R. Co. v. Texas & P. R. Co., C.C.A. Tex., 4 F.2d 904, 906, 907; Miller Engineering Co. v. Louisiana Ry. & Nav. Co., 144 La. 786, 81 So. 314, 317.

INDUSTRIAM, PER. Lat. A qualified property in animals *feræ naturæ* may be acquired *per industriam, i. e.*, by a man's reclaiming and making them tame by art, industry, and education; or by so confining them within his own immediate power that they cannot escape and use their natural liberty. 2 Steph.Comm. 5.

INDUSTRY. Any department or branch of art, occupation, or business conducted as a means of livelihood or for profit; especially, one which employs much labor and capital and is a distinct branch of trade. Chicago, R. I. & P. Ry. Co. v. State, 83 Okl. 161, 201 P. 260, 264; Dessen v. Department of Labor and Industries of Washington, 190 Wash. 69, 66 P.2d 867, 869.

INEBRIATE. A person addicted to the use of intoxicating liquors; an habitual drunkard. Taylor v. Koenigstein, 128 Neb. 809, 260 N.W. 544. Maher v. Brown, 225 Iowa 341, 280 N.W. 553, 554.

INE, CODE OF. A code of the West Saxons dating from 688 to 695. Adopted by Alford, probably with alterations. Seebohm, Tribal Customs, 386.

INEFFICIENCY. Quality of being incapable or indisposed to do the things required of an officer. Holmes v. Osborn, 57 Ariz. 522, 115 P.2d 775, 783.

INELIGIBILITY. Disqualification or legal incapacity to be elected to an office. Thus, an alien or naturalized citizen is ineligible to be elected president of the United States. Carroll v. Green, 148 Ind. 362, 47 N.E. 223.

This incapacity arises from various causes; and a person may be incapable of being elected to one office who may be elected to another; the incapacity may also be perpetual or temporary.

INELIGIBLE. Disqualified to be elected to an office; also disqualified to hold an office if elected or appointed to it. State v. Murray, 28 Wis. 99, 9 Am.Rep. 489; State ex rel. Graham v. Hall, 73 N. D. 428, 15 N.W.2d 736, 739.

INESSE POTEST DONATIONI, MODUS, CONDITIO SIVE CAUSA; UT MODUS EST; SI CONDITIO; QUIA CAUSA. In a gift there may be manner, condition, and cause; as [*ut*] introduces a manner; if, [*si*,] a condition; because, [*quia*,] a cause. Dyer, 138.

INESCAPABLE PERIL. Within last clear chance doctrine, means peril which the plaintiff is helpless to avoid by his own efforts, but which requires action on part of defendant to avert it. Melenson v. Howell, 344 Mo. 1137, 130 S.W.2d 555, 560.

INEST DE JURE. Lat. It is implied of right; it is implied by law.

INEVITABLE. Incapable of being avoided; fortuitous; transcending the power of human care, foresight, or exertion to avoid or prevent, and therefore suspending legal relations so far as to excuse from the performance of contract obligations, or from liability for consequent loss.

INEVITABLE ACCIDENT. An unavoidable accident; one produced by an irresistible physical cause; an accident which cannot be prevented by human skill or foresight, but results from natural causes, such as lightning or storms, perils of the sea, inundations or earthquakes, or sudden death or illness. By irresistible force is meant an interposition of human agency, from its nature and power absolutely uncontrollable. Brousseau v. The Hudson, 11 La.Ann. 428; Leland v. Empire Engineering Co., 108 A. 570, 575, 135 Md. 208.

An accident is "inevitable", so as to preclude recovery on ground of negligence, if person by whom it occurs neither has nor is legally bound to have sufficient power to avoid it or prevent its injuring another. Stephens v. Virginia Elec. & Power Co., 184 Va. 94, 34 S.E.2d 374, 377.

Inevitable accident occurs where a vessel is pursuing a lawful avocation in a lawful manner, using the proper precautions against danger, and an accident occurs. The highest degree of caution that can be used is not required. It is enough that it is reasonable under the circumstances; such as is usual in similar cases, and has been found by long experience to be sufficient to answer the end in view,—the safety of life and property. The Grace Girdler, 7 Wall. 196, 19 L.Ed. 113. Inevitable accident is only when the disaster happens from natural causes, without negligence or fault on either side, and when both parties have endeavored, by every means in their power, with due care and caution, and with a proper display of nautical skill, to prevent the occurrence of the accident. The Philip J. Kenny, C.C.A.N.J., 60 F.2d 457, 458.

INEWARDUS. A guard; a watchman. Domesday.

INFALISTATUS. In old English law. Exposed upon the sands, or seashore. A species of punishment mentioned in Hengham. Cowell.

INFAMIA. Lat. Infamy; ignominy or disgrace.

By *infamia juris* is meant infamy established by law as the consequence of crime; *infamia facti* is where the party is supposed to be guilty of such crime, but it has not been judicially proved. Comm. v. Green, 17 Mass. 515, 541.

INFAMIS. Lat. In Roman law. A person whose right of reputation was diminished (involving the loss of some of the rights of citizenship) either on account of his infamous avocation or because of conviction for crime. Mackeld. Rom. Law, § 135.

INFAMOUS. Shameful or disgraceful. Stevens v. Wilber, 136 Or. 599, 300 P. 329, 330.

INFAMOUS CRIME. See Crime.

INFAMOUS PUNISHMENT. See Punishment.

INFAMY. A qualification of a man's legal *status* produced by his conviction of an infamous crime and the consequent loss of honor and credit, which, at common law, rendered him incompetent as a witness, and by statute in some jurisdictions entails other disabilities. State v. Clark, 60 Kan. 450, 56 P. 767.

INFANCY. Minority; the state of a person who is under the age of legal majority,—at common law, twenty-one years. According to the sense in which this term is used, it may denote the condition of the person merely with reference to his years, or the contractual disabilities which nonage entails, or his *status* with regard to other powers or relations. Keating v. Railroad Co., 94 Mich. 219, 53 N.W. 1053.

Natural infancy. A period of non-responsible life, which ends with the seventh year. Wharton.

INFANGENTHEF. In old English law. A privilege of lords of certain manors to judge any thief taken within their fee. See Outfangthef.

INFANS. Lat. In the civil law. A child under the age of seven years; so called *"quasi impos fandi,"* (as not having the faculty of speech.) Cod. Theodos, 8, 18, 8.

INFANS NON MULTUM A FURIOSO DISTAT. An infant does not differ much from a lunatic. Bract. l. 3, c. 2, § 8; Dig. 50, 17, 5, 40; 1 Story, Eq. Jur. §§ 223, 224, 242.

INFANT. A person within age, not of age, or not of full age; a person under the age of twenty-one years; a minor. Co. Litt. 171*b;* 1 Bl.Comm. 463–466; 2 Kent, Comm. 233. Beavers v. Southern Ry. Co., 212 Ala. 600, 103 So. 887, 889.

INFANTIA. Lat. In the civil law. The period of infancy between birth and the age of seven years. Calvin.

INFANTICIDE. The murder or killing of an infant soon after its birth. The fact of the birth distinguishes this act from "feticide" or "procuring abortion," which terms denote the destruction of the *fetus* in the womb. See, also, Prolicide.

INFANTS' MARRIAGE ACT. The statute 18 & 19 Vict. c. 43. By virtue of this act every infant, (if a male, of twenty, or, if a female, of seventeen, years,—section 4,) upon or in contemplation of marriage, may, with the sanction of the chancery division of the high court, make a valid settlement or contract for a settlement of property. Wharton.

INFANZON. In Spanish law. A person of noble birth, who exercises within his domains and inheritance no other rights and privileges than those conceded to him. Escriche.

INFECTION. In medical jurisprudence. The transmission of disease or disease germs from one person to another, either directly by contact with morbidly affected surfaces, or more remotely through inhalation, absorption of food or liquid tainted with excremental matter, contact with contaminated clothing or bedding, or other agencies.

A distinction is sometimes made between "infection" and "contagion," by restricting the latter term to the communication of disease by direct contact. Grayson v. Lynch, 163 U.S. 468, 16 S.Ct. 1064, 41 L.Ed. 230. But "infection" is the wider term and in proper use includes "contagion," and is frequently extended so as to include the local inauguration of disease from other than human sources, as from miasmas, poisonous plants, etc. In another, and perhaps more accurate sense, contagion is the entrance or lodgment of pathogenic germs in the system as a result of direct contact; infection is their fixation in the system or the inauguration of disease as a consequence. In this meaning, infection does not always result from contagion, and on the other hand it may result from the introduction of disease germs into the system otherwise than by contagion.

Auto-infection. The communication of disease from one part of the body to another by mechanical transmission of virus from a diseased to a healthy part.

Infectious disease. One capable of being transmitted or communicated by means of infection.

INFEFT. In Scotch law. To give seisin or possession of lands; to invest or enfeoff. 1 Kames, Eq. 215.

INFEFTMENT. In Old Scotch law. Investiture or infeudation, including both charter and seisin. 1 Forb. Inst. pt. 2, p. 110.

In Later law. *Saisine,* or the instrument of possession. Bell.

INFENSARE CURIAM. Lat. An expression applied to a court when it suggested to an advocate something which he had omitted through mistake or ignorance. Spelman.

INFEOFFMENT. The act or instrument of feoffment. In Scotland it is synonymous with *"saisine,"* meaning the instrument of possession. Formerly it was synonymous with "investiture." Bell.

INFERENCE. In the law of evidence. A truth or proposition drawn from another which is supposed or admitted to be true. A process of reasoning by which a fact or proposition sought to be established is deduced as a logical consequence from other facts, or a state of facts, already proved or admitted. Whitehouse v. Bolster, 95 Me. 458, 50 A. 240; Joske v. Irvine, 91 Tex. 574, 44 S.W. 1059.

A deduction which the reason of the jury makes from the facts proved, without an express direction of law to that effect. Puget Sound Electric Ry. v. Benson, C.C.A. Wash., 253 F. 710, 714.

A "presumption" and an "inference" are not the same thing, a presumption being a deduction which the law requires a trier of facts to make, an inference being a deduction which the trier may or may not make, according to his own conclusions; a presumption is mandatory, an inference, permissible. Cross v. Passumpsic Fiber Leather Co., 90 Vt. 397, 98 A. 1010, 1014; Joyce v. Missouri & Kansas Telephone Co., Mo.App., 211 S.W. 900, 901.

INFERENCE ON INFERENCE, RULE OF. Means that one presumption or inference may not be based upon another. McManimen v. Public Service Co. of Northern Illinois, 317 Ill.App. 649, 47 N.E.2d 385.

INFERENTIAL. In the law of evidence. Operating in the way of inference; argumentative. Presumptive evidence is sometimes termed "inferential." Com. v. Harman, 4 Pa. 272.

INFERENTIAL FACTS. Such as are established not directly by testimony or other evidence, but by inferences or conclusions drawn from the evidence. Railway Co. v. Miller, 141 Ind. 533, 37 N.E. 343.

INFERIOR. One who, in relation to another, has less power and is below him; one who is bound to obey another. He who makes the law is the superior; he who is bound to obey it, the inferior. 1 Bouv. Inst. no. 8.

INFERIOR COURT. This term may denote any court subordinate to the chief appellate tribunal in the particular judicial system; but it is commonly used as the designation of a court of special, limited, or statutory jurisdiction, whose record must show the existence and attaching of jurisdiction in any given case, in order to give presumptive validity to its judgment. In re Heard's Guardianship, 174 Miss. 37, 163 So. 685, 687.

The English courts of judicature are classed generally under two heads,—the superior courts and the inferior courts; the former division comprising the courts at Westminster, the latter comprising all the other courts in general, many of which, however, are far from being of inferior importance in the common acceptation of the word. Brown.

INFEUDATION. The placing in possession of a freehold estate; also the granting of tithes to laymen.

INFICIARI. Lat. In the civil law. To deny; to deny one's liability; to refuse to pay a debt or restore a pledge; to deny the allegation of a plaintiff; to deny the charge of an accuser. Calvin.

INFICIATIO. Lat. In the civil law. Denial; the denial of a debt or liability; the denial of the claim or allegation of a party plaintiff. Calvin.

INFIDEL. One who does not believe in the existence of a God who will reward or punish in this world or that which is to come. Hale v. Everett, 53 N.H. 54, 16 Am.Rep. 82. One who professes no religion that can bind his conscience to speak the truth. 1 Greenl. Ev. § 368. One who does not recognize the inspiration or obligation of the Holy Scriptures, or generally recognized features of the Christian religion. Gibson v. Ins. Co., 37 N.Y. 580.

INFIDELIS. In Old English law. An infidel or heathen.

In Feudal law. One who violated fealty.

INFIDELITAS. In feudal law. Infidelity; faithlessness to one's feudal oath. Spelman.

INFIDUCIARE. In old European law. To pledge property. Spelman.

INFIHT. Sax. An assault made on a person inhabiting the same dwelling.

INFINITUM IN JURE REPROBATUR. That which is endless is reprobated in law. 12 Coke, 24. Applied to litigation.

INFIRM. Weak, feeble. The testimony of an "infirm" witness may be taken *de bene esse* in some circumstances. 1 P. Wms. 117.

INFIRMATIVE. In the law of evidence. Having the quality of diminishing force; having a tendency to weaken or render infirm. 3 Benth. Jud. Ev. 14; Best, Pres. § 217. Exculpatory is used by some authors as synonymous. Wills, Circ. Ev. 120; Best, Pres. § 217.

INFIRMATIVE CONSIDERATION. In the law of evidence. A consideration, supposition, or hypothesis of which the criminative facts of a case admit, and which tends to weaken the inference or presumption of guilt deducible from them. Burrill, Circ. Ev. 153–155.

INFIRMATIVE FACT. In the law of evidence. A fact set up, proved, or even supposed, in opposition to the criminative facts of a case, the tendency of which is to weaken the force of the inference of guilt deducible from them. 3 Benth. Jud. Ev. 14; Best, Pres. § 217, *et seq.*

INFIRMATIVE HYPOTHESIS. A term sometimes used in criminal evidence to denote an hypothesis or theory of the case which assumes the defendant's innocence, and explains the criminative evidence in a manner consistent with that assumption.

INFIRMITY. In an application for insurance an ailment or disease of a substantial character, which apparently in some material degree impairs the physical condition and health of the applicant and increases the chance of his death or sickness and which if known, would have been likely to deter the insurance company from issing the policy. Eastern Dist. Piece Dye Works v. Travelers" Ins. Co., 234 N.Y. 441, 138 N.E. 401, 404, 26 A.L.R. 1505.

INFLUENCE. See Undue Influence.

INFORMAL. Deficient in legal form; inartificially drawn up.

INFORMALITY. Want of legal form. State v. Gallimon, 24 N.C. 377; Franklin v. Mackey, 16 Serg. & R. (Pa.) 118; Hunt v. Curry, 37 Ark. 108.

INFORMATION. An accusation exhibited against a person for some criminal offense, without an indictment. 4 Bl.Comm. 308. An accusation in the nature of an indictment, from which it differs only in being presented by a competent public officer on his oath of office, instead of a grand jury on their oath. 1 Bish. Crim. Proc. § 141; People v. Sponsler, 46 N.W. 459, 1 Dak. 289; Howard v. State, 143 Tenn. 539, 227 S.W. 36. A written accusation sworn to before a magistrate, upon which an indictment is afterwards founded. Commonwealth v. Cooke, 55 Pa.Super.Ct. 435, 439.

The word is also frequently used in the law in its sense of communicated knowledge. Masline v. New York, N. H. & H. R. Co., 95 Conn. 702, 112 A. 639, 640. And affidavits are frequently made, and pleadings and other documents verified, on "information and belief."

In French Law. The act or instrument which contains the depositions of witnesses against the accused. Poth. Proc.Civil, § 2, art. 5.

Criminal information. A formal accusation of crime, differing from an indictment only in that it is preferred by a prosecuting officer instead of by a grand jury. People v. Gahagan, 368 Ill. 475, 14 N.E.2d 838, 839.

Information in the nature of a quo warranto. A proceeding against the usurper of a franchise or office. Jarman v. Mason, 102 Okl. 278, 229 P. 459, 460. See Quo Warranto.

Information of intrusion. A proceeding instituted by the state prosecuting officer against intruders upon the public domain. Gen. St. Mass. c. 141 (Gen. Laws, c. 245); Com. v. Hite, 6 Leigh (Va.) 588, 29 Am.Dec. 226.

INFORMATUS NON SUM. In practice. I am not informed. A formal answer made by the defendant's attorney in court to the effect that he has not been advised of any defense to be made to the action. Thereupon judgment by default passes.

INFORMER. A person who informs or prefers an accusation against another, whom he suspects of the violation of some penal statute.

Common informer. A common prosecutor. A person who habitually ferrets out crimes and offenses and lays information thereof before the ministers of justice, in order to set a prosecution on foot, not because of his office or any special duty in the matter, but for the sake of the share of the fine or penalty which the law allots to the informer in certain cases. Also used in a less invidious sense, as designating persons who were authorized and empowered to bring action for penalties. U. S. v. Stocking, D.C.Mont., 87 F. 861; In re Barker, 56 Vt. 20.

INFORTIATUM. The name given by the glossators to the second of the three parts or volumes into which the Pandects were divided. It commences with the third title of the twenty-fourth book and ends with the thirty-eighth book. The glossators at Bologna had at first only two parts, the first called *"Digestum Vetus,"* (the old Digest,) and the last called *"Digestum Novum,"* (the New Digest.) When they afterwards received the middle or second part, they separated from the *Digestum Novum* the beginning it had then, and added it to the second part, from which *enlargement* the latter received the name *"Infortiatum."* Mackeld. Rom. Law, § 110.

INFORTUNIUM, HOMICIDE PER. Where a man doing a lawful act, without intention of hurt, unfortunately kills another.

INFRA. (Lat.) Below, under, beneath, underneath. The opposite of *supra,* above. Thus, we say, *primo gradu est*—supra, *pater, mater,* infra, *filius, filia:* in the first degree of kindred in the ascending line, above is the father and the mother, below, in the descending line, son and daughter. Inst. 3. 6. 1.

In another sense, this word signifies *within:* as, *infra corpus civitatis,* within the body of the country; *infra præsidia,* within the guards. So of time, *during: infra furorem,* during the madness. This use is not classical. The use of *infra* for *intra* seems to have sprung up among the barbarians after the fall of the Roman empire.

INFRA ÆTATEM. Under age; not of age. Applied to minors.

INFRA ANNOS NUBILES. Under marriageable years; not yet of marriageable age.

INFRA ANNUM. Under or within a year. Bract. fol. 7.

INFRA ANNUM LUCTÛS. (Within the year of mourning.) The phrase is used in reference to the marriage of a widow within a year after her husband's death, which was prohibited by the civil law.

INFRA BRACHIA. Within her arms. Used of a husband *de jure,* as well as *de facto.* 2 Inst. 317. Also *inter brachia.* Bract. fol. 148*b*. It was in this sense that a woman could only have an appeal for murder of her husband *inter brachia sua.*

INFRA CIVITATEM. Within the state. 1 Camp. 23, 24.

INFRA CORPUS COMITATUS. Within the body (territorial limits) of a county. In English law, waters which are *infra corpus comitatus* are exempt from the jurisdiction of the admiralty. Waring v. Clarke, 5 How. 441, 451, 12 L.Ed. 226.

INFRA DIGNITATEM CURIÆ. Beneath the dignity of the court; unworthy of the consideration of the court. Where a bill in equity is brought upon a matter too trifling to deserve the attention of the court, it is demurrable, as being *infra dignitatem curiæ.* Smets v. Williams, 4 Paige, Ch. (N.Y.) 364.

INFRA FUROREM. During madness; while in a state of insanity. Bract. fol. 19*b*.

INFRA HOSPITIUM. Within the inn. When a traveler's baggage comes *infra hospitium, i. e.,* in the care and under the custody of the innkeeper, the latter's liability attaches. Davidson v. Madison Corporation, 247 N.Y.S. 789, 795, 231 App. Div. 421.

INFRA JURISDICTIONEM. Within the jurisdiction. 2 Strange, 827.

INFRA LIGEANTIAM REGIS. Within the king's ligeance. Comb. 212.

INFRA METAS. Within the bounds or limits. *Infra metas forestæ,* within the bounds of the forest. Fleta, lib. 2, c. 41, § 12. *Infra metas hospitii,* within the limits of the household; within the verge. Id. lib. 2, c. 2, § 2.

INFRA PRÆSIDIA. Within the protection; within the defenses. In international law, when a prize, or other captured property, is brought into a port of the captors, or within their lines, or otherwise under their complete custody, so that the chance of rescue is lost, it is said to be *infra præsidia.*

INFRA QUATUOR MARIA. Within the four seas; within the kingdom of England; within the jurisdiction.

INFRA QUATUOR PARIETES. Within four walls. 2 Crabb, Real Prop. p. 106, § 1089.

INFRA REGNUM. Within the realm.

INFRA SEX ANNOS. Within six years. Used in the Latin form of the plea of the statute of limitations.

INFRA TRIDUUM. Within three days. Formal words in old appeals. Fleta, lib. 1, c. 31, § 6; Id. c. 35, § 3.

INFRACTION. A breach, violation, or infringement; as of a law, a contract, a right or duty.

In French law, this term is used as a general designation of all punishable actions.

INFRINGEMENT. A breaking into; a trespass or encroachment upon; a violation of a law, regulation, contract, or right. Used especially of invasions of the rights secured by patents, copyrights, and trademarks. Goodyear Shoe Machinery Co. v. Jackson, C.C.A.Mass., 112 F. 146, 50 C.C.A. 159, 55 L.R.A. 692.

Infringement of patent. The unauthorized making, using, or selling for practical use, or for profit, of an invention covered by a valid claim of a patent during the life of the patent. It may involve any one or all of the acts of making, using, and selling. Johnston v. Davenport Brick & Tile Co., D.C.Iowa, 237 F. 668, 671. Celluloid Mfg. Co. v. American Zylonite Co., C.C.N.Y., 30 F. 437.

To constitute infringement of a patent claim there must be present in the infringing device or combination every element of such claim or its equivalent, so combined as to produce substantially the same result operating in substantially the same way. Safety Car Heating & Lighting Co. v. Gould Coupler Co., D.C.N.Y., 230 F. 848, 851; Montgomery Ward and Co. v. Clair, C.C.A.Mo., 123 F.2d 878, 881.

There is "infringement" where the departure is merely colorable. E. H. Bardes Range & Foundry Co. v. American Engineering Co., C.C.A.Ohio, 109 F.2d 696, 698; United States Rubber Co. v. General Tire & Rubber Co., C.C.A. Ohio, 128 F.2d 104, 108, 109; Swan Carburetor Co. v. General Motors Corporation, D.C.Ohio, 43 F.Supp. 499, 504.

Contributory infringement. The intentional aiding of one person by another in the unlawful making or selling of a patented invention; usually done by making or selling one part of the patented invention, or one element of the combination, with the intent and purpose of so aiding. Thomson-Houston Electric Co. v. Specialty Co., C.C. Conn., 72 F. 1016; Safety Car Heating & Lighting Co. v. Gould Coupler Co., D.C.N.Y., 229 F. 429, 439.

Infringement of copyright. A copy, more or less servile, of a copyrighted work. Mere likeness is insufficient, and an original treatment of a subject, open alike to treatment by the copyright holder and others does not constitute infringement. Pellegrini v. Allegrini, D.C.Pa., 2 F.2d 610, 612. There must be appropriation of substantial portions of the copyright matter. Roe-Lawton v. Hal E. Roach Studios, D.C.Cal., 18 F.2d 126, 127; Eggers v. Sun Sales Corporation, C.C.A.2, 263 F. 373, 375. But intention to infringe is not essential. Chappell & Co. v. Costa, D.C.N.Y., 45 F.Supp. 554, 555, 556; Towle v. Ross, D.C.Or., 32 F.Supp. 125, 127.

Under 17 U.S.C.A. § 1, one transmitting unauthorized performance of copyrighted musical composition by radio from a broadcasting station maintained and operated to stimulate sale of radio products is an "infringer," and is liable therefor. Jerome H. Remick & Co. v. General Electric Co., D.C.N.Y., 16 F.2d 829.

Infringement of trademark. The unauthorized use or colorable imitation of the mark already appropriated by another, on goods of a similar class. Block v. Jung Arch Brace Co., C.C.A.Ohio, 300 F. 308, 309. Weiss v. Tucker, 222 N.Y.S. 487, 488, 129 Misc. 648; Northam Warren Corporation v. Universal Cosmetic Co., C.C.A.Ill., 18 F.2d 774, 775. It exists if words or designs used by defendant are identical with or so similar to plaintiff's that they are likely to cause confusion, or deceive or mislead others. McGraw-Hill Pub. Co. v. American Aviation Associates, 117 F.2d 293, 294, 73 App.D.C. 131; Seattle Street Railway & Municipal Employees Relief Ass'n v. Amalgamated Ass'n of Street, Electric Railway & Motor Coach Employees of America, 101 P.2d 338, 344, 3 Wash.2d 520; California Fruit Growers Exchange v. Windsor Beverages, C.C.A.Ill., 118 F.2d 149, 152.

INFRINGER. One who appropriates another's patented invention. Stebler v. Riverside Heights Orange Growers' Ass'n, C.C.A.Cal., 205 F. 735, 739. One who affixes the trademark of another to similar articles in such way that his use of it is liable to cause confusion in the trade, or is calculated to mislead purchasers and induce them to buy infringer's articles as goods of the other thus depriving the latter of the full benefit of his property. James Heddon's Sons v. Millsite Steel & Wire Works, C.C.A.Mich., 128 F.2d 6, 8.

INFUGARE. Lat. To put to flight.

INFULA. A coif, or a cassock. Jacob.

INFUSION. In medical jurisprudence. The process of steeping in liquor; an operation by which the medicinal qualities of a substance may be extracted by a liquor without boiling. Also the product of this operation. "Infusion" and "decoction," though not identical, are *ejusdem generis* in law. 3 Camp. 74. Decoction. A pharmaceutical operation, which consists in pouring a hot or cold fluid upon a substance whose medical properties it is desired to extract. The product of this operation.

INGE. Meadow, or pasture. Jacob.

INGENIUM. (1) Artifice, trick, fraud; (2) an engine or device. Spelman. (3) A net or hook. (4) A machine, Spelman, Gloss., especially for warlike purposes; also, for navigation of a ship. Du Cange.

INGENUITAS. Lat. Freedom; liberty; the state or condition of one who is free. Also liberty given to a servant by manumission.

INGENUITAS REGNI. In old English law. The freemen, yeomanry, or commonalty of the kingdom. Cowell. Applied sometimes also to the barons.

INGENUITY. Acuteness of understanding. Tolfree v. Wetzler, D.C.N.J., 22 F.2d 214.

INGENUUS. In Roman law. A person who, immediately that he was born, was a free person. He was opposed to *libertinus,* or *libertus,* who, having been born a slave, was afterwards manumitted or made free. It is not the same as the English law term *"generosus,"* which denoted a person not merely free, but of good family. There were no distinctions among *ingenui;* but among *libertini* there were (prior to Justinian's abolition of the distinctions) three varieties, namely: Those of the highest rank, called *"Cives Romani;"* those of the second rank, called *"Latini Juniani;"* and those of the lowest rank, called *"Dediticii."* Brown.

INGRATITUDE. In Roman law, ingratitude was accounted a sufficient cause for revoking a gift or recalling the liberty of a freedman. Such is also the law of France, with respect to the first case. But the English law has left the matter entirely to the moral sense.

INGRESS, EGRESS, AND REGRESS. These words express the right of a lessee to enter, go upon, and return from the lands in question.

INGRESSU. In English law. An ancient writ of entry, by which the plaintiff or complainant sought an entry into his lands. Abolished in 1833.

INGRESSUS. In old English law. Ingress; entry. The relief paid by an heir to the lord was sometimes so called. Cowell.

INGROSSATOR. An engrosser. *Ingrossator magni rotuli,* engrosser of the great roll; afterwards called "clerk of the pipe." Spelman; Cowell.

INGROSSING. The act of making a fair and perfect copy of any document from a rough draft of it, in order that it may be executed or put to its final purpose.

INGUINAL. A term referring to the groin. Cavalier v. Chevrolet Motor Co. of New York, 178 N.Y.S. 489, 490, 189 App.Div. 412.

INHABIT. Synonymous with dwell, live, sojourn, stay, rest. MacLeod v. Stelle, 43 Idaho, 64, 249 P. 254, 256.

INHABITANT. One who resides actually and permanently in a given place, and has his domicile there. Ex parte Shaw, 12 S.Ct. 935, 145 U.S. 444, 36 L.Ed. 768; The Pizarro, 2 Wheat. 245, 4 L.Ed. 226.

"The words 'inhabitant,' 'citizen,' and 'resident,' as employed in different constitutions to define the qualifications of electors, mean substantially the same thing; and one is an inhabitant, resident, or citizen at the place where he has his domicile or home." Cooley, Const.Lim. *600; State ex rel. Sathre v. Moodie, 65 N.D. 340, 258 N.W. 558, 564. But the terms "resident" and "inhabitant" have also been held not synonymous, the latter implying a more fixed and permanent abode than the former, and importing privileges and duties to which a mere resident would not be subject. Tazewell County v. Davenport, 40 Ill. 197; State, to Use of Knox County Collector, v. Bunce, 187 Mo.App. 607, 173 S.W. 101, 102.

When relating to municipal rights, powers, or duties, the word inhabitant is almost universally used as signifying precisely the same as domiciled; Borland v. City of Boston, 132 Mass. 98, 42 Am.Rep. 424.

A corporation can be an inhabitant only in the state of its incorporation. Sperry Products v. Association of American Railroads, C.C.A.N.Y., 132 F.2d 408, 411; Vogel v. Crown Cork & Seal Co., D.C.Md., 36 F.Supp. 74, 75; International Union of Mine, Mill and Smelter Workers v. Tennessee Copper Co., D.C.Tenn., 31 F.Supp. 1015, 1017; Deutsch v. Times Pub. Corporation, D.C.N.Y., 33 F.Supp. 957, 958.

INHABITED HOUSE DUTY. A tax assessed in England on inhabited dwelling houses, according to their annual value, (St. 14 & 15 Vict. c. 36; 32 & 33 Vict. c. 14, § 11,) which is payable by the occupier, the landlord being deemed the occupier where the house is let to several persons. (St. 48 Geo. III. c. 55, Schedule B.) Houses occupied solely for business purposes are exempt from duty, although a care-taker may dwell therein, and houses partially occupied for business purposes are to that extent exempt. Sweet.

INHERE. To exist in and inseparable from something else; to stick fast. Majestic Theater Co. v. Lutz, 210 Ky. 92, 275 S.W. 16, 20.

INHERENT POWER. An authority possessed without its being derived from another. A right, ability, or faculty of doing a thing, without receiving that right, ability, or faculty from another. See, also, "Power."

INHERENT POWERS OF A COURT. Those reasonably necessary for administration of justice. State ex rel. Gentry v. Becker, 351 Mo. 769, 174 S.W.2d 181, 183. Ex parte Wetzel, 243 Ala. 130, 8 So.2d 824, 825.

INHERENTLY DANGEROUS. Danger inhering in instrumentality or condition itself at all times, so as to require special precautions to prevent injury, not danger arising from mere casual or collateral negligence of others with respect thereto under particular circumstances. Brown v. City of Craig, 350 Mo. 836, 168 S.W.2d 1080, 1082; Emery v. Thompson, 347 Mo. 494, 148 S.W.2d 479, 480; Hull v. Gillioz, 344 Mo. 1227, 130 S.W.2d 623, 628; Street v. W. E. Callahan Const. Co., Mo.App., 147 S.W.2d 153, 155.

INHERETRIX. The old term for "heiress." Co. Litt. 13*a*.

INHERIT. To take by inheritance; to take as heir on death of ancestor; to take by descent from ancestor; to take or receive, as right or title, by law from ancestor at his decease. Condren v. Marlin, 113 Okl. 259, 241 P. 826, 827. In re Buell's Estate, 167 Or. 295, 117 P.2d 832, 836. "To inherit *to*" a person is a common expression in the books. 2 Bl. Comm. 254, 255; 3 Coke, 41.

The word is also used in its popular sense, as the equivalent of to take or receive. Manchester v. Loomis, 191 Iowa 554, 181 N.W. 415, 442.

INHERITABLE BLOOD. Blood which has the purity (freedom from attainder) and legitimacy necessary to give its possessor the character of a lawful heir; that which is capable of being the medium for the transmission of an inheritance.

INHERITANCE. An estate in things real, descending to the heir. 2 Bl. Comm. 201; Rountree v. Pursell, 39 N.E. 747, 11 Ind.App. 522. Such an estate in lands or tenements or other things as may be inherited by the heir. Termes de la Ley. An estate or property which a man has by descent, as heir to another, or which he may transmit to another, as his heir. Litt. § 9.

A perpetuity in lands or tenements to a man and his heirs. Cowell; Blount. The method by which children or relatives take property from another at his death. Priddy v. Green, Tex.Civ.App., 220 S.W. 243, 248; Horner v. Webster, 33 N.J.L. 413.

Though "inheritance" in its restricted sense means something obtained through laws of descent and distribution from an intestate, in its popular use it includes property obtained by devise or descent. Pacheco v. Fernandez. Tex. Civ.App., 277 S.W. 197, 198; Higby v. Martin, 167 Okl. 10, 28 P.2d 1097, 1102.

"Inheritance" is also used in the old books where "hereditament" is now commonly employed. Thus, Coke divides inheritances into corporeal and incorporeal, into real, personal, and mixed, and into entire and several.

Civil Law

The succession of the heir to all the rights and property of the estate-leaver. It is either testamentary, where the heir is created by will, or *ab intestato*, where it arises merely by operation of law. Heinec. § 484.

In General

Estate of inheritance. See Estate.

Inheritance act. The English statute of 3 & 4 Wm. IV. c. 106, by which the law of inheritance or descent was considerably modified. 1 Steph. Comm. 359, 500.

Inheritance tax. A tax on the transfer or passing of estates or property by legacy, devise, or intestate succession; not a tax on the property itself, but on the right to acquire it by descent or testamentary gift. In re Gihon's Estate, 169 N.Y. 443; First Nat. Bank v. Commissioner of Corporations and Taxation, 258 Mass. 253, 154 N.E. 844, 845. A tax on the succession to, or transfer of, property occasioned by death. Waddell v. Doughton, 194 N.C. 537, 140 S.E. 160.

"Estate taxes" are based on the power to transmit or the transmission from the dead to the living, while "legacy taxes," or "inheritance taxes," are based on the transmission or right to receive the property. Frick v. Lewellyn, D.C.Pa., 298 F. 803, 810.

INHIBITION. In Ecclesiastical law. A writ issuing from a superior ecclesiastical court, forbidding an inferior judge to proceed further in a cause pending before him. In this sense it is closely analogous to the writ of *prohibition* at common law. Also the command of a bishop or ecclesiastical judge that a clergyman shall cease from taking any duty.

In English law. The name of a writ which forbids a judge from further proceeding in a cause depending before him; it is in the nature of a prohibition. *Termes de la Ley;* Fitzh. N. B. 39.

In Scotch law. A species of diligence or process by which a debtor is prohibited from contracting any debt which may become a burden on his heritable property, in competition with the creditor at whose instance the inhibition is taken out; and from granting any deed of alienation, etc., to the prejudice of the creditor. Brande.

In the Civil law. A prohibition which the law makes or a judge ordains to an individual. Hallifax, Civil Law, p. 126.

INHIBITION AGAINST A WIFE. In Scotch law. A writ in the sovereign's name, passing the signet, which prohibits all and sundry from having transactions with a wife or giving her credit. Bell; Ersk. Inst. 1, 6, 26.

INHOC. In old records. A nook or corner of a common or fallow field, inclosed and cultivated. Kennett, Par. Antiq. 297, 298; Cowell.

INHONESTUS. In old English law. Unseemly; not in due order. Fleta, lib. 1, c. 31, § 8.

INHUMAN TREATMENT. In the law of divorce. Such barbarous cruelty or severity as endangers the life or health of the party to whom it is addressed, or creates a well-founded apprehension of such danger. Whaley v. Whaley, 68 Iowa 647, 27 N.W. 809; Cole v. Cole, 23 Iowa 433. The phrase commonly employed in statutes is "cruel and inhuman treatment," from which it may be inferred that "inhumanity" is an extreme or aggravated "cruelty."

INIQUISSIMA PAX EST ANTEPONENDA JUSTISSIMO BELLO. The most unjust peace is to be preferred to the justest war. Root v. Stuyvesant, 18 Wend. (N.Y.) 257, 305.

INIQUITY. In Scotch practice. A technical expression applied to the decision of an inferior judge who has decided contrary to law; he is said to have committed iniquity. Bell.

INIQUUM EST ALIOS PERMITTERE, ALIOS INHIBERE MERCATURAM. It is inequitable to permit some to trade and to prohibit others. 3 Inst. 181.

INIQUUM EST ALIQUEM REI SUI ESSE JUDICEM. It is wrong for a man to be a judge in his own cause. Branch, Princ.; 12 Coke, 113.

INIQUUM EST INGENUIS HOMINIBUS NON ESSE LIBERAM RERUM SUARUM ALIENATIONEM. It is unjust that freemen should not have the free disposal of their own property. Co. Litt. 223*a*; 4 Kent, Comm. 131; Hob. 87.

INITIAL. That which begins or stands at the beginning. The first letter of a man's name. Elberson v. Richards, 42 N.J.L. 70.

INITIAL CARRIER. In the law of bailments. The carrier who first receives the goods and begins the process of their transportation, afterwards delivering them to another carrier for the further prosecution or completion of their journey. See Beard v. Railway Co., 79 Iowa 527, 44 N.W. 803.

But it has also been defined as the one contracting with the shipper, and not necessarily the one whose line constitutes the first link in transportation. Knapp v. Minneapolis, St. P. & S. S. M. Ry. Co., 33 N.D. 291, 156 N.W. 1019, 1023.

INITIALIA TESTIMONII. In Scotch law. Preliminaries of testimony. The preliminary examination of a witness, before examining him in chief, answering to the *voir dire* of the English law, though taking a somewhat wider range. Wharton.

INITIATE. Commenced; inchoate. *Curtesy initiate* is the interest which a husband has in the wife's lands after a child is born who may inherit, but before the wife dies.

To propose for approval—as schedule of rates. Idaho Power Co. v. Thompson, D.C.Idaho, 19 F.2d 547, 579.

INITIATION FEE. The sum paid on joining an organization for privileges of membership. Derby v. U. S., D.C.Mass., 17 F.2d 119, 120.

INITIATIVE. The power of the people to propose bills and laws, and to enact or reject them at the polls, independent of legislative assembly. City of Litchfield v. Hart, 306 Ill.App. 621, 29 N.E. 2d 678, 679.

In French law. The name given to the important prerogative conferred by the *charte constitutionnelle,* article 16, on the king to propose through his ministers projects of laws. 1 Toullier, no. 39.

INIURCOLLEGUIA. A body of Soviet lawyers in Moscow organized and constituted pursuant to statute under jurisdiction and control of the U. S. S. R. Ministry of Justice for the purpose of exclusive representation of Soviet nationals in foreign legal matters. In re Mitzkel's Estate, 233 N.Y.S.2d 519, 524, 36 Misc.2d 671; In re Kapocius' Estate, 234 N.Y.S.2d 346, 348, 36 Misc.2d 1087.

INJUNCTION. A prohibitive writ issued by a court of equity, at the suit of a party complainant, directed to a party defendant in the action, or to a party made a defendant for that purpose, forbidding the latter to do some act, or to permit his servants or agents to do some act, which he is threatening or attempting to commit, or restraining him in the continuance thereof, such act being unjust and inequitable, injurious to the plaintiff, and not such as can be adequately redressed by an action at law. Dupre v. Anderson, 45 La.Ann. 1134, 13 So. 743; City of Alma v. Loehr, 42 Kan. 368, 22 P. 424. A judicial process operating in personam, and requiring person to whom it is directed to do or refrain from doing a particular thing. Gainsburg v. Dodge, 193 Ark. 473, 101 S.W.2d 178, 180.

Final injunction

One granted when the rights of the parties are determined; distinguished from a preliminary injunction. Southern Pac. R. Co. v. Oakland, C.C.Cal., 58 F. 54.

Interlocutory injunction

One granted prior to the final hearing and determination of the matter in issue, and which is to continue until answer, or until the final hearing, or until the further order of the court. Gas & Electric Securities Co. v. Manhattan & Queens Traction Corporation. C.C.A.N.Y., 266 F. 625, 632.

Mandatory injunction

One which (1) commands the defendant to do some positive act or particular thing; (2) prohibits him from refusing (or persisting in a refusal) to do or permit some act to which the plaintiff has a legal right; or (3) restrains the defendant from permitting his previous wrongful act to continue operative, thus virtually compelling him to undo it. Bailey v. Schnitzius, 45 N.J.Eq. 178, 16 A. 680.

Permanent injunction

One intended to remain in force until the final termination of the particular suit. Riggins v. Thompson, 96 Tex. 154, 71 S.W. 14.

Perpetual injunction

An injunction which finally disposes of the suit, and is indefinite in point of time. Riggins v. Thompson, 96 Tex. 154, 71 S.W. 14.

Preliminary injunction

An injunction granted at the institution of a suit, to restrain the defendant from doing or continuing some act, the right to which is in dispute, and which may either be discharged or made perpetual, according to the result of the controversy, as soon as the rights of the parties are determined. Darlington Oil Co. v. Pee Dee Oil Co., 62 S.C. 196, 40 S.E. 169; Appeal of Mammoth Vein Consol. Coal Co., 54 Pa. 188.

Preventive injunction

One which prohibits the defendant from doing a particular act or commands him to refrain from it. Leaksville Woolen Mills v. Spray Water Power & Land Co., 183 N.C. 511, 112 S.E. 24, 25.

Provisional injunction

Another name for a preliminary or temporary injunction or an injunction pendente lite.

Special injunction

An injunction obtained only on motion and petition, usually with notice to the other party. Aldrich v. Kirkland, 6 Rich.Law S.C. 340; 4 Steph.Comm. 12, note z.

Temporary injunction

A preliminary or provisional injunction, or one granted pendente lite; as opposed to a final or perpetual injunction.

Jesse French Piano Co. v. Porter, 134 Ala. 302, 32 So. 678, 92 Am.St.Rep. 31.

INJURE. To violate the legal right of another or inflict an actionable wrong. Krom v. Antigo Gas Co., 154 Wis. 528, 143 N.W. 163, 164. To do harm to; to hurt; damage; impair; to hurt or wound, as the person; to impair the soundness of, as health. Ziolkowski v. Continental Casualty Co., 284 Ill.App. 505, 1 N.E.2d 410, 412. As applied to a building, "injure" means to materially impair or destroy any part of the existing structure. F. W. Woolworth Co. v. Nelson, 204 Ala. 172, 85 So. 449, 451, 13 A.L.R. 820.

INJURES GRAVES. Fr. In French law. Grievous insults or injuries, including personal insults and reproachful language, constituting a just cause of divorce. Butler v. Butler, 1 Pars. Eq. Cas. (Pa.) 344.

INJURIA. Lat. Injury; wrong; the privation or violation of right. 3 Bl. Comm. 2; J. A. & C. E. Bennett v. Winston-Salem Southbound R. Co., 170 N.C. 389, 87 S.E. 133, 134, L.R.A. 1916D, 1074.

INJURIA ABSQUE DAMNO. Injury or wrong without damage. A wrong done, but from which nc loss or damage results, and which, therefore, will not sustain an action.

INJURIA FIT EI CUI CONVICIUM DICTUM EST, VEL DE EO FACTUM CARMEN FAMOSUM. An injury is done to him of whom a reproachful thing is said, or concerning whom an infamous song is made. 9 Coke, 60.

INJURIA ILLATA JUDICI, SEU LOCUM TENENTI REGIS, VIDETUR IPSI REGI ILLATA MAXIME SI FIAT IN EXERCENTEM OFFICIUM. 3 Inst. 1. An injury offered to a judge, or person representing the king, is considered as offered to the king himself, especially if it be done in the exercise of his office.

INJURIA NON EXCUSAT INJURIAM. One wrong does not justify another. Broom, Max. 395. See 6 El. & Bl. 47.

INJURIA NON PRÆSUMITUR. Injury is not presumed. Co. Litt. 232. Cruel, oppressive, or tortious conduct will not be presumed. Best. Ev. p. 336, § 298.

INJURIA SERVI DOMINUM PERTINGIT. The master is liable for injury done by his servant. Lofft, 229.

INJURIA PROPRIA NON CADET IN BENEFICIUM FACIENTIS. One's own wrong shall not fall to the advantage of him that does it. A man will not be allowed to derive benefit from his own wrongful act. Branch, Princ.

INJURIOUS WORDS. In Louisiana. Slander, or libelous words. Civil Code La. art. 3501.

INJURY. Any wrong or damage done to another, either in his person, rights, reputation, or property. Woodruff v. Mining Co., C.C.Cal., 18 F. 781; Hitch v. Edgecombe County, 132 N.C. 573, 44 S.E. 30. An act which damages, harms, or hurts. Ritchie v. Standard Surety & Casualty Co. of New York, 13 N.Y.S.2d 1022, 1023, 257 App.Div. 545.

The words "damage," "loss," and "injury" are used interchangeably, and, within legislative meaning and judicial interpretation, import the same thing. In re City of Pittsburgh, 90 A. 329, 331, 243 Pa. 392, 52 L.R.A.,N.S., 262.

The term "injury," used to describe an error for which a reversal may be had, means an error which affects the result. Ryan v. State, 8 Okl.Cr. 623, 129 P. 685, 687.

Civil Law

A delict committed in contempt or outrage of any one, whereby his body, his dignity, or his reputation is maliciously injured. Voet, Com. ad Pand. 47, t. 10, no. 1.

In General

Absolute injuries. Injuries to those rights which a person possesses as being a member of society.

Accidental injury. A bodily injury by accident. Ideal Fuel Co. v. Industrial Commission, 298 Ill. 463, 131 N.E. 649, 650.

Within the Workmen's Compensation Act, one which occurs in the course of the employment, unexpectedly, and without the affirmative act or design of the employé; it being something which is unforeseen and not expected by the person to whom it happens. Jakub v. Industrial Commission, 288 Ill. 87, 123 N.E. 263, 264. Any injury to an employee in the course of his employment due to any occurrence referable to a definite time, and of the happening of which he can give notice to his employer, regardless of whether the injury is a visible hurt from external force, or disease or infection induced by sudden and castastrophic exposure. Lerner v. Rump Bros., 209 N.Y.S. 698, 701, 212 App.Div. 747. The term is to receive a broad and liberal construction with a view to compensating injured employés where injury resulted through some accidental means, was unexpected and undesigned and may be the result of mere mischance or miscalculation as to effect of voluntary action. Thomas v. Ford Motor Co., 114 Okl. 3, 242 P. 765, 766. It includes an accident causing injury to the physical structure of the body, notwithstanding a natural weakness predisposing to injury. Wilkins v. Ben's Home Oil Co., 166 Minn. 41, 207 N.W. 183. The words indicate, not so much the existence of an accident, but rather the idea that the injury was unexpected or unintended. Victory Sparkler & Specialty Co. v. Francks, 147 Md. 368, 128 A. 635, 639, 44 A.L.R. 363.

Civil injury. Injuries to person or property, resulting from a breach of contract, delict, or criminal offense, which may be redressed by means of a civil action. Cullinan v. Burkhard, 41 Misc.Rep. 321, 84 N.Y.S. 825.

An infringement or privation of the civil rights which belong to individuals, considered merely as individuals. State v. Magee Pub. Co., 29 N.M. 455, 224 P. 1028, 38 A.L.R. 142.

Irreparable injury. This phrase does not mean such an injury as is beyond the possibility of repair, or beyond possible compensation in damages, or necessarily great damage, but includes an injury, whether great or small, which ought not to be submitted to, on the one hand, or inflicted, on the other; and which, because it is so large or so small, or is of such constant and frequent occurrence, or because no certain pecuniary standard exists for the measurement of damages, cannot receive reasonable redress in a court of law.

Sanderlin v. Baxter, 76 Va. 306, 44 Am.Rep. 165. Wrongs of a repeated and continuing character, or which occasion damages that are estimated only by conjecture, and not by any accurate standard, are included. Johnson v. Kier, 3 Pittsb. R. (Pa.) 204; Scherman v. Stern, 117 A. 631, 633, 93 N.J.Eq. 626; Birchfield v. Bourland, Tex.Civ.App., 187 S.W. 422, 423.

Personal injury. A hurt or damage done to a man's *person,* such as a cut or bruise, a broken limb, or the like, as distinguished from an injury to his property or his reputation. The phrase is chiefly used in connection with actions of tort for negligence. Norris v. Grove, 100 Mich. 256, 58 N.W. 1006; State v. Clayborne, 14 Wash. 622, 45 P. 303. But the term is also used (chiefly in statutes) in a much wider sense, and as including any injury which is an invasion of personal rights, and in this signification it may include such injuries as libel or slander, criminal conversation with a wife, seduction of a daughter, and mental suffering. McDonald v. Brown, 23 R.I. 546, 51 A. 213, 58 L.R.A. 768, 91 Am.St.Rep. 659.

In Workmen's Compensation Acts, "personal injury" means any harm or damage to the health of an employee, however caused, whether by accident, disease, or otherwise, which arises in the course of and out of his employment, and incapacitates him in whole or in part. Hines v. Norwalk Lock Co., 100 Conn. 533, 124 A. 17, 20; Lane v. Horn & Hardart Baking Co., 261 Pa. 329, 104 A. 615, 616, 13 A.L.R. 963; Hanson v. Dickinson, 188 Iowa, 728, 176 N.W. 823, 824. A disease of mind or body which arises in the course of employment with nothing more is not within the Massachusetts act, but it must come from or by an injury, although that injury need not be a single definite act, but may extend over a continuous period of time. In re Maggelet, 228 Mass. 57, 116 N.E. 972, 973, L.R.A.1918F, 864; Taylor v. Swift & Co., 114 Kan. 431, 219 P. 516, 519. A "personal injury," as that term is used in the Workmen's Compensation Act, refers not to some break in some part of the body, or some wound thereon, or the like, but rather to the consequence or disability that results therefrom. Indian Creek Coal & Mining Co. v. Calvert, 68 Ind.App. 474, 119 N.E. 519, 525.

Permanent injury. An injury that, according to every reasonable probability, will continue throughout the remainder of one's life. Alabama Great Southern R. Co. v. Taylor, 196 Ala. 37, 71 So. 676, 678.

Private injuries. Infringements of the private or civil rights belonging to individuals considered as individuals.

Public injuries. Breaches and violations of rights and duties which affect the whole community as a community.

Real injury. A *real injury* is inflicted by any act by which a person's honor or dignity is affected.

Relative injuries. Injuries to those rights which a person possesses in relation to the person who is immediately affected by the wrongful act done.

Reparable injury. The general principle is that an injury, the damage from which is merely in the nature of pecuniary loss, and can be exactly and fully repaired by compensation in money, is a "reparable injury" for which a bond of sufficient amount and properly secured may afford an adequate indemnity. Barrow v. Duplantis, 148 La. 149, 86 So. 718, 723.

Verbal injury. A *verbal injury,* when directed against a private person, consists in the uttering contumelious words, which tend to injure his reputation by making him little or ridiculous.

INJUSTICE. The withholding or denial of justice. In law, almost invariably applied to the act, fault, or omission of a court, as distinguished from that of an individual. Holton v. Olcott, 58 N.H. 598; In re Moulton, 50 N.H. 532.

"Fraud" is deception practised by the party; "injustice" is the fault or error of the court. They are not equivalent words in substance, or in a statute authorizing a new trial on a showing of fraud or injustice. Fraud is always the result of contrivance and deception; injustice may be done by the negligence, mistake, or omission of the court itself. Silvey v. U. S., 7 Ct.Cl. 324.

INJUSTUM EST, NISI TOTA LEGE INSPECTA, DE UNA ALIQUA EJUS PARTICULA PROPOSITA JUDICARE VEL RESPONDERE. 8 Coke, 117*b*. It is unjust to decide or respond as to any particular part of a law without examining the whole of the law.

INLAGARE. In old English law. To restore to protection of law. To restore a man from the condition of outlawry. Opposed to *utlagare.* Bract. lib. 3, tr. 2, c. 14, § 1; Du Cange.

INLAGATION. Restoration to the protection of law. Restoration from a condition of outlawry.

INLAGH. A person within the law's protection; contrary to *utlagh,* an outlaw. Cowell.

INLAND. Within a country, state or territory; within the same country.

In old English law, inland was used for the demesne (*q. v.*) of a manor; that part which lay next or most convenient for the lord's mansion-house, as within the view thereof, and which, therefore, he kept in his own hands for support of his family and for hospitality; in distinction from outland or utland, which was the portion let out to tenants. Cowell; Kennett; Spelman.

INLAND BILL OF EXCHANGE. A bill of which both the drawer and drawee reside within the same state or country. Otherwise called a "domestic bill," and distinguished from a "foreign bill." Buckner v. Finley, 2 Pet. 589, 7 L.Ed. 528; Lonsdale v. Brown, 15 Fed.Cas. 857; Strawbridge v. Robinson, 10 Ill. 472, 50 Am.Dec. 420.

See Bill.

INLAND NAVIGATION. Within the meaning of the legislation of congress upon the subject, this phrase means navigation upon the rivers of the country, but not upon the great lakes. Moore v. American Transp. Co., 24 How. 38, 16 L.Ed. 674.

INLAND TRADE. Trade wholly carried on at home; as distinguished from commerce. See commerce.

INLAND WATERS. Such waters as canals, lakes, rivers, water-courses, inlets and bays, exclusive of the open sea, though the water in question may open or empty into the ocean. United States v. Steam Vessels of War, 1 S.Ct. 539, 106 U.S. 607, 27 L.Ed. 286; The Cotton Plant, 10 Wall. 581, 19 L.Ed. 983; Cogswell v. Chubb, 36 N.Y.S. 1076, 1 App.Div. 93.

INLANTAL, INLANTALE. Demesne or inland, opposed to *delantal,* or land tenanted. Cowell.

INLAUGHE. Sax. In old English law. Under the law, (*sub lege,*) in a frank-pledge, or decennary. Bract. fol. 125*b*.

INLAW. To place under the protection of the law. "Swearing obedience to the king in a leet, which doth *inlaw* the subject." Bacon.

INLEASED. In old English law. Entangled, or ensnared. 2 Inst. 247; Cowell; Blount.

INLIGARE. In old European law. To confederate; to join in a league, (*in ligam coire.*) Spelman.

INMATE. A person who lodges or dwells in the same house with another, occupying different rooms, but using the same door for passing in and out of the house. Webster; Jacob.

INMATE OF HOUSE OF PROSTITUTION. Those words apply only to the woman who goes there more or less regularly and who plies her trade there, and do not include a man found therein who has gone there for the purpose of illicit sexual intercourse. People v. Anonymous, 292 N.Y.S. 282, 285, 161 Misc. 379.

INN. An inn is a house where a traveler is furnished with everything which he has occasion for while on his way. Waitt Const. Co. v. Chase, 188 N.Y.S. 589, 592, 197 App.Div. 327. A house where all who conduct themselves properly, and who are able and ready to pay for their entertainment, are received, if there is accommodation for them, and who, without any stipulated engagement as to the duration of their stay, or as to the rate of compensation, are, while there, supplied at a reasonable charge with their meals, their lodging, and such services and attention as are necessarily incident to the use of the house as a temporary home. Ford v. Waldorf System, 57 R.I. 131, 188 A. 633, 635. A place where the public will be received and accommodations provided to guests for compensation. Edwards v. City of Los Angeles, 48 Cal.App.2d 62, 119 P.2d 370, 373, 374.

Under the term "inn" the law includes all taverns, hotels, and houses of public general entertainment for guests. Code Ga. 1882, § 2114 (Civ. Code 1910, § 3505).

See, also Hotel.

The words "inn," "tavern," and "hotel" are used synonymously to designate what is ordinarily and popularly known as an "inn" or "tavern," or place for the entertainment of travelers, and where all their wants can be supplied. A restaurant where meals only are furnished is not an inn or tavern. Carpenter v. Taylor, 1 Hilt., N.Y., 193. An inn is distinguished from a private boarding-house mainly in this: that the keeper of the latter is at liberty to choose his guests, while the innkeeper is obliged to entertain and furnish all travelers of good conduct and means of payment with what they may have occasion for, as such travelers, while on their way. Pinkerton v. Woodward, 33 Cal. 557, 91 Am.Dec. 657. Another distinction is that in a boarding-house the guest is under an express contract for a certain time at a certain rate, whereas, in an inn the guest is entertained from day to day upon an implied contract. Willard v. Reinhardt, 2 E.D.Smith, N.Y., 148. A lodging house does not become an "inn" because a register is kept. Roberts v. Case Hotel Co., 175 N.Y.S. 123, 127, 106 Misc. 481.

Common Inn. A house for the entertainment of travelers and passengers, in which lodging and necessaries are provided for them and for their horses and attendants. Cromwell v. Stephens, 2 Daly (N.Y.) 15. The word "common," in this connection, does not appear to add anything to the common-law definition of an inn, except in so far as it lays stress on the fact that the house is for the entertainment of the general public or for all suitable persons who apply for accommodations.

INNAMIUM. In old English law. A pledge.

INNAVIGABILITY. In insurance law. The condition of being *innavigable,* (*q. v.*) The foreign writers distinguish "innavigability" from "shipwreck." 3 Kent, Comm. 323, and note. The term is also applied to the condition of streams which are not large enough or deep enough, or are otherwise unsuited, for navigation.

INNAVIGABLE. As applied to streams, not capable of or suitable for navigation; impassable by ships or vessels.

As applied to vessels in the law of marine insurance, it means unfit for navigation; so damaged by misadventures at sea as to be no longer capable of making a voyage. See 3 Kent, Comm. 323, note.

INNER BARRISTER. A serjeant or king's counsel, in England, who is admitted to plead within the bar.

INNER HOUSE. The name given to the chambers in which the first and second divisions of the court of session in Scotland hold their sittings. See Outer House.

INNINGS. In old records. Lands recovered from the sea by draining and banking. Cowell.

INNKEEPER. One who keeps an *inn* or house for the lodging and entertainment of travelers. The keeper of a common inn for the lodging and entertainment of travelers and passengers, their horses and attendants, for a reasonable compensation. Story, Bailm. § 475. One who keeps a tavern or coffeehouse in which lodging is provided. 2 Steph. Comm. 133. See Inn.

One who receives as guests all who choose to visit his house, without any previous agreement as to the time of their stay, or the terms. His liability as innkeeper ceases when his guest pays his bill, and leaves the house with the declared intention of not returning, notwithstanding the guest leaves his baggage behind him. Wintermute v. Clark, 5 Sandf., N.Y., 242.

The words "innkeeper" and "hotel keeper" are synonymous, but each is distinct from a "boarding house keeper," in that the innkeeper has no right to select his guests, but must receive every one applying for accommodation who conducts himself in a proper manner, etc., while the keeper of a boarding house is one who maintains a house for the accommodation of those who enter under contract for entertainment at a certain rate for a certain period at an agreed compensation. McClaugherty v. Cline, 128 Tenn. 605, 163 S.W. 801. One who entertains strangers occasionally, although he may receive compensation for it, is not an innkeeper.

INNOCENCE. The absence of guilt.

INNOCENT. Free from guilt; acting in good faith and without knowledge of incriminatory circumstances, or of defects or objections.

INNOCENT AGENT. In criminal law. One who, being ignorant of any unlawful intent on the part of his principal, is merely the instrument of the guilty party in committing an offense; one who does an unlawful act at the solicitation or request of another, but who, from defect of understanding or ignorance of the inculpatory facts, incurs no legal guilt. Smith v. State, 21 Tex.App. 107, 17 S.W. 552; State v. Carr, 28 Or. 389, 42 P. 215.

INNOCENT CONVEYANCES. A technical term of the English law of conveyancing, used to designate such conveyances as may be made by a leasehold tenant without working a forfeiture. These are said to be lease and re-lease, bargain and sale, and, in case of a life-tenant, a covenant to stand seised. 1 Chit. Pr. 243.

INNOCENT PURCHASER. One who, by an honest contract or agreement, purchases property or acquires an interest therein, without knowledge, or means of knowledge sufficient to charge him in law with knowledge, of any infirmity in the title of the seller. Republic Power and Service Co. v. Continental Credit Corporation, 178 Ark. 966, 12 S.W.2d 906, 908.

INNOCENT TRESPASS. A trespass to land, committed, not recklessly, but through inadvertence or mistake, or in good faith, under an honest belief that the trespasser was acting within his legal rights. Elk Garden Big Vein Mining Co. v. Gerstell, 100 W.Va. 472, 131 S.E. 152, 153.

INNOCENT TRESPASSER. One who enters another's land unlawfully, but inadvertently or unintentionally, or in the honest, reasonable belief of his own right so to do, and removes sand or other material therefrom, is an "innocent trespasser." American Sand & Gravel Co. v. Spencer, 55 Ind. App. 523, 103 N.E. 426, 427.

INNOCENT WOMAN. One who has never had illicit intercourse with a man. State v. Cline, 170 N.C. 751, 87 S.E. 106, 107.

INNOMINATE. In the civil law. Not named or classed; belonging to no specific class; ranking under a general head. A term applied to those contracts for which no certain or precise remedy was appointed, but a general action on the case only. Dig. 2, 1, 4, 7, 2; Id. 19, 4, 5.

INNOMINATE CONTRACTS, literally, are the "unclassified" contracts of Roman law. They are contracts which are neither *re, verbis, literis,* nor *consensu* simply, but some mixture of or variation upon two or more of such contracts. They are principally the contracts of *permutatio, de æstimato, precarium,* and *transactio.* Brown.

INNONIA. In old English law. A close or inclosure, (*clausum, inclausura.*) Spelman.

INNOTESCIMUS. Lat. We make known. A term formerly applied to letters patent, derived from the emphatic word at the conclusion of the Latin forms. It was a species of exemplification of charters of feoffment or other instruments not of record. 5 Coke, 54*a*.

INNOVATION. In Scotch law. The exchange of one obligation for another, so as to make the second obligation come in the place of the first, and be the only subsisting obligation against the debtor. Bell. The same with "novation," (*q. v.*)

INNOXIARE. In old English law. To purge one of a fault and make him innocent.

INNS OF CHANCERY. So called because anciently inhabited by such clerks as chiefly studied the framing of writs, which regularly belonged to the cursitors, who were officers of the court of chancery. There are nine of them,—Clement's, Clifford's, and Lyon's Inn; Furnival's, Thavies', and Symond's Inn; New Inn; and Barnard's and Staples' Inn. These were formerly preparatory colleges for students, and many entered them before they were admitted into the inns of court. They consist chiefly of solicitors, and possess corporate property, hall, chambers, etc., but perform no public functions like the inns of court. Wharton.

INNS OF COURT. These are certain private unincorporated associations, in the nature of collegiate houses, located in London, and invested with the exclusive privilege of calling men to the bar; that is, conferring the rank or degree of a barrister. They were founded probably about the beginning of the fourteenth century. The principal inns of court are the Inner Temple, Middle Temple, Lincoln's Inn, and Gray's Inn. (The two former originally belonged to the Knights Templar; the two latter to the earls of Lincoln and Gray respectively.) These bodies now have a "common council of legal education," for giving lectures and holding examinations. The inns of chancery, distinguishable from the foregoing, but generally classed with them under the general name, are the buildings known as "Clifford's Inn," "Clement's Inn," "New Inn," "Staples' Inn," and "Barnard's Inn." They were formerly a sort of collegiate houses in which law students learned the elements of law before being admitted into the inns of court, but they have long ceased to occupy that position.

INNUENDO. This Latin word (commonly translated "meaning") was the technical beginning of that clause in a declaration or indictment for slander or libel in which the meaning of the alleged libelous words was explained, or the application of the language charged to the plaintiff was pointed out. Hence it gave its name to the whole clause; and this usage is still retained, although an equivalent English word is now substituted. Thus, it may be charged that the defendant said "he (*meaning* the said plaintiff) is a perjurer."

An "innuendo" in pleading in libel action is a statement by plaintiff of construction which he puts upon words which are alleged to be libelous and which meaning he will induce jury to adopt at trial. Burr v. Winnett Times Pub. Co., 80 Mont. 70, 258 P. 242, 244.

The word is also used, (though more rarely,) in other species of pleadings, to introduce an explanation of a preceding word, charge, or averment. Guide Pub. Co. v. Futrell, 175 Va. 77, 7 S.E.2d 133, 138.

It is said to mean no more than the words *"id est," "scilicet,"* or "meaning," or "aforesaid," as explanatory of a subject-matter sufficiently expressed before; as "such a one, *meaning* the defendant," or "such a subject, *meaning* the subject in question." Cowp. 683. It is only explanatory of some matter already expressed. It serves to point out where there is precedent matter, but never for a new charge. It may *apply* what is *already expressed,* but cannot add to or enlarge or change the sense of the previous words. See Grand v. Dreyfus, 122 Cal. 58, 54 P. 389; Kee v. Armstrong, Byrd & Co., 75 Okl. 84, 182 P. 494, 498, 5 A.L.R. 1349. The office of an "innuendo" is to explain the words published, and to give to them their true meaning, and it cannot introduce new matter, add to or enlarge the sense of those words, or impute to them a meaning not warranted by the publication, when taken alone, or read in connection with the inducement and colloquium. Bowie v. Evening News, 148 Md. 569, 129 A. 797, 800; Drebin v. Jewish World Pub. Co., 262 Pa. 169, 105 A. 58, 59. Its office is to set a meaning upon words or language of doubtful or ambiguous import which alone would not be actionable. Rail v. National Newspaper Ass'n, 198 Mo.App. 463, 192 S.W. 129, 134.

INOFFICIOSUM. In the civil law. Inofficious; contrary to natural duty or affection. Used of a will of a parent which disinherited a child without just cause, or that of a child which disinherited a parent, and which could be contested by *querela inofficiosi testamenti.* Dig. 2, 5, 3, 13; Paulus, lib. 4, tit. 5, § 1.

INOFFICIOUS TESTAMENT. A will not in accordance with the testator's natural affection and moral duties. In re Willford's Will (N.J.) 51 A. 502. But particularly, in the civil law, a will which deprives the heirs of that portion of the estate to which the law entitles them, and of which they cannot legally be disinherited. Mackeld. Rom. Law, § 714; Civ. Code La. art. 3556, subd. 16. A testament contrary to the natural duty of the parent, because it totally disinherited the child, without expressly giving the reason therefor.

INOFICIOCIDAD. In Spanish law. Every thing done contrary to a duty or obligation assumed, as well as in opposition to the piety and affection dictated by nature: *inofficiosum dicitur id omne quod contra pietatis officium factum est.* The term applies especially to testaments, donations, dower, etc., which may be either revoked or reduced when they affect injuriously the rights of creditors or heirs.

INOPS CONSILII. Lat. Destitute of counsel; without legal counsel. A term applied to the acts or condition of one acting without legal advice, as a testator drafting his own will.

INORDINATUS. An intestate.

INPENY and OUTPENY. In old English law. A customary payment of a penny on entering into and going out of a tenancy, (*pro exitu de tenura, et pro ingressu.*) Spelman.

INQUEST. A body of men appointed by law to inquire into certain matters. The grand jury is sometimes called the "grand inquest." The judicial inquiry made by a jury summoned for the purpose is called an "inquest." The finding of such men, upon an investigation, is also called an "inquest." People v. Coombs, 55 N.Y.S. 276, 36 App.Div. 284; Davis v. Bibb County, 116 Ga. 23, 42 S.E. 403.

The inquiry by a coroner, termed a "coroner's inquest," into the manner of the death of any one who has been slain, or has died suddenly or in prison.

This name is also given to a species of proceeding under the New York practice, allowable where the defendant in a civil action has not filed an affidavit of merits nor verified his answer. In such case the issue may be taken up, out of its regular order, on plaintiff's motion, and tried without the admission of any affirmative defense.

An inquest is a trial of an issue of fact where the plaintiff alone introduces testimony. The defendant is entitled to appear at the taking of the inquest, and to cross-examine the plaintiff's witnesses; and, if he do appear, the inquest must be taken before a jury, unless a jury be expressly waived by him. Haines v. Davis, 6 How.Prac., N.Y., 118.

The term "inquest," as applied to Surrogates' Courts, is a term of larger signification than as applied to proceedings at common law, and includes the exercise of the surrogate's function to determine all the circumstances concerning the genuineness of a will offered for probate, and the validity of its execution, without reference to whether there is a contest or not; his judicial power arising only after he has determined that the will is genuine and validly executed. In re Hermann's Will, 145 N.Y.S. 291, 297, 83 Misc. 283.

General

Coroner's inquest. See Coroner.

Inquest, arrest of. See Arrest.

Inquest of lunacy. See Inquisition (or Inquest) of Lunacy.

Inquest of office. In English practice. An inquiry made by the king's (or the queen's) officer, his sheriff, coroner, or escheator, *virtute officii,* or by writ sent to them for that purpose, or by commissioners specially appointed, concerning any matter that entitles the king to the possession of lands or tenements, goods or chattels; as to inquire whether the king's tenant for life died seised, whereby the reversion accrues to the king; whether A., who held immediately of the crown, died without heir, in which case the lands belong to the king by escheat; whether B. be attainted of treason, whereby his estate is forfeited to the crown; whether C., who has purchased land, be an alien, which is another cause of forfeiture, etc. 3 Bl. Comm. 258. These *inquests of office* were more frequent in practice during the continuance of the military tenures than at present; and were devised by law as an authentic means to give the king his right by solemn matter of record. Id. 258, 259; 4 Steph. Comm. 40, 41. Sometimes simply termed "*office*," as in the phrase "office found," (*q. v.*). Atlantic & P. R. Co. v. Mingus, 17 S.Ct. 348, 165 U.S. 413, 41 L.Ed. 770; Baker v. Shy, 9 Heisk. (Tenn.) 89.

Inquest of sheriffs. An inquest which directs a general inquiry as to the methods in which the sheriffs had been conducting the local government of the country (1170). 1 Holdsw. H. E. L. 21.

INQUILINUS. In Roman law. A tenant; one who hires and occupies another's house; but particularly, a tenant of a hired house in a city, as distinguished from *colonus*, the hirer of a house or estate in the country. Calvin.

INQUIRENDO. An authority given to some official person to institute an inquiry concerning the crown's interests.

INQUIRY, WRIT OF. A writ sued out by a plaintiff in a case where the defendant has let the proceedings go by default, and an interlocutory judgment has been given for damages generally, where the damages do not admit of calculation. It issues to the sheriff of the county in which the *venue* is laid, and commands him to inquire, by a jury of twelve men, concerning the amount of damages. The sheriff thereupon tries the cause in his sheriff's court, and some amount must always be returned to the court. But the return of the inquest merely informs the court, which may, if it choose, in all cases assess damages and thereupon give final judgment. 2 Archb. Pr., Waterman ed. 952; 3 Bla. Com. 398; 3 Chitty, Stat. 495, 497.

INQUISITIO. In old English law. An inquisition or inquest. *Inquisitio post mortem*, an inquisition after death. An inquest of office held, during the continuance of the military tenures, upon the death of every one of the king's tenants, to inquire of what lands he died seised, who was his heir, and of what age, in order to entitle the king to his marriage, wardship, relief, primer seisin, or other advantages, as the circumstances of the case might turn out. 3 Bl. Comm. 258. *Inquisitio patriæ*, the inquisition of the country; the ordinary jury, as distinguished from the grand assise. Bract. fol. 15*b*.

INQUISITION. In practice. An inquiry or inquest; particularly, an investigation of certain facts made by a sheriff, together with a jury impaneled by him for the purpose. The instrument of writing on which their decision is made is also called an inquisition.

In its broadest sense, "inquisition," includes any judicial inquiry. Phillips v. Vessells, 2 W.W.Harr. (Del.) 490, 126 A. 51.

INQUISITION AFTER DEATH. See Inquisitio.

INQUISITION (or INQUEST) OF LUNACY. A quasi-judicial examination into the sanity or insanity of a given person, ordered by a court having jurisdiction, on a proper application and sufficient preliminary showing of facts, held by the sheriff (or marshal, or a magistrate, or the court itself, according to the local practice) with the assistance of a special jury, usually of six men, who are to hear evidence and render a verdict in accordance with the facts. This is the usual foundation for an order appointing a guardian or conservator for a person adjudged to be insane, or for committing him to an insane asylum. See Hughes v. Jones, 116 N.Y. 67, 22 N.E. 446, 5 L.R.A. 637, 15 Am.St.Rep. 386; Hadaway v. Smith, 71 Md. 319, 18 A. 589.

INQUISITOR. A designation of sheriffs, coroners *super visum corporis*, and the like, who have power to inquire into certain matters.

In Ecclesiastical law. The name of an officer who is authorized to inquire into heresies, and the like, and to punish them. A judge.

INROLL. A form of "enroll," used in the old books. 3 Rep. Ch. 63, 73; 3 East, 410.

INROLLMENT. See Enrollment.

INSANE. Unsound in mind; of unsound mind; deranged, disordered, or diseased in mind. Violently deranged; mad.

INSANITY. Unsoundness of mind; madness; mental alienation or derangement; a morbid psychic condition resulting from disorder of the brain, whether arising from malformation or defective organization or morbid processes affecting the brain primarily or diseased states of the general system implicating it secondarily, which involves the intellect, the emotions, the will, and the moral sense, or some of these faculties, and which is characterized especially by their non-development, derangement, or perversion, and is manifested, in most forms, by delusions, incapacity to reason or to judge, or by uncontrollable impulses. In law, such a want of reason, memory, and intelligence as prevents a man from comprehending the nature and consequences of his acts or from distinguishing between right and wrong conduct. Crosswell v. People, 13 Mich. 427, 87 Am.Dec. 774; Johnson v. Insurance Co., 83 Me. 182, 22 A. 107; Frazer v. Frazer, 2 Del.Ch. 263.

"Insanity" does not include certain states of transitory mental disorder, such as trances, epilepsy, hysteria, and delirium. Martin v. Fraternal Reserve Life Ass'n, 200 Ill. App. 359, 364, and from both the pathologic and the legal definitions are to be excluded temporary mental aberrations caused by or accompanying alcoholic or other intoxication and the delirium of fever.

The distinction between the medical and the legal idea of insanity has, perhaps, not been better stated than by Ray, who is quoted by Ordronaux, and again by Witthaus & Becker: "*Insanity in medicine* has to do with a prolonged departure of the individual from his natural mental state arising from bodily disease." "*Insanity in law* covers nothing more than the relation of the person and the particular act which is the subject of judicial investigation. The legal problem must resolve itself into the inquiry, whether there was mental capacity and moral freedom to do or abstain from doing the particular act." 1 Whitth. & Beck.Med.Jur. 181; U. S. v. Faulkner, D.C.Tex., 35 F. 730.

Other definitions

Insanity is a manifestation of disease of the brain, characterized by a general or partial derangement of one or more faculties of the mind, and in which, while consciousness is not abolished, mental freedom is perverted, weakened, or destroyed. Hammond, Nervous System, 332. The prolonged departure, without any adequate cause, from the states of feeling and modes of thinking usual to the individual in health. Bouvier. By insanity is not meant (in law) a total deprivation of reason, but only an inability, from defect of perception, memory, and judgment, to do the act in question, [with an intelligent apprehension of its nature and consequences.] So, by a lucid interval is not meant a perfect restoration to reason, but a restoration so far as to be able, beyond doubt, to comprehend and to do the act with such reason, memory, and judgment as to make it a legal act. Frazer v. Frazer, 2 Del.Ch. 263.

Eccentricities and idiosyncracies, however gross, do not constitute "insanity." In re Hansen's Will, 50 Utah, 207, 167 P. 256, 261. And drunkenness is not insanity, nor does it answer to what is termed an unsound mind, unless the derangement which it causes becomes fixed and continued by the drunkenness being habitual, or by chronic alcoholism, and thereby rendering the party incapable of distinguishing between right and wrong, the same as insanity produced by any other cause. Rucker v. State, 119 Ohio St. 189, 162 N.E. 802, 805.

Synonyms

Delusion is sometimes loosely used as synonymous with insanity. But this is incorrect. Delusion is not the substance but the evidence of insanity. Ryan v. People, 60 Colo. 425, 153 P. 756, 757, L.R.A. 1917F, 646, Ann.Cas.1917C, 605.

The presence of an insane delusion is a recognized test of insanity in all cases except amentia and imbecility, and where there is no frenzy or raving madness; and in this sense an insane delusion is a fixed belief in the mind of the patient of the existence of a fact which has no objective existence but is purely the figment of his imagination, and which is so extravagant that no sane person would believe it under the circumstances of the case, the belief, nevertheless, being so unchangeable that the patient is incapable of being permanently disabused by argument or proof. Walker v. Struthers, 273 Ill. 387, 112 N.E. 961, 966. The characteristic which distinguishes an "insane" delusion from other mistaken beliefs is that it is not a product of the reason but of the imagination, that is, not a mistake of fact induced by deception, fraud, insufficient evidence, or erroneous reasoning, but the spontaneous conception of a perverted imagination, having no basis whatever in reason or evidence. Riggs v. Missionary Soc., 35 Hun, N.Y., 658; Buchanan v. Pierie, 205 Pa. 123, 54 Atl. 583, 97 Am.St.Rep. 725. An "insane delusion" is an idea or belief which springs spontaneously from a diseased or perverted mind without reason or without foundation in fact. It is distinguishable from a belief which is founded upon prejudice or aversion, no matter how unreasonable or unfounded the prejudice or aversion may be, and if it is the product of a reasoning mind, no matter how slight the evidence on which it is based, it cannot be classed as an insane delusion. Coffey v. Miller, 160 Ky. 415, 169 S.W. 852, 854, Ann.Cas.1916C, 30.

As to the distinctions between "Delusion" and "Illusion" and "Hallucination," see those titles.

Derangement. This term includes all forms of mental unsoundness, except of the natural born idiot. Hiett v. Shull, 36 W.Va. 563, 15 S.E. 147.

Idiocy is congenital amentia, that is, a want of reason and intelligence existing from birth and due to structural defect or malformation of the brain. It is a congenital obliteration of the chief mental powers, and is defined in law as that condition in which the patient has never had, from his birth, even the least glimmering of reason; for a man is not legally an "idiot" if he can tell his parents, his age, or other like common matters. This is not the condition of a deranged mind, but that of a total absence of mind, so that, while idiocy is generally classed under the general designation of "insanity," it is rather to be regarded as a natural defect than as a disease or as the result of a disease. It differs from "lunacy," because there are no lucid intervals or periods of ordinary intelligence. In re Beaumont, 1 Whart. (Pa.) 53, 29 Am.Dec. 33; Clark v. Robinson, 88 Ill. 502.

Imbecility. A more or less advanced decay and feebleness of the intellectual faculties; that weakness of mind which, without depriving the person entirely of the use of his reason, leaves only the faculty of conceiving the most common and ordinary ideas and such as relate almost always to physical wants and habits. It varies in shades and degrees from merely excessive folly and eccentricity to an almost total vacuity of mind or amentia, and the test of legal capacity, in this condition, is the stage to which the weakness of mind has advanced, as measured by the degree of reason, judgment, and memory remaining. It may proceed from paresis or general paralysis, from senile decay, or from the advanced stages of any of the ordinary forms of insanity; and the term is rather descriptive of the consequences of insanity than of any particular type of the disease. Campbell v. Campbell, 130 Ill. 466, 22 N.E. 620, 6 L.R.A. 167.

Mere imbecility or weakness of mind, however great, is not "insanity." There must be a total want of understanding. Johnson v. Millard, 110 Neb. 830, 195 N.W. 485, 487.

Lunacy. At the common law, was a term used to describe the state of one who, by sickness, grief, or other accident, has wholly lost his memory and understanding. Co. Litt. 246*b*, 247*a;* Com. v. Haskell, 2 Brewst. (Pa.) 496. It is distinguished from idiocy, an idiot being one who from his birth has had no memory or understanding, while lunacy implies the possession and subsequent loss of mental powers. Bicknell v. Spear, 77 N.Y.S. 920, 38 Misc. Rep. 389. On the other hand, lunacy is a total deprivation or suspension of the ordinary powers of the mind, and is to be distinguished from imbecility, where there is a more or less advanced decay and feebleness of the intellectual faculties. In re Vanauken, 10 N.J.Eq. 186, 195; Odell v. Buck, 21 Wend. (N.Y.) 142. As to all other forms of insanity, lunacy was originally distinguished by the occurrence of lucid intervals, and hence might be described as a periodical or recurrent insanity. In re Anderson, 132 N.C. 243, 43 S.E. 649. But while these distinctions are still observed in some jurisdictions, they are more generally disregarded; so that, at present, in inquisitions of lunacy and other such proceedings, the term "lunacy" has almost everywhere come to be synonymous with "insanity," Smith v. Hickenbottom, 57 Iowa, 733, 11 N.W. 664, 667, and is used as a general description of all forms of derangement or mental unsoundness, this rule being established by statute in many states and by judicial decisions in others, In re Clark, 175 N.Y. 139, 67 N. E. 212.

Cases of arrested mental development would come within the definition of lunacy, that is, where the patient was born with a normal brain, but the cessation of mental growth occurred in infancy or so near it that he never acquired any greater intelligence or discretion than belongs to a normally healthy child. Such a subject might be scientifically denominated an "idiot," but not legally, for in law the latter term is applicable only to congenital amentia. The term "lucid interval" means not an apparent tranquility or seeming repose, or cessation of the violent symptoms of the disorder, or a simple diminution or remission of the disease, but a temporary cure—an intermission so clearly marked that it perfectly resembles a return of health; and it must be such a restoration of the faculties as enables the patient beyond doubt to comprehend the nature of his acts and transact his affairs as usual; and it must be continued for a length of time sufficient to give certainty to the temporary restoration of reason. Godden v. Burke, 35 La.Ann. 160, 173; Frazer v. Frazer, 2 Del.Ch. 260.

Non compos mentis. Lat. Not of sound mind. A generic term applicable to all insane persons, of whatsoever specific type the insanity may be and from whatever cause arising, provided there be an entire loss of reason, as distinguished from mere weakness of mind. Somers v. Pumphrey, 24 Ind. 244. Potts v. House, 6 Ga. 350, 50 Am. Dec. 329.

Forms and Varieties of Insanity

Without attempting a scientific classification of the numerous types and forms of insanity, (as to which it may be said that there is as yet no final agreement among psychologists and alienists either as to analysis or nomenclature,) definitions and explanations will here be appended of the compound and descriptive terms most commonly met with in medical jurisprudence. And, first, as to the origins or causes of the disease:

Choreic insanity is insanity arising from chorea, the latter being a nervous disease, more commonly attacking children than adults, characterized by irregular and involuntary twitchings of the muscles of the limbs and face, popularly called "St. Vitus' dance."

Congenital insanity is that which exists from the birth of the patient, and is (in law) properly called "idiocy." See supra.

Cretinism is a form of imperfect or arrested mental development, which may amount to idiocy, with physical degeneracy or deformity or lack of development; endemic in Switzerland and some other parts of Europe, but the term is applied to similar states occurring elsewhere.

Delirium tremens. A disease of the nervous system, induced by the excessive and protracted use of intoxicating liquors. Ætna Life Ins. Co. v. Deming, 123 Ind. 384, 24 N.E. 86, 87, usually occurring in habitual drinkers after a few days' total abstinence from liquors, but sometimes resulting directly and immediately from drunkenness, Erwin v. State, 10 Tex.App. 700, 702; Knickerbocker Life Ins. Co. v. Foley, 105 U.S. 350, 354, 26 L.Ed. 1055; Evers v. State, 31 Tex.Cr.R. 318, 20 S.W. 744, 748, 18 L.R.A. 421, 37 Am.St.Rep. 811; and affecting the brain so as to produce incoherence and lack of continuity in the intellectual processes, a suspension or perversion of the power of volition, and delusions, particularly of a terrifying nature, but not generally prompting to violence except in the effort to escape from imaginary dangers. It is recognized in law as a form of insanity, and may be of such a nature or intensity as to render the patient legally incapable of committing a crime. United States v. McGlue, 1 Curt. 1, 26 Fed.Cas. 1093; Insurance Co. v. Deming, 123 Ind. 384, 24 N.E. 86; Maconnehey v. State, 5 Ohio St. 77; Erwin v. State, 10 Tex.App. 700.

In some states the insanity of alcoholic intoxication is classed as "temporary," where induced by the voluntary recent use of ardent spirits and carried to such a degree that the person becomes incapable of judging the consequences or the moral aspect of his acts, and "settled," where the condition is that of *delirium tremens*. Settled insanity, in this sense, excuses from civil or criminal responsibility; temporary insanity does not. The ground of the distinction is that the former is a remote effect of imbibing alcoholic liquors and is not voluntarily incurred, while the latter is a direct result voluntarily sought for. Evers v. State, 31 Tex.Cr.R. 318, 20 S.W. 744, 18 L.R.A. 421, 37 Am.St.Rep. 811; State v. Kidwell, 62 W.Va. 466, 59 S.E. 494, 495, 13 L.R.A.,N.S., 1024.

Folie brightique. A French term sometimes used to designate an access of insanity resulting from nephritis or "Bright's disease." In re McKean's Will, 66 N.Y.S. 44, 31 Misc. 703.

Idiopathic insanity is such as results from a disease of the brain itself, lesions of the cortex, cerebral anemia, etc.

Paranoia. A form of mental distress known as delusionary insanity, and a person afflicted with it has delusions which dominate, but do not destroy, the mental capacity, and, though sane as to other subjects, as to the delusion and its direct consequences the person is insane. Mounger v. Gandy, 110 Miss. 133, 69 So. 817, 818.

It is sometimes characterized as logical perversion, and is said to have "misplaced the antiquated term monomania, which not only implied that the delusion was restricted to one subject, but was otherwise insufficient and misleading." The memory, emotions, judgment, and conceptions are in most cases unimpaired, though each of these mental divisions may be involved. 2 Clevenger, Med.Jur. 860. It is characterized by systematized delusions, the term taking the place of "monomania" or "partial insanity". Taylor v. McClintock, 87 Ark. 243, 112 S.W. 405.

Pellagrous insanity. Insanity caused by or derived from pellagra, which is an endemic disease of southern Europe, (though not confined to that region,) characterized by erythema, digestive derangement, and nervous affections. (Cent. Dict.)

Polyneuritic insanity. Insanity arising from an inflammation of the nerves, of the kind called "polyneuritis" or "multiple neuritis" because it involves several nerves at the same time. This is often preceded by tuberculosis and almost always by alcoholism, and is characterized specially by delusions and falsification of the memory. It is otherwise called "Korssakoff's disease." (Kraepelin.)

Puerperal insanity. A mental derangement occurring in women at the time of child-birth or immediately after; it is also called *"eclampsia parturientium."*

Syphilitic insanity. A *paresis* or progressive imbecility resulting from the infection of *syphilis*.

It is sometimes called (as being a sequence or result of that disease) "*metasyphilis*" or "*parasyphilis*."

Tabetic dementia. A form of mental derangement or insanity complicated with "*tabes dorsalis*" or *locomotor ataxia*, which generally precedes, or sometimes follows, the mental attack. As to insanity resulting from cerebral embolism, see Embolism; from epilepsy, see Epilepsy. As to chronic alcoholism as a form of insanity, see Alcoholism.

Traumatic insanity is such as results from a wound or injury, particularly to the head or brain, such as fracture of the skull or concussion of the brain.

General Descriptive and Clinical Terms

Affective insanity. A modern comprehensive term descriptive of all those forms of insanity which affect or relate to the feelings and emotions and hence to the ethical and social relations of the individual.

Circular insanity. Another name for maniacal-depressive insanity, which see.

"Emotional insanity" or *mania transitoria* applies to the case of one in the possession of his ordinary reasoning faculties who allows his passions to convert him into a temporary maniac. Mutual L. Ins. Co. v. Terry, 15 Wall. 580, 583, 21 L.Ed. 236.

In a criminal case the law rejects the doctrine of what is called emotional insanity, which begins on the eve of the criminal act, and leaves off when it is committed. People v. Kernaghan, 72 Cal. 609, 14 P. 566, 568; Graves v. State, 45 N.J.L. (16 Vroom) 347, 350, 46 Am.Rep. 778.

Folie circulaire. The French name for circular insanity or maniacal-depressive insanity.

General paralysis. *Dementia paralytica* or paresis.

Habitual insanity. Such insanity as is, in its nature, continuous and chronic. Wright v. Market Bank, Tenn.Ch.App., 60 S.W. 623, 624.

Involutional insanity. That which sometimes accompanies the "involution" of the physical structure and physiology of the individual, the reverse of their "evolution," hence practically equivalent to the imbecility of old age or senile dementia.

Katatonia. A form of insanity distinguished by periods of acute mania and melancholia and especially by cataleptic states or conditions; the "insanity of rigidity." (Kahlbaum.) A type of insanity characterized particularly by "stereotypism," an instinctive inclination to purposeless repetition of the same expressions of the will, and "negativism," a senseless resistance against every outward influence. (Kraepelin.)

Legal insanity. Legal insanity is a disorder of the intellect, and is distinguished from "moral insanity," which is a disorder of the feelings and propensities. In re Forman's Will, 54 Barb. 274, 291; Bensberg v. Washington University, 251 Mo. 641, 158 S.W. 330, 336. A disease of the brain, rendering a person incapable of distinguishing between right and wrong with respect to the offense charged. State v. Privitt, 175 Mo. 207, 75 S.W. 457, 459.

Maniacal-depressive insanity. A form of insanity characterized by alternating periods of high maniacal excitement and of depressed and stuporous conditions in the nature of or resembling melancholia, often occurring as a series or cycle of isolated attacks, with more or less complete restoration to health in the intervals. (Kraepelin.) This is otherwise called "circular insanity" or "circular stupor."

Moral insanity. A morbid perversion of the feelings, affections, or propensities, but without any illusions or derangement of the intellectual faculties; irresistible impulse or an incapacity to resist the prompting of the passions, though accompanied by the power of discerning the moral or immoral character of the act. Moral insanity is not admitted as a bar to civil or criminal responsibility for the patient's acts, unless there is also shown to be intellectual disturbance, as manifested by insane delusions or the other recognized criteria of legal insanity. Taylor v. McClintock, 87 Ark. 243, 112 S.W. 405, 412; Bensberg v. Washington University, 251 Mo. 641, 158 S.W. 330, 336.

In a very few of the states where moral insanity is recognized as a defense, it means an incapacity of resistance, as where there was an entire destruction of the freedom of the will, although the person perceived the moral or immoral character of the act. State v. Leehman, 2 S.D. 171, 49 N.W. 3, 5.

Partial insanity, as a legal term, may mean either monomania (see *infra*) or an intermediate stage in the development of mental derangement. In the former sense, it does not relieve the patient from responsibility for his acts, except where instigated directly by his particular delusion or obsession. Trich v. Trich, 165 Pa. 586, 30 A. 1053. In the latter sense, it denotes a clouding or weakening of the mind, not inconsistent with some measure of memory, reason, and judgment. But the term, in this sense, does not convey any very definite meaning, since it may range from mere feeble-mindedness to almost the last stages of imbecility. Appeal of Dunham, 27 Conn. 205; State v. Jones, 50 N.H. 369, 383, 9 Am.Rep. 242.

Psychoneurosis. Mental disease without recognizable anatomical lesion, and without evidence and history of preceding chronic mental degeneration. Under this head come *melancholia, mania, primary acute dementia,* and *mania hallucinatoria*. Cent. Dict.

"Neurosis," in its broadest sense, may include any disease or disorder of the mind, and hence all the forms of insanity proper. But the term "psychoneurosis" is now employed by Freud and other European specialists to describe that class of exaggerated individual peculiarities or idiosyncrasies of thought towards special objects or topics which are absent from the perfectly normal mind, and which yet have so little influence upon the patient's conduct or his general modes of thought that they cannot properly be described as "insanity" or as any form of "mania," especially because ordinarily unaccompanied by any kind of delusions. At most, they lie on the debatable border-land between sanity and insanity. These idiosyncrasies or obsessions may arise from superstition, from a real incident in the patient's past history upon which he has brooded until it has assumed an unreal importance or significance, or from general neurasthenic conditions. Such, for example, are a terrified shrinking from certain kinds of animals, unreasonable dread of being shut up in some enclosed place or of being alone in a crowd, excessive fear of being poisioned, groundless conviction of irredeemable sinfulness, and countless other prepossessions, which may range from mere weak-minded superstition to actual monomania.

Recurrent insanity. Insanity which returns from time to time, hence equivalent to "lunacy" (see *supra*) in its common-law sense, as a mental disorder broken by lucid intervals. There is no presumption that fitful and exceptional attacks of insanity are continuous. Leache v. State, 22 Tex. App. 279, 3 S.W. 538, 58 Am.Rep. 638.

Settled insanity. The term applied to delirium tremens, which is a kind of insanity produced by alcoholism, caused by the breaking down of the person's system by long-continued or habitual drunkenness, and brought on by abstinence from drink. It is thus termed, to distinguish it from "temporary insanity," or drunkenness directly resulting from drink. Evers v. State, 31 Tex.Cr. R. 318, 20 S.W. 744, 748, 18 L.R.A. 421, 37 Am.St. Rep. 811.

Temporary delusion. The word implies unsoundness or derangement of mind or intellect, not a mere temporary or slight delusion, which might be occasioned by fever or accident. Karow v. New York Continental Ins. Co., 57 Wis. 56, 15 N.W. 27, 31, 46 Am.Rep. 17.

Other Forms of Insanity

Amentia, dementia, and mania. The classification of insanity into these three types or forms, though once common, has of late given way to a more scientific nomenclature, based chiefly on the origin or cause of the disease in the particular patient and its clinical history. These terms, however, are still occasionally encountered in medical jurisprudence, and the names of some of their subdivisions are in constant use.

Amentia. A total lack of intelligence, reason, or mental capacity. Sometimes so used as to cover imbecility or dotage, or even as applicable to all forms of insanity; but properly restricted to a lack of mental capacity due to original defective organization of the brain (idiocy) or arrested cerebral development, as distinguished from the degeneration of intellectual faculties which once were normal.

Dementia. A form of insanity resulting from degeneration or disorder of the brain (idiopathic or traumatic, but not congenital) and characterized by general mental weakness and decrepitude, forgetfulness, loss of coherence, and total inability to reason, but not accompanied by delusions or uncontrollable impulses. Dennett v. Dennett, 44 N.H. 531, 84 Am.Dec. 97; People v. Lake, 2 Parker, Cr.R. (N.Y.) 218; Graham v. Deuterman, 91 N.E. 61, 62, 244 Ill. 124; Hibbard v. Baker, 104 N.W. 399, 400, 141 Mich. 124.

Among the sub-divisions of dementia should be noticed the following: *Acute primary dementia* is a form of temporary dementia, though often extreme in its intensity, and occurring in young people or adolescents, accompanied by general physical debility or exhaustion and induced by conditions likely to produce that state, as malnutrition, overwork, dissipation, or too rapid growth. *Dementia paralytica* is a progressive form of insanity, beginning with slight degeneration of the physical, intellectual, and moral powers, and leading to complete loss of mentality, or imbecility, with general paralysis. Also called paresis, paretic dementia, or cirrhosis of the brain, or (popularly) "softening of the brain." *Dementia præcox.* A term applicable either to the early stages of dementia or to the dementia of adolescence, but more commonly applied to the latter. It is often (but not invariably) attributable to onanism or self-abuse, and is characterized by mental and moral stupidity, absence of any strong feeling of the impressions of life or interest in its events, blunting or obscuration of the moral sense, weakness of judgment, flightiness of thought, senseless laughter without mirth, automatic obedience, and apathetic despondency. (Kraepelin.) *Senile dementia.* Dementia occurring in persons of advanced age, and characterized by slowness and weakness of the mental processes and general physical degeneration, verging on or passing into imbecility, indicating the breaking down of the mental powers in advance of bodily decay. Hiett v. Shull, 36 W.Va. 563, 15 S.E. 146. *Toxic dementia.* Weakness of mind or feeble cerebral activity, approaching imbecility, resulting from continued administration or use of slow poisons or of the mere active poisons in repeated small doses, as in cases of lead poisoning and in some cases of addiction to such drugs as opium or alcohol.

Dementia præcox paranoid. A medical term indicating that form of dementia in which the patient exhibits ideas of persecution and has delusions. Rasmussen v. George Benz & Sons, 168 Minn. 319, 210 N.W. 75, 76.

Dipsomania. An irresistible impulse to indulge in intoxication, either alcohol or other drugs—opiums. This mania, or dipsomania, is classed as one of the minor forms of insanity. Repeated intoxication for a number of years, which is entirely voluntary, is not dipsomania. One having the power to refrain from the use of intoxicants, and who becomes intoxicated voluntarily, is not affected with dipsomania. Ballard v. State, 19 Neb. 609, 28 N.W. 271, 273. State v. Reidell, 14 A. 550, 9 Houst. (Del.) 470.

Erotomania. A form of mania similar to nymphomania, except that the present term is applied to patients of both sexes, and that (according to some authorities) it is applicable to all cases of excessive sexual craving irrespective of origin; while *nymphomania* is restricted to cases where the disease is caused by a local disorder of the sexual organs reacting on the brain. In erotomania, there is often an absence of any lesion of the intellectual powers. Krafft-Ebing, Psycopathia Sexualis, Chaddock's ed. And it is to be observed that the term *"erotomania"* is now often used, especially by French writers, to describe a morbid propensity for "falling in love" or an exaggerated and excited condition of amativeness or love-sickness, which may affect the general physical health, but is not necessarily correlated with any sexual craving, and which, though it may unnaturally color the imagination and distort the subject's view of life and affairs, does not at all amount to insanity, and should not be so considered when it leads to crimes of violence, as in the common case of a rejected lover who kills his mistress.

Fit of mania. A fit of mania includes a temporary depression or aberration of the mind, which sometimes accompanies or follows intoxication, and is often accompanied by delusions, hallucinations, and illusions. Gunter v. State, 3 So. 600, 607, 83 Ala. 96.

Homicidal mania. A form of mania in which the morbid state of the mind manifests itself in an irresistible inclination or impulse to commit homicide, prompted usually by an insane delusion either as to the necessity of self-defense or the avenging of injuries, or as to the patient being the appointed instrument of a superhuman justice. Com. v. Sayre, 5 Wkly. Notes Cas. (Pa.) 425.

Hypomania. A mild or slightly developed form or type of mania.

Kleptomania. See Kleptomania.

Mania. That form of insanity in which the patient is subject to hallucinations and illusions, accompanied by a high state of general mental excitement, sometimes amounting to fury. Hall v. Unger, 2 Abb. U. S. 510, 11 Fed.Cas. 261; People v. Lake, 2 Parker Cr.R., N.Y., 218.

In the case first above cited, the following description is given by Justice Field: "Mania is that form of insanity where the mental derangement is accompanied with more or less of excitement. Sometimes the excitement amounts to a fury. The individual in such cases is subject to hallucinations and illusions. He is impressed with the reality of events which have never occurred, and of things which do not exist, and acts more or less in conformity with his belief in these particulars. The mania may be general, and affect all or most of the operations of the mind; or it may be partial, and be confined to particular subjects. In the latter case it is generally termed 'monomania.'" In a more popular but less scientific sense, "mania" denotes a morbid or unnatural or excessive craving, issuing in impulses of such fixity and intensity that they cannot be resisted by the patient in the enfeebled state of the will and blurred moral concepts which accompany the disease. It is used in this sense in such compounds as "homicidal mania," "dipsomania," and the like.

Mania a potu. Delirium tremens, or a species of temporary insanity resulting as a secondary effect produced by the excessive and protracted indulgence in intoxicating liquors. See State v. Hurley, Houst.Cr.Cas. (Del.) 28, 35.

Mania fanatica. A form of insanity characterized by a morbid state of religious feeling. Ekin v. McCracken, 11 Phila., Pa. 540.

Mania transitoria. The term applies to the case of one in the possession of his ordinary reasoning faculties, who allows his passions to convert him into a temporary maniac. Mutual Life Ins. Co. v. Terry, 82 U.S. (15 Wall.) 580, 583, 21 L.Ed. 236.

Megalomania. The so-called "delirium of grandeur" or "folie de grandeur;" a form of mania in which the besetting delusion of the patient is that he is some person of great celebrity or exalted rank, historical or contemporary.

Melancholia. A form of insanity the characteristics of which are extreme mental depression, with delusions and hallucinations, the latter relating especially to the financial or social position of the patient or to impending or threatened dangers to his person, property, or reputation, or issuing in distorted conceptions of his relations to society or his family or of his rights and duties in general. State v. Reidell, 9 Houst., Del., 470, 14 A. 551; People v. Krist, 168 N.Y. 19, 60 N.E. 1057. *Hypochondria* or *hypochondriasis.* A form of melancholia in which the patient has exaggerated or causeless fears concerning his health or suffers from imaginary disease. *Toxiphobia.* Morbid dread of being poisoned; a form of insanity manifesting itself by an excessive and unfounded apprehension of death by poison.

Methomania. An irresistible craving for alcoholic or other intoxicating liquors, manifested by the periodical recurrence of drunken debauches. State v. Savage, 89 Ala. 1, 7 So. 183, 7 L.R.A. 426.

Monomania. A perversion of the understanding in regard to a single object or a small number of objects, with the predominance of mental excitement, as distinguished from "mania," which means a condition in which the perversion of the understanding embraces all kinds of objects, and is accompanied with general mental excitement. State v. John, 30 N.C. 330, 337, 49 Am.Dec. 396; Freed v. Brown, 55 Ind. 310, 317; People v. Lake, 2 Parker, Cr.R. (N.Y.) 215, 218. A perversion or derangement of the reason or understanding with reference to a single subject or small class of subjects, with considerable mental excitement and delusions, while, as to all matters outside the range of the peculiar infirmity, the intellectual faculties remain unimpaired and function normally. Hopps v. People, 31 Ill. 390, 83 Am.Dec. 231; Bohler v. Hicks, 120 Ga. 800, 48 S.E. 306, 307.

Necrophilism. A form of affective insanity manifesting itself in an unnatural and revolting fondness for corpses, the patient desiring to be in their presence, to caress them, to exhume them, or sometimes to mutilate them, and even (in a form of sexual perversion) to violate them.

Nymphomania. A form of mania characterized by a morbid, excessive, and uncontrollable craving for sexual intercourse. This term is applied only to women. The term for a corresponding mania in men is *"satyriasis."*

Oikei mania. A form of insanity manifesting itself in a morbid state of the domestic affections, as an unreasonable dislike of wife or child without cause or provocation. Ekin v. McCracken, 11 Phila. (Pa.) 540.

Paranoia. Monomania in general, or the obsession of a delusion or system of delusions which dominate without destroying the mental capacity, leaving the patient sane as to all matters outside their particular range, though subject to perverted ideas, false beliefs, and uncontrollable impulses within that range; and particularly, the form of monomania where the delusion is as to wrongs, injuries, or persecution inflicted upon the patient and his consequently justifiable resentment or revenge. Winters v. State, 61 N.J.L. 613, 41 Atl. 220; People v. Braun, 158 N.Y. 558, 53 N.E. 529. Paranoia is called by Kraepelin "progressive systematized insanity," because the delusions of being wronged or of persecution and of excessive self-esteem develop quite slowly, without independent disturbances of emotional life or of the will becoming prominent, and because there occurs regularly a mental working up of the delusion to form a delusionary view of the world,—in fact, a system,—leading to a derangement of the stand-point which the patient takes up towards the events of life.

Pyromania. Incendiarism; a form of affective insanity in which the mania takes the form of an irresistable impulse to burn or set fire to things.

Sebastomania. Religious insanity; demonomania.

Toxicomania. An excessive addiction to the use of toxic or poisonous drugs or other substances; a form of mania or affective insanity characterized by an irresistible impulse to indulgence in opium, cocaine, chloral, alcohol, etc.

Specific Definitions and Applications in Law

There are numerous legal proceedings where insanity may be shown, and the rule for establishing mental capacity or the want of it varies according to the object or purpose of the proceeding. Among these may be enumerated the following: A criminal prosecution where insanity is alleged as a defense; a proceeding to defeat a will on the ground of the insanity of the testator; a suit to avoid a contract (including that of marriage) for similar reasons; a proceeding to secure the commitment of a person alleged to be insane to an asylum; a proceeding to appoint a guardian or conservator for an alleged lunatic; a plea or proceeding to avoid the effect of the statute of limitations on account of insanity. What might be regarded as insanity in one of such cases would not necessarily be so regarded in another. No definite rule can be laid down which would apply to all cases alike. Snyder v. Snyder, 142 Ill. 60, 31 N.E. 303; Clarke v. Irwin, 63 Neb. 539, 88 N.W. 783. But the following rules or tests for specific cases have been generally accepted and approved:

In criminal law and as a defense to an accusation of crime, insanity means such a perverted and deranged condition of the mental and moral faculties as to render the person incapable of distinguishing between right and wrong, or to render him at the time unconscious of the nature of the act he is committing, or such that, though he may be conscious of it and also of its normal quality, so as to know that the act in question is wrong, yet his will or volition has been (otherwise than voluntarily) so completely destroyed that his actions are not subject to it but are beyond his control. Or, as otherwise stated, insanity is such a state of mental derangement that the subject is incompetent of having a criminal intent, or incapable of so controlling his will as to avoid doing the act in question. Davis v. U. S., 17 S.Ct. 360, 165 U.S. 373, 41 L.Ed. 750; Doherty v. State, 50 A. 1113, 73 Vt. 380; Butler v. State, 102 Wis. 364, 78 N.W. 590.

An insane person cannot be legally charged with a criminal intent; State v. Brown, 36 Utah, 46, 102 P. 641, 24 L.R.A.,N.S., 545.

In Coleman's case, in New York it was held that the "test of the responsibility for criminal acts, when insanity is asserted, is the capacity of the accused to distinguish between right and wrong at the time and with respect to the act which is the subject of inquiry." 1 N.Y.Cr.Rep. 1. With variations of expression this is the prevailing doctrine of the American courts. Mutual Life Ins. Co. v. Terry, 15 Wall. 590, 21 L.Ed. 236.

The capacity to distinguish between right and wrong has been held not to be a safe test in all cases. State v. Felter, 25 Iowa 67, per Dillon, C. J. See also Brown v. Com., 78 Pa. 122.

Insane delusion is of no avail as a defense unless, if true, the facts supposed to exist would have excused the crime. Thurman v. State, 32 Neb. 224, 49 N.W. 338; Smith v. State, 55 Ark. 259, 18 S.W. 237. Irresistible impulse to commit a crime is defined as that uncontrollable impulse produced by a disease of the mind, when that disease is sufficient to override judgment and obliterate the sense of right as to the acts done, and deprives the accused of power to choose between them. It was recognized as a defense in Stevens v. State, 31 Ind. 485, 99 Am.Dec. 634. But it is held that no impulse, however irresistible, is a defense, where there is a knowledge as to the particular act between right and wrong. State v. Brandon, 53 N.C. 463; State v. Miller, 141 Mo. 542, 20 S.W. 243, and that it was a crime morally, and punishable by the laws of the country; State v. Alexander, 30 S.C. 74, 8 S.E. 440, 14 Am.St.Rep. 879; Williams v. State, 50 Ark. 511, 9 S.W. 5.

Mere frenzy or ungovernable passion which controls the will and motives is not insanity sufficient to excuse crime. Garner v. State, 112 Miss. 317, 73 So. 50, 51.

What is sometimes called moral insanity, as distinguished from mental unsoundness, is not a defense to a charge of crime. Flanagan v. People, 52 N.Y. 467, 11 Am.Rep. 731; Andersen v. State, 43 Conn. 514, 21 Am.Rep. 669; St. Louis Mut. Life Ins. Co. v. Graves, 6 Bush, Ky., 268.

Testamentary capacity includes an intelligent understanding of the testator's property, its extent and items, and of the nature of the act he is about to perform, together with a clear understanding and purpose as to the manner of its distribution and the persons who are to receive it. Lacking these, he is not mentally competent. The presence of insane delusions is not inconsistent with testamentary capacity, if they are of such a nature that they cannot reasonably be supposed to have affected the dispositions made by the will; and the same is true of the various forms of monomania and of all kinds of eccentricity and personal idiosyncrasy. But imbecility, senile dementia, and all forms of systematized mania which affect the understanding and judgment generally disable the patient from making a valid will. Harrison v. Rowan, 3 Wash. C. C. 585, Fed. Cas. No. 6,141; Wilson v. Mitchell, 101 Pa. 495; Trustees of Epworth Memorial Methodist Church v. Overman, 185 Ky. 773, 215 S.W. 942, 944. To constitute "senile dementia," incapacitating one to make a will, there must be such a failure of the mind as to deprive the testator of intelligent action. Gates v. Cole, 137 Iowa 613, 115 N.W. 236, 237, 238.

As a ground for avoiding or annulling a contract or conveyance, insanity does not mean a total deprivation of reason, but an inability, from defect of perception, memory, and judgment, to do the act in question or to understand its nature and consequences. Frazer v. Frazer, 2 Del. Ch. 260; Durrett v. McWhorter, 161 Ga. 179, 129 S.E. 870, 874. The insanity must have entered into and induced the particular contract or conveyance; it must appear that it was not the act of the free and untrammeled mind, and that on account of the diseased condition of the mind the person entered into a contract or made a conveyance which he would not have made if he had been in the possession of his reason. Dewey v. Allgire, 37 Neb. 6, 55 N.W. 276, 40 Am.St.Rep. 468.

Insanity sufficient to justify the annulment of a marriage means such a want of understanding at the time of the marriage as to render the party incapable of assenting to the contract of marriage. The morbid propensity to steal, called "kleptomania," does not answer this description. Lewis v. Lewis, 44 Minn. 124, 46 N.W. 323, 9 L.R.A. 505, 20 Am.St.Rep. 559. The marriage of a person insane was held void in Inhabitants of Middleborough v. Inhabitants of Rochester, 12 Mass. 363. Powell v. Powell, 18 Kan. 371, 26 Am.Rep. 774; Waymire v. Jetmore, 22 Ohio St. 271. A marriage contracted while one party was insane from *delirium tremens* was held void, but mere weakness of mind not amounting to derangement is not sufficient. Rawdon v. Rawdon, 28 Ala. 565; and for that merely, or intoxication, a court has no power to declare a marriage null and void. The same degree of mental capacity which enables a person to make a valid deed or will is sufficient to enable him to marry; Inhabitants of Atkinson v. Inhabitants of Medford, 46 Me. 510.

Insanity is not a defense in an action of tort; but damages are compensatory and not punitive; McIntyre v. Sholty, 121 Ill. 660, 13 N.E. 239, 2 Am. St.Rep. 140. Williams v. Hays, 143 N.Y. 442, 38 N. E. 449, 26 L.R.A. 153, 42 Am.St.Rep. 743.

One is "insane," so as to make self-destruction an accident, within the meaning of an insurance policy compensating death by accident, where he is so mentally diseased as to be incapable of understanding the nature of the act and unable to distinguish between right and wrong. London Guarantee & Accident Co. v. Officer, 78 Colo. 441, 242 P. 989, 991.

As a ground for restraining the personal liberty of the patient, it may be said in general that the form of insanity from which he suffers should be such as to make his going at large a source of danger to himself or to others, though this matter is largely regulated by statute, and in many places the law permits the commitment to insane asylums and hospitals of persons whose insanity does not manifest itself in homicidal or other destructive forms of mania, but who are incapable of caring for themselves and their property or who are simply fit subjects for treatment in hospitals and other institutions specially designed for the care of such patients.

To constitute insanity such as will authorize the appointment of a guardian or conservator for the patient, there must be such a deprivation of reason and judgment as to render him incapable of understanding and acting with discretion in the ordinary affairs of life; a want of sufficient mental capacity to transact ordinary business and to take care of and manage his property and affairs. See Snyder v. Snyder, 142 Ill. 60, 31 N.E. 303.

Insanity as a plea or proceeding to avoid the effect of the statute of limitations means practically the same thing as in relation to the appointment of a guardian. On the one hand, it does not require a total deprivation of reason or absence of understanding. On the other hand, it does not include mere weakness of mind short of imbecility. It means such a degree of derangement as renders the subject incapable of understanding the nature of the particular affair and his rights and remedies in regard to it and incapable of taking discreet and intelligent action. Burnham v. Mitchell, 34 Wis. 134. The time of sanity required in order to allow the statute to begin to run is such as will enable the party to examine his affairs and institute an action, and is for the jury.

There are a few other legal rights or relations into which the question of insanity enters, such as the capacity of a witness or of a voter; but they are governed by the same general principles. The test is capacity to understand and appreciate the nature of the particular act and to exercise intelligence in its performance. A witness must understand the nature and purpose of an oath and have enough intelligence and memory to relate correctly the facts within his knowledge. So a voter must understand the nature of the act to be performed and be able to make an intelligent choice of candidates. In either case, eccentricity, "crankiness," feeble-mindedness not amounting to imbecility, or insane delusions which do not affect the matter in hand, do not disqualify. See District of Columbia v. Armes, 2 S.Ct. 840, 107 U.S. 521, 27 L.Ed. 618.

INSANUS EST QUI, ABJECTA RATIONE, OMNIA CUM IMPETU ET FURORE FACIT. He is insane who, reason being thrown away, does everything with violence and rage. 4 Coke, 128.

INSCRIBERE. Lat. In the civil law. To subscribe an accusation. To bind one's self, in case of failure to prove an accusation, to suffer the same punishment which the accused would have suffered had he been proved guilty. Calvin.

INSCRIPTIO. Lat. In the civil law. A written accusation in which the accuser undertakes to suffer the punishment appropriate to the offense charged, if the accused is able to clear himself of the accusation. Calvin; Cod. 9, 1, 10; Id. 9, 2, 16, 17.

INSCRIPTION. In Evidence. Anything written or engraved upon a metallic or other solid substance, intended for great durability; as upon a tombstone, pillar, tablet, medal, ring, etc.

In Civil law. An engagement which a person who makes a solemn accusation of a crime against another enters into that he will suffer the same punishment, if he has accused the other falsely, which would have been inflicted upon him had he been guilty. Code, 9. 1. 10; 9. 2. 16 and 17.

In Modern Civil law. The entry of a mortgage, lien, or other document at large in a book of public records; corresponding to "recording" or "registration."

INSCRIPTIONES. The name given by the old English law to any written instrument by which anything was granted. Blount.

INSECT POWDER. "Insect powder" is a dry powder used to kill or expel insects; an insecticide or insectifuge. Parke, Davis & Co. v. U. S., C.C.A.La., 255 F. 933, 935.

INSECURE. Unsafe and dangerous. Sabol v. St. Louis Cooperage Co., 313 Mo. 527, 282 S.W. 425, 430.

INSENSIBLE. In pleading. Unintelligible; without sense or meaning, from the omission of material words, etc. Steph. Pl. 377. See Union Sewer Pipe Co. v. Olson, 82 Minn. 187, 84 N.W. 756.

INSETENA. In old records. An inditch; an interior ditch; one made within another, for greater security. Spelman.

INSIDIATOR. Lat. A soldier lying in ambush. Hence, one who lies in wait, a lurker, waylayer (*rare*). Harpers' Lat. Dict.

INSIDIATORES VIARUM. Lat. Highwaymen; persons who lie in wait in order to commit some felony or other misdemeanor.

INSIGNIA. Ensigns or arms; distinctive marks; badges; *indicia;* characteristics.

INSILIARIUS. An evil counsellor. Cowell.

INSILIUM. Evil advice or counsel. Cowell.

INSIMUL. Lat. Together; jointly. Townsh. Pl. 44.

INSIMUL COMPUTASSENT. They accounted together. The name of the count in *assumpsit* upon an account stated; it being averred that the parties had settled their accounts together, and defendant engaged to pay plaintiff the balance. Fraley v. Bispham, 10 Pa. 325, 51 Am.Dec. 486; Loventhal v. Morris, 103 Ala. 332, 15 So. 672.

INSIMUL TENUIT. One species of the writ of *formedon* brought against a stranger by a coparcener on the possession of the ancestor, etc. Jacob.

INSINUACION. In Spanish law. The presentation of a public document to a competent judge, in order to obtain his approbation and sanction of the same, and thereby give it judicial authenticity. Escriche.

INSINUARE. Lat. In the civil law. To put into; to deposit a writing in court, answering nearly to the modern expression "to file." *Si non mandatum actis insinuatum est,* if the power or authority be not deposited among the records of the court. Inst. 4, 11, 3. To declare or acknowledge before a judicial officer; to give an act an official form.

INSINUATIO. Lat. In old English law. Information or suggestion. *Ex insinuatione,* on the information. Reg. Jud. 25, 50.

INSINUATION. In the civil law. The transcription of an act on the public registers like our recording of deeds. It was not necessary in any other alienation but that appropriated to the purpose of donation. Inst. 2, 7, 2.

INSINUATION OF A WILL. In the civil law. The first production of a will, or the leaving it with the registrar, in order to its probate. Cowell; Blount.

INSOLATION. In medical jurisprudence. Sunstroke or heat-stroke; heat prostration.

INSOLVENCY. The condition of a person who is insolvent; inability to pay one's debts; lack of means to pay one's debts. Such a relative condition of a man's assets and liabilities that the former, if all made immediately available, would not be sufficient to discharge the latter. Or the condition of a person who is unable to pay his debts as they fall due, or in the usual course of trade and business. Dewey v. St. Albans Trust Co., 56 Vt. 475, 48 Am.Rep. 803; Toof v. Martin, 13 Wall. 47, 20 L.Ed. 481; Frank v. Stearns, 111 Neb. 101, 195 N.W. 949, 951.

Independent of statute, it may generally be said that insolvency, when applied to a person, firm, or corporation engaged in trade, means inability to pay debts as they become due in the usual course of business. Parker v. First Nat. Bank, 96 Okl. 70, 220 P. 39; Bushman v. Bushman, 311 Mo. 551, 279 S.W. 122, 126. The mere fact that a corporation or an individual is unable to pay its debts upon a particular day does not constitute "insolvency." Wiggins Co. v. McMinnville Motor Car Co., 111 Or. 123, 225 P. 314, 317, and a bank is not "insolvent" if its assets are sufficient to meet its obligations within a reasonable time, although it did not have cash sufficient for its daily needs. Dunlap v. Seattle Nat. Bank, 93 Wash. 568, 161 P. 364, 368.

A man may be fully able to pay his debts, if he will, and yet in the eye of the law he is insolvent, if his property is so situated that it cannot be reached by process of law, and subjected, without his consent, to the payment of his debts. Pelham v. Chattahoochee Grocery Co., 156 Ala. 500, 47 So. 172.

Under Bankr.Act July 1, 1898, c. 541, § 1, cl. 19, as amended, (formerly 15), 30 Stat. 544 (11 U.S.C.A. § 1), and section 3a, cl. 4, as amended, (11 U.S.C.A. § 44), a person shall be deemed insolvent within the provisions of the act whenever the aggregate of his property, exclusive of any property which he may have conveyed, transferred, concealed, removed, or permitted to be concealed or removed, with intent to defraud, hinder, or delay his creditors, shall not at a fair valuation be sufficient in amount to pay his debts. In re Wm. S. Butler Co., C.C.A.Mass., 207 F. 705, 709; Anderson v. Myers, C.C.A.Fla., 296 F. 101, 103; Mountain States Power Co. v. A. L. Jordan Lumber Co., C.C.A. Mont., 293 F. 502, 507.

As to the distinction between bankruptcy and insolvency, see Bankruptcy.

Commercial Insolvency. See that title.

Insolvency fund. In English law. A fund, consisting of moneys and securities, which, at the time of the passing of the bankruptcy act, 1861, stood, in the Bank of England, to the credit of the commissioners of the insolvent debtors' court, and was, by the twenty-sixth section of that act, directed to be carried by the bank to the account of the accountant in bankruptcy. Provision has now been made for its transfer to the commissioners for the reduction of the national debt. Robs. Bankr. 20, 56.

Insolvency laws. *Insolvency laws* are generally statutory provisions by which the property of the debtor is surrendered for his debts; and upon this condition, and the assent of a certain proportion of his creditors, he is discharged from all further liabilities; Bartlet v. Prince, 9 Mass. 431; Otis v. Warren, 16 Mass. 53; 2 Kent 321; Ingr. Insolv. 9. Insolvency, according to some of the state statutes, may be of two kinds, voluntary and involuntary. *Voluntary insolvency* is the case in which the debtor institutes the proceedings, and is desirous of availing himself of the insolvent laws, and petitions for that purpose whereas *involuntary insolvency* is where the proceedings are instituted by the creditors *in invitum,* and so the debtor forced into insolvency.

Open insolvency. The condition of one who has no property, within the reach of the law, applicable to the payment of any debt. Hardesty v. Kinworthy, 8 Blackf. (Ind.) 305; Somerby v. Brown, 73 Ind. 356.

INSOLVENT. (Lat. *in,* privative, *solvo,* to pay). The condition of a person who is unable to pay his debts. 2 Bla.Com. 285, 471; Brouwer v. Harbeck, 9 N.Y. 589. One who cannot or does not pay; one who is unable to pay his debts; one who is not solvent; one who has not means or property sufficient to pay his debts. One who is unable to pay commercial paper in the due course of business. Warren v. Nat. Bank, 10 Blatchf. 493, Fed. Cas. No. 17,202; Clarke v. Mott, 4 Cal.Unrep.Cas. 80, 33 P. 884. See, also, Insolvency.

Other definitions

One who is unable to pay his debts as they fall due in the usual course of trade or business, 2 Kent 389; 1 M. & S. 338; Lee v. Kilbourn, 3 Gray, Mass., 600; Mitchell v. Bradstreet Co., 116 Mo. 226, 22 S.W. 358, 724, 20 L.R.A. 138, 38 Am.St.Rep. 592; although his assets in value exceed the amount of his liability, In re Ramazzina, 110 Cal. 488, 42 P. 970; or the embarrassment is only temporary, Langham v. Lanier, 7 Tex.Civ.App. 4, 26 S.W. 255; but it is held that mere inability to pay debts promptly as they mature is not conclusive, Mensing v. Atchison, Tex.Civ.App., 26 S.W. 509; and that one who has sufficient property subject to legal process to satisfy all legal demands is not insolvent. Smith v. Collins, 94 Ala. 394, 10 So. 334. A corporation is insolvent when its assets are insufficient for the payment of its debts, and it has ceased to do business, or has taken, or is in the act of taking, a step which will practically incapacitate it from conducting the corporate enterprise with reasonable prospect of success, or its embarrassments are such that early suspension and failure must ensue. Corey v. Wadsworth, 99 Ala. 68, 11 So. 350, 23 L.R.A. 618, 42 Am.St.Rep. 29. A bank is insolvent when the cash value of its assets realizable in a reasonable time is not equal to its liabilities exclusive of stock liabilities. Ellis v. State, 138 Wis. 513, 119 N.W. 1110, 20 L.R.A.,N.S., 444, 131 Am.St.Rep. 1022.

INSOLVENT LAW. See Insolvency Laws.

INSPECT. To look, to view or oversee for the purpose of ascertaining the quality or condition of the thing or for purpose of examination. U. S. v. A. Bentley & Sons Co., D.C.Ohio, 293 F. 229, 239; O'Hare v. Peacock Dairies, 26 Cal.App.2d 753, 79 P.2d 433, 438.

INSPECTATOR. A prosecutor or adversary.

INSPECTION. A critical examination, close or careful scrutiny, a strict or prying examination, or an investigation. In re Becker, 192 N.Y.S. 754, 756, 200 App.Div. 178. An examination or testing of food, fluids, or other articles made subject by law to such examination, to ascertain their fitness for use or commerce. People of the State of New York v. Compagnie Generale Transatlantique, C. C.N.Y., 10 F. 361; Id., 2 S.Ct. 87, 107 U.S. 59, 27 L. Ed. 383; Turner v. Maryland, 2 S.Ct. 44, 107 U.S. 38, 27 L.Ed. 370. An examination by a private person of public records and documents; or of the books and papers of his opponent in an action, for the purpose of better preparing his own case for trial.

Reasonable inspection. As relates to duty of employer to provide employee with proper instrumentalities with which to work, does not mean such an inspection as would necessarily or infallibly disclose a defect if one existed, but only such inspection as reasonably prudent man, in the exercise of ordinary care, would make. Alabama & V. R. Co. v. Fountain, 145 Miss. 515, 111 So. 153, 154.

INSPECTION LAWS. Laws authorizing and directing the inspection and examination of various kinds of merchandise intended for sale, especially food, with a view to ascertaining its fitness for use, and excluding unwholesome or unmarketable goods from sale, and directing the appointment of official inspectors for that purpose. Const.U.S. art. 1, § 10, cl. 2; Story, Const. § 1017, et seq. Gibbons v. Ogden, 9 Wheat. 202, 6 L.Ed. 23; Clintsman v. Northrop, 8 Cow. (N.Y.) 45; Patapsco Guano Co. v. Board of Agriculture, 18 S.Ct. 862, 171 U.S. 345, 41 L.Ed. 191; Turner v. State, 55 Md. 263.

INSPECTION OF DOCUMENTS. This phrase refers to the right of a party, in a civil action, to inspect and make copies of documents which are essential or material to the maintenance of his cause, and which are either in the custody of an officer of the law or in the possession of the adverse party.

INSPECTION, TRIAL BY. A mode of trial formerly in use in England, by which the judges of a court decided a point in dispute, upon the testimony of their own senses, without the intervention of a jury. This took place in cases where the fact upon which issue was taken must, from its nature, be evident to the court from ocular demonstration, or other irrefragable proof; and was adopted for the greater expedition of a cause. 3 Bl.Comm. 331.

INSPECTOR. The name given to certain officers whose duties are to examine and inspect things over which they have jurisdiction. Officers whose duty it is to examine the quality of certain articles of merchandise, food, weights and measures, etc.

INSPECTORSHIP, DEED OF. In English law. An instrument entered into between an insolvent debtor and his creditors, appointing one or more persons to inspect and oversee the winding up of such insolvent's affairs on behalf of the creditors.

INSPEXIMUS (Lat.). We have seen. A word sometimes used in letters patent, reciting a grant, *inspeximus* such former grant, and so reciting it verbatim; it then grants such further privileges as are thought convenient. 5 Co. 54.

INSTALL. To place in a seat, give a place to, to set, place, or instate in an office, rank, or order, etc. State ex rel. Slattery v. Raupp, 303 Mo. 684, 263 S.W. 834, 835. To set up or fix in position for use or service. King v. Elliott, 197 N.C. 93, 147 S.E. 701, 704.

INSTALLATION. The ceremony of inducting or investing with any charge, office, or rank, as the placing a bishop into his see, a dean or prebendary into his stall or seat, or a knight into his order. Wharton. The act by which an officer is put in public possession of the place he is to fill. The president of the United States, or a governor, is installed into office, by being sworn agreeably to the constitution and laws.

Installation of machinery means to place in position where it will reasonably accomplish purposes for which it is set up. Long v. Ulmer Machinery Co., 77 Cal.App. 66, 246 P. 113, 116.

INSTALLMENTS. Different portions of the same debt payable at different successive periods as agreed. Brown. Partial payments on account of a debt due. Kenney v. Los Feliz Inv. Co., 121 Cal.App. 378, 9 P.2d 225, 228.

INSTANCE. In pleading and practice. Solicitation, properly of an earnest or urgent kind. An act is often said to be done at a party's "special *instance* and request." Miller v. Mutual Grocery Co., 214 Ala. 62, 106 So. 396.

"Instance" does not imply the same degree of obligation to obey as does "command." Feore v. Trammel, 213 Ala. 293, 104 So. 808, 813.

In the civil and French law. A general term, designating all sorts of actions and judicial demands. Dig. 44, 7, 58.

In ecclesiastical law. Causes of *instance* are those proceeded in at the solicitation of some party, as opposed to causes of office, which run in the name of the judge. Hallifax, Civil Law, p. 156.

In Scotch law. That which may be insisted on at one diet or course of probation. Wharton.

INSTANCE COURT. In English law. That division or department of the court of admiralty which exercises all the ordinary admiralty jurisdiction, with the single exception of prize cases, the latter belonging to the branch called the "Prize Court." The term is sometimes used in American law for purposes of explanation, but has no proper application to admiralty courts in the United States, where the powers of both instance and prize courts are conferred without any distinction. 3 Kent, Comm. 355, 378; The Betsey, 3 Dall. 6, 1 L.Ed. 485; The Emulous, 1 Gall. 563, Fed.Cas.No.4,479.

INSTANCIA. In Spanish law. The institution and prosecution of a suit from its commencement until definitive judgment. The first instance, "*primera instancia,*" is the prosecution of the suit before the judge competent to take cognizance of it at its inception; the second instance, "*secunda instancia,*" is the exercise of the same action before the court of appellate jurisdiction; and the third instance, "*tercera instancia,*" is the prosecution of the same suit, either by an application of revision before the appellate tribunal that has already decided the cause, or before some higher tribunal, having jurisdiction of the same. Escriche.

INSTANS EST FINIS UNIUS TEMPORIS ET PRINCIPIUM ALTERIUS. An instant is the end of one time and the beginning of another. Co. Litt. 185.

INSTANT. Present, current, as instant case. Webster, Dict.

INSTANTANEOUS. An "instantaneous" crime is one which is fully consummated or completed in and by a single act (such as arson or murder) as distinguished from one which involves a series or repetition of acts. U. S. v. Owen, D.C.Or., 32 F. 537.

A death resulting within a few moments from a continuing injury is "instantaneous" within a statute respecting right of action for death. Beach v. City of St. Joseph, 192 Mich. 296, 158 N.W. 1045, 1046.

INSTANTER. Immediately; instantly; forthwith; without delay. Trial *instanter* was had where a prisoner between attainder and execution pleaded that he was not the same who was attainted.

When a party is ordered to plead *instanter,* he must plead the same day. The term is usually understood to mean within twenty-four hours. Fentress v. State, 16 Tex.App. 83; Champlin v. Champlin, 2 Edw.Ch., N.Y., 329.

INSTANTLY. Immediately; directly; without delay; at once.

INSTAR. Lat. Likeness; the likeness, size, or equivalent of a thing. *Instar dentium,* like teeth. 2 Bl.Comm. 295. *Instar omnium,* equivalent or tantamount to all. Id. 146; 3 Bl.Comm. 231.

INSTAURUM. In old English deeds. A stock or store of cattle, and other things; the whole stock upon a farm, including cattle, wagons, plows, and all other implements of husbandry. 1 Mon. Angl. 548*b*; Fleta, lib. 2, c. 72, § 7. *Terra instaurata,* land ready stocked.

INSTIGATE. To stimulate or goad to an action, especially a bad action; one of its synonyms is "abet". Hughes v. Van Bruggen, 44 N.M. 534, 105 P.2d 494, 499.

INSTIGATION. Incitation; urging; solicitation. The act by which one incites another to do something, as to commit some crime or to commence a suit. State v. Fraker, 148 Mo. 143, 49 S.W. 1017.

INSTIRPARE. To plant or establish.

INSTITOR. Lat. In the civil law. A clerk in a store; an agent.

INSTITORIA ACTIO. Lat. In the civil law. The name of an action given to those who had contracted with an *institor* (*q. v.*) to compel the principal to performance. Inst. 4, 7, 2; Dig. 14, 3, 1; Story, Ag. § 426.

INSTITORIAL POWER. The charge given to a clerk to manage a shop or store. 1 Bell, Comm. 506, 507.

INSTITUTE, *v.* To inaugurate or commence; as to institute an action. Post v. U. S., 16 S.Ct. 611, 161 U.S. 583, 40 L.Ed. 816; Ballard v. Cash, 191 Ky. 312, 230 S.W. 48, 49; Latham v. Latham, 178 N.C. 12, 100 S.E. 131, 132. To set up, to originate, to introduce. Brown v. City of Portland, 97 Or. 600, 190 P. 722, 724.

To nominate, constitute, or appoint; as to institute an heir by testament. Dig. 28, 5, 65.

INSTITUTE, *n.* In the civil law. A person named in the will as heir, but with a direction that he shall pass over the estate to another designated person, called the "substitute."

In Scotch law. The person to whom an estate is first given by destination or limitation; the others, or the heirs of tailzie, are called "substitutes."

INSTITUTED EXECUTOR. An instituted executor is one who is appointed by the testator without any condition.

INSTITUTES. A name sometimes given to textbooks containing the elementary principles of jurisprudence, arranged in an orderly and systematic manner. For example, the Institutes of Justinian, of Gaius, of Lord Coke.

Institutes of Gaius. An elementary work of the Roman jurist Gaius; important as having formed the foundation of the Institutes of Justinian, (*q. v.*). These Institutes were discovered by Niebuhr in 1816, in a *codex rescriptus* of the library of the cathedral chapter at Verona, and were first published at Berlin in 1820. Two editions have since appeared. Mackeld.Rom.Law, § 54.

Institutes of Justinian. One of the four component parts or principal divisions of the *Corpus Juris Civilis,* being an elementary treatise on the Roman law, in four books. This work was compiled from earlier sources, (resting principally on the Institutes of Gaius,) by a commission composed of Tribonian and two others, by command and under direction of the emperor Justinian, and was first published November 21, A. D. 533.

Institutes of Lord Coke. The name of four volumes by Lord Coke, published A. D. 1628. The first is an extensive comment upon a treatise on tenures, compiled by Littleton, a judge of the common pleas, *temp.* Edward IV. This comment is a rich mine of valuable common-law learning, collected and heaped together from the ancient reports and Year Books, but greatly defective in method. It is usually cited by the name of "Co. Litt.," or as "1 Inst." The second volume is a comment upon old acts of parliament, without systematic order; the third a more methodical treatise on the pleas of the crown; and the fourth an account of the several species of courts. These are cited as 2, 3, or 4 "Inst.," without any author's name. Wharton.

Theophilus' Institutes. A paraphrase of Justinian, made, it is believed, soon after A. D. 533. This paraphrase maintained itself as a manual of law until the eighth or tenth century. This text was used in the time of Hexabiblos of Harmenipulus, the last of the Greek jurists. It is also conjectured that Theophilus was not the editor of his own paraphrase, but that it was drawn up by some of his pupils after his explanations and lectures, inasmuch as it contains certain barbarous phrases, and the texts of the manuscripts vary greatly from each other.

INSTITUTIO HÆREDIS. Lat. In Roman law. The appointment of the *hæres* in the will. It corresponds very nearly to the nomination of an executor in English law. Without such an appointment the will was void at law, but the *prætor* (*i. e.,* equity) would, under certain circumstances, carry out the intentions of the testator. Brown.

INSTITUTION. The commencement or inauguration of anything. The first establishment of a law, rule, rite, etc. Any custom, system, organization, etc., firmly established. An elementary rule or principle.

An establishment, specially one of public character or one affecting a community. State v. Clausen, 85 Wash. 260, 148 P. 28, 32, Ann.Cas.1916B, 810. An established or organized society or corporation. It may be private in its character, designed for profit to those composing the organization, or public and charitable in its purposes. In re Peabody's Estate, 21 Cal.App.2d 690, 70 P.2d 249, 250. A foundation; as, a literary or charitable institution. Prescott Courier v. Board of Sup'rs of Yavapai County, 49 Ariz. 423, 67 P.2d 483, 486.

The term "institution" is sometimes used as descriptive of an establishment or place where the business or operations of a society or association is carried on; at other times it is used to designate the organized body. Benjamin Rose Institute v. Myers, 92 Ohio St. 252, 110 N.E. 924, 926, 927, L.R.A.1916D, 1170; Bartling v. Wait, 96 Neb. 532, 148 N.W. 507, 509.

Ecclesiastical Law

A kind of investiture of the spiritual part of the benefice, as induction is of the temporal; for by institution the care of the souls of the parish is committed to the charge of the clerk. Brown.

Civil Law

The appointment of an heir; the act by which a testator nominates one or more persons to succeed him in all his rights active and passive. Halifax, Anal. 39; Pothier, *Tr. des Donations testamentaires,* c. 2, s. 1, § 1; La Civ.Code, art. 1598 (Civ.Code, art. 1605); Dig. 28. 5; 1, 1; 28. 6. 1, 2, § 4.

Jurisprudence

The plural form of this word ("institutions") is sometimes used as the equivalent of "institutes," to denote an elementary textbook of the law.

Practice

The commencement of an action or prosecution; as, A. B. has instituted a suit against C. D. to recover damages for trespass.

Political Law

A law, rite, or ceremony enjoined by authority as a permanent rule of conduct or of government. Webster. An organized society, established either by law or the authority of individuals, for promoting any object, public or social. Dodge v. Williams, 46 Wis. 70, 1 N.W. 92, 50 N.W. 1103; State v. Edmondson, 88 Ohio St. 625, 106 N.E. 41, 44.

A system or body of usages, laws, or regulations, of extensive and recurring operation, containing within itself an organism by which it effects its own independent action, continuance, and generally its own further development. Its object is to generate, effect, regulate, or sanction a succession of acts, transactions, or productions of a peculiar kind or class. We are likewise in the habit of calling single laws or usages "institutions," if their operation is of vital importance and vast scope, and if their continuance is in a high degree independent of any interfering power. Lieb. Civil Lib. 300.

General

Public institution. One which is created and exists by law or public authority, e. g., an asylum, charity, college, university, schoolhouse, etc. Henderson v. Shreveport Gas, Electric Light & Power Co., 134 La. 39, 63 So. 616, 618, 51 L.R.A.,N.S., 448.

INSTITUTIONES. Lat. Works containing the elements of any science; institutions or institutes. One of Justinian's principal law collections, and a similar work of the Roman jurist Gaius, are so entitled. See Institutes.

INSTRUCT. To convey information as a client to an attorney, or as an attorney to a counsel; to authorize one to appear as advocate; to give a case in charge to the jury.

INSTRUCTION. In French criminal law. The first process of a criminal prosecution. It includes the examination of the accused, the preliminary interrogation of witnesses, collateral investigations, the gathering of evidence, the reduction of the whole to order, and the preparation of a document containing a detailed statement of the case, to serve as a brief for the prosecuting officers, and to furnish material for the indictment.

Juges d'instruction. In French law. Officers subject to the *procureur impérial* or *général,* who receive in cases of criminal offenses the complaints of the parties injured, and who summon and examine witnesses upon oath, and, after communication with the *procureur impérial,* draw up the forms of accusation. They have also the right, subject to the approval of the same superior officer, to admit the accused to bail. They are appointed for three years, but are re-eligible for a further period of office. They are usually chosen from among the regular judges. Brown.

Common Law

Order given by a principal to his agent in relation to the business of his agency.

Practice

A detailed statement of the facts and circumstances constituting a cause of action made by a client to his attorney for the purpose of enabling the latter to draw a proper declaration or procure it to be done by a pleader.

Trial Practice

A direction given by the judge to the jury concerning the law of the case; a statement made by the judge to the jury informing them of the law applicable to the case in general or some aspect of it; an exposition of the rules or principles of law applicable to the case or some branch or phase of it, which the jury are bound to accept and apply. Lehman v. Hawks, 121 Ind. 541, 23 N.E. 670; Boggs v. U. S., 10 Okl. 424, 63 P. 969; Lawler v. McPheeters, 73 Ind. 579; Davis v. State, 155 Ark. 245, 244 S.W. 750, 752; Kolkman v. People, 89 Colo. 8, 300 P. 575, 583.

The generally accepted meaning of the word instruction, when applied to courts, means a direction that is to be obeyed. State v. Downing, 23 Idaho, 540, 130 P. 461, 462.

Peremptory instruction. An instruction given by a court to a jury which the latter must obey implicitly; as an instruction to return a verdict for the defendant, or for the plaintiff, as the case may be.

INSTRUMENT. A written document; a formal or legal document in writing, such as a contract, deed, will, bond, or lease. State v. Phillips, 157 Ind. 481, 62 N.E. 12; Cardenas v. Miller, 108 Cal. 250, 39 P. 783, 49 Am.St.Rep. 84.

Anything reduced to writing, a document of a formal or solemn character, a writing given as a means of affording evidence. Smith v. Smith, Ind. App., 110 N.E. 1013, 1014. A document or writing which gives formal expression to a legal act or agreement, for the purpose of creating, securing, modifying, or terminating a right; a writing executed and delivered as the evidence of an act or agreement. Moore v. Diamond Dry Goods Co., 47 Ariz. 128, 54 P.2d 553, 554.

In the law of evidence. Anything which may be presented as evidence to the senses of the adjudicating tribunal. 1 Whart.Ev. § 615.

INSTRUMENT OF APPEAL. The document by which an appeal is brought in an English matrimonial cause from the president of the probate, divorce, and admiralty division to the full court. It is analogous to a petition. Browne, Div. 322.

INSTRUMENT OF EVIDENCE. Instruments of evidence are the *media* through which the evidence of facts, either disputed or required to be proved, is conveyed to the mind of a judicial tribunal; and they comprise persons and living things as well as writings. Best, Ev. § 123, 1 Whart.Ev. § 615.

INSTRUMENT OF SAISINE. An instrument in Scotland by which the delivery of "saisine" (*i. e.*, seisin, or the feudal possession of land) is attested. It is subscribed by a notary, in the presence of witnesses, and is executed in pursuance of a "precept of saisine," whereby the "grantor of the deed" desires "any notary public to whom these presents may be presented" to give saisine to the intended grantee or grantees. It must be entered and recorded in the registers of saisines. Mozley & Whiteley.

INSTRUMENTA. Lat. That kind of evidence which consists of writings not under seal; as court-rolls, accounts, and the like. 3 Co.Litt. 487.

INSTRUMENTAL. Serviceable, helpful. Culp v. Browne, Tex.Civ.App., 235 S.W. 675, 678.

INSTRUMENTALITY RULE. Under this rule, corporate existence will be disregarded where a corporation (subsidiary) is so organized and controlled and its affairs so conducted as to make it only an adjunct and instrumentality of another corporation (parent corporation). Jenkins Petroleum Process Co. v. Western Oil Corporation, D.C. Del., 21 F.Supp. 550, 551; and parent corporation will be responsible for the obligations of its subsidiary. Taylor v. Standard Gas & Electric Co., C.C.A.Okl., 96 F.2d 693, 704.

INSUBORDINATION. State of being insubordinate; disobedience to constituted authority. United States v. Krafft, C.C.A.N.J., 249 F. 919, 925, L.R.A.1918F, 402. Refusal to obey some order which a superior officer is entitled to give and have obeyed. Garvin v. Chambers, 195 Cal. 212, 232 P. 696, 701; Sheehan v. Board of Police Com'rs of City and County of San Francisco, 197 Cal. 70, 239 P. 844, 847. Not synonymous with incompetency. Cafferty v. Southern Tier Pub. Co., 173 N.Y.S. 774, 186 App.Div. 136.

"Insubordination" by a servant imports a willful disregard of express or implied directions of the employer and refusal to obey reasonable orders. MacIntosh v. Abbot, 231 Mass. 180, 120 N.E. 383.

INSUCKEN MULTURES. A quantity of corn paid by those who are thirled to a mill. See Thirlage.

INSUFFICIENT. Not sufficient; inadequate to some need, purpose, or use; wanting in needful value, ability, or fitness; incompetent; unfit; as insufficient food; insufficient means. It is the antonym of "sufficient." Nissen v. Miller, 44 N.M. 487, 105 P.2d 324, 325.

INSUFFICIENCY. In equity pleading. The legal inadequacy of an answer in equity which does not fully and specifically reply to some one or more of the material allegations, charges, or interrogatories set forth in the bill. White v. Joy, 13 N.Y. 89; Houghton v. Townsend, 8 How.Prac. (N.Y.) 446; Hill v. Fair Haven & W. R. Co., 75 Conn. 177, 52 A. 725.

INSUFFICIENCY OF EVIDENCE TO SUPPORT VERDICT. This phrase in a motion for new trial means that there is some evidence, but not enough in light of the evidence to the contrary to support a verdict. Arnold v. Haskins, 347 Mo. 320, 147 S. W.2d 469, 472. It means that there is no evidence which ought reasonably to satisfy jury that fact to be proved is established. Shtevelan v. Metropolitan Life Ins. Co., 295 N.Y.S. 735, 736, 162 Misc. 835.

INSULA. Lat. An island; a house not connected with other houses, but separated by a surrounding space of ground. Calvin.

INSULATE. To separate from conducting bodies by means of nonconductors, as to prevent the transfer of electricity or heat. Mauney v. Electric Const. Co., 210 Ala. 554, 98 So. 874, 877.

INSUPER. Lat. Moreover; over and above.

An old exchequer term, applied to a charge made *upon* a person in his account. Blount.

INSURABLE. Capable of being insured against loss, damage, death, etc.; proper to be insured; affording a sufficient ground for insurance. Greenberg v. Continental Casualty Co., 24 Cal.App.2d 506, 75 P.2d 644, 649.

INSURABLE INTEREST. Such a real and substantial interest in specific property as will prevent a contract to indemnify the person interested against its loss from being a mere wager policy. Mutual F. Ins. Co. v. Wagner, Pa., 7 A. 104; Insurance Co. v. Brooks, 131 Ala. 614, 30 So. 876; Berry v. Insurance Co., 132 N.Y. 49, 30 N.E. 254, 28 Am. St.Rep. 548; Strong v. Insurance Co., 10 Pick. (Mass.) 43, 20 Am.Dec. 507; Insurance Co. v. Winsmore, 124 Pa. 61, 16 A. 516. Such an interest as will make the loss of the property of pecuniary damage to the insured; a right, benefit, or advantage arising out of the property or dependent thereon, or any liability in respect thereof, or any relation thereto or concern therein, of such a nature that it might be so affected by the contemplated peril as to directly damnify the insured. 2 Joyce, Ins. §§ 887, 888. German Ins. Co. v. Hyman, 34 Neb. 704, 52 N.W. 401, 402. Tischendorf v. Lynn Mut. Fire Ins. Co., 190 Wis. 33, 208 N.W. 917, 919, 45 A.L.R. 856; Liverpool & London & Globe Ins. Co. v. Bolling, 176 Va. 182, 10 S.E.2d 518, 521.

Every interest in property, or any relation thereto, or liability in respect thereof, of such a nature that a contemplated peril might directly damnify the insured, is an insurable interest.

In the case of life insurance, a reasonable expectation of pecuniary benefit from the continued life of another; also, a reasonable ground, founded upon the relation of the parties to each other, either pecuniary or of blood or affinity, to expect some benefit or advantage from the continuance of the life of the assured. Insurance Co. v. Schaefer, 94 U.S. 460, 24 L.Ed. 251; National Life & Accident Ins. Co. v. Ball, 157 Miss. 163, 127 So. 268; Colgrove v. Lowe, 343 Ill. 360, 175 N.E. 569, 572. Essential thing being that policy be obtained in good faith, not for purpose of speculating on hazard of life in which insured has no interest. Alexander v. Griffith Brokerage Co., 228 Mo.App. 773, 73 S.W.2d 418, 423.

INSURANCE. A contract whereby, for a stipulated consideration, one party undertakes to compensate the other for loss on a specified subject by specified perils. The party agreeing to make the compensation is usually called the "insurer" or "underwriter;" the other, the "insured" or "assured;" the agreed consideration, the "premium;" the written contract, a "policy;" the events insured against, "risks" or "perils;" and the subject, right, or interest to be protected, the "insurable interest." 1 Phil.Ins. §§ 1–5. A contract whereby one undertakes to indemnify another against loss, damage, or liability arising from an unknown or contingent event and is applicable only to some contingency or act to occur in future. Com. v. Provident Bicycle Ass'n, 178 Pa. 636, 36 A. 197, 36 L.R.A. 589; Commonwealth v. Metropolitan Life Ins. Co., 254 Pa. 510, 98 A. 1072, 1073; and is applicable only to some contingency or act to occur in future. Clardy v. Grand Lodge of Oklahoma, A. O. U. W., 132 Okl. 165, 269 P. 1065, 1066. For "Family," see that title.

An agreement by which one party for a consideration promises to pay money or its equivalent or to do an act valuable to other party upon destruction, loss, or injury of something in which other party has an interest. Commissioner of Banking and Insurance v. Community Health Service, 129 N.J.L. 427, 30 A.2d 44, 46.

Classification

Accident insurance is that form of insurance which undertakes to indemnify the assured against expense, loss of time, and suffering resulting from accidents causing him physical injury, usually by payment at a fixed rate per week while the consequent disability lasts, and sometimes including the payment of a fixed sum to his heirs in case of his death by accident within the term of the policy. Employers' Liability Assur. Corp. v. Merrill, 155 Mass. 404, 29 N.E. 529.

Automobile insurance may embrace insurance against loss of or damage to a motor vehicle caused by fire, windstorm, theft, collision, or other insurable hazards, and also against legal liability for personal injuries or damage to property resulting from operation of the vehicle. 44 C.J.S. p. 492; Blashfield, Cyc. of Automobile Law and Prac., Perm. Ed., § 3461.

Burglary insurance. Insurance against loss of property by the depredations of burglars and thieves.

Casualty insurance. This term is generally used as equivalent to "accident" insurance. State v. Federal Inv. Co., 48 Minn. 110, 50 N.W. 1028. But in some states it means insurance against accidental injuries to property, as distinguished from accidents resulting in bodily injury or death. Employers' Liability Assur. Corp. v. Merrill, 155 Mass. 404, 29 N.E. 529.

Commercial insurance is a term applied to indemnity agreements, in the form of insurance bonds or policies, whereby parties to commercial contracts are to a designated extent guarantied against loss by reason of a breach of contractual obligations on the part of the other contracting party; to this class belong policies of contract credit and title insurance. Cowles v. Guaranty Co., 32 Wash. 120, 72 Pac. 1032, 98 Am.St.Rep. 838.

Employers' insurance. Employers' insurance policies are of two sorts, the "liability" contract, which obligates the insurer to pay the loss without first requiring that the assured do so, and the "indemnity" contract, which obligates the insurer to reimburse only after the employer has paid the debt to the injured employee. Davies v. Maryland Casualty Co., 89 Wash. 571, 154 P. 1116, 1117, L.R.A.1916D, 395, 398.

Employer's liability insurance. In this form of insurance the risk insured against is the liability of the assured to make compensation or pay damages for an accident, injury, or death occurring to a servant or other employee in the course of his employment, either at common law or under statutes imposing such liability on employers.

Fidelity insurance is that form of insurance in which the insurer undertakes to guaranty the fidelity of an officer, agent, or employee of the assured, or rather to indemnify the latter for losses caused by dishonesty or a want of fidelity on the part of such a person. People v. Rose, 174 Ill. 310, 51 N.E. 246, 44 L.R.A. 124.

Fire insurance. A contract of insurance by which the underwriter, in consideration of the premium, undertakes to indemnify the insured against all losses in his houses, buildings, furniture, ships in port, or merchandise, by means of accidental fire happening within a prescribed period. 3 Kent, Comm. 370; Mutual L. Ins. Co. v. Allen, 138 Mass. 27, 52 Am.Rep. 245; Durham v. Fire & Marine Ins. Co., C.C.Or., 22 F. 470.

Fraternal insurance. The form of life or accident insurance furnished by a fraternal beneficial association, consisting in the undertaking to pay to a member, or his heirs in case of death, a stipulated sum of money, out of funds raised for that purpose by the payment of dues or assessments by all the members of the association.

Guaranty or fidelity insurance is a contract whereby one, for a consideration, agrees to indemnify another against loss arising from the want of integrity or fidelity of employees and persons holding positions of trust, or embezzlements by them, or against the insolvency of debtors, losses in trade, loss by non-payment of notes, or against breaches of contract. People v. Rose, 174 Ill. 310, 51 N.E. 246, 44 L.R.A. 124; Cowles v. United States Fidelity & Guaranty Co., 32 Wash. 120, 72 P. 1032.

Indemnity insurance. This term has come to have a well defined and recognized meaning in insurance parlance, and is applied to contracts which provide indemnity against loss, and not the contracts which provide for indemnity against liability. The latter are known as liability contracts or policies, and the former as indemnity contracts or policies. 44 C.J.S. pp. 480, 482. As applied to motor vehicles, the distinctions between the two types of policies are discussed in Blashfield, Cyc. of Automobile Law and Prac., Perm. Ed., §§ 4011–4015.

Industrial insurance. Small policies issued in consideration of weekly premium payments. Life & Casualty Ins. Co. v. King, 137 Tenn. 685, 195 S.W. 585, 588.

Liability insurance is that form of insurance which indemnifies against liability on account of injuries to the person or property of another. It is distinguished from "indemnity insurance" (see that title, *supra*), and may be issued to cover the liability of, for example, carriers, contractors, employers, landlords, manufacturers, owners, and railroads. Liability insurance may extend to automobiles, elevators, fly wheels, libel, theaters, and vessels. 44 C.J.S. p. 481.

Life insurance. That kind of insurance in which the risk contemplated is the death of a particular person; upon which event (if it occurs within a prescribed term, or, according to the contract, whenever it occurs) the insurer engages to pay a stipulated sum to the legal representatives of such person, or to a third person having an insurable interest in the life of such person.

Straight life insurance or *whole life insurance* is insurance for which premiums are collected so long as the insured may live, whereas, *term insurance* is insurance which promises payment only within a stipulated number of years. Doty v. American Nat. Ins. Co., 350 Mo. 192, 165 S.W.2d 862, 869, 143 A.L.R. 1062.

Live-stock insurance. Insurance upon the lives, health, and good condition of domestic animals of the useful kinds, such as horses and cows.

Marine insurance. A contract whereby, for a consideration stipulated to be paid by one interested in a ship, freight, or cargo, subject to the risks of marine navigation, another undertakes to indemnify him against some or all of those risks during a certain period or voyage. 1 Phil.Ins. 1. A contract whereby one party, for a stipulated premium, undertakes to indemnify the other against certain perils or sea-risks to which his ship, freight, and cargo, or some of them, may be exposed during a certain voyage, or a fixed period of time. An insurance against risks connected with navigation, to which a ship, cargo, freightage, profits, or other insurable interest in movable property may be exposed during a certain voyage or a fixed period of time. Civ.Code Cal. § 2655.

Motor vehicle insurance. See *Automobile insurance, supra.*

Old line life insurance. Insurance on a level or flat rate plan where, for a fixed premium payable without condition at stated intervals, a certain sum is to be paid upon death without condition. Mattero v. Central Life Ins. Co., 202 Mo.App. 293, 215 S.W. 750, 751.

Plate-glass insurance. Insurance against loss from the accidental breaking of plate-glass in windows, doors, show-cases, etc.

Steam boiler insurance. Insurance against the destruction of steam boilers by their explosion, sometimes including indemnity against injuries to other property resulting from such explosion.

Title insurance. Insurance against loss or damage resulting from defects or failure of title to a particular parcel of realty, or from the enforcement of liens existing against it at the time of the insurance. This form of insurance is taken out by a purchaser of the property or one loaning money on mortgage, and is furnished by companies specially organized for the purpose, and which keep complete sets of abstracts or duplicates of the records, employ expert title-examiners, and prepare conveyances and transfers of all sorts. A "certificate of title" furnished by such a company is merely the formally expressed professional opinion of the company's examiner that the title is complete and perfect (or otherwise, as stated), and the company is liable only for a want of care, skill, or diligence on the part of its examiner; whereas an "insurance of title" warrants the validity of the title in any and all events. It is not always easy to distinguish between such insurance and a "guaranty of title" given by such a company, except that in the former case the maximum limit of liability is fixed by the policy, while in the latter case the undertaking is to make good any and all loss resulting from defect or failure of the title.

Tornado insurance. Insurance against injuries to crops, timber, houses, farm buildings, and other property from the effects of tornadoes, hurricanes, and cyclones.

Other Compound and Descriptive Terms

Additional insurance. To constitute prohibited "additional insurance" both policies must be on same subject-matter and on same interest therein. Clower v. Fidelity-Phenix Fire Ins. Co. of New York, 220 Mo.App. 1112, 296 S.W. 257, 260; Hurst Home Ins. Co. v. Deatley, 175 Ky. 728, 194 S.W. 910, 911, L.R.A.1917E, 750.

Assessment life insurance policy. A contract by which payments to insured are not unalterably fixed, but dependent on collection of assessments necessary to pay amounts insured, while an "old-line policy" unalterably fixes premiums and definitely and unchangeably fixes insurer's liability. Clark v. Metropolitan Life Ins. Co., 126 Me. 7, 135 A. 357, 358.

Comprehensive coverage. A simple and convenient form of indemnity now commonly available in contracts of automobile insurance. It includes not only the conventional coverages against loss caused by fire, theft, wind, water, or malicious mischief, but is generally designed to protect against all damage to the insured vehicle except by collision or upset. Blashfield, Cyc. of Automobile Law and Prac., Perm. Ed., § 3653. Among losses commonly incurred and paid under comprehensive policies are those caused by lighted cigarettes. Other examples of such losses include scratching of the finish by matches, thorns, or dust storms; damage to the upholstery caused by a child's loss of control of the urinary function, and by the clawing or chewing of the upholstery by a pet dog; and damage to the fenders resulting when a goat mistook them for hors d'oeuvres. Appleman, Ins. Law and Prac., § 3222.

Concurrent insurance. That which to any extent insures the same interest against the same casualty, at the same time, as the primary insurance, on such terms that the insurers would bear proportionately the loss happening within the provisions of both policies. Rubber Co. v. Assur. Co., 64 N.J. L. 580, 46 A. 777; Connecticut Fire Ins. Co. v. Union Mercantile Co., 161 Ky. 718, 171 S.W. 407, 409; Camden Fire Ins. Ass'n v. Sutherland, Tex. Civ.App., 278 S.W. 907, 914.

Double insurance. See Double.

Excess insurance. See Excess Insurance.

General and special insurance. In marine insurance a general insurance is effected when the perils insured against are such as the law would imply from the nature of the contract considered in itself and supposing none to be specified in the policy; in the case of special insurance, further perils (in addition to implied perils) are expressed in the policy. Vandenheuvel v. United Ins. Co., 2 Johns.Cas. (N.Y.) 127.

Loss. See Loss.

Insurance adjuster. One undertaking to ascertain and report the actual loss to the subject-matter of insurance due to the peril insured against. Laws Wash.1911, p. 163, § 2; Jensen v. Lincoln Hail Ins. Co., 125 Neb. 87, 249 N.W. 94.

Insurance agent. Person authorized to represent insurer in dealing with third parties in matters relating to insurance. American Casualty Co. of Reading, Pa., v. Ricas, 179 Md. 627, 22 A.2d 484, 487. An agent employed by an insurance company to solicit risks and effect insurances. Agents of insurance companies are called "general agents" when clothed with the general oversight of the companies' business in a state or large section of country, and "local agents" when their functions are limited and confined to some particular locality. McKinney v. Alton, 41 Ill.App. 512; State v. Accident Ass'n, 67 Wis. 624, 31 N.W. 229. See, also, Insurance broker, infra.

Insurance broker. One who acts as middleman between insured and company, and who solicits insurance from public under no employment from any special company and places order of insurance with company selected by insurer or, in absence of any selection, with company selected by such broker. Broker is agent for insured though at same time for some purposes he may be agent for insurer, and his acts and representations within scope of his authority as such agent are binding on insured. Pacific Fire Ins. Co. v. Bowers, 163 Va. 349, 175 S.E. 763.

An "insurance agent" is tied to his company, whereas an "insurance broker" is an independent middleman not tied to a particular company. Osborn v. Ozlin, Va., 310 U.S. 53, 60 S.Ct. 758, 761, 84 L.Ed. 1074.

Insurance commissioner. A public officer in several of the states, whose duty is to supervise the business of insurance as conducted in the state by foreign and domestic companies, for the protection and benefit of policy-holders, and especially to issue licenses, make periodical examinations into the condition of such companies, or receive, file, and publish periodical statements of their business as furnished by them.

Insurance company. A corporation or association whose business is to make contracts of insurance. They are either mutual companies or stock companies. A "mutual" insurance company is one whose fund for the payment of losses consists not of capital subscribed or furnished by outside parties, but of premiums mutually contributed by the parties insured, or in other words, one in which all persons insured become members of the association and contribute either cash or assessable premium notes, or both, to a common fund, out of which each is entitled to indemnity in case of loss. Mygatt v. Insurance Co., 21 N.Y. 65; Insurance Co. v. Hoge, 21 How. 35, 16 L.Ed. 61; Given v. Rettew, 162 Pa. 638, 29 A. 703. A "stock" company is one organized according to the usual form of business corporations, having a capital stock divided into shares, which, with current income and accumulated surplus, constitutes the fund for the payment of losses, policy-holders paying fixed premiums and not being members of the association unless they also happen to be stockholders.

Insurance policy. See Policy.

Insurance premium. The consideration paid by insured to insurer for insurance protection. Alyea-Nichols Co. v. U. S., D.C.Ill., 12 F.2d 998, 1005. See Premium.

Insurance trust. An agreement between insured and trustee, whereby proceeds of policy are paid directly to trustee for investment and distribution to designated beneficiaries in manner and at such time as insured has directed in trust agreement. In re Reynolds' Estate, 131 Neb. 557, 268 N.W. 480, 486, 487.

Interinsurance is insurance system whereby several individuals, partnerships, or corporations, through common attorney in fact, underwrite one another's risks against loss under agreement that underwriters act separately and severally. Wysong v. Automobile Underwriters, 204 Ind. 493, 184 N.E. 783, 785, 94 A.L.R. 826; Hoopeston Canning Co. v. Cullen, 63 S.Ct. 602, 604, 318 U.S. 313, 87 L.Ed. 777, 145 A.L.R. 1113.

It is distinguishable from all other forms of insurance, in that every insured is interinsurer, and every insurer is insured. Underwriters' Exchange v. Indianapolis St. Ry. Co., 204 Ind. 676, 185 N.E. 504, 506.

Mutual insurance. That form of insurance provided by mutual companies. An essential characteristic of a mutual insurance company is collective and entire ownership and control by its members, all of whom must be policyholders. A mutual company may collect cash premiums from members in advance or it may assess members to pay losses and overhead. An insurance company can be mutual even though policyholders are not subject to assessment. To be a mutual insurance company, it is also essential that the company provide insurance to its members substantially at cost. Ohio Farmers Indemnity Co. v. Commissioner of Internal Revenue, 108 F.2d 665; Union Ins. Co. v. Hoge, 62 U.S. 35, 16 L.Ed. 61; Mutual Fire Ins. Co. of Germantown v. United States, 142 F.2d 344.

Over-insurance. Insurance effected upon property, either in one or several companies, to an amount which, separately or in the aggregate, exceeds the actual value of the property.

Reinsurance. Insurance of an insurer; a contract by which an insurer procures a third person (usually another insurance company) to insure him against loss or liability by reason of the original insurance. Civ.Code Cal. § 2646; Insurance Co. v. Insurance Co., 38 Ohio St. 15, 43 Am.Rep. 413.

Specific insurance. That provided by a policy under the terms of which the insurance in the event of loss is to be distributed among the several items of property, a specific amount to each item. Wilson & Co. v. Hartford Fire Ins. Co., 300 Mo. 1, 254 S.W. 266, 282.

Term insurance. Insurance for a fixed time. Gilley v. Missouri State Life Ins. Co., 116 Tex. 43, 285 S.W. 807. Insurance covering only losses occurring before expiration of stated term. Ætna Casualty & Surety Co. v. Commercial State Bank of Rantoul, D.C.Ill., 13 F.2d 474, 476.

INSURE. To make sure or secure, to guarantee, as, to insure safety to any one. State v. Mutual Mortuary Ass'n, 166 Tenn. 260, 61 S.W.2d 664. To engage to indemnify a person against pecuniary loss from specified perils. To act as an insurer. U. S. Fidelity & Guaranty Co. v. Williams, 148 Md. 289, 129 A. 660, 664.

INSURED. The person who obtains insurance on his property, or upon whose life an insurance is effected. Kierce v. Lumbermen's Ins. Co. of Philadelphia, 162 Minn. 277, 202 N.W. 730, 731; Healy v. Prudential Ins. Co. of America, Sup., 140 N.Y.S. 505, 506; Thompson v. Northwestern Mut. Life Ins. Co., 161 Iowa 446, 143 N.W. 518.

INSURER. The underwriter or insurance company with whom a contract of insurance is made.

INSURGENT. One who participates in an insurrection; one who opposes the execution of law by force of arms, or who rises in revolt against the constituted authorities. Hearon v. Calus, 178 S.C. 381, 183 S.E. 13, 20.

A distinction is often taken between "insurgent" and "rebel," in this: that the former term is not necessarily to be taken in a bad sense, inasmuch as an insurrection, though extralegal, may be just and timely in itself; as where it is undertaken for the overthrow of tyranny or the reform of gross abuses.

INSURRECTION. A rebellion, or rising of citizens or subjects in resistance to their government. See Insurgent.

Insurrection shall consist in any combined resistance to the lawful authority of the state, with intent to the denial thereof, when the same is manifested, or intended to be manifested, by acts of violence. Allegheny County v. Gibson, 90 Pa. 417, 35 Am.Rep. 670.

INTAKERS. In old English law. A kind of thieves inhabiting Redesdale, on the extreme northern border of England; so called because they *took in* or received such booties of cattle and other things as their accomplices, who were called "out-parters," brought in to them from the borders of Scotland. Spelman; Cowell.

INTAKES. Temporary inclosures made by customary tenants of a manor under a special custom authorizing them to inclose part of the waste until one or more crops have been raised on it. Elton, Common, 277.

INTANGIBLE ASSET. Such values as accrue to a going business as good will, trademarks, copyrights, franchises, or the like. It exists only in connection with something else, as the good will of a business. In re Armour's Estate, 94 A. 284, 294, 11 N.J. 257.

INTANGIBLE PROPERTY. Used chiefly in the law of taxation, this term means such property as has no intrinsic and marketable value, but is merely the representative or evidence of value, such as certificates of stock, bonds, promissory notes, and franchises. Western Union Tel. Co. v. Norman, C.C.Ky., 77 F. 26; In re Hanson's Estate, 195 N.Y.S. 255, 119 Mich. 100; City of Richmond v. Drewry-Hughes Co., 122 Va. 178, 90 S.E. 635.

INTEGER. Lat. Whole; untouched. *Res integra* means a question which is new and undecided. 2 Kent, Comm. 177.

INTEGRATED. An agreement is integrated where the parties thereto adopt the writing or writings as the final and complete expression of the agreement and an "integration" is the writing or writings so adopted. Wilson v. Viking Corporation, 134 Pa.Super. 153, 3 A.2d 180, 183.

INTEGRATED BAR. See Integration, *infra.*

INTEGRATION. The act or process of making whole or entire. Webster.

The writing or writings adopted by the parties to an agreement as the final and complete expression of the agreement. Restatement, Contracts, § 228; Pettett v. Cooper, 62 Ohio App. 377, 24 N.E.2d 299, 302.

The act of organizing the bar of a state into an association, membership in which is a condition precedent to the right to practice law. Integration is accomplished by enactment of detailed statutes, by enactment of a short statute conferring authority upon the highest court of the state to integrate the bar, or by rule of court in the exercise of its inherent power. Integration of Bar Case, 244 Wis. 8, 11 N.W.2d 604, 608, 151 A.L.R. 586, rehearing denied 244 Wis. 8, 12 N.W. 2d 699; In re Integration of State Bar of Oklahoma, 185 Okl. 505, 95 P.2d 113.

Integrated Bar

"The integrated bar movement was initiated in this country about 35 years ago [i. e., about 1914] by the American Judicature Society and since that time at least 27 States have adopted it. None of them have returned to the old system of voluntary organization, but all commend the integrated bar highly. * * * When we say the bar is integrated we mean that every lawyer within a given area has membership in a cohesive organization. An organization of less than all the members of the bar in a given area would not be an integrated bar. The area may be the state, the county, or the city. The integrated bar has also been defined as the process by which every member of the bar is given an opportunity to do his part in performing the public service expected of him, and by which each member is obliged to bear his portion of the responsibility. * * * The integrated bar of California has promulgated the best pattern for an integrated bar program to which our attention has been directed." Terrell, J., writing for a majority of the Supreme Court of Florida on the Petition of Florida State Bar Ass'n (1949), 40 So.2d 902, 904.

INTEGRITY. As occasionally used in statutes prescribing the qualifications of public officers, trustees, etc., this term means soundness of moral principle and character, as shown by one person dealing with others in the making and performance of contracts, and fidelity and honesty in the discharge of trusts; it is synonymous with "probity," "honesty," and "uprightness." In re Bauquier's Estate, 88 Cal. 302, 26 Pac. 178; In re Gordon's Estate, 142 Cal. 125, 75 Pac. 672.

INTELLIGIBILITY. In pleading. The statement of matters of fact directly (excluding the necessity of inference or argument to arrive at the meaning) and in such appropriate terms, so arranged, as to be comprehensible by a person of common or ordinary understanding. Davis v. Trump, 43 W.Va. 191, 27 S.E. 397, 64 Am.St.Rep. 849.

INTEMPERANCE. Habitual intemperance is that degree of intemperance from the use of intoxicating drinks which disqualifies the person a great portion of the time from properly attending to business, or which would reasonably inflict a course of great mental anguish upon an innocent party. Hope v. The Maccabees, 91 N.J.L. 148, 102 A. 689, 691, 1 A.L.R. 455; Andrews v. United States Casualty Co., 154 Wis. 82, 142 N.W. 487, 490.

INTEND. To design, resolve, purpose. To apply a rule of law in the nature of presumption; to discern and follow the probabilities of like cases.

INTENDANT. One who has the charge, management, or direction of some office, department, or public business.

Used in the constitutional and statutory law of some European governments to designate a principal officer of state corresponding to the cabinet ministers or secretaries of the various departments of the United States government, as, "intendant of marine," "intendant of finance."

The term was also used in Alabama to designate the chief executive officer of a city or town, having practically the same duties and functions as a mayor. Const. Ala. 1901, § 176; Intendant and Council of Greensboro v. Mullins, 13 Ala. 341.

INTENDED TO BE RECORDED. This phrase is frequently used in conveyances, when reciting some other conveyance which has not yet been recorded, but which forms a link in the chain of title. In Pennsylvania, it has been construed to be a covenant, on the part of the grantor, to procure the deed to be recorded in a reasonable time. Penn v. Preston, 2 Rawle (Pa.) 14.

INTENDED WIFE. Betrothed. Mace v. Grand Lodge, A. O. U. W. of Massachusetts, 234 Mass. 299, 125 N.E. 569.

INTENDENTE. In Spanish law. The immediate agent of the minister of finance, or the chief and principal director of the different branches of the revenue, appointed in the various departments in each of the provinces into which the Spanish monarchy is divided. Escriche.

INTENDMENT OF LAW. The true meaning, the correct understanding or intention of the law; a presumption or inference made by the courts. Co. Litt. 78.

Common intendment. The natural and usual sense; the common meaning or understanding; the plain meaning of any writing as apparent on its face without straining or distorting the construction.

INTENT. Design, resolve, or determination with which person acts. Witters v. United States, 106 F.2d 837, 840, 70 App.D.C. 316, 125 A.L.R. 1031; being a state of mind, is rarely susceptible of direct proof, but must ordinarily be inferred from the facts. State v. Walker, 109 W.Va. 351, 154 S. E. 866, 867. It presupposes knowledge. Reinhard v. Lawrence Warehouse Co., 41 Cal.App.2d 741, 107 P.2d 501, 504.

"Intent" and "motive" are not in law one and the same thing. State v. Logan, 344 Mo. 351, 126 S.W.2d 256, 260, 122 A.L.R. 417. "Intent" in legal sense is purpose to use particular means to effect certain result; whereas, "motive" is reason which leads minds to desire that result. United Fidelity Life Ins. Co. v. Adair, Tex.Civ.App., 29 S.W.2d 940, 943.

"Intent" expresses mental action at its most advanced point, or as it actually accompanies an outward, corporal act which has been determined on. *Intent* shows the presence of *will* in the act which consummates a crime. It is the exercise of intelligent will, the mind being fully aware of the nature and consequences of the act which is about to be done, and with such knowledge, and with full liberty of action, willing and electing to do it. Burrill, Circ.Ev. 284, and notes.

General intent. An intention, purpose, or design, either without specific plan or particular object, or without reference to such plan or object.

Meaning; purpose; signification; intendment; applied to words or language. See Certainty.

Common intent. The natural sense given to words.

Estoppel. See Estoppel.

INTENTIO. Lat.

In the Civil law. The formal complaint or claim of a plaintiff before the prætor.

In Old English law. A count or declaration in a real action (*narratio*). Bract. lib. 4, tr. 2, c. 2; Fleta, lib. 4, c. 7; Du Cange.

INTENTIO CÆCA MALA. A blind or obscure meaning is bad or ineffectual. 2 Bulst. 179. Said of a testator's intention.

INTENTIO INSERVIRE DEBET LEGIBUS, NON LEGES INTENTIONI. The intention [of a party] ought to be subservient to [or in accordance with] the laws, not the laws to the intention. Co. Litt. 314*a*, 314*b*.

INTENTIO MEA IMPONIT NOMEN OPERI MEO. Hob. 123. My intent gives a name to my act.

INTENTION. Determination to act in a certain way or to do a certain thing. State ex rel. Verbon v. County of St. Louis, 216 Minn. 140, 12 N.W.2d 193, 196; In re McCafferty's Will, 254 N.Y.S. 789, 795, 142 Misc. 371. Meaning; will; purpose; design. 4 Kent, Comm. 534.

"Intention," when used with reference to the construction of wills and other documents, means the sense and meaning of it, as gathered from the words used therein. Parol evidence is not ordinarily admissible to explain this. When used with reference to civil and criminal responsibility, a person who contemplates any result, as not unlikely to follow from a deliberate act of his own, may be said to intend that result, whether he desire it or not. Thus, if a man should, for a wager, discharge a gun among a multitude of people, and any should be killed, he would be deemed guilty of intending the death of such person; for every man is presumed to intend the natural consequence of his own actions. Intention is often confounded with motive, as when we speak of a man's "good intentions." Mozley & Whitley.

INTENTIONAL. Willful. Jackson v. Edwards, 144 Fla. 187, 197 So. 833, 835.

INTENTIONE. A writ that lay against him who entered into lands after the death of a tenant in dower, or for life, etc., and held out to him in reversion or remainder. Fitzh. Nat. Brev. 203.

INTER. Lat. Among; between.

INTER ALIA. Among other things. A term anciently used in pleading, especially in reciting statutes, where the whole statute was not set forth at length. *Inter alia enactatum fuit,* among other things it was enacted. Plowd. 65.

INTER ALIAS CAUSAS ACQUISITIONIS, MAGNA, CELEBRIS, ET FAMOSA EST CAUSA DONATIONIS. Among other methods of acquiring property, a great, much-used, and celebrated method is that of gift. Bract. fol. 11.

INTER ALIOS. Between other persons; between those who are strangers to a matter in question.

INTER ALIOS RES GESTAS ALIIS NON POSSE PRÆJUDICIUM FACERE SÆPE CONSTITUTUM EST. It has been often settled that things which took place between other parties cannot prejudice. Code 7, 60, 1, 2.

INTER APICES JURIS. Among the subtleties of the law. See Apex Juris.

INTER ARMA SILENT LEGES. In time of war the laws are silent. Cicero, *pro Milone.* It applies as between the state and its external enemies; and also in cases of civil disturbance where extrajudicial force may supersede the ordinary process of law. Salmond, Jurispr. 641.

INTER BRACHIA. Between her arms. Fleta, lib. 1, c. 35, §§ 1, 2. See infra, Brachia.

INTER CÆTEROS. Among others; in a general clause; not by name (*nominatim*). A term applied in the civil law to clauses of disinheritance in a will. Inst. 2, 13, 1; Id. 2, 13, 3.

INTER CANEM ET LUPUM. (Lat. Between the dog and the wolf.) The twilight; because then the dog seeks his rest, and the wolf his prey. 3 Inst. 63.

INTER CONJUGES. Between husband and wife.

INTER CONJUNCTAS PERSONAS. Between conjunct persons. By the act 1621, c. 18, all conveyances or alienations between conjunct persons, unless granted for onerous causes, are declared, as in a question with creditors, to be null and of no avail. Conjunct persons are those standing in a certain degree of relationship to each other; such, for example, as brothers, sisters, sons, uncles, etc. These were formerly excluded as witnesses, on account of their relationship; but this, as a ground of exclusion, has been abolished. Tray. Lat. Max.

INTER FAUCES TERRÆ. (Between the jaws of the land.) A term used to describe a roadstead or arm of the sea enclosed between promontories or projecting headlands.

INTER PARES. Between peers; between those who stand on a level or equality, as respects diligence, opportunity, responsibility, etc.

INTER PARTES. Between parties. Instruments in which two persons unite, each making conveyance to, or engagement with, the other, are called "papers *inter partes.*" Smith v. Emery, 12 N.J. Law, 60.

Judgment Inter Partes

See Judgment in Personam.

INTER QUATUOR PARIETES. Between four walls. Fleta, lib. 6, c. 55, § 4.

INTER REGALIA. In English law. Among the things belonging to the sovereign. Among these are rights of salmon fishing, mines of gold and silver, forests, forfeitures, casualties of superiority, etc., which are called *"regalia minora,"* and may be conveyed to a subject. The *regalia majora* include the several branches of the royal prerogative, which are inseparable from the person of the sovereign. Tray. Lat. Max.

INTER RUSTICOS. Among the illiterate or unlearned.

INTER SE, INTER SESE. Among themselves. Story, Partn. § 405.

INTER VIRUM ET UXOREM. Between husband and wife.

INTER VIVOS. Between the living; from one living person to another. Where property passes by conveyance, the transaction is said to be *inter vivos*, to distinguish it from a case of succession or devise. So an ordinary gift from one person to another is called a "gift *inter vivos*," to distinguish it from a donation made in contemplation of death, (*mortis causa.*)

INTERCALARE. Lat. In the civil law. To introduce or insert among or between others; to introduce a day or month into the calendar; to intercalate. Dig. 50, 16, 98, pr.

INTERCEDERE. Lat. In the civil law. To become bound for another's debt.

INTERCEPTION. Within Federal Communications Act, prohibiting interception of communication by wire or radio, indicates taking or seizure by the way or before arrival at destined place, and does not ordinarily connote obtaining of what is to be sent before, or at the moment, it leaves the possession of the proposed sender, or after, or at the moment, it comes into possession of intended receiver. Communications Act of 1934, § 605, 47 U.S.C.A. § 605; Goldman v. United States, N.Y., 62 S.Ct. 993, 995, 316 U.S. 129, 86 L.Ed. 1322.

INTERCHANGEABLY. By way of exchange or interchange. This term properly denotes the method of signing deeds, leases, contracts, etc., executed in duplicate, where each party signs the copy which he delivers to the other. Roosevelt v. Smith, 40 N.Y.S. 381, 17 Misc.Rep. 323.

INTERCOMMON. To enjoy a common mutually or promiscuously with the inhabitants or tenants of a contiguous township, vill, or manor. 2 Bl. Comm. 33; 1 Crabb, Real Prop. p. 271, § 290.

INTERCOMMUNING. Letters of intercommuning were letters from the Scotch privy council passing (on their act) in the king's name, charging the lieges not to reset, supply, or intercommune with the persons thereby denounced; or to furnish them with meat, drink, house, harbor, or any other things useful or comfortable; or to have any intercourse with them whatever,—under pain of being reputed art and part in their crimes, and dealt with accordingly; and desiring all sheriffs, bailies, etc., to apprehend and commit such rebels to prison. Bell.

INTERCOURSE. Communication; literally, a *running* or passing *between* persons or places; commerce. As applied to two persons, the word standing alone, and without a descriptive or qualifying word, does not import sexual connection. People v. Howard, 143 Cal. 316, 76 P. 1116.

INTERDICT. In Roman law. A decree of the prætor by means of which, in certain cases determined by the edict, he himself directly commanded what should be done or omitted, particularly in causes involving the right of possession or a *quasi* possession. In the modern civil law, interdicts are regarded precisely the same as actions, though they give rise to a summary proceeding. Mackeld. Rom. Law, § 258.

Interdicts are either prohibitory, restorative, or exhibitory; the first being a prohibition, the second a decree for restoring possession lost by force, the third a decree for the exhibiting of accounts, etc. Heinec. § 1206.

An interdict was distinguished from an "action," *(actio,)* properly so called, by the circumstance that the prætor himself decided in the first instance, *(principaliter,)* on the application of the plaintiff, without previously appointing a *judex*, by issuing a decree commanding what should be done, or left undone. Gaius, 4, 139. It might be adopted as a remedy in various cases where a regular action could not be maintained, and hence interdicts were at one time more extensively used than were the *actiones* themselves. Afterwards, however, they fell into disuse, and in the time of Justinian were generally dispensed with. Mackeld. Rom.Law, § 258; Inst. 4, 15, 8.

In Ecclesiastical law. An ecclesiastical censure, by which divine services are prohibited to be administered either to particular persons or in particular places.

In Scotch law. An order of the court of session or of an inferior court, pronounced on cause shown, for stopping any act or proceedings complained of as illegal or wrongful. It may be resorted to as a remedy against any encroachment either on property or possession, and is a protection against any unlawful proceeding. Bell.

INTERDICTION. In French law. Every person who, on account of insanity, has become incapable of controlling his own interests, can be put under the control of a guardian, who shall administer his affairs with the same effect as he might himself. Such a person is said to be *"interdit,"* and his *status* is described as "interdiction." Arg. Fr. Merc. Law, 562.

In the Civil law. A judicial decree, by which a person is deprived of the *exercise* of his civil rights.

In French-Canadian law. A proceeding instituted for the purpose of obtaining a curator of the person and property, and includes the calling of a family council and a petition to the court or its prothonotary, followed by a hearing. In re Methot's Will, 98 A. 839, 840, 87 N.J.Eq. 256.

In International law. An "interdiction of commercial intercourse" between two countries is a governmental prohibition of commercial intercourse, intended to bring about an entire cessation for the time being of all trade whatever. The Edward, 1 Wheat. 272, 4 L.Ed. 86.

INTERDICTION OF FIRE AND WATER. Banishment by an order that no man should supply the person banished with fire or water, the two necessaries of life.

INTERDICTUM SALVIANUM. Lat. In Roman law. The Salvian interdict. A process which lay for the owner of a farm to obtain possession of the goods of his tenant who had pledged them to him for the rent of the land. Inst. 4, 15, 3.

INTERDUM EVENIT UT EXCEPTIO QUÆ PRIMA FACIE JUSTA VIDETUR, TAMEN INIQUE NOCEAT. It sometimes happens that a plea which seems *prima facie* just, nevertheless is injurious and unequal. Inst. 4, 14, 1, 2.

INTERESSE. Lat. Interest. The interest of money; also an interest in lands.

Interesse termini. An interest in a term. That species of interest or property which a lessee for years acquires in the lands demised to him, before he has actually become possessed of those lands; as distinguished from that property or interest vested in him by the demise, and also reduced into possession by an actual entry upon the lands and the assumption of ownership therein, and which is then termed an "estate for years." Brown.

Pro interesse suo. For his own interest; according to, or to the extent of, his individual interest. Used (in practice) to describe the intervention of a party who comes into a suit for the purpose of protecting interests of his own which may be involved in the dispute between the principal parties or which may be affected by the settlement of their contention.

INTEREST.

Property

The most general term that can be employed to denote a property in lands or chattels. In its application to lands or things real, it is frequently used in connection with the terms "estate," "right," and "title," and, according to Lord Coke, it properly includes them all. Co. Litt. 345*b*. State v. McKellop, 40 Mo. 185; Loventhal v. Home Ins. Co., 20 So. 419, 112 Ala. 116, 33 L.R.A. 258, 57 Am.St.Rep. 17.

More particularly it means a right to have the advantage accruing from anything; any right in the nature of property, but less than title; a partial or undivided right; a title to a share.

The terms "interest" and "title" are not synonymous. A mortgagor in possession, and a purchaser holding under a deed defectively executed, have, both of them, absolute as well as insurable interests in the property, though neither of them has the legal title. Hough v. City F. Ins. Co., 29 Conn. 20, 76 Am.Dec. 581.

Absolute or conditional. That is an absolute interest in property which is so completely vested in the individual that he can by no contingency be deprived of it without his own consent. So, too, he is the owner of such absolute interest who must necessarily sustain the loss if the property is destroyed. The terms "interest" and "title" are not synonymous. A mortgagor in possession, and a purchaser holding under a deed defectively executed, have, both of them, absolute, as well as insurable, interests in the property, though neither of them has the legal title. "Absolute" is here synonymous with "vested," and is used in contradistinction to contingent or conditional. Hough v. City F. Ins. Co., 29 Conn. 10, 76 Am.Dec. 581; Garver v. Hawkeye Ins. Co., 69 Iowa 202, 28 N. W. 555; Washington F. Ins. Co. v. Kelly, 32 Md. 421, 431, 3 Am.Rep. 149; Elliott v. Ashland Mut. F. Ins. Co., 12 A. 676, 117 Pa. 548, 2 Am.St.Rep. 703.

Insurance

Interest or no interest. These words, inserted in an insurance policy, mean that the question whether the insured has or has not an insurable interest in the subject-matter is waived, and the policy is to be good irrespective of such interest. The effect of such a clause is to make it a *wager* policy.

Interest policy. One which actually, or *prima facie,* covers a substantial and insurable interest; as opposed to a *wager* policy.

English Law

Interest suit. An action in the probate branch of the high court of justice, in which the question in dispute is as to which party is entitled to a grant of letters of administration of the estate of a deceased person. Wharton.

General

Joint interest. One owned by several persons in equal shares by a title created by a single will or transfer, when expressly declared in the will or transfer to be a joint tenancy, or when granted or devised to executors or trustees as joint tenants. Civ. Code Cal. § 683.

Law of Evidence

"Interest," in a statute that no witness shall be excluded by interest in the event of the suit, means "concern," "advantage," "good," "share," "portion," "part," or "participation." Morgan v. Johnson, 87 Ga. 382, 13 S.E. 710.

A relation to the matter in controversy, or to the issue of the suit, in the nature of a prospective gain or loss, which actually does, or presumably might, create a bias or prejudice in the mind, inclining the person to favor one side or the other.

For Money

Interest is the compensation allowed by law or fixed by the parties for the use or forbearance or detention of money. Beach v. Peabody, 188 Ill. 75, 58 N.E. 680, Shealy v. U. S., D.C.S.C., 37 F.2d 918, 919.

Conventional interest is interest at the rate agreed upon and fixed by the parties themselves, as distinguished from that which the law would prescribe in the absence of an explicit agreement. Fowler v. Smith, 2 Cal. 568; Vernon's Ann. Civ. St. art. 5069.

Legal interest. See Legal Interest.

Simple interest is that which is paid for the principal or sum lent, at a certain rate or allowance, made by law or agreement of parties.

Compound interest is interest upon interest, where accrued interest is added to the principal sum, and the whole treated as a new principal, for the calculation of the interest for the next period.

Ex-interest. In the language of stock exchanges, a bond or other interest-bearing security is said to be sold "ex-interest" when the vendor reserves to himself the interest already accrued and payable (if any) or the interest accruing up to the next interest day.

Interest, maritime. See Maritime Interest.

Interest upon interest. Compound interest.

INTEREST REIPUBLICÆ NE MALEFICIA REMANEANT IMPUNITA. It concerns the state that crimes remain not unpunished. Jenk. Cent. pp. 30, 31, case 59; Wing. Max. 501.

INTEREST REIPUBLICÆ NE SUA QUIS MALE UTATUR. It concerns the state that persons do not misuse their property. 6 Coke, 36*a*.

INTEREST REIPUBLICÆ QUOD HOMINES CONSERVENTUR. It concerns the state that [the lives of] men be preserved. 12 Coke, 62.

INTEREST REIPUBLICÆ RES JUDICATAS NON RESCINDI. It concerns the state that things adjudicated be not rescinded. 2 Inst. 360. It is matter of public concern that solemn adjudications of the courts should not be disturbed. Best, Ev. p. 41, § 44.

INTEREST REIPUBLICÆ SUPREMA HOMINUM TESTAMENTA RATA HABERI. It concerns the state that men's last wills be held valid, [or allowed to stand.] Co. Litt. 236b.

INTEREST REIPUBLICÆ UT CARCERES SINT IN TUTO. It concerns the state that prisons be safe places of confinement. 2 Inst. 589.

INTEREST (IMPRIMIS) REIPUBLICÆ UT PAX IN REGNO CONSERVETUR, ET QUÆCUNQUE PACI ADVERSENTUR PROVIDE DECLINENTUR. It especially concerns the state that peace be preserved in the kingdom, and that whatever things are against peace be prudently avoided. 2 Inst. 158.

INTEREST REIPUBLICÆ UT QUILIBET RE SUA BENE UTATUR. It is the concern of the state that every one uses his property properly.

INTEREST REIPUBLICÆ UT SIT FINIS LITIUM. It concerns the state that there be an end of lawsuits. Co. Litt. 303. It is for the general welfare that a period be put to litigation. Broom, Max. 331, 343.

INTERFERE. To check; hamper; hinder; disturb; intervene; intermeddle; interpose; to enter into, or to take part in, the concerns of others. State v. Estes, 185 N.C. 752, 117 S.E. 581, 582; Conger v. Italian Vineyard Co., 186 Cal. 404, 199 P. 503. People ex rel. Benefit Ass'n of Railway Employees v. Miner, 387 Ill. 393, 56 N.E.2d 353, 356.

INTERFERENCE. In patent law, this term designates a collision between rights claimed or granted; that is, where a person claims a patent for the whole or any integral part of the ground already covered by an existing patent or by a pending application. Milton v. Kingsley, 7 App.D.C. 540; Dederick v. Fox, C.C.Pa., 56 F. 717; Nathan Mfg. Co. v. Craig, C.C.Mass., 49 F. 370.

Strictly speaking, an "interference" is declared to exist by the patent office whenever it is decided by the properly constituted authority in that bureau that two pending applications (or a patent and a pending application), in their claims or essence, cover the same discovery or invention, so as to render necessary an investigation into the question of priority of invention between the two applications or the application and the patent, as the case may be. Lowrey v. Cowles Electric Smelting, etc., Co., C.C.Ohio, 68 F. 372.

INTERIM. Lat. In the meantime; meanwhile. An assignee *ad interim* is one appointed between the time of bankruptcy and appointment of the regular assignee. 2 Bell, Comm. 355.

INTERIM COMMITTITUR. "In the meantime, let him be committed." An order of court (or the docket-entry noting it) by which a prisoner is committed to prison and directed to be kept there until some further action can be taken, or until the time arrives for the execution of his sentence.

INTERIM CURATOR. In English law. A person appointed by justices of the peace to take care of the property of a felon convict, until the appointment by the crown of an administrator or administrators for the same purpose. Mozley & Whiteley.

INTERIM FACTOR. In Scotch law. A judicial officer elected or appointed under the bankruptcy law to take charge of and preserve the estate until a fit person shall be elected trustee. 2 Bell, Comm. 357.

INTERIM OFFICER. One appointed to fill the office during a temporary vacancy, or during an interval caused by the absence or incapacity of the regular incumbent.

INTERIM ORDER. One made in the meantime, and until something is done.

INTERIM RECEIPT. A receipt for money paid by way of premium for a contract of insurance for which application is made. If the risk is rejected, the money is refunded, less the *pro rata* premium.

INTERINSURANCE EXCHANGE. Reciprocal exchange. See that title.

INTERLAQUEARE. In old practice. To link together, or interchangeably. Writs were called "*interlaqueata*" where several were issued against several parties residing in different counties, each party being summoned by a separate writ to warrant the tenant, together with the other warrantors. Fleta, lib. 5, c. 4, § 2.

INTERLINEATION. The act of writing between the lines of an instrument; also what is written between lines. Morris v. Vanderen, 1 Dall. 67, 1 L.Ed. 38; Russell v. Eubanks, 84 Mo. 88.

INTERLOCUTOR. In Scotch practice. An order or decree of court; an order made in open court. 2 Swint. 362; Arkley, 32.

INTERLOCUTOR OF RELEVANCY. In Scotch practice. A decree as to the relevancy of a libel or indictment in a criminal case. 2 Alis. Crim. Pr. 373.

INTERLOCUTORY. Provisional; temporary; not final. Something intervening between the commencement and the end of a suit which decides some point or matter, but is not a final decision of the whole controversy. Mora v. Sun Mut. Ins. Co., 13 Abb. Prac. (N.Y.) 310.

As to interlocutory "Costs," "Decree," "Judgment," "Order," and "Sentence," see those titles.

INTERLOPERS. Persons who run into business to which they have no right, or who interfere wrongfully; persons who enter a country or place to trade without license. Webster.

INTERMARRIAGE. In the popular sense, this term denotes the contracting of a marriage relation between two persons considered as members of different nations, tribes, families, etc., as, between the sovereigns of two different countries, between an American and an alien, between Indians of different tribes, between the scions of different clans or families. But, in law, it is sometimes used (and with propriety) to emphasize the mutuality of the marriage contract and as importing a reciprocal engagement by which each of the parties "marries" the other. Thus, in a pleading, instead of averring that "the plaintiff was married to the defendant," it would be proper to allege that "the parties intermarried" at such a time and place.

INTERMEDDLE. To interfere with property or the conduct of business affairs officiously or without right or title. In re Shinn's Estate, 166 Pa. 121, 30 A. 1026, 45 Am.St.Rep. 656. Not a technical legal term, but sometimes used with reference to the acts of an executor *de son tort* or a *negotiorum gestor* in the civil law.

INTERMEDIARY. In modern civil law. A broker; one who is employed to negotiate a matter between two parties, and who for that reason is considered as the mandatary (agent) of both. Civ. Code La. art. 3016.

INTERMEDIATE. Intervening; interposed during the progress of a suit, proceeding, business, etc., or between its beginning and end.

INTERMEDIATE ACCOUNT. In probate law. An account of an executor, administrator, or guardian filed subsequent to his first or initial account and before his final account. Specifically in New York, an account filed with the surrogate for the purpose of disclosing the acts of the person accounting and the state or condition of the fund in his hands, and not made the subject of a judicial settlement. Code Civ.Proc. N.Y. 1899, § 2514, subd. 9 (Surrogate's Court Act, § 314, subd. 9).

INTERMEDIATE ORDER. An order made between the commencement of the action and its final determination, incident to and during its progress, which does not determine the cause but only some intervening matter relating thereto; one that is not directly appealable. Miami Copper Co. v. Strohl, 14 Ariz. 410, 130 P. 605, 608. People v. Priori, 163 N.Y. 99, 57 N.E. 85; Boyce v. Wabash Ry. Co., 63 Iowa 70, 18 N.W. 673, 50 Am.Rep. 730; State v. O'Brien, 18 Mont. 1, 43 P. 1091; Hymes v. Van Cleef, 61 Hun 618, 15 N.Y.S. 341.

INTERMEDIATE TOLL. Toll for travel on a toll road, paid or to be collected from persons who pass thereon at points between the toll gates, such persons not passing by, through, or around the toll gates. Hollingworth v. State, 29 Ohio St. 552.

INTERMITTENT EASEMENT. See Easement.

INTERMIXTURE OF GOODS. Confusion of goods; the confusing or mingling together of goods belonging to different owners in such a way that the property of neither owner can be separately identified or extracted from the mass. Smith v. Sanborn, 6 Gray (Mass.) 134. And see Confusion of Goods.

INTERN. To restrict or shut up a person, as a political prisoner, within a limited territory.

INTERNAL. Relating to the interior; comprised within boundary lines; of interior concern or interest; domestic, as opposed to foreign.

INTERNAL COMMERCE. See Commerce.

INTERNAL IMPROVEMENTS. With reference to governmental policy and constitutional provisions restricting taxation or the contracting of public debts, this term means works of general public utility or advantage, designed to promote facility of intercommunication, trade, and commerce, the transportation of persons and property, or the development of the natural resources of the state, such as railroads, public highways, turnpikes, and canals, bridges, the improvement of rivers and harbors, systems of artificial irrigation, and the improvement of water powers; but it does not include the building and maintenance of state institutions. State v. Froehlich, 115 Wis. 32, 91 N.W. 115, 58 L.R.A. 757, 95 Am.St.Rep. 894. State v. Knapp, 99 Kan. 852, 163 P. 181, 182, L.R.A. 1917C, 1034; State v. Donald, 160 Wis. 21, 151 N.W. 331, 346.

INTERNAL POLICE. A term sometimes applied to the police power, or power to enact laws in the interest of the public safety, health, and morality, which is inherent in the legislative authority of each state, is to be exercised with reference only to its domestic affairs and its own citizens, and is not surrendered to the federal government. Cheboygan Lumber Co. v. Delta Transp. Co., 100 Mich. 16, 58 N.W. 630.

INTERNAL REVENUE. In the legislation and fiscal administration of the United States, revenue raised by the imposition of taxes and excises on domestic products or manufactures, and on domestic business and occupations, inheritance taxes, and stamp taxes; as broadly distinguished from "customs duties," *i. e.*, duties or taxes on foreign commerce or on goods imported. Rev.St. U.S. tit. 35, § 3140 et seq.

INTERNAL WATERS. Such as lie wholly within the body of the particular state or country. The Garden City, D.C.N.Y., 26 F. 773.

INTERNATIONAL COMMERCE. See Commerce.

INTERNATIONAL COURT OF JUSTICE. An agency of the United Nations. It has jurisdiction to give advisory opinions on matters of law and treaty construction when requested by the General Assembly, Security Council or any other international agency authorized by the General Assembly to petition for such opinion. It has jurisdiction, also, to settle legal disputes between nations when voluntarily submitted to it. Its judgments may be enforced by the Security Council.

Every member of the United Nations is automatically a member of the court.

INTERNATIONAL LAW. The law which regulates the intercourse of nations; the law of nations. 1 Kent, Comm. 1, 4. The customary law which determines the rights and regulates the intercourse of independent states in peace and war. 1 Wildm. Int. Law, 1.

Public international law is the body of rules which control the conduct of independent states in their relations with each other.

Private international law is that branch of municipal law which determines before the courts of what nation a particular action or suit should be brought, and by the law of what nation it should be determined.

INTERNUNCIO. A minister of a second order, charged with the affairs of the papal court in countries where that court has no nuncio.

INTERNUNCIUS. A messenger between two parties; a go-between. Applied to a broker, as the agent of both parties. 4 C. Rob. Adm. 204.

INTERPELLATE. To address with a question, especially when formal and public; originally used with respect to proceedings in the French legislature; used in reference to questions by the court to counsel during an argument.

INTERPELLATION. In the civil law. The act by which, in consequence of an agreement, the party bound declares that he will not be bound beyond a certain time. Wolff, Inst. Nat. § 752.

INTERPLEA. A plea by which a person sued in respect to property disclaims any interest in it and demands that rival claimants shall litigate their titles between themselves and relieve him from responsibility. Bennett v. Wolverton, 24 Kan. 286. See Interpleader.

In Missouri, a statutory proceeding, serving as a substitute for the action of replevin, by which a third person intervenes in an action of attachment, sets up his own title to the specific property attached, and seeks to recover the possession of it. Rice v. Sally, 176 Mo. 107, 75 S.W. 398; Spooner v. Ross, 24 Mo.App. 603; State v. Barker, 26 Mo. App. 491; Brownwell, etc., Car. Co. v. Barnard, 139 Mo. 142, 40 S.W. 762.

INTERPLEADER. When two or more persons claim the same thing (or fund) of a third, and he, laying no claim to it himself, is ignorant which of them has a right to it, and fears he may be prejudiced by their proceeding against him to recover it, he may file a bill in equity against them, the object of which is to make them litigate their title between themselves, instead of litigating it with him, and such a bill is called a "bill of interpleader." Brown; Hall v. San Jacinto State Bank, Tex.Civ.App., 255 S.W. 506, 509; Alton & Peters v. Merritt, 145 Minn. 426, 177 N.W. 770, 771.

By the statute 1 & 2 Wm. IV. c. 58, summary proceedings at law were provided for the same purpose, in actions of assumpsit, debt, detinue, and trover. And the same remedy is known, in one form or the other, in most or all of the United States.

INTERPOLATE. To insert words in a complete document.

INTERPOLATION. The act of interpolating; the words interpolated.

INTERPOSITION. The doctrine that a state, in the exercise of its sovereignty, may reject a mandate of the federal government deemed to be unconstitutional or to exceed the powers delegated to the federal government. The doctrine denies constitutional obligation of states to respect Supreme Court decisions with which they do not agree. Bush v. Orleans Parish Sch. Bd., D.C.La., 188 F.Supp. 916.

The concept is based on the 10th Amendment of the Constitution of the United States reserving to the states powers not delegated to the United States. Historically, the doctrine emanated from Chisholm v. Georgia, 2 Dallas 419, wherein the state of Georgia, when sued in the Supreme Court by a private citizen of another state, entered a remonstrance and declined to recognize the court's jurisdiction. Amendment 11 validated Georgia's position.

Implementation of the doctrine may be peaceable, as by resolution, remonstrance or legislation, or may proceed ultimately to nullification, with forcible resistance.

The Constitution does contemplate and provide for the contingency of adverse state interposition or legislation to annul or defeat the execution of national laws. In re Charge to Grand Jury, Fed. Cas.No.18,274 [2 Spr. 292].

INTERPRET. To construe; to seek out the meaning of language; to translate orally from one tongue to another.

INTERPRETARE ET CONCORDARE LEGES LEGIBUS, EST OPTIMUS INTERPRETANDI MODUS. To interpret, and [in such a way as] to harmonize laws with laws, is the best mode of interpretation. 8 Coke, 169*a*.

INTERPRETATIO CHARTARUM BENIGNE FACIENDA EST, UT RES MAGIS VALEAT QUAM PEREAT. The interpretation of deeds is to be liberal, that the thing may rather have effect than fail. Broom, Max. 543.

INTERPRETATIO FIENDA EST UT RES MAGIS VALEAT QUAM PEREAT. Jenk. Cent. 198. Such an interpretation is to be adopted that the thing may rather stand than fall.

INTERPRETATIO TALIS IN AMBIGUIS SEMPER FIENDA EST UT EVITETUR INCONVENIENS ET ABSURDUM. In cases of ambiguity, such an interpretation should always be made that what is inconvenient and absurd may be avoided. 4 Inst. 328.

INTERPRETATION. The art or process of discovering and expounding the meaning of a statute, will, contract, or other written document. People v. Com'rs of Taxes, 95 N.Y. 559; Rome v. Knox, 14 How. Prac., N.Y., 272; Ming v. Pratt, 22 Mont. 262, 56 P. 279; Tallman v. Tallman, 3 Misc. 465, 23 N.Y.S. 734; Roberts v. Portland Water Dist., 124 Me. 63, 126 A. 162, 163; Cohn-Hall-Marx Co. v. Vanosdall, 25 Ohio App. 360, 157 N.E. 908, 909.

The discovery and representation of the true meaning of any signs used to convey ideas. Lieb. Herm.

"Construction" is a term of wider scope than "interpretation;" for, while the latter is concerned only with ascertaining the sense and meaning of the subject-matter, the former may also be directed to explaining the legal effects and consequences of the instrument in question. Hence interpretation precedes construction, but stops at the written text.

Interpretation and construction of written instruments are not the same. A rule of construction is one which either governs the effect of an ascertained intention, or points out what the court should do in the absence of express or implied intention, while a rule of interpretation is one which governs the ascertainment of the meaning of the maker of the instrument. In re Union Trust Co., 151 N.Y.S. 246, 249, 89 Misc. 69.

Close interpretation (*interpretatio restricta*) is adopted if just reasons, connected with the formation and character of the text, induce us to take the words in their narrowest meaning. This species of interpretation has generally been called "literal," but the term is inadmissible. Lieb. Herm. 54.

Extensive interpretation (*interpretatio extensiva,* called, also, "liberal interpretation") adopts a more comprehensive signification of the word. Lieb. Herm. 58.

Extravagant interpretation (*interpretatio excedens*) is that which substitutes a meaning evidently beyond the true one. It is therefore not genuine interpretation. Lieb. Herm. 59.

Free or unrestricted interpretation (*interpretatio soluta*) proceeds simply on the general principles of interpretation in good faith, not bound by any specific or superior principle. Lieb. Herm. 59.

Limited or restricted interpretation (*interpretatio limitata*) is when we are influenced by other principles than the strictly hermeneutic ones. Lieb. Herm. 60.

Predestined interpretation (*interpretatio predestinata*) takes place if the interpreter, laboring under a strong bias of mind, makes the text subservient to his preconceived views or desires. This includes artful interpretation, (*interpretatic vafer,*) by which the interpreter seeks to give a meaning to the text other than the one he knows to have been intended. Lieb. Herm. 60.

It is said to be either "legal," which rests on the same authority as the law itself, or "doctrinal," which rests upon its intrinsic reasonableness. Legal interpretation may be either "authentic," when it is expressly provided by the legislator, or "usual," when it is derived from unwritten practice. Doctrinal interpretation may turn on the meaning of words and sentences, when it is called "grammatical," or on the intention of the legislator, when it is described as "logical." When logical interpretation stretches the words of a statute to cover its obvious meaning, it is called "extensive;" when, on the other hand, it avoids giving full meaning to the words, in order not to go beyond the intention of the legislator, it is called "restrictive." Holl. Jur. 344.

As to *strict* and *liberal* interpretation, see Construction.

In the civil law, *authentic* interpretation of laws is that given by the legislator himself, which is obligatory on the courts. *Customary* interpretation (also called "usual") is that which arises from successive or concurrent decisions of the court on the same subject-matter, having regard to the spirit of the law, jurisprudence, usages, and equity; as distinguished from "authentic" interpretation, which is that given by the legislator himself. Houston v. Robertson, 2 Tex. 26.

INTERPRETATION CLAUSE. A section of a statute which defines the meaning of certain words occurring frequently in the other sections.

INTERPRETER. A person sworn at a trial to interpret the evidence of a foreigner or a deaf and dumb person to the court. Amory v. Fellowes, 5 Mass. 226; People v. Lem Deo, 132 Cal. 199, 64 P. 266.

INTERREGNUM. An interval between reigns. The period which elapses between the death of a sovereign and the election of another. The vacancy which occurs when there is no government.

INTERROGATOIRE. In French law. An act which contains the interrogatories made by the judge to the person accused, on the facts which are the object of the accusation, and the answers of the accused. Poth. Proc. Crim. c. 4, art. 2, § 1.

INTERROGATORIES. A set or series of written questions drawn up for the purpose of being propounded to a party in equity, a garnishee, or a witness whose testimony is taken on deposition; a series of formal written questions used in the judicial examination of a party or a witness. In taking evidence on depositions, the interrogatories are usually prepared and settled by counsel, and reduced to writing in advance of the examination.

Written questions propounded by one party and served on adversary, who must serve written answers thereto under oath. Neske v. Burns, 8 N.J. Misc. 160, 149 A. 761.

Interrogatories are either *direct* or *cross*, the former being those which are put on behalf of the party calling a witness; the latter are those which are interposed by the adverse party.

INTERRUPTIO. Lat. Interruption. A term used both in the civil and common law of prescription. Calvin.

INTERRUPTIO MULTIPLEX NON TOLLIT PRÆSCRIPTIONEM SEMEL OBTENTAM. 2 Inst. 654. Frequent interruption does not take away a prescription once secured.

INTERRUPTION. The occurrence of some act or fact, during the period of prescription, which is sufficient to arrest the running of the statute of limitations. It is said to be either "natural" or "civil," the former being caused by the act of the party; the latter by the legal effect or operation of some fact or circumstance. Innerarity v. Mims, 1 Ala. 674; Carr v. Foster, 3 Q.B. 588; Flight v. Thomas, 2 Adol. & El. 701.

Interruption of the possession is where the right is not enjoyed or exercised continuously; interruption of the right is where the person having or claiming the right ceases the exercise of it in such a manner as to show that he does not claim to be entitled to exercise it.

In Scotch law. The true proprietor's claiming his right during the course of prescription. Bell.

INTERSECTION. As applied to a street or highway means the space occupied by two streets at the point where they cross each other. Rodgers v. Commercial Casualty Ins. Co., 237 Ala. 301, 186 So. 684, 686. Space common to both streets or highways, formed by continuing the curb lines. Western Union Tel. Co. v. Dickson, 27 Tenn.App. 74, 173 S.W.2d 714, 718.

Point of intersection of two roads is the point where their middle lines intersect. In re Springfield Road, 73 Pa. 127. But the term may also mean the point which each of two approaching vehicles will reach at the same moment. Blashfield, Cyc. of Automobile Law and Prac., Perm.Ed., § 983.

"Intersection" may apply where street or highway runs into but without crossing another. Thrush v. Lingo Lumber Co., Tex.Civ.App., 262 S.W. 551, 553; Pangborn v. John Widdicomb Co., 223 Mich. 181, 193 N.W. 817, 31 A.L.R. 485; McCaa v. Thomas, 207 Ala. 211, 92 So. 414, 416; Mitchell v. Raymond, 181 Wis. 591, 195 N.W. 855, 857, 35 A.L.R. 1115; Rohde v. Knock, 101 Conn. 439, 126 A. 335, 336; Lawrence v. Goodwill, 44 Cal.App. 440, 186 P. 781, 783; York Ice Machinery Corporation v. Sachs, 167 Md. 113, 173 A. 240, 243.

INTERSTATE. Between two or more states; between places or persons in different states; concerning or affecting two or more states politically or territorially.

INTERSTATE COMMERCE. Traffic, intercourse, commercial trading, or the transportation of persons or property between or among the several states of the Union, or from or between points in one state and points in another state; commerce between two states, or between places lying in different states. Gibbons v. Ogden, 9 Wheat. 194, 6 L.Ed. 23; Wabash, etc. R. Co. v. Illinois, 118 U.S. 557, 7 S.Ct. 4, 30 L.Ed. 244; Louisville & N. R. Co. v. Railroad Com'rs, C.C.Tenn., 19 F. 701; Victor Talking Mach. Co. v. Lucker, 128 Minn. 171, 150 N.W. 790, 791; State v. Knights of Ku Klux Klan, 117 Kan. 564, 232 P. 254, 260, 37 A.L.R. 1267; Kirmeyer v. State of Kansas, 236 U.S. 568, 35 S.Ct. 419, 59 L.Ed. 721; Western Union Telegraph Co. v. Foster, 247 U.S. 105, 38 S.Ct. 438, 439, 62 L.Ed. 1006, 1 A.L.R. 1278. It comprehends all the component parts of commercial intercourse between different states. Furst v. Brewster, 282 U.S. 493, 51 S.Ct. 295, 296, 75 L.Ed. 478.

INTERSTATE COMMERCE ACT. The act of congress of February 4, 1887 (49 U.S.C.A. § 1 et seq.), designed to regulate commerce between the states, and particularly the transportation of persons and property, by carriers, between interstate points, prescribing that charges for such transportation shall be reasonable and just, prohibiting unjust discrimination, rebates, draw-backs, preferences, pooling of freights, etc., requiring schedules of rates to be published, establishing a commission to carry out the measures enacted, and prescribing the powers and duties of such commission and the procedure before it.

INTERSTATE COMMERCE COMMISSION. A commission created by the interstate commerce act (*q. v.*) to carry out the measures therein enacted, composed of eleven persons, appointed by the President, empowered to inquire into the business of the carriers affected, to enforce the law, to receive, investigate, and determine complaints made to them of any violation of the act, make annual reports, hold stated sessions, etc. 49 U.S.C.A. § 11.

INTERSTATE EXTRADITION. The reclamation and surrender, according to due legal proceedings, of a person who, having committed a crime in one of the states of the Union, has fled into another state to evade justice or escape prosecution.

INTERSTATE LAW. That branch of private international law which affords rules and principles for the determination of controversies between citizens of different states in respect to mutual rights or obligations, in so far as the same are affected by the diversity of their citizenship or by diversity in the laws or institutions of the several states.

INTERVENING ACT. Of third person in order to break chain of causation and obviate liability for original breach of duty must be a superseding cause and one which original wrongdoer was not bound to anticipate as the natural or ordinary result of his acts. Frazier v. Ayres, La.App., 20 So. 2d 754, 759; Littell v. Argus Production Co., C.C.A. Kan., 78 F.2d 955, 957.

INTERVENING AGENCY. To render an original wrong a remote cause, an "intervening agency," must be independent of such wrong, adequate to produce the injury, so interrupting the natural sequence of events as to produce a result different from what would have been produced, and one that could not have been reasonably expected from the original wrong. Lemos v. Madden, 28 Wyo. 1, 200 P. 791, 795.

An independent "intervening agency" which will protect the original wrongdoer must be the efficient cause of the injury of which complaint is made, and not a negligent act or omission of such agency concurring with or succeeding the original negligence permitted by the original wrongdoer to continue and which in the natural course of events results in such injury. In short, the result prevented by the intervening agency must be the injury complained of, and not the requital for that injury. Swanson v. Slagal, 212 Ind. 394, 8 N.E.2d 993, 1000.

An "intervening efficient cause" is a new and independent force which breaks the causal connection between the original wrong and injury, and itself becomes direct and immediate cause of injury. Phillabaum v. Lake Erie & W. R. Co., 315 Ill. 131, 145 N.E. 806, 808.

INTERVENING CAUSE. The "intervening cause," which will relieve of liability for an injury, is an independent cause which intervenes between the original wrongful act or omission and the injury, turns aside the natural sequence of events, and produces a result which would not otherwise have followed and which could not have been reasonably anticipated. Hartman v. Atchison, T. & S. F. Ry. Co., 94 Kan. 184, 146 P. 335, 336, L.R.A. 1915D, 563. An act of an independent agency which destroys the causal connection between the negligent act of the defendant and the wrongful injury; the independent act being the immediate cause, in which case damages are not recoverable because the original wrongful act is not the proximate cause. Davenport v. McClellan, 88 N.J.L. 653, 96 A. 921.

INTERVENING DAMAGES. See Damages.

INTERVENING FORCE. One which actively operates in producing harm to another after the actor's negligent act or omission has been committed. Walborn v. Epley, 148 Pa.Super. 417, 24 A.2d 668, 671; American Mut. Liability Ins. Co. v. Buckley & Co., C.C.A.Pa., 117 F.2d 845, 847.

INTERVENOR. An intervenor is a person who voluntarily interposes in an action or other proceeding with the leave of the court. Ladue v. Goodhead, 181 Misc. 807, 44 N.Y.S.2d 783, 787.

INTERVENTION. In international law. Intervention is such an interference between two or more states as may (according to the event) result in a resort to force; while mediation always is, and is intended to be and to continue, peaceful only. Intervention between a sovereign and his own subjects is not justified by anything in international law; but a remonstrance may be addressed to the sovereign in a proper case. Brown.

In English ecclesiastical law. The proceeding of a third person, who, not being originally a party to the suit or proceeding, but claiming an interest in the subject-matter in dispute, in order the better to protect such interest, interposes his claim. 2 Chit. Pr. 492; 3 Chit. Commer. Law, 633; 2 Hagg. Const. 137; 3 Phillim. Ecc. Law, 586; Stillwell Hotel Co. v. Anderson, 16 Cal.App.2d 636, 61 P.2d 71, 72.

In the civil law. The act by which a third party demands to be received as a party in a suit pending between other persons. Stillwell Hotel Co. v. Anderson, 16 Cal.App.2d 636, 61 P.2d 71, 73.

The intervention is made either for the purpose of being joined to the plaintiff, and to claim the same thing he does, or some other thing connected with it; or to join the defendant, and with him to oppose the claim of the plaintiff, which it is his interest to defeat. Poth. Proc. Civile, pt. 1, c. 2, § 7, no. 3.

In practice. A proceeding in a suit or action by which a third person is permitted by the court to make himself a party, either joining the plaintiff in claiming what is sought by the complaint, or uniting with the defendant in resisting the claims of the plaintiff, or demanding something adversely to both of them. Logan v. Greenlaw, C.C.Tenn., 12 F. 16; Fischer v. Hanna, 8 Colo.App. 471, 47 P. 303; Gale v. Frazier, 4 Dak. 196, 30 N.W. 138; Reay v. Butler, Cal., 7 P. 671; Gorham v. Hall, 172 Ark. 744, 290 S.W. 357, 358; Adler v. Seaman, C.C. A.Mo., 266 F. 828, 832; In re Prouty's Estate, 107 Vt. 496, 181 A. 134.

INTESTABILIS. Lat. A witness incompetent to testify. Calvin.

INTESTABLE. One who has not testamentary capacity; *e. g.*, an infant, lunatic, or person civilly dead.

INTESTACY. The state or condition of dying without having made a valid will, or without having disposed by will of a part of his property. In re Shestack's Estate, 267 Pa. 115, 110 A. 166; Brown v. Mugway, 15 N.J.L. 331.

Besides the strict meaning of the word as above given, there is also a sense in which intestacy may be partial; that is, where a man leaves a will which does not dispose of his whole estate, he is said to "die intestate" as to the property so omitted.

INTESTATE. Without making a will. A person is said to die intestate when he dies without making a will, or dies without leaving anything to testify what his wishes were with respect to the disposal of his property after his death. The word is also often used to signify the person himself. Thus, in speaking of the property of a person who died intestate, it is common to say "the intestate's property;" *i. e.*, the property of the person dying in an intestate condition. Brown. In re Cameron's Estate, 47 App.Div. 120, 62 N.Y.S. 187; Messmann v. Egenberger, 46 App.Div. 46, 61 N.Y.S. 556; Code Civ.Proc.N.Y. 1899, § 2514, subd. 1 (Surrogate's Court Act, § 314, subd. 1).

INTESTATE LAWS. Statutes which provide and prescribe the devolution of estates of persons who die without disposing of their estates by law, will or testament. Fullbright v. Boardman, 159 Ga. 162, 125 S.E. 44, 46, 37 A.L.R. 532; In re Rogers' Estate, Mo.Sup., 250 S.W. 576, 578; Ford v. U. S., C.C.A.N.Y., 205 F. 130, 134.

INTESTATE SUCCESSION. A succession is called "intestate" when the deceased has left no will, or when his will has been revoked or annulled as irregular. Therefore the heirs to whom a succession has fallen by the effects of law only are called "heirs *ab intestato.*" Civ. Code La. art. 1096.

INTESTATO. Lat. In the civil law. Intestate; without a will. Calvin.

INTESTATUS. Lat. In the civil and old English law. An intestate; one who dies without a will. Dig. 50, 17, 7.

INTESTATUS DECEDIT, QUI AUT OMNIO TESTAMENTUM NON FECIT; AUT NON JURE FECIT; AUT ID QUOD FECERAT RUPTUM IRRITUMVE FACTUM EST; AUT NEMO EX EO HÆRES EXSTITIT. A person dies intestate who either has made no testament at all or has made one not legally valid; or if the testament he has made be revoked, or made useless; or if no one becomes heir under it. Inst. 3, 1, pr.

INTIMACY. As generally applied to persons, it is understood to mean a proper, friendly relation of the parties, but it is frequently used to convey the idea of an improper relation; an intimacy at least disreputable and degrading. Collins v. Pub. Co., 152 Pa. 187, 25 A. 546, 34 Am.St.Rep. 636. See McCarty v. Coffin, 157 Mass. 478, 32 N.E. 649.

INTIMATE. Close in friendship or acquaintance, familiar, confidential; also near, close, direct, thorough, complete. Atkins Corporation v. Tourny, 6 Cal.2d 206, 57 P.2d 480, 484.

INTIMATION. In the civil law. A notification to a party that some step in a legal proceeding is asked or will be taken. Particularly, a notice given by the party taking an appeal, to the other party, that the court above will hear the appeal.

In Scotch law. A formal written notice, drawn by a notary, to be served on a party against whom a stranger has acquired a right or claim; *e. g.*, the assignee of a debt must serve such a notice on the debtor, otherwise a payment to the original creditor will be good.

INTIMIDATION. Unlawful coercion; duress; putting in fear. Michaels v. Hillman, 112 Misc. 395, 183 N.Y.S. 195, 200; Kayser v. Fitzgerald, 109 Misc. 27, 178 N.Y.S. 130, 134; Burns v. Lackey, 171 Ky. 21, 186 S.W. 909, 913; Southwick v. State, 126 Ark. 188, 189 S.W. 843, 844; Shehany v. Lowry, 170 Ga. 70, 152 S.E. 114, 115.

INTIMIDATION OF VOTERS. This, by statute in several of the states, is made a criminal offense. Under an early Pennsylvania act, it was held that, to constitute the offense of intimidation of voters, there must be a preconceived intention for the purpose of intimidating the officers or interrupting the election. Respublica v. Gibbs, 3 Yeates, Pa., 429.

INTITLE. An old form of *"entitle."* 6 Mod. 304.

INTO. A preposition signifying to the inside of; within. It expresses entrance, or a passage from the outside of a thing to its interior, and follows verbs expressing motion. It has been held equivalent to, or synonymous with, "at," "inside of," and "to," and has been distinguished from the words "from" and "through." 48 C.J.S. p. 120.

INTOL and UTTOL. In old records. Toll or custom paid for things imported and exported, or bought in and sold out. Cowell.

INTOLERABLE CRUELTY. In the law of divorce, this term denotes extreme cruelty, cruel and inhuman treatment, barbarous, savage, and inhuman conduct, and is equivalent to any of those phrases. Shaw v. Shaw, 17 Conn. 193; Morehouse v. Morehouse, 70 Conn. 420, 39 A. 516; Blain v. Blain, 45 Vt. 544.

INTOXICATED. Affected by an intoxicant, under the influence of an intoxicating liquor. Taylor v. Joyce, 4 Cal.App.2d 612, 41 P.2d 967, 968.

INTOXICATING LIQUOR. Any liquor used as a beverage, and which, when so used in sufficient quantities, ordinarily or commonly produces entire or partial intoxication; any liquor intended for use as a beverage or capable of being so used, which contains alcohol, either obtained by fermentation or by the additional process of distillation, in such proportion that it will produce intoxication when imbibed in such quantities as may practically be drunk. Intoxicating Liquor Cases, 25 Kan. 767, 37 Am.Rep. 284; Com'rs v. Taylor, 21 N.Y. 173; People v. Hawley, 3 Mich. 339; State v. Oliver, 26 W.Va. 431, 53 Am.Rep. 79; Frisvold v. Leahy, 15 Cal.App.2d 752, 60 P.2d 151, 153; Worley v. Spurgeon, 38 Iowa 465. See, also, Alcoholic Liquors.

INTOXICATION. The state of being poisoned; the condition produced by the administration or introduction into the human system of a poison. But in its popular use this term is restricted to *alcoholic* intoxication, that is, drunkenness or inebriety, or the mental and physical condition induced by drinking excessive quantities of alcoholic liquors, and this is its meaning as used in statutes, indictments, etc. Sapp v. State, 116 Ga. 182, 42 S.E. 410; State v. Pierce, 65 Iowa 85, 21 N.W. 195; Wadsworth v. Dunnam, 98 Ala. 610, 13 So. 599; Ring v. Ring, 112 Ga. 854, 38 S.E. 330; State v. Kelley, 47 Vt. 296; Com. v. Whitney, 11 Cush., Mass., 477.

INTOXIMETER. A trade name for scientific breath testing device that operates on assumption that concentration of blood alcohol bears fixed relation to concentration of alcohol in the deep lung, or alveolar air. City of Sioux Falls v. Kohler, S.D., 118 N.W.2d 14.

INTRA. Lat. In; near; within. *"Infra"* or *"inter"* has taken the place of *"intra"* in many of the more modern Latin phrases.

INTRA ANNI SPATIUM. Within the space of a year. Cod. 5, 9, 2. *Intra annale tempus.* Id. 6, 30, 19.

INTRA FIDEM. Within belief; credible. Calvin.

INTRA LUCTUS TEMPUS. Within the time of mourning. Cod. 9, 1, auth.

INTRA MŒNIA. Within the walls (of a house.) A term applied to domestic or *menial* servants. 1 Bl. Comm. 425.

INTRA PARIETES. Between walls; among friends; out of court; without litigation. Calvin.

INTRA PRÆSIDIA. Within the defenses. See Infra Præsidia.

INTRA QUATUOR MARIA. Within the four seas. Shep. Touch. 378.

INTRA VIRES. An act is said to be *intra vires* ("within the power") of a person or corporation when it is within the scope of his or its powers or authority. It is the opposite of *ultra vires,* (*q. v.*). Pittsburgh, etc., R. Co. v. Dodd, 115 Ky. 176, 72 S.W. 827.

INTRALIMINAL. In mining law, the term "intraliminal rights" denotes the right to mine, take, and possess all such bodies or deposits of ore as lie within the four planes formed by the vertical extension downward of the boundary lines of the claim; as distinguished from "extraliminal," or more commonly "extralateral," rights. Jefferson Min. Co. v. Anchoria-Leland Mill. & Min. Co., 32 Colo. 176, 75 P. 1073, 64 L.R.A. 925.

INTRAMURAL. Within the walls. The powers of a municipal corporation are "intramural" and "extramural"; the one being the powers exercised within the corporate limits, and the other being those exercised without. State v. Port of Astoria, 79 Or. 1, 154 P. 399, 404.

INTRARE MARISCUM. L. Lat. To drain a marsh or low ground, and convert it into herbage or pasture.

INTRASTATE COMMERCE. See Commerce.

INTRINSECUM SERVITIUM. Lat. Common and ordinary duties with the lord's court.

INTRINSIC EVIDENCE is that which is derived from a document without anything to explain it.

INTRODUCTION. The part of a writing which sets forth preliminary matter, or facts tending to explain the subject.

INTROMISSION. In Scotch law. The assumption of authority over another's property, either legally or illegally. The irregular intermeddling with the effects of a deceased person, which subjects the party to the whole debts of the deceased, is called *"vitious intromission."* Kames, Eq. b. 3, c. 8, § 2.

Necessary Intromission. That kind of intromission or interference where a husband or wife continues in possession of the other's goods after their decease, for preservation. Wharton.

In English law. Dealings in stock, goods, or cash of a principal coming into the hands of his agent, to be accounted for by the agent to his principal. Stewart v. McKean, 29 Eng.Law & Eq. 391.

INTRONISATION. In French ecclesiastical law. Enthronement. The installation of a bishop in his episcopal see.

INTRUDER. One who enters upon land without either right of possession or color of title. Miller v. McCullough, 104 Pa. 630; Russel v. Chambers, 43 Ga. 479. In a more restricted sense, a stranger who, on the death of the ancestor, enters on the land, unlawfully, before the heir can enter. Williams v. Alt, 226 N.Y. 283, 123 N.E. 499, 500. Also one who intrudes on office and assumes to exercise its functions without legal title or color of right thereto. State ex rel. City of Republic v. Smith, 345 Mo. 1158, 139 S.W.2d 929, 933; Alleger v. School Dist. No. 16, Newton County, Mo.App., 142 S.W.2d 660, 663.

INTRUSION. A species of injury by ouster or amotion of possession from the freehold, being an entry of a stranger, after a particular estate of freehold is determined, before him in remainder or reversion. Hulick v. Scovil, 9 Ill. 170; Boylan v. Deinzer, 45 N.J.Eq. 485, 18 A. 121.

The name of a writ brought by the owner of a fee-simple, etc., against an intruder. New Nat. Brev. 453. Abolished by 3 & 4 Wm. IV. c. 57.

INTRUST. To confer a trust upon; to deliver to another something in trust or to commit something to another with a certain confidence regarding his care, use or disposal of it. State v. Ugland, 48 N.D. 841, 187 N.W. 237, 239.

INTUITUS. Lat. A view; regard; contemplation. *Diverso intuitu,* (*q. v.,*) with a different view.

INUNDATION. The overflow of waters by coming out of their bed. See, also, Dam; Backwater; Irrigation; Waters; Water Course.

Inundations may arise from three causes: from public necessity, as in defence of a place it may be necessary to dam the current of a stream, which will cause an inundation to the upper lands; they may be occasioned by an invincible force, as by the accidental fall of a rock in the stream, or by a natural flood or freshet; or they may result from the erection of works on the stream. In the first case, the injury caused by the inundation is to be compensated as other injuries done in war; in the second, as there was no fault of any one, the loss is to be borne by the unfortunate owner of the estate; in the last, when the riparian proprietor is injured by such works as alter the level of the water where it enters or where it leaves the property on which they are erected, the person injured may recover damages for the injury thus caused to his property by the inundation, 9 Co. 59; 1 B. & Ald. 258; Sumner v. Tileston, 7 Pick., Mass., 198; Bailey v. City of New York, 3 Hill, N.Y., 531, 38 Am.Dec. 669; Tillotson v. Smith, 32 N.H. 90, 64 Am.Dec. 355; Merritt v. Parker, 1 N.J.L. 460; Williams v. Gale, 3 Har. & J., Md., 231; Ohio & M. R. Co. v. Nuetzel, 43 Ill.App. 108.

INURE. To take effect; to result. Cedar Rapids Water Co. v. Cedar Rapids, 118 Iowa 234, 91 N.W. 1081; Hinson v. Booth, 39 Fla. 333, 22 So. 687; Holmes v. Tallada, 125 Pa. 133, 17 A. 238, 3 L.R.A. 219, 11 Am.St.Rep. 880; Salyer v. Jackson, 105 Okl. 212, 232 P. 412, 414; Malachowski v. Varro, 76 Cal.App. 207, 244 P. 936, 938.

INUREMENT. Use; user; service to the use or benefit of a person. Dickerson v. Colgrove, 100 U.S. 583, 25 L.Ed. 618.

INUTILIS LABOR ET SINE FRUCTU NON EST EFFECTUS LEGIS. Useless and fruitless labor is not the effect of law. Co. Litt. 127*b*. The law forbids such recoveries whose ends are vain, chargeable, and unprofitable. Id.; Wing. Max. p. 110, max. 38.

INVADIARE. To pledge or mortgage lands.

INVADIATIO. A pledge or mortgage.

INVADIATUS. One who is under pledge; one who has had sureties or pledges given for him. Spelman.

INVALID. Vain; inadequate to its purpose; not of binding force or legal efficacy; lacking in authority or obligation. Hood v. Perry, 75 Ga. 312; State v. Casteel, 110 Ind. 174, 11 N.E. 219; Mutual Ben. L. Ins. Co. v. Winne, 20 Mont. 20, 49 P. 446; Avery & Co. v. Sorrell, 157 Ga. 476, 121 S.E. 828, 829; Dreidlein v. Manger, 69 Mont. 155, 220 P. 1107, 1108; Columbian Nat. Fire Ins. Co. v. Dixie Co-op. Mail Order House, Tex.Civ.App., 261 S.W. 174, 179.

INVASION. An encroachment upon the rights of another; the incursion of an army for conquest or plunder. Webster. See Ætna Ins. Co. v. Boon, 95 U.S. 129, 24 L.Ed. 395.

INVASIONES. The inquisition of serjeanties and knights' fees. Cowell.

INVECTA ET ILLATA. Lat. In the civil law. Things carried in and brought in. Articles brought into a hired tenement by the hirer or tenant, and which became or were pledged to the lessor as security for the rent. Dig. 2, 14, 4, pr. The phrase is adopted in Scotch law. See Bell.

INVENIENS LIBELLUM FAMOSUM ET NON CORRUMPENS PUNITUR. He who finds a libel and does not destroy it is punished. Moore, 813.

INVENT. To find out something new; to devise, contrive, and produce something not previously known or existing, by the exercise of independent investigation and experiment; particularly applied to machines, mechanical appliances, compositions, and patentable inventions of every sort. To create. E. W. Bliss Co. v. United States, 248 U.S. 37, 39 S. Ct. 42, 43, 63 L.Ed. 112.

INVENTIO. In the Civil law. Finding; one of the modes of acquiring title to property by occupancy. Heinecc. lib. 2, tit. 1, § 350.

In Old English law. A thing found; as goods or treasure-trove. Cowell. The plural, *"inventiones,"* is also used.

INVENTION. In patent law. The act or operation of finding out something new; the process of contriving and producing something not previously known or existing, by the exercise of independent investigation and experiment. Also the article or contrivance or composition so invented. Leidersdorf v. Flint, 15 Fed.Cas. 260; Smith v. Nichols, 21 Wall. 118, 22 L.Ed. 566; Hollister v. Manufacturing Co., 5 S.Ct. 717, 113 U.S. 72, 28 L. Ed. 901; Murphy Mfg. Co. v. Excelsior Car Roof Co., C.C.Mo., 70 F. 495.

A concept or thing evolved from the mind. "Invention" is not a revelation of something which existed and was unknown, but the creation of something which did not exist before, and possessing elements of novelty and utility in kind and measure different from, and greater than, what the art might expect from skilled workers. Pyrene Mfg. Co. v. Boyce, C.C.A.N.J., 292 F. 480, 481. The finding out—the contriving, the creating of something which did not exist, and was not known before, and which can be made useful and advantageous in the pursuits of life, or which can add to the enjoyment of mankind. Conover v. Roach, 4 Fish. 12. Fed.Cas.No.3,125. Not every improvement is invention; but to entitle a thing to protection it must be the product of some exercise of the inventive faculties, and it must involve something more than what is obvious to persons skilled in the art to which it relates. Rosenwasser v. Berry, C.C.Me., 22 F. 841. Mere adaptation of known process to clearly analogous use is not invention. Firestone Tire and Rubber Co. v. U. S. Rubber Co., C.C.A.Ohio, 79 F.2d 948, 952, 953.

"Invention" involves the exercise of the creative mind. Aeolian Co. v. Wanamaker, D.C., 221 F. 666, 668.

Inventive skill has been defined as that intuitive faculty of the mind put forth in the search for new results, or new methods, creating what had not before existed, or bringing to light what lay hidden from vision; it differs from a suggestion of that common experience which arose spontaneously and by a necessity of human reasoning in the minds of those who had become acquainted with the circumstances with which they had to deal. Hollister v. Mfg. Co., 113 U.S. 72, 5 S.Ct. 717, 28 L.Ed. 901. Invention, in the nature of improvements, is the double mental act of discerning, in existing machines, processes or articles, some deficiency, and pointing out the means of overcoming it. General Electric Co. v. Electric Co., Ill., 174 F. 246, 98 C.C.A. 154.

An "invention" differs from a "discovery." The former term is properly applicable to the contrivance and production of something that did not before exist; while discovery denotes the bringing into knowledge and use of something which, although it existed, was before unknown. Thus, we speak of the "discovery" of the properties of light, electricity, etc., while the telescope and the electric motor are the results of the process of "invention."

For "Examination of invention", see Examination.

INVENTIONES. See Inventio.

INVENTOR. One who finds out or contrives some new thing; one who devises some new art, manufacture, mechanical appliance, or process; one who invents a patentable contrivance. Sparkman v. Higgins, 22 Fed.Cas. 879; Henderson v. Tompkins, C.C.Mass., 60 F. 764.

INVENTORY. A detailed list of articles of property; a list or schedule of property, containing a designation or description of each specific article; an itemized list of the various articles constituting a collection, estate, stock in trade, etc., with their estimated or actual values. In law, the term is particularly applied to such a list made by an executor, administrator, or assignee in bankruptcy. See Silver Bow Min. Co. v. Lowry, 5 Mont. 618, 6 P. 62; Lloyd v. Wyckoff, 11 N.J.Law, 224; Roberts, etc., Co. v. Sun Mut. L. Ins. Co., 48 S.W. 559, 19 Tex.Civ.App. 338; Southern F. Ins. Co. v. Knight, 111 Ga. 622, 36 S.E. 821, 52 L.R.A. 70, 78 Am.St.Rep. 216.

INVENTUS. Lat. Found. *Thesaurus inventus,* treasure-trove. *Non est inventus,* [he] is not found.

INVERITARE. To make proof of a thing. Jacob.

INVERSE ORDER OF ALIENATION DOCTRINE. Under this doctrine, mortgagee or other lienor, where land subject to lien has been aliened in separate parcels successively, shall satisfy his lien out of land remaining in grantor or original owner if possible, and, if that be insufficient, he shall resort to parcels aliened in inverse order of their alienation. Fidelity & Casualty Co. of New York v. Massachusetts Mut. Life Ins. Co., C.C.A.N.C., 74 F.2d 881, 884.

INVEST. To loan money upon securities of a more or less permanent nature, or to place it in business ventures or real estate, or otherwise lay it out, so that it may produce a revenue or income. Drake v. Crane, 127 Mo. 85, 29 S.W. 990, 27 L.R.A. 653; Stramann v. Scheeren, 7 Colo.App. 1, 42 P. 191; Una v. Dodd, 39 N.J.Eq. 186.

To clothe one with the possession of a fief or benefice. See Investiture.

INVESTIGATION. To follow up step by step by patient inquiry or observation; to trace or track mentally; to search into; to examine and inquire into with care and accuracy; to find out by careful inquisition; examination; the taking of evidence; a legal inquiry. Lukert v. Eldridge, 49 Mont. 46, 139 P. 999, 1001; People ex rel. Fennell v. Wilmot, 217 N.Y.S. 477, 479, 127 Misc. 791. Application of Gilchrist, 130 Misc. 456, 224 N.Y.S. 210, 219.

INVESTITIVE FACT. The fact by means of which a right comes into existence; *e. g.*, a grant of a monopoly, the death of one's ancestor. Holl. Jur. 132.

INVESTITURE. A ceremony which accompanied the grant of lands in the feudal ages, and consisted in the open and notorious delivery of possession in the presence of the other vassals, which perpetuated among them the *æra* of their new acquisition at the time when the art of writing was very little known; and thus the evidence of the property was reposed in the memory of the neighborhood, who, in case of disputed title, were afterwards called upon to decide upon it. Brown.

In Ecclesiastical law. Investiture is one of the formalities by which the election of a bishop is confirmed by the archbishop. See Phillim. Ecc. Law, 42, et seq.

INVESTMENT. The placing of capital or laying out of money in a way intended to secure income or profit from its employment. Securities & Exchange Commission v. Wickham, D.C.Minn., 12 F. Supp. 245, 247.

INVIOLABILITY. The attribute of being secured against violation. The persons of ambassadors are inviolable.

INVITATION. In the law of negligence, and with reference to trespasses on realty, invitation is the act of one who solicits or incites others to enter upon, remain in, or make use of, his property or structures thereon, or who so arranges the property or the means of access to it or of transit over it as to induce the reasonable belief that he expects and intends that others shall come upon it or pass over it. Sweeney v. Old Colony & N. R. Co., 10 Allen, Mass., 373, 87 Am.Dec. 644; Wilson v. New York, N. H. & H. R. Co., 18 R.I. 491, 29 A. 258; Wright v. Boston & A. R. Co., 142 Mass. 300, 7 N.E. 866.

Thus the proprietor of a store, theatre or amusement park "invites" the public to come upon his premises for such purposes as are connected with its intended use. Again, the fact that safety gates at a railroad crossing, which should be closed in case of danger, are left standing open, is an "invitation" to the traveler on the highway to cross. Roberts v. Delaware & H. Canal Co., 177 Pa. 183, 35 A. 723. So, bringing a passenger train on a railroad to a full stop at a regular station is an "invitation to alight."

License distinguished

A license is a passive permission on the part of the owner of premises, with reference to other persons entering upon or using them, while an invitation implies a request, solicitation or desire that they should do so. An invitation may be inferred where there is a common interest or mutual advantage; while a license will be inferred where the object is the mere pleasure or benefit of the person using it. Bennett v. Louisville & N. R. Co., 102 U.S. 580, 26 L.Ed. 235; Weldon v. Philadelphia, W. & B. R. Co., 2 Pennewill, Del., 1, 43 A. 159; Babcock and Wilcox Co. v. Nolton, 58 Nev. 131, 71 P.2d 1051, 1053. An owner owes to a licensee no duty as to the condition of the premises (unless imposed by statute) save that he should not knowingly let him run upon a hidden peril or willfully cause him harm; while to one invited he is under the obligation to maintain the premises in a reasonably safe and secure condition. Beehler v. Daniels, 18 R.I. 563, 29 A. 6, 27 L.R.A. 512, 49 Am.St.Rep. 790.

Express and implied

An invitation may be *express*, when the owner or occupier of the land by words invites another to come upon it or make use of it or of something thereon; or it may be *implied* when such owner or occupier by acts or conduct leads another to believe that the land or something thereon was intended to be used as he uses them, and that such use is not only acquiesced in by the owner or occupier, but is in accordance with the intention or design for which the way or place or thing was adapted and prepared and allowed to be used. Turess v. New York, S. & W. R. Co., 61 N.J.L. 314, 40 A. 614; Furey v. New York Cent. R. Co., 67 N.J.L. 270, 51 A. 505; Lepnick v. Gaddis, 72 Miss. 200, 16 So. 213, 26 L.R.A. 686, 48 Am.St.Rep. 547; Plummer v. Dill, 156 Mass. 426, 31 N.E. 128, 32 Am.St.Rep. 463; Wilmes v. Chicago Great Western Ry. Co., 175 Iowa, 101, 156 N.W. 877, 880, L.R.A.1917F, 1024; Gasch v. Rounds, 93 Wash. 317, 160 P. 962, 964; Coburn v. Village of Swanton, 95 Vt. 320, 115 A. 153, 156; Bush v. Weed Lumber Co., 63 Cal.App. 426, 218 P. 618, 620; Polluck v. Minneapolis & St. L. R. Co., 44 S.D. 249, 183 N.W. 859, 862.

INVITED ERROR. See Error.

INVITEE. One who is at a place upon the invitation of another. Crossgrove v. Atlantic Coast Line R. Co., 30 Ga.App. 462, 118 S.E. 694, 695; Carr v. Wallace Laundry Co., 31 Idaho 266, 170 P. 107; Fleckenstein v. Great Atlantic & Pacific Tea Co., 91 N.J.L. 145, 102 A. 700, L.R.A.1918C, 179; Crossgrove v. Atlantic Coast Line R. Co., 30 Ga. App. 462, 118 S.E. 694; Campbell v. Sutliff, 193 Wis. 370, 214 N.W. 374, 375, 53 A.L.R. 771; Moohr v. Victoria Inv. Co., 144 Wash. 387, 258 P. 43, 46; Holm v. Investment & Securities Co., 195 Wash. 52, 79 P.2d 708, 711.

INVITO. Lat. Being unwilling. Against or without the assent or consent.

Ab invito

By or from an unwilling party. A transfer *ab invito* is a compulsory transfer.

Invito debitore

Against the will of the debtor.

Invito domino

The owner being unwilling; against the will of the owner; without the owner's consent. In order to constitute larceny, the property must be taken *invito domino*.

INVITO BENEFICIUM NON DATUR. A benefit is not conferred on one who is unwilling to receive it; that is to say, no one can be compelled to accept a benefit. Dig. 50, 17, 69; Broom, Max. 699, note.

INVOICE. In commercial law. A list or account of goods or merchandise sent by merchants to their correspondents at home or abroad, in which the marks of each package, with other particulars, are set forth. Marsh. Ins. 408; Jac. Sea Laws, 302; Dane Abr.; Merchants' Exch. Co. v. Weisman, 132 Mich. 353, 93 N.W. 870; Southern Exp. Co. v. Hess, 53 Ala. 22; Cramer v. Oppenstein, 16 Colo. 495, 27 P. 713; Stone v. First Nat. Bank, 100 Or. 528, 198 P. 244. Written itemized accounts sent to a purchaser by the seller of merchandise. Cobb & Seal Shoe Store v. Ætna Ins. Co., 78 S.C. 388, 58 S.E. 1099; Garner Mfg. Co. v. Cornelius Lumber Co., 165 Ark. 119, 262 S.W. 1011, 1014; Wilmot v. Minneapolis Automobile Trade Ass'n, 169 Minn. 140, 210 N.W. 861, 862; Larkin Co. v. New York, C. & St. L. R. Co., 98 Misc. 446, 162 N.Y. S. 870, 871. A list sent to a purchaser, factor, consignee, etc., containing the items, together with the prices and charges of merchandise sent or to be sent to him. State v. Standard Oil Co. of Indiana, 222 Iowa 1209, 271 N.W. 185, 187. A writing made on behalf of an importer, specifying the merchandise imported, and its true cost or value. And. Rev. Law, § 294.

INVOICE BOOK. A book in which invoices are copied.

INVOICE PRICE of goods means the prime cost. Le Roy v. United Ins. Co., 7 Johns., N.Y., 343. The cost or value of property at the shipping point. State v. Standard Oil Co. of Indiana, 222 Iowa 1209, 271 N.W. 185, 188.

In sale of retail stock of goods, this term ordinarily means wholesale cost at time goods were purchased by seller. Hamilton v. O'Rear, 224 Ala. 625, 141 So. 565, 567.

INVOLUNTARY. Without will or power of choice; opposed to volition or desire. Curry v. Federal Life Ins. Co., 221 Mo.App. 626, 287 S.W. 1053, 1056. An involuntary act is that which is performed with constraint (*q. v.*) or with repugnance, or without the will to do it. An action is involuntary, then, which is performed under duress. Wolff Inst. Nat. § 5.

As to involuntary "Bankruptcy," "Indebtedness," "Nonsuit," and "Trust," see those titles.

INVOLUNTARY DEPOSIT. In the law of bailments, one made by the accidental leaving or placing of personal property in the possession of another, without negligence on the part of the owner, or, in cases of fire, shipwreck, inundation, riot, insurrection, or the like extraordinary emergencies, by the owner of personal property committing it out of necessity to the care of any person. Civ. Code S. D. 1903, § 1354 (Rev. Codes 1919, § 971).

INVOLUNTARY DISCONTINUANCE. In practice. A discontinuance is involuntary where, in consequence of technical omission, mispleading, or the like, the suit is regarded as out of court, as where the parties undertake to refer a suit that is not referable, or omit to enter proper continuances. Hunt v. Griffin, 49 Miss. 748.

INVOLUNTARY MANSLAUGHTER. The unlawful killing of a human being in the commission of an unlawful act not amounting to felony, or in the commission of a lawful act which might produce death in an unlawful manner, or without due caution and circumspection. State v. Goodwin, 189 La. 443, 179 So. 591, 602; Salyer v. Commonwealth, 165 Va. 744, 181 S.E. 435, 436.

INVOLUNTARY PAYMENT. One obtained by fraud, oppression, or extortion, or to avoid the use of force to coerce it, or to obtain the release of the person or property from detention. Parcher v. Marathon County, 52 Wis. 388, 9 N.W. 23, 38 Am.Rep. 745; Wolfe v. Marshal, 52 Mo. 168; Corkle v. Maxwell, 6 Fed.Cas. 555.

INVOLUNTARY SERVITUDE. The condition of one who is compelled by force, coercion, or imprisonment, and against his will, to labor for another, whether he is paid or not. See State v. West, 42 Minn. 147, 43 N.W. 845; Ex parte Wilson, 114 U.S. 417, 5 S.Ct. 935, 29 L.Ed. 89; Thompson v. Benton, 117 Mo. 83, 22 S.W. 863, 20 L.R.A. 462; In re Slaughterhouse Cases, 16 Wall. 69, 21 L.Ed. 394; Robertson v. Baldwin, 165 U.S. 275, 17 S.Ct. 326, 41 L.Ed. 715.

IOTA. The minutest quantity possible. Iota is the smallest Greek letter. The word "jot" is derived therefrom.

IPSÆ LEGES CUPIUNT UT JURE REGANTUR. Co. Litt. 174. The laws themselves require that they should be governed by right.

IPSE. Lat. He himself; the same; the very person.

IPSE DIXIT. He himself said it; a bare assertion resting on the authority of an individual.

IPSISSIMIS VERBIS. In the identical words; opposed to "substantially." Townsend v. Jemison, 7 How. 719, 12 L.Ed. 880; Summons v. State, 5 Ohio St. 346.

IPSO FACTO. By the fact itself; by the mere fact. By the mere effect of an act or a fact. Barber Asphalt Paving Co. v. Hayward, 248 Mo. 280, 154 S.W. 140, 141.

In English ecclesiastical law. A censure of excommunication in the ecclesiastical court, immediately incurred for divers offenses, after lawful trial.

IPSO JURE. By the law itself; by the mere operation of law. Calvin.

IPSWICH, DOMESDAY OF. The earliest extant record of any borough court with elective officers sitting regularly and administering a customary law of the sea. Black Book of Admiralty, Vol. II. It was abolished by 5 & 6 Will. IV. c. 76. Its twelve "capital portmen" were elected from the most fit, wealthy and discreet of the judges.

IRA FUROR BREVIS EST. Anger is a short insanity. Beardsley v. Maynard, 4 Wend., N.Y., 336, 355.

IRA MOTUS. Lat. Moved or excited by anger or passion. A term sometimes formerly used in the plea of *son assault demesne.* 1 Tidd, Pr. 645.

IRADE. A decree of the Sultan.

IRE AD LARGUM. Lat. To go at large; to escape; to be set at liberty.

IRENARCHA. In Roman law. An officer whose duties are described in Dig. 5, 4, 18, 7. See Id. 48, 3, 6; Cod. 10, 75. Literally, a peace-officer or magistrate.

IRON-SAFE CLAUSE. A common clause in policies of fire insurance, requiring the insured to preserve his books and inventory in an iron or fireproof safe, or in some secure place not exposed to a fire which would destroy the building. This provision casts on the insured the responsibility for the loss of books and records if due to the wrongful act or negligence of himself or his employees in failing to comply with the requirement. 45 C.J.S. p. 358.

IRRATIONAL. Unreasonable, foolish, absurd; a person may be irrational in such sense, and still not be insane in the legal sense. Lee v. State, 30 Okl.Cr. 14, 234 P. 654, 655.

IRRECUSABLE. A term used to indicate a certain class of contractual obligations recognized by the law which are imposed upon a person without his consent and without regard to any act of his own. They are distinguished from recusable obligations which are the result of a voluntary act on the part of a person on whom they are imposed by law. A clear example of an irrecusable obligation is the obligation imposed on every man not to strike another without some lawful excuse. A recusable obligation is based upon some act of a person bound, which is a condition precedent to the genesis of the obligation. These terms were first suggested by Prof. Wigmore in 8 Harv. Law Rev. 200. See Harr. Contr. 6.

IRREGULAR. Not according to rule; improper or insufficient, by reason of departure from the prescribed course.

As to irregular "Deposit," "Indorsement," "Process," and "Succession," see those titles.

IRREGULAR JUDGMENT. One rendered contrary to the course and practice of the court. Duplin County v. Ezzell, 223 N.C. 531, 27 S.E.2d 448, 450.

IRREGULARITY. The doing or not doing that, in the conduct of a suit at law, which, conformably with the practice of the court, ought or ought not to be done. Doe ex dem. Cooper v. Harter, 2 Ind. 252. Violation or nonobservance of established rules and practices. The want of adherence to some prescribed rule or mode of proceeding; consisting either in omitting to do something that is necessary for the due and orderly conducting of a suit, or doing it in an unseasonable time or improper manner. Coulter v. Board of Com'rs of Bernalillo County, 22 N.M. 24, 158 P. 1086; Ex parte Davis, 118 Or. 693, 247 P. 809, 811; Emeric v. Alvarado, 64 Cal. 529, 2 P. 418; Hall v. Munger, 5 Lans., N.Y., 113; Corn Exch. Bank v. Blye, 119 N.Y. 414, 23 N.E. 805; Salter v. Hilgen, 40 Wis. 365; Turrill v. Walker, 4 Mich. 183. The technical term for every defect in practical proceedings, or the mode of conducting an action or defense, as distinguishable from defects in pleadings. 3 Chit. Gen. Pr. 509.

Not synonymous with illegality. City of Tampa v. Palmer, 89 Fla. 514, 105 So. 115, 117. "Irregularity" is a want of adherence to some prescribed rule or mode of proceeding, while "illegality" denotes a radical defect. United States v. Salomon, D.C.La., 231 F. 461, 463; U. S. v. Richmond, C.C.A.Pa., 17 F.2d 28, 32. "Illegality" in the assessment of a tax is a substantial defect contrary to law and leaving the proceeding with nothing to stand on, while an "irregularity" is a formal defect contrary only to the practice authorized by law, and relating rather to the manner of doing the act than to the act itself. Bunten v. Rock Springs Grazing Ass'n, 29 Wyo. 461, 215 P. 244, 254.

Under statutes authorizing the modification or setting aside of judgments, "irregularity" is some departure from the prescribed procedure in the trial, or in the determination of the action, not evidenced by a ruling or an order. Duncan v. Wilkins, 103 Okl. 221, 229 P. 801, 802; American Nat. Bank of Tucumcari v. Tarpley, 31 N.M. 667, 250 P. 18, 20. But under a statute providing for relief against an irregularity in obtaining a judgment, the term has no fixed legal meaning, and in every instance the question is one of fact, dependent upon the circumstances of each case. Nation v. Savely, 127 Okl. 117, 260 P. 32, 34.

Irregularity in the proceedings of the court, as used in a California statute pertaining to new trials, relates to matters occurring during the trial, and not after it. Diamond v. Superior Court of California in and for City and County of San Francisco, 189 Cal. 732, 210 P. 36, 37.

In Canon law. Any impediment which prevents a man from taking holy orders.

General

Legal Irregularity. An irregularity occurring in the course of some legal proceeding. A defect or informality which, in the technical view of the law, is to be accounted an irregularity.

IRRELEVANCY. The absence of the quality of relevancy, as in evidence or pleadings. The quality or state of being inapplicable or impertinent to a fact or argument.

Irrelevancy, in an answer, consists in statements which are not material to the decision of the case; such as do not form or tender any material issue. People v. McCumber, 18 N.Y. 321, 72 Am.Dec. 515; Walker v. Hewitt, 11 How.Prac., N.Y., 398; Carpenter v. Bell, 1 Rob., N.Y., 715; Smith v. Smith, 50 S.C. 54, 27 S.E. 545. See, also, Irrelevant.

IRRELEVANT. Not relevant; not relating or applicable to the matter in issue; not supporting the issue. Crump v. Lanham, 67 Okl. 33, 168 P. 43, 44. Evidence is irrelevant where it has no tendency to prove or disprove any issue involved. Malone v. State, 16 Ala.App. 185, 76 So. 469, 470.

IRRELEVANT ALLEGATION. One which has no substantial relation to the controversy between the parties to the suit, and which cannot affect the decision of the court. Wayte v. Bowker Chemical Co., 196 App.Div. 665, 187 N.Y.S. 276, 277; Commander Milling Co. v. Westinghouse Electric and Mfg. Co., C.C.A.Minn., 70 F.2d 469, 472; The test of any allegation being whether it tends to constitute a cause of action or a defense, Isaacs v. Solomon, 159 App.Div. 675, 144 N.Y.S. 876, 877.

An allegation is irrelevant, where the issue made by its denial has no effect upon the cause of action or no connection with the allegation. Germofert Mfg. Co. v. Castles, 97 S.C. 389, 81 S.E. 665, 666. In this connection, "redundant" is almost a synonym for "irrelevant." Plank v. Hopkins, 35 S.D. 243, 151 N.W. 1017, 1019.

IRRELEVANT ANSWER. See Answer.

IRREMOVABILITY. The status of a pauper in England, who cannot be legally removed from the parish or union in which he is receiving relief, notwithstanding that he has not acquired a settlement there. 3 Steph.Comm. 60. Thus a pauper who has resided in a parish during the whole of the preceding year is irremovable, in view of Stat. 28 and 29 Vict. c. 79, § 8.

IRREPARABLE DAMAGES. See Damages.

IRREPARABLE INJURY. See Injury.

IRREPLEVIABLE. That cannot be replevied or delivered on sureties. Spelled, also, "irreplevisable." Co. Litt. 145; 13 Edw. I. c. 2.

IRRESISTIBLE FORCE. A term applied to such an interposition of human agency as is, from its nature and power, absolutely uncontrollable; as the inroads of a hostile army. Story, Bailm. § 25; Noel Bros. v. Texas & P. Ry. Co., 16 La.App. 622, 133 So. 830, 832.

IRRESISTIBLE IMPULSE. Used chiefly in criminal law, this term means an impulse to commit an unlawful or criminal act which cannot be resisted or overcome by the patient because insanity or mental disease has destroyed the freedom of his will and his power of self-control and of choice as to his actions. McCarty v. Com., 114 Ky. 620, 71 S.W. 658; State v. Knight, 95 Me. 467, 50 A. 276, 55 L.R.A. 373; Leache v. State, 22 Tex.App. 279, 3 S.W. 539, 58 Am.Rep. 638; State v. Peel, 23 Mont. 358, 59 P. 169, 75 Am.St.Rep. 529. And see Insanity.

IRREVOCABLE. Which cannot be revoked or recalled. Commissioner of Internal Revenue v. Strong Mfg. Co., C.C.A.6, 124 F.2d 360, 363.

IRREVOCABLE LETTER. A confirmed irrevocable letter of credit, irrevocable letter, or a confirmed credit is a contract to pay on compliance with its terms, and needs no formal acknowledgment or acceptance other than is therein stated. Lamborn v. National Park Bank of New York, 240 N.Y. 520, 148 N.E. 664, 665.

IRRIGATION. The operation of watering lands for agricultural purposes by artificial means. In its primary sense, a sprinkling or watering; specifically, the application of water to lands for the raising of agricultural crops and other products of the soil. Platte Water Co. v. Irrigation Co., 12 Colo. 529, 21 P. 711; City and County of Denver v. Brown, 56 Colo. 216, 138 P. 44, 49.

IRRIGATION COMPANY. A private corporation, authorized and regulated by statute in several states, having for its object to acquire exclusive rights to the water of certain streams or other sources of supply, and to convey it by means of ditches or canals through a region where it can be beneficially used for agricultural purposes, and either dividing the water among stockholders, or making contracts with consumers, or furnishing a supply to all who apply at fixed rates.

IRRIGATION DISTRICT. A public and quasi-municipal corporation authorized by law in several states, comprising a defined region or area of land which is susceptible of one mode of irrigation from a common source and by the same system of works. These districts are created by proceedings in the nature of an election under the supervision of a court, and are authorized to purchase or condemn the lands and waters necessary for the system of irrigation proposed and to construct neccessary canals and other works, and the water is apportioned ratably among the landowners of the district. Nampa & Meridian Irr. Dist. v. Briggs, 27 Idaho 84, 147 P. 75, 82.

IRRITANCY. In Scotch law. The happening of a condition or event by which a charter, contract, or other deed, to which a clause irritant is annexed, becomes void.

IRRITANT. In Scotch law. Avoiding or making void; as an irritant clause. See Irritancy.

IRRITANT CLAUSE. In Scotch law. A provision by which certain prohibited acts specified in a deed are, if committed, declared to be null and void. A *resolutive* clause dissolves and puts an end to the right of a proprietor on his committing the acts so declared void.

IRROGARE. Lat. In the civil law. To impose or set upon, as a fine. Calvin. To inflict, as a punishment. To make or ordain, as a law.

IRROTULATIO. L. Lat. An enrolling; a record.

IS. This word, although normally referring to the present, Cunningham v. Moser, 91 Okl. 44, 215 P. 758, 759; Jenkins v. First Nat. Bank, 73 Mont. 110, 236 P. 1085, 1087; often has a future meaning, but is not synonymous with "shall have been." State v. Jorgenson, 25 N.D. 539, 142 N.W. 450, 462, 49 L.R.A.,N.S., 67. It may have, however, a past signification, as in the sense of "has been." 48 C.J.S. p. 774.

IS QUI COGNOSCIT. Lat. The cognizor in a fine. *Is cui cognoscitur,* the cognizee.

ISH. In Scotch law. The period of the termination of a tack or lease. 1 Bligh, 522.

ISLAND. A piece of land surrounded by water. Webber v. Pere Marquette Boom Co., 62 Mich. 626, 30 N.W. 469; Goff v. Cougle, 118 Mich. 307, 76 N.W. 489, 42 L.R.A. 161.

An island that arises in the bed of a stream usually first presents itself as a sand bar, Cox v. Arnold, 129 Mo. 337, 31 S.W. 592, 50 Am.St.Rep. 450; Glassell v. Hansen, 135 Cal. 547, 67 P. 964; Holman v. Hodges, 112 Iowa, 714, 84 N.W. 950, 58 L.R.A. 673, 84 Am.St.Rep. 367; a bar, before it will support vegetation of any kind, may become valuable for fishing, hunting, as a shooting park, for the harvest of ice, for pumping sand, etc. If further deposits of alluvion upon it would make it more valuable, the law of accretion should still apply, Fowler v. Wood, 73 Kan. 511, 85 P. 763, 6 L.R.A.,N.S., 162, 117 Am.St.Rep. 534. Land in a navigable stream which is surrounded by water only in times of high water is not an island within the rule that the state takes title to newly formed islands in navigable streams. Payne v. Hall, 192 Iowa, 780, 185 N.W. 912, 915.

ISOLATED TRANSACTION. This term, in connection with the rule that single or isolated transactions do not violate a statute prohibiting foreign corporations from doing business within a state without first filing a copy of their charter, may be inapplicable to a single transaction consummated in furtherance of a corporation's business, where it is shown that the corporation in question is a foreign corporation, with its principal office in a town in a sister state near the state line, and that it has solicited business generally in tributary territory within the adjoining state. Dahl Implement & Lumber Co. v. Campbell, 45 N.D. 239, 178 N.W. 197, 198.

ISSEI. Jap. A term used to describe alien Japanese residing in the United States. 1945 Report of the Tenney Joint Fact-Finding Committee on Un-American Activities to the California Legislature p. 48.

ISSINT. A law French term, meaning "thus," "so," giving its name to part of a plea in debt. A term formerly used to introduce a statement that special matter already pleaded amounts to a denial.

An example of this form of plea, which is sometimes called the special general issue, occurs in Bauer v. Roth, 4 Rawle, Pa., 83.

ISSUABLE. In practice. Leading or tending to, or producing, an issue; relating to an issue or issues. See Colquitt v. Mercer, 44 Ga. 433.

ISSUABLE DEFENSE. A technical expression meaning a plea to the merits, properly setting forth a legal defense, as distinguished from a plea in abatement, or any plea going only to delay the case. Adamson v. Reagin, 143 Ga. 306, 84 S. E. 965.

ISSUABLE PLEA. A plea to the merits; a traversable plea. A plea such that the adverse party can join issue upon it and go to trial. It is true a plea in abatement is a plea, and, if it be properly pleaded, issues may be found on it. In the ordinary meaning of the word "plea," and of the word "issuable," such pleas may be called "issuable pleas," but, when these two words are used together, "issuable plea," or "issuable defense," they have a technical meaning, to-wit, pleas to the merits. Colquitt v. Mercer, 44 Ga. 434.

ISSUABLE TERMS. In the former practice of the English courts, Hilary term and Trinity term were called "issuable terms," because the issues to be tried at the assizes were made up at those terms. 3 Bl.Comm. 353. But the distinction is superseded by the provisions of the judicature acts of 1873 and 1875.

ISSUE, *v.* To send forth; to emit; to promulgate; as, an officer *issues* orders, process *issues* from a court. To put into circulation; as, the treasury *issues* notes. To send out, to send out officially; to deliver, for use, or authoritatively; to go forth as authoritative or binding. Stokes v. Paschall, Tex.Civ.App., 243 S.W. 611, 614; Blythe v. Doheny, C.C.A.Cal., 73 F.2d 799, 803.

A writ is "issued" when it is delivered to an officer, with the intent to have it served, Wilkins v. Worthen, 62 Ark. 401, 36 S.W. 21; Michigan Ins. Bk. v. Eldred, 130 U.S. 693, 9 S.Ct. 690, 32 L.Ed. 1080; Webster v. Sharpe, 116 N.C. 466, 21 S.E. 912; Ferguson v. Estes & Alexander, Tex.Civ. App., 214 S.W. 465, 466.

When used with reference to a writ of error, State v. Brown, 103 N.J.L. 519, 138 A. 370; a writ of scire facias, In re Johns' Estate, 253 Pa. 532, 98 A. 719, 720; a writ of attachment, McMaster v. Ruby, 80 Or. 476, 157 P. 782, 784; corporate stock, Cattlemen's Trust Co. of Fort Worth v. Turner, Tex.Civ.App., 182 S.W. 438, 441; a bond, Klutts v. Jones, 20 N.M. 230, 148 P. 494, 499; Travis v. First Nat. Bank, 210 Ala. 620, 98 So. 890, 891; Steinbruck v. Milford Tp., 100 Kan. 93, 163 P. 647; State v. School Board of Tecumseh Rural High School Dist. No. 4, 110 Kan. 779, 204 P. 742, 744; a deed, Wyman v. Hageman, 318 Ill. 64, 148 N.E. 852, 855; a note, Foster v. Security Bank & Trust Co., Tex.Com.App., 288 S.W. 438, 440; an insurance policy, Coleman v. New England Mut. Life Ins. Co., 236 Mass. 552, 129 N.E. 288, 289; National Liberty Ins. Co. v. Norman, C.C.A.N.C., 11 F.2d 59, 61; and the like, the term is ordinarily construed as importing delivery to the proper person, or to the proper officer for service, etc. But it does not invariably have such a meaning. Estabrook & Co. v. Consolidated Gas, Electric Light & Power Co. of Baltimore, 122 Md. 643, 90 A. 523, 524.

In financial parlance the term "issue" seems to have two phases of meaning. "Date of issue" when applied to notes, bonds, etc., of a series, usually means the arbitrary date fixed as the beginning of the term for which they run, without reference to the precise time when convenience or the state of the market may permit of their sale or delivery. When the bonds are delivered to the purchaser, they will be "issued" to him, which is the other meaning of the term. Turner v. Roseberry Irr. Dist., 33 Idaho, 746, 198 P. 465, 467. See, also, Anderson v. Mutual Life Ins. Co. of New York, 164 Cal. 712, 130 P. 726, 727, Ann.Cas.1914B, 903.

ISSUE, *n.* The act of issuing, sending forth, emitting or promulgating; the giving a thing its first inception; as the issue of an order or a writ.

Pleading

A single, certain, and material point, deduced by the pleadings of the parties, which is affirmed on the one side and denied on the other. Whitney v. Borough of Jersey Shore, 266 Pa. 537, 109 A. 767, 769; Village of Oak Park v. Eldred, 265 Ill. 605, 107 N.E. 145, 146. A single certain and material point arising out of the allegations of the parties, and it should generally be made up of an affirmative and a negative. Cowen Co. v. Houck Mfg. Co.,

C.C.A.N.Y., 249 F. 285, 287; Simmons v. Hagner, 140 Md. 248, 117 A. 759, 760. A fact put in controversy by the pleadings. Shea v. Hillsborough Mills, 78 N.H. 57, 96 A. 293, 294.

The disputed point or question to which the parties in an action have narrowed their several allegations, and upon which they are desirous of obtaining the decision of the proper tribunal. When the plaintiff and defendant have arrived at some specific point or matter affirmed on the one side, and denied on the other, they are said to be at issue. Knaggs v. Cleveland-Cliffs Iron Co., C.C.A.Ohio, 287 F. 314, 316; First Nat. Bank v. District Court of Hardin County, 193 Iowa, 561, 187 N.W. 457, 458. (But as used in a rule of court, a case is not "at issue" where nothing but a demurrer has been filed, presenting no issue except a question of law as to the sufficiency of the complaint. Arnett v. Hardwick, 27 Ariz. 179, 231 P. 922, 923.) The question so set apart is called the "issue," and is designated, according to its nature, as an "issue in fact" or an "issue in law." Brown; Martin v. City of Columbus, 101 Ohio St. 1, 127 N.E. 411, 413.

Issues arise upon the pleadings, when a fact or conclusion of law is maintained by the one party and controverted by the other. They are of two kinds: (1) of law; and (2) of fact. Rev.Code Iowa 1880, § 2737 (Rules of Civil Procedure, Rule 176); Code Civ.Proc.Cal. § 588; Comp.St. Wyo.1910, § 4451 (Rev.St.1931, § 89-1202); Berglar v. University City, Mo.App., 190 S.W. 620, 622; General Electric Co. v. Sapulpa & I. Ry. Co., 49 Okl. 376, 153 P. 189, 193.

The entry of the pleadings. 1 Chitty, Pl. 630.

Issues are classified and distinguished as follows:

General and *special*. The former is a plea which traverses and denies, briefly and in general and summary terms, the whole declaration, indictment, or complaint, without tendering new or special matter. Steph. Pl. 155; Tilden v. E. A. Stevenson & Co., 3 W.W.Harr. 151, 132 A. 739, 740; McAllister v. State, 94 Md. 290, 50 A. 1046; Standard Loan & Acc. Ins. Co. v. Thornton, 97 Tenn. 1, 40 S.W. 136. Examples of the general issue are "not guilty," *"non assumpsit," "nil debet," "non est factum."* The latter is formed when the defendant chooses one single material point, which he traverses, and rests his whole case upon its determination.

Identical. Issues determined by same questions of fact and of law. Allbee v. Elms, 93 N.H. 202, 37 A.2d 790, 791.

Material and *immaterial*. They are so described according as they do or do not bring up some material point or question which, when determined by the verdict, will dispose of the whole merits of the case, and leave no uncertainty as to the judgment. Pearson v. Pearson, 104 Misc. 675, 173 N.Y. S. 563, 565.

Formal and *informal*. The former species of issue is one framed in strict accordance with the technical rules of pleading. The latter arises when the material allegations of the declaration are traversed, but in an inartificial or untechnical mode. In the latter case, the defect is cured by verdict, by the statute 32 Hen. VIII. c. 30.

A *collateral* issue is an issue taken upon matter *aside* from the intrinsic merits of the action, as upon a plea in abatement; or *aside* from the direct and regular order of the pleadings, as on a demurrer. 2 Archb. Pr. K. B. 1, 6, bk. 2, pts. 1, 2; Strickland v. Maddox, 4 Ga. 394. The term "collateral" is also applied in England to an issue raised upon a plea of diversity of person, pleaded by a criminal who has been tried and convicted, in bar of execution, viz., that he is not the same person who was attainted, and the like. 4 Bl. Comm. 396. Matters collateral to the main issue are those which do not constitute an essential element of the offense embraced within the charge. State v. English, 308 Mo. 695, 274 S.W. 470, 474.

Real or *feigned*. A real or actual issue is one formed in a regular manner in a regular suit for the purpose of determining an actual controversy. A feigned issue is one made up by direction of the court, upon a supposed case, for the purpose of obtaining the verdict of a jury upon some question of fact collaterally involved in the cause. Such issues are generally ordered by a court of equity, to ascertain the truth of a disputed fact. They are also used in courts of law, by the consent of the parties, to determine some disputed rights without the formality of pleading; and by this practice much time and expense are saved in the decision of a cause. 3 Bla.Comm. 452. The name is a misnomer, inasmuch as the *issue* itself is upon a real, material point in question between the parties, and the circumstances only are fictitious.

Common issue is the name given to the issue raised by the plea of *non est factum* to an action for breach of covenant.

Ultimate issue signifies either such an issue as within itself is sufficient and final for the disposition of the entire case or one which in connection with other issues will serve such end. First State Bank of Seminole v. Dillard, Tex.Civ.App., 71 S. W.2d 407, 410.

This is so called because it denies the deed only, and not the breach, and does not put the whole declaration in issue, and because there is no general issue to this form of action. 1 Chitty, Pl. 482; Gould, Pl. c. 6, pt. 1, § 7.

Realty Law

Descendants. All persons who have descended from a common ancestor. Edmundson v. Leigh, 189 N.C. 196, 126 S.E. 497, 499, Offspring; progeny; descent; lineage; lineal descendants. Gardner v. Anderson, 114 Kan. 778, 227 P. 743, 747; In re Schuster's Will, 111 Misc. 534, 181 N.Y.S. 500, 503; Wilkins v. Rowan, 107 Neb. 180, 185 N.W. 437, 439; Rhode Island Hospital Trust Co. v. Bridgham, 42 R.I. 161, 106 A. 149, 153, 5 A.L.R. 185; Hoadley v. Beardsley, 89 Conn. 270, 93 A. 535, 538; Turner v. Monteiro, 127 Va. 537, 103 S.E. 572, 575, 13 A.L.R. 383; In re Book's Will, 89 N.J.Eq. 509, 105 A. 878, 879; 3 Ves. 257; 17 Ves. 481; 19 Ves. 547; 1 Rop. Leg. 90.

In this sense, the word includes not only a child or children, but all other descendants in whatever degree; and it is so construed generally in deeds. But, when used in wills, it is, of course, subject to the rule of construction that the intention of the testator, as ascertained from the will, is to have effect, rather than the technical meaning of the language used by him; and hence issue may, in such a connection, be restricted to children, or to descendants living at the death of the testator, where such an intention clearly appears. Abbott; Sibley v. Perry, 7 Ves.Jun. 523, 529; Ralph v. Carrick, 11 Ch.D. 873, 883; Barmore v. Darragh, Tex.Civ.App., 231 S.W. 472, 479; Newcomb v. Newcomb, 197 Ky. 801, 248 S.W. 198, 200; Horner v Haase, 177

Iowa 115, 158 N.W. 548, 549; In re Rynear's Estate, 224 N.Y.S. 606, 607, 130 Misc. 804.

The word "issue" in a will is generally a word of limitation, In re Packer's Estate, 246 Pa. 116, 92 A. 70, 74; Baxter v. Early, 131 S.C. 374, 127 S.E. 607; Bonnycastle v. Lilly, 153 Ky. 834, 156 S.W. 874, L.R.A.1916B, 1076; and when so used, is sometimes said to be equivalent to "heirs of the body"; Rhode Island Hospital Trust Co. v. Bridgham, 42 R.I. 161, 106 A. 149, 152, 5 A.L.R. 185; Parrish v. Hodges, 178 N.C. 133, 100 S.E. 256; Middletown Trust Co. v. Gaffey, 96 Conn. 61, 112 A. 689, 690. But it has been pointed out in other cases that this word is not as strong a word of limitation as the words "heirs of the body," Adams v. Verner, 102 S.C. 7, 86 S.E. 211, 214; City Nat. Bank v. Slocum, C.C.A.Ohio, 272 F. 11, 18; and yields readily to a context indicating its use as a word of purchase, Stout v. Good, 245 Pa. 383, 91 A. 613, 615; Eversmeyer v. McCollum, 171 Ark. 117, 283 S.W. 379, 382; Ford v. McBrayer, 171 N.C. 420, 88 S.E. 736, 737; Yarrington v. Freeman, 201 Ky. 135, 255 S.W. 1034.

The word is commonly held to include only legitimate issue. Page v. Roddie, 92 Okl. 236, 218 P. 1092, 1095; King v. Thissell, 222 Mass. 140, 109 N.E. 880; Hardesty v. Mitchell, 302 Ill. 369, 134 N.E. 745, 746, 24 A.L.R. 565; Love v. Love, 179 N.C. 115, 101 S.E. 562, 563; *contra:* Eaton v. Eaton, 88 Conn. 286, 91 A. 196, 198.

Business Law

A class or series of bonds, debentures, etc., comprising all that are emitted at one and the same time.

ISSUE IN FACT. In pleading. An issue taken upon or consisting of matter of *fact,* the fact only, and not the law, being disputed, and which is to be tried by a jury. 3 Bl.Comm. 314, 315; Co. Litt. 126*a;* 3 Steph.Comm. 572. An issue which arises upon a denial in the answer of a material allegation of the complaint or in the reply of a material allegation in the answer. Rev. Codes, Mont. § 6793 (Rev. Code 1921, § 9395). See, also, Code Civ. Proc. Cal. § 590; Comp. St. Wyo. 1910, § 4452 (Rev. St. 1931, § 89–1203).

The "issues of fact" which, if presented by the pleadings and supported by evidence, must be submitted to the jury, where requested, are only the independent ultimate facts which go to make up plaintiff's cause of action and defendant's ground of defense. Texas City Transp. Co. v. Winters, Tex.Com.App., 222 S.W. 541, 542.

ISSUE IN LAW. In pleading. An issue upon matter of law, or consisting of matter of law, being produced by a demurrer on the one side, and a joinder in demurrer on the other. 3 Bl.Comm. 314; 3 Steph.Comm. 572, 580; Code Civ. Proc. Cal. § 589. The term "issue" may be so used as to include one of law raised by demurrer to the complaint, as well as one raised by answer. Fruth v. Bolt, 39 S.D. 371, 164 N.W. 270, 271.

ISSUE ROLL. In English practice. A roll upon which the issue in actions at law was formerly required to be entered, the roll being entitled of the term in which the issue was joined. 2 Tidd Pr. 733. It was not, however, the practice to enter the issue at full length, if triable by the country, until after the trial, but only to make an *incipitur* on the roll. Id. 734. It was abolished by the rules of Hilary Term, 1834. Moz. & W. Dict.

ISSUES. In English law. The goods and profits of the lands of a defendant against whom a writ of *distringas* or *distress infinite* has been issued, taken by virtue of such writ. 3 Bl.Comm. 280; 1 Chit. Crim. Law, 351.

ISSUES AND PROFITS, as applied to real estate, comprehend every available return therefrom, whether it arise above or below the surface. Minner v. Minner, 84 W.Va. 679, 100 S.E. 509, 510.

ISSUES ON SHERIFFS. Fines and amercements inflicted on sheriffs for neglects and defaults, levied out of the issues and profits of their lands. Toml.

ISTIMRAR. Continuance; perpetuity; especially a farm or lease granted in perpetuity by government or a zemindar (*q. v.*). Wilson's Gloss. Ind.

ISTIMRARDAR. The holder of a perpetual lease. Moz. & W.

ITA EST. Lat. So it is; so it stands. In modern civil law, this phrase is a form of attestation added to exemplifications from a notary's register when the same are made by the successor in office of the notary who made the original entries.

ITA LEX SCRIPTA EST. Lat. So the law is written. Dig. 40, 9, 12; Allen v. Cook, 26 Barb., N.Y., 374, 380; Hemphill's Appeal, 18 Pa. 306; Monson v. Chester, 22 Pick., Mass., 389. The law must be obeyed notwithstanding the apparent rigor of its application. 3 Bl.Comm. 430. We must be content with the law as it stands, without inquiring into its reasons. 1 Bl.Comm. 32.

ITA QUOD. Lat. In Old Practice. So that. Formal words in writs. *Ita quod habeas corpus,* so that you have the body. 2 Mod. 180. The name of the stipulation in a submission to arbitration which begins with the words "so as [*ita quod*] the award be made of and upon the premises."

In Old Conveyancing. So that. An expression which, when used in a deed, formerly made an estate upon condition. Litt. § 329. Sheppard enumerates it among the three words that are most proper to make an estate conditional. Shep. Touch. 121, 122.

ITA SEMPER FIAT RELATIO UT VALEAT DISPOSITIO. 6 Coke, 76. Let the interpretation be always such that the disposition may prevail.

ITA TE DEUS ADJUVET. Lat. So help you God. The old form of administering an oath in England, generally in connection with other words, thus: *Ita te Deus adjuvet, et sacrosancta Dei Evangelia,* So help you God, and God's holy Evangelists. *Ita te Deus adjuvet et omnes sancti,* So help you God and all the saints. Willes, 338.

ITA UTERE TUO UT ALIENUM NON LÆDAS. Use your own property and your own rights in such a way that you will not hurt your neighbor, or prevent him from enjoying his. Frequently written, "*Sic utere tuo,*" etc. (*q. v.*).

ITEM. Also; likewise; in like manner; again; a second time. This word was formerly used to mark the beginning of a new paragraph or division after the first, whence is derived the common application of it to denote a separate or distinct particular of an account or bill. Horwitz v. Norris, 60 Pa. 282; Baldwin v. Morgan, 73 Miss. 276, 18 So. 919; Callaghan v. Boyce, 17 Ariz. 433, 153 P. 773, 782; Innis, Pearce & Co. v. G. H. Poppenberg, Inc., 210 N.Y.S. 761, 762, 213 App.Div. 789, One of the portions, equal or unequal, into which anything is divided, or regarded as divided; something less than a whole; a number, quantity, mass, or the like, regarded as going to make up, with others or another, a larger number, quantity, mass, etc., whether actually separate or not; a piece, fragment, fraction, member, or constituent. State ex rel. Wisconsin Telephone Co. v. Henry, 218 Wis. 302, 260 N.W. 486, 99 A.L.R. 1267. An article; a single detail of any kind. Board of Education of Prince George's County v. County Com'rs of Prince George's County, 131 Md. 658, 102 A. 1007, 1010. A separate entry in an account or a schedule, or a separate particular in an enumeration of a total. People v. Brady, 277 Ill. 124, 115 N.E. 204, 206.

The word is sometimes used as a verb. "The whole [costs] in this case that was thus *itemed* to counsel." Bunb. p. 164, case 233.

An "item" in an appropriation bill is an indivisible sum of money dedicated to a stated purpose. Commonwealth v. Dodson, 176 Va. 281, 11 S.E.2d 120, 124, 125, 127, 130, 131.

ITEMIZE. To set down by items. People v. Lowden, 285 Ill. 618, 121 N.E. 188. To state each item or article separately. Hartford Fire Ins. Co. v. Walker, Tex.Civ.App., 153 S.W. 398, 400. Used almost entirely with reference to accounts. J. F. Rappell Co. v. City of Manitowoc, 182 Wis. 141, 195 N.W. 399, 401; Banner Oil & Gas Co. v. Gordon, Tex.Civ.App., 235 S.W. 945, 948; Dorough v. Reliance Ins. Co., Tex.Civ.App., 289 S.W. 703, 704; Board of Education of Prince George's County v. County Com'rs of Prince George's County, 131 Md. 658, 102 A. 1007, 1010; Lewis v. National Fire Ins. Underwriters, 136 Miss. 576, 101 So. 296, 297.

ITER. Lat.

In the Civil law. A way; a right of way belonging as a servitude to an estate in the country, (*prædium rusticum.*) The right of way was of three kinds: (1) *iter*, a right to walk, or ride on horseback, or in a litter; (2) *actus*, a right to drive a beast or vehicle; (3) *via*, a full right of way, comprising right to walk or ride, or drive beast or carriage. Heinec. § 408. Or, as some think, they were distinguished by the width of the objects which could be rightfully carried over the way; *e. g., via*, 8 feet; *actus*, 4 feet, etc. Mackeld. Rom. Law, § 290; Bract. fol. 232; 4 Bell, H. L. Sc. 390.

In old English law. A journey, especially a circuit made by a justice in eyre, or itinerant justice, to try causes according to his own mission. Du Cange; Bract. lib. 3, cc. 11, 12, 13.

In Maritime law. A way or route. The route or direction of a voyage; the route or way that is taken to make the voyage assured. Distinguished from the voyage itself.

ITER EST JUS EUNDI, AMBULANDI HOMINIS; NON ETIAM JUMENTUM AGENDI VEL VEHICULUM. A way is the right of going or walking, and does not include the right of driving a beast of burden or a carriage. Co. Litt. 56*a;* Inst. 2, 3, pr.; Mackeld. Rom. Law, § 318.

ITERATIO. Lat. Repetition. In the Roman law, a bonitary owner might liberate a slave, and the quiritary owner's repetition (*iteratio*) of the process effected a complete manumission. Brown.

ITINERA. Eyres, or circuits. 1 Reeve, Eng. Law, 52.

ITINERANT. Wandering; traveling; applied to justices who make circuits. Also applied in various statutory and municipal laws (in the sense of traveling from place to place) to certain classes of merchants, traders, and salesmen. Shiff v. State, 84 Ala. 454, 4 So. 419; Twining v. Elgin, 38 Ill.App. 357; Rev.Laws Mass. 1902, p. 595, c. 65, § 1 (Gen. Laws, c. 101, § 1); West v. Mt. Sterling, Ky., 65 S.W. 122.

ITINERANT PEDDLING. The going about of a merchant from place to place, meeting and dealing with his customers where he finds them. Good Humor Corporation v. City of New York, 264 App.Div. 620, 36 N.Y.S.2d 85, 91.

ITINERANT VENDOR. This term is variously defined in statutes; *e. g.*, a person engaged in transient business either in one locality or in traveling from place to place selling goods, who, for the purpose of carrying on such business, sells goods at retail from a car. Rev. St. Me. c. 45, § 15 (Rev.St.1930, c. 46, § 25). See, also, Laws Mont. 1911, c. 110, § 1; St. Cal. 1903, p. 284, § 3.

ITS. This term does not necessarily import legal ownership, but may signify merely possession, or the temporary use of. Campbell v. Canadian Northern Ry. Co., 124 Minn. 245, 144 N.W. 772, 773.

IULE. In old English law. Christmas.

J

J. The initial letter of the words "judge" and "justice," for which it frequently stands as an abbreviation. Thus, "J. A.," judge advocate; "J. J.," junior judge; "L. J.," law judge; "P. J.," president judge; "F. J.," first judge; "A. J.," associate judge; "C. J.," chief justice or judge; "J. P.," justice of the peace; "JJ.," judges or justices; "J. C. P.," justice of the common pleas; "J. K. B.," justice of the king's bench; "J. Q. B.," justice of the queen's bench; "J. U. B.," justice of the upper bench.

This letter is sometimes used for "I," as the initial letter of "Institutiones," in references to the Institutes of Justinian.

JAC. An abbreviation for *"Jacobus,"* the Latin form of the name James; used principally in citing statutes enacted in the reigns of the English kings of that name; *e. g.,* "St. 1 Jac. II." Used also in citing the second part of Croke's reports; thus, "Cro. Jac." denotes "Croke's reports of cases in the time of James I."

JACENS. Lat. Lying in abeyance, as in the phrase *"hæreditas jacens,"* which is an inheritance or estate lying vacant or in abeyance prior to the ascertainment of the heir or his assumption of the succession.

JACENS HÆREDITAS. See Hæreditas Jacens.

JACET IN ORE. Lat. In old English law. It lies in the mouth. Fleta, lib. 5, c. 5, § 49.

JACK. A kind of defensive coat-armor worn by horsemen in war; not made of solid iron, but of many plates fastened together. Some tenants were bound by their tenure to find it upon invasion. Cowell.

JACOB'S LADDER. A ladder with sides of rope and with wooden steps, frequently used on shipboard. Maloney v. Cunard S. S. Co., 217 N.Y. 278, 111 N.E. 835, 836.

JACOBUS. A gold coin an inch and three-eighths in diameter, in value about twenty-five shillings, so called from James I., in whose reign it was first coined. It was also called *broad, laurel,* and *broad-piece.* Its value is sometimes put at twenty-four shillings, but Macaulay speaks of a salary of eight thousand Jacobuses as equivalent to ten thousand pounds sterling. Hist. Eng. ch. xv.

JACTITATION. Boasting of something which is challenged by another. Moz. & W. A false boasting; a false claim; assertions repeated to the prejudice of another's right.

The species of defamation or disparagement of another's title to real estate known at common law as "slander of title" comes under the head of jactitation, and in some jurisdictions (as in Louisiana) a remedy for this injury is provided under the name of an "action of jactitation."

The action in jactitation of title is governed by the rules prescribed by the Code of Practice, under the title, "Possessory Actions," and differs materially from the common-law action of slander of title. Bill v. Saunders, 139 La. 1037, 72 So. 727, 729.

In medical jurisprudence. Involuntary convulsive muscular movement; restless agitation or tossing of the body to and fro. Leman v. Insurance Co., 46 La.Ann. 1189, 15 So. 388, 24 L.R.A. 589.

Jactitation of a right to a church sitting appears to be the boasting by a man that he has a right or title to a pew or sitting in a church to which he has legally no title.

Jactitation of marriage. In English ecclesiastical law. The boasting or giving out by a party that he or she is married to some other, whereby a common reputation of their matrimony may ensue. To defeat that result, the person may be put to a proof of the actual marriage, failing which proof, he or she is put to silence about it. 3 Bl. Comm. 93. The Scotch suit of a declarator of putting to silence is equivalent to jactitation of marriage.

Jactitation of tithes is the boasting by a man that he is entitled to certain tithes, to which he has legally no title. Rog. Ecc. L. 482.

JACTIVUS. Lost by default; tossed away. Cowell.

JACTURA. In the civil law. A throwing of goods overboard in a storm; jettison. Loss from such a cause. Calvin.

JACTUS. A throwing goods overboard to lighten or save the vessel, in which case the goods so sacrificed are a proper subject for general average. Dig. 14, 2, *"de lege Rhodia de Jactu;"* Barnard v. Adams, 10 How. 303, 13 L.Ed. 417.

JACTUS LAPILLI. The throwing down of a stone. One of the modes, under the civil law, of interrupting prescription. Where one person was building on another's ground, and in this way acquiring a right by *usucapio,* the true owner challenged the intrusion and interrupted the prescriptive right by throwing down one of the stones of the building before witnesses called for the purpose. Tray. Lat. Max.

JAIL. A gaol; a prison; a building designated by law, or regularly used, for the confinement of persons held in lawful custody. State v. Bryan, 89 N.C. 534; Adle v. Herald Co., Sup., 36 N.Y.S.2d 905, 907. See Gaol.

A "jail" is therefore distinguishable both in law and in common understanding from a temporary place of detention, like a police station or lockup. People ex rel. Murphy v. Holcomb, 181 N.Y.S. 780, 783, 111 Misc. 460. While the primary function of a "jail" is a place of detention for persons committed thereto, under sentence of a court, it is also the proper and usual place where persons under arrest or awaiting trial are kept until they appear in court and the charge is disposed of. Grab v. Lucas, 156 Wis. 504, 146 N.W. 504, 505.

JAIL DELIVERY. See Gaol.

JAIL LIBERTIES. See Gaol.

JAILER. A keeper or warden of a prison or jail. Lefman v. Schuler, 317 Mo. 671, 296 S.W. 808, 814.

JAKE. A low colloquialism applied to liquor reputed to be composed of a mixture of Jamaica ginger and some other beverage or beverages. Skelton v. State, 31 Okl.Cr. 343, 239 P. 189, 190.

JAMB. A side post or side of a doorway, window, opening, or fire place; a side or vertical piece of any opening or aperture in a wall which helps to bear an overhead member. Superior Skylight Co. v. Zerbe Const. Co., D.C.N.Y., 5 F.2d 982, 986.

JAMBEAUX. In old English and feudal law. Leg-armor. Blount.

JAMMA, JUMMA. In Hindu law. Total amount; collection; assembly. The total of a territorial assignment.

JAMMABUNDY, JUMMABUNDY. In Hindu law. A written schedule of the whole of an assessment.

JAMMUNDLING. See Jamunlingi.

JAMPNUM. Furze, or grass, or ground where furze grows; as distinguished from "arable," "pasture," or the like. Co. Litt. 5*a*.

JAMUNLINGI, JAMUNDILINGI. Freemen who delivered themselves and property to the protection of a more powerful person, in order to avoid military service and other burdens. Spelman. Also a species of serfs among the Germans. Du Cange. The same as *commendati*.

JANITOR. In old English law. A door-keeper. Fleta, lib. 2, c. 24.

In modern law. A person employed to take charge of rooms or buildings, to see that they are kept clean and in order, to lock and unlock them, and generally to care for them. Fagan v. New York, 84 N.Y. 352; Kramer v. Industrial Acc. Commission of State of California, 31 Cal.App. 673, 161 P. 278.

JANUS-FACED. An argument looking in both directions at the same time, e. g., urging jurors not to be swayed by sympathy, but adding that any sympathy should be in favor of the arguing counsel's client. Davis v. Franson, 296 P.2d 600, 606, 141 Cal.App.2d 263.

JAQUES. In old English law. Small money.

JASON CLAUSE. Clause in bills of lading which obligates cargo owners to contribute in general average in cases of danger, damage, or disaster resulting from faults or errors in navigation or in management of vessel, her machinery or appurtenances, provided that ship owner shall have exercised due diligence to make vessel in all respects seaworthy, and to have her properly manned, equipped, and supplied. Merklen v. Johnson & Higgins, D.C.N.Y., 3 F.Supp. 897, 898.

JAVELIN-MEN. Yeomen retained by the sheriff to escort the judge of assize.

JAVELOUR. In Scotch law. Jailer or gaoler. 1 Pitc. Crim. Tr. pt. 1, p. 33.

JAY WALKING. Proceeding diagonally across a street intersection. Gett v. Pacific Gas & Electric Co., 192 Cal. 621, 221 P. 376, 378.

Also, crossing a street between intersections, or at a place other than a crosswalk.

JEDBURGH JUSTICE. Summary justice inflicted upon a marauder or felon without a regular trial, equivalent to "lynch law." So called from a Scotch town, near the English border, where raiders and cattle lifters were often summarily hung. Also written "Jeddart" or "Jedwood" justice.

JEHOVAH'S WITNESSES. A religious sect whose members profess allegiance to a visionary heavenly kingdom and disclaim all duties of citizenship which they deem in conflict with such heavenly allegiance. U. S. ex rel. Hoce v. McGinnis, D.C.W.Va., 56 F.Supp. 668.

JEMAN. In old records. Yeoman. Cowell; Blount.

JENNY. With names of animals, often used to denote a female; also short for "jenny ass," "jenny wren," etc. Likewise short for "spinning jenny." Webster, Dict.; O'Rear v. Richardson, 17 Ala.App. 87, 81 So. 865, 866.

JEOFAILE. L. Fr. I have failed; I am in error. An error or oversight in pleading.

Certain statutes are called "statutes of amendments and jeofailes" because, where a pleader perceives any slip in the form of his proceedings, and acknowledges the error, (jeofaile,) he is at liberty, by those statutes, to amend it. 3 Bl.Comm. 407; 1 Saund. p. 228, no. 1.

Jeofaile is when the parties to any suit in pleading have proceeded so far that they have joined issue which shall be tried or is tried by a jury or inquest, and this pleading or issue is so badly pleaded or joined that it will be error if they proceed. Then some of the said parties may, by their counsel, show it to the court, as well after verdict given and before judgment as before the jury is charged. And the counsel shall say: "This inquest ye ought not to take." And if it be after verdict, then he may say: "To judgment you ought not to go." Termes de la Ley.

JEOPARDY. Danger; hazard; peril.

The danger of conviction and punishment which the defendant in a criminal action incurs when a valid indictment has been found, and a petit jury has been impaneled and sworn to try the case and give a verdict in a court of competent jurisdiction. State v. Nelson, 26 Ind. 368; State v. Emery, 59 Vt. 84, 7 A. 129; People v. Terrill, 132 Cal. 497, 64 P. 894; Mitchell v. State, 42 Ohio St. 383; Grogan v. State, 44 Ala. 9; Ex parte Glenn, C.C.W.Va., 111 F. 258; State v. McKee, 1 Bail., S.C., 655, 21 Am. Dec. 499; State v. Yokum, 155 La. 846, 99 So. 621, 631.

The peril in which a prisoner is put when he is regularly charged with a crime before a tribunal properly organized and competent to try him. Com. v. Fitzpatrick, 121 Pa. 109, 15 A. 466, 1 L.R.A. 451; Peavey v. State, 153 Ga. 119,

111 S.E. 420. The situation of a defendant when the jury is impaneled and sworn and the issues presented on a valid indictment or information in a court of competent jurisdiction. State v. Thompson, 58 Utah 291, 199 P. 161, 163, 38 A.L.R. 697. The condition of a person when he is put upon trial, before a court of competent jurisdiction, upon an indictment or information which is sufficient in form and substance to sustain a conviction, and a jury has been charged with his deliverance. Allen v. State, 13 Okl.Cr. 533, 165 P. 745, 748, L.R.A.1917E, 1085; State v. Runyon, 100 W.Va. 647, 131 S.E. 466, 467; Commonwealth v. Grey, 249 Ky. 36, 60 S.W.2d 133.

Defendant is not in "jeopardy" until jury has been duly impaneled and charged with his deliverance, but conviction or acquittal by any competent tribunal, whether after jury trial or not, satisfies requirement of jeopardy. Pepin v. State ex rel. Chambers, 217 Wis. 568, 259 N.W. 410.

The terms "jeopardy of life and liberty for the same offense," "jeopardy of life or limb," "jeopardy for the same offense," "in jeopardy of punishment," and other similar provisions used in the various Constitutions, are to be construed as meaning substantially the same thing. Stout v. State, 130 P. 553, 556, 36 Okl. 744, 45 L.R.A.,N.S., 884, Ann.Cas.1916E, 858.

JERGUER. In English law. An officer of the custom-house who oversees the waiters. Techn. Dict.

JERK. A sharply arrested pull, thrust, push, motion, a sudden movement or lurch;—"lurch" being used, however, with specific reference to sidewise movements. St. Louis Southwestern Ry. Co. of Texas v. Farris, Tex.Civ.App., 166 S.W. 463; Tritle v. Phillips Petroleum Co., 140 Kan. 671, 37 P.2d 996.

The ordinary jerks and jolts of a motorbus in starting or stopping are among the usual incidents of travel, and for injuries to passengers resulting from them the motor carrier is not liable. Blashfield, Cyc. of Automobile Law and Prac., Perm. Ed., § 2156.

JESSE. A large brass candlestick, usually hung in the middle of a church or choir. Cowell.

JET. Fr. In French law. Jettison. Ord. Mar. liv. 3, tit. 8; Emerig. Traité des Assur. c. 12, § 40.

JETSAM. Goods which, by the act of the owner, have been voluntarily cast overboard from a vessel, in a storm or other emergency, to lighten the ship. 1 C.B. 113.

Jetsam is where goods are cast into the sea, and there sink and remain under water. 1 Bl.Comm. 292.

The sense of "goods thrown overboard and sunk at sea" is an error arising apparently in the attempt to distinguish "jetsam" from "flotsam," the latter being properly wreckage of a ship or its cargo found floating on the sea. Webster, Dict.

JETTISON. The act of throwing overboard from a vessel part of the cargo, in case of extreme danger, to lighten the ship. The thing or things so cast out; jetsam. Gray v. Waln, 2 Serg. & R., Pa., 254, 7 Am.Dec. 642; Butler v. Wildman, 3 Barn. & Ald. 326; Barnard v. Adams, 10 How. 303, 13 L.Ed. 417.

A carrier by water may, when in case of extreme peril it is necessary for the safety of the ship or cargo, throw overboard, or otherwise sacrifice, any or all of the cargo or appurtenances of the ship. Throwing property overboard for such purpose is called "jettison," and the loss incurred thereby is called a "general average loss." Civil Code Cal. § 2148; Civil Code Dak. § 1245 (Comp. Laws 1913, N.D. § 6225; Rev.Code 1919, S.D. § 1147).

JETTY. A projection of stone or other material serving as a protection against the waves. Storm v. Town of Wrightsville Beach, 189 N.C. 679, 128 S.E. 17, 19.

JEUX DE BOURSE. Fr. In French law. Speculation in the public funds or in stocks; gambling speculations on the stock exchange; dealings in "options" and "futures."

A kind of gambling or speculation, which consists of sales and purchases which bind neither of the parties to deliver the things which are the object of the sale, and which are settled by paying the difference in the value of the things sold between the day of the sale and that appointed for delivery of such things. 1 Pardessus, *Droit Com.* n. 162.

JEWEL. An ornament of the person, such as ear-rings, pearls, diamonds, etc., prepared to be worn. Com. v. Stephens, 14 Pick., Mass., 373; Robbins v. Robertson, C.C.N.Y., 33 F. 710; Cavendish v. Cavendish, 1 Brown Ch. 409; Ramaley v. Leland, 43 N.Y. 541, 3 Am.Rep. 728; Gile v. Libby, 36 Barb., N.Y., 77. An ornament made of precious metal or a precious stone. Wagner v. Congress Square Hotel Co., 115 Me. 190, 98 A. 660, 662.

JEWELRY. Jewels collectively. Wagner v. Congress Square Hotel Co., 115 Me. 190, 98 A. 660, 662.

JEWISH SABBATH. A period which begins at sundown Friday night and ends at sundown Saturday night, and does not conform to a full statutory day according to the Christian calendar. Cohen v. Webb, 175 Ky. 1, 192 S.W. 828, 829.

JIGGER BOSS. In mining parlance, a "pusher" or kind of foreman engaged for the purpose of encouraging or hastening the men. Ryan v. Manhattan Big Four Mining Co., 38 Nev. 92, 145 P. 907, 908.

JITNEY. A self-propelled vehicle, other than a street car, traversing the public streets between certain definite points or termini, and, as a common carrier, conveying passengers at a five-cent or some small fare, between such termini and intermediate points, and so held out, advertised, or announced. City of Memphis v. State, 133 Tenn. 83, 179 S.W. 631, 634, L.R.A.1916B, 1151, Ann.Cas. 1917C, 1056. A motor vehicle carrying passengers for fare. Ft. Lee, etc., Transp. Co. v. Borough of Edgewater, 99 N.J.Eq. 850, 133 A. 424, 425. Also called "jitney bus." Huston v. City of Des Moines, 176 Iowa 455, 156 N.W. 883, 888.

JOB. The whole of a thing which is to be done. "To build by plot, or to work by the job, is to undertake a building for a certain stipulated price." Civ.Code La. art. 2727 (Civ.Code, art. 2756).

JOBBER. One who buys and sells goods for others; one who buys or sells on the stock exchange; a dealer in stocks, shares, or securities. One who buys and sells articles in bulk and resells them to dealers. A merchant buying and selling in job lots. Wasserstrom v. Cohen, Frank & Co., 165

App.Div. 171, 150 N.Y.S. 638, 639. A sort of middleman. Great Atlantic & Pacific Tea Co. v. Cream of Wheat Co., C.C.A.N.Y., 227 F. 46, 47.

JOBMASTER. In English law, one who carries on the business of letting out carriages and horses or other vehicles with drivers for hire; a livery stable keeper. Hyman v. Nye, 6 Queen's Bench, 685.

JOCALIA. In old English law. Jewels. This term was formerly more properly applied to those ornaments which women, although married, call their own. When these *jocalia* are not suitable to her degree, they are assets for the payment of debts. 1 Rolle, Abr. 911.

JOCELET. A little manor or farm. Cowell.

JOCKEY CLUB. An association of persons for the purpose of regulating all matters connected with horse racing. See Corrigan v. Jockey Club, 2 Misc. 512, 22 N.Y.S. 394.

JOCUS. In old English law. A game of hazard. Reg. Orig. 290.

JOCUS PARTITUS. In old English practice. A divided game, risk, or hazard. An arrangement which the parties to a suit were anciently sometimes allowed to make by mutual agreement upon a certain hazard, as that one should lose if the case turned out in a certain way, and, if it did not, that the other should gain. Bract. fols. 211*b*, 379*b*, 432, 434, 200*b*.

JOHN DOE. A fictitious name frequently used to indicate a person for the purpose of argument or illustration, or in the course of enforcing a fiction in the law. The name which was usually given to the fictitious lessee of the plaintiff in the mixed action of ejectment. He was sometimes called "Goodtitle." So the Romans had their fictitious personages in law proceedings, as *Titius, Seius.*

The name "John Doe" is, and for some centuries has been, used in legal proceedings as a fictitious name to designate a party until his real name can be ascertained. State v. Rossignol, 22 Wash.2d 19, 153 P.2d 882, 885.

JOIN. To unite; to come together; to combine or unite in time, effort, action; to enter into an alliance. Lowery v. Westheimer, 58 Okl. 560, 160 P. 496, 500.

JOINDER. Joining or coupling together; uniting two or more constituents or elements in one; uniting with another person in some legal step or proceeding; union; concurrence.

Joinder in demurrer. When a defendant in an action tenders an issue of law, (called a "demurrer,") the plaintiff, if he means to maintain his action, must accept it, and this acceptance of the defendant's tender, signified by the plaintiff in a set form of words, is called a "joinder in demurrer." Brown; Co. Litt. 71 *b;* Thompson v. Goudelock, 10 Rich., S.C., 49.

Joinder in issue. In pleading. A formula by which one of the parties to a suit joins in or accepts an issue in fact tendered by the opposite party. Steph. Pl. 57, 236. More commonly termed a "*similiter.*" (*q. v.*)

Joinder in pleading. Accepting the issue, and mode of trial tendered, either by demurrer, error, or issue, in fact, by the opposite party.

Joinder of actions. This expression signifies the uniting of two or more demands or rights of action in one action; the statement of more than one cause of action in a declaration. Sickler v. City of Broken Bow, 143 Neb. 542, 10 N.W.2d 462, 464.

Joinder of error. In proceedings on a writ of error in criminal cases, the joinder of error is a written denial of the errors alleged in the assignment of errors. It answers to a joinder of issue in an action.

Joinder of issue. The act by which the parties to a cause arrive at that stage of it in their pleadings, that one asserts a fact to be so, and the other denies it.

Joinder of offenses. The uniting of several distinct charges of crime in the same indictment or prosecution.

Joinder of parties. The uniting of two or more persons as co-plaintiffs or as co-defendants in one suit.

Misjoinder. The improper joining together of parties to a suit, as plaintiffs or defendants, or of different causes of action. Burstall v. Beyfus, 53 L.J.Ch. 567; Phenix Iron Foundry v. Lockwood, 21 R.I. 556, 45 A. 546.

Misjoinder of actions is the joining several demands which the law does not permit to be joined, to enforce by one proceeding several distinct, substantive rights of recovery. Gould, Pl. c. 4, § 98; Archb. Civ. Pl. 61; Dane, Abr. In equity, it is the joinder of different and distinct claims against one defendant; Adams, Eq. 309; 7 Sim. 241; Newland v. Rogers, 3 Barb. Ch., N.Y., 432.

Misjoinder of parties is the joining, as plaintiffs or defendants, parties who have not a joint interest. Billy v. McGill, 113 Okl. 153, 240 P. 119, 121; Gagle v. Besser, 162 Iowa 227, 144 N.W. 3, 4.

Misjoinder in a criminal prosecution is the charging in separate counts of separate and distinct offenses arising out of wholly different transactions having no connection or relation with each other. Optner v. U. S., C.C.A.Mich., 13 F.2d 11, 13.

Nonjoinder. The omission to join some person as party to a suit, whether as plaintiff or defendant, who ought to have been so joined, according to the rules of pleading and practice. Bardock Iron & Steel Co. v. Tenenbaum, 136 Va. 163, 118 S.E. 502, 505.

JOINT. United; combined; undivided; done by or against two or more unitedly; shared by or between two or more; coupled together in interest or liability.

The term is used to express a common property interest enjoyed or a common liability incurred by two or more persons. Thus, it is one in which the obligors (being two or more in number) bind themselves jointly but not severally, and which must therefore be prosecuted in a joint action against them all;—distinguished from "joint and several" obligation.

A place of meeting or resort for persons engaged in evil and secret practices of any kind, as a tramps' joint, an "opium joint," or, generally speaking, a rendezvous for persons of evil habits and practices. State v. Shoaf, 179 N.C. 744, 102 S.E. 705, 706, 9 A.L.R. 426.

In masonry, the permanent meeting surface of two bodies, as stones or bricks, held together by cement or otherwise, and, in paving blocks, the space between the side faces of the blocks brought together or nearly in touch. Central Union Stock Yards Co. v. Ualde Asphalt Paving Co., 82 N.J.Eq. 246, 87 A. 235, 239.

As used in income tax statute authorizing filing of joint return by spouses, means that both spouses should be liable for resulting tax. Moore v. United States, Ct.Cl., 37 F.Supp. 136, 140.

As to joint "Adventure," "Ballot," "Committee," "Contract," "Covenant," "Creditor," "Fiat," "Fine," "Indictment," "Obligation," "Obligee," "Obligor," "Owner," "Rate," "Resolution," "Session," "Tenancy," "Tenants," "Tortfeasor," "Trespass," "Trespassers," "Trustees," and "Will," see those titles. As to joint-stock banks, see Bank; joint-stock company, see Company; joint-stock corporation, see Corporation.

JOINT ACCOUNT. An account in two or more names. Harbour v. Harbour, 207 Ark. 551, 181 S.W.2d 805, 807.

In order to bank that "my checking account be made joint" with another "for him to check on only in case of my death," means that other person should take as survivor as joint tenant. First Nat. Bank v. Mulich, 83 Colo. 518, 266 P. 1110, 1111.

JOINT ACTION. An action brought by two or more as plaintiffs or against two or more as defendants.

JOINT AND SEVERAL. A liability is said to be joint and several when the creditor may sue one or more of the parties to such liability separately, or all of them together at his option. Dicey, Parties 230.

A joint and several bond or note is one in which the obligors or makers bind themselves both jointly and individually to the obligee or payee, so that all may be sued together for its enforcement, or the creditor may select one or more as the object of his suit. See Mitchell v. Darricott, 3 Brev., S.C., 145; Rice v. Gove, 22 Pick., Mass., 158, 33 Am.Dec. 724.

JOINT AUTHORSHIP. As to literary property, where there exists a common design to the execution of which several persons contribute. Mere alterations, additions or improvements, whether with or without the sanction of the author, will not entitle the person making them to claim to be a joint author of the work. 18 C.J.S., Copyright and Literary Property, § 11, p. 145.

Joint labor in furtherance of a common design. Edward B. Marks Music Corporation v. Jerry Vogel Music Co., C.C.A.N.Y., 140 F.2d 266, 267.

JOINT CAUSE OF ACTION. This term, as used in Equity Rule 26 (see Rules of Civil Procedure, Rules 18, 20, 82, 28 U.S.C.A.), does not mean a technical legal privity, such as a joint contract; but the rule will be satisfied where there is a single question of law and fact common to all the complainants, as where in a suit to quiet title they claim separate parcels of land under a common source of title. Commodores Point Terminal Co. v. Hudnall, D.C.Fla., 283 F. 150, 171.

JOINT DEBTORS. Persons united in a joint liability or indebtedness. Two or more persons jointly liable for the same debt. See Robertson v. Smith, 18 Johns., N.Y., 459, 9 Am.Dec. 227; Ex parte Zeigler, 83 S.C. 78, 64 S.E. 513, 916, 21 L.R.A., N.S., 1005.

JOINT DEBTORS' ACTS. Statutes enacted in many of the states, which provide that judgment may be given for or against one or more of several plaintiffs, and for or against one or more of several defendants, and that, "in an action against several defendants, the court may, in its discretion, render judgment against one or more of them, leaving the action to proceed against the others, whenever a several judgment is proper." The name is also given to statutes providing that where an action is instituted against two or more defendants upon an alleged joint liability, and some of them are served with process, but jurisdiction is not obtained over the others, the plaintiff may still proceed to trial against those who are before the court, and, if he recovers, may have judgment against all of the defendants whom he shows to be jointly liable. 1 Black, Judgm. §§ 208, 235. And see Hall v. Lanning, 91 U.S. 168, 23 L.Ed. 271.

JOINT ENTERPRISE. Also called "common enterprise." The joint prosecution of common purpose under such circumstances that each has authority express or implied to act for all in respect to the control, means or agencies employed to execute such common purpose. Hines v. Welch, Tex.Civ.App., 229 S.W. 681, 683. Greenwell's Adm'r v. Burba, 298 Ky. 255, 182 S.W.2d 436, 441; Illingworth v. Madden, 135 Me. 159, 192 A. 273, 276, 110 A.L.R. 1090. An enterprise participated in by associates acting together. Howard v. Zimmerman, 120 Kan. 77, 242 P. 131, 132. There must be a community of interests in the objects or purposes of the undertaking, and an equal right to direct and govern the movements and conduct of each other with respect thereto; each must have some voice and right to be heard in its control or management. St. Louis & S. F. R. Co. v. Bell, 58 Okl. 84, 159 P. 336, 337, L.R.A. 1917A, 543; Trumpfeller v. Crandall, 130 Me. 279, 155 A. 646, 650; Murphy v. Keating, 204 Minn. 269, 283 N.W. 389, 392, 393; Bloom v. Leech, 120 Ohio St. 239, 166 N.E. 137, 138.

JOINT ESTATE. "Joint estate" involves unity of interest, unity of title, unity of time, and unity of possession, and joint tenants must have the same interest accruing under the same conveyance, commencing at the same time, and held under the same undivided possession. Deslauriers v. Senesac, 331 Ill. 437, 163 N.E. 327, 329, 62 A.L.R. 511.

At common law, estates in which there were a plurality of tenants were described as "joint-estates" which designation includes estates in coparcenary, tenancies in common and joint tenancies, within which class are included tenancies by the entirety but the terms is not synonymous with "joint tenancies". Mosser v. Dolsay, 132 N.J.Eq. 121, 27 A.2d 155, 157.

JOINT EXECUTORS. Co-executors; two or more who are joined in the execution of a will. See, also, Coexecutor.

JOINT FEASORS IN PARI DELICTO. Phrase means as between persons who by concert of action intentionally commit the wrong complained of; there is no right of contribution. Commercial Cas. Ins. Co. v. Leonard, 210 Ark. 575, 196 S.W.2d 919, 920.

JOINT INDUSTRY OF HUSBAND AND WIFE. This phrase, as applied in Oklahoma statutes to property passing by descent, means the industry of a husband and wife each, in his or her recognized sphere of marital activity, and not that both must pursue jointly the same business or calling. In re Stone's Estate, 86 Okl. 33, 206 P. 246, 247. See, also, Chamberlain v. Chamberlain, 121 Okl. 145, 247 P. 684, 687.

JOINT INTEREST. This term within federal rule requiring persons having a joint interest to be made parties, refers to parties designated as necessary or indispensable under former practice, and means an interest which must be directly affected by adjudication in the case. Platte County v. New Amsterdam Cas. Co., D.C.Neb., 6 F.R.D. 475, 482.

JOINT INVENTIONS. These are made when two or more persons jointly work or collaborate in devising and putting into practical form the subject-matter of patent. Altoona Publix Theatres v. American Tri-Ergon Corporation, C.C.A.Pa., 72 F. 2d 53, 56.

JOINT LIABILITY. One wherein joint obligor has right to insist that co-obligor be joined as a codefendant with him, that is, that they be sued jointly. Schram v. Perkins, D.C.Mich., 38 F.Supp. 404, 407.

JOINT LIVES. This expression is used to designate the duration of an estate or right which is granted to two or more persons to be enjoyed so long as they both (or all) shall live. As soon as one dies, the interest determines. See Highley v. Allen, 3 Mo.App. 524.

JOINT NEGLIGENCE. In case of "joint negligence" of several people, proximately causing accident, they act together in concert and either do something together which they should not do or fail to do something which they are together obligated to do under circumstances. Russo v. Aucoin, La.App., 7 So.2d 744, 747.

JOINT OFFENSE. One offense committed by two or more persons jointly. Jacoby v. State, 212 Ind. 465, 8 N.E.2d 978, 979; State ex rel. Flaherty v. Ermston, 209 Ind. 117, 197 N.E. 908, 911.

JOINT POLICY. Insurance on lives of spouses, for benefit of survivor. O'Boyle v. Home Life Ins. Co. of America, D.C.Pa., 20 F.Supp. 33, 36; Kensington Nat. Bank of Philadelphia v. Sampson, 149 Pa.Super. 43, 26 A.2d 115, 118.

JOINT STOCK INSURANCE COMPANY. An insurance company having a subscribed capital and policyholders having nothing to do with management. Ohio Farmers Indemnity Co. v. Commissioner of Internal Revenue, C.C.A.6, 108 F.2d 665, 667.

JOINT TORT. Where two or more persons owe to another the same duty and by their common neglect such other is injured, the tort is "joint." Boyd v. Maxwell, 190 S.C. 103, 2 S.E.2d 395, 397; Leishman v. Brady, 9 W.W.Harr. 559, 3 A.2d 118, 120; Walder v. Manahan, 21 N.J.Misc. 1, 29 A.2d 395, 396.

JOINT VENTURE. See Adventure.

JOINTIST. A person established in a definite place of business, for the purpose of illegally selling intoxicants. Scriven v. City of Lebanon, 99 Kan. 602, 162 P. 307, 309, L.R.A.1917C, 460. One who opens up, conducts, or maintains any place for the unlawful sale of intoxicating liquors. Rem. Comp.Stat.Wash. § 7328; State v. Pistona, 127 Wash. 171, 219 P. 859, 860.

JOINTLY. Unitedly, combined or joined together in unity of interest or liability. Soderberg v. Atlantic Lighterage Corporation, D.C.N.Y., 15 F.2d 209. In a joint manner; in concert; not separately; in conjunction. Reclamation Dist. v. Parvin, 67 Cal. 501, 8 P. 43; Case v. Owen, 139 Ind. 22, 38 N.E. 395, 47 Am.St.Rep. 253; White v. Powell, 246 Ala. 356, 20 So.2d 467, 469. To be or become liable to a joint obligation; Arndt v. Brockhausen, 332 Pa. 416, 3 A.2d 384, 386; Kaspar American State Bank v. Oul Homestead Ass'n, 301 Ill.App. 326, 22 N.E.2d 785, 786; Creighton v. Continental Roll & Steel Foundry Co., 155 Pa.Super. 165, 38 A.2d 337, 342. Participated in or used by two or more, held or shared in common. Wunderlich v. Bleyle, 96 N. J.Eq. 135, 125 A. 386, 388. These are the non-technical meanings of the word, which it frequently has in wills, as opposed to its technical signification creating a joint tenancy. Overheiser v. Lackey, 207 N.Y. 229, 100 N.E. 738, Ann.Cas.1914C, 229.

Persons are "jointly bound" in a bond or note when both or all must be sued in one action for its enforcement, not either one at the election of the creditor.

JOINTLY ACQUIRED PROPERTY. Property accumulated by joint industry of husband and wife during marriage. Tobin v. Tobin, 89 Okl. 12, 213 P. 884; Bruce v. Bruce, 141 Okl. 160, 285 P. 30, 36.

JOINTLY AND SEVERALLY. See Joint and Several.

JOINTRESS, JOINTURESS. A woman who has an estate settled on her by her husband, to hold during her life, if she survive him. Co.Litt. 46.

JOINTURE. A freehold estate in lands or tenements secured to the wife, and to take effect on the decease of the husband, and to continue during her life at the least, unless she be herself the cause of its determination. Vance v. Vance, 21 Me. 369.

A competent livelihood of freehold for the wife, of lands and tenements, to take effect, in profit or possession, presently after the death of the husband, for the life of the wife at least. Comstock v. Comstock, 146 Ark. 266, 225 S.W. 621, 622; Co. Litt. 36*b*; 2 Bl.Comm. 137; Gercke v. Gercke, 331 Ill. 413, 163 N.E. 323, 325. A competent livelihood for the wife in the husband's property to take effect after his death; it is an estate conveyed or devised to the wife in lieu of dower and it must be in satisfaction of it. Maynard's Adm'r v. Maynard, 285 Ky. 75, 146 S.W.2d 343, 344.

A jointure strictly signifies a joint estate limited to both husband and wife, and such was its original form; but, in its more usual form, it is a sole estate limited to the wife only, expectant upon a life-estate in the husband. 2 Bl. Comm. 137; 1 Steph.Comm. 255.

In England, before the time of Henry VIII, in order to protect a wife who was deprived of dower by conveyances to uses, it was the usual custom of the husband before marriage to take an estate from his feoffees and limit it to himself and his intended wife for their lives in joint tenancy or jointure to protect the wife in case of his death, and St. 27 Henry VIII prohibited the widow from having both dower and jointure, which has been continued as part of law by Acts Va. 1785, c. 65 (1 Hening's St. at Large, p. 162), Rev. Code 1819, c. 107, and Code 1849, c. 110 (Code 1930, § 5117 et seq.). Jacobs v. Jacobs, 100 W. Va. 585, 131 S.E. 449, 453.

JOKER. In political usage, a clause in legislation that is ambiguous or apparently immaterial, inserted to render it inoperative or uncertain without arousing opposition at the time of passage. Bennet v. Commercial Advertiser Ass'n, 230 N.Y. 125, 129 N.E. 343, 344.

JOLT. A sudden shock or jerk; a jolting motion, as in a vehicle moving over a rough street or highway; the effect produced by a sudden start or quick increase in the speed of a vehicle. 48 C.J.S. p. 939. See Jerk, *supra*.

JONCARIA, or JUNCARIA. In old English law. Land where rushes grow. Co.Litt. 5*a*.

JORNALE. In old English law. As much land as could be plowed in one day. Spelman.

JOSH. To ridicule or tease, or make fun of in a joke, to lure or tease by misrepresenting the facts. State v. Powers, 181 Iowa 452, 164 N.W. 856, 861.

JOSTLE. To push or crowd in passing. Baker v. Chicago, B. & Q. R. Co., 327 Mo. 986, 39 S.W.2d 535, 543.

JOUIR. A French word, meaning to enjoy; to have enjoyment of; or to possess. Allison v. Maroun, 193 La. 286, 190 So. 408, 411.

JOUR. A French word, signifying "day."

It is used in our old law-books; as *"tout jours,"* forever. It is also frequently employed in the composition of words: as, *journal*, a daybook; *journey-man*, a man who works by the day; *journeys account*.

JOUR EN BANC. A day *in banc*. Distinguished from *"jour en pays,"* (a day in the country,) otherwise called *"jour en nisi prius."*

JOUR IN COURT. In old practice. Day in court; day to appear in court; appearance day. "Every process gives the defendant a day in court." Hale, Anal. § 8.

JOURNAL. A daily book; a book in which entries are made or events recorded from day to day.

In maritime law, the journal (otherwise called "log" or "log-book") is a book kept on every vessel, which contains a brief record of the events and occurrences of each day of a voyage, with the nautical observations, course of the ship, account of the weather, etc. In the system of double-entry bookkeeping, the journal is an account-book into which are transcribed, daily or at other intervals, the items entered upon the day-book, for more convenient posting into the ledger. In the usage of legislative bodies, the journal is a daily record of the proceedings of either house. It is kept by the clerk, and in it are entered the appointments and actions of committees, introduction of bills, motions, votes, resolutions, etc., in the order of their occurrence. See Montgomery Beer Bottling Works v. Gaston, 126 Ala. 425, 28 So. 497, 51 L.R.A. 396, 85 Am.St.Rep. 42.

The daily printed pamphlets which contain the record of the proceedings of each house of the Legislature are the "journals" of the respective houses. Amos v. Moseley, 74 Fla. 555, 77 So. 619, 621, L.R.A.1918C, 482.

A "journal" is a permanent record, and the daily minutes kept by the secretary of the Senate or the journal clerk from which the permanent record is finally made up, does not constitute a part of the journal. Niven v. Road Improvement Dist. No. 14 of Jefferson County, 132 Ark. 240, 200 S.W. 997, 998.

JOURNAL ENTRY RULE. Regularity of enactment of statute may be inquired into by examining legislative journals. Freeman v. Goff, 206 Minn. 49, 287 N.W. 238, 240.

JOURNEY. Originally, a day's travel. The word is now applied to a travel by land from place to place, without restriction of time. But, when thus applied, it is employed to designate a travel which is without the ordinary habits, business, or duties of the person, to a distance from his home, and beyond the circle of his friends or acquaintances. Gholson v. State, 53 Ala. 521, 25 Am.Rep. 652.

JOURNEY-HOPPERS. In English law. Regrators of yarn. 8 Hen. VI. c. 5.

JOURNEYMAN. A workman hired by the day, or other given time. Hart v. Aldridge, 1 Cowp. 56; Butler v. Clark, 46 Ga. 468.

JOURNEYS ACCOUNT. In English practice. A new writ which the plaintiff was permitted to sue out within a reasonable time after the abatement, without his fault, of the first writ. This time was computed with reference to the number of days which the plaintiff must spend in *journeying* to reach the court; hence the name of *journeys account*, that is, journeys *accomptes* or *counted*. Co.Litt. fol. 9*b*; English v. T. H. Rogers Lumber Co., 68 Okl. 238, 173 P. 1046, 1048.

This mode of proceeding has fallen into disuse, the practice now being to permit that writ to be quashed, and to sue out another. See *Termes de la Ley;* Bacon, Abr. *Abatement* (Q); 14 Viner, Abr. 558; 4 Com.Dig. 714; 7 M. & G. 762; Richards v. Ins. Co., 8 Cranch, 84, 3 L.Ed. 496.

JOUSTS. See Justs.

JUBERE. Lat. In the civil law. To order, direct, or command. Calvin. The word *jubeo* (I order,) in a will, was called a "word of direction," as distinguished from "precatory words." Cod. 6, 43, 2.

To assure or promise.

To decree or pass a law.

JUBILACION. In Spanish law. The privilege of a public officer to be retired, on account of infirmity or disability, retaining the rank and pay of his office (or part of the same) after twenty years of public service, and on reaching the age of fifty.

JUDÆUS, JUDEUS. Lat. A Jew.

JUDAISMUS. The religion and rites of the Jews. Du Cange. A quarter set apart for residence of Jews. Du Cange. A usurious rate of interest. 1 Mon.Angl. 839; 2 Mon.Angl. 10,665. *Sex marcus sterlingorum ad acquietandam terram prœdictum de Judaismo, in quo fuit impignorata.* Du Cange. An income anciently accruing to the king from the Jews. Blount.

JUDEX. Lat.

In Roman law. A private person appointed by the prætor, with the consent of the parties, to try and decide a cause of action commenced before him. He received from the prætor a written formula instructing him as to the legal principles according to which the action was to be judged. Calvin. Hence the proceedings before him were said to be *in judicio,* as those before the prætor were said to be *in jure.* A judge who conducted the trial from beginning to end; *magistratus.*

The practice of calling in *judices* was disused before Justinian's time: therefore, in the Code, Institutes, and Novels, *judex* means judge in its modern sense. Heineccius, Elem. Jur.Civ. § 1327. The term *judex* is used with very different significations at different periods of Roman law.

In later and modern Civil law. A judge in the modern sense of the term.

In old English law. A juror. A judge, in modern sense, especially—as opposed to *justiciarius, i. e.,* a common-law judge—to denote an ecclesiastical judge. Bract. fols. 401, 402.

JUDEX A QUO. In modern civil law. The judge *from* whom, as *judex ad quem* is the judge *to* whom, an appeal is made or taken. Halifax, Civil Law, b. 3, c. 11, no. 34.

JUDEX AD QUEM. A judge to whom an appeal is taken.

JUDEX ÆQUITATEM SEMPER SPECTARE DEBET. A judge ought always to regard equity. Jenk. Cent. p. 45, case 85.

JUDEX ANTE OCULOS ÆQUITATEM SEMPER HABERE DEBET. A judge ought always to have equity before his eyes. Jenk. Cent. p. 58.

JUDEX BONUS NIHIL EX ARBITRIO SUO FACIAT, NEO PROPOSITO DOMESTICÆ VOLUNTATIS, SED JUXTA LEGES ET JURA PRONUNCIET. A good judge should do nothing of his own arbitrary will, nor on the dictate of his personal inclination, but should decide according to law and justice. 7 Coke, 27*a.*

JUDEX DAMNATUR CUM NOCENS ABSOLVITUR. The judge is condemned when a guilty person escapes punishment.

JUDEX DATUS. In Roman law. A judge given, that is, assigned or appointed, by the prætor to try a cause.

JUDEX DEBET JUDICARE SECUNDUM ALLEGATA ET PROBATA. The judge ought to decide according to the allegations and the proofs.

JUDEX DELEGATUS. A delegated judge; a special judge.

JUDEX EST LEX LOQUENS. A judge is the law speaking, [the mouth of the law.] 7 Coke, 4*a.*

JUDEX FISCALIS. A fiscal judge; one having cognizance of matters relating to the *fiscus,* (*q. v.*).

JUDEX HABERE DEBET DUOS SALES,—SALEM SAPIENTIÆ, NE SIT INSIPIDUS; ET SALEM CONSCIENTIÆ, NE SIT DIABOLUS. A judge should have two salts,—the salt of wisdom, lest he be insipid [or foolish]; and the salt of conscience, lest he be devilish. 3 Inst. 147; Bart. Max. 189.

JUDEX NON POTEST ESSE TESTIS IN PROPRIA CAUSA. A judge cannot be a witness in his own cause. 4 Inst. 279.

JUDEX NON POTEST INJURIAM SIBI DATAM PUNIRE. A judge cannot punish a wrong done to himself. See 12 Coke, 114.

JUDEX NON REDDIT PLUS QUAM QUOD PETENS IPSE REQUIRIT. A judge does not give more than what the complaining party himself demands. 2 Inst. 286.

JUDEX ORDINARIUS. In the civil law. An ordinary judge; one who had the right of hearing and determining causes as a matter of his own proper jurisdiction, (*ex propria jurisdictione,*) and not by virtue of a delegated authority. Calvin. According to Blackstone judices ordinarii determined only questions of fact. 3 Bl.Comm. 315.

JUDEX PEDANEUS. In Roman law. Inferior judge; deputy judge. The judge who was commissioned by the prætor to hear a cause was socalled, from the low seat which he anciently occupied at the foot of the prætor's tribunal.

JUDEX QUÆSTIONIS. A magistrate who decided the law of a criminal case, when the *prœtor* himself did not sit as a magistrate. Morey, Rom. L. 88. The director of the criminal court under the presidency of the *prœtor.* Harper's Lat. Dict.; Cic. Brut. 76, 264.

JUDEX SELECTUS. A select or selected *judex* or judge. The judges in criminal suits selected by the *prœtor.* Harper's Lat.Dict.; Cic.Verr. 2, 2, 13, § 32. These *judices selecti* were used in criminal causes, and between them and modern *jurors* many points of resemblance have been noticed; 3 Bla.Comm. 366.

JUDGE. An officer so named in his commission, who presides in some court; a public officer, appointed to preside and to administer the law in a court of justice; the chief member of a court, and charged with the control of proceedings and the decision of questions of law or discretion. Todd v. U. S., 15 S.Ct. 889, 158 U.S. 278, 39 L.Ed. 982; Foot v. Stiles, 57 N.Y. 405; State v. Le Blond, 108 Ohio St. 126, 140 N.E. 510, 512. A public officer who, by virtue of his office, is clothed with judicial authority. State ex rel. Mayer v. City of Cincinnati, 60 Ohio App. 119, 19 N.E.2d 902. Presiding officer of court. State v. Horn, 336 Mo. 524, 79 S.W.2d 1044, 1045. Any officer authorized to function as or for judge in doing specified acts. In re Roberts' Estate, 49 Cal.App.2d 71, 120 P.2d 933, 937.

The term is sometimes held to include all officers appointed to decide litigated questions while acting in that capacity, including justices of the peace, and even jurors who are judges of the facts; Com. v. Dallas, 4 Dall. 229, 1 L.Ed. 812; In re Hess, 20 N.J.Misc. 12, 23 A.2d 298, 300, 301; Webster v. Boyer, 81 Or. 485, 159 P. 1166, Ann.Cas. 1918D, 988; but see, contra, Alcorn v. Fellows, 102 Conn. 22, 127 A. 911, 915; Vollmer v. Board of Com'rs of Dubois County, 53 Ind.App. 149, 101 N.E. 321, 322. In ordinary legal use, however, the term is limited to the sense of the first of the definitions here given, People v. Wilson, 15 Ill. 388; and it has been held that a surrogate is not a "judge" within a statute providing for additional compensation to a judge for his services in drawing jurors, People ex rel. Noble v. Mitchel, 170 App.Div. 379, 155 N.Y.S. 660, 662; nor are United States commissioners judges, although they at times act in a quasi judicial capacity and exercise the power of a court, in so far as an act of Congress has conferred specific authority or imposed the performance of a special duty, United States v. Jones, D.C.N.Y., 230 F. 262, 264.

As used in Chandler Act, means the judge of court of bankruptcy. London v. O'Dougherty, C.C.A.2, 102 F.2d 524, 525; Dickinson Industrial Site v. Cowan, Ill., 309 U.S. 382, 60 S.Ct. 595, 597, 84 L.Ed. 819. As used in statute authorizing introduction in criminal proceeding of a writing written for purpose of comparison under supervision of a judge, means judge of a court of record, and does not include a justice. State v. Shade, 119 W.Va. 600, 195 S.E. 338.

"Judge" and "court" are often synonymous or interchangeable. In re Slattery, 310 Mich. 458, 17 N.W.2d 251, 259; Commonwealth v. Shawell, 325 Pa. 497, 191 A. 17, 19, but see holding that a judge is not a court, State ex rel. Mayer v. City of Cincinnati, 60 Ohio App. 119, 19 N.E.2d 902.

"Judge" and "justice" *(q. v.)* are often used in substantially the same sense.

JUDGE ADVOCATE. An officer of a court-martial, whose duty is to swear in the other members of the court, to advise the court, and to act as the public prosecutor; but he is also so far the counsel for the prisoner as to be bound to protect him from the necessity of answering criminating questions, and to object to leading questions when propounded to other witnesses.

JUDGE ADVOCATE GENERAL. The adviser of the government in reference to courts-martial and other matters of military law. In England, he is generally a member of the house of commons and of the government for the time being.

JUDGE DE FACTO. One who holds and exercises the office of a judge under color of lawful authority and by a title valid on its face, though he has not full right to the office, as where he was appointed under an unconstitutional statute, or by an usurper of the appointing power, or has not taken the oath of office. State v. Miller, 111 Mo. 542, 20 S.W. 243; Walcott v. Wells, 21 Nev. 47, 24 P. 367, 9 L.R.A. 59, 37 Am.St.Rep. 478; Dredla v. Baache, 60 Neb. 655, 83 N.W. 916; Caldwell v. Barrett, 71 Ark. 310, 74 S.W. 748.

In Missouri, a special judge is a "judge de facto". State ex rel. McGaughey v. Grayston, 349 Mo. 700, 163 S.W.2d 335, 337.

JUDGE-MADE LAW. A phrase used to indicate judicial decisions which construe away the meaning of statutes, or find meanings in them the legislature never intended. It is sometimes used as meaning, simply, the law established by judicial precedent. Cooley, Const.Lim., 4th ed. 70, note.

JUDGE ORDINARY. By St. 20 & 21 Vict. c. 85, § 9, the judge of the court of probate was made judge of the court for divorce and matrimonial causes created by that act, under the name of the "judge ordinary."

In Scotland, the title "judge ordinary" is applied to all those judges, whether supreme or inferior, who, by the nature of their office, have a fixed and determinate jurisdiction in all actions of the same general nature, as contradistinguished from the old Scotch privy council, or from those judges to whom some special matter is committed; such as commissioners for taking proofs, and messengers at arms. Bell.

JUDGE PRO TEMPORE. One appointed for the term or some part thereof, during which time he exercises all the functions of the regular judge. State ex rel. Hodshire v. Bingham, 218 Ind. 490, 33 N.E.2d 771, 134 A.L.R. 1126.

JUDGER. A Cheshire juryman. Jacob.

JUDGE'S CERTIFICATE. In English practice. A certificate, signed by the judge who presided at the trial of a cause, that the party applying is entitled to costs. In some cases, this is a necessary preliminary to the taxing of costs for such party. A statement of the opinion of the court, signed by the judges, upon a question of law submitted to them by the chancellor for their decision. See 3 Bl.Comm. 453.

JUDGE'S MINUTES, OR NOTES. Memoranda usually taken by a judge, while a trial is proceeding, of the testimony of witnesses, of documents offered or admitted in evidence, of offers of evidence, and whether it has been received or rejected, and the like matters.

JUDGE'S ORDER. An order made by a judge at chambers, or out of court.

JUDGMENT. A sense of knowledge sufficient to comprehend nature of transaction. Thomas v. Young, 57 App.D.C. 282, 22 F.2d 588, 590.

An opinion or estimate. McClung Const. Co. v. Muncy, Tex.Civ.App., 65 S.W.2d 786, 790.

The conclusion in a syllogism having for its major and minor premises issues raised by the pleadings and the proofs thereon. Barlow v. Scott, Mo.Sup., 85 S.W.2d 504, 517.

The formation of an opinion or notion concerning some thing by exercising the mind upon it.

Cleveland Clinic Foundation v. Humphrys, C.C.A. Ohio, 97 F.2d 849, 857.

The official and authentic decision of a court of justice upon the respective rights and claims of the parties to an action or suit therein litigated and submitted to its determination. People v. Hebel, 19 Colo.App. 523, 76 P. 550; Bullock v. Bullock, 52 N.J.Eq. 561, 30 A. 676, 27 L.R.A. 213, 46 Am.St.Rep. 528; State v. Brown & Sharpe Mfg. Co., 18 R.I. 16, 25 A. 246, 17 L.R.A. 856.

Also it is, or may mean, adjudication, Horner v. Nerlinger, 304 Mich. 225, 7 N.W.2d 281, 284; Samuel Goldwyn, Inc., v. United Artists Corporation, C.C.A.Del., 113 F.2d 703, 706; Sutton v. Rhodes, 205 Iowa 227, 217 N.W. 626, 628; affirmance by court of compensation award. Lenon v. Standard Oil Co., 134 Kan. 289, 5 P.2d 853, 854; conclusion of law upon facts found or admitted by the parties or upon their default in the course of the suit. Tidd.Pr. 930; Ross v. C. D. Mallory Corporation, 37 A.2d 766, 768, 132 N.J.L. 1; Bell v. State Industrial Accident Commission, 157 Or. 653, 74 P.2d 55, 57; Siddall v. Jansen, 143 Ill. 537, 32 N.E. 384; conclusion that naturally follows from the premises of law and fact. Branch v. Branch, 5 Fla. 450; In re Sedgely Ave., 88 Pa. 513; debt which a court of law finds to be due and orders to be paid, Truscon Steel Co. of Canada, Limited, v. Biegler, 306 Ill.App. 180, 28 N.E.2d 623, 625; decision or determination on issues in any proceeding at law, Schmeizl v. Schmeizl, 184 Md. 584, 42 A.2d 106, 112; decision or sentence of the law, given by a court of justice or other competent tribunal, as the result of proceedings instituted therein, 3 Bla.Com. 395; Aetna Ins. Co. v. Swift, 12 Minn. 327 (Gil. 326); Allegheny County v. Maryland Casualty Co., C.C.A.Pa., 132 F.2d 894, 897; State v. Siglea, 196 Wash. 283, 82 P.2d 583, 584; decision or sentence of the law pronounced by the court and entered upon its docket, minutes or record, Clark v. State, 72 Ga. App. 603, 34 S.E.2d 608, 613; decision or sentence of the law pronounced by court or other competent tribunal upon the matter in record, Reed v. Howbert, C.C.A.Colo., 77 F. 2d 227, 228; Commonwealth ex rel. Kelley v. Brown, 527 Pa. 136, 193 A. 258, 260; determination of a court of competent jurisdiction upon matters submitted to it. State ex rel. Curran v. Brookes, 142 Ohio St. 107, 50 N.E.2d 995, 998; determination or sentence of the law, pronounced by a competent judge or court, as the result of an action or proceeding instituted in such court, affirming that, upon the matters submitted for its decision, a legal duty or liability does or does not exist, 1 Black, Judgm. § 1; Gunter v. Earnest, 68 Ark. 180, 56 S.W. 876; Danner v. Walker-Smith Co., Tex.Civ.App., 154 S.W. 295, 298; State v. King, 18 Wash.2d 747, 140 P.2d 283, 286; final determination of "any action or proceeding", Dahmen v. Gregory, 184 Misc. 724, 55 N.Y.S.2d 311, 313; final determination of rights of the parties in an action or proceeding, State v. McNichols, 62 Idaho 616, 115 P.2d 104, 107; California Machinery & Supply Co. v. University City Syndicate, Inc., 3 Cal.App.2d 425, 39 P.2d 853; Elliott v. Elliott, 154 Kan. 145, 114 P.2d 823, 825; final determination or action of the court. El Centro Grain Co. v. Bank of Italy Nat. Trust & Savings Ass'n, 123 Cal.App. 564, 11 P.2d 650, 651; Jackson v. Slaughter, Tex.Civ.App., 185 S.W.2d 759, 761; State ex rel. McDonald v. Lollis, 326 Mo. 644, 33 S.W.2d 98, 100; first order containing all necessary recitals which with finality dispose of cause, In re McLeod's Estate, 143 Or. 233, 21 P. 2d 1084; formal expression and evidence of the actual decision of a lawsuit, Gossman v. Gossman, 52 Cal.App.2d 184, 126 P.2d 178, 185; judicial determination of guilt based upon a verdict or a plea of guilty, People v. La Sasso, 182 Misc. 538, 44 N.Y.S.2d 93, 97; judicial determination or sentence of the court upon a matter within its jurisdiction, United States v. Hark, Mass., 320 U.S. 531, 64 S.Ct. 359, 360, 361, 88 L.Ed. 290; Schmeizl v. Schmeizl, 184 Md. 584, 42 A.2d 106, 112; law's last word in a judicial controversy, Pierce v. Pierce, 97 Colo. 39, 46 P.2d 748, 749; People ex rel. Toman v. Crane, 372 Ill. 228, 23 N.E.2d 337, 339; obligation especially of a debt created by decision or decree of court, Truscon Steel Co. of Canada, Limited, v. Biegler, 306 Ill.App. 180, 28 N.E.2d 623, 625; pronouncement by court from the bench, Walden v. Hudspeth, C.C.A.Kan., 115 F.2d 558, 559; pronouncement of judge, Bell Grocery v. Booth, 250 Ky. 1, 61 S.W.2d 879; Wilson v. Bell, C.C.A. Tenn., 137 F.2d 716, 720; record in the book, not the instrument typewritten and signed by the clerk, Groth v. Ness, 65 N.D. 580, 260 N.W. 700; sentence in criminal case, Attorney General ex rel. O'Hara v. Montgomery, 275 Mich. 504, 267 N.W. 550, 554; Moore v. Thorn, 154 Misc. 136, 277 N.Y.S. 544; Commonwealth v. Trunk, 320 Pa. 270, 182 A. 540, 541; sentence of the law on ultimate facts admitted by pleadings or proved by evidence, Kansas City Life Ins. Co. v. Anthony, 142 Kan. 670, 52 P.2d 1208, 1211, 104 A.L.R. 364; what the court pronounces, Corbett v. Rankin Independent School Dist., Tex.Civ.App., 100 S.W.2d 113, 115; De Leon v. Texas Employers Ins. Ass'n, Tex.Civ.App., 159 S.W.2d 574, 575.

The term "judgment" is also used to denote the reason which the court gives for its decision; but this is more properly denominated an "opinion."

A decree is a judgment. Fuller v. Fuller, 49 R.I. 45, 139 A. 662, 663; Knettle v. Knettle, 190 Wash. 395, 68 P.2d 218, 220; Spartan Mills v. Law, 186 S.C. 61, 194 S.E. 653, 655; National Surety Co. v. Mulligan, 105 N.J.L. 336, 146 A. 372, 375. As used in some statutes, judgment and decree are synonymous. Finnell v. Finnell, 113 Okl. 269, 230 P. 912, 913; Kline v. Murray, 79 Mont. 530, 257 P. 465, 467; Weeden v. Weeden, 116 Ohio St. 524, 156 N.E. 908, 909.

An allowance or disallowance of a claim may be a judgment. United States v. Paisley, D.C.Ill., 26 F.Supp. 237, 238; In re Hiller's Estate, 171 Or. 428, 137 P.2d 828, 830; State ex rel. Spellman v. Commercial State Bank of Omaha, 143 Neb. 490, 10 N.W.2d 268.

An award may be in the nature of, or equivalent of, a judgment. Traders & General Ins. Co. v. Baker, Tex.Civ. App., 111 S.W.2d 837, 839, 840; Holliday v. Salling, 54 Ariz. 496, 97 P.2d 221, 223, 126 A.L.R. 145; Wisconsin Compensation Bureau v. Mortensen, 227 Wis. 335, 277 N.W. 679, 684; Detroit Trust Co. v. Van Wagoner, 295 Mich. 449, 295 N.W. 222, 223.

An entry on court record may constitute a judgment. Nichols v. Chandler, Ohio App., 61 N.E.2d 239, 240.

An order may be a judgment: Compensation proceeding. Truax-Traer Coal Co. v. Compensation Com'r, 123 W. Va. 621, 17 S.E.2d 330, 334; Traders & General Ins. Co. v. Baker, Tex.Civ.App., 111 S.W.2d 837, 839, 840; State v. Thierfelder, 114 Mont. 104, 132 P.2d 1035, 1037; State v. McNichols, 62 Idaho 552, 115 P.2d 104, 107; Baumgartner v. United States, C.C.A.Mo., 138 F.2d 29, 33.

Commitment to institution, etc., as a judgment, People ex rel. McCarthy v. Snyder, Sup., 54 N.Y.S.2d 40, 41; Ex parte Herrera, 143 P.2d 345, 349, 23 Cal.2d 206.

The words "decision" and "judgment" may be used interchangeably. Smith v. State, 196 Ga. 595, 27 S.E.2d 369, 373; Gutierrez v. Brady, 45 N.M. 209, 113 P.2d 585, 587; but in a different context may not be synonymous. Mennel Milling Co. v. Slosser, 140 Ohio St. 445, 45 N.E.2d 306, 308. They are not the same thing under federal rules. Winkelman v. General Motors Corporation, D.C.N.Y., 48 F.Supp. 490, 494. A written decision that finally determines rights of parties is a "judgment". Zbikowski v. Straz, 236 Wis. 161, 294 N.W. 541, 543. Decisions by Secretary of the Interior on matters relating to public lands are equivalent of a "judgment" of a court. Elliott v. Thompson, 63 Idaho 395, 120 P.2d 1014, 1022. Decisions of administrative boards are not "judgments". Dal Maso v. Board of Com'rs of Prince George's County, 182 Md. 200, 34 A.2d 464, 466. The decision of the court, when filed, amounts to rendition of judgment. Lind v. Baker, 48 Cal.App.2d 234, 119 P.2d 806, 812.

To constitute act of bankruptcy, "judgment" suffered by debtor must be one that has become lien and, as such, a legal preference. Elkay Reflector Corporation v. Savory, Inc., C.C.A.N.Y., 57 F.2d 161, 162.

Judgments, considered with regard to the method of obtaining them, may be classified as follows.

Admission of facts by the parties, leaving only issues of law to be determined. Such judgments are: judgment upon a demurrer; judgment on a case stated; judgment on a general verdict subject to a special case; judgment on a special verdict.

Admissions or confessions of one only of the parties; judgments based on. Such judgments when for defendant upon the admissions of the plaintiff are: judgment of nolle prosequi; judgment of retraxit; judgment on leave of court to discontinue; a stet processus. Judgments for the plaintiff upon facts admitted by the defendant are: judgment by cognovit actionem; cognovit or confession.

Trial of an issue of fact. Judgments upon facts found are: Judgment of nul tiel record; judgment upon verdict; judgment non obstante veredicto; judgment of repleader.

Alternative judgment. One that by its terms might be satisfied by doing either of several acts at the election of the party or parties against whom the judgment is rendered and from whom performance is by the judgment required. Henderson v. Arkansas, 71 Okl. 253, 176 P. 751, 754. A judgment for one thing or another which does not specifically and in a definitive manner determine the rights of the parties. State v. Wilson, 216 N.C. 130, 4 S.E.2d 440, 442.

Assets in futuro, judgment of. One against an executor or heir, who holds at the time no property on which it can operate. See Quando Acciderint.

Case stated, judgment on. It sometimes happens that though the adverse parties are agreed as to the facts, and only differ as to the law arising out of them, still these facts do not so clearly appear on the pleadings as to enable them to obtain the opinion of the court by way of *demurrer;* for on demurrer the court can look at nothing whatever except the pleadings. In such circumstances the statute 3 & 4 Will. IV. c. 42, § 25, which has been imitated in most of the states, allows them after issue joined, and on obtaining the consent of a single judge, to state the facts in a *special case* for the opinion of the court, and agree that a judgment shall be entered for the plaintiff or defendant by *confession* or *nolle prosequi* immediately after the decision of the case; and judgment is entered accordingly, called judgment on a case stated.

Cassetur breve or billa, judgment of (that the writ or bill be quashed) is a judgment rendered in favor of a party pleading in abatement to a writ or action. Steph.Pl. 130, 131.

Cognovit. See Cognovit.

Cognovit actionem. See Cognovit Actionem.

Conditional judgment. One whose force depends upon the performance of certain acts to be done in the future by one of the parties; as, one which may become of no effect if the defendant appears and pleads according to its terms, or one which orders the sale of mortgaged property in a foreclosure proceeding unless the mortgagor shall pay the amount decreed within the time limited. Mahoney v. New South Building & Loan Ass'n, C.C.Va., 70 F. 513; Simmons v. Jones, 118 N.C. 472, 24 S.E. 114.

Confession. At common law, judgment entered where defendant, instead of entering plea, confessed action, or withdrew plea and confessed action. Information Buying Co. v. Miller, 173 Ga. 786, 161 S.E. 617, 618. Judgment where a defendant gives the plaintiff a cognovit or written confession of the action by virtue of which the plaintiff enters judgment. The act of a debtor in permitting judgment to be entered against him by his creditor, for a stipulated sum, by a written statement to that effect or by warrant of attorney, without the institution of legal proceedings of any kind; voluntary submission to court's jurisdiction. O'Hara v. Manley, 140 Pa.Super. 39, 12 A.2d 820, 822.

Consent judgment. A judgment, the provisions and terms of which are settled and agreed to by the parties to the action. Hargis v. Hargis, 252 Ky. 198, 66 S.W.2d 59; Andrews v. Indemnity Ins. Co. of North America, 55 R.I. 341, 181 A. 403; Matthews v. Looney, 132 Tex. 313, 123 S.W.2d 871, 872.

It is not the judgment of the court, it is the agreement of the parties, entered upon the record with the sanction and approval of the court, and is their act rather than that of the court. Andrews v. Indemnity Ins. Co. of North America, 55 R.I. 341, 181 A. 403; Cason v. Shutte, 211 N.C. 195, 189 S.E. 494, 495.

Consent judgments are, in effect, merely contracts acknowledged in open court and ordered to be recorded, but as such they bind the parties as fully as do other judgments. Prince v. Frost-Johnson Lumber Co., Tex.Civ.App., 250 S.W. 785, 789; Belcher v. Cobb, 169 N.C. 689, 86 S.E. 600, 602.

Contradictory judgment. A judgment which has been given after the parties have been heard, either in support of their claims or in their defense. Cox's Ex'rs v. Thomas, 11 La. 366.

It is used in Louisiana to distinguish such judgments from those rendered by default.

De melioribus damnis. See De Melioribus Damnis.

Default and inquiry, judgment by. It establishes right of action of kind properly pleaded in complaint, determines right of plaintiff to recover at least nominal damages and costs, and precludes defendant from offering any evidence on execution of inquiry to show that plaintiff has no right of action. De Hoff v. Black, 206 N.C. 687, 175 S.E. 179.

Default final, judgment by. It establishes allegations of complaint and concludes by way of estoppel. De Hoff v. Black, 206 N.C. 687, 175 S.E. 179.

Default judgment. A judgment rendered in consequence of the non-appearance of the defendant. Beard v. Sovereign Lodge, W. O. W., 184 N.C. 154, 113 S.E. 661; In re Smith, 38 Idaho, 746, 225 P. 495, 496; Brame v. Nolen, 139 Va. 413, 124 S.E. 299, 301. One entered upon the failure of a party to appear or plead at the appointed time. The term is also applied to judgments entered under statutes or rules of court, for want of affidavit of defense, plea, answer, and the like, or for failure to take some required step in the cause.

Judgments rendered on defendant's default are: Judgment *by default;* judgment by *non sum informatus;* judgment *nil dicit.* Judgments rendered on plaintiff's default are: Judgment of *non pros.* (from *non prosequitur)* and judgment of *nonsuit* (from *non sequitur,* or *ne suit pas).*

Deficiency judgment. See Deficiency.

Demurrer, judgment on. Concludes party demurring, because by demurring, a party admits the facts alleged in the pleadings of his adversary and relies on their insufficiency in law. See Demurrer.

Discontinuance. A "judgment of discontinuance" is one of dismissal of plaintiff's action based on interruption in proceedings occasioned by failure of plaintiff to continue suit regularly from time to time as he ought. Steele v. Beaty, 215 N.C. 680, 2 S.E.2d 854, 855.

A plaintiff sometimes, when he finds he has misconceived his action, obtains leave from the court to discontinue, on which there is a judgment against him and he has to pay costs; but he may commence a new action for the same cause.

Dismissal, judgment of. See Dismissal.

Domestic judgment. A judgment is *domestic* in the courts of the same state or country where it was originally rendered; in other states or countries it is called *foreign.* The federal court sitting for the state is a domestic court, and its judgments within the scope of its jurisdiction are domestic judgments. Louisville & N. R. Co. v. Tally, 203 Ala. 370, 83 So. 114, 117.

Dormant judgment. One which has not been satisfied or extinguished by lapse of time, but which has remained so long unexecuted that execution cannot now be issued upon it without first reviving the judgment. Draper v. Nixon, 93 Ala. 436, 8 So. 489; General Electric Co. v. Hurd, C.C.Or., 171 F. 984; Burlington State Bank v. Marlin Nat. Bank, Tex.Civ.App., 207 S.W. 954, 956. Or one which has lost its lien on land from the failure to issue execution on it or take other steps to enforce it within the time limited by statute. 1 Black, Judgm. (2d Ed.) § 462.

Error, judgment in. A judgment rendered by a court of error on a record sent up from an inferior court.

It is either in affirmance of the former judgment; in recall of it for error in fact; in reversal of it for error in law; that the plaintiff be barred of his writ of error, where a plea of release of errors or of the statute of limitations is found for the defendant; or that there be a *venire facias de novo,* which is an award of a new trial.

Execution of judgment. See Execution of Judgment or Decree.

Face of judgment. See Face of Judgment.

Final judgment. One which puts an end to a suit or action.

One which puts an *end* to an action at law by declaring that the plaintiff either has or has not entitled himself to recover the remedy he sues for. 3 Bl.Comm. 398; Frank P. Miller Paper Co. v. Keystone Coal & Coke Co., 275 Pa. 40, 118 A. 565, 566. So distinguished from *interlocutory* judgments, which merely establish the right of the plaintiff to recover, in general terms. Id. 397. A judgment which determines a particular cause. Bostwick v. Brinkerhoff, 106 U.S. 3, 1 S.Ct. 15, 27 L.Ed. 73; Pfeiffer v. Crane, 89 Ind. 487; Nelson v. Brown, 59 Vt. 601, 10 A. 721. A judgment which cannot be appealed from, which is perfectly conclusive upon the matter adjudicated. Snell v. Cotton Gin Mfg. Co., 24 Pick., Mass., 300; Foster v. Neilson, 2 Pet. 294, 7 L.Ed. 415; Forgay v. Conrad, 6 How. 201, 12 L.Ed. 404; State v. Harmon, 87 Ohio St. 364, 101 N.E. 286, 288. A judgment which disposes of the subject-matter of the controversy or determines the litigation as to all parties on its merits. Lamberton v. McCarthy, 30 Idaho, 707, 168 P. 11; Sanders v. May, 173 N.C. 47, 91 S.E. 526, 527; France & Canada S. S. Co. v. French Republic, C.C.A. N.Y., 285 F. 290, 294; Judson Lumber Co. v. Patterson, 68 Fla. 100, 66 So. 727, 728; Miller v. Farmers State Bank & Trust Co., Tex.Civ.App., 241 S.W. 540, 541. A judgment which terminates all litigation on the same right. For meaning of "final judgment", in the judiciary act of 1789, § 25, see 1 Kent., Comm. 316; Weston v. Charleston, 2 Pet. 494, 7 L.Ed. 481; Forgay v. Conrad, 6 How. 201, 209, 12 L.Ed. 404.

Foreign judgment. One rendered by the courts of a state or country politically and judicially distinct from that where the judgment or its effect is brought in question. One pronounced by a tribunal of a foreign country, or of a sister state. Karns v. Kunkle, 2 Minn. 313, Gil. 268; Gulick v. Loder, 13 N.J.L. 68, 23 Am.Dec. 711; Grover & B. Sewing Mach. Co. v. Radcliffe, 137 U.S. 287, 11 S. Ct. 92, 34 L.Ed. 670.

General verdict subject to a special case, judgment on. Where at the trial the parties agree on the facts and the only question is one of law and a verdict pro forma is taken and the jury find for the plaintiff generally but subject to the opinion of the court on a special case.

In personam or inter partes. See Judgment in Personam or Inter Partes.

In rem. See Judgment in Rem.

Interlocutory judgment. One given in the progress of a cause upon some plea, proceeding, or default which is only intermediate and does not finally determine or complete the suit. 3 Bl.Comm. 396. One which determines some preliminary or subordinate point or plea, or settles some step, question, or default arising in the progress of the cause, but does not adjudicate the ultimate rights of the parties, or finally put the case out of court. Thus, a judgment or order passed upon any provisional or accessory claim or contention is, in general, merely interlocutory, although it may finally dispose of that particular matter. 1 Black, Judgm. § 21; Hartford Fire Ins. Co. v. McDonald, 177 Ky. 838, 198 S.W. 225, 226; Frank P. Miller Paper Co. v. Keystone Coal & Coke Co., 275 Pa. 40, 118 A. 565, 566.

Junior judgment. One which was rendered or entered after the rendition or entry of another judgment, on a different claim, against the same defendant.

Merits, judgment on. One rendered after argument and investigation, and when it is determined which party is in the right, as distinguished from a judgment rendered upon some preliminary or formal or merely technical point, or by default and without trial. Bell Grocery Co. v. Booth, 250

Ky. 21, 61 S.W.2d 879; State ex rel. National Lead Co. v. Smith, Mo.App., 134 S.W.2d 1061, 1068.

Money judgment. One which adjudges the payment of a sum of money, as distinguished from one directing an act to be done or property to be restored or transferred. Fuller v. Aylesworth, Mich., 75 F. 694, 21 C.C.A. 505; Pendleton v. Cline, 85 Cal. 142, 24 P. 659.

Ordinary "judgment for money" merely determines amount due. State ex rel. Lang v. Superior Court for King County, 176 Wash. 472, 30 P.2d 237, 239.

Narr and cognovit, judgment on. Summons is unnecessary because maker of note authorizes appearance and waives summons. Schwartz v. Schwartz, 366 Ill. 247, 8 N.E.2d 668, 670, 112 A.L.R. 325.

Nihil dicit. See Nihil Dicit.

Nil capiat per breve or per billa (that he take nothing by his writ, or by his bill). A judgment in favor of the defendant upon an issue raised upon a declaration or peremptory plea.

Nil dicit, judgment by. One rendered where defendant fails to plead, or where, having pleaded, plea is stricken, withdrawn, or abandoned and no further defense is made. Grand Lodge Brotherhood of Railroad Trainmen v. Ware, Tex.Civ. App., 73 S.W.2d 1076, 1077; Reliance Equipment Co. v. Montgomery, 27 Ala.App. 539, 175 So. 703.

At common law, it may be taken against defendant who omits to plead or answer whole or any separable substantial portion of declaration. Clonts v. Spurway, 104 Fla. 340, 139 So. 896, 897. It amounts to judgment by confession with reference to cause of action stated, Grand Lodge Brotherhood of Railroad Trainmen v. Ware, Tex.Civ.App., 73 S.W.2d 1076, 1077. For judgment nihil dicit, see Nihil Dicit. Judgment rendered on plea of guilty is not judgment nil dicit, which is substantially identical with default judgment. Stevens v. State, 100 Vt. 214, 136 A. 387.

Nisi. At common law, judgment nisi was a judgment entered on the return of the nisi prius record, which, according to the terms of the postea indorsed thereon was to become absolute unless otherwise ordered by the court within the first four days of the next succeeding term. See U. S. v. Winstead, D.C.N.C., 12 F. 51; Young v. McPherson, 3 N.J.L. 897.

Nolle prosequi, judgment of. One entered against plaintiff when, after appearance and before judgment, he declares that he will not further prosecute his suit. Steph. Pl., Andr. Ed. § 97; Merchants Mut. Casualty Co. v. Kiley, 92 N.H. 323, 30 A.2d 681, 683.

Non obstante veredicto. See Non Obstante Veredicto.

Non pros (non prosequitur [he does not follow up, or pursue]). See Non Prosequitur.

Non sum informatus. See Non Sum Informatus.

Nonsuit. See Nonsuit.

Nul tiel record. See Nul Tiel Record.

Nunc pro tunc. One entered on a day subsequent to the time at which it should have been entered, as of the latter date. See Nunc Pro Tunc.

Personal judgment. One imposing on the defendant a personal liability to pay it, and which may therefore be satisfied out of any of his property which is within the reach of process, as distinguished from one which may be satisfied only out of a particular fund or the proceeds of particular property.

Thus, in a mortgage foreclosure suit, there may be a personal judgment against the mortgagor for any deficiency that may remain after the sale of the mortgaged premises. See Bardwell v. Collins, 44 Minn. 97, 46 N.W. 315, 9 L.R.A. 152.

Pocket judgment. A statute-merchant which was enforceable at any time after non-payment on the day assigned, without further proceedings. Wharton.

Pro retorno habendo. A judgment that the party have a return of the goods.

Quando acciderint. See Quando Acciderint.

Quod computet. See Quod Computet.

Quod partes replacitent. See Quod Partes Replacitent.

Quod partitio fiat. Interlocutory judgment in a writ of partition, that partition be made.

Quod recuperet. See Quod Recuperet.

Relicta verificatione. See Relicta Verificatione.

Repleader, judgment of. See Repleader.

Respondeat ouster. When the issue in law arises on a dilatory plea, and is determined for the plaintiff, the judgment is only that the defendant "do answer over," called a judgment of *respondeat ouster;* it is interlocutory only.

Retraxit. See Retraxit.

Special verdict, judgment on. Where *at the trial* the parties find that they agree on the facts and the only question is one of law and a verdict *pro forma* is taken, and the jury state the facts as they find them, concluding that the opinion of the court shall decide in whose favor the verdict shall be, and that they assess the damages accordingly.

Stet Processus. See Stet Processus.

Verdict, judgment on. The most usual of the judgments upon facts found, and is for the party obtaining the verdict.

Warrant of attorney. See Warrant.

JUDGMENT-BOOK. A book required to be kept by the clerk, among the records of the court, for the entry of judgments. In re Weber, 4 N.D. 119, 59 N.W. 523, 28 L.R.A. 621.

JUDGMENT CREDITOR. One who has obtained a judgment against his debtor, under which he can enforce execution. King v. Fraser, 23 S.C. 548; Baxter v. Moses, 77 Me. 465, 1 A. 350, 52 Am. Rep. 783; Chalmers & Williams v. Surprise, 70 Ind.App. 646, 123 N.E. 841, 844. Code Civ.Proc. N.Y.1899, § 3343 (Civ.Prac. Act, § 7). The owner of an unsatisfied judgment.

JUDGMENT DEBT. One which is evidenced by matter of record. Colonial Building-Loan Ass'n v. Mongiello Bros., 120 N.J.Eq. 270, 184 A. 635, 637. A debt, whether on simple contract or by specialty, for the recovery of which judgment has been entered up, either upon a *cognovit* or upon a warrant of attorney or as the result of a successful action. Brown.

JUDGMENT DEBTOR. A person against whom judgment has been recovered, and which remains unsatisfied. The term has been construed to include a judgment debtor's successors in interest. Bateman v. Kellogg, 59 Cal.App. 464, 211 P. 46, 51; but see, contra, Northwest Trust & Safe Deposit Co. v. Butcher, 98 Wash. 158, 167 P. 46, 47.

JUDGMENT DEBTOR SUMMONS. Under the English bankruptcy act, 1861, §§ 76–85, these summonses might be issued against both traders and non-traders, and, in default of payment of, or security or agreed composition for, the debt, the debtors might be adjudicated bankrupt. This act was repealed by 32 & 33 Vict. c. 83, § 20. The 32 & 33 Vict. c. 71, however, (bankruptcy act, 1869,) provides (section 7) for the granting of a "debtor's summons," at the instance of creditors, and, in the event of failure to pay or compound, a petition for adjudication may be presented, unless in the events provided for by that section. Wharton.

JUDGMENT DOCKET. A list or docket of the judgments entered in a given court, methodically kept by the clerk or other proper officer, open to public inspection, and intended to afford official notice to interested parties of the existence or lien of judgments.

JUDGMENT, ESTOPPEL BY. The estoppel raised by the rendition of a valid judgment by a court having jurisdiction. 2 Bl.Judgm. § 504; State v. Torinus, 28 Minn. 175, 9 N.W. 725. See, also, Verdict, Judgment By.

Final adjudication of any issue by court of competent jurisdiction binds parties and privies in any subsequent proceeding, irrespective of difference in forms or causes of action. Citizens' Loan & Trust Co. of Washington, Ind. v. Sanders, 99 Ind.App. 77, 187 N.E. 396, 398.

The essence of estoppel by judgment is that there has been a judicial determination of a fact. Price v. Clement, 187 Okl. 304, 102 P.2d 595, 597; Monteith Bros. Co. v. U. S., D.C.Ind., 48 F.Supp. 210, 212. It arises where a party litigant attempts to assume inconsistent and contradictory positions with respect to same matter. Elfman v. Glaser, 313 Mass. 370, 47 N.E.2d 925, 929. It rests upon principles forbidding one to relitigate matter in dispute between parties which has been determined by competent court, on ground that record of judgment imports absolute verity. Cauble v. Cauble, Tex.Civ.App., 2 S.W.2d 967, 970.

The doctrine extends to matters actually adjudicated, Hamlin v. Johns, 41 Ga.App. 91, 151 S.E. 815, 817; Penn Mut. Life Ins. Co. v. Childs, 189 Ga. 835, 7 S.E.2d 907; actually and necessarily included in judgment, MacDonnell v. Capital Co., C.C.A.Cal., 130 F.2d 311, 318; Panos v. Great Western Packing Co., Cal.App., 126 P.2d 889, 892; expressly or by necessary implication adjudicated, McKee v. Producers' & Refiners' Corporation, 170 Okl. 559, 41 P.2d 466, 469; necessarily adjudicated, Capps v. Toccoa Falls Light & Power Co., 46 Ga.App. 268, 167 S.E. 530, 532; Humble Oil & Refining Co. v. Webb, Tex.Civ.App., 177 S. W.2d 218, 223. It extends only to facts in issue as they existed at time judgment was rendered, Fort Worth Stockyards Co. v. Brown, Tex.Civ.App., 161 S.W.2d 549, 555. It extends to matters which might have been litigated in former case. Paine & Williams Co. v. Baldwin Rubber Co., C.C.A.Mich., 113 F.2d 840, 842, 843; Knabb v. Duner, 143 Fla. 92, 196 So. 456, 460. But it has been held that the doctrine does not apply where point at issue was not controverted in prior action but might have been. Haumesser v. Woodrich, 315 Ill.App. 475, 43 N.E.2d 193, 196; the estoppel does not extend to matter not directly in issue though it arose in case collaterally. Morrison v. Bank of Mount Hope, 124 W.Va. 478, 20 S.E.2d 790, 794.

Ordinarily, "estoppel" of judgment does not extend to matters not expressly adjudicated. Sonken-Galamba Corporation v. Atchison, T. & S. F. Ry. Co., C.C.A.Mo., 124 F.2d 952, 956; and a judgment or decree without prejudice does not work an "estoppel". In re McDermott, C.C.A. Ill., 115 F.2d 582, 584.

Elements or essentials are or may include former judgment between same parties or their privies. Postelneck v. Edbro Realty Co., 228 App.Div. 105, 239 N.Y.S. 173, 175; former judgment must relate to same question and must clearly decide it, First Nat. Bank of Atlanta v. Williams, 62 Ga.App. 203, 8 S.E.2d 562, 564, 565; former judgment on the merits, Stowers v. Harris, 194 Ga. 636, 22 S.E.2d 405, 408; Postelneck v. Edbro Realty Co., 228 App.Div. 105, 239 N.Y.S. 173, 175; identity of parties suing in same capacity, Ford v. Dania Lumber & Supply Co., 150 Fla. 435, 7 So.2d 594, 595; material facts necessary in arriving at conclusion must be properly in issue, Paine & Williams Co. v. Baldwin Rubber Co., C.C.A.Mich., 113 F.2d 840, 842, 843; matters litigated and determined in prior case must have been within scope of the pleadings, Slaughter v. Slaughter, 190 Ga. 229, 9 S.E.2d 70, 71, 129 A.L.R. 156; mutuality of estoppel, Stewart v. City of Springfield, 350 Mo. 234, 165 S.W.2d 626, 630; Elder v. New York & Pennsylvania Motor Express, 284 N.Y. 350, 31 N.E.2d 188, 189, 133 A.L.R. 176; precise facts or questions must have been determined by former judgment, Skolnik v. Petella, 376 Ill. 500, 34 N.E.2d 825, 826; Flint v. Kimbrough, 45 N.M. 342, 115 P.2d 84, 86; subsequent suit must be between same parties or their privies. Harris v. Jacksonville Paper Co., 67 Ga.App. 759, 21 S.E.2d 537, 541; Woods v. Duval, 151 Kan. 472, 99 P.2d 804, 808; substantial identity of parties, Curtis v. Maryland Baptist Union Ass'n, 176 Md. 430, 5 A.2d 836, 839, 121 A.L.R. 1516.

The estoppel may be based on consent judgment, Le Bire v. Department of Labor and Industries, 14 Wash.2d 407, 128 P.2d 308, 313; declaratory judgment, In re Patton's Estate, 170 Or. 186, 132 P.2d 402, 406; default judgment, Lawhorn v. Wellford, 179 Tenn. 625, 168 S.W.2d 790, 792; erroneous judgment regularly entered by court, Ex parte Young, 222 N.C. 708, 24 S.E.2d 539, 540; final judgment, Ramsey Tp., McCook County v. Lake County, 68 S.D. 67, 298 N.W. 356; final judgment in a criminal prosecution or proceeding, Ex parte Lewis, 152 Kan. 123, 102 P.2d 981, 982; judgment in rem, or quasi in rem, Saunders v. King, 69 Ohio App. 313, 37 N.E.2d 92, 93; judgment upon stipulation, Tillman v. National City Bank of New York, C.C.A.N.Y., 118 F.2d 631, 633, 634, 635; judgment upon the merits, Smith v. C. I. T. Corporation, 69 Ga.App. 516, 26 S.E.2d 146, 148; Fightmaster v. Tauber, 43 Ohio App. 266, 183 N.E. 116, 117.

When causes of action or claims or demands in prior and subsequent suits are different the estoppel exists with respect to matters actually decided and essential to or necessarily involved in judgment, Balcom v. Cain, Tex. Civ.App., 81 S.W.2d 827, 829; actually litigated, American Trust Co. v. Butler, C.C.A.Fla., 47 F.2d 482, 483; Vaughn's Adm'r v. Louisville & N. R. Co., 297 Ky. 309, 179 S.W.2d 441, 444, 152 A.L.R. 1060; common to both causes of action, McKee v. Producers' & Refiners' Corporation, 170 Okl. 559, 41 P.2d 466, 469; Guaranty Trust Co. of New York v. International Trust Co., 144 Misc. 127, 258 N.Y.S. 465; necessarily adjudicated, Bassick Mfg. Co. v. Larkin Automotive Parts Co., D.C.Ill., 23 F.2d 92, 94; McDowell v. Harris, Tex.Civ.App., 107 S.W.2d 647, 652.

Where subsequent proceeding is on same cause of action between same parties a former adjudication is conclusive. Kimpton v. Spellman, 351 Mo. 674, 173 S.W.2d 886, 891.

JUDGMENT EXECUTION. In the judgment on which it issues, it is a species of execution process, but as to the garnishee who becomes a party defendant therein it is an original process—a summons commanding him to appear and show cause, if any he has, why judgment in favor of the plaintiff should not be levied on the goods and effects of defendant in his hands. Shane v. Commercial Casualty Ins. Co., D.C.Pa., 48 F.Supp. 151, 156.

JUDGMENT IN PERSONAM OR INTER PARTES. A judgment against a particular person, as distinguished from a judgment against a thing or a right or *status*.

Judgments of the former class, though conclusive even against strangers, as to the fact of their rendition and the resultant legal consequences, are not binding as to the issues involved, except upon the parties and their privies, while judgments of the latter class are conclusive upon all the world. City of Huntsville v. Goodenrath, 13 Ala.App. 579, 68 So. 676, 680. See the title Judgment In Rem.

Decrees of divorce of other states recovered upon service by publication are not judgments in personam. Ball v. Cross, 106 Misc. 184, 174 N.Y.S. 259, 260.

JUDGMENT IN REM. An adjudication pronounced upon the status of some particular thing or subject matter. Perry v. Edmonds, 59 Nev. 60, 84 P.2d 711, 713; Consolidated Flour Mills Co. of Kansas v. Sayre Wholesale Grocer Co., 176 Okl. 482, 56 P.2d 781, 784; by a tribunal having competent authority. Booth v. Copley, 283 Ky. 23, 140 S.W.2d 662, 666. It is founded on proceeding instituted against or on some thing or subject matter whose status or condition is to be determined, McCormick v. Blaine, 345 Ill. 461, 178 N.E. 195, 197, 77 A.L.R. 1215; Eureka Building & Loan Ass'n v. Shultz, 139 Kan. 435, 32 P.2d 477, 480; or one brought to enforce a right in the thing itself, Federal Land Bank of Omaha v. Jefferson, 229 Iowa 1054, 295 N.W. 855, 857; Hobbs v. Lenon, 191 Ark. 509, 87 S.W.2d 6, 11. It operates directly upon the property. Federal Land Bank of Omaha v. Jefferson, 229 Iowa 1054, 295 N.W. 855, 857, 132 A.L.R. 1282; Hobbs v. Lenon, 191 Ark. 509, 87 S.W.2d 6, 11; Guild v. Wallis, 150 Or. 69, 40 P.2d 737, 742. It is a solemn declaration of the status of some person or thing. Jones v. Teat, Tex.Civ.App., 57 S.W.2d 617, 620. It is binding upon all persons in so far as their interests in the property are concerned. Federal Land Bank of Omaha v. Jefferson, 229 Iowa 1054, 295 N.W. 855, 857, 132 A.L.R. 1282. It is binding upon the world. Booth v. Copley, 283 Ky. 23, 140 S.W.2d 662, 666; Hobbs v. Lenon, 191 Ark. 509, 87 S.W.2d 6, 11.

Various definitions have been given of a judgment *in rem*, but all are criticised as either incomplete or comprehending too much.

"A very able writer says: 'The distinguishing characteristic of judgments *in rem* is that, wherever their obligation is recognized and enforced as against *any* person, it is equally recognized and enforced as against *all* persons.' It seems to us that the true definition of a 'judgment *in rem*' is 'an adjudication' against some person or thing, or upon the *status* of some subject-matter; which, wherever and whenever binding upon *any* person, is equally binding upon *all* persons." Bartero v. Real Estate Savings Bank, 10 Mo.App. 78.

In Pennoyer v. Neff, 95 U.S. 734, 24 L.Ed. 565, the court said: "It is true that, in a strict sense, a proceeding *in rem* is one taken directly against property, and has for its object the disposition of property, without reference to the title of individual claimants; but, in a larger and more general sense, the terms are applied to actions between parties, where the direct object is to reach and dispose of property owned by them, or of some interest therein. Such are cases commenced by attachment against the property of debtors, or instituted to partition real estate, foreclose a mortgage, or enforce a lien. So far as they affect property in this state, they are substantially proceedings *in rem* in the broader sense which we have mentioned."

JUDGMENT IN RETRAXIT. A "judgment" which is usually based upon and follows a settlement out of court, and like a judgment on the merits is a bar and estops plaintiff from again proceeding in another suit on same cause of action. Steele v. Beaty, 215 N.C. 680, 2 S.E.2d 854, 856, 857.

See Retraxit.

JUDGMENT LIEN. A lien binding the real estate of a judgment debtor, in favor of the holder of the judgment, and giving the latter a right to levy on the land for the satisfaction of his judgment to the exclusion of other adverse interests subsequent to the judgment. Ashton v. Slater, 19 Minn. 351 (Gil. 300); Shirk v. Thomas, 121 Ind. 147, 22 N.E. 976, 16 Am.St.Rep. 381; Jones v. Hall, 177 Va. 658, 15 S.E.2d 108, 111; right to subject land of judgment debtor to satisfaction of judgment, Jones v. Hall, 177 Va. 658, 15 S.E.2d 108, 110, 111.

JUDGMENT NOTE. A promissory note, embodying an authorization to any attorney, or to a designated attorney, or to the holder, or the clerk of the court, to enter an appearance for the maker and confess a judgment against him for a sum therein named, upon default of payment of the note. Sweeney v. Thickstun, 77 Pa. 131.

JUDGMENT OF BOARD OF DIRECTORS. Determination by corporate action. Du Bois v. Century Cement Products Co., 119 N.J.Eq. 472, 183 A. 188, 191.

JUDGMENT OF CONVICTION. Sentence in criminal case, entered in court's minutes. People v. Mellon, 261 App.Div. 400, 25 N.Y.S.2d 650, 651.

JUDGMENT OF HIS PEERS. A term of expression borrowed from Magna Charta and means trial by jury. Ex parte Wagner, 58 Okl.Cr. 161, 50 P.2d 1135, 1139. A trial by a jury of twelve men according to the course of the common law. Fetter v. Wilt, 46 Pa. 460; State v. Simons, 61 Kan. 752, 60 P. 1052; Newland v. Marsh, 19 Ill. 382.

JUDGMENT PAPER. In English practice. A sheet of paper containing an *incipitur* of the pleadings in an action at law, upon which final judgment is signed by the master. 2 Tidd, Pr. 930.

JUDGMENT RECORD. In English practice. A parchment roll, on which are transcribed the whole proceedings in the cause, deposited and filed of record in the treasury of the court, after signing of judgment. 3 Steph.Comm. 632. In American practice, the record is signed, filed, and docketed by the clerk.

Findings of fact and conclusions of law held part of "judgment record;" the phrases "judgment roll," "judgment record," and "face of the record" are synonymous. Permian Oil Co. v. Smith, 129 Tex. 413, 107 S.W.2d 564, 566, 111 A.L.R. 1152.

JUDGMENT ROLL. See Roll.

JUDGMENT RECOVERED. A plea by a defendant that the plaintiff has already recovered that which he seeks to obtain by his action. This was formerly a species of sham plea, often put in for the purpose of delaying a plaintiff's action.

JUDGMENT VOID ON ITS FACE. A judgment or order is "void on its face" when its invalidity is apparent upon inspection of judgment roll. Application of Behymer, 130 Cal.App. 200, 19 P.2d 829, 830.

JUDICANDUM EST LEGIBUS, NON EXEMPLIS. Judgment is to be given according to the laws, not according to examples or precedents. 4 Coke, 33*b*; 4 Bl.Comm. 405.

JUDICARE. Lat. In the civil and old English law. To judge; to decide or determine judicially; to give judgment or sentence.

JUDICATIO. Lat. In the civil law. Judging; the pronouncing of sentence after hearing a cause. Hallifax, Civil Law, b. 3, c. 8, no. 7.

JUDICATORES TERRARUM. Lat. Certain tenants in the county palatine of Chester, who were bound by their tenures to perform judicial functions.

In case of an erroneous judgment being given by them, the party aggrieved might obtain a writ of error out of Chancery, directing them to reform it. They then had a month to consider of the matter. If they declined to reform their judgment, the matter came on writ of error before the king's bench; and if the court of king's bench held the judgment to be erroneous they forfeited £100 to the crown by custom. Jenk.Cent. 71.

JUDICATORIES. The term as used designates that department of government which it was intended should interpret and administer the laws. In re Opinion of the Justices, 86 N.H. 597, 166 A. 640, 646.

JUDICATURE. The state or profession of those officers who are employed in administering justice; the judiciary.

A judicatory, tribunal, or court of justice.

Jurisdiction; the right of judicial action; the scope or extent of jurisdiction.

JUDICATURE ACTS (ENGLAND). The acts under which the present system of courts in England was organized and is continued.

The statutes of 36 & 37 Vict. c. 66, and 38 & 39 Vict. c. 77, which went into force November 1, 1875, with amendments in 1877, 40 & 41 Vict. c. 9; 1879, 42 & 43 Vict. c. 78; and 1881, 44 & 45 Vict. c. 68,—made most important changes in the organization of, and methods of procedure in, the superior courts of England, consolidating them together so as to constitute one supreme court of judicature, consisting of two divisions,—her majesty's high court of justice, having chiefly original jurisdiction; and her majesty's court of appeal, whose jurisdiction is chiefly appellate.

JUDICATURE ACTS (IRELAND). The act of 40 & 41 Vict. c. 57, which went into operation Jan. 1, 1878, established a supreme court of judicature in Ireland, under which acts and subsequent ones a system essentially similar in its constitution to that in England is in force.

JUDICES. Lat. Judges. See Judex.

JUDICES NON TENENTUR EXPRIMERE CAUSAM SENTENTIÆ SUÆ. Judges are not bound to explain the reason of their sentence. Jenk.Cent. 75.

JUDICES ORDINARII. Lat. Plural of *judex ordinarius* (*q. v.*).

JUDICES PEDANEI. Lat. Plural of *judex pedaneus* (*q. v.*).

JUDICES SELECTI. Lat. Plural of *judex selectus* (*q. v.*).

JUDICI OFFICIUM SUUM EXCEDENTI NON PARETUR. A judge exceeding his office (or jurisdiction) is not to be obeyed. Jenk.Cent. p. 139, case 84. Said of void judgments.

JUDICI SATIS PŒNA EST, QUOD DEUM HABET ULTOREM. It is punishment enough for a judge that he has God as his avenger. 1 Leon. 295.

JUDICIA; JUDICIA PUBLICA. Lat. In Roman law. Judicial proceedings; trials. *Judicia publica*, criminal trials. Dig. 48, 1. See, also, Judicium.

JUDICIA IN CURIA REGIS NON ADNIHILENTUR, SED STENT IN ROBORE SUO QUOUSQUE PER ERROREM AUT ATTINCTUM ADNULLENTUR. Judgments in the king's court are not to be annihilated, but to remain in force until annulled by error or attaint. 2 Inst. 539.

JUDICIA IN DELIBERATIONIBUS CREBRO MATURESCUNT, IN ACCELERATO PROCESSU NUNQUAM. Judgments frequently become matured by deliberations, never by hurried process or precipitation. 3 Inst. 210.

JUDICIA POSTERIORA SUNT IN LEGE FORTIORA. The later decisions are the stronger in law. 8 Coke, 97.

JUDICIA SUNT TANQUAM JURIS DICTA, ET PRO VERITATE ACCIPIUNTUR. Judgments are, as it were, the sayings of the law, and are received as truth. 2 Inst. 537.

JUDICIAL. Belonging to the office of a judge; as judicial authority.

Relating to or connected with the administration of justice; as a judicial officer.

Having the character of judgment or formal legal procedure; as a judicial act.

Proceeding from a court of justice; as a judicial writ, a judicial determination.

Involving the exercise of judgment or discretion; as distinguished from *ministerial*.

Of or pertaining or appropriate to the administration of justice, or courts of justice, or a judge thereof, or the proceedings therein; as, judicial power, judicial proceedings. State v. Freitag, 53 Idaho 726, 27 P.2d 68.

As to judicial "Confession," "Day," "Discretion," "Documents," "Estoppel," "Evidence," "Factor," "Mortgage," "Notice," "Process," "Record," "Sale," "Sequestration," and "Writ," see those titles.

As to quasi judicial, see Quasi Judicial.

JUDICIAL ACT. An act which involves exercise of discretion or judgment. State ex rel. Allen v. Rose, 123 Fla. 544, 167 So. 21, 24; In re McGarry, 380 Ill. 359, 44 N.E.2d 7, 10; Wicksel v. Cohen, 262 N.Y. 446, 187 N.E. 634, 635; Dovel v. Bertram, 184 Va. 19, 34 S.E.2d 369, 370.

It is also defined as an act by court or magistrate touching rights of parties or property brought before it or him by voluntary appearance, or by prior action of ministerial officers, Flournoy v. Jeffersonville, 17 Ind. 173, 79 Am.Dec. 468; Union Pac. R. Co. v. U. S., 99 U.S. 700, 761, 25 L.Ed. 496; United States v. Ward, C.C.A.Okl., 257 F. 372, 377; Board of Com'rs of Atoka County v. Cypert, 65 Okl. 168, 166 P. 195, 198; an act by member of judicial department in construing law or applying it to a particular state of facts, State ex rel. Tharel v. Board of Com'rs of Creek County, 188 Okl. 184, 107 P.2d 542, 549; an act of administrative board if it goes to determination of some right, protection of which is peculiar office of courts, Belk's Dept. Store v. Guilford County, 222 N.C. 441, 23 S.E.2d 897, 902; an act which imposes burdens or confers privileges according to finding of some person or body whether a general rule is applicable or according to discretionary judgment as to propriety, Stevens ex rel. Kuberski v. Haussermann, 113 N.J.L. 162, 172 A. 738, 741; an act which undertakes to determine a question of right or obligation or of property as foundation on which it proceeds, Pearson v. Reed, 6 Cal.App.2d 277, 44 P.2d 592, 597; determination of what the law is and what rights of parties are with reference to transactions already had or thing already done or happened, Nider v. Homan, 32 Cal.App.2d 11, 89 P.2d 136, 139; Nash v. Brooks, 251 App.Div. 616, 297 N.Y.S. 853, 855; State v. Ramirez, 34 Idaho 623, 203 P. 279, 282, 29 A.L.R. 297; the action of judge in trying a cause and rendering a decision, Application of Gleit, 178 Misc. 198, 33 N.Y.S.2d 629, 630, 631.

The act of an administrative or ministerial officer does not become judicial simply because it requires some discretion and judgment, but becomes judicial only when there is opportunity to be heard, and the production and weighing of evidence and a decision thereon. People ex rel. Argus Co. v. Hugo, 101 Misc. 48, 168 N.Y.S. 25, 27; Sweeney v. Young, 82 N.H. 159, 131 A. 155, 157, 42 A.L.R. 757.

Rendition or pronouncement of a judgment is a judicial act and entry thereof a ministerial act. Peoples Electric Co-op. v. Broughton, 191 Okl. 229, 127 P.2d 850, 853; O'Brien v. New York Edison Co., D.C.N.Y., 26 F.Supp. 290, 291; Bailer v. Dowd, 219 Ind. 624, 40 N.E.2d 325, 327. But if there are matters requiring exercise of court's discretion, entry of decree is judicial act. Stewart v. Superior Court in and for Los Angeles County, 3 Cal.App.2d 702, 40 P.2d 529.

JUDICIAL ACTION. An adjudication upon rights of parties who in general appear or are brought before tribunal by notice or process, and upon whose claims some decision or judgment is rendered. Southeastern Greyhound Lines v. Georgia Public Service Commission, 181 Ga. 75, 181 S.E. 834, 102 A.L.R. 517. Action of a court upon a cause, by hearing it, and determining what shall be adjudged or decreed between the parties, and with which is the right of the case. Rhode Island v. Massachusetts, 12 Pet. 718, 9 L.Ed. 1233; Kerosene Lamp Heater Co. v. Monitor Oil Stove Co., 41 Ohio St. 293. When an inferior officer or board is charged with an administrative act, the performance of which depends upon and requires the existence or ascertainment of facts, the investigation and determination of such facts is so-called judicial action. Austin v. Eddy, 41 S.D. 640, 172 N.W. 517, 518.

Every judicial action involves primary right of plaintiff and corresponding duty devolving on defendant, breach of such duty by defendant, remedial right and duty, and remedy itself. Vinson v. Graham, C.C.A.Okl., 44 F.2d 772, 777; Brice v. Glenn, 165 S.C. 509, 164 S.E. 302, 303; Radosevich v. Engle, 111 Mont. 504, 111 P.2d 299, 303.

JUDICIAL ADMISSION. See Admissions.

JUDICIAL AUTHORITY. The power and authority appertaining to the office of a judge; jurisdiction; the official right to hear and determine questions in controversy.

JUDICIAL BUSINESS. Such as involves the exercise of judicial power, or the application of the mind and authority of a court to some contested matter, or the conduct of judicial proceedings, as distinguished from such ministerial and other acts, incident to the progress of a cause, as may be performed by the parties, counsel, or officers of the court without application to the court or judge. See Heisen v. Smith, 138 Cal. 216, 71 P. 180, 94 Am.St.Rep. 39; Merchants' Nat. Bank v. Jaffray, 36 Neb. 218, 54 N.W. 258, 19 L.R.A. 316; State v. California Min. Co., 13 Nev. 214.

JUDICIAL CIRCUIT. As used in a state constitution, a term referring to the subdivisions of the state to each of which one judge shall be assigned to exercise therein the judicial power conferred by the constitution upon circuit courts. State v. Butler, 70 Fla. 102, 69 So. 771, 779.

JUDICIAL COGNIZANCE. Judicial notice, or knowledge upon which a judge is bound to act without having it proved in evidence.

JUDICIAL COMITY. Principle in accordance with which courts of one state or jurisdiction give effect to laws and judicial decisions of another state out of deference and respect, not obligation. Hartford Accident & Indemnity Co. v. City of Thomasville, 100 Fla. 748, 130 So. 7, 8.

JUDICIAL COMMITTEE OF THE PRIVY COUNCIL. In English law. A tribunal established in 1833, composed of members of the privy council, being judges or retired judges, which acts as the king's adviser in matters of law referred to it, and exercises a certain appellate jurisdiction, though its power in this respect was curtailed by the judicature act of 1873.

It consists of the Lord Chancellor, the six Lords of Appeal, if Privy Councillors, and such other members of the Privy Council as have held any high judicial office in the United Kingdom, India, or the colonies. It is the court of final appeal from the ecclesiastical courts, from the courts of India, the colonies, dominions, etc., the Channel Islands and the Isle of Man, administering all the different systems of law of the countries under its appellate jurisdiction, and exercising a notable influence on the tenor and course of law in some of those jurisdictions, especially Indian law.

JUDICIAL CONVENTION. An agreement entered into in consequence of an order of court; as, for example, entering into a bond on taking out a writ of sequestration. Penniman v. Barrymore, 6 Mart. N.S., La., 494.

JUDICIAL CY PRES.

Doctrine of "judicial cy pres" is a principle of construction based on a judicial finding of donor's intention as applied to new conditions. Rohlff v. German Old People's Home, 143 Neb. 636, 10 N.W.2d 686, 691.

When only minor features of a trust for charity become impossible or impracticable of performance and it cannot properly be said that general scheme of testator has failed, doctrine of "judicial cy pres" operates to avoid failure of charity. Noel v. Olds, 78 U.S.App.D.C. 155, 138 F.2d 581, 586, 587.

JUDICIAL DECISION. An opinion or determination of the judges in causes before them, particularly in appellate courts. Le Blanc v. Illinois Cent. R. Co., 73 Miss. 463, 19 So. 211. Application by a court or tribunal exercising judicial authority of competent jurisdiction of the law to a state of facts proved, or admitted to be true, and a declaration of the consequences which follow. In re Knofler's Estate, 73 Ohio App. 383, 52 N.E.2d 667, 668.

JUDICIAL DECLARATION OF LAW. A rule adopted as the basis of decision of issues involved. Trustees of Phillips Exeter Academy v. Exeter, 90 N.H. 472, 27 A.2d 569, 577.

JUDICIAL DEPARTMENT. The branch of government which is intended to interpret, construe and apply the law. Board of Com'rs of Wyandotte County v. General Securities Corporation, 157 Kan. 64, 138 P.2d 479, 487.

JUDICIAL DICTUM. A dictum made by a court or judge in the course of a judicial decision or opinion. Com. v. Paine, 207 Pa. 45, 56 A. 317. See Dictum.

JUDICIAL DISTRICT. One of the circuits or precincts into which a state is commonly divided for judicial purposes, a court of general original jurisdiction being usually provided in each of such districts, and the boundaries of the district marking the territorial limits of its authority; or the district may include two or more counties, having separate and independent county courts, but in that case they are presided over by the same judge. See Ex parte Gardner, 22 Nev. 280, 39 P. 570; Lindsley v. Coahoma County Sup'rs, 69 Miss. 815, 11 So. 336; Com. v. Hoar, 121 Mass. 377; Consolidated Flour Mills Co. v. Muegge, 127 Okl. 295, 260 P. 745, 752.

JUDICIAL DIVORCE. One granted by the sentence of a court of justice, pursuant to general law. Maclay v. Maclay, 147 Fla. 77, 2 So.2d 361, 363.

JUDICIAL DUTY. One that requires exercise of judgment or choice of alternatives in its performance. Board of Education of Nebo School Dist. v. Jeppson, 74 Utah 576, 280 P. 1065, 1069. One that requires exercise of judgment or decision of a question of fact. State ex rel. Coast Holding Co. v. Ekwall, 144 Or. 672, 26 P.2d 52. One that requires use of discretion or examination of evidence and decision of questions of law and fact. Taylor County Farm Bureau v. Board of Sup'rs of Taylor County, 218 Iowa 937, 252 N.W. 498. One that legitimately pertains to an officer in judicial department. Harding v. McCullough, 236 Iowa 556, 19 N.W.2d 613, 617; Ex parte Lewis, 328 Mo. 843, 42 S.W.2d 21, 22.

JUDICIAL ERRORS. Errors into which the court itself falls are "judicial errors." An error of this character occurs when the judgment rendered is erroneous in some particular, requiring it to be changed. Connecticut Mortgage & Title Guaranty Co. v. Di Francesco, 112 Conn. 673, 151 A. 491, 492.

JUDICIAL ESTOPPEL. Arises from sworn statements made in course of judicial proceedings. Clarke v. Ripley Sav. Bank & Trust Co., 27 Tenn. App. 387, 181 S.W.2d 386, 389; Helfer v. Mutual Benefit Health & Accident Ass'n, 170 Tenn. 630, 96 S.W.2d 1103, 1105, 113 A.L.R. 921. The doctrine of "judicial estoppel" is the doctrine of the conclusiveness of the judgments. State v. Ohio Oil Co., Tex.Civ.App., 173 S.W.2d 470, 478, 479.

It is based on bad faith, and cannot be asserted unless sworn statement was made knowingly, or with degree of negligence authorizing imputation of knowledge. Broyles v. Scottish Union & National Ins. Co., 16 Tenn.App. 331, 64 S.W. 517.

The rule may be invoked only where the prior and subsequent litigation involves the same parties and where one party has relied on the former testimony and changed his position by reason of it. Tracy Loan & Trust Co. v. Openshaw Inv. Co., 102 Utah 509, 132 P.2d 388, 390, 391. But see holding that judicial estoppel is based on public policy and not on prejudice to adverse party. Sartain v. Dixie Coal & Iron Co., 150 Tenn. 633, 266 S.W. 313, 316.

JUDICIAL EVIDENCE is the means, sanctioned by law, of ascertaining in a judicial proceeding the truth respecting a question.

JUDICIAL FUNCTION. The exercise of the judicial faculty or office. The capacity to act in the specific way which appertains to the judicial power, as one of the powers of government.

The term is used to describe generally those modes of action which appertain to the judiciary as a department of organized government, and through and by means of which it accomplishes its purposes and exercises its peculiar powers. See State v. Kelly, 27 N.M. 412, 202 P. 524, 528, 21 A.L.R. 156; Lyon v. City of Payette, 38 Idaho 705, 224 P. 793, 794; People v. Hersey, 69 Colo. 492, 196 P. 180, 181, 14 A.L.R. 631; Sauskelonis v. Herting, 89 Conn. 298, 94 A. 368, 369. While ordinarily a case or judicial controversy within the meaning of Const. art. 3, § 2, results in a judgment requiring award of process of execution to carry it into effect, such relief is not an indispensable adjunct to the exercise of the "judicial function." Fidelity Nat. Bank & Trust Co. of Kansas City v. Swope, 274 U.S. 123, 47 S.Ct. 511, 514, 71 L.Ed. 959.

JUDICIAL INQUIRY. Such inquiry investigates, declares, and enforces liabilities as they stand on present or past facts and under laws supposed already to exist. Oklahoma Gas & Electric Co. v. Wilson & Co. of Oklahoma, C.C.A.Okl., 54 F.2d

596, 598; In re Turnock's Estate, 238 Wis. 438, 300 N.W. 155, 156.

JUDICIAL KNOWLEDGE. Knowledge of that which is so notorious that everybody, including judges, knows it, and hence need not be proved. Ex parte Ferguson, 112 Tex.Cr.R. 152, 15 S.W.2d 650, 652.

JUDICIAL LEGISLATION. See Judge-Made Law.

JUDICIAL NOTICE. The act by which a court, in conducting a trial, or framing its decision, will, of its own motion, and without the production of evidence, recognize the existence and truth of certain facts, having a bearing on the controversy at bar, which, from their nature, are not properly the subject of testimony, or which are universally regarded as established by common notoriety, *e. g.*, the laws of the state, international law, historical events, the constitution and course of nature, main geographical features, etc. North Hempstead v. Gregory, 53 App.Div. 350, 65 N.Y.S. 867; State v. Main, 69 Conn. 123, 37 A. 80, 36 L.R. A. 623, 61 Am.St.Rep. 30. The cognizance of certain facts which judges and jurors may properly take and act upon without proof, because they already know them. United States v. Hammers, D. C.Fla., 241 F. 542, 543.

The true conception of what is "judicially known" is that of something which is not, or rather need not be, unless the tribunal wishes it, the subject of either evidence or argument. Chiulla de Luca v. Board of Park Com'rs of City of Hartford, 94 Conn. 7, 107 A. 611, 612. The limits of "judicial notice" cannot be prescribed with exactness, but notoriety is, generally speaking, the ultimate test of facts sought to be brought within the realm of judicial notice; in general, it covers matters so notorious that a production of evidence would be unnecessary, matters which the judicial function supposes the judge to be acquainted with actually or theoretically, and matters not strictly included under either of such heads. Gottstein v. Lister, 88 Wash. 462, 153 P. 595, 602, Ann.Cas.1917D, 1008.

JUDICIAL OATH. See Oath.

JUDICIAL OFFICE. Offices which relate to the administration of justice; Waldo v. Wallace, 12 Ind. 569; and which should be exercised by persons of sufficient skill and experience in the duties which appertain to them. A general term including courts of record and courts not of record. Buckley v. Holmes, 259 Pa. 176, 102 A. 497, 500.

A term used in 34 & 35 Vict. c. 91, to define qualifications of additional members of the judicial committee of the Privy Council.

JUDICIAL OFFICER. The term, in the popular sense, applies generally to an officer of a court, but in the strictly legal sense applies only to an officer who determines causes between parties or renders decision in a judicial capacity. Hitt v. State, 182 Miss. 184, 181 So. 331; Alexander v. Holmes, 180 Ga. 397, 179 S.E. 77, 78. One who exercises judicial function. Adams v. State, 214 Ind. 603, 17 N.E.2d 84, 118 A.L.R. 1095. A person in whom is vested authority to decide causes or exercise powers appropriate to a court. Settle v. Van Evrea, 49 N.Y. 284; People v. Wells, 2 Cal. 203; Reid v. Hood, 2 Nott & McC., S.C., 170, 10 Am. Dec. 582.

JUDICIAL OPINION. A term synonymous with what has been adjudged or decreed and final in its character. Alleghany Corporation v. Aldebaran Corporation, 173 Md. 472, 196 A. 418, 421. See, also, Opinion.

JUDICIAL ORDER. One which involves exercise of judicial discretion and affects final result of litigation. Happy Coal Co. v. Brashear, 263 Ky. 257, 92 S.W.2d 23, 27. See, also, Order.

JUDICIAL POWER. The authority exercised by that department of government which is charged with declaration of what law is and its construction. People v. Bruner, 343 Ill. 146, 175 N.E. 400, 404. The authority vested in courts and judges, as distinguished from the executive and legislative power. Gilbert v. Priest, 65 Barb., N.Y., 448; State ex rel. Jamison v. Denny, 118 Ind. 382, 21 N.E. 252, 4 L.R.A. 79.

It is a power that cannot be brought within ring fence of a definition, Batty v. Arizona State Dental Board, 57 Ariz. 239, 112 P.2d 870, 873. A power involving exercise of judgment and discretion in determination of questions of right in specific cases affecting interests of person or property, as distinguished from ministerial power involving no discretion, Stanton v. State Tax Commission, 114 Ohio St. 658, 151 N.E. 760, 764; Ward v. Board of Com'rs of Osfuskee County, 114 Okl. 246, 246 P. 376, 378; inherent authority not only to decide, but to make binding orders or judgments, Fewel v. Fewel, 23 Cal.2d 431, 144 P.2d 592, 594; power to decide and pronounce a judgment and carry it into effect between persons and parties who bring a case before court for decision, Miller, Const. U. S. 314; Stuart v. Norviel, 26 Ariz. 493, 266 P. 908, 909; Shea v. North-Butte Mining Co., 55 Mont. 522, 179 P. 499, 503; Rohde v. City of Newport, 246 Ky. 476, 55 S.W.2d 368, 87 A.L.R. 701; power to declare what law is or has been, Gorham v. Robinson, 57 R.I. 1, 186 A. 832, 842; State v. Leuders, 214 N.C. 558, 200 S.E. 22, 23; power to determine constitutionality and validity of legislative acts, Cohen v. Virginia, 6 Wheat. 264, 5 L.Ed. 257; Marbury v. Madison, 1 Cranch, 137, 2 L.Ed. 60; Wilentz v. Hendrickson, 133 N. J.Eq. 447, 33 A.2d 366, 390; although this is still sometimes challenged, power to determine what is the law applicable to a case, to apply that law to the case, and to render judgment accordingly, Kuhnert v. United States; D.C.Mo., 36 F.Supp. 798, 800; power to hear and determine, controversies between adverse parties and questions in litigation, In re Sanderson, 289 Mich. 165, 286 N.W. 198, 199; Citizen's Club v. Welling, 83 Utah 81, 27 P.2d 23; controversies between public officers, state, counties, cities, and other municipal corporations, subdivisions of state and state bonding board, Laverty v. Cochran, 132 Neb. 118, 271 N.W. 354; matters which affect the life, liberty, or property of the citizens of the state, Nash v. Brooks, 297 N.Y.S. 853, 856, 251 App.Div. 616; rights of persons or property, or the propriety of doing an act, In re McGarry, 44 N.E.2d 7, 10, 380 Ill. 359; Geauga Lake Improvement Ass'n v. Lozier, 182 N.E. 489, 491, 125 Ohio St. 565. Power that adjudicates upon and protects the rights and interests of persons or property, and to that end declares, construes and applies the law, In re Hunstiger, 130 Minn. 474, 153 N.W. 869, 870; People ex rel. Rusch v. White, 334 Ill. 465, 166 N.E. 100, 106, 64 A.L.R. 1006; In re Assessment of Kansas City Southern Ry. Co., 168 Okl. 495, 33 P.2d 772, 775; power that determines whether rules of action prescribed by the legislature have been transgressed in particular case, In re Manufacturer's Freight Forwarding Co., 294 Mich. 57, 292 N.W. 678, 680.

Power vested in a subordinate body to determine a question of fact is a "judicial power." Sheils v. Flynn, 164 Misc. 302, 299 N.Y.S. 64, 80.

JUDICIAL PROCEEDING. Any proceeding wherein judicial action is invoked and taken. Mannix v. Portland Telegram, 144 Or. 172, 23 P.2d 138, 90 A.L.R. 55. Any proceeding to obtain such remedy as the law allows. Treloar v. Harris, 66

Ind.App. 59, 117 N.E. 975, 978. Any step taken in a court of justice in the prosecution or defense of an action. National Homestead Ass'n v. Graham, 176 La. 1062, 147 So. 348, 352.

A general term for proceedings relating to, practiced in, or proceeding from, a court of justice; or the course prescribed to be taken in various cases for the determination of a controversy or for legal redress or relief. See Martin v. Simpkins, 20 Colo. 438, 38 P. 1092; Mullen v. Reed, 64 Conn. 240, 29 A. 478, 24 L.R.A. 664, 42 Am.St.Rep. 174; Aldrich v. Kinney, 4 Conn. 386, 10 Am.Dec. 151. A proceeding in a legally constituted court. Garrett v. State, 18 Ga.App. 360, 89 S.E. 380. A proceeding wherein there are parties, who have opportunity to be heard, and wherein the tribunal proceeds either to a determination of facts upon evidence or of law upon proved or conceded facts. Mitchel v. Cropsey, 177 App.Div. 663, 164 N.Y.S. 336, 339.

JUDICIAL QUESTION. One proper for the determination of a court of justice, as distinguished from such questions as belong to the decision of the legislative or executive departments of government and with which the courts will not interfere, called "political" or "legislative" questions. See Patton v. Chattanooga, 108 Tenn. 197, 65 S.W. 414.

JUDICIAL REMEDY. Such as is administered by the courts of justice, or by judicial officers empowered for that purpose by the constitution and laws of the state. Code Civ.Proc.Cal. § 20; Code Civ.Proc.Mont.1895, § 3469 (Rev.Codes 1921, § 8995).

JUDICIAL SEPARATION. A separation of man and wife by decree of court, less complete than an absolute divorce. A "limited divorce" or a "divorce a mensa et thoro," Maclay v. Maclay, 147 Fla. 77, 2 So.2d 361, 363.

JUDICIAL STATISTICS. In English law. Statistics, published by authority, of the civil and criminal business of the United Kingdom, and matters appertaining thereto. Annual reports are published separately for England and Wales, for Ireland, and for Scotland.

JUDICIARY, *adj.* Pertaining or relating to the courts of justice, to the judicial department of government, or to the administration of justice.

JUDICIARY, *n.* That branch of government invested with the judicial power; the system of courts in a country; the body of judges; the bench. That branch of government which is intended to interpret, construe and apply the law. Board of Com'rs of Wyandotte County v. General Securities Corporation, 157 Kan. 64, 138 P.2d 479, 487.

JUDICIARY ACT. The name commonly given to the act of congress of September 24, 1789, (1 St. at Large. 73,) by which the system of federal courts was organized, and their powers and jurisdiction defined.

JUDICIIS POSTERIORIBUS FIDES EST ADHIBENDA. Faith or credit is to be given to the later judgments. 13 Coke, 14.

JUDICIO SISTI. Lat. A caution, or security, given in Scotch courts for the defendant to abide judgment within the jurisdiction. Stim.Law Gloss.

JUDICIOUSLY. Directed by sound judgment. Shivers v. Stovall, Tex.Civ.App., 75 S.W.2d 276, 279.

JUDICIS EST IN PRONUNTIANDO SEQUI REGULAM, EXCEPTIONE NON PROBATA. The judge in his decision ought to follow the rule, when the exception is not proved.

JUDICIS EST JUDICARE SECUNDUM ALLEGATA ET PROBATA. Dyer, 12. It is the duty of a judge to decide according to facts alleged and proved.

JUDICIS EST JUS DICERE, NON DARE. It is the province of a judge to declare the law, not to give it. Lofft, Append. 42.

JUDICIS OFFICIUM EST OPUS DIEI IN DIE SUO PERFICERE. It is the duty of a judge to finish the work of each day within that day. Dyer, 12.

JUDICIS OFFICIUM EST UT RES, ITA TEMPORA RERUM, QUÆRERE. It is the duty of a judge to inquire into the times of things, as well as into things themselves. Co.Litt. 171.

JUDICIUM. Lat. Judicial authority or jurisdiction; a court or tribunal; a judicial hearing or other proceeding; a verdict or judgment; a proceeding before a judex or judge. State v. Whitford, 54 Wis. 150, 11 N.W. 424.

JUDICIUM A NON SUO JUDICE DATUM NULLIUS EST MOMENTI. 10 Coke, 70. A judgment given by one who is not the proper judge is of no force.

JUDICIUM CAPITALE. In old English law. Judgment of death; capital judgment. Fleta, lib. 1, c. 39, § 2. Called, also, "*judicium vitæ amissionis,*" judgment of loss of life. Id. lib. 2, c. 1, § 5.

JUDICIUM DEI. In old English and European law. The judgment of God; otherwise called "*divinum judicium,*" the "divine judgment."

A term particularly applied to the ordeals by fire or hot iron and water, and also to the trials by the cross, the eucharist, and the corsned, and the *duellum* or trial by battle, (*q. v.,*) it being supposed that the interposition of heaven was directly manifest, in these cases, in behalf of the innocent. Spelman; Burrill.

JUDICIUM EST QUASI JURIS DICTUM. Judgment is, as it were, a declaration of law.

JUDICIUM NON DEBET ESSE ILLUSORIUM; SUUM EFFECTUM HABERE DEBET. A judgment ought not to be illusory; it ought to have its proper effect. 2 Inst. 341.

JUDICIUM PARIUM. In old English law. Judgment of the peers; judgment of one's peers: trial by jury. Magna Charta, c. 39.

JUDICIUM REDDITUR IN INVITUM. Co.Litt. 248*b*. Judgment is given against one, whether he will or not.

JUDICIUM (SEMPER) PRO VERITATE ACCIPITUR. A judgment is always taken for truth [that is, as long as it stands in force it cannot be contradicted]. 2 Inst. 380; Co.Litt. 39*a*, 168*a*.

JUG. In old English law. A watery place. Domesday; Cowell.

JUGE. In French law. A judge.

JUGE DE PAIX. An inferior judicial functionary, appointed to decide summarily controversies of minor importance, especially such as turn mainly on questions of fact. He has also the functions of a police magistrate. Ferrière.

JUGE D'INSTRUCTION. See Instruction.

JUGERUM. An acre. Co.Litt. 5*b*. As much as a yoke (jugum) of oxen could plow in one day.

JUGULATOR. In old records. A cutthroat or murderer. Cowell.

JUGUM. Lat. In the civil law. A yoke; a measure of land; as much land as a yoke of oxen could plow in a day. Nov. 17, c. 8.

JUGUM TERRÆ. In old English law. A yoke of land; half a plow-land. Domesday; Co.Litt. 5*a*; Cowell.

JUICIO. In Spanish law. A trial or suit. White, New Recop. b. 3, tit. 4, c. 1.

JUICIO DE APEO. The decree of a competent tribunal directing the determining and marking the boundaries of lands or estates.

JUICIO DE CONCURSO DE ACREEDORES. The judgment granted for a debtor who has various creditors, or for such creditors, to the effect that their claims be satisfied according to their respective form and rank, when the debtor's estate is not sufficient to discharge them all in full. Escriche.

JULIAN LAW. See Lex Julia.

JUMENT. In old Scotch law. An ox used for tillage. 1 Pitc.Crim.Tr. pt. 2, p. 89.

JUMENTA. In the civil law. Beasts of burden; animals used for carrying burdens. This word did not include "oxen." Dig. 32, 65, 5.

JUMMABUNDY. See Jammabundy.

JUMP BAIL. To abscond, withdraw, or secrete one's self, in violation of the obligation of a bail-bond.

The expression is colloquial, and is applied only to the act of the principal.

JUNCARIA. In old English law. The soil where rushes grow. Co.Litt. 5*a*; Cowell.

JUNCTA JUVANT. United they aid. A portion of the maxim, "*Quæ non valeant singula juncta juvant,*" (*q. v.*,) frequently cited. 3 Man. & G. 99.

JUNGERE DUELLUM. In old English law. To join the *duellum;* to engage in the combat. Fleta, lib. 1, c. 21, § 10.

JUNIOR. Younger.

This has been held to be no part of a man's name, but an addition by use, and a convenient distinction between a father and son of the same name. Cobb v. Lucas, 15 Pick., Mass., 9; Padgett v. Lawrence, 10 Paige, N.Y., 177, 40 Am. Dec. 232; Prentiss v. Blake, 34 Vt. 460; Maxwell v. State, 65 So. 732, 734, 11 Ala.App. 53.

As to junior "Barrister," "Counsel," "Creditor," "Judgment," and "Writ," see those titles.

JUNIOR EXECUTION. One which was issued after the issuance of another execution, on a different judgment, against the same defendant.

JUNIOR RIGHT. A custom prevalent in some parts of England (also at some places on the continent) by which an estate descended to the youngest son in preference to his older brothers; the same as "Borough-English."

JUNIPERUS SABINA. In medical jurisprudence. This plant is commonly called "savin."

JUNK. Worn out and discarded material in general that may be turned to some use; especially old rope, chain, iron, copper, parts of machinery and bottles gathered or bought up by tradesmen called junk dealers; hence rubbish of any kind; odds and ends. City of Chicago v. Iroquois Steel & Iron Co., 284 Ill.App. 561, 1 N.E.2d 241, 243; Ex parte Scott, 130 Tex.Cr.R. 29, 91 S.W.2d 748, 749.

Articles that have outlived their usefulness in their original form, and are commonly gathered up and sold to be converted into another product, either of the same or of a different kind, City of Watseka v. Blatt, 320 Ill.App. 191, 50 N.E.2d 589, 594; old iron, or other base metals, old rope, rags, waste paper, etc., and empty bottles, and all articles discarded or no longer used as a manufactured article composed of any one or more of the materials mentioned. Beskin v. City of Chicago, 341 Ill. 489, 173 N.E. 364, 367.

JUNK-SHOP. A shop where old cordage and ships' tackle, old iron, rags, bottles, paper, etc., are kept and sold. A place or shop where odds and ends are purchased and sold. Charleston City Council v. Goldsmith, 12 Rich.Law (S.C.) 470; Grace Iron & Steel Corporation v. Ackerman, 123 N.J.L. 54, 7 A.2d 820, 821.

JUNTA, or JUNTO. A select council for taking cognizance of affairs of great consequence requiring secrecy; a cabal or faction.

This was a popular nickname applied to the Whig ministry in England, between 1693–1696. They clung to each other for mutual protection against the attacks of the so-called "Reactionist Stuart Party." In this sense, more properly called "junto."

JURA. Lat. Plural of "jus." Rights; laws. 1 Bl.Comm. 123. See Jus.

JURA ECCLESIASTICA LIMITATA SUNT INFRA LIMITES SEPARATOS. Ecclesiastical laws are limited within separate bounds. 3 Bulst. 53.

JURA EODEM MODO DESTITUUNTUR QUO CONSTITUUNTUR. Laws are abrogated by the same means [authority] by which they are made. Broom, Max. 878.

JURA FISCALIA. In English law. Fiscal rights; rights of the exchequer. 3 Bl.Comm. 45.

JURA IN RE. In the civil law. Rights in a thing; rights which, being separated from the *dominium,* or right of property, exist independently of it, and are enjoyed by some other person than him who has the *dominium.* Mackeld. Rom.Law, § 237.

JURA MAJESTATIS. Rights of sovereignty or majesty; a term used in the civil law to designate certain rights which belong to each and every sovereignty and which are deemed essential to its existence. Gilmer v. Lime Point, 18 Cal. 250.

JURA MIXTI DOMINII. In old English law. Rights of mixed dominion. The king's right or power of jurisdiction was so termed. Hale, Anal. § 6.

JURA NATURÆ SUNT IMMUTABILIA. The laws of nature are unchangeable. Branch, Princ.

JURA PERSONARUM. Rights of persons; the rights of persons. Rights which concern and are annexed to the persons of men. 1 Bl.Comm. 122.

JURA PRÆDIORUM. In the civil law. The rights of estates. Dig. 50, 16, 86.

JURA PUBLICA ANTEFERENDA PRIVATIS. Public rights are to be preferred to private. Co. Litt. 130*a*. Applied to protections.

JURA PUBLICA EX PRIVATO [PRIVATIS] PROMISCUE DECIDI NON DEBENT. Public rights ought not to be decided promiscuously with private. Co. Litt. 130*a*, 181*b*.

JURA REGALIA. In English law. Royal rights or privileges. 1 Bl.Comm. 117, 119; 3 Bl.Comm. 44.

JURA REGIA. In English law. Royal rights; the prerogatives of the crown. Crabb, Com.Law, 174.

JURA REGIS SPECIALIA NON CONCEDUNTUR PER GENERALIA VERBA. The special rights of the king are not granted by general words. Jenk. Cent. p. 103.

JURA RERUM. Rights of things; the rights of things; rights which a man may acquire over external objects or things, unconnected with his person. 1 Bl.Comm. 122; 2 Bl.Comm. 1.

JURA SANGUINIS NULLO JURE CIVILI DIRIMI POSSUNT. The right of blood and kindred cannot be destroyed by any civil law. Dig. 50, 17, 9; Bac.Max. reg. 11; Broom, Max. 533; Jackson v. Phillips, 14 Allen (Mass.) 562.

JURA SUMMI IMPERII. Rights of supreme dominion; rights of sovereignty. 1 Bl.Comm. 49; 1 Kent, Comm. 211.

JURAL. 1. Pertaining to natural or positive right, or to the doctrines of rights and obligations; as "jural relations."

2. Of or pertaining to jurisprudence; juristic; juridical.

3. Recognized or sanctioned by positive law; embraced within, or covered by, the rules and enactments of positive law.

4. Founded in law; organized upon the basis of a fundamental law, and existing for the recognition and protection of rights.

The "jural sphere" is to be distinguished from the "moral sphere;" the latter denoting the whole scope or range of ethics or the science of conduct, the former embracing only such portions of the same as have been made the subject of legal sanction or recognition.

The term "jural society" is used as the synonym of "state" or "organized political community."

JURAMENTÆ CORPORALES. Lat. Corporal oaths, *q. v.*

JURAMENTUM. Lat. In the civil law. An oath.

JURAMENTUM CALUMNIÆ. In the civil and canon law. The oath of calumny.

An oath imposed upon both parties to a suit, as a preliminary to its trial, to the effect that they are not influenced by malice or any sinister motives in prosecuting or defending the same, but by a belief in the justice of their cause. It was also required of the attorneys and proctors.

JURAMENTUM CORPORALIS. A corporal oath. See Corporal Oath.

JURAMENTUM EST INDIVISIBILE; ET NON EST ADMITTENDUM IN PARTE VERUM ET IN PARTE FALSUM. An oath is indivisible; it is not to be held partly true and partly false. 4 Inst. 274.

JURAMENTUM IN LITEM. In the civil law. An assessment oath; an oath, taken by the plaintiff in an action, that the extent of the damages he has suffered, estimated in money, amounts to a certain sum, which oath, in certain cases, is accepted in lieu of other proof. Mackeld. Rom.Law, § 376.

JURAMENTUM JUDICIALE. In the civil law. An oath which the judge, of his own accord, defers to either of the parties.

It is of two kinds: *First,* that which the judge defers for the decision of the cause, and which is understood by the general name *"juramentum judiciale,"* and is sometimes called "suppletory oath," *juramentum suppletorium; second,* that which the judge defers in order to fix and determine the amount of the condemnation which he ought to pronounce, and which is called *"juramentum in litem."* Poth. Obl. p. 4, c. 3, § 3, art. 3.

JURAMENTUM NECESSARIUM. In Roman law. A compulsory oath.

A disclosure under oath, which the prætor compelled one of the parties to a suit to make, when the other, applying for such an appeal, agreed to abide by what his adversary should swear. 1 Whart. Ev. § 458; Dig. 12, 2, 5, 2.

JURAMENTUM VOLUNTARIUM. In Roman law. A voluntary oath.

A species of appeal to conscience, by which one of the parties to a suit, instead of proving his case, offered to abide by what his adversary should answer under oath. 1 Whart. Ev. § 458; Dig. 12, 2, 34, 6.

JURARE. Lat. To swear; to take an oath.

JURARE EST DEUM IN TESTEM VOCARE, ET EST ACTUS DIVINI CULTUS. 3 Inst. 165. To swear is to call God to witness, and is an act of religion.

JURAT. Certificate of officer or person before whom writing was sworn to. Murphy v. State, 103 S.W.2d 765, 766, 132 Tex.Cr.R. 202; Gossard v. Vawter, 215 Ind. 581, 21 N.E.2d 416, 417. The clause written at the foot of an affidavit, stating when, where, and before whom such affidavit was sworn. See U. S. v. McDermott, 140 U.S. 151, 11 S.Ct. 746, 35 L.Ed. 391; U. S. v. Julian, 162 U.S. 324, 16 S.Ct. 801, 40 L.Ed. 984; Lutz v. Kinney, 46 P. 257, 23 Nev. 279.

JURATA. In old English law. A jury of twelve men sworn. Especially, a jury of the common law, as distinguished from the *assisa*.

The jury clause in a *nisi prius* record, so called from the emphatic words of the old forms: *"Jurata ponitur in respectum,"* the jury is put in respite. Townsh.Pl. 487.

Also a jurat, (which see.)

JURATION. The act of swearing; the administration of an oath.

JURATO CREDITUR IN JUDICIO. He who makes oath is to be believed in judgment. 3 Inst. 79.

JURATOR. A juror; a compurgator, (*q. v.*).

JURATORES DEBENT ESSE VICINI, SUFFICIENTES, ET MINUS SUSPECTI. Jurors ought to be neighbors of sufficient estate, and free from suspicion. Jenk. Cent. 141.

JURATORES SUNT JUDICES FACTI. Jenk. Cent. 61. Juries are the judges of fact.

JURATORY CAUTION. In Scotch law. A description of caution (security) sometimes offered in a suspension or advocation where the complainer is not in circumstances to offer any better. Bell.

JURATS. In English law. Officers in the nature of aldermen, sworn for the government of many corporations. The twelve assistants of the bailiff in Jersey are called "jurats."

JURE. Lat. By right; in right; by the law.

JURE BELLI. By the right or law of war. 1 Kent, Comm. 126; 1 C.Rob.Adm. 289.

JURE CIVILI. By the civil law. Inst. 1, 3, 4; 1 Bl.Comm. 423.

JURE CORONÆ. In right of the crown.

JURE DIVINO. By divine right. 1 Bl.Comm. 191.

JURE ECCLESIÆ. In right of the church. 1 Bl.Comm. 401.

JURE EMPHYTEUTICO. By the right or law of *emphyteusis.* 3 Bl.Comm. 232. See Emphyteusis.

JURE GENTIUM. By the law of nations. Inst. 1, 3, 4; 1 Bl.Comm. 423.

JURE NATURÆ ÆQUUM EST NEMINEM CUM ALTERIUS DETRIMENTO ET INJURIA FIERI LOCUPLETIOREM. By the law of nature it is not just that any one should be enriched by the detriment or injury of another. Dig. 50, 17, 206.

JURE PROPINQUITATIS. By right of propinquity or nearness. 2 Crabb, Real Prop. p. 1019, § 2398.

JURE REPRESENTATIONIS. By right of representation; in the right of another person. 2 Bl. Comm. 224, 517; 2 Crabb, Real Prop. p. 1019, § 2398.

JURE UXORIS. In right of a wife. 3 Bl.Comm. 210.

JURI NON EST CONSONUM QUOD ALIQUIS ACCESSORIUS IN CURIA REGIS CONVINCATUR ANTEQUAM ALIQUIS DE FACTO FUERIT ATTINCTUS. It is not consonant to justice that any accessary should be convicted in the king's court before any one has been attainted of the fact. 2 Inst. 183.

JURIDICAL. Relating to administration of justice, or office of a judge.

Regular; done in conformity to the laws of the country and the practice which is there observed.

JURIDICAL DAY. Day on which court is in session. Black v. National Bank of Kentucky, 226 Ky. 152, 10 S.W.2d 629, 630.

JURIDICUS. Lat. Relating to the courts or to the administration of justice; juridical; lawful.

JURIS. Lat. Of right; of law.

JURIS AFFECTUS IN EXECUTIONE CONSISTIT. The effect of the law consists in the execution. Co. Litt. 289*b*.

JURIS ET DE JURE. Of law and of right.

A presumption *juris et de jure,* or an irrebutable presumption, is one which the law will not suffer to be rebutted by any counter-evidence, but establishes as conclusive; while a presumption *juris tantum* is one which holds good in the absence of evidence to the contrary, but may be rebutted.

JURIS ET SEISINÆ CONJUNCTIO. The union of seisin or possession and the right of possession, forming a complete title. 2 Bl.Comm. 199, 311.

JURIS IGNORANTIA EST CUM JUS NOSTRUM IGNORAMUS. It is ignorance of the law when we do not know our own rights. Haven v. Foster, 9 Pick. (Mass.) 130, 19 Am.Dec. 353.

JURIS POSITIVI. Of positive law; a regulation or requirement of positive law, as distinguished from natural or divine law. 1 Bl.Comm. 439; 2 Steph.Comm. 286.

JURIS PRÆCEPTA SUNT HÆC: HONESTE VIVERE; ALTERUM NON LÆDERE; SUUM CUIQUE TRIBUERE. These are the precepts of the law: To live honorably; to hurt nobody; to render to every one his due. Inst. 1, 1, 3; 1 Bl. Comm. 40.

JURIS PRIVATI. Of private right; subjects of private property. Hale, Anal. § 23.

JURIS PUBLICI. Of common right; of common or public use; such things as, at least in their own use, are common to all the king's subjects; as common highways, common bridges, common rivers, and common ports. Hale, Anal. § 23.

JURIS UTRUM. In English law. An abolished writ which lay for the parson of a church whose predecessor had alienated the lands and tenements thereof. Fitzh. Nat. Brev. 48.

JURISCONSULT. A jurist; a person skilled in the science of law, particularly of international or public law.

JURISCONSULTUS. Lat. In Roman law. An expert in juridical science; a person thoroughly versed in the laws, who was habitually resorted to, for information and advice, both by private persons as his clients, and also by the magistrates, advocates, and others employed in administering justice. Abbreviated *i-ctus.*

JURISDICTIO EST POTESTAS DE PUBLICO INTRODUCTA, CUM NECESSITATE JURIS DICENDI. Jurisdiction is a power introduced for the public good, on account of the necessity of dispensing justice. 10 Coke, 73*a*.

JURISDICTION. The word is a term of large and comprehensive import, and embraces every kind of judicial action. Federal Land Bank of Louisville, Ky., v. Crombie, 258 Ky. 383, 80 S.W.2d 39, 40; McGowin v. McGowin, 122 Fla. 394, 165 So. 274, 275, 276. It is the authority by which courts and judicial officers take cognizance of and decide cases. Board of Trustees of Firemen's Relief and Pension Fund of City of Marietta v. Brooks, 179 Okl. 600, 67 P.2d 4, 6; Morrow v. Corbin, 122 Tex. 553, 62 S.W.2d 641; State v. Barnett, 110 Vt. 221, 3 A.2d 521, 526; the legal right by which judges exercise their authority. Max Ams, Inc. v. Barker, 293 Ky. 698, 170 S.W.2d 45, 48; It exists when court has cognizance of class of cases involved, proper parties are present, and point to be decided is within issues. Noxon Chemical Products Co. v. Leckie, C.C.A.N.J., 39 F.2d 318, 319; United Cemeteries Co. v. Strother, 342 Mo. 1155, 119 S.W.2d 762, 765; Harder v. Johnson, 147 Kan. 440, 76 P.2d 763, 764.

It is the authority, capacity, power or right to act, Campbell v. City of Plymouth, 293 Mich. 84, 291 N.W. 231, 232; Industrial Addition Ass'n v. Commissioner of Internal Revenue, Tenn., 323 U.S. 310, 65 S.Ct. 289, 291, 292, 89 L.Ed. 260; adjudicate, Morrow v. Corbin, 122 Tex. 553, 62 S.W. 2d 641; Iselin v. La Coste, C.C.A.La., 147 F.2d 791, 795; Sheldon v. Powell, 99 Fla. 782, 128 So. 258, 263; Broduer v. Broduer, 53 R.I. 450, 167 A. 104, 106; carry into execution or enforce sentence, judgment or decree, Morrow v. Corbin, 122 Tex. 553, 62 S.W.2d 641; U. S. v. Arredondo, 6 Pet. 691, 8 L.Ed. 547; Johnson v. Jones, 2 Neb. 135; Federal Land Bank of Louisville, Ky. v. Crombie, 258 Ky. 383, 80 S.W.2d 39, 40; compel parties to come before court or body, Great Lakes Stages v. Public Utilities Commission of Ohio, 120 Ohio St. 491, 166 N.E. 404, 406; deal with general abstract question, Thompson v. Terminal Shares, C.C.A.Mo., 89 F.2d 652, 655; deal with subject matter, U. S. v. Sanders, D.C.Tex., 42 F.Supp. 436, 439, 440; decide, Gossett v. Hensley, Tex.Civ.App., 94 S.W.2d 903, 906; Klancher v. Anderson, 113 Colo. 478, 158 P.2d 923, 925; Mattice v. Kingston Trust Co., 33 N.Y.S.2d 799, 801, 178 Misc. 256; including questions of law as well as of fact, Schlosser v. Welsh, D.C.S.D., 5 F.Supp. 993, 996; Atwood v. Cox, 88 Utah 437, 55 P.2d 377, 381; May Coal & Grain Co. v. Kansas City, Mo., C.C.A.Mo., 73 F.2d 345, 348; declare, expound, administer or apply the law, Long Flame Coal Co. v. State Compensation Com'r, 111 W.Va. 409, 163 S.E. 16, 19; Svitojus v. Kurant, 293 Mich. 291, 292 N.W. 637, 645; Johnson v. Harvey, 261 Ky. 522, 88 S.W.2d 42, 46; Max Ams, Inc., v. Barker, 293 Ky. 698, 170 S.W.2d 45, 48; Rasmusson v. Schmalenberger, 60 N.D. 527, 235 N.W. 496, 499; State ex rel. Moser v. District Court of Ninth Judicial Dist. in and for Pondera County, Mont., 116 Mont. 305, 151 P.2d 1002, 1006; determine action, controversy, or question, Fooks' Ex'rs v. Ghingher, 172 Md. 612, 192 A. 782, 786; U. S. v. Crittenden, D.C.N.Y., 24 F.Supp. 84, 88; Hawk v. Hollowell, D.C.Iowa, 1 F.Supp. 885, 887; People ex rel. Carlstrom v. Shurtleff, 355 Ill. 210, 189 N.E. 291; dispose of cause, Stewart v. Sampson, 285 Ky. 447, 148 S.W.2d 278, 280, 281; do justice, In re McMurray, D.C. Iowa, 8 F.Supp. 449, 452; Svitojus v. Kurant, 293 Mich. 291, 292 N.W. 637, 645; enter on inquiry, Berkman v. Levy, Tex.Civ.App., 129 S.W.2d 397, 398; American Co-op. Serum Ass'n v. Anchor Serum Co., D.C.Ill., 38 F.Supp. 313, 315; Janssen v. Tusha, 68 S.D. 639, 5 N.W.2d 684, 686; enter order, judgment, or decree, Harrison v. Barngrover, Tex.Civ.App., 72 S.W.2d 971, 975; People ex rel. Sokoll v. Municipal Court of Chicago, 359 Ill. 102, 194 N.E. 242; entertain suit or controversy, Walling v. Miller, C.C.A. Minn., 138 F.2d 629, 631, 633; In re Trustees of Milwaukee County Orphans' Board, 218 Wis. 518, 261 N.W. 676, 680; Mann v. Morrison, 106 Utah 15, 144 P.2d 543, 545; examine whether court has power to hear and determine controversy, Acadia Land Co. v. Horuff, C.C.A.La., 110 F.2d 354, 355; exercise judicial authority or power, Howe v. Lisbon Sav. Bank & Trust Co., 111 Vt. 201, 14 A.2d 3, 5; Thompson v. Short, 6 Wash.2d 71, 106 P.2d 720, 726, 728; Rhode Island v. Massachusetts, 12 Pet. 657, 717, 9 L.Ed. 1233; govern, People v. Pierce, 41 N.Y.S. 858, 860, 18 Misc. 83; hear and determine. Abbott; Ex parte Meisner, 30 Cal. App.2d 290, 86 P.2d 124, 125; State v. Hampson, 9 Wash.2d 278, 114 P.2d 992, 993; Roddy v. Fitzgerald's Estate, 113 Vt. 472, 35 A.2d 668, 670; hear without determining, Gray v. Hall, 203 Cal. 306, 265 P. 246, 251; inquire into facts, Rasmusson v. Schmalenberger, 60 N.D. 527, 235 N.W. 496, 499; McGowin v. McGowin, 122 Fla. 394, 165 So. 274, 275, 276; Arganbright v. Good, 46 Cal.App.2d Supp. 877, 116 P.2d 186; make laws. People v. Pierce, 41 N.Y.S. 858, 860, 18 Misc. 83; litigate controversy between parties, Morrow v. Corbin, 122 Tex. 553, 62 S.W.2d 641; pronounce sentence of law or award remedies provided by law, 1 Black, Judgm. § 215. State v. Barnett, 110 Vt. 221, 3 A.2d 521, 526; put wheels of justice in motion and to proceed to determination of cause, Employers Reinsurance Corporation v. Bryant, Tex., 299 U.S. 374, 57 S.Ct. 273, 277, 81 L.Ed. 289; render, declare or make judgment, order or decree, High v. Pearce, 220 N.C. 266, 17 S.E.2d 108, 112; McGowin v. McGowin, 122 Fla. 394, 165 So. 274, 275, 276; Reed v. Woodmen of the World, 94 Mont. 374, 22 P.2d 819; Thayer v. Village of Downers Grove, 369 Ill. 334, 16 N.E.2d 717, 719; take cognizance, Dailey v. Brennan, 123 W.Va. 261, 14 S.E.2d 617, 618; Western Grocer Co. v. Glenn, 226 Iowa 1374, 286 N.W. 441, 442; try, Robinette v. Price, 214 Minn. 521, 8 N.W.2d 800, 804; try dispute as to right to possession of property in replevin, Universal Credit Co. v. Antonsen, 374 Ill. 194, 29 N.E.2d 96, 99, 130 A.L.R. 626.

It is the power of him who has the right of judging, Gliptis v. Fifteen Oil Co., 204 La. 896, 16 So.2d 471, 477; the power of judicatories and courts, McGowin v. McGowin, 122 Fla. 394, 165 So. 274, 275, 276; Arganbright v. Good, 46 Cal.App.2d Supp. 877, 116 P.2d 186; Shaffer v. Bank, 201 N.C. 415, 160 S.E. 481, 482. It is power conferred by the Constitution or by law, Corby v. Dooley, 313 Ill.App. 509, 40 N.E.2d 581, 584; National Life Co. v. Rice, 140 Tex. 315, 167 S.W.2d 1021, 1024; State ex rel. Andrews v. Superior Court of Maricopa County, 39 Ariz. 242, 5 P. 2d 192, 194.

It is of three kinds, of the subject-matter, of the person, and to render particular judgment which was given. City of Phœnix v. Rodgers, 44 Ariz. 40, 34 P.2d 385, 388. The word may include or refer to jurisdiction of particular case, Brown v. State, 219 Ind. 251, 37 N.E.2d 73, 78, 137 A.L.R. 679; or jurisdiction of subject matter, Manning v. Baxter, 281 Ky. 659, 136 S.W.2d 1074, 1076; jurisdiction of subject matter and of the person, Stewart v. Sampson, 285

Ky. 447, 148 S.W.2d 278, 280, 281; Moffatt v. Cassimus, 28 Ala.App. 582, 190 So. 297, 298; State Board of Dental Examiners v. Savelle, 90 Colo. 177, 8 P.2d 693, 695; jurisdiction of subject matter, of the person, and to render the particular judgment which was given, Wall v. Superior Court of Yavapai County, 53 Ariz. 344, 89 P.2d 624, 628. Or it may mean only venue, Fiolat v. Minnesota-Atlantic Transit Co., D.C.Minn., 31 F.Supp. 219, 220. It does not depend either upon the regularity of exercise of power to hear and determine or upon correctness or rightfulness of decision made, Mattice v. Kingston Trust Co., 33 N.Y.S.2d 799, 801, 178 Misc. 256; Thompson v. Terminal Shares, C.C.A.Mo., 89 F.2d 652, 655; Klancher v. Anderson, 113 Colo. 478, 158 P.2d 923, 925; or on the ability of the judge to reason correctly or to act incorruptibly, In re Gardiner's Estate, 45 Cal.App.2d 559, 114 P.2d 643, 645.

The amount claimed in good faith is the test of jurisdiction, Gray v. Blight, C.C.A.Colo., 112 F.2d 696, 700; Schwartz v. California Claim Service, 52 Cal.App.2d 47, 125 P.2d 883, 889.

"Jurisdiction of subject-matter" means jurisdiction of class of cases to which particular case belongs. Honea v. Graham, Tex.Civ.App., 66 S.W.2d 802, 804; McFarlin v. McFarlin, 384 Ill. 428, 51 N.E.2d 520, 521; Ferree v. Ferree, 285 Ky. 825, 149 S.W.2d 719, 721; the nature of the cause of action and relief sought, Mid-City Bank & Trust Co. v. Myers, 343 Pa. 465, 23 A.2d 420, 423; Wilson v. State Highway Commissioner, 174 Va. 82, 4 S.E.2d 746, 751; or the amount for which a court of limited jurisdiction is authorized to enter judgment, Moffatt v. Cassimus, 28 Ala. App. 582, 190 So. 297, 298. It is power to: adjudge concerning general question involved, Parker Bros. v. Fagan, C.C.A.Fla., 68 F.2d 616, 617; Balzer v. Pyles, 350 Ill. 344, 183 N.E. 215, 217; In re Gibson's Will, Sur., 40 N.Y.S.2d 727, 733; adjudge whether facts make proper case for jurisdictional consideration by judge, Behee v. Beem, 156 Kan. 115, 131 P.2d 675, 677; Montgomery v. Equitable Life Assur. Soc. of U. S., C.C.A.Ill., 83 F.2d 758, 761; deal with general abstract question, to hear particular facts in any case relating to such question, and to determine whether they are sufficient to invoke exercise of power, Melton v. Jenkins, 50 Ga.App. 615, 178 S.E. 754; State ex rel. Campbell v. Chapman, 145 Fla. 647, 1 So.2d 278, 281; City of Phœnix v. Greer, 43 Ariz. 214, 29 P.2d 1062, 1064; decide rightly or wrongly, Montgomery v. Equitable Life Assur. Soc. of U. S., C.C.A.Ill., 83 F.2d 758, 761; determine every justiciable issue involved, Spencer v. Gypsy Oil Co., C.C.A. Okl., 142 F.2d 935, 937; hear and determine cases of general class to which proceeding belongs, Noxon Chemical Products Co. v. Leckie, C.C.A.N.J., 39 F.2d 318, 320; Brown v. Jacobs, 367 Ill. 545, 12 N.E.2d 10, 12.

"Jurisdiction of the person" is power to subject parties in a particular case to decisions and rulings made in such case, Collins v. Powell, 224 Iowa 1015, 277 N.W. 477, 481.

For "Appellate Jurisdiction," "Concurrent Jurisdiction," "Contentious Jurisdiction," "Co-Ordinate Jurisdiction," "Criminal Jurisdiction," "Excess of Jurisdiction," "Exclusive Jurisdiction," "Foreign Jurisdiction," "General Jurisdiction," "Limited Jurisdiction," "Pendent Jurisdiction," "Probate Jurisdiction," "Special Jurisdiction," "Summary Jurisdiction," "Territorial Jurisdiction," and "Voluntary Jurisdiction," see those titles. For equity jurisdiction, see "Equity." For original jurisdiction, see "Original."

JURISDICTION CLAUSE. In equity practice. That part of a bill which is intended to give jurisdiction of the suit to the court, by a general averment that the acts complained of are contrary to equity, and tend to the injury of the complainant, and that he has no remedy, or not a complete remedy, without the assistance of a court of equity, is called the "jurisdiction clause." Mitf. Eq.Pl. 43.

JURISDICTIONAL. Pertaining or relating to jurisdiction; conferring jurisdiction; showing or disclosing jurisdiction; defining or limiting jurisdiction; essential to jurisdiction.

JURISDICTIONAL AMOUNT. Amount involved in the particular case, Shabotzky v. Massachusetts Mut. Life Ins. Co., D.C.N.Y., 21 F.Supp. 166, 167; sum of all claims that are properly joined, Gray v. Blight, C.C.A.Colo., 112 F.2d 696, 700; value of the object sought to be attained in the litigation, Mountain States Power Co. v. City of Forsyth, D.C.Mont., 41 F.Supp. 389, 390; Ronzio v. Denver & R. G. W. R. Co., C.C.A.Utah, 116 F.2d 604, 606.

JURISDICTIONAL FACTS. Those matters of fact which must exist before the court can properly take jurisdiction of the particular case, as, that the defendant has been properly served with process, that the amount in controversy exceeds a certain sum, that the parties are citizens of different states, etc. Noble v. Railroad Co., 147 U.S. 165, 13 S.Ct. 271, 37 L.Ed. 123.

JURISDICTIONAL PLEA. While all dilatory pleas are sometimes referred to as "jurisdictional pleas," yet, strictly speaking, only those pleas to the jurisdiction of the court are "jurisdictional." Howe v. Lisbon Sav. Bank & Trust Co., 111 Vt. 201, 14 A.2d 3, 10.

JURISDICTIONAL STATEMENT. A statement in appellant's brief that concisely and clearly informs the Supreme Court of the exact ground on which the Supreme Court's jurisdiction is claimed to rest, and refers briefly to the constitutional provisions and decided cases sustaining such claim of jurisdiction. Andrew County v. Maxwell, 347 Mo. 156, 146 S.W.2d 621, 623.

JURISINCEPTOR. Lat. A student of the civil law.

JURISPERITUS. Lat. Skilled or learned in the law.

JURISPRUDENCE. The philosophy of law, or the science which treats of the principles of positive law and legal relations.

"The term is wrongly applied to actual systems of law, or to current views of law, or to suggestions for its amendment, but is the name of a science. This science is a formal, or analytical, rather than a material, one. It is the science of actual or positive law. It is wrongly divided into 'general' and 'particular,' or into 'philosophical' and 'historical.' It may therefore be defined as the formal science of positive law." Holl.Jur. 12.

In the proper sense of the word, "jurisprudence" is the science of law, namely, that science which has for its function to ascertain the principles on which legal rules are based, so as not only to classify those rules in their proper order, and show the relation in which they stand to one another, but also to settle the manner in which new or doubtful cases should be brought under the appropriate rules. Jurisprudence is more a formal than a material science. It has no direct concern with questions of moral or political policy, for they fall under the province of ethics and legislation; but, when a new or doubtful case arises to which two different rules seem, when taken literally, to be equally applicable, it may be, and often is, the function of jurisprudence to consider the ultimate effect which would be produced if each rule were applied to an indefinite number of similar cases, and to choose that rule which, when so applied, will produce the greatest advantage to the community. Sweet.

For "Comparative Jurisprudence" and "Medical Jurisprudence," see those titles. For equity jurisprudence, see "Equity."

JURISPRUDENTIA. Lat. In the civil and common law. Jurisprudence, or legal science.

JURISPRUDENTIA EST DIVINARUM ATQUE HUMANARUM RERUM NOTITIA, JUSTI ATQUE INJUSTI SCIENTIA. Jurisprudence is the knowledge of things divine and human, the science of what is right and what is wrong. Dig. 1, 1, 10, 2; Inst. 1, 1, 1. This definition is adopted by Bracton, word for word. Bract. fol. 3.

JURISPRUDENTIA LEGIS COMMUNIS ANGLIÆ EST SCIENTIA SOCIALIS ET COPIOSA. The jurisprudence of the common law of England is a science social and comprehensive. 7 Coke, 28*a*.

JURIST. One who is versed or skilled in law; answering to the Latin *"jurisperitus," (q. v.)*.

One who is skilled in the civil law, or law of nations. The term is now usually applied to those who have distinguished themselves by their *writings* on legal subjects.

JURISTIC. Pertaining or belonging to, or characteristic of, jurisprudence, or a jurist, or the legal profession.

JURISTIC ACT. One designed to have a legal effect, and capable thereof.

An act of a private individual directed to the origin, termination, or alteration of a right. Webster, Dict., citing T. E. Holland.

JURNEDUM. In old English law. A journey; a day's traveling. Cowell.

JURO. In Spanish law. A certain perpetual pension, granted by the king on the public revenues, and more especially on the salt-works, by favor, either in consideration of meritorious services, or in return for money loaned the government, or obtained by it through forced loans. Escriche.

JUROR. One member of a jury.

The term is not inflexible, and besides a person who has been accepted and sworn to try a cause "juror" may also mean a person selected for jury service. Green v. Smither, Ky., 199 S.W. 1056; People v. Newmark, 312 Ill. 625, 144 N.E. 338, 340. The term may apply to special jurors as well as members of regular panel. Beavers v. State, 187 Ark. 722, 61 S.W.2d 1113. Sometimes, one who takes an oath; as in the term "non-juror," a person who refuses certain oaths.

JUROR DESIGNATE. A juror who has been drawn as a juror. Summers v. State ex rel. Boykin, 66 Ga.App. 648, 19 S.E.2d 28, 31.

JUROR'S BOOK. A list of persons qualified to serve on juries.

JURY. In practice. A certain number of men, selected according to law, and *sworn (jurati)* to inquire of certain matters of fact, and declare the truth upon evidence to be laid before them. This definition embraces the various subdivisions of juries; as *grand jury, petit jury, common jury, special jury, coroner's jury, sheriff's jury, (q. v.)*

A jury is a body of men temporarily selected from the citizens of a particular district, and invested with power to present or indict a person for a public offense, or to try a question of fact. Code Civil Proc.Cal. § 190.

As understood at common law and as used in constitutional provision, "jury" imports body of twelve men. State v. Dalton, 206 N.C. 507, 174 S.E. 422, 424; People ex rel. Cooley v. Wilder, 255 N.Y.S. 218, 222, 234 App.Div. 256; Hall v. Brown, 129 Kan. 859, 284 P. 396.

"Jury trial" is not merely a trial by twelve men, but by twelve men selected by law, with judge who passes on many legal questions and has limited supervision over trial. Universal Truck Loading Co. v. Taylor, 178 Miss. 143, 172 So. 756, 757.

The right to "jury trial" guaranteed by Federal Constitution is the right of trial by jury as it existed at common law. Diederich v. American News Co., C.C.A.Okl., 128 F.2d 144, 145, 146.

The right to "jury trial" of controverted issues implies a trial by an impartial and qualified jury. Alexander v. R. D. Crier & Sons Co., 181 Md. 415, 30 A.2d 757, 759.

The "jury trial" guaranteed by Federal Constitution means trial by jury of 12 men in presence and under superintendence of judge empowered to instruct them on the law and advise them on the facts and, except on acquittal of criminal charge, to set aside their verdict if in judge's opinion it is contrary to law or evidence. Diederich v. American News Co., C.C.A.Okl., 128 F.2d 144, 145, 146.

The terms "jury" and "trial by jury," as used in the constitution, mean twelve competent men, disinterested and impartial, not of kin, nor personal dependents of either of the parties, having their homes within the jurisdictional limits of the court, drawn and selected by officers free from all bias in favor of or against either party, duly impaneled and sworn to render a true verdict according to the law and the evidence. State v. McClear, 11 Nev. 39; H. Wagman & Co. v. Schafer Motor Freight Service, 4 N.Y.S.2d 526, 529, 167 Misc. 681.

Common Jury

In practice. The ordinary kind of jury by which issues of fact are generally tried, as distinguished from a *special jury, (q. v.)*.

Fair and Impartial Jury

See Fair and Impartial Jury.

Foreign Jury

A jury obtained from a county other than that in which issue was joined.

Grand Jury

A jury of inquiry who are summoned and returned by the sheriff to each session of the criminal courts, and whose duty is to receive complaints and accusations in criminal cases, hear the evidence adduced on the part of the state, and find bills of indictment in cases where they are satisfied a trial ought to be had. They are first sworn, and instructed by the court.

This is called a "grand jury" because it comprises a greater number of jurors than the ordinary trial jury or "petit jury." At common law, a grand jury consisted of not less than twelve nor more than twenty-three men, and this is still the rule in many of the states, though in some the number is otherwise fixed by statute; thus in Oregon and Utah, the grand jury is composed of seven men; in South Dakota, not less than six nor more than eight; in Texas, twelve; in Idaho, sixteen; in Washington, twelve to seventeen; in North Dakota, sixteen to twenty-three; in California, nineteen; in New Mexico, twenty-one. See Ex parte Bain, 121 U.S. 1, 7 S.Ct. 781, 30 L.Ed. 849; In re Gardiner, 64 N.Y.S. 760, 31 Misc. 364; Finley v. State, 61

Ala. 204; People v. Duff, 65 How.Prac., N.Y., 365; English v. State, 31 Fla. 340, 12 So. 689; Jones v. McClaughry, 169 Iowa, 281, 151 N.W. 210, 216.

Mixed Jury

A bilingual jury; a jury of the half-tongue. See De Medietatæ Linguæ. Also a jury composed partly of negroes and partly of white men.

Petit Jury

The ordinary jury of twelve men for the trial of a civil or criminal action. So called to distinguish it from the grand jury.

A petit jury is a body of twelve men impaneled and sworn in a district court, to try and determine, by a true and unanimous verdict, any question or issue of fact, in any civil or criminal action or proceeding, according to law and the evidence as given them in the court. Gen.St. Minn.1878, c. 71, § 1 (M.S.A. § 593.01).

Pix Jury

See Pix.

Special Jury

A jury ordered by the court, on the motion of either party, in cases of unusual importance or intricacy. Called, from the manner in which it is constituted, a "struck jury." 3 Bl.Comm. 357. A jury composed of persons above the rank of ordinary freeholders; usually summoned to try questions of greater importance than those usually submitted to common juries. Brown.

Struck Jury

See Striking A Jury.

Trial Jury

The jury participating in the trial of a given case; or a jury summoned and impaneled for the trial of a case, and in this sense a petit jury as distinguished from a grand jury.

A body of men returned from the citizens of a particular district before a court or officer of competent jurisdiction, and sworn to try and determine, by verdict, a question of fact. Code Civ.Proc.Cal. § 193.

JURY ACTION. What was before adoption of Federal Rules of Civil Procedure an action at law is a "jury action". Ryan Distributing Corporation v. Caley, D.C.Pa., 51 F.Supp. 377, 379; Ransom v. Staso Milling Co., D.C.Vt., 2 F.R.D. 128, 131.

JURY-BOX. The place in court (strictly an inclosed place) where the jury sit during the trial of a cause. 1 Archb.Pr.K.B. 208; 1 Burrill, Pr. 455.

JURY COMMISSIONER. An officer charged with the duty of selecting the names to be put into the jury wheel, or of drawing the panel of jurors for a particular term of court.

JURY-LIST. A paper containing the names of jurors impaneled to try a cause, or it contains the names of all the jurors summoned to attend court.

JURY OF GOOD AND LAWFUL MEN. A jury of 12 good and lawful men. State v. Emery, 224 N.C. 581, 31 S.E.2d 858, 861.

JURY OF MATRONS. See Matrons, Jury Of.

JURY PROCESS. The process by which a jury is summoned in a cause, and by which their attendance is enforced.

JURY WHEEL. A machine containing the names of persons qualified to serve as grand and petit jurors, from which, in an order determined by the hazard of its revolutions, are drawn a sufficient number of such names to make up the panels for a given term of court.

JURYMAN. A juror; one who is impaneled on a jury.

JURYWOMAN. One member of a jury of matrons; a woman juror.

JUS. Lat. In Roman law. Right; justice; law; the whole body of law; also a right. The term is used in two meanings:

1. *"Jus"* means "law," considered in the abstract; that is, as distinguished from any specific enactment, the science or department of learning, or *quasi* personified factor in human history or conduct or social development, which we call, in a general sense, "the law." Or it means the law taken as a system, an aggregate, a whole; "the sum total of a number of individual laws taken together." Or it may designate some one particular system or body of particular laws; as in the phrases *"jus civile," "jus gentium," "jus prætorium."*

2. In a second sense, *"jus"* signifies "a right;" that is, a power, privilege, faculty, or demand inherent in one person and incident upon another; or a capacity residing in one person of controlling, with the assent and assistance of the state, the actions of another. This is its meaning in the expressions *"jus in rem," "jus accrescendi," "jus possessionis."*

It is thus seen to possess the same ambiguity as the words *"droit," "recht,"* and "right," (which see.)

Within the meaning of the maxim that *"ignorantia juris non excusat"* (ignorance of the law is no excuse), the word *"jus"* is used to denote the general law or ordinary law of the land, and not a private right. Churchill v. Bradley, 58 Vt. 403, 5 A. 189, 56 Am.Rep. 563; Cooper v. Fibbs, L.R. 2 H.L. 149; Freichnecht v. Meyer, 39 N.J.Eq. 561.

The continental jurists seek to avoid this ambiguity in the use of the word *"jus,"* by calling its former signification "objective," and the latter meaning "subjective." Thus Mackeldey (Rom.Law, § 2) says: "The laws of the first kind [compulsory or positive laws] form law *[jus]* in its objective sense, [*jus est norma agendi,* law is a rule of conduct.] The possibility resulting from law in this sense to do or require another to do is law in its subjective sense, [*jus est facultas agendi,* law is a license to act.] The voluntary action of man in conformity with the precepts of law is called 'justice,' *[justitia.]*"

Some further meanings of the word are:

An action. Bract. fol. 3. Or, rather, those proceedings in the Roman action which were conducted before the prætor.

Power or authority. *Sui juris,* in one's own power; independent. Inst. 1, 8, pr.; Bract. fol. 3. *Alieni juris,* under another's power. Inst. 1, 8, pr.

The profession *(ars)* or practice of the law. *Jus ponitur pro ipsa arte.* Bract. fol. 2b.

A court or judicial tribunal, *(locus in quo redditur jus.)* Id. fol. 3.

JUS ABSTINENDI. The right of renunciation; the right of an heir, under the Roman law, to renounce or decline the inheritance, as, for example, where his acceptance, in consequence of the necessity of paying the debts, would make it a burden to him. See Mackeld.Rom.Law, § 733.

JUS ABUTENDI. The right to abuse. By this phrase is understood the right to do exactly as one likes with property, or having full dominion over property. 3 Toullier, no. 86.

JUS ACCRESCENDI. The right of survivorship. In re Brogan's Estate, 165 Misc. 111, 300 N.Y.S. 447, 455. The right of the survivor or survivors of two or more joint tenants to the tenancy or estate, upon the death of one or more of the joint tenants. In re Capria's Estate, 89 Misc. 101, 151 N.Y.S. 385, 386.

JUS ACCRESCENDI INTER MERCATORES, PRO BENEFICIO COMMERCII, LOCUM NON HABET. The right of survivorship has no place between merchants, for the benefit of commerce. Co.Litt. 182*a*; 2 Story, Eq.Jur. § 1207; Broom, Max. 455. There is no survivorship in cases of partnership, as there is in joint-tenancy. Story, Partn. § 90.

JUS ACCRESCENDI PRÆFERTUR ONERIBUS. The right of survivorship is preferred to incumbrances. Co.Litt. 185*a*. Hence no dower or curtesy can be claimed out of a joint estate. 1 Steph. Comm. 316.

JUS ACCRESCENDI PRÆFERTUR ULTIMÆ VOLUNTATI. The right of survivorship is preferred to the last will. Co.Litt. 185*b*. A devise of one's share of a joint estate, by will, is no severance of the jointure; for no testament takes effect till after the death of the testator, and by such death the right of the survivor (which accrued at the original creation of the estate, and has therefore a priority to the other) is already vested. 2 Bl.Comm. 186; 3 Steph.Comm. 316.

JUS ACTUS. In Roman law. A rural servitude giving to a person a passage for carriages, or for cattle.

JUS AD REM. A term of the civil law, meaning "a right to a thing;" that is, a right exercisable by one person over a particular article of property in virtue of a contract or obligation incurred by another person in respect to it, and which is enforceable only against or through such other person. It is thus distinguished from *jus in re,* which is a complete and absolute dominion over a thing available against all persons.

The disposition of modern writers is to use the term *"jus ad rem"* as descriptive of a right without possession, and *"jus in re"* as descriptive of a right accompanied by possession. Or, in a somewhat wider sense, the former denotes an inchoate or incomplete right to a thing; the latter, a complete and perfect right to a thing. See The Carlos F. Roses, 177 U.S. 655, 20 S.Ct. 803, 44 L.Ed. 929; The Young Mechanic, 30 Fed.Cas. 873.

In canon law. A right to a thing. An inchoate and imperfect right, such as is gained by nomination and institution; as distinguished from *jus in re,* or complete and full right, such as is acquired by corporal possession. 2 Bl.Comm. 312.

JUS ÆLIANUM. A body of laws drawn up by Sextus Ælius, and consisting of three parts, wherein were explained, respectively: (1) The laws of the Twelve Tables; (2) the interpretation of and decisions upon such laws; and (3) the forms of procedure. In date, it was subsequent to the *jus Flavianum, (q. v.).* Brown.

JUS ÆQUUM. Equitable law. A term used by the Romans to express the adaptation of the law to the circumstances of the individual case as opposed to *jus strictum (q. v.).*

JUS ÆSNECIÆ. The right of primogeniture *(q. v.).*

JUS ALBINATUS. The *droit d'aubaine (q. v.).* See Albinatus Jus.

JUS ANGARIÆ. See Angaria; Angary, Right of.

JUS ANGLORUM. The laws and customs of the West Saxons, in the time of the Heptarchy, by which the people were for a long time governed, and which were preferred before all others. Wharton.

JUS AQUÆ HAUSTUS. In Roman law. A rural servitude giving to a person a right of watering cattle on another's field, or of drawing water from another's well.

JUS AQUÆDUCTUS. In the civil law. The name of a servitude which gives to the owner of land the right to bring down water through or from the land of another.

JUS BANCI. In old English law. The right of bench.

The right or privilege of having an elevated and separate *seat of judgment,* anciently allowed only to the king's judges, who hence were said to administer *high* justice, *(summam administrant justitiam.)* Blount.

JUS BELLI. The law of war. The law of nations as applied to a state of war, defining in particular the rights and duties of the belligerent powers themselves, and of neutral nations.

The right of war; that which may be done without injustice with regard to an enemy. Gro. de Jure B. lib. 1, c. 1, § 3.

JUS BELLUM DICENDI. The right of proclaiming war.

JUS CANONICUM. The canon law.

JUS CIVILE. Civil law. The system of law peculiar to one state or people. Inst. 1, 2, 1. Particularly, in Roman law, the civil law of the Roman people, as distinguished from the *jus gentium.* The term is also applied to the body of law called, emphatically, the "civil law."

The *jus civile* and the *jus gentium* are distinguished in this way. All people ruled by statutes and customs use a law partly peculiar to themselves, partly common to all men. The law each people has settled for itself is peculiar to the state itself, and is called *"jus civile,"* as being peculiar to that very state. The law, again, that natural reason has settled among all men,—the law that is guarded among all peoples quite alike,—is called the *"jus gentium,"* and all nations use it as if law. The Roman people, therefore, use a law that is partly peculiar to itself, partly common to all men. Hunter, Rom.Law, 38.

But this is not the only, or even the general, use of the words. What the Roman jurists had chiefly in view, when they spoke of *"jus civile,"* was not local as opposed to cosmopolitan law, but the old law of the city as contrasted with the newer law introduced by the prætor, *(jus prætorium, jus honorarium.)* Largely, no doubt, the *jus gentium* corresponds with the *jus prætorium;* but the correspondence is not perfect. Id. 39.

JUS CIVILE EST QUOD SIBI POPULUS CONSTITUIT. The civil law is what a people establishes for itself. Inst. 1, 2, 1; Jackson v. Jackson, 1 Johns., N.Y., 424, 426.

JUS CIVITATUS. The right of citizenship; the freedom of the city of Rome. It differs from *jus quiritium,* which comprehended all the privileges of a free native of Rome. The difference is much the same as between "denization" and "naturalization" with us. Wharton.

JUS CLOACÆ. In the civil law. The right of sewerage or drainage. An easement consisting in the right of having a sewer, or of conducting surface water, through the house or over the ground of one's neighbor. Mackeld. Rom. Law, § 317.

JUS COMMUNE.

In the Civil law. Common right; the common and natural rule of right, as opposed to *jus singulare, (q. v.).* Mackeld. Rom. Law, § 196.

In English law. The common law, answering to the Saxon *"folcright."* 1 Bl.Comm. 67.

JUS CONSTITUI OPORTET IN HIS QUÆ UT PLURIMUM ACCIDUNT NON QUÆ EX INOPINATO. Laws ought to be made with a view to those cases which happen most frequently, and not to those which are of rare or accidental occurrence. Dig. 1, 3, 3; Broom, Max. 43.

JUS CORONÆ. In English law. The right of the crown, or to the crown; the right of succession to the throne. 1 Bl.Comm. 191; 2 Steph. Comm. 434.

JUS CUDENDÆ MONETÆ. In old English law. The right of coining money. 2 How. State Tr. 118.

JUS CURIALITATIS. In English law. The right of curtesy. Spelman.

JUS DARE. To give or to make the law; the function and prerogative of the legislative department.

JUS DELIBERANDI. In the civil law. The right of deliberating.

A term granted by the proper officer at the request of him who is called to the inheritance, (the heir,) within which he has the right to investigate its condition and to consider whether he will accept or reject it. Mackeld.Rom. Law, § 742; Civ.Code La. art. 1026 (Civ.Code, art. 1033).

JUS DESCENDIT, ET NON TERRA. A right descends, not the land. Co. Litt. 345.

JUS DEVOLUTUM. The right of the church of presenting a minister to a vacant parish, in case the patron shall neglect to exercise his right within the time limited by law.

JUS DICERE. To declare the law; to say what the law is. The province of a court or judge. 2 Eden, 29; 3 P.Wms. 485.

JUS DICERE, ET NON JUS DARE. To declare the law, not to make it. 7 Term 696; *Arg.* Barry v. Mandell, 10 Johns., N.Y., 563, 566; 7 Exch. 543; 2 Eden 29; 4 C.B. 560, 561; Broom, Max. 140.

JUS DISPONENDI. The right of disposing.

An expression used either generally to signify the right of alienation, as when we speak of depriving a married woman of the *jus disponendi* over her separate estate, or specially in the law relating to sales of goods, where it is often a question whether the vendor of goods has the intention of reserving to himself the *jus disponendi; i. e.,* of preventing the ownership from passing to the purchaser, notwithstanding that he (the vendor) has parted with the possession of the goods. Sweet.

JUS DISTRAHENDI. The right of sale of goods pledged in case of non-payment. See Pledge; Distress.

JUS DIVIDENDI. The right of disposing of realty by will. Du Cange.

JUS DUPLICATUM. A double right; the right of possession united with the right of property; otherwise called *"droit-droit."* 2 Bl.Comm. 199.

JUS EDICERE, JUS EDICENDI. The right to issue edicts. It belonged to all the higher magistrates, but special interest is attached to the prætorian edicts in connection with the history of Roman law. See Prætor.

JUS EST ARS BONI ET ÆQUI. Law is the science of what is good and just. Dig. 1, 1, 1, 1; Bract. fol. 2*b*.

JUS EST NORMA RECTI; ET QUICQUID EST CONTRA NORMAM RECTI EST INJURIA. Law is a rule of right; and whatever is contrary to the rule of right is an injury. 3 Bulst. 313.

JUS ET FRAUS NUNQUAM COHABITANT. Right and fraud never dwell together. 10 Coke, 45*a*. Applied to the title of a statute. Id.; Best, Ev. p. 250, § 205.

JUS EX INJURIA NON ORITUR. A right does (or can) not rise out of a wrong. Broom, Max. 738, note; 4 Bing. 639.

JUS EX NON SCRIPTO. Law constituted by custom or such usage as indicates the tacit consent of the community.

JUS FALCANDI. The right of mowing or cutting. Fleta, lib. 4, c. 27, § 1. The right of cutting wood. Bract. fol. 231.

JUS FECIALE. In Roman law. The law of arms, or of heralds. A rudimentary species of international law founded on the rites and religious ceremonies of the different peoples.

JUS FIDUCIARIUM. In the civil law. A right in trust; as distinguished from *jus legitimum,* a legal right. 2 Bl.Comm. 328.

JUS FLAVIANUM. In old Roman law. A body of laws drawn up by Cneius Flavius, a clerk of Appius Claudius, from the materials to which he had access. It was a popularization of the laws. Mackeld. Rom. Law, § 39.

JUS FLUMINUM. In the civil law. The right to the use of rivers. Locc. de Jure Mar. lib. 1, c. 6.

JUS FODIENDI. In the civil and old English law. A right of digging on another's land. Inst. 2, 3, 2; Bract. fol. 222.

JUS FUTURUM. In the civil law. A future right; an inchoate, incipient, or expectant right, not yet fully vested.

It may be either *"jus delatum,"* when the subsequent acquisition or vesting of it depends merely on the will of the person in whom it is to vest, or *"jus nondum delatum,"* when it depends on the future occurrence of other circumstances or conditions. Mackeld.Rom.Law, § 191.

JUS GENTIUM. The law of nations. That law which natural reason has established among all men is equally observed among all nations, and is called the "law of nations," as being the law which all nations use. Inst. 1, 2, 1; Dig. 1, 1, 9; 1 Bl.Comm. 43; 1 Kent, Comm. 7; Mackeld. Rom. Law, § 125.

Although this phrase had a meaning in the Roman law which may be rendered by our expression "law of nations," it must not be understood as equivalent to what we now call "international law," its scope being much wider. It was originally a system of law, or more properly equity, gathered by the early Roman lawyers and magistrates from the common ingredients in the customs of the old Italian tribes,—those being the nations, *gentes,* whom they had opportunities of observing,—to be used in cases where the *jus civile* did not apply; that is, in cases between foreigners or between a Roman citizen and a foreigner. The principle upon which they proceeded was that any rule of law which was common to all the nations they knew of must be intrinsically consonant to right reason, and therefore fundamentally valid and just. From this it was an easy transition to the converse principle, viz., that any rule which instinctively commended itself to their sense of justice and reason must be a part of the *jus gentium.* And so the latter term came eventually to be about synonymous with "equity," (as the Romans understood it,) or the system of prætorian law.

Modern jurists frequently employ the term *"jus gentium privatum"* to denote private international law, or that subject which is otherwise styled the "conflict of laws;" and *"jus gentium publicum"* for public international law, or the system of rules governing the intercourse of nations with each other as persons.

JUS GLADII. The right of the sword; the executory power of the law; the right, power, or prerogative of punishing for crime. 4 Bl.Comm. 177.

JUS HABENDI. The right to have a thing. The right to be put in actual possession of property. Lewin, Trusts, 585.

JUS HABENDI ET RETINENDI. A right to have and to retain the profits, tithes, and offerings, etc., of a rectory or parsonage.

JUS HÆREDITATIS. The right of inheritance.

JUS HAURIENDI. In the civil and old English law. The right of drawing water. Fleta, lib. 4, c. 27, § 1.

JUS HONORARIUM. The body of Roman law, which was made up of edicts of the supreme magistrates, particularly the prætors.

JUS HONORUM. In Roman law. The right of holding offices. See Jus Suffragii.

JUS IMAGINIS. In Roman law. The right to use or display pictures or statues of ancestors; somewhat analogous to the right, in English law, to bear a coat of arms.

JUS IMMUNITATIS. In the civil law. The law of immunity or exemption from the burden of public office. Dig. 50, 6.

JUS IN PERSONAM. A right against a person; a right which gives its possessor a power to oblige another person to give or procure, to do or not to do, something.

JUS IN RE. A right in a thing. Denver Joint Stock Land Bank of Denver v. Dixon, 57 Wyo. 523, 122 P.2d 842, 847, 140 A.L.R. 1270. A right existing in a person with respect to an article or subject of property, inherent in his relation to it, implying complete ownership with possession, and available against all the world. See Jus ad Rem.

JUS IN RE ALIENA. An easement on servitude, or right in, or arising out of, the property of another.

JUS IN RE INHÆRIT OSSIBUS USUFRUCTUARII. A right in the thing cleaves to the person of the usufructuary.

JUS IN RE PROPRIA. The right of enjoyment which is incident to full ownership or property, and is often used to denote the full ownership or property itself. It is distinguished from *jus in re alienâ,* which is a mere easement or right in or over the property of another.

JUS INCOGNITUM. An unknown law. This term is applied by the civilians to obsolete laws. Bowyer, Mod.Civil Law, 33.

JUS INDIVIDUUM. An individual or indivisible right; a right incapable of division. 36 Eng.Law & Eq. 25.

JUS ITALICUM. A term of the Roman law descriptive of the aggregate of rights, privileges, and franchises possessed by the cities and inhabitants of Italy, outside of the city of Rome, and afterwards extended to some of the colonies and provinces of the empire, consisting principally in the right to have a free constitution, to be exempt from the land tax, and to have the title to the land regarded as Quiritarian property. See Gibbon, Rom.Emp. c. xvii; Mackeld.Rom.Law, § 43.

JUS ITINERIS. In Roman law. A rural servitude giving to a person the right to pass over an adjoining field, on foot or horseback.

JUS JURANDI FORMA VERBIS DIFFERT, RE CONVENIT; HUNC ENIM SENSUM HABERE DEBET: UT DEUS INVOCETUR. Grot. de Jur. B., l. 2, c. 13, § 10. The form of taking an oath differs in language, agrees in meaning; for it ought to have this sense: that the Deity is invoked.

JUS LATII. In Roman law. The right of Latium or of the Latins.

The principal privilege of the Latins seems to have been the use of their own laws, and their not being subject to the edicts of the prætor, and that they had occasional access to the freedom of Rome, and a participation in her sacred rites. Butl.Hor.Jur. 41.

JUS LATIUM. In Roman law. A rule of law applicable to magistrates in Latium.

It was either *majus Latium* or *minus Latium*,—the *majus Latium* raising to the dignity of Roman citizen not only the magistrate himself, but also his wife and children; the *minus Latium* raising to that dignity only the magistrate himself. Brown.

JUS LEGITIMUM. A legal right. In the civil law. A right which was enforceable in the ordinary course of law. 2 Bl.Comm. 328.

JUS LIBERORUM. In Roman law. The privilege conferred upon a woman who had three or four children.

Another author defines this privilege as one by which exemption was given from all troublesome offices. Brown, L.Dict.

In order that she should be able to take all the property given her by will, she must have had this privilege conferred upon her. Sohm, Inst.Rom.L. § 86. In the time of Hadrian, a decree was made conferring upon a mother, as such, who, being an *ingenua*, had the *jus trium liberorum*, or being a *libertina*, the *jus quatuor liberorum*, a civil law right to succeed her intestate children; *id.* § 98.

JUS MARITI. The right of a husband; especially the right which a husband acquires to his wife's movable estate by virtue of the marriage. 1 Forb. Inst. pt. 1, p. 63.

JUS MERUM. In old English law. Mere or bare right; the mere right of property in lands, without either possession or even the right of possession. 2 Bl.Comm. 197; Bract. fol. 23.

JUS MORIBUS CONSTITUTUM. See Jus Ex Non Scripto.

JUS NATURÆ. The law of nature. See Jus Naturale.

JUS NATURALE. The natural law, or law of nature; law, or legal principles, supposed to be discoverable by the light of nature or abstract reasoning, or to be taught by nature to all nations and men alike; or law supposed to govern men and peoples in a state of nature, *i. e.*, in advance of organized governments or enacted laws.

This concept originated with the philosophical jurists of Rome, and was gradually extended until the phrase came to denote a supposed basis or substratum common to all systems of positive law, and hence to be found, in greater or less purity, in the laws of all nations. And, conversely, they held that if any rule or principle of law was observed in common by all peoples with whose systems they were acquainted, it must be a part of the *jus naturale*, or derived from it. Thus the phrases *"jus naturale"* and *"jus gentium"* came to be used interchangeably.

JUS NATURALE EST QUOD APUD HOMINES EANDEM HABET POTENTIAM. Natural right is that which has the same force among all mankind. 7 Coke, 12.

JUS NAVIGANDI. The right of navigating or navigation; the right of commerce by ships or by sea. Locc. de Jure Mar. lib. 1, c. 3.

JUS NECIS. In Roman law. The right of death, or of putting to death. A right which a father anciently had over his children.

See Jus Vitæ Necisque.

JUS NON HABENTI TUTE NON PARETUR. One who has no right cannot be safely obeyed. Hob. 146.

JUS NON PATITUR UT IDEM BIS SOLVATUR. Law does not suffer that the same thing be twice paid.

JUS NON SACRUM. In Roman law. That portion of the *jus publicum* which regulated the duties of magistrates.

Non-sacred law; that which dealt with the duties of civil magistrates, the preservation of public order, and the rights and duties of persons in their relation to the state. Morey, Rom.L. 223. It was analogous to that which would now be called the police power.

JUS NON SCRIPTUM. The unwritten law. 1 Bl. Comm. 64.

JUS OFFERENDI. In Roman law, the right of subrogation, that is, the right of succeeding to the lien and priority of an elder creditor on tendering or paying into court the amount due to him. See Mackeld. Rom.Law, § 355.

JUS ONERIS FERENDI. An urban servitude in the Roman Law, the owner of which had the right of supporting and building upon the house wall of another.

JUS PAPIRIANUM. The civil law of Papirius.

The title of the earliest collection of Roman *leges curiatæ*, said to have been made in the time of Tarquin, the last of the kings, by a *pontifex maximus* of the name of Sextus or Publius Papirius. Very few fragments of this collection now remain, and the authenticity of these has been doubted. Mackeld.Rom.Law, § 21.

JUS PASCENDI. In the civil and old English law. The right of pasturing cattle. Inst. 2, 3, 2; Bract. fols. 53*b*, 222.

JUS PATRONATUS. In English ecclesiastical law. The right of patronage; the right of presenting a clerk to a benefice. Blount.

A commission from the bishop, where two presentations are offered upon the same avoidance, directed usually to his chancellor and others of competent learning, who are to summon a jury of six clergymen and six laymen to inquire into and examine who is the rightful patron. 3 Bl.Comm. 246; 3 Steph.Comm. 517.

JUS PERSONARUM. Rights of persons. Those rights which, in the civil law, belong to persons as such, or in their different characters and relations; as parents and children, masters and servants, etc.

JUS PŒNITENDI. In Roman law, the right of rescission or revocation of an executory contract on failure of the other party to fulfill his part of the agreement. See Mackeld. Rom. Law, § 444.

JUS PORTUS. In maritime law. The right of port or harbor.

JUS POSSESSIONIS. The right of possession.

JUS POSSIDENDI. The right of possessing, which is the legal consequence of ownership. It is to be distinguished from the *jus possessionis* (*q. v.*), which is a right to possess which may exist without ownership.

JUS POSTLIMINII. In the Civil law. The right of postliminy; the right or claim of a person who had been restored to the possession of a thing, or to a former condition, to be considered as though he had never been deprived of it. Dig. 49, 15, 5; 3 Bl.Comm. 107, 210.

In International law. The right by which property taken by an enemy, and recaptured or rescued from him by the fellow-subjects or allies of the original owner, is restored to the latter upon certain terms. 1 Kent, Comm. 108.

JUS PRÆSENS. In the civil law. A present or vested right; a right already completely acquired. Mackeld. Rom. Law, § 191.

JUS PRÆTORIUM. In the civil law. The discretion of the prætor, as distinct from the *leges*, or standing laws. 3 Bl.Comm. 49. That kind of law which the prætors introduced for the purpose of aiding, supplying, or correcting the civil law, for the public benefit. Dig. 1, 1, 7. Called, also, "*jus honorarium,*" (*q. v.*).

JUS PRECARIUM. In the civil law. A right to a thing held for another, for which there was no remedy by legal action, but only by entreaty or request. 2 Bl.Comm. 328.

JUS PRESENTATIONIS. The right of presentation.

JUS PRIVATUM. Private law; the law regulating the rights, conduct, and affairs of individuals, as distinguished from "public" law, which relates to the constitution and functions of government and the administration of criminal justice. See Mackeld. Rom. Law, § 124.

Also private ownership, or the right, title, or dominion of a private owner, as distinguished from "*jus publicum,*" which denotes public ownership, or the ownership of property by the government, either as a matter of territorial sovereignty or in trust for the benefit and advantage of the general public. In this sense, a state may have a double right in given property, *e. g.*, lands covered by navigable waters within its boundaries, including both "*jus publicum,*" a sovereign or political title, and "*jus privatum,*" a proprietary ownership. See Oakland v. Oakland Water Front Co., 118 Cal. 160, 50 P. 277; G. L. Webster Co. v. Steelman, 172 Va. 342, 1 S.E.2d 305, 311.

JUS PROJICIENDI. In the civil law. The name of a servitude which consists in the right to build a projection, such as a balcony or gallery, from one's house in the open space belonging to one's neighbor, but without resting on his house. Dig. 50, 16, 242; Id. 8, 2, 2; Mackeld. Rom. Law, § 317.

JUS PROPRIETATIS. The right of property, as distinguished from the *jus possessionis* or right of possession. Bract. fol. 3. Called by Bracton "*jus merum,*" the mere right. Id.; 2 Bl.Comm. 197; 3 Bl.Comm. 19, 176.

JUS PROTEGENDI. In the civil law. The name of a servitude. It is a right by which a part of the roof or tiling of one house is made to extend over the adjoining house. Dig. 50, 16, 242, 1; Id. 8, 2, 25; Id. 8, 5, 8, 5.

JUS PROTIMESEOS. The right of pre-emption of a landlord in case the tenant wishes to dispose of his rights as a perpetual lessee. Sohm. Inst. Rom.L. § 57. *Pactum protimeseos* was the right of pre-emption to the seller; *i. e.* in case the buyer should sell, he must sell to the former seller. Hunter. Rom. L., 503.

JUS PROVINCIARUM. A franchise conferred upon provincials much more limited than that conferred upon the people of Italy.

It has been described as "equivalent to the *jus italicum* minus the freedom from land taxation which the latter right involved. In short, the provincials possessed no status as Roman citizens; and even their capacity of ownership in their own land was qualified by their tributary obligations to Rome. The civil incapacity of the provincials had reference, however, merely to their exclusion from the strictly legal rights sanctioned by the *jus civile.*" Morey, Rom.L. 55.

JUS PUBLICUM. Public law, or the law relating to the constitution and functions of government and its officers and the administration of criminal justice. Also public ownership, or the paramount or sovereign territorial right or title of the state or government. See Jus Privatum.

It implies a right in a sovereign or public capacity to be exercised for the interest or benefit of the state or the public, as distinguished from the exercise in a proprietary capacity of a right of the sovereign or a right possessed by an individual in common with the public. G. L. Webster Co. v. Steelman, 172 Va. 342, 1 S.E.2d 305, 311.

Sovereign's right of jurisdiction and dominion for governmental purposes over all lands and waters within its territorial limits, including tidal waters and their bottoms, is sometimes termed "jus publicum." Commonwealth v. City of Newport News, 158 Va. 521, 164 S.E. 689, 696.

JUS PUBLICUM ET PRIVATUM QUOD EX NATURALIBUS PRÆCEPTIS AUT GENTIUM AUT CIVILIBUS EST COLLECTUM; ET QUOD IN JURE SCRIPTO JUS APPELLATUR, ID IN LEGE ANGLIÆ RECTUM ESSE DICITUR. Co. Litt. 185. Public and private law is that which is collected from natural principles, either of nations or in states; and that which in the civil law is called "*jus,*" in the law of England is said to be "right."

JUS PUBLICUM PRIVATORUM PACTIS MUTARI NON POTEST. A public law or right cannot be altered by the agreements of private persons.

JUS QUÆSITUM. A right to ask or recover; for example, in an obligation there is a binding of the obligor, and a *jus quœsitum* in the obligee. 1 Bell, Comm. 323.

JUS QUIRITIUM. The old law of Rome, that was applicable originally to patricians only, and, under the Twelve Tables, to the entire Roman people, was so called, in contradistinction to the *jus prœtorium,* (*q. v.,*) or equity. Brown.

JUS QUO UNIVERSITATES UTUNTUR EST IDEM QUOD HABENT PRIVATI. The law which governs corporations is the same which governs individuals. Foster v. Essex Bank, 16 Mass. 265, 8 Am.Dec. 135.

JUS RECUPERANDI. The right of recovering [lands.]

JUS RELICTÆ. In Scotch law. The right of a relict; the right or claim of a relict or widow to her share of her husband's estate, particularly the movables. 2 Kames, Eq. 340; 1 Forb. Inst. pt. 1, p. 67.

JUS REPRESENTATIONIS. The right of representing or standing in the place of another, or of being represented by another.

JUS RERUM. The law of things. The law regulating the rights and powers of persons over things; how property is acquired, enjoyed, and transferred.

JUS RESPICIT ÆQUITATEM. Law regards equity. Co. Litt. 24*b*; Broom, Max. 151.

JUS SACRUM. In Roman law. That portion of the public law which was concerned with matters relating to public worship and including the regulation of sacrifices and the appointment of priests. There was a general division of the *jus publicum* into *jus sacrum* and *jus non sacrum* (*q. v.*).

JUS SANGUINIS. The right of blood. See Jus Soli.

JUS SCRIPTUM. In English law. Written law, or statute law, otherwise called "*lex scripta,*" as distinguished from the common law, "*lex non scripta.*" 1 Bl.Comm. 62.

In Roman law. Written law. Inst. 1, 2, 3. All law that was actually committed to writing, whether it had originated by enactment or by custom, in contradistinction to such parts of the law of custom as were not committed to writing. Mackeld. Rom. Law, § 126.

After stating that the Roman law was written and unwritten just as it was among the Greeks, Justinian adds: "The written part consists of laws, *plebiscita, senatus-consulta,* enactments of emperors, edicts of magistrates, and answers of jurisprudents." Sand.Inst.Just. 1, 2, 3. See Jus Ex Non Scripto.

JUS SINGULARE. In the civil law. A peculiar or individual rule, differing from the *jus commune,* or common rule of right, and established for some special reason. Mackeld. Rom. Law, § 196.

JUS SOLI. The law of the place of one's birth as contrasted with *jus sanguinis,* the law of the place of one's descent or parentage. It is of feudal origin. Hershey, Int. L. 237.

JUS SPATIANDI. A right of way over land by the public by uses merely for the purposes of recreation and instruction.

It is usually limited to the cases of highways, parks, and squares. The public were denied any right in the grounds containing the ancient druidical monuments at Stonehenge; Attorney-General v. Antrobus, [1905] 2 Ch. 188. See 19 Harv.L.Rev. 55. See Du Cange, Glossarium, for a definition under the word *spatiare.*

JUS STAPULÆ. In old European law. The law of staple; the right of staple. A right or privilege of certain towns of stopping imported merchandise, and compelling it to be offered for sale in their own markets. Locc. de Jure Mar. lib. 1, c. 10.

JUS STILLICIDII VEL FLUMINIS RECIPIENDI. In Roman law. An urban servitude giving the owner a right to project his roof over the land of another or to open a house drain upon it.

JUS STRICTUM. Strict law; law interpreted without any modification, and in its utmost rigor.

JUS SUFFRAGII. In Roman law. The right of voting. This and the *jus honorum* (*q. v.*) were the public rights of the Roman citizen.

JUS SUPERVENIENS AUCTORI ACCRESCIT SUCCESSORI. A right growing to a possessor accrues to the successor. Halk. Lat. Max. 76.

JUS TERTII. The right of a third party.

A tenant, bailee, etc., who pleads that the title is in some person other than his landlord, bailor, etc., is said to set up a *jus tertii.* Dempsey Oil & Gas Co. v. Citizens' Nat. Bank, 110 Okl. 39, 235 P. 1104, 1107.

JUS TESTAMENTORUM PERTINET ORDINARIO. Y. B. 4 Hen. VII., 13*b*. The right of testaments belongs to the ordinary.

JUS TIGNI IMMITTENDI. In Roman law. An urban servitude which gave the right of inserting a beam into the wall of another.

JUS TRIPERTITUM. In Roman law. A name applied to the Roman law of wills, in the time of Justinian, on account of its three-fold derivation, viz., from the prætorian edict, from the civil law, and from the imperial constitutions. Maine, Anc. Law, 207.

JUS TRIPLEX EST,—PROPIETATIS, POSSESSIONIS, ET POSSIBILITATIS. Right is threefold,—of property, of possession, and of possibility.

JUS TRIUM LIBERORUM. In Roman law. A right or privilege allowed to the parent of three or more children. 2 Kent, Comm. 85; 2 Bl.Comm. 247. These privileges were an exemption from the trouble of guardianship, priority in bearing offices, and a treble proportion of corn. Adams, Rom. Ant. (Am. Ed.) 227.

JUS UTENDI. The right to use property without destroying its substance. It is employed in contradistinction to the *jus abutendi.* 3 Toullier, no. 86.

JUS VENANDI ET PISCANDI. The right of hunting and fishing.

JUS VENDIT QUOD USUS APPROBAVIT. Ellesm. Postn. 35. The law dispenses what use has approved.

JUS VITÆ NECISQUE. In Roman law. The right of life and death.

Originally a father, or his *pater-familias* if he was himself in domestic subjection, could decide—not arbitrarily, but judicially—whether or not to rear his child; and while this right became subject to certain restrictions, yet when the child had grown up, the father, in the exercise of his domestic jurisdiction, might visit his son's misconduct, both in private and public life, with such punishment as he though fit, even banishment, slavery, or death. In the early Empire these rights became relaxed, and they disappeared in the Justinian law. Murihead, Roman Law, 28, 346, 417. See Patria Potestas.

JUSJURANDI FORMA VERBIS DIFFERT, RE CONVENIT; HUNC ENIM SENSUM HABERE DEBET, UT DEUS INVOCETUR. The form of taking an oath differs in language, agrees in meaning; for it ought to have this sense, that the Deity is invoked. Grotius, b. 2, c. 13, s. 10.

JUSJURANDUM. Lat. An oath.

JUSJURANDUM INTER ALIOS FACTUM NEC NOCERE NEO PRODESSE DEBET. An oath made between others ought neither to hurt nor profit. 4 Inst. 279.

JUST. In the sense of "joust," see Justs, *infra.*

JUST. Conforming to or consonant with, what is legal or lawful, legally right, lawful. National Surety Corporation v. Mullins, 262 Ky. 465, 90 S.W.2d 707, 708. Correct, true, due. Wisdom v. Board of Sup'rs of Polk County, 236 Iowa 669, 19 N.W.2d 602, 606. Equitable. Carter v. Carter, 181 Okl. 204, 73 P.2d 404, 405. Reasonable. National Surety Corporation v. Mullins, 262 Ky. 465, 90 S.W.2d 707, 708; Wisdom v. Board of Sup'rs of Polk County, 236 Iowa 669, 19 N.W.2d 602, 606. Right; in accordance with law and justice. McKeon v. National Casualty Co., 216 Mo.App. 507, 270 S.W. 707, 712; New Haven Water Co. v. City of New Haven, 106 Conn. 562, 139 A. 99, 105; Lake Hancock & C. R. Co. v. Stinson, 77 Fla. 333, 81 So. 512.

"The words 'just' and 'justly' do not always mean 'just' and 'justly' in a moral sense, but they not unfrequently, in their connection with other words in a sentence, bear a very different signification. It is evident, however, that the word 'just' in the statute [requiring an affidavit for an attachment to state that plaintiff's claim is *just*] means 'just' in a moral sense; and from its isolation, being made a separate subdivision of the section, it is intended to mean 'morally just' in the most emphatic terms. The claim must be *morally* just, as well as *legally* just, in order to entitle a party to an attachment." Robinson v. Burton, 5 Kan. 300.

JUST BEYOND. Will directing erection of chapel "just beyond" the basin means barely beyond, scarcely beyond, or closely beyond, with the least practical space between it and the basin. Carroll v. Cave Hill Cemetery Co., 172 Ky. 204, 189 S.W. 186, 189.

JUST CAUSE. A cause outside legal cause, which must be based on reasonable grounds, and there must be a fair and honest cause or reason, regulated by good faith. Dubois v. Gentry, 182 Tenn. 103, 184 S.W.2d 369, 371; Quick v. Southern Churchman Co., 171 Va. 403, 199 S.E. 489, 494, 495. Fair, adequate, reasonable cause. In re Municipal Garage in and for City of Utica, 141 Misc. 15, 252 N.Y.S. 18, 32. Legitimate cause; legal or lawful ground for action; such reasons as will suffice in law to justify the action taken. State v. Langford, 90 Or. 251, 176 P. 197, 202; State v. Donzi, 133 La. 925, 63 So. 405, 406; State v. Wohlfort, 123 Kan. 62, 254 P. 317, 320; Boston Elevated Ry. Co. v. Commonwealth, 310 Mass. 528, 39 N.E.2d 87, 112, 124.

Under provision that no license shall be revoked without "just cause," the words imply that charges should be made and notice of hearing given and an opportunity to be heard afforded, Carroll v. California Horse Racing Board, 16 Cal.2d 164, 105 P.2d 110, 111.

JUST CAUSE OF PROVOCATION. That which will constitute the homicide murder in the second degree, as distinguished from a lawful provocation, which will reduce it to manslaughter. State v. McCracken, 341 Mo. 697, 108 S.W.2d 372, 376.

JUST COMPENSATION. As regards property taken for public use, the term is comprehensive and includes all elements. Jacobs v. U. S., Ala., 290 U.S. 13, 54 S.Ct. 26, 78 L.Ed. 142, 96 A.L.R. 1; Metropolitan Water Dist. of Southern California v. Adams, 16 Cal.2d 676, 107 P.2d 618, 621. But does not exceed market value. Sigurd City v. State, 105 Utah 278, 142 P.2d 154, 158; U. S. v. Waterhouse, C.C.A.Hawaii, 132 F.2d 699, 703. It means a settlement which leaves one no poorer or richer than he was before the property was taken. U. S. ex rel. Tennessee Valley Authority v. Indian Creek Marble Co., D.C.Tenn., 40 F.Supp. 811, 818, 819; adequate compensation, State v. Hale, Tex.Civ.App., 96 S.W.2d 135, 141; In re Board of Sup'rs of Chenango County, Co. Ct., 6 N.Y.S.2d 732, 739; fair market value, Cameron Development Co. v. United States, C.C.A.Fla., 145 F.2d 209, 210; U. S. ex rel. and for Use of Tennessee Valley Authority v. Davis, D.C.Tenn., 41 F.Supp. 595, 597, 598; United States v. Certain Parcels of Land in City of Baltimore, Parcel No. 12, D.C.Md., 43 F.Supp. 687, 689. Full and perfect equivalent of the property taken. Housing Authority of Shreveport v. Green, 200 La. 463, 8 So.2d 295, 298; U. S. v. 2.4 Acres of Land, More or Less, in Lake County, Ill., C.C.A.Ill., 138 F.2d 295, 297. It is the value of property taken at time of taking. United States v. 813.96 Acres of Land in Ouachita County, Ark., D.C.Ark., 45 F. Supp. 535, 538; Danforth v. U. S., Mo., 308 U.S. 271, 60 S.Ct. 231, 236, 84 L.Ed. 240; plus compensation for delay in payment. Kieselbach v. Commissioner of Internal Revenue, 317 U.S. 399, 63 S. Ct. 303, 305, 87 L.Ed. 358; or consequential damages to the owner. In re Board of Water Supply of City of New York, 277 N.Y. 452, 14 N.E.2d 789; or value of use of property from date of taking possession to date of judgment if possession is taken by condemnor prior to judgment. Los Angeles County Flood Control Dist. v. Hansen, 48 Cal.App.2d 314, 119 P.2d 734, 735. It requires that the owner be put in as good position pecuniarily as he would otherwise have been. Kansas City Southern Ry. Co. v. Commissioner of Internal Revenue, C.C.A.8, 52 F.2d 372, 379; In re Gratiot Ave., City of Detroit, 294 Mich. 569, 293 N.W. 755, 757; U. S. ex rel. and for Use of Tennessee Valley Authority v. Powelson, C.C.A.4, 118 F.2d 79, 87.

To arrive at fair indemnity, the interests of the public and of the owner, and all the circumstances of the particular appropriation, should be taken into consideration. Lewis, Em.Dom. § 462. And see Butler Hard Rubber Co. v. Newark, 61 N.J.L. 32, 40 A. 224; Bauman v. Ross, 167 U.S. 548, 17 S.Ct. 966, 42 L.Ed. 270; Newman v. Metropolitan El. R. Co., 118 N.Y. 623, 23 N.E. 901, 7 L.R.A. 289. Evidence of reproduction cost of structures affected by condemnation, less depreciation, improvements made on the property, consequential damage to portions not appropriated, and the fair market value of the property taken as of the date of the appropriation, may be relevant in determining "just compensation," according to the situation in a particular case. In re Board of Water Supply of City of New York, 277 N.Y. 452, 14 N.E.2d 789.

"Just compensation" is synonymous with "due process of law." Simms v. Dillon, 119 W.Va. 284, 193 S.E. 331, 337, 113 A.L.R. 787.

As regards public utility, just compensation is fair return on value of property. Fort Worth Gas Co. v. City of Fort Worth, D.C.Tex., 35 F.2d 743, 747; New York Edison Co. v. Maltbie, 150 Misc. 200, 270 N.Y.S. 409; State v. Tri-State Telephone & Telegraph Co., 204 Minn. 516, 284 N.W. 294, 306.

On government's cancellation of contract, "just compensation" recoverable consists of such sum as in court's judgment will fairly compensate contractor, Enright v. U. S., Ct.Cl., 54 F.2d 182, 190; it is the value of contract at time of cancellation, not profits which it would have produced. De Laval Steam Turbine Co. v. U. S., Ct.Cl., 284 U.S. 61, 52 S.Ct. 78, 79, 76 L.Ed. 168.

JUST DEBTS. As used in a will or a statute, this term means legal, valid, and incontestable obligations, not including such as are barred by the statute of limitations or voidable at the election of the party. See Burke v. Jones, 2 Ves. & B. 275; Peck v. Botsford, 7 Conn. 176, 18 Am.Dec. 92; Collamore v. Wilder, 19 Kan. 82; Smith v. Mayo, 9 Mass. 63, 6 Am.Dec. 28; Jones' Ex'r v. Jones, 275 Ky. 753, 122 S.W.2d 779, 780.

JUST PRIOR. "Immediately preceding", "just before", without appreciable lapse of time before. Jackson v. McCrary, Tex.Civ.App., 148 S.W.2d 942, 944. It means before the time and connotes nearness in point of time. Salmons v. Dun & Bradstreet, Mo.App., 153 S.W.2d 556, 562, modified on other grounds 349 Mo. 498, 162 S.W.2d 245, 141 A.L.R. 674. It means some period of time before. Hoelzel v. Chicago, R. I. & P. Ry. Co., 337 Mo. 61, 85 S.W.2d 126, 129.

JUST TITLE. By the term "just title," in cases of prescription, is meant a title which the possessor may have received from any person whom he honestly believed to be the real owner, provided the title were such as to transfer the ownership of the property. Civ.Code La. art. 3484; Davis v. Gaines, 104 U.S. 400, 26 L.Ed. 757; Johnson v. Sugar, 163 La. 785, 112 So. 721, 722; B. Fernandez & Bros. v. Ayllon, 266 U.S. 144, 45 S.Ct. 52, 69 L. Ed. 209. One good against all the world. Virginia & West Virginia Coal Co. v. Charles, C.C.A. Va., 254 F. 379, 387.

JUST VALUE. In taxation, the fair, honest, and reasonable value of property, without exaggeration or depreciation; its actual market value. State v. Smith, 158 Ind. 543, 63 N.E. 214, 63 L.R.A. 116; Winnipiseogee Lake, etc., Co. v. Gilford, 67 N.H. 514, 35 A. 945. Correct, honest and true value. Fruit Growers Express Co. v. Brett, 94 Mont. 281, 22 P.2d 171.

JUSTA. In old English law. A certain measure of liquor, being as much as was sufficient to drink at once. Mon. Angl. t. 1, c. 149.

JUSTA CAUSA. In the civil law. A just cause; a lawful ground; a legal transaction of some kind. Mackeld. Rom. Law, § 283.

JUSTICE, *v.* In old English practice. To do justice, to see justice done; to summon one to do justice.

JUSTICE, *n.* In common law. The title given in England to the judges of the king's bench and the common pleas, and in America to the judges of the supreme court of the United States and of the appellate courts of many of the states.

It is said that this word in its Latin form *(justitia)* was properly applicable only to the judges of common-law courts, while the term *"judex"* designated the judges of ecclesiastical and other courts. See Leg.Hen. I, §§ 24, 63; Co.Litt. 71*b*.

The same title is also applied to some of the judicial officers of the lowest rank and jurisdiction, such as police justices and justices of the peace.

A term used in the United States and England to designate judicial officers and magistrates of every grade. School Dist. No. 18 v. Grubbs Special School Dist., 184 Ark. 863, 43 S.W.2d 765, 766.

In Feudal law. Jurisdiction; judicial cognizance of causes or offenses.

High justice was the jurisdiction or right of trying crimes of every kind, even the highest. This was a privilege claimed and exercised by the great lords or barons of the middle ages. 1 Robertson's Car. V., appendix, note 23. *Low* justice was jurisdiction of petty offenses.

In Jurisprudence. The constant and perpetual disposition to render every man his due. Inst. 1, 1, pr.; 2 Inst. 56. See Borden v. State, 11 Ark. 528, 44 Am.Dec. 217; Collier v. Lindley, 203 Cal. 641, 266 P. 526, 530; The John E. Mulford, D.C. N.Y., 18 F. 455. The conformity of our actions and our will to the law. Toull. Droit Civil Fr. tit. prél. no. 5; Livingston Oil Corporation v. Henson, 90 Okl. 76, 215 P. 1057, 1059.

Commutative justice is that which should govern contracts. It consists in rendering to every man the exact measure of his dues, without regard to his personal worth or merits, *i. e.*, placing all men on an equality. *Distributive* justice is that which should govern the distribution of rewards and punishments. It assigns to each the rewards which his personal merit or services deserve, or the proper punishment for his crimes. It does not consider all men as equally deserving or equally blameworthy, but discriminates between them, observing a just proportion and comparison. This distinction originated with Aristotle. (Eth.Nic. V.) See Fonbl.Eq. 3; Toull.Droit Civil Fr. tit. prél. no. 7.

In the most extensive sense of the word "justice" differs little from "virtue;" for it includes within itself the whole circle of virtues. Yet the common distinction between them is that that which, considered positively and in itself, is called "virtue," when considered relatively and with respect to others has the name of "justice." But "justice," being in itself a part of "virtue," is confined to things simply good or evil, and consists in a man's taking such a proportion of them as he ought. Bouvier.

"Equity" and "Justice" are substantially equivalent terms, if not synonymous. In re Lessig's Estate, 6 N.Y. S.2d 720, 721, 168 Misc. 889.

Under constitutional provision guaranteeing right to obtain justice, the "justice" to be administered by courts is not an abstract justice as conceived of by the judge but justice according to law or, as it is phrased in the constitution, "conformably to the laws". State ex rel. Department of Agriculture v. McCarthy, 238 Wis. 258, 299 N.W. 58, 64.

In Norman French. Amenable to justice. Kelham.

JUSTICE AYRES (or AIRES). In Scotch law. Circuits made by the judges of the justiciary courts, through the country, for the distribution of justice. Bell.

JUSTICE IN EYRE. From the old French word *"eire," i. e.,* a journey. Those justices who in ancient times were sent by commission into various counties, to hear more especially such causes as were termed "pleas of the crown," were called "justices in eyre."

They differed from justices in oyer and terminer, inasmuch as the latter were sent to one place, and for the purpose of trying only a limited number of special causes; whereas the justices in eyre were sent through the various counties, with a more indefinite and general commission. In some respects they resembled our present justices of assize, although their authority and manner of proceeding differed much from them. Brown.

JUSTICE OF THE PEACE. In American law. A judicial officer of inferior rank having (usually) civil jurisdiction limited to that prescribed by statute in civil cases and in criminal proceedings, prosecutions and commitments of offenders. See Com. v. Frank, 21 Pa.Co.Ct.R. 120; Weikel v. Cate, 58 Md. 110; Smith v. Abbott, 17 N.J.L. 366; People v. Mann, 97 N.Y. 530, 49 Am.Rep. 556; Commonwealth, for Use and Benefit of Warren County, v. Cox's Adm'r, 264 Ky. 327, 94 S.W.2d 632.

In English law. Judges of record appointed by the crown to be justices within a certain district, (*e. g.*, a county or borough,) for the conservation of the peace, and for the execution of divers things, comprehended within their commission and within divers statutes, committed to their charge. Stone, J. Pr. 2.

JUSTICE SEAT. In English law. The principal court of the forest, held before the chief justice in eyre, or chief itinerant judge or his deputy; to hear and determine all trespasses within the forest, and all claims of franchises, liberties, and privileges, and all pleas and causes whatsoever therein arising. 3 Bl. Comm. 72; 4 Inst. 291; 3 Steph. Comm. 440.

JUSTICEMENTS. An old general term for all things appertaining to justice.

JUSTICER. The old form of *justice.* Blount.

JUSTICE'S CLERK. An amanuensis of the justice. A justice of the peace is regarded as his own clerk, and, in making entries on his docket, he acts in a ministerial capacity. State ex rel. Morris Bldg. & Inv. Co. v. Brown, 228 Mo.App. 760, 72 S.W.2d 859, 862.

JUSTICE'S COURTS. Inferior tribunals, not of record, with limited jurisdiction, both civil and criminal, held by justices of the peace. There are courts so called in many of the states. See Searl v. Shanks, 9 N.D. 204, 82 N.W. 734; Brownfield v. Thompson, 96 Mo.App. 340, 70 S.W. 378.

JUSTICES OF APPEAL. The title given to the ordinary judges of the English court of appeal. The first of such ordinary judges are the two former lords justices of appeal in chancery, and one other judge appointed by the crown by letters patent.

JUSTICES OF ASSIZE. These justices, or, as they are sometimes called, "justices of *nisi prius,"* are judges of the superior English courts, who go on circuit into the various counties of England and Wales for the purpose of disposing of such causes as are ready for trial at the assizes. See Assize.

JUSTICES OF GAOL DELIVERY. Those justices who are sent with a commission to hear and determine all causes appertaining to persons, who, for any offense, have been cast into gaol.

Part of their authority was to punish those who let to mainprise those prisoners who were not bailable by law, and they seem formerly to have been sent into the country upon this exclusive occasion, but afterwards had the same authority given them as the justices of assize. Brown.

JUSTICES OF LABORERS. In old English law. Justices appointed to redress the frowardness of laboring men, who would either be idle or have unreasonable wages. Blount.

JUSTICES OF NISI PRIUS. In English law. This title is now usually coupled with that of *justices of assize;* the judges of the superior courts acting on their circuits in both these capacities. 3 Bl. Comm. 58, 59.

JUSTICES OF OYER AND TERMINER. Certain persons appointed by the king's commission, among whom were usually two judges of the courts at Westminster, and who went twice in every year to every county of the kingdom, (except London and Middlesex,) and, at what was usually called the "assizes," heard and determined all treasons, felonies, and misdemeanors. Brown.

JUSTICES OF THE BENCH. The justices of the court of common bench or common pleas.

JUSTICES OF THE FOREST. In old English law. Officers who had jurisdiction over all offenses committed within the forest against vert or venison. The court wherein these justices sat and determined such causes was called the "justice seat of the forest." They were also sometimes called the "justices in eyre of the forest." Brown.

JUSTICES OF THE HUNDRED. Hundredors; lords of the hundreds; they who had the jurisdiction of hundreds and held the hundred courts.

JUSTICES OF THE JEWS. Justices appointed by Richard I. to carry into effect the laws and orders which he had made for regulating the money contracts of the Jews. Brown.

JUSTICES OF THE PAVILION. In old English law. Judges of a pyepowder court, of a most transcendant jurisdiction, anciently authorized by the bishop of Winchester, at a fair held on St. Giles' Hills near that city. Cowell; Blount.

JUSTICES OF THE QUORUM. See Quorum.

JUSTICES OF TRAIL-BASTON. See Trail-Baston.

JUSTICESHIP. Rank or office of a justice.

JUSTICIABLE. Proper to be examined in courts of justice. Subject to action of court of justice. International Harvest Hat Co. v. Caradine Hat Co., D.C.Mo., 17 F.Supp. 79, 80.

JUSTICIABLE CONTROVERSY. A controversy in which a claim of right is asserted against one who has an interest in contesting it. State ex rel. La Follette v. Dammann, 230 Wis. 17, 264 N.W. 627, 629, 103 A.L.R. 1089. A question as may properly come before a tribunal for decision. Duart Mfg. Co. v. Philad Co., D.C.Del., 30 F.Supp. 777, 779, 780.

JUSTICIAR. In old English law. A judge or justice. One of several persons learned in the law, who sat in the *aula regis,* and formed a kind of court of appeal in cases of difficulty. Also spelled *justicier.*

High Justicier

In old French and Canadian law. A feudal lord who exercised the right called "high justice." Guyot, Inst. Feod. c. 26.

JUSTICIARII ITINERANTES. In English law. Justices in eyre, who formerly went from county to county to administer justice. They were so called to distinguish them from justices residing at Westminster, who were called *"justicii residentes."* Co. Litt. 293.

JUSTICIARII RESIDENTES. In English law. Justices or judges who usually resided in Westminster. They were so called to distinguish them from justices in eyre. Co. Litt. 293.

JUSTICIARY. An old name for a judge or justice. The word is formed on the analogy of the Latin *"justiciarius"* and French *"justicier,"* and is a variant of *justiciar* (*q. v.*).

JUSTICIARY COURT. The chief criminal court of Scotland, consisting of five lords of session, added to the justice general and justice clerk; of whom the justice general, and in his absence, the justice clerk, is president. This court has a jurisdiction over all crimes, and over the whole of Scotland. Bell.

JUSTICIATUS. Judicature; prerogative.

The proceeding by which bail establish their ability to perform the undertaking of the bond or recognizance.

JUSTICIER. Fr. See Justiciar.

JUSTICIES. In English law. A writ directed to the sheriff, empowering him, for the sake of dispatch, to try an action in his county court for a larger amount than he has the ordinary power to do. It is so called because it is a commission to the sheriff to do the party justice, the word itself meaning, "You may do justice to ———." 3 Bl.Comm. 36; 4 Inst. 266.

JUSTIFIABLE. Rightful; defensible; warranted or sanctioned by law; that which can be shown to be sustained by law; as justifiable homicide. See Homicide.

JUSTIFIABLE CAUSE. "Justifiable cause" for prosecution is well-founded belief of person of ordinary caution, prudence, and judgment in existence of facts essential to prosecution. Dickerson v. Atlantic Refining Co., 201 N.C. 90, 159 S.E. 446, 449.

JUSTIFICATION. A maintaining or showing a sufficient reason in court why the defendant did what he is called upon to answer, particularly in an action of libel.

A defense of justification is a defense showing the libel to be true, or in an action of assault showing the violence to have been necessary. See Steph.Pl. 184. A sufficient lawful reason for acting or failing to act. Mercardo v. State, 86 Tex.Cr.R. 559, 218 S.W. 491, 492; State v. Rish, 104 S.C. 250, 88 S.E. 531, 534; Townsend v. U. S., 68 App. D.C. 223, 95 F.2d 352, 358.

Just cause or excuse. State v. Williams, 166 S.C. 63, 164 S.E. 415, 424. Just, lawful excuse for act. Louis Kamm, Inc., v. Flink, 113 N.J.L. 582, 175 A. 62, 67, 99 A.L.R. 1. Reasonable excuse. State v. Mueller, 208 Wis. 543, 243 N.W. 478, 479.

JUSTIFICATORS. A kind of compurgators, (*q. v.*,) or those who by oath justified the innocence or oaths of others; as in the case of wager of law.

JUSTIFIED. Done on adequate reasons sufficiently supported by credible evidence, when weighed by unprejudiced mind, guided by common sense and by correct rules of law. Selectmen of Wakefield v. Judge of First Dist. Court of Eastern Middlesex, 262 Mass. 477, 160 N.E. 427, 430.

JUSTIFYING BAIL consists in proving the sufficiency of bail or sureties in point of property, etc.

The production of bail in court, who there justify themselves against the exception of the plaintiff.

JUSTINIANIST. A civilian; one who studies the civil law.

JUSTINIAN'S INSTITUTES. See Institutes.

JUSTITIA. Lat. Justice. A jurisdiction, or the office of a judge.

JUSTITIA DEBET ESSE LIBERA, QUIA NIHIL INIQUIUS VENALI JUSTITIA; PLENA, QUIA JUSTITIA NON DEBET CLAUDICARE; ET CELERIS, QUIA DILATIO EST QUÆDAM NEGATIO. Justice ought to be free, because nothing is more iniquitous than venal justice; full, because justice ought not to halt; and speedy, because delay is a kind of denial. 2 Inst. 56.

JUSTITIA EST CONSTANS ET PERPETUA VOLUNTAS JUS SUUM CUIQUE TRIBUENDI. Justice is a steady and unceasing disposition to render to every man his due. Inst. 1, 1, pr.; Dig. 1, 1, 10.

JUSTITIA EST DUPLEX, VIZ., SEVERE PUNIENS ET VERE PRÆVENIENS. 3 Inst. Epil. Justice is double; punishing severely, and truly preventing.

JUSTITIA EST VIRTUS EXCELLENS ET ALTISSIMO COMPLACENS. 4 Inst. 58. Justice is excellent virtue and pleasing to the Most High.

JUSTITIA FIRMATUR SOLIUM. 3 Inst. 140. By justice the throne is established.

JUSTITIA NEMINI NEGANDA EST. Jenk. Cent. 178. Justice is to be denied to none.

JUSTITIA NON EST NEGANDA NON DIFFERENDA. Jenk. Cent. 93. Justice is neither to be denied nor delayed.

JUSTITIA NON NOVIT PATREM NEC MATREM; SOLAM VERITATEM SPECTAT JUSTITIA. Justice knows not father nor mother; justice looks at truth alone. 1 Bulst. 199.

JUSTITIA PIEPOUDROUS. Speedy justice. Bract. 333*b*.

JUSTITIUM. Lat. In the civil law. A suspension or intermission of the administration of justice in courts; vacation time. Calvin.

JUSTIZA. In Spanish law. The name anciently given to a high judicial magistrate, or supreme judge, who was the ultimate interpreter of the laws, and possessed other high powers.

JUSTNESS. Conformity to truth, propriety, accuracy, or the like. John W. Masury & Son v. Bisbee Lumber Co., 49 Ariz. 443, 68 P.2d 679, 693.

As used in statute providing for acknowledgment of "justness" of claim to remove bar of limitations, refers to moral obligation. John W. Masury & Son v. Bisbee Lumber Co., 49 Ariz. 443, 68 P.2d 679, 693.

JUSTS, or JOUSTS. Exercises between martial men and persons of honor, with spears, on horseback; different from *tournaments,* which were military exercises between many men in troops. 24 Hen. VIII. c. 13.

JUSTUM NON EST ALIQUEM ANTENATUM MORTUUM FACERE BASTARDUM, QUI PRO TOTA VITA SUA PRO LEGITIMO HABETUR. It is not just to make a bastard after his death one elder born who all his life has been accounted legitimate. 8 Coke, 101.

JUVENILE COURTS. A court having special jurisdiction, of a paternal nature, over delinquent and neglected children. Bryant v. Brown, 151 Miss. 398, 118 So. 184, 188, 60 A.L.R. 1325.

JUXTA. Lat. Near; following; according to.

JUXTA CONVENTIONEM. According to the covenant. Fleta lib. 4, c. 16, § 6.

JUXTA FORMAM STATUTI. According to the form of the statute.

JUXTA RATAM. At or after the rate. Dyer, 82.

JUXTA TENOREM SEQUENTEM. According to the tenor following. 2 Salk. 417. A phrase used in the old books when the very words themselves referred to were set forth. Id.; 1 Ld. Raym. 415.

JUXTAPOSITION. A placing or being placed in nearness or contiguity; or side by side; as a juxtaposition of words. Brown v. State, 126 Tex. Cr.R. 449, 72 S.W.2d 269, 270.

In patent law, "juxtaposition" is the English equivalent of "aggregation." Mesta Mach. Co. v. Federal Machine & Welder Co., C.C.A.Pa., 110 F.2d 479, 481.

JUZGADO. In Spanish law. The judiciary; the body of judges; the judges who concur in a decree.

K

K. B. An abbreviation for "King's Bench," (*q. v.*).

K. C. An abbreviation for "King's Counsel."

KABANI. A person who, in oriental states, supplies the place of our notary public.

KABOOLEAT. In Hindu law. A written agreement, especially one signifying assent, as the counterpart of a revenue lease, or the document in which a payer of revenue, whether to the government, the zamindar, or the farmer, expresses his consent to pay the amount assessed upon his land. Wils. Ind. Gloss.

KAHAKAI. Hawaiian. The junction or edge of the sea and land. See Andrew's Hawaiian Dictionary. Seashore, the sand of the beach, the region of country bordering on the sea. The word comes from kaha meaning scratch or mark and kai meaning sea or salt water.

KAHAWAI. Hawaiian. The flowing stream. It may include the bed or channel of the stream and may, also, include the portion of such channel covered only in times of high water or of freshets.

KAIA. A key, kay, or quay. Spelman.

KAIAGE, or KAIAGIUM. A wharfage-due.

KAIN. In Scotch law. Poultry renderable by a vassal to his superior, reserved in the lease as the whole or a part of the rent. Bell.

KALALCONNA. A duty paid by shopkeepers in Hindostan, who retail spirituous liquors; also the place where spirituous liquors are sold. Wharton.

KALENDÆ. In English ecclesiastical law. Rural chapters, or conventions of the rural deans and parochial clergy, which were formerly held on the calends of every month; hence the name. Paroch. Antiq. 604.

KALENDAR. An account of time, exhibiting the days of the week and month, the seasons, etc. More commonly spelled "calendar."

KALENDARIUM. In the civil law. A calendar; a book of accounts, memorandum-book, or debt-book; a book in which accounts were kept of moneys loaned out on interest. Dig. 32, 64. So called because the Romans used to let out their money and receive the interest on the calends of each month. Calvin.

KALENDS. See Calends.

KARL. In Saxon and old English law. A man; a serving man. *Buskarl,* a seaman. *Huskarl,* a house servant. Spelman.

KARRATA. In old records. A cart-load. Cowell; Blount.

KAST. In Swedish law. Jettison; a literal translation of the Latin *"jactus."*

KAST–GELD. Contribution for a jettison; average.

KATATONIA. See Insanity.

KAY. A quay, or key.

KAYAGE. See Cayagium.

KAZY. A Mohammedan judge or magistrate in the East Indies, appointed originally by the court at Delhi, to administer justice according to their written law.

KEELAGE. The right to demand money for the privilege of anchoring a vessel in a harbor; also the money so paid.

KEELHALE, KEELHAUL. To drag a person under the keel of a ship by means of ropes from the yard-arms, a punishment formerly practiced in the British navy. Enc. Lond.

KEELS. This word is applied, in England, to vessels employed in the carriage of coals. Jacob.

KEEP, *n.* A strong tower or hold in the middle of any castle or fortification, wherein the besieged make their last efforts of defense, was formerly, in England, called a "keep;" and the inner pile within the castle of Dover, erected by King Henry II. about the year 1153, was termed the "King's Keep;" so at Windsor, etc. It seems to be something of the same nature with what is called abroad a "citadel." Jacob.

KEEP, *v.* To continue. People v. Roseberry, 23 Cal.App.2d 13, 71 P.2d 944; Briggs v. U. S., C.C.A. Mich., 45 F.2d 479, 480.

To have or retain in one's power or possession; not to lose or part with; to preserve or retain. Deans v. Gay, 132 N.C. 227, 43 S.E. 643.

To maintain, carry on, conduct, or manage; as, to "keep" a liquor saloon, bawdy house, gaming table, nuisance, inn, hotel or policy game. State v. Irvin, 117 Iowa 469, 91 N.W. 760; State v. Cox, 52 Vt. 474; State v. Cieri, 128 Conn. 149, 20 A.2d 733, 734.

To maintain, tend, harbor, feed, and shelter; as, to "keep" a dangerous animal, to "keep" a horse at livery, to "keep" a dog. Allen v. Ham, 63 Me. 536; Skinner v. Caughey, 64 Minn. 375, 67 N.W. 203; Elender v. White, La.App., 14 So.2d 280.

To maintain continuously and methodically for the purposes of a record; as, to "keep" books. See Backus v. Richardson, 5 Johns., N.Y., 483; Hammond v. Niagara Fire Ins. Co., 92 Kan. 851, 142 P. 936, 937. Thus to "keep" records of court means, not only to preserve the manual possession of the records, books, and papers, but to correctly transcribe therein the proceedings of the court. Myers v. Colquitt, Tex.Civ.App., 173 S.W. 993, 997.

To maintain continuously and without stoppage or variation; as, when a vessel is said to "keep her course," that is, continue in motion in the same general direction in which she was previously sailing. See The Britannia, 153 U.S. 130, 14 S.Ct. 795, 38 L.Ed. 660; to maintain, to cause to continue without essential change of condition. Arden v. Boone, Tex.Com.App., 221 S.W. 265, 266.

To take care of and to preserve from danger, harm, or loss. Tannenbaum v. Seacoast Trust Co. of Asbury Park, 16 N.J.Misc. 234, 198 A. 855, 869.

A place where liquor is "possessed" is subject to abatement as place where liquor is "kept". Butler Hotel Co. v. U. S., C.C.A.Wash., 35 F.2d 76.

As applied to school refers to conduct of school activities. Borchers v. Taylor, 83 N.H. 564, 145 A. 666, 668, 63 A.L.R. 874.

As used in commitment order commanding marshal "to take and keep and safely deliver" prisoner to custody of penitentiary warden means to keep prisoner in local jail until time to take train for penitentiary. Smith v. Swope, C.C.A.Wash., 91 F.2d 260, 261.

As used in statute concerning voting by persons "kept" at public or charitable institutions, the word implies being beneficiaries of charity. Rathbun v. Smith, 23 N.Y. S.2d 95, 97, 175 Misc. 246.

As used in statute declaring it unlawful to keep a gaming house, implies duration. State v. Cieri, 128 Conn. 149, 20 A.2d 733, 734.

As used in statute that vehicles shall keep to right side of center of road or highway, means that drivers should get on right side of highway as quickly as possible and remain there. Mahoning Savings & Trust Co. v. Kellner, 131 Ohio St. 69, 1 N.E.2d 616, 619.

The word "kept" in policies providing that gasoline shall not be "kept, used, or allowed" on premises implies some degree of permanence of storage thereof, Bouchard v. Dirigo Mut. Fire Ins. Co., 113 Me. 17, 92 A. 899, 900, L.R. A.1915D, 187; D. I. Felsenthal Co. v. Northern Assur. Co., Limited, of London, 284 Ill. 343, 120 N.E. 268, 271, 1 A.L.R. 602; Home Ins. Co. of New York v. Bridges, 172 Ky. 161, 189 S.W. 6, 7, L.R.A.1917C, 276; while "keeping in possession" contraband liquors means to have habitually in possession, State v. Burns, 133 S.C. 238, 130 S.E. 641, 642. Within statutory provision defining common nuisance the word means kept for sale or barter or other commercial purposes. Burner v. Commonwealth, 140 Va. 508, 125 S.E. 324, 325; Singer v. U. S., C.C.A.N.J., 288 F. 695, 696; Ayers v. U. S., C.C.A.Ark., 58 F.2d 607, 610; Cuttera v. U. S., C.C.A.La., 31 F.2d 439. Within statute relating to slot machine for gaming, means holding the machine in readiness for purpose of obtaining bettors, or for gaming. Mooney v. State, 146 Tex.Cr.R. 64, 171 S.W.2d 494, 495.

KEEP DOWN INTEREST. The payment of interest periodically as it becomes due; it does not include the payment of all arrears of interest which may have become due on any security from the time when it was executed. 4 El. & Bl. 211.

KEEP HOUSE. As used in English bankrupt laws the phrase denotes an act of bankruptcy.

It is committed when a trader absents himself from his place of business and retires to his private residence to evade the importunity of creditors. The usual evidence of "keeping house" is refusal to see a creditor who has called on the debtor at his house for money. Robs.Bankr. 119.

KEEP IN REPAIR. When a lessee is bound to keep the premises in repair, he must have them in repair at all times during the term; and, if they are at any time out of repair, he is guilty of a breach of the covenant. 1 Barn. & Ald. 585.

KEEP OPEN. To allow general access to one's shop, for purposes of traffic, is a violation of a statute forbidding him to "keep open" his shop on the Lord's day, although the outer entrances are closed. Com. v. Harrison, 11 Gray, Mass., 308.

To "keep open," in the sense of such a law, implies a readiness to carry on the usual business in the store, shop, saloon, etc. Lynch v. People, 16 Mich. 472.

KEEPER. A custodian, manager, or superintendent; one who has the care, custody, or management of any thing or place; one who has or holds possession of anything. Schultz v. State, 32 Ohio St. 281; State v. Rozum, 8 N.D. 548, 80 N.W. 481; Fishell v. Morris, 57 Conn. 547, 18 A. 717, 6 L.R.A. 82; Stevens v. People, 67 Ill. 590; Janssen v. Voss, 189 Wis. 222, 207 N.W. 279, 280; State v. Weston, 235 Iowa 148, 15 N.W.2d 922, 923; People v. Dubinsky, Sp.Sess., 31 N.Y.S.2d 234, 238.

KEEPER OF DOG. A harborer of a dog. Elender v. White, La.App., 14 So.2d 280, 282. Any person, other than owner, harboring or having in his possession any dog. Hancock v. Finch, 9 A.2d 811, 126 Conn. 121. One who, either with or without owner's permission, undertakes to manage, control, or care for it as dog owners in general are accustomed to do. Raymond v. Bujold, 89 N. H. 380, 199 A. 91, 92.

KEEPER OF A BAWDY HOUSE or HOUSE OF ILL FAME. A person who has control, proprietorship, or management of the house in question. Jones v. State, 10 Okl.Cr. 79, 133 P. 1134, 1135; Gregg v. People, 65 Colo. 390, 176 P. 483, 485; State v. Weston, 235 Iowa 148, 15 N.W.2d 922, 923.

KEEPER OF THE FOREST. In old English law. An officer (called also chief warden of the forest) who had the principal government of all things relating to the forest, and the control of all officers belonging to the same. Cowell; Blount.

KEEPER OF THE GREAT SEAL. In English law. A high officer of state, through whose hands pass all charters, grants, and commissions of the king under the great seal.

He is styled "lord keeper of the great seal," and this office and that of lord chancellor are united under one person; for the authority of the lord keeper and that of the lord chancellor were, by St. 5 Eliz. c. 18, declared to be exactly the same; and, like the lord chancellor, the lord keeper at the present day is created by the mere delivery of the king's great seal into his custody. Brown.

KEEPER OF THE KING'S CONSCIENCE. A name sometimes applied to the chancellor of England, as being formerly an ecclesiastic and presiding over the royal chapel. 3 Bl. Comm. 48.

KEEPER OF THE PRIVY SEAL. In English law. An officer through whose hands pass all charters signed by the king before they come to the great seal. He is a privy councillor, and was anciently called "clerk of the privy seal," but is now generally called the "lord privy seal." Brown.

KEEPER OF THE TOUCH. The master of the assay in the English mint. 12 Hen. VI. c. 14.

KEEPING A GAMBLING HOUSE OR PLACE. A proprietor is guilty if with his knowledge, acquiescence, and consent, express or implied, gambling is carried on upon premises in his possession as owner or lessee, or under his management or control, by his associates or subordinates who are likewise guilty if they are present aiding and assisting in carrying on such gambling operations for him. Commonwealth v. Pinkenson, 138 Pa. Super. 485, 11 A.2d 176, 179. A proprietor of a place not kept for the purpose of gambling is guilty if he allows gambling to be carried on and participates in it or receives a benefit from it in some way. People v. Dubinsky, Sp.Sess., 31 N.Y. S.2d 234, 238.

KEEPING A GAMBLING TABLE OR BANK. If one has possession or custody of a gaming table, and authority over its use, and supervises the gaming, he is guilty. Smith v. State, 29 Ala.App. 302, 196 So. 132, 133.

KEEPING A LOOKOUT. Being watchful of movements of driver's own vehicle, as well as those of the thing seen by him. Rebmann v. Heesch, 227 Iowa 566, 288 N.W. 695, 701.

KEEPING BOOKS. Preserving an intelligent record of a merchant's or tradesman's affairs with such reasonable accuracy and care as may properly be expected from a man in that business.

KEEPING TERM. In English law. A duty performed by students of law, consisting in eating a sufficient number of dinners in hall to make the term count for the purpose of being called to the bar. Moz. & W.

KEEPING THE PEACE. Avoiding a breach of the peace; dissuading or preventing others from breaking the peace.

KEIKI. Hawaiian. Popular meaning is child, but the meaning of that word in any particular instance depends on context in which it is used, and it can mean "descendant of any generation." In re Kanoa's Trust Estate, 393 P.2d 753, 760, 47 Haw. 610; Kalakaua v. Parke, 8 Haw. 620, 621.

KELP-SHORE. The land between high and low water mark. Stroud. Jud. Dict.

KENILWORTH EDICT. An edict or award between Henry III. and those who had been in arms against him; so called because made at Kenilworth Castle, in Warwickshire, *anno* 51 Hen. III., A. D. 1266. It contained a composition of those who had forfeited their estates in that rebellion, which composition was five years' rent of the estates forfeited. Wharton.

KENNING TO THE TERCE. In Scotch law. The ascertainment by a sheriff of the just proportion of the husband's lands which belongs to the widow in virtue of her *terce* or third. An assignment of dower by sheriff. Erskine, Inst. 11. 9. 50; Bell, Dict.

KENTLAGE. In maritime law. A permanent ballast, consisting usually of pigs of iron, cast in a particular form, or other weighty material, which, on account of its superior cleanliness, and the small space occupied by it, is frequently preferred to ordinary ballast. Abb. Shipp. 5.

KENTREF. The division of a county; a hundred in Wales. See Cantred.

KENTUCKY RESOLUTIONS. A series of resolutions drawn up by Jefferson, and adopted by the legislature of Kentucky in 1799, protesting against the "alien and sedition laws," declaring their illegality, announcing the strict constructionist theory of the federal government, and declaring "nullification" to be "the rightful remedy."

KERF. The jagged end of a stick of wood made by the cutting. Pub. St. Mass. 1882, p. 1292.

KERHERE. A customary cart-way; also a commutation for a customary carriage-duty. Cowell.

KERNELLATUS. Fortified or embattled. Co. Litt. 5*a*.

KERNES. In English law. Idlers; vagabonds.

KEROSENE. A rock or earth oil. Morse v. Ins. Co., 30 Wis. 534, 11 Am.Rep. 587.

It is, in a commercial sense, a refined coal or earth oil, and is embraced within those terms as used in an insurance policy. Bennett v. Ins. Co., 81 N.Y. 273, 37 Am.Rep. 501. It is not petroleum, but made from the latter by a process of a distillation and refinement. Bennett v. Ins. Co., 81 N.Y. 273, 37 Am.Rep. 501.

Oil having a specific gravity of 34.2 degrees. Grosjean v. Chalmette Petroleum Corporation, La. App., 182 So. 142, 143.

KEY. A wharf for the lading and unlading of merchandise from vessels. More commonly spelled "quay."

An instrument for fastening and opening a lock.

Any descriptive words in a land contract which lead unerringly to the land. Blumberg v. Nathan, 190 Ga. 64, 8 S.E.2d 374, 375. Reference to something more definite by which an indefinite description of property is made certain. Erwin v. Hardin, 187 Ga. 275, 200 S.E. 159, 162.

KEYAGE. A toll paid for loading and unloading merchandise at a key or wharf. Rowan v. Portland, 8 B. Mon., Ky., 253.

KEYS, in the Isle of Man, are the twenty-four chief commoners, who form the local legislature. 1 Steph. Comm. 99.

In old English law. A guardian, warden, or keeper.

KEYS OF COURT. In old Scotch law. Certain officers of courts. See Claves Curiæ.

KEYUS. A guardian, warden, or keeper. Mon. Angl. tom. 2, p. 71.

KHALSA. In Hindu law. An office of government in which the business of the revenue department was transacted under the Mohammedan government, and during the early period of British rule. Khalsa lands are lands, the revenue of which is paid into the exchequer. Wharton.

KIBEI. *Jap.* A person born in the United States of Japanese parents and who has returned to Japan for education and training. 1945 Report of the Tenney Joint Fact-Finding Committee on Un-American Activities to the California Legislature, p. 48; Reader's Guide to Periodical Literature.

KIDDER. In English law. An engrosser of corn to enhance its price. Also a huckster.

KIDDLE. In old English law. A dam or open wear in a river, with a loop or narrow cut in it, accommodated for the laying of engines to catch fish. 2 Inst 38; Blount.

KIDNAPPING. At common law, the forcible abduction or stealing and carrying away of a person from own country to another. 4 Bl.Comm. 219, Collier v. Vaccaro, C.C.A.Md., 51 F.2d 17, 19; State v. Berry, 200 Wash. 495, 93 P.2d 782, 787, 792; Commonwealth v. Cartusciello, 100 Pa.Super. 473, 478; Doss v. State, 220 Ala. 30, 123 So. 231, 232, 60 A.L.R. 712; the unlawful seizure and removal of person from own country or state against his will, State v. Olsen, 76 Utah 181, 289 P. 92, 93. In American law, the intent to send the victim out of the country does not constitute a necessary part of the offense. The term includes false imprisonment plus the removal of the person to some other place. 2 Bish. Crim. Law, § 671. See State v. Rollins, 8 N.H. 567; State v. Sutton, 116 Ind. 527, 19 N.E. 602; Samson v. State, 37 Ohio App. 79, 174 N.E. 162, 163; People v. Fick, 89 Cal. 144, 26 P. 759; Furlong v. German-American Press Ass'n, Mo.Sup., 189 S.W. 385, 389.

It is the abduction and detention of person, to exact money or for other unlawful end. In re Dubroca y Paniagua, D.C.Pa., 33 F.2d 181, 182; asportation of victim, without authority of law, with intent of detaining victim, State v. Taylor, 70 N.D. 201, 293 N.W. 219, 223, 224; Keith v. State, 120 Fla. 847, 163 So. 136; carrying away person from his place of residence, forcibly or fradulently. Ex parte Kelsey, 19 N.J.Misc. 488, 21 A.2d 676, 678; intentional taking of person and compelling him to be detained against his will, State v. Taylor, 70 N.D. 201, 293 N.W. 219, 223, 224; restraint of victim with intent to cause him to be secretly confined or imprisoned against his will, or to be sent out of the state against his will, State v. Berry, 200 Wash. 495, 93 P.2d 782, 787; unlawful and forcible confinement of person with intent to cause him to be secretly confined, or imprisoned involuntarily or sent out of state against his will, Doss v. State, 23 Ala.App. 168, 123 So. 237, 241; unlawful detention or imprisonment regardless of purpose. State v. Berry, 200 Wash. 495, 93 P.2d 782, 787, 792; willful and unlawful seizing of person against his will with intent to cause him to be confined, imprisoned, or detained, People v. Weiss, 300 N.Y.S. 249, 254, 252 App. Div. 463. The essence of offense is the unlawful secret imprisonment. State v. Berry, 200 Wash. 495, 93 P.2d 782, 787, 792. Under the statutes of many states, one who enters another's automobile and, without lawful authority, compels the driver against his will to drive to some other place, is guilty of kidnapping. Blashfield, Cyc. of Automobile Law and Prac., Perm. Ed., § 5528.42.

KILDERKIN. A measure of eighteen gallons.

KILKETH. An ancient servile payment made by tenants in husbandry. Cowell.

KILL, *v.* To deprive of life; to destroy the life of an animal or person. The word "homicide" expresses the killing of a human being. See Carroll v. White, 33 Barb., N.Y., 620; Porter v. Hughey, 2 Bibb., Ky., 232; Com. v. Clarke, 162 Mass. 495, 39 N.E. 280; Fisher v. State, 109 Ark. 456, 160 S.W. 210, 213.

The word "kill" contains no implication of crime. Pilcher v. State, 16 Ala.App. 237, 77 So. 75.

KILL, *n.* A Dutch word, signifying a channel or bed of the river, and hence the river or stream itself. It is found used in this sense in descriptions of land in old conveyances. French v. Carhart, 1 N.Y. 96.

KILLED. The passive verb "to be killed" must generally impart to every one a meaning of some kind of external violence. City of Fort Smith v. Hairston, 196 Ark. 1005, 120 S.W.2d 689, 691.

KILLED INSTANTLY, in collision, may mean that death was instantaneous but not precisely coincidental with the impact. Cash v. Addington, 46 N.M. 451, 131 P.2d 265, 266; Justin v. Ketcham, 297 Mich. 592, 298 N.W. 294, 295.

KILLING BY MISADVENTURE. Accidental killing of a person where the slayer is doing a lawful act, unaccompanied by any criminal carelessness or reckless conduct, State v. Dean, 2 W.W.Harr., Del., 290, 122 A. 448, 449; excusable homicide occurring where one engaged in doing lawful act, without intention to do harm and, with proper precaution to avoid danger, unfortunately kills another. State v. Phillips, 7 W.W.Harr. 544, 187 A. 108, 111.

KILLYTH-STALLION. A custom by which lords of manors were bound to provide a stallion for the use of their tenants' mares. Spelman.

KIN. Relation or relationship by blood or consanguinity. "The nearness of *kin* is computed according to the civil law." 2 Kent, Comm. 413. See Keniston v. Mayhew, 169 Mass. 166, 47 N.E. 612; Lusby v. Cobb, 80 Miss. 715, 32 So. 6; State v. Bielman, 86 Wash. 460, 150 P. 1194; Poff v. Pennsylvania R. Co., D.C.N.Y., 57 F.Supp. 625, 626. As to "next of kin," see Next.

The primary and ordinary meaning of the word "kin" is related by ties of consanguinity, but the word "kin" is sometimes used in a general sense to include relationship by blood or by marriage. State v. Hooper, 140 Kan. 481, 37 P.2d 52.

KIND. Class, grade, or sort. City of St. Louis v. James Braudis Coal Co., Mo.App., 137 S.W.2d 668, 670. Genus; generic class; description. See In Kind.

KINDRED. Relation by birth or consanguinity. Relatives by blood. Next of kin. "Kindred of the whole blood, preferred to kindred of the half blood." 4 Kent, Comm. 404, notes. See In re Carroll's Estate, 153 Misc. 649, 275 N.Y.S. 911; Butler v. Elyton Land Co., 84 Ala. 384, 4 So. 675;

Wetter v. Walker, 62 Ga. 144; O'Connell v. Powers, 291 Mass. 153, 197 N.E. 162, 163; Frank v. Frank, 180 Tenn. 114, 172 S.W.2d 804, 806.

KING. The sovereign, ruler, or chief executive magistrate of a state or nation whose constitution is of the kind called "monarchical" is thus named if a man; if it be a woman, she is called "queen."

The word expresses the idea of one who rules singly over a whole people or has the highest executive power; but the office may be either hereditary or elective, and the sovereignty of the king may or may not be absolute, according to the constitution of the country.

See Emperor.

KING CAN DO NO WRONG. This maxim means that the king is not responsible legally for aught he may please to do, or for any omission. Aust. Jur. sect. VI.

It does not mean that everything done by the government is just and lawful, but that whatever is exceptionable in the conduct of public affairs is not to be imputed to the king, 2 Steph.Com., 11th ed. 486.

KING–CRAFT. The art of governing.

KINGDOM. A country where an officer called a "king" exercises the powers of government, whether the same be absolute or limited. Wolff, Inst. Nat. § 994. In some kingdoms, the executive officer may be a woman, who is called a "queen."

KING–GELD. A royal aid; an escuage (*q. v.*).

KING'S ADVOCATE. An English advocate who holds, in the courts in which the rules of the canon and civil law prevail, a similar position to that which the attorney general holds in the ordinary courts, *i. e.*, he acts as counsel for the crown in ecclesiastical, admiralty, and probate cases, and advises the crown on questions of international law. In order of precedence it seems that he ranks after the attorney general. 3 Steph. Comm. 275*n*.

KINGS–AT–ARMS. The principal herald of England was of old designated "king of the heralds," a title which seems to have been exchanged for "king-at-arms" about the reign of Henry IV.

The kings-at-arms at present existing in England are three—Garter, Clarencieux, and Norroy, besides Bath, who is not a member of the college. Scotland is placed under an officer called "Lyon King-at-Arms," and Ireland is the province of one named "Ulster." Wharton.

KING'S BENCH. The supreme court of common law in England, being so called because the king used formerly to sit there in person, the style of the court being "*coram ipso rege.*"

It was called the "queen's bench" in the reign of a queen, and during the protectorate of Cromwell it was styled the "upper bench." It consisted of a chief justice and three puisne justices, who were by their office the sovereign conservators of the peace and supreme coroners of the land. It was a remnant of the *aula regis,* and was not originally fixed to any certain place, but might follow the king's person, though for some centuries past it usually sat at Westminster. It had a very extended jurisdiction both in criminal and civil causes; the former in what was called the "crown side" or "crown office," the latter in the "plea side," of the court. Its civil jurisdiction was gradually enlarged until it embraced all species of personal actions. Since the judicature acts, this court constitutes the "king's bench division" of the "high court of justice." See 3 Bl.Comm. 41–43.

KING'S CHAMBERS. Those portions of the seas, adjacent to the coasts of Great Britain, which are inclosed within headlands so as to be cut off from the open sea by imaginary straight lines drawn from one promontory to another.

KING'S CORONER AND ATTORNEY. An officer of the court of king's bench, usually called "the master of the crown office," whose duty it is to file informations at the suit of a private subject by direction of the court. 4 Bl. Comm. 308, 309; 4 Steph. Comm. 374, 378.

KING'S COUNSEL. Barristers or serjeants who have been called within the bar and selected to be the king's counsel. They answer in some measure to the *advocati fisci,* or advocates of the revenue, among the Romans. They must not be employed against the crown without special leave, which is, however, always granted, at a cost of about nine pounds. 3 Bl. Comm. 27.

KING'S EVIDENCE. When several persons are charged with a crime, and one of them gives evidence against his accomplices, on the promise of being granted a pardon, he is said to be admitted king's or (in America) state's evidence. 4 Steph. Comm. 395; Sweet.

KING'S PROCTOR. A proctor or solicitor representing the crown in the former practice of the courts of probate and divorce.

In petitions for dissolution of marriage, or for declarations of nullity of marriage, the king's proctor may, under the direction of the attorney general, and by leave of the court, intervene in the suit for the purpose of proving collusion between the parties. Mozley & Whitley.

KING'S REMEMBRANCER. An officer of the central office of the English supreme court.

Formerly he was an officer of the exchequer, and had important duties to perform in protecting the rights of the crown; *e. g.,* by instituting proceedings for the recovery of land by writs of intrusion, *(q. v.,)* and for the recovery of legacy and succession duties; but of late years administrative changes have lessened the duties of the office. Sweet.

He was at the head of the department which had charge of all revenue suits, and of matters pertaining to the office of sheriff. He attended as the officer of the king's bench when the lord mayor made his appearance on November 9th, and as representing the old court of exchequer when the city of London did suit and service in discharge of quit-rents for certain lands anciently held under the crown. He presided at the Trial of the Pyx, the assaying and weighing of the coins of the realm. See Remembrances of Sir F. Pollock.

KING'S SILVER. In old English practice. A fine due the king *pro licentia concordandi,* (for leave to agree,) in the process of levying a fine. 5 Coke, 39, 43; 2 Inst. 511; 2 Bl. Comm. 350.

KING'S WIDOW. In feudal law. A widow of the king's tenant in chief, who was obliged to take oath in chancery that she would not marry without the king's leave.

KINSFOLK. Relations; those who are of the same family.

KINSHOTE. In Saxon law. A composition or satisfaction paid for killing a kinsman. Spelman.

KINSMAN. A man of the same race or family. Wood v. Mitcham, 92 N.Y. 379.

KINSWOMAN. A female relation.

KINTAL, or KINTLE. A hundred pounds in weight. See Quintal.

KINTLIDGE. A ship's ballast. See Kentlage.

KIPPER-TIME. In old English law. The space of time between the 3d of May and the Epiphany, in which fishing for salmon in the Thames, between Gravesend and Henley-on-Thames, was forbidden. Rot. Parl. 50 Edw. III.

KIRBY'S QUEST. In English law. An ancient record remaining with the remembrancer of the exchequer, being an inquisition or survey of all the lands in England, taken in the reign of Edward I. by John de Kirby, his treasurer. Blount; Cowell.

KIRK. In Scotch law. A church; the church; the established church of Scotland.

KIRK-MOTE. A meeting of parishioners on church affairs.

KIRK-OFFICER. The beadle of a church in Scotland.

KIRK-SESSION. A parochial church court in Scotland, consisting of the ministers and elders of each parish.

KISSING THE BOOK. The ceremony of touching the lips to a copy of the Bible, used in administering oaths. It is the external symbol of the witness' acknowledgment of the obligation of the oath.

KIST. In Hindu law. A stated payment; installment of rent.

KLEPTOMANIA. In medical jurisprudence. A species (or symptom) of mania, consisting in an irresistible propensity to steal. Looney v. State, 10 Tex.App. 525, 38 Am.Rep. 646; State v. Reidell, 9 Houst., Del., 470, 14 A. 550; Lowe v. State, 70 S.W. 206, 44 Tex.Cr.R. 224 (citing Hurst v. State, 40 Tex.Cr.R. 378, 46 S.W. 635, 50 S.W. 719).

It is said to be often shown in cases of women, laboring under their peculiar diseases or of those far advanced in pregnancy. A sharp distinction is made between kleptomania and the tendency to steal so commonly observed in the well defined forms of insanity; the former is a defective mental characteristic approaching the confines of insanity on one subject alone, while the individual, on all other subjects, is perfectly sane. It differs from shoplifting in that the shoplifter steals for a purpose, and only those articles which are of value, while the kleptomaniac takes goods of any description, often of no use to herself and with no motive for their possession; 4 Am.Lawy. 533.

KNACKER. One who slaughters useless or diseased animals or deals in such. Cent. Dict. A regular occupation in London and other large cities, regulated by act of parliament August 18, 1911.

KNAVE. A rascal; a false, tricky, or deceitful person. The word originally meant a boy, attendant, or servant, but long-continued usage has given it its present signification.

KNAVESHIP. A portion of grain given to a mill-servant from tenants who were bound to grind their grain at such mill.

KNEEL. To bend the knees in worship without resting on them is to kneel. 36 L.J.Ecc. 10.

KNIGHT. In English law. The next personal dignity after the nobility.

Of knights there are several orders and degrees. The first in rank are knights of the Garter, instituted by Richard I. and improved by Edward III. in 1344; next follows a knight banneret; then come knights of the Bath, instituted by Henry IV., and revived by George I.; and they were so called from a ceremony of bathing the night before their creation. The last order are knights bachelors, who, though the lowest, are yet the most ancient, order of knighthood; for we find that King Alfred conferred this order upon his son Athelstan. 1 Bl.Comm. 403.

KNIGHTENGUILD. An ancient guild or society formed by King Edgar.

KNIGHTHOOD. The rank, order, character, or dignity of a knight.

KNIGHT-MARSHAL. In English law. An officer in the royal household who has jurisdiction and cognizance of offenses committed within the household and verge, and of all contracts made therein, a member of the household being one of the parties. Wharton.

KNIGHTS BACHELORS. In English law. The most ancient, though lowest, order of knighthood. 1 Bl. Comm. 404.

KNIGHTS BANNERET. In English law. Those created by the sovereign in person on the field of battle. They rank, generally, after knights of the Garter. 1 Bl. Comm. 403.

KNIGHT'S FEE. The determinate quantity of land, (held by an estate of inheritance,) or of annual income therefrom, which was sufficient to maintain a knight.

In the time of Henry II. the estate was estimated at £20 a year; but Lord Coke in his time it to be an estate of 680 acres. See 1 Bl.Comm. 404, 410; 2 Bl.Comm. 62; Co.Litt. 69*a*; 1 Poll. & Maitl. 232.

KNIGHTS OF ST. MICHAEL AND ST. GEORGE. An English order of knighthood, instituted in 1818.

KNIGHTS OF ST. PATRICK. Instituted in Ireland by George III., A. D. 1763. They have no rank in England.

KNIGHTS OF THE BATH. An order supposed to have been instituted by Henry IV., and revived by George I. in 1725 to consist of the sovereign, a grand master and 36 knights companions. In 1815 the order was instituted in three classes. In 1847 the civil knights, commanders and companions were added. They are so called from the ceremony formerly observed of bathing the night before their creation.

KNIGHTS OF THE CHAMBER. Those created in the sovereign's chamber in time of peace, not in the field. 2 Inst. 666.

KNIGHTS OF THE GARTER. See Garter.

KNIGHTS OF THE POST. A term for hireling witnesses.

KNIGHTS OF THE SHIRE. In English law. Members of parliament representing counties or shires, in contradistinction to citizens or burgesses, who represent boroughs or corporations.

A knight of the shire is so called, because, as the terms of the writ for election still require, it was formerly necessary that he should be a knight. This restriction was coeval with the tenure of knight-service, when every man who received a knight's fee immediately of the crown was constrained to be a knight; but at present any person may be chosen to fill the office who is not an alien. The money qualification is abolished by 21 Vict. c. 26. Wharton.

KNIGHTS OF THE THISTLE. A Scottish order of knighthood.

This order is said to have been instituted by Achaius, king of Scotland, A. D. 819. The better opinion, however, is that it was instituted by James V. in 1534, was revived by James VII. (James II. of England) in 1687, and reestablished by Queen Anne in 1703. They have no rank in England. Wharton.

KNIGHT'S SERVICE. Upon the Norman conquest, all the lands in England were divided into knight's fees, in number above sixty thousand.

For every knight's fee, a knight was bound to attend the king in his wars forty days in a year, in which space of time a campaign was generally finished. If a man only held half a knight's fee, he was only bound to attend twenty days; and so in proportion. But this personal service, in process of time, grew into pecuniary commutations, or aids; until at last, with the military part of the feudal system, it was abolished at the restoration, by the statute of 12 Car. II. c. 24. 1 Bla.Com. 410; 2 *id.* 62; Will. Real Pr. 144; 1 Poll. & Maitl. 230.

KNOCK DOWN. To assign to a bidder at an auction by a knock or blow of the hammer.

Property is said to be "knocked down" when the auctioneer, by the fall of his hammer, or by any other audible or visible announcement, signifies to the bidder that he is entitled to the property on paying the amount of his bid, according to the terms of the sale. "Knocked down" and "struck off" are synonymous terms. Sherwood v. Reade, 7 Hill, N.Y., 439.

KNOT. In seamen's language, a "knot" is a division of the log-line serving to measure the rate of the vessel's motion.

The number of knots which run off from the reel in half a minute shows the number of miles the vessel sails in an hour. Hence when a ship goes 8 nautical miles an hour she is said to go "8 knots." Webster.

KNOW. To have knowledge; to possess information, instruction, or wisdom. State v. Ransberger, 106 Mo. 135, 17 S.W. 290. Horne v. Lewis, 160 Ga. 824, 129 S.E. 95; To perceive or apprehend, to understand. International-Great Northern R. Co. v. Pence, Tex.Civ.App., 113 S.W.2d 206, 210.

The word "familiar" is equivalent. Smiley v. Lenane, 363 Ill. 66, 1 N.E.2d 213, 216.

KNOW ALL MEN. In conveyancing. A form of public address, of great antiquity, and with which many written instruments, such as bonds, letters of attorney, etc., still commence.

KNOWINGLY. With knowledge; consciously; intelligently; willfully; intentionally. Atkinson v. State, 133 Ark. 341, 202 S.W. 709, 710; People v. Calvert, 93 Cal.App. 568, 269 P. 969, 971; Hutchman v. State, 61 Okl.Cr. 117, 66 P.2d 99, 102; Gottlieb v. Commonwealth, 126 Va. 807, 101 S.E. 872, 873; Cheffer v. Eagle Discount Stamp Co., 348 Mo. 1023, 156 S.W.2d 591, 595; and knowledge must be actual, not merely constructive, Parsons v. Rinard Grain Co., 186 Iowa 1017, 173 N.W. 276, 280.

The word imports a perception of facts requisite to make up crime, Commonwealth v. Altenhaus, 317 Mass. 270, 57 N.E.2d 921, 922; knowledge of act or thing done as well as evil intent or bad purpose, Erby v. State, 181 Tenn. 647, 184 S.W.2d 14, 16; a knowledge that facts exist which bring act or omission within provisions of Code. People v. Forbath, 5 Cal.App.2d Supp. 767, 42 P.2d 108, 109.

The use of the word in an indictment is equivalent to an averment that the defendant knew what he was about to do, and, with such knowledge, proceeded to do the act charged. U. S. v. Claypool, D.C.Mo., 14 F. 128; State v. Wilson, 41 Idaho 598, 242 P. 787, 788.

KNOWINGLY AND WILLFULLY. This phrase, in reference to violation of a statute, means consciously and intentionally. U. S. v. Lehigh Valley R. Co., C.C.A.N.J., 204 F. 705, 708; Oregon-Washington R. & Nav. Co. v. U. S., C.C.A.Idaho, 205 F. 337, 339; U. S. v. Philadelphia & R. Ry. Co., D.C. Pa., 238 F. 428, 430.

KNOWLEDGE. Acquaintance with fact or truth, United States Fire Ins. Co. v. Smith, 231 Ala. 169, 164 So. 70, 82, 103 A.L.R. 1468; People v. Henry, 23 Cal.App.2d 155, 72 P.2d 915, 921.

It has also been defined as act or state of knowing or understanding, Witters v. U. S., 70 App.D.C. 316, 106 F.2d 837, 840, 125 A.L.R. 1031; People v. Henry, 72 P.2d 915, 921, 23 Cal.App.2d 155; actual knowledge, notice or information, New York Underwriters Ins. Co. v. Central Union Bank of South Carolina, C.C.A.S.C., 65 F.2d 738, 739; Howard v. Whittaker, 250 Ky. 836, 64 S.W.2d 173; Cooper v. Independent Transfer & Storage Co., 19 P.2d 1057, 1058, 52 Idaho 747; assurance of fact or proposition founded on perception by senses, or intuition, Brooks v. Sessoms, 47 Ga.App. 554, 171 S.E. 222, 224; clear perception of that which exists, or of truth, fact or duty, People v. Steele, 179 Misc. 587, 37 N.Y.S.2d 199, 200; United States Fire Ins. Co. v. Smith, 231 Ala. 169, 164 So. 70, 82, 103 A.L.R. 1468; credible or reliable information, Sackett v. Farmers' State Bank of Boone, 209 Iowa 487, 228 N.W. 51, 54; Guardian Life Ins. Co. v. Weiser, Sup., 51 N.Y.S.2d 771, 773; firm belief, Witters v. U. S., 70 App.D.C. 316, 106 F. 2d 837, 840, 125 A.L.R. 1031; guilty knowledge, Goldsworthy v. Anderson, 92 Colo. 446, 21 P.2d 718, 87 A.L.R. 1396; information of fact, Green v. Stewart, 106 Cal.App. 518, 289 P. 940, 944; means of mental impression, Howard v. Whittaker, 250 Ky. 836, 64 S.W.2d 173; miscellaneous information and circumstances which engender belief to moral certainty or induce state of mind that one considers that he knows, Merritt v. American Stevedores, 15 N.J.Misc. 710, 195 A. 382; notice, Lally v. Cronen, 247 N. Y. 58, 159 N.E. 723, 725; Wise v. Curdes, 219 Ind. 606, 40 N.E.2d 122, 126; notice or knowledge sufficient to excite attention and put person on guard and call for inquiry, Iberville Land Co. v. Amerada Petroleum Corporation, C. C.A.La., 141 F.2d 384, 389; Hayward Lumber & Investment Co. v. Orondo Mines, 34 Cal.App.2d 697, 94 P.2d 380, 382, 383; Reynolds v. Moseley, C.C.A.Ark., 32 F.2d 979, 981; personal cognizance or knowledge or means of knowledge, The Chickie, D.C.Pa., 54 F.Supp. 19, 20; Taylor v. Moore, 87 Utah 493, 51 P.2d 222, 229; In re Eastern Transp. Co., D.C.Md., 37 F.2d 355, 363; state of being or having become aware of fact or truth; United States Fire Ins. Co. v. Smith, 231 Ala. 169, 164 So. 70, 82, 103 A.L.R. 1468; Howard v. Whittaker, 250 Ky. 836, 64 S.W.2d 173.

"Knowledge" consists in the perception of the truth of affirmative or negative propositions, while "belief" admits of all degrees, from the slightest suspicion to the fullest assurance. State v. Godette, 188 N.C. 497, 125 S.E. 24, 28; Franken v. State, 190 Wis. 424, 209 N.W. 766, 769. The difference between them is ordinarily merely in the degree, to be judged of by the court, when addressed to the court; by the jury, when addressed to the jury. Hatch v. Carpenter, 9 Gray, Mass., 271. See Utley v. Hill, 155 Mo.

232, 55 S.W. 1091, 49 L.R.A. 323, 78 Am.St.Rep. 569; Ohio Valley Coffin Co. v. Goble, 28 Ind.App. 362, 62 N.E. 1025.

Knowledge may be imputed, when the means of knowledge exists, known and accessible to the party, and capable of communicating positive information. Smith v. Industrial Acc. Commission of California, 174 Cal. 199, 162 P. 636, 637; Scheckells v. Ice Plant Mining Co., Mo.App., 180 S.W. 12, 15; Hopkins v. McCarthy, 121 Me. 27, 115 A. 513, 515. However closely actual notice may, in many instances, approximate knowledge, and constructive notice may be its equivalent in effect, there may be actual notice without knowledge; and, when constructive notice is made the test to determine priorities of right, it may fall far short of knowledge. Cleveland Woolen Mills v. Sibert, 81 Ala. 140, 1 So. 773; Dodge v. Grain Shippers' Mut. Fire Ins. Ass'n, 176 Iowa 316, 157 N.W. 955, 961; Stanton v. Hawkins, 41 R.I. 501, 103 A. 229, 230. Thus, oral notice to employer by employé of injury is not "knowledge" of the injury, excusing employé's failure to give notice of injury required by Workmen's Compensation Act. In re Brown, 228 Mass. 31, 116 N.E. 897, 898; In re Simmons, 117 Me. 175, 103 A. 68.

"Knowledge" of contents of an instrument must include understanding of its actual contents. Mitchell v. Slye, 137 Md. 89, 111 A. 814, 819.

Law regards as "knowledge" reckless misrepresentation, with intent to deceive, about that which party pretended to know but knew nothing. Holt v. Gloer, 44 Ga.App. 685, 162 S.E. 663, 664.

Carnal knowledge. See Carnal Knowledge.

Knowledge of another's peril. One has "knowledge of peril of another," within doctrine of discovered peril, whenever it reasonably appears from the known facts and circumstances that the latter is pursuing a course which will probably terminate in serious bodily injury to him, and that he probably will pursue it to the end. Galveston, H. & S. A. Ry. Co. v. Wagner, Tex.Com. App., 298 S.W. 552, 554.

Knowledge of law includes knowledge of the decisions of the courts, which are part of the law. Spitzer v. Board of Trustees for Regina Public School Dist. No. 4, of Saskatchewan, C.C.A.Ohio, 267 F. 121, 126.

Personal knowledge. Knowledge of the truth in regard to a particular fact or allegation, which is original, and does not depend on information or hearsay. Personal knowledge of an allegation in an answer is personal knowledge of its truth or falsity; and if the allegation is a negative one, this necessarily includes a knowledge of the truth or falsity of the allegation denied. West v. Home Ins. Co., C.C.Or., 18 F. 622.

KNOWN. Familiar; perceived; recognized; understood; especially, when used absolutely, familiar to all; generally understood or perceived, and term may, according to context, refer to both actual and constructive knowledge. Wolf v. Mallinckrodt Chemical Works, 336 Mo. 746, 81 S.W.2d 323, 333; McCullough v. National Bank of Union City, 127 Pa.Super. 452, 193 A. 65, 66.

KNOWN HEIRS. In a statute relating to the sale of property of unknown heirs, it has been held to mean those persons who are known, and whose right to inherit, or the extent of whose right, to inherit, is dependent on the non-existence of other persons nearer or as near as the ancestor in the line of descent. People v. Ryder, 65 Hun 175, 19 N.Y.S. 977.

KNOWN-MEN. A title formerly given to the Lollards. Cowell.

KORAN. The Mohammedan book of faith. It contains both ecclesiastical and secular laws.

KOSHUBA. The Jewish "Koshuba" is a marriage contract or marriage settlement. Hurwitz v. Hurwitz, 216 App.Div. 362, 215 N.Y.S. 184, 185.

KULEANA. The Hawaiian term "kuleana" means a small area of land, such as were awarded in fee by the Hawaiian monarch, about the year 1850, to all Hawaiians who made application therefor. De Fries v. Scott, C.C.A.Hawaii, 268 F. 952, 953.

KUT-KUBALA. In Hindu law. A mortgage-deed or deed of conditional sale, being one of the customary deeds or instruments of security in India as declared by regulation of 1806, which regulates the legal proceedings to be taken to enforce such a security. It is also called *"Byebil-Wuffa."* Wharton.

KYMORTHA. A Welsh term for a waster, rhymer, minstrel, or other vagabond who makes assemblies and collections. Barring. Ob. St. 360.

KYTH. Sax. Kin or kindred.

L

L. This letter, as a Roman numeral, stands for the number "fifty." It is also used as an abbreviation for "law," "*liber,*" (a book,) "lord," and some other words of which it is the initial.

L. 5. An abbreviation of *"Long Quinto,"* one of the parts of the Year Books.

L. C. An abbreviation which may stand either for "Lord Chancellor," "Lower Canada," or "Leading Cases."

L. J. An abbreviation for "Law Judge;" also for "Law Journal."

L. L. (also L. Lat.) and **L. F.** (also L. Fr.) are used as abbreviations of the terms "Law Latin" and "Law French."

L. R. An abbreviation for "Law Reports."

L. S. An abbreviation for *"Locus sigilli,"* the place of the seal, *i. e.,* the place where a seal is to be affixed, or a scroll which stands instead of a seal. See Smith v. Butler, 25 N.H. 524; Barnes v. Walker, 115 Ga. 108, 41 S.E. 243; McLaughlin v. Braddy, 63 S.C. 433, 41 S.E. 523, 90 Am.St.Rep. 681.

LL. The reduplicated form of the abbreviation "L." for "law," used as a plural. It is generally used in citing old collections of statute law; as "LL. Hen. I."

LL.B., LL.M., and LL.D. Abbreviations used to denote, respectively, the three academic degrees in law,—bachelor, master, and doctor of laws.

LA. Fr. The. The definite article in the feminine gender. Occurs in some legal terms and phrases; as *"Termes de la Ley,"* terms of the law.

LÀ. Fr. There. An adverb of time and place; whereas.

LA CHAMBRE DES ESTEILLES. The star-chamber.

LA CONSCIENCE EST LA PLUS CHANGEANTE DES RÈGIES. Conscience is the most changeable of rules.

LA LEY FAVOUR LA VIE D'UN HOME. The law favors the life of a man. Yearb. M. 10 Hen. VI. 51.

LA LEY FAVOUR L'ENHERITANCE D'UN HOME. The law favors the inheritance of a man. Yearb. M. 10 Hen. VI. 51.

LA LEY VOCT PLUS TOST SUFFER UN MISCHEIFE QUE UN INCONVENIENCE. The law will sooner suffer a mischief than an inconvenience. Litt. § 231. It is holden for an inconvenience that any of the maxims of the law should be broken, though a private man suffer loss. Co. Litt. 152*b*.

L'OBLIGATION SANS CAUSE, OU SUR UNE FAUSSE CAUSE, OU SUR CAUSE ILLICITE, NE PEUT AVOIR AUCUN EFFET. An obligation without consideration, or upon a false consideration (which fails), or upon unlawful consideration, cannot have any effect. Code 3. 3. 4; Chitty, Contr. 11th Am. ed. 25, note.

L'OU LE LAY DONE CHOSE, LA CEO DONE REMEDIE A VENER A CEO. Where the law gives a right, it gives a remedy to recover. 2 Rolle 17.

LAAS. In old records. A net, gin, or snare.

LABEL. Anything appended to a larger writing, as a codicil; a narrow slip of paper or parchment affixed to a deed or writ, in order to hold the appending seal.

An affixation to or markings on a manufactured article, giving information as to its nature or quality, or the contents of a package or container, name of the maker, etc. See State v. Reickenbach, 235 Iowa 731, 17 N.W.2d 530, 531; Higgins v. Keuffel, 140 U.S. 428, 11 S.Ct. 731, 35 L.Ed. 470; Burke v. Cassin, 45 Cal. 481, 13 Am.Rep. 204; U. S. v. Skilken, D.C.Ohio, 293 F. 916, 919.

A copy of a writ in the exchequer. 1 Tidd, Pr. 156.

A slip, mark or tag of paper, or other material. National Battery Co. v. Western Molded Products Co., D.C.Cal., 39 F.Supp. 954, 956.

An identification by inscription of the contents, ownership, etc. Graham v. Justice's Court of Colusa Judicial Tp., 20 Cal.App.2d 328, 67 P.2d 127, 128.

LABINA. In old records. Watery land.

LABOR. Work; toil; service.

Physical exertion. Leathers & Martin v. Conley, La.App., 157 So. 607, 609.

A Spanish land measure, in use in Mexico and formerly in Texas, equivalent to 177⅐ acres.

Continued exertion, of the more onerous and inferior kind, usually and chiefly consisting in protracted expenditure of muscular force. It is used in this sense in several legal phrases, such as "a count for work and labor," "wages of labor," etc., and is commonly construed as having such meaning when used in statutes giving liens to laborers, Road Supply & Metal Co. v. Bechtelheimer, 119 Kan. 560, 240 P. 846, 847; Stuart v. Camp Carson Mining & Power Co., 84 Or. 702, 165 P. 359, 362; Beakley v. Lind, Tex.Civ.App., 32 S.W.2d 671, 672; and in the Immigration Act excluding aliens coming to the United States under contract, "to perform labor." Ex parte Aird, D.C.Pa., 276 F. 954, 957; U. S. v. Union Bank of Canada, C.C.A.N.Y., 262 F. 91, 93. For "Farm Labor," see that title.

The word is sometimes construed to mean service rendered or part played in production of wealth, Britt v. Cotter Butte Mines, 108 Mont. 174, 89 P.2d 266, 267; or superintendence or supervision of work. Wandling v. Broaddus, Mo., 10 S.W.2d 651, 655; United States for Use and Benefit of Farwell, Ozmun, Kirk & Co. v. Shea-Adamson Co., D.C.Minn., 21 F.Supp. 831, 837. Or physical or mental toil, bodily or intellectual exertion. Christie v.

Commercial Casualty Ins. Co., 6 Cal.App.2d 710, 45 P.2d 263, 266; Crook v. Commonwealth, 147 Va. 593, 136 S.E. 565, 567, 50 A.L.R. 1043; United States, Fidelity & Guaranty Co., for Use of Reedy, v. American Surety Co., of New York, D.C.Pa., 25 F.Supp. 280, 284. This broad construction has been adopted in construing statutes limiting hours of labor. Commonwealth v. John T. Connor Co., 222 Mass. 299, 110 N.E. 301, 302, L.R.A.1916B, 1236; Ex parte Steiner, 68 Or. 218, 137 P. 204, 206.

As used in mechanic's lien law, an architect performs "labor", Cain v. Rea, 159 Va. 446, 166 S.E. 478, 480, 85 A.L.R. 945; Paterson v. Condos, 55 Nev. 134, 28 P.2d 499, 501; "labor" implies personal service, Hampton v. Incorporated Village of Freeport, 244 App.Div. 815, 279 N.Y.S. 776; and "labor" is not confined to physical or manual labor, Diffenbach v. H. H. Mahler Co., 167 Okl. 518, 30 P. 2d 907, 908.

As used in statute concerning labor for contractors or subcontractors or in contractor's bond, the word contemplates an architect or other skilled man who superintends work, U. S. for Use and Benefit of Farwell, Ozmun, Kirk & Co. v. Shea-Adamson Co., D.C.Minn., 21 F.Supp. 831, 837; claim for work done by man and team in highway construction, State ex rel. and to Use of Winebrenner v. Detroit Fidelity & Surety Co., 326 Mo. 684, 32 S.W.2d 572, 575, 71 A.L.R. 1131; manual labor, United States Fidelity & Guaranty Co. v. Ed Hockaday & Co., 182 Okl. 73, 76 P.2d 911, 912; mental effort, United States Fidelity & Guaranty Co., for Use of Reedy, v. American Surety Co., of New York, D.C.Pa., 25 F.Supp. 280, 284; repair work on automobiles and trucks used by highway contractors, Employers' Casualty Co. v. Rockwall County, 120 Tex. 441, 35 S.W.2d 690, 693; transportation of materials, State for Use of Pennsylvania R. Co. v. Ætna Casualty & Surety Co., 4 W.W.Harr. 158, 145 A. 172, 173; work of superintendent as well as labor in ordinary sense, Look v. City of Springfield, 292 Mass. 515, 198 N.E. 661, 662.

As used in statute concerning statement of claim by any person who has performed work, or rendered personal service on levy of attachment not founded on "labor" claim, the word includes services by salesmen, clerks, and persons who performed personal services for others, and not merely bodily exertion or physical toil. Levitt v. Faber, 20 Cal.App.2d, Supp., 758, 64 P.2d 498, 500.

"Labor" within arbitration statute applies where physical force or brawn and muscle constitute the principal effort to produce a given result. Levy v. Superior Court in and for Los Angeles County, 15 Cal.2d 692, 104 P.2d 770, 773, 129 A.L.R. 956.

"Labor," in connection with reference in Workmen's Compensation Act to manual or mechanical work, must mean actual physical contact with dangerous instruments and means used in carrying on business. Russell Flour & Feed Co. v. Walker, 148 Okl. 164, 298 P. 291, 293.

"Labor," "business," and "work" are not synonyms. Labor may be business, but it is not necessarily so; and business is not always labor. Labor implies toil; exertion producing weariness; manual exertion of a toilsome nature.

Common labor, within the meaning of Sunday laws, is not to be restricted to manual or physical labor, but includes the transaction of ordinary business, trading, and the execution of notes and other instruments. Bryan v. Watson, 127 Ind. 42, 26 N.E. 666, 11 L.R.A. 63; Link v. Clemmens, 7 Blackf., Ind., 480; Cincinnati v. Rice, 15 Ohio 225; Eitel v. State, 33 Ind. 201. But compare Bloom v. Richards, 2 Ohio St. 387; Horacek v. Keebler, 5 Neb. 355; State v. Somberg, 113 Neb. 761, 204 N.W. 788, 790. It does not include the transaction of judicial business or the acts of public officers. State v. Thomas, 61 Ohio St. 444, 56 N.E. 276, 48 L.R.A. 459; Hastings v. Columbus, 42 Ohio St. 585.

"Common labor" is unskilled manual labor, and is an "employment" within Workmen's Compensation Law. Leitz v. Labadie Ice Co., 211 Mich. 565, 179 N.W. 291, 293.

See, also, Laborer.

LABOR A JURY. In old practice. To tamper with a jury; to endeavor to influence them in their verdict, or their verdict generally.

LABOR CONDITIONS. The term "labor conditions" in a contract authorizing temporary suspension by the contractor for "strikes, labor conditions, and lockouts," refers to scarcity of labor alone, and bears no relation to the cost of labor. Robinson v. Solomon, 222 Mich. 618, 193 N.W. 209, 212. The term comprehends both wages and hours. Bumpus v. Continental Baking Co., C.C.A. Tenn., 124 F.2d 549, 552, 140 A.L.R. 1258.

LABOR DISPUTE. A controversy concerning terms or conditions of employment. Minnesota Council of State Emp., No. 19, v. American Federation of State, County and Municipal Emp., 220 Minn. 179, 19 N.W.2d 414, 419, 160 A.L.R. 533; Sandoval v. Industrial Commission, 110 Colo. 108, 130 P.2d 930, 932, 935, 937; Dallas Fuel Co. v. Horne, 230 Iowa 1148, 300 N.W. 303, 306. A controversy concerning wages. N. L. R. B. v. Indiana Desk Co., C.C.A.7, 149 F.2d 987, 990. A controversy related to purposes of collective bargaining. McKay v. Retail Automobile Salesmen's Local Union No. 1067, 16 Cal.2d 311, 106 P.2d 373, 380. A dispute between an employer and his employees about wages, hours, working conditions, or who shall speak for employees. Donnelly Garment Co. v. International Ladies' Garment Workers' Union, D.C.Mo., 20 F.Supp. 767.

LABOR ORGANIZATION. A combination of workmen usually, but not necessarily, of the same trade or of several allied trades, for securing by united action, the most favorable conditions as regards wages, hours of labor, etc., for its members. Keith Theatre v. Vachon, 134 Me. 392, 187 A. 692, 694; People v. Distributors Division, Smoked Fish Workers Union, Local No. 20377, 169 Misc. 255, 7 N.Y.S.2d 185, 187.

LABOR SEPARATION. Quits, discharges and lay-offs. International Ass'n of Machinists v. State ex rel. Watson, 153 Fla. 672, 15 So.2d 485, 490.

LABOR UNION. An organization, combination or association of employees or workmen. People v. Distributors Division, Smoked Fish Workers Union, Local No. 20377, 169 Misc. 255, 7 N.Y.S.2d 185, 187; Fertel v. Rosenzweig, Sup., 28 N.Y.S.2d 6, 9; for securing favorable wages, improved labor conditions, better hours of labor, etc., and righting grievances against employers. Com. v. Shipherd, 157 Pa.Super. 27, 41 A.2d 429, 431; Cole v. Commonwealth, 169 Va. 868, 193 S.E. 517, 519; People v. Graf, 261 App.Div. 188, 24 N.Y.S.2d 683, 685.

LABORARIIS. An ancient writ against persons who refused to serve and do labor, and who had no means of living; or against such as, having served in the winter, refused to serve in the summer. Reg. Orig. 189.

LABORER. The word ordinarily denotes one who subsists by physical labor. American Surety Co. of New York v. Stuart, Tex.Civ.App., 151 S.W.2d 886, 888. One who, as a means of livelihood, performs work and labor for another. Blanchard v. Railway Co., 87 Me. 241, 32 A. 890; Weymouth v.

Sanborn, 43 N.H. 171, 80 Am.Dec. 144; Missouri State Highway Commission to Use of Onstad v. Coopers' Const. Service Co., Mo.App., 268 S.W. 701, 702. One who furnishes his personal service, of a grade commonly performed by persons working by the day. Shefts Supply v. Brady, 170 Okl. 590, 41 P.2d 820, 822. A person without particular training employed at manual labor under a contract terminable at will. Morley v. McCaskey, 134 Okl. 50, 270 P. 1107, 1110; Devney v. City of Boston, 223 Mass. 270, 111 N.E. 788, 789; Cavanaugh v. Art Hardware & Mfg. Co., 124 Wash. 243, 214 P. 152, 154.

For "Farm Laborer," see that title.

A workman is a "laborer" within Longshoremen's Compensation Act, 33 U.S.C.A. §§ 901–950. Balaske v. Bassett, D.C.Mo., 35 F.Supp. 315, 316; and within Bankruptcy Act § 17 (11 U.S.C.A. § 35). In re Fabbri, D.C.N.Y., 8 F. Supp. 35, 36.

As used in laborers' or mechanics' lien law, the term means mechanics or skilled laborers, who perform work or labor under a verbal or written contract. Home Building & Loan Ass'n v. White, 141 Okl. 240, 284 P. 889, 890; one who performs manual labor, but includes employee whose regular duties include actual manual labor, although he performs other services, Aronoff v. Woodard, 47 Ga.App. 725, 171 S.E. 404, 405; all who work with their hands, crude implements, or teams in work demanding that character of service, Kansas City Southern Ry. Co. v. Wallace, 38 Okl. 233, 132 P. 908, 911, 46 L.R.A.,N.S., 112. Laborer under garnishment statute is unskilled laborer, Groves & Rosenblath v. Atkins, 160 La. 489, 107 So. 316, 317, but see Lames v. Armstrong, 162 Iowa 327, 144 N.W. 1, 2, 49 L.R.A.,N.S., 691, Ann.Cas.1916B, 511.

A laborer, as the word is used in the Pennsylvania act of 1872, giving a certain preference of lien, is one who performs, with his own hands, the contract which he makes with his employer. Appeal of Wentroth, 82 Pa. 469.

In English statutes, this term is generally understood to designate a servant employed in husbandry or manufactures, and not dwelling in the home of his employer. Wharton; Mozley & Whiteley.

See, also, Labor.

LABORERS, STATUTES OF. In English law. These are the statutes 23 Edw. III., 12 Rich. II, 5 Eliz. c. 4, and 26 & 27 Vict. c. 125, making various regulations as to laborers, servants, apprentices, etc.

LAC, LAK. In Indian computation, 100,000. The value of a lac of rupees is about £10,000 sterling. Wharton.

LACE. A measure of land equal to one pole. This term is widely used in Cornwall.

LACERTA. In old English law. A fathom. Co. Litt. 4*b*.

LACEY ACT. An act of congress, May 25, 1900, under which the states may enforce game laws against animals, birds, etc., imported from other states or countries. See Game Laws.

LACHES is principally a question of inequity of permitting claim to be enforced. Crowder v. Terhorst, 107 Ind.App. 288, 21 N.E.2d 141, 146; Brady v. Garrett, Tex.Civ.App., 66 S.W.2d 502, 504; Norman v. Boyer, 111 Colo. 531, 143 P.2d 1017, 1018; an inequity founded on some change in the condition or relations of the property or parties. Wallace v. Fiske, C.C.A.Mo., 80 F.2d 897, 912; Geiss v. Trinity Lutheran Church Congregation, 119 Neb. 745, 230 N.W. 658, 661; State v. Platte Valley Public Power and Irrigation Dist., 143 Neb. 661, 10 N.W.2d 631, 634.

Laches is, or is based on, delay attended by or inducing change of condition or relation. Jones v. McNabb, 184 Okl. 9, 84 P.2d 429, 430; Shea v. Shea, 269 Mass. 454, 4 N.E.2d 1015, 1018; Collier v. Caraway, Tex.Civ.App., 140 S.W.2d 910, 914, Poulin v. Poulin, 60 R.I. 264, 197 A. 878, 881; delay for such time as to constitute acquiescence, Mary Jane Stevens Co. v. First Nat. Bldg. Co., 89 Utah 456, 57 P.2d 1099, 1125; delay such as to preclude court from arriving at a safe conclusion as to truth, Grant v. Hart, 192 Ga. 153, 14 S.E.2d 860, 869, 870; delay that makes it inequitable to accord relief sought, Thorpe v. Wm. Filene's Sons Co., D.C.Mass., 40 F.2d 269; Cartmell v. Nigro, 19 Del.Ch. 231, 165 A. 625, 626; delay that warrants presumption that party has waived his right, Harrison v. Miller, 124 W.Va. 550, 21 S.E.2d 674, 679; Bank of Marlinton v. McLaughlin, 123 W.Va. 608, 17 S.E.2d 213, 218; delay that works or results in disadvantage, injury, injustice, detriment or prejudice. Marsh v. Marsh, Sup., 49 N.Y.S.2d 759, 761; Anderson v. Wyoming Development Co., 60 Wyo. 417, 154 P.2d 318, 345; Sample v. Romine, 193 Miss. 706, 8 So.2d 257, 263; failure to prosecute claim within reasonable and proper period, Burton v. Ryan, 88 Ind.App. 549, 165 N.E. 260, 261; implied waiver from knowledge of existing conditions and acquiescence in them, Jacksonville Public Service Corporation v. Profile Cotton Mills, 236 Ala. 4, 180 So. 583, 586; City of Lafayette v. Keen, 113 Ind.App. 552, 48 N.E.2d 63, 70; Pehlert v. Neff, 152 Pa. Super. 84, 31 A.2d 446, 448; inexcusable delay in assertion of rights, Winget v. Rockwood, C.C.A.Minn., 69 F.2d 326, 332, Lipsitz v. Parr, 164 Md. 222, 164 A. 743, 745; Johnson v. Umsted, C.C.A.Ark., 64 F.2d 316, 323; lack of diligence on part of plaintiff to injury, prejudice, or disadvantage of defendant. Rome Grader & Machinery Corporation v. J. D. Adams Mfg. Co., C.C.A.Ind., 135 F.2d 617, 619; Lamar v. Rivers, 235 Ala. 130, 178 So. 16, 18; Croyle v. Croyle, 184 Md. 126, 40 A.2d 374, 379, 380; lapse of time and acquiescence in alleged wrong, In re Associated Gas & Elec. Co., D.C.N.Y., 61 F.Supp. 11, 43; lapse of time together with change in condition or relation of parties, McKnight v. Basilides, 19 Wash.2d 391, 143 P.2d 307, 312; lapse of time together with prejudice or lapse such that prejudice will be presumed, Lindberg v. Linder, 133 Cal.App. 213, 23 P.2d 842; neglect for unreasonable and unexplained length of time under circumstances permitting diligence to do what could have or should have been done, Engel v. Mathley, 113 Ind.App. 458, 48 N.E.2d 463, 467; Columbia Theological Seminary v. Arnette, 168 S.C. 272, 167 S.E. 465, 468; Prudential Insurance Co. v. Sailors, 69 Ga.App. 628, 26 S.E.2d 557, 561; neglect for unreasonable length of time to do what should have been done, Bell v. Mackey, 191 S.C. 105, 3 S.E.2d 816, 824, 825, 830; Triangle Oil Co. v. City of New Orleans, La.App., 5 So.2d 558, 561, 562; neglect or omission for unexplained and unreasonable length of time, Pennington Engineering Co. v. Houde Engineering Corporation, D.C.N.Y., 43 F.Supp. 698, 705, 706; State ex rel. Phillips v. Ford, 116 Mont. 190, 151 P.2d 171, 176; neglect or omission to assert right as, taken in conjunction with lapse of time and other circumstances, causes prejudice to adverse party, McInnes v. McInnes, 163 Md. 303, 163 A. 85, 89; Hynes v. Silver Prince Min. Co., 86 Mont. 10, 281 P. 548; People ex rel. Mulvey v. City of Chicago, 292 Ill.App. 589, 12 N.E.2d 13, 16; neglect or omission to do what one should do as warrants presumption that one has abandoned right or claim, Shirley v. Van Every, 159 Va. 762, 167 S.E. 345, 350; Eldridge v. Idaho State Penitentiary, 54 Idaho 213, 30 P.2d 781, 784; negligence by which another has been led into changing his condition with respect to property or right, Heyburn Bldg. Co. v. Highland Motor Transfer Co., 245 Ky. 514, 53 S.W.2d 944, 946; negligence of complainant, good faith of defendant, and prejudice occasioned, or likelihood thereof, to defendant. Crandol v. Garrison, 115 N.J.Eq. 11, 169 A. 507, 511; negligence or omission seasonably to assert a right, Davidson v. Grady, C.C.A.Fla., 105 F.2d 405, 408; Sinell v. Town of Sharon, 206 Minn. 437, 289 N.W. 44, 45, 46; omission of something which a party might do and might reasonably be expected to do towards vindication or enforcement of his rights. Wynne v. Conrad, 220 N.C. 355, 17 S.E.2d 514, 518; McCauley v. Northern Texas Traction Co., Tex.Civ. App., 21 S.W.2d 309, 313; omission to do what law requires to protect one's rights under circumstances misleading or prejudicing adverse party, School Dist. No. 14, Fractional, Niles Tp. and Buchanan Tp. v. School Dist. No. 1, Buchanan Tp., 266 Mich. 479, 254 N.W. 174; unconscionable, undue, unexcused, unexplained or unreasonable delay in assertion of right, Loveland Camp No. 83, W. O. W., v. Woodmen Bldg. & Benev. Ass'n, 108 Colo. 297, 116 P.2d 195, 199; Calkin v. Hudson, 156 Kan. 308, 133 P.2d 177, 184, 185; Sample v. Natalby, 120 Fla. 161, 162 So. 493; City of Paducah v. Gillispie, 273 Ky. 101, 115 S.W.2d 574, 575; unreasonable or unexplained delay in asserting right which works disadvantage to another, Kennedy v. Denny, 237 Ky. 649, 36 S.W.2d 41, 42; Caswell v. Bathrick, 53 R.I. 114, 164 A. 505, 507; want of activity or diligence in making a claim or moving for the enforcement of a right, Wissler v. Craig, 80 Va. 30; Babb v. Sullivan, 43 S.C. 436, 21 S.E. 277; Graff v. Portland, etc., Co., 12 Colo.App. 106, 54 P. 854; In re Wallace's Estate, 299 Pa. 333, 149 A. 473, 475.

Conduct of party which has placed other party in a situation where his rights will be imperiled and his defenses embarrassed is a basis of laches. State v. Abernathy, 159 Tenn. 175, 17 S.W.2d 17, 19.

Knowledge, unreasonable delay, and change of position are essential elements. Shanik v. White Sewing Mach. Corporation, 25 Del.Ch. 371, 19 A.2d 831, 837.

Laches requires an element of estoppel or neglect which has operated to prejudice of defendant. Scarbrough v. Pickens, 26 Tenn.App. 213, 170 S.W.2d 585, 588; Mattison-Greenlee Service Corporation v. Culhane, D.C.Ill., 20 F. Supp. 882, 884.

"Limitations" and "laches" are not synonymous; but "limitations" signifies the fixed statutory period within which an action may be brought for some act done to preserve a right, while "laches" signifies delay independent of statute. In re Van Tassell's Will, 119 Misc. 478, 196 N.Y.S. 491, 494.

LACHES, ESTOPPEL BY. A failure to do something which should be done or to claim or enforce a right at a proper time. Hutchinson v. Kenney, C.C.A.N.C., 27 F.2d 254, 256. A neglect to do something which one should do, or to seek to enforce a right at a proper time. Jett v. Jett, 171 Ky. 548, 188 S.W. 669, 672. A species of "equitable estoppel" or "estoppel by matter in pais." See titles "Equitable Estoppel" and "In Pais, Estoppel In".

An element of the doctrine is that the defendant's alleged change of position for the worse must have been induced by or resulted from the conduct, misrepresentation, or silence of the plaintiff. Croyle v. Croyle, 184 Md. 126, 40 A.2d 374, 379. Delay in enforcement of rights until condition of other party has become so changed that he cannot be restored to his former state. Wisdom's Adm'r v. Sims, 284 Ky. 258, 144 S.W.2d 232, 235, 236; Oak Lawn Cemetery of Baltimore County v. Baltimore County Com'rs, 174 Md. 356, 198 A. 600, 605, 115 A.L.R. 1478. Essence of "laches" is estoppel. Burke v. Gunther, 128 N.J.Eq. 565, 17 A.2d 481, 487. Laches is a species of estoppel. Bankers' Trust Co. v. Rood, 211 Iowa 289, 233 N.W. 794, 802, 73 A.L.R. 1421; Stewart v. Pelt, 198 Ark. 776, 131 S.W.2d 644, 648. To create "estoppel by laches" party sought to be estopped must with knowledge of transaction have done something to mislead other party to his prejudice. Wisdom's Adm'r v. Sims, 144 S.W.2d 232, 235, 236, 284 Ky. 258.

LACK OF JURISDICTION. The phrase may mean lack of power to act in a particular manner or to give certain kinds of relief. In re Rowe's Estate, 66 Cal.App.2d 594, 152 P.2d 765, 770. It may consist in court's total want of power to act at all, or lack of power to act in particular case because conditions essential to exercise of jurisdiction have not been complied with. State v. Williams, 209 Wis. 541, 245 N.W. 663, 665.

LACTA. L. Lat. In old English law. Defect in the weight of money; *lack* of weight. This word and the verb *"lactare"* are used in an assise or statute of the sixth year of King John. Spelman.

LACUNA. In old records. A ditch or dyke; a furrow for a drain; a gap or blank in writing.

LACUS. In old English law. Allay or alloy of silver with base metal. Fleta, lib. 1, c. 22, § 6.

In the Civil law. A lake; a receptacle of water which is never dry. Dig. 43, 14, 1, 3.

LADA. In old English law. A court of justice; a lade or lath. Cowell.

In Saxon law. A purgation, or mode of trial by which one purged himself of an accusation; as by oath or ordeal. Spelman. A water-course; a trench or canal for draining marshy grounds. In old English, a *lade* or *load*. Spelman.

LADE, or LODE. The mouth of a river.

LADEN IN BULK. A term of maritime law, applied to a vessel which is freighted with a cargo which is neither in casks, boxes, bales, nor cases, but lies loose in the hold, being defended from wet or moisture by a number of mats and a quantity of dunnage. Cargoes of corn, salt, etc., are usually so shipped.

LADING, BILL OF. See Bill.

LADY. In English law. The title belonging to the wife of a peer, and (by courtesy) the wife of a baronet or knight, and also to any woman, married or sole, whose father was a nobleman of a rank not lower than that of earl.

LADY-COURT. In English law. The court of a lady of the manor.

LADY DAY. The 25th of March, the feast of the Annunciation of the Blessed Virgin Mary. In parts of Ireland, however, they so designate the 15th of August, the festival of the Assumption of the Virgin.

LADY'S FRIEND. The style of an officer of the English house of commons, whose duty was to secure a suitable provision for the wife, when her husband sought a divorce by special act of parliament. The act of 1857 abolished parliamentary divorces, and this office with them.

LÆN (Anglo-Saxon). A loan. See Beneficium.

LÆNLAND. Land held of a superior whether much or little. 1 Poll. & Maitl. 38.

Land given to the lessee and to two or three successive heirs of his; synonymous with loan land. This species of tenure seems to have been replaced by that of holding by book or bocland. See Maitl. Doomsday Book and Beyond 318. See Folcland.

LÆSA MAJESTAS. Lat. Leze-majesty, or injured majesty; high treason. It is a phrase taken from the civil law, and anciently meant any offense against the king's person or dignity.

LÆSIO ULTRA DIMIDIUM VEL ENORMIS. In Roman law. The injury sustained by one of the parties to an onerous contract when he had been overreached by the other to the extent of more than one-half of the value of the subject-matter; *e. g.*, when a vendor had not received half the value of property sold, or the purchaser had paid more than double value. Colq. Rom. Civil Law, § 2094.

LÆSIONE FIDEI, SUITS PRO. Suits in the ecclesiastical courts for spiritual offenses against conscience, for non-payment of debts, or breaches of civil contracts. This attempt to turn the ecclesiastical courts into courts of equity was checked by the constitutions of Clarendon, A. D. 1164. 3 Bl.Comm. 52.

LÆSIWERP. A thing surrendered into the hands or power of another; a thing given or delivered. Spelman.

LÆT. In old English law. One of a class between servile and free. Palgrave, i. 354.

LÆTARE JERUSALEM. Easter offerings, so called from these words in the hymn of the day. They are also denominated *"quadrage-simalia."* Wharton.

LÆTHE, or LATHE. A division or district peculiar to the county of Kent. Spelman.

LAFORDSWIC. In Saxon law. A betraying of one's lord or master.

LAGA. L. Lat., from the Saxon *"lag."* Law; a law.

LAGAN. See Ligan.

LAGE. Laws in early Saxon times; *e. g.*, "Danelage," "Mercen-Lage," and "West Saxon Lage" (see those titles).

LAGE DAY. In old English law. A law day; a time of open court; the day of the county court; a juridical day.

LAGE-MAN. A lawful man; a good and lawful man. A juror. Cowell.

LAGENA. L. Lat. In old English law. A measure of ale. Fleta, lib. 2, c. 11. Said to consist of six sextaries. Cowell.

LAGHDAY or LAHDY. A day of open court; a day of the county court. Cowell; Toml.

LAGU. In old English law. Law; also used to express the territory or district in which a particular law was in force, as *Dena lagu, Mercna lagu*, etc. See Lage.

LAHLSLIT. A breach of law. Cowell. A mulct for an offense, viz., twelve "ores."

LAHMAN, or LAGEMANNUS. An old word for a lawyer. Domesday, I. 189.

LAIA. A roadway in a wood. Mon. Angl. t. 1, p. 483.

LAICUS. Lat. A layman. One who is not in holy orders, or not engaged in the ministry of religion.

LAIRWITE, or LAIRESITE. A fine for adultery or fornication, anciently paid to the lords of some manors. 4 Inst. 206.

LAIS GENTS. L. Fr. Lay people; a jury.

LAITY. In English law. Those persons who do not make a part of the clergy.

They are divided into three states: (1) *Civil*, including all the nation, except the clergy, the army, and navy, and subdivided, into the *nobility* and the *commonalty;* (2) *military;* (3) *maritime*, consisting of the navy. Wharton.

LAIZ, LEEZ (O. Fr.). A legate. Kelh.

LAK. See Lac.

LAKE. A considerable body of standing water in a depression of land or expanded part of a river; an inland body of water or naturally enclosed basin serving to drain surrounding country; or a body of water of considerable size surrounded by land; a widened portion of a river or a lagoon. Wood v. Maitland, 169 Misc. 484, 8 N.Y.S.2d 146, 150.

Body of water, more or less, stagnant, in which the water is supplied from drainage. Amerada Petroleum Corporation v. State Mineral Board, 203 La. 473, 14 So.2d 61, 68, 69. An inland body of water of considerable size occupying natural basin or depression in earth's surface below ordinary drainage level of region. Keener v. Sharp, Mo.App., 95 S.W.2d 648, 652. A large body of water, contained in a depression of the earth's surface, and supplied from the drainage of a more or less extended area. Webster. See Jones v. Lee, 77 Mich. 35, 43 N.W. 855; Ne-pee-nauk Club v. Wilson, 96 Wis. 290, 71 N.W. 661.

The fact that there is a current from a higher to a lower level does not make that a river which would otherwise be a lake; and the fact that a river swells out into broad, pond-like sheets, with a current, does not make that a lake which would otherwise be a river. State v. Gilmanton, 14 N.H. 477.

LAMANEUR. Fr. In French marine law. A pilot. Ord. Mar. liv. 4, tit. 3.

LAMB. A sheep, ram or ewe under the age of one year. 4 Car. & P. 216.

LAMBARD'S ARCHAION. A discourse upon the high court of justice in England, by William Lambard, published in 1635. Marv. Leg. Bibl.

LAMBARD'S ARCHAIONOMIA. A work printed in 1568, containing the Anglo-Saxon laws, those of William the Conqueror, and of Henry I.

LAMBARD'S EIRENARCHA. A work upon the office of a justice of the peace, which, having gone through two editions, one in 1579, the other in 1581, was reprinted in English in 1599.

LAMBETH DEGREE. In English law. A degree conferred by the Archbishop of Canterbury, in prejudice of the universities. 3 Steph.Comm. 65; 1 Bl.Comm. 381.

LAME DUCK. A cant term on the stock exchange for a person unable to meet his engagements.

LAMMAS DAY. The 1st of August. It is one of the Scotch quarter days, and is what is called a "conventional term."

LAMMAS LANDS. Lands over which there is a right of pasturage by persons other than the owner from about Lammas, or reaping time, until sowing time. Wharton.

LANA. Lat. In the civil law. Wool. See Dig. 32, 60, 70, 88.

LANCASTER. A county of England, erected into a county palatine in the reign of Edward III., but now vested in the crown.

LANCETI. In feudal law. Vassals who were obliged to work for their lord one day in the week, from Michaelmas to autumn, either with fork, spade, or flail, at the lord's option. Spelman.

LAND, in the most general sense, comprehends any ground, soil, or earth whatsoever; as fields, meadows, pastures, woods, moors, waters, marshes, furzes, and heath. Co. Litt. 4*a;* Reynard v. City of Caldwell, 55 Idaho 342, 42 P.2d 292, 296; Holmes v. U. S., C.C.A.Okl., 53 F.2d 960, 963.

In its more limited sense, "land" denotes the quantity and character of the interest or estate which the tenant may own in land. Holmes v. U. S., C.C.A.Okl., 53 F.2d 960, 963. "Land" may include any estate or interest in lands, either legal or equitable, easements, incorporeal hereditaments. Reynard v. City of Caldwell, 55 Idaho 342, 42 P.2d 292, 297; Jones v. Magruder, D.C.Md., 42 F.Supp. 193, 198; Lynch v. Cunningham, 131 Cal. App. 164, 21 P.2d 154; Petition of Burnquist, 220 Minn. 48, 19 N.W.2d 394, 401; Cuff v. Koslosky, 165 Okl. 135, 25 P.2d 290. The land is one thing, and the estate in land is another thing, for an estate in land is a time in land or land for a time. Plowd. 555.

Technically land signifies everything which may be holden; and the term is defined as comprehending all things of a permanent and substantial nature, and even of an unsubstantial, provided they be permanent. Reynard v. City of Caldwell, 55 Idaho 342, 42 P.2d 292, 296.

Ordinarily, the term is used as descriptive of the subject of ownership and not the ownership. Southern Pac. Co. v. Riverside County, 35 Cal.App.2d 380, 95 P.2d 688, 692.

"Land" includes not only the soil or earth, but also things of a permanent nature affixed thereto or found therein, whether by nature, as water, trees, grass, herbage, other natural or perennial products, growing crops or trees, mineral under the surface, or by the hand of man, as buildings, fixtures, fences, bridges, as well as works constructed for use of water, such as dikes, canals, etc. Reynard v. City of Caldwell, 55 Idaho 342, 42 P.2d 292, 296; City of Newport News v. Warwick County, 159 Va. 571, 166 S.E. 570, 580; Morris Plan Bank of Fort Worth v. Ogden, Tex.Civ.App., 144 S.W.2d 998, 1002; 2 Bl.Comm. 16, 17; Sox v. Miracle, 35 N.D. 458, 160 N.W. 716, 719; Wynn v. Margate City, 9 N.J.Misc. 1324, 157 A. 565, 566. It embraces not only the surface of the earth, but everything under or over it. Gas Products Co. v. Rankin, 63 Mont. 372, 207 P. 993, 997, 24 A.L.R. 294; Garnsey Coal Co. v. Mudd, C.C.A.Ala., 281 F. 183, 184; Jones v. Vermont Asbestos Corporation, 108 Vt. 79, 182 A. 291, 303; Holloway's Unknown Heirs v. Whatley, Tex.Civ.App., 104 S.W.2d 646, 648. It has in its legal signification an indefinite extent upward and downward. Reynard v. City of Caldwell, 55 Idaho 342, 42 P.2d 292, 296; Bituminous Casualty Corporation v. Walsh & Wells, Mo.App., 170 S.W.2d 117, 121. It may include a franchise connected with land. Delaney v. Lowery, 25 Cal.2d 561, 154 P.2d 674, 679.

Land is or includes the solid material of the earth, whatever may be the ingredients of which it is composed, whether soil, rock, or other substance. Civ.Code Cal. § 659; Reynard v. City of Caldwell, 55 Idaho 342, 42 P.2d 292, 296.

Philosophically, it seems more correct to say that the word "land" means, in law, as in the vernacular, the soil, or portion of the earth's crust; and to explain or justify such expressions as that "whoever owns the land owns the buildings above and the minerals below," upon the view, not that these are within the extension of the term "land," but that they are so connected with it that by rules of law they pass by a conveyance of the land. This view makes "land," as a term, narrower in signification than "realty;" though it would allow an instrument speaking of land to operate co-extensively with one granting realty or real property by either of those terms. But many of the authorities use the expression "land" as including these incidents to the soil. Abbott.

The term "land" may be used interchangeably with "property;" it may include anything that may be classed as real estate or real property. Reynard v. City of Caldwell, 55 Idaho 342, 42 P.2d 292, 297.

The term "lands" designates all real estate. Enzor v. State, 167 So. 336, 338, 27 Ala.App. 60.

The word "lands" is ordinarily synonymous with "real estate" or "real property". Lincoln Nat. Bank & Trust Co. of Fort Wayne v. Nathan, 215 Ind. 178, 19 N.E.2d 243, 247; Southern Pac. Co. v. Riverside County, 35 Cal.App.2d 380, 95 P.2d 688, 692.

See, also, Lands.

Accommodation lands. See Accommodation Lands.

Bounty lands. See Bounty.

Certificate lands. See Certificate Lands.

Crown lands. See Crown Lands.

Demesne lands. See Demesne.

Donation lands. See Donation Lands.

Fabric lands. See Fabric Lands.

Farm land. See Farm Land.

General land office. See General Land Office.

Land patent. See Patent.

Mineral lands. See Mineral Lands.

Place lands. See Place Lands.

Public lands. See Public Lands.

School lands. See School.

Seated land. See Seated Land.

Swamp and overflowed lands. See Swamp and Overflowed Lands.

Tide lands. See Tide.

Unseated land. See Unseated Land.

LAND CERTIFICATE. An obligation of government entitling owner to secure designated quantity of land by following the requirements of law. State v. Balli, Tex.Civ.App., 173 S.W.2d 522, 538.

Upon the registration of freehold land under the English land transfer act, 1875, a certificate is given to the registered proprietor, and similarly upon every transfer of registered land. This registration supersedes the necessity of any further registration in the register counties. Sweet.

It contains a description of the land as it appears on the register and the name and address of the proprietor, and is *prima facie* evidence of the truth of the matters therein set forth.

LAND COP. The sale of land which was evidenced in early English law by the transfer of a rod or festuca (*q. v.*) as a symbol of possession which was handed by the seller to the reeve and by the reeve to the purchaser. The conveyance was made in court, it is supposed, for securing better evidence of it, and barring the claims of expectant heirs; Maitl. Domesd. B. 323.

LAND COURT. In American law. A court formerly existing in St. Louis, Mo., having a limited territorial jurisdiction over actions concerning real property, and suits for dower, partition, etc.

LAND DAMAGES. See Damages.

LAND DEPARTMENT. That office of the United States government which has jurisdiction and charge of the public lands, including the secretary of the interior and the commissioner of the general land office and their subordinate officers, and being in effect the department of the interior considered with reference to its powers and duties concerning the public lands. See U. S. v. Winona & St. P. R. Co., Minn., 67 F. 956, 15 C.C.A. 96; Northern Pac. R. Co. v. Barden, C.C.Mont., 46 F. 617.

LAND DISTRICT. A division of a state or territory, created by federal authority, in which is located a United-States land office, with a "register of the land office" and a "receiver of public money," for the disposition of the public lands within the district. See U. S. v. Smith, C.C.Or., 11 F. 491.

LAND GABEL. A tax or rent issuing out of land.

Spelman says it was originally a penny for every house. This *land-gabel*, or *land-gavel*, in the register of Domesday, was a quit-rent for the site of a house, or the land whereon it stood; the same with what we now call "ground-rent." Wharton.

LAND GRANT. A donation of public lands to a subordinate government, a corporation, or an individual; as, from the United States to a state, or to a railroad company to aid in the construction of its road.

LAND, LAW OF. See Law of the Land.

LAND OFFICES. Government offices, subordinate to the general land office, established in various parts of the United States, for the transaction of local business relating to the survey, location, settlement, pre-emption, and sale of the public lands. See General Land Office.

LAND-POOR. The term generally means that a man has a great deal of unproductive land, and perhaps is obliged to borrow money to pay taxes; but a man "land-poor" may be largely responsible. Matteson v. Blackmer, 46 Mich. 397, 9 N.W. 445.

LAND-REEVE. A person whose business it is to overlook certain parts of a farm or estate; to attend not only to the woods and hedge-timber, but also to the state of the fences, gates, buildings, private roads, driftways, and water-courses; and likewise to the stocking of commons, and encroachments of every kind, as well as to prevent or detect waste and spoil in general, whether by the tenants or others; and to report the same to the manager or land steward. Enc. Lond.

LAND REVENUES. This term denotes income derived from crown lands in Great Britain.

These lands have been so largely granted away to subjects that they are now contracted within very narrow limits. The crown was so much improverished in this manner by William III, that the stat. 1 Anne, c. 7, § 5, was passed, which, with stat. 34 George III, c. 75, which amends and continues it, makes void all grants or leases from the ground of royal manors or other possessions connected with land for a period exceeding thirty-one years, or three lives. Long prior to this a Scottish stat. 1445, c. 41, had made necessary the consent of parliament in case of the alienation of crown property. It is said that none of these statutes have succeeded in checking the practice. Early at the beginning of the reign of George III. the hereditary crown revenues derived from escheats, manors held *in capite*, estrays, fines, etc., were surrendered by the king to the general funds, and in the place of them he received a specified sum annually for the civil list.

LAND STEWARD. A person who overlooks or has the management of a farm or estate.

LAND TAX. A tax laid upon the legal or beneficial owner of real property, and apportioned upon the assessed value of his land. A tax on land. Texas Co. v. Moynier, 129 Cal.App. 738, 19 P.2d 280, 282.

LAND TENANT. The person actually in possession of land; otherwise styled the "terre-tenant."

LAND TITLES AND TRANSFER ACT. An English statute (38 & 39 Vict. c. 87) providing for the establishment of a registry for titles to real property, and making sundry provisions for the transfer of lands and the recording of the evidences thereof. It presents some analogies to the recording laws of the American states.

LAND WAITER. In English law. An officer of the customhouse, whose duty is, upon landing any merchandise, to examine, taste, weigh, or measure it, and to take an account thereof.

In some ports they also execute the office of a coast waiter. They are likewise occasionally styled "searchers" and are to attend and join with the patent searcher in the execution of all cockets for the shipping of goods to be exported to foreign parts; and, in cases where drawbacks on bounties are to be paid to the merchant on the exportation of any goods, they, as well as the patent searchers, are to certify the shipping thereof on the debentures. Enc. Lond.

LAND WARRANT. A warrant issued at the local land offices of the United States to purchasers of public lands, on the surrender of which at the general land office at Washington, they receive a conveyance from the general government.

The evidence which the state, on good consideration, gives that the person therein named is entitled to the quantity of land therein specified, the bounds and description of which the owner of the warrant may fix by entry and survey, in the section of country set apart for its location and satisfaction. Neal v. President, etc., of East Tennessee College, 6 Yerg., Tenn., 205.

LANDA. An open field without wood; a lawnd or lawn. Cowell; Blount.

LANDAGENDE, LANDHLAFORD, or LANDRICA. In Saxon law. A proprietor of land; lord of the soil. Anc. Inst. Eng.

LANDBOC. In Saxon law. A charter or deed by which lands or tenements were given or held. Spelman; Cowell; 1 Reeve, Eng. Law, 10.

LANDCHEAP. In old English law. An ancient customary fine, paid either in money or cattle, at every alienation of land lying within some manor, or within the liberty of some borough. Cowell; Blount.

LANDDAG. A convention of the Dutch in New Amsterdam. See 1 Fiske, Dutch & Quaker Colonies 328.

LANDEA. In old English law. A ditch or trench for conveying water from marshy grounds. Spelman.

LANDED. As used in a revenue act levying tolls on goods, the clear meaning and purport is "substantially imported." L. R. 4 Ex. 260.

Consisting in real estate or land; having an estate in land.

LANDED ESTATE OR PROPERTY. A colloquial or popular phrase to denote real property. Landed estate ordinarily means an interest in and pertaining to lands. Police Jury of Parish of St. Mary v. Harris, 10 La.Ann. 676.

In a tax law it "clearly embraces not only the land, but all houses, fixtures, and improvements of every kind thereon, and all machinery, neat cattle, horses, and mules, when attached to and used on a plantation or farm." A person holding such an estate is termed a landed proprietor. 10 La.Ann. 676. A devise of "all my landed property" carries the fee; Fogg v. Clark, 1 N.H. 163; and so does "my landed estate"; Bradstreet v. Clarke, 12 Wend., N.Y., 602.

Real estate in general, or sometimes, by local usage, suburban or rural land, as distinguished from real estate situated in a city. See Electric Co. v. Baltimore, 93 Md. 630, 49 A. 655, 52 L.R.A. 772; Sindall v. Baltimore, 93 Md. 526, 49 A. 645.

LANDED ESTATES COURT. In English law. Tribunals established by statute for the purpose of disposing more promptly and easily than could be done through the ordinary judicial machinery, of incumbered real estate.

These courts were first established in Ireland by the act of 11 & 12 Vict. c. 48, which being defective was followed by 12 & 13 Vict. c. 77. The purpose of these was to enable the owner, or a lessee for any less than 63 years unexpired, of land subject to incumbrance, to apply to commissioners who constituted a court of record to direct a sale. This court was called the Incumbered Estates Court. A new tribunal called the Landed Estates Court was created by 21 & 22 Vict. c. 72, which abolished the former court and established a permanent tribunal.

LANDED PROPRIETOR. Any person having an estate in lands whether highly improved or not. Police Jury of Parish of St. Mary v. Harris, 10 La.Ann. 677.

LANDED SECURITIES. Mortgages or other incumbrances affecting land. 3 Atk. 805, 808.

LANDEFRICUS. A landlord; a lord of the soil.

LANDEGANDMAN. Sax. In old English law. A kind of customary tenant or inferior tenant of a manor. Spelman.

LANDGRAVE. A name formerly given to those who executed justice on behalf of the German emperors, with regard to the internal policy of the country. It was applied, by way of eminence, to those sovereign princes of the empire who possessed by inheritance certain estates called *"landgravates,"* of which they received investiture from the emperor. Enc. Lond.

LANDHLAFORD. A proprietor of land; lord of the soil. Anc. Inst. Eng.

LANDIMER. In old Scotch law. A measurer of land. Skene.

LANDING. A place on a river or other navigable water for lading and unlading goods, or for the reception and delivery of passengers; the terminus of a road on a river or other navigable water, for the use of travelers, and the loading and unloading of goods. State v. Randall, 1 Strob., S.C., 111, 47 Am.Dec. 548; State v. Louisiana Terminal Co., 179 La. 671, 154 So. 731.

A place for loading or unloading boats, but not a harbor for them. Hays v. Briggs, 74 Pa. 373.

A place laid out by a town as a common landing place and used as such, but not designated as for the particular benefit of the town, is a public landing place.

LANDIRECTA. In Saxon law. Services and duties laid upon all that held land, including the three obligations called *"trinoda necessitas,"* (*q. v.;*) *quasi* land rights. Cowell.

LANDLOCKED. An expression sometimes applied to a piece of land belonging to one person and surrounded by land belonging to other persons, so that it cannot be approached except over their land. L. R. 13 Ch. Div. 798; Sweet.

LANDLORD. He of whom lands or tenements are holden. He who, being the owner of an estate in land, has leased it for a term of years, on a rent reserved, to another person, called the "tenant." Jackson v. Harsen, 7 Cow., N.Y., 326, 17 Am.Dec. 517; Becker v. Becker, 13 App.Div. 342, 43 N.Y.S. 17. Person letting land. Stone v. City of Los Angeles, 114 Cal.App. 192, 299 P. 838, 841.

When the absolute property in or fee-simple of the land belongs to a landlord, he is then sometimes denominated the "ground landlord," in contradistinction to such a one as is possessed only of a limited or particular interest in land, and who himself holds under a superior landlord. Brown.

"Landlord" is ordinarily referred to as owner of tenement, to whom tenant pays rent, but is also defined as master or proprietor of inn or of lodging or boarding house. Murray v. Hagens, La.App., 143 So. 505, 506.

LANDLORD AND TENANT. A phrase used to denote the familiar legal relation existing between lessor and lessee of real estate.

The relation is contractual, Renshaw v. Sullivan, Tex. Civ.App., 14 S.W.2d 919, 921; Story v. Lyon Realty Corporation, 308 Mass. 66, 30 N.E.2d 845, 847; Smith v. Royal Ins. Co., C.C.A.Cal., 111 F.2d 667, 670, 671, 130 A.L.R. 812. A lease (or agreement therefor) of lands for a term of years, from year to year, for life, or at will creates the relation. Dutton v. Dutton, 122 Kan. 640, 253 P. 553, 554; Minneapolis Iron Store Co. v. Branum, 36 N.D. 355, 162 N. W. 543, 545, L.R.A.1917E, 298. The relation exists where one person occupies premises of another in subordination to other's title or rights and with his permission or consent. Gates v. Herberger, 202 Minn. 610, 279 N.W. 711, 712; Wood v. Homelvig, 68 N.D. 735, 283 N.W. 278, 282; Marden v. Radford, 229 Mo.App. 789, 84 S.W.2d 947, 954; Coggins v. Gregoris, C.C.A.N.M., 97 F.2d 948, 950, 951. There must be reversion in landlord, an estate in tenant, transfer of possession and control of premises, and, generally, a contract, express or implied. Marden v. Radford, 229 Mo.App. 789, 84 S.W.2d 947, 954, 955; Coggins v. Gregorio, C.C.A.N.M., 97 F.2d 948, 950, 951.

LANDLORD'S WARRANT. A distress warrant; a warrant from a landlord to levy upon the tenant's goods and chattels, and sell the same at public sale, to compel payment of the rent or the observance of some other stipulation in the lease.

LANDMARK. A monument or erection set up on the boundary line of two adjoining estates, to fix such boundary. The removing of a landmark is a wrong for which an action lies. Collins v. Brittingham, 90 A. 420, 5 Boyce (Del.) 89.

LANDS. This term, the plural of "land," is said, at common law, to be a word of less extensive signification than either "tenements" or "hereditaments." But in some of the states it has been provided by statute that it shall include both those terms.

LANDS CLAUSES CONSOLIDATION ACTS. The name given to certain English statutes, (8 Vict. c. 8, amended by 23 & 24 Vict. c. 106, and 32 & 33 Vict. c. 18,) the object of which was to provide legislative clauses in a convenient form for incorporation by reference in future special acts of parliament for taking lands, with or without the consent of their owners, for the promotion of railways, and other public undertakings. Mozley & Whiteley.

LANDS, PUBLIC. See Public Lands.

LANDS, TENEMENTS, AND HEREDITAMENTS. The technical and most comprehensive description of real property, as "goods and chattels" is of personalty. Williams, Real Prop. 5.

The term refers to property in land. Denver Joint Stock Land Bank of Denver v. Dixon, 57 Wyo. 523, 122 P.2d 842, 846, 140 A.L.R. 1270. Under ancient law, the words comprehended only freehold estate and did not apply to easements or other incorporeal hereditaments. Hester v. Sawyers, 41 N.M. 497, 71 P.2d 646, 649, 112 A.L.R. 586.

LANDSLAGH. In Swedish law. A body of common law, compiled about the thirteenth century, out of the particular customs of every province; being analogous to the *common law* of England. 1 Bl.Comm. 66.

LANDWARD. In Scotch law. Rural. 7 Bell, App. Cas. 2.

LANGEMAN. A lord of a manor. 1 Inst. 5.

LANGEMANNI. The lords of manors. 1 Co. Inst. 5.

LANGEOLUM. An undergarment made of wool, formerly worn by the monks, which reached to their knees. Mon. Angl. 419.

LANGUAGE. Any means of conveying or communicating ideas; specifically, human speech, or the expression of ideas by written characters. The letter, or grammatical import, of a document or instrument, as distinguished from its spirit; as "the language of the statute." See Behling v. State, 110 Ga. 754, 36 S.E. 85; Stevenson v. State, 90 Ga. 456, 16 S.E. 95; Cavan v. Brooklyn, City Ct. Brook., 5 N.Y.S. 759. As to "offensive language," see Offensive Language.

LANGUIDUS. (Lat., sick.) In practice. The name of a return made by the sheriff when a defendant, whom he has taken by virtue of process, is so dangerously sick that to remove him would endanger his life or health. 3 Chit. Pr. 249, 358.

LANIS DE CRESCENTIA WALLIÆ TRADUCENDIS ABSQUE CUSTUMA, etc. An ancient writ that lay to the customer of a port to permit one to pass wool without paying custom, he having paid it before in Wales. Reg. Orig. 279.

LANNS MANUS (Old Fr.). A lord of the manor. Kelham.

LANO NIGER. A sort of base coin, formerly current in England. Cowell.

LANZAS. In Spanish law. A commutation in money, paid by the nobles and high officers, in lieu of the quota of soldiers they might be required to furnish in war. Trevino v. Fernandez, 13 Tex. 660.

LAPIDATION. The act of stoning a person to death.

LAPIDICINA. Lat. In the civil law. A stone-quarry. Dig. 7, 1, 9, 2.

LAPILLI. Lat. In the civil law. Precious stones. Dig. 34, 2, 19, 17. Distinguished from "gems," (*gemmæ.*) Id.

LAPIS MARMORIUS. A marble stone about twelve feet long and three feet broad, placed at the upper end of Westminster Hall, where was likewise a marble chair erected on the middle thereof, in which the English sovereigns anciently sat at their coronation dinner, and at other times the lord chancellor. Wharton.

LAPPAGE. A term synonymous with "interference," "conflict," "interlock," "lap" and "overlap" as regards adverse possession. It applies to a situation existing when a deed under which one party claims and grant under which another claims cover in large part the same land. Turk v. Wilson's Heirs, 265 Ky. 78, 98 S.W.2d 4, 8; Berry v. Coppersmith, 212 N.C. 50, 193 S.E. 3, 6.

LAPSE, *v.* To glide; to pass slowly, silently, or by degrees. To slip; to deviate from the proper path. Webster. To fall or fail. Life & Casualty Ins. Co. of Tennessee v. Wheeler, 265 Ky. 269, 96 S.W.2d 753, 755, 106 A.L.R. 1270.

LAPSE, *n.* The termination or failure of a right or privilege through neglect to exercise it within some limit of time, or through failure of some contingency. Wilmington Trust Co. v. Wilmington Trust Co., 25 Del.Ch. 204, 15 A.2d 830, 834.

In criminal proceedings. "Lapse" is used, in England, in the same sense as "abate" in ordinary procedure; *i. e.*, to signify that the proceedings came to an end by the death of one of the parties or some other event.

In ecclesiastical law. The transfer, by forfeiture of a right to present or collate to a vacant benefice from a person vested with such right to another, in consequence of some act of negligence by the former. Ayl.Par. 331.

In the law of wills. The failure of a testamentary gift. Wilmington Trust Co. v. Wilmington Trust Co., 25 Del.Ch. 204, 15 A.2d 830, 834; Gredig v. Sterling, C.C.A.Tex., 47 F.2d 832, 834.

LAPSE PATENT. A patent for land issued in substitution for an earlier patent to the same land, which was issued to another party, but has lapsed in consequence of his neglect to avail himself of it. Wilcox v. Calloway, 1 Wash., Va., 39.

LAPSED DEVISE. See Devise.

LAPSED LEGACY. See Legacy.

LAPSED POLICY. A policy on which there has been default in payment of premiums; policy remaining in force according to statutory provisions after such default. Metcalf v. Metropolitan Life Ins. Co., 1 Cal.App.2d 481, 37 P.2d 115.

LARBOARD. The left side of a ship or boat when one stands with his face towards the bow.

The opposite term is starboard, which is the right-hand side looking forward. The word is now, however, no longer used, the term port having been substituted for it. The change was made by order of the English admiralty, for the very obvious reason that larboard was apt to be confused with the opposite term.

LARCENOUS. Having the character of larceny; as a "larcenous taking." Contemplating or intending larceny; as a "larcenous purpose."

LARCENOUS INTENT. A larcenous intent exists where a man knowingly takes and carries away the goods of another without any claim or pretense of right, with intent wholly to deprive the owner of them or convert them to his own use. Wilson v. State, 18 Tex.App. 274, 51 Am.Rep. 309.

LARCENY. Felonious stealing, taking and carrying, leading, riding, or driving away another's personalty, 4 Bl.Comm. 229; People v. Brickey, 346 Ill. 273, 178 N.E. 483, 485; State v. Miller, 170 La. 51, 127 So. 361, 362; with intent to convert it or to deprive owner thereof, Ledbetter v. State, 24 Ala.App. 447, 136 So. 430; Globe & Rutgers Fire Ins. Co. v. House, 163 Tenn. 585, 45 S.W.2d 55, 56; Commonwealth v. Estes, 265 Ky. 186, 96 S.W. 2d 578, 580.

Larceny is fraudulent taking and carrying away of a thing without claim of right, with intention of converting it to a use other than that of the owner, without his consent. Thomas v. Kessler, 334 Pa. 7, 5 A.2d 187, 188; Fitch v. State, 135 Fla. 361, 185 So. 435, 437, 439, 440, 125 A.L.R. 360; Hanes Funeral Home v. Dixie Fire Ins. Co., 216 N.C. 562, 5 S.E.2d 820, 821, 822; receiving possession of personalty with intent to convert it to own use, and with intent of person parting with it to part merely with his possession, Hagan v. State, 76 Okl.Cr. 127, 134 P.2d 1042, 1047, 1048, 1050; taking and removing, by trespass, of personal property which trespasser knows to belong either generally or specially to another, with intent to deprive him of his ownership, State v. Broom, 135 Or. 641, 297 P. 340, 342; State v. Levy, 113 Vt. 459, 35 A.2d 853, 854, and, perhaps it should be added, for the sake of some advantage to the trespasser,—a proposition on which the decisions are not harmonious, 2 Bish.Crim.Law, §§ 757, 758; taking of personalty by fraud or stealth, and with intent to deprive another thereof, Pen. Code Dak. § 580 (Comp.Laws N.D. 1913, § 9913; Rev. Code S.D.1919, § 4210); Hughes v. State, 61 Okl.Cr. 40, 65 P.2d 544, 546; Bussart v. State, 128 Fla. 891, 176 So. 32, 33; unlawful acquisition of property with intent to convert to taker's use and appropriation by taker, State v. Smith, 2 Wash.2d 118, 98 P.2d 647, 648, 649; unlawful or felonious taking and carrying away of things personal with intent to deprive rightful owner of it, 4 Steph.Comm. 152; Globe & Rutgers Fire Ins. Co. v. House, 163 Tenn. 585, 45 S.W.2d 55, 56; Bowling v. Hamblen County Motor Co., 16 Tenn.App. 52, 66 S.W.2d 229; wrongful and fraudulent taking and carrying away by one of personal goods of another with felonious intent to convert them to his own use and make them his own property, or to deprive the owner permanently of his property, without owner's consent, Commonwealth v. Estes, 265 Ky. 186, 96 S.W.2d 578, 580; State v. Savage, Del., 7 W.W.Harr. 509, 186 A. 738, 739; State v. Delk, 212 N.C. 631, 194 S.E. 94; Hickman v. State, 25 Ala.App. 279, 145 So. 167, 168; wrongful or felonious taking property of another, without his consent and against his will, with intent to convert it to use of the taker, Hammon's Case, 2 Leach, 1089, State v. Boswell, 195 N.C. 496, 142 S.E. 583, 584; State v. Fulks, 114 W.Va. 785, 173 S.E. 888, 889.

Obtaining possession of property by fraud, trick or device with preconceived design or intent to appropriate, convert or steal is "larceny." John v. United States, 65 App.D.C. 11, 79 F.2d 136, People v. Cook, 10 Cal.App.2d 54, 51 P.2d 169, 170; State v. Wisman, 111 W.Va. 183, 161 S.E. 437, 438; Nugent v. Union Automobile Ins. Co., 140 Or. 61, 13 P.2d 343, 344.

Common-law distinctions between obtaining money under false pretenses, embezzlement, and larceny no longer exist in New York, but all such crimes are embraced within definition of "larceny." People v. Krumme, 161 Misc. 278, 292 N.Y.S. 657, 660.

Generally, one who unlawfully takes another's personal property, not intending to steal, and afterwards converts it, intending to steal, is guilty of "larceny". Calhoun v. State, 191 Miss. 82, 2 So.2d 802, 804, 805.

Every act of thief in the removal of property is in itself a complete "larceny". Schultz v. Lainson, 234 Iowa 606, 13 N.W.2d 326, 327, 156 A.L.R. 858.

Common Law Larceny

Felonious taking and carrying away of personal goods of another, Fowler v. Firth, 163 Misc. 942, 298 N.Y.S. 723, 726, with intent to convert it to taker's use. United States Fidelity & Guaranty Co. v. Peoples Bank & Trust Co. of Westfield, C.C.A.N.J., 79 F.2d 642, 644.

It is obtaining possession of another's property by fraudulent trick or device, with intent to convert it to own use. Powers v. State, 31 Ala.App. 614, 21 So.2d 282, 285; removal of personalty which trespasser knows to belong to another, with felonious intent to deprive him of his ownership, U. S. v. Patton, C.C.A.Pa., 120 F.2d 73, 75, 76; Austin v. State, 65 Ga.App. 733, 16 S.E.2d 497, 499; taking and carrying away personal property of another without his consent, feloniously, with intent to deprive owner of his property permanently, and to convert it to use of taker, or of some person other than the owner, Fowler v. Firth, 163 Misc. 942, 298 N.Y.S. 723, 726; trespassory taking and asportation, Crabb v. Zerbst, C.C.A.Ga., 99 F.2d 562, 564; unpermitted obtaining of possession of another's chattel and removal thereof, Crabb v. Zerbst, C.C.A.Ga., 99 F.2d 562, 564; wrongful or fraudulent taking and carrying away of the personal goods of another with felonious intent to convert them to the taker's own use and make them his own property without owner's consent. Riley v. State, 64

Okl.Cr. 183, 78 P.2d 712, 715, 716; Hatfield v. Guay, C.C.A. N.H., 87 F.2d 358, 363; Fowler v. Firth, 163 Misc. 942, 298 N.Y.S. 723, 726.

Compound Larceny

Larceny or theft accomplished by taking the thing stolen either from one's person or from his house; otherwise called "mixed" larceny, and distinguished from "simple" or "plain" larceny, in which the theft is not aggravated by such an intrusion either upon the person or the dwelling. Anderson v. Winfree, 85 Ky. 597, 4 S.W. 351; State v. Chambers, 22 W.Va. 786, 46 Am.Rep. 550.

Constructive Larceny

One where the felonious intent to appropriate the goods to his own use, at the time of the asportation, is made out by construction from the defendant's conduct, although, originally, the taking was not apparently felonious. 2 East, P.C. 685; 1 Leach, 212

False Pretense and Larceny Distinguished

See False Pretenses.

Grand Larceny

In criminal law. In England, simple larceny, was originally divided into two sorts,—*grand* larceny, where the value of the goods stolen was above twelve pence, and *petit* larceny, where their value was equal to or below that sum. 4 Bl. Comm. 229.

The distinction was abolished in England by St. 7 & 8 Geo. IV. c. 29, and is not generally recognized in the United States, although in a few states there is a statutory offense of grand larceny, one essential element of which is the value of the goods stolen, which value varies. See State v. Bean, 74 Vt. 111, 52 A. 269; People v. Murray, 8 Cal. 520; State v. Kennedy, 88 Mo. 343.

Larceny by Bailee

In Pennsylvania law. The crime of larceny committed where any person, being a bailee of any property, shall fraudulently take or convert the same to his own use, or to the use of any other person except the owner thereof, although he shall not break bulk or otherwise determine the bailment. Brightly's Purd. Dig. p. 436, § 177 (18 P.S. § 4816). And see Welsh v. People, 17 Ill. 339; State v. Skinner, 29 Or. 599, 46 P. 368.

Larceny from the Person

Act of taking property from the person by merely lifting it from the person or pocket. State v. Stanton, Mo., 68 S.W.2d 811, 812.

Larceny committed where the property stolen is on the person or in the immediate charge or custody of the person from whom the theft is made, but without such circumstances of force or violence as would constitute robbery, including pocket-picking and such crimes. Williams v. U. S., 3 App.D.C. 345; State v. Eno, 8 Minn. 220, Gil. 190.

Mixed Larceny

Otherwise called "compound" or "complicated larceny;" that which is attended with circumstances of aggravation or violence to the person, or taking from a house.

Petit Larceny

The larceny of things whose value was below a certain arbitrary standard, at common law twelve pence. See Ex parte Bell, 19 Fla. 612; Barnhart v. State, 154 Ind. 177, 56 N.E. 212; People v. Righetti, 66 Cal. 184, 4 P. 1185.

Simple Larceny

Felonious or wrongful taking and carrying away of personal goods of another. People v. Pace, 2 Cal.App.2d 464, 38 P.2d 202, 203. With intent to steal, Belmas v. State, 15 Ga.App. 288, 82 S.E. 819, unattended by acts of violence.

Larceny which is not complicated or aggravated with acts of violence. Larceny from the person, or with force and violence, is called "compound" larceny. See State v. Chambers, 22 W.Va. 786, 46 Am.Rep. 550; Anderson v. Winfree, 4 S.W. 351, 85 Ky. 597.

LARD. The clarified semi-solid oil of hog's fat. Cent. Dict. The pure fat of healthy swine. State v. Snow, 81 Iowa 642, 47 N.W. 777, 11 L.R.A. 355.

LARDARIUS REGIS. The king's larderer, or clerk of the kitchen. Cowell.

LARDING MONEY. In the manor of Bradford, in Wilts, the tenants pay to their lord a small yearly rent by this name, which is said to be for liberty to feed their hogs with the masts of the lord's wood, the fat of a hog being called "lard;" or it may be a commutation for some customary service of carrying salt or meat to the lord's larder. Mon. Angl. t. 1, p. 321.

LARGE. L. Fr. Broad; the opposite of *"estreyte,"* strait or strict. *Pures et larges.* Britt. c. 34.

LARONS. In old English law. Thieves.

LAS PARTIDAS. In Spanish law. The name of a code of laws, more fully described as *"Las Siete Partidas,"* ("the seven parts," from the number of its divisions,) which was compiled under the direction of Alphonso X., about the year 1250.

Its sources were the customary law of all the provinces, the canon law as there administered, and (chiefly) the Roman law. This work has always been regarded as of the highest authority in Spain and in those countries and states which have derived their jurisprudence from Spain.

LASCAR. A native Indian sailor; the term is also applied to tent pitchers, inferior artillery-men, and others.

LASCIVIOUS. Tending to excite lust; lewd; indecent; obscene; sexual impurity; tending to deprave the morals in respect to sexual relations; licentious. See Swearingen v. U. S., 161 U.S. 446, 16 S.Ct. 562, 40 L.Ed. 765; People on Complaint of Sumner v. Dial Press, 182 Misc. 416, 48 N.Y.S.2d 480, 481; Dunlop v. U. S., 165 U.S. 486, 17 S.Ct. 375, 41 L.Ed. 799; Purvis v. State, 117 Neb. 377, 220 N.W. 599, 600. Conduct which is wanton, lewd, and lustful, and tending to produce voluptuous or lewd emotions. Zeiner v. Zeiner, 120 Conn. 161, 179 A. 644, 646.

LASCIVIOUS CARRIAGE. In Connecticut. A term including those wanton acts between persons of different sexes that flow from the exercise of lustful passions, and which are not otherwise punished as crimes against chastity and public decency. 2 Swift, Dig. 343. It includes, also, indecent acts by one against the will of another. Fowler v. State, 5 Day, Conn., 81.

LASCIVIOUS COHABITATION. The offense committed by two persons (not married to each other) who live together in one habitation as man and wife and practice sexual intercourse.

LASHITE, or LASHLITE. A kind of forfeiture during the government of the Danes in England. Enc. Lond.

LAST, *n.* In old English law, signifies a burden; also a measure of weight used for certain commodities of the bulkier sort.

LAST, *adj.* Latest; ultimate; final; most recent.

LAST ANTECEDENT RULE. A canon of statutory construction that relative or qualifying words or phrases are to be applied to the words or phrases immediately preceding, and as not extending to or including other words, phrases, or clauses more remote, unless such extension or inclusion is clearly required by the intent and meaning of the context, or disclosed by an examination of the entire act. Stevens v. Illinois Cent. R. Co., 306 Ill. 370, 137 N.E. 859, 861; Nebraska State Ry. Commission v. Alfalfa Butter Co., 104 Neb. 797, 178 N.W. 766, 768; Wisconsin Power & Light Co. v. Public Service Commission of Wisconsin, 224 Wis. 286, 272 N.W. 50, 52.

LAST CLEAR CHANCE. The "last clear chance doctrine" is that a party who has last clear chance to avoid damage or injury to another is liable. Johnston v. Brewer, 40 Cal.App.2d 583, 105 P.2d 365, 367; Miami Beach Ry. Co. v. Dohme, 131 Fla. 171, 179 So. 166, 169; Virginia Electric & Power Co. v. Whitehurst, 175 Va. 339, 8 S.E.2d 296, 299; that negligence of party having last opportunity of avoiding accident is sole proximate cause of injury, Malfetano v. United Electric Rys. Co., 58 R.I. 129, 191 A. 491, 498; Gregory v. Maine Cent. R. Co., 317 Miss. 636, 59 N.E.2d 471, 476, 159 A.L.R. 714; that if one has opportunity of avoiding injuring another he must at his peril exercise the opportunity. Ferran v. Southern Pac. Co., 3 Cal. 2d 350, 44 P.2d 533, 534. It places liability upon him who commits the last proximate negligent act. Davis v. Cuesta, 146 Fla. 471, 1 So.2d 475, 476.

The doctrine is inapplicable unless injured party was guilty of negligence, Yellow Cab Corporation of Abingdon v. Henderson, 178 Va. 207, 16 S.E.2d 389, 393; Washam v. Peerless Automatic Staple Mach. Co., 45 Cal.App.2d 174, 113 P.2d 724, 728; and unless injured person is in an apparently helpless condition, Battle v. Southern Ry. Co., 223 N.C. 395, 26 S.E.2d 859.

The doctrine means that an injured party may recover, notwithstanding negligence: if defendant could have avoided injury after discovering or knowing of peril, Sprinkle v. Davis, C.C.A.Va., 111 F.2d 925, 928, 128 A.L.R. 1101; Weddle v. Virginian Ry. Co., 125 W.Va. 41, 22 S.E.2d 698, 701; Jones v. Yuma Motor Freight Terminal, 45 Cal.App.2d 497, 114 P.2d 438, 439, 440; Shea v. Pilette, 108 Vt. 446, 189 A. 154, 158, 109 A.L.R. 933, Stelter v. Northern Pac. Ry. Co., 71 N.D. 214, 299 N.W. 310, 313, 314; if injuring party, seeing or knowing or aware of peril, fails to use ordinary or due care and thereby causes injury, Underhill v. Peterson, 110 Cal.App. 221, 293 P. 861, 864; Groves v. Webster City, 222 Iowa 849, 270 N.W. 329, 332; Caplan v. Arndt, 123 Conn. 585, 196 A. 631, 633, 119 A.L.R. 1037; Kurn v. McCoy, 187 Okl. 210, 102 P.2d 177; if injury might have been avoided by exercise of reasonable care by defendant, Harstick v. Beckenhauer, 143 Neb. 179, 8 N.W.2d 834, 837; General Exchange Ins. Corporation v. Carp, La.App., 176 So. 145, 147; Kelley Furniture Co. v. Washington Ry. & Electric Co., 64 App.D.C. 215, 76 F.2d 985; Srogi v. New York Cent. R. Co., 247 App.Div. 95, 286 N.Y.S. 215; Mullins v. Cincinnati, N. & C. Ry. Co., 253 Ky. 156, 68 S.W.2d 790; Lovett v. Sandersville R. Co., 72 Ga.App. 692, 34 S.E.2d 664, 666; if, with knowledge of peril to plaintiff or plaintiff's property, another acts or omits to act and injury results, Parsons v. Berry, 130 Neb. 264, 264 N.W. 742, 744.

The doctrine implies thought, appreciation, mental direction, and a lapse of sufficient time to effectually act upon impulse to save another from injury, Colwell v. Nygaard, 8 Wash.2d 462, 112 P.2d 838, 845; Merchants' Transp. Co. v. Daniel, 109 Fla. 496, 149 So. 401, 403; or proof of circumstances which will put the one charged on implied notice of the situation, Schoen v. Western Union Telegraph Co., C.C.A.Fla., 135 F.2d 967, 968.

The doctrine imposes duty upon a party to exercise ordinary care in avoiding injury to another who has negligently placed himself in a situation of danger, Morris v. Seashore Transp. Co., 208 N.C. 807, 182 S.E. 487, duty to act when helpless peril is known and duty to exercise vigilance to discover helpless peril, if duty of vigilance exists toward class of which one in peril is member, Leinbach v. Pickwick Greyhound Lines, 138 Kan. 50, 23 P. 2d 449, 92 A.L.R. 1.

The doctrine is limited, according to some decisions, to cases in which defendant actually discovered person injured and his peril. Walker v. East St. Louis & Suburban Ry. Co., C.C.A.Mo., 25 F.2d 579, 580, Gauthier v. Foote, La. App., 12 So.2d 9, 11; or in which defendant had actual knowledge of plaintiff's peril or inability to extricate himself. Sarkise v. Boston & M. R. R., 88 N.H. 178, 186 A. 332, 334. But other decisions hold that the doctrine applies if defendant, aware of plaintiff's peril or unaware of it only through carelessness, has later opportunity than plaintiff to avert the accident, Cheek v. Thompson, D.C.La., 28 F. Supp. 391, 394; Linde Air Products Co. v. Cameron, C.C.A. W.Va., 82 F.2d 22, 24; or if defendant knew or could or should have known of peril, Arthur v. Rose, 289 Ky. 402, 158 S.W.2d 652, 653, 654; Ward v. City Fuel Oil Co., 147 Fla. 320, 2 So.2d 586, 587; Smith v. Pacific Greyhound Corporation, 139 Cal.App. 696, 35 P.2d 169, 172; or if defendant saw or discovered or should have seen or discovered the danger, Young v. Thompson, La.App., 189 So. 487, 489, 490, 491; Hartman v. Dyer, 298 Ky. 173, 182 S.W.2d 646, 647; Evansville Container Corporation v. McDonald, C.C.A. Tenn., 132 F.2d 80, 85; Harry v. Thompson, Mo.App., 166 S.W.2d 795, 798; or if injuring party was aware of peril or by reasonable care should have known of danger, Gardini v. Arakelian, 18 Cal.App.2d 424, 64 P.2d 181, 184; or if peril is realized by defendant or through culpable carelessness he is oblivious to it, Pedigo v. Osborne, 279 Ky. 85, 129 S.W.2d 996, 999; Johnson v. Southwestern Engineering Co., 41 Cal.App.2d 623, 107 P.2d 417, 418.

The doctrine is predicated, according to some decisions, upon the theory that negligence of injured party has ceased. Baltimore & O. R. Co. v. Joseph, C.C.A.Ohio, 112 F.2d 518, 521, 522; Cohen v. Smith, 26 Ohio App. 32, 159 N. E. 329, 333; Claggett v. Phillips Petroleum Co., 150 Kan. 191, 92 P.2d 52, 57; Becker v. Blum, 142 Fla. 60, 194 So. 275, 276.

Other decisions hold that, although plaintiff's negligence continued until accident he may recover if the defendant, after knowing of plaintiff's danger, or by exercise of ordinary care could have known, could have avoided injury by ordinary care, McLeod v. Charleston Laundry Co., 106 W.Va. 361, 145 S.E. 756, 757; Newbern v. Leary, 215 N.C. 134, 1 S.E.2d 384, 389, 393; Young v. Thompson, La.App., 189 So. 487, 489, 490, 491; that the doctrine applies where plaintiff's negligence continues up to time of injury, if defendant actually sees the peril, or if plaintiff's negligence has terminated and defendant should have seen it. Chadwick v. Ek, 1 Wash.2d 117, 95 P.2d 398, 404; that the doctrine applies where negligence of defendant with actual knowledge of situation stands over against continuing negligence of plaintiff without actual knowledge of situation, but not where plaintiff's negligence with knowledge of situation stands over against defendant's negligence also with such knowledge, Iverson v. Knorr, 68 S.D. 23, 298 N. W. 28, 31.

The doctrine is sometimes designated as the humanitarian doctrine, Blashfield's Cyc. of Automobile Law and Prac., Perm. Ed., § 2841; Gilbert v. Mississippi River & B. T. R. Co., Mo.App., 226 S.W. 263, 264; Iglesias v. Campbell, La. App., 175 So. 145, 147; and also the doctrine of discovered peril, Missouri Pac. R. Co. v. Skipper, 174 Ark. 1083, 298 S.W. 849, 854; Hines v. Foreman, Tex.Civ.App., 229 S.W. 630, 635; Soards v. Shreveport Rys. Co., La.App., 8 So.2d 343, 344. In Maryland, it is equivalent to "negligence in the third degree." State v. New York, P. & N. R. Co., 127 Md. 651, 96 A. 809, 811. The term "last fair chance" is synonymous. Nagel v. Bretthauer, 230 Iowa 707, 298 N. W. 852, 854.

LAST COURT. A court held by the twenty-four jurats in the marshes of Kent, and summoned by the bailiffs, whereby orders were made to lay and levy taxes, impose penalties, etc., for the preservation of the said marshes. Enc. Lond.

LAST HEIR. In English law. He to whom lands come by escheat for want of lawful heirs; that is, in some cases, the lord of whom the lands were held; in others, the sovereign. Cowell.

LAST ILLNESS. The illness terminating in person's death. Long v. Northrup, 225 Iowa 132, 279 N.W. 104, 106, 116 A.L.R. 1475; Proto v. Chenoweth, 40 Ariz. 312, 11 P.2d 950, 951.

LAST RESORT. A court from which there is no appeal is called the "court of last resort."

LAST SICKNESS. That illness of which a person dies is so called. Huse v. Brown, 8 Me: 169; Harrington v. Stees, 82 Ill. 54, 25 Am.Rep. 290; McVoy v. Percival, Dud. Law (S.C.) 337; Prince v. Hazelton, 20 Johns., N.Y., 513, 11 Am.Dec. 307.

LAST WILL. This term, according to Lord Coke, is most commonly used where lands and tenements are devised, and "testament" where it concerns chattels. Co. Litt. 111*a*. Both terms, however, are now generally employed in drawing a will either of lands or chattels. See Reagan v. Stanley, 11 Lea, Tenn., 322; Hill v. Hill, 7 Wash. 409, 35 P. 360.

The common usage the world over is to employ the words "will," "testament," and "last will and testament" as exactly synonymous. Occidental Life Ins. Co. v. Powers, 192 Wash. 475, 74 P.2d 27, 32, 114 A.L.R. 531.

LASTAGE. A custom exacted in some fairs and markets to carry things bought whither one will. But it is more accurately taken for the ballast or lading of a ship. Also custom paid for wares sold by the last, as herrings, pitch, etc. Wharton.

LATA CULPA. Lat. In the law of bailment. Gross fault or neglect; extreme negligence or carelessness (*nimia negligentia*). Dig. 50, 16, 213, 2.

LATA CULPA DOLO ÆQUIPARATUR. Gross negligence is equivalent to fraud.

LATCHING. An under-ground survey.

LATE. Defunct; existing recently, but now dead. Pleasant v. State, 17 Ala. 190. Formerly; recently; lately.

LATELY. This word has been held to have "a very large retrospect, as we say '*lately* deceased' of one dead ten or twenty years." Per. Cur. 2 Show. 294.

LATENS. Lat. Latent; hidden; not apparent. See Ambiguitas.

LATENT. Hidden; concealed; dormant; that does not appear upon the face of a thing; as, a latent ambiguity. See Ambiguity.

LATENT DEED. A deed kept for twenty years or more in a man's scrutoire or strongbox. Wright v. Wright, 7 N.J.L. 177, 11 Am.Dec. 546.

LATENT DEFECT. A hidden defect. Ross v. Tynes, La.App., 14 So.2d 80, 83. A defect in an article sold, which is known to the seller, but not to the purchaser, and is not discoverable by mere observation. See Hoe v. Sanborn, 21 N.Y. 552, 78 Am.Dec. 163. A defect which reasonably careful inspection will not reveal. Schaff v. Ellison, Tex.Civ.App., 255 S.W. 680, 682; Roberts v. Rogers, 129 Neb. 298, 261 N.W. 354; a defect which could not have been discovered by inspection. Roberts v. Rogers, 129 Neb. 298, 261 N.W. 354. A defect that could not be discovered by any known and customary test. The Bill, D.C.Md., 47 F.Supp. 969, 978. So, a latent defect in the title of a vendor of land is one not discoverable by inspection made with ordinary care. Newell v. Turner, 9 Port., Ala., 422.

LATENT EQUITY. See Equity.

LATERA. In old records. Sidesmen; companions; assistants. Cowell.

LATERAL RAILROAD. A lateral road is one which proceeds from some point on the main trunk between its termini; it is but another name for a branch road, both being a part of the main road. Newhall v. Railroad Co., 14 Ill. 273. An offshoot from main line of railroad. Union Pac. R. Co. v. Anderson, 167 Or. 687, 120 P.2d 578, 588.

LATERAL SUPPORT. The right of lateral and subjacent support is the right to have land supported by the adjoining land or the soil beneath. Stevenson v. Wallace, 27 Grat., Va., 77; Foley v. Wyeth, 2 Allen., Mass., 131, 79 Am.Dec. 771; In re Locust St. Subway, 117 Pa.Super. 86, 177 A. 599, 605; 12 Amer. & Eng. Enc. Law, 933.

LATERARE. To lie sideways, in opposition to lying endways; used in descriptions of lands.

LATH, LATHE. The name of an ancient civil division in England, intermediate between the county or shire and the hundred. Said to be the same as what, in other parts of the kingdom, was termed a "rape." 1 Bl.Comm. 116; Cowell; Spelman.

LATHREVE. An officer under the Saxon government, who had authority over a lathe. Cowell; 1 Bl.Comm. 116.

LATIFUNDIUM. Lat. In the civil law. Great or large possessions; a great or large field; a common. A great estate made up of smaller ones, (*fundis,*) which began to be common in the latter times of the empire.

LATIFUNDUS. A possessor of a large estate made up of smaller ones. Du Cange.

LATIMER. A word used by Lord Coke in the sense of an interpreter. 2 Inst. 515. Supposed to be a corruption of the French *"latinier,"* or *"latiner."* Cowell; Blount.

LATIN. The language of the ancient Romans.

There are three sorts of law Latin: (1) Good Latin, allowed by the grammarians and lawyers; (2) false or incongruous Latin, which in times past would abate original writs, though it would not make void any judicial writ, declaration, or plea, etc.; (3) words of art, known only to the sages of the law, and not to grammarians, called "Lawyers' Latin." Wharton.

LATINARIUS. An interpreter of Latin.

LATINI JUNIANI. Lat. In Roman law. A class of freedmen (*libertini*) intermediate between the two other classes of freedmen called, respectively, *"Cives Romani"* and *"Dediticii."*

Slaves under thirty years of age at the date of their manumission, or manumitted otherwise than by *vindicta, census,* or *testamentum,* or not the quiritary property of their manumissors at the time of manumission, were called *"Latini."* By reason of one or other of these three defects, they remained slaves by strict law even after their manumission, but were protected in their liberties first by equity, and eventually by the *Lex Junia Norbana,* A. D. 19, from which law they took the name of *"Juniani"* in addition to that of *"Latini."* Brown.

LATITAT. In old English practice. A writ which issued in personal actions, on the return of *non est inventus* to a bill of Middlesex; so called from the emphatic word in its recital, in which it was "testified that the defendant *lurks* [*latitat*] and wanders about" in the county. 3 Bl.Comm. 286. Abolished by St. 2 Wm. IV. c. 39.

LATITATIO. Lat. In the civil law and old English practice. A lying hid; lurking, or concealment of the person. Dig. 42, 4, 7, 5; Bract. fol. 126.

LATOR. Lat. In the civil law. A bearer; a messenger. Also a maker or giver of laws.

LATRO. Lat. In the civil and old English law. A robber. Dig. 50, 16, 118; Fleta, lib. 1, c. 38, § 1. A thief.

LATROCINATION. The act of robbing; a depredation.

LATROCINIUM. The prerogative of adjudging and executing thieves; also larceny; theft; a thing stolen.

LATROCINY. Larceny.

LATTER-MATH. A second mowing; the aftermath.

LAUDARE. Lat.

In Civil law. To name; to cite or quote; to show one's title or authority. Calvin.

In Feudal law. To determine or pass upon judicially. *Laudamentum,* the finding or award of a jury. 2 Bl.Comm. 285.

LAUDATIO. Lat. In Roman law. Testimony delivered in court concerning an accused person's good behavior and integrity of life. It resembled the practice which prevails in our trials of calling persons to speak to a prisoner's character. The least number of the *laudatores* among the Romans was ten. Wharton.

LAUDATOR. Lat. An arbitrator; a witness to character.

LAUDEMEO. In Spanish law. The tax paid by the possessor of land held by quit-rent or *emphyteusis* to the owner of the estate, when the tenant alienates his right in the property. Escriche.

LAUDEMIUM. Lat. In the civil law, a sum paid by a new *emphyteuta* (*q. v.*) who acquires the *emphyteusis,* not as heir, but as a singular successor, whether by gift, devise, exchange, or sale.

It was a sum equal to the fiftieth part of the purchase money, paid to the *dominus* or proprietor for his acceptance of the new *emphyteuta.* Mackeld.Rom.Law, § 328. Called, in old English law, "acknowledgment money." Cowell.

LAUDUM. Lat. An arbitrament or award.

In Old Scotch law. Sentence or judgment; dome or doom. 1 Pitc. Crim. Tr. pt. 2, p. 8.

LAUGHE. Frank-pledge. 2 Reeve, Eng. Law, 17.

LAUNCEGAY. A kind of offensive weapon, now disused, and prohibited by 7 Rich. II. c. 13.

LAUNCH. The act of launching a vessel; the movement of a vessel from the land into the water, especially the sliding on ways from the stocks on which it is built. Homer v. The Lady of the Ocean, 70 Me. 352.

A boat of the largest size belonging to a ship of war; an open boat of large size used in any service; a lighter.

LAUREATE. In English law. An officer of the household of the sovereign, whose business formerly consisted only in composing an ode annually, on the sovereign's birthday, and on the new year; sometimes also, though rarely, on occasion of any remarkable victory.

LAURELS. Pieces of gold, coined in 1619, with the king's head laureated; hence the name.

See Jacobus.

LAUS DEO. Lat. Praise be to God. An old heading to bills of exchange.

LAVATORIUM. A laundry or place to wash in; a place in the porch or entrance of cathedral churches, where the priest and other officiating ministers were obliged to wash their hands before they proceeded to divine service.

LAVOR NUEVA. In Spanish law. A new work. Las Partidas, pt. 3, tit. 32, l. 1.

LAW. That which is laid down, ordained, or established. A rule or method according to which phenomena or actions co-exist or follow each other. That which must be obeyed and followed by citizens, subject to sanctions or legal consequences, is a "law." Koenig v. Flynn, 258 N.Y. 292, 179 N.E. 705.

In old English jurisprudence, "law" is used to signify an oath, or the privilege of being sworn; as in the phrases "to wage one's law," "to lose one's law."

The term is also used in opposition to "fact." Thus questions of law are to be decided by the court, while it is the province of the jury to solve questions of fact.

The earliest notion of law was not an enumeration of a principle, but a judgment in a particular case. When pronounced in the early ages, by a king, it was assumed to be the result of direct divine inspiration. Afterwards came the notion of a custom which a judgment affirms, or punishes its breach. In the outset, however, the only authoritative statement of right and wrong is a judicial sentence rendered after the fact has occurred. It does not presuppose a law to have been violated, but is enacted for the first time by a higher form into the judge's mind at the moment of adjudication. Maine, Anc.Law, (Dwight's Ed.) pp. xv, 5.

The word may mean or embrace:

Act of the Legislature deposited in office of Secretary of State, properly authenticated by presiding officers of the two houses, and approved by Governor, State ex rel. Martin v. Zimmerman, 233 Wis. 16, 288 N.W. 454, 456; body of principles, standards and rules promulgated by government, State ex rel. Conway v. Superior Court within and for Greenlee County, 60 Ariz. 69, 131 P.2d 983, 986; city charter provision, Sykes v. City of Battle Creek, 288 Mich. 660, 286 N.W. 117, 118; command which obliges a person or persons and obliges generally to acts or forbearances of a class, Aust.Jur.; constitution or constitutional provision, Boston Elevated Ry. Co. v. Commonwealth, 310 Mass. 528, 39 N.E.2d 87, 109; Wickham v. Grand River Dam Authority, 189 Okl. 540, 118 P.2d 640, 643; Board of Public Instruction for Bay County v. State ex rel. Barefoot, 145 Fla. 482, 199 So. 760, 762; Hudson v. Cummard, 44 Ariz. 7, 33 P.2d 591, 593; county ordinance, People v. Ziady, 8 Cal.2d 149, 64 P.2d 425, 430, 108 A.L.R. 1234; distinct and complete act of positive law; doctrine or procedure of the common law, from which equity is a departure; enrolled bill attested by presiding officers of two branches of General Assembly, Shannon v. Dean, 279 Ky. 279, 130 S.W.2d 812, 815; Executive Order concerning alienation of Indians' land, United States v. Gilbertson, C.C.A.Wis., 111 F.2d 978, 980; Federal Communications Commission's regulations, Columbia Broadcasting System v. United States, N.Y., 316 U.S. 407, 62 S.Ct. 1194, 1200, 1201, 86 L.Ed. 1563; Federal Home Loan Bank Board's rules, Community Federal Sav. & Loan Ass'n of Independence, Mo. v. Fields, C.C.A.Mo., 128 F.2d 705, 707; Federal Trade Commission's rules, Kritzik v. Federal Trade Commission, C.C.A.7, 125 F.2d 351, 352; general rule of human action, taking cognizance only of external acts, enforced by a determinate authority, which authority is human, and among human authorities is that which is paramount in a political society, Holl.Jur. 36; governmental direction, In re Baldwin Tp., Allegheny County Annexation, 305 Pa. 490, 158 A. 272; grant by Legislature, City of Los Angeles v. Pacific Land Corporation, 41 Cal.App.2d 223, 106 P.2d 242, 244; Industrial Commission's Rules, State ex rel. Koger v. Industrial Commission, Ohio App., 48 N.E.2d 114, 118; Interstate Commerce Commission's Regulations, Columbia Broadcasting System v. United States, N.Y., 316 U.S. 407, 62 S.Ct. 1194, 1200, 86 L.Ed. 1563; judicial decisions, judgments or decrees, West v. American Telephone & Telegraph Co., Ohio, 311 U.S. 223, 61 S.Ct. 179, 183, 132 A.L.R. 956, 85 L.Ed. 139; Miller v. Huntington & Ohio Bridge Co., 123 W.Va. 320, 15 S.E.2d 687, 692; U. S. v. Pendergast, D.C.Mo., 35 F.Supp. 593, 599; Monteith Bros. Co. v. U. S., D.C.Ind., 48 F.Supp. 210, 211; law of the state, Plick v. Toye Bros. Auto & Taxicab Co., 169 La. 44, 124 So. 140, 141; legislation by initiative method, Opinion of the Justices, 309 Mass. 676, 35 N.E.2d 676, 680; local rules of decision, National Fruit Product Co. v. Dwinell-Wright Co., D.C.Mass., 47 F.Supp. 499, 502; long-established local custom which has the force of law, Dubois v. Hepburn, 10 Pet. 1, 9 L.Ed. 325, Bush v. Brenner, D.C.Minn., 29 F.2d 844, 845; municipal ordinance, Norfolk & W. Ry. Co. v. White, Va., 160 S.E. 218, 221; State v. Police Court of City of Deer Lodge, 86 Mont. 297, 283 P. 430, 433 (contra, Village of Brewster v. Hills, 128 Ohio St. 354, 191 N.E. 366; City of Cincinnati v. Correll, 141 Ohio St. 535, 49 N.E.2d 412, 413); prescribed rules of action or conduct, In re Baldwin Tp., Allegheny County Annexation, 305 Pa. 490, 158 A. 272; U. S. Fidelity & Guaranty Co. v. Guenther, 281 U.S. 34, 50 S.Ct. 165, 166, 74 L.Ed. 683, 72 A.L.R. 1064; proclamation of Governor, Williams v. State, 146 Tex.Cr.R. 430, 176 S.W.2d 177, 184; regulations, In re Baldwin Tp., Allegheny County Annexation, 305 Pa. 490, 158 A. 272; resolution passed by Legislature and approved by Governor, City of Bangor v. Inhabitants of Etna, 140 Me. 85, 34 A.2d 205, 208; revised statutes, W. R. McCullough Life Ins. Co. v. Armstrong, Tex. Civ.App., 158 S.W.2d 585, 586; rule of administrative authority, Inman v. Sandvig, 170 Wash. 112, 15 P.2d 696, 698; rule of civil conduct commanding what is right and prohibiting what is wrong, Rich Hill Coal Co. v. Bashore, 334 Pa. 449, 7 A.2d 302, 312; Maner v. Dykes, 183 Ga. 118, 187 S.E. 699, 701; City of Bangor v. Inhabitants of Etna, 140 Me. 85, 34 A.2d 205, 208; rule of civil conduct prescribed by the supreme power in a state, 1 Steph.Comm. 25; Civ.Code Dak. § 2 (Comp.Laws N.D.1913, § 4327; Rev. Code S.D.1919, § 1); Pol.Code Cal. § 4466; City of Bangor v. Inhabitants of Etna, 140 Me. 85, 34 A.2d 205, 208; rule of conduct prescribed by lawmaking power of state, Board of Education of Union Free School Dist. No. Six of Town of Greenburgh v. Town of Greenburgh, 277 N.Y. 193, 13 N.E.2d 768, 770; Maner v. Dykes, 183 Ga. 118, 187 S.E. 699, 701; rule prescribed by the sovereign power, Maner v. Dykes, 183 Ga. 118, 187 S.E. 699, 701; rules of court, Department of Finance v. Sheldon, 381 Ill. 256, 44 N.E.2d 863, 864; Goldston v. Karukas, 180 Md. 232, 23 A.2d 691, 692; State ex rel. Conway v. Superior Court within and for Greenlee County, 60 Ariz. 69, 131 P.2d 983, 986; rules of decision commonly accepted and acted upon by bar and inferior courts, West v. American Telephone & Telegraph Co., Ohio, 311 U.S. 223, 61 S.Ct. 179, 183, 132 A.L.R. 956, 85 L.Ed. 139; rules promulgated by government, State ex rel. Conway v. Superior Court within and for Greenlee County, 60 Ariz. 69, 131 P.2d 983, 986; science or system of principles or rules of human conduct; Secretary of the Treasury regulations, In re Deyo's Estate, 42 N.Y.S.2d 379, 386, 180 Misc. 32; solemn expressions of legislative will which generally relate to what passes in ordinary course of affairs, Civ.Code La. arts. 1, 2; statute laws as construed by highest courts of state, National City Bank v. National Sec. Co., C.C.A.Tenn., 58 F.2d 7, 9; statute or enactment of legislative body, Shute v. Frohmiller, 53 Ariz. 483, 90 P.2d 998, 1001; State v. Masnik, 123 N.J.L. 335, 8 A.2d 701, 704; State ex rel. McKittrick v. Missouri Public Service Commission, 252 Mo. 29, 175 S.W.2d 857, 861; United States law, U. S. v. Wagner, C.C.A.Cal., 93 F.2d 77, 79; War Department regulations, Standard Oil Co. of California v. Johnson, Cal., 316 U.S. 481, 62 S.Ct. 1168, 1169, 86 L.Ed. 1611.

A concurrent or joint resolution of legislature is not "a law", Koenig v. Flynn, 179 N.E. 705, 707, 258 N.Y. 292; Ex parte Hague, 105 N.J.Eq. 134, 147 A. 220, 222; Ward v. State, 176 Okl. 368, 56 P.2d 136, 137; Scudder v. Smith, 331 Pa. 165, 200 A. 601, 604; a resolution of the house of representatives is not a "law", State ex rel. Todd v. Yelle, 7 Wash.2d 443, 110 P.2d 162, 165; an unconstitutional statute is not a "law", John F. Jelke Co. v. Hill, 208 Wis. 650, 242 N.W. 576, 581; Flournoy v. First Nat. Bank of Shreveport, 197 La. 1067, 3 So.2d 244, 248.

When a statute is passed in violation of *law*, that is, of the fundamental *law* or constitution of a state, it is the prerogative of courts to declare it void, or, in other words, to declare it not to be *law*. Burrill.

When the term "law" is used to denote enactments of the legislative power, it is frequently confined, especially by English writers, to permanent rules of civil conduct, as distinguished from other acts, such as a divorce act, an appropriation bill, an estates act. Rep.Eng.St.L.Com.Mar. 1856.

With reference to its origin, "law" is derived either from judicial precedents, from legislation, or from custom. Sweet.

As to the different kinds of law, or law regarded in its different aspects, see Absolute Law; Adjective Law; Administrative Law; Admiralty; Arms, Law of; Bankrupt Law; Canon Law; Case Law; Citations, Law of; Civil Law; Commercial Law; Common Law; Constitutional Law; Criminal; Custom; Ecclesiastical Law; Enabling Statute; Equity; Evidence, Law of; Flag, Law of; Foreign Laws; Forest Law; International Law; Local Law; Maritime Law; Marque, Law of; Martial Law; Mercantile Law; Military Law; Moral Law; Municipal Law; Natural Law; Oleron, Laws of; Organic Law; Parliamentary Law; Penal Laws; Personal Law; Positive Law; Private Law; Probate; Prospective Law; Public Law; Remedial Statute; Retrospective Law; Revenue Law; Road, Law of; Roman Law; Special Law; Staple, Law of; Statute; Substantive Law; Unwritten Law; War; Wisby, Laws of; Written Law.

For "facts" and "law" as distinguishable, see Fact.

LAW AGENTS. Solicitors practicing in the Scotch courts.

LAW ALWAYS CONSTRUETH THINGS TO THE BEST. Wing. Max. p. 720, max. 193.

LAW ARBITRARY. Opposed to *immutable,* a law not founded in the nature of things, but imposed by the mere will of the legislature.

LAW BURROWS. In Scotch law. Security for the peaceable behavior of a party; security to keep the peace. Properly, a process for obtaining such security. 1 Forb. Inst. pt. 2, p. 198.

LAW CHARGES. This phrase is used, under the Louisiana Civil Code, to signify costs incurred in court in the prosecution of a suit, to be paid by the party cast. Rousseau v. His Creditors, 17 La. 206; Barkley v. His Creditors, 11 Rob. (La.) 28.

LAW CONSTRUETH EVERY ACT TO BE LAWFUL, WHEN IT STANDETH INDIFFERENT WHETHER IT SHOULD BE LAWFUL OR NOT. Wing. Max. p. 722, max. 194; Finch, Law, b. 1, c. 3, n. 76.

LAW CONSTRUETH THINGS ACCORDING TO COMMON POSSIBILITY OR INTENDMENT. Wing. Max. p. 705, max. 189.

LAW [THE LAW] CONSTRUETH THINGS WITH EQUITY AND MODERATION. Wing. Max. p. 685, max. 183; Finch, Law, b. 1, c. 3, n. 74.

LAW COURT OF APPEALS. In American law. An appellate tribunal, formerly existing in the state of South Carolina, for hearing appeals from the courts of law.

LAW DAY. See Day.

LAW DEPARTMENT. Department having charge of law business of government. People v. Board of Education of City of Chicago, 345 Ill. 486, 178 N.E. 154, 156.

LAW DISFAVORETH IMPOSSIBILITIES. Wing. Max. p. 606, max. 155.

LAW DISFAVORETH IMPROBABILITIES. Wing. Max. p. 620, max. 161.

LAW ENFORCEMENT OFFICER. Those whose duty it is to preserve the peace. Frazier v. Elmore, 180 Tenn. 232, 173 S.W.2d 563, 565.

LAW [THE LAW] FAVORETH CHARITY. Wing. Max. p. 497, max. 135.

LAW FAVORETH COMMON RIGHT. Wing. Max. p. 547, max. 144.

LAW FAVORETH DILIGENCE, AND THEREFORE HATETH FOLLY AND NEGLIGENCE. Wing. Max. p. 665, max. 172; Finch, Law, b. 1, c. 3, no. 70.

LAW FAVORETH HONOR AND ORDER. Wing. Max. p. 739, max. 199.

LAW FAVORETH JUSTICE AND RIGHT. Wing. Max. p. 502, max. 141.

LAW FAVORETH LIFE, LIBERTY, AND DOWER. 4 Bacon's Works, 345.

LAW FAVORETH MUTUAL RECOMPENSE. Wing. Max. p. 411, max. 108; Finch, Law, b. 1, c. 3, no. 42.

LAW [THE LAW] FAVORETH POSSESSION, WHERE THE RIGHT IS EQUAL. Wing. Max. p. 375, max. 98; Finch, Law, b. 1, c. 3, no. 36.

LAW FAVORETH PUBLIC COMMERCE. Wing. Max. p. 738, max. 198.

LAW FAVORETH PUBLIC QUIET. Wing. Max. p. 742, max. 200; Finch, Law, b. 1, c. 3, no. 54.

LAW FAVORETH SPEEDING OF MEN'S CAUSES. Wing. Max. p. 673, max. 175.

LAW [THE LAW] FAVORETH THINGS FOR THE COMMONWEALTH, [COMMON WEAL.] Wing. Max. p. 729, max. 197; Finch, Law, b. 1, c. 3, no. 53.

LAW FAVORETH TRUTH, FAITH, AND CERTAINTY. Wing. Max. p. 604, max. 154.

LAW FRENCH. The Norman French language, introduced into England by William the Conqueror.

For several centuries, it was, in an emphatic sense, the language of the English law. It is called by Blackstone a "barbarous dialect," and the later specimens of it fully warrant the appellation, but at the time of its introduction it was, as has been observed, the best form of the language spoken in Normandy. Burrill.

LAW HATETH DELAYS. Wing. Max. p. 674, max. 176; Finch, Law, b. 1, c. 3, no. 71.

LAW HATETH NEW INVENTIONS AND INNOVATIONS. Wing. Max. p. 756, max. 204.

LAW HATETH WRONG. Wing. Max. p. 563, max. 146; Finch, Law, b. 1, c. 3, no. 62.

LAW LATIN. The corrupt form of the Latin language employed in the old English lawbooks and legal proceedings.

LAW LIST. A publication compiling the names and addresses of those engaged in the practice of law and information of interest to the legal profession often including the courts, court calendars, lawyers engaged in specialized fields (as admiralty or patent law), public officers, stenographers, handwriting experts, private investigators, or abstracts of law; a legal directory.

An annual English publication of a *quasi* official character, comprising various statistics of interest in connection with the legal profession. Mozley & Whiteley.

LAW LORDS. Peers in the British parliament who have held high judicial office, or have been distinguished in the legal profession. Mozley & Whiteley.

LAW MARTIAL. See Martial Law.

LAW MERCHANT. See Mercantile Law.

LAW OF A GENERAL NATURE. One which relates to a subject that may exist throughout the state, Panhandle Eastern Pipe Line Co. v. Board of Com'rs of Miami County, 151 Kan. 533, 99 P.2d 828, 829, 830; one whose subject-matter is common to all the people. Panhandle Eastern Pipe Line Co. v. Board of Com'rs of Miami County, 151 Kan. 533, 99 P.2d 828, 829.

LAW OF ARMS. See Arms, Law Of.

LAW OF CITATIONS. See Citations, Law Of.

LAW OF EVIDENCE. See Evidence, Law Of.

LAW OF ITSELF PREJUDICETH NO MAN. Wing. Max. p. 575, max. 148; Finch, Law, b. 1, c. 3, no. 63.

LAW OF MARQUE. See Marque, Law Of.

LAW OF NATIONS. See International Law.

LAW OF NATURE. See Natural Law.

LAW OF THE CASE. The decision, judgment, opinion or rulings on former appeal or writ of error become "law of the case." Massachusetts Bonding & Insurance Co. v. Bankers' Surety Co., 96 Ind.App. 250, 179 N.E. 329, 332; City of Shreveport v. Kansas City Southern Ry. Co., 193 La. 277, 190 So. 404, 406; Nolan v. Nolan's Adm'rs, 234 Ky. 50, 27 S.W.2d 408, 409; Machenheimer v. Falknor, 151 Wash. 447, 276 P. 297, 298; Tressler Coal Min. Co. v. Klefeld, 125 W.Va. 301, 24 S.E.2d 98, 100; so, too, a holding of an appellate court on writ of certiorari. Goodkind v. Wolkowsky, 147 Fla. 415, 2 So.2d 723, 725; Atlantic Coast Line R. Co. v. Sperry Flour Co., 63 Ga.App. 611, 11 S.E.2d 809, 811; binding on subsequent appeal or writ of error. George v. Atlanta & C. A. L. Ry. Co., 210 N.C. 58, 185 S.E. 431, 432; Elliott v. Moffet, Tex.Civ.App., 165 S.W.2d 911, 912, 913; Moran v. Leccony Smokeless Coal Co., 124 W.Va. 54, 18 S.E.2d 808, 813; Hill v. Chappel Bros. of Montana, 97 Mont. 305, 33 P.2d 819, 820; or on subsequent proceedings or trials in trial court, Oliver v. Muncy, 271 Ky. 15, 111 S.W.2d 392, 393; Sarson v. Mueller, 105 N.J.L. 212, 143 A. 428; State of Kansas ex rel. Beck v. Occidental Life Ins. Co., C.C.A.Kan., 95 F.2d 935, 936; or in subsequent suit between same parties, Oglethorpe University v. City of Atlanta, 180 Ga. 152, 178 S.E. 156.

The doctrine expresses practice of courts generally to refuse to reopen what has been decided. White v. Higgins, C.C.A.Mass., 116 F.2d 312, 317, 318; Perkins v. Vermont Hydro-Electric Corporation, 106 Vt. 367, 177 A. 631, 653; Fleming v. Campbell, 148 Kan. 516, 83 P.2d 708, 709; it expresses the rule that final judgment of highest court is final determination of parties' rights. Atchison, T. & S. F. Ry. Co. v. Railroad Commission of California, 209 Cal. 460, 288 P. 775, 779.

The doctrine has reference to decisions on legal questions and principles of law announced. Haynes Drilling Co. v. Indian Territory Illuminating Oil Co., 185 Okl. 122, 90 P.2d 639, 640; and does not embrace questions of fact or decisions on questions of fact. McNeely v. Connell, 87 Cal. App. 87, 261 P. 754, 755. (But see holding that the decision of appellate court on facts proved becomes "law of the case". Cauldwell-Wingate Co. v. State, Ct.Cl., 31 N.Y.S.2d 211, 213).

The doctrine includes all errors relied on for reversal, whether mentioned in court's opinion or not, and all errors lurking in record on first appeal, which might have been, but were not, expressly relied on, Sowders v. Coleman, 223 Ky. 633, 4 S.W.2d 731, (but see holding that doctrine does not extend to facts or points of law which might have been but were not presented and determined on prior appeal, Steelduct Co. v. Henger-Seltzer Co., Cal., 26 Cal.2d 634, 160 P.2d 804, 809); all matters, issues or questions actually decided on former appeal. Fleming v. Buerkli, 164 Wash. 136, 1 P.2d 915; all questions involved in judgment, Helper State Bank v. Crus, 95 Utah 320, 81 P.2d 359, 361, 363; all questions involved on former appeal, whether or not expressly mentioned in opinion, unless expressly reserved, Martin v. Commonwealth, 265 Ky. 292, 96 S.W.2d 1011; all questions open expressly or by necessary implication decided on former appeal, Brown v. Brotherhood of Railroad Trainmen, 186 Okl. 275, 97 P.2d 62; Miller v. Sisters of St. Francis, 5 Wash.2d 204, 105 P.2d 32, 33; Kuhns v. Live Stock Nat. Bank of Omaha, 138 Neb. 797, 295 N.W. 818, 819, 820; decision on sufficiency of evidence, Wells v. Lloyd, 21 Cal.2d 452, 132 P.2d 471, 474; every applicable proposition of law actually applied to facts and pleadings involved, Union Central Life Ins. Co. v. Trundle, 65 Ga.App. 553, 15 S.E.2d 909, 913; only facts appearing in original opinion, Timm v. McCartney, 30 Cal.App.2d 241, 85 P.2d 920, 922; points presented on former appeal, Ætna Life Ins. Co. v. Wharton, C.C.A.Ark., 63 F.2d 378, 379; City of Sedalia ex rel. and to Use of Ferguson v. Shell Petroleum Corporation, C.C.A.Mo., 81 F.2d 193, 196, 106 A.L.R. 1327; ruling on point distinctly made on former appeal, People v. Marshall, 209 Cal. 540, 289 P. 629, 631; statements in opinion on former appeal, if necessary to decision of questions presented, Miller Cattle Co. v. Francis, Ariz., 298 P. 631, 632. It bars further adjudication in identical proceeding or on same or substantially identical facts or identical question, In re Norman's Estate, 161 Or. 450, 88 P.2d 977, 987.

The doctrine is generally deemed applicable whether former determination is right or wrong. Wells v. Lloyd, 21 Cal.2d 452, 132 P.2d 471, 474. But some cases hold that doctrine is inapplicable where prior decision is unsound, Standard Oil Co. of California v. Johnson, 56 Cal. App.2d 411, 132 P.2d 910, 913; Atchison T. & S. F. Ry. Co. v. Ballard, C.C.A.Tex., 108 F.2d 768, 772; or incorrect principles were announced or mistake of fact was made on first appeal. National Match Co. v. Empire Storage & Ice Co., 227 Mo.App. 1115, 58 S.W.2d 797; Morris v. E. I. Du Pont De Nemours & Co., 346 Mo. 126, 139 S.W.2d 984, 986, 129 A.L.R. 352.

The doctrine may be invoked unless evidence differs substantially, Chicago, St. P., M. & O. Ry. Co. v. Kuip, C.C.A. Minn., 102 F.2d 352, 354, 133 A.L.R. 1445; City of Louisville v. Redmon, 282 Ky. 1, 137 S.W.2d 350, 351; New York Life Ins. Co. v. Golightly, C.C.A.Ark., 94 F.2d 316, 319; new pleadings and new evidence adduced on subsequent trial call for different judgment, Maze v. Bennett, 117 W.Va. 165, 184 S.E. 564, 565; there has been a material change in record, Reynolds v. Virginian Ry. Co., 117 W.Va. 359, 185 S.E. 568, 569; there has been a substantial change in issues or evidence, Royal Collieries Co. v. Wells, 244 Ky. 303, 50 S.W.2d 948, 949.

It may be invoked where evidence or facts on subsequent appeal or subsequent trial is substantially the same, American Railway Express Co. v. Cole, 185 Ark. 532, 48 S.W.2d 223; State v. Loveless, 62 Nev. 312, 150 P.2d 1015, 1016, 1018; Clark v. Los Angeles & Salt Lake R. Co., 73 Utah, 486, 275 P. 582, 584; New York Life Ins. Co. v. Ittner, 62 Ga.App. 31, 8 S.E.2d 582, 586; Amerada Petroleum Corporation v. Elliff, 171 Okl. 38, 41 P.2d 850. General principle of law is declared as applicable to the facts of the case, Creason v. Harding, 344 Mo. 452, 126 S.W.2d 1179, 1183; pleadings and evidence were substantially the same, Lober v. Kansas City, 339 Mo. 1087, 100 S.W.2d 267, 268; questions of law and fact are the same. Helper State Bank v. Crus, 95 Utah 320, 81 P.2d 359, 361, 363; record is substantially identical with that in prior proceeding, Louisville Trust Co. v. National Bank of Kentucky, C.C.A.Ky., 102 F.2d 137, 139; City of San Antonio v. McKenzie Const. Co., Tex.Civ.App., 138 S.W.2d 568, 576; Stuart C. Irby Co. v. Smith, 205 Ark. 183, 168 S.W.2d 618, 619, 620.

The effect of "law of the case" is limited to court of co-ordinate jurisdiction. Walker v. Gerli, 12 N.Y.S.2d 942, 944, 257 App.Div. 249.

Where appeal is not pursued, decision of intermediate court is the "law of the case". State ex rel. Anderson Motor Service Co. v. Public Service Commission, 234 Mo. App. 470, 134 S.W.2d 1069, 1075.

"Law of the case" may signify, or be constituted by, other matters or things.

It has been held that "law of the case" may include, or be constituted by an agreement of arbitration, Acme Cut Stone Co. v. New Center Development Corporation, 281 Mich. 32, 274 N.W. 700, 706, 112 A.L.R. 865; allegation of complaint where not challenged below. Coulter v. Pomeroy, 38 N.Y.S.2d 22, 23, 265 App.Div. 51; answer to certified question, City of Brunswick v. King, 65 Ga.App. 44, 14 S.E.2d 760, 763; findings of fact or of law by an auditor unless excepted to, Brothers and Sisters of Charity v. Renfroe, 57 Ga.App. 646, 196 S.E. 135; finding on first hearing affirmed on appeal. Stonega Coke & Coal Co. v. Price, C.C.A. W.Va., 116 F.2d 618, 621; grant of temporary injunction and continuance by Appellate Division, Walker Memorial Baptist Church v. Saunders, 17 N.Y.S.2d 842, 847, 173 Misc. 455; holding in case not appealed from, Schul v. Clapp, 154 Kan. 372, 118 P.2d 570, 573; intention of testator as expressed in will, Clauss v. Rohde, 133 N.J.Eq. 105, 30 A.2d 695; judgment which remains unreversed or to which no exception has been taken, Palmer v. Jackson, 188 Ga. 336, 4 S.E.2d 28, 30; mandates of Supreme Court, People ex rel. McLaren v. DeBoice, 377 Ill. 634, 37 N.E.2d 337, 340; order not appealed, Foley v. Equitable Life Assur. Soc. of the United States, 33 N.Y.S.2d 917, 918, 263 App.Div. 605; Long v. Carolina Baking Co., 193 S.C. 225, 8 S.E.2d 326, 330, 331; order of trial court requiring amendment to petition, Martin v. Mayer, 63 Ga.App. 387, 11 S.E.2d 218, 226; order requiring judgment debtor to make monthly payments on judgment, Ryan v. Edgerton, 30 N.Y.S.2d 941, 942, 177 Misc. 421; order that case automatically stand dismissed unless plaintiff amends petition, Smith v. Atlanta Gas-Light Co., 181 Ga. 479, 182 S.E. 603; ordinance admitted by parties to be in force and to be accurately pleaded, with defendant reserving only the question of admissibility, Page v. Wieland, 137 Ohio St. 198, 28 N.E.2d 583, 585; plaintiffs' theory where adopted by trial justice, Ferrier v. City of White Plains, 28 N.Y.S.2d 218, 220, 262 App. Div. 94; portion of decree not appealed, Dawson County Irr. Co. v. Stuart, 142 Neb. 428, 8 N.W.2d 507, 508; prior decision of another judge of same court, United States Industrial Chemicals v. Carbide & Carbon Chemicals Corporation, D.C.N.Y., 52 F.Supp. 164, 165; referee's conclusions where no exceptions taken, Cooper v. Baxley, 194 S.C. 270, 9 S.E.2d 721, 722; ruling upon demurrer, Sanik v. Shryock Realty Co., 156 Kan. 641, 135 P.2d 545, 548; Darling stores Corporation v. Beatus, 197 Ga. 125, 28 S.E.2d 124, 126; Wilkinson v. Wilkinson, 192 S.C. 497, 7 S.E.2d 447, 449, 450; ruling of trial court as to applicable statute, Beck v. Baird, 238 Wis. 624, 300 N.W. 752, 754; ruling of trial court to which no exception is taken, Perkins v. Vermont Hydro-Electric Corporation, 106 Vt. 367, 177 A. 631, 654; ruling on motions to dismiss, Pathé Exchange v. International Alliance of Theatrical Stage Employés and Moving Picture Machine Operators of the United States and Canada, Local No. 306, D.C.N.Y., 3 F.Supp. 63, 64; ruling striking amendments to answer, Ford v. Jones, 66 Ga.App. 238, 17 S.E.2d 756, 757; stipulation, Mann v. R. Simpson & Co., 286 N.Y. 450, 36 N.E.2d 658, 662; theory acquiesced in by parties and court, Cote v. Boise, 111 Vt. 343, 16 A.2d 175, 177.

Instructions are the "law of the case." Douglas v. Manfree Realty Corporation, 263 App.Div. 998, 33 N.Y.S.2d 423, 424; Selfe v. Fuller, 179 Va. 30, 18 S.E.2d 254, 256; whether right or wrong, Rogers v. Jefferson, 223 Iowa 718, 272 N.W. 532, 533; McClelland v. Interstate Transit Lines, 142 Neb. 439, 6 N.W.2d 384, 391; Buckin v. Long Island R. Co., 286 N.Y. 146, 36 N.E.2d 88, 89.

It has been held that instructions are the "law of the case" where appealing defendant accepted instructions as correct, Ætna Life Ins. Co. v. McAdoo, C.C.A.Ark., 115 F.2d 369, 370; approved on former appeal and given at second trial, Whitehead v. Stith, 279 Ky. 556, 131 S.W.2d 455, 460; instruction given on first trial is corrected to meet criticism made by Court of Appeals, Waddle v. Williams, 294 Ky. 66, 170 S.W.2d 886, 888. Instruction is unappealed from, Stephenson v. W. R. Grimshaw Co., 148 Kan. 466, 83 P.2d 655, 656; instructions not challenged in any manner or in any particular, Madison v. Hood, 207 Iowa 495, 223 N.W. 178, 179; no exception is made and they are not assigned as error, New York Life Ins. Co. v. Stone, C.C.A.Mass., 80 F.2d 614, 616; Codd v. New York Underwriters Ins. Co., 19 Wash.2d 671, 144 P.2d 234, 237; no exceptions are taken, Miller v. Mohr, 198 Wash. 619, 89 P.2d 807, 814; Chancellor v. Hines Motor Supply Co., 104 Mont. 603, 69 P.2d 764, 769; Johnson v. Narragansett Filling Stations, R.I., 148 A. 901; no instructions are requested nor exceptions taken, U. S. v. Hossmann, C.C.A. Mo., 84 F.2d 808, 810; no objections are made, Brown v. Waltrip, 167 Va. 293, 189 S.E. 342, 343; Kovaniemi v. Sherman, 192 Minn. 395, 256 N.W. 661; Pankey v. First Nat. Bank, 40 N.M. 270, 58 P.2d 1186, 1188; only exception pressed before Supreme Court was exception to denial of motion for new trial based on usual grounds, Couture v. Industrial Trust Co., 66 R.I. 395, 19 A.2d 772, 775. An instruction excepted to by plaintiff is "law of the case" for purpose of trial only. Klimaszewski v. Herrick, 32 N.Y. S.2d 441, 442, 263 App.Div. 235. An instruction given at request of defendant is "law of the case" on defendant's appeal. Wood Towing Corporation v. West, 181 Va. 151, 23 S.E.2d 789, 791. Oral charge of court and special charges given at request of parties constitute "law of case". Franklin Fire Ins. Co. v. Slaton, 240 Ala. 560, 700 So. 564, 566. Portion of charge to which no exception was made became the "law of the case." Morrison v. Bitting, 60 R.I. 325, 198 A. 355, 359.

LAW OF THE FLAG. See Flag, Law of.

LAW OF THE LAND. Due process of law (*q. v.*). By the law of the land is most clearly intended the general law which hears before it condemns, which proceeds upon inquiry, and renders judgment only after trial. Dupuy v. Tedora, 204 La. 560, 15 So.2d 886, 891. The meaning is that every citizen shall hold his life, liberty, property, and immunities under the protection of general rules which govern society. Rich Hill Coal Co. v. Brashore, 334 Pa. 449, 7 A.2d 302, 316; In re Stobie's Estate, 30 Cal.App.2d 525, 86 P.2d 883, 885.

Everything which may pass under the form of an enactment is not the law of the land. Sedg.St. & Const.Law, (2d Ed.) 475. When first used in *Magna Charta*, the phrase probably meant the established law of the kingdom, in opposition to the civil or Roman law. It is now generally regarded as meaning general public laws binding on all members of the community. Janes v. Reynolds, 2 Tex. 251; Beasley v. Cunningham, 171 Tenn. 334, 103 S.W.2d 18, 20, 110 A.L.R. 306. It means due process of law warranted by the constitution, by the common law adopted by the constitution, or by statutes passed in pursuance of the constitution. Mayo v. Wilson, 1 N.H. 53.

LAW OF THE ROAD. See Road, Law of.

LAW OF THE STAPLE. See Staple, Law of.

LAW REPORTS. Published volumes containing the reports of cases argued and adjudged in the courts of law.

LAW RESPECTETH MATTER OF SUBSTANCE MORE THAN MATTER OF CIRCUMSTANCE. Wing. Max. p. 382, max. 101; Finch, Law, b. 1, c. 3, no. 39.

LAW RESPECTETH POSSIBILITY OF THINGS. Wing. Max. p. 403, max. 104; Finch, Law, b. 1, c. 3, no. 40.

LAW [THE LAW] RESPECTETH THE BONDS OF NATURE. Wing. Max. p. 268, max. 78; Finch, Law, b. 1, c. 3, no. 29.

LAW SPIRITUAL. The ecclesiastical law, or law Christian. Co. Litt. 344. See, also, Ecclesiastical Law.

LAW WORTHY. Being entitled to, or having the benefit and protection of, the law.

LAWFUL. Legal; warranted or authorized by the law; having the qualifications prescribed by law; not contrary to nor forbidden by the law. Ohio Automatic Sprinkler Co. v. Fender, 108 Ohio St. 149, 141 N.E. 269, 275; McDonnell v. Murnan Shipbuilding Corporation, 210 Ala. 611, 98 So. 887, 889; Hafner Mfg. Co. v. City of St. Louis, 262 Mo. 621, 172 S.W. 28, 33.

The principal distinction between the terms "lawful" and "legal" is that the former contemplates the substance of law, the latter the form of law. To say of an act that it is "lawful" implies that it is authorized, sanctioned, or at any rate not forbidden, by law. To say that it is "legal" implies that it is done or performed in accordance with the forms and usages of law, or in a technical manner. In this sense "illegal" approaches the meaning of "invalid." For example, a contract or will, executed without the required formalities, might be said to be invalid or illegal, but could not be described as unlawful. Further, the word "lawful" more clearly implies an ethical content than does "legal." The latter goes no further than to denote compliance, with positive, technical, or formal rules; while the former usually imports a moral substance or ethical permissibility. A further distinction is that the word "legal" is used as the synonym of "constructive," which "lawful" is not. Thus "legal fraud" is fraud implied or inferred by law, or made out by construction. "Lawful fraud" would be a contradiction of terms. Again, "legal" is used as the antithesis of "equitable." Thus, we speak of "legal assets," "legal estate," etc., but not of "lawful assets," or "lawful estate." But there are some connections in which the two words are used as exact equivalents. Thus, a "lawful" writ, warrant, or process is the same as a "legal" writ, warrant, or process.

LAWFUL AGE. Full age; majority; generally the age of twenty-one years, though sometimes eighteen as to a female. See McKim v. Handy, 4 Md.Ch. 237.

LAWFUL AUTHORITIES. The expression "lawful authorities," used in our treaty with Spain, refers to persons who exercised the power of making grants by authority of the crown. Mitchel v. U. S., 9 Pet. 711, 9 L.Ed. 283.

LAWFUL CAUSE. One supported by evidence (Pub.Laws 1931, c. 1818, § 3). Girouard v. Board of Police Com'rs of Central Falls, 52 R.I. 47, 157 A. 199, 200.

LAWFUL DAMAGES. Such damages as the law fixes and are ascertainable in a court of law. Carr v. U. S., D.C.Ky., 28 F.Supp. 236, 241.

LAWFUL DEPENDENTS. All dependents except those who might occupy an unlawful relation to individual. National Council Junior Order United American Mechanics v. Tate, 212 N.C. 305, 193 S.E. 397, 399, 113 A.L.R. 1514.

LAWFUL DISCHARGE. Such a discharge in insolvency as exonerates the debtor from his debts. Mason v. Haile, 12 Wheat. 370, 6 L.Ed. 660.

LAWFUL ENTRY. An entry on real estate, by one out of possession, under claim or color of right and without force or fraud. See Stouffer v. Harlan, 68 Kan. 135, 74 P. 613, 64 L.R.A. 320, 104 Am. St.Rep. 396.

LAWFUL GOODS. Whatever is not prohibited to be exported by the positive law of the country, even though it be contraband of war; for a neutral has a right to carry such goods at his own risk. Seton v. Low, 1 Johns.Cas., N.Y., 1; Skidmore v. Desdoity, 2 Johns.Cas., N.Y., 77; Juhel v. Rhinelander, 2 Johns.Cas., N.Y., 120.

LAWFUL HEIRS. See Heir.

LAWFUL ISSUE. As used in will the words primarily and generally mean descendants. In re Marsh's Will, 143 Misc. 609, 257 N.Y.S. 514, 521; they include descendants more remote than children. In re Woodcock's Will, Sur., 55 N.Y.S.2d 656, 658. At common law, the term includes only those who were children of legally recognized subsisting marriage. In re Sheffer's Will, 139 Misc. 519, 249 N.Y.S. 102, 105. Lawful descendants. In re Sheffer's Will, 139 Misc. 519, 249 N.Y.S. 102, 104.

LAWFUL MAN. A freeman, unattainted, and capable of bearing oath; a *legalis homo*.

LAWFUL MONEY. Money which is a legal tender in payment of debts. Vick v. Howard, 136 Va. 101, 116 S.E. 465, 467, 31 A.L.R. 240; Dunlap v. Whitmer, 133 La. 317, 62 So. 938, 942, Ann.Cas. 1915C, 990.

LAWFUL REPRESENTATIVES. Where real property is involved as subject-matter, term "lawful representatives" includes or means legal heirs. Where personal property is involved the term, when not qualified by context, is limited to executors and administrators. Conley v. Jamison, 205 Iowa 1326, 219 N.W. 485, 486, 59 A.L.R. 835.

LAWING OF DOGS. The cutting several claws of the forefeet of dogs in the forest, to prevent their running at deer. Expeditation (*q. v.*).

LAWLESS. Not subject to law; not controlled by law; not authorized by law; not observing the rules and forms of law. See Arkansas v. Kansas & T. Coal Co., C.C.Ark., 96 F. 362.

LAWLESS COURT. An ancient local English court, said to have been held in Essex once a year, at cock-crowing, without a light or pen and ink, and conducted in a whisper. Jacob.

LAWLESS MAN. An outlaw.

LAWNDE, LOWNDE. In old English law. A plain between woods. Co. Litt. 5*b*.

LAWS. Rules promulgated by government as a means to an ordered society. Miami Laundry Co. v. Florida Dry Cleaning & Laundry Board, 134 Fla. 1, 183 So. 759, 764, 119 A.L.R. 956. Session laws or statutes and not decisions of court. State ex rel. Helena Allied Printing Council v. Mitchell, Mont., 105 Mont. 326, 74 P.2d 417, 425. See, also, Law.

LAWS OF ANOTHER STATE. Statutory laws and laws established by judicial decisions. Holderness v. Hamilton Fire Ins. Co. of New York, D.C.Fla., 54 F.Supp. 145, 146.

LAWS OF THE SEVERAL STATES. As used in conformity act, means local statutes and decisions construing them, not decisions relating to matters of general jurisprudence. Ford v. Grocers' Mut. Ins. Co., D.C.Pa., 4 F.Supp. 911, 913. As used in statute requiring federal courts to apply laws of the several states, includes not only state statutory law, but also state decisions on questions of general law. Erie R. Co. v. Tompkins, N.Y., 304 U.S. 64, 58 S.Ct. 817, 822, 82 L.Ed. 1188, 114 A.L.R. 1487.

LAWS OF OLERON. See Oleron, Laws of.

LAWS OF WAR. See War.

LAWS OF WISBY. See Wisby, Laws of.

LAWSUIT. A vernacular term for a suit, action, or cause instituted or depending between two private persons in the courts of law. A suit at law or in equity; an action or proceeding in a civil court; a process in law instituted by one party to compel another to do him justice. Shepherd v. Standard Motor Co., 263 Ky. 329, 92 S.W.2d 337.

LAWYER. A person learned in the law; as an attorney, counsel, or solicitor; a person licensed to practice law.

Any person who, for fee or reward, prosecutes or defends causes in courts of record or other judicial tribunals of the United States, or of any of the states, or whose business it is to give legal advice in relation to any cause or matter whatever. Act of July 13, 1866, § 9, (14 St. at Large, 121.)

LAY, *n.* A share of the profits of a fishing or whaling voyage, allotted to the officers and seamen, in the nature of wages. Coffin v. Jenkins, 5 Fed.Cas. 1190; Thomas v. Osborn, 19 How. 33, 15 L.Ed. 534.

LAY, *adj.* Relating to persons or things not clerical or ecclesiastical; a person not in ecclesiastical orders. Also non-professional.

LAY, *v.* To state or allege in pleading.

LAY CORPORATION. See Corporation.

LAY DAMAGES. To state at the conclusion of the declaration the amount of damages which the plaintiff claims.

LAY DAYS. In the law of shipping. Days allowed to charter-parties for loading and unloading the cargo. 3 Kent, Comm. 202, 203.

LAY FEE. A fee held by ordinary feudal tenure, as distinguished from the ecclesiastical tenure of *frankalmoign,* by which an ecclesiastical corporation held of the donor. The tenure of *frankalmoign* is reserved by St. 12 Car. II., which abolished military tenures. 2 Bl.Comm. 101.

LAY IMPROPRIATOR. In English ecclesiastical law. A lay person holding a spiritual appropriation. 3 Steph.Comm. 72.

LAY INVESTITURE. In ecclesiastical law. The ceremony of putting a bishop in possession of the temporalities of his diocese.

LAY JUDGE. A judge who is not learned in the law, *i. e.*, not a lawyer; formerly employed in some of the states as assessors or assistants to the presiding judges in the nisi prius courts or courts of first instance.

LAY OUT. This term has come to be used technically in highway laws as embracing all the series of acts necessary to the complete establishment of a highway. Graham County v. Dowell, 50 Ariz. 221, 71 P.2d 1019, 1020; Hitchcock v. Aldermen of Springfield, 121 Mass. 382; Mansur v. County Com'rs, 83 Me. 514, 22 A. 358. See Borrowdale v. Board of County Com'rs of Socorro County, 23 N.M. 1, 163 P. 721, 723, L.R.A.1917E, 456; Patterson v. City of Baltimore, 130 Md. 645, 101 A. 589, 591.

LAY PEOPLE. Jurymen.

LAY SYSTEM. As applied to fishing vessels, the fish caught are sold at auction and from the proceeds is deducted charges for supplies furnished and balance distributed to the master and the crew. The Dirigo First, D.C.Mass., 60 F.Supp. 675.

LAYE. L. Fr. Law.

LAYING THE VENUE. Stating in the margin of a declaration the county in which the plaintiff proposes that the trial of the action shall take place.

LAYMAN. One of the people, and not one of the clergy; one who is not of the legal profession; one who is not of a particular profession.

LAYOFF. A termination of employment at the will of employer. International Ass'n of Machinists v. State ex rel. Watson, 153 Fla. 672, 15 So.2d 485, 490. Municipal employee who suffers a "lay-off" suffers a "suspension." State ex rel. Ausburn v. City of Seattle, 190 Wash. 222, 67 P.2d 913, 921, 111 A.L.R. 418.

LAYSTALL. A place for dung or soil.

LAZARET, or LAZARETTO. A pesthouse, or public hospital for persons affected with the more dangerous forms of contagious diseases; a quarantine station for vessels coming from countries where such diseases are prevalent.

LAZZI. A Saxon term for persons of a servile condition.

LE CONGRÈS. A species of proof on charges of impotency in France, *coitus coram testibus*. Abolished A.D. 1677.

LE CONTRAT FAIT LA LOI. The contract makes the law.

LE GUIDON DE LA MER. The title of a French work on marine insurance, by an unknown author, dating back, probably, to the sixteenth century, and said to have been prepared for the merchants of Rouen. It is noteworthy as being the earliest treatise on that subject now extant.

LE LEY DE DIEU ET LEY DE TERRE SONT TOUT UN; ET L'UN ET L'AUTRE PREFERRE ET FAVOUR LE COMMON ET PUBLIQUE BIEN DEL TERRE. The law of God and the law of the land are all one; and both preserve and favor the common and public good of the land. Keilw. 191.

LE LEY EST LE PLUS HAUT ENHERITANCE QUE LE ROY AD, CAR PER LE LEY IL MESME ET TOUTS SES SUJETS SONT RULES; ET, SI LE LEY NE FUIT, NUL ROY NE NUL ENHERITANCE SERRA. 1 J.H. 6, 63. The law is the highest inheritance that the king possesses, for by the law both he and all his subjects are ruled; and, if there were no law, there would be neither king nor inheritance.

LE ROI, or ROY. The old law-French words for "the king."

LE ROI VEUT EN DELIBERER. The king will deliberate on it. This is the formula which the king of the French used when he intended to veto an act of the legislative assembly. 1 Toullier, no. 42.

LE ROY (or LA REINE) LE VEUT. The king (or the queen) wills it. The form of the royal assent to public bills in parliament.

LE ROY (or LA REINE) REMERCIE SES LOYAL SUJETS, ACCEPTE LEUR BENEVOLENCE, ET AINSI LE VEUT. The king (or the queen) thanks his (or her) loyal subjects, accepts their benevolence, and therefore wills it to be so. The form of the royal assent to a bill of supply.

LE ROY (or LA REINE) S'AVISERA. The king (or queen) will advise upon it. The form of words used to express the refusal of the royal assent to public bills in parliament. 1 Bl.Comm. 184. This is supposed to correspond to the judicial phrase "*curia advisari vult*," (*q. v.*). 1 Chit.Bl.Comm. 184, note.

LE SALUT DU PEUPLE EST LA SUPREME LOI. Montesq. Esprit des Lois, l. xxvii, c. 23. The safety of the people is the highest law.

LEA, or LEY. A pasture. Co.Litt. 4*b*.

LEAD. The counsel on either side of a litigated action who is charged with the principal management and direction of the party's case, as distinguished from his juniors or subordinates, is said to "lead in the cause," and is termed the "leading counsel" on that side.

LEADING A USE. Where a deed was executed before the levy of a fine of land, for the purpose of specifying to whose use the fine should inure, it was said to "lead" the use. If executed after the fine, it was said to "declare" the use. 2 Bl.Comm. 363.

LEADING CASE. Among the various cases that are argued and determined in the courts, some, from their important character, have demanded more than usual attention from the judges, and from this circumstance are frequently looked upon as having settled or determined the law upon all points involved in such cases, and as guides for subsequent decisions, and from the importance they thus acquire are familiarly termed "leading cases." Brown.

LEADING COUNSEL. That one of two or more counsel employed on the same side in a cause who has the principal management of the cause.

LEADING QUESTION. One which instructs witness how to answer or puts into his mouth words to be echoed back, People v. Hamilton, Gen.Sess., 30 N.Y.S.2d 155, 158; one which suggests to witness answer desired. Little v. State, 79 Okl.Cr. 285, 154 P.2d 772, 777; State v. Scott, 20 Wash. 2d 696, 149 P.2d 152, 153, 154; Landers v. State, 118 Tex.Cr.R. 608, 39 S.W.2d 43, 44.

Questions are leading which suggest to the witness the answer desired, or which embody a material fact, and may be answered by a mere negative or affirmative, or which involve an answer bearing immediately upon the merits of the cause, and indicating to the witness a representation which will best accord with the interests of the party propounding them. Turney v. State, 8 Smedes & M., Miss., 104, 47 Am.Dec. 74.

A question is leading which puts into a witness' mouth the words that are to be echoed back, or plainly suggests the answer which the party wishes to get from him. People v. Mather, 4 Wend., N.Y., 229, 247, 21 Am.Dec. 122.

That question may be answered either yes or no does not necessarily make it leading, Foster v. Sol Greisler & Sons, 150 Pa.Super. 509, 29 A.2d 103, 106; Osterloh v. San Antonio Public Service Co., Tex.Civ.App., 77 S.W.2d 290, 292.

LEAGUE. 1. A treaty of alliance between different states or parties.

2. A measure of distance, varying in different countries.

It may be offensive or defensive, or both. It is *offensive* when the contracting parties agree to unite in attacking a common enemy; *defensive* when the parties agree to act in concert in defending each other against an enemy. Wharton.

The marine league, marking the limit of national jurisdiction on the high seas, is equal to three geographical (or marine) miles of 6,075 feet each.

In Spanish and Mexican law, the league, as a legal measure of length, consisted of 5,000 varas, and a vara was equivalent to 33⅓ English inches, making the league equal to a little more than 2.63 miles, and the square league equal to 4,428 acres. This is its meaning as used in Texas land grants. United States v. Perot, 98 U.S. 428, 25 L.Ed. 251; Hunter v. Morse, 49 Tex. 219. "League and labor," an area of land equivalent to 4,605 acres. Ammons v. Dwyer, 78 Tex. 639, 15 S.W. 1049. See Labor.

LEAKAGE. The waste or diminution of a liquid caused by its leaking from the cask, barrel, or other vessel in which it was placed.

Also an allowance made to an importer of liquids, at the custom-house, in the collection of duties, for his loss sustained by the leaking of the liquid from its cask or vessel.

LEAL. L. Fr. Loyal; that which belongs to the law.

LEALTE. L. Fr. Legality; the condition of a *legalis homo*, or lawful man.

LEAN. To incline in opinion or preference.

A court is sometimes said to "lean against" a doctrine, construction, or view contended for, whereby it is meant that the court regards it with disfavor or repugnance, because of its inexpedience, injustice, or inconsistency.

LEAP-YEAR. See Bissextile.

LEARN. To gain knowledge or information of; to ascertain by inquiry, study, or investigation. Fletcher Savings & Trust Co. v. American Surety Co. of New York, 92 Ind.App. 651, 175 N.E. 247, 251; Rambo v. Rambo, 245 Ala. 98, 16 So.2d 4, 5.

LEARNED. Possessing learning; erudite; versed in the law; informed.

In statutes prescribing the qualifications of judges, "learned in the law" designates one who has received a regular legal education, the almost invariable evidence of which is the fact of his admission to the bar. See Jamieson v. Wiggin, 12 S.D. 16, 80 N.W. 137, 46 L.R.A. 317, 76 Am.St.Rep. 585; O'Neal v. McKinna, 116 Ala. 620, 22 So. 905; Potter v. Robbins, 155 Tenn. 1, 290 S.W. 396, 399; Heard v. Moore, 154 Tenn. 566, 290 S.W. 15, 16, 50 A.L.R. 1152.

LEARNING. Legal doctrine. 1 Leon. 77.

LEASE. Any agreement which gives rise to relationship of landlord and tenant. Smith v. Royal Ins. Co., C.C.A.Cal., 111 F.2d 667, 671. Any grant of permissive use. People v. City of Chicago, 349 Ill. 304, 182 N.E. 419, 434.

Contract for exclusive possession of lands or tenements for determinate period. Barnett v. Lincoln, 162 Wash. 613, 299 P. 392, 394. Contract for possession and profits of lands and tenements either for life, or for certain period of time, or during the pleasure of the parties, Femmer v. City of Juneau, C.C.A.Alaska, 97 F.2d 649, 657; Smith v. Royal Ins. Co., D.C.Cal., 5 F.Supp. 435, 437; Intermountain Realty Co. v. Allen, 60 Idaho 228, 90 P.2d 704, 706, 122 A.L.R. 647. Contract for possession and profits of property for a recompense. White v. City of Grand Rapids, 244 N.W. 469, 260 Mich. 267; Stone v. City of Los Angeles, 114 Cal.App. 192, 299 P. 838, 840; Clark v. Harry, 182 Va. 410, 29 S.E.2d 231, 233. Conveyance, grant or devise of realty for designated period with reversion to grantor. Becker v. Manufacturers Trust Co., 262 App.Div. 525, 30 N.Y.S. 2d 542, 544; Moore v. Brandenberg, 234 Ky. 400, 28 S.W.2d 477, 478; Lewes Sand Co. v. Graves, Del., 1 Terry 189, 8 A.2d 21, 24. Conveyance of interest in real property for specified period or at will, Minneker v. Gardiner, 47 Ohio App. 203, 191 N.E. 793. Conveyance or grant of estate in real property for limited term with conditions attached, State ex rel. St. Louis County v. Evans, 246 Mo. 209, 139 S.W.2d 967, 969; Holcombe v. Lorino, 124 Tex. 446, 79 S.W.2d 307, 310; Dean v. Brower, 119 Cal.App. 412, 6 P.2d 580, 581. Conveyance, usually in consideration of rent or other recompense, for life, years, or at will. Smith v. Royal Ins. Co., C.C.A.Cal., 111 F.2d 667, 671; Clark v. Harry, 182 Va. 410, 29 S.E.2d 231, 233; but always for a less time than lessor has in the premises, Leonard v. Autocar Sales & Service Co., 325 Ill.App. 375, 60 N.E.2d 457, 462; Union Central Life Ins. Co. of Cincinnati, Ohio, v. Goode, 222 Iowa 716, 269 N.W. 762, 764. Grant of use and possession, in consideration of something to be rendered, Ottman v. Albert Co., 327 Pa. 49, 192 A. 897, 899.

A contract in writing, under seal, whereby a person having a legal estate in hereditaments, corporeal or incorporeal, conveys a portion of his interest to another, in consideration of a certain annual rent or render, or other recompense. Archb.Landl. & Ten. 2.

Instrument granting exclusive possession or control of premises, or portion, though use be restricted by reservations, will be considered lease, Barnett v. Lincoln, 162 Wash. 613, 299 P. 392, 394.

"Lease" or "hire" is a synallagmatic contract, to which consent alone is sufficient, and by which one party gives to the other the enjoyment of a thing, or his labor, at a fixed price. Civil Code La. art. 2669.

Oral agreement whereby property owner for fixed consideration gave another trapping privileges on his lands for trapping season held contract of "lease." Defelice v. Autin, La.App., 159 So. 648, 649.

The person who conveys is termed the "lessor," and the person to whom they are conveyed, the "lessee;" and when the lessor conveys lands or tenements to a lessee, he is said to lease, demise, or let them. 4 Cruise, Dig. 58; U. S. Nat. Bank of La Grande v. Miller, 122 Or. 285, 258 P. 205, 207, 58 A.L.R. 339; Howard v. Manning, 79 Okl. 165, 192 P. 358, 360, 79 A.L.R. 819. The word when used as verb, means to transfer for term specified therein from lessor to lessee property therein demised, also to let, to farm out, to rent; and there is authority for view that word "lease" may properly be used in two senses, first, in describing act of lessor in giving lease, and again in describing act of lessee in taking lease. Stone v. City of Los Angeles, 114 Cal.App. 192, 299 P. 838, 841.

The term embraces what are described as the covenants of the lease. Goldberg v. Grossman, 105 Pa.Super. 50, 160 A. 138, 139.

Whatever is sufficient to show that one party shall divest himself of possession and the other party shall come into it for a determinate time and for a fixed rental amounts to a lease. General American Life Ins. Co. v. North American Mfg. Co., 320 Ill.App. 488, 51 N.E.2d 619.

When the contract is bipartite the one part is called the "lease", the other the "counterclaim."

Concurrent Lease

One granted for a term which is to commence before the expiration or other determination of a previous lease of the same premises made to another person; or, in other words, an assignment of a part of the reversion, entitling the lessee to all the rents accruing on the previous lease after the date of his lease and to appropriate remedies against the holding tenant. Cargill v. Thompson, 57 Minn. 534, 59 N.W. 638.

Farm Lease

See Farm Lease.

Lease and Release

A species of conveyance much used in England, said to have been invented by Serjeant Moore, soon after the enactment of the statute of uses. It is thus contrived: A lease, or rather bargain and sale upon some pecuniary consideration for one year, is made by the tenant of the freehold to the lessee or bargainee. This, without any enrolment, makes the bargainor stand seised to the use of the bargainee, and vests in the bargainee the use of the term for one year, and then the statute immediately annexes the possession. Being thus in possession, he is capable of receiving a release of the freehold and reversion, which must be made to the tenant in possession, and accordingly the next day a release is granted to him. The lease and release, when used as a conveyance of the fee, have the joint operation of a single conveyance. 2 Bl. Comm. 339; 4 Kent, Comm. 482; Co.Litt. 207; Cruise, Dig. tit. 32, c. 11.

Mining Lease

See Mining.

Parol Lease

A lease of real estate not evidenced by writing, but resting in an oral agreement.

Perpetual Lease

A lease of lands which may last without limitation as to time; a grant of lands in fee with the reservation of a rent in fee; a fee-farm. Edwards v. Noel, 88 Mo.App. 434.

Sublease, or Underlease

One executed by the lessee of an estate to a third person, conveying the same estate for a shorter term than that for which the lessee holds it. The distinction between an assignment of a term for years and a sublease or subletting is that if the lessee parts with his entire interest in the term, it constitutes an assignment and not a subletting, although the transfer is in form a sublease; but if the lessee reserves to himself a reversionary interest in the term, it constitutes a sublease, whatever the form of the transfer. Johnson v. Thompson, 185 Ala. 666, 64 So. 554, 555; Weigle v. Rogers, 202 Mo.App. 520, 213 S.W. 501, 502; Holden v. Tidwell, 37 Okl. 553, 133 P. 54, 55, 49 L.R.A., N.S., 369, Ann.Cas.1915C, 394; Davis v. First Nat. Bank, Tex.Civ.App., 258 S.W. 241, 242.

For "Extension of lease," see Extension.

LEASEHOLD. An estate in realty held under a lease; an estate for a fixed term of years. See Stubbings v. Evanston, 136 Ill. 37, 26 N.E. 577, 11 L.R.A. 839, 29 Am.St.Rep. 300; Washington F. Ins. Co. v. Kelly, 32 Md. 421, 3 Am.Rep. 149; Greene Line Terminal Co. v. Martin, 122 W.Va. 483, 10 S.E. 2d 901, 903. Right of tenant at will is "leasehold." Public Service Co. of New Hampshire v. Voudoumas, 84 N.H. 387, 151 A. 81, 83, 70 A.L.R. 480.

LEASING, or LESING. Gleaning.

LEASING-MAKING. In old Scotch criminal law. An offense consisting in slanderous and untrue speeches, to the disdain, reproach, and contempt of the king, his council and proceedings, etc. Bell.

LEAUTE. L. Fr. Legality; sufficiency in law. Britt. c. 109.

LEAVE. Give. Grimes v. Crouch, 175 Va. 126, 7 S.E.2d 115, 117.

To allow or cause to remain; to let remain unmoved or undone; to refrain from or neglect taking, doing, or changing; to let stay or continue; to let be without interference; to suffer to remain subject to another's action, control, or the like; to suffer to be undisturbed in action. Collins v. Hartford Accident & Indemnity Co., 178 Va. 501, 17 S.E.2d 413, 418.

To give or dispose of by will; to bequeath or devise. Townsend v. Gordon, 308 Mich. 438, 14 N.W.2d 57, 60; Williams v. McPherson, 216 N.C. 565, 5 S.E.2d 830, 831. "The word 'leave,' as applied to the subject-matter, *prima facie* means a disposition by will." Thorley v. Thorley, 10 East, 438; Carr v. Effinger, 78 Va. 203.

To put, place, deposit, deliver, or the like. Jaggers v. Southeastern Greyhound Lines, D.C. Tenn., 34 F.Supp. 667, 668; Stafford v. Consolidated Bus Lines, 179 Tenn. 185, 164 S.W.2d 15, 16; Collins v. Hartford Accident & Indemnity Co., 178 Va. 501, 17 S.E.2d 413, 418, 137 A.L.R. 1046.

Willful departure with intent to remain away, and not temporary absence with intention of returning. Landreth v. Casey, 340 Ill. 519, 173 N.E. 84, 85.

LEAVE AND LICENSE. A defense to an action in trespass setting up the consent of the plaintiff to the trespass complained of.

LEAVE NO ISSUE. Not survived by a child or children or their descendants. A spouse of a deceased child is not "issue" (*q. v.*). In re Vigil's Estate, 38 N.M. 383, 34 P.2d 667, 668, 93 A.L.R. 1506.

LEAVE OF ABSENCE. Temporary absence from duty with intention to return during which time remuneration is suspended, State ex rel. McGaughey v. Grayston, 349 Mo. 700, 163 S.W.2d 335, 341.

LEAVE OF COURT. Permission obtained from a court to take some action which, without such permission, would not be allowable; as, to sue a receiver, to file an amended pleading, to plead several pleas. See Copperthwait v. Dummer, 18 N.J. L. 258.

LEAVE TO DEFEND. The bills of exchange act 1855 (18 & 19 Vict. c. 67) allowed actions on bills and notes commenced within six months after being due to be by writ of summons in a form provided by the act, and unless the defendant should within twelve days obtain leave to appear and defend the action, allowed the plaintiff to sign judgment on proof of service. This procedure was retained by the judicature act, but abolished in 1880. Whart. Lex.

LECCATOR. A debauched person. Cowell.

LECHERWITE, LAIRWITE, or LEGERWITE. A fine for adultery or fornication, anciently paid to the lords of certain manors. 4 Inst. 206.

LECTOR DE LETRA ANTIQUA. In Spanish law. A person appointed by competent authority to read and decipher ancient writings, to the end that they may be presented on the trial of causes as documents entitled to legal credit. Escriche.

LECTORES. A term applied to notaries in the Middle Ages. So.Afr.Law Dict.

LECTRINUM. A pulpit. Mon.Angl. tom. iii. p. 243.

LECTURER. An instructor; a reader of lectures; also a clergyman who assists rectors, etc., in preaching, etc.

LEDGE. In mining law. This term, as used in the mining laws of the United States (Rev.St. § 2322, 30 U.S.C.A. § 26) and in both legal and popular usage in the western American states, is synonymous with "lode," which see. Myers v. Lloyd, 4 Alaska, 263, 265.

LEDGER. A book of accounts in which a trader enters the names of all persons with whom he has dealings; there being two parallel columns in each account, one for the entries to the debit of the person charged, the other for his credits. Into this book are posted the items from the day-book or journal.

A "ledger" is the principal book of accounts of a business establishment in which all the transactions of each day are entered under appropriate heads so as to show at a glance the debits and credits of each account. Foothill Ditch Co. v. Wallace Ranch Water Co., 25 Cal.App.2d 555, 78 P.2d 215, 220.

LEDGER-BOOK. In ecclesiastical law. The name of a book kept in the prerogative courts in England. It is considered as a roll of the court, but, it seems, it cannot be read in evidence. Bac.Abr.

LEDGREVIUS. In old English law. A lathereeve, or chief officer of a lathe. Spelman.

LEDO. The rising water or increase of the sea.

LEEMAN'S ACTS. Acts 30 Vict. c. 29 and 35 & 36 Vict. c. 91, by which contracts for the sale of bank shares are void unless the number of the shares are set forth in the contract. 9 Q.B.D. 546; and by which are authorized the application of the funds of municipal corporations and other governing bodies under certain conditions towards promoting or opposing parliamentary and other proceedings for the benefit or protection of the inhabitants.

LEET. In English law. The name of a court of criminal jurisdiction, formerly of much importance, but latterly fallen into disuse. See Court-Leet.

LEETS. Meetings which were appointed for the nomination or election of ecclesiastical officers in Scotland. Cowell.

LEFT. To let remain or have remaining at death; to transmit, bequeath or give by will. Grimes v. Crouch, 175 Va. 126, 7 S.E.2d 115, 117.

LEGA, or LACTA. The alloy of money. Spelman.

LEGABILIS. In old English law. That which may be bequeathed. Cowell.

LEGACY. A disposition of personalty by will. In re Johnson's Estate, 220 Iowa 424, 262 N.W. 811; Hill v. Van Sant, 133 N.J.Eq. 133, 30 A.2d 904, 906; Stubbs v. Abel, 114 Or. 610, 233 P. 852, 858; State, for Use of Woodlands Cemetery Co. of Philadelphia v. Lodge, 2 Terry 125, 16 A.2d 250.

"Legacy" and "bequest" are equivalent terms. But in strict common-law terminology "legacy" and "devise" do not mean the same thing and are not interchangeable, latter being properly used only in relation to real estate. But by construction the word "legacy" may be so extended as to include realty or interests therein. See In re Ross's Estate, 140 Cal. 282, 73 P. 976; Bacon v. Bacon, 55 Vt. 247; Roth's Appeal, 94 Pa. 191; Williams v. McComb, 38 N.C. 455; In re Stuart's Will, 115 Wis. 294, 91 N.W. 688.

Absolute Legacy

One given without condition and intended to vest immediately.

Accumulative Legacy

A second, double, or additional legacy; a legacy given in addition to another given by the same instrument, or by another instrument.

Additional Legacy

One given to the same legatee in addition to (and not in lieu of) another legacy given before by the same will or in a codicil thereto.

Alternate Legacy

One by which the testator gives one of two or more things without designating which.

Conditional Legacy

One which is liable to take effect or to be defeated according to the occurrence or non-occurrence of some uncertain event. Harker v. Smith, 41 Ohio St. 238, 52 Am.Rep. 80; Markham v. Hufford, 123 Mich. 505, 82 N.W. 222, 48 L.R.A. 580, 81 Am.St.Rep. 222.

Contingent Legacy

A legacy given to a person at a future uncertain time, that may or may not arrive; as "at his age of twenty-one," or "if" or "when he attains twenty-one." 2 Bl. Comm. 513; 2 Steph.Comm. 259. A legacy made dependent upon some uncertain event. 1 Rop.Leg. 506. A legacy which has not vested. In re Engles' Estate, 166 Pa. 280, 31 A. 76; Andrews v. Russell, 127 Ala. 195, 28 So. 703; Rubencane v. McKee, 6 Del.Ch. 40, 6 A. 639.

Cumulative Legacies

These are legacies so called to distinguish them from legacies which are merely repeated. In the construction of testamentary instruments, the question often arises whether, where a testator has twice bequeathed a legacy to the same person, the legatee is entitled to both, or only to one of them; in other words, whether the second legacy must be considered as a mere repetition of the first, or as cumulative, *i. e.*, additional. In determining this question, the intention of the testator, if it appears on the face of the instrument, prevails. Wharton.

Demonstrative Legacy

A bequest of a certain sum of money, with a direction that it shall be paid out of a particular fund. It differs from a specific legacy in this respect: that, if the fund out of which it is payable fails for any cause, it is nevertheless entitled to come on the estate as a general legacy. And it differs from a general legacy in this: that it does not abate in that class, but in the class of specific legacies. Kenaday v. Sinnott, 179 U.S. 606, 21 S.Ct. 233, 45 L.Ed. 339; Spinney v. Eaton, 111 Me. 1, 87 A. 378, 380, 46 L.R.A.,N.S., 535; In re Douglas' Estate, 149 Minn. 276, 183 N.W. 355, 356; In re Wilson's Estate, 260 Pa. 407, 103 A. 880, 6 A.L.R. 1349; Baker v. Baker, 319 Ill. 320, 150 N.E. 284, 285, 42 A.L.R. 1514. A legacy of quantity is ordinarily a general legacy; but there are legacies of quantity in the nature of specific legacies, as of so much money, with reference to a particular fund for payment. This kind of legacy is called by the civilians a "demonstrative legacy," and it is so far general and differs so much in effect from one properly specific that, if the fund be called in or fail, the legatee will not be deprived of his legacy, but be permitted to receive it out of the general assets; yet the legacy is so far specific that it will not be liable to abate with general legacies upon a deficiency of assets. 2 Williams, Ex'rs, 1078.

General Legacy

A pecuniary legacy, payable out of the general assets of a testator. 2 Bl.Comm. 512; Ward.Leg. 1, 16. One so given as not to amount to a bequest of a particular thing or particular money of the testator, distinguished from others of the same kind; one of quantity merely, not specific. Evans v. Hunter, 86 Iowa 413, 53 N.W. 277, 17 L.R.A. 308, 41 Am.St.Rep. 503; Gardner v. Viall, 36 R.I. 436, 90 A. 760, 762; Spinney v. Eaton, 111 Me. 1, 87 A. 378, 380, 46 L.R.A.,N.S., 535; Guthie v. Guthrie's Ex'r, 168 Ky. 805, 183 S.W. 221, 224; School Dist. No. 1 in City and County of Denver v. International Trust Co., 59 Colo. 486, 149 P. 620, 623.

Indefinite Legacy

One which passes property by a general or collective term, without enumeration of number or quantity; as, a bequest of "all" the testator's "goods," or his "bank stock." Lown.Leg. 84.

Lapsed Legacy

Where the legatee dies before the testator, or before the legacy is payable, the bequest is said to *lapse,* as it then falls into the residuary fund of the estate.

Modal Legacy

A bequest accompanied by directions as to the mode or manner in which it shall be applied for the legatee's benefit, *e. g.,* a legacy to A. to buy him a house or a commission in the army. See Lown.Leg. 151.

Pecuniary Legacy

A bequest of a sum of money, or of an annuity. It may or may not specify the fund from which it is to be drawn. It is not the less a pecuniary legacy if it comprises the specific pieces of money in a designated receptacle, as a purse or chest. See Humphrey v. Robinson, 52 Hun, 200, 5 N.Y.S. 164; Lang v. Ropke, 10 N.Y.Leg.Obs. 75; Mathis v. Mathis, 18 N.J.L. 66.

Residuary Legacy

A bequest of all the testator's personal estate not otherwise effectually disposed of by his will; a bequest of "all the rest, residue, and remainder" of the personal property after payment of debts and satisfaction of the particular legacies. See In re Williams' Estate, 112 Cal. 521, 44 P. 808, 53 Am.St.Rep. 224; Stubbs v. Abel, 114 Or. 610, 233 P. 852, 857.

Special Legacy

A "specific legacy" *(q. v.)* is sometimes so called.

Specific Legacy

One which operates on property particularly designated. Hart v. Brown, 145 Ga. 140, 88 S.E. 670, 671; Spinney v. Eaton, 111 Me. 1, 87 A. 378, 380, 46 L.R.A.,N.S., 535; Bales v. Murray, 186 Iowa 649, 171 N.W. 747, 749; Baker v. Baker, 319 Ill. 320, 150 N.E. 284, 285, 42 A.L.R. 1514; School Dist. No. 1 in City and County of Denver v. International Trust Co., 59 Colo. 486, 149 P. 620, 623. A legacy or gift by will of a particular specified thing, as of a horse, a piece of furniture, a term of years, and the like. Morriss v. Garland, 78 Va. 222. In a strict sense, a legacy of a particular chattel, which is specified and distinguished from all other chattels of the testator of the same kind; as of a horse of a certain color. A legacy of a quantity of chattels described collectively; as a gift of all the testator's pictures. Ward, Leg. 16–18. A legacy is specific, when it is limited to a particular thing, subject, or chose in action, so identified as to render the bequest inapplicable to any other; as the bequest of a horse, a picture, or jewel, or a debt due from a person named, and, in special cases, even of a sum of money. In re Daniels' Estate, 192 Iowa 326, 184 N.W. 647, 650; Baker v. Baker, 319 Ill. 320, 150 N.E. 284, 285, 42 A.L.R. 1514; Carpenter's Estate v. Wiley, 166 Iowa, 48, 147 N.W. 175, 177; Langdon v. Astor, 3 Duer, N.Y., 477, 543.

Trust Legacy

A bequest of personal property to trustees to be held upon trust; as, to pay the annual income to a beneficiary for life.

Universal Legacy

In the civil law. A testamentary disposition by which the testator gives to one or several persons the whole of the property which he leaves at his decease. Civ.Code La., art. 1606.

LEGACY DUTY. A duty imposed in England upon personal property (other than leaseholds) devolving under any will or intestacy. Brown.

LEGACY OR SUCCESSION TAX. An excise, on privilege of taking property by will or inheritance or by succession on death of owner. In re Rosing's Estate, 337 Mo. 544, 85 S.W.2d 495, 496; State Tax Commission v. Backman, 88 Utah 424, 55 P.2d 171, 174.

LEGAL. 1. Conforming to the law; according to law; required or permitted by law; not forbidden or discountenanced by law; good and effectual in law. Freeman v. Fowler Packing Co., 135 Kan. 378, 11 P.2d 276, 277; General Motors Acceptance Corporation v. Schwartz, 118 N.J.L. 25, 190 A. 625, 627.

2. Proper or sufficient to be recognized by the law; cognizable in the courts; competent or adequate to fulfill the requirements of the law.

3. Cognizable in courts of law, as distinguished from courts of equity; construed or governed by the rules and principles of law, in contradistinction to rules of equity.

4. Posited by the courts as the inference or imputation of the law, as a matter of construction, rather than established by actual proof; *e. g.,* legal malice. See Lawful.

5. Created by law. De Vita v. Pianisani, 127 Misc. 611, 217 N.Y.S. 438, 440.

6. Lawful; of or pertaining to law. Kinsley v. Herald & Globe Ass'n, 113 Vt. 272, 34 A.2d 99, 101, 148 A.L.R. 1164.

As to legal "Consideration," "Damages," "Day," "Debts," "Demand," "Defense," "Disability," "Discretion," "Estate," "Incapacity," "Irregularity," "Memory," "Mortgage," "Process," "Relevancy," "Remedy," "Reversion," and "Tender," see those titles.

LEGAL ACUMEN. The doctrine of legal acumen is that if a defect in, or invalidity of, a claim to land is such as to require legal acumen to discover it, whether it appears upon the face of the record or proceedings, or is to be proved aliunde, then the powers or jurisdiction of a court of equity may be invoked to remove the cloud created by such defect or invalidity. Schwab v. City of St. Louis, 310 Mo. 116, 274 S.W. 1058, 1060.

LEGAL AGE. The age at which the person acquires full capacity to make his own contracts and deeds and transact business generally (age of majority) or to enter into some particular contract or relation, as, the "legal age of consent" to marriage. See Capwell v. Capwell, 21 R.I. 101, 41 A. 1005; Perkins v. Safe Deposit & Trust Co. of Baltimore, 138 Md. 299, 113 A. 877, 880.

Legal age may be full or partial. As respects the former, the common law fixes the beginning of such period on the day preceding the twenty-first anniversary of birth; as respects the latter, a person may be of legal age for certain purposes before arriving at the age of 21 years both at the common law and under the statutes. Montoya de Antonio v. Miller, 7 N.M. 289, 34 P. 40, 21 L.R.A. 699. Legal age to consent to marriage means age of consent to marriage at common law, to wit, 14 years in case of males, and 12 years in case of females. Capwell v. Capwell, 21 R.I. 101, 41 A. 1005. That age, when under the law duties imposed on trustees which were practically those of guardians were no longer regarded as necessary and when the beneficiaries could by their releases duly acquit the trustees for payments made to them, which in the case of boys is upon their arrival at the age of 21 years, and in the case of girls at the age of 18 years. Perkins v. Safe Deposit & Trust Co. of Baltimore, 138 Md. 299, 113 A. 877, 880. The expression "scholars of legal school age" includes all members of the schools under the age of 21 years. Needham v. Wellesley, 139 Mass. 372, 31 N.E. 732, 733.

LEGAL ASSETS. Such property of a testator in the hands of his executor as is liable to debts in temporal courts and to legacies in the spiritual, by course of law; equitable assets are such as are liable only by help of a court of equity. 2 Will.Ex. 1408–1431. The distinction is not important in the United States; In re Sperry's Estate, 1 Ashm. (Pa.) 347. That portion of the assets of a deceased party which by law is directly liable, in the hands of his executor or administrator, to the payment of debts and legacies. 1 Story, Eq.Jur. § 551. Such assets as can be reached in the hands of an executor or administrator, by a suit at law against him.

LEGAL CAPACITY TO SUE. Right to come into court, MacAffer v. Boston & M. R. R., 273 N.Y.S. 679, 242 App.Div. 140; American Home Benefit Ass'n v. United American Benefit Ass'n, 63 Idaho 754, 125 P.2d 1010, 1016.

LEGAL CAPITAL. Property sufficient to balance capital stock liability. Crocker v. Waltham Watch Co., 315 Mass. 397, 53 N.E.2d 230, 238.

LEGAL CAUSE. Proximate cause (*q. v.*). Substantial factor in bringing about harm. Krauss v. Greenbarg, C.C.A.Pa., 137 F.2d 569, 572; Giles v. Moundridge Milling Co., 351 Mo. 568, 173 S.W.2d 745, 750.

LEGAL CONCLUSION. A statement of legal duty without stating fact from which duty arises. Burton-Lingo Co. v. Morton, Tex.Civ.App., 126 S.W.2d 727, 733.

LEGAL CRUELTY. Such as will warrant the granting of a divorce to the injured party; as distinguished from such kinds or degrees of cruelty as do not, under the statutes and decisions, amount to sufficient cause for a decree. Such conduct on the part of a husband as will endanger the life, person, or health of his wife, or create a reasonable apprehension of bodily hurt; such acts as render cohabitation unsafe, or are likely to be attended with injury to the person or to the health of the wife; Odom v. Odom, 36 Ga. 286; 2 Curt. Eccl. 281; Singewald v. Singewald, 165 Md. 136, 166 A. 441, 446; the willful infliction of pain, bodily or mental, upon the complaining party, such as reasonably justified the apprehension of danger to life, limb, or health; Skellie v. Skellie, 152 Ga. 707, 111 S.E. 22, 24.

If acts of violence are not of frequent repetition, they must endanger life, limb, or health to constitute "cruelty." McKane v. McKane, 152 Md. 515, 137 A. 288, 289. To constitute "cruelty," within the divorce law, where there is no personal violence, the misconduct must be such as will impair the health or create a reasonable apprehension of bodily harm. Humber v. Humber, 109 Miss. 216, 68 So. 161, 163. The term is broad enough to include outrages upon the feelings inflicting mental pain and anguish, where the conduct has been studied, willful, and deliberate. McNabb v. McNabb, Tex.Civ.App., 207 S.W. 129, 130. See, also, as to "extreme cruelty" as a ground for divorce, Finnell v. Finnell, 113 Okl. 164, 240 P. 62, 63; Cavileer v. Cavileer, 94 N.J.Eq. 160, 119 A. 101, 103; Maloof v. Maloof, 175 Cal. 571, 166 P. 330, 331.

LEGAL DEPENDENT. Dependent according to law, Beard v. Rickert Rice Mills, La.App., 164 So. 636, 638. The term imports right to invoke aid of law to require support. National Council Junior Order United American Mechanics v. Tate, 193 S.E. 397, 212 N.C. 305, 399, 400, 113 A.L.R. 1514; Woodmen of the World Life Ins. Soc. v. Irick, D.C. S.C., 58 F.Supp. 202, 206.

LEGAL DETRIMENT. "Legal detriment" to promisee means that promisee changes his legal position, or assumes duties or liabilities not theretofore imposed on him. State ex rel. Kansas City v. State Highway Commission, 349 Mo. 865, 163 S.W.2d 948, 953.

LEGAL DISCRETION. See Discretion.

LEGAL DISTRIBUTEES, as used in will, is construed to mean persons who would be entitled to take under the law. Jackson v. Osborne, 108 W.Va. 480, 151 S.E. 709, 710.

LEGAL DUTY. An obligation arising from contract of the parties or the operation of the law. Riddell v. Ventilating Co., 27 Mont. 44, 69 P. 241. That which the law requires to be done or forborne to a determinate person or the public at large, correlative to a vested and coextensive right in such person or the public, and the breach of which constitutes negligence. Railroad Co. v. Ballentine, C.C.A.Ill., 84 F. 935, 28 C.C.A. 572; Toadvine v. Cincinnati, N. O. & T. P. Ry. Co., D.C.Ky., 20 F.Supp. 226, 227.

LEGAL ENTITY. Legal existence. Department of Banking v. Hedges, 136 Neb. 382, 286 N.W. 277, 281.

LEGAL ESTOPPEL. Estoppel by deed or record, as distinguished from estoppel by matter in pais. Lockhart State Bank v. Baker, Tex.Civ.App., 264 S.W. 566, 569. It excludes evidence of the truth and the equity of the particular case to support a strict rule of law on grounds of public policy. First Nat. Bank v. Boles, 231 Ala. 473, 165 So. 586, 592.

LEGAL ETHICS. Usages and customs among members of the legal profession, involving their moral and professional duties toward one another, toward clients, and toward the courts; that branch of moral science which treats of the duties which a member of the legal profession owes to the public, to the court, to his professional brethren, and to his client. Kraushaar v. La Vin, 42 N.Y.S.2d 857, 859, 181 Misc. 508.

LEGAL EVIDENCE. A broad general term meaning all admissible evidence, including both oral and documentary, but with a further implication that it must be of such a character as tends reasonably and substantially to prove the point, not to raise a mere suspicion or conjecture. Curtis v. Bradley, 65 Conn. 99, 31 A. 591, 594, 28 L.R.A. 143, 48 Am. St.Rep. 177.

LEGAL EXCUSE. The term "legal excuse," which will excuse observance of ordinance or statute concerning operating or equipping automobile, means anything that would make it impossible to comply with statute or ordinance; anything over which driver has no control in emergency not caused by driver; or excuse or exception specifically provided by statute. Edwards v. Perley, 223 Iowa 1119, 274 N.W. 910, 914; Herman v. Sladofsky, 301 Mass. 534, 17 N.E.2d 879, 881; Blashfield, Cyc. of Automobile Law and Prac., Perm. Ed., §§ 648 (care in general), and 752 (assured clear distance ahead).

LEGAL FRAUD. Contracts or acts as, though not originating in actual evil design to perpetrate fraud, yet by their tendency to mislead others or to violate confidence, are prohibited by law. Ruedy v. Toledo Factories Co., 61 Ohio App. 21, 22 N.E.2d 293, 297. Breach of duty which has tendency to deceive others and operates to their injury, even though there be no vicious intent. Charleroi Lumber Co. v. School Dist. of Borough of Bentleyville, 334 Pa. 424, 6 A.2d 88, 91.

Synonymous with "constructive fraud". Purcell v. Robertson, 122 W.Va. 287, 8 S.E.2d 881, 883; Tom Reed Gold Mines Co. v. United Eastern Mining Co., 39 Ariz. 533, 8 P.2d 449, 451. For definition of "Constructive Fraud," see Fraud.

LEGAL HEIRS. As used in deed, "Legal heirs" and "nearest kin" mean same thing. Weatherford v. Weatherford, 222 Ala. 102, 130 So. 890, 891. As used in will means, when applied to personalty, decedent's next of kin. In re Farkouh's Will, 235 N.Y.S. 165, 167, 134 Misc. 285; persons entitled under laws of descent and distribution. Daniels v. Daniels, 115 Conn. 239, 161 A. 94, 95; Ames v. Conry, 87 Ind.App. 149, 165 N.E. 435, 438. Person to whom law would give decedent's property if decedent died intestate. In re Wagar's Estate, 302 Mich. 243, 4 N.W.2d 535, 536.

"Heirs at law," "lawful heirs," "legal heirs," and similar expressions are synonymous. First & American Nat. Bank of Duluth v. Higgins, 208 Minn. 295, 293 N.W. 585, 590; Corwin v. Rheims, 390 Ill. 205, 61 N.E.2d 40, 48; In re Fahnestock's Estate, 384 Ill. 26, 50 N.E.2d 733, 736.

LEGAL HOLIDAY. A day designated by law as exempt from judicial proceedings, service of process, demand and protest of commercial paper, etc. A day designated by legislative enactment for purpose within meaning of term "holiday." Vidal v. Backs, 218 Cal. 99, 21 P.2d 952, 86 A.L.R. 1134.

LEGAL INJURY. Violation or invasion of legal right. Combs v. Hargis Bank & Trust Co., 234 Ky. 202, 27 S.W.2d 955, 956; American Indemnity Co. v. Ernst & Ernst, Tex.Civ.App., 106 S.W.2d 763, 765.

LEGAL INSANITY. See Insanity.

LEGAL INTEREST. That rate of interest prescribed by the laws of the particular state or country as the highest which may be lawfully contracted for or exacted, and which must be paid in all cases where the law allows interest without the assent of the debtor. American, etc., Ass'n v. Harn, Tex.Civ.App., 62 S.W. 75. Interest at the legal rate. People ex rel. Emigrant Industrial Sav. Bank v. Sexton, 20 N.Y.S.2d 41, 47, 259 App. Div. 566. Statutory interest allowed on open account. Oppenheim v. Hood, Tex.Civ.App., 33 S.W. 2d 265, 267. See, also, Legal Rate of Interest, *infra*.

LEGAL INVESTMENT. In re Froelich's Estate, 269 N.Y.S. 541, 150 Misc. 371. Sound investment. In re Public Parks, Borough of Queens, City of New York, 17 N.Y.S.2d 209, 216, 172 Misc. 877.

LEGAL ISSUE. When used in will and unexplained by context, means descendants. In re Mann's Will, 244 N.Y.S. 673, 680, 138 Misc. 42.

LEGAL JEOPARDY. A person is in "legal jeopardy" when he is put upon trial before a court of competent jurisdiction upon an indictment or information which is sufficient in form and substance to sustain a conviction, and a jury has been "charged with his deliverance," and a jury is thus charged when they have been impaneled and sworn. State v. Whitman, 93 Utah 557, 74 P.2d 696, 697.

LEGAL LIABILITY. A liability which courts recognize and enforce as between parties litigant. Abbott v. Ætna Casualty & Surety Co., D.C.Md., 42 F.Supp. 793, 806; Royal Ins. Co. v. St. Louis-San Francisco Ry. Co., C.C.A.Okl., 291 F. 358, 360. See, also, Brooklyn Clothing Corporation v. Fidelity-Phenix Fire Ins. Co., 200 N.Y.S. 208, 211, 205 App.Div. 743.

LEGAL MALICE. An expression used as the equivalent of "constructive malice," or "malice in law." Humphries v. Parker, 52 Me. 502. Inference of malice which can be reasonably drawn from wrongful act. Chrisman v. Terminal R. Ass'n of St. Louis, 237 Mo.App. 181, 157 S.W.2d 230, 235. Intentional doing of a wrongful act without just cause. State ex rel. United Factories v. Hostetter, 344 Mo. 386, 126 S.W.2d 1173, 1176; Ryan v. Wilson, 231 Iowa 33, 300 N.W. 707, 716; Hatton v. Carder Wholesale Grocery Co., 235 Mo. App. 1198, 150 S.W.2d 1096, 1101.

LEGAL NAME. Under common law consists of one Christian name and one surname, and the insertion, omission, or mistake in middle name or initial is immaterial. Langley v. Zurich General Accident & Liability Ins. Co., 97 Cal.App. 434, 275 P. 963, 965.

LEGAL NEGLIGENCE. Negligence per se; the omission of such care as ordinarily prudent persons exercise and deem adequate to the circumstances of the case. In cases where the common experience of mankind and the common judgment of prudent persons have recognized that to do or omit certain acts is prolific of danger, the doing or omission of them is "legal negligence." Johnson v. Railway Co., 49 Wis. 529, 5 N.W. 886. Failure to perform duty law imposes on one person for benefit of another. Sweeney v. Boston & M. R. R., 87 N.H. 90, 174 A. 676, 677.

LEGAL NOTICE. Such notice as is adequate in point of law; such notice as the law requires to be given for the specific purpose or in the particular case. See Sanborn v. Piper, 64 N.H. 335, 10 A. 680; Knowledge brought home to a party in a prescribed form. Worthen v. Kingsbury, 84 N.H. 304, 149 A. 869, 871.

LEGAL OBLIGATION. A legal obligation against state is an obligation which would form basis of judgment against state in court of competent jurisdiction should Legislature permit state to be sued. Fort Worth Cavalry Club, Inc., v. Sheppard, 125 Tex. 339, 83 S.W.2d 660, 663. Legal obligation to support parent exists if one is bound to support parent under statute. Anderson v. Hotel Cataract, 70 S.D. 376, 17 N.W.2d 913, 917.

LEGAL PERSONAL REPRESENTATIVE. Generally, when applied by testator to personalty, signifies "executors and administrators" and when applied to realty those upon whom law casts real estate immediately upon death of ancestor. Hogate v. Hogate, 132 N.J.Eq. 480, 28 A.2d 769, 771. As respects delivery of deposit on behalf of deceased seaman the public administrator, or executor or administrator appointed in state where seaman resided.

LEGAL POSSESSOR. One who, but for the reservation of strict legal title in conditional vendor, or the giving of a strict legal title in a conditional vendor, or the giving of a strict legal title to a chattel mortgagee, would have the status of a full and unqualified owner. General Motors Acceptance Corporation v. Baker, 291 N.Y.S. 1015, 1019, 161 Misc. 238.

LEGAL PREJUDICE. Legal prejudice which will defeat plaintiff's motion to dismiss is such as deprives defendant of substantive rights of property, or concerns his defense, which will not be available or may be endangered in a second suit. General Motors Acceptance Corporation v. Baker, 291 N.Y.S. 1015, 161 Misc. 238.

LEGAL PRESUMPTION. For "presumption of law," see Presumption.

LEGAL PRIVITY. "Legal privity", within rule that defense of usury is personal to debtor and those in legal privity with him, means those upon whom title or interest is cast by law. Fry v. Layton, 191 Miss. 17, 2 So.2d 561, 564, 134 A.L.R. 1330.

LEGAL PROCEEDING. Garrison v. Johnson, C.C.A.Kan., 66 F.2d 227, 229; Metropolitan Casualty Ins. Co. of New York v. Sloss-Sheffield Steel & Iron Co., 241 Ala. 545, 3 So.2d 306, 309. Any proceedings in court of justice, whether law or equity, interlocutory or final, by which property of debtor is seized and diverted from his general creditors. In re Rialto Properties Co., D.C.Cal., 8 F.Supp. 57, 59. Proceedings upon appeal to court of common pleas from action of Industrial Commission. Carson v. Beall, 55 Ohio App. 245, 9 N.E.2d 729, 731. This term includes all proceedings authorized or sanctioned by law, and brought or instituted in a court of justice or legal tribunal, for the acquiring of a right or the enforcement of a remedy. Griem v. Fidelity & Casualty Co., 99 Wis. 530, 75 N.W. 67; Mack v. Campau, 69 Vt. 558, 38 A. 149, 69 Am.St.Rep. 948.

LEGAL RATE OF INTEREST. A rate fixed by statute where it is not fixed by contract, and it is unless otherwise specifically provided the maximum rate which may be contracted for. City of Danville v. Chesapeake & O. Ry. Co., D.C.Va., 34 F.Supp. 620, 637. See Legal Interest, *supra*.

LEGAL REPRESENTATIVE. The term in its broadest sense, means one who stands in place of, and represents the interests of, another. Nudelman v. Thimbles, Inc., 225 Mo.App. 553, 40 S.W.2d 475, 477; Haney v. Farmers' Alliance Ins. Co., 134 Kan. 5, 4 P.2d 460, 461.

Primarily and usually the term connotes executors or administrators, Shiya v. Erickson, 282 N.Y.S. 812, 156 Misc. 738; Thompson v. Smith, 70 App.D.C. 65, 103 F.2d 936, 938, 123 A.L.R. 76; Commissioner of Corporations and Taxation v. Second Nat. Bank of Boston, 308 Mass. 1, 30 N.E.2d 889, 894.

But it will be given a different meaning when subject-matter or context shows that words are not used in ordinary sense, In re Olney Bank & Trust Co., 116 Pa.Super. 438, 176 A. 837, 839; Long v. Montgomery, Mo.App., 22 S.W.2d 206, 209; so that it may mean an assignee in bankruptcy or insolvency, an assignee for the benefit of creditors, a receiver, an assignee of a mortgage, a grantee of land, a guardian, a purchaser at execution sale, a widow, or a surviving partner (See Miller v. Metcalf, 77 Conn. 176, 58 A. 743; Mattson v. Wagstad, 188 Wis. 566, 206 N.W. 865, 868; Oldham's Trustee v. Boston Ins. Co., 189 Ky. 844, 226 S.W. 106, 107, 16 A.L.R. 305; Miller v. Miller, 200 Iowa, 1070, 205 N.W. 870, 874, 43 A.L.R. 567; Nobles v. Nobles, 177 N.C. 243, 98 S.E. 715); children, Caudle v. Eckles, 282 Ky. 295, 138 S.W.2d 468, 469, 471; Brooks Bank & Trust Co. v. Beers, 120 Conn. 477, 181 A. 391; children and children of deceased children. In re Blazej's Estate, 23 N.Y.S.2d 388, 393, 394, 175 Misc. 283; children or issue of deceased member, Stevenson v. Wachovia Bank & Trust Co., 202 N.C. 92, 161 S.E. 728, 730; descendants, per stirpes, of deceased next of kin of equal degree with living (remote) next of kin, In re Miller's Estate, 103 N.J.Eq. 86, 141 A. 676, 677; heirs, Long v. Montgomery, Mo.App., 22 S.W.2d 206, 209; Merchants Mut. Casualty Co. v. Egan, 91 N.H. 368, 20 A.2d 480, 482, 135 A.L.R. 745; lineal descendants, Caudle v. Eckles, 282 Ky. 295, 138 S.W.2d 468, 469, 471; Brooks Bank & Trust Co. v. Beers, 120 Conn. 477, 181 A. 391; Daniels v. Daniels, 115 Conn. 239, 161 A. 94, 95; next of kin, In re Ackerman's Will, 244 N.Y.S. 632, 634, 137 Misc. 910; persons entitled to take by descent or distribution, Caudle v. Eckles, 282 Ky. 295, 138 S.W.2d 468, 469, 471; In re Ackerman's Will, 244 N.Y.S. 632, 634, 137 Misc. 910; persons who succeed to benefits of fraternal policy by operation of law, Sovereign Camp, W. O. W. v. Snider, 227

Ala. 126, 148 So. 831, 833. Testamentary trustee, who is also executor, McMullen v. Sims, Tex.Com.App., 37 S.W.2d 141, 145.

LEGAL RESCISSION. Rescission by act of parties. Aron v. Mid-Continent Co., 141 Neb. 806, 4 N.W.2d 884, 886; Gifford v. Thur, 226 Wis. 630, 276 N.W. 348, 352.

LEGAL RESERVE. Reserve which life insurance companies are required by statute to set aside and maintain. Lubin v. Equitable Life Assur. Soc. of U. S., 326 Ill.App. 358, 61 N.E.2d 753, 754; Old Surety Life Ins. Co. of Alva, Okl., v. Morrow, 195 Okl. 442, 158 P.2d 715, 717.

LEGAL RESIDENCE. Actual dweller in place notwithstanding technical domicile elsewhere has "legal residence". City of New Haven v. Town of Torrington, 132 Conn. 194, 43 A.2d 455, 458. Actual residence at a place coupled with intent to remain. Nunn v. Hamilton, 233 Ky. 663, 26 S.W. 2d 526, 530. Domicile. Phillips v. South Carolina Tax Commission, 195 S.C. 472, 12 S.E.2d 13, 15, 19.

Township, city, or village in which poor relief applicant has resided continuously for more than year or in which he has longest resided within year, Burke County v. Brusven, 62 N.D. 1, 241 N.W. 82, 85; township wherein voter's family home was located though he occasionally lodged, ate and entertained elsewhere. In re Stabile, 348 Pa. 587, 36 A.2d 451, 452.

LEGAL RIGHT. Natural rights, rights existing as result of contract, and rights created or recognized by law. Fine v. Pratt, Tex.Civ.App., 150 S. W.2d 308, 311.

Claim enforceable by legal means against person or community; well-founded claim, enforced by sanctions, or right to which state gives sanction of remedies, Louis Kamm, Inc., v. Flink, 113 N.J.L. 582, 175 A. 62, 65, 99 A.L.R. 1; interest for infringement of which law gives a remedy. Norwood v. McDonald, 142 Ohio St. 299, 52 N.E.2d 67, 72. Personal interest or claim which society is willing to enforce, Greek Catholic Congregation of Borough of Olyphant v. Plummer, 347 Pa. 351, 32 A.2d 299, 300.

LEGAL STRIKE. A peaceable walkout, the voluntary cessation of striker's employment, in which employer and those desiring to remain in employer's employ are left free to continue operation of business in lawful manner and pursuit of their lawful employment unmolested. International Ticket Co. v. Wendrich, 122 N.J.Eq. 222, 193 A. 808, 813.

LEGAL SUBDIVISIONS. Divisions of land which result from application of ordinary methods used in making of a government survey. Greenblum v. Gregory, 160 Wash. 42, 294 P. 971, 972.

LEGAL SUBROGATION. A right arising by operation of law. Goodwin v. Schmidt, 149 Fla. 85, 5 So.2d 64, 66; Federal Land Bank of Baltimore v. Joynes, 179 Va. 394, 18 S.E.2d 917, 920. Where one having liability, right, or fiduciary relation pays another's debt under circumstances equitably entitling former to rights, remedies or securities held by creditor. Federal Union Life Ins. Co. v. Deitsch, 127 Ohio St. 505, 189 N.E. 440, 442; Ragland v. Board of Missions for Freedmen of Presbyterian Church, 224 Ala. 325, 140 So. 435; Western Union Telegraph Co. v. Smith, 50 Ga.App. 585, 178 S.E. 472. Where person pays in performance of legal duty imposed by contract, statute, or rule of law or where payment is favored by public policy. Western Union Telegraph Co. v. Smith, 50 Ga.App. 585, 178 S.E. 472; where person secondarily liable pays debt and becomes subrogated to creditor's rights, Lentz v. Stoflet, 280 Mich. 446, 273 N.W. 763, 766; Where person who pay stands in situation of a surety or is compelled to pay to protect his own right or property, Martin v. Hickenlooper, 90 Utah 150, 59 P.2d 1139, 1141, 107 A.L. R. 762; Lervold v. Republic Mut. Fire Ins. Co., 142 Kan. 43, 45 P.2d 839, 842, 106 A.L.R. 673.

"Legal subrogation" is generally confined to relation of principal and surety, to cases where person is compelled to remove title superior to that held by him in order to protect his own, and to cases of insurers, American Nat. Bank of Mt. Carmel v. Holsen, 331 Ill. 622, 163 N.E. 448, 453. The right of surety, though such relation is by construction, to pay debt on which he is bound, and thereby become equitable assignee from creditor of debt, Hall v. Hall, 241 Ala. 397, 2 So.2d 908, 914.

LEGAL TITLE. One cognizable or enforceable in a court of law, or one which is complete and perfect so far as regards the apparent right of ownership and possession, but which carries no beneficial interest in the property, another person being equitably entitled thereto; in either case, the antithesis of "equitable title." Tobin v. Gartiez, 44 Nev. 179, 191 P. 1063, 1064; Union Tanning Co. v. Lowe, 148 Tenn. 407, 255 S.W. 712, 714.

It may also mean appearance of title as distinguished from complete title, Southern Carbon Co. v. State, 13 N.Y. S.2d 7, 9, 171 Misc. 566; full and absolute title or apparent right of ownership with beneficial or equitable title in another; not necessarily record title. Barnes v. Boyd, D.C.W.Va., 8 F.Supp. 584, 597.

A tax title, which is prima facie valid, is a "legal title", Murray v. Holland, 108 Ind.App. 236, 27 N.E.2d 126, 128.

LEGAL USUFRUCT. Usufructs established by operation of law are legal usufructs. Hartford Accident & Indemnity Co. v. Abdalla, 203 La. 999, 14 So.2d 815; e. g., the usufruct colated for surviving spouse in necessitous circumstances. Taylor v. Taylor, 189 La. 1084, 181 So. 543, 549.

LEGAL VOTER. A person having constitutional requirements and who is registered. Public Service Electric & Gas Co. v. City of Camden, 13 N.J. Misc. 693, 180 A. 778. A person having constitutional qualifications, though not registered. Branstetter v. Heater, 269 Ky. 844, 108 S.W.2d 1040. A person invested by law with right to vote. Wright v. Lee, 125 N.J.L. 256, 15 A.2d 610, 611. A person qualified by Constitution and laws of state to vote. Lefler v. City of Dallas, Tex.Civ.App., 177 S.W.2d 231, 235.

One having right to vote in municipality is a "legal voter" within statute concerning call of special election on adoption of municipal manager form of government, Wright v. Lee, 125 N.J.L. 256, 15 A.2d 610, 611.

LEGAL WILLFULNESS. Intentional disregard of known duty necessary to safety of person or property of another and entire absence of care for life, person or property of others. Bartolucci v. Falleti, 314 Ill.App. 551, 41 N.E.2d 777, 780.

LEGALIS HOMO. Lat. A lawful man; a person who stands *rectus in curia;* a person not outlawed, excommunicated, or infamous. It occurs in the phrase, *"probi et legalès homines,"* (good and lawful men, competent jurors,) and "legality" designates the condition of such a man. Jacob.

LEGALIS MONETA ANGLIÆ. Lawful money of England. 1 Inst. 207.

LEGALITY, or LEGALNESS. Lawfulness.

LEGALIZATION. The act of legalizing or making legal or lawful.

LEGALIZE. To make legal or lawful. Wight v. New Jersey Racing Commission, 128 N.J.L. 517, 26 A.2d 709, 712. To confirm or validate what was before void or unlawful. To add the sanction and authority of law to that which before was without or against law.

LEGALIZED NUISANCE. A structure, erection, or other thing which would constitute a nuisance at common law, but which cannot be objected to by private persons because constructed or maintained under direct and sufficient legislative authority. Such, for example, are hospitals and pest-houses maintained by cities. See Baltimore v. Fairfield Imp. Co., 87 Md. 352, 39 A. 1081, 40 L.R.A. 494, 67 Am.St.Rep. 344.

LEGALLY. Lawfully; according to law.

LEGALLY ADOPTED. Adopted in accordance with laws of state. Wooster v. Iowa State Tax Commission, 230 Iowa 797, 298 N.W. 922, 924.

LEGALLY COMMITTED. Accused has been committed by magistrate who has jurisdiction to hold examination and who has actually heard evidence and determined probable cause exists for holding defendant. People v. Dal Porto, 17 Cal.App.2d 755, 63 P.2d 1199, 1200.

LEGALLY COMPETENT. Words "legally competent" in statute prescribing qualifications of executor mean fit or qualified to act according to judicial standards essential to proper course of justice. In re Haeffele's Estate, 145 Neb. 809, 18 N.W.2d 228, 231.

LEGALLY CONSTITUTED COURT. One known to and recognized by law. American Motorists' Ins. Co. v. Central Garage, 86 N.H. 362, 169 A. 121, 124.

LEGALLY CONTRIBUTING CAUSE OF INJURY. Substantial factor in bringing about injury. Farmer v. Central Mut. Ins. Co. of Chicago, Ill., 145 Kan. 951, 67 P.2d 511, 514.

LEGALLY DETERMINED. Determined by process of law. Black Diamond S. S. Corporation v. Fidelity & Deposit Co. of Maryland, D.C.Md., 33 F.2d 767, 769.

LEGALLY LIABLE. Liable under law as interpreted by courts. Beck v. Kansas City Public Service Co., Mo.App., 48 S.W.2d 213, 215. Liability imposed by law or liability which law fixed by contract. Home Ins. Co. of New York v. Moore & Rawls, 151 Miss. 189, 117 So. 524, 526.

LEGALLY OPERATING AUTOMOBILE. As used in liability policy, means operating automobile by right or by lawful authority. Universal Automobile Ins. Co. v. Benoit, C.C.A.Ariz., 67 F.2d 52, 53; Zurich General Accident & Liability Ins. Co. v. Thompson, C.C.A.Cal., 49 F.2d 860, 861.

See, generally, Blashfield, Cyc. of Automobile Law and Prac., Perm. Ed., § 3943.

LEGALLY QUALIFIED VOTER OR ELECTOR. As used in statute pertaining to voting in state elections by members of military forces, indicates legislative intent that such members be registered as prerequisite to right to vote. In re Donahay's Contested Election, 21 N.J.Misc. 360, 34 A.2d 299, 304.

LEGALLY RESIDE. Domicile. Mitchell v. Kinney, 242 Ala. 196, 5 So.2d 788, 793.

LEGALLY SUFFICIENT EVIDENCE. Competent, pertinent evidence coming from a legal source. Sun Cab Co. v. Reustle, 172 Md. 494, 192 A. 292, 296.

Evidence is "legally sufficient to sustain finding," if supported by substantial evidence, and record as whole does not clearly, convincingly, or even, possibly, indisputably require contrary conclusion. Tracy v. Commissioner of Internal Revenue, C.C.A.6, 53 F.2d 575, 579.

LEGALLY SUFFICIENT TENDER. A tender made under circumstances that fulfill obligations assumed by vendors. Kolling v. Martin, 109 Ind. App. 184, 33 N.E.2d 808, 815.

LEGALLY USING AUTOMOBILE. Using with "right," not "using in lawful manner." Blair v. Travelers Ins. Co., 291 Mass. 432, 197 N.E. 60, 63. The phrase refers to legality of consents. Witko v. Polito, 39 N.Y.S.2d 843, 845.

See Legally Operating Automobile, *supra.*

LEGANTINE CONSTITUTIONS. The name of a code of ecclesiastical laws, enacted in national synods, held under legates from Pope Gregory IX, and Clement IV., in the reign of Henry III., about the years 1220 and 1268. 1 Bl.Comm. 83.

LEGARE. Lat. In the civil and old English law. To bequeath; to leave or give by will; to give in anticipation of death. In Scotch phrase, to *legate.*

LEGATARIUS. Lat. In the civil law. One to whom a thing is bequeathed; a legatee or legatary. Inst. 2, 20, 2, 4, 5, 10; Bract. fol. 40. In old European law. A legate, messenger, or envoy. Spelman.

LEGATARY. One to whom anything is bequeathed; a legatee. This word is sometimes, though seldom, used to designate a legate or nuncio.

LEGATEE. The person to whom a legacy is given. See Legacy. Hobbs v. Brenneman, 94 W.Va. 320, 118 S.E. 546, 549; In re Lewis' Estate, 39 Nev. 445, 159 P. 961, 962, 4 A.L.R. 241.

The term may be used, however, to denominate those who take under will without any distinction between realty and personalty. Brooker v. Brooker, Tex.Civ.App., 76 S.W.2d 180, 183.

Residuary legatee. The person to whom a testator bequeaths the residue of his personal estate, after the payment of such other legacies as are specifically mentioned in the will. Laing v. Barbour, 119 Mass. 525; Lafferty v. People's Sav. Bank, 43 N.W. 34, 76 Mich. 35.

LEGATES. Nuncios, deputies, or extraordinary ambassadors sent by the pope to be his representatives and to exercise his jurisdiction in countries where the Roman Catholic Church is established by law.

LEGATION. An embassy; a diplomatic minister and his suite; the persons commissioned by one government to exercise diplomatic functions at the court of another, including the minister, secretaries, *attachés*, interpreters, etc., are collectively styled the "legation" of their government. The word also denotes the official residence of a foreign minister.

LEGATOR. One who makes a will, and leaves legacies.

LEGATORY. The third part of a freeman's personal estate, which by the custom of London, in case he had a wife and children, the freeman might always have disposed of by will. Bac.Abr. "Customs of London," D. 4.

LEGATOS VIOLARE CONTRA JUS GENTIUM EST. 4 Coke, pref. It is contrary to the law of nations to injure ambassadors.

LEGATUM. Lat. In old English law. A legacy given to the church, or an accustomed mortuary. Cowell. In the civil law. A legacy; a gift left by a deceased person, to be executed by the heir. Inst. 2, 20, 1.

LEGATUM MORTE TESTATORIS TANTUM CONFIRMATUR, SICUT DONATIO INTER VIVOS TRADITIONE SOLA. Dyer, 143. A legacy is confirmed by the death of a testator, in the same manner as a gift from a living person is by delivery alone.

LEGATUM OPTIONIS. In Roman law. A legacy to A. B. of any article or articles that A. B. liked to choose or select out of the testator's estate.

If A. B. died after the testator, but before making the choice or selection, his representative *(hæres)* could not, prior to Justinian, make the selection for him, but the legacy failed altogether. Justinian, however, made the legacy good, and enabled the representative to chose. Brown.

LEGATUS REGIS VICE FUNGITUR A QUO DESTINATUR ET HONORANDUS EST SICUT ILLE CUJUS VICEM GERIT. 12 Coke, 17. An ambassador fills the place of the king by whom he is sent, and is to be honored as he is whose place he fills.

LEGEM. Lat. Accusative of *lex*, law. Occurring in various legal phrases, as follows:

LEGEM AMITTERE. To lose one's law; that is, to lose one's privilege of being admitted to take an oath.

LEGEM FACERE. In old English law. To make law or oath.

LEGEM FERRE. In Roman law. To propose a law to the people for their adoption. Heinecc. Ant. Rom. lib. 1, tit. 2.

LEGEM HABERE. To be capable of giving evidence upon oath. Witnesses who had been convicted of crime were incapable of giving evidence, until 6 & 7 Vict. c. 85.

LEGEM JUBERE. In Roman law. To give consent and authority to a proposed law; to make or pass it. Tayl.Civil Law, 9.

LEGEM PONE. To propound or lay down the law. By an extremely obscure derivation or analogy, this term was formerly used as a slang equivalent for payment in cash or in ready money.

LEGEM SCISCERE. To give consent and authority to a proposed law; applied to the consent of the people.

LEGEM TERRÆ AMITTENTES, PERPETUAM INFAMIÆ NOTAM INDE MERITO INCURRUNT. Those who lose the law of the land, then justly incur the ineffaceable brand of infamy. 3 Inst. 221.

LEGEM VADIARE. In old English law. To wage law; to offer or to give pledge to make defense, by oath, with compurgators.

LEGENITA. A fine for criminal conversation with a woman. Whart.Lex. See Legruita.

LEGES. Lat. Laws. At Rome, the *leges* (the decrees of the people in a strict sense) were laws which were proposed by a magistrate presiding in the senate, and adopted by the Roman people in the *comitia centuriata.* Mackeld, Rom.Law, § 31.

LEGES ANGLIÆ. The laws of England, as distinguished from the civil law and other foreign systems.

LEGES ANGLIÆ SUNT TRIPARTITÆ,—JUS COMMUNE, CONSUETUDINES, AC DECRETA COMITIORUM. The laws of England are threefold,—common law, customs, and decrees of parliament.

LEGES BARBARORUM. A class name for the codes of mediæval European law. For a list, see Jenks, 2 Sel.Essays in Anglo-Amer. Leg. Hist. 154.

LEGES EDWARDI CONFESSORIS. A name used for a legal treatise written from 1130 to 1135, which presents the law in force toward the end of Henry I. Its authority is said to be undeserved. 2 Sel. Essays in Anglo-Am. Leg. Hist. 17.

LEGES ET CONSUETUDINI REGNI. The accepted name for the common law from an early time; Green, in 9 L.Q.R. 153; since the latter half of the 12th century at least; Pollock, First Book of Jurispr. 249.

LEGES FIGENDI ET REFIGENDI CONSUETUDO EST PERICULOSISSIMA. The practice of fixing and refixing [making and remaking] the laws is a most dangerous one. 4 Coke, pref.

LEGES HENRICI. A book written between 1114 and 1118 containing Anglo-Saxon and Norman law. It is said to be an invaluable source of knowledge of the period preceding the full development of the Norman law. 2 Sel.Essays in Anglo-Am. Leg. Hist. 16.

LEGES HUMANÆ NASCUNTUR, VIVUNT, ET MORIUNTUR. Human laws are born, live, and die. 7 Coke, 25; 2 Atk. 674; 11 C.B. 767; 1 Bl. Comm. 89.

LEGES JULIÆ. Laws enacted during the reign of Augustus or of Julius Cæsar which, with the *lex abutia,* effectually abolished the *legis actiones.*

LEGES NATURÆ PERFECTISSIMÆ SUNT ET IMMUTABILES; HUMANI VERO JURIS CONDITIO SEMPER IN INFINITUM DECURRIT, ET NIHIL EST IN EO QUOD PERPETUO STARE POSSIT. LEGES HUMANÆ NASCUNTUR, VIVUNT, MORIUNTUR. The laws of nature are most perfect and immutable; but the condition of human law is an unending succession, and there is nothing in it which can continue perpetually. Human laws are born, live, and die. 7 Coke, 25.

LEGES NON SCRIPTÆ. In English law. Unwritten or customary laws, including those ancient acts of parliament which were made before time of memory. Hale, Com.Law, 5. See 1 Bl. Comm. 63, 64.

LEGES NON VERBIS, SED REBUS, SUNT IMPOSITÆ. Laws are imposed, not on words, but things. 10 Coke, 101; Branch, Princ.

LEGES POSTERIORES PRIORES CONTRARIAS ABROGANT. Later laws abrogate prior laws that are contrary to them. Broom, Max. 27, 29.

LEGES SACRATÆ. All solemn compacts between the plebeians and patricians were so called.

LEGES SCRIPTÆ. In English law. Written laws; statute laws, or acts of parliament which are originally reduced into writing before they are enacted, or receive any binding power. Hale, Com.Law, 1, 2.

LEGES SUB GRAVIORI LEGE. Laws under a weightier law. Hale, Com.Law, 46, 44.

LEGES SUUM LIGENT LATOREM. Laws should bind their own maker. Fleta, lib. 1, c. 17, § 11.

LEGES TABELLARIÆ. Roman laws regulating the mode of voting by ballot, (*tabella.*) 1 Kent, Comm. 232, note.

LEGES VIGILANTIBUS, NON DORMIENTIBUS, SUBVENIUNT. The laws aid the vigilant, not the negligent. Smith v. Carll, 5 Johns.Ch. (N.Y.) 122, 145.

LEGIBUS SOLUTUS. Lat. Released from the laws; not bound by the laws. An expression applied in the Roman civil law to the emperor. Calvin.

LEGIBUS SUMPTIS DESINENTIBUS, LEGE NATURÆ UTENDUM EST. When laws imposed by the state fail, we must act by the law of nature. 2 Rolle, 298.

LEGIOSUS. In old records. Litigious, and so subjected to a course of law. Cowell.

LEGIS CONSTRUCTIO NON FACIT INJURIAM. Co.Litt. 183. The construction of law does no injury.

LEGIS INTERPRETATIO LEGIS VIM OBTINET. Ellesm. Postn. 55. The interpretation of law obtains the force of law.

LEGIS MINISTER NON TENETUR IN EXECUTIONE OFFICII SUI, FUGERE AUT RETROCEDERE. The minister of the law is bound, in the execution of his office, not to fly nor to retreat. Branch, Princ.

LEGISLATE. To enact laws or pass resolutions. State ex rel. Nunez v. Baynard, La.App., 15 So.2d 649, 655. To make or enact a law or laws. State ex rel. Porterie v. Louisiana State Board of Education, 190 La. 565, 182 So. 676, 678.

LEGISLATION. The act of giving or enacting laws; the power to make laws; the act of legislating; preparation and enactment of laws; the making of laws by express decree. State ex rel. Yancey v. Hyde, 121 Ind. 20, 22 N.E. 644. Formulation of rule for the future. Eastern Oil Refining Co. v. Court of Burgesses of Wallingford, 130 Conn. 606, 36 A.2d 586, 589; Oklahoma City, Okl., v. Dolese, C.C.A.Okl., 48 F.2d 734, 738.

Municipal ordinances are legislation. Doyle v. City of St. Paul, 206 Minn. 542, 289 N.W. 785, 788.

LEGISLATIVE. Actions which relate to subjects of permanent or general character are "legislative". Keigley v. Bench, 97 Utah, 69, 89 P.2d 480, 484, 485, 122 A.L.R. 756. Making or having the power to make a law or laws. State ex rel. Porterie v. Louisiana State Board of Education, 190 La. 565, 182 So. 676, 678. Making or giving laws; pertaining to the function of law-making or to the process of enactment of laws. See Evansville v. State, 118 Ind. 426, 21 N.E. 267, 4 L.R.A. 93.

LEGISLATIVE ACT. Enactment of laws. In re Manufacturer's Freight Forwarding Co., 294 Mich. 57, 292 N.W. 678, 680. One which prescribes a general rule of conduct. Stevens ex rel. Kuberski v. Haussermann, 113 N.J.Law 162, 172 A. 738, 741. One which prescribes what the law shall be in future cases arising under it. Nider v. Homan, 32 Cal.App.2d 11, 89 P.2d 136, 139; Mabray v. School Board of Carroll County, 162 Miss. 632, 137 So. 105, 106.

LEGISLATIVE COURTS. Courts created by Legislature not named or described by Constitution. Gorham v. Robinson, 57 R.I. 1. 186 A. 832.

Courts exercising judicial power created by Congress under constitutional authority to provide for government and administration of territories and tribunals created by Congress under general legislative power to perform administrative, or quasi judicial, functions. Gorham v. Robinson, 57 R.I. 1, 186 A. 832, 849, 850.

Court of Claims, Manion v. State, 303 Mich. 1, 5 N.W. 2d 527, 529; United States v. Sherwood, 61 S.Ct. 767, 770, 312 U.S. 584, 85 L.Ed. 1058; Court of Customs and Patent Appeals, Bland v. Commissioner of Internal Revenue, C.C. A.7, 102 F.2d 157, 159; Territorial courts; State ex rel. Ralston v. Turner, 141 Neb. 556, 4 N.W.2d 302, 306. O'Donoghue v. U. S., Ct.Cl., 53 S.Ct. 740, 289 U.S. 516, 77 L.Ed. 1356; United States Court for China, Casement v. Squier, D.C.Wash., 46 F.Supp. 296, 297.

LEGISLATIVE DEPARTMENT. That department of government whose appropriate function is the making or enactment of laws, as distinguished from the judicial department, which interprets and applies the laws, and the executive department, which carries them into execution and effect. See In re Davies, 168 N.Y. 89, 61 N.E. 118, 56 L.R.A. 855.

LEGISLATIVE EXPENSES. Distinction between "legislative expenses" and "personal expenses" is that legislative expenses are those that are necessary to enable the Legislature to properly perform its functions, while those that are personal are those that must be incurred by a member of the Legislature in order to be present at the place of meeting, expenses for his personal comfort and convenience, which have nothing to do with the performance of his duty as a member of the Legislature. Personal expenses are those incurred for rooms, meals, laundry, communications with their homes, and other things of like character. Scroggie v. Scarborough, 162 S.C. 218, 160 S.E. 596, 600.

LEGISLATIVE FUNCTION. The determination of legislative policy and its formulation as rule of conduct. Yakus v. United States, Mass., 64 S. Ct. 660, 667, 321 U.S. 414, 88 L.Ed. 834. The formation and determination of future rights and duties. Dal Maso v. Board of Com'rs of Prince George's County, 182 Md. 200, 34 A.2d 464, 466.

LEGISLATIVE OFFICER. A member of the legislative body or department of a state or municipal corporation. See Prosecuting Attorney v. Judge of Recorder's Court, 59 Mich. 529, 26 N.W. 694. One of those whose duties relate mainly to the enactment of laws, such as members of congress and of the several state legislatures.

These officers are confined in their duties by the constitution generally to make laws, though sometimes, in cases of impeachment, one of the houses of the legislature exercises judicial functions somewhat similar to those of a grand jury, by presenting to the other articles of impeachment, and the other house acts as a court in trying such impeachment.

LEGISLATIVE POWER. The lawmaking power; the department of government whose function is the framing and enactment of laws. Evansville v. State, 118 Ind. 426, 21 N.E. 267, 4 L.R.A. 93. Brown v. Galveston, 97 Tex. 1, 75 S.W. 495; O'Neil v. American F. Ins. Co., 166 Pa. 72, 30 A. 943, 26 L.R.A. 715, 45 Am.St.Rep. 650.

Authority to make, alter, amend, and repeal laws, Harsha v. City of Detroit, 261 Mich. 586, 246 N.W. 849, 850, 90 A.L.R. 853; Gregory v. Cockrell, 179 Ark. 719, 18 S.W.2d 362; authority to pass rules of law for government and regulation of people or property, Reif v. Barrett, 355 Ill. 104, 188 N.E. 889, 901; Schneberger v. State Board of Social Welfare, 228 Iowa 399, 291 N.W. 859, 861; power to declare what law shall be, Gorham v. Robinson, 57 R.I. 1, 186 A. 832, 842.

Power of home-rule city to fix its boundaries and to annex territory is a "legislative power". City of Houston v. State ex rel. City of West University Place, 142 Tex. 190, 176 S.W.2d 928, 931.

LEGISLATOR. One who makes laws; a member of a legislative body.

LEGISLATORUM EST VIVA VOX, REBUS ET NON VERBIS LEGEM IMPONERE. The voice of legislators is a living voice, to impose laws on things, and not on words. 10 Coke, 101.

LEGISLATURE. The department, assembly, or body of men that makes laws for a state or nation.

Body to declare public policy of state and to ordain changes therein, Commonwealth v. Hall, 291 Pa. 341, 140 A. 626, 630, 58 A.L.R. 1023; lawmaking body of state, Ex parte Hague, 105 N.J.Eq. 134, 147 A. 220, 221; legislative or lawmaking power including Governor, Koenig v. Flynn, 234 App.Div. 139, 254 N.Y.S. 339, 342; political body of persons organized for purpose of making laws and acting in official capacity, State ex rel. Carroll v. Becker, 329 Mo. 501, 45 S.W.2d 533, 536.

LEGISPERITUS. Lat. A person skilled or learned in the law; a lawyer or advocate. Feud. lib. 2, tit. 1.

LEGIT VEL NON? In old English practice, this was the formal question propounded to the ordinary when a prisoner claimed the benefit of clergy,—does he read or not? If the ordinary found that the prisoner was entitled to clergy, his formal answer was, *"Legit ut clericus,"* he reads like a clerk.

LEGITIM. In Scotch law. The children's share in the father's movables.

LEGITIMACY. Lawful birth; the condition of being born in wedlock; the opposite of illegitimacy or bastardy. Davenport v. Caldwell, 10 S.C. 337; Pratt v. Pratt, 5 Mo.App. 541.

LEGITIMATE, *v.* To make lawful; to confer legitimacy; to place a child born before marriage on the footing of those born in lawful wedlock. McKamie v. Baskerville, 86 Tenn. 459, 7 S.W. 194; Blythe v. Ayres, 96 Cal. 532, 31 P. 915, 19 L.R.A. 40.

LEGITIMATE, *adj.* That which is lawful, legal, recognized by law, or according to law; as legitimate children, legitimate authority, lawful power, legitimate sport or amusement. People v. Commons, 64 Cal.App.2d Supp. 925, 148 P.2d 724, 731. Real or genuine. United States v. Schenck, C.C.A. N.Y., 126 F.2d 702, 705, 707.

LEGITIMATION. The making legitimate or lawful that which was not originally so; especially the act of legalizing the *status* of a bastard.

LEGITIMATION PER SUBSEQUENS MATRIMONIUM. The legitimation of a bastard by the subsequent marriage of his parents. Bell.

LEGITIME. Lat. In the civil law. That portion of a parent's estate of which he cannot disinherit his children without a legal cause. That interest in a succession of which forced heirs may not be deprived. Alexander v. Gray, La.App., 181 So. 639, 643. Bauman v. Pennywell, 160 La. 555, 107 So. 425, 427. It may also apply to father or mother. Succession of Greenlaw, 148 La. 255, 86 So. 786, 791.

LEGITIME IMPERANTI PARERE NECESSE EST. Jenk. Cent. 120. One lawfully commanding must be obeyed.

LEGITIMI HÆREDES. Lat. In Roman law. Legitimate heirs; the agnate relations of the estate-leaver; so called because the inheritance was given to them by a law of the Twelve Tables.

LEGITIMUS. Lawful; legitimate. *Legitimus hæres et filius est quem nuptiæ demonstrant,* a lawful son and heir is he whom the marriage points out to be lawful. Bract. fol. 63.

LEGO. Lat. In Roman law. I bequeath. A common term in wills. Dig. 30, 36, 81, et seq.

LEGRUITA. In old records. A fine for criminal conversation with a woman. See Legenita.

LEGULEIUS. A person skilled in law, (*in legibus versatus;*) one versed in the forms of law. Calvin.

LEHURECHT. The German feudal law. 1 Poll. & Maitl. 214.

LEIDGRAVE. An officer under the Saxon government, who had jurisdiction over a lath. Enc. Lond. See Lath.

LEIPA. In old English law. A fugitive or runaway.

LEND. To put out for hire or compensation. In re Lalla's Estate, 362 Ill. 621, 1 N.E.2d 50, 53. To part with a thing of value to another for a time fixed or indefinite, yet to have some time in ending, to be used or enjoyed by that other, the thing itself or the equivalent of it to be given back at the time fixed, or when lawfully asked for, with or without compensation for the use as may be agreed upon. Kent v. Quicksilver Min. Co., 78 N. Y. 177. Term "lend" when used in a will means to "give" or "devise." Alexander v. Alexander, 210 N.C. 281, 186 S.E. 319; Allen v. Hewitt, 212 N.C. 367, 193 S.E. 275, 276.

LENDER. He from whom a thing is borrowed. The bailor of an article loaned.

LENDING OR LOANING MONEY OR CREDIT. Transactions creating customary relation of borrower and lender, in which money is borrowed for fixed time on borrower's promise to repay amount borrowed at stated time in future with interest at fixed rate. Bannock County v. Citizens' Bank & Trust Co., 53 Idaho 159, 22 P.2d 674.

LENT. In ecclesiastical law. The quadragesimal fast; a time of abstinence; the time from Ash-Wednesday to Easter.

LEOD. People; a people; a nation. Spelman.

LEODES. In old European law. A vassal, or leige man; service; a *were* or *weregild.* Spelman.

LEOHT-GESCEOT. A tax for supplying the church with lights. Anc.Inst.Eng.

LEONINA SOCIETAS. Lat. An attempted partnership, in which one party was to bear all the losses, and have no share in the profits. This was a void partnership in Roman law; and, apparently, it would also be void as a partnership in English law, as being inherently inconsistent with the notion of partnership. (Dig. 17, 2, 29, 2.) Brown.

LEP AND LACE. A custom in the manor of Writtle, in Essex, that every cart which goes over Greenbury within that manor (except it be the cart of a nobleman) shall pay 4d. to the lord. Blount.

LEPORARIUS. A greyhound. Cowell.

LEPORIUM. A place where hares are kept. Mon.Angl. t. 2, p. 1035.

LEPROSO AMOVENDO. An ancient writ that lay to remove a leper or lazar, who thrust himself into the company of his neighbors in any parish, either in the church or at other public meetings, to their annoyance. Reg.Orig. 237.

LEPROSUS. L. Lat. A leper.

LESCHEWES. Trees fallen by chance or windfalls. Brooke, Abr. 341.

LESE MAJESTY. The old English and Scotch translation of "*læsa majestas,*" or high treason. 2 Reeve, Eng.Law, 6. See Leze Majesty.

LES FICTIONS NAISSENT DE LA LOI, ET NON LA LOI DES FICTIONS. Fictions arise from the law, and not law from fictions.

LES LOIS NE SE CHARGENT DE PUNIR QUE LES ACTIONS EXTERIEURES. Laws do not undertake to punish other than outward actions. Montes. Esp. Lois, b. 12, c. 11; Broom, Max. 311.

LESING or LEASING. Gleaning.

LESION. Damage; injury; detriment. Gasperino v. Prudential Ins. Co. of America, Mo.App., 107 S.W.2d 819, 827; Kelham. Hurt, loss, or injury, Gasperino v. Prudential Ins. Co. of America, Mo. App., 107 S.W.2d 819, 827; Warbende v. Prudential Ins. Co. of America, C.C.A.Ill., 97 F.2d 749, 753, 117 A.L.R. 760; Order of United Commercial Travelers of America v. Sevier, C.C.A.Mo., 121 F.2d 650, 654. Any change in the structure of an organ due to injury or disease, whether apparent or diagnosed as the cause of a functional irregularity or disturbance. People v. Durand, 307 Ill. 611, 139 N.E. 78, 83. Morbid change in structure of organs or parts, Order of United Commercial Travelers of America v. Sevier, C.C.A.Mo., 121 F.2d 650, 654; Andrzejewski v. Prudential Ins. Co. of America, 321 Pa. 543, 184 A. 51, 53; Warbende v. Prudential Ins. Co. of America, C.C.A.Ill., 97 F.2d 749, 753, 117 A.L.R. 760. A term of the Scotch Law.

In the Civil law. The injury suffered by one who does not receive a full equivalent for what he gives in a commutative contract. Civil Code La. art. 1860. Inequality in contracts. Poth. Obl., no. 33; Fleming v. Irion, 132 La. 163, 61 So. 151, 152.

LESPEGEND. An inferior officer in forests to take care of the vert and venison therein, etc. Wharton.

LESSA. A legacy. Mon. Ang., t. 1, p. 562.

LESSEE. He to whom a lease is made. He who holds an estate by virtue of a lease. Viterbo v. Friedlander, 7 S.Ct. 962, 120 U.S. 707, 30 L.Ed. 776; Lang v. Hitt, 149 Ga. 667, 101 S.E. 795, 796; Dutton v. Dutton, 253 P. 553, 554, 122 Kan. 640; Boston Fish Market Corp. v. City of Boston, 224 Mass. 31, 112 N.E. 616, 617, one who has been given possession of land which is exclusive even of the landlord, except as the lease permits his entry, and except right to enter to demand rent or to make repairs. Seabloom v. Krier, 219 Minn. 362, 18 N.W.2d 88, 91.

LESSER OFFENSE. Though the term is used as synonymous with a "less serious offense" or a "minor offense" when one is considering quality of criminal act or severity of penalty imposed, such term as used in statute providing that defendant charged with one of offenses enumerated cannot be convicted or sentenced for lesser offense, means any offense necessarily included in offense charged, where offense charged is one of offenses defined in act. Witt v. State, 205 Ind. 499, 185 N.E. 645, 647.

LESSOR. He who grants a lease. Viterbo v. Friedlander, 7 S.Ct. 962, 120 U.S. 707, 30 L.Ed. 776; Dutton v. Dutton, 122 Kan. 640, 253 P. 553, 554.

One who has leased land for a definite or indefinite period, by a written or parol lease, irrespective of whether a statute of fraud requires the lease to be in writing. City of Tyler v. Ingram, 139 Tex. 600, 164 S.W.2d 516, 520. When a lessee subleases the res, he becomes "lessor" for purposes of sublease. Magnolia Petroleum Co. v. Carter, La.App., 2 So.2d 680, 682.

LESSOR OF THE PLAINTIFF. In the action of ejectment, this was the party who really and in effect prosecuted the action and was interested in its result.

The reason of his having been so called arose from the circumstance of the action having been carried on in the name of a nominal plaintiff, (John Doe,) to whom the real plaintiff had granted a fictitious lease, and thus had become his lessor.

LEST. Fr. In French maritime law. Ballast. Ord. Mar. liv. 4, tit. 4, art. 1.

LESTAGE, LASTAGE. A custom for carrying things in fairs and markets. Fleta, l. 1, c. 47; Termes de la Ley.

LESTAGEFRY. Lestage free, or exempt from the duty of paying ballast money. Cowell.

LESTAGIUM. Lastage or lestage; a duty laid on the cargo of a ship. Cowell.

LESWES. Pastures. Domesday; Co. Litt. 4*b*. A term often inserted in old deeds and conveyances. Cowell.

LET, *v.*

In contracts. To award to one of several persons, who have submitted proposals therefor, the contract for erecting public works or doing some part of the work connected therewith, or rendering some other service to government for a stipulated compensation.

Letting the contract is the choosing one from among the number of bidders, and the formal making of the contract with him. The letting, or putting out, is a different thing from the invitation to make proposals; the letting is subsequent to the invitation. It is the act of awarding the contract to the proposer, after the proposals have been received and considered. See Eppes v. Railroad Co., 35 Ala. 33, 55.

In conveyancing. To demise or lease. "To *let* and set" is an old expression.

In judicial orders and decrees. The word "let" (in the imperative) imports a positive direction or command.

Thus the phrase "let the writ issue as prayed" is equivalent to "it is hereby ordered that the writ issue," etc. See Ingram v. Laroussini, 50 La.Ann. 69, 23 So. 498.

In Practice. To deliver. "To *let* to bail" is to deliver to bail on arrest.

LET, *n.* In old conveyancing. Hindrance; obstruction; interruption. Still occasionally used in the phrase "without any *let,* suit, trouble," etc. Gustafson v. Ursales, 3 Ohio App. 136, 139.

LET IN. In practice. To admit a party as a matter of favor; as to open a judgment and "let the defendant in" to a defense.

LETHAL. Deadly, mortal, fatal. Vaughn v. Kansas City Gas Co., 236 Mo.App. 669, 159 S.W.2d 690, 698.

LETHAL WEAPON. In Scotch law. A deadly weapon. See State v. Godfrey, 17 Or. 300, 20 P. 625, 11 Am.St.Rep. 830.

LETRADO. In Spanish law. An advocate. White, New Recop. b. 1, tit. 1, c. 1, § 3, note.

LETTER. One of the arbitrary marks or characters constituting the alphabet, and used in written language as the representatives of sounds or articulations of the human organs of speech.

A dispatch or epistle; a written or printed message; a communication in writing from one person to another at a distance. Buchwald v. Buchwald, 199 A. 795, 799, 175 Md. 103.

In the imperial law of Rome, "letter" or "epistle" was the name of the answer returned by the emperor to a question of law submitted to him by the magistrates.

A communication inclosed, sealed, and stamped and being carried as first-class mail. Hyney v. U. S., C.C.A.Mich., 44 F.2d 134, 136; Wolpa v. U. S., C.C.A.Neb., 86 F.2d 35, 39.

A commission, patent, or written instrument containing or attesting the grant of some power, authority, or right.

The word appears in this generic sense in many compound phrases known to commercial law and jurisprudence; *e. g.*, letter of attorney, letter missive, letter of credit, letters patent. The plural is frequently used.

Metaphorically, the verbal expression; the strict literal meaning.

The *letter* of a statute, as distinguished from its *spirit*, means the strict and exact force of the language employed, as distinguished from the general purpose and policy of the law.

He who, being the owner of a thing, lets it out to another for hire or compensation. Story, Bailm. § 369.

As to letters of "Administration," "Advice," "Attorney," "Credit," "Horning," "Recommendation," see those titles. As to "Letters Patent," see Patent.

LETTER-BOOK. A book in which a merchant or trader keeps copies of letters sent by him to his correspondents.

LETTER-CARRIER. An employé of the post-office, whose duty it is to carry letters from the post-office to the persons to whom they are addressed.

LETTER MISSIVE. In English law. A letter from the king or queen to a dean and chapter, containing the name of the person whom he would have them elect as bishop. 1 Steph.Comm. 666. A request addressed to a peer, peeress, or lord of parliament against whom a bill has been filed desiring the defendant to appear and answer to the bill. In civil-law practice. The phrase "letters missive," or "letters dimissory," is sometimes used to denote the papers sent up on an appeal by the judge or court below to the superior tribunal, otherwise called the "apostles," (*q. v.*).

LETTER OF ADVOCATION. In Scotch law. The process or warrant by which, on appeal to the supreme court or court of session, that tribunal assumes to itself jurisdiction of the cause, and discharges the lower court from all further proceedings in the action. Ersk. Inst. 732.

LETTER OF CREDENCE. In international law. The document which accredits an ambassador, minister, or envoy to the court or government to which he is sent; *i. e.*, certifies to his appointment and qualification, and bespeaks credit for his official actions and representations.

LETTER OF EXCHANGE. A bill of exchange (*q. v.*).

LETTER OF LICENSE. In English law, a written instrument in the nature of an agreement, signed by all the creditors of a failing or embarrassed debtor in trade, granting him an extension of time for the payment of the debts, allowing him in the meantime to carry on the business in the hope of recuperation, and protecting him from arrest, suit, or other interference pending the agreement.

This form is not usual in America; but something similar to it is found in the "composition" or "extension agreement," by which all the creditors agree to fund their claims in the form of promissory notes, concurrent as to date and maturity, sometimes payable serially and sometimes extending over a term of years. Provision is often made for the supervision or partial control of the business, in the meantime, by a trustee or a committee of the creditors, in which case the agreement is sometimes called a "deed of inspectorship," though this term is more commonly used in England than in the United States.

LETTER OF MARQUE. A commission given to a private ship by a government to make reprisals on the ships of another state; hence, also, the ship thus commissioned. U. S. v. The Ambrose Light, D.C.N.Y., 25 F. 408; Gibbons v. Livingston, 6 N.J.Law, 255.

LETTER OF RECALL. A document addressed by the executive of one nation to that of another, informing the latter that a minister sent by the former has been recalled.

LETTER OF RECREDENTIALS. A document embodying the formal action of a government upon a letter of recall of a foreign minister. It, in effect, accredits him back to his own government. It is addressed to the latter government, and is delivered to the minister by the diplomatic secretary of the state from which he is recalled.

LETTERS AD COLLIGENDUM BONA DEFUNCTI. In Practice. In default of the representatives and creditors to administer to the estate of an intestate, the officer entitled to grant letters of administration may grant to such person as he approves, *letters to collect the goods of the deceased*, which neither make him executor nor administrator; his only business being to collect the goods and keep them in his safe custody. 2 Bla.Com. 505.

LETTERS CLOSE. In English law. Close letters are grants of the king, and, being of private concern, they are thus distinguished from letters patent.

LETTERS OF ABSOLUTION. Absolvatory letters, used in former times, when an abbot released any of his brethren *ab omnia subjectione et obedientia*, etc., and made them capable of entering into some other order of religion. Jacob.

LETTERS OF CORRESPONDENCE. In Scotch law. Letters are admissible in evidence against the panel, *i. e.*, the prisoner at the bar, in criminal trials. A letter written by the panel is evidence against him; not so one from a third party found in his possession. Bell.

LETTERS OF FIRE AND SWORD. See Fire and Sword.

LETTERS OF GUARDIANSHIP. A commission placing ward's property in the care of officer of court as custodian. Walker v. Graves, 174 Tenn. 336, 125 S.W.2d 154, 157.

LETTERS OF REQUEST. A formal instrument by which an inferior judge of ecclesiastical jurisdiction requests the judge of a superior court to take and determine any matter which has come before him, thereby waiving or remitting his own jurisdiction. This is a mode of beginning a suit originally in the court of arches, instead of the consistory court.

LETTERS OF SAFE CONDUCT. No subject of a nation at war with England can, by the law of nations, come into the realm, nor can travel himself upon the high seas, or send his goods and merchandise from one place to another, without danger of being seized, unless he has *letters of safe conduct.*

By divers old statutes these must be granted under the great seal, and enrolled in chancery, or else are of no effect; the sovereign being the best judge of such emergencies as may deserve exemption from the general law of arms. But passports or licenses from the ambassadors abroad are now more usually obtained, and are allowed to be of equal validity. Wharton.

LETTERS OF SLAINS, OR SLANES. Letters subscribed by the relatives of a person who had been slain, declaring that they had received an assythment, and concurring in an application to the crown for a pardon to the offender. These or other evidences of their concurrence were necessary to found the application. Bell.

LETTERS ROGATORY. A request by one court of another court in an independent jurisdiction, that a witness be examined upon interrogatories sent with the request. Magdanz v. District Court in and for Woodbury County, 222 Iowa 456, 269 N.W. 498, 499, 108 A.L.R. 377. The medium whereby one country, speaking through one of its courts, requests another country, acting through its own courts and by methods of court procedure peculiar thereto and entirely within the latter's control, to assist the administration of justice in the former country. The Signe, D.C.La., 37 F.Supp. 819, 820.

A formal communication in writing, sent by a court in which an action is pending to a court or judge of a foreign country, requesting that the testimony of a witness resident within the jurisdiction of the latter court may be there formally taken under its direction and transmitted to the first court for use in the pending action.

This process was also in use, at an early period, between the several states of the Union. The request rests entirely upon the comity of courts towards each other. See Union Square Bank v. Reichmann, 41 N.Y.S. 602, 9 App.Div. 596.

LETTERS TESTAMENTARY. The formal instrument of authority and appointment given to an executor by the proper court, empowering him to enter upon the discharge of his office as executor. It corresponds to letters of administration granted to an administrator.

LETTING. Leasing. City and County of San Francisco v. United States, C.C.A.Cal., 106 F.2d 569, 576.

LETTING OUT. The act of awarding a contract; *e. g.*, a construction contract, or contract for carrying the mails.

LETTRE. Fr. In French law. A letter. It is used, like our English "letter," for a formal instrument giving authority.

LETTRES DE CACHET. Letters issued and signed by the kings of France, and countersigned by a secretary of state, authorizing the imprisonment of a person.

Under them, persons were imprisoned for life or for a long period on the most frivolous pretexts, for the gratification of private pique or revenge, and without any reason being assigned for such punishment. They were also granted by the king for the purpose of shielding his favorites or their friends from the consequences of their crimes; and thus were as pernicious in their operation as the protection afforded by the church to criminals in a former age. Abolished during the Revolution of 1789. Wharton.

LEUCA.

In old French law. A league, consisting of fifteen hundred paces. Spelman.

In old English law. A league or mile of a thousand paces. Domesday; Spelman. A privileged space around a monastery of a league or mile in circuit. Spelman.

LEVANDÆ NAVIS CAUSA. Lat. For the sake of lightening the ship; denotes a purpose of throwing overboard goods, which renders them subjects of general average.

LEVANT ET COUCHANT. L. Fr. Rising up and lying down.

A term applied to trespassing cattle which have remained long enough upon land to have lain down to rest and risen up to fed; generally the space of a night and a day, or, at least, one night.

LEVANTES ET CUBANTES. Rising up and lying down. A term applied to cattle. 3 Bl.Comm. 9. The Latin equivalent of "*levant et couchant.*"

LEVARI FACIAS. Lat. A writ of execution directing the sheriff to cause to be made of the lands and chattels of the judgment debtor the sum recovered by the judgment. Pentland v. Kelly, 6 Watts & S. (Pa.) 484.

Also a writ to the bishop of the diocese, commanding him to enter into the benefice of a judgment debtor, and take and sequester the same into his possession, and hold the same until he shall have levied the amount of the judgment out of the rents, tithes, and profits thereof.

LEVARI FACIAS DAMNA DE DISSEISITORIBUS. A writ formerly directed to the sheriff for the levying of damages, which a disseisor had been condemned to pay to the disseisee. Cowell.

LEVARI FACIAS QUANDO VICECOMES RETURNAVIT QUOD NON HABUIT EMPTORES. An old writ commanding the sheriff to sell the goods of a debtor which he had already taken, and had returned that he could not sell them; and as much more of the debtor's goods as would satisfy the whole debt. Cowell.

LEVARI FACIAS RESIDUUM DEBITI. An old writ directed to the sheriff for levying the remnant of a partly-satisfied debt upon the lands and tenements or chattels of the debtor. Cowell.

LEVATO VELO. Lat. An expression used in the Roman law, and applied to the trial of wreck and salvage. Commentators disagree about the origin of the expression; but all agree that its general meaning is that these causes shall be heard summarily.

The most probable solution is that it refers to the place where causes were heard. A sail was spread before the door and officers employed to keep strangers from the tribunal. When these causes were heard, this sail was raised, and suitors came directly to the court, and their causes were heard immediately. As applied to maritime courts, its meaning is that causes should be heard without delay. These causes require dispatch, and a delay amounts practically to a denial of justice. (See Cod. 11, 4, 5.) Bouvier.

LEVEE. An embankment or artificial mound of earth constructed along the margin of a river, to confine the stream to its natural channel or prevent inundation or overflow. State v. New Orleans & N. E. R. Co., 7 So. 226, 42 La.Ann. 138; Royse v. Evansville & T. H. R. Co., 67 N.E. 446, 160 Ind. 592.

Also (probably by an extension of the foregoing meaning) a landing place on a river or lake; a place on a river or other navigable water for lading and unlading goods and for the reception and discharge of passengers to and from vessels lying in the contiguous waters, which may be either a wharf or pier or the natural bank. See Coffin v. Portland, C.C.Or., 27 F. 415; People v. Allen, 317 Ill. 92, 147 N.E. 479, 481.

LEVEE DISTRICT. A municipal subdivision of a state (which may or may not be a public corporation) organized for the purpose, and charged with the duty, of constructing and maintaining such levees within its territorial limits as are to be built and kept up at public expense and for the general public benefit. See People v. Levee Dist. No. 6, 131 Cal. 30, 63 P. 676.

LEVEL RATE, LEGAL RESERVE POLICY. Insurance which seeks to build up a reserve which will equal face value of policy at the end of insured's life. Helmer v. Equitable Reserve Ass'n, 214 Wis. 270, 252 N.W. 728.

LEVEL ROAD. Road with uniform grade, regardless of whether it is horizontal, up grade, or down grade. O'Rourke v. City of Washington, 304 Pa. 78, 155 A. 100, 102, 78 A.L.R. 811.

LEVIABLE. That which may be levied. That which is a proper or permissible subject for a levy; as, a "leviable interest" in land. See Bray v. Ragsdale, 53 Mo. 172.

LEVIR. In Roman law. A husband's brother; a wife's brother-in-law. Calvin.

LEVIS. Lat. Light; slight; trifling. *Levis culpa,* slight fault or neglect. *Levissima culpa,* the slightest neglect. *Levis nota,* a slight mark or brand. See Brand v. Schenectady & T. R. Co., 8 Barb. (N.Y.) 378.

LEVITICAL DEGREES. Degrees of kindred within which persons are prohibited to marry. They are set forth in the eighteenth chapter of Leviticus.

LEVITY. A term used in connection with collusion in a Pennsylvania divorce act. Lyon v. Lyon, 30 Pa.C.C. 359. See Collusion.

LEVY, *v.* To assess; raise; execute; exact; collect; gather; take up; seize. Thus, to levy (assess, exact, raise, or collect) a tax; to levy (raise or set up) a nuisance; to levy (acknowledge) a fine; to levy (inaugurate) war; to levy an execution, *i. e.,* to levy or collect a sum of money on an execution.

LEVY, *n.* A seizure. Farris v. Castor, 186 Okl. 668, 99 P.2d 900, 902; McBrien v. Harris, 39 Ga. App. 41, 145 S.E. 919; Radford v. Kachman, 27 Ohio App. 86, 160 N.E. 875, 877; Plaxico v. Webster, 175 S.C. 69, 178 S.E. 270. An actual making the money out of the property; the obtaining of money by seizure and sale of property. Farris v. Castor, 99 P.2d 900, 902, 186 Okl. 668. The mental act of determination to sell. Parker v. MacCue, 54 R.I. 270, 172 A. 725, 727. The raising of the money for which an execution has been issued. Plaxico v. Webster, 175 S.C. 69, 178 S.E. 270.

As used in Uniform Conditional Sales Act, "levy of execution" means the setting aside of specific property from the general property of the debtor and placing it in the custody of the law until it can be sold and applied to the payment of the execution. Bent v. H. W. Weaver, Inc., 106 W.Va. 164, 145 S.E. 594, 595.

In reference to taxation, the word may mean the legislative function and declaration of the subject and rate or amount of taxation, People v. Mahoney, 13 Cal.2d 729, 91 P.2d 1029; Atlantic Coast Line R. Co. v. Amos, 94 Fla. 588, 115 So. 315, 320; City of Richmond v. Eubank, 179 Va. 70, 18 S.E.2d 397, 403; or the rate of taxation rather than the physical act of applying the rate to the property, Lowden v. Texas County Excise Board, 187 Okl. 365, 103 P.2d 98, 100; or the formal order, by proper authority declaring property subject to taxation at fixed rate at its assessed valuation, State v. Davis, 335 Mo. 159, 73 S.W.2d 406, 407; or the ministerial function of assessing, listing and extending taxes, City of Plankinton v. Kieffer, 70 S.D. 329, 17 N.W.2d 494, 495, 496; or the extension of the tax, Syracuse Trust Co. v. Board of Sup'rs of Oneida County, 13 N.Y.S. 2d 390, 394; People ex rel. Oswego Falls Corporation v. Foster, 295 N.Y.S. 891, 895, 251 App.Div. 65; Day v. Inland Steel Co., 185 Minn. 53, 239 N.W. 776, 777; or the doing of whatever is necessary in order to authorize the collector to collect the tax, Syracuse Trust Co. v. Board of Sup'rs of Oneida County, 13 N.Y.S.2d 390, 394. The qualified electors "levy" a tax when they vote to impose it. Parker v. MacCue, 54 R.I. 270, 172 A. 725, 727.

Equitable levy. The lien in equity created by the filing of a creditors' bill to subject real property of the debtor, and of a lis pendens, is sometimes so called. Miller v. Sherry, 2 Wall. 249, 17 L.Ed. 827; Mandeville v. Campbell, 61 N.Y.S. 443, 45 App.Div. 512. The right to an equitable lien is sometimes called an "equitable levy." Hudson v. Wood, C.C.Ky., 119 F. 764, 776, 777.

LEVY COURT. A court formerly existing in the District of Columbia.

It was a body charged with the administration of the ministerial and financial duties of Washington county. It was charged with the duty of laying out and repairing roads, building bridges, providing poor-houses, laying and collecting the taxes necessary to enable it to discharge these and other duties, and to pay the other expenses of the county. It had capacity to make contracts in reference to any of these matters, and to raise money to meet such contracts. It had perpetual succession, and its functions were those which, in the several states, are performed by "county commissioners," "overseers of the poor," "county supervisors," and similar bodies with other designations. Levy Court v. Coroner, 2 Wall. 507, 17 L.Ed. 851.

In Delaware, the "levy court" is an administrative board.

The board is elected and organized in each county, composed of from five to thirteen "commissioners," who, in respect to taxation, perform the functions of a board of equalization and review and also of a board to supervise the assessors and collectors and audit and adjust their accounts, and who also have certain powers and special duties in respect to the administration of the poor laws, the system of public roads and the officers in charge of them, the care of insane paupers and convicts, the government and administration of jails, school districts, and various other matters of local concern. See Rev.St.Del. 1893, c. 8; Mealey v. Buckingham, 22 A. 357, 6 Del.Ch. 356.

LEVYING WAR. In criminal law. The assembling of a body of men for the purpose of effecting by force a treasonable object; and all who perform any part, however minute, or however remote from the scene of action, and who are leagued in the general conspiracy, are considered as engaged in levying war, within the meaning of the constitution. Const. art. 3, § 3; Ex parte Bollman, 4 Cranch, 75, 2 L.Ed. 554.

The words include forcible opposition, as the result of a combination of individuals, to the execution of any public law of the United States; and to constitute treason within the Federal Constitution, there must be a combination of individuals united for the common purpose of forcibly preventing the execution of some public law and the actual or threatened use of force by the combination to prevent its execution. Kegerreis v. Van Zile, 167 N.Y.S. 874, 876, 180 App.Div. 414.

LEWD. Obscene. People on Complaint of Sumner, v. Dial Press, Mag.Ct., 48 N.Y.S.2d 480, 481. Lustful, indecent, lascivious, lecherous. City of Shreveport v. Wilson, 145 La. 906, 83 So. 186, 188. The term imports a lascivious intent. It signifies that form of immorality which has relation to moral impurity. United States v. Barlow, D.C.Utah, 56 F.Supp. 795, 796, 797, or that carried on in a wanton manner. State v. Barnes, Mo.App., 256 S.W. 496, 498; Rebhuhn v. Cahill, D.C.N.Y., 31 F.Supp. 47, 49. Lewd and lascivious behavior of wife to authorize a divorce must be such conduct as proves the wife unchaste. Blackburn v. Blackburn, 294 Ky. 312, 171 S.W.2d 457.

LEWD AND LASCIVIOUS COHABITATION. Within statutes, the living together of a man and woman not married to each other, in the same house or apartment, as husband and wife. State v. Bridgeman, 88 W.Va. 231, 106 S.E. 708, 711. Habitual acts of illicit intercourse are necessary elements. State v. Tuttle, 129 Me. 125, 150 A. 490, 491; State v. Davenport, 225 N.C. 13, 33 S.E.2d 136, 139. See, also, Lewdness.

LEWD HOUSE. House may be a "lewd house," though chiefly devoted to carrying on business of boarding house or hotel, if lewd women are accustomed to frequent house and carry on their practices therein. Smith v. State, 52 Ga.App. 88, 182 S.E. 816, 818.

LEWD PERSON. One who is lawless, bad, vicious, unchaste. State v. Harlowe, 174 Wash. 227, 24 P.2d 601.

LEWDLY AND LASCIVIOUSLY PLAYING WITH A FEMALE CHILD. Playing or dallying with or touching or handling such child in indecent and obscene manner calculated to excite passions. State v. Martin, Del., 7 W.W.Harr. 342, 183 A. 334.

LEWDNESS. Gross and wanton indecency in sexual relations. State v. Brenner, 132 N.J.L. 607, 41 A.2d 532, 534, 535. Gross indecency so notorious as to tend to corrupt community's morals. Abbott v. State, 163 Tenn. 384, 43 S.W.2d 211, 212. Licentiousness; that form of immorality which has relation to sexual impurity. U. S. v. Males, D.C. Ind., 51 F. 41. Moral turpitude. Lane ex rel. Cronin v. Tillinghast, C.C.A.Mass., 38 F.2d 231, 232. Open and public indecency. State v. Brenner, 132 N.J.L. 607, 41 A.2d 532, 534, 535. Sensuality; debauchery. State v. Sullivan, 187 Iowa, 385, 174 N. W. 225. An offense against the public economy, when of an open and notorious character; as by frequenting houses of ill fame, which is an indictable offense, or by some grossly scandalous and public indecency, for which the punishment at common law is fine and imprisonment. Wharton. See Brooks v. State, 2 Yerg. (Tenn.) 483; State v. Bauguess, 106 Iowa, 107, 76 N.W. 508.

The term includes prostitution and assignation and other immoral or degenerate conduct or conversation between persons of opposite sexes, People v. Bay Side Land Co., 48 Cal.App. 257, 191 P. 994, 995. As well as between persons of the same sex, and signifies both illicit sexual intercourse and the irregular indulgence of lust, whether public or private, Commonwealth v. Porter, 237 Mass. 1, 129 N.E. 298, 299; State v. Rayburn, 170 Iowa 514, 153 N.W. 59, 60, L.R.A.1915F, 640. Holding that the living together of a man and woman unmarried, when generally known throughout the neighborhood, constitutes open and gross lewdness. *Contra:* City of Shreveport v. Wilson, 145 La. 906, 83 So. 186, 188.

Lewd or lascivious behavior practised without disguise, secrecy, or concealment. The adjective relates to the quality of the act, not to the place nor to the number of spectators. State v. Juneau, 88 Wis. 180, 59 N.W. 580, 24 L.R.A. 857, 43 Am.St.Rep. 877; Com. v. Wardell, 128 Mass. 52, 35 Am.Rep. 357. There must be present elements making the act shameless, aggressive, and defiant, rather than furtive and hiding away in shame; lewdness being deemed open when committed in the presence of another person, or in a place open to public view. State v. Pedigo, 190 Mo.App. 293, 176 S.W. 556, 557.

LEX. Lat.

In medieval jurisprudence. A body or collection of various laws peculiar to a given nation or people; not a code in the modern sense, but an aggregation or collection of laws not codified or systematized. See Mackeld.Rom.Law, § 98.

Also, a similar collection of laws relating to a general subject, and not peculiar to any one people.

In modern American and English jurisprudence. A system or body of laws, written or unwritten, or so much thereof as may be applicable to a particular case or question, considered as being local or peculiar to a given state, country, or jurisdiction, or as being different from the laws or rules relating to the same subject-matter which prevail in some other place.

In old English law. A body or collection of laws, and particularly the Roman or civil law.

Also a form or mode of trial or process of law, as the ordeal or battel, or the oath of a party with compurgators, as in the phrases *legem facere, legem vadiare,* etc. Also used in the sense of legal rights or civil rights or the protection of the law, as in the phrase *legem amittere.*

In Roman law. Law; a law; the law.

This term was often used as the synonym of *jus,* in the sense of a rule of civil conduct authoritatively prescribed for the government of the actions of the members of an organized jural society.

Lex is used in a purely juridical sense, law, and not also right; while *jus* has an ethical as well as a juridical meaning, not only law, but right. 15 L.Q.R. 367 (by Salmond). *Lex* is usually concrete, while *jus* is abstract. In English we have no term which combines the legal and ethical meanings, as do *jus* and its French equivalent, *droit*. Pollock, First Book of Jurispr. 14–18.

In a more limited and particular sense, it was a resolution adopted by the whole Roman *"populus"* (patricians and plebeians) in the *comitia*, on the motion of a magistrate of senatorial rank, as a consul, a prætor, or a dictator. Such a statute frequently took the name of the proposer; as the *lex Falcidia, lex Cornelia*, etc.

A rule of law which magistrates and people had agreed upon by means of a solemn declaration of consensus. Sohm, Inst.R.L. 28.

In a somewhat wider and more generic sense, a law (whatever its origin) or the aggregate of laws, relating to a particular subject-matter, thus corresponding to the meaning of the word "law" in some modern phrases, such as the "law of evidence," "law of wills," etc.

Other specific meanings of the word in Roman jurisprudence were as follows: Positive law, as opposed to natural. That system of law which descended from the Twelve Tables, and formed the basis of all the Roman law. The terms of a private covenant; the condition of an obligation. A form of words prescribed to be used upon particular occasions.

LEX ÆBUTIA. A statute which introduced and authorized new and more simple methods of instituting actions at law.

The law which, with the *leges Juliœ*, in part abolished the *legis actiones*. It provided that a judicium could be instituted in a city court without *legis actio*, merely by means of the formula or prætorian decree of appointment, and placed the *legis actio* and the formula, so far as the civil law was concerned, on a footing of equality. Sohm, Rom.L. 173.

LEX ÆLIA SENTIA. The Ælian Sentian law, respecting wills, proposed by the consuls Ælius and Sentius, and passed A. U. C. 756, restraining a master from manumitting his slaves in certain cases. Calvin.

LEX ÆMILIA. A law which reduced the official term of the censors at Rome from five years to a year and a half, and provided for the discharge of their peculiar functions by the consuls in the interim until the time for a new census. Mackeld. Rom.Law, § 29.

LEX ÆQUITATE GAUDET. Law delights in equity. Jenk.Cent. p. 36, case 69.

LEX ÆQUITATE GAUDET; APPETIT PERFECTUM; EST NORMA RECTI. The law delights in equity: it covets perfection; it is a rule of right. Jenk.Cent. 36.

LEX AGRARIA. The agrarian law. A law proposed by Tiberius Gracchus, A. U. C. 620, that no one should possess more than five hundred acres of land; and that three commissioners should be appointed to divide among the poorer people what any one had above that extent.

LEX ALAMANNORUM. The law of the Alemanni; first reduced to writing from the customs of the country, by Theodoric, king of the Franks, A. D. 512. Amended and reenacted by Clotaire II. Spelman.

LEX ALIQUANDO SEQUITUR ÆQUITATEM. Law sometimes follows equity. 3 Wils. 119.

LEX AMISSA. One who is an infamous, perjured, or outlawed person. Bract. lib. 4, c. 19.

LEX ANASTASIANA. The law admitting as agnati the children of emancipated brothers and sisters. Inst. 3, 5.

A law which provided that a third person who purchased a claim or debt for less than its true or nominal value should not be permitted to recover from the debtor more than the price paid with lawful interest. Mackeld.Rom. Law, § 369.

LEX ANGLIÆ. The law of England. The common law. Or, the curtesy of England.

LEX ANGLIÆ EST LEX MISERICORDIÆ. 2 Inst. 315. The law of England is a law of mercy.

LEX ANGLIÆ NON PATITUR ABSURDUM. 9 Coke, 22*a*. The law of England does not suffer an absurdity.

LEX ANGLIÆ NUNQUAM MATRIS SED SEMPER PATRIS CONDITIONEM IMITARI PARTUM JUDICAT. The law of England rules that the offspring shall always follow the condition of the father, never that of the mother. Co.Litt. 123; Bart.Max. 59.

LEX ANGLIÆ NUNQUAM SINE PARLIAMENTO MUTARI POTEST. 2 Inst. 218. The law of England cannot be changed but by parliament.

LEX APOSTATA. A thing contrary to law. Jacob.

LEX APPARENS. In old English and Norman law. Apparent or manifest law.

A term used to denote the trial by battel or duel, and the trial by ordeal, *"lex"* having the sense of process of law. Called "apparent" because the plaintiff was obliged to make his right *clear* by the testimony of witnesses, before he could obtain an order from the court to summon the defendant. Spelman.

LEX APULEJA, or APULEIA. A law giving to one of several joint sureties or guarantors, who had paid more than his proportion of the debt secured, a right of action for reimbursement against his co-sureties as if a partnership existed between them. See Mackeld.Rom.Law, § 454, note 2; Inst. 3, 20.

LEX AQUILIA. The Aquilian law; a celebrated law passed on the proposition of the tribune C. Aquilius Gallus, A. U. C. 672, superseding the earlier portions of the Twelve Tables, and regulating the compensation to be made for that kind of damage called "injurious," in the cases of killing or wounding the slave or beast of another. Inst. 4, 3; Calvin.

LEX ATILIA. The Atilian law. A law of Rome proposed by the tribune L. Atilius Regulus, A. U. C. 443, which conferred upon the magistrate the right of appointing guardians. It applied only to the city of Rome; Sohm, Inst.Rom.L. 400.

LEX ATINIA. The Atinian law. A law declaring that the property in things stolen should not be acquired by prescription, *(usucapione.)* Inst. 2, 6, 2; Adams, Rom.Ant. 207.

LEX BAIUVARIORUM, (BAIORIORUM, or BOIORUM). The law of the Bavarians, a barbarous nation of Europe, first collected (together with the law of the Franks and Alemanni) by Theodoric I., and finally completed and promulgated by Dagobert. Spelman.

LEX BARBARA. The barbarian law. The laws of those nations that were not subject to the Roman empire were so called. Spelman.

LEX BENEFICIALIS REI CONSIMILI REMEDIUM PRÆSTAT. 2 Inst. 689. A beneficial law affords a remedy for a similar case.

LEX BREHONIA. The Brehon or Irish law, overthrown by King John. See Brehon Law.

LEX BRETOISE. The law of the ancient Britons, or Marches of Wales. Cowell.

LEX BURGUNDIONUM. The law of the Burgundians, a barbarous nation of Europe, first compiled and published by Gundebald, one of the last of their kings, about A.D. 500. Spelman.

LEX CALPURNIA. A law relating to the form and prosecution of actions for the recovery of specific chattels other than money. See Mackeld. Rom.Law, § 203. The law which extended the scope of the action allowed by the *lex Silia* to all obligations for any certain definite thing.

LEX CANULEIA. The law which conferred upon the plebeians the *connubium,* or the right of intermarriage with Roman citizens. Morey, Rom.L. 48.

LEX CINCIA. A law which prohibited certain kinds of gifts and all gifts or donations of property beyond a certain measure, except in the case of near kinsmen.

LEX CITIUS TOLERARE VULT PRIVATUM DAMNUM QUAM PUBLICUM MALUM. The law will more readily tolerate a private loss than a public evil. Co.Litt. 152.

LEX CLAUDIA. A law which abolished the ancient guardianship of adult women by their male agnate relations. See Mackeld. Rom. Law, § 615.

LEX COMITATUS. The law of the county, or that administered in the county court before the earl or his deputy. Spelman.

LEX COMMISSORIA. See Commissoria Lex.

LEX COMMUNIS. The common law. See Jus Commune.

LEX CONTRA ID QUOD PRÆSUMIT, PROBATIONEM NON RECIPIT. The law admits no proof against that which it presumes. Lofft, 573.

LEX CORNELIA. The Cornelian law; a law passed by the dictator L. Cornelius Sylla, providing remedies for certain injuries, as for battery, forcible entry of another's house, etc. Calvin.

LEX CORNELIA DE ÆDICTIS. The law forbidding a prætor to depart during his term of office from the edict he had promulgated at its commencement. Sohm, Rom. L. 51.

LEX CORNELIA DE FALSO (or FALSIS). The Cornelian law respecting forgery or counterfeiting.

Passed by the dictator Sylla. Dig. 48, 10; Calvin. The law which provided that the same penalty should attach to the forgery of a testament of a person dying in captivity as to that of a testament made by a person dying in his own country. Inst. 2, 12, 5.

LEX CORNELIA DE INJURIIS. The law providing a civil action for the recovery of a penalty in certain cases of bodily injury. Sohm, R.L. 329.

LEX CORNELIA DE SICARIIS ET VENEFICIS. The Cornelian law respecting assassins and poisoners, passed by the dictator Sylla, and containing provisions against other deeds of violence.

It made the killing of the slave of another person punishable by death or exile, and the provisions of this law were extended by the Emperor Antoninus Pius to the case of a master killing his own slave. Inst. 1, 8; Dig. 48, 8; Calvin.

LEX CORNELIA DE SPONSU. A law prohibiting one from binding himself for the same debtor to the same creditor in the same year for more than a specified amount. Inst. 2, 20.

LEX DANORUM. The law of the Danes; Danelaw or Dane-lage. Spelman.

LEX DE FUTURO, JUDEX DE PRÆTERITO. The law provides for the future, the judge for the past.

LEX DE RESPONSIS PRUDENTUM. The law of citations.

LEX DEFICERE NON POTEST IN JUSTITIA EXHIBENDA. Co. Litt. 197. The law cannot be defective [or ought not to fail] in dispensing justice.

LEX DERAISNIA. The proof of a thing which one denies to be done by him, where another affirms it; defeating the assertion of his adversary, and showing it to be against reason or probability. This was used among the old Romans, as well as the Normans. Cowell.

LEX DILATIONES SEMPER EXHORRET. 2 Inst. 240. The law always abhors delays.

LEX DOMICILII. The law of the domicile. 2 Kent, Comm. 112, 433.

LEX EST AB ÆTERNO. Law is from everlasting.

A strong expression to denote the remote antiquity of the law. Jenk.Cent. p. 34, case 66; Branch, Princ.

LEX EST DICTAMEN RATIONIS. Law is the dictate of reason. Jenk.Cent. p. 117, case 33.

The common law will judge according to the law of nature and the public good.

LEX EST NORMA RECTI. Law is a rule of right. Branch, Princ.

LEX EST RATIO SUMMA, QUÆ JUBET QUÆ SUNT UTILIA ET NECESSARIA, ET CONTRARIA PROHIBET. Law is the perfection of reason, which commands what is useful and necessary, and forbids the contrary. Co. Litt. 319*b*; Id. 97*b*.

LEX EST SANCTIO SANCTA, JUBENS HONESTA, ET PROHIBENS CONTRARIA. Law is a sacred sanction, commanding what is right, and prohibiting the contrary. 2 Inst. 587; 1 Sharsw. Bla.Comm. 44, n.

LEX EST TUTISSIMA CASSIS; SUB CLYPEO LEGIS NEMO DECIPITUR. Law is the safest helmet; under the shield of the law no one is deceived. 2 Inst. 56.

LEX ET CONSUETUDO PARLIAMENTI. The law and custom (or usage) of parliament.

The houses of parliament constitute a court not only of legislation, but also of justice, and have their own rules, by which the court itself and the suitors therein are governed. May, Parl.Pr. (6th Ed.) 38–61.

LEX ET CONSUETUDO REGNI. The law and custom of the realm. One of the names of the common law. Hale, Com.Law, 52.

It was bad pleading to apply the term to law made by a statute. Pollock, First Book of Jurispr. 250.

LEX FABIA DE PLAGIARIIS. The law providing for the infliction of capital punishment in certain cases. Inst. 4, 18, 10.

LEX FALCIDIA. See Falcidian Law.

LEX FAVET DOTI. Jenk. Cent. 50. The law favors dower. 3 & 4 Will. IV. c. 105.

LEX FINGIT UBI SUBSISTIT ÆQUITAS. 11 Coke, 90. The law makes use of a fiction where equity subsists. Branch, Princ.

LEX FORI. The law of the forum, or court; that is, the positive law of the state, country, or jurisdiction of whose judicial system the court where the suit is brought or remedy sought is an integral part. 2 Kent, Comm. 462.

"Remedies upon contracts and their incidents are regulated and pursued according to the law of the place where the action is instituted, and the *lex loci* has no application." 2 Kent, Comm. 462. "The remedies are to be governed by the laws of the country where the suit is brought; or, as it is compendiously expressed, by the *lex fori.*" Bank of United States v. Donnally, 8 Pet. 361, 372, 8 L.Ed. 974. "So far as the law affects the remedy, the *lex fori,* the law of the place where that remedy is sought, must govern. But, so far as the law of the construction, the legal operation and effect, of the contract, is concerned, it is governed by the *law of the place* where the *contract* is made." Warren v. Copelin, 4 Metc. (Mass.) 594, 597. The lex fori, or law of jurisdiction in which relief is sought controls as to all matters pertaining to remedial as distinguished from substantive rights. Shimonek v. Tillman, 150 Okl. 177, 1 P.2d 154, 156; Sullivan v. McFetridge, Sup., 55 N.Y.S.2d 511, 516. See Lex Loci Contractus.

LEX FRANCORUM. The law of the Franks; promulgated by Theodoric I., son of Clovis I., at the same time with the law of the Alemanni and Bavarians. Spelman. This was a different collection from the Salic law.

LEX FRISIONUM. The law of the Frisians, promulgated about the middle of the eighth century. Spelman.

LEX FURIA CANINIA. The Furian Caninian law.

A law passed in the consulship of P. Furius Camillus and C. Caninius Gallus, A.U.C. 752, prohibiting masters from manumitting by will more than a certain number or proportion of their slaves. This law was abrogated by Justinian. Inst. 1, 7; Heinecc.Elem. lib. 1, tit. 7.

LEX FURIA DE SPONSU. The law limiting the liability of sponsors and fide-promissors to two years, and providing that as between several co-sponsors or co-fide-promissors, the debt should be, *ipso jure,* divided according to the number of the sureties without taking the solvency of individual sureties into account. It applied only to Italy. Sohm, Rom.L. 299, n.; Inst. 3, 20.

LEX FURIA TESTAMENTARIA. A law enacting that a testator might not bequeath as a legacy more than one thousand asses.

LEX GABINIA. A law introducing the ballot in elections.

LEX GENUCIA. A law which entirely forbade the charging or taking of interest for the use of money among Roman citizens, but which was usually and easily evaded, as it did not declare an agreement for interest to be a nullity. See Mackeld. Rom.Law, § 382*n*.

LEX GOTHICA. The Gothic law, or law of the Goths. First promulgated in writing A.D. 466. Spelman.

LEX HORATIA VALERIA. A law which assured to the tribal assembly its privilege of independent existence. See Lex Horatii.

LEX HORATII. An important constitutional statute, taking its name from the consul who secured its enactment, to the effect that all decrees passed in the meetings of the plebeians should be laws for the whole people; formerly they were binding only on the plebeians. Mackeld. Rom.Law, § 32.

LEX HORTENSIA. The law giving the plebeians a full share in the *jus publicum* and the *jus sacrum.* Sand. Just. Introd. § 9.

LEX HOSTILIA DE FURTIS. A Roman law, which provided that a prosecution for theft might be carried on without the owner's intervention. 4 Steph.Comm. (7th Ed.) 118.

LEX IMPERATORIA. The Imperial or Roman law. Quoted under this name, by Fleta, lib. 1, c. 38, § 15; Id. lib. 3, c. 10, § 3.

LEX INTENDIT VICINUM VICINI FACTA SCIRE. The law intends [or presumes] that one neighbor knows what another neighbor does. Co. Litt. 78*b*.

LEX JUDICAT DE REBUS NECESSARIO FACIENDIS QUASI RE IPSA FACTIS. The law judges of things which must necessarily be done as if actually done. Branch, Princ.

LEX JUDICIALIS. An ordeal.

LEX JULIA. Several statutes bore this name, being distinguished by the addition of words descriptive of their subject matter.

The *"lex Julia de adulteriis"* related to marriage, dower, and kindred subjects. The *lex Julia de ambitu* was a law to repress illegal methods of seeking office. Inst. 4, 18. The *lex Julia de annona* was designed to repress combinations for heightening the price of provisions. The *"lex Julia de cessione bonorum"* related to bankruptcies. The *lex Julia de majestate* inflicted the punishment of death on all who attempted anything against the emperor or state. Inst. 4, 18. The *lex Julia de maritandis ordinibus* forbade senators and their children to intermarry with freedmen or infames, and freedmen to marry infames. Sohm, Rom.L. 497. The *lex Julia de residuis* was a law punishing those who gave an incomplete account of public money committed to their charge. Inst. 4, 18. The *lex Julia de peculatu* punished those who had stolen public money or property or anything sacred or religious. Magistrates and those who had aided them in stealing public money during their administration were punished capitally; other persons were deported. Inst. 4, 18, 9. As to *lex Julia et Papia Poppœa,* See Lex Papia Poppæa.

LEX JULIA MAJESTATIS. The Julian law of majesty.

A law promulgated by Julius Cæsar, and again published with additions by Augustus, comprehending all the laws before enacted to punish transgressors against the state. Calvin.

LEX JUNIA NORBANA. The law conferring legal freedom on all such freedmen as were *tuitione prœtoris.* See Latini Juniani.

Lex Junia Velleja conferred the same right on pósthumous children born in the lifetime of the testator, but after the execution of the will, as were enjoyed by those born after the death of the testator. Sohm, Rom.L. 463.

LEX JUNIA VELLEJA. A law providing that descendants who became *sui heredes* of the testator otherwise than by birth, as by the death of their father, must be disinherited or instituted heirs in the same way as posthumous children. Campbell, Rom.L. 77.

LEX KANTIÆ. The body of customs prevailing in Kent during the time of Edward I.

A written statement of these customs was sanctioned by the king's justices *in eyre.* They were mainly concerned with the maintenance of a form of land tenure known as gavelkind *(q. v.).* 1 Poll. & Maitl. 166.

LEX LOCI. The law of the place. This may be of several descriptions but, in general, *lex loci* is only used for *lex loci contractus.*

The "lex loci" furnishes the standard of conduct, Russ v. Atlantic Coast Line R. Co., 220 N.C. 715, 18 S.E.2d 130, 131; it governs as to all matters going to the basis of the right of action itself, State of Maryland, for Use of Joynes, v. Coard, 175 Va. 571, 9 S.E.2d 454, 458.

The substantive rights of parties to action are governed by "lex loci" or law of place where rights were acquired or liabilities incurred. Sullivan v. McFetridge, Sup., 55 N.Y.S.2d 511, 516; Gray v. Blight, C.C.A.Colo., 112 F.2d 696, 699.

LEX LOCI ACTUS. The law of the place where the act was done.

LEX LOCI CELEBRATIONIS. The law of the place where a contract is made.

LEX LOCI CONTRACTUS. Used sometimes to denote the law of the place where the contract was made, and at other times to denote the law by which the contract is to be governed, which may or may not be the same as that of the place where it was made. The earlier cases do not regard this distinction. See Pritchard v. Norton, 1 S.Ct. 102, 106 U.S. 124, 27 L.Ed. 104; Pickering v. Fisk, 6 Vt. 102; Speed v. May, 17 Pa. 91, 55 Am.Dec. 540; Hayward v. Le Baron, 4 Fla. 404; Scudder v. Bank, 91 U.S. 406, 23 L.Ed. 245. See an elaborate collection of cases on conflict of laws, 5 Eng.Rul.Cas. 703–975. The phrase is used, in a double sense, to mean, sometimes, the law of the place where a contract is entered into; sometimes that of the place of its performance. Security Trust & Savings Bank of Charles City, Iowa v. Gleichmann, 50 Okl. 441, 150 P. 908, 911, L.R.A.1915F, 1203; Farm Mortgage & Loan Co. v. Beale, 113 Neb. 293, 202 N.W. 877, 878; Bullington v. Angel, 220 N.C. 18, 16 S.E.2d 411, 412, 136 A.L.R. 1054; it is the place of acceptance. Sterrett v. Stoddard Lumber Co., 150 Or. 491, 46 P.2d 1023, 1029.

LEX LOCI DELICTUS. The law of the place where the crime or wrong took place. More fully expressed by the words *lex loci delicti commissi* (law of the place where a tort is committed), usually written more briefly as *lex loci delicti,* or, sometimes, simply *lex delicti.*

LEX LOCI DOMICILII. The law of the place of domicile.

LEX LOCI REI SITÆ. The law of the place where a thing or subject-matter is situated.

"It is equally settled in the law of all civilized countries that real property, as to its tenure, mode of enjoyment, transfer, and descent, is to be regulated by the *lex loci rei sitœ.*" 2 Kent, Comm. 429. The title to realty or question of real estate law can be affected only by the law of the place where the realty is situated. Colden v. Alexander, 171 S.W.2d 328, 335, 141 Tex. 134; United States v. Becktold Co., C.C.A.Mo., 129 F.2d 473, 477.

LEX LOCI SOLUTIONIS. The law of the place of solution; the law of the place where payment or performance of a contract is to be made.

LEX LONGOBARDORUM. The law of the Lombards. The name of an ancient code of laws among that people, framed, probably, between the fifth and eighth centuries. It continued in force after the incorporation of Lombardy into the empire of Charlemagne, and traces of its laws and institutions are said to be still discoverable in some parts of Italy.

LEX MANIFESTA. Manifest or open law; the trial by duel or ordeal.

The same with *lex apparens, (q. v.).* In King John's charter (chapter 38) and the articles of that charter (chapter 28) the word *"manifestam"* is omitted.

LEX MERCATORIA. The law-merchant.

That system of laws which is adopted by all commercial nations, and constitutes a part of the law of the land. It is part of the common law. Gates v. Fauvre, 74 Ind.App. 382, 119 N.E. 155.

LEX NATURALE. Natural law. See Jus Naturale.

LEX NECESSITATIS EST LEX TEMPORIS; i. e., INSTANTIS. The law of necessity is the law of the time; that is, of the instant, or present moment. Hob. 159.

LEX NEMINEM COGIT AD VANA SEU INUTILIA PERAGENDA. The law compels no one to do vain or useless things. Co.Litt. 197*b*; Broom,

Max. 252; 5 Coke, 21*a*; Wing. Max. 600; 3 Sharsw.Bla.Comm. 144; 2 Bingh.N.C. 121; 13 East 420; Trustees of Huntington v. Nicoll, 3 Johns. (N.Y.) 598; Lucas v. Board of Canvassers of Lincoln County, 116 W.Va. 427, 181 S.E. 77, 78; Baker v. Happ, 114 Ind.App. 591, 54 N.E.2d 123, 126.

LEX NEMINEM COGIT OSTENDERE QUOD NESCIRE PRÆSUMITUR. Lofft, 569. The law compels no one to show that which he is presumed not to know.

LEX NEMINI FACIT INJURIAM. The law does injury to no one. Branch, Princ.; Brown's Appeal, 66 Pa. 157.

LEX NEMINI OPERATUR INIQUUM. The law works injustice to no one. Jenk.Cent. p. 18, case 33.

LEX NEMINI OPERATUR INIQUUM, NEMINI FACIT INJURIAM. The law never works an injury, or does a wrong. Jenk.Cent. 22.

LEX NIL FACIT FRUSTRA. The law does nothing in vain. Jenk.Cent. p. 12, case 19; Broom, Max. 252; 1 Ventr. 417.

LEX NIL FACIT FRUSTRA, NIL JUBET FRUSTRA. The law does nothing and commands nothing in vain. 3 Bulstr. 279; Jenk. Cent. 17.

LEX NIL FRUSTRA JUBET. The law commands nothing vainly. 3 Bulst. 280.

LEX NON A REGE EST VIOLANDA. Jenk. Cent. 7. The law is not to be violated by the king.

LEX NON COGIT AD IMPOSSIBILIA. The law does not compel the doing of impossibilities. Broom, Max. 242; Hob. 96; Co. Litt. 231*b*; 1 Bouv. Inst. n. 851; Wells v. Burbank, 17 N.H. 411.

LEX NON CURAT DE MINIMIS. Hob. 88. The law cares not about trifles. The law does not regard small matters.

LEX NON DEFICIT IN JUSTITIA EXHIBENDA. The law does not fail in showing justice. Jenk. Cent. p. 31, case 61.

LEX NON EXACTE DEFINIT, SED ARBITRIO BONI VIRI PERMITTIT. The law does not define exactly, but trusts in the judgment of a good man. Bissell v. Briggs, 9 Mass. 475, 6 Am.Dec. 88.

LEX NON FAVET DELICATORUM VOTIS. The law favors not the wishes of the dainty. Broom, Max. 379; 9 Coke, 58.

LEX NON INTENDIT ALIQUID IMPOSSIBILE. The law does not intend anything impossible. 12 Coke, 89*a*. For otherwise the law should not be of any effect.

LEX NON PATITUR FRACTIONES ET DIVISIONES STATUUM. The law does not suffer fractions and divisions of estates. Branch, Princ.; 1 Coke, 87*a*.

LEX NON PRÆCIPIT INUTILIA, QUIA INUTILIS LABOR STULTUS. The law commands not useless things, because useless labor is foolish. Co. Litt. 197; 5 Co. 89*a*; Mowry's Case, 112 Mass. 400.

LEX NON REQUIRIT VERIFICARI QUOD APPARET CURIÆ. The law does not require that to be verified [or proved] which is apparent to the court. 9 Coke, 54*b*.

LEX NON SCRIPTA. The unwritten or common law, which includes general and particular customs, and particular local laws. 1 Steph.Com. 40–68.

LEX ORDINANDI. The same as *lex fori, (q. v.)*.

LEX PAPIA POPPÆA. The Papian Poppæan law.

A law proposed by the consuls Papius and Poppæus at the desire of Augustus, A.U.C. 762, enlarging the *Lex Prætoria (q. v.)* Inst. 3, 8, 2. The law which exempted from tutelage women who had three children. It is usually considered with the *Lex Julia de maritandis ordinibus* as one law.

LEX PATRIÆ. National law. See Meili, Intern. Law 119.

LEX PETRONIA. The law forbidding masters to expose their slaves to contests with wild beasts. Inst. 1, 8.

LEX PLÆTORIA. A law designed for the protection of minors against frauds and allowing them in certain cases to apply for the appointment of a guardian. Inst. 1, 23.

LEX PLAUTIA. The law which conferred the full rights of citizenship on Italy below the Po. Sand. Just. Introd. § 11.

LEX PLUS LAUDATUR QUANDO RATIONE PROBATUR. The law is the more praised when it is approved by reason. Broom, Max. 159; 3 Term 146; 7 Term 252; 7 A. & E. 657.

LEX POETELIA. The law abolishing the right of a creditor to sell or kill his debtor. Sohm. Rom. L. 210.

LEX POMPEIA DE PARRICIDIIS. The law which inflicted a punishment on one who had caused the death of a parent or child.

The offender was by this law to be sewn up in a sack with a dog, a cock, a viper, and an ape, and thrown into the sea or a river, so that even in his lifetime he might begin to be deprived of the use of the elements; that the air might be denied him whilst he lived and the earth when he died. Inst. 4, 18, 6.

LEX POSTERIOR DEROGAT PRIORI. A later statute takes away the effect of a prior one. But the later statute must either expressly repeal, or be manifestly repugnant to, the earlier one. Broom, Max. 29; Mackeld. Rom. Law, § 7.

LEX PRÆTORIA. The prætorian law. A law by which every freedman who made a will was commanded to leave a moiety to his patron. Inst. 3, 8, 1. The term has been applied to the rules that govern in a court of equity. Gilb.Ch. pt. 2.

LEX PROSPICIT, NON RESPICIT. Jenk.Cent. 284. The law looks forward, not backward.

LEX PUBLILIA. The law providing that the *plebiscita* should bind the whole people. Inst. 1, 2.

The *lex Publilia de sponsu* allowed sponsores, unless reimbursed within six months, to recover from their principal by a special *actio* what they had paid.

LEX PUNIT MENDACIUM. The law punishes falsehood. Jenk.Cent. p. 15, case 26.

LEX REGIA. The royal or imperial law. A law enacted (or supposed or claimed to have been enacted) by the Roman people, constituting the emperor a source of law, conferring the legislative power upon him, and according the force and obligation of law to the expression of his mere will or pleasure. See Inst. 1, 2, 6; Gaius, 1, 5; Mackeld. Rom. Law, § 46; Heinecc. Rom. Ant. l. 1, tit. 2, §§ 62–67; 1 Kent, Comm. 544, note.

LEX REI SITÆ. The law of the place of situation of the thing. It is said to be an inexact mode of expression; *lex situs,* or *lex loci rei sitæ* are better. 29 L.Q.R. 2 (H. Gondy).

LEX REJICIT SUPERFLUA, PUGNANTIA, INCONGRUA. Jenk.Cent. 133. The law rejects superfluous, contradictory, and incongruous things.

LEX REPROBAT MORAM. Jenk.Cent. 35. The law dislikes delay.

LEX RESPICIT ÆQUITATEM. Co.Litt. 24*b*. The law pays regard to equity. See 14 Q.B. 504, 511, 512; Broom, Max. 151.

LEX RHODIA. See Rhodian Laws.

LEX ROMANA. See Civil Law; Roman Law.

LEX SACRAMENTALIS. Purgation by oath.

LEX SALICA. See Salic Law.

LEX SCRIBONIA. The law abolishing the *usucapio servitutis.* Sohm, Rom.L. 265.

LEX SCRIPTA. Written law; law deriving its force, not from usage, but from express legislative enactment; statute law. 1 Bl.Comm. 62, 85.

LEX SCRIPTA SI CESSET, ID CUSTODIRI OPORTET QUOD MORIBUS ET CONSUETUDINE INDUCTUM EST; ET, SI QUA IN RE HOC DEFECERIT, TUNC ID QUOD PROXIMUM ET CONSEQUENS EI EST; ET, SI ID NON APPAREAT, TUNC JUS QUO URBS ROMANA UTITUR SERVARI OPORTET. 7 Coke, 19. If the written law be silent, that which is drawn from manners and custom ought to be observed; and, if that is in any manner defective, then that which is next and analogous to it; and, if that does not appear, then the law which Rome uses should be followed.

This maxim of Lord Coke is so far followed at the present day that, in cases where there is no precedent of the English courts, the civil law is always heard with respect, and often, though not necessarily, followed. Wharton.

LEX SEMPER DABIT REMEDIUM. The law will always give a remedy. Branch, Princ.; Broom, Max. 192; Bac.Abr. *Actions in general* (B); 12 A. & E. 266; 7 Q.B. 451.

LEX SEMPER INTENDIT QUOD CONVENIT RATIONI. Co.Litt. 78*b*. The law always intends what is agreeable to reason.

LEX SEMPRONIA. The law preventing senators from being judges and allowing the office to the knights. Sand.Just. Introd. § 12.

LEX SILIA. A law concerning personal actions. Sohm, Rom.L. 155.

LEX SITUS. Modern law Latin for "the law of the place where property is situated." The general rule is that lands and other immovables are governed by the *lex situs*; *i. e.,* by the law of the country in which they are situated. Westl.Priv. Int.Law, 62.

LEX SPECTAT NATURÆ ORDINEM. The law regards the order of nature. Co.Litt. 197*b*; Broom, Max. 252.

LEX SUCCURRIT IGNORANTI. Jenk. Cent. 15. The law assists the ignorant.

LEX SUCCURRIT MINORIBUS. The law aids minors. Jenk. Cent. p. 51, case 97.

LEX TALIONIS. The law of retaliation; which requires the infliction upon a wrongdoer of the same injury which he has caused to another.

Expressed in the Mosaic law by the formula, "an eye for an eye; a tooth for a tooth," etc. In modern international law, the term describes the rule by which one state may inflict upon the citizens of another state death, imprisonment, or other hardship, in retaliation for similar injuries imposed upon its own citizens.

LEX TERRÆ. The law of the land. The common law, or the due course of the common law; the general law of the land. Bract. fol. 17*b*. Equivalent to "due process of law." In the strictest sense, trial by oath; the privilege of making oath.

Bracton uses the phrase to denote a freeman's privilege of being sworn in court as a juror or witness, which jurors convicted of perjury forfeited, *(legem terræ amittant.)* Bract. fol. 292*b*. The phrase means "the procedure of the old popular law." Thayer, Evid. 201, quoting Brunner, Schw. 254, and Fortesq. *de Laud.* c. 26 (Selden's notes).

LEX UNO ORE OMNES ALLOQUITUR. The law addresses all with one [the same] mouth or voice. 2 Inst. 184.

LEX VIGILANTIBUS, NON DORMIENTIBUS, SUBVENIT. Law assists the wakeful, not the sleeping. 1 Story, Cont. § 529.

LEX VOCONIA. A *plebiscitum* forbidding a legatee to receive more than each heir had. Inst. 2, 22.

LEX WALLENSICA. The Welsh law; the law of Wales. Blount.

LEX WISIGOTHORUM. The law of the Visigoths, or Western Goths who settled in Spain;

first reduced to writing A. D. 466. A revision of these laws was made by Egigas. Spelman.

LEY. L. Fr. (A corruption of *loi.*) Law; the law. For example, *Termes de la Ley,* Terms of the Law.

In another, and an old technical, sense, ley signifies an oath, or the oath with compurgators; as, il tend sa *ley* aiu pleyntiffe. Britton, c. 27.

In Spanish law. A law; the law; law in the abstract.

LEY CIVILE. In old English law. The civil or Roman law. Yearb. H. 8 Edw. III. 42. Otherwise termed *"ley escripte,"* the written law. Yearb. 10 Edw. III. 24.

LEY GAGER. Law wager; wager of law; the giving of gage or security by a defendant that he would make or perfect his law at a certain day. Litt. § 514; Co. Litt. 294*b*, 295*a*.

An offer to make an oath denying the cause of action of the plaintiff, confirmed by compurgators, which oath was allowed in certain cases. When it was accomplished, it was called the "doing of the law," *"fesans de ley." Termes de la Ley;* 2 B. & C. 538; 3 B. & P. 297.

LEYES DE ESTILO (or ESTILLO). In Spanish law. Laws of the age.

A collection of laws usually published as an appendix to the Fuero Real; treating of the mode of conducting suits, prosecuting them to judgment, and entering appeals. Schm. Civil Law, Introd. 74. Formed under the authority of Alonzo X. and his son Sancho, and of Fernando el Emplazado, and published at the end of the 13th century or beginning of the 14th; some of them are inserted in the New Recopilacion. 1 New Recop. 354.

LEZE MAJESTY, or LESE MAJESTY. An offense against sovereign power; treason; rebellion.

LIABILITY. The word is a broad legal term. Mayfield v. First Nat. Bank of Chattanooga, Tenn., C.C.A.Tenn., 137 F.2d 1013, 1019. It has been referred to as of the most comprehensive significance, including almost every character of hazard or responsibility, absolute, contingent, or likely. Wentz v. State, 108 Neb. 597, 188 N.W. 467, 468.

It has been defined to mean: all character of municipal debts and obligations, Washington Water Power Co. v. City of Coeur d'Alene, Idaho, D.C.Idaho, 9 F.Supp. 263, 271; Public Market Co. of Portland v. City of Portland, 171 Or. 522, 130 P.2d 624, 643, 646; amenability or responsibility, Eberhard v. Ætna Ins. Co., 235 N.Y.S. 445, 447, 134 Misc. 386; an obligation, one is bound in law or justice to perform, Murphy v. Chicago League Ball Club, 221 Ill.App. 120, 126; State ex rel. Diederichs v. Board of Trustees of Missoula County High School, 91 Mont. 300, 7 P.2d 543, 545. An obligation which may or may not ripen into a debt, Brogan v. Ferguson, 101 Fla. 1306, 131 So. 171, 173. Any kind of debt or liability, either absolute or contingent, express or implied, Public Market Co. of Portland v. City of Portland, 171 Or. 522, 130 P.2d 624, 643, 646; any liability whatsoever, In re Tatnall, 102 N.J. Eq. 445, 141 A. 174, 175; condition of being actually or potentially subject to an obligation, Enyeart v. City of Lincoln, 136 Neb. 146, 285 N.W. 314, 318; condition of being exposed to the upspringing of an obligation to discharge or make good an undertaking of another, or a loss or deficit, or the being exposed or subject to a given contingency, risk, or casualty which is more or less probable, First National Bank of East Islip v. National Surety Co., 228 N.Y. 469, 127 N.E. 478, 480; United States Fidelity & Guaranty Co. v. Haney, 166 Minn. 403, 208 N.W. 17; condition of being responsible for a possible or actual loss, penalty, evil, expense, or burden, Wentz v. State, 108 Neb. 597, 188 N.W. 467, 468; condition which creates a duty to perform an act immediately or in the future, Union Oil Co. of California v. Basalt Rock Co., 30 Cal.App.2d 317, 86 P. 2d 139, 141; duty to pay money or perform some other service, Dehne v. Hillman Inv. Co., C.C.A.Pa., 110 F.2d 456, 458; duty which must at least eventually be performed, Vandegrift v. Riley, Cal.Sup., 16 P.2d 734, 736; estate tax, Lyeth v. Hoey, C.C.A.N.Y., 112 F.2d 4, 6; every kind of legal obligation, responsibility, or duty, Mayfield v. First Nat. Bank of Chattanooga, Tenn., C.C.A.Tenn., 137 F.2d 1013, 1019; fixed liability, Vandegrift v. Riley, Cal.Sup., 16 P.2d 734, 736; Ivester v. State ex rel. Gillum, 183 Okl. 519, 83 P.2d 193, 196; legal responsibility, Clark v. Lowden, D.C.Minn., 43 F.Supp. 261, 263; McCullough v. National Bank of Union City, 127 Pa.Super. 452, 193 A. 65, 66; penalty for failure to pay tax when due, State v. Fischl, 94 Mont. 92, 20 P.2d 1057, 1059; present, current, future, fixed or contingent debts, Erickson v. Grande Ronde Lumber Co., 162 Or. 556, 92 P.2d 170, 174; punishment, Holliman v. Cole, 168 Okl. 473, 34 P.2d 597, 599; responsibility for torts, Italiani v. Metro-Goldwyn-Mayer Corporation, 45 Cal.App.2d 464, 114 P.2d 370, 372; tax, State ex rel. DuFresne v. Leslie, 100 Mont. 449, 50 P.2d 959, 963, 101 A.L.R. 1329; Thompson v. Smith, 189 Okl. 217, 114 P.2d 922, 924; that which one is under obligation to pay, or for which one is liable, Reconstruction Finance Corporation v. Gossett, Tex., 111 S.W.2d 1066; Boney v. Central Mut. Ins. Co. of Chicago, 213 N.C. 470, 196 S.E. 837, 842; the state of being bound or obliged in law or justice to do, pay, or make good something. Feil v. City of Cœur d'Alene, 23 Idaho 32, 129 P. 643, 649, 43 L.R.A.,N. S., 1095; Breslaw v. Rightmire, 196 N.Y.S. 539, 541, 119 Misc. 833; the state of one who is bound in law and justice to do something which may be enforced by action. Fidelity Coal Co. v. Diamond, 310 Ill.App. 387, 34 N.E.2d 123; Clark v. Lowden, D.C.Minn., 48 F.Supp. 261, 263; McCullough v. National Bank of Union City, 127 Pa.Super. 452, 193 A. 65, 66; unliquidated claim, Stephens v. Duckworth, 188 Miss. 626, 196 So. 219, 221; unpaid debt, Comstock v. Morgan Park Trust & Savings Bank, 367 Ill. 276, 11 N.E.2d 394. 396.

The term is therefore broader than the word "debt," or "indebtedness," and includes in addition existing obligations, which may or may not in the future eventuate in an indebtedness. Daniels v. Goff, 192 Ky. 15, 232 S.W. 66, 67; Irving Bank-Columbia Trust Co. v. New York Rys. Co., D.C.N.Y., 292 F. 429, 433.

The word is not synonymous with "loss" or "damage," and under an automobile insurance policy insuring against "liabilities," there may be recovery without allegation or proof that insured has been required to pay any sum, whereas under a policy covering "actual loss or damage," no obligation arises till insured has suffered loss or damage. Ducommun v. Strong, 193 Wis. 179, 214 N.W. 616; Stag Mining Co. v. Missouri Fidelity & Casualty Co., Mo. App., 209 S.W. 321, 323.

Existing liability. See Existing Liabilities.

Legal liability. See Legal Liability.

Liability bond. See Bond.

Limited liability. See Limited Liability.

Personal liability. See Personal Liability.

Secondary liability. See Secondary Liability.

Strict liability. See Strict Liability.

LIABILITY CREATED BY STATUTE. One depending for its existence on the enactment of the statute, and not on the contract of the parties. Dietrich v. Copeland Lumber Co., 154 P. 626, 628, 28 Idaho 312. One which would not exist but for the statute. Frank Shepard Co. v. Zachary P. Taylor Pub. Co., 138 N.E. 409, 410, 234 N.Y. 465; Cannon v. Miller, 22 Wash.2d 227, 155 P.2d 500, 507, 508, 157 A.L.R. 530.

LIABILITY FOR DAMAGES. Liability for an amount to be ascertained by trial of the facts in particular cases. Hurt v. Pennsylvania Threshermen & Farmers' Casualty Ins. Co., 175 Md. 403, 2 A.2d 402, 406.

Liability Imposed by Law. Liability imposed in a definite sum by a final judgment against assured. Girard v. Commercial Standard Ins. Co., 66 Cal. App.2d 483, 152 P.2d 509, 513; total liability imposed by law upon a person. Schwartz v. Merola Bros. Const. Corporation, 290 N.Y. 145, 48 N.E.2d 299, 303.

LIABILITY INSURANCE. Indemnity against liability, Zieman v. U. S. Fidelity & Guaranty Co. of Baltimore, Md., 214 Iowa 468, 238 N.W. 100, 102. Twichell v. Hetzel, 145 Kan. 139, 64 P.2d 557, 559; Indemnity against loss or liability. Employers' Liability Assur. Corporation, Limited, of London, England v. C. E. Carnes & Co., D.C.La., 24 F.Supp. 128, 135; State ex rel. Travelers' Indemnity Co. v. Knott, 114 Fla. 820, 153 So. 304, indemnity against loss through liability. Trandum v. Trandum, 187 Minn. 327, 245 N.W. 380, 381. Martin v. Zurich General Accident & Liability Ins. Co., C.C.A.R.I., 84 F.2d 618. See, also, Insurance.

LIABLE. **1.** Bound or obliged in law or equity; responsible; chargeable; answerable; compellable to make satisfaction, compensation, or restitution. Homan v. Employers Reinsurance Corporation, 345 Mo. 650, 136 S.W.2d 289, 298, 127 A.L.R. 163; State v. Albert, 125 Me. 325, 133 A. 693, 694. Obligated; accountable for or chargeable with. Wilhelm v. Parkersburg, M. & I. Ry. Co., 74 W.Va. 678, 82 S.E. 1089, 1091.

2. Exposed or subject to a given contingency, risk, or casualty, which is more or less probable. Jennings v. National American, Mo.App., 179 S.W. 789; Pacific Fire Ins. Co. v. Murdoch Cotton Co., 193 Ark. 327, 99 S.W.2d 233, 235. Exposed, as to damage, penalty, expense, burden, or anything unpleasant or dangerous; justly or legally responsible or answerable. Breslaw v. Rightmire, 196 N.Y.S. 539, 541, 119 Misc. 833.

3. Condition of being bound to respond because a wrong has occurred. State v. Grand Forks County, 71 N.D. 355, 300 N.W. 827, 831. Condition out of which a legal liability might arise. Pacific Fire Ins. Co. v. Murdoch Cotton Co., 193 Ark. 327, 99 S.W.2d 233, 235.

4. Future possible or probable happening which may not actually occur, and relates to an occurrence within the range of possibility. Alabama Great Southern R. Co. v. Smith, 209 Ala. 301, 96 So. 239, 240; Pacific Fire Ins. Co. v. Murdoch Cotton Co., 99 S.W.2d 233, 235, 193 Ark. 327.

5. In all probability. Neely v. Chicago Great Western R. Co., Mo.App., 14 S.W.2d 972, 978.

LIABLE FOR SUCH TAX. Subject to a tax. Houston Street Corporation v. Commissioner of Internal Revenue, C.C.A.Tex., 84 F.2d 821, 822.

LIABLE TO ACTION. Liable to judgment in given action. Haas v. New York Post Graduate Medical School and Hospital, 226 N.Y.S. 617, 620, 131 Misc. 395.

LIABLE TO PENALTY. Subject to penalty. The Motorboat, D.C.N.J., 53 F.2d 239, 241.

LIARD. An old French coin, of silver or copper, formerly current to a limited extent in England, and there computed as equivalent to a farthing.

LIBEL, *v.*

Admiralty Practice. To proceed against, by filing a libel; to seize under admiralty process, at the commencement of a suit

Torts. To defame or injure a person's reputation by a published writing.

LIBEL, *n.*

In Practice. The initiatory pleading on the part of the plaintiff or complainant in an admiralty or ecclesiastical cause, corresponding to the declaration, bill, or complaint.

A written statement by a plaintiff of his cause of action, and of the relief he seeks to obtain in a suit. Ayliffe, Par. 346; Shelf.Marr. & D. 506; Dunl.Adm.Pr. 111.

In Scotch Law. The form of the complaint or ground of the charge on which either a civil action or criminal prosecution takes place. Bell. A libel of accusation is the instrument which contains the charge against a person accused of a crime. Libels are of two kinds, namely, indictments and criminal letters.

In Torts. A method of defamation expressed by print, writing, pictures, or signs. Spence v. Johnson, 142 Ga. 267, 82 S.E. 646, 647, Ann.Cas.1916A, 1195. In its most general sense any publication that is injurious to the reputation of another. Ajouelo v. Auto-Soler Co., 61 Ga.App. 216, 6 S.E. 2d 415, 418. Flake v. Greensboro News Co., 212 N.C. 780, 195 S.E. 55, 60. Libel is written defamation. Locke v. Gibbons, 299 N.Y.S. 188, 192, 193, 164 Misc. 877. Defamatory words read aloud by speaker from written article and broadcast by radio constitute libel. Sorensen v. Wood, 123 Neb. 348, 243 N.W. 82; Hartman v. Winchell, 73 N.E.2d 30, 296 N.Y. 296.

Accusation in writing or printing against the character of a person which affects his reputation, in that it tends to hold him up to ridicule, contempt, shame, disgrace, or obloquy, to degrade him in the estimation of the community, to induce an evil opinion of him in the minds of right-thinking persons, to make him an object of reproach, to diminish his respectability or abridge his comforts, to change his position in society for the worse, to dishonor or discredit him in the estimation of the public, or his friends and acquaintances, or to deprive him of friendly intercourse in society, or cause him to be shunned or avoided, or where it is charged that one has violated his public duty as a public officer. Stevens v. Wright, 107 Vt. 337, 179 A. 213, 217.

Almost any language which upon its face has a natural tendency to injure a man's reputation, either generally or with respect to his occupation. Washer v. Bank of America Nat. Trust & Savings Ass'n, 21 Cal.2d 822, 136 P.2d 297, 300, 155 A.L.R. 1338.

Censorious or ridiculing writing, picture, or sign made with a mischievous intent. People v. Croswell, 3 Johns. Cas. (N.Y.) 354; Steele v. Southwick, 9 Johns. (N.Y.) 215; McCorkle v. Binns, 5 Bin. (Pa.) 348, 6 Am.Dec. 420.

Disparagement of goods is a form of libel. Black & Yates v. Mahogany Ass'n, D.C.Del., 34 F.Supp. 450, 456.

False accusation which dishonors or discredits a man in estimate of public or his friends and acquaintances or has a reasonable tendency to do so. Stoll v. Long Islander Pub. Co., Sup., 40 N.Y.S.2d 412, 413.

False and malicious publication, which charges an offense punishable by indictment, or which tends to bring individual into public hatred, contempt, or ridicule, or charges an act odious and disgraceful in society. White v. Birmingham Post Co., 233 Ala. 547, 172 So. 649, 651.

False and malicious publication intended to injure reputation or expose person to public contempt or ridicule. Woolf v. Scripps Pub. Co., 35 Ohio App. 343, 172 N.E. 389, 390; O'Brien v. Clement, 15 Mees. & W. 435. Or a written statement, injurious to his trade. 7 App.Cas. 741.

False and malicious publication which tends to blacken the memory of one who is dead or to degrade or injure one who is alive, or bring him in contempt, hatred, or ridicule, or which accuses him of any crime punishable by law, or of any act odious and disgraceful to society. Cole v. Commonwealth, 222 Ky. 350, 300 S.W. 907, 910; Wells v. Times Printing Co., 77 Wash. 171, 137 P. 457, 459.

False and malicious writing published of another when its tendency is to render him contemptible or ridiculous in public estimation, or expose him to public hatred or contempt; Wood v. Hannett, 35 N.M. 23, 289 P. 590, 592; Talbot v. Mack, 41 Nev. 245, 169 P. 25, 30, or hinder virtuous men from associating with him. Wood v. Hannett, 35 N. M. 23, 289 P. 590, 592; Burns v. Telegram Pub. Co., 89 Conn. 549, 94 A. 917, 918.

False publication that humiliates a person and degrades one in the estimation of others and subjects a person to loss of social prestige. Ransom v. Matson Nav. Co., D.C. Wash., 1 F.Supp. 244, 247.

False and unprivileged publication by writing, printing, pictures, effigy or other fixed representation to the eye which exposes any person to hatred, contempt, ridicule or obloquy or which causes him to be shunned or avoided, or which has a tendency to injure him in his occupation. Civ.Code Cal. § 45; Penal Law N.Y. (Consol.Laws, c. 40) § 1340; Civ.Code S.D. § 29 (Rev.Code 1919, § 95); Comp. Laws N.D. 1913, § 4352; Ajouelo v. Auto-Soler Co., 61 Ga. App. 216, 6 S.E.2d 415, 418.

False and unprivileged publication, which tends to impair the social standing of a man, to make him contemptible or ridiculous, or to deprive him of the confidence, good will, or esteem of his fellow men. Robinson v. Johnson, C.C.A.Mo., 239 F. 671, 673.

Malicious defamation, expressed either by writing, printing, or by signs or pictures, or the like, tending to blacken the memory of one who is dead, or to impeach the honesty, integrity, virtue, or reputation, or publish the natural or alleged defects, of one who is alive, and thereby to expose him to public hatred, contempt, or ridicule. Pen.Code Cal. § 248; Bac.Abr. tit. "Libel;" 1 Hawk.P.C. 1, 73, § 1; Brown v. Elm City Lumber Co., 167 N.C. 9, 82 S.E. 961, 962, L.R.A.1915E, 275, Ann.Cas.1916E, 631; Ilitzky v. Goodman, 57 Ariz. 216, 112 P.2d 860, 862, 863.

Malicious defamation of person by printing, writing, sign, picture, representation, or effigy tending to provoke him to wrath or expose him to public hatred, contempt, or ridicule, or to deprive him of benefits of public confidence and social intercourse. Hylsky v. Globe Democrat Pub. Co., 348 Mo. 83, 152 S.W.2d 119, 122; Shaw Cleaners & Dyers v. Des Moines Dress Club, 215 Iowa 1130, 245 N.W. 231, 234, 86 A.L.R. 839.

Malicious falsehood expressed by writing, printing, or by signs or pictures, which tends to bring any person into disrepute, contempt or ridicule. Ilitzky v. Goodman, 57 Ariz. 216, 112 P.2d 860, 862, 863.

Malicious publication tending either to blacken or injure the memory of one dead or the reputation of one alive and expose him to public hatred, contempt or ridicule. Sarkees v. Warner-West Corporation, 349 Pa. 365, 37 A.2d 544, 546; Renfro Drug Co. v. Lawson, 138 Tex. 434, 160 S.W.2d 246, 248, 146 A.L.R. 732; Hinson v. Pollock, 159 Tenn. 1, 15 S.W.2d 737, 738.

Printed or written article which has a tendency to expose one to public contempt, scorn, obloquy, ridicule, shame or disgrace, or tending to induce an evil opinion of him in the minds of right thinking persons, or injure him in his profession, occupation, or trade. Dall v. Time, Inc., 300 N.Y.S. 680, 684, 685, 252 App.Div. 636.

Printed or written article which tends to expose plaintiff to public contempt, ridicule, aversion, or disgrace, or induce an evil opinion of him in the minds of right-thinking persons and deprives him of their friendly intercourse in society. Neaton v. Lewis Apparel Stores, 48 N.Y.S.2d 492, 495, 267 App.Div. 728.

Printed or written statement which falsely and maliciously charges another with the commission of a crime. Duncan v. Record Pub. Co., 145 S.C. 196, 143 S.E. 31, 58; Peinhardt v. West, 217 Ala. 12, 115 So. 88, 89.

Publication by any means other than words orally spoken of any false and scandalous matter with intent to injure or defame another. L.O.L. Or. § 1930 (Code 1930, § 14–238).

Publication that tends to disgrace, degrade, or injure reputation of person or bring him into contempt, hatred, or ridicule. Cummins v. State, 166 N.E. 155, 157, 89 Ind. App. 256; Axton Fisher Tobacco Co. v. Evening Post Co., 169 Ky. 64, 183 S.W. 269, 274, L.R.A.1916E, 667, Ann.Cas. 1918B, 560.

Publication which falsely charges or imputes dishonesty, or engagement in fraudulent enterprises of such a nature as reflects on the character and integrity of a person, and to subject him to the loss of public confidence and respect. Smith v. Pure Oil Co., 278 Ky. 430, 128 S.W.2d 931, 932.

That which is written or printed, and published, calculated to injure the character or reputation of another by bringing him into ridicule, hatred, or contempt. Palmer v. Concord, 48 N.H. 211, 97 Am.Dec. 605; Collins v. Dispatch Pub. Co., 152 Pa. 187, 25 A. 546, 34 Am.St.Rep. 636; Hartford v. State, 96 Ind. 463, 49 Am.Rep. 185; 15 M. & W. 344; Hughes v. Samuels Bros., 179 Iowa, 1077, 159 N.W. 589, 590, L.R.A.1917F, 1088.

Writing that discredits plaintiff in minds of any considerable and respectable class in the community. Streeter v. Eldridge, 311 Mass. 180, 40 N.E.2d 254, 255.

Libels have been classified according to their objects: (1) Libels which impute to a person the commission of a crime; (2) libels which have a tendency to injure him in his office, profession, calling, or trade; (3) libels which hold him up to scorn and ridicule and to feelings of contempt or execration, impair him in the enjoyment of general society, and injure those imperfect rights of friendly intercourse and mutual benevolence which man has with respect to man. Newell, Slan. & L. 67.

Criminal libel. See Criminal.

Seditious libel. See Seditious Libel.

LIBEL OF REVIEW. New proceeding instituted to attack final decree after expiration of term and right to appeal. The Astorian, C.C.A.Cal., 57 F.2d 85, 87.

LIBELANT. The complainant or party who files a libel in an ecclesiastical or admiralty case, corresponding to the plaintiff in actions at law.

LIBELEE. A party against whom a libel has been filed in an ecclesiastical court or in admiralty, corresponding to the defendant in a common-law action.

LIBELLUS. Lat.

In civil law. A little book.

Libellus supplex, a petition, especially to the emperor, all petitions to whom must be in writing. *Libellum rescribere,* to mark on such petition the answer to it. *Libellum agere,* to assist or counsel the emperor in regard to such petitions. *Libellus accusatorius,* an information and accusation of a crime. *Libellus divortii,* a writing of divorcement. *Libellus rerum,* an inventory. Calvin. *Libellus* or *oratio consultoria,* a message by which emperors laid matters before the senate. Calvin. *Libellus appellatorius,* an appeal. Calvin.

A writing in which are contained the names of the plaintiff *(actor)* and defendant, *(reus,)* the thing sought, the right relied upon, and name of the tribunal before which the action is brought. Calvin.

In Feudal law. An instrument of alienation or conveyance, as of a fief, or a part of it.

Also, a bill. Bracton, fol. 112. Sometimes called *libellus conventionis* (*q. v.*).

LIBELLUS CONVENTIONIS. In the civil law. The statement of a plaintiff's claim in a petition presented to the magistrate, who directed an officer to deliver it to the defendant.

LIBELLUS FAMOSUS. In the civil law. A defamatory publication; a publication injuriously affecting character; a libel. Inst. 4, 4, 1; Dig. 47, 10; Cod. 9, 36.

LIBELOUS. Defamatory; of the nature of a libel; constituting or involving libel. See, also, Libel.

LIBELOUS PER QUOD. Expressions "libelous per quod" are such as require that their injurious character or effect be established by allegation and proof. Talbot v. Mack, 41 Nev. 245, 169 P. 25, 32. They are those expressions which are not actionable upon their face, but which become so by reason of the peculiar situation or occasion upon which the words are written. Oliveros v. Henderson, 116 S.C. 77, 106 S.E. 855, 857; Norton v. Great Atlantic & Pacific Tea Co., 184 S.C. 525, 193 S.E. 126, 128. Publications which are susceptible of two reasonable interpretations, one of which is defamatory and the other is not, or publications which are not obviously defamatory, but which become so when considered in connection with innuendo, colloquium, and explanatory circumstances, Flake v. Greensboro News Co., 212 N.C. 780, 195 S.E. 55, 59.

LIBELOUS PER SE. A publication is libelous *per se* when the words are of such a character that an action may be brought upon them without the necessity of showing any special damage, the imputation being such that the law will presume that any one so slandered must have suffered damage. See Mayrant v. Richardson, 1 Nott. & McC. (S.C.) 349, 9 Am.Dec. 707; Woolworth v. Star Co., 97 App.Div. 525, 90 N.Y.S. 147; Morse v. Times-Republican Printing Co., 124 Iowa 707, 100 N.W. 867. To render words "libelous per se," the words must be of such character that a presumption of law will arise therefrom that the plaintiff has been degraded in the estimation of his friends or of the public or has suffered some other loss either in his property, character, reputation, or business or in his domestic or social relations. Whitaker v. Sherbrook Distributing Co., 189 S.C. 243, 200 S.E. 848, 849. See, also, Actionable Words.

Publications or words have been held libelous per se which charge a public officer with a crime or misdemeanor in office, Sweeney v. Philadelphia Record Co., C.C.A.Pa., 126 F.2d 53, 54, 55; disparage a man in his profession, office, trade or occupation, De Pasquale v. Westchester Newspapers, 8 N.Y.S.2d 829, 831, 170 Misc. 268; Washer v. Bank of America Nat. Trust & Savings Ass'n, 21 Cal.2d 822, 136 P.2d 297, 301, 155 A.L.R. 1338; dishonor or discredit a man in estimate of the public or his friends and acquaintances, or expose him to ridicule, or have a reasonable tendency to do so, O'Leary v. Hearst Magazines, 4 N.Y.S.2d 79, 167 Misc. 481; expose a person to hatred, distrust, contempt, ridicule, or obloquy, or tend to cause him to be shunned or avoided, or to injure him in office, occupation, business, or employment. Layne v. Tribune Co., 108 Fla. 177, 146 So. 234, 236, 86 A.L.R. 466; Harris v. Curtis Pub. Co., 49 Cal.App.2d 340, 121 P.2d 761, 763, 764; impute crime, Martin v. Markley, 202 La. 291, 11 So.2d 593, 596, 597; Le Moine v. Spicer, 146 Fla. 758, 1 So.2d 730, 731, 732; impute dishonesty, Ripps v. Herrington, 241 Ala. 209, 1 So.2d 899, 902; impute infectious disease, Flake v. Greensboro News Co., 212 N.C. 780, 195 S.E. 55; impute insolvency, Kirkman v. Westchester Newspapers, 24 N.Y.S. 2d 860, 864, 261 App.Div. 181; Impute to public officer misconduct in office, want of official integrity or fidelity to public trust, Ziebell v. Lumbermens Printing Co., 14 Wash.2d 261, 127 P.2d 677, 680, 681; may well lead right thinking people to believe public official unworthy of public trust and confidence, Sweeney v. Schenectady Union Pub. Co., C.C.A.N.Y., 122 F.2d 288, 290, 291; tend either to blacken the memory of one dead or the reputation of one who is alive and expose him to public hatred, contempt, or ridicule, Flake v. Greensboro News Co., 212 N.C. 780, 195 S.E. 55; tend to alienate from a business the good will and patronage of a large class of its customers, Emde v. San Joaquin County Central Labor Council, Cal.App., 132 P.2d 279, 286, 287; tend to degrade or disgrace plaintiff or to subject him to public distrust, ridicule, or contempt, Judevine v. Benzies-Montanye Fuel & Warehouse Co., 222 Wis. 512, 269 N.W. 295, 298, 299, 106 A.L.R. 1443; Towles v. Travelers Ins. Co., 282 Ky. 147, 137 S.W.2d 1110, 1111; tend to expose one to public hatred, shame, obloquy, contumely, odium, contempt, ridicule, aversion, ostracism, degradation, or disgrace, or to induce an evil opinion of one in the minds of right-thinking persons, and to deprive one of their confidence and friendly intercourse, Harris v. Twentieth Century Fox Film Corporation, D.C.N.Y., 43 F.Supp. 119, 121, 122; Adle v. Herald Co., Sup., 36 N.Y.S.2d 905, 907; tend to injure plaintiff in his business and occupation and to ruin his name and reputation for honesty, integrity and virtue, and thereby expose him to public hatred, contempt or ridicule, Browder v. Cook, D.C.Idaho, 59 F. Supp. 225, 231, 232; tend to injure reputation and to expose to public hatred, contempt, or shame, Hall v. Binghamton Press Co., Sup., 29 N.Y.S.2d 760, 769, 772.

LIBER, *adj.* Lat. Free; open and accessible, as applied to courts, places, etc.; of the state or condition of a freeman, as applied to persons. Exempt from the service or jurisdiction of another.

LIBER, *n.* Lat. A book, of whatever material composed; a main division of a literary work.

LIBER ASSISARUM. The Book of Assizes or pleas of the crown.

A collection of cases that arose on assizes and other trials in the country. It was the fourth volume of the reports of the reign of Edward III. 3 Reeve, Eng.Law, 148.

LIBER AUTHENTICORUM. The authentic collection of the novels of Justinian, so called to distinguish them from the Epitome Juliani. Sohm, Rom. L. 14.

LIBER BANCUS. In old English law. Free bench. Bract. fol. 97*b*.

LIBER ET LEGALIS HOMO. In old English law. A free and lawful man. A term applied to a juror, or to one worthy of being a juryman, from the earliest period.

LIBER FEUDORUM. See Feudorum Liber.

LIBER HOMO. See Homo Liber.

LIBER JUDICIALIS OF ALFRED. Alfred's dome-book. See Dombec; Dome-Book.

LIBER JUDICIARUM. The book of judgment, or doom-book. The Saxon Domboc. Conjectured to be a book of statutes of ancient Saxon kings. See Jacob, *Domboc;* 1 Bla. Comm. 64.

LIBER NIGER. Black book or register in the exchequer. Chartularies of abbeys, cathedrals, etc. A name given to several ancient records. See Niger Liber.

LIBER NIGER DOMÛS REGIS. The black book of the king's household.

The title of a book in which there is an account of the household establishment of King Edward IV., and of the several musicians retained in his service, as well for his private amusement as for the service in his chapel. Enc. Lond.

LIBER NIGER SCACCARII. The black book of the exchequer, attributed to Gervase of Tilbury. 1 Reeve, Eng. Law, 220, note.

LIBER RUBER SCACCARII. The red book of the exchequer. 1 Reeve, Eng. Law, 220, note.

LIBERA. Lat. (Feminine of *liber, adj.*) Free; at liberty; exempt; not subject to toll or charge.

It is also a livery or delivery of so much corn or grass to a customary tenant, who cut down or prepared the said grass or corn, and received some part or small portion of it as a reward or gratuity. Cowell.

LIBERA BATELLA. In old records. A free boat; the right of having a boat to fish in a certain water; a species of free fishery.

LIBERA CHASEA HABENDA. A judicial writ granted to a person for a free chase belonging to his manor after proof made by inquiry of a jury that the same of right belongs to him. Wharton.

LIBERA ELEEMOSYNA. In old English law. Free alms; frankalmoigne. Bract. fol. 27*b*.

LIBERA FALDA. In old English law. Frank fold; free fold; free foldage. 1 Leon. 11.

LIBERA LEX. In old English law. Free law; frank law; the law of the land.

The law enjoyed by free and lawful men, as distinguished from such men as have lost the benefit and protection of the law in consequence of crime. Hence this term denoted the *status* of a man who stood guiltless before the law, and was *free*, in the sense of being entitled to its full protection and benefit. *Amittere liberam legem* (to lose one's free law) was to fall from that *status* by crime or infamy. See Co.Litt. 94*b*.

LIBERA PISCARIA. In old English law. A free fishery. Co. Litt. 122*a*.

LIBERA WARRENA. In old English law. Free warren, (*q. v.*).

LIBERAL. Free in giving; generous; not mean or narrow-minded; not literal or strict.

LIBERAL CONSTRUCTION OR INTERPRETATION. See Construction.

LIBERAL SYSTEM OF PUBLIC SCHOOLS. Constitutional provision requiring "liberal system of public schools" means that schools shall be liberally maintained and be open to common and general use. Vincent v. County Board of Education of Talladega County, 222 Ala. 216, 131 So. 893, 894.

LIBERAM LEGEM AMITTERE. To lose one's free law, (called the villainous judgment,) to become discredited or disabled as juror and witness, to forfeit goods and chattels and lands for life, to have those lands wasted, houses razed, trees rooted up, and one's body committed to prison. It was anciently pronounced against conspirators, but is now disused, the punishment substituted being fine and imprisonment. Hawk. P. C. 61, c. lxxii., s. 9; 3 Inst. 221; Jones v. Brinkley, 174 N.C. 23, 93 S.E. 372, 374.

LIBERARE. Lat.

In old English law. To deliver, transfer, or hand over. Applied to writs, panels of jurors, etc. Bract. fols. 116; 176*b*.

In the civil law. To free or set free; to liberate; to give one his liberty. Calvin.

LIBERATA PECUNIA NON LIBERAT OFFERENTEM. Co. Litt. 207. Money being restored does not set free the party offering.

LIBERATE. In old English practice. An original writ issuing out of chancery to the treasurer, chamberlains, and barons of the exchequer, for the payment of any annual pension, or other sum. Reg. Orig. 193; Cowell.

A writ issued to a sheriff, for the delivery of any lands or goods taken upon forfeits of recognizance. 4 Coke, 64*b*.

A writ issued to a gaoler for the delivery of a prisoner that had put in bail for his appearance. Cowell.

A writ which issues on lands, tenements, and chattels, being returned under an extent on a statute staple, commanding the sheriff to deliver them to the plaintiff, by the extent and appraisement mentioned in the writ of extent and in the sheriff's return thereto. See Com.Dig. *Statute Staple* (D 6).

LIBERATIO.

In old English law. Livery; money paid for the delivery or use of a thing.

In old Scotch law. Livery; a fee given to a servant or officer. Skene.

Money, meat, drink, clothes, etc., yearly given and delivered by the lord to his domestic servants. Blount.

LIBERATION. In Civil Law. The extinguishment of a contract, by which he who was bound becomes free or liberated. Wolff, *Dr. de la Nat.* § 749. Synonymous with payment. Dig. 50, 16, 47.

LIBERI.

In Saxon law. Freemen; the possessors of allodial lands. 1 Reve, Eng. Law, 5.

In the Civil law. Children. The term included "grandchildren."

LIBERTAS. Lat. Liberty; freedom; a privilege; a franchise.

LIBERTAS ECCLESIASTICA. Church liberty, or ecclesiastical immunity.

LIBERTAS EST NATURALIS FACULTAS EJUS QUOD CUIQUE FACERE LIBET, NISI QUOD DE JURE AUT VI PROHIBETUR. Co. Litt. 116. Liberty is that natural faculty which permits every one to do [or the natural power of doing] anything he pleases except that which is restrained by law or force.

LIBERTAS INESTIMABILIS RES EST. Liberty is an inestimable thing; a thing above price. Dig. 50, 17, 106; Fleta, lib. 2, c. 51, § 13.

LIBERTAS NON RECIPIT ÆSTIMATIONEM. Freedom does not admit of valuation. Bract. fol. 14.

LIBERTAS OMNIBUS REBUS FAVORABILIOR EST. Liberty is more favored than all things, [anything.] Dig. 50, 17, 122.

LIBERTATES REGALES AD CORONAM SPECTANTES EX CONCESSIONE REGUM À CORONÂ EXIERUNT. 2 Inst. 496. Royal franchises relating to the crown have emanated from the crown by grant of kings.

LIBERTATIBUS ALLOCANDIS. A writ lying for a citizen or burgess, impleaded contrary to his liberty, to have his privilege allowed. Reg. Orig. 262.

LIBERTATIBUS EXIGENDIS IN ITINERE. An ancient writ whereby the king commanded the justices in eyre to admit of an attorney for the defense of another's liberty. Reg. Orig. 19.

LIBERTI, LIBERTINI. Lat. In Roman law. Freedmen. The condition of those who, having been slaves, had been made free. 1 Brown, Civ. Law 99.

There seems to have been some difference in the use of these two words; the former denoting the manumitted slaves considered in their relations with their former master, who was now called their "patron;" the latter term applying to them in their *status* in the general social economy of Rome subsequent to manumission. *Lec. El. Dr. Rom.* § 93. See Morey, Rom.L. 236.

LIBERTICIDE. A destroyer of liberty.

LIBERTIES. Privileged districts exempt from the sheriff's jurisdiction; as, "gaol liberties." See Gaol.

In colonial times, laws, or legal rights resting upon them. The early colonial ordinances in Massachusetts were termed laws and liberties, and the code of 1641 the "Body of Liberties." Com. v. Alger, 7 Cush. (Mass.) 70.

Formerly, political subdivisions of Philadelphia; as, Northern Liberties.

"Liberties" referred to in statute concerning indecent liberties with female child are such as common sense of society would regard as indecent and improper. People v. Lakin, 286 Mich. 282, 282 N.W. 149, 150.

LIBERTINUM INGRATUM LEGES CIVILES IN PRISTINAM SERVITUTEM REDIGUNT; SED LEGES ANGLIÆ SEMEL MANUMISSUM SEMPER LIBERUM JUDICANT. Co. Litt. 137. The civil laws reduce an ungrateful freedman to his original slavery; but the laws of England regard a man once manumitted as ever after free.

LIBERTY. Freedom; exemption from extraneous control.

Freedom from all restraints except such as are justly imposed by law. Ex parte Kreutzer, 187 Wis. 463, 204 N.W. 595, 604. Freedom from restraint, under conditions essential to the equal enjoyment of the same right by others; freedom regulated by law. Kelly v. James, 37 S.D. 272, 157 N.W. 990, 991. The absence of arbitrary restraint, not immunity from reasonable regulations and prohibitions imposed in the interests of the community. Southern Utilities Co. v. City of Palatka, 86 Fla. 583, 99 So. 236, 240; Nelsen v. Tilley, 137 Neb. 327, 289 N.W. 388, 392, 126 A.L.R. 729; Arnold v. Board of Barber Examiners, 45 N.M. 57, 109 P.2d 779, 785.

The power of the will to follow the dictates of its unrestricted choice, and to direct the external acts of the individual without restraint, coercion, or control from other persons. See Booth v. Illinois, 22 S.Ct. 425, 184 U.S. 425, 46 L.Ed. 623; Munn v. Illinois, 94 U.S. 142, 24 L.Ed. 77; People v. Warden of City Prison, 51 N.E. 1006, 157 N.Y. 116, 43 L.R.A. 264, 68 Am.St.Rep. 763.

The word "liberty" includes and comprehends all personal rights and their enjoyment. Rosenblum v. Rosenblum, 42 N.Y.S.2d 626, 630, 181 Misc. 78. It embraces freedom from duress, In re Miner, D.C.Ill., 9 F.Supp. 1, 7; freedom from governmental interference in exercise of intellect, in formation of opinions, in the expression of them, and in action or inaction dictated by judgment, Zavilla v. Masse, 112 Colo. 183, 147 P.2d 823, 827; freedom from servitude, imprisonment or restraint, Committee for Industrial Organization v. Hague, D.C.N.J., 25 F.Supp. 127, 131, 141; People v. Wood, 272 N.Y.S. 258, 151 Misc. 66; freedom in enjoyment and use of all of one's powers, faculties and property, Grosjean v. American Press Co., La., 56 S.Ct. 444, 446, 297 U.S. 233, 80 L.Ed. 660; City of Mt. Vernon v. Julian, 369 Ill. 447, 17 N.E.2d 52, 55, 119 A.L.R. 747; freedom of assembly, Rosenblum v. Rosenblum, 42 N.Y.S. 2d 626, 630, 181 Misc. 78; freedom of citizen from banishment, Committee for Industrial Organization v. Hague, D.C.N.J., 25 F.Supp. 127, 141; freedom of conscience, Gobitis v. Minersville School Dist., D.C.Pa., 21 F.Supp. 581, 584, 587; freedom of contract, State ex rel. Hamby v. Cummings, 166 Tenn. 460, 63 S.W.2d 515; State v. Henry, 37 N.M. 536, 25 P.2d 204, 90 A.L.R. 805; freedom of locomotion or movement, Commonwealth v. Doe, 109 Pa.Super. 187, 167 A. 241, 242; Committee for Industrial Organization v. Hague, D.C.N.J., 25 F.Supp. 127, 131, 141; freedom of occupation, Koos v. Saunders, 349 Ill. 442, 182 N.E. 415, 418; freedom of press, Commonwealth v. Nichols, 301 Mass. 584, 18 N.E.2d 166, 167; Near v. State of Minnesota ex rel. Olson (Minn.) 51 S.Ct. 625, 628, 283 U.S. 697, 75 L.Ed. 1357; freedom of religion, Gabrielli v. Knickerbocker, 12 Cal.2d 85, 82 P.2d 391, 393; Hamilton v. City of Montrose, 109 Colo. 228, 124 P.2d 757, 759; Cantwell v. State of Connecticut, Conn., 60 S.Ct. 900, 903, 310 U.S. 296, 84 L.Ed. 1213, 128 A.L.R. 1352; freedom of speech, Ghadiali v. Delaware State Medical Soc., D.C.Del., 28 F.Supp. 841, 844; Carpenters and Joiners Union of America, Local No. 213, v. Ritter's Cafe, Tex., 62 S.Ct. 807, 809, 315 U.S. 722, 86 L.Ed. 1143. It also embraces right of self-defense against unlawful violence, Rohrer v. Milk Control Board, 121 Pa. Super. 281, 184 A. 133, 136; right to acquire and enjoy property, Rohrer v. Milk Control Board, 121 Pa.Super. 281, 184 A. 133, 136; right to acquire useful knowledge, Rosenblum v. Rosenblum, 42 N.Y.S.2d 626, 630, 181 Misc. 78; right to carry on business, Mlle. Reif, Inc., v. Randau, 1 N.Y.S.2d 515, 518, 166 Misc. 247; right to earn livelihood in any lawful calling. Saidel v. Village of Tupper Lake, 4 N.Y.S.2d 814, 818, 254 App.Div. 22; right to emigrate, and if a citizen, to return, Committee for Industrial Organization v. Hague, D.C.N.J., 25 F.Supp. 127, 141; right to engage in a lawful business, to determine the price of one's labor, and to fix the hours when one's place of business shall be kept open, State Board of Barber Examiners v. Cloud, 220 Ind. 552, 44 N.E.2d 972, 980; right to enjoy to the fullest extent the privileges and immunities given or assured by law to people living within the country, McGrew v. Industrial Commission, 96 Utah 203, 85 P.2d 608, 611; right to forswear allegiance and expatriate oneself, Committee for Industrial Organization v. Hague, D.C. N.J., 25 F.Supp. 127, 141; right to freely buy and sell as others may, Rohrer v. Milk Control Board, 121 Pa.Super. 281, 184 A. 133, 136; right to labor, Simon v. Schwachman, 301 Mass. 573, 18 N.E.2d 1, 3; right to live and work where one will, People v. Wood, 272 N.Y.S. 258, 151 Misc. 66; right to marry and have a family, Committee for Industrial Organization v. Hague, D.C.N.J., 25 F.Supp. 127, 141; Rosenblum v. Rosenblum, 42 N.Y.S.2d 626, 630, 181 Misc. 78; right to pursue chosen calling, State v. Chisesi, 187 La. 675, 175 So. 453; People v. Cohen, 8 N.Y.S.2d 70, 72, 255 App.Div. 485; right to use property according owner's will, State Bank & Trust Co. v. Village of Wilmette, 358 Ill. 311, 193 N.E. 131, 133, 96 A.L.R. 1327.

Liberty, on its positive side, denotes the fullness of individual existence; on its negative side it denotes the necessary restraint on all, which is needed to promote the greatest possible amount of liberty for each. Amos, Science of Law, p. 90.

The word "liberty" as used in the state and federal Constitutions means, in a negative sense, freedom from restraint, but in a positive sense, it involves the idea of freedom secured by the imposition of restraint, and it is in this positive sense that the state, in the exercise of its police powers, promotes the freedom of all by the imposition upon particular persons of restraints which are deemed necessary for the general welfare. Fitzsimmons v. New York State Athletic Commission, Sup., 146 N.Y.S. 117, 121.

"Liberty," in so far as it is noticed by government, is restraint, rather than license. It is a yielding of the individual will to that of the many, subject to such constitutional guarantees or limitations as will preserve those rights and privileges which are admitted of all men to be fundamental. "Liberty" in the civil state is a giving up of natural right in consideration of equal protection and opportunity. Weber v. Doust, 84 Wash. 330, 146 P. 623, 625.

The "personal liberty" guaranteed by Const. U. S. Amend. 13 consists in the power of locomotion without imprisonment or restraint unless by due course of law, except those restraints imposed to prevent commission of threatened crime or in punishment of crime committed, those in punishment of contempts of courts or legislative bodies or to render their jurisdiction effectual, and those necessary to enforce the duty citizens owe in defense of the state to protect community against acts of those who by reason of mental infirmity are incapable of self-control. Ex parte Hudgins, 86 W.Va. 526, 103 S.E. 327, 329, 9 A.L.R. 1361.

The "liberty" safeguarded by Fourteenth Amendment is liberty in a social organization which requires the protection of law against the evils which menace the health, safety, morals, and welfare of the people. West Coast Hotel Co. v. Parrish, Wash., 57 S.Ct. 578, 581, 582, 300 U.S. 379, 81 L.Ed. 703, 108 A.L.R. 1330.

Also, a franchise or personal privilege, being some part of the sovereign power, vested in an individual, either by grant or prescription.

The term is used in the expression, rights, liberties, and franchises, as a word of the same general class and meaning with those words and privileges. This use of the term is said to have been strictly conformable to its sense as used in Magna Charta and in English declarations of rights, statutes, grants, etc.; Com. v. Alger, 7 Cush. (Mass.) 70.

In a derivative sense, the place, district, or boundaries within which a special franchise is enjoyed, an immunity claimed, or a jurisdiction exercised. In this sense, the term is commonly used in the plural; as the "liberties of the city."

Civil Liberty

The liberty of a member of society, being a man's natural liberty, so far restrained by human laws (and no further) as is necessary and expedient for the general advantage of the public. 1 Bl. Comm. 125; 2 Steph. 487

The power of doing whatever the laws permit. 1 Bl. Comm. 6; Inst. 1, 3, 1. See Dennis v. Moses, 18 Wash. 537, 52 P. 333, 40 L.R.A. 302. The greatest amount of absolute liberty which can, in the nature of things, be equally possessed by every citizen in a state. Guarantied protection against interference with the interests and rights held dear and important by large classes of civilized men, or by all the members of a state, together with an effectual share in the making and administration of the laws, as the best apparatus to secure that protection. Lieber, Civ.Lib. 24.

Liberty of a Port

In marine insurance. A license or permission incorporated in a marine policy allowing the vessel to touch and trade at a designated port other than the principal port of destination. See Allegre v. Maryland Ins. Co., 8 Gill & J. (Md.) 200, 29 Am.Dec. 536.

Liberty of Conscience

Liberty for each individual to decide for himself what is to him religious. Gobitis v. Minersville School Dist., D.C.Pa., 21 F.Supp. 581, 584. See, also, Religious Liberty, as defined below.

Liberty of Contract

The ability at will, to make or abstain from making, a binding obligation enforced by the sanctions at the law. Judson, Liberty of Contract, Rep. Am. Bar Ass'n (1891) 233.

The right to contract about one's affairs, including the right to make contracts of employment, and to obtain the best terms one can as the result of private bargaining. Adkins v. Children's Hospital of District of Columbia, 43 S. Ct. 394, 396, 261 U.S. 525, 67 L.Ed. 785, 24 A.L.R. 1238. It includes the corresponding right to accept a contract proposed. St. Louis Southwestern Ry. Co. of Texas v. Griffin, 106 Tex. 477, 171 S.W. 703, 704, L.R.A.1917B, 1108. There is, however, no absolute freedom of contract. The government may regulate or forbid any contract reasonably calculated to affect injuriously public interest. Atlantic Coast Line R. Co. v. Riverside Mills, 31 S.Ct. 164, 219 U.S. 186, 55 L.Ed. 167, 31 L.R.A.,N.S., 7; Carleton Screw Products Co. v. Fleming, C.C.A.Minn., 126 F.2d 537, 541. It means freedom from arbitrary or unreasonable restraint, not immunity from reasonable regulation to safeguard public interest, Saucier v. Life & Casualty Ins. Co. of Tennessee, 189 Miss. 693, 198 So. 625, 631; or the right to make contracts with competent persons on a plane of relative parity or freedom of choice and within the limits allowed or not forbidden by law. McGrew v. Industrial Commission, 96 Utah 203, 85 P.2d 608, 612.

Liberty of Speech

Freedom accorded by the constitution or laws of a state to express opinions and facts by word of mouth, uncontrolled by any censorship or restrictions of government.

But language tending to the violation of the rights of personal security and private property, and toward breaches of the public peace, is an abuse of the right, State v. Boyd, 86 N.J.L. 75, 91 A. 586, 587; which is not license, nor lawlessness, but rather the right to fairly criticize and comment, State v. Pape, 90 Conn. 98, 96 A. 313, 315. Liberty never has meant the unrestricted right to say what one pleases at all times and under all circumstances. Fraina v. U. S., C.C.A.N.Y., 255 F. 28, 35. It is not an absolute right. State v. Chaplinsky, 91 N.H. 310, 18 A.2d 754, 760. It has been thought that the liberty to speak includes the corresponding right to be silent, and that this right is infringed by a statute compelling a corporation to give a discharged employee a statement of the cause of discharge. St. Louis Southwestern Ry. Co. of Texas v. Griffin, 106 Tex. 477, 171 S.W. 703, 705, L.R.A.1917B, 1108. As used in Constitution, "freedom of speech" means freedom of speech as it was understood by the common law when the Constitution was adopted. State v. Boloff, 138 Or. 568, 7 P.2d 775, 781.

Liberty of the Globe

In marine insurance. A license or permission incorporated in a marine policy authorizing the vessel to go to any part of the world, instead of being confined to a particular port of destination. See Eyre v. Marine Ins. Co., 6 Whart. (Pa.) 254.

Liberty of the Press

The right to print and publish the truth, from good motives and for justifiable ends. People v. Croswell, 3 Johns. Cas. 394. Kline v. Robert M. McBride & Co., 11 N.Y.S.2d 674, 679, 170 Misc. 974.

The right to print without any previous license, subject to the consequences of the law. 3 Term 431; Respublica v. Dennie, 4 Yeates, Pa., 267, 2 Am.Dec. 402; Williams Printing Co. v. Saunders, 113 Va. 156, 73 S.E. 472, Ann.Cas. 1913E, 693. The right to publish whatever one may please. Knapp v. Post Printing & Publishing Co., 111 Colo. 492, 144 P.2d 981, 985; Howard Sports Daily v. Weller, 179 Md. 355, 18 A.2d 210, 215; and to be protected against any responsibility for so doing except so far as such publications, from their blasphemy, obscenity, or scandalous character, may be a public offense, or as by their falsehood and malice they may injuriously affect the standing, reputation, or pecuniary interests of individuals, Cooley, Const. Lim. p. 422. It is said to consist in this: "That neither courts of justice, nor any judges whatever, are authorized to take notice of writings *intended* for the press, but are confined to those which are actually printed." De Lolme, Eng.Const. 254. Immunity from previous restraints or [from] censorship. Grosjean v. American Press Co., La., 297 U.S. 233, 56 S.Ct. 444, 449, 80 L.Ed. 660.

Liberty of the Rules

A privilege to go out of the Fleet and Marshalsea prisons within certain limits, and there reside. Abolished by 5 & 6 Vict. c. 22.

Liberty to Hold Pleas

The liberty of having a court of one's own. Thus certain lords had the privilege of holding pleas within their own manors.

Natural Liberty

The power of acting as one thinks fit, without any restraint or control, unless by the law of nature. 1 Bl. Comm. 125.

The right which nature gives to all mankind of disposing of their persons and property after the manner they judge most consistent with their happiness, on condition of their acting within the limits of the law of nature, and so as not to interfere with an equal exercise of the same rights by other men. Burlamaqui, c. 3, § 15; 1 Bl.Comm. 125. It is called by Lieber *social* liberty, and is defined as the protection or unrestrained action in as high a degree as the same claim of protection of each individual admits of.

Personal Liberty

The right or power of locomotion; of changing situation, or moving one's person to whatsoever place one's own inclination may direct, without imprisonment or restraint, unless by due course of law. 1 Bl. Comm. 134. Civil Rights Cases, 3 S.Ct. 42, 109 U.S. 3, 27 L.Ed. 835; Pinkerton v. Verberg, 78 Mich. 573, 44 N.W. 579, 7 L.R.A. 507, 18 Am.St.Rep. 473.

Political Liberty

Liberty of the citizen to participate in the operations of government, and particularly in the making and administration of the laws.

Religious Liberty

Freedom from dictation, constraint, or control in matters affecting the conscience, religious beliefs, and the practice of religion; freedom to entertain and express any or no system of religious opinions, and to engage in or refrain from any form of religious observance or public or private religious worship, not inconsistent with the peace and good order of society and the general welfare. See Frazee's Case, 63 Mich. 396, 30 N.W. 72, 6 Am.St.Rep. 310; State v. White, 64 N.H. 48, 5 A. 828.

LIBERUM CORPUS NULLAM RECIPIT ÆSTIMATIONEM. Dig. 9, 3, 7. The body of a freeman does not admit of valuation.

LIBERUM EST CUIQUE APUD SE EXPLORARE AN EXPEDIAT SIBI CONSILIUM. Every one is free to ascertain for himself whether a recommendation is advantageous to his interest. Upton v. Vail, 6 Johns. (N.Y.) 181, 184, 5 Am.Dec. 210.

LIBERUM MARITAGIUM. In old English law. Frank-marriage. Bract. fol. 21; Littleton, § 17.

LIBERUM SERVITIUM. Free service. Service of a warlike sort by a feudatory tenant; sometimes called *"servitium liberum armorum."* Jacob. See, also, Servitium Liberum.

Service not unbecoming the character of a freeman and a soldier to perform; as to serve under the lord in his wars, to pay a sum of money, and the like. 2 Bl.Comm. 60.

The tenure of free service does not make a villein a freeman, unless homage or manumission precede, any more than a tenure by villein services makes a freeman a villein. Bract. fol. 24.

LIBERUM SOCAGIUM. In old English law. Free socage. Bract. fol. 207; 2 Bl. Comm. 61, 62.

LIBERUM TENEMENTUM.

In Pleading. A plea of freehold. A plea by the defendant in an action of trespass to real property that the *locus in quo* is his freehold, or that of a third person, under whom he acted. 1 Tidd, Pr. 645; 2 Salk. 453; 7 Term 355; 1 Wms. Saund. 299*b*.

In Realty Law. Freehold. Frank-tenement.

LIBLAC. In Saxon law. Witchcraft, particularly that kind which consisted in the compounding and administering of drugs and philters. Sometimes occurring in the Latinized form *liblacum*.

LIBRA. In old English law. A pound; also a sum of money equal to a pound sterling.

LIBRA ARSA. A pound burned; that is, melted, or assayed by melting, to test its purity. *Libræ arsæ et pensatæ*, pounds burned and weighed. A frequent expression in Domesday, to denote the purer coin in which rents were paid. Spelman; Cowell.

LIBRA NUMERATA. A pound of money counted instead of being weighed. Spelman.

LIBRA PENSA. A pound of money by weight.

It was usual in former days not only to sell the money, but to weigh it; because many cities, lords, and bishops, having their mints, coined money, and often very bad money, too, for which reason, though the pound consisted of 20 shillings, they weighed it. Enc.Lond.

LIBRARIUS. In Roman law. A writer or amanuensis; a copyist. Dig. 50, 17, 92.

LIBRARY. While word "library" is at times used as meaning both a collection of books and the building or room in which such collection is housed, it is also used as meaning a collection of books not kept for sale. In re Mead's Estate, 227 Wis. 311, 277 N.W. 694, 701.

LIBRATA TERRÆ. A portion of ground containing four oxgangs, and every oxgang fourteen acres. Cowell. This is the same with what in Scotland was called "pound-land" of old extent. Wharton. See Oxgang; Pound of Land.

LIBRIPENS. In Roman law. A weigher or balance-holder. The person who held a brazen balance in the ceremony of emancipation *per æs et libram*. Inst. 2, 10, 1.

A neutral person or balance holder, who was present at a conveyance of real property. He held in his hand the symbolic balance, which was struck by the purchaser with a piece of bronze as a sign of the completion of the conveyance. The bronze was then transferred to the seller as a sign of the purchase money. Morey, Rom.L. 21, 80.

LIBRORUM APPELLATIONE CONTINENTUR OMNIA VOLUMINA, SIVE IN CHARTA, SIVE IN MEMBRANA SINT, SIVE IN QUAVIS ALIA MATERIA. Under the name of books are contained all volumes, whether upon paper, or parchment, or any other material. Dig. 32, 52, *pr.*

LICENCIADO. In Spanish law. An attorney or advocate; particularly, a person admitted to the degree of "Licentiate in Jurisprudence" by any of the literary universities of Spain and who is thereby authorized to practice in all the courts. Escriche.

LICENSE. Certificate or the document itself which gives permission. Aldrich v. City of Syracuse, 236 N.Y.S. 614, 617, 134 Misc. 698. Permission or authority. Independent School Dist., Class A, No. 1, Cassia County v. Pfost, 51 Idaho 240, 4 P.2d 893, 897; Monsour v. City of Shreveport, 194 La. 625, 194 So. 569, 571; Platt v. Bender, La.App., 178 So. 678, 682.

Authority or liberty given to do or forbear any act. Monsour v. City of Shreveport, 194 La. 625, 194 So. 569, 571. Leave to do thing which licensor could prevent. Western Electric Co. v. Pacent Reproducer Corporation, C.C.A.N.Y., 42 F.2d 116, 118. Permission by some competent authority to do some act which, without such permission, would be illegal. State ex rel. Zugravu v. O'Brien, 130 Ohio St. 23, 196 N.E. 664; Solberg v. Davenport, 211 Iowa, 612, 232 N.W. 477, 480; Standard Oil Co. (Indiana) v. State Board of Equalization, 110 Mont. 5, 99 P.2d 229, 234. Permission to do a particular thing, to exercise a certain privilege or to carry on a particular business or to pursue a certain occupation. Blatz Brewing Co. v. Collins, Cal.App., 160 P.2d 37, 39, 40. Permission to do something which without the license would not be allowable. City of Shreveport v. Brister, 194 La. 615, 194 So. 566, 567. Great Atlantic & Pacific Tea Co. v. City of Lexington, 256 Ky. 595, 76 S.W.2d 894, 896. Privilege from state or sovereign. M. Itzkowitz & Sons v. Geraghty, 247 N.Y.S. 703, 704, 139 Misc. 163; Alabama Power Co. v. Federal Power Commission, 75 U.S.App.D.C. 315, 128 F.2d 280, 289. Revocable certificate of convenience and necessity. Ex parte Lockhart, 350 Mo. 1220, 171 S.W.2d 660, 666. To "license" means to confer right or power which does not exist without it. Inter-City Coach Lines v. Harrison, 172 Ga. 390 157 S.E. 673, 676; S. S. Kresge Co. v. City of Bluefield, 117 W.Va. 17, 183 S.E. 601, 602.

Admission to Practice

Accountant's certificate is a license to practice accountancy. Jaeger Mfg. Co. v. Maryland Casualty Co., 231 Iowa 151, 300 N.W. 680, 683.

Permission to pursue calling of veterinary surgery and medicine. Staniforth v. State, 34 Ohio App. 239, 170 N.E. 578, 580.

The words "admit" and "license" as used in statute providing that power to admit and license persons to practice as attorneys is vested exclusively in the Supreme Court are inseparable and refer to the same thing. In re H—— S——, 236 Mo.App. 1296, 165 S.W.2d 300, 302.

Burial

Right of burial as license, Bockel v. Fidelity Development Co., Tex.Civ.App., 101 S.W.2d 628.

Constitutional Law and Law of Contracts

A permission, by a competent authority to do some act which without such authorization would be illegal, or would be a trespass or a tort. State v. Hipp, 38 Ohio St. 226; Hubman v. State, 61 Ark. 482, 33 S.W. 843, Chicago v. Collins, 175 Ill. 445, 51 N.E. 907, 49 L.R.A. 408, 67 L.R.A. 224. A permit or privilege to do what otherwise would be unlawful. Palmetto Fire Ins. Co. v. Beha, D.C. N.Y., 13 F.2d 500, 505; La Plante v. State Board of Public Roads, 47 R.I. 258, 131 A. 641, 642; State ex rel. Biscayne Kennel Club v. Stein, 130 Fla. 517, 178 So. 133, 135. Also, the written evidence of permission.

A permit, granted by the sovereign, generally for a consideration (Smith v. Commonwealth, 175 Ky. 286, 194 S.W. 367, 370), to a person, firm, or corporation to pursue some occupation or to carry on some business subject to regulation under the police power. State ex rel. Guillot v. Central Bank & Trust Co., 143 La. 1053, 79 So. 857, 858.

A "license" is not a contract between the state and the licensee, but is a mere personal permit. Rosenblatt v. California State Board of Pharmacy, 69 Cal.App.2d 69, 158 P.2d 199, 203. Neither is it property or a property right. American States Water Service Co. of California v. Johnson, 31 Cal.App.2d 606, 88 P.2d 770, 774; Garford Trucking v. Hoffman, 114 N.J.L. 522, 177 A. 882, 887; nor does it create a vested right. State ex rel. Biscayne Kennel Club v. Stein, 130 Fla. 517, 178 So. 133, 135; Asbury Hospital v. Cass County, 72 N.D. 359, 7 N.W.2d 438, 452.

Exclusive License

See Exclusive License.

High License

A system for the regulation and restriction of the traffic in intoxicating liquors, of which the distinguishing feature is the grant of licenses only to carefully selected persons and the charging of a license fee so great in amount as automatically to limit the number of retailers.

Inflammable Articles

A license to keep, store, and sell inflammable articles, is not merely a personal privilege, but is essentially a grant. Street Com'rs of Boston, 307 Mass. 495, 30 N.E.2d 380, 381, 131 A.L.R. 1336.

International Law

Permission granted by a belligerent state to its own subjects, or to the subjects of the enemy, to carry on a trade interdicted by war. Wheat. Int. Law, 447.

Letter of License

See Letter of License.

Liquor

A license is a permission to do something which without such permission would have been unauthorized or prohibited. Collier v. State, 54 Ga. App. 346, 187 S.E. 843, 845.

A license to sell liquor is merely permit to do that which otherwise would be unlawful to do and is not property. Oval Bar & Restaurant v. Bruckman, 30 N.Y.S.2d 394, 395, 177 Misc. 244; State Board of Equalization of California v. Superior Court in and for City and County of San Francisco, 5 Cal.App.2d 374, 42 P.2d 1076, 1077. Such license is a mere privilege. State v. Wipke, 345 Mo. 283, 133 S.W.2d 354, 357. Permits to carry on liquor business are mere "licenses" revocable as provided in such act and do not create a property right. State ex rel. Gutter v. Hawley, Ohio App., 44 N.E.2d 815, 820.

Marriage License

See Marriage License.

Motor Carriers

A grant by state commerce commission of petition for certificate of convenience and necessity to operate as motor carrier is the grant of a license. Railway Express Agency v. Illinois Commerce Commission, 374 Ill. 151, 28 N.E.2d 116, 118.

City having right to regulate use of its streets by motor vehicles for hire may issue licenses, a license being permission. Ex parte Schutte, 118 Tex.Cr.R. 182, 42 S.W.2d 252, 255.

Motor Vehicles

License to operate motor vehicle is mere privilege, and not a contract or property right. Garford Trucking v. Hoffman, 114 N.J.L. 522, 177 A. 882, 887; Blashfield, Cyc. of Automobile Law and Prac., Perm. Ed., § 580.

Patent Law

A written authority granted by the owner of a patent to another person empowering the latter to make or use the patented article for a limited period or in a limited territory.

A permission to make, use or sell articles embodying invention. De Forest Radio Telephone & Telegraph Co. v. Radio Corporation of America, D.C.Del., 9 F.2d 150, 151. A transfer which does not affect the monopoly, except by estopping licensor from exercising his prohibitory powers in derogation of privileges conferred upon licensee. L. L. Brown Paper Co. v. Hydroiloid, Inc., D.C.N.Y., 32 F.Supp. 857, 867, 868; De Forest Radio Telephone & Telegraph Co. v. Radio Corporation of America, D.C.Del., 9 F.2d 150, 151. An assignment by the patentee to another of rights less in degree than the patent itself. Arnold v. North American Chemical Co., 232 Mass. 196, 122 N.E. 283, 284. Any right to make, use, or sell the patented invention, which is less than an undivided part interest in the patent itself. Baker v. Murray Tool & Supply Co., 137 Okl. 288, 279 P. 340, 343. Any transfer of patent rights short of assignment. Wayman v. Louis Lipp Co., D.C.Ohio, 222 F. 679, 681. Language used by owner of patent, or any conduct on his part exhibited to another, from which that other may properly infer that owner consents to his use of patent, on which the other acts, constitutes a license. General Motors Corporation v. Dailey, C.C.A.Mich., 93 F.2d 938, 941; Finley v. Asphalt Paving Co. of St. Louis, C.C.A.Mo., 69 F.2d 498, 504. The right not to be sued. L. L. Brown Paper Co. v. Hydroiloid, Inc., D.C.N.Y., 32 F.Supp. 857, 867, 868. Transfer of exclusive right to do merely two of the three rights under patent to make, use, and vend invention. Overman Cushion Tire Co. v. Goodyear Tire & Rubber Co., C.C.A.N.Y., 59 F.2d 998, 1000.

Pleading

A plea of justification to an action of trespass that the defendant was authorized by the owner of the freehold to commit the trespass complained of.

It is generally revocable at will of owner of land, Messer v. City of Birmingham, 243 Ala. 520, 10 So.2d 760, 763; Stanolind Pipe Line Co. v. Ellis, 142 Kan. 102, 45 P.2d 846, 848.

Real Property Law

Permission or authority to do particular act or series of acts on land of another without possessing any estate or interest therein. Lang v. Dupuis, 382 Ill. 101, 46 N.E.2d 21, 23, 24; Sisters of Mercy of Cedar Rapids v. Lightner, 223 Iowa 1049, 274 N.W. 86, 94; Stanolind Pipe Line Co. v. Ellis, 142 Kan. 102, 45 P.2d 846, 848. A permissive use. Novinger v. Shoop, Mo.Sup., 201 S.W. 64, 66; Caldwell v. Gem Packing Co., 52 Cal.App.2d 80, 125 P. 2d 901, 903.

Also, the written evidence of authority accorded.

Executed license. That which exists when the licensed act has been done.

Executory license. That which exists where the licensed act has not been performed.

Express license. One which is granted in direct terms.

Implied license. One which is presumed to have been given from the acts of the party authorized to give it.

Simple license. One revocable at the will of the grantor; *i. e.*, one not coupled with a grant. Cook v. Stearnes, 11 Mass. 533; Mumford v. Whitney, 15 Wend. (N.Y.) 380, 30 Am.Dec. 60; Fluker v. Banking Co., 81 Ga. 461, 8 S.E. 529, 2 L.R.A. 843, 12 Am.St.Rep. 328; Wheeler v. West, 78 Cal. 95, 20 P. 45; Cowles v. Kidder, 24 N.H. 364, 57 Am. Dec. 287.

A license is a personal privilege, Minnesota Valley Gun Club v. Northline Corporation, 207 Minn. 126, 290 N.W. 222, 224; Burnham v. Burnham, 130 Me. 409, 156 A. 823, 825; a personal, revocable, and unassignable privilege, Schnuerle v. Gilbert, 43 S.D. 535, 180 N.W. 953, 954; Morrison v. Fellman, 271 N.Y.S. 436, 150 Misc. 772; Beckett v. City of Paris Dry Goods Co., 14 Cal.2d 633, 96 P.2d 122, 124; a privilege to occupy under the owner, Rhode Island Marine Transp. Co. v. Interstate Nav. Co., 52 R.I. 322, 161 A. 108, 109; San Juan Gold Co. v. San Juan Ridge Mut. Water Ass'n, 34 Cal.App.2d 159, 93 P.2d 582, 589; an authority to do a particular act or series of acts which would amount to a trespass without permission, Barnett v. Lincoln, 162 Wash. 613, 299 P. 392, 394. It does not operate to confer upon or vest in licensee any title, interest or estate in property and licensee is "estopped" during time that license exists to deny title of licensor or of any one claiming under him, Wood v. Gregory, Mo., 155 S.W.2d 168, 171, 172. It is unassignable, Sweeney v. Bird, 293 Mich. 624, 292 N.W. 506, 508, 509.

A license is distinguished from an "easement," which implies an interest in the land, and a "lease," or right to take the profits of land. It may be, however, and often, is, coupled with a grant of some interest in the land itself, or right to take the profits. 1 Washb.Real Prop. *398; Davis v. Tway, 16 Ariz. 566, 147 P. 750, L.R.A.1915E, 604; National Memorial Park v. C. I. R., C.C.A.4, 145 F.2d 1008, 1015.

A license is an authority to enter on land which is generally granted by parol and may be revoked by the licensor at pleasure and is not assignable, being a personal privilege, while an easement confers an interest in the land and may not be terminated at the pleasure of the servient owner. Louisville Chair & Furniture Co. v. Otter, 219 Ky. 757, 294 S.W. 483, 485.

The distinction between an easement and a license is often so metaphysical, subtle, and shadowy as to elude analysis. But there are certain fundamental principles underlying most cases which enable courts to distinguish an easement from a license when construed in the light of surrounding circumstances. East Jersey Iron Co. v. Wright, 32 N.J.Eq. 254; Nunnelly v. Iron Co., 94 Tenn. 397, 29 S.W. 361, 28 L.R.A. 421.

A "tenancy" implies some interest in the land leased, while a "license" conveys only a temporary privilege in the use of property usually revocable at the will of the licensor. Klein v. City of Portland, 106 Or. 686, 213 P. 147, 150; Vicker v. Byrne, 155 Wis. 281, 143 N.W. 186, 188. But see Mitchell v. Probst, 52 Okl. 10, 152 P. 597, 598.

An "invitation" is inferred where there is a common interest or mutual advantage, or where an owner or occupant of premises, by acts or conduct, leads another to believe the premises or something thereon were intended to be used by such other person, that such use is not only acquiesced in by the owner or occupant, but is in accordance with the intention or design for which the way, place, or thing was adapted or prepared or allowed to be used; while a "license" is implied where the object is the mere pleasure, convenience, or benefit of the person enjoying the privilege. Kruntorad v. Chicago, R. I. & P. Ry. Co., 111 Neb. 753, 197 N.W. 611, 612. Polluck v. Minneapolis & St. L. R. Co., 44 S.D. 249, 183 N.W. 859, 862.

Registrar's License

See Registrar's License.

Rod License

See Rod License.

Special License

In English law. One granted by the archbishop of Canterbury to authorize a marriage at any time or place whatever. 2 Steph. Comm. 247, 255.

Streets and Ways

A permit to use street is a mere license revocable at pleasure. City of Boston v. A. W. Perry, Inc., 304 Mass. 18, 22 N.E.2d 627, 630; Lanham v. Forney, 196 Wash. 62, 81 P.2d 777, 779.

City having right to regulate use of its streets by motor vehicles for hire may issue licenses; license being permission. Ex parte Schutte, 118 Tex.Cr.R. 182, 42 S.W.2d 252, 255. Permissive use and license as synonymous. Aldine Realty Co. of Pittsburgh v. Manor Real Estate & Trust Co., 297 Pa. 583, 148 A. 56, 58. Street railway location or elevated railway location as license. Boston Elevated Ry. Co. v. Commonwealth, 310 Mass. 528, 39 N.E.2d 87, 103, 106, 108.

The privilege of using the streets and highways by the operation thereon of motor carriers for hire can be acquired only by permission or license from the state or its political subdivisions. Blashfield, Cyc. of Automobile Law and Prac., Perm. Ed., § 331.

Trade, Business or Calling

Authority or permission to do or carry on some trade or business which would otherwise be unlawful. Solberg v. Davenport, 211 Iowa 612, 232 N.W. 477, 480; S. S. Kresge Co. v. City of Bluefield, 117 W.Va. 17, 183 S.E. 601, 602; Standard Oil Co. (Indiana) v. State Board of Equalization, 110 Mont. 5, 99 P.2d 229, 234. Permission conferred by proper authority, to pursue certain trade, profession, or calling. Staniforth v. State, 34 Ohio App. 239, 170 N.E. 578, 580. Privilege to carry on a business. Johnson v. Liquor Control Commission, 266 Mich. 682, 254 N.W. 557; Lloyds of Texas v. Bobbitt, Tex.Civ.App., 40 S.W.2d 897, 901.

A license confers upon licensee neither contractual nor vested rights. Rosenblatt v. California State Board of Pharmacy, 69 Cal.App.2d 69, 158 P.2d 199, 203. Asbury Hospital v. Cass County, 72 N.D. 359, 7 N.W.2d 438, 452. Nor does it create a property right. State ex rel. Zugravu v. O'Brien, 130 Ohio St. 23, 196 N.E. 664.

Trade-Mark

Permission to use a trade-mark in an area where the purported owner's goods have not become known and identified by his use of mark is a naked "license". E. F. Prichard Co. v. Consumers Brewing Co., C.C.A.Ky., 136 F.2d 512, 521.

LICENSE CASES. The name given to the group of cases including Peirce v. New Hampshire, 5 How. 504, 12 L.Ed. 256, decided by the United States supreme court in 1847, to the effect that state laws requiring a license or the payment of a tax for the privilege of selling intoxicating liquors were not in conflict with the constitutional provision giving to congress the power to regulate interstate commerce, even as applied to liquors imported from another state and remaining in the original and unbroken packages. This decision was overruled in Leisy v. Hardin, 10 Sup.Ct. 681, 135 U.S. 100, 34 L.Ed. 128, which in turn was counteracted by the act of congress of August 8, 1890, commonly called the "Wilson law."

LICENSE FEE or TAX. Charge imposed by sovereign for a privilege. Pennsylvania Liquor Control Board v. Publicker Commercial Alcohol Co., 347 Pa. 555, 32 A.2d 914, 917. Stone v. General Contract Purchase Corporation, 193 Miss. 301, 7 So.2d 806, 808, 140 A.L.R. 1029.

Charge or fee imposed primarily for the discouragement of dangerous employments, the protection of the safety of the public, or the regulation of relative rights, privileges, or duties as between individuals, Conard v. State, Del. Super., 2 Terry 107, 16 A.2d 121, 125. Price paid to governmental or municipal authority for a license to engage in and pursue a particular calling or occupation. See Home Ins. Co. v. Augusta, 50 Ga. 537; Levi v. Louisville, 97 Ky. 394, 30 S.W. 973, 28 L.R.A. 480. Tax on privilege of exercising corporate franchise. City Investments v. Johnson, 6 Cal.2d 150, 56 P.2d 939, 940. The term "license tax" includes both charge imposed under police power for privilege of obtaining license to conduct particular business, and tax imposed upon business for sole purpose of raising revenue; "license tax" being defined as sum exacted for privilege of carrying on particular occupation. City of Waycross v. Bell, 169 Ga. 57, 149 S.E. 641, 642. Where a fee is exacted and something is required or permitted in addition to the payment of the sum, either to be done by the licensee, or by some regulation or restriction imposed on him, then the fee is a "license fee". Conard v. State, Del.Super., 2 Terry 107, 16 A.2d 121, 125.

LICENSE IN AMORTIZATION. A license authorizing a conveyance of property which, without it, would be invalid under the statutes of mortmain.

LICENSE TAX. A license, strictly so-called, imposed in exercise of the ordinary police power of the state, or a tax, laid in the exercise of the power of taxation. State v. Commercial Loan Co., 251 Ala. 672, 38 So.2d 571, 573.

See License Fee or Tax, *supra*.

LICENSED VICTUALLER. A term applied, in England, to all persons selling any kind of intoxicating liquor under a license from the justices of the peace. Wharton.

LICENSEE. A person licensed; one who holds a license. Texas-Louisiana Power Co. v. Webster, 127 Tex. 126, 91 S.W.2d 302. A social guest. Biggs v. Bear, 320 Ill.App. 597, 51 N.E.2d 799, 800; Kalinowski v. Young Women's Christian Ass'n, 17 Wash.2d 380, 135 P.2d 852, 857; Gregory v. Loder, 116 N.J.L. 451, 185 A. 360; an invitee stepping beyond limits of his invitation, Wilson v. Goodrich, 252 N.W. 142, 218 Iowa 462; McGenty v. John A. Stephenson & Co., 218 Minn. 311, 15 N.W.2d 874, 875; person entering or using premises by permission or by operation of law but without express or implied invitation. Boneau v. Swift & Co., Mo.App., 66 S.W.2d 172, 175; Texas-Louisiana Power Co. v. Webster, 127 Tex. 126, 91 S.W.2d 302; Texas Co. v. Haggard, 23 Tenn. App. 475, 134 S.W.2d 880, 884, 885; person entering premises by permission only, without invitation, enticement, or allurement. Brody v. Cudahy Packing Co., 233 Mo.App. 973, 127 S.W.2d 7, 10. Person entering premises either without invitation, or for purpose not connected with business conducted on premises, but with permission or toleration. Kalinowski v. Young Women's Christian Ass'n, 17 Wash.2d 380, 135 P.2d 852, 857; Person granted express permission to use premises of another, Dye v. Montgomery Ward & Co., 175 Okl. 567, 54 P.2d 182, 183; person on another's premises only through acquiescence or sufferance. Karns v. Trostel, 44 Ohio App. 498, 186 N.E. 405; Foley v. H. F. Farnham Co., 135 Me. 29, 188 A. 708, 712; person on another's premises solely in pursuit or furtherance of own business, pleasure, or convenience. Sulhoff v. Everett, 235 Iowa 396, 16 N.W.2d 737, 739; Connole v. Floyd Plant Food Co., Mo.App., 96 S.W.2d 655, 657, 658; person on another's premises by invitation, Atlantic Greyhound Corporation v. Newton, C.C.A.N.C., 131 F.2d 845, 847; person permitted on another's premises merely for his own interest, or for that of a third person. Keesecker v. G. M. McKelvey Co., 141 Ohio St. 162, 47 N.E.2d 211, 214; Fraters v. Keeling, 20 Cal. App.2d 490, 67 P.2d 118; person privileged to enter or remain on land by virtue of possessor's consent, whether given by invitation or permission. Smith v. Southwest Missouri R. Co., 333 Mo. 314, 62 S.W.2d 761; Manley v. Haus, 113 Vt. 217, 32 A.2d 668, 671; Hashim v. Chimiklis, 91 N.H. 456, 21 A.2d 166, 167; person using premises through owner's sufferance only, without any enticement, allurement, or inducement and for his own personal benefit, convenience, and pleasure. Boneau v. Swift & Co., Mo.App., 66 S.W.2d 172, 175; person who has mere permission to use land, dominion over it remaining in owner, and no interest in nor exclusive possession of it being given to occupant. Seabloom v. Krier, 219 Minn. 362, 18 N.W.2d 88, 91; person who is neither passenger, servant, nor trespasser and does not stand in any contractual relation with owner, and is permitted to come upon premises for his own interest, convenience, and gratification, Hyde v. Atlanta & W. P. R. Co., 47 Ga.App. 139, 169 S.E. 854, 855; Buss v. Wachsmith, 190 Wash. 673, 70 P.2d 417, 421; Platt v. Bender, La.App., 178 So. 678, 682; person whose presence upon the premises of another is tolerated, Malolepszy v. Central Market, 143 Neb. 356, 9 N.W.2d 474, 477. Third person on vehicle on the invitation, or with the knowledge and acquiescence, of employee. Wurtzburger v. Oglesby, 222 Ala. 151, 131 So. 9, 10; Brown v. Standard Casket Mfg. Co., 234 Ala. 512, 175 So. 358, 361; volunteer or person on premises with permission of owner from motives of curiosity or private convenience. Armour & Co. v. Rose, 183 Ark. 413, 36 S.W.2d 70, 74.

Exclusive Licensee

See Exclusive Licensee.

Patent Law

One who has had transferred to him, either in writing or orally, a less or different interest than either the interest in the whole patent, or an undivided part of such whole interest, or an exclusive sectional interest. Potter v. Holland, 4 Blatchf. 211, Fed.Cas.No.11,329.

LICENSEE BY INVITATION. A person who goes upon the lands of another with express or implied invitation to transact business with the owner or occupant or do some act to his advantage or to the mutual advantage of both the licensee and the owner or occupant. Samuel E. Pentecost Const. Co. v. O'Donnell, 112 Ind.App. 47, 39 N.E.2d 812.

A licensee by express invitation is one who is directly invited by the owner of the land to enter upon it. Mann v. Des Moines Ry. Co., 232 Iowa 1049, 7 N.W.2d 45, 51.

A licensee by implied invitation is one who has been invited to enter upon the land either by the owner or occupier of the same by some affirmative act done by such owner or occupier or by appearances which justify persons generally in believing that such owner or occupier had given his consent to the public generally to enter upon or to cross over his premises. Mann v. Des Moines Ry. Co., 232 Iowa 1049, 7 N.W.2d 45, 51.

LICENSEE BY PERMISSION. One who, for his own convenience, curiosity, or entertainment, goes upon the premises of another by the owner's or occupant's permission or sufferance. Samuel E. Pentecost Const. Co. v. O'Donnell, 112 Ind.App. 47, 39 N.E.2d 812, 817.

LICENSING ACTS. This expression is applied by Hallam (Const. Hist. c. 13) to acts of parliament for the restraint of printing, except by license.

It may also be applied to any act of parliament passed for the purpose of requiring a license for doing any act whatever. But, generally, when we speak of the licensing acts, we mean the acts regulating the sale of intoxicating liquors. Mozley & Whiteley.

LICENSOR. The person who gives or grants a license.

LICENTIA. Lat. License; leave; permission.

LICENTIA CONCORDANDI. In old practice and conveyancing. License or leave to agree; one of the proceedings on levying a fine of lands. 2 Bl. Comm. 350.

LICENTIA LOQUENDI. In old practice. Leave to speak, (*i. e.*, with the plaintiff;) an imparlance; or rather leave to imparl. 3 Bl. Comm. 299.

LICENTIA SURGENDI. In old English practice. License to arise; permission given by the court to a tenant in a real action, who had cast an essoin *de malo lecti*, to *arise* out of his bed. Also, the writ thereupon.

If the demandant can show that the tenant was seen abroad before leave of court, and before being viewed by the knights appointed by the court for that purpose, such tenant shall be taken to be deceitfully essoined, and to have made default. Bract. lib. 5; Fleta, lib. 6, c. 10.

LICENTIA TRANSFRETANDI. A writ or warrant directed to the keeper of the port of Dover, or other seaport, commanding him to let such persons pass over sea as have obtained the royal license thereunto. Reg. Orig. 193.

LICENTIATE. One who has license to practice any art or faculty.

LICENTIOUSNESS. The indulgence of the arbitrary will of the individual, without regard to ethics or law, or respect for the rights of others.

In this it differs from "liberty;" for the latter term may properly be used only of the exercise of the will in its *moral* freedom, with justice to all men and obedience to the laws, Welch v. Durand, 36 Conn. 184, 4 Am.Rep. 55; State v. Brigman, 94 N.C. 889; liberty is restrained by natural or positive law, and consists in doing whatever we please not inconsistent with the rights of others, whereas licentiousness does not respect those rights. Wolff, Inst. § 84.

Also, lewdness or lasciviousness. Holton v. State, 28 Fla. 303, 9 So. 716; Purvis v. State, 117 Neb. 377, 220 N.W. 599, 600.

LICERE. Lat. To be lawful; to be allowed or permitted by law. Calvin.

LICERE, LICERI. Lat. In Roman law. To offer a price for a thing; to bid for it.

LICET. Lat. From the verb *"licere,"* (*q. v.*). It is allowed; it is permissible; it is lawful; not forbidden by law.

Although; notwithstanding. Calvin. Importing, in this sense, a direct affirmation. Plowd. 127.

LICET DISPOSITIO DE INTERESSE FUTURO SIT INUTILIS, TAMEN POTEST FIERI DECLARATIO PRÆCEDENS QUÆ SORTIATUR EFFECTUM, INTERVENIENTE NOVO ACTU. Although the grant of a future interest be inoperative, yet a declaration precedent may be made, which may take effect provided a new act intervene. Bac. Max. pp. 60, 61, reg. 14; Broom, Max. 498.

LICET SÆPIUS REQUISITUS. (Although often requested.)

In pleading. A phrase used in the old Latin forms of declarations, and literally translated in the modern precedents. Yel. 66; 2 Chit.Pl. 90; 1 Chit.Pl. 331. The clause in a declaration which contains the general averment of a request by the plaintiff of the defendant to pay the sums claimed is still called the *"licet sœpius requisitus."*

LICITA BENE MISCENTUR, FORMULA NISI JURIS OBSTET. Lawful acts [done by several authorities] are well mingled, [*i. e.*, become united or consolidated into one good act,] unless some form of law forbid. Bac. Max. p. 94, reg. 24 (*E. g.*, Two having a right to convey, each a moiety, may unite and convey the whole.)

LICITACION. In Spanish law. The offering for sale at public auction of an estate or property held by co-heirs or joint proprietors, which cannot be divided up without detriment to the whole. See, also, Licitation.

LICITARE. Lat. In Roman law. To offer a price at a sale; to bid; to bid often; to make several bids, one above another. Calvin.

LICITATION. In the civil law. An offering for sale to the highest bidder, or to him who will give most for a thing.

An act by which co-heirs or other co-proprietors of a thing in common and undivided between them put it to bid between them, to be adjudged and to belong to the highest and last bidder, upon condition that he pay to each of his co-proprietors a part in the price equal to the undivided part which each of the said co-proprietors had in the estate *licited*, before the adjudication. Poth.Cont.Sale, nn. 516, 638. See Barbarich v. Meyer, 154 La. 325, 97 So. 459, 460.

LICITATOR. In Roman law. A bidder at a sale.

LICKING OF THUMBS. An ancient formality by which bargains were completed.

LIDFORD LAW. A sort of lynch law, whereby a person was first punished and then tried. Wharton.

LIE, *n.* An untruth deliberately told; the uttering or acting of that which is false for the purpose of deceiving; intentional mistatement. Brothers v. Brothers, 208 Ala. 258, 94 So. 175, 177.

LIE, *v.* To subsist; to exist; to be sustainable; to be proper or available.

Thus the phrase "an action will not *lie*" means that an action cannot be sustained, or that there is no ground upon which to found the action.

LIE DETECTOR. A machine which records by a needle on a graph varying emotional disturbances when answering questions truly or falsely, as indicated by fluctuations in blood pressure, respiration or perspiration. State v. Cole, 354 Mo. 181, 188 S.W.2d 43, 51. A pathometer. People v. Forte, 4 N.Y.S.2d 913, 919, 167 Misc. 868.

LIE IN FRANCHISE. Property is said to "lie in franchise" when it is of such a nature that the persons entitled thereto may seize it without the aid of a court; *e. g.*, wrecks, waifs, estrays.

LIE IN GRANT. Incorporeal hereditaments are said to "lie in grant;" that is, they pass by force of the grant (deed or charter) without livery.

LIE IN LIVERY. A term applied to corporeal hereditaments, freeholds, etc., signifying that they pass by livery, not by the mere force of the grant.

LIE IN WAIT. See Lying in Wait.

LIE TO. To adjoin. A cottage must have had four acres of land *laid to* it. See 2 Show. 279.

LIEFTENANT. An old form of "lieutenant," and still retained as the vulgar pronunciation of the word.

LIEGE.

In feudal law. Bound by a feudal tenure; bound in allegiance to the lord paramount, who owned no superior.

The term was applied to the lord, or liege lord, to whom allegiance was due, since he was *bound* to protection and a just government, and also to the feudatory, liegeman, or subject bound to allegiance, for he was *bound* to tribute and due subjection. 34 & 35 Hen. VIII. So *lieges* are the king's subjects. Stat. 8 Hen. VI. c. 10; 14 Hen. VIII. c. 2. So in Scotland. Bell, Dict.

In old records. Full; absolute; perfect; pure. *Liege* widowhood was pure widowhood. Cowell. *Ligius* was also used; *e. g. ligia potestas,* full and free power of disposal. Paroch. Antiq. 280.

LIEGE HOMAGE. Homage which, when performed by one sovereign prince to another, included fealty and services, as opposed to *simple homage,* which was a mere acknowledgment of tenure. (1 Bl. Comm. 367; 2 Steph. Comm. 400.) Mozley & Whiteley.

LIEGE LORD. A sovereign; a superior lord.

LIEGE POUSTIE. In Scotch law. That state of health which gives a person full power to dispose of, *mortis causâ* or otherwise, his heritable property. Bell. A deed executed at the time of such a state of health, as opposed to a death-bed conveyance. The term seems to be derived from the Latin *"legitima potestas."*

LIEGEMAN. He that oweth allegiance. Cowell.

LIEGER, or LEGER. A resident ambassador.

LIEGES, or LIEGE PEOPLE. Subjects.

LIEN. A charge or security or incumbrance upon property. Theatre Realty Co. v. Aronberg-Fried Co., C.C.A.Mo., 85 F.2d 383, 388, McCarty v. Robinson, 222 Ala. 287, 131 So. 895, 896; Springer v. J. R. Clark Co., C.C.A.Minn., 138 F.2d 722, 726.

A claim or charge on property for payment of some debt, obligation or duty, Shipley v. Metropolitan Life Ins. Co., 25 Tenn.App. 452, 158 S.W.2d 739, 741; Williams v. Greer, Tex.Civ.App., 122 S.W.2d 247, 248; Ross v. Franko, 139 Ohio St. 395, 40 N.E.2d 664, 665; Gray v. Horne, 48 Cal.App.2d 372, 119 P.2d 779, 780; Willard v. Stauffer, 91 Ind.App. 119, 170 N.E. 332, 335; hold or claim which one person has upon the property of another for some debt or charge, Sissman v. Chicago Title & Trust Co., 303 Ill.App. 620, 25 N.E.2d 599, 600; Marquette Nat. Bank of Minneapolis v. Mullin, 205 Minn. 562, 287 N.W. 233, 238; Bent v. H. W. Weaver, Inc., 106 W.Va. 164, 145 S.E. 594, 595; obligation, tie, duty or claim annexed to or attaching upon property by the common law, equity, contract or statute, without satisfying which such property cannot be lawfully demanded by another, Landis Mach. Co. v. Omaha Merchants Transfer Co., 142 Neb. 389, 9 N.W.2d 198, 203; pledging of the assets available to pay the corporate liabilities, Andrew v. Bevington Sav. Bank, 206 Iowa, 869, 221 N.W. 668. Preferred or privileged claims given by statute or by admiralty law. American Legion Post No. 279 v. Barrett, 371 Ill. 78, 20 N.E.2d 45, 50; Marshall v. People of State of New York, 254 U.S. 380, 41 S.Ct. 143, 145, 65 L.Ed. 315; qualified right of property which a creditor has in or over specific property of his debtor, as security for the debt or charge or for performance of some act, 6 East 25, n; right to detain property, O'Brien v. Buxton, 156 A. 17, 18, 9 N.J.Misc.R. 876; right or claim against some interest in property created by law as an incident of contract, Van Camp v. Van Camp, 291 Mich. 688, 289 N.W. 297, 300; right to enforce charge upon property of another for payment or satisfaction of debt or claim, Vaughan v. John Hancock Mut. Life Ins. Co., Tex.Civ.App., 61 S.W.2d 189, 190; Day v. Ostergard, 146 Pa.Super. 27, 21 A.2d 586, 588. Right to retain property for payment of debt or demand, Samuels v. Public Nat. Bank & Trust Co. of New York, 251 N.Y.S. 671, 674, 140 Misc. 744; Bell v. Dennis, 43 N.M. 350, 93 P.2d 1003, 1006; Huie v. Soo Hoo, 132 Cal.App.Supp. 787, 22 P.2d 808. Security for a debt, duty or other obligation, Hurley v. Boston R. Holding Co., 315 Mass. 591, 54 N.E.2d 183, 193; tie that binds property to a debt or claim for its satisfaction. United States v. 1364.76875 Wine Gallons, More or Less, of Spirituous Liquors, D.C.Mo., 60 F.Supp. 389, 392; Baranofsky v. Weiss, 120 Pa.Super. 126, 182 A. 47, 48.

A "claim" is generally a liability in personam but capable of embracing both a personal liability and a lien on property, while a lien is a liability in rem. Fairbanks, Morse & Co. v. Cape Charles, 144 Va. 56, 131 S.E. 437, 439.

A lien is a charge imposed upon specific property, whereas an assignment, unless in some way qualified, is properly the transfer of one's whole interest in an estate, or chattel, or other thing. Guaranteed State Bank of Durant v. D'Yarmett, 67 Okl. 164, 169 P. 639, 641; Millsap v. Sparks, 21 Ariz. 317, 188 P. 135, 136.

A "lien" is not a property in or right to the thing itself, but constitutes a charge or security thereon. Koenig v. Leppert-Roos Fur Co., Mo.App., 260 S.W. 756, 758; Steagall-Cheairs Fertilizer Co. v. Bethume Mule Co., 181 Ala. 250, 61 So. 274, 275; Powers v. Fidelity & Deposit Co. of Maryland, 180 S.C. 501, 186 S.E. 523, 530.

An "estate" in land is the right to the possession and enjoyment of it, while a "lien" on land is the right to have it sold or otherwise applied in satisfaction of a debt. State Bank of Decatur v. Sanders, 114 Ark. 440, 170 S.W. 86, 89.

Liens are "property rights". In re Pennsylvania Central Brewing Co., C.C.A.Pa., 114 F.2d 1010, 1013; Smith v. Russell, 223 Iowa 123, 272 N.W. 121, 125.

The word "lien" is a generic term and, standing alone, includes liens acquired by contract or by operation of law. Egyptian Supply Co. v. Boyd, C.C.A.Ky., 117 F.2d 608, 612.

Some transactions or agreements held to constitute a "lien" are conditional sales contract, General Motors Acceptance Corporation v. Hamlin, 25 Ala.App. 522, 149 So. 864, 865; interest of a purchaser on execution sale during redemption period, Local Realty Co. v. Lindquist, 92 Utah. 297, 85 P.2d 770, 773; levy made on tax assessment, City of Salem v. Marion County, 171 Or. 254, 137 P.2d 977. Mortgage or deed of trust, Tracy v. Costa, 132 N.J.Eq. 455, 28 A.2d 523, 524; State v. Sheridan County, 72 N.D. 254, 6 N.W.2d 51, 54; Fickling v. Jackman, 203 Cal. 657, 265 P. 810, 812; Klika v. Albert Wemzlick Real Estate Co., Mo. App., 150 S.W.2d 18, 24; street improvement assessment, City of Orangeburg v. Southern Ry. Co., D.C.S.C., 45 F.Supp. 734, 738; taxes, Harrell v. Burch, 195 Ga. 96, 23 S.E.2d 434, 436; In re Empire Granite Co., D.C.Ga., 42 F.Supp. 450, 455, 457; Cowen v. Wassman, 64 Ohio App. 84, 28 N.E.2d 201, 204; title retention contract. Franklin Savings & Loan Corporation v. Snapp, 179 Tenn. 151, 163 S.W.2d 332, 333; unrecorded trust deed. Wasco Creamery & Construction Co. v. Coffee, 117 Cal.App. 298, 3 P.2d 588, 589.

Lien *by operation of law.* Where the law itself, without the stipulation of the parties, raises a lien, as an implication or legal consequence from the relation of the parties or the circumstances of their dealings. Liens of this species may arise either under the rules of common law or of equity or under a statute. In the first case they are called "common-law liens;" in the second, "equitable liens;" in the third, "statutory liens."

Roman or Civil Law

The peculiar securities which, in the common and maritime law and equity, are termed "liens," are embraced under the head of "mortgage and privilege."

Scotch Law

The doctrine of lien is known by the name of "retention," and that of set-off by the name of "compensation"; though certain rights of retention are also called liens. Ersk. Prin. 374.

As to "Attorney's Lien," "Charging Lien," "Common Law Lien," "Concurrent Liens," "Consummate Lien," "Conventional Lien," "Equitable Liens," "Execution Lien," "First Lien," "General Lien," "Inchoate Lien," "Judgment Lien," "Maritime Lien," "Mechanic's Lien," "Municipal Lien," "Particular Lien," "Possessory Lien," "Prior Lien," "Second Lien," "Secret Lien," "Special Lien" and "Vendor's Lien," see those titles.

LIEN ACCOUNT. Such statement of claim as fairly apprises property owner and public of nature and amount of demand asserted as lien. Hanenkamp v. Hagedorn, Mo.App., 110 S.W.2d 826, 829.

LIEN CREDITOR. One whose debt or claim is secured by a lien on particular property, as distinguished from a "general" creditor, who has no such security.

LIEN OF A COVENANT. The commencement of a covenant stating the names of the covenantors and covenantees, and the character of the covenant, whether joint or several. Wharton.

LIEN OF FACTOR AT COMMON LAW. Lien not created through statutory enactment, but lien of ordinary factor as known to common law. Irving Trust Co. v. B. Lindner & Bro., Inc., 264 N.Y. 165, 190 N.E. 332, 336.

LIENEE. One whose property is subject to a lien. Webster.

It was held that "lienee" as used in statute providing that failure to have required notice of suit affecting realty entered in lis pendens records shall not affect rights of a bona fide purchaser-mortgagee or other lienee in absence of actual notice means the person having or owning a lien; one who has a right of lien on property of another. Lee v. Macon County Bank, 233 Ala. 522, 172 So. 662, 670.

LIENOR. The person having or owning a lien; one who has a right of lien upon property of another.

LIEU. Fr. Place; room. It is only used with "in;" *in lieu,* instead of. Enc. Lond.

LIEU CONUS. L. Fr. In old pleading. A known place; a place well known and generally taken notice of by those who dwell about it, as a castle, a manor, etc. Whishaw; 1 Ld. Raym. 259.

LIEU LANDS. A term used to indicate public lands within the indemnity limits granted in *lieu* of those lost within place limits. See Weyerhaeuser v. Hoyt, 31 S.Ct. 300, 219 U.S. 380, 55 L.Ed. 258.

LIEU TAX. A lieu tax means instead of or a substitute for, and it is not an additional tax. Lebeck v. State, 62 Ariz. 171, 156 P.2d 720, 721.

LIEUTENANCY, COMMISSION OF. See Commission of Array.

LIEUTENANT. **1.** A deputy; substitute; an officer who supplies the place of another; one acting by vicarious authority. Etymologically, one who holds the post or office of another, in the place and stead of the latter.

2. The word is used in composition as part of the title of several civil and military officers, who are subordinate to others, and especially where the duties and powers of the higher officer may, in certain contingencies, devolve upon the lower; as lieutenant governor, lieutenant colonel, etc. See *infra.*

3. In the army, a lieutenant is a commissioned officer, ranking next below a captain. In the United States navy, he is an officer whose rank is intermediate between that of an ensign and that of a lieutenant commander. In the British navy, his rank is next below that of a commander.

LIEUTENANT COLONEL. An officer of the army whose rank is above that of a major and below that of a colonel.

LIEUTENANT COMMANDER. A commissioned officer of the United States navy, whose rank is above that of lieutenant and below that of commander.

LIEUTENANT GENERAL. An officer in the army, whose rank is above that of major general and below that of "general of the army." In the United States, this rank is not permanent, being usually created for special persons or in times of war.

LIEUTENANT GOVERNOR. In English law. A deputy-governor, acting as the chief civil officer of one of several colonies under a governor general. Webster. In American law. An officer of a state, sometimes charged with special duties, but chiefly important as the deputy or substitute of the governor, acting in the place of the governor upon the latter's death, resignation, or disability.

LIFE. That state of animals and plants or of an organized being, in which its natural functions and motions are performed, or in which its organs are capable of performing their functions. Webster. The sum of the forces by which death is resisted. Bichat.

"Life" begins in contemplation of law as soon as an infant is able to stir in the mother's womb. State v. Forte, 222 N.C. 537, 23 S.E.2d 842, 843.

"Life" protected by the Federal Constitution includes all personal rights and their enjoyment embracing the use and enjoyment of the faculties, acquiring useful knowledge, the right to marry, establish a home, and bring up children, freedom of worship, conscience, contract, occupation, speech, assembly and press. Rosenblum v. Rosenblum, 42 N.Y.S.2d 626, 630, 181 Misc. 78.

Natural life. See Natural Life.

LIFE ANNUITY. An engagement to pay an income yearly during the life of some person; also the sum thus promised.

An annuity contract which contemplated monthly payments until death of annuitant or surrender of policy by him was a life annuity. Bodine v. Commissioner of Internal Revenue, C.C.A.3, 103 F.2d 982, 985. An annuity, depending on the continuance of an assigned life or lives, is sometimes called a life annuity. Bodine v. Commissioner of Internal Revenue, C.C.A.3, 103 F.2d 982, 985.

LIFE ESTATE. An estate whose duration is limited to the life of the party holding it, or of some other person. Williams v. Ratcliff, 42 Miss. 154; Civ.Code Ga. 1895, § 3087 (Civ.Code 1910, § 3663).

Estates for life may be created by act of law or by act of the parties: in the former case they are called legal, in the latter conventional. The legal life estates are estates-tail after possibility of issue extinct, estates by dower, estates by curtesy, jointures; Mitch.R.P. 118, 133; Dejarnatte v. Allen, 5 Grat., Va., 499; Irwin v. Covode, 24 Pa. 162; 3 E.L. & Eq.R. 345; Gourley v. Woodbury, 51 Vt. 37; Brooks v. Brooks, 12 S.C. 422; Rountree v. Talbot, 89 Ill. 246.

A freehold estate, not of inheritance, but which is held by the tenant for his own life or the life or lives of one or more other persons, or for an indefinite period, which may endure for the life or lives of persons in being, and not beyond the period of a life. 1 Washb.Real Prop. 88; Brandenburg v. Petroleum Exploration, 218 Ky. 557, 291 S.W. 757, 759; Co.Litt. 42*a;* Bract. lib. 4, c. 28, § 207. Measure of duration is the tenant's own life, it is called simply an estate "for life;" when the measure of duration is the life of another person, it is called an estate *"per (or pur) autre vie."* 2 Bl.Comm. 120; Co.Litt. 41*b;* 4 Kent 23, 24.

A devise of a life estate to terminate upon devisee's remarriage constitutes a devise of a "life estate", Lydick v. Tate, 380 Ill. 616, 44 N.E.2d 583, 589. A devise to a devisee and her children in fee simple passes a "life estate" in named devisee with remainder in fee to the children, Meily v. Meily, 147 Pa.Super. 140, 24 A.2d 25, 27, 28. A gift, though not expressly for life, but with a limitation over of any part of the estate remaining at the death of the immediate devisee, creates a "life estate." Shelton v. Shelton, 348 Mo. 820, 155 S.W.2d 187, 188.

LIFE IN BEING. A phrase used in the common-law and statutory rules against perpetuities, meaning the remaining duration of the life of a person who is in existence at the time when the deed or will takes effect. See McArthur v. Scott, 5 S.Ct. 652, 113 U.S. 340, 28 L.Ed. 1015.

LIFE INSURANCE. See Insurance.

LIFE INSURANCE COMPANY. Any corporation writing life insurance, whether with or without capital stock, and on whatever plan (Rev.St. 1925, art. 4716). National Mut. Ben. Ass'n v. Aaron, Tex.Civ.App., 45 S.W.2d 371, 373.

LIFE INTEREST. A claim or interest, not amounting to ownership, and limited by a term of life, either that of the person in whom the right is vested or that of another.

LIFE-LAND, or LIFE-HOLD. Land held on a lease for lives.

LIFE OF A WRIT. The period during which a writ (execution, etc.) remains effective and can lawfully be served or levied, terminating with the day on which, by law or by its own terms, it is to be returned into court.

LIFE OF BONDS. Within statute respecting their maturity dates, commenced upon their issuance and sale. Shamblin v. Board of Sup'rs of Prentiss County, 192 Miss. 267, 5 So.2d 675, 676.

LIFE OR LIMB. The phrase "life or limb" within constitutional provision that no person shall be subject for the same offense to be twice put in jeopardy of life or limb is not construed strictly but applies to any criminal penalty. U.S.C.A. Const.Amend. 5. Clawans v. Rives, 104 F.2d 240, 242, 70 App.D.C. 107, 122 A.L.R. 1436.

LIFE PEERAGE. Letters patent, conferring the dignity of baron for life only, do not enable the grantee to sit and vote in the house of lords, not even with the usual writ of summons to the house. Wharton.

LIFE POLICY. A policy of life insurance; a policy of insurance upon the life of an individual.

Contract to pay money to beneficiaries on death of insured. Cohen v. Metropolitan Life Ins. Co., 112 Pa. Super. 314, 171 A. 106, 109. Contract to pay a fixed sum at death, Kahn v. Continental Cas. Co., 325 Ill.App. 1, 59 N.E.2d 524, 533. Without regard to value of his life to beneficiary, First-Columbus Nat. Bank v. D. S. Pate Lumber Co., 163 Miss. 691, 141 So. 767, 768. Contract which insures a beneficiary or beneficiaries against financial hardships which may otherwise result from death of the insured. In re Sothern's Estate, 14 N.Y.S.2d 509, 511, 170 Misc. 805.

Insurance policy including a death benefit and a health or accident disability benefit constituted a "life insurance policy", it being immaterial that in some policy forms the health and disability feature was more valuable absent a showing that death provision was inserted to avoid the higher tax. Universal Life Ins. Co. v. State, 155 Miss. 358, 121 So. 849, 850.

LIFE-RENT. In Scotch law. An estate for life; a right to the use and enjoyment of an estate or thing for one's life, but without destruction of its substance. They are either *legal,* such as terce and curtesy, (*q. v.,*) or *conventional, i. e.,* created by act of the parties. Conventional life-rents are either *simple,* where the owner of an estate grants a life-interest to another, or *by reservation,* where the owner, in conveying away the fee, reserves a life-estate to himself.

LIFE-RENTER. In Scotch law. A tenant for life without waste. Bell.

LIFE TABLES. Statistical tables exhibiting the probable proportion of persons who will live to reach different ages. Cent. Dict.

Such tables are used for many purposes, such as the computation of the present value of annuities, dower rights, etc.; and for the computation of damages resulting from injuries which destroy the earning capacity of a person, or those resulting from the death of a person to those who are dependent upon him.

LIFE TENANT. One who holds an estate in lands for the period of his own life or that of another certain person.

LIFT. To raise; to take up.

To "lift" a promissory note is to discharge its obligation by paying its amount or substituting another evidence of debt. To "lift the bar" of the statute of limitations, or of an estoppel, is to remove the obstruction which it interposes, by some sufficient act or acknowledgment.

LIGA. In old European law. A league or confederation. Spelman.

LIGAN, LAGAN. Goods cast into the sea tied to a buoy, so that they may be found again by the owners, are so denominated.

When goods are cast into the sea in storms or shipwrecks, and remain there, without coming to land, they are distinguished by the barbarous names of "jetsam," "flotsam," and "ligan." 5 Coke, 108; Harg.State Tr. 48; 1 Bl.Comm. 292.

LIGARE. To tie or bind. Bract. fol. 369*b*. To enter into a league or treaty. Spelman.

LIGEA. In old English law. A liege-woman; a female subject. Reg. Orig. 312*b*.

LIGEANCE. Allegiance; the faithful obedience of a subject to his sovereign, of a citizen to his government. Also, derivatively, the territory of a state or sovereignty.

LIGEANTIA. Lat. Ligeance; allegiance.

LIGEANTIA EST QUASI LEGIS ESSENTIA; EST VINCULUM FIDEI. Co. Litt. 129. Allegiance is, as it were, the essence of law; it is the chain of faith.

LIGEANTIA NATURALIS NULLIS CLAUSTRIS COERCETUR, NULLIS METIS REFRÆNATUR, NULLIS FINIBUS PREMITUR. 7 Coke, 10. Natural allegiance is restrained by no barriers, reined by no bounds, compressed by no limits.

LIGEAS. In old records. A liege.

LIGHT. A window, or opening in the wall for the admission of light.

Also a privilege or easement to have light admitted into one's building by the openings made for that purpose, without obstruction or obscuration by the walls of adjacent or neighboring structures. Also an instrument through which illumination is projected. Santos v. Dondero, 11 Cal.App.2d 720, 54 P.2d 764, 766.

LIGHT AND POWER. "Light and power" is a generic term describing companies which furnish electricity. Union Electric Co. v. City of St. Charles, 352 Mo. 1194, 181 S.W.2d 526, 528.

LIGHT-HOUSE. A structure, usually in the form of a tower, containing signal-lights for the guidance of vessels at night, at dangerous points of a coast, shoals, etc. They are usually erected by government, and subject to governmental regulation.

As term applied to rugs may mean that rugs were made by blind in charitable or quasi charitable institutions called lighthouses, Lighthouse Rug Co. v. Federal Trade Commission, C.C.A.7, 35 F.2d 163, 165.

LIGHT-HOUSE BOARD. A commission authorized by congress, consisting of two officers of the navy, two officers of the corps of engineers of the army, and two civilians, together with an officer of the navy and an officer of engineers of the army as secretaries, attached to the office of the secretary of the treasury, at Washington, and charged with superintending the construction and management of light-houses, light-ships, and other maritime signals for protection of commerce. Abbott.

LIGHT-SHIP, LIGHT-VESSEL. A vessel serving the purpose of a light-house, usually at a place where the latter could not well be built.

LIGHTER. A small vessel used in loading and unloading ships and steamers. The Mamie (D.C.) 5 Fed. 818; Reed v. Ingham, 26 Eng.Law & Eq. 167.

LIGHTERAGE. The business of transferring merchandise to and from vessels by means of lighters; also the compensation or price demanded for such service. Western Transp. Co. v. Hawley, 1 Daly (N.Y.) 327.

The loading, unloading and transfer of freight between a car and a ship's side. Loading, unloading, or transportation by means of a lighter. Hoboken Manufacturers' R. Co. v. United States, D.C.N.J., 47 F.Supp. 779, 782.

LIGHTERMAN. The master or owner of a lighter. He is liable as a common carrier.

LIGHTS. 1. Windows; openings in the wall of a house for the admission of light.

2. Signal-lamps on board a vessel or at particular points on the coast, required by the navigation laws to be displayed at night.

LIGIUS. A person bound to another by a solemn tie or engagement. Now used to express the relation of a subject to his sovereign.

See, also, Liege.

LIGNA ET LAPIDES SUB "ARMORUM" APPELLATIONE NON CONTINENTUR. Sticks and stones are not contained under the name of "arms." Bract. fol. 144*b*.

LIGNAGIUM. A right of cutting fuel in woods; also a tribute or payment due for the same. Jacob.

LIGNAMINA. Timber fit for building. Du Fresne.

LIGULA. In old English law. A copy, exemplification, or transcript of a court roll or deed. Cowell.

LIKE. Equal in quantity, quality, or degree or exactly corresponding. Bader v. Coale, 48 Cal. App.2d 276, 119 P.2d 763, 765; Braren v. Horner, Cust. & Pat. App., 47 F.2d 358, 365.

Also means having the same, or nearly the same, appearance, qualities, or characteristics, Japan Import Co. v. United States, Cust. & Pat.App., 86 F.2d 124, 131; Clarke v. Johnson, 119 Ga. 163, 33 S.E.2d 425, 427; resembling, Clarke v. Johnson, 199 Ga. 163, 33 S.E.2d 425, 427; same manner, Seilaz v. Seilaz, 24 Tenn.App. 611, 148 S.W.2d 23, 25; similar, Castell v. United States, D.C.N.Y., 20 F.Supp. 175, 179; substantially similar, Jones v. H. D. & J. K. Crosswell, C.C.A.S.C., 60 F.2d 827, 829.

LIKE A SHOT. Quickly, instantaneously. McNulty v. Joseph Horne Co., 298 Pa. 244, 148 A. 105, 106.

LIKE BENEFITS. Similar in salient features. MacKay v. City of Port Huron, 288 Mich. 129, 284 N.W. 671, 672.

LIKE CHARACTER. Similarity. Bader v. Coale, 48 Cal.App.2d 276, 119 P.2d 763, 765.

LIKELIHOOD. Probability. Clark v. Welch, C.C. A.Mass., 140 F.2d 271, 273. The word imports something less than reasonably certain. Ottgen v. Garey, 41 Ohio App. 499, 181 N.E. 485, 487.

LIKELY. Probable. Horning v. Gerlach, 139 Cal. App. 470, 34 P.2d 504, 505; In all probability. Neely v. Chicago Great Western R. Co., Mo.App., 14 S.W.2d 972, 978.

LIKEWISE. In like manner. Reece v. McCrary, 51 Ga.App. 746, 181 S.E. 697.

LIMB. A member of the human body. In the phrase "life and limb," the latter term appears to denote bodily integrity in general; but in the definition of "mayhem" it refers only to those members or parts of the body which may be useful to a man in fighting. 1 Bl.Comm. 130.

LIMENARCHA. In Roman law. An officer who had charge of a harbor or port. Dig. 50, 4, 18, 10; Cod. 7, 16, 38.

LIMIT, *v.* To abridge, confine, and restrict. Brown v. Board of Appeals of City of Springfield, 227 Ill. 644, 159 N.E. 225, 226, 56 A.L.R. 242. To circumscribe. Orme v. Atlas Gas & Oil Co., 217 Minn. 27, 13 N.W.2d 757, 761. To mark out; to define; to fix the extent of. Brown.

Thus, to limit an estate means to mark out or to define the period of its duration, and the words employed in deeds for this purpose are thence termed "words of limitation," and the act itself is termed "limiting the estate." Brown.

LIMIT, *n.* A bound; a restraint; a circumscription; a boundary. Casler v. Connecticut Mut. L. Ins. Co., 22 N.Y. 429. Boundary, border or outer line of thing. State v. Jones, 133 Me. 387, 178 A. 719, 720. Extreme boundary. Lane v. Lukens, 48 Idaho 517, 283 P. 532, 533.

Within act giving injured party right of direct action against automobile liability insurer within terms and limits of policy, word "limits" refers not only to amount of policy, but to time in which notice of accident must be given. Duncan v. Pedare, La.App., 161 So. 221, 228.

LIMITATION. Restriction or circumspection; settling an estate or property; a certain time allowed by a statute for litigation.

The provisions of State Constitution are not a "grant" but a "limitation" of legislative power. Ellerbe v. David, 193 S.C. 332, 8 S.E.2d 518, 520; Mulholland v. Ayers, 109 Mont. 558, 99 P.2d 234, 239.

Corporations

Under the statute providing that all corporations expiring by their own "limitation" shall for certain purposes be continued as bodies corporate for a term of three years, the word "limitation" is an act of limiting, a restriction of power, a qualification. Porter v. Tempa Min. & Mill. Co., 59 Nev. 332, 93 P.2d 741, 743.

Estates

The restriction or circumscription of an estate, in the conveyance by which it is granted, in respect to the interest of the grantee or its duration; the specific curtailment or confinement of an estate, by the terms of the grant, so that it cannot endure beyond a certain period or a designated contingency.

A "limitation" on a grant determines an estate upon the happening of the event itself without the necessity of doing any act to regain the estate, such as re-entry. Gulf Production Co. v. Continental Oil Co., Tex., 132 S.W.2d 553, 563.

A limitation, whether made by the express words of the party or existing in intendment of law, circumscribes the continuance of time for which the property is to be enjoyed, and by positive and certain terms, or by reference to some event which possibly may happen, marks the period at which the time of enjoyment shall end. Smith v. Smith, 23 Wis. 181, 99 Am.Dec. 153; Hoselton v. Hoselton, 166 Mo. 182, 65 S.W. 1005; Stearns v. Godfrey, 16 Me. 160.

The "unless" provisions of oil and gas lease which provided that if no well should be commenced within one year, lease should terminate unless privilege of commencement should be deferred by payment of rental, were a "limitation" on the grant. Gulf Production Co. v. Continental Oil Co., 139 Tex. 183, 132 S.W.2d 553, 563.

The word "limitation" defines the extent or quality of an estate conveyed or devised. Richardson v. Roney, 382 Ill. 528, 47 N.E.2d 714.

Collateral limitation. One which gives an interest in an estate for a specified period, but makes the right of enjoyment to depend on some collateral event, as an estate to A. till B. shall go to Rome. Templeman v. Gibbs, 86 Tex. 358, 24 S.W. 792; 4 Kent, Comm. 128.

Conditional limitation. A condition followed by a limitation over to a third person in case the condition be not fulfilled or there be a breach of it. Stearns v. Godfrey, 16 Me. 158; Hess v. Kernen Bros., 169 Iowa 646, 149 N.W. 847, 851; Yarbrough v. Yarbrough, 151 Tenn. 221, 209 S.W. 36, 38. Board of Education of Borough of West Paterson v. Brophy, 90 N.J.Eq. 57, 106 A. 32, 34. A conditional limitation is where an estate is so expressly defined and limited by the words of its creation that it cannot endure for any longer time than till the contingency happens upon which the estate is to fail. 1 Steph.Comm. 309. Between conditional limitations and estates depending on conditions subsequent there is this difference: that in the former the estate determines as soon as the contingency happens; but in the latter it endures until the grantor or his heirs take advantage of the breach. 1 Steph.Comm. 310.

Contingent limitation. When a remainder in fee is limited upon any estate which would by the common law be adjudged a fee tail, such a remainder is valid as a contingent limitation upon a fee, and vests in possession on the death of the first taker without issue living at the time of his death. Rev.Codes N.D.1899, § 3328 (Comp.Laws 1913, § 5307).

Limitation in law. A limitation in law, or an estate limited, is an estate to be holden only during the continuance of the condition under which it was granted, upon the determination of which the estate vests immediately in him in expectancy. 2 Bl.Comm. 155.

Limitation over. This term includes any estate in the same property created or contemplated by the conveyance, to be enjoyed after the first estate granted expires or is exhausted. Lane v. Citizens & Southern Nat. Bank, 195 Ga. 828, 25 S.E.2d 800, 802, 803. Thus, in a gift to A. for life, with remainder to the heirs of his body, the remainder is a "limitation over" to such heirs. Ewing v. Shropshire, 80 Ga. 374, 7 S.E. 554.

Limitation title. Full title, precluding all claims. Free v. Owen, 131 Tex. 281, 113 S.W.2d 1221, 1224.

Special limitation. A qualification serving to mark out the bounds of an estate, so as to determine it *ipso facto* in a given event, without action, entry, or claim, before it would, or might, otherwise expire by force of, or according to, the general limitation. Henderson v. Hunter, 59 Pa. 340.

Title by limitation. A prescriptive title; one which is indefeasible because of the expiration of the time prescribed by the statute of limitations for the bringing of actions to test or defeat it. See Dalton v. Rentaria, 2 Ariz. 275, 15 P. 37.

Words of limitation. In a conveyance or will, words which have the effect of marking the duration of an estate are termed "words of limitation." Thus, in a grant to A. and his heirs, the words "and his heirs" are words of limitation, because they show that A. is to take an estate in fee-simple and do not give his heirs anything. Fearne, Rem. 78. And see Ball v. Payne, 6 Rand., Va., 75; Summit v. Yount, 109 Ind. 506, 9 N.E. 582.

Limitation of Actions

The term "limitation" means the time at the end of which no action at law or suit in equity can be maintained. Uscienski v. National Sugar Refining Co., 18 A.2d 611, 612, 19 N.J.Misc. 240. American Nat. Ins. Co. v. Hicks, Tex.Com.App., 35 S.W.2d 128, 130, 75 A.L.R. 623.

The restriction by statute of the right of action to certain periods of time, after the accruing of the cause of action, beyond which, except in certain specified cases, it will not be allowed. Also the period of time so limited by law for the bringing of actions. See Keyser v. Lowell, 117 F. 404, 54 C.C.A. 574; Battle v. Shivers, 39 Ga. 409; Baker v. Kelley, 11 Minn. 493 (Gil. 358); Riddelsbarger v. Hartford F. Ins. Co., 7 Wall. 390, 19 L.Ed. 257.

Limitation of Assize

In old practice. A certain time prescribed by statute, within which a man was required to allege himself or his ancestor to have been seised of lands sued for by a writ of assize. Cowell.

Statute of Limitations

A statute prescribing limitations to the right of action on certain described causes of action; that is, declaring that no suit shall be maintained on such causes of action unless brought within a specified period after the right accrued. Statutes of limitation are statutes of repose. Philadelphia, B. & W. R. Co. v. Quaker City Flour Mills Co., 282 Pa. 362, 127 A. 845, 846, and are such legislative enactments as prescribe the periods within which actions may be brought upon certain claims or within which certain rights may be enforced. People v. Kings County Development Co., 48 Cal. App. 72, 191 P. 1004, 1005. In criminal cases, however, a statute of limitation is an act of grace, a surrendering by sovereign of its right to prosecute. People v. Ross, 325 Ill. 417, 156 N.E. 303, 304.

LIMITED. Restricted; bounded; prescribed. Confined within positive bounds; restricted in duration, extent, or scope.

As to limited "Company," "Divorce," "Fee," and "Partnership," see those titles.

LIMITED ADMINISTRATION. An administration of a temporary character, granted for a particular period, or for a special or particular purpose. Holthouse.

LIMITED APPEAL. An appeal from only adverse portions of a decree; it is limited to the particular portions of the decree appealed from. Fox v. River Heights, 22 Tenn.App. 166, 118 S.W.2d 1104, 1114.

LIMITED COURT. Where special authority, in derogation of common law, is conferred by statute on a court of general jurisdiction, it becomes an "inferior or limited court". Partlow v. Partlow, 246 Ala. 259, 20 So.2d 517, 518.

LIMITED EXECUTOR. An executor whose appointment is qualified by limitations as to the time or place wherein, or the subject-matter whereon, the office is to be exercised; as distinguished from one whose appointment is absolute, *i. e.*, certain and immediate, without any restriction in regard to the testator's effects or limitation in point of time. 1 Williams, Ex'rs, 249, *et seq.*

LIMITED GUARANTY. A limited guaranty is ordinarily one restricted in its application to a single transaction. Cooling v. Springer, 3 Terry 228, 30 A.2d 466, 469.

LIMITED JURISDICTION. This term is ambiguous, and the books sometimes use it without due precision. It is sometimes carelessly employed instead of "special." The true distinction between courts is between such as possess a general and such as have only a special jurisdiction for a particular purpose, or are clothed with special powers for the performance. Obert v. Hammel, 18 N.J.Law, 73.

LIMITED LIABILITY. The liability of the members of a joint-stock company may be either unlimited or limited; and, if the latter, then the limitation of liability is either the amount, if any, unpaid on the shares, (in which case the limit is said to be "by shares,") or such an amount as the members guaranty in the event of the company being wound up, (in which case the limit is said to be "by guaranty.") Brown.

LIMITED OR SPECIAL JURISDICTION. Jurisdiction which is confined to particular causes, or which can be exercised only under the limitations and circumstances prescribed by the statute. Midwest Piping & Supply Co. v. Thomas Spacing Mach. Co., 109 Pa.Super. 571, 167 A. 636, 638.

LIMITED OWNER. A tenant for life, in toil, or by the curtesy, or other person not having a fee-simple in his absolute disposition.

LIMITED PAYMENT PLAN. A policy upon a "limited payment plan" is a paid-up policy, and insurance upon which no further premium is to be paid. Bankers Life & Loan Ass'n v. Chase, Tex.Civ.App., 114 S.W.2d 374, 376.

LIMITED PERIOD. As used in statutes authorizing assignment in actions for divorce and separate maintenance, of homestead selected from separate property of either, to innocent party for limited period, means period of natural life of such innocent party. Greenlee v. Greenlee, 7 Cal. 2d 579, 61 P.2d 1157, 1159.

LIMITED POLICY. Is one specifically excluding certain classes or types of loss. State Compensation Ins. Fund v. Industrial Accident Commission, 56 Cal.App.2d 443, 132 P.2d 890, 894.

LIMITED POWER OF APPOINTMENT. Power of appointment is limited when it is exercisable only in favor of persons or a class of persons designated in the instrument creating the power. Johnstone v. Commissioner of Internal Revenue, C.C.A.9, 76 F.2d 55, 57.

LIMITED PUBLICATION. Communication to a select number on condition, express or implied, that it is not intended to be thereafter common property. Berry v. Hoffman, 125 Pa.Super. 261, 189 A. 516, 519. Waring v. WDAS Broadcasting Station, 327 Pa. 433, 194 A. 631, 636.

LIMOGIA. Enamel. Du Cange.

LINARIUM. In old English law. A flax plat, were flax is grown. Du Cange.

LINCOLN'S INN. An inn of court. See Inns of Court.

LINE.

Lineal measure, containing the one-twelfth part of an inch.

The boundary or line of division between two estates.

Route. Menut & Parks Co. v. Cray, 114 Vt. 41, 39 A.2d 342, 347, 156 A.L.R. 404.

When a particular type of silver plate has gone through several patterns and has gained recognition, it is often called in the trade a "line". Oneida, Limited, v. National Silver Co., Sup., 25 N.Y.S.2d 271, 277.

Line by Line Budget. A detailed itemization of all expenditures by budget line. Block v. Sprague, Sup., 24 N.Y.S.2d 245, 247.

Line of an Intersection. A straight line substantially at right angles to bounds of highway at a point where, to the reasonable perception of a driver, the highway starts to widen as the result of the outcurving of its bounds to form the junction. Beck v. Sosnowitz, 125 Conn. 553, 7 A.2d 389, 391.

Line of credit. A margin or fixed limit of credit granted by one to another, to the full extent of which the latter may avail himself in his dealings with the former, but which he must not exceed; usually intended to cover a series of transactions, in which case, when the customer's line of credit is nearly or quite exhausted, he is expected to reduce his indebtedness by payments before drawing upon it further. Pittinger v. Southwestern Paper Co. of Fort Worth, Tex.Civ.App., 151 S.W.2d 922, 925.

Line of duty. In military law and usage, an act is said to be done, or an injury sustained, "in the line of duty," when done or suffered in the performance or discharge of a duty incumbent upon the individual in his character as a member of the military or naval forces. See Rhodes v. U. S., 79 F. 743, 25 C.C.A. 186. An injury suffered or disease contracted by a sailor is considered to have been in "line of duty" unless actually caused by something for which sailor is responsible which intervenes between his performance of duty and the injury or disease. Meyer v. Dollar S. S. Line, C.C.A.Wash., 49 F.2d 1002, 1003.

Line of electrically infinite length. "Reflectionless line" and "traveling wave" are synonymous terms. Radio Corporation of America v. Mackay Radio & Telegraph Co., D.C.N.Y., 16 F.Supp. 610, 612.

Line of ordinary high tide. Ordinary high tide may, for practical purposes, within a restricted area, be conceived as a level plane; the "line of ordinary high tide" is the intersection of said plane with the surface of the land. Swarzwald v. Cooley, 39 Cal.App.2d 306, 103 P.2d 580, 584.

Building line. See Building Line.

Collateral line. See Descent.

Descent. See Descent.

Direct line. See Descent.

Maternal line. See Maternal Line.

Paternal line. See Paternal Line.

Public utilities. See Public Utility.

LINEA. Lat. A line; line of descent. See Descent.

LINEA OBLIQUA. In the civil law. The oblique line. More commonly termed *"linea transversalis."*

LINEA RECTA. The direct line; the vertical line.

In computing degrees of kindred and the succession to estates, this term denotes the direct line of ascendants and descendants. Where a person springs from another immediately, or mediately through a third person, they are said to be in the direct line, *(linea recta,)* and are called "ascendants" and "descendants." Mackeld.Rom.Law, § 129.

LINEA RECTA EST INDEX SUI ET OBLIQUI; LEX EST LINEA RECTI. Co. Litt. 158. A right line is a test of itself, and of an oblique; law is a line of right.

LINEA RECTA SEMPER PRÆFERTUR TRANSVERSALI. The right line is always preferred to the collateral. Co. Litt. 10; Broom, Max. 529.

LINEA TRANSVERSALIS. A collateral, transverse, or oblique line. Where two persons are descended from a third, they are called "collaterals," and are said to be related in the collateral line, (*linea transversa* or *obliqua.*)

LINEAGE. Race; progeny; family, ascending or descending. Lockett v. Lockett, 94 Ky. 289, 22 S. W. 224. Line of descent from an ancestor, hence, family, race, stock. In re Herrick's Estate, 273 N. Y.S. 803, 152 Misc. 9.

LINEAL. That which comes in a line; especially a direct line, as from father to son. Collateral relationship is not called "lineal," though the expression "collateral line," is not unusual. Proceeding in direct or unbroken line, hereditary, unbroken in course, distinguished from collateral, as lineal descent, lineal succession, having an ancestral basis or right. In re Herrick's Estate, 273 N. Y.S. 803, 152 Misc. 9.

LINEAL CONSANGUINITY. That kind of consanguinity which subsists between persons of whom one is descended in a *direct line* from the other; as between a particular person and his father, grandfather, great-grandfather, and so upward, in the direct ascending line; or between the same person and his son, grandson, great-grandson, and so downwards in the direct descending line. 2 Bl.Comm. 203; Willis Coal & Min. Co. v. Grizzell, 198 Ill. 313, 65 N.E. 74.

LINEAL DESCENT. See Descent.

LINEAL HEIR. One who inherits in a line either ascending or descending from the common source, as distinguished from a collateral heir. Rocky Mountain Fuel Co. v. Kovaics, 26 Colo.App. 554, 144 P. 863, 865.

The words "lineal heirs" like "heirs of the body" mean all lineal descendants to the remotest posterity and are words of "inheritance" and not of "purchase," unless the instrument clearly shows that they were used in a restricted sense to denote "children." Sims v. Clayton, 193 S.C. 98, 7 S.E.2d 724, 727.

LINEAL WARRANTY. A warranty by an ancestor from whom the title did or might have come to the heir. 2 Bl.Comm. 301; Rawle, Cov. 30.

LINES AND CORNERS. *In deeds and surveys.* Boundary-lines and their angles with each other. Nolin v. Parmer, 21 Ala. 66.

LINK. A unit in a connected series; anything which serves to connect or bind together the things which precede and follow it. Thus, we speak of a "link in the chain of title." Something which binds together, or connects, separate things; a part of a connected series; a tie, a bond. City of Independence v. Board of Com'rs of Montgomery County, 140 Kan. 661, 38 P.2d 105, 106.

LIQUERE. Lat. In the civil law. To be clear, evident, or satisfactory.

When a *judex* was in doubt how to decide a case, he represented to the prætor, under oath, *sibi non liquere*, (that it was not clear to him,) and was thereupon discharged. Calvin.

LIQUET. It is clear or apparent; it appears. *Satis liquet*, it sufficiently appears. 1 Strange, 412.

LIQUID DEBT. A debt immediately and unconditionally due. In re Brock, 312 Pa. 7, 166 A. 778, 780.

LIQUIDATE. To pay and settle. Gibson v. American Ry. Express Co., 195 Iowa 1126, 193 N.W. 274; Farmers State Bank & Trust Co. v. Brady, 137 Tex. 39, 152 S.W.2d 729, 732; Fleckner v. Bank of U. S., La., 8 Wheat. 338, 362, 5 L.Ed. 631.

Also to liquidate means to adjust. State ex rel. Banister v. Cantley, 330 Mo. 943, 52 S.W.2d 397, 399. Belden v. Modern Finance Co., Ohio App., 61 N.E.2d 801, 804; to ascertain the amount, or the several amounts, of the liabilities of insolvent and apportion the assets toward discharge of the indebtedness, Farmers State Bank & Trust Co. v. Brady, 137 Tex. 39, 152 S.W.2d 729, 732; to ascertain the balance due and to whom payable, State ex rel Banister v. Cantley, 330 Mo. 943, 52 S.W.2d 397, 399; to assemble and mobilize the assets, settle with the creditors and the debtors and apportion the remaining assets, if any, among the stockholders or owners. United States v. Metcalf, C.C.A.Cal., 131 F.2d 677, 679; State ex rel. Gibson v. American Bonding & Casualty Co., 225 Iowa 638, 281 N.W. 172, 175; to clear up, State ex rel. Banister v. Cantley, 330 Mo. 943, 52 S.W.2d 397, 399; Fleckner v. Bank of U. S., La., 8 Wheat. 338, 362, 5 L.Ed. 631; to determine by agreement or litigation precise amount of indebtedness, Continental Ins. Co. v. Harris, 190 Ark. 1110, 82 S.W.2d 841, 843; to discharge, Continental Ins. Co. v. Harris, 190 Ark. 1110, 82 S.W.2d 841, 843; to extinguish an indebtedness, Gibson v. American Ry. Express Co., 195 Iowa 1126, 193 N.W. 274, 278; Belden v. Modern Finance Co., Ohio App., 61 N.E.2d 801, 804; to gather in the assets, convert them into cash and distribute them according to the legal rights of the parties interested, Browne v. Hammett, 133 S.C. 446, 131 S.E. 612, 614; to lessen, Fleckner v. Bank of U. S., La., 8 Wheat. 338, 362, 5 L.Ed. 631; to make amount of indebtedness clear and certain, Continental Ins. Co. v. Harris, 190 Ark. 1110, 82 S.W.2d 841, 843; to reduce to precision in amount and to satisfy, State ex rel. Banister v. Cantley, 330 Mo. 943, 52 S.W.2d 397, 399; to sell, Esser v. Chimel, Del.Ch., 30 A.2d 685, 687; to "wind up" affairs of a business, Ex parte Amos, 94 Fla. 1023, 114 So. 760, 765; State ex rel. Gibson v. American Bonding & Casualty Co., 225 Iowa 638, 281 N.W. 172, 175.

LIQUIDATED. Ascertained; determined; fixed; settled; made clear or manifest. Cleared away; paid; discharged. Canda v. Canda, 92 N.J.Eq. 423, 112 A. 727, 728, 13 A.L.R. 1029; State Bank of Stratford v. Young, 159 Iowa 375, 140 N.W. 376, 380; Sinclair Refining Co. v. Unadilla Motor & Supply Co., 213 N.Y.S. 81, 83, 126 Misc. 292.

Adjusted, certain, or settled. Murchison v. Levy Plumbing Co., Tex.Civ.App., 73 S.W.2d 967, 968; McMurray v. Faust, 224 Iowa 50, 276 N.W. 95, 100. Declared by the parties as to amount, U. S. v. Skinner & Eddy Corporation, D.C.Wash., 28 F.2d 373, 386; made certain as to what and how much is due, Gasper v. Mayer, 171 Okl. 457, 43 P.2d 467, 471; Electrical Products Corporation of Oregon v. Ziegler Drug Stores, 157 Or. 267, 71 P.2d 583, 584.

Made certain or fixed by agreement of parties or by operation of law, Sawyer v. Somers Lumber Co., 86 Mont. 169, 282 P. 852, 854; Miller v. Prince Street Elevator Co., 41 N.M. 330, 68 P.2d 663, 666. "Settled, paid, discharged," Trenton Banking Co. v. Kennedy, 17 N.J.Misc. 222, 8 A.2d 232, 234. "Settlement," "arrangement," "agreement," "to clear from obscurity," Davies v. Turner, 61 Ga.App. 531, 6 S.E.2d 356, 359.

LIQUIDATED ACCOUNT. An account whereof the amount is certain and fixed, either by the act and agreement of the parties or by operation of law; a sum which cannot be changed by the proof; it is so much or nothing; but the term does not necessarily refer to a writing. Gasper v. Mayer, 171 Okl. 457, 43 P.2d 467, 471. Williamson v. City of Eastland, Tex.Civ.App., 65 S.W.2d 774, 775.

LIQUIDATED CLAIM. Claim, amount of which has been agreed on by parties to action or is fixed by operation of law. Tapp v. Tapp's Trustee, 299 Ky. 345, 185 S.W.2d 534, 535; United States Fidelity & Guaranty Co. v. American Bldg. Maintenance Co. of Los Angeles, 7 Cal.App.2d 683, 46 P.2d 984, 988.

A claim which can be determined with exactness from parties' agreement or by arithmetical process or application of definite rules of law, Huo Chin Yin v. Amino Products Co., 141 Ohio St. 21, 46 N.E.2d 610, 614; Petersen v. Graham, 7 Wash.2d 464, 110 P.2d 149, 154.

LIQUIDATED DAMAGES. See Damages.

LIQUIDATED DEBT. A debt is liquidated when it is certain what is due and how much is due.

Roberts v. Prior, 20 Ga. 562; Nelson v. Zahn Grain Co., 191 Okl. 181, 127 P.2d 803, 805. That which has been made certain as to amount due by agreement of parties or by operation of law. Gasper v. Mayer, 171 Okl. 457, 43 P.2d 467, 471.

LIQUIDATED DEMAND. A demand the amount of which has been ascertained or settled by agreement of the parties, or otherwise. Williamson v. City of Eastland, Tex.Civ.App., 65 S.W.2d 774, 775; Mitchell v. Addison, 20 Ga. 53.

Amount claimed is a "liquidated demand" if it is susceptible of being made certain in amount by mathematical calculations from factors which are or ought to be in possession or knowledge of party to be charged. Rifkin v. Safenovitz, 131 Conn. 411, 40 A.2d 188, 189.

LIQUIDATING DISTRIBUTION. A distribution of stock pursuant to reorganization plan. Dworsky v. Buzza Co., 215 Minn. 282, 9 N.W.2d 767, 769.

LIQUIDATING PARTNER. The partner who upon the dissolution or insolvency of the firm, is appointed to settle its accounts, collect assets, adjust claims, and pay debts. Garretson v. Brown, 185 Pa. 447, 40 A. 300.

LIQUIDATION. The act or process of settling or making clear, fixed, and determinate that which before was uncertain or unascertained.

Payment, satisfaction, or collection, Bassett v. City Bank & Trust Co., 116 Conn. 617, 165 A. 557; realization on assets and discharge of liabilities, In re Burger's Estate, 276 Mich. 485, 267 N.W. 887, 891. To clear away—to lessen—a debt, Craddock-Terry Co. v. Powell, 180 Va. 242, 22 S.E.2d 30, 34; to pay or settle, In re Klink's Estate, 310 Ill.App. 609, 35 N.E.2d 684, 687. To take over for collection, Belden v. Modern Finance Co., Ohio App., 61 N.E.2d 801, 804.

As applied to a bank or other corporation (or sometimes to the affairs of an individual) liquidation means winding up. People ex rel. Palmer v. Acme Plate Glass Mut. Ins. Co., 292 Ill.App. 275, 10 N.E.2d 988, 991; Luikart v. Flannigan, 130 Neb. 901, 267 N.W. 165, 167. It is also defined as winding up affairs by realizing upon assets, paying liabilities, and appropriating the profit or loss. Horn & Hardart Banking Co. v. United States, D.C.Pa., 34 F.Supp. 89, 90; Young v. Blandin, 215 Minn. 111, 9 N.W.2d 313, 316; Northwest Bancorporation v. Commissioner of Internal Revenue, C.C.A.8, 88 F.2d 293, 296; winding up and distribution of assets among creditors and stockholders, United States v. Bank of New York & Trust Co., D.C.N.Y., 10 F.Supp. 269, 271; winding up affairs and settlement with creditors, New York Title & Mortgage Co. v. Friedman, 276 N.Y.S. 72, 153 Misc. 697; winding up or settling with creditors and debtors, Wilson v. Superior Court in and for Santa Clara County, 2 Cal.2d 632, 43 P.2d 286, 288.

LIQUIDATION DIVIDEND. Act or operation in winding up affairs of firm or corporation, a settling with its debtors and creditors, and an appropriation and distribution to its stockholders ratably of the amount of profit and loss. Hellman v. Helvering, App.D.C., 68 F.2d 763, 765.

LIQUIDATION TAXABLE. Distribution to their own stockholders of cash and stock received by selling corporations for their assets. Commissioner of Internal Revenue v. Sussman, C.C.A.2, 102 F.2d 919, 921.

LIQUIDATOR. A person appointed to carry out the winding up of a company.

Official Liquidator. In English law. A person appointed by the judge in chancery, in whose court a joint-stock company is being wound up to bring and defend suits and actions in the name of the company, and generally to do all things necessary for winding up the affairs of the company, and distributing its assets. 3 Steph.Comm. 24.

LIQUOR. Spirituous or intoxicating liquor. McCoy v. State, 177 Ark. 1053, 9 S.W.2d 241, 242; Wooten v. State, 47 Ga.App. 301, 170 S.E. 392; State v. Hickey, 198 N.C. 45, 150 S.E. 615, 617; People v. Crilley, 20 Barb. (N.Y.) 248.

All kinds of intoxicating decoctions, liquids, or beverages, Newton v. State ex rel. Atty. Gen., 234 Ala. 91, 175 So. 563, 564. Any alcoholic or intoxicating liquid, People v. Draper, 134 Cal.App. 1, 22 P.2d 604.

Any beverage, as temperance liquors, or those not intoxicating. Benton v. State, 24 Ala.App. 441, 136 So. 428, 429.

Any liquid substance, Newton v. State ex rel. Atty. Gen., 234 Ala. 91, 175 So. 563, 564.

Distilled spirits stronger than malt beverages and fermented wines, Peurifoy v. State, 53 Ga.App. 515, 186 S.E. 461, 462.

Such as is prohibited by prohibition law, Newton v. State, 27 Ala.App. 492, 175 So. 562, 563.

Whisky, Bolivar v. Monnat, 248 N.Y.S. 722, 727, 232 App. Div. 33; Jones v. State, 23 Ala.App. 339, 125 So. 382, 383.

See Alcoholic Liquors; Intoxicating Liquor; Spirituous Liquors.

LIQUOR DEALER. One who carries on the business of selling intoxicating liquors, either at wholesale or retail and irrespective of whether the liquor sold is produced or manufactured by himself or by others; but there must be more than a single sale. See Timm v. Harrison, 109 Ill. 601; U. S. v. Allen, D.C.Iowa, 38 F. 738; State v. Dow, 21 Vt. 484; Mansfield v. State, 17 Tex.App. 472.

LIQUOR-SHOP. A house where spirituous liquors are kept and sold. Wooster v. State, 6 Baxt. (Tenn.) 534.

LIQUOR TAX CERTIFICATE. Under the excise laws of New York a certificate of payment of the tax imposed upon the business of liquor-selling, entitling the holder to carry on that business, and differing from the ordinary form of license in that it does not confer a mere personal privilege but creates a species of property which is transferable by the owner. See In re Lyman, 160 N.Y. 96, 54 N.E. 577; In re Cullinan, 82 App.Div. 445, 81 N.Y.S. 567.

LIRA. The name of an Italian coin, of the value of about eighteen cents.

LIS. Lat. A controversy or dispute; a suit or action at law.

LIS ALIBI PENDENS. A suit pending elsewhere.

The fact that proceedings are pending between a plaintiff and defendant in one court in respect to a given matter is frequently a ground for preventing the plaintiff from taking proceedings in another court against the same defendant for the same object and arising out of the same cause of action. Sweet.

LIS MOTA. A controversy moved or begun.

By this term is meant a dispute which has arisen upon a point or question which afterwards forms the issue upon which legal proceedings are instituted. Westfelt v. Adams, 131 N.C. 379, 42 S.E. 823. After such controversy has arisen, *(post litem motam,)* it is held, declarations as to pedigree, made by members of the family since deceased, are not admissible. See 4 Camp. 417; 6 Car. & P. 560.

LIS PENDENS. A pending suit. Moore v. Zelic, 338 Ill. 583, 170 N.E. 664, 666; People ex rel. O'Connor v. City of Chicago, 299 Ill.App. 504, 20 N.E.2d 306, 307; jurisdiction, power, or control which courts acquire over property in suit pending action and until final judgment, Commonwealth ex rel. Kelley v. Kelly, 322 Pa. 178, 185 A. 307, 310; Coleman v. Law, 170 Ga. 906, 154 S.E. 445, 448, 74 A.L.R. 684; notice of all facts apparent on face of pleadings and exhibits and of all other facts of which they would put a person of ordinary prudence on inquiry, Ben Williamson & Co. v. Hall, 290 Ky. 672, 161 S.W.2d 905, 907; notice of pendency of suit and warning to anyone interested to examine proceedings, Harris v. Lipson, 167 Va. 365, 189 S.E. 349, 352, 108 A.L.R. 912; a suit or controversy in court, Mayne v. St. Louis Union Trust Co., C.C.A.Mo., 64 F.2d 843, 845; that legal process, in a suit regarding land, which amounts to legal notice to all the world that there is a dispute as to the title. Stim. Law Gloss.

The filing of the bill and serving a subpœna creates a *lis pendens,* except when statutes require some record. Stim.Law Gloss. Tinsley v. Rice, 105 Ga. 285, 31 S.E. 174; Hines v. Duncan, 79 Ala. 117, 58 Am.Rep. 580; Troll v. City of St. Louis, 257 Mo. 626, 168 S.W. 167, 177; Heckmann v. Detlaff, 283 Ill. 505, 119 N.E. 639, 640. In the civil law. A suit pending. A suit was not said to be pending before that stage of it called *"litis contestatio" (q. v.).* Mackeld.Rom.Law, § 219; Calvin.

Notice of lis pendens. A notice filed for the purpose of warning all persons that the title to certain property is in litigation, and that, if they purchase the defendant's claim to the same, they are in danger of being bound by an adverse judgment. See Empire Land & Canal Co. v. Engley, 18 Colo. 388, 33 P. 153.

The notice is for the purpose of preserving rights pending litigation. Mitchell v. Federal Land Bank of St. Louis, 206 Ark. 253, 174 S.W.2d 671, 674.

LIST. A docket or calendar of causes ready for trial or argument, or of motions ready for hearing.

Entering or enrolling in a list; to enter in an official list or schedule; as, to list property for taxation; to put into a list or catalogue; register; enroll. Baldrige v. Flothow, 123 Neb. 218, 242 N.W. 414, 417.

Legal voters. Official registry of voters. Commonwealth v. Ballou, 283 Mass. 304, 186 N.E. 494, 497.

LISTED. Included in a list; put on a list, particularly on a list of taxable persons or property.

LISTERS. This word is used in some of the states to designate the persons appointed to make lists of taxables. See Rev. St. Vt. 538.

LISTING. An alleged oral agreement to sell to any purchaser procured by broker for certain amount was a "listing" of the property. Zeligson v. Hartman-Blair, Inc., C.C.A.Kan., 135 F.2d 874, 876.

"Listing property for taxation" is the making of a schedule or inventory of such property, whereby owner makes statement of property in response to assessor's inquiries, Templing v. Bennett, 156 Kan. 68, 131 P.2d 904, 907. The word listing ordinarily implies an official listing of the persons and property to be taxed, and a valuation of the property of each person as a basis of apportionment. Buser v. Kriechbaum, 229 Iowa 888, 295 N.W. 455, 460.

LITE PENDENTE. Lat. Pending the suit. Fleta, lib. 2, c. 54, § 23.

LITEM DENUNCIARE. Lat. In the civil law. To cast the burden of a suit upon another; particularly used with reference to a purchaser of property who, being sued in respect to it by a third person, gives notice to his vendor and demands his aid in its defense. See Mackeld. Rom. Law, § 403.

LITEM SUAM FACERE. Lat. To make a suit his own. Where a *judex,* from partiality or enmity, evidently favored either of the parties, he was said *litem suam facere.* Calvin.

LITERA. Lat. A letter. The letter of a law, as distinguished from its spirit. See Letter.

LITERA PISANA. The Pisan letter. A term applied to the old character in which the copy of the Pandects formerly kept at Pisa, in Italy, was written. Spelman.

LITERÆ. Letters. A term applied in old English law to various instruments in writing, public and private.

LITERÆ DIMISSORIÆ. Dimissory letters *(q. v.).*

LITERÆ HUMANIORES. A term including Greek, Latin, general philology, logic, moral philosophy, metaphysics; the name of the principal course of study in the University of Oxford. Wharton.

LITERÆ MORTUÆ. Dead letters; fulfilling words of a statute.

Lord Bacon observes that "there are in every statute certain words which are as veins, where the life and blood of the statute cometh, and where all doubts do arise, and the rest are *literæ mortuæ,* fulfilling words." Bac.St.Uses, (Works, iv. 189).

LITERÆ PATENTES. Letters patent; literally, open letters.

LITERÆ PATENTES REGIS NON ERUNT VACUÆ. 1 Bulst. 6. The king's letters patent shall not be void.

LITERÆ PROCURATORIÆ. In old English law. Letters procuratory; letters of procuration; letters of attorney. Bract. fols. 40, 43.

LITERÆ RECOGNITIONIS. In maritime law. A bill of lading. Jac. Sea Laws, 172.

LITERÆ SCRIPTÆ MANENT. Written words last.

LITERÆ SIGILLATÆ. In old English law. Sealed letters. The return of a sheriff was so called. Fleta, lib. 2, c. 64, § 19.

LITERAL. According to language; following expression in words.

A literal construction of a document adheres closely to its words, without making differences for extrinsic circumstances; a literal performance of a condition is one which complies exactly with its terms.

LITERAL CONTRACT. In Roman law. A species of written contract, in which the formal act by which an obligation was superinduced on the convention was an entry of the sum due, where it should be specifically ascertained, on the debit side of a ledger. Maine, Anc. Law, 320. A contract, the whole of the evidence of which is reduced to writing, and binds the party who subscribed it, although he has received no consideration. Lec. El. Dr. Rom. § 887.

LITERAL PROOF. In the civil law. Written evidence.

LITERARY. Pertaining to polite learning; connected with the study or use of books and writings.

The word "literary," having no legal signification, is to be taken in its ordinary and usual meaning. We speak of literary persons as learned, erudite; of literary property, as the productions of ripe scholars, or, at least, of professional writers; of literary institutions, as those where the positive sciences are taught, or persons eminent for learning associate, for purposes connected with their professions. This we think the popular meaning of the word; and that it would not be properly used as descriptive of a school for the instruction of youth. Indianapolis v. McLean, 8 Ind. 332.

LITERARY COMPOSITION. In copyright law. An original result of mental production, developed in a series of written or printed words, arranged for an intelligent purpose, in an orderly succession of expressive combinations. Keene v. Wheatley, 14 Fed.Cas. 192; Woolsey v. Judd, 4 Duer (N. Y.) 396.

LITERARY PROPERTY. May be described as the right which entitles an author and his assigns to all the use and profit of his composition, to which no independent right is, through any act or omission on his or their part, vested in another person. 9 Amer. Law Reg. 44. And see Keene v. Wheatley, 14 Fed.Cas. 192; Palmer v. De Witt, 32 N.Y.Super.Ct. 552.

A distinction is to be taken between "literary property" (which is the natural, common-law right a person has in the form of written expression to which he has, by labor and skill, reduced his thoughts) and "copyright," (which is a statutory monopoly, above and beyond natural property, conferred upon an author to encourage and reward a dedication of his literary property to the public.) Abbott.

LITERATE. In English ecclesiastical law. One who qualifies himself for holy orders by presenting himself as a person accomplished in classical learning, etc., not as a graduate of Oxford, Cambridge, etc.

LITERATURA. *"Ad literaturam ponere"* means to put children to school.

This liberty was anciently denied to those parents who were servile tenants, without the lord's consent. The prohibition against the education of sons arose from the fear that the son, being bred to letters, might enter into holy orders, and so stop or divert the services which he might otherwise do as heir to his father. Paroch.Antiq. 401.

LITERIS OBLIGATIO. In Roman law. The contract of *nomen,* which was constituted by writing, (*scripturâ.*)

It was of two kinds, viz.: (1) *A re in personam,* when a transaction was transferred from the daybook *(adversaria)* into the ledger *(codex)* in the form of a debt under the name or heading of the purchaser or debtor, *(nomen;)* and (2) *a personâ in personam,* where a debt already standing under one *nomen* or heading was transferred in the usual course of *novatio* from that *nomen* to another and substituted *nomen.* By reason of this transferring, these obligations were called *"nomina transcriptia."* No money was, in fact, paid to constitute the contract. If ever money was paid, then the *nomen* was *arcarium, (i. e.,* a real contract, *re contractus,)* and not a *nomen proprium.* Brown.

LITIGANT. A party to a lawsuit; one engaged in litigation; usually spoken of active parties, not of nominal ones.

LITIGARE. Lat. To litigate; to carry on a suit, (*litem agere,*) either as plaintiff or defendant; to claim or dispute by action; to test or try the validity of a claim by action.

LITIGATE. To dispute or contend in form of law; to carry on a suit.

To bring into or engage in litigation, the act of carrying on a suit in a law court, a judicial contest; hence, any controversy that must be decided upon evidence. In re Loudenslager's Estate, N.J.Prerog., 13 N.J.Eq. 418, 167 A. 194, 195.

LITIGATION. Contest in a court of justice for the purpose of enforcing a right. Summerour v. Fortson, 174 Ga. 862, 164 S.E. 809; a judicial contest, a judicial controversy, a suit at law. In re Loudenslager's Estate, Prerog., 113 N.J.Eq. 418, 167 A. 194; civil actions. Sunshine Mining Co. v. Carver, D.C.Idaho, 34 F.Supp. 274, 280.

LITIGIOSITY. In Scotch law. The pendency of a suit; it is a tacit legal prohibition of alienation, to the disappointment of an action, or of diligence, the direct object of which is to obtain possession, or to acquire the property of a particular subject. The effect of it is analogous to that of inhibition. Bell.

LITIGIOSO. Span. Litigious; the subject of litigation; a term applied to property which is the subject of dispute in a pending suit. White v. Gay, 1 Tex. 388.

LITIGIOUS. That which is the subject of a suit or action; that which is contested in a court of justice. In another sense, "litigious" signifies fond of litigation; prone to engage in suits.

LITIGIOUS CHURCH. In ecclesiastical law, a church is said to be litigious where two presentations are offered to the bishop upon the same avoidance. Jenk. Cent. 11.

LITIGIOUS RIGHT. In the civil law. A right which cannot be exercised without undergoing a lawsuit. Civil Code La. art. 3556, par. 18.

A right, to be considered "litigious" under Louisiana law, must be in litigation at time of the sale thereof, and ceases to be litigious if at time of the sale judgment has become final. Caucier v. Crichton, C.C.A.La., 147 F.2d 430, 435.

LITIS ÆSTIMATIO. Lat. The measure of damages.

LITIS CONTESTATIO. Lat.

Admiralty Practice. The general issue. 2 Browne, Civil & Adm. Law, 358, and note.

Civil and Canon Law. Contestation of suit; the process of contesting a suit by the opposing statements of the respective parties; the process of coming to an issue; the attainment of an issue; the issue itself.

Ecclesiastical Courts. The general answer made by the defendant, in which he denies the matter charged against him in the libel. Hallifax, Civil Law, b. 3, c. 11, no. 9.

LITIS DENUNCIATIO. Lat. In the civil law. The process by which a purchaser of property, who is sued for its possession or recovery by a third person, falls back upon his vendor's covenant of warranty, by giving the latter notice of the action and demanding his aid in defending it. See Mackeld. Rom. Law, § 403.

LITIS DOMINIUM. Lat. In the civil law. Ownership, control, or direction of a suit. A fiction of law by which the employment of an attorney or proctor (*procurator*) in a suit was authorized or justified, he being supposed to become, by the appointment of his principal (*dominus*) or client, the *dominus litis*. Heinecc. Elem. lib. 4, tit. 10, §§ 1246, 1247.

LITIS NOMEN OMNEM ACTIONEM SIGNIFICAT, SIVE IN REM, SIVE IN PERSONAM SIT. Co. Litt. 292. A lawsuit signifies every action, whether it be *in rem* or *in personam*.

LITISPENDENCE. An obsolete term for the time during which a lawsuit is going on.

LITISPENDENCIA. In Spanish law. Litispendency. The condition of a suit pending in a court of justice.

LITRE. Fr. A measure of capacity in the metric system, being a cubic decimetre, equal to 61.022 cubic inches, or 2.113 American pints, or 1.76 English pints. Webster.

LITTLE MORE THAN. About. Pierce v. Lefort, 197 La. 1, 200 So. 801, 803.

LITTORAL. Belonging to the shore, as of seas and great lakes. Webster.

Corresponding to riparian proprietors on a stream or small pond are littoral proprietors on a sea or lake. But "riparian" is also used coextensively with "littoral." Commonwealth v. Alger, 7 Cush., Mass., 94. See Boston v. Lecraw, 17 How. 426, 15 L.Ed. 118. One whose lands abuts on lake is a "littoral owner". Darling v. Christensen, 166 Or. 17, 109 P.2d 585, 592; Peck v. Alfred Olsen Const. Co., 216 Iowa 519, 245 N.W. 131, 137, 89 A.L.R. 1147.

LITURA. Lat. In the civil law. An obliteration or blot in a will or other instrument. Dig. 28, 4, 1, 1.

LITUS. In Civil law. The bank of a stream or shore of the sea; the coast.

In old European law. A kind of servant; one who surrendered himself into another's power. Spelman.

LITUS EST QUOUSQUE MAXIMUS FLUCTUS A MARI PERVENIT. The shore is where the highest wave from the sea has reached. Dig. 50, 16, 96. Ang. Tide-Waters, 67.

LITUS MARIS. The sea-shore.

"It is certain that that which the sea overflows, either at high spring tides or at extraordinary tides, comes not, as to this purpose, under the denomination of '*litus maris*,' and consequently the king's title is not of that large extent, but only to land that is usually overflowed at ordinary tides. That, therefore, I call the '*shore*' that is between the common high-water and low-water mark, and no more." Hale de Jure Mar. c. 4.

LITVINOV ASSIGNMENT. An assignment to the United States as an incident to its recognition of the Union of Soviet Socialist Republics as the de jure government of Russia, of the Soviet government's claims against American nationals, as clarified by subsequent correspondence between officials of the two countries. United States v. Pink, N.Y., 62 S.Ct. 552, 562, 315 U.S. 203, 86 L.Ed. 796.

LIVE. In possession of all those limbs and faculties by which life is enjoyed and not mere animal existence. In re Healy's Will, 8 N.Y.S.2d 394, 399, 255 App.Div. 361. To live in a place, is to reside there, to abide there, to have one's home. Leroux v. Industrial Accident Commission of California, 140 Cal.App. 569, 35 P.2d 624, 626.

LIVE AND COHABIT TOGETHER AS HUSBAND AND WIFE. As applied to common-law marriages, means a living together, claiming to be married, in the relationship of husband and wife. Drummond v. Benson, Tex.Civ.App., 133 S.W.2d 154, 159.

LIVE OIL. Oil that has gas in it. Crow v. Continental Oil Co., C.C.A.Tex., 100 F.2d 292, 293.

LIVE STOCK. Domestic animals used or raised on a farm. Boland v. Cecil, 65 Cal.App.2d 832, 150 P.2d 819, 822.

The term in its generic sense includes all domestic animals. Meader v. Unemployment Compensation Division of Industrial Accident Board, 64 Idaho 716, 136 P.2d 984, 987. It includes fur bearing animals raised in captivity. Fromm Bros. v. United States, D.C.Wis., 35 F.Supp. 145, 147.

LIVE-STOCK INSURANCE. See Insurance.

LIVE STORAGE. As applied to storage of automobiles in garages, "dead storage" is where cars not in use are deposited or put away, sometimes for the season, and "live storage" is the storage of cars in active daily use. Hogan v. O'Brien, 206 N.Y.S. 831, 832, 123 Misc. 865, affirmed 208 N.Y.S. 477, 212 App.Div. 193.

"The extent of responsibility of a garage keeper for cars put in his garage sometimes depends on whether they are in 'dead storage' or 'live storage'. * * * In some jurisdictions where, according to the general custom of the patrons of a garage, their cars kept at the garage can be taken out and returned at will, day or night, the garage keeper will be liable for a loss caused by a failure to exercise ordinary care for the protection of such cars, notwithstanding he may not know that the specific car has been returned." Blashfield, Cyc. of Automobile Law and Prac., Perm. Ed., § 5023.

LIVELODE. Maintenance; support.

LIVERY. 1. In English law. Delivery of possession of their lands to the king's tenants *in capite* or tenants by knight's service.

2. A writ which may be sued out by a ward in chivalry, on reaching his majority, to obtain delivery of the possession of his lands out of the hands of the guardian. 2 Bl.Comm. 68.

3. A particular dress or garb appropriate or peculiar to certain persons, as the members of a guild, or, more particularly, the servants of a nobleman or gentleman.

4. The privilege of a particular guild or company of persons, the members thereof being called "livery-men."

5. A contract of hiring of work-beasts, particularly horses, to the use of the hirer. It is seldom used alone in this sense, but appears in the compound, "livery-stable."

6. Feeding, stabling, and care of horses for pay; boarding; as, to keep one's horses at livery, the keeping of horses, and hence of vehicles, boats, etc., in readiness to be hired; the state of being so kept. Biehler v. Great American Indemnity Co., 127 N.J.L. 114, 21 A.2d 225, 226.

LIVERY CONVEYANCE. A vehicle used indiscriminately in conveying the public, without limitation to certain persons or particular occasions or without being governed by special terms. Elliott v. Behner, 150 Kan. 876, 96 P.2d 852, 857.

LIVERY IN CHIVALRY. In feudal law. The delivery of the lands of a ward in chivalry out of the guardian's hands, upon the heir's attaining the requisite age,—twenty-one for males, sixteen for females. 2 Bl.Comm. 68.

LIVERY OF SEISIN. The appropriate ceremony, at common law, for transferring the corporal possession of lands or tenements by a grantor to his grantee.

It was livery *in deed* where the parties went together upon the land, and there a twig, clod, key, or other symbol was delivered in the name of the whole. Livery *in law* was where the same ceremony was performed, not upon the land itself, but in sight of it. 2 Bl.Comm. 315, 316; Micheau v. Crawford, 8 N.J.Law, 108; Northern Pac. R. Co. v. Cannon, C.C.Mont., 46 F. 232.

LIVERY OFFICE. An office appointed for the delivery of lands.

LIVERY STABLE. A place where horses are groomed, fed, and hired, and where vehicles are let. Williams v. Garignes, 30 La.Ann. 1095; Grimes v. State, 82 Tex.Cr.R. 512, 200 S.W. 378, 379.

LIVERY STABLE KEEPER. One whose business it is to keep horses for hire or to let, or to keep, feed, or board horses for others. Kittanning Borough v. Montgomery, 5 Pa.Super. 198.

LIVERYMAN. A member of some company in the city of London; also called a "freeman."

LIVES IN BEING. As used in rule against perpetuities, means any lives in being at any time future interest is created, regardless of personal interest therein. In re Friday's Estate, 313 Pa. 328, 170 A. 123, 125, 91 A.L.R. 766.

LIVING. Existing, surviving, or continuing in operation. In re Lydig's Estate, 260 N.Y.S. 147, 145 Misc. 321.

Also means to abide, to dwell, to reside and literally signifies the pecuniary resources by means of which one exists. Leroux v. Industrial Accident Commission of California, 140 Cal.App. 569, 35 P.2d 624, 626.

A child in the mother's womb is living, In re Holthausen's Will, 26 N.Y.S.2d 140, 143, 175 Misc. 1022. A child born two months after death of father was a "living child" at death of father. Barnett v. Pinkston, 238 Ala. 327, 191 So. 371, 374. Person born within three months after testator's death held "living," at that time. In re Abbe's Estate, 245 N.Y.S. 291, 293, 138 Misc. 210. Under testamentary gift, life tenant's daughter or survivor, word "survivor" is synonymous with word "living." In re Dyckman's Will, 245 N.Y.S. 631, 635, 138 Misc. 253.

LIVING APART. To live in a separate abode. McDaniel v. McDaniel, 292 Ky. 56, 165 S.W.2d 966, 967.

LIVING AT TIME OF ANOTHER'S DEATH. Remaining in life after such other person's death. Sabit v. Safe Deposit & Trust Co. of Baltimore, 184 Md. 24, 40 A.2d 231, 238.

LIVING IN ADULTERY. An act of intercourse between parties and a continuation of such relation or an intention or agreement that it be continued. Brown v. State, 31 Ala.App. 233, 14 So.2d 596, 597.

LIVING IN OPEN AND NOTORIOUS ADULTERY. To constitute, parties must dwell together openly and notoriously as if conjugal relation existed between them. People v. Potter, 319 Ill.App. 409, 49 N.E.2d 307, 309.

The parties must reside together in face of society as if conjugal relations existed between them, and fact of their so living and that they are not husband and wife must be known in community in which they reside. Mathis v. State, 60 Okl.Cr. 58, 61 P.2d 261, 267.

LIVING SEPARATE AND APART. Exists where the spouses have come to a parting of the ways and have no present intention of resuming marital relations and taking up life together under the same roof, not where they are residing temporarily in different places for economic or social reasons. Woodall v. Commissioner of Internal Revenue, C.C.A.9, 105 F.2d 474, 477.

LIVING TOGETHER. As respects court's right to allow suit money to wife in divorce action, means dwelling together in same house, eating at same table, the two parties holding themselves out to world and conducting themselves toward each other as husband and wife. Lipp v. Lipp, Mo.App., 117 S.W.2d 364, 365, 366.

As used in adultery, statute means that parties must dwell or reside together in same habitation as a common or joint residing place. Polous v. State, 117 Tex.Cr.R. 1, 36 S.W.2d 754, 755.

As used in compensation law the words were intended to cover cases where no break in marriage relation existed, and therefore physical dwelling together is not necessary. Harris v. Louisiana Oil Refining Corporation, 127 So. 40, 42, 13 La.App. 416; Berg v. Industrial Commission, 236 Wis. 172, 294 N.W. 506, 509.

LIVING WITH HUSBAND. Means to dwell, to reside, to make one's abiding place or home with him, and may also mean to cohabit, and means living together as husband and wife in ordinary acceptation of words in common understanding, maintaining a home and living together in same household or actually cohabiting under conditions which would be regarded as constituting a family relation. McPadden v. Morris, 126 Conn. 654, 13 A.2d 679, 680.

Wife continuing to occupy homestead premises after husband abandoned, Reymond v. Louisiana Trust & Savings Bank, 177 La. 409, 148 So. 663, 667. Wife involuntarily confined in asylum for insane. Harrison v. Cargill Commission Co., 126 Neb. 185, 252 N.W. 899.

LIVRE TOURNOIS. A coin used in France before the Revolution. It is to be computed in the *ad valorem* duty on goods, etc., at eighteen and a half cents. Act Cong. March 2, 1798, § 61; 1 Story, Laws, 629.

LLOYD'S. An association in the city of London, originally for the transaction of marine insurance, the members of which underwrite one another's policies. See Durbrow v. Eppens, 65 N.J.L. 10, 46 A. 585.

LLOYD'S BONDS. The name of a class of evidences of debt, used in England; being acknowledgments, by a borrowing company made under its seal, of a debt incurred and actually due by the company to a contractor or other person for work done, goods supplied, or otherwise, as the case may be, with a covenant for payment of the principal and interest at a future time. Brown.

LLOYD'S INSURANCE. Insurers are such as individuals and not as a corporate insurance company and the liability for loss is several and not joint. Jones v. Hollywood Style Shop, Tex.Civ. App., 62 S.W.2d 167. The "Lloyds' Plan," contemplates individual liability of the several underwriters. Harris v. Prince, 132 Tex. 231, 121 S.W. 2d 983, 986.

LOAD LINE. The depth to which a ship will sink in salt water when loaded.

A design, painted on each side of vessel, intended as a guide to determine safe loading depth under various conditions. The Indien, C.C.A.Cal., 71 F.2d 752, 759.

Every British ship must be marked on each side amidships with a loadline indicating the maximum loadline in salt water, to which it is lawful to load the ship. Sailing ships under eighty tons, fishing ships, and pleasure yachts, also ships employed exclusively in trading in any river or inland water wholly or partly in any British possession, and tugs and passenger steamers plying in smooth water or in excursion limits are excepted. This mark is called Plimsoll's Mark or Line, from Samuel Plimsoll, by whose efforts the passage of an act of parliament to prevent overloading was procured. The law applies to foreign ships while within any port of the United Kingdom, other than such as come into any such port to which they are not bound and for any purpose other than embarking or landing passengers or taking in or discharging cargo or taking in bunker coal. There must also be a mark on each side amidships indicating the position of each deck above water.

LOADING. The act of putting a load on or in; as to load a beast of burden, a car or a vessel; hence, to charge as with a load or burden. American Oil & Supply Co. v. United States Casualty Co., 19 N.J.Misc. 7, 18 A.2d 257, 259.

The difference between gross and net premiums on policies. Commissioner of Insurance v. Massachusetts Accident Co., 314 Mass. 558, 50 N.E.2d 801, 809; Metropolitan Life Ins. Co. v. Rouillard, 92 N.H. 16, 24 A.2d 264, 266; Magers v. Northwestern Mut. Life Ins. Co., 348 Mo. 96, 152 S.W.2d 148, 150.

LOADMANAGE. The pay to loadsmen; that is, persons who sail or row before ships, in barks or small vessels, with instruments for towing the ship and directing her course, in order that she may escape the dangers in her way. Poth. Des Avaries, no. 137.

LOAF. To spend time in idleness, to lounge or loiter about or along. City of Olathe v. Lauck, 156 Kan. 637, 135 P.2d 549, 551.

LOAN. A lending, In re Lalla's Estate, 362 Ill. 621, 1 N.E.2d 50, 53.

Also means advance of money with an absolute promise to repay, Bankers Mortgage Co. v. Commissioner of Internal Revenue, C.C.A.Tex., 142 F.2d 130, 131. Bailment without reward, consisting of the delivery of an article by the owner to another person, to be used by the latter gratuitously, and returned either *in specie* or in kind. A sum of money confided to another. Nichols v. Fearson, 7 Pet. 109, 8 L.Ed. 623; Booth v. Terrell, 16 Ga. 20, 25; a borrowing of money or other personal property by a person who promises to return it, State v. Moltzner, 141 Or. 355, 17 P.2d 555, 556; contract whereby one delivers money to another who agrees to return equivalent sum. Easter Oil Corporation v. Strauss, Tex.Civ.App., 52 S.W.2d 336, 340; Shaw v. McShane, Tex.Com.App., 50 S.W.2d 278, 282; debts arising from borrowing of money, Lawrie v. Miller, Tex.Com.App., 45 S.W.2d 172, 173; delivery by one party and receipt by another party of money on agreement, express or implied, to repay money with or without interest, Parsons v. Fox, 179 Ga. 605, 176 S.E. 642; O. A. Graybeal Co. v. Cook, 111 Cal.App. 518, 295 P. 1088, 1092; deposit of money by a customer with banker, Gimbel Bros. v. White, 10 N.Y.S.2d 666, 667, 256 App.Div. 439; deposit on time certificates, Carroll v. Eblen, 178 Tenn. 146, 156 S.W.2d 412, 415; payment of money by one to another to be repaid some future day, In re Arbuckle's Estate, 324 Pa. 501, 188 A. 758, 761; that which one lends or borrows, In re Lalla's Estate, 362 Ill. 621, 1 N.E.2d 50, 53; transaction creating customary relation of borrower and lender, Bannock County v. Citizens' Bank & Trust Co., 53 Idaho 159, 22 P.2d 674. Transaction wherein one party transfers to the other a sum of money which that other agrees to repay absolutely. Yezek v. Delaware, L. & W. R. Co., 28 N.Y.S.2d 35, 36, 176 Misc. 553.

The four elements of a "loan" are, a principal sum, a placing of the sum with a safe borrower, an agreement that interest is to be paid, and a recognition by receiver of money of his liability for return of the principal amount with accrued interest. McLendon v. Johnson, 71 Ga.App. 424, 31 S.E.2d 89, 92.

LOAN ASSOCIATION. See Building and Loan Association.

LOAN CERTIFICATES. Certificates issued by a clearing-house to the associated banks to the amount of seventy-five per cent. of the value of the collaterals deposited by the borrowing banks with the loan committee of the clearing-house. Anderson.

LOAN FOR CONSUMPTION. A loan for consumption is where the article is not to be returned in specie, but in kind. This is a sale and not a bailment. Code Ga. 1882, § 2125 (Civ. Code 1910, § 3516).

The loan for consumption is an agreement by which one person delivers to another a certain quantity of things which are consumed by the use, under the obligation, by the borrower, to return to him as much of the same kind and quality. Civ.Code La. art. 2910.

LOAN FOR EXCHANGE. A loan for exchange is a contract by which one delivers personal property to another, and the latter agrees to return to the lender a similar thing at a future time, without reward for its use. Civ. Code Cal. § 1902.

LOAN FOR USE. Occurs where a chattel is to be used by bailee without reward and then specifically returned to bailor. Slack v. Bryan, 299 Ky. 132, 184 S.W.2d 873, 876.

The loan for use is an agreement by which a person delivers a thing to another, to use it according to its natural destination, or according to the agreement, under the obligation on the part of the borrower, to return it after he shall have done using it. Civ.Code La. art. 2893. A loan for use is a contract by which one gives to another the temporary possession and use of personal property, and the latter agrees to return the same thing to him at a future time, without reward for its use. Civ.Code Cal. § 1884. A loan for use is the gratuitous grant of an article to another for use, to be returned *in specie*, and may be either for a certain time or indefinitely, and at the will of the grantor. Code Ga.1882, § 2126 (Civ.Code 1910, § 3517). Loan for use (called *"commodatum"* in the civil law) differs from a loan for consumption, (called *"mutuum"* in the civil law,) in this: that the *commodatum* must be specifically returned; the *mutuum* is to be returned in kind. In the case of a *commodatum*, the property in the thing remains in the lender; in a *mutuum*, the property passes to the borrower. Bouvier.

LOAN, GRATUITOUS, (or COMMODATE.) A class of bailment which is called *"commodatum"* in the Roman law, and is denominated by Sir William Jones a "loan for use," (*prêt-à-usage*,) to distinguish it from *"mutuum,"* a loan for consumption. It is the gratuitous lending of an article to the borrower for his own use. Wharton.

LOAN SOCIETIES. In English law. A kind of club formed for the purpose of advancing money on loan to the industrial classes.

LOANED EMPLOYEE. Whether an employee should be regarded as a "loaned employee" in the service of a special employer, or whether he should be regarded as remaining in the service of his general employer, depends upon in whose work the employee was engaged at the time of injury. Owen v. St. Louis Spring Co., 175 Tenn. 543, 136 S.W.2d 498, 499, 500.

Under the "loaned servant doctrine", when one lends his servant to another for a particular employment, servant, for anything done in that employment, must be dealt with as servant of one to whom he is lent. Blair v. Durham, C.C.A.Tenn., 134 F.2d 729, 732.

Under the "loaned servant" rule, a loaned servant does not become the servant of the borrower unless the borrower has exclusive control over him for the period covered. Walter v. Everett School Dist. No. 24, 195 Wash. 45, 79 P.2d 689.

LOBBYING. "Lobbying" is defined to be any personal solicitation of a member of a legislative body during a session thereof, by private interview, or letter or message, or other means and appliances not addressed solely to the judgment, to favor or oppose, or to vote for or against, any bill, resolution, report, or claim pending, or to be introduced by either branch thereof, by any person who misrepresents the nature of his interest in the matter to such member, or who is employed for a consideration by a person or corporation interested in the passage or defeat of such bill, resolution, report, or claim, for the purpose of procuring the passage or defeat thereof. But this does not include such services as drafting petitions, bills, or resolutions, attending to the taking of testimony, collecting facts, preparing arguments and memorials, and submitting them orally or in writing to a committee or member of the legislature, and other services of like character, intended to reach the reason of legislators. Code Ga. 1882, § 4486. And see Colusa County v. Welch, 122 Cal. 428, 55 P. 248; Houlton v. Nichol, 93 Wis. 393, 67 N.W. 715, 33 L.R.A. 166, 57 Am.St.Rep. 928.

LOBBYING CONTRACT. A contract to secure the passage of legislation by any other means than the use of reason and presentation of facts, making arguments and submitting them orally or in writing. Ewing v. National Airport Corporation, C.C.A.Va., 115 F.2d 859, 860, 861.

LOBBYIST. One who makes it a business to procure the passage of bills pending before a legislative body.

One "who makes it a business to 'see' members and procure, by persuasion, importunity, or the use of inducements, the passing of bills, public as well as private, which involve gain to the promoters." 1 Bryce, Am. Com. 156.

L'OBLIGATION SANS CAUSE, OU SUR UNE FAUSSE CAUSE, OU SUR CAUSE ILLICITE, NE PEUT AVOIR AUCUN EFFET. An obligation without consideration, or upon a false consideration, (which fails,) or upon unlawful consideration, cannot have any effect. Code Civil, 3, 4; Chit. Cont. (11th Am. Ed.) 25, note.

LOCAL. Relating to place, expressive of place; belonging or confined to a particular place. Distinguished from "general," "personal," and "transitory."

As to local "Allegiance," "Custom," "Government," "Taxes," and "Venue," see those titles.

LOCAL ACT. See Local Law.

LOCAL ACT OF PARLIAMENT. An act which has for its object the interest of some particular locality as the formation of a road, the alteration of the course of a river, the formation of a public market in a particular district, etc. Brown.

LOCAL ACTIONS. Embrace all actions in which the subject or thing sought to be recovered is in its nature local. Hesselbrock v. Burlington County, 111 N.J.L. 177, 168 A. 45, 46. If action could only have arisen in one place, then it is a "local action." Employers' Casualty Co. v. Ponton, Tex. Civ.App., 41 S.W.2d 147, 149; Barnett v. National Surety Corporation, 195 Miss. 528, 15 So.2d 775, 776, 777.

Actions are "local" when the transactions on which they are based could not occur except in some particular place. Bunting v. Henderson, 220 N.C. 194, 16 S.E.2d 836, 837. "Local," within statute providing where suits of local nature must be brought, is fixed place or determinate zone identified with given region. Hills v. F. S. Harmon & Co., D.C.Wash., 56 F.2d 662, 663.

One wherein all principal facts on which it is founded are of a local nature; as where possession of land is to be recovered, or damages for an actual trespass, or for waste affecting land, because in such case the cause of action relates to some particular locality, which usually also constitutes the venue of the action. Miller & Lux v. Rickey, C.C.Nev., 127 F. 577; Crook v. Pitcher, 61 Md. 513. Where subject-matter is situated in a county other than one in which the parties reside and the primary and principal relief sought relates to such subject-matter; such action must be brought and tried in the county where such subject-matter is situated. State v. District Court of Blue Earth County, 150 Minn. 512, 185 N.W. 953. And where the cause in its nature could only have arisen in one place. Taylor v. Sommers Bros. Match Co., 35 Idaho, 30, 204 P. 472, 474. See *transitory* actions, post, in this note.

LOCAL AFFAIRS. The "local affairs" over which regulation, management and control are delegated to cities are affairs within the jurisdiction of the city by the law of its being. Robia Holding Corporation v. Walker, 239 N.Y.S. 659, 662, 136 Misc. 358.

LOCAL AGENT. An agent at a given place or within a definite district. Sharp & Dohme v. Waybourne, Tex.Civ.App., 74 S.W.2d 413.

An agent may be a general agent as to his powers, although he represents the company only in a particular locality or within a limited territory, and in the latter aspect is called a "local agent", Prudential Ins. Co. of America v. Jenkins, 290 Ky. 802, 162 S.W.2d 791, 795. An agent placed in charge of corporation's local business for purpose of winding it up, National Hardware & Stove Co. v. Walters, Tex.Civ.App., 58 S.W.2d 146, 147; an employee whose duties were to keep books, to write sales letters, to sell merchandise, to audit claims, and, in absence of president, to look after office details of business, State Trust & Savings Bank v. Ferguson Seed Farms, Inc., Tex.Civ.App., 80 S.W.2d 417, 418; one appointed to act as the representative of a corporation and transact its business generally (or business of a particular character) at a given place or within a defined district, Moore v. Freeman's Nat. Bank, 92 N.C. 590, 594; Western Cottage Piano & Organ Co. v. Anderson, 97 Tex. 432, 79 S.W. 517; one who represents corporation in promotion of business for which it was incorporated, in county in which suit is filed, National Hardware & Stove Co. v. Walters, Tex.Civ.App., 58 S.W.2d 146; one who stands in shoes of corporation in relation to particular matters committed to his care and represents corporation in its business in either a general or limited capacity. McDonald Service Co. v. Peoples Nat. Bank of Rock Hill, S.C., 218 N.C. 533, 11 S.E.2d 556, 558, 559. A "local agent" to receive and collect money means an agent residing either permanently or temporarily within the state for purpose of his agency. McDonald Service Co. v. Peoples Nat. Bank of Rock Hill, S.C., 218 N.C. 533, 11 S.E.2d 556, 558.

City manager is the "managing or local agent of city". Grimes v. City of Lexington, 216 N.C. 735, 6 S.E.2d 505, 506.

LOCAL AND SPECIAL LEGISLATION. Applies to special or particular places or special and particular person, and is distinguished from statute general in operation and relating to classes of persons or subjects. Madison County Board of Education v. Smith, 250 Ky. 495, 63 S.W.2d 620.

LOCAL ASSESSMENT. A charge in the nature of tax, levied to pay the whole or part of the cost of local improvements, and assessed upon the various parcels of property specially benefited thereby. Gould v. Baltimore, 59 Md. 380.

LOCAL CHATTEL. A thing is local that is fixed to the freehold. Kitchin, 180.

LOCAL CONCERN. An activity is of "local concern" if it is exercised by the municipality in its proprietary capacity. Luhrs v. City of Phoenix, 52 Ariz. 438, 83 P.2d 283, 285.

LOCAL COURTS. Courts whose jurisdiction is limited to a particular territory or district. The expression often signifies the courts of the state, in opposition to the United States courts. People v. Porter, 90 N.Y. 75.

LOCAL FREIGHT. Freight shipped from either terminus of a railroad to a way station, or *vice versa*, or from one way station to another; that is, over a part of the road only. Mobile & M. R. Co. v. Steiner, 61 Ala. 579.

LOCAL FREIGHT TRAIN. One which stops at any siding or depot and loads or unloads freight as differentiated from one which takes and leaves freight only at certain stops. Arizona Eastern R. Co. v. State, 29 Ariz. 446, 242 P. 870, 871; Oregon, C. & E. Ry. Co. v. Blackmer, 154 Or. 388, 59 P.2d 694, 695.

LOCAL IMPROVEMENT. A public improvement made in a particular locality, by which the real property adjoining or near such locality is specially benefited. Floyd v. Parker Water & Sewer Sub-District, 203 S.C. 276, 17 S.E.2d 223, 227; Bragdon v. City of Muskogee, 133 Okl. 224, 271 P. 1006, 1008.

LOCAL IMPROVEMENT ASSESSMENT. A charge placed upon lands within a given district to pay the benefits which the respective parcels of land derive from the improvement. Wells v. Union Oil Co. of California, 25 Cal.App.2d 165, 76 P.2d 696, 697. An assessment for construction of improvement. University Nat. Co. v. Grays Harbor County, 12 Wash.2d 549, 122 P.2d 501, 502.

LOCAL IMPROVEMENT BONDS. Bonds issued to pay for improvements. State ex rel. Kuehl v. City of Seattle, 195 Wash. 110, 79 P.2d 974, 979.

LOCAL INFLUENCE. As a statutory ground for the removal of a cause from a state court to a federal court, this means influence enjoyed and wielded by the plaintiff, as a resident of the place where the suit is brought, in consequence of his wealth, prominence, political importance, business or social relations, or otherwise, such as might affect the minds of the court or jury and prevent the defendant from winning the case, even though the merits should be with him. See Neale v. Foster, C.C.Or., 31 F. 53.

LOCAL LAW. A law which is special as to place. Leuthold v. Brandjord, 100 Mont. 96, 47 P.2d 41, 45; City of Mt. Olive v. Braje, 366 Ill. 132, 7 N.E. 2d 851, 853.

One applicable exclusively to special or particular places, or special and particular persons, Stevenson v. Hardin, 238 Ky. 600, 38 S.W.2d 462, 463; State v. First State Bank of Jud, 52 N.D. 231, 202 N.W. 391, 399; one applicable only to a particular part of the legislative jurisdiction, Handy v. Johnson, D.C.Tex., 51 F.2d 809, 812; one limited in its operation to certain districts of the territorial jurisdiction of the law-making power or to certain individual persons or corporations, one which pertains to a particular place or to a definite region or portion of space or is restricted to one place. State v. Johnson, 170 N.C. 685, 86 S.E. 788, 792; State v. Daniel, 87 Fla. 270, 99 So. 804, 809; one operating only in a limited territory or specified locality, State v. Dixon, 215 N.C. 161, 1 S.E.2d 521, 522; Douglas v. Foley, 36 N.Y.S.2d 657, 660, 178 Misc. 767; one operating only in a part of domain of state, Tribbett v. Village of Marcellus, 294 Mich. 607, 293 N.W. 872, 877; Punke v. Village of Elliott, 364 Ill. 604, 5 N.E.2d 389, 393; one that affects private persons, private property, and private or local private interests, State ex rel. Porterie v. Smith, 184 La. 263, 166 So. 72, 79, 80, 81; one that in fact, if not in form, is directed only to a specific spot, City of Fort Worth v. Bobbitt, 121 Tex. 14, 36 S.W.2d 470, 472; one that rests on false or deficient classifications, its vice being that it does not embrace all the class to which it is naturally related. State ex rel. Atty. Gen. v. Lee, 193 Ark. 270, 99 S.W.2d 835, 837; School Dist. No. 85 of Kay County v. School Dist. No. 71 of Kay County, 135 Okl. 270, 276 P. 186, 189; one which embraces less than the entire class of persons or places to whose condition such legislation would be necessary or appropriate, State v. Clement, 188 La. 923, 178 So. 493, 496; one which in its subjects relates to but a portion of the people of the state, or to their property, and may not, either in its subject, operation, or immediate and necessary results, affect the people of the state, or their property in general, State v. Clement, 188 La. 923, 178 So. 493, 496; one which relates to particular locality, Iowa Motor Vehicle Ass'n v. Board of Railroad Com'rs, 207 Iowa 461, 221 N.W. 364; one which relates to particular persons or things or to particular persons or things of a class or which operates on or over a portion of a class instead of all of the class, In re Annexation of Reno Quartermaster Depot Military Reservation to Independent School Dist. No. 34, Canadian County, Okl., 180 Okl. 274, 69 P.2d 659, 662; one whose operation is confined within territorial limits, other than those of the whole state or any properly constituted class or locality therein. State v. Kallas, 97 Utah 492, 94 P.2d 414, 420; Ravitz v. Steurele, 257 Ky. 108, 77 S.W.2d 360, 364.

Act is not "local" because it operates in only one place or on particular class of persons or things, provided there is reasonable basis for legislative classification. People v. City of Chicago, 349 Ill. 304, 182 N.E. 419, 430.

Exemption of one or more counties from law makes law "local." Leonard v. Luxora-Little River Road Maintenance Dist. No. 1, 187 Ark. 599, 61 S.W.2d 70.

Municipal ordinances and regulations are "local laws". Orme v. Atlas Gas & Oil Co., 217 Minn. 27, 13 N.W.2d 757, 761.

There must be a reasonable basis for a classification of counties by population, else an act affecting counties within a certain range in population will be declared a "local act". Waybright v. Duval County, 142 Fla. 875, 196 So. 430, 432.

LOCAL OPTION. "Prohibition" in a particular locality. Keeling v. Coker, 294 Ky. 199, 171 S.W.2d 263, 267. Prohibition of the sale and traffic in alcoholic beverages. Neff v. Moberly, 296 Ky. 319, 177 S.W.2d 78.

A privilege accorded by the legislature of a state to the several counties or other districts of the state to determine, each for itself, by popular vote, whether or not licenses should be issued for the sale of intoxicating liquors within such districts. See Wilson v. State, 35 Ark. 416; State v. Brown, 19 Fla. 598.

LOCAL PREJUDICE. The "prejudice or local influence" which will warrant the removal of a cause from a state court to a federal court may be either prejudice and influence existing against the party seeking such removal or existing in favor of his adversary. Neale v. Foster, C.C.Or., 31 F. 53.

LOCAL RULES. Those promulgated in view of local physical conditions in the state, the character of the people, their peculiar customs, usages, and beliefs. Farmers Bank & Trust Co. v. Public Service Co. of Indiana, D.C.Ky., 13 F.Supp. 548, 552.

LOCAL STATUTE. See Local Law.

LOCALITY. Is a definite region in any part of space; geographical position. Warnock v. Kraft, 30 Cal.App.2d 1, 85 P.2d 505, 506. "Place", "vicinity", "neighborhood" and "community". Conley v. Valley Motor Transit Co., C.C.A.Ohio, 139 F.2d 692, 693; Lukens Steel Co. v. Perkins, 107 F.2d 627, 631, 70 App.D.C. 354.

Word "localities" in act prohibiting carrier from giving undue preference to any locality or subjecting it to undue prejudice denotes origin or destination of traffic and shipping, producing, and consuming areas affected by carrier's rates and practices, Texas & P. Ry. Co. v. U. S., Tex., 53 S.Ct. 768, 289 U.S. 627, 77 L.Ed. 1410.

In Scotch law. This name is given to a life-rent created in marriage contracts in favor of the wife, instead of leaving her to her legal life-rent of tierce. 1 Bell, Comm. 55.

LOCALITY OF A LAW SUIT. Place where judicial authority may be exercised. Graver Tank & Manufacturing Corporation v. New England Terminal Co., C.C.A.R.I., 125 F.2d 71, 73; Neirbo Co. v. Bethlehem Shipbuilding Corporation, N. Y., 60 S.Ct. 153, 154, 308 U.S. 165, 84 L.Ed. 167.

LOCARE. To let for hire; to deliver or bail a thing for a certain reward or compensation. Bract. fol. 62.

LOCARIUM. In old European law. The price of letting; money paid for the hire of a thing; rent. Spelman.

LOCATAIRE. In French law. A lessee, tenant, or renter.

LOCATARIUS. Lat. A depositee.

LOCATE. Discovery by survey. Guardian Trust Co. of Houston, Tex., v. Jefferson Lake Oil Co., C.C.A.La., 85 F.2d 465, 467.

Also means to ascertain place in which something belongs, Town of Underhill v. Town of Jericho, 101 Vt. 41, 140 A. 156, 157. To ascertain and fix the position of something, the place of which was before uncertain or not manifest, as to locate the calls in a deed. To decide upon the place or direction to be occupied by something not yet in being, as to locate a road; or to define location or limits, Delaware, L. & W. R. Co. v. Chiara, C.C.A.N.J., 95 F.2d 663, 668; to designate site or place, Union Pac. R. Co. v. City of Los Angeles, 53 Cal.App.2d 825, 128 P.2d 408, 410; Board of Sup'rs of Marshall County v. Stephenson, 160 Miss. 372, 134 So. 142, 144.

LOCATED. A bank is "located" in the place specified in its organization certificate. Raiola v. Los Angeles First Nat. Trust & Savings Bank, 233 N.Y.S. 301, 304, 133 Misc. 630.

Commissioner of Agriculture and Markets or any head of bureau is "located" not only in principal office, but in authorized branch office, Dairy Sealed v. Ten Eyck, 288 N.Y.S. 641, 649, 159 Misc. 716; as used in articles of association of corporation, refers only to place where governing power of corporation is exercised, Carter v. Spring Perch Co., 113 Conn. 636, 155 A. 832, 834; as used in gift tax law provision that no tax shall be imposed upon certain property when located without the state, refers to situs and not to mere physical presence, Van Dyke v. Wisconsin Tax Commission, 235 Wis. 128, 292 N.W. 313, 318; as used in special appearance of corporation, meant the place where defendant had its place of business, Thomas v. Hector Const. Co.,

216 Minn. 207, 12 N.W.2d 769; as used in statute imposing inheritance tax on devises to certain organizations "located" without the state or to such organizations "located" within the state if devise is for use without the state, is used in sense of domicile or residence. San Jacinto Nat. Bank v. Sheppard, Tex.Civ.App., 125 S.W.2d 715, 716, 717.

LOCATIO. Lat. In the civil law. Letting for hire.

The term is also used by text-writers upon the law of bailment at common law. Hanes v. Shapiro & Smith, 168 N.C. 24, 84 S.E. 33, 35. In Scotch law it is translated "location." Bell.

LOCATIO-CONDUCTIO. In the civil law. A compound word used to denote the contract of bailment for hire, expressing the action of *both* parties, viz., a letting by the one and a hiring by the other. 2 Kent, Comm. 586, note; Story, Bailm. § 368; Coggs v. Bernard, 2 Ld. Raym. 913.

LOCATIO CUSTODIÆ. A letting to keep; a bailment or deposit of goods for hire. Story, Bailm. § 442.

According to the classification of bailments at civil law, a "locatio custodiæ" is the hiring of care and services to be bestowed on the thing delivered. Hanes v. Shapiro & Smith, 168 N.C. 24, 84 S.E. 33, 35.

LOCATIO OPERIS. In the civil law. The contract of hiring work, *i. e.*, labor and services.

It is a contract by which one of the parties gives a certain work to be performed by the other, who binds himself to do it for the price agreed between them, which he who gives the work to be done promises to pay to the other for doing it. Poth.Louage, no. 392; Zell v. Dunkle, 27 Atl. 38, 156 Pa. 353.

LOCATIO OPERIS FACIENDI. A letting out of work to be done; a bailment of a thing for the purpose of having some work and labor or care and pains bestowed on it for a pecuniary recompense. 2 Kent, Com. 586, 588; Story, Bailm. §§ 370, 421, 422; Hanes v. Shapiro & Smith, 168 N.C. 24, 84 S.E. 33, 35. Metal Package Corporation of New York v. Osborn, 145 Md. 371, 125 A. 752, 754.

LOCATIO OPERIS MERCIUM VEHENDARUM. A letting of work to be done in the carrying of goods; a contract of bailment by which goods are delivered to a person to carry for hire. 2 Kent, Comm. 597; Story, Bailm. §§ 370, 457; Hanes v. Shapiro & Smith, 168 N.C. 24, 84 S.E. 33, 35.

LOCATIO REI. A letting of a thing to hire. 2 Kent, Comm. 586.

The bailment or letting of a thing to be used by the bailee for a compensation to be paid by him. Story, Bailm. § 370; Hanes v. Shapiro & Smith, 168 N.C. 24, 84 S.E. 33, 35.

LOCATION. Site or place. Board of Sup'rs of Marshall County v. Stephenson, 160 Miss. 372, 134 So. 142, 144.

The "location" of administration of a trust means place of performance of active duties of trustee. In re Risher's Will, 227 Wis. 104, 277 N.W. 160, 164, 115 A.L.R. 790; Campbell v. Albers, 313 Ill.App. 152, 39 N.E.2d 672, 676.

American land law. The designation of the boundaries of a particular piece of land, either upon record or on the land itself. Mosby v. Carland, 1 Bibb, Ky., 84. The finding and marking out the bounds of a particular tract of land, upon the land itself, in conformity to a certain description contained in an entry, grant, map, etc.; such description consisting in what are termed "locative calls." Cunningham v. Browning, 1 Bland, Md., 329.

Corporations. Place where governing power of corporation is exercised. Carter v. Spring Perch Co., 113 Conn. 636, 155 A. 832, 834.

Mining law. Continuous possession of mining claim for five years before adverse rights exist is equivalent to "location." Dalton v. Clark, 129 Cal.App. 136, 18 P.2d 752, 754.

The act of appropriating a "mining claim" (parcel of land containing precious metal in its soil or rock) according to certain established rules. It usually consists in placing on the ground, in a conspicuous position, a notice setting forth the name of the locator, the fact that it is thus taken or located, with the requisite description of the extent and boundaries of the parcel. St. Louis Smelting, etc., Co. v. Kemp, 104 U.S. 649, 26 L.Ed. 875; Producers' Oil Co. v. Hanszen, 132 La. 691, 61 So. 754, 759; Cole v. Ralph, 252 U.S. 286, 40 S.Ct. 321, 326, 64 L.Ed. 567.

In a secondary sense, the mining claim covered by a single act of appropriation or location.

The act or series of acts whereby the boundaries of the claim are marked, etc., but it confers no right in the absence of discovery, both being essential to a valid claim. United States v. Mobley, D.C.Cal., 45 F.Supp. 407, 410.

To constitute a valid "location" of a lode of quartz, "discovery" of a vein or lode of quartz is necessary. Dalton v. Clark, 129 Cal.App. 136, 18 P.2d 752, 754.

Scotch law. A contract by which the temporary use of a subject, or the work or service of a person, is given for an ascertained hire. 1 Bell, Comm. 255.

Street railways. A location, except on private premises, is in the nature of a privilege or permit to use the public ways, Boston Elevated Ry. Co. v. Commonwealth, 310 Mass. 528, 39 N.E.2d 87, 99. A "location" on private lands means a location in the nature of an "easement" or of ownership thereof with permission from public authorities to construct and maintain railway. Boston Elevated Ry. Co. v. Commonwealth, 310 Mass. 528, 39 N.E.2d 87, 99.

LOCATIVE CALLS. In a deed, patent, or other instrument containing a description of land, locative calls are specific calls, descriptions, or marks of location, referring to landmarks, physical objects, or other points by which the land can be exactly located and identified.

In harmonizing conflicting calls in a deed or survey of public lands, courts will ascertain which calls are locative and which are merely directory, and conform the lines to the locative calls; "directory calls" being those which merely direct the neighborhood where the different calls may be found, whereas "locative calls" are those which serve to fix boundaries. Cates v. Reynolds, 143 Tenn. 667, 228 S.W. 695, 696.

LOCATOR.

American land law. One who locates land, or intends or is entitled to locate. See Location.

Civil and Scotch law. A letter; one who lets; he who, being the owner of a thing, lets it out to another for hire or compensation. Coggs v. Bernard, 2 Ld. Raym. 913.

LOCATUM. A hiring. See Bailment.

LOCKED. Iron-safe clause providing that safe be kept securely "locked" required merely that safe door be securely closed so as to preserve fireproof quality of safe, regardless whether combination lock was set. British General Ins. Co., Limited, of London, England v. Boone, Tex.Civ.App., 67 S.W.2d 353.

LOCKMAN. An officer in the Isle of Man, to execute the orders of the governor, much like our under-sheriff. Wharton.

LOCKOUT. A cessation of the furnishing of work to employees in an effort to get for the employer more desirable terms. Jeffery-DeWitt Insulator Co. v. National Labor Relations Board, C.C.A.4, 91 F.2d 134, 137; Sandoval v. Industrial Commission, 110 Colo. 108, 130 P.2d 930, 935; Barnes v. Hall, 285 Ky. 160, 146 S.W.2d 929, 936; The act of locking out; refusal of an employer to furnish work to employees, used as a means of coercion. Agostini v. State, 40 N.Y.S.2d 598, 605.

LOCK-UP HOUSE. A place used temporarily as a prison.

LOCMAN. Fr. In French marine law. A local pilot whose business was to assist the pilot of the vessel in guiding her course into a harbor, or through a river or channel. Martin v. Farnsworth, 33 N.Y.Super.Ct. 260.

LOCO PARENTIS. See In Loco Parentis.

LOCOCESSION. The act of giving place.

LOCOMOTIVE. An engine constructed and used for traction purposes on a railroad track. United States v. Fort Worth & Denver City Ry. Co., D.C. Tex., 21 F.Supp. 916, 917, 918.

Other definitions and examples are gasoline engine or tractor used in yards for switching and frequently hauling long line of cars. Hoffman v. New York, N. H. & H. R. Co., C.C.A.N.Y., 74 F.2d 227, 232; locomotive crane used to convey materials loaded on cars to scene of construction work, United States v. Fort Worth & Denver City Ry. Co., D.C.Tex., 21 F.Supp. 916; motor engines generating and driven by steam power. Libby v. New York, N. H. & H. R. Co., 273 Mass. 522, 174 N.E. 171, 174, 73 A.L.R. 101; quasi public corporations and agencies engaged in serving public in transportation of passengers and goods. Cain v. Bowlby, C.C.A.N.M., 114 F.2d 519, 523; self-propelled engine or vehicle, Smith v. Atchison, T. & S. F. Ry. Co., 145 Kan. 615, 66 P.2d 562, 566; New York Cent. R. Co. v. Public Utilities Commission, 121 Ohio St. 383, 169 N.E. 299, 300.

LOCULUS. In old records. A coffin; a purse.

LOCUM TENENS. Lat. Holding the place. A deputy, substitute, lieutenant, or representative.

LOCUPLES. Lat. In the civil law. Able to respond in an action; good for the amount which the plaintiff might recover. Dig. 50, 16, 234, 1.

LOCUS. Lat. A place; the place where a thing is done.

LOCUS CONTRACTUS. The place of a contract; the place where a contract is made.

That place where last act which makes agreement binding contract is performed. Sun Ins. Office, Limited, of London v. Mallick, 160 Md. 71, 153 A. 35, 39.

LOCUS CONTRACTUS REGIT ACTUM. The place of the contract governs the act. 2 Kent 458; L.R. 1 Q.B. 119; Scudder v. Union Nat. Bank, 91 U.S. 406, 23 L.Ed. 245. See Lex Loci.

LOCUS CRIMINIS. The locality of a crime; the place where a crime was committed.

LOCUS DELICTI. The place of the offense; the place where an offense was committed. 2 Kent, Comm. 109.

State where last event necessary to make actor liable occurs. Hunter v. Derby Foods, C.C.A.N.Y., 110 F.2d 970, 972.

LOCUS IN QUO. The place in which. The place in which the cause of action arose, or where anything is alleged, in pleadings, to have been done. The phrase is most frequently used in actions of trespass *quare clausum fregit.*

LOCUS PARTITUS. In old English law. A place divided.

A division made between two towns or counties to make out in which the land or place in question lies. Fleta, lib. 4, c. 15, § 1; Cowell.

LOCUS PŒNITENTIÆ. A place for repentance; an opportunity for changing one's mind; an opportunity to undo what one has done (Pope v. Safe Deposit & Trust Co., 163 Md. 239, 161 A. 404); a chance to withdraw from a contemplated bargain or contract before it results in a definite contractual liability; a right to withdraw from an incompleted transaction (Alford v. Henderson, 237 Ala. 27, 185 So. 368, 369). Also used of a chance afforded to a person, by the circumstances, of relinquishing the intention which he has formed to commit a crime, before the perpetration thereof.

LOCUS PRO SOLUTIONE REDITUS AUT PECUNIÆ SECUNDUM CONDITIONEM DIMISSIONIS AUT OBLIGATIONIS EST STRICTE OBSERVANDUS. 4 Coke, 73. The place for the payment of rent or money, according to the condition of a lease or bond, is to be strictly observed.

LOCUS PUBLICUS. In the civil law. A public place. Dig. 43, 8, 1; Id. 43, 8, 2, 3.

LOCUS REGIT ACTUM. In private international law. The rule that, when a legal transaction complies with the formalities required by the law of the country where it is done, it is also valid in the country where it is to be given effect, although by the law of that country other formalities are required. 8 Sav. Syst. § 381; Westl. Priv. Int. Law, 159.

LOCUS REI SITÆ. The place where a thing is situated. In proceedings *in rem,* or the real actions of the civil law, the proper forum is the *locus rei sitœ.* The Jerusalem, 2 Gall. 191, 197, Fed.Cas.No.7,293.

LOCUS SIGILLI. The place of the seal; the place occupied by the seal of written instruments. Usually abbreviated to "L. S."

LOCUS STANDI. A place of standing; standing in court. A right of appearance in a court of justice, or before a legislative body, on a given question.

LODE. This term, as used in the legislation of congress, is applicable to any zone or belt of mineralized rock lying within boundaries clearly separating it from the neighboring rock. It includes all deposits of mineral matter found through a mineralized zone or belt coming from the same source, impressed with the same forms, and appearing to have been created by the same processes. Myers v. Lloyd, 4 Alaska, 263, 265; Inyo Marble Co. v. Loundagin, 120 Cal.App. 298, 7 P.2d 1067.

A body of mineral-bearing rock lying within walls of neighboring rock usually of a different kind, although sometimes of the same kind, and extending longitudinally between the walls in a continuous zone or belt. McMullin v. Magnuson, 102 Colo. 230, 78 P.2d 964, 968, 970. A line or aggregation of metal embedded in quartz or other rock in place; the presence of metal in rock, Inyo Marble Co. v. Loundagin, 120 Cal.App. 298, 7 P.2d 1067, 1072.

LODEMAN, or LOADSMAN. The pilot conducts the ship up the river or into port; but the loadsman is he that undertakes to bring a ship through the haven, after being brought thither by the pilot, to the quay or place of discharge. Jacob.

LODEMANAGE. The hire of a pilot for conducting a vessel from one place to another. Cowell.

LODGER. An occupant who has mere use without actual or exclusive possession. Roberts v. Casey, 36 Cal.App.2d, Supp. 767, 93 P.2d 654, 657, 658, 659; Coggins v. Gregorio, C.C.A.N.M., 97 F. 2d 948, 951; Marden v. Radford, 229 Mo.App. 789, 84 S.W.2d 947, 955, 957, 959.

A tenant, with the right of exclusive possession of a part of a house, the landlord, by himself or an agent, retaining general dominion over the house itself, Wansey v. Perkins, 7 Man. & G. 155; Pollock v. Landis, 36 Iowa, 652; one obtaining room in residence hotel by special arrangement with proprietor at fixed rate for permanent stay and having merely use of room, Brams v. Briggs, 272 Mich. 38, 260 N.W. 785; one who has no interest in the realty but who occupies part of a tenement which is under the control of another, Edwards v. City of Los Angeles, 48 Cal.App.2d 62, 119 P.2d 370, 373; one who occupies hired apartment in another's house; a tenant of part of another's house, Smith v. Dorchester Hotel Co., 145 Wash. 344, 259 P. 1085, 1086; Dewar v. Minneapolis Lodge, No. 44, B. P. O. E., 155 Minn. 98, 192 N.W. 358, 359, 32 A.L.R. 1012; one who occupies room or portion of tenement under control or in occupancy of another and has no interest in real estate, Stone v. City of Los Angeles, 114 Cal.App. 192, 299 P. 838, 841.

If proprietor retains to himself any supervision or control of premises of one who has taken room or rooms for hire, or if possession of occupant is anything less than that enjoyed by tenant or if relation between proprietor and occupant possesses features inconsistent with that of landlord and tenant, occupant is a "lodger." Warden v. Radford, 229 Mo.App. 789, 84 S.W.2d 947, 955, 957, 959.

"Lodger" has been defined as a tenant of part of another's house, one who for time being has his home at his lodging place, one who has leave to inhabit another man's house, one who inhabits portion of a house of which another has general possession and custody, one who lives at board or in a hired room or who has a bed in another's house, one who lives in a hired room or rooms in house of another, one who occupies hired apartments in another's house. The term is also defined as a person who lives and sleeps in a place, a person whose occupancy is a part of a house and subordinate to and in some degree under the control of a landlord or his representative. The term is used to indicate a personal relationship of some one lodging somewhere with somebody. Marden v. Radford, 229 Mo.App. 789, 84 S.W.2d 947, 955, 957, 959.

LODGING HOUSE. A house where lodgings are let; houses containing furnished apartments which are let out by the week or by the month, without meals, or with breakfast simply. Marden v. Radford, 229 Mo.App. 789, 84 S.W.2d 947, 955.

LODGING PLACE. A place of rest for a night or a residence for a time; a temporary habitation. Marden v. Radford, 229 Mo.App. 789, 84 S.W.2d 947, 955.

LODGINGS. Habitation in another's house; apartments in another's house, furnished or unfurnished, occupied for habitation; the occupier being termed a "lodger."

LODS ET VENTES. In old French and Canadian law. A fine payable by a *roturier* on every change of ownership of his land; a mutation or alienation fine. Steph. Lect. 351.

LOGATING. An unlawful game mentioned in St. 33 Hen. VIII. c. 9.

LOG ROLLING. A mischievous legislative practice, of embracing in one bill several distinct matters, none of which, perhaps, could singly obtain the assent of the legislature, and then procuring its passage by a combination of the minorities in favor of each of the measures into a majority that will adopt them all. Walker v. Griffith, 60 Ala. 369; Com. v. Barnet, 199 Pa. 161, 48 A. 976, 55 L.R.A. 882; O'Leary v. Cook County, 28 Ill. 534; St. Louis v. Tiefel, 42 Mo. 590.

Practice of including in one statute or constitutional amendment more than one proposition, inducing voters to vote for all, notwithstanding they might not have voted for all if amendments or statutes had been submitted separately. Kerby v. Luhrs, 44 Ariz. 208, 36 P.2d 549, 552, 94 A.L.R. 1502.

LOGBOOK. A ship's journal.

It contains a minute account of the ship's course, with a short history of every occurrence during the voyage. 1 Marsh.Ins. 312.

The part of the logbook relating to transactions in the harbor is termed the "harbor log;" that relating to what happens at sea, the "sea log." Young, Naut.Dict.

Official Logbook. A logbook in a certain form, and containing certain specified entries required by 17 & 18 Vict. c. 104, §§ 280–282, to be kept by all British merchant ships, except those exclusively engaged in the coasting trade.

LOGGING. Includes felling and preparation of logs for transport, log assemblage, and main log haul; it includes also production of large quantities of pulpwood, cross ties, poles, piling, mine timbers, veneer logs, bolts and miscellaneous other forms. Cherry River Boom & Lumber Co. v. United States, D.C.W.Va., 37 F.Supp. 887, 888, 889.

Cutting and hauling or dealing in or with logs, Brasher v. Industrial Lumber Co., La.App., 165 So. 524, 526; felling trees, cutting them into logs, and transporting them to mill or market, Middlebusher v. State Industrial Accident Commission, 147 Or. 459, 34 P.2d 325, 327.

Felling trees of merchantable size for lumber, cutting them into suitable lengths and hauling them to some point for manufacture or transportation; felling trees for subsequent use as stovewood. Peterson v. State Industrial Accident Commission, 140 Or. 326, 12 P.2d 564, 565.

LOGIA. A small house, lodge, or cottage. Mon. Angl. tom. 1, p. 400.

LOGIC. The science of reasoning, or of the operations of the understanding which are subservient to the estimation of evidence. The term includes both the process itself of proceeding from known truths to unknown, and all other intellectual operations, in so far as auxiliary to this.

LOGICAL RELEVANCY. Existence of such a relationship in logic between the fact of which evidence is offered and a fact in issue that the existence of the former renders probable or improbable the existence of the latter. State v. Knox, 236 Iowa 499, 18 N.W.2d 716, 723.

LOGIUM. In old records. A lodge, hovel, or outhouse.

LOGOGRAPHUS. In Roman law. A public clerk, register, or book-keeper; one who wrote or kept books of accounts. Dig. 50, 4, 18, 10; Cod. 10, 69.

LOGS. Stems or trunks of trees cut into convenient lengths for the purpose of being afterwards manufactured into lumber of various kinds; not including manufactured lumber of any sort, nor timber which is squared or otherwise shaped for use without further change in form. Kolloch v. Parcher, 52 Wis. 393, 9 N.W. 67. And see Haynes v. Hayward, 40 Me. 148; State v. Addington, 121 N.C. 538, 27 S.E. 988; Brasher v. Industrial Lumber Co., La.App., 165 So. 524, 526.

As used in subcontract for clearing and grubbing highway right of way, meant merchantable logs, that is, logs not less than nine inches by thirty-two feet. McBride v. Callahan, 173 Wash. 609, 24 P.2d 105.

LOITER. To be dilatory; to be slow in movement; to stand around or move slowly about; to stand idly around; to spend time idly; to saunter; to delay; to idle; to linger; to lag behind. City of Columbus v. Aldrich, 69 Ohio App. 396, 42 N.E.2d 915, 917; State v. Jasmin, 105 Vt. 631, 168 A. 545, 546, Phillips v. Municipal Court of Los Angeles, 24 Cal.App.2d 453, 75 P.2d 548, 549; City of Olathe v. Lauck, 156 Kan. 637, 135 P.2d 549, 551; State v. Starr, 57 Ariz. 270, 113 P.2d 356, 357.

LOLLARDS. A body of primitive Wesleyans, who assumed importance about the time of John Wycliffe, (1360,) and were very successful in disseminating evangelical truth; but, being implicated (apparently against their will) in the insurrection of the villeins in 1381, the statute *De Hœretico Comburendo* (2 Hen. IV. c. 15) was passed against them, for their suppression. However, they were not suppressed, and their representatives survive to the present day under various names and disguises. Brown.

LOMBARDIAN LAW. See Lex Longobardorum.

LOMBARDS. A name given to the merchants of Italy, numbers of whom, during the twelfth and thirteenth centuries, were established as merchants and bankers in the principal cities of Europe.

LONDON LLOYDS. Voluntary association of merchants, shipowners, underwriters, and brokers, which writes no policies, but, when broker for one wishing insurance posts particulars of risk, underwriting members wishing to so subscribe name and share of total that each wishes to take, and policy is issued when total is reached containing names of underwriters bound thereby and name of attorney in fact who handles insurance affairs of the group. Ell Dee Clothing Co. v. Marsh, 247 N. Y. 392, 160 N.E. 651, 653.

LONDRES. L. Fr. London. Yearb. P. 1 Edw. II. p. 4.

LONG. In various compound legal terms (see *infra*) this word carries a meaning not essentially different from its signification in the vernacular.

In the language of the stock exchange, a broker or speculator is said to be "long" on stock, or as to a particular security, when he has in his possession or control an abundant supply of it, or a supply exceeding the amount which he has contracted to deliver, or, more particularly, when he has bought a supply of such stock or other security for future delivery, speculating on a considerable future advance in the market price. See Kent v. Miltenberger, 13 Mo.App. 506; Corner. A trader is said to be "long" on the market when he takes the full price risk, gains if the market price goes up, and loses if it goes down. Valley Waste Mills v. Page, C.C.A.Ga., 115 F.2d 466, 467.

As applied to an antenna, means a wire which is long in relation to the wave length used. Mackay Radio & Telegraph Co. v. Radio Corporation of America, N.Y., 306 U.S. 86, 618, 59 S.Ct. 427, 430, 83 L.Ed. 506.

LONG ACCOUNT. An account involving numerous separate items or charges, on one side or both, or the statement of various complex transactions, such as a court of equity will refer to a master or commissioner or a court of law to a referee under the codes of procedure. Druse v. Horter, 57 Wis. 644, 16 N.W. 14. Reed v. Young, 248 Mo. 606, 154 S.W. 766, 768, Fry v. Pomona Mills Inc., 206 N.C. 768, 175 S.E. 156.

For "Examination of a long account," see Examination.

LONG PARLIAMENT. The name usually given to the parliament which met in November, 1640, under Charles I., and was dissolved by Cromwell on the 10th of April, 1653.

The name "Long Parliament" is, however, also given to the parliament which met in 1661, after the restoration of the monarchy, and was dissolved on the 30th of December, 1678. This latter parliament is sometimes called, by way of distinction, the "long parliament of Charles II." Mozley & Whiteley.

LONG QUINTO, THE. An expression used to denote part second of the year-book which gives reports of cases in 5 Edw. IV.

LONG ROBE. A metaphorical expression designating the practice of profession of the law; as, in the phrase "gentlemen of the long robe."

LONG TON. A measure of weight equivalent to 20 hundred-weight of 112 pounds each, or 2,240 pounds, as distinguished from the "short" ton of 2,000 pounds. See Rev.St.U.S. § 2951 (19 U.S.C.A. § 420). But see Jones v. Giles, 10 Exch. 119, as to an English custom of reckoning a ton of iron "long weight" as 2,400 pounds.

LONG VACATION. The recess of the English courts from August 10th to October 24th.

LONGA PATIENTIA TRAHITUR AD CONSENSUM. Long sufferance is construed as consent. Fleta, lib. 4, c. 26, § 4.

LONGA POSSESSIO EST PACIS JUS. Long possession is the law of peace. Branch, Princ.; Co. Litt. 6.

LONGA POSSESSIO JUS PARIT. Long possession begets right. Fleta, lib. 3, c. 15, § 6.

LONGA POSSESSIO PARIT JUS POSSIDENDI, ET TOLLIT ACTIONEM VERO DOMINO. Long possession produces the right of possession, and takes away from the true owner his action. Co. Litt. 110*b*.

LONGEVITY PAY. Extra compensation for longevity in actual service in the army or navy. Thornley v. U. S., 18 Ct.Cl. 111; Barton v. U. S., 9 Sup.Ct. 285, 129 U.S. 249, 32 L.Ed. 663; U. S. v. Alger, 14 Sup.Ct. 346, 151 U.S. 362, 38 L.Ed. 192; U. S. v. Stahl, 14 Sup.Ct. 347, 151 U.S. 366, 38 L.Ed. 194.

LONGSHOREMAN. A laborer, such as a stevedore or loader, who works about wharves of a seaport. Duke v. Helena-Glendale Ferry Co., 203 Ark. 865, 159 S.W.2d 74, 77, 139 A.L.R. 1404.

LONGUM TEMPUS ET LONGUS USUS QUI EXCEDIT MEMORIA HOMINUM SUFFICIT PRO JURE. Co. Litt. 115*a*. Long time and long use, exceeding the memory of men, suffices for right.

LOOK AND LISTEN. The requirement that a man shall "look and listen" before crossing street railroad track means only that he shall observe and estimate with reasonable accuracy his distance from the car and the speed of its oncoming, and then make calculation and comparison of the time it will take the car to come and the time it will take to cross the track. Kansas City Public Service Co. v. Knight, C.C.A.Kan., 116 F.2d 233, 234.

LOOKOUT. A person who is specially charged with the duty of observing the lights, sounds, echoes, or any obstruction to navigation, with the thoroughness which the circumstances admit. The Tillicum (D.C.) 217 F. 976, 978; The Wilbert L. Smith (D.C.) 217 F. 981, 984.

A proper lookout on a vessel is some one in a favorable position to see, stationed near enough to the helmsman to communicate with him, and to receive communications from him, and exclusively employed in watching the movements of vessels which they are meeting or about to pass. The Genesee Chief v. Fitzhugh, 12 How. 462, 13 L.Ed. 1058. Proper "lookouts" are competent persons other than the master and helmsman, properly stationed to look out, on the forward part of the vessel. The Catalina, C.C.A.Cal., 95 F.2d 283, 285.

LOPWOOD. A right in the inhabitants of a parish within a manor, in England, to lop for fuel, at certain periods of the year, the branches of trees growing upon the waste lands of the manor. Sweet.

LOQUELA. Lat. A colloquy; talk.

In old English law, this term denoted the oral altercations of the parties to a suit, which led to the issue, now called the "pleadings." It also designated an "imparlance," *(q. v.,)* both names evidently referring to the talking together of the parties. *Loquela sine die,* a postponement to an indefinite time.

LOQUENDUM UT VULGUS; SENTIENDUM UT DOCTI. We must speak as the common people; we must think as the learned. 7 Coke, 11*b*.

This maxim expresses the rule that, when words are used in a technical sense, they must be understood technically; otherwise, when they may be supposed to be used in their ordinary acceptation.

LORD. A feudal superior or proprietor; one of whom a fee or estate is held.

A title of honor or nobility belonging properly to the degree of baron, but applied also to the whole peerage, as in the expression "the house of lords." 1 Bl. Comm. 396–400.

A title of office, as lord mayor, lord commissioner, etc.

Law lords

See Law.

Lord advocate

The chief public prosecutor of Scotland. 2 Alis.Crim. Pr. 84.

Lord and vassal

In the feudal system, the grantor, who retained the dominion or ultimate property, was called the "lord," and the grantee, who had only the use or possession, was called the "vassal" or "feudatory."

Lord chief baron

The chief judge of the English court of exchequer, prior to the judicature acts.

Lord chief justice

See Justice.

Lord high chancellor

See Chancellor.

Lord high steward

In England, when a person is impeached, or when a peer is tried on indictment for treason or felony before the house of lords, one of the lords is appointed lord high steward, and acts as speaker *pro tempore.* Sweet.

Lord high treasurer

An officer formerly existing in England, who had the charge of the royal revenues and customs duties, and of leasing the crown lands. His functions are now vested in the lords commissioners of the treasury. Mozley & Whitley.

Lord in gross

In feudal law. He who is lord, not by reason of any manor, but as the king in respect of his crown, etc. "Very lord" is he who is immediate lord to his tenant; and "very tenant," he who holds immediately of that lord. So that, where there is lord paramount, lord mesne, and tenant, the lord paramount is not very lord to the tenant. Wharton.

Lord justice clerk

The second judicial officer in Scotland.

Lord keeper

Originally another name for the lord chancellor. After Henry II.'s reign they were sometimes divided, but now there cannot be a lord chancellor and lord keeper at the same time, for by St. 5 Eliz. c. 18, they are declared to be the same office. Com.Dig. "Chancery," B. 1.

Lord lieutenant

In English law. The viceroy of the crown in Ireland. The principal military officer of a county, originally appointed for the purpose of mustering the inhabitants for the defense of the country.

Lord mayor

The chief officer of the corporation of the city of London is so called. The origin of the appelation of "lord," which the mayor of London enjoys, is attributed to the fourth charter of Edward III., which conferred on that officer the honor of having maces, the same as royal, carried before him by the sergeants. Pull.Laws & Cust.Lond.

Lord mayor's court

In English law. This is a court of record, of law and equity, and is the chief court of justice within the corporation of London. Theoretically the lord mayor and aldermen are supposed to preside, but the recorder is in fact the acting judge. It has jurisdiction of all personal and mixed actions arising within the city and liberties without regard to the amount in controversy. See 3 Steph.Comm. 449, note *l*.

Lord of a manor

The grantee or owner of a manor.

Lord ordinary

The judge of the court of session in Scotland, who officiates for the time being as the judge of first instance. Darl.Pr.Ct.Sess.

Lord paramount

A term applied to the King of England as the chief feudal proprietor, the theory of the feudal system being that all lands in the realm were held mediately or immediately from him. See De Peyster v. Michael, 6 N.Y. 495, 57 Am.Dec. 470; Opinion of Justices, 66 N.H. 629, 33 A. 1076.

Lord privy seal

Before the 30 Hen. VIII., was generally an ecclesiastic. The office has since been usually conferred on temporal peers above the degree of barons. He is appointed by letters patent. The lord privy seal, receiving a warrant from the signet office, issues the privy seal, which is an authority to the lord chancellor to pass the great seal where the nature of the grant requires it. But the privy seals for money begin in the treasury, whence the first warrant issues, countersigned by the lord treasurer. The lord privy seal is a member of the cabinet council. Enc.Lond.

Lord warden of Cinque Ports

See Cinque Ports.

Lords appellants

Five peers who for a time superseded Richard II. in his government, and whom, after a brief control of the government, he in turn superseded in 1397, and put the survivors of them to death. Richard II.'s eighteen commissioners (twelve peers and six commoners) took their place, as an embryo privy council acting with full powers, during the parliamentary recess. Brown.

Lords commissioners

In English law. When a high public office in the state, formerly executed by an individual, is put into commission, the persons charged with the commission are called "lords commissioners," or sometimes "lords" or "commissioners" simply. Thus, we have, in lieu of the lord treasurer and lord high admiral of former times, the lords commissioners of the treasury, and the lords commissioners of the admiralty; and, whenever the great seal is put into commission, the persons charged with it are called "commissioners" or "lords commissioners" of the great seal. Mozley & Whiteley.

Lord's day

A name sometimes given to Sunday. Co.Litt. 135.

Lords justices of appeal

In English law. The title of the ordinary judges of the court of appeal, by Jud.Act 1877, § 4. Prior to the judicature acts, there were two "lords justices of appeal in chancery," to whom an appeal lay from a vice-chancellor, by 14 & 15 Vict. c. 83.

Lords marchers

Those noblemen who lived on the marches of Wales or Scotland, who in times past had their laws and power of life and death, like petty kings. Abolished by 27 Hen. VIII. c. 26, and 6 Edw. VI. c. 10. Wharton.

Lords of appeal

Those members of the house of lords of whom at least three must be present for the hearing and determination of appeals. They are the lord chancellor, the lords of appeal in ordinary, and such peers of parliament as hold, or have held, high judicial offices, such as ex-chancellors and judges of the superior courts in Great Britain and Ireland. App.Jur. Act 1876, §§ 5, 25.

Lords of appeal in ordinary

These are appointed, with a salary of £6,000 a year, to aid the house of lords in the hearing of appeals. They rank as barons for life, but sit and vote in the house of lords during the tenure of their office only. App.Jur. Act 1876, § 6.

Lords of erection

On the Reformation in Scotland, the king, as proprietor of benefices formerly held by abbots and priors, gave them out in temporal lordships to favorites, who were termed "lords of erection." Wharton.

Lords of parliament

Those who have seats in the house of lords. During bankruptcy, peers are disqualified from sitting or voting in the house of lords. 34 & 35 Vict. c. 50.

Lords of regality

In Scotch law. Persons to whom rights of civil and criminal jurisdiction were given by the crown.

Lords ordainers

Lords appointed in 1312, in the reign of Edward II., for the control of the sovereign and the court party, and for the general reform and better government of the country. Brown.

Lords spiritual

The archbishops and bishops who have seats in the house of lords.

Lords temporal

Those lay peers who have seats in the house of lords.

LORD CAMPBELL ACT. An act which fixes the maximum amount recoverable for wrongful death.

LORDSHIP. In English law. Dominion, manor, seigniory, domain; also a title of honor used to a nobleman not being a duke.

It is also the customary titulary appellation of the judges, and some other persons in authority and office.

LOSE. To bring to destruction; to ruin; to destroy; to suffer the loss of; to be deprived of; to part with, especially in an accidental or unforeseen manner; as to lose an eye. Logan v. Johnson, 218 N.C. 200, 10 S.E.2d 653, 655.

LOSE HIS LIFE. Die. Hershey v. Agnew, 83 Colo. 89, 262 P. 526, 528.

LOSS is a generic and relative term; it is not a word of limited, hard and fast meaning. Boney v. Central Mut. Ins. Co. of Chicago, 213 N.C. 470, 196 S.E. 837, 841; United Service Automobile Ass'n v. Miles, 139 Tex. 138, 161 S.W.2d 1048, 1050.

It may mean act of losing, or the thing lost, Fidelity Union Casualty Co. v. Wilkinson, Tex.Civ.App., 94 S.W. 2d 763, 766; United States v. City Nat. Bank of Duluth, D.C.Minn., 31 F.Supp. 530, 534, 535; actual losses, Cheney v. National Surety Corporation, 10 N.Y.S.2d 706, 256 App. Div. 1041; N. L. R. B. v. Cowell Portland Cement Co., C. C.A.9, 148 F.2d 237, 246; bad and uncollectible accounts, Duke v. Cregan, 91 Colo. 120, 12 P.2d 354, 355; bereaved, Lytle v. Southern Ry.-Carolina Division, 171 S.C. 221, 171 S.E. 42, 44, 90 A.L.R. 915; damage, Glinz v. State, 70 N.D. 776, 298 N.W. 238, 239; Wilbur v. U. S. ex rel. C. L. Wold Co., 30 F.2d 871, 872, 58 App.D.C. 347; a decrease in value of resources or increase in liabilities, Boney v. Central Mut. Ins. Co. of Chicago, 213 N.C. 470, 196 S.E. 837, 841; depletion or depreciation or destruction of value, Malley v. American Indemnity Corporation, 297 Pa. 216, 146 A. 571,

572; deprivation, Lytle v. Southern Ry.-Carolina Division, 171 S.C. 221, 171 S.E. 42, 44, 90 A.L.R. 915; Smith v. Federal Surety Co., 60 S.D. 100, 243 N.W. 664, 666; destruction, Malley v. American Indemnity Corporation, 297 Pa. 216, 146 A. 571, 572; Wells v. Thomas W. Garland, Inc., Mo.App., 39 S.W.2d 409, 411; detriment, Fidelity Union Casualty Co. v. Wilkinson, Tex.Civ.App., 94 S.W.2d 763, 766; United States v. City Nat. Bank of Duluth, D.C. Minn., 31 F.Supp. 530, 534, 535; failure to keep that which one has or thinks he has, First Nat. Bank & Trust Co. of Port Chester v. New York Title Ins. Co., 12 N.Y.S.2d 703, 711, 171 Misc. 854; In re Gordon, 317 Pa. 161, 176 A. 494, 498; injury, United Service Automobile Ass'n v. Miles, 139 Tex. 138, 161 S.W.2d 1048; United States v. City Nat. Bank of Duluth, D.C.Minn., 31 F.Supp. 530, 534, 535; privation, United States v. City Nat. Bank of Duluth, D. C.Minn., 31 F.Supp. 530, 534, 535; ruin, Logan v. Johnson, 218 N.C. 200, 10 S.E.2d 653, 655; shrinkage in value of estate or property, Malley v. American Indemnity Corporation, 297 Pa. 216, 146 A. 571, 572; Boney v. Central Mut. Ins. Co. of Chicago, 213 N.C. 470, 196 S.E. 837, 841; state or fact of being lost or destroyed, Logan v. Johnson, 218 N.C. 200, 10 S.E.2d 653, 655; that which is gone and cannot be recovered or that which is withheld or that of which a party is dispossessed, Walker v. Thomas, 75 F.2d 667, 669, 64 App.D.C. 148; Smith v. Federal Surety Co., 60 S.D. 100, 243 N.W. 664, 666; unintentional parting with something of value, Providence Journal Co. v. Broderick, C.C.A.R.I., 104 F.2d 614, 616.

Loss provided against by bank deposit guarantee was total and permanent loss of deposit. Wood v. Utter, 229 Mo.App. 309, 77 S.W.2d 832, 838.

Statute for payment of claims for "loss" on account of fire from operation of railroads by United States was intended for relief of all who suffered "loss" of whatsoever nature, United States v. City Nat. Bank of Duluth, D.C. Minn., 31 F.Supp. 530, 534, 535.

Compensation acts and compensation insurance

Amputation of foot held compensable as "loss of foot," Marshall v. Octavia J. Coal Mining Co., 252 Ky. 460, 67 S. W.2d 697; claimant's eye or foot or the use of it is not lost unless it is useless in any employment for which claimant is fitted. Zellner v. Haddock Mining Co., 139 Pa. Super. 16, 10 A.2d 918, 919; Novak v. State Workmen's Ins. Fund, 113 Pa.Super. 555, 173 A. 827; Injury rendering testicles useless for performance of normal functions is compensable as "loss" thereof. Northwestern Barb Wire Co. v. Industrial Commission, 353 Ill. 371, 187 N.E. 468, 469.

"Loss of an eye" and "total loss of vision of an eye" indicate state or fact of loss of eye or total destruction of vision as distinguished from partial loss of vision. Logan v. Johnson, 218 N.C. 200, 10 S.E.2d 653, 655.

Loss of eye means destruction of sight to extent that no vision useful in industry remains, Henderson v. Consumers Power Co., 301 Mich. 564, 4 N.W.2d 10, 17; loss of physical organ, State ex rel. Gilmore v. Industrial Commission of Ohio, 127 Ohio St. 214, 187 N.E. 770, 771; loss of sight or vision of eye, Powers v. Motor Wheel Corporation, 252 Mich. 639, 234 N.W. 122, 124, 73 A.L.R. 702; loss of use of eye for work which claimant was accustomed to perform, Baugh v. Glassell-Rogers Drilling Co., La.App., 190 So. 130, 132; loss of vision which is subnormal due to prior injury or natural defects, Hamilton v. P. E. Johnson & Sons, 224 Iowa 1097, 276 N.W. 841, 845; removal of a partially or totally sightless eye as result of accident, McCadden v. West End Building & Loan Ass'n, 18 N.J.Misc. 395, 13 A.2d 665, 666.

Loss of more than one phalange of a thumb requires merely loss of more of thumb than one phalange, Ciotti v. Jarecki Mfg. Co., 128 Pa.Super. 233, 193 A. 323, 324.

Loss of use of arm means substantial and material impairment of its use in practicable performance of its functions, Traders & General Ins. Co. v. Porter, Tex.Civ.App., 124 S.W.2d 900, 903; loss was "sustained" within policy agreeing to indemnify employer against "loss from liability," where judgment was rendered against employer for medical services, E. M. Cummings & Co. v. American Mut. Liability Ins. Co., 262 N.Y.S. 611, 146 Misc. 621; Substantial loss of phalange is essential for loss of first phalange of thumb or any finger, Decicco v. John Morrell & Co., 152 Kan. 601, 106 P.2d 1053, 1056.

Earnings

"Loss of earnings" is synonymous with loss of profits. Beyer v. Coca-Cola Bottling Co. of St. Louis, Mo.App., 75 S.W.2d 642, 648.

Fidelity Bond

Deprivation or dispossession of money or property due to dishonest, criminal, or fraudulent acts of officers, Smith v. Federal Surety Co., 60 S.D. 100, 243 N.W. 664, 666; pecuniary damage for which insurer may be liable, though extent may not be immediately ascertainable, Fletcher Savings & Trust Co. v. American Surety Co. of New York, 92 Ind.App. 651, 175 N.E. 247, 252; wrongful abstraction, willful misapplication, or fraudulent or dishonest acts. Pacific Coast Adjustment Bureau v. Indemnity Ins. Co. of North America, 115 Cal.App. 583, 2 P.2d 218, 219.

Indemnity bond or contract

Condition in which insured would be subjected to claim or demand, and not to adjudge liability, National City Bank v. National Sec. Co., C.C.A.Tenn., 58 F.2d 7, 8; deprivation or dispossession of money or property of bank due to dishonored criminal or fraudulent acts of officers, Fitchburg Sav. Bank v. Massachusetts Bonding & Insurance Co., 274 Mass. 135, 174 N.E. 324, 328, 74 A.L.R. 274; payment of legal liability caused by dishonest act of an employee was a "loss of money". Hooker v. New Amsterdam Casualty Co., D.C.Ky., 33 F.Supp. 672, 673.

Insurance

Ascertained liability of insurer, Michel v. American Fire & Casualty Co., C.C.A. Fla., 82 F.2d 583, 586; decrease in value of resources or increase in liabilities, Goerss v. Indemnity Co. of America, 223 Mo.App. 316, 3 S.W.2d 272, 275; depletion or depreciation or destruction or shrinkage of value, Malley v. American Indemnity Corporation, 297 Pa. 216, 146 A. 571, 572; injury, damage, etc., to property or persons injured; Miles v. United Services Automobile Ass'n, Tex.Civ.App., 149 S.W.2d 233, 235, 236; injury or damage sustained by insured in consequence of happening of one or more of the accidents or misfortunes against which insurer has undertaken to indemnify the insured, 1 Bouv.Inst. no. 1215; pecuniary injury resulting from the occurrence of the contingency insured against, Ocean Accident & Guarantee Corporation v. Southwestern Bell Telephone Co., C.C.A.Mo., 100 F.2d 441, 446; word "loss" implies that property is no longer in existence. Littrell v. Allemannia Fire Ins. Co. of Pittsburgh, Pa., 226 N.Y.S. 243, 244, 222 App.Div. 302.

Liability assumed and paid by insured under policy provision authorizing insured to provide injured person "imperative medical relief" held "loss". Employers' Liability Assur. Corporation v. Manget Bros. Co., 45 Ga.App. 721, 165 S.E. 770, 773.

"Loss by fire" includes loss directly resulting from ignition or burning or from bona fide efforts, Fogarty v. Fidelity & Casualty Co., 122 Conn. 245, 188 A. 481, 483; loss necessarily following from occurrence of fire to amount of actual injury to subject of risk, Freed's, Inc., v. American Home Fire Assur. Co., 305 Mich. 89, 8 N.W.2d 923, 925. It means a "hostile fire". Pacific Fire Ins. Co. v. C. C. Anderson Co. of Nampa, D.C. Idaho, 47 F.Supp. 90, 91.

Loss by severance means loss of use due to substantial severance, King v. Metropolitan Life Ins. Co., 20 Tenn.App. 246, 97 S.W.2d 651, 654; Loss from liability is loss which arises when liability becomes fixed, Cormier v. Hudson, 284 Mass. 231, 187 N.E. 625, 627; Boney v. Central Mut. Ins. Co. of Chicago, 213 N.C. 470, 196 S.E. 837, 842.

"Loss of eye" means loss of use for any practical purpose, Order of United Commercial Travelers of America v. Knorr, C.C.A.Kan., 112 F.2d 679, 682; loss of member or loss of an entire member means destruction of usefulness of member or entire member for purposes to which in its normal condition it is susceptible of application, in absence of more specific definition, Molnor v. Commercial Casualty Ins. Co., 114 W.Va. 402, 171 S.E. 894, 896; Bowling v. Life Ins. Co. of Virginia, 39 Ohio App. 491, 177 N.E. 531, 532; loss of use of hand means substantial and material impairment of use in practical performance of its function, E. K. Local Ins. Co. No. 1 of Seymour v. Lilly, Tex.Civ.App., 1 S.W.2d 490, 492; loss of use of member is equivalent to loss of member, Continental Casualty Co. v. Linn, 10 S.W.2d 1079, 1082, 226 Ky. 328; Noel v. Continental Casualty Co., 138 Kan. 136, 23 P.2d 610; loss of vision to extent that one cannot perceive and distinguish objects is "loss of sight", Locomotive Engineers' Mut. Life & Accident Ins. Co. v. Meeks, 157 Miss. 97, 127 So. 699, 701; loss under indemnity policy limiting liability to amount paid by carrier in respect of stolen merchandise could not occur until carrier paid shipper for merchandise. Savin Exp. Co. v. Hanover Fire Ins. Co., 132 Conn. 181, 43 A.2d 69, 70; provision limiting liability for loss of foot to "loss by severance" refers to manner rather than to extent of injury. Brittain v. Prudential Ins. Co. of America, 29 Ala.App. 57, 191 So. 794, 799.

To constitute "loss or damage by fire" existence of actual fire, which becomes uncontrollable or breaks out from where it was intended to be and becomes a hostile element, is sufficient. Princess Garment Co. v. Fireman's Fund Ins. Co. of San Francisco, Cal., C.C.A.Ohio, 115 F.2d 380, 382; Coryell v. Old Colony Ins. Co., 118 Neb. 303, 229 N.W. 326, 328, 68 A.L.R. 222.

Revenue Acts

Difference between cost of assets and the sale price, Weil v. State, 237 Ala. 293, 186 So. 467, 469; failure to keep that which one has, A. Giurlani & Bro. v. Commissioner of Internal Revenue, C.C.A.9, 119 F.2d 852, 857, 858; loss means actual loss, Brandon v. State Revenue Commission, 54 Ga. App. 62, 186 S.E. 872, 874.

Losses deductible are those occasioned by casualties, Buffalo Union Furnace Co. v. Helvering, C.C.A.2, 72 F.2d 399, 402; physical losses by fire, flood or other like causes which are not covered by insurance. W. F. Young, Inc. v. Commissioner of Internal Revenue, C.C.A.1, 120 F.2d 159, 166; First Nat. Bank of Sharon v. Heiner, D.C.Pa., 2 F. Supp. 960, 961; Brown v. United States, D.C.Pa., 19 F. Supp. 825, 827; unintentional parting with something of value. A. Giurlani & Bro. v. Commissioner of Internal Revenue, C.C.A.9, 119 F.2d 852, 857, 858; McDonald v. Commissioner of Internal Revenue, C.C.A.3, 139 F.2d 400, 401, 402.

Time

"Loss of time" as used in connection with damages recoverable for personal injuries means "loss of earnings." Sinclair Refining Co. v. Tompkins, C.C.A.Miss., 117 F.2d 596, 598.

As to "Actual Loss," "Constructive Loss," "Direct Loss," "Partial Loss," and "Total Loss," see those titles. As to "Loss of Consortium," see Consortium. As to "Salvage Loss," see Salvage.

LOST. An article is "lost" when the owner has lost the possession or custody of it, involuntarily and by any means, but more particularly by accident or his own negligence or forgetfulness, and when he is ignorant of its whereabouts or cannot recover it by a ordinarily diligent search. See In re O'Neil, 39 N.Y.S.2d 82, 179 Misc. 455; Belote v. State, 36 Miss. 120, 72 Am.Dec. 163; Hoagland v. Amusement Co., 170 Mo. 335, 70 S.W. 878, 94 Am.St.Rep. 740.

Involuntary change of location or inability to find, State v. Brewster, 72 N.D. 409, 7 N.W.2d 742, 744. See, also, Lost Property.

As applied to ships and vessels, the term means "lost at sea," and a vessel lost is one that has totally gone from the owners against their will, so that they know nothing of it, whether it still exists or not, or one which they know is no longer within their use and control, either in consequence of capture by enemies or pirates, or an unknown foundering, or sinking by a known storm, or collision, or destruction by shipwreck. Bennett v. Garlock, *10 Hun (N.Y.) 338; Collard v. Eddy, 17 Mo. 355; Insurance Co. v. Gossler, 7 Fed.Cas. 406.

LOST CORNER. See Corner.

LOST OR NOT LOST. A phrase sometimes inserted in policies of marine insurance.

It signifies that the contract is meant to relate back to the beginning of a voyage now in progress, or to some other antecedent time, and to be valid and effectual even if, at the moment of executing the policy, the vessel should have already perished by some of the perils insured against, provided that neither party has knowledge of that fact or any advantage over the other in the way of superior means of information. See Hooper v. Robinson, 98 U.S. 537, 25 L.Ed. 219; Insurance Co. v. Folsom, 18 Wall. 251, 21 L.Ed. 827.

LOST PAPERS. Papers which have been so mislaid that they cannot be found after diligent search.

LOST PROPERTY. Property which the owner has involuntarily parted with and does not know where to find or recover it, not including property which he has intentionally concealed or deposited in a secret place for safe-keeping. See Pritchett v. State, 2 Sneed (Tenn.) 288, 62 Am.Dec. 468; State v. Cummings, 33 Conn. 260, 89 Am.Dec. 208; Danielson v. Roberts, 44 Or. 108, 74 Pac. 913, 65 L.R.A. 526, 102 Am.St.Rep. 627. But see: Foster v. Fidelity Safe Deposit Co., 264 Mo. 89, 174 S.W. 376, 377, L.R.A. 1916A, 655, Ann.Cas.1917D, 798; State v. Courtsol, 89 Conn. 564, 94 A. 973, 975, L.R. A. 1916A, 465.

Goods are "lost" only when possession has been casually and involuntarily parted with, so that mind has no impress of, and can have no recourse to, the event, Automobile Ins. Co. of Hartford, Conn., v. Kirby, 25 Ala.App. 245, 144 So. 123, 124; when property is stolen and then abandoned at place unknown to owner, property is lost, Automobile Ins. Co. of Hartford, Conn. v. Kirby, 25 Ala.App. 245, 144 So. 123, 124.

LOT. A number of associated persons or things taken collectively. Hitchcock v. United States, D. C.Mich., 36 F.Supp. 507, 510.

A share; one of several parcels into which property is divided.

Any portion, piece, division or parcel of land. Lehmann v. Revell, 188 N.E. 531, 537, 354 Ill. 262; Corden v. Zoning Bd. of Appeals of City of Waterbury, 131 Conn. 654, 41 A.2d 912, 915, 916, 159 A.L. R. 849.

Fractional part or subdivision of block, according to plat or survey, Lehmann v. Revell, 354 Ill. 262, 188 N.E. 531, 537; Mawson-Peterson Lumber Co. v. Sprinkle, 59 Wyo. 334, 140 P.2d 588, 591, 147 A.L.R. 1089; portion of platted territory measured and set apart for individual and private use and occupancy, Hunter v. Roman Catholic Bishop of Los Angeles and San Diego Corporation Sole, 128 Cal.App. 90, 16 P.2d 1048, 1049; right of way of street railway abutting a public highway, Sterling Nat. Bank & Trust Co. of New York v. Charleston Transit Co., 126 W.Va. 42, 27 S.E. 2d 256, 259; small tract or parcel of land in a village, town, or city, suitable for building, or for a garden, or other similar uses. See Pilz v. Killingsworth, 20 Or. 432, 26 P. 305; Webster v. Little Rock, 44 Ark. 551; Diamond Mach. Co. v. Ontonagon, 72 Mich. 261, 40 N.W. 448.

The arbitrament of chance; hazard. That which fortuitously determines what course shall be taken or what disposition be made of property or rights.

The thirteenth dish of lead in the mines of Derbyshire, which belonged to the crown.

LOT AND SCOT. In English law. Certain duties which must be paid by those who claim to exercise the elective franchise within certain cities and boroughs, before they are entitled to vote.

It is said that the practice became uniform to refer to the poor-rate as a register of "scot and lot" voters; so that the term, when employed to define a right of election, meant only the payment by a parishioner of the sum to which he was assessed on the poor-rate. Brown.

LOT BOOK. Plat book. National Surety Corporation v. Monroe County, 239 Ala. 35, 193 So. 173, 175.

LOTHERWITE, or LEYERWIT. In old English law. A liberty or privilege to take amends for lying with a bondwoman without license.

LOTTERY. A chance for a prize for a price. Iris Amusement Corporation v. Kelly, 366 Ill. 256, 8 N.E.2d 648; Commonwealth v. McLaughlin, 307 Mass. 230, 29 N.E.2d 821, 822. To constitute a "lottery," there must be a prize, a chance and a price, State v. Dorau, 124 Conn. 160, 198 A. 573, 576, 577; State ex rel. Cowie v. La Crosse Theaters Co., 232 Wis. 153, 286 N.W. 707, 710.

Also defined as device whereby anything of value is for a consideration allotted by lot or chance. State ex Inf. McKittrick v. Globe-Democrat Pub. Co., 341 Mo. 862, 110 S.W.2d 705, 713, 714, 717, 718, 113 A.L.R. 1104; distribution of prizes and blanks by lot or chance, Shanchell v. Lewis Amusement Co., La.App., 171 So. 426, 429; game by which a person paying money becomes entitled to money or other thing of value on certain contingencies, determinable by lot cast in a particular way by the manager of the game, Lee v. City of Miami, 121 Fla. 93, 163 So. 486, 492, 101 A.L.R. 1115, game of hazard in which small sums of money are ventured for chance of obtaining a larger value in money or other articles; State v. Jones, 44 N.M. 623, 107 P.2d 324, 326; Darlington Theatres v. Coker, 190 S.C. 282, 2 S.E.2d 782, 786; game of hazard wherein several lots of merchandise are deposited in prizes for benefit of the fortunate, Lee v. City of Miami, 121 Fla. 93, 163 So. 486, 493, 101 A.L.R. 1115; game which, played or operated once, destroys the value of ticket provided as the prizes are distributed, D'Alessandro v. State, 114 Fla. 70, 153 So. 95, gaming contract by which for a valuable consideration one may by favor of the lot obtain a prize of value superior to the amount or value of that which he risks; Dorman v. Publix-Saenger-Sparks Theatres, 135 Fla. 284, 184 So. 886, 890, 891, 120 A.L.R. 403; Troy Amusement Co. v. Attenweiler, 64 Ohio App. 105, 28 N.E.2d 207, 212; hazard in which sums are ventured for a chance of obtaining a greater value, People v. Hines, 284 N.Y. 93, 29 N.E.2d 483, 488; plan whereby anything of value is disposed of by lot or chance, State v. Emerson, 318 Mo. 633, 1 S.W.2d 109, 112. Scheme by which one or more prizes are distributed by chance. State v. Wersebe, 107 Vt. 529, 181 A. 299. Scheme by which result is reached by some action or means taken, and in which result man's choice or will has no part nor can human reason, foresight, sagacity, or design enable him to know or determine such result until the same has been accomplished, State v. Schwemler, 154 Or. 533, 60 P.2d 938, 940; scheme for distribution of prizes or things of value by lot or chance. State v. Horn, 16 N.J.Misc. 319, 1 A.2d 51, 54; Engle v. State, 53 Ariz. 458, 90 P.2d 988, 992, 993, scheme for raising money by selling chances to share in distribution of prizes, Lee v. City of Miami, 121 Fla. 93, 163 So. 486, 488, 101 A.L.R. 1115. Scheme where money is paid for chance of receiving money or a prize in return. People v. Psallis, Mag.Ct.N.Y., 12 N.Y.S.2d 796, 797, 798, 799; scheme whereby one on paying money or other valuable thing to another becomes entitled to receive from him such a return in value or nothing as some formula of chance may determine, Commonwealth v. Banks, 98 Pa.Super. 432, 436; State v. Hundling, 220 Iowa 1369, 264 N.W. 608, 609, 610, 103 A.L.R. 861; scheme which, played or operated once, destroys the value of ticket provided as the prizes are distributed, D'Alessandro v. State, 114 Fla. 70, 153 So. 95. Scheme which tends to induce one to pay or agree to pay a valuable consideration for a chance to draw a prize. State ex rel. Hunter v. Omaha Motion Picture Exhibitors Ass'n, 139 Neb. 312, 297 N.W. 547, 548, 549, 550.

—**Dutch lottery.** See that title.

—**Genoese lottery.** See that title.

LOU LE LEY DONE CHOSE, LA CEO DONE REMEDIE A VENER A CEO. 2 Rolle, 17. Where the law gives a right, it gives a remedy to recover.

LOUAGE. Fr. This is the contract of hiring and letting in French law, and may be either of things or of labor.

The varieties of each are the following:

1. Letting of things,—*bail à loyer* being the letting of houses; *bail à ferme* being the letting of lands.

2. Letting of labor,—*loyer* being the letting of personal service; *bail à cheptel* being the letting of animals. Brown.

LOURCURDUS. A ram or bell-wether. Cowell.

LOVE-DAY. In old English law. The day on which any dispute was amicably settled between neighbors; or a day on which one neighbor helps another without hire. Wharton.

LOW JUSTICE. In old European law, jurisdiction of petty offenses, as distinguished from "high justice," (*q. v.*).

LOW-WATER. The furthest receding point of ebb-tide. Howard v. Ingersoll, 13 How. 417, 14 L. Ed. 189.

LOW-WATER MARK. See Water-Mark.

LOWBOTE. A recompense for the death of a man killed in a tumult. Cowell.

LOWERS. Fr. In French maritime law. Wages. Ord.Mar. liv. 1, tit. 14, art. 16.

LOYAL. Legal; authorized by or conforming to law. Also faithful in one's political relations; giving faithful support of one's prince or sovereign or to the existing government.

LOYALTY. Adherence to law. Faithfulness to one's prince or sovereign or to the existing government.

LUBRICUM LINGUÆ NON FACILE TRAHENDUM EST IN PŒNAM. Cro. Car. 117. A slip of the tongue ought not lightly to be subjected to punishment.

LUCID INTERVAL. A temporary cure, Succession of Tyler, 193 La. 480, 190 So. 651, 656; a temporary restoration to sanity, Abercrombie v. McLarty, 173 Ga. 414, 160 S.E. 611, 612.

A full return of mind to sanity as places the party in possession of the powers of his mind enabling him to understand and transact his affairs as usual, Succession of Tyler, 193 La. 480, 190 So. 651, 656; an interval in which the mind, having thrown off the disease, has recovered from its general habit, Melody v. Hamblin, 21 Tenn.App. 687, 115 S.W.2d 237, 245; Intervals occurring in the mental life of an insane person during which he is completely restored to the use of his reason, or so far restored that he has sufficient intelligence, judgment, and will to enter into contractual relations, or perform other legal acts, without disqualification by reason of his disease, Roberts v. Pacific Telephone & Telegraph Co., 93 Wash. 274, 160 P. 965, 970; Oklahoma Natural Gas Corporation v. Lay, 175 Okl. 75, 51 P.2d 580, 583; period of time during which person had sufficient mental capacity to know and understand nature and consequence of marriage relation, and the reciprocal and mutual duties and obligations thereof, Carter v. Bacle, Tex.Civ.App., 94 S.W.2d 817, 819.

LUCRA NUPTIALIA. Lat. In Roman law. A term including everything which a husband or wife, as such, acquires from the estate of the other, either before the marriage, or on agreeing to it, or during its continuance, or after its dissolution, and whether the acquisition is by pure gift, or by virtue of the marriage contract, or against the will of the other party by law or statute. See Mackeld. Rom. Law, § 580.

LUCRATIVA CAUSA. Lat. In Roman law. A consideration which is voluntary; that is to say, a gratuitous gift, or such like.

It was opposed to *onerosa causa,* which denoted a valuable consideration. It was a principle of the Roman law that two lucrative causes could not concur in the same person as regarded the same thing; that is to say, that, when the same thing was bequeathed to a person by two different testators, he could not have the thing (or its value) twice over. Brown.

LUCRATIVA USUCAPIO. Lat. This species of *usucapio* was permitted in Roman law only in the case of persons taking possession of property upon the decease of its late owner, and in exclusion or deforcement of the heir, whence it was called *"usucapio pro hœrede."*

The adjective *"lucrativa"* denoted that property was acquired by this *usucapio* without any consideration or payment for it by way of purchase; and, as the possessor who so acquired the property was a *malâ fide* possessor, his acquisition, or *usucapio,* was called also *"improba," (i. e.,* dishonest;) but this dishonesty was tolerated (until abolished by Hadrian) as an incentive to force the *hœres to* take possession, in order that the debts might be paid and the sacrifices performed; and, as a further incentive to the *hœres,* this *usucapio* was complete in one year. Brown.

LUCRATIVE. Yielding gain or profit; profitable; bearing or yielding a revenue or salary.

LUCRATIVE BAILMENT. See Bailment.

LUCRATIVE OFFICE. One which yields a revenue (in the form of fees or otherwise) or a fixed salary to the incumbent; according to some authorities, one which yields a compensation supposed to be adequate to the services rendered and in excess of the expenses incidental to the office. See State v. Kirk, 44 Ind. 405, 15 Am.Rep. 239; Crawford v. Dunbar, 52 Cal. 39; Hodge v. State, 135 Tenn. 525, 188 S.W. 203, 206. One the pay of which is affixed to performance of duties of office. Holman v. Lutz, 132 Or. 185, 284 P. 825, 827.

LUCRATIVE SUCCESSION. In Scotch law. A kind of passive title by which a person accepting from another, without any onerous cause, (or without paying value,) a disposition of any part of his heritage, to which the receiver would have succeeded as heir, is liable to all the grantor's debts contracted before the said disposition. 1 Forb. Inst. pt. 3, p. 102.

LUCRATUS. In Scotch law. A gainer.

LUCRE. Gain in money or goods; profit; usually in an ill sense, or with the sense of something base or unworthy. Webster.

LUCRI CAUSA. Lat. In criminal law. A term descriptive of the intent with which property is taken in cases of larceny, the phrase meaning "for the sake of lucre" or gain. State v. Ryan, 12 Nev. 403, 28 Am.Rep. 802; State v. Slingerland, 19 Nev. 135, 7 P. 280; Groover v. State, 82 Fla. 427, 90 So. 473, 475, 26 A.L.R. 375.

LUCRUM. A small slip or parcel of land.

LUCRUM CESSANS. Lat. In Scotch law. A ceasing gain, as distinguished from *damnum datum,* an actual loss.

LUCRUM FACERE EX PUPILLI TUTELA TUTOR NON DEBET. A guardian ought not to make money out of the guardianship of his ward. Manning v. Manning's Ex'rs, 1 Johns. Ch. (N.Y.) 527, 535.

LUCTUOSA HÆREDITAS. A mournful inheritance. See Hæreditas Luctuosa.

LUCTUS. In Roman law. Mourning. See Annus Luctus.

LUGGAGE. Luggage may consist of any articles intended for the use of a passenger while traveling, or for his personal equipment. Civ.Code Cal. § 2181.

This term is synonymous with "baggage," but is more commonly used in England than in America. Choctaw, etc., R. Co. v. Zwirtz, 13 Okl. 411, 73 P. 941.

If a bus company or other motor carrier, "to suit its own convenience, takes possession of the luggage of a passenger for hire, to care for it on the trip, and becomes a bailee under a special contract, its liability as special bailee is broader than that of a common carrier and includes liability for articles that might not be classed as ordinary baggage." Blashfield, Cyc. of Automobile Law and Prac., Perm. Ed., § 2195.

LUMBER. Used to describe both trees suitable to saw and products into which they are sawed. Brasher v. Industrial Lumber Co., La.App., 165 So. 524, 526.

LUMBER PORTS. Openings in the bow of the barge which are used when long pieces of lumber are put on board are lumber ports. The Chehaw, D.C.N.Y., 54 F.2d 645, 648.

LUMEN. Lat. In the civil law. Light; the light of the sun or sky; the privilege of receiving light into a house.

A light or window.

LUMINA. Lat. In the civil law. Lights; windows; openings to obtain light for one's building.

LUMINARE. A lamp or candle set burning on the altar of any church or chapel, for the maintenance whereof lands and rent-charges were frequently given to parish churches, etc. Kennett, Gloss.

LUMP SUM PAYMENT within compensation act is a payment before it becomes due under monthly payments. Verban v. State Industrial Accident Commission, 169 Or. 394, 123 P.2d 988, 996.

LUMP-SUM SETTLEMENT within compensation act, means that the entire amount of compensation due the employee is paid at one and the same time. Puchner v. Employers' Liability Assur. Corporation, 198 La. 921, 5 So.2d 288, 296.

LUMPING SALE. As applied to judicial sales, this term means a sale in mass, as where several distinct parcels of real estate, or several articles of personal property, are sold together for a "lump" or single gross sum. Anniston Pipeworks v. Williams, 106 Ala. 324, 18 So. 111, 54 Am.St. Rep. 51.

LUNACY. Lunacy is that condition or habit in which the mind is directed by the will, but is wholly or partially misguided or erroneously governed by it; or it is the impairment of any one or more of the faculties of the mind, accompanied with or inducing a defect in the comparing faculty. Owings' Case, 1 Bland (Md.) 386, 17 Am.Dec. 311.

The term includes every kind of unsoundness of mind except idiocy. De Nardo v. De Nardo, 293 N.Y. 550, 59 N. E.2d 241. See Insanity.

For "Commission of Lunacy," and "Inquisition (or Inquest) of Lunacy," see those titles.

LUNAR. Belonging to or measured by the revolutions of the moon.

LUNAR MONTH. See Month.

LUNATIC. A person of deranged or unsound mind; a person whose mental faculties are in the condition called "lunacy"; one who possessed reason, but through disease, grief, or other cause has lost it. May mean all insane persons or persons of unsound mind, sometimes including and sometimes excluding idiots. Oklahoma Natural Gas Corporation v. Lay, 175 Okl. 75, 51 P.2d 580, 582.

A "lunatic" is distinguished from an "idiot" in that the lunatic has lucid intervals, while the idiot has no power of mind whatever. Weinberg v. Weinberg, 8 N.Y.S.2d 341, 344, 255 App.Div. 366.

LUNATICUS, QUI GAUDET IN LUCIDIS INTERVALLIS. He is a lunatic who enjoys lucid intervals. 1 Story, Cont. § 73.

LUNDRESS. In old English law. A silver penny, so called because it was to be coined only at London, (*à Londres,*) and not at the country mints. Lown. Essay Coins, 17; Cowell.

LUPANATRIX. A bawd or strumpet. 3 Inst. 206.

LUPINUM CAPUT GERERE. Lat. To be outlawed, and have one's head exposed, like a wolf's, with a reward to him who should take it. Cowell.

LURCH. See Jerk.

LURGULARY. Casting any corrupt or poisonous thing into the water. Wharton.

LUSHBOROW. In old English law. A base sort of money, coined beyond sea in the likeness of English coin, and introduced into England in the reign of Edward III. Prohibited by St. 25 Edw. III. c. 4. Spelman; Cowell.

LUXURY. Excess and extravagance which was formerly an offense against the public economy, but is not now punishable. Wharton.

LYCH-GATE. The gate into a church-yard, with a roof or awning hung on posts over it to cover the body brought for burial, when it rests underneath. Wharton.

LYEF-GELD. Sax. In old records. Lief silver or money; a small fine paid by the customary tenant to the lord for *leave* to plow or sow, etc. Somn. Gavelkind, 27.

LYING BY. A person who, by his presence and silence at a transaction which affects his interests, may be fairly supposed to acquiesce in it, if he afterwards propose to disturb the arrangement, is said to be prevented from doing so by reason that he has been lying by.

LYING IN FRANCHISE. A term descriptive of waifs, wrecks, estrays, and the like, which may be seized without suit or action.

LYING IN GRANT. A phrase applied to incorporeal rights, incapable of manual tradition, and which must pass by mere delivery of a deed.

LYING IN WAIT. Lying in ambush; lying hid or concealed for the purpose of making a sudden and unexpected attack upon a person when he shall arrive at the scene.

In some jurisdictions, where there are several degrees of murder, lying in wait is made evidence of that deliberation and premeditated intent which is necessary to characterize murder in the first degree. Commonwealth v. Mondollo, 247 Pa. 526, 93 A. 612.

This term is not synonymous with "concealed." If a person conceals himself for the purpose of shooting another unawares, he is lying in wait; but a person may, while concealed, shoot another without committing the crime of murder. People v. Miles, 55 Cal. 207.

LYNCH LAW. A term descriptive of the action of unofficial persons, organized bands, or mobs, who seize persons charged with or suspected of crimes, or take them out of the custody of the law, and inflict summary punishment upon them, without legal trial, and without the warrant or authority of law. See State v. Aler, 39 W.Va. 549, 20 S.E. 585; Bates' Ann.St.Ohio, 1904, § 4426 (Gen. Code, § 6278).

LYNDHURST'S (LORD) ACT. This statute (5 & 6 Wm. IV. c. 54) renders marriages within the prohibited degrees absolutely null and void. Theretofore such marriages were voidable merely.

LYON KING OF ARMS. In Scotch law. The ancient duty of this officer was to carry public messages to foreign states, and it is still the practice of the heralds to make all royal proclamations at the Cross of Edinburgh. The officers serving under him are heralds, pursuivants, and messengers. Bell. See Kings–at–Arms.

LYTÆ. In old Roman law. A name given to students of the civil law in the fourth year of their course, from their being supposed capable of *solving* any difficulty in law. Tayl. Civil Law, 39.

M

M'NAGHTEN RULE. The right-wrong test of criminal responsibility. The rule states essentially that if accused was possessed of sufficient understanding when he committed criminal act to know what he was doing and to know that it was wrong, he is responsible therefor, but if he did not know the nature and quality of the act or did know what he was doing but did not know that it was wrong, he is not responsible. Hixon v. State, Fla.App., 165 So.2d 436, 439; Spurlock v. State, 368 S.W.2d 299, 301, 212 Tenn. 132; Dunn v. State, 174 A.2d 185, 188, 226 Md. 463.

McNABB DOCTRINE. Evidence obtained during an illegal detention; that is, one in which the prisoner has not been promptly taken before a committing magistrate as required by law, is inadmissible in a criminal trial. McNabb v. United States, 318 U.S. 332, 63 S.Ct. 608, 87 L.Ed. 819; Mullican v. U. S., C.A.Tex., 252 F.2d 398.

M. This letter, used as a Roman numeral, stands for one thousand.

It was also, in old English law, a brand or stigma impressed upon the brawn of the thumb of a person convicted of manslaughter and admitted to the benefit of clergy.

This letter was sometimes put on the face of treasury notes of the United States, and signifies that the treasury note bears interest at the rate of one mill per centum, and not one per centum interest. U. S. v. Hardyman, 13 Pet. 176, 10 L.Ed. 113.

M. D. An abbreviation for "Middle District," in reference to the division of the United States into judicial districts. Also an abbreviation for "Doctor of Medicine."

M. F. B. M. An abbreviation meaning 1,000 feet board measure. T. L. James & Co. v. Galveston County, Tex., C.C.A.Tex., 74 F.2d 313.

M. R. An abbreviation for "Master of the Rolls."

M. T. An abbreviation for "Michaelmas Term."

MACE. A large staff, made of the precious metals, and highly ornamented.

It is used as an emblem of authority, and carried before certain public functionaries by a mace-bearer. In many legislative bodies, the mace is employed as a visible symbol of the dignity and collective authority of the house. In the house of lords and house of commons of the British parliament, it is laid upon the table when the house is in session. In the United States house of representatives, it is borne upright by the sergeant-at-arms on extraordinary occasions, as when it is necessary to quell a disturbance or bring refractory members to order.

MACE-BEARER. In English law. One who carries the mace before certain functionaries. In Scotland, an officer attending the court of session, and usually called a "macer."

MACE-GREFF. In old English law. One who buys stolen goods, particularly food, knowing it to have been stolen.

MACE-PROOF. Secure against arrest.

MACEDONIAN DECREE. In Roman law. This was the *Senatus-consultum Macedonianum*, a decree of the Roman senate, first given under Claudius, and renewed under Vespasian by which it was declared that no action should be maintained to recover a loan of money made to a child who was under the *patria potestas*.

It was intended to strike at the practice of usurers in making loans, on unconscionable terms, to family heirs who would mortgage their future expectations from the paternal estate. The law is said to have derived its name from that of a notorious usurer. See Mackeld.Rom. Law, § 432; Inst. 4, 7, 1; Dig. 14, 6.

MACER. A mace-bearer; an officer attending the court of session in Scotland.

MACHECOLLARE. To make a warlike device over a gate or other passage like to a grate, through which scalding water or ponderous or offensive things may be cast upon the assailants. Co. Litt. 5*a*.

MACHINATION. The act of planning or contriving a scheme for executing some purpose, particularly an evil purpose; an artful design formed with deliberation.

MACHINE. Combination of inanimate mechanism for utilizing or applying power, Northern New York Trust Co. v. Bano, 273 N.Y.S. 694, 151 Misc. 684.

Also means construction or contrivance of mechanical sort, Monroe Calculating Mach. Co. v. Department of Labor and Industries, 11 Wash.2d 636, 120 P.2d 466, 471; contrivance composed of cooperating elements which act under the law imposed upon them to regulate or modify the relations between force, motion and weight; Contrivance used to regulate or augment force or motion; a complex structure, consisting of a combination, or peculiar modification, of mechanical powers to perform some function. Simon, Buhler & Baumann v. U. S., 8 Ct.Cust.App. 273, 277; device consisting of two or more resistant, relatively constrained parts, which, by certain predetermined intermotion, may serve to transmit and modify force and motion so as to produce some given effect or to do some desired kind of work, Blankenship v. Cox, 204 Ark. 427, 162 S.W.2d 918, 923. Device or combination of devices by means of which energy can be utilized for useful operation to be performed. Nestle-Le Mur Co. v. Eugene, Limited, C.C.A.Ohio, 55 F.2d 854, 857; mechanical device, or combination of mechanical powers and devices, to perform some function and produce a certain effect or result. Corning v. Burden, 15 How. 252, 267, 14 L.Ed. 683.

For "Dangerous Machine" and "Perfect Machine," see those titles.

MACHINERY. Complex combination of mechanical parts, Blankenship v. Cox, 204 Ark. 427, 162 S.W.2d 918, 923.

A more comprehensive term than "machine"; including the appurtenances necessary to the working of a machine. Shaleen v. Central Coal & Coke Co., 127 Ark. 397, 192 S.W. 225, 227. Parts of a machine considered collectively. Haddad v. Commercial Motor Truck Co., 146 La. 897, 84 So. 197, 198, 9 A.L.R. 1380.

Machines, in general, or collectively; also, the working parts of a machine, engine or instrument; as the machinery of a watch. Monroe Calculating Mach. Co. v. Department of Labor and Industries, 11 Wash.2d 636, 120 P.2d 466, 471.

MACHOLUM. In old English law. A barn or granary open at the top; a rick or stack of corn. Spelman.

MACTATOR. L. Lat. In old European law. A murderer.

MACULARE. In old European law. To wound. Spelman.

MAD PARLIAMENT. Henry III, in 1258, at the desire of the Great Council in Parliament, consented to the appointment of a committee of twenty-four, of whom twelve were appointed by the Barons and twelve by the King, in a parliament which was stigmatized as the "Mad Parliament." Unlimited power was given to it to carry out all necessary reforms. It drew up the Provisions of Oxford.

MAD POINT. A term used to designate the idea or subject to which is confined the derangement of the mental faculties of one suffering from monomania. Owing's Case, 1 Bland (Md.) 388, 17 Am. Dec. 311. See Insanity.

MADE. Filed. St. Louis Law Printing Co. v. Aufderheide, 226 Mo.App. 680, 45 S.W.2d 543, 545; Peavy v. Peavy, 145 S.E. 55, 56, 167 Ga. 219. Produced artificially. United States v. Anderson, D.C. Cal., 45 F.Supp. 943, 946. To require or compel, Dickinson v. Mingea, 191 Ark. 946, 88 S.W.2d 807, 809.

MADE KNOWN. Where a writ of *scire facias* has been actually served upon a defendant, the proper return is that its contents have been "made known" to him.

A crime is "made known" to an officer when facts which come to knowledge of the officer are such as to indicate to him that it is his official duty to act or to see that an investigation of the alleged crime is instituted within his jurisdiction. State v. Young, 194 La. 1061, 195 So. 539, 540.

MADMAN. An insane person, particularly one suffering from mania in any of its forms.

Said to be inapplicable to idiots (Com. v. Haskell, 2 Brewst. [Pa.] 497); Bensberg v. Washington University, 251 Mo. 641, 158 S.W. 330, 336, but it is not a technical term either of medicine or the law, and is incapable of being applied with scientific precision. See Insanity.

MADNESS. See Insanity.

MADRAS REGULATIONS. Certain regulations prescribed for the government of the Madras presidency. Mozley & Whiteley.

MÆC-BURGH. In Saxon law. Kindred; family.

MÆG. A kinsman. 2 Poll. & Maitl. 241.

MÆGBOTE. In Saxon law. A recompense or satisfaction for the slaying or murder of a kinsman. Spelman.

MÆRE. Famous; great; noted; as *Ælmere,* all famous. Gibs, Camd.

MÆREMIUM. Timber; wood suitable for building purposes.

MAGIC. In English statutes. Witch-craft and sorcery.

MAGIS. Lat. More; more fully; more in number; rather.

MAGIS DE BONO QUAM DE MALO LEX INTENDIT. Co. Litt. 78*b*. The law favors a good rather than a bad construction.

Where the words used in an agreement are susceptible of two meanings, the one agreeable to, the other against, the law, the former is adopted. Thus, a bond conditioned "to assign all offices" will be construed to apply to such offices only as are assignable. Chit.Cont. 78.

MAGIS DIGNUM TRAHIT AD SE MINUS DIGNUM. The more worthy draws to itself the less worthy. Yearb. 20 Hen. VI. 2, arg.

MAGISTER. Lat.

Civil law. A title of several offices under the Roman Empire.

English law. A master or ruler; a person who has attained to some eminent degree in science. Cowell.

MAGISTER AD FACULTATES. In English ecclesiastical law. The title of an officer who grants dispensations; as to marry, to eat flesh on days prohibited, and the like. Bac. Abr. "Ecclesiastical Courts," A, 5.

MAGISTER BONORUM VENDENDORUM. In Roman law, a person appointed by judicial authority to inventory, collect, and sell the property of an absent or absconding debtor for the benefit of his creditors.

He was generally one of the creditors, and his functions corresponded generally to those of a receiver or an assignee for the benefit of creditors under modern practice. See Mackeld.Rom. Law § 521.

MAGISTER CANCELLARIÆ. In old English law. Master of the chancery; master in chancery. These officers were said to be called *"magistri,"* because they were priests. Latch. 133.

MAGISTER EQUITUM. Master of the horse. A title of office under the Roman Empire.

MAGISTER LIBELLORUM. Master of requests. A title of office under the Roman Empire.

MAGISTER LITIS. Master of the suit; the person who controls the suit or its prosecution, or has the right so to do.

MAGISTER NAVIS. In the civil law. The master of a ship or vessel. He to whom the care of the whole vessel is committed. Dig. 14, 1, 1, 1, 5.

MAGISTER PALATII. Master of the palace or of the offices. An officer under the Roman Empire bearing some resemblance to the modern lord chamberlain. Tayl. Civil Law, 37.

MAGISTER RERUM USUS. Use is the master of things. Co. Litt. 229*b*. Usage is a principal guide in practice.

MAGISTER RERUM USUS; MAGISTRA RERUM EXPERIENTIA. Use is the master of things; experience is the mistress of things. Co. Litt. 69, 229; Wing. Max. 752.

MAGISTER SOCIETATIS. In the civil law. The master or manager of a partnership; a managing partner or general agent; a manager specially chosen by a firm to administer the affairs of the partnership. Story Partn. § 95.

MAGISTERIAL. Relating or pertaining to the character, office, powers, or duties of a magistrate or of the magistracy.

MAGISTERIAL PRECINCT. In some American states, a local subdivision of a county, defining the territorial jurisdiction of justices of the peace and constables, Breckinridge Co. v. McCracken, C.C.A.Ky., 61 F. 194, 9 C.C.A. 442; also called magisterial district. State v. Mingo County Court, 97 W.Va. 615, 125 S.E. 576, 577.

MAGISTRACY. This term may have a more or less extensive signification according to the use and connection in which it occurs. In its widest sense it includes the whole body of public functionaries, whether their offices be legislative, judicial, executive, or administrative. In a more restricted (and more usual) meaning, it denotes the class of officers who are charged with the application and execution of the laws. In a still more confined use, it designates the body of judicial officers of the lowest rank, and more especially those who have jurisdiction for the trial and punishment of petty misdemeanors or the preliminary steps of a criminal prosecution, such as police judges and justices of the peace. The term also denotes the office of a magistrate. Golden v. Golden, 41 N.M. 356, 68 P.2d 928, 930.

MAGISTRALIA BREVIA. In old English practice. Magisterial writs; writs adapted to special cases, and so called from being framed by the *masters* or principal clerks of the chancery. Bract. fol. 413*b*; Crabb, Com. Law, 547, 548.

MAGISTRATE. Person clothed with power as a public civil officer. State ex rel. Miller v. McLeod, 142 Fla. 254, 194 So. 628, 630.

A public officer belonging to the civil organization of the state, and invested with powers and functions which may be either judicial, legislative, or executive. But the term is commonly used in a narrower sense, designating, in England, a person intrusted with the commission of the peace, and, in America, one of the class of inferior judicial officers, such as justices of the peace and police justices. Martin v. State, 32 Ark. 124; Ex parte White, 15 Nev. 146, 37 Am.Rep. 466; State v. Allen, 83 Fla. 655, 92 So. 155, 156; Merritt v. Merritt, 193 Iowa 899, 188 N.W. 32, 34.

A magistrate is an officer having power to issue a warrant for the arrest of a person charged with a public offense. Pen. Code Cal. § 807.

The word "magistrate" does not necessarily imply an officer exercising any judicial functions, and might very well be held to embrace notaries and commissioners of deeds. Schultz v. Merchants' Ins. Co., 57 Mo. 336.

For "Chief Magistrate," "Committing Magistrate," "Police Magistrate" and "Stipendiary Magistrates," see those titles.

MAGISTRATE'S COURT. In American law. Courts in the state of South Carolina, having exclusive jurisdiction in matters of contract of and under twenty dollars.

A local court in the city of Philadelphia, possessing the criminal jurisdiction of a police court and civil jurisdiction in actions involving not more than one hundred dollars. It is not a court of record. See Const.Pa. art. 4, § 12.

MAGISTRATUS. Lat. In the civil law. A magistrate. Calvin.

A judicial officer who had the power of hearing and determining causes, but whose office properly was to inquire into matters of law, as distinguished from fact. Hallifax, Civil Law, b. 3, c. 8.

MAGNA ASSISA. In old English law. The grand assize. Glanv. lib. 2, cc. 11, 12.

MAGNA ASSISA ELIGENDA. An ancient writ to summon four lawful knights before the justices of assize, there to choose twelve others, with themselves to constitute the *grand assize* or great jury, to try the matter of right. The trial by grand assize was instituted by Henry II. in parliament, as an alternative to the duel in a writ of right. Abolished by 3 & 4 Wm. IV. c. 27. Wharton.

MAGNA AVERIA. In old pleading. Great beasts, as horses, oxen, etc. Cro. Jac. 580.

MAGNA CENTUM. The great hundred, or six score. Wharton.

MAGNA CHARTA. The great charter.

The name of a charter (or constitutional enactment) granted by King John of England to the barons, at Runnymede, on June 15, 1215, and afterwards, with some alterations, confirmed in parliament by Henry III. and Edward I. This charter is justly regarded as the foundation of English constitutional liberty. Among its thirty-eight chapters are found provisions for regulating the administration of justice, defining the temporal and ecclesiastical jurisdictions, securing the personal liberty of the subject and his rights of property, and the limits of taxation, and for preserving the liberties and privileges of the church. *Magna Charta* is so called, partly to distinguish it from the *Charta de Foresta,* which was granted about the same time, and partly by reason of its own transcendent importance.

MAGNA CHARTA ET CHARTA DE FORESTA SONT APPELÈS LES "DEUX GRANDES CHARTERS." 2 Inst. 570. *Magna Charta* and the Charter of the Forest are called the "two great charters."

MAGNA COMPONERE PARVIS. To compare great things with small things.

MAGNA CULPA. Great fault; gross negligence.

MAGNA NEGLIGENTIA. In the civil law. Great or gross negligence.

MAGNA NEGLIGENTIA CULPA EST; MAGNA CULPA DOLUS EST. Gross negligence is fault; gross fault is fraud. Dig. 50, 16, 226.

MAGNA PRECARIA. In old English law. A great or general reap-day. Cowell; Blount.

MAGNA SERJEANTIA. In old English law. Grand serjeanty. Fleta, lib. 2, c. 4, § 1.

MAGNUM CAPE. In old Practice. Great or grand *cape.* 1 Reeve, Eng. Law, 418. See Grand Cape.

MAGNUM CONCILIUM. In old English law. The great council; the general council of the realm; afterwards called "parliament." 1 Bl. Comm. 148; 1 Reeve, Eng. Law, 62; Spelman.

The king's great council of barons and prelates. Spelman; Crabb, Com. Law 228.

MAGNUS ROTULUS STATUTORUM. The great statute roll. The first of the English statute rolls, beginning with *Magna Charta,* and ending with Edward III. Hale, Com. Law, 16, 17.

MAHA-GEN. In Hindu law. A banker or any great shop-keeper.

MAHAL. In Hindu law. Any land or public fund producing a revenue to the government of Hindostan. *"Mahalaat"* is the plural.

MAHLBRIEF. In maritime law. The German name for the contract for the building of a vessel.

This contract contains a specification of the kind of vessel intended, her dimensions, the time within which she is to be completed, the price and times of payment, etc., with reservation generally that the contractor or his agent (usually the master of a vessel) may reject uncontractworthy materials, and oblige the builder to supply others. Jac. Sea Laws 2-8.

MAIDEN. A young unmarried woman. In an indictment for adultery, not necessarily a virgin. State v. Shedrick, 69 Vt. 428, 38 A. 75.

In Scotch law. An instrument formerly used in beheading criminals. It resembled the French guillotine, of which it is said to have been the prototype. Wharton.

MAIDEN ASSIZE. In English law. Originally an assize at which no person was condemned to die. Now a session of a criminal court at which there are no prisoners to be tried.

MAIDEN RENTS. In old English law. A fine paid to lords of some manors, on the marriage of tenants, originally given in consideration of the lord's relinquishing his customary right of lying the first night with the bride of a tenant. Cowell.

MAIGNAGIUM. A brasier's shop, or, perhaps, a house. Cowell.

MAIHEM. See Mayhem; Maim.

MAIHEMATUS. Maimed or wounded.

MAIHEMIUM. In old English law. Mayhem (*q. v.*).

MAIHEMIUM EST HOMICIDIUM INCHOATUM. 3 Inst. 118. Mayhem is incipient homicide.

MAIHEMIUM EST INTER CRIMINA MAJORA MINIMUM, ET INTER MINORA MAXIMUM. Co.Litt. 127. Mayhem is the least of great crimes, and the greatest of small.

MAIHEMIUM EST MEMBRI MUTILATIO, ET DICI POTERIT, UBI ALIQUIS IN ALIQUA PARTE SUI CORPORIS EFFECTUS SIT INUTILIS AD PUGNANDUM. Co.Litt. 126. Mayhem is the mutilation of a member, and can be said to take place when a man is injured in any part of his body so as to be useless in fight.

MAIL. As applied to the post-office, the carriage of letters, whether applied to the bag into which they are put, the coach or vehicle by means of which they are transported, or any other means employed for their carriage and delivery by public authority. Wynen v. Schappert, 6 Daly (N.Y.) 560. It may also denote the letters or other matter so carried.

The term "mail," as used in Rev. St. U. S. § 5469, 18 U.S.C.A. §§ 1702, 1708, relative to robbing the mails, may mean either the whole body of matter transported by the postal agents, or any letter or package forming a component part of it. U. S. v. Inabnet, D.C.S.C., 41 F. 130.

Mail also denotes armor, as in the phrase a "coat of mail."

Scotch law. Rent; a rent or tribute. A tenant who pays a rent is called a "mail-payer," "mailer," or "mail-man." Skene.

MAIL MATTER. This term includes letters, packets, etc., received for transmission, and to be transmitted by post to the person to whom such matter is directed. U. S. v. Huggett, C.C.Ohio, 40 F. 641; U. S. v. Rapp, C.C.Ga., 30 F. 820.

Mail and mail matter are used interchangeably in statute, and both stamps and money can be mail matter. Kelly v. Johnston, C.C.A.Cal., 128 F.2d 793, 794.

MAILABLE. Suitable or admissible for transmission by the mail; belonging to the classes of articles which, by the laws and postal regulations, may be sent by post.

MAILE. In old English law. A kind of ancient money, or silver half-pence; a small rent.

MAILED. Mailing with appropriate address on envelope. Societa Principessa Iolanda Margherita Di Savoia (Fondata Dai Bonitesi) v. Broderick, 260 N.Y. 260, 183 N.E. 382, 383.

This word, as applied to a letter, means that the letter was properly prepared for transmission by the postal department, and that it was put in the custody of the officer charged with the duty of forwarding the mail. Pier v. Heinrichshoffen, 67 Mo. 163, 29 Am.Rep. 501, and testimony that a letter was "mailed" to the addressee implies that it was properly addressed, stamped, and deposited in a proper place for the receipt of mail. Dawson Farmer's Elevator Co. v. Opp, 57 N.D. 598, 223 N.W. 350, 353. Model Mill Co. v. Webb, 164 N.C. 87, 80 S.E. 232, 233. But some courts limit this implication. See W. T. Rawleigh Medical Co. v. Burney, 25 Ga.App. 20, 102 S.E. 358; Feder Silberberg Co. v. McNeil, 18 N.M. 44, 133 P. 975, 49 L.R.A., N.S., 458.

MAILLS AND DUTIES. In Scotch law. The rents of an estate. Bell.

MAIM. As now used signifies to cripple or mutilate in any way, to inflict upon a person any injury which deprives him of the use of any limb or member of the body, or renders him lame or defective in bodily vigor; to inflict bodily injury; to seriously wound or disfigure; disable. See Shackelford v. Com., 183 Va. 423, 32 S.E.2d 682, 684; State v. Thomas, 157 Kan. 526, 142 P.2d 692, 693; State v. Deso, 1 A.2d 710, 715; Phillips v. State, 140 Tex.Cr.R. 84, 143 S.W.2d 591, 592.

At common law, to deprive a person of a member or part of the body, the loss of which renders him less capable of fighting; or of defending himself; to commit mayhem *(q. v.)*. State v. Johnson, 58 Ohio St. 417, 51 N.E. 40, 65 Am.St.Rep. 769.

To "maim" an animal permanent injury must have been inflicted. State v. Benson, 91 Mont. 21, 5 P.2d 223, 224; Williams v. State, 51 Ga.App. 53, 179 S.E. 600.

MAIN. L. Fr. A hand. More commonly written "*meyn.*"

Principal, chief, most important in size, extent, or utility.

First or chief in size, rank, importance, strength, extent; principal, chief, leading. Oregon, C. & E. Ry. Co. v. Blackmer, 154 Or. 388, 59 P.2d 694, 696.

Utilities, chief or primary conductors, Jersey Central Power & Light Co. v. State Board of Tax Appeals, 131 N.J.L. 565, 37 A.2d 111, 112, 113; main or principal conduits, Jersey Central Power & Light Co. v. State Board of Tax Appeals, 130 N.J.L. 364, 33 A.2d 355, 356.

MAIN CHANNEL. The main channel of a river is that bed over which the principal volume of water flows. See St. Louis, etc., Packet Co. v. Keokuk & H. Bridge Co., C.C.Iowa, 31 F. 757; Cessill v. State, 40 Ark. 504; Dunlieth & D. Bridge Co. v. Dubuque County, 55 Iowa 558, 8 N.W. 443. See, also, Thalweg.

MAIN LINE. Line which would develop sufficient traffic to necessitate operation of more than one train in same or opposite direction at any one time within division terminals. Oregon, C. & E. Ry. Co. v. Blackmer, 154 Or. 388, 59 P.2d 694, 696; principal line, Union Pac. R. Co. v. Anderson, 167 Or. 687, 120 P.2d 578, 588.

MAIN SEA. See Sea.

MAIN SEWER. That portion of sewers which serves as outlet for laterals. Boswell v. Chambless, 189 Okl. 112, 113 P.2d 832, 834.

MAIN STAIRWAY in tenement houses means staircase designated as main stairway by building commissioner. Steele v. Lifland, 265 Mass. 233, 163 N.E. 898.

MAINAD. In old English law. A false oath; perjury. Cowell. Probably from Sax. "*manath*" or "*mainath*" a false or deceitful oath.

MAIN-A-MAIN. Immediately. Kelham.

MAINE-PORT. A small tribute, commonly of loaves of bread, which in some places the parishioners paid to the rector in lieu of small tithes. Cowell.

MAINLY. Principally, chiefly, in the main. McGill v. Baumgart, 233 Wis. 86, 288 N.W. 799, 802.

MAINOUR. In criminal law. An article stolen, when found in the hands of the thief.

A thief caught with the stolen goods in his possession is said to be taken "with the mainour," that is, with the property *in manu*, in his hands. 4 Bl.Comm. 307.

The word seems to have corresponded with the Saxon "*handhabend*," *(q. v.)*. In modern law it has sometimes been written as an English word "manner," and the expression "taken in the manner" occurs in the books. Crabb, Eng. Law, 154.

MAINOVRE, or MAINŒUVRE. A trespass committed by hand. See 7 Rich. II. c. 4.

MAINPERNABLE. Capable of being bailed; bailable; admissible to bail on giving surety by mainpernors.

MAINPERNOR. In old practice. A surety for the appearance of a person under arrest, who is delivered out of custody into the hands of his bail.

MAINPRISE. The delivery of a person into the custody of *mainpernors* *(q. v.)*. Also the name of a writ (now obsolete) commanding the sheriff to take the security of mainpernors and set the party at liberty.

"Mainpernors" differ from "bail" in that a man's bail may imprison or surrender him up before the stipulated day of appearance; mainpernors can do neither, but are barely sureties for his appearance at the day. Bail are only sureties that the party be answerable for the special matter for which they stipulate; mainpernors are bound to produce him to answer all charges whatsoever. 3 Bl. Comm. 128. Other distinctions are made in the old books. See Cowell.

MAIN-RENT. Vassalage.

MAINSWORN. Forsworn, by making false oath with *hand (main)* on book. Used in the north of England. Brownl. 4; Hob. 125.

MAINTAIN, as its structure indicates, signifies literally to hold by the hand.

It is variously defined as acts of repairs and other acts to prevent a decline, lapse or cessation from existing state or condition; bear the expense of; carry on; commence; continue; furnish means for subsistence or existence of; hold; hold or keep in an existing state or condition; hold or preserve in any particular state or condition; keep; keep from change; keep from falling, declining, or ceasing; keep in existence or continuance; keep in force; keep in good order; keep in proper condition; keep in repair; keep up; preserve; preserve from lapse, decline, failure, or cessation; provide for; rebuild; repair; replace; supply with means of support; supply with what is needed; support; sustain; uphold. Negatively stated, it is defined as not to lose or surrender; not to suffer or fail or decline. Tennessee Electric Power Co. v. White County, C.C.A.Tenn., 52 F.2d 1065, 1066; Maryland Casualty Co. v. City of Seattle, 11 Wash.2d 69, 118 P.2d 416, 418; State ex rel. Rose Bros. Lumber & Supply Co. v. Clousing, 198 Minn. 35, 268 N.W. 844; City of New York v. Long Island R. Co., 289 N.Y.S. 217, 219, 248 App.Div. 820; Owens v. Greenville News-Piedmont, D.C.S.C., 43 F.Supp. 785, 789; In re Klein, D.C.Minn., 9 F.Supp. 57, 58; Ponsler v. Union Traction Co. of Indiana, 76 Ind.App. 616, 132 N.E. 708, 709.

To "maintain" a suit is to uphold, continue on foot, and keep from collapse a suit already begun, or to prosecute a suit with effect. George Moore Ice Cream Co. v. Rose, Ga., 53 S.Ct. 620, 289 U.S. 373, 77 L.Ed. 1265. To maintain an action or suit may mean to commence or institute it; the term imports the existence of a cause of action. Boutiller v. The Milwaukee, 8 Minn. 105, (Gil. 80, 81). Maintain, however, is applied to actions already brought, but not yet reduced to judgment, Bruenn v. North Yakima School Dist. No. 7, Yakima County, 101 Wash. 374, 172 P. 569, 571; Smallwood v. Gallardo, 48 S.Ct. 23, 275 U.S. 56, 72 L.Ed. 152. In this connection it means to continue or preserve in or with; to carry on. In re Charles Nelson Co., D.C.Cal., 294 F. 926, 928; Roullard v. Gray, 38 Cal. App. 79, 175 P. 479, 480.

The words "maintains" and "maintaining" in statutes denouncing maintenance of a liquor nuisance denote continuous or recurrent acts approaching permanence. Keeth v. State, 193 Ind. 549, 139 N.E. 589, 590; the term "maintaining government" means providing money to enable government to perform duties which it is required by law to perform. Winebrenner v. Salmon, 155 Md. 563, 142 A. 723, 725.

To "maintain an airport" is to keep it in state of efficiency for the furnishing of those facilities and the rendition of those services which air transportation and communication demand. Concordia-Arrow Flying Service Corporation v. City of Concordia, 131 Kan. 247, 289 P. 955, 957.

MAINTAINED. Carried on, kept possession of, F. W. Woolworth Co. v. Erickson, 221 Ala. 5, 127 So. 534, 536. To hold possession of; to keep effectively; commenced. Ricciardi v. Lazzara Baking Corporation, D.C.N.J., 32 F.Supp. 956, 958.

In pleading. A technical word indispensable in an indictment for maintenance. 1 Wils. 325.

MAINTAINOR. In criminal law. One that maintains or seconds a cause depending in suit between others, either by disbursing money or making friends for either party towards his help. Blount. One who is guilty of *maintenance (q. v.)*.

MAINTENANCE. Act of maintaining, keeping up, supporting; livelihood; means of sustenance. Federal Land Bank of St. Louis v. Miller, 184 Ark. 415, 42 S.W.2d 564, 566.

The upkeep, or preserving the condition of property to be operated. Orleans Parish School Board v. Murphy, 156 La. 925, 101 So. 268, 269.

Sustenance; support; assistance; aid. The furnishing by one person to another, for his support, of the means of living, or food, clothing, shelter, etc., particularly where the legal relation of the parties is such that one is bound to support the other, as between father and child, or husband and wife. State ex rel. Blume v. State Board of Education of Montana, 97 Mont. 371, 34 P.2d 515, 519. The supplying of the necessaries of life. Federal Land Bank of St. Louis v. Miller, 184 Ark. 415, 42 S.W.2d 564, 566.

Criminal law. An unauthorized and officious interference in a suit in which the offender has no interest, to assist one of the parties to it, against the other, with money or advice to prosecute or defend the action. Hawk.P.C. 393; Wickham v. Conklin, 8 Johns. (N.Y.) 220.

Roads. "Maintenance" of public roads and highways includes all necessary powers to provide and keep up a system of highways. Handy v. Johnson, D.C.Tex., 51 F.2d 809, 813.

Sick or injured seaman. "Maintenance" to which such seaman is entitled means food and lodging. Fegan v. Lykes Bros. S. S. Co., La.App., 195 So. 392, 398; Socony Vacuum Oil Co. v. Premeaux, Tex.Civ.App., 187 S.W.2d 690, 695.

Suits. A layman's furnishing money to permit a lawyer to provide, in part, costs and expenses in carrying on litigation for a third party, Kane v. Sesac, Inc., D.C.N.Y., 54 F.Supp. 853, 859; aid a party, with money or otherwise, to prosecute or defend his suit without expectation of personal profit, Sampliner v. Motion Picture Patents Co., C.C.A., 255 F. 242, 247; Whisman v. Wells, 206 Ky. 59, 266 S.W. 897, 899; contract must tend or be intended to stir up litigation, multiply contentions, unsettle peace and quiet of a community or set one neighbor against another or give one litigant advantage over another, Fordson Coal Co. v. Garrard, 277 Ky. 218, 125 S.W.2d 977, 981, 121 A.L.R. 841; maintaining, supporting, or promoting the litigation of another, Draper v. Zebec, Ind., 219 Ind. 362, 37 N.E.2d 952, 956; Whelchel v. Stennett, 192 Miss. 241, 5 So.2d 418, 420. Malicious or officious intermeddling with a suit that does not belong to one, by assisting either party with money or otherwise to prosecute or defend, Markarian v. Bartis, 89 N.H. 370, 199 A. 573, 575; Merrell v. Stuart, 220 N.C. 326, 17 S.E.2d 458, 460; Bayard v. McLane, 3 Har. (Del.) 208; something done which tends to obstruct court of justice or is against good policy in tending to promote unnecessary litigation and is performed under a bad motive, Fordson Coal Co. v. Garrard, 277 Ky. 218, 125 S.W.2d 977, 981, 121 A.L.R. 841; unlawful taking in hand or upholding of quarrels or sides to the disturbance or hindrance of common right. Fordson Coal Co. v. Garrard, 277 Ky. 218, 125 S.W.2d 977, 981, 121 A.L.R. 841; Richardson v. Rowland, 40 Conn. 570.

MAINTENANCE ASSESSMENT. One for purpose of keeping an improvement in working order. University Nat. Co. v. Grays Harbor County, 12 Wash.2d 549, 122 P.2d 501, 502.

MAIOR. An old form of "mayor."

MAIRE. In French law. A mayor.

In old Scotch law. An officer to whom process was directed. Otherwise called "mair of fie" (fee), and classed with the "serjand." Skene.

MAIRIE. In French law. The government building of each commune. It contains the record office of all civil acts and the list of voters; and it is there that political and municipal elections take place. Arg.Fr.Merc.Law, 566.

MAISON DE DIEU. Fr. A hospital; an almshouse; a monastery. St. 39 Eliz. c. 5. Literally, "house of God."

MAISTER. An old form of "master."

MAISURA. A house, mansion, or farm. Cowell.

MAÎTRE. Fr. In French maritime law. Master; the master or captain of a vessel. Ord.Mar. liv. 2, tit. 1, art. 1.

MAJESTAS. Lat. In Roman law. The majesty, sovereign authority, or supreme prerogative of the state or prince.

Also a shorter form of the expression *"crimen majestatis,"* or *"crimen læsæ majestatis,"* an offense against sovereignty, or against the safety or organic life of the Roman people; *i. e.*, high treason.

MAJESTY. Royal dignity. A term used of kings and emperors as a title of honor.

MAJOR. A minor emancipated by marriage. Rice v. Kansas City Southern Ry. Co., La.App., 194 So. 444, 447. A person of full age; one who is no longer a minor; one who has attained the management of his own concerns and the enjoyment of his civic rights.

Greater or larger. Zenith Radio Distributing Corporation v. Mateer, 311 Ill.App. 263, 35 N.E.2d 815, 816.

Military law. The officer next in rank above a captain.

MAJOR AND MINOR FAULT RULE. Vessel guilty of gross fault has burden of showing that other vessel committed a plain fault. General Seafoods Corporation v. J. S. Packard Dredging Co., C.C.A.Mass., 120 F.2d 117, 119, 120. Where fault on part of one vessel is established by uncontradicted testimony and such fault is, of itself, sufficient to account for the disaster, it is not enough for such vessel to raise a doubt with regard to management of other vessel and any reasonable doubt with regard to propriety of conduct of such other vessel should be resolved in its favor. Intagliata v. Shipowners & Merchants T vboat Co., 26 Cal.2d 365, 159 P.2d 1, 10; General Seafoods Corporation v. J. S. Packard Dredging Co., C.C.A.Mass., 120 F.2d 117, 119, 120.

MAJOR ANNUS. The greater year; the bissextile year, consisting of 366 days. Bract. fol. 359*b*.

MAJOR CONTINET IN SE MINUS. The greater includes the less. 19 Vin.Abr. 379.

MAJOR GENERAL. In military law. An officer next in rank above a brigadier general, and next below a lieutenant general, and who usually commands a division or an army corps.

MAJOR HÆREDITAS VENIT UNICUIQUE NOSTRUM A JURE ET LEGIBUS QUAM A PARENTIBUS. 2 Inst. 56. A greater inheritance comes to every one of us from right and the laws than from parents.

MAJOR NUMERUS IN SE CONTINET MINOREM. Bract. fol. 16. The greater number contains in itself the less.

MAJORA REGALIA. The king's dignity, power, and royal prerogative, as opposed to his revenue, which is comprised in the *minora* regalia. 2 Steph. Comm. 475; 1 Bl.Comm. 240.

MAJORE PŒNA AFFECTUS QUAM LEGIBUS STATUTA EST, NON EST INFAMIS. One affected with a greater punishment than is provided by law is not infamous. 4 Inst. 66.

MAJORES.

Old English law. Greater persons; persons of higher condition or estate.

Roman law and genealogical tables. The male ascendants beyond the sixth degree.

MAJORI SUMMÆ MINOR INEST. In the greater sum the less is included. 2 Kent, Comm. 618; Story, Ag. § 172.

MAJORITY. Full age; the age at which, by law, a person is entitled to the management of his own affairs and to the enjoyment of civic rights. The opposite of minority. Also the *status* of a person who is a major in age.

The greater number.

The number greater than half of any total. Application of McGovern, 44 N.Y.S.2d 132, 137, 180 Misc. 508.

Elections. Majority signifies the greater number of votes. In re Todd, 208 Ind. 168, 193 N.E. 865.

When there are only two candidates, he who receives the greater number of the votes cast is said to have a majority; when there are more than two competitors for the same office, the person who receives the greatest number of votes has a *plurality,* but he has not a majority unless he receives a greater number of votes than those cast for all his competitors combined.

It relates to voters voting at election, not those qualified and not voting. Hevelone v. City of Beatrice, 120 Neb. 648, 234 N.W. 791, 795.

Military affairs. Majority denotes the rank and commission of a major.

MAJORITY OF QUALIFIED ELECTORS. Refers to those who actually vote on election day. Harris v. Baden, 154 Fla. 373, 17 So.2d 608, 609.

MAJORITY OF STOCKHOLDERS. A majority in interest of the stockholders, and not a majority in number only. Bank of Los Banos v. Jordan, 139 P. 691, 167 Cal. 327. "Majority of stockholders" means majority per capita when the right to vote is per capita, and a majority of stock when each share of stock is entitled to a vote, each particular case being determined by provisions of charter regulating voting. Simon Borg & Co. v. New Orleans City R. Co., D.C.La., 244 F. 617, 619.

MAJORITY RULE. Rule by the choice of the majority of those who actually vote, irrespective of whether a majority of those entitled participate. N. L. R. B. v. Standard Lime & Stone Co., C.C.A.4, 149 F.2d 435, 437.

MAJORITY VOTE. Where question is required to be submitted at certain regular election and is made to depend on "majority of votes" cast at "such election," a majority of all votes cast at election is meant, and not merely majority of votes cast on that particular question. In re Todd, 208 Ind. 168, 193 N.E. 865.

Where legislative body provides that proposition shall be submitted to voters and those in favor of proposition shall cast affirmative vote, while those opposed shall cast negative vote, and that "majority of votes" given shall be requisite to adoption of measure, only votes to be counted in determining whether measure was adopted are those given on particular question involved. In re Todd, 208 Ind. 168, 193 N.E. 865.

MAJUS DIGNUM TRAHIT AD SE MINUS DIGNUM. The more worthy draws to itself the less worthy. Co.Litt. 43, 355*b*; Bract. fol. 175; Noy, Max. p. 6, max. 18.

MAJUS EST DELICTUM SEIPSUM OCCIDERE QUAM ALIUM. It is a greater crime to kill one's self than another. Bart.Max. 108. See Suicide.

MAJUS JUS. In old practice, greater right or more right. A plea in the old real actions. 1 Reeve, Eng.Law, 476. *Majus jus merum,* more mere right. Bract. fol. 31.

A writ proceeding in some customary manors to try a right to land. Cow.

MAJUS LATIUM. See Jus Latium.

MAKE. To cause to exist. United States v. Giles, Tex., 57 S.Ct. 340, 344, 300 U.S. 41, 81 L.Ed. 493. To form, fashion, or produce; to do, perform, or execute; as to make an issue, to make oath, to make a presentment.

To do in form of law; to perform with due formalities; to execute in legal form; as to make answer, to make a return or report. Ex parte Lockhart, 72 Mont. 136, 232 P. 183, 185.

To execute as one's act or obligation; to prepare and sign; to issue; to sign, execute, and deliver; as to make a conveyance, to make a note. Heinbach v. Heinbach, 274 Mo. 301, 202 S.W. 1123, 1130; Spaulding v. First Nat. Bank, 205 N.Y.S. 492, 493, 210 App.Div. 216.

To conclude, determine upon, agree to, or execute; as to make a contract. MacIntyre v. McLean, 162 Ga. 280, 133 S.E. 471, 475. Tourtlott v. West Bangor & Hermon Mut. Fire Ins. Co., 126 Me. 118, 136 A. 481, 482.

To cause to happen by one's neglect or omission; as to make default.

To make acquisition of; to procure; to collect; as to make the money on an execution or to make a loan. Fidelity Trust Co. v. Fowler, Tex.Civ.App., 217 S.W. 953, 954.

To have authority or influence; to support or sustain; as in the phrase, "This precedent makes for the plaintiff."

MAKE AN ASSIGNMENT. To transfer one's property to an assignee for the benefit of one's creditors.

MAKE AN AWARD. To form and publish a judgment on the facts. Hoff v. Taylor, 5 N.J.Law, 833.

MAKE A CONTRACT. To agree upon, and conclude or adopt, a contract. In case of a written contract, to reduce it to writing, execute it in due form, and deliver it as binding.

MAKE DEFAULT. To fail or be wanting in some legal duty; particularly to omit the entering of an appearance when duly summoned in an action at law or other judicial proceeding, to neglect to obey the command of a subpœna, etc.

MAKE ONE'S FAITH. A Scotch phrase, equivalent to the old English phrase, "to make one's law."

MAKER. One who makes, frames, or ordains; as a "law-maker." One who makes or executes; as the maker of a promissory note. See Aud v. Magruder, 10 Cal. 290; Sawyers v. Campbell, 107 Iowa 397, 78 N.W. 56.

Accommodation maker. See Accommodation.

MAKING LAW. In old practice, the formality of denying a plaintiff's charge under oath, in open court, with compurgators. One of the ancient methods of trial, frequently, though inaccurately, termed "waging law," or "wager of law." 3 Bl. Comm. 341.

MAL. A prefix meaning bad, wrong, fraudulent; as maladministration, malpractice, malversation, etc.

MAL GREE. L. Fr. Against the will; without the consent. Hence the single word "*malgre,*" and more modern "*maugre,*" (*q. v.*).

MAL-TOLTE. Fr. In old French law, a term said to have arisen from the usurious gains of the Jews and Lombards in their management of the public revenue. Steph.Lect. 372.

MALA. Lat. Bad; evil; wrongful.

MALA FIDES. Bad faith. The opposite of *bona fides* (*q. v.*). *Malâ fide,* in bad faith. *Malœ fidei possessor,* a possessor in bad faith. Mackeld.Rom. Law, § 297.

MALA GRAMMATICA NON VITIAT CHARTAM. SED IN EXPOSITIONE INSTRUMENTORUM MALA GRAMMATICA QUOAD FIERI POSSIT EVITANDA EST. Bad grammar does not vitiate a deed. But in the exposition of instruments, bad grammar, as far as it can be done, is to be avoided. 6 Coke, 39; Broom, Max. 686.

MALA IN SE. Wrongs in themselves; acts morally wrong; offenses against conscience. 1 Bl. Comm. 57, 58; 4 Bl.Comm. 8; Com. v. Adams, 114 Mass. 323, 19 Am.Rep. 362; Turner v. Merchants' Bank, 126 Ala. 397, 28 So. 469.

MALA PRAXIS. Malpractice; unskillful management or treatment. Particularly applied to the neglect or unskillful management of a physician, surgeon, or apothecary. 3 Bl.Comm. 122.

MALA PROHIBITA. Prohibited wrongs or offenses; acts which are made *offenses* by positive laws, and *prohibited* as such. 1 Bl.Comm. 57, 58; 4 Bl. Comm. 8.

MALADMINISTRATION. This term is used, in the law-books, interchangeably with *misadministration,* and both words mean "wrong administration." Minkler v. State, 14 Neb. 183, 15 N.W. 331.

MALANDRINUS. In old English law, a thief or pirate. Wals. 338.

MALARY. In Hindu law, judicial; belonging to a judge or magistrate.

MALBERGE. A hill where the people assembled at a court, like the English assizes; which by the Scotch and Irish were called "parley hills." Du Cange.

MALCONDUCT. Ill conduct, especially dishonest conduct, maladministration, or, as applied to officers, official misconduct. Sausbier v. Wheeler, 299 N.Y.S. 466, 473, 252 App.Div. 267.

MALCONNA. In Hindu law, a treasury or storehouse.

MALE. Of the masculine sex; of the sex that begets young.

MALE CREDITUS. In old English law, unfavorably thought of; in bad repute or credit. Bract. fols. 116, 154.

MALEDICTA EST EXPOSITIO QUÆ CORRUMPIT TEXTUM. That is a cursed interpretation which corrupts the text. 4 Coke, 35*a*; Broom, Max. 622.

MALEDICTION. A curse, which was anciently annexed to donations of lands made to churches or religious houses, against those who should violate their rights. Cowell.

MALEFACTION. A crime; an offense.

MALEFACTOR. He who is guilty, or has been convicted, of some crime or offense.

MALEFICIA NON DEBENT REMANERE IMPUNITA; ET IMPUNITAS CONTINUUM AFFECTUM TRIBUIT DELINQUENTI. 4 Coke, 45. Evil deeds ought not to remain unpunished; and impunity affords continual incitement to the delinquent.

MALEFICIA PROPOSITIS DISTINGUUNTUR. Jenk.Cent. 290. Evil deeds are distinguished from evil purposes, or *by* their purposes.

MALEFICIUM. In the civil law, waste; damage; tort; injury. Dig. 5, 18, 1.

MALESON, or MALISON. A curse.

MALESWORN, or MALSWORN. Forsworn. Cowell.

MALFEASANCE. Evil doing; ill conduct; the commission of some act which is positively unlawful; the doing of an act which is wholly wrongful and unlawful; the doing of an act which person ought not to do at all or the unjust performance of some act which the party had no right or which he had contracted not to do. Comprehensive term including any wrongful conduct that affects, interrupts or interferes with the performance of official duties. State ex rel. Knabb v. Frater, 198 Wash. 675, 89 P.2d 1046, 1048.

It differs from "misfeasance" and "non-feasance," (which titles see.) See 1 Chit.Pr. 9; 1 Chit. Pl. 134; Dudley v. Flemingsburg, 72 S.W. 327, 115 Ky. 5, 60 L.R.A. 575, 103 Am.St.Rep. 253.

MALFETRIA. In Spanish law, offense. White, New Recop. b. 2, tit. 19, c. 1, § 1.

MALICE. The intentional doing of a wrongful act without just cause or excuse, with an intent to inflict an injury or under circumstances that the law will imply an evil intent. Luikart v. Miller, Mo., 48 S.W.2d 867, 871. Cottle v. Johnson, 179 N.C. 426, 102 S.E. 769, 770.

A conscious violation of the law (or the prompting of the mind to commit it) which operates to the prejudice of another person. Seaboard Air Line Ry. Co. v. Glenn, 213 Ala. 284, 104 So. 548, 549. A condition of the mind showing a heart regardless of social duty and fatally bent on mischief. Cockrell v. State, 135 Tex.Cr.R. 218, 117 S.W. 2d 1105, 1109, 1110.

In murder, that condition of mind which prompts one to take the life of another without just cause or provocation. State v. Smith, 26 N.M. 482, 194 P. 869, 870; State v. Moynihan, 93 N.J.L. 253, 106 A. 817, 818; a willful or corrupt intention of the mind. Pembrook v. State, 117 Neb. 759, 222 N.W. 956. It includes not only anger, hatred and revenge, but also every other unlawful and unjustifiable motive. State v. Scherr, 243 Wis. 65, 9 N.W.2d 117, 119.

"Malice," in its common acceptation, means ill will towards some person. In its legal sense, it applies to a wrongful act done intentionally, without legal justification or excuse. Dunn v. Hall, 1 Ind. 344.

It includes intent and will. State v. Robbins, 66 Me. 328.

"Malice" in law is not necessarily personal hate or ill will, but it is that state of mind which is reckless of law and of the legal rights of the citizen. Evers-Jordan Furniture Co. v. Hartzog, 237 Ala. 407, 187 So. 491, 493.

"Malice," in legal sense, characterizes all acts done with an evil disposition, a wrong and unlawful motive or purpose, or the willful doing of an injurious act without a lawful excuse. Giguere v. Rosselot, 110 Vt. 173, 3 A.2d 538, 542.

In libel and slander, as to privileged communications, "malice" involves an evil intent or motive arising from spite or ill will; personal hatred or ill will; or culpable recklessness or a willful and wanton disregard of the rights and interests of the person defamed. McDonald v. Brown, 23 R.I. 546, 51 A. 213, 58 L.R.A. 768, 91 Am.St.Rep. 659; Cherry v. Des Moines Leader, 86 N.W. 323, 114 Iowa 298, 54 L.R.A. 855, 89 Am.St.Rep. 365.

In a libel case it consists in intentionally publishing, without justifiable cause, any written or printed matter which is injurious to the character of another. Becker v. Brinkop, 230 Mo.App. 871, 78 S.W.2d 538, 541. And in a legal sense, as an ingredient of actions for slander or libel, it signifies nothing more than a wrongful act done intentionally, without just cause or excuse. Ambruster v. National Bank of Westfield, 116 N.J.L. 122, 182 A. 613, 614.

In the law of malicious prosecution, it means that the prosecution was instituted primarily because of a purpose other than that of bringing an offender to justice. Brown v. Kisner, 192 Miss. 746, 6 So.2d 611, 617.

Actual malice. Express malice, or malice in fact. Gee v. Culver, 13 Or. 598, 11 P. 302; Eteenpain Co-op. Soc. v. Lillback, C.C.A.Mass., 18 F.2d 912, 917.

Constructive malice. Implied malice; malice inferred from acts; malice imputed by law; malice which is not shown by direct proof of an intention to do injury, (express malice,) but which is inferentially established by the necessarily injurious results of the acts shown to have been committed. State v. Harrigan, 31 Atl. 1052, 9 Houst. (Del.) 369; Caldwell v. Raymond, 2 Abb.Prac. (N.Y.) 196.

Express malice. Actual malice; malice in fact; ill will or wrongful motive; a deliberate intention to commit an injury, evidenced by external circumstances. Sparf v. U. S., 15 S.Ct. 273, 156 U.S. 51, 39 L.Ed. 343; Weir v. McEwan, 94 N.J.L. 92, 109 A. 355, 356; People v. Scalisi, 324 Ill. 131, 154 N.E. 715, 722.

General malice. General malice is wickedness, a disposition to do wrong, a "black and diabolical heart, regardless of social duty and fatally bent on mischief." Neal v. Nelson, 117 N.C. 393, 23 S.E. 428, 53 Am.St.Rep. 590.

Implied malice. Malice inferred by legal reasoning and necessary deduction from the *res gestæ* or the conduct of the party. Malice inferred from any deliberate cruel act committed by one person against another, however sudden. Whart.Hom. 38. What is called "general malice" is often thus inferred. Sparf v. U. S., 15 S.Ct. 273, 156 U.S. 51, 39 L.Ed. 343.

Legal malice. See Legal Malice.

Particular malice. Malice directed against a particular individual; ill will; a grudge; a desire to be revenged on a particular person. Brooks v. Jones, 33 N.C. 261; State v. Long, 117 N.C. 791, 23 S.E. 431.

Preconceived malice. Malice prepense or aforethought. See State v. Reidell, 9 Houst. (Del.) 470, 14 A. 550.

Premeditated malice. An intention to kill unlawfully, deliberately formed in the mind as the result of a determination meditated upon and fixed before the act. State v. Gin Pon, 16 Wash. 425, 47 P. 961; State v. Rutten, 13 Wash. 211, 43 P. 30.

Special malice. Particular or personal malice; that is, hatred, ill will, or a vindictive disposition against a particular individual.

Universal malice. By this term is not meant a malicious purpose to take the life of all persons, but it is that depravity of the human heart which determines to take life upon slight or insufficient provocation, without knowing or caring who may be the victim. Mitchell v. State, 60 Ala. 30.

MALICE AFORETHOUGHT. A predetermination to commit an act without legal justification or excuse. Harrison v. Commonwealth, 279 Ky. 510, 131 S.W.2d 454, 455. A malicious design to injure. State v. Thomas, 157 Kan. 526, 142 P.2d 692, 693.

In the definition of "murder," malice aforethought exists where the person doing the act which causes death has an intention to cause death or grievous bodily harm to any person, (whether the person is actually killed or not) or to commit any felony whatever, or has the knowledge that the act will probably cause the death of or grievous bodily harm to some person, although he does not desire it, or even wishes that it may not be caused. Steph.Crim.Dig. 144; 1 Russ.Crimes. 641. The words "malice aforethought" long ago acquired in law a settled meaning, somewhat different from the popular one. In their legal sense they do not import an actual intention to kill the deceased. The idea is not spite or malevolence to the deceased in particular, but evil design in general, the dictate of a wicked, depraved, and malignant heart; not premeditated personal hatred or revenge towards the person killed, but that kind of unlawful purpose which, if persevered in, must produce mischief. State v. Pike, 49 N.H. 399, 6 Am. Rep. 533.

MALICE IN FACT. Express or actual malice. Railway Co. v. Behee, 2 Tex.Civ.App. 107, 21 S.W. 384, Hotchkiss v. Porter, 30 Conn. 414.

It implies desire or intent to injure, while "malice in law," or "implied malice," means wrongful act done intentionally, without just cause or excuse, and jury may infer it as a deduction from want of probable cause. Glieberman v. Fine, 248 Mich. 8, 226 N.W. 669, 670.

MALICE IN LAW. The intentional doing of a wrongful act without just cause or excuse. Lyons v. St. Joseph Belt Ry. Co., Mo.App., 84 S.W.2d 933, 944. Implied, inferred, or legal malice. Smith v. Rodecap, 5 Ind.App. 78, 31 N.E. 479; Bacon v. Railroad Co., 66 Mich. 166, 33 N.W. 181.

As distinguished from malice in fact, it is presumed from tortious acts, deliberately done without just cause, excuse, or justification, which are reasonably calculated to injure another or others. Betts v. Jones, 208 N.C. 410, 181 S.E. 334.

MALICE PREPENSE. Malice aforethought; deliberate, predetermined malice. 2 Rolle, 461.

MALICIOUS. Characterized by, or involving, malice; having, or done with, wicked or mischievous intentions or motives; wrongful and done intentionally without just cause or excuse. People v. Knapp, 274 N.Y.S. 85, 152 Misc. 368.

In its broad sense it does not necessarily mean ill will or hatred. In a legal sense, any act done willfully and purposely to the prejudice and injury of another, which is unlawful, is, as against that person, "malicious." Pollard v. Phelps, 56 Ga.App. 408, 193 S.E. 102, 108.

MALICIOUS ABANDONMENT. In criminal law, the desertion of a wife or husband without just cause.

MALICIOUS ABUSE OF LEGAL PROCESS. Willfully misapplying court process to obtain object not intended by law. Atlanta Finance Co. v. Cain, 42 Ga.App. 819, 157 S.E. 337.

The willful misuse or misapplication of process to accomplish a purpose not warranted or commanded by the writ; the malicious perversion of a regularly issued process, whereby a result not lawfully or properly obtained on a writ is secured; not including cases where the process was procured maliciously but not abused or misused after its issuance. King v. Yarbray, 136 Ga. 212 (1), 71 S.E. 131.

MALICIOUS ACCUSATION. Procuring accusation or prosecution of another from improper motive and without probable cause. McKenzie v. State, 113 Neb. 576, 204 N.W. 60, 63.

MALICIOUS ACT. A wrongful act intentionally done without legal justification or excuse; an unlawful act done willfully or purposely to injure another. La Plante v. Johnson, 297 N.Y.S. 318, 321, 163 Misc. 96.

MALICIOUS ARREST. An arrest made willfully and without probable cause, but in the course of a regular proceeding.

MALICIOUS INJURY. An injury committed against a person at the prompting of malice or hatred towards him, or done spitefully or wantonly. State v. Huegin, 110 Wis. 189, 85 N.W. 1046, 62 L.R.A. 700; Wing v. Wing, 66 Me. 62, 22 Am. Rep. 548.

The willful doing of an act with knowledge it is liable to injure another and regardless of consequences. In re Kalk, D.C.N.Y., 270 F. 627, 629.

Injury involving element of fraud, violence, wantonness and willfulness, or criminality. Braxton v. Matthews, 199 N.C. 484, 154 S.E. 735.

An injury that is intentional, wrongful and without just cause or excuse, even in the absence of hatred, spite or ill will. Panchula v. Kaya, 59 Ohio App. 556, 18 N.E.2d 1003, 1005.

MALICIOUS KILLING. Any intentional killing without a legal justification or excuse and not within the realm of voluntary manslaughter. State v. Cope, 78 Ohio App. 429, 67 N.E.2d 912, 920.

MALICIOUS MISCHIEF. Willful destruction of personal property, from actual ill will or resentment towards its owner or possessor. People v. Petheram, 31 N.W. 188, 64 Mich. 252; First Nat. Bank v. Burkett, 101 Ill. 394, 40 Am.Rep. 209; State v. Waltz, 158 Iowa 191, 139 N.W. 458, 459. Though only a trespass at the common law, it is now, by several statutes, made severely penal. Jacob.

MALICIOUS MOTIVE. Any motive for instituting a prosecution, other than a desire to bring an offender to justice. Lounder v. Jacobs, 119 Colo. 511, 205 P.2d 236, 238.

MALICIOUS PROSECUTION. One begun in malice without probable cause to believe the charges can be sustained. Eustace v. Dechter, 28 Cal.App. 2d 706, 83 P.2d 523, 525. Instituted with intention of injuring defendant and without probable cause, and which terminates in favor of the person prosecuted. For this injury an action on the case lies, called the "action of malicious prosecution." Hicks v. Brantley, 29 S.E. 459, 102 Ga. 264; Eggett v. Allen, 96 N.W. 803, 119 Wis. 625.

MALICIOUS TRESPASS. The act of one who maliciously or mischievously injures or causes to be injured any property of another or any public property. State v. McKee, 109 Ind. 497, 10 N.E. 405; Hannel v. State, 4 Ind.App. 485, 30 N.E. 1118.

MALICIOUS USE OF PROCESS. Exists where plaintiff proceeds maliciously and without probable cause to execute object which law intends process to subserve. Davison-Paxon Co. v. Walker, 45 Ga.App. 395, 165 S.E. 160, 163.

MALICIOUSLY. Imports a wish to vex, annoy, or injure another, or an intent to do a wrongful act, and may consist in direct intention to injure, or in reckless disregard of another's rights. Briggs v. Coykendall, 57 N.D. 785, 224 N.W. 202, 205.

MALICIOUSNESS. "Maliciousness" does not necessarily mean actual malice or ill will, but intentional doing of a wrongful act without legal or social justification. Dorrington v. Manning, 135 Pa.Super. 194, 4 A.2d 886, 890.

MALIGNARE. To malign or slander; also to maim.

MALINGER. To feign sickness or any physical disablement or mental lapse or derangement, especially for the purpose of escaping the performance of a task, duty, or work.

MALITIA. Lat. Actual evil design; express malice.

MALITIA EST ACIDA; EST MALI ANIMI AFFECTUS. Malice is sour; it is the quality of a bad mind. 2 Bulst. 49.

MALITIA PRÆCOGITATA. Malice aforethought.

MALITIA SUPPLET ÆTATEM. Malice supplies [the want of] age. Dyer, 104*b*; Broom Max. 316.

MALITIIS HOMINUM EST OBVIANDUM. The wicked or malicious designs of men must be thwarted. 4 Coke, 15*b*.

MALLEABLE. Capable of being drawn out and extended by beating; capable of extension by hammering; reducible to laminated form by beating. Farris v. Magone, C.C.N.Y., 46 F. 845.

MALLUM. In old European law, a court of the higher kind in which the more important business of the county was dispatched by the count or earl. Spelman. A public national assembly.

MALO ANIMO. Lat. With an evil mind; with a bad purpose or wrongful intention; with malice.

MALO GRATO. Lat. In spite; unwillingly.

MALO SENSU. Lat. In an evil sense or meaning; with an evil signification.

MALPRACTICE. Any professional misconduct, unreasonable lack of skill or fidelity in professional or fiduciary duties, evil practice, or illegal or immoral conduct. Gregory v. McInnis, 140 S.C. 52, 134 S.E. 527, 529.

As applied to physicians and surgeons, this term means, generally, professional misconduct towards a patient which is considered reprehensible either because immoral in itself or because contrary to law or expressly forbidden by law.

In a more specific sense, it means bad, wrong, or injudicious treatment of a patient, professionally and in respect to the particular disease or injury, resulting in injury, unnecessary suffering, or death to the patient, and proceeding from ignorance, carelessness, want of proper professional skill, disregard of established rules or principles, neglect, or a malicious or criminal intent. Rodgers v. Kline, 56 Miss. 816, 31 Am.Rep. 389; Hibbard v. Thompson, 109 Mass. 288; Napier v. Greenzweig, C.C.A.N.Y., 256 F. 196, 197.

The term is occasionally applied to lawyers, and then means generally any evil practice in a professional capacity, but rather with reference to the court and its practice and process than to the client. In re Baum, 8 N.Y.S. 771, 55 Hun, 611; Cowley v. O'Connell, 54 N.E. 558, 174 Mass. 253.

MALT. A substance produced from barley or other grain by a process of steeping in water until germination begins and then drying in a kiln, thus converting the starch into saccharine matter. Hollender v. Magone, C.C.N.Y., 38 F. 915; U. S. v. Cohn, 52 S.W. 38, 2 Ind.T. 474.

MALT BEVERAGES. Consists of beer, ale, porter, and the like, and do not include distilled alcoholic beverages, or fermented juices from grapes, fruits, and berries. McCaffrey v. State, 183 Ga. 827, 189 S.E. 825, 826.

MALT LIQUOR. A general term including all alcoholic beverages prepared essentially by the fermentation of an infusion of malt (as distinguished from such liquors as are produced by the process of distillation), and particularly such beverages as are made from malt and hops, like beer, ale, and porter. Allred v. State, 89 Ala. 112, 8 So. 56; State v. Gill, 89 Minn. 502, 95 N.W. 449; Claunch v. State, 82 Tex.Cr. 355, 199 S.W. 483, 484.

MALT MULNA. A quern or malt-mill.

MALT-SHOT, or MALT-SCOT. A certain payment for making malt. Somner.

MALT-TAX. An excise duty upon malt in England. 1 Bl.Comm. 313; 2 Steph.Comm. 581.

MALTOTE. In French history, an oppressive tax levied in 1292 and later. Cassell's New Fr. Dict.

MALTREATMENT. In reference to the treatment of his patient by a surgeon, this term signifies improper or unskillful treatment; it may result either from ignorance, neglect, or willfulness; but the word does not necessarily imply that the conduct of the surgeon, in his treatment of the patient, is either willfully or grossly careless. Com. v. Hackett, 2 Allen (Mass.) 142.

MALUM, *n.* Lat. In Roman law, a mast; the mast of a ship. Dig. 50, 17, 242, pr. Held to be part of the ship. Id.

MALUM, *adj.* Lat. Wrong; evil; wicked; reprehensible.

MALUM IN SE. A wrong in itself; an act or case involving illegality from the very nature of the transaction, upon principles of natural, moral, and public law. Story, Ag. § 346. State v. Shedoudy, 45 N.M. 516, 118 P.2d 280, 287.

An act is said to be *malum in se* when it is inherently and essentially evil, that is, immoral in its nature and injurious in its consequences, without any regard to the fact of its being noticed or punished by the law of the state. Such are most or all of the offenses cognizable at common law, (without the denouncement of a statute;) as murder, larceny, etc.

MALUM NON HABET EFFICIENTEM, SED DEFICIENTEM, CAUSAM. 3 Inst.Proem. Evil has not an efficient, but a deficient, cause.

MALUM NON PRÆSUMITUR. Wickedness is not presumed. Branch, Princ.; 4 Coke, 72*a*.

MALUM PROHIBITUM. A wrong prohibited; a thing which is wrong *because* prohibited; an act which is not inherently immoral, but becomes so because its commission is expressly forbidden by positive law; an act involving an illegality resulting from positive law. Contrasted with *malum in se*. Story, Ag. § 346; People v. Pavlic, 227 Mich. 562, 199 N.W. 373, 374, 35 A.L.R. 741.

MALUM QUO COMMUNIUS EO PEJUS. The more common an evil is, the worse it is. Branch, Princ.

MALUS USUS ABOLENDUS EST. A bad or invalid custom is [ought] to be abolished. Litt. § 212; Co.Litt. 141; 1 Bl.Comm. 76; Broom, Max. 921.

MALVEILLES. In old English law, ill will; crimes and misdemeanors; malicious practices. Cowell.

MALVEIS PROCURORS. L. Fr. Such as used to pack juries, by the nomination of either party in a cause, or other practice. Cowell.

MALVEISA. A warlike engine to batter and beat down walls.

MALVERSATION. In French law, this word is applied to all grave and punishable faults committed in the exercise of a charge or commission, (office,) such as corruption, exaction, concussion, larceny. Merl. Répert.

MAN. A human being. A person of the male sex. A male of the human species above the age of puberty.

In its most extended sense the term includes not only the adult male sex of the human species, but women and children.

In feudal law, a vassal; a tenant or feudatory. The Anglo-Saxon relation of *lord and man* was originally purely personal, and founded on mutual contract. 1 Spence, Ch. 37.

MAN OF STRAW. See Men of Straw.

MANACLES. Chain for the hands; shackles.

MANAGE. To control and direct, to administer, to take charge of. Fluet v. McCabe (1938), 299 Mass. 173, 12 N.E.2d 89, 93. To conduct; to carry on the concerns of a business or establishment. Generally applied to affairs that are somewhat complicated and that involve skill and judgment. Com. v. Johnson, 144 Pa. 377, 22 A. 703.

MANAGEMENT. Government, control, superintendence, physical or manual handling or guidance; act of managing by direction or regulation, or administration, as management of family, or of household, or of servants, or of great enterprises, or of great affairs. Branch v. Veterans' Administration, 189 Ark. 662, 74 S.W.2d 800, 804. Discretionary power of direction; J. T. Camp Transfer Co. v. Davenport, 15 Ala.App. 507, 74 So. 156, 159; Browne v. City of New York, 210 N.Y.S. 786, 795, 125 Misc. 1.

MANAGER. One who has charge of corporation and control of its business or branch establishment, and who is vested with a certain amount of discretion and independent judgment. Braniff v. McPherren, 177 Okl. 292, 58 P.2d 871, 872. A person chosen or appointed to manage, direct, or administer the affairs of another person or of a corporation or company. Com. v. Johnson, 144 Pa. 377, 22 A. 703. Also one of the persons appointed on the part of the house of representatives to prosecute impeachments before the senate.

MANAGERS OF A CONFERENCE. Members of the houses of parliament appointed to represent each house at a conference between the two houses. It is an ancient rule that the number of commons named for a conference should be double those of the lords. May, Parl.Pr. c. 16.

MANAGING AGENT. See Agent.

MANAGING OWNER OF SHIP. The managing owner of a ship is one of several co-owners, to whom the others, or those of them who join in the adventure, have delegated the management of the ship. He has authority to do all things usual and necessary in the management of the ship and the delivery of the cargo, to enable her to prosecute her voyage and earn freight, with the right to appoint an agent for the purpose. 6 Q.B.Div. 93; Sweet.

MANAGIUM. A mansion-house or dwelling-place. Cowell.

MANAS MEDIÆ. Men of a mean condition, or of the lowest degree.

MANBOTE. In Saxon law, a compensation or recompense for homicide, particularly due to the lord for killing his man or vassal, the amount of which was regulated by that of the *were*.

MANCA, MANCUS, or MANCUSA. A square piece of gold coin, commonly valued at thirty pence. Cowell.

MANCEPS. Lat. In Roman law, a purchaser; one who took the article sold in his hand; a formality observed in certain sales. Calvin. A farmer of the public taxes.

MANCHE-PRESENT. A bribe; a present from the donor's own hand.

MANCIPARE. Lat. In Roman law, to sell, alienate, or make over to another; to sell with certain formalities; to sell a person; one of the forms observed in the process of emancipation.

MANCIPATE. To enslave; to bind; to tie.

MANCIPATIO. Lat. In Roman law, a certain ceremony or formal process anciently required to be performed, to perfect the sale or conveyance of *res mancipi*, (land, houses, slaves, horses, or cattle.)

The parties were present, (vendor and vendee,) with five witnesses and a person called *"libripens,"* who held a balance or scales. A set form of words was repeated on either side, indicative of transfer of ownership, and certain prescribed gestures made, and the vendee then struck the scales with a piece of copper, thereby symbolizing the payment, or weighing out, of the stipulated price.

The ceremony of *mancipatio* was used, in later times, in one of the forms of making a will. The testator acted as vendor, and the heir (or *familiæ emptor*) as purchaser, the latter symbolically *buying* the whole estate or succession, of the former. The ceremony was also used by a father in making a fictitious sale of his son, which sale, when three times repeated, effectuated the emancipation of the son.

MANCIPI RES. Lat. In Roman law, certain classes of things which could not be aliened or transferred except by means of a certain formal ceremony of conveyance called *"mancipatio"* (*q. v.*). These included land, houses, slaves, horses, and cattle. All other things were called *"res nec mancipi."*

The distinction was abolished by Justinian. The distinction corresponded as nearly as may be to the early distinction of English law into real and personal property; *res mancipi* being objects of a military or agricultural character, and *res nec mancipi* being all other subjects of property. Like personal estate, *res nec mancipi* were not originally either valuable *in se* or valued. Brown.

MANCIPIUM. Lat. In Roman law, the momentary condition in which a *filius*, etc., might be when in course of emancipation from the *potestas*, and before that emancipation was absolutely complete. The condition was not like the *dominica potestas* over slaves, but slaves are frequently called *"mancipia"* in the non-legal Roman authors. Brown.

To form a clear conception of the true import of the word in the Roman jurisprudence, it is necessary to advert to the four distinct powers which were exercised by the *pater familias*, viz.: the *manus*, or martial power; the *mancipium*, resulting from the *mancipatio*, or *alienatio per æs et libram*, of a freeman; the *dominica potestas*, the power of the master over his slaves, and the *patria potestas*, the paternal power. When the *pater familias* sold his son, *venum dare, mancipare*, the paternal power was succeeded by the *mancipium*, or the power acquired by the purchaser over the person whom he held *in mancipio*, and whose condition was assimilated to that of a slave. What is most remarkable is, that on the emancipation from the *mancipium* he fell back into the paternal power, which was not entirely exhausted until he had been sold three times by the *pater familias*. *Si pater filium ter venum dat, filius a patre liber esto*. Gaius speaks of the *mancipatio* as *imaginaria quædam venditio*, because in his times it was only resorted to for the purpose of adoption or emancipation. See 1 Ortolan 112; Morey, Rom.L. 23, 32; Sohm, Inst.R.L. 124, 390.

MANCIPLE. A clerk of the kitchen, or caterer, especially in colleges. Cowell.

MANCOMUNAL. In Spanish law, an obligation is said to be *mancomunal* when one person assumes the contract or debt of another, and makes himself liable to pay or fulfill it. Schm.Civil Law, 120.

MANCUS. See Manca.

MANDAMIENTO. In Spanish law, commission; authority or power of attorney. A contract of good faith, by which one person commits to the gratuitous charge of another his affairs, and the latter accepts the charge. White, New Recop. b. 2, tit. 12, c. 1.

MANDAMUS. Lat. We command. This is the name of a writ (formerly a high prerogative writ) which issues from a court of superior jurisdiction, and is directed to a private or municipal corporation, or any of its officers, or to an executive, administrative or judicial officer, or to an inferior court, commanding the performance of a particular act therein specified, and belonging to his or their public, official, or ministerial duty, or directing the restoration of the complainant to rights or privileges of which he has been illegally deprived. Lahiff v. St. Joseph, etc., Soc., 76 Conn. 648, 57 A. 692, 65 L.R.A. 92, 100 Am.St.Rep. 1012.

The action of *mandamus* is one, brought in a court of competent jurisdiction, to obtain an order of such court commanding an inferior tribunal, board, corporation, or person to do or not to do an act the performance or omission of which the law enjoins as a duty resulting from an office, trust, or station. Where discretion is left to the inferior tribunal or person, the *mandamus*, can only compel it to act, but cannot control such discretion. Rev.Code Iowa, 1880, § 3373 (Code 1931, § 12440).

Writ of "mandamus" is summary writ issued from court of competent jurisdiction to command performance of specific duty which relator is entitled to have performed. People v. Nelson, 346 Ill. 247, 178 N.E. 485, 487.

It is legal, not equitable, remedy, and, when issued, is an inflexible peremptory command to do a particular thing. State ex rel. Onion v. Supreme Temple Pythian Sisters, 227 Mo.App. 557, 54 S.W.2d 468, 469.

The writ of *mandamus* is either *peremptory* or *alternative*, according as it requires the defendant absolutely to obey its behest, or gives him an opportunity to show cause to the contrary. It is the usual practice to issue the alternative writ first. This commands the defendant to do the particular act, or else to appear and show cause against it at a day named. If he neglects to obey the writ, and either makes default in his appearance or fails to show good cause against the application, the peremptory *mandamus* issues, which commands him absolutely and without qualification to do the act.

MANDANS. Lat. In the civil law, the employing party in a contract of mandate. One who gives a thing in charge to another; one who requires, requests, or employs another to do some act for him. Inst. 3, 27, 1, et seq.

MANDANT. In French and Scotch law, the employing party in the contract of *mandatum*, or mandate. Story, Bailm. § 138.

MANDATA LICITA RECIPIUNT STRICTAM INTERPRETATIONEM, SED ILLICITA LATAM EX EXTENSAM. Lawful commands receive a strict interpretation, but unlawful commands a broad and extended one. Bac.Max. reg. 16.

MANDATAIRE. Fr. In French law, a person employed by another to do some act for him; a mandatary.

MANDATARIUS TERMINOS SIBI POSITOS TRANSGREDI NON POTEST. A mandatary cannot exceed the limits assigned him. Jenk.Cent. 53.

MANDATARY. He to whom a mandate, charge, or commandment is given; also, he that obtains a benefice by *mandamus*. Briggs v. Spaulding, 11 S.Ct. 924, 141 U.S. 132, 35 L.Ed. 662.

MANDATE. A command, order, or direction, written or oral, which court is authorized to give and person is bound to obey. Silverman v. Seneca Realty Co., 276 N.Y.S. 466, 154 Misc. 35. A judicial command or precept proceeding from a court or judicial officer, directing the proper officer to enforce a judgment, sentence, or decree. Seaman v. Clarke, 69 N.Y.S. 1002, 60 App.Div. 416; Horton v. State, 63 Neb. 34, 88 N.W. 146.

A precept or order issued upon the decision of an appeal or writ of error, directing action to be taken, or disposition to be made of case, by inferior court. Egbert v. St. Louis & S. F. R. Co., 50 Okl. 623, 151 P. 228, 230.

In some of the state jurisdictions, the name "mandate" has been substituted for "*mandamus*" as the formal title of that writ. Chrisman v. Superior Court in and for Fresno County, 63 Cal. App. 477, 219 P. 85, 86; Davies v. Board of Com'rs of Nez Perce County, 26 Idaho, 450, 143 P. 945, 946.

A bailment of property in regard to which the bailee engages to do some act without reward. Story, Bailm. § 137; Maddock v. Riggs, 106 Kan. 808, 190 P. 12, 16, 12 A.L.R. 216.

Mandates and deposits closely resemble each other; the distinction being that in mandates the care and service are the principal, and the custody the accessory, while in deposits the custody is the principal thing, and the care and service are merely accessory. Story, Bailm. § 140.

A contract by which a lawful business is committed to the management of another, and by him undertaken to be performed gratuitously. The mandatary is bound to the exercise of slight diligence, and is responsible for gross neglect. Richardson v. Futrell, 42 Miss. 525; Williams v. Conger, 8 S.Ct. 933, 125 U.S. 397, 31 L.Ed. 778. A mandate, procuration, or letter of attorney is an act by which one person gives power to another to transact for him and in his name one or several affairs.

The mandate may take place in five different manners,—for the interest of the person granting it only; for the joint interest of both parties; for the interest of a third person; for the interest of a third person and that of the party granting it; and, finally, for the interest of the mandatary and a third person. Civ.Code La. arts. 2985, 2986.

The word may also denote a request or direction. Thus, a check is a *mandate* by the drawer to his banker to pay the amount to the transferee or holder of the check. 1 Q.B.Div. 33.

Civil Law. The instructions which the emperor addressed to a public functionary, and which were rules for his conduct. These mandates resembled those of the proconsuls, the *mandata jurisdictio*, and were ordinarily binding on the legates or lieutenants of the emperor in the imperial provinces and there they had the authority of the principal edicts. Sav.Dr.Rom. c. 3, § 24, no. 4.

MANDATO. In Spanish law, the contract of mandate. Escriche.

MANDATO, PANES DE. Loaves of bread given to the poor upon Maundy Thursday.

MANDATOR. The person employing another to perform a mandate.

MANDATORY, *adj.* Containing a command; preceptive; imperative; peremptory.

A "mandatory" provision in the statute is one the omission to follow which renders the proceedings to which it relates void, while a "directory" provision is one the observance of which is not necessary to validity of the proceeding. Siedschlag v. May, 363 Ill. 538, 2 N.E.2d 836, 838. So the mandatory part of a writ is that which commands the person to do the act specified. State v. Barnell, 109 Ohio St. 246, 142 N.E. 611, 613; Williams v. Sherwood, 51 N.D. 520, 200 N.W. 782, 784.

It is also said that when the provision of a statute is the essence of the thing required to be done, it is mandatory, Kavanaugh v. Fash, C.C.A.Okl., 74 F.2d 435, 437; otherwise, when it relates to form and manner; and where an act is incident, or after jurisdiction acquired, it is directory merely, Davis v. Smith, 58 N.H. 17.

"Mandatory" statutory provision is one which must be observed, as distinguished from "directory" provision, which leaves it optional with department or officer to which addressed to obey it or not. State ex rel. Dworken v. Court of Common Pleas of Cuyahoga County, 131 Ohio St. 23, 1 N.E.2d 138, 139.

MANDATORY, *n.* One to whom a mandate is given; one who undertakes without compensation to perform certain duties. Swords v. Simineo, 216 P. 806, 809, 68 Mont. 164; Smith v. State, 199 Ind. 217, 156 N.E. 513, 515.

MANDATORY INJUNCTION. See Injunction.

MANDATUM. Lat. In the civil law, the contract of mandate (*q. v.*).

MANDATUM NISI GRATUITUM NULLUM EST. Unless a mandate is gratuitous, it is not a mandate. Dig. 17. 1. 1. 4; Inst. 3, 27; 1 Bouv.Inst. n. 1070.

MANDAVI BALLIVO. (I have commanded or made my mandate to the bailiff.) In English practice, the return made by a sheriff, where the bailiff of a liberty has the execution of a writ, that he has commanded the bailiff to execute it. 1 Tidd, Pr. 309; 2 Tidd, Pr. 1025.

MANENTES. Tenants. Obsolete. Cowell.

MANERA. In Spanish law, manner or mode. Las Partidas, pt. 4, tit. 4, l. 2.

MANERIUM. In old English law, a manor.

MANERIUM DICITUR A MANENDO, SECUNDUM EXCELLENTIAM, SEDES MAGNA, FIXA, ET STABILIS. Co.Litt. 58. A manor is so called from *manendo,* according to its excellence, a seat, great, fixed, and firm.

MANGONARE. In old English law, to buy in a market.

MANGONELLUS. A warlike instrument for casting stones against the walls of a castle. Cowell.

MANIA A POTU. Insanity resulting as a secondary effect produced by excessive and protracted indulgence in intoxicating liquors in which the patient becomes a madman fully deprived of reason while the fit is upon him. State v. Wallace, 170 Or. 60, 131 P.2d 222, 233.

MANHOOD. In feudal law, a term denoting the ceremony of doing homage by the vassal to his lord. The formula used was, *"Devenio vester homo,"* I become your man. 2 Bl.Comm. 54.

To arrive at manhood means to arrive at twenty-one years of age. Felton v. Billups, 21 N.C. 585.

MANIA. See Insanity.

MANIFEST. Evident to the senses, especially to the sight, obvious to the understanding, evident to the mind, not obscure or hidden, and is synonymous with open, clear, visible, unmistakable, indubitable, indisputable, evident, and self-evident. London Guarantee & Accident Co. v. Coffeen, 96 Colo. 375, 42 P.2d 998, 1001.

In evidence, that which is clear and requires no proof; that which is notorious.

In maritime law. A sea-letter; a written document required to be carried by merchant vessels, containing an account of the cargo, with other particulars, for the facility of the customs officers. The Sylvia II, D.C.Mass., 28 F.2d 215, 216.

MANIFEST LAW. See Lex manifesta, *s. v.* Lex.

MANIFESTA PROBATIONE NON INDIGENT. 7 Coke, 40. Things manifest do not require proof.

MANIFESTO. A formal written declaration, promulgated by a prince, or by the executive authority of a state or nation, proclaiming its reasons and motives for declaring a war, or for any other important international action.

MANIPULUS. In canon law, a handkerchief, which the priest always had in his left hand. Blount.

MANKIND. The race or species of human beings. In law, females, as well as males, may be included under this term. Fortesc. 91.

MANNER. A way, mode, method of doing anything, or mode of proceeding in any case or situation. Ducre v. Milner, La.App., 146 So. 734, 736.

A word of large signification, but cannot exceed the subject to which it belongs. The incident cannot be extended beyond its principal. Wells v. Bain, 75 Pa. 39, 54, 15 Am. Rep. 563.

Also a thing stolen, in the hand of the thief; a corruption of *"mainour" (q. v.).*

MANNER AND FORM; MODO ET FORMA. Formal words introduced at the conclusion of a traverse.

Their object is to put the party whose pleading is traversed not only to the proof that the matter of fact denied is, in its general effect, true as alleged, but also that the manner and form in which the fact or facts are set forth are also capable of proof. Brown.

MANNING. A day's work of a man. Cowell. A summoning to court. Spelman.

MANNIRE. To cite any person to appear in court and stand in judgment there. It is different from *bannire;* for, though both of them are citations, this is by the adverse party, and that is by the judge. Du Cange.

MANNOPUS. In old English law, goods taken in the hands of an apprehended thief. The same as *"mainour,"* (*q. v.*).

MANNUS. A horse. Cowell.

MANOR. A house, dwelling, seat, or residence.

In English law, the manor was originally a tract of land granted out by the king to a lord or other great person, in fee. It was otherwise called a "barony" or "lordship," and appendant to it was the right to hold a court, called the "court-baron." The lands comprised in the manor were divided into *terræ tenementales* (tenemental lands or bocland) and *terræ dominicales,* or demesne lands. The former were given by the lord of the manor to his followers or retainers in freehold. The latter were such as he reserved for his own use; but of these part were held by tenants in copyhold, *i. e.,* those holding by a copy of the record in the lord's court; and part, under the name of the "lord's waste," served for public roads and commons of pasture for the lord and tenants. The tenants, considered in their relation to the court-baron and to each other, were called *"pares curiæ."* The word also signified the franchise of having a manor, with jurisdiction for a court-baron and the right to the rents and services of copyholders.

In American law, a manor is a tract held of a proprietor by a fee-farm rent in money or in kind, and descending to the oldest son of the proprietor, who in New York is called a "patroon." People v. Van Rensselaer, 9 N.Y. 291.

Reputed Manor. Whenever the demesne lands and the services become absolutely separated, the manor ceases to be a manor in reality, although it may (and usually does) continue to be a manor in reputation, and is then called a "reputed manor," and it is also sometimes called a "seigniory in gross." Brown.

MANORIAL EXTENT. A survey of a manor made by a jury of tenants, often of unfree men sworn to sit for the particulars of each tenancy, and containing the smallest details as to the nature of the service due. These manorial extents "were made in the interest of the lords, who were anxious that all due services should be done; but they imply that other and greater services are not due, that the customary tenants, even though they be unfree men, owe these services for their tenements, no less and no more. Statements that the tenants are not bound to do services of a particular kind are not very uncommon"; 1 Poll. & Maitl. 343. The "extents" of manors are descriptions which give the numbers and names of the tenants, the size of their holdings, the legal kind of their tenure and the kind and amount of their service; Maitland, Material for Hist. E. L. in 2 Sel.Essays in Anglo-Amer. Leg. Hist. 87.

MANQUELLER. In Saxon law, a murderer.

MANRENT. In Scotch law, the service of a man or vassal. A bond of manrent was an instrument by which a person, in order to secure the protection of some powerful lord, bound himself to such lord for the performance of certain services.

MANSE. In old English law, a habitation or dwelling, generally with land attached. Spelman.

A residence or dwelling-house for the parish priest; a parsonage or vicarage house. Cowell. Still used in Scotch law in this sense.

MANSER. A bastard. Cowell.

MANSIO. In Anglo-Saxon times the amount of land which would support a man and his family, called by various names: Mansio, familia, hide. 2 Holdsw. Hist.E.L. 54.

MANSION. A dwelling-house or place of residence, including its appurtenant outbuildings. 2 East, P.C. 492; Thompson v. People, 3 Parker, Cr. R. (N.Y.) 214; Armour v. State, 3 Humph. (Tenn.) 385.

In old English law, residence; dwelling.

MANSION-HOUSE. In the law of burglary, etc., any species of dwelling-house. 3 Inst. 64.

MANSLAUGHTER. The unlawful killing of another without malice, either express or implied; which may be either voluntarily, upon a sudden heat, or involuntarily, but in the commission of some unlawful act. 1 Hale, P.C. 466; 4 Bl.Comm. 191.

The unlawful killing of a human creature without any deliberation, which may be involuntary, in the commission of a lawful act without due caution and circumspection. Wallace v. U. S., 16 S. Ct. 859, 162 U.S. 466, 40 L.Ed. 1039; High v. State, 10 S.W. 238, 26 Tex.App. 545, 8 Am.St.Rep. 488; U. S. v. Lewis, C.C.Tex., 111 F. 632.

The distinction between "manslaughter" and "murder" consists in the following: In the former, though the act which occasions the death be unlawful or likely to be attended with bodily mischief, yet the malice, either express or implied, which is the very essence of murder, is presumed to be wanting in manslaughter. 1 East, P.C. 218; Comm. v. Webster, 5 Cush., Mass., 304, 52 Am.Dec. 711. No time for premeditation. 1 Hale, P.C. 437; 1 Russ. Crimes, 485; 1 Bish.Crim.Law, 678; People v. Crenshaw, 298 Ill. 412, 131 N.E. 576, 577, 15 A.L.R. 671.

There are various degrees of manslaughter recognized by different states, viz.: First degree: Roohano v. State, 167 Wis. 500, 167 N.W. 741, 742. Second degree: State v. Staples, 126 Minn. 396, 148 N.W. 283. Third degree: State v. Prince, 258 Mo. 315, 167 S.W. 535, 538. Fourth degree: State v. Schwenk, 101 Kan. 408, 167 P. 743, 744.

Voluntary manslaughter. Manslaughter committed voluntarily upon a sudden heat of the passions; as if, upon a sudden quarrel, two persons fight, and one of them kills the other. 4 Bl.Comm. 190, 191; State v. Disalvo, 121 A. 661, 663, 2 W.W. Harr. (Del.) 232; Wiley v. State, 19 Ariz. 346, 170 P. 869, 873, L.R.A.1918D, 373. It is the unlawful taking of human life under circumstances falling short of willful or deliberate intent to kill and approaching too near thereto to be justifiable homicide. State v. McVay, 47 R.I. 292, 132 A. 436, 438, 44 A.L.R. 572.

Involuntary manslaughter. It exists where a person in committing an unlawful act not felonious or tending to great bodily harm, or in committing a lawful act without proper caution or requisite skill, unguardedly or undesignedly kills another. State v. Disalvo, 2 W.W.Harr. (Del.) 232, 121 A. 661, 663; State v. McVay, 47 R.I. 292, 132 A. 436, 437, 44 A.L.R. 572.

The absence of intention to kill or to commit any unlawful act which might reasonably produce death or great bodily harm is the distinguishing feature between voluntary and involuntary homicide. State v. Weisengoff, 85 W.Va. 271, 101 S.E. 450, 455; State v. Pond, 125 Me. 453, 134 A. 572, 573.

MANSO, or MANSUM. In old English law, a mansion or house. Spelman.

MANSTEALING. A word sometimes used synonymously with "kidnapping," (*q. v.*).

MANSUETAE NATURA. Tamed and domesticated animals. Andrews v. Smith, 324 Pa. 455, 188 A. 146, 148.

MANSUETUS. Lat. Tame; as though accustomed to come to the hand. 2 Bl.Comm. 391.

MANSUM CAPITALE. The manor-house or lord's court. Paroch.Antiq. 150.

MANTEA. In old records, a long robe or mantle.

MANTHEOFF. In Saxon law, a horse-stealer.

MANTICULATE. To pick pockets.

MANTLE CHILDREN. See Pallio Cooperire.

MAN-TRAPS. Engines to catch trespassers, now unlawful unless set in a dwelling-house for defense between sunset and sunrise. 24 & 25 Vict. c. 100, § 31.

MANU BREVI. Lat. With a short hand. A term used in the civil law, signifying shortly; directly; by the shortest course; without circuity.

MANU FORTI. Lat. With strong hand. A term used in old writs of trespass. *Manu forti et cum multitudine gentium,* with strong hand and multitude of people. Reg.Orig. 183.

MANU LONGA. Lat. With a long hand. A term used in the civil law, signifying indirectly or circuitously. Calvin.

MANU OPERA. Lat. Cattle or implements of husbandry; also stolen goods taken from a thief caught in the fact. Cowell.

MANUAL. Of, or pertaining to, the hand or hands; done, made, or operated by or used with the hand or hands; or as manual labor. McErlain v. Taylor, 207 Ind. 240, 192 N.E. 260, 262, 94 A.L.R. 1284. Performed by the hand; used or employed by the hand; held in the hand.

MANUAL DELIVERY. Delivery of personal property sold, donated, mortgaged, etc., by passing it into the "hand" of the purchaser or transferee, that is, by an actual and corporeal change of possession.

MANUAL GIFT. The manual gift, that is, the giving of corporeal movable effects, accompanied by a real delivery, is not subject to any formality. Civil Code La. art. 1539.

MANUAL LABOR. Work done with the hand. State v. Ash, 53 Ariz. 197, 87 P.2d 270, 272. Labor performed by hand or by the exercise of physical force, with or without the aid of tools and of horses or other beasts of burden, but depending for its effectiveness chiefly upon personal muscular exertion rather than upon skill, intelligence or adroitness. Lew Jim v. U. S., C.C.A.Cal., 66 F. 954, 14 C.C.A. 281; Martin v. Wakefield, 42 Minn. 176, 43 N.W. 966, 6 L.R.A. 362.

MANUAL RATES. The Oklahoma Inspection Bureau is a private enterprise maintained by the insurance companies and its function is to compile the general basis schedule which sets out the rates for the risks insured. These rates are commonly referred to as "manual rates." Commercial Standard Ins. Co. v. Remer, C.C.A.Okl., 119 F. 2d 66, 67.

MANUALIA BENEFICIA. The daily distributions of meat and drink to the canons and other members of cathedral churches for their present subsistence. Cowell.

MANUALIS OBEDIENTIA. Sworn obedience or submission upon oath. Cowell.

MANUCAPTIO. In old English practice, a writ which lay for a man taken on suspicion of felony, and the like, who could not be admitted to bail by the sheriff, or others having power to let to mainprise. Fitzh.Nat.Brev. 249.

MANUCAPTORS. Same as mainpernors (*q. v.*).

MANUFACTORY. A physical plant, or a place or building where manufacturing is carried on. (Plant wherein electric power was generated.) Duke Power Co. v. Bell, 156 S.C. 299, 152 S.E. 865, 868. What in common understanding is known as a "factory." Halpin v. Insurance Co., 23 N.E. 989, 120 N.Y. 73, 8 L.R.A. 79; In re I. Rheinstrom & Sons Co., D.C.Ky., 207 F. 119, 134.

MANUFACTURE, *v.* From Latin words manus and factura, literally, put together by hand. Now it means the process of making products by hand or machinery. United States v. Anderson, D.C. Cal., 45 F.Supp. 943, 946.

The primary meaning of this word is "making with the hand," but this definition is too narrow for its present use. Meaning of word "manufacture," which is defined as the making of goods or wares by manual labor or by machinery, especially on a large scale, has expanded as workmanship and art have advanced, so that now nearly all artificial products of human industry, nearly all such materials as have acquired changed conditions or new and specific combinations, whether from the direct action of the human hand, from chemical processes devised and directed by human skill, or by the employment of machinery, are now commonly designated as "manufactured." Mayor and City Council of Baltimore v. Price, 168 Md. 174, 177 A. 160, 163.

Ordinarily does not include building or construction of outdoor structures. Morrison-Knudson Co. v. State Board of Equalization, 58 Wyo. 500, 135 P.2d 927, 931, 932.

MANUFACTURE, *n.* The process or operation of making wares or any material produced by hand, by machinery or by other agency; anything made from raw materials by the hand, by machinery, or by art. Jones Bros. Co. v. Underkoffler, D.C.Pa., 16 F.Supp. 729, 730. The production of articles for use from raw or prepared materials by giving such materials new forms, qualities, properties or combinations, whether by hand labor or machine. Cain's Coffee Co. v. City of Muskogee, 171 Okl. 635, 44 P.2d 50, 52.

In patent law, any useful product made directly by human labor, or by the aid of machinery directed and controlled by human power, and either from raw materials, or from materials worked up into a new form. Also the process by which such products are made or fashioned. Turner v. Quincy Market Cold Storage & Warehouse Co., C.C.A.Mass., 225 F. 41; International Mausoleum Co. v. Sievert, C.C.A.Ohio, 213 F. 225, 227; Riter-Conley Mfg. Co. v. Aiken, C.C.A.Pa., 203 F. 699, 702.

An instrument created by the exercise of mechanical forces and designed for the production of mechanical effects, but not capable, when set in motion, of attaining, by its own operation, to any predetermined results. It receives its rule of action from the external source which furnishes its motive power.

A manufacture requires the constant guidance and control of some separate intelligent agent; a machine operates under the direction of that intelligence with which it was endowed by its inventor when he imposed on it its structural law. The parts of a machine, considered separately from the machine itself, all kinds of tools and fabrics, and every other vendible substance, which is neither a complete machine nor produced by the mere union of ingredients, is included under the title "manufacture." Rob.Pat. § 182.

Domestic manufactures. Generally, manufactures within a state's jurisdiction. Com. v. Giltinan, 64 Pa. 100.

MANUFACTURER. One who by labor, art, or skill transforms raw material into some kind of a finished product or article of trade. Henry v. Markesan State Bank, C.C.A.Minn., 68 F.2d 554, 557.

MANUFACTURERS LIABILITY DOCTRINE. The foundation for the liability is knowledge of the danger attending use of manufactured or assembled product and negligence in failing to give appropriate warning, or negligence in failing to discover and appreciate the danger, and the probable consequences that injury will proximately result from the use of such product for the purposes for which it was intended. Crane Co. v. Davies, 242 Ala. 570, 8 So.2d 196, 199.

MANUFACTURING CORPORATION. A corporation engaged in the production of some article, thing, or object, by skill or labor, out of raw material, or from matter which has already been subjected to artificial forces, or to which something has been added to change its natural condition. People v. Knickerbocker Ice Co., 99 N.Y. 181, 1 N.E. 669. The term does not include a mining corporation. Byers v. Franklin Coal Co., 106 Mass. 135. But includes a corporation engaged in generation and distribution of electricity. Curry v. Alabama Power Co., 8 So.2d 521, 526, 243 Ala. 53.

MANUFACTURING ESTABLISHMENT. Any place where machinery is used for manufacturing purposes. Lilley v. Eberhardt, Mo., 37 S.W.2d 599, 601.

MANUMISSION. The act of liberating a slave from bondage and giving him freedom. In a wider sense, releasing or delivering one person from the power or control of another. See Fenwick v. Chapman, 9 Pet. 472, 9 L.Ed. 193; State v. Prall, 1 N.J.Law, 4.

MANUMITTERE IDEM EST QUOD EXTRA MANUM VEL POTESTATEM PONERE. Co.Litt. 137. To manumit is the same as to place beyond hand and power.

MANUNG, or MONUNG. In old English law, the district within the jurisdiction of a reeve, apparently so called from his power to exercise therein one of his chief functions, viz., to exact (*amanian*) all fines.

MANUPES. In old English law, a foot of full and legal measure.

MANUPRETIUM. Lat. In Roman law, the hire or wages of labor; compensation for labor or services performed. See Mackeld.Rom.Law, § 413.

MANURABLE. In old English law, capable of being had or held in hand; capable of manual occupation; capable of being cultivated; capable of being touched; tangible; corporeal. Hale, Anal. § 24.

MANURE. In old English law, to occupy; to use or cultivate; to have in manual occupation; to bestow manual labor upon. Cowell.

MANUS. Lat. A hand.

In the civil law, this word signified power, control, authority, the right of physical coercion, and was often used as synonymous with "*potestas.*"

In old English law, it signified an oath or the person taking an oath; a compurgator.

MANUS MORTUA. A dead hand; mortmain. Spelman.

MANUSCRIPT. A writing; a paper written with the hand; a writing that has not been printed. Parton v. Prang, 18 Fed.Cas. 1275; Leon Loan & Abstract Co. v. Equalization Board, 86 Iowa 127, 53 N.W. 94, 17 L.R.A. 199, 41 Am.St.Rep. 486.

MANUTENENTIA. The old writ of maintenance. Reg.Orig. 182.

MANWORTH. In old English law, the price or value of a man's life or head. Cowell.

MANY. The word "many" is defined as consisting of a great number, numerous, not few. Many is a word of very indefinite meaning, and, though it is defined to be numerous and multitudinous, it is also recognized as synonymous with "several", "sundry", "various" and "divers". Goslin v. Kurn, 351 Mo. 395, 173 S.W.2d 79, 87.

MANZIE. In old Scotch law, mayhem; mutilation of the body of a person. Skene.

MAP. A representation of the earth's surface, or of some portion of it, showing the relative position of the parts represented, usually on a flat surface. Webster. "A map is but a transcript of the region which it portrays, narrowed in compass so as to facilitate an understanding of the original." Banker v. Caldwell, 3 Minn. 103 (Gil. 55).

MAR. To make defective; to do serious injury to; to damage greatly; to impair, spoil, ruin; to do physical injury to, especially by cutting off or defacing a part; to mutilate; mangle, disfigure; deface. Maxwell v. City of Buhl, 236 P. 122, 123, 40 Idaho 644; Borden v. Hirsh, 249 Mass. 205, 143 N.E. 912, 914, 33 A.L.R. 526.

MARA. In old records, a mere or moor; a lake, pool, or pond; a bog or marsh that cannot be drained. Cowell; Blount; Spelman.

MARAJUANA PLANT. The plant scientifically known as cannabis indica or cannabis americana, though there possibly may be some slight and unimportant botanical difference between the two, but apparently none in its effect upon the human system. See Mariguana.

MARATHON. Modern meaning is any race or physical endurance contest. Sportatorium, Inc., v. State, Tex.Civ.App., 104 S.W.2d 912, 916.

MARAUDER. "A marauder is defined in the law to be 'one who, while employed in the army as a soldier, commits larceny or robbery in the neighborhood of the camp, or while wandering away from the army.' But in the modern and metaphorical sense of the word, as now sometimes used in common speech, it seems to be applied to a class of persons who are not a part of any regular army, and are not answerable to any military discipline, but who are mere lawless banditti, engaged in plundering, robbery, murder, and all conceivable crimes." Curry v. Collins, 37 Mo. 328.

MARC-BANCO. The name of a piece of money formerly coined at Hamburg. Its value was thirty-five cents.

MARCA. A mark; a coin of the value of 13s. 4d. Spelman.

MARCATUS. The rent of a mark by the year anciently reserved in leases, etc.

MARCH. In Scotch law, a boundary line or border. Bell. The word is also used in composition; as *march-dike, march-stone.*

MARCHANDISES AVARIEES. In French mercantile law. Damaged goods.

MARCHERS. In old English law, noblemen who lived on the marches of Wales or Scotland, and who, according to Camden, had their private laws, as if they had been petty kings; which were abolished by the statute 27 Hen. VIII. c. 26. Called also "lords marchers." Cowell.

MARCHES. An old English term for boundaries or frontiers, particularly the boundaries and limits between England and Wales, or between England and Scotland, or the borders of the dominions of the crown, or the boundaries of properties in Scotland. Mozley & Whitley.

MARCHES, COURT OF. An abolished tribunal in Wales, where pleas of debt or damages, not above the value of £50, were tried and determined. Cro.Car. 384.

MARCHETA.

In old Scotch law, a custom for the lord of a fee to lie the first night with the bride of his tenant. Abolished by Malcolm III. Spelman; 2 Bl. Comm. 83. A fine paid by the tenant for the remission of such right, originally a mark or half a mark of silver. Spelman.

In old English law, a fine paid for leave to marry, or to bestow a daughter in marriage. Cowell.

MARCHIONESS. A dignity in a woman answerable to that of marquis in a man, conferred either by creation or by marriage with a marquis. Wharton.

MARE. Lat. The sea.

MARE CLAUSUM. The sea closed; that is, not open or free. The title of Selden's great work, intended as an answer to the *Mare Liberum* of Grotius; in which he undertakes to prove the sea to be capable of private dominion. 1 Kent, Comm. 27.

MARE LIBERUM. The sea free. The title of a work written by Grotius against the Portuguese claim to an exclusive trade to the Indies, through the South Atlantic and Indian oceans; showing that the sea was not capable of private dominion. 1 Kent, Comm. 27.

MARESCALLUS. In old English law, a marshal; a master of the stables; an officer of the exchequer; a military officer of high rank, having powers and duties similar to those of a constable. Du Cange. See Marshal.

MARESCHAL. L. Fr. Marshal; a high officer of the royal household, Britt. fol. 1*b*.

MARETTUM. Marshy ground overflowed by the sea or great rivers. Co.Litt. 5.

MARGIN. The edge or border; the edge of a body of water where it meets the land. As applied to a boundary line of land, the "margin" of a river, creek, or other watercourse means the center of the stream. Varick v. Smith, 9 Paige, N.Y., 551. But in the case of a lake, bay, or natural pond, the "margin" means the line where land and water meet. Fowler v. Vreeland, 44 N.J.Eq. 268, 14 A. 116; Lembeck v. Andrews, 47 Ohio St. 336, 24 N.E. 686, 8 L.R.A. 578.

A sum of money, or its equivalent, placed in the hands of a stockbroker by the principal or person on whose account a purchase or sale is to be made, as a security to the former against losses to which he may be exposed by subsequent fluctuations in the market value of the stock. Sheehy v. Shinn, 103 Cal. 325, 37 P. 393; Memphis Brokerage Ass'n v. Cullen, 11 Lea, Tenn., 77.

MARGINAL NOTE. In Scotch law, a note inserted on the margin of a deed, embodying either some clause which was omitted in transcribing or some change in the agreement of the parties. Bell.

An abstract of a reported case, a summary of the facts, or brief statement of the principle decided, which is prefixed to the report of the case, sometimes in the margin, is also spoken of by this name.

MARGINAL STREET. Dock or wharf used in conjunction with and in furtherance of commerce and navigation. In re Triborough Bridge Approach, City of New York, 159 Misc. 617, 288 N.Y.S. 697, 711, 716.

MARGIN OF PROFIT. Difference between purchase price and selling price of merchandise. Kelley v. Baisch, 59 Idaho 798, 87 P.2d 468, 469.

MARIGUANA, MARIHUANA, MARIJUANA. "Mariguana" is an annual herb, cannabis sativa, having angular rough stem and deeply lobed leaves. The bast fibres of cannabis are the hemp of commerce. A drug prepared from "cannabis sativa," designated in technical dictionaries as "cannabis" and commonly known as marijuana, mariahuana, marajuana, maraguana, or marihuana, in Southern and Western states. State v. Navaro, 83 Utah 6, 26 P.2d 955; People v. Savage, 148 P.2d 654, 64 Cal.App.2d 314. For the history of cannabis, see Simpson v. State, 176 So. 515, 129 Fla. 127.

"Marihuana" is referred to by Brundage's Toxicology as a drug, the use of which results in a "sense of exhilaration; pleasurable intoxication; peculiar prolongation of time; sense of double consciousness followed by drowsiness; anæthesia; loss of power, particularly of the lower extremities; pupils dilated; pulse rapid; respiration slow; may cause increased sexual desires; catalepsy; sometimes convulsions." It is known most generally in the United States by the Mexican name, "Marihuana," because it was introduced into this country by Mexicans. State v. Navaro, 83 Utah 6, 26 P.2d 955.

"Marihuana" is the Mexican term for cannabis indica. The plant or drug known as cannabis indica, or marihuana, has as its parent the plant known as cannabis sativa. It is popularly known in India as cannabis indica; in America, as cannabis americana; in Mexico, as cannabis mexicana, or marihuana. It is all the same drug, and is known in different countries by different names. It is scientifically known as cannabis sativa, and is popularly called cannabis americana, cannabis indica, or cannabis mexicana, in accordance with the geographical origin of the particular plant. In the East, it is known as charras, as gunga, as hasheesh, as bhang, or siddi, and goes by a variety of names in the countries of Continental Europe. In America, particularly in the South and Southwestern portions of the United States, it is called marihuana. It is popularly known among the criminal element as "muggles," or "mooter," and addicts are commonly termed "muggle heads." State v. Navaro, 83 Utah 6, 26 P.2d 955.

MARINARIUS. An ancient word which signified a mariner or seaman. In England, *marinarius capitaneus* was the admiral or warden of the ports.

MARINE. Naval; relating or pertaining to the sea; transacted at sea; doing duty or service on the sea.

This is also a general name for the navy of a kingdom or state; as also the whole economy of naval affairs, or whatever respects the building, rigging, arming, equipping, navigating, and fighting ships. It comprehends also the government of naval armaments, and the state of all the persons employed therein, whether civil or military. Also one of the marines. Wharton. Doughten v. Vandever, 5 Del.Ch. 73.

MARINE BELT. That portion of the main or open sea, adjacent to the shores of a given country, over which the jurisdiction of its municipal laws and local authorities extends; defined by international law as extending out three miles from the shore. The Alexander, D.C.Alaska, 60 F. 918.

MARINE CARRIER. By statutes of several states this term is applied to carriers plying upon the ocean, arms of the sea, the Great Lakes, and other navigable waters within the jurisdiction of the United States. Civ.Code Cal. § 2087; Rev. Codes N.D.1899, § 4176, Comp.Laws 1913, § 6187.

MARINE CONTRACT. One relating to maritime affairs, shipping, navigation, marine insurance, affreightment, maritime loans, or other business to be done upon the sea or in connection with navigation.

MARINE CORPS. A body of soldiers enlisted and equipped for service on board vessels of war; also the naval forces of the nation. U. S. v. Dunn, 120 U.S. 249, 7 S.Ct. 507, 30 L.Ed. 667.

MARINE COURT IN THE CITY OF NEW YORK. Formerly, a local court of New York City, originally created as a tribunal for the settlement of causes betwen seamen. It was the predecessor of the present city court of the city of New York. 15 C.J. 1003. The history of this court may be found in McAdam, Mar.Ct.Pr., 2d Ed. 1872.

MARINE INSURANCE. See Insurance.

MARINE INTEREST. Interest, allowed to be stipulated for at an extraordinary rate, for the use and risk of money loaned on *respondentia* and bottomry bonds.

MARINE LEAGUE. A measure of distance commonly employed at sea, being equal to one-twentieth part of a degree of latitude, or three geographical or nautical miles. Rockland, etc., S. Co. v. Fessenden, 79 Me. 140, 8 A. 552.

MARINE RISK. The perils of the sea; the perils necessarily incident to navigation.

MARINE SOCIETY. In English law, a charitable institution for the purpose of apprenticing boys to the naval service, etc., incorporated by 12 Geo. III. c. 67.

MARINER. A seaman or sailor; one engaged in navigating vessels upon the sea; every person employed aboard ships or vessels. Pacific Mail S. S. Co. v. Schmidt, C.C.A.Cal., 214 F. 513, 518.

MARINES. A body of infantry soldiers, trained to serve on board of vessels of war when in commission and to fight in naval engagements. See Marine Corps.

MARIS ET FŒMINÆ CONJUNCTIO EST DE JURE NATURÆ. 7 Coke, 13. The connection of male and female is by the law of nature.

MARISCHAL. An officer in Scotland, who, with the lord high constable, possessed a supreme itinerant jurisdiction in all crimes committed within a certain space of the court, wherever it might happen to be. Wharton.

MARISCUS. A marshy or fenny ground. Co. Litt. 5*a*.

MARITAGIO AMISSO PER DEFALTAM. An obsolete writ for the tenant in frank-marriage to recover lands, etc., of which he was deforced.

MARITAGIUM. The portion which is given with a daughter in marriage. Also the power which the lord or guardian in chivalry had of disposing of his infant ward in matrimony.

MARITAGIUM EST AUT LIBERUM AUT SERVITIO OBLIGATUM; LIBERUM MARITAGIUM DICITUR UBI DONATOR VULT QUOD TERRA SIC DATA QUIETA SIT ET LIBERA AB OMNI SECULARI SERVITIO. Co.Litt. 21. A marriage portion is either free or bound to service; it is called "frank-marriage" when the giver wills that land thus given be exempt from all secular service.

MARITAGIUM HABERE. To have the free disposal of an heiress in marriage.

MARITAL. Relating to, or connected with, the *status* of marriage; pertaining to a husband; incident to a husband.

MARITAL COERCION. Coercion of the wife by the husband.

MARITAL FOURTH. A gift or bounty bestowed by law in favor of surviving spouse left in penurious circumstances. Maddox v. Butchee, 203 La. 299, 14 So.2d 4, 8.

MARITAL PORTION. In Louisiana, the name given to that part of a deceased husband's estate to which the widow is entitled. Abercrombie v. Caffray, 3 Mart.N.S., La., 1.

MARITAL RIGHTS AND DUTIES. Those arising from marriage contract and constituting its object, and therefore embracing what the parties agree to perform towards each other and to society. Alexander v. Alexander, 107 Conn. 101, 139

A. 685, 688. Rights of husband and wife to a specified share of other's personal estate upon death of other. In re Dean's Estate, 350 Mo. 494, 166 S.W.2d 529, 534, 535.

MARITIMA ANGLIÆ. In old English law, the emolument or revenue coming to the king from the sea, which the sheriffs anciently collected, but which was afterwards granted to the admiral. Spelman.

MARITIMA INCREMENTA. In old English law, marine increases. Lands gained from the sea. Hale, de Jure Mar. pt. 1, c. 4.

MARITIME. Pertaining to the sea or ocean or the navigation thereof; or to commerce conducted by navigation of the sea or (in America) of the great lakes and rivers.

It is nearly equivalent to "marine" in many connections and uses; in others, the two words are used as quite distinct.

MARITIME BELT. That part of the sea which, in contradistinction to the open sea, is under the sway of the riparian states. Louisiana v. Mississippi, 202 U.S. 1, 26 S.Ct. 408, 571, 50 L.Ed. 913.

MARITIME CAUSE. A cause of action originating on the high seas, or growing out of a maritime contract. 1 Kent, Comm. 367, *et seq.*

MARITIME CONTRACT. A contract relating to business of navigation. Massman Const. Co. v. Bassett, D.C.Mo., 30 F.Supp. 813, 815. A contract whose subject-matter has relation to the navigation of the seas or to trade or commerce to be conducted by navigation or to be done upon the sea or in ports. Edwards v. Elliott, 21 Wall. 553, 22 L.Ed. 487; Doolittle v. Knobeloch, D.C.S.C., 39 F. 40; Holt v. Cummings, 102 Pa. 215, 48 Am.Rep. 199; Rounds v. Cloverport Foundry & Machine Co., 159 Ky. 414, 167 S.W. 384, 387, Ann.Cas.1915D, 40.

MARITIME COURT. A court exercising jurisdiction in maritime causes; one which possesses the powers and jurisdiction of a court of admiralty.

MARITIME INTEREST. An expression equivalent to marine interest (*q. v.*).

MARITIME JURISDICTION. Jurisdiction in maritime causes; such jurisdiction as belongs to a court of admiralty on the instance side.

MARITIME LAW. The traditional body of rules, precepts, and practices known as the "maritime law". O'Donnell v. Great Lakes Dredge & Dock Co., 318 U.S. 36, 63 S.Ct. 488, 490, 87 L.Ed. 596. That system of law which particularly relates to commerce and navigation, to business transacted at sea or relating to navigation, to ships and shipping, to seamen, to the transportation of persons and property by sea, and to marine affairs generally. The law relating to harbors, ships, and seamen, divided into a variety of departments, such as those about harbors, property of ships, duties and rights of masters and seamen, contracts of affreightment, average, salvage, etc. Wharton; The Lottawanna, 21 Wall. 572, 22 L.Ed. 654; The Unadilla, D.C.Ill., 73 F. 351.

MARITIME LIEN. A privileged claim on a vessel for some service rendered to it to facilitate its use in navigation, or an injury caused by it in navigable waters, to be carried into effect by legal process in the admiralty court. The Westmoor, D.C.Or., 27 F.2d 886, 887.

It attaches to the vessel and freight, and is to be enforced by an action *in rem.* Paxson v. Cunningham, C.C.A.1, 63 F. 134, 11 C.C.A. 111.

The word "lien" is used in maritime law not in the strict legal sense in which we understand it in courts of common law, in which case there could be no lien where there was no possession, actual or constructive, but to express, as if by analogy, the nature of claims which neither presuppose nor originate in possession. 22 Eng.Law & Eq. 62. A distinction is sometimes made, however, between qualified maritime liens, which depend upon possession, and absolute maritime liens, which do not require nor depend upon possession. Cutler v. Rae, 7 How. 729, 12 L.Ed. 890; 21 Am.Law Reg. 1. A "maritime lien" is a special property right in a ship given to a creditor by law as security for a debt or claim subsisting from the moment the debt arises with right to have the ship sold and debt paid out of proceeds. The Poznan, C.C.A.N.Y., 9 F.2d 838, 842. Such a lien is a proprietary interest or right of property in the vessel itself, and not a cause of action or demand for personal judgment against the owner. The Theodore Roosevelt, D.C.Ohio, 291 F. 453, 461; The River Queen, D.C.Va., 8 F.2d 426, 427.

MARITIME LOAN. A contract or agreement by which one, who is the lender, lends to another, who is the borrower, a certain sum of money, upon condition that if the thing upon which the loan has been made should be lost by any peril of the sea, or *vis major,* the lender shall not be repaid unless what remains shall be equal to the sum borrowed; and if the thing arrive in safety, or in case it shall not have been injured but by its own defects or the fault of the master or mariners, the borrower shall be bound to return the sum borrowed, together with a certain sum agreed upon as the price of the hazard incurred. Emerig. Mar. Loans, c. 1, s. 2. The Draco, 7 Fed.Cas. 1,042.

MARITIME PROFIT. A term used by French writers to signify any profit derived from a maritime loan.

MARITIME SERVICE. In admiralty law, a service rendered upon the high seas or a navigable river, and which has some relation to commerce or navigation,—some connection with a vessel employed in trade, with her equipment, her preservation, or the preservation of her cargo or crew. Thackarey v. The Farmer, 23 F.Cas. 877; The Atlantic, D.C.S.C., 53 F. 609; Newham v. Chile Exploration Co., 133 N.E. 120, 232 N.Y. 37, 25 A.L.R. 1018.

MARITIME STATE, in English law, consists of the officers and mariners of the British navy, who are governed by express and permanent laws, or the articles of the navy, established by act of parliament.

MARITIME TORT. Civil wrongs committed on navigable waters. Berwind-White Coal Mining Co. v. City of New York, C.C.A.N.Y., 135 F.2d 443, 446. The term is never applied to a tort committed upon land, though relating to maritime matters. The Plymouth, 3 Wall. 33, 18 L.Ed. 125; Holmes v. Oregon & C. Ry. Co., D.C.Or., 5 F. 77; Butler v. Robins Dry Dock & Repair Co., 147 N.E. 235, 236, 240 N.Y. 23; Kuhlman v. W. & A. Fletcher Co., C.C.A.N.J., 20 F.2d 465, 466.

MARITUS. Lat. A husband; a married man. Calvin.

MARK. A character, usually in the form of a cross, made as a substitute for his signature by a person who cannot write, in executing a conveyance or other legal document.

It is commonly made as follows: A third person writes the name of the marksman, leaving a blank space between the Christian name and surname; in this space the latter traces the mark, or crossed lines, and above the mark is written "his," (or "her,") and below it, "mark."

The sign, writing, or ticket put upon manufactured goods to distinguish them from others, appearing thus in the compound, "trade-mark."

A token, evidence, or proof; as in the phrase "a mark of fraud."

A weight used in several parts of Europe, and for several commodities, especially gold and silver. When gold and silver are sold by the *mark*, it is divided into twenty-four carats.

A money of accounts in England, and in some other countries a coin. The English mark is two-thirds of a pound sterling, or 13s. 4d.; and the Scotch mark is of equal value in Scotch money of account. Enc.Amer.

The word is sometimes used as another form of "*marque*," a license of reprisals.

In early Teutonic and English law, a species of village community, being the lowest unit in the political system; one of the forms of the *gens* or clan, variously known as the "*mark*," "*gemeinde*," "*commune*," or "*parish*." Also the land held in common by such a community. The union of several such village communities and their *marks*, or common lands, forms the next higher political union, the hundred. Freem. Compar. Politics, 116, 117.

Demi-mark. Half a mark; a sum of money which was anciently required to be tendered in a writ of right, the effect of such tender being to put the demandant, in the first instance, upon proof of the seisin as stated in his count; that is, to prove that the seisin was in the king's reign there stated. Rosc. Real Act. 216.

High and low water-mark. See Water-Mark.

Mark banco. See Marc–Banco.

MARKEPENNY. A penny anciently paid at the town of Maldon by those who had gutters laid or made out of their houses into the streets. Wharton.

MARKET. Place of commercial activity in which articles are bought and sold. Zemel v. Commercial Warehouses, 132 N.J.L. 341, 40 A.2d 642, 643. The region in which any commodity can be sold; the geographical or economic extent of commercial demand. State v. Auclair, 110 Vt. 147, 4 A.2d 107, 116. A public time and appointed place of buying and selling; also purchase and sale. Caldwell v. Alton, 33 Ill. 419, 75 Am.Dec. 282; Strickland v. Pennsylvania R. Co., 154 Pa. 348, 26 A. 431, 21 L.R.A. 224; State v. Burkett, 119 Md. 609, 87 A. 514, 518, Ann.Cas.1914D, 345. It differs from the *forum*, or market of antiquity, which was a public market-place on one side only, or during one part of the day only, the other sides being occupied by temples, theaters, courts of justice, and other public buildings. Wharton.

The liberty, privilege, or franchise by which a town holds a market, which can only be by royal grant or immemorial usage. In re Certain Lands on North Shore of Harlem River in City of New York, 127 Misc.Rep. 710, 217 N.Y.S. 544, 557.

By the term "market" is also understood the demand there is for any particular article; as, "the cotton market in Europe is dull."

Clerk of the Market. See Clerk of the Market.

Public market. A market which is not only open to the resort of the general public as purchasers, but also available to all who wish to offer their wares for sale, stalls, stands, or places being allotted to those who apply, to the limits of the capacity of the market, on payment of fixed rents or fees. American Live Stock Commission Co. v. Chicago Live Stock Exchange, 143 Ill. 210, 32 N.E. 274, 18 L.R.A. 190; State v. Fernandez, 39 La.Ann. 538, 2 So. 233.

MARKET GELD. The toll of a market.

MARKET OVERT. In English law, an open and public market. The market-place or spot of ground set apart by custom for the sale of particular goods is, in the country, the only market *overt;* but in London every shop in which goods are exposed publicly to sale is market overt, for such things only as the owner professes to trade in. 2 Bl.Comm. 449; Godb. 131; 5 Coke, 83. Fawcett v. Osborn, 32 Ill. 426, 83 Am.Dec. 278.

MARKET PRICE. The price at which a seller is ready and willing to sell and a buyer ready and willing to buy in the ordinary course of trade. Bourjois, Inc., v. McGowan, D.C.N.Y., 12 F.Supp. 787, 790. The price actually given in current market dealings, and actual price at which given commodity is currently sold, or has recently been sold in open market, that is, not at forced sale, but in the usual and ordinary course of trade and competition between sellers and buyers equally free to bargain, as established by records of late sales. Wall v. United Gas Public Service Co., 178 La. 908, 152 So. 561, 563.

The actual price at which the given commodity is currently sold, or has recently been sold, in the open market, that is, not at a forced sale, but in the usual and ordinary course of trade and competition, between sellers and buyers equally free to bargain, as established by records of late sales. Lovejoy v. Michels, 88 Mich. 15, 49 N.W. 901, 13 L.R.A. 770; Sanford v. Peck, 63 Conn. 486, 27 A. 1057; McGarry v. Superior Portland Cement Co.,

95 Wash. 412, 163 P. 928, 929, Ann.Cas.1918A, 572. The term also means, when price at the place of exportation is in view, the price at which articles are sold and purchased, clear of every charge but such as is laid upon it at the time of sale. Goodwin v. United States, 2 Wash.C.C. 493, F.Cas.No.5,554.

For "Fair Market Price," see that title.

MARKET TOWNS. Those towns which are entitled to hold markets. 1 Steph.Comm., 7th Ed., 130.

MARKET VALUE. The price property would command in the market. State Highway Board v. Bridges, 60 Ga.App. 240, 3 S.E.2d 907, 910.

For "Fair and Reasonable Market Value" and "Fair Cash Market Value", see those titles.

The market value of an article or piece of property is the price which it might be expected to bring if offered for sale in a fair market; not the price which might be obtained on a sale at public auction or a sale forced by the necessities of the owner, but such a price as would be fixed by negotiation and mutual agreement, after ample time to find a purchaser, as between a vendor who is willing (but not compelled) to sell and a purchaser who desires to buy but is not compelled to take the particular article or piece of property. Winnipiseogee Lake, etc., Co. v. Gilford, 67 N.H. 514, 35 A. 945; Muser v. Magone, 155 U.S. 240, 15 S.Ct. 77, 39 L.Ed. 135; Little Rock Junction Ry. v. Woodruff, 49 Ark. 381, 5 S.W. 792, 4 Am.St.Rep. 51; William H. Lowe Estate Co. v. Lederer Realty Corporation, 35 R.I. 352, 86 A. 881, 883, Ann.Cas.1916A, 341.

Same meaning as "reasonable market value," or "fair market value." Sanders v. Pinney, 103 Wash. 162, 174 P. 471, 472; Hubbell v. City of Des Moines, 166 Iowa 581, 147 N.W. 908, 910, Ann.Cas.1916E, 592.

MARKET ZELD. Properly *market geld.* In old records. The toll of a market. Cowell.

MARKETABLE. Such things as may be sold in the market; those for which a buyer may be found; merchantable. Hinton v. Martin, 151 Ark. 343, 236 S.W. 267, 268; Pryor v. Fruit Distributors' Service Co., 73 Cal.App. 467, 238 P. 825, 827.

MARKETABLE TITLE. A "marketable title" to land is such a title as a court of equity, when asked to decree specific performance of the contract of sale, will compel the vendee to accept as sufficient. It is said to be not merely a defensible title, but a title which is free from plausible or reasonable objections. Austin v. Barnum, 52 Minn. 136, 53 N.W. 1132; Brokaw v. Duffy, 165 N.Y. 391, 59 N.E. 196; Wilson v. Korte, 91 Wash. 30, 157 P. 47, 48.

Such a title as is free from reasonable doubt in law and in fact; not merely a title valid in fact, but one which readily can be sold or mortgaged to a reasonably prudent purchaser or mortgagee; one acceptable to a reasonable purchaser, informed as to the facts and their legal meaning, willing to perform his contract, in the exercise of that prudence which business men usually bring to bear on such transactions; one under which a purchaser may have quiet and peaceful enjoyment of the property; one that is free from material defects, or grave doubts, and reasonably free from litigation. Myrick v. Austin, 141 Kan. 778, 44 P.2d 266, 268.

MARKSMAN. In practice and conveyancing. One who makes his mark; a person who cannot write, and only makes his mark in executing instruments. Arch.N.Pr. 13; 2 Chit. 92.

MARKUSH DOCTRINE. The doctrine permits an applicant for a patent where there is no known subgeneric term which would include elements which applicant found useful and exclude those which are not, to employ a generic term limited to the elements found to be operative and recognizes as unobjectionable as to form, claims containing a coined subgeneric expression. In re Swenson, C.C.P.A., 132 F.2d 336.

MARLBRIDGE, STATUTE OF. An English statute enacted in 1267 (52 Hen. III.) at Marlbridge, (now called "Marlborough,") where parliament was then sitting. It related to land tenures, and to procedure, and to unlawful and excessive distresses.

MARQUE AND REPRISAL, LETTERS OF. These words, "marque" and "reprisal," are frequently used as synonymous, but, taken in their strict etymological sense, the latter signifies a "taking in return;" the former, the passing the frontiers (*marches*) in order to such taking. Letters of marque and reprisal are grantable, by the law of nations, whenever the subjects of one state are oppressed and injured by those of another, and justice is denied by that state to which the oppressor belongs; and the party to whom these letters are granted may then seize the bodies or the goods of the subjects of the state to which the offender belongs, until satisfaction be made, wherever they happen to be found. Reprisals are to be granted only in case of a clear and open denial of justice. At the present day, in consequence partly of treaties and partly of the practice of nations, the making of reprisals is confined to the seizure of commercial property on the high seas by public cruisers, or by private cruisers specially authorized thereto. Brown.

MARQUE, LAW OF. A sort of law of reprisal, which entitles him who has received any wrong from another and cannot get ordinary justice to take the shipping or goods of the wrong-doer, where he can find them within his own bounds or precincts, in satisfaction of the wrong. Cowell; Brown.

MARQUIS, or MARQUESS. In English law, one of the second order of nobility; next in order to a duke.

MARQUISATE. The seigniory of a marquis.

MARRIAGE. Marriage, as distinguished from the agreement to marry and from the act of becoming married, is the civil status, condition, or relation of one man and one woman united in law for life, for the discharge to each other and the community of the duties legally incumbent on those whose association is founded on the distinction of sex. 1 Bish.Mar. & Div. § 3; Collins v. Hoag & Rollins, 121 Neb. 716, 238 N.W. 351, 355; Allen v. Allen, 73 Conn. 54, 46 A. 242, 49 L.R.A. 142.

A contract, according to the form prescribed by law, by which a man and woman, capable of entering into such contract, mutually engage with each other to live their whole lives together in the state of union which ought to exist between a husband and wife. Shelf. Mar. & Div. 1; Seuss v. Schukat, 358 Ill. 27, 192 N.E. 668, 671, 95 A.L.R. 1461.

The word also signifies the act, ceremony, or formal proceeding by which persons take each other for husband and wife. Davis v. Davis, 119 Conn. 194, 175 A. 574, 575.

In old English law, marriage is used in the sense of "*maritagium*," (*q. v.*,) or the feudal right enjoyed by the lord or guardian in chivalry of disposing of his ward in marriage.

Avail of marriage. See that title.

Consensual marriage. See that title.

Common-law marriage. See Common Law.

Fleet marriages. There were in the neighborhood of the Fleet prison about sixty marriage houses, some of which were public houses and others not. They were known by having a sign-board, with joined hands, in addition to the public house sign. At the doors of these houses persons called Pliers solicited the passers-by to come in and be married, and in these houses persons who were, or pretended to be, clergymen performed the marriage ceremony and made entries in registers that were kept at the respective houses. There is little doubt that many entries had false dates, that persons who were married personated others, and that women who wished to plead a plea of coverture or hide their shame were married to men who, for a trifling gratuity, married any woman who would pay them, though they had previously married others. Such marriages also took place in the neighborhood of the King's Bench prison, at the Savoy, in the Mint, in the Borough, and at the Mayfair Chapel.

It is said in 1 Peake N.P.C. 303, that a marriage in the Fleet was considered *at that time* good and legal. In 8 Carr. & P. 581 (34 E.C.L.R.), Patteson, J., said: "I shall not receive the Fleet Registry in evidence for any purpose whatever." They were refused in 1 Peake N.P.C. 303. A collection of over a thousand Fleet registers have been deposited in the Registry of the Bishop of London.

See Extracts from these registers and a historical note in 34 E.C.L.R. 534; Burns, Fleet Registers.

Jactitation of marriage. See Jactitation.

Manus marriage. A form of marriage in early Rome; it formed a relation called *manus* (hand) and brought the wife into the husband's power, placing her as to legal rights in the position of a daughter. Bryce, Marr. & Divorce, in 3 Sel. Essays in Anglo-Amer.L.H. 787.

Mixed marriage. A marriage between persons of different nationalities; or, more particularly, between persons of different racial origin; as between a white person and a negro or an Indian.

Morganatic marriage. The lawful and inseparable conjunction of a man, of noble or illustrious birth, with a woman of inferior station, upon condition that neither the wife nor her children shall partake of the titles, arms, or dignity of the husband, or succeed to his inheritance, but be contented with a certain allowed rank assigned to them by the morganatic contract. But since these restrictions relate only to the rank of the parties and succession to property, without affecting the nature of a matrimonial engagement, it must be considered as a just marriage. The marriage ceremony was regularly performed; the union was indissoluble; the children legitimate. Wharton.

Plural marriage. In general, any bigamous or polygamous union, but particularly, a second or subsequent marriage of a man who already has one wife living under system of polygamy. See Freil v. Wood, 1 Utah 165.

Scotch marriage. A marriage contracted without any formal solemnization or religious ceremony, by the mere mutual agreement of the parties *per verba de præsenti* in the presence of witnesses, recognized as valid by the Scottish law.

MARRIAGE ACT, ROYAL. An act of 12 Geo. III, c. 1 (1772), by which members of the royal family are forbidden to marry without the king's consent, or except on certain onerous conditions.

MARRIAGE ARTICLES. Articles of agreement between parties contemplating marriage, intended as preliminary to a formal marriage settlement, to be drawn after marriage. Ath.Mar.Sett. 92.

MARRIAGE BROKERAGE. The act by which a third person, for a consideration, negotiates a marriage between a man and woman. The money paid for such services is also known by this name. Hellen v. Anderson, 83 Ill.App. 509; White v. Equitable Nuptial Ben. Union, 76 Ala. 251, 52 Am. Rep. 325.

MARRIAGE CEREMONY. The form, religious or civil, for the solemnization of a marriage.

MARRIAGE CERTIFICATE. An instrument which certifies a marriage, and is executed by the person officiating at the marriage; it is not intended to be signed by the parties. Spencer v. Spencer, 84 Misc.Rep. 264, 147 N.Y.S. 111, 113.

MARRIAGE CONSIDERATION. The consideration furnished by an intended marriage of two persons. It is the highest consideration known to the law.

MARRIAGE LICENSE. A license or permission granted by public authority to persons who intend to intermarry, usually addressed to the minister or magistrate who is to perform the ceremony, or, in general terms, to any one authorized to solemnize marriages. By statute in some jurisdictions, it is made an essential prerequisite to the lawful solemnization of the marriage.

MARRIAGE-NOTICE BOOK. A book kept, in England, by the registrar, in which applications for and issue of registrar's licenses to marry are recorded.

MARRIAGE PER VERBA DE PRAESENTI. To constitute such a marriage, there must be an agreement to become husband and wife immediately from the time when the mutual consent is given. Pitney v. Pitney, 151 Kan. 848, 101 P.2d 933, 935.

MARRIAGE PORTION. Dowry; a sum of money or other property which is given to or settled on a woman on her marriage. In re Croft, 162 Mass. 22, 37 N.E. 784.

MARRIAGE PROMISE. Betrothal; engagement to intermarry with another. Perry v. Orr, 35 N. J.L. 296.

MARRIAGE SETTLEMENT. A written agreement in the nature of a conveyance, called a "settlement," which is made in contemplation of a proposed marriage and in consideration thereof, either by the parties about to intermarry, or one of them, or by a parent or relation on their behalf, by which the title to certain property is settled, *i. e.*, fixed or limited to a prescribed course of succession; the object being, usually, to provide for the wife and children. Thus, the estate might be limited to the husband and issue, or to the wife and issue, or to husband and wife for their joint lives, remainder to the survivor for life, remainder over to the issue, or otherwise. Such settlements may also be made after marriage, in which case they are called "postnuptial."

MARRIED WOMAN. A woman who has a husband living and not divorced; a *feme covert*.

MARSHAL. In old English law, the title borne by several officers of state and of the law, of whom the most important were the following: (1) The earl-marshal, who presided in the court of chivalry; (2) the marshal of the king's house, or knight-marshal, whose special authority was in the king's palace, to hear causes between members of the household, and punish faults committed within the verge; (3) the marshal of the king's bench prison, who had the custody of that jail; (4) the marshal of the exchequer, who had the custody of the king's debtors; (5) the marshal of the judge of assize, whose duty was to swear in the grand jury.

In American law, an officer pertaining to the organization of the federal judicial system, whose duties are similar to those of a sheriff. He is to execute the process of the United States courts within the district for which he is appointed, etc.

Also, in some of the states, this is the name of an officer of police, in a city or borough, having powers and duties corresponding generally to those of a constable or sheriff.

MARSHAL OF THE QUEEN'S BENCH. An officer who had the custody of the queen's bench prison. The St. 5 & 6 Vict. c. 22, abolished this office, and substituted an officer called "keeper of the queen's prison."

MARSHALING. Arranging, ranking, or disposing in order; particularly, in the case of a group or series of conflicting claims or interests, arranging them in such an order of sequence, or so directing the manner of their satisfaction, as shall secure justice to all persons concerned and the largest possible measure of satisfaction to each. See sub-titles *infra*.

MARSHALING ASSETS. In equity, the arranging or ranking of assets in the due order of administration. Such an arrangement of the different funds under administration as shall enable all the parties having equities therein to receive their due proportions, notwithstanding any intervening interests, liens, or other claims of particular persons to prior satisfaction out of a portion of these funds. In re Van Zandt's Estate, 142 Misc. 663, 255 N.Y.S. 359, 366. The arrangement or ranking of assets in a certain order towards the payment of debts. 1 Story, Eq.Jur. § 558; 4 Kent, Comm. 421. The arrangement of assets or claims so as to secure the proper application of the assets to the various claims; especially when there are two classes of assets, and some creditors can enforce their claims against both, and others against only one, and the creditors of the former class are compelled to exhaust the assets against which they alone have a claim before having recourse to other assets, thus providing for the settlement of as many claims as possible. Pub.St.Mass. p. 1292.

MARSHALING LIENS. The ranking or ordering of several estates or parcels of land, for the satisfaction of a judgment or mortgage to which they are all liable, though successively conveyed away by the debtor. The rule is that, where lands subject to the lien of a judgment or mortgage have been sold or incumbered by the owner at different times to different purchasers, the various tracts are liable to the satisfaction of the lien in the inverse order of their alienation or incumbrance, the land last sold being first chargeable. 1 Black, Judgm. § 440.

MARSHALING REMEDIES. The basis for "marshaling of remedies" is that where one creditor has security on two funds of common debtor and another creditor has security on only one of such funds, second creditor has right in equity to compel first creditor to resort to the other fund, if it is necessary for satisfaction of both creditors and will not prejudice rights or interests of party entitled to double fund, do injustice to debtor, or operate inequitably on other persons' interests. Greenwich Trust Co. v. Tyson, 129 Conn. 211, 27 A.2d 166, 174.

MARSHALING SECURITIES. An equitable practice, which consists in so ranking or arranging classes of creditors, with respect to the assets of the common debtor, as to provide for satisfaction of the greatest number of claims. The process is this: Where one class of creditors have liens or securities on *two* funds, while another class of creditors can resort to only *one* of those funds, equity will compel the doubly-secured creditors to first exhaust that fund which will leave the single security of the other creditors intact. See 1 Story, Eq.Jur. § 633; Dilworth v. Federal Reserve Bank of St. Louis, 170 Miss. 373, 154 So. 535, 540, 92 A. L.R. 1076.

MARSHALSEA. In English law, a prison belonging to the king's bench. It has now been consolidated with others, under the name of the "King's Prison."

MARSHALSEA, COURT OF. In English law, the court or seat of the marshal. A court originally held before the steward and marshal of the king's house, instituted to administer justice between the king's domestic servants. It had jurisdiction of all trespasses committed within the verge of the king's court, where one of the parties was of the royal household; and of all debts and contracts, when both parties were of that establishment. It was abolished by 12 & 13 Vict. c. 101, § 13. Mozley & Whitley.

MART. A place of public traffic or sale.

MARTE SUO DECURRERE. Lat. To run by its own force. A term applied in the civil law to a suit when it ran its course to the end without any impediment. Calvin.

MARTIAL LAW. Exists when military authorities carry on government or exercise various degrees of control over civilians or civilian authorities in domestic territory. Ochikubo v. Bonesteel, D.C.Cal., 60 F.Supp. 916, 928, 929, 930. A system of law, obtaining only in time of actual war and growing out of the exigencies thereof, arbitrary in its character, and depending only on the will of the commander of an army, which is established and administered in a place or district of hostile territory held in belligerent possession, or, sometimes, in places occupied or pervaded by insurgents or mobs, and which suspends all existing civil laws, as well as the civil authority and the ordinary administration of justice. In re Ezeta, D. C.Cal., 62 F. 972; Com. v. Shortall, 206 Pa. 165, 55 A. 952, 65 L.R.A. 193. See, also, Military Law.

"Martial law, which is built upon no settled principles, but is entirely arbitrary in its decisions, is in truth and reality no law, but something indulged rather than allowed as a law. The necessity of order and discipline in an army is the only thing which can give it countenance, and therefore it ought not to be permitted in time of peace, when the king's courts are open for all persons to receive justice according to the laws of the land." 1 Bl. Comm. 413.

Martial law is neither more nor less than the will of the general who commands the army. It overrides and suppresses all existing civil laws, civil officers, and civil authorities, by the arbitrary exercise of military power; and every citizen or subject—in other words, the entire population of the country, within the confines of its power—is subjected to the mere will or caprice of the commander. He holds the lives, liberty, and property of all in the palm of his hand. Martial law is regulated by no known or established system or code of laws, as it is over and above all of them. The commander is the legislator, judge, and executioner. In re Egan, 5 Blatchf. 321, F.Cas. No.4,303.

MARTINMAS. The feast of St. Martin of Tours, on the 11th of November; sometimes corrupted into "Martilmas" or "Martlemas." It is the third of the four cross quarter-days of the year. Wharton.

MARUS. In old Scotch law, a maire; an officer or executor of summons. Otherwise called "*prœco regis.*" Skene.

MASAGIUM. L. Lat. A messuage.

MASH. "Mash" means crushed malt, meal, rye, and the like steeped and mixed in hot water to form wort; a mixture of grain, meal, or the like, and hot water fed to animals; to subject crushed malt to action of hot water by heating and stirring to prepare extract known as wort; to convert into a mass; to reduce to soft pulpy state by heating or pressure; to bruise; to crush. Whisnant v. State, 39 Okl.Cr. 214, 264 P. 837, 839.

MASHGIACH. A qualified supervisor designated by rabbinical authority to supervise the receipt and handling of kosher meat. People on Complaint of Waller v. Jacob Branfman & Son, 147 Misc. 290, 263 N.Y.S. 629.

MASOCHISM. [From Leopold von Sacher-Masoch, a nineteenth-century Austrian novelist and historian.] A form of perversion in which sexual pleasure is heightened when one is beaten and maltreated at the hands of the other party; the opposite of sadism. Stedman's Med.Dict. (11th Ed.1930). Sexual perversion, in which a member of one sex takes delight in being dominated, even to the extent of violence or cruelty, by one of the other sex. Dunglison's Med.Dict. (1893), quoted in Murray's (Oxford) New English Dict.

MASON AND DIXON'S LINE. The boundary line between Pennsylvania on the north and Maryland on the south, celebrated before the extinction of slavery as the line of demarcation between the slave and the free states. It was run by Charles Mason and Jeremiah Dixon, commissioners in a dispute between the Penn Proprietors and Lord Baltimore. The line was carried 244 miles from the Delaware river where it was stopped by Indians. A resurvey was made in 1849, and in 1900 a new survey was authorized by the two states.

MASS PICKETING. The use of a large number of pickets. Lilly Dache, Inc., v. Rose, Sup., 28 N.Y.S.2d 303, 305.

MASS STRIKE. The striking or ceasing to work by concerted action of all working classes, thus paralyzing and bringing to an end government and its functions. People v. Gitlow, 234 N.Y. 132, 136 N.E. 317, 320.

MASSA. In civil law, a mass; an unwrought substance, such as gold or silver, before it is wrought into cups or other articles. Dig. 47, 2, 52, 14; Fleta, lib. 2, c. 60, §§ 17, 22.

MASSACHISM. See Masochism.

MASSACHUSETTS RULE. As regards sending out checks through banks for collection, the "Massachusetts rule" is that each bank that receives the item acts as an agent for the depositor; but in some other states, the "New York rule" prevails, under which only the bank first receiving the item is responsible to, or is the agent of, the depositor, the other banks being the agent of the bank, in the process of the collection. People's Gin Co. v. Canal Bank & Trust Co., 168 Miss. 630, 144 So. 858, 860.

MASSACHUSETTS TRUST. A business organization wherein property is conveyed to trustees and managed for benefit of holders of certificates like corporate stock certificates. Enochs & Flowers v. Roell, 170 Miss. 44, 154 So. 299.

MASSES. Religious ceremonials or observances of the Roman Catholic Church.

MAST. To fatten with mast (acorns, etc.). 1 Leon. 186.

MAST-SELLING. In old English law, the practice of selling the goods of dead seamen at the mast. Held void. 7 Mod. 141.

MASTER. A principal who employs another to perform service in his affairs and who controls or has right to control physical conduct of other in performance of the service. King v. Ransburg, 111 Ind.App. 523, 39 N.E.2d 822, 829.

One having authority; one who rules, directs, instructs, or superintends; a head or chief; an instructor; an employer. Applied to several judicial officers. See *infra.*

In Scotland, the title of the eldest son of a viscount or baron. Cent. Dict.

Special master. A master in chancery appointed to act as the representative of the court in some particular act or transaction, as, to make a sale of property under a decree. Guaranty Trust, etc., Co. v. Delta & Pine Land Co., C.C.A.Miss., 104 F. 5, 43 C.C.A. 396; Pewabic Min. Co. v. Mason, 145 U.S. 349, 12 S.Ct. 887, 36 L.Ed. 732.

Taxing masters. Officers of the English supreme court, who examine and allow or disallow items in bills of costs.

MASTER AND SERVANT. The relation of master and servant exists where one person, for pay or other valuable consideration, enters into the service of another and devotes to him his personal labor for an agreed period. Sweet.

It usually contemplates employer's right to prescribe end and direct means and methods of doing work. Holleman v. Taylor, 200 N.C. 618, 158 S.E. 88, 89.

MASTER AT COMMON LAW. The title of officers of the English superior courts of common law appointed to record the proceedings of the court to which they belong; to superintend the issue of writs and the formal proceedings in an action; to receive and account for the fees charged on legal proceedings, and moneys paid into court. There are five to each court. They are appointed under St. 7 Wm. IV. and 1 Vict. c. 30, passed in 1837. Mozley & Whitley.

MASTER IN CHANCERY. An officer of a court of chancery who acts as an assistant to the judge or chancellor. His office is to inquire into such matters as may be referred to him by the court, examine causes, take testimony, take accounts, compute damages, etc., reporting his findings to the court in such shape that a decree may be made; also to take oaths and affidavits and acknowledgments of deeds. In modern practice, many of the functions of a master are performed by clerks, commissioners, auditors, and referees, and in some jurisdictions the office has been superseded. Kimberly v. Arms, 129 U.S. 512, 9 S.Ct. 355, 32 L.Ed. 764; Schuchardt v. People, 99 Ill. 501, 39 Am.Rep. 34.

MASTER IN LUNACY. In English law, the masters in lunacy are judicial officers appointed by the lord chancellor for the purpose of conducting inquiries into the state of mind of persons alleged to be lunatics. Such inquiries usually take place before a jury. 2 Steph.Comm. 511–513.

MASTER OF A SHIP. In maritime law, the commander of a merchant vessel, who has the chief charge of her government and navigation and the command of the crew, as well as the general care and control of the vessel and cargo, as the representative and confidential agent of the owner. He is commonly called the "captain." Martin v. Farnsworth, 33 N.Y.Super.Ct. 260; Hubbell v. Denison, 20 Wend., N.Y., 181.

MASTER OF THE CROWN OFFICE. The king's coroner and attorney in the criminal department of the court of king's bench, who prosecutes at the relation of some private person or common informer, the crown being the nominal prosecutor. St. 6 & 7 Vict. c. 20; Wharton.

MASTER OF THE FACULTIES. In English law, an officer under the archbishop, who grants licenses and dispensations, etc.

MASTER OF THE HORSE. In English law, the third great officer of the royal household, being next to the lord steward and lord chamberlain. He has the privilege of making use of any horses, footmen, or pages belonging to the royal stables.

MASTER OF THE MINT. In English law, an officer who receives bullion for coinage, and pays for it, and superintends everything belonging to the mint. He is usually called the "warden of the mint." It is provided by St. 33 Vict. c. 10, § 14, that the chancellor of the exchequer for the time being shall be the master of the mint.

MASTER OF THE ORDNANCE. In English law, a great officer, to whose care all the royal ordnance and artillery were committed.

MASTER OF THE ROLLS. In English law, an assistant judge of the court of chancery, who holds a separate court ranking next to that of the lord chancellor, and has the keeping of the rolls and grants which pass the great seal, and the records of the chancery.

He was originally appointed only for the superintendence of the writs and records appertaining to the common-law department of the court, and is still properly the chief of the masters in chancery. 3 Steph.Comm. 417. Under the act constituting the supreme court of judicature, the master of the rolls becomes a judge of the high court of justice and *ex officio* a member of the court of appeal. The same act, however, provides for the abolition of this office, under certain conditions, when the next vacancy occurs. See 36 & 37 Vict. c. 66, §§ 5, 31, 32.

MASTERS OF THE SUPREME COURT. In English law, officials deriving their title from Jud. (Officers') Act 1879, and being, or filling the places of, the sixteen masters of the common-law courts, the queen's coroner and attorney, the master of the crown office, the two record and writ clerks, and the three associates. Wharton.

MASTER OF THE TEMPLE. The chief ecclesiastical functionary of the Temple Church.

MASTER'S REPORT. The formal report or statement made by a master in chancery of his decision on any question referred to him, or of any facts or action he has been directed to ascertain or take.

MASURA. In old records, a decayed house; a wall; the ruins of a building; a certain quantity of land about four oxgangs.

MATE. The officer second in command on a merchant vessel. Ely v. Peck, 7 Conn. 242; Millaudon v. Martin, 6 Rob., La., 539.

MATELOTAGE. In French law, the hire of a ship or boat.

Seamanship; seaman's wages, pay.

MATER-FAMILIAS. Lat. In civil law, the mother or mistress of a family. A chaste woman, married or single. Calvin.

MATERIA. Lat. In Civil law, materials; as distinguished from *species*, or the *form* given by labor and skill. Dig. 41, 1, 7, 7–12; Fleta lib. 3, c. 2, § 14.

Materials (wood) for building, as distinguished from *"lignum."* Dig. 32, 55, pr.

In English law, matter; substance; subject-matter. 3 Bl.Comm. 322.

MATERIAL. Important; more or less necessary; having influence or effect; going to the merits; having to do with matter, as distinguished from form.

Representation relating to matter which is so substantial and important as to influence party to whom made is "material." McGuire v. Gunn, 133 Kan. 422, 300 P. 654, 656. Any misrepresentation bringing about issuance of policy on reduced premium rate is "material." Brooks Transp. Co. v. Merchants' Mut. Casualty Co., 6 W.W.Harr. 40, 171 A. 207.

MATERIAL ALLEGATION. An allegation is said to be material when it forms a substantive part of the case presented by the pleading. A material allegation in a pleading is one essential to the claim or defense, and which could not be stricken from the pleading without leaving it insufficient. Lusk v. Perkins, 48 Ark. 247, 2 S.W. 847; Wheeler v. Hurley, 49 Nev. 70, 236 P. 559, 560. A material alteration in any written instrument is one which changes its tenor, or its legal meaning and effect; one which causes it to speak a language different in effect from that which it originally spoke. White v. Harris, 69 S.C. 65, 48 S.E. 41, 104 Am.St.Rep. 791; Foxworthy v. Colby, 64 Neb. 216, 89 N.W. 800, 62 L.R.A. 393.

MATERIAL ALTERATION. Alteration of instrument is "material" if legal effect thereof is changed notwithstanding triviality of change or whether it may be beneficial or detrimental to party to be charged on contract. Cook v. Parks, 46 Ga.App. 749, 169 S.E. 208, 210.

MATERIAL EVIDENCE. Such as is relevant and goes to the substantial matters in dispute, or has a legitimate and effective influence or bearing on the decision of the case. Porter v. Valentine, 18 Misc. 213, 41 N.Y.S. 507; Connecticut Fire Ins. Co. of Hartford, Conn., v. George, 52 Okl. 432, 153 P. 116, 119. "Materiality," with reference to evidence does not have the same signification as "relevancy." Pangburn v. State, Tex.Cr.App., 56 S.W. 72, 73.

MATERIAL FACT. (In contracts.) One which constitutes substantially the consideration of the contract, or without which it would not have been made. Lyons v. Stephens, 45 Ga. 143.

(In pleading and practice.) One which is essential to the case, defense, application, etc., and without which it could not be supported. Sandheger v. Hosey, 26 W.Va. 223; Davidson v. Hackett, 49 Wis. 186, 5 N.W. 459; Hansen v. Sandvik, 128 Wash. 60, 222 P. 205, 207.

One which tends to establish any of issues raised. Sherwood Bros. v. Yellow Cab Co. of Philadelphia, 283 Pa. 488, 129 A. 563, 564. The "material facts" of an issue of fact are such as are necessary to determine the issue. Woolman Const. Co. v. Sampson, 219 Mich. 125, 188 N.W. 420, 422.

(In insurance.) A fact which, if communicated to the agent or insurer, would induce him either to decline the insurance altogether, or not accept it unless a higher premium is paid. Berry v. Equitable Fire & Marine Ins. Co., Mo.App., 263 S.W. 884, 886; Franklin Life Ins. Co. v. Dossett, Tex.Civ.App., 265 S.W. 259, 262. One which necessarily has some bearing on the subject-matter. Wittels Loan & Mercantile Co. v. American Cent. Ins. Co., Mo. App., 273 S.W. 1084, 1086. A fact which increases the risk, or which, if disclosed, would have been a fair reason for demanding a higher premium; any fact the knowledge or ignorance of which would naturally influence the insurer in making or refusing the contract, or in estimating the degree and character of the risk, or in fixing the rate. Boggs v. Insurance Co., 30 Mo. 68; Clark v. Insurance Co., 40 N.H. 338, 77 Am.Dec. 721; Murphy v. Insurance Co., 205 Pa. 444, 55 A. 19; Penn Mut. L. Ins. Co. v. Mechanics' Sav. Bank, 19 C.C.A. 286, 72 F. 413, 38 L.R.A. 33.

MATERIALMAN. A person who has furnished materials used in the construction or repair of a building, structure, or vessel. Hihn-Hammond Lumber Co. v. Elsom, 171 Cal. 570, 154 P. 12, 13, Ann.Cas.1917C, 798; Royal Indemnity Co. v. Day & Maddock Co., 114 Ohio St. 58, 150 N.E. 426, 427, 44 A.L.R. 374.

MATERIALS. The substance or matter of which anything is made. Mutual Lumber Co. v. Sheppard, Tex.Civ.App., 173 S.W.2d 494, 498. Matter furnished for the erection of a house, ship, or other structure which enters into and becomes a part thereof. Moyer v. Pennsylvania Slate Co., 71 Pa. 293; Standard Oil Co. v. Detroit Fidelity & Surety Co., 24 Ohio App. 237, 157 N.E. 418, 420; Royal Indemnity Co. v. Day & Maddock Co., 114 Ohio St. 58, 150 N.E. 426, 427, 44 A.L.R. 374; Fay v. Bankers' Surety Co., 125 Minn. 211, 146 N.W. 359, 360, Ann.Cas.1915C, 688.

MATERNA MATERNIS. Lat. A maxim of the French law, signifying that property of a decedent acquired by him through his mother descends to the relations on the mother's side.

MATERNAL. That which belongs to, or comes from, the mother; as maternal authority, maternal relation, maternal estate, maternal line.

MATERNAL LINE. A line of descent or relationship between two persons which is traced through the mother of the younger.

MATERNAL PROPERTY. That which comes from the mother of the party, and other ascendants of the maternal stock. Dom.Liv.Prél. t. 3, s. 2, no. 12.

MATERNITY. The character, relation, state, or condition of a mother.

MATERTERA. Lat. In civil law, a maternal aunt; a mother's sister. Inst. 3, 6, 1; Bract. fol. 68*b*.

MATERTERA MAGNA. A great aunt; a grandmother's sister, (*aviæ soror.*) Dig. 38, 10, 10, 15.

MATERTERA MAJOR. A greater aunt; a great-grandmother's sister, (*proaviæ soror;*) a father's or mother's great-aunt, (*patris vel matris matertera magna.*) Dig. 38, 10, 10, 16.

MATERTERA MAXIMA. A greatest aunt; a great-great-grandmother's sister, (*abaviæ soror;*) a father's or mother's greater aunt, (*patris vel matris matertera major.*) Dig. 38, 10, 10, 17.

MATHEMATICAL EVIDENCE. Demonstrative evidence; such as establishes its conclusions with absolute necessity and certainty. It is used in contradistinction to *moral* evidence.

MATIMA. A godmother.

MATRICIDE. The murder of a mother; or one who has slain his mother.

MATRICULA. In civil and old English law, a register of the admission of officers and persons entered into any body or society, whereof a list was made. Hence those who are admitted to a college or university are said to be "matriculated." Also a kind of almshouse, which had revenues appropriated to it, and was usually built near the church, whence the name was given to the church itself. Wharton.

MATRICULATE. To enroll; to enter in a register; specifically, to enter or admit to membership in a body or society, particularly in a college or university, by enrolling the name in a register; to go through the process of admission to membership, as by examination and enrollment, in a society or college. State v. Regents of University System of Georgia, 179 Ga. 210, 175 S.E. 567.

MATRIMONIA DEBENT ESSE LIBERA. Marriages ought to be free. A maxim of the civil law. 2 Kent, Comm. 102.

MATRIMONIAL. Of or pertaining to matrimony or the estate of marriage.

MATRIMONIAL ACTION. An action seeking a determination of the marital status of the parties and brought or defended in an endeavor to sustain or prevent the destruction of such marital status. Kraunz v. Kraunz, 183 Misc. 724, 51 N.Y.S. 2d 433, 436.

MATRIMONIAL CAUSES. In English ecclesiastical law, causes of action or injuries respecting the rights of marriage. One of the three divisions of causes or injuries cognizable by the ecclesiastical courts, comprising suits for jactitation of marriage, and for restitution of conjugal rights, divorces, and suits for alimony. 3 Bl.Comm. 92–94; 3 Steph.Comm. 712–714.

MATRIMONIAL COHABITATION. The living together of a man and woman ostensibly as husband and wife. Cox v. State, 117 Ala. 103, 23 So. 806, 41 L.R.A. 760. Also the living together of those who are legally husband and wife, the term carrying with it, in this sense, an implication of mutual rights and duties as to sharing the same habitation. Forster v. Forster, 1 Hagg.Consist. 144; U. S. v. Cannon, 4 Utah, 122, 7 P. 369.

MATRIMONIAL DOMICILE. Place where parties live together as husband and wife either actually or constructively. Ex parte Allan, 220 Ala. 482, 125 So. 612, 614.

MATRIMONIAL RES. The marriage state. Usen v. Usen, 136 Me. 480, 13 A.2d 738, 749, 128 A.L.R. 1449.

MATRIMONIUM. Lat. In Roman law, a legal marriage, contracted in strict accordance with the forms of the older Roman law, *i. e.*, either with the *farreum*, the *coemptio*, or by *usus*.

This was allowed only to Roman citizens and to those neighboring peoples to whom the right of *connubium* had been conceded. The effect of such a marriage was to bring the wife into the *manus*, or marital power, of the husband, and to create the *patria potestas* over the children.

MATRIMONIUM SUBSEQUENS TOLLIT PECCATUM PRÆCEDENS. Subsequent marriage cures preceding criminality.

MATRIMONY. Marriage, (*q. v.*,) in the sense of the relation or *status*, not of the ceremony.

MATRIX. In civil law, the protocol or first draft of a legal instrument, from which all copies must be taken. Downing v. Diaz, 80 Tex. 436, 16 S.W. 53.

MATRIX ECCLESIA. Lat. A mother church. This term was anciently applied to a cathedral, in relation to the other churches in the same see, or to a parochial church, in relation to the chapels or minor churches attached to it or depending on it. Blount.

MATRON. A married woman; an elderly woman. The female superintendent of an establishment or institution, such as a hospital, an orphan asylum, etc., is often so called. Fisher v. Gardnier, 183 Mich. 660, 150 N.W. 358.

MATRONS, JURY OF. In common-law practice, a jury of twelve matrons or discreet women, impaneled upon a writ *de ventre inspiciendo*, or where a female prisoner, being under sentence of death, pleaded her pregnancy as a ground for staying execution. In the latter case, such jury inquired into the truth of the plea.

MATTER. Substantial facts forming basis of claim or defense; facts material to issue; substance as distinguished from form; transaction, event, occurrence; subject-matter of controversy; special proceeding. Parker v. Bowen, 98 Vt. 115, 126 A. 522, 523; Bishop v. Shurly, 237 Mich. 76, 211 N.W. 75, 78; Rubin v. Sheldon, 130 Misc. 588, 224 N.Y.S. 340, 341; People v. Anderson, 62 Cal.App. 222, 216 P. 401, 402; Franklin Buggy Co. v. Carter, 21 Ga.App. 576, 94 S.E. 820.

MATTER IN CONTROVERSY, or IN DISPUTE. Subject of litigation, matter on which action is brought and issue is joined and in relation to which, if issue be one of fact, testimony is taken. Golden v. Sixth Judicial Dist. Ct. in and for Pershing County, 57 Nev. 114, 58 P.2d 1042, 1044. Rights which plaintiffs assert and seek to have protected and enforced. Gavica v. Donaugh, C.C.A.Or., 93 F.2d 173, 175.

MATTER IN DEED. Such matter as may be proved or established by a deed or specialty. Matter of fact, in contradistinction to matter of law. Co.Litt. 320; Steph.Pl. 197.

MATTER IN ISSUE. That matter on which plaintiff proceeds by his action, and which defendant controverts by his pleadings. MacKenzie v. Union Guardian Trust Co., 262 Mich. 563, 247 N.W. 914. Not including facts offered in evidence to establish the matters in issue. King v. Chase, 15 N.H. 9, 41 Am.Dec. 675. That ultimate fact or state of facts in dispute upon which the verdict or finding is predicated. Clark v. Arizona Mut. Savings & Loan Ass'n, D.C.Ariz., 217 F. 640, 644. See 2 Black, Judgm. § 614, and cases cited.

MATTER IN LEY NE SERRA MISE IN BOUTCHE DEL JURORS. Jenk.Cent. 180. Matter of law shall not be put into the mouth of the jurors.

MATTER IN PAIS. Matter of fact that is not in writing; thus distinguished from matter in deed and matter of record; matter that must be proved by parol evidence.

MATTER OF COURSE. Anything done or taken in the course of routine or usual procedure, which is permissible and valid without being specially applied for and allowed.

MATTER OF FACT. That which is to be ascertained by the senses, or by the testimony of witnesses describing what they have perceived. Distinguished from matter of law and matter of opinion. Moses v. United States, C.C.A.Vt., 221 F. 863, 871.

MATTER OF FORM. See Form.

MATTER OF LAW. Whatever is to be ascertained or decided by the application of statutory rules or the principles and determinations of the law, as distinguished from the investigation of particular facts, is called "matter of law."

MATTER OF RECORD. Any judicial matter or proceeding entered on the records of a court, and to be proved by the production of such record. It differs from matter in deed, which consists of facts which may be proved by specialty.

MATTER OF RECORD, ESTOPPEL BY. See Record, Estoppel By.

MATTER OF SUBSTANCE. That which goes to the merits. The opposite of matter of form.

MATTERS OF SUBSISTENCE FOR MAN. This phrase comprehends all articles or things, whether animal or vegetable, living or dead, which are used for food, and whether they are consumed in the form in which they are bought from the producer or are only consumed after undergoing a process of preparation, which is greater or less, according to the character of the article. Sledd v. Com., 19 Grat., Va., 813.

MATURE; MATURED. A claim is "matured" for receivership purposes if it has become absolutely due without contingency, although not necessarily liquidated nor presently payable. In re L. P. Hollander Co., 301 Mass. 278, 16 N.E.2d 35, 36.

MATURIORA SUNT VOTA MULIERUM QUAM VIRORUM. 6 Coke, 71. The desires of women are more mature than those of men; *i. e.*, women arrive at maturity earlier than men.

MATURITY. Termination of period a note or other obligation has to run. Pacific States Savings & Loan Co. v. Hollywood Knickerbocker, 11 Cal.App.2d 56, 52 P.2d 1014, 1017. In mercantile law, the time when a bill of exchange or promissory note becomes due. Story, Bills, § 329. Gilbert v. Sprague, 88 Ill.App. 508; Wheeless v. Williams, 62 Miss. 371, 52 Am.Rep. 190.

MAUGRE. L. Fr. In spite of; against the will of. Litt. § 672.

MAUNDY THURSDAY. The day preceding Good Friday, on which princes gave alms.

See Mandato, Panes De.

MAXIM. "Maxims" are but attempted general statements of rules of law and are law only to extent of application in adjudicated cases. Swetland v. Curtiss Airports Corporation, D.C.Ohio, 41 F. 2d 929, 936. An established principle or proposition. A principle of law universally admitted, as being a correct statement of the law, or as agreeable to reason.

Coke defines a maxim to be "conclusion of reason," and says that it is so called "*quia maxima ejus dignitas et certissima auctoritas, et quod maxime omnibus probetur.*" Co.Litt. 11*a*. He says in another place: "A maxime is a proposition to be of all men confessed and granted without proofe, argument, or discourse." Id. 67*a*.

The maxims of the law, in Latin, French, and English, will be found distributed through this book in their proper alphabetical order.

MAXIME PACI SUNT CONTRARIA VIS ET INJURIA. The greatest enemies to peace are force and wrong. Co.Litt. 161*b*.

MAXIMUM. The highest or greatest amount, quality, value, or degree. Moweaqua Coal Corporation v. Industrial Commission, 360 Ill. 194, 195 N.E. 607.

MAXIMUS ERRORIS POPULUS MAGISTER. Bacon. The people is the greatest master of error.

MAY. An auxiliary verb qualifying the meaning of another verb by expressing ability, competency, liberty, permission, possibility, probability or contingency. U. S. v. Lexington Mill & E. Co., 232 U.S. 399, 34 S.Ct. 337, 340, 58 L.Ed. 658, L.R.A. 1915B, 774; Carson v. Turrish, 140 Minn. 445, 168 N.W. 349, 352, L.R.A.1918F, 154. Regardless of the instrument, however, whether constitution, statute, deed, contract or whatnot, courts not infrequently construe "may" as "shall" or "must" to the end that justice may not be the slave of grammar. Minor v. Mechanics' Bank, 1 Pet. 46, 64, 7 L.Ed. 47; Appeal of Burnap, 94 Conn. 286, 108 A. 802, 804; Stapler v. El Dora Oil Co., 27 Cal.App. 516, 150 P. 643, 645.

MAYHEM. Unlawfully and violently depriving another of the use of such of his members as may render him the less able in fighting, either to defend himself, or to annoy his adversary. 4 Bl.Comm. 205. State v. Deso, 110 Vt. 1, 1 A.2d 710, 714.

Every person who unlawfully and maliciously deprives a human being of a member of his body, or disables, disfigures, or renders it useless, or cuts or disables the tongue, or puts out an eye, or slits the nose, ear, or lip, is guilty of mayhem. Pen.Code Cal. § 203.

MAYHEMAVIT. Maimed. This was a term of art which could not be supplied in pleading by any other word, as *mutilavit, truncavit,* etc. 3 Thom. Co. Litt. 548; Com. v. Newell, 7 Mass. 247.

MAYN. L. Fr. A hand; handwriting. Britt. c. 28.

MAYNOVER. L. Fr. A work of the hand; a thing produced by manual labor. Yearb. M. 4 Edw. III. 38.

MAYOR. The executive head of a municipal corporation; the governor or chief magistrate of a city. Waldo v. Wallace, 12 Ind. 577; People v. New York, 25 Wend., N.Y., 36.

MAYOR'S COURT. A court established in some cities, in which the mayor sits with the powers of a police judge or committing magistrate in respect to offenses committed within the city, and sometimes with civil jurisdiction in small causes, or other special statutory powers.

MAYOR'S COURT OF LONDON. An inferior court having jurisdiction in civil cases where the whole cause of action arises within the city of London.

MAYORALTY. The office or dignity of a mayor.

MAYORAZGO. In Spanish law, the right to the enjoyment of certain aggregate property, left with the condition thereon imposed that they are to pass in their integrity, perpetually, successively to the eldest son. Schm. Civil Law, 62.

MAYORESS. The wife of a mayor.

MEAD. Ground somewhat watery, not plowed, but covered with grass and flowers. Enc. Lond.

MEADOW. A tract of low or level land producing grass which is mown for hay. Webster.

A tract which lies above the shore, and is overflowed by spring and extraordinary tides only, and yields grasses which are good for hay. Church v. Meeker, 34 Conn. 429. State v. Crook, 132 N.C. 1053, 44 S.E. 32.

MEAL-RENT. A rent formerly paid in meal.

MEAN, or MESNE. A middle between two extremes, whether applied to persons, things, or time.

Average, having an intermediate value between two extremes or between the several successive values of variable quantity during one cycle of variation. Western & Southern Life Ins. Co. v. Huwe, C.C.A.Ohio, 116 F.2d 1008, 1009.

MEAN LOW TIDE. The average of all low tides both low and lower low over a fixed period of time. State v. Edwards, 188 Wash. 467, 62 P.2d 1094, 1095.

As applied to Puget Sound, the "Harmonic plane" is the zero adopted by the United States Coast and Geodetic Survey of the Department of Commerce upon which its tidal tables, charts, and maps are based. It is an arbitrary plane, and is the lowest plane of the tide in the Sound recognized by that department, being approximately two feet lower than mean lower low tide, and approximately four feet lower than mean low tide. State v. Scott, 89 Wash. 63, 154 P. 165, 168.

MEAN LOWER LOW TIDE. The average of lower low tides over a fixed period of time. State v. Edwards, 188 Wash. 467, 62 P.2d 1094, 1095.

MEAN RESERVE. The mean of the reserve at the beginning of the policy year, after the premium for such year is paid, and the terminal reserve at end of such policy year. Kentucky Home Life Ins. Co. v. Leisman, 268 Ky. 825, 105 S.W.2d 1046, 1047.

MEANDER. To meander means to follow a winding or flexuous course; and when it is said, in a description of land, "thence with the meander of the river," it must mean a meandered line,—a line which follows the sinuosities of the river,—or, in other words, that the river is the boundary between the points indicated. Turner v. Parker, 14 Or. 341, 12 P. 495; Schurmeier v. St. Paul & P. R. Co., 10 Minn. 100, Gil. 75, 88 Am.Dec. 59.

This term is used in some jurisdictions with the meaning of surveying and mapping a stream according to its meanderings, or windings and turnings. See Jones v. Pettibone, 2 Wis. 317.

MEANDER LINES. Lines run in surveying particular portions of the public lands which border on navigable rivers, not as boundaries of the tract, but for the purpose of defining the sinuosities of the banks of the stream, and as the means of ascertaining the quantity of land in the fraction subject to sale, and which is to be paid for by the purchaser. In preparing the official plat from the field notes, the meander line is represented as the border line of the stream, and shows that the watercourse, and not the meander line as naturally run on the ground, is the boundary. St. Paul & P. R. Co. v. Schurmeier, 7 Wall. 286, 19 L.Ed. 74; Niles v. Cedar Point Club, 175 U.S. 300, 20 S.Ct. 124, 44 L.Ed. 171; Producers' Oil Co. v. Hanszen, 61 So. 754, 132 La. 691.

MEANING. That which is, or is intended to be, signified or denoted by act or language; signification; sense; import. Webster, Dict.

Secondary Meaning. While generic names, geographical names, and names composed of words which are merely descriptive are incapable of exclusive appropriation, words or names, which have a primary meaning of their own, such as words descriptive of the goods, service, or place where they are made, or the name of the maker, may nevertheless, by long use in connection with the business of the particular trade, come to be understood by the public as designating the goods, service, or business of a particular trader. This is what is known as the doctrine of "secondary meaning"; and is the origin of the law of unfair competition, as distinguished from technical trademarks or trade-names. Saunders System Atlanta Co. v. Drive It Yourself Co., 158 Ga. 1, 123 S.E. 132, 135; Richmond Remedies Co. v. Dr. Miles Medical Co., C.C.A.Mo., 16 F.2d 598, 602.

MEANS. That through which, or by the help of which, an end is attained; something tending to an object desired; intermediate agency or measure; necessary condition or co-agent; instrument. Pope v. Business Men's Assur. Co. of America, 235 Mo.App. 263, 131 S.W.2d 887, 892; Under insurance policy, equivalent to cause. Pope v. Business Men's Assur. Co. of America, 235 Mo.App. 263, 131 S.W.2d 887, 892.

Enactments and initiative and referendum measures. State ex rel. Bylander v. Hoss, 143 Or. 383, 22 P.2d 883.

Resources; available property; money or property, as an available instrumentality for effecting a purpose, furnishing a livelihood, paying a debt, or the like.

MEASURE. That by which extent or dimension is ascertained, either length, breadth, thickness, capacity, or amount. Webster. The rule by which anything is adjusted or proportioned.

MEASURE OF DAMAGES. The rule, or rather the system of rules, governing the adjustment or apportionment of damages as a compensation for injuries in actions at law.

MEASURE OF VALUE. In the ordinary sense of the word, "measure" would mean something by comparison with which we may ascertain what is the value of anything. When we consider, further, that value itself is relative, and that two things are necessary to constitute it, independently of the third thing, which is to measure it, we may define a "measure of value" to be something by comparing with which any two other things we may infer their value in relation to one another. 2 Mill, Pol. Econ. 101.

MEASURER, or METER. An officer in the city of London, who measured woolen clothes, coals, etc.

MEASURING MONEY. In old English law, a duty which some persons exacted, by letters patent, for every piece of cloth made, besides alnage. Now abolished.

MEAT. Specifically, animal flesh, though in one sense, the word includes other foods. Gardner v. State, 183 Ind. 101, 108 N.E. 230. Food in general; anything eaten for nourishment, either by man or beast; especially, solid food; hence, the edible part of anything. Webster, Dict.

MECHANIC. A person skilled in the practical use of tools. Warner Memorial University v. Ritenour, Tex.Civ.App., 56 S.W.2d 236, 237. A workman employed in shaping and uniting materials, such as wood, metal, etc., into some kind of structure, machine, or other object, requiring the use of tools. Story v. Walker, 11 Lea, Tenn., 517, 47 Am.Rep. 305; In re Osborn, D.C.N.Y., 104 F. 781; Baker v. Maxwell, 183 Iowa 1192, 168 N.W. 160, 2 A.L.R. 814.

MECHANIC'S LIEN. A claim created by law for the purpose of securing priority of payment of the price or value of work performed and materials furnished in erecting or repairing a building or other structure, and as such attaches to the land as well as buildings and improvements erected thereon. In re Louisville Daily News & Enquirer, D.C.Ky., 20 F.Supp. 465, 466.

MECHANICAL. Having relation to, or produced or accomplished by, the use of mechanism or machinery. Used chiefly in patent law. Of, pertaining to, or concerned with, manual labor; engaged in manual labor; of the artisan class; of, pertaining to, or concerned with, machinery or mechanism; made or formed by a machine or with tools. State v. Crounse, 105 Neb. 672, 181 N.W. 562, 563, 16 A.L.R. 533.

MECHANICAL ARM. In the artificial limb trade. An arm provided with fingers which can be moved by some mechanical contrivance, together with mechanism for rotating the wrist, simulating, as nearly as possible the motion of the human wrist, hand, and fingers. Carnes Artificial Limb Co. v. Dilworth Arm Co., D.C.Conn., 273 F. 838, 839.

MECHANICAL EQUIVALENT. If two devices do the same work in substantially the same way, and accomplish substantially the same result, they are "mechanical equivalents." Wire Tie Machinery Co. v. Pacific Box Corporation, C.C.A.Cal., 107 F.2d 54, 56. A device which may be substituted or adopted, instead of another, by any person skilled in the particular art from his knowledge of the art, and which is competent to perform the same functions or produce the same result, without introducing an original idea or changing the general idea of means. Smith v. Marshall, 22 F.Cas. 595; Alaska Packers' Ass'n v. Letson, C.C.Wash., 119 F. 611. The test of equivalency is whether the substituted element operates in substantially the same way to produce substantially the same result. Palmer v. Mach. Co., C.C.N.Y., 186 F. 496.

MECHANICAL MOVEMENT. A mechanism transmitting power or motion from a driving part to a part to be driven; a combination and arrangement of mechanical parts intended for the translation or transformation of motion. Campbell Printing Press Co. v. Miehle Printing Press Co., 42 C.C.A. 235, 102 F. 159.

MECHANICAL PROCESS. See Process.

MECHANICAL SKILL. As distinguished from invention or inventive capacity, this term means such skill, intelligence, ingenuity, or constructive ability in the adaptation of means to ends as would be possessed and exhibited by an ordinarily clever mechanic in the practice of his particular art or trade. Hollister v. Benedict & B. Mfg. Co., 113 U. S. 59, 5 S.Ct. 717, 28 L.Ed. 901; Johnson Co. v. Pennsylvania Steel Co., C.C.Pa., 67 F. 942.

MEDERIA. In old records, a house or place where metheglin, or mead, was made.

MEDFEE. In old English law, a bribe or reward; a compensation given in exchange, where the things exchanged were not of equal value. Cowell.

MEDIA ANNATA. In Spanish law, half-yearly profits of land. McMullen v. Hodge, 5 Tex. 34, 79.

MEDIA CONCLUDENDI. The steps of an argument. Thus "a judgment is conclusive as to all the *media concludendi.*" Fauntleroy v. Lum, 210 U.S. 230, 28 S.Ct. 641, 52 L.Ed. 1039. The theory or basis of facts upon which a legal conclusion is reached, per Holmes, C. J., in Hoseason v. Keegen, 178 Mass. 250, 59 N.E. 627. Grounds for asserting the right known when the suit was brought. Mendez v. Baetjer, C.C.A.Puerto Rico, 106 F.2d 163, 166.

MEDIA NOX. In old English law, midnight. *Ad mediam noctem,* at midnight. Fleta, lib. 5, c. 5, § 31.

MEDIÆ ET INFIRMÆ MANUS HOMINES. Men of a middle and base condition. Blount.

MEDIANUS HOMO. A man of middle fortune.

MEDIATE DATUM. A fact from whose existence may be rationally inferred the existence of ultimate facts. The Evergreens v. Nunan, C.C.A. 2, 141 F.2d 927, 928.

MEDIATE DESCENT. See Descent.

MEDIATE POWERS. Those incident to primary powers given by a principal to his agent.

For example, the general authority given to collect, receive, and pay debts due by or to the principal is a primary power. In order to accomplish this, it is frequently required to settle accounts, adjust disputed claims, resist those which are unjust, and answer and defend suits. These subordinate powers are sometimes called "mediate powers." Story, Ag. § 58.

MEDIATE TESTIMONY. Secondary evidence (*q. v.*).

MEDIATION. Intervention; interposition; the act of a third person who interferes between two contending parties with a view to reconcile them or persuade them to adjust or settle their dispute. In international law and diplomacy, the word denotes the friendly interference of a state in the controversies of others, for the purpose, by its influence and by adjusting their difficulties, of keeping the peace in the family of nations.

MEDIATOR. One who interposes between parties at variance for purpose of reconciling them. People v. Lindsey, 86 Colo. 458, 283 P. 539, 544.

MEDIATORS OF QUESTIONS. In English law, six persons authorized by statute, (27 Edw. III. St. 2, c. 24,) who, upon any question arising among merchants relating to unmerchantable wool, or undue packing, etc., might, before the mayor and officers of the staple upon their oath certify and settle the same; to whose determination therein the parties concerned were to submit. Cowell.

MEDICAL. Pertaining, relating, or belonging to the study and practice of medicine, or the science and art of the investigation, prevention, cure, and alleviation of disease.

MEDICAL EVIDENCE. Evidence furnished by medical men, testifying in their professional capacity as experts, or by standard treatises on medicine or surgery.

MEDICAL JURISPRUDENCE. The science which applies the principles and practice of the different branches of medicine to the elucidation of doubtful questions in a court of justice. Otherwise called "forensic medicine," (*q. v.*). A sort of mixed science, which may be considered as common ground to the practitioners both of law and physics. 1 Steph.Comm. 8.

MEDICAL SERVICES. Include all services rendered to deceased because of illness, upon advice of his physician, which were reasonably necessary for his care and comfort and proper treatment by his physicians. Park View Hospital Ass'n v. Peoples Bank & Trust Co., 211 N.C. 244, 189 S.E. 766, 769.

MEDICINE. The science and art dealing with the prevention, cure and alleviation of diseases; in a narrower sense that part of the science and art of restoring and preserving health which is the province of the physician as distinguished from the surgeon and obstetrician. Burke v. Kansas State Osteopathic Ass'n, C.C.A.Kan., 111 F.2d 250, 253. The term is not limited to substances supposed to possess curative or remedial properties. People v. Kabana, 321 Ill.App. 158, 52 N.E.2d 320.

Forensic Medicine. Another name for medical jurisprudence. See Forensic Medicine.

Schools of Medicine. See Osteopathy; Psychotherapy.

MEDICINE-CHEST. A box containing an assortment of medicines, required by statute to be carried by all vessels above a certain tonnage.

MEDICO-LEGAL. Relating to the law concerning medical questions.

MEDIETAS LINGUÆ. In old practice, moiety of tongue; half-tongue. Applied to a jury impaneled in a cause consisting the one half of natives, and the other half of foreigners. See De Medietate Linguæ.

MEDIO ACQUIETANDO. A judicial writ to distrain a lord for the acquitting of a mesne lord from a rent, which he had acknowledged in court not to belong to him. Reg. Jur. 129.

MEDITATIO FUGÆ. In Scotch law, contemplation of flight; intention to abscond. 2 Kames, Eq. 14, 15.

MEDITERRANEAN PASSPORT. A pass issued by the admiralty of Great Britain under various treaties with the Barbary States in the eighteenth century. They were granted to British built ships and were respected by the Barbary pirates. See 2 Halleck, Int. L., Baker's ed. 100. They were also issued by the United States. The term is still retained in R. S. § 4191, 46 U.S.C.A. § 62.

MEDIUM TEMPUS. In old English law, meantime; mesne profits. Cowell.

MEDLETUM. In old English law, a mixing together; a medley or *mêlée;* an affray or sudden encounter. An offense suddenly committed in an affray. The English word "medley" is preserved in the term "chance-medley." An intermeddling, without violence, in any matter of business. Spelman.

MEDLEY. An affray; a sudden or casual fighting; a hand to hand battle; a *mêlée*. See Chance-Medley; Chaud-Medley.

MEDSCEAT. In old English law, a bribe; hush money.

MEDSYPP. A harvest supper or entertainment given to laborers at harvest-home. Cowell.

MEETING. A coming together of persons; an assembly. Particularly, in law, an assembling of a number of persons for the purpose of discussing and acting upon some matter or matters in which they have a common interest. People v. Mintz, 106 Cal.App. 725, 290 P. 93, 100.

Called meeting. In the law of corporations, a meeting not held at a time specially appointed for it by the charter or by-laws, but assembled in pursuance of a "call" or summons proceeding from some officer, committee or group of stockholders, or other persons having authority in that behalf.

Family meeting. See Family.

General meeting. A meeting of all the stockholders of a corporation, all the creditors of a bankrupt, etc. In re Bonnaffe, 23 N.Y. 177; Mutual F. Ins. Co. v. Farquhar, 86 Md. 668, 39 A. 527.

Regular meeting. In the law of public and private corporations, a meeting (of directors, trustees, stockholders, etc.) held at the time and place appointed for it by statute, by-law, charter or other positive direction. State v. Wilkesville Tp., 20 Ohio St. 293.

Special meeting. In the law of corporations. A meeting called for special purposes; one limited to particular business; a meeting for those purposes of which the parties have had special notice. Mutual F. Ins. Co. v. Farquhar, 86 Md. 668, 39 A. 527; Warren v. Mower, 11 Vt. 385.

Stated meeting. A meeting held at a stated or duly appointed time and place; a regular meeting, (*q. v.*).

Town meeting. See Town.

MEETING OF MINDS. The "meeting of the minds" required to make a contract is not based on secret purpose or intention on the part of one of the parties, stored away in his mind and not brought to the attention of the other party, but must be based on purpose and intention which has been made known or which from all the circumstances should be known. McClintock v. Skelly Oil Co., 232 Mo.App. 1204, 114 S.W.2d 181, 189.

MEGALOMANIA. See Insanity.

MEGBOTE. In Saxon law, a recompense for the murder of a relation.

MEIGNE, or MAISNADER. In old English law, a family.

MEILICKE SYSTEM. Consists of computing fractions on the basis of a 30-day month, and does not charge interest for the 31st day of any month. Swistak v. Personal Finance Co., 175 Misc. 791, 24 N.Y.S.2d 80, 81.

MEINDRE AGE. L. Fr. Minority; lesser age. Kelham.

MEINY, MEINE, or MEINIE. In old English law, a household; staff or suite of attendants; a retinue; particularly, the royal household.

MEJORADO. In Spanish law, preferred; advanced. White, New Recop. l. 3, tit. 10, c. 1, § 4.

MELANCHOLIA. In medical jurisprudence, a kind of mental unsoundness characterized by extreme depression of spirits, ill-grounded fears, delusions, and brooding over one particular subject or train of ideas. Webster. See Insanity.

MELDFEOH. In Saxon law, the recompense due and given to him who made discovery of any breach of penal laws committed by another person, called the "promoter's [*i e.,* informer's] fee." Wharton.

MELIOR. Lat. Better; the better. *Melior res,* the better (best) thing or chattel. Bract. fol. 60.

MELIOR EST CAUSA POSSIDENTIS. The cause of the possessor is preferable. Dig. 50. 17. 126. 2.

MELIOR EST CONDITIO DEFENDENTIS. The condition of the party in possession is the better one, *i. e.,* where the right of the parties is equal. Broom, Max. 715, 719.

MELIOR EST CONDITIO POSSIDENTIS, ET REI QUAM ACTORIS. The condition of the possessor is the better, and the condition of the defendant is better than that of the plaintiff. 4 Inst. 180; Broom, Max. 714, 719.

MELIOR EST CONDITIO POSSIDENTIS UBI NEUTER JUS HABET. Jenk. Cent. 118. The condition of the possessor is the better where neither of the two has a right.

MELIOR EST JUSTITIA VERE PRÆVENIENS QUAM SEVERE PUNIENS. That justice which absolutely prevents [a crime] is better than that which severely punishes it. 3 Inst. Epil.

MELIORATIONS. In Scotch law, improvements of an estate, other than mere repairs; betterments. 1 Bell, Comm. 73. Occasionally used in English and American law in the sense of valuable and lasting improvements or betterments. See Green v. Biddle, 8 Wheat. 84, 5 L.Ed. 547.

MELIOREM CONDITIONEM ECCLESIÆ SUÆ FACERE POTEST PRÆLATUS, DETERIOREM NEQUAQUAM. Co. Litt. 101. A bishop can make the condition of his own church better, but by no means worse.

MELIOREM CONDITIONEM SUAM FACERE POTEST MINOR, DETERIOREM NEQUAQUAM. Co. Litt. 337. A minor can make his own condition better, but by no means worse.

MELIUS EST IN TEMPORE OCCURRERE, QUAM POST CAUSAM VULNERATUM REMEDIUM QUÆRERE. 2 Inst. 299. It is better to meet a thing in time than after an injury inflicted to seek a remedy.

MELIUS EST JUS DEFICIENS QUAM JUS INCERTUM. Law that is deficient is better than law that is uncertain. Lofft, 395.

MELIUS EST OMNIA MALA PATI QUAM MALO CONSENTIRE. 3 Inst. 23. It is better to suffer every ill than to consent to ill.

MELIUS EST PETERE FONTES QUAM SECTARI RIVULOS. It is better to go to the fountain head than to follow little streamlets.

MELIUS EST RECURRERE QUAM MALE CURRERE. It is better to run back than to run badly; it is better to retrace one's steps than to proceed improperly. 4 Inst. 176.

MELIUS INQUIRENDUM. To be better inquired into.

In old English law, the name of a writ commanding a further inquiry respecting a matter; as, after an imperfect inquisition in proceedings in outlawry, to have a new inquest as to the value of lands.

MEMBER. One of the persons constituting a family, Grant v. Louisiana Sawmill Co., 6 La.App. 673, 675; a partnership, association, corporation, guild, etc. In re Sixth Ward Building & Loan Ass'n of Newark, 134 N.J.Eq. 98, 34 A.2d 292, 294.

One of the persons constituting a court, a legislative assembly, etc. In re Heafy, 247 App.Div. 277, 285 N.Y.S. 188, 193.

A part or organ of the animal body; especially a limb or other separate part. California Casualty Indemnity Exchange v. Industrial Accident Commission, Cal.App., 82 P.2d 1115, 1116.

MEMBER OF CONGRESS. A member of the senate or house of representatives of the United States. In popular usage, particularly the latter.

MEMBER OF PARLIAMENT. One having the right to sit in either house of the British parliament.

MEMBERS. In English law, places where a custom-house has been kept of old time, with officers or deputies in attendance; and they are lawful places of exportation or importation. 1 Chit. Com. Law, 726.

MEMBERSHIP CORPORATION. One organized for purposes other than that of pecuniary gain. In re William McKinley Lodge No. 840, F. & A. M., D.C.N.Y., 4 F.Supp. 280, 282.

MEMBRANA. Lat.

In Civil law, parchment. Dig. 32, 52.

In old English law, a skin of parchment. The ancient rolls usually consist of several of these skins, and the word *"membrana"* is used, in citations to them, in the same way as "page" or "folio," to distinguish the particular skin referred to.

MEMBRUM. A slip or small piece of land.

MÉMOIRE. In French law, a document in the form of a petition, by which appeals to the court of cassation are initiated.

MEMORANDUM. Lat. To be remembered; be it remembered. A formal word with which the body of a record in the court of king's bench anciently commenced. Townsh. Pl. 486; 2 Tidd, Pr. 719.

Also an informal note or instrument embodying something that the parties desire to fix in memory by the aid of written evidence, or that is to serve as the basis of a future formal contract or deed. Plott v. Kittelson, 58 N.D. 881, 228 N.W. 217, 221.

This word is used in the statute of frauds as the designation of the written agreement, or note or evidence thereof, which must exist in order to bind the parties in the cases provided. The memorandum must be such as to disclose the parties, the nature and substance of the contract, the consideration and promise, and be signed by the party to be bound or his authorized agent. See 2 Kent, Comm. 510; Des Brisay v. Foss, 264 Mass. 102, 162 N.E. 4, 6.

The whole clause is now, in practice, termed, from this initial word, the "memorandum," and its use is supposed to have originated from the circumstance that proceedings "by bill" (in which alone it has been employed) were formerly considered as the by-business of the court. Gilb. Com.Pl. 47, 48.

MEMORANDUM ARTICLES. In the law of marine insurance, this phrase designates the articles of merchandise which are usually mentioned in the memorandum clause, (*q. v.,*) and for which the underwriter's liability is thereby limited. See Waln v. Thompson, 9 Serg. & R., Pa., 120, 11 Am. Dec. 675.

MEMORANDUM CHECK. See Check.

MEMORANDUM CLAUSE. In a policy of marine insurance the memorandum clause is a clause inserted to prevent the underwriters from being liable for injury to goods of a peculiarly perishable nature, and for minor damages. It begins as follows: "N. B. Corn, fish, salt, fruit, flour, and seed are warranted free from average, unless general, or the ship be stranded,"—meaning that the underwriters are not to be liable for damage to these articles caused by seawater or the like. Maude & P. Shipp. 371; Sweet.

MEMORANDUM IN ERROR. A document alleging error in fact, accompanied by an affidavit of such matter of fact.

MEMORANDUM OF ALTERATION. Formerly, in England, where a patent was granted for two inventions, one of which was not new or not useful, the whole patent was bad, and the same rule applied when a material part of a patent for a single invention had either of those defects. To remedy this the statute 5 & 6 Wm. IV. c. 83, empowers a patentee (with the fiat of the attorney general) to enter a disclaimer (*q. v.*) or a memorandum of an alteration in the title or specification of the patent, not being of such a nature as to extend the exclusive right granted by the patent, and thereupon the memorandum is deemed to be part of the letters patent or the specification. Sweet.

MEMORANDUM OF ASSOCIATION. A document to be subscribed by seven or more persons associated for a lawful purpose, by subscribing which, and otherwise complying with the requisitions of the companies' acts in respect of registration, they may form themselves into an incorporated company, with or without limited liability. 3 Steph.Comm. 20.

MEMORANDUM SALE. See Sale.

MEMORIAL. A document presented to a legislative body, or to the executive, by one or more individuals, containing a petition or a representation of facts.

In English law, that which contains the particulars of a deed, etc., and is the instrument registered, as in the case of an annuity which must be registered. Wharton.

In practice, a short note, abstract, memorandum, or rough draft of the orders of the court, from which the records thereof may at any time be fully made up. State v. Shaw, 73 Vt. 149, 50 A. 863.

MEMORITER. Lat. From memory; by or from recollection. Thus, *memoriter* proof of a written instrument is such as is furnished by the recollection of a witness who had seen and known it.

MEMORIZATION. Committing anything to memory. Used to describe the act of one who listens to a public representation of a play or drama, and then, from his recollection of its scenes, incidents, or language, reproduces it, substantially or in part, in derogation of the rights of the author. 5 Term R. 245; 14 A.L.R., N.S. 207.

MEMORY. The word as used in Blackstone and other ancient authorities, appeared to be synonymous with "mind", whereas the word "memory" in modern times is used in a more restricted sense of recollection of past events rather than the general state of one's mental power. United States v. Boylen, D.C.Or., 41 F.Supp. 724, 725.

Mental capacity; the mental power to review and recognize the successive states of consciousness in their consecutive order.

This word, as used in jurisprudence to denote one of the psychological elements necessary in the making of a valid will or contract or the commission of a crime, implies the mental power to conduct a consecutive train of thought, or an orderly planning of affairs, by recalling correctly the past states of the mind and past events, and arranging them in their due order of sequence and in their logical relations with the events and mental states of the present.

The phrase "sound and disposing mind and memory" means not merely distinct recollection of the items of one's property and the persons among whom it may be given, but entire power of mind to dispose of property by will. Abbott.

The reputation and name, good or bad, which a man leaves at his death.

Legal memory. An ancient usage, custom, supposed grant (as a foundation for prescription) and the like, are said to be immemorial when they are really or fictitiously of such an ancient date that "the memory of man runneth not to the contrary," or, in other words, "beyond legal memory." And legal memory or "time out of mind," according to the rule of the common law, commenced from the reign of Richard I., A. D. 1189. But under the statute of limitation of 32 Hen. VIII. this was reduced to 60 years, and again by that of 2 & 3 Wm. IV. c. 71, to 20 years. In the American states, by statute, the time of legal memory is generally fixed at a period corresponding to that prescribed for actions for the recovery of real property, usually about 20 years. See 2 Bl.Comm. 31; Miller v. Garlock, 8 Barb., N.Y. 153.

MEN OF STRAW. Men who used in former days to ply about courts of law, so called from their manner of making known their occupation, (*i. e.*, by a straw in one of their shoes,) recognized by the name of "straw-shoes." An advocate or lawyer who wanted a convenient witness knew by these signs where to meet with one, and the colloquy between the parties was brief. "Don't you remember?" said the advocate; to which the ready answer was, "To be sure I do." "Then come into court and swear it." And straw-shoes went into court and swore. Athens abounded in straw-shoes. Quart. Rev. vol. 33, p. 344.

MENACE. A threat; the declaration or show of a disposition or determination to inflict an evil or injury upon another. Cumming v. State, 99 Ga. 662, 27 S.E. 177; Morrill v. Nightingale, 93 Cal. 452, 28 Pac. 1068, 27 Am.St.Rep. 207.

MENETUM. In old Scotch law, a stockhorn; a horn made of wood, "with circles and girds of the same." Skene.

MENIAL. A servant of the lowest order; more strictly, a domestic servant living under his master's roof. Boniface v. Scott, 3 Serg. & R., Pa. 354.

MENS. Lat. Mind; intention; meaning; understanding; will.

MENS LEGIS. The mind of the law; that is, the purpose, spirit, or intention of a law or the law generally.

MENS LEGISLATORIS. The intention of the law-maker.

MENS REA. A guilty mind; a guilty or wrongful purpose; a criminal intent.

Guilty knowledge and wilfulness. United States v. Greenbaum, C.C.A.N.J., 138 F.2d 437, 438.

MENS TESTATORIS IN TESTAMENTIS SPECTANDA EST. Jenk. Cent. 277. The intention of the testator is to be regarded in wills.

MENSA. Lat. Patrimony or goods and necessary things for livelihood. Jacob. A table; the table of a money-changer. Dig. 2, 14, 47.

MENSA ET THORO. From bed and board. See Divorce.

MENSALIA. Parsonages or spiritual livings united to the tables of religious houses, and called "mensal benefices" amongst the canonists. Cowell.

MENSIS. Lat. In the civil and old English law, a month. *Mensis vetitus,* the prohibited month; fence-month (*q. v.*).

MENSOR. In civil law, a measurer of land; a surveyor. Dig. 11, 6; Id. 50, 6, 6; Cod. 12, 28.

MENSULARIUS. In civil law, a money-changer or dealer in money. Dig. 2, 14, 47, 1.

MENSURA. In old English law, a measure.

MENSURA DOMINI REGIS. "The measure of our lord the king," being the weights and measures established under King Richard I. in his parliament at Westminster, 1197. 1 Bl.Comm. 275; Mozley & Whiteley.

MENTAL. Relating to or existing in the mind; intellectual, emotional, or psychic, as distinguished from bodily or physical.

MENTAL ALIENATION. A phrase sometimes used to describe insanity (*q. v.*).

MENTAL ANGUISH. When connected with a physical injury, this term includes both the resultant mental sensation of pain and also the accompanying feelings of distress, fright, and anxiety. Railway Co. v. Miller, 25 Tex.Civ.App. 460, 61 S.W. 978. In other connections, and as a ground for damages or an element of damages, it includes the mental suffering resulting from the excitation of the more poignant and painful emotions, such as grief, severe disappointment, indignation, wounded pride, shame, public humiliation, despair, etc. Western Union Telegraph Co. v. Taylor, 94 Fla. 841, 114 So. 529, 532; Western Union Telegraph Co. v. Chamberlain, Tex.Civ.App., 169 S.W. 370, 371.

MENTAL CAPACITY OR COMPETENCE. Contemplates the ability to understand the nature and effect of the act in which a person is engaged and the business he is transacting. Jones v. Traders & General Ins. Co., Tex.Civ.App., 144 S.W.2d 689, 694. Such a measure of intelligence, understanding, memory, and judgment (relative to the particular transaction) as will enable the person to understand the nature of his act. Davren v. White, 42 N.J.Eq. 569, 7 A. 682; Conley v. Nailor, 118 U.S. 127, 6 S.Ct. 1001, 30 L.Ed. 112.

MENTAL CRUELTY. A course of conduct on the part of one spouse toward the other spouse which can endanger the mental and physical health and efficiency of the other spouse to such an extent as to render continuance of the marital relation intolerable. Burns v. Burns, 153 Fla. 73, 13 So.2d 599, 602.

MENTAL DEFECT. As applied to the qualification of a juror, this term must be understood to embrace either such gross ignorance or imbecility as practically disqualifies any person from performing the duties of a juror. Caldwell v. State, 41 Tex. 94.

MENTAL INCAPACITY; MENTAL INCOMPETENCY. Established when there is found to exist an essential privation of reasoning faculties, or when a person is incapable of understanding and acting with discretion in the ordinary affairs of life. In re Blochowitz' Guardianship, 135 Neb. 163, 280 N.W. 438, 441.

MENTAL RESERVATION. A silent exception to the general words of a promise or agreement not expressed, on account of a general understanding on the subject. But the word has been applied to an exception existing in the mind of the one party only, and has been degraded to signify a dishonest excuse for evading or infringing a promise. Wharton.

MENTE CAPTUS. Persons who are habitually insane. Clanton v. Shattuck, 211 La. 750, 30 So.2d 823, 824.

MENTIRI. Lat. To lie; to assert a falsehood. Calvin; 3 Bulst. 260.

MENTITION. The act of lying; a falsehood.

MENU, LAWS OF. A collection or institute of the earliest laws of ancient India. The work is of very remote antiquity.

MER, or MERE. A fenny place. Cowell.

MERA NOCTIS. Midnight. Cowell.

MERANNUM. In old records, timbers; wood for building.

MERCABLE. Merchantable; to be sold or bought.

MERCANTANT. A foreign trader.

MERCANTILE. Of, pertaining to, or characteristic of, merchants, or the business of merchants; having to do with trade or commerce or the business of buying and selling merchandise; trading; commercial; conducted or acting on business principles. In re Wanamaker's Estate, 312 Pa. 362, 167 A. 592, 594.

MERCANTILE AGENCIES. Establishments which make a business of collecting information relating to the credit, character, responsibility and reputation of merchants, for the purpose of furnishing the information to subscribers. Brookfield v. Kitchen, 163 Mo. 546, 63 S.W. 825; State v. Morgan, 2 S.D. 32, 48 N.W. 314.

MERCANTILE LAW. An expression substantially equivalent to the law-merchant or commercial law. It designates the system of rules, customs, and usages generally recognized and adopted by merchants and traders, and which, either in its simplicity or as modified by common law or statutes, constitutes the law for the regulation of their transactions and the solution of their controversies.

MERCANTILE LAW AMENDMENT ACTS. The statutes 19 & 20 Vict. cc. 60, 97, passed mainly for the purpose of assimilating the mercantile law of England, Scotland, and Ireland.

MERCANTILE PAPER. Commercial paper; such negotiable paper (bills, notes, checks, etc.) as is made or transferred by and between merchants or traders, and is governed by the usages of the business world and the law-merchant.

MERCANTILE PARTNERSHIP. One which habitually buys and sells; one which buys for the purpose of afterwards selling. Com. v. Natural Gas Co., 32 Pittsb.Leg.J., O.S. 310.

MERCAT. A market. An old form of the latter word common in Scotch law, formed from the Latin *"mercatum."*

MERCATIVE. Belonging to trade.

MERCATUM. Lat. A market. A contract of sale. Supplies for an army (*commeatus*).

MERCATURE. The practice of buying and selling.

MERCEDARY. A hirer; one that hires.

MERCEN-LAGE. The law of the Mercians. One of the three principal systems of laws which prevailed in England about the beginning of the eleventh century. It was observed in many of the midland counties, and those bordering on the principality of Wales. 1 Bl.Comm. 65.

"Upon the expulsion of these intruders [the Danish invaders], the English returned to their ancient law, retaining a few customs of their late visitants, which were termed *Dane Lage,* as the code compiled by Alfred was called *West-Saxon Lage,* and the laws of the kingdom of Mercia, which obtained in the countries next to Wales, were termed the *Mercen Lage.*" 4 Bl. Comm. 412 (quoted from Browne's Abr., p. 735 [Gavit's Ed., p. 939]).

MERCENARIUS. A hireling or servant. Jacob.

MERCES. Lat. In the civil law, reward of labor in money or other things. As distinguished from *"pensio,"* it means the rent of farms, (*prœdia rustici.*) Calvin.

MERCHANDISE. All commodities which merchants usually buy and sell, whether at wholesale or retail; wares and commodities such as are ordinarily the objects of trade and commerce. But the term is never understood as including real estate, and is rarely applied to provisions such as are purchased day by day, or to such other articles as are required for immediate consumption. Passaic Mfg. Co. v. Hoffman, 3 Daly, N.Y. 512; Hein v. O'Connor, Tex.App., 15 S.W. 414; Elliott v. Swartwout, 10 Pet. 137, 9 L.Ed. 373; Smith v. Boyer, 119 S.C. 176, 112 S.E. 71, 74, 41 A.L.R. 1466.

Stock of Merchandise. See Stock.

MERCHANDISE BROKER. One who negotiates the sale of merchandise without having it in his possession or control, being simply an agent with very limited powers. Hughes v. Young, 17 Tenn. App. 24, 65 S.W.2d 858.

MERCHANDISE MARKS ACT, 1862. The statute 25 & 26 Vict. c. 88, designed to prevent the fraudulent marking of merchandise and the fraudulent sale of merchandise falsely marked.

MERCHANT. One who is engaged in the purchase and sale of goods; a trafficer; a trader. Fischbach Brewing Co. v. City of St. Louis, 231 Mo.App. 793, 95 S.W.2d 335, 340.

A man who traffics or carries on trade with foreign countries, or who exports and imports goods and sells them by wholesale. Webster. Merchants of this description are commonly known by the name of "shipping merchants."

Commission merchant. See Commission.

Law merchant. See Mercantile Law.

Statute merchant. See Statute.

MERCHANT APPRAISER. See Appraiser.

MERCHANT SEAMAN. A sailor employed in a private vessel, as distinguished from one employed in the navy or public ships. U. S. v. Sullivan, C.C.Or., 43 F. 604; The Ben Flint, 3 F.Cas. 184.

MERCHANT SHIPPING ACTS. Certain English statutes, beginning with the St. 16 & 17 Vict. c. 131, whereby a general superintendence of merchant shipping is vested in the board of trade.

MERCHANTABILITY. Means that the article sold shall be of the general kind described and reasonably fit for the general purpose for which it shall have been sold, and where the article sold is ordinarily used in but one way, its fitness for use in that particular way is impliedly warranted unless there is evidence to the contrary. D'Onofrio v. First Nat. Stores, 68 R.I. 144, 26 A.2d 758, 760.

MERCHANTABLE. Salable and fit for the market; sound and undamaged; such as is generally sold in the market; vendible in the market, Nettles v. Lichtman, 228 Ala. 52, 152 So. 450, 453, 91 A.L.R. 1455; possessing an ordinary or medium quality of goodness, Martin's Fork Coal Co. v. Harlan-Wallins Coal Corporation, D.C.Ky., 14 F. Supp. 902, 907; of a quality such as will bring the ordinary market price. Riggs v. Armstrong, 23 W. Va. 773; Wallace v. L. D. Clark & Sons, 74 Okl. 208, 174 P. 557, 558, 21 A.L.R. 361. It may include reasonable fitness for general purpose for which article is manufactured and sold. Outhwaite v. A. B. Knowlson Co., 259 Mich. 224, 242 N.W. 895, 896.

MERCHANTABLE TITLE. One that can be held without reasonable apprehension of being assailed and readily transferable in market. Crow Creek Gravel & Sand Co. v. Dooley, 182 Ark. 1009, 33 S. W.2d 369, 370.

MERCHANTMAN. A ship or vessel employed in foreign or domestic commerce or in the merchant service.

MERCHANTS' ACCOUNTS. Accounts between merchant and merchant, which must be current, mutual, and unsettled, consisting of debts and credits for merchandise. Fox v. Fisk, 6 How., Miss. 328.

MERCHANTS, STATUTE OF. The English statute 13 Edw. I. St. 3, repealed by 26 & 27 Vict. c. 125.

MERCHET. In feudal law, a fine or composition paid by inferior tenants to the lord for liberty to dispose of their daughters in marriage. Cowell. The same as *marcheta* (*q. v.*).

MERCIAMENT. An amerciament, penalty, or fine (*q. v.*).

MERCIAN LAW. One of the main bodies of customs (with the Dane law and the West Saxon law and perhaps an admixture of Norman laws and customs) which composed the law in the early Norman days. 1 Holdsw. Hist. E. L. 3. See Mercen-Lage.

MERCIMONIA. In old writs, wares. *Mercimonia et merchandizas,* wares and merchandises. Reg. Brev. Append. 10.

MERCIMONINATUS ANGLIÆ. In old records, the impost of England upon merchandise. Cowell.

MERCIS APPELLATIO AD RES MOBILES TANTUM PERTINET. The term "merchandise" belongs to movable things only. Dig. 50, 16, 66.

MERCIS APPELLATIONE HOMINES NON CONTINERI. Men are not included under the denomination of "merchandise." Dig. 50, 16, 207.

MERCNA LAGU. See Lagu; Mercen-Lage.

MERCY. In practice. The arbitrament of the king or judge in punishing offenses not directly censured by law. Jacob. So, "to be in mercy" signifies to be amerced or fined for bringing or defending an unjust suit, or to be liable to punishment in the discretion of the court.

In criminal law. The discretion of a judge, within the limits prescribed by positive law, to remit altogether the punishment to which a convicted person is liable, or to mitigate the severity of his sentence; as when a jury recommends the prisoner to the *mercy* of the court.

MERE. Sax. A marsh. Spelman.

MERE. L. Fr. Mother. *Æle, mere, fille,* grandmother, mother, daughter. Britt. c. 89. *En ventre sa mere,* in its mother's womb.

MERE LICENSEE. One who enters upon the land or property of another without objection, or by the mere permission, sufferance, or acquiescence of the owner or occupier. Mann v. Des Moines Ry. Co., 232 Iowa 1049, 7 N.W.2d 45, 50.

MERE MOTION. The free and voluntary act of a party himself, done without the suggestion or influence of another person, is said to be done of his mere motion, *ex mero motu* (*q. v.*). Brown.

The phrase is used of an interference of the courts of law, who will, under some circumstances, of their own motion, object to an irregularity in the proceedings, though no objection has been taken to the informality by the plaintiff or defendant in the suit. 3 Chit. Gen. Pr. 430.

MERE RIGHT. The mere right of property in land; the *jus proprietatis,* without either possession or even the right of possession. 2 Bl. Comm. 197. The abstract right of property.

MERE-STONE. In old English law, a stone for bounding or dividing lands. Yearb. P. 18 Hen. VI. 5.

MERELY. Without including anything else; purely; only; solely; absolute; wholly. In re Plymouth Motor Corporation, Cust. & Pat. App., 46 F.2d 211, 212.

MERENNIUM. In old records, timber. Cowell.

MERETRICIOUS. Of the nature of unlawful sexual connection. The term is descriptive of the relation sustained by persons who contract a marriage that is void by reason of legal incapacity. 1 Bl. Comm. 436.

MERGER. The fusion or absorption of one thing or right into another; generally spoken of a case where one of the subjects is of less dignity or importance than the other. Here the less important ceases to have an independent existence. Marfield v. Cincinnati, D. & T. Traction Co., 111 Ohio St. 139, 144 N.E. 689, 696, 40 A.L.R. 357.

Conglomerate merger. Merger of corporations which are neither competitors nor potential or actual customers or suppliers of each other. U. S. v. General Dynamics Corp., D.C.N.Y., 258 F.Supp. 36, 56.

Contract law. Extinguishment of one contract by absorption into another. Clark v. Compania Granadera de Cananera, S.A., 385 P.2d 691, 695, 94 Ariz. 391; Whiddon v. General Mills, Inc., Tex. Civ.App., 347 S.W.2d 7, 10.

Corporations. The union of two or more corporations by the transfer of property of all to one of them, which continues in existence, the others being swallowed up or merged therein. Metropolitan Edison Co. v. Commissioner of Internal Revenue, C.C.A.3, 98 F.2d 807, 810, 811. It differs from a consolidation wherein all the corporations terminate their existence and become parties to a new one. Murphy v. Niehus, 50 Ohio App. 299, 198 N.E. 197.

Criminal Law. When a man commits a great crime which includes a lesser, or commits a felony which includes a tort against a private person, the latter is merged in the former. 1 East, P. C. 411.

Divorce law. Substitution of rights and duties under judgment or decree for those under property settlement agreement. Roesberry v. Roesberry, 401 P.2d 805, 807, 88 Idaho 514.

Horizontal merger. Merger of corporate competitors. U. S. v. General Dynamics Corp., D.C. N.Y., 258 F.Supp. 36, 56; U. S. v. Manufacturers Hanover Trust Co., D.C.N.Y., 240 F.Supp. 867, 930.

Real-Property Law. It is a general principle of law that where a greater estate and a less coincide and meet in one and the same person, without any intermediate estate, the less is immediately annihilated, or, in the law phrase, is said to be *merged,* that is, sunk or drowned, in the greater. Thus, if there be tenant for years, and the reversion in fee-simple descends to or is purchased by him, the term of years is *merged* in the inheritance, and shall never exist any more. 2 Bl. Comm. 177; 1 Steph. Comm. 293; 4 Kent, Comm. 99. Duncan v. Smith, 31 N.J.L. 327.

Rights. This term, as applied to rights, is equivalent to *"confusio"* in the Roman law, and indicates that where the qualities of debtor and creditor become united in the same individual, there arises a confusion of rights which extinguishes both qualities; whence, also, merger is often called "extinguishment." Brown.

Rights of Action. In the law relating to rights of action, when a person takes or acquires a remedy or security of a higher nature, in legal estimation, than the one which he already possesses for the same right, then his remedies in respect of the minor right or security merge in those attaching to the higher one. Leake, Cont. 506; 10 C.B. 561. As where a claim is merged in the judgment recovered upon it. Frost v. Thompson, 219 Mass. 360, 106 N.E. 1009, 1010.

Vertical merger. Union with corporate customer or supplier. U. S. v. General Dynamics Corp., D.C.N.Y., 258 F.Supp. 36, 56.

MERIDIES. In old English law, noon. Fleta, lib. 5, c. 5, § 31.

MERINO. A fine long staple wool, which commands the highest price. Federal Trade Commission v. Winsted Hosiery Co., 258 U.S. 483, 42 S.Ct. 384, 385, 66 L.Ed. 729.

MERIT SYSTEM. A system of appointing employees to office in the civil service, and of promoting them for competency only; opposed, in the United States, to the spoils system. Heck v. Hall, 238 Ala. 274, 190 So. 280, 285.

MERITORIOUS. Possessing or characterized by "merit" in the legal sense of the word. See Merits.

MERITORIOUS CAUSE OF ACTION. This description is sometimes applied to a person with whom the ground of action, or the consideration, originated or from whom it moved. For example, where a cause of action accrues to a woman while sole, and is sued for, after her marriage, by her husband and herself jointly, she is called the "meritorious cause of action."

MERITORIOUS CONSIDERATION. One founded upon some moral obligation; a valuable consideration in the second degree.

MERITORIOUS DEFENSE. See Defense.

MERITS. The word "merit" as a legal term is to be regarded as referring to the strict legal rights of the parties. Mink v. Keim, 266 App.Div. 184, 41 N.Y.S.2d 769, 771.

MERO MOTU. See Ex Mero Motu; Mere Motion.

MERSCUM. A lake; also a marsh or fenland.

MERTLAGE. A church calendar or rubric. Cowell.

MERTON, STATUTE OF. An old English statute, relating to dower, legitimacy, wardships, procedure, inclosure of common, and usury. It was passed in 1235, (20 Hen. III.,) and was named from Merton, in Surrey, where parliament sat that year. See Barring. St. 41, 46.

MERUM. In old English law, mere; naked or abstract. *Merum jus,* mere right. Bract. fol. 31.

MERX. Lat. Merchandise; movable articles that are bought and sold; articles of trade.

MERX EST QUICQUID VENDI POTEST. Merchandise is whatever can be sold. Com. 355; 3 Wood. Lect. 263.

MESCREAUNTES. L. Fr. Apostates; unbelievers.

MESCROYANT. A term used in the ancient books to designate an infidel or unbeliever.

MESE. A house and its appurtenance. Cowell.

MESNALTY, or MESNALITY. A manor held under a superior lord. The estate of a mesne.

MESNE. Intermediate; intervening; the middle between two extremes, especially of rank or time.

An intermediate lord; a lord who stood between a tenant and the chief lord; a lord who was also a tenant. "Lord, *mesne,* and tenant; the tenant holdeth by four pence, and the mesne by twelve pence." Co. Litt 23*a*.

As to mesne "Conveyance," "Process," and "Profits," see those titles.

MESNE ASSIGNMENT. If A. grant a lease of land to B., and B. assign his interest to C., and C. in his turn assign his interest therein to D., in this case the assignments so made by B. and C. would be termed "mesne assignments;" that is, they would be assignments intervening between A.'s original grant and the vesting of D.'s interest in the land under the last assignment. Brown.

MESNE INCUMBRANCE. An intermediate charge, burden, or liability; an incumbrance which has been created or has attached to property between two given periods.

MESNE LORD. In old English law, a middle or intermediate lord; a lord who held of a superior lord. 2 Bl. Comm. 59. More commonly termed a "mesne" (*q. v.*).

MESNE, WRIT OF. An ancient and abolished writ, which lay when the lord paramount distrained on the tenant paravail. The latter had a writ of mesne against the mesne lord.

MESS BRIEF. In Danish sea law, one of a ship's papers; a certificate of admeasurement granted at the home port of a vessel by the government or by some other competent authority. Jac. Sea Laws, 51.

MESSAGE. Any notice, word, or communication, written or oral, sent from one person to another. Webster, Dict.

President's message. An annual communication from the president of the United States to congress, made at or near the beginning of each session, embodying his views on the state and exigencies of national affairs, suggestions and recommendations for legislation, and other matters. Const. U. S. art. 2, § 3.

Repeated message. Within the meaning of restricted liability clauses printed on the back of blank telegraph forms, one telegraphed back to the sending office for comparison; the object being to guard against mistakes in transmission. Dettis v. Western Union Telegraph Co., 141 Minn. 361, 170 N.W. 334, 338.

MESSAGE FROM THE CROWN. In English law, the method of communicating between the sovereign and the house of parliament. A written message under the royal sign-manual is brought by a member of the house, being a minister of the crown or one of the royal household. Verbal messages are also sometimes delivered. May, Parl. Pr. c. 17.

MESSARIUS. In old English law, a chief servant in husbandry; a bailiff.

MESSE THANE. One who said mass; a priest. Cowell.

MESSENGER. One who bears messages or errands; a ministerial officer employed by executive officers, legislative bodies, and courts of justice, whose service consists principally in carrying verbal or written communications or executing other orders. In Scotland there are officers attached to the courts, called "messengers at arms."

An officer attached to a bankruptcy court, whose duty consists, among other things, in seizing and taking possession of the bankrupt's estate during the proceedings in bankruptcy.

The messenger of the English court of chancery has the duty of attending on the great seal, either in person or by deputy, and must be ready to execute all such orders as he shall receive from the lord chancellor, lord keeper, or lords commissioners. Brown.

MESSIS SEMENTEM SEQUITUR. The crop belongs to [follows] the sower. A maxim in Scotch law. Where a person is in possession of land which he has reason to believe is his own, and sows that land, he will have a right to the crops, although before it is cut down it should be discovered that another has a preferable title to the land. Bell.

MESSUAGE. This term is now synonymous with "dwelling-house," but had once a more extended signification. Marmet Co. v. Archibald, 37 W.Va. 778, 17 S.E. 300; Grimes v. Wilson, 4 Blackf. Ind. 333. Dwelling-house with the adjacent buildings and curtilage. Hall v. Philadelphia Co., 72 W.Va. 573, 78 S.E. 755, 757.

Although the word "messuage" may, there is no necessity that it must, import more than the word "dwelling-house," with which word it is frequently put in apposition and used synonymously. 2 Bing.N.C. 617.

In Scotland, the principal dwelling-house within a barony. Bell.

MESTIZO. A mongrel or person of mixed blood; sometimes used as equivalent to "octoroon," that is, the child of a white person and a quadroon, sometimes as denoting a person one of whose parents was a Spaniard and the other an American Indian.

META. Lat. A goal, bound, or turning-point. In old English law, the term was used to denote a bound or boundary line of land; a landmark; a material object, as a tree or a pillar, marking the position or beginning of a boundary line.

METABOLISM. The sum total of all processes of the human body by which food is transformed into chemicals which are absorbed into blood stream and lymphatic system for purpose of so nourishing body that it can continue to function. United States v. 62 Packages, More or Less, of Marmola Prescription Tablets, C.C.A.Wis., 142 F.2d 107, 109.

METACHRONISM. An error in computation of time.

METALLIC. "Consisting of or having the characters of a metal. * * * Having one or more properties resembling those of metals." Trussell Mfg. Co. v. S. E. & M. Vernon, Inc., D.C.N.Y., 11 F.2d 289, 290, 291.

METALLUM. Lat. In Roman law, metal; a mine. Labor in mines, as a punishment for crime. Dig. 40, 5, 24, 5; Calvin.

METAPHYSICS. The science of being; the science which deals with ultimate reality. Vineland Trust Co. v. Westendorf, 86 N.J.Eq. 343, 98 A. 314.

METATUS. In old European law, a dwelling; a seat; a station; quarters; the place where one lives or stays. Spelman.

METAYER SYSTEM. A system of agricultural holdings, under which the land is divided, in small farms, among single families, the landlord generally supplying the stock which the agricultural system of the country is considered to require, and receiving, in lieu of rent and profit, a fixed proportion of the produce. This proportion, which is generally paid in kind, is usually one-half. 1 Mill, Pol. Econ. 296, 363; and 2 Smith, Wealth Nat. 3, c. ii. The system prevails in some parts of France and Italy.

METECORN. A measure or portion of corn, given by a lord to customary tenants as a reward and encouragement for labor. Cowell.

METEGAVEL. A tribute or rent paid in victuals. Cowell.

METER. An instrument of measurement; as a coal-meter, a gas-meter, a land-meter.

Also see Metre.

METES AND BOUNDS. The boundary lines of land, with their terminal points and angles. Lefler v. City of Dallas, Tex.Civ.App., 177 S.W.2d 231, 234.

METEWAND, or METEYARD. A staff of a certain length wherewith measures are taken.

METHEL. Sax. Speech; discourse. *Mathlian*, to speak; to harangue. Anc. Inst. Eng.

METHOD. The mode of operating, or the means of attaining an object. In patent law, "Engine" and "method" mean the same thing, and may be the subject of a patent. Method, properly speaking, is only placing several things, or performing several operations, in the most convenient order, but it may signify a contrivance or device. Fessen. Pat. 127; Hornblower v. Boulton, 8 Term R. 106.

METHOMANIA. See Insanity.

METRE. The unit of measure in the "metric system" of weights and measures. It is a measure of length, being the ten-millionth part of the distance from the equator to the north pole, and equivalent to 39.37 inches. From this unit all the other denominations of measure, as well as of weight, are derived. The metric system was first adopted in France in 1795.

METRIC SYSTEM. A system of measures for length, surface, weight, and capacity, founded on the *metre* as a unit. It originated in France, has been established by law there and in some other countries, and is recommended for general use by other governments.

METROPOLIS. A mother city; one from which a colony was sent out. The capital of a province. Calvin.

METROPOLITAN. In English law, one of the titles of an archbishop. Derived from the circumstance that archbishops were consecrated at first in the metropolis of a province. 4 Inst. 94.

In England, the word is frequently used to designate a statute, institution, governmental agency, etc., relating exclusively or especially to the city of London; *e. g.*, the metropolitan board of works, metropolitan buildings act, etc.

METROPOLITAN BOARD OF WORKS. A board constituted in 1855 by St. 18 & 19 Vict. c. 120, for the better sewering, draining, paving, cleansing, lighting, and improving the metropolis (London.) The board is elected by vestries and district boards, who in their turn are elected by the ratepayers. Wharton.

METROPOLITAN POLICE DISTRICT. A region composed of New York city and some adjacent territory, which was, for police purposes, organized as one district, and provided with a police force common to the whole.

METTESHEP, or METTENSCHEP. In old records, an acknowledgment paid in a certain measure of corn; or a fine or penalty imposed on tenants for default in not doing their customary service in cutting the lord's corn.

METUS. Lat. Fear; terror. In a technical sense, a reasonable and well-grounded apprehension of some great evil, such as death or mayhem, and not arising out of mere timidity, but such as might fall upon a man of courage. Fear must be of this description in order to amount to duress avoiding a contract. See Bract. lib. 2, c. 5; 1 Bl. Comm. 131; Calvin.

MEUBLES. In French law, the movables of English law. Things are *meubles* from either of two causes: (1) From their own nature, *e. g.*, tables, chairs; or (2) from the determination of the law, *e. g.*, obligations.

MEUBLES MEUBLANS. In French law, the utensils and articles of ornament usual in a dwelling-house. Brown.

MEUM EST PROMITTERE, NON DIMITTERE. It is mine to promise, not to discharge. 2 Rolle, 39.

MICHAELMAS. The feast of the Archangel Michael, celebrated in England on the 29th of September, and one of the usual quarter days.

MICHAELMAS HEAD COURT. A meeting of the heritors of Scotland, at which the roll of freeholders used to be revised. See Bell.

MICHAELMAS TERM. One of the four terms of the English courts of common law, beginning on the 2d day of November and ending on the 25th. 3 Steph. Comm. 562.

MICHE, or MICH. O. Eng. To practice crimes requiring concealment or secrecy; to pilfer articles secretly. *Micher,* one who practices secret crime. Webster.

MICHEL-GEMOT. One of the names of the general council immemorially held in England. The *Witenagemote.*

One of the great councils of king and noblemen in Saxon times. Jacob.

MICHEL-SYNOTH. Great council. One of the names of the general council of the kingdom in the times of the Saxons. 1 Bl. Comm. 147.

MICHERY. In old English law, theft; cheating.

MID-CHANNEL. In international law and by the usage of European nations, the terms "middle of the stream" and "mid-channel" of a navigable river are synonymous and interchangeably used. Hill City Compress Co. v. West Kentucky Coal Co., 155 Miss. 55, 122 So. 747, 748.

MIDDLE LINE OF MAIN CHANNEL. The equidistant point in the main channel of the river between the well-defined banks on either shore. Hearne v. State, 121 Ark. 460, 181 S.W. 291, 295.

MIDDLE OF THE RIVER. The phrases "middle of the river" and "middle of the main channel" are equivalent expressions, and both mean the main line of the channel or the middle thread of the current. Western Union Tel. Co. of Illinois v. Louisville & N. R. Co., 270 Ill. 399, 110 N.E. 583, 591, Ann.Cas.1917B, 670. See Thalweg.

Terms "middle of the Mississippi river," "middle of the main channel of the Mississippi river," and "center of the main channel of the Mississippi river," are synonymous and mean middle of broad and distinctly defined bed of main river, as distinguished from changing line of navigation, in determining location of boundaries between states. Hill City Compress Co. v. West Kentucky Coal Co., 155 Miss. 55, 122 So. 747, 748.

MIDDLE TERM. A phrase used in logic to denote the term which occurs in both of the premises in the syllogism, being the means of bringing together the two terms in the conclusion.

MIDDLE THREAD. The middle thread of a stream is an imaginary line drawn lengthwise through the middle of its current.

MIDDLEMAN. One who merely brings parties together in order to enable them to make their own contracts. Crane v. Colonial Holding Corporation, Tex.Civ.App., 57 S.W.2d 316, 320.

An agent between two parties, an intermediary who performs the office of a broker or factor between seller and buyer, producer and consumer, land-owner and tenant, etc. Southack v. Lane, 65 N.Y.Supp. 629, 32 Misc.Rep. 141. Brokers are "middlemen" only where, without having undertaken to act as agents for either party, or to exercise their skill, knowledge, or influence, they merely bring the parties together to deal for themselves, and stand indifferent between them. Geddes v. Rhee, 126 Minn. 517, 148 N.W. 549, 550.

One who has been employed as an agent by a principal, and who has employed a subagent under him by authority of the principal, either express or implied.

A person who is employed both by the seller and purchaser of goods, or by the purchaser alone, to receive them into his possession, for the purpose of doing something in or about them.

In Ireland, a person who takes land in large tracts from the proprietors, and then rents it out to the peasantry in small portions at a greatly enhanced price. Wharton.

MIDDLESEX, BILL OF. See Bill.

MIDSHIPMAN. In ships of war, a kind of naval cadet, whose business is to second or transmit the orders of the superior officers and assist in the necessary business of the vessel, but understood to be in training for a commission. A *passed* midshipman is one who has passed an examination and is a candidate for promotion to the rank of lieutenant. See U. S. v. Cook, 128 U.S. 254, 9 S.Ct. 108, 32 L.Ed. 464.

MIDSUMMER-DAY. The summer solstice, which is about June Twenty-Second, and the feast of St. John the Baptist, a festival first mentioned by Maximus Tauricensis, A. D. 400. It is generally a quarter-day for the payment of rents, etc. Wharton.

MIDWAY. See Thalweg.

MIDWIFE. In medical jurisprudence, a woman who assists at childbirth; an *accoucheuse.*

MIESES. In Spanish law, crops of grain. White, New Recop. b. 1, tit. 7, c. 5, § 2.

MIGHT, *v.* The preterit of the word "may". Equivalent to "had power" or "was possible" or "have the physical or moral opportunity to be contingently possible." In re Weidberg's Estate, 172 Misc. 524, 15 N.Y.S.2d 252, 257.

MIGRANS JURA AMITTAT AC PRIVILEGIA ET IMMUNITATES DOMICILII PRIORIS. One who emigrates will lose the rights, privileges, and immunities of his former domicile. Voet, Com. ad. Pand. tom. i. 347; 1 Kent, Comm. 76.

MILE. A measure of length or distance, containing 8 furlongs, or 1,760 yards, or 5,280 feet. This is the measure of an ordinary or statute mile; but the nautical or geographical mile contains 6,080 feet.

MILEAGE. Allowance for traveling expenses at certain rate per mile, Reed v. Gallet, 50 Idaho 638, 299 P. 337, 338. Especially to members of legislative bodies, witnesses, sheriffs, and bailiffs. Richardson v. State, 66 Ohio St. 108, 63 N.E. 593; State v. Clausen, 142 Wash. 450, 253 P. 805, 807.

MILEAGE TAX. License tax imposed upon intrastate business of transportation for compensation on public roads of state. State ex rel. Five Transp. Co. v. Lee, 132 Fla. 183, 181 So. 179, 181.

MILES. Lat. In civil law, a soldier.

In old English law, a knight, because military service was part of the feudal tenure. Also a tenant by military service, not a knight. 1 Bl. Comm. 404; Seld. Tit. Hon. 334.

MILESTONES. Stones set up to mark the miles on a road or railway.

MILITARE. To be knighted.

MILITARY. Pertaining to war or to the army; concerned with war. Also the whole body of soldiers; an army.

MILITARY BASE. See Base.

MILITARY BOUNTY LAND. See Bounty.

MILITARY CAUSES. In English law, causes of action or injuries cognizable in the court military, or court of chivalry. 3 Bl. Comm. 103.

MILITARY COMMISSIONS. Courts whose procedure and composition are modeled upon courts-martial, being the tribunals by which alleged violations of martial law are tried and determined. The membership of such commissions is commonly made up of civilians and army officers. They are probably not known outside of the United States, and were first used by General Scott during the Mexican war. 15 Amer. & Eng. Enc. Law, 473.

MILITARY COURTS. In England the court of chivalry and courts-martial, in America courts-martial and courts of inquiry, are called by this general name.

MILITARY FEUDS. See Feud.

MILITARY FORCES. Under Espionage Act June 15, 1917, included persons subject to be called into active service under Selective Service Act May 18, 1917. Anderson v. U. S., C.C.A.S.D., 264 F. 75, 76; White v. United States, C.C.A.Ohio, 263 F. 17, 19, but see contra, United States v. Hall, D.C.Mont., 248 F. 150, 152.

MILITARY GOVERNMENT. Exercised by military commander under direction of President in time of foreign war without the boundaries of the United States, or in time of rebellion and civil war within states or districts occupied by rebels. Hammond v. Squier, D.C.Wash., 51 F.Supp. 227, 230.

MILITARY JURISDICTION. There are under the Constitution, three kinds of military jurisdiction: one to be exercised both in peace and war; another to be exercised in time of foreign war without the boundaries of the United States or in time of rebellion and civil war within states or districts occupied by rebels treated as belligerents; and a third to be exercised in time of invasion or insurrection within the limits of the United States or during rebellion within the limits of states maintaining adhesion to the National Government, when the public danger requires its exercise. The first of these may be called jurisdiction under "military law" and is found in acts of Congress prescribing rules and articles of war, or otherwise providing for the government of the national forces; the second may be distinguished as "military government" superseding, as far as may be deemed expedient the local law, and exercised by the military commander under the direction of the President, with the express or implied sanction of Congress; while the third may be denominated "martial law", and is called into action by Congress, or temporarily when the action of Congress cannot be invited, and in the face of justifying or excusing peril, by the President in times of insurrection or invasion, or of civil or foreign war, within districts or localities where ordinary law no longer adequately secures public safety and private rights. United States v. Minoru Yasui, D.C. Or., 48 F.Supp. 40, 46, 47.

MILITARY LAW. A system of regulations for the government of an army. 1 Kent, Comm. 341, note. That branch of the laws which respects military discipline and the government of persons employed in the military service. De Hart, Mil. Law, 16. Johnson v. Jones, 44 Ill. 153, 92 Am.Dec. 159. Military is distinct from martial law, in that it applies only to persons in the military or naval service of the government; whereas, martial law, when once established, applies alike to citizens and soldiers and supersedes civil law. U. S. ex rel. Wessels v. McDonald, D.C.N.Y., 265 F. 754, 761; Bishop v. Vandercook, 228 Mich. 299, 200 N. W. 278, 280.

MILITARY OFFENSES. Those offenses which are cognizable by the courts military, as insubordination, sleeping on guard, desertion, etc.

MILITARY OFFICE. See Office.

MILITARY OFFICER. See Officer.

MILITARY SERVICE. Every branch of service in either the armies or navies of the United States. Maclean v. Brodigan, 41 Nev. 468, 172 P. 375, 377; In re Opinion to the Governor. 41 R.I. 118, 102 A. 913.

"Active military service" within exemption provision of life policy is service in garrison or at sea in time of peace or before an enemy in time of war. Redd v. American Cent. Life Ins. Co., 200 Mo.App. 383, 207 S.W. 74, 75; Rex Health & Accident Ins. Co. v. Pettiford, 74 Ind.App. 507, 129 N.E. 248.

MILITARY STATE. The soldiery of the kingdom of Great Britain.

MILITARY TENURES. The various tenures by knight-service, grand-serjeanty, cornage, etc., are frequently called "military tenures," from the nature of the services which they involved. 1 Steph. Comm. 204.

MILITARY TESTAMENT. See Testament.

MILITES. Lat. Knights; and, in Scotch law, freeholders.

MILITIA. The body of citizens in a state, enrolled for discipline as a military force, but not engaged in actual service except in emergencies, as distinguished from regular troops or a standing army. Ex parte McCants, 39 Ala. 112; Worth v. Craven County, 118 N.C. 112, 24 S.E. 778; Story v. Perkins, D.C.Ga., 243 F. 997, 999.

MILITIAMEN. Comprehends every temporary citizen-soldier who in time of war or emergency enters active military service of the country. Critchlow v. Monson, 102 Utah 378, 131 P.2d 794, 798.

MILK. In England milk means, commercially speaking, skimmed milk.

MILL. A complicated engine or machine for grinding and reducing to fine particles grain, fruit, or other substance, or for performing other operations by means of wheels and a circular motion; also the building containing such machinery. State v. Livermore, 44 N.H. 387; Lamborn v. Bell, 18 Colo. 346, 32 P. 989, 20 L.R.A. 241.

The word as used in Employers' Liability Act has been extended to include not only the building in which the business of manufacturing is carried on, but the dam, flume, and ways which the master provides for the use of those employés. Boody v. K. & C. Mfg. Co., 77 N.H. 208, 90 A. 859, 860, L.R.A.1916A, 10.

An American money of account, of the value of the tenth part of a cent.

MILL-HOLMS. Low meadows and other fields in the vicinity of mills, or watery places about mill-dams. Enc. Lond.

MILL OATS. A species of wild oats of volunteer growth with a dark brown or almost black kernel incased in hard cover with stiff beard, having low food value. Gibson v. State, 214 Ala. 38, 106 So. 231, 238.

MILL POWER. An expression designating a unit of water power. It is the descriptive term frequently used to rate water power for the purpose of renting it. It indicates the amount of power due to a stated quantity of water used on the particular fall. It is a term of practical convenience in defining the quantity and weight of water available for use by the lessee. The actual amount of horse power developed may vary with the efficiency of the water wheels and other appliances supplied by the lessee. Holyoke Water Power Co. v. Whiting & Co., 276 Mass. 528, 177 N.E. 568, 572.

MILL PRIVILEGE. The right of a riparian proprietor to erect a mill on his land and to use the power furnished by the stream for the purpose of operating the mill, with due regard to the rights of other owners above and below him on the stream. Hutchinson v. Chase, 39 Me. 511, 63 Am. Dec. 645; Rome Ry. & Light Co. v. Loeb, 141 Ga. 202, 80 S.E. 785, 787, Ann.Cas.1915C, 1023.

MILL RUN. The lumber that comes from the mill in the ordinary process of its operation. Pye v. Eagle Lake Lumber Co., 66 Cal.App. 584, 227 P. 193, 194.

MILL SITE. A parcel of land on or contiguous to a water-course, suitable for the erection and operation of a mill operated by the power furnished by the stream. Occum Co. v. Sprague Mfg. Co., 35 Conn. 512; Mandeville v. Comstock, 9 Mich. 537. Specifically, in American mining law, a parcel of land constituting a portion of the public domain, located and claimed by the owner of a mining claim under the laws of the United States (or purchased by him from the government and patented,) not exceeding five acres in extent, not including any mineral land, not contiguous to the vein or lode, and occupied and used for the purpose of a mill or for other uses directly connected with the operation of the mine; or a similiar parcel of land located and actually used for the purpose of a mill or reduction plant, but not by the owner of an existing mine nor in connection with any particular mining claim. See U.S.Rev.St. § 2337, 30 U.S.C.A. § 42.

MILLBANK PRISON. Formerly called the "Penitentiary at Millbank." A prison at Westminster, for convicts under sentence of transportation, until the sentence or order shall be executed, or the convict be entitled to freedom, or be removed to some other place of confinement. Wharton.

MILLEATE, or MILL-LEAT. A trench to convey water to or from a mill. St. 7 Jac. I. c. 19.

MILLED MONEY. This term means merely coined money; and it is not necessary that it should be marked or rolled on the edges. Leach, 708.

MILLING IN TRANSIT. A special privilege allowable at certain designated points, whereby the carrier, having transported grain to a shipper's mill, agrees that the shipper may reship the meal without charge and for which extra compensation is usually exacted by interstate carriers under control of the Interstate Commerce Commission. Priebe v. Southern Ry. Co., 189 Ala. 427, 66 So. 573, 574.

MIL-REIS. The name of a piece of money in the coinage of Portugal, and the Azores and Madeira islands. Its value at the customhouse, according as it is coined in the first, second, or third of the places named, is $1.12, or 83 1/3 cents, or $1.

MINA. In old English law, a measure of corn or grain. Cowell; Spelman.

MINABLE COAL. Coal that can be profitably mined by judicious methods. Martin's Fork Coal Co. v. Harlan-Wallins Coal Corporation, D.C.Ky., 14 F.Supp. 902, 908.

MINAGE. A toll or duty paid for selling corn by the mina. Cowell.

MINARE. In old records, to mine or dig mines. *Minator*, a miner. Cowell.

MINATOR CARUCÆ. A plowman. Cowell.

MINATUR INNOCENTIBUS QUI PARCIT NOCENTIBUS. 4 Coke, 45. He threatens the innocent who spares the guilty.

MIND. In its legal sense, "mind" means only the ability to will, to direct, to permit, or to assent. McDermott v. Evening Journal Ass'n, 43 N.J.L. 492, 39 Am.Rep. 606.

MIND AND MEMORY. A phrase applied to testators, denoting the possession of mental capacity to make a will. In other words, one ought to be capable of making his will, with an understanding of the nature of the business in which he is engaged, a recollection of the property he means to dispose of, of the persons who are the objects of his bounty, and the manner in which it is to be distributed between them. Harrison v. Rowan, 3 Wash. C.C. 585, F.Cas.No.6,141.

MINE. An excavation in the earth from which ores, coal, or other mineral substances are removed by digging or other mining methods, and in its broader sense it denotes the vein, lode, or deposit of minerals. Atlas Milling Co. v. Jones, C.C.A.Okl., 115 F.2d 61, 63. It may include open cut, strip, or hydraulic methods of mining. Rudd v. Hayden, 265 Ky. 495, 97 S.W.2d 35, 37.

MINE RUN COAL. Fine broken coal and dust obtained by removing lumps and using fine coal underneath. Brodmeier v. Lamb, 170 Minn. 143, 212 N.W. 187, 188.

MINER. One who mines; a digger for metals and other minerals. While men of scientific attainments, or of experience in the use of machinery, are to be found in this class, yet the word by which the class is designated imports neither learning nor skill. Watson v. Lederer, 11 Colo. 577, 19 P. 604, 1 L.R.A. 854; Barton v. Wichita River Oil Co., Tex.Civ.App., 187 S.W. 1043, 1046.

MINER'S INCH. See Inch.

MINERAL, *adj.* Relating to minerals or the process and business of mining; bearing or producing valuable minerals.

MINERAL, *n.* Any valuable inert or lifeless substance formed or deposited in its present position through natural agencies alone, and which is found either in or upon the soil of the earth or in the rocks beneath the soil. Barringer & Adams, Mines, p. lxxvi.

Any natural constituent of the crust of the earth, inorganic or fossil, homogeneous in structure, having a definite chemical composition and known crystallization. See Webster; Cent.Dict.

The term includes all fossil bodies or matters dug out of mines or quarries, whence anything may be dug, such as beds of stone which may be quarried. Earl of Rosse v. Wainman, 14 Mees. & W. 872.

The word is not a definite term and is susceptible of limitations or extensions according to intention with which it is used. Standing alone it might by itself embrace the soil, hence include sand and gravel, or, under a strict definition, it might be limited to metallic substances. Puget Mill Co. v. Duecy, 1 Wash.2d 421, 96 P.2d 571, 573, 574.

MINERAL DEED. A realty conveyance involving a severance from fee of present title to minerals in place, either effecting such severance in first instance or conveying part of such mineral ownership previously severed from the fee. Hickey v. Dirks, 156 Kan. 326, 133 P.2d 107, 109, 110.

MINERAL DISTRICT. A term occasionally used in acts of congress, designating in a general way those portions or regions of the country where valuable minerals are mostly found, or where the business of mining is chiefly carried on, but carrying no very precise meaning and not a known term of the law. See U. S. v. Smith, C.C.Or., 11 F. 490.

MINERAL LAND ENTRY. See Entry.

MINERAL LANDS. Lands containing deposits of valuable, useful, or precious minerals in such quantities as to justify expenditures in the effort to extract them, and which are more valuable for the minerals they contain than for agricultural or other uses. Northern Pac. R. Co. v. Soderberg, 188 U.S. 526, 23 S.Ct. 365, 47 L.Ed. 575; Deffeback v. Hawke, 115 U.S. 392, 6 S.Ct. 95, 29 L.Ed. 423.

Lands on which metals or minerals have been discovered in rock in place. State v. Field, 31 N.M. 120, 241 P. 1027, 1042. "Mineral lands" include not merely metalliferous lands, but all such as are chiefly valuable for their deposits of mineral character, which are useful in arts or valuable for purposes of manufacture, Dunbar Lime Co. v. Utah-Idaho Sugar Co., C.C.A.Utah, 17 F.2d 351, 354; and embrace not only those which the lexicon defines as "mineral", but, in addition, such as are valuable for deposits of marble, slate, petroleum, asphaltum, and even guano. United States v. Northern Pac. R. Co., 311 U.S. 317, 61 S.Ct. 264, 284, 85 L.Ed. 210.

MINERAL LEASE. An agreement permitting use of land to explore, and then, if mineral is discovered, giving right to take mineral either for definite term or so long as it can be produced in paying quantities upon reserved royalty. Gordon v. Empire Gas & Fuel Co., C.C.A.Tex., 63 F.2d 487, 488.

MINERAL LODE. A mineral bed of rock with definite boundaries in a general mass of the mountain and also any zone or belt of mineralized rock lying within boundaries clearly separating it from the neighboring rock. Duffield v. San Francisco Chemical Co., C.C.A.Idaho, 205 F. 480, 484.

MINERAL RIGHT. An interest in minerals in land. A right to take minerals or a right to receive a royalty. Missouri Pac. R. Co. v. Strohacker, 202 Ark. 645, 152 S.W.2d 557, 561; Sheppard v. Stanolind Oil & Gas Co., Tex.Civ.App., 125 S.W. 2d 643, 648.

"Mineral rights" is a much broader term and is more inclusive than the term "oil and gas". Federal Gas, Oil & Coal Co. v. Moore, 290 Ky. 284, 161 S.W.2d 46, 49.

MINERAL ROYALTY. Income received from lessees of mineral land. Logan Coal & Timber Ass'n v. Helvering, C.C.A.3, 122 F.2d 848, 850. The term is distinguished from mineral interest. Maddox v. Butchee, 203 La. 299, 14 So.2d 4, 9.

MINERAL SERVITUDE. The right to exploit or develop. Frost Lumber Industries v. Republic Production Co., C.C.A.La., 112 F.2d 462, 466.

MINERATOR. In old records, a miner.

MINIMA PŒNA CORPORALIS EST MAJOR QUALIBET PECUNIARIA. The smallest corporal punishment is greater than any pecuniary one. 2 Inst. 220.

MINIME MUTANDA SUNT QUÆ CERTAM HABUERUNT INTERPRETATIONEM. Things which have had a certain interpretation [whose interpretation has been settled, as by common opinion] are not to be altered. Co. Litt. 365; Wing. Max. p. 748, max. 202.

MINIMENT. An old form of *muniment* (*q. v.*). Blount.

MINIMUM CHARGE. A "minimum charge" in connection with public utilities rate-fixing means the minimum monthly bill which will be rendered regardless of whether or not a customer has used sufficient of the commodity to make up that sum at the agreed rate. Ashtabula Gas Co. v. Public Utilities Commission, 102 Ohio St. 678, 133 N.E. 915, 916, 20 A.L.R. 217.

MINIMUM EST NIHILO PROXIMUM. The smallest is next to nothing.

MINIMUM WAGE. Such an amount as will maintain a normal standard of living, including the preservation of the health and efficiency of the worker.

The least wage on which an ordinary individual can be self-sustaining and obtain the ordinary requirements of life. Associated Industries of Oklahoma v. Industrial Welfare Commission, 185 Okl. 177, 90 P.2d 899, 913.

MINING. The process or business of extracting from the earth the precious or valuable metals, either in their native state or in their ores. In re Rollins Gold Min. Co., D.C.N.Y., 102 F. 985.

As ordinarily used, the term does not include the extraction from the earth of rock, marble, or slate, which is commonly described as "quarrying," although coal and salt are "mined;" nor does it include sinking wells or shafts for petroleum or natural gas, unless expressly so declared by statute, as is the case in Indiana. State v. Indiana, etc., Min. Co., 120 Ind. 575, 22 N.E. 778, 6 L.R.A. 579; Williams v. Citizens' Enterprise Co., 153 Ind. 496, 55 N.E. 425.

MINING CLAIM. A parcel of land, containing precious metal in its soil or rock, and appropriated by an individual, according to established rules, by the process of "location." St. Louis Smelting & Refining Co. v. Kemp, 104 U.S. 649, 26 L.Ed. 875; Northern Pac. R. Co. v. Sanders, C.C.A.Mont., 49 F. 135, 1 C.C.A. 192.

MINING COMPANIES. This designation was formerly applied in England to the associations formed in London in 1825 for working mines in Mexico and South America; but at present it comprises, both in England and America, all mining projects carried on by joint-stock associations or corporations. Rapalje & Lawrence.

MINING DISTRICT. A section of country usually designated by name and described or understood as being confined within certain natural boundaries, in which the precious metals (or their ores) are found in paying quantities, and which is worked therefor, under rules and regulations prescribed or agreed upon by the miners therein. U. S. v. Smith, C.C.Or., 11 F. 490.

MINING LEASE. A lease of a mine or mining claim or a portion thereof, to be worked by the lessee, usually under conditions as to the amount and character of work to be done, and reserving compensation to the lessor either in the form of a fixed rent or a royalty on the tonnage of ore mined, and which (as distinguished from a license) conveys to the lessee an interest or estate in the land, and (as distinguished from an ordinary lease) conveys not merely the temporary use and occupation of the land, but a portion of the land itself, that is, the ore in place and unsevered and to be extracted by the lessee. Austin v. Huntsville Min. Co., 72 Mo. 541, 37 Am.Rep. 446; Knight v. Indiana Coal Co., 47 Ind. 113, 17 Am.Rep. 692.

MINING LOCATION. The act of appropriating and claiming, according to certain established rules and local customs, a parcel of land of defined area, upon or in which one or more of the precious metals or their ores have been discovered, and which constitutes a portion of the public domain, with the declared intention to occupy and work it for mining purposes under the implied license of the United States. Also the parcel of land so occupied and appropriated. Poire v. Wells, 6 Colo. 412; St. Louis Smelting & Refining Co. v. Kemp, 104 U.S. 649, 26 L.Ed. 875; Golden Fleece, etc., Min. Co v. Cable, etc., Min. Co., 12 Nev. 328.

MINING PARTNERSHIP. A special type of partnership different in many respects from ordinary or trading partnerships. Meister v. Farrow, 109 Mont. 1, 92 P.2d 753, 757, 758, 760, 761.

An association of several owners of a mine for co-operation in working the mine. Kahn v. Central Smelting Co., 102 U.S. 645, 26 L.Ed. 266; Skillman v. Lachman, 23 Cal. 203, 83 Am.Dec. 96; Kimberly v. Arms, 129 U.S. 512, 9 S.Ct. 355, 32 L.Ed. 764.

Generally, where the parties co-operate in developing a lease for oil and gas, each agreeing to pay his part of the expenses and to share in the profits or losses, a "mining partnership" exists. Continental Supply Co. v. Dickson Oil Co., 94 Okl. 660, 153 P.2d 1017, 1019.

MINING RENT. In practice, the term is used to designate consideration given for a mining lease, whether such lease creates a tenancy, conveys a fee, or grants an incorporeal right or a mere license. Miller v. Carr, 137 Fla. 114, 188 So. 103, 107.

MINISTER. Ecclesiastical law. A person ordained according to the usages of some church or associated body of Christians for the preaching of the gospel and filling the pastoral office.

Foreign minister. An ambassador, minister, or envoy from a foreign government. Cherokee Nation v. Georgia, 5 Pet. 56, 8 L.Ed. 25.

International law. An officer appointed by the government of one nation as a mediator or arbitrator between two other nations who are engaged in a controversy, with their consent, with a view to effecting an amicable adjustment of the dispute.

A general name given to the diplomatic representatives sent by one state to another, including ambassadors, envoys, and residents.

Practice. An officer of justice, charged with the execution of the law, and hence termed a "ministerial officer;" such as a sheriff, bailiff, coroner, sheriff's officer. Britt. c. 21.

An agent; one who acts not by any inherent authority, but under another.

Public law. One of the highest functionaries in the organization of civil government, standing next to the sovereign or executive head, acting as his immediate auxiliary, and being generally charged with the administration of one of the great bureaus or departments of the executive branch of government. Otherwise called a "cabinet minister," "secretary of state," or "secretary of a department."

Public minister. A general term comprehending all the higher classes of diplomatic representatives,—as ambassadors, envoys, residents,—but not including the commercial representatives, such as consuls.

MINISTERIAL. That which is done under the authority of a superior; opposed to *judicial;* that which involves obedience to instructions, but demands no special discretion, judgment, or skill. State Tax Commission of Utah v. Katsis, 90 Utah 406, 62 P.2d 120, 123, 107 A.L.R. 1477; Blalock v. Johnston, 180 S.C. 40, 185 S.E. 51, 54, 105 A.L.R. 1115; First Nat. Bank v. Filer, 107 Fla. 526, 145 So. 204, 207, 87 A.L.R. 267.

MINISTERIAL ACT. One which a person performs in a given state of facts in a prescribed manner in obedience to the mandate of legal authority, without regard to or the exercise of his own judgment upon the propriety of the act being done. State Tax Commission of Utah v. Katsis, 90 Utah 406, 62 P.2d 120, 123, 107 A.L.R. 1477.

MINISTERIAL ACT OF MUNICIPAL CORPORATION. See Corporate Act of Municipal Corporation.

MINISTERIAL DUTY. One regarding which nothing is left to discretion—a simple and definite duty, imposed by law, and arising under conditions admitted or proved to exist. City of Tacoma v. Peterson, 165 Wash. 461, 5 P.2d 1022, 1024. Mott v. Hull, 51 Okl. 602, 152 P. 92, L.R.A.1916B, 1184. It arises when an individual has such a legal interest in its performance that neglect of performance becomes a wrong to such individual. Morton v. Comptroller General, 4 S.C. 473.

MINISTERIAL OFFICE. See Office.

MINISTERIAL OFFICER. One whose duties are purely ministerial, as distinguished from executive, legislative, or judicial functions, requiring obedience to the mandates of superiors and not involving the exercise of judgment or discretion. U. S. to Use of Kinney v. Bell, C.C.Pa., 127 F. 1002; State v. Loechner, 65 Neb. 814, 91 N.W. 874, 59 L.R.A. 915; Reid v. Hood, 2 Nott & McC., S.C., 169, 10 Am.Dec. 582.

MINISTERIAL POWER. See Power.

MINISTERIAL TRUST. See Trust.

MINISTERS PLENIPOTENTIARY. *Ministers plenipotentiary* possess full powers, and are of much greater distinction than simple ministers. These are without any particular attribution of rank and character, but by custom are now placed immediately below the ambassador, or on a level with the envoy extraordinary; Vattel, liv. 4, c. 5, § 74; 1 Kent 48; Merlin, *Répert.*

MINISTRANT. The party cross-examining a witness was so called, under the old system of the ecclesiastical courts.

MINISTRI REGIS. Lat. In old English law, ministers of the king, applied to the judges of the realm, and to all those who hold ministerial offices in the government. 2 Inst. 208.

MINISTRY. The term as used in England is wider than Cabinet and includes all the holders of public office who come in and go out with the Prime Minister. In this respect it may be contrasted with the Permanent Civil Service, whose tenure is independent of public changes. The first English Ministry as now understood was formed after the general election of 1696. Macaulay, Hist. Engl., ch. 24.

"Ecclesiastical functions," or "duties." Rector, etc., of St. George's Church in City of New York v. Morgan, 88 Misc. 702, 152 N.Y.S. 497, 498.

MINOR. An infant or person who is under the age of legal competence. One under twenty-one. A term derived from the civil law, which described a person under a certain age as *less than* so many years. *Minor viginti quinque annis,* one less than twenty-five years of age. Inst. 1, 14, 2; Audsley v. Hale, 303 Mo. 451, 261 S.W. 117, 123.

Also, less; of less consideration; lower; a person of inferior condition. Fleta, 2, 47, 13, 15; Calvin.

MINOR ÆTAS. Lat. Minority or infancy. Cro. Car. 516. Literally, lesser age.

MINOR ANTE TEMPUS AGERE NON POTEST IN CASU PROPRIETATIS NEC ETIAM CONVENIRE; DIFFERETUR USQUE ÆTATEM; SED NON CADIT BREVE. 2 Inst. 291. A minor before majority cannot act in a case of property, nor even agree; it should be deferred until majority; but the writ does not fail.

MINOR FACT. In the law of evidence, a relative, collateral, or subordinate fact; a circumstance. Wills, Circ.Ev. 27; Burrill, Circ.Ev. p. 121, note, 582.

MINOR JURARE NON POTEST. A minor cannot make oath. Co.Litt. 172*b*. An infant cannot be sworn on a jury. Litt. 289.

MINOR MINOREM CUSTODIRE NON DEBET, ALIOS ENIM PRÆSUMITUR MALE REGERE QUI SEIPSUM REGERE NESCIT. A minor ought not to be guardian to a minor, for he who knows not how to govern himself is presumed to be unfit to govern others. Fleta, lib. 1, c. 10; Co.Litt. 88*b*.

MINOR NON TENETUR RESPONDERE DURANTE MINORI ÆTATE, NISI IN CAUSA DOTIS, PROPTER FAVOREM. 3 Bulst. 143. A minor is not bound to reply during his minority, except as a matter of favor in a cause of dower.

MINOR QUI INFRA ÆTATEM 12 ANNORUM FUERIT UITAGARI NON POTEST, NEC EXTRA LEGEM PONI, QUIA ANTE TALEM ÆTATEM, NON EST SUB LEGE ALIQUA, NEC IN DECENNA. Co.Litt. 128. A minor who is under twelve years of age cannot be outlawed, nor placed without the law, because before such age he is not under any law, nor in a decennary.

MINOR SEPTEMDECIM ANNIS NON ADMITTITUR FORE EXECUTOREM. A person under seventeen years is not admitted to be an executor. 6 Coke, 67. A rule of ecclesiastical law.

MINORA REGALIA. In English law, the lesser prerogatives of the crown, including the rights of the revenue. 1 Bl.Comm. 241.

MINORITY. The state or condition of a minor; infancy.

The smaller number of votes of a deliberative assembly; opposed to majority, (which see.)

MINT. The place designated by law where bullion is coined into money under authority of the government.

Also a place of privilege, in Southwark, near the king's prison, where persons formerly sheltered themselves from justice under the pretext that it was an ancient palace of the crown. The privilege is now abolished. Wharton.

MINT-MARK. The masters and workers of the English mint, in the indentures made with them, agreed "to make a privy mark in the money they make, of gold and silver, so that they may know which moneys were of their own making." After every trial of the pix, having proved their moneys to be lawful, they were entitled to their *quietus* under the great seal, and to be discharged from all suits or actions. Wharton.

MINT-MASTER. One who manages the coinage.

MINTAGE. The charge or commission taken by the mint as a consideration for coining into money the bullion which is brought to it for that purpose; the same as "seigniorage."

Also that which is coined or stamped as money; the product of the mint.

MINUS. Lat. In the civil law, less; less than. The word had also, in some connections, the sense of "not at all." For example, a debt remaining wholly unpaid was described as *"minus solutum."*

MINUS LATIUM. See Jus Latium.

MINUS SOLVIT, QUI TARDIUS SOLVIT. He does not pay who pays too late. Dig. 50, 16, 12, 1.

MINUTE. In measures of time or circumference, a minute is the sixtieth part of an hour or degree.

MINUTE-BOOK. A book kept by the clerk or prothonotary of a court for entering memoranda of its proceedings.

MINUTE TITHES. Small tithes, usually belonging to the vicar; *e. g.* eggs, honey, wax, etc. 3 Burn, Eccl.Law 680; 6 & 7 Will. IV. c. 71, §§ 17, 18, 27.

MINUTES. Business law. Memoranda or notes of a transaction or proceeding. Thus, the record of the proceedings at a meeting of directors or shareholders of a company is called the "minutes."

Practice. A memorandum of what takes place in court, made by authority of the court. Moore v. State, 3 Heisk., Tenn., 509.

Scotch Practice. A pleading put into writing before the lord ordinary, as the ground of his judgment. Bell.

MINUTIO. Lat. In the civil law, a lessening; diminution or reduction. Dig. 4, 5, 1.

MIRANDA RULE. Prior to any custodial interrogation; that is, questioning initiated by law enforcement officers after a person is taken into custody or otherwise deprived of his freedom in any significant way, the person must be warned:

1. That he has a right to remain silent;
2. That any statement he does make may be used as evidence against him;
3. That he has a right to the presence of an attorney;
4. That if he cannot afford an attorney, one will be appointed for him prior to any questioning if he so desires.

Unless and until these warnings or a waiver of these rights are demonstrated at the trial, no evidence obtained in the interrogation may be used against the accused. Miranda v. Arizona, 384 U.S. 436, 444, 478, 479, 86 S.Ct. 1602, 1612, 1630, 16 L.Ed.2d 294.

MIRROR. The Mirror of Justice, or of the Justices, commonly spoken of as the "Mirror," is an ancient treatise on the laws of England, supposedly written during the reign of Edward II., and attributed to one Andrew Horne. But it has been thought that the germ of it was written before the Conquest and that Horne only made additions to it.

MIS. An inseparable particle used in composition, to mark an ill sense or depravation of the meaning; as "miscomputation" or "misaccompting," *i. e.*, false reckoning.

MISA. In old English law, the mise or issue in a writ of right. Spelman.

In old records, a compact or agreement; a form of compromise. Cowell.

MISADVENTURE. A mischance or accident; a casualty caused by the act of one person inflicting injury upon another. Homicide "by misadventure" occurs where a man, doing a lawful act, without any intention of hurt, unfortunately kills another. 4 Bl.Comm. 182; Williamson v. State, 2 Ohio Cir. Ct.R. 292.

MISALLEGE. To cite falsely as a proof or argument.

MISAPPLICATION. Improper, illegal, wrongful, or corrupt use or application of funds, property, etc. Jewett v. U. S., C.C.A.Mass., 100 F. 840, 41 C.C.A. 88; Kansas Flour Mills Co. v. American Surety Co. of New York, 98 Kan. 618, 158 P. 1118.

MISAPPROPRIATION. The act of misappropriating or turning to a wrong purpose; wrong appropriation; a term which does not necessarily mean peculation, although it may mean that. Bannon v. Knauss, 57 Ohio App. 288, 13 N.E.2d 733, 735.

MISBEHAVIOR. Ill conduct; improper or unlawful behavior. Smith v. Cutler, 10 Wend., N.Y., 590, 25 Am.Dec. 580; State v. Arnold, 100 Tenn. 307, 47 S.W. 221.

MISBRANDING. False or misleading labeling. People v. Rosenbloom, Cal., 119 Cal.App. 759, 2 P.2d 228, 231.

MISCARRIAGE. Medical jurisprudence. The expulsion of the *ovum* or embryo from the *uterus* within the first six weeks after conception. Between that time, and before the expiration of the sixth month, when the child may possibly live, it is termed "abortion." When the delivery takes place soon after the sixth month, it is denominated "premature labor." But the criminal act of destroying or bringing forth prematurely the *fœtus* or unborn offspring of a pregnant woman, at any time before birth, is termed, in law, "procuring miscarriage." Chit.Med.Jur. 410. Smith v. State, 33 Me. 59, 54 Am.Dec. 607; People v. Rankin, 10 Cal.2d 198, 74 P.2d 71, 73.

The failure of a woman, from causes beyond her control to carry a fetus to maturity. Flory v. Supreme Tribe of Ben Hur, 98 Neb. 160, 152 N.W. 295.

Practice. As used in the statute of frauds, ("debt, default, or miscarriage of another,") this term means any species of unlawful conduct or wrongful act for which the doer could be held liable in a civil action. Gansey v. Orr, 173 Mo. 532, 73 S.W. 477.

MISCARRIAGE OF JUSTICE. Prejudice to substantial rights of a party. See the cases of State v. Cluff, 48 Utah, 102, 158 P. 701, 703; State v. Nell, 117 Wash. 142, 202 P. 7, 8.

MISCASTING. An error in auditing and numbering. It does not include any pretended miscasting or misvaluing. 4 Bouvier, Inst. n. 4128.

MISCEGENATION. Mixture of races; marriage between persons of different races; as between a white person and a Negro.

Living together in state of adultery or fornication, by white person and Negro, or descendant of Negro Jackson v. State, 23 Ala.App. 555, 129 So. 306.

MISCHARGE. An erroneous charge; a charge, given by a court to a jury, which involves errors for which the judgment may be reversed.

MISCHIEF. In legislative parlance, the word is often used to signify the evil or danger which a statute is intended to cure or avoid.

In the phrase "malicious mischief," (which see,) it imports a wanton or reckless injury to persons or property.

MISCOGNISANT. Ignorant; uninformed. The word is obsolete.

MISCONDUCT. A transgression of some established and definite rule of action, a forbidden act, a dereliction from duty, unlawful behavior, willful in character, improper or wrong behavior; its synonyms are misdemeanor, misdeed, misbehavior, delinquency, impropriety, mismanagement, offense, but not negligence or carelessness. Mandella v. Mariano, 61 R.I. 163, 200 A. 478, 479.

MISCONDUCT IN OFFICE. Any unlawful behavior by a public officer in relation to the duties of his office, willful in character. Wysong v. Walden, 120 W.Va. 122, 196 S.E. 573, 575.

MISCONTINUANCE. In practice, an improper continuance; want of proper form in a continuance; the same with "discontinuance." Cowell.

MISCREANT. In old English law, an apostate; an unbeliever; one who totally renounced Christianity. 4 Bl.Comm. 44.

MISDATE. A false or erroneous date affixed to a paper or document.

MISDELIVERY. The delivery of property by a carrier or warehouseman to a person not authorized by the owner or person to whom the carrier or warehouseman is bound by his contract to deliver it. Cleveland, etc., R. Co. v. Potts, 33 Ind. App. 564, 71 N.E. 689; Forbes v. Boston & L. R. Co., 133 Mass. 156.

MISDEMEANANT. A person guilty of a misdemeanor; one sentenced to punishment upon conviction of a misdemeanor. See First-Class Misdemeanant.

MISDEMEANOR. Offenses lower than felonies and generally those punishable by fine or imprisonment otherwise than in penitentiary. People v. Harshbarger, 296 Ill.App. 397, 16 N.E.2d 247, 248.

An act committed or omitted in violation of a public law either forbidding or commanding it. State v. Magee Pub. Co., 29 N.M. 455, 224 P. 1028, 1031, 38 A.L.R. 142; State v. Jackson, 142 La. 540, 77 So. 196, 197, L.R.A.1918B, 1178.

In the English law, "misdemeanor" is generally used in contradistinction to "felony;" and misdemeanors comprehend all indictable offenses which do not amount to felony, as libels, conspiracies, attempts, and solicitations to commit felonies, etc. Brown. People v. Upson, 79 Hun 87, 29 N.Y.Supp. 615; In re Bergin, 31 Wis. 386; Walsh v. People, 65 Ill. 65, 16 Am.Rep. 569.

Under modern statutes the distinction between felonies and misdemeanors is not whether the offense is infamous, but whether it is punishable by imprisonment in the penitentiary or capitally, in which case it is a "felony"; otherwise a "misdemeanor." Jones v. Brinkley, 174 N.C. 23, 93 S.E. 372, 373; Lee Lewis, Inc., v. Dosch, 193 Ky. 163, 235 S.W. 355, 356.

MISDESCRIPTION. An error or falsity in the description of the subject-matter of a contract which deceives one of the parties to his injury, or is misleading in a material or substantial point.

MISDIRECTION. In practice, an error made by a judge in instructing the jury upon the trial of a cause.

MISE. The issue in a writ of right. When the tenant in a writ of right pleads that his title is better than the demandant's, he is said to join the *mise* on the mere right.

Also expenses; costs; disbursements in an action.

MISE-MONEY. Money paid by way of contract or composition to purchase any liberty, etc. Blount.

MISERA EST SERVITUS, UBI JUS EST VAGUM AUT INCERTUM. It is a wretched state of slavery which subsists where the law is vague or uncertain. 4 Inst. 245; Broom, Max. 150.

MISERABILE DEPOSITUM. Lat. In the civil law, the name of an involuntary deposit, made under pressing necessity; as, for instance, shipwreck, fire, or other inevitable calamity. Poth. Proc. Civile, pt. 5, c. 1, § 1; Code La. art. 2935, Civ. Code, art. 2964.

MISERERE. The name and first word of one of the penitential psalms, being that which was commonly used to be given by the ordinary to such condemned malefactors as were allowed the benefit of clergy; whence it is also called the "psalm of mercy." Wharton.

MISERICORDIA. Lat. Mercy; a fine or amerciament; an arbitrary or discretionary amercement.

MISERICORDIA COMMUNIS. In old English law, a fine set on a whole county or hundred.

MISFEASANCE. A misdeed or trespass. The improper performance of some act which a man may lawfully do. 3 Steph.Comm. 460. Bell v. Josselyn, 3 Gray, Mass. 309, 63 Am.Dec. 741.

"Nonfeasance" means the omission of an act which a person ought to do; "misfeasance" is the improper doing of an act which a person might lawfully do; and "malfeasance" is the doing of an act which a person ought not to do at all. Proksch v. Bettendorf, 218 Iowa 1376, 257 N.W. 383. But "misfeasance" is often used in the sense of "malfeasance." Coite v. Lynes, 33 Conn. 109; Brooks v. Hornbeck, Tex.Civ.App., 274 S.W. 162, 163.

MISFEAZANCE. See Misfeasance.

MISFORTUNE. An adverse event, calamity, or evil fortune, arising by accident, (or without the will or concurrence of him who suffers from it,) and not to be foreseen or guarded against by care or prudence. 20 Q.B.Div. 816. Swetland v. Swetland, 100 N.J.Eq. 196, 134 A. 822, 829. In its application to the law of homicide, this term always involves the further idea that the person causing the death is not at the time engaged in any unlawful act. 4 Bl.Comm. 182. Gaunce v. State, 22 Okl.Cr. 361, 211 P. 517, 518.

MISJOINDER. See Joinder.

MISKENNING. In Saxon and old English law, an unjust or irregular summoning to court; to speak unsteadily in court; to vary in one's plea. Cowell; Blount; Spelman.

MISLAY. To deposit in a place not afterwards recollected; to lose anything by forgetfulness of the place where it was laid. Shehane v. State, 13 Tex.App. 535.

MISLEADING. Delusive; calculated to lead astray or to lead into error. Diamond Drill Contracting Co. v. International Diamond Drill Contracting Co., 106 Wash. 72, 179 P. 120, 122. Instructions which are of such a nature as to be misunderstood by the jury, or to give them a wrong impression, are said to be "misleading."

MISNOMER. Mistake in name; giving incorrect name to person in accusation, indictment, pleading, deed or other instrument. Culpepper v. State, 173 Ga. 799, 161 S.E. 623.

MISPLEADING. Pleading incorrectly, or omitting anything in pleading which is essential to the support or defense of an action, is so called; as in the case of a plaintiff not merely stating his title in a defective manner, but setting forth a title which is essentially defective in itself; or if, to an action of debt, the defendant pleads "not guilty" instead of *nil debet*. Brown. Lovett v. Pell, 22 Wend., N.Y., 376; Chicago & A. R. Co. v. Murphy, 198 Ill. 462, 64 N.E. 1011.

MISPRISION. A word used to describe a misdemeanor which does not possess a specific name. 3 Inst. 36; United States v. Perlstein, C.C.A.N.J., 126 F.2d 789, 798. But more particularly and properly the term denotes either (1) a contempt against the sovereign, the government, or the courts of justice, including not only contempts of court, properly so called, but also all forms of seditious or disloyal conduct and leze-majesty; (2) maladministration of high public office, including peculation of the public funds; (3) neglect or light account made of a crime, that is, failure in the duty of a citizen to endeavor to prevent the commission of a crime, or, having knowledge of its commission, to reveal it to the proper authorities. 4 Bl.Comm. 119–126; State v. Biddle, 124 A. 804, 805, 2 W.W.Harr., Del. 401.

Negative misprision. The concealment of something which ought to be revealed; that is, misprision in the third of the specific meanings given above.

Positive misprision. The commission of something which ought not to be done; that is, misprision in the first and second of the specific meanings given above.

Practice. A clerical error or mistake made in writing or keeping records. State v. Ryan, 146 Wash. 114, 261 P. 775, 776.

MISPRISION OF FELONY. The offense of concealing a felony committed by another, but without such previous concert with or subsequent assistance to the felon as would make the party concealing an accessory before or after the fact. 4 Steph.Comm. 260; 4 Bl.Comm. 121; United States v. Perlstein, C.C.A.N.J., 126 F.2d 789, 798.

MISPRISION OF TREASON. The bare knowledge and concealment of an act of treason or treasonable plot, that is, without any assent or participation therein, for if the latter elements be present the party becomes a principal. 4 Bl.Comm. 120; Pen.Code Cal. § 38.

MISREADING. Reading a deed or other instrument to an illiterate or blind man (who is a party to it) in a false or deceitful manner, so that he conceives a wrong idea of its tenor or contents. 5 Coke, 19; 6 East, 309; Hallenbeck v. Dewitt, 2 Johns., N.Y. 404.

MISRECITAL. The erroneous or incorrect recital of a matter of fact, either in an agreement, deed, or pleading.

MISREPRESENTATION. Any manifestation by words or other conduct by one person to another that, under the circumstances, amounts to an assertion not in accordance with the facts. A. P. Landis, Inc., v. Mellinger, 116 Pa.Super. 167, 175 A. 745, 746.

An untrue statement of fact. An incorrect or false representation. That which, if accepted, leads the mind to an apprehension of a condition other and different from that which exists. Colloquially it is understood to mean a statement made to deceive or mislead. Haigh v. White Way Laundry Co., 164 Iowa 143, 145 N.W. 473, 474, 50 L.R.A.,N.S., 1091; Zackwik v. Hanover Fire Ins. Co., Mo. App., 225 S.W. 135, 138.

In a limited sense, an intentional false statement respecting a matter of fact, made by one of the parties to a contract, which is material to the contract and influential in producing it. Wise v. Fuller, 29 N.J.Eq. 262; Hicks v. Wynn, 137 Va. 186, 119 S.E. 133, 135.

A "misrepresentation," which justifies the rescission of a contract, is a false statement of a substantive fact, or any conduct which leads to a belief of a substantive fact material to proper understanding of the matter in hand, made with intent to deceive or mislead. Rhodes v. Uhl, 189 Iowa 408, 178 N.W. 394, 400.

Misrepresentation such as will amount to false pretense is not confined to mere oral misstatements of fact but includes distribution of printed matter, or a course of conduct, manifestly intended to deceive as to conditions actually existing. Commonwealth v. Dougherty, 84 Pa.Super. Ct. 319, 321.

False or *fraudulent* misrepresentation is a representation contrary to the fact, made by a person with a knowledge of its falsehood, and being the cause of the other party's entering into the contract. 6 Clark & F. 232.

Negligent misrepresentation is a false representation made by a person who has no reasonable grounds for believing it to be true, though he does not know that it is untrue, or even believes it to be true. L.R. 4 H.L. 79.

Innocent misrepresentation occurs where the person making the representation had reasonable grounds for believing it to be true. L.R. 2 Q.B. 580.

Insurance law. A statement of something as a fact which is untrue and material to the risk, and which assured states knowing it to be untrue and with intent to deceive, or which insured states positively as true, not knowing it to be true, and which has a tendency to mislead. Lawson v. Southwestern Voluntary Ass'n, 168 Va. 294, 191 S. E. 648, 649.

Material misrepresentation. In insurance law, one that would influence a prudent insurer in determining whether or not to accept the risk, or in fixing the amount of the premium in the event of such acceptance. Sovereign Camp, W. O. W., v. Parker, 36 Ga.App. 695, 138 S.E. 86, 87.

MISSA. Lat. The mass.

MISSÆ PRESBYTER. A priest in orders. Blount.

MISSAL. The mass-book.

MISSILIA. In Roman law, gifts or liberalities, which the prætors and consuls were in the habit of throwing among the people. Inst. 2, 1, 45.

MISSING SHIP. In maritime law, a vessel is so called when, computed from her known day of sailing, the time that has elapsed exceeds the average duration of similar voyages at the same season of the year. 2 Duer, Ins. 469.

MISSIONARIES. The term "missionaries," as used in the liquor trade, applies to men employed to visit saloons throughout the country and puff liquors of particular manufacture, so that salesmen of wholesalers and jobbers will find the way prepared for them. Hiram Walker & Sons v. Corning & Co., D.C.Ill., 255 F. 129, 130.

MISSIONS. In church parlance, the establishment of churches and schools and relief depots through which are taught the principles of Christianity, the afflicted cared for, and the needy supplied. Hitchcock v. Board of Home Missions, 259 Ill. 288, 102 N.E. 741, 744, Ann.Cas.1915B, 1.

MISSIVES. In Scotch law, writings passed between parties as evidence of a transaction. Bell.

MISSTAICUS. In old records, a messenger.

MISSURA. The ceremonies used in a Roman Catholic church to recommend and dismiss a dying person.

MISTAKE. Some unintentional act, omission, or error arising from ignorance, surprise, imposition, or misplaced confidence. Code Ga. § 3117, Civ. Code 1910, § 4570; 1 Story, Eq. Jur. § 110.

A mistake exists when a person, under some erroneous conviction of law or fact, does, or omits to do, some act which, but for the erroneous conviction, he would not have done or omitted. Jeremy, Eq. Jur. 358; Ward v. Lyman, 108 Vt. 464, 188 A. 892, 896. It may arise either from unconsciousness, ignorance, forgetfulness, imposition, or misplaced confidence. Bisph. Eq. § 185; Salazar v. Steelman, 22 Cal.App.2d 402, 71 P.2d 79, 82.

Mistake of fact is a mistake not caused by the neglect of a legal duty on the part of the person making the mistake, and consisting in (1) an unconscious ignorance or forgetfulness of a fact, past or present, material to the contract; or (2) belief in the present existence of a thing material to the contract which does not exist, or in the past existence of such a thing which has not existed. Callan Court Co. v. Citizens & Southern Nat. Bank, 184 Ga. 87, 190 S.E. 831, 854.

A *mistake of law* happens when a party, having full knowledge of the facts, comes to an erroneous conclusion as to their legal effect. It is a mistaken opinion or inference, arising from an imperfect or incorrect exercise of the judgment, upon facts, Page v. Provines, 179 Okl. 391, 66 P.2d 7, 10; and necessarily presupposes that the person forming it is in full possession of the facts. The facts precede the law, and the true and false opinion alike imply an acquaintance with them. The one is the result of a correct application of legal principles, which every man is presumed to know, and is called "law;" the other, the result of a faulty application, and is called a "mistake of law." Hurd v. Hall, 12 Wis. 124; Barnett v. Douglas, 102 Okl. 85, 226 P. 1035, 1037, 39 A.L.R. 188.

Mutual mistake is where the parties have a common intention, but it is induced by a common or mutual mistake. Paine-Fishburn Granite Co. v. Reynoldson, 115 Neb. 520, 213 N.W. 750, 751; Northwest Thresher Co. v. McNinch, 42 Okl. 155, 140 P. 1170, 1172. "Mutual" as used in the expression mutual mistake of fact expresses a thought of reciprocity and distinguishes it from a mistake which is a common mistake of both parties. There is something of the thought of a common mistake because it must affect both parties. Mistake of fact as ground for relief may be neither "mutual" nor common in the strict sense because it may be wholly the mistake of one of the parties, the other being wholly ignorant both of the fact upon the faith of which the other has mistakenly acted and that the other has acted upon such an understanding of the fact situation. United States Fidelity & Guaranty Co. v. Heller, D.C.Pa., 259 F. 885, 890; Litteral v. Bevins, 186 Ky. 514, 217 S.W. 369, 370.

MISTER. A title of courtesy. A trade, craft, occupation, employment, office. Webster.

MISTERY. A trade or calling. Cowell.

MISTRESS. The proper style of the wife of an esquire or a gentleman in England.

MISTRIAL. An erroneous, invalid, or nugatory trial; a trial of an action which cannot stand in law because of want of jurisdiction, or a wrong drawing of jurors, or disregard of some other fundamental requisite. C. W. Hunt Co. v. Boston Elevated Ry. Co., 217 Mass. 319, 104 N.E. 728, 729; Illinois Oil Co. v. Grandstaff, 118 Okl. 101, 246 P. 832, 833.

MISUSER. An unlawful use of a right. Abuse of an office or franchise. 2 Bl.Comm. 153.

MITIGATING CIRCUMSTANCES. Such as do not constitute a justification or excuse of the offense in question, but which, in fairness and mercy, may be considered as extenuating or reducing the degree of moral culpability. Heaton v. Wright, 10 How.Prac., N.Y. 82. Those that affect basis for award of exemplary damages, or reduce actual damages by showing, not that they were never suffered, but that they have been partially extinguished. McClelland v. Climax Hosiery Mills, 252 N.Y. 347, 169 N.E. 605, 608. And in actions for libel and slander, circumstances bearing on defendant's liability for exemplary damages by reducing moral culpability, or on liability for actual damages by showing partial extinguishment thereof. Civil Practice Act, §§ 262, 338. Fleckenstein v. Friedman, 266 N.Y. 19, 193 N.E. 537, 539.

MITIGATION. Alleviation; abatement or diminution of a penalty or punishment imposed by law.

Reduction, diminishing, or lessening amount of penalty or punishment. People v. Fook, 206 Cal. 64, 273 P. 779, 782.

MITIGATION OF DAMAGES. A reduction of the amount of damages, not by proof of facts which are a bar to a part of the plaintiff's cause of action, or a justification, nor yet of facts which constitute a cause of action in favor of the defendant, but rather facts which show that the plaintiff's conceded cause of action does not entitle him to so large an amount as the showing on his side would otherwise justify the jury in allowing him. 1 Suth. Dam. 226.

MITIOR SENSUS. Lat. The more favorable acceptation.

MITIUS IMPERANTI MELIUS PARETUR. The more mildly one commands, the better is he obeyed. 3 Inst. 24.

MITOYENNETÉ. In French law, the joint ownership of two neighbors in a wall, ditch, or hedge which separates their estates.

MITTENDO MANUSCRIPTUM PEDIS FINIS. An abolished judicial writ addressed to the treasurer and chamberlain of the exchequer to search for and transmit the foot of a fine acknowledged before justices in eyre into the common pleas. Reg. Orig. 14.

MITTER. L. Fr. To put, to send, or to pass; as, *mitter l'estate,* to pass the estate; *mitter le droit,* to pass a right. These words are used to distinguish different kinds of releases.

MITTER AVANT. L. Fr. In old practice, to put before; to present before a court; to produce in court.

MITTIMUS. Criminal practice. The name of a precept in writing, issuing from a court or magistrate, directed to the sheriff or other officer, commanding him to convey to the prison the person named therein, and to the jailer, commanding him to receive and safely keep such person until he shall be delivered by due course of law. Pub. St. Mass. 1882, p. 1293. Connolly v. Anderson, 112 Mass. 62; Saunders v. U. S., D.C.Me., 73 F. 786. Transcript of minutes of conviction and sentence duly certified by court clerk. United States ex rel. Chasteen v. Denemark, C.C.A.Ill., 138 F.2d 289, 291.

Old English law. A writ enclosing a record sent to be tried in a county palatine; it derives its name from the Latin word *mittimus,* "we send." It is the jury process of these counties, and commands the proper officer of the county palatine to command the sheriff to summon the jury for the trial of the cause, and to return the record, etc. Territory v. Hattick, 2 Mart. O. S., La., 88.

MIXED. Formed by admixture or commingling; partaking of the nature, character, or legal attributes of two or more distinct kinds or classes.

As to mixed "Action," "Blood," "Contract," "Government," "Jury," "Larceny," "Marriage," "Nuisance," "Policy," "Presumption," "Property," "Tithes," and "War," see those titles.

MIXED ESTATE. Leasehold estates created by ground rent leases for 99 years renewable forever, both at common law and in Maryland, are sometimes called "mixed estates". Jones v. Magruder, D.C.Md., 42 F.Supp. 193, 198.

MIXED INSURANCE COMPANY. One which has, at least in part, the nature of both stock and mutual companies, and in which a certain portion of the profits is divided among the stockholders and distribution of other funds is made among the insured. Ohio Farmers Indemnity Co. v. Commissioner of Internal Revenue, C.C.A.6, 108 F.2d 665, 667; Pink v. Town Taxi Co., 138 Me. 44, 21 A.2d 656, 658, 659.

MIXED LAWS. A name sometimes given to those which concern both persons and property.

MIXED QUESTION OF LAW AND FACT. A question depending for solution on questions of both law and fact, but is really a question of either law or fact to be decided by either judge or jury. State v. Hayes, 162 La. 917, 111 So. 327, 329.

MIXED QUESTIONS. This phrase may mean either those which arise from the conflict of foreign and domestic laws, or questions arising on a trial involving both law and fact. Bennett v. Eddy, 120 Mich. 300, 79 N.W. 481.

MIXED SUBJECTS OF PROPERTY. Such as fall within the definition of things real, but which are attended, nevertheless, with some of the legal qualities of things personal, as emblements, fixtures, and shares in public undertakings, connected with land. Besides these, there are others which, though things personal in point of definition, are, in respect of some of their legal qualities, of the nature of things real; such are animals *feræ naturæ,* charters and deeds, court rolls, and other evidences of the land, together with the chests in which they are contained, ancient family pictures, ornaments, tombstones, coats of armor, with pennons and other ensigns, and especially heirlooms. Wharton.

MIXED TRAIN. "Mixed train" is one carrying both passengers and freight. State v. Chicago, St. P., M. & O. Ry. Co., 115 Neb. 306, 212 N.W. 535, 536; Arizona Eastern R. Co. v. State, 29 Ariz. 446, 242 P. 870, 871.

MIXED TRIBUNALS. A name given to an international jurisdiction introduced into Egypt in 1878, after negotiations with the various Christian Powers of Europe.

This tribunal made the administration of civil justice quite independent of the government of Egypt. They have jurisdiction over cases between persons of different nationalities, whether native or European, but criminal charges against natives are heard in the native criminal courts and those against Europeans in the proper consular courts. There are three first instance courts, one at Alexandria with eighteen judges, of whom twelve are foreign, one at Cairo with nineteen judges, of whom thirteen are foreign, and one at Mansurah with nine judges, of whom six are foreign, and a Court of Appeal sitting at Alexandria, composed of fifteen judges. The jurisdiction cannot be invoked unless one party is a foreigner, but it is said to be not uncommon for Egyptian merchants to assign their claims to foreigners, so as to get them into these courts. Ann.Bull. of Comp.Law Bureau, 1911, p. 43. The judges are subjects of various European states, and of the United States and Brazil. They are appointed by their respective governments; Milner, England in Egypt.

These courts were instituted for a period of five years only, and have been renewed at various times. Bonfils, Manual of Int.Law 460; 23 L.Q.R. 409; 8 Encyc.Laws of Eng. 445.

MIXTION. The mixture or confusion of goods or chattels belonging severally to different owners, in such a way that they can no longer be separated or distinguished; as where two measures of wine belonging to different persons are poured together into the same cask.

MIXTUM IMPERIUM. Lat. In old English law, mixed authority; a kind of civil power. A term applied by Lord Hale to the "power" of certain subordinate civil magistrates as distinct from "jurisdiction." Hale, Anal. § 11.

MOB. An assemblage of many people, acting in a violent and disorderly manner, defying the law, and committing, or threatening to commit, depredations upon property or violence to persons. Alexander v. State, 40 Tex.Cr.R. 395, 50 S.W. 716; Marshall v. Buffalo, 50 App.Div. 149, 64 N.Y.S. 411; Champaign County v. Church, 62 Ohio St. 318, 57 N.E. 50, 48 L.R.A. 738.

The word, in legal use, is practically synonymous with "riot," but the latter is the more correct term. Koska v. Kansas City, 123 Kan. 362, 255 P. 57, 58; Blakeman v. City of Wichita, 93 Kan. 444, 144 P. 816, L.R.A.1915C, 578.

MOBBING AND RIOTING. In Scotch law, a general term including all those convocations of the lieges for violent and unlawful purposes, which are attended with injury to the persons or property of the lieges, or terror and alarm to the neighborhood in which it takes place. The two phrases are usually placed together; but, nevertheless, they have distinct meanings, and are sometimes used separately in legal language, the word "mobbing" being peculiarly applicable to the unlawful assemblage and violence of a number of persons, and that of "rioting" to the outrageous behavior of a single individual. Alis. Crim. Law, c. 23, p. 509.

MOBILIA. Lat. Movables; movable things; otherwise called *"res mobiles."*

MOBILIA NON HABENT SITUM. Movables have no *situs* or local habitation. Holmes v. Remsen, 4 Johns., N.Y., Ch. 472, 8 Am.Dec. 581.

MOBILIA SEQUUNTUR PERSONAM. Movables follow the [law of the] person. Story, Confl. Law, § 378; Broom, Max. 522.

MOCK. To deride, to laugh at, to ridicule, to treat with scorn and contempt. State v. Warner, 34 Conn. 279.

MOCKADOES. A kind of cloth made in England, mentioned in St. 23 Eliz. c. 9.

MODAL LEGACY. See Legacy.

MODE. The manner in which a thing is done; as the mode of proceeding, the mode of process. Anderson's L. Dict.

MODEL. A pattern or representation of something to be made. A *fac simile* of something invented, made on a reduced scale, in compliance with the patent laws. State v. Fox, 25 N.J.L. 566; Montana Ore Purchasing Co. v. Boston, etc., Min. Co., 27 Mont. 288, 70 P. 1126.

MODERAMEN INCULPATÆ TUTELÆ. Lat. In Roman law, the regulation of justifiable defense. A term used to express that degree of force in defense of the person or property which a person might safely use, although it should occasion the death of the aggressor. Calvin; Bell.

MODERATA MISERICORDIA. A writ founded on *Magna Charta,* which lies for him who is amerced in a court, not of record, for any transgression beyond the quality or quantity of the offense. It is addressed to the lord of the court, or his bailiff, commanding him to take a moderate amerciament of the parties. New Nat. Brev. 167; Fitzh. Nat. Brev. 76.

MODERATE CASTIGAVIT. Lat. In pleading, he moderately chastised. The name of a plea in trespass which justifies an alleged battery on the ground that it consisted in a moderate chastisement of the plaintiff by the defendant, which, from their relations, the latter had a legal right to inflict.

MODERATE SPEED. In admiralty law, as applied to a steam-vessel, "such speed only is moderate as will permit the steamer reasonably and effectually to avoid a collision by slackening speed, or by stopping and reversing, within the distance at which an approaching vessel can be seen." The City of New York, C.C.N.Y., 35 F. 609; The Allianca, D.C.N.Y., 39 F. 480. As to sailing vessel, see The Robert M. Thompson, C.C.A.N.Y., 244 F. 662, 671.

MODERATOR. A chairman or president of an assembly. A person appointed to preside at a popular meeting. The presiding officer of town-meetings in New England is so called. See Wheeler v. Carter, 180 Mass. 382, 62 N.E. 471.

MODIATIO. In old English law, a certain duty paid for every tierce of wine.

MODICA CIRCUMSTANTIA FACTI JUS MUTAT. A small circumstance attending an act may change the law.

MODIFICATION. A change; an alteration which introduces new elements into the details, or cancels some of them, but leaves the general purpose and effect of the subject-matter intact. Wiley v. Corporation of Bluffton, 111 Ind. 152, 12 N.E. 165; State v. Tucker, 36 Or. 291, 61 P. 894, 51 L.R.A. 246.

"Modification" is not exactly synonymous with "amendment," for the former term denotes some minor change in the substance of the thing, without reference to its improvement or deterioration thereby, while the latter word imports an amelioration of the thing (as by changing the phraseology of an instrument, so as to make it more distinct or specific) without involving the idea of any change in substance or essence.

Scotch law. The term usually applied to the decree of the teind court, awarding a suitable stipend to the minister of a parish. Bell.

MODIFY. To alter; to change in incidental or subordinate features; enlarge, extend; limit, reduce. State v. Lincoln, 133 Minn. 178, 158 N.W. 50, 52; U. S. v. Felder, D.C.N.Y., 13 F.2d 527, 528. See Modification.

MODIUS. Lat. A measure. Specifically, a Roman dry measure having a capacity of about 550 cubic inches; but in medieval English law used as an approximate translation of the word "bushel."

MODIUS TERRÆ VEL AGRI. In old English law, a quantity of ground containing in length and breadth 100 feet.

MODO ET FORMA. Lat. In manner and form. Words used in the old Latin forms of pleadings by way of traverse, and literally translated in the modern precedents, importing that the party traversing denies the allegation of the other party, not only in its general effect, but in the exact *manner and form* in which it is made. Steph.Pl. 189, 190.

MODUS. Lat. Civil law. Manner; means; way.

Old conveyancing. Mode; manner; the arrangement or expression of the terms of a contract or conveyance.

Also a consideration; the consideration of a conveyance, technically expressed by the word "*ut.*"

A qualification, involving the idea of variance or departure from some general rule or form, either by way of restriction or enlargement, according to the circumstances of a particular case, the will of a donor, the particular agreement of parties, and the like. Burrill.

Criminal pleading. The *modus* of an indictment is that part of it which contains the narrative of the commission of the crime; the statement of the mode or manner in which the offense was committed. Tray. Lat. Max.

Ecclesiastical law. A peculiar manner of tithing, growing out of custom.

Rank modus. One that is too large. Rankness is a mere rule of evidence, drawn from the improbability of the fact, rather than a rule of law. 2 Steph.Comm. 729.

MODUS DE NON DECIMANDO. In ecclesiastical law, a custom or prescription of entire exemption from the payment of tithes; this is not valid, unless in the case of abbey-lands.

MODUS DE NON DECIMANDO NON VALET. A *modus* (prescription) not to pay tithes is void. Lofft, 427; Cro.Eliz. 511; 2 Shars.Bl.Comm. 31.

MODUS DECIMANDI. In ecclesiastical law, a manner of tithing; a partial exemption from tithes, or a pecuniary composition prescribed by immemorial usage, and of reasonable amount; for it will be invalid as a *rank modus* if greater than the value of the tithes in the time of Richard I. Stim.Law Gloss.

MODUS ET CONVENTIO VINCUNT LEGEM. Custom and agreement overrule law. This maxim forms one of the first principles relative to the law of contracts. The exceptions to the rule here laid down are in cases against public policy, morality, etc. 2 Coke, 73; Broom, Max. 689, 691–695.

MODUS HABILIS. A valid manner.

MODUS LEGEM DAT DONATIONI. Custom gives law to the gift. Co.Litt. 19; Broom, Max. 459.

MODUS LEVANDI FINES. The manner of levying fines. The title of a short statute in French passed in the eighteenth year of Edward I. 2 Inst. 510; 2 Bl.Comm. 349.

MODUS TENENDI. The manner of holding; *i. e.*, the different species of tenures by which estates are held.

MODUS TRANSFERRENDI. The manner of transferring.

MODUS VACANDI. The manner of vacating. How and why an estate has been relinquished or surrendered by a vassal to his lord might well be referred to by this phrase. Tray.Lat.Max. *s. v.*

MOEBLE. L. Fr. Movablè. *Biens moebles*, movable goods. Britt. c. 11.

MOERDA. The secret killing of another; murder. 4 Bl.Comm. 194.

MOFUSSIL. In Hindu law, separated; particularized; the subordinate divisions of a district in contradistinction to *Sadder* or *Sudder*, which implies the chief seat of government. Wharton.

MOHAMMEDAN LAW. A system of native law prevailing among the Mohammedans in India, and administered there by the British government.

MOHATRA. In French law, a transaction covering a fraudulent device to evade the laws against usury.

It takes place where an individual buys merchandise from another on a credit at a high price, to sell it immediately to the first seller, or to a third person who acts as his agent, at a much less price for cash. 16 Toullier, no. 44.

MOIDORE. A gold coin of Portugal, valued at twenty-seven English shillings.

MOIETY. The half of anything. Joint tenants are said to hold by moieties. Litt. 125; 3 C.B. 274, 283; Young v. Smithers, 181 Ky. 847, 205 S.W. 949, 950.

MOIETY ACTS. A name sometimes applied to penal and criminal statutes which provide that half the penalty or fine shall inure to the benefit of the informer.

MOLENDINUM. In old records, a mill.

MOLENDUM. A grist; a certain quantity of corn sent to a mill to be ground.

MOLESTATION. In Scotch law, a possessory action calculated for continuing proprietors of landed estates in the lawful possession of them till the point of right be determined against all who shall attempt to disturb their possession. It is chiefly used in questions of commonty or of controverted marches. Ersk.Inst. 4, 1, 48.

MOLITURA. The toll or multure paid for grinding corn at a mill. Jacob.

MOLITURA LIBERA. Free grinding; a liberty to have a mill without paying tolls to the lord. Jacob.

MOLLITER MANUS IMPOSUIT. Lat. He gently laid hands upon. Formal words in the old Latin pleas in actions of trespass and assault where a defendant justified laying hands upon the plaintiff, as where it was done to keep the peace, etc. The phrase is literally translated in the modern precedents, and the original is retained as the name of the plea in such cases. 3 Bl.Comm. 21; 1 Chit.Pl. 501, 502; Id. 1071.

MOLMUTIAN LAWS. The laws of Dunvallo Molmutuis, a legendary or mythical king of the Britons, who is supposed to have begun his reign about 400 B. C. These laws were famous in the land till the Conquest. Tomlins; Mozley & Whiteley.

MOMENTUM. In the civil law, an instant; an indivisible portion of time. Calvin.

A portion of time that might be measured; a division or subdivison of an hour; answering in some degree to the modern *minute*, but of longer duration. Calvin.

MONACHISM. The state of monks.

MONARCHY. A government in which the supreme power is vested in a single person.

Where a monarch is invested with absolute power, the monarchy is termed "despotic;" where the supreme power is virtually in the laws, though the majesty of government and the administration are vested in a single person, it is a "limited" or "constitutional" monarchy. It is hereditary where the regal power descends immediately from the possessor to the next heir by blood, as in England; or elective, as was formerly the case in Poland. Wharton.

MONASTERIUM. A monastery; a church. Spelman.

MONASTICON. A book giving an account of monasteries, convents, and religious houses.

MONETA. Lat. Money, (*q. v.*).

MONETA EST JUSTUM MEDIUM ET MENSURA RERUM COMMUTABILIUM, NAM PER MEDIUM MONETÆ FIT OMNIUM RERUM CONVENIENS ET JUSTA ÆSTIMATIO. Dav. Ir. K. B. 18. Money is the just medium and measure of commutable things, for by the medium of money a convenient and just estimation of all things is made.

MONETAGIUM. Mintage, or the right of coining money. Cowell. Hence, anciently, a tribute payable to a lord who had the prerogative of coining money, by his tenants, in consideration of his refraining from changing the coinage.

MONETANDI JUS COMPREHENDITUR IN REGALIBUS QUÆ NUNQUAM A REGIO SCEPTRO ABDICANTUR. The right of coining money is comprehended among those royal prerogatives which are never relinquished by the royal scepter. Dav. Ir. K. B. 18.

MONETARY. The usual meaning is "pertaining to coinage or currency or having to do with money", but it has been held to include personal property. In re Kipp's Will, Sur., 37 N.Y.S.2d 541, 543.

MONEY. In usual and ordinary acceptation it means gold, silver, or paper money used as circulating medium of exchange, and does not embrace notes, bonds, evidences of debt, or other personal or real estate. Lane v. Railey, 280 Ky. 319, 133 S.W.2d 74, 79, 81. Currency; the circulating medium; cash.

The term "moneys" is not of more extensive signification than "money," and means only cash, and not things in action. Mann v. Mann, 14 Johns., N.Y., 1, 7 Am.Dec. 416.

In its strict technical sense, "money" means coined metal, usually gold or silver, upon which the government stamp has been impressed to indicate its value. In its more popular sense, "money" means any currency, tokens, bank-notes, or other circulating medium in general use as the representative of value. Kennedy v. Briere, 45 Tex. 305; Cook v. State, 130 Ark. 90, 196 S.W. 922, 924; Vick v. Howard, 136 Va. 101, 116 S.E. 465, 467, 31 A.L.R. 240.

The simple meaning of "money" is current coin, but it may mean possessions expressible in money values. "Money" has no technical meaning, but is of ambiguous import, and may be interpreted having regard to all surrounding circumstances under which it is used. "Money" is often and popularly used as equivalent to "property." "Money" means wealth reckoned in terms of money; capital considered as a cash asset; specifically such wealth or capital dealt in as a commodity to be loaned, invested, or the like; wealth considered as a cash asset. Salt Lake County v. Utah Copper Co., C.C.A.Utah, 93 F.2d 127, 132.

In its more comprehensive and general sense, it means wealth,—the representative of commodities of all kinds, of lands, and of everything that can be transferred in commerce. Paul v. Ball, 31 Tex. 10. A general, indefinite term for the measure and representative of value.

Public Money. Revenue. Hays v. State, 22 Okl.Cr. 99, 210 P. 728, 730. Money received by officers of the state in the ordinary processes of taxation, etc. Beaumont S. L. & W. Ry. Co. v. State, Tex.Civ.App., 173 S.W. 641, 642; Wardell v. Town of Killingly, 97 Conn. 423, 117 A. 520, 522. Under a municipal charter, money or funds belonging to a city; moneys which are owing or payable to the city in its corporate capacity, such as assessments, license fees, or moneys derived from the sales of property, wharfage charges, and such like, City of Sacramento v. Simmons, 66 Cal.App. 18, 225 P. 36, 39. Under a statute, all money which by law the sheriff in his capacity as such and as treasurer of the county and district is authorized to collect, receive, and disburse for public purposes. Bunch v. Short, 78 W.Va. 764, 90 S.E. 810, 812. As used in the United States statutes, the money of the federal government received from the public revenues, or intrusted to its fiscal officers, wherever it may be. See Branch v. U. S., 12 Ct.Cl. 281.

As to money "Broker," "Count," "Judgment," and "Scrivener," see those titles.

MONEY-BILL. In parliamentary language, an act by which revenue is directed to be raised, for any purpose or in any shape whatsoever, either for governmental purposes, and collected from the whole people generally, or for the benefit of a particular district, and collected in that district, or for making appropriations. Opinion of Justices, 126 Mass. 547; Northern Counties Inv. Trust v. Sears, 30 Or. 388, 41 P. 931, 35 L.R.A. 188.

MONEY CHANGERS. A money changer is one whose occupation is the exchanging of kinds or denominations of currency, and the common meaning of the term pertained to those persons who, in early history, engaged in the business of foreign exchange and it includes the business of a banker and buying and selling of uncurrent funds and the exchanging of one kind of money for another. Arnold v. City of Chicago, 387 Ill. 532, 56 N.E.2d 795, 799.

MONEY CLAIMS. In English practice, under the judicature act of 1875, claims for the price of goods sold, for money lent, for arrears of rent, etc., and other claims where money is directly payable on a contract express or implied, as opposed to the cases where money is claimed by way of damages for some independent wrong, whether by breach of contract or otherwise. These "money claims" correspond very nearly to the "money counts" hitherto in use. Mozley & Whitley.

MONEY DEMAND. A claim for a fixed and liquidated amount of money, or for a sum which can be ascertained by mere calculation; in this sense, distinguished from a claim which must be passed upon and liquidated by a jury, called "damages." Roberts v. Nodwift, 8 Ind. 341; Mills v. Long, 58 Ala. 460.

MONEY HAD AND RECEIVED. In pleading, the technical designation of a form of declaration in *assumpsit,* wherein the plaintiff declares that the defendant *had and received* certain money, etc.

Gist of action for "money had and received" is that defendant has received money which, in equity and good conscience, should have been paid to plaintiff and under such circumstances that he ought to pay it over. Bosworth v. Wolfe, 146 Wash. 615, 264 P. 413, 417, 56 A.L.R. 1117.

MONEY LAND. A phrase descriptive of money which is held upon a trust to convert it into land.

MONEY LENT. In pleading, the technical name of a declaration in an action of *assumpsit* for that the defendant promised to pay the plaintiff for money lent.

MONEY MADE. The return made by a sheriff to a writ of execution, signifying that he has collected the sum of money required by the writ.

MONEY OF ADIEU. In French law, earnest money; so called because given at parting in completion of the bargain. *Arrhes* is the usual French word for earnest money; "money of adieu" is a provincialism found in the province of Orleans. Poth.Cont. 507.

MONEY ORDER. Under the postal regulations of the United States, a money order is a species of draft drawn by one post-office upon another for an amount of money deposited at the first office by the person purchasing the money order, and payable at the second office to a payee named in the order. U. S. v. Long, C.C.Ga., 30 F. 679.

MONEY-ORDER OFFICE. One of the post-offices authorized to draw or pay money orders.

MONEY PAID. In pleading, the technical name of a declaration in *assumpsit,* in which the plaintiff declares for money paid for the use of the defendant.

MONEYED CAPITAL. This term has a more limited meaning than the term "personal property," and applies to such capital as is readily solvable in money. Mercantile Nat. Bank v. New York, 121 U.S. 138, 7 S.Ct. 826, 30 L.Ed. 895.

MONEYED CORPORATION. See Corporation.

MONGER. A dealer or seller. It is seldom or never used alone, or otherwise than after the name of any commodity, to express a seller of such commodity.

MONIERS, or MONEYEERS. Ministers of the mint; also bankers. Cowell.

MONIMENT. A memorial, superscription, or record.

MONITION. Admiralty. The summons to appear and answer, issued on filing the libel; which is either a simple monition *in personam* or an attachment and monition *in rem.* Ben.Adm. 228, 239.

It is sometimes termed "monition *viis et modis,*" and has been supposed to be derived from the old Roman practice of summoning a defendant. Manro v. Almeida, 10 Wheat. 490, 6 L.Ed. 369.

The monition, in American admiralty practice, is, in effect, a summons, citation, or notice, though in form a command to the marshal to cite and admonish the defendant to appear and answer, and not a summons addressed to the party. 2 Conk.Adm., 2d Ed., 147.

General monition. In civil law and admiralty practice, a monition or summons to all parties in interest to appear and show cause against the decree prayed for.

Practice. A monition is a formal order of the court commanding something to be done by the person to whom it is directed, and who is called the "person monished." Thus, when money is decreed to be paid, a monition may be obtained commanding its payment. In ecclesiastical procedure, a monition is an order monishing or warning the party complained against to do or not to do a certain act "under pain of the law and contempt thereof." A monition may also be appended to a sentence inflicting a punishment for a past offense; in that case the monition forbids the repetition of the offense. Sweet.

MONITORY LETTERS. Communications of warning and admonition sent from an ecclesiastical judge, upon information of scandal and abuses within the cognizance of his court.

MONOCRACY. A government by one person.

MONOCRAT. A monarch who governs alone; an absolute governor.

MONOGAMY. The marriage of one wife only, or the state of such as are restrained to a single wife. Webster.

A marriage contracted between one man and one woman, in exclusion of all the rest of mankind. The term is used in opposition to "bigamy" and "polygamy." Wolff, Dr. de la Nat. § 857.

MONOGRAM. A character or cipher composed of one or more letters interwoven, being an abbreviation of a name.

MONOGRAPH. A special treatise upon a particular subject of limited range; a treatise or commentary upon a particular branch or division of a general subject.

MONOMACHY. A duel; a single combat.

It was anciently allowed by law for the trial or proof of crimes. It was even permitted in pecuniary causes, but it is now forbidden both by the civil law and canon laws.

MONOMANIA. In medical jurisprudence, derangement of a single faculty of the mind, or with regard to a particular subject, the other faculties being in regular exercise. See Insanity.

MONOPOLIA DICITUR, CUM UNUS SOLUS ALIQUOD GENUS MERCATURÆ UNIVERSUM EMIT, PRETIUM AD SUUM LIBITUM STATUENS. 11 Coke, 86. It is said to be a monopoly when one person alone buys up the whole of one kind of commodity, fixing a price at his own pleasure.

MONOPOLIUM. The sole power, right, or privilege of sale; monopoly; a monopoly. Calvin.

MONOPOLY. A privilege or peculiar advantage vested in one or more persons or companies, consisting in the exclusive right (or power) to carry on a particular business or trade, manufacture a particular article, or control the sale of the whole supply of a particular commodity.

Defined in English law to be "a license or privilege allowed by the king for the sole buying and selling, making, working, or using, of anything whatsoever; whereby the subject in general is restrained from that liberty of manufacturing or trading which he had before." 4 Bl. Comm. 159; 4 Steph.Comm. 291; State v. Duluth Board of Trade, 107 Minn. 506, 121 N.W. 395, 23 L.R.A.,N.S., 1260.

A monopoly consists in the ownership or control of so large a part of the market-supply or output of a given commodity as to stifle competition, restrict the freedom of commerce, and give the monopolist control over prices. State v. Atlantic Ice & Coal Co., 210 N.C. 742, 188 S.E. 412, 416.

MONSTER. A prodigious birth; a human birth or offspring not having the shape of mankind, which cannot be heir to any land, albeit it be brought forth in marriage. Bract. fol. 5; Co.Litt. 7, 8; 2 Bl.Comm. 246.

MONSTRANS DE DROIT. L. Fr. In English law, a showing or manifestation of right; one of the common law methods of obtaining possession or restitution from the crown, of either real or personal property.

It is the proper proceeding when the right of the party, as well as the right of the crown, appears upon record, and consists in putting in a claim of right grounded on facts already acknowledged and established, and praying the judgment of the court whether upon these facts the king or the subject has the right. 3 Bl.Comm. 256; 4 Coke, 54*b*.

MONSTRANS DE FAITS. L. Fr. In old English practice, a showing of deeds; a species of profert. Cowell.

MONSTRAVERUNT, WRIT OF. In English law, a writ which lies for the tenants of ancient demesne who hold by free charter, and not for those tenants who hold by copy of court roll, or by the rod, according to the custom of the manor. Fitzh. Nat. Brev. 14.

MONSTRUM. A box in which relics are kept; also a muster of soldiers. Cowell.

MONTES. In Spanish law, forests or woods. White, New Recop. b. 2, tit. 1, c. 6, § 1.

MONTES PIETATIS. Public pawnbroking establishments; institutions established by government, in some European countries, for lending small sums of money on pledges of personal property. In France they are called *"monts de piété."*

MONTH. Word "month," unless otherwise defined, means "calendar month," or time from any day of any of the months as adjudged in the calendar to corresponding day, if any, if not any, to last day, of next month. Daniel v. Ormand, 26 Ala.App. 441, 163 So. 361.

The space of time denoted by this term varies according as one or another of the following varieties of months is intended.:

Astronomical, containing one-twelfth of the time occupied by the sun in passing through the entire zodiac.

Calendar, civil, or *solar,* which is one of the months in the Gregorian calendar,—January, February, March, etc., —which are of unequal length.

Lunar, being the period of one revolution of the moon, or twenty-eight days.

The word "month," when used in a statute or contract without qualification, meant at common law a lunar month of 28 days. State v. White, 73 Fla. 426, 74 So. 486, 487.

The matter is generally regulated by statute now. In re McNamara's Estate, 181 Cal. 82, 183 P. 552, 556, 7 A.L.R. 313.

MONUMENT. Anything by which the memory of a person, thing, idea, art, science or event is preserved or perpetuated. A tomb where a dead body has been deposited. In re Ogden, 25 R.I. 373, 55 A. 933; Rhode Island Hospital Trust Co. v. Benedict, 41 R.I. 143, 103 A. 146, 147.

In real-property law and surveying, monuments are visible marks or indications left on natural or other objects indicating the lines and boundaries of a survey. In this sense the term includes not only posts, pillars, stone markers, cairns, and the like, but also fixed natural objects, blazed trees, and even a watercourse. Grier v. Pennsylvania Coal Co., 128 Pa. 79, 18 A. 480; Cox v. Freedley, 33 Pa. 124, 75 Am.Dec. 584.

MONUMENTA QUÆ NOS RECORDA VOCAMUS SUNT VERITATIS ET VETUSTATIS VESTIGIA. Co.Litt. 118. Monuments, which we call "records," are the vestiges of truth and antiquity.

MONUNG. See Manung.

MONYA. In Norman law, moneyage. A tax or tribute of one shilling on every hearth, payable to the duke every three years, in consideration that he should not alter the coin. Hale, Com.Law, 148, and note.

MOOKTAR. In Hindu law, an agent or attorney.

MOOKTARNAMA. In Hindu law, a written authority constituting an agent; a power of attorney.

MOONSHINE. Intoxicating liquor illicitly produced or smuggled into community for beverage purposes, or spirituous liquor, illegally distilled or manufactured. State v. King, 331 Mo. 268, 53 S.W.2d 252, 254.

MOOR. An officer in the Isle of Man, who summons the courts for the several sheadings. The office is similar to the English bailiff of a hundred.

MOORAGE. A sum due by law or usage for mooring or fastening of ships to trees or posts at the shore, or to a wharf. Wharf Case, 3 Bland, Md., 373.

MOORING. In maritime law, anchoring or making fast to the shore or dock; the securing or confining a vessel in a particular station, as by cables and anchors or by a line or chain run to the wharf.

A vessel is "moored in safety," within the meaning of a policy of marine insurance, when she is thus moored to a wharf or dock, free from any immediate danger from any of the perils insured against. 1 Phil.Ins. 968; Bramhall v. Sun Mut. Ins. Co., 104 Mass. 516, 6 Am.Rep. 261.

MOOT, *n.* English law. Moots are exercises in pleading, and in arguing doubtful cases and questions, by the students of an inn of court before the benches of the inn. Sweet.

Saxon law. A meeting or assemblage of people, particularly for governmental or judicial purposes. The more usual forms of the word were "mote" and "gemot." See those titles.

MOOT, *adj.* A subject for argument; unsettled; undecided. A moot point is one not settled by judicial decisions. A moot case is one which seeks to determine an abstract question which does not arise upon existing facts or rights. Adams v. Union R. Co., 21 R.I. 134, 42 A. 515, 44 L.R.A. 273.

One which seeks to get a judgment on a pretended controversy, or a decision in advance about a right before it has been actually asserted and contested, or a judgment on some matter which, when rendered, for any reason, cannot have any practical legal effect upon a then existing controversy. Smith v. Smith, 209 Wis. 605, 245 N.W. 644, 645.

MOOT COURT. A court held for the arguing of moot cases or questions.

MOOT HALL. The place where moot cases were argued. Also a council-chamber, hall of judgment, or town-hall.

MOOT HILL. Hill of meeting, (*gemot*,) on which the Britons used to hold their courts, the judge sitting on the eminence; the parties, etc., on an elevated platform below. Enc.Lond.

MOOT MAN. One of those who used to argue the reader's cases in the inns of court.

MOOTA CANUM. In old English law, a pack of dogs. Cowell.

MOOTER. Marihuana is popularly known among the criminal element as "muggles," or "mooter" and addicts are commonly termed "muggle heads." State v. Navaro, 83 Utah 6, 26 P.2d 955.

MOOTING. The exercise of arguing questions of law or equity, raised for the purpose. See Moot.

MORA. Lat. In the civil law, delay; default; neglect; culpable delay or default. Calvin.

MORA. Sax. A moor; barren or unprofitable ground; marsh; a heath; a watery bog or moor. Co.Litt. 5; Fleta, 1, 2, c. 71.

MORA MUSSA. A watery or boggy moor; a morass.

MORA REPROBATUR IN LEGE. Delay is reprobated in law. Jenk.Cent. p. 51, case 97.

MORAL. Pertains to character, conduct, intention, social relations, etc. United States v. Carrollo, D.C.Mo., 30 F.Supp. 3, 6.

1. Pertaining or relating to the conscience or moral sense or to the general principles of right conduct.

2. Cognizable or enforceable only by the conscience or by the principles of right conduct, as distinguished from positive law.

3. Depending upon or resulting from probability; raising a belief or conviction in the mind independent of strict or logical proof.

4. Involving or affecting the moral sense; as in the phrase "moral insanity."

MORAL ACTIONS. Those only in which men have knowledge to guide them, and a will to choose for themselves. Ruth, Inst. lib. 1, c. 1.

MORAL CERTAINTY. That degree of assurance which induces a man of sound mind to act, without doubt, upon the conclusions to which it leads. Wills, Circ.Ev. 7. A high degree of impression of the truth of a fact, falling short of absolute certainty, but sufficient to justify a verdict of guilty, even in a capital case. Burrill, Circ.Ev. 198–200.

As explained in the Century Dictionary, it signifies a probability sufficiently strong to justify action on it. In Webster's International, the first definition given is, "a very high degree of probability, although not demonstrable, as a certainty." It has also been used as indicating a conclusion of the mind established beyond a reasonable doubt. Gray v. State, 56 Okl.Cr. 208, 38 P.2d 967.

The phrase "moral certainty" has been introduced into our jurisprudence from the publicists and metaphysicians, and signifies only a very high degree of probability. It was observed by Puffendorf that, "when we declare such a thing to be morally certain, because it has been confirmed by credible witnesses, this moral certitude is nothing else but a strong presumption grounded on probable reasons, and which very seldom fails and deceives us." "Probable evidence," says Bishop Butler, in the opening sentence of his Analogy, "is essentially distinguished from demonstrative by this: that it admits of degrees, and of all variety of them, from the highest moral certainty to the very lowest presumption." Com. v. Costley, 118 Mass. 23.

MORAL CONSIDERATION. See Consideration.

MORAL DURESS. Consists in imposition, oppression, undue influence, or the taking of undue advantage of the business or financial stress or extreme necessity or weakness of another. Lafayette Dramatic Productions v. Ferentz, 305 Mich. 193, 9 N.W.2d 57, 66, 145 A.L.R. 1158.

MORAL EVIDENCE. As opposed to "mathematical" or "demonstrative" evidence, this term denotes that kind of evidence which, without developing an absolute and necessary certainty, generates a high degree of probability or persuasive force. It is founded upon analogy or induction, experience of the ordinary course of nature or the sequence of events, and the testimony of men.

MORAL FRAUD. This phrase is one of the less usual designations of "actual" or "positive" fraud or "fraud in fact," as distinguished from "constructive" fraud or "fraud in law." It means fraud which involves actual guilt, a wrongful purpose, or moral obliquity.

MORAL HAZARD. See Hazard.

MORAL INSANITY. See Insanity.

MORAL LAW. The law of conscience; the aggregate of those rules and principles of ethics which relate to right and wrong conduct and prescribe the standards to which the actions of men should conform in their dealings with each other. Moore v. Strickling, 46 W.Va. 515, 33 S.E. 274, 50 L.R.A. 279.

MORAL OBLIGATION. See Obligation.

MORAL TURPITUDE. An act of baseness, vileness, or depravity in the private and social duties which a man owes to his fellow men, or to society in general, contrary to the accepted and customary rule of right and duty between man and man. Traders & General Ins. Co. v. Russell, Tex.Civ. App., 99 S.W.2d 1079, 1084; Jordan v. De George, 341 U.S. 223, 71 S.Ct. 703, 706.

Conduct contrary to justice, honesty, modesty, or good morals. Marsh v. State Bar of California, 210 Cal. 303, 291 P. 583, 584.

MORANDÆ SOLUTIONIS CAUSA. Lat. For the purpose of delaying or postponing payment or performance.

MORATORIUM. A term designating suspension of all or of certain legal remedies against debtors, sometimes authorized by law during financial distress. Brown v. State Nat. Bank of Shawnee, 133 Okl. 173, 271 P. 833, 834. A period of permissive or obligatory delay; specifically, a period during which an obligor has a legal right to delay meeting an obligation. State ex rel. Jensen Livestock Co. v. Hyslop, 111 Mont. 122, 107 P.2d 1088, 1092.

MORATUR IN LEGE. Lat. He delays in law. The phrase describes the action of one who demurs, because the party does not proceed in pleading, but rests or abides upon the judgment of the court on a certain point, as to the legal sufficiency of his opponent's pleading. The courts deliberate and determine thereupon.

MORAVIANS. Otherwise called "Herrnhutters" or "United Brethren." A sect of Christians whose social polity is particular and conspicuous. It sprung up in Moravia and Bohemia, on the opening of that reformation which stripped the chair of St. Peter of so many votaries, and gave birth to so many denominations of Christians. They give evidence on their solemn affirmation. 2 Steph.Comm. 338*n*.

MORBUS SONTICUS. Lat. In the civil law, a sickness which rendered a man incapable of attending to business.

MORE COLONICO. Lat. In old pleading, in husband-like manner. Townsh.Pl. 198.

MORE OR LESS. About; substantially; or approximately; implying that both parties assume the risk of any ordinary discrepancy. Alexander v. Hicks, 242 Ala. 243, 5 So.2d 781, 782, 783.

The words are intended to cover slight or unimportant inaccuracies in quantity, Carter v. Finch, 186 Ark. 954, 57 S.W.2d 408; and are ordinarily to be interpreted as taking care of unsubstantial differences or differences of small importance compared to the whole number of items transferred. Crowl v. Box, 144 Okl. 25, 288 P. 942, 946.

MOREOVER. In addition thereto, also, furthermore, likewise, beyond this, besides this. Pagano v. Cerri, 93 Ohio St. 345, 112 N.E. 1037, 1040, L.R.A. 1917A, 486; Aldersley v. McCloud, 35 Cal.App. 17, 168 P. 1153, 1155.

MORGANATIC-MARRIAGE. See Marriage.

MORGANGINA, or MORGANGIVA. A gift on the morning after the wedding; dowry; the husband's gift to his wife on the day after the wedding. Du Cange; Cowell.

MORGEN. Anglo-Dutch. In old New York law, a measure of land, equal to about two acres.

MORGUE. A place where the bodies of persons found dead are kept for a limited time and exposed to view, to the end that their friends may identify them.

MORMON. A member of the Church of Jesus Christ of Latter-day Saints. The Church was organized in 1830 at Seneca, New York, by Joseph Smith, and today its headquarters are in Salt Lake City, Utah.

MORON. One whose intellectual development proceeds normally up to about the 8th year of age, then is arrested, and never exceeds that of a normal child of about 12 years. People v. Joyce, 233 N.Y. 61, 134 N.E. 836, 840.

MORPHINOMANIA, or MORPHINISM. The opium habit. An excessive desire for morphia.

MORRIS PLAN COMPANY. An industrial bank which accepts money from the public for investment in "investment certificates" which draw interest periodically payable to the investor, and which bank lends money principally to steadily employed salaried people who are required to secure repayment with the endorsement of two other employed salaried people, the contract calling for installment payments over a one year period. Other secured loans are also made. Board of Com'rs of Tulsa County v. Remedial Finance Corporation, 186 Okl. 648, 100 P.2d 240, 242.

MORS. Lat. Death. State v. Logan, 344 Mo. 351, 126 S.W.2d 256, 259, 122 A.L.R. 417.

MORS DICITUR ULTIMUM SUPPLICIUM. Death is called the "last punishment," the "extremity of punishment." 3 Inst. 212.

MORS OMNIA SOLVIT. Death dissolves all things. Jenk.Cent. p. 160, case 2. Applied to the case of the death of a party to an action.

MORSELLUM, or MORSELLUS, TERRÆ. In old English law, a small parcel or bit of land.

MORT CIVILE. In French law, civil death, as upon conviction for felony.

It was nominally abolished by a law of the 31st of May, 1854, but something very similar to it, in effect at least, still remains. Thus, the property of the condemned, possessed by him at the date of his conviction, goes and belongs to his successors, *(héritiers,)* as in case of an intestacy; and his future acquired property goes to the state by right of its prerogative, *(par droit de déshérence,)* but the state may, as a matter of grace, make it over in whole or in part to the widow and children. Brown.

MORT D'ANCESTOR. An ancient and now almost obsolete remedy in the English law. An assize of *mort d'ancestor* was a writ which lay for a person whose ancestor died seised of lands in fee-simple, and after his death a stranger abated; and this writ directed the sheriff to summon a jury or assize, who should view the land in question and recognize whether such ancestor were seised thereof on the day of his death, and whether the demandant were the next heir.

MORTAL. Destructive to life; causing or occasioning death; exposing to or deserving death, especially spiritual death; deadly; fatal; as, a mortal wound, State v. Logan, 344 Mo. 351, 126 S.W.2d 256, 259, 122 A.L.R. 417; or mortal sin; of or pertaining to time of death. State v. Baker, 122 Kan. 552, 253 P. 221, 223.

MORTALITY. This word, in its ordinary sense, never means violent death, but death arising from natural causes. Lawrence v. Aberdein, 5 Barn. & Ald. 110.

MORTALITY TABLES. A means of ascertaining the probable number of years any man or woman of a given age and of ordinary health will live. Butler v. Butler, 180 Minn. 134, 230 N.W. 575, 579.

MORTGAGE. An estate created by a conveyance absolute in its form, but intended to secure the performance of some act, such as the payment of money, and the like, by the grantor or some other person, and to become void if the act is performed agreeably to the terms prescribed at the time of making such conveyance. 1 Washb.Real Prop. *475.

A conditional conveyance of land. Mitchell v. Burnham, 44 Me. 299.

A transfer of property passing conditionally as security for debt. Potter v. Vernon, 129 Okl. 251, 264 P. 611, 613.

A debt by specialty, secured by a pledge of lands, of which the legal ownership is vested in the creditor, but of which, in equity, the debtor and those claiming under him remain the actual owners, until debarred by judicial sentence or their own laches. Coote, Mortg. 1.

The foregoing definitions are applicable to the common-law conception of a mortgage. But in many states in modern times, it is regarded as a mere lien, and not as creating a title or estate. Zeigler v. Sawyer, Tex.Civ.App., 16 S.W.2d 894, 896. It is a pledge or security of particular property for the payment of a debt or the performance of some other obligation, whatever form the transaction may take, but is not now regarded as a conveyance in effect, though it may be cast in the form of a conveyance. Muth v. Goddard, 28 Mont. 237, 72 P. 621, 98 Am.St.Rep. 553; Johnson v. Robinson, 68 Tex. 399, 4 S.W. 625; Killebrew v. Hines, 104 N.C. 182, 10 S.E. 159, 17 Am.St.Rep. 672; Stockel v. Elich, 297 P. 595, 597, 112 Cal.App. 588; In re Morgan, D.C.N.J., 39 F.2d 489, 490.

Chattel mortgage. A mortgage of goods, chattels, or personal property. See Chattel Mortgage.

Conventional mortgage. The conventional mortgage is a contract by which a person binds the whole of his property, or a portion of it only, in favor of another, to secure the execution of some engagement, but without divesting himself of possession. Civ.Code La. art. 3290; Succession of Benjamin, 39 La.Ann. 612, 2 So. 187. It is distinguished from the "legal" mortgage, which is a privilege which the law alone in certain cases gives to a creditor over the property of his debtor, without stipulation of the parties. This last is very much like a general lien at common law, created by the law rather than by the act of the parties, such as a judgment lien.

Equitable mortgage. A specific lien upon real property to secure the payment of money or the performance of some other obligation, which a court of equity will recognize and enforce, in accordance with the clearly ascertained intent of the parties to that effect, but which lacks the essential features of a legal mortgage, either because it grows out of the transactions of the parties without any deed or express contract to give a lien, or because the instrument used for that purpose is wanting in some of the characteristics of a common-law mortgage, or, being absolute in form, is accompanied by a collateral reservation of a right to redeem, or because an explicit agreement to give a mortgage has not been carried into effect. 4 Kent, Comm. 150; 2 Story, Eq.Jur. § 1018; Ketchum v. St. Louis, 101 U.S. 306, 25 L.Ed. 999; Gessner v. Palmateer, 89 Cal. 89, 26 P. 789, 13 L.R.A. 187.

In English law, the following mortgages are equitable: (1) Where the subject of a mortgage is trust property, which security is effected either by a formal deed or a written memorandum, notice being given to the trustees in order to preserve the priority. (2) Where it is an equity of redemption, which is merely a right to bring an action in the chancery division to redeem the estate. (3) Where there is a written agreement only to make a mortgage, which creates an equitable lien on the land. (4) Where a debtor deposits the title-deeds of his estate with his creditor or some person on his behalf, without even a verbal communication. The deposit itself is deemed evidence of an executed agreement or contract for a mortgage for such estate. Wharton.

First mortgage. The first (in time or right) of a series of two or more mortgages covering the same property and successively attaching as liens upon it; also, in a more particular sense, a mortgage which is a first lien on the property, not only as against other mortgages, but as against any other charges or incumbrances. Green's Appeal, 97 Pa. 347.

First mortgage bonds. Bonds the payment of which is secured by a first mortgage on property. Bank of Atchison County v. Byers, 139 Mo. 627, 41 S.W. 325; Com. v. Williamstown, 156 Mass. 70, 30 N.E. 472.

General mortgage. Mortgages are sometimes classified as general and special, a mortgage of the former class being one which binds all property, present and future, of the debtor (sometimes called a "blanket" mortgage); while a special mortgage is limited to certain particular and specified property. Barnard v. Erwin, 2 Rob., La., 415.

Judicial mortgage. In the law of Louisiana, the lien resulting from judgments, whether rendered on contested cases or by default, whether final or provisional, in favor of the person obtaining them. Civ.Code La. art. 3321.

Legal mortgage. A term used in Louisiana. The law alone in certain cases gives to the creditor a mortgage on the property of his debtor, without it being requisite that the parties should stipulate it. This is called "legal mortgage." Civ.Code La. art. 3311.

Mortgage of goods. A conveyance of goods in gage or mortgage by which the whole legal title passes conditionally to the mortgagee; and, if the goods are not redeemed at the time stipulated, the title becomes absolute in law, although equity will interfere to compel a redemption. It is distinguished from a "pledge" by the circumstance that possession by the mortgagee is not or may not be essential to create or to support the title. Story, Bailm. § 287. See Chattel Mortgage.

Purchase-money mortgage. A mortgage given, concurrently with a conveyance of land, by the vendee to the vendor, on the same land, to secure the unpaid balance of the purchase price. Baker v.

Clepper, 26 Tex. 629, 84 Am.Dec. 591; Keefe v. Cropper, 196 Iowa 1179, 194 N.W. 305, 306; Ladd & Tilton Bank v. Mitchell, 93 Or. 668, 184 P. 282, 284, 6 A.L.R. 1420.

Second mortgage. One which takes rank immediately after a first mortgage on the same property, without any intervening liens, and is next entitled to satisfaction out of the proceeds of the property. Green's Appeal, 97 Pa. 347. Properly speaking, however, the term designates the second of a series of mortgages, not necessarily the second lien. For instance, the lien of a judgment might intervene between the first and second mortgages; in which case, the second mortgage would be the third lien.

Tacit mortgage. In Louisiana, the same as a "legal" mortgage. See *supra*.

Welsh mortgage. In English law, a species of security which partakes of the nature of a mortgage, as there is a debt due, and an estate is giyen as security for the repayment, but differs from it in the circumstances that the rents and profits are to be received without account till the principal money is paid off, and there is no remedy to enforce payment, while the mortgagor has a perpetual power of redemption. It is now rarely used. 1 Pow.Mortg. 373*a;* Bentley v. Phelps, 3 F.Cas. 250.

MORTGAGE POOLS. Groups of mortgages. In re D'Happart's Estate, 132 Pa.Super. 326, 200 A. 927, 929.

MORTGAGEE. He that takes or receives a mortgage.

MORTGAGEE IN POSSESSION. A mortgagee of real property who is in possession of it with the agreement or assent of the mortgagor, express or implied, and in recognition of his mortgage and because of it, and under such circumstances as to make the satisfaction of his lien an equitable prerequisite to his being dispossessed. Rogers v. Benton, 39 Minn. 39, 38 N.W. 765, 12 Am.St.Rep. 613; Stouffer v. Harlan, 68 Kan. 135, 74 P. 610, 64 L.R.A. 320.

MORTGAGOR. One who, having all or some part of title to property, by written instrument pledges that property for some particular purpose such as security for a debt. Goodell v. Silver Creek Nat. Bank, Sup., 48 N.Y.S.2d 572, 576.

MORTH. Sax. Murder, answering exactly to the French *"assassinat"* or *"muertre de guet-apens."*

MORTHLAGA. A murderer. Cowell.

MORTHLAGE. Murder. Cowell.

MORTIFICATION. In Scotch law, a term nearly synonymous with "mortmain." Bell. Lands are said to be *mortified* for a charitable purpose.

MORTIS CAUSA. Lat. By reason of death; in contemplation of death. Thus used in the phrase *"Donatio mortis causa,"* (*q. v.*).

MORTIS MOMENTUM EST ULTIMUM VITÆ MOMENTUM. The last moment of life is the moment of death. Terrill v. Public Adm'r, 4 Bradf. Sur., N.Y., 245, 250.

MORTMAIN. A term applied to denote the alienation of lands or tenements to any corporation, sole or aggregate, ecclesiastical or temporal. These purchases having been chiefly made by religious houses, in consequence of which lands became perpetually inherent in one dead hand, this has occasioned the general appellation of "mortmain" to be applied to such alienations. 2 Bl.Comm. 268; Co.Litt. 2*b;* Perin v. Carey, 24 How. 495, 16 L.Ed. 701.

MORTMAIN ACTS. These acts had for their object to prevent lands getting into the possession or control of religious corporations, or, as the name indicates, *in mortua manu.* After numerous prior acts dating from the reign of Edward I., it was enacted by the statute 9 Geo. II. c. 36, (called the "Mortmain Act" *par excellence*), that no lands should be given to charities unless certain requisites should be observed. Brown. Yates v. Yates, 9 Barb., N.Y., 324.

MORTON TOE. "Morton toe" is neuralgia of the fourth toe. State v. Armstrong, 38 Idaho 493, 225 P. 491, 493, 33 A.L.R. 835.

MORTUARY. In ecclesiastical law, a burial-place.

Modern term applied to undertaking and embalming establishments. City of Tucson v. Arizona Mortuary, 34 Ariz. 495, 272 P. 923, 924.

A kind of ecclesiastical heriot, being a customary gift of the second best living animal belonging to the deceased, claimed by and due to the minister in many parishes, on the death of his parishioners, whether buried in the church-yard or not. 2 Bl. Comm. 425. Ayrton v. Abbott, 14 Q.B. 19.

It has been sometimes used in a civil as well as in an ecclesiastical sense, and applied to a payment to the lord of the fee. Paroch.Antiq. 470.

MORTUARY TABLES. Tables for estimating the probable duration of the life of a party at a given age. Gallagher v. Market St. Ry. Co., 67 Cal. 16, 6 P. 871, 51 Am.Rep. 680.

MORTUUM VADIUM. A dead pledge; a mortgage (*q. v.*); a pledge where the profits or rents of the thing pledged are not applied to the payment of the debt.

MORTUUS. Lat. Dead. So in sheriff's return. *mortuus est,* he is dead.

MORTUUS CIVILITER. Civil death.

This incident attended every attainder of treason or other felony, whereby in the language of Lord Coke the attainted person "is disabled to bring any action, for he is *extra legem mortuus*"; Co.Litt. 199. He could be heard in court only for the direct purpose of reversing the attainder, and not in prosecution of a civil right; 1 B. & A. 159. He could be grantor or grantee after attainder, and the grant would be good against all persons except the king; Shepard, Touch. 231.

MORTUUS EXITUS NON EST EXITUS. A dead issue is no issue. Co.Litt. 29. A child born dead is not considered as issue.

MORTUUS SINE PROLE. Dead without issue. In genealogical tables often abbreviated to "*m. s. p.*"

MOS RETINENDUS EST FIDELISSIMÆ VETUSTATIS. 4 Coke, 78. A custom of the truest antiquity is to be retained.

MOSCOW INTERNATIONAL. See Third International.

MOSLEM LAW. One of the two great systems of customary law which the English found in India. It regulated the life and relations of all Moslems, and parts of it, especially its penal provisions, were applied to both Moslems and Hindus. Bryce, Extension of the Law.

MOST FAVORED NATION CLAUSE. A clause found in most treaties providing that the citizens or subjects of the contracting states may enjoy the privileges accorded by either party to those of the most favored nations. It is said that the general design of such clauses is to establish the principle of equality of international treatment. The test of whether this principle is violated by the concession of advantages to a particular nation is, not the form in which such concession is made, but the condition on which it is granted; whether it is given for a price, or whether this price is in the nature of a substantial equivalent, and not of a mere evasion. The United States has always taken the stand that reciprocal commercial concessions are given for a valuable consideration and are not within the scope of this clause. Whitney v. Robertson, 124 U.S. 190, 8 S.Ct. 456, 31 L.Ed. 386. Great Britain has taken the opposite position.

See Consular Treaty Rights and Comments on the "Most Favored Nation" Clause, by Ernest Ludwig; 3 Amer.Journ.Int.L. 57; Herod, Most Favored Nation Treatment; Moore's Dig.Int.Law; 3 Amer. Journ.Int.Law 395.

MOSTRENCOS. In Spanish law, strayed goods; estrays. White, New Recop. b. 2, tit. 2, c. 6.

MOTE. Sax. A meeting; an assembly. Used in composition, as *burgmote, folkmote,* etc.

MOTE-BELL. The bell which was used by the Saxons to summon people to the court. Cowell.

MOTEER. A customary service or payment at the mote or court of the lord, from which some were exempted by charter or privilege. Cowell.

MOTHER. A woman who has borne a child. Gardner v. Hall, 132 N.J.Eq. 64, 26 A.2d 799, 807. A female parent, Guide Pub. Co. v. Futrell, 175 Va. 77, 7 S.E.2d 133, 138. Correlative to "son" or "daughter." The term includes maternity during prebirth period. Watson v. Independent Banner of Love Soc., 54 Ga.App. 370, 187 S.E. 897, 898.

MOTHER-IN-LAW. The mother of one's wife or of one's husband.

MOTION. Parliamentary law. The formal mode in which a member submits a proposed measure or resolve for the consideration and action of the meeting.

Practice. Primarily an application for a rule or order made viva voce to a court or judge, but the term is generally employed with reference to all such applications, whether written or oral. Irwin v. Gilson Realty Co., 117 Fla. 394, 158 So. 77.

Special motion. A motion addressed to the discretion of the court, and which must be heard and determined; as distinguished from one which may be granted of course. Merchants' Bank v. Crysler, Mo., 14 C.C.A. 444, 67 F. 390.

MOTION FOR DECREE. Under the chancery practice, the most usual mode of bringing on a suit for hearing when the defendant has answered is by motion for decree. Hunter, Suit Eq. 59; Daniell, Ch.Pr. 722.

MOTION FOR JUDGMENT. In English practice, a proceeding whereby a party to an action moves for the judgment of the court in his favor. S.Ct. Rules 1883, ord. 40.

MOTION IN ARREST OF JUDGMENT. It is intended to avoid judgment because of unamendable defect appearing on record. Turner v. Shackleford, 43 Ga.App. 271, 158 S.E. 439, 440.

MOTION IN ERROR. A motion in error stands on the same footing as a writ of error; the only difference is that, on a motion in error, no service is required to be made on the opposite party, because, being before the court when the motion is filed, he is bound to take notice of it at his peril. Treadway v. Coe, 21 Conn. 283.

MOTION TO SET ASIDE JUDGMENT. This is a step taken by a party in an action who is dissatisfied with the judgment directed to be entered at the trial of the action.

MOTIVE. Cause or reason that moves the will and induces action. Commonwealth v. Trunk, 311 Pa. 555, 167 A. 333, 338. An inducement, or that which leads or tempts the mind to indulge a criminal act. People v. Lewis, 275 N.Y. 33, 9 N.E.2d 765, 768.

In the popular mind intent and "motive" are not infrequently regarded as one and the same thing. In law there is a clear distinction between them. "Motive" is the moving power which impels to action for a definite result. Intent is the purpose to use a particular means to effect such result. "Motive" is that which incites or stimulates a person to do an act. People v. Weiss, 252 App.Div. 463, 300 N.Y.S. 249, 255.

MOTOR VEHICLE. In the Uniform Act Regulating Traffic on Highways, 11 U.L.A., and similar statutes, any self-propelled "vehicle," defined as including every device in, upon, or by which any person or property is or may be transported or drawn upon a highway, except devices moved by human or muscular power or used exclusively upon stationary rails or tracks. The term "motor vehicles," although sometimes regarded as synonymous with or limited to "automobiles," often has a broader meaning, and includes not only ordinary automobiles, but also motorbusses and trucks, as well as motorcycles. Blashfield, Cyc. of Automobile Law and Prac., Perm. Ed., § 2.

Motor vehicle insurance. See Insurance.

MOTORCYCLE. A bicycle propelled by a gasoline engine located in the frame between the wheels. Ellett v. Klein, C.C.A.Pa., 252 F. 805, 806, certiorari denied Harley-Davidson Motor Co. v. Ellett, 39 S.Ct. 8, 248 U.S. 563, 63 L.Ed. 423; Bonds v. State, 16 Ga.App. 401, 85 S.E. 629, 630.

A motorcycle is not a "motor-driven car" as that term is used in insurance policies. Generally, however, a motorcycle is included in the term "motor vehicle," although under some statutes the words "automobile" and "motorcycle" are separately defined and the regulations and liabilities with respect thereto differ in material ways. Blashfield, Cyc. of Automobile Law and Prac., Perm. Ed., § 2.

MOTU PROPRIO. Lat. Of his own motion. The commencing words of a certain kind of papal rescript.

MOUNTINGS. Used in the Tariff Act of 1913, in connection with optical instruments such as the microscope and polariscope, in the sense of accessories, adjuncts, or parts thereof. U. S. v. International Forwarding Co., 9 Ct.Cust.App. 156, 159.

MOURNING. The dress or apparel worn by mourners at a funeral and for a time afterwards. Also the expenses paid for such apparel.

As to "year of mourning," see that title.

MOUTH OF RIVER. By statute in some states, the mouth of a river or creek, which empties into another river or creek, is defined as the point where the middle of the channel of each intersects the other. Pol.Code Cal. § 3908; Rev.St.Ariz.1901, par. 931, Rev.Code 1928, § 742.

MOVABLE. That which can be changed in place, as movable property; or in time, as movable feasts or terms of court. Goddard v. Winchell, 86 Iowa 71, 52 N.W. 1124, 17 L.R.A. 788.

MOVABLE ESTATE. A term equivalent to "personal estate" or "personal property." Den v. Sayre, 3 N.J.L. 187.

MOVABLE FREEHOLD. A term applied by Lord Coke to real property which is capable of being increased or diminished by natural causes; as where the owner of seashore acquires or loses land as the waters recede or approach. Holman v. Hodges, 112 Iowa 714, 84 N.W. 950, 58 L.R.A. 673.

MOVABLES. Things movable; movable or personal chattels which may be annexed to or attendant on the person of the owner, and carried about with him from one part of the world to another. 2 Bl.Comm. 387.

Movables consist—*First,* of inanimate things, as goods, plate, money, jewels, implements of war, garments, and the like or vegetable productions, as the fruit or other parts of a plant when severed from the body of it or the whole plant itself when severed from the ground; *secondly,* of animals, which have in themselves a principle and power of motion. 2 Steph.Comm. 67.

Movables are further distinguished into such as are in possession, or which are in the power of the owner, as a horse in actual use, a piece of furniture in a man's own house; and such as are in the possession of another, and can only be recovered by action, which are therefore said to be in action, as a debt.

But it has been held that movable property, in a legacy, strictly includes only such as is corporeal and tangible; not, therefore, rights in action, as judgment or bond debts; Strong v. White, 19 Conn. 238, 245; 1 Wm. Jones 225; but see Penniman v. French, 17 Pick., Mass., 404, 28 Am.Dec. 309; and that, in a will, "movables" is used in its largest sense, but will not pass growing crops, nor building materials on ground; Jackson v. Vanderspreigle, 2 Dall. 142, 1 L.Ed. 323.

Civil law. Movables (*mobilia,*) properly denoted inanimate things; animals being distinguished as *moventia,* things moving. Calvin. But these words *mobilia* and *moventia* are also used synonymously, and in the general sense of "movables." *Id.*

Scotch law. "Movables" are opposed to "heritage." So that every species of property, and every right a man can hold, is by that law either heritable or movable. Bell.

MOVANT. One who moves; one who makes a motion before a court; the applicant for a rule or order.

MOVE. To make an application to a court for a rule or order, or to take action in any matter. To ask. Harris v. Chicago House-Wrecking Co., 314 Ill. 500, 145 N.E. 666, 669. The term comprehends all things necessary to be done by a litigant to obtain an order of the court directing the relief sought. O'Hanion v. Great Northern Ry. Co., 76 Mont. 128, 245 P. 518, 519.

To propose a resolution, or recommend action in a deliberate body.

To pass over; to be transferred; as when the consideration of a contract is said to "move" from one party to the other.

To occasion; to contribute to; to tend or lead to. The forewheel of a wagon was said "to *move* to the death of a man." Sayer, 249.

MOVE OUT. To vacate; to yield up possession. Polich v. Severson, 68 Mont. 225, 216 P. 785, 787.

MOVEMENT. In relating to train, the word "movement" was not restricted to actual revolution of wheels of train or locomotive engaged in interstate commerce, but could apply to a train tied up on a siding. Great Northern Ry. Co. v. United States, C.C.A.Idaho, 211 F. 309, 312. Similarly, as regards vehicles, the term could comprehend the control and management of vehicles, including power to require that motor be closed down when a motor vehicle was left on street. White v. District of Columbia, 55 App.D.C. 197, 4 F.2d 163, 164.

MOVENT. An alternative spelling of *movant.*

MOVING FOR AN ARGUMENT. Making a motion on a day which is not motion day in virtue of having argued a special case; used in the exchequer after it became obsolete in the queen's bench. Wharton.

MOVING PAPERS. Such papers as are made the basis of some motion in court proceedings, *e. g.* a bill in equity with supporting affidavits.

MOVING PICTURE SHOW. A place where motion pictures are exhibited for the purpose of public amusement and entertainment. State v. Morris, 28 Idaho 599, 155 P. 296, 297, L.R.A.1916D, 573.

MRS. Title of courtesy prefixed to name of woman to indicate that she has been married. Guide Pub. Co. v. Futrell, 175 Va. 77, 7 S.E.2d 133, 138.

MUCIANA CAUTIO. See Cautio.

MUEBLES. In Spanish law, movables; all sorts of personal property. White, New Recop. b. 1, tit. 3, c. 1, § 2.

MUFFLER. Any of various devices to deaden the noise of escaping gases or vapors, such as a tube filled with obstructions, through which the exhaust gases of an internal combustion engine, as an automobile, are passed (called also a silencer), or an attachment usually consisting of a series of perforated baffles for a locomotive pop safety valve. Hines v. Foreman, Tex.Com.App., 243 S.W. 479, 484.

MUGGLE; MUGGLE HEADS. Marihuana is popularly known among the criminal element as "muggles" or "mooter," and addicts are commonly termed "muggle heads." State v. Navaro, 83 Utah, 6, 26 P.2d 955.

MUIRBURN. In Scotch law, the offense of setting fire to a muir or moor. 1 Brown, Ch. 78, 116.

MULATTO. A person that is the offspring of a negress by a white man, or of a white woman by a negro. Thurman v. State, 18 Ala. 276. In a more general sense, a person of mixed Caucasian and negro blood, or Indian and negro blood. Webster, Dict. See, also, Mustizo.

Properly a mulatto is a person one of whose parents is wholly black and the other wholly white; but the word does not always, though perhaps it does generally, require so exactly even a mixture of blood, nor is its signification alike in all the states. 1 Bish.Mar. & D. § 308.

MULCT. A penalty or punishment imposed on a person guilty of some offense, tort, or misdemeanor, usually a pecuniary fine or condemnation in damages. Cook v. Marshall County, 119 Iowa 384, 93 N.W. 372, 104 Am.St.Rep. 283. A forfeit, fine, or penalty. Kleinath, Schuster & Hudson v. Reed, 18 N.M. 358, 137 P. 841, 844. To sentence to a pecuniary penalty or forfeiture as a punishment; fine; hence to fine unjustly; to punish. Gorton v. Doty, 57 Idaho 792, 69 P.2d 136, 142.

Formerly, an imposition laid on ships or goods by a company of trade for the maintenance of consuls and the like.

MULCTA DAMNUM FAMÆ NON IRROGAT. Cod. 1, 54; Calvin. A fine does not involve loss of character.

MULE. A hybrid between the horse and the ass; especially, the offspring of a male ass and a mare. Webster, Dict.

MULIER. Lat. A woman; a wife; a widow; a virgin; a legitimate child. 1 Inst. 243; Co.Litt. 170, 253; 2 Bla.Com. 248.

The term is used always in contradistinction to a bastard, *mulier* being always legitimate. Co. Litt. 243.

MULIER PUISNÉ. L. Fr. When a man has a bastard son, and afterwards marries the mother, and by her has also a legitimate son, the elder son is *bastard eigné,* and the younger son is *mulier puisné.*

MULIERATUS. A legitimate son. Glanvil.

MULIERTY. In old English law, the state or condition of a *mulier,* or lawful issue. Co.Litt. 352*b*. The opposite of bastardy. Blount.

MULTA. A fine or final satisfaction, anciently given to the king by the bishops, that they might have power to make their wills, and that they might have the probate of other men's wills, and the granting of administration. 2 Inst. 291. Called, also, *multura episcopi.*

A fine imposed *ex arbitrio* by magistrates on the *præsides probinciarum.* Inst. 4, 1.

MULTA CONCEDUNTUR PER OBLIQUUM QUÆ NON CONCEDUNTUR DE DIRECTO. Many things are allowed indirectly which are not allowed directly. 6 Coke, 47.

MULTA FIDEM PROMISSA LEVANT. Many promises lessen confidence. Brown v. Castles, 11 Cush. (Mass.) 350.

MULTA IGNORAMUS QUÆ NOBIS NON LATERENT SI VETERUM LECTIO NOBIS FUIT FAMILIARIS. 10 Coke, 73. We are ignorant of many things which would not be hidden from us if the reading of old authors was familiar to us.

MULTA IN JURE COMMUNI CONTRA RATIONEM DISPUTANDI, PRO COMMUNI UTILITATE INTRODUCTA SUNT. Many things have been introduced into the common law, with a view to the public good, which are inconsistent with sound reason. Co.Litt. 70*b*; Broom, Max. 158; 2 Co. 75. See 3 Term 146; 7 *id.* 252.

MULTA MULTO EXERCITATIONE FACILIUS QUAM REGULIS PERCIPIES. 4 Inst. 50. You will perceive many things much more easily by practice than by rules.

MULTA NON VETAT LEX, QUÆ TAMEN TACITE DAMNAVIT. The law forbids not many things which yet it has silently condemned.

MULTA TRANSEUNT CUM UNIVERSITATE QUÆ NON PER SE TRANSEUNT. Many things pass with the whole which do not pass separately. Co.Litt. 12*a*.

MULTI MULTA, NEMO OMNIA NOVIT. 4 Inst. 348. Many men have known many things; no one has known everything.

MULTIFARIOUSNESS. Equity pleading. The misjoinder of causes of action in a bill. Van Antwerp v. Van Antwerp, 242 Ala. 92, 5 So.2d 73, 77.

The fault of improperly joining in one bill distinct and independent matters, and thereby confounding them; as, for example, the uniting in one bill of several matters perfectly distinct and unconnected against one defendant (more commonly called misjoinder of claims), or the demand of several matters of a distinct and independent nature against several defendants, in the same bill. Story, Eq.Pl. § 271; Essen v. Adams, 342 Mo. 1196, 119 S.W.2d 773, 777, 118 A.L.R. 1393.

"Multifariousness" as to matter consists in uniting in the same bill distinct and disconnected subjects, matters, or causes, and "multifariousness" as to parties consists in joining in same suit parties who are without a common interest in subject of litigation and have no connection with each other. Essen v. Adams, 342 Mo. 1196, 119 S.W.2d 773, 777, 118 A.L.R. 1393.

The joining of distinct and independent matters, each of which would constitute a cause of action. Otto F. Stifel's Union Brewing Co. v. Weber, 194 Mo.App. 605, 186 S.W. 1119, 1122; Johnson v. Benbow, 93 Fla. 124, 111 So. 504, 507.

"Multifariousness" abstractly is incapable of an accurate definition, but includes those cases where a party is brought as a defendant on a record with a large portion of which, and, in the case made by which, he has no connection whatever. Stamey v. Fortner, 230 Ala. 204, 160 So. 116.

The vice of multifariousness is the union of causes of action which, or of parties whose claims, it is either impractical or inconvenient to adjudicate in a single suit. Where it is as practical and convenient for court and parties to deal with the claims, and parties joined, in one suit as in many, there is no multifariousness. Westinghouse Air Brake Co. v. R. Co., C.C.A.Mo., 71 C.C.A. 1, 137 F. 26; Schell v. Leander Clark College, C.C.A.Iowa, 2 F.2d 17, 21. And it is not essential that every defendant have an interest in or concern for all matters or phases of the controversy. Mitchell v. Cudd, 196 Ala. 162, 71 So. 660; Norfolk Southern R. Co. v. Stricklin, D.C.N.C., 264 F. 546, 555.

A bill is not multifarious which seeks alternative or inconsistent relief growing out of the same subject-matter or founded on the same contract or transaction, or relating to the same property between the same parties. Code Ala. § 3095, Code 1923, § 6526; Szabo v. Speckman, 73 Fla. 374, 74 So. 411, 412, L.R.A. 1917D, 357.

Legislation. The joining, in a single legislative act, of dissimilar and discordant subjects, which, by no fair intendment, can be considered as having a legitimate connection or relation to the subject of the act. Boise City v. Baxter, 41 Idaho 368, 238 P. 1029, 1033.

MULTIPARTITE. Divided into many or several parts.

MULTIPLE EVIDENCE. That which is admissible for a specific purpose to which it must be confined and inadmissible to prove a different fact. Green v. Atlantic Coast Line R. Co., 136 S.C. 337, 134 S.E. 385, 386.

MULTIPLE POINDING. In Scotch law, double distress; a name given to an action, corresponding to proceedings by way of interpleader, which may be brought by a person in possession of goods claimed by different persons pretending a right thereto, calling the claimants and all others to settle their claims, so that the party who sues may be liable only "in once and single payment." Bell.

MULTIPLEX ET INDISTINCTUM PARIT CONFUSIONEM; ET QUÆSTIONES, QUO SIMPLICIORES, EO LUCIDIORES. Hob. 335. Multiplicity and indistinctness produce confusion; and questions, the more simple they are, the more lucid.

MULTIPLICATA TRANSGRESSIONE CRESCAT PŒNÆ INFLICTIO. As transgression is multiplied, the infliction of punishment should increase. 2 Inst. 479.

MULTIPLICITY. A state of being many. That quality of a pleading which involves a variety of matters or particulars; undue variety. 2 Saund. 410. A multiplying or increasing. Story, Eq.Pl. § 287.

MULTIPLICITY OF ACTIONS, or SUITS. Numerous and unnecessary attempts to litigate the same right. A phrase descriptive of the state of affairs where several different suits or actions are brought upon the same issue. The actions must be against a single defendant. Prospect Park & C. I. R. Co. v. Morey, 155 App.Div. 347, 140 N.Y.S. 380, 385; Williams v. Millington, 1 H.Bl. 81.

MULTITUDE. An assemblage of many people. According to Coke it is not a word of very precise meaning; for some authorities hold that there must be at least ten persons to make a multitude, while others maintain that no definite number is fixed by law. Co.Litt. 257. Two cannot constitute a multitude. Pike v. Witt, 104 Mass. 595. Three or more constitute. State v. Earp, 196 N.C. 164, 145 S.E. 23, 25.

MULTITUDINEM DECEM FACIUNT. Co.Litt. 257. Ten make a multitude.

MULTITUDO ERRANTIUM NON PARIT ERRORI PATROCINUM. The multitude of those who err furnishes no countenance or excuse for error. 11 Coke, 75*a*. It is no excuse for error that it is entertained by numbers.

MULTITUDO IMPERITORUM PERDIT CURIAM. A great number of unskillful practitioners ruins a court. 2 Inst. 219.

MULTO. In old records, a wether sheep.

MULTO UTILIUS EST PAUCA IDONEA EFFUNDERE QUAM MULTIS INUTILIBUS HOMINES GRAVARI. 4 Coke, 20. It is more useful to pour forth a few useful things than to oppress men with many useless things.

MULTURA EPISCOPI. See Multa.

MULTURE. In Scotch law, the quantity of grain or meal payable to the proprietor of a mill, or to the multurer, his tacksman, for manufacturing the corns. Ersk.Inst. 2, 9, 19.

MUMMIFICATION. In medical jurisprudence, the complete drying up of the body as the result of burial in a dry, hot soil, or the exposure of the body to a dry, cold atmosphere. 15 Amer. & Eng. Enc. Law, 261.

MUMMING. Antic diversions in the Christmas holidays, suppressed in Queen Anne's time.

MUND. In old English law, peace; whence *mundbryc,* a breach of the peace.

MUNDBYRD, MUNDEBURDE. A receiving into favor and protection. Cowell.

MUNDIUM. In old French law, a tribute paid by a church or monastery to their seignorial *avoués* and *vidames,* as the price of protecting them. Steph.Lect. 236.

MUNERA. In the early ages of the feudal law, the name given to the grants of land made by a king or chieftain to his followers, which were held by no certain tenure, but merely at the will of the lord. Afterwards they became life-estates, and then hereditary, and were called first "benefices," and then "feuds." See Wright, Ten. 19.

MUNICEPS. Lat. In Roman Law, eligible to office. A provincial person; a countryman. This was the designation of one born in the provinces or in a city politically connected with Rome, who had come to Rome, and though a Roman citizen, yet was looked down upon as a provincial, and not allowed to hold the higher offices.

In the provinces the term seems to have been applied to the freemen of any city who were eligible to the municipal offices. Calvin.

MUNICIPAL. In narrower sense, it means pertaining to a local governmental unit, commonly, a city or town or other governmental unit. In its broader sense, it means pertaining to the public or governmental affairs of a state or nation or of a people. Chadwick v. City of Crawfordsville, 216 Ind. 399, 24 N.E.2d 937, 941, 942, 129 A.L.R. 469. Sometimes, pertaining to a county. State ex rel. Schneider v. Midland Investment & Finance Corporation, 219 Wis. 161, 262 N.W. 711, *contra,* State ex rel. City of Missoula v. Holmes, 100 Mont. 256, 47 P.2d 624, 628, 100 A.L.R. 581; local, particular, independent; Horton v. Mobile School Com'rs, 43 Ala. 598; also, pertaining to local self-government in general; Woodward v. Livermore Falls Water Dist., 116 Me. 86, 100 A. 317, 319, L.R.A. 1917D, 678.

Relating to a state or nation, particularly when considered as an entity independent of other states or nations. Hammel v. Little, 66 App.D.C. 356, 87 F.2d 907, 910.

Among the Romans, cities were called *municipia;* these cities voluntarily joined the Roman republic in relation to their sovereignty only, retaining their laws, their liberties, and their magistrates, who were thence called *municipal magistrates.* With us this word has a more extensive meaning: for example, we call *municipal law* not the law of a city only, but the law of the state. 1 Bla.Comm. 44.

MUNICIPAL ACTION. Exercise of governmental power by a municipality. Orme v. Atlas Gas & Oil Co., 217 Minn. 27, 13 N.W.2d 757, 761.

MUNICIPAL AFFAIRS. A term referring to the internal business affairs of a municipality. Griffin v. City of Los Angeles, 134 Cal.App. 763, 26 P. 2d 655.

The term is frequently used in constitutional and statutory provisions concerning the power to legislate as to the concerns of municipalities. City of Los Angeles v. Central Trust Co. of New York, 173 Cal. 323, 159 P. 1169, 1171; State v. Cummings, 47 Okl. 44, 147 P. 161, 163. And it has come to include public service activities, such as supplying water to the inhabitants, the construction of a reservoir for their benefit, the sale and distribution of electrical energy, and the establishment and operation of transportation service, which were once regarded as being of a strictly private nature. In re Bonds of Orosi Public Utility Dist., 196 Cal. 43, 235 P. 1004, 1010.

MUNICIPAL AID. A contribution or assistance granted by a municipal corporation towards the execution or progress of some enterprise, undertaken by private parties, but likely to be of benefit to the municipality; *e. g.,* a railroad.

MUNICIPAL AUTHORITIES. As used in statutes contemplating the consent of such authorities, the term means the consent by the legislative authorities of the city acting by ordinance; Holland Realty & Power Co. v. City of St. Louis, 282 Mo. 180, 221 S.W. 51, 53, for example, in a town, the members of the town board; Farnsworth v. Boro Oil & Gas Co., 216 N.Y. 40, 109 N.E. 860.

MUNICIPAL BONDS. Evidences of indebtedness issued by cities or other corporate public body, negotiable in form, payable at designated future time, and intended for sale in market with object of raising money for municipal expense, which is beyond immediate resources of reasonable taxation, as distinguished from temporary evidences of debt, such as vouchers, certificates of indebtedness, orders, or drafts drawn by one officer on another and similar devices for liquidating current obligations in anticipation of collection of taxes. City of Stamford v. Town of Stamford, 107 Conn. 596, 141 A. 891, 896.

MUNICIPAL CHARTER. A legislative enactment conferring governmental powers of the state upon its local agencies. State v. Thompson, 193 Ala. 561, 69 So. 461, 464.

MUNICIPAL CLAIMS. In Pennsylvania law, claims filed by a city against property owners therein, for taxes, rates, levies, or assessments for local improvements, such as the cost of grading, paving, or curbing the streets, or removing nuisances.

MUNICIPAL CORPORATION. A public corporation, created by government for political purposes, and having subordinate and local powers of legislation. 2 Kent, Comm. 275; Bonaparte v. Camden & A. R. Co., Baldw. 222, F.Cas.No.1617.

An incorporation of persons, inhabitants of a particular place, or connected with a particular district, enabling them to conduct its local civil government Glov.Mun.Corp. 1.

A legal institution formed by charter from sovereign power erecting a populous community of prescribed area into a body politic and corporate with corporate name and continuous succession and for the purpose and with the authority of subordinate self-government and improvement and local administration of affairs of state. State v. Cheyenne County, 127 Neb. 619, 256 N.W. 67.

A body corporate consisting of the inhabitants of a designated area created by the legislature with or without the consent of such inhabitants for governmental purposes, possessing local legislative and administrative power, also power to exercise within such area so much of the administrative power of the state as may be delegated to it and possessing limited capacity to own and hold property, and to act in purveyance of public conveniences. Van Gilder v. City of Madison, 222 Wis. 58, 268 N.W. 108, 109.

Cities, towns, and villages are municipal corporations proper. Strickfaden v. Green Creek Highway Dist., 42 Idaho 738, 248 P. 456, 458, 49 A.L.R. 1057. On the other hand, such term in many instances does not extend so far as to include counties; Hersey v. Nelson, 47 Mont. 132, 131 P. 30, 31, Ann.Cas.1914C, 963; or drainage districts; Sawyer v. Camden Run Drainage Dist., 179 N.C. 182, 102 S.E. 273, 274; or irrigation districts; Crawford v. Imperial Irr. Dist., 200 Cal. 318, 253 P. 726, 729; or road districts; William T. Joyce Co. v. Police Jury of Parish of Tangipahoa, 146 La. 322, 83 So. 587, 588; or school districts; Dickson v. Brewer, 180 N.C. 403, 104 S.E. 887, 889; nor does it include the state; Herkimer Lumber Co. v. State, 196 App. Div. 708, 189 N.Y.S. 119, 122; but see *contra*, as to the District of Columbia, Stoutenburgh v. Hennick, 129 U.S. 141, 9 S.Ct. 256, 32 L.Ed. 637. Nevertheless, it has been held in other cases, often under different circumstances or in different contexts, that the term may include counties; Van Hess v. Board of Com'rs of St. Joseph County, 190 Ind. 347, 129 N.E. 305, 307; and, in Louisiana, parishes; State v. Hagen, 136 La. 868, 67 So. 935; drainage districts; State v. Little River Drainage Dist., 291 Mo. 267, 236 S.W. 848, 849; irrigation districts; Peters v. Union Gap Irr. Dist., 98 Wash. 412, 167 P. 1085, 1086; road districts; State ex rel. Little Prairie Special Road Dist. of Pemiscot County v. Thompson, 315 Mo. 56, 285 S.W. 57, 61; and the like; Milheim v. Moffat-Tunnel Improvement Dist., 72 Colo. 268, 211 P. 649, 653; Drum v. University Place Water Dist. 144 Wash. 585, 258 P. 505, 506.

English law. A body of persons in a town having the powers of acting as one person, of holding and transmitting property, and of regulating the government of the town. Such corporations existed in the chief towns of England (as of other countries) from very early times, deriving their authority from "incorporating" charters granted by the crown. Wharton.

Quasi municipal corporations. Bodies politic and corporate, created for the sole purpose of performing one or more municipal functions. Woodward v. Livermore Falls Water Dist., 116 Me. 86, 100 A. 317, 319, L.R.A.1917D, 678.

Public corporations organized for governmental purposes and having for most purposes the status and powers of municipal corporations (such as counties, townships, school districts, drainage districts, irrigation districts, etc.), but not municipal corporations proper, such as cities and incorporated towns. Snider v. St. Paul, 51 Minn. 466, 53 N.W. 763, 18 L.R.A. 151; Plumbing Supply Co. v. Board of Education of Independent School Dist. of City of Canton, 32 S.D. 270, 142 N.W. 1131, 1132; Melin v. Community Consol. School Dist. No. 76, 312 Ill. 376, 144 N.E. 13, 16.

MUNICIPAL CORPORATION DE FACTO. One which exists when there is (1) some law under which a corporation with the powers assumed might lawfully have been created; (2) a colorable and bona fide attempt to perfect an organization under such a law; (3) user of the rights claimed to have been conferred by the law. Evens v. Anderson, 132 Minn. 59, 155 N.W. 1040, 1041.

MUNICIPAL CORPORATIONS ACT. In English law, a general statute, (5 & 6 Wm. IV. c. 76,) passed in 1835, prescribing general regulations for the incorporation and government of boroughs.

MUNICIPAL COURTS. In the judicial organization of several states, courts are established under this name, whose territorial authority is confined to the city or community in which they are erected. Such courts usually have a criminal jurisdiction corresponding to that of a police court, and, in some cases, possess civil jurisdiction in small causes. Ex parte Gownlock, 13 Okl.Cr. 293, 164 P. 130, 131.

MUNICIPAL DOMICILE. Sometimes used in contradistinction to "national domicile" and "quasi national domicile" to refer to residence in a county, township, or municipality; called also "domestic domicile." Hayward v. Hayward, 65 Ind.App. 440, 115 N.E. 966, 970.

MUNICIPAL ELECTION. One at which municipal officers are chosen. Hutchins v. City of Des Moines, 176 Iowa, 189, 157 N.W. 881, 883. Compare Johnson v. Luers, 129 Md. 521, 99 A. 710, 714.

MUNICIPAL FUNCTION. One created or granted for the special benefit and advantage of the urban community embraced within the corporate boundaries. State ex rel. Gebhardt v. City Council of Helena, 102 Mont. 27, 55 P.2d 671, 673.

Sometimes called a private function, as distinguished from a public or governmental function, which is one conferred or imposed on the municipality as a local agency of limited and prescribed jurisdiction to be employed in administering the affairs of the state, and promoting the public welfare generally. Bryan v. City of West Palm Beach, 75 Fla. 19, 77 So. 627; Griffith v. City of Butte, 72 Mont. 552, 234 P. 829, 831.

Logically all those are strictly municipal functions which specially and peculiarly promote the comfort, convenience, safety and happiness of the citizens of the municipality, rather than the welfare of the general public. Under this class of functions are included, in most jurisdictions, the proper care of streets and alleys, parks and other public places, and the erection and maintenance of public utilities and improvements generally. Chardkoff Junk Co. v. City of Tampa, 102 Fla. 501, 135 So. 457, 459.

MUNICIPAL GOVERNMENT. Instrumentalities of state for purpose of local government. Moore v. State, 159 Tenn. 468, 19 S.W.2d 233.

This term, in certain state constitutions, embraces the governmental affairs of counties; State v. Touchberry, 121 S.C. 5, 113 S.E. 345; and includes all forms of representative municipal government; In re Opinion of the Justices, 229 Mass. 601, 119 N.E. 778, 781.

MUNICIPAL LAW. Not the law of a city only but the law of the state. People ex rel. Ray v. Martin, 181 Misc. 925, 47 N.Y.S.2d 883, 891.

In contradistinction to international law, it is the law of an individual state or nation. It is the rule or law by which a particular district, community, or nation is governed. 1 Bl.Comm. 44. That which pertains solely to the citizens and inhabitants of a state, and is thus distinguished from political law, commercial law, and the law of nations. Wharton; City of Louisville v. Babb, C.C.A. Ind., 75 F.2d 162, 165. In its more modern and narrower connotation it means those laws which pertain to towns, cities and villages and their local government. People ex rel. Ray v. Martin, 294 N.Y. 61, 60 N.E.2d 541, 547, 548.

MUNICIPAL LIEN. A lien or claim existing in favor of a municipal corporation against a property owner for his proportionate share of a public improvement, made by the municipality, whereby his property is specially and individually benefited.

MUNICIPAL OFFICER. One who holds an office of a municipality. Danculovic v. Zimmerman,

184 Minn. 370, 238 N.W. 695. A city, town, or borough;—not including a county. State v. Cooney, 70 Mont. 355, 225 P. 1007, 1010, but the term often bears a special or limited sense, in which it may not apply even to members of the city council. Lambert v. Barrett, 115 Va. 136, 78 S.E. 586, 587, Ann.Cas.1914D, 1226.

MUNICIPAL ORDINANCE. A law, rule, or ordinance enacted or adopted by a municipal corporation for the proper conduct of its affairs or the government of its inhabitants. Rutherford v. Swink, 96 Tenn. 564, 35 S.W. 554. Particularly a regulation under a delegation of power from the state. Harris v. City of Des Moines, 202 Iowa 53, 209 N.W. 454, 456, 46 A.L.R. 1429.

MUNICIPAL PURPOSES. Public or governmental purposes as distinguished from private purposes; Georgia Ry. & Power Co. v. City of Atlanta, 154 Ga. 731, 115 S.E. 263, 271. It may comprehend all activities essential to the health, morals, protection, and welfare of the municipality. State ex rel. Harper v. McDavid, 145 Fla. 605, 200 So. 100, 102, 133 A.L.R. 360.

For example, the taking of land for a school; Byfield v. City of Newton, 247 Mass. 46, 141 N.E. 658, 661; lighting the streets; City of Colorado Springs v. Pike's Peak Hydro-Electric Co., 57 Colo. 169, 140 P. 921, 927; supplying water to the inhabitants; Marin Water & Power Co. v. Town of Sausalito, 168 Cal. 587, 143 P. 767, 772; The collection and disposal of garbage and refuse; N. Ward Co. v. Board of Street Com'rs of City of Boston, 217 Mass. 381, 104 N.E. 965, 966; or the building of a subway; In re Montague Street in Borough of Brooklyn in City of New York, 87 Misc. 120, 150 N.Y.S. 382, 385.

MUNICIPAL SECURITIES. The evidences of indebtedness issued by cities, towns, counties, townships, school-districts, and other such territorial divisions of a state. They are of two general classes: (1) Municipal warrants, orders, or certificates; (2) municipal negotiable bonds. 15 Amer. & Eng. Enc. Law, 1206.

MUNICIPAL TAXATION. Refers to municipal purposes that are beneficial to municipality as a whole. Klemm v. Davenport, 100 Fla. 627, 129 So. 904, 910, 70 A.L.R. 156.

This term may have reference to any tax collected by the city tax collector, including state, county, and city or town taxes. Boston Fish Market Corp. v. City of Boston, 224 Mass. 31, 112 N.E. 616.

MUNICIPAL WARRANTS. A municipal warrant or order is an instrument, generally in the form of a bill of exchange, drawn by an officer of a municipality upon its treasurer, directing him to pay an amount of money specified therein to the person named or his order, or to bearer. 15 Amer. & Eng. Enc. Law, 1206.

MUNICIPALITY. A legally incorporated or duly authorized association of inhabitants of limited area for local governmental or other public purposes. State ex rel. Attorney General v. City of Avon Park, 108 Fla. 641, 149 So. 409, 412.

A body politic created by the incorporation of the people of a prescribed locality invested with subordinate powers of legislation to assist in the civil government of the state and to regulate and administer local and internal affairs of the community. State ex rel. McIntire v. City Council of City of Libby, 107 Mont. 216, 82 P.2d 587, 588.

Though sometimes limited in its application to cities only; City of Bangor v. Ridley, 117 Me. 297, 104 A. 230, 232; it ordinarily includes towns as well as cities of all classes; Goodman Warehouse Corporation v. Jersey City, 102 N.J.L. 294, 132 A. 503, 506; and may on occasion include townships; Whittingham v. Milburn Tp., 90 N.J.L. 344, 100 A. 854; counties; Murphy v. Freeholders of Hudson, 91 N.J.L. 40, 102 A. 896; school districts; Scobee v. Board of Education of Clark County, 157 Ky. 510, 163 S.W. 472, 473; and every kind and character of public corporations which are created by statute or the Constitution of the state, and which are dependent for their support and maintenance from taxes imposed and collected; Joint School Dist. No. 132 in Major County and Alfalfa County v. Dabney, 127 Okl. 234, 260 P. 486, 487. But neither townships; Petition of Herrington, 266 Pa. 88, 109 A. 791, 793; nor school districts; Long v. School Dist. of Cheltenham Tp., 269 Pa. 472, 112 A. 545, 546; nor drainage districts or the like are necessarily included; Witty v. Ellsberry Drainage Dist., 126 Miss. 645, 89 So. 268, 270.

Also, the body of officers taken collectively, belonging to a city, who are appointed to manage its affairs and defend its interests.

MUNICIPIUM. In Roman law, a foreign town to which the freedom of the city of Rome was granted, and whose inhabitants had the privilege of enjoying offices and honors there. Adams, Rom. Ant. 47, 77. A free town which retained its original right of self-government, but whose inhabitants also acquired certain rights of Roman citizens. Morey, Rom.L. 51.

MUNIMENT-HOUSE, or MUNIMENT-ROOM. A house or room of strength, in cathedrals, collegiate churches, castles, colleges, public buildings, etc., purposely made for keeping deeds, charters, writings, etc. 3 Inst. 170; Cowell.

MUNIMENTS. Documentary evidence of title. Merrill v. Rocky Mountain Cattle Co., 26 Wyo. 219, 181 P. 964, 971. The instruments of writing and written evidences which the owner of lands, possessions, or inheritances has, by which he is enabled to defend the title of his estate. Termes de la Ley; 3 Inst. 170.

MUNITIONS OF WAR. In international law and United States statutes, this term includes not only ordnance, ammunition, and other material directly useful in the conduct of a war, but also whatever may contribute to its successful maintenance, such as military stores of all kinds and articles of food. U. S. v. Sheldon, 2 Wheat. 119, 4 L.Ed. 199.

MUNUS. Lat. A gift; an office; a benefice or feud. A gladiatorial show or spectacle. Calvin.; Du Cange.

MURAGE. A toll formerly levied in England for repairing or building public walls.

MURAL MONUMENTS. Monuments made in walls.

MURDER. The unlawful killing of a human being by another with malice aforethought, either express or implied. State v. Hutter, 145 Neb. 798, 18 N.W.2d 203, 206.

The crime committed where a person of sound mind and discretion (that is, of sufficient age to form and execute a criminal design and not legally "insane") kills any human creature in being (excluding quick but unborn children) and in the peace of the state or nation (including all persons except the military forces of the public enemy in time of war or battle) without any warrant, justification, or excuse in law, with malice aforethought, express or implied, that is, with a deliberate purpose or a design or determination distinctly formed in the mind before the commission of the act, provided generally that death results from the injury inflicted within one year and a day after its infliction. Kilpatrick v. Com., 31 Pa. 198; Hotema v. U. S., 186 U.S. 413, 22 S.Ct. 895, 46 L.Ed. 1225; Clarke v. State, 117 Ala. 1, 23 So. 671, 67 Am.St.Rep. 157.

The term implies a felonious homicide, while the word "kill" does not necessarily mean any more than to deprive of life, as a man may kill another by accident, or in self-defense, and in many other ways, without the imputation of crime. Pilcher v. State, 16 Ala.App. 237, 77 So. 75, 76.

For the distinction between murder and manslaughter and other forms of homicide, see Homicide; Manslaughter.

Statutory Definitions. Murder is the unlawful killing of a human being with malice aforethought. Pen.Code Cal. § 187; Arizona Code Ann.1939, § 43–2901, Pen.Code Ariz. 1901, § 172. Whoever kills any human being with malice aforethought, either express or implied, is guilty of murder. I.C.A. § 690.1. Murder is the unlawful killing of a human being, in the peace of the State, by a person of sound memory and discretion, with malice aforethought, either express or implied. Georgia Code Ann. § 26–1002. The killing of a human being, without the authority of law, by any means, or in any manner shall be murder in the following cases: When done with deliberate design to effect the death of the person killed, or of any human being; when done in the commission of an act eminently dangerous to others, and evincing a depraved heart, regardless of human life, although without any premeditated design to effect the death of any particular individual; when done without any design to effect death, by any person engaged in the commission of the crime of rape, burglary, arson, or robbery, or in any attempt to commit such felonies. Mississippi Code 1942 § 2215. Every homicide, perpetrated by poison, lying in wait, or any other kind of willful, deliberate, malicious, and premeditated killing; or committed in the perpetration of, or the attempt to perpetrate, any arson, rape, robbery, or burglary; or perpetrated from a premeditated design unlawfully and maliciously to effect the death of any human being other than him who is killed; or perpetrated by any act greatly dangerous to the lives of others, and evidencing a depraved mind, regardless of human life, although without any preconceived purpose to deprive any particular person of life, is murder in the first degree; and every other homicide, committed under such circumstances as would have constituted murder at common law, is murder in the second degree. Code Ala. 1940, § 314. Murder is the unlawful killing of a human being, in the peace of the people, with malice aforethought, either expressed or implied. The unlawful killing may be perpetrated by poisoning, striking, starving, drowning, stabbing, shooting, or by any other of the various forms or means by which human nature may be overcome, and death thereby occasioned. S.H.A. ch. 38, § 358.

Common-Law. The willful killing of any subject whatever, with malice aforethought, whether the person slain shall be an Englishman or a foreigner. Hawk. P.C. b. 1, c. 13, § 3. The killing of any person under the king's peace, with malice prepense or aforethought, either express, or implied by law. 1 Russ. Crimes, 421; Com. v. Webster, 5 Cush., Mass., 304, 52 Am.Dec. 711. When a person of sound mind and discretion unlawfully killeth any reasonable creature in being, and under the king's peace, with malice aforethought, either express or implied. 3 Inst. 47; State v. Robinson, 143 La. 543, 78 So. 933, 935.

Degrees. These were unknown at common law, but have been introduced in many states by statutes, the terms of which are too variant to be here discussed in detail. In general, however, it may be said that most states only divide the crime into "murder in the first degree" and "murder in the second degree," though in some there are three degrees; and that the general purport of these statutes is to confine murder in the first degree to homicide committed by poison, lying in wait, and other killings committed in pursuance of a deliberate and premeditated design, and to those which accompany the commission of some of the more atrocious felonies, such as burglary, arson, rape, and robbery; while murder in the second degree occurs where there is no such deliberately formed design to take life or to perpetrate one of the enumerated felonies as is required for the first degree, but where, nevertheless, there was a purpose to kill (or at least a purpose to inflict the particular injury without caring whether it caused death or not) formed instantaneously in the mind, and where the killing was without justification or excuse, and without any such provocation as would reduce the crime to the grade of manslaughter. State v. Nelson, 148 Minn. 285, 181 N.W. 850, 851; State v. Liolios, 285 Mo. 1, 225 S.W. 941, 947; Commonwealth v. Divomte, 262 Pa. 504, 105 A. 821, 822. In a few states, there is a crime of "murder in the third degree," which is defined as the killing of a human being without any design to effect death by a person who is engaged in the commission of a felony. Tillman v. State, 81 Fla. 558, 88 So. 377, 378.

MURDRUM. In old English law, the killing of a man in a secret manner.

When a man was thus killed, and he was unknown, by the laws of Canute he was presumed to be a Dane, and the vill was compelled to pay forty marks to the king for his death. After the conquest, a similar law was made in favor of Normans, which was abolished by 3 Edw. III.

The fine formerly imposed in England upon a person who had committed homicide *per infortunium* or *se defendendo.* Prin.Pen.Law 219, note.

MURORUM OPERATIO. Lat. The service of work and labor done by inhabitants and adjoining tenants in building or repairing the walls of a city or castle; their personal service was commuted into *murage (q. v.).* Cowell.

MURTHRUM. In old Scotch law, murther or murder. Skene.

MUSEUM. A building or institution for the cultivation of science or the exhibition of curiosities or works of art. The term embraces not only collections of curiosities for the entertainment of the sight, but also such as would interest, amuse, and instruct the mind. Bostick v. Purdy, 5 Stew. & P., Ala., 109.

MUSICAL INSTRUMENT. An instrument having the capacity in and of itself when properly operated to produce or initiate the musical sound. Dunbar v. Spratt-Snyder Co., 208 Iowa 490, 226 N. W. 22, 63 A.L.R. 1016.

MUSICAL TABLOID. As distinguished from vaudeville, a condensation of a musical comedy in which the plot and the characters taken by different actors are preserved, to produce just one whole play by itself, without any special independent features brought into it; it classifies as vaudeville only when other features are put on during the intermissions between the scenes or acts. Princess Amusement Co. v. Well, C.C.A. Tenn., 271 F. 226, 231.

MUSSA. In old English law, a moss or marsh ground, or a place where sedges grow; a place overrun with moss. Cowell.

MUSSEL. A fresh water shellfish capable of locomotion, usually living in the bed of streams partially covered with mud. Gratz v. McKee, C. C.A.Mo., 258 F. 335, 336.

MUST. This word, like the word "shall," is primarily of mandatory effect; State ex rel. McCabe v. District Court of Third Judicial Dist. in and for Deer Lodge County, 106 Mont. 272, 76 P.2d 634,

637; and in that sense is used in antithesis to "may"; Emery v. First Nat. Bank, 32 N.D. 575, 156 N.W. 105, 109; Reinert Bros. Const. Co. v. Tootle, 200 Mo.App. 284, 206 S.W. 422, 424. But this meaning of the word is not the only one, and it is often used in a merely directory sense. Robinson v. City of Saginaw, 267 Mich. 557, 255 N.W. 396; Munro v. State, 223 N.Y. 208, 119 N.E. 444, 445; State v. Barnell, 109 Ohio St. 246, 142 N.E. 611, 614; and consequently is a synonym for the word "may" not only in the permissive sense of that word; Tosti v. Sbano, 170 Misc. 828, 11 N.Y.S.2d 321, 323; Pleasant Grove Union School Dist. v. Algeo, 61 Cal.App. 660, 215 P. 726; but also in the mandatory sense which it sometimes has; People v. Highway Com'rs of Town of Anchor, 279 Ill. 542, 117 N.E. 56, 57.

MUSTER. To assemble together troops and their arms, whether for inspection, drill, or service in the field. To take recruits into the service in the army and inscribe their names on the muster-roll or official record. To summon together; to enroll in service. Bannister v. Soldiers' Bonus Board, 43 R.I. 346, 112 A. 422, 423, 13 A.L.R. 589. In the latter sense the term implies that the persons mustered are not already in the service. Tyler v. Pomeroy, 8 Allen, Mass., 480.

MUSTER-MASTER. One who superintended the muster to prevent frauds. St. 35 Eliz. c. 4.

MUSTER-BOOK. A book in which the forces are registered. Termes de la Ley.

MUSTER-ROLL. In maritime law, a list or account of a ship's company, required to be kept by the master or other person having care of the ship, containing the name, age, national character, and quality of every person employed in the ship. Abb.Shipp. 191, 192; Jac. Sea Laws, 161. It is of great use in ascertaining the ship's neutrality. Marsh.Ins. p. 407; Ketland v. Lebering, 2 Wash. C.C. 201, F.Cas.No.7,744.

MUSTIZO. A name given in a South Carolina Act of 1740 to the issue of an Indian and a negro. Miller v. Dawson, Dudl., S.C., 174.

MUTA-CANUM. A kennel of hounds; one of the mortuaries to which the crown was entitled at a bishop's or abbot's decease. 2 Bl.Comm. 426.

MUTATIO NOMINIS. Lat. In the civil law, change of name. Cod. 9, 25.

MUTATION. In French law, this term is synonymous with "change," and is especially applied to designate the change which takes place in the property of a thing in its transmission from one person to another. Mutation, therefore, happens when the owner of the thing sells, exchanges, or gives it. Merl.Répert.

MUTATION OF LIBEL. In practice, an amendment allowed to a libel, by which there is an alteration of the substance of the libel, as by propounding a new cause of action, or asking one thing instead of another. Dunl.Adm.Pr. 213; U. S. v. Four Part Pieces of Woollen Cloth, 1 Paine 435, F.Cas.No.15,150.

MUTATIS MUTANDIS. Lat. With the necessary changes in points of detail, meaning that matters or things are generally the same, but to be altered when necessary, as to names, offices, and the like. Housman v. Waterhouse, 191 App.Div. 850, 182 N.Y.S. 249, 251.

MUTE. Speechless; dumb; that cannot or will not speak.

In English criminal law, a prisoner is said to *stand mute* when, being arraigned for treason or felony, he either makes no answer at all, or answers foreign to the purpose or with such matter as is not allowable, and will not answer otherwise, or, upon having pleaded not guilty, refuses to put himself upon the country. 4 Bl.Comm. 324.

MUTILATION. As applied to written documents, such as wills, court records, and the like, this term means rendering the document imperfect by the subtraction from it of some essential part, as, by cutting, tearing, burning, or erasure, but without totally destroying it. Woodfill v. Patton, 76 Ind. 583, 40 Am.Rep. 269; Tinsley v. Carwile, 212 Ind. 675, 10 N.E.2d 597, 600. Also, the alteration in the writing, as in a negotiable instrument, so as to make it another and different instrument and no longer evidence of the contract which the parties made. Clem v. Chapman, Tex.Civ.App., 262 S.W. 168, 171.

In criminal law, the depriving a man of the use of any of those limbs which may be useful to him in fight, the loss of which amounts to *mayhem*. 1 Bl.Comm. 130; People v. Bullington, 27 Cal.App. 2d 396, 80 P.2d 1030, 1032.

MUTINOUS. Insubordinate; disposed to mutiny; tending to incite or encourage mutiny.

MUTINY, *v.* To rise against lawful or constituted authority, particularly in the naval or military service. United States v. Krafft, C.C.A.N.J., 249 F. 919, 925, L.R.A.1918F, 402.

MUTINY, *n.* In criminal law, an insurrection of soldiers or seamen against the authority of their commanders; a sedition or revolt in the army or navy. The Stacey Clarke, D.C.Ala., 54 F. 533; U. S. v. Smith, 1 Mas. 147, F.Cas.No.16,337.

MUTINY ACT. In English law, an act of parliament annually passed to punish mutiny and desertion, and for the better payment of the army and their quarters. It was first passed April 12, 1689, and was the only provision for the payment of the army. 1 Bl.Comm. 415.

MUTUAL. Common to both parties. Kansas Amusement Co. v. Maryland Casualty Co., 126 Kan. 354, 267 P. 968, 969.

Interchangeable; reciprocal; each acting in return or correspondence to the other; given and received;—spoken of an engagement or relation in which like duties and obligations are exchanged; *e. g.*, the marital relation. O'Malley v. O'Malley, 46 Mont. 549, 129 P. 501, 502, Ann.Cas.1914B, 662; Canal-Commercial Trust & Savings Bank v. Brewer, 143 Miss. 146, 108 So. 424, 431, 47 A.L.R. 45.

As to mutual "Accounts," "Assent," "Combat," "Conditions," "Contracts," "Covenants," "Credits,"

"Debts," "Insurance," "Insurance Company," "Mistake," "Promise," and "Testaments," see those titles.

MUTUAL AFFRAY. A fight in which both parties willingly enter and is similar to a duel. Taylor v. Commonwealth, 281 Ky. 442, 136 S.W.2d 544.

MUTUAL BENEFIT ASSOCIATION. One based on reciprocal contracts and requires that a member receive benefits as a matter of right. In re Henderson's Estate, 17 Cal.2d 853, 112 P.2d 605, 609.

MUTUAL COMPANY. One in which the members are both the insurers and the insured. Pink v. Town Taxi Co., 138 Me. 44, 21 A.2d 656, 659.

MUTUAL DEMANDS. Those between the same parties and due in the same capacity or right. Thompson v. Prince, Tex.Civ.App., 126 S.W.2d 574, 576.

MUTUAL ENTERPRISE. Building and loan association is generally a "mutual enterprise," all members being under same rules, sharing in profits equally, and bearing proportionate share of losses. Griffin v. White, 182 S.C. 219, 189 S.E. 127, 131.

MUTUAL RELIEF ASSOCIATION. An insurer, chartered under a designated statute, having no capital stock, having relief funds created and sustained by assessments made upon the members, which files reports with insurance commissioner evidencing that it is not conducted for profit of its officers. State v. Texas Mut. Life Ins. Co. of Texas, Tex.Civ.App., 51 S.W.2d 405, 412.

MUTUAL RESERVE COMPANY. A company issuing "benefit thrift certificates" containing both savings features and renewable term insurance features, paid for by a single premium, with cash and loan values and limitation upon the expense liable for cost of supervision and management, was a "mutual reserve company". State ex rel. Smrha v. Cosmopolitan Old Line Life Ins. Co., 137 Neb. 742, 291 N.W. 72, 79.

MUTUAL SAVINGS BANK. A bank organized by depositors, whose interest is shown by certificates of deposit, for the purpose of furnishing a safe depositary for money of members. It need not be incorporated or under supervision unless state law so requires. A-C Investment Ass'n v. Helvering, 62 App.D.C. 339, 68 F.2d 386, 387.

MUTUAL WILLS. Those made as the separate wills of two people which are reciprocal in provision. Child v. Smith, 225 Iowa 1205, 282 N.W. 316, 321. Or those executed pursuant to agreement or compact between two or more persons to dispose of their property in particular manner, each in consideration of the other. Maloney v. Rose, 224 Iowa 1071, 277 N.W. 572, 574.

MUTUALITY. Reciprocation; interchange. An acting by each of two parties; an acting in return.

Contracts and obligations. "Mutuality of contract" means that obligation rests on each party to do or permit doing of something in consideration of other party's act or promise; neither party being bound unless both are bound. Aden v. Dalton, 341 Mo. 454, 107 S.W.2d 1070, 1073. Called, also, mutuality of obligation. Warren v. Ray County Coal Co., 200 Mo.App. 442, 207 S.W. 883, 884; United Appliance Corporation v. Boyd, Tex. Civ.App., 108 S.W.2d 760, 764.

As to mutuality of "Assent," "Mistake," etc., see those titles.

MUTUANT. The person who lends chattels in the contract of *mutuum*, (*q. v.*).

MUTUARI. To borrow; *mutuatus*, a borrowing. 2 Arch.Pr. 25.

MUTUARY. A person who borrows personal chattels to be consumed by him and returned to the lender in kind and quantity; the borrower in a contract of *mutuum*.

MUTUATUS. A loan of money. See Gilbert, Com. Pleas 5.

MUTUS ET SURDUS. Lat. In civil and old English law, dumb and deaf.

MUTUUM. Lat. A loan for consumption; a loan of chattels, upon an agreement that the borrower may consume them, returning to the lender an equivalent in kind and quantity; as, a loan of corn, wine, or money which is to be used or consumed, and is to be replaced by other corn, wine, or money. Story, Bailm. § 228; In re Ellis' Estate, 24 Del.Ch. 393, 6 A.2d 602, 611. At common law, such a transaction is regarded as a sale or exchange, and not a bailment. Hanes v. Shapiro & Smith, 168 N.C. 24, 84 S.E. 33, 35; New Domain Oil & Gas Co. v. Hayes, 202 Ky. 377, 259 S.W. 715, 717, 38 A.L.R. 172.

MYNSTER-HAM. Monastic habitation; perhaps the part of a monastery set apart for purposes of hospitality, or as a sanctuary for criminals. Anc. Inst.Eng.

MYSTERIOUS DISAPPEARANCE. Theft insurance policy provision covering any disappearance or loss under unknown, puzzling or baffling circumstances which arouse wonder, curiosity or speculation, or circumstances which are difficult to understand or explain. Claiborne v. U. S. Fire Ins. Co., La.App., 193 So.2d 315, 317.

MYSTERY. A trade, art, or occupation. 2 Inst. 668. Masters frequently bind themselves in the indentures with their apprentices to teach them their art, trade, and *mystery*. State v. Bishop, 15 Me. 122; Barger v. Caldwell, 2 Dana, Ky., 131.

MYSTIC TESTAMENT. In the law of Louisiana, a closed or sealed will, required by statute to be executed in a particular manner and to be signed (on the outside of the paper or of the envelope containing it) by a notary and seven witnesses as well as the testator. See Civ.Code La. art. 1584.

N

N. An abbreviation of *"Novellæ,"* the Novels of Justinian, used in citing them. Tayl.Civil Law, 24.

In English, a common and familiar abbreviation for the word "north," as used in maps, charts, conveyances, etc. Burr v. Broadway Ins. Co., 16 N.Y. 271; Village of Bradley v. New York Cent. R. Co., 296 Ill. 383, 129 N.E. 744, 746.

N. A. An abbreviation for *"non allocatur,"* it is not allowed.

N. A. S. A. National Aeronautics and Space Administration.

N. B. An abbreviation for *"nota bene,"* mark well, observe; also *"nulla bona,"* no goods.

N. C. D. *Nemine contra dicente.* No one dissenting.

N. D. An abbreviation for "Northern District."

N. E. I. An abbreviation for *"non est inventus,"* he is not found.

N. I. H. National Institutes of Health.

N. L. An abbreviation of *"non liquet,"* (which see.)

N. L. R. B. National Labor Relations Board.

N. O. I. B. N. Abbreviation, used under terms of tariffs, filed with Interstate Commerce Commission, meaning not otherwise indexed by name. Pennsylvania R. Co. v. U. S., Ct.Cl., 42 F.2d 600, 602.

N. O. V. See Non Obstante Veredicto.

N. P. An abbreviation for "notary public," Rowley v. Berrian, 12 Ill. 200; also for *"nisi prius,"* (*q. v.*).

N. R. An abbreviation for "New Reports;" also for "not reported," and for "nonresident."

N. S. An abbreviation for "New Series;" also for "New Style."

NAAM. Sax. The attaching or taking of movable goods and chattels, called *"vif"* or *"mort"* according as the chattels were living or dead. Termes de la Ley.

NABOB. Originally the governor of a province under the Mogul government of Hindostan, whence it became a mere title of any man of high rank, upon whom it was conferred without any office being attached to it. Wils. Indian Gloss.

NAIF. L. Fr. A villein; a born slave; a bondwoman.

NAIL. A lineal measure of two inches and a quarter.

NAKED. Bare; wanting in necessary conditions; incomplete, as a naked contract, (*nudum pactum,*) *i. e.*, a contract devoid of consideration, and therefore invalid; or simple, unilateral, comprising but a single element, as a naked authority, *i. e.*, one which is not coupled with any interest in the agent, but subsists for the benefit of the principal alone.

As to naked "Confession," "Deposit," "Possession," "Possibility," "Power," "Promise," and "Trust," see those titles.

NAM. In old English law, a distress or seizure of chattels.

As a Latin conjunction, for; because. Often used by the old writers in introducing the quotation of a Latin maxim.

NAMARE. L. Lat. In old records, to take, seize or distrain.

NAMATIO. L. Lat. In old English and Scotch law, a distraining or taking of a distress; an impounding. Spelman.

NAME. The designation of an individual person, or of a firm or corporation. Riley v. Litchfield, 168 Iowa 187, 150 N.W. 81, 83, Ann.Cas.1917B, 172.

A person's "name" consists of one or more Christian or given names and one surname or family name. Blakeney v. Smith, 183 Miss. 151, 183 So. 920, 921. It is the distinctive characterization in words by which one is known and distinguished from others, and description, or abbreviation, is not the equivalent of a "name." Putnam v. Bessom, 291 Mass. 217, 197 N.E. 147, 148. Custom gives one his father's family name, and such prænomina as his parents choose to put before it, but this is only general rule, from which individual may depart, if he choose. In re Cohen, 142 Misc. 852, 255 N.Y.S. 616, 617. As to the history of Christian names and surnames and their use and relative importance in law, see In re Snook, 2 Hilt., N.Y., 566.

Distinctive Name. As used in regulation of United States Department of Agriculture, a trade, arbitrary, or fancy name which clearly distinguishes a food product, mixture, or compound from any other food product, mixture, or compound. Crescent Mfg. Co. v. Wilson, D.C.N.Y., 233 F. 282, 285; U. S. v. Forty Barrels and Twenty Kegs of Coca Cola, 241 U.S. 265, 36 S.Ct. 573, 580, 60 L.Ed. 995, Ann.Cas.1917C, 487.

NAME AND ARMS CLAUSE. The popular name in English law for the clause, sometimes inserted in a will or settlement by which property is given to a person, for the purpose of imposing on him the condition that he shall assume the surname and arms of the testator or settlor, with a direction that, if he neglects to assume or discontinues the use of them, the estate shall devolve on the next person in remainder, and a provision for preserving contingent remainders. 3 Dav.Prec.Conv. 277; Sweet.

NAMELY. A difference, in grammatical sense, in strictness exists between the words namely and including. Namely imports interpretation, *i. e.*, indicates what is included in the previous term; but including imports addition, *i. e.*, indicates something not included. 2 Jarm.Wills 222.

NAMIUM. L. Lat. In old English law, a taking; a distress. Spelman. Things, goods, or animals taken by way of distress. *Simplex namium,* a simple taking or pledge. Bract. fol. 205b.

NAMIUM VETITUM. An unjust taking of the cattle of another and driving them to an unlawful place, pretending damage done by them. 3 Bl. Comm. 149.

NANTES, EDICT OF. A celebrated law for the security of Protestants, made by Henry IV. of France, and revoked by Louis XIV., October 2, 1685.

NANTISSEMENT. In French law, the contract of pledge; if of a movable, it is called *"gage;"* and if of an immovable, it is called *"antichrèse."* Brown.

NARR. A common abbreviation of *"narratio,"* (*q. v.*). A declaration in an action. Jacob.

NARR AND COGNOVIT LAW. Law providing that judgment may be had for plaintiff on notes by confession of any attorney that amount shown on notes, together with interest and costs, constitutes legal and just claim; word "narr" being an abbreviation of Latin word "narratio," meaning complaint or petition, and word "cognovit" meaning that defendant has confessed judgment and justice of claim. Dyer v. Johnson, Tex.Civ.App., 19 S.W.2d 421, 422.

NARRATIO. Lat. One of the common law names for a plaintiff's count or declaration, as being a narrative of the facts on which he relies.

NARRATIVE. In Scotch conveyancing, that part of a deed which describes the grantor, and person in whose favor the deed is granted, and states the cause (consideration) of granting. Bell.

NARRATOR. A countor; a pleader who draws *narrs. Serviens narrator,* a serjeant at law. Fleta, l. 2, c. 37.

NARROW SEAS. Those seas which run between two coasts not far apart. The term is sometimes applied to the English channel. Wharton.

NASCITURUS. Lat. That shall hereafter be born. A term used in marriage settlements to designate the future issue of the marriage, as distinguished from *"natus,"* a child already born.

NATALE. The state and condition of a man acquired by birth.

NATI ET NASCITURI. Born and to be born. All heirs, near and remote.

NATIO. In old records, a native place. Cowell.

NATION. A people, or aggregation of men, existing in the form of an organized jural society, usually inhabiting a distinct portion of the earth, speaking the same language, using the same customs, possessing historic continuity, and distinguished from other like groups by their racial origin and characteristics, and generally, but not necessarily, living under the same government and sovereignty. Montoya v. U. S., 180 U.S. 261, 21 S. Ct. 358, 45 L.Ed. 521; Worcester v. Georgia, 6 Pet. 539, 8 L.Ed. 483; Republic of Honduras v. Soto, 112 N.Y. 310, 19 N.E. 845, 2 L.R.A. 642.

Besides the element of autonomy or self-government, that is, the independence of the community as a whole from the interference of any foreign power in its affairs or any subjection to such power, it is further necessary to the constitution of a nation that it should be an organized jural society, that is, both governing its own members by regular laws, and defining and protecting their rights, and respecting the rights and duties which attach to it as a constituent member of the family of nations. Such a society, says Vattel, has her affairs and her interests; she deliberates and takes resolutions in common: thus becoming a moral person, who possesses an understanding and will peculiar to herself, and is susceptible of obligations and rights. Vattel, §§ 1, 2.

The words "nation" and "people" are frequently used as synonyms, but there is a great difference between them. A nation is an aggregation of men speaking the same language, having the same customs, and endowed with certain moral qualities which distinguish them from other groups of a like nature. It would follow from this definition that a nation is destined to form only one *state,* and that it constitutes one indivisible whole. Nevertheless, the history of every age presents us with nations divided into several states. Thus, Italy was for centuries divided among several different governments. The *people* is the collection of all citizens without distinction of rank or order. All men living under the same *government* compose the *people* of the *state.* In relation to the state, the citizens constitute the people; in relation to the human race, they constitute the nation. A free nation is one not subject to a foreign government, whatever be the constitution of the state; a *people* is free when all the citizens can participate in a certain measure in the direction and in the examination of public affairs. The people is the political body brought into existence by community of laws, and the people may perish with these laws. The nation is the moral body, independent of political revolutions, because it is constituted by inborn qualities which render it indissoluble. The *state* is the people organized into a political body. Lalor, Pol.Enc. *s. v.*

In American constitutional law the word "state" is applied to the several members of the American Union, while the word "nation" is applied to the whole body of the people embraced within the jurisdiction of the federal government. Cooley, Const.Lim. 1; Texas v. White, 7 Wall. 720, 19 L. Ed. 227.

NATIONAL. Pertaining or relating to a nation as a whole; commonly applied in American law to institutions, laws, or affairs of the United States or its government, as opposed to those of the several states.

The term "national" as used in the phrase "national of the United States" is broader than the term "citizen". Brassert v. Biddle, D.C.Conn., 59 F.Supp. 457, 462.

NATIONAL AGENCY. That Mexican government contributed to capital of association, and was represented on governing board and even subsidized association did not render association a "national agency" that it might claim sovereign immunity. The Uxmal, D.C.Mass., 40 F.Supp. 258, 261.

NATIONAL BANK. A bank incorporated and doing business under the laws of the United States, as distinguished from a *state* bank, which derives its powers from the authority of a particular state.

NATIONAL CURRENCY. Notes issued by national banks, and by the United States government.

NATIONAL DEBT. The money owing by government to some of the public, the interest of which is paid out of the taxes raised by the whole of the public.

NATIONAL DEFENSE. A generic concept and refers to the military and naval establishments and the related activities of national preparedness and includes all matters directly and reasonably connected with the defense of the nation against its enemies. Gorin v. United States, Cal., 312 U. S. 19, 61 S.Ct. 429, 434, 436, 85 L.Ed. 488.

NATIONAL DOMAIN. See Domain.

NATIONAL DOMICILE. See Domicile.

NATIONAL EMERGENCY. A state of national crisis; a situation demanding immediate and extraordinary national or federal action.

Congress has made little or no distinction between a "state of national emergency" and a "state of war". Brown v. Bernstein, D.C.Pa., 49 F.Supp. 728, 732.

NATIONAL GOVERNMENT. The government of a whole nation, as distinguished from that of a local or territorial division of the nation, and also as distinguished from that of a league or confederation.

"A *national* government is a government of the people of a single state or nation, united as a community by what is termed the 'social compact,' and possessing complete and perfect supremacy over persons and things, so far as they can be made the lawful objects of civil government. A *federal* government is distinguished from a national government, by its being the government of a community of independent and sovereign states, united by compact." Piqua Branch Bank v. Knoup, 6 Ohio St. 393.

NATIONALITY. That quality or character which arises from the fact of a person's belonging to a nation or state.

Nationality determines the political *status* of the individual, especially with reference to allegiance; while domicile determines his civil *status*. Nationality arises either by birth or by naturalization. According to Savigny, "nationality" is also used as opposed to "territoriality," for the purpose of distinguishing the case of a nation having no national territory; *e. g.*, the Jews. 8 Sav. Syst. § 346; Westl.Priv.Int. Law, 5.

NATIONALIZACION. In Spanish and Mexican law, nationalization.

"The nationalization of property is an act which denotes that it has become that of the nation by some process of law, whereby private individuals or corporations have been for specified reasons deprived thereof." Hall, Mex. Law, § 749.

NATIONS, LAW OF. See International Law.

NATIVE. A natural-born subject or citizen; a denizen by birth; one who owes his domicile or citizenship to the fact of his birth within the country referred to. The term may also include one born abroad, if his parents were then citizens of the country, and not permanently residing in foreign parts. U. S. v. Wong Kim Ark, 169 U.S. 649, 18 S.Ct. 456, 42 L.Ed. 890; New Hartford v. Canaan, 54 Conn. 39, 5 A. 360; Oken v. Johnson, 160 Minn. 217, 199 N.W. 910.

The word "natives", as used in Alien Enemy Act, refers to person's place of birth, so that a person remains a native of country of his birth, though he has moved away therefrom. United States ex rel. D'Esquiva v. Uhl, C.C.A. N.Y., 137 F.2d 903, 905.

One who was born in Germany and later become a citizen of France was a "native" of Germany. Ex parte Gregoire, D.C.Cal., 61 F.Supp. 92, 93.

But a person born in Alsace which at time of his birth was part of Germany but which was restored to French sovereignty by the treaty of Versailles of 1918, was a "native" of France. United States ex rel. Umecker v. McCoy, D.C.N.D., 54 F.Supp. 679, 681, 682.

NATIVA. A niefe or female villein. So called because for the most part bound by nativity. Co. Litt. 122*b*.

NATIVI CONVENTIONARII. Villeins or bondmen by contract or agreement.

NATIVI DE STIPITE. Villeins or bondmen by birth or stock. Cowell.

NATIVITAS. Villenage; that state in which men were born slaves. 2 Mon. Angl. 643.

NATIVO HABENDO. A writ which lay for a lord when his villein had run away from him. It was directed to the sheriff, and commanded him to apprehend the villein, and to restore him together with his goods to the lord. Brown.

NATIVUS. Lat. In old English law, a native; specifically, one born into a condition of servitude; a born serf or villein.

NATURA APPETIT PERFECTUM; ITA ET LEX. Nature covets perfection; so does law also. Hob. 144.

NATURA BREVIUM. The name of an ancient collection of original writs, accompanied with brief comments and explanations, compiled in the time of Edward III. This is commonly called "*Old* Natura Brevium," (or "O. N. B.,") to distinguish it from Fitzherbert's Natura Brevium, a later work, cited as "F. N. B.," or "Fitzh. Nat. Brev."

NATURA FIDE JUSSIONIS SIT STRICTISSIMI JURIS ET NON DURAT VEL EXTENDATUR DE RE AD REM, DE PERSONA AD PERSONAM, DE TEMPORE AD TEMPUS. The nature of the contract of suretyship is *strictissimi juris*, and cannot endure nor be extended from thing to thing, from person to person, or from time to time. Burge, Sur. 40.

NATURA NON FACIT SALTUM; ITA NEC LEX. Nature makes no leap, [no sudden or irregular movement;] so neither does law. Co. Litt. 238. Applied in old practice to the regular observance of the degrees in writs of entry, which could not be passed over *per saltum*.

NATURA NON FACIT VACUUM, NEC LEX SUPERVACUUM. Nature makes no vacuum, the law nothing purposeless. Co. Litt. 79.

NATURÆ VIS MAXIMA; NATURA BIS MAXIMA. The force of nature is greatest; nature is doubly great. 2 Inst. 564.

NATURAL. The juristic meaning of this term does not differ from the vernacular, except in the cases where it is used in opposition to the term "legal;" and then it means proceeding from or determined by physical causes or conditions, as distinguished from positive enactments of law, or attributable to the nature of man rather than to the commands of law, or based upon moral rather than legal considerations or sanctions.

As to natural "Allegiance," "Boundary," "Channel," "Child," "Day," "Death," "Domicile," "Equity," "Fruits," "Guardian," "Heir," "Infancy," "Liberty," "Obligation," "Person," "Possession," "Presumption," "Rights," "Succession," "Watercourse," and "Year," see those titles.

NATURAL AFFECTION. Such as naturally subsists between near relatives, as a father and child, brother and sister, husband and wife. This is regarded in law as a good consideration.

NATURAL-BORN SUBJECT. In English law, one born within the dominions, or rather within the allegiance, of the king of England.

NATURAL FLOOD CHANNEL. A channel beginning at some point on banks of stream and ending at some other point lower down stream, through which flood waters naturally flow at times of high water. C. M. Bott Furniture Co. v. City of Buffalo, 131 Misc. 624, 227 N.Y.S. 660, 665.

NATURAL FOOL. A person born without understanding; a born fool or idiot. Sometimes called, in the old books, a "natural." In re Anderson, 132 N.C. 243, 43 S.E. 649.

NATURAL LAW. This expression, "natural law," or *jus naturale,* was largely used in the philosophical speculations of the Roman jurists of the Antonine age, and was intended to denote a system of rules and principles for the guidance of human conduct which, independently of enacted law or of the systems peculiar to any one people, might be discovered by the rational intelligence of man, and would be found to grow out of and conform to his *nature,* meaning by that word his whole mental, moral, and physical constitution. The point of departure for this conception was the Stoic doctrine of a life ordered "according to nature," which in its turn rested upon the purely supposititious existence, in primitive times, of a "state of nature;" that is, a condition of society in which men universally were governed solely by a rational and consistent obedience to the needs, impulses, and promptings of their true nature, such nature being as yet undefaced by dishonesty, falsehood, or indulgence of the baser passions. Maine, Anc.Law, 50, et seq.; Jus Naturale.

NATURAL LIFE. The period of a person's existence considered as continuing until terminated by physical dissolution or death occurring in the course of nature; used in contradistinction to that juristic and artificial conception of life as an aggregate of legal rights or the possession of a legal personality, which could be terminated by "civil death," (*q. v.*), that is, that extinction of personality which resulted from entering a monastery or being attainted of treason or felony. See People v. Wright, 89 Mich. 70, 50 N.W. 792.

NATURAL MARKETING AREA. A region within which milk is ordinarily sold in response to commercial demand. State v. Auclair, 110 Vt. 147, 4 A.2d 107, 116.

NATURAL MILK SHED. The milk producing area which normally produces milk for a given milk consuming area or market.

Milk producer whose milk could be preserved and transported to Connecticut in time to be usable as fresh milk was within the "natural milk shed" of Connecticut. Bryant & Chapman & Co. v. Lowell, 129 Conn. 321, 27 A.2d 637, 638.

NATURAL MONUMENT. Objects permanent in character which are found on the land as they were placed by nature, such as streams, lakes, ponds, shores, and beaches. Timme v. Squires, 199 Wis. 178, 225 N.W. 825, 828. Sometimes including highways and streets, walls, fences, trees, hedges, springs, and rocks, and the like. Parran v. Wilson, 160 Md. 604, 154 A. 449, 451.

NATURAL OBJECT OF TESTATOR'S BOUNTY. In testamentary law, term comprises whoever would take, in the absence of a will, because they are the persons whom the law has so designated, and in the ordinary case the law follows the normal condition of near relationship. Page v. Phelps, 108 Conn. 572, 143 A. 890, 893.

NATURAL OBJECTS. In interpretation of boundaries term includes mountains, lakes, rivers, etc. Earhart v. Rosenwinkel, 108 Ind.App. 281, 25 N.E. 2d 268, 273.

NATURAL PREMIUM. Actual sum necessary to meet maturing death claims each year and is necessarily exceeded by the "net premium". Fox v. Mutual Ben. Life Ins. Co., C.C.A.Mo., 107 F.2d 715, 718.

NATURAL RESOURCE. The term includes not only timber, gas, oil, coal, minerals, lakes, and submerged lands, but also, features which supply a human need and contribute to the health, welfare, and benefit of a community, and are essential to the well-being thereof and proper enjoyment of property devoted to park and recreational purposes. Snyder v. Board of Park Com'rs of Cleveland Metropolitan Park Dist., 125 Ohio St. 336, 181 N.E. 483, 484.

NATURALE EST QUIDLIBET DISSOLVI EO MODO QUO LIGATUR. It is natural for a thing to be unbound in the same way in which it was bound. Jenk. Cent. 66; Broom, Max. 877.

NATURALEZA. In Spanish law, the state of a natural-born subject. White, New Recop. b. 1, tit. 5, c. 2.

NATURALIZATION. The act of adopting a foreigner and clothing him with the privileges of native citizen. U. S. v. Harbanuk, C.C.A.Conn., 62 F.2d 759, 761.

Collective Naturalization. This takes place where a government, by treaty or cession, acquires the whole or part of the territory of a foreign nation and takes to itself the inhabitants thereof, clothing them with the rights of citizenship either by the terms of the treaty or by subsequent legislation. State v. Boyd, 31 Neb. 682, 48 N.W. 739; Opinion of Justices, 68 Me. 589.

NATURALIZE. To confer citizenship upon an alien; to make a foreigner the same, in respect to rights and privileges, as if he were a native citizen or subject.

NATURALIZED CITIZEN. One who, being an alien by birth, has received citizenship under the laws of the state or nation.

NATUS. Lat. Born, as distinguished from *nasciturus,* about to be born. *Ante natus,* one born before a particular person or event, *e. g.,* before the death of his father, before a political revolution, etc. *Post natus,* one born after a particular person or event.

NAUCLERUS. Lat. In the civil law, the master or owner of a merchant vessel. Calvin.

NAUFRAGE. In French maritime law, shipwreck.

"The violent agitation of the waves, the impetuous force of the winds, storm, or lightning, may swallow up the vessel, or shatter it, in such a manner that nothing remains of it but the wreck; this is called 'making shipwreck,' *(faire naufrage.)* The vessel may also strike or run aground upon a bank, where it remains grounded, which is called *'échouement;'* it may be dashed against the coast or a rock, which is called *'bris;'* an accident of any kind may sink it in the sea, where it is swallowed up, which is called *'sombrer.'* " 3 Pard. Droit Commer, § 643.

NAUFRAGIUM. Lat. Shipwreck.

NAUGHT. In old practice, bad; defective. "The bar is *naught.*" 1 Leon. 77. "The avowry is *naught.*" 5 Mod. 73. "The plea is undoubtedly *naught.*" 10 Mod. 329. See 11 Mod. 179.

NAULAGE. The freight of passengers in a ship. Johnson; Webster.

NAULUM. In the civil law, the freight or fare paid for the transportation of cargo or passengers over the sea in a vessel. This is a Latinized form of a Greek word.

NAUTA. Lat. In the civil and maritime law, a sailor; one who works a ship. Calvin. Any one who is on board a ship for the purpose of navigating her. The employer of a ship. Dig. 4, 9, 1, 2.

NAUTICA PECUNIA. A loan to a shipowner, to be repaid only upon the successful termination of the voyage, and therefore allowed to be made at an extraordinary rate of interest (*nauticum fœnus*). Holland, Jurispr. 250.

NAUTICAL. Pertaining to ships or to the art of navigation or the business of carriage by sea.

NAUTICAL ASSESSORS. Experienced shipmasters, or other persons having special knowledge of navigation and nautical affairs, who are called to the assistance of a court of admiralty, in difficult cases involving questions of negligence, and who sit with the judge during the argument, and give their advice upon questions of seamanship or the weight of testimony. The Empire, D.C.Mich., 19 F. 559; The Clement, 2 Curt. 369, F.Cas.No.2,879.

NAUTICAL MILE. See Mile.

NAUTICUM FŒNUS. Lat. In the civil law, nautical or maritime interest; an extraordinary rate of interest agreed to be paid for the loan of money on the hazard of a voyage; corresponding to interest on contracts of bottomry or respondentia in English and American maritime law. Mackeld. Rom.Law, § 433; 2 Bl.Comm. 458.

NAVAGIUM. In old English law, a duty on certain tenants to carry their lord's goods in a ship.

NAVAL. Appertaining to the navy, (*q. v.*).

NAVAL BASE. See Base.

NAVAL COURTS. Courts held abroad in certain cases to inquire into complaints by the master or seamen of a British ship, or as to the wreck or abandonment of a British ship.

A naval court consists of three, four, or five members, being officers in her majesty's navy, consular officers, masters of British merchant ships, or British merchants. It has power to supersede the master of the ship with reference to which the inquiry is held, to discharge any of the seamen, to decide questions as to wages, send home offenders for trial, or try certain offenses in a summary manner. Sweet.

NAVAL COURTS-MARTIAL. Tribunals for the trial of offenses arising in the management of public war vessels.

NAVAL LAW. The system of regulations and principles for the government of the navy.

NAVAL OFFICER. An officer in the navy. Also an important functionary in the United States custom-houses, who estimates duties, signs permits and clearances, certifies the collectors' returns, etc.

NAVARCHUS. In the civil law, the master or commander of a ship; the captain of a man-of-war.

NAVICULARIUS. In the civil law, the master or captain of a ship. Calvin.

NAVIGABLE. Capable of being navigated; that may be navigated or passed over in ships or vessels. Natcher v. City of Bowling Green, 264 Ky. 584, 95 S.W.2d 255, 259. But the term is often, particularly at common law, understood in a more restricted sense, viz., subject to the ebb and flow of the tide. Luscher v. Reynolds, 153 Or. 625, 56 P.2d 1158, 1162.

"The doctrine of the common law as to the navigability of waters has no application in this country. * * *

There [In England] no waters are navigable in fact, or at least to any considerable extent, which are not subject to the tide, and from this circumstance tide-water and navigable water there signify substantially the same thing. But in this country the case is widely different. * * * Those rivers must be regarded as public navigable rivers, in law, which are navigable in fact." The Daniel Ball, 10 Wall. 563, 19 L.Ed. 999.

Waters are "navigable" when they are used, or are susceptible of being used, in their ordinary condition, as highways for commerce, over which trade and travel are or may be conducted in customary modes of trade and travel on water. United States v. Appalachian Electric Power Co., D.C.Va., 23 F.Supp. 83.

NAVIGABLE IN FACT. Streams or lakes are navigable in fact when they are used or are susceptible of being used in their natural and ordinary condition as highways for commerce over which trade and travel are or may be conducted in the customary modes of trade and travel on water. Taylor Fishing Club v. Hammett, Tex.Civ.App., 88 S.W.2d 127, 129.

NAVIGABLE RIVER OR STREAM. At common law, a river or stream in which the tide ebbs and flows, or as far as the tide ebbs and flows. 3 Kent, Comm. 412, 414, 417, 418; 2 Hil. Real Prop. 90, 91. But as to the definition in American law, see Navigable, *supra*.

NAVIGABLE WATERS. Those waters which afford a channel for useful commerce. The Montello, 20 Wall. 430, 22 L.Ed. 391.

See, also, Navigable, supra.

In several states so long as a stream or body of water may be put to public use it is "navigable" whether it can be used for commercial navigation or not. U. S. v. Holt State Bank, C.C.A.Minn., 294 F. 161, 166; State v. Korrer, 127 Minn. 60, 148 N.W. 617, 618, L.R.A.1916C, 139; State v. Akers, 92 Kan. 169, 140 P. 637, 640, Ann.Cas.1916B, 543. Any natural waters that are usable for rowing or canoeing are "navigable," and as such open to the public for hunting or fishing, notwithstanding water is a shallow, muddy lake or marsh. Baker v. Voss, 217 Wis. 415, 259 N.W. 413. Contra: To be "navigable," waters must be navigable for some purpose useful to trade or agriculture and susceptible of use for purposes of commerce, or possess capacity for valuable floatage in transportation to market of products of country through which it runs, a mere theoretical or potential navigability, or one that is temporary, precarious, unprofitable, or which requires artificial improvement, being insufficient. St. Paul Fire & Marine Ins. Co. v. Carroll, Tex.Civ.App., 106 S.W.2d 757, 759. The test of "navigability" is whether there is in the stream capacity for use for the purpose of transportation valuable to the public. American Red Cross v. Hinson, 173 Tenn. 667, 122 S.W.2d 433, 435. Navigability is not imparted by ability to float small boats, such as skiffs or canoes. United States v. Appalachian Electric Power Co., D.C.Va., 23 F.Supp. 83. Generally, a lake that is chiefly valuable for fishing or pleasure boats of small size is not "navigable." Taylor Fishing Club & Hammett, Tex.Civ.App., 88 S.W.2d 127, 129, 130.

NAVIGABLE WATERS OF THE UNITED STATES. Waters are "navigable waters of the United States" when they form in their ordinary condition by themselves, or by uniting with other waters, a continued highway over which commerce is or may be carried on with other states or foreign countries in the customary modes in which such commerce is conducted by water. United States v. Appalachian Electric Power Co., D.C. Va., 23 F.Supp. 83.

NAVIGATE. To journey by water; to go in a vessel; to sail or manage a vessel; to use the waters as a highway for commerce or communication; ply. Hence, to direct one's course through any medium; to steer, especially to operate an airplane or airship. United States v. Monstad, C.C.A.Cal., 134 F.2d 986, 987, 988.

NAVIGATION. The act or the science or the business of traversing the sea or other waters in ships or vessels. Pollock v. Cleveland Ship Building Co., 56 Ohio St. 655, 47 N.E. 582; The Silvia, 171 U.S. 462, 19 S.Ct. 7, 43 L.Ed. 241; Laurie v. Douglass, 15 Mees. & W. 746.

Regular navigation. In this phrase, the word "regular" may be used in contradistinction to "occasional," rather than to "unlawful," and refer to vessels that, alone or with others, constitute lines, and not merely to such as are regular in the sense of being properly documented under the laws of the country to which they belong. The Steamer Smidt, 16 Op.Attys.Gen. 276.

Rules of navigation. Rules and regulations adopted by commercial nations to govern the steering and management of vessels approaching each other at sea so as to avoid the danger of collision or fouling.

NAVIGATION ACTS. Various English enactments passed for the protection of British shipping and commerce as against foreign countries. For a sketch of their history and operation, see 3 Steph. Comm. They are now repealed. See 16 & 17 Vict. c. 107, and 17 & 18 Vict. cc. 5, 120. Wharton.

NAVIGATION SERVITUDE. Public right of navigation for the use of the people at large. United States v. 412.715 Acres of Land, Contra Costa County, Cal., D.C.Cal., 53 F.Supp. 143, 148, 149.

NAVIGATIONAL VISIBILITY. Visibility as affecting speed with reference to distance within which boat in fog could be brought to stop, before any course of any vessel emerging from fog on either side would cross her projected course alongside the fog bank at its nearest point. The Silver Palm, C.C.A.Cal., 94 F.2d 754, 767.

NAVIRE. Fr. In French law, a ship. Emerig. Traité des Assur. c. 6, § 1.

NAVIS. Lat. A ship; a vessel.

NAVIS BONA. A good ship; one that was staunch and strong, well caulked, and stiffened to bear the sea, obedient to her helm, swift, and not unduly affected by the wind. Calvin.

NAVY. A fleet of ships; the aggregate of vessels of war belonging to an independent nation. In a broader sense, and as equivalent to "naval forces," the entire corps of officers and men enlisted in the naval service and who man the public ships of war, including in this sense, in the United States, the officers and men of the Marine Corps. Wilkes v. Dinsman, 7 How. 124, 12 L.Ed. 618; U. S. v. Dunn, 120 U.S. 249, 7 S.Ct. 507, 30 L.Ed. 667.

NAVY BILLS. Bills drawn by officers of the English navy for their pay, etc.

NAVY DEPARTMENT. One of the executive departments of the United States, presided over by the secretary of the navy, and having in charge the defense of the country by sea, by means of ships of war and other naval appliances.

NAVY PENSION. A pecuniary allowance made in consideration of past services of some one in the navy.

NAZERANNA. A sum paid to government as an acknowledgment for a grant of lands, or any public office. Enc. Lond.

NAZIM. In Hindu law, composer, arranger, adjuster. The first officer of a province, and minister of the department of criminal justice.

NE ADMITTAS. Lat. In ecclesiastical law, the name of a prohibitory writ, directed to the bishop, at the request of the plaintiff or defendant, where a *quare impedit* is pending, when either party fears that the bishop will admit the other's clerk pending the suit between them. Fitzh. Nat. Brev. 37.

NE BAILA PAS. L. Fr. He did not deliver. A plea in detinue, denying the delivery to the defendant of the thing sued for.

NE DISTURBA PAS. L. Fr. (Does or did not disturb.) In English practice, the general issue or general plea in *quare impedit.* 3 Steph.Comm. 663.

NE DONA PAS, or NON DEDIT. The general issue in a formedon, now abolished. It denied the gift in tail to have been made in manner and form as alleged; and was therefore the proper plea, if the tenant meant to dispute the fact of the gift, but did not apply to any other case. 5 East, 289.

NE EXEAT. A writ which forbids the person to whom it is addressed to leave the country, the state, or the jurisdiction of the court; available in some cases to keep a defendant within the reach of the court's process, where the ends of justice would be frustrated if he should escape from the jurisdiction.

Sometimes a ne exeat writ is issued only to restrain a person from leaving the jurisdiction, and sometimes it is issued against a person who is removing or attempting to remove property beyond the jurisdiction. August v. August, 65 Ga.App. 883, 16 S.E.2d 784, 785.

NE EXEAT BOND. In wife's suit for divorce and alimony, "ne exeat bond" conditioned on husband's appearance on hearing of bill of complaint was in effect an appearance bond to abide the decree of the court. Muckelrath v. Chezem, 184 Miss. 511, 186 So. 621, 623.

NE EXEAT REGNO. Lat. In English practice, a writ which issues to restrain a person from leaving the kingdom. It was formerly used for political purposes, but is now only resorted to in equity when the defendant is about to leave the kingdom; it is only in cases where the intention of the party to leave can be shown that the writ is granted.

NE EXEAT REPUBLICA. Lat. In American practice, a writ similar to that of *ne exeat regno,* (*q. v.*) available to the plaintiff in a civil suit, under some circumstances, when the defendant is about to leave the state. Dean v. Smith, 23 Wis. 483, 99 Am.Dec. 198; Adams v. Whitcomb, 46 Vt. 712; Cable v. Alvord, 27 Ohio St. 664.

NE GIST PAS EN BOUCHE. L. Fr. It does not lie in the mouth. A common phrase in the old books. Yearb. M. 3 Edw. II. 50.

NE INJUSTE VEXES. Lat. In old English practice, a prohibitory writ, commanding a lord not to demand from the tenant more services than were justly due by the tenure under which his ancestors held.

NE LUMINIBUS OFFICIATUR. Lat. In the civil law, the name of a servitude which restrains the owner of a house from making such erections as obstruct the light of the adjoining house. Dig. 8, 4, 15, 17.

NE QUID IN LOCO PUBLICO VEL ITINERE FIAT. Lat. That nothing shall be done (put or erected) in a public place or way. The title of an interdict in the Roman law. Dig. 43, 8.

NE RECIPIATUR. Lat. That it be not received. A *caveat* or warning given to a law officer, by a party in a cause, not to receive the next proceedings of his opponent. 1 Sell. Pr. 8.

NE RECTOR PROSTERNET ARBORES. L. Lat. The statute 35 Edw. I. § 2, prohibiting rectors, *i. e.*, parsons, from cutting down the trees in churchyards. In Rutland v. Green, 1 Keb. 557, it was extended to prohibit them from opening new mines and working the minerals therein. Brown.

NE RELESSA PAS. L. Fr. Did not release. Where the defendant had pleaded a release, this was the proper replication by way of traverse.

NE UNQUES ACCOUPLE. L. Fr. Never married. More fully, *ne unques accouple en loiall matrimonie,* never joined in lawful marriage. The name of a plea in the action of dower *unde nihil habet,* by which the tenant denied that the dowress was ever lawfully married to the decedent.

NE UNQUES EXECUTOR. L. Fr. Never executor. The name of a plea by which the defendant denies that he is an executor, as he is alleged to be; or that the plaintiff is an executor, as he claims to be.

NE UNQUES SEISE QUE DOWER. L. Fr. (Never seised of a dowable estate.) In pleading, the general issue in the action of dower *unde nil habet,* by which the tenant denies that the demandant's husband was *ever seised* of an estate of which dower might be had. Rosc. Real Act. 219, 220.

NE UNQUES SON RECEIVER. L. Fr. In pleading, the name of a plea in an action of account-render, by which the defendant denies that he ever was receiver of the plaintiff. 12 Vin. Abr. 183.

NE VARIETUR. Lat. It must not be altered. A phrase sometimes written by a notary upon a bill or note, for the purpose of establishing its identity, which, however, does not affect its negotiability. Fleckner v. Bank of United States, 8 Wheat. 338, 5 L.Ed. 631.

NEAP TIDE. When the moon is in its first and third quarters, the tides do not rise as high, nor fall as low, as on the average; at such times the tides are known as "neap tides." Borax Consolidated v. City of Los Angeles, Cal., 296 U.S. 10, 56 S.Ct. 23, 80 L.Ed. 9.

NEAR. The word as applied to space is a relative term without positive or precise meaning, depending for its signification on the subject-matter in relation to which it is used and the circumstances under which it becomes necessary to apply it to surrounding objects. Case-Fowler Lumber Co. v. Winslett, 168 Ga. 808, 149 S.E. 211, 213.

NEAT, NET. The clear weight or quantity of an article, without the bag, box, keg, or other thing in which it may be enveloped.

NEAT CATTLE. Oxen or heifers. "Beeves" may include neat stock, but all neat stock are not beeves. Castello v. State, 36 Tex. 324; Hubotter v. State, 32 Tex. 479. Straight-backed, domesticated animals of the bovine genus regardless of sex, and is not generally but may be, taken to mean calves, or animals younger than yearlings. It includes cows, bulls, and steers, but not horses, mares, geldings, colts, mules, jacks, or jennies, goats, hogs, sheep, shoats, or pigs. State v. District Court of Fifth Judicial Dist. in and for Nye County, 42 Nev. 218, 174 P. 1023, 1025; State v. Swager, 110 Wash. 431, 188 P. 504, 506.

NEAT-LAND. Land let out to the yeomanry. Cowell.

NEATNESS. In pleading, the statement in apt and appropriate words of all the necessary facts, and no more. Lawes, Pl. 62.

NEC CURIA DEFICERET IN JUSTITIA EXHIBENDA. Nor should the court be deficient in showing justice. 4 Inst. 63.

NEC NON. A clause so called which was used as a fiction to give jurisdiction to the common pleas in connection with the writ of *quare clausum fregit*. 1 Holdsw. Hist. E. L. 89, note. See Bill of Middlesex.

NEC TEMPUS NEC LOCUS OCCURRIT REGI. Jenk. Cent. 190. Neither time nor place affects the king.

NEC VENIAM EFFUSO SANGUINE CASUS HABET. Where blood is spilled, the case is unpardonable. 3 Inst. 57.

NEC VENIAM, LÆSO NUMINE, CASUS HABET. Where the Divinity is insulted the case is unpardonable. Jenk. Cent. 167.

NECATION. The act of killing.

NECESSARIES. An article which a party actually needs. State v. Earnest, Mo.App., 162 S.W. 2d 338, 341. Things indispensable, or things proper and useful, for the sustenance of human life.

The word has no hard and fast meaning, but varies with the accustomed manner of living of the parties. Smitti v. Roth Cadillac Co., 145 Pa.Super. 292, 21 A.2d 127, 130.

"Necessaries" consist of food, drink, clothing, medical attention, and a suitable place of residence, and they are regarded as necessaries in the absolute sense of the word; however, liability for necessaries is not limited to articles required to sustain life; it extends to articles which would ordinarily be necessary and suitable, in view of the rank, position, fortune, earning capacity, and mode of living of the husband or father. Caruso v. Caruso, 102 N.J.Eq. 393, 141 A. 16, 19.

Such things as are suited to wife's and children's condition and station in life, their needs and wants, in so far as ability of parties will permit. Rice v. Mercantile Bank & Trust Co. of Texas, Tex.Civ.App., 86 S.W.2d 54, 56.

Including funeral expenses of wife and children. Colovos' Adm'r v. Gouvas, 269 Ky. 752, 108 S.W.2d 820, 827, 113 A.L.R. 871. And children's insurance. Sanker v. Humborg, 48 Cal.App.2d 205, 119 P.2d 433, 434.

Whether attorney's services are to be considered "necessaries" depends on whether there is necessity therefor. Fenn v. Hart Dairy Co., 231 Mo.App. 1005, 83 S.W.2d 120, 124. But such services are usually "necessaries". Leonard v. Alexander, 50 Cal.App.2d 385, 122 P.2d 984, 986.

What constitutes "necessaries" for which an admiralty lien will attach depends upon what is reasonably needed in the ship's business, regard being had to the character of the voyage and the employment in which the vessel is being used. Walker Skageth Food Stores v. The Bavois, D.C. N.Y., 43 F.Supp. 109, 110, 111.

In the case of ships the term "necessaries" means such things as are fit and proper for the service in which the ship is engaged, and such as the owner, being a prudent man, would have ordered if present; *e. g.*, anchors, rigging, repairs, victuals. Maude & P. Shipp. 71, 113. The master may hypothecate the ship for necessaries supplied abroad so as to bind the owner. Sweet; The Plymouth Rock, 19 F.Cas. 898; Hubbard v. Roach, C.C.Ill., 2 F. 394; The Gustavia, 11 Fed.Cas. 126.

NECESSARIUM EST QUOD NON POTEST ALITER SE HABERE. That is necessary which cannot be otherwise.

NECESSARIUS. Lat. Necessary; unavoidable; indispensable; not admitting of choice or the action of the will; needful.

NECESSARY. This word must be considered in the connection in which it is used, as it is a word susceptible of various meanings. It may import absolute physical necessity or inevitability, or it may import that which is only convenient, useful, appropriate, suitable, proper, or conducive to the end sought. It is an adjective expressing degrees, and may express mere convenience or that which is indispensable or an absolute physical necessity. It may mean something which in the accomplishment of a given object cannot be dispensed with, or it may mean something reasonably useful and proper, and of greater or lesser benefit or convenience, and its force and meaning must be determined with relation to the particular object sought. Kay County Excise Board v. Atchison, T. & S. F. R. Co., 185 Okl. 327, 91 P.2d 1087, 1088.

In eminent domain proceedings, it means land reasonably requisite and proper for accomplishment of end in view, not absolute necessity of particular location. State v. Whitcomb, 94 Mont. 415, 22 P.2d 823.

As to necessary "Damages," "Deposit," "Domicile," "Implication," "Intromission," "Parties," "Repairs," and "Way," see those titles.

NECESSARY INFERENCE. One which is inescapable or unavoidable from the standpoint of reason. Taylor v. Twiner, 193 Miss. 410, 9 So.2d 644, 646.

NECESSARY INJURY. Under Wrongful Death Statute the words mean pecuniary injury and include any damages whether present, prospective, or proximate which may be estimated according to a pecuniary standard, and the jury is not confined to precise calculation as to amount of loss to survivors of deceased, but has large discretion in determining such damages. Polk v. Krenning, Mo. App., 2 S.W.2d 107, 109.

NECESSITAS. Lat. Necessity; a force, power, or influence which compels one to act against his will. Calvin.

NECESSITAS CULPABILIS. Culpable necessity; unfortunate necessity; necessity which, while it excuses the act done under its compulsion, does not leave the doer entirely free from blame. The necessity which compels a man to kill another in self-defense is thus distinguished from that which requires the killing of a felon. See 4 Bl. Comm. 187.

NECESSITAS EST LEX TEMPORIS ET LOCI. Necessity is the law of time and of place. 1 Hale, P. C. 54.

NECESSITAS EXCUSAT AUT EXTENUAT DELICTUM IN CAPITALIBUS, QUOD NON OPERATUR IDEM IN CIVILIBUS. Necessity excuses or extenuates a delinquency in capital cases, which has not the same operation in civil cases. Bac. Max.

NECESSITAS FACIT LICITUM QUOD ALIAS NON EST LICITUM. 10 Coke, 61. Necessity makes that lawful which otherwise is not lawful.

NECESSITAS INDUCIT PRIVILEGIUM QUOAD JURA PRIVATA. Bac. Max. 25. Necessity gives a privilege with reference to private rights. The necessity involved in this maxim is of three kinds, viz.: (1) Necessity of self-preservation; (2) of obedience; and (3) necessity resulting from the act of God, or of a stranger. Noy, Max. 32.

NECESSITAS NON HABET LEGEM. Necessity has no law. Plowd. 18*a*. "Necessity shall be a good excuse in our law, and in every other law." Id.

NECESSITAS PUBLICA MAJOR EST QUAM PRIVATA. Public necessity is greater than private. "Death," it has been observed, "is the last and furthest point of particular necessity, and the law imposes it upon every subject that he prefer the urgent service of his king and country before the safety of his life." Noy, Max. 34; Broom, Max. 18.

NECESSITAS QUOD COGIT, DEFENDIT. Necessity defends or justifies what it compels. 1 Hale, P. C. 54. Applied to the acts of a sheriff, or ministerial officer, in the execution of his office. Broom, Max. 14.

NECESSITAS SUB LEGE NON CONTINETUR, QUIA QUOD ALIAS NON EST LICITUM NECESSITAS FACIT LICITUM. 2 Inst. 326. Necessity is not restrained by law; since what otherwise is not lawful necessity makes lawful.

NECESSITAS VINCIT LEGEM. Necessity overrules the law. Hob. 144; Cooley, Const. Lim. 4th Ed. 747.

NECESSITAS VINCIT LEGEM; LEGUM VINCULA IRRIDET. Hob. 144. Necessity overcomes law; it derides the fetters of laws.

NECESSITOUS. Indigent or pressed by poverty. St. Cyr v. Wills, 87 N.H. 277, 178 A. 257.

NECESSITOUS CIRCUMSTANCES. In the civil code of Louisiana the words are used relative to the fortune of the deceased and to the condition in which the claimant lived during the marriage. Smith v. Smith, 43 La.Ann. 1140, 10 So. 248.

Needing the necessaries of life, which cover not only primitive physical needs, things absolutely indispensable to human existence and decency, but those things, also, which are in fact necessary to the particular person left without support. State v. Waller, 90 Kan. 829, 136 P. 215, 216, 49 L.R.A., N.S., 588.

NECESSITUDO. Lat. In the civil law, an obligation; a close connection; relationship by blood. Calvin.

NECESSITY. Controlling force; irresistible compulsion; a power or impulse so great that it admits no choice of conduct.

When it is said that an act is done "under necessity," it may be, in law, either of three kinds of necessity: (1) The necessity of preserving one's own life, which will excuse a homicide; (2) the necessity of obedience, as to the laws, or the obedience of one not *sui juris* to his superior; (3) the necessity caused by the act of God or a stranger. See Jacob; Mozley & Whiteley.

That which makes the contrary of a thing impossible.

The quality or state of being necessary, in its primary sense signifying that which makes an act or event unavoidable. Spreckels v. City and County of San Francisco, 76 Cal.App. 267, 244 P. 919, 922; In re Washington Ave. in Borough of Chatham, 5 N.J.Misc. 858, 139 A. 239, 240.

A constraint upon the will whereby a person is urged to do that which his judgment disapproves, and which, it is to be presumed, his will (if left to itself) would reject. A man, therefore, is excused for those actions which are done through unavoidable force and compulsion. Wharton.

In determining what is a work of "necessity" excepted from the operation of the Sunday law, the necessity meant is not a physical or absolute necessity, but a moral fitness or propriety of the work and labor done under the circumstances of the particular case, and whether or not the act is morally fit and proper is usually a question of fact for the jury under proper instructions. Lakeside Inn Corporation v. Commonwealth, 134 Va. 696, 114 S.E. 769, 771; Natural Gas Products Co. v. Thurman, 205 Ky. 100, 265 S.W. 475, 477. The term "necessity" means an economical and moral necessity, rather than an unavoidable physical necessity. Rosenbaum v. State, 131 Ark. 251, 199 S.W. 388, 392, L.

R.A.1918B, 1109. The necessity which must exist depends on what the general public in its ordinary modes of doing business regards as necessary. Gray v. Commonwealth, 171 Ky. 269, 188 S.W. 354, 355, L.R.A. 1917B, 93. "Works of necessity" include whatever is needful for the good health, order, or comfort of the community. State v. Dean, 149 Minn. 410, 84 N.W. 275.

The word "necessity", within certificate of public convenience and necessity, is not used in the sense of being essential or absolutely indispensable but merely that certificate is reasonably necessary for public good. Alabama Public Service Commission v. Crow, 247 Ala. 120, 22 So.2d 721, 724.

To fulfill requirements for easement of right of way of necessity, the necessity must be actual, real, and reasonable, as distinguished from inconvenience, but it need not be absolute and irresistible necessity. Brasington v. Williams, 143 S.C. 223, 141 S.E. 375, 383.

"Necessity" when used in relation to power of eminent domain does not mean absolute necessity, but only reasonable necessity. Chicago & N. W. R. Co. v. City of Racine, 200 Wis. 170, 227 N.W. 859, 861.

The "necessity" of and appurtenance for the beneficial use of leased premises, which will entitle the lessee thereto, is not an absolute necessity in the sense that it must be completely indispensable, but is a real necessity and not a mere convenience or advantage. Raynes v. Stevens, 219 Mass. 556, 107 N.E. 398, 399.

Public necessity. Of a municipal improvement, needed for reasonable convenience, facility, and completeness in accomplishing a public purpose. In re Washington Ave. in Borough of Chatham, 5 N.J.Misc. 858, 139 A. 239, 240. With reference to common carriers, great or urgent public convenience. Delaware, L. & W. R. Co. v. Van Santvoord, D.C.N.Y., 232 F. 978, 983.

NECK-VERSE The Latin sentence, *"Miserere mei, Deus,"* was so called, because the reading of it was made a test for those who claimed benefit of clergy.

NECROPHILISM. See Insanity.

NECROPSY. An autopsy, or *post-mortem* examination of a human body.

NEED. A relative term, the conception of which must, within reasonable limits, vary with the personal situation of the individual employing it. In re Skuse's Estate, 165 Misc. 554, 1 N.Y.S.2d 202, 205.

NEEDFUL. Necessary, requisite, essential, indispensable. Riddell v. Pennsylvania R. Co., 262 Pa. 582, 106 A. 80, 81.

NEEDLESS. In a statute against "needless" killing or mutilation of any animal, this term denotes an act done without any useful motive, in a spirit of wanton cruelty, or for the mere pleasure of destruction. Grise v. State, 37 Ark. 460; Hunt v. State, 3 Ind.App. 383, 29 N.E. 933; State v. Bogardus, 4 Mo.App. 215.

NEEDY. Indigent, necessitous, very poor. Moore v. State Social Security Commission, 233 Mo.App. 536, 122 S.W.2d 391, 393; Nichols v. State Social Security Commission of Missouri, 349 Mo. 1148, 164 S.W.2d 278, 280.

NEFAS. Lat. That which is against right or the divine law. A wicked or impious thing or act. Calvin.

NEFASTUS. Lat. Inauspicious. Applied, in the Roman law, to a day on which it was unlawful to open the courts or administer justice.

NEGATIO CONCLUSIONIS EST ERROR IN LEGE. Wing. 268. The denial of a conclusion is error in law.

NEGATIO DESTRUIT NEGATIONEM, ET AMBÆ FACIUNT AFFIRMATIONEM. A negative destroys a negative, and both make an affirmative. Co. Litt. 146*b*. Lord Coke cites this as a rule of grammatical construction, not always applying in law.

NEGATIO DUPLEX EST AFFIRMATIO. A double negative is an affirmative.

NEGATIVE. A denial; a proposition by which something is denied; a statement in the form of denial. Two negatives do not make a good issue. Steph. Pl. 386, 387.

As to negative "Covenant," "Easement," "Servitude," "Statute," and "Testimony," see those titles.

NEGATIVE AVERMENT. As opposed to the traverse or simple denial of an affirmative allegation, a negative averment is an allegation of some substantive fact, *e. g.*, that premises are not in repair, which, although negative in form, is really affirmative in substance, and the party alleging the fact of non-repair must prove it. Brown. An averment in some of the pleadings in a case in which a negative is asserted. U. S. v. Eisenminger, D.C. Del., 16 F.2d 816, 819.

NEGATIVE CONDITION. One by which it is stipulated that a given thing shall not happen.

NEGATIVE EVIDENCE. Testimony that an alleged fact did not exist. K. B. Johnson & Sons v. Southern Ry. Co., 214 N.C. 484, 199 S.E. 704, 706.

NEGATIVE HEAD. As used in connection with a filtration plant it means the force that comes into play when a partial vacuum is created either within or below the filter bed. City of Harrisburg v. New York Continental Jewell Filtration Co., C.C. A.Pa., 217 F. 366, 368.

NEGATIVE PREGNANT. In pleading, a negative implying also an affirmative. Cowell. Such a form of negative expression as may imply or carry within it an affirmative. Steph. Pl. 318; Fields v. State, 134 Ind. 46, 32 N.E. 780; Stone v. Quaal, 36 Minn. 46, 29 N.W. 326.

As if a man be said to have aliened land *in fee*, and he says *he has not aliened in fee*, this is a negative pregnant; for, though it be true that he has not aliened in fee, yet it may be that he has made an estate *in tail*. Cowell. A "negative pregnant," is a denial in form, but is in fact an admission, as where the denial in hæc verba includes the time and place, which are usually immaterial. Hall & Lyon Furniture Co. v. Torrey, 196 App.Div. 804, 188 N.Y. S. 486, 487; Green v. Commercial Bank & Trust Co., D.C. Wyo., 277 F. 527, 528; McIntosh Livestock Co. v. Buffington, 108 Or. 358, 217 P. 635, 636.

A denial in such form as to imply or express an admission of the substantial fact which apparently is controverted; or a denial which, although in the form of a traverse, really admits the important facts contained in the allegations to which it relates. Cramer v. Aiken, 63 App.D.C. 16, 68 F.2d 761, 762.

NEGGILDARE. To claim kindred. Jac. L. Dict.

NEGLECT. May mean to omit, fail, or forbear to do a thing that can be done, or that is required to be done, but it may also import an absence of care or attention in the doing or omission of a given act. State v. Sheldon, 135 Okl. 278, 276 P. 468, 472; Same v. Butterfield, 138 Okl. 112, 276 P. 473.

And it may mean a designed refusal or unwillingness to perform one's duty. In re Perkins, 234 Mo.App. 716, 117 S.W.2d 686, 692.

The term is used in the law of bailment as synonymous with "negligence." But the latter word is the closer translation of the Latin *"negligentia."*

Failure to pay money which the party is bound to pay without demand. Kimball v. Rowland, 6 Gray, Mass., 224. An omission to do or perform some work, duty, or act. Esposito v. St. George Swimming Club, 143 Misc. 15, 255 N.Y.S. 794, 801. Failure to perform or discharge a duty, covering positive official misdoing or official misconduct as well as negligence. Commonwealth ex rel. and to Use of Allegheny County v. De Luca, 131 Pa.Super. 451, 200 A. 712, 714.

Culpable Neglect. In this phrase, the word "culpable" means not only criminal, but censurable. As he has merely lost a right of action which he might voluntarily relinquish, and has wronged nobody but himself, culpable neglect to preserve rights conveys the idea of neglect which exists where the loss can fairly be ascribed to the party's own carelessness, improvidence, or folly. State ex rel. Fulton v. Coburn, 133 Ohio St. 192, 12 N.E.2d 471, 477.

Willful Neglect. The neglect of the husband to provide for his wife the common necessaries of life, he having the ability to do so; or it is the failure to do so by reason of idleness, profligacy, or dissipation. Civil Code Cal. § 105.

NEGLECTED MINOR. One suffering from neglect and in state of want. People v. De Pue, 217 N.Y.S. 205, 206, 217 App.Div. 321.

NEGLIGENCE. The omission to do something which a reasonable man, guided by those ordinary considerations which ordinarily regulate human affairs, would do, or the doing of something which a reasonable and prudent man would not do. Schneeweisz v. Illinois Cent. R. Co., 196 Ill.App. 248, 253; Schneider v. C. H. Little Co., 184 Mich. 315, 151 N.W. 587, 588; Hulley v. Moosbrugger, 88 N.J.L. 161, 95 A. 1007, 1010, L.R.A. 1916C, 1203.

The term refers only to that legal delinquency which results whenever a man fails to exhibit the care which he ought to exhibit, whether it be slight, ordinary, or great. Hazzard v. Chase Nat. Bank of City of New York, 159 Misc. 57, 287 N.Y.S. 541, 552. It is characterized chiefly by inadvertence, thoughtlessness, inattention, and the like, while "wantonness" or "recklessness" is characterized by willfulness. People v. Orr, 243 Mich. 300, 220 N.W. 777, 779. The law of "negligence" is founded on reasonable conduct or reasonable care under all circumstances of particular case. Charbonneau v. MacRury, 84 N.H. 501, 153 A. 457, 462, 73 A.L.R. 1266. Doctrine of negligence rests on duty of every person to exercise due care in his conduct toward others from which injury may result. Johnson v. Grand Trunk Western R. Co., 246 Mich. 52, 224 N.W. 448, 449. "Negligence" is not intentional conduct. Gunther v. Morey Larue Laundry Co., 129 N.J.L. 345, 29 A.2d 713, 714. Inaction as well as action may be "negligence". Public Service Co. of New Hampshire v. Elliott, C.C.A.N.H., 123 F.2d 2, 5. It is not act itself, but fact which defines character of act and makes it legal wrong. Metzger v. Gambill, Tex.Civ.App., 37 S.W.2d 1077, 1078. It is immaterial to the question of "negligence" whether violated standard of conduct is established by statute or by the common law. Armit v. Loveland, C.C.A.Pa., 115 F.2d 308, 311, 312. It is the failure to do that which a person of ordinary prudence, Ottenheimer v. Molohan, 146 Md. 175, 126 A. 97, 100; an ordinarily prudent person, Wichita Valley Ry. Co. v. Meyers, Tex.Civ.App., 248 S.W. 444, 447; a reasonable and prudent person, Chickasha Cotton Oil Co. v. Brown, 39 Okl. 245, 134 P. 850; Baltimore & P. R. Co. v. Jones, 95 U.S. 441, 24 L.Ed. 506; a person of ordinary care. Citizens' Nat. Bank of Jasper v. Ratcliff & Lanier, Tex.Civ.App., 238 S.W. 362, 365; a reasonable, prudent person, Boswell v. Whitehead Hosiery Mills, 191 N.C. 549, 132 S.E. 598, 602; a person of ordinary prudence and care, Illinois Cent. R. Co. v. Nelson, C.C.A.Iowa, 203 F. 956, 959; an ordinarily reasonable, careful, and prudent person, Johnson v. Omaha & Council Bluffs Street Ry. Co., 194 Iowa 1230, 190 N.W. 977, 978; or a reasonably prudent person, guided by those considerations which ordinarily regulate conduct of human affairs, would do, or doing something which such a person would not do, under like or similar circumstances. McKee v. Iowa Ry. & Light Co., 204 Iowa 44, 214 N.W. 564, 565; Bowers v. J. D. Halstead Lumber Co., 28 Ariz. 122, 236 P. 124, 125.

The failure to use ordinary care, Curtis v. Mauger, 186 Ind. 118, 114 N.E. 408, 409; reasonable care, Crowley v. Chicago, B. & Q. R. Co., 204 Iowa 1385, 213 N.W. 403, 407, 53 A.L.R. 964; or ordinary or reasonable care under the circumstances, Thrasher v. St. Louis & S. F. Ry. Co., 826 Okl. 88, 206 P. 212, 214.

The failure to exercise that degree of care which a prudent person, Getsinger v. Corbell, 188 N.C. 553, 125 S.E. 180, 181; an ordinarily prudent person, Faulk v. Kansas City Rys. Co., Mo.App., 247 S.W. 253; a reasonably prudent person, Moir v. Hart, 189 Ill.App. 566, 567; City of Decatur v. Eady, 186 Ind. 205, 115 N.E. 577, 579, L.R.A. 1917E, 242; a reasonable and prudent person, Heller v. New York, N. H. & H. R. Co., C.C.A.N.Y., 265 F. 192, 198, 17 A.L.R. 823; a reasonably careful person, Behen v. Philadelphia, B. & W. R. Co., 93 A. 903, 904, 5 Boyce, Del., 389; an ordinary prudent person, Donahue v. R. A. Sherman's Sons Co., 39 R.I. 373, 98 A. 109, 114, L.R.A.1917A, 76; a reasonably prudent, careful person, Gray v. Pennsylvania R. Co., 3 W.W.Harr., Del., 450, 139 A. 66, 75; a reasonably prudent and careful person, Lemmon v. Broadwater, 108 A. 273, 274, 7 Boyce, Del., 472; or an ordinarily prudent and careful person would exercise under like circumstances, Clayton v. Philadelphia, B. & W. R. Co., 106 A. 577, 579, 7 Boyce, Del., 343.

The failure to exercise ordinary care. Anderson v. Atlantic Coast Line R. Co., 161 N.C. 462, 77 S.E. 402, 404. Ordinary or reasonable care being that care which ordinarily prudent persons, Travis v. Louisville & N. R. Co., 183 Ala. 415, 62 So. 851, 854; reasonably prudent persons, Burns v. Polar Wave Ice & Fuel Co., Mo.App., 187 S.W. 145, 148; persons of ordinary prudence, Shirley Hill Coal Co. v. Moore, 181 Ind. 513, 103 N.E. 802, 804; ordinary careful, prudent persons, Yellow Pine Paper Mill Co. v. Wright, Tex., 154 S.W. 1168, 1171; or ordinarily careful or prudent persons, would exercise under like or similar circumstances. Loverage v. Carmichael, 164 Minn. 76, 204 N.W. 921, 922.

The breach of a legal duty. Taylor v. Neuse Lumber Co., 173 N.C. 112, 91 S.E. 719, 720; Jones v. Atchison, T. & S. F. Ry. Co., 98 Kan. 133, 157 P. 399, 400; Pickett v. Waldorf System, 241 Mass. 569, 136 N.E. 64, 65, 23 A.L.R. 1014; Schell v. Du Bois, 94 Ohio St. 93, 113 N.E. 664, 668, L.R.A.1917A, 710.

Negligence usually consists in the "involuntary and casual"—that is, "accidental"—doing or omission to do something which results in an injury, Root v. Topeka Ry. Co., 96 Kan. 694, 153 P. 550; and is synonymous with heedlessness, carelessness, thoughtlessness, disregard, inattention, inadvertence, remissness and oversight, Payne v. Vance, 103 Ohio St. 59, 133 N.E. 85, 87.

"Negligence" in official conduct is ordinarily the failure to use such reasonable care and caution as would be expected of a prudent man. Hamrick v. McCutcheon, 101 W. Va. 485, 133 S.E. 127, 129.

Negligence is any culpable omission of a positive duty. It differs from heedlessness, in that heedlessness is the doing of an act in violation of a negative duty, without adverting to its possible consequences. In both cases there is inadvertence, and there is breach of duty. Aust. Jur. § 630.

Negligence or carelessness signifies want of care, caution, attention, diligence, or discretion in one having no positive intention to injure the person complaining thereof. The words "reckless," "indifferent," "careless," and "wanton" are never understood to signify positive will or intention, unless when joined with other words which show that they are to receive an artificial or unusual, if not an unnatural, interpretation. Lexington v. Lewis, 10 Bush, Ky., 677.

"Negligence" is not synonymous with "incompetency," since the competent may be negligent. Alabama City, G. & A. Ry. Co. v. Bessiere, 190 Ala. 59, 66 So. 805, 806; Barclay v. Wetmore & Morse Granite Co., 92 Vt. 195, 102 A. 493, 495.

See Care.

Actionable Negligence. See Actionable Negligence.

Collateral Negligence. In the law relating to the responsibility of an employer or principal for the negligent acts or omissions of his employee, the term "collateral" negligence is sometimes used to describe negligence attributable to a contractor employed by the principal and for which the latter is not responsible, though he would be responsible for the same thing if done by his servant. Weber v. Railway Co., 20 App.Div. 292, 47 N.Y.S. 11.

Comparative Negligence. See Comparative Negligence.

Concurrent Negligence. Arises where the injury is approximately caused by the concurrent wrongful acts or omissions of two or more persons acting independently. Carr v. St. Louis Auto Supply Co., 293 Mo. 562, 239 S.W. 827, 828.

Contributory Negligence. The act or omission amounting to want of ordinary care on part of complaining party, which, concurring with defendant's negligence, is proximate cause of injury. Honaker v. Crutchfield, 247 Ky. 495, 57 S.W.2d 502.

Any want of ordinary care on the part of the person injured, (or on the part of another whose negligence is imputable to him,) which combined and concurred with the defendant's negligence, and contributed to the injury as a proximate cause thereof, and as an element without which the injury would not have occurred. Railroad Co. v. Young, 153 Ind. 163, 54 N.E. 791; Barton v. Railroad Co., 52 Mo. 253, 14 Am.Rep. 418; McLaughlin v. Electric Light Co., 100 Ky. 173, 37 S.W. 851, 34 L.R.A. 812; 25 C.J. S. Damages; Townsend v. Missouri Pac. R. Co., 163 La. 872, 113 So. 130, 132, 54 A.L.R. 538.

The negligent act of plaintiff which, concurring and cooperating with negligent act of defendant, becomes real, efficient, and proximate cause of injury, or cause without which the injury would not have occurred. Elder v. Plaza Ry., 194 N.C. 617, 140 S.E. 298, 299; James v. Delaware, L. & W. R. Co., 92 N.J.L. 149, 104 A. 328, 333.

"Assumption of risk" and "contributory negligence" are not synonymous. Chicago, R. I. & P. R. Co. v. Rogers, 60 Okl. 249, 159 P. 1132, 1136.

Concurrent Contributory Negligence. Knowledge of specific danger and negligent failure to avoid it. Sprinkle v. St. Louis & S. F. R. Co., 215 Ala. 191, 110 So. 137, 140.

Mutual Contributory Negligence. Exists when injury would not have happened but for negligence of both parties. Alexander v. Missouri, K. & T. R. Co. of Texas, Tex.Civ.App., 287 S.W. 153, 155.

Criminal Negligence. Criminal negligence which will render killing a person manslaughter is the omission on the part of the person to do some act which an ordinarily careful and prudent man would do under like circumstances, or the doing of some act which an ordinarily careful, prudent man under like circumstances would not do by reason of which another person is endangered in life or bodily safety; the word "ordinary" being synonymous with "reasonable" in this connection. State v. Coulter, Mo.Sup., 204 S.W. 5.

Negligence of such a character, or occurring under such circumstances, as to be punishable as a crime by statute; or (at common law) such a flagrant and reckless disregard of the safety of others, or wilful indifference to the injury liable to follow, as to convert an act otherwise lawful into a crime when it results in personal injury or death. 4 Bl. Comm. 192, note; Cook v. Railroad Co., 72 Ga. 48; Rankin v. Transportation Co., 73 Ga. 229, 54 Am.Rep. 874; Railroad Co. v. Chollette, 33 Neb. 143, 49 N.W. 1114.

Culpable Negligence. Failure to exercise that degree of care rendered appropriate by the particular circumstances, and which a man of ordinary prudence in the same situation and with equal experience would not have omitted. Carter v. Lumber Co., 129 N.C. 203, 39 S.E. 828; Woodman v. Nottingham, 49 N.H. 387, 6 Am.Rep. 526; Kimball v. Palmer, C.C.A.Va., 25 C.C.A. 394, 80 F. 240.

Degrees of Negligence. There are degrees of care, and failure to exercise proper degree of care is "negligence," but there are no degrees of negligence. Murray v. De Luxe Motor Stages of Illinois, Mo.App., 133 S.W.2d 1074, 1078.

Classification of "negligence" as "gross," "ordinary," and "slight" indicates only that under special circumstances great care and caution, or ordinary care, or slight care are required, but failure to exercise care demanded is "negligence." 38 Del.Laws, c. 26. Gallegher v. Davis, 7 W.W.Harr. 380, 183 A. 620.

Gross Negligence. The intentional failure to perform a manifest duty in reckless disregard of the consequences as affecting the life or property of another; such a gross want of care and regard for the rights of others as to justify the presumption of willfulness and wantonness. Seelig v. First Nat. Bank, D.C.Ill., 20 F.Supp. 61, 68.

The failure to exercise slight care. Jones v. Atchison, T. & S. F. Ry. Co., 98 Kan. 133, 157 P. 399, 400; Burton Const. Co. v. Metcalfe, 162 Ky. 366, 172 S.W. 698, 701.

The want of slight diligence. The want of that care which every man of common sense, how inattentive soever, takes of his own property. The omission of that care which even inattentive and thoughtless men never fail to take of their own property. Litchfield v. White, 7 N.Y. 442, 57 Am.Dec. 534; Seybel v. National Currency Bank, 54 N.Y. 299, 13 Am.Rep. 583; Briggs v. Spaulding, 141 U. S. 132, 11 S.Ct. 925, 35 L.Ed. 662; The want of ordinary diligence and care which usually prudent man takes of his own property of like description. Dalton v. Hamilton Hotel Operating Co., 242 N.Y. 481, 152 N.E. 268, 270. In the law of torts (and especially with reference to personal injury cases), the term means such negligence as evidences a reckless disregard of human life, or of the safety of persons exposed to its dangerous effects, or that entire want of care which would raise the presumption of a conscious indifference to the rights of others which is equivalent to an intentional violation of them. McDonald v. Railroad Co., Tex.Civ.App., 21 S.W. 775; Railroad Co. v. Bodemer, 139 Ill. 596, 29 N.E. 692, 32 Am.St.Rep. 218; Colt v. Western Union Tel. Co., 130 Cal. 657, 63 P. 83, 53 L.R.A. 678; Bremer v. Lake Erie & W. R. Co., 318 Ill. 11, 148 N. E. 862, 866, 41 A.L.R. 1345.

Indifference to present legal duty and utter forgetfulness of legal obligations, so far as other persons may be affected, and a manifestly smaller amount of watchfulness and circumspection than the circumstances require of a person of ordinary prudence. Burke v. Cook, 246 Mass. 518, 141 N.E. 585, 586. Negligence bordering on recklessness. People v. Adams, 289 Ill. 339, 124 N.E. 575, 577.

"Gross negligence," is substantially higher in magnitude than simple inadvertence, but falls short of intentional wrong. Young v. City of Worcester, 253 Mass. 481,

149 N.E. 204, 205. Words "gross negligence," are equivalent to words "reckless and wanton." Jones v. Commonwealth, 213 Ky. 356, 281 S.W. 164, 167.

Hazardous Negligence. Such careless or reckless conduct as exposes one to very great danger of injury or to imminent peril. Riggs v. Standard Oil Co., C.C.Minn., 130 F. 204.

Legal Negligence. See Legal Negligence.

Ordinary Negligence. The omission of that care which a man of common prudence usually takes of his own concerns. Ouderkirk v. Central Nat. Bank, 119 N.Y. 263, 23 N.E. 875; Scott v. Depeyster, 1 Edw. Ch., N.Y., 543; Briggs v. Spaulding, 141 U. S. 132, 11 Sup.Ct. 924, 35 L.Ed. 662. Failure to exercise care of an ordinarily prudent person in same situation. Avery v. Thompson, 117 Me. 120, 103 A. 4, 5, L.R.A. 1918D 205. A want of that care and prudence that the great majority of mankind exercise under the same or similar circumstances. Clemens v. State, 176 Wis. 289, 185 N.W. 209, 212, 21 A.L.R. 1490. Wherever distinctions between gross, ordinary and slight negligence are observed, "ordinary negligence" is said to be the want of ordinary care. Saxe v. Terry, 250 P. 27, 28, 140 Wash. 503.

"Ordinary negligence" is based on fact that one ought to have known results of his acts, while "gross negligence" rests on assumption that one knew results of his acts, but was recklessly or wantonly indifferent to results. All negligence below that called gross by courts and text-book writers is "slight negligence" and "ordinary negligence." People v. Campbell, 237 Mich. 424, 212 N.W. 97, 99. The distinction between "ordinary negligence" and "gross negligence" is that the former lies in the field of inadvertence and the latter in the field of actual or constructive intent to injure. Bentson v. Brown, 191 Wis. 460, 211 N.W. 132, 133.

Passive Negligence. Negligence which permits defects, obstacles or pitfalls to exist upon premises; which causes dangers arising from physical condition of land itself. Perry v. St. Jean, 218 A.2d 484, 485; Cunag v. McCarthy, 191 N.E.2d 404, 407, 42 Ill.App.2d 36.

Slight Negligence. "A slight want of ordinary care." 7 A. & E. Enc. Law 2d Ed. 373(2), 375(4), 377(5); Macon & Western R. Co. v. Davis, 13 Ga. 68(10). Slight negligence is not slight want of ordinary care contributing to the injury, which would defeat an action for negligence. Slight negligence is defined to be only an absence of that degree of care and vigilance which persons of extraordinary prudence and foresight are accustomed to use. Briggs v. Spaulding, 141 U.S. 132, 11 S.Ct. 924, 35 L.Ed. 662; Litchfield v. White, 7 N.Y. 438, 57 Am.Dec. 534.

Subsequent Negligence. Exists where defendant sees plaintiff in a position of danger and fails to exercise due and proper precaution to prevent injury to plaintiff. Holman v. Brady, 241 Ala. 487, 3 So.2d 30, 33.

Wanton Negligence. Reckless indifference to the consequences of an act or omission, where the party acting or failing to act is conscious of his conduct and, without any actual intent to injure, is aware, from his knowledge of existing circumstances and conditions, that his conduct will inevitably or probably result in injury to another. Alabama G. S. R. Co. v. Hall, 105 Ala. 599, 17 So. 176.

Willful Negligence. Though rejected by some courts and writers as involving a contradiction of terms, this phrase is occasionally used to describe a higher or more aggravated form of negligence than "gross." It then means a willful determination not to perform a known duty, or a reckless disregard of the safety or the rights of others, as manifested by the conscious and intentional omission of the care proper under the circumstances. Victor Coal Co. v. Muir, 20 Colo. 320, 38 P. 378, 26 L.R.A. 435; Holwerson v. Railway Co., 157 Mo. 216, 57 S.W. 770, 50 L.R.A. 850.

Also, the failure to exercise ordinary care after discovering a person to be in a position of peril. Cowan v. Minneapolis, St. P. & S. S. M. Ry. Co., 42 N.D. 170, 172 N.W. 322, 323. It involves deliberation and malice. Schwartz v. Johnson, 152 Tenn. 586, 280 S.W. 32, 33, 47 A.L.R. 323. "Willful negligence" implies an act intentionally done in disregard of another's rights, or omission to do something to protect the rights of another after having had such notice of those rights as would put a prudent man on his guard to use ordinary care to avoid injury. Covert v. Rockford & I. Ry. Co., 299 Ill. 288, 132 N.E. 504, 505. There is no proof of what is called "willful negligence," unless it is shown that defendant discovered plaintiff's peril at such a time and under such circumstances as offered an opportunity, and in consequence imposed a duty on defendant, to take some step to prevent the injury. It is the failure in such a duty that is willful negligence, so called. Westerberg v. Motor Truck Service Co., 158 Minn. 202, 197 N.W. 98, 99. A charge of "willful and wanton negligence" does not signify degrees of negligence, but the words have reference to the intent, which must have been to do the wrongful act, but not to inflict the resulting injury; otherwise, it would be a willful and not a negligent injury. Westre v. Chicago, M. & St. P. Ry. Co., C.C.A.S.D., 2 F.2d 227, 229.

NEGLIGENCE, ESTOPPEL BY. An estoppel which occurs when one who is under a legal duty, either to the person injured or to the public, to act with due care, fails to do so, and such failure is the natural and proximate cause of misleading that person to alter his position. Bradford v. Ins. Co., C.C.A.Pa., 102 F. 48, 43 C.C.A. 310, 49 L.R.A. 530; Central R. R. Co. of New Jersey v. McCartney, 68 N.J.Law, 165, 52 Atl. 575; Brown & Co. v. Ins. Co., 42 Md. 384, 20 Am.Rep. 90; 1 C. P. D. 578; 1905, 1 K. B. 677; Bigelow, Est. 6th Ed. 711.

An estoppel arises when one by acts, representations, intentionally or negligently, induces another to change his position for the worse. Smith v. Vara, 136 Misc. 500, 241 N.Y.S. 202, 209.

An estoppel arises when one by acts, representations, or admissions, or by silence when he ought to speak, intentionally or through culpable negligence, induces another to believe certain facts to exist and such other rightfully relies and acts on such belief so that he will be prejudiced if the former is permitted to deny the existence of such facts. Postal v. Home State Bank for Savings, 284 Mich. 220, 279 N.W. 488, 491. American Exchange Nat. Bank v. Winder, 198 N.C. 18, 150 S.E. 489, 491.

Estoppel may exist where a party has led another into the belief of a certain state of facts by conduct of culpable negligence, calculated to have that result, and the other party has acted upon such belief to his prejudice. Scott v. First Nat. Bank, 343 Mo. 77, 119 S.W.2d 929, 938.

The phrase "estoppel by negligence" has been characterized as "an expression usual but not accurate, since negligence prevents a right of action accruing, estoppel a right that has accrued from being set up"; 2 Beven, Negl. 1332. See a discussion of the doctrine, with critical examination of the English cases, in 15 L. Q. R. 384.

NEGLIGENCE IN LAW. "Actionable negligence" or "negligence in law" grows out of nonobservance of a duty prescribed by law. Kingery v. Donnell, 222 Iowa 241, 268 N.W. 617, 620.

NEGLIGENCE PER SE. Conduct, whether of action or omission, which may be declared and treated as negligence without any argument or proof as to the particular surrounding circumstances, either because it is in violation of a statute or valid municipal ordinance, or because it is so palpably opposed to the dictates of common prudence that it can be said without hesitation or doubt that no careful person would have been guilty of it. Missouri Pac. Ry. Co. v. Lee, 70 Tex. 496, 7 S.W. 857; Murray v. Missouri Pac. R. Co., 101 Mo. 236, 13 S.W. 817, 20 Am.St.Rep. 601. As a general rule, the violation of a public duty, enjoined by law for the protection of person or property, constitutes. Chicago, R. I. & P. Ry. Co. v. Pitchford, 44 Okl. 197, 143 P. 1146, 1150; Kavanagh v. New York, O. & W. Ry. Co., 196 App.Div. 384, 187 N.Y.S. 859, 860.

NEGLIGENT. One is not "negligent" unless he fails to exercise that degree of reasonable care that would be exercised by person of ordinary prudence under all the existing circumstances in view of probable danger of injury. Pulford v. Mouw, 279 Mich. 376, 272 N.W. 713, 714.

Synonymous with "careless." Delmore v. Kansas City Hardwood Flooring Co., 90 Kan. 29, 133 P. 151, 47 L.R.A., N.S., 1220. Sometimes regarded as synonymous with "wrongful." Belmont v. City of New York, 191 App.Div. 717, 182 N.Y.S. 173, 175.

The word is often used to include all conduct which, although not intended to invade any legally protected interest, has the element of social fault. Universal Concrete Pipe Co. v. Bassett, 130 Ohio St. 567, 200 N.E. 843, 847.

NEGLIGENT ESCAPE. Where prisoner escapes through officer's negligence. Hershey v. People, 91 Colo. 113, 12 P.2d 345, 347.

Where a party arrested or imprisoned escapes against the will of him who arrests or imprisons him, and is not freshly pursued and taken again before he has been lost sight of. State v. Wedin, 85 N.J.L. 399, 89 A. 753, 754.

NEGLIGENT OFFENSE. One which ensues from a defective discharge of a duty, which defect could have been avoided by the exercise of that care which is usual, under similar circumstances, with prudent persons of the same class. People v. Gaydica, 122 Misc.Rep. 31, 203 N.Y.S. 243, 258.

NEGLIGENT VIOLATION OF STATUTE. One occasioned by or accompanied with negligent conduct. Hamrick v. McCutcheon, 101 W.Va. 485, 133 S.E. 127, 128.

NEGLIGENTIA. Lat. In the civil law, carelessness; inattention; the omission of proper care or forethought. The term is not exactly equivalent to our "negligence," inasmuch as it was not any *negligentia,* but only a high or gross degree of it, that amounted to *culpa,* (actionable or punishable fault.)

NEGLIGENTIA SEMPER HABET INFORTUNIUM COMITEM. Negligence always has misfortune for a companion. Co. Litt. 246*b;* Shep. Touch. 476.

NEGLIGENTLY. Without due caution and circumspection. People v. Pociask, 96 P.2d 788, 791, 14 Cal.2d 679.

The absence of ordinary care, which is such care as an ordinarily prudent person would exercise for his own protection. Jones v. Commonwealth, 213 Ky. 356, 281 S.W. 164, 167. Equivalent of improperly. Cairnes v. Hillman Drug Co., 214 Ala. 545, 108 So. 362, 364. "Inadvertently" and "negligently" are synonymous. Meyerstein v. Burke, 193 Cal. 105, 222 P. 810.

NEGLIGENTLY DONE. The doing of an act where ordinary care required that it should not have been done at all, or that it should have been done in some other way, and where the doing of the act was not consistent with the exercise of ordinary care under the circumstances. Curtis v. Mauger, 186 Ind. 118, 114 N.E. 408, 409.

NEGOCE. Fr. Business; trade; management of affairs.

NEGOTIABILITY. In mercantile law, transferable quality. That quality of bills of exchange and promissory notes which renders them transferable from one person to another, and from possessing which they are emphatically termed "negotiable paper." 3 Kent, Comm. 74, 77, 89, et seq. Story, Bills, § 60.

NEGOTIABLE. Capable of being transferred by indorsement or delivery so as to pass to holder the right to sue in his own name and take free of equities against assignor payee. Fischbach & Moore v. Philadelphia Nat. Bank, 134 Pa.Super. 84, 3 A.2d 1011, 1012.

An instrument embodying an obligation for the payment of money is called "negotiable" when the legal title to the instrument itself and to the whole amount of money expressed upon its face, with the right to sue therefor in his own name, may be transferred from one person to another without a formal assignment, but by mere indorsement and delivery by the holder or by delivery only. 1 Daniel, Nego. Inst. § 1; Walker v. Ocean Bank, 19 Ind. 247; Robinson v. Wilkinson, 38 Mich. 299.

Quasi Negotiable. "Quasi negotiable" describes the nature of instruments which, while not negotiable, in sense of law merchant, are so framed and dealt with as frequently to convey as good title to transferee as if they were negotiable. A bill of lading is a quasi negotiable instrument. National Bank of Savannah v. Kershaw Oil Mill, C.C.A.S.C., 202 F. 90, 94.

NEGOTIABLE INSTRUMENTS. Any written securities which may be transferred by indorsement and delivery or by delivery merely, so as to vest in the indorsee the legal title, and thus enable him to sue thereon in his own name. Or, more technically, those instruments which not only carry the legal title with them by indorsement or delivery, but carry as well, when transferred before maturity, the right of the transferee to demand the full amounts which their faces call for. Daniel, Neg. Inst. § 1*a*.

A negotiable instrument is a written promise or request for the payment of a certain sum of money to order or bearer. Civ.Code Cal. § 3087.

A general name for bills, First Nat. Bank v. Rochamora, 193 N.C. 1, 136 S.E. 259, 261; notes, checks, Kansas City Casualty Co. v. Westport Ave. Bank, 191 Mo.App. 287, 177 S.W. 1092, 1094; Santa Marina Co. v. Canadian Bank of Commerce, C.C.A.Cal., 254 F. 391, 393; trade acceptances, Federal Commercial & Savings Bank v. International Clay Machinery Co., 230 Mich. 33, 203 N.W. 166, 43 A.L.R. 1245; certain bonds, Grosfield v. First Nat. Bank, 73 Mont. 219, 236 P. 250, 254; Stevens v. Berkshire St. Ry. Co., 247 Mass. 399, 142 N.E. 59, 60; letters of credit, and other negotiable written securities.

Under the Uniform Negotiable Instruments Act, an instrument, to be negotiable, must be in writing and signed; must contain an unconditional promise or order to pay a certain sum of money on demand, or at a fixed and determinable future time; it must be payable to order or to bearer, and where it is addressed to the drawee, he must be named or otherwise indicated with reasonable certainty; its negotiability is not affected by the fact that it is not dated, or that it bears a seal, or that it does not specify the value given or that any value was given.

NEGOTIABLE WORDS. Words and phrases which impart the character of negotiability to bills, notes, checks, etc., in which they are inserted; for instance, a direction to pay to A. "or order" or "bearer."

NEGOTIATE. To transact business, to treat with another respecting a purchase and sale, to hold intercourse, to bargain or trade, to conduct communications or conferences. It is that which passes between parties or their agents in the course of or incident to the making of a contract and is also conversation in arranging terms of contract. Werner v. Hendricks, 121 Pa.Super. 46, 182 A. 748, 749.

To discuss or arrange a sale or bargain; to arrange the preliminaries of a business transaction. Also to sell or discount negotiable paper, or assign or transfer it by indorsement and delivery. Palmer v. Ferry, 6 Gray, Mass., 420; Newport Nat. Bank v. Board of Education, 114 Ky. 87, 70 S.W. 186.

To conclude by bargain, treaty, or agreement. Morton Furniture Co. v. Dubuque Fire & Marine Ins. Co., 287 Mass. 170, 191 N.E. 637, 638.

An instrument is "negotiated" when transferred from one person to another so as to constitute transferee holder thereof. Ficklin v. Nickles, 238 Ky. 591, 38 S.W.2d 456, 459.

NEGOTIATION. The deliberation, discussion, or conference upon the terms of a proposed agreement; the act of settling or arranging the terms and conditions of a bargain, sale, or other business transaction.

The act by which a bill of exchange or promissory note is put into circulation by being passed by one of the original parties to another person.

NEGOTIORUM GESTIO. Lat. In the civil law, literally, a doing of business or businesses. A species of spontaneous agency, or an interference by one in the affairs of another, in his absence, from benevolence or friendship, and without authority. 2 Kent, Comm. 616, note; Inst. 3, 28, 1.

NEGOTIORUM GESTOR. Lat. In the civil law, a transactor or manager of business; a person voluntarily constituting himself agent for another; one who, without any mandate or authority, assumes to take charge of an affair or concern for another person, in the latter's absence, but for his interest.

One who spontaneously, and without the knowledge or consent of the owner, intermeddles with his property, as to do work on it, or to carry it to another place, etc. Story, Bailm. § 189.

NEGRO. The word "negro" means a black man, one descended from the African race, and does not commonly include a mulatto. Felix v. State, 18 Ala. 720. But the laws of the different states are not uniform in this respect, some including in the description "negro" one who has one-eighth or more of African blood.

Term "Negro" means necessarily person of color, but not every person of color is "negro." Rice v. Gong Lum, 139 Miss. 760, 104 So. 105, 109.

NEIFE, NAIF, NATIVUS. In old English law, a woman who was born a villein, or a bond-woman. 1 Steph. Com. 133.

NEIGHBOR. One who lives in close proximity to another. In a grant relating to the use of water by neighbors, it was limited to the next adjoining farm; 1 A. C., 22 (So. Africa).

NEIGHBORHOOD. A place near; an adjoining or surrounding district; a more immediate vicinity; vicinage. Langley v. Barnstead, 63 N.H. 246; Madison v. Morristown Gaslight Co., 65 N.J.Eq. 356, 54 A. 439; Connally v. General Const. Co., 269 U.S. 385, 46 S.Ct. 126, 129, 70 L.Ed. 322.

It is not synonymous with territory or district, but is a collective noun, with the suggestion of proximity, and refers to the units which make up its whole, as well as to the region which comprehends those units. A district or locality, especially when considered with relation to its inhabitants or their interests. Lindsay Irr. Co. v. Mehrtens, 97 Cal. 676, 32 P. 803.

In ordinary and common usage "locality" is synonymous in meaning with "neighborhood," and neither connote large geographical areas with widely diverse interests. Lukens Steel Co. v. Perkins, 70 App.D.C. 354, 107 F.2d 627, 631.

As used with reference to a person's reputation, "neighborhood" means in general any community or society where person is well known and has established a reputation. Craven v. State, 22 Ala.App. 39, 111 So. 767, 769.

NEITHER PARTY. An abbreviated form of docket entry, meaning that, by agreement, neither of the parties will further appear in court in that suit. Gendron v. Hovey, 98 Me. 139, 56 A. 583; White v. Beverly Bldg. Ass'n, 221 Mass. 15, 108 N.E. 921, 922.

NEMBDA. In Swedish and Gothic law, a jury. 3 Bl. Comm. 349, 359.

NEMINE CONTRADICENTE. Lat. No one dissenting; no one voting in the negative. A phrase used to indicate the unanimous consent of a court or legislative body to a judgment, resolution, vote, or motion. Commonly abbreviated "*nem. con.*"

NEMINEM LÆDIT QUI JURE SUO UTITUR. He who stands on his own rights injures no one.

NEMINEM OPORTET ESSE SAPIENTIOREM LEGIBUS. Co. Litt. 97*b*. No man ought to be wiser than the laws.

NEMO. Lat. No one; no man. The initial word of many Latin phrases and maxims, among which are the following:

NEMO ADMITTENDUS EST INHABILITARE SEIPSUM. Jenk. Cent. 40. No man is to be admitted to incapacitate himself.

NEMO AGIT IN SEIPSUM. No man acts against himself. Jenk. Cent. p. 40, case 76. A man cannot be a judge and a party in his own cause. Id.; Broom, Max. 216*n*.

NEMO ALIENÆ REI, SINE SATISDATIONE, DEFENSOR IDONEUS INTELLIGITUR. No man is considered a competent defender of another's property, without security. A rule of the Roman law, applied in part in admiralty cases. 1 Curt. 202.

NEMO ALIENO NOMINE LEGE AGERE POTEST. No one can sue in the name of another. Dig. 50, 17, 123.

NEMO ALIQUAM PARTEM RECTE INTELLIGERE POTEST, ANTEQUAM TOTUM ITERUM ATQUE ITERUM PERLEGERIT. No one can properly understand any part of a thing till he has read through the whole again and again. 3 Co. 59; Broom, Max. 593.

NEMO ALLEGANS SUAM TURPITUDINEM AUDIEN DUS EST. No one alleging his own turpitude is to be heard as a witness. 4 Inst. 279; 12 Pick., Mass., 567. This is not a rule of evidence, but applies to a party seeking to enforce a right founded on an illegal consideration; 94 U.S. 426, 24 L.Ed. 204.

NEMO BIS PUNITUR PRO EODEM DELICTO. No man is punished twice for the same offense. 4 Bl. Comm. 315; 2 Hawk. P. C. 377.

NEMO COGITATIONIS PŒNAM PATITUR. No one suffers punishment on account of his thoughts. Tray. Lat. Max. 362.

NEMO COGITUR REM SUAM VENDERE, ETIAM JUSTO PRETIO. No man is compelled to sell his own property, even for a just price. 4 Inst. 275.

NEMO CONTRA FACTUM SUUM VENIRE POTEST. No man can contravene or contradict his own deed. 2 Inst. 66. The principle of estoppel by deed. Best, Ev. p. 408, § 370.

NEMO DAMNUM FACIT, NISI QUI ID FECIT QUOD FACERE JUS NON HABET. No one is considered as doing damage, unless he who is doing what he has no right to do. Dig. 50, 17, 151.

NEMO DARE POTEST QUOD NON HABET. No man can give that which he has not. Fleta, lib. 3, c. 15, § 8.

NEMO DAT QUI NON HABET. He who hath not cannot give. Jenk. Cent. 250; Broom, Max. 499*n*; 6 C. B., N. S., 478.

NEMO DE DOMO SUA EXTRAHI POTEST. No one can be dragged out of his own house. In other words, every man's house is his castle. Dig. 50, 17, 103.

NEMO DEBET ALIENA JACTURA LOCUPLETARI. No one ought to gain by another's loss. 2 Kent 336.

NEMO DEBET BIS PUNIRI PRO UNO DELICTO. No man ought to be punished twice for one offense. 4 Coke, 43*a*; 11 Coke, 59*b*. No man shall be placed in peril of legal penalties more than once upon the same accusation. Broom, Max. 348.

NEMO DEBET BIS VEXARI PRO EADEM CAUSA. No one should be twice harassed for the same cause. 2 Johns., N.Y., 182; 13 Johns., N.Y., 153.

NEMO DEBET BIS VEXARI [SI CONSTET CURLÆ QUOD SIT] PRO UNA ET EADEM CAUSA. No man ought to be twice troubled or harassed [if it appear to the court that it is] for one and the same cause. 5 Coke, 61*a*; 5 Pet. 61, 8 L.Ed. 25; 2 Mass. 355; 17 Mass. 425. No man can be sued a second time for the same cause of action, if once judgment has been rendered. See Broom, Max. 327, 348. No man can be held to bail a second time at the suit of the same plaintiff for the same cause of action. 1 Chit. Archb. Pr. 476.

NEMO DEBET ESSE JUDEX IN PROPRIA CAUSA. No man ought to be a judge in his own cause. 12 Coke, 114*a*. A maxim derived from the civil law. Cod. 3, 5. Called a "fundamental rule of reason and of natural justice." Burrows, Sett. Cas. 194, 197.

NEMO DEBET IMMISCERE SE REI AD SE NIHIL PERTINENTI. No one should intermeddle with a thing that in no respect concerns him. Jenk. Cent. p. 18, case 32.

NEMO DEBET IN COMMUNIONE INVITUS TENERI. No one should be retained in a partnership against his will. Selden v. Vermilya, 2 Sandf., N.Y., 568, 593; United Ins. Co. v. Scott, 1 Johns., N.Y., 106, 114.

NEMO DEBET LOCUPLETARI ALIENA JACTURA. No one ought to be enriched by another's loss. Dig. 6, 1, 48, 65; 2 Kent, Comm. 336; 1 Kames, Eq. 331.

NEMO DEBET LOCUPLETARI EX ALTERIUS INCOMMODO. No one ought to be made rich out of another's loss. Jenk. Cent. 4; Taylor v. Baldwin, 10 Barb., N.Y., 626, 633.

NEMO DEBET REM SUAM SINE FACTO AUT DEFECTU SUO AMITTERE. No man ought to lose his property without his own act or default. Co. Litt. 263*a*.

NEMO DUOBUS UTATUR OFFICIIS. 4 Inst. 100. No one should hold two offices, *i. e.*, at the same time.

NEMO EJUSDEM TENEMENTI SIMUL POTEST ESSE HÆRES ET DOMINUS. No one can at the same time be the heir and the owner of the same tenement. See 1 Reeve, Eng. Law, 106.

NEMO ENIM ALIQUAM PARTEM RECTE INTELLIGERE POSSIT ANTEQUAM TOTUM ITERUM ATQUE ITERUM PERLEGERIT. No one is able rightly to understand one part before he has again and again read through the whole. Broom, Max. 593.

NEMO EST HÆRES VIVENTIS. No one is the heir of a living person. Co. Litt. 8*a*, 22*b*. No one can be heir during the life of his ancestor. Broom, Max. 522, 523; 99 Mass. 456; 118 Mass. 345. No person can be the actual complete heir of another till the ancestor is previously dead. 2 Bl. Comm. 208.

NEMO EST SUPRA LEGES. No one is above the law. Lofft, 142.

NEMO EX ALTERIUS FACTO PRÆGRAVARI DEBET. No man ought to be burdened in consequence of another's act. 2 Kent, Comm. 646.

NEMO EX CONSILIO OBLIGATUR. No man is bound in consequence of his advice. Mere advice will not create the obligation of a mandate. Story, Bailm. § 155.

NEMO EX DOLO SUO PROPRIO RELEVETUR, AUT AUXILIUM CAPIAT. Let no one be relieved or gain an advantage by his own fraud. A civil law maxim.

NEMO EX PROPRIO DOLO CONSEQUITUR ACTIONEM. No one maintains an action arising out of his own wrong. Broom, Max. 297.

NEMO EX SUO DELICTO MELIOREM SUAM CONDITIONEM FACERE POTEST. No one can make his condition better by his own misdeed. Dig. 50, 17, 134, 1.

NEMO IN PROPRIA CAUSA TESTIS ESSE DEBET. No one ought to be a witness in his own cause. 3 Bl. Comm. 371.

NEMO INAUDITUS CONDEMNARI DEBET SI NON SIT CONTUMAX. No man ought to be condemned without being heard unless he be contumacious. Jenk. Cent. p. 18, case 12, in marg.

NEMO JUS SIBI DICERE POTEST. No one can declare the law for himself. No one is entitled to take the law into his own hands. Tray. Lat. Max. 366.

NEMO MILITANS DEO IMPLICETUR SECULARIBUS NEGOTIIS. No man who is warring for [in the service of] God should be involved in secular matters. Co. Litt. 70*b*. A principle of the old law that men of religion were not bound to go in person with the king to war.

NEMO NASCITUR ARTIFEX. Co. Litt. 97. No one is born an artificer.

NEMO PATRIAM IN QUA NATUS EST EXUERE, NEC LIGEANTIÆ DEBITUM EJURARE POSSIT. No man can renounce the country in which he was born, nor abjure the obligation of his allegiance. Co. Litt. 129*a;* Broom, Max. 75; Fost. Cr. Law, 184.

NEMO PLUS COMMODI HÆREDI SUO RELINQUIT QUAM IPSE HABUIT. No one leaves a greater benefit to his heir than he had himself. Dig. 50, 17, 120.

NEMO PLUS JURIS AD ALIUM TRANSFERRE POTEST QUAM IPSE HABET. No one can transfer more right to another than he has himself. Dig. 50, 17, 54; Broom, Max. 467, 469; 2 Kent 324; 5 Co. 113; 10 Pet. 161, 175, 9 L.Ed. 382.

NEMO POTEST CONTRA RECORDUM VERIFICARE PER PATRIAM. No one can verify by the country against a record. 2 Inst. 380. The issue upon matter of record cannot be to the jury. A maxim of old practice.

NEMO POTEST ESSE DOMINUS ET HÆRES. No man can be both owner and heir. Hale, Com. Law, c. 7.

NEMO POTEST ESSE SIMUL ACTOR ET JUDEX. No one can be at once suitor and judge. Broom, Max. 117.

NEMO POTEST ESSE TENENS ET DOMINUS. No man can be both tenant and lord [of the same tenement.] Gilb. Ten. 142.

NEMO POTEST EXUERE PATRIAM. No man can renounce his own country. 18 L. Q. R. 51.

NEMO POTEST FACERE PER ALIUM QUOD PER SE NON POTEST. No one can do that by another which he cannot do of himself. Jenk. Cent. p. 237, case 14. A rule said to hold in original grants, but not in descents; as where an office descended to a woman, in which case, though she could not exercise the office in person, she might by deputy. Id.

NEMO POTEST FACERE PER OBLIQUUM QUOD NON POTEST FACERE PER DIRECTUM. No man can do that indirectly which he cannot do directly. 1 Eden, 512.

NEMO POTEST MUTARE CONSILIUM SUUM IN ALTERIUS INJURIAM. No man can change his purpose to another's injury. Dig. 50, 17, 75; Broom, Max. 34.

NEMO POTEST NISI QUOD DE JURE POTEST. No one is able to do a thing, unless he can do it lawfully. 67 Ill.App. 80.

NEMO POTEST PLUS JURIS AD ALIUM TRANSFERRE QUAM IPSE HABET. Co. Litt. 309; Wing. Max. 56. No one can transfer a greater right to another than he himself has.

NEMO POTEST SIBI DEBERE. No one can owe to himself.

NEMO PRÆSENS NISI INTELLIGAT. One is not present unless he understands.

NEMO PRÆSUMITUR ALIENAM POSTERITATEM SUÆ PRÆTULISSE. No man is presumed to have preferred another's posterity to his own. Wing. Max. p. 285, max. 79.

NEMO PRÆSUMITUR DONARE. No one is presumed to give. Haren v. Foster, 9 Pick., Mass., 128, 19 Am.Dec. 353.

NEMO PRÆSUMITUR ESSE IMMEMOR SUÆ ÆTERNÆ SALUTIS, ET MAXIME IN ARTICULO MORTIS. 6 Coke, 76. No one is presumed to be forgetful of his own eternal welfare, and particularly at the point of death.

NEMO PRÆSUMITUR LUDERE IN EXTREMIS. No one is presumed to trifle at the point of death.

NEMO PRÆSUMITUR MALUS. No one is presumed to be bad.

NEMO PROHIBETUR PLURES NEGOTIATIONES SIVE ARTES EXERCERE. No one is prohibited from following several kinds of business or several arts. 11 Coke, 54*a*. The common law doth not prohibit any person from using several arts or mysteries at his pleasure. Id.

NEMO PROHIBETUR PLURIBUS DEFENSIONIBUS UTI. Co. Litt. 304*a*. No one is prohibited from making use of several defenses.

NEMO PRUDENS PUNIT UT PRÆTERITA REVOCENTUR, SED UT FUTURA PRÆVENIANTUR. No wise man punishes in order that past things may be recalled, but that future wrongs may be prevented. 2 Bulst. 173.

NEMO PUNITUR PRO ALIENO DELICTO. Wing. Max. 336. No one is punished for another's wrong.

NEMO PUNITUR SINE INJURIA, FACTO, SEU DEFALTA. No one is punished unless for some wrong, act, or default. 2 Inst. 287.

NEMO QUI CONDEMNARE POTEST, ABSOLVERE NON POTEST. No one who may condemn is unable to acquit. Dig. 50, 17, 37.

NEMO SIBI ESSE JUDEX VEL SUIS JUS DICERE DEBET. No man ought to be his own judge, or to administer justice in cases where his relations are concerned. 12 Co. 113; Cod. 3, 5, 1; Broom, Max. 116, 124.

NEMO SINE ACTIONE EXPERITUR, ET HOC NON SINE BREVE SIVE LIBELLO CONVENTIONALI. No one goes to law without an action, and no one can bring an action without a writ or bill. Bract. fol. 112.

NEMO TENETUR AD IMPOSSIBILE. No one is bound to an impossibility. Jenk. Cent. 7; Broom, Max. 244.

NEMO TENETUR ARMARE ADVERSARIUM CONTRA SE. Wing. Max. 665. No one is bound to arm his adversary against himself.

NEMO TENETUR DIVINARE. No man is bound to divine, or to have foreknowledge of, a future event. 10 Coke, 55*a*.

NEMO TENETUR EDERE INSTRUMENTA CONTRA SE. No man is bound to produce writings against himself. A rule of the Roman law, adhered to in criminal prosecutions, but departed from in civil questions. Bell.

NEMO TENETUR INFORMARE QUI NESCIT, SED QUISQUIS SCIRE QUOD INFORMAT. Branch, Princ. No one is bound to give information about things he is ignorant of, but every one is bound to know that which he gives information about.

NEMO TENETUR JURARE IN SUAM TURPITUDINEM. No one is bound to swear to the fact of his own criminality; no one can be forced to give his own oath in evidence of his guilt. Bell; Halk. 100.

NEMO TENETUR PRODERE SEIPSUM. No one is bound to betray himself. In other words, no one can be compelled to criminate himself. Broom, Max. 968.

NEMO TENETUR SEIPSUM ACCUSARE. Wing. Max. 486. No one is bound to accuse himself; 14 M. & W. 286; 107 Mass. 181.

NEMO TENETUR SEIPSUM INFORTUNIIS ET PERICULIS EXPONERE. No one is bound to expose himself to misfortunes and dangers. Co. Litt. 253*b*.

NEMO TENETUR SEIPSUM PRODERE. No one is bound to betray himself. 10 N.Y. 10; 7 How. Prac., N.Y., 57, 58; Broom, Max. 968.

NEMO UNQUAM JUDICET IN SE. No one can ever be a judge in his own cause.

NEMO UNQUAM VIR MAGNUS FUIT, SINE ALIQUO DIVINO AFFLATU. No one was ever a great man without some divine inspiration. Cicero.

NEMO VIDETUR FRAUDARE EOS QUI SCIUNT ET CONSENTIUNT. No one seems [is supposed] to defraud those who know and assent [to his acts.] Dig. 50, 17, 145.

NEMY. L. Fr. Not. Litt. § 3.

NEPHEW. In legal usage only children of brothers and sisters are called "nephews" and "nieces," children of husband's or wife's brothers and sisters being so called only by courtesy. In re Lamberton's Estate, 105 Pa.Super. 348, 161 A. 596, 597.

The term, as used in wills and other documents, may include the children of half brothers and sisters and also grandnephews, if such be the apparent intention, but not the nephew of a husband or wife, and not (presumptively) a nephew who is illegitimate. Shephard v. Shephard, 57 Conn. 24, 17 A. 173; Lyon v. Lyon, 88 Me. 395, 34 A. 180; In re Logan, 131 N.Y. 456, 30 N.E. 485.

NEPOS. Lat. A grandson.

NEPOTISM. Bestowal of patronage by public officers in appointing others to positions by reason of blood or marital relationship to appointing authority. State ex rel. Robinson v. Keefe, 111 Fla. 701, 149 So. 638.

NEPTIS. Lat. A granddaughter; sometimes great-granddaughter.

NEPUOY. In Scotch law, a grandson. Skene.

NEQUE LEGES NEQUE SENATUS CONSULTA ITA SCRIBI POSSUNT UT OMNIS CASUS QUI QUANDOQUE IN SEDIRIUNT COMPREHENDATUR; SED SUFFICIT EA QUAE PLAERUMQUE ACCIDUNT CONTINERI. Means that neither laws nor acts of a parliament can be so written as to include all actual or possible cases; it is sufficient if they provide for those things which frequently or ordinarily may happen. State ex rel. Dowling v. Butts, 111 Fla. 630, 149 So. 746, 757, 89 A.L.R. 946.

NERVINE. A descriptive word meaning a nerve tonic or a remedy for disorder of the nerves. Richmond Remedies Co. v. Dr. Miles Medical Co., C.C.A.Mo., 16 F.2d 598, 601.

NERVOUSNESS. A species of mental suffering. Southern Ry. in Kentucky v. Owen, 156 Ky. 827, 162 S.W. 110, 111.

NET. Clear of anything extraneous, with all deductions, such as charges, expenses, discounts, commissions, taxes, etc., made. Cleveland v. Glassell, 117 Cal.App. 713, 4 P.2d 596, 598.

That which remains after deducting all charges and outlay. John Fink Agency v. Dougherty, 90 Pa.Super. 443, 445.

NET ASSETS. A bookkeeping balance obtained by subtracting company's liabilities from its gross assets. Commonwealth v. Union Trust Co. of Pittsburgh, 345 Pa. 298, 27 A.2d 15, 17.

NET BALANCE. The proceeds of sale, after deducting expenses. Evans v. Waln, 71 Pa. 69; Meserve v. Smith Bros., 56 Cal.App. 683, 206 P. 105.

NET EARNINGS. See Earnings.

NET ESTATE. Under estate tax statute the term means that which is left of the gross estate after the deduction of proper and lawful items in the course of settlement. United States Trust Co. of New York v. Sears, D.C.Conn., 29 F.Supp. 643, 649.

NET INCOME. Amount remaining after proper current charges have been made against gross income. In re Matthews' Estate, 210 Wis. 109, 245 N.W. 122.

NET LEVEL ANNUAL PREMIUM. An amount which, if exacted from a group of policyholders and increased by interest, will yield a sum sufficient to satisfy all death claims. The result is generally referred to as the "net" or "net level premium" of the policy. Fox v. Mutual Ben. Life Ins. Co., C.C.A.Mo., 107 F.2d 715, 718.

NET LOSS. Any deficit from operations, plus any shrinkage in value of plant investment. War Minerals Relief Act March 2, 1919, § 5, 50 U.S.C.A. § 80 note; Act Feb. 13, 1929, c. 182, 45 Stat. 1166. Ickes v. U. S. ex rel. Chestatee Pyrites & Chemical Corporation, D.C., 289 U.S. 510, 53 S.Ct. 700, 77 L.Ed. 1352.

NET PREMIUM. In the business of life insurance, this term is used to designate that portion of the premium which is intended to meet the cost of the insurance, both current and future; its amount is calculated upon the basis of the mortality tables and upon the assumption that the company will receive a certain rate of interest upon all its assets; it does not include the entire premium paid by the assured, but does include a certain sum for expenses. Fuller v. Metropolitan L. Ins. Co., 70 Conn. 647, 41 A. 4.

NET PRICE. The lowest price, after deducting all discounts.

NET PROCEEDS. Gross proceeds, less charges which may be rightly deducted. Pflueger v. United States, 73 App.D.C. 364, 121 F.2d 732, 736.

NET PROFITS. What remains after deducting all liabilities, including capital stock, from present value of all assets of corporation, or that which remains as clear gain of corporation, after deducting from its income all expenses incurred and losses sustained in the conduct and prosecution of its business. Guaranty Trust Co. of New York v. Grand Rapids, G. H. & M. Ry. Co., D.C.Mich., 7 F.Supp. 511, 517.

NET REVENUES. Revenues remaining after providing for the sinking fund, interest, and current expenses of the plant. City of Raymondville v. McCann, Tex.Civ.App., 54 S.W.2d 1049, 1050.

NET SINGLE PREMIUM. Aggregate of future yearly costs of insurance, severally discounted to age from which computation is made. Magers v. Northwestern Mut. Life Ins. Co., 348 Mo. 96, 152 S.W.2d 148, 152.

Premium which, if exacted from a group of policyholders and immediately invested at the assumed rate of interest, will yield in the aggregate a sum exactly sufficient to pay all death claims as they mature providing the mortality rate is in accord with the table used. Fox v. Mutual Ben. Life Ins. Co., C.C.A.Mo., 107 F.2d 715, 718.

NET TONNAGE. The cubic contents of the interior of a vessel, when the spaces occupied by the crew and by propelling machinery are deducted, numbered in tons. Kiessig v. San Diego County, 51 Cal.App.2d 47, 124 P.2d 163, 165.

NET VALUE. Accumulation of balances of past net premiums not absorbed in carrying risk. Fox v. Mutual Ben. Life Ins. Co., C.C.A.Mo., 107 F.2d 715, 718, 719. Policy "reserve". Magers v. Northwestern Mut. Life Ins. Co., 348 Mo. 96, 152 S.W.2d 148, 152, 153.

NET WEIGHT. The weight of an article or collection of articles, after deducting from the gross weight the weight of the boxes, coverings, casks, etc., containing the same. The weight of an animal dressed for sale, after rejecting hide, offal, etc.

NET WORTH. Remainder after deduction of liabilities from assets. W. H. Miner, Inc. v. Peerless Equipment Co., C.C.A.Ill., 115 F.2d 650, 655.

NETHER HOUSE OF PARLIAMENT A name given to the English house of commons in the time of Henry VIII.

NEURASTHENIA. In medical jurisprudence, a condition of weakness or exhaustion of the general nervous system, giving rise to various forms of mental and bodily inefficiency.

NEUTRAL. In international law, indifferent; impartial; not engaged on either side; not taking an active part with either of the contending states. In an international war, the principal hostile powers are called "belligerents;" those actively co-operating with and assisting them, their "allies;" and those taking no part whatever, "neutrals."

NEUTRAL PROPERTY. Property which belongs to citizens of neutral powers, and is used, treated, and accompanied by proper *insignia* as such.

NEUTRALITY. The state of a nation which takes no part between two or more other nations at war. U. S. v. The Three Friends, 166 U.S. 1, 17 S.Ct. 495, 41 L.Ed. 897; O'Neill v. Central Leather Co., 87 N.J.L. 552, 94 A. 789, 790, L.R.A. 1917A, 276.

NEUTRALITY LAWS. Acts of congress which forbid the fitting out and equipping of armed vessels, or the enlisting of troops, for the aid of either of two belligerent powers with which the United States is at peace.

NEUTRALITY PROCLAMATION. A proclamation by the president of the United States, issued on the outbreak of a war between two powers with both of which the United States is at peace, announcing the neutrality of the United States and warning all citizens to refrain from any breach of the neutrality laws.

NEVER INDEBTED, PLEA OF. A species of traverse which occurs in actions of debt on simple contract, and is resorted to when the defendant means to deny in point of fact the existence of any express contract to the effect alleged in the declaration, or to deny the matters of fact from which such contract would by law be implied. Steph. Pl. 153, 156; Wharton.

NEW. As an element in numerous compound terms and phrases of the law, this word may denote novelty, or the condition of being previously unknown or of recent or fresh origin, but ordinarily it is a purely relative term and is employed in contrasting the date, origin, or character of one thing with the corresponding attributes of another thing of the same kind or class.

Of New. See that title.

NEW ACQUISITION. An estate derived from any source other than descent, devise, or gift from father or mother or any relative in the paternal or maternal line. Webb v. Caldwell, 198 Ark. 331, 128 S.W.2d 691, 694, 122 A.L.R. 814.

NEW AND USEFUL. The phrase used in the patent laws to describe the two qualities of an invention or discovery which are essential to make it patentable, viz., novelty, or the condition of having been previously unknown, and practical utility. In re Gould, 1 MacArthur, D.C. 410; Adams v. Turner, 73 Conn. 38, 46 A. 247; Lowell v. Lewis, 1 Mason, 182, F.Cas.No.8,568.

To accomplish a new and useful result within meaning of Rev.St. § 4886, 35 U.S.C.A. § 31, it is not necessary that result before unknown should be brought about, but it is sufficient if an old result is accomplished in a new and more effective way. Hirschy v. Wisconsin-Minnesota Gas & Electric Household Appliances Co., D.C.Minn., 18 F.2d 347, 354. An invention achieves a new result, where a function which had been performed by other means was performed to an efficient degree by an association of means never before combined, though all of them were old, and some of the changes seemed to be only in degree. American Ball Bearing Co. v. Finch, C.C.A.Ohio, 239 F. 885, 889.

NEW ASSETS. In the law governing the administration of estates, this term denotes assets coming into the hands of an executor or administrator after the expiration of the time when, by statute, claims against the estate are barred so far as regards recourse against the assets with which he was originally charged. Littlefield v. Eaton, 74 Me. 521; Chenery v. Webster, 8 Allen, Mass., 77.

NEW ASSIGNMENT. Under the common-law practice, where the declaration in an action is ambiguous, and the defendant pleads facts which are literally an answer to it, but not to the real claim set up by the plaintiff, the plaintiff's course is to reply by way of new assignment; *i. e.*, allege that he brought his action not for the cause supposed by the defendant, but for some other cause to which the plea has no application. 3 Steph.Comm. 507; Sweet. Bishop v. Travis, 51 Minn. 183, 53 N.W. 461.

NEW CAUSE OF ACTION. With reference to the amendment of pleadings, this term may refer to a new state of facts out of which liability is claimed to arise, or it may refer to parties who are alleged to be entitled under the same state of facts, or it may embrace both features. Love v. Southern R. Co., 108 Tenn. 104, 65 S.W. 475, 55 L.R.A. 471; Nelson v. First Nat. Bank, 139 Ala. 578, 36 So. 707, 101 Am.St.Rep. 52.

NEW FOR OLD. In making an adjustment of a partial loss under a policy of marine insurance, the rule is to apply the old materials towards the payment of the new, by deducting the value of them from the gross amount of the expenses for repairs, and to allow the deduction of one-third *new for old* upon the balance. 3 Kent, Comm. 339.

NEW INN. An inn of chancery. See Inns of Chancery.

NEW MATTER. In pleading, matter of fact not previously alleged by either party in the pleadings. Walters v. Battenfield, 21 N.M. 413, 155 P. 721, 723; Continental Gin Co. v. Arnold, 52 Okl. 569, 153 P. 160, 163.

NEW PROMISE. See Promise.

NEW STYLE. The modern system of computing time was introduced into Great Britain A.D. 1752, the 3d of September of that year being reckoned as the 14th.

NEW TRIAL. See Trial.

NEW WORKS. In the civil law, by a new work is understood every sort of edifice or other work which is newly commenced on any ground whatever. When the ancient form of work is changed, either by an addition being made to it or by some part of the ancient work being taken away, it is styled also a "new work." Civ.Code La. art. 856.

NEW YEAR'S DAY. The first day of January.

The 25th of March was the civil and legal New Year's Day, till the alteration of the style in 1752, when it was permanently fixed at the 1st of January. In Scotland the year was, by a proclamation, which bears date 27th of November, 1599, ordered thenceforth to commence in that kingdom on the 1st of January instead of the 25th of March. Enc.Lond.

NEWGATE. The name of a prison in London, said to have existed as early as 1207. For centuries the condition of the place was horrible, but it has been greatly improved since 1808.

NEWLY-DISCOVERED EVIDENCE. Evidence of a new and material fact, or new evidence in relation to a fact in issue, discovered by a party to a cause after the rendition of a verdict or judgment therein. Wynne v. Newman, 75 Va. 816; People v. Priori, 164 N.Y. 459, 58 N.E. 668. Testimony discovered after trial, not discoverable before trial by exercise of due diligence. Mode v. State, 169 Ark. 356, 275 S.W. 700, 701; State v. Blackwood, 103 Wash. 529, 175 P. 168, 169; Murphy v. Skelly, 101 N.J.Eq. 793, 138 A. 882, 884, any evidence newly discovered, whether the facts existed at the time of the trial or not. In re Wood, 140 Minn. 130, 167 N.W. 358, 359. For the requirements which such evidence must meet before a new trial will be granted, State v. Luttrell, 28 N.M. 393, 212 P. 739, 741; Sanchez v. State, 199 Ind. 235, 157 N.E. 1, 3; Gonirenki v. American Steel & Wire Co., 106 Conn. 1, 137 A. 26, 28.

NEWSPAPER. A publication, usually in sheet form, intended for general circulation, and published regularly at short intervals, containing intelligence of current events and news of general interest. 4 Op.Attys.Gen. 10; Garden City News v. Hurst, 129 Kan. 365, 282 P. 720, 722.

Official Newspaper. One designated by a state or municipal legislative body, or agents empowered by them, in which the public acts, resolves, advertisements, and notices are required to be published. Albany County v. Chaplin, 5 Wyo. 74, 37 P. 370.

NEXI. Lat. In Roman law, bound; bound persons. A term applied to such insolvent debtors as were delivered up to their creditors, by whom they might be held in bondage until their debts were discharged. Calvin.; Adams, Rom.Ant. 49.

NEXT. Nearest; closest; immediately following. Green v. McLaren, 7 Ga. 107; State v. Asbell, 57 Kan. 398, 46 P. 770.

Nearest or nighest, not in the sense of propinquity alone, as, for example, three persons on three chairs, one in the midst, those on each side of the middle one are equally near, each "next" to the middle one; but it signifies also order, or succession, or relation as well as propinquity. 27 L.J.Ch. 654. 3 Q.B. 723; Couch v. Turnpike Co., 4 Johns.Ch., N.Y., 26.

NEXT DEVISEE. Person to whom remainder is given by will. Young v. Robinson, 5 N.J.L. 689.

NEXT EVENTUAL ESTATE. Estate taking effect upon happening of the event terminating accumulation. In re Shupack's Estate, 158 Misc. 873, 287 N.Y.S. 184, 196.

NEXT FRIEND. One acting for benefit of infant, married woman, or other person not sui juris, without being regularly appointed guardian. In re Boulware's Will, 144 Misc. 235, 258 N.Y.S. 522.

"Next friend" or "prochein ami" is one admitted to court to prosecute for infant. Crawford v. Amusement Syndicate Co., Mo., 37 S.W.2d 581, 584.

NEXT OF KIN. In the law of descent and distribution, this term properly denotes the persons nearest of kindred to the decedent, that is, those who are most nearly related to him by blood; but it is sometimes construed to mean only those who are entitled to take under the statute of distributions, and sometimes to include other persons. 2 Story, Eq.Jur. § 1065*b*; Barrett v. Egbertson, 92 N.J.Eq. 118, 111 A. 326, 327; Godfrey v. Epple, 100 Ohio St. 447, 126 N.E. 886, 11 A.L.R. 317; Close v. Benham, 97 Conn. 102, 115 A. 626, 627, 20 A.L.R. 351; Hamilton v. Erie R. Co., 219 N.Y. 343, 114 N.E. 399, 403, Ann.Cas.1918A, 928; Arnold v. O'Connor, 37 R.I. 557, 94 A. 145, L.R.A.1916C, 898; Mostenbocker v. Shawnee Gas & Electric Co., 49 Okl. 304, 152 P. 82, 83, L.R.A.1916B, 910. The words "next of kin," used *simpliciter* in a deed or will, mean, not nearest of kindred, but those relatives who share in the estate according to the statute of distributions, including those claiming *per stirpes* or by representation. Slosson v. Lynch, 43 Barb., N.Y., 147.

NEXT PRESENTATION. In the law of advowsons, the right of next presentation is the right to present to the first vacancy of a benefice.

NEXUM. Lat. In Roman law, in ancient times the *nexum* seems to have been a species of formal contract, involving a loan of money, and attended with peculiar consequences, solemnized with the "copper and balance." Later, it appears to have been used as a general term for any contract struck with those ceremonies, and hence to have included the special form of conveyance called "*mancipatio*." In a general sense it means the obligation or *bond* between contracting parties. Maine, Anc.Law, 305, *et seq.*; Hadl.Rom. Law, 247.

In Roman law, this word expressed the tie or obligation involved in the old conveyance by *mancipatio;* and came latterly to be used interchangeably with (but less frequently than) the word "*obligatio*" itself. Brown.

NICHILLS. In English practice, debts due to the exchequer which the sheriff could not levy, and as to which he returned *nil.* These sums were transcribed once a year by the clerk of the nichills, and sent to the treasurer's remembrancer's office, whence process was issued to recover the "nichill" debts. Both of these offices were abolished in 1833. Mozley & Whitley.

NICKNAME. A short name; one *nicked* or cut off for the sake of brevity, without conveying an idea of opprobrium, and frequently evincing the strongest affection or the most perfect familiarity. North Carolina Inst. v. Norwood, 45 N.C. 74.

NIDERLING, NIDERING, or NITHING. A vile, base person, or sluggard; chicken-hearted. Spelman.

NIECE. The daughter of one's brother or sister. Ambl. 514. Capps v. State, 87 Fla. 388, 100 So. 172, 173.

In legal usage only children of brothers and sisters are called "nephews" and "nieces," children of husband's or wife's brothers and sisters being so called only by courtesy. In re Lamberton's Estate, 105 Pa.Super. 348, 161 A. 596, 597.

NIEFE. In old English law, a woman born in vassalage; a bondwoman.

NIENT. L. Fr. Nothing; not.

NIENT COMPRISE. Not comprised; not included. An exception taken to a petition because the thing desired is not contained in that deed or proceeding whereon the petition is founded. Tomlins.

NIENT CULPABLE. Not guilty. The name in law French of the general issue in tort or in a criminal action.

NIENT DEDIRE. To say nothing; to deny nothing; to suffer judgment by default.

NIENT LE FAIT. In pleading, not the deed; not his deed. The same as the plea of *non est factum.*

NIENT SEISI. In old pleading, not seised. The general plea in the writ of annuity. Crabb, Eng. Law, 424.

NIGER LIBER. See Liber Niger.

NIGHT. At common-law, that period between sunset and sunrise during which there is not daylight enough to discern a man's face. 1 Hale, P. C. 350; State v. Perkins, 342 Mo. 560, 116 S.W.2d 80, 81, 82.

The rule is often followed that "nighttime" begins thirty minutes after sunset and ends thirty minutes before sunrise. State v. Perkins, 342 Mo. 560, 116 S.W.2d 80, 82.

However, the limit of 9 p. m. to 6 a. m. has been fixed by statute, in England, as the period of night, in prosecutions for burglary and larceny. St. 24 & 25 Vict. c. 96, § 1; Brown. In American law, the common-law definition is still adhered to in some states, but in others "night" has been defined by statute. U. S. v. Lepper, D.C.N.Y., 288 F. 136, 137; Weatherred v. State, 101 Tex.Cr.R. 520, 276 S.W. 436, 437.

NIGHT MAGISTRATE. A constable of the night; the head of a watch-house.

NIGHT WALKERS. Described in the statute 5 Edw. III. c. 14, as persons who sleep by day and walk by night. Persons who prowl about at night, and are of a suspicious appearance and behavior. Persons whose habit is to be abroad at night for the purpose of committing some crime or nuisance or mischief or disturbing the peace; not now generally subject to the criminal laws except in respect to misdemeanors actually committed, or in the character of vagrants or suspicious persons. Thomas v. State, 55 Ala. 260, 261; State v. Dowers, 45 N.H. 543. In a narrower sense, a night walker is a prostitute who walks the streets at night for the purpose of soliciting men for lewd purposes. Stokes v. State, 92 Ala. 73, 9 So. 400, 25 Am.St.Rep. 22; People v. Berger, Gen.Sess., 169 N.Y.S. 319, 321.

NIGRUM NUNQUAM EXCEDERE DEBET RUBRUM. The black should never go beyond the red, [*i. e.*, the text of a statute should never be read in a sense more comprehensive than the rubric, or title.] Tray. Lat. Max. 373.

NIHIL. Lat. Nothing. Often contracted to *"nil."* The word standing alone is the name of an abbreviated form of return to a writ made by a sheriff or constable, the fuller form of which would be *"nihil est"* or *"nihil habet,"* according to circumstances.

NIHIL ALIUD POTEST REX QUAM QUOD DE JURE POTEST. 11 Coke, 74. The king can do nothing except what he can by law do.

NIHIL CAPIAT PER BREVE. In practice, that he take nothing by his writ. The form of judgment against the plaintiff in an action, either in bar or in abatement. When the plaintiff has commenced his proceedings by bill, the judgment is *nihil capiat per billam.* Co.Litt. 363.

NIHIL CONSENSUI TAM CONTRARIUM EST QUAM VIS ATQUE METUS. Nothing is so opposed to consent as force and fear. Dig. 50, 17, 116.

NIHIL DAT QUI NON HABET. He gives nothing who has nothing.

NIHIL DE RE ACCRESCIT EI QUI NIHIL IN RE QUANDO JUS ACCRESCERET HABET. Co. Litt. 188. Nothing of a matter accrues to him who, when the right accrues, has nothing in that matter.

NIHIL DICIT. He says nothing.

This is the name of the judgment which may be taken as of course against a defendant who omits to plead or answer the plaintiff's declaration or complaint within the time limited. In some jurisdictions it is otherwise known as judgment "for want of a plea." Gilder v. McIntyre, 29 Tex. 91; Falken v. Housatonic R. Co., 63 Conn. 258, 27 A. 1117; Wilbur v. Maynard, 6 Colo. 486.

Judgment taken against party who withdraws his answer is *judgment nihil dicit,* which amounts to confession of cause of action stated, and carries with it, more strongly than judgment by default, admission of justice of plaintiff's case. Howe v. Central State Bank of Coleman, Tex. Civ.App., 297 S.W. 692, 694.

NIHIL DICTUM QUOD NON DICTUM PRIUS. Nothing is said which was not said before. Said of a case where former arguments were repeated. Hardr. 464.

NIHIL EST. There is nothing. A form of return made by a sheriff when he has been unable to serve the writ.

"Although *non est inventus* is the more frequent return in such a case, yet it is by no means as full in answer to the command of the writ as is the return of *nihil*. That amounts to an averment that the defendant has nothing in the bailiwick, no dwelling-house, no family, no residence, and no personal presence to enable the officer to make the service required by the act of assembly. It is therefore a full answer to the exigency of the writ." Sherer v. Easton Bank, 33 Pa. 139.

NIHIL EST ENIM LIBERALE QUOD NON IDEM JUSTUM. For there is nothing generous which is not at the same time just. 2 Kent, Comm. 441, note *a*.

NIHIL EST MAGIS RATIONI CONSENTANEUM QUAM EODEM MODO QUODQUE DISSOLVERE QUO CONFLATUM EST. Nothing is more consonant to reason than that a thing should be dissolved or discharged in the same way in which it was created. Shep.Touch. 323.

NIHIL FACIT ERROR NOMINIS CUM DE CORPORE CONSTAT. 11 Coke, 21. An error as to a name is nothing when there is certainty as to the person.

NIHIL HABET. He has nothing. The name of a return made by a sheriff to a *scire facias* or other writ which he has been unable to serve on the defendant.

NIHIL HABET FORUM EX SCENA. The court has nothing to do with what is not before it. Bac.Max.

NIHIL IN LEGE INTOLERABILIUS EST [QUAM] EANDEM REM DIVERSO JURE CENSERI. Nothing is more intolerable in law than that the same matter, thing, or case should be subject to different views of law. Applied to the difference of opinion entertained by different courts, as to the law of a particular case. 4 Coke 93a.

NIHIL INFRA REGNUM SUBDITOS MAGIS CONSERVAT IN TRANQUILITATE ET CONCORDIA QUAM DEBITA LEGUM ADMINISTRATIO. Nothing preserves in tranquillity and concord those who are subjected to the same government better than a due administration of the laws. 2 Inst. 158.

NIHIL INIQUIUS QUAM ÆQUITATEM NIMIS INTENDERE. Nothing is more unjust than to extend equity too far. Halk. 103.

NIHIL MAGIS JUSTUM EST QUAM QUOD NECESSARIUM EST. Nothing is more just than that which is necessary. Dav.Ir.K.B. 12; Branch, Princ.

NIHIL NEQUAM EST PRÆSUMENDUM. Nothing wicked is to be presumed. 2 P.Wms. 583.

NIHIL PERFECTUM EST DUM ALIQUID RESTAT AGENDUM. Nothing is perfect while anything remains to be done. 9 Coke, 9*b*.

NIHIL PETI POTEST ANTE ID TEMPUS QUO PER RERUM NATURAM PERSOLVI POSSIT. Nothing can be demanded before the time when, by the nature of things, it can be paid. Dig. 50, 17, 186.

NIHIL POSSUMUS CONTRA VERITATEM. We can do nothing against truth. Doct. & Stud. dial. 2, c. 6.

NIHIL PRÆSCRIBITUR NISI QUOD POSSIDETUR. There is no prescription for that which is not possessed. 5 Barn. & Ald. 277.

NIHIL QUOD EST CONTRA RATIONEM EST LICITUM. Nothing that is against reason is lawful. Co.Litt. 97*b*.

NIHIL QUOD EST INCONVENIENS EST LICITUM. Nothing that is inconvenient is lawful. Co.Litt. 66*a*, 97*b*. A maxim very frequently quoted by Lord Coke, but to be taken in modern law with some qualification. Broom, Max. 186, 366.

NIHIL SIMUL INVENTUM EST ET PERFECTUM. Co.Litt. 230. Nothing is invented and perfected at the same moment.

NIHIL TAM CONVENIENS EST NATURALI ÆQUITATI QUAM UNUMQUODQUE DISSOLVI EO LIGAMINE QUO LIGATUM EST. Nothing is so consonant to natural equity as that a thing should be dissolved by the same means by which it was bound. 2 Inst. 359; Broom, Max. 877.

NIHIL TAM CONVENIENS EST NATURALI ÆQUITATI QUAM VOLUNTATEM DOMINI REM SUAM IN ALIUM TRANSFERRE RATAM HABERE. 1 Coke, 100. Nothing is so consonant to natural equity as to regard the intention of the owner in transferring his own property to another.

NIHIL TAM NATURALE EST, QUAM EO GENERE QUIDQUE DISSOLVERE, QUO COLLIGATUM EST; IDEO VERBORUM OBLIGATIO VERBIS TOLLITUR; NUDI CONSENSUS OBLIGATIO CONTRARIO CONSENSU DISSOLVITUR. Nothing is so natural as to dissolve anything in the way in which it was bound together; therefore the obligation of words is taken away by words; the obligation of mere consent is dissolved by the contrary consent. Dig. 50, 17, 35; Broom, Max. 887.

NIHIL TAM PROPRIUM IMPERIO QUAM LEGIBUS VIVERE. Nothing is so becoming to authority as to live in accordance with the laws. Fleta, lib. 1, c. 17, § 11.

NIHILIST. One advocating doctrine of nihilism. Webster. One devoted to the destruction of the present political, religious, and social institutions.

NIL. Lat. Nothing. A contracted form of *"nihil,"* which see.

NIL AGIT EXEMPLUM LITEM QUOD LITE RESOLVIT. An example does no good which settles one question by another. Hatch v. Mann, 15 Wend. (N.Y.) 44, 49.

NIL CONSENSUI TAM CONTRARIUM EST QUAM VIS ATQUE METUS. Nothing is so opposed to consent as force and fear. Dig. 50, 17, 116.

NIL DEBET. He owes nothing. The form of the general issue in all actions of debt on simple contract.

NIL FACIT ERROR NOMINIS CUM DE CORPORE VEL PERSONA CONSTAT. A mistake in the name does not matter when the body or person is manifest. 11 Coke, 21; Broom, Max. 634.

NIL HABUIT IN TENEMENTIS. He had nothing [no interest] in the tenements. A plea in debt on a lease indented, by which the defendant sets up that the person claiming to be landlord had no title or interest.

NIL LIGATUM. Nothing bound; that is, no obligation has been incurred. Tray. Lat.Max.

NIL SINE PRUDENTI FECIT RATIONE VETUSTAS. Antiquity did nothing without a good reason. Co.Litt. 65.

NIL TEMERE NOVANDUM. Nothing should be rashly changed. Jenk.Cent. 163.

NIMIA CERTITUDO CERTITUDINEM IPSAM DESTRUIT. Too great certainty destroys certainty itself. Lofft, 244.

NIMIA SUBTILITAS IN JURE REPROBATUR. Wing.Max. 26. Too much subtlety in law is discountenanced.

NIMIUM ALTERCANDO VERITAS AMITTITUR. Hob. 344. By too much altercation truth is lost.

NIMMER. A thief; a pilferer.

NISEI. Jap. Second generation. Particularly a person born in the United States of Japanese parents. 1945 Report of the Tenney Joint Fact-Finding Committee on Un-American Activities to the California Legislature; Reader's Guide to Periodical Literature. See also *Kibei.*

NISI. Lat. Unless.

The word is often affixed, as a kind of elliptical expression, to the words "rule," "order," "decree," "judgment," or "confirmation," to indicate that the adjudication spoken of is one which is to stand as valid and operative *unless* the party affected by it shall appear and show cause against it, or take some other appropriate step to avoid it or procure its revocation. Thus a "decree *nisi*" is one which will definitely conclude the defendant's rights unless, within the prescribed time, he shows cause to set it aside or successfully appeals. The word, in this sense, is opposed to "absolute." And when a rule *nisi* is finally confirmed, for the defendant's failure to show cause against it, it is said to be "made absolute."

NISI FECERIS. The name of a clause commonly occurring in the old manorial writs, commanding that, if the lords failed to do justice, the king's court or officer should do it. By virtue of this clause, the king's court usurped the jurisdiction of the private, manorial, or local courts. Stim. Law Gloss.

NISI PRIUS. The *nisi prius* courts are such as are held for the trial of issues of fact before a jury and one presiding judge. In America the phrase is familiarly used to denote the forum (whatever may be its statutory name) in which the cause was tried to a jury, as distinguished from the appellate court. See 3 Bl.Comm. 58.

NISI PRIUS CLAUSE. In practice, a clause entered on the record in an action at law, authorizing the trial of the cause at *nisi prius* in the particular county designated. It was first used by way of continuance.

NISI PRIUS ROLL. In practice, the roll or record containing the pleadings, issue, and jury process of an action, made up for use in the *nisi prius* court.

NISI PRIUS WRIT. The old name of the writ of *venire*, which originally, in pursuance of the statute of Westminster 2, contained the *nisi prius* clause. Reg.Jud. 28, 75. Cowell.

NIVICOLLINI BRITONES. In old English law, Welshmen, because they live near high mountains covered with snow. Du Cange.

NO ARRIVAL NO SALE. If goods do not arrive at destination buyer acquires no property therein and does not become liable for price. Cundill v. A. W. Millhauser Corporation, 257 N.Y. 416, 178 N.E. 680, 681.

NO AWARD. The name of a plea in an action on an award, by which the defendant traverses the allegation that an award was made.

NO BILL. This phrase, when indorsed by a grand jury on an indictment, is equivalent to "not found," "not a true bill," or "*ignoramus.*"

NO FUNDS. See Fund.

NO GOODS. This is the English equivalent of the Latin term "*nulla bona,*" being the form of the return made by a sheriff or constable, charged with an execution, when he has found no property of the debtor on which to levy.

NO MAN CAN HOLD THE SAME LAND IMMEDIATELY OF TWO SEVERAL LANDLORDS. Co.Litt. 152.

NO MAN IS PRESUMED TO DO ANYTHING AGAINST NATURE. 22 Vin.Abr. 154.

NO MAN MAY BE JUDGE IN HIS OWN CAUSE.

NO MAN SHALL SET UP HIS INFAMY AS A DEFENSE. 2 W.Bl. 364.

NO MAN SHALL TAKE ADVANTAGE OF HIS OWN WRONG. Lightbody v. Russell, Sup., 45 N.Y.S.2d 15, 17.

NO MAN SHALL TAKE BY DEED BUT PARTIES, UNLESS IN REMAINDER.

NO ONE CAN GRANT OR CONVEY WHAT HE DOES NOT OWN. Seymour v. Canandaigua & N. F. R. Co., 25 Barb., N.Y., 284, 301; Saltus v. Everett, 20 Wend., N.Y., 267, 32 Am.Dec. 541.

NO ONE WILL BE PERMITTED TO TAKE THE BENEFIT UNDER A WILL AND AT THE SAME TIME DEFEAT ITS PROVISIONS. 25 Wash.L. Rep. 50.

NO RECOURSE. No access to; no return; no coming back upon; no assumption of any liability whatsoever; no looking to the party using the term for any reimbursement in case of loss or damage or failure of consideration in that which was the cause, the motive, the object, of the undertaking or contract. Guardian Homestead Ass'n v. Mazerat, 182 La. 710, 162 So. 574.

NOBILE OFFICIUM. In Scotch law, an equitable power of the court of session, to give relief when none is possible at law. Ersk.Inst. 1, 3, 22; Bell.

NOBILES MAGIS PLECTUNTUR PECUNIA; PLEBES VERO IN CORPORE. 3 Inst. 220. The higher classes are more punished in money; but the lower in person.

NOBILES SUNT, QUI ARMA GENTILITIA ANTECESSORUM SUORUM PROFERRE POSSUNT. 2 Inst. 595. The gentry are those who are able to produce armorial bearings derived by descent from their own ancestors.

NOBILIORES ET BENIGNIORES PRÆSUMPTIONES IN DUBIIS SUNT PRÆFERENDÆ. In cases of doubt, the more generous and more benign presumptions are to be preferred. A civil-law maxim.

NOBILITAS EST DUPLEX, SUPERIOR ET INFERIOR. 2 Inst. 583. There are two sorts of nobility, the higher and the lower.

NOBILITY. In English law, a division of the people, comprehending dukes, marquises, earls, viscounts, and barons.

These had anciently duties annexed to their respective honors. They are created either by writ, *i. e.*, by royal summons to attend the house of peers, or by letters patent, *i. e.*, by royal grant of any dignity and degree of peerage; and they enjoy many privileges, exclusive of their senatorial capacity. 1 Bl.Comm. 396.

NOCENT. From Latin *"nocere,"* guilty. "The *nocent* person." 1 Vern. 429.

NOCTANTER. By night; an abolished writ which issued out of chancery, and returned to the queen's bench, for the prostration of inclosures, etc.

NOCTES and NOCTEM DE FIRMA. Entertainment of meat and drink for so many nights. Domesday.

NOCUMENTUM. Lat. In old English law, a nuisance. *Nocumentum damnosum,* a nuisance occasioning loss or damage. *Nocumentum injuriosum,* an injurious nuisance. For the latter only a remedy was given. Bract. fol. 221.

NOLENS VOLENS. Lat. Whether willing or unwilling; consenting or not.

NOLIS. Fr. In French law, freight. The same with *"fret."* Ord. Mar. liv. 3, tit. 3.

NOLISSEMENT. Fr. In French marine law, affreightment. Ord. Mar. liv. 3, tit. 1.

NOLLE PROSEQUI. Lat. In practice, a formal entry upon the record, by the plaintiff in a civil suit (Hewitt v. International Shoe Co., 110 Fla. 37, 148 So. 533, 536), or the prosecuting officer in a criminal action, (Commonwealth v. Shields, 89 Pa. Super. 266, 268) by which he declares that he "will no further prosecute" the case, either as to some of the counts, or some of the defendants, or altogether. State v. Primm, 61 Mo. 171; Com. v. Casey, 12 Allen, Mass., 214; Scheibler v. Steinburg, 129 Tenn. 614, 167 S.W. 866, Ann.Cas.1915D, 1162.

A *nolle prosequi* is in the nature of an acknowledgment or undertaking by the plaintiff in an action to forbear to proceed any further either in the action altogether, or as to some part of it, or as to some of the defendants; and is different from a *non pros.*, by which the plaintiff is put out of court with respect to all the defendants. Brown.

NOLO CONTENDERE. Lat. I will not contest it. The name of a plea in a criminal action, having the same legal effect as a plea of guilty, so far as regards all proceedings on the indictment, and on which the defendant may be sentenced. U. S. v. Hartwell, 3 Cliff. 221, F.Cas.No.15,318.

Like a demurrer this plea admits, for the purposes of the case, all the facts which are well pleaded, but is not to be used as an admission elsewhere. Com. v. Tilton, 8 Metc., Mass., 232. Not available as an estoppel in a civil action. Com. v. Horton, 9 Pick., Mass., 206; Olszewski v. Goldberg, 223 Mass. 27, 111 N.E. 404; Hudson v. U. S., 272 U.S. 451, 47 S.Ct. 127, 129, 71 L.Ed. 347.

See, also, Plea.

NOMEN. Lat. In the civil law, a name; the name, style, or designation of a person. Properly, the name showing to what *gens* or tribe he belonged, as distinguished from his own individual name, (*the prœnomen,*) from his surname or family name, (*cognomen,*) and from any name added by way of a descriptive title, (*agnomen.*) The name or style of a class or genus of persons or objects. A debt or a debtor. Ainsworth; Calvin.

NOMEN COLLECTIVUM. A collective name or term; a term expressive of a class; a term including several of the same kind; a term expressive of the plural, as well as singular, number.

NOMEN EST QUASI REI NOTAMEN. A name is, as it were, the note of a thing. 11 Coke, 20.

NOMEN GENERALE. A general name; the name of a *genus.* Fleta, lib. 4, c. 19, § 1.

NOMEN GENERALISSIMUM. A name of the most general kind; a name or term of the most general meaning. By the name of "land," which is *nomen generalissimum,* everything terrestrial will pass. 2 Bl.Comm. 19; 3 Bl.Comm. 172.

NOMEN JURIS. A name of the law; a technical legal term.

NOMEN NON SUFFICIT, SI RES NON SIT DE JURE AUT DE FACTO. A name is not sufficient if there be not a thing [or subject for it] *de jure* or *de facto.* 4 Coke, 107*b*.

NOMEN TRANSCRIPTITIUM. See Nomina Transcriptitia.

NOMINA MUTABILIA SUNT, RES AUTEM IMMOBILES. Names are mutable, but things are immovable, [immutable.] A name may be true or false, or may change, but the thing itself always maintains its identity. 6 Coke, 66.

NOMINA SI NESCIS PERIT COGNITIO RERUM; ET NOMINA SI PERDAS, CERTE DISTINCTIO RERUM PERDITUR. Co.Litt. 86. If you know not the names of things, the knowledge of things themselves perishes; and, if you lose the names, the distinction of the things is certainly lost.

NOMINA SUNT NOTÆ RERUM. 11 Coke, 20. Names are the notes of things.

NOMINA SUNT SYMBOLA RERUM. Godb. Names are the symbols of things.

NOMINA TRANSCRIPTITIA. In Roman law, obligations contracted by *literæ* (*i. e., literis obligationes*) were so called because they arose from a peculiar *transfer* (*transcriptio*) from the creditor's day-book (*adversaria*) into his ledger, (*codex.*)

NOMINA VILLARUM. In English law, an account of the names of all the villages and the possessors thereof, in each county, drawn up by several sheriffs, (9 Edw. II.,) and returned by them into the exchequer, where it is still preserved. Wharton.

NOMINAL. Titular; existing in name only; not real or substantial; connected with the transaction or proceeding in name only, not in interest. Park Amusement Co. v. McCaughn, D.C.Pa., 14 F.2d 553, 556; not real or actual; merely named, stated, or given, without reference to actual conditions; often with the implication that the thing named is so small, slight, or the like, in comparison to what might properly be expected, as scarcely to be entitled to the name; a nominal price. Lehman v. Tait, C.C.A.Md., 58 F.2d 20, 23.

NOMINAL CAPITAL. Very small or negligible capital, whose use in particular business is incidental. Strayer's Business College v. Commissioner of Internal Revenue, C.C.A.4, 35 F.2d 426, 429. Capital in name only and which is not substantial; not real or actual; merely named, stated, or given, without reference to actual conditions. Feeders' Supply Co. v. Commissioner of Internal Revenue, C.C.A.8, 31 F.2d 274, 276.

NOMINAL CONSIDERATION. See Consideration.

NOMINAL DAMAGES. See Damages.

NOMINAL DEFENDANT. A person who is joined as defendant in an action, not because he is immediately liable in damages or because any specific relief is demanded as against him, but because his connection with the subject-matter is such that the plaintiff's action would be defective, under the technical rules of practice, if he were not joined.

NOMINAL PARTNER. A person who appears to be a partner in a firm, or is so represented to persons dealing with the firm, or who allows his name to appear in the style of the firm or to be used in its business, in the character of a partner, but who has no actual interest in the firm or business. Story, Partn. § 80.

NOMINAL PARTY. Those who are joined as parties or defendants merely because the technical rules of pleading require their presence in the record. Yellow Cab & Baggage Co. v. Smith, Tex.Civ. App., 30 S.W.2d 697, 702. Those having no interest in immediate controversy, but having interest in subject-matter which may be conveniently settled in suit. Medico v. Employers' Liability Assur. Corporation, 132 Me. 422, 172 A. 1, 3.

NOMINAL PLAINTIFF. One who has no interest in the subject-matter of the action, having assigned the same to another, (the real plaintiff in interest, or "use plaintiff,") but who must be joined as plaintiff, because, under technical rules of practice, the suit cannot be brought directly in the name of the assignee.

NOMINATE. To name, designate by name, or appoint. Wilson v. Stump, 310 Mass. 614, 39 N.E.2d 416, 418; to name, designate, or propose for election or appointment. State ex rel. Pittman v. Barker, 113 Fla. 865, 152 So. 682, 683, 94 A.L.R. 1481, for an office, a privilege, a living, etc.

NOMINATE CONTRACTS. In the civil law, contracts having a proper or peculiar name and form, and which were divided into four kinds, expressive of the ways in which they were formed, viz.: (1) Real, which arose *ex re,* from something done; (2) verbal, *ex verbis,* from something said; (3) literal, *ex literis,* from something written; and (4) consensual, *ex consensu,* from something agreed to. Calvin.

NOMINATIM. Lat. By name; expressed one by one.

NOMINATING AND REDUCING. A mode of obtaining a panel of special jurors in England, from which to select the jury to try a particular action.

The proceeding takes place before the under-sheriff or secondary, and in the presence of the parties' solicitors. Numbers denoting the persons on the sheriff's list are put into a box and drawn until forty-eight unchallenged persons have been nominated. Each party strikes off twelve, and the remaining twenty-four are returned as the "panel," (*q. v.*). This practice is now only employed by order of the court or judge. (Sm.Ac. 130; Juries Act 1870, § 17.) Sweet.

NOMINATIO AUCTORIS. Lat. In Roman law, a form of plea or defense in an action for the recovery of real estate, by which the defendant, sued as the person apparently in possession, alleges that he holds only in the name or for the benefit of another, whose name he discloses by the plea, in order that the plaintiff may bring his action against such other. Mackeld. Rom.Law, § 297.

NOMINATION. An appointment or designation of a person to fill an office or discharge a duty. The act of suggesting or proposing a person by name as a candidate for an office.

NOMINATION PAPER. A paper used for selection of candidates by a political body which is not a political party and is not entitled to use a "nomination petition". Commonwealth v. Antico, 146 Pa.Super. 293, 22 A.2d 204, 209.

NOMINATION TO A LIVING. In English ecclesiastical law, the rights of nominating and of presenting to a living are distinct, and may reside in different persons. Presentation is the offering a clerk to the bishop. Nomination is the offering a clerk to the person who has the right of presentation. Brown.

NOMINATIVUS PENDENS. Lat. A nominative case grammatically unconnected with the rest of the sentence in which it stands. The opening words in the ordinary form of a deed *inter partes*, "This indenture," etc., down to "whereas," though an intelligible and convenient part of the deed, are of this kind. Wharton.

NOMINE. Lat. By name; by the name of; under the name or designation of.

NOMINE PŒNÆ. In the name of a penalty.

In the civil law, a legacy was said to be left *nomine pœnæ* where it was left for the purpose of coercing the heir to do or not to do something. Inst. 2, 20, 36.

The term has also been applied, in English law, to some kinds of covenants, such as a covenant inserted in a lease that the lessee shall forfeit a certain sum on non-payment of rent, or on doing certain things, as plowing up ancient meadow, and the like. 1 Crabb, Real Prop. p. 171, § 155.

NOMINEE. One who has been nominated or proposed for an office.

One designated to act for another as his representative in a rather limited sense. It is used sometimes to signify an agent or trustee. It has no connotation, however, other than that of acting for another, in representation of another, or as the grantee of another. Schuh Trading Co. v. Commissioner of Internal Revenue, C.C.A.7, 95 F.2d 404, 411.

NOMOCANON. (1) A collection of canons and imperial laws relative or conformable thereto. The first nomocanon was made by Johannes Scholasticus in 554. Photius, patriarch of Constantinople, in 883, compiled another nomocanon, or collation of the civil laws with the canons; this is the most celebrated. Balsamon wrote a commentary upon it in 1180. (2) A collection of the ancient canons of the apostles, councils, and fathers, without regard to imperial constitutions. Such is the nomocanon by M. Cotelier. Enc. Lond.

NOMOGRAPHER. One who writes on the subject of laws.

NOMOGRAPHY. A treatise or description of laws.

NOMOTHETA. A lawgiver; such as Solon and Lycurgus among the Greeks, and Cæsar, Pompey, and Sylla among the Romans. Calvin.

NON. Lat. Not. The common prefix of negation. Geronime v. German Roman Catholic Aid Ass'n of America, 127 Minn. 247, 149 N.W. 291, 292.

NON ACCEPTAVIT. In pleading, the name of a plea to an action of *assumpsit* brought against the drawee of a bill of exchange by which he denies that he *accepted* the same.

NON ACCIPI DEBENT VERBA IN DEMONSTRATIONEM FALSAM, QUÆ COMPETUNT IN LIMITATIONEM VERAM. Words ought not to be taken to import a false demonstration which may have effect by way of true limitation. Bac.Max. p. 59, reg. 13; Broom, Max. 642.

NON ACCREVIT INFRA SEX ANNOS. It did not accrue within six years. The name of a plea by which the defendant sets up the statute of limitations against a cause of action which is barred after six years.

NON ALIO MODO PUNIATUR ALIQUIS QUAM SECUNDUM QUOD SE HABET CONDEMNATIO. 3 Inst. 217. A person may not be punished differently than according to what the sentence enjoins.

NON ALITER A SIGNIFICATIONE VERBORUM RECEDI OPORTET QUAM CUM MANIFESTUM EST, ALIUD SENSISSE TESTATOREM. We must never depart from the signification of words, unless it is evident that they are not conformable to the will of the testator. Dig. 32, 69, pr.; Broom, Max. 568.

NON ASSUMPSIT. The general issue in the action of *assumpsit*; being a plea by which the defendant avers that "he did not undertake" or promise as alleged. Standard Fashion Co. v. Morgan, 48 Okl. 217, 149 P. 1160.

NON ASSUMPSIT INFRA SEX ANNOS. He did not undertake within six years. The name of the plea of the statute of limitations, in the action of *assumpsit*.

NON AUDITUR PERIRE VOLENS. He who is desirous to perish is not heard. Best, Ev. 423, § 385. He who confesses himself guilty of a crime, with the view of meeting death, will not be heard. A maxim of the foreign law of evidence. Id.

NON BIS IN IDEM. Not twice for the same; that is, a man shall not be twice tried for the same crime. This maxim of the civil law (Code 9, 2, 9, 11) expresses the same principle as the familiar rule of our law that a man shall not be twice "put in jeopardy" for the same offense.

NON CEPIT. He did not take. The general issue in replevin, where the action is for the wrongful *taking* of the property; putting in issue not only the taking, but the *place* in which the taking is stated to have been made. Steph.Pl. 157, 167.

NON COMPOS MENTIS. Lat. Not sound of mind; insane. This is a very general term, embracing all varieties of mental derangement. See Insanity.

Coke has enumerated four different classes of persons who are deemed in law to be *non compotes mentis: First*, an idiot, or fool natural; *second*, he who was of good and sound mind and memory, but by the act of God has lost it; *third*, a lunatic, *lunaticus qui gaudet lucidis intervallis*, who sometimes is of good sound mind and memory, and sometimes *non compos mentis; fourth*, one who is *non compos mentis* by his own act, as a drunkard, Co.Litt. 247*a*; 4 Coke, 124.

NON CONCEDANTUR CITATIONES PRIUSQUAM EXPRIMATUR SUPER QUA RE FIERI DEBET CITATIO. 12 Coke, 47. Summonses should not be granted before it is expressed on what matter the summons ought to be made.

NON CONCESSIT. Lat. He did not grant. The name of a plea denying a grant, which could be made only by a stranger.

NON CONSENTIT QUI ERRAT. Bract. fol. 44. He who mistakes does not consent.

NON CONSTAT. Lat. It does not appear; it is not clear or evident. A phrase used in general to state some conclusion as not necessarily following although it may appear on its face to follow.

NON CULPABILIS. Lat. In pleading, not guilty. It is usually abbreviated "*non cul.*"

NON DAMNIFICATUS. Lat. Not injured.

This is a plea in an action of debt on an indemnity bond, or bond conditioned "to keep the plaintiff harmless and indemnified," etc. It is in the nature of a plea of performance, being used where the defendant means to allege that the plaintiff has been kept harmless and indemnified, according to the tenor of the condition. Steph.Pl., 7th Ed., 300, 301. State Bank v. Chetwood, 8 N.J.L. 25.

NON DAT QUI NON HABET. He who has not does not give. Lofft, 258; Broom, Max. 467.

NON DEBEO MELIORIS CONDITIONIS ESSE, QUAM AUCTOR MEUS A QUO JUS IN ME TRANSIT. I ought not to be in better condition than he to whose rights I succeed. Dig. 50, 17, 175, 1.

NON DEBERET ALII NOCERE QUOD INTER ALIOS ACTUM ESSET. No one ought to be injured by that which has taken place between other parties. Dig. 12, 2, 10.

NON DEBET ACTORI LICERE QUOD REO NON PERMITTITUR. A plaintiff ought not to be allowed what is not permitted to a defendant. A rule of the civil law. Dig. 50, 17, 41.

NON DEBET ADDUCI EXCEPTIO EJUS REI CUJUS PETITUR DISSOLUTIO. A plea of the same matter the dissolution of which is sought [by the action] ought not to be brought forward. Broom, Max. 166.

NON DEBET ALII NOCERE, QUOD INTER ALIOS ACTUM EST. A person ought not to be prejudiced by what has been done between others. Dig. 12, 2, 10.

NON DEBET ALTERI PER ALTERUM INIQUA CONDITIO INFERRI. A burdensome condition ought not to be brought upon one man by the act of another. Dig. 50, 17, 74.

NON DEBET CUI PLUS LICET, QUOD MINUS EST NON LICERE. He to whom the greater is lawful ought not to be debarred from the less as unlawful. Dig. 50, 17, 21; Broom, Max. 176.

NON DEBET DICI TENDERE IN PRÆJUDICIUM ECCLESIASTICÆ LIBERATATIS QUOD PRO REGE ET REPUBLICA NECESSARIUM VIDETUR. 2 Inst. 625. That which seems necessary for the king and the state ought not to be said to tend to the prejudice of spiritual liberty.

NON DECET HOMINES DEDERE CAUSA NON COGNITA. It is unbecoming to surrender men when no cause is shown. In re Washburn, 4 Johns.Ch., N.Y., 106, 114, 8 Am.Dec. 548; Id., 3 Wheeler, Cr.Cas., N.Y., 473, 482.

NON DECIMANDO. See De Non Decimando.

NON DECIPITUR QUI SCIT SE DECIPI. 5 Coke, 60. He is not deceived who knows himself to be deceived.

NON DEDIT. Lat. In pleading, he did not grant. The general issue in formedon.

NON DEFINITUR IN JURE QUID SIT CONATUS. What an attempt is, is not defined in law. 6 Co. 43. See Attempt.

NON DEMISIT. Lat. He did not demise.

A plea proper to be pleaded to an action of debt for rent, when the plaintiff declares on a parol lease. Gilb.Debt 436; Bull.N.P. 177; 1 Chitty, Pl. 477. A plea in bar, in replevin, to an avowry for arrears of rent, that the avowant did not demise. Morris, Repl. 179. It cannot be pleaded when the demise is stated to have been by indenture. 12 Viner, Abr. 178; Com.Dig. *Pleader* (2 W 48).

NON DETINET. Lat. He does not detain.

The name of the general issue in the action of detinue. 1 Tidd, Pr. 645; Berlin Mach. Works v. Alabama City Furniture Co., 112 Ala. 488, 20 So. 418.

The general issue in the action of replevin, where the action is for the wrongful detention only. 2 Burrill, Pr. 14.

NON DIFFERUNT QUÆ CONCORDANT RE, TAMETSI NON IN VERBIS IISDEM. Those things do not differ which agree in substance, though not in the same words. Jenk.Cent. p. 70, case 32.

NON DIMISIT. L. Lat. He did not demise.

A plea resorted to where a plaintiff declared upon a demise without stating the indenture in an action of debt for rent. Also, a plea in bar, in replevin, to an avowry for arrears of rent, that the avowant did not demise.

NON DISTRINGENDO. A writ not to distrain.

NON DUBITATUR, ETSI SPECIALITER VENDITOR EVICTIONEM NON PROMISERIT, RE EVICTA, EX EMPTO COMPETERE ACTIONEM. It is certain that, although the vendor has not given a special guaranty, an action *ex empto* lies against him, if the purchaser is evicted. Code, 8, 45, 6; Broom, Max. 768.

NON EFFICIT AFFECTUS NISI SEQUATUR EFFECTUS. The intention amounts to nothing unless the effect follow. 1 Rolle, 226.

NON ERIT ALIA LEX ROMÆ, ALIA ATHÆNIS; ALIA NUNC, ALIA POSTHAC; SED ET OMNES GENTES, ET OMNI TEMPORE, UNA LEX, ET SEMPITERNA, ET IMMORTALIS CONTINEBIT. There will not be one law at Rome, another at

Athens; one law now, another hereafter; but one eternal and immortal law shall bind together all nations throughout all time. Cic.Frag. de Repub. lib. 3; 3 Kent, Comm. 1.

NON EST ARCTIUS VINCULUM INTER HOMINES QUAM JUSJURANDUM. There is no closer [or firmer] bond between men than an oath. Jenk.Cent. p. 126, case 54.

NON EST CERTANDUM DE REGULIS JURIS. There is no disputing about rules of law.

NON EST CONSONUM RATIONI, QUOD COGNITIO ACCESSORII IN CURIA CHRISTIANITATIS IMPEDIATUR, UBI COGNITIO CAUSÆ PRINCIPALIS AD FORUM ECCLESIASTICUM NOSCITUR PERTINERE. 12 Coke, 65. It is unreasonable that the cognizance of an accessory matter should be impeded in an ecclesiastical court, when the cognizance of the principal cause is admitted to appertain to an ecclesiastical court.

NON EST DISPUTANDUM CONTRA PRINCIPIA NEGANTEM. Co. Litt. 343. We cannot dispute against a man who denies first principles.

NON EST FACTUM. Lat. A plea denying execution of instrument sued on, Blair v. Lockwood, 226 Ky. 412, 11 S.W.2d 107, 109.

A plea by way of traverse, which occurs in debt on bond or other specialty, and also in covenant. It denies that the deed mentioned in the declaration is the defendant's deed Under this, the defendant may contend at the trial that the deed was never executed in point of fact; but he cannot deny its validity in point of law. Wharton; Haggart v. Morgan, 5 N.Y. 422, 55 Am.Dec. 350; Evans v. Southern Turnpike Co., 18 Ind. 101.

The plea of *non est factum* is a denial of the execution of the instrument sued upon, and applies to notes or other instruments, as well as deeds, and applies only when the execution of the instrument is alleged to be the act of the party filing the plea, or adopted by him. Code Ga.1882, § 3472 (Civ.Code 1910, § 5676).

Special Non Est Factum. A form of the plea of *non est factum,* in debt on a specialty, by which the defendant alleges that, although he executed the deed, yet it is in law "not his deed," because of certain special circumstances which he proceeds to set out: as, where he delivered the deed as an escrow, and it was turned over to the plaintiff prematurely or without performance of the condition.

NON EST INVENTUS. Lat. He is not found. The sheriff's return to process requiring him to arrest the body of the defendant, when the latter is not found within his jurisdiction. It is often abbreviated, "*n. e. i.*," or written, in English, "not found." The Bremena v. Card, D.C.Wash., 38 F. 144.

NON EST JUSTUM ALIQUEM ANTENATUM POST MORTEM FACERE BASTARDUM QUI TOTO TEMPORE VITÆ SUÆ PRO LEGITIMO HABEBATUR. It is not just to make an elder-born a bastard after his death, who during his lifetime was accounted legitimate. 12 Coke, 44.

NON EST NOVUM UT PRIORES LEGES AD POSTERIORES TRAHANTUR. It is no new thing that prior statutes should give place to later ones. Dig. 1, 3, 36; Broom, Max. 28.

NON EST RECEDENDUM A COMMUNI OBSERVANTIA. There should be no departure from a common observance. 2 Co. 74.

NON EST REGULA QUIN FALLET. There is no rule but what may fail. Off.Exec. 212.

NON EST REUS NISI MENS SIT REA. One is not guilty unless his intention be guilty. Chisholm v. Chisholm, 105 Fla. 402, 141 So. 302, 303. This maxim is much criticised. See *actus non reum facit,* etc.; Mens Rea.

NON EST SINGULIS CONCEDENDUM, QUOD PER MAGISTRATUM PUBLICE POSSIT FIERI, NE OCCASIO SIT MAJORIS TUMULTUS FACIENDI. That is not to be conceded to private persons which can be publicly done by the magistrate, lest it be the occasion of greater tumults. Dig. 50, 17, 176.

NON EX OPINIONIBUS SINGULORUM, SED EX COMMUNI USI, NOMINA EXAUDIRI DEBENT. The names of things ought to be understood, not according to the opinions of individuals, but according to common usage. Dig. 33, 10, 7, 2.

NON EXEMPLIS SED LEGIBUS JUDICANDUM EST. Not by the facts of the case, but by the law must judgment be made. Dig. 7, 45, 13. (called by Albericus Gentilis *lex aurea*).

NON FACIAS MALUM, UT INDE FIAT BONUM. You are not to do evil, that good may be or result therefrom. 11 Coke, 74*a*; 5 Coke, 30*b*.

NON FECIT. Lat. He did not make it. A plea in an action of *assumpsit* on a promissory note. 3 Man. & G. 446.

NON FECIT VASTUM CONTRA PROHIBITIONEM. He did not commit waste against the prohibition. A plea to an action founded on a writ of estrepement for waste. 3 Bl.Comm. 226, 227.

NON HÆC IN FŒDERA VENI. I did not agree to these terms.

NON IMPEDIT CLAUSULA DEROGATORIA QUO MINUS AD EADEM POTESTATE RES DISSOLVANTUR A QUA CONSTITUUNTUR. A derogatory clause does not impede things from being dissolved by the same power by which they are created. Broom, Max. 27.

NON IMPEDIVIT. Lat. He did not impede. The plea of the general issue in *quare impedit.* The Latin form of the law French "*ne disturba pas.*"

NON IMPLACITANDO ALIQUEM DE LIBERO TENEMENTO SINE BREVI. A writ to prohibit bailiffs, etc., from distraining or impleading any man touching his freehold without the king's writ. Reg. Orig. 171.

NON IN LEGENDO SED IN INTELLIGENDO LEGIS CONSISTUNT. The laws consist not in being read, but in being understood. 8 Coke, 167*a*.

NON INFREGIT CONVENTIONEM. Lat. He did not break the contract. The name of a plea sometimes pleaded in the action of covenant, and intended as a general issue, but held to be a bad plea; there being, properly speaking, no general issue in that action. 1 Tidd, Pr. 356.

NON INTERFUI. I was not present. A reporter's note. T.Jones, 10.

NON INTROMITTANT CLAUSE. In English law, a clause of a charter of a municipal borough, whereby the borough is exempted from the jurisdiction of the justices of the peace for the county.

NON INTROMITTENDO, QUANDO BREVE PRÆCIPE IN CAPITE SUBDOLE IMPETRATUR. A writ addressed to the justices of the bench, or in eyre, commanding them not to give one, who, under color of entitling the king to land, etc., as holding of him *in capite,* had deceitfully obtained the writ called *"præcipe in capite,"* any benefit thereof, but to put him to his writ of right. Reg. Orig. 4.

NON JURIDICUS. Not judicial; not legal. *Dies non juridicus* is a day on which legal proceedings cannot be had.

NON JUS EX REGULA, SED REGULA EX JURE. The law does not arise from the rule (or maxim,) but the rule from the law. Tray.Lat.Max. 384.

NON JUS, SED SEISINA, FACIT STIPITEM. Not right, but seisin, makes a stock. Fleta, lib. 6, c. 2, § 2. It is not a mere *right* to enter on lands, but actual *seisin,* which makes a person the root or *stock* from which all future inheritance by right of blood must be derived. 2 Bl.Comm. 209, 312. See Broom, Max. 525, 527.

NON LICET QUOD DISPENDIO LICET. That which may be [done only] at a loss is not allowed [to be done.] The law does not permit or require the doing of an act which will result only in loss. The law forbids such recoveries whose ends are vain, changeable, and unprofitable. Co.Litt. 127*b*.

NON LIQUET. Lat. It is not clear.

In the Roman courts, when any of the judges, after the hearing of a cause, were not satisfied that the case was made clear enough for them to pronounce a verdict, they were privileged to signify this opinion by casting a ballot inscribed with the letters "N. L.," the abbreviated form of the phrase *"non liquet."*

NON MERCHANDIZANDA VICTUALIA. An ancient writ addressed to justices of assize, to inquire whether the magistrates of a town sold victuals in gross or by retail during the time of their being in office, which was contrary to an obsolete statute; and to punish them if they did. Reg. Orig. 184.

NON MOLESTANDO. A writ that lay for a person who was molested contrary to the king's protection granted to him. Reg.Orig. 184.

NON NASCI, ET NATUM MORI, PARIA SUNT. Not to be born, and to be dead-born, are the same.

NON OBLIGAT LEX NISI PROMULGATA. A law is not obligatory unless it be promulgated.

NON OBSERVATA FORMA, INFERTUR ADNULLATIO ACTUS. Where form is not observed, an annulling of the act is inferred or follows. 12 Coke, 7.

NON OBSTANTE. Lat. Notwithstanding.

Words anciently used in public and private instruments, intended to preclude, in advance, any interpretation contrary to certain declared objects or purposes. Burrill.

A clause frequent in old English statutes and letters patent, (so termed from its initial words,) importing a license from the crown to do a thing which otherwise a person would be restrained by act of parliament from doing. Crabb, Com.Law, 570; Plowd. 501; Cowell.

A power in the crown to dispense with the laws in any particular case. This was abolished by the bill of rights at the Revolution. 1 Bl.Comm. 342.

NON OBSTANTE VEREDICTO. Notwithstanding the verdict. A judgment entered by order of court for the plaintiff, although there has been a verdict for the defendant, is so called. German Ins. Co. v. Frederick, Kan., 58 F. 144, 7 C.C.A. 122; Wentworth v. Wentworth, 2 Minn. 282, Gil. 238, 72 Am.Dec. 97

Judgment *non obstante veredicto* originally, at common law, was a judgment entered for plaintiff "notwithstanding the verdict" for defendant; which could be done only, after verdict and before judgment, where it appeared that defendant's plea confessed the cause of action and set up matters in avoidance which, although verified by the verdict, were insufficient to constitute a defense or bar to the action. But either by statutory enactment or because of relaxation of the early common-law rule, the generally prevailing rule now is that either plaintiff or defendant may have a judgment *non obstante veredicto* in proper cases. 49 C.J.S.Judgments § 60.

Judgment *non obstante veredicto* in its broadest sense is a judgment rendered in favor of one party notwithstanding the finding of a verdict in favor of the other party, 49 C.J.S.Judgments § 59.

NON OFFICIT CONATUS NISI SEQUATUR EFFECTUS. An attempt does not harm unless a consequence follow. 11 Coke, 98.

NON OMITTAS. A clause usually inserted in writs of execution, in England, directing the sheriff "not to omit" to execute the writ by reason of any liberty, because there are many liberties or districts in which the sheriff has no power to execute process unless he has special authority. 2 Steph.Comm. 630.

NON OMNE DAMNUM INDUCIT INJURIAM. It is not every loss that produces an injury. Bract. fol. 45*b*.

NON OMNE QUOD LICET HONESTUM EST. It is not everything which is permitted that is honorable. Dig. 50, 17, 144; Howell v. Baker, 4 Johns. Ch., N.Y., 121.

NON OMNIUM QUÆ A MAJORIBUS NOSTRIS CONSTITUTA SUNT RATIO REDDI POTEST. There cannot be given a reason for all the things which have been established by our ancestors. Branch, Princ.; 4 Coke, 78; Broom, Max. 157.

NON PERTINET AD JUDICEM SECULAREM COGNOSCERE DE IIS QUÆ SUNT MERE SPIRITUALIA ANNEXA. 2 Inst. 488. It belongs not to the secular judge to take cognizance of things which are merely spiritual.

NON PLEVIN. In old English law, default in not replevying land in due time, when the same was taken by the king upon a default. The consequence thereof (loss of seisin) was abrogated by St. 9 Edw. III. c. 2.

NON PONENDIS IN ASSISIS ET JURATIS. A writ formerly granted for freeing and discharging persons from serving on assizes and juries. Fitzh.Nat.Brev. 165.

NON POSSESSORI INCUMBIT NECESSITAS PROBANDI POSSESSIONES AD SE PERTINERE. A person in possession is not bound to prove that the possessions belong to him. Broom, Max. 714.

NON POTEST ADDUCI EXCEPTIO EJUS REI CUJUS PETITUR DISSOLUTIO. An exception of the same thing whose avoidance is sought cannot be made. Broom, Max. 166.

NON POTEST PROBARI QUOD PROBATUM NON RELEVAT. 1 Exch. 91, 92. That cannot be proved which, if proved, is immaterial.

NON POTEST QUIS SINE BREVI AGERE. No one can sue without a writ. Fleta, lib. 2, c. 13, § 4. A fundamental rule of old practice.

NON POTEST REX GRATIAM FACERE CUM INJURIA ET DAMNO ALIORUM. The king cannot confer a favor on one subject which occasions injury and loss to others. 3 Inst. 236; Broom, Max. 63.

NON POTEST REX SUBDITUM RENITENTEM ONERARE IMPOSITIONIBUS. The king cannot load a subject with imposition against his consent. 2 Inst. 61.

NON POTEST VIDERI DESISSE HABERA QUI NUNQUAM HABUIT. He cannot be considered as having ceased to have a thing who never had it Dig. 50, 17, 208.

NON PRÆSTAT IMPEDIMENTUM QUOD DE JURE NON SORTITUR EFFECTUM. A thing which has no effect in law is not an impediment. Jenk.Cent. 162; Wing.Max. 727.

NON PROCEDENDO AD ASSISSAM REGE INCONSULTO. A writ to put a stop to the trial of a cause appertaining unto one who is in the king's service, etc., until the king's pleasure respecting the same be known. Cowell.

NON PROS. Abbreviation of non prosequitur. Bucci v. Detroit Fire & Marine Ins. Co., 109 Pa. Super. 167, 167 A. 425, 427. At common law, a judgment entered at instance of defendant when plaintiff at any stage of proceedings fails to prosecute his action, or any part of it, in due time. Steele v. Beaty, 215 N.C. 680, 2 S.E.2d 854, 856.

NON PROSEQUITUR. Lat. He does not follow up, or pursue.

If, in the proceedings in an action at law, the plaintiff neglects to take any of those steps which he ought to take within the time prescribed by the practice of the court for that purpose, the defendant may enter judgment of *non pros.* against him, whereby it is adjudged that the plaintiff does not follow up *(non prosequitur)* his suit as he ought to do, and therefore the defendant ought to have judgment against him. Smith, Act. 96; Com. v. Casey, 12 Allen, Mass., 218.

NON QUIETA MOVERE. Lat. Not to disturb what is settled. A rule expressing the same principle as that of *stare decisis* (*q. v.*).

NON QUOD DICTUM EST, SED QUOD FACTUM EST INSPICITUR. Not what is said, but what is done, is regarded. Co.Litt. 36*a*.

NON REFERT AN QUIS ASSENSUM SUUM PRÆFERT VERBIS, AUT REBUS IPSIS ET FACTIS. 10 Coke, 52. It matters not whether a man gives his assent by his words or by his acts and deeds.

NON REFERT QUID EX ÆQUIPOLLENTIBUS FIAT. 5 Coke, 122. It matters not which of [two] equivalents happen.

NON REFERT QUID NOTUM SIT JUDICI, SI NOTUM NON SIT IN FORMA JUDICII. It matters not what is known to a judge, if it be not known in judicial form. 3 Bulst. 115. A leading maxim of modern law and practice. Best, Ev.Introd. 31, § 38.

NON REFERT VERBIS AN FACTIS FIT REVOCATIO. Cro.Car. 49. It matters not whether a revocation is made by words or deeds.

NON RESIDENTIO PRO CLERICO REGIS. A writ, addressed to a bishop, charging him not to molest a clerk employed in the royal service, by reason of his nonresidence; in which case he is to be discharged. Reg.Orig. 58.

NON RESPONDEBIT MINOR NISI IN CAUSA DOTIS, ET HOC PRO FAVORE DOTI. 4 Coke, 71. A minor shall not answer unless in a case of dower, and this in favor of dower.

NON SANÆ MENTIS. Lat. Of unsound mind. Fleta, lib. 6, c. 40, § 1.

NON SEQUITUR. Lat. It does not follow.

NON SOLENT QUÆ ABUNDANT VITIARE SCRIPTURAS. Superfluities [things which abound] do not usually vitiate writings. Dig. 50, 17, 94.

NON SOLUM QUID LICET, SED QUID EST CONVENIENS, EST CONSIDERANDUM; QUIA NIHIL QUOD EST INCONVENIENS EST LICITUM. Not only what is lawful, but what is proper or convenient, is to be considered; because nothing that is inconvenient is lawful. Co.Litt. 66*a*.

NON SOLVENDO PECUNIAM AD QUAM CLERICUS MULCTATUR PRO NON-RESIDENTIA. A writ prohibiting an ordinary to take a pecuniary mulct imposed on a clerk of the sovereign for nonresidence. Reg.Writ. 59.

NON SUBMISSIT. Lat. He did not submit. A plea to an action of debt, on a bond to perform an award, to the effect that the defendant did not submit to the arbitration.

NON SUI JURIS. Lat. Not his own master. The opposite of *sui juris (q. v.)*.

NON SUM INFORMATUS. Lat. I am not informed; I have not been instructed.

The name of a species of judgment by default, which is entered when the defendant's attorney announces that he is not informed of any answer to be given by him; usually in pursuance of a previous arrangement between the parties. Steph.Pl. 130.

NON SUNT LONGA UBI NIHIL EST QUOD DEMERE POSSIS. There is no prolixity where there is nothing that can be omitted. Vaugh. 138.

NON TEMERE CREDERE EST NERVUS SAPIENTIÆ. 5 Coke, 114. Not to believe rashly is the nerve of wisdom.

NON TENENT INSIMUL. Lat. In pleading, a plea to an action in partition, by which the defendant denies that he and the plaintiff are joint tenants of the estate in question.

NON TENUIT. Lat. He did not hold. A plea in bar in replevin, by which the plaintiff alleges that he did not hold in manner and form as averred, being given in answer to an avowry for rent in arrear. Rosc. Real Act. 638.

NON USURPAVIT. Lat. He has not usurped. A form of traverse, in an action or proceeding against one alleged to have usurped an office or franchise, denying the usurpation charged. Com. v. Cross Cut R. Co., 53 Pa. 62.

NON VALEBIT FELONIS GENERATIO, NEC AD HÆREDITATEM PATERNAM VEL MATERNAM; SI AUTEM ANTE FELONIAM GENERATIONEM FECERIT, TALIS GENERATIO SUCCEDIT IN HÆREDITATE PATRIS VEL MATRIS A QUO NON FUERIT FELONIA PERPETRATA. 3 Coke, 41. The offspring of a felon cannot succeed either to a maternal or paternal inheritance; but, if he had offspring before the felony, such offspring may succeed as to the inheritance of the father or mother by whom the felony was not committed.

NON VALENTIA AGERE. Inability to sue. 5 Bell, App.Cas. 172.

NON VALET CONFIRMATIO, NISI ILLE, QUI CONFIRMAT, SIT IN POSSESSIONE REI VEL JURIS UNDE FIERI DEBET CONFIRMATIO; ET EODEM MODO, NISI ILLE CUI CONFIRMATIO FIT SIT IN POSSESSIONE. Co.Litt. 295. Confirmation is not valid unless he who confirms is either in possession of the thing itself or of the right of which confirmation is to be made, and, in like manner, unless he to whom confirmation is made is in possession.

NON VALET DONATIO NISI SUBSEQUATUR TRADITIO. A gift is not valid unless accompanied by possession. Bract. 39*b*.

NON VALET EXCEPTIO EJUSDEM REI CUJUS PETITUR DISSOLUTIO. A plea of the same matter the dissolution of which is sought, is not valid. Called a "maxim of law and common sense." 2 Eden, 134.

NON VALET IMPEDIMENTUM QUOD DE JURE NON SORTITUR EFFECTUM. 4 Coke, 31*a*. An impediment which does not derive its effect from law is of no force.

NON VERBIS, SED IPSIS REBUS, LEGES IMPONIMUS. Cod. 6, 43, 2. We impose laws, not upon words, but upon things themselves.

NON VIDENTUR QUI ERRANT CONSENTIRE. They are not considered to consent who commit a mistake. Dig. 50, 17, 116, § 2; Broom, Max. 262.

NON VIDENTUR REM AMITTERE QUIOUS PROPRIA NON FUIT. They are not considered as losing a thing whose own it was not. Dig. 50, 17, 85.

NON VIDETUR CONSENSUM RETINUISSE SI QUIS EX PRÆSCRIPTO MINANTIS ALIQUID IMMUTAVIT. He does not appear to have retained consent, who has changed anything through menaces. Broom, Max. 278.

NON VIDETUR PERFECTE CUJUSQUE ID ESSE, QUOD EX CASU AUFERRI POTEST. That does not seem to be completely one's own which can be taken from him on occasion. Dig. 50, 17, 139, 1.

NON VIDETUR QUISQUAM ID CAPERE QUOD EI NECESSE EST ALII RESTITUTERE. Dig. 50, 17, 51. No one is considered entitled to recover that which he must give up to another.

NON VIDETUR VIM FACERE, QUI JURE SUO UTITUR ET ORDINARIA ACTIONE EXPERITUR. He is not deemed to use force who exercises his own right, and proceeds by ordinary action. Dig. 50, 17, 155, 1.

NON VULT CONTENDERE. Lat. He (the defendant in a criminal case) will not contest it. A plea legally equivalent to that of guilty, being a variation of the form "*nolo contendere,*" (*q. v.*,) and sometimes abbreviated "*non vult.*"

NON-ABILITY. Want of ability to do an act in law, as to sue. A plea founded upon such cause. Cowell.

NON-ACCEPTANCE. The refusal to accept anything.

NON-ACCESS. Absence of opportunities for sexual intercourse between husband and wife; or the absence of such intercourse.

NON-ADMISSION. The refusal of admission.

NON-AGE. Lack of requisite legal age. The condition of a person who is under twenty-one years of age, in some cases, and under fourteen or twelve in others; minority.

NON-ANCESTRAL ESTATE. Realty coming to deceased in any way other than by descent or devise from a now dead ancestor, or by deed of actual gift from a living one, there being no other consideration than that of blood. In re Yahola's Heirship, 142 Okl. 79, 285 P. 946, 948. One acquired by purchase or by act or agreement of the parties, as distinguished from one acquired by descent or by operation of law. Gray v. Chapman, 122 Okl. 130, 243 P. 522, 524.

NON-APPARENT EASEMENT. A non-continuous or discontinuous easement. Fetters v. Humphreys, 18 N.J.Eq. 262. See Easement.

NON-APPEARANCE. A failure of appearance; the omission of the defendant to appear within the time limited.

NON-ASSESSABLE. This word, placed upon a certificate of stock, does not cancel or impair the obligation to pay the amount due upon the shares created by the acceptance and holding of such certificate. At most its legal effect is a stipulation against liability from further assessment or taxation after the entire subscription of one hundred per cent. shall have been paid. Upton v. Tribilcock, 91 U.S. 45, 23 L.Ed. 203; Porter v. Northern Fire & Marine Ins. Co., 36 N.D. 199, 161 N.W. 1012, 1014.

NON-BAILABLE. Not admitting of bail; not requiring bail.

NON-CANCELLABLE. The term merely limited the right of assurer to cancel after an illness or accident, so long as the premium was paid. Dudgeon v. Mutual Ben. Health & Accident Ass'n, C.C. A.W.Va., 70 F.2d 49, 52.

NON-CLAIM. The omission or neglect of him who ought to claim his right within the time limited by law; as within a year and a day where a continual claim was required, or within five years after a fine had been levied. Termes de la Ley.

Covenant of Non-Claim. See Covenant.

NON-COMBATANT. A person connected with an army or navy, but for purposes other than fighting; such as the surgeons and chaplains. Also a neutral.

NON-COMMISSIONED. A non-commissioned officer of the army or militia is a subordinate officer who holds his rank, not by commission from the executive authority of the state or nation, but by appointment by a superior officer.

NON-COMPETITIVE TRAFFIC. Traffic which originates at a point served by a single haul carrier, or which is consigned to an industry on a line whose switching charge is not absorbed by a competing line-haul carrier. Northern Pac. Ry. Co. v. United States, D.C.Minn., 41 F.Supp. 439, 441.

NON-CONFORMING USES. Uses permitted by zoning statutes or ordinances to continue notwithstanding similar uses are not permitted in area in which they are located. Beyer v. Mayor and Council of Baltimore City, 182 Md. 444, 34 A.2d 765, 766.

NON-CONFORMIST. In English law, one who refuses to comply with others; one who refuses to join in the established forms of worship.

Non-conformists are of two sorts: (1) such as absent themselves from divine worship in the Established Church through total irreligion, and attend the service of no other persuasion; (2) such as attend the religious service of another persuasion. Wharton.

NON-CONTESTABLE. A non-contestable clause secures to insured indemnity by way of short limitations by contract against belated charges of fraud and mistake and rescission therefor, when he has acted thereon to his detriment by payment of premiums and foregoing other insurance. Pacific Mut. Life Ins. Co. of California v. Strange, 226 Ala. 98, 145 So. 425, 426.

NON-CONTINUOUS EASEMENT. "Continuous easement" is one which may be enjoyed without any act by party claiming it, while "noncontinuous easement," such as right of way, is one to enjoyment of which party's act is essential. Waubun Beach Ass'n v. Wilson, 274 Mich. 598, 265 N. W. 474, 477, 103 A.L.R. 983. A non-apparent or discontinuous easement. Fetters v. Humphreys, 18 N.J.Eq. 262. See Easement.

NON-CUMULATIVE DIVIDENDS. "Cumulative dividends" must be paid regardless of the year in which they are earned, whereas "noncumulative dividends" paid in a year are dependent upon earnings of that year. Barclay v. Wabash Ry. Co., C. C.A.N.Y., 30 F.2d 260, 262.

NON-DELIVERY. Neglect, failure, or refusal to deliver goods, on the part of a carrier, vendor, bailee, etc.

NONDESCRIPT. A "nondescript" in the labor market is unfitted to do even light work of general character, but fitted to do odd jobs not generally obtainable. Babcock v. Babcock & Wilcox Co., 137 Pa.Super. 517, 9 A.2d 492, 494, 496.

NON-DETACHABLE FACILITIES. Facilities which may not be put back into channels of commerce. Briggs Mfg. Co. v. U. S., D.C.Conn., 30 F.2d 962, 967.

NON-DIRECTION. Omission on the part of a judge to properly instruct the jury upon a necessary conclusion of law.

NON-DISCLOSURE. A failure to reveal facts, which may exist when there is no "concealment." State v. Watson, 145 Kan. 792, 67 P.2d 515, 517, 110 A.L.R. 998.

NON-ENUMERATED DAY. A motion day in New York on which the court hears motions classified as "non-enumerated motions." Jackson v. ———, 2 Caines (N.Y.) 259. For a collection of cases holding particular motions to be either enumerated or non-enumerated motions, see 66 C.J.S. Non, p. 603, n. 36(26).

NON-FORFEITABLE. Not subject to forfeiture. Columbian Nat. Life Ins. Co. v. Griffith, C.C.A.Mo., 73 F.2d 244, 246.

NON-FUNCTIONAL. A feature of goods is "non-functional" if it does not affect their purpose, action or performance, or the facility or economy of processing, handling or using them. In effect a mere form of merchandising or a business method. J. C. Penney Co. v. H. D. Lee Mercantile Co., C.C.

A.Mo., 20 F.2d 949, 954. A feature if, when omitted, nothing of substantial value in the goods is lost. Ainsworth v. Gill Glass & Fixture Co., D.C. Pa., 26 F.Supp. 183, 187.

NON-INTERCOURSE. The refusal of one state or nation to have commercial dealings with another; similar to an embargo (*q. v.*).

The absence of access, communication, or sexual relations between husband and wife.

NON-INTERVENTION WILL. A term sometimes applied to a will which authorizes the executor to settle and distribute the estate without the intervention of the court and without giving bond. In re Macdonald's Estate, 29 Wash. 422, 69 P. 1111.

NON-ISSUABLE PLEAS. Those upon which a decision would not determine the action upon the merits, as a plea in abatement. 1 Chit.Archb.Pr. 12th Ed., 249.

NON-JOINDER. See Joinder.

NON-JUDICIAL DAY. Day on which process cannot ordinarily issue or be executed or returned, and on which courts do not usually sit. Vidal v. Backs, 218 Cal. 99, 21 P.2d 952, 86 A.L.R. 1134.

NON-JURORS. In English law, persons who refuse to take the oaths, required by law, to support the government.

NON-LEVIABLE. Not subject to be levied upon. Non-leviable assets are assets upon which an execution cannot be levied. Farmers' F. Ins. Co. v. Conrad, 102 Wis. 387, 78 N.W. 582.

NON-MAILABLE. A term applied to all letters and parcels which are by law excluded from transportation in the United States mails, whether on account of the size of the package, the nature of its contents, its obscene character, or for other reasons. U. S. v. Nathan, D.C.Iowa, 61 F. 936.

NON-MEDICAL POLICY. One issued without medical examination of an applicant. Reserve Loan Life Ins. Co. of Texas v. Brown, Tex.Civ. App., 159 S.W.2d 179, 180.

NON-MERCHANTABLE TITLE. The title to realty need not be bad in fact to render it "nonmerchantable", but it is sufficient, if an ordinarily prudent man with knowledge of facts and aware of legal questions involved would not accept it in ordinary course of business. Ghormley v. Kleeden, 155 Kan. 319, 124 P.2d 467, 470.

NON-NAVIGABLE. At common law, streams or bodies of water not affected by tide were "nonnavigable". Luscher v. Reynolds, 153 Or. 625, 56 P.2d 1158, 1162.

NON-NEGOTIABLE. Not negotiable; not capable of passing title or property by indorsement and delivery.

NON-OCCUPATIONAL. Not of or pertaining to an occupation, trade, or work. Morgan v. Equitable Life Assur. Soc. of U. S., La.App., 22 So.2d 595, 597.

NON-PERFORMANCE. Neglect, failure, or refusal to do or perform an act stipulated to be done. Failure to keep the terms of a contract or covenant, in respect to acts or doings agreed upon.

NON-PROFIT. A "non-profit" corporation is one not designed primarily to pay dividends on invested capital. Greene County Rural Electric Co-operative v. Nelson, 234 Iowa 362, 12 N.W.2d 886, 888.

NON-RESIDENCE. Residence beyond the limits of the particular jurisdiction.

In ecclesiastical law. The absence of spiritual persons from their benefices.

NON-RESIDENT. One who is not a dweller within jurisdiction in question; not an inhabitant of the state of the forum. Gardner v. Meeker, 169 Ill. 40, 48 N.E. 307; Nagel v. Loomis, 33 Neb. 499, 50 N.W. 441. For the distinction between "residence" and "domicile," see Domicile.

NON-SANE. As "sane," when applied to the mind, means whole, sound, in a healthful state, "non-sane" must mean not whole, not sound, not in a healthful state; that is, broken, impaired, shattered, infirm, weak, diseased, unable, either from nature or accident, to perform the rational functions common to man upon the objects presented to it. Den v. Vancleve, 5 N.J.L. 589, 661.

NON-SANE MEMORY. Unsound memory; unsound mind. In re Beaumont, 1 Whart., Pa., 52, 29 Am.Dec. 33; In re Forman's Will, 54 Barb., N. Y., 286.

NON-SUMMONS, WAGER OF LAW OF. The mode in which a tenant or defendant in a real action pleaded, when the summons which followed the original was not served within the proper time.

NON-TENURE. A plea in a real action, by which the defendant asserts, either as to the whole or as to some part of the land mentioned in the plaintiff's declaration, that he does not hold it. Pub. St.Mass.1882, p. 1293.

NON-TERM. The vacation between two terms of a court.

NON-TERMINUS. The vacation between term and term, formerly called the time of days of the king's peace.

NON-TRADER. Person not engaged in buying and selling so as to be required to establish credit in commercial world. First Nat. Bank v. Ducros, 27 Ala.App. 193, 168 So. 704, 706.

NON-USER. Neglect to use. Neglect to use a franchise; neglect to exercise an office. 2 Bl. Comm. 153. Neglect or omission to use an easement or other right. 3 Kent, Comm. 448. A right acquired by use may be lost by *non-user*.

NON-WAIVER AGREEMENT. A "nonwaiver agreement" reserves to insurer every right under fire policy not previously waived, and to the insured every right which had not been forfeited. Ætna Ins. Co. of Hartford, Conn., v. Powers, 190 Okl. 116, 121 P.2d 599, 602.

NONÆ ET DECIMÆ. Payments made to the church, by those who were tenants of church-farms. The first was a rent or duty for things belonging to husbandry; the second was claimed in right of the church. Wharton.

NONAGIUM, or NONAGE. A ninth part of movables which was paid to the clergy on the death of persons in their parish, and claimed on pretense of being distributed to pious uses. Blount.

NONES. In the Roman calendar, the fifth, and, in March, May, July, and October, the seventh, day of the month. So called because, counting inclusively, they were *nine* days from the ides. Adams, Rom.Ant. 355, 357.

Under the word "Ides" in Bouvier's Law Dict., Rawle's 3d Rev., p. 1486, will be found a complete table of the calends, nones, and ides.

NONFEASANCE. Nonperformance of some act which ought to be performed, omission to perform a required duty at all, or total neglect of duty. Brooks v. Jacobs, 139 Me. 371, 31 A.2d 414, 416.

The term is not generally used to denote a breach of contract, but rather the failure to perform a duty towards the public whereby some individual sustains special damage, as where a sheriff fails to execute a writ. Sweet. Coite v. Lines, 33 Conn. 115; Gregor v. Cady, 82 Me. 131, 19 A. 108, 17 Am.St.Rep. 466.

There is a distinction between "nonfeasance" and "misfeasance" or "malfeasance"; and this distinction is often of great importance in determining an agent's liability to third persons. "Nonfeasance" means the total omission or failure of an agent to enter upon the performance of some distinct duty or undertaking which he has agreed with his principal to do; "misfeasance" means the improper doing of an act which the agent might lawfully do, or, in other words, it is the performing of his duty to his principal in such a manner as to infringe upon the rights and privileges of third persons; and "malfeasance" is a doing of an act which he ought not to do at all. Owens v. Nichols, 139 Ga. 475, 77 S.E. 635, 636; Maddock v. Riggs, 106 Kan. 808, 190 P. 12, 14, 12 A.L.R. 216.

NONNA. In old ecclesiastical law. A nun. *Nonnus,* a monk. Spelman.

NONPAYMENT. The neglect, failure, or refusal of payment of a debt or evidence of debt when due.

NONSENSE. Unintelligible matter in a written agreement or will.

NONSUIT. A term broadly applied to a variety of terminations of an action which do not adjudicate issues on the merits. McColgan v. Jones, Hubbard & Donnell, 11 Cal.2d 243, 78 P.2d 1010, 1011. Name of a judgment given against the plaintiff when he is unable to prove a case, or when he refuses or neglects to proceed to trial and leaves the issue undetermined. Carolina Transportation & Distributing Co. v. American Alliance Ins. Co., 214 N.C. 596, 200 S.E. 411, 413.

Judgment of *Nonsuit* is of two kinds,—*voluntary* and *involuntary.* When plaintiff abandons his case, and consents that judgment go against him for costs, it is *voluntary.* But when he, being called, neglects to appear, or when he has given no evidence on which a jury could find a verdict, or when his case is put out of court by some adverse ruling precluding a recovery, it is *involuntary.* Freem.Judgm. § 6.

A *peremptory* nonsuit is a compulsory or involuntary nonsuit, ordered by the court upon a total failure of the plaintiff to substantiate his claim by evidence. Jacques v. Fourthman, 137 Pa. 428, 20 A. 802.

Motion for Nonsuit. A motion in the nature of a demurrer to the evidence. Woods v. Wikstrom, 67 Or. 581, 135 P. 192, 195; Biurrun v. Elizalde, 75 Cal.App. 44, 242 P. 109, 113.

NOOK OF LAND. In English law, twelve acres and a half.

NORI TSUKUDANI. Seaweed. Togasaki & Co. v. U. S., 12 Ct.Cust.App. 463, 465.

NORMAL. According to, constituting, or not deviating from an established norm, rule, or principle; conformed to a type, standard or regular form; performing the proper functions; regular; natural. Webster; Railroad Commission v. Konowa Operating Co., Tex.Civ.App., 174 S.W.2d 605, 609.

NORMAL LAW. A term employed by modern writers on jurisprudence to denote the law as it affects persons who are in a normal condition; *i. e., sui juris* and sound in mind.

NORMAL MIND. One which in strength and capacity ranks reasonably well with the average of the great body of men and women who make up organized human society in general and are by common consent recognized as sane and competent to perform the ordinary duties and assume the ordinary responsibilities of life. State v. Haner, 186 Iowa, 2159, 173 N.W. 225, 226.

NORMAL SCHOOL. See School.

NORMALLY. As a rule; regularly; according to rule, general custom, etc. Palmer v. Jordan Mach. Co., C.C.N.Y., 186 F. 496, 504.

NORMAN FRENCH. The tongue in which several formal proceedings of state in England are still carried on. The language, having remained the same since the date of the Conquest, at which it was introduced into England, is very different from the French of this day, retaining all the peculiarities which at that time distinguished every province from the rest. A peculiar mode of pronunciation (considered authentic) is handed down and preserved by the officials who have, on particular occasions, to speak the tongue. Norman French was the language of English legal procedure till the 36 Edw. III. (A.D.1362). Wharton.

NORROY. In English law, the title of the third of the three kings-at-arms, or provincial heralds.

NORTH. Means due north. Same with word *northerly.* Brandt v. Ogden, 1 Johns., N.Y., 156; Currier v. Nelson, 96 Cal. 505, 31 P. 531, 746, 31 Am.St.Rep. 239.

NORTHAMPTON, ASSIZE OF. An assize held in 1176; in it, the king confirmed and perfected the judicial legislation which he had begun ten years before in the Assize of Clarendon. Stephen, Cr.Proc. in 2 Essays in Anglo-Amer. L.H. 445; Mrs. J. R. Green in 1 *id.*

NORTHAMPTON TABLES. Longevity and annuity tables compiled from bills of mortality kept in All Saints parish, England, in 1735–1780.

NORTHWEST TERRITORY. A name formerly applied to the territory northwest of the Ohio river.

NOSCITUR A SOCIIS. It is known from its associates. 1 Vent. 225. The meaning of a word is or may be known from the accompanying words. 3 Term R. 87; Broom, Max. 588. Morecock v. Hood, 202 N.C. 321, 162 S.E. 730, 731; Louis Pizitz Dry Goods Co. v. Fidelity & Deposit Co. of Maryland, 223 Ala. 385, 136 So. 800, 801.

The doctrine means that general and specific words are associated with and take color from each other, restricting general words to sense analogous to less general. Dunham v. State, 140 Fla. 754, 192 So. 324, 325, 326.

NOSCITUR EX SOCIO, QUI NON COGNOSCITUR EX SE. Moore, 817. He who cannot be known from himself may be known from his associate.

NOSOCOMI. In the civil law, persons who have the management and care of hospitals for paupers.

NOSTRUM. A quack, patent, or proprietary medicine recommended by its proprietor, or one the ingredients of which are kept secret for the purpose of restricting the profits of sale to the inventor or proprietor. World's Dispensary Medical Ass'n v. Collier, 86 Misc. 217, 148 N.Y.S. 405, 409.

NOT EXCEEDING. Usually a term of limitation only, denoting uncertainty of amount. Stuyvesant Ins. Co. v. Jacksonville Oil Mill, C.C.A.Tenn., 10 F.2d 54, 56.

NOT FOUND. These words, indorsed on a bill of indictment by a grand jury, have the same effect as the indorsement "Not a true bill" or "*Ignoramus.*"

See, also, Non Est Inventus.

NOT GUILTY. A plea of the general issue in the actions of trespass and case and in criminal prosecutions.

The form of the verdict in criminal cases, where the jury acquit the prisoner. 4 Bl.Comm. 361.

NOT GUILTY BY STATUTE. In English practice, a plea of the general issue by a defendant in a civil action, when he intends to give special matter in evidence by virtue of some act or acts of parliament, in which case he must add the reference to such act or acts, and state whether such acts are public or otherwise. But, if a defendant so plead, he will not be allowed to plead any other defense, without the leave of the court or a judge. Mozley & Whiteley.

NOT LATER THAN. "Within" or "not beyond" time specified. Hansen v. Bacher, Tex.Com.App., 299 S.W. 225, 227.

NOT LESS THAN. The words "not less than" signify in the smallest or lowest degree, at the lowest estimate; at least. Watson v. City of Salem, 84 Or. 666, 164 P. 567, 568; Miller v. Rodd, 285 Pa. 16, 131 A. 482, 483.

NOT POSSESSED. A special traverse used in an action of trover, alleging that defendant was not possessed, at the time of action brought, of the chattels alleged to have been converted by him.

NOT PROVEN. A verdict in a Scotch criminal trial, to the effect that the guilt of the accused is not made out, though his innocence is not clear.

NOT SATISFIED. A return sometimes made by sheriffs or constables to a writ of execution; but it is not a technical formula, and is condemned by the courts as ambiguous and insufficient. Martin v. Martin, 50 N.C. 346; Langford v. Few, 146 Mo. 142, 47 S.W. 927, 69 Am.St.Rep. 606.

NOT TO BE PERFORMED WITHIN ONE YEAR. The clause "not to be performed within one year" includes any agreement which by a reasonable interpretation in view of all the circumstances does not admit of its performance, according to its language and intention, within one year from the time of its making. Mrs. K. Edwards & Sons v. Farve, 110 Miss. 864, 71 So. 12, 13.

NOT TRANSFERABLE. These words, when written across the face of a negotiable instrument, operate to destroy its negotiability. Durr v. State, 59 Ala. 24.

NOTA. Lat. In the civil law, a mark or brand put upon a person by the law. Mackeld. Rom. Law, § 135.

NOTÆ. In civil and old European law, short-hand characters or marks of contraction, in which the emperors' secretaries took down what they dictated. Spelman; Calvin.

NOTARIAL. Taken by a notary; performed by a notary in his official capacity; belonging to a notary and evidencing his official character, as, a notarial seal.

NOTARIAL WILL. A will executed by the testator in the presence of a Notary Public and two witnesses.

NOTARIUS. Lat.

In old English law. A scribe or scrivener who made short draughts of writings and other instruments; a notary. Cowell.

In Roman law. A draughtsman; an amanuensis; a shorthand writer; one who took notes of the proceedings in the senate or a court, or of what was dictated to him by another; one who prepared draughts of wills, conveyances, etc.

NOTARY PUBLIC. A public officer whose function it is to administer oaths; to attest and certify, by his hand and official seal, certain classes of documents, in order to give them credit and authenticity in foreign jurisdictions; to take acknowledgments of deeds and other conveyances, and certify the same; and to perform certain official acts, chiefly in commercial matters, such as the protesting of notes and bills, the noting of foreign drafts, and marine protests in cases of loss or damage. Kip v. People's Bank & Trust Co., 110 N.J.L. 178, 164 A. 253, 254.

NOTATION. In English probate practice, the act of making a memorandum of some special circumstance on a probate or letters of administration.

Thus, where a grant is made for the whole personal estate of the deceased within the United Kingdom, which can only be done in the case of a person dying domiciled in England, the fact of his having been so domiciled is noted on the grant. Coote, Prob.Pr. 36; Sweet.

NOTCHELL, or NOCHELL. "Crying the wife's Notchell" seems to have been a means of preventing her running up debts against her husband. 20 Law Mag. & Rev. 280.

It is the custom in Lancashire for a man to advertise that he will not be responsible for debts contracted by her [his wife] after that date. He is thus said to *notchel* her, and the advertisement is termed a notchel notice. N. and Q., 7th ser., VIII, 268, quoted in Cent.Dict.

NOTE, *v.* To make a brief written statement; to enter a memorandum; as to note an exception.

NOTE, *n.* A unilateral instrument containing an express and absolute promise of signer to pay to a specified person or order, or bearer, a definite sum of money at a specified time. Shawano Finance Corporation v. Julius, 214 Wis. 637, 254 N.W. 355. An abstract, a memorandum; an informal statement in writing. Road Improvement Dist. No. 4 of Cleveland County v. Southern Trust Co., 152 Ark. 422, 239 S.W. 8, 11; American Nat. Bank v. Marshall, 122 Kan. 793, 253 P. 214, 215. See Bought Note; Notes; Judgment Note; Promissory Note; Sold Note.

NOTE A BILL. When a foreign bill has been dishonored, it is usual for a notary public to present it again on the same day, and, if it be not then paid, to make a minute, consisting of his initials, the day, month, and year, and reason, if assigned, of non-payment. The making of this minute is called "noting the bill." Wharton.

NOTE OF A FINE. In old conveyancing, one of the parts of a fine of lands, being an abstract of the writ of covenant, and the concord; naming the parties, the parcels of land, and the agreement. 2 Bl.Comm. 351.

NOTE OF ALLOWANCE. In English practice, a note delivered by a master to a party to a cause, who alleged that there was error in law in the record and proceedings, allowing him to bring error.

NOTE OF HAND. A popular name for a promissory note. Perry v. Maxwell, 17 N.C. 496; Hopkins v. Holt, 9 Wis. 230.

NOTE OF PROTEST. A memorandum of the fact of protest, indorsed by the notary upon the bill, at the time, to be afterwards written out at length.

NOTE OR MEMORANDUM. Under statute of frauds, an informal minute or memorandum made on the spot. Clason v. Bailey, 14 Johns., N.Y. 492. It must contain all the essential elements and substantial parts of the contract. Stanley v. A. Levy & J. Zentner Co., 60 Nev. 432, 112 P.2d 1047, 1053.

NOTES. In practice, memoranda made by a judge on a trial, as to the evidence adduced, and the points reserved, etc. A copy of the judge's notes may be obtained from his clerk.

NOTHUS. Lat. In Roman law, a natural child or a person of spurious birth.

NOTICE. Information; the result of observation, whether by the senses or the mind; knowledge of the existence of a fact or state of affairs; the means of knowledge. Abercrombie v. Virginia-Carolina Chemical Co., 206 Ala. 615, 91 So. 311, 312; Knights and Ladies of Security v. Bell, 93 Okl. 272, 220 P. 594, 597.

Knowledge of facts which would naturally lead an honest and prudent person to make inquiry constitutes "notice" of everything which such inquiry pursued in good faith would disclose. Twitchell v. Nelson, 131 Minn. 375, 155 N.W. 621, 624; German-American Nat. Bank of Lincoln v. Martin, 277 Ill. 629, 115 N.E. 721, 729.

In another sense, "notice" means information, an advice, or written warning, in more or less formal shape, intended to apprise a person of some proceeding in which his interests are involved, or informing him of some fact which it is his right to know and the duty of the notifying party to communicate.

Under the Negotiable Instrument Law "notice" of infirmity of instrument is actual knowledge or knowledge of such facts that taking note amounts to bad faith. Glendo State Bank v. Abbott, 30 Wyo. 98, 216 P. 700, 702, 34 A.L.R. 294.

Notice is either (1) statutory, *i. e.,* made so by legislative enactment; (2) actual, which brings the knowledge of a fact directly home to the party; or (3) constructive. Constructive notice may be subdivided into: *(a)* Where there exists actual notice of matter, to which equity has added constructive notice of facts, which an inquiry after such matter would have elicited; and *(b)* where there has been a designed abstinence from inquiry for the very purpose of escaping notice. Wharton.

Actual notice has been defined as notice expressly and actually given, and brought home to the party directly. Jordan v. Pollock, 14 Ga. 145; McCray v. Clar, 82 Pa. 457; Morey v. Milliken, 86 Me. 464, 30 A. 102. The term "actual notice," however, is generally given a wider meaning as embracing two classes, express and implied; the former includes all knowledge of a degree above that which depends upon collateral inference, or which imposes upon the party the further duty of inquiry; the latter imputes knowledge to the party because he is shown to be conscious of having the means of knowledge. In this sense actual notice is such notice as is positively proved to have been given to a party directly and personally, or such as he is presumed to have received personally because the evidence within his knowledge was sufficient to put him upon inquiry. Picklesimer v. Smith, 164 Ga. 600, 139 S.E. 72, 74; White v. Fisher, 77 Ind. 65, 40 Am.Rep. 287.

Constructive notice is information or knowledge of a fact imputed by law to a person, (although he may not actually have it), because he could have discovered the fact by proper diligence, and his situation was such as to cast upon him the duty of inquiring into it. Baltimore v. Whittington, 78 Md. 231, 27 A. 984; Acer v. Westcott, 46 N.Y. 384, 7 Am. Rep. 355.

Notice is also further classified as *express* or *implied.* Express notice embraces not only knowledge, but also that which is communicated by direct information, either written or oral, from those who are cognizant of the fact communicated. Baltimore v. Whittington, 78 Md. 231, 27 A. 984. Implied notice is one of the varieties of actual notice (not constructive) and is distinguished from "express" actual notice. It is notice inferred or imputed to a party by reason of his knowledge of facts or circumstances collateral to the main fact, of such a character as to put him upon inquiry, and which, if the inquiry were followed up with due diligence, would lead him definitely to the knowledge of the main fact. Rhodes v. Outcalt, 48 Mo. 370; Baltimore v. Whittington, 78 Md. 231, 27 A. 984; Wells v. Sheerer, 78 Ala. 147.

"Constructive notice" is a presumption of law, making it impossible for one to deny the matter concerning which notice is given, while "implied notice" is a presumption of fact, relating to what one can learn by reasonable inquiry, and arises from actual notice of circumstances, and not from constructive notice. Charles v. Roxana Petroleum Corporation, C.C.A.Okl., 282 F. 983, 988. Or as otherwise defined, implied notice may be said to exist where the fact in question lies open to the knowledge of the party, so that the exercise of reasonable observation and watchfulness would not fail to apprise him of it, although no one has told him of it in so many words. See City of Philadelphia v. Smith, Pa., 16 A. 493.

Averment of Notice. The statement in a pleading that notice has been given.

Immediate Notice. Under an insurance policy, notice of loss within reasonable time under circumstances of case. National Surety Co. v. Western Pac. Ry. Co., Cal., 119 C.C.A. 91, 200 F. 675, 687; Southern States Fire Ins. Co. v. Hand-Jordan Co., 112 Miss. 565, 73 So. 578, 579.

Judicial Notice. See Judicial Notice.

Legal Notice. See Legal Notice.

Personal Notice. Communication of notice orally or in writing (according to the circumstances) directly to the person affected or to be charged, as distinguished from constructive or implied notice, and also from notice imputed to him because given to his agent or representative. Loeb v. Huddleston, 105 Ala. 257, 16 So. 714; Pearson v. Lovejoy, 53 Barb., N.Y., 407.

Presumptive Notice. Implied actual notice. The difference between "presumptive" and "constructive" notice is that the former is an inference of fact which is capable of being explained or contradicted, while the latter is a conclusion of law which cannot be contradicted. Brown v. Baldwin, 121 Mo. 106, 25 S.W. 858; Brush v. Ware, 15 Pet. 98, 10 L.Ed. 672.

Public Notice. Notice given to the public generally, or to the entire community, or to all whom it may concern. Pennsylvania Training School v. Independent Mut. F. Ins. Co., 127 Pa. 559, 18 A. 392.

Reasonable Notice. Such notice or information of a fact as may fairly and properly be expected or required in the particular circumstances. Sterling Mfg. Co. v. Hough, 49 Neb. 618, 68 N.W. 1019; Mallory v. Leiby, 1 Kan. 102.

NOTICE IN LIEU OF SERVICE. In lieu of personally serving a writ of summons (or other legal process,) in English practice, the court occasionally allows the plaintiff (or other party) to give notice in lieu of service, such notice being such as will in all probability reach the party. This notice is peculiarly appropriate in the case of a foreigner out of the jurisdiction, whom it is desired to serve with a writ of summons. Sweet.

NOTICE OF ACTION. When it is intended to sue certain particular individuals, as in the case of actions against justices of the peace, it is necessary in some jurisdictions to give them notice of the action some time before.

NOTICE OF APPEARANCE. See Appearance.

NOTICE OF DISHONOR. See Dishonor.

NOTICE OF JUDGMENT. It is required by statute in several of the states that the party for whom the verdict in an action has been given shall serve upon the other party or his attorney a written notice of the time when judgment is entered.

NOTICE OF LIS PENDENS. See Lis Pendens.

NOTICE OF MOTION. A substitute for writ and declaration in common-law actions, which notifies defendant when and where he is to appear and sets forth cause of complaint. Baldwin v. Norton Hotel, 163 Va. 76, 175 S.E. 751. A notice in writing, entitled in a cause, stating that, on a certain day designated, a motion will be made to the court for the purpose or object stated. Field v. Park, 20 Johns., N.Y., 140.

NOTICE OF PROTEST. See Protest.

NOTICE OF TRIAL. A notice given by one of the parties in an action to the other, after an issue has been reached, that he intends to bring the cause forward for trial at the next term of the court.

NOTICE TO ADMIT. In the practice of the English high court, either party to an action may call on the other party by notice to admit the existence and execution of any document, in order to save the expense of proving it at the trial; and the party refusing to admit must bear the costs of proving it unless the judge certifies that the refusal to admit was reasonable. Rules of Court, xxxii. 2; Sweet.

NOTICE TO PLEAD. This is a notice which, in the practice of some states, is prerequisite to the taking judgment by default. It proceeds from the plaintiff, and warns the defendant that he must plead to the declaration or complaint within a prescribed time.

NOTICE TO PRODUCE. In practice, a notice in writing, given in an action at law, requiring the opposite party to produce a certain described paper or document at the trial. Chit.Archb.Pr. 230; 3 Chit.Gen.Pr. 834.

NOTICE TO QUIT. A written notice given by a landlord to his tenant, stating that the former desires to repossess himself of the demised premises, and that the latter is required to quit and remove from the same at a time designated, either at the expiration of the term, if the tenant is in under a lease, or immediately, if the tenancy is at will or by sufferance. The term is also sometimes applied to a written notice given by the tenant to the landlord, to the effect that he intends to quit the demised premises and deliver possession of the same on a day named. Garner v. Hannah, 6 Duer, N.Y., 270; Oakes v. Munroe, 8 Cush., Mass., 287.

NOTIFY. To give notice to; to inform by words or writing, in person or by message, or by any signs which are understood; to make known; to "notify" one of a fact is to make it known to him; to inform him by notice. Fast v. Scruggs, 164 Okl. 196, 23 P.2d 383.

In legal proceedings, and in respect to public matters, this word is generally, if not universally, used as importing a notice *given* by some person, whose duty it was to give it, in some manner prescribed, and to some person entitled to receive it, or be notified. Appeal of Potwine, 31 Conn. 384; Home Benefit Ass'n of Angelina County v. Jordan, Tex.Civ.App., 191 S.W. 725, 728.

NOTING. The act of a notary in minuting on a bill of exchange, after it has been presented for acceptance or payment, the initials of his name, the date of the day, month, and year when such presentment was made, and the reason, if any has been assigned, for non-acceptance or non-payment, together with his charge. 4 Term 175.

NOTIO. Lat. In the civil law, the power of hearing and trying a matter of fact; the power or authority of a *judex*; the power of hearing causes and of pronouncing sentence, without any degree of jurisdiction. Calvin.

NOTITIA. Lat. Knowledge; information; intelligence; notice.

NOTITIA DICITUR A NOSCENDO; ET NOTITIA NON DEBET CLAUDICARE. Notice is named from a knowledge being had; and notice ought not to halt, [*i. e.*, be imperfect.] 6 Coke, 29.

NOTORIAL. The Scotch form of "notarial," (*q. v.*). Bell.

NOTORIETY. The state of being notorious or universally well known.

Proof by Notoriety. In Scotch law, dispensing with positive testimony as to matters of common knowledge or general notoriety, the same as the "judicial notice" of English and American law. See Judicial Notice.

NOTORIOUS. Generally known and talked of, well or widely known, forming a part of common knowledge, or universally recognized. Mathis v. State, 60 Okl.Cr. 58, 61 P.2d 261, 267. Open; generally or commonly known and spoken of. McNeill v. McNeill, 166 Iowa, 680, 148 N.W. 643, 651; Record v. Ellis, 97 Kan. 754, 156 P. 712, 713, L.R.A.1916E, 654; Spicer v. Spicer, 249 Mo. 582, 155 S.W. 832, 835, Ann.Cas.1914D, 238.

In the law of evidence, matters deemed notorious do not require to be proved. There does not seem to be any recognized rule as to what matters are deemed notorious. Cases have occurred in which the state of society or public feeling has been treated as notorious; *e. g.*, during times of sedition. Best, Ev. 354; Sweet.

NOTORIOUS INSOLVENCY. A condition of insolvency which is generally known throughout the community or known to the general class of persons with whom the insolvent has business relations.

NOTORIOUS POSSESSION. Possession that is so conspicuous that it is generally known and talked of by the public or the people in the neighborhood. Terral v. Brooks, 194 Ark. 311, 108 S.W. 2d 489, 493. Possession or character of holding in its nature having such elements of notoriety that the owner may be presumed to have notice of it and of its extent. Watrous v. Morrison, 33 Fla. 261, 14 So. 805, 39 Am.St.Rep. 139.

NOTOUR. In Scotch law, open; notorious. A *notour* bankrupt is a debtor who, being under diligence by horning and caption of his creditor, retires to sanctuary or absconds or defends by force, and is afterwards found insolvent by the court of session. Bell.

NOVA CONSTITUTIO FUTURIS FORMAM IMPONERE DEBET NON PRÆTERITIS. A new state of the law ought to affect the future, not the past. 2 Inst. 292; Broom, Max. 34, 37.

NOVA CUSTUMA. The name of an imposition or duty. See Antiqua Custuma.

NOVA STATUTA. New statutes. An appellation sometimes given to the statutes which have been passed since the beginning of the reign of Edward III. 1 Steph.Comm. 68.

NOVÆ NARRATIONES. New counts. The collection called "*Novæ Narrationes*" contains pleadings in actions during the reign of Edward III. It consists principally of declarations, as the title imports; but there are sometimes pleas and subsequent pleadings. The *Articuli ad Novas Narrationes* is usually subjoined to this little book, and is a small treatise on the method of pleading. It first treats of actions and courts, and then goes through each particular writ, and the declaration upon it, accompanied with directions, and illustrated by precedents. 3 Reeve, Eng. Law, 152; Wharton.

NOVALE. Land newly plowed and converted into tillage, and which has not been tilled before within the memory of man; also fallow land.

NOVALIS. In the civil law, land that rested a year after the first plowing. Dig. 50, 16, 30, 2.

NOVATIO NON PRÆSUMITUR. Novation is not presumed. Halk. Lat. Max. 109.

NOVATION. Substitution of new contract between same or different parties. Alexander v. Manza, 22 N.J.Misc. 88, 36 A.2d 142, 148. The substitution of a new debt or obligation for an existing one. Hard v. Burton, 62 Vt. 314, 20 A. 269; McCartney v. Kipp, 171 Pa. 644, 33 A. 233. The substitution by mutual agreement of one debtor for another or of one creditor for another, whereby the old debt is extinguished. Pierce Fordyce Oil Ass'n v. Woods, Tex.Civ.App., 180 S.W. 1181, 1183; Peters v. Poro's Estate, 96 Vt. 95, 117 A. 244, 249, 25 A.L.R. 615.

The requisites of a "novation" are a previous valid obligation, an agreement of all the parties to a new contract, the extinguishment of the old obligation, and the validity of the new one. Alkire v. Acuff, 134 Okl. 43, 272 P. 405, 406; Tulsa Ice Co. v. Liley, 157 Okl. 86, 10 P.2d 1090, 1091; Cox v. Baltimore & O. S. W. R. Co., 180 Ind. 495, 103 N.E. 337, 342, 50 L.R.A.,N.S., 453.

The term was originally a technical term of the civil law, but is now in very general use in English and American jurisprudence.

In the civil law, there are three kinds of novation: Where the debtor and creditor remain the same, but a new debt takes the place of the old one; where the debt remains the same, but a new debtor is substituted; where the debt and debtor remain, but a new creditor is substituted. Wheeler v. Wardell, 173 Va. 168, 3 S.E.2d 377, 380.

NOVEL ASSIGNMENT. See New Assignment.

NOVEL DISSEISIN. See Assise of Novel Disseisin.

NOVELLÆ (or NOVELLÆ CONSTITUTIONES.) New constitutions; generally translated in English, "Novels." The Latin name of those constitutions which were issued by Justinian after the publication of his Code; most of them being originally written in Greek. After his death, a collection of 168 Novels was made, 154 of which had been issued by Justinian, and the rest by his successors. These were afterwards included in the *Corpus Juris Civilis,* (*q. v.,*) and now constitute one of its four principal divisions. Mackeld. Rom. Law, § 80; 1 Kent, Comm. 541.

NOVELLÆ LEONIS. The ordinances of the Emperor Leo, which were made from the year 887 till the year 893, are so called. These Novels changed many rules of the Justinian law. This collection contains 113 Novels, written originally in Greek, and afterwards, in 1560, translated into Latin by Agilæus. Mackeld. Rom. Law, § 84.

NOVELS. The title given in English to the New Constitutions (*Novellæ Constitutiones*) of Justinian and his successors, now forming a part of the *Corpus Juris Civilis.* See Novellæ.

NOVELTY. In order that there may be "novelty" so as to sustain a patent, the thing must not have been known to any one before, mere novelty of form being insufficient. Seaver v. Wm. Filene's Sons Co., D.C.Mass., 37 F.Supp. 762, 765. An objection to a patent or claim for a patent on the ground that the invention is not new or original is called an objection "for want of novelty."

NOVERCA. Lat. In the civil law, a stepmother.

NOVERINT UNIVERSI PER PRÆSENTES. Know all men by these presents. Formal words used at the commencement of deeds of release in the Latin forms.

NOVI OPERIS NUNCIATIO. Lat. Denunciation of, or protest against, a new work.

This was a species of remedy in the civil law, available to a person who thought his rights or his property were threatened with injury by the act of his neighbor in erecting or demolishing any structure, which was called a "new work." In such case, he might go upon the ground, while the work was in progress, and publicly protest against or forbid its completion, in the presence of the workmen or of the owner or his representative.

NOVIGILD. In Saxon law, a pecuniary satisfaction for an injury, amounting to nine times the value of the thing for which it was paid. Spelman.

NOVISSIMA RECOPILACION. (Latest Compilation.) The title of a collection of Spanish law compiled by order of Don Carlos IV. in 1805. 1 White, Recop. 355.

NOVITAS. Lat. Novelty; newness; a new thing.

NOVITAS NON TAM UTILITATE PRODEST QUAM NOVITATE PERTURBAT. A novelty does not benefit so much by its utility as it disturbs by its novelty. Jenk. Cent. p. 167, case 23.

NOVITER PERVENTA, or NOVITER AD NOTITIAM PERVENTA. In ecclesiastical procedure, facts "newly come" to the knowledge of a party to a cause. Leave to plead facts *noviter perventa* is generally given, in a proper case, even after the pleadings are closed. Phillim. Ecc. Law, 1257; Rog. Ecc. Law, 723.

NOVODAMUS. In old Scotch law, we give anew. The name given to a charter, or clause in a charter, granting a renewal of a right. Bell.

NOVUM JUDICIUM NON DAT NOVUM JUS, SED DECLARAT ANTIQUUM; QUIA JUDICIUM EST JURIS DICTUM ET PER JUDICIUM JUS EST NOVITER REVELATUM QUOD DIU FUIT VELATUM. A new adjudication does not make a new law, but declares the old; because adjudication is the utterance of the law, and by adjudication the law is newly revealed which was for a long time hidden. 10 Coke, 42.

NOVUM OPUS. Lat. In the civil law, a new work. See Novi Operis Nunciatio.

NOVUS HOMO. Lat. A new man. This term is applied to a man who has been pardoned of a crime, and so made, as it were, a "new man."

NOW. At this time, or at the present moment; or at a time contemporaneous with something done. Pike v. Kennedy, 15 Or. 426, 15 P. 637. At the present time. Nutt v. U. S., 26 Ct.Cl. 15. Shubert v. Rosenberger, C.C.A.Mo., 204 F. 934, 935; Walker v. Dwelle, 187 Iowa, 1384, 175 N.W. 957, 960.

"Now" as used in a statute ordinarily refers to the date of its taking effect, but the word is sometimes used, not with reference to the moment of speaking but to a time contemporaneous with something done, and may mean at the time spoken of or referred to as well as at the time of speaking. State v. City of St. Lawrence, 101 Kan. 225, 165 P. 826.

Word "now" used in will refers to time of testator's death, Tate v. Tate, 160 Ga. 449, 128 S.E. 393, 395; but, in light of context, may apply to date of will, Merrill v. Winchester, 120 Me. 203, 113 A. 261, 264.

NOXA. Lat. In the civil law, any damage or injury done to persons or property by an unlawful act committed by a man's slave or animal. An action for damages lay against the master or owner, who, however, might escape further responsibility by delivering up the offending agent to the party injured. *"Noxa"* was also used as the designation of the offense committed, and of its punishment, and sometimes of the slave or animal doing the damage.

NOXA SEQUITUR CAPUT. The injury [*i. e.*, liability to make good an injury caused by a slave] follows the head or person, [*i. e.*, attaches to his master.] Heinecc. Elem. l. 4, t. 8, § 1231.

NOXÆ DEDITIO. The surrender of a slave who has committed a misdeed. The master may elect whether he will pay the damages assessed or surrender the slave. Hunter, Rom. Law, 166.

NOXAL ACTION. An action for damage done by slaves or animals. Sandars, Just. Inst. (5th Ed.) 457.

NOXALIS ACTIO. Lat. In the civil law, an action which lay against the master of a slave, for some offense (as theft or robbery) committed or damage or injury done by the slave, which was called *"noxa."* Usually translated "noxal action."

NOXIA. Lat. In the civil law, an offense committed or damage done by a slave. Inst. 4, 8, 1.

NOXIOUS. Hurtful; offensive; offensive to the smell. Rex v. White, 1 Burrows, 337. The word "noxious" includes the complex idea both of insalubrity and offensiveness. Id. That which causes or tends to cause injury, especially to health or morals. Moubray v. G. & M. Improvement Co., 178 App.Div. 737, 165 N.Y.S. 842, 843.

NUBILIS. Lat. In the civil law, marriageable; one who is of a proper age to be married.

NUCES COLLIGERE. Lat. To collect nuts. This was formerly one of the works or services imposed by lords upon their inferior tenants. Paroch. Antiq. 495.

NUDA PACTIO OBLIGATIONEM NON PARIT. A naked agreement [*i. e.*, without consideration] does not beget an obligation. Dig. 2, 14, 7, 4; Broom, Max. 746.

NUDA PATIENTIA. Lat. Mere sufferance.

NUDA POSSESSIO. Lat. Bare or mere possession.

NUDA RATIO ET NUDA PACTIO NON LIGANT ALIQUEM DEBITOREM. Naked reason and naked promise do not bind any debtor. Fleta, l. 2, c. 60, § 25.

NUDE. Naked. This word is applied metaphorically to a variety of subjects to indicate that they are lacking in some essential legal requisite.

NUDE CONTRACT. One made without any consideration; upon which no action will lie, in conformity with the maxim *"ex nudo pacto non oritur actio."* 2 Bl.Comm. 445.

NUDE MATTER. A bare allegation of a thing done, unsupported by evidence.

NUDE PACT. One without consideration; an executory contract without a consideration; a naked promise. Oliver v. Home Service Ice Co., La.App., 161 So. 766, 770.

NUDUM PACTUM. A voluntary promise, without any other consideration than mere good will, or natural affection. Grimes v. Baker, 133 Neb. 517, 275 N.W. 860, 863.

A naked pact; a bare agreement; a promise or undertaking made without any consideration for it. Justice v. Lang, 42 N.Y. 493, 1 Am.Rep. 576; Wardell v. Williams, 62 Mich. 50, 28 N.W. 800, 4 Am.St.Rep. 814.

In Roman law. Informal agreements not coming within any of the privileged classes. They could not be sued on. The term was sometimes used with a special and rather different meaning to express the rule that a contract without delivery will not pass property. Pollock, Contracts 743. Salmond, Jurisprudence 640.

NUDUM PACTUM EST UBI NULLA SUBEST CAUSA PRÆTER CONVENTIONEM; SED UBI SUBEST CAUSA, FIT OBLIGATIO, ET PARIT ACTIONEM. A naked contract is where there is no consideration except the agreement; but, where there is a consideration, it becomes an obligation and gives a right of action. Plowd. 309; Broom, Max. 745, 750.

NUDUM PACTUM EX QUO NON ORITUR ACTIO. *Nudum pactum* is that upon which no action arises. Cod. 2, 3, 10; Id. 5, 14, 1; Broom, Max. 676.

NUEVA RECOPILACION. New Compilation. The title of a code of Spanish law, promulgated in the year 1567. Schm. Civil Law, Introd. 79–81.

NUGATORY. Futile; ineffectual; invalid; destitute of constraining force or vitality. A legislative act may be "nugatory" because unconstitutional. Avery & Co. v. Sorrell, 157 Ga. 476, 121 S. E. 828, 829.

NUISANCE. That which annoys and disturbs one in possession of his property, rendering its ordinary use or occupation physically uncomfortable to him. Yaffe v. City of Ft. Smith, 178 Ark. 406, 10 S.W.2d 886, 890, 61 A.L.R. 1138. Everything that endangers life or health, gives offense to senses, violates the laws of decency, or obstructs reasonable and comfortable use of property. Hall v. Putney, 291 Ill.App. 508, 10 N.E.2d 204, 207. Annoyance; anything which essentially interferes with enjoyment of life or property. Holton v. Northwestern Oil Co., 201 N.C. 744, 161 S.E. 391, 393. That class of wrongs that arise from the unreasonable, unwarrantable, or unlawful use by a person of his own property, either real or personal, or from his own improper, indecent, or unlawful personal conduct, working an obstruction of or injury to the right of another or of the public, and producing such material annoyance, inconvenience, discomfort, or hurt, that the law will presume resulting damage. City of Phoenix v. Johnson, 51 Ariz. 115, 75 P.2d 30; Wood, Nuis. § 1; District of Columbia v. Totten, 55 App.D.C. 312, 5 F.2d 374, 380, 40 A.L.R. 1461. Anything that unlawfully worketh hurt, inconvenience, or damage. 3 Bl.Comm. 216; City of Birmingham v. Hood-McPherson Realty Co., 233 Ala. 352, 172 So. 114, 120, 108 A.L.R. 1140. Anything which is injurious to health, or is indecent or offensive to the senses, or an obstruction to the free use of property, so as to interfere with the comfortable enjoyment of life or property, or which unlawfully obstructs the free passage or use, in the customary manner, of any navigable lake or river, bay, stream, canal, or basin, or any public park, square, street, or highway, is a nuisance. Civ. Code Cal. § 3479; Veazie v. Dwinel, 50 Me. 479; Bohan v. Port Jervis Gaslight Co., 122 N.Y. 18, 25 N.E. 246, 9 L.R.A. 711; Baltimore & P. R. Co. v. Fifth Baptist Church, 137 U.S. 568, 11 S.Ct. 185, 34 L.Ed. 784; Ex parte Foote, 70 Ark. 12, 65 S.W. 706, 91 Am.St.Rep. 63.

In determining what constitutes a "nuisance," the question is whether the nuisance will or does produce such a condition of things as in the judgment of reasonable men is naturally productive of actual physical discomfort to persons of ordinary sensibility and ordinary tastes and habits. Meeks v. Wood, 66 Ind.App. 594, 118 N.E. 591, 592.

Nuisances are commonly classed as *public* and *private*, and *mixed*. A public nuisance is one which affects an indefinite number of persons, or all the residents of a particular locality, or all people coming within the extent of its range or operation, although the extent of the annoyance or damage inflicted upon individuals may be unequal. Burnham v. Hotchkiss, 14 Conn. 317; Chesbrough v. Com'rs, 37 Ohio St. 508; Lansing v. Smith, 4 Wend., N.Y., 30, 21 Am.Dec. 89. A private nuisance was originally defined as anything done to the hurt or annoyance of the lands, tenements, or hereditaments of another. 3 Bl. Comm. 216; Whittemore v. Baxter Laundry Co., 181 Mich. 564, 148 N.W. 437, 52 L.R.A.,N.S., 930, Ann.Cas.1916C, 818. As distinguished from public nuisance, it includes any wrongful act which destroys or deteriorates the property of an individual or of a few persons or interferes with their lawful use or enjoyment thereof, or any act which unlawfully hinders them in the enjoyment of a common or public right and causes them a special injury different from that sustained by the general public. Therefore, although the ground of distinction between public and private nuisances is still the injury to the community at large or, on the other hand, to a single individual, it is evident that the same thing or act may constitute a public nuisance and at the same time a private nuisance. Heeg v. Licht, 80 N.Y. 582, 36 Am.Rep. 654; Baltzeger v. Carolina Midland R. Co., 54 S.C. 242, 32 S.E. 358, 71 Am.St.Rep. 789; Willcox v. Hines, 100 Tenn. 538, 46 S.W. 297, 41 L.R.A. 278; Harris v. Poulton, 99 W.Va. 20, 127 S.E. 647, 650, 651, 40 A.L.R. 334. A *mixed* nuisance is of the kind last described; that is, it is one which is both public and private in its effects,—public because it injures many persons or all the community, and private in that it also produces special injuries to private rights. Kelley v. New York, 27 N.Y.S. 164, 6 Misc. 516.

Abatement of a nuisance. The removal, prostration, or destruction of that which causes a nuisance, whether by breaking or pulling it down, or otherwise removing, disintegrating, or effacing it. Ruff v. Phillips, 50 Ga. 130.

The remedy which the law allows a party injured by a nuisance of destroying or removing it by his own act, so as he commits no riot in doing it, nor occasions (in the case of a private nuisance) any damage beyond what the removal of the inconvenience necessarily requires. 3 Bl. Comm. 5, 168; 3 Steph.Comm. 361; 2 Salk. 458.

Actionable nuisance. See Actionable.

Assize of nuisance. In old practice, this was a judicial writ directed to the sheriff of the county in which a nuisance existed, in which it was stated that the party injured complained of some particular fact done *ad nocumentum liberi tenementi sui*, (to the nuisance of his freehold,) and commanding the sheriff to summon an assize (that is, a jury) to view the premises, and have them at the next commission of assizes, that justice might be done, etc. 3 Bl.Comm. 221.

Common nuisance. One which affects the public in general, and not merely some particular person; a public nuisance. 1 Hawk.P.C. 197; State v. Rodgers, 91 N.J.L. 212, 102 A. 433, 434.

Continuing nuisance. An uninterrupted or periodically recurring nuisance; not necessarily a constant or unceasing injury, but a nuisance which occurs so often and is so necessarily an incident of the use of property complained of that it can fairly be said to be continuous. Farley v. Gaslight Co., 105 Ga. 323, 31 S.E. 193; Kafka v. Bozio, 191 Cal. 746, 218 P. 753, 755, 29 A.L.R. 833.

Permanent nuisance. A nuisance of such a character that its continuance is necessarily an injury which will continue without change. Norfolk & W. Ry. Co. v. Allen, 118 Va. 428, 87 S.E. 558, 560. One that cannot be readily abated at small expense. Cumberland Torpedo Co. v. Gaines, 201 Ky. 88, 255 S.W. 1046, 1048

NUISANCE AT LAW. Nuisance per se (*q. v.*).

NUISANCE IN FACT. Acts, occupations or structures which are not nuisances per se but may become nuisances by reason of the circumstances or the location and surroundings. Asphalt Products Co. v. Marable, 65 Ga.App. 877, 16 S.E.2d 771, 772.

NUISANCE PER ACCIDENS. Nuisances in fact (*q. v.*).

NUISANCE PER SE. An act, occupation, or structure which is a nuisance at all times and under all circumstances, regardless of location or surroundings. Kays v. City of Versailles, 224 Mo.App. 178, 22 S.W.2d 182, 183. As, things prejudicial to public morals or dangerous to life or injurious to public rights; distinguished from things declared to be nuisances by statute, and also from things which constitute nuisances only when considered with reference to their particular location or other individual circumstances. Hundley v. Harrison, 123 Ala. 292, 26 So. 294; Whitmore v. Paper Co., 91 Me. 297, 39 A. 1032, 40 L.R.A. 377; Simpson v. Du Pont Powder Co., 143 Ga. 465, 85 S.E. 344, 345, L.R.A.1915E, 430.

NUL. No; none. A law French negative particle commencing many phrases.

NUL AGARD. No award. The name of a plea in an action on an arbitration bond, by which the defendant traverses the making of any legal award.

NUL CHARTER, NUL VENTE, NE NUL DONE VAULT PERPETUALMENT, SI LE DONOR N'EST SEISE AL TEMPS DE CONTRACTS DE DEUX DROITS, SC. DEL DROIT DE POSSESSION ET DEL DROIT DE PROPERTIE. Co. Litt. 266. No grant, no sale, no gift, is valid forever, unless the donor, at the time of the contract, is seised of two rights, namely, the right of possession, and the right of property.

NUL DISSEISIN. In pleading, no disseisin. A plea of the general issue in a real action, by which the defendant denies that there was any desseisin.

NUL NE DOIT S'ENRICHIR AUX DEPENS DES AUTRES. No one ought to enrich himself at the expense of others.

NUL PRENDRA ADVANTAGE DE SON TORT DEMESNE. No one shall take advantage of his own wrong. 2 Inst. 713; Broom, Max. 290.

NUL SANS DAMAGE AVERA ERROR OU ATTAINT. Jenk. Cent. 323. No one shall have error or attaint unless he has sustained damage.

NUL TIEL CORPORATION. No such corporation [exists]. The form of a plea denying the existence of an alleged corporation. Rialto Co. v. Miner, 183 Mo.App. 119, 166 S.W. 629, 632.

NUL TIEL RECORD. No such record. A plea denying the existence of any such record as that alleged by the plaintiff. It is the general plea in an action of debt on a judgment. Hoffheimer v. Stiefel, 17 Misc. 236, 39 N.Y.S. 714; Watters v. Freeman Bros., 16 Ga.App. 595, 85 S.E. 931.

Judgment of *nul tiel record* occurs when some pleading denies the existence of a record and issue is joined thereon; the record being produced is compared by the court with the statement in the pleading which alleges it; and if they correspond, the party asserting its existence obtains judgment; if they do not correspond, the other party obtains judgment of *nul tiel record* (no such record).

NUL TORT. In pleading, a plea of the general issue to a real action, by which the defendant denies that he committed any wrong.

NUL WASTE. No waste. The name of a plea in an action of waste, denying the committing of waste, and forming the general issue.

NULL. Naught; of no validity or effect. Usually coupled with the word "void;" as "null and void." Forrester v. Boston, etc., Min. Co., 29 Mont. 397, 74 P. 1088; Hume v. Eagon, 73 Mo.App. 276. The words "null and void," when used in a contract or statute are often construed as meaning "voidable." Burns Mortg. Co. v. Schwartz, C.C.A.N.J., 72 F.2d 991, 992; Metropolitan Life Ins. Co. v. Hall, 191 Ga. 294, 12 S.E.2d 53, 61.

NULLA BONA. Lat. No goods. The name of the return made by the sheriff to a writ of execution, when he has not found any goods of the defendant within his jurisdiction on which he could levy. Woodward v. Harbin, 1 Ala. 108; Reed v. Lowe, 163 Mo. 519, 63 S.W. 687, 85 Am.St.Rep. 578.

NULLA CURIA QUÆ RECORDUM NON HABET POTEST IMPONERE FINEM NEQUE ALIQUEM MANDARE CARCERI; QUIA ISTA SPECTANT TANTUMMODO AD CURIAS DE RECORDO. 8 Coke, 60. No court which has not a record can impose a fine or commit any person to prison; because those powers belong only to courts of record.

NULLA EMPTIO SINE PRETIO ESSE POTEST. There can be no sale without a price. Brown v. Bellows, 4 Pick., Mass., 189.

NULLA IMPOSSIBILIA AUT INHONESTA SUNT PRÆSUMENDA; VERA AUTEM ET HONESTA ET POSSIBILIA. No things that are impossible or dishonorable are to be presumed; but things that are true and honorable and possible. Co.Litt. 78*b*.

NULLA PACTIONE EFFICI POTEST UT DOLUS PRÆSTETUR. By no agreement can it be effected that a fraud shall be practiced. Fraud will not be upheld, though it may seem to be authorized by express agreement. 5 Maule & S. 466; Broom, Max. 696.

NULLA VIRTUS, NULLA SCIENTIA, LOCUM SUUM ET DIGNITATEM CONSERVARE POTEST SINE MODESTIA. Co.Litt. 394. Without modesty, no virtue, no knowledge, can preserve its place and dignity.

NULLE RÈGLE SANS FAUTE. There is no rule without a fault.

NULLE TERRE SANS SEIGNEUR. No land without a lord. A maxim of feudal law. Guyot, Inst. Feod. c. 28.

NULLI ENIM RES SUA SERVIT JURE SERVITUTIS. No one can have a servitude over his own property. Dig. 8, 2, 26; 2 Bouv.Inst. no. 1600; Grant v. Chase, 17 Mass. 443, 9 Am.Dec. 161.

NULLI VENDEMUS, NULLI NEGABIMUS, AUT DIFFEREMUS RECTUM VEL JUSTITIAN. We neither sell nor deny, nor delay, to any person, equity or justice. State ex rel. Macri v. City of Bremerton, 8 Wash.2d 93, 111 P.2d 612, 619.

NULLITY. Nothing; no proceeding; an act or proceeding in a cause which the opposite party may treat as though it had not taken place, or which has absolutely no legal force or effect. Salter v. Hilgen, 40 Wis. 363; Jenness v. Lapeer County Circuit Judge, 42 Mich. 469, 4 N.W. 220.

Absolute Nullity. In Spanish law, nullity is either absolute or relative. The former is that which arises from the law, whether civil or criminal, the principal motive for which is the public interest, while the latter is that which affects one certain individual. Sunol v. Hepburn, 1 Cal. 281. No such distinction, however, is recognized in American law, and the term "absolute nullity" is used more for emphasis than as indicating a degree of invalidity. As to the ratification or subsequent validation of "absolute nullities," see Means v. Robinson, 7 Tex. 502, 516.

NULLITY OF MARRIAGE. The entire invalidity of a supposed, pretended, or attempted marriage, by reason of relationship or incapacity of the parties or other diriment impediments. An action seeking a decree declaring such an assumed marriage to be null and void is called a suit of "nullity of marriage." It differs from an action for divorce, because the latter supposes the existence of a valid and lawful marriage. 2 Bish. Mar. & Div. §§ 289–294.

NULLIUS FILIUS. Lat. The son of nobody; a bastard. A bastard is considered *nullius filius* as far as regards his right to inherit. But the rule of *nullius filius* does not apply in other respects, and has been changed by statute in most states so as to make him the child of his mother, in respect of inheritance. State v. Chavez, 42 N.M. 569, 82 P.2d 900, 902.

NULLIUS HOMINIS AUCTORITAS APUD NOS VALERE DEBET, UT MELIORA NON SEQUEREMUR SI QUIS ATTULERIT. The authority of no man ought to prevail with us, so far as to prevent our following better [opinions] if any one should present them. Co.Litt. 383*b*.

NULLIUS IN BONIS. Lat. Among the property of no person.

NULLIUS JURIS. Lat. In old English law, of no legal force. Fleta, lib. 2, c. 60, § 24.

NULLUM ARBITRIUM. L. Lat. No award. The name of a plea in an action on an arbitration bond, for not fulfilling the award, by which the defendant traverses the allegation that there was an award made.

NULLUM CRIMEN MAJUS EST INOBEDIENTIA. No crime is greater than disobedience. Jenk.Cent. p. 77, case 48. Applied to the refusal of an officer to return a writ.

NULLUM EXEMPLUM EST IDEM OMNIBUS. No example is the same for all purposes. Co.Litt. 212*a*. No one precedent is adapted to all cases. A maxim in conveyancing.

NULLUM FECERUNT ARBITRIUM. L. Lat. The name of a plea to an action of debt upon an obligation for the performance of an award, by which the defendant denies that he submitted to arbitration, etc. Bac.Abr. "*Arbitr.*" etc., G.

NULLUM INIQUUM EST PRÆSUMENDUM IN JURE. 7 Coke, 71. No iniquity is to be presumed in law.

NULLUM MATRIMONIUM, IBI NULLA DOS. No marriage, no dower. Wait v. Wait, 4 Barb., N.Y., 192, 194.

NULLUM SIMILE EST IDEM NISI QUATUOR PEDIBUS CURRIT. Co. Litt. 3. No like is identical, unless it run on all fours.

NULLUM SIMILE QUATOUR PEDIBUS CURRIT. No simile runs upon four feet, (or *all fours*, as it is otherwise expressed.) No simile holds in everything. Co. Litt. 3*a*; Ex parte Foster, 2 Story, 143, Fed.Cas.No.4960.

NULLUM TEMPUS ACT. A name given to the statute 3 Geo. III. c. 16, because that act, in contravention of the maxim "*Nullum tempus occurrit regi,*" (no lapse of time bars the king,) limited the crown's right to sue, etc., to the period of sixty years.

NULLUM TEMPUS AUT LOCUS OCCURRIT REGI. No time or place affects the king. 2 Inst. 273; Jenk. Cent. 83; Broom, Max. 65.

NULLUM TEMPUS OCCURRIT REGI. Time does not run against the king. The rule refers to the king in his official capacity as representing the sovereignty of the nation and not to the king as an individual. City of Bisbee v. Cochise County, 52 Ariz. 1, 78 P.2d 982, 984.

NULLUM TEMPUS OCCURRIT REIPUBLICAE. No time runs [time does not run] against the commonwealth or state. Covington County v. O'Neal, 239 Ala. 322, 195 So. 234, 238.

NULLUS ALIUS QUAM REX POSSIT EPISCOPO DEMANDARE INQUISITIONEM FACIENDAM. Co. Litt. 134. No other than the king can command the bishop to make an inquisition.

NULLUS COMMODUM CAPERE POTEST DE INJURIA SUA PROPRIA. No one can obtain an advantage by his own wrong. Co. Litt. 148; Broom, Max. 279; De Zotell v. Mutual Life Ins. Co. of New York, 60 S.D. 532, 245 N.W. 58, 59.

NULLUS DEBET AGERE DE DOLO, UBI ALIA ACTIO SUBEST. Where another form of action is given, no one ought to sue in the action *de dolo*. 7 Coke, 92.

NULLUS DICITUR ACCESSORIUS POST FELONIAM, SED ILLE QUI NOVIT PRINCIPALEM FELONIAM FECISSE, ET ILLUM RECEPTAVIT ET COMFORTAVIT. 3 Inst. 138. No one is called an "accessary" after the fact but he who knew the principal to have committed a felony, and received and comforted him.

NULLUS DICITUR FELO PRINCIPALIS NISI ACTOR, AUT QUI PRÆSENS EST, ABETTANS AUT AUXILIANS AD FELONIAM FACIENDAM. No one is called a "principal felon" except the party actually committing the felony, or the party present aiding and abetting in its commission.

NULLUS IDONEUS TESTIS IN RE SUA INTELLIGITUR. No person is understood to be a competent witness in his own cause. Dig. 22, 5, 10.

NULLUS JUS ALIENUM FORISFACERE POTEST. No man can forfeit another's right. Fleta, lib. 1, c. 28, § 11.

NULLUS RECEDAT E CURIA CANCELLARIA SINE REMEDIO. No person should depart from the court of chancery without a remedy. 4 Hen. VII. 4; Branch, Princ.

NULLUS SIMILE EST IDEM, NISI QUATUOR PEDIBUS CURRIT. No like is exactly identical unless it runs on all fours.

NULLUS VIDETUR DOLO FACERE QUI SUO JURE UTITUR. No one is considered to act with guile who uses his own right. Dig. 50, 17, 55; Broom, Max. 130.

NUMBERS GAME. A game of chance in which player selects any number and makes a bet on that number and gives amount of bet and number to the "runner" who enters it on a pad, player receiving a copy, and whereby winning number is determined each day by computation based upon prices paid on parimutuel betting machine at a designated track for horse racing as published in a newspaper, the holder of winning number receiving through the number 600 times the amount of his bet. State v. Mola, 128 Conn. 407, 23 A.2d 126, 127.

NUMERATA PECUNIA. Lat. In the civil law, money told or counted; money paid by tale. Inst. 3, 24, 2; Bract. fol. 35.

NUMERICAL LOTTERY. See Genoese Lottery.

NUMMATA. The price of anything in money, as *denariata* is the price of a thing by computation of pence, and *librata* of pounds.

NUMMATA TERRÆ. An acre of land. Spelman.

NUN. A woman who lives in a convent under vows of poverty, chastity, and obedience. Scott Co. v. Roman Catholic Archbishop for Diocese of Oregon, A. Christie, 83 Or. 97, 163 P. 88, 91.

NUNC PRO TUNC. Lat. Now for then. In re Peter's Estate, 175 Okl. 90, 51 P.2d 272, 274. A phrase applied to acts allowed to be done after the time when they should be done, with a retroactive effect, *i. e.*, with the same effect as if regularly done. Perkins v. Hayward, 132 Ind. 95, 31 N.E. 670; Secou v. Leroux, 1 N.M. 388.

"Nunc pro tunc" entry is an entry made now of something actually previously done to have effect of former date; office being not to supply omitted action, but to supply omission in record of action really had but omitted through inadvertence or mistake. Mallory v. Ward Baking Co., 270 Mich. 94, 258 N.W. 414; People v. Rosenwald, 266 Ill. 548, 107 N.E. 854, 856, Ann.Cas.1915D, 688; Grizzard v. Fite, 137 Tenn. 103, 191 S.W. 969, 971, L.R.A.1917D, 652.

NUNCIATIO. Lat. In the civil law, a solemn declaration, usually in prohibition of a thing; a protest.

NUNCIO. The permanent official representative of the pope at a foreign court or seat of government. Webster. They are called "ordinary" or "extraordinary," according as they are sent for general purposes or on a special mission.

NUNCIUS. In international law, a messenger; a minister; the pope's legate, commonly called a "nuncio."

NUNCUPARE. Lat. In the civil law, to name; to pronounce orally or in words without writing.

NUNCUPATE. To declare publicly and solemnly.

NUNCUPATIVE WILL. An oral will declared or dictated by the testator in his last sickness before a sufficient number of witnesses, and afterwards reduced to writing. Ex parte Thompson, 4 Bradf. Sur., N.Y., 154; Sykes v. Sykes, 2 Stew., Ala., 367, 20 Am.Dec. 40.

A will made by the verbal declaration of the testator, and usually dependent merely on oral testimony for proof. Cent. Dict.

NUNDINÆ. Lat. In the civil and old English law, a fair. *In nundinis et mercatis,* in fairs and markets. Bract. fol. 56.

NUNDINATION. Traffic at fairs and markets; any buying and selling.

NUNQUAM CRESCIT EX POST FACTO PRÆTERITI DELICTI ÆSTIMATIO. The character of a past offense is never aggravated by a subsequent act or matter. Dig. 50, 17, 139, 1; Bac. Max. p. 38, reg. 8; Broom, Max. 41.

NUNQUAM DECURRITUR AD EXTRAORDINARIUM SED UBI DEFICIT ORDINARIUM. We are never to resort to what is extraordinary, but [until] what is ordinary fails. 4 Inst. 84.

NUNQUAM FICTIO SINE LEGE. There is no fiction without law.

NUNQUAM INDEBITATUS. Lat. Never indebted. The name of a plea in an action of *indebitatus assumpsit,* by which the defendant alleges that he is not indebted to the plaintiff.

NUNQUAM NIMIS DICITUR QUOD NUNQUAM SATIS DICITUR. What is never sufficiently said is never said too much. Co. Litt. 375.

NUNQUAM PRÆSCRIBITUR IN FALSO. There is never a prescription in case of falsehood or forgery. A maxim in Scotch law. Bell.

NUNQUAM RES HUMANÆ PROSPERE SUCCEDUNT UBI NEGLIGUNTUR DIVINÆ. Co. Litt. 15. Human things never prosper where divine things are neglected.

NUNTIUS. In old English practice, a messenger. One who was sent to make an excuse for a party summoned, or one who explained as for a friend the reason of a party's absence. Bract. fol. 345. An officer of a court; a summoner, apparitor, or beadle. Cowell.

NUPER OBIIT. Lat. In practice, the name of a writ (now abolished) which, in the English law, lay for a sister coheiress dispossessed by her coparcener of lands and tenements whereof their father, brother, or any common ancestor died seised of an estate in fee-simple. Fitzh. Nat. Brev. 197.

NUPTIÆ SECUNDÆ. Lat. A second marriage. In the canon law, this term included any marriage subsequent to the first.

NUPTIAL. Pertaining to marriage; constituting marriage; used or done in marriage.

NUPTIAS NON CONCUBITUS SED CONSENSUS FACIT. Co. Litt. 33. Not cohabitation but consent makes the marriage.

NURTURE. To give nourishment to, to feed, to bring up, or train, to educate. Pieretti v. Pieretti, Ch., 13 N.J.Misc. 98, 176 A. 589, 592. The act of taking care of children, bringing them up, and educating them. Regina v. Clarke, 7 El. & Bl. 193.

NURUS. Lat. In the civil law, a son's wife; a daughter-in-law. Calvin.

NYCTHEMERON. The whole natural day, or day and night, consisting of twenty-four hours. Enc. Lond.

NYMPHOMANIA. See Insanity.

O

O. C. An abbreviation, in the civil law, for *"ope consilio"* (*q. v.*). In American law, these letters are used as an abbreviation for "Orphans' Court."

O. E. O. Office of Economic Opportunity.

O. K. A conventional symbol, of obscure origin much used in commercial practice and occasionally in indorsements on legal documents, signifying "correct," "approved," "accepted," "satisfactory," or "assented to." Getchell & Martin Lumber Co. v. Peterson, 124 Iowa, 599, 100 N.W. 550; Morganton Mfg. Co. v. Ohio River, etc., Ry. Co., 121 N.C. 514, 28 S.E. 474, 61 Am.St.Rep. 679.

O. N. B. An abbreviation for "Old Natura Brevium." See Natura Brevium.

O. NI. It was the course of the English exchequer, as soon as the sheriff entered into and made up his account for issues, amerciaments, etc., to mark upon each head *"O. Ni.,"* which denoted *oneratur, nisi habeat sufficientem exonerationem,* and presently he became the king's debtor, and a *debet* was set upon his head; whereupon the parties *paravaile* became debtors to the sheriff, and were discharged against the king, etc. 4 Inst. 116; Wharton.

O. S. An abbreviation for "Old Style," or "Old Series."

OATH. Any form of attestation by which a person signifies that he is bound in conscience to perform an act faithfully and truthfully. Vaughn v. State, 146 Tex.Cr.R. 586, 177 S.W.2d 59, 60. An affirmation of truth of a statement, which renders one willfully asserting untrue statements punishable for perjury. U. S. v. Klink, D.C.Wyo., 3 F. Supp. 208, 210. An outward pledge by the person taking it that his attestation or promise is made under an immediate sense of responsibility to God. Morrow v. State, 140 Neb. 592, 300 N.W. 843, 845. A solemn appeal to the Supreme Being in attestation of the truth of some statement. State v. Jones, 28 Idaho 428, 154 P. 378, 381; Tyler, Oaths 15. An external pledge or asseveration, made in verification of statements made, or to be made, coupled with an appeal to a sacred or venerated object, in evidence of the serious and reverent state of mind of the party, or with an invocation to a supreme being to witness the words of the party, and to visit him with punishment if they be false. June v. School Dist. No. 11, Southfield Tp., 283 Mich. 533, 278 N.W. 676, 677, 116 A.L. R. 581. In its broadest sense, the term is used to include all forms of attestation by which a party signifies that he is bound in conscience to perform the act faithfully and truly. In a more restricted sense, it excludes all those forms of attestation or promise which are not accompanied by an imprecation.

The term has been variously defined: as, "a solemn invocation of the vengeance of the Deity upon the witness if he do not declare the whole truth, so far as he knows it," 1 Stark.Ev. 22; or, "a religious asseveration by which a person renounces the mercy and imprecates the vengeance of Heaven if he do not speak the truth," 1 Leach 430; or, as "a religious act by which the party invokes God not only to witness the truth and sincerity of his promise, but also to avenge his imposture or violated faith, or, in other words, to punish his perjury if he shall be guilty of it," 10 Toullier, n. 343; Puffendorff, b. 4, c. 2, § 4. The essential idea of an oath would seem to be, however, that of a recognition of God's authority by the party taking it, and an undertaking to accomplish the transaction to which it refers as required by his laws.

See Kissing the Book.

Assertory Oath. One relating to a past or present fact or state of facts, as distinguished from a "promissory" oath which relates to future conduct; particularly, any oath required by law other than in judicial proceedings and upon induction to office, such, for example, as an oath to be made at the custom-house relative to goods imported.

Corporal Oath. See Corporal.

Decisive or Decisory Oath. In the civil law, where one of the parties to a suit, not being able to prove his charge, offered to refer the decision of the cause to the oath of his adversary, which the adversary was bound to accept, or tender the same proposal back again, otherwise the whole was taken as confessed by him. Cod. 4, 1, 12.

Extrajudicial Oath. One not taken in any judicial proceeding, or without any authority or requirement of law, though taken formally before a proper person. State v. Scatena, 84 Minn. 281, 87 N.W. 764.

False Oath. See titles "False Oath" and "Perjury."

Judicial Oath. One taken in some judicial proceeding or in relation to some matter connected with judicial proceedings. One taken before an officer in open court, as distinguished from a "non-judicial" oath, which is taken before an officer ex parte or out of court. State v. Dreifus, 38 La.Ann. 877.

Official Oath. One taken by an officer when he assumes charge of his office, whereby he declares that he will faithfully discharge the duties of the same, or whatever else may be required by statute in the particular case.

Poor Debtor's Oath. See Poor.

Promissory Oaths. Oaths which bind the party to observe a certain course of conduct, or to fulfill certain duties, in the future, or to demean himself thereafter in a stated manner with reference to specified objects or obligations; such, for example, as the oath taken by a high executive officer, a legislator, a judge, a person seeking naturalization, an attorney at law. Case v. People, 6 Abb. N. C., N.Y., 151. A solemn appeal to God, or, in a wider sense, to some superior sanction or a sacred or revered person in witness of the inviolability of a promise or undertaking. People ex rel. Bryant v. Zimmerman, 241 N.Y. 405, 150 N.E. 497, 499, 43 A.L.R. 909.

Purgatory Oath. An oath by which a person *purges* or clears himself from presumptions, charges or suspicions standing against him, or from a contempt.

Qualified Oath. One the force of which as an affirmation or denial may be qualified or modified by the circumstances under which it is taken or which necessarily enter into it and constitute a part of it; especially thus used in Scotch law.

Solemn Oath. A corporal oath. Jackson v. State, 1 Ind. 184.

Suppletory Oath. In the civil and ecclesiastical law, the testimony of a single witness to a fact is called "half-proof," on which no sentence can be founded; in order to supply the other half of proof, the party himself (plaintiff or defendant) is admitted to be examined in his own behalf, and the oath administered to him for that purpose is called the "suppletory oath," because it supplies the necessary *quantum* of proof on which to found the sentence. 3 Bl. Comm. 370.

This term, although without application in American law in its original sense, is sometimes used as a designation of a party's oath required to be taken in authentication or support of some piece of documentary evidence which he offers, for example, his books of account.

Voluntary Oath. Such as a person may take in extrajudicial matters, and not regularly in a court of justice, or before an officer invested with authority to administer the same. Brown.

OATH AGAINST BRIBERY. One which could have been administered to a voter at an election for members of parliament. Abolished in 1854. Wharton.

OATH EX OFFICIO. The oath by which a clergyman charged with a criminal offense was formerly allowed to swear himself to be innocent; also the oath by which the compurgators swore that they believed in his innocence. 3 Bl. Comm. 101, 447; Mozley & Whiteley.

OATH IN LITEM. In the civil law, an oath permitted to be taken by the plaintiff, for the purpose of proving the value of the subject-matter in controversy, when there was no other evidence on that point, or when the defendant fraudulently suppressed evidence which might have been available. Greenl. Ev. § 348; 1 Eq. Cas. Abr. 229; Herman v. Drinkwater, 1 Greenl., Me., 27.

OATH OF ALLEGIANCE. An oath by which a person promises and binds himself to bear true allegiance to a particular sovereign or government, *e. g.*, the United States; administered generally to high public officers and to soldiers and sailors, also to aliens applying for naturalization, and, occasionally, to citizens generally as a prerequisite to their suing in the courts or prosecuting claims before government bureaus. Rev.St. U.S. §§ 3478, 31 U.S.C.A. § 204.

OATH OF CALUMNY. In the civil law, an oath which a plaintiff was obliged to take that he was not prompted by malice or trickery in commencing his action, but that he had *bona fide* a good cause of action. Poth. Pand. lib. 5, tt. 16, 17, s. 124.

OATH-RITE. The form used at the taking of an oath.

OB. Lat. On account of; for. Several Latin phrases and maxims, commencing with this word, are more commonly introduced by *"in"* (*q. v.*).

OB CAUSAM ALIQUAM A RE MARITIMA ORTAM. For some cause arising out of a maritime matter. 1 Pet. Adm. 92. Said to be Selden's translation of the French definition of admiralty jurisdiction, *"pour le fait de la mer."* Id.

OB CONTINENTIAM DELICTI. On account of contiguity to the offense, *i. e.*, being contaminated by conjunction with something illegal.

For example, the cargo of a vessel, though not contraband or unlawful, may be condemned in admiralty, along with the vessel, when the vessel has been engaged in some service which renders her liable to seizure and confiscation. The cargo is then said to be condemned *ob continentiam delicti*, because found in company with an unlawful service. 1 Kent, Comm. 152.

OB CONTINGENTIAM. On account of connection; by reason of similarity. In Scotch law, this phrase expresses a ground for the consolidation of actions.

OB FAVOREM MERCATORUM. In favor of merchants. Fleta, lib. 2, c. 63, § 12.

OB INFAMIAM NON SOLET JUXTA LEGEM TERRÆ ALIQUIS PER LEGEM APPARENTEM SE PURGARE, NISI PRIUS CONVICTUS FUERIT VEL CONFESSUS IN CURIA. Glan. lib. 14, c. ii. On account of evil report, it is not usual, according to the law of the land, for any person to purge himself, unless he have been previously convicted, or confessed in court.

OB TURPEM CAUSAM. For an immoral consideration. Dig. 12, 5.

OBÆRATUS. Lat. In Roman law, a debtor who was obliged to serve his creditor till his debt was discharged. Adams, Rom. Ant. 49.

OBEDIENCE. Compliance with a command, prohibition, or known law and rule of duty prescribed; the performance of what is required or enjoined by authority, or the abstaining from what is prohibited, in compliance with the command or prohibition. Webster.

OBEDIENTIA. An office, or the administration of it; a kind of rent; submission; obedience.

OBEDIENTIA EST LEGIS ESSENTIA. 11 Coke, 100. Obedience is the essence of the law.

OBEDIENTIAL OBLIGATION. See Obligation.

OBEDIENTIARIUS; OBEDIENTIARY. A monastic officer. Du Cange; see 1 Poll. & Maitl. 417.

OBIT. A funeral solemnity, or office for the dead. Cowell. The anniversary of a person's death; the anniversary office. Cro. Jac. 51.

OBIT SINE PROLE. Lat. [He] died without issue. Yearb. M. 1 Edw. II. 1.

OBITER. Lat. By the way; in passing; incidentally; collaterally.

OBITER DICTUM. Words of a prior opinion entirely unnecessary for the decision of the case. Noel v. Olds, 78 U.S.App.D.C. 155, 138 F.2d 581, 586.

Statements in opinions wherein courts indulged in generalities that had no actual bearing on issues involved. Graham v. Jones, 198 La. 507, 3 So. 2d 761, 774.

A remark made, or opinion expressed, by a judge, in his decision upon a cause, "by the way," that is, incidentally or collaterally, and not directly upon the question before him, or upon a point not necessarily involved in the determination of the cause, or introduced by way of illustration, or analogy or argument. See Dictum.

OBJECT, *v.* In legal proceedings, to object (*e. g.*, to the admission of evidence) is to interpose a declaration to the effect that the particular matter or thing under consideration is not done or admitted with the consent of the party objecting, but is by him considered improper or illegal, and referring the question of its propriety or legality to the court.

OBJECT, *n.* End aimed at, the thing sought to be accomplished, the aim or purpose, the thing sought to be attained. State v. Banks, 33 Idaho 765, 198 P. 472, 474; Miller v. Tucker, 142 Miss. 146, 105 So. 774, 777.

Anything which comes within the cognizance or scrutiny of the senses, especially anything tangible or visible. Moore v. Union Mut. Fire Ins. Co., 112 Vt. 218, 22 A.2d 503, 505. That which is perceived, known, thought of, or signified; that toward which a cognitive act is directed. Cent. Dict.

The term includes whatever may be presented to the mind as well as to the senses; whatever, also, is acted upon or operated upon affirmatively, or intentionally influenced by anything done, moved, or applied thereto, Wells v. Shook, 8 Blatchf. 257, Fed.Cas.No.17,406; it may be used as having the sense of effect, Harland v. Territory, 3 Wash.T. 131, 13 P. 453.

OBJECT OF AN ACTION. Legal relief to prevent or redress the wrong. Ophuls & Hill v. Carolina Ice & Fuel Co., 160 S.C. 441, 158 S.E. 824, 827. The thing sought to be obtained by the action; the remedy demanded or the relief or recovery sought or prayed for; not the same thing as the cause of action or the subject of the action. Scarborough v. Smith, 18 Kan. 406; Lassiter v. Norfolk & C. R. Co., 136 N.C. 89, 48 S.E. 643.

OBJECT OF A STATUTE. Aim or purpose of its enactment. Pinder v. Board of Sup'rs of Election of Calcasieu Parish, La.App., 146 So. 715, 718; Nichols v. Yandre, 151 Fla. 87, 9 So.2d 157, 158, 144 A.L.R. 1351. End or design which it is meant to accomplish, while the "subject" is the matter to which it relates and with which it deals. Medical Examiners v. Fowler, 50 La.Ann. 1358, 24 So. 809; McNeely v. South Penn Oil Co., 52 W.Va. 616, 44 S.E. 508, 62 L.R.A. 562. Matter or thing forming groundwork of statute. Moats v. Cook, 113 W.Va. 151, 167 S.E. 137, 138.

OBJECTION. Act of objecting; that which is, or may be, presented in opposition; an adverse reason or argument; a reason for objecting or opposing; a feeling of disapproval. 131 Ken Ave. Co. v. Gross, 125 N.J.L. 513, 16 A.2d 469, 470.

The act of a party who objects to some matter or proceeding in the course of a trial, (see Object, *v.*:) or an argument or reason urged by him in support of his contention that the matter or proceeding objected to is improper or illegal.

By the term "objections" by the Governor to a statute, as used in a state constitution, is meant his disapproval. State v. Forsyth, 21 Wyo. 359, 133 P. 521, 529.

It is directed to thing done by one other than judge or court, and "exception" going to action or ruling of court. State ex rel. Brockman Mfg. Co. v. Miller, 241 S.W. 920, 922.

OBJECTIVE SYMPTOM. Those which a surgeon or physician discovers from an examination of his patient, "subjective symptoms" being those which he learns from what his patient tells him. Schroeder v. Western Union Telegraph Co., Mo.App., 129 S.W.2d 917, 922.

OBJECTS OF A POWER. Those among whom donee is given power to appoint. Restatement, Property, § 319(3); Mozley & Whiteley.

OBJURGATRIX. In old English law, scolds or unquiet women were referred to as objurgatrices and were punished with the cucking-stool (*q. v.*).

OBLATA. Gifts or offerings made to the king by any of his subjects; old debts, brought, as it were, together from preceding years, and put on the present sheriff's charge. Wharton.

OBLATA TERRÆ. Half an acre, or, as some say, half a perch, of land. Spelman.

OBLATE. See Oblati.

OBLATE ROLLS. Chancery Rolls (1199–1641), called also Fine Rolls, containing records of payments to the king by way of oblate or fine for the grant of privileges, or by way of amercement for breach of duty. 2 Holdsw. Hist. E. L. 141.

OBLATI. In old European law, voluntary slaves of churches or monasteries.

OBLATI ACTIO. In the civil law, an action given to a party against another who had *offered* to him a stolen thing, which was found in his possession. Inst. 3, 1, 4.

OBLATIO. Lat. In the civil law, a tender of money in payment of a debt made by debtor to creditor. Whatever is offered to the church by the pious. Calvin.

OBLATION. Oblations, or obventions, are offerings or customary payments made, in England, to the minister of a church, including fees on marriages, burials, mortuaries, etc., (*q. v.*) and Easter offerings. 2 Steph. Comm. 740; Phillim. Ecc. Law, 1596. They may be commuted by agreement.

OBLATIONES DICUNTUR QUÆCUNQUE A PIIS FIDELIBUSQUE CHRISTIANIS OFFERUNTUR DEO ET ECCLESIÆ, SIVE RES SOLIDÆ SIVE MOBILES. 2 Inst. 389. Those things are called "oblations" which are offered to God and to the Church by pious and faithful Christians, whether they are movable or immovable.

OBLIGATE. To bind or constrain; to bind to the observance or performance of a duty; to place under an obligation. To bind one's self by an obligation or promise; to assume a duty; to execute a written promise or covenant; to make a writing obligatory. Wachter v. Famachon, 62 Wis. 117, 22 N.W. 160; Maxwell v. Jacksonville Loan & Imp. Co., 45 Fla. 425, 34 So. 255.

OBLIGATIO. Lat. In Roman law, a legal bond which obliges the performance of something in accordance with the law of the land. Ortolan, Inst. 2, § 1179. It corresponded nearly to our word contract. The legal relation existing between two certain persons whereby one (the creditor) is authorized to demand of the other (the debtor) a certain performance which has a money value. In this sense *obligatio* signifies not only the duty of the debtor, but also the right of the creditor. The fact establishing such claim and debt, as also the instrument evidencing it, is termed "obligation." Mackeld. Rom. Law, § 360.

That legal relation subsisting between two persons by which one is bound to the other for a certain performance. The passive relation sustained by the debtor to the creditor is likewise called an "obligation." Sometimes, also, the term *"obligatio"* is used for the *causa obligationis,* and the contract itself is designated an "obligation." There are passages in which even the document which affords the proof of a contract is called an "obligation." Such applications, however, are but a loose extension of the term, which, according to its true idea, is only properly employed when it is used to denote the debt relationship, in its totality, active and passive, subsisting between the creditor and the debtor. Tomk. & J.Mod.Rom.Law, 301.

OBLIGATIO CIVILIS. An obligation enforceable by action, whether it derives its origin from the *jus civile,* as the obligation engendered by formal contracts or the obligation enforceable by bilaterally penal suits, or from such portion of the *jus gentium* as had been completely naturalized in the civil law and protected by all its remedies, such as the obligation engendered by formless contracts.

OBLIGATIO EX CONTRACTU. An obligation arising from contract, or an antecedent *jus in personam.* In this there are two stages,—first, a primary or sanctioned personal right antecedent to wrong, and, afterwards, a secondary or sanctioning personal right consequent on a wrong. Poste's Gaius' Inst. 359.

OBLIGATIO EX DELICTO, or OBLIGATIO EX MALEFICIO. An obligation founded on wrong or tort, or arising from the invasion of a *jus in rem.* In this there is the second stage, a secondary or sanctioning personal right consequent on a wrong, but the first stage is not a personal right, (*jus in personam,*) but a real right, (*jus in rem,*) whether a primordial right, right of *status,* or of property. Poste's Gaius' Inst. 359.

OBLIGATIO NATURALIS. An obligation not immediately enforceable by action; one deriving its validity from the law of nature, or one imposed by that portion of the *jus gentium* which is only imperfectly recognized by civil law.

These had not the binding force of the other classes, not being capable of enforcement by action, and are, therefore, not noticed by Justinian in his classification; but they had, nevertheless, a certain efficacy even in the civil law: for instance, though a debt founded upon a natural obligation could not be recovered by an action, yet if it was voluntarily paid by the debtor he could not recover it back, as he might do in the case of money paid by mistake, etc., where no natural obligation existed. L. 38, pr. D. 12. 6; Ortolan 2, § 1180.

OBLIGATIO PRÆTORIÆ. The Romans considered that obligations derived their validity solely from positive law. At first the only ones recognized were those established in special cases in accordance with the forms prescribed by the strict *jus civile.* In the course of time, however, the prætorian jurisdiction, in mitigation of the primtive rigor of the law, introduced new modes of contracting obligations and provided the means of enforcing them; hence the twofold division made by Justinian of *obligationes civiles* and *obligationes prœtoriœ.* Inst. 1. 3. 13.

OBLIGATION. A generic word, derived from the Latin substantive "obligatio," having many, wide, and varied meanings, according to the context in which it is used. Enyeart v. City of Lincoln, 136 Neb. 146, 285 N.W. 314, 318. That which a person is bound to do or forbear; any duty imposed by law, promise, contract, relations of society, courtesy, kindness, etc. Goodwin v. Freadrich, 135 Neb. 203, 280 N.W. 917, 923. Duty. Rucks-Brandt Const. Co. v. Price, 165 Okl. 178, 23 P.2d 690. Duty imposed by law. Helvering v. British-American Tobacco Co., C.C.A., 69 F.2d 528, 530. Law or duty binding parties to perform their agreement. An undertaking to perform. State v. Citrus County, 116 Fla. 676, 157 So. 4, 97 A.L.R. 431. That which constitutes a legal or moral duty and which renders a person liable to coercion and punishment for neglecting it; a word of broad meaning, and the particular meaning intended is to be gained by consideration of its context. An obligation or debt may exist by reason of a judgment as well as an express contract, in either case there being a legal duty on the part of the one bound to comply with the promise. Schwartz v. California Claim Service, 52 Cal.App.2d 47, 125 P.2d 833, 888. Liabilities created by contract or law, Rose v. W. B. Worthen Co., 186 Ark. 205, 53 S.W.2d 15, 16, 85 A.L.R. 212; or tort. Exchange Bank v. Ford, 3 P. 449, 451, 7 Colo. 314. As legal term word originally meant a sealed bond, but it now extends to any certain written promise to pay money or do a specific thing. Lee v. Kenan, C.C.A.Fla., 78 F.2d 425, 100 A.L.R. 869. A formal and binding agreement or acknowledgment of a liability to pay a certain sum or do a certain thing. United States v. One Zumstein Briefmarken Katalog 1938, D.C. Pa., 24 F.Supp. 516, 519.

The binding power of a vow, promise, oath, or contract, or of law, civil, political, or moral, independent of a promise; that which constitutes legal or moral duty, and which renders a person liable to coercion and punishment for neglecting it. Webster.

A tie which binds us to pay or do something agreeably to the laws and customs of the country in which the obligation is made. Inst. 3, 14.

Obligation is (1) legal or moral duty, as opposed to physical compulsion; (2) a duty incumbent upon an individual, or a specific and limited number of individuals, as opposed to a duty imposed upon the world at large; (3) the right to enforce such a duty, *(jus in personam,)* as opposed to such a right as that of property, *(jus in rem,)* which avails against the world at large; (4) a bond containing a penalty, with a condition annexed, for the payment of money, performance of covenants, or the like. Mozley & Whitley.

"Obligation" is the correlative of "right." Taking the latter word in its politico-ethical sense, as a power of free action lodged in a person, "obligation" is the corresponding duty, constraint, or binding force which should prevent all other persons from denying, abridging, or obstructing such right, or interfering with its exercise. And the same is its meaning as the correlative of a *"jus in rem."* Taking "right" as meaning a *"jus in personam,"* (a power, demand, claim, or privilege inherent in one person, and incident upon another,) the "obligation" is the coercive force or control imposed upon the person of incidence by the moral law and the positive law, (or the moral law as recognized and sanctioned by the positive law,) constraining him to accede to the demand, render up the thing claimed, pay the money due, or otherwise perform what is expected of him with respect to the subject-matter of the right.

A penal bond or "writing obligatory," that is, a bond containing a penalty, with a condition annexed for the payment of money, performance of covenants, or the like, and which differs from a bill, the latter being generally without a penalty or condition, though it may be obligatory. Co.Litt. 172.

A deed whereby a man binds himself under a penalty to do a thing. Com.Dig. *Obligation* (A); Taylor v. Glaser, 2 Serg. & R., Pa., 502; Denton v. Adams, 6 Vt. 40. The word has a very broad and comprehensive legal signification and embraces all instruments of writing, however informal, whereby one party contracts with another for the payment of money or the delivery of specific articles. State v. Campbell, 103 N.C. 344, 9 S.E. 410; Morrison v. Lovejoy, 6 Minn. 353, Gil. 224; Sinton v. Carter Co., 23 F. 535.

In English expositions of the Roman law, and works upon general jurisprudence, "obligation" is used to translate the Latin *"obligatio."* In this sense its meaning is much wider than as a technical term of English law. See Obligatio.

Absolute obligation. One which gives no alternative to the obligor, but requires fulfillment according to the engagement.

Conjunctive or alternative obligation. The former is one in which the several objects in it are connected by a copulative, or in any other manner which shows that all of them are severally comprised in the contract. This contract creates as many different obligations as there are different objects; and the debtor, when he wishes to discharge himself, may force the creditor to receive them separately. But where the things which form the object of the contract are separated by a disjunctive, then the obligation is alternative, and the performance of either of such things will discharge the obligor. The choice of performing one of the obligations belongs to the obligor, unless it is expressly agreed that it shall belong to the creditor. Civ.Code La. art. 2068; Dougl. 14; 1 Ld. Raym. 279; Galloway v. Legan, 4 Mart. N. S. (La.) 167. A promise to deliver a certain thing or to pay a specified sum of money is an example of an alternative obligation. Civ.Code La. arts. 2063, 2066, 2067.

Contractual obligation. One which arises from a contract or agreement.

Determinate or indeterminate obligation. A determinate obligation is one which has for its object a certain thing: as, an obligation to deliver a certain horse named Bucephalus, in which case the obligation can be discharged only by delivering the identical horse. An indeterminate obligation is one where the obligor binds himself to deliver one of a certain species: as, to deliver a horse, where the delivery of any horse will discharge the obligation.

Divisible or indivisible obligation. A divisible obligation is one which, being a unit, may nevertheless be lawfully divided, with or without the consent of the parties. An indivisible obligation is one which is not susceptible of division: as, for example, if I promise to pay you one hundred dollars, you cannot assign one-half of this to another, so as to give him a right of action against me for his share.

Express or implied obligation. Express or conventional obligations are those by which the obligor binds himself in express terms to perform his obligation, while implied obligations are such as are raised by the implication or inference of the law from the nature of the transaction.

Failure to meet obligations. See Failure to Meet Obligations.

Joint or several obligation. A joint obligation is one by which two or more obligors bind themselves jointly for the performance of the obligation. France v. France, 94 Or. 414, 185 P. 1108. A several obligation is one where the obligors promise, each for himself, to fulfill the engagement.

Moral obligation. A duty which is valid and binding in conscience and according to natural justice, but is not recognized by the law as adequate to set in motion the machinery of justice; that is, one which rests upon ethical considerations alone, and is not imposed or enforced by positive law. Taylor v. Hotchkiss, 81 App.Div. 470, 80 N.Y.S. 1042; Bailey v. Philadelphia, 167 Pa. 569, 31 A. 925, 46 Am.St.Rep. 691. A duty which would be enforceable by law, were it not for some positive rule, which, with a view to general benefit, exempts the party in that particular instance from legal liability. Backhaus v. Lee, 49 N.D. 821, 194 N.W. 887, 890; Longstreth v. City of Philadelphia, 245 Pa. 233, 91 A. 667.

Natural or civil obligation. A natural obligation is one which cannot be enforced by action, but which is binding on the party who makes it in conscience and according to natural justice; Blair v. Williams, 4 Litt., Ky., 41. As, for instance, when the action is barred by the act of limitation, a natural obligation still subsists, although the civil obligation is extinguished; Sturges v. Crowninshield, 4 Wheat. 197, 4 L.Ed. 529; Ogden v.

Saunders, 12 Wheat. 318, 337, 6 L.Ed. 606. A civil obligation is a legal tie, which gives the party with whom it is contracted the right of enforcing its performance by law. Civ.Code La. art. 1757; Poth. Obl. 173, 191.

Obediential obligation. One incumbent on parties in consequence of the situation or relationship in which they are placed. Ersk. Prin. 60.

Perfect or imperfect obligation. A perfect obligation is one recognized and sanctioned by positive law; one of which the fulfillment can be enforced by the aid of the law. Aycock v. Martin, 37 Ga. 124, 92 Am.Dec. 56. But if the duty created by the obligation operates only on the moral sense, without being enforced by any positive law, it is called an "imperfect obligation," and creates no right of action, nor has it any legal operation. The duty of exercising gratitude, charity, and the other merely moral duties are examples of this kind of obligation. Civ.Code La. art. 1757; Edwards v. Kearzey, 96 U.S. 600, 24 L.Ed. 793.

Personal or heritable obligation. An obligation is heritable when the heirs and assigns of one party may enforce the performance against the heirs of the other. Civ.Code La. art. 1997. It is personal when the obligor binds himself only, not his heirs or representatives. An obligation is strictly personal when none but the obligee can enforce the performance, or when it can be enforced only against the obligor. Civ.Code La. art. 1997. An obligation may be personal as to the obligee, and heritable as to the obligor, and it may in like manner be heritable as to the obligee, and personal as to the obligor. Civ.Code La. art. 1998. For the term *personal obligation,* as used in a different sense, see the next paragraph.

Personal or real obligation. A personal obligation is one by which the obligor binds himself to perform an act, without directly binding his property for its performance. A real obligation is one by which real estate, and not the person, is liable to the obligee for the performance.

Thus, when an estate owes an easement, as a right of way, it is the thing, and not the owner, who owes the easement. Another instance of a real obligation occurs when a person buys an estate which has been mortgaged, subject to the mortgage; he is not liable for the debt, though the estate is. In these cases the owner has an interest only because he is seized of the servient estate or the mortgaged premises, and he may discharge himself by abandoning or parting with the property. The obligation is both personal and real when the obligor has bound himself and pledged his estate for the fulfilment of the obligations. In the civil law and in Louisiana, a real obligation is one which is attached to immovable property, and it passes with such property into whatever hands the property may come, without making the third possessor personally responsible. Civ.Code La. art. 1997.

Primary obligation. An obligation which is the principal object of the contract.

For example, the primary obligation of the seller is to deliver the thing sold, and to transfer the title to it. It is distinguished from the accessory or secondary obligation to pay damages for not doing so. 1 Bouv.Inst. no. 702. The words "primary" and "direct," contrasted with "secondary," when spoken with reference to an obligation, refer to the remedy provided by law for enforcing the obligation, rather than to the character and limits of the obligation itself. Kilton v. Providence Tool Co., 22 R.I. 605, 48 A. 1039.

Primitive or secondary obligation. A primitive obligation, which in one sense may also be called a principal obligation, is one which is contracted with a design that it should itself be the first fulfilled. A secondary obligation is one which is contracted and is to be performed in case the primitive cannot be. For example, if one sells his house, he binds himself to give a title; but if he finds he cannot as when the title is in another, then his secondary obligation is to pay damages for nonperformance of the obligation.

Principal or accessory obligation. A principal obligation is one which arises from the principal object of the engagement of the contracting parties; while an accessory obligation depends upon or is collateral to the principal. See Poth. Obl. no. 182.

For example, in the case of the sale of a house and lot of ground, the principal obligation on the part of the vendor is to make title for it; the accessory obligation is to deliver all the title-papers which the vendor has relating to it, to take care of the estate until it is delivered, and the like. See, further, the title Accessory Obligation.

Pure obligation. One which is not suspended by any condition, whether it has been contracted without any condition, or, when thus contracted, the condition has been accomplished. Poth. Obl. no. 176. See simple obligation.

Simple or conditional obligation. Simple obligations are such as are not dependent for their execution on any event provided for by the parties, and which are not agreed to become void on the happening of any such event. Conditional obligations are such as are made to depend on an uncertain event. If the obligation is not to take effect until the event happens, it is a suspensive condition; if the obligation takes effect immediately, but is liable to be defeated when the event happens, it is then a resolutory condition. Civ.Code La. arts. 2020, 2021; Moss v. Smoker, 2 La.Ann. 989. A simple obligation is also defined as one which is not suspended by any condition, either because it has been contracted without condition, or, having been contracted with one, the condition has been fulfilled; and a conditional obligation is also defined as one the execution of which is suspended by a condition which has not been accomplished, and subject to which it has been contracted.

Single or penal obligation. A penal obligation is one to which is attached a penal clause, which is to be enforced if the principal obligation be not performed. A single obligation is one without any penalty: as where one simply promises to pay another one hundred dollars. This is called a single bill, when it is under seal.

Solidary obligation. In the law of Louisiana, one which binds each of the obligors for the whole debt, as distinguished from a "joint" obligation, which binds the parties each for his separate proportion of the debt. Groves v. Sentell, 14 S.Ct. 898, 153 U.S. 465, 38 L.Ed. 785. See Solidary.

OBLIGATION OF A CONTRACT. That which law in force when contract is made obliges parties to do or not to do, and remedy and legal means to carry it into effect. Harris v. Monroe Building & Loan Ass'n, La.App., 154 So. 503, 505.

As used in Const.U.S. art. 1, § 10, the term means the binding and coercive force which constrains every man to perform the agreements he has made; a force grounded in the ethical principle of fidelity to one's promises, but deriving its legal efficacy from its recognition by positive law, and sanctioned by the law's providing a remedy for the infraction of the duty or for the enforcement of the correlative right. Story, Const. § 1378; Black, Const.Prohib. § 139; Ogden v. Saunders, 12 Wheat. 213, 6 L.Ed. 606.

The "obligation of a contract" is its binding force according to the standards of law in existence when it was made. Colby v. City of Medford, 85 Or. 485, 167 P. 487, 499. The "obligation of a contract" is the duty of performance. Hays v. Port of Seattle, D.C.Wash., 226 F. 287, 293. The term includes everything within the obligatory scope of the contract, and it includes the means of enforcement. E. J. Lander & Co. v. Deemy, 46 N.D. 273, 176 N.W. 922, 925; Franklin Sugar Refining Co. v. Martin-Nelly Grocery Co., 94 W.Va. 504, 119 S.E. 473, 476.

OBLIGATION SOLIDAIRE. This, in French law, corresponds to joint and several liability in English law, but is applied also to the joint and several rights of the creditors parties to the obligation.

OBLIGATIONES EX DELICTO or EX MALEFICIO. Obligations arising from the commission of a wrongful injury to the person or property of another.

"Delictum" is not exactly synonymous with "tort," for, while it includes most of the wrongs known to the common law as torts, it is also wide enough to cover some offenses (such as theft and robbery) primarily injurious to the individual, but now only punished as crimes. Such acts gave rise to an *obligatio,* which consisted in the liability to pay damages.

OBLIGATIONES EX VARIIS CAUSARUM FIGURIS. Athough Justinian confined the divisions of obligations to four classes, namely *obligationes ex contractu, quasi ex contractu, ex maleficio* and *quasi ex maleficio,* there are many species of obligations which cannot properly be reduced within any of these classes. Some authorities have, consequently, established a fifth class, to receive the odds and ends which belonged nowhere else, and have given to this class the above designation, borrowed from Gaius, l. 1, pr. § 1, D. 44, 7; Mackeldey § 474; Hadley, Rom. Law 209, etc.

OBLIGATIONES QUASI EX CONTRACTU. Often persons who have not contracted with each other, under a certain state of facts, are regarded by the Roman law as if they had actually concluded a convention between themselves. The legal relation which then takes place between these persons, which has always a similarity to a contract obligation, is therefore termed *obligatio quasi ex contractu.*

Such a relation arises from the conducting of affairs without authority, *(negotiorum gestio)* or unauthorized agency; from the management of property that is in common when the community arose from casualty, *(communio incidens);* from the payment of what was not due *(solutio indebiti);* from tutorship and curatorship *(tutela* and *cura),* resembling the relation of guardian and ward; from taking possession of an inheritance *(additio hereditatis* and *agnitio bonorum possessionis);* and in many other cases. Mackeld.Rom.Law, § 491.

OBLIGATIONES QUASI EX DELICTO, or OBLIGATIONES QUASI EX MALIFICIO. This class embraces all torts not coming under the denomination of *delicta* and not having a special form of action provided for them by law. They differed widely in character, and at common law would in some cases give rise to an action on the case, in others to an action on an implied contract. Ort. Inst. §§ 1781–1792.

OBLIGATORY PACT. See Pact.

OBLIGATORY RIGHTS. See Right.

OBLIGATORY WRITING. See Writing Obligatory.

OBLIGEE. The person in favor of whom some obligation is contracted, whether such obligation be to pay money or to do or not to do something. Code La. art. 3522, no. 11 (Civ.Code, art. 3556, subd. 20). Jenkins v. Williams, 191 Ky. 165, 229 S.W. 94, 95. The party to whom a bond is given.

Obligees are either *several* or *joint.* An obligee is several when the obligation is made to him alone; obligees are joint when the obligation is made to two or more; and in that event each is not a creditor for his separate share, unless the nature of the subject or the particularity of the expression in the instrument lead to a different conclusion. 2 Pothier, Obl., Evans ed. 56; Hob. 172; Cro.Jac. 251.

The words obligee and payee have been held to have a technical and definite meaning under an act relative to promissory notes, bonds, etc., and apply only to notes, bonds, or bills whether given for the payment of money or for the performance of covenants and conditions, and not to mortgages; Hall v. Bryne, 1 Scam., Ill., 142.

OBLIGOR. The person who has engaged to perform some obligation. Code La. art. 3522, no. 12, Civ.Code, art. 3556, subd. 21. One who makes a bond.

Includes person liable for tort. Sarine v. American Lumbermen's Casualty Co. of Illinois, 258 App.Div. 653, 17 N.Y.S.2d 754, 756.

Obligors are *joint* and *several.* They are joint when they agree to pay the obligation jointly. They are several when one or more bind themselves and each of them separately to perform the obligation. In order to become an obligor, the party must actually, either himself or by his attorney, enter into the obligation and execute it as his own.

OBLIQUUS. Lat.

In the old law of descents, oblique; cross; transverse; collateral. The opposite of *rectus,* right, or upright.

In the law of evidence, indirect; circumstantial.

OBLITERATED CORNER. See Corner.

OBLITERATION. Erasure or blotting out of written words.

Lines drawn through the signatures of the witnesses to a will amount to an "obliteration," though the signatures be discernible. In re Kutzner's Will, 19 N.Y.S.2d 13, 16, 173 Misc. 776. Same where line is drawn through writing. Glass v. Scott, 14 Colo.App. 377, 60 P. 186; Evans' Appeal, 58 Pa. 244; Townshend v. Howard, 86 Me. 285, 29 A. 1077.

When the testator of a holographic will wrote across its face "Will revoked," and "This will is hereby revoked," and signed his name with lines beneath the signature, the will was canceled, defaced, and obliterated, within Decedent Estate Law, § 34, subds. 5, 6 (Consol.Laws, c. 13). In re Parsons' Will, 195 N.Y.S. 742, 745, 119 Misc. 26.

OBLIVION. Act of forgetting, or fact of having forgotten; forgetfulness. Official ignoring of offenses; amnesty, or general pardon; as, an act of oblivion. State or fact of being forgotten. Webster, Dict. A kind of annihilation. Gilbert v. Missouri Pac. Ry. Co., 92 Kan. 281, 140 P. 883.

OBLIVIOUS. Evincing oblivion; forgetful; forgetting. Webster, Dict. Where thing is extinguished from mind. Gilbert v. Missouri Pac. Ry. Co., 92 Kan. 281, 140 P. 883.

OBLOQUY. Censure and reproach. Bettner v. Holt, 70 Cal. 275, 11 Pac. 716. Blame, reprehension, being under censure, a cause or object of reproach, a disgrace. Burr v. Winnett Times Pub. Co., 80 Mont. 70, 258 P. 242, 246.

OBNOXIOUS. "Obnoxious" and "offensive" in ordinary use are synonymous, and mean objectionable, disagreeable, displeasing, and distasteful. City of Muskogee v. Morton, 128 Okl. 17, 261 P. 183, 184.

OBRA. In Spanish law, work. *Obras,* works or trades; those which men carry on in houses or covered places. White, New Recop. b. 1, tit. 5, c. 3, § 6.

OBREPTIO. Lat. The obtaining a thing by fraud or surprise. Calvin. Called, in Scotch law, *"obreption."*

OBREPTION. Obtaining anything by fraud or surprise. Acquisition of escheats, etc., from the sovereign, by making false representations. Bell. See, also, Subreption.

OBROGARE. Lat. In the civil law, to pass a law contrary to a former law, or to some clause of it; to change a former law in some part of it. Calvin.

OBROGATION. In the civil law, the annulling a law, in whole or in part, by passing a law contrary to it. The alteration of a law. Calvin.

OBSCENE. Material is "obscene" if to average person, applying contemporary community standards, dominant theme of material taken as a whole appeals to prurient interest, if it is utterly without redeeming social importance, if it goes substantially beyond customary limits of candor in description or representation, if it is characterized by patent offensiveness, and if it is hard-core pornography. Roth v. United States, 354 U.S. 476, 77 S.Ct. 1304; Jacobellis v. Ohio, 378 U.S. 184, 84 S.Ct. 1676; Manual Enterprises, Inc. v. Day, 370 U.S. 478, 82 S.Ct. 1432; U. S. v. Klaw, C.A.N.Y., 350 F.2d 155, 164.

Offensive to chastity of mind or to modesty, expressing or presenting to the mind or view something that delicacy, purity, and decency forbids to be exposed; calculated to corrupt, deprave, and debauch the morals of the people, and promote violation of law; licentious and libidinous and tending to excite feelings of an impure or unchaste character; tending to stir the sex impulses or to lead to sexually impure and lustful thoughts; tending to corrupt the morals of youth or to lower the standards of right and wrong especially as to the sexual relation. Parmelee v. United States, 72 App.D.C. 203, 113 F.2d 729, 730.

OBSCENE BOOK or PAPER. An obscene book or paper within the act relating to nonmailable matter means one which contains immodest and indecent matter, the reading whereof would have a tendency to deprave and corrupt the minds of those in whose hands the publication might fall, and whose minds are open to such immoral influences; U. S. v. Clarke, D.C.Mo., 38 Fed. 732.

OBSCENITY. The character or quality of being obscene; conduct tending to corrupt the public morals by its indecency or lewdness. State v. Pfenninger, 76 Mo.App. 313; U. S. v. Males, D.C. Ind., 51 Fed. 41.

OBSCURE. When applied to words, statements or meanings, it signifies not perspicuous, not clearly expressed, hard to understand. Western Union Telegraph Co. v. Geo. F. Fish, Inc., 148 Md. 210, 129 A. 14, 16.

OBSERVE. In the civil law, to perform that which has been prescribed by some law or usage. Dig. 1, 3, 32; Marshall County v. Knoll, 102 Iowa 573, 69 N.W. 1146.

OBSES. Lat. In the law of war, a hostage. *Obsides,* hostages.

OBSIGNARE. Lat. In the civil law, to seal up; as money that had been tendered and refused.

OBSIGNATORY. Ratifying and confirming.

OBSOLESCENCE. Condition or process of falling into disuse. State Line & Sullivan R. Co. v. Phillips, D.C.Pa., 17 F.Supp. 607, 609, 610.

OBSOLESCENT. Becoming obsolete; going out of use; not entirely disused, but gradually becoming so.

OBSOLETE. That which is no longer used. Becker v. Anheuser-Busch, Inc., C.C.A.Mo., 120 F. 2d 403, 416. Disused; neglected; not observed.

The term is applied to statutes which have become inoperative by lapse of time, either because the reason for their enactment has passed away, or their subject-matter no longer exists, or they are not applicable to changed circumstances, or are tacitly disregarded by all men, yet without being expressly abrogated or repealed. Lemen v. Kansas Flour Mills Co., 122 Kan. 574, 253 P. 547, 548.

OBSTA PRINCIPIIS. Lat. Withstand beginnings; resist the first approaches or encroachments. Bradley, J., Boyd v. U. S., 116 U.S. 635, 6 Sup.Ct. 535, 29 L.Ed. 746.

OBSTANTE. Withstanding; hindering. See Non Obstante.

OBSTETRICS. The branch of medical science which has to do with the care of women during pregnancy and parturition. Stoike v. Weseman, 167 Minn. 266, 208 N.W. 993.

OBSTINATE DESERTION. "Obstinate" as used of desertion, which is a ground for divorce, means determined, fixed, persistent. Mitchell v. Mitchell, 91 Fla. 427, 107 So. 630, 631. Persisted in against the willingness of the injured party to have it concluded. Laing v. Laing, 110 N.J.Eq. 411, 160 A. 510, 511.

OBSTRICTION. Obligation; bond.

OBSTRUCT. To hinder or prevent from progress, check, stop, also to retard the progress of, make accomplishment of difficult and slow. Conley v. United States, C.C.A.Minn., 59 F.2d 929, 936. To be or come in the way of or to cut off the sight of an object. Silva v. Waldie, 42 N.M. 514, 82 P.2d 282, 286. To block up; to interpose obstacles; to render impassable; to fill with barriers or impediments; as to obstruct a road or way. U. S. v. Williams, 28 Fed.Cas. 633; Chase v. Oshkosh, 81 Wis. 313, 51 N.W. 560, 15 L.R.A. 553, 29 Am.St.Rep. 898. To impede; to interpose impediments, to the hindrance or frustration of some act or service; as to obstruct an officer in the execution of his duty. Davis v. State, 76 Ga. 722; Lamon v. Gold, 72 W.Va. 618, 79 S.E. 728, 730, 51 L.R.A.,N.S., 883.

As applied to navigable waters, to "obstruct" them is to interpose such impediments in the way of free and open navigation that vessels are thereby prevented from going where ordinarily they have a right to go or where they may find it necessary to go in their maneuvers. The City of Richmond, D.C.S.D.N.Y., 43 F. 88; Terre Haute Drawbridge Co. v. Halliday, 4 Ind. 36; The Vancouver, 28 F. Cas. 960.

OBSTRUCTING JUSTICE. Impeding or obstructing those who seek justice in a court, or those who have duties or powers of administering justice therein. People v. Ormsby, 310 Mich. 291, 17 N.W. 2d 187, 190.

The act by which one or more persons attempt to prevent, or do prevent, the execution of lawful process. The term applies also to obstructing the administration of justice in any way—as by hindering witnesses from appearing. Melton v. Commonwealth, 160 Ky. 642, 170 S.W. 37, 42, L.R.A.1915B, 689; People v. Hebbard, 162 N.Y.S. 80, 89, 96 Misc.Rep. 617. Any act, conduct, or directing agency pertaining to pending proceedings, intended to play on human frailty and to deflect and deter court from performance of its duty and drive it into compromise with its own unfettered judgment by placing it, through medium of knowingly false assertion, in wrong position before public, constitutes an obstruction to administration of justice. State v. Shumaker, 200 Ind. 623, 157 N.E. 769, 774, 58 A.L.R. 954; Toledo Newspaper Co. v. U. S., 247 U.S. 402, 38 S.Ct. 560, 564, 62 L.Ed. 1186.

OBSTRUCTING AN OFFICER. Implies forcible resistance; State v. Le Blanc, 115 Me. 142, 98 A. 119, 120; contra, State v. Estes, 185 N.C. 752, 117 S.E. 581, 582.

To "obstruct" a public officer means to oppose that officer. It does not mean to oppose or impede the process with which the officer is armed, or to defeat its execution, but that the officer himself shall be obstructed. Knoff v. State, 18 Okl.Cr. 36, 192 P. 596, 597; Ratcliff v. State, 12 Okl.Cr. 448, 158 P. 293, 294.

OBSTRUCTING PROCEEDINGS OF LEGISLATURE. The term embraces not only things done in the presence of the legislature, but those done in disobedience of a committee. Ex parte Youngblood, 94 Tex.Cr.R. 330, 251 S.W. 509, 512.

OBSTRUCTING PROCESS. In criminal law, the act by which one or more persons attempt to prevent or do prevent the execution of lawful process.

OBSTRUCTING THE RECRUITING OR ENLISTMENT SERVICE. The phrase in Espionage Act, tit. 1, § 3 (50 USCA § 33 note), should be given a broad meaning, and includes to hinder, impede, embarrass, and retard, in whole or in part. Doe v. U. S., C.C.A.Colo., 253 F. 903, 906. The term does not necessarily mean actual prevention of enlistments or recruiting, it being sufficient if one interferes with such service or renders it more difficult. Rhuberg v. United States, C.C.A.Or., 255 F. 865, 869; U. S. v. Pierce, D.C.N.Y., 245 F. 878, 884. It contemplates more than a physical obstruction. O'Hare v. U. S., C.C.A.N.D., 253 F. 538, 540.

OBSTRUCTION. A hindrance, obstacle, or barrier. Carder v. City of Clarksburg, 100 W.Va. 605, 131 S.E. 349, 352. Delay, impeding or hindering. State v. Malpass, 189 N.C. 349, 127 S.E. 248, 250.

This is the word properly descriptive of an injury to any-one's incorporeal hereditament, *e. g.*, his right to an easement, or *profit à prendre;* an alternative word being "disturbance." On the other hand, "infringement" is the word properly descriptive of an injury to any one's patent-rights or to his copyright. But "obstruction" is also a very general word in law, being applicable to every hindrance of a man in the discharge of his duty, (whether official, public, or private.) Brown.

"Obstruction" in highway includes anything interfering with highway easement. Andrew B. Hendryx Co. v. City of New Haven, 104 Conn. 632, 134 A. 77, 79.

"Obstruction," within a statute requiring certain precautions by those in charge of train on appearance of obstruction, means obstacle, impediment, hindrance, bar, barrier, clog, or check. Howard & Herrin v. Nashville, C. & St. L. Ry. Co., 153 Tenn. 649, 284 S.W. 894, 896, 46 A.L.R. 1530; Turner v. Southern Ry. Co., 112 Miss. 359, 73 So. 62, 63.

As applied to the operation of railroads, an "obstruction" may be either that which obstructs or hinders the free and safe passage of a train, or that which may receive an injury or damage, such as it would be unlawful to inflict, if run over or against by the train, as in the case of cattle or a man approaching on the track. Louisville N. & G. R. Co. v. Reidmond, 11 Lea, Tenn., 205; South & North Alabama R. Co. v. Williams, 65 Ala. 77.

OBSTRUCTION TO NAVIGATION. Any unnecessary interference with the free movements of vessels. The Steam Dredge No. 6, D.C.N.Y., 222 F. 576, 579.

OBTAIN. To get hold of by effort; to get possession of; to procure; to acquire, in any way. State v. Bowdry, 346 Mo. 1090, 145 S.W.2d 127, 129.

The word in statute relating to obtaining money or property by false pretenses, is not limited to getting, securing, or appropriating money or property as owner. It includes as well the getting or securing of money or property by way of a loan. Tingue v. State, 90 Ohio St. 368, 108 N.E. 222, 223, Ann.Cas.1916C, 1156. As used in a confidence game statute it means to acquire the possession of, or control of, and not necessarily to acquire title to. People v. Miller, 278 Ill. 490, 116 N.E. 131, 138, L.R.A.1917E, 797.

OBTAINING MONEY BY FALSE PRETENSES. See False Pretenses.

OBTEMPER. See Obtemperare.

OBTEMPERANDUM EST CONSUETUDINI RATIONABILI TANQUAM LEGI. A reasonable custom is to be obeyed as a law. 4 Coke, 38.

OBTEMPERARE. Lat. To obey. Hence the Scotch *"obtemper,"* to obey or comply with a judgment of a court.

OBTEST. To protest.

OBTORTO COLLO. In Roman law, taken by the neck or collar; as a plaintiff was allowed to drag a reluctant defendant to court. Adams, Rom. Ant. 242.

OBTULIT SE. Offered himself. In old practice, the emphatic words of entry on the record where one party *offered himself* in court against the other, and the latter did not appear. 1 Reeve, Eng. Law, 417.

OBVENTIO. Lat. (from *obvenire,* to fall in).

In the civil law, rent; profits; income; the return from an investment or thing owned; as the earnings of a vessel. Generally used in the plural.

In old English law, the revenue of a spiritual living, so called. Also, in the plural, "offerings."

OBVENTION. See Obventio; Oblation.

OBVIOUS. Easily discovered, seen, or understood, readily perceived by the eye or the intellect, plain, synonymous with the words "plain," "clear," and "evident." Combs v. Colonial Casualty Co., 73 W. Va. 473, 80 S.E. 779, 781, 50 L.R.A.,N.S., 1218. Apparent; evident; manifest. Fandeck v. Barnett & Record Co., 161 Wis. 55, 150 N.W. 537, 541; Tolfree v. Wetzler, D.C.N.J., 22 F.2d 214.

OBVIOUS DANGER. Apparent in exercise of ordinary observation and disclosed by use of eyes and other senses. Patterson v. Cleveland Cliffs Iron Co., 37 Ohio App. 316, 174 N.E. 592, 594. Plain and apparent to a reasonably observant person. Combs v. Colonial Casualty Co., 73 W.Va. 473, 80 S.E. 779, 780, 50 L.R.A.,N.S., 1218.

OBVIOUS RISK. One so plain that it would be instantly recognized by a person of ordinary intelligence. City of Atlanta v. Trussell, 21 Ga.App. 340, 94 S.E. 649, 653. Within an accident policy, one which would be plain and apparent to a reasonably prudent and cautious person in the use of his faculties. Christensen v. National Travelers' Ben. Ass'n of Des Moines, Iowa, 196 Iowa 375, 194 N.W. 194, 196, 29 A.L.R. 709. It does not mean an unnecessary risk. Hickman v. Ohio State Life Ins. Co., 92 Ohio St. 87, 110 N.E. 542, 543.

OCASION. In Spanish law, accident. Las Partidas, pt. 3, tit. 32, l. 21; White, New Recop. b. 2, tit. 9, c. 2.

OCCASIO. In feudal law, a tribute which the lord imposed on his vassals or tenants for his necessity. Hindrance; trouble; vexation by suit. See, also, Occasiones.

OCCASION, *n.* That which provides an opportunity for the causal agency to act. Weinberg v. Richardson, 291 Ill.App. 618, 10 N.E.2d 893. Meaning not only particular time but carrying idea of opportunity, necessity, or need, or even cause in a limited sense, under G. L. c. 4, § 6, subd. 3. Commonwealth v. Tsouprakakis, 267 Mass. 496, 166 N.E. 855, 856. Condition of affairs; juncture entailing need; exigency; or juncture affording ground or reason for something. Ridout v. State, 161 Tenn. 248, 30 S.W.2d 255, 259, 71 A.L.R. 830.

OCCASION, *v.* To cause or bring about by furnishing the condition or opportunity for the action of some other cause. Smart v. Raymond, Mo.App., 142 S.W.2d 100, 104. To give occasion to, to produce; to cause incidentally or indirectly; bring about or be the means of bringing about or producing. Industrial Commission of Ohio v. Weigandt, 102 Ohio St. 1, 130 N.E. 38, 39.

OCCASIONARI. To be charged or loaded with payments or occasional penalties.

OCCASIONES. In old English law, assarts. Spelman.

OCCUPANCY. Occupancy is a mode of acquiring property by which a thing which belongs to nobody becomes the property of the person who took possession of it with the intention of acquiring a right of ownership in it. Civ. Code La. art. 3412; Goddard v. Winchell, 86 Iowa, 71, 52 N.W. 1124, 17 L.R.A. 788, 41 Am.St.Rep. 481. The taking possession of things which before belonged to nobody, with an intention of appropriating them to one's own use. To constitute occupancy, there must be a taking of a thing corporeal, belonging to nobody, with an intention of becoming the owner of it; Co. Litt. 416.

Occupancy is sometimes used in the sense of occupation or holding possession; indeed it has come to be very generally so used in this country in homestead laws, public-land laws, and the like, Walters v. People, 21 Ill. 178; Redfield v. R. Co., 25 Barb., N.Y., 54; Act of Cong. May 29, 1830, 4 Stat. 420; but this does not appear to be a common legal use of the term, as recognized by English authorities.

There is a use of the word in public-land laws, homestead laws, "occupying-claimant" laws, cases of landlord and tenant, and like connections, which seems to require the broader sense of possession, although there is, in most of these uses, a shade of meaning discarding any prior title as a foundation of right. Perhaps both uses or views may be harmonized, by saying that in jurisprudence occupancy or occupation is possession, presented independent of the idea of a chain of title, of any earlier owner. Or "occupancy" and "occupant" might be used for assuming property which has no owner, and "occupation" and "occupier" for the more general idea of possession. Judge Bouvier's definitions seem partly founded on such a distinction, and there are indications of it in English usage. It does not appear generally drawn in American books. Abbott.

"Possession" and "occupancy," when applied to land, are nearly synonymous terms, and may exist through a tenancy. Thus, occupancy of a homestead, such as will satisfy the statute, may be by means other than that of actual residence on the premises by the widow or child. Walters v. People, 21 Ill. 178. Occupancy is always actual, as distinguished from possession, which may be actual or constructive. Occupancy is never constructive, save in the sense that land may be occupied through the actual possession of another. Davis v. State, 20 Ga.App. 68, 92 S.E. 550, 551. "Occupancy" is act of taking or holding possession and does not necessarily include residence. Kornhauser v. National Surety Co., 114 Ohio St. 24, 150 N.E. 921, 923.

Under fire policy, it must be such as ordinarily pertains to purpose to which property is adapted or devoted as described in policy. Continental Ins. Co. of New York v. Dunning, 249 Ky. 234, 60 S.W. 2d 577.

Under burglary policy it implies an actual use of the house as a dwelling place not absolutely continuous, but as a place of usual return. Young v.

Fidelity & Casualty Co. of New York, 202 Mo.App. 319, 215 S.W. 496, 498.

Under statute respecting adverse possession, the term was synonymous with "actual possession," as distinguished from "constructive possession." Hart v. All Persons, 26 Cal.App. 664, 148 P. 236, 240.

See Occupation; Occupy.

In International law. The taking possession of a newly discovered or conquered country with the intention of holding and ruling it.

OCCUPANT. Person having possessory rights, who can control what goes on on premises. United States v. Fox, C.C.A.N.Y., 60 F.2d 685, 688.

One who takes the first possession of a thing of which there is no owner.

One who occupies and takes possession, one who has the actual use, possession or control of a thing. Lechler v. Chapin, 12 Nev. 65; Wittkop v. Garner, 4 N.J.Misc. 234, 132 A. 339, 340.

In a special sense, one who takes possession of lands held *pur autre vie,* after the death of the tenant, and during the life of the *cestui que vie.*

Common occupant. See *general occupant,* below.

General occupant. At common law where a man was tenant *pur autre vie,* or had an estate granted to himself only (without mentioning his heirs) for the life of another man, and died without alienation during the life of *cestui que vie,* or him by whose life it was holden, he that could first enter on the land might lawfully retain the possession, so long as *cestui que vie* lived, by right of occupancy, and was hence termed a "general" or common "occupant." 1 Steph.Comm. 415.

Special occupant. A person having a special right to enter upon and occupy lands granted *pur autre vie,* on the death of the tenant, and during the life of *cestui que vie.*

Where the grant is to a man *and his heirs* during the life of *cestui que vie,* the *heir,* succeeds as special occupant, having a special exclusive right by the terms of the original grant. 2 Bl.Comm. 259; 1 Steph.Comm. 416.

In the United States the statute provisions of the different states vary considerably upon this subject. In New York and New Jersey, special occupancy is abolished. Virginia, and probably Maryland, follow the English statutes. In Massachusetts and other states, where the real and personal estates of intestates are distributed in the same way and manner, the question does not seem to be material. 4 Kent 27.

OCCUPANTIS FIUNT DERELICTA. Things abandoned become the property of the (first) occupant. Taylor v. The Cato, 1 Pet.Adm. 53, Fed. Cas.No.13,786.

OCCUPARE. Lat. In the civil law, to seize or take possession of; to enter upon a vacant possession; to take possession before another. Calvin.

OCCUPATILE. That which has been left by the right owner, and is now possessed by another.

OCCUPATIO. "The advisedly taking possession of that which is at the moment the property of no man, with a view of acquiring property in it for yourself." Maine, Anc.L. 245. The advised assumption of physical possession. *Id.* 256. See Occupancy.

OCCUPATION. Possession. Sweet; Kinneer v. Southwestern Mut. Fire Ass'n, 118 Pa.Super. 312, 179 A. 800. Where a person exercises physical control over land. Lancaster County Bank v. Marshel, 130 Neb. 141, 264 N.W. 470, 475. Control; tenure; use.

"Occupation" of a dwelling house means living in it. The use for which premises are intended should be considered in determining what is meant by the word "unoccupied" as contained in a policy. Hoover v. Mercantile Town Mut. Ins. Co., 93 Mo.App. 111, 69 S.W. 42. As used in a fire insurance policy the word *unoccupied,* is not synonymous with *vacant,* but is that condition where no one has the actual use or possession of the thing or property in question, Yost v. Ins. Co., 38 Pa.Super.Ct. 594; Hardiman v. Fire Ass'n, 212 Pa. 383, 61 A. 990.

A putting out of a man's freehold in time of war. Co.Litt. s. 412.

Actual occupation. An open, visible occupancy as distinguished from the constructive one which follows the legal title. Cutting v. Patterson, 82 Minn. 375, 85 N.W. 172; People v. Ambrecht, 11 Abb.Prac., N.Y., 97; Bennett v. Burton, 44 Iowa 550.

Vocation. That which principally takes up one's time, thought, and energies; especially, one's regular business or employment; also whatever one follows as the means of making a livelihood. Dorrell v. Norida Land & Timber Co., 53 Idaho, 793, 27 P.2d 960; Texas Co. v. Amos, 77 Fla. 327, 81 So. 471, 472; Childers v. Brown, 81 Or. 1, 158 P. 166, 168, Ann.Cas.1918D, 170. Particular business, profession, trade, or calling which engages individual's time and efforts, employment in which one regularly engages or vocation of his life. Harris v. Southern Carbon Co., La.App., 162 So. 430, 434; Evans v. Woodman Acc. Ass'n, 171 P. 643, 644, 102 Kan. 556, L.R.A.1918D, 122; Industrial Commission of Ohio v. Roth, 120 N.E. 172, 173, 98 Ohio St. 34, 6 A.L.R. 1463.

OCCUPATION TAX. A tax imposed upon an occupation or the prosecution of a business, trade, or profession; not a tax on property, or even the capital employed in the business, but an excise tax on the business itself; to be distinguished from a "license tax," which is a fee or exaction for the privilege of engaging in the business, not for its prosecution. Adler v. Whitbeck, 44 Ohio St. 539, 9 N.E. 672; Appeal of Banger, 109 Pa. 95; Pullman Palace Car Co. v. State, 64 Tex. 274, 53 Am. Rep. 758.

OCCUPATIONAL. Of or pertaining to an occupation, trade or work. Morgan v. Equitable Life Assur. Soc. of U. S., La.App., 22 So.2d 595, 597.

OCCUPATIONAL DISEASE. Disease gradually contracted in usual and ordinary course of employment, because thereof, and incidental thereto. Travelers Ins. Co. v. Lancaster, Tex.Civ.App., 71 S.W.2d 318, 319.

OCCUPATIONAL DUTIES. Those of insured's ordinary and usual occupation, and not those of unusual, casual and temporary employment. Federal Life Ins. Co. v. Lorton, 97 Colo. 545, 51 P.2d 693, 694.

OCCUPATIVE. Pertaining to or involving occupation or the right of occupation. Webster.

OCCUPAVIT. Lat. In old English law, a writ that lay for one who was ejected out of his land or tenement in time of war. Cowell.

OCCUPIER. An occupant; one who is in the enjoyment of a thing.

A tenant, though absent, is, generally speaking, the occupier of premises; 1 B. & C. 178; but not a servant or other person who may be there *virtute officii*; 26 L.J.C.P. 12; 47 L.J.Ex. 112; L.R. 1 Q.B. 72.

OCCUPY. To take or enter upon possession of; to hold possession of; to hold or keep for use; to possess; to tenant; to do business in. People v. Roseberry, 23 Cal.App.2d 13, 71 P.2d 944. Actual use, possession, and cultivation. Jackson v. Sill, 11 Johns., N.Y., 202, 6 Am.Dec. 363.

The term, under fire policy, implies use by some person according to purpose for which it is designed, and does not imply that some one shall remain in building all of the time without interruption, but merely that there shall not be a cessation of occupancy for any considerable length of time. Washington Fire Ins. Co. v. Cobb, Tex.Civ.App., 163 S.W. 608, 612; Southern Nat. Ins. Co. v. Cobb, Tex.Civ.App., 180 S.W. 155, 156. As used in connection with a homestead, it does not always require an actual occupancy, but may sometimes permit a constructive occupancy. Kerns v. Warden, 88 Okl. 297, 213 P. 70, 72.

See Occupation; Occupancy.

OCCUPYING CLAIMANT. An occupant claiming right under statute to recover for improvements he has placed on the land subsequently found not to be his. Kelly v. Watkins, 135 Okl. 276, 276 P. 191, 192.

OCCUPYING CLAIMANT ACTS. Statutes providing for the reimbursement of a *bona fide* occupant and claimant of land, on its recovery by the true owner, to the extent to which lasting improvements made by him have increased the value of the land, and generally giving him a lien therefor. Jones v. Great Southern Hotel Co., 86 F. 370, 30 C.C.A. 108.

OCCUR. To meet one's eye; to be found or met with; to present itself; to appear; hence, to befall in due course; to happen. Grenada Bank v. Petty, 174 Miss. 415, 164 So. 316, 318. To arise; begin. Murphy v. People, 78 Colo. 276, 242 P. 57, 59.

OCCURRENCE. A coming or happening; any incident or event, especially one that happens without being designed or expected. Farmers & Merchants Nat. Bank v. Arrington, Tex.Civ.App., 98 S.W.2d 378, 382.

OCEAN. The main or open sea; the high sea; that portion of the sea which does not lie within the body of any country and is not subject to the territorial jurisdiction or control of any country, but is open, free, and common to the use of all nations. U. S. v. Rodgers, 14 S.Ct. 109, 150 U.S. 249, 37 L.Ed. 1071; U. S. v. New Bedford Bridge, 27 Fed.Cas. 120.

OCHIERN. In old Scotch law, a name of dignity; a freeholder. Skene's de Verb. Sign.

OCHLOCRACY. Government by the multitude. A form of government wherein the populace has the whole power and administration in its own hands. The abuse of a democracy. Mob rule.

OCTAVE. In old English law, the eighth day inclusive after a feast; one of the return days of writs. 3 Bl.Comm. 278.

OCTO TALES. Lat. Eight such; eight such men; eight such jurors. The name of a writ, at common law, which issues when upon a trial at bar, *eight* more jurors are necessary to fill the panel, commanding the sheriff to summon the requisite number. 3 Bl.Comm. 364; Decem Tales.

OCTROI. Fr. In French law, originally, a toll or duty, which, by the permission of the *seigneur,* any city was accustomed to collect on liquors and some other goods, brought within its precincts, for the consumption of the inhabitants. Afterwards appropriated to the use of the king. Steph. Lect. p. 361.

OCULIST. A duly licensed physician specializing in the diseases of the eye. Stern v. Flynn, 154 Misc. 609, 278 N.Y.S. 598.

ODD LOT BUSINESS. The dealing in a smaller number of shares than the unit of trading on the floor of the stock exchange. People ex rel. Berdan v. Goldfogle, 213 App.Div. 702, 211 N.Y.S. 107.

ODD LOT DOCTRINE. Under this doctrine, if the effects of an accident have not been removed, it is not sufficient, to entitle an employer to have a reduction in the weekly compensation ordered by the court under the Workmen's Compensation Act, that it appears the workman has the physical capacity to do some kind of work different from the general kind of work which he was engaged in at the time of the accident, but it must also be shown that the workman, either by his own efforts or that of his employer, can actually get such work. Olneyville Wool Combing Co. v. Di Donato, 65 R.I. 154, 13 A.2d 817. Zelinckas v. Ford Motor Co., 294 Mich. 494, 293 N.W. 732.

ODERUNT PECCARE BONI, VIRTUTIS AMORE; ODERUNT PECCARE MALI, FORMIDINE PŒNÆ. Good men hate to sin through love of virtue; bad men, through fear of punishment.

ODHAL. Complete property, as opposed to feudal tenure. The transposition of the syllables of *"odhal"* makes it *"allodh,"* and hence, according to Blackstone, arises the word *"allod"* or *"allodial,"* (*q. v.*). *"Allodh"* is thus put in contradistinction to *"feeodh."* Mozley & Whiteley.

ODHAL RIGHT. An allodial right.

ODIO ET ATIA. See De Odio et Atia.

ODIOSA ET INHONESTA NON SUNT IN LEGE PRÆSUMANDA. Odius and dishonest acts are not presumed in law. Co. Litt. 78; Jackson v. Miller, 6 Wend. (N. Y.) 228, 231, 21 Am.Dec. 316.

ODIOSA NON PRÆSUMUNTUR. Odius things are not presumed. Burrows, Sett. Cas. 190.

ODIUM. Means hatred and dislike. In venue statute, it implies such a general ill feeling toward a party to an action as will render it uncertain whether the cause can be tried by impartial triers, free from an atmosphere impregnated with malice or corrupting prejudices. Brow v. Levy, 3 Ind.App. 464, 29 N.E. 417.

ODIOUS. Synonymous with infamous. Polson v. Polson, 140 Ind. 310, 39 N.E. 498.

ŒCONOMICUS. L. Lat. In old English law. The executor of a last will and testament. Cowell.

ŒCONOMUS. Lat. In the civil law. A manager or administrator. Calvin.

OEDEMA. A bogging down of the kidneys, heart and lungs because of heavy load of gas poison entering through the lungs and infecting the tissues and organs of the whole system. Ogletree v. Jones, 44 N.M. 567, 106 P.2d 302.

OF. A term denoting that from which anything proceeds; indicating origin, source, descent, and the like; as, he is of a race of kings; he is of noble blood. Stone v. Riggs, 43 Okl. 209, 142 P. 298, 299. Associated with or connected with, usually in some causal relation, efficient, material, formal, or final. Harlan v. Industrial Accident Commission, 194 Cal. 352, 228 P. 654, 657.

The word has been held equivalent to after, 10 L.J.Q.B. 10; at, or belonging to, Davis v. State, 38 Ohio St. 506; in possession of, Bell County v. Hines, Tex.Civ.App., 219 S.W. 556, 557; Stokes v. Great Southern Lumber Co., D.C.Miss., 21 F.2d 185, 186; manufactured by, 2 Bing. N.C. 668; by, Hannum v. Kingsley, 107 Mass. 355; residing at, Porter v. Miller, 3 Wend. (N.Y.) 329; 8 A. & E. 232; from, State v. Wong Fong, 75 Mont. 81, 241 P. 1072, 1074; in, Kellogg v. Ford, 70 Or. 213, 139 P. 751, 752.

OF COUNSEL. A phrase commonly applied in practice to the counsel employed by a party in a cause, and particularly to one employed to assist in the preparation or management of a cause, or its presentation on appeal, but who is not the principal attorney of record for the party.

OF COURSE. As a matter of right. Stoddard v. Treadwell, 29 Cal. 281; Jones v. McGonigle, 327 Mo. 457, 37 S.W.2d 892, 74 A.L.R. 550. Any action or step taken in the course of judicial proceedings which will be allowed by the court upon mere application, without any inquiry or contest, or which may be effectually taken without even applying to the court for leave. Merchants' Bank of St. Joseph v. Crysler, C.C.A.Mo., 67 F. 390, 14 C.C.A 444; Petit v. Petit, 45 Misc. 155, 91 N.Y.S. 979.

OF FORCE. In force; extant; not obsolete; existing as a binding or obligatory power.

OF GRACE. This phrase had its origin in an age when kings dispensed their royal favors at the hands of chancellors, but has no rightful place in American jurisprudence. Sullivan v. Jones & Laughlin Steel Co., 208 Pa. 540, 57 A. 1065, 66 L.R. A. 712. A term applied to any permission or license granted to a party in the course of a judicial proceeding which is not claimable as a matter of course or of right, but is allowed by the favor or indulgence of the court. See Walters v. McElroy, 151 Pa. 549, 25 A. 125.

OF NEW. A Scotch expression, closely translated from the Latin *"de novo,"* (*q. v.*).

OF RECORD. Recorded; entered on the records; existing and remaining in or upon the appropriate records.

A mortgage to be "of record" must be recorded in the county in which it is properly and legally recordable for purpose of constructive notice. Riley v. Commonwealth, 275 Ky. 370, 121 S.W.2d 921.

Under statute providing that recognizances shall be "of record", the term means of record in the sense that it is taken by inferior tribunals—that they have been taken and certified to the clerk of the court of record and by him recorded. King v. State, 18 Neb. 375, 25 N.W. 519.

OF RIGHT. As a matter of course. Atkins v. Garrett, D.C.La., 252 F. 280, 282. See "Of Course."

OF THE BLOOD. A technical legal phrase meaning to be descended from the person referred to or from the same common stock and from a common ancestor. In re Easter's Estate, 24 Cal.2d 191, 148 P.2d 601.

OFFA EXECRATA. In old English law. The morsel of execration; the corsned, (*q. v.*). 1 Reeve, Eng. Law, 21.

OFFENDER. Commonly used in statutes to indicate person implicated in the commission of a crime and includes person guilty of a misdemeanor. State ex rel. Smith v. Jameson, 70 S.D. 503, 19 N.W.2d 505, 508.

OFFENSE. A crime or misdemeanor; a breach of the criminal laws. People v. Brenta, 64 Cal. App. 91, 220 P. 447; State v. Hirsch, 91 Vt. 330, 100 A. 877, 879; Ex parte Brady, 116 Ohio St. 512, 157 N.E. 69, 70. State v. Johnson, 212 N.C. 566, 194 S.E. 319, 322.

It is used as a *genus*, comprehending every crime and misdemeanor, or as a *species*, signifying a crime not indictable, but punishable summarily or by the forfeiture of a penalty. In re Terry, C.C.Cal., 37 F. 649.

The word "offense," while sometimes used in various senses, generally implies a crime or a misdemeanor infringing public as distinguished from mere private rights, and punishable under the criminal laws, though it may also include the violation of a criminal statute for which the remedy is merely a civil suit to recover the penalty. Commonwealth v. Brown, 264 Pa. 85, 107 A. 676, 678.

Under a statute, declaring that one guilty of an offense or fault causing another damage is obliged to repair it, "offense or fault" has the same meaning as "tort"; Panama R. Co. v. Rock, C.C.A.Canal Zone, 272 F. 649, 651; and a criminal contempt has been held to be an "offense." Creekmore v. U. S., C.C.A.Okl., 237 F. 743, 754, L.R.A. 1917C, 845; Ex parte Grossman, 267 U.S. 87, 45 S.Ct. 332, 335, 69 L.Ed. 527, 38 A.L.R. 131.

Continuing offense. A transaction or a series of acts set on foot by a single impulse, and operated by an unintermittent force, no matter how long a time it may occupy. State v. Brown, 10 Okl.Cr. 52, 133 P. 1143, 1144; Ex parte Dunn, 33 Okl.Cr. 190, 242 P. 574.

Criminal offense. Includes misdemeanors as well as felonies. People v. Scalisi, 324 Ill. 131, 154 N.E. 715, 721. It is an offense which subjects the offender to indictment. Latimer v. Wilson, 103 N.J.L. 159, 134 A. 750, 751.

Quasi offense. One which is imputed to the person who is responsible for its injurious consequences, not because he himself committed it, but because the perpetrator of it is presumed to have acted under his commands.

Same offense. As used in a provision against double jeopardy, the term means the same crime, not the same transaction, acts, circumstances, or situation. State v. Billotto, 104 Ohio St. 13, 135 N.E. 285, 287; U. S. v. Bostow, D.C.Ala., 273 F. 535, 538.

Second offense. One committed after conviction for a first offense. Holst v. Owen, C.C.A.Fla., 24 F. 2d 100. See State v. Snyder, 30 N.M. 40, 227 P. 613, 618; Meyers v. State, 193 Wis. 126, 213 N.W. 645, 646; Staniforth v. State, 24 Ohio App. 208, 156 N.E. 924.

It is the previous conviction, and not the indictment, which is the basis of the charge of a second offense. People v. Boardman, 172 App.Div. 733, 159 N.Y.S. 577.

OFFENSIVE. In the law relating to nuisances and similar matters, this term means noxious, causing annoyance, discomfort, or painful or disagreeable sensations. In ordinary use, the term is synonymous with "obnoxious" and means objectionable, disagreeable, displeasing and distasteful. Moller v. Presbyterian Hospital, 65 App.Div. 134, 72 N.Y.S. 483; City of Muskogee v. Morton, 128 Okl. 17, 261 P. 183, 184.

OFFENSIVE AND DEFENSIVE LEAGUE. In international law. A league binding the contracting powers not only to aid each other in case of aggression upon either of them by a third power, but also to support and aid each other in active and aggressive measures against a power with which either of them may engage in war.

OFFENSIVE LANGUAGE. Language adapted to give offense; displeasing or annoying language. People v. Whitman (Co. Ct.) 157 N.Y.S. 1107, 1109.

OFFENSIVE WEAPON. As occasionally used in criminal law and statutes, a weapon primarily meant and adapted for attack and the infliction of injury, but practically the term includes anything that would come within the description of a "deadly" or "dangerous" weapon. State v. Dineen, 10 Minn. 411 (Gil. 325); Rex v. Grice, 7 Car. & P. 803; Rex v. Noakes, 5 Car. & P. 326. Pistol has been held to be "offensive weapon" within statute punishing assault with intent to rob. Reed v. Commonwealth, 281 Ky. 189, 135 S.W.2d 867, 870, 872.

OFFER, *v.* To bring to or before; to present for acceptance or rejection; to hold out or proffer; to make a proposal to; to exhibit something that may be taken or received or not. Morrison v. Springer, 15 Iowa 346; People v. Ah Fook, 62 Cal. 494.

To attempt or endeavor; to make an effort to effect some object, as, to offer to bribe; in this sense used principally in criminal law. State v. Armijo, 19 N.M. 345, 142 P. 1126, 1127.

In trial practice, to "offer" evidence is to state its nature and purport, or to recite what is expected to be proved by a given witness or document, and demand its admission. Unless under exceptional circumstances, the term is not to be taken as equivalent to "introduce." Harris v. Tomlinson, 130 Ind. 426, 30 N.E. 214.

The word "offer," as used in a statute providing that the buyer, to rescind a sale, must offer within a reasonable time to return the goods, is synonymous with the word "tender." Collins v. Skillings, 224 Mass. 275, 112 N.E. 938, 939, Ann.Cas.1918D, 424.

OFFER, *n.* A proposal; a proposal to do a thing.

An attempt; endeavor. Webster.

An offer of evidence. See the verb "offer," supra.

An act on the part of one person whereby he gives to another the legal power of creating the obligation called contract. In re Larney's Estate, 148 Misc. 871, 266 N.Y.S. 564.

An offer, as an element of a contract, is a proposal to make a contract. It must be made by the person who is to make the promise, and it must be made to the person to whom the promise is made. It may be made either by words or by signs, either orally or in writing, and either personally or by a messenger; but in whatever way it is made, it is not in law an offer until it comes to the knowledge of the person to whom it is made; Langd.Contr. § 151; 6 H.L.Cas. 112. See Sunburst Oil & Gas Co. v. Neville, 79 Mont. 550, 257 P. 1016, 1019.

An "offer" must be so definite in its terms, or require such definite terms in acceptance, that the promises and performances to be rendered by each party are reasonably certain. Wadge v. Crestwood Acres, 128 N.J.L. 551, 27 A.2d 148, 150.

An "offer to sell" merely contemplates the proffer, proposal, presentation, or exhibition of something to another for acceptance or rejection. Frissell v. Nichols, 94 Fla. 403, 114 So. 431, 433.

OFFER OF COMPROMISE. An offer to settle a dispute or difference amicably for the purpose of avoiding a lawsuit and without admitting liability. Freeman v. Vandruff, 126 Okl. 238, 259 P. 257, 259.

OFFERINGS. In English ecclesiastical law. Personal tithes, payable by custom to the parson or vicar of a parish, either occasionally, as at sacraments, marriages, churching of women, burials, etc., or at constant times, as at Easter, Christmas, etc. See Obventio.

OFFERTORIUM. In English ecclesiastical law. The offerings of the faithful, or the place where they are made or kept; the service at the time of the Communion.

OFFICE. Right to exercise public or private employment, and to take the fees and emoluments thereunto belonging, whether public, as those of magistrates, or private, as of bailiffs, receivers, or the like. 2 Bl.Comm. 36. Blair v. Marye, 80 Va. 495; Worthy v. Barrett, 63 N.C. 202; Shelf. Mortm. 797; Cruise, Dig. Index; Com. v. Sutherland, 3 S. & R., Pa., 149. A right, and correspondent duty, to exercise a public trust. Whitehead v. Clark, 146 Tenn. 660, 244 S.W. 479, 482. A public charge or employment; U. S. v. Maurice, 2 Brock. 102, Fed. Cas. No. 15,747, per Marshall, C. J.; Lamar v. Splain, 42 App.D.C. 300, 305. An employment on behalf of the government in any station or public trust, not merely transient, occasional, or incidental. See Eason v. Majors, 111 Neb. 288, 196 N.W. 133, 134, 30 A.L.R. 1419.

An "assigned duty" or "function." Synonyms are "post", "appointment", "situation", "place", "position", and "office" commonly suggests a position of (especially public) trust or authority. Also right to exercise a public function or employment, and to take the fees and emoluments belonging to it. Frazier v. Elmore, 180 Tenn. 232, 173 S.W.2d 563, 565. A public charge or employment, and he who performs the duties of the office is an officer. Although an office is an employment, it does not follow that every employment is an office. A man may be employed under a contract, express or implied, to do an act, or to perform a service, without becoming an officer. But, if the duty be a continuing one, which is defined by rule prescribed by the government, which an individual is appointed by the government to perform, who enters upon the duties appertaining to his status, without any contract defining them, it seems very difficult to distinguish such a charge or employment from an office, or the person who performs the duty from an officer. Lacy v. State, 13 Ala. App. 212, 68 So. 706, 710. In the constitutional sense, the term implies an authority to exercise some portion of the sovereign power, either in making, executing, or administering the laws. State v. Christmas, 126 Miss. 358, 88 So. 881, 882.

The most frequent occasions to use the word arise with reference to a duty and power conferred on an individual by the government; and, when this is the connection, "public office" is a usual and more discriminating expression. But a power and duty may exist without immediate grant from government, and may be properly called an "office;" as the office of executor, the office of steward. Here the individual acts towards legatees or towards tenants in performance of a duty, and in exercise of a power not derived from their consent, but devolved on him by an authority which *quoad hoc* is superior. Abbott.

A place for the regular transaction of business. Bradley v. Certigue Mining & Dredging Co., 157 N.Y.S. 275, 276, 93 Misc. 519. For the word "office" as used of a place for transacting public business, see Com. v. White, 6 Cush., Mass., 181.

"Office" is frequently used in the old books as an abbreviation for "inquest of office," (*q. v.*).

As to various particular offices, see Land Office, Petty Bag Office, Post Office, etc.

Civil office. Distinguished from military. Waldo v. Wallace, 12 Ind. 569.

County office. As used in a primary election law, an office filled by the electorate of the entire county. Hamilton v. Monroe, Tex.Civ.App., 287 S.W. 304, 306.

District office. As used in a primary election law, an office filled by the electorate of a district. Hamilton v. Monroe, Tex.Civ.App., 287 S.W. 304, 306.

Judicial office. See Judicial.

Lucrative office. See Lucrative.

Military office. Such as are held by soldiers and sailors for military purposes.

Ministerial office. One which gives the officer no discretion as to the matter to be done, and requires him to obey mandates of a superior. Vose v. Deane, 7 Mass. 280; Savacool v. Boughton, 5 Wend., N.Y., 170, 21 Am.Dec. 181; Waldo v. Wallace, 12 Ind. 569. It is a general rule that a judicial office cannot be exercised by deputy, while a ministerial office may.

Office book. Any book for the record of official or other transactions, kept under authority of the state, in public offices not connected with the courts.

Office copy. A copy or transcript of a deed or record or any filed document, made by the officer having it in custody or under his sanction, and by him sealed or certified.

A copy made by an officer of the court, bound by law to make it, is equivalent to an exemplification, though it is sometimes called an "office copy"; Steph.Dig.Ev. art. 77. Copies of public records, whether judicial or otherwise, made by a public officer authorized by law to make them, are often termed "office copies," *e. g.* copies of recorded deeds; Elwell v. Cunningham, 74 Me. 127. A copy made by an officer of the court, who is authorized to make it by a rule of court, but not required by law to make it, is equivalent to an exemplification in the same cause and court, but in other causes or courts is not admissible unless it can be proved as an examined copy; Steph.Dig.Ev. art. 78. These are called "office copies"; Kellogg v. Kellogg, 6 Barb. (N.Y.) 130.

Office found. In English law. Inquest of office found; the finding of certain facts by a jury on an inquest or inquisition of office. 3 Bl.Comm. 258, 259. This phrase has been adopted in American law. 2 Kent, Comm. 61. See Phillips v. Moore, 100 U.S. 212, 25 L.Ed. 603; Finch v. Goldstein, 245 N.Y. 300, 157 N.E. 146, 147.

Office grant. A designation of a conveyance made by some officer of the law to effect certain purposes, where the owner is either unwilling or unable to execute the requisite deeds to pass the title; such, for example, as a tax-deed. 3 Washb. Real Prop. *537.

Office hours. That portion of the day during which public offices are usually open for the transaction of business.

Officer of honor. See Honor.

Office of judge. A criminal suit in an ecclesiastical court, not being directed to the reparation of a private injury, is regarded as a proceeding emanating from the *office of the judge,* and may be instituted by the mere motion of the judge. But, in practice, these suits are instituted by private individuals, with the permission of the judge or his surrogate; and the private prosecutor in any such case is, accordingly, said to "promote the office of the judge." Mozley & Whiteley.

Political office. Civil offices are usually divided into three classes,—political, judicial, and ministerial. Political offices are such as are not immediately connected with the administration of justice, or with the execution of the mandates of a superior, such as the president or the head of a department. Fitzpatrick v. U. S., 7 Ct.Cl. 293.

Principal office. The principal office of a corporation is its headquarters, or the place where the chief or principal affairs and business of the corporation are transacted. Usually it is the office where the company's books are kept, where its meetings of stockholders are held, and where the directors, trustees, or managers assemble to discuss and transact the important general business of the company; but no one of these circumstances is a controlling test. See Jossey v. Georgia & A. Ry., 102 Ga. 706, 28 S.E. 273; Middletown Ferry Co. v. Middletown, 40 Conn. 69; In re Lone Star Shipbuilding Co., C.C.A.N.Y., 6 F.2d 192, 196. Synonymous with "principal place of business," being the place where the principal affairs of a corporation are transacted. Foreman & Clark Mfg. Co. v. Bartle, 125 Misc.Rep. 759, 211 N.Y.S. 602, 604.

Public office. The right, authority, and duty created and conferred by law, by which for a given period, either fixed by law or enduring at the pleasure of the creating power, an individual is invested with some portion of the sovereign functions of government for the benefit of the public. Walker v. Rich, 79 Cal.App. 139, 249 P. 56, 58. An agency for the state, the duties of which involve in their performance the exercise of some portion of the sovereign power, either great or small. Yaselli v. Goff, C.C.A., 12 F.2d 396, 403, 56 A.L.R. 1239; Lacey v. State, 13 Ala.App. 212, 68 So. 706, 710; Curtin v. State, 61 Cal.App. 377, 214 P. 1030, 1035; Shelmadine v. City of Elkhart, 75 Ind.App. 493, 129 N.E. 878. State ex rel. Colorado River Commission v. Frohmiller, 46 Ariz. 413, 52 P.2d 483, 486.

Where, by virtue of law, a person is clothed, not as an incidental or transient authority, but for such time as denotes duration and continuance, with independent power to control the property of the public, or with public functions to be exercised in the supposed interest of the people, the service to be compensated by a stated yearly salary, and the occupant having a designation or title, the position so created is a public office. State v. Brennan, 49 Ohio St. 33, 29 N.E. 593.

State office. This term as used in a primary election law, means offices to be filled by the electorate of the entire state. Hamilton v. Monroe, Tex.Civ.App., 287 S.W. 304, 306.

OFFICER. The incumbent of an office; one who is lawfully invested with an office. Evans v. Beattie, 137 S.C. 496, 135 S.E. 538, 554; State v. Bratton, 148 Tenn. 174, 253 S.W. 705, 706. One who is charged by a superior power (and particularly by government) with the power and duty of exercising certain functions.

One who is invested with some portion of the functions of the government to be exercised for the public benefit. Fox v. Lantrip, 162 Ky. 178, 172 S.W. 133, 136; In a popular sense, an officer is one holding a position of trust and authority in any kind of an organization—civil, military, political, ecclesiastical, or social. Illinois Commerce Commission v. Cleveland, C., C. & St. L. Ry. Co., 320 Ill. 214, 150 N.E. 678, 682. The word "officer," as used in state statutes or constitutions, is sometimes held to refer only to elective officers; Cunningham v. Rockwood, 222 Mass. 574, 111 N. E. 409, 411, Ann.Cas.1917C, 1100; and sometimes to both appointive and elective officers; State v. Campbell, 94 Ohio St. 403, 115 N.E. 29, 31.

An "officer" is distinguished from an "employee" in the greater importance, dignity, and independence of his position, in requirement of oath, bond, more enduring tenure, and fact of duties being prescribed by law. Bowden v. Cumberland County, 123 Me. 359, 123 A. 166, 169; McClendon v. Board of Health of City of Hot Springs, 141 Ark. 114, 216 S.W. 289, 290; Jefferson County v. Case, 244 Ala. 56, 12 So.2d 343, 346.

In determining whether one is an "officer" or "employee," important tests are the tenure by which a position is held, whether its duration is defined by the statute or ordinance creating it, or whether it is temporary or transient or for a time fixed only by agreement; whether it is created by an appointment or election, or merely by a contract of employment by which the rights of the parties are regulated; whether the compensation is by a salary or fees fixed by law, or by a sum agreed upon by the contract of hiring. Hyde v. Board of Com'rs of Wells County, 209 Ind. 245, 198 N.E. 333, 337.

For *obstructing an officer*, see that title.

For definitions of the various classes and kinds of officers, see the titles "Commissioned Officers," "Executive," "Fiscal," "Judicial," "Legislative," "Ministerial," "Municipal," "Naval," "Non-Commissioned," "Peace," "State," and "Subordinate".

Civil officer. The word "civil," as regards civil officers, is commonly used to distinguish those officers who are in public service but not of the military. U. S. v. American Brewing Co., D.C.Pa., 296 F. 772, 776; State v. Clarke, 21 Nev. 333, 31 P. 545, 18 L.R.A. 313, 37 Am.St.Rep. 517. Hence, any officer of the United States who holds his appointment under the national government, whether his duties are executive or judicial, in the highest or the lowest departments of the government, with the exception of officers of the army and navy, is a "civil officer." 1 Story, Const. § 792. See, also, Com'rs v. Goldsborough, 90 Md. 193, 44 A. 1055.

Military officer. Officer who has command in the army. Non-commissioned officer is not officer in the sense in which that word is generally used; Babbitt v. U. S., 16 Ct.Cl. 214.

Officer de facto. As distinguished from an officer *de jure;* this is the designation of one who is in the actual possession and administration of the office, under some colorable or apparent authority, although his title to the same, whether by election or appointment, is in reality invalid or at least formally questioned. Norton v. Shelby County, 6 S.Ct. 1121, 118 U.S. 425, 30 L.Ed. 78; State v. Carroll, 38 Conn. 449, 9 Am.Rep. 409. One who has the reputation of being the officer he assumes to be, and yet is not a good officer in point of law. 6 East 368; City of Terre Haute v. Burns, 69 Ind. App. 7, 116 N.E. 604, 608; Johnson v. State, 27 Ga. App. 679, 109 S.E. 526, 527.

Official acts of officer de facto are binding on others. McNatt v. State, 130 Tex.Cr.R. 42, 91 S.W.2d 1068, 1069.

A *de facto* officer is also distinguished from a "usurper" who has neither lawful title nor color of right. Smith v. City of Jefferson, 75 Or. 179, 146 P. 809, 812.

To constitute an officer de facto it is not a necessary prerequisite that there shall have been an attempted exercise of competent prima facie power of appointment or election; a de facto officer being one whose title is not good in law, but who is in fact in the unobstructed possession of an office and is discharging its duties in full view of the public, in such manner and under such circumstances as not to present the appearance of being an intruder or usurper. U. S. v. Royer, 45 S.Ct. 519, 520, 268 U.S. 394, 69 L.Ed. 1011. A person is a "de facto officer" where the duties of the officer are exercised—First, without a known appointment or election, but under such circumstances of reputation or acquiescence as were calculated to induce people, without inquiry, to submit to or invoke his action, supposing him to be the officer he assumed to be. Second, under color of a known and valid appointment or election, but where the officer has failed to conform to some precedent requirement or condition, as to take an oath, give a bond, or the like. Third, under color of a known election or appointment, void because the officer was not eligible, or because there was a want of power in the electing or appointing body, or by reason of some defect or irregularity in its exercise, such ineligibility, want of power, or defect being unknown to the public. Fourth, under color of an election or appointment by or pursuant to a public unconstitutional law, before the same is adjudged to be such. Wendt v. Berry, 154 Ky. 586, 157 S.W. 1115, 1118, 45 L.R.A.,N.S., 1101, Ann.Cas.1915C, 493.

Officer de jure. One who is in all respects legally appointed and qualified to exercise the office. People v. Brautigan, 310 Ill. 472, 142 N.E. 208, 211.

Officer of justice. A general name applicable to all persons connected with the administration of the judicial department of government, but commonly used only of the class of officers whose duty is to serve the process of the courts, such as sheriffs, constables, bailiffs, marshals, sequestrators, etc.

Officer of United States. An officer nominated by the president and confirmed by the senate or one who is appointed under an act of congress, by the president alone, a court of law, or a head of a department. U. S. v. Germaine, 99 U.S. 508, 25 L. Ed. 482; see U. S. v. Mouat, 8 S.Ct. 505, 124 U.S. 303, 31 L.Ed. 463.

Public officer. An officer of a public corporation; that is, one holding office under the government of a municipality, state, or nation. One occupying a public office created by law. Shanks v. Howes, 214 Ky. 613, 283 S.W. 966, 967; Schmitt v. Dooling, 145 Ky. 240, 140 S.W. 197, 36 L.R.A.,N.S., 881, Ann.Cas.1913B, 1078. One of necessary characteristics of "public officer" is that he perform public function for public benefit and in so doing he be vested with exercise of some sovereign power of state. Leymel v. Johnson, 105 Cal.App. 694, 288 P. 858, 860.

In English law. An officer appointed by a joint-stock banking company, under the statutes regulating such companies, to prosecute and defend suits in its behalf.

Warrant officer. One who holds as evidence of right a warrant signed by the Secretary of War or of the Navy. Stephens v. Civil Service Commission of New Jersey, 101 N.J.L. 192, 127 A. 808, 811.

OFFICIA JUDICIALIA NON CONCEDANTUR ANTEQUAM VACENT. Judicial offices should not be granted before they are vacant. 11 Coke, 4.

OFFICIA MAGISTRATUS NON DEBENT ESSE VENALIA. The offices of magistrates ought not to be sold. Co. Litt. 234.

OFFICIAL, *n.* An officer; a person invested with the authority of an office.

In Canon law. A person to whom a bishop commits the charge of his spiritual jurisdiction.

In Civil law. The minister or apparitor of a magistrate or judge.

In Common and Statute law. The person whom the archdeacon substitutes in the execution of his jurisdiction. Cowell.

OFFICIAL, *adj.* Pertaining to an office; invested with the character of an officer; proceeding from, sanctioned by, or done by, an officer. Cohn v. U. S., 169 C.C.A. 371, 258 F. 355, 358.

As to official "Bonds," "Liquidator," "Log-Book," "Newspaper," "Oath," and "Use," see those titles.

Demi-official. Partly official or authorized. Having color of official right.

Official act. One done by an officer in his official capacity under color and by virtue of his office. Lammon v. Feusire, 4 S.Ct. 286, 111 U.S. 17, 28 L.Ed. 337; Meek v. Tilghman, 55 Okl. 208, 154 P. 1190, 1191; Miles v. Wright, 22 Ariz. 73, 194 P. 88, 91, 12 A.L.R. 970. Weidler v. Arizona Power Co., 39 Ariz. 390, 7 P.2d 241, 243.

Official assignee. In English practice. An assignee in bankruptcy appointed by the lord chancellor to co-operate with the other assignees in administering a bankrupt's estate.

Official managers. Persons formerly appointed, under English statutes now repealed, to superintend the winding up of insolvent companies under the control of the court of chancery. Wharton.

Official misconduct. Any unlawful behavior by a public officer in relation to the duties of his office, willful in its character, including any willful or corrupt failure, refusal, or neglect of an officer to perform any duty enjoined on him by law. Kesling v. Moore, 102 W.Va. 251, 135 S.E. 246, 248; State on Inf. of Barker v. Crandall, 269 Mo. 44, 190 S.W. 889, 892; Bolton v. State, 69 Tex.Cr.R. 582, 154 S.W. 1197.

Official principal. An ecclesiastical officer whose duty it is to hear causes between party and party as the delegate of the bishop or archbishop by whom he is appointed. He generally also holds the office of vicar general and (if appointed by a bishop) that of chancellor. The official principal of the province of Canterbury is called the "dean of arches." Phillim. Ecc. Law, 1203, *et seq.;* Sweet.

Official solicitor to the court of chancery. An officer in England whose functions are to protect the suitors' fund, and to administer, under the direction of the court, so much of it as now comes under the spending power of the court. He acts for persons suing or defending *in forma pauperis,* when so directed by the judge, and for those who, through ignorance or forgetfulness, have been guilty of contempt of court by not obeying process. He also acts generally as solicitor in all cases in which the chancery division requires such services. The office is transferred to the high court by the judicature acts, but no alteration in its name appears to have been made. Sweet.

Official trustee of charity lands. The secretary of the English charity commissioners. He is a corporation sole for the purpose of taking and holding real property and leaseholds upon trust for an endowed charity in cases where it appears to the court desirable to vest them in him. He is a bare trustee, the possession and management of the land remaining in the persons acting in the administration of the charity. Sweet.

OFFICIALTY. The court or jurisdiction of which an official is head.

OFFICIARIIS NON FACIENDIS VEL AMOVENDIS. A writ addressed to the magistrates of a corporation, requiring them not to make such a man an officer, or to put one out of the office he has, until inquiry is made of his manners, etc. Reg. Orig. 126.

OFFICINA JUSTITIÆ. The workshop or office of justice. The chancery was formerly so called. 3 Bl.Comm. 273; Yates v. People, 6 Johns. (N. Y.) 363.

OFFICIO, EX, OATH. An oath whereby a person may be obliged to make any presentment of any crime or offense, or to confess or accuse himself of any criminal matter or thing whereby he may be liable to any censure, penalty, or punishment. 3 Bl.Comm. 447.

OFFICIOUS WILL. A testament by which a testator leaves his property to his family. Sandars, Just. Inst. 207; Inofficious Testament.

OFFICIT CONATUS SI EFFECTUS SEQUATUR. The attempt becomes of consequence, if the effect follows. Jenk. Cent. 55.

OFFICIUM NEMINI DEBET ESSE DAMNOSUM. Office ought not to be an occasion of loss to any one. A maxim in Scotch law. Bell.

OFFSET. A deduction; a counterclaim; a contrary claim or demand by which a given claim may be lessened or canceled. Leonard v. Charter Oak L. Ins. Co., 65 Conn. 529, 33 A. 511; Cable Flax Mills v. Early, 72 App.Div. 213, 76 N.Y.S. 191. The more usual form of the word is "set-off," (*q. v.*).

OFFSPRING. This term is synonymous with "issue." Barber v. Railroad Co., 17 S.Ct. 488, 166 U.S. 83, 41 L.Ed. 925; Powell v. Brandon, 2 Cushm. (Miss.) 343.

OIKEI MANIA. See Insanity.

OIR. In Spanish law. To hear; to take cognizance. White, New Recop. b. 3, tit. 1, c. 7.

OKAY. The colloquial expression means correct, all right, to approve, and is of such common usage that it immediately conveys to the mind of person to whom it is addressed that a proposition submitted is agreed to. Muegler v. Crosthwait, 239 Mo.App. 801, 179 S.W.2d 761, 763. See, also, O. K.

OKER. In Scotch law. Usury; the taking of interest for money, contrary to law. Bell.

OLD NATURA BREVIUM. The title of a treatise written in the reign of Edward III., containing the writs which were then most in use, annexing to each a short comment concerning their nature and the application of them, with their various properties and effects. 3 Reeve, Eng. Law, 152.

OLD STYLE. The ancient calendar or method of reckoning time, whereby the year commenced on March 25th. It was superseded by the new style (that now in use) in most countries of Europe in 1582 and in England in 1752.

OLD TENURES. A treatise, so called to distinguish it from Littleton's book on the same subject, which gives an account of the various tenures by which land was holden, the nature of estates, and some other incidents to landed property in the reign of Edward III. It is a very scanty tract, but has the merit of having led the way to Littleton's famous work. 3 Reeve, Eng. Law, 151.

OLEOMARGARINE. An artificial imitation of butter, made chiefly from animal fats. Its sale is prohibited or restricted by statute in several of the states. Powell v. Pennsylvania, 8 S.Ct. 992. 127 U.S. 678, 32 L.Ed. 253.

OLERON, LAWS OF. A code of maritime laws published at the island of Oleron in the twelfth century by Eleanor of Guienne. They were adopted in England successively under Richard I., Henry III., and Edward III. and are often cited before the admiralty courts.

OLIGARCHY. A form of government wherein the administration of affairs is lodged in the hands of a few persons.

OLIGOPOLY. Economic climate existing where a few sellers sell only a standardized product. U. S. v. E. I. DuPont de Nemours & Co., D.C.Del., 118 F.Supp. 41, 49.

OLOGRAPH. An instrument (*e. g.,* a will) wholly written by the person from whom it emanates. Lovskog v. American Nat. Red Cross, C.C.A.Alaska, 111 F.2d 88, 91.

OLOGRAPHIC TESTAMENT. The olographic testament is that which is written by the testator himself. In order to be valid it must be entirely written, dated, and signed by the hand of the testator. It is subject to no other form, and may be made anywhere, even out of the state. Civil Code La. art. 1588. Succession of Butterworth, 195 La. 115, 196 So. 39, 41.

OLYMPIAD. A Grecian epoch; the space of four years.

OMBUDSMAN CONCEPT. A citizen aggrieved by an official's action or inaction should be able to state his grievance to an influential functionary empowered to investigate and to express conclusions.

OME BUENO. In Spanish law. A good man; a substantial person. Las Partidas, pt. 5, tit. 13, l. 38.

OMISSIO EORUM QUÆ TACITE INSUNT NIHIL OPERATUR. The omission of those things which are tacitly implied is of no consequence. 2 Bulst. 131.

OMISSION. The neglect to perform what the law requires. People v. Hughey, 382 Ill. 136, 47 N.E. 2d 77, 80.

OMISSIS OMNIBUS ALIIS NEGOTIIS. Lat. Laying aside all other businesses. 9 East, 347.

OMITTANCE. Forbearance; omission.

OMNE ACTUM AB INTENTIONE AGENTIS EST JUDICANDUM. Every act is to be judged by the intention of the doer. Branch, Princ.

OMNE CRIMEN EBRIETAS ET INCENDIT ET DETEGIT. Drunkenness both inflames (or aggravates) and reveals every crime. Co. Litt. 247*a*; 4 Bl.Comm. 26; Broom, Max. 17.

OMNE JUS AUT CONSENSUS FECIT, AUT NECESSITAS CONSTITUIT AUT FIRMAVIT CONSUETUDO. Every right is either made by consent, or is constituted by necessity, or is established by custom. Dig. 1, 3, 40.

OMNE MAGIS DIGNUM TRAHIT AD SE MINUS DIGNUM, QUAMVIS MINUS DIGNUM SIT ANTIQUIUS. Every worthier thing draws to it the less worthy, though the less worthy be the more ancient. Co. Litt. 355*b*.

OMNE MAGNUM EXEMPLUM HABET ALIQUID EX INIQUO, QUOD PUBLICA UTILITATE COMPENSATUR. Hob. 279. Every great example has some portion of evil, which is compensated by the public utility.

OMNE MAJUS CONTINET IN SE MINUS. Every greater contains in itself the less. 5 Coke, 115*a*. The greater always contains the less. Broom, Max. 174.

OMNE MAJUS DIGNUM CONTINET IN SE MINUS DIGNUM. Co. Litt. 43. The more worthy contains in itself the less worthy.

OMNE MAJUS MINUS IN SE COMPLECTITUR. Every greater embraces in itself the less. Jenk. Cent. 208.

OMNE PRINCIPALE TRAHIT AD SE ACCESSORIUM. Every principal thing draws to itself the accessory. Parsons v. Welles, 17 Mass. 425; Green v. Hart, 1 Johns. (N.Y.) 580.

OMNE QUOD SOLO INÆDIFICATUR SOLO CEDIT. Everything which is built upon the soil belongs to the soil. Dig. 47, 3, 1; Broom, Max. 401.

OMNE SACRAMENTUM DEBET ESSE DE CERTA SCIENTIA. Every oath ought to be of certain knowledge. 4 Inst. 279.

OMNE TESTAMENTUM MORTE CONSUMMATUM EST. 3 Coke, 29. Every will is completed by death.

OMNES ACTIONES IN MUNDO INFRA CERTA TEMPORA HABENT LIMITATIONEM. All actions in the world are limited within certain periods. Bract. fol. 52.

OMNES HOMINES AUT LIBERI SUNT AUT SERVI. All men are freemen or slaves. Inst. 1, 3, pr.; Fleta, l. 1, c. 1, § 2.

OMNES LICENTIAM HABERE HIS QUÆ PRO SE INDULTA SUNT, RENUNCIARE. [It is a rule of the ancient law that] all persons shall have liberty to renounce those privileges which have been conferred for their benefit. Cod. 1, 3, 51; Cod. 2, 3, 29; Broom, Max. 699.

OMNES PRUDENTES ILLA ADMITTERE SOLENT QUÆ PROBANTUR IIS QUI ARTE SUA BENE VERSATI SUNT. All prudent men are accustomed to admit those things which are approved by those who are well versed in the art. 7 Coke, 19.

OMNES SORORES SUNT QUASI UNUS HÆRES DE UNA HÆREDITATE. Co.Litt. 67. All sisters are, as it were, one heir to one inheritance.

OMNI EXCEPTIONE MAJUS. 4 Inst. 262. Above all exception.

OMNIA DELICTA IN APERTO LEVIORA SUNT. All crimes that are committed openly are lighter, [or have a less odious appearance than those committed secretly.] 8 Coke, 127*a*.

OMNIA PERFORMAVIT. He has done all. In pleading. A good plea in bar where all the covenants are in the affirmative. Bailey v. Rogers, 1 Me. 189.

OMNIA PRÆSUMUNTUR CONTRA SPOLIATOREM. All things are presumed against a despoiler or wrong-doer. A leading maxim in the law of evidence. Best, Ev. p. 340, § 303; Broom, Max. 938.

OMNIA PRÆSUMUNTUR LEGITIME FACTA DONEC PROBETUR IN CONTRARIUM. All things are presumed to be lawfully done, until proof be made to the contrary. Co.Litt. 232*b*; Best, Ev. p. 337, § 300.

OMNIA PRÆSUMUNTUR RITE ET SOLEMNITER ESSE ACTA DONEC PROBETUR IN CONTRARIUM. All things are presumed to have been rightly and duly performed until it is proved to the contrary. Co.Litt. 232; Broom, Max. 944.

OMNIA PRÆSUMUNTUR SOLEMNITER ESSE ACTA. Co.Litt. 6. All things are presumed to have been done rightly.

OMNIA PRESUMUNTUR RITA ESSE ACTA. A prima facie presumption of the regularity of the acts of public officers exists until the contrary appears. Beacom v. Robison, 157 Pa.Super. 515, 43 A.2d 640, 643.

OMNIA QUÆ JURE CONTRAHUNTUR CONTRARIO JURE PEREUNT. Dig. 50, 17, 100. All things which are contracted by law perish by a contrary law.

OMNIA QUÆ SUNT UXORIS SUNT IPSIUS VIRI. All things which are the wife's are the husband's. Bract. fol. 32; Co.Litt. 112*a*; 2 Kent, Comm. 130–143.

OMNIA RITE ACTA PRÆSUMUNTUR. All things are presumed to have been rightly done. Broom, Max. 944.

OMNIBUS. For all; containing two or more independent matters. Applied to a count in a declaration, and to a bill of legislation, and perhaps to a clause in a will, which comprises more than one general subject. Yeager v. Weaver, 64 Pa. 428; Parkinson v. State, 14 Md. 193, 74 Am.Dec. 522. See In Omnibus.

OMNIBUS AD QUOS PRÆSENTES LITERÆ PERVENERINT, SALUTEM. To all to whom the present letters shall come, greeting. A form of address with which charters and deeds were anciently commenced.

OMNIBUS BILL. In legislative practice, a bill including in one act various separate and distinct matters, and particularly one joining a number of different subjects in one measure in such a way as to compel the executive authority to accept provisions which he does not approve or else defeat the whole enactment. Com. v. Barnett, 199 Pa. 161, 48 A. 977, 55 L.R.A. 882; Yeager v. Weaver, 64 Pa. 425.

In equity pleading, a bill embracing the whole of a complex subject-matter by uniting all parties in interest having adverse or conflicting claims, thereby avoiding circuity or multiplicity of action.

OMNIS ACTIO EST LOQUELA. Every action is a plaint or complaint. Co.Litt. 292*a*.

OMNIS CONCLUSIO BONI ET VERI JUDICII SEQUITUR EX BONIS ET VERIS PRÆMISSIS ET DICTIS JURATORUM. Every conclusion of a good and true judgment follows from good and true premises, and the verdicts of jurors. Co.Litt. 226*b*.

OMNIS CONSENSUS TOLLIT ERROREM. Every consent removes error. Consent always removes the effect of error. 2 Inst. 123.

OMNIS DEFINITIO IN JURE CIVILI PERICULOSA EST, PARUM EST ENIM UT NON SUBVERTI POSSIT. Every definition in the civil law is dangerous, for there is very little that cannot be overthrown. (There is no rule in the civil law which is not liable to some exception; and the least difference in the facts of the case renders its application useless.) Dig. 50. 17. 202; 2 Woodd. Lect. 196.

OMNIS DEFINITIO IN LEGE PERICULOSA. All definition in law is hazardous. 2 Wood.Lect. 196.

OMNIS EXCEPTIO EST IPSA QUOQUE REGULA. Every exception is itself also a rule.

OMNIS INDEMNATUS PRO INNOXIS LEGIBUS HABETUR. Every uncondemned person is held by the law as innocent. Lofft, 121.

OMNIS INNOVATIO PLUS NOVITATE PERTURBAT QUAM ULTILITATE PRODEST. Every innovation occasions more harm by its novelty than benefit by its utility. 2 Bulst, 338; Broom, Max. 147.

OMNIS INTERPRETATIO SI FIERI POTEST ITA FIENDA EST IN INSTRUMENTIS, UT OMNES CONTRARIETATES AMOVEANTUR. Jenk. Cent. 96. Every interpretation, if it can be done, is to be so made in instruments that all contradictions may be removed.

OMNIS INTERPRETATIO VEL DECLARAT, VEL EXTENDIT, VEL RESTRINGIT. Every interpretation either declares, extends, or restrains.

OMNIS NOVA CONSTITUTIO FUTURIS FORMAM IMPONERE DEBET, NON PRÆTERITIS. Every new statute ought to prescribe a form to future, not to past, acts. Bract. fol. 228; 2 Inst. 95.

OMNIS PERSONA EST HOMO, SED NON VICISSIM. Every person is a man, but not every man a person. Calvin.

OMNIS PRIVATIO PRÆSUPPONIT HABITUM. Every privation presupposes a former enjoyment. Co.Litt. 339*a*. A "rule of philosophie" quoted by Lord Coke, and applied to the discontinuance of an estate.

OMNIS QUEREIA ET OMNIS ACTIO INJURIARUM LIMITA EST INFRA CERTA TEMPORA. Co.Litt. 114*b*. Every plaint and every action for injuries is limited within certain times.

OMNIS RATIHABITIO RETROTRAHITUR ET MANDATO PRIORI ÆQUIPARATUR. Every ratification relates back and is equivalent to a prior authority. Broom, Max. 757, 871; Chit. Cont. 196.

OMNIS REGULA SUAS PATITUR EXCEPTIONES. Every rule is liable to its own exceptions.

OMNIUM. In mercantile law. A term used to express the aggregate value of the different stock in which a loan is usually funded. Tomlins.

OMNIUM CONTRIBUTIONE SARCIATUR QUOD PRO OMNIBUS DATUM EST. 4 Bing. 121. That which is given for, all is recompensed by the contribution of all. A principle of the law of general average.

OMNIUM RERUM QUARUM USUS EST, POTEST ESSE ABUSUS, VIRTUTE SOLO EXCEPTA. There may be an abuse of everything of which there is a use, virtue only excepted. Dav.Ir.K.B. 79.

ON. Upon; as soon as; near to; along; along side of; adjacent to; contiguous to; at the time of; following upon; in; during; at or in contact with upper surface of a thing. Slaughter v. Robinson, 52 Utah, 273, 173 P. 456, 458; Hinton v. Vinson, 180 N.C. 393, 104 S.E. 897, 900; Stuckey v. Jones, Tex.Civ.App., 240 S.W. 565, 566.

ON ACCOUNT. In part payment; in partial satisfaction of an account. The phrase is usually contrasted with "in full."

See, also, *On or About* and *On the Person*.

ON ACCOUNT OF WHOM IT MAY CONCERN. When a policy of insurance expresses that the insurance is made "on account of whom it may concern," it will cover all persons having an insurable interest in the subject-matter at the date of the policy and who were then contemplated by the party procuring the insurance. 2 Pars.Mar.Law, 30.

ON ALL FOURS. A phrase used to express the idea that a case at bar is in all points similar to another. The one is said to be on all fours with the other when the facts are similar and the same questions of law are involved.

ON CALL. There is no legal difference between an obligation payable "when demanded" or "on demand" and one payable "on call" or "at any time called for." In each case the debt is payable immediately. Bowman v. McChesney, 22 Grat. (Va.) 609; Citizens' Bank of Waynesboro v. Mobley, 166 Ga. 543, 144 S.E. 119, 121, 58 A.L.R. 1383.

The term "on call," according to the evidence, is a term known to persons engaged in the cotton business, and means that cotton placed "on call" is sold, but the price remains unfixed, and that the owner has until a certain set date in the future to name the market price of the cotton on any day between the day the cotton is placed "on call" and the set day as the price at which the owner is entitled to a settlement for the cotton. Bennett v. Weil Bros., 28 Ga.App. 266, 110 S.E. 744.

ON DEFAULT. In case of default; upon failure of stipulated action or performance; upon the occurrence of a failure, omission, or neglect of duty.

ON DEMAND. A promissory note payable "on demand" is a present debt, and is payable without any demand. Dominion Trust Co. v. Hildner, 243 Pa. 253, 90 A. 69.

ON FILE. Filed; entered or placed upon the files; existing and remaining upon or among the proper files. Slosson v. Hall, 17 Minn. 95 (Gil. 71); Snider v. Methvin, 60 Tex. 487.

ON OR ABOUT. A phrase used in reciting the date of an occurrence or conveyance, or the location of it to escape the necessity of being bound by the statement of an exact date, or place; approximately; about; without substantial variance from; near. Parker v. State, 63 Ind.App. 671, 113 N.E. 763, 764; Render v. Commonwealth, 206 Ky. 1, 266 S.W. 914, 916; Thompson v. U. S., C.C.A.N.J., 283 F. 895, 897; Pillsbury Flour Mills Co. v. Erie R. Co., 216 N.Y.S. 486, 489, 127 Misc.Rep. 466; Petty v. Giles, 29 C.C.P.A. (Patents) 804, 125 F.2d 177, 181.

As used in statutes making it an offense to carry a weapon "on or about" the person, it is generally held that the word "on" means connected with or attached to, and that "about" is a comprehensive term having a broader meaning than "on," and conveying the idea of being near by, in close proximity, within immediate reach, or conveniently accessible. As applied to motor vehicles, therefore, it is commonly held that an occupant of the front seat of an automobile is carrying a weapon "about" his person where the weapon is on or under the seat, or between the cushion and the back of the seat, or on a shelf behind the seat, or in a pocket on the door or on the back of the seat, or in the glove compartment, or on the floor. There are, however, a few decisions to the contrary. The cases are collected and analyzed in Blashfield, Cyc. of Automobile Law and Prac., Perm. Ed. § 5528.90.

ON OR BEFORE. These words, inserted in a stipulation to do an act or pay money, entitle the party stipulating to perform at any time before the day; and upon performance, or tender and refusal, he is immediately vested with all the rights which would have attached if performance were made on the day. Davis v. Burns, Tex.Civ.App., 173 S.W. 476, 480; McGrory Stores Corporation v. Goldberg, 95 N.J.Eq. 152, 122 A. 113.

ON STAND. A term used in the law of landlord and tenant. A tenant of a farm who cannot carry away manure but has the right to sell it to his successor, is said to have the right of *on stand* on the farm for it till he can sell it; he may maintain trespass for the taking of it by the incoming tenant before it is sold. 16 East 116.

ON THE PERSON. In common parlance, when it is said that someone has an article on his person, it means that it is either in contact with his person or is carried in his clothing. Com. v. Lanzetti, 97 Pa.Super. 126.

Accordingly, where a statute punishes the carrying of a weapon "on the person," an occupant of an automobile does not violate the statute by carrying therein a weapon detached from his person, as, *e. g.*, where the weapon is under the cushion of the seat. Blashfield, Cyc. of Automobile Law and Prac., Perm. Ed., § 5528.88.

ONCE A FRAUD, ALWAYS A FRAUD. 13 Vin. Abr. 539.

ONCE A MORTGAGE, ALWAYS A MORTGAGE. This rule signifies that an instrument originally intended as a mortgage, and not a deed, cannot be converted into anything else than a mortgage by any subsequent clause or agreement.

ONCE A RECOMPENSE, ALWAYS A RECOMPENSE. 19 Vin.Abr. 277.

ONCE IN JEOPARDY. A phrase used to express the condition of a person charged with crime, who has once already, by legal proceedings, been put in danger of conviction and punishment for the same offense. Com. v. Fitzpatrick, 121 Pa. 109, 15 A. 466, 1 L.R.A. 451, 6 Am.St.Rep. 757.

ONCE QUIT AND CLEARED, EVER QUIT AND CLEARED. (Scotch, anis quit and clenged, ay quit and clenged.) Skene, de Verb. Sign. voc. "Iter.," ad fin.

ONCUNNE. L. Fr. Accused. Du Cange.

ONE HUNDRED THOUSAND POUNDS CLAUSE. A precautionary stipulation inserted in a deed making a good tenant to the *præcipe* in a common recovery. 1 Prest.Conv. 110.

ONE PERSON, ONE VOTE. State legislative districting which gives equal legislative representation to all citizens of all places. The rule was established in Reynolds v. Sims, 377 U.S. 533, 568, 84 S.Ct. 1362, 1385, which required that the seats in both houses of a bicameral state legislature be apportioned on a population basis.

ONE THIRD NEW FOR OLD. See New for Old.

ONE YEAR. A calendar year, regardless of whether it be a leap year or otherwise. Rev.St. 1925, art. 23. Douglas v. Acacia Mut. Life Ins. Co., Tex.Civ.App., 118 S.W.2d 643.

ONERANDO PRO RATA PORTIONIS. A writ that lay for a joint tenant or tenant in common who was distrained for more rent than his proportion of the land comes to. Reg.Orig. 182.

ONERARI NON. In pleading. The name of a plea, in an action of debt, by which the defendant says that he ought not to be charged.

ONERATIO. Lat. A lading; a cargo.

ONERATUR NISI. See O. Ni.

ONERIS FERENDI. Lat. In the civil law. The servitude of support; a servitude by which the wall of a house is required to sustain the wall or beams of the adjoining house.

ONEROUS. A contract, lease, share, or other right is said to be "onerous" when the obligations attaching to it counter-balance or exceed the advantage to be derived from it, either absolutely or with reference to the particular possessor. Sweet.

As used in the civil law and in the systems derived from it, (French, Scotch, Spanish, Mexican,) the term also means based upon, supported by, or relating to a good and valuable consideration, *i. e.*, one which imposes a burden or charge in return for the benefit conferred.

ONEROUS CAUSE. In Scotch law. A good and legal consideration.

ONEROUS CONTRACT. See Contract.

ONEROUS DEED. In Scotch law. A deed given for a valuable consideration. Bell.

ONEROUS GIFT. A gift made subject to certain charges imposed by the donor on the donee.

ONEROUS TITLE. A title acquired by the giving of a valuable consideration, as the payment of money or rendition of services or the performance of conditions or assumption or discharge of liens or charges. Scott v. Ward, 13 Cal. 458; Kircher v. Murray, C.C.Tex., 54 F. 617; Noe v. Card, 14 Cal. 576; Civ.Code La. 1900, art. 3556.

ONLY. Solely; merely; for no other purpose; at no other time; in no otherwise; alone; of or by itself; without anything more; exclusive; nothing else or more.

ONOMASTIC. A term applied to the signature of an instrument, the body of which is in a different handwriting from that of the signature. Best, Ev. 315.

ONROERENDE AND VAST STAAT. Dutch. Immovable and fast estate, that is, land or real estate. The phrase is used in Dutch wills, deeds, and antenuptial contracts of the early colonial period in New York. Spraker v. Van Alstyne, 18 Wend., N.Y., 208.

ONUS. Lat. A burden or load; a weight. The lading, burden, or cargo of a vessel. A charge; an incumbrance. *Cum onere, (q. v.,)* with the incumbrance.

ONUS EPISCOPALE. Ancient customary payments from the clergy to their diocesan bishop, of synodals, pentecostals, etc.

ONUS IMPORTANDI. The charge of importing merchandise, mentioned in St. 12 Car. II. c. 28.

ONUS PROBANDI. Burden of proving; the burden of proof. The strict meaning of the term "*onus probandi*" is that, if no evidence is adduced by the party on whom the burden is cast, the issue must be found against him. Davis v. Rogers, 1 Houst. (Del.) 44.

OPE CONSILIO. Lat. By aid and counsel. A civil law term applied to accessaries, similar in import to the "aiding and abetting" of the common law. Often written "*ope et consilio.*" Burrill.

OPEN, *v.* To render accessible, visible, or available; to submit or subject to examination, inquiry, or review, by the removal of restrictions or impediments.

Open a case. In practice. To open a case is to begin it; to make an initiatory explanation of its features to the court, jury, referee, etc., by outlining the nature of the transaction on which it is founded, the questions involved, and the character and general course of the evidence to be adduced.

Open a commission. To enter upon the duties under a commission, or commence to act under a commission, is so termed in English law. Thus, the judges of assize and *nisi prius* derive their authority to act under or by virtue of commissions directed to them for that purpose; and, when they commence acting under the powers so committed to them, they are said to open the commissions; and the day on which they so commence their proceedings is thence termed the "commission day of the assizes." Brown.

Open a court. To open a court is to make a formal announcement, usually by the crier or bailiff, that its session has now begun and that the business before the court will be proceeded with.

Open a credit. To accept or pay the draft of a correspondent who has not furnished funds. Pardessus, no. 296.

Open a deposition. To break the seals by which it was secured, and lay it open to view, or to bring it into court ready for use.

Open a judgment. To lift or relax the bar of finality and conclusiveness which it imposes so as to permit a re-examination of the merits of the action in which it was rendered. This is done at the instance of a party showing good cause why the execution of the judgment would be inequitable. It so far annuls the judgment as to prevent its enforcement until the final determination upon it, but does not in the meantime release its lien upon real estate. Insurance Co. v. Beale, 110 Pa. 321, 1 A. 926.

Open a rule. To restore or recall a rule which has been made absolute to its conditional state, as a rule *nisi*, so as to readmit of cause being shown against the rule. Thus, when a rule to show cause has been made absolute under a mistaken impression that no counsel had been instructed to show cause against it, it is usual for the party at whose instance the rule was obtained to consent to have the rule opened, by which all the proceedings subsequent to the day when cause ought to have been shown against it are in effect nullified, and the rule is then argued in the ordinary way. Brown.

Open a street or highway. To establish it by law and make it passable and available for public travel. Wilcoxon v. San Luis Obispo, 101 Cal. 508, 35 P. 988; Patterson v. City of Baltimore, 130 Md. 645, 101 A. 589, 591; Royal v. City of Des Moines, 195 Iowa, 23, 191 N.W. 377, 383.

Open bids. To open bids received on a foreclosure or other judicial sale is to reject or cancel them for fraud, mistake, or other cause, and order a resale of the property. Andrews v. Scotton, 2 Bland (Md.) 644.

Open the door. If one party to litigation puts in evidence part of document or correspondence or conversation which is detrimental to the opposing party, the latter may introduce balance of document, correspondence or conversation in order to explain or rebut adverse inferences which might arise from the fragmentary or incomplete character of evidence introduced by his adversary. U. S. v. Corrigan, C.C.A.N.Y., 168 F.2d 641, 645.

Open the pleadings. To state briefly at a trial before a jury the substance of the pleadings. This is done by the junior counsel for the plaintiff at the commencement of the trial.

OPEN, *adj.* Patent; visible; apparent; notorious; not clandestine; not closed, settled, fixed, or terminated. Pratt v. Boggs, 171 Ky. 106, 186 S.W. 901, 902; Dale v. Hartson, D.C.Wash., 289 F. 493, 495.

As to open "Account," "Corporation," "Entry," "Insolvency," "Lewdness," "Policy," "Possession," and "Verdict," see those titles.

Open bulk. In the mass; exposed to view; not tied or sealed up. In re Sanders, C.C.N.C., 52 F. 802, 18 L.R.A. 549.

Open court. This term may mean either a court which has been formally convened and declared open for the transaction of its proper judicial business, or a court which is freely open to the approach of all decent and orderly persons in the character of spectators. Conover v. Bird, 56 N.J.Law, 228, 28 A. 428. Gomes v. Ulibarri, 23 N.M. 501, 169 P. 301, 302; U. S. v. Ginsberg, 243 U.S. 472, 37 S.Ct. 422, 425, 61 L.Ed. 853; Gillham v. St. Louis Southwestern Ry. Co. of Texas, Tex. Civ.App., 241 S.W. 512, 514.

Open doors. In Scotch law. "Letters of open doors" are process which empowers the messenger, or officer of the law, to break open doors of houses or rooms in which the debtor has placed his goods. Bell.

Open-end agreement. An agreement between employer and injured employee for compensation for indefinite period, approved by the labor commissioner, having effect of judgment so long as facts on which the award was predicated continue. Healey's Case, 124 Me. 54, 126 A. 21, 22.

Open fields, or meadows. In English law. Fields which are undivided, but belong to separate owners; the part of each owner is marked off by boundaries until the crop has been carried off, when the pasture is shared promiscuously by the joint herd of all the owners. Elton, Commons, 31; Sweet.

Open law. The making or waging of law. Magna Charta, c. 21.

Open lot. One bounded upon all sides by streets. Illinois Surety Co. v. O'Brien, C.C.A.Ohio, 223 F. 933, 938.

Open mortgage clause. See Union Mortgage Clause.

Open sea. The expanse and mass of any great body of water, as distinguished from its margin or coast, its harbors, bays, creeks, inlets. The Cuzco, D.C.Wash., 225 F. 169, 176.

Open season. That portion of the year wherein the laws for the preservation of game and fish permit the killing of a particular species of game or the taking of a particular variety of fish.

Open shop. In trade union cant, one where nonunion men are employed. George J. Grant Const. Co. v. St. Paul Bldg. Trades Council, 136 Minn. 167, 161 N.W. 520, 521. A shop in which union and nonunion workmen are employed indiscriminately. Shine v. Fox Bros. Mfg. Co., 156 F. 357, 86 C.C.A. 311. The term is frequently used in a depreciatory sense, as implying that the operator of such a shop, by employing nonunion men, is in effect discriminating against trade unions, and hampering their advancement.

Open theft. In Saxon law. The same with the Latin *"furtum manifestum,"* (*q. v.*).

OPENING. In American practice. The beginning; the commencement; the first address of the counsel.

OPENING STATEMENT OF COUNSEL. Outline of anticipated proof. Speer v. Shipley, 149 Kan. 15, 85 P.2d 999, 1001. Its purpose is to advise the jury of facts relied upon and of issues involved, and to give jury a general picture of the facts and the situations so that jury will be able to understand the evidence. State v. Erwin, 101 Utah 365, 120 P.2d 285, 313.

OPENTIDE. The time after corn is carried out of the fields.

OPERA. A composition of a dramatic kind, set to music and sung, accompanied with musical instruments, and enriched with appropriate costumes, scenery, etc. The house in which operas are represented is termed an "opera-house." Rowland v. Kleber, 1 Pittsb.R. (Pa.) 71.

OPERARII. Such tenants, under feudal tenures, as held some little portions of land by the duty of performing bodily labor and servile works for their lord.

OPERATE. This word, when used with relation to automobiles, signifies a personal act in working the mechanism of the automobile; that is, the driver operates the automobile for the owner, but the owner does not operate the automobile unless he drives it himself. Beard v. Clark, Tex.Civ. App., 83 S.W.2d 1023, 1025.

Similarly, as used in some statutes authorizing substituted service on the nonresident owner of an automobile, the word "operate" is limited to the personal act of the owner; but under other statutes, substituted service is authorized when the automobile was being operated by another with the owner's consent, whether express or implied. Blashfield, Cyc. of Automobile Law and Prac., Perm.Ed., § 5914. In the context of some automobile liability policies, the word "operate" may be construed as describing the personal act of the insured owner in working the mechanism of the automobile. Id., § 3941. As used in accident policies insuring against injuries while operating a motor vehicle "operate" does not contemplate a constant and unceasing motion but includes those stops which an automobile driver ordinarily makes, such as a stop to change or repair a tire. Id., § 4127.

OPERATIO. One day's work performed by a tenant for his lord.

OPERATION. Exertion of power; the process of operating or mode of action; an effect brought about in accordance with a definite plan; action; activity. Little Rock v. Parish, 36 Ark. 166; Fleming Oil Co. v. South Penn Oil Co., 37 W.Va. 653, 17 S.E. 203, National Exchange Bank and Trust Co. of Steubenville v. New York Life Ins. Co., D.C.Pa., 19 F.Supp. 790, 791. In surgical practice, the term is of indefinite import, but may be approximately defined as an act or succession of acts performed upon the body of a patient, for his relief or restoration to normal conditions, either by manipulation or the use of surgical instruments or both, as distinguished from therapeutic treatment by the administration of drugs or other remedial agencies. See Akridge v. Noble, 114 Ga. 949, 41 S.E. 78.

Criminal operation. In medical jurisprudence. An operation to procure an abortion. Miller v. Bayer, 94 Wis. 123, 68 N.W. 869.

Operation of law. This term expresses the manner in which rights, and sometimes liabilities, devolve upon a person by the mere application to the particular transaction of the established rules of law, without the act or co-operation of the party himself.

OPERATIVE. A workman; a laboring man; an artisan; particularly one employed in factories. Cocking v. Ward, Tenn.Ch.App., 48 S.W. 287; In re City Trust Co., 121 F. 706, 58 C.C.A. 126.

OPERATIVE PART. That part of a conveyance, or of any instrument intended for the creation or transference of rights, by which the main object of the instrument is carried into effect. It is distinguished from introductory matter, recitals, formal conclusion, etc.

OPERATIVE WORDS, in a deed or lease, are the words which effect the transaction intended to be consummated by the instrument.

OPERIS NOVI NUNTIATIO. Lat. In the civil law. A protest or warning against [of] a new work. Dig. 39, 1.

OPETIDE. The ancient time of marriage, from Epiphany to Ash-Wednesday.

OPHTHALMOLOGIST. One who is skilled in, or practices, ophthalmology. Practice of "oculists" and "ophthalmologists" has relation to practice of medicine and surgery in treatment of diseases of eye, while practice of "optometry" relates to measurement of powers of vision and adaptation of lenses for aid thereof. New Jersey State Board of Optometrists v. S. S. Kresge Co., 113 N.J.L. 287, 174 A. 353, 357. See Oculist.

OPINIO EST DUPLEX, SCILICET, OPINIO VULGARIS, ORTA INTER GRAVES ET DISCRETOS, ET QUÆ VULTUM VERITATIS HABET; ET OPINIO TANTUM ORTA INTER LEVES ET VULGARES HOMINES, ABSQUE SPECIE VERITATIS. 4 Coke, 107. Opinion is of two kinds, namely, common opinion, which springs up among grave and discreet men, and which has the appearance of truth, and opinion which springs up only among light and foolish men, without the semblance of truth.

OPINIO QUÆ FAVET TESTAMENTO EST TENENDA. The opinion which favors a will is to be followed. 1 W.Bl. 13, arg.

OPINION. A document prepared by an attorney for his client, embodying his understanding of the law as applicable to a state of facts submitted to him for that purpose.

The statement by a judge or court of the decision reached in regard to a cause tried or argued before them, expounding the law as applied to the case, and detailing the reasons upon which the judgment is based. Craig v. Bennett, 158 Ind. 9, 62 N.E. 273; Coffey v. Gamble, 117 Iowa, 545, 91 N.W. 813.

The words "decision" and "opinion" do not have same meaning, a "decision" of a court being its judgment, and its "opinion" being reasons given for judgment. Robertson v. Vandergrift, 119 W.Va. 219, 193 S.E. 62, 63; In re Brown's Guardianship, 6 Wash.2d 215, 107 P.2d 1104, 1106, 1107, 1108; Mosley v. Magnolia Petroleum Co., 45 N.M. 230, 114 P.2d 740, 747.

Concurring opinion. An opinion, separate from that which embodies the views and decision of the majority of the court, prepared and filed by a judge who agrees in the general result of the decision, and which either reinforces the majority opinion by the expression of the particular judge's own views or reasoning, or (more commonly) voices his disapproval of the grounds of the decision or the arguments on which it was based, though approving the final result.

Dissenting opinion. A separate opinion in which a particular judge announces his dissent from the conclusion held by a majority of the court, and expounds his own views.

Per curiam opinion. One concurred in by the entire court, but expressed as being "*per curiam*" or "by the court," without disclosing the name of any particular judge as being its author.

OPINION EVIDENCE. Evidence of what the witness thinks, believes, or infers in regard to facts in dispute, as distinguished from his personal knowledge of the facts themselves; not admissible except (under certain limitations) in the case of experts. Britt v. Carolina Northern R. Co., 148 N.C. 37, 61 S.E. 601, 603. That which is given by a person of ordinary capacity who has by opportunity for practice acquired special knowledge outside limits of common observation, of value in illucidating a matter under consideration. Crosby v. Wells, 73 N.J.L. 790, 67 A. 295, 298.

In the law of evidence, opinion is an inference or conclusion drawn by a witness from facts some of which are known to him and others assumed, or drawn from facts which, though lending probability to the inference, do not evolve it by a process of absolutely necessary reasoning. Lipscomb v. State, 75 Miss. 559, 23 So. 210.

An inference necessarily involving certain facts may be stated without the facts, the inference being an equivalent to a specification of the facts; but, when the facts are not necessarily involved in the inference (*e. g.*, when the inference may be sustained upon either of several distinct phases of fact, neither of which it necessarily involves,) then the facts must be stated. Whart.Ev. § 510.

OPIUM. Drug consisting of inspissated juice of opium poppy. State v. Brennan, 89 Mont. 479, 300 P. 273, 275.

OPIUM JOINT. A "joint" is usually regarded as a place of meeting or resort for persons engaged in evil and secret practices of any kind, as a tramps' joint, such a place as is usually kept by Chinese for the accommodation of persons addicted to the habit of opium smoking, and where they are furnished with pipes, opium, etc., for that purpose, and called an "opium joint," or, generally speaking, a rendezvous for persons of evil habits and practices. State v. Shoaf, 179 N.C. 744, 102 S.E. 705, 706, 9 A.L.R. 426.

OPORTET QUOD CERTA RES DEDUCATUR IN DONATIONEM. It is necessary that a certain thing be brought into the gift, or made the subject of the conveyance. Bract. fol. 15*b*.

OPORTET QUOD CERTA RES DEDUCATUR IN JUDICIUM. Jenk.Cent. 84. A thing certain must be brought to judgment.

OPORTET QUOD CERTA SIT RES QUÆ VENDITUR. It is necessary that there should be a certain thing which is sold. To make a valid sale, there must be certainty as to the thing which is sold. Bract. fol. 61*b*.

OPORTET QUOD CERTÆ PERSONÆ, TERRÆ, ET CERTI STATUS COMPREHENDANTUR IN DECLARATIONE USUUM. 9 Coke, 9. It is necessary that given persons, lands, and estates should be comprehended in a declaration of uses.

OPPIGNERARE. Lat. In the civil law. To pledge. Calvin.

OPPOSER. An officer formerly belonging to the green-wax in the exchequer.

OPPOSITE. An old word for "opponent."

OPPOSITE PARTY. Within statutes providing that opposite party shall be incompetent to testify as to matters equally within knowledge of deceased is one whose personal and financial interests, either immediate or remote, are antagonistic to like interests of protected party. Salsbury v. Sackrider, 284 Mich. 493, 280 N.W. 926.

OPPOSITION. Act of opposing or resisting; antagonism; state of being opposite or opposed; antithesis; also, a position confronting another or placing in contrast; that which is or furnishes an obstacle to some result; political party opposed to ministry or administration; or might be construed to include peaceful and orderly opposition to government. People v. Mintz, 106 Cal.App. 725, 290 P. 93, 97.

In Bankruptcy Practice. Opposition is the refusal of a creditor to assent to the debtor's discharge under the bankrupt law.

In French law. A motion to open a judgment by default and let the defendant in to a defense.

OPPRESSION. The misdemeanor committed by a public officer, who under color of his office, wrongfully inflicts upon any person any bodily harm, imprisonment, or other injury. 1 Russ. Crimes, 297; Steph.Dig.Crim.Law, 71. See U. S. v. Deaver, D.C.N.C., 14 F. 597. An act of cruelty, severity, unlawful exaction, or excessive use of authority. Ramsbacker v. Hohman, 80 Mont. 480, 261 P. 273, 276, an act of subjecting to cruel and unjust hardship; an act of domination. Baker v. Peck, 1 Cal.App.2d 231, 36 P.2d 404, 406.

OPPRESSOR. A public officer who unlawfully uses his authority by way of oppression, (*q. v.*).

OPPROBRIUM. In the civil law. Ignominy; infamy; shame.

OPTICIAN. Persons engaged in optometry, who confine themselves entirely to the work of making lenses in accordance with prescriptions given by physicians or oculists, are known as "opticians"; others, who manufacture the lenses, either according to their own judgment or the prescription of physicians, and also examine the eyes to ascertain whether there are any such defects visible as can be corrected by the application of lenses, are known as "optometrists." Martin v. Baldy, 249 Pa. 253, 94 A. 1091, 1092.

OPTIMA EST LEGIS INTERPRES CONSUETUDO. Custom is the best interpreter of the law. Dig. 1, 3, 37; Broom, Max. 931; Lofft, 237.

OPTIMA EST LEX QUÆ MINIMUM RELINQUIT ARBITRIO JUDICIS; OPTIMUS JUDEX QUI MINIMUM SIBI. That law is the best which leaves least to the discretion of the judge; that judge is the best who leaves least to his own. Bac. Aphorisms, 46; 2 Dwar.St. 782. That system of law is best which confides as little as possible to the discretion of the judge; that judge the best who relies as little as possible on his own opinion. Broom, Max. 84; 1 Kent, Comm. 478.

OPTIMA STATUTI INTERPRETATRIX EST (OMNIBUS PARTICULIS EJUSDEM INSPECTIS) IPSUM STATUTUM. The best interpreter of a statute is (all its parts being considered) the statute itself. Wing.Max. p. 239, max. 68; 8 Coke, 117*b*.

OPTIMACY. Nobility; men of the highest rank.

OPTIMAM ESSE LEGEM, QUÆ MINIMUM RELINQUIT ARBITRIO JUDICIS; ID QUOD CERTITUDO EJUS PRÆSTAT. That law is the best which leaves the least discretion to the judge; and this is an advantage which results from its certainty. Bac.Aphorisms, 8.

OPTIMUS INTERPRES RERUM USUS. Use or usage is the best interpreter of things. 2 Inst. 282; Broom, Max. 917, 930, 931.

OPTIMUS INTERPRETANDI MODUS EST SIC LEGES INTERPRETARI UT LEGES LEGIBUS CONCORDANT. 8 Coke, 169. The best mode of interpretation is so to interpret laws that they may accord with each other.

OPTIMUS JUDEX, QUI MINIMUM SIBI. He is the best judge who relies as little as possible on his own discretion. Bacon, Aph. 46; Broom, Max. 84.

OPTIMUS LEGUM INTERPRES CONSUETUDO. 4 Inst. 75. Custom is the best interpreter of the laws.

OPTION. In English ecclesiastical law. A customary prerogative of an archbishop, when a bishop is consecrated by him, to name a clerk or chaplain of his own to be provided for by such suffragan bishop; in lieu of which it is now usual for the bishop to make over by deed to the archbishop, his executors and assigns, the next presentation of such dignity or benefice in the bishop's disposal within that see, as the archbishop himself shall *choose*, which is therefore called his "option." 1 Bl.Comm. 381; 3 Steph.Comm. 63, 64; Cowell.

In contracts. A privilege existing in one person, for which he has paid money, which gives him the right to *buy* certain merchandise or certain specified securities from another person, if he chooses, at any time within an agreed period, at a fixed price, or to *sell* such property to such other person at an agreed price and time. If the option gives the choice of buying or not buying, it is denominated a "call." If it gives the choice of selling or not, it is called a "put." If it is a combination of both these, and gives the privilege of *either* buying or selling or not, it is called a "straddle" or a "spread eagle." These terms are used on the stock-exchange. Plank v. Jackson, 128 Ind. 424, 26 N.E. 568; Osgood v. Bauder, 75 Iowa, 550, 39 N.W. 887, 1 L.R.A. 655.

A continuing offer or contract by which owner stipulates with another that latter shall have right to buy property at fixed price within certain time, and an agreement is only an "option" when no obligation rests on party to make any payment except such as may be agreed on between parties as consideration to support option until he has made up his mind within time specified to complete purchase. Gibbs v. Piper, Del., 153 A. 674, 676.

It is but continuing offer, which is merged in contract resulting from acceptance thereof. Helvering v. Bartlett, C.C.A. 4, 71 F.2d 598, 599.

OPTIONAL WRIT. In old England practice. That species of original writ, otherwise called a "*præcipe*," which was framed in the alternative, commanding the defendant to do the thing required, *or* show the reason wherefore he had not done it. 3 Bl.Comm. 274.

OPTOMETRIST. One who is skilled in, or practices, optometry. Webster, Dict. See Oculist.

OPTOMETRY. The employment of any means other than the use of drugs for the measurement of the powers of vision and the adaptation of lenses for the correction and aid thereof. Martin v. Baldy, 249 Pa. 253, 94 A. 1091, 1092; People v. Griffith, 280 Ill. 18, 117 N.E. 195, 196; New Jersey State Board of Optometrists v. S. S. Kresge Co., 113 N.J.Law, 287, 174 A. 353, 356.

OPUS. Lat. Work; labor; the product of work or labor.

OPUS LOCATUM. The product of work let for use to another; or the hiring out of work or labor to be done upon a thing.

OPUS MANIFICUM. In old English law. Labor done by the hands; manual labor; such as making a hedge, digging a ditch. Fleta, lib. 2, c. 48, § 3.

OPUS NOVUM. In the civil law. A new work. By this term was meant something newly built upon land, or taken from a work already erected. He was said *opus novum facere* (to make a new work) who, either by building or by taking anything away, changed the former appearance of a work. Dig. 39, 1, 1, 11.

OR, *n.* A term used in heraldry, and signifying gold; called "sol" by some heralds when it occurs in the arms of princes, and "topaz" or "carbuncle" when borne by peers. Engravers represent it by an indefinite number of small points. Wharton.

OR, *conj.* A disjunctive particle used to express an alternative or to give a choice of one among two or more things. It is also used to clarify what has already been said, and in such cases, means "in other words," "to-wit," or "that is to say." Peck v. Board of Directors of Public Schools for Parish of Catahoula, 137 La. 334, 68 So. 629, 630; Travelers' Protective Ass'n v. Jones, 75 Ind. App. 29, 127 N.E. 783, 785.

Or is frequently misused; and courts will construe it to mean "and" where it was so used. State v. Circuit Court of Dodge County, 176 Wis. 198, 186 N.W. 732, 734; Northern Commercial Co. v. U. S., C.C.A.Alaska, 217 F. 33, 36; Spillman v. Succession of Spillman, 147 La. 47, 84 So. 489, 490; Smiley v. Lenane, 363 Ill. 66, 1 N.E.2d 213, 216. However, where the word "or" is preceded by the word "either," it is never given a conjunctive meaning. Smith v. Farley, 155 App.Div. 813, 140 N.Y.S. 990, 992.

ORA. A Saxon coin, valued at sixteen pence, and sometimes at twenty pence.

ORACULUM. In the civil law. The name of a kind of response or sentence given by the Roman emperors.

ORAL. Uttered by the mouth or in words; spoken, not written.

ORAL CONTRACT. One which is partly in writing and partly depends on spoken words, or none of which is in writing; one which, so far as it has been reduced to writing, is incomplete or expresses only a part of what is intended, but is completed by spoken words; or one which, originally written, has afterwards been changed orally. Railway Passenger, etc., Ass'n v. Loomis, 142 Ill. 560, 32 N.E. 424; Moore v. Ohl, 65 Ind.App. 691, 116 N.E. 9, 10.

ORAL EVIDENCE. Evidence given by word of mouth; the oral testimony of a witness. Bates' Ann.St.Ohio 1904, § 5262 (Gen.Code, § 11522); Rev.St.Wyo.1899, § 3704 (Rev.St.1931, § 89-1725). See, also, Parol Evidence.

ORAL PLEADING. Pleading by word of mouth, in the actual presence of the court. This was the ancient mode of pleading in England, and continued to the reign of Edward III. Steph.Pl. 23–26.

ORANDO PRO REGE ET REGNO. An ancient writ which issued, while there was no standing collect for a sitting parliament, to pray for the peace and good government of the realm.

ORANGEMEN. A party in Ireland who keep alive the views of William of Orange. Wharton.

ORATOR. The plaintiff in a cause or matter in chancery, when addressing or petitioning the court, used to style himself "orator," and, when a woman, "oratrix." But these terms have long gone into disuse, and the customary phrases now are "plaintiff" or "petitioner."

In Roman law, the term denoted an advocate.

ORATRIX. A female petitioner; a female plaintiff in a bill in chancery was formerly so called.

ORBATION. Deprivation of one's parents or children, or privation in general. Little used.

ORCINUS LIBERTUS. Lat. In Roman law. A freedman who obtained his liberty by the direct operation of the will or testament of his deceased master was so called, being the freedman of the deceased, (*orcinus,*) not of the *hœres.* Brown.

ORDAIN. To institute or establish; to make an ordinance; to enact a constitution or law. State v. Dallas City, 72 Or. 337, 143 P. 1127, 1131, Ann. Cas.1916B, 855. To confer on a person the holy orders of priest or deacon. Kibbe v. Antram, 4 Conn. 134.

ORDAINERS. An elected body of 21 members appointed by Parliament in 1310 to make ordinances for the good of the realm. The whole administration passed into their hands. Stubbs, Early Plantagenets.

ORDEAL. The most ancient species of trial, in Saxon and old English law, being peculiarly distinguished by the appellation of "*judicium Dei,*" or "judgment of God," it being supposed that supernatural intervention would rescue an innocent person from the danger of physical harm to which he was exposed in this species of trial. The ordeal was of two sorts,—either fire ordeal or water ordeal; the former being confined to persons of higher rank, the latter to the common people. 4 Bl.Comm. 342.

Fire ordeal. The ordeal by fire or red-hot iron, which was performed either by taking up in the hand a piece of red-hot iron, of one, two, or three pounds weight, or by walking barefoot and blindfolded over nine red-hot plowshares, laid lengthwise at unequal distances. 4 Bl.Comm. 343; Cowell.

Water Ordeal

In Saxon and old English law. The ordeal or trial by water. The *hot-water* ordeal was performed by plunging the bare arm up to the elbow in boiling water, and escaping unhurt thereby. The *cold-water* ordeal was performed by casting the person suspected into a river or pond of cold water, when, if he floated therein, without any action of swimming it was deemed an evidence of his guilt; but, if he sunk, he was acquitted. 4 Bl.Comm. 343.

ORDEFFE, or ORDELFE. A liberty whereby a man claims the ore found in his own land; also, the ore lying under land. Cowell.

ORDELS. In old English law. The right of administering oaths and adjudging trials by ordeal within a precinct or liberty. Cowell.

ORDENAMIENTO. In Spanish law. An order emanating from the sovereign, and differing from a *cedula* only in form and in the mode of its promulgation. Schm.Civil Law, Introd. 93, note.

ORDENAMIENTO DE ALCALA. A collection of Spanish law promulgated by the Cortes in the year 1348. Schm.Civil Law, Introd. 75.

ORDER. A mandate, precept; a command or direction authoritatively given; a rule or regulation. Brady v. Interstate Commerce Commission, D.C. W.Va., 43 F.2d 847, 850.

The distinction between "order" and "requisition" is that the first is a mandatory act, the latter a request. Mills v. Martin, 19 Johns. (N.Y.) 7.

An informal bill of exchange or letter of request whereby the party to whom it is addressed is directed to pay or deliver to a person therein named the whole or part of a fund or other property of the person making the order, and which is in the possession of the drawee. People v. Smith, 112 Mich. 192, 70 N.W. 466, 67 Am.St.Rep. 392; State v. Nevins, 23 Vt. 521. A designation of the person to whom a bill of exchange or negotiable promissory note is to be paid.

It is also used to designate a rank, class, or division of men; as the order of nobles, order of knights, order of priests, etc.

Orders are also issued by subordinate legislative authorities. Such are the English orders in council, or orders issued by the privy council in the name of the king, either in exercise of the royal prerogative or in pursuance of an act of parliament. The rules of court under the judicature act are grouped together in the form of orders, each order dealing with a particular subject-matter. Sweet.

In French law. The name order (*ordre*) is given to the operation which has for its object to fix the rank of the preferences claimed by the creditors in the distribution of the price [arising from the sale] of an immovable affected by their liens. Dalloz, *mot* "Ordre."

Practice

Every direction of a court or judge made or entered in writing, and not included in a judgment. An application for an order is a motion. Code Civ. Proc.Cal. § 1003; Code N.Y. § 400 (Civil Practice Act, § 113). Tyvand v. McDonne, 37 N.D. 251, 164 N.W. 1, 3; First Nat. Bank v. Poling, 42 Idaho 636, 248 P. 19, 20.

General

Agreed order. See Agreed.

Charging order. The name bestowed, in English practice, upon an order allowed by St. 1 & 2 Vict. c. 110, § 14, and 3 & 4 Vict. c. 82, to be granted to a judgment creditor, that the property of a judgment debtor in government stock, or in the stock of any public company in England, corporate or otherwise, shall (whether standing in his own name or in the name of any person in trust for him) stand charged with the payment of the amount for which judgment shall have been recovered, with interest. 3 Steph.Comm. 587, 588.

Decretal order. In chancery practice. An order made by the court of chancery, in the nature of a decree, upon a motion or petition. Thompson v. McKim, 6 Har. & J. Md. 319; Bissell Carpet Sweeper Co. v. Goshen Sweeper Co., 19 C.C.A. 25, 72 F. 545. An order in a chancery suit made on motion or otherwise not at the regular hearing of a cause, and yet not of an interlocutory nature, but finally disposing of the cause, so far as a decree could then have disposed of it. Mozley & Whiteley.

Final order. One which either terminates the action itself, or decides some matter litigated by the parties, or operates to divest some right; or one which completely disposes of the subject-matter and the rights of the parties. Salem King's Products Co. v. La Follette, 100 Or. 11, 196 P. 416, 417; Stockham v. Knollenberg, 133 Md. 337, 105 A. 305, 307; Marchant & Taylor v. Mathews County, 139 Va. 723, 124 S.E. 420, 423.

General orders. Orders or rules of court, promulgated for the guidance of practitioners and the regulation of procedure in general, or in some general branch of its jurisdiction; as opposed to a rule or an order made in an individual case; the rules of court.

Interlocutory order. An order which decides not the cause, but only settles some intervening matter relating to it; as when an order is made, on a motion in chancery, for the plaintiff to have an injunction to quiet his possession till the hearing of the cause. Termes de la Ley; Gas & Electric Securities Co. v. Manhattan & Queens Traction Corporation, C.C.A.N.Y., 266 F. 625, 632; Johnson v. Roberson, 171 N.C. 194, 88 S.E. 231; Theo. Hirsch Co. v. Scott, 87 Fla. 336, 100 So. 157, 158; Salmons v. Rugyeri, 103 N.J.Law, 596, 137 A. 568, 569; Simons v. Morris, 325 Ill. 199, 156 N.E. 280; Joyce v. Nona Mills Co., 142 La. 934, 77 So. 854.

Money order. See Money.

Restraining order. In equity practice. An order which may issue upon the filing of an application for an injunction forbidding the defendant to do the threatened act until a hearing on the application can be had. Though the term is sometimes used as a synonym of "injunction," a restraining order is properly distinguishable from an injunction, in that the former is intended only as a restraint upon the defendant until the propriety of granting an injunction, temporary or perpetual, can be determined, and it does no more than restrain the proceedings until such determination. Wetzstein v. Boston, etc., Min. Co., 25 Mont. 135, 63 P. 1043. Mason v. Milligan, 185 Ind. 319, 114 N.E. 3; Labbitt v. Bunston, 80 Mont. 293, 260 P. 727, 730. In English law, the term is specially applied to an order restraining the Bank of England, or any public company, from allowing any dealing with some stock or shares specified in the order. It is granted on motion or petition. Hunt, Eq. p. 216.

Speaking order. An order which contains matter which is explanatory or illustrative of the mere direction which is given by it is sometimes thus called. Duff v. Duff, 101 Cal. 1, 35 P. 437.

Stop order. The meaning of a stop order given to a broker is to wait until the market price of the particular security reaches a specified figure, and then to "stop" the transaction by either selling or buying, as the case may be, as well as possible. Porter v. Wormser, 94 N.Y. 431.

Order and disposition of goods and chattels. When goods are in the "order and disposition" of a bankrupt, they go to his trustee, and have gone so since the time of James I. Wharton.

Order nisi. A provisional or conditional order, allowing a certain time within which to do some required act, on failure of which the order will be made absolute.

Order of discharge. In England. An order made under the bankruptcy act of 1869, by a court of bankruptcy, the effect of which is to discharge a bankrupt from all debts, claims, or demands provable under the bankruptcy.

Order of filiation. An order made by a court or judge having jurisdiction, fixing the paternity of a bastard child upon a given man, and requiring him to provide for its support.

Order of revivor. In English practice. An order as of course for the continuance of an abated suit. It superseded the bill of revivor.

ORDERLY. A hospital attendant who does general work. Phillips v. Buffalo General Hospital, 239 N.Y. 188, 146 N.E. 199, 200.

ORDERS. The directions as to the course and purpose of a voyage given by the owner of the vessel to the captain or master. For other meanings, see Order.

ORDERS OF THE DAY. Any member of the English house of commons who wishes to propose any question, or to "move the house," as it is termed, must, in order to give the house due notice of his intention, state the form or nature of his motion on a previous day, and have it entered in a book termed the "order-book;" and the motions so entered, the house arranges, shall be considered on particular days, and such motions or matters, when the day arrives for their being considered, are then termed the "orders of the day." Brown. A similar practice obtains in the legislative bodies of this country.

ORDINANCE. A rule established by authority; a permanent rule of action; a law or statute. In a more limited sense, the term is used to designate the enactments of the legislative body of a municipal corporation. State v. Swindell, 146 Ind. 527, 45 N.E. 700, 58 Am.St.Rep. 375; Bills v. Goshen, 117 Ind. 221, 20 N.E. 115, 3 L.R.A. 261.

The name has also been given to certain enactments, more general in their character than ordinary statutes, and serving as organic laws, yet not exactly to be called "constitutions." Such was the "Ordinance for the government of the North-West Territory," enacted by congress in 1787.

Strictly, a bill or law which might stand with the old law, and did not alter any statute in force at the time, and which became complete by the royal assent on the *parliament roll,* without any entry on the *statute roll.* A bill or law which might at any time be amended by the parliament, without any statute. Hale, Com. Law. An ordinance was otherwise distinguished from a statute by the circumstance that the latter required the threefold assent of king, lords, and commons, while an ordinance might be ordained by one or two of these constituent bodies. See 4 Inst. 25.

ORDINANCE OF 1647. A law passed by the Colony of Massachusetts, still in force, in a modified form, whereby the state owns the great ponds within its confines, which are held in trust for public uses. Watuppa Reservoir Co. v. Fall River, 147 Mass. 548, 18 N.E. 465, 1 L.R.A. 466.

ORDINANCE OF 1648. A law of England relating to admiralty jurisdiction. See Bened. Adm. § 99. It expired in 1660.

ORDINANCE OF 1681. An ordinance of France relating to maritime affairs. See Bened. Adm. § 173.

ORDINANCE OF 1787. A statute for the government of the Northwest Territory. Religious and legal freedom, encouragement of education, just treatment of the Indians, the future division into States, and the exclusion of slavery were ordained. Webster, Dict.

ORDINANCE OF THE FOREST. In English law. A statute made touching matters and causes of the forest. 33 & 34 Edw. 1.

ORDINANCES OF EDWARD I. Two laws and ordinances published by Edward I. in the second year of his reign, at Hastings, relating to admiralty jurisdiction. These are said to have been the foundation of a consistent usage for a long time. See Bened. Adm. § 55.

ORDINANDI LEX. Lat. The law of procedure, as distinguished from the substantial part of the law.

ORDINARIUS ITA DICITUR QUIA HABET ORDINARIAM JURISDICTIONEM, IN JURE PROPRIO, ET NON PROPTER DEPUTATIONEM. Co.Litt. 96. The ordinary is so called because he has an ordinary jurisdiction in his own right, and not a deputed one.

ORDINARY, *n.* At common law. One who has exempt and immediate jurisdiction in causes ecclesiastical. Also a bishop; and an archbishop is the ordinary of the whole province, to visit and receive appeals from inferior jurisdictions. Also a commissary or official of a bishop or other ecclesiastical judge having judicial power; an archdeacon; officer of the royal household. Wharton.

In American law. A judicial officer, in several of the states, clothed by statute with powers in regard to wills, probate, administràtion, guardianship, etc. Darrow v. Darrow, 201 Ala. 477, 78 So. 383, 384. A public house where food and lodging are furnished to the traveler and his beast, at fixed rates, open to whoever may apply for accommodation, and where intoxicating liquor is sold at retail. Talbott v. Southern Seminary, 131 Va. 576, 109 S.E. 440, 441, 19 A.L.R. 534; City of Chicago v. R. & X. Restaurant, 369 Ill. 65, 15 N.E.2d 725, 727, 117 A.L.R. 1313.

In Scotch law. A single judge of the court of session, who decides with or without a jury, as the case may be. Brande.

In the civil law. A judge who has authority to take cognizance of causes in his own right, and not by deputation. Murden v. Beath, 1 Mill. Const., S.C., 269.

Ordinary of assize and sessions. In old English law. A deputy of the bishop of the diocese, anciently appointed to give malefactors their neck-verses, and judge whether they read or not; also to perform divine services for them, and assist in preparing them for death. Wharton.

Ordinary of Newgate. The clergyman who is attendant upon condemned malefactors in that prison to prepare them for death; he records the behavior of such persons. Formerly it was the custom of the ordinary to publish a small pamphlet upon the execution of any remarkable criminal. Wharton.

ORDINARY, *adj.* Regular; usual; normal; common; often recurring; according to established order; settled; customary; reasonable; not characterized by peculiar or unusual circumstances; belonging to, exercised by, or characteristic of, the normal or average individual. Albrecht v. Schultz Belting Co., 299 Mo. 12; 252 S.W. 400, 402; State v. Coulter, Mo.Sup., 204 S.W. 5; Albrecht v. Schultz Belting Co., 299 Mo. 12, 252 S.W. 400, 402; Wiener v. Mutual Life Ins. Co. of New York, Mo. App., 170 S.W.2d 174, 178.

As to ordinary "Care," "Diligence," "Negligence," see those titles.

Ordinary calling. Those things which are repeated daily or weekly in the course of business. Ellis v. State, 5 Ga.App. 615, 63 S.E. 588.

Ordinary conveyances. Those deeds of transfer which are entered into between two or more persons, without an assurance in a superior court of justice. Wharton.

Ordinary course of business. The transaction of business according to the usages and customs of the commercial world generally or of the particular community or (in some cases) of the particular individual whose acts are under consideration. Rison v. Knapp, 20 Fed.Cas. 835; Christianson v. Farmers' Warehouse Ass'n, 5 N.D. 438, 67 N.W. 300, 32 L.R.A. 730.

Ordinary dangers incident to employment. Those commonly and usually pertaining to and incident to it, which a reasonably prudent person might anticipate, and do not include danger by acts of negligence, unless habitual and known to the servant. Chicago, R. I. & G. Ry. Co. v. Smith, Tex. Civ.App., 197 S.W. 614, 618.

Ordinary expense. An expense is "ordinary" if it is in an ordinary class, if in the ordinary course of the transaction of municipal business or the maintenance of municipal property it may and is likely to become necessary; and it will be assumed that if by law a specific duty is imposed, and the mode of performance is prescribed, so that no discretion is left with the officer, the expense necessarily incurred in discharging the duty is a "necessary expense." Dexter Horton Trust & Savings Bank v. Clearwater County, D.C.Idaho, 235 F. 743, 750; Arthur v. Horwege, 28 Cal.App. 738, 153 P. 980, 981; State v. Carter, 31 Wyo. 401, 226 P. 690, 693.

Ordinary handling. As in a railroad's baggage tariff, providing that cases marked "Fragile" and likely to be damaged by ordinary handling will not be accepted, except at owner's risk, means merely ordinary wear and tear necessarily incidental to transportation of such articles, where reasonable care is used. Perkins v. New York, N. H. & H. R. Co., 232 Mass. 336, 122 N.E. 306, 307.

Ordinary hazards of occupation. Those arising without negligence on part of master. Chesapeake & O. Ry. Co. v. Coleman, 220 Ky. 64, 294 S.W. 809, 810.

Ordinary inspection. As applied to railroad equipment. That degree of care and of inspection which ordinarily prudent railroad companies, their officers and employees, commonly use under similar circumstances. Canadian Northern Ry. Co. v. Senske, C.C.A.Minn., 201 F. 637, 642.

Ordinary kerosene. The kerosene sold in the open market, kerosene of a lawful grade and quality ordinarily sold for the general use of the public for illuminating purposes. Standard Oil Co. v. Reagan, 15 Ga.App. 571, 84 S.E. 69, 76.

Ordinary persons. Men of ordinary care and diligence in relation to any particular thing. Ford v. Engleman, 118 Va. 89, 86 S.E. 852, 855.

Ordinary proceeding. Such a proceeding as was known to the common law and was formerly conducted in accordance with the proceedings of the common-law courts, and as is generally known under the modern Codes to be such a proceeding as is started by the issuance of a summons, and results in a judgment enforceable by execution. Dow v. Lillie, 26 N.D. 512, 144 N.W. 1082, 1084, L.R.A.1915D, 754.

Ordinary repairs. Such as are necessary to make good the usual wear and tear or natural and unavoidable decay and keep the property in good condition. Abell v. Brady, 79 Md. 94, 28 A. 817; Clark Civil Tp. v. Brookshire, 114 Ind. 437, 16 N.E. 132; Syracuse Malleable Iron Works v. Travelers' Ins. Co., 94 Misc. 411, 157 N.Y.S. 572, 574; Farmers' Handy Wagon Co. v. Casualty Co. of America, 184 Iowa, 773, 169 N.W. 178; Springfield Light, Heat & Power Co. v. Philadelphia Casualty Co., 184 Ill.App. 175, 178.

Ordinary risks. Those incident to the business, and do not imply the result of the master's negligence. The expression "extraordinary risks" is generally used to describe risks arising from the negligence of the master, and they are generally held not to be assumed unless known or obvious. Emanuel v. Georgia & F. Ry. Co., 142 Ga. 543, 83 S.E. 230, 231; Arundell v. American Oilfields Co.,

31 Cal.App. 218, 160 P. 159, 165; Emerick v. Slavonian Roman Greek Catholic Union, 93 N.J.Law, 282, 108 A. 223; Neary v. Georgia Public Service Co., 27 Ga.App. 238, 107 S.E. 893, 896.

Ordinary seaman. A sailor who is capable of performing the ordinary or routine duties of a seaman, but who is not yet so proficient in the knowledge and practice of all the various duties of a sailor at sea as to be rated as an "able" seaman.

Ordinary services of administrators include all the services incident to the closing and distribution of an estate, and not merely the receiving and disbursing of the funds and to justify an allowance of further compensation the administrator must have rendered services of an extraordinary character necessary to the protection of the estate, and, if he employs another to perform services which he is required to perform under the law, he cannot charge such services as an expense of administration. In re Carmody's Estate, 163 Iowa, 463, 145 N.W. 16, 17.

Ordinary skill in an art. That degree of skill which men engaged in that particular art usually employ; not that which belongs to a few men only, of extraordinary endowments and capacities. Baltimore Baseball Club Co. v. Pickett, 78 Md. 375, 28 A. 279, 22 L.R.A. 690, 44 Am.St.Rep. 304. Burrichter v. Bell, 196 Iowa 529, 194 N.W. 947, 948.

Ordinary travel. Moving a house along a village street is not using the street for the purpose of ordinary travel; and the statutory requirement that a telephone company shall locate its lines so as not to interfere with the safety and convenience of "ordinary travel" does not make it the duty of the company to remove its wires from the street to permit the passage of a house along the same. Collar v. Bingham Lake Rural Telephone Co., 132 Minn. 110, 155 N.W. 1075, 1076, L.R.A.1916C, 1249.

Ordinary written law. Law made, within constitutional restrictions, by the Legislature. State v. Marcus, 160 Wis. 354, 152 N.W. 419, 422.

ORDINATION. Ceremony by which a bishop confers on a person the privileges and powers necessary for the execution of sacerdotal functions in the church. Phillim.Ecc.Law, 110.

ORDINATIONE CONTRA SERVIENTES. A writ that lay against a servant for leaving his master contrary to the ordinance of St. 23 & 24 Edw. III. Reg.Orig. 189.

ORDINATUM EST. In old practice. It is ordered. The initial words of rules of court when entered in Latin.

ORDINE PLACITANDI SERVATO, SERVATUR ET JUS. When the order of pleading is observed, the law also is observed. Co.Litt. 303*a*; Broom, Max. 188.

ORDINES. A general chapter or other solemn convention of the religious of a particular order.

ORDINES MAJORES ET MINORES. In ecclesiastical law. The holy orders of priest, deacon, and subdeacon, any of which qualified for presentation and admission to an ecclesiastical dignity or cure were called "*ordines majores;*" and the inferior orders of chanters, psalmists, ostiary, reader, exorcist, and acolyte were called "*ordines minores.*" Persons ordained to the *ordines minores* had their *prima tonsura,* different from the *tonsura clericalis.* Cowell.

ORDINIS BENEFICIUM. Lat. In the civil law. The benefit or privilege of order; the privilege which a surety for a debtor had of requiring that his principal should be discussed, or thoroughly prosecuted, before the creditor could resort to him. Nov. 4, c. 1; Heinecc.Elem. lib. 3, tit. 21, § 883.

ORDINUM FUGITIVI. In old English law. Those of the religious who deserted their houses, and, throwing off the habits, renounced their particular order in contempt of their oath and other obligations. Paroch.Antiq. 388.

ORDO. Lat. That rule which monks were obliged to observe. Order; regular succession. An order of a court.

ORDO ALBUS. The white friars or Augustines. Du Cange.

ORDO ATTACHIAMENTORUM. In old practice. The order of attachments. Fleta, lib. 2, c. 51, § 12.

ORDO GRISEUS. The gray friars, or order of Cistercians. Du Cange.

ORDO JUDICIORUM. In the canon law. The order of judgments; the rule by which the due course of hearing each cause was prescribed. 4 Reeve, Eng.Law, 17.

ORDO NIGER. The black friars, or Benedictines. The Cluniacs likewise wore black. Du Cange.

ORDONNANCE. Fr. In French law, an ordinance; an order of a court; a compilation or systematized body of law relating to a particular subject-matter, as, commercial law or maritime law. Particularly, a compilation of the law relating to prizes and captures at sea. Coolidge v. Inglee, 13 Mass. 43.

ORE-LEAVE. A license or right to dig and take ore from land. Ege v. Kille, 84 Pa. 340.

ORE TENUS. Lat. By word of mouth; orally. Pleading was anciently carried on *ore tenus,* at the bar of the court. 3 Bl.Comm. 293.

ORFGILD. In Saxon law. The price or value of a beast. A payment for a beast. The payment or forfeiture of a beast. A penalty for taking away cattle. Spelman.

ORGANIC ACT. An act of congress conferring powers of government upon a territory. In re Lane, 10 S.Ct. 760, 135 U.S. 443, 34 L.Ed. 219.

A statute by which a municipal corporation is organized and created is its "organic act" and the limit of its power, so that all acts beyond the scope of the powers there granted are void. Tharp v. Blake, Tex.Civ.App., 171 S.W. 549, 550.

ORGANIC LAW. The fundamental law, or constitution, of a state or nation, written or unwritten; that law or system of laws or principles which defines and establishes the organization of its government. St. Louis v. Dorr, 145 Mo. 466, 46 S.W. 976, 42 L.R.A. 686, 68 Am.St.Rep. 575.

ORGANIZE. To establish or furnish with organs; to systematize; to put into working order; to arrange in order for the normal exercise of its appropriate functions. City of Beaumont v. City of Beaumont Independent School Dist., Tex.Civ. App., 164 S.W.2d 753, 756.

The word "organize," as used in railroad and other charters, ordinarily signifies the choice and qualification of all necessary officers for the transaction of the business of the corporation. This is usually done after all the capital stock has been subscribed for. New Haven & D. R. Co. v. Chapman, 38 Conn. 66.

ORGANIZED COUNTY. A county which has its lawful officers, legal machinery, and means for carrying out the powers and performing the duties pertaining to it as a quasi municipal corporation. In re Section No. 6, 66 Minn. 32, 68 N.W. 323; City of Beaumont v. City of Beaumont Independent School Dist., Tex.Civ.App., 164 S.W.2d 753, 757.

ORGILD. In Saxon law. Without recompense; as where no satisfaction was to be made for the death of a man killed, so that he was judged lawfully slain. Spelman.

ORIGINAL. Primitive; first in order; bearing its own authority, and not deriving authority from an outside source; as *original* jurisdiction, *original* writ, etc. As applied to documents, the original is the first copy or archetype; that from which another instrument is transcribed, copied, or imitated. Arenson v. Jackson, 97 Misc.Rep. 606, 162 N.Y.S. 142, 143; State v. Lee, 173 La. 770, 138 So. 662.

A carbon impression of a letter written on a typewriter, made by the same stroke of the keys as the companion impression, is an "original." Either impression is primary evidence of the contents of the letter, and notice to produce the original mailed letter in order to introduce one of the retained copies in evidence is not necessary. U. S. Fire Ins. Co. of City of New York v. L. C. Adam Mercantile Co., 117 Okl. 73, 245 P. 885, 887.

Original appointment. Within statute providing for suspension of civil servants in inverse order of original appointment, means appointment for probationary term ripening into permanent appointment, and not mere provisional or temporary appointment. Civil Service Law, § 31; Const. art. 5, § 6, amended in 1929. Koso v. Greene, 260 N.Y. 491, 184 N.E. 65, 66.

Original bill. In equity pleading. A bill which relates to some matter not before litigated in the court by the same persons standing in the same interests. Mitf.Eq.Pl. 33; Christmas v. Russell, 14 Wall. 69, 20 L.Ed. 762. In old practice. The ancient mode of commencing actions in the English court of king's bench. See Bill.

Original charter. In Scotch law. One by which the first grant of land is made. On the other hand, a charter by progress is one renewing the grant in favor of the heir or singular successor of the first or succeeding vassals. Bell.

Original contractor. One who for a fixed price agrees with owner to perform certain work or furnish certain material. East Arkansas Lumber Co. v. Bryant, Mo.App., 247 S.W. 496, 497; Hihn-Hammond Lumber Co. v. Elsom, 171 Cal. 570, 154 P. 12, 13, Ann.Cas.1917C, 798.

Original conveyances. Those conveyances at common law, otherwise termed "primary," by which a benefit or estate is created or first arises; comprising feoffments, gifts, grants, leases, exchanges, and partitions. 2 Bl.Comm. 309.

Original entry. The first entry of an item of an account made by a trader or other person in his account-books, as distinguished from entries posted into the ledger or copied from other books. Keller Electric Co. v. Burg, 140 Minn. 360, 168 N.W. 98; Shea v. Biddle Improvement Co., 188 Iowa, 952, 176 N.W. 948, 949; Lewis Mears Co. v. Norfolk County Creamery, 48 R.I. 221, 137 A. 149, 150.

When multiplicate instruments are made at one writing, each is "original entry," as regards best evidence rule. Gus Dattilo Fruit Co. v. Louisville & N. R. Co., 238 Ky. 322, 37 S.W.2d 856, 858.

Original estates. See Estate.

Original evidence. An original document, writing, or other material object introduced in evidence as distinguished from a copy of it or from extraneous evidence of its content or purport. Or.Laws, 1920, § 691 (Code 1930, § 9—106).

Original inventor. In patent law. A pioneer in the art; one who evolves the original idea and brings it to some successful, useful and tangible result; as distinguished from an improver. Norton v. Jensen, 33 C.C.A. 141, 90 F. 415.

Original jurisdiction. Jurisdiction in the first instance; jurisdiction to take cognizance of a cause at its inception, try it, and pass judgment upon the law and facts. Distinguished from *appellate* jurisdiction.

Original package. A package prepared for interstate or foreign transportation, and remaining in the same condition as when it left the shipper, that is, unbroken and undivided; a package of such form and size as is used by producers or shippers for the purpose of securing both convenience in handling and security in transportation of merchandise between dealers in the ordinary course of actual commerce. Austin v. Tennessee, 21 S.Ct. 132, 179 U.S. 343, 45 L.Ed. 224; Haley v. State, 42 Neb. 556, 60 N.W. 962, 47 Am.St.Rep. 718. Mexican Petroleum Corporation v. City of South Portland, 121 Me. 128, 115 A. 900, 901, 26 A. L.R. 965.

Original plat. The first plat of a town from the subsequent additions, and "original town" is employed in the same way. State v. City of Victoria, 97 Kan. 638, 156 P. 705, 708.

Original promise. An original promise, without the statute of frauds, is one in which the direct and leading object of the promisor is to further or promote some purpose or interest of his own, although the incidental effect may be the payment of the debt of another. Umpqua Valley Bank of Roseburg v. Wilson, 120 Or. 396, 252 P. 563, 565; Olson v. McQueen, 24 N.D. 212, 139 N.W. 522, 524.

Original process. See Process.

Original vein. Is used to describe the different veins found within the same surface boundaries and may refer to the relative importance or value of the different veins, or the relations to each other, or to the time of discovery, but most frequently is used to distinguish between the discovery vein and other veins within the same surface boundaries. Northport Smelting & Refining Co. v. Lone Pine-Surprise Consol. Mines Co., D.C. Wash., 271 F. 105, 111.

Original Writ. See Writ.

Single original. An original instrument which is executed singly, and not in duplicate.

ORIGINALIA. In English law. Transcripts sent to the remembrancer's office in the exchequer out of the chancery, distinguished from *recorda*, which contain the judgments and pleadings in actions tried before the barons. The treasurer-remembrancer's office was abolished in 1833.

ORIGINE PROPRIA NEMINEM POSSE VOLUNTATE SUA EXIMI MANIFESTUM EST. It is evident that no one is able of his own pleasure, to do away with his proper origin. Code 10, 38, 4; Broom, Max. 77.

ORIGO REI INSPICI DEBET. The origin of a thing ought to be regarded. Co.Litt. 248*b*.

ORNEST. In old English law. The trial by battle, which does not seem to have been usual in England before the time of the Conqueror, though originating in the kingdoms of the north, where it was practiced under the name of "*holmgang*," from the custom of fighting duels on a small island or *holm*. Wharton.

ORPHAN. Any person (but particularly a minor or infant) who has lost both (or one) of his or her parents. More particularly, a fatherless child. Chicago Guaranty Fund Life Soc. v. Wheeler, 79 Ill.App. 241; Stewart v. Morrison, 38 Miss. 419; Downing v. Shoenberger, 9 Watts, Pa., 299.

ORPHANAGE PART. That portion of an intestate's effects which his children were entitled to by the custom of London. This custom appears to have been a remnant of what was once a general law all over England, namely, that a father should not by his will bequeath the entirety of his personal estate away from his family, but should leave them a third part at least, called the "children's part," corresponding to the "bairns' part" or *legitim* of Scotch law, and also (although not in amount) to the *legitima quarta* of Roman law. (Inst. 2, 18.) This custom of London was abolished by St. 19 & 20 Vict. c. 94. Brown.

ORPHANOTROPHI. In the civil law. Managers of houses for orphans.

ORPHANS' COURT. In American law. Courts of probate jurisdiction, in Delaware, Maryland, New Jersey, and Pennsylvania.

ORTELLI. The claws of a dog's foot. Kitch.

ORTHOPEDIST. A surgeon engaged in branch of medicine dealing with correction of deformities and chronic diseases of the joints and spine. Sansom v. Ross-Loos Medical Group, 57 Cal.App.2d 549, 134 P.2d 927, 931.

ORTOLAGIUM. A garden plot or hortilage.

ORWIGE, SINE WITÂ. In old English law. Without war or feud, such security being provided by the laws, for homicides under certain circumstances, against the *foehth*, or deadly feud, on the part of the family of the slain. Anc.Inst.Eng.

OSCULI, JUS. The right to kiss. According to the old phraseology there could be no marriage within the circle of the *jus osculi*—the seventh degree. Second cousins (sixth degree) could not marry. Muirhead, Rom.L. 26.

OSTENDIT VOBIS. Lat. In old pleading. Shows to you. Formal words with which a demandant began his count. Fleta, lib. 5, c. 38, § 2.

OSTENSIBLE AGENCY. An implied or presumptive agency, which exists where one, either intentionally or from want of ordinary care, induces another to believe that a third person is his agent, though he never in fact employed him. First Nat. Bank v. Elevator Co., 11 N.D. 280, 91 N.W. 437. It is, strictly speaking, no agency at all, but is in reality based entirely upon estoppel. Hartford Accident & Indemnity Co. v. Bear Butte Valley Bank, 63 S.D. 262, 257 N.W. 642.

OSTENSIBLE AUTHORITY. Such authority as a principal, intentionally or by want of ordinary care, causes or allows a third person to believe that the agent possesses. National Cash Register Co. v. Wichita Frozen Food Lockers, Tex.Civ.App., 172 S.W.2d 781, 787.

OSTENSIBLE PARTNER. One whose name appears to the world as such, though he have no interest in the firm. Civ.Code 1910, § 3157. Roberts v. Curry Grocery Co., 18 Ga.App. 53, 88 S.E. 796.

OSTENSIO. A tax anciently paid by merchants, etc., for leave to show or expose their goods for sale in markets. Du Cange.

OSTENTUM. Lat. In the civil law. A monstrous or prodigious birth. Dig. 50, 16, 38.

OSTEOPATH. One who practices osteopathy. State v. Chase, 76 N.H. 553, 86 A. 144.

OSTEOPATHY. A method or system of treating various diseases of the human body without the use of drugs, by manipulation applied to various nerve centers, rubbing, pulling, and kneading parts of the body, flexing and manipulating the limbs, and the mechanical readjustment of any bones, muscles, or ligaments not in the normal position, with a view to removing the cause of the disorder and aiding the restorative force of nature in cases where the trouble originated in misplacement of parts, irregular nerve action, or defective circulation. State v. Liffring, 61 Ohio St. 39, 55 N.E. 168, 76 Am.St.Rep. 358; Parks v. State, 159 Ind. 211, 64 N.E. 862, 59 L.R.A. 190.

A system of treatment based on the theory that diseases are chiefly due to deranged mechanism of the bones, nerves, blood vessels, and other tissues, and can be remedied by manipulations of these parts. Special attention is given to the readjustment of any bones, muscles, or ligaments not in the normal position. Waldo v. Poe, D.C. Wash., 14 F.2d 749, 751; Arnold v. Schmidt, 155 Wis. 55, 143 N.W. 1055, 1058; State ex rel. Wheat v. Moore, 154 Kan. 193, 117 P.2d 598, 602. The term does not include the practice of optometry. Ex parte Rust, 181 Cal. 73, 183 P. 548, 550, nor, at least under some statutes, the practice of medicine or surgery. State v. Sawyer, 36 Idaho, 814, 214 P. 222.

OSTIA REGNI. Lat. Gates of the kingdom. The ports of the kingdom of England are so called by Sir Matthew Hale. De Jure Mar. pt. 2, c. 3.

OSTIUM ECCLESIÆ. Lat. In old English law. The door or porch of the church, where dower was anciently conferred.

OSWALD'S LAW. The law by which was effected the ejection of married priests, and the introduction of monks into churches, by Oswald, bishop of Worcester, about A.D. 964. Wharton.

OSWALD'S LAW HUNDRED. An ancient hundred in Worcestershire, so called from Bishop Oswald, who obtained it from King Edgar, to be given to St. Mary's Church in Worcester. It was exempt from the sheriff's jurisdiction, and comprehends 300 hides of land. Camd. Brit.

OTER LA TOUAILLE. In the laws of Oleron. To deny a seaman his mess. Literally, to deny the table-cloth or victuals for three meals.

OTHER. Different or distinct from that already mentioned; additional, or further. City of Ft. Smith v. Gunter, 106 Ark. 371, 154 S.W. 181, 183; State v. Blumenthal, 136 Ark. 532, 203 S.W. 36, 37, L.R.A.1918E, 482.

Following an enumeration of particular classes "other" must be read as "other such like," and includes only others of like kind and character. Van Pelt v. Hilliard, 75 Fla. 792, 78 So. 693, 697, L.R.A.1918E, 639; Baker v. Baker, 82 N.J.Eq. 150, 91 A. 729, 730; George H. Dingledy Lumber Co. v. Erie R. Co., 102 Ohio St. 236, 131 N.E. 723, 726.

OTHERWISE. In a different manner; in another way, or in other ways. Safe Deposit & Trust Co. of Baltimore v. New York Life Ins. Co., D.C. Md., 14 F.Supp. 721, 726.

OTHESWORTHE. In Saxon law. Oathsworth; oathworthy; worthy or entitled to make oath. Bract. fols. 185, 292*b*.

OUGHT. This word, though generally directory only, will be taken as mandatory if the context requires it. Pract. fol. 185, 292*b*; Life Ass'n v. St. Louis County Assessors, 49 Mo. 518.

OUNCE. The twelfth part; the twelfth part of a pound troy or the sixteenth part of a pound avoirdupois.

OUNCE LANDS. Certain districts or tracts of lands in the Orkney Islands were formerly so called, because each paid an annual tax of one ounce of silver.

OURLOP. The lierwite or fine paid to the lord by the inferior tenant when his daughter was debauched. Cowell.

OUST. To put out; to eject; to remove or deprive; to deprive of the possession or enjoyment of an estate or franchise.

OUSTER. In practice. A putting out; dispossession; amotion of possession. A species of injuries to things real, by which the wrong-doer gains actual occupation of the land, and compels the rightful owner to seek his legal remedy in order to gain possession. 2 Crabb, Real Prop. p. 1063, § 2454*a*; Pursel v. Reading Iron Co., C.C.A. Pa., 232 F. 801, 807; Lucas v. Ferris, 95 Conn. 619, 112 A. 165, 167; Hardman v. Brown, 77 W. Va. 478, 88 S.E. 1016, 1019.

Actual Ouster. Does not mean a physical eviction, but a possession attended with such circumstances as to evince a claim of exclusive right and title, and a denial of the right of the other tenants to participate in the profits. Burns v. Byrne, 45 Iowa 287; Miller v. State, 121 Conn. 43, 183 A. 17, 20.

OUSTER LE MAIN. L. Fr. Literally, out of the hand.

1. A delivery of lands out of the king's hands by judgment given in favor of the petitioner in a *monstrans de droit.*

2. A delivery of the ward's lands out of the hands of the guardian, on the former arriving at the proper age, which was twenty-one in males, and sixteen in females. Abolished by 12 Car. II. c. 24. Mozley & Whiteley.

OUSTER LE MER. L. Fr. Beyond the sea; a cause of excuse if a person, being summoned, did not appear in court. Cowell.

OUT-BOUNDARIES. A term used in early Mexican land laws to designate certain boundaries within which grants of a smaller tract, which designated such out-boundaries, might be located by the grantee. U. S. v. Maxwell Land Grant Co., 7 S.Ct. 1015, 121 U.S. 325, 30 L.Ed. 949.

OUT OF BENEFIT. A term descriptive of insurance policy holders who have been suspended for nonpayment of premiums. American Nat. Ins. Co. v. Otis, 122 Ark. 219, 183 S.W. 183, 184, L.R.A. 1916E, 875.

OUT OF COURT. He who has no legal status in court is said to be "out of court," *i. e.*, he is not before the court. Thus, when the plaintiff in an action, by some act of omission or commission, shows that he is unable to maintain his action, he is frequently said to put himself "out of court." Brown. The expression is colloquially applied to a litigant party when his case breaks down, equivalent to saying, "he has not a leg to stand on;" Moz. & W.

The phrase is also used with reference to agreements and transactions in regard to a pending suit which are arranged or take place between the parties or their counsel privately and without being referred to the judge or court for authorization or approval. Thus, a case which is compromised, settled, and withdrawn by private agreement of the parties, after its institution, is said to be settled "out of court." So attorneys may make agreements with reference to the conduct of a suit or the course of proceedings therein; but if these are made "out of court," that is, not made in open court or with the approval of the judge, it is a general rule that they will not be noticed by the court unless reduced to writing. Welsh v. Blackwell, 14 N.J.Law, 345.

OUT OF POCKET RULE. Determination for damages for fraudulent misrepresentations which permits recovery of difference between price paid and actual value of property acquired. Zeliff v. Sabatino, 104 A.2d 54, 55, 15 N.J. 70; Zeliff v. Sabatino, 98 A.2d 679, 681, 27 N.J.Super. 13; Jacobs v. Levin, 137 P.2d 500, 501, 58 Cal.App.2d Supp. 913.

Also called out-of-pocket loss rule.

OUT OF REPAIR. In a West Virginia statute relating to streets, sidewalks, and the like, this term means unsafe for reasonable use in the ordinary modes of travel by day or night, whether the danger exists overhead or on the surface.

OUT OF TERM. At a time when no term of the court is being held; in the vacation or interval which elapses between terms of the court. See McNeill v. Hodges, 99 N.C. 248, 6 S.E. 127.

OUT OF THE STATE. In reference to rights, liabilities, or jurisdictions arising out of the common law, this phrase is equivalent to "beyond sea," which see.

In other connections, it means physically beyond the territorial limits of the particular state in question, or constructively so, as in the case of a foreign corporation. Foster v. Givens, 67 F. 684, 14 C.C.A. 625; Larson v. Aultman & Taylor Co., 80 Wis. 281, 56 N.W. 915, 39 Am.St.Rep. 893. But a foreign corporation maintaining an agent within the state is not deemed to be "out of the state," within various statutes. Hamilton v. North. Pac. S. S. Co., 84 Or. 71, 164 P. 579, 581; American Surety Co. of New York v. Blake, 45 Idaho 159, 261 P. 239, 240.

OUT OF TIME. A mercantile phrase applied to a ship or vessel that has been so long at sea as to justify the belief of her total loss. In another sense, a vessel is said to be *out of time* when, computed from her known day of sailing, the time that has elapsed exceeds the average duration of similar voyages at the same season of the year. The phrase is identical with "missing ship." 2 Duer, Ins. 469.

OUTAGE. A tax or charge formerly imposed by the state of Maryland for the inspection and marking of hogsheads of tobacco intended for export. Turner v. Maryland, 2 S.Ct. 44, 107 U.S. 38, 27 L. Ed. 370.

OUTBUILDING. Something used in connection with a main building. Com. v. Intoxicating Liquors, 140 Mass. 287, 3 N.E. 4. A small building appurtenant to a main building, and generally separated from it; an outhouse. Bruce v. McClees, 110 N.J.Eq. 92, 158 A. 849, 850.

OUTCAST. This term, applied to a person, has been held to be libelous per se, because it represents him as being a degraded and disgraced character. Herald Pub. Co. v. Feltner, 158 Ky. 35, 164 S.W. 370, 372.

OUTCROP. In mining law. The edge of a stratum which appears at the surface of the ground; that portion of a vein or lode which appears at the surface or immediately under the soil and surface débris. Duggan v. Davey, 4 Dak. 110, 26 N.W. 887; Stevens v. Williams, 23 Fed.Cas. 40. The term is not, in itself, definitive of quantity or area in respect of the mineral involved. Sloss-Sheffield Iron & Steel Co. v. Payne, 186 Ala. 341, 64 So. 617, 618.

OUTER BAR. In the English courts, barristers at law have been divided into two classes, viz., king's counsel, who are admitted within the bar of the courts, in seats specially reserved for themselves, and junior counsel, who sit without the bar; and the latter are thence frequently termed barristers of the "outer bar," or "utter bar," in contradistinction to the former class. Brown.

OUTER DOOR. In connection with the rule, statutory or otherwise, forbidding an officer to break open the outer door to serve civil process, this term designates the door of each separate apartment, where there are different apartments having a common outer door. Fourette v. Griffin, 92 Conn. 388, 103 A. 123, 124, L.R.A.1918D, 876; Schork v. Calloway, 205 Ky. 346, 265 S.W. 807, 808.

OUTER HOUSE. The name given to the great hall of the parliament house in Edinburgh, in which the lords ordinary of the court of session sit as single judges to hear causes. The term is used colloquially as expressive of the business done there in contradistinction to the "Inner House," the name given to the chambers in which the first and second divisions of the court of session hold their sittings. Bell.

OUTFANGTHEF. A liberty or privilege in the ancient common law, whereby a lord was enabled to call any man dwelling in his manor, and taken for felony in another place out of his fee, to judgment in his own court. Du Cange. See Infangenthef.

OUTFIT. Originally, as applying to ships, those objects connected with a ship which were necessary for the sailing of her, and without which she would not in fact be navigable. But in ships engaged in whaling voyages the word has acquired a much more extended signification. Macy v. Whaling Ins. Co., 9 Metc. (Mass.) 364.

An allowance made by the United States government to one of its diplomatic representatives, as an ambassador, a minister plenipotentiary, or *chargé d'affaires,* but not a consul, for the expense of his equipment on going from the United States to any foreign country.

Equipment. U. S. v. Richard & Co., 8 Ct.Cust. App. 231, 233.

OUTGO. In taxation, a flow of disservice (negative service) or negative income;—distinguished from "income," or the flow of capital service. U. S. v. Guggenheim Exploration Co., D.C.N.Y., 238 F. 231, 234.

OUTHEST, or OUTHOM. A calling men out to the army by sound of horn. Jacob.

OUTHOUSE. Any house necessary for the purposes of life, in which the owner does not make his constant or principal residence. State v. O'Brien, 2 Root (Conn.) 516. A building subservient to, yet distinct from, the principal mansion-house, located either within or without the curtilage. State v. Brooks, 4 Conn. 446; Jones v. Hungerford, 4 Gill. & J. (Md.) 402, 2 Cr. & D. 479. Parks v. State, 22 Ga.App. 621, 96 S.E. 1050, 1051.

A smaller or subordinate building connected with a dwelling, usually detached from it and standing at a little distance from it, not intended for persons to live in, but to serve some purpose of convenience or necessity; as a barn, a dairy, a toolhouse, and the like.

Under statutes, such a building may be subservient to and adjoin a business building as well as a dwelling house. State v. Marks, 45 Idaho, 92, 260 P. 697, 698.

OUTLAND. The Saxon thanes divided their hereditary lands into inland, such as lay nearest their dwelling, which they kept to their own use, and outland, which lay beyond the demesnes, and was granted out to tenants, at the will of the lord, like copyhold estates. This outland they subdivided into two parts. One part they disposed among those who attended their persons, called "theodans," or lesser thanes; the other part they allotted to their husbandmen, or churls. Jacob.

OUTLAW. In English law. One who is put out of the protection or aid of the law. 22 Viner, Abr. 316; Bacon Abr. *Outlawry*; 2 Sell.Pr. 277; Doctr. Plac. 331; 3 Bla.Comm. 283, 284.

Popularly, a person violating the law. Oliveros v. Henderson, 116 S.C. 77, 106 S.E. 855, 859.

OUTLAWED. With reference to a debt means barred by the statute of limitations. Brady v. Tarr, 145 Pa.Super. 316, 21 A.2d 131, 133.

OUTLAWRY. In English law. A process by which a defendant or person in contempt on a civil or criminal process was declared an outlaw. If for treason or felony, it amounted to conviction and attainder. Stim.Law Gloss. See Respublica v. Doan, 1 Dall. (Pa.) 86, 1 L.Ed. 47; Dale County v. Gunter, 46 Ala. 138; Drew v. Drew, 37 Me. 391; 3 Bla.Comm. 283; Co.Litt. 128. Outlawry for a misdemeanor does not amount to a conviction for the offense itself. 4 Steph.Com. 317. The "minor outlawry" for "trespasses" did not involve sentence of death; otherwise of the higher crimes. 2 Poll. & Maitl. 581.

In the United States, the process of outlawry seems to be unknown, at least in civil cases. Dane, Abr. ch. 193 *a*, 34; Hall v. Lanning, 91 U.S. 160, 23 L.Ed. 271; 37 Harvard Law Review, 799.

OUTLINE. The line which marks the outer limits of an object or figure; an exterior line or edge; contour. Taggart v. Great Northern Ry. Co., D.C. Wash., 208 F. 455, 456.

OUTLOT. In early American land law, (particularly in Missouri,) a lot or parcel of land lying outside the corporate limits of a town or village but subject to its municipal jurisdiction or control. Kissell v. St. Louis Public Schools, 16 Mo. 592; St. Louis v. Toney, 21 Mo. 243; Eberle v. St. Louis Public Schools, 11 Mo. 265; Vasquez v. Ewing, 42 Mo. 256.

OUTPARTERS. Stealers of cattle. Cowell.

OUTPUTERS. Such as set watches for the robbing of any manor-house. Cowell.

OUTRAGE. A grave injury; injurious violence; in general, any species of serious wrong offered to the person, feelings, or rights of another. McKinley v. Railroad Co., 44 Iowa, 314, 24 Am.Rep. 748; Aldrich v. Howard, 8 R.I. 246; Mosnat v. Snyder, 105 Iowa, 500, 75 N.W. 356. Synonyms are affront, insult, and abuse. State ex rel. and to Use of Donelon v. Deuser, 345 Mo. 628, 134 S.W.2d 132, 133.

OUTRIDERS. In English law. Bailiffs-errant employed by sheriffs or their deputies to ride to the extremities of their counties or hundreds to summon men to the county or hundred court. Wharton.

OUTRIGHT. Free from reserve or restraint; direct; positive; down-right; altogether; entirely; openly. Hughes v. First State Bank of Wagoner, 106 Okl. 146, 235 P. 1097, 1099.

OUTROPER. A person to whom the business of selling by auction was confined by statute. 2 H. Bl. 557.

OUTS. In banking parlance, are conditions or warranties, failure to comply with which by the prospect give the banker a right to escape from a contract and to terminate negotiations. Cray, McFawn & Co. v. Hegarty, Conroy & Co., D.C.N.Y., 27 F.Supp. 93, 100.

OUTSETTER. In Scotch law. Publisher. 3 How. State Tr. 603.

OUTSIDE. To the exterior of; without; outward from. Union Fishermen's Co-operative Packing

Co. v. Shoemaker, 98 Or. 659, 193 P. 476, 480. See, also, Frankel v. Massachusetts Bonding & Ins. Co., Mo.App., 177 S.W. 775.

OUTSTANDING. Remaining undischarged; unpaid; uncollected; as an outstanding debt. New York Trust Co. v. Portland Ry. Co., 197 App.Div. 422, 189 N.Y.S. 346, 350. Constituting an effective obligation; as, outstanding stock. Borg v. International Silver Co., C.C.A.N.Y., 11 F.2d 147, 150; Scheirich v. Otis-Hidden Co., 204 Ky. 289, 264 S. W. 755, 756.

Existing as an adverse claim or pretension; not united with, or merged in, the title or claim of the party; as an outstanding title.

OUTSTANDING AND OPEN ACCOUNT. In legal and commercial transactions it is an unsettled debt arising from items of work and labor, goods sold and delivered, and other open transactions, not reduced to writing, and subject to future settlement and adjustment and usually disclosed by account books of the owner of the demand and does not include express contracts or obligations which have been reduced to writing such as bonds, bills of exchange, or notes. Lee v. De Forest, 22 Cal.App.2d 351, 71 P.2d 285, 291. Checotah Hardware Co. v. Housel, 169 Okl. 112, 35 P.2d 966, 967.

OUTSTANDING CROP. One not harvested or gathered. It is outstanding from the day it commences to grow until gathered and taken away. Sullins v. State, 53 Ala. 474.

OUTSTANDING TERM. A term in gross at law, which, in equity, may be made attendant upon the inheritance, either by express declaration or by implication.

OUTSTROKE. To mine by outstroke is to take out mineral from adjoining property through the tunnels and shafts of the demised premises. Percy La Salle Mining & Power Co. v. Newman Mining, Milling & Leasing Co., D.C.Colo., 300 F. 141, 142.

OUTSUCKEN MULTURES. In Scotch law. Outtown multures; multures, duties, or tolls paid by persons voluntarily grinding corn at any mill to which they are not *thirled,* or bound by tenure. 1 Forb.Inst. pt. 2, p. 140.

OUVERTURE DES SUCCESSIONS. In French law. The right of succession which arises to one upon the death, whether natural or civil, of another.

OVE. L. Fr. With. Modern French *avec.*

OVELL. L. Fr. Equal.

OVELTY. In old English law. Equality.

OVER. Above; overhead. Detamore v. Hindley, 83 Wash. 322, 145 P. 462, 464. Through. Kynerd v. Hulen, C.C.A.Tex., 5 F.2d 160, 161. More than; in excess of. People v. Shupe, 306 Ill. 31, 137 N.E. 515, 516.

Continued;—sometimes written on one page or sheet to indicate a continuation of matter on a separate sheet. In re Johnston's Estate, 64 Cal. App. 197, 221 P. 382, 384.

In conveyancing. The word is used to denote a contingent limitation intended to take effect on the failure of a prior estate. Thus, in what is commonly called the "name and arms clause" in a will or settlement there is generally a proviso that if the devisee fails to comply with the condition the estate is to go to some one else. This is a limitation or gift over. Wats.Comp.Eq. 1110; Sweet.

OVER SEA. Beyond the sea; outside the limits of the state or country. Gustin v. Brattle, Kirby, Conn. 300. See Beyond Sea.

OVERAWE. To subjugate or restrain by awe, or profound reverence. Collum v. State, 21 Ala.App. 220, 107 So. 35.

OVERBRAIDED. Of ropes, made by having a certain number of strands laid over a center already braided. Macomber & Whyte Rope Co. v. Hazard Mfg. Co., C.C.A.N.Y., 211 F. 976, 979.

OVERBREAK. In blasting, that portion of material removed which is outside and beyond slopes indicated by slope stakes. Porter v. State, 141 Wash. 51, 250 P. 449.

OVERCHARGE. Of public utilities, a charge collected above a lawful tariff rate, a charge of more than is permitted by law. Taylor-Williams Coal Co. v. Public Utilities Commission of Ohio, 97 Ohio St. 224, 119 N.E. 459, 460; Crook v. Baltimore & O. R. Co., 32 Ohio App. 263, 167 N.E. 899, 900. An unreasonable or discriminatory charge. Postal Telegraph-Cable Co. v. Associated Press, 228 N.Y. 370, 127 N.E. 256, 259; Cleveland, C., C. & St. L. Ry. Co. v. Mills Bros., 101 Ohio St. 173, 128 N.E. 81, 82.

OVERCOME. As used in a statute providing that a presumption may be overcome by other evidence, this term is not synonymous with overbalance or outweigh, but requires merely that such evidence counterbalance the presumption, where the party relying on it has the burden of proof. Hansen v. Oregon-Washington R. & Nav. Co., 97 Or. 190, 191 P. 655, 656.

OVERCYTED, or OVERCYHSED. Proved guilty or convicted. Blount.

OVERDRAFT. The act of checking out more money than one has on deposit in a bank. Bank of Jeanerette v. Druilhet, 149 La. 505, 89 So. 674, 678; State v. Larson, 119 Wash. 259, 205 P. 373, 374. It is in the nature of a loan made at the request of the depositor, and implies a promise to pay. Becker v. Fuller, 99 Misc.Rep. 672, 164 N.Y.S. 495.

OVERDRAW. To draw upon a person or a bank, by bills or checks, to an amount in excess of the funds remaining to the drawer's credit with the drawee, or to an amount greater than what is due. See State v. Jackson, 21 S.D. 494, 113 N.W. 880, 16 Ann.Cas. 87.

The term has a definite and well-understood meaning. Money is drawn from the bank by him who draws the check, not by him who receives the money; and it is drawn upon the account of the individual by whose check it is drawn, though it be paid to and for the benefit of another. No one can draw money from bank upon his own account, except by means of his own check or draft, nor can he overdraw his account with the bank in any other manner. State v. Stimson, 24 N.J.Law, 478, 484.

OVERDUE. Due and more than due; delayed or unpaid. Bliss v. California Co-op. Producers, Cal. App., 156 P.2d 259, 260.

A negotiable instrument or other evidence of debt is overdue when the day of its maturity is past and it remains unpaid. La Due v. First Nat. Bank, 31 Minn. 33, 16 N.W. 426.

A vessel is said to be overdue when she has not reached her destination at the time when she might ordinarily have been expected to arrive.

OVERFLOWED LANDS. Those that are covered by nonnavigable waters (not including lands between high and low water mark of navigable streams or bodies of water, nor lands covered and uncovered by ordinary daily ebb and flow of normal tides of navigable waters). Miller v. Bay-To-Gulf, 141 Fla. 452, 193 So. 425, 427.

OVERHAUL. To inquire into; to review; to disturb. "The merits of a judgment can never be *overhauled* by an original suit." 2 H.Bl. 414.

To examine thoroughly, as machinery, with a view to repairs. Holloway v. Wheeler, Tex.Civ. App., 261 S.W. 467, 468.

OVERHEAD. All administrative or executive costs incident to the management, supervision, or conduct of the capital outlay, or business;—distinguished from "operating charges," or those items that are inseparably connected with the productive end and may be seen as the work progresses, and are the subject of knowledge from observation. Lytle, Campbell & Co. v. Somers, Fitler & Todd Co., 276 Pa. 409, 120 A. 409, 410, 27 A.L.R. 41. Continuous expenses of a business: the expenses and obligations incurred in connection with operation; expenses necessarily incurred in organization. office expenses, engineering, inspection, supervision, and management during construction; and general expenditures in financial or industrial enterprise which cannot be attributed to any one department or product, excluding cost of materials, labor, and selling. Guillot v. State Highway Commission of Montana, 102 Mont. 149, 56 P.2d 1072, 1075.

"Overhead charges" is a term which, as applied to a public service corporation, includes the expense that would necessarily be incurred in the reproduction of the property; the legal expenses of organization and expenses for office, engineering, inspection, supervision, and management during construction; fire and casualty insurance, taxes and interest during the period. contractors profits, and other minor expenses of like character. Bonbright v. Geary, D.C.Ariz., 210 F. 44, 54.

OVERHERNISSA. In Saxon law. Contumacy or contempt of court. Leg. Æthel, c. 25.

OVER-INSURANCE. See Double Insurance.

OVERISSUE. To issue in excessive quantity; to issue in excess of fixed legal limits. Thus, "overissued stock" of a private corporation is capital stock issued in excess of the amount limited and prescribed by the charter or certificate of incorporation. Hayden v. Charter Oak Driving Park, 63 Conn. 142, 27 A. 232.

OVERLIVE. To survive; to live longer than another. Finch, Law, b. 1, c. 3, no. 58; 1 Leon. 1.

OVERLOAD. To cause to bear too heavy a burden; to load too heavily. But to say of a business, such as an insurance business, that it is overloaded, implies nothing defamatory on its face in the sense of imputing dishonesty, lack of fair dealing, want of fidelity, integrity, or business ability. Talbot v. Mack, 41 Nev. 245, 169 P. 25, 29.

OVERLYING RIGHT. Right of owner of land to take water from ground underneath for use on his land within basin or watershed. Right is based on ownership of land and is appurtenant thereto. City of Pasadena v. City of Alhambra, 207 P.2d 17, 28, 33 Cal.2d 908.

OVERPLUS. What is left beyond a certain amount; the residue; the surplus; the remainder of a thing. Lyon v. Tomkies, 1 Mees. & W. 603.

OVERRATE. In its strictest signification, a rating by way of excess and not one which ought not to have been made at all. 2 Ex. 352.

OVERREACHING CLAUSE. In a resettlement, a clause which saves the powers of sale and leasing annexed to the estate for life created by the original settlement, when it is desired to give the tenant for life the same estate and powers under the resettlement. The clause is so called because it provides that the resettlement shall be overreached by the exercise of the old powers. If the resettlement were executed without a provision to this effect, the estate of the tenant for life and the annexed powers would be subject to any charges for portions, etc., created under the original settlement. 3 Dav.Conv. 489; Sweet.

OVERRIDE. An estate carved out of working interest under an oil or gas lease. Youngblood v. Seewald, D.C.Okl., 194 F.Supp. 417, 420.

OVERRIDING ROYALTY. As applied to an existing oil and gas lease is a given percentage of the gross production payable to some person other than the lessor or persons claiming under him. Homestake Exploration Corporation v. Schoregge, 81 Mont. 604, 264 P. 388, 392. An interest carved out of the lessee's share of the oil. Wright v. Brush, C.C.A.Kan., 115 F.2d 265, 267.

OVERRULE. To supersede; annul; make void; reject by subsequent action or decision. A judicial decision is said to be overruled when a later decision, rendered by the same court or by a superior court in the same system, expresses a judgment upon the same question of law directly opposite to that which was before given, thereby depriving the earlier opinion of all authority as a precedent. The term is not properly applied to conflicting decisions on the same point by co-ordinate or independent tribunals. It also signifies that a majority of the judges of a court have decided against the opinion of the minority, in which case the minority judges are said to be overruled.

To refuse to sustain, or recognize as sufficient, an objection made in the course of a trial, as to the introduction of particular evidence, etc.

OVERS. In the meat packing business, the increase in the weight of meat resulting from salt put on it. G. H. Hammond Co. v. Joseph Mercantile Co., 144 Ark. 108, 222 S.W. 27, 28.

OVERSAMESSA. In old English law. A forfeiture for contempt or neglect in not pursuing a malefactor. 3 Inst. 116.

OVERSEER. A superintendent or supervisor; a public officer whose duties involve general superintendence of routine affairs.

OVERSEERS OF HIGHWAYS. The name given, in some of the states, to a board of officers of a city, township, or county, whose special function is the construction and repair of the public roads or highways.

OVERSEERS OF THE POOR. Persons appointed or elected to take care of the poor with moneys furnished to them by the public authority. Their duties are regulated by local statutes.

OVERSMAN. In Scotch law. An umpire appointed by a submission to decide where two arbiters have differed in opinion, or he is named by the arbiters themselves, under powers given them by the submission. Bell.

OVERT. Open; manifest; public; issuing in action, as distinguished from that which rests merely in intention or design. Commonwealth v. Barnes, 107 Pa.Super. 46, 162 A. 670, 675.

Market Overt. See Market.

OVERT ACT. In criminal law. An open, manifest act from which criminality may be implied. An outward act done in pursuance and manifestation of an intent or design. An open act, which must be manifestly proved. 3 Inst. 12. United States v. Haupt, D.C.Ill., 47 F.Supp. 836, 839.

An overt act essential to establish an attempt to commit a crime is an act done to carry out the intention, and it must be such as would naturally effect that result unless prevented by some extraneous cause. People v. Mills, 178 N.Y. 274, 70 N.E. 786, 67 L.R.A. 131; State v. Enanno, 96 Conn. 420, 114 A. 386, 389. It must be something done that directly moves toward the crime, and brings the accused nearer to its commission than mere acts of preparation or of planning, and will apparently result, in the usual and natural course of events, if not hindered by extraneous causes, in the commission of the crime itself. Powell v. State, 128 Miss. 107, 90 So. 625, 626; State v. Roby, 194 Iowa 1032, 188 N.W. 709, 714.

In reference to the crime of treason, and the provision of the federal constitution that a person shall not be convicted thereof unless on the testimony of two witnesses to the same "overt act," the term means a step, motion, or action really taken in the execution of a treasonable purpose, as distinguished from mere words, and also from a treasonable sentiment, design, or purpose not issuing in action. It is an act in furtherance of the crime. U. S. v. Fricke, D.C.N.Y., 259 F. 673, 676. One which manifests the intention of the traitor to commit treason. Archb. Cr.Pl. 379; 4 Bla.Comm. 79; Co. 3d Inst. 12; Re Bollman, 4 Cranch, 75, 2 L.Ed. 554; U. S. v. Pryor, 3 Wash.C.C. 234, Fed.Cas.No.16,096.

An overt act which will justify the exercise of the right of self-defense is such as would manifest to the mind of a reasonable person a present intention to kill him or do him great bodily harm. Cooke v. State, 18 Ala.App. 416, 93 So. 86, 88.

An overt act which completes crime of conspiracy to violate federal law is something apart from conspiracy and is an act to effect the object of the conspiracy, and need be neither a criminal act, nor crime that is object of conspiracy, but must accompany or follow agreement and must be done in furtherance of object of agreement. Marino v. United States, C.C.A.Cal., 91 F.2d 691, 694, 695, 113 A.L.R. 975.

OVERT WORD. An open, plain word, not to be misunderstood. Cowell.

OVERTAKE. To come or catch up with in a course of motion. Ringwald v. Beene, 170 Tenn. 116, 92 S.W.2d 411, 413.

OVERTIME. After regular working hours; beyond the regular fixed hours. Ferguson v. Port Huron & Sarnia Ferry Co., D.C.Mich., 13 F.2d 489, 492; Goodman v. Moss, 43 N.Y.S.2d 381, 385.

OVERTIME WAGE. Portion of wages paid employee for services rendered beyond regularly fixed working hours. Goodman v. Moss, 43 N.Y.S.2d 381, 385.

OVERTURE. An opening; a proposal.

OWE. To be bound to do or omit something, especially to pay a debt. Robinson v. Ramsey, 161 Ga. 1, 129 S.E. 837, 839; Humphreys v. County Court, 90 W.Va. 315, 110 S.E. 701, 703.

OWELTY. Equality; an equalization charge. Bagg v. Osborn, 169 Minn. 126, 210 N.W. 862, 863.

This word is used in law in several compound phrases, as follows:

Owelty of exchange. A sum of money given, when two persons have exchanged lands, by the owner of the less valuable estate to the owner of the more valuable, to equalize the exchange.

Owelty of partition. A sum of money paid by one of two coparceners or co-tenants to the other, when a partition has been effected between them, but, the land not being susceptible of division into exactly equal shares, such payment is required to make the portions respectively assigned to them of equal value. Littleton, § 251; Co. Litt. 169*a;* Long v. Long, 1 Watts (Pa.) 265; 16 Viner, Abr. 223, pl. 3. Reed v. Deposit Co., 113 Pa. 578, 6 A. 163. The power to grant owelty has been exercised by the courts of equity from time immemorial. Town of Morganton v. Avery, 179 N.C. 551, 103 S.E. 138.

Owelty of services. In the feudal law, the condition obtaining when there is lord, mesne, and tenant, and the tenant holds the mesne by the same service that the mesne holds over the lord above him. Tomlins.

OWING. Unpaid. A debt, for example, is owing while it is unpaid, and whether it be due or not. Coquard v. Bank of Kansas City, 12 Mo.App. 261; Musselman v. Wise, 84 Ind. 248; Jones v. Thompson, 1 El., Bl. & El. 64; Succession of Guidry, 40 La.Ann. 671, 4 So. 893.

OWLERS. In English law. Persons who carried wool, etc., to the sea-side by night, in order that it might be shipped off contrary to law. Jacob.

OWLING. In English law. The offense of transporting wool or sheep out of the kingdom; so called from its being usually carried on in the night. 4 Bl. Comm. 154.

OWN. To have a good legal title; to hold as property; to have a legal or rightful title to; to have; to possess. Shepherd v. Maine Cent. R. Co., 112 Me. 350, 92 A. 189; McKennon v. Warnick, 115 Or. 163, 236 P. 1051, 1052; Miller-Link Lumber Co. v. Stephenson, Tex.Civ.App., 265 S.W. 215, 220; Melvin v. Scowley, 213 Ala. 414, 104 So. 817, 820. The term does not necessarily signify absolute ownership in fee. Rydeen v. Clearwater County, 139 Minn. 329, 166 N.W. 334, 335; Makemson v. Dillon, 24 N.M. 302, 171 P. 673, 676; Bush v. State, 128 Ark. 448, 194 S.W. 857. It is not synonymous with "acquire." State v. District Court of Third Judicial Dist. in and for Granite County, 79 Mont. 1, 254 P. 863, 865.

OWNED BY. Although these words may be used synonymously with "belonging to" or "forming part of"; Gilpatric v. City of Hartford, 98 Conn. 471, 120 A. 317, 319; in a stricter sense they denote an absolute and unqualified title, whereas the words "belonging to" do not import that the whole title to property or thing is meant, for a thing may belong to one who has less than an unqualified and absolute title; Baltimore Dry Docks & Ship Building Co. v. New York & P. R. S. S. Co., C.C.A.Md., 262 F. 485, 488.

OWNER. The person in whom is vested the ownership, dominion, or title of property; proprietor. Garver v. Hawkeye Ins. Co., 69 Iowa 202, 28 N.W. 555; McGowan v. Morgan, 145 N.Y.S. 787, 160 App. Div. 588; Cayce Land Co. v. Southern Ry. Co., 111 S.C. 115, 96 S.E. 725, 727; Staples v. Adams, Payne & Gleaves, C.C.A.Va., 215 F. 322, 325. He who has dominion of a thing, real or personal, corporeal or incorporeal, which he has a right to enjoy and do with as he pleases, even to spoil or destroy it, as far as the law permits, unless he be prevented by some agreement or covenant which restrains his right. Miller-Link Lumber Co. v. Stephenson, Tex.Civ.App., 265 S.W. 215, 220; Newborn v. Peart, 121 Misc.Rep. 221, 200 N.Y.S. 890, 892; Hare v. Young, 26 Idaho, 682, 146 P. 104, 106; Johnson v. Crookshanks, 21 Or. 339, 28 P. 78.

The word is not infrequently used to describe one who has dominion or control over a thing, the title to which is in another. Robinson v. State, 7 Ala.App. 172, 62 So. 303, 306. Thus, it may denote the buyer under a conditional sale agreement; Lennon v. L. A. W. Acceptance Corporation of Rhode Island, 48 R.I. 363, 138 A. 215, 217; a lessee; E. Corey & Co. v. H. P. Cummings Const. Co., 118 Me. 34, 105 A. 405, 407; Texas Bank & Trust Co. of Beaumont v. Smith, 108 Tex. 265, 192 S.W. 533, 534, 2 A.L.R. 771; Hacken v. Isenberg, 288 Ill. 589, 124 N.E. 306, 308; Grattan v. Trego, C.C.A.Kan., 225 F. 705, 708; a pledgee; American Nat. Bank of Tucumcari v. Tarpley, 31 N.M. 667, 250 P. 18, 20; Baxter v. Moore, 56 Ind.App. 472, 105 N.E. 588, 589; and a person for whose benefit a ship is operated on a particular voyage, and who directs and controls it, its officers and crew; Potter v. American Union Line, 185 N.Y.S. 842, 843, 114 Misc.Rep. 101 (see, also, Petition of E. I. Du Pont de Nemours & Co., D.C.N.Y., 18 F.2d 782, 784).

The term is, however, a nomen generalissimum, and its meaning is to be gathered from the connection in which it is used, and from the subject-matter to which it is applied. Warren v. Lower Salt Creek Drainage Dist. of Logan County, 316 Ill. 345, 147 N.E. 248, 249. The primary meaning of the word as applied to land is one who owns the fee and who has the right to dispose of the property, but the term also includes one having a possessory right to land or the person occupying or cultivating it. Dunbar v. Texas Irr. Co., Tex.Civ. App., 195 S.W. 614, 616; McCarthy v. Hansel, 4 Ohio App. 425; Thompson v. Thompson, 79 Or. 513, 155 P. 1190, 1191; McLevis v. St. Paul Fire & Marine Ins. Co., 165 Minn. 468, 206 N.W. 940, 942; Great Northern Ry. Co. v. Oakley, 135 Wash. 279, 237 P. 990, 992; In re Opinion of the Justices, 234 Mass. 597, 127 N.E. 525, 529. Sometimes it includes a lessee; Tobin v. Gartiez, 44 Nev. 179, 191 P. 1063, 1064; but not always; Smith v. Improvement Dist. No. 14 of Texarkana, 108 Ark. 141, 156 S.W. 455, 456, 44 L.R.A.,N.S., 696. A mortgagee may be deemed an "owner"; Lindholm v. Hamilton, 159 Minn. 81, 198 N.W. 289, 290; Blaine County Bank v. Noble, 55 Okl. 361, 155 P. 532, 534; Burrill Nat. Bank v. Edminister, 119 Me. 367, 111 A. 423, 424; Merriman v. City of New York, 227 N.Y. 279, 125 N.E. 500, 502; but under different statutes or circumstances, an opposite result may be reached; Huebner v. Lashley, 239 Mich. 50, 214 N.W. 107, 108. The term may likewise, on occasion, include mortgagors; Hendricks v. Town of Julesburg, 55 Colo. 59, 132 P. 61, 63; Smith v. Craver, 89 Wash. 243, 154 P. 156, 158; Borough of Princeton v. State Board of Taxes and Assessments, 96 N.J. L. 334, 115 A. 342, 344.

In theft and burglary cases, the "owner" is the person in possession, having care, control, and management at the time. Cantrell v. State, 105 Tex.Cr.R. 560, 289 S.W. 406, 407; Allen v. State, 94 Tex.Cr.R. 646, 252 S.W. 505; Carson v. State, 30 Okl.Cr. 438, 236 P. 627, 628.

In embezzlement, the principal to whom an agent looks for authority, under whose control he acts, and from whom he receives compensation and takes direction, is the owner within the meaning of statute. Coney v. State, 100 Tex.Cr.R. 380, 272 S.W. 197, 199.

Equitable owner. One who is recognized in equity as the owner of property, because the real and beneficial use and title belong to him, although the bare legal title is vested in another, *e. g.*, a trustee for his benefit. One who has a present title in land which will ripen into legal ownership upon the performance of conditions subsequent. Hawkins v. Stiles, Tex.Civ.App., 158 S.W. 1011, 1021. There may therefore be two "owners" in respect of the same property, one the nominal or legal owner, the other the beneficial or equitable owner. In re Fulham's Estate, 96 Vt. 308, 119 A. 433, 437.

General owner. He who has the primary or residuary title to it; as distinguished from a *special* owner, who has a special interest in the same thing, amounting to a qualified ownership, such, for example, as a bailee's lien. Farmers' & Mechanics' Nat. Bank v. Logan, 74 N.Y. 581. One who has both the right of property and of possession.

General and beneficial owner. The person whose interest is primarily one of possession and enjoyment in contemplation of an ultimate absolute ownership;—not the person whose interest is primarily in the enforcement of a collateral pecuniary claim, and does not contemplate the use or enjoyment of the property as such. Ex parte State, 206 Ala. 575, 90 So. 896.

Joint owners. Two or more persons who jointly own and hold title to property, *e. g.*, joint tenants, and also partners and tenants in common. In re Huggins' Estate, 96 N.J.Eq. 275, 125 A. 27, 30. In its most comprehensive sense, the term embraces all cases where the property in question is owned by two or more persons regardless of the special nature of their relationship or how it came into being. Halferty v. Karr, 188 Mo.App. 241, 175 S W. 146, 147.

An estate by entirety is a "joint ownership" of a husband and wife as at common law notwithstanding legislative enactments touching joint tenancy. Cullum v. Rice, 236 Mo.App. 1113, 162 S.W.2d 342, 344.

Legal owner. One who is recognized and held responsible by the law as the owner of property. In a more particular sense, one in whom the legal title to real estate is vested, but who holds it in trust for the benefit of another, the latter being called the "equitable" owner.

Part owners. Joint owners; co-owners; those who have shares of ownership in the same thing, particularly a vessel.

Real owners. Those who must be joined in actions of scire facias sur mortgage under Pennsylvania statutes are the present owners of the title under which the mortgagor claimed when he executed the mortgages, and do not include persons claiming by titles antagonistic to the mortgagor. Orient Building & Loan Ass'n v. Gould, 239 Pa. 335, 86 A. 863.

Record owner. This term, particularly used in statutes requiring notice of tax delinquency or sale, means the owner of record, not the owner described in the tax roll; Okanogan Power & Irrigation Co. v. Quackenbush, 107 Wash. 651, 182 P. 618, 619, 5 A.L.R. 966; the owner of the title at time of notice; Hunt v. State, 110 Tex. 204, 217 S. W. 1034, 1035.

Reputed owner. One who has to all appearances the title to, and possession of, property; one who, from all appearances, or from supposition, is the owner of a thing. Lowell Hardware Co. v. May, 59 Colo. 475, 149 P. 831, 832. He who has the general credit or reputation of being the owner or proprietor of goods. Santa Cruz Rock Pav. Co. v. Lyons, 5 Cal.Unrep.Cas. 260, 43 P. 601.

This phrase is chiefly used in English bankruptcy practice, where the bankrupt is styled the "reputed owner" of goods lawfully in his possession, though the real owner may be another person. The word "reputed" has a much weaker sense than its derivation would appear to warrant; importing merely a supposition or opinion derived or made up from outward appearances, and often unsupported by fact. The term "reputed owner" is frequently employed in this sense. 2 Steph.Comm. 206.

Riparian owner. See Riparian.

Sole and unconditional owner. An expression commonly used in fire insurance policies, in which the word "sole" means that no one else has any interest in the property as owner, and "unconditional" means that the quality of the estate is not limited or affected by any condition. Globe & Rutgers Fire Ins. Co. v. Creekmore, 69 Okl. 238, 171 P. 874, 876; Hartford Fire Ins. Co. v. McCain, 141 Miss. 394, 106 So. 529. To be "unconditional and sole," the interest or ownership of the insured must be completely vested, not contingent or conditional, nor in common or jointly with others, but of such nature that the insured must alone sustain the entire loss if the property is destroyed; and this is so whether the title is legal or equitable. Socicero v. National Union Fire Ins. Co. of Pittsburgh, Pa., 90 Fla. 820, 106 So. 879; Livingstone v. Boston Ins. Co., 255 Pa. 1, 99 A. 212, 213.

It is sufficient to satisfy the requirements of "sole and unconditional ownership" that the insured is the sole equitable owner and has the full equitable title. Turner v. Home Ins. Co., 195 Mo.App. 138, 189 S.W. 626, 628; Alliance Ins. Co. v. Enders, C.C.A.Idaho, 293 F. 485, 489. It is enough that the insured is equitably entitled to immediate and absolute legal ownership. Exchange Underwriters' Agency of Royal Exchange Assur. of London, England, v. Bates, 195 Ala. 161, 69 So. 956, 960. The term contemplates beneficial and practical proprietorship and not necessarily technical title. Royal Ins. Co. v. Drury, 150 Md. 211, 132 A. 635, 640, 43 A.L.R. 582. See Giles v. Citizens' Ins. Co. of Missouri, 32 Ga.App. 207, 122 S.E. 890, 891.

Special owner. One who has a special interest in an article of property, amounting to a qualified ownership of it, such, for example, as a bailee's lien; as distinguished from the *general* owner, who has the primary or residuary title to the same thing. Frazier v. State, 18 Tex.App. 441. Some person holding property with the consent of, and as representative of, the actual owner. Mathieu v. Roberts, 31 N.M. 469, 247 P. 1066, 1068.

OWNER'S RISK. An expression employed by carriers with the object of relieving them from responsibility. See [1906] T. S. 973 (So. Afr.); Heiskell v. Furness, Withy & Co., C.C.A.N.Y., 4 F.2d 977, 978.

OWNERSHIP. Collection of rights to use and enjoy property, including right to transmit it to others. Trustees of Phillips Exeter Academy v. Exeter, 92 N.H. 473, 33 A.2d 665, 673. The complete dominion, title, or proprietary right in a thing or claim. The entirety of the powers of use and disposal allowed by law. See Property.

The right of one or more persons to possess and use a thing to the exclusion of others. Civ. Code Cal. § 654. The right by which a thing belongs to some one in particular, to the exclusion of all other persons. Civ. Code La. art. 488. The exclusive right of possession, enjoyment, and disposal; Thompson v. Kreutzer, 112 Miss. 165, 72 So. 891; involving as an essential attribute the right to control, handle, and dispose; Hardinge v. Empire Zinc Co., 17 Ariz. 75, 148 P. 306, 310.

Ownership is divided into *perfect* and *imperfect*. Ownership is perfect when it is perpetual, and when the thing is unincumbered with any real right towards any other person than the owner. On the contrary, ownership is imperfect when it is to terminate at a certain time or on a condition, or if the thing which is the object of it, being an immovable, is charged with any real right towards a third person; as a usufruct, use, or servitude. When an immovable is subject to a usufruct, the owner of it is said to possess the naked ownership. Civ.Code La. art. 490; Maestri v. Board of Assessors, 110 La. 517, 34 So. 658.

In criminal law. In connection with burglary, "ownership" means any possession which is rightful as against the burglar. Seaba v. State, 33 Okl. Cr. 59, 242 P. 779, 780; State v. Bige, 195 Iowa, 1342, 193 N.W. 17, 21. It is synonymous with occupancy. State v. Harrison, Mo.Sup., 285 S.W. 83, 87; Carneal v. State, 86 Tex.Cr.R. 274, 216 S.W. 626. When considered as an element of larceny, "ownership" means the same as "possession." People v. Edwards, 72 Cal.App. 102, 236 P. 944, 950.

Exclusive ownership. See Exclusive Ownership.

OXFILD. A restitution anciently made by a hundred or county for any wrong done by one that was within the same. Lamb.Arch. 125.

OXGANG. In old English law. As much land as an ox could till. Co. Litt. 5*a*. A measure of land of uncertain quantity. In the north of England a division of a carucate. According to some, fifteen acres. Co. Litt. 69*a;* Crompton, Jurisd. 220. According to Balfour, the Scotch *oxengang,* or *oxgate,* contained twelve acres; but this does not correspond with ancient charters. Bell, Dict. *Ploughgate.* Skene and Spelman say thirteen acres. Cowell; 1 Poll. & Maitl. 347.

See Librata Terrae.

OYER. In Old Practice. Hearing; the hearing a deed read, which a party sued on a bond, etc., might pray or demand, and it was then *read* to him by the other party; the entry on the record being, *"et ei legitur in hœc verba,"* (and it is read to him in these words). Steph. Pl. 67, 68; 3 Bl. Comm. 299; 3 Salk. 119.

In Modern practice. A *copy* of a bond or specialty sued upon, given to the opposite party, in lieu of the old practice of reading it.

OYER AND TERMINER. A half French phrase applied in England to the assizes, which are so called from the commission of *oyer and terminer* directed to the judges, empowering them to "inquire, *hear, and determine*" all treasons, felonies, and misdemeanors. This commission is now issued regularly, but was formerly used only on particular occasions, as upon sudden outrage or insurrection in any place. In the United States, the higher criminal courts are called "courts of oyer and terminer." Burrill.

OYER DE RECORD. A petition made in court that the judges, for better proof's sake, will hear or look upon any record. Cowell.

OYEZ. Hear ye. A word used in courts by the public crier to command attention when a proclamation is about to be made. Usually pronounced "O yes." 4 Bla.Comm. 340, n.

P

P. An abbreviation for "page;" also for "Paschalis," (Easter term,) in the Year Books, and for numerous other words of which it is the initial.

P. C. An abbreviation for "Pleas of the Crown;" sometimes also for "Privy Council," "Parliamentary Cases," "Patent Cases," "Practice Cases," "Penal Code," or "Political Code."

P. H. A. Public Housing Administration.

P. H. V. An abbreviation for *"pro hac vice,"* for this turn, for this purpose or occasion.

P. J. An abbreviation for "president" (or presiding) "judge," (or justice).

P. L. An abbreviation for "Pamphlet Laws" or "Public Laws."

P. M. An abbreviation for "postmaster;" also for *"post-meridiem,"* afternoon.

P. O. An abbreviation of "public officer;" also of "post-office."

P. P. An abbreviation for *"propria persona,"* in his proper person, in his own person, and for *per procuration* (*q. v.*).

P. P. I. Policy proof of interest, *i. e.,* in the event of loss, the insurance policy is to be deemed sufficient proof of interest. Frank B. Hall & Co. v. Jefferson Ins. Co., D.C.N.Y., 279 F. 892, 893.

P. S. An abbreviation for "Public Statutes;" also for "postscript."

P. S. I. A. An abbreviation for "pounds per square inch absolute." Application of Corneil, 347 F.2d 563, 564, 52 C.C.P.A. 1718.

PAAGE. In old English law. A toll for passage through another's land. The same as "pedage."

PACARE. L. Lat. To pay.

PACATIO. Payment. Mat. Par. A. D. 1248.

PACE. A measure of length containing two feet and a half, being the ordinary length of a step. The geometrical pace is five feet long, being the length of two steps, or the whole space passed over by the same foot from one step to another.

PACEATUR. Lat. Let him be freed or discharged.

PACI SUNT MAXIME CONTRARIA VIS ET INJURIA. Co. Litt. 161. Violence and injury are the things chiefly hostile to peace.

PACIFICATION. The act of making peace between two hostile or belligerent states; reestablishment of public tranquillity.

PACIFIST. One who seeks to maintain peace and to abolish war; one who refuses or is unwilling for any purpose to bear arms because of conscientious considerations, and who is disposed to encourage others in such refusal. U. S. v. Schwimmer, Ill., 49 S.Ct. 448, 451, 279 U.S. 644, 73 L.Ed. 889.

PACK. To deceive by false appearances; to counterfeit; to delude; to put together in sorts with a fraudulent design. To pack a jury is to use unlawful, improper, or deceitful means to have the jury made up of persons favorably disposed to the party so contriving, or who have been or can be improperly influenced to give the verdict he seeks. The term imports the improper and corrupt selection of a jury sworn and impaneled for the trial of a cause. Mix v. Woodward, 12 Conn. 289.

PACK OF WOOL. A horse load, which consists of seventeen stone and two pounds, or two hundred and forty pounds weight. Fleta, l. 2, c. 12; Cowell.

PACKAGE. A bundle put up for transportation or commercial handling; a thing in form to become, as such, an article of merchandise or delivery from hand to hand. A parcel is a small package; "parcel" being the diminutive of "package." Each of the words denotes a thing in form suitable for transportation or handling, or sale from hand to hand. Haley v. State, 42 Neb. 556, 60 N.W. 962, 47 Am.St.Rep. 718; State v. Parsons, 124 Mo. 436, 27 S.W. 1102, 46 Am.St.Rep. 457. As ordinarily understood in the commercial world, it means a shipping package. Noble v. People, 67 Colo. 429, 180 P. 562, 563. Where a bale of cotton was held not a package; *contra,* Lamb v. Transp. Co., 2 Daly (N. Y.) 454.

In old English law. One of various duties charged in the port of London on the goods imported and exported by aliens, or by denizens the sons of aliens. Tomlins. Now abolished. Whart. Lex.

Original package. See Original.

PACKED PARCELS. The name for a consignment of goods, consisting of one large parcel made up of several small ones, (each bearing a different address,) collected from different persons by the immediate consignor, (a carrier,) who unites them into one for his own profit, at the expense of the railway by which they are sent, since the railway company would have been paid more for the carriage of the parcels singly than together. Wharton.

PACKER. A person employed in England by merchants to receive and (in some instances) to select goods from manufacturers, dyers, calenders, etc., and pack the same for exportation. Arch. Bankr., 11th ed. 37.

In the United States, one engaged in the business of slaughtering and packing cattle, sheep, and hogs, and preparing their products for sale. See Williams v. Schehl, 84 W.Va. 499, 100 S.E. 280, 282.

PACT. A bargain; compact; agreement. This word is used in writings on Roman law and on general jurisprudence as the English form of the Latin *"pactum,"* (which see.)

Nude Pact. A translation of the Latin *"nudum pactum,"* a bare or naked pact, that is, a promise or agreement made without any consideration on the other side, which is therefore not enforceable.

Obligatory Pact. In Civil Law. An informal obligatory declaration of consensus, which the Roman law refused to acknowledge. Sohm, Rom. L. 321.

Pact De Non Alienando. An agreement not to alienate incumbered (particularly mortgaged) property. This stipulation, sometimes found in mortgages made in Louisiana, and derived from the Spanish law, binds the mortgagor not to sell or incumber the mortgaged premises to the prejudice of the mortgagee; it does not avoid a sale made to a third person, but enables the mortgagee to proceed directly against the mortgaged property in a proceeding against the mortgagor alone and without notice to the purchaser. See Dodds v. Lanaux, 45 La.Ann. 287, 12 So. 345.

PACTA CONVENTA QUÆ NEQUE CONTRA LEGES NEQUE DOLO MALO INITA SUNT OMNI MODO OBSERVANDA SUNT. Agreements which are not contrary to the laws nor entered into with a fraudulent design are in all respects to be observed. Cod. 2, 3, 39; Broom, Max. 698, 732.

PACTA DANT LEGEM CONTRACTUI. Hob. 118. The stipulations of parties constitute the law of the contract. Agreements give the law to the contract. Halkers, Max. 118.

PACTA PRIVATA JURI PUBLICO DEROGARE NON POSSUNT. 7 Coke, 23. Private compacts cannot derogate from public right.

PACTA QUÆ CONTRA LEGES CONSTITUTIONESQUE, VEL CONTRA BONOS MORES FIUNT, NULLAM VIM HABERE, INDUBITATI JURIS EST. That contracts which are made against law or against good morals have no force is a principle of undoubted law. Cod. 2, 3, 6; Broom, Max. 695.

PACTA QUÆ TURPEM CAUSAM CONTINENT NON SUNT OBSERVANDA. Agreements founded upon an immoral consideration are not to be observed. Dig. 2, 14, 27, 4; Broom, Max. 732; 2 Pet. 539, 7 L.Ed. 508.

PACTIO. Lat. In the civil law. A bargaining or agreeing of which *pactum* (the agreement itself) was the result. Calvin. It is used, however, as the synonym of *"pactum."*

PACTIONAL. Relating to or generating an agreement; by way of bargain or covenant.

PACTIONS. In international law. Contracts between nations which are to be performed by a single act, and of which execution is at an end at once. 1 Bouv. Inst. no. 100.

PACTIS PRIVATORUM JURI PUBLICO NON DEROGATUR. Private contracts do not derogate from public law. Broom, Max. 695; per Dr. Lushington, Arg. 4 Cl. & F. 241; Arg. 3 Id. 621.

PACTITIOUS. Settled by covenant.

PACTO ALIQUOD LICITUM EST, QUOD SINE PACTO NON ADMITTITUR. Co. Litt. 166. By special agreement things are allowed which are not otherwise permitted.

PACTUM. Lat.

In the civil law. A pact. An agreement or convention without specific name, and without consideration, which, however, might, in its nature, produce a civil obligation. Heinecc. Elem. lib. 3, tit. 14, § 775; Merlin, *Rép. Pacte.*

In Roman law. With some exceptions, those agreements that the law does not directly enforce, but which it recognizes only as a valid ground of defense, were called *"pacta."* Those agreements that are enforced, in other words, are supported by actions, are called *"contractus."* The exceptions are few, and belong to a late period. Hunter, Rom. Law, 546.

Nudum Pactum. A bare or naked pact or agreement; a promise or undertaking made without any consideration for it, and therefore not enforceable.

PACTUM COMMISSORIUM. An agreement of forfeiture. See Lex Commissoria.

PACTUM CONSTITUTÆ PECUNIÆ. In the Civil Law. An agreement by which a person appointed to his creditor a certain day, or a certain time, at which he promised to pay; or it may be defined simply an agreement by which a person promises a creditor to pay him. There is a striking conformity between the *pactum constitutæ pecuniæ*, as above defined, and our *indebitatus assumpsit.* 4 Co. 91, 95. See 1 H.Bla. 550, 850; Brooke, Abr. *Action sur le Case* (Pl. 7, 69, 72); 4 B. & B. 295; 1 Chitty, Pl. 89.

PACTUM DE NON ALIENANDO. A pact or agreement binding the owner of property not to alienate it, intended to protect the interests of another; particularly an agreement by the mortgagor of real estate that he will not transfer the title to a third person until after satisfaction of the mortgage. Mackeld. Rom. Law, § 461. A clause inserted in mortgages in Louisiana to secure to the mortgage creditor the right to foreclose his mortgage by executory process directed solely against the mortgagor, and to give him the right to seize and sell the mortgaged property, regardless of any subsequent alienations. Avegno v. Schmidt, 35 La.Ann. 585; Shields v. Schiff, 124 U.S. 355, 8 S.Ct. 510, 31 L.Ed. 445.

PACTUM DE NON PETENDO. In the civil law. An agreement not to sue. A simple convention whereby a creditor promises the debtor that he will not enforce his claim. Mackeld. Rom. Law, § 542.

PACTUM DE QUOTA LITIS. In the civil law. An agreement by which a creditor promised to pay a portion of a debt difficult to recover to a person who undertook to recover it. Wharton.

PAD. To stuff or furnish with padding. A charge that a contractor padded his pay roll would imply a charge of deceit or artifice. Smith v. Aultman, 30 Ga.App. 507, 118 S.E. 459.

PADDER. A robber; a foot highwayman; a foot-pad.

PADDOCK. A small inclosure for deer or other animals.

PAGA. In Spanish law. Payment. Las Partidas, pt. 5, tit. 14, l. 1. *Pagamento,* satisfaction.

PAGARCHUS. A petty magistrate of a *pagus* or little district in the country.

PAGE. One side of a leaf, as of a book, manuscript or letter. Roberts Bros. Co. v. Grein, 129 Misc. 406, 221 N.Y.S. 321, 322.

PAGODA. A gold or silver coin, of several kinds and values, formerly current in India. It was valued at the United States custom-house, at $1.94.

PAGUS. A county. Jacob.

PAIN. A disagreeable feeling, usually in its intenser degrees, resulting from, or accompanying, deranged or otherwise abnormal action of the physical powers. Merriam v. Hamilton, 64 Or. 476, 130 P. 406, 407.

PAINE FORTE ET DURE. See Peine Forte et Dure.

PAINS AND PENALTIES, BILLS OF. The name given to acts of parliament to attaint particular persons of treason or felony, or to inflict pains and penalties beyond or contrary to the common law, to serve a special purpose. They are in fact new laws, made *pro re nata.* See, also, Bill of Pains and Penalties.

PAINTING. A likeness, image, or scene depicted with paints. Cent. Dict. The term does not necessarily mean anything upon which painting has been done by a workman, but rather something of value as a painting and something on which skill has been bestowed in producing it. Colored imitations of rugs and carpets and colored working designs, each of them valuable and designed by skilled persons and hand painted, but having no value as works of art, are not "paintings," within the meaning of a statute on the liability of carriers. 3 Ex. Div. 121.

PAIRING-OFF. In the practice of legislative bodies, a species of negative proxies, by which two members, who belong to opposite parties or are on opposite sides with regard to a given question, mutually agree that they will both be absent from voting, either for a specified period or when a division is had on the particular question. By this mutual agreement a vote is neutralized on each side of the question, and the relative numbers on the division are precisely the same as if both members were present. May, Parl. Pr. 370. It is said to have originated in the house of commons in Cromwell's time.

PAIS, PAYS. Fr. The country; the neighborhood.

A trial *per pais* signifies a trial by the country; that is, by jury.

An assurance by matter *in pais* is an assurance transacted between two or more private persons "in the country;" that is, upon the very spot to be transferred.

Matter *in pais* signifies matter of fact, probably because matters of fact are triable by the country; *i. e.,* by jury.

Estoppels *in pais* are estoppels by conduct, as distinguished from estoppels by deed or by record.

Conveyances *in pais* are ordinary conveyances between two or more persons *in the country; i. e.,* upon the land to be transferred.

See, also, In Pais; Matter In Pais.

PALACE COURT. See Court of the Steward and Marshal.

PALAGIUM. A duty to lords of manors for exporting and importing vessels of wine at any of their ports. Jacob.

PALAM. Lat. In the civil law. Openly; in the presence of many. Dig. 50, 16, 33.

PALATINE. Possessing royal privileges. See County Palatine.

PALATINE COURTS. Formerly, the court of common pleas at Lancaster, the chancery court of Lancaster, and the court of pleas at Durham, the second of which alone now exists. Sweet. (See the respective titles.)

PALATIUM. Lat. A palace. The emperor's house in Rome was so called from the *Mons Palatinus* on which it was built. Adams, Rom. Ant. 613.

PALFRIDUS. A palfrey; a horse to travel on.

PALINGMAN. In old English law. A merchant denizen; one born within the English *pale.* Blount.

PALLIO COOPERIRE. In old English law. An ancient custom, where children were born out of wedlock, and their parents afterwards intermarried. The children, together with the father and mother, stood under a cloth extended while the marriage was solemnized. It was in the nature of adoption. The children were legitimate by the civil, but not by the common, law. Jacob. They were called "mantle children" in Germany, France, and Normandy. 2 Poll. & Maitl. 397. The custom existed in Scotland almost to our own time. Bryce, Studies in Hist. etc., Essay xvi.

PALM OFF. To impose by fraud; to put off by unfair means. Sayre v. McGill Ticket Punch Co., D.C.Ill., 200 F. 771, 773.

PALMARIUM. In civil law. A conditional fee for professional services in addition to the lawful charge.

PALMER ACT. A name given to the English statute 19 & 20 Vict. c. 16, enabling a person accused of a crime committed out of the jurisdiction of the central criminal court, to be tried in that court.

PALMING OFF DOCTRINE. Rule of law itself by which it is determined whether a given state of facts constitutes "unfair competition." Soft-Lite Lens Co. v. Ritholz, 301 Ill.App. 100, 21 N.E. 2d 835, 838.

PALMISTRY. The practice of telling fortunes by a feigned interpretation of the lines and marks on the hand. Also, a trick with the hand. 2 Exch. Div. 268.

PALPABLE. Easily perceptible, plain, obvious, readily visible, noticeable, patent, distinct, manifest. State v. Department of Public Works, 143 Wash. 67, 254 P. 839, 844; Alabama Fuel & Iron Co. v. Minyard, 210 Ala. 299, 97 So. 918, 921. People v. Hughey, 382 Ill. 136, 47 N.E.2d 77, 80.

PAMPHLET. A small book, bound in paper covers, usually printed in octavo form, and stitched. U. S. v. Chase, 10 S.Ct. 756, 135 U.S. 255, 34 L.Ed. 117.

PAMPHLET LAWS. The name given in some states, such as Pennsylvania, to the publication, in pamphlet or book form, containing the acts passed by the state legislature at each of its biennial sessions.

PANDECTS. A compilation of Roman law, consisting of selected passages from the writings of the most authoritative of the older jurists, methodically arranged, prepared by Tribonian with the assistance of sixteen associates, under a commission from the emperor Justinian. This work, which is otherwise called the "Digest," because in his compilation the writings of the jurists were reduced to order and condensed *quasi digestiœ*, comprises fifty books, and is one of the four great works composing the *Corpus Juris Civilis*. It was first published in A. D. 533, when Justinian gave to it the force of law.

PANDER, *n.* One who caters to the lust of others; a male bawd, a pimp, or procurer. Hewitt v. State, 71 Tex.Cr.R. 243, 158 S.W. 1120, 1125.

PANDER, *v.* To pimp; to cater to the gratification of the lust of another. State v. Thibodeaux, 136 La. 935, 67 So. 973, 974. To entice or procure a female, by promises, threats, fraud, or artifice, to enter any place in which prostitution is practiced, for the purpose of prostitution. Boyle v. State, 110 Ark. 318, 161 S.W. 1049, 1051; Crawford & Moses' Dig. § 2707; Humphries v. State, 79 Tex.Cr.R. 637, 186 S.W. 332, 334; To take and detain a female for the purpose of sexual intercourse, on pretense of marriage. Crawford & Moses' Dig. (Ark.) § 2703.

PANDERER. One who solicits for prostitute or lewd woman. Lutes v. Commonwealth, 236 Ky. 549, 33 S.W.2d 620, 622, 74 A.L.R. 304.

PANDOXATOR. In old records. A brewer.

PANDOXATRIX. An ale-wife; a woman that both brewed and sold ale and beer.

PANEL. The roll or slip of parchment returned by the sheriff in obedience to a *venire facias*, containing the names of the persons whom he has summoned to attend the court as jurymen. Beasley v. People, 89 Ill. 571; People v. Coyodo, 40 Cal. 592; Co. Litt. 158*b*.

A list of jurors returned by a sheriff, to serve at a particular court or for the trial of a particular action. Pen.Code Cal. § 1057. The word may be used to denote either the whole body of persons summoned as jurors for a particular term of court, or those selected by the clerk by lot. State v. Gurlagh, 76 Iowa, 141, 40 N.W. 141.

In Scotch law. The prisoner at the bar, or person who takes his trial before the court of justiciary for any crime. This name is given to him after his appearance. Bell.

PANIER, in the parlance of the English bar societies, is an attendant or domestic who waits at table and gives bread, *(panis,)* wine, and other necessary things to those who are dining. The phrase was in familiar use among the knights templar, and from them has been handed down to the learned societies of the inner and middle temples, who at the present day occupy the halls and buildings once belonging to that distinguished order, and who have retained a few of their customs and phrases. Brown.

PANIS. Lat. In old English law. Bread; loaf; a loaf. Fleta, lib. 2, c. 9. See Mandato, Panes De.

PANNAGE. A common of pannage is the right of feeding swine on mast and acorns at certain seasons in a commonable wood or forest. Elton, Commons, 25; Williams, Common, 168.

PANNAGIUM EST PASTUS PORCORUM, IN NEMORIBUS ET IN SILVIS, UT PUTA, DE GLANDIBUS, ETC. 1 Bulst. 7. A pannagium is a pasture of hogs, in woods and forests, upon acorns, and so forth.

PANNELLATION. The act of impaneling a jury.

PANTOMIME. A dramatic performance in which gestures take the place of words. See 3 C. B. 871.

PAPAL SUPREMACY. The supremacy which the Pope claimed not only over the Emperor of the Holy Roman Empire, but over all other Christian princes. The theory was that they stood to the Pope as feudal vassals to a supreme lord; as such, the Pope claimed the right to enforce the duties due to him from his feudal subordinates through an ascending scale of penalties culminating in the absolution of the prince's subjects from the bonds of allegiance, and in the disposition of the sovereign himself. The papal supremacy was overthrown in England by acts of the Parliament which met in 1529 and was dissolved in 1536, ending in the Act of Supremacy. Hannis Taylor, Science of

Jurispr.; Boyce, Holy Rom. Emp.; Freeman, Sel. Hist. Essays; 2 Phill. Intern. Law.

PAPER. A manufactured substance composed of fibres (whether vegetable or animal) adhering together in forms consisting of sheets of various sizes and of different thicknesses, used for writing or printing or other purposes to which flexible sheets are applicable. 4 H. & N. 470.

A written or printed document or instrument. A document filed or introduced in evidence in a suit at law, as, in the phrase "papers in the case" and in "papers on appeal." Any writing or printed document, including letters, memoranda, legal or business documents, and books of account, as in the constitutional provision which protects the people from unreasonable searches and seizures in respect to their "papers" as well as their houses and persons. A written or printed evidence of debt, particularly a promissory note or a bill of exchange, as in the phrases "accommodation paper" and "commercial paper."

Books are not paper within the meaning of the tariff act; Pott v. Arthur, 104 U.S. 735, 26 L.Ed. 909.

The term "papers" does not mean newspapers or perhaps even include them within the meaning of a statute, the object of which is to prevent a jury from receiving any evidence, papers, or documents not authorized by the court. State v. Jackson, 9 Mont. 508, 24 P. 216. But the word includes photographs of deceased showing the nature of his wounds. People v. Balestieri, 23 Cal.App. 708, 139 P. 821, 823.

Generally, the words "documents" and "papers" refer to particular instruments and writings bearing upon specific transactions, whereas "books of accounts" and "records" have reference to serial, continuous, and more permanent memorials of a concern's business and affairs. Cudahy Packing Co. v. U. S., C.C.A.Ill., 15 F.2d 133, 136.

In English practice. The list of causes or cases intended for argument, called "the paper of causes." 1 Tidd, Pr. 504. See Paper Days.

In General

Accommodation paper. See that title.

Commercial paper. See Commercial.

Paper blockade. See Blockade.

Paper book. In practice. A printed collection or abstract, in methodical order, of the pleadings, evidence, exhibits, and proceedings in a cause, or whatever else may be necessary to a full understanding of it, prepared for the use of the judges upon a hearing or argument on appeal. Copies of the proceedings on an issue in law or demurrer, of cases, and of the proceedings on error, prepared for the use of the judges, and delivered to them previous to bringing the cause to argument. 3 Bl. Comm. 317; Archb. New Pr. 353; 5 Man. & G. 98. In proceedings on appeal or error in a criminal case, copies of the proceedings with a note of the points intended to be argued, delivered to the judges by the parties before the argument. Archb. Crim. Pl. 205; Sweet.

Paper credit. Credit given on the security of any written obligation purporting to represent property.

Paper days. In English law. Certain days in term-time appointed by the courts for hearings or arguments in the cases set down in the various special papers.

Paper hangings. In tariff acts, tinted or decorative paper used for covering walls, ceiling, etc.;—distinguished from "hanging paper," meaning such paper, whether or not tinted or decorative. Downing & Co. v. U. S., 12 Ct.Cust.App. 451, 454.

Paper mill. See Paper office.

Paper money. Bills drawn by a government against its own credit, engaging to pay money, but which do not profess to be immediately convertible into specie, and which are put into compulsory circulation as a substitute for coined money.

Paper office. In English law. An ancient office in the palace of Whitehall, where all the public writings, matters of state and council, proclamations, letters, intelligences, negotiations of the queen's ministers abroad, and generally all the papers and dispatches that pass through the offices of the secretaries of state, are deposited. Also an office or room in the court of queen's bench where the records belonging to that court are deposited; sometimes called "paper-mill." Wharton.

Paper title. See Title.

PAPIAN POPPÆAN LAW. See Lex Papia Poppæa.

PAPIST. One who adheres to the communion of the Church of Rome. The word seems to be considered by the Roman Catholics themselves as a nickname of reproach, originating in their maintaining the supreme ecclesiastical power of the pope. Wharton.

PAR. In commercial law. Equal; equality. An equality subsisting between the nominal or face value of a bill of exchange, share of stock, etc., and its actual selling value. When the values are thus equal, the instrument or share is said to be "at par;" if it can be sold for more than its nominal worth, it is "above par;" if for less, it is "below par." Conover v. Smith, 83 Cal.App. 227, 256 P. 835, 838; Town of Buffalo v. Walker, 126 Okl. 6, 257 P. 766, 770; Boston & M. R. R. v. U. S., C.C.A.Mass., 265 F. 578, 579.

Par of exchange. In mercantile law. The precise equality or equivalency of any given sum or quantity of money in the coin of one country, and the like sum or quantity of money in the coin of any other foreign country into which it is to be exchanged, supposing the money of such country to be of the precise weight and purity fixed by the mint standard of the respective countries. Story, Bills, § 30. Murphy v. Kastner, 50 N.J.Eq. 220, 24 A. 564; Blue Star S. S. Co. v. Keyser, D.C.Fla., 81 F. 510; Delafield v. Illinois, 26 Wend., N.Y., 224. The par of the currencies of any two countries means the equivalence of a certain amount of the currency of the one in the currency of the other, supposing the currency of both to be of the precise weight and purity fixed by their respective mints. The exchange between the two countries is said to be at par when bills are negotiated on this footing; *i. e.,* when a bill for £100 drawn on London sells in Paris for 2,520 frs., and *vice versa.* Bowen, Pol. Econ. 284, 11 East, 267.

PAR. Lat. Equal.

Par delictum. Equal guilt. "This is not a case of *par delictum.* It is oppression on one side and submission on the other. It never can be predicated as *par delictum* when one holds the rod and the other bows to it." 6 Maule & S. 165. See In Pari Delicto.

Par oneri. Equal to the burden or charge, or to the detriment or damage.

PAR IN PAREM IMPERIUM NON HABET. Jenk.Cent. 174. An equal has no dominion over an equal.

PARACHRONISM. Error in the computation of time.

PARACIUM. The tenure between parceners, viz., that which the youngest owes to the eldest without homage or service. Domesday.

PARAGE, or PARAGIUM. An equality of blood or dignity, but more especially of land, in the partition of an inheritance between co-heirs. Co. Litt. 166*b*. More properly, however, an equality of condition among nobles, or persons holding by a noble tenure. Thus, when a fief is divided among brothers, the younger hold their part of the elder by parage; *i. e.,* without any homage or service. Also the portion which a woman may obtain on her marriage. Cowell.

PARAGRAPH. A distinct part of a discourse or writing, any section or subdivision of writing or chapter which relates to particular point, whether consisting of one or many sentences. Lehmann v. Revell, 354 Ill. 262, 188 N.E. 531, 540.

An entire or integral statement of a cause of action equivalent to a count at common law. Bailey v. Mosher, 11 C.C.A. 304, 63 F. 488.

A part or section of a statute, pleading, affidavit, etc., which contains one article, the sense of which is complete. McClellan v. Hein, 56 Neb. 600, 77 N.W. 120; Hill v. Fairhaven & W. R. Co., 75 Conn. 177, 52 A. 725; Marine v. Packham, 3 C.C.A. 210, 52 F. 579. The term in an act of congress will be construed to mean section whenever to do so accords with the legislative intent; Alfrey v. Colbert, 93 C.C.A. 517, 168 F. 231.

PARALLEL. Extending in the same direction and in all parts equidistant; having the same direction or tendency. Postal Tel. C. Co. v. R. Co., 88 Va. 920, 14 S.E. 803.

In the specification of a patent the word has been construed in its popular sense of going side by side and not in its purely mathematical sense; 2 App.Cas. 423; and so in Fratt v. Woodward, 32 Cal. 231, 91 Am.Dec. 573; Williams v. Jackson, 5 Johns. (N.Y.) 489; where it was held that parallel lines were not necessarily straight lines. For two lines of street railway to be "parallel," within the meaning of a statute, it may not be necessary that the two lines should be parallel for the whole length of each or either route. Exact parallelism is not contemplated. Cronin v. Highland St. Ry. Co., 144 Mass. 254, 10 N.E. 833. And see East St. Louis Connecting Ry. Co. v. Jarvis, 34 C.C.A. 639, 92 F. 735; Louisville & N. R. Co. v. Kentucky, 16 S.Ct. 714, 161 U.S. 677, 40 L.Ed. 849.

PARALYSIS. In its popular rather than medical sense, signifies that the part of the body so afflicted, as an arm, is numb. Hudson v. Kansas City Rys. Co., Mo.Sup., 246 S.W. 576, 578.

PARAMOUNT. Above; upwards. Kelh. Norm. Dict. *Paramount especifié,* above specified. Plowd. 209*a*. Higher; superior; pre-eminent; of the highest rank or nature. Board of Com'rs of Big Horn County v. Bench Canal Drainage Dist., 56 Wyo. 285, 108 P.2d 590, 594. Malone v. Kansas City Rys. Co., Mo.App., 232 S.W. 782, 785. That which is superior; usually applied to the highest lord of the fee of lands, tenements, or hereditaments, as distinguished from the *mesne* (or intermediate) lord. Fitzh. Nat. Brev. 135.

PARAMOUNT EQUITY. An equitable right or claim which is prior, superior, or preferable to that with which it is compared.

PARAMOUNT TITLE. In the law of real property, properly one which is superior to the title with which it is compared, in the sense that the former is the source or origin of the latter. It is, however, frequently used to denote a title which is simply better or stronger than another, or will prevail over it. Isaacs v. Maupin, 191 Ky. 527, 231 S.W. 49, 51. But this use is scarcely correct, unless the superiority consists in the seniority of the title spoken of as "paramount." Hoopes v. Meyer, 1 Nev. 444; Jones & Brindisi, Inc., v. Bernstein, 119 Misc.Rep. 697, 197 N.Y.S. 263, 265.

PARANOIA. See Insanity.

PARAPH. A flourish at the end of a signature. In the Middle Ages this was a sort of rude safeguard against forgery. Webster, Dict.

Also, as in Louisiana, the signature itself, such as the official signature of a notary. Harz v. Gowland, 126 La. 674, 52 So. 986–988.

PARAPHERNA. In the civil law. Goods brought by wife to husband over and above her dowry (*dos*). Voc. Jur. Utr.; Fleta, lib. 5, c. 23, § 6; Mack. C. L. § 529.

In mediæval times the *"res parapherna"* were all the goods other than the *"dos."* These the husband did not own and of them the wife could make her will. 3 Holdsw. Hist.E.L. 426.

PARAPHERNAL PROPERTY. See Paraphernalia.

PARAPHERNALIA. The separate property of a married woman, other than that which is included in her dowry, or *dos*.

The separate property of the wife is divided into dotal and extradotal. Dotal property is that which the wife brings to the husband to assist him in bearing the expenses of the marriage establishment. Extradotal property, otherwise called "paraphernal property," is that which forms no part of the dowry. Civ. Code La. art. 2335. It is property brought to the marriage by one of the spouses.

There can be no such thing as paraphernal property prior to marriage; Le Boeuf v. Melancon, 131 La. 148, 59 So. 102.

Those goods which a woman is allowed to have, after the death of her husband, *besides* her *dower,* consisting of her apparel and ornaments, suitable to her rank and degree. 2 Bl. Comm. 436.

Those goods which a wife could bequeath by her testament. 2 Poll. & Maitl. 427.

PARAPHERNAUX, BIENS. Fr. In French law. All the wife's property which is not subject to the *régime dotal;* and of these articles the wife has the entire administration; but she may allow the husband to enjoy them, and in that case he is not liable to account. Brown.

PARASCEVE. The sixth day of the last week in Lent, particularly called "Good Friday." In English law, it is a *dies non juridicus.*

PARASYNEXIS. In the civil law. A conventicle, or unlawful meeting.

PARATITLA. In the civil law. Notes or abstracts prefixed to titles of law, giving a summary of their contents. Cod. 1, 17, 1, 12. An abbreviated explanation of some titles or books of the Code or Digest.

PARATUM HABEO. Lat. I have him in readiness. The return by the sheriff to a *capias ad respondendum,* signifying that he has the defendant in readiness to be brought into court. This was a fiction, where the defendant was at large. Afterwards he was required, by statute, to take bail from the defendant, and he returned *cepi corpus* and bailbond. But still he might be ruled to bring in the body; White v. Fitler, 7 Pa. 533.

PARATUS EST VERIFICARE. Lat. He is ready to verify. The Latin form for concluding a pleading with a *verification, (q. v.).*

PARAVAIL. Inferior; subordinate. Tenant paravail signified the lowest tenant of land, being the tenant of a mesne lord. He was so called because he was supposed to make "avail" or profit of the land for another. Cowell; 2 Bl. Comm. 60.

PARCEL, *v.* To divide an estate. Bac. Abr. *Conditions* (O).

PARCEL, *n.* A small package or bundle. See Package.

The word "parcel" is not a sufficient description of the property alleged in an indictment to have been stolen. The prisoner was indicted for stealing "one parcel, of the value of one shilling, of the goods," etc. The parcel in question was taken from the hold of a vessel, out of a box broken open by the prisoner. Held an insufficient description; 7 Cox, C.C. 13.

A part or portion of land. State v. Jordan, 36 Fla. 1, 17 So. 742; Johnson v. Sirret, 153 N.Y. 51, 46 N.E. 1035; Chicago, M. & St. P. Ry. Co. v. Town of Churdan, 196 Iowa 1057, 195 N.W. 996, 997. A part of an estate. Martin v. Cole, 38 Iowa, 141; 1 Comyns, Dig. *Abatement* (H 51), *Grant* (E 10). It may be synonymous with lot. Terre Haute v. Mack, 139 Ind. 99, 38 N.E. 468.

PARCEL MAKERS. Two officers in the exchequer who formerly made the parcels or items of the escheators' accounts, wherein they charged them with everything they had levied for the king during the term of their office. Cowell.

PARCELLA TERRÆ. A parcel of land.

PARCELS. A description of property, formally set forth in a conveyance, together with the boundaries thereof, in order to its easy identification.

PARCELS, BILL OF. An account of the items composing a parcel or package of goods, transmitted with them to the purchaser. See, further, Bill of Parcels under "Bill," 8.

PARCENARY. The state or condition of holding title to lands jointly by parceners, before the common inheritance has been divided. Center v. Kramer, 112 Ohio St. 269, 147 N.E. 602, 605.

PARCENER. A joint heir; one who, with others, holds an estate in co-parcenary, *(q. v.).* Gibson v. Johnson, 331 Mo. 1198, 56 S.W.2d 783, 88 A.L.R. 369.

PARCHMENT. Sheep-skins dressed for writing, so called from *Pergamus,* Asia Minor, where they were invented. Used for deeds, and used for writs of summons in England previous to the judicature act, 1875. Wharton.

The skin of a lamb, sheep, goat, young calf, or other animal, prepared for writing on; also, any of various papers made in imitation thereof. Webster, Dict.

PARCO FRACTO. Pound-breach; also the name of an old English writ against one who violently breaks a pound and takes beasts which, for some trespass done, or some other just cause, were lawfully impounded.

PARCUS. A park, *(q. v.).* A pound for stray cattle. Spelman.

PARDON. An act of grace, proceeding from the power intrusted with the execution of the laws, which exempts the individual on whom it is bestowed from the punishment the law inflicts for a crime he has committed. U. S. v. Wilson, 7 Pet. 160, 8 L.Ed. 640; Ex parte Garland, 4 Wall. 380, 18 L.Ed. 366; Ex parte Wells, 18 How. 307, 15 L. Ed. 421; Moore v. State, 43 N.J.Law, 241, 39 Am. Rep. 558; Ex parte Rice, 72 Tex.Cr.R. 587, 162 S. W. 891, 899; People v. Hale, 64 Cal.App. 523, 222 P. 148, 151; Ex parte Miers, 124 Tex.Cr.R. 592, 64 S.W.2d 778.

It releases punishment and blots out the existence of guilt, so that in the eyes of the law the offender is as innocent as if he had never committed the offense. U. S. ex rel. Palermo v. Smith, C.C.A.N.Y., 17 F.2d 534, 535; Ex parte Jones, 25 Okl.Cr. 347, 220 P. 978, 34 A.L.R. 206. It implies guilt and does not proceed on the theory of innocence of the person pardoned. State v. Cullen, 14 Wash.2d 105, 127 P.2d 257, 259.

A "pardon" releases the offender from the entire punishment prescribed for the offense, and from all the disabilities consequent on his conviction, while by a "parole" a convict is merely released before the expiration of his term, to remain subject during the remainder thereof to supervision by the public authority, and to return to imprisonment on violation of the condition of the parole. Board of Prison Com'rs v. De Moss, 157 Ky. 289, 163 S.W. 183, 187.

A pardon, to be effective, must be accepted; Burdick v. U. S., 35 S.Ct. 267, 268, 236 U.S. 79, 59 L.Ed. 476; but a commutation is merely a cessation of the exercise of sovereign authority, and does not obliterate guilt nor restore civil rights, and need not be accepted by the convict to be operative; Chapman v. Scott, D.C.Conn., 10 F.2d 156, 159; In re Charles, 115 Kan. 323, 222 P. 606, 608. A commutation is simply a remission of a part of the punishment, a substitution of a less penalty for the one originally imposed; State v. District Court of Eighteenth Judicial Dist. in and for Blaine County, 73 Mont. 541, 237 P. 525, 527; while a "pardon" avoids or terminates punishment for crime; U. S. v. Commissioner of Immigration at Port of New York, C.C.A.N.Y., 5 F.2d 162, 165.

The distinction between amnesty and pardon is one rather of philological interest than of legal importance. Knote v. U. S., 95 U.S. 149, 153, 24 L.Ed. 442, 443. This is so as to their ultimate effect, but there are incidental differences of importance. They are of different character and have different purposes. The one overlooks offense; the other remits punishment. The first is usually addressed to crimes against the sovereignty of the state, to political offenses, forgiveness being deemed more expedient for the public welfare than prosecution and punishment. The second condones infractions of the peace of the state. Amnesty is usually general, addressed to classes or even communities—a legislative act, or under legislation, constitutional or statutory—the act of the supreme magistrate. There may or may not be distinct acts of acceptance. If other rights are dependent upon it and are asserted, there is affirmative evidence of acceptance. Burdick v. U. S., 35 S.Ct. 267, 236 U.S. 79, 271, 59 L.Ed. 476. "Pardon" applies only to the individual, releases him from the punishment fixed by law for his specific offense, but does not affect the criminality of the same or similar acts when performed by other persons or repeated by the same person.

Absolute or Unconditional Pardon. One which frees the criminal without any condition whatever. That which reaches both the punishment prescribed for the offense and the guilt of the offender. It obliterates in legal contemplation the offense itself. Ex parte Collins, 32 Okl.Cr. 6, 239 P. 693, 696. It goes no further than to restore the accused to his civil rights and remit the penalty imposed for the particular offense of which he was convicted in so far as it remains unpaid. State v. Cullen, 14 Wash.2d 105, 127 P.2d 257, 259.

Conditional Pardon. One to which a condition is annexed, performance of which is necessary to the validity of the pardon. Ex parte Hunt, 10 Ark. 284; State v. Fuller, 1 McCord, S.C., 178. A pardon which does not become operative until the grantee has performed some specific act, or where it becomes void when some specific event transpires. Ex parte Collins. 32 Okl.Cr. 6, 239 P. 693, 697. One granted on the condition that it shall only endure until the voluntary doing of some act by the person pardoned, or that it shall be revoked by a subsequent act on his part, as that he shall leave the state and never return. Ex parte Janes, 1 Nev. 319; State v. Wolfer, 53 Minn. 135, 54 N.W. 1065, 19 L.R.A. 783, 39 Am.St. Rep. 582; State v. Barnes, 32 S.C. 14, 10 S.E. 611, 6 L.R.A. 743, 17 Am.St.Rep. 832; People v. Burns, 77 Hun, 92, 28 N.Y.S. 300.

Full pardon. One freely and unconditionally absolving party from all legal consequences, direct and collateral, of crime and conviction. Warren v. State, 127 Tex.Cr.R. 71, 74 S.W.2d 1006, 1008.

Executive pardon. See Executive Pardon.

General Pardon. One granted to all the persons participating in a given criminal or treasonable offense (generally political), or to all offenders of a given class or against a certain statute or within certain limits of time. But "amnesty" is the more appropriate term for this. It may be express, as when a general declaration is made that all offenders of a certain class shall be pardoned, or implied, as in case of the repeal of a penal statute. Roberts v. State, 2 Over. (Tenn.) 423.

Partial pardon. That which remits only portion of punishment or absolves from only portion of legal consequences of crime. Warren v. State, 127 Tex.Cr.R. 71, 74 S.W.2d 1006, 1008.

PARDONERS. In old English law. Persons who carried about the pope's indulgences, and sold them to any who would buy them.

PARENS. Lat. In Roman law. A parent; originally and properly only the father or mother of the person spoken of; but also, by an extension of its meaning, any relative, male or female, in the line of direct ascent.

"PARENS" EST NOMEN GENERALE AD OMNE GENUS COGNATIONIS. "Parent" is a name general for every kind of relationship. Co. Litt. 80; Littleton § 108; Mag. Cart. Joh. c. 50.

PARENS PATRIÆ. Father of his country; parent of the country. In England, the king. In the United States, the state, as a sovereign—referring to the sovereign power of guardianship over persons under disability; In re Turner, 94 Kan. 115, 145 P. 871, 872, Ann.Cas.1916E, 1022; such as minors, and insane and incompetent persons; McIntosh v. Dill, 86 Okl. 1, 205 P. 917, 925.

PARENT. The lawful father or the mother of a person. Appeal of Gibson, 154 Mass. 378; 28 N.E. 296; Ellis v. Hewitt, 15 Ga.App. 693, 84 S.E. 185, 187; In re Tombo, 86 Misc. 361, 149 N.Y.S. 219, 221; One who procreates, begets, or brings forth offspring. McDonald v. Texas Employers' Ins. Ass'n, Tex.Civ.App., 267 S.W. 1074, 1075.

This word is distinguished from "ancestors" in including only the immediate progenitors of the person, while the latter embraces his more remote relatives in the ascending line. The word "parents" should therefore not ordinarily be construed to include grandparents. In re Spooner's Estate, 172 Wis. 174, 177 N.W. 598, 600. But by the civil law, grandfathers and grandmothers, and other ascendants, were, in certain cases, considered parents. *Dict. de Jur. Parents;* Com. v. Anderson, 1 Ashm. (Pa.) 55; 2 Kent 159; 5 East 223.

The term literally can apply only to a father or mother related by blood, including the parent of an illegitimate child; Commonwealth v. Wibner, 73 Pa.Super.Ct. 349, 351; and excluding a stepfather or stepmother or one standing in loco parentis; State v. District Court of Second Judicial Dist. of Montana in and for Silver Bow County, 66 Mont. 427, 213 P. 802, 804; State v. Barger, 14 Ohio App. 127, 128; In re Remske, 95 Misc. 330, 160 N.Y.S. 715, 716; Coakley v. Coakley, 216 Mass. 71, 102 N.E. 930, 932, Ann. Cas.1915A, 867. In statutes, however, the word is commonly construed as including a stepmother; State v. Juvenile Court of Ramsey County, 163 Minn. 312, 204 N.W.

21, 22, (see, also, Sovereign Camp, W. O. W., v. Cole, 124 Miss. 299, 86 So. 802, 804); and likewise adopting parents; Ransom v. New York C. & St. L. Ry. Co., 93 Ohio St. 223, 112 N.E. 586, L.R.A.1916E, 704; Commonwealth v. Kirk, 212 Ky. 646, 279 S.W. 1091, 1092, 44 A.L.R. 816; In re Yates' Estate, 108 Kan. 721, 196 P. 1077; but not as including the father of an illegitimate child; People v. Rupp, 219 Ill.App. 269, 271; Howard v. U. S., D.C.Ky., 2 F.2d 170, 173; Ex parte Newsome, 212 Ala. 168, 102 So. 216, 218; People v. Fitzgerald, 167 App.Div. 85, 152 N.Y.S. 641, 643; State ex rel. Canfield v. Porterfield, 222 Mo.App. 553, 292 S.W. 85, 86.

PARENTAGE. Kindred in the direct ascending line. See 2 Bouv. Inst. n. 1955.

PARENTELA. The sum of those persons who trace descent from one ancestor. 2 Poll. & Maitl. 296.

In old English law. Parentela, or *de parentela se tollere*, signified a renunciation of one's kindred and family. This was, according to ancient custom, done in open court, before the judge, and in the presence of twelve men, who made oath that they believed it was done for a just cause. We read of it in the laws of Henry I. After such abjuration, the person was incapable of inheriting anything from any of his relations, etc. Enc. Lond.

PARENTHESIS. Part of a sentence occurring in the middle thereof, and inclosed between marks like ( ), the omission of which part would not injure the *grammatical* construction of the rest of the sentence. Wharton; In re Schilling, 53 Fed. 81, 3 C.C.A. 440. A word, phrase, or sentence, by way of comment or explanation, inserted in, or attached to, a sentence which would be grammatically complete without it. State v. Morgan, 133 La. 1033, 63 So. 509, 512.

PARENTICIDE. One who murders a parent; also the crime so committed.

PARENTUM EST LIBEROS ALERE ATIAM NOTHOS. It is the duty of parents to support their children even when illegitimate. Lofft, 222.

PARERGON. One work executed in the intervals of another; a subordinate task. Particularly, the name of a work on the Canons, in great repute, by Ayliffe.

PARES. Lat. A person's peers or equals; as the jury for the trial of causes, who were originally the vassals or tenants of the lord, being the equals or peers of the parties litigant; and, as the lord's vassals judged each other in the lord's courts, so the sovereign's vassals, or the lords themselves, judged each other in the sovereign's courts. 3 Bl. Comm. 349.

PARES CURIÆ. Peers of the court. Vassals who were bound to attend the lord's court.

PARES REGNI. Peers of the realm. Spelman.

PARESIS. In medical jurisprudence. Progressive general paralysis, involving or leading to the form of insanity known as *"dementia paralytica."* Popularly, but not very correctly, called "softening of the brain." See Insanity.

The term is applied to a group of mental and bodily symptoms, developing usually late in life and as a result of previous syphilis. The condition differs from the various insanities, in that definite alterations of the surface of the brain and its membranes are found, in the form of chronic inflammation. Loss of memory, passionate outbursts, delusions of grandeur, restlessness and insomnia, with final absolute dementia, are the chief mental symptoms, while physically muscular weakness, tremor, particularly of the lips and tongue, ataxia, and various convulsive seizures are seen. Losh v. Winters Nat. Bank & Trust Co., Ohio App., 46 N.E.2d 443, 448.

PARI CAUSA. Lat. With equal right; upon an equal footing; equivalent in rights or claims.

PARI DELICTO. Lat. In equal fault; in a similar offense or crime; equal in guilt or in legal fault. See In Pari Delicto.

PARI MATERIA. Lat. Of the same matter; on the same subject; as, laws *pari materia* must be construed with reference to each other. Bac.Abr. "Statute," I, 3; Dupont v. Mills, Del., 196 A. 168, 177, 119 A.L.R. 174.

PARI MUTUEL. A mutual stake or wager; a betting pool. Utah State Fair Ass'n v. Green, 68 Utah, 251, 249 P. 1016, 1028. See, also, Pompano Horse Club v. State, 93 Fla. 415, 111 So. 801, 813, 52 A.L.R. 51. A form of betting on horses or dogs in which those who bet on winner share total stakes less a small percent to the management. Donovan v. Eastern Racing Ass'n, 324 Mass. 393, 86 N.E.2d 903, 906.

PARI PASSU. Lat. By an equal progress; equably; ratably; without preference. Coote, Mortg. 56. Used especially of creditors who, in marshalling assets, are entitled to receive out of the same fund without any precedence over each other.

PARI PASSU BONDS. A name given in Scotland to certain bonds secured upon lands which share an equal benefit of the security. Where several securities are created over the same lands by separate bonds and dispositions in security, they would ordinarily have priority according to the date of registration of the sasine or bond, as the case may be. If it is intended to have them rank as *pari passu*, it is usual to insert a clause in each bond declaring that they shall be so ranked without regard to their priority of registration. 9 Jurid. Rev. 74.

PARI RATIONE. Lat. For the like reason; by like mode of reasoning.

PARIA COPULANTUR PARIBUS. Like things unite with like. Bac. Max.

PARIBUS SENTENTIIS REUS ABSOLVITUR. Where the opinions are equal, [where the court is equally divided,] the defendant is acquitted. 4 Inst. 64.

PARIENTES. In Spanish law. Relations. White, New Recop. b. 1, tit. 7, c. 5, § 2.

PARIES. Lat. In the civil law. A wall. *Paries est, sive murus, sive maceria est.* Dig. 50, 16, 157.

PARIES COMMUNIS. A common wall; a party-wall. Dig. 29, 2, 39.

PARIS, DECLARATION OF. See Declaration.

PARISH. In English ecclesiastical law. A circuit of ground, committed to the charge of one parson or vicar, or other minister having cure of souls therein. 1 Bl. Comm. 111. Wilson v. State, 34 Ohio St. 199. The precinct of a parish church, and the particular charge of a secular priest. Cowell. An ecclesiastical division of a town or district, subject to the ministry of one pastor. Brande.

In New England. A division of a town, originally territorial, but which now constitutes a *quasi*-corporation, consisting of those connected with a certain church. Weston v. Hunt, 2 Mass. 501. Synonymous with church and used in the same sense as society. Ayres v. Weed, 16 Conn. 299. A corporation established for the maintenance of public worship, which may be coterminous with a town, or include only part of it. A precinct or parish is a corporation established solely for the purpose of maintaining public worship, and its powers are limited to that object. It may raise money for building and keeping in repair its meetinghouse and supporting its minister, but for no other purpose. A town is a civil and political corporation, established for municipal purposes. They may both subsist together in the same territory, and be composed of the same persons. Milford v. Godfrey, 1 Pick. (Mass.) 91.

In Pennsylvania the term has no legal signification and is used merely in its general sense. If used there in ecclesiastical divisions, it has just such importance and significance as may be given it under ecclesiastical regulations. In re St. Casimir's Polish Roman Catholic Church of Shenandoah, 273 Pa. 494, 117 A. 219, 220.

In Louisiana. A territorial division of the state corresponding to what is elsewhere called a "county." Sherman v. Parish of Vermillion, 51 La.Ann. 880, 25 So. 538; Attorney General v. Detroit Common Council, 112 Mich. 148, 70 N.W. 450, 37 L.R.A. 211.

PARISH APPRENTICE. In English law. The children of parents unable to maintain them may, by law, be apprenticed, by the guardians or overseers of their parish, to such persons as may be willing to receive them as apprentices. Such children are called "parish apprentices." 2 Steph. Comm. 230.

PARISH CHURCH. This expression has various significations. It is applied sometimes to a select body of Christians, forming a local spiritual association, and sometimes to the building in which the public worship of the inhabitants of a parish is celebrated; but the true legal notion of a parochial church is a consecrated place, having attached to it the rights of burial and the administration of the sacraments. Story, J., Pawlet v. Clark, 9 Cranch, 326, 3 L.Ed. 735.

PARISH CLERK. In English law. An officer, in former times often in holy orders, and appointed to officiate at the altar; now his duty consists chiefly in making responses in church to the minister. By common law he has a freehold in his office, but it seems now to be falling into desuetude. 2 Steph. Comm. 700; Mozley & Whiteley.

PARISH CONSTABLE. A petty constable exercising his functions within a given parish. Mozley & Whiteley. See Constable.

PARISH COURT. The name of a court established in each parish in Louisiana, and corresponding to the county courts or common pleas courts in the other states. It has a limited civil jurisdiction, besides general probate powers.

PARISH OFFICERS. Church-wardens, overseers, and constables.

PARISH PRIESTS. In English law. The parson; a minister who holds a parish as a benefice. If the predial tithes are appropriated, he is called "rector;" if impropriated, "vicar." Wharton.

PARISHIONERS. Members of a parish. In England, for many purposes they form a body politic.

PARITOR. A beadle; a summoner to the courts of civil law.

PARITY. Equality. Arkansas State Highway Commission v. Otis & Co., 182 Ark. 242, 31 S.W.2d 427, 431.

PARIUM EADEM EST RATIO, IDEM JUS. Of things equal, the reason is the same, and the same is the law.

PARIUM JUDICIUM. The judgment of peers; trial by a jury of one's peers or equals.

PARK, *v.* Voluntarily and temporarily to leave an automobile, especially on a street or highway, when not in use. Kastler v. Tures, 191 Wis. 120, 210 N.W. 415, 417; Ex parte Corvey, 220 Mo.App. 602, 287 S.W. 879, 881; Blashfield, Cyc. of Automobile Law and Prac., Perm. Ed., §§ 1191–1212, 2160.50, 5963.

PARK, *n.* In American law. An inclosed pleasure-ground in or near a city, set apart for the recreation of the public. Riverside v. MacLain, 210 Ill. 308, 71 N.E. 408, 66 L.R.A. 288, 102 Am.St. Rep. 164; People v. Green, 52 How. Prac., N.Y., 440; Archer v. Salinas City, 93 Cal. 43, 28 P. 839, 16 L.R.A. 145; Ehmen v. Gothenburg, 50 Neb. 715, 70 N.W. 237. A pleasure ground for the recreation of the public to promote its health and enjoyment. Booth v. City of Minneapolis, 163 Minn. 223, 203 N.W. 625, 626; Williams v. Gallatin, 229 N.Y. 248, 128 N.E. 121, 122, 18 A.L.R. 1238.

A piece of ground enclosed for purposes of pleasure, exercise, amusement, or ornament. Perrin v. R. Co., 36 N. Y. 120; Blank v. Browne, 216 N.Y.S. 664, 668, 217 App.Div. 624. A place for the resort of the public for recreation, air, and light; a place open for everyone. Price v. Plainfield, 40 N.J.L. 613; Kennedy v. City of Nevada, 222 Mo.App.

459, 281 S.W. 56, 58; Baird v. Board of Recreation Com'rs of Village of South Orange, 108 N.J.Eq. 91, 154 A. 204, 208.

A detached tract of ground set apart and maintained for public use, generally of quite sizable proportions devoted to purposes of ornamentation and recreation, usually platted out with trees and ornamented in a way pleasing to the eye as well as furnishing an opportunity for open-air recreation. Kupelian v. Andrews, 233 N.Y. 278, 135 N.E. 502, 503; Ramstad v. Carr, 31 N.D. 504, 154 N.W. 195, 200, L.R.A.1916B, 1160; Los Angeles County v. Dodge, 51 Cal.App. 492, 197 P. 403, 409.

As applied to pleasure grounds and spaces or open places for public use or public recreation owned by towns, the term is largely one of quite modern usage, and until recent years such places were in popular speech spoken of as "squares" and "commons." Woodward v. City of Des Moines, 182 Iowa 1102, 165 N.W. 313, 314.

In English law. A tract of inclosed ground privileged for keeping wild beasts of the chase, particularly deer; an inclosed chase extending only over a man's own grounds. 2 Bl. Comm. 38; 13 Car. II, c. 10. A pound. Reg. Orig. 166; Cowell.

PARK-BOTE. To be quit of inclosing a park or any part thereof.

PARKER. A park-keeper.

PARKING. In municipal law and administration. A strip of land, lying either in the middle of the street or in the space between the building line and the sidewalk, or between the sidewalk and the driveway, intended to be kept as a park-like space, that is, not built upon, but beautified with turf, trees, flowerbeds, etc. See Downing v. Des Moines, 124 Iowa 289, 99 N.W. 1066. See, also, Parkway.

PARKING METER. A clock set on a post, measuring time of parking. It provides mechanical assistance in the enforcement of parking limitation. Cassidy v. City of Waterbury, 130 Conn. 237, 33 A.2d 142, 144; Blashfield, Cyc. of Automobile Law and Prac., Perm. Ed., § 78.10.

PARKING PLACE. A place where motor vehicles may be left parked or standing and removed by the owner at pleasure. Mobile Light & R. Co., 211 Ala. 525, 101 So. 177, 178, 34 A.L.R. 921.

PARKWAY. An ornamental part of a street which may be used for recreation purposes. Kupelian v. Andrews, 233 N.Y. 278, 135 N.E. 502. In that sense, substantially synonymous with "parking" (*q. v.*). Also, an attractive street or highway, ornamented with shrubbery and the like. Municipal Securities Corporation v. Kansas City, 265 Mo. 252, 177 S.W. 856, 860.

PARLE HILL, or PARLING HILL. A hill where courts were anciently held. Cowell.

PARLIAMENT. The supreme legislative assembly of Great Britain and Ireland, consisting of the king or queen and the three estates of the realm, viz., the lords spiritual, the lords temporal, and the commons. 1 Bl. Comm. 153.

High Court of Parliament. In English law. The English parliament, as composed of the house of peers and house of commons; or the house of lords sitting in its judicial capacity.

PARLIAMENTARY. Relating or belonging to, connected with, enacted by or proceeding from, or characteristic of, the English parliament in particular, or any legislative body in general.

PARLIAMENTARY AGENTS. Persons who act as solicitors in promoting and carrying private bills through parliament. They are usually attorneys or solicitors, but they do not usually confine their practice to this particular department. Brown.

PARLIAMENTARY COMMITTEE. A committee of members of the house of peers or of the house of commons, appointed by either house for the purpose of making inquiries, by the examination of witnesses or otherwise, into matters which could not be conveniently inquired into by the whole house. Wharton.

PARLIAMENTARY LAW. The general body of enacted rules and recognized usages which governs the procedure of legislative assemblies and other deliberative bodies.

PARLIAMENTARY TAXES. See Tax.

PARLIAMENTUM. L. Lat. A legislative body in general or the English parliament in particular.

PARLIAMENTUM DIABOLICUM. A parliament held at Coventry, 38 Hen. VI., wherein Edward, Earl of March, (afterwards King Edward IV.,) and many of the chief nobility were attainted, was so called; but the acts then made were annulled by the succeeding parliament. Jacob.

PARLIAMENTUM INDOCTUM. Unlearned or lack-learning parliament. A name given to a parliament held at Coventry in the sixth year of Henry IV. under an ordinance requiring that no lawyer should be chosen knight, citizen, or burgess; "by reason whereof," says Sir Edward Coke, "this parliament was fruitless, and never a good law made thereat." 4 Inst. 48; 1 Bl. Comm. 177.

PARLIAMENTUM INSANUM. A parliament assembled at Oxford, 41 Hen. III., so styled from the madness of their proceedings, and because the lords came with armed men to it, and contentions grew very high between the king, lords, and commons, whereby many extraordinary things were done. Jacob.

PARLIAMENTUM RELIGIOSORUM. In most convents there has been a common room into which the brethren withdrew for conversation; conferences there being termed *"parliamentum."* Likewise, the societies of the two temples, or inns of court, call that assembly of the benchers or governors wherein they confer upon the common affairs of their several houses a "parliament." Jacob.

PAROCHIA EST LOCUS QUO DEGIT POPULUS ALICUJUS ECCLESIÆ. 5 Coke, 67. A parish is a place in which the population of a certain church resides.

PAROCHIAL. Relating or belonging to a parish.

PAROCHIAL CHAPELS. In English law. Places of public worship in which the rites of sacrament and sepulture are performed.

PAROL. A word; speech; hence, oral or verbal; expressed or evidenced by speech only; not expressed by writing; not expressed by sealed instrument.

The pleadings in an action are also, in old law French, denominated the "parol," because they were formerly actual *viva voce* pleadings in court, and not mere written allegations, as at present. Brown.

As to parol "Agreement," "Arrest," "Demurrer," "Lease," and "Promise," see those titles.

PAROL EVIDENCE. Oral or verbal evidence; that which is given by word of mouth; the ordinary kind of evidence, given by witnesses in court. 3 Bl.Comm. 369. In a particular sense, and with reference to contracts, deeds, wills, and other writings, parol evidence is the same as extraneous evidence or evidence *aliunde*. See, also, Aliunde; Extraneous Evidence; Oral Evidence.

PAROL EVIDENCE RULE. Under this rule, when parties put their agreement in writing, all previous oral agreements merge in the writing and a contract as written cannot be modified or changed by parol evidence, in the absence of a plea of mistake or fraud in the preparation of the writing. Russell v. Halteman's Adm'x, 287 Ky. 404, 153 S.W.2d 899, 904. But rule does not forbid a resort to parol evidence not inconsistent with the matters stated in the writing. Elkins v. Super-Cold Southwest Co., Tex.Civ.App., 157 S.W. 2d 946, 947.

Under this rule, parol or extrinsic evidence is not admissible to add to, subtract from, vary or contradict judicial or official records or documents, or written instruments which dispose of property or are contractual in nature, and which are valid, complete, unambiguous and unaffected by accident or mistake. Wheeler, Kelly & Hagny Inv. Co. v. Curts, 158 Kan. 312, 147 P.2d 737, 740.

PAROLE. In military law. A promise given by a prisoner of war, when he has leave to depart from custody, that he will return at the time appointed, unless discharged. Webster.

An engagement by a prisoner of war, upon being set at liberty, that he will not again take up arms against the government by whose forces he was captured, either for a limited period or while hostilities continue.

In criminal law. A conditional release; condition being that, if prisoner makes good, he will receive an absolute discharge from balance of sentence, but, if he does not, he will be returned to serve unexpired time. In re Eddinger, 236 Mich. 668, 211 N.W. 54, 55; Crooks v. Sanders, 123 S.C. 28, 115 S.E. 760, 762, 28 A.L.R. 940; Board of Prison Com'rs v. De Moss, 157 Ky. 289, 163 S.W. 183, 187; Duehay v. Thompson, C.C.A. Wash., 223 F. 305, 307; In re Sutton, 50 Mont. 88, 145 P. 6, 8, Ann.Cas.1917A, 1223. Release of convict from imprisonment on certain conditions to be observed by him, and suspension of sentence during liberty thus granted. Ex parte Foster, 60 Okl.Cr.App. 50, 61 P.2d 37, 39.

PAROLS DE LEY. L. Fr. Words of law; technical words.

PAROLS FONT PLEA. Words make the plea. 5 Mod. 458.

PARQUET. In French law. The magistrates who are charged with the conduct of proceedings in criminal cases and misdemeanors. That part of the *bourse* which is reserved for stock-brokers.

PARRICIDE. The crime of killing one's father; also a person guilty of killing his father.

PARRICIDIUM. Lat. In the civil law. Parricide; the murder of a parent. Dig. 48, 9, 9.

PARS. Lat. A part; a party to a deed, action, or legal proceeding.

PARS ENITIA. In old English law. The privilege or portion of the eldest daughter in the partition of lands by lot.

PARS GRAVATA. In old practice. A party aggrieved; the party aggrieved. Hardr. 50; 3 Leon. 237.

PARS PRO TOTO. Part for the whole; the name of a part used to represent the whole; as the roof for the house, ten spears for ten armed men, etc.

PARS RATIONABILIS. That part of a man's goods which the law gave to his widow and children. 2 Bl.Comm. 492.

PARS REA. A party defendant. St. Marlbr. c. 13.

PARS VISCERUM MATRIS. Part of the bowels of the mother; *i. e.*, an unborn child.

PARSON. The rector of a church; one that has full possession of all the rights of a parochial church. The appellation of "parson," however it may be depreciated by familiar, clownish, and indiscriminate use, is the most legal, most beneficial, and most honorable title that a parish priest can enjoy, because such a one, Sir Edward Coke observes, and he only, is said *vicem seu personam ecclesiæ gerere*, (to represent and bear the person of the church.) 1 Bl.Comm. 384.

PARSON IMPARSONEE. In English law. A clerk or parson in full possession of a benefice. Cowell.

PARSON MORTAL. A rector instituted and inducted for his own life. But any collegiate or conventional body, to whom a church was forever appropriated, was termed *"persona immortalis."* Wharton.

PARSONAGE. A certain portion of lands, tithes, and offerings, established by law, for the maintenance of the minister who has the cure of souls. Tomlins.

The word is more generally used for the house set apart for the residence of the minister. Mozley & Whiteley. See Wells' Estate v. Congregational Church, 63 Vt. 116, 21 A. 270; Everett v. First Presbyterian Church, 53 N.J.Eq. 500, 32 A. 747; State v. Kittle, 87 W.Va. 526, 105 S.E. 775, 776; St. Joseph's Church v. City of Detroit, 189 Mich. 408, 155 N.W. 588, 590.

PART. An integral portion, something essentially belonging to a larger whole; that which together with another or others makes up a whole. First-Mechanics Nat. Bank of Trenton v. Norris, 134 N.J.Eq. 229, 34 A.2d 746, 749. A portion, share, or purpart. One of two duplicate originals of a conveyance or covenant, the other being called "counterpart." Also, in composition, partial or incomplete; as part payment, part performance. Cairo v. Bross, 9 Ill.App. 406.

PART AND PERTINENT. In the Scotch law of conveyancing. Formal words equivalent to the English "appurtenances." Bell.

As to part "Owner," "Payment," and "Performance," see those titles.

PARTAGE. In French law. A division made between co-proprietors of a particular estate held by them in common. It is the operation by means of which the goods of a succession are divided among the co-heirs; while licitation (*q. v.*) is an adjudication to the highest bidder of objects which are not divisible. Duverger.

PARTE INAUDITA. Lat. One side being unheard. Spoken of any action which is taken *ex parte.*

PARTE NON COMPARENTE. Lat. The party not having appeared. The condition of a cause called "default."

PARTE QUACUMQUE INTEGRANTE SUBLATA, TOLLITUR TOTUM. An integral part being taken away, the whole is taken away. 8 Coke, 41.

PARTEM ALIQUAM RECTE INTELLIGERE NEMO POTEST, ANTEQUAM TOTUM, ITERUM ATQUE ITERUM, PERLEGERIT. 3 Coke, 52. No one can rightly understand any part until he has read the whole again and again.

PARTES FINIS NIHIL HABUERUNT. In old pleading. The parties to the fine had nothing; that is, had no estate which could be conveyed by it. A plea to a fine which had been levied by a stranger. 2 Bl.Comm. 357; 1 P.Wms. 520.

PARTIAL. Relating to or constituting a part; not complete; not entire or universal; not general or total. United States Fidelity & Guaranty Co. v. Baker, Tex.Civ.App., 65 S.W.2d 344, 346.

PARTIAL ACCOUNT. An account of an executor, administrator, guardian, etc., not exhibiting his entire dealings with the estate or fund from his appointment to final settlement, but covering only a portion of the time or of the estate. Marshall v. Coleman, 187 Ill. 556, 58 N.E. 628.

PARTIAL AVERAGE. Another name for particular average. Peters v. Warren Ins. Co., 19 Fed. Cas. 370. See Average.

PARTIAL DEPENDENCY. Test as to existence of such dependency for purpose of workmen's compensation is whether contributions were relied on by claimants to aid and maintain them in present position in life and whether they were to substantial degree depending on support or aid of employee at time of death. Ritzman v. Industrial Commission, 353 Ill. 34, 186 N.E. 545, 546. Federal Underwriters Exchange v. Hinkle, Tex.Civ.App., 187 S.W.2d 122, 124.

PARTIAL EVICTION. That which takes place when the possessor is deprived of only a portion of his rights in the premises.

PARTIAL EVIDENCE. That which goes to establish a detached fact, in a series tending to the fact in dispute.

It may be received, subject to be rejected as incompetent, unless connected with the fact in dispute by proof of other facts; for example, on an issue of title to real property, evidence of the continued possession of a remote occupant is partial, for it is of a detached fact, which may or may not be afterwards connected with the fact in dispute. Code Civ.Proc.Cal. § 1834; Or. Laws 1920, § 696 (Code 1930, § 9–111).

PARTIAL INSANITY. Mental unsoundness always existing, although only occasionally manifest; monomania. 3 Add. 79.

PARTIAL LOSS. A loss of a part of a thing or of its value, or any damage not amounting (actually or constructively) to its entire destruction; as contrasted with *total* loss.

Partial loss is one in which the damage done to the thing insured is not so complete as to amount to a total loss, either actual or constructive. In every such case the underwriter is liable to pay such proportion of the sum which would be payable on total loss as the damage sustained by the subject of insurance bears to the whole value at the time of insurance. 2 Steph.Comm. 132, 133; Crump. Ins. § 331; Mozley & Whiteley. Partial loss implies a damage sustained by the ship or cargo, which falls upon the respective owners of the property so damaged; and, when happening from any peril insured against by the policy, the owners are to be indemnified by the underwriters, unless in cases excepted by the express terms of the policy. Padelford v. Boardman, 4 Mass. 548; Globe Ins. Co. v. Sherlock, 25 Ohio St. 65; Willard v. Insurance Co., 30 Mo. 35.

PARTIAL PAYMENT. See Payment.

PARTIAL VERDICT. See Verdict.

PARTIARIUS. Lat. In Roman law. A legatee who was entitled, by the directions of the will, to receive a share or portion of the inheritance left to the heir.

PARTIBLE LANDS. Lands which might be divided; lands held in gavelkind. See 2 Poll. & Maitl. 268, 271; Gavelkind.

PARTICEPS. Lat. A participant; a sharer; anciently, a part owner, or parcener.

PARTICEPS CRIMINIS. A participant in a crime; an accomplice. One who shares or co-operates in a criminal offense, tort, or fraud. Alberger v. White, 117 Mo. 347, 23 S.W. 92; State v. Fox, 70 N.J.L. 353, 57 A. 270.

PARTICIPATE. To receive or have a part or share of; to partake of; experience in common with others; to have or enjoy a part or share in common with others; partake; as to "participate" in a discussion. To take a part in; as to participate in joys or sorrows. Bew v. Travelers' Ins. Co., 95 N.J.L. 533, 112 A. 859, 860, 14 A.L.R. 983. To take equal shares and proportions; to share or divide. 6 Ch. 696. *Participate in an estate.* To take as tenants in common. 28 Beav. 266.

PARTICIPES PLURES SUNT QUASI UNUM CORPUS IN EO QUOD UNUM JUS HABENT, ET OPORTET QUOD CORPUS SIT INTEGRUM, ET QUOD IN NULLA PARTE SIT DEFECTUS. Co. Litt. 4. Many parceners are as one body, inasmuch as they have one right, and it is necessary that the body be perfect, and that there be a defect in no part.

PARTICULA. A small piece of land.

PARTICULAR. Relating to a part or portion of anything; separate; sole; single; individual; specific; local; comprising a part only; partial in extent; not universal. Opposed to general. State v. Patterson, 60 Idaho 67, 88 P.2d 493, 497. Minneapolis Steel & Machinery Co. v. Casey Land Agency, 51 N.D. 832, 201 N.W. 172, 175.

As to particular "Average," "Custom," "Estate," "Malice," and "Partnership," see those titles.

PARTICULAR LIEN. A particular lien is a right to retain a thing for some charge or claim growing out of, or connected with, the identical thing.

Right to retain property of another on account of labor employed or money expended on that specific property, and such lien may arise by implication of law, usages of a trade, or by express contract, General Motors Acceptance Corporation v. Vaughn, 358 Ill. 541, 193 N.E. 483, 485.

PARTICULAR STATEMENT. This term, in use in Pennsylvania, denotes a statement which a plaintiff may be required to file, exhibiting in detail the items of his claim, (or its nature, if single,) with the dates and sums. It is a species of declaration, but is informal and not required to be methodical. Dixon v. Sturgeon, 6 Serg. & R. (Pa.) 28.

PARTICULAR TENANT. The tenant of a particular estate. 2 Bl.Comm. 274. See Estate.

PARTICULARITY, in a pleading, affidavit, or the like, is the detailed statement of particulars.

PARTICULARS. The details of a claim, or the separate items of an account. When these are stated in an orderly form, for the information of a defendant, the statement is called a "bill of particulars," (*q. v.*).

PARTICULARS OF BREACHES AND OBJECTIONS. In an action brought, in England, for the infringement of letters patent, the plaintiff is bound to deliver with his declaration (now with his statement of claim) particulars (*i. e.*, details) of the breaches which he complains of. Sweet.

PARTICULARS OF CRIMINAL CHARGES. A prosecutor, when a charge is general, is frequently ordered to give the defendant a statement of the acts charged, which is called, in England, the "particulars" of the charges.

PARTICULARS OF SALE. When property such as land, houses, shares, reversions, etc., is to be sold by auction, it is usually described in a document called the "particulars," copies of which are distributed among intending bidders. They should fairly and accurately describe the property. Dart, Vend. 113; 1 Dav. Conv. 511.

PARTIDA. Span. Part; a part. See Las Partidas.

PARTIES. The persons who take part in the performance of any act, or who are directly interested in any affair, contract, or conveyance, or who are actively concerned in the prosecution and defense of any legal proceeding. U. S. to Use of Edward Hines Lumber Co. v. Henderlong, C.C.Ind., 102 F. 2; Robbins v. Chicago, 4 Wall. 672, 18 L. Ed. 427; Green v. Bogue, 15 S.Ct. 975, 158 U.S. 478, 39 L.Ed. 1061; Hughes v. Jones, 116 N.Y. 67, 22 N. E. 446, 5 L.R.A. 637, 15 Am.St.Rep. 386. See also Party.

In the Roman civil law, the parties were designated as *"actor"* and *"reus."* In the common law, they are called "plaintiff" and "defendant;" in real actions, "demandant" and "tenant;" in equity, "complainant" or "plaintiff" and "defendant;" in Scotch law, "pursuer" and "defender;" in admiralty practice, "libelant" and "respondent;" in appeals, "appellant" and "respondent," sometimes, "plaintiff in error" and "defendant in error;" in criminal proceedings, "prosecutor" and "prisoner."

Classification

Formal, or *proper* parties are those who have no interest in the controversy between the immediate litigants, but have an interest in the subject-matter which may be conveniently settled in the suit, and thereby prevent further litigation; they may be made parties or not, at the option of the complainant. Chadbourne v. Coe, 2 C.C.A. 327, 51 F. 479; Sexton v. Sutherland, 37 N.D. 500, 164 N.W. 278, 281; Consolidated Gas Co. of New York v. Newton, D.C.N.Y., 256 F. 238, 245; State v. Municipal Savings & Loan Co., 111 Ohio St. 178, 144 N.E. 736, 740. *Necessary* parties are those parties who have such an interest in the subject-matter of a suit in equity, or whose rights are so involved in the controversy, that no complete and effective decree can be made, disposing of the matters in issue and dispensing complete justice, unless they are before the court in such a manner as to entitle them to be heard in vindication or protection of their interests. Chandler v. Ward, 188 Ill. 322, 58 N.E. 919; Chadbourne v. Coe, 2 C. C.A. 327, 51 F. 480; Burrill v. Garst, 19 R.I. 38, 31 A. 436; Castle v. Madison, 113 Wis. 346, 89 N. W. 156; Iowa County Sup'rs v. Mineral Point R.

Co., 24 Wis. 132. *Nominal* parties are those who are joined as plaintiffs or defendants, not because they have any real interest in the subject-matter or because any relief is demanded as against them, but merely because the technical rules of pleading require their presence on the record. It should be noted that some courts make a further distinction between "necessary" parties and "indispensable" parties. Thus, it is said that the supreme court of the United States divides parties in equity suits into three different classes: (1) Formal parties, who have no interest in the controversy between the immediate litigants, but have such an interest in the subject-matter as may be conveniently settled in the suit, and thereby prevent further litigation; (2) necessary parties, who have an interest in the controversy, but whose interests are separable from those of the parties before the court, and will not be directly affected by a decree which does complete and full justice between them; (3) indispensable parties, who not only have an interest in the subject-matter of the controversy, but an interest of such a nature that a final decree cannot be made without either affecting their interests or leaving the controversy in such a condition that its final determination may be wholly inconsistent with equity and good conscience. Hicklin v. Marco, 6 C.C.A.10, 56 F. 552, citing Shields v. Barrow, 17 How. 139, 15 L.Ed. 158; Ribon v. Railroad Co., 16 Wall. 450, 21 L.Ed. 367; Williams v. Bankhead, 19 Wall. 571, 22 L.Ed. 184; Kendig v. Dean, 97 U.S. 425, 24 L.Ed. 1061; Barmore v. Darragh, Tex.Civ.App., 227 S.W. 522, 523; Jones v Bryant, 204 Ill.App. 609; Sexton v. Sutherland, 37 N.D. 500, 164 N.W. 278, 281; Hughes v. Yates, 195 Ind. 182, 144 N.E. 863, 864; Hyams v. Old Dominion Co., 113 Me. 337, 93 A. 899; Tupelo Townsite Co. v. Cook, 52 Okl. 703, 153 P. 164, 167; Shedd v. American Maize Products Co., 60 Ind. App. 146, 108 N.E. 610, 621.

PARTIES AND PRIVIES. Parties to a deed or contract are those with whom the deed or contract is actually made or entered into. By the term "privies," as applied to contracts, is frequently meant those between whom the contract is mutually binding, although not literally parties to such contract. Thus, in the case of a lease, the lessor and lessee are both parties and privies, the contract being literally made between the two, and also being mutually binding; but, if the lessee assign his interest to a third party, then a privity arises between the assignee and the original lessor, although such assignee is not literally a party to the original lease. Brown.

PARTIES IN INTEREST. Under General Order 6 (11 U.S.C.A. § 53) respecting transfer of bankruptcy proceedings for the greatest convenience of "parties in interest," the term "parties in interest" includes not only general creditors, but prior and secured creditors as well, and also the bankrupt and every other party, whose pecuniary interest is affected by the proceedings. In re Devonian Mineral Spring Co., D.C.Ohio, 272 F. 527, 532.

PARTITIO. Lat. In the civil law. Partition; division. This word did not always signify *dimidium*, a dividing into halves. Dig. 50, 16, 164, 1.

PARTITIO LEGATA. A testamentary partition. This took place where the testator, in his will, directed the heir to divide the inheritance and deliver a designated portion thereof to a named legatee. See Mackeld. Rom. Law, §§ 781, 785.

PARTITION. The dividing of lands held by joint tenants, coparceners, or tenants in common, into distinct portions, so that they may hold them in severalty. And, in a less technical sense, any division of real or personal property between co-owners or co-proprietors. Meacham v. Meacham, 91 Tenn. 532, 19 S.W. 757; Hudgins v. Sansom, 72 Tex. 229, 10 S.W. 104; Weiser v. Weiser, 5 Watts, Pa., 279, 30 Am.Dec. 313; Thomason v. Thompson, 123 Okl. 218, 253 P. 99, 102; Gillespie v. Jackson, 153 Tenn. 150, 281 S.W. 929, 932.

Partition does not create or convey a new or additional title or interest but merely severs the unity of possession. Noble v. Beach, 21 Cal.2d 91, 130 P.2d 426, 430. Cleveland v. Milner, 141 Tex. 120, 170 S.W.2d 472, 475.

Owelty of partition. See Owelty.

Partition, deed of. In conveyancing. A species of primary or original conveyance between two or more joint tenants, coparceners, or tenants in common, by which they divide the lands so held among them in severalty, each taking a distinct part. 2 Bl.Comm. 323, 324.

Partition of a Succession. The partition of a succession is the division of the effects of which the succession is composed, among all the co-heirs, according to their respective rights. Partition is voluntary or judicial. It is voluntary when it is made among all the co-heirs present and of age, and by their mutual consent. It is judicial when it is made by the authority of the court, and according to the formalities prescribed by law. Every partition is either definitive or provisional. Definitive partition is that which is made in a permanent and irrevocable manner. Provisional partition is that which is made provisionally, either of certain things before the rest can be divided, or even of everything that is to be divided, when the parties are not in a situation to make an irrevocable partition. Civ. Code La. art. 1293, *et seq.*

PARTNER. A member of copartnership or firm; one who has united with others to form a partnership in business. See Partnership.

Parties intending to do a thing which in law constitutes partnership are "partners," whether their purpose was to create or avoid relation. Pearl Bowling & Co. v. Hensley & Hensley, 259 Ky. 651, 83 S.W.2d 31, 32.

Dormant Partners

Those whose names are not known or do not appear as partners, but who nevertheless are silent partners, and partake of the profits, and thereby become partners, either absolutely to all intents and purposes, or at all events in respect to third parties. Dormant partners, in strictness of language, mean those who are merely passive in the firm, whether known or unknown, in contradistinction to those who are active and conduct the business of the firm, as principals. Story, Partn. § 80; Rowland v. Estes, 190 Pa. 111, 42 A. 528; National Bank of Salem v. Thomas, 47 N.Y. 15; Metcalf v. Officer, C.C.Iowa, 2 F. 640; Pooley v. Driver, 5 Ch.Div. 458.

Liquidating Partner

The partner who, upon the dissolution or insolvency of the firm, is appointed to settle its accounts, collect assets, adjust claims, and pay debts.

Nominal Partner

One whose name appears in connection with the business as a member of the firm, but who has no real interest in it.

Ostensible Partner

One whose name appears to the world as such, or who is held out to all persons having dealings with the firm in the character of a partner, whether or not he has any real interest in the firm. Civ.Code Ga.1910, § 3157.

Quasi Partners

Partners of lands, goods, or chattels who are not actual partners are sometimes so called. Poth. de Société, App. no. 184.

Secret Partner

A dormant partner; one whose connection with the firm is really or professedly concealed from the world. In re Victor, D.C.Ga., 246 F. 727, 731.

Silent Partner, Sleeping Partner

Popular names for dormant partners or special partners.

Solvent Partner

This term does not mean one who has assets sufficient to pay his debts, but one who is not in bankruptcy, so that his property is open to joint creditors' appropriation by legal action and not subject to distribution in bankruptcy proceedings. Robinson v. Security Co., 87 Conn. 268, 87 A. 879, 881, Ann.Cas.1915C, 1170.

Special Partner

A member of a limited partnership, who furnishes certain funds to the common stock, and whose liability extends no further than the fund furnished. A partner whose responsibility is restricted to the amount of his investment. 3 Kent, Comm. 34.

Surviving Partner

The partner who, on the dissolution of the firm by the death of his copartner, occupies the position of a trustee to settle up its affairs.

PARTNERSHIP. A voluntary contract between two or more competent persons to place their money, effects, labor, and skill, or some or all of them, in lawful commerce or business, with the understanding that there shall be a proportional sharing of the profits and losses between them. Story, Partn. § 2; Colly. Partn. § 2; 3 Kent, Comm. 23. Preston v. State Industrial Accident Commission, 174 Or. 553, 149 P.2d 957, 961, 962. An association of two or more persons to carry on as co-owners a business for profit. Uniform Partnership Act, § 6(1). Schleicker v. Krier, 218 Wis. 376, 261 N.W. 413. A synallagmatic and commutative contract made between two or more persons for the mutual participation in the profits which may accrue from property, credit, skill, or industry, furnished in determined proportions by the parties. Civ. Code La. art. 2801.

Partnership is where two or more persons agree to carry on any business or adventure together, upon the terms of mutual participation in its profits and losses. Mozley & Whitley. And see Macomber v. Parker, 13 Pick., Mass., 181; Bucknam v. Barnum, 15 Conn. 71; Farmers' Ins. Co. v. Ross, 29 Ohio St. 431; In re Gibb's Estate, 157 Pa. 59, 27 A. 383, 22 L.R.A. 276; Wild v. Davenport, 48 N.J.L. 129, 7 A. 295, 57 Am.Rep. 552; Morse v. Pacific Ry. Co., 191 Ill. 356, 61 N.E. 104. It is in effect a contract of mutual agency, each partner acting as a principal in his own behalf and as agent for his copartners, and general rules of law applicable to agents apply with equal force in determining rights and liabilities of partners. Lindley v. Seward, Ind. App., 5 N.E.2d 998, 1006.

Commercial partnership. Trading partnership (*q. v.*).

General partnership. A partnership in which the parties carry on all their trade and business, whatever it may be, for the joint benefit and profit of all the parties concerned, whether the capital stock be limited or not, or the contributions thereto be equal or unequal. Story, Partn. § 74; Bigelow v. Elliot, 3 Fed.Cas. 351; Eldridge v. Troost, 3 Abb.Prac., N.S. (N.Y.) 23.

Limited partnership. A partnership consisting of one or more general partners, jointly and severally responsible as ordinary partners, and by whom the business is conducted, and one or more special partners, contributing in cash payments a specific sum as capital to the common stock, and who are not liable for the debts of the partnership beyond the fund so contributed. 1 Rev.St.N.Y. 764; Moorhead v. Seymour (City Ct. N.Y.) 77 N.Y.S. 1054; Taylor v. Webster, 39 N.J.Law, 104.

Mining partnership. See that title.

Particular partnership. One existing where the parties have united to share the benefits of a single individual transaction or enterprise. Spencer v. Jones, Tex.Civ.App., 47 S.W. 665.

Partnership assets. Property of any kind belonging to the firm as such (not the separate property of the individual partners) and available to the recourse of the creditors of the firm in the first instance.

Partnership at will. One designed to continue for no fixed period of time, but only during the pleasure of the parties, and which may be dissolved by any partner without previous notice.

Partnership debt. One due from the partnership or firm as such and not (primarily) from one of the individual partners.

Partnership in commendam. A partnership formed by a contract by which one person or partnership agrees to furnish another person or partnership a certain amount, either in property or money, to be employed by the person or partnership to whom it is furnished, in his or their own name or firm, on condition of receiving a share in the profits, in the proportion determined by the contract, and of being liable to losses and expenses to the amount furnished and no more. Civ. Code La. art. 2839.

Secret partnership. One where the existence of certain persons as partners is not avowed to the public by any of the partners. Deering v. Flanders, 49 N.H. 225.

Special partnership. At common law. One formed for the prosecution of a special branch of business, as distinguished from the general business of the parties, or for one particular venture or subject. Bigelow v. Elliot, 3 Fed.Cas. 351. A joint adventure. McDaniel v. State Fair of Texas, Tex.Civ.App., 286 S.W. 513, 517. Under statutes. A limited partnership (*q. v.*).

Subpartnership. One formed where one partner in a firm makes a stranger a partner with him in his share of the profits of that firm.

Trading partnership. See that title.

Universal partnership. One in which the partners jointly agree to contribute to the common fund of the partnership the whole of their property, of whatever character, and future, as well as present. Poth. Société, 29; Civ. Code La. art. 2829.

PARTURITION. The act of giving birth to a child.

PARTUS. Lat. Child; offspring; the child just before it is born, or immediately after its birth.

PARTUS EX LEGITIMO THORO NON CERTIUS NOSCIT MATREM QUAM GENITOREM SUUM. Fortes. 42. The offspring of a legitimate bed knows not his mother more certainly than his father.

PARTUS SEQUITUR VENTREM. The offspring follows the mother; the brood of an animal belongs to the owner of the dam; the offspring of a slave belongs to the owner of the mother, or follow the condition of the mother. A maxim of the civil law, which has been adopted in the law of England in regard to animals, though never allowed in the case of human beings. 2 Bl.Comm. 390, 94; Fortes. 42.

PARTY, *n.* A person concerned or having or taking part in any affair, matter, transaction, or proceeding, considered individually. See Parties.

"Party" is a technical word, and has a precise meaning in legal parlance. By it is understood he or they by or against whom a suit is brought, whether in law or equity; the party plaintiff or defendant, whether composed of one or more individuals, and whether natural or legal persons, (they are parties in the writ, and parties on the record;) and all others who may be affected by the suit, indirectly or consequentially, are persons interested, but not parties. Merchants' Bank v. Cook, 4 Pick. 405.

"Party" is not restricted to strict meaning of plaintiff or defendant in a lawsuit, being defined as one concerned in or privy to a matter as in the relation of accessory or confidant, and again a partial person, one who takes sides. State v. Orr, 53 Idaho 452, 24 P.2d 679.

Party aggrieved. Under statutes permitting any party aggrieved to appeal, one whose right has been directly and injuriously affected by action of court. Freeman v. Thompson, 216 N.C. 484, 5 S.E.2d 434, 436. Singer v. Allied Factors, 216 Minn. 443, 13 N.W.2d 378, 380.

Party and party. This phrase signifies the contending parties in an action; *i. e.*, the plaintiff and defendant, as distinguished from the attorney and his client. It is used in connection with the subject of costs, which are differently taxed between party and party and between attorney and client. Brown.

Party injured. As used in divorce statute giving right of action only to party injured means party wronged by action of the other. Byers v. Byers, 223 N.C. 85, 25 S.E.2d 466, 469.

Party to be charged. A phrase used in the statute of frauds, meaning the party against whom the contract is sought to be enforced. Dominion Oil Co. v. Pou, Tex.Civ.App., 253 S.W. 317, 320; Kingfisher Mill & Elevator Co. v. Westbrook, 79 Okl. 188, 192 P. 209, 212. The party to be charged in the action—that is, the defendant. Jones v. School Dist. No. 48, 137 Ark. 414, 208 S.W. 798, 799; Graham v. Henderson Elevator Co., 60 Ind.App. 697, 111 N.E. 332, 335; Also, the vendor. Henry v. Reeser, 153 Ky. 8, 154 S.W. 371, 373; Kaiser v. Jones, 157 Ky. 607, 163 S.W. 741, 742; The owner of the realty rather than the party attempted to be charged or held liable in an action based on the memorandum. Lusky v. Keiser, 128 Tenn. 705, 164 S.W. 777, 778, L.R.A.1915C, 400.

Real party. In statutes requiring suits to be brought in the name of the "real party in interest," this term means the person who is actually and substantially interested in the subject-matter, as distinguished from one who has only a nominal, formal, or technical interest in it or connection with it. Hoagland v. Van Etten, 22 Neb. 681, 35 N.W. 870; Gruber v. Baker, 20 Nev. 453, 23 P. 858, 9 L.R.A. 302; Chew v. Brumagen, 13 Wall. 504, 20 L.Ed. 663. Gay v. Jackson County Board of Education, 205 Ky. 277, 265 S.W. 772, 773; Taylor v. Hurst, 186 Ky. 71, 216 S.W. 95, 96; Rothwell v. Knight, 37 Wyo. 11, 258 P. 576, 582.

Third parties. A term used to include all persons who are not parties to the contract, agreement, or instrument of writing by which their interest in the thing conveyed is sought to be affected. Morrison v. Trudeau (La.) 1 Mart., N.S., 384. But it is difficult to give a very definite idea of *third persons;* for sometimes those who are not parties to the contract, but who represent the rights of the original parties, as executors, are not to be considered third persons. 1 Bouvier, Inst. n. 1335. In statutes the words may have special meanings, and are often used to refer to creditors. Flemming v. Drake, 163 Ga. 872, 137 S.E. 268, 270; For other uses, see Behr v. Soth, 170 Minn. 278, 212 N.W. 461, 463; In re Thomas, D.C.N.Y., 283 F. 676; Cartwright v. Ennis, 215 Ky. 3, 284 S.W. 87; Oakdale Bank & Trust Co. v. Young & Leggett, 2 La. App. 586, 589; Bogdon v. Fort, 75 Colo. 231, 225 P. 247, 248; Churchill v. Stephens, 91 N.J.Law, 195, 102 A. 657, 658.

PARTY, *adj.* Relating or belonging to, or composed of, two or more parts or portions, or two or more persons or classes of persons.

Party jury. A jury *de medietate linguæ*; (which title see.)

Party structure. A structure separating buildings, stories, or rooms which belong to different owners, or which are approached by distinct staircases or separate entrances from without, whether the same be a partition, arch, floor, or other structure. (St. 18 & 19 Vict. c. 122, § 3.) Mozley & Whiteley.

Party-wall. A wall built partly on the land of one owner, and partly on the land of another, for the common benefit of both in supporting timbers used in the construction of contiguous buildings. Brown v. Werner, 40 Md. 19. In the primary and most ordinary meaning of the term, a party-wall is (1) a wall of which the two adjoining owners are tenants in common. But it may also mean (2) a wall divided longitudinally into two strips, one belonging to each of the neighboring owners; (3) a wall which belongs entirely to one of the adjoining owners, but is subject to an easement or right in the other to have it maintained as a dividing wall between the two tenements, (the term is so used in some of the English building acts;) or (4) a wall divided longitudinally into two moieties, each moiety being subject to a cross-easement in favor of the owner of the other moiety. Sweet. Gates v. Friedman, 83 W.Va. 710, 98 S. E. 892, 893; Carroll Blake Const. Co. v. Boyle, 140 Tenn. 166, 203 S.W. 945, 946; Smoot v. Heyl, 33 S. Ct. 336, 337, 227 U.S. 518, 57 L.Ed. 621; Feder v. Solomon, 3 N.J.Misc. 1189, 131 A. 290; Freedman v. Kensico Realty Co., 99 N.J.Eq. 115, 131 A. 916, 917.

PARUM. Lat. Little; but little.

PARUM CAVET NATURA. Nature takes little heed. Vandenheuvel v. United Ins. Co., 2 Johns. Cas. (N.Y.) 127, 166.

PARUM CAVISSE VIDETUR. Lat. In Roman law. He seems to have taken too little care; he seems to have been incautious, or not sufficiently upon his guard. A form of expression used by the judge or magistrate in pronouncing sentence of death upon a criminal. Festus, 325; Tayl. Civil Law, 81; 4 Bl.Comm. 362, note.

PARUM DIFFERUNT QUÆ RE CONCORDANT. 2 Bulst. 86. Things which agree in substance differ but little.

PARUM EST LATAM ESSE SENTENTIAM NISI MANDETUR EXECUTIONI. It is little [or to little purpose] that judgment be given unless it be committed to execution. Co. Litt. 289.

PARUM PROFICIT SCIRE QUID FIERI DEBET, SI NON COGNOSCAS QUOMODO SIT FACTURUM. 2 Inst. 503. It profits little to know what ought to be done, if you do not know how it is to be done.

PARVA SERJEANTIA. Petty serjeanty (*q. v.*).

PARVISE. An afternoon's exercise or moot for the instruction of young students, bearing the same name originally with the *Parvisiœ* (little-go) of Oxford. Wharton.

PARVUM CAPE. See Petit Cape.

PAS. In French. Precedence; right of going foremost.

PASCH. The passover; Easter.

PASCHA. In old English law and practice. Easter. *De termino Paschœ,* of the term of Easter. Bract. fol. 246*b*.

PASCHA CLAUSUM. The octave of Easter, or Low-Sunday, which closes that solemnity.

PASCHA FLORIDUM. The Sunday before Easter, called "Palm-Sunday."

PASCHA RENTS. In English ecclesiastical law. Yearly tributes paid by the clergy to the bishop or archdeacon at their Easter visitations.

PASCUA. A particular meadow or pasture land set apart to feed cattle.

PASCUA SILVA. In the civil law. A feeding wood; a wood devoted to the feeding of cattle. Dig. 50, 16, 30, 5.

PASCUAGE. The grazing or pasturage of cattle.

PASS, *v.* In practice. To utter or pronounce; as when the court *passes* sentence upon a prisoner. Also to proceed; to be rendered or given; as when judgment is said to *pass* for the plaintiff in a suit.

In legislative parlance, a bill or resolution is said to *pass* when it is agreed to or enacted by the house, or when the body has sanctioned its adoption by the requisite majority of votes; in the same circumstances, the body is said to *pass* the bill or motion.

When an auditor appointed to examine into any accounts certifies to their correctness, he is said to *pass* them; *i. e.,* they pass through the examination without being detained or sent back for inaccuracy or imperfection. Brown.

The term also means to examine into anything and then authoritatively determine the disputed questions which it involves. In this sense a jury is said to *pass upon* the rights or issues in litigation before them.

In the language of conveyancing, the term means to move from one person to another; to be transferred or conveyed from one owner to another; as in the phrase "the word 'heirs' will *pass* the fee."

To publish; utter; transfer; circulate; impose fraudulently. This is the meaning of the word when the offense of *passing* counterfeit money or a forged paper is spoken of.

"Pass," "utter," "publish," and "sell" are in some respects convertible terms, and, in a given case, "pass" may include utter, publish, and sell. The words "uttering" and "passing," used of notes, do not necessarily import that they are transferred as genuine. The words include any delivery of a note to another for value, with intent that it shall be put into circulation as money. U. S. v. Nelson, 1 Abb. 135, Fed. Cas. No. 15,861; Smith v. State, 13 Ga.App. 663, 79 S.E. 764, 766.

Passing a paper is putting it off in payment or exchange. Uttering it is a declaration that it is good, with an intention to pass, or an offer to pass it.

PASS, *n.* Permission to pass; a license to go or come; a certificate, emanating from authority, wherein it is declared that a designated person is permitted to go beyond certain boundaries which, without such authority, he could not lawfully pass. Also a ticket issued by a railroad or other transportation company, authorizing a designated person to travel free on its lines, between certain points or for a limited time.

PASSAGE. A way over water; an easement giving the right to pass over a piece of private water. Travel by sea; a voyage over water; the carriage of passengers by water; money paid for such carriage.

Enactment; the act of carrying a bill or resolution through a legislative or deliberative body in accordance with the prescribed forms and requisites; the emergence of the bill in the form of a law, or the motion in the form of a resolution. Passage may mean when bill has passed both houses of legislature or when it is signed by Governor. People v. Coffin, 279 Ill. 401, 117 N.E. 85, 87; Board of Education of School Dist. No. 41 v. Morgan, 316 Ill. 143, 147 N.E. 34; Jemison v. Town of Ft. Deposit, 21 Ala.App. 331, 108 So. 396.

PASSAGE COURT. An ancient court of record in Liverpool, once called the "mayor's court of *pays sage,*" but now usually called the "court of the passage of the borough of Liverpool." This court was formerly held before the mayor and two bailiffs of the borough, and had jurisdiction in actions where the amount in question exceeded forty shillings. Mozley & Whitley.

PASSAGE MONEY. The fare of a passenger by sea; money paid for the transportation of persons in a ship or vessel; as distinguished from "freight" or "freight-money," which is paid for the transportation of goods and merchandise.

PASSAGIO. An ancient writ addressed to the keepers of the ports to permit a man who had the king's leave to pass over sea. Reg. Orig. 193.

PASSAGIUM REGIS. A voyage or expedition to the Holy Land made by the kings of England in person. Cowell.

PASSATOR. He who has the interest or command of the passage of a river; or a lord to whom a duty is paid for passage. Wharton.

PASS-BOOK. A book in which a bank or banker enters the deposits made by a customer, and which is retained by the latter. Also a book in which a merchant enters the items of sales on credit to a customer, and which the latter carries or keeps with him.

PASSENGER. A person whom a common carrier has contracted to carry from one place to another, and has, in the course of the performance of that contract, received under his care either upon the means of conveyance, or at the point of departure of that means of conveyance. Bricker v. Philadelphia & R. R. Co., 132 Pa. 1, 18 A. 983, 19 Am.St. Rep. 585; Schepers v. Union Depot R. Co., 126 Mo. 665, 29 S.W. 712; Pennsylvania R. Co. v. Price, 96 Pa. 256; The Main v. Williams, 14 S.Ct. 486, 152 U.S. 122, 38 L.Ed. 381; Horne v. Southern Ry. Co., 186 S.C. 525, 197 S.E. 31, 35, 116 A.L.R. 745.

The above definition is not exhaustive. For one who goes to a railroad station to take the next train in a reasonable time before the time for the arrival of the train is a passenger, though he has not purchased a ticket, and the duties imposed by the relation of carrier and passenger are obligatory on the railroad. Clark v. Bland, 181 N.C. 110, 106 S.E. 491, 492; Garricott v. New York State Rys., 223 N.Y. 9, 119 N.E. 94, L.R.A.1918B, 929; Dillahunty v. Chicago, R. I. & P. Ry. Co., 119 Ark. 392, 178 S.W. 420, 422; Kidwell v. Chesapeake & O. Ry. Co., 71 W.Va. 664, 77 S.E. 285, 43 L.R.A.,N.S., 999; Youngerman v. New York, N. H. & H. R. Co., 223 Mass. 29, 111 N.E. 607, 608; Mobile Light & R. Co. v. Hughes, 190 Ala. 216, 67 So. 278, 281. And a child about nine months old, who accompanies her mother, who is a passenger, is a passenger, though riding free. Southern Ry. Co. v. Herron, 12 Ala.App. 415, 68 So. 551, 552. Railway mail clerks, required by 39 U.S.C.A. § 523, to be carried by railroad without compensation, held to be "passengers." Pittsburgh, C., C. & St. L. R. Co. v. Jones, 82 Ind.App. 569, 146 N.E. 864; Carter v. Washington & O. D. Ry., 122 Va. 458, 95 S.E. 464, 465; Missouri, K. & T. Ry. Co. v. Edmonds, 73 Okl. 2, 174 P. 1052, 1054; Baltimore & O. R. Co. v. Davis, 152 Md. 427, 137 A. 30, 33. When a person ceases to be a passenger depends upon the particular facts of each case. Louisville Ry. Co. v. Kennedy, 162 Ky. 560, 172 S.W. 970, 971, Ann.Cas.1916E, 996; Will v. Milwaukee Electric Ry. & Light Co., 169 Wis. 38, 171 N.W. 658, 659; Lackey v. Missouri & K. I. Ry. Co., 305 Mo. 260, 264 S.W. 807, 808; Gillis v. Duluth Casualty Ass'n, 133 Minn. 238, 158 N.W. 252, 253; Moffit v. Grand Rapids Ry. Co., 228 Mich. 349, 200 N.W. 274, 275.

One carried for hire, or reward, as distinguished from a "guest" who is one carried gratuitously, that is, without any financial return except such slight benefit as is customary as part of the ordinary courtesy of the road. Duncan v. Hutchinson, 139 Ohio St. 185, 39 N.E.2d 140, 142.

PASSENGER TRAIN. Any train used to carry members of the general public for hire. Nadler v. Illinois Commercial Men's Ass'n, 188 Ill.App. 459, 460; Chicago, B. & Q. R. Co. v. Railroad Commission of Wisconsin, 152 Wis. 654, 140 N.W. 296, 299.

A passenger train is one which carries passengers, their baggage, mail and express only, while a freight train is one which carries freight alone, having a caboose attached for the use of the crew. Arizona Eastern R. Co. v. State, 29 Ariz. 446, 242 P. 870, 871.

PASSIAGIARIUS. A ferryman. Jacob.

PASSIM (Lat). Everywhere. Often used to indicate a very general reference to a book or legal authority.

PASSING-TICKET. In English law. A kind of permit, being a note or check which the toll-clerks on some canals give to the boatmen, specifying the lading for which they have paid toll. Wharton.

PASSIO. Pannage; a liberty for hogs to run in forests or woods to feed upon mast. Mon. Angl. 1, 682.

PASSION. In the definition of manslaughter as homicide committed without premeditation but under the influence of sudden "passion," this term means any of the emotions of the mind known as rage, anger, hatred, furious resentment, or terror, rendering the mind incapable of cool reflection. Stell v. State, Tex.Cr.App., 58 S.W. 75; State v. Johnson, 23 N.C. 362, 35 Am.Dec. 742; Winton v. State, 151 Tenn. 177, 268 S.W. 633, 637; Collins v. State, 88 Fla. 578, 102 So. 880, 882. Commonwealth v. Flax, 331 Pa. 145, 200 A. 632, 636.

PASSIVE. As used in law, this term means inactive; permissive; consisting in endurance or submission, rather than action; and in some connections it carries the implication of being subjected to a burden or charge.

As to passive "Debt," "Negligence," "Title," "Trust," and "Use," see those titles.

PASSPORT.

Maritime. A document issued to a neutral merchant vessel, by her own government, during the progress of a war, to be carried on the voyage, to evidence her nationality and protect her against the cruisers of the belligerent powers. This paper is otherwise called a "pass," "sea-pass," "sea-letter," "sea-brief." It usually contains the captain's or master's name and residence, the name, property, description, tonnage, and destination of the ship, the nature and quantity of the cargo, the place from whence it comes, and its destination, with such other matters as the practice of the place requires.

In international law. A license or safe-conduct, issued during the progress of a war, authorizing a person to remove himself or his effects from the territory of one of the belligerent nations to another country, or to travel from country to country without arrest or detention on account of the war.

In American law. A special instrument intended for the protection of American vessels against the Barbary powers, usually called a "Mediterranean pass." Jac. Sea Laws, 69. Also a document addressed to foreign powers, which certifies that the person therein described is a citizen of the United States and which requests for him while abroad permission to come and go as well as lawful aid and protection. United States v. Browder, C.C.A.N.Y., 113 F.2d 97, 98.

In Modern law. A warrant of protection and authority to travel, granted by the competent officer to persons moving from place to place. Brande.

PASTO. In Spanish law. Feeding; pasture; a right of pasture. White, New Recop. b. 2, tit. 1, c. 6, § 4.

PASTOR. Lat. A shepherd. Applied to a minister of the Christian religion, who has charge of a congregation or parish, hence called his "flock." First Presbyterian Church v. Myers, 5 Okl. 809, 50 P. 70, 38 L.R.A. 687; Griswold v. Quinn, 97 Kan. 611, 156 P. 761, 762; Dupont v. Pelletier, 120 Me. 114, 113 A. 11, 13.

PASTURE. Ground for the grazing of domestic animals, and includes also the grass growing upon the ground. State v. Cornett, 199 N.C. 634, 155 S. E. 451, 452. Also the right of pasture. Co. Litt. 4*b*.

PASTUS. In feudal law. The procuration or provision which tenants were bound to make for their lords at certain times, or as often as they made a progress to their lands. It was often converted into money.

PATEAT UNIVERSIS PER PRÆSENTES. Know all men by these presents. Words with which letters of attorney anciently commenced. Reg. Orig. 305*b*, 306.

PATENT, *adj.* Open; manifest; evident; unsealed. Used in this sense in such phrases as "patent ambiguity," "patent writ," "letters patent."

Letters patent. Open letters, as distinguished from letters close. An instrument proceeding from the government, and conveying a right, authority, or grant to an individual, as a patent for a tract of land, or for the exclusive right to make and sell a new invention. Familiarly termed a "patent." International Tooth Crown Co. v. Hanks Dental Ass'n, C.C.N.Y., 111 F. 918; Ulman v. Thompson, 57 Ind.App. 126, 106 N.E. 611, 613.

Patent ambiguity. See Ambiguity.

Patent defect. In sales of personal property, one which is plainly visible or which can be discovered by such an inspection as would be made in the exercise of ordinary care and prudence. Lawson v. Baer, 52 N.C. 461.

Patent writ. In old practice. An open writ; one not closed or sealed up. See Close Writs.

PATENT, *n.* A grant of some privilege, property, or authority, made by the government or sovereign of a country to one or more individuals. Phil. Pat. 1.

In American law. The instrument by which a state or government grants public lands to an individual. Bovey-Shute Lumber Co. v. Erickson, 41 N.D. 365, 170 N.W. 628, 630; McCarty v. Helbling, 73 Or. 356, 144 P. 499, 503. A grant made by the government to an inventor, conveying and securing to him the exclusive right to make, use and sell his invention for a term of years. Atlas Glass Co. v. Simonds Mfg. Co., 42 C.C.A. 554, 102 F. 647; Société Anonyme v. General Electric Co., C.C.N.Y., 97 F. 605; Pegram v. American Alkali Co., C.C. Pa., 122 F. 1000; Luten v. Kansas City Bridge Co., C.C.A.Mo., 285 F. 840, 844; American Foundry and Mfg. Co. v. Josam Mfg. Co., C.C.A.Mo., 79 F.2d 116, 117.

In English law. A grant by the sovereign to a subject or subjects, under the great seal, conferring some authority, title, franchise, or property; termed "letters patent" from being delivered open, and not closed up from inspection.

General

Design patent. Granted for giving a new and pleasing appearance to an article of manufacture whereby its sale is enhanced. Viehmann v. D. F. H. Novelty Furniture Co., D.C.N.Y., 27 F.Supp. 566, 567; 35 U.S.C.A. § 171 et seq.

Land patent. A muniment of title issued by a government or state for the conveyance of some portion of the public domain.

Patent bill office. The attorney general's patent bill office is the office in which were formerly prepared the drafts of all letters patent issued in England, other than those for inventions. The draft patent was called a "bill," and the officer who prepared it was called the "clerk of the patents to the queen's attorney and solicitor general." Sweet.

Patent of precedence. Letters patent granted, in England, to such barristers as the crown thinks fit to honor with that mark of distinction, whereby they are entitled to such rank and preaudience as are assigned in their respective patents, which is sometimes next after the attorney general, but more usually next after her majesty's counsel then being. These rank promiscuously with the king's (or queen's) counsel, but are not the sworn servants of the crown. 3 Bl.Comm. 28; 3 Steph.Comm. 274.

Patent-office. In the administrative system of the United States, this is one of the bureaus of the department of commerce. It has charge of the issuing of patents to inventors and of such business as is connected therewith.

Patent-right. A right secured by patent; usually meaning a right to the exclusive manufacture and sale of an invention or patented article. Avery v. Wilson, C.C.N.C., 20 F. 856; Crown Cork & Seal Co. v. State, 87 Md. 687, 40 A. 1074, 53 L.R.A. 417; Com. v. Central, etc., Tel. Co., 145 Pa. 121, 22 A. 841, 27 Am.St.Rep. 677.

Patent-right dealer. Any one whose business it is to sell, or offer for sale, patent-rights. 14 St. at Large, 118.

Patent rolls. The official records of royal charters and grants; covering from the reign of King John to recent times. They contain grants of offices and lands, restitutions of temporalities to ecclesiastical persons, confirmations of grants made to bodies corporate, patents of creation of peers, and licenses of all kinds. Hubb. Succ. 617; 32 Phila. Law Lib. 429.

Patent suit. A suit with issues affecting the legality or infringement of a patent. Rubens v. Bowers, C.C.A.Cal., 136 F.2d 887, 889.

Pioneer patent. A patent for an invention covering a function never before performed, or a wholly novel device, or one of such novelty and importance as to mark a distinct step in the progress of the art, as distinguished from a mere improvement or perfecting of what has gone before. Westinghouse v. Boyden Power-Brake Co., 18 S.Ct. 707, 170 U.S. 537, 42 L.Ed. 1136; Yancey v. Enright, C.C.A.La., 230 F. 641, 645; Spengler Core Drilling Co. v. Spencer, D.C.Cal., 10 F.2d 579, 582.

Plant patent. Granted to person who invents or discovers and asexually reproduces a distinct and new variety of plant; word "plant" being used in the popular sense. Kim Bros. v. Hagler, D.C. Cal., 167 F.Supp. 665, 667; 35 U.S.C.A. § 161 et seq.

Reissued patent. A patent securing rights of an inventor more definitely in some particular wherein the original patent was defective. Ingersoll v. Holt, 104 F. 682, 683.

PATENTABLE. Suitable to be patented; entitled by law to be protected by the issuance of a patent. Heath Cycle Co. v. Hay, C.C.Ind., 67 F. 246; Maier v. Bloom, C.C.N.J., 95 F. 166; Boyd v. Cherry, C.C. Iowa, 50 F. 282; Providence Rubber Co. v. Goodyear, 9 Wall. 796, 19 L.Ed. 566. And to be "patentable," a device must embody some new idea or principle not before known, and it must be a discovery as distinguished from mere mechanical skill or knowledge. Hobart Mfg. Co. v. Landers, Frary & Clark, D.C.Conn., 26 F.Supp. 198, 202; In re Herthel, Cust. & Pat.App., 104 F.2d 824, 826.

PATENTEE. He to whom a patent has been granted. The term is usually applied to one who has obtained letters patent for a new invention.

PATER. Lat. A father; the father. In the civil law, this word sometimes included *avus*, (grandfather.) Dig. 50, 16, 201.

PATER PATRIÆ. Father of the country. See Parens Patriæ.

PATER IS EST QUEM NUPTIÆ DEMONSTRANT. The father is he whom the marriage points out. 1 Bl.Comm. 446; Tate v. Penne, 7 Mart. (N. S. La.) 548, 553; Dig. 2, 4, 5; Broom, Max. 516.

PATERFAMILIAS. The father of a family.

In Roman law. The head or master of a family.

This word is sometimes employed, in a wide sense, as equivalent to *sui juris*. A person *sui juris* is called "*paterfamilias*" even when under the age of puberty. In the narrower and more common use, a *paterfamilias* is any one invested with *potestas* over any person. It is thus as applicable to a grandfather as to a father. Hunter, Rom. Law, 49.

PATERNA PATERNIS. Lat. Paternal estates to paternal heirs. A rule of the French law, signifying that such portion of a decedent's estate as came to him from his father must descend to his heirs on the father's side.

PATERNAL. That which belongs to the father or comes from him.

PATERNAL LINE. A line of descent or relationship between two persons which is traced through the father.

PATERNAL POWER. The authority lawfully exercised by parents over their children. This phrase is also used to translate the Latin *"patria potestas,"* (*q. v.*).

PATERNAL PROPERTY. That which descends or comes to one from his father, grandfather, or other ascendant or collateral on the paternal side of the house.

PATERNITY. The state or condition of a father; the relationship of a father.

The Latin *"paternitas"* is used in the canon law to denote a kind of spiritual relationship contracted by baptism. Heinecc. Elem. lib. 1, tit. 10, § 161, note.

PATHOLOGY. In medical jurisprudence. The science or doctrine of diseases. That part of medicine which explains the nature of diseases, their causes, and their symptoms. Bacon v. U. S. Mut. Acc. Ass'n, 123 N.Y. 304, 25 N.E. 399, 9 L.R.A. 617, 20 Am.St.Rep. 748; Williams v. Scudder, 102 Ohio St. 305, 131 N.E. 481, 483.

PATIBULARY. Belonging to the gallows.

PATIBULATED. Hanged on a gibbet.

PATIBULUM. In old English law. A gallows or gibbet. Fleta, lib. 2, c. 3, § 9.

PATIENS. Lat. One who suffers or permits; one to whom an act is done; the passive party in a transaction.

PATIENT. One who has been committed to the asylum and has remained there for care and treatment. Edwards v. West Texas Hospital, Tex.Civ. App., 89 S.W.2d 801, 811.

PATRIA. Lat. The country, neighborhood, or vicinage; the men of the neighborhood; a jury of the vicinage. Synonymous, in this sense, with *"pais."*

PATRIA LABORIBUS ET EXPENSIS NON DEBET FATIGARI. A jury ought not to be harassed by labors and expenses. Jenk. Cent. 6.

PATRIA POTESTAS. Lat. In Roman law. Paternal authority; the paternal power. This term denotes the aggregate of those peculiar powers and rights which, by the civil law of Rome, belonged to the head of a family in respect to his wife, children, (natural or adopted,) and any more remote descendants who sprang from him through males only. Anciently, it was of very extensive reach, embracing even the power of life and death, but was gradually curtailed, until finally it amounted to little more than a right in the *paterfamilias* to hold as his own any property or acquisitions of one under his power. Mackeld. Rom. Law, § 589.

PATRIA POTESTAS IN PIETATE DEBET, NON IN ATROCITATE, CONSISTERE. Paternal power should consist [or be exercised] in affection, not in atrocity.

PATRIMONY. Any kind of property. Such estate as has descended in the same family; estates which have descended or been devised in a direct line from the father, and, by extension, from the mother or other ancestor. It has been held that the word is not necessarily restricted to property inherited directly from the father. 5 Ir. Ch.Rep. 525.

PATRIARCH. The chief bishop over several countries or provinces, as an archbishop is of several dioceses. Godb. 20.

PATRICIDE. One who has killed his father. As to the punishment of that offense by the Roman law, see Sandars' Just.Inst. (5th Ed.) 496.

PATRICIUS. In the civil law. A title of the highest honor, conferred on those who enjoyed the chief place in the emperor's esteem.

PATRIMONIAL. Pertaining to a patrimony; inherited from ancestors, but strictly from the direct male ancestors.

PATRIMONIUM. In civil law. That which is capable of being inherited. The private and exclusive ownership or dominion of an individual. Things capable of being possessed by a single person to the exclusion of all others (or which are actually so possessed) are said to be *in patrimonio;* if not capable of being so possessed, (or not actually so possessed,) they are said to be *extra patrimonium.* See Gaius, bk. 2, § 1.

PATRINUS. In old ecclesiastical law. A godfather. Spelman.

PATRITIUS. An honor conferred on men of the first quality in the time of the English Saxon kings.

PATROCINIUM. In Roman law. Patronage; protection; defense. The business or duty of a patron or advocate.

PATROLMAN. A policeman assigned to duty in patrolling a certain beat or district; also the designation of a grade or rank in the organized police force of large cities, a patrolman being generally a private in the ranks, as distinguished from roundsmen, sergeants, lieutenants, etc. See State v. Walbridge, 153 Mo. 194, 54 S.W. 447.

PATRON. In ordinary usage one who protects, countenances, or supports some person or thing; one who habitually extends material assistance; a regular customer; a protector or benefactor. State v. Board of Trust of Vanderbilt University, 129 Tenn. 279, 164 S.W. 1151, 1170; Carroll v. Leemon Special School Dist., 175 Ark. 274, 299 S.W. 11, 12.

In ecclesiastical law. He who has the right, title, power, or privilege of presenting to an ecclesiastical benefice.

In Roman law. The former master of an emancipated slave.

In French marine law. The captain or master of a vessel.

PATRONAGE. In English ecclesiastical law. The right of presentation to a church or ecclesiastical benefice; the same with advowson (*q. v.*). 2 Bl.Comm. 21. The right of appointing to office, considered as a perquisite, or personal right; not in the aspect of a public trust.

PATRONATUS. Lat.

In Roman law. The condition, relation, right, or duty of a patron.

In ecclesiastical law. Patronage, (*q. v.*).

PATRONIZE. To act as a patron, extend patronage, countenance, encourage, favor. State v. Board of Trust of Vanderbilt University, 129 Tenn. 279, 164 S.W. 1151, 1170.

PATRONUM FACIUNT DOS, ÆDIFICATIO, FUNDUS. Dod. Adv. 7. Endowment, building, and land make a patron.

PATRONUS (Lat.).

In Roman law. A modification of the Latin word *pater,* father. A denomination applied by Romulus to the first senators of Rome, and which they always afterwards bore. A person who stood in the relation of protector to another who was called his "client." One who advised his client in matters of law, and advocated his causes in court. Gilb. Forum Rom. 25.

PATROON. The proprietors of certain manors created in New York in colonial times were so called.

PATRUELIS. Lat. In the civil law. A cousin-german by the father's side; the son or daughter of a father's brother. Wharton.

PATRUUS. Lat. An uncle by the father's side; a father's brother.

PATRUUS MAGNUS. A grandfather's brother; granduncle.

PATRUUS MAJOR. A great-grandfather's brother.

PATRUUS MAXIMUS. A great-grandfather's father's brother.

PAUPER. A person so poor that he must be supported at public expense; also a suitor who, on account of poverty, is allowed to sue or defend without being chargeable with costs. In re Hoffen's Estate, 70 Wis. 522, 36 N.W. 407; Hutchings v. Thompson, 10 Cush., Mass., 238; Charleston v. Groveland, 15 Gray, Mass., 15; Lee County v. Lackie, 30 Ark. 764; Allegheny County v. City of Pittsburgh, 281 Pa. 300, 127 A. 72, 73. For "Family," see that title.

Dispauper. To deprive one of the status of a pauper and of any benefits incidental thereto: particularly, to take away the right to sue *in forma pauperis* because the person so suing, during the progress of the suit, has acquired money or property which would enable him to sustain the costs of the action.

PAUPERIES. Lat. In Roman law. Damage or injury done by an irrational animal, without active fault on the part of the owner, but for which the latter was bound to make compensation. Inst. 4, 9; Mackeld.Rom.Law, § 510.

PAVAGE. Money paid towards paving the streets or highways.

PAVE. To cover with stone, brick, concrete, or any other substantial matter, making a smooth and level surface. A sidewalk is paved when it is laid or flagged with flat stones, as well as when paved with brick, as is frequently done. In re Phillips, 60 N.Y. 22; Buell v. Ball, 20 Iowa 282; Harrisburg v. Segelbaum, 151 Pa. 172, 24 A. 1070, 20 L.R.A. 834.

PAVING. Any substance on a street forming an artificial roadway or wearing surface. Heath v. Seattle Taxicab Co., 73 Wash. 177, 131 P. 843, 844.

PAWN, *v.* To deliver personal property to another in pledge, or as security for a debt or sum borrowed.

PAWN, *n.* A bailment of goods to a creditor, as security for some debt or engagement; a pledge. Story, Bailm. § 7; Coggs v. Bernard, 2 Ld.Raym. 913; Commercial Bank v. Flowers, 116 Ga. 219, 42 S.E. 474; Jacobs v. Grossman, 310 Ill. 247, 141 N.E. 714, 715.

Pawn, or pledge, is a bailment of goods by a debtor to his creditor, to be kept till the debt is discharged. Wharton. In common usage pawn means a pledge of chattels as distinguished from pledges of choses in action, and in more limited sense means a deposit of personal property made to a pawnbroker as security for a loan; that sort of bailment when goods or chattels are delivered to another as security to him for money borrowed of him by the bailor. In re Rogers, D.C.W.Va., 20 F.Supp. 120, 126.

Also the specific chattel delivered to the creditor as a pledge.

In the law of Louisiana, *pawn* is known as one species of the contract of *pledge,* the other being *antichresis;* but the word "pawn" is sometimes used as synonymous with "pledge," thus including both species. Civ.Code La. art. 3134.

PAWNBROKER. A person whose business is to lend money, usually in small sums, on security of personal property deposited with him or left in pawn. Schaul v. Charlotte, 118 N.C. 733, 24 S.E. 526; Chicago v. Hulbert, 118 Ill. 632, 8 N.E. 812, 59 Am.Rep. 400.

Any person engaged in the business of lending money on deposit or pledges of personal property or other valuable thing, other than securities or printed evidence of indebtedness, or in the business of purchasing personal property, or choses in action, or other valuable thing, and selling or agreeing to sell the same back to the seller at a price other than the original price of purchase, or in the business of purchasing personal property such as articles containing gold, silver, platinum or other precious metals or jewels for the purpose of reducing or smelting them into a different form and reselling the product. Gen. Code Ohio, § 6338.

PAWNEE. The person receiving a pawn, or to whom a pawn is made; the person to whom goods are delivered by another in pledge.

PAWNOR. The person pawning goods or delivering goods to another in pledge.

PAX ECCLESIÆ. Lat. In old English law. The peace of the church. A particular privilege attached to a church; sanctuary (*q. v.*). Crabb, Eng. Law, 41; Cowell.

PAX REGIS. Lat. The peace of the king; that is, the peace, good order, and security for life and property which it is one of the objects of government to maintain, and which the king, as the personification of the power of the state, is supposed to guaranty to all persons within the protection of the law.

This name was also given, in ancient times, to a certain privileged district or sanctuary. The *pax regis*, or verge of the court, as it was afterwards called, extended from the palace-gate to the distance of three miles, three furlongs, three acres, nine feet, nine palms, and nine barleycorns. Crabb, Eng. Law, 41.

PAY, *n*. Compensation. Smith v. Jones, 102 Conn. 471, 129 A. 50, 51, 43 A.L.R. 952; Christopherson v. Reeves, 44 S.D. 634, 184 N.W. 1015, 1017. A fixed and definite amount given by law to persons in military service in consideration of and as compensation for their personal services. Sherburne v. U. S., 16 Ct.Cl. 496.

PAY, *v*. To discharge a debt; to deliver to a creditor the value of a debt, either in money or in goods, for his acceptance. Beals v. Home Ins. Co., 36 N.Y. 522. Carpenter v. Dummit, 221 Ky. 67, 297 S.W. 695, 700; Vollmer v. Automobile Fire Ins. Co. of Hartford, Conn., 207 App.Div. 67, 202 N.Y.S. 374, 375.

The term, however, is sometimes limited to discharging an indebtedness by the use of money. Krahn v. Goodrich, 164 Wis. 600, 160 N.W. 1072, 1075. In re Bailey's Estate, 276 Pa. 147, 119 A. 907, 909.

PAYABLE. Capable of being paid; suitable to be paid; admitting or demanding payment; justly due; legally enforceable. In re Advisory Opinion to the Governor, 74 Fla. 250, 77 So. 102, 103.

A sum of money is said to be payable when a person is under an obligation to pay it. "Payable" may therefore signify an obligation to pay at a future time, but, when used without qualification, "payable" means that the debt is payable at once, as opposed to "owing." Sweet. And see First Nat. Bank v. Greenville Nat. Bank, 84 Tex. 40, 19 S.W. 334; Easton v. Hyde, 13 Minn. 91, Gil. 83.

PAYABLE AFTER SIGHT. Payable after acceptance of bill or protest for nonacceptance. Waggoner Banking Co. v. Gray County State Bank, Tex.Civ.App., 165 S.W. 922, 925.

PAYABLE ON DEMAND. A bill payable on demand is payable on its date or within a reasonable time without grace. Waggoner Banking Co. v. Gray County State Bank, Tex.Civ.App., 165 S.W. 922, 925.

At common law an instrument is payable on demand where no time for payment is expressed, unless the circumstances show a different intention. Coleman v. Page's Estate, 202 S.C. 486, 25 S.E.2d 559.

PAYEE. In mercantile law. The person in whose favor a bill of exchange, promissory note, or check is made or drawn; the person to whom or to whose order a bill, note, or check is made payable. 3 Kent, Comm. 75; Thomson v. Findlater Hardware Co., Tex.Civ.App., 156 S.W. 301, 303.

PAYER, or PAYOR. One who pays, or who is to make a payment; particularly the person who is to make payment of a bill or note. Correlative to "payee."

PAYING QUANTITIES. This phrase, as used in oil and gas leases, when applied to the production of oil, means such a quantity as will pay a profit on the cost of operating the well. Pine v. Webster, 118 Okl. 12, 246 P. 429, 430; Waring v. Lockett, Tex.Civ.App., 118 S.W.2d 1000. Sufficient quantities to pay a reasonable profit on the whole sum required to be expended, including the cost of drilling, equipping, and operating the well Pelham Petroleum Co. v. North, 78 Okl. 39, 188 P. 1069, 1073; Aycock v. Paraffine Oil Co., Tex Civ.App., 210 S.W. 851, 853.

If the well pays a profit, even small, over operating expenses, it produces in paying quantities, though it may never repay its cost, and the operation as a whole may prove unprofitable. Gypsy Oil Co. v. Marsh, 121 Okl. 135, 248 P. 329, 333, 48 A.L.R. 876; Masterson v. Amarillo Oil Co., Tex.Civ.App., 253 S.W. 908, 915.

PAYMASTER. An officer of the army or navy whose duty is to keep the pay-accounts and pay the wages of the officers and men. Any official charged with the disbursement of public money.

PAYMASTER GENERAL. In English law. The officer who makes the various payments out of the public money required for the different departments of the state by issuing drafts on the Bank of England. Sweet. In American law, the officer at the head of the pay corps of the army is so called, also the naval officer holding corresponding office and rank with reference to the pay department of the navy.

PAYMENT. The fulfilment of a promise, or the performance of an agreement.

A discharge of an obligation or debt, and part payment, if accepted, is a discharge pro tanto. Hattrem v. Burdick, 138 Or. 660, 6 P.2d 18, 19.

In a more restricted legal sense payment is the performance of a duty, promise, or obligation, or discharge of a debt or liability, by the delivery of money or other value by a debtor to a creditor, where the money or other valuable thing is tendered and accepted as extinguishing debt or obligation in whole or in part. Also the money or other thing so delivered. Root v. Kelley, 39 Misc. 530, 80 N.Y.Supp. 482; Moulton v. Robison, 27 N.H. 554; Clay v. Lakenan, 101 Mo.App. 563, 74 S.W. 391; Roberts v. Vonnegut, 58 Ind.App. 142,

104 N.E. 321, 326; Buhl Highway Dist. v. Allred, 41 Idaho 54, 238 P. 298, 304.

Satisfaction of a debt in coin of the realm. Hettrick Mfg. Co. v. Barish, 120 Misc.Rep. 673, 199 N.Y.S. 755, 760.

"Payment" implies discharge of an obligation according to its terms or by something given or received of agreed value equal to the debt or liability. Crutchfield v. Johnson & Latimer, 243 Ala. 73, 8 So.2d 412, 414. "Payment" of a debt involves both tender by debtor with intention to pay debt, and acceptance by creditor. In re McElmurray, D.C. S.C., 47 F.Supp. 15, 19. Anything delivered and accepted in discharge of obligation is payment of debt. Barret v. Clarke, 226 Ky. 109, 9 S.W.2d 1091, 1093.

Though "payment" in a broad sense includes money or anything else of value which the creditor accepts in satisfaction of his debt, it means in its restricted sense full satisfaction paid by money and not by exchange or compromise or by an accord and satisfaction. Roach v. McDonald, 187 Ala. 64, 65 So. 823. "Payment" is generally understood to mean a discharge by a compliance with the terms of the obligation or its equivalent, while in an "accord and satisfaction" the discharge is effected by the performance of terms other than those originally agreed on. Barcus v. J. I. Case Threshing Mach. Co., Tex.Civ.App., 197 S.W. 478, 480.

The execution and delivery of negotiable papers is not payment unless it is accepted by the parties in that sense. Seamen v. Muir, 72 Or. 583, 144 P. 121, 123; Cleve v. Craven Chemical Co., C.C.A.N.C., 18 F.2d 711, 712, 52 A.L.R. 980; Morrison v. Chapman, 155 App.Div. 509, 140 N.Y.S. 700, 702; Reid v. Topper, 32 Ariz. 381, 259 P. 397, 399; People v. Davis, 237 Mich. 165, 211 N.W. 36, 37.

Pleading. When the defendant alleges that he has paid the debt or claim laid in the declaration, this is called a "plea of payment."

General

Part payment. The reduction of any debt or demand by the payment of a sum less than the whole amount originally due. Young v. Perkins, 29 Minn. 173, 12 N.W. 515; Moffitt v. Carr, 48 Neb. 403, 67 N.W. 150, 58 Am.St.Rep. 696.

Partial payments. The United States rule of partial payments is to apply the payment, in the first place, to the discharge of the interest then due. If the payment exceeds the interest, the surplus goes toward discharging the principal, and the subsequent interest is to be computed on the balance of principal remaining due. If the payment be less than the interest, the surplus of the interest must not be taken to augment the principal; but interest continues on the former principal until the period of time when the payments, taken together, exceed the interest then due, to discharge which they are applied, and the surplus, if any, is to be applied towards the discharge of the principal, and the interest is to be computed on the balance as aforesaid, and this process continues until final settlement. Langton v. Kops, 41 N.D. 442, 171 N.W. 334, 336.

Payment into court. In practice. The act of a defendant in depositing the amount which he admits to be due, with the proper officer of the court, for the benefit of the plaintiff and in answer to his claim.

Voluntary payment. A payment made by a debtor of his own will and choice, as distinguished from one exacted from him by process of execution or other compulsion. Redmond v. New York, 125 N.Y. 632, 26 N.E. 727; Rumford Chemical Works v. Ray, 19 R.I. 456, 34 A. 814; St. Johns Electric Co. v. City of St. Augustine, 81 Fla. 588, 88 So. 387; Greene v. E. H. Taylor, Jr. & Sons, 184 Ky. 739, 212 S.W. 925, 928. Payments may be voluntary which are made unwillingly as a choice of evils. Singer Sewing Mach. Co. v. Teasley, 198 Ala. 673, 73 So. 969, 971. But money paid under a mistake of the facts is not ordinarily treated as falling within the rule that money paid with full knowledge of all the facts relating to the claim paid constitutes a voluntary payment, and cannot be recovered back. Strong & Jarvis v. Oldsmobile Co. of Vermont, 96 Vt. 355, 120 A. 100, 102.

PAYS. Fr. Country. Trial *per pays,* trial by jury, (the country.) See Pais.

PEACE. The concord or final agreement in a fine of land. 18 Edw. I. *modus levandi finis.*

The tranquility enjoyed by a political society, internally by the good order which reigns among its members, and externally by the good understanding it has with all other nations. Applied to the internal regulations of a nation, peace imports, in a technical sense, not merely a state of repose and security as opposed to one of violence or warfare, but likewise a state of public order and decorum. Hamm.N.P. 139; 12 Mod. 566; People v. Johnson, 86 Mich. 175, 48 N.W. 870, 13 L.R.A. 163, 24 Am.St.Rep. 116; State v. Reichman, 135 Tenn. 685, 188 S.W. 597, 601, Ann.Cas. 1918B, 889; Catlette v. U. S., C.C.A.W.Va., 132 F.2d 902, 906.

Articles of the peace. See Articles.

Bill of peace. See Bill.

Breach of peace. See Breach.

Conservator of the peace. See Conservator.

Justice of the peace. See that title.

Peace and quietude. Public tranquillity and obedience to law, and that public order and security which is commanded by the laws of a particular sovereign, lord or superior. Weakley v. State, 168 Ark. 1087, 273 S.W. 374, 377.

Peace of God. The words, "in the peace of God and the said commonwealth, then and there being," as used in indictments for homicide and in the definition of murder, mean merely that it is not murder to kill an alien enemy in time of war, provided such killing occur in the actual exercise of war. Whart.Cr.Law, § 310; State v. Gut, 13 Minn. 341 (Gil. 315).

Peace of God and the church. In old English law. That rest and cessation which the king's subjects had from trouble and suit of law between the terms and on Sundays and holidays. Cowell; Spelman.

Peace of the state. The protection, security, and immunity from violence which the state undertakes to secure and extend to all persons within its jurisdiction and entitled to the benefit of its laws. This is part of the definition of murder, it being necessary that the victim should be "in the peace of the state," which now practically includes all persons except armed public enemies. See Murder. And see State v. Dunkley, 25 N.C. 121.

Peace officers. This term is variously defined by statute in the different states; but generally it includes sheriffs and their deputies, constables, marshals, members of the police force of cities, and other officers whose duty is to enforce and preserve the public peace. People v. Clinton, 28 App.Div. 478, 51 N.Y.S. 115; Jones v. State, Tex.Cr.App., 65 S.W. 92.

Public peace. The peace or tranquillity of the community in general; the good order and repose of the people composing a state or municipality. State v. Mancini, 91 Vt. 507, 101 A. 581, 583; State ex rel. Pollock v. Becker, 289 Mo. 660, 233 S.W. 641, 649. That invisible sense of security which every man feels so necessary to his comfort, and for which all governments are instituted. Redfield, J., in State v. Benedict, 11 Vt. 236, 34 Am.Dec. 688.

Public peace and quiet. Peace, tranquillity, and order and freedom from agitation or disturbance, the security, good order, and decorum guaranteed by civil society and by the law. State v. Brooks, 146 La. 325, 83 So. 637, 639.

PEACEABLE. Free from the character of force, violence, or trespass; as, a "peaceable entry" on lands. "Peaceable possession" of real estate is such as is acquiesced in by all other persons, including rival claimants, and not disturbed by any forcible attempt at ouster nor by adverse suits to recover the possession or the estate. Stanley v. Schwalby, 13 S.Ct. 418, 147 U.S. 508, 37 L.Ed. 259; Allaire v. Ketcham, 55 N.J.Eq. 168, 35 A. 900; North Fort Worth Townsite Co. v. Taylor, Tex.Civ.App., 262 S.W. 505; Mascall v. Murray, 76 Or. 637, 149 P. 517, 519.

PECCATA CONTRA NATURAM SUNT GRAVISSIMA. 3 Inst. 20. Crimes against nature are the most heinous.

PECCATUM PECCATO ADDIT QUI CULPÆ QUAM FACIT PATROCINIA DEFENSIONIS ADJUNGIT. 5 Coke, 49. He adds fault to fault who sets up a defense of a wrong committed by him.

PECK. A measure of two gallons; a dry measure.

PECIA. A piece or small quantity of ground. Paroch.Antiq. 240.

PECORA. Lat. In Roman law. Cattle; beasts. The term included all quadrupeds that fed in flocks. Dig. 32, 65, 4.

PECULATION. The unlawful appropriation, by a depositary of public funds, of the property of the government intrusted to his care, to his own use, or that of others. Domat.Supp. au Droit Public, l. 3, tit. 5; Bork v. People, 91 N.Y. 16.

The fraudulent misappropriation by one to his own use of money or goods intrusted to his care. White v. Commonwealth, 158 Va. 462, 164 S.E. 375, 378.

PECULATUS. Lat. In the civil law. The offense of stealing or embezzling the public money. 4 Bl.Comm. 121, 122.

PECULIAR, *adj.* Particular or special. Wolf v. Mallinckrodt Chemical Works, 336 Mo. 746, 81 S.W.2d 323, 330.

PECULIAR, *n.* In ecclesiastical law. A parish or church in England which has jurisdiction of ecclesiastical matters within itself, and independent of the ordinary, and is subject only to the metropolitan.

PECULIARS, COURT OF. In English law. A branch of and annexed to the court of arches. It has a jurisdiction over all those parishes dispersed through the province of Canterbury, in the midst of other dioceses, which are exempt from the ordinary's jurisdiction, and subject to the metropolitan only.

PECULIUM. Lat. In Roman law. Such private property as might be held by a slave, wife, or son who was under the *patria potestas*, separate from the property of the father or master, and in the personal disposal of the owner.

PECULIUM CASTRENSE. In Roman law. That kind of *peculium* which a son acquired in war, or from his connection with the camp, (*castrum.*) Heinecc. Elem. lib. 2, tit. 9, § 474.

PECUNIA. Lat. Originally and radically, property in cattle, or cattle themselves. So called because the wealth of the ancients consisted in cattle. Co.Litt. 207*b*.

In old English law. Goods and chattels. Spelman.

In the civil law. Property in general, real or personal; anything that is actually the subject of private property. In a narrower sense, personal property; fungible things. In the strictest sense, money. This has become the prevalent, and almost the exclusive, meaning of the word.

PECUNIA CONSTITUTA. In Roman law. Money owing (even upon a moral obligation) upon a day being fixed (*constituta*) for its payment, became recoverable upon the implied promise to pay on that day, in an action called "*de pecunia constituta,*" the implied promise not amounting (of course) to a *stipulatio*. Brown.

PECUNIA DICITUR A PECUS, OMNES ENIM VETERUM DIVITIÆ IN ANIMALIBUS CONSISTEBANT. Co.Litt. 207. Money (*pecunia*) is so called from cattle, (*pecus,*) because all the wealth of our ancestors consisted in cattle.

PECUNIA NON NUMERATA. In the civil law. Money not paid. The subject of an exception or plea in certain cases. Inst. 4, 13, 2.

PECUNIA NUMERATA. Money numbered or counted out; *i. e.*, given in payment of a debt.

PECUNIA SEPULCHRALIS. Money anciently paid to the priest at the opening of a grave for the good of the deceased's soul.

PECUNIA TRAJECTITIA. In the civil law. A loan in money, or in wares which the debtor purchases with the money to be sent by sea, and whereby the creditor, according to the contract, assumes the risk of the loss from the day of the departure of the vessel till the day of her arrival at her port of destination. Interest does not necessarily arise from this loan, but when is stipulated for it is termed "*nauticum fœnus*," (maritime interest,) and, because of the risk which the creditor assumes, he is permitted to receive a higher interest than usual. Mackeld.Rom.Law, § 433.

PECUNIARY. Monetary; relating to money; financial; consisting of money or that which can be valued in money. El Paso Electric Ry. Co. v. Benjamin, Tex.Civ.App., 202 S.W. 996, 998; In re Foster's Will, 143 Misc. 191, 256 N.Y.S. 383, 387.

As to pecuniary "Consideration," "Damages," and "Legacy," see those titles.

PECUNIARY BENEFITS. Include such things only as can be valued in money. Dallas Ry. & Terminal Co. v. Moore, Tex.Civ.App., 52 S.W.2d 104.

PECUNIARY CAUSES. In English ecclesiastical practice. Causes arising from the withholding of ecclesiastical dues, or the doing or neglecting some act relating to the church whereby some damage accrues to the plaintiff. 3 Bl.Comm. 88.

PECUNIARY CONDITION. Within statute relative to obtaining goods by false pretenses, comprehends, not only money in hand, but property and all other assets of value constituting an existing fact that go to make up financial responsibility as a basis of credit. Dennis v. State, 16 Ala. App. 115, 75 So. 707, 708.

PECUNIARY LOSS. A loss of money, or of something by which money or something of money value may be acquired. Green v. Hudson River R. Co., 32 Barb. (N.Y.) 33.

As applied to a dependent's loss from death pecuniary loss means the reasonable expectation of pecuniary benefit from the continued life of the deceased, to be inferred from proof of assistance by way of money, services, or other material benefits rendered prior to death. Standard Forgings Co. v. Holmstrom, 58 Ind.App. 306, 104 N.E. 872, 875; Louisville & N. R. Co. v. Holloway's Adm'r, 168 Ky. 262, 181 S.W. 1126, 1129. "Pecuniary loss" is a term employed judicially to discriminate between a material loss which is susceptible of pecuniary valuation, and that inestimable loss of the society and companionship of the deceased relative upon which, in the nature of things, it is not possible to set a pecuniary valuation. Michigan Cent. R. Co. v. Vreeland, 33 S.Ct. 192, 196, 227 U.S. 59, 57 L.Ed. 417, Ann.Cas.1914C, 176.

PECUS. Lat. In Roman law. Cattle; a beast. Under a bequest of *pecudes* were included oxen and other beasts of burden. Dig. 32, 81, 2.

PEDAGE. In old English law. A toll or tax paid by travelers for the privilege of passing, on foot or mounted, through a forest or other protected place. Spelman.

PEDAGIUM. L. Lat. Pedage, (*q. v.*)

PEDANEUS. Lat. In Roman law. At the foot; in a lower position; on the ground. See Judex Pedaneus.

PEDAULUS (Lat. *pes* foot). In civil law. A judge who sat at the foot of the tribunal, *i. e.* on the lowest seats, ready to try matters of little moment at command of the prætor. Calvinus, Lex.; Vicat, Voc.Jur.

PEDDLER. An itinerant trader; a person who sells small wares, which he carries with him in traveling about from place to place. In re Wilson, 19 D.C. 341, 12 L.R.A. 624; Hall v. State, 39 Fla. 637, 23 So. 119; Graffty v. Rushville, 107 Ind. 502, 8 N.E. 609, 57 Am.Rep. 128; In re Pringle, 67 Kan. 364, 72 P. 864; State ex rel. Brittain v. Hayes, 143 La. 39, 78 So. 143, 144; De Witt v. State, 155 Wis. 249, 144 N.W. 253. Persons, except those peddling newspapers, Bibles, or religious tracts, who sell, or offer to sell, at retail, goods, wares, or other commodities, traveling from place to place, in the street, or through different parts of the country are peddlers. 12 U.S. St. at Large, p. 458, § 27.

Distinguished from "trader" who has goods for sale and sells them in a fixed place of business. Commonwealth v. Bergeron, 296 Mass. 60, 5 N.E.2d 31, 32.

PEDESTRIAN. A person traveling on foot. Leopold v. Williams, 54 Ohio App. 540, 8 N.E.2d 476; Maletis v. Portland Traction Co., 160 Or. 30, 83 P.2d 141, 143.

PEDE PULVEROSUS. In old English and Scotch law. Dusty-foot. A term applied to itinerant merchants, chapmen, or peddlers who attended fairs.

PEDERASTY. In criminal law. The unnatural carnal copulation of male with male, particularly of a man with a boy; a form of sodomy, (*q. v.*)

PEDIGREE. Lineage, descent, and succession of families; line of ancestors from which a person descends; genealogy. An account or register of a line of ancestors. Family relationship. Swink v. French, 11 Lea, Tenn., 80, 47 Am.Rep. 277; People v. Mayne, 118 Cal. 516, 50 P. 654, 62 Am. St.Rep. 256; In re Wood's Estate, 164 Misc. 425, 299 N.Y.S. 195, 202.

The rule admitting hearsay evidence in matters of "pedigree" embraces, not only descent and relationship, but also facts and dates of birth, marriage, and death. Lincoln Reserve Life Ins. Co. v. Morgan, 126 Ark. 615, 191 S.W. 236; In re Paulsen's Estate, 179 Cal. 528, 178 P. 143, 145; Tuite v. Supreme Forest Woodmen Circle, 193 Mo. App. 619, 187 S.W. 137, 140.

PEDIS ABSCISSIO. Lat. In old criminal law. The cutting off a foot; a punishment anciently inflicted instead of death. Fleta, lib. 1, c. 38.

PEDIS POSITIO. Lat. In the civil and old English law. A putting or placing of the foot. A term used to denote the possession of lands by actual corporal entry upon them. Waggoner v. Hastings, 5 Pa. 303.

PEDIS POSSESSIO. Lat. A foothold; an actual possession. To constitute adverse possession there must be *pedis possessio*, or a substantial inclosure. 2 Bouv.Inst. no. 2193; Bailey v. Irby, 2 Nott & McC. (S.C.) 343, 10 Am.Dec. 609.

PEDONES. Foot-soldiers.

PEEPING TOM. A person who makes it a habit of sneaking up to windows and peeping in, for the purpose generally of seeing the women of the household in the nude. Browder v. Cook, D.C. Idaho, 59 F.Supp. 225, 231.

PEERAGE. The rank or dignity of a peer or nobleman. Also the body of nobles taken collectively.

PEERESS. A woman who belongs to the nobility, which may be either in her own right or by right of marriage.

PEERS. In feudal law. The vassals of a lord who sat in his court as judges of their co-vassals, and were called "peers," as being each other's equals, or of the same condition. The nobility of Great Britain, being the lords temporal having seats in parliament, and including dukes, marquises, earls, viscounts, and barons.

Equals; those who are a man's equals in rank and station; thus "trial by a jury of his peers" means trial by jury of citizens. In re Grilli, 110 Misc. 45, 179 N.Y.S. 795, 797. For "judgment of his peers," see Judgment.

PEERS OF FEES. Vassals or tenants of the same lord, who were obliged to serve and attend him in his courts, being equal in function. These were termed "peers of fees," because holding fees of the lord, or because their business in court was to sit and judge, under their lords, of disputes arising upon fees; but, if there were too many in one lordship, the lord usually chose twelve, who had the title of peers, by way of distinction; whence, it is said, we derive our common juries and other peers. Cowell.

PEINE FORTE ET DURE. L. Fr. In old English law. A special form of punishment for those who, being arraigned for felony, obstinately "stood mute," that is, refused to plead or to put themselves upon trial. It is described as a combination of solitary confinement, slow starvation, and crushing the naked body with a great load of iron. This atrocious punishment was vulgarly called "pressing to death." See 4 Bl.Comm. 324–328; Britt. cc. 4, 22; 2 Reeve, Eng.Law 134; Cowell.

PELA. A peal, pile, or fort. Cowell.

PELES. Issues arising from or out of a thing. Jacob.

PELFE, or PELFRE. Booty; also the personal effects of a felon convict. Cowell.

PELLAGE. The custom or duty paid for skins of leather.

PELLEX. Lat. In Roman law. A concubine. Dig. 50, 16, 144.

PELLICIA. A pilch or surplice. Spelman.

PELLIPARIUS. A leather-seller or skinner. Jacob.

PELLOTA. The ball of a foot. 4 Inst. 308.

PELLS, CLERK (or MASTER) OF THE. Formerly, an officer in the English exchequer, who entered every teller's bill on the parchment rolls, *i. e.*, "pells," commonly two in number, one being the pell or roll of receipts, and the other the pell or roll of disbursements.

PELT-WOOL. The wool pulled off the skin or pelt of dead sheep. 8 Hen. VI. c. 22.

PENAL. Punishable; inflicting a punishment; containing a penalty, or relating to a penalty. Missouri, K. & T. Ry. Co. v. Dewey Portland Cement Co., 113 Okl. 142, 242 P. 257.

PENAL ACTION. In practice. An action upon a penal statute; an action for the recovery of a penalty given by statute. 3 Steph. 535, 536; Smith Engineering Works v. Custer, 194 Okl. 318, 151 P.2d 404, 407, 408. An action which enforces a forfeiture or penalty for transgressing the law. The term "penal" is broader than "criminal," and relates to actions which are not necessarily criminal as well. The term "penalty" in its broad sense is a generic term which includes fines as well as other kinds of punishment, but in its narrowest sense is the amount recovered for violation of the statute law of the state or a municipal ordinance, which violation may or may not be a crime, and the term applies mostly to a pecuniary punishment. The word "forfeiture" is frequently used in civil as well as criminal law, and it is also used in actions for a penalty, although the action is a civil one. Silberman v. Skouras Theatres Corporation, 11 N.J.Misc. 907, 169 A. 170, 171.

Distinguished from a popular or *qui tam* action, in which the action is brought by the informer, to whom part of the penalty goes. A penal action or information is brought by an officer, and the penalty goes to the king. 1 Chit. Gen.Pr. 25, note; 2 Archb. Pr. 188. But in American law, the term includes actions brought by informers or other private persons, as well as those instituted by governments or public officers. In a broad sense, the term has been made to include all actions in which there may be a recovery of exemplary or vindictive damages, as suits for libel and slander, or in which special, double, or treble damages are given by statute, such as actions to recover money paid as usury or lost in gaming. See Bailey v. Dean, 5 Barb., N.Y., 303; Ashley v. Frame, 4 Kan.App. 265, 45 P. 927; Cole v. Groves, 134 Mass. 472. But in a more particular sense it means (1) an action on a statute which gives a certain penalty to be recovered by any person who will sue for it. Gawthrop v. Fairmont Coal Co., 74 W.Va. 39, 81 S.E. 560, 561; McNeely v. City of Natchez, 148 Miss. 268, 114 So. 484, 487, or (2) an action in which the judgment against the defendant is in the nature of a fine or is intended as a punishment, actions in which the recovery is to be compensatory in its purpose and effect not being penal actions but civil suits, though they may carry special damages by statute. Moller v. U. S., 6 C.C.A. 459, 57 F. 490; Atlanta v. Chattanooga Foundry & Pipe Works, 61 C.C.A. 387, 127 F. 23, 64 L.R.A. 721.

PENAL BILL. An instrument formerly in use, by which a party bound himself to pay a certain sum or sums of money, or to do certain acts, or, in default thereof, to pay a certain specified sum by way of penalty; thence termed a "penal sum." These instruments have been superseded by the use of a bond in a penal sum, with conditions. Brown.

PENAL BOND. A promise to pay a named sum of money, the penalty, with a condition underwritten that, if a stipulated collateral thing, other than the payment of money, be done or forborne, the obligation shall be void. Maryland Casualty Co. v. Kansas City, Mo., C.C.A.Mo., 128 F.2d 998, 1004.

PENAL CLAUSE. A secondary obligation entered into for purpose of enforcing performance of a primary obligation, and nature of penalty is by way of compensation for damages and not as punishment for failure to perform obligation. Civ.Code, art. 2117. Reimann v. New Orleans Public Service, 191 La. 1079, 187 So. 30, 31, 32. Also a clause in a statute declaring a penalty for a violation of the preceding clauses.

PENAL LAWS. Those which prohibit an act and impose a penalty for the commission of it. 2 Cro.Jac. 415. Strictly and properly speaking, a penal law is one imposing a penalty or punishment (and properly a pecuniary fine or mulct) for some offense of a public nature or wrong committed against the state. Kilton v. Providence Tool Co., 22 R.I. 605, 48 A. 1039; Wellman v. Mead, 93 Vt. 322, 107 A. 396, 397; Atlantic Coast Line R. Co. v. State, 73 Fla. 609, 74 So. 595, 600. Strictly speaking, statutes giving a private action against a wrongdoer are not penal in their nature, neither the liability imposed nor the remedy given being penal. If the wrong done is to the individual, the law giving him a right of action is remedial, rather than penal, though the sum to be recovered may be called a "penalty" or may consist in double or treble damages. See Huntington v. Attrill, 13 S.Ct. 224, 146 U.S. 657, 36 L.Ed. 1123; Diversey v. Smith, 103 Ill. 390, 42 Am.Rep. 14; Cullinan v. Burkhard, 41 Misc. 321, 84 N.Y.S. 825; Credit Men's Adjustment Co. v. Vickery, 62 Colo. 214, 161 P. 297, 298.

Where a statute is both penal and remedial, as where it is penal in one part and remedial in the other, it should be considered as a "penal statute" when it is sought to enforce the penalty, and as a "remedial statute" when it is sought to enforce the remedy. Collins v. Kidd, D.C.Tex., 38 F.Supp. 634, 637.

PENAL SERVITUDE. In English criminal law, is a punishment which consists in keeping an offender in confinement, and compelling him to labor. Steph.Crim.Dig. 2.

PENAL STATUTES. See Penal Laws.

PENAL SUM. A sum agreed upon in a bond, to be forfeited if the condition of the bond is not fulfilled.

PENALTY. The sum of money which the obligor of a bond undertakes to pay in the event of his omitting to perform or carry out the terms imposed upon him by the conditions of the bond. Brown. Stennick v. J. K. Lumber Co., 85 Or. 444, 161 P. 97, 106. An agreement to pay a greater sum, to secure the payment of a less sum. It is conditional, and can be avoided by the payment of the less sum before the contingency agreed upon shall happen. By what name it is called is immaterial. McClain v. Continental Supply Co., 66 Okl. 225, 168 P. 815, 816. A punishment; a punishment imposed by statute as a consequence of the commission of an offense. People v. Nedrow, 122 Ill. 363, 13 N.E. 533; State of Iowa v. Chicago, etc., R. Co., C.C., 37 F. 497, 3 L.R.A. 554; Miller v. Bopp, 136 La. 788, 67 So. 831. Also money recoverable by virtue of a statute imposing a payment by way of punishment. City of Buffalo v. Neubeck, 209 App.Div. 386, 204 N.Y.S. 737, 738. State v. Franklin, 63 Utah, 442, 226 P. 674, 676. Brown v. Commins Distilleries Corporation, D.C.Ky., 56 F.Supp. 941, 942.

To constitute a "punishment" or "penalty" there must be a deprivation of property or some right, such as the enjoyment of liberty. State v. Cowen, 231 Iowa 1117, 3 N.W.2d 176, 179, 182.

PENANCE. In ecclesiastical law. An ecclesiastical punishment inflicted by an ecclesiastical court for some spiritual offense. Ayl.Par. 420.

PENCIL. An instrument made of plumbago, red chalk, or other suitable substance, for writing without ink.

PENDENCY. Suspense; the state of being pendent or undecided; the state of an action, etc., after it has been begun, and before the final disposition of it.

PENDENS. Lat. Pending; as *lis pendens*, a pending suit.

PENDENT JURISDICTION. Original jurisdiction resting under federal claim extends to any nonfederal claim against same defendant if the federal question is substantial and the federal and nonfederal claims constitute a single cause of action. Fullerton v. Monongahela Connecting R. Co., D.C.Pa., 242 F.Supp. 622, 626. Such jurisdiction exists, even though it is determined that no cause of action is made out under federal grounds. Taussig v. Wellington Fund, Inc., D.C.Del., 187 F.Supp. 179, 191. The test is whether substantially the same evidence will prove both the federal and nonfederal claims. Wagner v. World Wide Automobiles Corp., D.C.N.Y., 201 F.Supp. 22, 24.

PENDENTE LITE. Lat. Pending the suit; during the actual progress of a suit; during litigation. In re Morrissey's Will, 91 N.J.Eq. 289, 107 A. 70, 71.

PENDENTE LITE NIHIL INNOVETUR. Co. Litt. 344. During a litigation nothing new should be introduced.

PENDENTES. In the civil law. The fruits of the earth not yet separated from the ground; the fruits hanging by the roots. Ersk.Inst. 2, 2, 4.

PENDICLE. In Scotch law. A piece or parcel of ground.

PENDING. Begun, but not yet completed; during; before the conclusion of; prior to the completion of; unsettled; undetermined; in process of settlement or adjustment. Thus, an action or suit is "pending" from its inception until the rendition of final judgment. Midkiff v. Colton, C.C.A.W.Va., 242 F. 373, 381; Ex parte Craig, C.C.A. N.Y., 274 F. 177, 187; United States v. 2,049.85 Acres of Land, More or Less, in Nueces County, Tex., D.C.Tex., 49 F.Supp. 20, 22. A criminal case is pending, in the sense that a court may correct its records, until the judgment is fully satisfied. Dunn v. State, 18 Okl.Cr. 493, 196 P. 739, 741.

The term "pending appeal" may refer to the time before appeal, and while an appeal is impending. Cincinnati, H. & D. Ry. Co. v. McCullom, 183 Ind. 556, 109 N.E. 206, 209, Ann.Cas.1917E, 1165.

PENETRATION. A term used in criminal law, and denoting (in cases of alleged rape) the insertion of the male part into the female parts to however slight an extent; and by which insertion the offense is complete without proof of emission. Brown.

PENITENTIALS. A compilation or list of sins and other penances, compiled in the Eastern Church and in the extreme west about the sixth century. Stubbs, Canon Law, in 1 Sel.Essays in Anglo-Amer. L. H. 252.

PENITENTIARY. A prison or place of punishment; the place of punishment in which convicts sentenced to confinement and hard labor are confined by the authority of the law. Millar v. State, 2 Kan. 175; Bowers v. Bowers, 114 Ohio St. 568, 151 N.E. 750, 751; State v. Rardon, 221 Ind. 154, 46 N.E.2d 605, 609.

PENNON. A standard, banner, or ensign carried in war.

PENNY. An English coin, being the twelfth part of a shilling. It was also used in America during the colonial period.

PENNYWEIGHT. A Troy weight, equal to twenty-four grains, or one-twentieth part of an ounce.

PENSAM. The full weight of twenty ounces.

PENSIO. Lat. In the civil law. A payment, properly, for the use of a thing. A rent; a payment for the use and occupation of another's house.

PENSION. A stated allowance out of the public treasury granted by government to an individual, or to his representatives, for his valuable services to the country, or in compensation for loss or damage sustained by him in the public service. Frisbie v. U. S., 15 S.Ct. 586, 157 U.S. 160, 39 L.Ed. 657; State ex rel. Wander v. Kimmel, 256 Mo. 611, 165 S.W. 1067, 1072; Dickey v. Jackson, 181 Iowa, 1155, 165 N.W. 387, 389; Hawkins v. Randolph, 149 Ark. 124, 231 S.W. 556, 559.

"Pensions" are in the nature of bounties of the government, which it has the right to give, withhold, distribute, or recall at its discretion. Pecoy v. City of Chicago, 265 Ill. 78, 106 N.E. 435, 436; Rohe v. City of Covington, 255 Ky. 164, 73 S.W.2d 19, 20.

In civil, Scotch, and Spanish law. A rent; an annual rent.

In English practice. An annual payment made by each member of the inns of court. Cowell; Holthouse. Also an assembly of the members of the society of Gray's Inn, to consult of their affairs.

PENSION OF CHURCHES. In English ecclesiastical law. Certain sums of money paid to clergymen in lieu of tithes. A spiritual person may sue in the spiritual court for a pension originally granted and confirmed by the ordinary, but, where it is granted by a temporal person to a clerk, he cannot; as, if one grant an annuity to a parson, he must sue for it in the temporal courts. Cro. Eliz. 675.

PENSION WRIT. A peremptory order against a member of an inn of court who is in arrear for his pensions, (that is, for his periodical dues), or for other duties. Cowell.

PENSIONARY PARLIAMENT. A parliament of Charles II which was prolonged for nearly 18 years.

PENSIONER. One who is supported by an allowance at the will of another; a dependent. It is usually applied (in a public sense) to those who receive pensions or annuities from government, who are chiefly such as have retired from places of honor and emolument. Jacob.

Persons making periodical payments are sometimes so called. Thus, resident undergraduates of the university of Cambridge, who are not on the foundation of any college, are spoken of as "pensioners." Mozley & Whiteley.

The head of one of the Inns of Court, otherwise the Treasurer. *Pension* was used to designate meetings of the Benchers in Gray's Inn.

PENT-ROAD. A road shut up or closed at its terminal points. Wolcott v. Whitcomb, 40 Vt. 41.

PENTECOSTALS. In ecclesiastical law. Pious oblations made at the feast of Pentecost by parishioners to their priests, and sometimes by inferior churches or parishes to the principal mother churches. They are also called "Whitsun farthings." Wharton.

PEON. In Mexico. A debtor held by his creditor in a qualified servitude to work out the debt; a serf. Webster.

In India. A footman; a soldier; an inferior officer; a servant employed in the business of the revenue, police, or judicature.

PEONAGE. The state or condition of a peon as above defined; a condition of enforced servitude, by which the servitor is restrained of his liberty and compelled to labor in liquidation of some debt or obligation, real or pretended, against his will. Peonage Cases, D.C.Ala., 123 F. 671; In re Lewis,

C.C.Fla., 114 F. 963; Pierce v. U. S., C.C.A.Ga., 146 F.2d 84, 86.

PEONIA. In Spanish law. A portion of land which was formerly given to a simple soldier on the conquest of a country. It is now a quantity of land of different size in different provinces. In the Spanish possessions in America it measured fifty feet front and one hundred feet deep. 2 White, N.Rec. 49; Strother v. Lucas, 12 Pet., U.S. 444, 9 L.Ed. 1137. See Caballeria.

PEOPLE. A state; as the people of the state of New York. A nation in its collective and political capacity. Nesbitt v. Lushington, 4 Term R. 783; U. S. v. Quincy, 6 Pet. 467, 8 L.Ed. 458; U. S. v. Trumbull, D.C.Cal., 48 F. 99. The aggregate or mass of the individuals who constitute the state. Solon v. State, 54 Tex.Cr.R. 261, 114 S.W. 349; Loi Hoa v. Nagle, C.C.A.Cal., 13 F.2d 80, 81.

In a more restricted sense, and as generally used in constitutional law, the entire body of those citizens of a state or nation who are invested with political power for political purposes, that is, the qualified voters or electors. Koehler v. Hill, 60 Iowa 543, 15 N.W. 609; Boyd v. Nebraska, 12 S.Ct. 375, 143 U.S. 135, 36 L.Ed. 103; In re Incurring of State Debts, 19 R.I. 610, 37 A. 14; In re Opinion of the Justices, 226 Mass. 607, 115 N.E. 921, 922; State v. City of Albuquerque, 31 N.M. 576, 249 P. 242, 247.

In neutrality laws, a government recognized by the United States. The Three Friends, D.C.Fla., 78 F. 175.

The word "people" may have various significations according to the connection in which it is used. When we speak of the rights of the people, or of the government of the people by law, or of the people as a non-political aggregate, we mean all the inhabitants of the state or nation, without distinction as to sex, age, or otherwise. But when reference is made to the people as the repository of sovereignty, or as the source of governmental power, or to popular government, we are in fact speaking of that selected and limited class of citizens to whom the constitution accords the elective franchise and the right of participation in the offices of government. Black, Const. Law 3d Ed. p. 30.

PEPPERCORN. A dried berry of the black pepper. In English law, the reservation of a merely nominal rent, on a lease, is sometimes expressed by a stipulation for the payment of a peppercorn.

PER. Lat. By, through, or by means of. Lea v. Helgerson, Tex.Civ.App., 228 S.W. 992, 993. When a writ of entry is sued out against the alienee of the original intruder or disseisor, or against his heir to whom the land has descended, it is said to be brought "in the *per*," because the writ then states that the tenant had not entry but by (*per*) the original wrong-doer. 3 Bl.Comm. 181.

Words "by," "per," "pro," used to signature and adding description thereto, such as agent, shows that person signed official name alone and not personally. Agricultural Bond & Credit Corporation v. Courtenay Farmers' Co-op. Ass'n, 64 N.D. 253, 251 N.W. 881.

PER ÆS ET LIBRAM. Lat. In Roman law. The sale *per æs et libram* (with copper and scales) was a ceremony used in transferring *res mancipi*, in the emancipation of a son or slave, and in one of the forms of making a will. The parties having assembled, with a number of witnesses, and one who held a balance or scales, the purchaser struck the scales with a copper coin, repeating a formula by which he claimed the subject-matter of the transaction as his property, and handed the coin to the vendor.

PER ALLUVIONEM. Lat. In the civil law. By alluvion, or the gradual and imperceptible increase arising from deposit by water.

PER ALLUVIONEM ID VIDETUR ADJICI QUOD ITA PAULATIM ADJICITUR UT INTELLIGERE NON POSSUMUS QUANTUM QUOQUO MOMENTO TEMPORIS ADJICIATUR. That is said to be added by alluvion which is so added little by little that we cannot tell how much is added at any one moment of time. Dig. 41, 1, 7, 1; Fleta, l. 3, c. 2, § 6.

PER AND CUI. When a writ of entry is brought against a second alienee or descendant from the disseisor, it is said to be in the *per* and *cui*, because the form of the writ is that the tenant had not entry but *by* and *under* a prior alienee, *to* whom the intruder himself demised it. 3 Bl. Comm. 181.

PER AND POST. To come in in the *per* is to claim by or through the person last entitled to an estate; as the heirs or assigns of the grantee. To come in in the *post* is to claim by a paramount and prior title; as the lord by escheat.

PER ANNULUM ET BACULUM. L. Lat. In old English law. By ring and staff, or crozier. The symbolical mode of conferring an ecclesiastical investure. 1 Bl.Comm. 378, 379.

PER ANNUM. Lat. By the year. A phrase still in common use. Ramsdell v. Hulett, 50 Kan. 440, 31 P. 1092; Matheson v. Marion County Lumber Co., 95 S.C. 352, 78 S.E. 970, 971.

PER AUTRE VIE. L. Fr. For or during another's life; for such period as another person shall live.

PER AVERSIONEM. Lat. In the civil law. By turning away. A term applied to that kind of sale where the goods are taken in bulk, and not by weight or measure, and for a single price; or where a piece of land is sold as containing in gross, by estimation, a certain number of acres. Poth.Cont.Sale, nn. 256, 309. So called because the buyer acts without particular examination or discrimination, *turning* his face, as it were, *away*. Calvin.

PER BOUCHE. L. Fr. By the mouth; orally. 3 How. State Tr. 1024.

PER CAPITA. Lat. By the heads or polls; according to the number of individuals; share and share alike. This term, derived from the civil law, is much used in the law of descent and distribution, and denotes that method of dividing an intestate estate by which an equal share is given to each of a number of persons, all of whom stand in equal degree to the decedent, without reference to their stocks or the right of representation. It is the antithesis of *per stirpes*, (*q. v.*). Buxton v. Noble, 146 Kan. 671, 73 P.2d 43, 47. MacGregor v. Roux, 198 Ga. 520, 32 S.E.2d 289, 291.

PER CENT. An abbreviation of the Latin *"per centum,"* meaning by the hundred, or so many parts in the hundred, or so many hundredths. Blakeslee v. Mansfield, 66 Ill.App. 119.

PER CONSEQUENS. Lat. By consequence; consequently. Yearb. M. 9 Edw. III. 8.

PER CONSIDERATIONEM CURIÆ. Lat. In old practice. By the consideration (judgment) of the court. Yearb. M. 1 Edw. II. 2.

PER CURIAM. Lat. By the court. A phrase used in the reports to distinguish an opinion of the whole court from an opinion written by any one judge. Sometimes it denotes an opinion written by the chief justice or presiding judge. Clarke v. Western Assur. Co., 146 Pa. 561, 23 A. 248, 15 L.R.A. 127, 28 Am.St.Rep. 821.

PER DIEM. By the day; an allowance or amount of so much per day. Webster.

Generally, as used in connection with compensation, wages or salary, means pay for a day's service. Scroggie v. Scarborough, 162 S.C. 218, 160 S.E. 596, 599.

Constitution held to limit compensation which any legislature may fix for its successors to mileage and "per diem"; hence, statute authorizing allowance of personal expenses to legislature was unconstitutional. Gallarno v. Long, 214 Iowa 805, 243 N.W. 719, 725.

Per diem is sometimes and by some courts held to be included in the term fees and sometimes otherwise, and the two terms are not always synonymous. Anderson v. Beadle County, 51 S.D. 6, 211 N.W. 968, 969.

Term "per diem" as used in constitutional provision fixing compensation of members is synonymous with salary. Peay v. Nolan, 157 Tenn. 222, 7 S.W.2d 815, 817, 60 A.L.R. 408.

PER EUNDEM. Lat. By the same. This phrase is commonly used to express "by, or from the mouth of, the same judge." So *"per eundem in eadem"* means "by the same judge in the same case."

PER EXTENSUM. Lat. In old practice. At length.

PER FORMAM DONI. L. Lat. In English law. By the form of the gift; by the designation of the giver, and not by the operation of law. 2 Bl. Comm. 113, 191.

PER FRAUDEM. Lat. By fraud. Where a plea alleges matter of discharge, and the replication avers that the discharge was fraudulently obtained and is therefore invalid, it is called a "replication *per fraudem.*"

PER INCURIAM. Lat. Through inadvertence. 35 Eng. Law & Eq. 302.

PER INDUSTRIAM HOMINIS. Lat. In old English law. By human industry. A term applied to the reclaiming or taming of wild animals by art, industry, and education. 2 Bl.Comm. 391.

PER INFORTUNIUM. Lat. By misadventure. In criminal law, homicide *per infortunium* is committed where a man, doing a lawful act, without any intention of hurt, unfortunately kills another. 4 Bl.Comm. 182. See Homicide.

PER LEGEM ANGLIÆ. Lat. By the law of England; by the curtesy. Fleta, lib. 2, c. 54, § 18.

PER LEGEM TERRÆ. Lat. By the law of the land; by due process of law. U. S. v. Kendall, 26 Fed.Cas. 748; Appeal of Ervine, 16 Pa. 263, 55 Am. Dec. 499.

PER METAS ET BUNDAS. L. Lat. In old English law. By metes and bounds.

PER MINAS. Lat. By threats. See Duress.

PER MISADVENTURE. In old English law. By mischance. 4 Bl.Comm. 182. The same with *per infortunium (q. v.).*

PER MITTER LE DROIT. L. Fr. By passing the right. One of the modes by which releases at common law were said to inure was *"per mitter le droit,"* as where a person who had been disseised released to the disseisor or his heir or feoffee. In such case, by the release, the right which was in the releasor was added to the possession of the releasee, and the two combined perfected the estate. Miller v. Emans, 19 N.Y. 387.

PER MITTER L'ESTATE. L. Fr. By passing the estate. At common law, if two or more are seised, either by deed, devise, or descent, as joint tenants or coparceners of the same estate, and one of them releases to the other, this is said to inure by way of *"per mitter l'estate."* Miller v. Emans, 19 N.Y. 388.

PER MY ET PER TOUT. L. Fr. By the half and by the whole. A phrase descriptive of the mode in which joint tenants hold the joint estate, the effect of which, technically considered, is that for purposes of tenure and survivorship each is the holder of the whole, but for purposes of alienation each has only his own share, which is presumed in law to be equal. 1 Washb.Real Prop. 406.

PER PAIS, TRIAL. Trial by the country; *i. e.,* by jury.

PER PROCURATION. By proxy; by one acting as an agent with special powers; as under a letter of attorney. These words "give notice to all persons that the agent is acting under a special and limited authority." 10 C.B. 689. The phrase is commonly abbreviated to *"per proc.,"* or *"p. p.,"* and is more used in the civil law and in England than in American law.

PER QUÆ SERVITIA. Lat. A real action by which the grantee of a seigniory could compel the tenants of the grantor to attorn to himself. It was abolished by St. 3 & 4 Wm. IV, c. 27, § 35.

PER QUOD. Lat. Whereby. When the declaration in an action of tort, after stating the acts complained of, goes on to allege the consequences of those acts as a ground of special damage to the plaintiff, the recital of such consequences is prefaced by these words, *"per quod,"* whereby;

and sometimes the phrase is used as the name of that clause of the declaration.

Words "actionable per quod" are those not actionable per se upon their face, but are only actionable in consequence of extrinsic facts showing circumstances under which they were said or the damages resulting to slandered party therefrom. Smith v. Mustain, 210 Ky. 445, 276 S.W. 154, 155, 44 A.L.R. 386.

PER QUOD CONSORTIUM AMISIT. Lat. In old pleading. Whereby he lost the company [of his wife.] A phrase used in the old declarations in actions of trespass by a husband for beating or ill using his wife, descriptive of the special damage he had sustained. 3 Bl.Comm. 140; Cro.Jac. 501, 538; Crocker v. Crocker, C.C.Mass., 98 F. 703.

PER QUOD SERVITIUM AMISIT. Lat. In old pleading. Whereby he lost the service [of his servant.] A phrase used in the old declarations in actions of trespass by a master, for beating or ill using his servant, descriptive of the special damage he had himself sustained. 3 Bl.Comm. 142; 9 Coke, 113*a*; Callaghan v. Lake Hopatcong Ice Co., 69 N.J.Law, 100, 54 A. 223. This action is commonly brought by the father for the seduction of his daughter, in which case very slight evidence of the relation of master and servant is necessary; but still some loss of service, or some expense, must be shown; 5 B. & P. 466; 5 Price, 641; Kendrick v. McCrary, 11 Ga. 603; Phelin v. Kenderdine, 20 Pa. 354.

PER RATIONES PERVENITUR AD LEGITIMAM RATIONEM. Litt. § 386. By reasoning we come to true reason.

PER RERUM NATURAM FACTUM NEGANTIS NULLA PROBATIO EST. It is in the nature of things that he who denies a fact is not bound to give proof.

PER SALTUM. Lat. By a leap or bound; by a sudden movement; passing over certain proceedings. 8 East, 511.

PER SAMPLE. By sample. A purchase so made is a collateral engagement that the goods shall be of a particular quality. 4 B. & Ald. 387.

PER SE. Lat. By himself or itself; in itself; taken alone; inherently; in isolation; unconnected with other matters. Findley v. Wilson, 115 Okl. 280, 242 P. 565, 568; Rowan v. Gazette Printing Co., 74 Mont. 326, 239 P. 1035, 1037.

PER STIRPES. Lat. By roots or stocks; by representation. This term, derived from the civil law, is much used in the law of descents and distribution, and denotes that method of dividing an intestate estate where a class or group of distributees take the share which their deceased would have been entitled to, taking thus by their right of representing such ancestor, and not as so many individuals. In re Shoch's Estate, 271 Pa. 165, 114 A. 505, 506; Petition of Gee, 44 R.I. 132, 115 A. 716, 717; Buxton v. Noble, 146 Kan. 671, 73 P.2d 43, 47.

PER TOTAM CURIAM. L. Lat. By the whole court. A common phrase in the old reports.

PER TOUT ET NON PER MY. L. Fr. By the whole, and not by the moiety. Where an estate in fee is given to a man and his wife, they cannot take the estate by moieties, but both are seised of the entirety, *per tout et non per my*. 2 Bl.Comm. 182.

PER UNIVERSITATEM. Lat. In the civil law. By an aggregate or whole; as an entirety. The term described the acquisition of an entire estate by one act or fact, as distinguished from the acquisition of single or detached things.

PER VADIUM. L. Lat. In old practice. By gage. Words in the old writs of attachment or *pone*. 3 Bl.Comm. 280.

PER VARIOS ACTUS LEGEM EXPERIENTIA FACIT. By various acts experience frames the law. 4 Inst. 50.

PER VERBA DE FUTURO. Lat. By words of the future [tense.] A phrase applied to contracts of marriage. 1 Bl.Comm. 439; 2 Kent, Comm. 87.

PER VERBA DE PRÆSENTI. Lat. By words of the present [tense.] A phrase applied to contracts of marriage. 1 Bl.Comm. 439.

PER VISUM ECCLESIÆ. Lat. In old English law. By view of the church; under the supervision of the church. The disposition of intestates' goods *per visum ecclesiœ* was one of the articles confirmed to the prelates by King John's *Magna Charta*. 3 Bl.Comm. 96.

PER VIVAM VOCEM. Lat. In old English law. By the living voice; the same with *viva voce*. Bract. fol. 95.

PER YEAR, in a contract, is equivalent to the word "annually." Curtiss v. Howell, 39 N.Y. 211; Larson v. Augustana Colonization Ass'n of North America, 155 Minn. 1, 192 N.W. 108.

PERAMBULATION. The act or custom of walking over the boundaries of a district or piece of land, either for the purpose of determining them or of preserving evidence of them. Thus, in many parishes in England, it is the custom for the parishioners to perambulate the boundaries of the parish in rogation week in every year. Such a custom entitles them to enter any man's land and abate nuisances in their way. Phillim.Ecc. Law, 1867; Hunt, Bound. 103; Sweet; Greenville v. Mason, 57 N.H. 385.

The custom has now largely fallen into disuse. Cent. Dict.

PERAMBULATIONE FACIENDA, WRIT DE. In English law. The name of a writ which is sued by consent of both parties when they are in doubt as to the bounds of their respective estates. It is directed to the sheriff to make perambulation, and to set the bounds and limits between them in certainty. Fitzh.Nat.Brev. 133.

PERCA. A perch of land; sixteen and one-half feet. See Perch.

PERCEIVABLE RISK. Risk which indefinite and uncertain. Martin v. Hodson, 93 N.H. 66, 35 A.2d 402, 404.

PERCEPTION. Taking into possession. Thus, perception of crops or of profits is reducing them to possession. Used of money, it means the counting out and payment of a debt. Also used for food due to soldiers. Vicat, Voc.Jur.

PERCEPTURA. In old records. A wear; a place in a river made up with banks, dams, etc., for the better convenience of preserving and taking fish. Cowell.

PERCH. A measure of land containing five yards and a half, or sixteen feet and a half in length; otherwise called a "rod" or "pole." Cowell.

As a unit of solid measure, a perch of masonry or stone or brick work contains, according to some authorities and in some localities, sixteen and one-half cubic feet, but elsewhere, or according to others, twenty-five. Unless defined by statute, it is a very indefinite term and must be explained by evidence. Harris v. Rutledge, 19 Iowa 388, 87 Am. Dec. 441; Sullivan v. Richardson, 33 Fla. 1, 14 So. 692.

PERCOLATE. As used in the cases relating to the right of land-owners to use water on their premises, designates any flowage of sub-surface water other than that of a running stream, open, visible, clearly to be traced. Mosier v. Caldwell, 7 Nev. 363.

PERCOLATING WATERS. See Water.

PERDIDA. A synonym of damages. Ponce De Leon v. Coca Cola Bottling Co., D.C.Puerto Rico, 75 F.Supp. 966.

PERDONATIO UTLAGARIÆ. L. Lat. A pardon for a man who, for contempt in not yielding obedience to the process of a court, is outlawed, and afterwards of his own accord surrenders. Reg.Orig. 28.

PERDUELLIO. Lat. In Roman law. Hostility or enmity towards the Roman republic; traitorous conduct on the part of a citizen, subversive of the authority of the laws or tending to overthrow the government. Calvin; Vicat.

PERDURABLE. As applied to an estate, perdurable signifies lasting long or forever. Thus, a disseisor or tenant in fee upon condition has as high and great an estate as the rightful owner or tenant in fee-simple absolute, but not so perdurable. The term is chiefly used with reference to the extinguishment of rights by unity of seisin, which does not take place unless both the right and the land out of which it issues are held for equally high and perdurable estates. Co.Litt. 313*a*, 313*b*; Gale Easem. 582; Sweet.

PEREGRINI. Lat. The name given to aliens in Rome. The class of *peregrini* embraced at the same time both those who had no capacity in law (capacity for rights or jural relations,) namely, the slaves, and the members of those nations which had not established amicable relations with the Roman people. Sav. Dr. Rom. § 66.

PEREMPT. In ecclesiastical procedure, to waive or bar an appeal by one's own act so as partially to comply with or acquiesce in a sentence of a court. Phill.Eccl.L. 1275; Rog.Eccl.L. 47.

PEREMPTION. A nonsuit; also a quashing or killing.

PEREMPTORIUS. Lat. In the civil law. That which takes away or destroys forever; hence, *exceptio peremptoria*, a plea which is a perpetual bar. Calvin.

PEREMPTORY. Imperative; absolute; conclusive; positive; not admitting of question, delay, or reconsideration. Positive; final; decisive; not admitting of any alternative. Self-determined; arbitrary; not requiring any cause to be shown. Wolfe v. State, 147 Tex.Cr.R. 62, 178 S.W.2d 274, 279.

As to peremptory "Challenge," "Defense," "Instruction," "Mandamus," "Nonsuit," "Plea," and "Writ," see those titles.

PEREMPTORY DAY. A day assigned for trial or hearing in court, absolutely and without further opportunity for postponement.

PEREMPTORY EXCEPTIONS. In the civil law. Any defense which denies entirely the ground of action. Those exceptions which tend to the dismissal of the action.

PEREMPTORY PAPER. A list of the causes which were enlarged at the request of the parties, or which stood over from press of business in court.

PEREMPTORY RULE. In practice. An absolute rule; a rule without any condition or alternative of showing cause.

PEREMPTORY UNDERTAKING. An undertaking by a plaintiff to bring on a cause for trial at the next sittings or assizes. Lush, Pr. 649.

PERFECT. Complete; finished; executed; enforceable; without defect; merchantable; marketable. Sliosberg v. New York Life Ins. Co., 217 App.Div. 67, 216 N.Y.S. 215, 220; Tucker v. Thraves, 50 Okl. 691, 702, 151 P. 598, 601; Satterthwaite v. Van Dissen, 99 Okl. 233, 226 P. 583, 584.

As to perfect "Equity," "Obligation," "Ownership," "Title," and "Usufruct," see those titles.

PERFECT ATTESTATION CLAUSE. One that asserts performance of all acts required to be done to make valid testamentary disposition. In re Johnson's Will, Prerog., 115 N.J.Eq. 249, 171 A. 307, 309.

PERFECT CONDITION. In a statement of the rule that, when two claims exist in "perfect condition" between two persons, either may insist on a set-off, this term means that state of a demand when it is of right demandable by its terms. Taylor v. New York, 82 N.Y. 17.

PERFECT INSTRUMENT. An instrument such as a deed or mortgage is said to become perfect when recorded (or registered) or filed for record, because it then becomes good as to all the world. Wilkins v. McCorkle, 112 Tenn. 688, 80 S.W. 834.

PERFECT MACHINE. In patent law. A perfected invention; not a perfectly constructed machine, but a machine so constructed as to embody all the essential elements of the invention, in a form that would make them practical and operative so as to accomplish the result.

But it is not necessary that it should accomplish that result in the most perfect manner, and be in a condition where it was not susceptible of a higher degree of perfection in its mere mechanical construction. American Hide, etc., Co. v. American Tool, etc., Co., 4 Fish.Pat.Cas. 299, 1 Fed.Cas. 647.

PERFECT TRUST. An executed trust, (*q. v.*).

PERFECTED. Brought to a state of perfection, completed. Krause v. Henry, Ohio App., 35 N.E. 2d 169, 170.

PERFECTING BAIL. Certain qualifications of a property character being required of persons who tender themselves as bail, when such persons have justified, *i. e.*, established their sufficiency by satisfying the court that they possess the requisite qualifications, a rule or order of court is made for their allowance, and the bail is then said to be perfected, *i. e.*, the process of giving bail is finished or completed. Brown.

PERFECTUM EST CUI NIHIL DEEST SECUNDUM SUÆ PERFECTIONIS VEL NATURÆ MODUM. That is perfect to which nothing is wanting, according to the measure of its perfection or nature. Hob. 151.

PERFIDY. The act of one who has engaged his faith to do a thing, and does not do it, but does the contrary. Wolff, Inst. § 390. Faithlessness, treachery, violation of a promise or vow or a trust reposed. Streeter v. Emmons County Farmers' Press, 57 N.D. 438, 222 N.W. 455, 458.

PERFORM. To perform an obligation or contract is to execute, fulfill, or accomplish it according to its terms. This may consist either in action on the part of the person bound by the contract or in omission to act, according to the nature of the subject-matter; but the term is usually applied to any action in discharge of a contract other than payment.

PERFORMANCE. The fulfillment or accomplishment of a promise, contract, or other obligation according to its terms.

Part Performance. The doing some portion, yet not the whole, of what either party to a contract has agreed to do. Borrow v. Borrow, 34 Wash. 684, 76 P. 305.

The "part performance" necessary to take oral contract to sell realty out of the statute of frauds must be of such character that it is impossible or impracticable to place the parties in status quo and payment in full is not sufficient. Rork v. Orcutt, 53 N.Y.S.2d 354, 356. The possession necessary to constitute "part performance" which will take an oral agreement, purporting to convey an interest in land, out of the operation of the statute of frauds must be unequivocal and in consequence of the contract. Guckenberger v. Shank, 110 Ind.App. 442, 37 N.E.2d 708, 714.

Specific Performance. Performance of a contract in the specific form in which it was made, or according to the precise terms agreed upon. This is frequently compelled by a bill in equity filed for the purpose. 2 Story, Eq.Pl. § 712, *et seq.* The actual accomplishment of a contract by a party bound to fulfill it. Guadalupe County Board of Education v. O'Bannon, 26 N.M. 606, 195 P. 801, 803; Municipal Gas Co. v. Lone Star Gas Co., Tex. Civ.App., 259 S.W. 684, 689. The doctrine of specific performance is that, where damages would be an inadequate compensation for the breach of an agreement, the contractor will be compelled to perform specifically what he has agreed to do. Sweet. As the exact fulfillment of an agreement is not always practicable, the phrase may mean, in a given case, not literal, but substantial performance. Waterm.Spec.Perf. § 1.

PERGAMENUM. In old practice. Parchment. *In pergameno scribi facit.* 1 And. 54.

PERICARDITIS. In medical jurisprudence. An inflammation of the lining membrane of the heart.

PERICULOSUM EST RES NOVAS ET INUSITATAS INDUCERE. Co.Litt. 379*a*. It is perilous to introduce new and untried things.

PERICULOSUM EXISTIMO QUOD BONORUM VIRORUM NON COMPROBATUR EXEMPLO. 9 Coke, 97*b*. I consider that dangerous which is not approved by the example of good men.

PERICULOSUS. Lat. Dangerous; perilous.

PERICULUM. Lat. In the civil law. Peril; danger; hazard; risk.

PERICULUM REI VENDITÆ, NONDUM TRADITÆ, EST EMPTORIS. The risk of a thing sold, and not yet delivered, is the purchaser's. 2 Kent, Comm. 498, 499.

PERIL. The risk, hazard, or contingency insured against by a policy of insurance.

Peril within humanitarian doctrine means certain peril, not bare possibility of injury. Thomasson v. Henwood, 235 Mo.App. 1211, 146 S.W.2d 88, 91.

PERILS OF THE LAKES. As applied to navigation of the Great Lakes, this term has the same meaning as "perils of the sea." See *infra.*

PERILS OF THE SEA. In maritime and insurance law. Natural accidents peculiar to the sea, which do not happen by the intervention of man, nor are to be prevented by human prudence. 3 Kent, Comm. 216. Hence to recover on marine policy insuring against loss by perils of sea, vessel must be seaworthy when it is sent to sea. Read v. Agricultural Ins. Co., 219 Wis. 580, 263

N.W. 632. Perils of the sea are from (1) storms and waves; (2) rocks, shoals, and rapids; (3) other obstacles, though of human origin; (4) changes of climate; (5) the confinement necessary at sea; (6) animals peculiar to the sea; (7) all other dangers peculiar to the sea. Civ.Code Cal. § 2199. All losses caused by the action of wind and water acting on the property insured under extraordinary circumstances, either directly or mediately, without the intervention of other independent active external causes, are losses by "perils of the sea or other perils and dangers," within the meaning of the usual clause in a policy of marine insurance. Baily, Perils of Sea, 6. In an enlarged sense, all losses which occur from maritime adventure may be said to arise from the perils of the sea; but underwriters are not bound to this extent. They insure against losses from extraordinary occurrences only; such as stress of weather, winds and waves, lightning, tempests, etc. These are understood to be meant by the phrase "the perils of the sea," in a marine policy, and not those ordinary perils which every vessel must encounter. American-Hawaiian S. S. Co. v. Bennett & Goodall, 125 C.C.A. 172, 207 F. 510, 513; The Mary F. Barrett, C.C.A.Pa., 279 F. 329, 331; Delanty v. Yang Tsze Ins. Ass'n, 127 Wash. 238, 220 P. 754, 758; Western Assur. Co. of Toronto, Canada, v. Shaw, C.C.A.Pa., 11 F.2d 495, 496; Union Marine Ins. Co. v. Chas. D. Stone & Co., C.C.A.Ill., 15 F.2d 937, 939.

" 'Perils of the sea' means all marine casualties resulting from the violent action of the elements, as distinguished from their natural, silent influence upon the fabric of the vessel; casualties which may, and not consequences which must, occur." Pillsbury Flour Mills Co. v. Becker S. S. Co., D.C.N.Y., 49 F.2d 648, 650.

PERINDE VALERE. A dispensation granted to a clerk, who, being defective in capacity for a benefice or other ecclesiastical function, is *de facto* admitted to it. Cowell.

PERIOD. Any point, space, or division of time.

"The word has its etymological meaning, but it also has a distinctive signification, according to the subject with which it may be used in connection. It may mean any portion of complete time, from a thousand years or less to the period of a day; and when used to designate an act to be done or to be begun, though its completion may take an uncertain time, as, for instance, the act of exportation, it must mean the day on which the exportation commences, or it would be an unmeaning and useless word in its connection in the statute. Sampson v. Peaslee, 20 How. 579, 15 L.Ed. 1022.

PERIODICAL. Recurring at fixed intervals; to be made or done, or to happen, at successive periods separated by determined intervals of time; as periodical payments of interest on a bond.

PERIPHRASIS. Circumlocution; use of many words to express the sense of one.

PERISH. To come to an end; to cease to be; to die.

PERISHABLE. Subject to speedy and natural decay. But, where the time contemplated is necessarily long, the term may embrace property liable merely to material depreciation in value from other causes than such decay. Callahan v. Danziger, 172 Cal. 738, 158 P. 760, 761; Marston v. Rue, 92 Wash. 129, 159 P. 111, 113; In re Pedlow, C.C.A.N.Y., 209 F. 841, 842; Falmouth Co-op. Marketing Ass'n v. Pennsylvania R. Co., 237 Mich. 406, 212 N.W. 84, 85.

PERISHABLE COMMODITY. A relative term used ordinarily by courts and lawyers to describe a product, like fruit or fresh vegetables, which quickly deteriorates in quality and value. In re Rosenbaum Grain Corporation, C.C.A.Ill., 83 F. 2d 391, 393.

PERISHABLE GOODS. Goods which decay and lose their value if not speedily put to their intended use. Kleinpeter v. Ferrara, 179 La. 193, 153 So. 689.

PERJURI SUNT QUI SERVATIS VERBIS JURAMENTI DECIPIUNT AURES EORUM QUI ACCIPIUNT. 3 Inst. 166. They are perjured, who, preserving the words of an oath, deceive the ears of those who receive it.

PERJURY. In criminal law. The willful assertion as to a matter of fact, opinion, belief, or knowledge, made by a witness in a judicial proceeding as part of his evidence, either upon oath or in any form allowed by law to be substituted for an oath, whether such evidence is given in open court, or in an affidavit, or otherwise, such assertion being material to the issue or point of inquiry and known to such witness to be false. 2 Whart.Crim.Law, § 1244; People v. Glenn, 294 Ill. 333, 128 N.E. 532, 533; Mathes v. State, 15 Okl.Cr. 382, 177 P. 120; Commonwealth v. Hinkle, 177 Ky. 22, 197 S.W. 455, 456; People v. Rendigs, 123 Misc.Rep. 32, 205 N.Y.S. 133, 136.

To constitute "perjury" an oath must be administered by one authorized to do so. People v. Gade, City Ct., 6 N.Y.S.2d 1018, 1021.

Perjury shall consist in willfully, knowingly, absolutely, and falsely swearing, either with or without laying the hand on the Holy Evangelist of Almighty God, or affirming, in a matter material to the issue or point in question, in some judicial proceeding, by a person to whom a lawful oath or affirmation is administered. Code Ga. 1882, § 4460 (Pen. Code 1910, § 259). Every person who, having taken an oath that he will testify, declare, depose, or certify truly before any competent tribunal, officer, or person, in any of the cases in which such an oath may by law be administered, willfully, and contrary to such oath, states as truth any material matter which he knows to be false, is guilty of perjury. Pen. Code Cal. § 118. The willful giving, under oath, in a judicial proceeding or course of justice, oi false testimony material to the issue or point of inquiry. 2 Bish.Crim. Law, § 1015. Perjury, at common law, is the "taking of a willful false oath by one who, being lawfully sworn by a competent court to depose the truth in any judicial proceeding, swears absolutely and falsely in a matter material to the point in issue, whether he believed or not." Comm. v. Powell, 2 Metc. (Ky.) 10; Cothran v. State, 39 Miss. 541. It will be observed that, at common law, the crime of perjury can be committed only in the course of a suit or judicial proceeding. But statutes have very generally extended both the definition and the punishment of this offense to willful false swearing in many different kinds of affidavits and depositions, such as those required to be made in tax returns, pension proceedings, transactions at the custom house, and various other administrative or non-judicial proceedings.

PERMANENT. Fixed, continuing, lasting, stable, enduring, abiding, not subject to change. Generally opposed in law to "temporary," but not always meaning "perpetual." Penn Mut. Life Ins. Co. v. Milton, 160 Ga. 168, 127 S.E. 140, 141, 40 A.L.R. 1382; Roseburg Nat. Bank v. Camp, 89 Or. 67, 173 P. 313, 316. Richards v. Metropolitan Life Ins. Co., 184 Wash. 595, 55 P.2d 1067, 1071.

As to permanent "Alimony," "Injunction," and "Trespass," see those titles.

PERMANENT ABODE. A domicile or fixed home, which the party may leave as his interest or whim may dictate, but which he has no present intention of abandoning. Moffett v. Hill, 131 Ill. 239, 22 N.E. 821; Berry v. Wilcox, 44 Neb. 82, 62 N.W. 249, 48 Am.St.Rep. 706.

PERMANENT BUILDING AND LOAN ASSOCIATION. One which issues its stock, not all at once or in series, but at any time when application is made therefor. Cook v. Equitable B. & L. Ass'n, 104 Ga. 814, 30 S.E. 911.

PERMANENT DISABILITY. Within insurance policies does not mean that disability must continue throughout life of insured, but it connotes idea that disability must be something more than temporary, and at least presumably permanent. Commonwealth Life Ins. Co. v. Ovesen, 257 Ky. 622, 78 S.W.2d 745, 746; Equitable Life Ins. Co. of Iowa v. Gerwick, 50 Ohio App. 277, 197 N.E. 923, 926; Equitable Life Assur. Soc. of U. S. v. Preston, 253 Ky. 459, 70 S.W.2d 18.

PERMANENT EMPLOYMENT. Provided for by contract, means only that employment is to continue indefinitely and until either party wishes to sever relation for some good reason. Speegle v. Board of Fire Underwriters of Pacific, Cal.App., 158 P.2d 426, 429; Alabama Mills v. Smith, 237 Ala. 296, 186 So. 699, 701.

PERMISSION. A license to do a thing; an authority to do an act which, without such authority, would have been unlawful.

PERMISSIONS. Negations of law, arising either from the law's silence or its express declaration. Ruth.Inst. b. 1, c. 1.

PERMISSIVE. Allowed; allowable; that which may be done.

PERMISSIVE USE. See Use.

PERMISSIVE WASTE. See Waste.

PERMIT, *v.* To suffer, allow, consent, let; to give leave or license; to acquiesce, by failure to prevent, or to expressly assent or agree to the doing of an act. State v. Waxman, 93 N.J.Law, 27, 107 A. 150; State v. Peters, 112 Ohio St. 249, 147 N.E. 81, 84; Little Falls Fibre Co. v. Henry Ford & Son, 126 Misc. 126, 212 N.Y.S. 630, 634; Lemery v. Leonard, 99 Or. 670, 196 P. 376, 378; Armstrong's Adm'r v. Sumne & Ratterman Co., 211 Ky. 750, 278 S.W. 111, 113; Atwater v. Lober, 133 Misc. 652, 233 N.Y.S. 309, 313.

PERMIT, *n.* A license or instrument granted by the officers of excise (or customs), certifying that the duties on certain goods have been paid, or secured, and permitting their removal from some specified place to another. Wharton. A written license or warrant, issued by a person in authority, empowering the grantee to do some act not forbidden by law, but not allowable without such authority.

PERMUTATIO. Lat. In the civil law. Exchange; barter. Dig. 19, 4.

PERMUTATION. The exchange of one movable subject for another; barter.

PERMUTATIONE. A writ to an ordinary, commanding him to admit a clerk to a benefice upon exchange made with another. Reg.Orig. 307.

PERNANCY. Taking; a taking or receiving; as of the profits of an estate. Actual pernancy of the profits of an estate is the taking, perception, or receipt of the rents and other advantages arising therefrom. 2 Bl.Comm. 163.

PERNOR OF PROFITS. He who receives the profits of lands, etc.; he who has the actual pernancy of the profits.

PERNOUR. L. Fr. A taker. *Le pernour ou le detenour,* the taker or the detainer. Britt. c. 27.

PERPARS. L. Lat. A purpart; a part of the inheritance.

PERPETRATOR. Generally, this term denotes the person who actually commits a crime or delict, or by whose immediate agency it occurs. But, where a servant of a railroad company is killed through the negligence of a co-employee, the company itself may be regarded as the "perpetrator" of the act, within the meaning of a statute giving an action against the perpetrator. Philo v. Illinois Cent. R. Co., 33 Iowa, 47.

PERPETUA LEX EST NULLAM LEGEM HUMANAM AC POSITIVAM PERPETUAM ESSE, ET CLAUSULA QUÆ ABROGATIONEM EXCLUDIT AB INITIO NON VALET. It is a perpetual law that no human and positive law can be perpetual, and a clause [in a law] which precludes the power of abrogation is void *ab initio.* Bac. Max. p. 77, in reg. 19.

PERPETUAL. Never ceasing; continuous; enduring; lasting; unlimited in respect of time; continuing without intermission or interval. Scanlan v. Crawshaw, 5 Mo.App. 337.

As to perpetual "Curacy," "Injunction," "Lease," and "Statute," see those titles.

PERPETUAL EDICT. In Roman law. Originally the term "perpetual" was merely opposed to "occasional" and was used to distinguish the general edicts of the prætors from the special edicts or orders which they issued in their judicial capacity. But under Hadrian the edict was revised by the jurist Julianus, and was republished as a permanent act of legislation. It was then styled "perpetual," in the sense of being calculated to endure *in perpetuum,* or until abrogated by competent authority. Aust.Jur. 855.

PERPETUAL SUCCESSION. That continuous existence which enables a corporation to manage its affairs, and hold property without the necessity of perpetual conveyances, for the purpose of transmitting it. By reason of this quality, this ideal and artificial person remains, in its legal entity and personality, the same, though frequent changes may be made of its members. Field, Corp. § 58; Scanlan v. Crawshaw, 5 Mo.App. 340.

PERPETUATING TESTIMONY. A proceeding for taking and preserving the testimony of witnesses, which otherwise might be lost before the trial in which it is intended to be used. It is usually allowed where the witnesses are aged and infirm or are about to remove from the state. 3 Bl.Comm. 450.

PERPETUITY. Any limitation or condition which may take away or suspend the power of alienation for a period beyond life or lives in being and 21 years thereafter. Loud v. St. Louis Union Trust Co., 298 Mo. 148, 249 S.W. 629, 634; Barton v. Thaw, 246 Pa. 348, 92 A. 312, 313, Ann. Cas.1916D, 570; True Real Estate Co. v. True, 115 Me. 533; 99 A. 627, 630; Melvin v. Hoffman, 290 Mo. 464, 235 S.W. 107, 115. Any limitation tending to take the subject of it out of commerce for a longer period than a life or lives in being, and twenty-one years beyond, and, in case of a posthumous child, a few months more, allowing for the term of gestation. Rand.Perp. 48. Such a limitation of property as renders it unalienable beyond the period allowed by law. Gilb. Uses, (Sugd. Ed.) 260. Ould v. Washington Hospital, 95 U.S. 303, 24 L.Ed. 450; Duggan v. Slocum, 34 C.C.A. 676, 92 F. 806; Stevens v. Annex Realty Co., 173 Mo. 511, 73 S.W. 505; Griffin v. Graham, 8 N.C. 130, 9 Am.Dec. 619; In re John's Will, 30 Or. 494, 47 P. 341, 36 L.R.A. 242. See, also, Rule Against Perpetuities.

PERPETUITY OF THE KING. That fiction of the English law which for certain political purposes ascribes to the king in his political capacity the attribute of immortality; for, though the reigning monarch may die, yet by this fiction the king never dies, *i. e.*, the office is supposed to be reoccupied for all political purposes immediately on his death. Brown.

PERQUISITES. Anything obtained by industry or purchased with money, different from that which descends from a father or ancestor. Bract. l. 2, c. 30, n. 3.

Profits accruing to a lord of a manor by virtue of his court-baron, over and above the yearly profits of his land; also other things that come casually and not yearly. Mozley & Whiteley.

In Modern Use. Emoluments or incidental profits attaching to an office or official position, beyond the salary or regular fees. Harris County v. Hammond, Tex.Civ.App., 203 S.W. 445, 448; Christopherson v. Reeves, 44 S.D. 634, 184 N.W. 1015; State v. Reeves, 44 S.D. 568, 184 N.W. 993, 998.

PERQUISITIO. Purchase. Acquisition by one's own act or agreement, and not by descent.

PERQUISITOR. In old English law. A purchaser; one who first acquired an estate to his family; one who acquired an estate by sale, by gift, or by any other method, except only that of descent. 2 Bl.Comm. 220.

PERSECUTIO. Lat. In the civil law. A following after; a pursuing at law; a suit or prosecution. Properly that kind of judicial proceeding before the prætor which was called "extraordinary." In a general sense, any judicial proceeding, including not only "actions," (*actiones,*) properly so called, but other proceedings also. Calvin.

PERSEQUI. Lat. In the civil law. To follow after; to pursue or claim in form of law. An action is called a "*jus persequendi.*"

PERSON. A man considered according to the rank he holds in society, with all the right to which the place he holds entitles him, and the duties which it imposes. People v. R. Co., 134 N.Y. 506, 31 N.E. 873.

The word in its natural and usual signification includes women as well as men. Commonwealth v. Welosky, 276 Mass. 398, 177 N.E. 656.

Term may include artificial beings, as corporations, 1 Bla.Com. 123; 4 Bingh. 669; People v. Com'rs of Taxes, 23 N.Y. 242; *quasi*-corporations, Sedgw. Stat. & Const. L. 372; L. R. 5 App. Cas. 857; territorial corporations, Seymour v. School District, 53 Conn. 507, 3 A. 552; and foreign corporations, People v. McLean, 80 N.Y. 259; under statutes, forbidding the taking of property without due process of law and giving to all persons the equal protection of the laws, Smyth v. Ames, 18 S.Ct. 418, 169 U.S. 466, 42 L.Ed. 819; Gulf, C. & S. F. R. Co. v. Ellis, 17 S.Ct. 255, 165 U.S. 150, 41 L.Ed. 666; concerning claims arising from Indian depredations, U. S. v. Transp. Co., 17 S.Ct. 206, 164 U.S. 686, 41 L.Ed. 599; relating to taxation and the revenue laws, People v. McLean, 80 N.Y. 254; to attachments, Bray v. Wallingford, 20 Conn. 416; usurious contracts, Philadelphia Loan Co. v. Towner, 13 Conn. 249; applying to limitation of actions, Olcott v. R. Co., 20 N.Y. 210, 75 Am.Dec. 393; North Mo. R. Co. v. Akers, 4 Kan. 453, 96 Am.Dec. 183; and concerning the admissibility as a witness of a party in his own behalf when the opposite party is a living person, La Farge v. Ins. Co., 22 N.Y. 352. A corporation is also a person under a penal statute; U. S. v. Amedy, 11 Wheat. 392, 6 L.Ed. 502. Corporations are "persons" as that word is used in the first clause of the XIVth Amendment; Covington & L. Turnp. Co. v. Sandford, 17 S.Ct. 198, 164 U.S. 578, 41 L.Ed. 560; Smyth v. Ames, 18 S.Ct. 418, 169 U.S. 466, 42 L.Ed. 819; People v. Fire Ass'n, 92 N.Y. 311, 44 Am.Rep. 380; U. S. v. Supply Co., 30 S.Ct. 15, 215 U.S. 50, 54 L.Ed. 87; *contra,* Central P. R. Co. v. Board, 60 Cal. 35. But a corporation of another state is not a "person" within the jurisdiction of the state until it has complied with the conditions of admission to do business in the state, Fire Ass'n of Phila. v.

New York, 7 S.Ct. 108, 119 U.S. 110, 30 L.Ed. 342; and a statutory requirement of such conditions is not in conflict with the XIVth Amendment; Pembina Consol. S. M. & M. Co. v. Pennsylvania, 8 S.Ct. 737, 125 U.S. 181, 189, 31 L.Ed. 650.

It may include partnerships. In re Julian, D. C.Pa., 22 F.Supp. 97, 99. Also firms. State ex rel. Joseph R. Peebles Sons Co. v. State Board of Pharmacy, 127 Ohio St. 513, 189 N.E. 447, 448.

"Persons" are of two kinds, natural and artificial. A natural person is a human being. Artificial persons include a collection or succession of natural persons forming a corporation; a collection of property to which the law attributes the capacity of having rights and duties. The latter class of artificial persons is recognized only to a limited extent in our law. Examples are the estate of a bankrupt or deceased person. Hogan v. Greenfield, 58 Wyo. 13, 122 P.2d 850, 853.

It has been held that when the word person is used in a legislative act, *natural* persons will be intended unless something appear in the context to show that it applies to artificial persons, Blair v. Worley, 1 Scam., Ill., 178; Appeal of Fox, 112 Pa. 337; 4 A. 149; but as a rule corporations will be considered persons within the statutes unless the intention of the legislature is manifestly to exclude them. Stribbling v. Bank, 5 Rand., Va., 132.

A county is a person in a legal sense, Lancaster Co. v. Trimble, 34 Neb. 752, 52 N.W. 711; but a sovereign is not; In re Fox, 52 N.Y. 535, 11 Am.Rep. 751; U. S. v. Fox, 94 U.S. 315, 24 L.Ed. 192, but *contra* within the meaning of a statute, providing a penalty for the fraudulent alteration of a public record with intent that any "person" be defrauded, Martin v. State, 24 Tex. 61; and within the meaning of a covenant for quiet and peaceful possession against all and every person or persons; Giddings v. Holter, 19 Mont. 263, 48 P. 8. An Indian is a person, U. S. v. Crook, 5 Dill. 459, Fed.Cas.No.14,891; and a slave was so considered, in so far, as to be capable of committing a riot in conjunction with white men, State v. Thackam, 1 Bay, S.C., 358. The estate of a decedent is a person, Billings v. State, 107 Ind. 54, 6 N.E. 914, 7 N.E. 763, 57 Am. Rep. 77; and where the statute makes the owner of a dog liable for injuries to any person, it includes the property of such person, Brewer v. Crosby, 11 Gray, Mass., 29; but where the statute provided damages for the bite of a dog which had previously bitten a person, it was held insufficient to show that the dog had previously bitten a goat, [1896] 2 Q.B. 109; a dog will not be included in the word in an act which authorizes a *person* to kill dogs running at large, Heisrodt v. Hackett, 34 Mich. 283, 22 Am.Rep. 529.

Where the statute prohibited any person from pursuing his usual vocation on the Lord's Day, it was held to apply to a judge holding court. Bass v. Irvin, 49 Ga. 436.

A child *en ventre sa mere* is not a person. Dietrich v. Northampton, 138 Mass. 14, 52 Am.Rep. 242; but an infant is so considered; Madden v. Springfield, 131 Mass. 441.

In the United States bankrupty act of 1898, it is provided that the word "persons" shall include corporations, except where otherwise specified, and officers, partnerships, and women, and, when used with reference to the commission of acts which are therein forbidden, shall include persons who are participants in the forbidden acts, and the agents, officers, and members of the board of directors or trustees, or their controlling bodies, of corporations. 11 U.S.C.A. § 1.

Persons are the subject of rights and duties; and, as a subject of a right, the person is the object of the correlative duty, and conversely. The subject of a right has been called by Professor Holland, the person of inherence; the subject of a duty, the person of incidence. "Entitled" and "bound" are the terms in common use in English and for most purposes they are adequate. Every full citizen is a person; other human beings, namely, subjects who are not citizens, may be persons. But not every human being is necessarily a person, for a person is capable of rights and duties, and there may well be human beings having no legal rights, as was the case with slaves in English law. * * *

A person is such, not because he is human, but because rights and duties are ascribed to him. The person is the legal subject or substance of which the rights and duties are attributes. An individual human being considered as having such attributes is what lawyers call a *natural* person. Pollock, First Book of Jurispr. 110. Gray, Nature and Sources of Law, ch. II.

PERSONA. Lat.

In the civil law. Character, in virtue of which certain rights belong to a man and certain duties are imposed upon him. Thus one man may unite many characters, (*personœ,*) as, for example, the characters of father and son, of master and servant. Mackeld.Rom.Law, § 129.

In Ecclesiastical Law. The rector of a church instituted and inducted, for his own life, was called *"persona mortalis;"* and any collegiate or conventual body, to whom the church was forever appropriated, was termed *"persona immortalis."* Jacob.

PERSONA CONJUNCTA ÆQUIPARATUR INTERESSE PROPRIO. A personal connection [literally, a united person, union with a person] is equivalent to one's own interest; nearness of blood is as good a consideration as one's own interest. Bac.Max. 72, reg.

PERSONA DESIGNATA. A person pointed out or described as an individual, as opposed to a person ascertained as a member of a class, or as filling a particular character.

PERSONA ECCLESIÆ. The parson or personation of the church.

PERSONA EST HOMO CUM STATU QUODAM CONSIDERATUS. A person is a man considered with reference to a certain *status.* Heinecc. Elem. l. 1, tit. 3, § 75.

PERSONA NON GRATA. In international law and diplomatic usage, a person not acceptable (for reasons peculiar to himself) to the court or government to which it is proposed to accredit him in the character of an ambassador or minister.

PERSONA REGIS MERGITUR PERSONA DUCIS. Jenk.Cent. 160. The person of duke merges in that of king.

PERSONA STANDI IN JUDICIO. Capacity of standing in court or in judgment; capacity to be a party to an action; capacity or ability to sue.

PERSONABLE. Having the rights and powers of a person; able to hold or maintain a plea in court; also capacity to take anything granted or given.

PERSONÆ VICE FUNGITUR MUNICIPIUM ET DECURIA. Towns and boroughs act as if persons. Warner v. Beers, 23 Wend., N.Y., 103, 144.

PERSONAL. Appertaining to the person; belonging to an individual; limited to the person; having the nature or partaking of the qualities of human beings, or of movable property. In re Steimes' Estate, 150 Misc. 279, 270 N.Y.S. 339.

As to personal "Action," "Assets," "Chattels," "Contract," "Covenant," "Credit," "Demand," "Disability," "Franchise," "Injury," "Judgment,"

"Knowledge," "Liberty," "Notice," "Obligation," "Property," "Replevin," "Representatives," "Rights," "Security," "Service," "Servitude," "Statute," "Tax," "Tithes," "Tort," and "Warranty," see those titles.

PERSONAL EFFECTS. Articles associated with person, as property having more or less intimate relation to person of possessor; "effects" meaning movable or chattel property of any kind. Ettlinger v. Importers' & Exporters' Ins. Co. of New York, 138 Misc. 743, 247 N.Y.S. 260, 261.

Term when used in will, includes only such tangible property as attended the person, or such tangible property as is worn or carried about the person. In re Sorensen's Estate, 46 Cal.App.2d 35, 115 P.2d 241, 243.

PERSONAL LAW. As opposed to territorial law, is the law applicable to persons not subject to the law of the territory in which they reside.

It is only by permission of the territorial law that personal law can exist at the present day; *e. g.*, it applies to British subjects resident in the Levant and in other Mohammedan and barbarous countries. Under the Roman Empire, it had a very wide application. Brown.

PERSONAL LIABILITY. The liability of the stockholders in corporations, under certain statutes, by which they may be held individually responsible for the debts of the corporation, either to the extent of the par value of their respective holdings of stock, or to twice that amount, or without limit, or otherwise, as the particular statute directs.

PERSONAL THINGS CANNOT BE DONE BY ANOTHER. Finch, Law, b. 1, c. 3, n. 14.

PERSONAL THINGS CANNOT BE GRANTED OVER. Finch, Law, b. 1, c. 3, n. 15.

PERSONAL THINGS DIE WITH THE PERSON. Finch, Law, b. 1, c. 3, n. 16.

PERSONALIA PERSONAM SEQUUNTUR. Personal things follow the person. Flanders v. Cross, 10 Cush. (Mass.) 516.

PERSONALIS ACTIO. Lat.

In the civil law. A personal action; an action against the person, (*in personam.*) Dig. 50, 16, 178, 2.

In old English law. A personal action. In this sense, the term was borrowed from the civil law by Bracton. The English form is constantly used as the designation of one of the chief divisions of civil actions.

PERSONALITER. In old English law. Personally; in person.

PERSONALITY. In modern civil law. The incidence of a law or statute upon persons, or that quality which makes it a *personal* law rather than a *real* law. "By the personality of laws, foreign jurists generally mean all laws which concern the condition, state, and capacity of persons." Story, Confl. Laws, § 16.

PERSONALTY. Personal property; movable property; chattels.

In old practice, an action was said to be in the personalty, where it was brought against the right person or the person against whom in law it lay. Old Nat.Brev. 92; Cowell.

Quasi personalty. Things which are movable in point of law, though fixed to things real, either actually, as emblements, (*fructus industriales,*) fixtures, etc.; or fictitiously, as chattels-real, leases for years, etc.

PERSONATE. In criminal law. To assume the person (character) of another, without his consent or knowledge, in order to deceive others, and, in such feigned character, to fraudulently do some act or gain some advantage, to the harm or prejudice of the person counterfeited. 2 East, P.C. 1010. To pass one's self off as another having a certain identity. Lane v. U. S., C.C.A.Ohio, 17 F.2d 923.

PERSONERO. In Spanish law. An attorney. So called because he represents the *person* of another, either in or out of court. Las Partidas, pt. 3, tit. 5, l. 1.

PERSONNE. Fr. A person. This term is applicable to men and women, or to either. Civ.Code Lat. art. 3556, par. 23.

PERSPICUA VERA NON SUNT PROBANDA. Co.Litt. 16. Plain truths need not be proved.

PERSUADE. To induce one by argument, entreaty, or expostulation into a determination, decision, conclusion, belief, or the like; to win over by an appeal to one's reason and feelings, as into doing or believing something; to bring oneself or another to belief, certainty or conviction; to argue into an opinion or procedure. La Page v. U. S., C.C.A.Minn., 156 A.L.R. 965, 146 F.2d 536, 538.

PERSUASION. The act of persuading; the act of influencing the mind by arguments or reasons offered, or by anything that moves the mind or passions, or inclines the will to a determination. Marx v. Threet, 131 Ala. 340, 30 So. 831. For "Fair Persuasion," see that title.

PERTAIN. To belong or relate to, whether by nature, appointment, or custom. People v. Chicago Theological Seminary, 174 Ill. 177, 51 N.E. 198.

PERTENENCIA. In Spanish law. The claim or right which one has to the property in anything; the territory which belongs to any one by way of jurisdiction or property; that which is accessory or consequent to a principal thing, and goes with the ownership of it. Escriche, Castillero v. United States, 2 Black. 17, 17 L.Ed. 360.

PERTICATA TERRÆ. The fourth part of an acre. Cowell.

PERTICULAS. A pittance; a small portion of alms or victuals. Also certain poor scholars of the Isle of Man. Cowell.

PERTINENT. Applicable; relevant. Evidence is called "pertinent" when it is directed to the issue or matters in dispute, and legitimately tends to prove the allegations of the party offering it; otherwise it is called "impertinent." A pertinent hypothesis is one which, if sustained, would logically influence the issue. Whitaker v. State, 106 Ala. 30, 17 So. 456; Vaughn v. State, 136 Tex.Cr.R. 455, 125 S.W.2d 568, 570.

PERTINENTS. In Scotch law. Appurtenances. "Parts and pertinents" are formal words in old deeds and charters. 1 Forb. Inst. pt. 2, pp. 112, 118.

PERTURBATION. In the English ecclesiastical courts, a "suit for perturbation of seat" is the technical name for an action growing out of a disturbance or infringement of one's right to a pew or seat in a church. 2 Phillim.Ecc.Law, 1813.

PERTURBATRIX. A woman who breaks the peace.

PERVERSE VERDICT. A verdict whereby the jury refuse to follow the direction of the judge on a point of law. Callahan v. Chicago & N. W. Ry. Co., 161 Wis. 288, 154 N.W. 449, 452.

PERVISE, PARVISE. In old English law. The court or yard of the king's palace at Westminster. Also an afternoon exercise or moot for the instruction of students. Cowell; Blount.

PESA. A weight of two hundred and fifty-six pounds. Cowell.

PESAGE. In England. A toll charged for weighing avoirdupois goods other than wool. 2 Chit. Com.Law, 16.

PESQUISIDOR. In Spanish law. Coroner. White, New Recop. b. 1, tit. 1, § 3.

PESSIMI EXEMPLI. Lat. Of the worst example.

PESSONA. Mast of oaks, etc., or money taken for mast, or feeding hogs. Cowell.

PESSURABLE WARES. Merchandise which takes up a good deal of room in a ship. Cowell.

PETENS. Lat. In old English law. A demandant; the plaintiff in a real action. Bract. fols. 102, 106*b*.

PETER-PENCE. An ancient levy or tax of a penny on each house throughout England, paid to the pope. It was called "Peter-pence," because collected on the day of St. Peter, *ad vincula*; by the Saxons it was called "Romefeoh," "Rome-scot," and "Rome-pennying," because collected and sent to Rome; and, lastly, it was called "hearth money," because every dwelling-house was liable to it, and every religious house, the abbey of St. Albans alone excepted. Wharton.

PETIT. Fr. Small; minor; inconsiderable. Used in several compounds, and sometimes written "petty." People v. Sprado, 72 Cal.App. 582, 237 P. 1087, 1089.

As to petit "Jury," "Larceny," "Sergeanty," and "Treason," see those titles.

PETIT CAPE. A judicial writ, issued in the old actions for the recovery of land, requiring the sheriff to take possession of the estate, where the tenant, after having appeared in answer to the summons, made default in a subsequent stage of the proceedings.

PETITE ASSIZE. Used in contradistinction from the *grand assize*, which was a jury to decide on questions of property. *Petite assize*, a jury to decide on questions of possession. Britt. c. 42; Glan. lib. 2, cc. 6, 7.

PETITIO. Lat.

In the civil law. The plaintiff's statement of his cause of action in an action *in rem*. Calvin.

In old English law. Petition or demand; the count in a real action; the form of words in which a title to land was stated by the demandant, and which commenced with the word *"peto."* 1 Reeve, Eng.Law, 176.

PETITIO PRINCIPII. In logic. Begging the question, which is the taking of a thing for true or for granted, and drawing conclusions from it as such, when it is really dubious, perhaps false, or at least wants to be proved, before any inferences ought to be drawn from it.

PETITION. A written address, embodying an application or prayer from the person or persons preferring it, to the power, body, or person to whom it is presented, for the exercise of his or their authority in the redress of some wrong, or the grant of some favor, privilege, or license. Enderson v. Hildenbrand, 52 N.D. 533, 204 N.W. 356; Benton Coal Mining Co. v. Industrial Commission, 321 Ill. 208, 151 N.E. 520, 522; In re L. M. Axle Co., C.C.A.Ohio, 3 F.2d 581, 582; State v. American Sugar Refining Co., 138 La. 1005, 71 So. 137, 140.

In practice. An application made to a court *ex parte*, or where there are no parties in opposition, praying for the exercise of the judicial powers of the court in relation to some matter which is not the subject for a suit or action, or for authority to do some act which requires the sanction of the court; as for the appointment of a guardian, for leave to sell trust property, etc.

The word "petition" is generally used in judicial proceedings to describe an application in writing, in contradistinction to a motion, which may be *viva voce*. Bergen v. Jones, 4 Metc., Mass., 371. The principal distinction between motions and petitions lies in the fact that motions, though usually made in writing, may sometimes be made orally, while a petition is always in writing. So, also, motions can usually be made only by a party to the record, while petitions may in some cases be presented by persons not parties. Gibbs v. Ewing, 94 Fla. 236, 113 So. 730, 735.

In the practice of some of the states, the word "petition" is adopted as the name of that initiatory pleading in an action which is elsewhere called a "declaration" or "complaint."

In equity practice. An application in writing for an order of the court, stating the circumstances upon which it is founded; a proceeding resorted to whenever the nature of the application to the court requires a fuller statement than can be conveniently made in a notice of motion. 1 Barb. Ch.Pr. 578.

PETITION DE DROIT. L. Fr. In English practice. A petition of right; a form of proceeding to obtain restitution from the crown of either real or personal property, being of use where the crown is in possession of any hereditaments or chattels, and the petitioner suggests such a right as controverts the title of the crown, grounded on facts disclosed in the petition itself. 3 Bl.Comm. 256.

PETITION IN BANKRUPTCY. A paper filed in a court of bankruptcy, or with the clerk, by a debtor praying for the benefits of the bankruptcy act, or by creditors alleging the commission of an act of bankruptcy by their debtor and praying an adjudication of bankruptcy against him.

PETITION OF RIGHT. In English law. A proceeding in chancery by which a subject may recover property in the possession of the king. See Petition de Droit.

PETITION OF RIGHTS. A parliamentary declaration of the liberties of the people, assented to by King Charles I, in 1629. It is to be distinguished from the bill of rights, (1689), which has passed into a permanent constitutional statute. Brown.

PETITIONER. One who presents a petition to a court, officer, or legislative body. In legal proceedings begun by petition, the person against whom action or relief is prayed, or who opposes the prayer of the petition, is called the "respondent."

PETITIONING CREDITOR. The creditor at whose instance an adjudication of bankruptcy is made against a bankrupt.

PETITORY ACTION. A droitural action; that is, one in which the plaintiff seeks to establish and enforce, by an appropriate legal proceeding, his right of property, or his title, to the subject-matter in dispute; as distinguished from a *possessory* action, where the right to the possession is the point in litigation, and not the mere right of property. The term is chiefly used in admiralty. 1 Kent, Comm. 371; The Tilton, 5 Mason, 465, Fed.Cas.No.14,054.

In Louisiana, an action brought by an alleged owner out of possession against one having possession to determine ownership, in which plaintiff must recover on strength of his own title, not on weakness of defendant's title. Saucier v. Crichton, C.C.A.La., 147 F.2d 430, 433.

In Scotch law. Actions in which damages are sought.

PETO. Lat. In Roman law. I request. A common word by which a *fideicommissum*, or trust, was created in a will. Inst. 2, 24, 3.

PETRA. A stone weight. Cowell.

PETRONIAN LAW. See Lex Petronia.

PETTIFOGGER. A lawyer who is employed in a small or mean business, or who carries on a disreputable business by unprincipled or dishonorable means.

PETTIFOGGING SHYSTER. This "combination of epithets every lawyer and citizen knows belongs to none but unscrupulous practitioners who disgrace their profession by doing mean work, and resort to sharp practice to do it." Bailey v. Kalamazoo Pub. Co., 40 Mich. 251, 256.

PETTY. Small, minor, of less or inconsiderable importance. The English form of *"petit,"* and sometimes used instead of that word in such compounds as "petty jury," "petty larceny," and "petty treason." See Petit.

As to petty "Average," "Constable," and "Sessions," see those titles.

PETTY BAG OFFICE. In English law. An office in the court of chancery, for suits against attorneys and officers of the court, and for process and proceedings by extent on statutes, recognizances, *ad quod damnum*, and the like. Termes de la Ley.

PETTY OFFICERS. Inferior officers in the naval service, of various ranks and kinds, corresponding to the non-commissioned officers in the army. U. S. v. Fuller, 16 S.Ct. 386, 160 U.S. 593, 40 L.Ed. 549.

PEW. An inclosed seat in a church. O'Hear v. De Goesbriand, 33 Vt. 606, 80 Am.Dec. 653; Trustees of Third Presbyterian Congregation v. Andruss, 21 N.J.Law, 328; Gay v. Baker, 17 Mass. 435, 9 Am.Dec. 159.

PHARMACIST. One skilled in pharmacy; druggist. Webster.

Registered Pharmacist. One who has qualified by training, education, and experience and is so certified. Reppert v. Utterback, 206 Iowa 314, 217 N.W. 545.

PHARMACY. The science and art of preserving drugs and of compounding and dispensing medicines according to prescriptions of physicians; the occupation of an apothecary or pharmaceutical chemist. Ballard v. Goldsby, 142 La. 15, 76 So. 219. Ex parte Sarros, 116 Fla. 86, 156 So. 396. Place where medicines are compounded or dispensed; a drug store; an apothecary shop. Carroll Perfumers v. State, Ind., 7 N.E.2d 970, 972.

PHAROS. A watch-tower, light-house, or sea-mark.

PHLEBITIS. In medical jurisprudence. An inflammation of the veins, which may originate in *septicœmia* (bacterial blood-poisoning) or *pyœmia* (poisoning from *pus*), and is capable of being transmitted to other tissues, as, the brain or the muscular tissue of the heart. In the latter case, an inflammation of the heart is produced which is called "*endocarditis*" and which may result fatally. Succession of Bidwell, 52 La.Ann. 744, 27 So. 281.

PHOTOGRAPHER. An artist, not an artisan. A photographer is not a mechanic and his apparatus is not exempt as the tools of a mechanic. Story v. Walker, 79 Tenn. (11 Lea) 515, 517, 47 Am.Rep. 305. See, also, City of New Orleans v. Robira, 8 So. 402, 403, 42 La.Ann. 1098, 11 L.R.A. 141; Mullinix v. State, 60 S.W. 768, 42 Tex.Cr.R. 526.

PHOTOGRAPHY. The science which relates to the action of light on sensitive bodies in the production of pictures; the fixation of images and the like. Frankel v. German Tyrolean Alps, 97 S.W. 961, 962, 121 Mo.App. 51, citing Webst. Dict.

PHYLASIST. A jailer.

PHYSICAL. Relating or pertaining to the body, as distinguished from the mind or soul or the emotions; material, substantive, having an objective existence, as distinguished from imaginary or fictitious; real, having relation to facts, as distinguished from moral or constructive.

PHYSICAL DEPRECIATION. Reduction in value of structure due to actual wear and tear or physical deterioration. People ex rel. Union Bag & Paper Corporation v. Fitzgerald, 166 Misc. 237, 2 N.Y.S.2d 290, 295.

PHYSICAL DISABILITY. See Disability.

PHYSICAL FACT. In the law of evidence. A fact having a physical existence, as distinguished from a mere conception of the mind; one which is visible, audible, or palpable; such as the sound of a pistol shot, a man running, impressions of human feet on the ground. Burrill, Circ. Ev. 130. A fact considered to have its seat in some inanimate being, or, if in an animate being, by virtue, not of the qualities by which it is constituted animate, but of those which it has in common with the class of inanimate beings. 1 Benth. Jud. Ev. 45.

PHYSICAL FORCE. Force applied to the body; actual violence. State v. Wells, 31 Conn. 212.

PHYSICAL IMPOSSIBILITY. Practical impossibility according to the knowledge of the day. State v. Hillis, 79 Ind.App. 599, 124 N.E. 515, 516.

PHYSICAL INCAPACITY. In the law of marriage and divorce, impotence, inability to accomplish sexual coition, arising from incurable physical imperfection or malformation. Anonymous, 89 Ala. 291, 7 So. 100, 7 L.R.A. 425, 18 Am.St.Rep. 116; Franke v. Franke, Cal., 31 P. 574, 18 L.R.A. 375.

PHYSICAL INJURY. Bodily harm or hurt, excluding mental distress, fright, or emotional disturbance. Deming v. Chicago, etc., R. Co., 80 Mo. App. 157.

PHYSICAL NECESSITY. A condition in which a person is absolutely compelled to act in a particular way by overwhelming superior force; as distinguished from *moral* necessity, which arises where there is a duty incumbent upon a rational being to perform, which he ought at the time to perform. The Fortitude, 3 Sumn. 248, Fed.Cas. No. 4,953.

PHYSICIAN. A practitioner of medicine; a person duly authorized or licensed to treat diseases; one lawfully engaged in the practice of medicine, without reference to any particular school. State v. Beck, 21 R.I. 288, 43 A. 366, 45 L.R.A. 269; Raynor v. State, 62 Wis. 289, 22 N.W. 430; Nelson v. State Board of Health, 108 Ky. 769, 57 S.W. 501, 50 L.R.A. 383; Millsap v. Alderson, 63 Cal. App. 518, 219 P. 469, 472. But see: Isaacson v. Wisconsin Casualty Ass'n, 187 Wis. 25, 203 N.W. 918, 920; Le Grand v. Security Ben. Ass'n, 210 Mo.App. 700, 240 S.W. 852, 853.

PHYSICIAN'S PRESCRIPTION. A physician's order for morphine issued to a habitual user, not in the course of professional treatment for a cure, but to keep him comfortable by maintaining his customary use, is not a "physician's prescription" within 26 U.S.C.A. § 2554 (c) (2). Webb v. U. S., 39 S.Ct. 217, 218, 249 U.S. 96, 63 L.Ed. 497.

PHYSIOTHERAPY. Treatment of disease by physical remedies rather than drugs. People v. Mari, 260 N.Y. 383, 183 N.E. 858, 859.

PIA FRAUS. Lat. A pious fraud; a subterfuge or evasion considered morally justifiable on account of the ends sought to be promoted. Particularly applied to an evasion or disregard of the laws in the interests of religion or religious institutions, such as circumventing the statutes of mortmain.

PIACLE. An obsolete term for an enormous crime.

PICAROON. A robber; a plunderer.

PICK OF LAND. A narrow slip of land running into a corner.

PICKAGE. Money paid at fairs for breaking ground for booths.

PICKERY. In Scotch law. Petty theft; stealing of trifles, punishable arbitrarily. Bell.

PICKET. A person posted by a labor organization at an approach to a place of work affected by strike to ascertain the workmen going and coming, and to persuade or otherwise influence them to quit working there. Evening Times Printing & Publishing Co. v. American Newspaper Guild, 124 N.J.Eq. 71, 199 A. 598, 603.

PICKETING, by members of a trade union on strike, consists in posting members at all the approaches to the works struck against, for the purpose of observing and reporting the workmen going to or coming from the works, and of using such influence as may be in their power to prevent the workmen from accepting work there. See Beck v. Railway Teamsters' Protective Union,

118 Mich. 497, 77 N.W. 13, 42 L.R.A. 407, 74 Am. St.Rep. 421; Cumberland Glass Mfg. Co. v. Glass Bottle Blowers' Ass'n, 59 N.J.Eq. 49, 46 A. 208.

Peaceable picketing, in which laboring men and women have right to participate during labor dispute, means tranquil conduct, conduct devoid of noise or tumult, the absence of a quarrelsome demeanor, and a course of conduct that does not violate or disturb the public peace. Lilly Dache, Inc., v. Rose, 28 N.Y.S.2d 303, 305; Ex parte Bell, 37 Cal.App.2d 582, 100 P.2d 339, 340. It connotes peaceable methods of presenting a cause to the public in the vicinity of the employer's premises. Music Hall Theatre v. Moving Picture Mach. Operators Local No. 165, 249 Ky. 639, 61 S.W.2d 283.

Unlawful picketing. See that title.

PICKLE, PYCLE, or PIGHTEL. A small parcel of land inclosed with a hedge, which, in some countries, is called a "pingle." Enc. Lond.

PICK-LOCK. An instrument by which locks are opened without a key.

PICKPOCKET. A thief who secretly steals money or other property from the person of another.

PIECE WORK. Work done or paid for by the piece or quantity. Calascibett v. Highway Freight Co., 18 N.J.Misc. 144, 11 A.2d 408, 409.

PIEPOUDRE. See Court of Piepoudre.

PIER. A structure extending from the solid land out into the water of a river, lake, harbor, etc., to afford convenient passage for persons and property to and from vessels along the sides of the pier. Seabright v. Allgor, 69 N.J.Law, 641, 56 A. 287.

PIERAGE. The duty for maintaining piers and harbors.

PIGNORATIO. Lat. In the civil law. The contract of pledge; and also the obligation of such contract. L. 9 D. *de pignor.* Sealing up (*obsignatio*). A shutting up of an animal caught in one's field and keeping it till the expenses and damage have been paid by its master. New Decis. 1, 34, 13.

PIGNORATITIA ACTIO. Lat. In the civil law. An action of pledge, or founded on a pledge, which was either *directa,* for the debtor, after payment of the debt, or *contraria,* for the creditor. Heinecc. Elem. lib. 3, tit. 13, §§ 824–826.

PIGNORATIVE CONTRACT. In the civil law. A contract of pledge, hypothecation, or mortgage of realty.

PIGNORIS CAPIO. Lat. In Roman law. This was the name of one of the *legis actiones.* It was employed only in certain particular kinds of pecuniary cases, and consisted in that the creditor, without preliminary suit and without the co-operation of the magistrate, by reciting a prescribed formula, took an article of property from the debtor to be treated as a pledge or security. The proceeding bears a marked analogy to distress at common law. Mackeld. Rom. Law, § 203; Gaius, bk. 4, §§ 26–29.

PIGNUS. Lat. In the civil law. A pledge or pawn; a delivery of a thing to a creditor, as security for a debt. Also a thing delivered to a creditor as security for a debt. Hanes v. Shapiro & Smith, 168 N.C. 24, 84 S.E. 33, 35.

PILA. In old English law. That side of coined money which was called "pile," because it was the side on which there was an impression of a church built on piles. Fleta, lib. 1, c. 39.

PILETTUS. In the ancient forest laws. An arrow which had a round knob a little above the head, to hinder it from going far into the mark. Cowell.

PILFER. To pilfer, in the plain and popular sense, means to steal. To charge another with pilfering is to charge him with stealing, and is slander. Becket v. Sterrett, 4 Blackf. (Ind.) 499.

PILFERAGE. Some form of stealing. Felgar v. Home Ins. Co. of New York, 207 Ill.App. 492; Ledvinka v. Home Ins. Co. of New York, 139 Md. 434, 115 A. 596, 598, 19 A.L.R. 167. Petty larceny. Stuht v. Maryland Motor Car Ins. Co., 90 Wash. 576, 156 P. 557, 558; Hartford Fire Ins. Co. v. Wimbish, 12 Ga.App. 712, 78 S.E. 265, 266; Illinois Automobile Ins. Exch. v. Southern Motor Sales Co., 207 Ala. 265, 92 So. 429, 430, 24 A.L.R. 734.

The word "pilferage," in a policy against theft of trunks of merchandise in transit, excluding all pilferage, must be construed as having been used in the sense of filching; of taking a small part only, rather than the whole; of stealing privily. Tamarin v. Insurance Co. of North America, 68 Pa.Super.Ct. 614, 615; Goldman v. Insurance Co. of North America, 185 N.Y.S. 210, 211, 194 App.Div. 266.

PILFERER. One who steals petty things, or a small part of a thing.

PILLAGE. Plunder; the forcible taking of private property by an invading or conquering army from the enemy's subjects. American Ins. Co. v. Bryan, 26 Wend. (N. Y.) 573, 37 Am.Dec. 278.

PILLAR-AND-STALL SYSTEM. In mining of limestone. Beginning at mine opening, cutting tunnels or entries in the limestone ledge and taking off rooms therefrom leaving limestone roof of varying thickness, theoretically sufficient to sustain the hundred foot overburden when pillars of sufficient size are allowed to remain and when boundary is reached such part of pillars and roof is taken as is practicable as the work recedes. Marquette Cement Mining Co. v. Oglesby Coal Co., D.C.Ill., 253 F. 107, 109.

PILLORY. A frame erected on a pillar, and made with holes and movable boards, through which the heads and hands of criminals were put.

PILOT. A particular officer serving on board a ship during the course of a voyage, and having the charge of the helm and the ship's route; or a person taken on board at any particular place for the purpose of conducting a ship through a river, road, or channel, or from or into a port. State v. Turner, 34 Or. 173, 55 P. 92; State v. Jones, 16 Fla. 306; The Maren Lee, C.C.A.N.Y., 278 F. 918, 920.

Branch pilot. One possessing a license, commission, or certificate of competency issued by the proper authority and usually after an examination. U. S. v. Forbes, 25 Fed.Cas. 1141; Petterson v. State, Tex.Cr.R., 58 S.W. 100; State v. Follett, 33 La.Ann. 228; Davis v Heide & Co., 161 N.C. 476, 77 S.E. 691, 693.

PILOTAGE. The navigation of a vessel by a pilot; the duty of a pilot. The charge or compensation allowed for piloting a vessel.

PILOTAGE AUTHORITIES. In English law. Boards of commissioners appointed and authorized for the regulation and appointment of pilots, each board having jurisdiction within a prescribed district.

PIMP. One who provides for others the means of gratifying lust; a procurer; a panderer. The word pimp is not a technical one, nor has it acquired any peculiar or appropriate meaning in the law; and is therefore to be construed and understood according to the common and approved usage of the language; People v. Gastro, 75 Mich. 127, 42 N.W. 937, where the court disapproved the action of the judge at *nisi prius* who defined the term to mean a man who has intercourse with a loose woman, who usually is supporting him. It is frequently defined by ordinance or statute. Fleming v. City of Atlanta, 21 Ga.App. 797, 95 S.E. 271; Powell v. State, 108 Miss. 497, 66 So. 979, 980; People v. Simpson, 79 Cal.App. 555, 250 P. 403, 404; State v. Thibodeaux, 136 La. 935, 67 So. 973, 974.

PIMP-TENURE. A very singular and odious kind of tenure mentioned by the old writers. *Wilhelmus Hoppeshort tenet dimidiam virgatam terræ per servitium custodiendi sex damisellas, scil. meretrices ad usum domini regis.* Wharton.

PINCERNA. In old English law. Butler; the king's butler, whose office it was to select out of the cargo of every vessel laden with wine, one cask at the prow and another at the stern, for the king's use. Fleta, lib. 2, c. 22.

PIN-MONEY. An allowance set apart by a husband for the personal expenses of his wife, for her dress and pocket money.

PINNAGE. Poundage of cattle.

PINNER. A pounder of cattle; a poundkeeper.

PINT. A liquid measure of half a quart, or the eighth part of a gallon.

PIONEER PATENT. See Patent.

PIOUS USES. See Charitable Uses.

PIPE. A roll in the exchequer; otherwise called the "great roll." A liquid measure containing two hogsheads.

PIPE LINE. A connected series of pipes for the transportation of oil, gas, or water.

PIPE ROLLS. These were the Great Rolls of the Exchequer and contained the account of the king's profits and rents in all the counties of England. They exist in a continuous series (676 rolls) from 1156 to 1833 (except 1216 and 1403). The Chancellor's Roll from 1255 to 1833 is a duplicate of the Pipe Rolls. A single roll of Henry I, but not complete, is extant. 2 Holdsw. Hist.E.L. 129. The Pipe Rolls are our earliest records; *id.* 138. They are said to be most instructive as to legal rules and institutions; Brunner, 2 Sel.Essays in Anglo-Amer. L. H. 24.

PIRACY. In criminal law. A robbery or forcible depredation on the high seas, without lawful authority, done *animo furandi,* in the spirit and intention of universal hostility. United States v. Palmer, 3 Wheat. 610, 4 L.Ed. 471. This is the definition of this offense by the law of nations. 1 Kent, Comm. 183. And see Talbot v. Janson, 3 Dall. 152, 1 L.Ed. 540; U. S. v. The Ambrose Light, D.C.N.Y., 25 F. 408; Davison v. Seal-skins, 7 Fed.Cas. 192.

There is a distinction between the offense of piracy, as known to the law of nations, which is justiciable anywhere, and offenses created by statutes of particular nations, cognizable only before the municipal tribunals of such nations. Dole v. Insurance Co., 2 Cliff. 394, 418, Fed.Cas.No.3,966.

The term is also applied to the illicit reprinting or reproduction of a copyrighted book or print or to unlawful plagiarism from it.

PIRATA EST HOSTIS HUMANI GENERIS. 3 Inst. 113. A pirate is an enemy of the human race.

PIRATE. A person who lives by piracy; one guilty of the crime of piracy. A sea-robber, who, to enrich himself, by subtlety or open force, setteth upon merchants and others trading by sea, despoiling them of their loading, and sometimes bereaving them of life and sinking their ships. Ridley, Civil & Ecc.Law, pt. 2, c. 1, § 3. One who acts solely on his own authority, without any commission or authority from a sovereign state, seizing by force, and appropriating to himself without discrimination, every vessel he meets with. Robbery on the high seas is piracy; but to constitute the offense the taking must be felonious. Consequently the *quo animo* may be inquired into. Davison v. Seal-skins, 2 Paine, 324, Fed.Cas. No.3,661.

Pirates are common sea-rovers, without any fixed place of residence, who acknowledge no sovereign and no law, and support themselves by pillage and depredations at sea; but there are instances wherein the word *"pirata"* has been formerly taken for a sea-captain. Spelman.

PIRATICALLY. A technical word which must always be used in an indictment for piracy. 3 Inst. 112.

PISCARY. The right of fishing. Thus, common of piscary is the right of fishing in waters belonging to another person.

PISTAREEN. A small Spanish coin. It is not made current by the laws of the United States. United States v. Gardner, 10 Pet. 618, 9 L.Ed. 556.

PISTOL. A short firearm, intended to be aimed and fired from one hand. Campbell v. Commonwealth, 295 Ky. 511, 174 S.W.2d 778, 779.

PIT. In old Scotch law. An excavation or cavity in the earth in which women who were under sentence of death were drowned.

A cavity or hole in the ground, natural or artificial; a large hole from which some mineral deposit is dug or quarried, as a gravel pit, a stone pit. Walker v. Dwelle, 187 Iowa, 1384, 175 N.W. 957, 964.

PIT AND GALLOWS. In Scotch law. A privilege of inflicting capital punishment for theft, given by King Malcolm, by which a woman could be drowned in a pit, (*fossa,*) or a man hanged on a gallows, (*furca.*) Bell.

PITCHING-PENCE. In old English law. Money, commonly a penny, paid for pitching or setting down every bag of corn or pack of goods in a fair or market. Cowell.

PITTANCE. A slight repast or refection of fish or flesh more than the common allowance; and the pittancer was the officer who distributed this at certain appointed festivals. Cowell.

PIX. A mode of testing coin. The ascertaining whether coin is of the proper standard is in England called "pixing" it; and there are occasions on which resort is had for this purpose to an ancient mode of inquisition called the "trial of the pix," before a jury of members of the Goldsmiths' Company. 2 Steph.Comm. 540, note.

PIX JURY. A jury consisting of the members of the corporation of the goldsmiths of the city of London, assembled upon an inquisition of very ancient date, called the "trial of the pix." Such juries were abolished in 1930.

PLACARD. An edict; a declaration; a manifesto. Also an advertisement or public notification.

PLACE. An old form of the word "pleas." Thus the "Court of Common Pleas" was sometimes called the "Court of Common Place."

PLACE. This word is a very indefinite term. It is applied to any locality, limited by boundaries, however large or however small. It may be used to designate a country, state, county, town, or a very small portion of a town. The extent of the locality designated by it must generally be determined by the connection in which it is used. Robinson v. State, 143 Miss. 247, 108 So. 903, 905; Hammell v. State, 198 Ind. 45, 152 N.E. 161, 163; State v. Cahalan, 204 Iowa, 410, 214 N.W. 612, 613. In its primary and most general sense means locality, situation, or site, and it is also used to designate an occupied situation or building. Burns v. McDaniel, Fla., 140 So. 314, 316.

PLACE LANDS. Lands granted in aid of a railroad company which are within certain limits on each side of the road, and which become instantly fixed by the adoption of the line of the road. There is a well-defined difference between place lands and "indemnity lands." See Indemnity. See Jackson v. La Moure County, 1 N.D. 238, 46 N.W. 449.

PLACE OF CONTRACT. The place (country or state) in which a contract is made, and whose law must determine questions affecting the execution, validity, and construction of the contract. Scudder v. Union Nat. Bank, 91 U.S. 412, 23 L.Ed. 245.

PLACE OF DELIVERY. The place where delivery is to be made of goods sold. If no place is specified in the contract, the articles sold must, in general, be delivered at the place where they are at the time of the sale. Hatch v. Standard Oil Co., 100 U.S. 134, 25 L.Ed. 554.

PLACE OF EMPLOYMENT. Within the safe place statutes, a place where active work, either temporary or permanent, is being conducted in connection with a business for profit, that is, where some process or operation related to such industry, trade or business is carried on and where any person is directly or indirectly employed by another. Padley v. Village of Lodi, 233 Wis. 661, 290 N.W. 136, 137.

PLACE WHERE. A phrase used in the older reports, being a literal translation of *locus in quo* (*q. v.*).

PLACEMAN. One who exercises a public employment, or fills a public station.

The distinction between an officer and a placeman is that the former must take an oath of office, the latter not. Worthy v. Barrett, 63 N.C. 199.

PLACER. In mining law. A superficial deposit of sand, gravel, or disintegrated rock, carrying one or more of the precious metals, along the course or under the bed of a water-course, ancient or current, or along the shore of the sea. Under the acts of congress, the term includes all forms of mineral deposits, except veins of quartz or other rock in place. 30 U.S.C.A. § 35. Montana Coal & Coke Co. v. Livingston, 21 Mont. 59, 52 P. 780; Gregory v. Pershbaker, 73 Cal. 109, 14 P. 401; Duffield v. San Francisco Chemical Co., C.C.A. Idaho, 205 F. 480, 484; San Francisco Chemical Co. v. Duffield, C.C.A.Wyo., 201 F. 830, 835.

PLACER CLAIM. A mining claim located on the public domain for the purpose of placer mining, that is, ground within the defined boundaries which contains mineral in its earth, sand, or gravel; ground which includes valuable deposits not "in place," that is, not fixed in rock, or which are in a loose state. U. S. v. Iron Silver Min. Co., 9 S.Ct. 195, 128 U.S. 673, 32 L.Ed. 571; Clipper Min. Co. v. Eli Min. Co., 24 S.Ct. 632, 194 U.S. 220, 48 L.Ed. 944; U. S. v. Ohio Oil Co., D.C.Wyo., 240 F. 996, 999; Duffield v. San Francisco Chemical Co., C.C.A.Idaho, 205 F. 480, 483.

PLACER LOCATION. A placer claim located and occupied on the public domain.

PLACET. (Fr.) The name of a document in French practice requesting an audience of the court. Outside of Paris the request is made orally, in Paris the *avouè* of the plaintiff sends his request to the clerk of the court who puts the case on the list.

PLACIT, or PLACITUM. Decree; determination.

PLACITA. See Placitum.

PLACITA COMMUNIA. Common pleas. All civil actions between subject and subject. 3 Bl. Comm. 38, 40.

PLACITA CORONÆ. Pleas of the crown. All trials for crimes and misdemeanors, wherein the king is plaintiff, on behalf of the people. 3 Bl. Comm. 40; Cowell, *Plea.*

PLACITA DE TRANSGRESSIONE CONTRA PACEM REGIS, IN REGNO ANGLIÆ VI ET ARMIS FACTA, SECUNDUM LEGEM ET CONSUETUDINEM ANGLIÆ SINE BREVI REGIS PLACITARI NON DEBENT. 2 Inst. 311. Pleas of trespass against the peace of the king in the kingdom of England, made with force and arms, ought not, by the law and custom of England, to be pleaded without the king's writ.

PLACITA JURIS. Pleas or rules of law; "particular and positive learnings of laws;" "grounds and positive learnings received with the law and set down;" as distinguished from maxims or the formulated conclusions of legal reason. Bac.Max. pref., and reg. 12.

PLACITA NEGATIVA DUO EXITUM NON FACIUNT. Two negative pleas do not form an issue. Lofft, 415.

PLACITABILE. In old English law. Pleadable. Spelman.

PLACITAMENTUM. In old records. The pleading of a cause. Spelman.

PLACITARE. To plead.

PLACITATOR. In old records. A pleader. Cowell; Spelman.

PLACITORY. Relating to pleas or pleading.

PLACITUM. In civil law. An agreement of parties; that which is their *pleasure* to arrange between them.

An imperial ordinance or constitution; literally, the prince's pleasure. Inst. 1, 2, 6.

A judicial decision; the judgment, decree, or sentence of a court. Calvin.

In old English law. A public assembly at which the king presided, and which comprised men of all degrees, met for consultation about the great affairs of the kingdom. Cowell.

A court; a judicial tribunal; a lord's court. *Placita* was the style or title of the courts at the beginning of the old *nisi prius* record.

A suit or cause in court; a judicial proceeding; a trial. *Placita* were divided into *placita coronæ* (crown cases or pleas of the crown, *i. e.*, criminal actions) and *placita communia,* (common cases or common pleas, *i. e.*, private civil actions.)

A fine, mulct, or pecuniary punishment.

A pleading or plea. In this sense, the term was not confined to the defendant's answer to the declaration, but included all the pleadings in the cause, being *nomen generalissimum.* 1 Saund. 388, n. 6.

In the old reports and abridgments, *"placitum"* was the name of a paragraph or subdivision of a title or page where the point decided in a cause was set out separately. It is commonly abbreviated, "pl."

PLACITUM ALIUD PERSONALE, ALIUD REALE, ALIUD MIXTUM. Co.Litt. 284. Pleas [*i. e.*, actions] are personal, real, and mixed.

PLACITUM FRACTUM. A day past or lost to the defendant. 1 Hen. I. c. 59.

PLACITUM NOMINATUM. The day appointed for a criminal to appear and plead and make his defense. Cowell.

PLAGIARISM. The act of appropriating the literary composition of another, or parts or passages of his writings, or the ideas or language of the same, and passing them off as the product of one's own mind.

To be liable for "plagiarism" it is not necessary to exactly duplicate another's literary work, it being sufficient if unfair use of such work is made by lifting of substantial portion thereof, but even an exact counterpart of another's work does not constitute "plagiarism" if such counterpart was arrived at independently. O'Rourke v. RKO Radio Pictures, D.C.Mass., 44 F.Supp. 480, 482, 483.

PLAGIARIST, or PLAGIARY. One who publishes the thoughts and writings of another as his own.

PLAGIARIUS. Lat. In the civil law. A man-stealer; a kidnapper. Dig. 48, 15, 1; 4 Bl.Comm. 219.

PLAGIUM. Lat. In the civil law. Man-stealing; kidnapping. The offense of enticing away and stealing men, children, and slaves. Calvin. The persuading a slave to escape from his master, or the concealing or harboring him without the knowledge of his master. Dig. 48, 15, 6.

PLAGUE. Pestilence; a contagious and malignant fever.

PLAIDEUR. Fr. An obsolete term for an attorney who pleaded the cause of his client; an advocate.

PLAINT. In civil law. A complaint; a form of action, particularly one for setting aside a testament alleged to be invalid. This word is the English equivalent of the Latin *"querela."*

In English practice. A private memorial tendered in open court to the judge, wherein the party injured sets forth his cause of action. A proceeding in inferior courts by which an action is commenced without original writ. 3 Bl.Comm.

373. This mode of proceeding is commonly adopted in cases of replevin. 3 Steph.Comm. 666.

PLAINTIFF. A person who brings an action; the party who complains or sues in a personal action and is so named on the record. Gulf, etc., R. Co. v. Scott, Tex.Civ.App., 28 S.W. 458; Carmody v. Land, 207 La. 625, 21 So.2d 764, 768.

Plaintiff in error. The party who sues out a writ of error to review a judgment or other proceeding at law.

Use plaintiff. One for whose use (benefit) an action is brought in the name of another. Thus, where the assignee of a chose in action is not allowed to sue in his own name, the action would be entitled "A. B. (the assignor) for the use of C. D. (the assignee) against E. F." In this case, C. D. is called the "use plaintiff."

PLAN. A delineation; a design; a draft, a draft or form or representation; the representation of anything drawn on a plane, as a map or chart; a scheme; a sketch; also a method of action, procedure, or arrangement. Shainwald v. City of Portland, 153 Or. 167, 55 P.2d 1151, 1156; Jenney v. Des Moines, 103 Iowa, 347, 72 N.W. 550.

PLANE. Surface in which, if any two points are taken, straight line that joins them lies wholly in that surface. In re Vincent, Cust. & Pat.App., 40 F.2d 573, 574.

PLANT. The fixtures, tools, machinery, and apparatus which are necessary to carry on a trade or business. Wharton. Southern Bell Tel. Co. v. D'Alemberte, 39 Fla. 25, 21 So. 570; Sloss-Sheffield Steel Co. v. Mobley, 139 Ala. 425, 36 So. 181; Maxwell v. Wilmington Dental Mfg. Co., C.C.Del., 77 F. 941; State Public Utilities Commission v. Noble, 275 Ill. 121, 113 N.E. 910, 912; McKeon v. Proctor & Gamble Mfg. Co., 154 App.Div. 740, 139 N.Y.S. 805, 806; Tennessee Coal, Iron & R. Co. v. Wiggins, 198 Ala. 346, 73 So. 516, 517. An organized physical equipment to produce any desired result, or an operating unit. Otis Elevator Co. v. Arey-Hauser Co., D.C.Pa., 22 F.Supp. 4, 6.

PLANTATION. In English law. A colony; an original settlement in a new country. See 1 Bl. Comm. 107.

In American law. A farm; a large cultivated estate. Used chiefly in the southern states.

In North Carolina, "plantation" signifies the land a man owns which he is cultivating more or less in annual crops. Strictly, it designates the place planted; but in wills it is generally used to denote more than the inclosed and cultivated fields, and to take in the necessary woodland, and, indeed, commonly all the land forming the parcel or parcels under culture as one farm, or even what is worked by one set of hands. Stowe v. Davis, 32 N.C. 431.

PLAT, or PLOT. A map, or representation on paper, of a piece of land subdivided into lots, with streets, alleys, etc., usually drawn to a scale. McDaniel v. Mace, 47 Iowa, 510; Burke v. McCowen, 115 Cal. 481, 47 P. 367.

PLATA. Under Roumanian law, on the sale of a Roumanian ship, the owners become liable to the seamen only for repatriation at the expense of the ship, and "plata salariilor," or payment of salaries; the word "plata" meaning payment, and "salariilor" being the genitive plural of "salariu," which, like the English word "salary," means fixed compensation regularly paid. The Prahova, D.C.Cal., 38 F.Supp. 418, 425.

PLAY-DEBT. Debt contracted by gaming.

PLAZA. A Spanish word, meaning a public square in a city or town. Sachs v. Towanda, 79 Ill.App. 441; Kelly v. Town of Hayward, 192 Cal. 242, 219 P. 749.

PLEA. Common-law practice. A pleading; any one in the series of pleadings. More particularly, the first pleading on the part of the defendant. In the strictest sense, the answer which the defendant in an action at law makes to the plaintiff's declaration, and in which he sets up matter of *fact* as defense, thus distinguished from a demurrer, which interposes objections on grounds of *law*.

Equity. A special answer showing or relying upon one or more things as a cause why the suit should be either dismissed or delayed or barred. Mitf.Eq.Pl. 219; Coop.Eq.Pl. 223.

A short statement, in response to a bill in equity, of facts which, if inserted in the bill, would render it demurrable; while an answer is a complete statement of the defendant's case, and contains answers to any interrogatories the plaintiff may have administered. Hunt, Eq. pt. 1, c. 3.

Old English Law

A suit or action.

Thus, the power to "hold pleas" is the power to take cognizance of actions or suits; so "common pleas" are actions or suits between private persons. And this meaning of the word still appears in the modern declarations, where it is stated, *e. g.*, that the defendant "has been summoned to answer the plaintiff in a *plea* of debt."

General

Affirmative plea. One which sets up a single fact, not appearing in the bill, or sets up a number of circumstances all tending to establish a single fact, which fact, if existing, destroys the complainant's case. Potts v. Potts, N.J.Ch., 42 A. 1055.

Anomalous plea. One which is partly affirmative and partly negative. Baldwin v. Elizabeth, 42 N.J.Eq. 11, 6 A. 275; Potts v. Potts, N.J.Ch., 42 A. 1055.

Bad plea. One which is unsound or insufficient in form or substance, or which does not technically answer or correspond with the pleading which preceded it in the action.

Common pleas. Common causes or suits; civil actions brought and prosecuted between subjects or citizens, as distinguished from pleas of the crown or criminal cases.

Counter-plea. A plea to some matter incidental to the main object of the suit, and out of the direct line of pleadings. In the more ancient system of pleading, counter-plea was applied to what was, in effect, a replication to aid prayer, (*q. v.*;) that is, where a tenant for life or other limited interest in land, having an action brought against him in respect to the title to such land, prayed in aid of the lord or reversioner for his better defense, that which the demandant alleged against either request was called a "counter-plea." Cowell.

Dilatory pleas. See Dilatory.

Double plea. One having the technical fault of duplicity; one consisting of several distinct and independent matters alleged to the same point and requiring different answers.

False plea. A sham plea; (which title see infra.)

Foreign plea. A plea objecting to the jurisdiction of a judge, on the ground that he had not cognizance of the subject-matter of the suit. Cowell.

Negative plea. One which does not undertake to answer the various allegations of the bill, but specifically denies some particular fact or matter the existence of which is essential to entitle the complainant to any relief. Potts v. Potts, N.J. Ch., 42 A. 1056.

Peremptory pleas. "Pleas in bar" are so termed in contradistinction to that class of pleas called "dilatory pleas." The former, viz., peremptory pleas, are usually pleaded to the merits of the action, with the view of raising a material issue between the parties; while the latter class, viz., dilatory pleas, are generally pleaded with a view of retarding the plaintiff's proceedings, and not for the purpose of raising an issue upon which the parties may go to trial and settle the point in dispute. Peremptory pleas are also called "pleas in bar," while dilatory pleas are said to be in abatement only. Brown.

Plea in abatement. In practice. A plea which, without disputing justice of plaintiff's claim, objects to place, mode, or time of asserting it; it allows plaintiff to renew suit in another place or form, or at another time, and does not assume to answer action on its merits, or deny existence of particular cause of action on which plaintiff relies. Dickenson v. Hawes, 32 Ga.App. 173, 122 S.E. 811, 812; Harris v. North, 78 W.Va. 76, 88 S.E. 603, 604, 1 A.L.R. 356; Hurst v. Everett, C.C.N.C., 21 F. 221; Wilson v. Winchester & P. R. Co., C.C. W.Va., 82 F. 18.

Plea in bar. In practice. A plea which goes to *bar* the plaintiff's action; that is, to defeat it absolutely and entirely. 1 Burrill, Pr. 162; 3 Bl. Comm. 303; Rawson v. Knight, 71 Me. 102; Norton v. Winter, 1 Or. 48, 62 Am.Dec. 297; Wilson v. Knox County, 132 Mo. 387, 34 S.W. 45.

Plea in discharge. One which admits that the plaintiff had a cause of action, but shows that it was discharged by some subsequent or collateral matter, as, payment or accord and satisfaction. Nichols v. Cecil, 106 Tenn. 455, 61 S.W. 768.

Plea in reconvention. In the civil law. A plea which sets up new matter, not in defense to the action, but by way of cross-complaint, set-off, or counterclaim.

Plea of confession and avoidance. One which admits that plaintiff had a cause of action, but which avers that it has been discharged by some subsequent or collateral matter. De Lissa v. Fuller Coal and Mining Co., 59 Kan. 319, 52 P. 886, 888.

Plea of guilty. A confession of guilt in open court. Griffin v. State, 12 Ga.App. 615, 77 S.E. 1080, 1084; Stokes v. State, 122 Ark. 56, 182 S.W. 521; Accardi v. U. S., C.C.A.Mo., 15 F.2d 619, 621.

Plea of nolo contendere. One which has the same effect as a "plea of guilty" in so far as regards the proceedings on the indictment, and it is a confession only for the purposes of the criminal prosecution and does not bind the defendant in a civil suit for the same wrong. Schireson v. State Board of Medical Examiners of New Jersey, 129 N.J.L. 203, 28 A.2d 879, 881. See, also, Nolo Contendere.

Plea of release. One which admits the cause of action, but sets forth a release subsequently executed by the party authorized to release the claim. Landis v. Morrissey, 69 Cal. 83, 10 P. 258.

Plea side. The plea side of a court is that branch or department of the court which entertains or takes cognizance of civil actions and suits, as distinguished from its criminal or crown department. Thus the court of king's bench is said to have a plea side and a crown or criminal side; the one branch or department of it being devoted to the cognizance of civil actions, the other to criminal proceedings and matters peculiarly concerning the crown. So the court of exchequer is said to have a plea side and a crown side; the one being appropriated to civil actions, the other to matters of revenue. Brown.

Pleas in short by consent. Pleas which are intended to be nothing more than a mere outline, or sketch of the defense they respectively set up. Steele v. Walker, 115 Ala. 485, 21 So. 942, 943, 67 Am.St.Rep. 62.

Pleas of the crown. In English law. A phrase now employed to signify criminal causes, in which the king is a party. Formerly it signified royal causes for offenses of a greater magnitude than mere misdemeanors.

Pleas roll. In English practice. A record upon which are entered all the pleadings in a cause, in their regular order, and the issue.

Pure plea. One which relies wholly on some matter outside those referred to in the bill; as a plea of a release on a settled account.

Pleas not pure are so called in contradistinction to pure pleas; they are sometimes also denominated negative pleas. 4 Bouvier, Inst. n. 4275.

Sham plea. A false plea; a plea of false or fictitious matter, subtly drawn so as to entrap an opponent, or create delay. 3 Chit.Pr. 729, 730. A vexatious or false defense, resorted to under the old system of pleading for purposes of delay and annoyance. Steph.Pl. 383.

Mr. Chitty defines sham pleas to be pleas so palpably and manifestly untrue that the court will assume them to be so; pleas manifestly absurd. When answers or defenses admit of lawyer-like argument, such as courts should listen to, they are not "sham," in the sense of the statute. When it needs argument to prove that an answer or demurrer is frivolous, it is not frivolous, and should not be stricken off. To warrant this summary mode of disposing of a defense, the mere reading of the pleadings should be sufficient to disclose, without deliberation and without a doubt, that the defense is sham or irrelevant. Cottrill v. Cramer, 40 Wis. 559. A "sham plea" is one good on its face, but false in fact. In re Beam, 93 N.J.Eq. 593, 117 A. 613, 614. At common law a plea was considered sham when it was palpably or inherently false, and from the plain or conceded facts in the case must have been known to the party interposing it to be false. Fidelity Mut. Life Ins. Co. v. Wilkes Barre & H. R. Co., 98 N.J.Law, 507, 120 A. 734, 735.

Special plea. A special kind of plea in bar, distinguished by this name from the general issue, and consisting usually of some new affirmative matter, though it may also be in the form of a traverse or denial. Steph.Pl. 52, 162; Allen v. New Haven & N. Co., 49 Conn. 245.

Special plea in bar. One which advances new matter. It differs from the general, in this; that the latter denies some material allegation, but never advances new matter. Gould, Pl. c. 2, § 38.

PLEAD. To make, deliver, or file any pleading; to conduct the pleadings in a cause. To interpose any pleading in a suit which contains allegations of fact; in this sense the word is the antithesis of "demur." More particularly, to deliver in a formal manner the defendant's answer to the plaintiff's declaration, or to the indictment, as the case may be.

To appear as a pleader or advocate in a cause; to argue a cause in a court of justice. But this meaning of the word is not technical, but colloquial.

PLEAD A STATUTE. Pleading a statute is stating the facts which bring the case within it; and "counting" on it, in the strict language of pleading, is making express reference to it by apt terms to show the source of right relied on. McCullough v. Colfax County, 4 Neb. (Unof.) 543, 95 N.W. 31.

PLEAD ISSUABLY. This means to interpose such a plea as is calculated to raise a material issue, either of law or of fact.

PLEAD OVER. To pass over, or omit to notice, a material allegation in the last pleading of the opposite party; to pass by a defect in the pleading of the other party without taking advantage of it. In another sense, to plead the general issue, after one has interposed a demurrer or special plea which has been dismissed by a judgment of *respondeat ouster*.

PLEAD TO THE MERITS. This is a phrase of long standing and accepted usage in the law, and distinguishes those pleas which answer the cause of action and on which a trial may be had from all pleas of a different character. Rahn v. Gunnison, 12 Wis. 529.

PLEADED. Alleged or averred, in form, in a judicial proceeding.

It more often refers to matter of defense, but not invariably. To say that matter in a declaration or replication is not well pleaded would not be deemed erroneous. Abbott.

PLEADER. A person whose business it is to draw pleadings. Formerly, when pleading at common law was a highly technical and difficult art, there was a class of men known as "special pleaders not at the bar," who held a position intermediate between counsel and attorneys. The class is now almost extinct, and the term "pleaders" is generally applied, in England, to junior members of the common-law bar. Sweet.

Special pleader. In English practice. A person whose professional occupation is to give verbal or written opinions upon statements made verbally or in writing, and to draw pleadings, civil or criminal, and such practical proceedings as may be out of the usual course. 2 Chit.Pr. 42.

Special pleaders were not necessarily at the bar; but those that were not required to take out annual certificates under 33 & 34 Vict. c. 97, §§ 60, 63; Moz. & W.

PLEADING. The peculiar science or system of rules and principles, established in the common law, according to which the pleadings or responsive allegations of litigating parties are framed, with a view to preserve technical propriety and to produce a proper issue.

The process performed by the parties to a suit or action, in alternately presenting written statements of their contention, each responsive to that which precedes, and each serving to narrow the field of controversy, until there evolves a single point, affirmed on one side and denied on the other, called the "issue," upon which they then go to trial.

The act or step of interposing any one of the pleadings in a cause, but particularly one on the part of the defendant; and, in the strictest sense, one which sets up allegations of fact in defense to the action.

The name "a pleading" is also given to any one of the formal written statements of accusation or defense presented by the parties alternately in an action at law; the aggregate of such statements filed in any one cause are termed "the pleadings."

The oral advocacy of a client's cause in court, by his barrister or counsel, is sometimes called "pleading;" but this is a popular, rather than technical, use.

Chancery Practice

It consists in making the formal written allegations or statements of the respective parties on the record to maintain the suit, or to defeat it, of which, when contested in matters of fact, they propose to offer proofs, and in matters of law to offer arguments to the court. Story, Eq.Pl. § 4, note.

In General

Articulated pleading. The stating in separate paragraphs, separately numbered, of each material fact of the petition. Newspaper Feature Service v. Southern Pub. Co., 140 La. 702, 73 So. 777.

Double pleading. This is not allowed either in the declaration or subsequent pleadings. Its meaning with respect to the former is that the declaration must not, in support of a single demand, allege several distinct matters, by any one of which that demand is sufficiently supported. With respect to the subsequent pleadings, the meaning is that none of them is to contain several distinct answers to that which preceded it; and the reason of the rule in each case is that such pleading tends to several issues in respect of a single claim. Wharton.

Special pleading. When the allegations (or "pleadings," as they are called) of the contending parties in an action are not of the general or ordinary form, but are of a more complex or special character, they are denominated "special pleadings;" and, when a defendant pleads a plea of this description, (*i. e.*, a special plea,) he is said to plead specially, in opposition to pleading the general issue. These terms have given rise to the popular denomination of that science which, though properly called "pleading," is generally known by the name of "special pleading." Brown. The allegation of special or new matter in opposition or explanation of the last previous averments on the other side, as distinguished from a direct denial of matter previously alleged by the opposite party. Gould, Pl. c. 1, § 18; Gelston v. Hoyt, 3 Wheat. 246, 4 L.Ed. 381; Com.Dig. *Pleader* (E 15); Steph.Pl., And. ed. 240, n. In popular language, the adroit and plausible advocacy of a client's case in court. Stimson, Law Gloss.

PLEADINGS. The formal allegations by the parties of their respective claims and defenses, for the judgment of the court. Smith v. Jacksonville Oil Mill Co., 21 Ga.App. 679, 94 S.E. 900, 901; Wilkinson v. Stone, 82 Okl. 296, 200 P. 196, 199; Treadgold v. Willard, 81 Or. 658, 160 P. 803, 805.

The individual allegations of the respective parties to an action at common law, proceeding from them alternately, in the order and under the distinctive names following: The plaintiff's *declaration*, the defendant's *plea*, the plaintiff's *replication*, the defendant's *rejoinder*, the plaintiff's *surrejoinder*, the defendant's *rebutter*, the plaintiff's *surrebutter*; after which they have no distinctive names. Burrill.

The term "pleadings" has a technical and well-defined meaning. Pleadings are written allegations of what is affirmed on the one side, or denied on the other, disclosing to the court or jury having to try the cause the real matter in dispute between the parties. Desnoyer v. Hereux, 1 Minn. 17 (Gil. 1).

PLEBANUS. In old English ecclesiastical law. A rural dean. Cowell.

PLEBEIAN. One who is classed among the common people, as distinguished from the nobles.

PLEBEITY, or PLEBITY. The common or meaner sort of people; the plebeians.

PLEBEYOS. In Spanish law. Commons; those who exercise any trade, or who cultivate the soil. White, New Recop. b. 1, tit. 5, c. 3, § 6, and note.

PLEBIANA. In old records. A mother church.

PLEBISCITE. In modern constitutional law, the name *"plebiscite"* has been given to a vote of the entire people, (that is, the aggregate of the enfranchised individuals composing a state or nation,) expressing their choice for or against a proposed law or enactment, submitted to them, and which, if adopted, will work a radical change in the constitution, or which is beyond the powers of the regular legislative body. The proceeding is extraordinary, and is generally revolutionary in its character; an example of which may be seen in the *plebiscites* submitted to the French people by Louis Napoleon, whereby the Second Empire was established. But the principle of the *plebiscite* has been incorporated in the modern Swiss constitution, (under the name of *"referendum,"*) by which a revision of the constitution must be undertaken when demanded by the vote of fifty thousand Swiss citizens. Maine Popular Govt. 40, 96.

PLEBISCITUM. Lat. In Roman law. A law enacted by the *plebs* or commonalty, (that is, the citizens, with the exception of the patricians and senators,) at the request or on the proposition of a plebeian magistrate, such as a "tribune." Inst. 1, 2, 4.

PLEBS. Lat. In Roman law. The commonalty or citizens, exclusive of the patricians and senators. Inst. 1, 2, 4.

PLEDABLE. L. Fr. That may be brought or conducted; as an action or "plea," as it was formerly called. Britt. c. 32.

PLEDGE. In the law of bailment. A bailment of goods to a creditor as security for some debt or engagement. A bailment or delivery of goods by a debtor to his creditor, to be kept till the debt be discharged. Story, Bailm. § 7; Civ. Code La. art. 3133; 2 Kent, Comm. 577; Stearns v. Marsh, 4 Denio, N.Y., 229, 47 Am.Dec. 248; Sheridan v. Presas, 18 Misc. 180, 41 N.Y.S. 451; Bank of Rochester v. Jones, 4 N.Y. 507, 55 Am.Dec. 290; Gloucester Bank v. Worcester, 10 Pick., Mass., 531; Lilienthal v. Ballou, 125 Cal. 183, 57 P. 897.

The necessary elements to constitute a contract one of "pledge" are: Possession of the pledged property must pass from the pledgor to the pledgee; the legal title to the property must remain in the pledgor; and the pledgee must have a lien on the property for the payment of a debt or the performance of an obligation due him by the pledgor or some other person—while, in a "chattel mortgage," the legal title passes to the mortgagee subject to a defeasance. Rice v. Garnett, 17 Ala.App. 239, 84 So. 557, 558; Campbell v. Redwine Bros., 22 Ga.App. 455, 96 S.E. 347; Sneeden v. Nurnberger's Market, 192 N.C. 439, 135 S.E.

328, 330; McAndrews v. Idawa Gold Mining Co., 54 N.D. 734, 210 N.W. 514, 519, 51 A.L.R. 1123.

A bailment of personal property as security for a debt or other obligation. Thoen v. First Nat. Bank, 199 Minn. 47, 271 N.W. 111, 112; Travers v. Stevens, 108 Fla. 11, 145 So. 851, 854.

The specific article delivered to the creditor in security is also called a "pledge" or "pawn."

There is a clear distinction between mortgages and pledges. In a pledge the legal title remains in the pledgor; in a mortgage it passes to the mortgagee. In a mortgage the mortgagee need not have possession; in a pledge the pledgee must have possession, though it be only constructive. In a mortgage, at common law, the property on non-payment of the debt passes wholly to the mortgagee; in a pledge the property is sold, and only so much of the proceeds as will pay his debt passes to the pledgee. A mortgage is a conditional conveyance of property, which becomes absolute unless redeemed at a specified time. A pledge is not strictly a conveyance at all, nor need any day of redemption be appointed for it. A mortgagee can sell and deliver the thing mortgaged, subject only to the right of redemption. A pledgee cannot sell and deliver his pawn until the debt is due and payment denied. Bouvier.

There are two varieties of the contract of pledge known to the law of Louisiana, viz., *pawn* and *antichresis;* the former relating to chattel securities, the latter to landed securities. Civ.Code La. art. 3134; and see those titles.

PLEDGEE. The party to whom goods are pledged, or delivered in pledge. Story, Bailm. § 287.

PLEDGERY. Suretyship, or an undertaking or answering for another. Gloucester Bank v. Worcester, 10 Pick., Mass., 531.

PLEDGES. In pleading. Those persons who became sureties for the prosecution of the suit. Their names were anciently appended at the foot of the declaration. In time it became purely a formal matter, because the plaintiff was no longer liable to be amerced for a false claim, and the fictitious persons John Doe and Richard Roe became the universal pledges, or they might be omitted altogether, 1 Tidd, Pr. 455; Archb. Civ. Pl. 171; or inserted at any time before judgment; they are now omitted.

PLEDGES TO RESTORE. In England, before the plaintiff in foreign attachment can issue execution against the property in the hands of the garnishee, he must find "pledges to restore," consisting of two householders, who enter into a recognizance for the restoration of the property, as a security for the protection of the defendant; for, as the plaintiff's debt is not proved in any stage of the proceedings, the court guards the rights of the absent defendant by taking security on his behalf, so that if he should afterwards disprove the plaintiff's claim he may obtain restitution of the property attached. Brand. For. Attachm. 93; Sweet.

PLEDGOR. The party delivering goods in pledge; the party pledging. Story, Bailm. § 287.

PLEGIABILIS. In old English law. That may be pledged; the subject of pledge or security. Fleta, lib. 1, c. 20, § 98.

PLEGII DE PROSEQUENDO. Pledges to prosecute with effect an action of replevin.

PLEGII DE RETORNO HABENDO. Pledges to return the subject of distress, should the right be determined against the party bringing the action of replevin. 3 Steph. Comm. (7th Ed.) 422*n*.

PLEGIIS ACQUIETANDIS. A writ that anciently lay for a surety against him for whom he was surety, if he paid not the money at the day. Fitzh. Nat. Brev. 137.

PLENA ÆTAS. Lat. In old English law. Full age.

PLENA ET CELERIS JUSTITIA FIAT PARTIBUS. 4 Inst. 67. Let full and speedy justice be done to the parties.

PLENA FORISFACTURA. A forfeiture of all that one possesses.

PLENA PROBATIO. In the civil law. A term used to signify full proof, (that is, proof by two witnesses,) in contradistinction to *semi-plena probatio,* which is only a presumption. Cod. 4, 19, 5.

PLENARTY. In English law. Fullness; a state of being full. A term applied to a benefice when full, or possessed by an incumbent. The opposite state to a *vacation,* or vacancy. Cowell.

PLENARY. Full, entire, complete, absolute, perfect, unqualified. Mashunkashey v. Mashunkashey, 191 Okl. 501, 134 P.2d 976, 979.

PLENARY CONFESSION. A full and complete confession. An admission or confession, whether in civil or criminal law, is said to be "plenary" when it is, if believed, conclusive against the person making it. Best, Ev. 664; Rosc. Crim. Ev. 39.

PLENARY SUIT. One that proceeds on formal pleadings. Central Republic Bank and Trust Co. v. Caldwell, C.C.A.Mo., 58 F.2d 721.

In the ecclesiastical courts, (and in admiralty practice,) causes are divided into plenary and summary. The former are those in whose proceedings the order and solemnity of the law is required to be exactly observed, so that if there is the least departure from that order, or disregard of that solemnity, the whole proceedings are annulled. Summary causes are those in which it is unnecessary to pursue that order and solemnity. Brown.

PLENE. Lat. Completely; fully; sufficiently.

PLENE ADMINISTRAVIT. In practice. A plea by an executor or administrator that he has fully administered all the assets that have come to his hands, and that no assets remain out of which the plaintiff's claim could be satisfied.

PLENE ADMINISTRAVIT PRÆTER. In practice. A plea by an executor or administrator that he has "fully administered" all the assets that have come to his hands, "except" assets to a certain amount, which are not sufficient to satisfy the plaintiff. 1 Tidd, Pr. 644.

PLENE COMPUTAVIT. He has fully accounted. A plea in an action of account render, alleging that the defendant has fully accounted.

PLENIPOTENTIARY. One who has full power to do a thing; a person fully commissioned to act for another. A term applied in international law to ministers and envoys of the second rank of public ministers. Wheat. Hist. Law Nat. 266.

PLENUM DOMINIUM. Lat. In the civil law. Full ownership; the property in a thing united with the usufruct. Calvin.

PLEVIN. A warrant, or assurance.

PLEYTO. In Spanish law. The pleadings in a cause. White, New Recop. b. 3, tit. 7.

PLIGHT. In old English law. An estate, with the habit and quality of the land; extending to a rent charge and to a possibility of dower. Co. Litt. 221*b*; Cowell.

PLOK-PENNIN. A kind of earnest used in public sales at Amsterdam. Wharton.

PLOTTAGE. A term used in appraising land values and particularly in eminent domain proceedings, to designate the additional value given to city lots by the fact that they are contiguous, which enables the owner to utilize them as large blocks of land. Erlanger v. New York Theatre Co., 206 App.Div. 148, 200 N.Y.S. 696, 698; People ex rel. Frederick Loeser & Co. v. Goldfogle, 220 App.Div. 326, 221 N.Y.S. 342, 346.

PLOW-ALMS. The ancient payment of a penny to the church from every plow-land. 1 Mon. Angl. 256.

PLOW-BOTE. An allowance of wood which tenants are entitled to, for repairing their plows and other implements of husbandry.

PLOW-LAND. A quantity of land "not of any certain content, but as much as a plow can, by course of husbandry, plow in a year." Co. Litt. 69*a*.

Tillable. Govier v. Brechler, 159 Wis. 157, 149 N.W. 740, 742.

PLOW-MONDAY. The Monday after twelfth-day.

PLOW-SILVER. Money formerly paid by some tenants, in lieu of service to plow the lord's lands.

PLUMBATURA. Lat. In the civil law. Soldering. Dig. 6, 1, 23, 5.

PLUMBER. A tradesman who furnishes, fits, and repairs gas, water and soil pipes, cisterns, tanks, baths, water closets, their fittings, and other sanitary and fire protection apparatus for a house or other building, including junctions to mains and sewers. Com. v. Dougherty, 156 Pa.Super. 520, 40 A.2d 902, 903; People v. Osborne, 149 Misc. 676, 269 N.Y.S. 409.

PLUMBUM. Lat. In the civil law. Lead. Dig. 50, 16, 242, 2.

PLUNDER, *v.* To take property from persons or places by open force, and this may be in course of a lawful war, or by unlawful hostility, as in the case of pirates or banditti. The term is also used to express the idea of taking property from a person or place, without just right, but not expressing the nature or quality of the wrong done. Carter v. Andrews, 16 Pick., Mass., 9; U. S. v. Stone, C.C.Tenn., 8 F. 246; U. S. v. Pitman, 27 Fed.Cas. 540.

PLUNDER, *n.* Personal property belonging to an enemy, captured and appropriated on land; booty. Also the act of seizing such property. See Booty; Prize.

PLUNDERAGE. In maritime law. The embezzlement of goods on board of a ship is so called.

PLURAL. Containing more than one; consisting of or designating two or more. Webster.

PLURAL MARRIAGE. See Marriage.

PLURALIS NUMERUS EST DUOBUS CONTENTUS. 1 Rolle, 476. The plural number is satisfied by two.

PLURALIST. One that holds more than one ecclesiastical benefice, with cure of souls.

PLURALITER. In the plural. 10 East, 158, arg.

PLURALITY. In the law of elections. The excess of the votes cast for one candidate over those cast for any other. Where there are only two candidates, he who receives the greater number of the votes cast is said to have a *majority;* when there are more than two competitors for the same office, the person who receives the greatest number of votes has a *plurality,* but he has not a majority unless he receives a greater number of votes than those cast for all his competitors combined, or, in other words, more than one-half of the total number of votes cast.

In ecclesiastical law, "plurality" means the holding two, three, or more benefices by the same incumbent; and he is called a "pluralist." Pluralities are now abolished, except in certain cases. 2 Steph.Comm. 691, 692.

PLURES COHÆREDES SUNT QUASI UNUM CORPUS PROPTER UNITATEM JURIS QUOD HABENT. Co. Litt. 163. Several co-heirs are, as it were, one body, by reason of the unity of right which they possess.

PLURES PARTICIPES SUNT QUASI UNUM CORPUS, IN EO QUOD UNUM JUS HABENT. Co. Litt. 164. Several parceners are as one body, in that they have one right.

PLURIES. Lat. Often; frequently. When an original and *alias* writ have been issued and proved ineffectual, a third writ, called a "*pluries* writ," may frequently be issued. It is to the same effect as the two former, except that it contains the words, "as we have often commanded you," ("*sicut pluries præcepimus,*") after the usual commencement, "We command you." 3 Bl. Comm. 283; Archb. Pr. 585.

PLURIES FI. FA. A writ issued where other commands of the court have proved ineffectual. U. S. v. Bd of Dir., C.C.A.La., 229 F. 1, 3.

PLURIS PETITIO. Lat. In Scotch practice. A demand of more than is due. Bell.

PLUS EXEMPLA QUAM PECCATA NOCENT. Examples hurt more than crimes.

PLUS PECCAT AUTHOR QUAM ACTOR. The originator or instigator of a crime is a worse offender than the actual perpetrator of it. Applied to the crime of subornation of perjury. 5 Coke, 99*a*.

PLUS PETITIO. In Roman law. A phrase denoting the offense of claiming more than was just in one's pleadings. This more might be claimed in four different respects, viz.: (1) *Re, i. e.*, in amount, (*e. g.*, £50 for £5;) (2) *loco, i. e.*, in place (*e. g.*, delivery at some place more difficult to effect than the place specified;) (3) *tempore, i. e.*, in time, (*e. g.*, claiming payment on the 1st of August of what is not due till the 1st of September;) and (4) *causa, i. e.*, in quality, (*e. g.*, claiming a dozen of champagne, when the contract was only for a dozen of wine generally.) Prior to Justinian's time, this offense was in general fatal to the action; but, under the legislation of the emperors Zeno and Justinian, the offense (if *re, loco*, or *causa*) exposed the party to the payment of three times the damage, if any, sustained by the other side, and (if *tempore*) obliged him to postpone his action for double the time, and to pay the costs of his first action before commencing a second. Brown.

PLUS VALET CONSUETUDO QUAM CONCESSIO. Custom is more powerful than grant.

PLUS VALET UNUS OCULATUS TESTIS QUAM AURITI DECEM. One eye-witness is of more weight than ten ear-witnesses, [or those who speak from hearsay.] 4 Inst. 279.

PLUS VIDENT OCULI QUAM OCULUS. Several eyes see more than one. 4 Inst. 160.

PNEUMOCONIOSIS. A generic term including all lung diseases caused by dust particles of any sort. Genesco, Inc. v. Greeson, 125 S.E.2d 786, 789, 105 Ga.App. 798.

PO. LO. SUO. An old abbreviation for the words *"ponit loco suo,"* (puts in his place,) used in warrants of attorney. Townsh. Pl. 431.

POACH. To steal game on a man's land.

POACHING. In English criminal law. The unlawful entry upon land for the purpose of taking or destroying game; the taking or destruction of game upon another's land, usually committed at night. Steph. Crim. Law 119, et seq.; 2 Steph. Comm. 82.

POBLADOR. In Spanish law. A colonizer; he who peoples; the founder of a colony.

POCKET. This word is used as an adjective in several compound legal phrases, carrying a meaning suggestive of, or analogous to, its signification as a pouch, bag, or secret receptacle. For these phrases, see "Borough," "Judgment," "Record," "Sheriff," and "Veto."

PŒNA. Lat. Punishment; a penalty. Inst. 4, 6, 18, 19.

POD NET. See Pound Net.

PŒNA AD PAUCOS, METUS AD OMNES PERVENIAT. If punishment be inflicted on a few, a dread comes to all.

PŒNA CORPORALIS. Corporal punishment.

PŒNA EX DELICTO DEFUNCTI HÆRES TENERI NON DEBET. The heir ought not to be bound by a penalty arising out of the wrongful act of the deceased. 2 Inst. 198.

PŒNA NON POTEST, CULPA PERENNIS ERIT. Punishment cannot be, crime will be, perpetual. 21 Vin. Abr. 271.

PŒNA PILLORALIS. In old English law. Punishment of the pillory. Fleta, lib. 1, c. 38, § 11.

PŒNA SUOS TENERE DEBET ACTORES ET NON ALIOS. Punishment ought to bind the guilty, and not others. Bract. fol. 380*b*.

PŒNA TOLLI POTEST, CULPA PERENNIS ERIT. The punishment can be removed, but the crime remains. 1 Park.Cr.Rep. (N.Y.) 241.

PŒNÆ POTIUS MOLLIENDÆ QUAM EXASPARANDÆ SUNT. 3 Inst. 220. Punishments should rather be softened than aggravated.

PŒNÆ SINT RESTRINGENDÆ. Punishments should be restrained. Jenk. Cent. 29.

PŒNÆ SUOS TENERE DEBET ACTORES ET NON ALIOS. Punishment ought to be inflicted upon the guilty, and not upon others. Bract. 380*b*; Fleta, l. 1, c. 38, § 12; l. 4, c. 17, § 17.

PŒNALIS. Lat. In the civil law. Penal; imposing a penalty; claiming or enforcing a penalty. *Actiones pœnales*, penal actions. Inst. 4, 6, 12.

PŒNITENTIA. Lat. In the civil law. Repentance; reconsideration; changing one's mind; drawing back from an agreement already made, or rescinding it.

Locus pœnitentiæ. Room or place for repentance or reconsideration; an opportunity to withdraw from a negotiation before finally concluding the contract or agreement. Also, in criminal law, an opportunity afforded by the circumstances to a person who has formed an intention to kill or to commit another crime, giving him a chance to reconsider and relinquish his purpose.

POINDING. The process of the law of Scotland which answers to the distress of the English law. Poinding is of three kinds:

Real poinding or poinding of the ground. This is the action by which a creditor, having a security on the land of his debtor, is enabled to appropriate the rents of the land, and the goods of the debtor or his tenants found thereon, to the satisfaction of the debt.

Personal poinding. This consists in the seizure of the goods of the debtor, which are sold under the direction of a court of justice, and the net amount of the sales paid over to the creditor in satisfaction of his debt; or, if no purchaser appears, the goods themselves are delivered.

Poinding of *stray cattle*, committing depredations on corn, grass, or plantations, until satisfaction is made for the damage. Bell.

POINT. A distinct proposition or question of law arising or propounded in a case. Gulf, C. & S. F. Ry. Co. v. Tarver, Steele & Co., Tex.Civ. App., 295 S.W. 320, 323.

POINT RESERVED. When, in the progress of the trial of a cause, an important or difficult point of law is presented to the court, and the court is not certain of the decision that should be given, it may *reserve* the point, that is, decide it provisionally as it is asked by the party, but reserve its more mature consideration for the hearing on a motion for a new trial, when, if it shall appear that the first ruling was wrong, the verdict will be set aside. The point thus treated is technically called a "point reserved."

POINTS. The distinct propositions of law, or chief heads of argument, presented by a party in his paper-book, and relied upon on the argument of the cause. Also the marks used in punctuation. Duncan v. Kohler, 37 Minn. 379, 34 N.W. 594; Commonwealth Ins. Co. v. Pierro, 6 Minn. 570 (Gil. 404).

POISON. In medical jurisprudence. A substance having an inherent deleterious property which renders it, when taken into the system, capable of destroying life. 2 Whart. & S. Med. Jur. § 1. A substance which, on being applied to the human body, internally or externally, is capable of destroying the action of the vital functions, or of placing the solids and fluids in such a state as to prevent the continuance of life. Wharton. Boswell v. State, 114 Ga. 40, 39 S.E. 897; United States Mut. Acc. Ass'n v. Newman, 84 Va. 52, 3 S.E. 805.

POLAR STAR RULE. The rule that the intent of the maker of a written document, as gathered from its four corners, shall prevail unless such intent conflicts with some statutory provision within the jurisdiction, or is against public policy. Hanks v. McDanell, 307 Ky. 243, 210 S.W.2d 784, 786.

POLE. A measure of length, equal to five yards and a half.

POLICE. The function of that branch of the administrative machinery of government which is charged with the preservation of public order and tranquillity, the promotion of the public health, safety, and morals, and the prevention, detection, and punishment of crimes. State v. Hine, 59 Conn. 50, 21 A. 1024, 10 L.R.A. 83; People v. Squire, 107 N.Y. 593, 14 N.E. 820, 1 Am.St.Rep. 893.

The police of a state, in a comprehensive sense, embraces its whole system of internal regulation, by which the state seeks not only to preserve the public order and to prevent offenses against the state, but also to establish for the intercourse of citizen with citizen those rules of good manners and good neighborhood which are calculated to prevent a conflict of rights, and to insure to each the uninterrupted enjoyment of his own, so far as is reasonably consistent with a like enjoyment of rights by others. Cooley, Const. Lim. *572. It is defined by Jeremy Bentham in his works: "Police is in general a system of precaution, either for the prevention of crime or of calamities. Its business may be distributed into eight distinct branches: (1) police for the prevention of offenses; (2) police for the prevention of calamities; (3) police for the prevention of epidemic diseases; (4) police of charity; (5) police of interior communications; (6) police of public amusements; (7) police for recent intelligence; (8) police for registration." Canal Com'rs v. Willamette Transp. Co., 6 Or. 222.

The term "police" has also been divided into "administrative police", which has for its object to maintain constantly public order in every part of the general administration, and "judiciary police" which is intended principally to prevent crimes by punishing the criminals. Its object is to punish crimes which the administrative police has not been able to prevent. Green v. City of Bennettsville, 197 S.C. 313, 15 S.E.2d 334, 337.

POLICE COURT. The name of a kind of inferior court in several of the states, which has a summary jurisdiction over minor offenses and misdemeanors of small consequence, and the powers of a committing magistrate in respect to more serious crimes, and, in some states, a limited jurisdiction for the trial of civil causes. In English law. Courts in which stipendiary magistrates, chosen from barristers of a certain standing, sit for the dispatch of business. Their general duties and powers are the same as those of the unpaid magistracy, except that one of them may usually act in cases which would require to be heard before two other justices. Wharton.

POLICE DE CHARGEMENT. Fr. In French law. A bill of lading. Ord. Mar. liv. 3, tit. 2.

POLICE JURY. In Louisiana. The governing bodies of the "parishes," which are political subdivisions of the state, comparable to counties in other states. National Liberty Ins. Co. of America v. Police Jury of Natchitoches Parish, C.C.A. La., 96 F.2d 261, 262.

POLICE JUSTICE. A magistrate charged exclusively with the duties incident to the common-law office of a conservator or justice of the peace; the prefix "police" serving merely to distinguish them from justices having also civil jurisdiction. Wenzler v. People, 58 N.Y. 530.

POLICE MAGISTRATE. An inferior judicial officer having jurisdiction of minor criminal offenses, breaches of police regulations, and the like; so called to distinguish them from magistrates who have jurisdiction in civil cases also, as justices of the peace. People v. Curley, 5 Colo. 416; McDermont v. Dinnie, 6 N.D. 278, 69 N.W. 295.

POLICE OFFICER. One of the staff of men employed in cities and towns to enforce the municipal police, *i. e.*, the laws and ordinances for preserving the peace and good order of the community. Otherwise called "policeman."

POLICE POWER. The power vested in a state to establish laws and ordinances for the regulation and enforcement of its police as above defined. The power vested in the legislature to make, ordain, and establish all manner of wholesome and reasonable laws, statutes, and ordinances, either with penalties or without, not repugnant to the constitution, as they shall judge to be for the good and welfare of the commonwealth, and of the subjects of the same. Com. v. Alger, 7 Cush. (Mass.) 85. An authority conferred by the American constitutional system upon the individual states, through which they are enabled to establish a special department of police; adopt such regulations as tend to prevent the commission of fraud, violence, or other offenses against the state; aid in the arrest of criminals; and secure generally the comfort, health, and prosperity of the state, by preserving the public order, preventing a conflict of rights in the common intercourse of the citizens, and insuring to each an uninterrupted enjoyment of all the privileges conferred upon him by the laws of his country. Lalor, Pol. Enc. s. v.

That inherent and plenary power in state over persons and property which enables the people to prohibit all things inimical to comfort, safety, health, and welfare of society. Drysdale v. Prudden, 195 N.C. 722, 143 S.E. 530, 536.

It is true that the legislation which secures to all protection in their rights, and the equal use and enjoyment of their property, embraces an almost infinite variety of subjects. Whatever affects the peace, good order, morals, and health of the community comes within its scope; and every one must use and enjoy his property subject to the restrictions which such legislation imposes. What is termed the "police power" of the state, which, from the language often used respecting it, one would suppose to be an undefined and irresponsible element in government, can only interfere with the conduct of individuals in their intercourse with each other, and in the use of their property, so far as may be required to secure these objects. Munn v. Illinois, 94 U.S. 145, 24 L.Ed. 77. For other definitions, see Slaughterhouse Cases, 16 Wall. 62, 21 L.Ed. 394; Stone v. Mississippi, 101 U.S. 818, 25 L.Ed. 1079; Thorpe v. Rutland & B. R. Co., 27 Vt. 140, 62 Am.Dec. 625; People v. Steele, 231 Ill. 340, 83 N.E. 236, 14 L.R.A.,N.S., 361, 121 Am.St.Rep. 321; In re Clark, 65 Conn. 17, 31 A. 522, 28 L.R.A. 242; Mathews v. Board of Education, 127 Mich. 530, 86 N.W. 1036, 54 L.R.A. 736; In re Main, 162 Okl. 65, 19 P.2d 153, 156.

POLICE REGULATIONS. Laws of a state, or ordinances of a municipality, which have for their object the preservation and protection of public peace and good order, and of the health, morals, and security of the people. Ex parte Bourgeois, 60 Miss. 663, 45 Am.Rep. 420; Sonora v. Curtin, 137 Cal. 583, 70 P. 674; Roanoke Gas Co. v. Roanoke, 88 Va. 810, 14 S.E. 665.

POLICE SUPERVISION. In England, subjection to police supervision is where a criminal offender is subjected to the obligation of notifying the place of his residence and every change of his residence to the chief officer of police of the district, and of reporting himself once a month to the chief officer or his substitute. Offenders subject to police supervision are popularly called "habitual criminals." Sweet.

POLICIES OF INSURANCE, COURT OF. A court established in pursuance of the statutes 43 Eliz. c. 12, and 13 & 14 Car. II. c. 23. Composed of the judge of the admiralty, the recorder of London, two doctors of the civil law, two common lawyers, and eight merchants; any three of whom, one being a civilian or a barrister, could determine in a summary way causes concerning policies of assurance in London, with an appeal to chancery. No longer in existence. 3 Bl.Comm. 74.

POLICY. The general principles by which a government is guided in its management of public affairs, or the legislature in its measures.

This term, as applied to a law, ordinance, or rule of law, denotes its general purpose or tendency considered as directed to the welfare or prosperity of the state or community.

In gaming. A species of "lottery" whereby the chance is determined by numbers; "numbers game" also being a lottery. People v. Hines, 258 App.Div. 466, 17 N.Y.S.2d 141, 142.

Policy of a statute, or legislature. As applied to a penal or prohibitive statute, means the intention of discouraging conduct of a mischievous tendency. See L.R. 6 P.C. 134; 5 Barn. & Ald. 335; Pol. Cont. 235.

Policy of the law. By this phrase is understood the disposition of the law to discountenance certain classes of acts, transactions, or agreements, or to refuse them its sanction, because it considers them immoral, detrimental to the public welfare, subversive of good order, or otherwise contrary to the plan and purpose of civil regulations.

Public policy. That principle of the law which holds that no subject can lawfully do that which has a tendency to be injurious to the public or against the public good. 4 H. L. Cas. 1; Greenh. Pub. Pol. 2. The principles under which the freedom of contract or private dealings is restricted by law for the good of the community. Wharton. The term "policy," as applied to a statute, regulation, rule of law, course of action, or the like, refers to its probable effect, tendency, or object, considered with reference to the social or political well-being of the state. Thus, certain classes of acts are said to be "against public policy," when the law refuses to enforce or recognize them, on the ground that they have a mischievous tendency, so as to be injurious to the interests of the state, apart from illegality or immorality. Sweet Egerton v. Earl Brownlow, 4 H.L.Cas. 235; Smith v. Railroad Co., 115 Cal. 584, 47 P. 582. Workmen's Compensation Board of Kentucky v. Abbott, 212 Ky. 123, 278 S.W. 533, 536, 47 A.L.R. 789; Driver v. Smith, 89 N.J.Eq. 339, 104 A. 717, 725; Nashville Ry. & Light Co. v. Lawson, 144 Tenn. 78, 229 S.W. 741, 743; American Nat. Ins. Co. v. Coates, 112 Tex. 267, 246 S.W. 356, 359;

People v. Herrin, 284 Ill. 368, 120 N.E. 274, 275; Fidelity & Deposit Co. of Maryland v. Moore, D. C.Or., 3 F.2d 652, 653.

"Public policy" is the community common sense and common conscience extended and applied throughout the state to matters of public morals, public health, public safety, public welfare, and the like; it is that general and well-settled public opinion relating to man's plain, palpable duty to his fellow men having due regard to all the circumstances of each particular relation and situation. Pittsburgh, C., C. & St. L. Ry. Co. v. Kinney, 95 Ohio St. 64, 115 N.E. 505, 506, L.R.A.1917D, 641, Ann.Cas.1918B, 286. Public policy properly cognizable by courts is that derived or derivable by clear implication from its Constitution, statutes, and judicial decisions. Brown v. American Ry. Express Co., 128 S.C. 428, 123 S.E. 97, 98; In re Rahn's Estate, 316 Mo. 492, 291 S.W. 120, 122, 51 A.L.R. 877; Hogston v. Bell, 185 Ind. 536, 112 N.E. 883, 886; New York Life Ins. Co. v. Hamburger, 174 Mich. 254, 140 N.W. 510, 512. "Public policy is a variable quantity; it must and does vary with the habits, capacities, and opportunities of the public." 36 Ch.Div. 359; Chaffee v. Farmers' Co-op. Elevator Co., 39 N.D. 585, 168 N.W. 616, 618.

POLICY OF INSURANCE. A mercantile instrument in writing, by which one party, in consideration of a premium, engages to indemnify another against a contingent loss, by making him a payment in compensation, whenever the event shall happen by which the loss is to accrue. 2 Steph. Comm. 172. Contract whereby insurer, in return for premiums, engages, on happening of designated event, to pay certain sum as provided. In re O'Neill's Estate, 143 Misc. 733, 255 N.Y.S. 767, 771.

The written instrument in which a contract of insurance is set forth. Civ. Code Cal. § 2586.

Blanket policy. A policy of fire insurance which contemplates that the risk is shifting, fluctuating, or varying, and is applied to a class of property rather than to any particular article or thing. Insurance Co. v. Baltimore Warehouse Co., 93 U.S. 541, 23 L.Ed. 868; Insurance Co. v. Landau, 62 N.J.Eq. 73, 49 A. 738.

The term "specific" as applied in insurance phraseology is frequently used in contrast with "blanket insurance" and denotes coverage of a particular piece of property or property at a specific location, as contrasted with blanket insurance which covers the same and other property in several different locations. Davis Yarn Co. v. Brooklyn Yarn Dye Co., 293 N.Y. 236, 56 N.E.2d 564, 571.

Class of life insurance policies. Those policies issued in the same calendar year, upon the lives of persons of the same age, and on the same plan of insurance. Miller v. New York Life Ins. Co., 179 Ky. 246, 200 S.W. 482, 484.

Endowment policy. In life insurance. A policy the amount of which is payable to the assured himself at the end of a fixed term of years, if he is then living, or to his heirs or a named beneficiary if he shall die sooner.

Floating policy. A policy of fire insurance not applicable to any specific described goods, but to any and all goods which may at the time of the fire be in a certain building.

Interest policy. One where the assured has a real, substantial, and assignable interest in the thing insured; as opposed to a wager policy.

Mixed policy. A policy of marine insurance in which not only the time is specified for which the risk is limited, but the voyage also is described by its local termini; as opposed to policies of insurance for a particular voyage, without any limits as to time, and also to purely time policies, in which there is no designation of local termini at all. Mozley & Whitley. And see Wilkins v. Tobacco Ins. Co., 30 Ohio, 340, 27 Am.Rep. 455.

Open policy. One in which the value of the subject insured is not fixed or agreed upon in the policy as between the assured and the underwriter, but is left to be estimated in case of loss. The term is opposed to "valued policy," in which the value of the subject insured is fixed for the purpose of the insurance, and expressed on the face of the policy. Mozley & Whitley. Riggs v. Fire Protection Ass'n, 61 S.C. 448, 39 S.E. 614; Cox v. Insurance Co., 3 Rich. Law, 331, 45 Am.Dec. 771; Insurance Co. v. Butler, 38 Ohio St. 128. But this term is also sometimes used in America to describe a policy in which an aggregate amount is expressed in the body of the policy, and the specific amounts and subjects are to be indorsed from time to time. London Assur. Corp. v. Paterson, 106 Ga. 538, 32 S.E. 650.

Paid-up policy. In life insurance. A policy on which no further payments are to be made in the way of annual premiums.

Policy loan. An advancement on life policy without a personal obligation on the part of the policy holder as to repayment. Board of Assessors of the Parish of Orleans v. New York Life Ins. Co., 30 S.Ct. 385, 216 U.S. 517, 54 L.Ed. 597.

Time policy. In fire insurance, one made for a defined and limited time, as, one year. In marine insurance, one made for a particular period of time, irrespective of the voyage or voyages upon which the vessel may be engaged during that period. Wilkins v. Tobacco Ins. Co., 30 Ohio St. 339, 27 Am.Rep. 455; Greenleaf v. St. Louis Ins. Co., 37 Mo. 29.

Valued policy. One in which the value of the thing insured is settled by agreement between the parties and inserted in the policy. Riggs v. Insurance Co., 61 S.C. 448, 39 S.E. 614; Luce v. Insurance Co., 15 Fed.Cas. 1071.

Voyage policy. A policy of marine insurance effected for a particular voyage or voyages of the vessel, and not otherwise limited as to time. Wilkins v. Tobacco Ins. Co., 30 Ohio St. 339, 27 Am.Rep. 455.

Wager policy. An insurance upon a subject-matter in which the party assured has no real, valuable, or insurable interest. A mere wager policy is that in which the party assured has no interest in the thing assured, and could sustain no possible loss by the event insured against, if he had not made such wager. Gambs v. Insurance Co., 50 Mo. 47; Moving Picture Co. of America v. Scottish Union & National Ins. Co. of Edinburg, 244 Pa. 358, 90 A. 642, 644; Avery v. Mechanics' Ins. Co. of Philadelphia, Mo.App., 295 S. W. 509, 512.

POLITIÆ LEGIBUS NON LEGES POLITIIS ADAPTANDÆ. Politics are to be adapted to the laws, and not the laws to politics. Hob. 154.

POLITICAL. Pertaining or relating to the policy or the administration of government, state or national. People v. Morgan, 90 Ill. 558. Pertaining to, or incidental to, the exercise of the functions vested in those charged with the conduct of government; relating to the management of affairs of state; as political theories; of or pertaining to exercise of rights and privileges or the influence by which individuals of a state seek to determine or control its public policy; having to do with organization or action of individuals, parties, or interests that seek to control appointment or action of those who manage affairs of a state. State ex rel. Maley v. Civic Action Committee, 238 Iowa 851, 28 N.W.2d 467, 470.

POLITICAL ARITHMETIC. An expression sometimes used to signify the art of making calculations on matters relating to a nation; the revenues, the value of land and effects; the produce of lands and manufactures; the population, and the general statistics of a country. Wharton.

POLITICAL COMMITTEE. Exists whenever three or more persons co-operate to bring about election or defeat of candidate or proposition at election. Empire City Job Print v. Harbord, 148 Misc. 331, 265 N.Y.S. 450.

POLITICAL CORPORATION. A public or municipal corporation; one created for political purposes, and having for its object the administration of governmental powers of a subordinate or local nature. Auryansen v. Hackensack Imp. Com'n, 45 N.J.L. 115; Curry v. District Tp., 62 Iowa 102, 17 N.W. 191.

POLITICAL ECONOMY. The science which describes the methods and laws of the production, distribution, and consumption of wealth, and treats of economic and industrial conditions and laws, and the rules and principles of rent, wages, capital, labor, exchanges, money, population, etc. The science which determines what laws men ought to adopt in order that they may, with the least possible exertion, procure the greatest abundance of things useful for the satisfaction of their wants, may distribute them justly, and consume them rationally. De Laveleye, Pol. Econ. The science which treats of the administration of the revenues of a nation, or the management and regulation of its resources, and productive property and labor. Wharton.

POLITICAL LAW. That branch of jurisprudence which treats of the science of politics, or the organization and administration of government.

POLITICAL LIBERTY. See Liberty.

POLITICAL OFFENSES. As a designation of a class of crimes usually excepted from extradition treaties, this term denotes crimes which are incidental to and form a part of political disturbances; but it might also be understood to include offenses consisting in an attack upon the political order of things established in the country where committed, and even to include offenses committed to obtain any political object. 2 Steph. Crim. Law, 70.

POLITICAL OFFICE. See Office.

POLITICAL PARTY. A number of persons united in opinion and organized in the manner usual to the then existing political parties. Swindall v. State Election Board, 168 Okl. 97, 32 P.2d 691, 695. An unincorporated, voluntary association of persons sponsoring certain ideas of government or maintaining certain political principles or beliefs in public policies of government, not a governmental agency or instrumentality. Robinson v. Holman, 181 Ark. 428, 26 S.W.2d 66, 68, 70 A.L.R. 1480.

POLITICAL QUESTIONS. Questions of which the courts of justice will refuse to take cognizance, or to decide, on account of their purely political character, or because their determination would involve an encroachment upon the executive or legislative powers; *e. g.*, what sort of government exists in a state, whether peace or war exists, whether a foreign country has become an independent state, etc. Kenneth v. Chambers, 14 How. 38, 14 L.Ed. 316.

POLITICAL RIGHTS. Those which may be exercised in the formation or administration of the government. People v. Morgan, 90 Ill. 563. Rights of citizens established or recognized by constitutions which give them the power to participate directly or indirectly in the establishment or administration of government. People v. Barrett, 203 Ill. 99, 67 N.E. 742, 96 Am.St.Rep. 296; Winnett v. Adams, 71 Neb. 817, 99 N.W. 684.

POLITICS. The science of government; the art or practice of administering public affairs.

POLITY. The form of government; civil constitution.

POLL, *v.* In practice. To single out, one by one, of a number of persons. To examine each juror separately, after a verdict has been given, as to his concurrence in the verdict. 1 Burrill, Pr. 238; State v. Boger, 202 N.C. 702, 163 S.E. 877, 878.

POLL, *n.* A head; an individual person; a register of persons. In the law of elections, a list or register of heads or individuals who may vote in an election; the aggregate of those who actually cast their votes at the election, excluding those who stay away. De Soto Parish v. Williams, 49 La.Ann. 422, 21 So. 647, 37 L.R.A. 761. See, also, Polls.

POLL, *adj.* Cut or shaved smooth or even; cut in a straight line without indentation. A term anciently applied to a deed, and still used, though with little of its former significance. 2 Bl.Comm. 296.

POLL–MONEY. A tax ordained by act of parliament (18 Car. II. c. 1), by which every subject in the kingdom was assessed by the head or poll, according to his degree. Cowell. A similar personal tribute was more anciently termed "poll-silver."

POLL-TAX. A capitation tax; a tax of a specific sum levied upon each person within the jurisdiction of the taxing power and within a certain class (as, all males of a certain age, etc.) without reference to his property or lack of it. Southern Ry. Co. v. St. Clair County, 124 Ala. 491, 27 So. 23; Short v. State, 80 Md. 392, 31 A. 322, 29 L.R.A. 404; Marion Foundry Co. v. Landes, 112 Ohio St. 166, 147 N.E. 302, 304. Breedlove v. Suttles, Ga., 58 S.Ct. 205, 207, 302 U.S. 277, 82 L.Ed. 252.

POLLARDS. A foreign coin of base metal, prohibited by St. 27 Edw. I. c. 3, from being brought into the realm, on pain of forfeiture of life and goods. 4 Bl.Comm. 98. It was computed at two pollards for a sterling or penny. Dyer, 82*b*.

POLLENGERS. Trees which have been lopped; distinguished from timber-trees. Plowd. 649.

POLLICITATION. In the civil law. An offer not yet accepted by the person to whom it is made. Langd. Cont. § 1. See McCulloch v. Eagle Ins. Co., 1 Pick. (Mass.) 283.

POLLIGAR, POLYGAR. In Hindu law. The head of a village or district; also a military chieftain in the peninsula, answering to a hill *zemindar* in the northern *circars*. Wharton.

POLLING THE JURY. A practice whereby the jurors are asked individually whether they assented, and still assent, to the verdict. To poll a jury is to call the names of the persons who compose a jury and require each juror to declare what his verdict is before it is recorded. Silak v. Hudson & M. R. Co., 114 N.J.L. 428, 176 A. 674, 675.

POLLS. The place where electors cast in their votes. Adams v. Corwin, 118 Misc. 701, 195 N.Y.S. 41, 42.

Heads; individuals; persons singly considered. A challenge to the *polls* (*in capita*) is a challenge to the individual jurors composing the panel, or an exception to one or more particular jurors. 3 Bl.Comm. 358, 361.

POLLUTE. To corrupt or defile. Young v. State, 194 Ind. 221, 141 N.E. 309, 311.

POMACE WINE. Any product made by the addition of water and sugar to the pomace of grapes from which the juice has been partially expressed, and by fermenting the mixture until a fermented beverage is produced. United States v. Sixty Barrels of Wine, D.C.Mo., 225 F. 846, 848.

POLYANDRY. The civil condition of having more husbands than one to the same woman; a social order permitting plurality of husbands.

POLYGAMIA EST PLURIUM SIMUL VIRORUM UXORUMVE CONNUBIUM. 3 Inst. 88. Polygamy is the marriage with many husbands or wives at one time.

POLYGAMY. In criminal law. The offense of having several wives or husbands at the same time, or more than one wife or husband at the same time. 3 Inst. 88. And see Reynolds v. U. S., 98 U.S. 145, 25 L.Ed. 244; McBride v. Graeber, 16 Ga.App. 240, 85 S.E. 86, 89.

The offense committed by a layman in marrying while any previous wife is living and undivorced; as distinguished from bigamy in the sense of a breach of ecclesiastical law involved in any second marriage by a clerk.

Polygamy, or bigamy, shall consist in knowingly having a plurality of husbands or wives at the same time. Code Ga.1882, § 4530 (Pen.Code 1910, § 367).

A bigamist or polygamist is a man who, having contracted a bigamous or polygamous marriage, and become the husband at one time, of two or more wives, maintains that relation and *status* at the time when he offers to be registered as a voter (8 U.S.C.A. § 136); and this without reference to the question whether he was at any time guilty of the offense of bigamy or polygamy, or whether any prosecution for such offense was barred by the lapse of time; neither is it necessary that he should be guilty of polygamy under the first section of the act of March 22, 1882. Murphy v. Ramsey, 5 S.Ct. 747, 114 U.S. 16, 29 L.Ed. 47; Cannon v. U. S., 6 S.Ct. 278, 116 U.S. 55, 29 L.Ed. 561.

Bigamy literally means a second marriage distinguished from a third or other; while polygamy means many marriages,—implies more than two.

POLYGARCHY. A term sometimes used to denote a government of many or several; a government where the sovereignty is shared by several persons; a collegiate or divided executive.

POMARIUM. In old pleading. An apple tree; an orchard.

POND. A body of stagnant water without an outlet, larger than a puddle and smaller than a lake; or a like body of water with a small outlet. Webster. Rockland Water Co. v. Camden & R. Water Co., 80 Me. 544, 15 A. 785, 1 L.R.A. 388; Concord Mfg. Co. v. Robertson, 66 N.H. 1, 25 A. 718, 18 L.R.A. 679; Munn v. Board of Sup'rs of Greene County, 161 Iowa 26, 141 N.W. 711, 714; Humphreys-Mexia Co. v. Arseneaux, 116 Tex. 603, 297 S.W. 225, 229, 53 A.L.R. 1147.

A standing ditch cast by labor of man's hand, in his private grounds, for his private use, to serve his house and household with necessary waters; but a *pool* is a low plat of ground by nature, and is not cast by man's hand. Call.Sew. 103.

Great ponds. In Maine and Massachusetts, natural ponds having a superficial area of more than ten acres, and not appropriated by the proprietors to their private use prior to a certain date. Barrows v. McDermott, 73 Me. 441; West Roxbury v. Stoddard, 7 Allen (Mass.) 158.

Public pond. In New England, a great pond; a pond covering a superficial area of more than ten acres. Brastow v. Rockport Ice Co., 77 Me. 100; West Roxbury v. Stoddard, 7 Allen (Mass.) 170.

Private pond. A body of water wholly on the lands of a single owner, or of a single group of joint owners or tenants in common, which did not have any such connection with any public waters that fish could pass from one to the other. If pond was so connected with public waters that at time of high water, fish could go in and out, it was not "private pond" from which defendants could seine fish whether fish might go out same day or next season. State v. Lowder, 198 Ind. 234, 153 N.E. 399, 400.

PONDERANTUR TESTES, NON NUMERANTUR. Witnesses are weighed, not counted. 1 Starkie, Ev. 554; Best, Ev. p. 426, § 389; Bakeman v. Rose, 14 Wend. (N.Y.) 105, 109.

PONDUS. In old English law. Poundage; *i. e.*, a duty paid to the crown according to the weight of merchandise.

PONDUS REGIS. The king's weight; the standard weight appointed by the king. Cowell.

PONE. In English practice. An original writ formerly used for the purpose of removing suits from the court-baron or county court into the superior courts of common law. It was also the proper writ to remove all suits which were before the sheriff by writ of justices. But this writ is now in disuse, the writ of *certiorari* being the ordinary process by which at the present day a cause is removed from a county court into any superior court. Brown.

PONE PER VADIUM. In English practice. An obsolete writ to the sheriff to summon the defendant to appear and answer the plaintiff's suit, on his putting in sureties to prosecute. It was so called from the words of the writ, "*pone per vadium et salvos plegios,*" "put by gage and safe pledges, A. B., the defendant."

PONENDIS IN ASSISIS. An old writ directing a sheriff to impanel a jury for an assize or real action.

PONENDUM IN BALLIUM. A writ commanding that a prisoner be bailed in cases bailable. Reg. Orig. 133.

PONENDUM SIGILLUM AD EXCEPTIONEM. A writ by which justices were required to put their seals to exceptions exhibited by a defendant against a plaintiff's evidence, verdict, or other proceedings, before them, according to the statute Westm. 2, (13 Edw. I. St. 1, c. 31).

PONERE. Lat. To put, place, lay, or set. Often used in the Latin terms and phrases of the old law.

PONIT SE SUPER PATRIAM. Lat. He puts himself upon the country. The defendant's plea of not guilty in a criminal action is recorded, in English practice, in these words, or in the abbreviated form "*po. se.*"

PONTAGE. In old English law. Duty paid for the reparation of bridges; also a due to the lord of the fee for persons or merchandises that pass over rivers, bridges, etc. Cowell.

PONTIBUS REPARANDIS. An old writ directed to the sheriff, commanding him to charge one or more to repair a bridge.

POOL. A combination of persons or corporations engaged in the same business, or for the purpose of engaging in a particular business or commercial or speculative venture, where all contribute to a common fund, or place their holdings of a given stock or other security in the hands and control of a managing member or committee, with the object of eliminating competition as between the several members of the pool, or of establishing a monopoly or controlling prices or rates by the weight and power of their combined capital, or of raising or depressing prices on the stock market, or simply with a view to the successful conduct of an enterprise too great for the capital of any member individually, and on an agreement for the division of profits or losses among the members, either equally or pro rata. Also, a similar combination not embracing the idea of a pooled or contributed capital, but simply the elimination of destructive competition between the members by an agreement to share or divide the profits of a given business or venture, as, for example, a contract between two or more competing railroads to abstain from "rate wars" and (usually) to maintain fixed rates, and to divide their earnings from the transportation of freight in fixed proportions. Green v. Higham, 161 Mo. 333, 61 S.W. 798; Mollyneaux v. Wittenberg, 39 Neb. 547, 58 N.W. 205; Kilbourn v. Thompson, 103 U.S. 195, 26 L.Ed. 377; American Biscuit Co. v. Klotz, C.C.La., 44 F. 725; U. S. v. Trans-Missouri Freight Ass'n, 7 C.C.A. 15, 58 F. 65, 24 L.R.A. 73; Georgia Fruit Exchange v. Turnipseed, 9 Ala. App. 123, 62 So. 542, 546.

In various methods of gambling, a "pool" is a sum of money made up of the stakes contributed by various persons, the whole of which is then wagered as a stake on the event of a race, game, or other contest, and the winnings (if any) are divided among the contributors to the pool pro rata. Or it is a sum similarly made up by the contributions of several persons, each of whom then makes his guess or prediction as to the event of a future contest or hazard, the successful better taking the entire pool. Ex parte Powell, 43 Tex.Cr.R. 391, 66 S.W. 298; Com. v. Ferry, 146 Mass. 203, 15 N.E. 484; Lacey v. Palmer, 93 Va. 159, 24 S.E. 930, 31 L.R.A. 822, 57 Am.St.Rep. 795; People v. McCue, 87 App.Div. 72, 83 N.Y.S. 1088; Commonwealth v. Sullivan, 218 Mass. 281, 105 N.E. 895, Ann.Cas.1916B, 98.

A body of standing water, without a current or issue, accumulated in a natural basin or depression in the earth, and not artificially formed. Stephens v. State, 81 Tex.Cr.R. 177, 194 S.W. 400, 401. See Pond.

POOLING CONTRACTS. Agreements between competing railways for a division of the traffic, or for a *pro rata* distribution of their earnings united into a "pool" or common fund. 15 Fed. 667, note. See Pool.

POOLROOM. A room in which pools on races are sold. In another sense, a room where the game of pool is played. Town of Eros v. Powell, 137 La. 342, 68 So. 632, 634.

POOR. As used in law, this term denotes those who are so destitute of property or of the means of support, either from their own labor or the care of relatives, as to be a public charge, that is, dependent either on the charity of the general public or on maintenance at the expense of the public. The term is synonymous with "indigent persons" and "paupers." State v. Osawkee Tp., 14 Kan. 421, 19 Am.Rep. 99; In re Hoffen's Estate, 70 Wis. 522, 36 N.W. 407; Polk County v. Owen, 187 Iowa 220, 174 N.W. 99, 107.

POOR DEBTOR'S OATH. An oath allowed, in some jurisdictions, to a person who is arrested for debt. On swearing that he has not property enough to pay the debt, he is set at liberty.

POOR LAW. That part of the law which relates to the public or compulsory relief of paupers.

POOR RATE. In English law. A tax levied by parochial authorities for the relief of the poor.

POOR-LAW BOARD. The English official body appointed under St. 10 & 11 Vict. c. 109, passed in 1847, to take the place of the poor-law commissioners, under whose control the general management of the poor, and the funds for their relief throughout the country, had been for some years previously administered. The poor-law board is now superseded by the local government board, which was established in 1871 by St. 34 & 35 Vict. c. 70. 3 Steph.Comm. 49.

POOR-LAW GUARDIANS. See Guardians of the Poor.

POP SHOTS. The explosion of light charges of dynamite to break up large fragments of rock. Brede v. Minnesota Crushed Stone Co., 146 Minn. 406, 178 N.W. 820, 821.

POPE. The bishop of Rome, and supreme head of the Roman Catholic Church. 4 Steph.Comm. (7th Ed.) 168–185.

POPE NICHOLAS' TAXATION. The first fruits (*primitiæ* or *annates*) were the first year's profits of all the spiritual preferments in the kingdom according to a rate made by Walter, bishop of Norwich, in the time of Pope Innocent II., and afterwards advanced in value in the time of Pope Nicholas IV. This last valuation was begun A. D. 1288, and finished 1292, and is still preserved in the exchequer. The taxes were regulated by it till the survey made in the twenty-sixth year of Henry VIII. 2 Steph.Comm. 567.

POPERY. The religion of the Roman Catholic Church, comprehending doctrines and practices.

POPULACE, or POPULACY. The vulgar; the multitude.

POPULAR ACTION. An action for a statutory penalty or forfeiture, given to any such person or persons as will sue for it; an action given to the *people* in general. 3 Bl.Comm. 161.

POPULAR SENSE. In reference to the construction of a statute, this term means that sense which people conversant with the subject-matter with which the statute is dealing would attribute to it. 1 Exch.Div. 248; Westerlund v. Black Bear Mining Co., C.C.A.Colo., 203 F. 599, 605.

POPULISCITUM. Lat. In Roman law. A law enacted by the people; a law passed by an assembly of the Roman people, in the *comitia centuriata*, on the motion of a senator; differing from a *plebiscitum*, in that the latter was always proposed by one of the tribunes.

POPULUS. Lat. In Roman law. The people; the whole body of Roman citizens, including as well the patricians as the plebeians.

PORCION. In Spanish law. A part or portion; a lot or parcel; an allotment of land. Downing v. Diaz, 80 Tex. 436, 16 S.W. 49.

PORNOGRAPHIC. That which is of or pertaining to obscene literature; obscene; licentious. People on Complaint of Savery v. Gotham Book Mart, 158 Misc. 240, 285 N.Y.S. 563, 567.

PORRECTING. Producing for examination or taxation, as porrecting a bill of costs, by a proctor.

PORT. A place for the lading and unlading of the cargoes of vessels, and the collection of duties or customs upon imports and exports. A place, either on the seacoast or on a river, where ships stop for the purpose of loading and unloading, from whence they depart, and where they finish their voyages. Devato v. Barrels of Plumbago, D.C.N.Y., 20 F. 515; Petrel Guano Co. v. Jarnette, C.C.N.C., 45 F. 675.

While Rev.St. §§ 4178, 4334 (46 U.S.C.A. §§ 47, 287), declare that the word "port" may mean the place where a vessel is built, or where one or more of the owners reside, a "port," in ordinary significance, is a place where ships are accustomed to load and unload goods, or to take on and let off passengers, and where persons and merchandise are allowed to pass into and out of the realm, and implies that it is something more than a roadstead; therefore a place on the high seas, fixed by latitude and longitude, where vessels were to be met and provisioned and coaled, is not a port. Hamburg-American Steam Packet Co. v. United States, C.C.A.N.Y., 250 F. 747, 759.

French Maritime Law

Burden, (of a vessel;) size and capacity.

General

Foreign port. One exclusively within the jurisdiction of a foreign nation, hence one without the United States. Bigley v. New York & P. R. S. S. Co., D.C.N.Y., 105 F. 74. But the term is also applied to a port in any state other than the state where the vessel belongs or her owner resides. The Canada, D.C.Or., 7 F. 124; The Lulu, 10 Wall. 200, 19 L.Ed. 906; Negus v. Simpson, 99 Mass. 393.

Home port. The port at which a vessel is registered or enrolled or where the owner resides.

Port charges, dues, or tolls. Pecuniary exactions upon vessels availing themselves of the commercial conveniences and privileges of a port. Wilkins v. Trafikaktiebolaget Grangesbert Okelosund, C.C.A., 10 F.2d 129, 131; The Vigo, D.C. N.Y., 257 F. 586, 587; Dampskibs Aktieselskabet Jeanette Skinner v. Munson S. S. Line, C.C.A. N.Y., 20 F.2d 345, 347; Christianssand Shipping Co. v. Marshall, D.C.Pa., 22 F.2d 192, 194.

Port-greve. The chief magistrate of a sea-port town is sometimes so called.

Port of delivery. In maritime law. The port which is to be the terminus of any particular voyage, and where the vessel is to unlade or deliver her cargo, as distinguished from any port at which she may touch, during the voyage, for other purposes. The Two Catharines, 24 Fed. Cas. 429.

Port of departure. As used in the United States statutes requiring a ship to procure a bill of health from the consular officer at the place of departure, is not the last port at which the ship stops while bound for the United States, but the port from which she cleared. The Dago, 10 C.C.A. 224, 61 F. 986.

Port of destination. In maritime law and marine insurance, the term includes both ports which constitute the termini of the voyage, the home port and the foreign port to which the vessel is consigned as well as any usual stopping places for the receipt or discharge of cargo. Gookin v. New England Mut. Marine Ins. Co., 12 Gray, Mass., 501, 74 Am.Dec. 609.

Port of discharge, in a policy of marine insurance, means the place where the substantial part of the cargo is discharged, although there is an intent to complete the discharge at another basin. Bramhall v. Sun Mut. Ins. Co., 104 Mass. 510, 6 Am.Rep. 261.

Port of entry. One of the ports designated by law, at which a custom-house or revenue office is established for the execution of the laws imposing duties on vessels and importations of goods. Cross v. Harrison, 16 How. 164, 14 L.Ed. 889.

Port-reeve, or port-warden. An officer maintained in some ports to oversee the administration of the local regulations; a sort of harbor-master.

Port-risk. In marine insurance. A risk upon a vessel while lying in port, and before she has taken her departure upon another voyage. Nelson v. Sun Mut. Ins. Co., 71 N.Y. 459.

Port toll. The toll paid for bringing goods into a port.

PORTATICA. In English law. The generic name for port duties charged to ships. Harg.Law Tract, 64.

PORTEOUS. In old Scotch practice. A roll or catalogue containing the names of indicted persons, delivered by the justice-clerk to the coroner, to be attached and arrested by him. Otherwise called the "Porteous Roll." Bell.

PORTER. In old English law, this title was given to an officer of the courts who carried a rod or staff before the justices.

A person who keeps a gate or door; as the door-keeper of the houses of parliament.

One who carries or conveys parcels, luggage, etc., particularly from one place to another in the same town.

PORTERAGE. A kind of duty formerly paid at the English custom-house to those who attended the water-side, and belonged to the package-office; but it is now abolished. Also the charge made for sending parcels.

PORTIO LEGITIMA. Lat. In the civil law. The birthright portion; that portion of an inheritance to which a given heir is entitled, and of which he cannot be deprived by the will of the decedent, without special cause, by virtue merely of his relationship to the testator.

PORTION. The share falling to a child from a parent's estate or the estate of any one bearing a similar relation. Lewis's Appeal, 108 Pa. 136; In re Miller's Will, 2 Lea, Tenn., 57; Stubbs v. Abel, 114 Or. 610, 233 P. 852, 857. An allotted part; a share, a parcel; a division in a distribution; a share of an estate or the like, received by gift or inheritance. Lecompte v. Davis' Ex'r, 285 Ky. 433, 148 S.W.2d 292, 295.

Portion is especially applied to payments made to younger children out of the funds comprised in their parents' marriage settlement, and in pursuance of the trusts thereof. Mozley & Whiteley.

PORTION DISPONIBLE. Fr. In French law. That part of a man's estate which he may bequeath to other persons than his natural heirs. A parent leaving one legitimate child may dispose of one-half only of his property; one leaving two, one-third only; and one leaving three or more, one-fourth only; and it matters not whether the disposition is *inter vivos* or by will.

PORTIONER.

Old English law. A minister who serves a benefice, together with others; so called because he has only a portion of the tithes or profits of the living; also an allowance which a vicar commonly has out of a rectory or impropriation. Cowell.

Scotch law. The proprietor of a small feu or portion of land. Bell.

PORTIONIBUS. Is properly employed to mean a portion of the tithes of one parish claimed by the rector of another parish. 4 Cl. & F. 1.

PORTIONIST. One who receives a portion; the allottee of a portion. One of two or more incumbents of the same ecclesiastical benefice.

PORTMEN. The burgesses of Ipswich and of the Cinque Ports were so called.

PORTMOTE. In old English law. A court held in ports or haven towns, and sometimes in inland towns also. Cowell; Blount.

PORTORIA. In the civil law. Duties paid in ports on merchandise. Taxes levied in old times at city gates. Tolls for passing over bridges.

PORTSALE. In old English law. An auction; a public sale of goods to the highest bidder; also a sale of fish as soon as it is brought into the haven. Cowell.

PORTSOKA, or PORTSOKEN. The suburbs of a city, or any place within its jurisdiction. Somner; Cowell.

PORTUS EST LOCUS IN QUO EXPORTANTUR ET IMPORTANTUR MERCES. 2 Inst. 148. A port is a place where goods are exported or imported.

POSITIVE. Laid down, enacted, or prescribed. Express or affirmative. Direct, absolute, explicit.

As to positive "Condition," "Fraud," "Proof," and "Servitude," see those titles.

POSITIVE EVIDENCE. Direct proof of the fact or point in issue; evidence which, if believed, establishes the truth or falsehood of a fact in issue, and does not arise from any presumption. It is distinguished from circumstantial evidence. 3 Bouv. Inst. no. 3057; Cooper v. Holmes, 71 Md. 20, 17 A. 711; Com. v. Webster, 5 Cush., Mass., 310, 52 Am.Dec. 711.

POSITIVE LAW. Law actually and specifically enacted or adopted by proper authority for the government of an organized jural society.

"A 'law,' in the sense in which that term is employed in jurisprudence, is enforced by a sovereign political authority. It is thus distinguished not only from all rules which, like the principles of morality and the so-called laws of honor and of fashion, are enforced by an indeterminate authority, but also from all rules enforced by a determinate authority which is either, on the one hand, superhuman, or, on the other hand, politically subordinate. In order to emphasize the fact that 'laws,' in the strict sense of the term, are thus authoritatively imposed, they are described as *positive* laws." Holl.Jur. 37.

POSITIVE WRONG. A wrongful act, wilfully committed. Padgett v. Missouri Motor Distributing Corporation, Mo., 177 S.W.2d 490, 492.

POSITIVI JURIS. Lat. Of positive law. "That was a rule *positivi juris*; I do not mean to say an unjust one." Lord Ellenborough, 12 East, 639.

POSITO UNO OPPOSITORUM, NEGATUR ALTERUM. One of two opposite positions being affirmed, the other is denied. 3 Rolle, 422.

POSSE. Lat. A possibility. A thing is said to be *in posse* when it may possibly be; *in esse* when it actually is. Guidry v. Caire, 181 La. 895, 160 So. 622.

POSSE COMITATUS. Lat. The power or force of the county. The entire population of a county above the age of fifteen, which a sheriff may summon to his assistance in certain cases; as to aid him in keeping the peace, in pursuing and arresting felons, etc. 1 Bl.Comm. 343; Com. v. Martin, 7 Pa.Dist.R. 224.

POSSESS. To occupy in person; to have in one's actual and physical control; to have the exclusive detention and control of; to have and hold as property; to have a just right to; to be master of; to own or be entitled to. Fuller v. Fuller, 84 Me. 475, 24 A. 946; Bingham's Adm'r v. Commonwealth, 196 Ky. 318, 244 S.W. 781, 785; Davis v. State, 102 Tex.Cr.R. 546, 278 S.W. 848, 849; Ex parte Okahara, 191 Cal. 353, 216 P. 614, 617; Melvin v. Scowley, 213 Ala. 414, 104 So. 817, 820; Nevin v. Louisville Trust Co., 258 Ky. 187, 79 S.W. 2d 688, 689.

POSSESSED. This word is applied to the right and enjoyment of a termor, or a person having a term, who is said to be possessed, and not seised. Bac.Tr. 335; Poph. 76; Dyer, 369.

"Possessed" is a variable term in the law, and has different meanings as it is used in different circumstances. It sometimes implies a temporary interest in lands; as we say a man is possessed, in contradistinction to being seised. It sometimes implies the corporal having; as we say a man is seised and possessed. But it sometimes implies no more than that one has a property in a thing; that he has it as owner; that it is his. Thompson v. Moran, 44 Mich. 603, 7 N.W. 180; In re Dillingham's Estate, 196 Cal. 525, 238 P. 367, 369; O'Connor v. Halpin, 166 Iowa, 101, 147 N.W. 185, 186; United States Trust Co. v. Gulick, 179 N.Y.S. 769, 771, 107 Misc. 316; Thomson v. Fidelity Trust Co., 268 Pa. 203, 110 A. 770, 773.

POSSESSIO. Lat.

Civil Law

That condition of fact under which one can exercise his power over a corporeal thing at his pleasure, to the exclusion of all others. This condition of fact is called "detention," and it forms the substance of possession in all its varieties. Mackeld. Rom. Law, § 238.

"Possession," in the sense of "detention," is the actual exercise of such a power as the owner has a right to exercise. The term *"possessio"* occurs in the Roman jurists in various senses. There is *possessio* simply, and *possessio civilis,* and *possessio naturalis.* *Possessio* denoted, originally, bare detention. But this detention, under certain conditions, becomes a legal state, inasmuch as it leads to ownership, through *usucapio.* Accordingly, the word *"possessio,"* which required no qualification so long as there was no other notion attached to *possessio,* requires such qualification when detention becomes a legal state. This detention, then, when it has the conditions necessary to *usucapio,* is called *"possessio civilis;"* and all other *possessio* as opposed to *civilis* is *naturalis.* Sandars, Just.Inst. 274. Wharton.

Old English law. Possession; seisin. The detention of a corporeal thing by means of a physical act and mental intent, aided by some support of right. Bract. fol. 38*b*.

General

Pedis possessio. A foothold; an actual possession of real property, implying either actual occupancy or enclosure and use. Lawrence v. Fulton, 19 Cal. 690; Porter v. Kennedy, 1 McMul., S.C., 357.

Possessio bona fide. Possession in good faith. *Possessio mala fide,* possession in bad faith. A possessor *bona fide* is one who believes that no other person has a better right to the possession than himself. A possessor *mala fide* is one who knows that he is not entitled to the possession. Mackeld. Rom. Law, § 243.

Possessio bonorum. In the civil law. The possession of goods. More commonly termed *"bonorum possessio."* (*q. v.*).

Possessio civilis. In Roman law. A legal possession, *i. e.*, a possessing accompanied with the intention to be or to thereby become owner; and, as so understood, it was distinguished from *"possessio naturalis,"* otherwise called *"nuda detentio,"* which was a possessing without any such intention. *Possessio civilis* was the basis of *usucapio* or of *longi temporis possessio*, and was usually (but not necessarily) adverse possession. Brown.

Possessio fratris. The possession or seisin of a brother; that is, such possession of an estate by a brother as would entitle his sister of the whole blood to succeed him as heir, to the exclusion of a half-brother. Hence, derivatively, that doctrine of the older English law of descent which shut out the half-blood from the succession to estates; a doctrine which was abolished by the descent act, 3 & 4 Wm. IV. c. 106. 1 Steph.Comm. 385; Broom, Max. 532.

Possessio longi temporis. See Usucapio.

Possessio naturalis. See Possessio Civilis.

POSSESSIO EST QUASI PEDIS POSITIO. Possession is, as it were, the position of the foot. 3 Co. 42.

POSSESSIO FRATRIS DE FEODO SIMPLICI FACIT SORORUM ESSE HÆREDEM. The brother's possession of an estate in fee-simple makes the sister to be heir. 3 Coke, 41; Broom, Max. 532.

POSSESSIO PACIFICA PER ANNOS 60 FACIT JUS. Peaceable possession for sixty years gives a right. Jenk. Cent. 26.

POSSESSION. The detention and control, or the manual or ideal custody, of anything which may be the subject of property, for one's use and enjoyment, either as owner or as the proprietor of a qualified right in it, and either held personally or by another who exercises it in one's place and name. Act or state of possessing. That condition of facts under which one can exercise his power over a corporeal thing at his pleasure to the exclusion of all other persons. Starits v. Avery, 204 Iowa 401, 213 N.W. 769, 771; Schenk v. State, 106 Tex.Cr.R. 564, 293 S.W. 1101, 1102; State v. Compton, Mo.App., 297 S.W. 413, 414; Nevin v. Louisville Trust Co., 258 Ky. 187, 79 S.W.2d 688, 689.

In the older books, "possession" is sometimes used as the synonym of "seisin;" but, strictly speaking, they are entirely different terms. "The difference between possession and seisin is: Lessee for years is possessed, and yet the lessor is still seised; and therefore the terms of law are that of chattels a man is possessed, whereas in feoffments, gifts in tail, and leases for life he is described as 'seised.' " Noy.Max. 64.

"Possession" is used in some of the books in the sense of property. "A possession is an hereditament or chattel." Finch,Law, b. 2, c. 3.

Possession of liquor which is made unlawful is possession under some claim of right, control, or dominion, with knowledge of facts. Schwartz v. State, 192 Wis. 414, 212 N.W. 664, 665. Taking a drink of intoxicating liquor on invitation of owner thereof does not constitute criminal "possession." Colbaugh v. U. S., C.C.A.Okl., 15 F.2d 929, 931; State v. Williams, 117 Or. 238, 243 P. 563; Sizemore v. Commonwealth, 202 Ky. 273, 259 S.W. 337, 342; Brazeale v. State, 133 Miss. 171, 97 So. 525, 526; Harness v. State, 130 Miss. 673, 95 So. 64; State v. McAllister, 187 N.C. 400, 121 S.E. 739, 740; People v. Leslie, 239 Mich. 334, 214 N.W. 128.

Actual possession. Exists where the thing is in the immediate occupancy of the party. Simpson v. Blount, 14 N.C. 34; Field Furniture Co. v. Community Loan Co., 257 Ky. 825, 79 S.W.2d 211, 215.

Adverse possession. The actual, open, and notorious possession and enjoyment of real property, or of any estate lying in grant, continued for a certain length of time, held adversely and in denial and opposition to the title of another claimant, or under circumstances which indicate an assertion or color of right or title on the part of the person maintaining it, as against another person who is out of possession. Hall v. Lavat, 301 Mo. 675, 257 S.W. 108, 111; W. T. Carter & Bro. v. Richardson, Tex.Civ.App., 225 S.W. 816, 817; Baxter v. Girard Trust Co., 288 Pa. 256, 135 A. 620, 621, 49 A.L.R. 1011; Mendel v. Poland, 200 Mich. 571, 166 N.W. 910, 912.

Chose in possession. A thing (subject of personal property) in actual possession, as distinguished from a "chose in action," which is not presently in the owner's possession, but which he has a right to demand, receive, or recover by suit.

Civil possession. In modern civil law and in the law of Louisiana, that possession which exists when a person ceases to reside in a house or on the land which he occupied, or to detain the movable which he possessed, but without intending to abandon the possession. It is the detention of a thing by virtue of a just title and under the conviction of possessing as owner. Civ.Code La. art. 3429 et seq. A fiction resulting from the registry of the title of the original owner. Baldwin Lumber Co. v. Dalferes, 138 La. 507, 70 So. 493, 499; Maisonneuve v. Dalferes, 138 La. 527, 70 So. 500, 501.

Constructive possession. Possession not actual but assumed to exist, where one claims to hold by virtue of some title, without having the actual occupancy, as, where the owner of a tract of land, regularly laid out, is in possession of a part, he is constructively in possession of the whole. Fleming v. Maddox, 30 Iowa 241.

Corporeal possession. The continuing exercise of a claim to the exclusive use of a material thing. The elements of this possession are first, the mental attitude of the claimant, the intent to possess, to appropriate to oneself; and second, the effective realization of this attitude. All the authorities agree that an intent to exclude others must coexist with the external facts, and must be fulfilled in the external physical facts in order to constitute possession. State v. Wagoner, 123 Kan. 591, 256 P. 957, 958.

Derivative possession. The kind of possession of one who is in the lawful occupation or custody of the property, but not under a claim of title of his own, but under a right derived from another, as, for example, a tenant, bailee, licensee, etc.

Dispossession. The act of ousting or removing one from the possession of property previously held by him, which may be tortious and unlawful, as in the case of a forcible amotion, or in pursuance of law, as where a landlord "dispossesses" his tenant at the expiration of the term or for other cause by the aid of judicial process.

Estate in possession. An estate whereby a present interest passes to and resides in the tenant, not depending on any subsequent circumstance or contingency. 2 Bl.Comm. 163. An estate where the tenant is in actual pernancy, or receipt of the rents and other advantages arising therefrom. 2 Crabb, Real Prop. p. 958, § 2322. Eberts v. Fisher, 44 Mich. 551, 7 N.W. 211; Sage v. Wheeler, 3 App.Div. 38, 37 N.Y.S. 1107.

Exclusive possession. See Exclusive Possession.

Hostile possession. This term, as applied to an occupant of real estate holding adversely, is not construed as implying actual enmity or ill will, but merely means that he claims to hold the possession in the character of an owner, and therefore denies all validity to claims set up by any and all other persons. Ballard v. Hansen, 33 Neb. 861, 51 N.W. 295; Mittet v. Hansen, 178 Wash. 541, 35 P.2d 93, 95.

Naked possession. The actual occupation of real estate, but without any apparent or colorable right to hold and continue such possession; spoken of as the lowest and most imperfect degree of title. 2 Bl.Comm. 195; Birdwell v. Burleson, 31 Tex.Civ.App. 31, 72 S.W. 446.

Natural possession. That by which a man detains a thing corporeally, as, by occupying a house, cultivating ground, or retaining a movable in possession; natural possession is also defined to be the corporeal detention of a thing which we possess as belonging to us, without any title to that possession or with a title which is void. Civ. Code La. arts. 3428, 3430. Railroad Co. v. Le Rosen, 52 La.Ann. 192, 26 So. 854.

Open possession. Possession of real property is said to be "open" when held without concealment or attempt at secrecy, or without being covered up in the name of a third person, or otherwise attempted to be withdrawn from sight, but in such a manner that any person interested can ascertain who is actually in possession by proper observation and inquiry. See Bass v. Pease, 79 Ill.App. 318

Peaceable possession. See Peaceable.

Pedal possession. In establishing title by adverse possession this means actual possession; that is, living upon or actually occupying the land, or placing improvements directly upon it. Schaeffer v. Williams, Tex., 208 S.W. 220, 224.

Possession money. In English law. The man whom the sheriff puts in possession of goods taken under a writ of *fieri facias* is entitled, while he continues so in possession, to a certain sum of money *per diem*, which is thence termed "possession money." The amount is 3s. 6d. per day if he is boarded, or 5s. per day if he is not boarded. Brown.

Possession, writ of. Where the judgment in an action of ejectment is for the delivery of the land claimed, or its possession, this writ is used to put the plaintiff in possession. It is in the nature of execution.

Quasi possession. Is to a right what possession is to a thing, it is the exercise or enjoyment of the right, not necessarily the continuous exercise, but such an exercise as shows an intention to exercise it at any time when desired. Sweet.

Scrambling possession. By this term is meant a struggle for possession on the land itself, not such a contest as is waged in the courts, or possession gained by an act of trespass, such as building a fence. Lobdell v. Keene, 85 Minn. 90, 88 N.W. 426.

Unity of possession. Joint possession of two rights by several titles, as where a lessee of land acquires the title in fee-simple, which extinguishes the lease. The term also describes one of the essential properties of a joint estate, each of the tenants having the entire possession as well of every parcel as of the whole. 2 Bl.Comm. 182.

Vacant possession. An estate which has been abandoned, vacated, or forsaken by the tenant. The abandonment must be complete in order to make the possession vacant, and, therefore, if the tenant have goods on the premises it will not be so considered. 2 Chitty, Bail. 177; 2 Stra. 1064.

POSSESSION IS A GOOD TITLE WHERE NO BETTER TITLE APPEARS. 20 Vin.Abr. 278.

POSSESSION IS NINE-TENTHS OF THE LAW. This adage is not to be taken as true to the full extent, so as to mean that the person in possession can only be ousted by one whose title is nine times better than his, but it places in a strong light the legal truth that every claimant must succeed by the strength of his own title, and not by the weakness of his antagonist's. Wharton.

POSSESSION VAUT TITRE. Fr. In English law, as in most systems of jurisprudence, the fact of possession raises a *prima facie* title or a presumption of the right of property in the thing possessed. In other words, the possession is as good as the title (about.) Brown.

POSSESSOR. One who possesses; one who has possession.

POSSESSOR BONA FIDE. He is a *bona fide* possessor who possesses as owner by virtue of an act sufficient in terms to transfer property, the defects of which he was ignorant of. He ceases to be a *bona fide* possessor from the moment these defects are made known to him, or are declared to him by a suit instituted for the recovery of the thing by the owner. Civ.Code La. art. 503.

POSSESSOR MALA FIDE. The possessor in bad faith is he who possesses as master, but who assumes this quality, when he well knows that he has no title to the thing, or that his title is vicious and defective. Civ.Code La. art. 3452.

POSSESSORY. Relating to possession; founded on possession; contemplating or claiming possession.

Possessory action. See next title.

Possessory claim. The title of a pre-emptor of public lands who has filed his declaratory statement but has not paid for the land. Enoch v. Spokane Falls & N. Ry. Co., 6 Wash. 393, 33 P. 966.

Possessory judgment. In Scotch practice. A judgment which entitles a person who has uninterruptedly been in possession for seven years to continue his possession until the question of right be decided in due course of law. Bell.

Possessory lien. A lien is possessory where the creditor has the right to hold possession of the specific property until satisfaction of the debt.

One which attaches to such articles of another's as may be at the time in the possession of the lienor, as, for example, an attorney's lien on the papers and documents of the client in his possession. Wood Sewing Mach. Co. v. Boutelle, 56 Vt. 570, 48 Am.Rep. 821.

POSSESSORY ACTION. An action which has for its immediate object to obtain or recover the actual *possession* of the subject-matter; as distinguished from an action which merely seeks to vindicate the plaintiff's *title*, or which involves the bare right only; the latter being called a "petitory" action.

An action founded on possession. Trespass for injuries to personal property is called a "possessory" action, because it lies only for a plaintiff who, at the moment of the injury complained of, was in actual or constructive, immediate, and exclusive possession. 1 Chit.Pl. 168, 169.

Admiralty practice. One which is brought to recover the possession of a vessel, had under a claim of title. The Tilton, 5 Mason, 465, Fed.Cas. No.14,054; 1 Kent, Comm. 371.

Louisiana. An action by which one claims to be maintained in the possession of an immovable property, or of a right upon or growing out of it, when he has been disturbed, or to be reinstated to that possession, when he has been divested or evicted. Code Prac.La. art. 6.

Old English law. A real action which had for its object the regaining possession of the freehold, of which the demandant or his ancestors had been unjustly deprived by the present tenant or possessor thereof.

Scotch law. An action for the vindication and recovery of the possession of heritable or movable goods; *e. g.*, the action of molestation. Paters. Comp.

POSSIBILITAS. Lat. Possibility; a possibility. *Possibilitas post dissolutionem executionis nunquam reviviscatur*, a possibility will never be revived after the dissolution of its execution. 1 Rolle, 321. *Post executionem status, lex non patitur possibilitatem,* after the execution of an estate the law does not suffer a possibility. 3 Bulst. 108.

POSSIBILITY. An uncertain thing which may happen. A contingent interest in real or personal estate. Kinzie v. Winston, 14 Fed.Cas. 651; Bodenhamer v. Welch, 89 N.C. 78; Needles v. Needles, 7 Ohio St. 442, 70 Am.Dec. 85.

It is either *near,* (or *ordinary,*) as where an estate is limited to one after the death of another, or *remote,* (or *extraordinary,*) as where it is limited to a man, provided he marries a certain woman, and that she shall die and he shall marry another.

Bare possibility. The same as a "naked" possibility. See *infra.*

Naked possibility. A bare chance or expectation of acquiring a property or succeeding to an estate in the future, but without any present right in or to it which the law would recognize as an estate or interest. Rogers v. Felton, 98 Ky. 148, 32 S.W. 406.

Possibility coupled with an interest. An expectation recognized in law as an estate or interest, such as occurs in executory devises and shifting or springing uses: such a possibility may be sold or assigned.

Possibility of reverter. This term denotes no estate, but only a possibility to have the estate at a future time. Of such possibilities there are several kinds, of which two are usually denoted by the term under consideration, (1) the possibility that a common-law fee may return to the grantor by breach of a condition subject to which it was granted, (2) the possibility that a common-law fee other than a fee simple may revert to the grantor by the natural determination of the fee. Sorrels v. McNally, 89 Fla. 457, 105 So. 106, 109; Des Moines City Ry. Co. v. City of Des Moines, 183 Iowa, 1261, 159 N.W. 450, 452, L.R.A.1918D, 839; Trustees of Calvary Presbyterian Church of Buffalo v. Putnam, 221 App.Div. 502, 224 N.Y.S. 651, 654.

Possibility on a possibility. A remote possibility, as if a remainder be limited in particular to A.'s son John, or Edward, it is bad if he have no son of that name, for it is too remote a possibility that he should not only have a son, but a son of that particular name. 2 Coke, 51.

POSSIBLE. Capable of existing, happening, being, becoming or coming to pass; feasible, not contrary to nature of things; neither necessitated nor precluded; free to happen or not; contrasted with necessary and impossible. In another sense, the word denotes extreme improbability, without excluding the idea of feasibility. It is also sometimes equivalent to "practicable" or "reasonable," as in some cases where action is required to be taken "as soon as possible." Norris v. Elmdale Elevator Co., 216 Mich. 548, 185 N.W. 696, 698; Miller v. Southern Express Co., 99 S.C. 333, 83 S. E. 449, 451; National Enameling & Stamping Co. v. Zirkovics, C.C.A.Mo., 251 F. 184, 189. Guidry v. Caire, 181 La. 895, 160 So. 622.

POST. Lat. After; occurring in a report or a text-book, is used to send the reader to a subsequent part of the book.

POST, *n.* A conveyance for letters or dispatches. The word is derived from "*positi,*" the horses carrying the letters or dispatches being kept or placed at fixed stations. The word is also applied to the person who conveys the letters to the houses where he takes up and lays down his charge, and to the stages or distances between house and house. Hence the phrases, post-boy, post-horse, post-house, etc. Wharton.

A military establishment where a body of troops is permanently fixed. Caldwell's Case, 19 Wall. 268, 22 L.Ed. 114; a military post is synonymous with military station. U. S. v. Phisterer, 94 U.S. 219, 24 L.Ed. 116; Hines v. Mikell, C.C.A.S.C., 259 F. 28, 31.

A landmark. Cornelious v. State, 22 Ala.App. 150, 113 So. 475, 476; U. S. v. Sherman, C.C.A.S.D., 288 F. 497, 501.

POST, *v.* To bring to the notice or attention of the public by affixing to a post or wall, or putting up in some public place; to placard. City of Pittsburgh v. Pittsburgh Rys. Co., 259 Pa. 558, 103 A. 372, 373; Stanford v. State, 99 Tex.Cr.R. 111, 268 S.W. 161, 162; Iowa-Missouri Grain Co. v. Powers, 198 Iowa, 208, 196 N.W. 979, 980, 33 A.L.R. 1268.

POST–ACT. An after-act; an act done afterwards.

POST CONQUESTUM. After the Conquest. Words inserted in the king's title by King Edward I., and constantly used in the time of Edward III. Tomlins.

POST–DATE. To date an instrument as of a time later than that at which it is really made.

POST–DATED CHECK. One delivered prior to its date, generally payable at sight or on presentation on or after day of its date. It differs from an ordinary check by carrying on its face implied notice that there is no money presently on deposit available to meet it, but with implied assurance that such funds will exist when check becomes due. Lovell v. Eaton, 99 Vt. 255, 133 A. 742, 743; State v. Langer, 46 N.D. 462, 177 N.W. 408, 419.

POST DIEM. After the day; as, a plea of payment *post diem,* after the day when the money became due. Com.Dig. "Pleader," 2.

Old Practice. The return of a writ after the day assigned. A fee paid in such case. Cowell.

POST DISSEISIN. In English law. The name of a writ, which lies for him who, having recovered lands and tenements by force of a novel disseisin, is again disseised by a former disseisor. Jacob.

POST ENTRY. When goods are weighed or measured, and the merchant has got an account thereof at the custom-house, and finds his entry already made too small, he must make a post or additional entry for the surplusage, in the same manner as the first was done. As a merchant is always in time, prior to the clearing of the vessel, to make his post, he should take care not to over-enter, to avoid as well the advance as the trouble of getting back the overplus. McCul.Dict.

POST EXCHANGE. A voluntary association of companies, detachments, or other army units at military posts, permitted by a special regulation of the War Department for the purpose of conducting for the benefit of the members of such units what is in effect a co-operative store and place of entertainment. Keane v. U. S., C.C.A.Va., 272 F. 577, 578.

POST EXECUTIONEM STATUS LEX NON PATITUR POSSIBILITATEM. 3 Bulst. 108. After the execution of the estate the law suffers not a possibility.

POST FACTO. After the fact. See Ex Post Facto.

POST–FACTUM, or POSTFACTUM. An after-act; an act done afterwards; a post-act.

POST–FINE. In old conveyancing. A fine or sum of money, (otherwise called the "king's silver") formerly due on granting the *licentia concordandi,* or leave to agree, in levying a fine of lands. It amounted to three-twentieths of the supposed annual value of the land, or ten shillings for every five marks of land. 2 Bl.Comm. 350.

POST HAC. Lat. After this; after this time; hereafter.

POST LITEM MOTAM. Lat. After suit moved or commenced. Depositions in relation to the subject of a suit, made after litigation has commenced, are sometimes so termed. 1 Starkie, Ev. 319.

POST–MARK. A stamp or mark put on letters received at the post-office for transmission through the mails.

POST–MORTEM. After death. A term generally applied to an autopsy or examination of a dead body, to ascertain the cause of death, or to the inquisition for that purpose by the coroner. Wehle v. United States Mut. Acc. Ass'n, 11 Misc. Rep. 36, 31 N.Y.Supp. 865; Stephens v. People, 4 Parker Cr. R., N.Y., 475.

POST NATUS. Born afterwards. A term applied by old writers to a second or younger son. It is used in private international law to designate a person who was born *after* some historic event, (such as the American Revolution or the act of union between England and Scotland,) and whose rights or *status* will be governed or affected by the question of his birth before or after such event.

POST-NOTES. A species of bank-notes payable at a distant period, and not on demand.

They are a species of obligation resorted to by banks when the exchanges of the country, and especially of the banks, have become embarrassed by excessive speculations. Much concern is then felt for the country, and through the newspapers it is urged that post-notes be issued by the banks "for aiding domestic and foreign exchanges," as a "mode of relief," or a "remedy for the distress," and "to take the place of the southern and foreign exchanges." And so presently this is done. Post-notes are therefore intended to enter into the circulation of the country as a part of its medium of exchanges; the smaller ones for ordinary business, and the larger ones for heavier operations. They are intended to supply the place of demand notes, which the banks cannot afford to issue or reissue, to relieve the necessities of commerce or of the banks, or to avoid a compulsory suspension. They are under seal, or without seal, and at long or short dates, at more or less interest, or without interest, as the necessities of the bank may require. Appeal of Hogg, 22 Pa. 488.

POST-NUPTIAL. After marriage. Thus, an agreement entered into by a father after the marriage of his daughter, by which he engages to make a provision for her, would be termed a "post-nuptial agreement." Brown.

POST-NUPTIAL SETTLEMENT. A settlement made after marriage upon a wife or children; otherwise called a "voluntary" settlement. 2 Kent, Comm. 173.

POST-OBIT. (Lat.) An agreement by which the obligor borrows a certain sum of money and promises to pay a larger sum, exceeding the lawful rate of interest, upon the death of a person from whom he has some expectation, if the obligor be then living. Boynton v. Hubbard, 7 Mass. 119; 6 Madd. 111; 5 Ves. 57; 19 Ves. 628.

POST OBIT BOND. A bond given by an expectant, to become due on the death of a person from whom he will have property. A bond or agreement given by a borrower of money, by which he undertakes to pay a larger sum, exceeding the legal rate of interest, on or *after the death* of a person from whom he has expectations, in case of surviving him. Crawford v. Russell, 62 Barb., N.Y., 92; Boynton v. Hubbard, 7 Mass. 119.

POST-OFFICE. A bureau or department of government, or under governmental superintendence, whose office is to receive, transmit, and deliver letters, papers, and other mail-matter sent by post. Also the office established by government in any city or town for the local operations of the postal system, for the receipt and distribution of mail from other places, the forwarding of mail there deposited, the sale of postage stamps, etc.

POST-OFFICE DEPARTMENT. The name of one of the departments of the executive branch of the government of the United States, which has charge of the transmission of the mails and the general postal business of the country.

POST-OFFICE ORDER. A letter of credit furnished by the government, at a small charge, to facilitate the transmission of money.

POST PROLEM SUSCITATAM. After issue born, (raised.) Co.Litt. 19*b*.

POST ROADS. The roads or highways, by land or sea, designated by law as the avenues over which the mails shall be transported. Railway Mail Service Cases, 13 Ct.Cl. 204. A "post route," on the other hand, is the appointed course or prescribed line of transportation of the mail. U. S. v. Kochersperger, 26 Fed.Cas. 803; Blackham v. Gresham, C.C.N.Y., 16 Fed. 611.

POST-TERMINAL SITTINGS. Sittings after term. See Sittings.

POST TERMINUM. After term, or post-term. The return of a writ not only after the day assigned for its return, but after the term also, for which a fee was due. Cowell.

POST, WRIT OF ENTRY IN. In English law. An abolished writ given by statute of Marlbridge, 52 Hen. III. c. 30, which provided that when the number of alienations or descents exceeded the usual degrees, a new writ should be allowed, without any mention of degrees at all.

POSTAGE. The fee charged by law for carrying letters, packets, and documents by the public mails.

POSTAGE STAMP. A ticket issued by government, to be attached to mail-matter, that represents the postage or fee paid for the transmission of such matter through the public mails.

POSTAL. Relating to the mails; pertaining to the post-office.

POSTAL CURRENCY. During a brief period following soon after the commencement of the civil war in the United States, when specie change was scarce, postage stamps were popularly used as a substitute; and the first issues of paper representatives of parts of a dollar, issued by authority of congress, were called "postal currency." This issue was soon merged in others of a more permanent character, for which the later and more appropriate name is "fractional currency." Abbott.

POSTAL SAVINGS DEPOSITORIES. The act of congress of June 25, 1910, c. 386, 36 Stat. 814 (39 U.S.C.A. § 751 et seq.), created a board of trustees (the postmaster general, the secretary of the treasury, and the attorney general) to establish such depositories. Deposits may be made by any person of ten years or over, in his or her name, or by a married woman in her own name and free from her husband's control. Deposits may be made of $1 or multiples thereof, and any person may purchase for 10 cents "postal savings stamps" and attach them to a card furnished for the purpose, and a card with ten stamps affixed will be accepted as a deposit of $1, or may be redeemed in cash. Interest at the rate of 2 per cent. a year is paid, but not on fractions of a dollar. No balance shall exceed $2,500.

Deposits may be withdrawn, in whole or in part, on demand. A depositor may surrender his deposit in sums of $20, $40, $60, $80, $100, and multiples of $100 and of $500, and receive United States bonds of corresponding denominations, bearing interest at 2½ per cent. per annum, payable half-yearly and redeemable at the pleasure of the United States after one year, and payable in gold at the end of twenty years.

By 39 U.S.C.A. § 766, "the faith of the United States is solemnly pledged to the payment of the deposits."

POSTAL UNION. A treaty made at Berne in October, 1874, for the regulation of rates of postage and other matters connected with the post-office between England and various other countries. See 38 & 39 Vict. c. 22; 1 Hall.Int.L. 286. Several international conferences have since been held on the subject: Paris, 1878; Lisbon, 1885; Vienna, 1891; Washington, 1897; Rome, 1906.

POSTEA. In the common-law practice, a formal statement, indorsed on the *nisi prius* record, which gives an account of the proceedings at the trial of the action. Smith, Act. 167.

POSTED WATERS. In Vermont. Waters flowing through or lying upon inclosed or cultivated lands, which are preserved for the exclusive use of the owner or occupant by his posting notices (according to the statute) prohibiting all persons from shooting, trapping, or fishing thereon, under a prescribed penalty. See State v. Theriault, 70 Vt. 617, 41 A. 1030, 43 L.R.A. 290, 67 Am.St.Rep. 695.

POSTERIORA DEROGANT PRIORIBUS. Posterior things derogate from things prior. 1 Bouv. Inst. n. 90.

POSTERIORES. Lat. This term was used by the Romans to denote the descendants in a direct line beyond the sixth degree.

POSTERIORITY. This is a word of comparison and relation in tenure, the correlative of which is the word "priority." Thus, a man who held lands or tenements of two lords was said to hold of his more ancient lord by priority, and of his less ancient lord by posteriority. Old Nat.Brev. 94. It has also a general application in law consistent with its etymological meaning, and, as so used, it is likewise opposed to priority. Brown.

POSTERITY. All the descendants of a person in a direct line to the remotest generation. Breckinridge v. Denny, 8 Bush (Ky.) 527.

POSTHUMOUS CHILD. One borne after the death of its father; or, when the Cæsarean operation is performed, after that of the mother.

Quasi-posthumous child. In civil law. One who, born during the life of his grandfather or other male ascendant, was not his heir at the time he made his testament, but who by the death of his father became his heir in his lifetime. Inst. 2, 13, 2; Dig. 28, 3, 13.

POSTHUMUS PRO NATO HABETUR. A posthumous child is considered as though born, [at the parent's death.] Hall v. Hancock, 15 Pick. (Mass.) 258, 26 Am.Dec. 598.

POSTHUMOUS WORK. Work on which original copyright has been taken out by someone to whom literary property passed before publication. Shapiro, Bernstein & Co. v. Bryan, C.C.A.N.Y., 123 F.2d 697, 699.

POSTLIMINIUM. Lat. In the civil law. A doctrine or fiction of the law by which the restoration of a person to any *status* or right formerly possessed by him was considered as relating back to the time of his original loss or deprivation; particularly in the case of one who, having been taken prisoner in war, and having escaped and returned to Rome, was regarded, by the aid of this fiction, as having never been abroad, and was thereby reinstated in all his rights. Inst. 1, 12, 5.

The term is also applied, in international law, to the recapture of property taken by an enemy, and its consequent restoration to its original owner.

POSTLIMINIUM FINGIT EUM QUI CAPTOS EST IN CIVITATE SEMPER FUISSE. Postliminy feigns that he who has been captured has never left the state. Inst. 1, 12, 5; Dig. 49, 51.

POSTLIMINY. See Postliminium.

POSTMAN. A senior barrister in the court of exchequer, who has precedence in motions, so called from the place where he sits. 2 Bl.Comm. 28. A letter-carrier.

POSTMASTER. An officer of the United States, appointed to take charge of a local post-office and transact the business of receiving and forwarding the mails at that point, and such other business as is committed to him under the postal laws.

POSTMASTER GENERAL. The head of the post-office department. He is one of the president's cabinet.

POSTNATI. Those born after. See Post Natus.

POSTPONE. To put off; defer; delay; continue: adjourn; as when a hearing is *postponed.* Also to place after; to set below something else; as when an earlier lien is for some reason *postponed* to a later lien.

The word "postpone" carries with it the idea of deferring the doing of something or the taking effect of something until a future or later time. Gartner v. Roth, Cal., 157 P.2d 361, 363.

The word "postponement," in speaking of legal proceedings, is nearly equivalent to "continuance;" except that the former word is generally preferred when describing an adjournment of the cause to another day during the term, and the latter when the case goes over to another term. State v. Underwood, 76 Mo. 639; State v. Nathaniel, 52 La.Ann. 558, 26 So. 1008.

POSTREMO-GENITURE. Borough-English (*q. v.*).

POSTULATIO. Lat. Old English ecclesiastical law. A species of petition for transfer of a bishop.

Roman law. A request or petition. This was the name of the first step in a criminal prosecution, corresponding somewhat to "swearing out a warrant" in modern criminal law. The accuser appeared before the prætor, and stated his desire to institute criminal proceedings against a designated person, and prayed the authority of the magistrate therefor.

POSTULATIO ACTIONIS. In Roman law. The demand of an action; the request made to the prætor by an *actor* or plaintiff for an action or formula of suit; corresponding with the application for a writ in old English practice. Or, as otherwise explained, the *actor's* asking of leave to institute his action, on appearance of the parties before the prætor. Hallifax, Civil Law, b. 3, c. 9, no. 12.

POTABLE. Suitable for drinking; drinkable. State v. Mairs, Mo.App., 272 S.W. 992, 995; Huddleston v. State, 103 Tex.Cr.R. 108, 280 S.W. 218.

POT-DE-VIN. In French law. A sum of money frequently paid, at the moment of entering into a contract, beyond the price agreed upon. It differs from *arrha,* in this: that it is no part of the price of the thing sold, and that the person who has received it cannot, by returning double the amount, or the other party by losing what he has paid, rescind the contract. 18 Toullier, no. 52.

POTENTATE. A person who possesses great power or sway; a prince, sovereign, or monarch.

By the naturalization law of the United States, an alien is required to renounce all allegiance to any foreign "prince, potentate, or sovereign whatever."

POTENTIA. Lat. Possibility; power.

POTENTIA PROPINQUA. Common possibility. See Possibility.

POTENTIA DEBET SEQUI JUSTITIAM, NON ANTECEDERE. 3 Bulst. 199. Power ought to follow justice, not go before it.

POTENTIA EST DUPLEX, REMOTA ET PROPINQUA; ET POTENTIA REMOTISSIMA ET VANA EST QUÆ NUNQUAM VENIT IN ACTUM. 11 Coke, 51. Possibility is of two kinds, remote and near; that which never comes into action is a power the most remote and vain.

POTENTIA INUTILIS FRUSTRA EST. Useless power is to no purpose. Branch, Princ.

POTENTIA NON EST NISI AD BONUM. Power is not conferred but for the public good.

POTENTIAL. Existing in possibility but not in act; naturally and probably expected to come into existence at some future time, though not now existing; for example, the future product of grain or trees already planted, or the successive future installments or payments on a contract or engagement already made. Things having a "potential existence" may be the subject of mortgage, assignment, or sale. Campbell v. Grant Co., 36 Tex. Civ.App. 641, 82 S.W. 796; Dickey v. Waldo, 97 Mich. 255, 56 N.W. 608, 23 L.R.A 449; Long v. Hines, 40 Kan. 220, 19 P. 796, 10 Am.St.Rep. 192; Carter v. Rector, 88 Okl. 12, 210 P. 1035, 1037.

POTEST QUIS RENUNCIARE PRO SE ET SUIS JURI QUOD PRO SE INTRODUCTUM EST. Bract. 20. One may relinquish for himself and his heirs a right which was introduced for his own benefit.

POTESTAS. Lat. In the civil law. Power; authority; domination; empire. *Imperium,* or the jurisdiction of magistrates. The power of the father over his children, *patria potestas.* The authority of masters over their slaves. Inst. 1, 9, 12; Dig. 2, 1, 13, 1; Dig. 14, 1; Dig. 14, 4, 1, 4.

POTESTAS STRICTE INTERPRETATUR. A power is strictly interpreted. Jenk.Cent. p. 17, case 29, in marg.

POTESTAS SUPREMA SEIPSUM DISSOLVERE POTEST, LIGARE NON POTEST. Supreme power can dissolve [unloose] but cannot bind itself. Branch, Princ.; Bacon.

POTIOR EST CONDITIO DEFENDENTIS. Better is the condition of the defendant, [than that of the plaintiff.] Broom, Max. 740; Cowp. 343; Williams v. Ingell, 21 Pick., Mass., 289; White v. Franklin Bank, 22 Pick., Mass., 186, 187; Cranson v. Goss, 107 Mass. 440, 9 Am.Rep. 45.

POTIOR EST CONDITIO POSSIDENTIS. Better is the condition of the possessor. Broom, Max. 215, n. 719; 6 Mass. 84; 21 Pick.,Mass., 140.

POTTS' FRACTURE. A fracture of the lower part of the fibula, accompanied with injury to the ankle joint, so that the foot is dislocated outward. Stockham v. Hall, 145 Kan. 291, 65 P.2d 348.

POTWALLOPER. A term formerly applied to voters in certain boroughs of England, where all who boil (*wallop*) a *pot* were entitled to vote. Webster.

POULTRY COUNTER. The name of a prison formerly existing in London. See Counter.

POUND. A place, inclosed by public authority, for the temporary detention of stray animals. Chenango County Humane Soc. v. Polmatier, 188 App.Div. 419, 177 N.Y.S. 101, 103.

A pound-*overt* is said to be one that is open overhead; a pound-*covert* is one that is close, or covered over, such as a stable or other building.

"There is no more ancient institution in the country than the Village *Pound.* It is far older than the King's Bench, and probably older than the kingdom." Maine, Early Hist. of Inst., p. 263.

A measure of weight. The pound avoirdupois contains 7,000 grains; the pound troy 5,760 grains.

In New York, the unit or standard of weight from which all other weights shall be derived and ascertained, is declared to be the *pound,* of such magnitude that the weight of a cubic foot of distilled water, at its maximum density, weighed in a vacuum with brass weights, shall be equal to sixty-two and a half such pounds. 1 Rev.St.N.Y. p. 617, § 8.

Name of a denomination of English money, containing twenty shillings. It was also used in the United States, in computing money, before the introduction of the federal coinage.

POUND BREACH. The act or offense of breaking a pound, for the purpose of taking out the cattle or goods impounded. 3 Bl.Comm. 12, 146; State v. Young, 18 N.H. 544.

POUND NET. A kind of fishing net also known as a "dutch" net and sometimes, formerly, as a "pod" net. N. Car. G. S. § 113–278; Hettrick v. Page, 82 N.C. 65; Rea v. Hampton, 7 S.E. 649, 101 N.C. 51, 9 Am.St.Rep. 21. It is a wall net with wings, and a leader, together with a pocket, bowl, pot, or pound, into which the fish are guided by the wings and the leader, which is an upright net extended in a straight line to the shore. The wings are in many cases a thousand yards in length. Cent. Dict.

POUND OF LAND. An uncertain quantity of land, said to be about fifty-two acres.

See Librata Terræ.

POUNDAGE. Old English law. A subsidy to the value of twelve pence in the *pound,* granted to the king, of all manner of merchandise of every merchant, as well denizen as alien, either exported or imported. Cowell.

Practice. An allowance to the sheriff of so much in the pound upon the amount levied under an execution. Bowe v. Campbell, 2 Civ.Proc.R., N.Y., 234. The money which an owner of animals impounded must pay to obtain their release.

POUNDKEEPER. An officer charged with the care of a pound, and of animals confined there.

POUR ACQUIT. Fr. In French law. The formula which a creditor prefixes to his signature when he gives a receipt.

POUR APPUYER. For the support of, or "in the support of." Collins v. Collins, 193 So. 702, 703, 194 La. 446.

POUR APPUYER NOUVELLE DEMANDE. In support of his new action. Collins v. Collins, 194 La. 446, 193 So. 702, 703.

POUR COMPTE DE QUI IL APPARTIENT. Fr. For account of whom it may concern.

POUR FAIRE PROCLAIMER. L. Fr. An ancient writ addressed to the mayor or bailiff of a city or town, requiring him to make proclamation concerning nuisances, etc. Fitzh.Nat.Brev. 176.

POUR SEISIR TERRES. L. Fr. An ancient writ whereby the crown seized the land which the wife of its deceased tenant, who held *in capite,* had for her dower, if she married without leave. It was grounded on the statute *De Prærogativa Regis,* 7 (17 Edw. II. St. 1, c. 4). It is abolished by 12 Car. II. c. 24.

POURPARLER. Fr. In French law. The preliminary negotiations or bargainings which lead to a contract between the parties. As in English law, these form no part of the contract when completed. The term is also used in this sense in international law and the practice of diplomacy.

POURPARTY. To make *pourparty* is to divide and sever the lands that fall to parceners, which, before partition, they held jointly and *pro indiviso.* Cowell.

POURPRESTURE. An inclosure. Anything done to the nuisance or hurt of the public demesnes, or the highways, etc., by inclosure or building, endeavoring to make that private which ought to be public. The difference between a *pourpresture* and a public nuisance is that *pourpresture* is an invasion of the *jus privatum* of the crown; but where the *jus publicum* is violated it is a nuisance. Skene makes three sorts of this offense: (1) Against the crown; (2) against the lord of the fee; (3) against a neighbor. 2 Inst. 38; 1 Reeve, Eng.Law, 156.

POURSUIVANT. The king's messenger; a royal or state messenger. In the heralds' college, a functionary of lower rank than a herald, but discharging similar duties, called also "poursuivant at arms."

POURVEYANCE. In old English law. The providing corn, fuel, victuals, and other necessaries for the king's house. Cowell.

POURVEYOR, or PURVEYOR. A buyer; one who provided for the royal household.

POUSTIE. In Scotch law. Power. See Liege Poustie. A word formed from the Latin *"potestas."*

POVERTY AFFIDAVIT. An affidavit, made and filed by one of the parties to a suit, that he is not able to furnish security for the final costs. The use of the term is confined to a few states. Cole v. Hoeburg, 36 Kan. 263, 13 P. 275.

POWER. The right, ability, or faculty of doing something. Clifford v. Helvering, C.C.A.8, 105 F. 2d 586, 591. Authority to do any act which the grantor might himself lawfully perform. In re Morrison's Estate, 173 Misc. 503, 18 N.Y.S.2d 235, 241.

In a restricted sense a "power" is a liberty or authority reserved by, or limited to, a person to dispose of real or personal property, for his own benefit, or benefit of others, or enabling one person to dispose of interest which is vested in another. In re Vanatta's Estate, 99 N.J.Eq. 339, 131 A. 515, 518; Hupp v. Union Coal & Coke Co., 284 Pa. 529, 131 A. 364, 365; Security Trust & Safe Deposit Co. v. Ward, 10 Del.Ch. 408, 93 A. 385, 388.

Real property law. An authority to do some act in relation to real property, or to the creation or revocation of an estate therein, or a charge thereon, which the owner granting or reserving such power might himself perform for any purpose. Civ.Code Dak. § 298 (Comp.Laws N.D.1913, § 5383; Rev.Code S.D.1919, § 390); How.St.Mich. § 5591 (Comp.Laws 1929, § 12996).

"Power" is sometimes used in the same sense as "right," as when we speak of the powers of user and disposition which the owner of property has over it, but, strictly speaking, a power is that which creates a special or exceptional right, or enables a person to do something which he could not otherwise do. Sweet.

Technically, an authority by which one person enables another to do some act for him. 2 Lil. Abr. 339.

An authority enabling a person to dispose, through the medium of the statute of uses, of an interest, vested either in himself or in another person. Sugd. Powers, 82. An authority expressly reserved to a grantor, or expressly given to another, to be exercised over lands, etc., granted or conveyed at the time of the creation of such power. Watk.Conv. 157. A proviso, in a conveyance under the statute of uses, giving to the grantor or grantee, or a stranger, authority to revoke or alter by a subsequent act the estate first granted. 1 Steph.Comm. 505; Burleigh v. Clough, 52 N.H. 267, 13 Am.Rep. 23; Griffith v. Maxfield, 66 Ark. 513, 51 S.W. 832, Bouton v. Doty, 69 Conn. 531, 37 A. 1064; Law Guarantee & Trust Co. v. Jones, 103 Tenn. 245, 58 S.W. 219.

There is a clear distinction between a power and a trust, since "powers" are never imperative, but leave the act to be done at the will of the donee of the power, while "trusts" are always imperative, and are obligatory on the conscience of the trustee. People v. Kaiser, 306 Ill. 313, 137 N.E. 826, 828; Hirschmann v. Gantt, 136 S.C. 1, 134 S.E. 230, 231.

General

Appendant or appurtenant powers. Those existing where the donee of the power has an estate in the land and the power is to take effect wholly or in part out of that estate, and the estate created by its exercise affects the estate and interest of the donee of the power. Baker v. Wilmert, 288 Ill. 434, 123 N.E. 627, 629; Taylor v. Phillips, 147 Ga. 761, 95 S.E. 289.

Collateral powers. Those in which the donee of the power has no interest or estate in the land which is the subject of the power. Also called "naked powers." 2 Washb.R.P. 305; Baker v. Wilmert, 288 Ill. 434, 123 N.E. 627, 629.

Executive power. See Executive Power.

Exclusive power. See Exclusive Power.

General and special powers. A power is general when it authorizes the alienation in fee, by means of a conveyance, will, or charge, of the lands embraced in the power to any alienee whatsoever. It is special (1) when the persons or class of persons to whom the disposition of the lands under the power is to be made are designated, or (2) when the power authorizes the alienation, by means of a conveyance, will, or charge, of a particular estate or interest less than a fee. Coster v. Lorillard, 14 Wend. (N.Y.) 324; Thompson v. Garwood, 3 Whart. (Pa.) 305, 31 Am.Dec. 502.

General and special powers in trust. A general power is in trust when any person or class of persons other than the grantee of such power is designated as entitled to the proceeds or any portion of the proceeds or other benefits to result from the alienation. A special power is in trust (1) when the disposition or charge which it authorizes is limited to be made to any person or class of persons other than the holder of the power, or (2) when any person or class of persons other than the holder is designated as entitled to any benefit from the disposition or charge authorized by the power. Cutting v. Cutting, 20 Hun (N.Y.) 360; Dana v. Murray, 122 N.Y. 612, 26 N.E. 23; 60 Okl. St.Ann. §§ 191, 192.

Inherent powers. Those which are enjoyed by the possessors of natural right, without having been received from another. Such are the powers of a people to establish a form of government, of a father to control his children. Some of these are regulated and restricted in their exercise by law, but are not technically considered in the law as powers.

Ministerial powers. A phrase used in English conveyancing to denote powers given for the good, not of the donee himself exclusively, or of the donee himself necessarily at all, but for the good of several persons, including or not including the donee also. They are so called because the donee of them is as a minister or servant in his exercise of them. Brown.

Naked power. One which is simply collateral and without interest in the donee, which arises when, to a mere stranger, authority is given of disposing of an interest, in which he had not before, nor has by the instrument creating the power, any estate whatsoever. Bergen v. Bennett, 1 Caines Cas. (N.Y.) 15, 2 Am.Dec. 281; Hunt v. Ennis, 12 Fed.Cas. 915; Atzinger v. Berger, 151 Ky. 800, 152 S.W. 971, 972, 50 L.R.A.,N.S., 622.

Power of revocation. A power which is to divest or abridge an existing estate. Distinguished from those of appointment; but the distinction is of doubtful exactness, as every new appointment must divest or revoke a former use. Sanders, Uses 154.

Power of visitation. A power vested by the founder in an appointed visitor, or the trustees or governors of an institution, to regulate its internal affairs and to appoint professors, elect scholarships, officers, and the like. In re Norton, 97 Misc.Rep. 289, 161 N.Y.S. 710, 717.

Powers in gross. Those which give a donee of the power, who has an estate in the land, authority to create such estates only as will not attach on the interest limited to him or take effect out of his interest, but will take effect after donee's estate has terminated. Baker v. Wilmert, 288 Ill. 434, 123 N.E. 627; Taylor v. Phillips, 147 Ga. 761, 95 S.E. 289, 290.

Constitutional Law

The right to take action in respect to a particular subject-matter or class of matters, involving more or less of discretion, granted by the constitutions to the several departments or branches of the government, or reserved to the people. Powers in this sense are generally classified as legislative, executive, and judicial. See those titles.

Implied powers are such as are necessary to make available and carry into effect those powers which are expressly granted or conferred, and which must therefore be presumed to have been within the intention of the constitutional or legislative grant. First M. E. Church v. Dixon, 178 Ill. 260, 52 N.E. 887; In re Board of Com'rs of Cook County, 146 Minn. 103, 177 N.W. 1013, 1014; Skelly Oil Co. v. Pruitt & McCrory, 94 Okl. 232, 221 P. 709, 710; Citizens' Electric Illuminating Co. v. Lackawanna & W. V. Power Co., 255 Pa. 176, 99 A. 465, 467.

Law of Corporations

The right or capacity to act or be acted upon in a particular manner or in respect to a particular subject; as, the power to have a corporate seal, to sue and be sued, to make by-laws, to carry on a particular business or construct a given work. See Freligh v. Saugerties, 70 Hun, 589, 24 N.Y.S. 182; In re Lima & H. F. Ry. Co., 68 Hun, 252, 22 N.Y.S. 967.

For other compound terms, such as "Power of Appointment," "Power of Sale," etc., see the following titles.

POWER COUPLED WITH AN INTEREST. A right or power to do some act, together with an interest in the subject-matter on which the power is to be exercised. It is distinguished from a *naked* power, which is a mere authority to act, not accompanied by any interest of the donee in the subject-matter of the power. Arcweld Mfg. Co. v. Burney, 12 Wash.2d 212, 121 P.2d 350, 355.

Is it an interest in the subject on which the power is to be exercised, or is it an interest in that which is produced by the exercise of the power? We hold it to be clear that the interest which can protect a power after the death of a person who creates it must be an interest in the thing itself. In other words, the power must be engrafted on an estate in the thing. The words themselves would seem to import this meaning. "A power coupled with an interest" is a power which accompanies or is connected with an interest. The power and the interest are united in the same person. But, if we are to understand by the word "interest" an interest in that which is to be produced by the exercise of the power, then they are never united. The power to produce the interest must be exercised, and by its exercise is extinguished. The power ceases when the interest commences, and therefore cannot, in accurate law language, be said to be "coupled" with it. And see Missouri v. Walker, 8 S.Ct. 929, 125 U.S. 339, 31 L.Ed. 769; Griffith v. Maxfield, 66 Ark. 513, 51 S.W. 832; Hunt v. Ennis, 12 Fed.Cas. 915; Chase Nat. Bank of New York v. Sayles, C.C.A.R.I., 11 F.2d 948, 957; Sphier v. Michael, 112 Or. 229, 229 P. 1100, 1101; Drake v. O'Brien, 99 W.Va. 582, 130 S.E. 276, 278.

POWER OF APPOINTMENT. A power or authority conferred by one person by deed or will upon another (called the "donee") to appoint, that is, to select and nominate, the person or persons who are to receive and enjoy an estate or an income therefrom or from a fund, after the testator's death, or the donee's death, or after the termination of an existing right or interest. Heinemann v. De Wolf, 25 R.I. 243, 55 A. 707; People v. Kaiser, 306 Ill. 313, 137 N.E. 826, 828.

The distinction between a "will" and a "power of appointment" is that a will concerns the estate of the testator, while an appointment under a power concerns that of the donor of the power. Thompson v. Pew, 214 Mass. 520, 102 N.E. 122, 125.

Powers are either: *Collateral*, which are given to strangers; *i. e.*, to persons who have neither a present nor future estate or interest in the land. These are also called simply "collateral," or powers not coupled with an interest, or powers not being interests. Or they are powers relating to the land. These are called "appendant" or "appurtenant," because they strictly depend upon the estate limited to the person to whom they are given. Thus, where an estate for life is limited to a man, with a power to grant leases in possession, a lease granted under the power may operate wholly out of the life-estate of the party executing it, and must in every case have its operation out of his estate during his life. Such an estate must be created, which will attach on an interest actually vested in himself. Or they are called "in gross," if given to a person who had an interest in the estate at the execution of the deed creating the power, or to whom an estate is given by the deed, but which enabled him to create such estates only as will not attach on the interest limited to him. Of necessity, therefore, where a man seised in fee settles his estate on others, reserving to himself only a particular power, the power is in gross.

A power to a tenant for life to appoint the estate after his death among his children, a power to jointure a wife after his death, a power to raise a term of years to commence from his death, for securing younger children's portions, are all powers in gross. An important distinction is established between *general* and *particular* powers. By a general power we understand a right to appoint to whomsoever the donee pleases. By a particular power it is meant that the donee is restricted to some objects designated in the deed creating the power, as to his own children. Wharton.

A general power is *beneficial* when no person other than the grantee has, by the terms of its creation, any interest in its execution. A general power is *in trust* when any person or class of persons, other than the grantee of such power, is designated as entitled to the proceeds, or any portion of the proceeds, or other benefits to result from the alienation. Cutting v. Cutting, 20 Hun, N.Y., 364.

When a power of appointment among a class requires that each shall have a share, it is called a "distributive" or "non-exclusive" power; when it authorizes, but does not direct, a selection of one or more to the exclusion of the others, it is called an "exclusive" power, and is also distributive; when it gives the power of appointing to a certain number of the class, but not to all, it is exclusive only, and not distributive. Leake, 389. A power authorizing the donee either to give the whole to one of a class or to give it equally among such of them as he may select (but not to give one a larger share than the others) is called a "mixed" power. Sugd.Powers, 448. Sweet.

POWER OF ATTORNEY. An instrument authorizing another to act as one's agent or attorney. A letter of attorney. Arcweld Mfg. Co. v. Burney, 12 Wash.2d 212, 121 P.2d 350, 354; Olive-Sternenberg Lumber Co. v. Gordon, Tex.Civ.App., 143 S.W.2d 694, 698. See Attorney.

POWER OF DISPOSITION. Every power of disposition is deemed absolute, by means of which the donee of such power is enabled in his life-time to dispose of the entire fee for his own benefit; and, where a general and beneficial power to devise the inheritance is given to a tenant for life or years, it is absolute, within the meaning of the statutes of some of the states. See Power of Appointment.

POWER OF SALE. A clause sometimes inserted in mortgages and deeds of trust, giving the mortgagee (or trustee) the right and power, on default in the payment of the debt secured, to advertise and sell the mortgaged property at public auction (but without resorting to a court for authority), satisfy the creditor out of the net proceeds, convey by deed to the purchaser, return the surplus, if any, to the mortgagor, and thereby divest the latter's estate entirely and without any subsequent right of redemption. Capron v. Attleborough Bank, 11 Gray (Mass.) 493; Appeal of Clark, 70 Conn. 195, 39 A. 155.

POYNDING. See Poinding.

POYNINGS' ACT. An act of parliament, made in Ireland, (10 Hen. VII. c. 22, A.D. 1495;) so called because Sir Edward Poynings was lieutenant there when it was made, whereby all general statutes before then made in England were declared of force in Ireland, which, before that time, they were not. 1 Broom & H.Comm. 112.

PRACTICABLE, PRACTICABLY. Practicable is that which may be done, practiced, or accomplished, that which is performable, feasible, possible; and the adverb practicably means in a practicable manner. Streeter v. Streeter, 43 Ill. 165; Lauck v. Reis, 310 Mo. 184, 274 S.W. 827, 832; Unverzagt v. Prestera, 339 Pa. 141, 13 A.2d 46, 48.

PRACTICAL. A practical construction of a constitution or statute is one determined not by judicial decision, but practice sanctioned by general consent. Bloxham v. Consumers' Electric Light, etc., Co., 36 Fla. 519, 18 So. 444, 29 L.R.A. 507, 51 Am.St.Rep. 44.

PRACTICE. Repeated or customary action; habitual performance; a succession of acts of similar kind; habit; custom; usage; application of science to the wants of men; the exercise of any profession. Marker v. Cleveland, 212 Mo.App. 467, 252 S.W. 95, 96; Columbia Life Ins. Co. v. Tousey, 152 Ky. 447, 153 S.W. 767, 768.

The form or mode or proceeding in courts of justice for the enforcement of rights or the redress of wrongs, as distinguished from the substantive law which gives the right or denounces the wrong. The form, manner, or order of instituting and conducting a suit or other judicial proceeding, through its successive stages to its end, in accordance with the rules and principles laid down by law or by the regulations and precedents of the courts. The term applies as well to the conduct of criminal actions as to civil suits, to proceedings in equity as well as at law, and to the defense as well as the prosecution of any proceeding. Wells Lamont Corp. v. Bowles, Em.App., 149 F.2d 364, 366.

Practice of a profession implies a continuing occupation, and a practitioner of veterinary science is one who habitually held himself out to the public as such. Beaver Brook Resort Co. v. Stevens, 76 Colo. 133, 230 P. 121, 122.

It may include pleading, but is usually employed as excluding both pleading and evidence, and to designate all the incidental acts and steps in the course of bringing matters pleaded to trial and proof, and procuring and enforcing judgment on them.

Practice of law. Not limited to appearing in court, or advising and assisting in the conduct of litigation, but embracing the preparation of pleadings, and other papers incident to actions and special proceedings, conveyancing, the preparation of legal instruments of all kinds, and the giving of all legal advice to clients. State v. Chamberlain, 132 Wash. 520, 232 P. 337, 338. It embraces all advice to clients and all actions taken for them in matters connected with the law. Rhode Island Bar Ass'n v. Lesser, 68 R.I. 14, 26 A.2d 6, 7.

Practice of medicine. The discovery of the cause and nature of disease, and the administration of remedies, or the prescribing of treatment therefor. State v. Heffernan, 40 R.I. 121, 100 A. 55, 60. Statutes, regulating the "practice of medicine" and providing penalties for failure to comply therewith, include all who practice the art of healing, State v. Collins, 178 Iowa, 73, 159 N.W. 604, 607, and diagnosing, prescribing and treating ailments are constituent parts of "practice of medicine." People v. T. Wah Hing, 79 Cal.App. 286, 249 P. 229, 230.

PRACTICE COURT. In English law. A court attached to the court of king's bench, which heard and determined common matters of business and ordinary motions for writs of *mandamus*, prohibition, etc. It was usually called the "bail court." It was held by one of the puisne justices of the king's bench.

PRACTICES. A succession of acts of a similar kind or in a like employment.

PRACTICKS. In Scotch law. The decisions of the court of session, as evidence of the *practice* or custom of the country. Bell.

PRACTITIONER. He who is engaged in the exercise or employment of any art or profession.

PRÆCEPTORES. Lat. Masters. The chief clerks in chancery were formerly so called, because they had the direction of making out remedial writs. 2 Reeve, Eng.Law, 251.

PRÆCEPTORIES. In feudal law. A kind of benefices, so called because they were possessed by the more eminent templars whom the chief master by his authority created and called *"Præceptores Templi."*

PRÆCIPE. Lat. In practice. An original writ, drawn up in the alternative, commanding the defendant to do the thing required, or show the reason why he had not done it. 3 Bl.Comm. 274.

A slip of paper upon which the particulars of a writ are written. It is lodged in the office out of which the required writ is to issue. Wharton. Dict.

Also an order, written out and signed, addressed to the clerk of a court, and requesting him to issue a particular writ.

PRÆCIPE IN CAPITE. When one of the king's immediate tenants *in capite* was deforced, his writ of right was called a writ of *"præcipe in capite."*

PRÆCIPE QUOD REDDAT. Command that he render. A writ directing the defendant to restore the possession of land, employed at the beginning of a common recovery.

PRÆCIPE QUOD TENEAT CONVENTIONEM. The writ which commenced the action of covenant in fines, which are abolished by 3 & 4 Wm. IV. c. 74.

PRÆCIPE, TENANT TO THE. A person having an estate of freehold in possession, against whom the *præcipe* was brought by a tenant in tail, seeking to bar his estate by a recovery.

PRÆCIPITIUM. The punishment of casting headlong from some high place.

PRÆCIPUT CONVENTIONNEL. In French law. Under the *régime en communauté,* when that is of the conventional kind, if the surviving husband or wife is entitled to take any portion of the common property by a paramount title and before partition thereof, this right is called by the somewhat barbarous title of the conventional *"præciput,"* from *"præ,"* before, and *"capere,"* to take. Brown.

PRÆCO. Lat. In Roman law. A herald or crier.

PRÆCOGNITA. Things to be previously known in order to the understanding of something which follows. Wharton.

PRÆDIA. In the civil law. Lands; estates; tenements; properties. See Prædium.

PRÆDIA BELLICA. Booty. Property seized in war.

PRÆDIA STIPENDIARIA. In the civil law. Provincial lands belonging to the people.

PRÆDIA TRIBUTARIA. In the civil law. Provincial lands belonging to the emperor.

PRÆDIA VOLANTIA. In the duchy of Brabant, certain things movable, such as beds, tables, and other heavy articles of furniture, were ranked among immovables, and were called *"prædia volantia,"* or "volatile estates." 2 Bl.Comm. 428.

PRÆDIAL. That which arises immediately from the ground: as, grain of all sorts, hay, wood, fruits, herbs, and the like.

PRÆDIAL SERVITUDE. A right which is granted for the advantage of one piece of land over another, and which may be exercised by every possessor of the land entitled against every possessor of the servient land. It always presupposes two pieces of land (*prædia*) belonging to different proprietors; one burdened with the servitude, called *"prædium serviens,"* and one for the advantage of which the servitude is conferred, called *"prædium dominans."* Mackeld. Rom. Law, § 314.

PRÆDIAL TITHES. Such as arise merely and immediately from the ground; as grain of all sorts, hops, hay, wood, fruit, herbs. 2 Bl.Comm. 23; 2 Steph.Comm. 722.

PRÆDICTUS. Lat. Aforesaid. Hob. 6. Of the three words, *"idem," "prædictus,"* and *"præfatus," "idem"* was most usually applied to plaintiffs or demandants; *"prædictus,"* to defendants or tenants, places, towns, or lands; and *"præfatus,"* to persons named, not being *actors* or parties. Townsh.Pl. 15. These words may all be rendered in English by "said" or "aforesaid."

PRÆDIUM. Lat. In the civil law. Land; an estate; a tenement; a piece of landed property. Dig. 50, 16, 115.

PRÆDIUM DOMINANS. In the civil law. The name given to an estate to which a servitude is due; the dominant tenement. Morgan v. Mason, 20 Ohio, 409, 55 Am.Dec. 464.

PRÆDIUM RUSTICUM. In Roman law. A rustic or rural estate. Primarily, this term denoted an estate lying in the country, *i. e.,* beyond the limits of the city, but it was applied to any landed estate or heritage other than a dwelling-house, whether in or out of the town. Thus, it included gardens, orchards, pastures, meadows, etc. Mackeld. Rom. Law, § 316. A rural or country estate; an estate or piece of land principally destined or devoted to agriculture; an empty or vacant space of ground without buildings.

PRÆDIUM SERVIENS. In the civil law. The name of an estate which suffers a servitude or easement to another estate; the servient tenement. Morgan v. Mason, 20 Ohio, 409, 55 Am. Dec. 464.

PRÆDIUM SERVIT PRÆDIO. Land is under servitude to land, [*i. e.,* servitudes are not personal rights, but attach to the dominant tenement.] Tray. Lat. Max. 455.

PRÆDIUM URBANUM. In the civil law. A building or edifice intended for the habitation and use of man, whether built in cities or in the country. Colq. Rom. Civil Law, § 937.

PRÆDO. Lat. In Roman law. A robber. Dig. 50, 17, 126.

PRÆFATUS. Lat. Aforesaid. Sometimes abbreviated to *"præfat,"* and *"p. fat."*

PRÆFECTI APOSTOLICI. Officers of the same character as the Vicarius Apostolicus (*q. v.*), but without the power of exercising episcopal functions. 2 Phill.Int.L. 529.

PRÆFECTURÆ. In Roman law. Conquered towns, governed by an officer called a "prefect," who was chosen in some instances by the people, in others by the prætors. Butl.Hor.Jur. 29.

PRÆFECTUS URBI. Lat. In Roman law. An officer who, from the time of Augustus, had the superintendence of the city and its police, with jurisdiction extending one hundred miles from the city, and power to decide both civil and criminal cases. As he was considered the direct representative of the emperor, much that previously belonged to the *prætor urbanus* fell gradually into his hands. Colq.Rom. Civil Law, § 2395.

PRÆFECTUS VIGILUM. Lat. In Roman law. The chief officer of the night watch. His jurisdiction extended to certain offenses affecting the public peace, and even to larcenies; but he could inflict only slight punishments. Colq. Rom. Civil Law, § 2395.

PRÆFECTUS VILLÆ. The mayor of a town.

PRÆFINE. The fee paid on suing out the writ of covenant, on levying fines, before the fine was passed. 2 Bl.Comm. 350.

PRÆJURAMENTUM. In old English law. A preparatory oath.

PRÆLEGATUM. Lat. In Roman law. A payment in advance of the whole or part of the share which a given heir would be entitled to receive out of an inheritance; corresponding generally to "advancement" in English and American law. Mackeld. Rom. Law, § 762.

PRÆMIUM. Lat. Reward; compensation. *Præmium assecurationis,* compensation for insurance; premium of insurance. Locc. de Jur. Mar. lib. 2, c. 5, § 6.

PRÆMIUM EMANCIPATIONIS. In Roman law. A reward or compensation anciently allowed to a father on emancipating his child, consisting of one-third of the child's separate and individual property, not derived from the father himself. Mackeld. Rom. Law, § 605.

PRÆMIUM PUDICITIÆ. The price of chastity; or compensation for loss of chastity. A term applied to bonds and other engagements given for the benefit of a seduced female. Sometimes called "*præmium pudoris.*" 2 Wils. 339, 340.

PRÆMUNIRE. In English law. An offense against the king and his government, though not subject to capital punishment. So called from the words of the writ which issued preparatory to the prosecution: "*Præmunire facias A. B. quod sit coram nobis,*" etc.; "Cause A. B. to be forewarned that he appear before us to answer the contempt with which he stands charged." The statutes establishing this offense, the first of which was made in the thirty-first year of the reign of Edward I., were framed to encounter the papal usurpations in England; the original meaning of the offense called "*præmunire*" being the introduction of a foreign power into the kingdom, and creating *imperium in imperio,* by paying that obedience to papal process which constitutionally belonged to the king alone. The penalties of *præmunire* were afterwards applied to other heinous offenses. 4 Bl.Comm. 103–117; 4 Steph. Comm. 215–217.

PRÆNOMEN. Lat. Forename, or first name. The first of the three names by which the Romans were commonly distinguished. It marked the individual, and was commonly written with one letter; as "A." for "Aulus;" "C." for "Caius,' etc. Adams, Rom.Ant. 35.

PRÆPOSITUS. In old English law. An officer next in authority to the alderman of a hundred, called "*præpositus regius;*" or a steward or bailiff of an estate, answering to the "*wicnere.*"

Also the person from whom descents are traced under the old canons.

PRÆPOSITUS ECCLESIÆ. A church-reeve, or warden. Spelman.

PRÆPOSITUS VILLÆ. A constable of a town, or petty constable.

PRÆPROPERA CONSILIA RARO SUNT PROSPERA. 4 Inst. 57. Hasty counsels are rarely prosperous.

PRÆSCRIPTIO. Lat. In the civil law. That mode of acquisition whereby one becomes proprietor of a thing on the ground that he has for a long time possessed it as his own; prescription. Dig. 41, 3. It was anciently distinguished from "*usucapio,*" (*q. v.,*) but was blended with it by Justinian.

PRÆSCRIPTIO EST TITULUS EX USU ET TEMPORE SUBSTANTIAM CAPIENS AB AUCTORITATE LEGIS. Co.Litt. 113. Prescription is a title by authority of law, deriving its force from use and time.

PRÆSCRIPTIO ET EXECUTIO NON PERTINENT AD VALOREM CONTRACTUS, SET AD TEMPUS ET MODUM ACTIONIS INSTITUENDÆ. Prescription and execution do not affect the validity of the contract, but the time and manner of bringing an action. Pearsall v. Dwight, 2 Mass. 84, 3 Am.Dec. 35; Decouche v. Savetier, 3 Johns.Ch. (N.Y.) 190, 219, 8 Am.Dec. 478.

PRÆSCRIPTIONES. Lat. In Roman law. Forms of words (of a qualifying character) inserted in the *formulæ* in which the claims in actions were expressed; and, as they occupied an early place in the *formulæ,* they were called by this name, *i. e.,* qualifications *preceding* the claim. For example, in an action to recover the arrears of an annuity, the claim was preceded by the words "so far as the annuity is due and unpaid," or words to the like effect, ("*cujus rei dies fuit.*") Brown.

PRÆSENTARE NIHIL ALIUD EST QUAM PRÆSTO DARE SEU OFFERE. To present is no more than to give or offer on the spot. Co.Litt. 120.

PRÆSENTIA CORPORIS TOLLIT ERROREM NOMINIS; ET VERITAS NOMINIS TOLLIT ERROREM DEMONSTRATIONIS. The presence of the body cures error in the name; the truth of the name cures an error of description. Broom, Max. 637, 639, 640.

PRÆSES. Lat. In Roman law. A president or governor. Called a "*nomen generale*," including pro-consuls, legates, and all who governed provinces.

PRÆSTARE. Lat. In Roman law. "*Prœstare*" meant to make good, and, when used in conjunction with the words "*dare,*" "*facere,*" "*oportere,*" denoted obligations of a personal character, as opposed to real rights.

PRÆSTAT CAUTELA QUAM MEDELA. Prevention is better than cure. Co.Litt. 304*b*.

PRÆSTITA ROLLS. In these were entered the sums of money which issued out of the royal treasury, by way of imprest, advance, or accommodation, in the 12th year of King John; also roll of the 7th, and one of the 14th, 15th and 16th years of the same reign. See Record Commission (1844).

PRÆSUMATUR PRO JUSTITIA SENTENTIÆ. The presumption should be in favor of the justice of a sentence. Best, Ev. Introd. 42.

PRÆSUMITUR PRO LEGITIMATIONE. The presumption is in favor of legitimacy. 1 Bl. Comm. 457; 5 Coke, 98*b*.

PRÆSUMITUR PRO NEGANTE. It is presumed for the negative. The rule of the house of lords when the numbers are equal on a motion. Wharton.

PRÆSUMPTIO. Lat. Presumption; a presumption. Also intrusion, or the unlawful taking of anything.

PRÆSUMPTIO, EX EO QUOD PLERUMQUE FIT. Presumptions arise from what generally happens. Post v. Pearsall, 22 Wend. (N.Y.) 425, 475.

PRÆSUMPTIO FORTIOR. A strong presumption; a presumption of fact entitled to great weight. One which determines the tribunal in its belief of an alleged fact, without, however, excluding the belief of the possibility of its being otherwise; the effect of which is to shift the burden of producing evidence to the opposite party, and, if this proof be not made, the presumption is held for truth. Hub.Præl.J.C. lib. 22, tit. 3, n. 16; Burrill, Circ.Ev. 66.

PRÆSUMPTIO HOMINIS. The presumption of the man or individual; that is, natural presumption unfettered by strict rule.

PRÆSUMPTIO JURIS. A legal presumption or presumption of law; that is, one in which the law assumes the existence of something until it is disproved by evidence; a conditional, inconclusive, or rebuttable presumption. Best, Ev. § 43.

PRÆSUMPTIO JURIS ET DE JURE. A presumption of law and of right; a presumption which the law will not suffer to be contradicted; a conclusive or irrebuttable presumption.

PRÆSUMPTIO MUCIANA. In Roman law. A presumption of law that property in the hands of a wife came to her as a gift from her husband and was not acquired from other sources; available only in doubtful cases and until the contrary is shown. Mackeld. Rom. Law, § 560.

PRÆSUMPTIO VIOLENTA PIENA PROBATIO. Co.Litt. 6*b*. Strong presumption is full proof.

PRÆSUMPTIO VIOLENTA VALET IN LEGE. Strong presumption is of weight in law. Jenk. Cent. p. 56, case 3.

PRÆSUMPTIONES SUNT CONJECTURÆ EX SIGNO VERISIMILI AD PROBANDUM ASSUMPTÆ. Presumptions are conjectures from probable proof, assumed for purposes of evidence. J. Voet, Com. ad Pand. l. 22, tit. 3, n. 14.

PRÆTERITIO. Lat. A passing over or omission. Used in the Roman law to describe the act of a testator in excluding a given heir from the inheritance by silently passing him by, that is, neither instituting nor formally disinheriting him. Mackeld. Rom. Law, § 711.

PRÆTEXTU LICITI NON DEBET ADMITTI ILLICITUM. Under pretext of legality, what is illegal ought not to be admitted. Wing. Max. p. 728, max. 196.

PRÆTEXTUS. Lat. A pretext; a pretense or color. *Prœtextu cujus*, by pretense, or under pretext whereof. 1 Ld.Raym. 412.

PRÆTOR. Lat. In Roman law. A municipal officer of the city of Rome, being the chief judicial magistrate, and possessing an extensive equitable jurisdiction.

PRÆTOR FIDEI-COMMISSARIUS. In the civil law. A special prætor created to pronounce judgment in cases of trusts or *fidei-commissa.* Inst. 2, 23, 1.

PRÆTORIAN LAW. See Lex Prætoria.

PRÆVARICATOR. Lat. In the civil law. One who betrays his trust, or is unfaithful to his trust. An advocate who aids the opposite party by betraying his client's cause. Dig. 47, 15, 1.

PRÆVENTO TERMINO. In old Scotch practice. A form of action known in the forms of the court of session, by which a delay to discuss a suspension or advocation was got the better of. Bell.

PRAGMATIC SANCTION. In French law. A solemn ordinance or decree of a sovereign dealing with matters of primal importance and regarded as constituting a part of the fundamental law of the land. It originated in the Byzantine Empire; in later European history it was especially used to designate an ordinance of Charles VI, emperor of Germany, issued April, 1713, to settle the succession on his daughter, Maria Theresa. It was ratified by the Great Powers. On the death of the emperor, it was repudiated by Prussia, France and others, which led to the War of the Austrian Succession. Int. Encycl.

In the civil law. The answer given by the emperors on questions of law, when consulted by a corporation or the citizens of a province or of a municipality. Lec.El.Dr.Rom. § 53.

PRAGMATICA. In Spanish colonial law. An order emanating from the sovereign, and differing from a *cedula* only in form and in the mode of promulgation. Schm.Civil Law, Introd. 93, note.

PRAIRIE. An extensive tract of level or rolling land, destitute of trees, covered with coarse grass, and usually characterized by a deep, fertile soil. Webster. Buxton v. Railroad Co., 58 Mo. 45; Brunell v. Hopkins, 42 Iowa, 429.

PRATIQUE. A license for the master of a ship to traffic in the ports of a given country, or with the inhabitants of a given port, upon the lifting of quarantine or production of a clean bill of health.

PRAXIS. Lat. Use; practice.

PRAXIS JUDICUM EST INTERPRES LEGUM. Hob. 96. The practice of the judges is the interpreter of the laws.

PRAY IN AID. In old English practice. To call upon for assistance. In real actions, the tenant might *pray in aid* or call for assistance of another, to help him to plead, because of the feebleness or imbecility of his own estate. 3 Bl.Comm. 300.

PRAYER. The request contained in a bill in equity that the court will grant the process, aid, or relief which the complainant desires. Also, by extension, the term is applied to that part of the bill which contains this request.

PRAYER OF PROCESS. A petition with which a bill in equity used to conclude, to the effect that a writ of subpœna might issue against the defendant to compel him to answer upon oath all the matters charged against him in the bill.

PREAMBLE. A clause at the beginning of a constitution or statute explanatory of the reasons for its enactment and the objects sought to be accomplished. Townsend v. State, 147 Ind. 624, 47 N.E. 19, 37 L.R.A. 294, 62 Am.St.Rep. 477; Fenner v. Luzerne County, 167 Pa. 632, 31 A. 862.

It is not essential part of act, and neither enlarges nor confers powers. Portland Van & Storage Co. v. Hoss, 139 Or. 434, 9 P.2d 122, 126, 81 A.L.R. 1136.

PREAPPOINTED EVIDENCE. The kind and degree of evidence prescribed in advance (as, by statute) as requisite for the proof of certain facts or the establishment of certain instruments. It is opposed to *casual* evidence, which is left to grow naturally out of the surrounding circumstances.

PREAUDIENCE. The right of being heard before another. A privilege belonging to the English bar, the members of which are entitled to be heard in their order, according to rank, beginning with the king's attorney general, and ending with barristers at large. 3 Steph.Comm. 387, note.

PREBEND. In English ecclesiastical law. A stipend granted in cathedral churches; also, but improperly, a prebendary. A simple prebend is merely a revenue; a prebend with dignity has some jurisdiction attached to it. The term "prebend" is generally confounded with "canonicate;" but there is a difference between them. The former is the stipend granted to an ecclesiastic in consideration of his officiating and serving in the church; whereas the canonicate is a mere title or spiritual quality which may exist independently of any stipend. 2 Steph.Comm. 674, note.

PREBENDARY. An ecclesiastical person serving on the staff of a cathedral, and receiving a stated allowance or stipend from the income or endowment of the cathedral, in compensation for his services.

PRECARIÆ, or PRECES. Day-works which the tenants of certain manors were bound to give their lords in harvest time. *Magna precaria* was a great or general reaping day. Cowell.

PRECARIOUS. Liable to be returned or rendered up at the mere demand or request of another; hence held or retained only on sufferance or by permission; and by an extension of meaning, doubtful, uncertain, dangerous, very liable to break, fail, or terminate.

PRECARIOUS CIRCUMSTANCES. The circumstances of an executor are *precarious*, within the meaning and intent of a statute, only when his character and conduct present such evidence of improvidence or recklessness in the management of the trust-estate, or of his own, as in the opinion of prudent and discreet men endangers its security. Shields v. Shields, 60 Barb. (N.Y.) 56.

PRECARIOUS LOAN. A bailment by way of loan which is not to continue for any fixed time, but may be recalled at the mere will and pleasure of the lender.

PRECARIOUS POSSESSION. In modern civil law, possession is called "precarious" which one enjoys by the leave of another and during his pleasure. Civ.Code La. art. 3556, subd. 25.

PRECARIOUS RIGHT. The right which the owner of a thing transfers to another, to enjoy the same until it shall please the owner to revoke it.

PRECARIOUS TRADE. In international law. Such trade as may be carried on by a neutral between two belligerent powers by the mere sufferance of the latter.

PRECARIUM. Lat. In the civil law. A convention whereby one allows another the use of a thing or the exercise of a right gratuitously till revocation. The bailee acquires thereby the lawful possession of the thing, except in certain cases. The bailor can redemand the thing at any time, even should he have allowed it to the bailee for a designated period. Mackeld. Rom. Law, § 447.

PRECATORY. Having the nature of prayer, request, or entreaty; conveying or embodying a recommendation or advice or the expression of a wish, but not a positive command or direction. United States v. 15,883.55 Acres of Land in Spartanburg County, S. C., D.C.S.C., 40 F.Supp. 558, 561.

PRECATORY TRUST. A trust created by certain words, which are more like words of entreaty and permission than of command or certainty. Examples of such words, which the courts have held sufficient to constitute a trust, are "wish and request," "have fullest confidence," "heartily beseech," and the like. Rapalje & Lawrence. Keplinger v. Keplinger, 185 Ind. 81, 113 N.E. 292, 293; Simpson v. Corder, 185 Mo.App. 398, 170 S.W. 357, 358. Thomas v. Reynolds, 234 Ala. 212, 174 So. 753, 757.

PRECATORY WORDS. Words of entreaty, request, desire, wish, or recommendation, employed in wills, as distinguished from direct and imperative terms. 1 Williams, Ex'rs, 88, 89, and note; Pratt v. Miller, 23 Neb. 496, 37 N.W. 263; Wemme v. First Church of Christ, Scientist, of Portland, 110 Or. 179, 219 P. 618, 627.

PRECAUTION. Previous action; proven foresight; care previously employed to prevent mischief or to secure good result; or a measure taken beforehand; an active foresight designed to ward off possible evil or secure good results. Fegan v. Lykes Bros. S. S. Co., 198 La. 312, 3 So.2d 632, 635; Rincon v. Berg Co., Tex.Civ.App., 60 S.W.2d 811, 813.

PRECEDENCE, or PRECEDENCY. The act or state of going before; adjustment of place. The right of being first placed in a certain order.

PRECEDENCE, PATENT OF. In English law. A grant from the crown to such barristers as it thinks proper to honor with that mark of distinction, whereby they are entitled to such rank and preaudience as are assigned in their respective patents. 3 Steph.Comm. 274.

PRECEDENT. An adjudged case or decision of a court of justice, considered as furnishing an example or authority for an identical or similar case afterwards arising or a similar question of law.

It means that a principle of law actually presented to a court of authority for consideration and determination has, after due consideration, been declared to serve as a rule for future guidance in the same or analogous cases, but matters which merely lurk in the record and are not directly advanced or expressly decided are not precedents. Empire Square Realty Co. v. Chase Nat. Bank of City of New York, 43 N.Y.S.2d 470, 473, 181 Misc. 752; Kvos, Inc. v. Associated Press, 299 U.S. 269, 279, 57 S.Ct. 197, 81 L.Ed. 183.

A draught of a conveyance, settlement, will, pleading, bill, or other legal instrument, which is considered worthy to serve as a pattern for future instruments of the same nature.

PRECEDENT CONDITION. Such as must happen or be performed before an estate can vest or be enlarged. See Condition Precedent.

PRECEDENTS SUB SILENTIO. Silent uniform course of practice, uninterrupted though not supported by legal decisions. Calton v. Bragg, 15 East, 226; Thompson v. Musser, 1 Dall. 464, 1 L. Ed. 222.

PRECEDENTS THAT PASS SUB SILENTIO ARE OF LITTLE OR NO AUTHORITY. 16 Vin. Abr. 499.

PRECEDING. Next before. Smith v. Gibson, 191 Ala. 305, 68 So. 143.

PRECEPARTIUM. The continuance of a suit by consent of both parties. Cowell.

PRECEPT. In English and American law. An order or direction, emanating from authority, to an officer or body of officers, commanding him or them to do some act within the scope of their powers. A commandment in writing, sent out by a justice of the peace or other like officer, for the bringing of a person or record before him. Cowell. The direction formerly issued by a sheriff to the proper returning officers of cities and boroughs within his jurisdiction for the election of members to serve in parliament. 1 Bl.Comm. 178. The direction by the judges or commissioners of assize to the sheriff for the summoning a sufficient number of jurors. 3 Steph.Comm. 516. The direction issued by the clerk of the peace to the overseers of parishes for making out the jury lists. 3 Steph.Comm. 516, note.

Precept is not to be confined to civil proceedings, and is not of a more restricted meaning than "process." It includes warrants and processes in criminal as well as civil proceedings. Adams v. Vose, 1 Gray, Mass., 51, 58.

In old English criminal law. Instigation to commit a crime. Bract. fol. 138*b*; Cowell.

In Scotch law. An order, mandate, or warrant to do some act. The precept of seisin was the order of a superior to his bailie, to give infeftment of certain lands to his vassal. Bell.

In old French law. A kind of letters issued by the king in subversion of the laws, being orders to the judges to do or tolerate things contrary to law.

PRECEPT OF CLARE CONSTAT. A deed in the Scotch law by which a superior acknowledges the title of the heir of a deceased vassal to succeed to the lands.

PRECES. Lat. In Roman law. Prayers. One of the names of an application to the emperor. Tayl. Civil Law, 230.

PRECES PRIMARIÆ. In English ecclesiastical law. A right of the crown to name to the first prebend that becomes vacant after the accession of the sovereign, in every church of the empire. This right was exercised by the crown of England in the reign of Edward I. 2 Steph.Comm. 670, note.

PRECINCT. A constable's or police district. The immediate neighborhood of a palace or court. A small geographical unit of government. An election district created for convenient localization of polling places. Union Pac. Ry. Co. v. Ryan, 5 S.Ct. 601, 113 U.S. 516, 28 L.Ed. 1098; Railway Co. v. Oconto, 50 Wis. 189, 6 N.W. 607, 36 Am.Rep. 840; Rich v. Industrial Commission, 80 Utah, 511, 15 P.2d 641, 645.

PRECIPE. Another form of the name of the written instructions to the clerk of court; also spelled "*præcipe,*" (*q. v.*).

PRECIPITATION. Hastening occurrence of event or causing to happen or come to crisis suddenly, unexpectedly or too soon. Knock v. Industrial Acc. Commission of California, 200 Cal. 456, 253 P. 712, 714.

PRECIPITIN TEST. Precipitins are formations in the blood of an animal induced by repeated injections into its veins of the blood-serum of an animal of another species; and their importance in diagnosis lies in the fact that when the blood-serum of an animal so treated is mixed with that of any animal of the second species (or a closely related species) and the mixture kept at a temperature of about 98 degrees for several hours, a visible precipitate will result, but not so if the second ingredient of the mixture is drawn from an animal of an entirely different species. In medico-legal practice, therefore, a suspected stain or clot having been first tested by other methods and demonstrated to be blood, the question whether it is the blood of a human being or of other origin is resolved by mixing a solution of it with a quantity of blood-serum taken from a rabbit or some other small animal which has been previously prepared by injections of human blood-serum. After treatment as above described, the presence of a precipitate will furnish strong presumptive evidence that the blood tested was of human origin. The test is not absolutely conclusive, for the reason that blood from an anthropoid ape would produce the same result, in this experiment, as human blood. But if the alternative hypothesis presented attributed the blood in question to some animal of an unrelated species (as, a dog, sheep, or horse) the precipitin test could be fully relied on, as also in the case where no precipitate resulted.

PRÉCIPUT. In French law. A portion of an estate or inheritance which falls to one of the coheirs over and above his equal share with the rest, and which is to be taken out before partition is made.

PRECISE. Having determinate limitations. Wall v. Pierpont, 119 Kan. 420, 240 P. 251, 258.

PRECLUDE. Estop. Morris Plan Bank of Fort Worth v. Continental Nat. Bank of Fort Worth, Tex.Civ.App., 155 S.W.2d 407, 409.

PRECLUDI NON. Lat. In pleading. The commencement of a replication to a plea in bar, by which the plaintiff "says that, by reason of anything in the said plea alleged, he *ought not to be barred* from having and maintaining his aforesaid action against him, the said defendant, because he says," etc. Steph.Pl. 440.

PRECOGNITION. In Scotch practice. Preliminary examination. The investigation of a criminal case, preliminary to committing the accused for trial. 2 Alis.Crim.Pr. 134.

PRECOGNOSCE. In Scotch practice. To examine beforehand. Arkley, 232.

PRECONIZATION. Proclamation.

PRECONTRACT. A contract or engagement made by a person, which is of such a nature as to preclude him from lawfully entering into another contract of the same nature. 1 Bish.Mar. & Div. §§ 112, 272.

PREDECESSOR. One who goes or has gone before; the correlative of "successor." One who has filled an office or station before the present incumbent. Applied to a body politic or corporate, in the same sense as "ancestor" is applied to a natural person. Lorillard Co. v. Peper, C.C. Mo., 65 F. 597, 598.

In Scotch law. An ancestor. 1 Kames, Eq. 371.

PREDIAL SERVITUDE. A charge laid on an estate for the use and utility of another estate belonging to another owner. Civil Code La. art. 647. See Prædial Servitude.

PREDICATE. In logic. That which is said concerning the subject in a logical proposition; as, "The law is the perfection of common sense." "Perfection of common sense," being affirmed concerning the law, (the subject,) is the predicate or thing predicated. Wharton, Bourland v. Hildreth, 26 Cal. 232.

PREDOMINANT. Something greater or superior in power and influence to others with which it is connected or compared. Matthews v. Bliss, 22 Pick. (Mass.) 53.

PRE-EMPTION. In international law. The right of pre-emption is the right of a nation to detain the merchandise of strangers passing through her territories or seas, in order to afford to her subjects the preference of purchase. 1 Chit.Com. Law, 103.

According to general modern usage the doctrine of pre-emption, as applied in time of war rests upon the distinction between articles which are contraband *(q. v.) universally,* and those which are contraband only under the particular circumstances of the case. The carrying of the former class entails the penalty of confiscation, either of ship or cargo or both. The latter class, while confiscable according to strict law, are sometimes merely subjected to the milder belligerent right of *pre-emption,* which is regarded as a fair compromise between the right of the belligerent to seize, and the claim of the neutral to export his *native commodities,* though immediately subservient to the purpose of hostility; 3 Phill.Int.L. 450; 1 C.Rob. 241. The right of pre-emption is said to be rather a waiver of a greater right than a right itself; an indulgence to the neutral rather than a right of the belligerent; Ward, Contraband 196.

In English law. The first buying of a thing. A privilege formerly enjoyed by the crown, of buying up provisions and other necessaries, by the intervention of the king's purveyors, for the use of his royal household, at an appraised valuation, in preference to all others, and even without consent of the owner. 1 Bl.Comm. 287; Garcia v. Callender, 125 N.Y. 307, 26 N.E. 283.

In the United States. A privilege accorded by the government to the actual settler upon a certain limited portion of the public domain, to purchase such tract at a fixed price to the exclusion of all other applicants. Nix v. Allen, 5 S.Ct. 70, 112 U.S. 129, 28 L.Ed. 675.

PRE–EMPTION CLAIMANT. One who has settled upon land subject to pre-emption, with the intention to acquire title to it, and has complied, or is proceeding to comply, in good faith, with the requirements of the law to perfect his right to it. Hosmer v. Wallace, 97 U.S. 575, 581, 24 L. Ed. 1130.

PRE–EMPTION ENTRY. See Entry.

PRE–EMPTION RIGHT. The right given to settlers upon the public lands of the United States to purchase them at a limited price in preference to others.

PRE–EMPTIONER. One who, by settlement upon the public land, or by cultivation of a portion of it, has obtained the right to purchase a portion of the land thus settled upon or cultivated, to the exclusion of all other persons. Dillingham v. Fisher, 5 Wis. 480; Doe v. Beck, 108 Ala. 71, 19 So. 802.

PREFECT. In French law. The name given to the public functionary who is charged in chief with the administration of the laws, in each department of the country. Merl. Répert. See Crespin v. U. S., 18 S.Ct. 53, 168 U.S. 208, 42 L. Ed. 438. The term is also used, in practically the same sense, in Mexico. But in New Mexico, a prefect is a probate judge.

PREFER. To bring before; to prosecute; to try; to proceed with. Thus, preferring an indictment signifies prosecuting or trying an indictment.

To give advantage, priority, or privilege; to select for first payment, as to prefer one creditor over others.

PREFERENCE. The paying or securing to one or more of his creditors, by an insolvent debtor, the whole or a part of their claim, to the exclusion of the rest. The act of an insolvent debtor who, in distributing his property or in assigning it for the benefit of his creditors, pays or secures to one or more creditors the full amount of their claims or a larger amount than they would be entitled to receive on a *pro rata* distribution. Citizens' State Bank of Chautauqua v. First Nat. Bank of Sedan, 98 Kan. 109, 157 P. 392, 394, L.R. A.1917A, 696. Jackson v. Coons, 285 Ky. 154, 147 S.W.2d 45, 47, 132 A.L.R. 1403. It imports the relation of existing creditors having equal equities at the time of the transfer whereby the rights of one are advanced over those of another. Adams v. City Bank & Trust Co. of Macon, Ga., C.C.A.Ga., 115 F.2d 453, 454.

The trustee in bankruptcy, to establish a recoverable "preference" under the Federal Bankruptcy Act, must show a transfer of property or money to the creditor, during insolvency and within four months of bankruptcy, that the creditor had reasonable grounds for believing that the bankrupt was then insolvent, and that the effect of the transfer was to give the creditor a greater percentage of his debt than other creditors of the same class. Walker v. Wilkinson, C.C.A.Tex., 296 F. 850, 852. There must be a parting with the bankrupt's property for the benefit of the creditor and a subsequent diminution of his estate; Continental & Commercial T. & S. Bk. v. Trust Co., 33 S.Ct. 829, 229 U.S. 435, 57 L.Ed. 1268; N. Bk. of Newport v. Bank, 32 S.Ct. 633, 225 U.S. 178, 56 L.Ed. 1042.

Also the right held by a creditor, in virtue of some lien or security, to be preferred above others (*i. e.*, paid first) out of the debtor's assets constituting the fund for creditors. Chadbourne v. Harding, 80 Me. 580, 16 A. 248; In re Ratliff, D.C. N.C., 107 F. 80; In re Stevens, 38 Minn. 432, 38 N. W. 111.

PREFERENCE SHARE. One giving its holder a preference, either as to receipt of dividends, as to payment in case of winding up, or both. In re Schaffer Stores Co., 229 N.Y.S. 735, 739, 224 App. Div. 268.

A term used in English law to designate a new issue of shares of stock in a company, which, to facilitate the disposal of them, are accorded a priority or preference over the original shares.

PREFERENTIAL ASSIGNMENT. An assignment of property for the benefit of creditors, made by an insolvent debtor, in which it is directed that a preference (right to be paid first in full) shall be given to a creditor or creditors therein named.

PREFERENTIAL DEBTS. In bankruptcy. Those which are prior to all others; as, wages of a clerk, servant, or workman, rates due and taxes. Brett, Comm. 890.

PREFERRED. Possessing or accorded a priority, advantage, or privilege. Generally denoting a prior or superior claim or right of payment as against another thing of the same kind or class. State v. Cheraw & C. R. Co., 16 S.C. 528.

PREFERRED DEBT. A demand which has priority; which is payable in full before others are paid at all.

PREFERRED DIVIDEND. See Dividend.

PREFERRED DOCKETS. Lists of preference cases prepared by the clerks when the cases are set for trial. King v. New Orleans Ry. & Light Co., 140 La. 843, 74 So. 168, 169.

PREFERRED STOCK. See Stock.

PRÉFET. In French law. A chief officer invested with the superintendence of the administration of the laws in each department. Merlin, Répert.

PREGNANCY. In medical jurisprudence. The state of a female who has within her ovary or womb a fecundated germ. Dungl. Med. Dict. The existence of the condition beginning at the moment of conception and terminating with delivery of the child. State v. Loomis, 90 N.J.Law, 216, 100 A. 160, 161.

Extra uterine or ectopic pregnancy is the development of the ovum outside of the uterine cavity, as in the Fallopian tubes or ovary. Extra uterine pregnancy commonly terminates by rupture of the sac, profuse internal hemorrhage, and death if not relieved promptly by a surgical operation.

PREGNANCY, PLEA OF. A plea which a woman capitally convicted may plead in stay of execution; for this, though it is no stay of judgment, yet operates as a respite of execution until she is delivered. Brown.

PREGNANT NEGATIVE. See Negative Pregnant.

PREJUDICE. A forejudgment; bias; preconceived opinion. A leaning towards one side of a cause for some reason other than a conviction of its justice. Tegeler v. State, 130 P. 1164, 1167, 9 Okl.Cr. 138; Taylor v. F. W. Woolworth Co., 146 Kan. 841, 73 P.2d 1102, 1103.

Of judge. That which disqualifies judge is condition of mind, which sways judgment and renders judge unable to exercise his functions impartially in particular case. Evans v. Superior Court in and for Los Angeles County, 107 Cal. App. 372, 290 P. 662, 665. It refers to mental attitude or disposition of the judge toward a party to the litigation, and not to any views that he may entertain regarding the subject matter involved. State ex rel. Mitchell v. Sage Stores Co., 157 Kan. 622, 143 P.2d 652, 655.

Without prejudice. Where an offer or admission is made "without prejudice," or a motion is denied or a bill in equity dismissed "without prejudice," it is meant as a declaration that no rights or privileges of the party concerned are to be considered as thereby waived or lost, except in so far as may be expressly conceded or decided. See, also, Dismissal Without Prejudice.

PREJUDICIAL ERROR. Error substantially affecting appellant's legal rights and obligations. Erskine v. Upham, 56 Cal.App.2d 235, 132 P.2d 219, 228; Trepanier v. Standard Min. & Mill. Co., 58 Wyo. 29, 123 P.2d 378, 380.

PRELATE. A clergyman of a superior order, as an archbishop or a bishop, having authority over the lower clergy; a dignitary of the church. Webster.

PRÉLÈVEMENT. Fr. In French law. A preliminary deduction; particularly, the portion or share which one member of a firm is entitled to take out of the partnership assets before a division of the property is made between the partners.

PRELIMINARY. Introductory; initiatory; preceding; temporary and provisional; as preliminary examination, injunction, articles of peace, etc.

PRELIMINARY ACT. In English admiralty practice. A document stating the time and place of a collision between vessels, the names of the vessels, and other particulars, required to be filed by each solicitor in actions for damage by such collision, unless the court or a judge shall otherwise order. Wharton.

PRELIMINARY EXAMINATION OR HEARING. See Hearing.

PRELIMINARY INJUNCTION. See Injunction.

PRELIMINARY PROOF. In insurance. The first proof offered of a loss occurring under the policy, usually sent in to the underwriters with the notification of claim.

PREMATURE LABOR. See Miscarriage.

PREMEDITATE. To think of an act beforehand, to contrive and design; to plot or lay plans for the execution of a purpose. See Deliberate.

PREMEDITATED DESIGN. In homicide cases. The mental purpose, the formed intent, to take human life. Radej v. State, 152 Wis. 503, 140 N. W. 21, 22.

PREMEDITATEDLY. Thought of beforehand, for any length of time, however short. State v. Johnson, 92 Kan. 441, 140 P. 839, 840.

PREMEDITATION. The act of meditating in advance; deliberation upon a contemplated act; plotting or contriving; a design formed to do something before it is done. State v. Spivey, 132 N.C. 989, 43 S.E. 475; Parker v. State, 24 Wyo. 491, 161 P. 552, 554.

A prior determination to do an act, but such determination need not exist for any particular period before it is carried into effect. Commonwealth v. Dreher, 274 Pa. 325, 118 A. 215, 216.

Premeditation differs essentially from *will*, which constitutes the crime; because it supposes, besides an *actual* will, a *deliberation*, and a *continued persistence*.

PREMIER. A principal minister of state; the prime minister.

PREMIER SERJEANT, THE QUEEN'S. This officer, so constituted by letters patent, has preaudience over the bar after the attorney and solicitor general and queen's advocate. 3 Steph. Comm. (7th Ed.) 274, note.

PREMISES. That which is put before; that which precedes; the foregoing statements. Thus, in logic, the two introductory propositions of the syllogism are called the "premises," and from them the conclusion is deduced. So, in pleading, the expression "in consideration of the premises" means in consideration of the matters hereinbefore stated. Alaska Imp. Co. v. Hirsch, 119 Cal. 249, 47 P. 124; Meese v. Northern Pac. Ry. Co., C.C.A.Wash., 211 F. 254, 259.

In conveyancing. That part of a deed which precedes the *habendum*, in which are set forth the names of the parties with their titles and additions, and in which are recited such deeds, agreements, or matters of fact as are necessary to explain the reasons upon which the present transaction is founded; and it is here, also, the consideration on which it is made is set down and the certainty of the thing granted. 2 Bl. Comm. 298. Liles v. Pitts, 145 La. 650, 82 So. 735, 738.

In equity pleading. The stating part of a bill. It contains a narrative of the facts and circumstances of the plaintiff's case, and the wrongs of which he complains, and the names of the persons by whom done and against whom he seeks redress. Story, Eq. Pl. § 27.

In estates. Lands and tenements; an estate; land and buildings thereon; the subject-matter of a conveyance. F. F. Proctor Troy Properties Co. v. Dugan Store, 181 N.Y.S. 786, 788, 191 App.Div. 685. The area of land surrounding a house, and actually or by legal construction forming one inclosure with it. Ratzell v. State, Okl.Cr.App., 228 P. 166, 168. A distinct and definite locality, and may mean a room, shop, building, or other definite area. Robinson v. State, 143 Miss. 247, 108 So. 903, 905, or a distinct portion of real estate. Ruble v. Ruble, Tex.Civ.App., 264 S.W. 1018, 1020.

The term "premises" is used in common parlance to signify land, with its appurtenances; but its usual and appropriate meaning in a conveyance is the interest or estate demised or granted by the deed. State v. French, 120 Ind. 229, 22 N.E. 108; Cooper v. Robinson, 302 Ill. 181, 134 N.E. 119, 120.

"Premises" of the employer as used in Workmen's Compensation Acts means on the property owned, leased, or controlled by the employer and so connected with the business in which the employee is engaged as to form a component or integral part of it. Werner v. Allegheny County, 153 Pa.Super. 10, 33 A.2d 451, 453.

The words "premises" and "plant" are sometimes distinguished; "premises" refers to place and territory, while "plant" includes place and territory, together with the appliances and things which go to make the facilities for the execution of the design and purposes of the enterprise. Martin v. Matson Nav. Co., D.C.Wash., 244 F. 976, 977.

In insurance law. The subject-matter insured in a policy. 4 Campb. 89.

PREMIUM. A reward for an act done. Brown v. Board of Police Com'rs of City of Los Angeles, 58 Cal.App.2d 473, 136 P.2d 617, 619.

A bounty or bonus; a consideration given to invite a loan or a bargain; as the consideration paid to the assignor by the assignee of a lease, or to the transferrer by the transferee of shares of stock, etc. So stock is said to be "at a premium" when its market price exceeds its nominal or face value. Boston & M. R. R. v. U. S., C.C.A. Mass., 265 F. 578, 579. See Par.

In granting a lease, part of the rent is sometimes capitalized and paid in a lump sum at the time the lease is granted. This is called a "premium."

The sum paid or agreed to be paid by an assured to the underwriter as the consideration for the insurance. Wade v. National Bank of Commerce, 144 Minn. 187, 174 N.W. 889, 890.

Premium note. A promissory note given by the insured for part or all of the amount of the premium.

Unearned premium. That portion which must be returned to insured on cancellation of policy. Ætna Ins. Co. v. Hyde, 315 Mo. 113, 285 S.W. 65, 71.

PREMIUM PUDICITIÆ. The price of chastity. A compensation for the loss of chastity, paid or promised to, or for the benefit of, a seduced female.

PREMUNIRE. See Præmunire.

PRENDA. In Spanish law. Pledge. White, New Recop. b. 2, tit. 7.

PRENDER, PRENDRE. L. Fr. To take. The power or right of taking a thing without waiting for it to be offered. See À Prendre.

PRENDER DE BARON. L. Fr. In old English law. A taking of husband; marriage. An exception or plea which might be used to disable a woman from pursuing an appeal of murder against the killer of her former husband. Staundef. P. C. lib. 3, c. 59.

PRENOMEN. (Lat.) The first or Christian name of a person. See Cas. Hardw. 286; 1 Tayl. 148.

PREPARATION. For offense consists in devising or arranging means or measures necessary for its commission, while attempt is direct movement toward commission after preparations are made. People v. George, 74 Cal.App. 440, 241 P. 97, 100. State v. Quick, 199 S.C. 256, 19 S.E.2d 101, 103.

PREPARE. To provide with necessary means; to make ready; to provide with what is appropriate or necessary. Brennan v. Northern Electric Co., 72 Mont. 35, 231 P. 388, 389.

PREPARED COAL. In anthracite coal trade means sizes of coal above pea. New York, N. H. & H. R. Co. v. Salter, 104 Conn. 728, 134 A. 220, 222.

PREPENSE. Forethought; preconceived; premeditated. See Territory v. Bannigan, 1 Dak. 451, 46 N.W. 597; People v. Clark, 7 N.Y. 385.

PREPONDERANCE. Greater weight of evidence, or evidence which is more credible and convincing to the mind. Button v. Metcalf, 80 Wis. 193, 49 N.W. 809. That which best accords with reason and probability. U. S. v. McCaskill, D.C.Fla., 200 F. 332. The word "preponderance" means something more than "weight"; it denotes a superiority of weight, or outweighing. The words are not synonymous, but substantially different. There is generally a "weight" of evidence on each side in case of contested facts. But juries cannot properly act upon the weight of evidence, in favor of the one having the *onus,* unless it overbear, in some degree, the weight upon the other side. Mathes v. Aggler & Musser Seed Co., 178 P. 713, 715, 179 Cal. 697; Barnes v. Phillips, 184 Ind. 415, 111 N.E. 419. See, also, Weight of Evidence.

It rests with that evidence which, when fairly considered, produces the stronger impression, and has the greater weight, and is more convincing as to its truth when weighed against the evidence in opposition thereto. S. Yamamoto v. Puget Sound Lumber Co., 84 Wash. 411, 146 P. 861, 863; but it does not mean greater number of witnesses. Heerdink v. Kohmescher, 94 Ind.App. 296, 180 N.E. 683, 684.

Preponderance of evidence may not be determined by the number of witnesses, but by the greater weight of all evidence, which does not necessarily mean the greater number of witnesses, but opportunity for knowledge, information possessed, and manner of testifying determines the weight of testimony. Garver v. Garver, 52 Colo. 227, 121 P. 165, 166, Ann.Cas.1913D, 674.

PREROGATIVE. An exclusive or peculiar privilege. The special power, privilege, immunity, or advantage vested in an official person, either generally, or in respect to the things of his office, or in an official body, as a court or legislature. Attorney General v. Blossom, 1 Wis. 317; Attorney General v. Eau Claire, 37 Wis. 443.

In English law. A power or will which is discretionary, and above and uncontrolled by any other will. That special pre-eminence which the king (or queen) has over and above all other persons, in right of his (or her) regal dignity. A term used to denote those rights and capacities which the sovereign enjoys alone, in contradistinction to others. 1 Bl.Comm. 239. It is sometimes applied by law writers to the thing over which the power or will is exercised, as fiscal prerogatives, meaning king's revenues; 1 Halleck, Int. L. 147.

PREROGATIVE COURT. In English law. A court established for the trial of all testamentary causes, where the deceased left *bona notabilia* within two different dioceses; in which case the probate of wills belonged to the archbishop of the province, by way of special prerogative. And all causes relating to the wills, administrations, or legacies of such persons were originally cognizable herein, before a judge appointed by the archbishop, called the "judge of the prerogative court," from whom an appeal lay to the privy council. 3 Bl.Comm. 66; 3 Steph.Comm. 432.

In New Jersey the prerogative court is the court of appeal from decrees of the orphans' courts in the several counties of the state. The court is held before the chancellor, under the title of the "ordinary." Flanigan v. Guggenheim Smelting Co., 63 N.J.L. 647, 44 A. 762; Robinson v. Fair, 128 U.S. 53, 9 S.Ct. 30, 32 L.Ed. 415.

PREROGATIVE LAW. That part of the common law of England which is more particularly applicable to the king. Com. Dig. tit. "Ley," A.

PREROGATIVE WRITS. In English law, the name is given to certain judicial writs issued by the courts only upon proper cause shown, never as a mere matter of right, the theory being that they involve a direct interference by the government with the liberty and property of the subject, and therefore are justified only as an exercise of the extraordinary power (prerogative) of the crown. In America, a theory has sometimes been advanced that these writs should issue only in cases *publici juris* and those affecting the sovereignty of the state, or its franchises or prerogatives, or the liberties of the people. But their issuance is now generally regulated by statute, and the use of the term "prerogative," in describing them, amounts only to a reference to their origin and history. These writs are the writs of mandamus, procedendo, prohibition, quo warranto, habeas corpus, and certiorari. Click v. Click, 98 W. Va. 419, 127 S.E. 194, 195.

PRES. L. Fr. Near. *Cy pres,* so near; as near. See Cy Pres.

PRESBYTER. Lat. In civil and ecclesiastical law. An elder; a presbyter; a priest. Cod. 1, 3, 6, 20; Nov. 6.

PRESBYTERIANISM. One of the principal systems of church polity known as the "Christian Protestant Church", occupying an intermediate position between episcopacy and congregationalism. Trustees of Pencader Presbyterian Church in Pencader Hundred v. Gibson, Del., 22 A.2d 782, 788. A religious faith or doctrine, based on the Westminster Confession of Faith and the Larger and Shorter Catechisms. In re McKean's Estate, 152 Pa.Super. 613, 33 A.2d 51, 52.

PRESBYTERIAN SYSTEM. That type of church organization in which the congregation is but a unit in a larger body which governs. Doughty v. Herr, 97 Ind.App. 427, 185 N.E. 657, 658.

PRESBYTERIUM. That part of the church where divine offices are performed; formerly applied to the choir or chancel, because it was the place appropriated to the bishop, priest, and other clergy, while the laity were confined to the body of the church. Jacob.

PRESCRIBABLE. That to which a right may be acquired by prescription.

PRESCRIBE. To assert a right or title to the enjoyment of a thing, on the ground of having hitherto had the uninterrupted and immemorial enjoyment of it.

To lay down authoritatively as a guide, direction, or rule; to impose as a peremptory order; to dictate; to point; to direct; to give as a guide, direction, or rule of action; to give law. State v. Truax, 130 Wash. 69, 226 P. 259, 260, 33 A.L.R. 1206; McMahon v. Devlin, 254 N.Y. 397, 173 N.E. 560, 561.

To direct; define; mark out. Field v. Marye, 83 Va. 882, 3 S.E. 707.

In modern statutes relating to matters of an administrative nature, such as procedure, registration, etc., it is usual to indicate in general terms the nature of the proceedings to be adopted, and to leave the details to be *prescribed* or regulated by rules or orders to be made for that purpose in pursuance of an authority contained in the act. Sweet. Mansfield v. People, 164 Ill. 611, 45 N.E. 976.

In a medical sense prescribe means to direct, designate, or order use of a remedy. State v. Whipple, 143 Minn. 403, 173 N.W. 801, 802.

PRESCRIPTION. A direction of remedy or remedies for a disease and the manner of using them; a formula for the preparation of a drug and medicine. People v. Cohen, 94 Misc. 355, 157 N.Y.S. 591, 593.

International Law

Acquisition of sovereignty over a territory through continuous and undisputed exercise of sovereignty over it during such a period as is necessary to create under the influence of historical development the general conviction that the present condition of things is in conformity with international order. State of Arkansas v. State of Tennessee, Ark. & Tenn., 60 S.Ct. 1026, 1030, 310 U.S. 563, 84 L.Ed. 1362.

Real Property Law

The name given to a mode of acquiring title to incorporeal hereditaments by immemorial or long-continued enjoyment. Zetrouer v. Zetrouer, 89 Fla. 253, 103 So. 625, 627. Hester v. Sawyers, 41 N.M. 497, 71 P.2d 646, 649, 112 A.L.R. 536.

To create an easement by "prescription," the use must have been open, continuous, exclusive, and under claim of right for statutory period. Burk v. Diers, 102 Neb. 721, 169 N.W. 263, 264.

"Prescription" is the term usually applied to incorporeal hereditaments, while "adverse possession" is applied to lands. Hindley v. Metropolitan El. R. Co., 85 N.Y.S. 561, 42 Misc. 56.

In Louisiana, prescription is defined as a manner of acquiring the ownership of property, or discharging debts, by the effect of time, and under the conditions regulated by law. Each of these prescriptions has its special and particular definition. The prescription by which the ownership of property is acquired, is a right by which a mere possessor acquires the ownership of a thing which he possesses by the continuance of his possession during the time fixed by law. The prescription by which debts are released, is a peremptory and perpetual bar to every species of action, real or personal, when the creditor has been silent for a certain time without urging his claim. Civ. Code La. arts. 3457–3459. In this sense of the term it is very nearly equivalent to what is elsewhere expressed by "limitation of actions," or rather, the "bar of the statute of limitations."

There is a distinction between title by "limitation" and a "prescriptive title," in that the latter is based upon a presumed grant to the property or use, while the former is not, Abel v. Love, 81 Ind.App. 328, 143 N.E. 515, 520, while the distinction between a highway by prescription and one by dedication is that "prescription" is an adverse holding under color of right, while a "dedication," whether expressed or implied, rests upon the consent of the owner. Hatch Bros. Co. v. Black, 25 Wyo. 416, 171 P. 267, 270.

"Prescription" and "custom" are frequently confounded in common parlance, arising perhaps from the fact that immemorial usage was essential to both of them; but, strictly, they materially differ from one another, in that custom is properly a local impersonal usage, such as borough-English, or postremogeniture, which is annexed to a given estate, while prescription is simply personal, as that a certain man and his ancestors, or those whose estate he enjoys, have immemorially exercised a right of pasture-common in a certain parish, and usage differs from both, for it may be either to persons or places. Again, prescription has its origin in a grant, evidenced by usage, and is allowed on account of its loss, either actual or supposed, and therefore only those things can be prescribed for which could be raised by a grant previously to 8 & 9 Vict. c. 106, § 2; but this principle does not necessarily hold in the case of a custom. Wharton; Olin v. Kingsbury, 168 N.Y.S. 766, 770, 181 App.Div. 348.

In General

Corporations by prescription. In English law. Those which have existed beyond the memory of man, and therefore are looked upon in law to be well created, such as the city of London.

Prescription act. The statute 2 & 3 Wm. IV. c. 71, passed to limit the period of prescription in certain cases.

Prescription in a que estate. A claim of prescription based on the immemorial enjoyment of the right claimed, by the claimant and those former owners "whose estate" he has succeeded to and holds. Donnell v. Clark, 19 Me. 182.

Time of prescription. The length of time necessary to establish a right claimed by prescription or a title by prescription. Before the act of 2 & 3 Wm. IV. c. 71, the possession required to constitute a prescription must have existed "time out of mind" or "beyond the memory of man," that is, before the reign of Richard I.; but the time of prescription, in certain cases, was much shortened by that act. 2 Steph.Comm. 35.

PRESENCE. Act, fact, or state of being in a certain place and not elsewhere, or within sight or call, at hand, or in some place that is being thought of. London v. Maryland Casualty Co., 10 Minn. 581, 299 N.W. 193, 194; the existence of a person in a particular place at a given time particularly with reference to some act done there and then. Besides actual presence, the law recognizes *constructive* presence, which latter may be predicated of a person who, though not on the very spot, was near enough to be accounted present by the law, or who was actively co-operating with another who was actually present. Mitchell v. Com., 33 Grat., Va., 868.

PRESENCE OF AN OFFICER. An offense is committed in "presence" or "view" of officer, within rule authorizing arrest without warrant, when officer sees act constituting it, though at distance, or when circumstances within his observation give probable cause for belief that defendant has committed offense, or when he hears disturbance created by offense and proceeds at once to scene, or if offense is continuing, or has not been fully consummated when arrest is made. Kennington-Saenger, Inc., v. Wicks, 168 Miss. 566, 151 So. 549, 551. Mantei v. State, 210 Wis. 1, 245 N.W. 683, 684.

PRESENCE OF THE COURT. A contempt is in the "presence of the court," if it is committed in the ocular view of the court, or where the court has direct knowledge of the contempt. People v. Cochrane, 307 Ill. 126, 138 N.E. 291, 293.

PRESENCE OF THE TESTATOR. Will is attested in presence of testator if witnesses are within range of any of testator's senses. In re Demaris' Estate, 166 Or. 36, 110 P.2d 571, 585, 586.

PRESENT, *v.* In English ecclesiastical law. To offer a clerk to the bishop of the diocese, to be instituted. 1 Bl.Comm. 389.

In criminal law. To find or represent judicially; used of the official act of a grand jury when they take notice of a crime or offense from their own knowledge or observation, without any bill of indictment laid before them. To lay before judge, magistrate, or governing body for action or consideration; submit as a petition or remonstrance for a decision or settlement to proper authorities. Haynes v. State, 108 Tex.Cr.R. 62, 299 S.W. 234, 235.

In the law of negotiable instruments. Primarily, to present is to tender or offer. Thus, to present a bill of exchange for acceptance or payment is to exhibit it to the drawee or acceptor, (or his authorized agent,) with an express or implied demand for acceptance or payment. Byles, Bills, 183, 201.

Claims are "presented" to the probate court when placed in the custody of the court, or filed or made a matter of record therein, State v. Probate Court of Hennepin County, 145 Minn. 344, 177 N.W. 354, 11 A.L.R. 242; and to present claim against city, within statute providing that claims for damages against the city must be "presented" to the city or town council and filed with the city or town clerk, means to hand to and leave with. Titus v. City of Montesano, 106 Wash. 608, 181 P. 43, 46.

PRESENT, *n.* A gift; a gratuity; anything presented or given.

PRESENT, *adj.* Now existing; at hand; relating to the present time; considered with reference to the present time.

Present conveyance. A conveyance made with the intention that it take effect at once and not at a future time. Prior v. Newsom, 144 Ark. 593, 223 S.W. 21, 22.

Present enjoyment. The immediate or present possession and use of an estate or property, as distinguished from such as is postponed to a future time.

Present estate. An estate in immediate possession; one now existing, or vested at the present time; as distinguished from a *future* estate, the enjoyment of which is postponed to a future time.

Present interest. One which entitles the owner to the immediate possession of the property.

Present time. A period of appreciable and generally considerable duration within which certain transactions are to take place. Corscot v. State, 178 Wis. 661, 190 N.W. 465, 468.

Present use. One which has an immediate existence, and is at once operated upon by the statute of uses.

PRESENTATION. In ecclesiastical law. The act of a patron or proprietor of a living in offering or presenting a clerk to the ordinary to be instituted in the benefice.

PRESENTATION OFFICE. The office of the lord chancellor's official, the secretary of presentations, who conducts all correspondence having reference to the twelve canonries and six hundred and fifty livings in the gift of the lord chancellor, and draws and issues the fiats of appointment. Sweet.

PRESENTATIVE ADVOWSON. See Advowson.

PRESENTEE. In ecclesiastical law. A clerk who has been presented by his patron to a bishop in order to be instituted in a church.

PRESENTER. One that presents.

PRESENTLY. Immediately; now; at once. A right which may be exercised "presently" is opposed to one in reversion or remainder.

PRESENTMENT.

Criminal Practice

The written notice taken by a grand jury of any offense, from their own knowledge or observation, without any bill of indictment laid before them at the suit of the government. 4 Bl. Comm. 301; Bennett v. Kalamazoo Circuit Judge, 183 Mich. 200, 150 N.W. 141, 142, Ann.Cas.1916E, 223. Presentments are also made in courts-leet and courts-baron, before the stewards. Steph. Comm. 644.

The writing which contains the accusation so presented by a grand jury. U. S. v. Hill, 1 Brock. 156, Fed.Cas.No.15,364.

In an extended sense, the term includes not only presentments properly so called, but also inquisitions of office and indictments found by a grand jury. 2 Hawk. Pl. Cr. c. 25, § 1.

An informal statement in writing, by the grand jury, representing to the court that a public offense has been committed which is triable in the county, and that there is reasonable ground for believing that a particular individual named or described therein has committed it. Eason v. State, 11 Ark. 482; State v. Kiefer, 90 Md. 165, 44 A. 1043. An accusation of crime, made by a grand jury from their own knowledge or from evidence furnished them by witnesses or by one or more of their members. In re Report of Grand Jury of Baltimore City, 152 Md. 616, 137 A. 370, 372.

The difference between a presentment and an inquisition is this: that the former is found by a grand jury authorized to inquire of offenses generally, whereas the latter is an accusation found by a jury specially returned to inquire concerning the particular offense. 2 Hawk.Pl.Cr. c. 25, § 6.

An indictment differs from a presentment in that the former must be indorsed "A true bill," followed by the signature of the grand jury foreman; a presentment is to be signed by all the grand jurors, and hence does not have to be indorsed "A true bill." Martin v. State, 127 Tenn. 324, 155 S.W. 129, 130.

The distinction between a special presentment and a bill of indictment, even under the old practice, was very thin; and in Georgia even this distinction has been abolished in practice for many years. The solicitor is not now required to frame any indictment on a special presentment, but the special presentment of the grand jury is returned into court, and upon it the defendant is arraigned and tried. It has the same force and effect as a bill of indictment. The only formal difference between the two is that a prosecutor prefers a bill of indictment, and a special presentment has no prosecutor, but, in theory, originates with the grand jury (Progress Club v. State, 12 Ga.App. 174, 76 S.E. 1029, 1030). Even this difference between a bill of indictment and a special presentment no longer exists, and the finding of the grand jury is prepared by the solicitor-general and called a bill of indictment, or a special presentment, at his will. Head v. State, 32 Ga.App. 331, 123 S.E. 34.

Negotiable Instruments

The production of a bill of exchange to the drawee for his acceptance, or to the drawer or acceptor for payment; or of a promissory note to the party liable, for payment of the same.

PRESENTS. The present instrument. The phrase "these presents" is used in any legal document to designate the instrument in which the phrase itself occurs.

PRESERVATION. Keeping safe from harm; avoiding injury, destruction, or decay. This term always presupposes a real or existing danger. State ex rel. Pollock v. Becker, 289 Mo. 660, 233 S.W. 641, 649. It is not creation, but the saving of that which already exists, and implies the continuance of what previously existed. McKeon v. Central Stamping Co., C.C.A.N.J., 264 F. 385, 387.

PRESERVE. With reference to foodstuffs, to prepare in such a manner as to resist decomposition or fermentation; to prevent from spoiling by the use of preservative substances with or without the use of the agency of heat. U. S. v. Dodson, D.C.Cal., 268 F. 397, 403. The word "preserved," when applied to meat, implies that it has been so processed that its preservation is of permanent character. U. S. v. Conkey & Co., 12 Ct.Cust.App. 552, 554.

PRESIDE. To occupy the place of authority or of president, chairman, moderator, etc., to direct, control or regulate proceedings as chief officer or to preside at public meetings, to preside over the senate. Drake v. Drake, 187 Ga. 423, 1 S.E.2d 573, 575. To preside over a court is to "hold" it,—to direct, control, and govern it as the chief officer. A judge may "preside" whether sitting as a sole judge or as one of several judges. Smith v. People, 47 N.Y. 334.

PRESIDENT. One placed in authority over others; a chief officer; a presiding or managing officer; a governor, ruler, or director. The chairman, moderator, or presiding officer of a legislative or deliberative body, appointed to keep order, manage the proceedings, and govern the administrative details of their business.

The chief officer of a corporation, company, board, committee, etc., generally having the main direction and administration of their concerns. Roe v. Bank of Versailles, 167 Mo. 406, 67 S.W. 303. The term does not ordinarily include "vice president." First Nat. Bank v. C. H. Meyers & Co., Tex.Civ.App., 283 S.W. 265, 266.

The chief executive magistrate of a state or nation, particularly under a democratic form of government; or of a province, colony, or dependency.

In the United States, the word is commonly used in reference to the private as well as public character of the nation's chief executive. U. S. v. Metzdorf, D.C.Mont., 252 F. 933, 937.

In English law. A title formerly given to the king's lieutenant in a province; as the president of Wales. Cowell.

This word is also an old though corrupted form of "precedent," (*q. v.*,) used both as a French and English word. *Le president est rare.* Dyer, 136.

PRESIDENT JUDGE. A title sometimes given to the presiding judge. It was formerly used in England and is now used in the courts of common pleas in Pennsylvania. So in the old Virginia court of appeals. The lord chief justice is now permanent president of the high court of justice in England. The title president is said to have a high Norman flavor. Inderwick, King's Peace 225.

PRESIDENT OF THE COUNCIL. In English law. A great officer of state; a member of the cabinet. He attends on the sovereign, proposes business at the council-table, and reports to the sovereign the transactions there. 1 Bl. Comm. 230.

PRESIDENT OF THE UNITED STATES. The official title of the chief executive officer of the federal government in the United States.

PRESIDENTIAL ELECTORS. A body of electors chosen in the different states, whose sole duty it is to elect a president and vice-president of the United States. Each state appoints, in such manner as the legislature thereof may direct, a number of electors equal to the whole number of senators and representatives to which the state is entitled in congress. Const. U. S. art. 2, § 1; McPherson v. Blacker, 13 S.Ct. 3, 146 U.S. 1, 36 L.Ed. 869. The usual method of appointment is by general ballot, so that each voter in a state votes for the whole number of electors to which his state is entitled.

PRESIDING JUDGE. This term, in statutes requiring exceptions to be signed by the judge who presides at the trial, means the judge presiding at the trial of which a review is sought; hence exceptions saved at a first trial, contained in bill of exceptions signed by the judge presiding at a second trial, are not reviewable. Tucker v. Yandow, 100 Vt. 169, 135 A. 600, 601.

PRESS. In old practice. A piece or skin of parchment, several of which used to be sewed together in making up a roll or record of proceedings. 1 Bl. Comm. 183; Townsh. Pl. 486.

Metaphorically, the aggregate of publications issuing from the press, or the giving publicity to one's sentiments and opinions through the medium of printing; as in the phrase "liberty of the press."

PRESSING SEAMEN. See Impressment.

PRESSING TO DEATH. See Peine Forte et Dure.

PREST. In old English law. A duty in money to be paid by the sheriff upon his account in the exchequer, or for money left or remaining in his hands. Cowell.

PREST MONEY. A payment which binds those who receive it to be ready at all times appointed, being meant especially of soldiers. Cowell.

PRESTATION. In old English law. A presting or payment of money. Cowell. A payment or performance; the rendering of a service.

In international law. The term is sometimes used of a right by which neutral vessels may be appropriated by way of hire by a belligerent on payment of freight beforehand. In 1870 the Prussian troops sank six British vessels to obstruct navigation in the river Seine. Indemnification was subsequently made. 1 Halleck, Int. L. Baker's Ed. 520.

PRESTATION MONEY. A sum of money paid by archdeacons yearly to their bishop; also purveyance. Cowell.

PRESTIMONY, or PRÆSTIMONIA. In canon law. A fund or revenue appropriated by the founder for the subsistence of a priest, without being erected into any title or benefice, chapel, prebend, or priory. It is not subject to the ordinary; but of it the patron, and those who have a right from him, are the collators. Wharton.

PRESUMABLY. Fit to be assumed as true in advance of conclusive evidence; credibly deduced; fair to suppose; by reasonable supposition or inference; what appears to be entitled to belief without direct evidence. Kurth v. Continental Life Ins. Co., 234 N.W. 201, 202, 211 Iowa 736; Mitchell v. Equitable Life Assur. Soc. of U. S., 205 N.C. 726, 172 S.E. 495, 496.

PRESUME. To assume beforehand. Hickman v. Union Electric Light & Power Co., Mo.Sup., 226 S.W. 570, 576. In a more technical sense, to believe or accept upon probable evidence. It is not so strong a word as "infer"; Morford v. Peck, 46 Conn. 385; though often used with substantially the same meaning; State v. Schuck, 51 N.D. 875, 201 N.W. 342, 345.

PRESUMPTIO. See Præsumptio; Presumption.

PRESUMPTION. Of fact. An inference affirmative or disaffirmative of the truth or falsehood of any proposition or fact drawn by a process of probable reasoning in the absence of actual certainty of its truth or falsehood, or until such certainty can be ascertained. Best, Pres. § 3.

An inference affirmative or disaffirmative of the existence of a disputed fact, drawn by a judicial tribunal, by a process of probable reasoning, from some one or more matters of fact, either admitted in the cause or otherwise satisfactorily established. Best, Pres. § 12. An inference as to the existence of a fact not known, arising from its connection with the facts that are known, and founded upon a knowledge of human nature and the motives which are known to influence human conduct. Hawes v. State of Georgia, 42 S.Ct. 204, 258 U.S. 1, 66 L.Ed. 431. An inference as to the existence of some fact drawn from the existence of some other fact; an inference which common sense draws from circumstances usually occurring in such cases. 1 Phil.Ev. 436; 3 B. & Ad. 890. A strong probability or reasonable supposition. In re Van Tassell's Will, 196 N.Y.S. 491, 494, 119 Misc. 478. That which may be assumed without proof or taken for granted as self-evident result of human reason and experience. Watkins v. Prudential Ins. Co. of America, 315 Pa. 497, 173 A. 644, 647, 95 A.L.R. 869.

A conclusion reached by means of the weight of proved circumstances. Marquet v. Ætna Life Ins. Co., 128 Tenn. 213, 159 S.W. 733, 736, L.R.A.1915B, 749, Ann.Cas.1915B, 677.

Presumptions of fact are not the subject of fixed rules, but are merely natural presumptions, such as appear, from common experience, to arise from the particular circumstances of any case. Some of these are "founded upon a knowledge of the human character, and of the motives, passions, and feelings by which the mind is usually influenced." 1 Stark.Ev. 27. They may be said to be the conclusions drawn by the mind from the natural connection of the circumstances disclosed in each case, or, in other words, from circumstantial evidence.

Of Law. A rule of law that courts and judges shall draw a particular inference from a particular fact, or from particular evidence, unless and until the truth of such inference is disproved. Steph. Ev. 4; Lane v. Missouri Pac. Ry. Co., 132 Mo. 4, 33 S.W. 645. A rule which, in certain cases, either forbids or dispenses with any ulterior inquiry. 1 Greenl. Ev. § 14.

A consequence which the law or the judge draws from a known fact to a fact unknown. In re Cowdry's Will, 77 Vt. 359, 60 A. 141, 142. A rule of law laid down by the judge and attaching to evidentiary facts certain procedural consequences as to the duty of production of other evidence by the opponent. If the opponent does offer evidence to the contrary, the presumption disappears, and the case stands upon the facts and the reasonable inferences to be drawn therefrom. Kramer v. Nichols-Chandler Home Building & Brokerage Co., 103 Okl. 208, 229 P. 767, 768. A conclusion, which, in the absence of evidence upon the exact question, the law draws from other proof made or from facts judicially noticed or both, the burden of proof cast by it being satisfied by the presentation of evidence sufficient to convince the jury that the probabilities of truth are against the party whom the presumption relieves of the burden of proof. State ex rel. Detroit Fire & Marine Ins. Co. v. Ellison, 268 Mo. 239, 187 S.W. 23, 26. Presumptions of law are divided into *conclusive* presumptions and *disputable* presumptions.

A conclusive presumption, called also an "absolute" or "irrebuttable" presumption, is a rule of law determining the quantity of evidence requisite for the support of a particular averment which is not permitted to be overcome by any proof that the fact is otherwise. 1 Greenl.Ev. § 15; U. S. v. Clark, 5 Utah, 226, 14 P. 288. It is an inference which the court will draw from the proof, which no evidence, however strong, will be permitted to overturn. Lyon v. Guild, 5 Heisk., Tenn., 175, 182; Best, Pres. § 20.

A disputable presumption, called also an "inconclusive" or "rebuttable" presumption, is an inference of law which holds good until it is invalidated by proof or a stronger presumption. Best, Pres. § 29; Livingston v. Livingston, 4 Johns.Ch., N.Y., 287, 8 Am.Dec. 562.

Mixed. There are also certain mixed presumptions, or presumptions of fact recognized by law, or presumptions of mixed law and fact. These are certain presumptive inferences, which, from their strength, importance, or frequent occurrence, attract, as it were, the observation of the law. The presumption of a "lost grant" falls within this class. Best, Ev. 436. See Dickson v. Wilkinson, 3 How. 57, 11 L.Ed. 491.

Distinction. The distinctions between presumptions of law and presumptions of fact are, first, that in regard to presumptions of law a certain inference must be made whenever the facts appear which furnish the basis of the inference; while in case of other presumptions a discretion more or less extensive is vested in the tribunal as to drawing the inference. 9 B. & C. 643. Second, in case of presumptions of law, the court may draw the inference whenever the requisite facts are developed in pleading; Steph. Pl. 382; while other presumptions can be made only by the intervention of a jury. Presumptions of law are reduced to fixed rules, and form a part of the system of jurisprudence to which they belong; presumptions of fact are derived wholly and directly from the circumstances of the particular case, by means of the common experience of mankind. 2 Stark. Ev. 684; Douglass v. Mitchell's Ex'r, 35 Pa. 440.

It has been suggested as the characteristic distinction between presumptions of law and presumptions of fact, either simple or mixed, that when the former are disregarded by a jury, a new trial is granted as matter of right, but that the disregard of any of the latter, however strong and obvious, is only ground for a new trial at the discretion of the court; Chamb.Best, Ev. § 327; 1 Term 167; Turnley v. Black, 44 Ala. 159; Goggans v. Monroe, 31 Ga. 331. A presumption of law is a juridical postulate that a particular predicate is universally assignable to a particular subject. A presumption of fact is a logical argument from a fact to a fact; or, as the distinction is sometimes put, it is an argument which infers a fact otherwise doubtful from a fact which is proved. 2 Whart.Ev. § 1226; Smith v. Gardner, 36 Neb. 741, 55 N.W. 245.

Presumptions are divided into *præsumptiones juris et de jure,* otherwise called "irrebuttable presumptions," (often, but not necessarily, fictitious,) which the law will not suffer to be rebutted by any counter-evidence; as, that an infant under seven years is not responsible for his actions; *præsumptiones juris tantum,* which hold good in the absence of counter-evidence, but against which counter-evidence may be admitted; and *præsumptiones hominis,* which are not necessarily conclusive, though no proof to the contrary be adduced. Mozley & Whiteley.

A *natural* presumption is that species of presumption, or process of probable reasoning, which is exercised by persons of ordinary intelligence, in inferring one fact from another, without reference to any technical rules. Otherwise called *"præsumptio hominis."* Burrill, Circ. Ev. 11, 12, 22, 24.

Legitimate presumptions have been denominated "violent" or "probable," according to the amount of weight which attaches to them. Such presumptions as are drawn from inadequate grounds are termed "light" or "rash" presumptions. Brown.

Evidence and Presumptions

Presumptions are evidence or have the effect of evidence. Brill v. Brill, 38 Cal.App.2d 741, 102 P. 2d 534, 537. Westberg v. Willde, 14 Cal.2d 360, 94 P.2d 590, 593.

Examples are disputable presumptions. Clary v. Lindley, 30 Cal.App.2d 571, 86 P.2d 920, 921; Equitable Life Assur. Soc. of United States v. Irelan, C.C.A.Mont., 123 F.2d 462, 464; legal presumption, Asbury v. Goldberg, 8 Cal.App.2d 70, 47 P.2d 311, 313. Presumption against suicide, Brown v. Metropolitan Life Ins. Co., 233 Iowa 5, 7 N.W.2d 21, 24; presumption arising from doctrine of res ipsa loquitur, Vonault v. O'Rourke, 97 Mont. 92, 33 P.2d 535, 540; presumption from facts that automobile was driven by agent acting within scope of employment, Judson v. Bee Hive Auto Service Co., 136 Or. 1, 294 P. 588, 589; presumption of due execution of will in will contest, In re Stone's Estate, 59 Cal.App.2d 263, 138 P.2d 710, 713; presumption of exercise of care for own safety, Eastman v. Atchison, T. & S. F. Ry. Co., 51 Cal.App.2d 653, 125 P.2d 564, 570; presumption of fairness and regularity of private transactions, Ross v. Real Estate Inv. Co., 135 Cal.App. 563, 28 P.2d 52, 54.

Presumption of innocence, Williams v. State, 30 Ala.App. 495, 8 So.2d 271, 274; presumption of negligence from driving on left side of highway, Temple v. De Mirjian, 51 Cal. App.2d 559, 125 P.2d 544, 546.

Presumption of ownership arising from possession, Lane v. Whitaker, 50 Cal.App.2d 327, 123 P.2d 53, 55; presumption that insured's wound causing death was not intentionally inflicted, Brown v. Metropolitan Life Ins. Co., 233 Iowa 5, 7 N.W.2d 21, 24; rebuttable presumption, Graybiel v. Consolidated Ass'ns, 16 Cal.App.2d 20, 60 P.2d 164, 167.

Presumptions are not "evidence". Walters v. Western & Southern Life Ins. Co., 318 Pa. 382, 178 A. 499, 501; McKiver v. Theo. Hamm Brewing Co., 67 S.D. 613, 297 N.W. 445; Equitable Life Assur. Soc. of United States v. MacDonald, C.C.A.Wash., 96 F.2d 437, 439. Examples are presumption against partial intestacy, Heffenger v. Heffenger, 89 N.H. 530, 3 A.2d 95, 97; presumption against suicide, Jefferson Standard Life Ins. Co. v. Clemmer, C.C.A.Va., 79 F.2d 724, 730, 103 A.L.R. 171; Reliance Life Ins. Co. v. Burgess, C.C.A.Mo., 112 F.2d 234, 238; presumption arising under law, Dunn v. Goldman, 11 N.J.Misc. 833, 168 A. 299, 300; presumption of continuance of condition or status, State ex rel. Northwestern Development Corporation v. Gehrz, 230 Wis. 412, 283 N.W. 827, 832; Rupp v. Guardian Life Ins. Co. of America, Mo.App., 170 S.W.2d 123, 128; presumption of due care, Morris v. Chicago, M., St. P. & P. R. Co., 1 Wash.2d 587, 97 P.2d 119, 127; Silvia v. Caizz, 63 R.I. 172, 7 A.2d 704, 707; presumption of fact, American Alliance Ins. Co. v. Brady Transfer & Storage Co., C.C.A. Iowa, 101 F.2d 144, 149; presumption of innocence, United States v. Nimerick, C.C.A.Vt., 118 F.2d 464, 467; British America Assur. Co. of Toronto, Canada v. Bowen, C.C.A. Okl., 134 F.2d 256, 259; presumption of negligence of railroad, St. Louis-San Francisco Ry. Co. v. Mangum, 199 Ark. 767, 136 S.W.2d 158, 160; Carter v. Kurn, C.C.A.Ark., 127 F.2d 415, 420; presumption of ownership from registration of motor vehicle, Pioneer Mut. Compensation Co. v. Diaz, 142 Tex. 184, 177 S.W.2d 202, 204; presumption that driver failed to see automobile because he was not looking, Page v. Lockley, Tex.Civ.App., 176 S.W.2d 991, 997; presumption that employee was acting in course of employment arising from evidence of ownership of automobile causing accident, Frick v. Bickel, 115 Ind.App. 114, 54 N.E.2d 436, 440; presumption that tax assessors in making valuation have done their duty, People ex rel. Wallington Apartments v. Miller, 288 N.Y. 31, 41 N.E.2d 445, 446; statutory presumptions, Kelly v. Hudson Coal Co., 119 Pa.Super. 405, 179 A. 753, 754; Allstaedt v. Ochs, 302 Mich. 232, 4 N.W.2d 530, 532.

A presumption is a substitute for evidence, Siler v. Siler, 152 Tenn. 379, 277 S.W. 886, 887; U. S. ex rel. Scharlon v. Pulver, C.C.A.N.Y., 54 F.2d 261, 263; but is not itself evidence, being rather an aid to legal reasoning applied to particular subjects; Van Ausdall v. Van Ausdall, 48 R.I. 106, 135 A. 850, 851. It is a rule about the duty of producing evidence. Duggan v. Bay State St. Ry. Co., 230 Mass. 370, 119 N.E. 757, 760, L.R.A.1918E, 680; 4 Wigm.Ev. §§ 2490, 2491, 2511. Presumptions will serve in the place of "evidence". Bohmont v. Moore, 138 Neb. 784, 295 N.W. 419, 424. While presumptions, in tort actions, that automobile was in possession of owner at time of accident and that taxicab was being operated in usual course of cab company's business, are not "evidence," they serve as evidence in proper case until overcome by competent evidence to contrary. Van Court v. Lodge Cab Co., 198 Wash. 530, 89 P.2d 206, 211.

PRESUMPTION OF INNOCENCE. Conclusion drawn by law in favor of one brought to trial on criminal charge, requiring acquittal unless guilt is established by sufficient evidence. Blim v. United States, C.C.A.Ill., 68 F.2d 484, 487.

PRESUMPTION OF SURVIVORSHIP. A presumption of fact, to the effect that one person survived another, applied for the purpose of determining a question of succession or similar matter, in a case where the two persons perished in the same catastrophe, and there are no circumstances extant to show which of them actually died first, except those on which the presumption is founded, viz., differences of age, sex, strength, or physical condition.

PRESUMPTIVE. Resting on presumption; created by or arising out of presumption; inferred; assumed; supposed; as, "presumptive" damages, evidence, heir, notice, or title. See those titles.

PRESUMPTIVE EVIDENCE. This term has several meanings in law. 1 Wig. Evi. § 25, n. 3.

(1) Any evidence which is not direct and positive; the proof of minor or other facts incidental to or usually connected with the fact sought to be proved which, when taken together, inferentially establish or prove the fact in question to a reasonable degree of certainty; evidence drawn by human experience from the connection of cause and effect and observation of human conduct; the proof of facts from which, with more or less certainty, according to the experience of mankind of their more or less universal connection, the existence of other facts can be deduced. In this sense the term is nearly equivalent to "circumstantial" evidence. See 1 Starkie, Ev. 558; 2 Saund. Pl. & Ev. 673; State v. Kornstett, 62 Kan. 221, 61 P. 805, 808; Ezzard v. U. S., C.C.A.Okl., 7 F.2d 808, 810. Best says presumptive evidence is as original as direct, and that presumption of a fact is as good as any other proof when it is legitimate. Jones v. Granite State Fire Ins. Co., 90 Me. 40, 37 A. 326, 328. "Circumstantial evidence" is sometimes used as synonymous with presumptive evidence, but not with strict accuracy; for presumptive evidence is not necessarily and in all cases what is usually understood by circumstantial evidence. See 1 Stark.Ev. 478; Whart.Ev. 1, 2, 15. The word presumption imports an inference from facts known, based upon previous experience of the ordinary connection between the two, and, the word itself implies a certain relation between fact and inference. Circumstances, however, generally but not necessarily lead to particular inferences; for the facts may be indisputable, and yet their relation to the principal fact may be only apparent, not real; and even where the connection is real, the deduction may be erroneous. Circumstantial and presumptive evidence differ therefore as genus and species. Will, Cir.Ev. 17.

(2) Evidence which must be received and treated as true and sufficient until rebutted by other testimony; as, where a statute provides that certain facts shall be presumptive evidence of guilt, of title, etc. State v. Mitchell, 119 N.C. 784, 25 S.E. 783; State v. Intoxicating Liquors, 80 Me. 57, 12 A. 794.

(3) Also, it means evidence that admits of explanation or contradiction by other evidence, as distinguished from conclusive evidence. Burrill, Circ.Ev. 89. "Presumptive evidence" is synonymous with prima facie evidence. State v. Simon, 163 Minn. 317, 203 N.W. 989, 990; Watson v. Rollins, 18 Ala.App. 125, 90 So. 60, 61. See, also, Presumption; Prima Facie Evidence.

PRÊT. In French law. Loan. A contract by which one of the parties delivers an article to the other, to be used by the latter, on condition of his returning, after having used it, the same article in nature or an equivalent of the same species and quality. Duverger.

PRÊT À INTÉRÊT. Loan at interest. A contract by which one of the parties delivers to the other a sum of money, or commodities, or other movable or fungible things, to receive for their use a profit determined in favor of the lender. Duverger.

PRÊT À USAGE. Loan to use. A contract by which one of the parties delivers an article to the other, to be used by the latter, the borrower agreeing to return the specific article after having used it. Duverger. A contract identical with the *commodatum* (*q. v.*) of the civil law.

PRÊT DE CONSOMMATION. Loan for consumption. A contract by which one party delivers to the other a certain quantity of things, such as are consumed in the use, on the undertaking of the borrower to return to him an equal quantity of the same species and quality. Duverger. A contract identical with the *mutuum* (*q. v.*) of the civil law.

PRÊTE-NOM. One who lends his name. Peterson v. Moresi, 191 La. 932, 186 So. 737, 739.

PRETEND. To feign or simulate; to hold that out as real which is false or baseless. Brown v. Perez, Tex.Civ.App., 25 S.W. 983; King v. U. S., C.C.A.Fla., 279 F. 103. As to the rule against the buying and selling of "any pretended right or title," see Pretensed Right or Title.

PRETENSE. See False Pretenses.

PRETENSED, or PRETENDED, TITLE STATUTE. The English statute 32 Hen. VIII. c. 9, § 2. It enacts that no one shall sell or purchase any pretended right or title to land, unless the vendor has received the profits thereof for one whole year before such grant, or has been in actual possession of the land, or of the reversion or remainder, on pain that both purchaser and vendor shall each forfeit the value of such land to the king and the prosecutor. See 4 Broom & H. Comm. 150.

PRETENSED RIGHT or TITLE. Where one is in possession of land, and another, who is out of possession, claims and sues for it. Here the pretensed right or title is said to be in him who so claims and sues for the same. Mod. Cas. 302.

PRETENSES. Allegations sometimes made in a bill in chancery for the purpose of negativing an anticipated defense. Hunt, Eq. pt. I. c. 1.

False pretenses. See that title.

PRÉTENTION. In French law. The claim made to a thing which a party believes himself entitled to demand, but which is not admitted or adjudged to be his.

The words *right, action,* and *prétention* are usually joined; not that they are synonymous, for *right* is something positive and certain, *action* is what is demanded, while *prétention* is sometimes not even accompanied by a demand.

PRETER LEGAL. Not agreeable to law; exceeding the limits of law; not legal.

PRETERMIT. To "pretermit" is to pass by, to omit or to disregard, e. g., failure of testator to mention his children in his will.

PRETERMITTED HEIR. A child or other descendant omitted by a testator. Where a testator unintentionally fails to mention in his will, or make provision for, a child, either living at the date of the execution of the will or born thereafter, a statute may provide that such child, or the issue of a deceased child, shall share in the estate as though the testator had died intestate. In re Price's Estate, 56 Cal.App.2d 335, 132 P.2d 485.

PRETEXT. Ostensible reason or motive assigned or assumed as a color or cover for the real reason or motive; false appearance, pretense. State v. Ball, 27 Neb. 604, 43 N.W. 398.

In international law. A reason alleged as justificatory, but which is so only in appearance, or which is even absolutely destitute of all foundation. The name of "pretexts" may likewise be applied to reasons which are in themselves true and well-founded, but, not being of sufficient importance for undertaking a war, [or other international act,] are made use of only to cover ambitious views. Vatt. Law Nat. bk. 3, c. 3, § 32.

PRETIUM. Lat. Price; cost; value; the price of an article sold.

PRETIUM AFFECTIONIS. An imaginary value put upon a thing by the fancy of the owner, and growing out of his attachment for the specific article, its associations, his sentiment for the donor, etc. Bell; The H. F. Dimock, C.C.A.Mass., 77 F. 233, 23 C.C.A. 123; Burr v. Bloomsburg, 101 N.J. Eq. 615, 138 A. 876, 878.

PRETIUM PERICULI. The price of the risk, *e. g.* the premium paid on a policy of insurance; also the interest paid on money advanced on bottomry or respondentia.

PRETIUM SEPULCHRI. A mortuary (*q. v.*).

PRETIUM SUCCEDIT IN LOCUM REI. The price stands in the place of the thing sold. 1 Bouv. Inst. no. 939; 2 Bulst. 312.

PRETORIAL COURT. In the colony of Maryland, a court for the trial of capital crimes, consisting of the lord proprietor or his lieutenant-general, and the council. Also called *Pretorial.* Murray, New English Dict.

PRETORIUM. In Scotch law. A courthouse, or hall of justice. 3 How. State Tr. 425.

PREUVE. Fr. "Evidence" in the sense of the term in English law, and of *probatio* in the canon and civil law. The French word *évidence,* Latin *evidentia,* is commonly restricted to the testimony of the senses. 1 Best, Evid. § 11.

PREVAIL. To be or become effective or effectual, to be in force, to obtain, to be in general use or practice, to be commonly accepted or adopted; to exist. Atlantic Coast Line R. Co. v. Gamble, 155 Fla. 678, 21 So.2d 348, 350.

PREVAILING PARTY. That one of the parties to a suit who successfully prosecutes the action or successfully defends against it, prevailing on the main issue, even though not to the extent of his original contention. Weston v. Cushing, 45 Vt. 531; Hawkins v. Nowland, 53 Mo. 329; Huggins v. Hill, Mo.Sup., 236 S.W. 1054, 1055.

The one in whose favor the decision or verdict is rendered and judgment entered. United States v. Minneapolis, St. P. & S. S. M. Ry. Co., D.C.Minn., 235 F. 951, 955; Dunne v. New York Telephone Co., 176 N.Y.S. 519, 520, 107 Misc. 439; O'Hare v. Peacock Dairies, 28 Cal.App.2d 562, 82 P.2d 1112, 1113. The party ultimately prevailing when the matter is finally set at rest. Comparri v. James Reading, Inc., 121 N.J.L. 591, 3 A.2d 802, 803. The party prevailing in interest, and not necessarily the prevailing person. Gertz v. Milwaukee Electric Ry. & Light Co., 153 Wis. 475, 140 N.W. 312, 316. To be such does not depend upon the degree of success at different stages of the suit, but whether, at the end of the suit, or other proceeding, the party who has made a claim against the other, has successfully maintained it. Bangor & P. R. Co. v. Chamberlain, 60 Me. 286. Thus, where the court grants defendant a new trial after verdict for plaintiff, defendant is the "prevailing party" on that trial, and entitled to costs, although the plaintiff again gets verdict on retrial. Klock Produce Co. v. Diamond Ice & Storage Co., 98 Wash. 676, 168 P. 476, 478.

PREVAILING PRICES. This term, as used in a contract for the sale of paper which had no market price, as it required special manufacture and came only from one source, means such prices as were set by that source in the usual course of business, without undue enlargement of cost, and with a reasonable profit in addition. New York Oversea Co. v. China, Japan & South American Trading Co., 200 N.Y.S. 449, 451, 206 App.Div. 242.

PREVARICATION. In the civil law. The acting with unfaithfulness and want of probity; deceitful, crafty, or unfaithful conduct; particularly, such as is manifested in concealing a crime. Dig. 47, 15, 6.

In English law. A collusion between an informer and a defendant, in order to a feigned prosecution. Cowell. Any secret abuse committed in a public office or private commission; willful concealment or misrepresentation of truth, by giving evasive or equivocating evidence.

PREVENT. To hinder, frustrate, prohibit, impede, or preclude; to obstruct; to intercept. Burr v. Williams, 20 Ark. 185; Orme v. Atlas Gas and Oil Co., 217 Minn. 27, 13 N.W.2d 757, 761. To stop or intercept the approach, access, or performance of a thing. Webster, Dict.; U. S. v. Souders, 27 Fed.Cas.1,269; Green v. State, 109 Ga. 536, 35 S. E. 97.

PREVENTION. In the civil law. The right of a judge to take cognizance of an action over which he has concurrent jurisdiction with another judge.

In canon law. The right which a superior person or officer has to lay hold of, claim, or transact an affair prior to an inferior one, to whom otherwise it more immediately belongs. Wharton.

PREVENTION OF CRIMES ACT. The statute 34 & 35 Vict. c. 112, passed for the purpose of securing a better supervision over habitual criminals. This act provides that a person who is for a second time convicted of crime may, on his second conviction, be subjected to police supervision for a period of seven years after the expiration of the punishment awarded him. Penalties are imposed on lodging-house keepers, etc., for harboring thieves or reputed thieves. There are also provisions relating to receivers of stolen property, and dealers in old metals who purchase the same in small quantities. This act repeals the habitual criminals act of 1869, (32 & 33 Vict. c. 99.) Brown.

PREVENTIVE JUSTICE. The system of measures taken by government with reference to the direct prevention of crime. It generally consists in obliging those persons whom there is probable ground to suspect of future misbehavior to give full assurance to the public that such offense as is apprehended shall not happen, by finding pledges or securities to keep the peace, or for their good behavior. 4 Bl. Comm. 251; 4 Steph. Comm. 290; Bradley v. Malen, 37 N.D. 295, 164 N.W. 24, 25.

PREVENTIVE SERVICE. The name given in England to the coast-guard, or armed police, forming a part of the customs service, and employed in the prevention and detection of smuggling.

PREVIOUS. Antecedent; prior. Webster, Dict. Sometimes limited in meaning to "next prior to" or "next preceding." Syracuse Sav. Bank v. Brown, 42 N.Y.S.2d 156, 158, 181 Misc. 999.

PREVIOUS INTENTIONS ARE JUDGED BY SUBSEQUENT ACTS. Dumont v. Smith, 4 Denio (N.Y.) 319, 320.

PREVIOUS QUESTION. In parliamentary practice, the question whether a vote shall be taken on the main issue, or not, brought forward before the main or real question is put by the speaker and for the purpose of avoiding, if the vote is in the negative, the putting of this question. The motion is in the form "that the question be now put," and the mover and seconder vote against it. It is described in May, Parl. Prac. 277.

In the house of representatives of the United States and in many state legislatures the object of moving the previous question is to cut off debate and secure immediately a vote on the question under consideration. Hinds, Precedents in the House of Repr.

PREVIOUSLY. An adverb of time, used in comparing an act or state named with another act or state, subsequent in order of time, for the purpose of asserting the priority of the first. Lebrecht v. Wilcoxon, 40 Iowa 94.

PREVISORS, STATUTE OF. A statute of 25 Edw. III. St. 6, for the protection of spiritual patrons against the pope. Maitl. Canon L. 69.

PRICE. Something which one ordinarily accepts voluntarily in exchange for something else. Herb v. Hallowell, 304 Pa. 128, 154 A. 582, 584. The consideration given for the purchase of a thing; Hibernia Bank & Trust Co. v. McCall Bros. Planting & Mfg. Co., 140 La. 763, 73 So. 857, 858;—usually in money; Embden State Bank v. Boyle, 50 N.D. 573, 196 N.W. 820, 821.

For "Fair Market Price," see that title.

Sum of money which an article is sold for; but this is simply because property is generally sold for money, not because the word has necessarily such a restricted meaning. Among writers on political economy, who use terms with philosophical accuracy, the word "price" is not always or even generally used as denoting the moneyed equivalent of property sold. They generally treat and regard price as the equivalent or compensation, in whatever form received, for property sold. The Latin word from which "price" is derived sometimes means "reward," "value," "estimation," "equivalent." Hudson Iron Co. v. Alger, 54 N.Y. 177. Amount which a prospective seller indicates as the sum for which he is willing to sell; market value. Ara v. Rutland, Tex.Civ.App., 172 S.W. 993, 994. The term may be synonymous with cost, Williams v. Hybskmann, 311 Mo. 332, 278 S.W. 377, 379; and with value, Southeastern Express Co. v. Nightingale, 33 Ga.App. 515, 126 S.E. 915, as well as with consideration, though price is not always identical either with consideration, Oregon Home Builders v. Crowley, 87 Or. 517, 170 P. 718, 721; or with value, Chicago, K. & W. R. Co. v. Parsons, 51 Kan. 408, 32 P. 1083.

"Price" within ceiling price regulations of the Office of Price Administration is the amount paid by the purchaser. Boyles v. Stapleton, D.C.Colo., 53 F.Supp. 336, 340.

PRICE CURRENT. A list or enumeration of various articles of merchandise, with their prices, the duties, if any, payable thereon, when imported or exported, with the drawbacks occasionally allowed upon their exportation, etc. Wharton.

PRICE DISCRIMINATION. Within anti-trust laws selling to one at a price and refusing to sell to another at any price by one engaged in interstate commerce, in absence of reason for refusal to sell. Sherman Anti-Trust Act, 15 U.S.C.A. § 1 et seq.; Shaw's v. Wilson-Jones Co., D.C.Pa., 26 F. Supp. 713, 714.

PRICE EXPECTANCY. In the moving picture industry, the minimum receipts which distributors expect to realize from the exhibition of pictures;—used interchangeably with "minimum sale" and "exhibition value." Export & Import Film Co. v. B. P. Schulberg Productions, 125 Misc. 756, 211 N.Y.S. 838, 839.

PRICKING FOR SHERIFFS. In England, when the yearly list of persons nominated for the office of sheriff is submitted to the sovereign, he takes a pin, and to insure impartiality, as it is said, lets the point of it fall upon one of the three names nominated for each county, etc., and the person upon whose name it chances to fall is sheriff for the ensuing year. This is called "pricking for sheriffs." Atk. Sher. 18.

PRICKING NOTE. Where goods intended to be exported are put direct from the station of the warehouse into a ship alongside, the exporter fills up a document to authorize the receiving the goods on board. This document is called a "pricking note," from a practice of pricking holes in the paper corresponding with the number of packages counted into the ship. Hamel, Cust. 181.

PRIDE GAVEL. A rent or tribute. Tayl. Gavelk. 112.

PRIEST. A minister of a church. A person in the second order of the ministry, as distinguished from bishops and deacons.

A pastor is a permanent official of a parish, and more than a priest, who holds a position of spiritual power without reference to locality. Dupont v. Pettelier, 120 Me. 114, 113 A. 11, 13.

PRIMA FACIE. Lat. At first sight; on the first appearance; on the face of it; so far as can be judged from the first disclosure; presumably; a fact presumed to be true unless disproved by some evidence to the contrary. State ex rel. Herbert v. Whims, 68 Ohio App. 39, 38 N.E.2d 596, 599.

PRIMA FACIE CASE. Such as will suffice until contradicted and overcome by other evidence. Pacific Telephone & Telegraph Co. v. Wallace, 158 Or. 210, 75 P.2d 942, 947. A case which has proceeded upon sufficient proof to that stage where it will support finding if evidence to contrary is disregarded. In re Hoagland's Estate, 126 Neb. 377, 253 N.W. 416.

A litigating party is said to have a *prima facie* case when the evidence in his favor is sufficiently strong for his opponent to be called on to answer it. A *prima facie* case, then, is one which is established by sufficient evidence, and can be overthrown only by rebutting evidence adduced on the other side. In some cases the only question to be considered is whether there is a *prima facie* case or no. Thus a grand jury are bound to find a true bill of indictment, if the evidence before them creates a *prima facie* case against the accused; and for this purpose, therefore, it is not necessary for them to hear the evidence for the defense. Mozley & Whitley. And see State v. Hardelein, 169 Mo. 579, 70 S.W. 130; State v. Lawlor, 28 Minn. 216, 9 N.W. 698.

PRIMA FACIE EVIDENCE. Evidence good and sufficient on its face; such evidence as, in the judgment of the law, is sufficient to establish a given fact, or the group or chain of facts constituting the party's claim or defense, and which if not rebutted or contradicted, will remain sufficient. State v. Burlingame, 146 Mo. 207, 48 S.W. 72.

Evidence which suffices for the proof of a particular fact until contradicted and overcome by other evidence. Dodson v. Watson, 110 Tex. 355, 220 S.W. 771, 772, 11 A.L.R. 583. Evidence which, standing alone and unexplained, would maintain the proposition and warrant the conclusion to support which it is introduced. Gilmore v. Modern Brotherhood of America, 186 Mo.App. 445, 171 S.W. 629, 632. An inference or presumption of law, affirmative or negative of a fact, in the absence of proof, or until proof can be obtained or produced to overcome the inference. People v. Thacher, 1 Thomp. & C., N.Y., 167. A litigating party is said to have a *prima facie* case when the evidence in his favor is sufficiently strong for his opponent to be called on to answer it. A *prima facie* case, then, is one which is established by sufficient evidence, and can be overthrown only by rebutting evidence adduced on the other side. Mozley & Whitley. State v. Lawlor, 28 Minn. 216, 9 N.W. 698. A "prima facie case" is one which is apparently established by evidence adduced by plaintiff in support of his case up to the time such evidence stands unexplained and uncontradicted. Morrison v. Flowers, 308 Ill. 189, 139 N.E. 10, 12. A "prima facie case" is one in which the evidence in favor of a proposition is sufficient to support a finding in its favor, if all of the evidence to the contrary be disregarded. Schallert v. Boggs, Tex.Civ.App., 204 S.W. 1061, 1062. See, also, Presumptive Evidence.

PRIMA PARS ÆQUITATIS ÆQUALITAS. The radical element of equity is equality.

PRIMA TONSURA. The first mowing; a grant of a right to have the first crop of grass. 1 Chit. Pr. 181.

PRIMÆ IMPRESSIONIS. A case *primœ impressionis* (of the first impression) is a case of a new kind, to which no established principle of law or precedent directly applies, and which must be decided entirely by reason as distinguished from authority.

PRIMÆ PRECES. Lat. In the civil law. An imperial prerogative by which the emperor exercised the right of naming to the first prebend that became vacant after his accession, in every church of the empire. 1 Bl. Comm. 381.

PRIMAGE. In mercantile law. Formerly, a small allowance or compensation payable to the master and mariners of a ship or vessel; to the former for the use of his cables and ropes to discharge the goods of the merchant; to the latter for lading and unlading in any port or haven. Abb. Shipp. 404; Peters v. Speights, 4 Md. Ch. 381; Blake v. Morgan, 3 Mart. O. S. (La.) 381. It is sometimes called the master's hat-money.

It is no longer, however, a gratuity to the master, unless especially stipulated; but it belongs to the owners or freighters, and is nothing but an increase of the freight rate. Carr v. Austin & N. W. R. Co., C.C.Tex., 14 F. 419.

PRIMARIA ECCLESIA. The mother church. 1 Steph. Comm. (7th Ed.) 118.

PRIMARY. First; principal; chief; leading. First in order of time, or development, or in intention. State v. Erickson, 44 S.D. 63, 182 N.W. 315, 316, 13 A.L.R. 1189.

As to primary "Conveyance," "Election," "Obligation," and "Vein," see those titles.

PRIMARY ALLEGATION. The opening pleading in a suit in the ecclesiastical court. It is also called a "primary plea."

PRIMARY DISPOSAL OF THE SOIL. In acts of congress admitting territories as states, and providing that no laws shall be passed interfering with the primary disposal of the soil, this means the disposal of it by the United States government when it parts with its title to private persons or corporations acquiring the right to a patent or deed in accordance with law. See Oury v. Goodwin, 3 Ariz. 255, 26 P. 377; Topeka Commercial Security Co. v. McPherson, 7 Okl. 332, 54 P. 489.

PRIMARY EVIDENCE. That kind of evidence which, under every possible circumstance, affords the greatest certainty of the fact in question. Thus, a written instrument is itself the best possible evidence of its existence and contents.

Primary evidence means original or first-hand evidence; the best evidence that the nature of the case admits of; the evidence which is required in the first instance, and which must fail before secondary evidence can be admitted. That evidence which the nature of the case or question suggests as the proper means of ascertaining the truth. See Cross v. Baskett, 17 Or. 84, 21 P. 47; Scott v. State, 3 Tex. App. 103, 104. It is the particular means of proof which is the most natural and satisfactory of which the case admits, and includes the best evidence which is available to a party and procurable under the existing situation, and all evidence falling short of such standard, and which in its nature suggests there is better evidence of the same fact, is "secondary evidence." Best v. Equitable Life Assur. Soc., Mo.App., 299 S.W. 118, 120. See, also, Best Evidence.

PRIMARY POWERS. The principal authority given by a principal to his agent. It differs from "mediate powers." Story, Ag. § 58.

PRIMARY PURPOSE. That which is first in intention; which is fundamental. State v. Erickson, 44 S.D. 63, 182 N.W. 315, 317, 13 A.L.R. 1189. The principal or fixed intention with which an act or course of conduct is undertaken. Carlson v. Carpenter Contractors' Ass'n, 224 Ill.App. 430, 447.

PRIMATE. A chief ecclesiastic; an archbishop who has jurisdiction over his province, or one of several metropolitans presiding over others. Exarch comes nearest to it in the Greek church. Thus the archbishop of Canterbury is styled "Primate of all England;" the archbishop of York is "Primate of England." Wharton.

PRIME, *n.* In French law. The price of the risk assumed by an insurer; premium of insurance. Emerig. Traite des Assur. c. 3, § 1, nn. 1, 2.

PRIME, *v.* To stand first or paramount; to take precedence or priority of; to outrank; as, in the sentence "taxes prime all other liens."

PRIME COST. The true price paid for goods upon a *bona fide* purchase. U. S. v. Sixteen Packages, 2 Mas. 53, Fed.Cas.No.16,303.

PRIME MINISTER. The responsible head of a ministry or executive government, especially of a monarchical government. Webster, Dict. In England, he is the head of the cabinet, and usually holds the office of First Lord of the Treasury. The office was unknown to the law until 1906, when the prime minister was accorded a place in the order of precedence. Lowell, Gov. of Engl. 68. "He is the principal executive of the British constitution, and the sovereign a cog in the mechanism." Bagehot.

PRIME SERJEANT. In English law. The king's first serjeant at law.

PRIMER. A law French word, signifying first; primary.

PRIMER ELECTION. A term used to signify first choice; *e. g.*, the right of the eldest co-parcener to first choose a purpart.

PRIMER FINE. On suing out the writ or *præcipe* called a "writ of covenant," there was due to the crown, by ancient prerogative, a *primer fine*, or a noble for every five marks of land sued for. That was one-tenth of the annual value. 1 Steph. Comm. (7th Ed.) 560.

PRIMER SEISIN. See Seisin.

PRIMICERIUS. In old English law. The first of any degree of men. 1 Mon. Angl. 838.

PRIMITIÆ. In English law. First fruits; the first year's whole profits of a spiritual preferment. 1 Bl. Comm. 284.

PRIMITIVE OBLIGATION. See Obligation.

PRIMO BENEFICIO. Lat. A writ directing a grant of the first benefice in the sovereign's gift. Cowell.

PRIMO EXECUTIENDA EST VERBI VIS, NE SERMONIS VITIO OBSTRUATUR ORATIO, SIVE LEX SINE ARGUMENTIS. Co. Litt. 68. The full meaning of a word should be ascertained at the outset, in order that the sense may not be lost by defect of expression, and that the law be not without reasons [or arguments].

PRIMO VENIENTI. Lat. To the one first coming. An executor anciently paid debts as they were presented, whether the assets were sufficient to meet all debts or not. Stim. Law Gloss.

PRIMOGENITURE. The state of being the first-born among several children of the same parents; seniority by birth in the same family. The superior or exclusive right possessed by the eldest son, and particularly, his right to succeed to the estate of his ancestor, in right of his seniority by birth, to the exclusion of younger sons.

PRIMOGENITUS. Lat. In old English law. A first-born or eldest son. Bract. fol. 33; 1 Ves. 290; 3 Maule & S. 25; 8 Taunt. 468.

PRIMUM DECRETUM. Lat. In the canon law. The first decree; a preliminary decree granted on the non-appearance of a defendant, by which the plaintiff was put in possession of his goods, or of the thing itself which was demanded. Gilb. Forum Rom. 32, 33. In the courts of admiralty, this name is given to a provisional decree. Bacon, Abr. *The Court of Admiralty* (E).

PRINCE. In a general sense, a sovereign; the ruler of a nation or state. More particularly, the son of a king or emperor, or the issue of a royal family; as princes of the blood. The chief of any body of men. Webster; The Lucy H., D.C.Fla., 235 F. 610, 612.

Prince of Wales. A title given to the eldest son of the British sovereign or to the heir apparent to the crown. He is so created by letters patent, and is also created Earl of Chester. He is Duke of Cornwall by inheritance. Mary and Elizabeth, though each, at the time, was only heiress presumptive, were created Princesses of Wales by Henry VIII.

Princes and princesses of the royal blood. In English law. The younger sons and daughters of the sovereign, and other branches of the royal family who are not in the immediate line of succession.

PRINCEPS. Lat. In the civil law. The prince; the emperor.

PRINCEPS ET RESPUBLICA EX JUSTA CAUSA POSSUNT REM MEAM AUFERRE. 12 Coke, 13. The prince and the commonwealth, for a just cause, can take away my property.

PRINCEPS LEGIBUS SOLUTUS EST. The emperor is released from the laws; is not bound by the laws. Dig. 1, 3, 31; Halifax, Anal. prev. vi, vii, note.

PRINCEPS MAVULT DOMESTICOS MILITES QUAM STIPENDIARIOS BELLICIS OPPONERE CASIBUS. Co. Litt. 69. A prince, in the chances of war, had better employ domestic than stipendiary troops.

PRINCESS ROYAL. In English law. The eldest daughter of the sovereign. 3 Steph. Comm. 450.

PRINCIPAL, *adj.* Chief; leading; most important or considerable; primary; original. Highest in rank, authority, character, importance, or degree. Bland v. Board of Trustees of Galt Joint Union High School Dist., 67 Cal.App. 784, 228 P. 395, 397.

As to principal "Challenge," "Contract," "Obligation," "Office," and "Vein," see those titles.

Principal establishment. In the law concerning domicile, the principal domestic establishment. Mosely v. Dabezies, 142 La. 256, 76 So. 705, 706.

Principal fact. In the law of evidence. A fact sought and proposed to be proved by evidence of other facts (termed "evidentiary facts") from which it is to be deduced by inference. A fact which is the principal and ultimate object of an inquiry, and respecting the existence of which a definite belief is required to be formed. 3 Benth. Jud. Ev. 3; Burrill, Circ. Ev. 3, 119.

PRINCIPAL, *n.* The source of authority or right. A superintendent, as of a school district. Williams v. School Dist. No. 189, 104 Wash. 659, 177 P. 635, 636. The capital sum of a debt or obligation, as distinguished from interest or other additions to it. Christian v. Superior Court, 122 Cal. 117, 54 P. 518. The corpus or capital of an estate in contradistinction to the income; "income" being merely the fruit of capital. Carter v. Rector, 88 Okl. 12, 210 P. 1035, 1037.

Criminal Law

A chief actor or perpetrator, or an aider and abettor actually or constructively present at the commission of the crime, as distinguished from an "accessory." At common law, a principal in the first degree is he that is the actor or absolute perpetrator of the crime; and, in the second degree, he who is present, aiding and abetting the fact to be done. 4 Bl. Comm. 34. Cooney v. Burke, 11 Neb. 258, 9 N.W. 57.

Neither a principal in the first degree nor one in the second degree need be actually present when the offense is consummated, Smith v. State, 21 Tex.App. 107, 17 S.W. 552; State v. Morey, 126 Me. 323, 138 A. 474, 475; for the presence of a principal in the second degree may be merely constructive; *e. g.*, where he stays outside and keeps watch or guard, Pierce v. State, 130 Tenn. 24, 168 S.W. 851, 855, Ann.Cas.1916B, 137. In misdemeanors, anyone participating is a principal, Boggs v. Commonwealth, 218 Ky. 782, 292 S.W. 324, 325.

All persons acting together in commission of offense, and persons advising or agreeing to commission thereof and present when committed, though not aiding therein, are principals. Stringfellow v. State, 111 Tex.Cr.R. 504, 14 S.W.2d 1031, 1032. A criminal offender is either a principal or an accessory. A principal is either the actor (*i. e.*, the actual perpetrator of the crime) or else is present, aiding and abetting, the fact to be done; an accessory is he who is not the chief actor in the offense, nor yet present at its performance, but is some way concerned therein, either before or after the fact committed. 1 Hale, P.C. 613, 618; People v. Ah Gee, 37 Cal.App. 1, 174 P. 371, 372. All persons concerned in the commission of crime, whether it be felony or misdemeanor, and whether they directly commit the act constituting the offense, or aid and abet in its commission, though not present, are principals. State v. Curtis, 30 Idaho 537, 165 P. 999, 1000. Some of these statutes, and other similar ones, expressly abrogate the common-law distinction between a principal and an accessory before the fact. People v. Wood, 56 Cal.App. 431, 205 P. 698. All persons are principals who are guilty of acting together in the commission of an offense. Vernon's Ann.P.C. art. 66. A principal is one who advises or agrees to the commission of an offense, and is present when it is done. Vernon's Ann.P.C. art. 69. See Pizana v. State, 81 Tex.Cr.R. 81, 193 S.W. 671, 673; Middleton v. State, 86 Tex.Cr.R. 307, 217 S.W. 1046, 1052. "Accomplice," by virtue of statute in Vernon's Ann.P.C. art. 70, means one who is not present at the commission of the offense, Serrato v. State, 74 Tex.Cr.R. 413, 171 S.W. 1133, 1144, and is practically synonymous with the common-law accessory before the fact. McKeen v. State, 7 Tex.Cr.R. 631; Strong v. State, 52 Tex.Cr.R. 133, 105 S.W. 785. But the ordinary meaning of "accomplice" includes all the *particeps criminis*, whether principals in the first or second degree or mere accessories. It means one who at common law might have been convicted either as principal or accessory before the fact. People v. Crossman, 241 N.Y. 138, 149 N.E. 330, 331.

Law of Agency

The employer or constitutor of an agent; the person who gives authority to an agent or attorney to do some act for him. Adams v. Whittlesey, 3 Conn. 567. Called also constituent or chief. Mech. Agency § 3. One, who, being competent *sui juris* to do any act for his own benefit or on his own account, confides it to another person to do for him. 1 Domat, b. 1, tit. 15.

Law of Guaranty and Suretyship

The person primarily liable, for whose performance of his obligation the guarantor or surety has become bound. See Rollings v. Gunter, 211 Ala. 671, 101 So. 446, 448.

Old English Law

An heir-loom, mortuary, or corse-present. Wharton.

Property Law

A term used as the correlative of "accessory" or "incident" to denote the more important or valuable subject, with which others are connected in a relation of dependence or subservience, or to which they are incident or appurtenant. Thus, it is said that the incident shall pass by the grant of the principal; but not the principal by the grant of the incident. Co. Litt. 152*a*.

General

Principal of the house. In English law. The chief person in some of the inns of chancery.

Undisclosed principal. One not disclosed in the contract. Unruh v. Roemer, 135 Minn. 127, 160 N.W. 251, 252.

Vice principal. In the law of master and servant, this term means one to whom the employer has confided the entire charge of the business or of a distinct branch of it, giving him authority to superintend, direct, and control the workmen and make them obey his orders, the master himself exercising no particular oversight and giving no particular orders, or one to whom the master has delegated a duty of his own, which is a direct, personal, and absolute obligation. Durkin v. Kingston Coal Co., 171 Pa. 193, 33 A. 237, 29 L.R.A. 808, 50 Am.St.Rep. 801.

The term "vice principal," as used in the fellow-servant law, includes any servant who represents the master in the discharge of those personal or absolute duties which every master owes to his servants; such duties being often referred to as the nonassignable duties of the master, among which are, providing suitable machinery and appliances, a safe place to work, the proper inspection and repair of premises and appliances, the selection and retention of suitable servants, the establishment of proper rules and regulations, and the instruction of servants as to the kind and manner of work to be done by them. International Cotton Mills v. Webb, 22 Ga.App. 309, 96 S.E. 16; Wolverine Oil Co. v. Kingsbury, 66 Okl. 271, 168 P. 1021, 1022. To make a servant a vice principal, it is only necessary that he have authority to direct and supervise the work and to hire and discharge subordinate servants engaged in the work. Modern Order of Praetorians v. Nelson, Tex.Civ.App., 162 S.W. 17, 18; Daggett v. American Car & Foundry Co., Mo.App., 284 S.W. 855, 856. However, a servant may be a vice principal, though he has no power to employ and discharge men under him. Wilson v. Counsell, 182 Ill.App. 79, 84.

PRINCIPALIS. Lat. Principal; a principal debtor; a principal in a crime.

PRINCIPALIS DEBET SEMPER EXCUTI ANTEQUAM PERVENIATUR AD FIDEIJUSSORES. The principal should always be exhausted before coming upon the sureties. 2 Inst. 19.

PRINCIPIA DATA SEQUUNTUR CONCOMITANTIA. Given principles are followed by their concomitants.

PRINCIPIA PROBANT, NON PROBANTUR. Principles prove; they are not proved. Fundamental principles require no proof; or, in Lord Coke's words, "they ought to be approved, because they cannot be proved." 3 Coke, 50a.

PRINCIPIIS OBSTA. Withstand beginnings; oppose a thing in its early stages, if you would do so with success. Branch, Princ.

PRINCIPIORUM NON EST RATIO. There is no reasoning of principles; no argument is required to prove fundamental rules. 2 Bulst. 239.

PRINCIPIUM EST POTISSIMA PARS CUJUSQUE REI. 10 Coke, 49. The principle of anything is its most powerful part.

PRINCIPLE. A fundamental truth or doctrine, as of law; a comprehensive rule or doctrine which furnishes a basis or origin for others; a settled rule of action, procedure, or legal determination. A truth or proposition so clear that it cannot be proved or contradicted unless by a proposition which is still clearer. That which constitutes the essence of a body or its constituent parts. 8 Term 107. That which pertains to the theoretical part of a science. Hemler v. Richland Parish School Board, 142 La. 133, 76 So. 585, 587.

In patent law. The principle of a machine is the particular means of producing a given result by a mechanical contrivance. Parker v. Stiles, 5 McLean 44, 63, Fed.Cas.No.10,749. It is the *modus operandi*, or that which applies, modifies, or combines mechanical powers to produce a certain result; and, so far, a principle, if new in its application to a useful purpose, may be patentable. Barrett v. Hall, 1 Mason, 470, Fed.Cas.No. 1,047. The word "principles," as applied to inventions, designate those elements which in combination compose the claims. Schweyer Electric & Mfg. Co. v. Regan Safety Devices Co., C.C.A. N.Y., 4 F.2d 970, 973.

PRINT, *n.* A term which includes most of the forms of figures or characters or representations, colored or uncolored, that may be impressed on a yielding surface. U. S. v. Harman, D.C.Kan., 38 F. 827, 829.

PRINT, *v.* To stamp by direct pressure as from the face of types, plates, or blocks covered with ink or pigments, or to impress with transferred characters or delineations by the exercise of force as with a press or other mechanical agency. Acme Coal Co. v. Northrup Nat. Bank of Iola, Kan., 23 Wyo. 66, 146 P. 593, L.R.A. 1915D, 1084.

The term properly refers to the mechanical work of production, whereas "publish" pertains to the issuance from the place where printed. In re Monrovia Evening Post, 199 Cal. 263, 248 P. 1017, 1018; In re McDonald, 187 Cal. 158, 201 P. 110, 111. But a finding that a newspaper is "published" in a certain county may be deemed sufficient to show that it was "printed" in such county. McCormick v. Higgins, 190 Ill.App. 241, 261. Similarly, a requirement that matter be "printed" in a particular county may be construed as a direction that it be "published" there. In re Publication of Docket of Supreme Court, Mo. Sup., 232 S.W. 454, 455.

PRINTING. The impress of letters or characters upon paper, or upon other substance;—implying a mechanical act. Daly v. Beery, 178 N.W. 104, 106, 45 N.D. 287. The art of impressing letters; the art of making books or papers by impressing legible characters. Arthur v. Moller, 97 U.S. 365, 24 L.Ed. 1046; Le Roy v. Jamison, 15 Fed.Cas. 373; Forbes Lithograph Mfg. Co. v. Worthington, C.C.Mass., 25 F. 899, 900.

The term may include typewriting. Sunday v. Hagenbuch, 18 Pa.Co.Ct. 540, 541. Compare State v. Oakland, 69 Kan. 784, 77 P. 696. It may also include mimeographing within the meaning of the copyright statutes. Macmillan Co. v. King, D.C.Mass., 223 F. 862, 867.

Printing paper. This term does not necessarily include news print paper. Davis v. Age-Herald Pub. Co., C.C.A.Ala., 293 F. 591, 593 (tariff of an interstate carrier).

Public printing. Such as is directly ordered by the legislature, or performed by the agents of the government authorized to procure it to be done. Ellis v. State, 4 Ind. 1.

PRIOR. Lat. The former; earlier; preceding; preferable or preferred.

Prior petens. The person first applying.

PRIOR, *n.* The chief of a convent; next in dignity to an abbot.

PRIOR, *adj.* Earlier; elder; preceding; superior in rank, right, or time; as, a prior lien, mortgage, or judgment. See Fidelity Insurance, Trust & Safe Deposit Co. v. Roanoke Iron Co., C.C.Va., 81 F. 439, 447.

Prior creditor. Generally, the creditor who is accorded priority in payment from the assets of his debtor. Richey v. Ferguson, 93 Kan. 152, 143 P. 497.

PRIOR LIEN. This term commonly denotes a first or superior lien, and not one necessarily antecedent in time. Titus v. United States Smelting, Refining & Mining Exploration Co., D.C.N.Y., 231 F. 205, 210.

PRIOR TEMPORE POTIOR JURE. He who is first in time is preferred in right. Co. Litt. 14*a;* Broom, Max. 354, 358; 2 P. Wms. 491; 1 Term 733; 9 Wheat. 24, 6 L.Ed. 23; 15 A. (Pa.) 730.

PRIORI PETENTI. To the person first applying. In probate practice, where there are several persons equally entitled to a grant of administration, (*e. g.*, next of kin of the same degree,) the rule of the court is to make the grant *priori petenti*, to the first applicant. Browne, Prob. Pr. 174; Coote, Prob. Pr. 173, 180.

PRIORITY. Precedence; going before. A legal preference or precedence. When two persons have similar rights in respect of the same subject-matter, but one is entitled to exercise his right to the exclusion of the other, he is said to have priority.

In old English law. An antiquity of tenure, in comparison with one not so ancient. Cowell.

PRISAGE. An ancient hereditary revenue of the crown, consisting in the right to take a certain quantity from cargoes of wine imported into England. In Edward I.'s reign it was converted into a pecuniary duty called "butlerage." 2 Steph. Comm. 561.

PRISE. Fr. In French law. Prize; captured property. Ord. Mar. liv. 3, tit. 9. Dole v. Insurance Co., 6 Allen (Mass.) 373.

PRISEL EN AUTER LIEU. L. Fr. A taking in another place. A plea in abatement in the action of replevin. 2 Ld. Raym. 1016, 1017.

PRISON. A public building or other place for the confinement or safe custody of persons, whether as a punishment imposed by the law or otherwise in the course of the administration of justice. Sturtevant v. Com., 158 Mass. 598, 33 N.E. 648; Copeland v. Commonwealth, 214 Ky. 209, 282 S.W. 1077.

The words "prison" and "penitentiary" are used synonymously to designate institutions for the imprisonment of persons convicted of the more serious crimes, as distinguished from reformatories and county or city jails. State v. Delmonto, 110 Conn. 298, 147 A. 825, 826.

Originally it was distinguished from jail, which was a place for confinement, not for punishment, and the popular modern tendency is to use the term in contradistinction to jail, to denote particularly a state penitentiary. Copeland v. Commonwealth, 282 S.W. 1077, 214 Ky. 209. But the term may also properly apply to a county jail. State v. Killian, 173 N.C. 792, 92 S.E. 499, 501.

As used in a statute pertaining to escapes, the word may include territory outside a state prison, where an inmate, when at work outside, is under the surveillance of prison guards. People v. Vanderburg, 67 Cal.App. 217, 227 P. 621.

PRISON BOUNDS. The limits of the territory surrounding a prison, within which an imprisoned debtor, who is out on bonds, may go at will. See Gaol.

PRISON BREAKING, or BREACH. The common-law offense of one who, being lawfully in custody, escapes from the place where he is confined, by the employment of force and violence. This offense is to be distinguished from "rescue," (*q. v.*,) which is a deliverance of a prisoner from lawful custody by a third person. 2 Bish. Crim. Law, § 1065.

PRISONAM FRANGENTIBUS, STATUTE DE. The English statute 1 Edw. II. St. 2, (in Rev. St. 23 Edw. I.,) whereby it is felony for a felon to break prison, but misdemeanor only for a misdemeanant to do so. 1 Hale, P. C. 612.

PRISONER. One who is deprived of his liberty; one who is against his will kept in confinement or custody. U. S. v. Curran, C.C.A.N.Y., 297 F. 946, 950. A person restrained of his liberty upon any action, civil or criminal, or upon commandment. Cowell.

A person on trial for crime. "The *prisoner* at the bar." The jurors are told to "look upon the *prisoner*." The court, after passing sentence, gives orders to "remove the *prisoner*." Hairston v. Com., 97 Va. 754, 32 S.E. 797.

PRISONER AT THE BAR. An accused person, while on trial before the court, is so called. One accused of crime, who is actually on trial, is in legal effect a "prisoner at the bar," notwithstanding he has given bond for his appearance at the trial. He is a "prisoner" if held in custody either under bond or other process of law, or when physically held under arrest, and when actually on trial he is a "prisoner at the bar." The term is as applicable to one on trial for a misdemeanor as for a felony. Allen v. State, 18 Ga.App. 1, 88 S.E. 100.

PRISONER OF WAR. One who has been captured in war while fighting in the army of the public enemy.

PRIST. L. Fr. Ready. In the old forms of oral pleading, this term expressed a tender or joinder of issue.

PRIUS VITIIS LABORAVIMUS, NUNC LEGIBUS. 4 Inst. 76. We labored first with vices, now with laws.

PRIVACY, RIGHT OF. The right to be let alone, the right of a person to be free from unwarranted publicity. Holloman v. Life Ins. Co. of Virginia, 192 S.C. 454, 7 S.E.2d 169, 171, 127 A.L.R. 110. The right of an individual (or corporation) to withhold himself and his property from public scrutiny, if he so chooses. It is said to exist only so far as its assertion is consistent with law or public policy, and in a proper case equity will interfere, if there is no remedy at law, to prevent an injury threatened by the invasion of, or infringement upon, this right from motives of curiosity, gain, or malice. Federal Trade Commission v. American Tobacco Co., 44 S.Ct. 336, 264 U.S. 298, 68 L.Ed. 696, 32 A.L.R. 786.

PRIVATE. Affecting or belonging to private individuals, as distinct from the public generally. Not official; not clothed with office. People v. Powell, 280 Mich. 699, 274 N.W. 372, 373, 111 A.L.R. 721.

As to private "Act," "Agent," "Bill," "Boundary," "Bridge," "Business," "Carrier," "Chapel," "Corporation," "Detective," "Dwelling House," "Easement," "Examination," "Ferry," "Nuisance," "Pond," "Property," "Prosecutor," "Rights," "Road," "Sale," "School," "Seal," "Statute," "Stream," "Trust," "Water," "War," "Way," 'Wharf," and "Wrongs," see those titles.

PRIVATE BILL OFFICE. An office of the British parliament where the business of securing private acts of parliament is conducted.

PRIVATE EXAMINATION. An examination or interrogation, by a magistrate, of a married woman who is grantor in a deed or other conveyance, held out of the presence of her husband, for the purpose of ascertaining whether her will in the matter is free and unconstrained. Hadley v. Geiger, 9 N.J.L. 233.

PRIVATE INTERNATIONAL LAW. A name used by some writers to indicate that branch of the law which is now more commonly called "Conflict of Laws" (*q. v.*).

PRIVATE LAW. As used in contradistinction to public law, the term means all that part of the law which is administered between citizen and citizen, or which is concerned with the definition, regulation, and enforcement of rights in cases where both the person in whom the right inheres and the person upon whom the obligation is incident are private individuals. See Public Law.

PRIVATE PERSON. An individual who is not the incumbent of an office.

PRIVATE STREET. Literally speaking, this is an impossibility, for no way can be both private and a street. It may be one or the other, but not both. Greil v. Stollenwerck, 201 Ala. 303, 78 So. 79, 82.

PRIVATEER. A vessel owned, equipped, and armed by one or more private individuals, and duly commissioned by a belligerent power to go on cruises and make war upon the enemy, usually by preying on his commerce. A private vessel commissioned by the state by the issue of a letter of marque to its owner to carry on all hostilities by sea, presumably according to the laws of war. Formerly a state issued letters of marque to its own subjects, and to those of neutral states as well, but a privateersman who accepted letters of marque from both belligerents was regarded as a pirate. By the Declaration of Paris (April, 1856), privateering was abolished, but the United States, Spain, Mexico, and Venezuela did not accede to this declaration. It has been thought that the constitutional provision empowering Congress to issue letters of marque deprives it of the power to join in a permanent treaty abolishing privateering. 28 Am.L.Rev. 615; 24 Am.L.Rev. 902; 19 Law Mag. & Rev. 35.

PRIVATIO PRÆSUPPONIT HABITUM. 2 Rolle, 419. A deprivation presupposes a possession.

PRIVATION. A taking away or withdrawing. Co. Litt. 239.

PRIVATIS PACTIONIBUS NON DUBIUM EST NON LÆDI JUS CÆTERORUM. There is no doubt that the rights of others [third parties] cannot be prejudiced by private agreements. Dig. 2, 15, 3, pr.; Broom, Max. 697.

PRIVATORUM CONVENTIO JURI PUBLICO NON DEROGAT. The agreement of private individuals does not derogate from the public right, [law.] Dig. 50, 17, 45, 1; 9 Coke, 141; Broom, Max. 695.

PRIVATUM. Lat. Private. *Privatum jus,* private law. Inst. 1, 1, 4.

PRIVATUM COMMODUM PUBLICO CEDIT. Private good yields to public. The interest of an individual should give place to the public good. Jenk. Cent. p. 223, case 80.

PRIVATUM INCOMMODUM PUBLICO BONO PENSATUR. Private inconvenience is made up for by public benefit. Jenk. Cent. p. 85, case 65; Broom, Max. 7.

PRIVEMENT ENCEINTE. Fr. Pregnant privately. A term used to signify that a woman is pregnant, but not yet quick with child.

PRIVIES. Those who are partakers or have an interest in any action or thing, or any relation to another. Harrington v. Harrington, 3 Miss. (2 How.) 701, 717; Brown v. Fidelity Union Trust Co., 126 N.J.Eq. 406, 9 A.2d 311, 326; Hamelik v. Sypek, 274 N.Y.S. 875, 152 Misc. 799. They are of six kinds:

(1) Privies of blood; such as the heir to his ancestor.

(2) Privies in representation; as executors or administrators to their deceased testator or intestate.

(3) Privies in estate; as grantor and grantee, lessor and lessee, assignor and assignee, etc.

(4) Privies in respect to contract.

(5) Privies in respect of estate and contract; as where the lessee assigns his interest, but the contract between lessor and lessee continues, the lessor not having accepted of the assignee.

(6) Privies in law; as the lord by escheat, a tenant by the curtesy, or in dower, the incumbent of a benefice, a husband suing or defending in right of his wife, etc. Wharton; H. Weston Lumber Co. v. Lacey Lumber Co., 85 So. 193, 195, 123 Miss. 208, 10 A.L.R. 436.

"Privies," in the sense that they are bound by the judgment, are those who acquired an interest in the subject-matter after the rendition of the judgment. Village Mills Co. v. Houston Oil Co. of Texas, Tex.Civ.App., 186 S.W. 785, 790; Central Oregon Irr. Co. v. Young, 107 Or. 39, 213 P. 782, 784. "Privies" to a judgment are those whose succession to the rights of property affected occurs after the institution of the suit and form a party to it. Gill v. Porter, 176 N.C. 451, 97 S.E. 381, 382; Lancaster v. Borkowski, 179 Wis. 1, 190 N.W. 852, 854.

PRIVIGNA. Lat. In the civil law. A step-daughter.

PRIVIGNUS. Lat. In the civil law. A son of a husband or wife by a former marriage; a stepson. Calvin.

PRIVILEGE. A particular and peculiar benefit or advantage enjoyed by a person, company, or class, beyond the common advantages of other citizens. An exceptional or extraordinary power or exemption. A right, power, franchise, or immunity held by a person or class, against or beyond the course of the law. Waterloo Water Co. v. Village of Waterloo, 193 N.Y.S. 360, 362, 200 App.Div. 718; Colonial Motor Coach Corporation v. City of Oswego, 215 N.Y.S. 159, 163, 126 Misc. 829; Cope v. Flanery, 234 P. 845, 849, 70 Cal.App. 738; Bank of Commerce & Trust Co. v. Senter, 260 S.W. 144, 147, 149 Tenn. 569; State v. Betts, 24 N.J.L. 557.

An exemption from some burden or attendance, with which certain persons are indulged, from a supposition of law that the stations they fill, or the offices they are engaged in, are such as require all their time and care, and that, therefore, without this indulgence, it would be impracticable to execute such offices to that advantage which the public good requires. Dike v. State, 38 Minn. 366, 38 N.W. 95; International Trust Co. v. American L. & T. Co., 62 Minn. 501, 65 N.W. 78. State v. Gilman, 33 W.Va. 146, 10 S.E. 283, 6 L.R.A. 847. That which releases one from the performance of a duty or obligation, or exempts one from a liability which he would otherwise be required to perform, or sustain in common with all other persons. State v. Grosnickle, 189 Wis. 17, 206 N.W. 895, 896. A peculiar advantage, exemption, or immunity. Sacramento Orphanage & Children's Home v. Chambers, 25 Cal.App. 536, 144 P. 317, 319.

Civil Law

A right which the nature of a debt gives to a creditor, and which entitles him to be preferred before other creditors. Civil Code La. art. 3186. It is merely an accessory of the debt which it secures, and falls with the extinguishment of the debt. A. Baldwin & Co. v. McCain, 159 La. 966, 106 So. 459, 460. The civil-law privilege became, by adoption of the admiralty courts, the admiralty lien. Howe, Stud. Civ. L. 89; The J. E. Rumbell, 148 U.S. 1, 13 S.Ct. 498, 37 L.Ed. 345.

Exclusive Privilege

See Exclusive Privilege or Franchise.

Law of Libel and Slander

An exemption from liability for the speaking or publishing of defamatory words concerning another, based on the fact that the statement was made in the performance of a duty, political, judicial, social, or personal. Privilege is either *absolute* or *conditional.* The former protects the speaker or publisher without reference to his motives or the truth or falsity of the statement. This may be claimed in respect, for instance, to statements made in legislative debates, in reports of military officers to their superiors in the line of their duty, and statements made by judges, witnesses, and jurors in trials in court. Conditional privilege (called also "qualified privilege") will protect the speaker or publisher unless actual malice and knowledge of the falsity of the statement is shown. This may be claimed where the communication related to a matter of public interest, or where it was necessary to protect one's private interest and was made to a person having an interest in the same matter. Hill v. Drainage Co., 79 Hun, 335, 29 N.Y.S. 427; Cooley v. Galyon, 109 Tenn. 1, 70 S.W. 607, 60 L.R.A. 139, 97 Am.St.Rep. 823.

"Absolute privilege" is confined to cases in which the public service or the administration of justice requires complete immunity from being called to account for language used. Taber v. Aransas Harbor Terminal Ry., Tex. Civ.App., 219 S.W. 860, 861. It is based upon the theory that the publication of defamatory matter must be protected in the interest of and for the necessities of society, even though it be both false and malicious. Light Pub. Co. v. Huntress, Tex.Civ.App., 199 S.W. 1168, 1171.

"Qualified privilege" extends to all communications made in good faith upon any subject-matter in which the party communicating has an interest or in reference to which he has a duty to a person having a corresponding interest or duty, although the duty be not a legal one, but of a moral or social character of imperfect obligation; and it arises from the necessity of full and unrestricted communication concerning a matter in which the parties have an interest or duty. Southern Ice Co. v. Black, 136 Tenn. 391, 189 S.W. 861, 863, Ann.Cas.1917E, 695.

Maritime Law

An allowance to the master of a ship of the same general nature with primage, being compensation, or rather a gratuity, customary in certain trades, and which the law assumes to be a fair and equitable allowance, because the contract on both sides is made under the knowledge of such usage by the parties. 3 Chit. Commer. Law, 431.

Parliamentary Law

The right of a particular question, motion, or statement to take precedence over all other business before the house and to be considered immediately, notwithstanding any consequent interference with or setting aside the rules of procedure adopted by the house. The matter may be one of "personal privilege," where it concerns one member of the house in his capacity as a legislator, or of the "privilege of the house," where it concerns the rights, immunities, or dignity of the entire body, or of "constitutional privilege," where it relates to some action to be taken or some order of proceeding expressly enjoined by the constitution.

General

Privilege from arrest. A privilege extended to certain classes of persons, either by the rules of international law, the policy of the law, or the necessities of justice or of the administration of government, whereby they are exempted from arrest on civil process, and, in some cases, on criminal charges, either permanently, as in the case of a foreign minister and his suite, or temporarily, as in the case of members of the legislature, parties and witnesses engaged in a particular suit, etc. 1 Kent 243; 8 R. I. 43; 2 Stra. 985; 1 M. & W. 488; Parker v. Marco, 136 N.Y. 585, 32 N.E. 989, 20 L.R.A. 45, 32 Am.St.Rep. 770.

Privilege of transit. In railroading, the right of a shipper to have a car stopped at some intermediate point, the commodity shipped unloaded and treated or changed into some other form, and then reloaded and shipped to its destination as though it had been a continuous shipment and at the same rate as originally billed. Chicago, M. & St. P. Ry. Co. v. Board of Railroad Com'rs, 47 S.D. 395, 199 N.W. 453, 454.

Privilege tax. A tax on the privilege of carrying on a business for which a license or franchise is required. Southeastern Express Co. v. City of Charlotte, 186 N.C. 668, 120 S.E. 475, 477; Gulf & Ship Island R. Co. v. Hewes, 183 U.S. 66, 22 S. Ct. 26, 46 L.Ed. 86.

Privileges and immunities. Within the meaning of the 14th amendment of the United States constitution, such privileges as are fundamental, which belong to the citizens of all free governments and which have at all times been enjoyed by citizens of the United States. La Tourette v. McMaster, 104 S.C. 501, 89 S.E. 398, 399. They are only those which owe their existence to the federal government, its national character, its Constitution, or its laws. Ownbey v. Morgan, 256 U. S. 94, 41 S.Ct. 433, 65 L.Ed. 837, 17 A.L.R. 873; Prudential Ins. Co. of America v. Cheek, 25 U.S. 530, 42 S.Ct. 516, 520, 66 L.Ed. 1044, 27 A.L.R. 27; Rosenthal v. New York, 33 S.Ct. 27, 226 U.S. 260, 57 L.Ed. 212, Ann.Cas.1914B, 71.

Real privilege. In English law. A privilege granted to, or concerning, a particular place or locality.

Special privilege. In constitutional law. A right, power, franchise, immunity, or privilege granted to, or vested in, a person or class of persons, to the exclusion of others, and in derogation of common right. Plattsmouth v. Nebraska Teleph. Co., 80 Neb. 460, 114 N.W. 588, 14 L.R.A., N.S., 654, 127 Am.St.Rep. 779.

Writ of privilege. A process to enforce or maintain a privilege; particularly to secure the release of a person arrested in a civil suit contrary to his privilege.

PRIVILEGED. Possessing or enjoying a privilege; exempt from burdens; entitled to priority or precedence.

PRIVILEGED COMMUNICATIONS. See Communication.

PRIVILEGED COPYHOLDS. See Copyhold.

PRIVILEGED DEBTS. Those which an executor or administrator, trustee in bankruptcy, and the like, may pay in preference to others; such as funeral expenses, servants' wages, and doctors' bills during last sickness, etc.

PRIVILEGED DEED. In Scotch law. An instrument, for example, a testament, in the execution of which certain statutory formalities usually required are dispensed with, either from necessity or expediency. Ersk.Inst. 3, 2, 22; Bell.

PRIVILEGED VESSEL. That one of two vessels which, as against the other, ordinarily has the right or duty to hold her course and speed. Under International Rules, arts. 20, 22 (33 U.S.C.A. §§ 105, 107), a sailing vessel, except when the overtaking vessel, is always the privileged vessel, as against a steamer. The Buenos Aires, C.C.A. N.Y., 5 F.2d 425, affirming, D.C.N.Y., The Windrush, 286 F. 251. But the fact that a vessel is privileged does not excuse her from failing to observe the rules, inattention to signals, or failure to answer where an answer is required, or from adopting such precautions as may be necessary to avoid a collision. The West Hartland, C.C.A.Wash., 2 F. 2d 834.

PRIVILEGED VILLENAGE. In old English law. A species of villenage in which the tenants held by certain and determinate services; otherwise called "villein-socage." Bract. fol. 209. Now called "privileged copyhold," incuding the tenure in ancient demesne. 2 Bl.Comm. 99, 100.

PRIVILEGIA QUÆ RE VERA SUNT IN PRÆJUDICIUM REIPUBLICÆ, MAGIS TAMEN HABENT SPECIOSA FRONTISPICIA, ET BONI PUBLICI PRÆTEXTUM, QUAM BONÆ ET LEGALES CONCESSIONES; SED PRÆTEXTU LICITI NON DEBET ADMITTI ILLICTUM. 11 Coke, 88. Privileges which are truly in prejudice of public good have, however, a more specious front and pretext of public good than good and legal grants; but, under pretext of legality, that which is illegal ought not to be admitted.

PRIVILEGIUM. In Roman law. A special constitution by which the Roman emperor conferred on some single person some anomalous or irregular right, or imposed upon some single person some anomalous or irregular obligation, or inflicted on some single person some anomalous or irregular punishment. When such *privilegia* conferred anomalous rights, they were styled "favorable." When they imposed anomalous obligations, or inflicted anomalous punishments, they were styled "odious." Aust.Jur. § 748. A private law inflicting a punishment or conferring a reward. Calvinus, Lex.; Cicero, *de Lege*, 3, 19; *pro Domo* 17; Vicat, Voc.Jur.

In modern civil law. Every peculiar right or favor granted by the law, contrary to the common rule. Mackeld. Rom. Law, § 197. A species of lien or claim upon an article of property, not dependent upon possession, but continuing until either satisfied or released. Such is the lien, recognized by modern maritime law, of seamen upon the ship for their wages. 2 Pars. Mar. Law, 561.

PRIVILEGIUM CLERICALE. The benefit of clergy, (*q. v.*).

PRIVILEGIUM EST BENEFICIUM PERSONALE, ET EXTINGUITUR CUM PERSONA. 3 Bulst. 8. A privilege is a personal benefit, and dies with the person.

PRIVILEGIUM EST QUASI PRIVATA LEX. 2 Bulst. 189. Privilege is, as it were, a private law.

PRIVILEGIUM NON VALET CONTRA REMPUBLICAM. Privilege is of no force against the commonwealth. Even necessity does not excuse, where the act to be done is against the commonwealth. Bac. Max. p. 32, in reg. 5; Broom, Max. 18; Noy, Max., 9th ed. 34.

PRIVILEGIUM, PROPERTY PROPTER. A qualified property in animals *feræ naturæ*; *i. e.*, a privilege of hunting, taking, and killing them, in exclusion of others. 2 Bl.Comm. 394; 2 Steph. Comm. 9.

PRIVITY. Mutual or successive relationship to the same rights of property. 1 Greenl.Ev. § 189; Duffy v. Blake, 91 Wash. 140, 157 P. 480, 482; Haverhill v. International Ry. Co., 217 App.Div. 521, 217 N.Y.S. 522, 523.

Thus, the executor is in privity with the testator, the heir with the ancestor, the assignee with the assignor, the donee with the donor, and the lessee with the lessor. Litchfield v. Crane, 8 S.Ct. 210, 123 U.S. 549, 31 L.Ed. 199.

Derivative interest founded on, or growing out of, contract, connection, or bond of union between parties; mutuality of interest. Hodgson v. Midwest Oil Co., C.C.A.Wyo., 17 F.2d 71, 75.

Private knowledge; joint knowledge with another of a private concern; cognizance implying a consent or concurrence. Taylor v. Ferroman Properties, 103 Fla. 960, 139 So. 149, 150.

In a strict and technical sense a judgment creditor does not occupy such a relation to his debtor as to fall within the meaning of the word "privity," for there is no succession to the property of the debtor until a sale under execution is had and the judgment creditor has become vested with the title thereof. But a majority of the courts have enlarged the meaning of the word, and consequently have held that there is privity between the two before there is an actual devolution of the title of the property owned by the debtor. Buss v. Kemp Lumber Co., 23 N.M. 567, 170 P. 54, 56, L.R.A.1918C, 1015.

Privity of blood exists between an heir and his ancestor, (privity in blood inheritable,) and between coparceners. This privity was formerly of importance in the law of descent cast. Co. Litt. 271*a*, 242*a*; 2 Inst. 516; 8 Coke, 42*b*.

Privity of contract is that connection or relationship which exists between two or more contracting parties. It is essential to the maintenance of an action on any contract that there should subsist a privity between the plaintiff and defendant in respect of the matter sued on. Brown.

Privity of estate is that which exists between lessor and lessee, tenant for life and remainderman or reversioner, etc., and their respective assignees, and between joint tenants and coparceners. Privity of estate is required for a release by enlargement. Sweet.

PRIVITY OR KNOWLEDGE. Under Rev.St. §§ 4283–4286 (46 U.S.C.A. §§ 183–186) withholding the right to limit liability if the shipowner had "privity or knowledge" of the fault which occasioned damages, privity or knowledge must be actual and not merely constructive, and must involve a personal participation of the owner in some fault or act of negligence causing or contributing to the injury suffered. The 84–H, C.C. A.N.Y., 296 F. 427, 431. The words import actual knowledge of the things causing or contributing to the loss, or knowledge or means of knowledge of a condition of things likely to produce or contribute to the loss without adopting proper means to prevent it. Petition of Canadian Pac. Ry. Co., D.C.Wash., 278 F. 180, 189.

PRIVY. A person who is in privity with another. One who is a partaker or has any part or interest in any action, matter, or thing. See Privies; Privity.

Also, a water-closet. Louisville & N. R. Co. v. Commonwealth, 175 Ky. 282, 194 S.W. 313, 314.

As an adjective, the word has practically the same meaning as "private."

PRIVY COUNCIL. In English law. The principal council of the sovereign, composed of the cabinet ministers, and other persons chosen by the king or queen as privy councillors. 2 Steph. Comm. 479, 480. The judicial committee of the privy council acts as a court of ultimate appeal in various cases.

PRIVY COUNCILLOR. A member of the privy council.

PRIVY PURSE. In English law. The income set apart for the sovereign's personal use.

PRIVY SEAL. In English law. A seal used in making out grants or letters patent, preparatory to their passing under the great seal. 2 Bl.Comm. 347. A seal which the king uses to such grants or things as pass the great seal. Co. 2d Inst. 554. A seal of the British government which is affixed to documents not requiring the great seal. Encycl. Br.

PRIVY SIGNET. In English law. The signet or seal which is first used in making out grants and letters patent, and which is always in the custody of the principal secretary of state. 2 Bl.Comm. 347.

PRIVY TOKEN. A false mark or sign, forged object, counterfeited letter, key, ring, etc., used to deceive persons, and thereby fraudulently get possession of property. St. 33 Hen. VIII. c. 1. A false privy token is a false privy document or sign, not such as is calculated to deceive men generally, but designed to defraud one or more individuals. Cheating by such false token was not indictable at common law. Pub. St. Mass. 1882, p. 1294.

PRIVY VERDICT. In practice. A verdict given privily to the judge out of court, but which was of no force unless afterwards affirmed by a public verdict given openly in court. 3 Bl.Comm. 377. Kramer v. Kister, 187 Pa. 227, 40 A. 1008, 44 L.R.A. 432. Now generally superseded by the "sealed verdict," *i. e.*, one written out, sealed up, and delivered to the judge or the clerk of the court.

PRIZE. Anything offered as a reward of contest; a reward offered to the person who, among several persons or among the public at large, shall first (or best) perform a certain undertaking or accomplish certain conditions.

An award or recompense for some act done; some valuable thing offered by a person for something done by others. It is distinguished from a "bet" or "wager" in that it is known before the event who is to give either the premium or the prize, and there is but one operation until the accomplishment of the act, thing, or purpose for which it is offered. People v. Cohen, 289 N.Y.S. 397, 400, 160 Misc. 10.

In admiralty law. A vessel or cargo, belonging to one of two belligerent powers, apprehended or forcibly captured at sea by a war-vessel or privateer of the other belligerent, and claimed as enemy's property, and therefore liable to appropriation and condemnation under the laws of war. 1 C.Rob.Adm. 228. The apprehension and detention at sea of a ship or other vessel, by authority of a belligerent power, either with the design of appropriating it, with the goods and effects it contains, or with that of becoming master of the whole or a part of its cargo. 1 C.Rob. 228.

Captured property regularly condemned by the sentence of a competent prize court. 1 Kent, Comm. 102.

Goods taken on land from a public enemy are called "booty"; and the distinction between a prize and booty consists in this, that the former is taken at sea and the latter on land.

PRIZE COURTS. Courts having jurisdiction to adjudicate upon captures made at sea in time of war, and to condemn the captured property as prize if lawfully subject to that sentence. In England, the admiralty courts have jurisdiction as prize courts, distinct from the jurisdiction on the instance side. A special commission issues in time of war to the judge of the admiralty court, to enable him to hold such court. In America, the federal district courts have jurisdiction in cases of prize. 1 Kent, Comm. 101–103, 353–360. See Penhallow v. Doane, 3 Dall. 91, 1 L.Ed. 507.

PRIZE-FIGHT. A bout between two persons who fight each other by means of their fists, by consent, and who have an expectation of reward to be gained by the contest or competition, either to be won from the contestant or to be otherwise awarded, where there is an intent to inflict some degree of bodily harm on the contestant. Magness v. Isgrig, 145 Ark. 232, 225 S.W. 332, 334. An exhibition contest of pugilists for a stake or reward. Sampson v. State, 18 Okl.Cr. 191, 194 P. 279, 280; Fitzsimmons v. New York State Athletic Commission, Sup., 146 N.Y.S. 117, 120. It is not essential that the fight should be with the naked fist or hand. Sampson v. State, 18 Okl.Cr. 191, 194 P. 279, 280.

PRIZE GOODS. Goods which are taken on the high seas, *jure belli,* out of the hands of the enemy. The Adeline, 9 Cranch 244, 284, 3 L.Ed. 719.

PRIZE LAW. The system of laws and rules applicable to the capture of prize at sea; its condemnation, rights of the captors, distribution of the proceeds, etc. The Buena Ventura, D.C.Fla., 87 F. 927, 929.

PRIZE MONEY. A dividend from the proceeds of a captured vessel, etc., paid to the captors. U. S. v. Steever, 5 S.Ct. 765, 113 U.S. 747, 28 L.Ed. 1133.

PRO. For; in respect of; on account of; in behalf of. The introductory word of many Latin phrases.

PRO AND CON. For and against. A phrase descriptive of the presentation of arguments or evidence on both sides of a disputed question.

PRO BONO ET MALO. For good and ill; for advantage and detriment.

PRO BONO PUBLICO. For the public good; for the welfare of the whole.

PRO CONFESSO. For confessed; as confessed. A term applied to a bill in equity, and the decree founded upon it, where no answer is made to it by the defendant. 1 Barb.Ch.Pr. 96; The Richmond, D.C.Del., 2 F.2d 903.

PRO CONSILIO. For counsel given. An annuity *pro consilio* amounts to a condition, but in a feoffment or lease for life, etc., it is the consideration, and does not amount to a condition; for the state of the land by the feoffment is executed, and the grant of the annuity is executory. Plowd. 412.

PRO CORPORE REGNI. In behalf of the body of the realm. Hale, Com. Law, 32.

PRO DEFECTU EMPTORUM. For want (failure) of purchasers.

PRO DEFECTU EXITUS. For, or in case of, default of issue. 2 Salk. 620.

PRO DEFECTU HÆREDIS. For want of an heir.

PRO DEFECTU JUSTITIÆ. For defect or want of justice. Fleta, lib. 2, c. 62, § 2.

PRO DEFENDENTE. For the defendant. Commonly abbreviated *"pro def."*

PRO DERELICTO. As derelict or abandoned. A species of usucaption in the civil law. Dig. 41, 7.

PRO DIGNITATE REGALI. In consideration of the royal dignity. 1 Bl.Comm. 223.

PRO DIVISO. As divided; *i. e.,* in severalty.

PRO DOMINO. As master or owner; in the character of master. Calvin.

PRO DONATO. As a gift; as in case of gift; by title of gift. A species of usucaption in the civil law. Dig. 41, 6. See Id. 5, 3, 13, 1.

PRO DOTE. As a dowry; by title of dowry. A species of usucaption. Dig. 41, 9. See Id. 5, 3, 13, 1.

PRO EMPTORE. As a purchaser; by the title of a purchaser. A species of usucaption. Dig. 41, 4, 5, 3, 13, 1.

PRO EO QUOD. In pleading. For this that. This is a phrase of affirmation, and is sufficiently direct and positive for introducing a material averment. 1 Saund. 117, no. 4; 2 Chit.Pl. 369–393.

PRO FACTO. For the fact; as a fact; considered or held as a fact.

PRO FALSO CLAMORE SUO. A nominal amercement of a plaintiff for *his false claim,* which used to be inserted in a judgment for the defendant. Obsolete.

PRO FORMA. As a matter of form. 3 East, 232; 2 Kent, Comm. 245.

The phrase "pro forma," in an appealable decree or judgment, usually means that the decision was rendered, not on a conviction that it was right, but merely to facilitate further proceedings. Cramp & Sons S. & E. Bldg. Co. v. Turbine Co., 33 Sup.Ct. 722, 228 U.S. 645, 57 L.Ed. 1003.

PRO HAC VICE. For this turn; for this one particular occasion.

PRO ILLA VICE. For that turn. 3 Wils. 233, arg.

PRO INDEFENSO. As undefended; as making no defense. A phrase in old practice. Fleta, lib. 1, c. 41, § 7.

PRO INDIVISO. As undivided; in common. The joint occupation or possession of lands. Thus, lands held by coparceners are held *pro indiviso;*

that is, they are held undividedly, neither party being entitled to any specific portions of the land so held, but both or all having a joint interest in the undivided whole. Cowell; Bract. 1, 5.

PRO INTERESSE SUO. According to his interest; to the extent of his interest. Thus, a third party may be allowed to intervene in a suit *pro interesse suo.*

Examination pro interesse suo. When a person claims to be entitled to an estate or other property sequestered, whether by mortgage, judgment, lease, or otherwise, or has a title paramount to the sequestration, he should apply to the court to direct an inquiry whether the applicant has any, and what, interest in the property; and this inquiry is called an "examination pro interesse suo." Krippendorf v. Hyde, 4 S.Ct. 27, 110 U.S. 276, 28 L.Ed. 145; Hitz v. Jenks, 22 S.Ct. 598, 185 U.S. 155, 46 L.Ed. 851.

PRO LÆSIONE FIDEI. For breach of faith. 3 Bl.Comm. 52.

PRO LEGATO. As a legacy; by the title of a legacy. A species of usucaption. Dig. 41, 8.

PRO MAJORI CAUTELA. For greater caution; by way of additional security. Usually applied to some act done, or some clause inserted in an instrument, which may not be really necessary, but which will serve to put the matter beyond any question.

PRO NON SCRIPTO. As not written; as though it had not been written; as never written. Ambl. 139.

PRO OPERE ET LABORE. For work and labor. 1 Comyns, 18.

PRO PARTIBUS LIBERANDIS. An ancient writ for partition of lands between co-heirs. Reg. Orig. 316.

PRO POSSE SUO. To the extent of his power or ability. Bract. fol. 109.

PRO POSSESSIONE PRÆSUMITUR DE JURE. From possession arises a presumption of law.

PRO POSSESSORE. As a possessor; by title of a possessor. Dig. 41, 5. See Id. 5, 3, 13.

PRO POSSESSORE HABETUR QUI DOLO INJURIAVE DESIIT POSSIDERE. He is esteemed a possessor whose possession has been disturbed by fraud or injury. Off. Exec. 166.

PRO QUERENTE. For the plaintiff; usually abbreviated *pro quer.*

PRO RATA. Proportionately; according to a certain rate, percentage, or proportion. According to measure, interest, or liability. Chaplin v. Griffin, 252 Pa. 271, 97 A. 409, 411, Ann.Cas.1918C, 787. According to a certain rule or proportion. 19 Am.L.Reg.N.S. 355, n. (U.S.D.C.Cal.).

Thus, the creditors (of the same class) of an insolvent estate are to be paid *pro rata;* that is, each is to receive a dividend bearing the same ratio to the whole amount of his claim that the aggregate of assets bears to the aggregate of debts.

PRO RE NATA. For the affair immediately in hand; for the occasion as it may arise; adapted to meet the particular occasion. Thus, a course of judicial action adopted under pressure of the exigencies of the affair in hand, rather than in conformity to established precedents, is said to be taken *pro re nata.*

PRO SALUTE ANIMÆ. For the good of his soul. All prosecutions in the ecclesiastical courts are *pro salute animæ;* hence it will not be a temporal damage founding an action for slander that the words spoken put any one in danger of such a suit. 3 Steph.Comm. (7th Ed.) 309*n*, 437; 4 Steph.Comm. 207.

PRO SE. For himself; in his own behalf; in person.

PRO SOCIO. For a partner; the name of an action in behalf of a partner. A title of the civil law. Dig. 17, 2; Cod. 4, 37.

PRO SOLIDO. For the whole; as one; jointly; without division. Dig. 50, 17, 141, 1.

PRO TANTO. For so much; for as much as may be; as far as it goes. Donley v. Hays, 17 Serg. & R. (Pa.) 400.

PRO TEMPORE. For the time being; temporarily; provisionally.

PROAMITA. Lat. In the civil law. A great paternal aunt; the sister of one's grandfather.

PROAMITA MAGNA. Lat. In the civil law. A great-great-aunt.

PROAVIA. Lat. In the civil law. A great-grandmother. Inst. 3, 6, 3; Dig. 38, 10, 1, 5.

PROAVUNCULUS. Lat. In the civil law. A great-grandfather's or great-grandmother's brother. Inst. 3, 6, 3; Bract. fol. 68*b*; Ainsworth, Dict.

PROAVUS. Lat. In the civil law. A great-grandfather. Inst. 3, 6, 1; Bract. fols. 67, 68. Employed in making genealogical tables.

PROBABILITY. Likelihood; appearance of reality or truth; reasonable ground of presumption; verisimilitude; consonance to reason. The likelihood of a proposition or hypothesis being true, from its conformity to reason or experience, or from superior evidence or arguments adduced in its favor. People v. O'Brien, 130 Cal. 1, 62 P. 297; Shaw v. State, 125 Ala. 80, 28 So. 390. Coppinger v. Broderick, 39 Ariz. 473, 295 P. 780, 781. Inference; assumption; presumption. Ohio Bldg. Safety Vault Co. v. Industrial Board, 277 Ill. 96, 115 N.E. 149, 154. A condition or state created when there is more evidence in favor of the existence of a given proposition than there is against it. Harris v. State, 8 Ala.App. 33, 62 So. 477, 479.

High probability rule. A rule relating to the right of insured to abandon a vessel, by virtue of which the right of abandonment does not depend upon the certainty, but upon the high probability of a total loss, either of the property, or voyage, or both. The result is to act not upon certainties, but upon probabilities; and if the facts present a case of extreme hazard, and of probable expense, exceeding half the value of the ship, the insured may abandon, though it should happen that she was afterwards recovered at a less expense. Fireman's Fund Ins. Co. v. Globe Nav. Co., C.C.A.Wash., 236 F. 618, 635. In re Salomon's Estate, 287 N.Y.S. 814, 821, 159 Misc. 379.

PROBABLE. Having the appearance of truth; having the character of probability; appearing to be founded in reason or experience. State v. Thiele, 119 Iowa, 659, 94 N.W. 256. Having more evidence for than against; supported by evidence which inclines the mind to believe, but leaves some room for doubt; likely. Barrett v. Green River & Rock Springs Live Stock Co., 28 Wyo. 379, 205 P. 742, 743. Apparently true, yet possibly false. Spadra Creek Coal Co. v. Harger, 130 Ark. 374, 197 S.W. 705.

PROBABLE CAUSE. Reasonable cause. State v. Baltes, 183 Wis. 545, 198 N.W. 282, 284. Having more evidence for than against. Ex parte Souza, 65 Cal.App. 9, 222 P. 869, 870. A reasonable ground for belief in the existence of facts warranting the proceedings complained of. Owens v. Graetzel, 149 Md. 689, 132 A. 265, 267. An apparent state of facts found to exist upon reasonable inquiry, (that is, such inquiry as the given case renders convenient and proper,) which would induce a reasonably intelligent and prudent man to believe, in a criminal case, that the accused person had committed the crime charged, or, in a civil case, that a cause of action existed. Brand v. Hinchman, 68 Mich. 590, 36 N.W. 664, 13 Am. St.Rep. 362; Cook v. Singer Sewing Mach. Co., 138 Cal.App. 418, 32 P.2d 430, 431.

In malicious prosecution the existence of such facts and circumstances as would excite the belief in a reasonable mind, acting on the facts within the knowledge of the prosecutor, that the person charged was guilty of the crime for which he was prosecuted. Lunsford v. Dietrich, 86 Ala. 250, 5 So. 461, 11 Am.St.Rep. 37. A reasonable ground of suspicion, supported by circumstances sufficiently strong in themselves to warrant a prudent and cautious man to believe that the accused is guilty of the offense with which he is charged. Sanders v. Palmer, N.Y., 55 F. 217, 5 C.C. A. 77. Such a state of facts and circumstances known to the prosecutor personally or by information from others as would, in the judgment of the court, lead a man of ordinary caution, acting conscientiously in the light of such facts and circumstances, to believe that the person charged is guilty. Keebey v. Stifft, 145 Ark. 8, 224 S.W. 396, 400. See, also, Galley v. Brennan, 216 N.Y. 118, 110 N.E. 179, 180. Where defendant in an action for malicious prosecution shows that before commencing the prosecution he, in good faith, consulted an attorney of good standing and made a full disclosure of all of the facts reasonably obtainable, and in good faith acted upon such advice, this of itself constitutes "probable cause." Gustason v. Speak, 85 Cal.App. 18, 258 P. 725, 726; Treloar v. Harris, 66 Ind. App. 159, 117 N.E. 975, 976.

As justifying arrest without a warrant by one believed guilty of felony or to be engaged in commission of a felony, is a belief fairly arising out of facts and circumstances known to officer that a party is engaged in commission of a crime. Day v. U. S., C.C.A.Neb., 37 F.2d 80, 81.

For search warrant means reasonable ground of suspicion, supported by circumstances sufficiently strong to warrant cautious man in believing party is guilty of offense charged. Shore v. U. S., 49 F.2d 519, 521, 60 App.D. C. 137.

For arrest which must be shown as justification by defendants in action for false imprisonment is reasonable ground of suspicion supported by circumstances sufficient in themselves to warrant cautious man in believing accused to be guilty, but does not depend on actual state of case in point of fact, as it may turn out upon legal investigation, but on knowledge of facts which would be sufficient to induce reasonable belief in truth of accusation. Christ v. McDonald, 152 Or. 494, 52 P.2d 655, 658.

PROBABLE CONSEQUENCE. One that is more likely to follow its supposed cause than it is not to follow it. See, also, Collins v. Pecos & N. T. Ry. Co., 110 Tex. 577, 212 S.W. 477, 478.

PROBABLE EVIDENCE. Presumptive evidence is so called, from its foundation in probability.

PROBABLE FUTURE PAYMENTS. This expression in the Workmen's Compensation Act, providing for commutation at an amount which will equal the total sum of the probable future payments capitalized at their present value upon the basis of interest calculated at 3 per cent. per annum, means such payments as would ordinarily become payable in the natural course of events, taking into consideration the expectancy of the beneficiary. H. W. Clark Co. v. Industrial Commission, 291 Ill. 561, 126 N.E. 579, 582.

PROBABLE GROUND. As used in the Illinois Quo Warranto Act, requiring the judge to be satisfied there is probable ground for the proceeding before granting leave to file the information in quo warranto, means a reasonable ground of presumption that a charge is or may be well founded. People v. Hartquist, 311 Ill. 127, 142 N.E. 475, 476.

PROBABLE REASONING. In the law of evidence. Reasoning founded on the probability of the fact or proposition sought to be proved or shown; reasoning in which the mind exercises a discretion in deducing a conclusion from premises. Burrill.

PROBABLY. In all probability; so far as the evidence shows; presumably; likely. In re Salomon's Estate, 287 N.Y.S. 814, 820, 159 Misc. 379.

PROBANDI NECESSITAS INCUMBIT ILLI QUI AGIT. The necessity of proving lies with him who sues. Inst. 2, 20, 4. In other words, the burden of proof of a proposition is upon him who advances it affirmatively.

PROBARE. In Saxon law. To claim a thing as one's own. Jacob.

In modern law language. To make proof, as in the term *"onus probandi,"* the burden or duty of making proof.

PROBATE. Originally, relating to proof; afterwards, relating to the proof of wills.

The act or process of proving a will. Ross' Estate v. Abrams, Tex.Civ.App., 239 S.W. 705, 707. The proof before an ordinary, surrogate, register, or other duly authorized person that a document produced before him for official recognition and registration, and alleged to be the last will and testament of a certain deceased person, is such in reality. A judicial act or determination of a court having competent jurisdiction establishing the validity of a will. Simpson v. Anderson, 305 Ill. 172, 137 N.E. 88, 89; Peterson v. Demmer, D. C.Tex., 34 F.Supp. 697, 700.

Also, the copy of the will, made out in parchment or due form, under the seal of the ordinary or court of probate, and usually delivered to the executor or administrator of the deceased, together with a certificate of the will's having been proved.

In American law, now a general name or term used to include all matters of which probate courts have jurisdiction. Johnson v. Harrison, 47 Minn. 575, 50 N.W. 923, 28 Am.St.Rep. 382.

In the canon law, "probate" consisted of *probatio,* the proof of the will by the executor, and *approbatio,* the approbation given by the ecclesiastical judge to the proof. 4 Reeve, Eng. Law, 77. McCay v. Clayton, 119 Pa. 133, 12 A. 860; Reno v. McCully, 65 Iowa 629, 22 N.W. 902; Appeal of Dawley, 16 R.I. 694, 19 A. 248.

The term is used, particularly in Pennsylvania, but not in a strictly technical sense, to designate the proof of his claim made by a non-resident plaintiff (when the same is on book-account, promissory note, etc.) who swears to the correctness and justness of the same, and that it is due, before a notary or other officer in his own state; also of the copy or statement of such claim filed in court, with the jurat of such notary attached. Stevens v. D. R. Dunlap Mercantile Co., 108 Miss. 690, 67 So. 160, 161.

Common and solemn form of probate. In English law, there are two kinds of probate, namely, probate in common form, and probate in solemn form. Probate in common form is granted in the registry, without any formal procedure in court, upon an *ex parte* application made by the executor. Probate in solemn form is in the nature of a final decree pronounced in open court, all parties interested having been duly cited. The difference between the effect of probate in common form and probate in solemn form is that probate in common form is revocable, whereas probate in solemn form is irrevocable, as against all persons who have been cited to see the proceedings, or who can be proved to have been privy to those proceedings, except in the case where a will of subsequent date is discovered, in which case probate of an earlier will, though granted in solemn form, would be revoked. Coote, Prob. Pr. (5th Ed.) 237–239; Mozley & Whitley. And see Luther v. Luther, 122 Ill. 558, 13 N.E. 166.

PROBATE BOND. One required by law to be given to the probate court or judge, as incidental to proceedings in such courts, such as the bonds of executors, administrators, and guardians. Thomas v. White, 12 Mass. 367.

PROBATE CODE. The body or system of law relating to all matters of which probate courts have jurisdiction. Johnson v. Harrison, 47 Minn. 575, 50 N.W. 923, 28 Am.St.Rep. 382.

PROBATE COURT. See Court of Probate.

PROBATE, DIVORCE, AND ADMIRALTY DIVISION. That division of the English high court of justice which exercises jurisdiction in matters formerly within the exclusive cognizance of the court of probate, the court for divorce and matrimonial causes, and the high court of admiralty. (Judicature Act 1873, § 34.) It consists of two judges, one of whom is called the "President." The existing judges are the judge of the old probate and divorce courts, who is president of the division, and the judge of the old admiralty court, and of a number of registrars. Sweet.

PROBATE DUTY. A tax laid by government on every will admitted to probate or on the gross value of the personal property of the deceased testator, and payable out of the decedent's estate.

PROBATE HOMESTEAD. See Homestead.

PROBATE JUDGE. The judge of a court of probate.

PROBATE JURISDICTION. The exercise of the ordinary, generally understood power of a probate court, which includes the establishment of wills, settlement of decedents' estates, supervision of guardianship of infants, control of their property, allotment of dower, and other powers pertaining to such subjects. Clark v. Carolina Homes, 189 N.C. 703, 128 S.E. 20, 25.

PROBATE MATTERS. Matters pertaining to the settlement of estates of deceased persons. In re Bishop's Estate, 370 Ill. 173, 18 N.E.2d 218, 219.

PROBATE PROCEEDING. A general designation of the actions and proceedings whereby the law is administered upon the various subjects within probate jurisdiction. Jackson v. Porter, 87 Okl. 112, 209 P. 430, 435. Specifically, a proceeding in rem for the determination of the disposition of decedents' property. Lillard v. Tolliver, 154 Tenn. 304, 285 S.W. 576, 578. A proceeding to contest the validity, as a will, of a paper which had been admitted to probate as such, or to have a paper probated as a will. Jackson v. Porter, 87 Okl. 112, 209 P. 430, 435.

PROBATIO. Lat. Proof; more particularly direct, as distinguished from indirect or circumstantial evidence.

PROBATIO MORTUA. Dead proof; that is proof by inanimate objects, such as deeds or other written evidence.

PROBATIO PLENA. In the civil law. Full proof; proof by two witnesses, or a public instrument. Hallifax, Civil Law, b. 3, c. 9, no. 25; 3 Bl. Comm. 370.

PROBATIO SEMI-PLENA. In the civil law. Half-full proof; half-proof. Proof by one witness, or a private instrument. Hallifax, Civil Law, b. 3, c. 9, no. 25; 3 Bl.Comm. 370.

PROBATIO VIVA. Living proof; that is, proof by the mouth of living witnesses.

PROBATION. The evidence which proves a thing; the act of proving; proof. Trial; test; the time of novitiate. Used in the latter sense in the monastic orders, and sometimes in civil service laws and the like. People ex rel. Walter v. Woods, 168 App.Div. 3, 153 N.Y.S. 872.

In modern criminal administration, allowing a person convicted of some minor offense (particularly juvenile offenders) to go at large, under a suspension of sentence, during good behavior, and generally under the supervision or guardianship of a probation officer. People ex rel. Schindler v. Kaiser, 95 Misc. 681, 159 N.Y.S. 322, 325. An act of grace and clemency which may be granted by the trial court to a seemingly deserving defendant whereby such defendant may escape the extreme rigors of the penalty imposed by law for the offense of which he stands convicted. People v. Leach, 22 Cal.App.2d 525, 71 P.2d 594, 595.

PROBATION OFFICER. An officer or assistant of the court to assist in the exercise of the jurisdiction which courts of chancery have exercised from time immemorial to protect the financial, social, and moral welfare of infants within their jurisdiction, or to assist in the administration of the probation system for offenders against the criminal laws. State v. Monongalia County Court, 82 W.Va. 564, 96 S.E. 966, 968.

PROBATION SYSTEM. A system of administering the criminal laws, based on the effort to encourage good behavior in a convicted criminal by granting a deduction from his sentence or in case of its being his first offense, releasing him on condition that, for a stated period, he lead an orderly life.

PROBATIONER. One who is upon trial. A convicted offender who is allowed to go at large, under suspension of sentence, during good behavior.

PROBATIONES DEBENT ESSE EVIDENTES, ID EST, PERSPICUÆ ET FACILES INTELLIGI. Co. Litt. 283. Proofs ought to be evident, that is, perspicuous and easily understood.

PROBATIS EXTREMIS, PRÆSUMUNTUR MEDIA. The extremes being proved, the intermediate proceedings are presumed. 1 Greenl. Ev. § 20.

PROBATIVE. In the law of evidence. Having the effect of proof; tending to prove, or actually proving.

Testimony carrying quality of proof and having fitness to induce conviction of truth, consisting of fact and reason co-operating as co-ordinate factors. Globe Indemnity Co. v. Daviess, 243 Ky. 356, 47 S.W.2d 990, 992.

PROBATIVE FACTS. In the law of evidence. Facts which actually have effect of proving facts sought; evidentiary facts. 1 Benth. Ev. 18. Matters of evidence required to prove ultimate facts. Johnson v. Inter-Southern Life Ins. Co., 244 Ky. 83, 50 S.W.2d 16.

PROBATOR. In old English law. Strictly, an accomplice in felony who to save himself confessed the fact, and charged or accused any other as principal or accessory, against whom he was bound to make good his charge. It also signified an approver, or one who undertakes to prove a crime charged upon another. Jacob. See State v. Graham, 41 N.J.L. 16, 32 Am.Rep. 174.

PROBATORY TERM. In the practice of the English admiralty courts, the space of time allowed for the taking of testimony in an action, after issue formed. It is common to both parties, and either party may examine his witnesses. 2 Brown, Civ. Law 418.

PROBATUM EST. Lat. It is tried or proved.

PROBUS ET LEGALIS HOMO. Lat. A good and lawful man. A phrase particularly applied to a juror or witness who was free from all exception, and competent in point of law to serve on juries. Cro. Eliz. 654, 751; Cro. Jac. 635; Mart. & Y. 147; Bac. Abr. *Juries* (A); 3 Bl.Comm. 102. In the plural form: *probi et legales homines.*

PROCEDENDO. In practice. A writ by which a cause which has been removed from an inferior to a superior court by *certiorari* or otherwise is sent down again to the same court, *to be proceeded in* there, where it appears to the superior court that it was removed on insufficient grounds. Cowell; Yates v. People, 6 Johns. (N. Y.) 446; 2 W.Bla. 1060; 6 Term 365.

A writ (*procedendo ad judicium*) which issued out of the common-law jurisdiction of the court of chancery, when judges of any subordinate court delayed the parties for that they would not give judgment either on the one side or on the other, when they ought so to do. In such a case, a writ of *procedendo ad judicium* was awarded, commanding the inferior court in the sovereign's name to proceed to give judgment, but without specifying any particular judgment. Wharton. McCord v. Briggs and Turivas, 338 Ill. 158, 170 N. E. 320, 324. It was the earliest remedy for the refusal or neglect of justice on the part of the courts. In re Press Printers & Publishers, C.C.A. N.J., 12 F.2d 660, 664.

A writ by which the commission of a justice of the peace is revived, after having been suspended. 1 Bl.Comm. 353.

PROCEDENDO ON AID PRAYER. If one pray in aid of the crown in real action, and aid be granted, it shall be awarded that he sue to the sovereign in chancery, and the justices in the common pleas shall stay until this writ of *procedendo de loquela* come to them. So, also, on a personal action. New Nat. Brev. 154.

PROCEDURAL LAW. That which prescribes method of enforcing rights or obtaining redress for their invasion; machinery for carrying on a suit. Barker v. St. Louis County, 340 Mo. 986, 104 S.W.2d 371, 377, 378, 379.

As relating to crimes, that which provides or regulates the steps by which one who violates a criminal statute is punished. State v. Elmore, 179 La. 1057, 155 So. 896.

PROCEDURE. The mode of proceeding by which a legal right is enforced, as distinguished from the law which gives or defines the right, and which, by means of the proceeding, the court is to administer; the machinery, as distinguished from its product. Per Lush, L. J., in 7 Q. B. Div. 333. That which regulates the formal steps in an action or other judicial proceeding; a form, manner, and order of conducting suits or prosecutions. Mahoning Valley Ry. Co. v. Santoro, 93 Ohio St. 53, 112 N.E. 190, 191. The judicial process for enforcing rights and duties recognized by substantive law and for justly administering redress for infraction of them. Sims v. United Pacific Ins. Co., D.C.Idaho, 51 F.Supp. 433, 435.

This term is commonly opposed to the sum of legal principles constituting the substance of the law, and denotes the body of rules, whether of practice or of pleading, whereby rights are effectuated through the successful application of the proper remedies. It is also generally distinguished from the law of evidence. Brown; Sackheim v. Pigueron, 215 N.Y. 62, 109 N.E. 109, 111. Cochran v. Ward, 5 Ind.App. 89, 29 N.E. 795, 31 N.E. 581, 51 Am.St.Rep. 229.

Procedure is the machinery for carrying on the suit, including pleading, process, evidence, and practice, whether in the trial court or the appellate court, or in the processes by which causes are carried to appellate courts for review, or in laying the foundation for such review. Jones v. Erie R. Co., 106 Ohio St. 408, 140 N.E. 366, 367. It not only embraces practice in courts, but regulation of the conduct of the court itself wherein such practice takes place. State v. Greenwald, 186 Ind. 321, 116 N.E. 296, 297.

The law of procedure is what is now commonly termed by jurists "adjective law," (*q. v.*).

PROCEDURE ACTS. Three acts of parliament passed in 1852, 1854, and 1860, for the amendment of procedure at common law. Moz. & W. They have been largely superseded by the Judicature Acts of 1873 and 1875. See Judicature Acts.

PROCEED. To carry on some series of motions and to set oneself to work and go on in a certain way and for some particular purpose. Hodson v. O'Keeffe, 71 Mont. 322, 229 P. 722, 724; To sue. Brabon v. Gladwin Light & Power Co., 201 Mich. 697, 167 N.W. 1024, 1026; Planters' Bank v. Houser, 57 Ga. 140; Iliff v. Weymouth, 40 Ohio St. 101.

PROCEEDING. In a general sense, the form and manner of conducting juridical business before a court or judicial officer; regular and orderly progress in form of law; including all possible steps in an action from its commencement to the execution of judgment. Erwin v. U. S., D.C.Ga., 37 F. 470, 488, 2 L.R.A. 229. Sometimes, merely the record history of a case. See Uhe v. Railway Co., 3 S.D. 563, 54 N.W. 601.

An act which is done by the authority or direction of the court, express or implied; an act necessary to be done in order to obtain a given end; a prescribed mode of action for carrying into effect a legal right. Green v. Board of Com'rs of Lincoln County, 126 Okl. 300, 259 P. 635, 637; Marblehead Land Co. v. Superior Court in and for Los Angeles County, 60 Cal.App. 644, 213 P. 718, 723. All the steps or measures adopted in the prosecution or defense of an action. Statter v. United States, C.C.A.Alaska, 66 F.2d 819, 822. The word may be used synonymously with "action" or "suit" to describe the entire course of an action at law or suit in equity from the issuance of the writ or filing of the bill until the entry of a final judgment, or may be used to describe any act done by authority of a court of law and every step required to be taken in any cause by either party. Gonzales v. Gonzales, 240 Mass. 159, 133 N.E. 855, 856. The proceedings of a suit embrace *all* matters that occur in its progress judicially. Morewood v. Hollister, 6 N.Y. 320. For illustrative cases, see Venator v. Edwards, 126 Okl. 296, 259 P. 596, 599; Dixie Guano Co. v. Alpha Process Co., 5 Boyce (Del.) 277, 92 A. 1013, 1014; State v. Kerr, 117 Me. 254, 103 A. 585, 587. It is a prescribed mode of action for carrying into effect a legal right W. S. Tyler Co. v. Rebic, 118 Ohio St. 522, 161 N.E. 790, 791.

In a more particular sense, any application to a court of justice, however made, for aid in the enforcement of rights, for relief, for redress of injuries, for damages, or for any remedial object. See Coca-Cola Co. v. City of Atlanta, 152 Ga. 558, 110 S.E. 730, 732, 23 A.L.R. 1339. People v. Raymond, 186 Ill. 407, 57 N.E. 1066.

The term is properly applicable, in a legal sense, only to judicial acts before some judicial tribunal. Nelson v. Dunn, 56 Ind.App. 645, 104 N.E. 45. Lait v. Sears, 226 Mass. 119, 115 N.E. 247, 248.

Collateral proceeding. One in which the particular question may arise or be involved incidentally, but which is not instituted for the very purpose of deciding such question; as in the rule that a judgment cannot be attacked, or a corporation's right to exist be questioned, in any collateral proceeding. Peyton v. Peyton, 28 Wash. 278, 68 P. 757.

Executory proceeding. In the law of Louisiana, a proceeding which is resorted to in the following cases: When the creditor's right arises from an act importing a confession of judgment, and which contains a privilege or mortgage in his favor; or when the creditor demands the execution of a judgment which has been rendered by a tribunal different from that within whose jurisdiction the execution is sought. Code Prac. La. art. 732.

Legal proceedings. See Legal Proceedings.

Ordinary proceedings. Those founded on the regular and usual mode of carrying on a suit by due course at common law.

Proceedings in bankruptcy. As used in Bankr. Act July 1, 1898, c. 541, §§ 23–25, 30 Stat. 552, 553 (11 U.S.C.A. §§ 74–76), this term covers questions between the alleged bankrupt or the receiver or trustee on the one hand and the general creditors as such on the other, commencing with the petition for adjudication and ending with the discharge, including matters of administration generally, and is distinguished from "controversies, at law and in equity arising in the course of bankruptcy proceedings," which involve questions between the receiver or trustee, representing the bankrupt and his general creditors as such, on the one hand, and adverse claimants, on the other, concerning property in the possession of the receiver or trustee or of the claimants, to be litigated in appropriate plenary suits, and not affecting directly administrative orders and judgments, but only the extent of the estate to be distributed ultimately among general creditors. In re Breyer Printing Co., C.C.A.Ill., 216 F. 878, 880.

The phrase "controversy arising in bankruptcy proceedings" includes those matters arising in the course of a bankruptcy proceeding which are not mere steps in the ordinary administration of the bankrupt estate, but present distinct and separable issues between the trustee and adverse claimants concerning the right and title to the bankrupt's estate. Gibbons v. Goldsmith, 222 F. 826, 828, 138 C.C.A. 252.

Proceeding in error. One by way of writ of error. State v. Scott, 34 Wyo. 163, 242 P. 322, 324.

Special proceeding. This phrase has been used in the New York and other codes of procedure as a generic term for all civil remedies which are not ordinary actions. An action is an ordinary proceeding in a court of justice, by which one party prosecutes another party for the enforcement or protection of a right, the redress or prevention of a wrong, or the punishment of a public offence. Every other remedy is a special proceeding. State v. Rosenwald Bros. Co., 23 N.M. 578, 170 P. 42, 44.

Summary proceeding. Any proceeding by which a controversy is settled, case disposed of, or trial conducted, in a prompt and simple manner, without the aid of a jury, without presentment or indictment, or in other respects out of the regular course of the common law. In procedure, proceedings are said to be summary when they are short and simple in comparison with regular proceedings; *i. e.,* in comparison with the proceedings which alone would have been applicable, either in the same or analogous cases, if summary proceedings had not been available. Sweet. And see Phillips v. Phillips, 8 N.J.L. 122.

Supplementary proceeding. A separate proceeding in an original action, in which the court where the action is pending is called upon to exercise its jurisdiction in aid of the judgment in the action. Bryant v. Bank of California, 7 Pac. 128, 130, 2 Cal.Unrep. 475. In a more particular sense, a proceeding in aid of execution, authorized by statute in some states in cases where no leviable property of the judgment debtor is found. It is a statutory equivalent in actions at law of the creditor's bill in equity, and in states where law and equity are blended, is provided as a substitute therefor. In this proceeding the judgment debtor is summoned to appear before the court (or a referee or examiner) and submit to an oral examination touching all his property and effects, and if property subject to execution and in his possession or control is thus discovered, he is ordered to deliver it up, or a receiver may be appointed. Eikerberry v. Edwards, 67 Iowa 619, 25 N.W. 832, 56 Am.Rep. 360.

PROCEEDS. Issues; income; yield; receipts; produce; money or articles or other thing of value arising or obtained by the sale of property; the sum, amount, or value of property sold or converted into money or into other property. Wharton; Blackford v. Boak, 73 Or. 61, 143 P. 1136, 1137. Thus, goods purchased with money arising from the sale of other goods, or obtained on their credit, are proceeds of such goods. 2 Pars.Marit. L. 201; Bened.Adm. 290. Proceeds does not necessarily mean cash or money. Phelps v. Harris, 25 L.Ed. 855, 101 U.S. 380.

The word when applied to the income to be derived from real estate embraces the idea of issues, rents, profits, or produce. Gorin Sav. Bank v. Early, Mo.App., 260 S.W. 480, 483. It is synonymous with avails, use, and profits. In re Coughlin's Estate, 53 N.D. 188, 205 N.W. 14, 16.

PROCERES. Nobles; lords. The house of lords in England is called, in Latin, "*Domus Procerum.*"

Formerly, the chief magistrates in cities. St. Armand, Hist. Eq. 88.

PROCÈS-VERBAL. In French law. A true relation in writing in due form of law, of what has been done and said verbally in the presence of a public officer, and what he himself does upon the occasion. It is a species of inquisition of office, and must be signed by the officer. Dalloz, Dict.; Hall v. Hall, 11 Tex. 526, 539.

A written report, which is signed, setting forth a statement of facts. This term is applied to the report proving the meeting and the resolutions passed at a meeting of shareholders, or to the report of a commission to take testimony. It can also be applied to the statement drawn up by a *huissier* in relation to any facts which one of the parties to a suit can be interested in proving; for instance the sale of a counterfeited object. Statements, drawn up by other competent authorities, of misdemeanors or other criminal acts, are also called by this name. Arg. Fr. Merc. Law, 570.

PROCESS. A series of actions, motions, or occurrences; progressive act or transaction; continuous operation; method, mode or operation, whereby a result or effect is produced; normal or actual course of procedure; regular proceeding, as, the process of vegetation or decomposition; a chemical process; processes of nature. Sokol v. Stein Fur Dyeing Co., 216 App.Div. 573, 216 N.Y.S. 167, 169; Kelley v. Coe, App.D.C., 99 F.2d 435, 441.

Patent Law

An art or method by which any particular result is produced. An act or series of acts performed upon the subject-matter to be transformed or reduced to a different state or thing. American Graphophone Co. v. Gimbel Bros. (D.C.) 234 F. 361, 368; Nestle Patent Holding Co. v. E. Frederics, Inc. (C.C.A.) 261 F. 780, 783. A means or method employed to produce a certain result or effect, or a mode of treatment of given materials to produce a desired result, either by chemical action, by the operation or application of some element or power of nature, or of one substance to another, irrespective of any machine or mechanical device; in this sense a "process" is patentable, though, strictly speaking, it is the art and not the process which is the subject of patent. Rohm v. Martin Dennis Co., D.C.N.J., 263 F. 106, 107.

Broadly speaking, a "process" is a definite combination of new or old elements, ingredients, operations, ways, or means to produce a new, improved or old result, and any substantial change therein by omission, to the same or better result, or by modification or substitution, with different function, to the same or better result, is a new and patentable process. Minerals Separation v. Hyde, D.C. Mont., 207 F. 956, 960.

Mechanical process. A process involving solely the application of mechanism or mechanical principles; an aggregation of functions; not patentable considered apart from the mechanism employed or the finished product of manufacture. Risdon Iron, etc., Works v. Medart, 15 S.Ct. 745, 158 U.S. 68, 39 L.Ed. 899; Cochrane v. Deener, 94 U.S. 780, 24 L.Ed. 139.

Practice

This word is generally defined to be the means of compelling the defendant in an action to appear in court; Gondas v. Gondas, 99 N.J.Eq. 473, 134 A. 615, 618; or a means whereby a court compels a compliance with its demands. Frank Adam Electric Co. v. Witman, 16 Ga.App. 574, 85 S.E. 819, 820. Stevens v. Associated Mortg. Co. of New Jersey, 107 N.J.Eq. 297, 152 A. 461, 462. And when actions were commenced by original writ, instead of, as at present, by writ of summons, the method of compelling the defendant to appear was by what was termed "original process," being founded on the original writ, and so called also to distinguish it from "mesne" or "intermediate" process, which was some writ or process which issued during the progress of the suit. The word "process," however, as now commonly understood, signifies those formal instruments called "writs." The word "process" is in common-law practice frequently applied to the writ of summons, which is the instrument now in use for commencing personal actions. Farmers' Implement Co. of Hallock, Minn., v. Sandberg, 132 Minn. 389, 157 N.W. 642. But in its more comprehensive signification it includes not only the writ of summons, but all other writs which may be issued during the progress of an action. Those writs which are used to carry the judgments of the courts into effect, and which are termed "writs of execution" are also commonly denominated "final process," because they usually issue at the end of a suit. Anderson v. Dewey, 91 Conn. 510, 100 A. 99, 100.

A writ, summons, or order issued in a judicial proceeding to acquire jurisdiction of a person or his property, to expedite the cause or enforce the judgment. Royal Exchange Assurance of London v. Bennettsville & C. R. Co., 95 S.C. 375, 79 S.E. 104, 105. A writ or summons issued in the course of judicial proceedings. Radovich v. French, 36 Nev. 341, 135 P. 920, 921. The term in statutes may be used with the meaning of procedure. Safford v. United States, C.C.A.N.Y., 252 F. 471, 472.

In the practice of the English privy council in ecclesiastical appeals, "process" means an official copy of the whole proceedings and proofs of the court below, which is transmitted to the registry of the court of appeal by the registrar of the court below in obedience to an order or requisition requiring him so to do, called a "monition for process," issued by the court of appeal. Macph. Jud. Com. 173.

Abuse of process. See Abuse.

Compulsory process. See Compulsory.

Executory process. In the law of Louisiana, a summary process in the nature of an order of seizure and sale, which is available when the right of the creditor arises from an act or instrument which includes or imports a confession of judgment and a privilege or lien in his favor, and also to enforce the execution of a judgment rendered in another jurisdiction. Code Prac. art. 732.

Final process. The last process in a suit; that is, writs of execution. Thus distinguished from *mesne* process, which includes all writs issued during the progress of a cause and before final judgment. Collier v. Blake, 16 Ga.App. 382, 85 S.E. 354. A distress warrant is final process, unless arrested by the interposition of a counter affidavit. Long v. Clark, 16 Ga.App. 355, 85 S.E. 358.

Irregular process. Sometimes defined to mean process absolutely void, and not merely erroneous and voidable; but that term is usually applied to all process not issued in strict conformity with the law, whether the defect appears upon the face of the process, or by reference to extrinsic facts, and whether such defects render the process absolutely void or only voidable. And see Bryan v. Congdon, 86 F. 221, 29 C.C.A. 670.

Judicial process. In a wide sense, this term may include all the acts of a court from the beginning to the end of its proceedings in a given cause; but more specifically it means the writ, summons, mandate, or other process which is used to inform the defendant of the institution of proceedings against him and to compel his appearance, in either civil or criminal cases. Blair v. Maxbass Security Bank of Maxbass, 44 N.D. 12, 176 N.W. 98, 100; In re Smith & Shuck, D.C. Iowa, 132 F. 301, 303.

Legal process. This term is sometimes used as equivalent to "lawful process." Cooley v. Davis, 34 Iowa 130. Thus, it is said that legal process means process not merely fair on its face, but in fact valid. State v. Wagoner, 123 Kan. 586, 256 P. 959, 960. But properly it means a writ, warrant, mandate, or other process issuing from a court of justice, such as an attachment, execution, injunction, etc. Grossman v. Weiss, 221 N.Y.S. 266, 267, 129 Misc. 234.

Mesne process. As distinguished from *final* process, this signifies any writ or process issued between the commencement of the action and the suing out of execution. 3 Bla.Comm. 279. This is substantially the meaning of the term as used in admiralty rule 1 (29 S.Ct. xxxix; 28 U.S.C.A. §§ 2071, 2073), providing that no mesne process shall issue until the libel shall be filed in the clerk's office. The City of Philadelphia, D.C.Pa., 263 F. 234, 235. "Mesne" in this connection may be defined as intermediate; intervening; the middle between two extremes. L. N. Dantzler Lumber Co. v. Texas & P. Ry. Co., 119 Miss. 328, 80 So. 770, 775, 49 A.L.R. 1669. Mesne process includes the writ of summons, (although that is now the usual commencement of actions,) because anciently that was preceded by the original writ. The writ of *capias ad respondendum* was called "mesne" to distinguish it, on the one hand, from the original process by which a suit was formerly commenced; and, on the other, from the final process of execution. Birmingham Dry Goods Co. v. Bledsoe, 21 So. 403, 113 Ala. 418.

Original process. That by which a judicial proceeding is instituted; process to compel the appearance of the defendant. Distinguished from "mesne" process, which issues, during the progress of a suit, for some subordinate or collateral purpose; and from "final" process, which is process of execution. Appeal of Hotchkiss, 32 Conn. 353.

Process of interpleader. A means of determining the right to property claimed by each of two or more persons, which is in the possession of a third.

Process of law. See Due Process of Law.

Process roll. In practice. A roll used for the entry of process to save the statute of limitations. 1 Tidd, Pr. 161, 162.

Regular process. Such as is issued according to rule and the prescribed practice, or which emanates, lawfully and in a proper case, from a court or magistrate possessing jurisdiction.

Summary process. Such as is immediate or instantaneous, in distinction from the ordinary course, by emanating and taking effect without intermediate applications or delays. Gaines v. Travis, 8 N.Y.Leg.Obs. 49.

Trustee process. The name given in some states (particularly in New England) to the process of garnishment or foreign attachment.

Void process. Such as was issued without power in the court to award it, or which the court had not acquired jurisdiction to issue in the particular case, or which fails in some material respect to comply with the requisite form of legal process. Bryan v. Congdon, C.C.A.Kan., 86 F. 221, 223, 29 C.C.A. 670.

PROCESSION. To beat the bounds of (a parish, lands, etc.). Webster's New Int. Dict. In some of the North American colonies (and still in the states of North Carolina and Tennessee), to make a procession around a piece of land in order formally to determine its bounds. Murray's New English Dict.

The ceremony of perambulating the boundaries of a parish ("processioning," as it was commonly called in later times) is an extremely old one. Blomfield, *Hist. Fritwell,* quoted in Murray's New English Dict. *s. v.* "Processioning" *(q. v.).*

PROCESSIONING. A survey and inspection of boundaries periodically performed in some of the American colonies by the local authorities. It was analogous in part to the English perambulation (*q. v.*), and was superseded by the introduction of the practice of accurate surveying and of recording. The term is still used of some official surveys in North Carolina and Tennessee. Cent. Dict. See Code Tenn.1858, § 2020 et seq.; Rhodes v. Ange, 173 N.C. 25, 91 S.E. 356.

PROCESUM CONTINUANDO. In English practice. A writ for the continuance of process after the death of the chief justice or other justices in the commission of *oyer* and *terminer*. Reg. Orig. 128.

PROCESSUS LEGIS EST GRAVIS VEXATIO; EXECUTIO LEGIS CORONAT OPUS. The process of the law is a grievous vexation; the execution of the law crowns the work. Co.Litt. 289*b*. The proceedings in an action while in progress are burdensome and vexatious; the execution, being the end and object of the action, crowns the labor, or rewards it with success.

PROCHEIN. L. Fr. Next. A term somewhat used in modern law, and more frequently in the old law; as *prochein ami, prochein cousin.* Co. Litt. 10.

PROCHEIN AMI. (Spelled, also, *prochein amy* and *prochain amy.*) Next friend. As an infant cannot legally sue in his own name, the action must be brought by his *prochein ami*; that is, some friend (not being his guardian) who will appear as plaintiff in his name.

PROCHEIN AVOIDANCE. Next vacancy. A power to appoint a minister to a church when it shall next become void.

PROCHRONISM. An error in chronology, consisting in dating a thing before it happened.

PROCINCTUS. Lat. In the Roman law. A girding or preparing for battle. *Testamentum in procinctu,* a will made by a soldier, while girding himself, or preparing to engage in battle. Adams, Rom.Ant. 62; Calvin.

PROCLAIM. To promulgate; to announce; to publish, by governmental authority, intelligence of public acts or transactions or other matters important to be known by the people. To give wide publicity to; to disclose. Simon v. Moore, D.C.Mo., 261 F. 638, 643.

PROCLAMATION. The act of proclaiming or publishing; a formal declaration; an avowal. Dickinson v. Page, 120 Ark. 377, 179 S.W. 1004, 1006; State v. Oregon-Washington R. & Nav. Co., 128 Wash. 365, 223 P. 600, 608. The act of causing some state matters to be published or made generally known. A written or printed document in which are contained such matters, issued by proper authority. 3 Inst. 162; 1 Bl.Comm. 170.

Also, the public nomination made of any one to a high office; as, such a prince was *proclaimed* emperor.

In practice. The declaration made by the crier, by authority of the court, that something is about to be done.

It usually commences with the French word *Oyez, do you hear, hear ye,* in order to attract attention; it is particularly used on the opening of the court, and at its adjournment; it is also frequently employed to discharge persons who have been accused of crimes or misdemeanors.

In equity practice. Proclamation made by a sheriff upon a writ of attachment, summoning a defendant who has failed to appear personally to appear and answer the plaintiff's bill. 3 Bl.Comm. 444.

PROCLAMATION BY LORD OF MANOR. A proclamation made by the lord of a manor (thrice repeated) requiring the heir or devisee of a deceased copyholder to present himself, pay the fine, and be admitted to the estate; failing which appearance, the lord might seize the lands *quousque* (provisionally.)

PROCLAMATION OF A FINE. The notice or proclamation which was made after the engrossment of a fine of lands, and which consisted in its being openly read in court sixteen times, viz., four times in the term in which it was made, and four times in each of the three succeeding terms, which, however, was afterwards reduced to one reading in each term. Cowell. See 2 Bl.Comm. 352.

PROCLAMATION OF EXIGENTS. In old English law. When an *exigent* was awarded, a writ of proclamation issued, at the same time, commanding the sheriff of the county wherein the defendant dwelt to make three proclamations thereof in places the most notorious, and most likely to come to his knowledge, a month before the outlawry should take place. 3 Bl.Comm. 284.

PROCLAMATION OF REBELLION. In old English law. A proclamation to be made by the sheriff commanding the attendance of a person who had neglected to obey a subpœna or attachment in chancery. If he did not surrender himself after this proclamation, a commission of rebellion issued. 3 Bl.Comm. 444.

PROCLAMATION OF RECUSANTS. A proclamation whereby recusants were formerly convicted, on non-appearance at the assizes. Jacob.

PROCLAMATOR. An officer of the English court of common pleas.

PRO–CONSUL. Lat. In the Roman law. Originally a consul whose command was prolonged after his office had expired. An officer with consular authority, but without the title of "consul." The governor of a province. Calvin.

PROCREATION. The generation of children. It is said to be one of the principal ends of marriage. Inst. tit. 2, in pr.

PROCTOR. One appointed to manage the affairs of another or represent him in judgment. A procurator, proxy, or attorney. More particularly, an officer of the admiralty and ecclesiastical courts whose duties and business correspond exactly to those of an attorney at law or solicitor in chancery.

A proctor, strictly speaking, conducts the proceeding out of court, as an English solicitor does in common-law courts; while the advocate conducts those in court. But in this country the distinction is not observed. The fees of proctors are fixed by statute (see 28 U.S.C.A. § 1923).

An ecclesiastical person sent to the lower house of convocation as the representative of a cathedral, a collegiate church, or the clergy of a diocese. Also certain administrative or magisterial officers in the universities.

PROCTORS OF THE CLERGY. They who are chosen and appointed to appear for cathedral or other collegiate churches; as also for the common clergy of every diocese, to sit in the convocation house in the time of parliament. Wharton.

PROCURACY. The writing or instrument which authorizes a procurator to act. Cowell; Termes de la Ley.

PROCURADOR DEL COMUN. Sp. In Spanish law, an officer appointed to make inquiry, put a petitioner in possession of land prayed for, and execute the orders of the executive in that behalf. Lecompte v. U. S., 11 How. 115, 126, 13 L.Ed. 627.

PROCURARE. Lat. To take care of another's affairs for him, or in his behalf; to manage; to take care of or superintend.

PROCURATIO. Lat. Management of another's affairs by his direction and in his behalf; procuration; agency.

PROCURATIO EST EXHIBITIO SUMPTUUM NECESSARIORUM FACTA PRÆLATIS, QUI DIŒCESES PERAGRANDO, ECCLESIAS SUBJECTAS VISITANT. Dav. Ir. K. B. 1. Procuration is the providing necessaries for the bishops, who, in traveling through their dioceses, visit the churches subject to them.

PROCURATION. Agency; proxy; the act of constituting another one's attorney in fact. The act by which one person gives power to another to act in his place, as he could do himself. Clinton v. Hibb's Ex'x, 259 S.W. 356, 358, 202 Ky. 304, 35 A. L.R. 462. Action under a power of attorney or other constitution of agency. Indorsing a bill or note "by procuration" is doing it as proxy for another or by his authority. The use of the word procuration (usually, *per procuratione*, or abbreviated to *per proc.* or *p. p.*) on a promissory note by an agent is notice that the agent has but a limited authority to sign. Neg.Instr.Act. § 21.

An *express* procuration is one made by the express consent of the parties. An *implied* or *tacit* procuration takes place when an individual sees another managing his affairs and does not interfere to prevent it. Dig. 17, 1, 6, 2; 50, 17, 60; Code 7, 32, 2. Procurations are also divided into those which contain absolute power, or a general authority, and those which give only a limited power. Dig. 3, 3, 58; 17, 1, 60, 4.

Also, the act or offence of procuring women for lewd purposes. Odgers, C.L. 214.

In ecclesiastical law. In the plural, the term denotes certain sums of money which parish priests pay yearly to the bishops or archdeacons, *ratione visitationis*. Dig. 3, 39, 25; Ayliffe, Parerg. 429; 17 Viner, Abr. 544.

PROCURATION FEE, or MONEY. In English law. Brokerage or commission allowed to scriveners and solicitors for obtaining loans of money. 4 Bl.Comm. 157.

PROCURATIONEM ADVERSUS NULLA EST PRÆSCRIPTIO. Dav. Ir. K. B. 6. There is no prescription against procuration.

PROCURATOR. In the civil law. A proctor; a person who acts for another by virtue of a procuration. Dig. 3, 3, 1.

In old English law. An agent or attorney; a bailiff or servant. A proxy of a lord in parliament.

In ecclesiastical law. One who collected the fruits of a benefice for another. An advocate of a religious house, who was to solicit the interest and plead the causes of the society. A proxy or representative of a parish church.

PROCURATOR FISCAL. In Scotch law, this is the title of the public prosecutor for each district, who institutes the preliminary inquiry into crime within his district. The office is analogous, in some respect, to that of "prosecuting attorney," "district attorney," or "state's attorney" in America.

PROCURATOR IN REM SUAM. Proctor (attorney) in his own affair, or with reference to his own property. This term is used in Scotch law to denote that a person is acting under a procuration (power of attorney) with reference to a thing which has become his own property. Ersk.Inst. 3, 5, 2.

PROCURATOR LITIS. In the civil law. One who by command of another institutes and carries on for him a suit. Vicat, Voc.Jur. *Procurator* is properly used of the attorney of *actor* (the plaintiff), *defensor* of the attorney of *reus* (the defendant). It is distinguished from *advocatus*, who was one who undertook the defence of persons, not things, and who was generally the patron of the person whose defence he prepared, the person himself speaking it. It is also distinguished from *cognitor* who conducted the cause in the presence of his principal, and generally in cases of citizenship; whereas the procurator conducted the cause in the absence of his principal. Calvinus, Lex.

PROCURATOR NEGOTIORUM. In the civil law. An attorney in fact; a manager of business affairs for another person.

PROCURATOR PROVINCIÆ. In Roman law. A provincial officer who managed the affairs of the revenue, and had a judicial power in matters that concerned the revenue. Adams, Rom.Ant. 178.

PROCURATORES ECCLESIÆ PAROCHIALIS. The old name for church-wardens. Paroch.Antiq. 562.

PROCURATORIUM. In old English law. The procuratory or instrument by which any person or community constituted or delegated their *procurator* or proctors to represent them in any judicial court or cause. Cowell.

PROCURATORY OF RESIGNATION. In Scotch law. A form of proceeding by which a vassal authorizes the feu to be returned to his superior. Bell. It is analogous to the surrender of copyholds in England.

PROCURATRIX. In old English law. A female agent or attorney in fact. Fleta, lib. 3, c. 4, § 4.

PROCURE. To initiate a proceeding; to cause a thing to be done; to instigate; to contrive, bring about, effect, or cause. Marcus v. Bernstein, 117 N.C. 31, 23 S.E. 38. Rosenbarger v. State, 154 Ind. 425, 56 N.E. 914. To persuade, induce, prevail upon, or cause. Hines v. State, 16 Ga.App. 411, 85 S.E. 452, 454. To obtain, as intoxicating liquor, for another. State v. Desmarais, 81 N.H. 199, 123 A. 582, 583. Compare, however, People v. Robertson, 284 Ill. 620, 120 N.E. 539, 541. To find or introduce;—said of a broker who obtains a customer. Low v. Paddock, Mo.App., 220 S.W. 969, 972. To bring the seller and the buyer together so that the seller has an opportunity to sell. Fritsch v. Hess, 162 P. 70, 71, 49 Utah, 75. See, also, Miller v. Eldridge, Tex.Civ.App., 286 S.W. 999, 1000.

To "procure" an act to be done is not synonymous with to "suffer" it to be done. 2 Ben. 196.

PROCURER. One who procures for another the gratification of his lusts; a pimp; a panderer; one who solicits trade for a prostitute or lewd woman. State v. Smith, 149 La. 700, 90 So. 28, 30. One that procures the seduction or prostitution of girls. The offense is punishable by statute in England and America. One who uses means to bring anything about, especially one who does so secretly and corruptly. U. S. v. Richmond, C.C.A. Pa., 17 F.2d 28, 30.

PROCUREUR. In French law. An attorney; one who has received a commission from another to act on his behalf. There were in France two classes of *procureurs: Procureurs ad negotia*, appointed by an individual to act for him in the administration of his affairs; persons invested with a power of attorney; corresponding to "attorneys in fact." *Procureurs ad lites* were persons appointed and authorized to act for a party in a court of justice. These corresponded to attorneys at law, (now called, in England, "solicitors of the supreme court.") The order of *procureurs* was abolished in 1791, and that of *avoués* established in their place. Mozley & Whitley.

PROCUREUR DE LA RÉPUBLIQUE. (Formerly *procureur du roi.*) In French law. A public prosecutor, with whom rests the initiation of all criminal proceedings. In the exercise of his office (which appears to include the apprehension of offenders) he is entitled to call to his assistance the public force, (*posse comitatus*;) and the officers of police are auxiliary to him.

PROCUREUR GENERAL, or IMPERIAL. In French law. An officer of the imperial court, who either personally or by his deputy prosecuted every one who was accused of a crime according to the forms of French law. His functions were apparently confined to preparing the case for trial at the assizes, assisting in that trial, demanding the sentence in case of a conviction, and being present at the delivery of the sentence. He had a general superintendence over the officers of police and of the *juges d'instruction*, and he required from the *procureur du roi* a general report once in every three months. Brown.

PROCURING CAUSE. The approximate cause; the cause originating a series of events, which, without break in their continuity, result in the accomplishment of the prime object. Averill v. Hart & O'Farrell, 101 W.Va. 411, 132 S.E. 870, 875; The inducing cause. Moseley-Comstock Realty Co. v. McClelland, Mo.App., 294 S.W. 103, 106. The direct or proximate cause. Custer v. Thaxton, Tex.Civ.App., 287 S.W. 528, 529. Substantially synonymous with "efficient cause." Bagley v. Foley, 82 Wash. 222, 144 P. 25.

A broker will be regarded as the "procuring cause" of a sale, so as to be entitled to commission, if his efforts are the foundation on which the negotiations resulting in a sale are begun. Cales v. Pattison, 189 Okl. 160, 114 P.2d 457, 458.

PRODES HOMINES. A term said by Tomlins to be frequently applied in the ancient books to the barons of the realm, particularly as constituting a council or administration or government. It is probably a corruption of "probi homines."

PRODIGAL. In civil law. A person who, though of full age, is incapable of managing his affairs, and of the obligations which attend them, in consequence of his bad conduct, and for whom a curator is therefore appointed. See Prodigus.

According to the Code Napoléon, a French subject of full age, who is of extravagant habits, when adjudged to be a "prodigal," is restrained from dealing with his movables without the consent of a legal adviser.

PRODIGUS. Lat. In Roman law. A prodigal; a spendthrift; a person whose extravagant habits manifested an inability to administer his own affairs, and for whom a guardian might therefore be appointed.

PRODITION. Treason; treachery.

PRODITOR. A traitor.

PRODITORIE. Treasonably. This is a technical word formerly used in indictments for treason, when they were written in Latin. Tomlins.

PRODUCE, *n.* The product of natural growth labor, or capital. Articles produced or grown from or on the soil, or found in the soil. Newhoff Packing Co. v. Sharpe, 240 S.W. 1101, 1103, 146 Tenn. 293.

The produce of a farm has been held not to include beef raised and killed thereon. Philadelphia v. Davis, 6 Watts & S. (Pa.) 269. But See City of Higbee v. Burgin, 197 Mo. App. 682, 201 S.W. 558.

PRODUCE, *v.* To bring forward; to show or exhibit; to bring into view or notice; as, to present a play, including its presentation in motion pictures. Manners v. Morosco, D.C.N.Y., 254 F. 737, 740; to present testimony, In re McGuire's Will, 220 N.Y.S. 773, 776, 128 Misc. 679; to produce books or writings at a trial in obedience to a *subpœna duces tecum.*

To produce, for the purpose of use in a legal hearing, within the meaning of a subpœna ordering a witness to produce a public record, means more than an appearance with the document in his possession, and implies the handing of it to the tribunal for perusal, and, if that is not asked, the reading aloud of it by witness or counsel. Langley v. F. W. Woolworth Co., 46 R.I. 394, 129 A. 1, 2.

To make, originate, or yield, as gasoline. Gay Oil Co. v. State, 170 Ark. 587, 280 S.W. 632, 634. To bring to the surface, as oil. Tedrow v. Shaffer, 23 Ohio App. 343, 155 N.E. 510, 511.

To yield, as revenue. Thus, sums are "produced" by taxation, not when the tax is levied, but when the sums are collected. Board of Education of Louisville v. Sea, 167 Ky. 772, 181 S.W. 670, 673.

PRODUCE BROKER. A person whose occupation it is to buy or sell agricultural or farm products. U. S. v. Simons, 1 Abb. (U.S.) 470, Fed.Cas. No.16,291.

PRODUCENT. The party calling a witness under the old system of the English ecclesiastical courts.

PRODUCER. One who produces, brings, forth, or generates. Boland v. Cecil, 150 P.2d 819, 822, 65 Cal.App.2d Supp. 832.

PRODUCING. Bring about, to cause to happen or take place, as an effect or result. Strong v. Aetna Casualty & Surety Co., Tex.Civ.App., 170 S.W.2d 786, 788.

PRODUCING CAUSE. Respecting broker's commission, is act which, continuing in unbroken chain of cause and effect, produces result. Schebesta v. Stewart, Tex.Civ.App., 37 S.W.2d 781, 786.

A "producing cause" of an employee's death for which compensation is sought is that cause which, in a natural and continuous sequence, produces the death, and without which death would not have occurred. Jones v. Traders & General Ins. Co., 140 Tex. 599, 169 S.W.2d 160, 162.

PRODUCT. With reference to property, proceeds; yield; income; receipts; return. Gibbs v. Barkley, Tex.Com.App., 242 S.W. 462, 465.

The "products" of a farm may include the increase of cattle on the premises. Case v. Ploutz, 154 N.Y.S. 914, 915, 90 Misc. 568.

PRODUCTIO SECTÆ. In old English law. Production of suit; the production by a plaintiff of his *secta* or witnesses to prove the allegations of his count. 3 Bl.Comm. 295.

PRODUCTION. That which is produced or made product; fruit of labor; as the productions of the earth, comprehending all vegetables and fruits; the productions of intellect, or genius, as poems and prose compositions; the productions of art, as manufactures of every kind. Dano v. R. Co., 27 Ark. 567.

In political economy. The creation of objects which constitute wealth. The requisites of production are labor, capital, and the materials and motive forces afforded by nature. Of these, labor and the raw material of the globe are primary and indispensable. Natural motive powers may be called in to the assistance of labor, and are a help, but not an essential, of production. The remaining requisite, capital, is itself the product of labor. Its instrumentality in production is therefore, in reality, that of labor in an indirect shape. Mill, Pol. Econ.; Wharton.

PRODUCTION FOR COMMERCE. Within Fair Labor Standards Act includes production of goods which, at time of production, employer, according to normal course of his business, intends or expects to move in interstate commerce immediately following initial sale. Fair Labor Standards Act of 1938, §§ 6, 7, 29 U.S.C.A. §§ 206, 207. Hill v. Jones, D.C.Ky., 59 F.Supp. 569, 572.

PRODUCTION OF SUIT. In pleading. The formula, "and therefore [or thereupon] he brings his suit," etc., with which declarations always conclude. Steph.Pl. 428, 429. In old pleading, this referred to the production by the plaintiff of his *secta* or suit, *i. e.* persons prepared to confirm what he had stated in the declaration. The phrase has remained; but the practice from which it arose is obsolete. 3 Bla.Comm. 295.

PROFANE. Irreverent toward God or holy things; written or spoken; acting or acted, in manifest or implied contempt of sacred things. Town of Torrington v. Taylor, 59 Wyo. 109, 137 P.2d 621, 624; Duncan v. U. S., C.C.A.Or., 48 F.2d 128, 133. That which has not been consecrated. Dig. 11, 7, 2, 4.

PROFANE PLACE. A place which is neither sacred nor sanctified nor religious. Dig. 11, 7, 2, 4.

PROFANELY. In a profane manner. In Pennsylvania, a technical word in indictments for the statutory offense of profanity. Updegraph v. Com., 11 Serg. & R. (Pa.) 394.

PROFANITY. Irreverence towards sacred things; particularly, an irreverent or blasphemous use of the name of God; punishable by statute in some jurisdictions. Orf v. State, 147 Miss. 160, 113 So. 202. Cason v. Baskin, 155 Fla. 198, 20 So.2d 243, 247, 168 A.L.R. 430.

PROFECTITIUS. Lat. In the civil law. That which descends to us from our ascendants. Dig. 23, 3, 5.

PROFER. In old English law. An offer or proffer; an offer or endeavor to proceed in an action, by any man concerned to do so. A return made by a sheriff of his accounts into the exchequer; a payment made on such return. Cowell.

PROFERT IN CURIA. L. Lat. (Sometimes written *profert in curiam.*) He produces in court. In old practice, these words were inserted in a declaration, as an allegation that the plaintiff was ready to produce, or did actually produce, in court, the deed or other written instrument on which his suit was founded, in order that the court might inspect the same and the defendant hear it read. The same formula was used where the defendant pleaded a written instrument.

In modern practice. An allegation formally made in a pleading, where a party alleges a deed, that he shows it in court, it being in fact retained in his own custody. Steph.Pl. 67. But by virtue of the allegation, the deed is then constructively in possession of the court. 6 M. & G. 277; Tucker v. State, 11 Md. 322; Germain v. Wilgus, 67 F. 597, 14 C.C.A. 561. The profert of any recorded instrument, as letters patent, is equivalent to annexing a copy. American Bell Tel. Co. v. Southern Tel. Co., C.C.Ark., 34 F. 803. This result does not occur, however, in the case of other documents, such as a note. Waterhouse v. Sterchi Bros. Furniture Co., 139 Tenn. 117, 201 S.W. 150, 151.

Profert and oyer are abolished in England by the Common Law Procedure Act, 15 & 16 Vict. c. 76; and a provision exists, 14 & 15 Vict. c. 99, for allowing inspection of all documents in the possession or under the control of the party against whom the inspection is asked. 25 E. L. & E. 304. In many of the states profert has been abolished, and in some instances the instrument must be set forth in the pleading of the party relying upon it.

PROFESS. To make open declaration of, to make public declaration or avowal. Wristen v. Wristen, Tex.Civ.App., 119 S.W.2d 1104, 1106.

PROFESSION. A public declaration respecting something. Cod. 10, 41, 6.

A vocation, calling, occupation or employment involving labor, skill, education, special knowledge and compensation or profit, but the labor and skill involved is predominantly mental or intellectual, rather than physical or manual. Maryland Casualty Co. v. Crazy Water Co., Tex.Civ.App., 160 S.W.2d 102, 104. The method or means pursued by persons of technical or scientific training. Board of Sup'rs of Amherst County v. Boaz, 176 Va. 126, 10 S.E.2d 498, 499.

The term originally contemplated only theology, law, and medicine, but as applications of science and learning are extended to other departments of affairs, other vocations also receive the name, which implies professed attainments in special knowledge as distinguished from mere skill. Aulen v. Triumph Explosive, D.C.Md., 58 F.Supp. 4, 8.

In ecclesiastical law. The act of entering into a religious order. See 17 Vin.Abr. 545.

PROFESSIONAL. A term applied in the Immigration Law, 8 U.S.C.A. § 137c, to an alien instrumental musician who is of distinguished merit and ability or is a member of a musical organization of distinguished merit and is applying for admission as such. It is opposed to amateur, and as used in the statute refers to one who pursues an art and makes his living therefrom. U. S. ex rel. Liebmann v. Flynn, D.C.N.Y., 16 F.2d 1006, 1007; U. S. v. Commissioner of Immigration at Port of New York, C.C.A.N.Y., 298 F. 449, 450.

PROFESSIONAL EMPLOYMENT. Within the meaning of a statute authorizing actions for misconduct or neglect, professional services by an attorney are not limited to litigation, but include giving advice, managing a business, devising plans, and making collections, and the employment may be recognized as professional, although including services not ordinarily classed as professional services; whether the attorney is professionally employed depending on the relations and mutual understanding of what was said and done, and on all the facts and circumstances of the particular undertaking. Case v. Ranney, 174 Mich. 673, 140 N.W. 943, 946.

PROFESSOR. Public teacher of any science or branch of learning. U. S. ex rel. Jacovides v. Day, C.C.A.N.Y., 32 F.2d 542, 543.

PROFICUA. L. Lat. In old English law. Profits; especially the "issues and profits" of an estate in land. Co.Litt. 142.

PROFILE. In civil engineering, a drawing representing the elevation of the various points on the plan of a road, or the like, above some fixed elevation. Pub.St.Mass.1882, p. 1294. A side or sectional elevation, or a drawing showing a vertical section of the ground along a surveyed line or graded work. Also, an outline or contour. Taggart v. Great Northern Ry. Co., D.C.Wash., 208 F. 455, 456. As used in Act March 3, 1875, c. 152, § 1, 18 St. 482 (43 U.S.C.A. § 934), granting rights of way through the public lands to railroads, the term, in view of regulations of the general land office, may be deemed to mean a map of alignment or of definite location. Taggart v. Great Northern Ry. Co., C.C.A.Wash., 211 F. 288, 292.

PROFIT. The advance in the price of goods sold beyond the cost of purchase. The gain made by the sale of produce or manufactures, after deducting the value of the labor, materials, rents, and all expenses, together with the interest of the capital employed. Webster. Lapham v. Tax Com'r, 244 Mass. 40, 138 N.E. 708, 710; McCready v. Bullis, 59 Cal.App. 286, 210 P. 638, 640. Gain realized from business or investment over and above expenditures. Citizens Nat. Bank v. Corl, 225 N.C. 96, 33 S.E.2d 613, 616. Fairchild v. Gray, 242 N.Y.S. 192, 196, 136 Misc. 704. An excess of the value of returns over the value of advances. The same as net profits. Crawford v. Surety Inv. Co., 91 Kan. 748, 139 P. 481, 484.

The term "profit," as applied to a corporation, has a larger meaning than "dividends," and covers benefits of any kind, the excess of value over cost, acquisition beyond expenditure, gain or advance. Booth v. Gross, Kelley & Co., 30 N.M. 465, 238 P. 829, 831, 41 A.L.R. 868. Dividends are properly declared only from profits after they have been earned. Indiana Veneer & Lumber Co. v. Hageman, 57 Ind.App. 668, 105 N.E. 253, 256. This is a word of very extended signification. In commerce, it means the advance in the price of goods sold beyond the cost of purchase. In distinction from the wages of labor, it is well understood to imply the net return to the capital of stock employed, after deducting all the expenses, including not only the wages of those employed by the capitalist, but the wages of the capitalist himself for superintending the employment of his capital or stock. Columbus Mining Co. v. Ross, 218 Ky. 98, 290 S.W. 1052, 1053, 50 A.L.R. 1394. After indemnifying the capitalist for his outlay, there commonly remains a surplus, which is his profit, the net income from his capital. 1 Mill, Polit. Econ. c. 15.

Profits have been divided by writers on political economy into gross and net,—gross profits being the whole difference between the value of advances and the value of returns made by their employment, and net profits being so much of that difference as is attributable solely to the capital employed. Malthus, Political Econ.; M'Culloch, Political Econ. 563. For judicial criticism of the expression "gross profits," see the opinion of Jessel, M. R., 10 App.Cas. 446. See, also, Buie v. Kennedy, 164 N.C. 290, 80 S.E. 445, 446.

The benefit, advantage, or pecuniary gain accruing to the owner or occupant of land from its actual use; as in the familiar phrase "rents, issues and profits," or in the expression "mesne profits."

A devise of the rents and profits of land is equivalent to a devise of the land itself, and will carry the legal as well as the beneficial interest therein. 2 B. & Ald. 42; Earl v. Rowe, 35 Me. 414, 58 Am.Dec. 714; 1 Bro.C.C. 310.

A division sometimes made of incorporeal hereditaments. 2 Steph.Comm. 2. Profits are divided into *profits à prendre* and *profits à rendre.* See those titles, *infra.*

Clear profit. A net profit, or a profit above the price paid. Kreitz v. Gallenstein, 170 Ky. 16, 185 S.W. 132, 134.

Mesne profits. Intermediate profits; that is, profits which have been accruing between two given periods. Thus, after a party has recovered the land itself in an action of ejectment, he frequently brings another action for the purpose of recovering the profits which have been accruing or arising out of the land between the time when his title to the possession accrued or was raised and the time of his recovery in the action of ejectment, and such an action is thence termed an "action for mesne profits." Brown; New York, O. & W. Ry. Co. v. Livingston, 206 App.Div. 589, 201 N.Y.S. 629, 633.

Mesne profits, action of. An action of trespass brought to recover profits derived from land, while the possession of it has been improperly withheld; that is, the yearly value of the premises. Worthington v. Hiss, 70 Md. 172, 16 A. 534; Thompson v. Bower, 60 Barb. (N.Y.) 477.

Net profits. Theoretically all profits are "net." Buie v. Kennedy, 164 N.C. 290, 80 S.E. 445, 446. But as the expression "gross profits" is sometimes used to describe the mere excess of present value over former value, or of returns from sales over prime cost, the phrase "net profits" is appropriate to describe the gain which remains after the further deduction of all expenses, charges, costs, allowance for depreciation, etc.

Paper profits. Speculative or prospective profits. Tooey v. C. L. Percival Co., 192 Iowa, 267, 182 N.W. 403, 404.

Profit à prendre. Called also "right of common." A right exercised by one man in the soil of another, accompanied with participation in the profits of the soil thereof. A right to take a part of the soil or produce of the land. Gadow v. Hunholtz, 160 Wis. 293, 151 N.W. 810, 811, Ann.Cas. 1917D, 91.

The term includes the right to take soil, gravel, minerals, and the like from another's land, Munsey v. Mills & Garitty, 115 Tex. 469, 283 S.W. 754, 759; Mathews Slate Co. of New York v. Advance Industrial Supply Co., 172 N.Y.S. 830, 832, 185 App.Div. 74; the right to take seaweed, Hill v. Lord, 48 Me. 100; and to take coal or timber, Huff v. McCauley, 53 Pa. 206, 91 Am.Dec. 203; the right to hunt, St. Helen Shooting Club v. Mogle, 234 Mich. 60, 207 N.W. 915, 917; or fish, Turner v. Hebron, 22 A. 951, 61 Conn. 175, 14 L.R.A. 386; and the right to cut grass, Baker v. Kenney, 145 Iowa 638, 124 N.W. 901, 139 Am.St.Rep. 456; but not the right to take running water, since it is not a product of the soil. Hill v. Lord, 48 Me. 83. Profits à prendre differ from easements, in that the former are rights of profit, and the latter are mere rights of convenience without profit. Gale, Easem. 1; Hall. Bingham v. Salene, 15 Or. 208, 14 P. 523, 3 Am.St.Rep. 152; Pierce v. Keator, 70 N.Y. 422, 26 Am.Rep. 612. A profit à prendre is considered an interest or estate in the land itself, 28 C.J.S., Easements, 628, 631, § 3, whereas an easement is a privilege without profit. Walker v. Dwelle, 187 Iowa 1384, 175 N.W. 957. Saratoga State Waters Corporation v. Pratt, 227 N.Y. 429, 125 N.E. 834, 838. But a profit à prendre is sometimes spoken of as an easement, especially when appurtenant to a dominant tenement. Grubb v. Grubb, 74 Pa. 25, 33. The right can be acquired only by grant or prescription, and not by custom or parol. 28 C.J.S., Easements, 628, 633, § 3. Council v. Sanderlin, 183 N.C. 253, 111 S.E. 365, 367, 32 A. L.R. 1527.

Profit à rendre. Such as is received at the hands of and rendered by another. The term comprehends rents and services. Ham.N.P. 192.

Profit and loss. The gain or loss arising from goods bought or sold, or from carrying on any other business, the former of which, in book-keeping, is placed on the creditor's side; the latter on the debtor's side.

Surplus profits. Within the meaning of a statute prohibiting the declaration of corporate dividends other than from such profits, the excess of receipts over expenditures, or net earnings or receipts, or gross receipts, less expenses of operation. Southern California Home Builders v. Young, 45 Cal.App. 679, 188 P. 586, 591. Of a corporation, the difference over and above the capital stock, debts, and liabilities. Western & Southern Fire Ins. Co. v. Murphey, 56 Okl. 702, 156 P. 885, 890.

PROFITEERING. The acquisition of excessive profits;—usually used as a term of reproach and dishonor. Mount v. Welsh, 118 Or. 568, 247 P. 815, 822.

PROGENER. Lat. In the civil law. A grandson-in-law. Dig. 38, 10, 4, 6.

PROGRESSION. That state of a business which is neither the commencement nor the end. Some act done after the matter has commenced, and before it is completed. Plowd. 343.

PROHIBETUR NE QUIS FACIAT IN SUO QUOD NOCERE POSSIT ALIENO. It is forbidden for any one to do or make on his own [land] what may injure another's. 9 Coke, 59a.

PROHIBIT. To forbid by law; to prevent;—not synonymous with "regulate." Simpkins v. State, 35 Okl.Cr. 143, 249 P. 168, 170; Arkansas Railroad Commission v. Independent Bus Lines, 172 Ark. 3, 285 S.W. 388, 390.

PROHIBITED DEGREES. Those degrees of relationship by consanguinity which are so close that marriage between persons related to each other in any of such degrees is forbidden by law. State v. Guiton, 51 La.Ann. 155, 24 So. 784.

PROHIBITIO DE VASTO, DIRECTA PARTI. A judicial writ which was formerly addressed to a tenant, prohibiting him from waste, pending suit. Reg.Jud. 21; Moore, 917.

PROHIBITION. Inhibition; interdiction. Talbott v. Casualty Co., 74 Md. 545, 22 A. 395, 13 L.R.A. 584.

In practice. The name of a writ issued by a superior court, directed to the judge and parties of a suit in an inferior court, commanding them to cease from the prosecution of the same, upon a suggestion that the cause originally, or some collateral matter arising therein, does not belong to that jurisdiction, but to the cognizance of some other court. 3 Bl.Comm. 112; Alexander v. Crollott, 199 U.S. 580, 26 S.Ct. 161, 50 L.Ed. 317. It is only issued in cases of extreme necessity where the grievance cannot be redressed by ordinary proceedings at law, or in equity, or by appeal. Niagara Falls Power Co. v. Halpin, 45 N.Y.S.2d 421, 424, 181 Misc. 13; State ex rel. Levy v. Savord, 143 Ohio St. 451, 55 N.E.2d 735, 736.

An extraordinary writ, issued by a superior court to an inferior court to prevent the latter from exceeding its jurisdiction, either by prohibiting it from assuming jurisdiction in a matter over which it has no control, or from going beyond its legitimate powers in a matter of which it has jurisdiction. State v. Medler, 19 N.M. 252, 142 P. 376, 377. An extraordinary judicial writ issuing out of a court of superior jurisdiction, directed to an inferior court or tribunal exercising judicial powers, for the purpose of preventing the inferior tribunal from usurping a jurisdiction with which it is not lawfully vested, State v. Stanfield, 11 Okl.Cr. 147, 143 P. 519, 522; from assuming or exercising jurisdiction over matters beyond its cognizance, Jackson v. Calhoun, 156 Ga. 756, 120 S.E. 114, 115; or from exceeding its jurisdiction in matters of which it has cognizance. Jackson v. Calhoun, 156 Ga. 756, 120 S.E. 114, 115.

The writ of prohibition is the counterpart of the writ of mandate. It arrests the proceedings of any tribunal, corporation, board, or person, when such proceedings are without or in excess of the jurisdiction of such tribunal, corporation, board, or person. Code Civ.Proc.Cal. § 1102. State v. Packard, 32 N.D. 301, 155 N.W. 666, 667. Johnston v. Hunter, 50 W.Va. 52, 40 S.E. 448. State v. Evans, 88 Wis. 255, 60 N.W. 433.

Prohibition may, where the action sought to be prohibited is judicial in its nature, be exercised against public officers. State ex rel. United States Fidelity & Guaranty Co. v. Harty, 276 Mo. 583, 208 S.W. 835, 838.

The term *prohibition* is also applied to the interdiction of making, possessing, selling or giving away, intoxicating liquors, either absolutely, or for beverage purposes, or for other than medicinal, scientific, and sacramental purposes.

PROHIBITIVE IMPEDIMENTS. Those impediments to a marriage which are only followed by a punishment, but do not render the marriage null. Bowyer, Mod. Civil Law, 44. See Impediments.

PROJECTIO. Lat. In old English law. A throwing up of earth by the sea.

PROJET. Fr. In international law. The draft of a proposed treaty or convention.

PROJET DE LOI. A bill in a legislative body.

PROLEM ANTE MATRIMONIUM NATAM, ITA UT POST LEGITIMAM, LEX CIVILIS SUCCEDERE FACIT IN HÆREDITATE PARENTUM; SED PROLEM, QUAM MATRIMONIUM NON PARIT, SUCCEDERE NON SINIT LEX ANGLORUM. Fortesc. c. 39. The civil law permits the offspring born before marriage, provided such offspring be afterwards legitimized, to be the heirs of their parents; but the law of the English does not suffer the offspring not produced by the marriage to succeed.

PROLES. Lat. Offspring; progeny; the issue of a lawful marriage. In its enlarged sense, it signifies any children.

PROLES SEQUITUR SORTEM PATERNAM. The offspring follows the condition of the father. Lynch v. Clarke, 1 Sandf.Ch. (N.Y.) 583, 660.

PROLETARIAT, PROLETARIATE. The class or body of proletarians. Webster, Dict. The class of unskilled laborers, without property or capital, engaged in the lower grades of work. People v. Gitlow, 234 N.Y. 132, 136 N.E. 317, 322. The class of *proletarii* (see the next title); the lowest stratum of the people of a country, consisting mainly of the waste of other classes, or of those fractions of the population who, by their isolation and their poverty, have no place in the established order of society.

PROLETARIUS. Lat. In Roman law. A proletary; a person of poor or mean condition; one among the common people whose fortunes were below a certain valuation; one of a class of citizens who were so poor that they could not serve the state with money, but only with their children, (*proles.*) Calvin.; Vicat.

PROLICIDE. In medical jurisprudence. A word used to designate the destruction of the human offspring. Jurists divide the subject into *feticide,* or the destruction of the *fetus in utero,* and *infanticide,* or the destruction of the new-born infant. Ry.Med.Jur. 280.

PROLIXITY. The unnecessary and superfluous statement of facts in pleading or in evidence. This will be rejected as impertinent. 7 Price, 278, note.

PROLOCUTOR. In ecclesiastical law. The president or chairman of a convocation. The speaker of the house of lords is called the prolocutor. The office belongs to the lord chancellor by prescription; 3 Steph.Comm. 347.

PROLONGATION. Time added to the duration of something; an extension of the time limited for the performance of an agreement.

PROLYTÆ. In Roman law. A term applied to students of law in the fifth and last year of their course; as being in advance of the Lytæ, or students of the fourth year. Calvin. They were left during this year very much to their own direction, and took the name prolytæ, *omnio soluti.* They studied chiefly the Code and the imperial constitutions.

PROMATERTERA. Lat. In the civil law. A maternal great-aunt; the sister of one's grandmother. Inst. 3. 6. 3; Dig. 38. 10. 10. 14.

PROMATERTERA MAGNA. Lat. In the civil law. A great-great-aunt.

PROMISE. A declaration which binds the person who makes it, either in honor, conscience, or law, to do or forbear a certain specific act, and which gives to the person to whom made a right to expect or claim the performance of some particular thing. Hoskins v. Black, 190 Ky. 98, 226 S.W. 384, 385. A declaration, verbal or written, made by one person to another for a good or valuable consideration, in the nature of a covenant by which the promisor binds himself to do or forbear some act, and gives to the promisee a legal right to demand and enforce a fulfillment. Scott v. S. H. Kress & Co., Tex.Civ.App., 191 S.W. 714, 716. An express undertaking, or agreement to carry a purpose into effect. E. I. Du Pont De Nemours & Co. v. Claiborne-Reno Co., C.C.A.Iowa, 64 F.2d 224, 89 A.L.R. 238.

While a "promise" is sometimes loosely defined as a declaration by any person of his intention to do or forbear from anything at the request or for the use of another. Finlay v. Swirsky, 103 Conn. 624, 131 A. 420, 423; Beck v. Wilkins-Ricks Co., 186 N.C. 210, 119 S.E. 235, 236; it is to be distinguished, on the one hand, from a mere declaration of intention involving no engagement or assurance as to the future. Scott v. S. H. Kress & Co., Tex.Civ.App., 191 S.W. 714, 716. And, on the other, from "agreement," which is an obligation arising upon reciprocal promises, or upon a promise founded on a consideration. Abbott.

Strictly speaking a promise is not a representation; the failure to make it good may give a cause of action, but it is not a false representation, which will authorize the rescission of a contract. Cunyus v. Guenther, 96 Ala. 564, 11 So. 649.

Fictitious promise. Sometimes called "implied promises," or "promises implied in law," occur in the case of those contracts which were invented to enable persons in certain cases to take advantage of the old rules of pleading peculiar to contracts, and which are not now of practical importance. Sweet.

Mutual promises. Promises simultaneously made by and between two parties; each promise being the consideration for the other. Anson Contr. 72; 14 M. & W. 855.

Naked promise. One given without any consideration, equivalent, or reciprocal obligation, and for that reason not enforceable at law. Arend v. Smith, 151 N.Y. 502, 45 N.E. 872.

New promise. An undertaking or promise, based upon and having relation to a former promise which, for some reason, can no longer be enforced, whereby the promisor recognizes and revives such former promise and engages to fulfill it.

Parol promise. A simple contract; a verbal promise. 2 Steph.Comm. 109.

Promise of marriage. A contract mutually entered into by a man and a woman that they will marry each other.

Promise to pay the debt of another. Within the statute of frauds, a promise to pay the debt of another is an undertaking by a person not before liable, for the purpose of securing or performing the same duty for which the party for whom the undertaking is made, continues liable. Dillaby v. Wilcox, 60 Conn. 71, 22 A. 491, 13 L.R.A. 643, 25 Am.St.Rep. 299.

PROMISEE. One to whom a promise has been made.

PROMISOR. One who makes a promise.

PROMISSOR. Lat. In the civil law. A promiser; properly the party who undertook to do a thing in answer to the interrogation of the other party, who was called the "stipulator."

PROMISSORY. Containing or consisting of a promise; in the nature of a promise; stipulating or engaging for a future act or course of conduct.

As to promissory "Oath," "Representation," and "Warranty," see those titles.

PROMISSORY ESTOPPEL. That which arises when there is a promise which promisor should reasonably expect to induce action or forbearance of a definite and substantial character on part of promisee, and which does induce such action or forbearance, and such promise is binding if injustice can be avoided only by enforcement of promise. New Eureka Amusement Co. v. Rosinsky, 126 Pa.Super. 444, 191 A. 412, 415.

To constitute "waiver without consideration," there must be promise or permission, express or implied in fact, supported only by action in reliance thereon, to excuse performance in future of condition or obligation not due at time when promise is made, or to give up defense not yet arisen, and such facts do not constitute "estoppel" because there is no misrepresentation of existing facts, but it may be called "promissory estoppel." Colbath v. H. B. Stebbins Lumber Co., 127 Me. 406, 144 A. 1, 5.

PROMISSORY NOTE. A promise or engagement, in writing, to pay a specified sum at a time therein limited, or on demand, or at sight, to a person therein named, or to his order, or bearer. Byles, Bills, 1, 4; Hall v. Farmer, 5 Denio, N.Y., 484. A written promise made by one or more to pay another, or order, or bearer, at a specified time, a specific amount of money, or other articles of value. Pryor v. American Trust & Banking Co., 15 Ga.App. 822, 84 S.E. 312, 314. An unconditional written promise, signed by the maker, to pay absolutely and at all events a sum certain in money, either to the bearer or to a person therein designated or his order, Benj. Chalm. Bills & N. art. 271; Harrison v. Beals, 111 Or. 563, 222 P. 728, 730; at a time specified therein, or at a time which must certainly arrive. Iowa State Savings Bank v. Wignall, 53 Okl. 641, 157 P. 725; Lanum v. Harrington, 267 Ill. 57, 107 N.E. 826, 828.

A written promise to pay a certain sum of money, at a future time, unconditionally. Brooks v. Owen, 112 Mo. 251, 19 S.W. 723, 20 S.W. 492. By the Uniform Negotiable Instruments Act, a *negotiable promissory note* is defined as an unconditional promise in writing made by one person to another signed by the maker engaging to pay on demand, or at a fixed or determinable future time, a sum certain in money to order or to bearer. Where a note is drawn to the maker's own order, it is not complete until indorsed by him. Section 184.

PROMOTE. To contribute to growth, enlargement, or prosperity of; to forward; to further; to encourage; to advance. People v. Augustine, 232 Mich. 29, 204 N.W. 747, 749.

PROMOTER. One who promotes, urges on, encourages, incites, advances, etc. Martin v. Street Improvement Dist. No. 324 of City of Little Rock, 167 Ark. 108, 266 S.W. 941, 942. One promoting a plan by which it is hoped to insure the success of a business venture. Caskie v. State Corporation Commission, 145 Va. 459, 134 S.E. 583, 584.

Corporation Law

The persons who, for themselves or others, take the preliminary steps to the organization of a corporation. 1 Thompson on Corporations, § 81. McRee v. Quitman Oil Co., 16 Ga.App. 12, 84 S.E. 487; Alkire v. Acuff, 134 Okl. 43, 272 P. 405, 407. Those persons who first associate themselves together for the purpose of organizing the company, issuing its prospectus, procuring subscriptions to the stock, securing a charter, etc. See Dickerman v. Northern Trust Co., 20 S.Ct. 311, 176 U.S. 181, 44 L.Ed. 423.

Ecclesiastical Law

One who puts in motion an ecclesiastical tribunal, for the purpose of correcting the manners of any person who has violated the laws ecclesiastical; and one who takes such a course is said to "promote the office of the judge." See Mozley & Whiteley.

England

The term is also applied to persons or corporations at whose instance private bills are introduced into and passed through parliament, especially those who press forward bills for the taking of land for railways and other public purposes, who are then called promoters of the undertaking.

English Practice

Those persons who, in popular and penal actions, prosecute offenders in their own names and that of the king, and are thereby entitled to part of the fines and penalties for their pains. Brown.

PROMOVENT. A plaintiff in a suit of *duplex querela* (*q. v.*). 2 Prob.Div. 192.

PROMPT. To act immediately, responding on the instant. In re Peene's Will, 279 N.Y.S. 131, 155 Misc. 155.

PROMPT DELIVERY. This term means within a few days at most. Acme-Evans Co. v. Hunter, 194 Ill.App. 542, 543. Delivery as promptly as possible, all things considered. Meyer Bros. Drug Co. v. Callison, 120 Wash. 378, 207 P. 683, 684.

PROMPT SHIPMENT. Shipment within a reasonable time. Kelley-Clarke Co. v. Leslie, 61 Cal. App. 559, 215 P. 699, 702.

PROMPTLY. Adverbial form of the word "prompt," which means ready and quick to act as occasion demands. Missouri, K. & T. Ry. Co. v. Missouri Pac. Ry. Co., 103 Kan. 1, 175 P. 97, 103. The meaning of the word depends largely on the facts in each case. Irvin v. Koehler, C.C.A.N.Y., 230 F. 795, 796; Stovall & Strickland v. McBrayer, 20 Ga.App. 93, 92 S.E. 543.

PROMULGARE. Lat. In Roman law. To make public; to make publicly known; to promulgate. To publish or make known a law after its enactment.

PROMULGATE. To publish; to announce officially; to make public as important or obligatory. Price v. Supreme Home of the Ancient Order of Pilgrims, Tex.Com.App., 285 S.W. 310, 312.

PROMULGATION. The order given to cause a law to be executed, and to make it public; it differs from publication. 1 Bl.Comm. 45; Stat. 6 Hen. VI. c. 4. In modern practice, it is usually by publishing one or more volumes of the laws and circulating them among public officials and selling them. As to the practice in England at various times, see Record Com. in 7 Sel. Essays in Anglo-Amer. L. H. 168.

As to the rules of a railway company it means made known; brought to the attention of the service affected thereby, so that a servant is bound to take notice. Wooden v. R. Co., Super., 18 N.Y.S. 768.

Formerly promulgation meant introducing a bill to the senate; Aust. Jur. Lect. 28.

PROMUTUUM. Lat. In the civil law. A *quasi* contract, by which he who receives a certain sum of money, or a certain quantity of fungible things, which have been paid to him through mistake, contracts towards the payer the obligation of returning him as much. Poth. de l'Usure, pt. 3, s. 1, a. 1.

This contract is called *promutuum,* because it has much resemblance to that of *mutuum.* This resemblance consists in this: *first,* that in both a sum of money or some fungible things are required; *second,* that in both there must be a transfer of the property in the thing; *third,* that in both there must be returned the same amount or quantity of the thing received. But, though there is this general resemblance between the two, the *mutuum* differs essentially from the *promutuum.* The former is the actual contract of the parties, made expressly, but the latter is a *quasi*-contract, which is the effect of an error or mistake. 1 Bouvier, Inst. n. 1125.

PRONEPOS. Lat. In the civil law. A great-grandson. Inst. 3, 6, 1; Bract. fol. 67.

PRONEPTIS. Lat. In the civil law. A great-granddaughter. Inst. 3, 6, 1; Bract. fol. 67. Also, a niece's daughter. Ainsworth, Dict.

PRONOTARY. First notary. See Prothonotary.

PRONOUNCE. To utter formally, officially, and solemnly; to declare or affirm; to declare aloud and in a formal manner. In this sense a court is said to "pronounce" judgment or a sentence. Griffin v. State, 12 Ga.App. 615(2), 618, 77 S.E. 1080; Sanders v. State, 18 Ga.App. 786, 90 S.E. 728.

PRONUNCIATION. L. Fr. A sentence or decree. Kelham.

PRONURUS. Lat. In the civil law. The wife of a grandson or great-grandson. Dig. 38, 10, 4, 6.

PROOF. The effect of evidence; the establishment of a fact by evidence. Nevling v. Com., 98 Pa. 328; Powell v. State, 101 Ga. 9, 29 S.E. 309, 65 Am.St.Rep. 277. New England Newspaper Pub. Co. v. Bonner, C.C.A.Mass., 77 F.2d 915, 916. Any fact or circumstance which leads the mind to the affirmative or negative of any proposition. Nauful v. National Loan & Exchange Bank of Columbia, 111 S.C. 309, 97 S.E. 843, 845. The conviction or persuasion of the mind of a judge or jury, by the exhibition of evidence, of the reality of a fact alleged. Ellis v. Wolfe-Shoemaker Motor Co., 227 Mo.App. 508, 55 S.W.2d 309.

"Testimony" is a more restricted term. For "Testimony," see that title.

Ayliffe defines "judicial proof" to be a clear and evident declaration or demonstration of a matter which was before doubtful, conveyed in a judicial manner by fit and proper arguments, and likewise by all other legal methods—*First,* by fit and proper arguments, such as conjectures, presumptions, *indicia,* and other adminicular ways and means; *secondly,* by legal methods, or methods according to law, such as witnesses, public instruments, and the like. Ayl. Par. 442.

Evidence and Proof Distinguished

"Proof" is the logically sufficient reason for assenting to the truth of a proposition advanced. In its juridical sense it is a term of wide import, and comprehends everything that may be adduced at a trial, within the legal rules, for the purpose of producing conviction in the mind of judge or jury, aside from mere argument; that is, everything that has a probative force intrinsically, and not merely as a deduction from, or combination of, original probative facts. But "evidence" is a narrower term, and includes only such kinds of proof as may be legally presented at a trial, by the act of the parties, and through the aid of such concrete facts as witnesses, records, or other documents. Thus, to urge a presumption of law in support of one's case is adducing proof, but it is not offering evidence. "Belief" is a subjective condition resulting from proof. It is a conviction of the truth of a proposition, existing in the mind, and induced by persuasion, proof, or argument addressed to the judgment.

The word "proof" seems properly to mean anything which serves, either immediately or mediately, to convince the mind of the truth or falsehood of a fact or proposition. It is also applied to the conviction generated in the mind by proof properly so called. The word "evidence" signifies, in its original sense, the state of being evident, *i. e.,* plain, apparent, or notorious. But by an almost peculiar inflection of our language, it is applied to that which tends to render evident or to generate proof. Best, Ev. §§ 10, 11; Dupont v. Pelletier, 120 Me. 114, 113 A. 11, 12. "Evidence" differs from "proof" in that former may be false and of no probative value. State v. Howard, 162 La. 719, 111 So. 72, 75.

Proof in a strictly accurate and technical sense is the result or effect of evidence, while evidence is the medium or means by which a fact is proved or disproved, but the words "proof" and "evidence" may be used interchangeably. Walker v. State, 138 Ark. 517, 212 S.W. 319, 324; Latikos v. State, 17 Ala.App. 592, 88 So. 45, 47.

"Proof" is only link in chain of evidence relating to single thing or statement of single witness, and it is these links relating to entire proof which go to make up evidence. Cleveland Metal Bed Co. v. Kutz, 27 Ohio App. 245, 160 N.E. 725, 726.

Proof is the conclusion drawn from the evidence, Jones v. Clements, Tex.Civ.App., 41 S.W.2d 1069, 1070; it is the effect of evidence. State v. Crutcher, 231 Iowa 418, 1 N.W. 2d 195, 198. Sims v. Clayton, 193 S.C. 98, 7 S.E.2d 724, 728.

Proof is the perfection of evidence; for without evidence there is no proof, although there may be evidence which does not amount to proof: for example, if a man is found murdered at a spot where another has been seen walking but a short time before, this fact will be *evidence* to show that the latter was the murderer, but, standing alone, will be very far from *proof* of it.

"Proof," when used in a legislative enactment means competent and legal evidence, testimony conforming to fundamental rules of proof, excluding hearsay evidence, however trustworthy. Hand v. Nolan, 1 N.J.Misc. 428, 136 A. 430, 431.

No material difference between terms exists for purposes of instruction. Merrick v. United Rys. & Electric Co. of Baltimore City, 163 Md. 641, 163 A. 816, 818.

Affirmative proof. Evidence establishing the fact in dispute by a preponderance of the evidence. Boardman v. Lorentzen, 155 Wis. 566, 145 N.W. 750, 755, 52 L.R.A.,N.S., 476.

Burden of proof. See that title.

Conclusive proof. As used in a statute providing for an action against a county for injury to cattle resulting from dipping for eradication of cattle ticks, it has been held to be equivalent to the expression, "to a moral certainty" or "beyond a reasonable doubt," meaning a higher degree of proof than by a preponderance of the evidence. Covington County v. Fite, 120 Miss. 421, 82 So. 308, 309.

Degree of proof. Refers to effect of evidence rather than medium by which truth is established, and in this sense expressions "preponderance of evidence" and "proof beyond reasonable doubt" are used. Sowle v. Sowle, 115 Neb. 795, 215 N.W. 122, 123.

Full proof. See Full.

Half proof. See Half.

Negative proof. See *Positive Proof,* infra.

Positive proof. Direct or affirmative proof; that which directly establishes the fact in question; as opposed to *negative* proof, which establishes the fact by showing that its opposite is not or cannot be true. Schrack v. McKnight, 84 Pa. 30.

Preliminary proof. See Preliminary.

Proof beyond a reasonable doubt. Such proof as precludes every reasonable hypothesis except that which it tends to support and which is wholly consistent with defendant's guilt and inconsistent with any other rational conclusion. State v. McDonough, 129 Conn. 483, 29 A.2d 582, 583.

Proof evident or presumption great. As used in constitutional provisions that accused shall be bailable unless for capital offenses when the "proof is evident" or "presumption great," means evidence clear and strong, and which leads well guarded, dispassionate judgment to conclusion that accused committed offense and will be punished capitally. Ex parte Coward, 145 Tex.Cr.R. 593, 170 S.W.2d 754, 755. Ex parte Goode, 123 Tex.Cr.R. 492, 59 S.W.2d 841; Ex parte Tully, 70 Fla. 1, 66 So. 296, 297.

Proof of debt. The formal establishment by a creditor of his debt or claim, in some prescribed manner, (as, by his affidavit or otherwise,) as a preliminary to its allowance, along with others, against an estate or property to be divided, such as the estate of a bankrupt or insolvent, a deceased person or a firm or company in liquidation.

Proof of spirits. Testing the strength of alcoholic spirits, also the degree of strength; as high proof, first proof, second, third, and fourth proofs. In the internal revenue law it is used in the sense of degree of strength. Louisville P. W. Co. v. Collector of Customs, C.C.A.Ky., 49 F. 561, 1 C.C.A. 371, 6 U.S.App. 53.

Proof of will. A term having the same meaning as "probate," (*q. v.*), and used interchangeably with it.

PROP. An upright post wedged between the roof and the floor of a mine to support the roof. Big Branch Coal Co. v. Wrenchie, 160 Ky. 668, 170 S.W. 14, 16.

PROPAGATE. To cause to spread. In re Atkinson's Will, 197 N.Y.S. 831, 832, 120 Misc.Rep. 186.

PROPATRUUS. Lat. In the civil law. A great-grandfather's brother. Inst. 3, 6, 3; Bract. fol. 68*b*.

PROPATRUUS MAGNUS. In the civil law. A great-great-uncle.

PROPER. That which is fit, suitable, appropriate, adapted, correct. Knox v. Lee, 12 Wall. 457, 20 L.Ed. 287; Reasonably sufficient. Houston & T. C. Ry. Co. v. Kujawa, Tex.Civ.App., 265 S.W. 186, 187; Freedom Casket Co. v. McManus, C.C.A. Pa., 218 F. 323, 326.

Peculiar; naturally or essentially belonging to a person or thing; not common; appropriate; one's own.

PROPER CARE. That degree of care which a prudent man should use under like circumstances. Baskin v. Montgomery Ward & Co., C.C.A.N.C., 104 F.2d 531, 533.

PROPER EVIDENCE. Such evidence as may be presented under the rules established by law and recognized by the courts. The Betsey, 49 Ct.Cl. 125, 131.

PROPER FEUDS. In feudal law, the original and genuine feuds held by purely military service.

PROPER INDEPENDENT ADVICE. As to donor means that he had preliminary benefit of conferring upon subject of intended gift with a person who was not only competent to inform him correctly of its legal effect, but who was so disassociated from interests of donee as to be in position to advise with donor impartially and confidentially as to consequences to donor of his proposed gift. Blume v. Blume, 90 N.J.Eq. 258, 106 A. 367, 368; Zwirtz v. Dorl, 123 Okl. 284, 253 P. 75, 77.

PROPER LOOKOUT. Duty imposed on motorist to keep such lookout requires motorist to use care, prudence, watchfulness, and attention of an ordinarily prudent person under same or similar circumstances. Pazen v. Des Moines Transp. Co.,

223 Iowa 23, 272 N.W. 126, 130; Southern Motor Lines v. Creamer, Tex.Civ.App., 113 S.W.2d 624, 627.

PROPER PARTY. As distinguished from a necessary party, is one who has an interest in the subject-matter of the litigation, which may be conveniently settled therein; one without whom a substantial decree may be made, but not a decree which shall completely settle all the questions which may be involved in the controversy and conclude the rights of all the persons who have any interest in the subject of the litigation. See Kelley v. Boettcher, C.C.A.Colo., 85 F. 55, 29 C.C.A. 14; Tatum v. Roberts, 59 Minn. 52, 60 N.W. 848.

PROPERTY. That which is peculiar or proper to any person; that which belongs exclusively to one; in the strict legal sense, an aggregate of rights which are guaranteed and protected by the government. Fulton Light, Heat & Power Co. v. State, 65 Misc.Rep. 263, 121 N.Y.S. 536. The term is said to extend to every species of valuable right and interest. McAlister v. Pritchard, 230 S.W. 66, 67, 287 Mo. 494. More specifically, ownership; the unrestricted and exclusive right to a thing; the right to dispose of a thing in every legal way, to possess it, to use it, and to exclude every one else from interfering with it. Mackeld. Rom. Law, § 265. That dominion or indefinite right of use or disposition which one may lawfully exercise over particular things or subjects. Transcontinental Oil Co. v. Emmerson, 298 Ill. 394, 131 N.E. 645, 647, 16 A.L.R. 507. The exclusive right of possessing, enjoying, and disposing of a thing. Barnes v. Jones, 139 Miss. 675, 103 So. 773, 775, 43 A.L.R. 673; Tatum Bros. Real Estate & Investment Co. v. Watson, 92 Fla. 278, 109 So. 623, 626. The highest right a man can have to anything; being used for that right which one has to lands or tenements, goods or chattels, which no way depends on another man's courtesy. Jackson ex dem. Pearson v. Housel, 17 Johns. 281, 283.

The right of property is that sole and despotic dominion which one man claims and exercises over the external things of the world, in total exclusion of the right of any other individual in the universe. It consists in the free use, enjoyment, and disposal of all a person's acquisitions, without any control or diminution save only by the laws of the land. 1 Bl.Comm. 138; 2 Bl.Comm. 2, 15; Great Northern Ry. Co. v. Washington Elec. Co., 197 Wash. 627, 86 P.2d 208, 217.

The word is also commonly used to denote everything which is the subject of ownership, corporeal or incorporeal, tangible or intangible, visible or invisible, real or personal; everything that has an exchangeable value or which goes to make up wealth or estate. It extends to every species of valuable right and interest, and includes real and personal property, easements, franchises, and incorporeal hereditaments. Samet v. Farmers' & Merchants' Nat. Bank of Baltimore, C.C.A.Md., 247 F. 669, 671; Globe Indemnity Co. v. Bruce, C.C.A. Okl., 81 F.2d 143, 150.

Absolute property. In respect to chattels personal property is said to be "absolute" where a man has, solely and exclusively, the right and also the possession of movable chattels. 2 Bl.Comm. 389. In the law of wills, a bequest or devise "to be the absolute property" of the beneficiary may pass a title in fee simple. Fackler v. Berry, 93 Va. 565, 25 S.E. 887, 57 Am.St.Rep. 819. Or it may mean that the property is to be held free from any limitation or condition or free from any control or disposition on the part of others. Wilson v. White, 133 Ind. 614, 33 N.E. 361, 19 L.R.A. 581.

Common property. A term sometimes applied to lands owned by a municipal corporation and held in trust for the common use of the inhabitants. Also property owned jointly by husband and wife under the community system. See Community.

Community property. See that title.

Ganancial property. See that title.

General property. The right and property in a thing enjoyed by the *general owner*. See Owner.

Literary property. See Literary.

Mixed property. Property which is personal in its essential nature, but is invested by the law with certain of the characteristics and features of real property. Heirlooms, tombstones, monuments in a church, and title-deeds to an estate are of this nature. 2 Bl.Comm. 428, 3 Barn. & Adol. 174; 4 Bing. 106; Minot v. Thompson, 106 Mass. 585.

Personal property. In broad and general sense, everything that is the subject of ownership, not coming under denomination of real estate. A right or interest in things personal, or right or interest less than a freehold in realty, or any right or interest which one has in things movable. Elkton Electric Co. v. Perkins, 145 Md. 224, 125 A. 851, 858. The term is generally applied to property of a personal or movable nature, as opposed to property of a local or immovable character, (such as land or houses,) the latter being called "real property," but is also applied to the right or interest less than a freehold which a man has in realty. Boyd v. Selma, 96 Ala. 144, 11 So. 393, 16 L.R.A. 729; In re Bruckman's Estate, 195 Pa. 363, 45 A. 1078.

That kind of property which usually consists of things temporary and movable, but includes all subjects of property not of a freehold nature, nor descendible to the heirs at law. 2 Kent, Comm. 340.

Personal property is divisible into (1) corporeal personal property, which includes movable and tangible things, such as animals, ships, furniture, merchandise, etc.; and (2) incorporeal personal property, which consists of such rights as personal annuities, stocks, shares, patents, and copyrights. Sweet.

Private property. As protected from being taken for public uses, is such property as belongs absolutely to an individual, and of which he has the exclusive right of disposition; property of a specific, fixed and tangible nature, capable of being had in possession and transmitted to another, such as houses, lands, and chattels. Homochitto River Com'rs v. Withers, 29 Miss. 21, 64 Am.Dec. 126; Scranton v. Wheeler, 21 S.Ct. 48, 179 U.S. 141, 45 L.Ed. 126.

Property tax. In English law, this is understood to be an income tax payable in respect to landed property. In America, it is a tax imposed on property, whether real or personal, as distinguished from poll taxes, and taxes on successions, transfers, and occupations, and from license taxes. Garrett v. St. Louis, 25 Mo. 510, 69 Am.Dec. 475; In re Swift's Estate, 137 N.Y. 77, 32 N.E. 1096, 18 L.R.A. 709.

Public property. This term is commonly used as a designation of those things which are *publici juris*, (*q. v.*,) and therefore considered as being owned by "the public," the entire state or community, and not restricted to the dominion of a private person. It may also apply to any subject of property owned by a state, nation, or municipal corporation as such.

Qualified property. Property in chattels which is not in its nature permanent, but may at some times subsist and not at other times; such for example, as the property a man may have in wild animals which he has caught and keeps, and which are his only so long as he retains possession of them. 2 Bl.Comm. 389. Any ownership not absolute.

Real property. Land, and generally whatever is erected or growing upon or affixed to land. Lanpher v. Glenn, 37 Minn. 4, 33 N.W. 10. Also rights issuing out of, annexed to, and exercisable within or about land; a general term for lands, tenements, and hereditaments; property which, on the death of the owner intestate, passes to his heir. Ralston Steel Car Co. v. Ralston, 112 Ohio St. 306, 147 N.E. 513, 516, 39 A.L.R. 334. In respect to property, *real* and *personal* correspond very nearly with *immovables* and *movables* of the civil law. Guyot, *Répert. Biens.*

Separate property. See that title.

Special property. Property of a qualified, temporary, or limited nature; as distinguished from absolute, general, or unconditional property. Such is the property of a bailee in the article bailed, of a sheriff in goods temporarily in his hands under a levy, of the finder of lost goods while looking for the owner, of a person in wild animals which he has caught. Stief v. Hart, 1 N.Y. 20, 24.

PROPINQUI ET CONSANGUINEI. Lat. The nearest of kin to a deceased person.

PROPINQUIOR EXCLUDIT PROPINQUUM; PROPINQUUS REMOTUM; ET REMOTUS REMOTIOREM. Co.Litt. 10. He who is nearer excludes him who is near; he who is near, him who is remote; he who is remote, him who is remoter.

PROPINQUITY. Kindred; parentage.

PROPIOR SOBRINO, PROPIOR SOBRINA. Lat. In the civil law. The son or daughter of a great-uncle or great-aunt, paternal or maternal. Inst. 3, 6, 3.

PROPIOS, PROPRIOS. In Spanish law. Certain portions of ground laid off and reserved when a town was founded in Spanish America as the unalienable property of the town, for the purpose of erecting public buildings, markets, etc., or to be used in any other way, under the direction of the municipality, for the advancement of the revenues or the prosperity of the place. 12 Pet. 442, note.

Thus, there are *solares*, or house lots of a small size, upon which dwellings, shops, stores, etc., are to be built. There are *suertes*, or sowing grounds of a larger size, for cultivating or planting; as gardens, vineyards, orchards, etc. There are *ejidos*, which are quite well described by our word "commons," and are lands used in common by the inhabitants of the place for pasture, wood, threshing ground, etc.; and particular names are assigned to each, according to its particular use. Sometimes additional *ejidos* were allowed to be taken outside of the town limits. There are also *propios* or municipal lands, from which revenues are derived to defray the expenses of the municipal administration. Hart v. Burnett, 15 Cal. 554.

PROPONE. In Scotch law. To state. To *propone* a defense is to state or move it. 1 Kames, Eq. pref.

In ecclesiastical and probate law. To bring forward for adjudication; to exhibit as basis of a claim; to proffer for judicial action.

PROPONENT. The propounder of a thing. Thus, the proponent of a will is the party who offers it for probate (*q. v.*).

PROPORTIONATE. Adjusted to something else according to certain rate of comparative relation. Hochsprung v. Stevenson, 82 Mont. 222, 266 P. 406, 408.

PROPORTUM. In old records. Purport; intention or meaning. Cowell.

PROPOSAL. An offer; something proffered. An offer, by one person to another, of terms and conditions with reference to some work or undertaking, or for the transfer of property, the acceptance whereof will make a contract between them. Eppes v. Mississippi, G. & T. R. Co., 35 Ala. 33. Signification by one person to another of his willingness to enter into a contract with him on the terms specified in the offer. Salisbury v. Credit Service, Del.Super., 199 A. 674, 681.

In English practice. A statement in writing of some special matter submitted to the consideration of a chief clerk in the court of chancery, pursuant to an order made upon an application *ex parte*, or a decretal order of the court. It is either for maintenance of an infant, appointment of a guardian, placing a ward of the court at the university or in the army, or apprentice to a trade; for the appointment of a receiver, the establishment of a charity, etc. Wharton.

PROPOSITIO INDEFINITA ÆQUIPOLLET UNIVERSALI. An indefinite proposition is equivalent to a general one.

PROPOSITION. A single logical sentence; also an offer to do a thing. Perry v. Dwelling House Ins. Co., 67 N.H. 291, 33 A. 731, 68 Am.St.Rep. 668.

PROPOSITUS. Lat. The person proposed; the person from whom a descent is traced.

PROPOUND. To offer; to propose. An executor or other person is said to propound a will when he takes proceedings for obtaining probate in solemn form. The term is also technically used, in England, to denote the allegations in the statement of claim, in an action for probate, by which the plaintiff alleges that the testator executed the will with proper formalities, and that he was of sound mind at the time. Sweet.

PROPRES. In French law. The term "*propres*" or "*biens propres*" as distinguished from "*acquets*" denotes all property inherited by a person, whether by devise or *ab intestato*, from his direct or collateral relatives, whether in the ascending or descending line; that is, in terms of the common law, property acquired by "descent" as distinguished from that acquired by "purchase."

PROPRIA PERSONA. See In Propria Persona.

PROPRIEDAD. In Spanish law. Property. White, New Recop. b. 1, tit. 7, c. 5, § 2.

PROPRIETARY, *n.* A proprietor or owner; one who has the exclusive title to a thing; one who possesses or holds the title to a thing in his own right. The grantees of Pennsylvania and Maryland and their heirs were called the proprietaries of those provinces. Webster.

PROPRIETARY, *adj.* Belonging to ownership; belonging or pertaining to a proprietor; relating to a certain owner or proprietor. State v. F. W. Woolworth Co., 184 Minn. 51, 237 N.W. 817, 818.

Proprietary articles. Goods manufactured under some exclusive individual right to make and sell them. The term is chiefly used in the internal revenue laws of the United States. See Ferguson v. Arthur, 6 S.Ct. 861, 117 U.S. 482, 29 L. Ed. 979.

Proprietary chapel. See Chapel.

Proprietary duties. Those duties of a municipality which are not governmental duties. City of Miami v. Oates, 152 Fla. 21, 10 So.2d 721, 723. See Governmental Duties.

Proprietary governments. This expression is used by Blackstone to denote governments granted out by the crown to individuals, in the nature of feudatory principalities, with inferior regalities and subordinate powers of legislation such as formerly belonged to the owners of counties palatine. 1 Bl.Comm. 108.

Proprietary rights. Those rights which an owner of property has by virtue of his ownership. When proprietary rights are opposed to acquired rights, such as easements, franchises, etc., they are more often called "natural rights." Sweet.

PROPRIETAS. Lat. In the civil and old English law. Property; that which is one's own; ownership.

Proprietas plena, full property, including not only the title, but the usufruct, or exclusive right to the use. Calvin.

Proprietas nuda, naked or mere property or ownership; the mere title, separate from the usufruct.

PROPRIETAS TOTIUS NAVIS CARINÆ CAUSAM SEQUITUR. The property of the whole ship follows the condition of the keel. Dig. 6, 1, 61. If a man builds a vessel from the very keel with the materials of another, the vessel belongs to the owner of the materials. 2 Kent, Comm. 362.

PROPRIETAS VERBORUM EST SALUS PROPIETATUM. Jenk.Cent. 16. Propriety of words is the salvation of property.

PROPRIETATE PROBANDA, DE. A writ addressed to a sheriff to try by an inquest in whom certain property, previous to distress, subsisted. Finch, Law, 316.

PROPRIETATES VERBORUM SERVANDÆ SUNT. The proprieties of words [proper meanings of words] are to be preserved or adhered to. Jenk.Cent. p. 136, case 78.

PROPRIÉTÉ. The French law term corresponding to our "property," or the right of enjoying and of disposing of things in the most absolute manner, subject only to the laws. Brown.

PROPRIETOR. One who has the legal right or exclusive title to anything. In many instances it is synonymous with owner. State v. F. W. Woolworth Co., 184 Minn. 51, 237 N.W. 817, 818, 76 A.L.R. 1202.

A person entitled to a trade-mark or a design under the acts for the registration or patenting of trade-marks and designs *(q. v.)* is called "proprietor" of the trade-mark or design. Sweet; Louisville Planing Mill Co. v. Weir Sheet Iron Works, 199 Ky. 361, 251 S.W. 176, 177.

PROPRIETY. In Massachusetts colonial ordinance of 1741 is nearly, if not precisely, equivalent to property. Com. v. Alger, 7 Cush. (Mass.) 53, 70.

In old English law. Property; propriety in action; propriety in possession; mixed propriety. Hale, Anal. § 26.

PROPRIO VIGORE. Lat. By its own force; by its intrinsic meaning.

PROPRIOS. In Spanish and Mexican law. Productive lands, the usufruct of which had been set apart to the several municipalities for the purpose of defraying the charges of their respective governments. Sheldon v. Milmo, 90 Tex. 1, 36 S.W. 413. See Arbitrios.

PROPTER. For; on account of. The initial word of several Latin phrases.

PROPTER AFFECTUM. For or on account of some affection or prejudice. The name of a species of *challenge* (*q. v.*).

PROPTER DEFECTUM. On account of or for some defect. The name of a species of *challenge* (*q. v.*).

PROPTER DEFECTUM SANGUINIS. On account of failure of blood.

PROPTER DELICTUM. For or on account of crime. The name of a species of *challenge*, (*q. v.*).

PROPTER HONORIS RESPECTUM. On account of respect of honor or rank. See Challenge.

PROPTER IMPOTENTIAM. On account of helplessness. The term describes one of the grounds of a qualified property in wild animals, consisting in the fact of their inability to escape; as is the case with the young of such animals before they can fly or run. 2 Bl.Comm. 394.

PROPTER PRIVILEGIUM. On account of privilege. The term describes one of the grounds of a qualified property in wild animals, consisting in the special privilege of hunting, taking and killing them, in a given park or preserve, to the exclusion of other persons. 2 Bl.Comm. 394.

PRORATE. To divide, share, or distribute proportionally; to assess or apportion pro rata. Formed from the Latin phrase "pro rata," and said to be a recognized English word. Diamond Alkali Co. v. Henderson Coal Co., 287 Pa. 232, 134 A. 386, 388.

PROROGATED JURISDICTION. In Scotch law. A power conferred by consent of the parties upon a judge who would not otherwise be competent.

PROROGATION. Prolonging or putting off to another day. In English law, a prorogation is the continuance of the parliament from one session to another, as an adjournment is a continuation of the session from day to day. Wharton.

In the civil law. The giving time to do a thing beyond the term previously fixed. Dig. 2, 14, 27, 1.

PROROGUE. To direct suspension of proceedings of parliament; to terminate a session.

PROSCRIBED. In the civil law. Among the Romans, a man was said to be "proscribed" when a reward was offered for his head; but the term was more usually applied to those who were sentenced to some punishment which carried with it the consequences of civil death. Cod. 9, 49.

PROSECUTE. To follow up; to carry on an action or other judicial proceeding; to proceed against a person criminally. To "prosecute" an action is not merely to commence it, but includes following it to an ultimate conclusion. Service & Wright Lumber Co. v. Sumpter Valley Ry. Co., 81 Or. 32, 152 P. 262, 264.

PROSECUTING ATTORNEY. The name of the public officer (in several states) who is appointed in each judicial district, circuit, or county, to conduct criminal prosecutions on behalf of the state or people. Holder v. State, 58 Ark. 473, 25 S.W. 279.

PROSECUTING WITNESS. The private person upon whose complaint or information a criminal accusation is founded and whose testimony is mainly relied on to secure a conviction at the trial; in a more particular sense, the person who was chiefly injured, in person or property, by the act constituting the alleged crime, (as in cases of robbery, assault, criminal negligence, bastardy, and the like,) and who instigates the prosecution and gives evidence.

PROSECUTIO LEGIS EST GRAVIS VEXATIO; EXECUTIO LEGIS CORONAT OPUS. Litigation is vexatious, but an execution crowns the work. Co.Litt. 289*b*.

PROSECUTION. In criminal law. A criminal action; a proceeding instituted and carried on by due course of law, before a competent tribunal, for the purpose of determining the guilt or innocence of a person charged with crime. U. S. v. Reisinger, 9 S.Ct. 99, 128 U.S. 398, 32 L.Ed. 480; Sigsbee v. State, 43 Fla. 524, 30 So. 816; People v. Ellis, 204 Mich. 157, 169 N.W. 930, 931. The continuous following up, through instrumentalities created by law, of a person accused of a public offense with a steady and fixed purpose of reaching a judicial determination of the guilt or innocence of the accused. Davenport v. State, 20 Okl. Cr. 253, 202 P. 18, 24.

The means adopted to bring a supposed offender to justice and punishment by due course of law, carried on in the name of the government. Summerour v. Fortson, 174 Ga. 862, 164 S.E. 809.

By an easy extension of its meaning "prosecution" is sometimes used to designate the state as the party proceeding in a criminal action, or the prosecutor, or counsel; as when we speak of "the evidence adduced by the prosecution."

The term is also frequently used respecting civil litigation, Eastman Marble Co. v. Vermont Marble Co., 236 Mass. 138, 128 N.E. 177, 182; and includes every step in action, from its commencement to its final determination. Ray Wong v. Earle C. Anthony, Inc., 199 Cal. 15, 247 P. 894, 895; The Brazil, C.C.A.Ill., 134 F.2d 929, 930.

Malicious prosecution. See Malicious.

PROSECUTOR. In practice. One who prosecutes another for a crime in the name of the government; one who instigates a prosecution by making affidavit charging a named person with the commission of a penal offense on which a warrant is issued or an indictment or accusation is based. State v. Snelson, 13 Okl.Cr. 88, 162 P. 444, 445; Ethridge v. State, 164 Ga. 53, 137 S.E. 784, 785. One who instigates the prosecution upon which an accused is arrested or who prefers an accusation against the party whom he suspects to be guilty. People v. Lay, 193 Mich. 476, 160 N.W. 467, 470. One who takes charge of a case and performs function of trial lawyer for the people. People v. Lee, 272 N.Y.S. 817, 151 Misc. 431.

Private prosecutor. One who sets in motion the machinery of criminal justice against a person whom he suspects or believes to be guilty of a crime, by laying an accusation before the proper authorities, and who is not himself an officer of justice. Heacock v. State, 13 Tex.App. 129; State v. Millain, 3 Nev. 425.

Prosecutor of the pleas. This name is given, in New Jersey, to the county officer who is charged with the prosecution of criminal actions, corresponding to the "district attorney" or "county attorney" in other states.

Public prosecutor. An officer of government (such as a state's attorney or district attorney) whose function is the prosecution of criminal actions, or suits partaking of the nature of criminal actions.

PROSECUTRIX. In criminal law. A female prosecutor.

PROSEQUI. Lat. To follow up or pursue; to sue or prosecute. See Nolle Prosequi.

PROSEQUITUR. Lat. He follows up or pursues; he prosecutes. See Non Pros.

PROSOCER. Lat. In the civil law. A father-in-law's father; a grandfather of wife.

PROSOCERUS. Lat. In the civil law. A wife's grandmother.

PROSPECTIVE. Looking forward; contemplating the future.

PROSPECTIVE DAMAGES. See Damages.

PROSPECTIVE LAW. One applicable only to cases which shall arise after its enactment.

PROSPECTUS. A document published by a company or corporation, or by persons acting as its agents or assignees, setting forth the nature and objects of an issue of shares, debentures, or other securities created by the company or corporation, and inviting the public to subscribe to the issue. A prospectus is also usually published on the issue, in England, of bonds or other securities by a foreign state or corporation. Sweet.

In the civil law. Prospect; the view of external objects. Dig. 8, 2, 3, 15.

PROSTITUTION. Common lewdness of a woman for gain; whoredom; the act or practice of a woman who permits any man who will pay her price to have sexual intercourse with her. Com. v. Cook, 12 Metc., Mass., 97; State v. Anderson, 284 Mo. 657, 225 S.W. 896, 897; U. S. ex rel. Mittler v. Curran, C.C.A.N.Y., 18 F.2d 355, 356. The act or practice of a female of prostituting or offering her body to an indiscriminate intercourse with men for money or its equivalent. People v. Rice, 277 Ill. 521, 115 N.E. 631, 632.

PROSTITUTE. A woman who indiscriminately consorts with men for hire. State v. Stoyell, 54 Me. 24, 89 Am.Dec. 716. A woman who has given herself up to indiscriminate lewdness. Wilson v. State, 17 Ala.App. 307, 84 So. 783. A woman submitting to indiscriminate sexual intercourse, which she solicits. Trent v. Commonwealth, 181 Va. 338, 25 S.E.2d 350, 352.

The word in its most general sense means the act of setting one's self to sale, or of devoting to infamous purposes what is in one's power: as, the prostitution of talents or abilities; the prostitution of the press, etc. Carpenter v. People, 8 Barb., N.Y., 610.

PROTECTIO TRAHIT SUBJECTIONEM, ET SUBJECTIO PROTECTIONEM. Protection draws with it subjection, and subjection protection. 7 Coke, 5*a*. The protection of an individual by government is on condition of his submission to the laws, and such submission on the other hand entitles the individual to the protection of the government. Broom, Max. 78.

PROTECTION. In English law. A writ by which the king might, by a special prerogative, privilege a defendant from all personal and many real suits for one year at a time, and no longer, in respect of his being engaged in his service out of the realm. 3 Bl.Comm. 289.

In former times the name "protection" was also given to a certificate given to a sailor to show that he was exempt from impressment into the royal navy.

In mercantile law. The name of a document generally given by notaries public to sailors and other persons going abroad, in which it is certified that the bearer therein named is a citizen of the United States.

In public commercial law. A system by which a government imposes customs duties upon commodities of foreign origin or manufacture when imported into the country, for the purpose of stimulating and developing the home production of the same or equivalent articles, by discouraging the importation of foreign goods, or by raising the price of foreign commodities to a point at which the home producers can successfully compete with them.

PROTECTION OF INVENTIONS ACT. The statute 33 & 34 Vict. c. 27. By this act it is provided that the exhibition of new inventions shall not prejudice patent rights, and that the exhibition of designs shall not prejudice the right to registration of such designs.

PROTECTION OF THE LAWS. See Equal.

PROTECTION ORDER. In English practice. An order for the protection of the wife's property, when the husband has willfully deserted her, issuable by the divorce court under statutes on that subject.

PROTECTIONIBUS DE. The English statute 33 Edw. I. St. 1, allowing a challenge to be entered against a protection, etc.

PROTECTIVE TARIFF. A law imposing duties on imports, with the purpose and the effect of discouraging the use of products of foreign origin, and consequently of stimulating the home production of the same or equivalent articles. R. E. Thompson, in Enc.Brit.

PROTECTOR OF SETTLEMENT. In English law. By the statute 3 & 4 Wm. IV. c. 74, § 32, power is given to any settlor to appoint any person or persons, not exceeding three, the "protector of the settlement." The object of such appointment is to prevent the tenant in tail from barring any subsequent estate, the consent of the protector being made necessary for that purpose.

PROTECTORATE. A state which has transferred the management of its more important international affairs to a stronger state. 1 Opp. 144; Salmond, Juris. 210. It implies only a partial loss of sovereignty, so that the protected state still retains a position in the family of nations. Moreover, the protected state remains so far independent of its protector that it is not obliged to be a party to a war carried on by the protector against a third state, nor are treaties concluded by the protector *ipso facto* binding upon the protected state; 1 Opp. 145–146.

The period during which Oliver Cromwell ruled in England. Also the office of protector.

PROTEST. A formal declaration made by a person interested or concerned in some act about to be done, or already performed, whereby he expresses his dissent or disapproval, or affirms the act against his will. The object of such a declaration is generally to save some right which would be lost to him if his implied assent could be made out, or to exonerate himself from some responsibility which would attach to him unless he expressly negatived his assent.

A notarial act, being a formal statement in writing made by a notary under his seal of office, at the request of the holder of a bill or note, in which it is declared that the bill or note described was on a certain day presented for payment, (or acceptance,) and that such payment or acceptance was refused, and stating the reasons, if any, given for such refusal, whereupon the notary *protests* against all parties to such instrument, and declares that they will be held responsible for all loss or damage arising from its dishonor. Annville Nat. Bank v. Kettering, 106 Pa. 531, 51 Am. Rep. 536; Dennistoun v. Stewart, 17 How. 607, 15 L.Ed. 228. It denotes also all the steps or acts accompanying dishonor necessary to charge an indorser. Townsend v. Lorain Bank, 2 Ohio St. 345; Piedmont Carolina Ry. Co. v. Shaw, C.C.A.N.C., 223 F. 973, 977; Maury v. Winlock & Toledo Logging & R. Co., 148 Wash. 572, 269 P. 815, 817.

A formal declaration made by a minority (or by certain individuals) in a legislative body that they dissent from some act or resolution of the body, usually adding the grounds of their dissent. The term, in this sense, seems to be particularly appropriate to such a proceeding in the English house of lords. Auditor General v. Board of Sup'rs, 51 N.W. 483, 89 Mich. 552.

The formal statement, usually in writing, made by a person who is called upon by public authority to pay a sum of money, in which he declares that he does not concede the legality or justice of the claim or his duty to pay it, or that he disputes the amount demanded; the object being to save his right to recover or reclaim the amount, which right would be lost by his acquiescence. Thus, taxes may be paid under "protest." Meyer v. Clark, 2 Daly (N.Y.) 509.

The name of a paper served on a collector of customs by an importer of merchandise, stating that he believes the sum charged as duty to be excessive, and that, although he pays such sum for the purpose of getting his goods out of the custom-house, he reserves the right to bring an action against the collector to recover the excess. U. S. v. Lian, C.C.A.N.Y., 10 F.2d 41, 42.

In maritime law. A written statement by the master of a vessel, attested by a proper judicial officer or a notary, to the effect that damage suffered by the ship on her voyage was caused by storms or other perils of the sea, without any negligence or misconduct on his own part. Marsh. Ins. 715. And see Cudworth v. South Carolina Ins. Co., 4 Rich.Law, S.C., 416, 55 Am.Dec. 692.

Notice of protest. A notice given by the holder of a bill or note to the drawer or indorser that the bill has been protested for refusal of payment or acceptance. First Nat. Bank v. Hatch, 78 Mo. 23; Roberts v. State Bank, 9 Port. (Ala.) 315.

Supra protest. In mercantile law. A term applied to an acceptance of a bill by a third person, after protest for nonacceptance by the drawee. 3 Kent, Comm. 87.

Waiver of protest. As applied to a note or bill, a waiver of protest implies not only dispensing with the formal act known as "protest," but also with that which ordinarily must precede it, viz., demand and notice of non-payment. Baker v. Scott, 29 Kan. 136, 44 Am.Rep. 628; First Nat. Bank v. Hartman, 110 Pa. 196, 2 A. 271.

PROTESTANDO. L. Lat. Protesting. The emphatic word formerly used in pleading by way of protestation. 3 Bl.Comm. 311. See Protestation.

PROTESTANTS. Those who adhered to the doctrine of Luther; so called because, in 1529, they protested against a decree of the emperor Charles V. and of the diet of Spires, and declared that they appealed to a general council. The name is now applied indiscriminately to all the sects, of whatever denomination, who have seceded from the Church of Rome. Enc.Lond. See Hale v. Everett, 53 N.H. 9, 16 Am.Rep. 82.

PROTESTATION. In pleading. The indirect affirmation or denial of the truth of some matter which cannot with propriety or safety be positively affirmed, denied, or entirely passed over. 3 Bl. Comm. 311. The exclusion of a conclusion. Co. Litt. 124.

In practice. An asseveration made by taking God to witness. A protestation is a form of asseveration which approaches very nearly to an oath. Wolff.Inst.Nat. § 375.

PROTHONOTARY. The title given to an officer who officiates as principal clerk of some courts. Vin. Abr. Trebilcox v. McAlpine, 46 Hun, N.Y., 469; Whitney v. Hopkins, 19 A. 1075, 135 Pa. 246.

PROTOCOL. A record or register. Among the Romans, *protocollum* was a writing at the head of the first page of the paper used by the notaries or tabelliones. Nov. 44.

In France, the minutes of notarial acts were formerly transcribed on registers, which were called "protocols." Toullier, Droit Civil Fr. liv. 3, t. 3, c. 6, s. 1, no. 413.

By the German law it signifies the minutes of any transaction. Encyc.Amer.

International Law

The first draft or rough minutes of an instrument or transaction; the original copy of a dispatch, treaty, or other document. Brande. A document serving as the preliminary to, or opening of, any diplomatic transaction.

Old Scotch Practice

A book, marked by the clerk-register, and delivered to a notary on his admission, in which he was directed to insert all the instruments he had occasion to execute; to be preserved as a record. Bell.

PROTOCOLIZE. A term in Cuban law meaning to copy in the records of a notary. In re Moran's Will, 39 N.Y.S.2d 929, 934, 180 Misc. 469.

PROTOCOLO. In Spanish law. The original draft or writing of an instrument which remains in the possession of the *escribano,* or notary. White, New Recop. lib. 3, tit. 7, c. 5, § 2.

The term *"protocolo,"* when applied to a single paper, means the first draft of an instrument duly executed before a notary—the matrix,—because it is the source from which must be taken copies to be delivered to interested parties as their evidence of right; and it also means a bound book in which the notary places and keeps in their order instruments executed before him, from which copies are taken for the use of parties interested. Downing v. Diaz, 80 Tex. 436, 16 S.W. 53.

PROTUTOR. Lat. In the civil law. He who, not being the tutor of a minor, has administered his property or affairs as if he had been, whether he thought himself legally invested with the authority of a tutor or not. Mackeld. Rom. Law, § 630. He who marries a woman who is tutrix becomes, by the marriage, a protutor. The protutor is equally responsible with the tutor.

PROUT PATET PER RECORDUM. As appears by the record. In the Latin phraseology of pleading, this was the proper formula for making reference to a record.

PROVABLE. Susceptible of being proved. City Hall Building & Loan Ass'n of Newark v. Star Corporation, 110 N.J.L. 570, 166 A. 223, 224.

PROVE. To establish or make certain; to establish a fact or hypothesis as true by satisfactory and sufficient evidence. Blackstone Hall Co. v. Rhode Island Hospital Trust Co., 97 A. 484, 487, 39 R.I. 69.

To present a claim or demand against a bankrupt or insolvent estate, and establish by evidence or affidavit that the same is correct and due, for the purpose of receiving a dividend on it. Tibbetts v. Trafton, 80 Me. 264, 14 A. 71; In re California Pac. R. Co., 4 Fed.Cas. 1060; In re Bigelow, 3 Fed.Cas. 343.

To establish the genuineness and due execution of a paper, propounded to the proper court or officer, as the last will and testament of a deceased person. See Probate.

PROVEN TERRITORY. In oil prospecting "proven territory" means territory so situated with reference to known producing wells as to establish the general opinion that, because of its location in relation to them, oil is contained in it. Minchew v. Morris, Tex.Civ.App., 241 S.W. 215, 217.

PROVER. In old Englsh law. A person who, on being indicted of treason or felony, and arraigned for the same, confessed the fact before plea pleaded, and appealed or accused others, his accomplices, in the same crime, in order to obtain his pardon. 4 Bl.Comm. 329, 330.

PROVIDE. To make, procure, or furnish for future use, prepare. Booth v. State, 179 Ind. 405, 100 N.E. 563, 566, L.R.A.1915B, 420, Ann.Cas. 1915D, 987. To supply; to afford; to contribute. Keith v. Rust Land & Lumber Co., 167 Wis. 528, 167 N.W. 432, 435.

PROVIDED. The word used in introducing a proviso (which see.) Ordinarily it signifies or expresses a condition; but this is not invariable, for, according to the context, it may import a covenant, or a limitation or qualification, or a restraint, modification, or exception to something which precedes. Stanley v. Colt, 5 Wall. 166, 18 L.Ed. 502; Robertson v. Caw, 3 Barb., N.Y., 418; Attorney General v. City of Methuen, 129 N.E. 662, 665, 236 Mass. 564.

PROVIDED BY LAW. This phrase when used in a constitution or statute generally means prescribed or provided by some statute. Lawson v. Kanawha County Court, 80 W.Va. 612, 92 S.E. 786, 789.

PROVINCE. The district into which a country has been divided; as, the province of Canterbury, in England; the province of Languedoc, in France. A dependency or colony, as, the province of New Brunswick. Figuratively, power or authority; as, it is the province of the court to judge of the law; that of the jury to decide on the facts. 1 Bl.Comm. 111; Tomlins.

PROVINCIAL CONSTITUTIONS. The decrees of provincial synods held under divers archbishops of Canterbury, from Stephen Langton, in the reign of Henry III., to Henry Chichele, in the reign of Henry V., and adopted also by the province of York in the reign of Henry VI. Wharton.

PROVINCIAL COURTS. In English law. The several archi-episcopal courts in the two ecclesiastical provinces of England.

PROVINCIALE. A work on ecclesiastical law, by William Lyndwode, official principal to Archbishop Chichele in the reign of Edward IV. 4 Reeve, Eng.Law, c. 25, p. 117.

PROVINCIALIS. Lat. In the civil law. One who has his domicile in a province. Dig. 50, 16, 190.

PROVING OF THE TENOR. In Scotch practice. An action for proving the tenor of a lost deed. Bell.

PROVISION. Foresight of the chance of an event happening, sufficient to indicate that any present undertaking upon which its assumed realization might exert a natural and proper influence was entered upon in full contemplation of it as a future possibility. Appeal of Blake, 95 Conn. 194, 110 A. 833, 834.

In commercial law. Funds remitted by the drawer of a bill of exchange to the drawee in order to meet the bill, or property remaining in the drawee's hands or due from him to the drawer, and appropriated to that purpose.

In ecclesiastical law. A nomination by the pope to an English benefice before it became void; the term was afterwards indiscriminately applied to any right of patronage exerted or usurped by the pope.

In French law. An allowance or alimony granted by a judge to one of the parties in a cause for his or her maintenance until a definite judgment is rendered. Dalloz.

In English history. A name given to certain statutes or acts of parliament, particularly those intended to curb the arbitrary or usurped power of the sovereign, and also to certain other ordinances or declarations having the force of law. See *infra*.

A term used in the reign of Henry III. to designate enactments of the King in Council, perhaps less solemn than statutes. The term "statutes" was a later term, with a changed conception of the solemnity of a statute, and is one that cannot easily be defined. It came into use in Edward I.'s reign, supplanting "provisions," which is characteristic of Henry III.'s reign, which had supplanted "assize," characteristic of the reigns of Henry II., Richard and John Maitland, 2 Sel. Essays in Anglo-Am. Leg. Hist. 80.

Provisions of Merton. Another name for the statute of Merton. See Merton, Statute of.

Provisions of Oxford. Legislative provisions (1258) forbidding the Chancellor to issue writs, other than those "of course" without the approval of the executive council, as well as the king. Certain provisions made in the Parliament of Oxford, 1258, for the purpose of securing the execution of the provisions of *Magna Charta*, against the invasions thereof by Henry III. The government of the country was in effect committed by these provisions to a standing committee of twenty-four, whose chief merit consisted in their representative character, and their real desire to effect an improvement in the king's government. Brown.

Provisions of Westminster. A name given to certain ordinances or declarations promulgated by the barons in A. D. 1259, for the reform of various abuses.

PROVISIONAL. Temporary; preliminary; tentative; taken or done by way of precaution or *ad interim*.

PROVISIONAL ASSIGNEES. In the former practice in bankruptcy in England. Assignees to whom the property of a bankrupt was assigned until the regular or permanent assignees were appointed by the creditors.

PROVISIONAL COMMITTEE. A committee appointed for a temporary occasion.

PROVISIONAL COURT. A federal court with jurisdiction and powers governed by the order from which it derives its authority.

A provisional court established in conquered or occupied territory by military authorities, or the provisional government, is a federal court deriving its existence and all its powers from the federal government. 36 C.J.S., Federal Courts, § 320.

PROVISIONAL GOVERNMENT. One temporarily established in anticipation of and to exist and continue until another (more regular or more permanent) shall be organized and instituted in its stead. Chambers v. Fisk, 22 Tex. 535.

PROVISIONAL INJUNCTION. Sometimes, though not correctly, used for interlocutory injunction.

PROVISIONAL ORDER. In English law. Under various acts of parliament, certain public bodies and departments of the government are authorized to inquire into matters which, in the ordinary course, could only be dealt with by a private act of parliament, and to make orders for their regulation. These orders have no effect unless they are confirmed by an act of parliament, and are hence called "provisional orders." Several orders may be confirmed by one act. The object of this mode of proceeding is to save the trouble and expense of promoting a number of private bills. Sweet.

PROVISIONAL REMEDY. A remedy provided for present need or for the immediate occasion; one adapted to meet a particular exigency. Particularly, a temporary process available to a plaintiff in a civil action, which secures him against loss, irreparable injury, dissipation of the property, etc., while the action is pending. Such are the remedies by injunction, appointment of a receiver, attachment, or arrest. The term is chiefly used in the codes of practice. Snavely v. Abbott Buggy Co., 36 Kan. 106, 12 P. 522.

PROVISIONAL SEIZURE. A remedy known under the law of Louisiana, and substantially the same in general nature as attachment of property in other states. Code Prac. La. 284, *et seq.* See Nolte v. His Creditors, 6 Mart. N. S. (La.) 168.

PROVISIONES. Lat. In English history. Those acts of parliament which were passed to curb the arbitrary power of the crown. See Provision.

PROVISIONS. Food; victuals; articles of food for human consumption. State v. Angelo, 71 N.H. 224, 51 A. 905; Clatsop County v. Feldschau, 99 Or. 680, 196 P. 379, 380. The word does not include a milch cow; Wilson v. McMillan, 80 Ga. 733, 6 S.E. 182; nor cotton; Butler v. Shiver, 79 Ga. 172, 4 S.E. 115.

PROVISO. A condition or provision which is inserted in a deed, lease, mortgage, or contract, and on the performance or nonperformance of which the validity of the instrument frequently depends; it usually begins with the word "provided."

It always implies a condition, unless subsequent words change it to a covenant, Rich v. Atwater, 16 Conn. 419; but when a proviso contains the mutual words of the parties to a deed, it amounts to a covenant. 2 Co. 72; Cro.Eliz. 242.

The word "proviso" is generally taken for a condition, but it differs from it in several respects; for a condition is usually created by the grantor or lessor, but a proviso by the grantee or lessee. Jacob.

The mere use of technical terms which ordinarily denote a limitation or a condition subsequent is an unsafe test of the true nature of the estate granted; the word "proviso" or "provided" itself being sometimes taken as a condition, sometimes as a limitation, and sometimes as a covenant. Stevens v. Galveston H. & S. A. Ry. Co., Tex.Com.App., 212 S.W. 639, 644.

A limitation or exception to a grant made or authority conferred, the effect of which is to declare that the one shall not operate, or the other be exercised, unless in the case provided. Clearwater Tp. v. Board of Sup'rs of Kalkaska County, 187 Mich. 516, 153 N.W. 824, 827.

A clause or part of a clause in a statute, the office of which is either to except something from the enacting clause, or to qualify or restrain its generality, or to exclude some possible ground of misinterpretation of its extent. Cox v. Hart, 260 U.S. 427, 43 S.Ct. 154, 157, 67 L.Ed. 332; Riley Pennsylvania Oil Co. v. Symmonds, 195 Mo.App. 111, 190 S.W. 1038, 1040. Strain v. East Bay Municipal Utility Dist., 21 Cal.App.2d 281, 69 P.2d 191, 193.

A proviso is sometimes misused to introduce independent pieces of legislation. Cox v. Hart, 43 S.Ct. 154, 157, 260 U.S. 427, 67 L.Ed. 332. Its proper use, however, is to qualify what is affirmed in the body of the act, section, or paragraph preceding it, or to except something from the act, but not to enlarge the enacting clause. State Public Utilities Commission v. Early, 285 Ill. 469, 121 N.E. 63, 66; And it cannot be held to enlarge the scope of the statute; Jordan v. Town of South Boston, 138 Va. 838, 122 S.E. 265, 267.

While a proviso is commonly found at the end of the act or section, and is usually introduced by the word "provided," that word is not necessary, the matter and not the form of the succeeding words controlling. Mackenzie v. Douglas County, 81 Or. 442, 159 P. 625, 627.

The proper use of provisoes in drafting acts is explained by Coode on Legislative Construction. The early, and, as he thinks, the correct use, is by way of taking special cases out of general enactments and *providing for them*. The courts have generally assumed that such was the proper mode of using a proviso. It is incorrectly used to introduce mere exceptions to the operation of the enactment where no special provision is made for the exception; these are better expressed as exceptions.

Exception and proviso distinguished. See Exception.

PROVISO EST PROVIDERE PRÆSENTIA ET FUTURA, NON PRÆTERITA. Coke, 72; Vaugh. 279. A proviso is to provide for the present or future, not the past.

PROVISO, TRIAL BY. In English practice. A trial brought on by the defendant, in cases where the plaintiff, after issue joined, neglects to proceed to trial; so called from a clause in the writ to the sheriff, which directs him, in case two writs come to his hands, to execute but one of them. 3 Bl. Comm. 357. The defendant may take out a *venire facias* to the sheriff, which hath in it these words, *Proviso quod*, etc., provided that if the plaintiff shall take out any writ to that purpose, the sheriff shall summon but one jury on them both. Jacob; Old Nat. Brev. 159.

PROVISOR. In old English law. A provider, or purveyor. Spelman. Also a person nominated to be the next incumbent of a benefice (not yet vacant) by the pope. 4 Bl.Comm. 111. He that hath the care of providing things necessary; but more especially one who sued to the court of Rome for a provision. Jacob; 25 Edw. III.

PROVISORS, STATUTE OF. A statute passed in 25 Edw. III. forbidding the Pope to nominate to benefices, and declaring that the election of bishops and other dignitaries should be free, and all rights of patrons preserved. Taswell-Langmead, Engl. Constit. Hist. 322. See Præmunire.

PROVOCATION. The act of inciting another to do a particular deed. That which arouses, moves, calls forth, causes, or occasions. Manson v. State, 14 Ga.App. 837, 82 S.E. 763, 764.

Such conduct or actions on the part of one person towards another as tend to arouse rage, resentment, or fury in the latter against the former, and thereby cause him to do some illegal act against or in relation to the person offering the provocation. State v. Byrd, 52 S.C. 480, 30 S.E. 482.

"Provocation" which will reduce killing to manslaughter must be of such character as will, in mind of average reasonable man, stir resentment likely to cause violence, obscure the reason, and lead to action from passion rather than judgment. Wooten v. State, 171 Tenn. 362, 103 S.W. 2d 324, 326. There must be a state of passion without time to cool placing defendant beyond control of his reason. Commonwealth v. Gelfi, 282 Pa. 434, 128 A. 77, 79. Provocation carries with it the idea of some physical aggression or some assault which suddenly arouses heat and passion in the person assaulted. State v. Hollis, 108 S.C. 442, 95 S.E. 74, 76.

PROVOKE. To excite; to stimulate; to arouse. To irritate, or enrage. State v. Milosovich, 42 Nev. 263, 175 P. 139, 141.

PROVOKING A DIFFICULTY. The law on this point arises only where deceased was the attacking party, and his attack was brought about by the words or acts of accused, intended to bring on the attack, in order that advantage might be taken thereof by him to slay his adversary and escape the consequences. Carter v. State, 87 Tex.Cr.R. 200, 220 S.W. 335, 336.

PROVOST. The principal magistrate of a royal burgh in Scotland. A governing officer of certain universities or colleges. The chief dignitary of a cathedral or collegiate church.

In France, this title was formerly given to some presiding judges.

PROVOST-MARSHAL. In English law, an officer of the royal navy who had the charge of prisoners taken at sea, and sometimes also on land.

In military law, the officer acting as the head of the military police of any post, camp, city or other place in military occupation, or district under the reign of martial law. He or his assistants may, at any time, arrest and detain for trial, persons subject to military law committing offenses, and may carry into execution any punishments to be inflicted in pursuance of a court martial.

PROXENETA. Lat. In the civil law. A broker; one who negotiated or arranged the terms of a contract between two parties, as between buyer and seller; one who negotiated a marriage; a match-maker. Calvin.; Dig. 50, 14, 3.

PROXIMATE. Immediate; nearest; direct, next in order. In its legal sense, closest in causal connection. Menger v. Laur, 55 N.J.L. 205, 26 A. 180, 20 L.R.A. 61. Poore v. Edgar Bros. Co., 33 Cal. App.2d 6, 90 P.2d 808, 810. Next in relation to cause and effect. Godfrey v. Vinson, 215 Ala. 166, 110 So. 13, 16.

PROXIMATE CAUSE. That which, in a natural and continuous sequence, unbroken by any efficient intervening cause, produces the injury, and without which the result would not have occurred. Swayne v. Connecticut Co., 86 Conn. 439, 85 A. 634, 635; Lemos v. Madden, 28 Wyo. 1, 200 P. 791, 793. That which is nearest in the order of responsible causation. Butcher v. R. Co., 37 W. Va. 180, 16 S.E. 457, 18 L.R.A. 519. That which stands next in causation to the effect, not necessarily in time or space but in causal relation. Cundiff v. City of Owensboro, 193 Ky. 168, 235 S.W. 15, 16; Carlock v. Denver & R. G. R. Co., 55 Colo. 146, 133 P. 1103, 1104. The last negligent act contributory to an injury, without which such injury would not have resulted. Estep v. Price, 93 W.Va. 81, 115 S.E. 861, 863. The dominant cause. Ballagh v. Interstate Business Men's Acc. Ass'n, 176 Iowa 110, 155 N.W. 241, 244, L.R.A.1917A, 1050; The moving or producing cause. Eberhardt v. Glasco Mut. Tel. Ass'n, 91 Kan. 763, 139 P. 416, 417, Buchanan v. Hurd Creamery Co., 215 Iowa 415, 246 N.W. 41. The efficient cause; the one that necessarily sets the other causes in operation. Baltimore & O. R. Co. v. Ranier, 84 Ind.App. 542, 149 N.E. 361, 364. The causes that are merely incidental or instruments of a superior or controlling agency are not the proximate causes and the responsible ones, though they may be nearer in time to the result. It is only when the causes are independent of each other that the nearest is, of course, to be charged with the disaster. Blythe v. Railway Co., 15 Colo. 333, 25 P. 702, 11 L.R.A. 615, 22 Am.St.Rep. 403; act or omission immediately causing or failing to prevent injury; act or omission occurring or concurring with another, which, had it not happened, injury would not have been inflicted. Herron v. Smith Bros., 116 Cal.App. 518, 2 P.2d 1012, 1013.

"Proximate cause" is distinguishable from "immediate cause." Missouri, K. & T. Ry. Co. of Texas v. Cardwell, Tex.Civ.App., 187 S.W. 1073, 1076. The immediate cause is generally referred to in the law as the nearest cause in point of time and space, while an act or omission may be the proximate cause of an injury without being the immediate cause. Thus, where several causes combine to produce an injury, the last intervening cause is commonly referred to as the immediate cause, although some other agency more remote in time or space may, in causal relation, be the nearer to the result, and thus be the proximate responsible cause. Dunbar v. Davis, 32 Ga.App. 192, 122 S. E. 895, citing, among others, Insurance Co. v. Boon, 95 U. S. 117, 130, 24 L.Ed. 395; Terry Shipbuilding Corp. v. Griffian, 112 S.E. 374, 153 Ga. 390. Moreover, there may be two or more proximate causes, but only one immediate cause. Thomas v. Chicago Embossing Co., 307 Ill. 134, 138 N.E. 285, 287; American Stone Ballast Co. v. Marshall's Adm'r, 206 Ky. 133, 266 S.W. 1051, 1052. But the two terms are sometimes used interchangeably. Wilczynski v. Milwaukee Electric Ry. & Light Co., 171 Wis. 508, 177 N.W. 876, 877; but see Wright v. Greenwood Telephone Co., 108 S.C. 84, 93 S.E. 398, 399; Knight v. Wessler, 67 Utah, 354, 248 P. 132, 133. See, also, Immediate Cause.

PROXIMATE CONSEQUENCE OR RESULT. One which succeeds naturally in the ordinary course of things. Swaim v. Chicago, R. I. & P. Ry. Co., 187 Iowa 466, 174 N.W. 384, 386. A consequence which, in addition to being in the train of physical causation, is not entirely outside the range of expectation or probability, as viewed by ordinary men. The Mars, D.C.N.Y., 9 F.2d 183, 184. One ordinarily following from the negligence complained of, unbroken by any independent cause, which might have been reasonably foreseen. One which a prudent and experienced man, fully acquainted with all the circumstances which in fact existed, would, at time of the negligent act, have thought reasonably possible to follow, if it had occurred to his mind. Coast S. S. Co. v. Brady, C.C.A.Ala., 8 F.2d 16, 19. A mere possibility of the injury is not sufficient, where a reasonable man would not consider injury likely to result from the act as one of its ordinary and probable results.

PROXIMATE DAMAGES. See Damages.

PROXIMATELY. Directly or immediately. Kentucky Traction & Terminal Co. v. Bain, 161 Ky. 44, 170 S.W. 499, 501. Pertaining to that which in an ordinary natural sequence produces a specific result, no independent disturbing agency intervening. Weaver v. Landis, 66 Cal.App.2d 34, 151 P.2d 884, 886.

PROXIMITY. Kindred between two persons. Dig. 38, 16, 8. Quality or state of being next in time, place, causation, influence, etc.; immediate nearness. Webster, Dict.

PROXIMUS EST CUI NEMO ANTECEDIT, SUPREMUS EST QUEM NEMO SEQUITUR. He is next whom no one precedes; he is last whom no one follows. Dig. 50, 16, 92.

PROXY. (Contracted from procuracy.) A person who is substituted or deputed by another to represent him and act for him, particularly in some meeting or public body. An agent representing and acting for principal. Also the instrument containing the appointment of such person. Manson v. Curtis, 223 N.Y. 313, 119 N.E. 559, 561, Ann.Cas.1918E, 247; Cliffs Corporation v. United States, C.C.A.Ohio, 103 F.2d 77, 80.

In ecclesiastical law. A person who is appointed to manage another man's affairs in the ecclesiastical courts; a judicial proctor.

Also an annual payment made by the parochial clergy to the bishop, on visitations. Tomlins.

PRUDENCE. Carefulness, precaution, attentiveness, and good judgment, as applied to action or conduct. That degree of care required by the exigencies or circumstances under which it is to be exercised. Cronk v. Railway Co., 52 N.W. 420, 3 S.D. 93. This term, in the language of the law, is commonly associated with "care" and "diligence" and contrasted with "negligence." See those titles.

PRUDENT. Sagacious in adapting means to end, circumspect in action, or in determining any line of conduct, practically wise, judicious, careful, discreet, circumspect, sensible. Tureen v. Peoples Motorbus Co. of St. Louis, Mo.App., 97 S.W.2d 847, 848. In defining negligence, practically synonymous with cautious. Malcolm v. Mooresville Cotton Mills, 191 N.C. 727, 133 S.E. 7, 9; Hurley v. Gus Blass Co., 191 Ark. 917, 88 S.W.2d 850, 851.

PRUDENTER AGIT QUI PRÆCEPTO LEGIS OBTEMPERAT. 5 Coke, 49. He acts prudently who obeys the command of the law.

PRUDENTIAL AFFAIRS. Within the meaning of a statute authorizing the making of by-laws by municipalities for the directing and managing of their prudential affairs, this term includes those matters for the necessary convenience of the inhabitants. Clarke v. City of Fall River, 219 Mass. 580, 107 N.E. 419, 421.

PRUDHOMMES, PRODES HOMMES. This word was used in early Norman times, and before, in a general sense to signify freeholders or respectable burgesses; sometimes a special body of such persons acting as magistrates or judges. Black Book of Adm. IV, 186. There were prudhommes of the sea; of merchants; of the corporation of Barcelona; and of the gild of coopers. Usually two sat.

PRYK. A kind of service of tenure. Blount says it signifies an old-fashioned spur with one point only, which the tenant, holding land by this tenure, was to find for the king. Wharton.

PSEUDO. False, counterfeit, pretended, spurious. State v. Skinner, 37 Nev. 107, 139 P. 773, 776.

PSEUDOCYESIS. In medical jurisprudence. A frequent manifestation of hysteria in women, in which the abdomen is inflated, simulating pregnancy; the patient aiding in the deception.

PSEUDOGRAPH. False writing.

PSYCHO-DIAGNOSIS. In medical jurisprudence. A method of investigating the origin and cause of any given disease or morbid condition by examination of the mental condition of the patient, the application of various psychological tests, and an inquiry into the past history of the patient, with a view to its bearing on his present psychic state.

PSYCHOLOGICAL FACT. In the law of evidence. A fact which can only be perceived mentally; such as the motive by which a person is actuated. Burrill, Circ. Ev. 130, 131.

PSYCHONEUROSIS. See Insanity.

PSYCHOPATH. Person having mental disorder. More commonly, mental disorder not amounting to insanity or taking the specific form of a psychoneurosis, but characterized by a defect of character or personality, eccentricity, emotional instability, inadequacy or perversity of conduct, under conceit and suspiciousness, or lack of common sense, social feeling, self-control, truthfulness, energy, or persistence. Mutual Life Ins. Co. v. Frost, C.C.A.R.I., 164 F.2d 542, 545.

Synonymous with "sociopathic personality"

PSYCHOSIS. A disease of the mind; especially, a functional mental disorder, that is, one unattended with structural changes in the brain. Davis v. State, 153 Ga. 154, 112 S.E. 280, 282. See Insanity.

PSYCHOTHERAPY. A method or system of alleviating or curing certain forms of disease, particularly diseases of the nervous system or such as are traceable to nervous disorders, by suggestion, persuasion, encouragement, the inspiration of hope or confidence, the discouragement of morbid memories, associations, or beliefs, and other similar means addressed to the mental state of the patient, without (or sometimes in conjunction with) the administration of drugs or other physical remedies.

PTOMAINE. In medical jurisprudence. An alkaloidal product of the decomposition or putrefaction of albuminous substances, as, in animal and vegetable tissues. Ptomaines are sometimes poisonous, but not invariably. Examples of poisonous ptomaines are those occurring in putrefying fish and the tyrotoxicons of decomposing milk and milk products. They are sometimes found in a less harmful form in preserved vegetable matter. Drury v. Armour & Co., 140 Ark. 371, 216 S.W. 40, 42.

PUBERTY. The earliest age at which persons are capable of begetting or bearing children. Webster, Dict.

In the civil and common law, the age at which one becomes capable of contracting marriage. It is in boys fourteen, and in girls twelve years. Ayliffe, Pand. 63; Toullier, *Dr. Civ. Fr.* tom. 5, p. 100; Inst. 1, 22; Dig. 1, 7, 40, 1; Code 5, 60, 3;

1 Bl.Comm. 436; 2 Kent, Comm. 78; State v. Pierson, 44 Ark. 265. Otherwise called the "age of consent to marriage."

PUBLIC, *n.* The whole body politic, or the aggregate of the citizens of a state, district, or municipality. Knight v. Thomas, 93 Me. 494, 45 A. 499. The inhabitants of a state, county, or community. People v. Turnbull, 184 Ill.App. 151, 155; Commonwealth v. Bosworth, 257 Mass. 212, 153 N.E. 455, 457. In one sense, everybody; and accordingly the body of the people at large; the community at large, without reference to the geographical limits of any corporation like a city, town, or county; the people. In another sense the word does not mean all the people, nor most of the people, nor very many of the people of a place, but so many of them as contradistinguishes them from a few. Accordingly, it has been defined or employed as meaning the inhabitants of a particular place; all the inhabitants of a particular place; the people of the neighborhood. People v. Powell, 280 Mich. 699, 274 N.W. 372, 373, 111 A.L.R. 721; State ex rel. Maher v. Baker, 88 Ohio St. 165, 102 N.E. 732, 736. Also, a part of the inhabitants of a community. Davis v. People, 79 Colo. 642, 247 P. 801, 802.

PUBLIC, *adj.* Pertaining to a state, nation, or whole community; proceeding from, relating to, or affecting the whole body of people or an entire community. Open to all; notorious. Common to all or many; general; open to common use. Morgan v. Cree, 46 Vt. 786, 14 Am.Rep. 640; Crane v. Waters, C.C.Mass., 10 F. 621. Belonging to the people at large; relating to or affecting the whole people of a state, nation, or community; not limited or restricted to any particular class of the community. People v. Powell, 280 Mich. 699, 274 N.W. 372, 373, 111 A.L.R. 721.

A distinction has been made between the terms "public" and "general." They are sometimes used as synonymous. The former term is applied strictly to that which concerns all the citizens and every member of the state; while the latter includes a lesser, though still a large, portion of the community. 1 Greenl.Ev. § 128.

As to public "Accounts," "Acknowledgment," "Act," "Administrator," "Agent," "Attorney," "Auction," "Breach," "Blockade," "Boundary," "Bridge," "Business," "Capacity," "Carrier," "Chapel," "Charge," "Charity," "Company," "Corporation," "Debt," "Document," "Domain," "Easement," "Enemy," "Ferry," "Funds," "Good," "Grant," "Health," "Highway," "Holiday," "Hospital," "House," "Indecency," "Institution," "Market," "Minister," "Money," "Necessity," "Notice," "Nuisance," "Office," "Officer," "Peace," "Policy," "Pond," "Printing," "Property," "Prosecutor," "Record," "Revenue," "River," "Road," "Sale," "School," "Seal," "Sewer," "Square," "Stock," "Store," "Tax," "Things," "Thoroughfare," "Trial," "Trust," "Trustee," "Verdict," "Vessel," "War," "Works," "Worship," and "Wrongs," see those titles.

Public appointments. Public offices or stations which are to be filled by the appointment of individuals, under authority of law, instead of by election.

Public building. One of which the possession and use, as well as the property in it, are in the public. Pancoast v. Troth, 34 N.J.Law, 383. Any building held, used, or controlled exclusively for public purposes by any department or branch of government, state, county, or municipal, without reference to the ownership of the building or of the realty upon which it is situated. Shepherd v. State, 16 Ga.App. 248, 85 S.E. 83. A building belonging to or used by the public for the transaction of public or quasi public business. Lewis v. Commonwealth, 197 Ky. 449, 247 S.W. 749, 750.

Public character. An individual who asks for and desires public recognition, such as a statesman, author, artist, or inventor. Corliss v. E. W. Walker Co., C.C.Mass., 64 F. 280, 31 L.R.A. 283.

Public convenience. In a statute requiring the issuance of a certificate of public convenience and necessity by the Public Utilities Commission for the operation of a motorbus line, "convenience" is not used in its colloquial sense as synonymous with handy or easy of access, but in accord with its regular meaning of suitable and fitting, and "public convenience" refers to something fitting or suited to the public need. Abbott v. Public Utilities Commission, 48 R.I. 196, 136 A. 490, 491.

Public interest. Something in which the public, the community at large, has some pecuniary interest, or some interest by which their legal rights or liabilities are affected. It does not mean anything so narrow as mere curiosity, or as the interests of the particular localities, which may be affected by the matters in question. State v. Crockett, 86 Okl. 124, 206 P. 816, 817.

If by public permission one is making use of public property and he chances to be the only one with whom the public can deal with respect to the use of that property, his business is affected with a public interest which requires him to deal with the public on reasonable terms. Cooley, Const.Lim. 746. The circumstances which clothe a particular kind of business with a "public interest," as to be subject to regulation, must be such as to create a peculiarly close relation between the public and those engaged in it and raise implications of an affirmative obligation on their part to be reasonable in dealing with the public. One does not devote his property or business to a public use, or clothe it with a public interest, merely because he makes commodities for and sells to the public in common callings such as those of the butcher, baker, tailor, etc. Chas. Wolff Packing Co. v. Court of Industrial Relations of State of Kansas, 43 S.Ct. 630, 633, 262 U.S. 522, 67 L.Ed. 1103, 27 A.L.R. 1280. A business is not affected with a public interest merely because it is large, or because the public has concern in respect of its maintenance, or derives benefit, accommodation, ease, or enjoyment from it. Tyson & Bro.-United Theatre Ticket Offices v. Banton, 47 S.Ct. 426, 273 U.S. 418, 71 L.Ed. 718, 58 A.L.R. 1236.

Public lands. The general public domain; unappropriated lands; lands belonging to the United States and which are subject to sale or other disposal under general laws, and not reserved or held back for any special governmental or public purpose. Newhall v. Sanger, 92 U.S. 763, 23 L.Ed. 769; State v. Telegraph Co., 52 La.Ann. 1411, 27 So. 796. See Lands.

Public laundry. This term, in Labor Law, N. Y. § 296 (Consol. Laws, c. 31), includes a laundry doing laundry work that is ultimately distributed to the public, and is not limited to laundry doing custom work only. Van Zandt's, Inc., v. Department of Labor of State of New York, 129 Misc. 747, 222 N.Y.S. 450, 451.

Public lavatories. Such as are open to all who may choose to use them. Irvine v. Commonwealth, 124 Va. 817, 97 S.E. 769.

The term may, however, include a washroom in a lodging house for men guests only. City of Chicago v. McGuire, 185 Ill.App. 589, 590.

Public law. That branch or department of law which is concerned with the state in its political or sovereign capacity, including constitutional and administrative law, and with the definition, regulation, and enforcement of rights in cases where the state is regarded as the subject of the right or object of the duty,—including criminal law and criminal procedure,—and the law of the state, considered in its *quasi* private personality, *i. e.*, as capable of holding or exercising rights, or acquiring and dealing with property, in the character of an individual. Holl. Jur. 106, 300. That portion of law which is concerned with political conditions; that is to say, with the powers, rights, duties, capacities, and incapacities which are peculiar to political superiors, supreme and subordinate. Aust. Jur. In one sense, a designation given to international law, as distinguished from the laws of a particular nation or state. In another sense, a law or statute that applies to the people generally of the nation or state adopting or enacting it, is denominated a public law, as contradistinguished from a private law, affecting only an individual or a small number of persons. Morgan v. Cree, 46 Vt. 773, 14 Am.Rep. 640.

Public offense. An act or omission forbidden by law, and punishable as by law provided. Ford v. State, 7 Ind.App. 567, 35 N.E. 34.

Public passage. A right, subsisting in the public, to pass over a body of water, whether the land under it be public or owned by a private person. This term is synonymous with public highway, with this difference: by the latter is understood a right to pass over the land of another; by the former is meant the right of going over the water which is on another's land. Carth. 193; Hamm. N. P. 195.

Public place. A place to which the general public has a right to resort; not necessarily a place devoted solely to the uses of the public, but a place which is in point of fact public rather than private, a place visited by many persons and usually accessible to the neighboring public. People v. Whitman, 178 App.Div. 193, 165 N.Y.S. 148, 149. Roach v. Eugene, 23 Or. 376, 31 P. 825. Any place so situated that what passes there can be seen by any considerable number of persons, if they happen to look. Steph. Cr. L. 115. Also, a place in which the public has an interest as affecting the safety, health, morals, and welfare of the community. A place exposed to the public, and where the public gather together or pass to and fro. Lewis v. Commonwealth, 197 Ky. 449, 247 S.W. 749, 750.

Public purpose. In the law of taxation, eminent domain, etc., this is a term of classification to distinguish the objects for which, according to settled usage, the government is to provide, from those which, by the like usage, are left to private interest, inclination, or liberality. People v. Salem Tp. Board, 20 Mich. 485, 4 Am.Rep. 400; Black, Const. Law (3d Ed.) p. 454, *et seq.*; Hagler v. Small, 307 Ill. 460, 138 N.E. 849, 854. The term is synonymous with governmental purpose. State v. Dixon, 66 Mont. 76, 213 P. 227, 231. As employed to denote the objects for which taxes may be levied, it has no relation to the urgency of the public need or to the extent of the public benefit which is to follow; the essential requisite being that a public service or use shall affect the inhabitants as a community, and not merely as individuals. Stevenson v. Port of Portland, 82 Or. 576, 162 P. 509, 511. A public purpose or public business has for its objective the promotion of the public health, safety, morals, general welfare, security, prosperity, and contentment of all the inhabitants or residents within a given political division, as, for example, a state, the sovereign powers of which are exercised to promote such public purpose or public business. Green v. Frazier, 44 N.D. 395, 176 N.W. 11, 17. See, also, City of Tombstone v. Macia, 30 Ariz. 218, 245 P. 677, 679, 46 A.L.R. 828.

Public service. A term applied in modern usage to the objects and enterprises of certain kinds of corporations, which specially serve the needs of the general public or conduce to the comfort and convenience of an entire community, such as railroad, gas, water, and electric light companies; and companies furnishing motor vehicle transportation. Harrison v. Big Four Bus Lines, 217 Ky. 119, 288 S.W. 1049. A public service or quasi public corporation is one private in its ownership, but which has an appropriate franchise from the state to provide for a necessity or convenience of the general public, incapable of being furnished by private competitive business, and dependent for its exercise on eminent domain or governmental agency. Attorney General v. Haverhill Gaslight Co., 215 Mass. 394, 101 N.E. 1061, 1063, Ann.Cas.1914C, 1266. It is one of a large class of private corporations which on account of special franchises conferred on them owe a duty to the public which they may be compelled to perform. State ex rel. Coco v. Riverside Irr. Co., 142 La. 10, 76 So. 216, 218.

Public service commission. A board or commission created by the legislature to exercise power of supervision or regulation over public utilities or public service corporations. Railroad Commission of Alabama v. Northern Alabama Ry. Co., 182 Ala. 357, 62 So. 749. Such a commission is a legal, administrative body, provided for the administration of certain matters within the police power, with power to make regulations as to certain matters when required for the public safety and convenience, and to determine facts on which existing laws shall operate. Bessette v. Goddard, 87 Vt. 77, 88 A. 1, 3. People ex rel. New York Telephone Co. v. Public Service Commission,

Second District, 141 N.Y.S. 1018, 1022, 157 App. Div. 156.

Public, true, and notorious. The old form by which charges in the *allegations* in the ecclesiastical courts were described at the end of each particular.

Public use, in constitutional provisions restricting the exercise of the right to take private property in virtue of eminent domain, means a use concerning the whole community as distinguished from particular individuals. But each and every member of society need not be equally interested in such use, or be personally and directly affected by it; if the object is to satisfy a great public want or exigency, that is sufficient. Rindge Co. v. Los Angeles County, 43 S.Ct. 689, 692, 262 U.S. 700, 67 L.Ed. 1186. The term may be said to mean public usefulness, utility, or advantage, or what is productive of general benefit. Williams v. City of Norman, 85 Okl. 230, 205 P. 144, 148. But it is not synonymous with public benefit. Ferguson v. Illinois Cent. R. Co., 202 Iowa, 508, 210 N.W. 604, 606. It may be limited to the inhabitants of a small or restricted locality, but must be in common, and not for a particular individual. Pocantico Water Works Co. v. Bird, 130 N.Y. 249, 29 N.E. 246. The use must be a needful one for the public, which cannot be surrendered without obvious general loss and inconvenience. Jeter v. Vinton-Roanoke Water Co., 114 Va. 769, 76 S.E. 921, 925, Ann.Cas.1914C, 1029.

In patent law, a public use is entirely different from a use by the public. Los Angeles Lime Co. v. Nye, C.C.A.Cal., 270 F. 155, 162. If an inventor allows his machine to be used by other persons generally, either with or without compensation, or if it is, with his consent, put on sale for such use, then it will be in "public use" and on public sale. David E. Kennedy v. United Cork Cos., C. C.A.N.Y., 225 F. 371, 372. Experimental use is never "public use" if conducted in good faith to test the qualities of the invention, and for no other purpose not naturally incidental. Union Sulphur Co. v. Freeport Texas Co., D.C.Del., 251 F. 634, 651.

PUBLIC UTILITY. A business or service which is engaged in regularly supplying the public with some commodity or service which is of public consequence and need, such as electricity, gas, water, transportation, or telephone or telegraph service. Gulf States Utilities Co. v. State, Tex.Civ.App., 46 S.W.2d 1018, 1021. Any agency, instrumentality, business industry or service which is used or conducted in such manner as to affect the community at large, that is which is not limited or restricted to any particular class of the community. State Public Utilities Commission v. Monarch Refrigerating Co., 267 Ill. 528, 108 N.E. 716, Ann.Cas. 1916A, 528. The test for determining if a concern is a public utility is whether it has held itself out as ready, able and willing to serve the public. Humbird Lumber Co. v. Public Utilities Commission, 39 Idaho, 505, 228 P. 271. The term implies a public use of an article, product, or service, carrying with it the duty of the producer or manufacturer, or one attempting to furnish the service, to serve the public and treat all persons alike, without discrimination. Highland Dairy Farms Co. v. Helvetia Milk Condensing Co., 308 Ill. 294, 139 N.E. 418, 420. It is synonymous with "public use," and refers to persons or corporations charged with the duty to supply the public with the use of property or facilities owned or furnished by them. Buder v. First Nat. Bank in St. Louis, C.C.A.Mo., 16 F.2d 990, 992. To constitute a true "public utility," the devotion to public use must be of such character that the public generally, or that part of it which has been served and which has accepted the service, has the legal right to demand that that service shall be conducted, so long as it is continued, with reasonable efficiency under reasonable charges. Richardson v. Railroad Commission of California, 191 Cal. 716, 218 P. 418, 420. The devotion to public use must be of such character that the product and service is available to the public generally and indiscriminately, or there must be the acceptance by the utility of public franchises or calling to its aid the police power of the state. Southern Ohio Power Co. v. Public Utilities Commission of Ohio, 110 Ohio St. 246, 143 N.E. 700, 701, 34 A.L.R. 171.

Line

Chief or primary conductors to exclusion of subsidiary transmission facilities. Jersey Central Power & Light Co. v. State Board of Tax Appeals, 131 N.J.L. 565, 37 A.2d 111, 112, 113; "lines" as used in sense of "mains". Jersey Central Power & Light Co. v. State Board of Tax Appeals, 130 N.J.L. 364, 33 A.2d 355, 356; main or principal conduit. Jersey City v. Martin, 20 N.J.Misc. 270, 26 A.2d 574, 576.

Electric company's line as referring to poles. Central States Electric Co. v. Pocahontas County, Iowa, 223 N.W. 236, 240.

Railroad or Other Carriers

A line is a series of public conveyances, as coaches, steamers, packets and the like passing to and fro between places with regularity. The word is broad enough to include line of motor freight trucks operating between fixed termini on regular schedule and route. "Stage line," "railroad line" and "automobile line" are expressions which are ordinarily understood to mean a regular line of vehicles for public use operating between distant points or between different cities. Bruce Transfer Co. v. Johnston, 227 Iowa 50, 287 N.W. 278, 280. A "line" is an operating unit under one management over a designated way or right of way. Regenhardt Const. Co. v. Southern Ry. in Kentucky, 297 Ky. 840, 181 S.W.2d 441, 444. A number of public conveyances, as carriages or vessels plying regularly under one management over a certain route, is a "line." Tuggle v. Parker, 159 Kan. 572, 156 P.2d 533, 534. Everything essential to the operation and maintenance of a railroad transportation system is a constituent part of the "line." City of Pocatello v. Ross, 51 Idaho

395, 6 P.2d 481, 482. The words "lines" and "property" are convertible terms. In re Central States Freight Corporation, C.C.A.Mich., 45 F.2d 73, 74.

Telephone or telegraph company's "lines" include not only wires and poles, but also right to have them supported by land to which they are attached. City of Fort Worth v. Southwestern Bell Telephone Co., C.C.A.Tex., 80 F.2d 972, 976.

Public ways. Highways (*q. v.*).

Public weigher. This term in a statute refers to the official who has been elected, appointed, or qualified and holding office. Interstate Compress Co. v. Colley, 88 Okl. 42, 211 P. 413, 414.

Public welfare. The prosperity, well-being, or convenience of the public at large, or of a whole community, as distinguished from the advantage of an individual or limited class. Shaver v. Starrett, 4 Ohio St. 499. It embraces the primary social interests of safety, order, morals, economic interest, and non-material and political interests. State v. Hutchinson Ice Cream Co., 168 Iowa, 1, 147 N.W. 195, 199, L.R.A.1917B, 198. In the development of our civic life, the definition of "public welfare" has also developed until it has been held to bring within its purview regulations for the promotion of economic welfare and public convenience. Pettis v. Alpha Alpha Chapter of Phi Beta Pi, 115 Neb. 525, 213 N.W. 835, 838.

PUBLICAN. In the civil law. A farmer of the public revenue; one who held a lease of some property from the public treasury. Dig. 39, 4, 1, 1; Dig. 39, 4, 12, 3; Dig. 39, 4, 13.

In English law. A person authorized by license to keep a public house, and retail therein, for consumption on or off the premises where sold, all intoxicating liquors; also termed "licensed victualler." Wharton. A victualer; one who serves food or drink prepared for consumption on the premises. Friend v. Childs Dining Hall Co., 231 Mass. 65, 120 N.E. 407, 409, 5 A.L.R. 1100.

PUBLICANUS. Lat. In Roman law. A farmer of the customs; a publican. Calvin.

PUBLICATION. To make public; to make known to people in general; to bring before public; to exhibit, display, disclose or reveal. Tiffany Productions v. Dewing, D.C.Md., 50 F.2d 911, 914. The act of publishing anything; offering it to public notice, or rendering it accessible to public scrutiny. Linley v. Citizens' Nat. Bank of Anderson, 108 S.C. 372, 94 S.E. 874, 877, National Geographic Soc. v. Classified Geographic, D.C. Mass., 27 F.Supp. 655, 659. An advising of the public; a making known of something to them for a purpose. Associated Press v. International News Service, C.C.A.N.Y., 245 F. 244, 250. It implies the means of conveying knowledge or notice. Daly v. Beery, 45 N.D. 287, 178 N.W. 104, 106.

As descriptive of the publishing of laws and ordinances, it means printing or otherwise reproducing copies of them and distributing them in such a manner as to make their contents easily accessible to the public; it forms no part of the enactment of the law. "Promulgation," on the other hand, seems to denote the proclamation or announcement of the edict or statute as a preliminary to its acquiring the force and operation of law. But the two terms are often used interchangeably. Chicago v. McCoy, 136 Ill. 344, 26 N.E. 363, 11 L.R.A. 413; For the distinction between them, see Toullier, *Dr. Civ. Fr.* titre *Préliminaire*, n. 59.

In connection with the publication of rates, the term may include both the promulgation and the distribution of the rates in printed form. City of Pittsburg v. Pittsburg Rys. Co., 259 Pa. 558, 103 A. 372, 374.

Copyright Law

The act of making public a book, writing, chart, map, etc.; that is, offering or communicating it to the public by the sale or distribution of copies. Keene v. Wheatley, 14 Fed.Cas. 180; Jewelers' Mercantile Agency v. Jewelers' Weekly Pub. Co., 155 N.Y. 241, 49 N.E. 872, 41 L.R.A. 846, 63 Am.St.Rep. 666. As employed in the Copyright Law, means a general publication rather than a limited one. Copyright Act 1909, § 2, 17 U.S.C.A. § 2.

"Limited publication" is communication of a literary composition to a select number upon condition, express or implied, that it is not intended to be thereafter common property. To constitute "publication," within Copyright Law, there must be such a dissemination of the work of art itself among the public as to justify the belief that it took place with the intention of rendering such work common property. Copyright Law 1909, § 2, 17 U.S.C.A. § 2. Berry v. Hoffman, 125 Pa.Super. 261, 189 A. 516.

Law of Libel

The act of making the defamatory matter known publicly, of disseminating it, or communicating it to one or more persons. Wilcox v. Moon, 63 Vt. 481, 22 A. 80; Gambrill v. Schooley, 93 Md. 48, 48 A. 730, 52 L.R.A. 87, 86 Am.St.Rep. 414. The reduction of libelous matter to writing and its delivery to any one other than the person injuriously affected thereby.

The dictation to a stenographer of a libelous letter is ordinarily a publication of the libel. Nelson v. Whitten, D.C.N.Y., 272 F. 135, 139; But see Owen v. Pub. Co., 32 App.Div. 465, 53 N.Y.S. 1033. Every repetition of defamatory words is a new publication and constitutes a new cause of action.

Law of Wills

The formal declaration made by a testator at the time of signing his will that it is his last will and testament. 4 Kent, Comm. 515, and note. In re Simpson, 56 How.Prac. (N.Y.) 134; Compton v. Mitton, 12 N.J.Law, 70. The act or acts of the testator by which he manifests that it is his intention to give effect to the paper as his last will and testament; any communication indicating to the witness that the testator intends to give effect to the paper as his will, by words, sign, motion, or conduct. In re Spier's Estate, 99 Neb. 853, 157 N.W. 1014, 1016, L.R.A.1916E, 692.

Practice

In the practice of the states adopting the reformed procedure, and in some others, publication of a summons is the process of giving it currency as an advertisement in a newspaper, under the conditions prescribed by law, as a means of giving notice of the suit to a defendant upon whom personal service cannot be made.

In equity practice. The making public the depositions taken in a suit, which have previously been kept private in the office of the examiner. *Publication* is said to *pass* when the depositions are so made public, or openly shown, and copies of them given out, in order to the hearing of the cause. 3 Bl.Comm. 450.

PUBLICI JURIS. Lat. Of public right. The word "public" in this sense means pertaining to the people, or affecting the community at large; that which concerns a multitude of people; and the word "right," as so used, means a well-founded claim; an interest; concern; advantage; benefit. State v. Lyon, 63 Okl. 285, 165 P. 419, 420.

This term, as applied to a thing or right, means that it is open to or exercisable by all persons. It designates things which are owned by "the public;" that is, the entire state or community, and not by any private person. When a thing is common property, so that any one can make use of it who likes, it is said to be *publici juris;* as in the case of light, air, and public water. Sweet.

PUBLICIANA. In the civil law. The name of an action introduced by the prætor Publicius, the object of which was to recover a thing which had been lost. Its effects were similar to those of our action of trover. Mackeld. Rom. Law, § 298. See Inst. 4, 6, 4; Dig. 6, 2, 1, 16.

PUBLICIST. One versed in, or writing upon, public law, the science and principles of government, or international law.

PUBLICITY. The doing of a thing in the view of all persons who choose to be present.

PUBLICLY. Openly. Winters v. Duncan, Tex. Civ.App., 220 S.W. 219, 220. In public, well known, open, notorious, common, or general, as opposed to private, secluded, or secret. Fairchild v. U. S., C.C.A.S.D., 265 F. 584, 586.

PUBLICUM JUS. Lat. In the civil law. Public law; that law which regards the state of the commonwealth. Inst. 1, 1, 4.

PUBLISH. To make public; to circulate; to make known to people in general. U. S. v. Baltimore Post Co., D.C.Md., 2 F.2d 761, 764; In re Willow Creek, 74 Or. 592, 144 P. 505, 515. To issue; to put into circulation. In re Willow Creek, 74 Or. 592, 144 P. 505, 515. To utter; to present (a forged instrument) for payment. Smith v. State, 13 Ga.App. 663, 79 S.E. 764, 766; State v. Hobl, 108 Kan. 261, 194 P. 921, 924. To declare or assert, directly or indirectly, by words or actions, that a forged instrument is genuine. People v. Bradford, 84 Cal.App. 707, 258 P. 660, 662. An advising of the public or making known of something to the public for a purpose. Estill County v. Noland, 295 Ky. 753, 175 S.W.2d 341, 346.

To "publish" a libel is to make it known to any person other than the person libeled. Age-Herald Pub. Co. v. Huddleston, 207 Ala. 40, 92 So. 193, 197, 37 A.L.R. 898; to exhibit or expose the libelous matter. State v. Moore, 140 La. 281, 72 So. 965, 971.

To "publish" a newspaper ordinarily means to compose, print, issue, and distribute it to the public, and especially its subscribers, at and from a certain place. To "print" may therefore refer only to the mechanical work of production. In re Monrovia Evening Post, 199 Cal. 263, 248 P. 1017, 1019, and constitute a narrower term than "publish." In re Publishing Docket in Local Newspaper, 266 Mo. 48, 187 S.W. 1174, 1175.

PUBLISHER. One who by himself or his agent makes a thing publicly known. One whose business is the manufacture, promulgation, and sale of books, pamphlets, magazines, newspapers, or other literary productions. One who publishes, especially one who issues, or causes to be issued, from the press, and offers for sale or circulation matter printed, engraved, or the like. Brokaw v. Cottrell, 114 Neb. 858, 211 N.W. 184, 187.

PUDENDUM. The external female sexual organ. State v. Wisdom, 122 Or. 148, 257 P. 826, 830.

PUDICITY. Chastity; purity; continence; modesty; the abstaining from all unlawful carnal commerce or connection.

PUDZELD. In old English law. Supposed to be a corruption of the Saxon *"wudgeld,"* (woodgeld,) a freedom from payment of money for taking *wood* in any forest. Co. Litt. 233*a*.

PUEBLO. In Spanish law. People; all the inhabitants of any country or place, without distinction. A town, township, or municipality. White, New Recop. b. 2, tit. 1, c. 6, § 4. A small settlement or gathering of people, a steady community; the term applies equally whether the settlement be a small collection of Spaniards or Indians. Pueblo of Santa Rosa v. Fall, App.D.C., 12 F.2d 332, 335.

This term *"pueblo,"* in its original signification, means "people" or "population," but is used in the sense of the English word "town." It has the indefiniteness of that term, and, like it, is sometimes applied to a mere collection of individuals residing at a particular place, a settlement or village, as well as to a regularly organized municipality. Trenouth v. San Francisco, 100 U.S. 251, 25 L.Ed. 626.

PUER. Lat. In the civil law. A child; one of the age from seven to fourteen, including, in this sense, a girl. But it also meant a "boy," as distinguished from a "girl;" or a servant. Dy. 337*b*; Hob. 33.

PUERI SUNT DE SANGUINE PARENTUM, SED PATER ET MATER NON SUNT DE SANGUINE PUERORUM. 3 Coke, 40. Children are of the blood of their parents, but the father and mother are not of the blood of the children.

PUERILITY. In the civil law. A condition intermediate between infancy and puberty, continuing in boys from the seventh to the fourteenth year of their age, and in girls from seven to twelve.

The ancient Roman lawyers divided puerility into *proximus infantiæ,* as it approached infancy, and *proximus pubertati,* as it became nearer to puberty. 6 Toullier, n. 100.

PUERITIA. Lat. In the civil law. Childhood; the age from seven to fourteen. 4 Bl.Comm. 22. The age from birth to fourteen years in the male, or twelve in the female. Calvinus, Lex. The age from birth to seventeen. Vicat, Voc. Jur.

PUFFER. A person employed by the owner of property which is sold at auction to attend the sale and run up the price by making spurious bids. Peck v. List, 23 W.Va. 375, 48 Am.Rep. 398. Beasley v. Burton, 32 Ga.App. 727, 124 S.E. 368.

PUFFING. An expression of opinion by seller not made as a representation of fact. Gulf Oil Corp. v. Federal Trade Commission, C.C.A.5, 150 F.2d 106, 109.

PUGILIST. One who fights with his fists. Reisler v. Dempsey, 207 Mo.App. 182, 232 S.W. 229, 230.

PUIS. Fr. In law. Afterwards; since.

PUIS DARREIN CONTINUANCE. Since the last continuance. The name of a plea which a defendant is allowed to put in, after having already pleaded, where some *new* matter of defense arises after issue joined; such as payment, a release by the plaintiff, the discharge of the defendant under an insolvent or bankrupt law, and the like. 3 Bl.Comm. 316; Waterbury v. McMillan, 46 Miss. 640; Woods v. White, 97 Pa. 227.

PUISNE. L. Fr. Younger; junior; subordinate; associate. The title by which the justices and barons of the several common-law courts at Westminster are distinguished from the *chief* justice and *chief* baron.

PUISSANCE PATERNELLE. Fr. Paternal power. In the French law, the male parent has the following rights over the person of his child: (1) If child is under sixteen years of age, he may procure him to be imprisoned for one month or under. (2) If child is over sixteen and under twenty-one he may procure an imprisonment for six months or under with power in each case to procure a second period of imprisonment. The female parent, being a widow, may, with the approval of the two nearest relations on the father's side, do the like. The parent enjoys also the following rights over the property of his child, viz., a right to take the income until the child attains the age of eighteen years, subject to maintaining the child and educating him in a suitable manner. Brown.

PULLING. In terminology associated with oil wells, the withdrawing from the well of the casing placed therein, after it has been demonstrated that the well is a nonproducer. Texas Granite Oil Co. v. Williams, 199 Ky. 146, 250 S.W. 818, 820.

PULSARE. Lat. In the civil law. To beat; to accuse or charge; to proceed against at law. Calvin.

PULSATOR. The plaintiff, or actor.

PUMMY. Possibly a provincialism peculiar to Ochiltree county, Tex., presumably meaning a farm product or the residue of a farm product which has some value as a stock food. Cudd v. Whippo, Tex.Civ.App., 234 S.W. 706, 708.

An obsolete or dialectic variant of "pomace." Webster's New Int. Dict.

PUNCTUATION. The division of a written or printed document into sentences by means of periods; and of sentences into smaller divisions by means of commas, semicolons, colons, etc.

PUNCTUM TEMPORIS. Lat. A point of time; an indivisible period of time; the shortest space of time; an instant. Calvin.

PUNCTURED WOUND. In medical jurisprudence. A wound made by the insertion into the body of any instrument having a sharp point. The term is practically synonymous with "stab."

PUNDBRECH. In old English law. Pound-breach; the offense of breaking a pound. The illegal taking of cattle out of a pound by any means whatsoever. Cowell.

PUNDIT. An interpreter of the Hindu law; a learned Brahmin.

PUNISHABLE. Deserving of or capable or liable to punishment; capable of being punished by law or right. People v. Superior Court of City and County of San Francisco, 116 Cal.App. 412, 2 P.2d 843, 844.

PUNISHMENT. In criminal law. Any pain, penalty, suffering, or confinement inflicted upon a person by the authority of the law and the judgment and sentence of a court, for some crime or offense committed by him, or for his omission of a duty enjoined by law. Cummings v. Missouri, 4 Wall. 320, 18 L.Ed. 356. State v. Hondros, 100 S. C. 242, 84 S.E. 781, 783; Orme v. Rogers, 32 Ariz. 502, 260 P. 199; Cardigan v. White, C.C.A. 18 F. 2d 572, 573. A deprivation of property or some right. State v. Cowen, 231 Iowa 1117, 3 N.W.2d 176, 179. But does not include a civil penalty redounding to the benefit of an individual, such as a forfeiture of interest. People v. Vanderpool, 20 Cal.2d 746, 128 P.2d 513, 515.

Cruel and Unusual Punishment

Such punishment as would amount to torture or barbarity, and any cruel and degrading punishment not known to the common law, and also any punishment so disproportionate to the offense as to shock the moral sense of the community. State v. Driver, 78 N.C. 423; In re Kemmler, 136 U.S. 436, 10 S.Ct. 930, 34 L.Ed. 519; Sustar v. County Court of Marion County, 101 Or. 657, 201 P. 445, 448.

Cumulative Punishment

An increased punishment inflicted for a second or third conviction of the same offense, under the statutes relating to habitual criminals. State v. Hambly, 126 N.C. 1066, 35 S.E. 614. To be distinguished from a "cumulative sentence," as to which see Sentence.

Infamous Punishment

Punishment by imprisonment, Lee v. Stanfill, 171 Ky. 71, 186 S.W. 1196, 1198; in a penitentiary, Maxey v. United States, C.C.A.Ark., 207 F. 327, 331. Also, imprisonment at hard labor, Flannagan v. Jepson, 177 Iowa 393, 158 N.W. 641, 643, L.R.A.1918E, 548, particularly if in a penitentiary or state prison. Hull v. Donze, 164 La. 199, 113 So. 816. Sometimes, imprisonment at hard labor regardless of the place of imprisonment. U. S. v. Moreland, 42 S.Ct. 368, 258 U.S. 433, 66 L.Ed. 700, 24 A.L.R. 992.

PUNITIVE. Relating to punishment; having the character of punishment or penalty; inflicting punishment or a penalty.

PUNITIVE DAMAGES. See Damages.

PUNITIVE POWER. The power and authority of a state, or organized jural society, to inflict punishments upon those persons who have committed actions inherently evil and injurious to the public, or actions declared by the laws of that state to be sanctioned with punishments.

PUNITIVE STATUTE. One which creates forfeiture or imposes penalty. Peterson v. Ball, 211 Cal. 461, 296 P. 291, 300, 74 A.L.R. 187.

PUPIL. A youth or scholar of either sex under care of an instructor, tutor, or teacher. Kruse v. Independent School Dist. of Pleasant Hill, 209 Iowa 64, 227 N.W. 594, 595.

In the civil law. One who is in his or her minority. Particularly, one who is in ward or guardianship.

PUPILLARIS SUBSTITUTIO. Lat. In the civil law. Pupillar substitution; the substitution of an heir to a pupil or infant under puberty. The substitution by a father of an heir to his children under his power, disposing of his own estate and theirs, in case the child refused to accept the inheritance, or died before the age of puberty. Hallifax, Civil Law, b. 2, c. 6, no. 64.

PUPILLARITY. In Scotch law. That period of minority from the birth to the age of fourteen in males, and twelve in females. Bell.

PUPILLUS. Lat. In the civil law. A ward or infant under the age of puberty; a person under the authority of a *tutor*, (*q. v.*).

PUPILLUS PATI POSSE NON INTELLIGITUR. A pupil or infant is not supposed to be able to suffer, *i. e.*, to do an act to his own prejudice. Dig. 50, 17, 110, 2.

PUR. L. Fr. By or for. Used both as a separable particle, and in the composition of such words as "purparty," "purlieu."

PUR AUTRE VIE. For (or during) the life of another. An estate *pur autre vie* is an estate in lands which a man holds for the life of another person. 2 Bl.Comm. 120; Litt. § 56.

PUR CAUSE DE VICINAGE. By reason of neighborhood. See Common.

PUR FAIRE PROCLAMER. An ancient writ addressed to the mayor or bailiff of a city or town, requiring him to make proclamation concerning nuisances, etc. Fitz. Nat. B. 392.

PUR TANT QUE. Forasmuch as; because; to the intent that. Kelham.

PURCHASE. Transmission of property from one person to another by voluntary act and agreement, founded on a valuable consideration. Spur Independent School Dist. v. W. A. Holt Co., Tex. Civ.App., 88 S.W.2d 1071, 1073. In a technical and broader meaning relative to land generally means the acquisition of real estate by any means whatever except by descent. Kelly v. Southworth, 38 Wyo. 414, 267 P. 691, 692. Lindburg v. Bennett, 117 Neb. 66, 219 N.W. 851, 855. Oklahoma City v. Board of Education of Oklahoma City, 181 Okl. 539, 75 P.2d 201.

Quasi purchase. In the civil law. A purchase of property not founded on the actual agreement of the parties, but on conduct of the owner which is inconsistent with any other hypothesis than that he intended a sale.

Words of purchase. Words which denote the person who is to take the estate. Thus, if I grant land to A. for twenty-one years, and after the determination of that term to A.'s heirs, the word "heirs" does not denote the duration of A.'s estate, but the person who is to take the remainder on the expiration of the term, and is therefore called a "word of purchase." Williams, Real Prop.; Fearne, Rem. 76, *et seq.*

PURCHASE AND LIQUIDATION. Of savings bank means undertaking to wind up affairs and pay off obligations of savings bank. Wasmann v. City Nat. Bank of Knoxville, Tenn., C.C.A. Tenn., 52 F.2d 705, 707.

PURCHASE MONEY. The consideration in money paid or agreed to be paid by the buyer to the seller of property, particularly of land. It means money stipulated to be paid by a purchaser to his vendor, and does not include money the purchaser may have borrowed to complete his purchase. Purchase money, as between vendor and vendee only, is contemplated; as between purchaser and lender, the money is "borrowed money." Williams v. American Slicing Mach. Co., 148 Ga. 770, 98 S. E. 270, 271. As used with reference to part performance under statute of frauds comprehends consideration, whether it be money or property or services, for which lands are to be conveyed. Hall v. Haer, 160 Okl. 118, 16 P.2d 83, 84.

PURCHASE-MONEY MORTGAGE. See Mortgage.

PURCHASE PRICE. Price agreed upon as a consideration for which property is sold and purchased. Byrd v. Babin, 196 La. 902, 200 So. 294, 300.

PURCHASER. One who acquires real property in any other mode than by descent. One who acquires either real or personal property by buying it for a price in money; a buyer; vendee. Hodge Ship Bldg. Co. v. City of Moss Point, 144 Miss. 657, 110 So. 227, 229. Also, a successful bidder at judicial sale. In re Spokane Sav. Bank, 198 Wash. 665, 89 P.2d 802, 806.

In the construction of registry acts, the term "purchaser" is usually taken in its technical legal sense. It means a complete purchaser, or, in other words, one clothed with the legal title. Steele v. Spencer, 1 Pet. 552, 559, 7 L.Ed. 259.

Bona fide purchaser. See Bona Fide.

First purchaser. In the law of descent, this term signifies the ancestor who first acquired (in any other manner than by inheritance) the estate which still remains in his family or descendants.

Innocent purchaser. See Innocent.

Purchaser of a note or bill. The person who buys a promissory note or bill of exchange from the holder without his indorsement.

PURCHASER WITHOUT NOTICE IS NOT OBLIGED TO DISCOVER TO HIS OWN HURT. See 4 Bouv. Inst. note 4336.

PURE. Absolute; complete; simple; unmixed; unqualified; free from conditions or restrictions; as in the phrases pure charity, pure debt, pure obligation, pure plea, pure villenage, as to which see the nouns.

PURE ACCIDENT. Implies that accident was caused by some unforeseen and unavoidable event over which neither party to the action had control, and excludes the idea that it was caused by carelessness or negligence of defendant. Maletis v. Portland Traction Co., 160 Or. 30, 83 P.2d 141, 142. Unavoidable accident synonymous. Brewer v. Berner, 15 Wash.2d 644, 131 P.2d 940, 942.

PURGATION. The act of cleansing or exonerating one's self of a crime, accusation, or suspicion of guilt, by denying the charge on oath or by ordeal.

Canonical purgation was made by the party's taking his own oath that he was innocent of the charge, which was supported by the oath of twelve compurgators, who swore they believed he spoke the truth. To this succeeded the mode of purgation by the single oath of the party himself, called the "oath *ex officio*," of which the modern defendant's oath in chancery is a modification. 3 Bl. Comm. 447; 4 Bl.Comm. 368.

Vulgar purgation consisted in ordeals or trials by hot and cold water, by fire, by hot irons, by battel, by corsned, etc.

PURGE. To cleanse; to clear; to clear or exonerate from some charge or imputation of guilt, or from a contempt.

PURGE DES HYPOTHÈQUES. Fr. In French law. An expression used to describe the act of freeing an estate from the mortgages and privileges with which it is charged, observing the formalities prescribed by law. Duverger.

PURGED OF PARTIAL COUNSEL. In Scotch practice. Cleared of having been partially advised. A term applied to the preliminary examination of a witness, in which he is sworn and examined whether he has received any bribe or promise of reward, or has been told what to say, or whether he bears malice or ill will to any of the parties. Bell.

PURGING A TORT. Is like the ratification of a wrongful act by a person who has power of himself to lawfully do the act. But, unlike ratification, the purging of the tort may take place even after commencement of the action. 1 Brod. & B. 282.

PURGING CONTEMPT. Atoning for, or clearing one's self from, contempt of court, (*q. v.*). It is generally done by apologizing and paying fees, and is generally admitted after a moderate time in proportion to the magnitude of the offense.

PURLIEU. In English law. A space of land near a royal forest, which, being severed from it, was made *purlieu;* that is pure or free from the forest laws.

PURLIEU-MEN. Those who have ground within the purlieu to the yearly value of 40s. a year freehold are licensed to hunt in their own purlieus. Manw. c. 20, § 8.

PURLOIN. To steal; to commit larceny or theft. McCann v. U. S., 2 Wyo. 298.

PURPART. A share; a part in a division; that part of an estate, formerly held in common, which is by partition allotted to any one of the parties. The ward was anciently applied to the shares falling separately to co-parceners upon a division or partition of the estate, and was generally spelled "purparty;" but it is now used in relation to any kind of partition proceedings. Seiders v. Giles, 141 Pa. 93, 21 A. 514.

PURPARTY. That part of an estate which, having been held in common by parceners, is by partition allotted to any of them. To make purparty is to divide and sever the lands which fall to parceners. Old, N. B. 11. Formerly *pourparty*. See Jacob. The word *purpart* is commonly used to indicate a part of an estate in any connection.

PURPORT, *n.* Meaning; import; substantial meaning; substance; legal effect. The "purport" of an instrument means the substance of it as it appears on the face of the instrument, and is distinguished from "tenor," which means an exact copy. Dana v. State, 2 Ohio St. 93. Deskin v. U. S. Reserve Ins. Corporation, 221 Mo.App. 1151, 298 S.W. 103, 106.

PURPORT, *v.* To convey, imply, or profess outwardly; to have the appearance of being, intending, claiming, etc. United States v. 306 Cases Containing Sandford Tomato Catsup with Preservative, D.C.N.Y., 55 F.Supp. 725, 727.

PURPOSE. That which one sets before him to accomplish; an end, intention, or aim, object, plan, project. State v. Patch, 64 Mont. 565, 210 P. 748, 750; Macomber v. State, 137 Neb. 882, 291 N.W. 674, 680.

PURPOSELY. Intentionally; designedly; consciously; knowingly. Holt v. State, 107 Ohio St. 307, 140 N.E. 349, 350.

PURPRESTURE. An inclosure by a private party of a part of that which belongs to and ought to be open and free to the enjoyment of the public at large. It is not necessarily a public nuisance. A public nuisance must be something which subjects the public to some degree of inconvenience or annoyance; but a purpresture may exist without putting the public to any inconvenience whatever. Attorney General v. Evart Booming Co., 34 Mich. 462. And see Cobb v. Lincoln Park Com'rs, 202 Ill. 427, 67 N.E. 5, 63 L.R.A. 264, 95 Am.St.Rep. 258.

PURPRISE. L. Fr. A close or inclosure; as also the whole compass of a manor.

PURPURE, or PORPRIN. A term used in heraldry; the color commonly called "purple," expressed in engravings by lines in bend sinister. In the arms of princes it was formerly called "mercury," and in those of peers "amethyst."

PURSE. Some valuable thing, offered by a person for the doing of something by others, into strife for which he does not enter; prize; premium. He has not a chance of gaining the thing offered; and, if he abide by his offer, that he must lose it and give it over to some of those contending for it is reasonably certain. Harris v. White, 81 N.Y. 539.

PURSER. The person appointed by the master of a ship or vessel, whose duty it is to take care of the ship's books, in which everything on board is inserted, as well the names of mariners as the articles of merchandise shipped. Roccus, Ins. note.

PURSUANT. A following after or following out; line in accordance with or by reason of something; conformable; in accordance; agreeably, conformably; a carrying out or with effect, the act of executing; that which is pursuant; consequence; acting or done in consequence or in prosecution of anything; hence, agreeable. Suppiger v. Enking, 60 Idaho 292, 91 P.2d 362, 366.

PURSUE. To follow a matter judicially, as a complaining party.

To pursue a warrant or authority, in the old books, is to execute it or carry it out. Co. Litt. 52*a*.

To pursue the practice of any profession or business, contemplates a course of business or professional practice, and not single isolated acts arising from unusual circumstances. Dane v. Brown, C.C.A.Mass., 70 F.2d 164, 165.

PURSUER. One who pursues; one who follows in order to overtake. Tatum v. State, 57 Ga.App. 849, 197 S.E. 51, 53.

The name by which the complainant or plaintiff is known in the ecclesiastical courts, and in the Scotch law.

PURSUIT. That which one engages in as an occupation, trade, or profession; that which is followed as a continued or at least extended and prolonged employment. Dorrell v. Norida Land & Timber Co., 53 Idaho 793, 27 P.2d 960.

PURSUIT OF HAPPINESS. As used in constitutional law, this right includes personal freedom, freedom of contract, exemption from oppression or invidious discrimination, the right to follow one's individual preference in the choice of an occupation and the application of his energies, liberty of conscience, and the right to enjoy the domestic relations and the privileges of the family and the home. Black, Const. Law (3d Ed.) p. 544. Butchers' Union, etc., Co. v. Crescent City Live Stock, etc., Co., 111 U.S. 746, 4 S.Ct. 652, 28 L.Ed. 585. The right to follow or pursue any occupation or profession without restriction and without having any burden imposed upon one that is not imposed upon others in a similar situation. Myers v. City of Defiance, 67 Ohio App. 159, 36 N.E.2d 162.

PURUS IDIOTA. Lat. A congenital idiot.

PURVEYANCE. In old English law. A providing of necessaries for the king's house. Cowell.

PURVEYOR. In old English law. An officer who procured or purchased articles needed for the king's use at an arbitrary price. In the statute 36 Edw. III. c. 2, this is called a "*heignous nome*," (heinous or hateful name,) and changed to that of "*achator*." Barring. Ob. St. 289.

PURVIEW. Enacting part of a statute, in contradistinction to the preamble. Schaffer v. State, 202 Ind. 318, 173 N.E. 229, 231. That part of a statute commencing with the words "Be it enacted," and continuing as far as the repealing clause; and hence, the design, contemplation, purpose, or scope of the act. Smith v. Hickman, Cooke (Tenn.) 337; Olson v. Heisen, 90 Or. 176, 175 P. 859.

PUT. In pleading. To confide to; to rely upon; to submit to. As in the phrase, "the said defendant puts himself upon the country;" that is, he trusts his case to the arbitrament of a jury.

As used by speculators in the stock market, a contract by which one of the parties thereto purchases at a fixed sum the privilege to deliver certain stock or grain within a definite period of time. Colston v. Burnet, 59 F.2d 867, 61 App.D.C. 192. See, also, Puts and Calls.

PUT IN. In practice. To place in due form before a court; to place among the records of a court.

PUT OFF. To postpone. In a bargain for the sale of goods, it may mean to postpone its completion or to procure a resale of the goods to a third person. 11 Ex. 302.

PUT OUT. To open. To put out lights; to open or cut windows. 11 East, 372.

PUTAGIUM HÆREDITATEM NON ADIMIT. 1 Reeve, Eng. Law, c. 3, p. 117. Incontinence does not take away an inheritance.

PUTATIVE. Reputed; supposed; commonly esteemed. Applied in Scotch law to creditors and proprietors. 2 Kames, Eq. 105, 107, 109.

PUTATIVE FATHER. The alleged or reputed father of an illegitimate child. State v. Nestaval, 72 Minn. 415, 75 N.W. 725.

PUTATIVE MARRIAGE. A marriage contracted in good faith and in ignorance (on one or both sides) that impediments exist which render it unlawful. Mackeld. Rom. Law, § 556; In re Hall, 61 App.Div. 266, 70 N.Y.S. 410; Smith v. Smith, 1 Tex. 628, 46 Am.Dec. 121; United States Fidelity and Guaranty Co. v. Henderson, Tex.Civ.App., 53 S.W.2d 811, 816.

PUTS AND CALLS. A "put" in the language of the grain or stock market is a privilege of delivering or not delivering the subject-matter of the sale; and a "call" is a privilege of calling or not calling for it. Pixley v. Boynton, 79 Ill. 351.

PUTS AND REFUSALS. In English law. Time-bargains, or contracts for the sale of supposed stock on a future day.

PUTTING IN FEAR. These words are used in the definition of a robbery from the person: The offense must have been committed by *putting in fear* the person robbed. 3 Inst. 68; 4 Bl. Comm. 243.

No matter how slight the cause creating the fear may be, if transaction is attended with such circumstances of terror, such threatening by word or gesture, as in common experience is likely to create an apprehension of danger and induce a man to part with his property for sake of his person, victim is put in fear. State v. Sawyer, 224 N.C. 61, 29 S.E.2d 34, 37.

PUTTING IN SUIT. As applied to a bond, or any other legal instrument, signifies bringing an action upon it, or making it the subject of an action.

PUTURE. In old English law. A custom claimed by keepers in forests, and sometimes by bailiffs of hundreds, to take man's meat, horse's meat, and dog's meat of the tenants and inhabitants within the perambulation of the forest, hundred, etc. The land subject to this custom was called *"terra putura."* Others, who call it *"pulture,"* explain it as a demand in general; and derive it from the monks, who, before they were admitted, *pulsabant,* knocked at the gates for several days together. 4 Inst. 307; Cowell.

PYKE, PAIK. In Hindu law. A foot-passenger; a person employed as a night-watch in a village, and as a runner or messenger on the business of the revenue. Wharton.

PYKERIE. In old Scotch law. Petty theft. 2 Pitc. Crim. Tr. 43.

PYROMANIA. See Insanity.

PYX, TRIAL OF THE. Under the British Coinage Acts this occurs annually at Goldsmiths' Hall. The coins of the realm are assayed and weighed by a jury of goldsmiths over which the King's Remembrancer is usually appointed by the treasury to preside. Formerly the specimen coins put into the Pyx or box were produced at Westminster, from the treasure-house of the Abbey, where the Pyx was kept; the duty of presiding at the trial belonged to the office of the Remembrancer.

See Remembrances of Sir F. Pollock.

Also spelled "pix" (*q. v.*).

Q

Q. B. An abbreviation of "Queen's Bench."

Q. B. D. An abbreviation of "Queen's Bench Division."

Q. C. An abbreviation of "Queen's Counsel."

Q. C. F. An abbreviation of *"quare clausum fregit," (q. v.)*.

Q. D. An abbreviation of *"quasi dicat,"* as if he should say. Webster, New Int. Dict.

Q. E. N. An abbreviation of *"quare executionem non,"* wherefore execution [should] not [be issued.]

Q. S. An abbreviation for "Quarter Sessions."

Q. T. An abbreviation of *"qui tam," (q. v.)*.

Q. V. An abbreviation of *"quod vide,"* used to refer a reader to the word, chapter, etc., the name of which it immediately follows.

QUA. Lat. Considered as; in the character or capacity of. For example, "the trustee *qua* trustee [that is, in his character as trustee] is not liable," etc.

QUACK. A pretender to medical skill which he does not possess; one who practices as a physician or surgeon without adequate preparation or due qualification. Elmergreen v. Horn, 115 Wis. 385, 91 N.W. 973.

QUACUNQUE VIA DATA. Lat. Whichever way you take it.

QUADRAGESIMA. Lat. The fortieth. The first Sunday in Lent is so called because it is about the fortieth day before Easter. Cowell.

QUADRAGESIMALS. Offerings formerly made, on Mid-Lent Sunday, to the mother church.

QUADRAGESMS. The third volume of the year books of the reign of Edward III. So called because beginning with the *fortieth* year of that sovereign's reign. Crabb, Eng. Law, 327.

QUADRANS. Lat.

In Roman law. The fourth part; the quarter of any number, measure, or quantity. Hence an heir to the fourth part of the inheritance was called *"hœres ex quadrante."* Also a Roman coin, being the fourth part of an *as*, equal in value to an English half-penny.

In old English law. A farthing; a fourth part or quarter of a penny.

QUADRANT. An angular measure of ninety degrees.

QUADRANTATA TERRÆ. In old English law. A measure of land, variously described as a quarter of an acre or the fourth part of a yard-land.

QUADRARIUM. In old records. A stone-pit or quarry. Cowell.

QUADRIENNIUM. Lat. In the civil law. The four-year course of study required to be pursued by law-students before they were qualified to study the Code or collection of imperial constitutions. See Inst. Proem.

QUADRIENNIUM UTILE. In Scotch law. The term of four years allowed to a minor, after his majority, in which he may by suit or action endeavor to annul any deed to his prejudice, granted during his minority. Bell.

QUADRIPARTITE. Divided into four parts. A term applied in conveyancing to an indenture executed in four parts.

QUADRIPARTITUS. The name of an Anglo-Latin legal treatise. The two extant books were completed in 1114. The compiler was a secular clerk who entered into relations with the archbishop of York; his name is unknown. Brunner, Sources of English Law in 2 Sel. Essays in Anglo-Amer. L. H. 8.

QUADROON. A person who is descended from a white person and another person who has an equal mixture of the European and African blood. State v. Davis, 2 Bailey (S. C.) 558.

QUADRUPLATORES. Lat. In Roman law. Informers who, if their information were followed by conviction, had the fourth part of the confiscated goods for their trouble.

QUADRUPLICATIO. Lat. In the civil law. A pleading on the part of a defendant, corresponding to the *rebutter* at common law. The third pleading on the part of the defendant. Inst. 4, 14, 3; 3 Bl. Comm. 310.

QUADRUPLICATION. In pleading. A pleading in admiralty, third in order after a replication; now obsolete. Formerly this word was used instead of surrebutter. 1 Brown, Civ.Law, 469, n.

QUÆ AB HOSTIBUS CAPIUNTUR, STATIM CAPIENTIUM FIUNT. 2 Burrows, 693. Things which are taken from enemies immediately become the property of the captors.

QUÆ AB INITIO INUTILIS FUIT INSTITUTIO, EX POST FACTO CONVALESCERE NON POTEST. An institution which was at the beginning of no use or force cannot acquire force from after matter. Dig. 50, 17, 210.

QUÆ AB INITIO NON VALENT, EX POST FACTO CONVALESCERE NON POSSUNT. Things invalid from the beginning cannot be made valid by subsequent act. Tray. Lat. Max. 482.

QUÆ ACCESSIONUM LOCUM OBTINENT, EXTINGUUNTUR CUM PRINCIPALES RES PEREMPTÆ FUERINT. Things which hold the place of accessories are extinguished when the principal things are destroyed. 2 Poth. Obl. 202; Broom, Max. 496.

QUÆ AD UNUM FINEM LOQUUTA SUNT, NON DEBENT AD ALIUM DETORQUERI. 4 Coke, 14. Those words which are spoken to one end ought not to be perverted to another.

QUÆ COHÆRENT PERSONÆ A PERSONA SEPARARI NEQUEUNT. Things which cohere to, or are closely connected with, the person, cannot be separated from the person. Jenk. Cent. p. 28, case 53.

QUÆ COMMUNI LEGE DEROGANT STRICTE INTERPRETANTUR. [Statutes] which derogate from the common law are strictly interpreted. Jenk. Cent. p. 221, case 72.

QUÆ CONTRA RATIONEM JURIS INTRODUCTA SUNT, NON DEBENT TRAHI IN CONSEQUENTIAM. 12 Coke, 75. Things introduced contrary to the reason of law ought not to be drawn into a precedent.

QUÆ DUBITATIONIS CAUSA TOLLENDÆ INSERUNTUR COMMUNEM LEGEM NON LÆDUNT. Co. Litt. 205. Things which are inserted for the purpose of removing doubt hurt not the common law.

QUÆ DUBITATIONIS TOLLENDÆ CAUSA CONTRACTIBUS INSERUNTUR, JUS COMMUNE NON LÆDUNT. Particular clauses inserted in agreements to avoid doubts and ambiguity do not prejudice the general law. Dig. 50, 17, 81.

QUÆ EST EADEM. Lat. Which is the same. Words used for alleging that the trespass or other fact mentioned in the plea is the same as that laid in the declaration, where, from the circumstances, there is an apparent difference between the two. 1 Chit. Pl. *582.

QUÆ IN CURIA REGIS ACTA SUNT RITE AGI PRÆSUMUNTUR. 3 Bulst. 43. Things done in the king's court are presumed to be rightly done.

QUÆ IN PARTES DIVIDI NEQUEUNT SOLIDA A SINGULIS PRÆSTANTUR. 6 Coke, 1. Services which are incapable of division are to be performed in whole by each individual.

QUÆ IN TESTAMENTO ITA SUNT SCRIPTA UT INTELLIGI NON POSSINT, PERINDE SUNT AC SI SCRIPTA NON ESSENT. Things which are so written in a will that they cannot be understood, are the same as if they had not been written at all. Dig. 50, 17, 73, 3.

QUÆ INCONTINENTI FIUNT INESSE VIDENTUR. Things which are done incontinently [or simultaneously with an act] are supposed to be inherent [in it; to be a constituent part of it.] Co. Litt. 236*b*.

QUÆ INTER ALIOS ACTA SUNT NEMINI NOCERE DEBENT, SED PRODESSE POSSUNT. 6 Coke, 1. Transactions between strangers ought to hurt no man, but may benefit.

QUÆ LEGI COMMUNI DEROGANT NON SUNT TRAHENDA IN EXEMPLUM. Things derogatory to the common law are not to be drawn into precedent. Branch, Princ.

QUÆ LEGI COMMUNI DEROGANT STRICTE INTERPRETANTUR. Jenk. Cent. 29. Those things which are derogatory to the common law are to be strictly interpreted.

QUÆ MALA SUNT INCHOATA IN PRINCIPIO VIX BONO PERAGUNTUR EXITU. 4 Coke, 2. Things bad in principle at the commencement seldom achieve a good end.

QUÆ NIHIL FRUSTRA. Lat. Which [does or requires] nothing in vain. Which requires nothing to be done, that is, to no purpose. 2 Kent, Comm. 53.

QUÆ NON FIERI DEBENT, FACTA, VALENT. Things which ought not to be done are held valid when they have been done. Tray. Lat. Max. 484.

QUÆ NON VALEANT SINGULA, JUNCTA JUVANT. Things which do not avail when separate, when joined avail. 3 Bulst. 132; Broom, Max. 588.

QUÆ PLURA. Lat. In old English practice. A writ which lay where an inquisition had been made by an escheator in any county of such lands or tenements as any man died seised of, and all that was in his possession was imagined not to be found by the office; the writ commanding the escheator to inquire *what more (quæ plura)* lands and tenements the party held on the day when he died, etc. Fitzh. Nat. Brev. 255*a;* Cowell.

QUÆ PRÆTER CONSUETUDINEM ET MOREM MAJORUM FIUNT NEQUE PLACENT NEQUE RECTA VIDENTUR. Things which are done contrary to the custom of our ancestors neither please nor appear right. 4 Coke, 78.

QUÆ PROPTER NECESSITATEM RECEPTA SUNT, NON DEBENT IN ARGUMENTUM TRAHI. Things which are admitted on the ground of necessity ought not to be drawn into question. Dig. 50, 17, 162.

QUÆ RERUM NATURA PROHIBENTUR NULLA LEGE CONFIRMATA SUNT. Things which are forbidden by the nature of things are [can be] confirmed by no law. Branch, Princ. Positive laws are framed after the laws of nature and reason. Finch, Law, 74.

QUÆ SINGULA NON PROSUNT, JUNCTA JUVANT. Things which taken singly are of no avail afford help when taken together. Tray. Lat. Max. 486.

QUÆ SUNT MINORIS CULPÆ SUNT MAJORIS INFAMIÆ. [Offenses] which are of a lower grade of guilt are of a higher degree of infamy. Co. Litt. 6*b*.

QUÆCUNQUE INTRA RATIONEM LEGIS INVENIUNTUR INTRA LEGEM IPSAM ESSE JUDICANTUR. Things which are found within the reason of a law are supposed to be within the law itself. 2 Inst. 689.

QUÆLIBET CONCESSIO DOMINI REGIS CAPI DEBET STRICTE CONTRA DOMINUM REGEM, QUANDO POTEST INTELLIGI DUABUS VIIS. 3 Leon. 243. Every grant of our lord the king ought to be taken strictly against our lord the king, when it can be understood in two ways.

QUÆLIBET CONCESSIO FORTISSIME CONTRA DONATOREM INTERPRETANDA EST. Every grant is to be interpreted most strongly against the grantor. Co. Litt. 183*a*.

QUÆLIBET JURISDICTIO CANCELLOS SUOS HABET. Jenk. Cent. 137. Every jurisdiction has its own bounds.

QUÆLIBET PARDONATIO DEBET CAPI SECUNDUM INTENTIONEM REGIS, ET NON AD DECEPTIONEM REGIS. 3 Bulst. 14. Every pardon ought to be taken according to the intention of the king, and not to the deception of the king.

QUÆLIBET PŒNA CORPORALIS, QUAMVIS MINIMA, MAJOR EST QUALIBET PŒNA PECUNIARIA. 3 Inst. 220. Every corporal punishment, although the very least, is greater than any pecuniary punishment.

QUÆRAS DE DUBIIS LEGEM BENE DISCERE SI VIS. Inquire into doubtful points if you wish to understand the law well. Litt. § 443.

QUÆRE. A query; question; doubt. This word, occurring in the syllabus of a reported case or elsewhere, shows that a question is propounded as to what follows, or that the particular rule, decision, or statement is considered as open to question.

QUÆRE DE DUBIIS, QUIA PER RATIONES PERVENITUR AD LEGITIMAM RATIONEM. Inquire into doubtful points, because by reasoning we arrive at legal reason. Litt. § 377.

QUÆRENS. Lat. A plaintiff; the plaintiff.

QUÆRENS NIHIL CAPIAT PER BILLAM. The plaintiff shall take nothing by his bill. A form of judgment for the defendant. Latch, 133.

QUÆRENS NON INVENIT PLEGIUM. L. Lat. The plaintiff did not find a pledge. A return formerly made by a sheriff to a writ requiring him to take security of the plaintiff to prosecute his claim. Cowell.

QUÆRERE DAT SAPERE QUÆ SUNT LEGITIMA VERE. Litt. § 443. To inquire into them, is the way to know what things are truly lawful.

QUÆSTA. An indulgence or remission of penance, sold by the pope.

QUÆSTIO.

Medieval Law

The question; the torture; inquiry or inquisition by inflicting the torture.

Roman Law

Anciently a species of commission granted by the *comitia* to one or more persons for the purpose of inquiring into some crime or public offense and reporting thereon. In later times, the *quæstio* came to exercise plenary criminal jurisdiction, even to pronouncing sentence, and then was appointed periodically, and eventually became a *permanent* commission or regular criminal tribunal, and was then called *"quæstio perpetua."* Maine, Anc. Law, 369–372.

General

Cadit quæstio. The question falls; the discussion ends; there is no room for further argument.

Quæstio vexata. A vexed question or mooted point; a question often agitated or discussed but not determined; a question or point which has been differently decided, and so left doubtful.

QUÆSTIONARII. Those who carried *quæsta* about from door to door.

QUÆSTIONES PERPETUÆ, in Roman law, were commissions (or courts) of inquisition into crimes alleged to have been committed. They were called *"perpetuæ,"* to distinguish them from *occasional* inquisitions, and because they were permanent courts for the trial of offenders. Brown.

QUÆSTOR. Lat. A Roman magistrate, whose office it was to collect the public revenue. Varro de L. L. iv. 14.

QUÆSTOR SACRI PALATII. Quæstor of the sacred palace. An officer of the imperial court at Constantinople, with powers and duties resembling those of a chancellor. Calvin.

QUÆSTORES CLASSICI. Lat. In Roman law. officers entrusted with the care of the public money.

Their duties consisted in making the necessary payments from the *ærarium,* and receiving the public revenues. Of both they had to keep correct accounts in their *tabulæ publicæ.* Demands which any one might have on the *ærarium,* and outstanding debts were likewise registered by them. Fines to be paid to the public treasury were registered and exacted by them. They were likewise to provide proper accommodations for foreign ambassadors and such persons as were connected with the republic by ties of public hospitality. Lastly, they were charged with the care of the burials and monuments of distinguished men, the expenses for which had been decreed by the senate to be paid by the treasury. Their number at first was confined to two; but this was afterwards increased as the empire became extended. There were quæstors of cities and of provinces, and quæstors of the army; the latter were in fact paymasters.

QUÆSTORES PARRICIDII. See Questores Parricidii.

QUÆSTUS. L. Lat. That estate which a man has by acquisition or purchase, in contradistinction to "*hœreditas,*" which is what he has by descent. Glan. 1, 7, c. 1.

QUAKER. In England, the statutory, as well as the popular, name of a member of a religious society, by themselves denominated "Friends."

QUALE JUS. Lat. In old English law. A judicial writ, which lay where a man of religion had judgment to recover land before execution was made of the judgment. It went forth to the escheator between judgment and execution, to inquire what *right* the religious person had to recover, or whether the judgment were obtained by the collusion of the parties, to the intent that the lord might not be defrauded. Reg. Jud. 8.

QUALIFICATION. The possession by an individual of the qualities, properties, or circumstances, natural or adventitious, which are inherently or legally necessary to render him eligible to fill an office or to perform a public duty or function. Thus, the ownership of a freehold estate may be made the qualification of a voter; so the possession of a certain amount of stock in a corporation may be the qualification necessary to enable one to serve on its board of directors. Cummings v. Missouri, 4 Wall. 319, 18 L.Ed. 356; Hyde v. State, 52 Miss. 665.

Qualification for office is "endowment, or accomplishment that fits for an office; having the legal requisites, endowed with qualities suitable for the purpose." State v. Seay, 64 Mo. 89, 27 Am.Rep. 206.

Also a modification or limitation of terms or language; usually intended by way of restriction of expressions which, by reason of their generality, would carry a larger meaning than was designed.

QUALIFIED. Adapted; fitted; entitled; susceptible; capable; competent; fitting; possessing legal power or capacity; eligible; as an elector to vote. Applied to one who has taken the steps to prepare himself for an appointment or office, as by taking oath, giving bond, etc. Gibbany v. Ford, 29 N.M. 621, 225 P. 577, 578; Board of Com'rs of Guadalupe County v. District Court of Fourth Judicial Dist., 29 N.M. 244, 223 P. 516, 522. Also limited; restricted; confined; modified; imperfect, or temporary.

The term is also applied in England to a person who is enabled to hold two benefices at once.

QUALIFIED ACCEPTANCE. See Acceptance.

QUALIFIED ELECTOR. A person who is legally qualified to vote. Minges v. Board of Trustees of City of Merced, 27 Cal.App. 15, 148 P. 816, 817.

See Qualified Voter.

QUALIFIED ESTATE. See Estate.

QUALIFIED FEE. See Fee.

QUALIFIED INDORSEMENT. See Indorsement.

QUALIFIED OATH. See Oath.

QUALIFIED PRIVILEGE. In the law of libel and slander, the same as conditional privilege. See Privilege.

QUALIFIED PROPERTY. See Property.

QUALIFIED VOTER. A person qualified to vote generally. In re House Bill No. 166, 9 Colo. 629, 21 P. 473. A person qualified and actually voting. Carroll County v. Smith, 4 S.Ct. 539, 111 U.S. 565, 28 L.Ed. 517. A legal voter. Branstetter v. Heater, 269 Ky. 844, 108 S.W.2d 1040. See Qualified Elector.

QUALIFY. To make one's self fit or prepared to exercise a right, office, or franchise. To take the steps necessary to prepare one's self for an office or appointment, as by taking oath, giving bond, etc. Archer v. State, 74 Md. 443, 22 A. 8, 28 Am.St.Rep. 261. State v. Albert, 55 Kan. 154, 40 P. 286.

Also to limit; to modify; to restrict. Thus, it is said that one section of a statute qualifies another.

QUALITAS QUÆ INESSE DEBET, FACILE PRÆSUMITUR. A quality which ought to form a part is easily presumed.

QUALITY. In respect to persons, this term denotes comparative rank; state or condition in relation to others; social or civil position or class. In pleading, it means an attribute or characteristic by which one thing is distinguished from another.

Adoptiveness, suitableness, fitness; grade; condition. Macy v. Browne, D.C.N.Y., 215 F. 456, 458.

Under Uniform Sales Act, "quality of goods" includes their state or condition. Ford v. Waldorf System, 57 R.I. 131, 188 A. 633, 636.

QUALITY OF ESTATE. The period when, and the manner in which, the right of enjoying an estate is exercised. It is of two kinds: (1) The period when the right of enjoying an estate is conferred upon the owner, whether at present or in future; and (2) the manner in which the owner's right of enjoyment of his estate is to be exercised, whether solely, jointly, in common, or in coparcenary. Wharton.

QUAM LONGUM DEBET ESSE RATIONABILE TEMPUS NON DEFINITUR IN LEGE, SED PENDET EX DISCRETIONE JUSTICIARIORUM. Co. Litt. 56. How long *reasonable time* ought to be is not defined by law, but depends upon the discretion of the judges.

QUAM RATIONABILIS DEBET ESSE FINIS, NON DEFINITUR, SED OMNIBUS CIRCUMSTANTIIS INSPECTIS PENDET EX JUSTICIARIORUM DISCRETIONE. What a reasonable fine ought to be is not defined, but is left to the discretion of the judges, all the circumstances being considered. 11 Coke, 44.

QUAMDIU. Lat. As long as; so long as. A word of limitation in old conveyances. Co. Litt. 235*a*.

QUAMDIU SE BENE GESSERIT. As long as he shall behave himself well; during good behavior; a clause frequent in letters patent or grants of certain offices, to secure them so long as the persons to whom they are granted shall not be guilty of abusing them, the opposite clause being "*durante bene placito,*" (during the pleasure of the grantor.)

QUAMVIS ALIQUID PER SE NON SIT MALUM, TAMEN, SI SIT MALI EXEMPLI, NON EST FACIENDUM. Although a thing may not be bad in itself, yet, if it is of bad example, it is not to be done. 2 Inst. 564.

QUAMVIS LEX GENERALITER LOQUITUR, RESTRINGENDA TAMEN EST, UT, CESSANTE RATIONE, IPSA CESSAT. Although a law speaks generally, yet it is to be restrained, so that when its reason ceases, it should cease also. 4 Inst. 330.

QUANDO ABEST PROVISIO PARTIS, ADEST PROVISIO LEGIS. When the provision of the party is wanting, the provision of the law is at hand. 6 Vin. Abr. 49; 13 C. B. 960.

QUANDO ACCIDERINT. Lat. When they shall come in.

In practice. When a defendant, executor, or administrator pleads *plene administravit,* the plaintiff may pray to have judgment of assets *quando acciderint;* Bull. N. P. 169; Bac. Abr. Executor (M). A similar judgment may be taken at plaintiff's election, in an action against an heir, on a plea of *riens per descent*, instead of taking issue on the plea. In either of these cases if assets afterwards come to the hands of the executor or heir a *scire facias* must be sued out before execution can issue, or there may be an action of debt, suggesting a *devastavit;* 2 Bouv. Inst. 3708. It is also sometimes termed a judgment of *assets in futuro*. By taking a judgment in this form the plaintiff admits that defendant has fully administered to that time; 1 Pet. C. C. 442, n; and therefore the plaintiff will not be allowed to give evidence of effects come to defendant's hands before judgment. For this reason the *scire facias* on a judgment of assets *quando acciderint* must only pray execution of such assets as have come to the defendant's hands since former judgment, and if it prays judgment of assets generally, it cannot be supported. 2 Com. Dig. Pleader (2D9).

QUANDO ALIQUID MANDATUR, MANDATUR ET OMNE PER QUOD PERVENITUR AD ILLUD. 5 Coke 116. When anything is commanded, everything by which it can be accomplished is also commanded.

QUANDO ALIQUID PER SE NON SIT MALUM, TAMEN SI SIT MALI EXEMPLII, NON EST FACIENDUM. When anything by itself is not evil, and yet may be an example for evil, it is not to be done. 2 Inst. 564.

QUANDO ALIQUID PROHIBETUR EX DIRECTO, PROHIBETUR ET PER OBLIQUUM. Co. Litt. 223. When anything is prohibited directly, it is prohibited also indirectly.

QUANDO ALIQUID PROHIBETUR, PROHIBETUR ET OMNE PER QUOD DEVENITUR AD ILLUD. When anything is prohibited, everything by which it is reached is prohibited also. 2 Inst. 48. That which cannot be done directly shall not be done indirectly. Broom, Max. 489.

QUANDO ALIQUIS ALIQUID CONCEDIT, CONCEDERE VIDETUR ET ID SINE QUO RES UTI NON POTEST. When a person grants anything, he is supposed to grant that also without which the thing cannot be used. When the use of a thing is granted, everything is granted by which the grantee may have and enjoy such use. 3 Kent, Comm. 421.

QUANDO CHARTA CONTINET GENERALEM CLAUSULAM, POSTEAQUE DESCENDIT AD VERBA SPECIALIA QUÆ CLAUSULÆ GENERALI SUNT CONSENTANEA, INTERPRETANDA EST CHARTA SECUNDUM VERBA SPECIALIA. When a deed contains a general clause, and afterwards descends to special words which are agreeable to the general clause, the deed is to be interpreted according to the special words. 8 Coke 154*b*.

QUANDO DE UNA ET EADEM RE DUO ONERABILES EXISTUNT, UNUS, PRO INSUFFICIENTIA ALTERIUS, DE INTEGRO ONERABITUR. When there are two persons liable for one and the same thing, one of them, in case of default of the other, shall be charged with the whole. 2 Inst. 277.

QUANDO DISPOSITIO REFERRI POTEST AD DUAS RES ITA QUOD SECUNDUM RELATIONEM UNAM VITIETUR ET SECUNDUM ALTERAM UTILIS SIT, TUM FACIENDA EST RELATIO AD ILLAM UT VALEAT DISPOSITIO. 6 Coke 76. When a disposition may refer to two things, so that by the former it would be vitiated, and by the latter it would be preserved, then the relation is to be made to the latter, so that the disposition may be valid.

QUANDO DIVERSI DESIDERANTUR ACTUS AD ALIQUEM STATUM PERFICIENDUM, PLUS RESPICIT LEX ACTUM ORIGINALEM. When different acts are required to the formation of any estate, the law chiefly regards the original act. When to the perfection of an estate or interest divers acts or things are requisite, the law has more regard to the original act, for that is the fundamental part on which all the others are founded. 10 Coke 49*a*.

QUANDO DUO JURA CONCURRUNT IN UNA PERSONA, ÆQUUM EST AC SI ESSENT IN DIVERSIS. When two rights concur in one person, it is the same as if they were in two separate persons. 4 Co. 118; Broom, Max. 531.

QUANDO JUS DOMINI REGIS ET SUBDITI CONCURRUNT, JUS REGIS PRÆFERRI DEBET. 9 Coke 129. When the right of king and of subject concur, the king's right should be preferred.

QUANDO LEX ALIQUID ALICUI CONCEDIT, CONCEDERE VIDETUR ET ID SINE QUO RES IPSÆ ESSE NON POTEST. 5 Coke 47. When the law gives a man anything, it gives him that also without which the thing itself cannot exist.

QUANDO LEX ALIQUID ALICUI CONCEDIT, OMNIA INCIDENTIA TACITE CONCEDUNTUR. 2 Inst. 326. When the law gives anything to any one, all incidents are tacitly given.

QUANDO LEX EST SPECIALIS, RATIO AUTEM GENERALIS, GENERALITER LEX EST INTELLIGENDA. When a law is special, but its reason [or object] general, the law is to be understood generally. 2 Inst. 83.

QUANDO LICET ID QUOD MAJUS, VIDETUR ET LICERE ID QUOD MINUS. Shep. Touch. 429. When the greater is allowed, the less is to be understood as allowed also.

QUANDO MULIER NOBILIS NUPSERIT IGNOBILI, DESINIT ESSE NOBILIS NISI NOBILITAS NATIVA FUERIT. 4 Coke, 118. When a noble woman marries a man not noble, she ceases to be noble, unless her nobility was born with her.

QUANDO PLUS FIT QUAM FIERI DEBET, VIDETUR ETIAM ILLUD FIERI QUOD FACIENDUM EST. When more is done than ought to be done, that at least shall be considered as performed which should have been performed, [as, if a man, having a power to make a lease for ten years, make one for twenty years, it shall be void only for the surplus.] Broom, Max. 177; 5 Coke, 115; 8 Coke, 85*a*.

QUANDO QUOD AGO NON VALET UT AGO, VALEAT QUANTUM VALERE POTEST. When that which I do does not have effect as I do it, let it have as much effect as it can. Vandervolgen v. Yates, 3 Barb. Ch. (N. Y.) 242, 261.

QUANDO RES NON VALET UT AGO, VALEAT QUANTUM VALERE POTEST. When a thing is of no effect as I do it, it shall have effect as far as [or in whatever way] it can. Cowp. 600.

QUANDO VERBA ET MENS CONGRUUNT, NON EST INTERPRETATIONI LOCUS. When the words and the mind agree, there is no place for interpretation.

QUANDO VERBA STATUTI SUNT SPECIALIA, RATIO AUTEM GENERALIS, GENERALITER STATUTUM EST INTELLIGENDUM. When the words of a statute are special, but the reason or object of it general, the statute is to be construed generally. 10 Coke 101*b*.

QUANTI MINORIS. Lat. The name of an action in the civil law, (and in Louisiana,) brought by the purchaser of an article, for a reduction of the agreed price on account of defects in the thing which diminish its value.

QUANTUM DAMNIFICATUS? How much damnified? The name of an issue directed by a court of equity to be tried in a court of law, to ascertain the amount of compensation to be allowed for damage.

QUANTUM MERUIT. As much as he deserved. In pleading. The common count in an action of *assumpsit* for work and labor, founded on an implied *assumpsit* or promise on the part of the defendant to pay the plaintiff *as much as he* reasonably *deserved* to have for his labor. 3 Bl. Comm. 161; 1 Tidd, Pr. 2; Viles v. Kennebec Lumber Co., 118 Me. 148, 106 A. 431.

It refers to class of obligations imposed by law, without regard to intention or assent of parties bound, for reasons dictated by reason and justice; such obligations not being contracts though form of action is contract. Carpenter v. Josey Oil Co., C.C.A.Okl., 26 F.2d 442, 443. Amount of recovery being only the reasonable value of the services rendered regardless of any agreement as to value. Smith v. Bliss, 44 Cal.App.2d 171, 112 P.2d 30, 33.

QUANTUM TENENS DOMINO EX HOMAGIO, TANTUM DOMINUS TENENTI EX DOMINIO DEBET PRÆTER SOLAM REVERENTIAM; MUTUA DEBET ESSE DOMINII ET HOMAGII FIDELITATIS CONNEXIO. Co. Litt. 64. As much as the tenant by his homage owes to his lord, so much is the lord, by his lordship, indebted to the tenant, except reverence alone; the tie of dominion and of homage ought to be mutual.

QUANTUM VALEBANT. As much as they were worth. In pleading. The common count in an action of *assumpsit* for goods sold and delivered, founded on an implied *assumpsit* or promise, on the part of the defendant, to pay the plaintiff *as much as* the goods *were* reasonably *worth.* 3 Bl. Comm. 161; 1 Tidd, Pr. 2.

QUARANTINE. A period of time (theoretically forty days) during which a vessel, coming from a place where a contagious or infectious disease is prevalent, is detained by authority in the harbor of her port of destination, or at a station near it, without being permitted to land or to discharge her crew or passengers. Quarantine is said to have been first established at Venice in 1484. Baker, Quar. 3.

The space of forty days during which a widow has a right to remain in her late husband's principal mansion immediately after his death. The right of the widow is also called her "quarantine." See Davis v. Lowden, 56 N.J.Eq. 126, 38 A. 648; Falvey v. Hicks, 315 Mo. 442, 286 S.W. 385, 392.

A provision or interest given in law to the widow in her husband's estate, such as the privilege of occupying the mansion house and curtilage without charge until her dower is assigned, and technically is a dower right, or more broadly is a part of the dower estate. Amiss v. Hiteshew, 106 W.Va. 703, 147 S.E. 26, 28.

QUARE. Lat. Wherefore; for what reason; on what account. Used in the Latin form of several common-law writs.

QUARE CLAUSUM FREGIT. Lat. Wherefore he broke the close. That species of the action of trespass which has for its object the recovery of damages for an unlawful entry upon another's land is termed "trespass *quare clausum fregit;*" "breaking a close" being the technical expression for an unlawful entry upon land. The language of the declaration in this form of action is "that the defendant, with force and arms, broke and entered the close" of the plaintiff. The phrase is often abbreviated to "*qu. cl. fr.*" Brown.

QUARE EJECIT INFRA TERMINUM. Wherefore he ejected within the term. In old practice. A writ which lay for a lessee where he was ejected before the expiration of his term, in cases where the wrong-doer or ejector was not himself in possession of the lands, but his feoffee or another claiming under him. 3 Bl. Comm. 199, 206; Reg. Orig. 227; Fitzh. Nat. Brev. 197 S.

QUARE IMPEDIT. Wherefore he hinders. In English practice. A writ or action which lies for the patron of an advowson, where he has been disturbed in his right of patronage; so called from the emphatic words of the old form, by which the disturber was summoned to answer *why he hinders* the plaintiff. 3 Bl.Comm. 246, 248.

QUARE INCUMBRAVIT. In English law. A writ which lay against a bishop who, within six months after the vacation of a benefice, conferred it on his clerk, while two others were contending at law for the right of presentation, calling upon him to show cause why he had incumbered the church. Reg. Orig. 32. Abolished by 3 & 4 Wm. IV. c. 27.

QUARE INTRUSIT. A writ that formerly lay where the lord proffered a suitable marriage to his ward, who rejected it, and entered into the land, and married another, the value of his marriage not being satisfied to the lord. Abolished by 12 Car. II. c. 24.

QUARE NON ADMISIT. In English law. A writ to recover damages against a bishop who does not admit a plaintiff's clerk. It is, however, rarely or never necessary; for it is said that a bishop, refusing to execute the writ *ad admittendum clericum*, or making an insufficient return to it, may be fined. Wats.Cler.Law, 302.

QUARE NON PERMITTIT. An ancient writ, which lay for one who had a right to present to a church for a turn against the proprietary. Fleta, l. 5, c. 6.

QUARE OBSTRUXIT. Wherefore he obstructed. In old English practice. A writ which lay for one who, having a liberty to pass through his neighbor's ground, could not enjoy his right because the owner had so obstructed it. Cowell.

QUARENTENA TERRÆ. A furlong. Co.Litt. 5*b*.

QUARREL. This word is said to extend not only to real and personal actions, but also to the causes of actions and suits; so that by the release of all "quarrels," not only actions pending, but also causes of action and suit, are released; and "quarrels," "controversies," and "debates" are in law considered as having the same meaning. Co.Litt. 8, 153; Termes de la Ley.

In an untechnical sense, it signifies an altercation, an angry dispute, an exchange of recriminations, taunts, threats or accusations between two persons. Carr v. Conyers, 84 Ga. 287, 10 S.E. 630, 20 Am.St.Rep. 357; Accident Ins. Co. v. Bennett, 90 Tenn. 256, 16 S.W. 723, 25 Am.St. Rep. 685.

QUARRY. In mining law. An open excavation where the works are visible at the surface; a place or pit where stone, slate, marble, etc., is dug out or separated from a mass of rock. Bainb. Mines, 2. See Marvel v. Merritt, 116 U.S. 11, 6 S.Ct. 207, 29 L.Ed. 550.

QUART. A liquid measure, containing one-fourth part of a gallon.

QUARTA DIVI PII. In Roman law. That portion of a testator's estate which he was required by law to leave to a child whom he had adopted and afterwards emancipated or unjustly disinherited, being one-fourth of his property. Mackeld. Rom. Law, § 594.

QUARTA FALCIDIA. In Roman law. That portion of a testator's estate which, by the Falcidian law, was required to be left to the heir, amounting to at least one-fourth. Mackeld. Rom. Law, § 771.

QUARTER. The fourth part of anything, especially of a year. Also a length of four inches. In England, a measure of corn, generally reckoned at eight bushels, though subject to local variations. Hospital St. Cross v. Lord Howard De Walden, 6 Term, 343. In American land law, a quarter section of land. See *infra*. And see McCartney v. Dennison, 101 Cal. 252, 35 P. 766. In a military sense, the usual term applied to stations, buildings, lodgings, etc., in the regular occupation of military troops. State ex rel. Charlton v. French, 44 N.M. 169, 99 P.2d 715, 727.

In the Law of War. The sparing of the life of a fallen or captured enemy on the battlefield. By the end of the seventeenth century quarter became a recognized usage of war. It is forfeited only under exceptional circumstances. 1. In case of absolute and overwhelming necessity, as where a small force is incumbered with a large number of prisoners in a savage and hostile country, and may be justified in killing them for their own self-preservation. 2. Where belligerents violate the laws of war they may be refused quarter. 3. By way of retaliation against an enemy who has denied quarter without a cause. Risley, The Law of War; Spaight, War Rights on Land, 88–95.

QUARTER CHEST OF TEA. A chest containing from 25 to 30 pounds. Japan Tea Co. v. Franklin MacVeagh & Co., 142 Minn. 152, 171 N.W. 305, 307.

QUARTER OF A YEAR. Ninety-one days. Co. Litt. 135*b*.

QUARTER-DAY. The four days in the year upon which, by law or custom, moneys payable in quarter-yearly installments are collectible, are called "quarter-days."

QUARTER-DOLLAR. A copper-nickel clad (formerly silver) coin of the United States, of the value of twenty-five cents.

QUARTER-EAGLE. A gold coin of the United States, of the value of two and a half dollars.

QUARTER-SALES. In New York law. A species of fine on alienation, being one-fourth of the purchase money of an estate, which is stipulated to be paid back on alienation by the grantee. The expressions "tenth-sales," etc., are also used, with similar meanings. Jackson ex dem. Livingston v. Groat, 7 Cow. (N.Y.) 285.

QUARTER SEAL. See Seal.

QUARTER SECTION. In American land law. The quarter of a section of land according to the divisions of the government survey, laid off by dividing the section into four equal parts by north-and-south and east-and-west lines, and containing 160 acres.

QUARTER SESSIONS. In English law. A criminal court held before two or more justices of the peace, (one of whom must be of the quorum), in every county, once in every quarter of a year. 4 Bl.Comm. 271; 4 Steph.Comm. 335.

In American law. Courts established in some of the states, to be holden four times in the year, invested with criminal jurisdiction, usually of offenses less than felony, and sometimes with the charge of certain administrative matters, such as the care of public roads and bridges.

QUARTERING. In English criminal law. The dividing a criminal's body into quarters, after execution. A part of the punishment of high treason. 4 Bl.Comm. 93.

QUARTERING SOLDIERS. The act of a government in billeting or assigning soldiers to private houses, without the consent of the owners of such houses, and requiring such owners to supply them with board or lodging or both.

QUARTERIZATION. Quartering of criminals.

QUARTERLY. Quarter yearly; once in a quarter year. Dickenson v. Cox, 118 Or. 88, 244 P. 877, 878; Leonard v. St. Clair, 27 Idaho, 568, 149 P. 1058, 1060.

QUARTERLY COURTS. A system of courts in Kentucky possessing a limited original jurisdiction in civil cases and appellate jurisdiction from justices of the peace. Hamilton v. Spalding, 76 S.W. 517, 25 Ky.Law Rep. 847. They are not county courts, but separate and independent courts created and established by the constitution. Perry County v. McIntosh, 280 Ky. 223, 133 S.W. 2d 90, 91.

QUARTERONE. In the Spanish and French West Indies, a quadroon, that is, a person one of whose parents was white and the other a mulatto. Daniel v. Guy, 19 Ark. 131.

QUARTO DIE POST. Lat. On the fourth day after. Appearance day, in the former English practice, the defendant being allowed four days, inclusive, from the return of the writ, to make his appearance.

QUASH. To overthrow; to abate; to vacate; to annul; to make void. Spelman; 3 Bl.Comm. 303. Bosley v. Bruner, 2 Cushm. (Miss.) 462; Wilson v. Commonwealth, 157 Va. 776, 162 S.E. 1, 2.

QUASI. Lat. As if; almost as it were; analogous to. This term is used in legal phraseology to indicate that one subject resembles another, with which it is compared, in certain characteristics, but that there are intrinsic and material differences between them. Bicknell v. Garrett, 1 Wash.2d 564, 96 P.2d 592, 595, 126 A.L.R. 258; Cannon v. Miller, 22 Wash.2d 227, 155 P.2d 500, 503, 507, 157 A.L.R. 530. Marker v. State, 25 Ala.App. 91, 142 So. 105, 106. It is often prefixed to English words, implying mere appearance or want of reality. State v. Jeffrey, 188 Minn. 476, 247 N.W. 692, 693.

It is exclusively a term of classification. Prefixed to a term of Roman law, it implies that the conception to which it serves as an index is connected with the conception with which the comparison is instituted by a strong superficial analogy or resemblance. It negatives the notion of identity, but points out that the conceptions are sufficiently similar for one to be classed as the sequel to the other. Maine, Anc. Law, 332. Civilians use the expressions *"quasi contractus," "quasi delictum," "quasi possessio," "quasi traditio,"* etc.

As to quasi "Affinity," "Contract," "Corporation," "Crime," "Delict," "Deposit," "Derelict," "Easement," "Entail," "Fee," "In Rem," "Municipal Corporation," "Offense," "Partners," "Personalty," "Possession," "Posthumous Child," "Purchase," "Realty," "Tenant," "Tort," "Traditio," "Trustee," and "Usufruct," see those titles.

QUASI ADMISSION. An act or utterance, usually extrajudicial, which creates an inconsistency with and discredits to a greater or lesser degree, present claim or other evidence of person creating the inconsistency, and person who enacted or uttered it may nevertheless disprove its correctness by introduction of other evidence. Sutherland v. Davis, 151 Ky. 743, 151 S.W.2d 1021, 1024.

QUASI-CONTRACTUS (Lat.). In civil law. An obligation similar in character to that of a contract, which arises not from an agreement of parties but from some relation between them, or from a voluntary act of one of them. An obligation springing from voluntary and lawful acts of parties in the absence of any agreement. Howe. Stud. Civ. L. 171.

QUASI ESTOPPEL. The principle which precludes a party from asserting, to another's disadvantage, a right inconsistent with a position previously taken by him. Philadelphia County v. Sheehan, 263 Pa. 449, 107 A. 14, 16.

A term used by Bigelow to cover a group of cases in which a party is precluded from occupying inconsistent positions, either in litigations or in ordinary dealings; Big.Est. (6th ed.) 732. Pickett v. Bank, 32 Ark. 346; Robinson v. Pebworth, 71 Ala. 240. It is to be noted that in the cases grouped under this title the courts have generally used the simple term "estoppel" which, it has been suggested, is a questionable use of terms, since many of the cases are mere instances of ratification or acquiescence; Big.Est. 755.

"Equitable estoppel" and "estoppel in pais" are convertible terms embracing "quasi estoppel" and embody doctrine that one may not repudiate an act done or position assumed by him, where such course would work injustice to another rightfully relying thereon. Brown v. Corn Exchange Nat. Bank & Trust Co., 136 N.J.Eq. 430, 42 A.2d 474, 480.

QUASI JUDICIAL. A term applied to the action, discretion, etc., of public administrative officers, who are required to investigate facts, or ascertain the existence of facts, and draw conclusions from them, as a basis for their official action, and to exercise discretion of a judicial nature. Bair v. Struck, 29 Mont. 45, 74 P. 69, 63 L.R.A. 481; Mitchell v. Clay County, 69 Neb. 779, 96 N.W. 678.

The actions of the National Labor Relations Board are "quasi-judicial" in character. Thompson Products v. National Labor Relations Board, C.C.A.6, 133 F.2d 637, 640.

QUASI JUDICIAL ACT. A judicial act performed by one not a judge. State Tax Commission of Utah v. Katsis, 90 Utah 406, 62 P.2d 120, 123, 107 A.L.R. 1477.

QUASI-TRADITIO (Lat.). In civil law. A term used to designate that a person is in the use of the property of another, which the latter suffers and does not oppose. *Lec.Elem.* § 396. It also signifies the act by which the right of property is ceded in a thing to a person who is in possession of it; as, if I loan a boat to Paul, and deliver it to him, and afterwards I sell him the boat, it is not requisite that he should deliver the boat to me to be again delivered to him: there is a *quasi*-tradition or delivery.

QUATER COUSIN. See Cousin.

QUATUOR PEDIBUS CURRIT. Lat. It runs upon four feet; it runs upon all fours. See All-Fours.

QUATUORVIRI. In Roman law. Magistrates who had the care and inspection of roads. Dig. 1, 2, 3, 30.

QUAY. A wharf for the loading or unloading of goods carried in ships. This word is sometimes spelled "key."

The popular and commercial signification of the word "quay" involves the notion of a space of ground appropriated to the public use; such use as the convenience of commerce requires. New Orleans v. U. S., 10 Pet. 662, 715, 9 L.Ed. 573.

QUE EST LE MESME. L. Fr. Which is the same. A term used in actions of trespass, etc. See Quæ est Eadem.

QUE ESTATE. L. Fr. Whose estate. A term used in pleading, particularly in claiming prescription, by which it is alleged that the plaintiff and those former owners *whose estate* he has have immemorially exercised the right claimed. This was called "prescribing in a *que* estate."

QUEAN. A worthless woman; a strumpet. Obsolete.

QUEEN. A woman who possesses the sovereignty and royal power in a country under a monarchical form of government. The wife of a king.

Queen consort. In English law. The wife of a reigning king. 1 Bl.Comm. 218.

Queen dowager. In English law. The widow of a king. 1 Bl.Comm. 223.

Queen-gold. A royal revenue belonging to every queen consort during her marriage with the king, and due from every person who has made a voluntary fine or offer to the king of ten marks or upwards, in consideration of any grant or privilege conferred by the crown. It is now quite obsolete. 1 Bl.Comm. 220–222.

Queen regnant. In English law. A queen who holds the crown in her own right; as the first Queen Mary, Queen Elizabeth, Queen Anne, and Queen Victoria. 1 Bl.Comm. 218; 2 Steph.Comm. 465.

For the titles and descriptions of various officers in the English legal system, called "Queen's Advocate," "Queen's Coroner," "Queen's Counsel," "Queen's Proctor," "Queen's Remembrancer," etc., during the reign of a female sovereign, as in the time of Queen Victoria, see, now, under King and the following titles.

QUEEN ANNE'S BOUNTY. A fund created by a charter of Queen Anne, (confirmed by St. 2 Ann. c. 11), for the augmentation of poor livings, consisting of all the revenue of first fruits and tenths, which was vested in trustees forever. 1 Bl.Comm. 286.

QUEEN'S BENCH. The English court of king's bench is so called during the reign of a queen. 3 Steph.Comm. 403. See King's Bench.

QUEEN'S PRISON. A jail which used to be appropriated to the debtors and criminals confined under process or by authority of the superior courts at Westminster, the high court of admiralty, and also to persons imprisoned under the bankrupt law.

QUEM REDITUM REDDIT. L. Lat. An old writ which lay where a rent-charge or other rent which was not rent service was granted by fine holding of the grantor. If the tenant would not attorn, then the grantee might have had this writ. Old Nat. Brev. 126.

QUEMADMODUM AD QUÆSTIONEM FACTI NON RESPONDENT JUDICES, ITA AD QUÆSTIONEM JURIS NON RESPONDENT JURATORES. In the same manner that judges do not answer to questions of fact, so jurors do not answer to questions of law. Co.Litt. 295.

QUERELA. Lat. An action preferred in any court of justice. The plaintiff was called "*querens,*" or complainant and his brief, complaint, or declaration was called "*querela.*" Jacob.

QUERELA CORAM REGE A CONCILIO DISCUTIENDA ET TERMINANDA. A writ by which one is called to justify a complaint of a trespass made to the king himself, before the king and his council. Reg.Orig. 124.

QUERELA INOFFICIOSI TESTAMENTI. Lat. In the civil law. A species of action allowed to a child who had been unjustly disinherited, to set aside the will, founded on the presumption of law, in such cases, that the parent was not in his right mind. Calvin.; 2 Kent, Comm. 327; Bell.

QUERENS. Lat. A plaintiff; complainant; inquirer.

QUERULOUS. Apt to find fault; habitually complaining; disposed to murmur. Expressing, or suggestive of complaint; fretful; whining. Crounse v. Booth Fisheries, 111 Neb. 6, 195 N.W. 462, 463

QUESTA. In old records. A quest; an inquest, inquisition, or inquiry, upon the oaths of an impaneled jury. Cowell.

QUESTION. A subject or point of investigation, examination or debate; theme of inquiry; problem; matter to be inquired into; as a delicate or doubtful question. Pitts v. Howe Scale Co., 110 Vt. 27, 1 A.2d 695, 697.

A method of criminal examination heretofore in use in some of the countries of continental Europe, consisting of the application of torture to the supposed criminal, by means of the rack or other engines, in order to extort from him, as the condition of his release from the torture, a confession of his own guilt or the names of his accomplices.

Evidence

An interrogation put to a witness, for the purpose of having him declare the truth of certain facts as far as he knows them.

Practice

A point on which the parties are not agreed, and which is submitted to the decision of a judge and jury.

General

Categorical question. One inviting a distinct and positive statement of fact; one which can be answered by "yes" or "no." In the plural, a series of questions, covering a particular subject-matter, arranged in a systematic and consecutive order.

Federal question. See Federal.

Hypothetical question. See that title.

Judicial question. See Judicial.

Leading question. See that title.

Political question. See Political.

QUESTMAN, or QUESTMONGER. In old English law. A starter of lawsuits, or prosecutions; also a person chosen to inquire into abuses, especially such as relate to weights and measures; also a church-warden.

QUESTORES PARRICIDII. Lat. In Roman law. Certain officers, two in number, who were deputed by the *comitia*, as a kind of commission, to search out and try all cases of parricide and murder. They were probably appointed annually. Maine, Anc.Law, 370. They ceased to be appointed at an early period. Smith, Dict. Gr. & Rom. Antiq.

QUESTUS EST NOBIS. Lat. A writ of nuisance, which, by 15 Edw. I., lay against him to whom a house or other thing that caused a nuisance descended or was alienated; whereas, before that statute the action lay only against him who first levied or caused the nuisance to the damage of his neighbor. Cowell.

QUI ABJURAT REGNUM AMITTIT REGNUM, SED NON REGEM; PATRIAM, SED NON PATREM PATRIÆ. 7 Coke, 9. He who abjures the realm leaves the realm, but not the king; the country, but not the father of the country.

QUI ACCUSAT INTEGRÆ FAMÆ SIT, ET NON CRIMINOSUS. Let him who accuses be of clear fame, and not criminal. 3 Inst. 26.

QUI ACQUIRIT SIBI ACQUIRIT HÆREDIBUS. He who acquires for himself acquires for his heirs. Tray. Lat.Max. 496.

QUI ADIMIT MEDIUM DIRIMIT FINEM. He who takes away the mean destroys the end. He that deprives a man of the mean by which he ought to come to a thing deprives him of the thing itself. Co.Litt. 161a; Litt. § 237.

QUI ALIQUID STATUERIT, PARTE INAUDITA ALTERA ÆQUUM LICET DIXERIT, HAUD ÆQUUM FECERIT. He who determines any matter without hearing both sides, though he may have decided right, has not done justice. 6 Coke, 52*a*; 4 Bl.Comm. 283.

QUI ALTERIUS JURE UTITUR, EODEM JURE UTI DEBET. He who uses the right of another ought to use the same right. Poth. Traité De Change, pt. 1, c. 4, § 114; Broom, Max. 473.

QUI APPROBAT NON REPROBAT. He who approbates does not reprobate, [*i. e.*, he cannot both accept and reject the same thing.]

QUI BENE DISTINGUIT BENE DOCET. 2 Inst. 470. He who distinguishes well teaches well.

QUI BENE INTERROGAT BENE DOCET. He who questions well teaches well. Information or express averment may be effectually conveyed in the way of interrogation. 3 Bulst. 227.

QUI CADIT A SYLLABA CADIT A TOTA CAUSA. He who fails in a syllable fails in his whole cause. Bract. fol. 211.

QUI CONCEDIT ALIQUID, CONCEDERE VIDETUR ET ID SINE QUO CONCESSIO EST IRRITA, SINE QUO RES IPSA ESSE NON POTUIT. 11 Coke, 52. He who concedes anything is considered as conceding that without which his concession would be void, without which the thing itself could not exist.

QUI CONCEDIT ALIQUID CONCEDIT OMNE ID SINE QUO CONCESSIO EST IRRITA. He who grants anything grants everything without which the grant is fruitless. Jenk. Cent. p. 32, case 63.

QUI CONFIRMAT NIHIL DAT. He who confirms does not give. 2 Bouv. Inst. no. 2069.

QUI CONTEMNIT PRÆCEPTUM CONTEMNIT PRÆCIPIENTEM. He who contemns [contemptuously treats] a command contemns the party who gives it. 12 Coke 97.

QUI CUM ALIO CONTRAHIT, VEL EST, VEL ESSE DEBET NON IGNARUS CONDITIONIS EJUS. He who contracts with another either is or ought to be not ignorant of his condition. Dig. 50, 17, 19; Story, Confl. Laws, § 76.

QUI DAT FINEM, DAT MEDIA AD FINEM NECESSARIA. He who gives an end gives the means to that end. Commonwealth v. Andrews, 3 Mass. 129.

QUI DESTRUIT MEDIUM DESTRUIT FINEM. He who destroys the mean destroys the end. 10 Coke, 51*b*; Co. Litt. 161*a*; Shep. Touch. 342.

QUI DOIT INHERITER AL PERE DOIT INHERITER AL FITZ. He who would have been heir to the father shall be heir to the son. 2 Bl. Comm. 223; Broom, Max. 517.

QUI EVERTIT CAUSAM, EVERTIT CAUSATUM FUTURUM. He who overthrows the cause overthrows its future effects. 10 Coke, 51.

QUI EX DAMNATO COITU NASCUNTUR INTER LIBEROS NON COMPUTENTUR. Those who are born of an unlawful intercourse are not reckoned among the children. Co. Litt. 8*a*; Broom, Max. 519.

QUI FACIT ID QUOD PLUS EST, FACIT ID QUOD MINUS EST, SED NON CONVERTITUR. He who does that which is more does that which is less, but not *vice versa*. Bracton 207*b*.

QUI FACIT PER ALIUM FACIT PER SE. He who acts through another acts himself, [*i. e.*, the acts of an agent are the acts of the principal.] Broom, Max. 818, et seq.; 1 Bl.Comm. 429; Story, Ag. § 440.

QUI HABET JURISDICTIONEM ABSOLVENDI, HABET JURISDICTIONEM LIGANDI. He who has jurisdiction to loosen, has jurisdiction to bind. Applied to writs of prohibition and consultation, as resting on a similar foundation. 12 Coke, 60.

QUI HÆRET IN LITERA HÆRET IN CORTICE. He who considers merely the letter of an instrument goes but skin deep into its meaning. Co. Litt. 289; Broom, Max. 685.

QUI IGNORAT QUANTUM SOLVERE DEBEAT, NON POTEST IMPROBUS VIDERE. He who does not know what he ought to pay, does not want probity in not paying. Dig. 50, 17, 99.

QUI IMPROVIDE. A *supersedeas* granted where a writ was erroneously sued out or misawarded.

QUI IN JUS DOMINIUMVE ALTERIUS SUCCEDIT JURE EJUS UTI DEBET. He who succeeds to the right or property of another ought to use his right, [*i. e.*, holds it subject to the same rights and liabilities as attached to it in the hands of the assignor.] Dig. 50, 17, 177; Broom, Max. 473, 478.

QUI IN UTERO EST PRO JAM NATO HABETUR, QUOTIES DE EJUS COMMODO QUÆRITUR. He who is in the womb is held as already born, whenever a question arises for his benefit.

QUI JURE SUO UTITUR, NEMINI FACIT INJURIAM. He who uses his legal rights harms no one. Carson v. Western R. Co., 8 Gray (Mass.) 424. See Broom, Max. 379.

QUI JUSSU JUDICIS ALIQUOD FECERIT NON VIDETUR DOLO MALO FECISSE, QUIA PARERE NECESSE EST. Where a person does an act by command of one exercising judicial authority, the law will not suppose that he acted from any wrongful or improper motive, because it was his bounden duty to obey. 10 Coke, 76; Broom, Max. 93.

QUI MALE AGIT ODIT LUCEM. He who acts badly hates the light. 7 Coke, 66.

QUI MANDAT IPSE FECISSI VIDETUR. He who commands [a thing to be done] is held to have done it himself. Story, Bailm. § 147.

QUI MELIUS PROBAT MELIUS HABET. He who proves most recovers most. 9 Vin. Abr. 235.

QUI MOLITUR INSIDIAS IN PATRIAM ID FACIT QUOD INSANUS NAUTA PERFORANS NAVEM IN QUA VEHITUR. He who betrays his country is like the insane sailor who bores a hole in the ship which carries him. 3 Inst. 36.

QUI NASCITUR SINE LEGITIMO MATRIMONIO, MATREM SEQUITUR. He who is born out of lawful matrimony follows the condition of the mother.

QUI NON CADUNT IN CONSTANTEM VIRUM VANI TIMORES SUNT ÆSTIMANDI. 7 Coke, 27. Those fears are to be esteemed vain which do not affect a firm man.

QUI NON HABET, ILLE NON DAT. He who has not, gives not. He who has nothing to give, gives nothing. A person cannot convey a right that is not in him. If a man grant that which is not his, the grant is void. Shep. Touch. 243; Watk. Conv. 191.

QUI NON HABET IN ÆRE, LUAT IN CORPORE, NE QUIS PECCETUR IMPUNE. He who cannot pay with his purse must suffer in his person, lest he who offends should go unpunished. 2 Inst. 173; 4 Bl.Comm. 20.

QUI NON HABET POTESTATEM ALIENANDI HABET NECESSITATEM RETINENDI. Hob. 336. He who has not the power of alienating is obliged to retain.

QUI NON IMPROBAT, APPROBAT. 3 Inst. 27. He who does not blame, approves.

QUI NON LIBERE VERITATEM PRONUNCIAT PRODITOR EST VERITATIS. He who does not freely speak the truth is a betrayer of the truth.

QUI NON NEGAT FATETUR. He who does not deny, admits. A well-known rule of pleading. Tray. Lat. Max. 503.

QUI NON OBSTAT QUOD OBSTARE POTEST, FACERE VIDETUR. He who does not prevent [a thing] which he can prevent, is considered to do [as doing] it. 2 Inst. 146.

QUI NON PROHIBET ID QUOD PROHIBERE POTEST ASSENTIRE VIDETUR. 2 Inst. 308. He who does not forbid what he is able to prevent, is considered to assent.

QUI NON PROPULSAT INJURIAM QUANDO POTEST, INFERT. Jenk. Cent. 271. He who does not repel an injury when he can, induces it.

QUI OBSTRUIT ADITUM, DESTRUIT COMMODUM. He who obstructs a way, passage, or entrance destroys a benefit or convenience. He who prevents another from entering upon land destroys the benefit which he has from it. Co. Litt. 161*a*.

QUI OMNE DICIT NIHIL EXCLUDIT. 4 Inst. 81. He who says all excludes nothing.

QUI PARCIT NOCENTIBUS INNOCENTES PUNIT. Jenk. Cent. 133. He who spares the guilty punishes the innocent.

QUI PECCAT EBRIUS LUAT SOBRIUS. He who sins when drunk shall be punished when sober. Cary, 133; Broom, Max. 17.

QUI PER ALIUM FACIT PER SEIPSUM FACERE VIDETUR. He who does a thing by an agent is considered as doing it himself. Co. Litt. 258; Broom, Max. 817.

QUI PER FRAUDEM AGIT FRUSTRA AGIT. 2 Rolle, 17. What a man does fraudulently he does in vain.

QUI POTEST ET DEBET VETARE, JUBET. He who can and ought to forbid a thing [if he do not forbid it] directs it. 2 Kent, Comm. 483, note.

QUI PRIMUM PECCAT ILIE FACIT RIXAM. Godb. He who sins first makes the strife.

QUI PRIOR EST TEMPORE POTIOR EST JURE. He who is before in time is the better in right. Priority in time gives preference in law. Co. Litt. 14*a*; 4 Coke, 90*a*. A maxim of very extensive application, both at law and in equity. Broom, Max. 353–362; 1 Story, Eq. Jur. § 64*d*; Story, Bailm. § 312.

QUI PRO ME ALIQUID FACIT NIHI FECISSE VIDETUR. 2 Inst. 501. He who does anything for me appears to do it to me.

QUI PROVIDET SIBI PROVIDET HÆREDIBUS. He who provides for himself provides for his heirs.

QUI RATIONEM IN OMNIBUS QUÆRUNT RATIONEM SUBVERTUNT. They who seek a reason for everything subvert reason. 2 Coke, 75; Broom, Max. 157.

QUI SCIENS SOLVIT INDEBITUM DONANDI CONSILIO ID VIDETUR FECISSE. One who knowingly pays what is not due is supposed to have done it with the intention of making a gift. Walker v. Hill, 17 Mass. 388.

QUI SEMEL ACTIONEM RENUNCIAVERIT AMPLIUS REPETERE NON POTEST. He who has once relinquished his action cannot bring it again. 8 Coke, 59*a*. A rule descriptive of the effect of a *retraxit* and *nolle prosequi*.

QUI SEMEL EST MALUS, SEMPER PRÆSUMITUR ESSE MALUS IN EODEM GENERE. He who is once criminal is presumed to be always criminal in the same kind or way. Cro. Car. 317; Best, Ev. 345.

QUI SENTIT COMMODUM SENTIRE DEBET ET ONUS. He who receives the advantage ought also to suffer the burden. 1 Coke, 99; Broom, Max. 706–713.

QUI SENTIT ONUS SENTIRE DEBET ET COMMODUM. 1 Coke, 99*a*. He who bears the burden of a thing ought also to experience the advantage arising from it.

QUI TACET, CONSENTIRE VIDETUR. He who is silent is supposed to consent. The silence of a party implies his consent. Jenk. Cent. p. 32, case 64; Broom, Max. 138, 787.

QUI TACET CONSENTIRE VIDETUR, UBI TRACTATUR DE EJUS COMMODO. 9 Mod. 38. He who is silent is considered as assenting, when his interest is at stake.

QUI TACET NON UTIQUE FATETUR, SED TAMEN VERUM EST EUM NON NEGARE. He who is silent does not indeed confess, but yet it is true that he does not deny. Dig. 50, 17, 142.

QUI TAM. Lat. "Who as well ———." An action brought by an informer, under a statute which establishes a penalty for the commission or omission of a certain act, and provides that the same shall be recoverable in a civil action, part of the penalty to go to any person who will bring such action and the remainder to the state or some other institution, is called a "*qui tam* action"; because the plaintiff states that he sues *as well* for the state as for himself. See In re Barker, 56 Vt. 14; Grover v. Morris, 73 N.Y. 478.

QUI TARDIUS SOLVIT, MINUS SOLVIT. He who pays more tardily [than he ought] pays less [than he ought.] Jenk. Cent. 58.

QUI TIMENT, CAVENT VITANT. They who fear, take care and avoid. Branch, Princ.

QUI TOTUM DICIT NIHIL EXCIPIT. He who says all excepts nothing.

QUI VULT DECIPI, DECIPIATUR. Let him who wishes to be deceived, be deceived. Broom, Max. 782, note; 1 De Gex, M. & G. 687, 710; Shep. Touch. 56.

QUIA. Lat. Because; whereas; inasmuch as.

QUIA DATUM EST NOBIS INTELLIGI. Because it is given to us to understand. Formal words in old writs.

QUIA EMPTORES. Lat. "Because the purchasers." The title of the statute of Westm. 3, (18 Edw. I. c. 1.) This statute took from the tenants of common lords the feudal liberty they claimed of disposing of part of their lands to hold of themselves, and, instead of it, gave them a general liberty to sell all or any part, to hold of the next superior lord, which they could not have done before without consent. The effect of this statute was twofold: (1) To facilitate the alienation of fee-simple estates; and (2) to put an end to the creation of any new manors, *i. e.*, tenancies in fee-simple of a subject. Brown.

QUIA ERRONICE EMANAVIT. Because it issued erroneously, or through mistake. A term in old English practice. Yel. 83.

QUIA NON REFERT AUT QUIS INTENTIONEM SUAM DECLARET, VERBIS, AUT REBUS IPSIS VEL FACTIS. It is immaterial whether the intention be collected from the words used or the acts done. Tocci v. Nowfall, 220 N.C. 550, 18 S. E.2d 225, 228.

QUIA TIMET. Lat. Because he fears or apprehends. In equity practice. The technical name of a bill filed by a party who seeks the aid of a court of equity, *because he fears* some future probable injury to his rights or interests, and relief granted must depend upon circumstances. 2 Story, Eq. Jur. § 826; Pell v. McCabe, D.C.N.Y., 254 F. 356, 357; Estate of Gilbert Smith v. Cohen, 123 N.J.Eq. 419, 196 A. 361, 364.

QUIBBLE. A cavilling or verbal objection. A slight difficulty raised without necessity or propriety.

QUICK. Living; alive. "*Quick* chattels must be put in pound-overt that the owner may give them sustenance; dead need not." Finch, Law, b. 2, c. 6.

QUICK CHILD. One that has developed so that it moves within the mother's womb. State v. Timm, 244 Wis. 508, 12 N.W.2d 670, 671.

QUICK WITH CHILD. Having conceived. Evans v. People, 49 N.Y. 86, 1 Cow.Cr.R. 494.

QUICKENING. In medical jurisprudence. The first motion of the *fœtus* in the womb felt by the mother, occurring usually about the middle of the term of pregnancy. State v. Patterson, 105 Kan. 9, 181 P. 609, 610.

QUICQUID ACQUIRITUR SERVO ACQUIRITUR DOMINO. Whatever is acquired by the servant is acquired for the master. Pull. Accts. 38, note. Whatever rights are acquired by an agent are acquired for his principal. Story, Ag. § 403.

QUICQUID DEMONSTRATÆ REI ADDITUR SATIS DEMONSTRATÆ FRUSTRA EST. Whatever is added to demonstrate anything already sufficiently demonstrated is surplusage. Dig. 33, 4, 1, 8; Broom, Max. 630.

QUICQUID EST CONTRA NORMAM RECTI EST INJURIA. 3 Bulst. 313. Whatever is against the rule of right is a wrong.

QUICQUID IN EXCESSU ACTUM EST, LEGE PROHIBETUR. 2 Inst. 107. Whatever is done in excess is prohibited by law.

QUICQUID JUDICIS AUCTORITATI SUBJICITUR NOVITATI NON SUBJICITUR. Whatever is subject to the authority of a judge is not subject to innovation. 4 Inst. 66.

QUICQUID PLANTATUR SOLO, SOLO CEDIT. Whatever is affixed to the soil belongs to the soil. Broom, Max. 401–431.

QUICQUID RECIPITUR, RECIPITUR SECUNDUM MODUM RECIPIENTIS. Whatever is received is received according to the intention of the recipient. Broom, Max. 810; Halkers. Max. 149; 14 Sim. 522; 2 Cl. & F. 681; 2 Cr. & J. 678; 14 East, 239, 243 *c.*

QUICQUID SOLVITUR, SOLVITUR SECUNDUM MODUM SOLVENTIS; QUICQUID RECIPITUR, RECIPITUR SECUNDUM MODUM RECIPIENTIS. Whatever money is paid, is paid according to the direction of the payer; whatever money is received, is received according to that of the recipient. 2 Vern. 606; Broom, Max. 810.

QUICUNQUE HABET JURISDICTIONEM ORDINARIAM EST ILLIUS LOCI ORDINARIUS. Co. Litt. 344. Whoever has an ordinary jurisdiction is ordinary of that place.

QUICUNQUE JUSSU JUDICIS ALIQUID FECERIT NON VIDETUR DOLO MALO FECISSE, QUIA PARERE NECESSE EST. 10 Coke, 71. Whoever does anything by the command of a judge is not reckoned to have done it with an evil intent, because it is necessary to obey.

QUID JURIS CLAMAT. In old English practice. A writ which lay for the grantee of a reversion or remainder, where the particular tenant would not attorn, for the purpose of compelling him. Termes de la Ley; Cowell.

QUID PRO QUO. What for what; something for something. Used in law for the giving one valuable thing for another. It is nothing more than the mutual consideration which passes between the parties to a contract, and which renders it valid and binding. Cowell.

QUID SIT JUS, ET IN QUO CONSISTIT INJURIA, LEGIS EST DEFINIRE. What constitutes right, and what injury, it is the business of the law to declare. Co.Litt. 158*b*.

QUID TURPI EX CAUSA PROMISSUM EST NON VALET. A promise arising out of immoral circumstances is invalid.

QUIDAM. Lat. Somebody. This term is used in the French law to designate a person whose name is not known.

QUIDQUID ENIM SIVE DOLO ET CULPA VENDITORIS ACCIDIT IN EO VENDITOR SECURUS EST. For concerning anything which occurs without deceit and wrong on the part of the vendor, the vendor is secure. Brown v. Bellows, 4 Pick. (Mass.) 198.

QUIET, *v.* To pacify; to render secure or unassailable by the removal of disquieting causes or disputes. This is the meaning of the word in the phrase "action to quiet title," which is a proceeding to establish the plaintiff's title to land by bringing into court an adverse claimant and there compelling him either to establish his claim or be forever after estopped from asserting it. Wright v. Mattison, 18 How. 56, 15 L.Ed. 280.

QUIET, *adj.* Unmolested; tranquil; free from interference or disturbance.

Covenant of quiet enjoyment. A covenant, usually inserted in leases and conveyances on the part of the grantor, promising that the tenant or grantee shall enjoy the possession of the premises in peace and without disturbance.

QUIETA NON MOVERE. Not to unsettle things which are established. Green v. Hudson River R. Co., 28 Barb. (N.Y.) 9, 22.

QUIETARE. L. Lat. To quit, acquit, discharge, or save harmless. A formal word in old deeds of donation and other conveyances. Cowell.

QUIETE CLAMANTIA. L. Lat. In old English law. Quitclaim. Bract. fol. 33*b*.

QUIETE CLAMARE. L. Lat. To quitclaim or renounce all pretensions of right and title. Bract. fols. 1, 5.

QUIETUS. In old English law. Quit; acquitted; discharged. A word used by the clerk of the pipe, and auditors in the exchequer, in their acquittances or discharges given to accountants; usually concluding with an *abinde recessit quietus,* (hath gone quit thereof,) which was called a "*quietus est.*" Cowell.

In modern law. A final discharge or acquittance, as from a debt or obligation; that which silences claims. State ex rel. Jones v. Edwards, 203 La. 1039, 14 So.2d 829, 834.

QUIETUS REDDITUS. In old English law. Quitrent. Spelman. See Quitrent.

QUILIBET POTEST RENUNCIARE JURI PRO SE INTRODUCTO. Every one may renounce or relinquish a right introduced for his own benefit. 2 Inst. 183; Wing. Max. p. 483, max. 123; 4 Bl. Comm. 317.

QUILLE. In French marine law. Keel; the keel of a vessel. Ord. Mar. liv. 3, tit. 6, art. 8.

QUINQUE PORTUS. In old English law. The Cinque Ports. Spelman.

QUINQUEPARTITE. Consisting of five parts; divided into five parts.

QUINSTEME, or QUINZIME. Fifteenths; also the fifteenth day after a festival. 13 Edw. I. See Cowell.

QUINTAL, or KINTAL. A weight of one hundred pounds. Cowell.

QUINTERONE. A term used in the West Indies to designate a person one of whose parents was a white person and the other a quadroon. Also spelled "quintroon." Daniel v. Guy, 19 Ark. 131.

QUINTO EXACTUS. In old practice. Called or exacted the fifth time. A return made by the sheriff, after a defendant had been proclaimed, required, or exacted in five county courts successively, and failed to appear, upon which he was outlawed by the coroners of the county. 3 Bl. Comm. 283.

QUIRE OF DOVER. In English law. A record in the exchequer, showing the tenures for guarding and repairing Dover Castle, and determining the services of the Cinque Ports. 3 How.State Tr. 868.

QUIRITARIAN OWNERSHIP. In Roman law. Ownership held by a title recognized by the municipal law, in an object also recognized by that law, and in the strict character of a Roman citizen. "Roman law originally only recognized one kind of dominion, called, emphatically, 'quiritary dominion.' Gradually, however, certain real rights arose which, though they failed to satisfy all the elements of the definition of quiritary dominion, were practically its equivalent, and received from the courts a similar protection. These real rights might fall short of quiritary dominion in three respects: (1) Either in respect of the persons in whom they resided; (2) or of the subjects to which they related; or (3) of the title by which they were acquired." In the latter case, the ownership was called "bonitarian," *i. e.*, "the property of a Roman citizen, in a subject capable of quiritary property, acquired by a title not known to the civil law, but introduced by the prætor and protected by his *imperium* or supreme executive power;" *e. g.*, where *res mancipi* had been transferred by mere tradition. Poste's Gaius' Inst. 186.

QUISQUIS ERIT QUI VULT JURIS–CONSULTUS HABERI CONTINUET STUDIUM, VELIT A QUOCUNQUE DOCERI. Jenk. Cent. Whoever wishes to be a juris-consult, let him continually study, and desire to be taught by every one.

QUISQUIS PRÆSUMITUR BONUS; ET SEMPER IN DUBIIS PRO REO RESPONDENDUM. Every one is presumed good; and in doubtful cases the resolution should be ever for the accused.

QUIT, *v.* To leave; remove from; surrender possession of; as when a tenant "quits" the premises or receives a "notice to quit." Schotter v. Carnegie Steel Co., 272 Pa. 437, 116 A. 358, 359.

Notice to Quit

A written notice given by a landlord to his tenant, stating that the former desires to repossess himself of the demised premises, and that the latter is required to quit and remove from the same at a time designated, either at the expiration of the term, if the tenant is in under a lease, or immediately, if the tenancy is at will or by sufferance.

QUIT, *adj.* Clear; discharged; free; also spoken of persons absolved or acquitted of a charge.

QUITCLAIM, *v.* In conveyancing. To release or relinquish a claim; to execute a deed of quitclaim. See Quitclaim, *n.*

QUITCLAIM, *n.* A release or acquittance given to one man by another, in respect of any action that he has or might have against him. Also acquitting or giving up one's claim or title. Termes de la Ley; Cowell.

Quitclaim deed. A deed of conveyance operating by way of release; that is, intended to pass any title, interest, or claim which the grantor may have in the premises, but not professing that such title is valid, nor containing any warranty or covenants for title. Cook v. Smith, 107 Tex. 119, 174 S.W. 1094, 1095, 3 A.L.R. 940; Pierson v. Bill, 133 Fla. 81, 182 So. 631, 634.

QUIT RENT. A rent paid by the tenant of the freehold, by which he goes quit and free,—that is, discharged from any other rent. 2 Bla.Com. 42.

QUITTANCE. An abbreviation of "acquittance;" a release, (*q. v.*).

QUO ANIMO. Lat. With what intention or motive. Used sometimes as a substantive, in lieu of the single word "*animus*," design or motive. "The *quo animo* is the real subject of inquiry." 1 Kent, Comm. 77.

QUO JURE. Lat. In old English practice. A writ which lay for one that had land in which another claimed common, to compel the latter to show *by what title* he claimed it. Cowell; Fitzh. Nat.Brev. 128, F.

QUO LIGATUR, EO DISSOLVITUR. 2 Rolle, 21. By the same mode by which a thing is bound, by that is it released.

QUO MINUS. Lat. A writ upon which all proceedings in the court of exchequer were formerly grounded. In it the plaintiff suggests that he is the king's debtor, and that the defendant has done him the injury or damage complained of, *quo minus sufficiens existit,* by which *he is less able* to pay the king's debt. This was originally requisite in order to give jurisdiction to the court of exchequer; but now this suggestion is a mere form. 3 Bl.Comm. 46.

Also, a writ which lay for him who had a grant of house-bote and hay-bote in another's woods, against the grantor making such waste as that the grantee could not enjoy his grant. Old Nat. Brev. 148.

QUO MODO QUID CONSTITUITUR EODEM MODO DISSOLVITUR. Jenk.Cent. 74. In the same manner by which anything is constituted by that it is dissolved.

QUO WARRANTO. In old English practice. A writ, in the nature of a writ of right for the king, against him who claimed or usurped any office, franchise, or liberty, to inquire *by what authority* he supported his claim, in order to determine the right. It lay also in case of non-user, or long neglect of a franchise, or misuser or abuse of it; being a writ commanding the defendant to show *by what warrant* he exercises such a franchise, having never had any grant of it, or having forfeited it by neglect or abuse. 3 Bl.Comm. 262.

In England, and quite generally throughout the United States, this writ has given place to an "information in the nature of a *quo warranto,*" which, though in form a criminal proceeding, is in effect a civil remedy similar to the old writ, and is the method now usually employed for trying the title to a corporate or other franchise, or to a public or corporate office. Ames v. Kansas, 111 U.S. 449, 4 S.Ct. 437, 28 L.Ed. 482; People v. Londoner, 13 Colo. 303, 22 P. 764, 6 L.R.A. 444; An extraordinary proceeding, prerogative in nature, addressed to preventing a continued exercise of authority unlawfully asserted. Johnson v. Manhattan Ry. Co., N.Y., 53 S.Ct. 721, 289 U.S. 479, 77 L.Ed. 1331.

It is intended to prevent exercise of powers that are not conferred by law, and is not ordinarily available to regulate the manner of exercising such powers. State ex rel. Johnson v. Conservative Savings & Loan Ass'n, 143 Neb. 805, 11 N.W.2d 89, 92, 93.

QUOAD HOC. Lat. As to this; with respect to this; so far as this in particular is concerned.

A prohibition *quoad hoc* is a prohibition as to certain things among others. Thus, where a party was complained against in the ecclesiastical court for matters cognizable in the temporal courts, a prohibition *quoad* these matters issued, *i. e., as to such matters* the party was prohibited from prosecuting his suit in the ecclesiastical court. Brown.

QUOAD SACRA. Lat. As to sacred things; for religious purposes.

QUOCUMQUE MODO VELIT; QUOCUMQUE MODO POSSIT. In any way he wishes; in any way he can. Clason v. Bailey, 14 Johns., N.Y., 484, 492.

QUOD A QUOQUE PŒNÆ NOMINE EXACTUM EST ID EIDEM RESTITUERE NEMO COGITUR. That which has been exacted as a penalty no one is obliged to restore. Dig. 50, 17, 46.

QUOD AB INITIO NON VALET IN TRACTU TEMPORIS NON CONVALESCET. That which is bad in its commencement improves not by lapse of time. Broom, Max. 178; 4 Coke, 2.

QUOD AD JUS NATURALE ATTINET OMNES HOMINES ÆQUALES SUNT. All men are equal as far as the natural law is concerned. Dig. 50, 17, 32.

QUOD ÆDIFICATUR IN AREA LEGATA CEDIT LEGATO. Whatever is built on ground given by will goes to the legatee. Broom, Max. 424.

QUOD ALIAS BONUM ET JUSTUM EST, SI PER VIM VEL FRAUDEM PETATUR, MALUM ET INJUSTUM EFFICITUR. 3 Coke, 78. What otherwise is good and just, if it be sought by force and fraud, becomes bad and unjust.

QUOD ALIAS NON FUIT LICITUM, NECESSITAS LICITUM FACIT. What otherwise was not lawful, necessity makes lawful. Fleta, lib. 5, c. 23, § 14.

QUOD APPROBO NON REPROBO. What I approve I do not reject. I cannot approve and reject at the same time. I cannot take the benefit of an instrument, and at the same time repudiate it. Broom, Max. 712.

QUOD ATTINET AD JUS CIVILE, SERVI PRO NULLIS HABENTUR, NON TAMEN ET JURE NATURALI, QUIA, QUOD AD JUS NATURALE ATTINET, OMNES HOMINES ÆQUALL SUNT. So far as the civil law is concerned, slaves are not reckoned as persons, but not so by natural law, for, so far as regards natural law, all men are equal. Dig. 50, 17, 32.

QUOD BILLA CASSETUR. That the bill be quashed. The common-law form of a judgment sustaining a plea in abatement, where the proceeding is by bill, *i. e.*, by a *capias* instead of by original writ.

QUOD CLERICI BENEFICIATI DE CANCELLARIA. A writ to exempt a clerk of the chancery from the contribution towards the proctors of the clergy in parliament, etc. Reg.Orig. 261.

QUOD CLERICI NON ELIGANTUR IN OFFICIO BALLIVI, etc. A writ which lay for a clerk, who, by reason of some land he had, was made, or was about to be made, bailiff, beadle, reeve, or some such officer, to obtain exemption from serving the office. Reg.Orig. 187.

QUOD COMPUTET. That he account.

Judgment quod computet. A preliminary or interlocutory judgment given in the action of account-render (also in the case of creditors' bills against an executor or administrator,) directing that accounts be taken before a master or auditor.

QUOD CONSTAT CLARE NON DEBET VERIFICARI. What is clearly apparent need not be proved. 10 Mod. 150.

QUOD CONSTAT CURIÆ OPERE TESTIUM NON INDIGET. That which appears to the court needs not the aid of witnesses. 2 Inst. 662.

QUOD CONTRA LEGEM FIT PRO INFECTO HABETUR. That which is done against law is regarded as not done at all. 4 Coke, 31*a*.

QUOD CONTRA RATIONEM JURIS RECEPTUM EST, NON EST PRODUCENDUM AD CONSEQUENTIAS. That which has been received against the reason of the law is not to be drawn into a precedent. Dig. 1, 3, 14.

QUOD CUM. In pleading. For that whereas. A form of introducing matter of inducement in certain actions, as *assumpsit* and case.

QUOD DATUM EST ECCLESIÆ, DATUM EST DEO. 2 Inst. 2. What is given to the church is given to God.

QUOD DEMONSTRANDI CAUSA ADDITUR REI SATIS, DEMONSTRATÆ, FRUSTRA FIT. 10 Coke, 113. What is added to a thing sufficiently palpable, for the purpose of demonstration, is vain.

QUOD DUBITAS, NE FECERIS. What you doubt of, do not do. In a case of moment, especially in cases of life, it is safest to hold that in practice which hath least doubt and danger. 1 Hale, P.C. 300.

QUOD EI DEFORCEAT. In English law. The name of a writ given by St. Westm. 2, 13 Edw. I. c. 4, to the owners of a particular estate, as for life, in dower, by the curtesy, or in fee-tail, who were barred of the right of possession by a recovery had against them through their default or nonappearance in a possessory action, by which the right was restored to him who had been thus unwarily deforced by his own default. 3 Bl.Comm. 193.

QUOD ENIM SEMEL AUT BIS EXISTIT, PRÆTEREUNT LEGISLATORES. That which never happens but once or twice, legislators pass by. Dig. 1, 3, 17.

QUOD EST EX NECESSITATE NUNQUAM INTRODUCITUR, NISI QUANDO NECESSARIUM. 2 Rolle, 502. That which is of necessity is never introduced, unless when necessary.

QUOD EST INCONVENIENS AUT CONTRA RATIONEM NON PERMISSUM EST IN LEGE. Co. Litt. 178*a*. That which is inconvenient or against reason is not permissible in law.

QUOD EST NECESSARIUM EST LICITUM. What is necessary is lawful. Jenk.Cent. p. 76, case 45.

QUOD FACTUM EST, SUM IN OBSCURO SIT, EX AFFECTIONE CUJUSQUE CAPIT INTERPRETATIONEM. When there is doubt about an act, it receives interpretation from the (known) feelings of the actor. Dig. 50, 17, 68, 1.

QUOD FIERI DEBET FACILE PRÆSUMITUR. Halk. 153. That which ought to be done is easily presumed.

QUOD FIERI NON DEBET, FACTUM VALET. That which ought not to be done, when done, is valid. Broom, Max. 182.

QUOD FUIT CONCESSUM. Which was granted. A phrase in the reports, signifying that an argument or point made was conceded or acquiesced in by the court.

QUOD IN JURE SCRIPTO "JUS" APPELLATUR, ID IN LEGE ANGLIÆ "RECTUM" ESSE DICITUR. What in the civil law is called *"jus,"* in the law of England is said to be *"rectum,"* (right.) Co.Litt. 260; Fleta, l. 6, c. 1, § 1.

QUOD IN MINORI VALET VALEBIT IN MAJORI; ET QUOD IN MAJORI NON VALET NEC VALEBIT IN MINORI. Co. Litt. 260*a*. That which is valid in the less shall be valid in the greater; and that which is not valid in the greater shall neither be valid in the less.

QUOD IN UNO SIMILIUM VALET VALEBIT IN ALTERO. That which is effectual in one of two like things shall be effectual in the other. Co. Litt. 191*a*.

QUOD INCONSULTO FECIMUS, CONSULTIUS REVOCEMUS. Jenk.Cent. 116. What we have done without due consideration, upon better consideration we may revoke.

QUOD INITIO NON VALET, TRACTU TEMPORIS NON VALET. A thing void in the beginning does not become valid by lapse of time.

QUOD INITIO VITIOSUM EST NON POTEST TRACTU TEMPORIS CONVALESCERE. That which is void from the beginning cannot become valid by lapse of time. Dig. 50, 17, 29.

QUOD IPSIS QUI CONTRAXERUNT OBSTAT, ET SUCCESSORIBUS EORUM OBSTABIT. That which bars those who have made a contract will bar their successors also. Dig. 50, 17, 143.

QUOD JUSSU. Lat. In the civil law. The name of an action given to one who had contracted with a son or slave, *by order* of the father or master, to compel such father or master to stand to the agreement. Hallifax, Civil Law, b. 3, c. 2, no. 3; Inst. 4, 7, 1.

QUOD JUSSU ALTERIUS SOLVITUR PRO EO EST QUASI IPSI SOLUTUM ESSET. That which is paid by the order of another is the same as though it were paid to himself. Dig. 50, 17, 180.

QUOD MEUM EST SINE FACTO MEO VEL DEFECTU MEO AMITTI VEL IN ALIUM TRANSFERRI NON POTEST. That which is mine cannot be lost or transferred to another without my alienation or forfeiture. Broom, Max. 465.

QUOD MEUM EST SINE ME AUFERRI NON POTEST. That which is mine cannot be taken away without me, [without my assent.] Jenk. Cent. p. 251, case 41.

QUOD MINUS EST IN OBLIGATIONEM VIDETUR DEDUCTUM. That which is the less is held to be imported into the contract; (*e. g.*, A offers to hire B.'s house at six hundred dollars, at the same time B. offers to let it for five hundred dollars; the contract is for five hundred dollars.) 1 Story, Cont. 481.

QUOD NATURALIS RATIO INTER OMNES HOMINES CONSTITUIT, VOCATUR JUS GENTIUM. That which natural reason has established among all men is called the "law of nations." 1 Bl.Comm. 43; Dig. 1, 1, 9; Inst. 1, 2, 1.

QUOD NECESSARIE INTELLIGITUR NON DEEST. 1 Bulst. 71. That which is necessarily understood is not wanting.

QUOD NECESSITAS COGIT, DEFENDIT. Hale, P. C. 54. That which necessity compels, it justifies.

QUOD NON APPARET NON EST; ET NON APPARET JUDICIALITER ANTE JUDICIUM. 2 Inst. 479. That which appears not is not; and nothing appears judicially before judgment.

QUOD NON CAPIT CHRISTUS, CAPIT FISCUS. What Christ [the church] does not take the treasury takes. Goods of a *felo de se* go to the king. A maxim in old English law. Yearb. P. 19 Hen. VI. 1.

QUOD NON FUIT NEGATUM. Which was not denied. A phrase found in the old reports, signifying that an argument or proposition was not denied or controverted by the court. Latch, 213.

QUOD NON HABET PRINCIPIUM NON HABET FINEM. Wing. Max. 79; Co. Litt. 345*a*. That which has not beginning has not end.

QUOD NON LEGITUR, NON CREDITUR. What is not read is not believed. 4 Coke, 304.

QUOD NON VALET IN PRINCIPALI, IN ACCESSORIO SEU CONSEQUENTI NON VALEBIT; ET QUOD NON VALET IN MAGIS PROPINQUO NON VALEBIT IN MAGIS REMOTO. 8 Coke, 78. That which is not good against the principal will not be good as to accessories or consequences; and that which is not of force in regard to things near it will not be of force in regard to things remote from it.

QUOD NOTA. Which note; which mark. A reporter's note in the old books, directing attention to a point or rule. Dyer, 23.

QUOD NULLIUS ESSE POTEST ID UT ALICUJUS FIERET NULLA OBLIGATIO VALET EFFICERE. No agreement can avail to make that the property of any one which cannot be acquired as property. Dig. 50, 17, 182.

QUOD NULLIUS EST, EST DOMINI REGIS. That which is the property of nobody belongs to our lord the king. Fleta, lib. 1, c. 3; Broom, Max. 354.

QUOD NULLIUS EST, ID RATIONE NATURALI OCCUPANTI CONCEDITUR. That which is the property of no one is, by natural reason, given to the [first] occupant. Dig. 41, 1, 3; Inst. 2, 1, 12. Adopted in the common law. 2 Bl.Comm. 258.

QUOD NULLUM EST, NULLUM PRODUCIT EFFECTUM. That which is null produces no effect. Tray. Leg.Max. 519.

QUOD OMNES TANGIT AB OMNIBUS DEBET SUPPORTARI. That which touches or concerns all ought to be supported by all. 3 How.State Tr. 878, 1087.

QUOD PARTES REPLACITENT. That the parties do replead.

Judgment quod partes replacitent. A judgment for repleader which is given if an issue is formed on so immaterial a point that the court cannot know for whom to give judgment. The parties must then reconstruct their pleadings.

QUOD PARTITIO FIAT. That partition be made. The name of the judgment in a suit for partition, directing that a partition be effected.

QUOD PENDET NON EST PRO EO QUASI SIT. What is in suspense is considered as not existing during such suspense. Dig. 50, 17, 169, 1.

QUOD PER ME NON POSSUM, NEC PER ALIUM. What I cannot do by myself, I cannot by another. 4 Coke, 24*b*; 11 Coke, 87*a*.

QUOD PER RECORDUM PROBATUM, NON DEBET ESSE NEGATUM. What is proved by record ought not to be denied.

QUOD PERMITTAT. That he permit. In old English law. A writ which lay for the heir of him that was disseised of his common of pasture, against the heir of the disseisor. Cowell.

QUOD PERMITTAT PROSTERNERE. That he permit to abate. In old practice. A writ, in the nature of a writ of right, which lay to abate a nuisance. 3 Bl.Comm. 221. Conhocton Stone Road v. Buffalo, etc., R. Co., 51 N.Y. 579, 10 Am. Rep. 646.

QUOD PERSONA NEC PREBENDARII, etc. A writ which lay for spiritual persons, distrained in their spiritual possessions, for payment of a fifteenth with the rest of the parish. Fitzh. Nat. Brev. 175. Obsolete.

QUOD POPULUS POSTREMUM JUSSIT, ID JUS RATUM ESTO. What the people have last enacted, let that be the established law. A law of the Twelve Tables, the principle of which is still recognized. 1 Bl.Comm. 89.

QUOD PRIMUM EST INTENTIONE ULTIMUM EST IN OPERATIONE. That which is first in intention is last in operation. Bac.Max.

QUOD PRINCIPI PLACUIT, LEGIS HABET VIGOREM; UT POTE CUM LEGE REGIA, QUÆ DE IMPERIO EJUS LATA EST, POPULUS EI ET IN EUM OMNE SUUM IMPERIUM ET POTESTATEM CONFERAT. The will of the emperor has the force of law; for, by the royal law which has been made concerning his authority, the people have conferred upon him all its sovereignty and power. Dig. 1. 4. 1; Inst. 1. 2. 1; Fleta, l. 1, c. 17, § 7; Brac. 107; Selden, *Diss. ad Flet.* c. 3, § 2.

QUOD PRIUS EST VERIUS EST; ET QUOD PRIUS EST TEMPORE POTIUS EST JURE. Co.Litt. 347. What is first is true; and what is first in time is better in law.

QUOD PRO MINORE LICITUM EST ET PRO MAJORE LICITUM EST. 8 Coke, 43. That which is lawful as to the minor is lawful as to the major.

QUOD PROSTRAVIT. That he do abate. The name of a judgment upon an indictment for a nuisance, that the defendant abate such nuisance.

QUOD PURE DEBETUR PRÆSENTI DIE DEBETUR. That which is due unconditionally is due now. Tray. Leg. Max. 519.

QUOD QUIS EX CULPA SUA DAMNUM SENTIT NON INTELLIGITUR DAMNUM SENTIRE. The damage which one experiences from his own fault is not considered as his damage. Dig. 50, 17, 203.

QUOD QUIS SCIENS INDEBITUM DEBIT HAC MENTE, UT POSTEA REPETERET, REPETERE NON POTEST. That which one has given, knowing it not to be due, with the intention of redemanding it, he cannot recover back. Dig. 12, 6, 50.

QUOD QUISQUIS NORIT IN HOC SE EXERCEAT. Let every one employ himself in what he knows. 11 Coke, 10.

QUOD RECUPERET. That he recover. The ordinary form of judgments for the plaintiff in actions at law. 1 Archb.Pr.K.B. 225; 1 Burrill, Pr. 246.

Judgment of quod recuperet. When an issue in fact, or an issue in law arising on a peremptory plea, is determined for the plaintiff, the judgment is "that the plaintiff do recover," etc., which is called a judgment quod recuperet; Steph.Pl. 126. It is either final or interlocutory, according as the quantum of damages is or is not ascertained at the rendition of the judgment.

QUOD REMEDIO DESTITUITUR IPSA RE VALET SI CULPA ABSIT. That which is without remedy avails of itself, if there be no fault in the party seeking to enforce it. Broom, Max. 212.

QUOD SEMEL AUT BIS EXISTIT PRÆTERUNT LEGISLATORES. Legislators pass over what happens [only] once or twice. Dig. 1, 3, 6; Broom, Max. 46.

QUOD SEMEL MEUM EST AMPLIUS MEUM ESSE NON POTEST. Co. Litt. 49*b*. What is once mine cannot be more fully mine.

QUOD SEMEL PLACUIT IN ELECTIONE, AMPLIUS DISPLICERE NON POTEST. Co. Litt. 146. What a party has once determined, in a case where he has an election, cannot afterwards be disavowed.

QUOD SI CONTINGAT. That if it happen. Words by which a condition might formerly be created in a deed. Litt. § 330.

QUOD SOLO INÆDIFICATUR SOLO CEDIT. Whatever is built on the soil is an accessory of the soil. Inst. 2. 1. 29; 16 Mass. 449; 2 Bouv.Inst. n. 1571.

QUOD SUB CERTA FORMA CONCESSUM VEL RESERVATUM EST NON TRAHITUR AD VALOREM VEL COMPENSATIONEM. That which is granted or reserved under a certain form is not [permitted to be] drawn into valuation or compensation. Bac.Max. 26, reg. 4. That which is granted or reserved in a certain specified form must be taken as it is granted, and will not be permitted to be made the subject of any adjustment or compensation on the part of the grantee. Ex parte Miller, 2 Hill (N.Y.) 423.

QUOD SUBINTELLIGITUR NON DEEST. What is understood is not wanting. 2 Ld.Raym. 832.

QUOD TACITE INTELLIGITUR DEESSE NON VIDETUR. What is tacitly understood is not considered to be wanting. 4 Coke, 22*a*.

QUOD VANUM ET INUTILE EST, LEX NON REQUIRIT. Co.Litt. 319. The law requires not what is vain and useless.

QUOD VERO CONTRA RATIONEM JURIS RECEPTUM EST, NON EST PRODUCENDUM AD CONSEQUENTIAS. But that which has been admitted contrary to the reason of the law, ought not to be drawn into precedents. Dig. 1. 3. 14; Broom, Max. 158.

QUOD VIDE. Which see. A direction to the reader to look to another part of the book, or to another book, there named, for further information. Usually abbreviated "*q. v.*"

QUOD VOLUIT NON DIXIT. What he intended he did not say, or express. An answer sometimes made in overruling an argument that the law-maker or testator *meant* so and so. 1 Kent, Comm. 468, note; Mann v. Mann's Ex'rs, 1 Johns. Ch. (N.Y.) 235.

QUODCUNQUE ALIQUIS OB TUTELAM CORPORIS SUI FECERIT, JURE ID FECISSE VIDETUR. 2 Inst. 590. Whatever any one does in defense of his person, that he is considered to have done legally.

QUODQUE DISSOLVITUR EODEM MODO QUO LIGATUR. 2 Rolle, 39. In the same manner that a thing is bound, in the same manner it is unbound.

QUONIAM ATTACHIAMENTA. (Since the attachments.) One of the oldest books in the Scotch law. So called from the two first words of the volume. Jacob; Whishaw.

QUORUM. A majority of the entire body; *e. g.*, a quorum of a state supreme court. Mountain States Telephone & Telegraph Co. v. People, 68 Colo. 487, 190 P. 513, 517.

Such a number of the members of a body as is competent to transact business in the absence of the other members. Morton v. Talmadge, 166 Ga. 620, 144 S.E. 111.

The idea of a quorum is that, when that required number of persons goes into a session as a body, such as directors of a corporation, the votes of a majority thereof are sufficient for binding action. Benintendi v. Kenton Hotel, 294 N.Y. 112, 60 N.E.2d 829, 831.

When a committee, board of directors, meeting of shareholders, legislature or other body of persons cannot act unless a certain number at least of them are present, that number is called a "quorum." Sweet. In the absence of any law or rule fixing the quorum, it consists of a majority of those entitled to act. Ex parte Willcocks, 7 Cow. (N.Y.) 409, 17 Am.Dec. 525; Snider v. Rinehart, 18 Colo. 18, 31 P. 716; In re Webster Loose Leaf Filing Co., D.C. N.J., 240 F. 779, 784; Application of McGovern, 44 N.Y.S. 2d 132, 137, 180 Misc. 508.

Justices of the Quorum

In English law, those justices of the peace whose presence at a session is necessary to make a lawful bench. All the justices of the peace for a county are named and appointed in one commission, which authorizes them all, jointly and severally, to keep the peace, but provides that some particular named justices or one of them shall always be present when business is to be transacted, the ancient Latin phrase being "*quorum unum A. B. esse volumus.*" These designated persons are the "justices of the quorum." But the distinction is long since obsolete. 1 Bl.Comm. 351; Snider v. Rinehart, 18 Colo. 18, 31 P. 716.

QUORUM PRÆTEXTU NEC AUGET NEC MINUIT SENTENTIAM, SED TANTUM CONFIRMAT PRÆMISSA. Plowd. 52. "*Quorum prœtextu*" neither increases nor diminishes a sentence, but only confirms that which went before.

QUOT. In old Scotch law. A twentieth part of the movable estate of a person dying, which was due to the bishop of the diocese within which the person resided. Bell.

QUOTA. A proportional part or share, the proportional part of a demand or liability, falling upon each of those who are collectively responsible for the whole.

QUOTATION. The production to a court or judge of the exact language of a statute, precedent, or other authority, in support of an argument or proposition advanced.

The transcription of part of a literary composition into another book or writing.

A statement of the market price of one or more commodities; or the price specified to a correspondent.

QUOTIENS DUBIA INTERPRETATIO LIBERTATIS EST, SECUNDUM LIBERTATEM RESPONDENDUM ERIT. Whenever there is a doubt between liberty and slavery, the decision must be in favor of liberty. Dig. 50. 17. 20.

QUOTIENS IDEM SERMO DUAS SENTENTIAS EXPRIMIT, EA POTISSIMUM ACCIPIATUR, QUÆ REI GERENDÆ APTIOR EST. Whenever the same words express two meanings, that is to be taken which is the better fitted for carrying out the proposed end. Dig. 50. 17. 67.

QUOTIENT VERDICT. A money verdict the amount of which is fixed by the following process: Each juror writes down the sum he wishes to award by the verdict; these amounts are all added together, and the total is divided by twelve, (the number of the jurors,) and the quotient stands as the verdict of the jury by their agreement. Hamilton v. Owego Waterworks, 48 N.Y.S. 106, 22 App.Div. 573. Such verdict is invalid. Hoffman v. City of St. Paul, 187 Minn. 320, 245 N.W. 373, 374, 86 A.L.R. 198; Stone v. State, 24 Ala.App. 395, 135 So. 646, 647; Killion v. Dinklage, 121 Neb. 322, 236 N.W. 757, 759.

QUOTIES DUBIA INTERPRETATIO LIBERTATIS EST, SECUNDUM LIBERTATEM RESPONDENDUM ERIT. Whenever the interpretation of liberty is doubtful, the answer should be on the side of liberty. Dig. 50, 17, 20.

QUOTIES IDEM SERMO DUAS SENTENTIAS EXPRIMIT, EA POTISSIMUM EXCIPIATUR, QUÆ REI GERENDÆ APTIOR EST. Whenever the same language expresses two meanings that should be adopted which is the better fitted for carrying out the subject-matter. Dig. 50, 17, 67.

QUOTIES IN STIPULATIONIBUS AMBIGUA ORATIO EST, COMMODISSIMUM EST ID ACCIPI QUO RES DE QUA AGITUR IN TUTO SIT. Whenever the language of stipulations is ambiguous, it is most fitting that that [sense] should be taken by which the subject-matter may be protected. Dig. 45, 1, 80.

QUOTIES IN VERBIS NULLA EST AMBIGUITAS, IBI NULLA EXPOSITIO CONTRA VERBA FIENDA EST. Co. Litt. 147. When in the words there is no ambiguity, then no exposition contrary to the words is to be made.

QUOTUPLEX. Lat. Of how many kinds; how many fold. A term of frequent occurrence in Sheppard's Touchstone.

QUOUSQUE. Lat. How long; how far; until. In old conveyances it is used as a word of limitation. 10 Coke, 41.

QUOVIS MODO. Lat. In whatever manner.

QUUM DE LUCRO DUORUM QUÆRATUR, MELIOR EST CAUSA POSSIDENTIS. When the question is as to the gain of two persons, the title of the party in possession is the better one. Dig. 50, 17, 126, 2.

QUUM IN TESTAMENTO AMBIGUE AUT ETIAM PERPERAM SCRIPTUM EST, BENIGNE INTERPRETARI ET SECUNDUM ID QUOD CREDIBLE ET COGITATUM, CREDENDUM EST. When in a will an ambiguous or even an erroneous expression occurs, it should be construed liberally and in accordance with what is thought the probable meaning of the testator. Dig. 34, 5, 24; Broom, Max. 437.

QUUM PRINCIPALIS CAUSA NON CONSISTIT NE EA QUIDEM QUÆ SEQUUNTUR LOCUM HABENT. When the principal does not hold, the incidents thereof ought not to obtain. Broom, Max. 496.

QUUM QUOD AGO NON VALET UT AGO, VALEAT QUANTUM VALERE POTEST. 1 Vent. 216. When what I do is of no force as to the purpose for which I do it, let it be of force to as great a degree as it can.

R

R. In the signatures of royal persons, "R." is an abbreviation for *"rex"* (king) or *"regina"* (queen.) In descriptions of land, according to the divisions of the governmental survey, it stands for "range." Ottumwa, etc., R. Co. v. McWilliams, 71 Iowa 164, 32 N.W. 315; Simms v. Rolfe, 177 Ark. 52, 5 S.W.2d 718, 719.

R. E. A. Rural Electrification Administration.

R. G. An abbreviation for *Regula Generalis,* a general rule or order of court; or for the plural of the same.

R. L. This abbreviation may stand either for "Revised Laws" or "Roman law."

R. S. An abbreviation for "Revised Statutes."

RACE. An ethnical stock; a great division of mankind having in common certain distinguishing physical peculiarities constituting a comprehensive class appearing to be derived from a distinct primitive source. A tribal or national stock, a division or subdivision of one of the great racial stocks of mankind distinguished by minor peculiarities. Descent. In re Halladjian, C.C.Mass., 174 F. 834; Ex parte (Ng.) Fung Sing, D.C.Wash., 6 F.2d 670.

RACE-WAY. An artificial canal dug in the earth; a channel cut in the ground. Wilder v. De Cou, 26 Minn. 17, 1 N.W. 48. The channel for the current that drives a waterwheel. Webster.

RACHAT. In French law. The right of repurchase which, in English and American law, the vendor may reserve to himself. It is also called *"réméré."* Brown.

RACHATER. L. Fr. To redeem; to repurchase, (or buy back.) Kelham.

RACHETUM. In Scotch law. Ransom; corresponding to Saxon *"weregild,"* a pecuniary composition for an offense. Skene; Jacob.

RACHIMBURGII. In the legal polity of the Salians and Ripuarians and other Germanic peoples, the name given to the judges or assessors who sat with the count in his *mallum,* (court,) and were generally associated with him in other matters. Spelman.

RACING TIP. A false assumption of vaticination concerning the result of a speed contest between animals justly termed thoroughbred. Armstrong Racing Publications v. Moss, 43 N.Y.S.2d 171, 173, 181 Misc. 966.

RACK. An engine of torture anciently used in the inquisitorial method of examining persons charged with crime, the office of which was to break the limbs or dislocate the joints.

RACK-RENT. A rent of the full value of the tenement, or near it. 2 Bl.Comm. 43.

RACK-VINTAGE. Wines drawn from the lees. Cowell.

RACKET. Engaging in an operation to make money illegitimately, implying continuity of behavior. Bradley v. Conners, 7 N.Y.S.2d 294, 295, 169 Misc. 442.

RACKETEER. A person who makes money by violations of the Penal Law, particularly those violations accompanied by violence. Continental Bank & Trust Co. of New York v. 200 Madison Avenue Corporation, Sup., 43 N.Y.S.2d 402, 407.

RACKETEERING. An organized conspiracy to commit the crimes of extortion or coercion, or attempts to commit extortion or coercion. From the standpoint of extortion, it is the obtaining of money or property from another, with his consent, induced by the wrongful use of force or fear. The fear which constitutes the legally necessary element in extortion is induced by oral or written threats to do an unlawful injury to the property of the threatened person by means of explosives, fire, or otherwise; and to kill, kidnap, or injure him or a relative of his or some member of his family. From the standpoint of coercion, it usually takes the form of compelling by use of similar threats to person or property a person to do or abstain from doing an act which such other person has the legal right to do or abstain from doing, such as joining a so-called protective association to protect his right to conduct a business or trade. United States v. McGlone, D.C. Pa., 19 F.Supp. 285, 287.

RADICALS. A political party. The term arose in England, in 1818, when the popular leaders, Hunt, Cartwright, and others, sought to obtain a radical reform in the representative system of parliament. Bolingbroke (Disc. Parties, Let. 18) employs the term in its present accepted sense: "Such a remedy might have wrought a *radical* cure of the evil that threatens our constitution," etc. Wharton.

RADIUS. A straight line drawn from the centre of a circle to any point of the circumference. Its length is half the diameter of that circle, or is the space between the centre and the circumference. State v. Berard, 40 La.App. 174, 3 So. 463.

RADOUR. In French law. A term including the repairs made to a ship, and a fresh supply of furniture and victuals, munitions, and other provisions required for the voyage. Pardessus, n. 602.

RAFFLE. A kind of lottery in which several persons pay, in shares, the value of something put up as a stake, and then determine by chance (as by casting dice) which one of them shall become the sole possessor of it. Webster; Prendergast v. State, 41 Tex.Cr.R. 358, 57 S.W. 850. People v. American Art Union, 7 N.Y. 241.

RAGEMAN. A statute, so called, of justices assigned by Edward I. and his council, to go a circuit through all England, and to hear and determine all complaints of injuries done within five years next before Michaelmas, in the fourth year of his reign. Spelman. Also a rule, form, regimen, or precedent.

RAGMAN'S ROLL, or RAGIMUND'S ROLL. A roll, called from one Ragimund or Ragimont, a legate in Scotland, who, summoning all the beneficed clergymen in that kingdom, caused them on oath to give in the true value of their benefices, according to which they were afterwards taxed by the court of Rome. Wharton.

RAIL CHAIR. A device used where the ends of rails come together; it holds the separate rails firmly together and in alignment and so gives them the effect of being one continuous rail. Railroad Supply Co. v. Hart Steel Co., C.C.A.Ill., 222 F. 261, 269.

RAILROAD, *v.* With respect to legislation, to force through legislation over the objection of a minority. Roane v. Columbian Pub. Co., 126 Wash. 416, 218 P. 213, 214.

RAILROAD, *n.* A road or way on which iron or steel rails are laid for wheels to run on, for the conveyance of heavy loads in cars or carriages propelled by steam or other motive power; a road or way on which iron rails are laid for transportation purposes, as incident to the possession or ownership of which important franchises and rights affecting the public are attached. A railway. New Deemer Mfg. Co. v. Kilpatrick, 129 Miss. 268, 92 So. 71, 73; Muskogee Electric Traction Co. v. Doering, 70 Okl. 21, 172 P. 793, 794, 2 A.L.R. 94. An enterprise created and operated to carry on a fixed track passengers and freight, or passengers or freight, for rates or tolls, without discrimination as to those who demand transportation. Bradley v. Degnon Contracting Co., 224 N.Y. 60, 120 N.E. 89, 91. In a strictly accurate sense, it is a generic term, and includes all kinds of railroads, whether street railways, horse car lines, cable car lines, electric trolley lines, suburban lines, interurban lines, or steam railroads engaged in general transportation. In re Columbia Ry., Gas & Electric Co., D.C.S.C., 24 F.2d 828, 831.

The term "railroad" or "railway" may in a broad sense include all structures which are necessary to operation of railroad. Smith v. Northern Pac. Ry. Co., 50 Mont. 539, 148 P. 393, 394.

Whether or not "railroad" includes roads operated by horse-power, electricity, cable-lines, etc., will generally depend upon the context of the statute in which it is found. The decisions on this point are at variance. Frisco Lumber Co. v. Spivey, 40 Okl. 633, 140 P. 157, 158; Morgan v. Grande Ronde Lumber Co., 76 Or. 440, 148 P. 1122, 1123.

If scope of a statute relating to railroads shows that both railroads and street railroads were within the legislative contemplation, the word "railroad" will include street railroads; but, if act was aimed at railroads proper, street railroads are excluded from its provisions. In re Columbia Ry., Gas & Electric Co., D.C.S.C., 24 F.2d 828, 831.

Railroad is usually limited to roads for heavy steam transportation and also to steam roads partially or wholly electrified or roads for heavy traffic designed originally for electric traction. The lighter electric street-car lines and the like are usually termed *railways*. In Great Britain and the British colonies, except Canada, all such roads, whether for heavy or light traffic, are usually called *railways*. Webster, Dict.

See, also, Railway.

Branch Railroad

A road connected with the main line, not as a mere incident thereto, to facilitate the business of the main line, but to do a business of its own by transporting persons and property to and from places not reached by the main line. Illinois Cent. R. Co. v. East Sioux Falls Quarry Co., 33 S.D. 63, 144 N.W. 724, 726.

Railroad Car

Any vehicle constructed for operation over railroad tracks. State v. Tardiff, 111 Me. 552, 90 A. 424, L.R.A.1915A, 817.

Railroad Commission

A body of commissioners, appointed in several of the states, to regulate railway traffic within the state, with power, generally, to regulate and fix rates, see to the enforcement of police ordinances, and sometimes assess the property of railroads for taxation. Southern Pac. Co. v. Board of Railroad Com'rs, C.C.Cal., 78 F. 236, 252.

Railroad Company

A company which is principally engaged in operating a railroad. Crowley v. Polleys Lumber Co., 92 Mont. 27, 9 P.2d 1068, 1070.

Railroad Division

A unit of management established for convenience in operation. Day v. Louisville & N. R. Co., 295 Ky. 679, 175 S.W.2d 347, 349.

Railroad Line

A regular line of railroad vehicles for public use operating between distant points or between different cities. Bruce Transfer Co. v. Johnston, 227 Iowa 50, 287 N.W. 278, 280.

Railroad Property

The property which is essential to a railroad company to enable it to discharge its functions and duties as a common carrier by rail. It includes the road bed, right of way, tracks, bridges, stations, rolling stock, and such like property. Northern Pac. R. Co. v. Walker, C.C.N.D., 47 F. 681.

Railroad Relief Funds

A term applied to funds raised by periodical contributions of corporation employees, or by them jointly with the corporation, for the purpose of providing relief to the employees in case of injury, and the payment of money to their families in case of death, in the service.

RAILWAY. In law, this term is usually of exactly equivalent import to "railroad" (*q. v.*). State v. Brin, 30 Minn. 522, 16 N.W. 406; Millvale

Borough v. Evergreen Ry. Co., 131 Pa. 1, 18 A. 993, 7 L.R.A. 369.

Interurban Railways

A sort of hybrid, having in some respects the characteristics of the ordinary railroad and in others those of the street railroad. Within the limits of the cities which they enter, they usually pass along the streets, and perform the ordinary functions of street railroads, stopping where desired to let passengers on or off, and serving the public need for local street travel. Outside the cities, on their way from one city or town to another, they frequently travel upon a roadway obtained from private persons, not upon a public road, and stop, as in case of ordinary railroads, only at stations established by them for that purpose. They also often convey freight as well as passengers. San Francisco and S. M. Electric Ry. Co. v. Scott, 142 Cal. 222, 75 P. 575, 576, 583.

Railway Commissioners

A body of three commissioners appointed under the English regulation of railways act, 1873, principally to enforce the provisions of the railway and canal traffic act, 1854, by compelling railway and canal companies to give reasonable facilities for traffic, to abstain from giving unreasonable preference to any company or person, and to forward through traffic at through rates. They also have the supervision of working agreements between companies. Sweet.

Railway Depot

A station at which trains stop for transaction of ordinary business of railroad company, the receiving and delivering of freight and passengers. Brenner v. Amrine, 151 Kan. 788, 100 P.2d 688, 690.

Street Railway

One constructed and operated on or along the streets of a city or town to carry persons from one point to another in such city or town, or to and from its suburbs. It is peculiarly to accommodate people in cities and towns; its tracks are ordinarily laid to conform to street grades, its cars run at short intervals, stopping at street crossings to receive and discharge passengers, and its business is confined to the carriage of passengers and not freight. Muskogee Electric Traction Co. v. Doehring, 70 Okl. 21, 172 P. 793, 795, 2 A.L.R. 94. An enterprise created and operated to carry on a fixed track passengers and freight, or passengers or freight, for rates or tolls, without discrimination as to those who demand transportation. Bradley v. Degnon Contracting Co., 224 N.Y. 60, 120 N.E. 89, 91. The term "street railroad" is used interchangeably with "street railway." Metropolitan West Side Electric Ry. Co. v. City of Chicago, 261 Ill. 624, 104 N.E. 165, 167. The term is sometimes distinguished from "railway," meaning one of those larger institutions employed in general freight and passenger traffic from one city, town, or place to another, and usually denominated "commercial railways," while a "street railway" is built upon streets and avenues for the accommodation of street traffic. Anhalt v. Waterloo, C. F. & N. Ry. Co., 166 Iowa 479, 147 N.W. 928, 931. See Railroad. "Street railway" may include both urban and interurban lines. City of Milwaukee v. Railroad Commission of Wisconsin, 169 Wis. 559, 173 N.W. 329, 330. See, also, Interurban Railways.

Trunk Railway

A commercial railway connecting towns, cities, counties, or other points within the state or in different states, which has the legal capacity, under its charter or the general law, of constructing, purchasing, and operating branch lines or feeders connecting with its main stem or trunk; the main or trunk line bearing the same relation to its branches that the trunk of a tree bears to its branches, or the main stream of a river to its tributaries. Oregon, C. & E. Ry. Co. v. Blackmer, 154 Or. 388, 59 P.2d 694, 696.

RAIN-WATER. The water which naturally falls from the clouds.

RAINY DAYS. Where a charter party (a cargo of wheat) provided that rainy days should not be counted as lay days, it excludes only rainy days on which, with reference to the facilities of the port in the way of covered docks, etc., the cargo could not be safely landed. Kerr v. Schwaner, 101 C.C.A. 285, 177 F. 659.

RAISE. To create; to infer; to create or bring to light by construction or interpretation. To cause or procure to be produced, bred or propagated. To bring together; to get together or obtain for use or service; to gather; to collect; to levy; as to raise money to raise an army. Town of Amherst v. Erie County, 256 N.Y.S. 785, 143 Misc. 540; Miller Hatcheries v. Boyer, C.C.A. Iowa, 131 F.2d 283, 287.

RAISE A PRESUMPTION. To give occasion or ground for a presumption; to be of such a character, or to be attended with such circumstances, as to justify an inference or presumption of law. Thus, a person's silence, in some instances, will "raise a presumption" of his consent to what is done.

RAISE AN ISSUE. To bring pleadings to an issue; to have the effect of producing an issue between the parties pleading in an action.

RAISE REVENUE. To levy a tax, as a means of collecting revenue; to bring together, collect, or levy revenue. The phrase does not imply an increase of revenue. Perry County v. Selma, etc., R. Co., 58 Ala. 557.

RAISING A PROMISE. The act of the law in extracting from the facts and circumstances of a particular transaction a promise which was implicit therein, and postulating it as a ground of legal liability.

RAISING A USE. Creating, establishing, or calling into existence a use. Thus, if a man conveyed land to another in fee, without any consideration, equity would presume that he meant it to be to the use of himself, and would, therefore, raise an implied use for his benefit. Brown.

RAISING AN ACTION, in Scotland, is the institution of an action or suit.

RAISING MONEY. Realizing money by subscription, loan, or otherwise. New York & R. Cement Co. v. Davis, 173 N.Y. 235, 66 N.E. 9; New London Literary Inst. v. Prescott, 40 N.H. 333.

RAISING PORTIONS. When a landed estate is settled on an eldest son, it is generally burdened with the payment of specific sums of money in favor of his brothers and sisters. A direction to this effect is called a direction for "raising portions for younger children;" and, for this purpose, it is usual to demise or lease the estate to trustees for a term of years, upon trust to raise the required portions by a sale or mortgage of the same. Mozley & Whitley.

RAN. Sax. In Saxon and old English law. Open theft, or robbery.

RANCHO. Sp. A small collection of men or their dwellings; a hamlet. As used, however, in Mexico and in the Spanish law formerly prevailing in California, the term signifies a ranch or large tract of land suitable for grazing purposes where horses or cattle are raised, and is distinguished from *hacienda,* a cultivated farm or plantation.

RANCID. Having a rank smell or taste from chemical change or decomposition. Spry v. Kiser, 179 N.C. 417, 102 S.E. 708, 709.

RAND, or RAND LIFT. In the nomenclature of the art of building heels, the cup-shaped piece attached to the top of the heel, fitting it to the heel seat of the shoe. Brockton Heel Co. v. International Shoe Co., D.C.N.H., 19 F.2d 145.

RANGE, *v.* To have or extend in certain direction, to correspond in direction or line, or to trend or run. Lilly v. Marcum, 214 Ky. 514, 283 S.W. 1059, 1060.

RANGE, *n.* In the government survey of the United States, one of the divisions of a state, a row or tier of townships as they appear on the map.

A tract or district of land within which domestic animals in large numbers range for subsistence; an extensive grazing ground. The term is used on the great plains of the United States to designate a tract commonly of many square miles occupied by one or different proprietors and distinctively called a cattle range, stock range, or sheep range. The animals on a range are usually left to take care of themselves during the whole year without shelter, except when periodically gathered in a round-up for counting and selection, and for branding, when the herds of several proprietors run together. State v. Omaechevviaria, 27 Idaho, 797, 152 P. 280, 282; Missoula Trust & Savings Bank v. Northern Pac. Ry. Co., 76 Mont. 201, 245 P. 949, 951.

RANGER. In forest law. A sworn officer of the forest, whose office chiefly consists in three points: To walk daily through his charge to see, hear, and inquire as well of trespasses as trespassers in his bailiwick; to drive the beasts of the forest, both of venery and chace, out of the deafforested into the forested lands; and to present all trespassers of the forest at the next courts holden for the forest. Cowell.

RANK, *n.* Grade of official standing. The order or place in which certain officers are placed in the army and navy, in relation to others. Wood v. U. S., 15 Ct.Cl. 158.

Rank is often used to express something different from *office.* It then becomes a designation or title of honor, dignity, or distinction conferred upon an officer in order to fix his relative position in reference to other officers in matters of privilege, precedence, and sometimes of command, or by which to determine his pay and emoluments. This is the case with the staff officers of the army. Wood v. U. S., 15 Ct.Cl. 159.

RANK, *adj.* In English law. Excessive; too large in amount; as a *rank modus.* 2 Bl.Comm. 30.

RANKING OF CREDITORS. The Scotch term for the arrangement of the property of a debtor according to the claims of the creditors, in consequence of the nature of their respective securities. Bell. The corresponding process in England is the marshalling of securities in a suit or action for redemption or foreclosure. Paterson.

RANSOM. The money, price, or consideration paid or demanded for redemption of a captured person or persons, a payment that releases from captivity. Acts 1933, c. 16063. Keith v. State, 120 Fla. 847, 163 So. 136.

In international law. The redemption of captured property from the hands of an enemy, particularly of property captured at sea. 1 Kent, Comm. 104. A sum paid or agreed to be paid for the redemption of captured property. 1 Kent, Comm. 105.

Strictly speaking, not a recapture of the captured property. It is rather a purchase of the right of the captors at the time, be it what it may; or, more properly, it is a relinquishment of all the interest and benefit which the captors might acquire or consummate in the property, by a regular adjudication of a prize tribunal, whether it be an interest *in rem,* a lien, or a mere title to expenses. In this respect, there seems to be no difference between the case of a ransom of an enemy or a neutral. Maisonnaire v. Keating, 2 Gall. 325, Fed.Cas.No.8,978.

In old English law. A sum of money paid for the pardoning of some great offense. The distinction between ransom and amerciament is said to be that ransom was the redemption of a corporal punishment, while amerciament was a fine or penalty directly imposed, and not in lieu of another punishment. Cowell; 4 Bl.Comm. 380; U. S. v. Griffin, 6 D.C. 57. A sum of money paid for the redemption of a person from captivity or imprisonment. Thus one of the feudal "aids" was to ransom the lord's person if taken prisoner. 2 Bl.Comm. 63.

RANSOM BILL. A contract by which a captured vessel, in consideration of her release and of safe-conduct for a stipulated course and time, agrees to pay a certain sum as ransom.

RAPE. In criminal law. The unlawful carnal knowledge of a woman by a man forcibly and against her will. Gore v. State, 119 Ga. 418, 46 S.E. 671, 100 Am.St.Rep. 182; People v. Cieslak, 319 Ill. 221, 149 N.E. 815, 816. State ex rel. Moffitt v. Zupnik, Ohio App., 50 N.E.2d 427, 429. That is, without her consent and against her utmost resistance. State v. Cottengim, Mo., 12 S.W.2d 53, 57.

Hence, if she consent to the sexual intercourse, although that consent may be reluctantly given, and although there may be some force used to obtain her consent, the offense cannot be "rape." Opposition to the sexual act by mere words is not sufficient. Welch v. State, 58 Ga.App. 447, 198 S.E. 810, 811. While slightest penetration is sufficient, it must be shown that private parts of male entered at least to some extent in those of female, and emission without penetration is insufficient. Kitchen v. State, 61 Okl.Cr. 435, 69 P.2d 411, 415.

Under modern statutes which often materially change the common-law definition and create an offense commonly known as "statutory rape," where the offense consists in having sexual intercourse with a female under statutory age, the offense may be either with or without the female's consent. State v. Ellison, 19 N.M. 428, 144 P. 10, 13.

In English law. An intermediate division between a shire and a hundred; or a division of a county, containing several hundreds. 1 Bl.Comm. 116; Cowell. Apparently peculiar to the county of Sussex. See, however, *Lath.*

RAPE OF THE FOREST. In old English law. Trespass committed in a forest by violence. Cowell.

RAPE-REEVE. In English law. The chief officer of a rape, (*q. v.*). 1 Bl.Comm. 116.

RAPINE. The felonious taking of another man's personal property, openly and by violence, against his will.

In the civil law, *rapina* is defined as the forcible and violent taking of another man's movable property with the criminal intent to appropriate it to the robber's own use. A prætorian action lay for this offense, in which quadruple damages were recoverable. Gaius, lib. 3, § 209; Inst. 4, 2; Mackeld. Rom. Law, § 481; Heinecc. Elem. § 1071.

RAPPORT À SUCCESSION. In French law and in Louisiana. A proceeding similar to hotchpot; the restoration to the succession of such property as the heir may have received by way of advancement from the decedent, in order that an even division may be made among all the co-heirs. Civ.Code La. art. 1227.

RAPTOR. In old English law. A ravisher. Fleta, lib. 2, c. 52, § 12.

RAPTU HÆREDIS. In old English law. A writ for taking away an heir holding in socage, of which there were two sorts: One when the heir was married; the other when he was not. Reg. Orig. 163.

RAPUIT. Lat. In old English law. Ravished. A technical word in old indictments. 2 East, 30.

RASURE. The act of scraping, scratching, or shaving the surface of a written instrument, for the purpose of removing certain letters or words from it. It is to be distinguished from "obliteration," as the latter word properly denotes the crossing out of a word or letter by drawing a line through it with ink. But the two expressions are often used interchangeably. Penny v. Corwithe, 18 Johns., N.Y. 499.

RASUS. In old English law. A rase; a measure of onions, containing twenty flones, and each flonis twenty-five heads. Fleta, lib. 2, c. 12, § 12.

RATABLE. Proportional; proportionately rated upon a constant ratio adjusted to due relation. Glucksman v. Board of Education of City of New York, Mun.Ct., 164 N.Y.S. 351, 359. According to a measure which fixes proportions. It has no meaning unless referable to some rule or standard, and never means equality or equal division but implies unequal division as between different persons. Chenoweth v. Nordan & Morris, Tex. Civ.App., 171 S.W.2d 386, 387.

RATABLE ESTATE OR PROPERTY. Property in its quality and nature capable of being rated, *i. e.* appraised, assessed. 10 B. & S. 323; Coventry Co. v. Assessors, 16 R.I. 240, 14 A. 877; Burdick v. Pendleton, 46 R.I. 125, 125 A. 278, 279. Taxable estate; the real and personal property which the legislature designates as "taxable." Marshfield v. Middlesex, 55 Vt. 546.

RATAM REM HABERE. Lat. In the civil law. To hold a thing ratified; to ratify or confirm it. Dig. 46, 8, 12, 1.

RATE. Proportional or relative value, measure, or degree; the proportion or standard by which quantity or value is adjusted. Shropshire v. Commerce Farm Credit Co., Tex.Civ.App., 266 S.W. 612, 614.

Thus, the *rate* of interest is the proportion or ratio between the principal and interest. So the buildings in a town are *rated* for insurance purposes; *i. e.*, classified and individually estimated with reference to their insurable qualities. In this sense also we speak of articles as being in "first-rate" or "second-rate" condition.

A fixed relation of quantity, amount or degree; also, a charge, valuation, payment or price fixed according to ratio, scale or standard; comparative price or amount of demands. E. C. Miller Cedar Lumber Co. v. United States, Cust. & Pat.App., 86 F.2d 429, 434. Webster.

Thus, we speak of the *rate* at which public lands are sold, *rates* of fare upon railroads, etc. Georgia R. & B. Co. v. Maddox, 116 Ga. 64, 42 S.E. 315; Naylor v. Board of Education of Fulton County, 216 Ky. 766, 288 S.W. 690, 692.

In connection with public utilities, a charge to the public for a service open to all and upon the same terms. State v. Spokane & I. E. R. Co., 89 Wash. 599, 154 P. 1110, 1113, L.R.A.1918C, 675;

City of Detroit v. Public Utilities Commission, 288 Mich. 267, 286 N.W. 368, 373.

As used in the interstate commerce law, it means the net cost to the shipper of the transportation of his property; that is to say, the net amount the carrier receives from the shipper and retains. Elliott v. Empire Natural Gas Co., 123 Kan. 558, 256 P. 114, 117. Great Northern Ry. Co. v. Armour & Co., D.C.Ill., 26 F.Supp. 964, 967.

The term is also used as the synonym of "tax;" that is, a sum assessed by governmental authority upon persons or property, by proportional valuation, for public purposes. It is chiefly employed in this sense in England, but is there usually confined to taxes of a local nature, or those raised by the parish; such as the poor-rate, borough rate, etc.

It sometimes occurs in a connection which gives it a meaning synonymous with "assessment;" that is, the apportionment of a tax among the whole number of persons who are responsible for it, by estimating the value of the taxable property of each, and making a proportional distribution of the whole amount. Thus we speak of "rating" persons and property.

In marine insurance, the term refers to the classification or scaling of vessels based on their relative state and condition in regard to insurable qualities; thus, a vessel in the best possible condition and offering the best risk from the underwriter's standpoint, is "rated" as "A 1." Insurance Companies v. Wright, 1 Wall. 472, 17 L.Ed. 505.

Class Rate

A single rate applying to the transportation of a number of articles of the same general character. Norfolk Southern R. Co. v. Freeman Supply Corporation, 145 Va. 207, 133 S.E. 817, 818.

Commodity Rate

A rate which applies to the transportation of a specific commodity alone. Norfolk Southern R. Co. v. Freeman Supply Corporation, 145 Va. 207, 133 S.E. 817, 818.

Joint Rate

As applied to railroads, a rate prescribed to be charged for the transportation of goods or passengers over the connecting lines of two or more railroads, and to be divided among them for the service rendered by each respectively. Southern Bell Telephone & Telegraph Co. v. Railroad Commission of Georgia, D.C.Ga., 274 F. 438, 441.

Rate of Exchange

In commercial law. The actual price at which a bill, drawn in one country upon another country, can be bought or obtained in the former country at any given time. Story, Bills, § 31.

Rate Tariff

Statement by carrier to possible shippers that it will furnish certain services under certain conditions for certain price. Union Wire Rope Corporation v. Atchison, T. & S. F. Ry. Co., C.C.A.Mo., 66 F.2d 965, 966.

Rate-tithe

In English law. When any sheep, or other cattle, are kept in a parish for less time than a year, the owner must pay tithe for them *pro rata*, according to the custom of the place. Fitzh.Nat. Brev. 51.

RATIFICATION. In a broad sense, the confirmation of a previous act done either by the party himself or by another; confirmation of a voidable act. Story, Ag. §§ 250, 251; 2 Kent, Comm. 237; Norton v. Shelby County, 6 S.Ct. 1121, 118 U.S. 425, 30 L.Ed. 178; Gallup v. Fox, 30 A. 756, 64 Conn. 491. The affirmance by a person of a prior act which did not bind him, but which was done or professedly done on his account, whereby the act, as to some or all persons, is given effect as if originally authorized by him. Goldfarb v. Reicher, 112 N.J.L. 413, 171 A. 149, 151; The adoption by one, as binding upon himself, of an act done in such relations that he may claim it as done for his benefit, although done under such circumstances as would not bind him except for his subsequent assent. Samstag & Hilder Bros. v. Ottenheimer & Weil, 90 Conn. 475, 97 A. 865, 867; It is equivalent to a previous authorization and relates back to time when act ratified was done, except where intervening rights of third persons are concerned. Petray v. First Nat. Bank, 92 Cal.App. 86, 267 P. 711, 713.

In the law of principal and agent, the adoption and confirmation by one person with knowledge of all material facts, of an act or contract performed or entered into in his behalf by another who at the time assumed without authority to act as his agent. Maryland Casualty Co. v. First State Bank of Dewar, 101 Okl. 71, 223 P. 701, 705; Gould v. Maine Farmers' Mut. Fire Ins. Co., 114 Me. 416, 96 A. 732, 734, L.R.A.1917A, 604.

Ratification of transaction involves same elements as making of new contract, and understanding of material facts necessary to an intelligent assent is essential to "ratification." State ex rel. Robertson v. Johnson County Bank, 18 Tenn.App. 232, 74 S.W.2d 1084, 1087.

Essence of "ratification" by principal of act of agent is manifestation of mental determination by principal to affirm the act, and this may be manifested by written word or by spoken word or by conduct, or may be inferred from known circumstances and principal's acts in relation thereto. Miller v. Chatsworth Sav. Bank, 203 Iowa, 411, 212 N.W. 722, 724.

To constitute ratification of voidable contract the act relied on must be performed with full knowledge of its consequences and with an express intention of ratifying what is known to be voidable. Coe v. Moon, 260 Ill. 76, 102 N.E. 1074, 1076; Fletcher v. A. W. Koch Co., Tex.Civ.App., 189 S.W. 501, 503.

Express ratifications are those made in express and direct terms of assent. *Implied* ratifications are such as the law presumes from the acts of the principal.

Estoppel and ratification distinguished. See Estoppel.

RATIFY. To approve and sanction; to make valid; to confirm; to give sanction to. Short v. Metz Co., 165 Ky. 319, 176 S.W. 1144, 1149; Farmers' Co-op. Exch. Co. of Good Thunder v. Fidelity & Deposit Co. of Maryland, 149 Minn. 171, 182 N.W. 1008, 1009.

Though sometimes used synonymously, from a strictly lexical standpoint, the word "adopt" should be used to apply to void transactions, while the word "ratify" should be limited to the final approval of a voidable transaction by one who theretofore had the optional right to relieve himself from its obligations. Cosden Oil & Gas Co. v. Hendrickson, 96 Okl. 206, 221 P. 86, 89.

RATIHABITIO. Lat. Confirmation, agreement, consent, approbation of a contract. Saltmarsh v. Candia, 51 N.H. 76.

RATIHABITIO MANDATO ÆQUIPARATUR. Ratification is equivalent to express command. Dig. 46, 3, 12, 4; Broom, Max. 867; Palmer v. Yates, 3 Sandf. (N.Y.) 151.

RATIO. Rate; proportion; degree. Reason, or understanding. Also a cause, or giving judgment therein.

RATIO DECIDENDI. The ground of decision. The point in a case which determines the judgment.

RATIO EST FORMALIS CAUSA CONSUETUDINIS. Reason is the formal cause of custom.

RATIO EST LEGIS ANIMA; MUTATA LEGIS RATIONE MUTATUR ET LEX. 7 Coke, 7. Reason is the soul of law; the reason of law being changed the law is also changed.

RATIO EST RADIUS DIVINI LUMINIS. Co. Litt. 232. Reason is a ray of the divine light.

RATIO ET AUCTORITAS, DUO CLARISSIMA MUNDI LUMINA. 4 Inst. 320. Reason and authority, the two brightest lights of the world.

RATIO IN JURE ÆQUITAS INTEGRA. Reason in law is perfect equity.

RATIO LEGIS. The reason or occasion of a law; the occasion of making a law. Bl.Law Tracts, 3.

RATIO LEGIS EST ANIMA LEGIS. Jenk.Cent. 45. The reason of law is the soul of law.

RATIO NON CLAUDITUR LOCO. Reason is not confined to any place.

RATIO POTEST ALLEGARI DEFICIENTE LEGE; SED RATIO VERA ET LEGALIS, ET NON APPARENS. Co. Litt. 191. Reason may be alleged when law is defective; but it must be true and legal reason, and not merely apparent.

RATIONABILE ESTOVERIUM. A Latin phrase equivalent to "alimony."

RATIONABILI PARTE BONORUM. A writ that lay for the wife against the executors of her husband, to have the third part of his goods after his just debts and funeral expenses had been paid. Fitzh.Nat.Brev. 122.

RATIONAL DOUBT. A doubt based upon reasonable inferences such as are ordinarily drawn by ordinary men in the light of their experiences in ordinary life. Hicks v. State, 66 Ga.App. 577, 18 S.E.2d 637, 640, 66 Ga.App. 577.

RATIONALIBUS DIVISIS. An abolished writ which lay where two lords, in divers towns, had seigniories adjoining, for him who found his waste by little and little to have been encroached upon, against the other, who had encroached, thereby to rectify their bounds. Cowell.

RATIONE IMPOTENTIÆ. Lat. On account of inability. A ground of qualified property in some animals *feræ naturæ*; as in the young ones, while they are unable to fly or run. 2 Bl.Comm. 3, 4.

RATIONE MATERIÆ. Lat. By reason of the matter involved; in consequence of, or from the nature of, the subject-matter.

RATIONE PERSONÆ. Lat. By reason of the person concerned; from the character of the person.

RATIONE PRIVILEGII. Lat. This term describes a species of property in wild animals, which consists in the right which, by a peculiar franchise anciently granted by the English crown, by virtue of its prerogative, one man may have of killing and taking such animals on the land of another. 106 E. C. L. 870.

RATIONE SOLI. Lat. On account of the soil; with reference to the soil. Said to be the ground of ownership in bees. 2 Bl. Comm. 393.

RATIONE TENURÆ. L. Lat. By reason of tenure; as a consequence of tenure. 3 Bl. Comm. 230.

RATIONES. In old law. The pleadings in a suit. *Rationes exercere*, or *ad rationes stare*, to plead.

RATTENING. The offense on the part of members of a trade union, of causing the tools, clothes, or other property of a workman to be taken away or hidden, in order to compel him to join the union or cease working. It is, in England, an offense punishable by fine or imprisonment. 38 & 39 Vict. c. 86, § 7. Sweet.

RAVINE. A long, deep, and narrow hollow, worn by a stream or torrent of water; a long, deep, and narrow hollow or pass through the mountains. Long v. Boone Co., 36 Iowa 60.

RAVISH. To have carnal knowledge of a woman by force and against her will; to rape. State v. Heyer, 89 N.J.L. 187, 98 A. 413, 414, Ann.Cas.1918 D, 284.

RAVISHED. In criminal practice. A material word in indictments for rape. Whart. Crim.Law, § 401.

RAVISHER. One who has carnal knowledge of a woman by force and against her consent. Hart v. State, 144 Tex.Cr.R. 161, 161 S.W.2d 791, 793.

RAVISHMENT. In criminal law. An unlawful taking of a woman, or of an heir in ward. Rape, which see.

RAVISHMENT DE GARD. L. Fr. An abolished writ which lay for a guardian by knight's service or in socage, against a person who took from him the body of his ward. Fitzh. Nat. Brev. 140; 12 Car. II. c. 3.

RAVISHMENT OF WARD. In English law. The marriage of an infant ward without the consent of the guardian.

RAW. Not cooked, or refined. Fleming v. Farmers Peanut Co., C.C.A.Ga., 128 F.2d 404, 407.

RAW FRUITS. Fruits which are in their natural state, or so nearly in that condition that they retain substantially unimpaired qualities and characteristics of the fruit as it came from the tree. U. S. v. Meyer Co., 12 Ct.Cust.App. 124, 125.

RAW MATERIAL. As used in definitions of "manufacture," denotes merely material from which final product is made, not necessarily material in its natural state. State v. Hennessy Co., 71 Mont. 301, 230 P. 64, 65.

When raw material is converted into a finished product complete and ready for the final use intended, it ceases to be "raw material". Stearns Coal & Lumber Co. v. Thomas, 295 Ky. 808, 175 S.W.2d 505, 507.

RAZE. To erase. 3 How. State Tr. 156.

RAZON. In Spanish law. Cause, (*causa.*) Las Partidas, pt. 4, tit. 4, l. 2.

RE. Lat. In the matter of; in the case of. A term of frequent use in designating judicial proceedings, in which there is only one party. Thus, "*Re* Vivian" signifies "In the matter of Vivian," or in "Vivian's Case."

RE. FA. LO. The abbreviation of *"recordari facias loquelam,"* (*q. v.*).

RE, VERBIS, SCRIPTO, CONSENSU, TRADITIONE, JUNCTURA VESTES SUMERE PACTA SOLENT. Compacts usually take their clothing from the thing itself, from words, from writing, from consent, from delivery. Plowd. 161.

READERS. In the middle temple, those persons were so called who were appointed to deliver lectures or "readings" at certain periods during term. The clerks in holy orders who read prayers and assist in the performance of divine service in the chapels of the several inns of court are also so termed. Brown.

READING. The act of pronouncing aloud, or of acquiring by actual inspection, a knowledge of the contents of a writing or of a printed document.

The act or art of perusing written or printed matter and considering its contents or meaning. U. S. v. Tod, C.C.A.N.Y., 294 F. 820, 822.

READING-IN. In English ecclesiastical law. The title of a person admitted to a rectory or other benefice will be divested unless within two months after actual possession he publicly read in the church of the benefice, upon some Lord's day, and at the appointed times, the morning and evening service, according to the book of common prayer; and afterwards, publicly before the congregation, declare his assent to such book; and also publicly read the thirty-nine articles in the same church, in the time of common prayer, with declaration of his assent thereto; and moreover, within three months after his admission, read upon some Lord's day in the same church, in the presence of the congregation, in the time of divine service, a declaration by him subscribed before the ordinary, of conformity to the Liturgy, together with the certificate of the ordinary of its having been so subscribed. 2 Steph. Comm. (7th Ed.) 687; Wharton.

READY. Prepared for what one is about to do or experience; equipped or supplied with what is needed for some act or event; prepared for immediate movement or action. Terrell v. Harris, 42 Ga.App. 760, 157 S.E. 387, 391. Fitted, arranged, or placed for immediate use; causing no delay for lack of being prepared or furnished. Woodley Petroleum Co. v. Arkansas Louisiana Pipeline Co., 179 La. 136, 153 So. 539.

READY AND WILLING. Implies capacity to act as well as disposition. 11 L. J. Ex. 322; 5 Bing. N. C. 399; Tout Temps Prist.

REAFFORESTED. Where a deafforested forest is again made a forest. 20 Car. II. c. 3.

REAL.

Civil Law

Relating to a *thing,* (whether movable or immovable,) as disinguished from a person.

Common Law

Relating to *land,* as distinguished from personal property. This term is applied to lands, tenements, and hereditaments.

As to real "Action," "Assets," "Chattels," "Composition," "Contract," "Covenant," "Estate," "Issue," "Obligation," "Party," "Poinding," "Privilege," "Property," "Representative," "Right," "Security," "Servitude," "Statute," "Warrandice," and "Wrong," see those titles.

REAL BURDEN. In Scotch law. Where a right to lands is expressly granted under the burden of a specific sum, which is declared a burden on the lands themselves, or where the right is declared null if the sum be not paid, and where the amount of the sum, and the name of the creditor in it, can be discovered from the records, the burden is said to be real. Bell.

REAL CHYMIN. L. Fr. In old English law. The royal way; the king's highway, (*regia via.*)

REAL EVIDENCE. Evidence furnished by things themselves, on view or inspection, as distinguished from a description of them by the mouth of a witness; *e. g.*, the physical appearance of a person when exhibited to the jury, marks, scars, wounds, finger-prints, etc., also the weapons or implements used in the commission of a crime, and other inanimate objects, and evidence of the physical appearance of a place (the scene of an accident or of the commission of a crime or of property to be taken under condemnation proceedings) as obtained by a jury when they are taken to view it. See Chamb. Best, Ev. 16; Riggie v. Grand Trunk Ry. Co., 93 Vt. 282, 107 A. 126, 127.

REAL INJURY. In the civil law. An injury arising from an unlawful *act,* as distinguished from a verbal injury, which was done by words. Hallifax, Civil Law, b. 2, c. 15, nn. 3, 4.

REAL LAW. At common law. The body of laws relating to real property. This use of the term is popular rather than technical.

In the civil law. A law which relates to specific property, whether movable or immovable.

If real law in any given case relates to immovable property, it is limited in its operation to the territory within which the property is situate, real estate being both by common and continental laws, subject exclusively to the laws of the government within whose territory it is situate. Story, Confl.L. 426.

REAL THINGS (or THINGS REAL). In common law. Such things as are permanent, fixed, and immovable, which cannot be carried out of their place; as lands and tenements. 2 Bl.Comm. 15. Things substantial and immovable, and the rights and profits annexed to or issuing out of them. 1 Steph.Comm. 156.

REALITY. In foreign law. That quality of laws which concerns property or things, (*quæ ad rem spectant.*) Story, Confl. Laws, § 16.

REALIZE. To convert any kind of property into money; but especially to receive the returns from an investment. Weldon v. Newsom, 67 Colo. 502, 186 P. 516, 517.

REALM. A kingdom; a country. 1 Taunt. 270; 4 Camp. 289.

REALTY. A brief term for real property; also for anything which partakes of the nature of real property.

Quasi realty. Things which are fixed in contemplation of law to realty, but movable in themselves, as heir-looms, (or limbs of the inheritance,) title-deeds, court rolls, etc. Wharton.

REAPPRAISER. A person who, in certain cases, is appointed to make a revaluation or second appraisement of imported goods at the customhouse.

REAPTOWEL. See Riptowell.

REAR. The word has been held not necessarily to mean directly behind. Hinds v. Hinsdale, 80 N.H. 346, 116 A. 635, 636.

REARGUMENT. Its purpose is to demonstrate to court that there is some decision or principle of law which would have a controlling effect and which has been overlooked, or that there has been a misapprehension of facts. In re Hooker's Estate, 18 N.Y.S.2d 107, 110, 173 Misc. 515.

REASON. A faculty of the mind by which it distinguishes truth from falsehood, good from evil, and which enables the possessor to deduce inferences from facts or from propositions. Webster. Also an inducement, motive, or ground for action, as in the phrase "reasons for an appeal." Miller v. Miller, 8 Johns. (N.Y.) 77.

REASONABLE. Just; proper. Ordinary or usual. Fit and appropriate to the end in view. Parkes v. Bartlett, 236 Mich. 460, 210 N.W. 492, 494, 47 A.L.R. 1128; Having the faculty of reason; rational; governed by reason; under the influence of reason; agreeable to reason. Claussen v. State, 21 Wyo. 505, 133 P. 1055, 1056. Thinking, speaking, or acting according to the dictates of reason; not immoderate or excessive, being synonymous with rational; honest; equitable; fair; suitable; moderate; tolerable. Cass v. State, 124 Tex.Cr.R. 208, 61 S.W.2d 500.

As applied to rates of public service companies, a reasonable rate is one not so low as to be destructive of the company's property or so high, either intrinsically or because discriminatory, as to be an unjust exaction from the public. Turner v. Connecticut Co., 91 Conn. 692, 101 A. 88, 90.

As to reasonable "Aids," "Care," "Diligence," "Doubt," "Fair and Reasonable Compensation," "Fair and Reasonable Contract," "Fair and Reasonable Market Value," "Fair and Reasonable Tolls," "Fair and Reasonable Value," "Notice," "Skill," and "Time," see those titles.

REASONABLE ACT. Such as may fairly, justly, and reasonably be required of a party.

REASONABLE AND PROBABLE CAUSE. Such grounds as justify any one in suspecting another of a crime, and giving him in custody thereon. It is a suspicion founded upon circumstances sufficiently strong to warrant reasonable man in belief that charge is true. Murphy v. Murray, 74 Cal.App. 726, 241 P. 938, 940.

REASONABLE CAUSE TO BELIEVE A DEBTOR INSOLVENT. Knowledge of facts of a character calculated to induce a belief in the mind of an ordinarily intelligent and prudent business man. Putnam v. United States Trust Co., 223 Mass. 199, 111 N.E. 969, 972.

REASONABLE CERTAINTY, RULE OF. Permits recovery of damages only for such future pain and suffering as is reasonably certain to result from the injury received. Prettyman v. Topkis, 3 A.2d 708, 710, 9 W.W.Harr. (Del.) 568. To authorize recovery under such rule for permanent injury, permanency of injury must be shown with reasonable certainty, which is not mere conjecture or likelihood or even a probability of such injury. State ex rel. Kansas City Public Service Co. v. Shain, 350 Mo. 316, 165 S.W.2d 428, 430.

REASONABLE CREATURE. Under the common-law rule that murder is taking the life of a "reasonable creature" under the king's peace, with malice aforethought, the phrase means a human being, and has no reference to his mental condition, as it includes a lunatic, an idiot, and even an unborn child. State v. Jones, Walk. (Miss.) 85.

REASONABLE PART. In old English law. That share of a man's goods which. the law gave to his wife and children after his decease. 2 Bl. Comm. 492.

REASSURANCE. This is where an insurer procures the whole or a part of the sum which he has insured (*i. e.,* contracted to pay in case of loss, death, etc.) to be insured again to him by another person. Sweet.

REATTACHMENT. A second attachment of him who was formerly attached, and dismissed the court without day, by the not coming of the justices, or some such casualty. Reg. Orig. 35.

REBATE. Discount; reducing the interest of money in consideration of prompt payment. A deduction from a stipulated premium on a policy of insurance, in pursuance of an antecedent contract. A deduction or drawback from a stipulated payment, charge, or rate, (as, a rate for the transportation of freight by a railroad,) not taken out in advance of payment, but handed back to the payer after he has paid the full stipulated sum. U. S. v. Lehigh Valley R. Co., D.C.N.Y., 222 F. 685; New York Cent. & H. R. R. Co. v. General Electric Co., 219 N.Y. 227, 114 N.E. 115, 117, 1 A. L.R. 1417.

REBEL. A citizen or subject who unjustly and unlawfully takes up arms against the constituted authorities of the nation, to deprive them of the supreme power, either by resisting their lawful and constitutional orders in some particular matter or to impose on them conditions. Vattel, Droit des Gens, liv. 3, § 328. In another sense, it signifies a refusal to obey a superior or the commands of a court.

REBELLION. Deliberate, organized resistance, by force and arms, to the laws or operations of the government, committed by a subject. Crashley v. Press Pub. Co., 74 App.Div. 118, 77 N.Y.S. 711.

In old English law, also a contempt of a court manifested by disobedience to its process, particularly of the court of chancery. If a defendant refused to appear, after attachment and proclamation, a "commission of rebellion" issued against him. 3 Bl.Comm. 444.

REBELLION, COMMISSION OF. In equity practice. A process of contempt issued on the non-appearance of a defendant.

REBELLIOUS ASSEMBLY. In English law. A gathering of twelve persons or more, intending, going about, or practicing unlawfully and of their own authority to change any laws of the realm; or to destroy the inclosure of any park or ground inclosed, banks of fish-ponds, pools, conduits, etc., to the intent the same shall remain void; or that they shall have way in any of the said grounds; or to destroy the deer in any park, fish in ponds, coneys in any warren, dovehouses, etc.; or to burn sacks of corn; or to abate rents or prices of victuals, etc. Cowell.

REBOUTER. To repel or bar. The action of the heir by the warranty of his ancestor is called "to rebut or repel." 2 Co. Litt. 247.

REBUS SIC STANTIBUS. Lat. At this point of affairs; in these circumstances. A name given to a tacit condition, said to attach to all treaties, that they shall cease to be obligatory so soon as the state of facts and conditions upon which they were founded has substantially changed. Taylor, Int. L. § 394; 1 Oppenheim, Int. L. 550; Grotius, ch. XVI, § XXV.

The change of government from a monarchy to a republic was treated as not terminating treaties, nor a successful revolution; nor an alliance of one of the treaty powers with a third power. As the result, however, of the changes in the state of Europe effected by the wars of Napoleon, all the treaties of the United States with European powers were considered as terminated, excepting only one with Spain of 1795. 5 Moore, Dig. Int. L. 335, 337, 338.

REBUT. In pleading and evidence. To defeat or take away the effect of something. Sweet.

When a plaintiff in an action produces evidence which raises a presumption of the defendant's liability, and the defendant adduces evidence which shows that the presumption is ill-founded, he is said to "rebut it." Sweet.

In the old law of real property, to repel or bar a claim. Co. Litt. 365*a*; Termes de la Ley.

Thus, when a person was sued for land which had been warranted to him by the plaintiff or his ancestor, and he pleaded the warranty as a defense to the action, this was called a "rebutter." Co.Litt. 365*a;* Termes de la Ley.

REBUT AN EQUITY. To defeat an apparent equitable right or claim, by the introduction of evidence showing that, in the particular circumstances, there is no ground for such equity to attach, or that it is overridden by a superior or countervailing equity. 2 Whart. Ev. § 973.

REBUTTABLE PRESUMPTION. In the law of evidence. A presumption which may be rebutted by evidence. Otherwise called a "disputable" presumption. A species of legal presumption which holds good until disproved. Best, Pres. § 25; 1 Greenl. Ev. § 33; Beck v. Kansas City Public Service Co., Mo.App., 48 S.W.2d 213, 215. It shifts burden of proof. Heiner v. Donnan, 52 S.Ct. 358, 362, 285 U.S. 312, 76 L.Ed. 772. And which standing alone will support a finding against contradictory evidence. Lieber v. Rigby, 34 Cal.App.2d 582, 94 P.2d 49, 50.

REBUTTAL. The introduction of rebutting evidence; the showing that statement of witnesses as to what occurred is not true; the stage of a trial at which such evidence may be introduced; also the rebutting evidence itself. Lux v. Haggin, 69 Cal. 255, 10 P. 674. State v. Monroe, 205 La. 285, 17 So.2d 331, 332.

REBUTTER. In pleading. A defendant's answer of fact to a plaintiff's surrejoinder; the third pleading in the series on the part of the defendant. Steph. Pl. 59; 3 Bl.Comm. 310.

REBUTTING EVIDENCE. Evidence given to explain, repel, counteract, or disprove facts given in evidence by the adverse party. State v. Martinez, 43 Idaho 180, 250 P. 239, 244; State v. Fourchy, 25 So. 109, 51 La.Ann. 228.

Also evidence given in opposition to a presumption of fact or a *prima facie* case; in this sense, it may be not only counteracting evidence, but evidence sufficient to counteract, that is, conclusive. Fain v. Cornett, 25 Ga. 186.

RECALL. A method of removal of official in which power of removal is either granted to or reserved by the people. Jones v. Harlan, Tex.Civ. App., 109 S.W.2d 251, 254.

Constitutional Law

To retire an elected officer, by a vote of the electorate. In 1911 the right to recall was provided in Idaho, Montana, North and South Dakota, Washington, Wisconsin, Wyoming, and California. Like provisions were adopted in 1912 in Ohio, Arizona, and Nebraska. The recall of judges was adopted in Oregon in 1908; in California in 1911; in Colorado, Arizona, and Nevada in 1912.

International Law

To summon a diplomatic minister back to his home court, at the same time depriving him of his office and functions.

RECALL A JUDGMENT. To revoke, cancel, vacate, or reverse a judgment for matters of fact; when it is annulled by reason of errors of law, it is said to be "reversed."

RECANT. To withdraw or repudiate formally and publicly. Pradlik v. State, 131 Conn. 682, 41 A.2d 906, 907.

RECAPITALIZATION. An arrangement whereby stock, bonds or other securities of a corporation are adjusted as to amount, income or priority. United Gas Improvement Co. v. Commissioner of Internal Revenue, C.C.A.3, 142 F.2d 216, 218, 219. Reshuffling of capital structure within framework of existing corporation. Helvering v. Southwest Consol. Corporation, La., 62 S.Ct. 546, 552, 315 U. S. 194, 86 L.Ed. 789.

RECAPTION. A retaking, or taking back. A species of remedy by the mere act of the party injured, (otherwise termed "reprisal,") which happens when any one has deprived another of his property in goods or chattels personal, or wrongfully detains one's wife, child, or servant. In this case, the owner of the goods, and the husband, parent, or master may lawfully claim and retake them, wherever he happens to find them, so it be not in a riotous manner, or attended with a breach of the peace. 3 Inst. 134; 3 Bl.Comm. 4; 3 Steph.Comm. 358; Prigg v. Pennsylvania, 16 Pet. 612, 10 L.Ed. 1060. It also signifies the taking a second distress of one formerly distrained during the plea grounded on the former distress.

Also a writ to recover damages for him whose goods, being distrained for rent in service, etc., are distrained again for the same cause, pending the plea in the county court, or before the justice. Fitzh. Nat. Brev. 71.

RECAPTURE. The taking from an enemy, by a force friendly to the former owner, of a vessel previously taken for prize by such enemy.

RECEDITUR A PLACITIS JURIS, POTIUS QUAM INJURIÆ ET DELICTA MANEANT IMPUNITA. Positive rules of law [as distinguished from maxims or conclusions of reason] will be receded from, [given up or dispensed with,] rather than that crimes and wrongs should remain unpunished. Bac. Max. 55, reg. 12.

RECEIPT. Written acknowledgment of the receipt of money, or a thing of value, without containing any affirmative obligation upon either party to it; a mere admission of a fact, in writing. Krutz v. Craig, 53 Ind. 574; Stone v. Steil, 230 Mich. 249, 202 N.W. 982, 983. And being a mere acknowledgment of payment, is subject to parol explanation or contradiction. Cappel v. Evansville Oil Corporation, La.App., 195 So. 104, 105; Adams v. Camden Safe Deposit & Trust Co., 15 N.J.Misc. 48, 188 A. 913, 914.

Act of receiving; also, the fact of receiving or being received; that which is received; that which comes in, in distinction from what is expended, paid out, sent away, and the like. State v. Texas Co., 173 Tenn. 154, 116 S.W.2d 583, 584.

In old practice. Admission of a party to defend a suit, as of a wife on default of the husband in certain cases. Litt. § 668; Co. Litt. 352*b*.

RECEIPTOR. A name given in some of the states to a person who receives from the sheriff goods which the latter has seized under process of garnishment, on giving to the sheriff a bond conditioned to have the property forthcoming when demanded or when execution issues. Story, Bailm. § 124.

RECEIVE. To take into possession and control; accept custody of. Young v. Alexander, 123 Miss. 708, 86 So. 461; Northwestern Consol. Milling Co. v. Rosenberg, C.C.A.Pa., 287 F. 785, 788.

RECEIVER. An indifferent person between the parties to a cause, appointed by the court to receive and preserve the property or fund in litigation, and receive its rents, issues, and profits, and apply or dispose of them at the direction of the court when it does not seem reasonable that either party should hold them. Or where a party is incompetent to do so, as in the case of an infant. The remedy of the appointment of a receiver is one of the very oldest in the court of chancery, and is founded on the inadequacy of the remedy to be obtained in the court of ordinary jurisdiction. Bisp. Eq. § 576; In re Guaranty Indemnity Co., 256 Mich. 671, 240 N.W. 78. A fiduciary of the court, appointed as an incident to other proceedings wherein certain ultimate relief is prayed. In re Granada Hotel Corporation, D. C.Ill., 9 F.Supp. 909. He is a trustee or ministerial officer representing court, and all parties in interest in litigation, and property or fund intrusted to him. Dallas Bank & Trust Co. v. Thompson, Tex.Civ.App., 87 S.W.2d 307, 308. See also Receiver Pendente Lite and Receivership.

One who receives money to the use of another to render an account. Story, Eq. Jur. § 446.

In criminal law. One who receives stolen goods from thieves, and conceals them. Cowell. This was always the prevalent sense of the word in the common as well as the civil law.

RECEIVER GENERAL OF THE DUCHY OF LANCASTER. An officer of the duchy court, who collects all the revenues, fines, forfeitures, and assessments within the duchy.

RECEIVER GENERAL OF THE PUBLIC REVENUE. In English law. An officer appointed in every county to receive the taxes granted by parliament, and remit the money to the treasury.

RECEIVER OF FINES. An English officer who receives the money from persons who compound with the crown on original writs sued out of chancery. Wharton.

RECEIVERS AND TRIERS OF PETITIONS. The mode of receiving and trying petitions to parliament was formerly judicial rather than legislative, and the triers were committees of prelates, peers, and judges, and, latterly, of the members generally. Brown.

RECEIVER'S CERTIFICATE. A non-negotiable evidence of debt, or debenture, issued by authority of a court of chancery, as a first lien upon the property of a debtor corporation in the hands of a receiver. Beach, Rec. § 379.

RECEIVERS OF WRECK. Persons appointed by the English board of trade. The duties of a receiver of wreck are to take steps for the preservation of any vessel stranded or in distress within his district; to receive and take possession of all articles washed on shore from the vessel; to use force for the suppression of plunder and disorder; to institute an examination on oath with respect to the vessel; and, if necessary, to sell the vessel, cargo, or wreck. Sweet.

RECEIVER PENDENTE LITE. A person appointed to take charge of the fund or property to which the receivership extends while the case remains undecided. The title to the property is not changed by the appointment. The receiver acquires no title, but only the right of possession as the officer of the court. The title remains in those in whom it was vested when the appointment was made. The object of the appointment is to secure the property pending the litigation, so that it may be appropriated in accordance with the rights of the parties, as they may be determined by the judgment in the action. Title Guarantee & Trust Co. v. 457 Schenectady Ave., 257 N.Y.S. 413, 417, 235 App.Div. 509.

RECEIVERSHIP. An extraordinary remedy of an ancillary character; chief reason for its allowance being to husband property in litigation for benefit of person who may ultimately be found entitled thereto. Pereira v. Wulf, 83 Mont. 343, 272 P. 532, 533. See, also, Receiver.

RECEIVING STOLEN GOODS. The short name usually given to the offense of receiving any property with the knowledge that it has been feloniously, or unlawfully stolen, taken, extorted, obtained, embezzled, or disposed of. Sweet; Underwood v. State, 36 Okl.Cr. 21, 251 P. 507, 508; Winters v. State, 80 Tex.Cr.R. 85, 188 S.W. 982.

RECENS INSECUTIO. In old English law. Fresh suit; fresh pursuit. Pursuit of a thief immediately after the discovery of the robbery. 1 Bl.Comm. 297.

RÉCÉPISSÉ DE COTISATION. In French law. A receipt setting forth the extent of the interest subscribed by a member of a mutual insurance company. Arg. Fr. Merc. Law, 571.

RECEPTUS. Lat. In the civil law. The name sometimes given to an arbitrator, because he had been received or chosen to settle the differences between the parties. Dig. 4, 8; Cod. 2, 56.

RECESS. In the practice of the courts, a short interval or period of time during which the court suspends business, but without adjourning. In re Gannon, 69 Cal. 541, 11 P. 240. In legislative practice, the interval, occurring in consequence of an adjournment, between the sessions of the same continuous legislative body; not the interval between the final adjournment of one body and the convening of another at the next regular session. Tipton v. Parker, 71 Ark. 193, 74 S.W. 298; Reynolds v. Cropsey, 241 N.Y. 389, 150 N.E. 303, 307.

RECESSION. The act of ceding back; the restoration of the title and dominion of a territory, by the government which now holds it, to the government from which it was obtained by cession or otherwise. 2 White, Recop. 516.

RECESSUS MARIS. Lat. In old English law. A going back; reliction or retreat of the sea.

RECHT. Ger. Right; justice; equity; the whole body of law; unwritten law; law; also a right.

There is much ambiguity in the use of this term, an ambiguity which it shares with the French *"droit,"* the Italian *"diritto,"* and the English "right." On the one hand, the term *"Recht"* answers to the Roman *"jus,"* and thus indicates law in the abstract, considered as the foundation of all rights, or the complex of underlying moral principles which impart the character of justice to all positive law, or give it an ethical content. Taken in this abstract sense, the term may be an adjective, in which case it is equivalent to the English "just," or a noun, in which case it may be paraphrased by the expressions "justice," "morality," or "equity." On the other hand, it serves to point out a right; that is, a power, privilege, faculty, or demand, inherent in one person, and incident upon another. In the latter signification *"Recht"* (or *"droit,"* or *"diritto,"* or "right") is the correlative of "duty" or "obligation." In the former sense, it may be considered as opposed to wrong, injustice, or the absence of law. The word *"Recht"* has the further ambiguity that it is used in contradistinction to *"Gesetz,"* as *"jus"* is opposed to *"lex,"* or the unwritten law to enacted law. See Droit; Jus; Right.

RECIDIVE. In French law. The state of an individual who having been convicted of a crime or misdemeanor, commits one again. A relapse. Dalloz.

RECIDIVIST. A habitual criminal. An incorrigible criminal. One who makes a trade of crime. McDonald, Criminology, ch. viii; People v. Rave, 364 Ill. 72, 3 N.E.2d 972, 976.

RECIPROCAL CONTRACT. A contract, the parties to which enter into mutual engagements. A mutual or bilateral contract.

RECIPROCAL or INTERINSURANCE EXCHANGE. Group or association of persons cooperating through an attorney in fact for purpose of insuring themselves and each other. In re Minnesota Ins. Underwriters, D.C.Minn., 36 F.2d 371, 372.

RECIPROCAL WILLS. Wills made by two or more persons in which they make reciprocal testamentary provisions in favor of each other, whether they unite in one will or each executes a separate one. In re Cawley's Estate, 136 Pa. 628, 20 A. 567, 10 L.R.A. 93.

RECIPROCITY. Mutuality. The term is used in international law to denote the relation existing between two states when each of them gives the subjects of the other certain privileges, on condition that its own subjects shall enjoy similar privileges at the hands of the latter state. Sweet.

RECITAL. The formal statement or setting forth of some matter of fact, in any deed or writing, in order to explain the reasons upon which the transaction is founded. The recitals are situated in the premises of a deed, that is, in that part of a deed between the date and the *habendum,* and they usually commence with the formal word "whereas." Brown.

The formal preliminary statement in a deed or other instrument, of such deeds, agreements, or matters of fact as are necessary to explain the reasons upon which the transaction is founded. 2 Bl.Comm. 298.

In pleading. The statement of matter as introductory to some positive allegation, beginning in declarations with the words, "For that *whereas.*" Steph. Pl. 388, 389.

RECITE. To state in a written instrument facts connected with its inception, or reasons for its being made. Also to quote or set forth the words or the contents of some other instrument or document; as, to "recite" a statute. See Hart v. Baltimore & O. R. Co., 6 W.Va. 348.

RECK. To take heed; have a care, mind, heed. Lancaster v. Carter, Tex.Com.App., 255 S.W. 392, 394.

RECKLESS. Not recking; careless, heedless, inattentive; indifferent to consequences. According to circumstances it may mean desperately heedless, wanton or willful, or it may mean only careless, inattentive, or negligent. People v. Sweet, 130 Misc.Rep. 612, 225 N.Y.S. 182, 183.

Reckless conduct, as respects common-law manslaughter, must evince disregard of consequences under circumstances involving danger to life or safety. State v. Custer, 129 Kan. 381, 282 P. 1071, 1078, 67 A.L.R. 909.

RECKLESS DISREGARD OF RIGHTS OF OTHERS. As used in automobile guest law, mean the voluntary doing by motorist of an improper or wrongful act, or with knowledge of existing conditions, the voluntary refraining from doing a proper or prudent act when such act or failure to act evinces an entire abandonment of any care, and heedless indifference to results which may follow and the reckless taking of chance of accident happening without intent that any occur. Albert McGann Securities Co. v. Coen, 114 Ind.App. 60, 48 N.E.2d 58, 60. Gill v. Hayes, 188 Okl. 434, 108 P.2d 117, 120.

RECKLESS DRIVING. Operation of automobile manifesting reckless disregard of possible consequences and indifference to others' rights. People v. Whitby, 44 N.Y.S.2d 76, 77.

RECKLESSNESS. Rashness; heedlessness; wanton conduct. The state of mind accompanying an act, which either pays no regard to its probably or possibly injurious consequences, or which, though forseeing such consequences, persists in spite of such knowledge. Railroad Co. v. Bodemer, 139 Ill. 596, 29 N.E. 692, 32 Am.St.Rep. 218; St. Louis, I. M. & S. Ry. Co. v. Plott, 108 Ark. 292, 157 S.W. 385, 386. Conduct amounting to more than negligence. Barnard v. Heather, 135 Neb. 513, 282 N.W. 534, 537.

RECLAIM. To claim or demand back; to ask for the return or restoration of a thing; to insist upon one's right to recover that which was one's own, but was parted with conditionally or mistakenly; as, to *reclaim* goods which were obtained from one under false pretenses. Witson v. Succession of Staring, La.App., 175 So. 495, 498.

Feudal Law

It was used of the action of a lord pursuing, prosecuting, and recalling his vassal, who had gone to live in another place, without his permission.

International Law

The demanding of a thing or person to be delivered up or surrendered to the government or state to which either properly belongs, when, by an irregular means, it has come into the possession of another. Wharton.

Law of Property

Spoken of animals, to reduce from a wild to a tame or domestic state; to tame them. In an analogous sense, to reclaim land is to reduce marshy or swamp land to a state fit for cultivation and habitation.

Scotch Law

To appeal. The reclaiming days in Scotland are the days allowed to a party dissatisfied with the judgment of the lord ordinary to appeal therefrom to the inner house; and the petition of appeal is called the reclaiming "bill," "note," or "petition." Mozley & Whitley; Bell.

RECLAIMED ANIMALS. Those that are made tame by art, industry, or education, whereby a qualified property may be acquired in them.

RECLAIMING BILL. In Scotch law. A petition of appeal or review of a judgment of the lord ordinary or other inferior court. Bell.

RECLAMATION DISTRICT. A subdivision of a state created by legislative authority, for the purpose of reclaiming swamp, marshy, or desert lands within its boundaries and rendering them fit for habitation or cultivation, generally with funds raised by local taxation or the issue of bonds, and sometimes with authority to make rules or ordinances for the regulation of the work in hand.

RECLUSION. In French law and in Louisiana. Incarceration as a punishment for crime; a temporary, afflictive, and infamous punishment, consisting in being confined at hard labor in a penal institution, and carrying civil degradation. Phelps v. Reinach, 38 La.Ann. 551; Jurgens v. Ittman, 47 La.Ann. 367, 16 So. 952.

RECOGNITION. Ratification; confirmation; an acknowledgment that something done by another person in one's name had one's authority.

An inquiry conducted by a chosen body of men, not sitting as part of the court, into the facts in dispute in a case at law; these "recognitors" preceded the jurymen of modern times, and reported their recognition or verdict to the court. Stim. Law Gloss.

RECOGNITIONE ADNULLANDA PER VIM ET DURITIEM FACTA. A writ to the justices of the common bench for sending a record touching a recognizance, which the recognizor suggests was acknowledged by force and duress; that if it so appear the recognizance may be annulled. Reg. Orig. 183.

RECOGNITORS. In English law. The name by which the jurors impaneled on an assize are known. See Recognition.

The word is sometimes met in modern books, as meaning the person who enters into a recognizance, being thus another form of recognizor.

RECOGNIZANCE. An obligation of record, entered into before some court of record, or magistrate duly authorized, with condition to do some particular act; as to appear at the assizes, or criminal court, to keep the peace, to pay a debt, or the like. It resembles a bond, but differs from it in being an acknowledgment of a former debt upon record. 2 Bl.Comm. 341; Albrecht v. State, 132 Md. 150, 103 A. 443, 444; Modern Finance Co. v. Martin, 311 Mass. 509, 42 N.E.2d 533, 534.

In the practice of several of the states, a species of bail bond or security, given by the prisoner either on being bound over for trial or on his taking an appeal.

In criminal law, a person who has been found guilty of an offense may, in certain cases, be required to enter into a recognizance by which he binds himself to keep the peace for a certain period. Sweet.

In criminal cases, a "bail bond" is a contract under seal, executed by accused, and from its nature requiring sureties or bail, to whose custody he is committed, while a "recognizance" is an obligation of record, entered into before some court or magistrate authorized to take it, with condition to do some particular act, and a prisoner is often allowed so to obligate himself to answer to the charge. State v. Bradsher, 189 N.C. 401, 127 S.E. 349, 351, 38 A.L.R. 1102.

RECOGNIZE. To try; to examine in order to determine the truth of a matter. Also to enter into a recognizance.

RECOGNIZED. Actual and publicly known. Commonwealth v. Kimball, 299 Mass. 353, 13 N.E. 2d 18, 22, 114 A.L.R. 1440.

RECOGNIZEE. He to whom one is bound in a recognizance.

RECOGNIZOR. He who enters into a recognizance.

RÉCOLEMENT. In French law. This is the process by which a witness, who has given his deposition, reads the same over and scrutinizes it, with a view to affirming his satisfaction with it as it stands, or to making such changes in it as his better recollection may suggest to him as necessary to the truth. This is necessary to the validity of the deposition. Poth. Proc. Crim. § 4, art. 4.

RECOMMEND. To advise or counsel. Kirby v. Nolte, 351 Mo. 525, 173 S.W.2d 391.

RECOMMENDATION. In feudal law. A method of converting allodial land into feudal property. The owner of the allod surrendered it to the king or a lord, doing homage, and received it back as a benefice or feud, to hold to himself and such of his heirs as he had previously nominated to the superior.

The act of one person in giving to another a favorable account of the character, responsibility, or skill of a third.

Letter of Recommendation

A writing whereby one person certifies concerning another that he is of good character, solvent, possessed of commercial credit, skilled in his trade or profession, or otherwise worthy of trust, aid, or employment. It may be addressed to an individual or to whom it may concern, and is designed to aid the person commended in obtaining credit, employment, etc. McDonald v. Illinois Cent. R. Co., 187 Ill. 529, 58 N.E. 463.

RECOMMENDATORY. Precatory, advisory, or directory.

Recommendatory words in a will are such as do not express the testator's command in a peremptory form, but advise, counsel, or suggest that a certain course be pursued or disposition made.

RECOMPENSATION. In Scotland, where a party sues for a debt, and the defendant pleads compensation, *i. e.,* set-off, the plaintiff may allege a compensation on his part; and this is called a "recompensation." Bell.

RECOMPENSE. A reward for services; remuneration for goods or other property.

RECOMPENSE OR RECOVERY IN VALUE. That part of the judgment in a "common recovery" by which the tenant is declared entitled to recover lands of equal value with those which were warranted to him and lost by the default of the vouchee. 2 Bl.Comm. 358–359.

RECONCILIATION. The renewal of amicable relations between two persons who had been at enmity or variance; usually implying forgiveness of injuries on one or both sides. It is sometimes used in the law of divorce as a term synonymous or analogous to "condonation." Martin v. Martin, 151 La. 530, 92 So. 46, 48.

RECONDUCTION. In the civil law. A renewing of a former lease; relocation. Dig. 19, 2, 13, 11; Code Nap. arts. 1737–1740.

RECONSTRUCT. To construct again, to rebuild, either in fact or idea, or to remodel, to form again or anew as in the imagination or to restore again as an entity the thing which was lost or destroyed. City of Seattle v. Northern Pac. Ry. Co., 12 Wash. 2d 247, 121 P.2d 382, 386.

RECONSTRUCTION. Act of constructing again. It presupposes the nonexistence of the thing to be reconstructed, as an entity; that the thing before existing has lost its entity. McCarty v. Boulevard Com'rs of Hudson County, 91 N.J.Law, 137, 106 A. 219, 220; Miller Hatcheries v. Buckeye Incubator Co., C.C.A.Mo., 41 F.2d 619.

Also the name commonly given to the process of reorganizing, by acts of congress and executive action, the governments of the states which had passed ordinances of secession, and of re-establishing their constitutional relations to the national government, restoring their representation in congress, and effecting the necessary changes in their internal government, after the close of the civil war. Black, Const. Law (3d Ed.) 48; Texas v. White, 7 Wall. 700, 19 L.Ed. 227.

RECONTINUANCE. Used to signify that a person has recovered an incorporeal hereditament of which he had been wrongfully deprived. Thus, A. is disseised of a mannor, whereunto an advowson is appendant, an estranger [*i. e.,* neither A. nor the disseisor] usurpes to the advowson; if the disseisee [A.] enter into the mannor, the advowson is recontinued again, which was severed by the usurpation. * * * And so note a diversitie between a recontinuance and a remitter; for a remitter cannot be properly, unless there be two titles; but a recontinuance may be where there is but one. Co. Litt. 363*b*; Sweet.

RECONVENIRE. Lat. In the canon and civil law. To make a cross-demand upon the actor, or plaintiff. 4 Reeve, Eng. Law, 14, and note, (*r*).

RECONVENTION. In the civil law. An action by a defendant against a plaintiff in a former action; a cross-bill or litigation.

The term is used in practice in the states of Louisiana and Texas, derived from the *reconventio* of the civil law. Reconvention is not identical with set-off, but more extensive. Pacific Exp. Co. v. Malin, 132 U.S. 531, 10 S.Ct. 166, 33 L.Ed. 450; Suberville v. Adams, 47 La.Ann. 68, 16 So. 652; Gimbel v. Gomprecht, 89 Tex. 497, 35 S.W. 470.

RECONVENTIONAL DEMAND. Any plea by a defendant which constitutes more than mere defense and amounts to counterclaim. Alfonso v. Ruiz, La.App., 2 So.2d 480, 483, 484.

RECONVERSION. That imaginary process by which a prior constructive conversion is annulled and the property restored in contemplation of equity to its original actual quality. Seagle v. Harris, 214 N.C. 339, 199 S.E. 271, 273.

RECONVEYANCE. It takes place where a mortgage debt is paid off, and the mortgaged property is conveyed again to the mortgagor or his representatives free from the mortgage debt. Sweet.

RECOPILACION DE INDIAS. A collection of Spanish colonial law, promulgated A. D. 1680. See Schm. Civil Law, Introd. 94.

RECORD, *v.* To commit to writing, to printing, to inscription, or the like, to make an official note of, to write, transcribe, or enter in a book or on parchment, for the purpose of preserving authentic evidence of, or on a wax cylinder, rubber disk, etc., for reproduction, as by a phonograph, or to register or enroll. To transcribe a document, or enter the history of an act or series of acts, in an official volume, for the purpose of giving notice of the same, of furnishing authentic evidence, and for preservation. Cady v. Purser, 131 Cal. 552, 63 P. 844, 82 Am.St.Rep. 391; Shimmel v. People, 108 Colo. 592, 121 P.2d 491, 493.

RECORD, *n.* A written account of some act, transaction, or instrument, drawn up, under authority of law, by a proper officer, and designed to remain as a memorial or permanent evidence of the matters to which it relates. People ex rel. Simons v. Dowling, 146 N.Y.S. 919, 920, 84 Misc. 201. A memorandum public or private, of what has been done, ordinarily applied to public records only, in which sense it is a written memorial made by a public officer. Nogueira v. State, 123 Tex.Cr.R. 449, 59 S.W.2d 831.

The act or fact of recording or being recorded, reduction to writing as evidence, also, the writing so made, a register, a family record, official contemporaneous writing, an authentic official copy of document entered in book or deposited in keeping of officer designated by law, an official contemporaneous memorandum stating the proceedings of a court or official copy of legal papers used in a case. Shimmel v. People, 108 Colo. 592, 121 P.2d 491, 493.

There are three kinds of records, viz.: (1) *judicial,* as an attainder; (2) *ministerial,* on oath, being an office or inquisition found; (3) by way of *conveyance,* as a deed enrolled. Wharton.

Practice

A written memorial of all the acts and proceedings in an action or suit, in a court of record. The official and authentic history of the cause, consisting in entries of each successive step in the proceedings, chronicling the various acts of the parties and of the court, couched in the formal language established by usage, terminating with the judgment rendered in the cause, and intended to remain as a perpetual and unimpeachable memorial of the proceedings and judgment. State v. Brewer, 19 Ala.App. 291, 97 So. 160, 161.

At common law, a *roll of parchment* upon which the proceedings and transactions of a court are entered or drawn up by its officers, and which is then deposited in its treasury *in perpetuam rei memoriam.* 3 Steph.Comm. 583; 3 Bl.Comm. 24. A court of record is that where the acts and judicial proceedings are enrolled in parchment for a perpetual memorial and testimony, which rolls are called the "records of the court," and are of such high and supereminent authority that their truth is not to be called in question. Hahn v. Kelly, 34 Cal. 422, 94 Am.Dec. 742. O'Connell v. Hotchkiss, 44 Conn. 53; Murrah v. State, 51 Miss. 656; State v. Anders, 64 Kan. 742, 68 P. 668; Wilkinson v. Railway Co., C.C., 23 F. 562; In re Christern, 43 N.Y.Super.Ct. 531.

In the practice of appellate tribunals, the history of the proceedings on the trial of the action below, (with the pleadings, offers, objections to evidence, rulings of the court, exceptions, charge, etc.,) in so far as the same appears in the record furnished to the appellate court in the paper-books or other transcripts. Hence, derivatively, it means the aggregate of the various judicial steps taken on the trial below, in so far as they were taken, presented, or allowed in the formal and proper manner necessary to put them upon the record of the court. This is the meaning in such phrases as "no error in the record," "contents of the record," "outside the record," etc. Le Clair v. Calls Him, 106 Okl. 247, 233 P. 1087, 1091.

General

Conveyances by record. Extraordinary assurances; such as private acts of parliament and royal grants.

Courts of record. Those whose judicial acts and proceedings are enrolled in parchment, for a perpetual memorial and testimony, which rolls are called the "records of the court," and are of such high and supereminent authority that their truth is not to be called in question. Every court of record has authority to fine and imprison for contempt of its authority. 3 Broom & H. Comm. 21, 30. Page v. Turcott, 179 Tenn. 491, 167 S.W.2d 350, 354.

Debts of record. Those which appear to be due by the evidence of a court of record; such as a judgment, recognizance, etc.

Diminution of record. Incompleteness of the record sent up on appeal. See Diminution.

Face of record. See Face of Record.

False record. See False Record.

Judicial record. A precise history of suit from commencement to termination, including conclusion of law. People v. Fox, 346 Ill. 374, 178 N.E. 907, 910.

Matter of record. See Matter.

Nul tiel record. See Nul.

Of record. See that title.

Pocket record. A statute so called. Brownl. pt. 2, p. 81.

Public record. A record, memorial of some act or transaction, written evidence of something done, or document, considered as either concerning or interesting the public, affording notice or information to the public, or open to public inspection. Keefe v. Donnell, 92 Me. 151, 42 A. 345; Colnon v. Orr, 71 Cal. 43, 11 P. 814.

Record and writ clerk. Four officers of the court of chancery were designated by this title, whose duty it was to file bills brought to them for that purpose. Business was distributed among them according to the initial letter of the surname of the first plaintiff in a suit. Hunt, Eq. These officers are now transferred to the high court of justice under the judicature acts.

Record commission. The name of a board of commissioners appointed for the purpose of searching out, classifying, indexing, or publishing the public records of a state or county.

Records of a corporation. Import the transcript of its charter and by-laws, the minutes of its meetings—the books containing the accounts of its official doings and the written evidence of its contracts and business transactions. U. S. v. Louisville & N. R. Co., 35 S.Ct. 363, 368, 236 U.S. 318, 59 L.Ed. 598; Maremont v. Old Colony Life Ins. Co., 189 Ill.App. 231, 232.

Record of nisi prius. In English law. An official copy or transcript of the proceedings in an action, entered on parchment and "sealed and passed," as it is termed, at the proper office; it serves as a warrant to the judge to try the cause, and is the only document at which he can judicially look for information as to the nature of the proceedings and the issues joined. Brown.

Title of record. A title to real estate, evidenced and provable by one or more conveyances or other instruments all of which are duly entered on the public land records.

Trial by record. A species of trial adopted for determining the existence or non-existence of a record. When a record is asserted by one party to exist, and the opposite party denies its existence under the form of a traverse that there is no such record remaining in court as alleged, and issue is joined thereon, this is called an "issue of *nul tiel record,*" and in such case the court awards a trial by inspection and examination of the record. Upon this the party affirming its existence is bound to produce it in court on a day given for the purpose, and, if he fails to do so, judgment is given for his adversary. Co. Litt. 117*b*, 260*a*; 3 Bl. Comm. 331.

RECORD, ESTOPPEL BY. An estoppel founded upon matter of record; as a confession, or admission made in pleading in a court of record, which precludes the party from afterwards contesting the same fact in the same suit. Steph. Pl. 197.

It arises from or is founded upon the adjudication of a competent court. Smith v. Urquhart, 129 Fla. 742, 176 So. 787, 789. Confessions or admissions made in pleadings in a court of record, decrees, and other final determinations work estoppels. Bradner v. Howard, 75 N.Y. 417; Butterfield v. Smith, 101 U.S. 570, 25 L.Ed. 868; Denver City Irr. & Water Co. v. Middaugh, 12 Colo. 434, 21 Pac. 565, 13 Am.St.Rep. 234. An "estoppel by record" is the preclusion to deny the truth of a matter set forth in a record, whether judicial or legislative, also to deny the facts adjudicated by a court of competent jurisdiction. Swofford Bros. Dry Goods Co. v. Owen, 37 Okl. 616, 133 P. 193, 198, L.R.A.1916C, 189; Watson v. Goldsmith, 205 S.C. 215, 31 S.E.2d 317, 320.

An "estoppel by record" cannot be invoked where allegations or recitals did not conclude pleader in prior proceeding. Blackburn v. Blackburn, Tex.Civ.App., 163 S.W.2d 251, 255. It bars a second action between the same parties on an issue necessarily raised and decided in the first action. Woods v. Duval, 151 Kan. 472, 99 P.2d 804, 808. It exists only as between the same parties, or those in privity with them, in same case on same issues. Smith v. Maine, 260 N.Y.S. 425, 145 Misc. 521. The doctrine prevents a party not only from litigating again what was actually litigated in the former case, but litigating what might have been litigated therein. Kuchenreuther v. Chicago, M. St. P. & P. R. Co., 225 Wis. 613, 275 N.W. 457.

Defense of res judicata a plea of "estoppel by record". Hull v. Hercules Powder Co., 20 N.J.Misc. 168, 26 A.2d 164, 168.

RECORDA SUNT VESTIGIA VETUSTATIS ET VERITATIS. Records are vestiges of antiquity and truth. 2 Rolle, 296.

RECORDARE. In American practice. A writ to bring up judgments of justices of the peace. Halcombe v. Loudermilk, 48 N.C. 491.

RECORDARI FACIAS LOQUELAM. In English practice. A writ by which a suit or plaint in replevin may be removed from a county court to one of the courts of Westminster Hall. 3 Bl. Comm. 149; 3 Steph. Pl. 522, 666. So termed from the emphatic words of the old writ, by which the sheriff was commanded to *cause the plaint to be recorded*, and to have the record before the superior court. Reg. Orig. 5*b*.

RECORDATUR. In old English practice. An entry made upon a record, in order to prevent any alteration of it. 1 Ld. Raym. 211. An order or allowance that the verdict returned on the *nisi prius* roll be recorded.

RECORDER, *v.* L. Fr. In Norman law. To recite or testify on recollection what had previously passed in court. This was the duty of the judges and other principal persons who presided at the *placitum;* thence called *"recordeurs."* Steph. Pl., Append. note 11.

RECORDER, *n.* In old English law. A barrister or other person learned in the law, whom the mayor or other magistrate of any city or town corporate, having jurisdiction or a court of record within their precincts, associated to him for his better direction in matters of justice and proceedings according to law. Cowell.

A magistrate, in the judicial systems of some of the states, who has a criminal jurisdiction analogous to that of a police judge or other committing magistrate, and usually a limited civil jurisdiction, and sometimes authority conferred by statute in special classes of proceedings. Leigeber v. State, 17 Ala.App. 551, 86 So. 126; City of Colton v. Superior Court in and for San Bernardino County, 84 Cal.App. 303, 257 P. 909, 911.

An officer appointed to make record or enrolment of deeds and other legal instruments authorized by law to be recorded.

RECORDER OF LONDON. One of the justices of oyer and terminer, and a justice of the peace of the *quorum* for putting the laws in execution for the preservation of the peace and government of the city. Being the mouth of the city, he delivers the sentences and judgments of the court therein, and also certifies and records the city customs, etc. He is chosen by the lord mayor and aldermen, and attends the business of the city when summoned by the lord mayor, etc. Wharton.

RECORDING ACTS. Statutes enacted in the several states relative to the official recording of deeds, mortgages, bills of sale, chattel mortgages, etc., and the effect of such records as notice to creditors, purchasers, incumbrancers, and others interested.

RECORDS, EARLY ENGLISH. A record commission was appointed in 1800 by parliament, which in 37 years of service printed many records of England, Wales and Scotland. See their reports. Extracts from that on the "Statutes of the Realm" will be found in 2 Sel. Essays in Anglo. Amer. L. H. 171. See 2 Holdsw. Hist. E. L.

RECORDUM. A record; a judicial record. It is used in the phrase *prout patet per recordum,* which is a formula employed, in pleading, for reference to a record, signifying as it appears from the record. 1 Chit. Pl. 385; Philpot v. McArthur, 10 Me. 127.

RECOUP, or RECOUPE. To deduct, defalk, discount, set off, or keep back; to withhold part of a demand.

RECOUPMENT. In practice. Defalcation or discount from a demand. A keeping back something which is due, because there is an equitable reason to withhold it. Tomlins. A right of the defendant to have a deduction from the amount of the plaintiff's damages, for the reason that the plaintiff has not complied with the cross-obligations or independent covenants arising under the same contract. Hoover Commercial Co. v. Humphrey, 107 Miss. 810, 66 So. 214, 216.

It implies that plaintiff has cause of action, but asserts that defendant has counter cause of action growing out of breach of some other part of same contract on which plaintiff's action is founded, or for some cause connected with contract. Marianna Lime Products Co. v. McKay, 109 Fla. 275, 147 So. 264, 267; Storrs v. Storrs, 130 Fla. 717, 178 So. 841, 843.

It is keeping back something which is due because there is an equitable reason to withhold it; and is now uniformly applied where a man brings an action for breach of a contract between him and the defendant; and where the latter can show that some stipulation in the same contract was made by the plaintiff, which he has violated, the defendant may, if he choose, instead of suing in his turn, *recoupe* his damages arising from the breach committed by the plaintiff, whether they be liquidated or not. Ives v. Van Eppes, 22 Wend., N.Y., 156. And see Barber v. Chapin, 28 Vt. 413.

In speaking of matters to be shown in defense, the term "recoupment" is often used as synonymous with "reduction." The term is of French origin, and signifies cutting again, or cutting back, and, as a defense, means the cutting back on the plaintiff's claim by the defendant. Like reduction, it is of necessity limited to the amount of the plaintiff's claim. It is properly applicable to a case where the same contract imposes mutual duties and obligations on the two parties, and one seeks a remedy for the breach of duty by the second, and the second meets the demand by a claim for the breach of duty by the first. Davenport v. Hubbard, 46 Vt. 207, 14 Am.Rep. 620.

"Recoupment" differs from "set-off" in this respect: that any claim or demand the defendant may have against the plaintiff may be used as a set-off, while it is not a subject for recoupment unless it grows out of the very same transaction which furnishes the plaintiff's cause of action. The term is, as appears above, synonymous with "*reduction;*" but the latter is not a technical term of the law; the word "defalcation," in one of its meanings, expresses the same idea, and is used interchangeably with recoupment. Recoupment, as a remedy, corresponds to the *reconvention* of the civil law. Dexter-Portland Cement Co. v. Acme Supply Co., 147 Va. 758, 133 S.E. 788, 790; Lovett v. Lovett, 93 Fla. 611, 112 So. 768, 780.

"Recoupment" is the right to set off unliquidated damages, while the right of "set-off," comprehends only liquidated damages, or those capable of being ascertained by calculation. Alley v. Bessemer Gas Engine Co., Tex. Civ.App., 228 S.W. 963, 966. Recoupment is confined to matters arising out of the transaction or contract upon which suit is brought, not depending upon whether the matter be liquidated or unliquidated. J. C. Lysle Milling Co. v. North Alabama Grocery Co., 201 Ala. 222, 77 So. 748, 749. While there is a well-defined distinction between set-off and recoupment, they are each, in a sense, set-offs. Lehman v. Austin, 195 Ala. 244, 70 So. 653, 655.

RECOURSE. To recur. As to "Without Recourse," see that title.

RECOUSSE. Fr. In French law. Recapture. Emerig. Traité des Assur. c. 12, § 23.

RECOVER. To get or obtain again, to collect, to get renewed possession of; to win back; to regain, as lost property, territory, appetite, health, courage. In a narrower sense, to be successful in a suit, to collect or obtain amount, to have judgment, to obtain a favorable or final judgment, to obtain in any legal manner in contrast to voluntary payment. Covert v. Randles, 53 Ariz. 225, 87 P.2d 488, 490. Olds v. General Acc. Fire and Life Assur. Corp., 67 Cal.App.2d 812, 155 P.2d 676, 680.

RECOVEREE. In old conveyancing. The party who suffered a common recovery.

RECOVERER. The demandant in a common recovery, after judgment has been given in his favor.

RECOVERY. In its most extensive sense, the restoration or vindication of a right existing in a person, by the formal judgment or decree of a competent court, at his instance and suit, or the obtaining, by such judgment, of some right or property which has been taken or withheld from him. This is also called a "true" recovery, to distinguish it from a "feigned" or "common" recovery. See Common Recovery.

The obtaining of a thing by the judgment of a court, as the result of an action brought for that purpose. Vaughan v. Humphreys, 153 Ark. 140, 239 S.W. 730, 22 A.L.R. 1201.

The amount finally collected, or the amount of judgment. In re Lahm, 179 App.Div. 757, 167 N.Y.S. 217, 219.

Final Recovery

The final judgment in an action. Also the final verdict in an action, as distinguished from the judgment entered upon it. Fisk v. Gray, 100 Mass. 193.

RECREANT. Coward or craven. The word pronounced by a combatant in the trial by battel, when he acknowledged himself beaten. 3 Bl. Comm. 340.

RECRIMINATION. A charge made by an accused person against the accuser; in particular a counter-charge of adultery or cruelty made by one charged with the same offense in a suit for divorce, against the person who has charged him or her. Wharton. A showing by the defendant of any cause of divorce against the plaintiff, in bar of the plaintiff's cause of divorce. Morrison v. Morrison, 38 Idaho 45, 221 P. 156, 158. And to bar divorce, complainant's misconduct need not be of equal degree with that of defendant, but must be of same general character. Carter v. Carter, Tex. Civ.App., 151 S.W.2d 884, 885.

RECRUIT. A newly-enlisted soldier.

RECRUITING. Within 50 U.S.C.A. § 2388(a), denouncing the offense of obstructing the "recruiting or enlistment service," "recruiting" is gaining fresh supplies for the forces, as well by draft as otherwise, and put as an alternative to enlistment or voluntary enrollment. U. S. v. Prieth, D.C.N.J., 251 F. 946, 951.

RECTA PRISA REGIS. In old English law. The king's right to prisage, or taking of one butt or pipe of wine before and another behind the mast, as a custom for every ship laden with wines. Cowell.

RECTIFICATION OF BOUNDARIES. The action to rectify or ascertain the boundaries of two adjoining pieces of land. Sweet.

RECTIFICATION OF REGISTER. The process by which a person whose name is wrongly entered on (or omitted from) a register may compel the keeper of the register to remove (or enter) his name. Sweet.

RECTIFIER. As used in the United States internal revenue laws, this term is not confined to a person who runs spirits through charcoal, but is applied to any one who rectifies or purifies spirits in any manner whatever, or who makes a mixture of spirits with anything else, and sells it under any name. Quantity of Distilled Spirits, 3 Ben. 73, Fed.Cas.No.11,494.

RECTIFY. To correct or define something which is erroneous or doubtful. Sweet.

Thus, where the parties to an agreement have determined to embody its terms in the appropriate and conclusive form, but the instrument meant to effect this purpose (*e. g.*, a conveyance, settlement, etc.) is, by mutual mistake, so framed as not to express the real intention of the parties, an action may be brought in the chancery division of the high court to have it rectified. Sweet.

RECTITUDO. Lat. Right or justice; legal dues; tribute or payment. Cowell.

RECTO, BREVE DE. A writ of right, which was of so high a nature that as other writs in real actions were only to recover the possession of the land, etc., in question, this aimed to recover the seisin and the property, and thereby both the rights of possession and property were tried together. Cowell.

RECTO DE ADVOCATIONE ECCLESIÆ. A writ which lay at common law, where a man had right of advowson of a church, and, the parson dying, a stranger had presented. Fitzh. Nat. Brev. 30.

RECTO DE CUSTODIA TERRÆ ET HÆREDIS. A writ of right of ward of the land and heir. Abolished.

RECTO DE DOTE. A writ of right of dower, which lay for a widow who had received part of of her dower, and demanded the residue, against the heir of the husband or his guardian. Abolished. 23 & 24 Vict. c. 126, § 26.

RECTO DE DOTE UNDE NIHIL HABET. A writ of right of dower whereof the widow had nothing, which lay where her deceased husband, having divers lands or tenements, had assured no dower to his wife, and she thereby was driven to sue for her thirds against the heir or his guardian. Abolished.

RECTO DE RATIONABILI PARTE. A writ of right, of the reasonable part, which lay between privies in blood; as brothers in gavelkind, sisters, and other coparceners, for land in fee-simple. Fitzh. Nat. Brev. 9.

RECTO QUANDO (or QUIA) DOMINUS REMISIT CURIAM. A writ of right, when or because the lord had remitted his court, which lay where lands or tenements in the seignory of any lord were in demand by a writ of right. Fitzh. Nat. Brev. 16.

RECTO SUR DISCLAIMER. An abolished writ on disclaimer.

RECTOR. In ecclesiastical law. One who rules or governs. A name given to certain officers of the Roman church. Dict. Canonique.

The spiritual head and presiding officer of church. A clergyman elected by the members of the parish to have permanent charge of it. He is the official head of the parish and ex officio head of all parochial organizations. Hunter v. Rector, Wardens and Vestrymen of St. Anna's Chapel, 185 La. 217, 168 So. 780, 783.

In English law. He that has full possession of a parochial church. A rector (or parson) has, for the most part, the whole right to all the ecclesiastical dues in his parish; while a *vicar* has an appropriator over him, entitled to the best part of the profits, to whom the vicar is, in effect, perpetual curate, with a standing salary. 1 Bl. Comm. 384, 388; Bird v. St. Mark's Church, 62 Iowa 567, 17 N.W. 747.

RECTOR PROVINCIÆ. Lat. In Roman law. The governor of a province. Cod. 1, 40.

RECTOR SINECURE. A rector of a parish who has not the cure of souls. 2 Steph. Comm. 683.

RECTORIAL TITHES. Great or predial tithes.

RECTORY. An entire parish church, with all its rights, glebes, tithes, and other profits whatsoever; otherwise commonly called a "benefice." Gibson v. Brockway, 8 N.H. 470, 31 Am.Dec. 200; Pawlet v. Clark, 9 Cranch, 326, 3 L.Ed. 735. A rector's manse, or parsonage house. Spelman.

RECTUM. Lat. Right; also a trial or accusation. Bract.; Cowell.

RECTUM ESSE. To be right in court.

RECTUM ROGARE. To ask for right; to petition the judge to do right.

RECTUM, STARE AD. To stand trial or abide by the sentence of the court.

RECTUS. In the old law of descents. Right; upright; the opposite of obliquus (*q. v.*).

RECTUS IN CURIA. Lat. Right in court. The condition of one who stands at the bar, against whom no one objects any offense. When a person outlawed has reversed his outlawry, so that he can have the benefit of the law, he is said to be "*rectus in curia.*" Jacob.

RECUPERATIO. Lat. In old English law. Recovery; restitution by the sentence of a judge of a thing that has been wrongfully taken or detained. Co. Litt. 154*a*.

RECUPERATIO, i. e., AD REM, PER INJURIAM EXTORTAM SIVE DETENTAM, PER SENTENTIAM JUDICIS RESTITUTIO. Co. Litt. 154*a*. Recovery, *i. e.*, restitution by sentence of a judge of a thing wrongfully extorted or detained.

RECUPERATIO EST ALICUJUS REI IN CAUSAM, ALTERIUS ADDUCTÆ PER JUDICEM ACQUISITIO. Co. Litt. 154*a*. Recovery is the acquisition by sentence of a judge of anything brought into the cause of another.

RECUPERATORES. In Roman law. A species of judges first appointed to decide controversies between Roman citizens and strangers concerning rights requiring speedy remedy, but whose jurisdiction was gradually extended to questions which might be brought before ordinary judges. Mackeld. Rom. Law, § 204.

RECURRENDUM EST AD EXTRAORDINARIUM QUANDO NON VALET ORDINARIUM. We must have recourse to what is extraordinary, when what is ordinary fails.

RECUSANTS. In English law. Persons who willfully absent themselves from their parish church, and on whom penalties were imposed by various statutes passed during the reigns of Elizabeth and James I. Wharton. Those persons who separate from the church established by law. Termes de la Ley. The term was practically restricted to Roman Catholics.

RECUSATIO TESTIS. Lat. In the civil law. Rejection of a witness, on the ground of incompetency. Best, Ev. Introd. 60, § 60.

RECUSATION. In the civil law. A species of exception or plea to the jurisdiction, to the effect that the particular judge is disqualified from hearing the cause by reason of interest or prejudice. Poth. Proc. Civile, pt. 1, c. 2, § 5. The challenge of jurors. Code Prac. La. arts. 499, 500. An act, of what nature soever it may be, by which a strange heir, by deeds or words, declares he will not be heir. Dig. 29, 2, 95.

RED, RAED, or REDE. Sax. Advice; counsel.

RED. A color.

A communist; radical. The term contemplates a follower of the red flag of the Russian revolution. A name of opprobrium sometimes given to those with a liberal political outlook, especially to those advocating social, political or economic reform.

RED BOOK OF THE EXCHEQUER. An ancient record, wherein are registered the holders of lands *per baroniam* in the time of Henry II., the number of hides of land in certain counties before the Conquest, and the ceremonies on the coronation of Eleanor, wife of Henry III. Jacob; Cowell.

RED FLAG. The recognized standard or symbol of an extreme revolutionary party or of those who seek social as well as political revolution and anarchy; as the red flag of the Commune. People v. Chambers, 22 Cal.App.2d 687, 72 P.2d 746, 758.

RED HANDED. With the marks of crime fresh on him.

RED INTERNATIONAL. See Third International.

RED LIGHTS AHEAD DOCTRINE. Under this doctrine, third party obtaining securities is required to investigate only under exceptional circumstances which arise when a party to a transaction has knowledge that some fact or facts exist with respect to transaction which would prevent action by commercially honest men for whom law is made. Thomas v. Atkins, D.C.Minn., 52 F.Supp. 405, 410.

RED TAPE. In a derivative sense, order carried to fastidious excess; system run out into trivial extremes. Webster v. Thompson, 55 Ga. 434.

REDDENDO SINGULA SINGULIS. Lat. By referring each to each; referring each phrase or expression to its appropriate object. A rule of construction.

REDDENDUM. Lat. In conveyancing. Rendering; yielding. The technical name of that clause in a conveyance by which the grantor creates or reserves some new thing to himself, out of what he had before granted; as "*rendering* therefor yearly the sum of ten shillings, or a pepper-corn," etc. That clause in a lease in which a rent is reserved to the lessor, and which commences with the word "*yielding.*" 2 Bl.Comm. 299; Freudenberger Oil Co. v. Simmons, 75 W.Va. 337, 83 S.E. 995, 997, Ann.Cas.1918A, 873.

REDDENS CAUSAM SCIENTIÆ. Lat. Giving the reason of his knowledge.

In Scotch practice. A formal phrase used in depositions, preceding the statement of the reason of the witness' knowledge. 2 How. State Tr. 715.

REDDERE, NIL ALIUD EST QUAM ACCEPTUM RESTITUERE; SEU, REDDERE EST QUASI RETRO DARE, ET REDDITUR DICITUR A REDEUNDO, QUIA RETRO IT. Co. Litt. 142. To render is nothing more than to restore that which has been received; or, to render is as it were to give back, and it is called "rendering" from "returning," because it goes back again.

REDDIDIT SE. Lat. He has rendered himself.

In old English practice. A term applied to a principal who had rendered himself in discharge of his bail. Holthouse.

REDDITARIUM. In old records. A rental, or rent-roll. Cowell.

REDDITARIUS. In old records. A renter; a tenant. Cowell.

REDDITION. A surrendering or restoring; also a judicial acknowledgment that the thing in demand belongs to the demandant, and not to the person surrendering. Cowell.

REDEEM. To buy back. To liberate an estate or article from mortgage or pledge by paying the debt for which it stood as security. To repurchase in a literal sense; as, to redeem one's land from a tax-sale. Maxwell v. Foster, 67 S.C. 377, 45 S.E. 927; Miller v. Ratterman, 47 Ohio St. 141, 24 N.E. 496; Layton v. Thayne, C.C.A.Utah, 144 F.2d 94, 96. It implies the existence of a debt and means to rid property of that incumbrance. Talley v. Eastland, 259 Ky. 241, 82 S.W.2d 368, 372.

REDEEMABLE. Subject to an obligation of redemption; embodying, or conditioned upon, a promise or obligation of redemption; convertible into coin; as, a "redeemable currency." U. S. v. North Carolina, 136 U.S. 211, 10 S.Ct. 920, 34 L.Ed. 336. Subject to redemption; admitting of redemption or repurchase; given or held under conditions admitting of reacquisition by purchase; as, a "redeemable pledge."

REDEEMABLE RIGHTS. Rights which return to the conveyor or disposer of land, etc., upon payment of the sum for which such rights are granted. Jacob.

REDELIVERY. A yielding and delivering back of a thing. American Brake Shoe & Foundry Co. v. New York Rys. Co., D.C.N.Y., 293 F. 612, 623.

REDELIVERY BOND. A bond given to a sheriff or other officer, who has attached or levied on personal property, to obtain the release and repossession of the property, conditioned to redeliver the property to the officer or pay him its value in case the levy or attachment is adjudged good. Drake v. Sworts, 24 Or. 198, 33 P. 563.

REDEMISE. A regranting of land demised or leased.

REDEMPTIO OPERIS. Lat. In Roman law, a contract for the hiring or letting of services, or for the performance of a certain work in consideration of the payment of a stipulated price. It is the same contract as "*locatio operis*," but regarded from the standpoint of the one who is to do the work, and who is called "*redemptor operis*," while the hirer is called "*locator operis*." Mackeld. Rom. Law, § 408.

REDEMPTION. A repurchase; a buying back. The act of a vendor of property in buying it back again from the purchaser at the same or an enhanced price. Murphy v. Casselman, 24 N.D. 336, 139 N.W. 802, 803; Venner v. Public Utilities Commission, 302 Ill. 232, 134 N.E. 17, 18.

The process of annulling and revoking a conditional sale of property, by performance of the conditions on which it was stipulated to be revocable.

The process of cancelling and annulling a defeasible title to land, such as is created by a mortgage or a tax-sale, by paying the debt or fulfilling the other conditions.

The liberation of an estate from a mortgage. Webb v. Williamson, 202 Ark. 763, 152 S.W.2d 312, 314.

The liberation of a chattel from pledge or pawn, by paying the debt for which it stood as security.

Repurchase of notes, bills, or other evidences of debt, (particularly bank-notes and paper-money,) by paying their value in coin to their holders.

Redemption, equity of. See Equity of Redemption.

Redemption of land tax. In English law. The payment by the landowner of such a lump sum as shall exempt his land from the land tax. Mozley & Whitley.

The right of redemption. An agreement or paction, by which the vendor reserves to himself the power of taking back the thing sold by returning the price paid for it. Civil Code La. art. 2567.

Voluntary redemption. In Scotch law, is when a mortgagee receives the sum due into his own hands, and discharges the mortgage, without any consignation. Bell.

REDEMPTIONES. In old English law. Heavy fines. Distinguished from *misericordia*, (which see.)

REDEUNDO. Lat. Returning; in returning; while returning. 2 Strange, 985.

REDEVANCE. In old French and Canadian law. Dues payable by a tenant to his lord, not necessarily in money.

REDHIBERE. Lat. In the civil law. To have again; to have back; to cause a seller to have again what he had before.

REDHIBITION. In the civil law. The avoidance of a sale on account of some vice or defect in the thing sold, which renders it either absolutely useless or its use so inconvenient and imperfect that it must be supposed that the buyer would not have purchased it had he known of the vice. Civ.Code La. art. 2520.

REDHIBITORY ACTION. In the civil law. An action for redhibition. An action to avoid a sale on account of some vice or defect in the thing sold, which renders its use impossible, or so inconvenient and imperfect that it must be supposed the buyer would not have purchased it had he known of the vice. Civ. Code La. art. 2520. An action in which buyer, alleging seller's breach of express or implied warranty, seeks to return thing sold or part thereof and to recover back all or part of price paid. Hermanos v. Matos, C.C.A. Puerto Rico, 81 F.2d 930, 931.

REDHIBITORY DEFECT or VICE. In the civil law. A defect in an article sold, for which the seller may be compelled to take it back; a defect against which the seller is bound to warrant. Poth. Cont. Sale, no. 203.

REDIMERE. Lat. In Roman law. To buy back. Talley v. Eastland, 259 Ky. 241, 82 S.W.2d 368, 372.

REDISSEISIN. In old English law. A second disseisin of a person of the same tenements, and by the same disseisor, by whom he was before disseised. 3 Bl. Comm. 188.

REDISTRIBUTION. In gambling. Pay-off to holders of winning tickets. Delaware Steeplechase & Race Ass'n v. Wise, 27 A.2d 357, 361, 2 Terry (Del.) 587.

REDITUS. Lat. A revenue or return, income or profit; specifically, rent.

REDITUS ALBI. White rent; blanche farm; rent payable in silver or other money.

REDITUS ASSISUS. A set or standing rent.

REDITUS CAPITALES. Chief rent paid by freeholders to go quit of all other services.

REDITUS NIGRI. Black rent; black mail; rent payable in provisions, corn, labor, etc.; as distinguished from "money rent," called "*reditus albi.*"

REDITUS QUIETI. Quitrents (*q. v.*).

REDITUS SICCUS. Rent seck (*q. v.*).

REDMANS. In feudal law. Men who, by the tenure or custom of their lands, were to ride with or for the lord of the manor, about his business. Domesday.

REDOBATORES. In old English law. Those that buy stolen cloth and turn it into some other color or fashion that it may not be recognized. Redubbers.

REDRAFT. In commercial law. A draft or bill drawn in the place where the original bill was made payable and where it went to protest, on the place where such original bill was drawn, or, when there is no regular commercial intercourse rendering that practicable, then in the next best or most direct practicable course. 1 Bell, Comm. 406.

REDRESS. The receiving satisfaction for an injury sustained.

REDUBBERS. In criminal law. Those who bought stolen cloth and dyed it of another color to prevent its being identified were anciently so called. Cowell; 3 Inst. 134.

REDUCE. In Scotch law. To rescind or annul.

REDUCTIO AD ABSURDUM. Lat. In logic. The method of disproving an argument by showing that it leads to an absurd consequence.

REDUCTION. In Scotch law. An action brought for the purpose of rescinding, annulling, or cancelling some bond, contract, or other instrument in writing. 1 Forb. Inst. pt. 4, pp. 158, 159.

In French law, abatement. When a parent gives away, whether by gift *inter vivos* or by legacy, more than his *portion disponible,* (*q. v.*) the donee or legatee is required to submit to have his gift reduced to the legal proportion.

REDUCTION EX CAPITE LECTI. By the law of Scotland the heir in heritage was entitled to reduce all voluntary deeds granted to his prejudice by his predecessor within sixty days preceding the predecessor's death; provided the maker of the deed, at its date, was laboring under the disease of which he died, and did not subsequently go to kirk or market unsupported. Bell.

REDUCTION IMPROBATION. In Scotch law. One form of the action of reduction in which falsehood and forgery are alleged against the deed or document sought to be set aside.

REDUCTION INTO POSSESSION. The act of exercising the right conferred by a chose in action, so as to convert it into a chose in possession; thus, a debt is reduced into possession by payment. Sweet.

REDUCTION OF CAPITAL. Voluntary liquidation of retired corporate capital. Jay Ronald Co. v. Marshall Mortg. Corporation, 40 N.Y.S.2d 391, 399, 265 App.Div. 622.

REDUCTION TO POSSESSION. Conversion of a right existing as a claim into actual custody and enjoyment. Newell v. McLaughlin, 126 Conn. 138, 9 A.2d 815, 819.

REDUCTION TO PRACTICE. As respects priority of invention for purposes of patentability is accomplished when inventor's conception is embodied in such form as to render it capable of practical and successful use. Pyrene-Minimax Corporation v. Palmer, 89 F.2d 505, 510, 67 App.D.C. 33. But device need not be perfect or commercial success. Pierson v. Beck, Cust. & Pat.App., 40 F.2d 769, 770.

REDUNDANCY. This is the fault of introducing superfluous matter into a legal instrument; particularly the insertion in a pleading of matters foreign, extraneous, and irrelevant to that which it is intended to answer. Carpenter v. Reynolds, 58 Wis. 666, 17 N.W. 300; In re Wise's Estate, 144 Neb. 273, 13 N.W.2d 146, 151.

RE-ENACT. To enact again; to revive. Police Jury of Caddo Parish v. City of Shreveport, 137 La. 1032, 69 So. 828, 831.

RE-ENTRY. The act of resuming the possession of lands or tenements in pursuance of a right which party exercising it reserved to himself when he quit his former possession. Sokolow v. Meyer, 248 N.Y.S. 405, 409, 139 Misc. 424. Fleisher v. Friob, 161 N.Y.S. 940, 944, 97 Misc.Rep. 343.

RE-ESTABLISH. To restore to its former position. Baron v. Prudence Life Ins. Co., 315 Ill. App. 129, 42 N.E.2d 137, 138.

RE-EXAMINATION. An examination of a witness after a cross-examination, upon matters arising out of such cross-examination.

RE-EXCHANGE. The damages or expenses caused by the dishonor and protest of a bill of exchange in a foreign country, where it was payable, and by its return to the place where it was drawn or indorsed, and its being there taken up. Bangor Bank v. Hook, 5 Me. 175; Simonoff v. Granite City Nat. Bank, 279 Ill. 248, 116 N.E. 636, 639.

RE-EXTENT. In English practice. A second extent made upon lands or tenements, upon complaint made that the former extent was partially performed. Cowell.

REEF. In mining law. A vein or lode containing or supposed to contain minerals.

REEVE. An ancient English officer of justice inferior in rank to an alderman. He was a ministerial officer appointed to execute process, keep the King's peace, and put the laws in execution. He witnessed all contracts and bargains, brought offenders to justice and delivered them to punishment, took bail for such as were to appear at the county court, and presided at the court or folcmote. He was also called *gerefa*.

There were several kinds of reeves, as, the *shire-gerefa*, shire-reeve or sheriff; the *heh-gerefa*, or high-sheriff; *tithing-reeve*, burghor or borough-reeve.

Land Reeve

See Land.

REFALO. A word composed of the three initial syllables *"re." "fa." "lo.,"* for *"recordari facias loquelam,"* (*q. v.*). 2 Sell. Pr. 160.

REFARE. To bereave, take away, rob. Cowell.

REFECTION. In the civil law. Reparation; reestablishment of a building. Dig. 19, 1, 6, 1.

REFER. When a case or action involves matters of account or other intricate details which require minute examination, and for that reason are not fit to be brought before a jury, it is usual to *refer* the whole case, or some part of it, to the decision of an auditor or referee, and the case is then said to be referred.

Taking this word in its strict, technical use, it relates to a mode of determining questions which is distinguished from "arbitration," in that the latter word imports submission of a controversy without any lawsuit having been brought, while "reference" imports a lawsuit pending, and an issue framed or question raised which (and not the controversy itself) is sent out. Thus, arbitration is resorted to instead of any judicial proceeding; while reference is one mode of decision employed in the course of a judicial proceeding. And "reference" is distinguished from "hearing or trial," in that these are the ordinary modes of deciding issues and questions in and by the courts with aid of juries when proper; while reference is an employment of non-judicial persons—individuals not integral parts of the court—for the decision of particular matters inconvenient to be heard in actual court. Abbott.

To point, allude, direct, or make reference to. This is the use of the word in conveyancing and in literature, where a word or sign introduced for the purpose of directing the reader's attention to another place in the deed, book, document, etc., is said to "refer" him to such other connection.

REFEREE. In practice. A person to whom a cause pending in a court is referred by the court, to take testimony, hear the parties, and report thereon to the court. Central Trust Co. of New York v. Wabash, etc., R. Co., C.C.Mo., 32 F. 684, 685. He is an officer exercising judicial powers, and is an arm of the court for a specific purpose. Segal v. Jackson, 48 N.Y.S.2d 877, 879, 183 Misc. 460.

REFEREE IN BANKRUPTCY. An officer appointed by the courts of bankruptcy under the act of 1898 (11 U.S.C.A. § 1) corresponding to the "registers in bankruptcy" under earlier statutes having administrative and quasi-judicial functions under the bankruptcy law, and who assists the court in such cases and relieves the judge of attention to matters of detail or routine, by taking charge of all administrative matters and the preparation or preliminary consideration of questions requiring judicial decision, subject at all times to the supervision and review of the court. In re Carl Dernburg & Son, C.C.A.N.Y., 5 F.2d 37, 38. He is an officer of the bankruptcy court but not a judge. Fish v. East, C.C.A.Colo., 114 F.2d 177, 200. His status is substantially that of a master whose findings to extent adopted are considered findings of District Court. Stewart v. Ganey, C.C.A.Ala., 116 F.2d 1010, 1012.

REFEREES, COURT OF. In the passage of private bills through the house of commons, the practice was adopted in 1864 of the appointment of referees on such bills, consisting of the chairman of ways and means and not less than three other persons to be appointed by the speaker. The referees were formed into one or more courts, three at least being required to constitute each court, a member in every case being chairman, but receiving no salary. The referees inquired into the proposed works, etc., and reported to the house. The committees of the house on any bill might also refer any question to the referees for their decision. It was also ordered in 1864 that the referees should decide on all petitions as to the right of the petitioner to be heard, *i. e.*, his *locus standi*. A court of referees was specially constituted for the adjudication of this right, called *locus standi*. A series of reports of the court of referees on private bills in parliament, called *Locus Standi* reports, has been published since 1867.

REFEREES, OFFICIAL. Officials in the King's Bench Division of the High Court of Justice in England, created by the judicature acts. They are three in number. They try such questions and actions as may be referred to them, and act as arbitrators in certain cases.

REFERENCE. In contracts. An agreement to submit to arbitration; the act of parties in submitting their controversy to chosen referees or arbitrators.

In practice. The act of sending a cause pending in court to a referee for his examination and decision. State v. Innes, 89 Kan. 168, 130 P. 677, 680; Jones v. Jones, 188 Mo.App. 220, 175 S.W. 227, 230. See Refer.

In commercial law. The act of sending or directing one person to another, for information or advice as to the character, solvency, standing, etc., of a third person, who desires to open business relations with the first, or to obtain credit with him.

REFERENCE IN CASE OF NEED. When a person draws or indorses a bill of exchange, he sometimes adds the name of a person to whom it may be presented "in case of need;" *i. e.*, in case it is dishonored by the original drawee or acceptor. Byles, Bills, 261.

REFERENCE STATUTES. Statutes which refer to other statutes and make them applicable to the subject of legislation. Their object is to incorporate into the act of which they are a part the provisions of other statutes by reference and adoption. State ex rel. School Dist. of Kansas City v. Lee, 334 Mo. 513, 66 S.W.2d 521; Van Pelt v. Hilliard, 75 Fla. 792, 78 So. 693, 698, L.R.A. 1918E, 639.

REFERENCE TO RECORD. Under the English practice, when an action is commenced, an entry of it is made in the cause-book according to the year, the initial letter of the surname of the first plaintiff, and the place of the action, in numerical order among those commenced in the same year, *e. g.*, "1876, A. 26;" and all subsequent documents in the action (such as pleadings and affidavits) bear this mark, which is called the "reference to the record." Sweet.

REFERENDARIUS. An officer by whom the order of causes was laid before the Roman emperor, the desires of petitioners made known, and answers returned to them. Vicat, Voc. Jur.; Calvin.

REFERENDARY. In Saxon law. A master of requests; an officer to whom petitions to the king were referred. Spelman.

REFERENDO SINGULA SINGULIS. Lat. Referring individual or separate words to separate subjects; making a distributive reference of words in an instrument; a rule of construction.

REFERENDUM. In international law. A communication sent by a diplomatic representative to his home government, in regard to matters presented to him which he is unable or unwilling to decide without further instructions.

In the modern constitutional law of Switzerland and elsewhere, a method of submitting an important legislative measure to a direct vote of the whole people. Pacific States Telephone & Telegraph Co. v. Oregon, 32 S.Ct. 224, 223 U.S. 118, 56 L.Ed. 377; Kiernan v. Portland, 32 Sup.Ct. 231, 223 U.S. 151, 56 L.Ed. 386; Plebiscite; Initiative. Right reserved to the people to adopt or reject any act or measure which has been passed by a legislative body, and which, in most cases, would without action on the part of the electors become a law. Whitmore v. Carr, 2 Cal. App.2d 590, 38 P.2d 802, 803. City of Litchfield v. Hart, 306 Ill.App. 621, 29 N.E.2d 678, 679.

REFINANCE. To finance again or anew. In automobile parlance, signifying that notes executed for the purchase price of an automobile have been negotiated by the original vendor to some corporation dealing in that character of securities. American Indemnity Co. v. Allen, for Use and Benefit of Commerce Union Bank, 176 Tenn. 134, 138 S.W.2d 445, 446.

REFINEMENT. A term sometimes employed to describe verbiage inserted in a pleading or indictment, over and above what is necessary to be set forth; or an objection to a plea or indictment on the ground of its failing to include such superfluous matter. State v. Peak, 130 N.C. 711, 41 S.E. 887.

REFORM. To correct, rectify, amend, remodel. Instruments *inter partes* may be *reformed,* when defective, by a court of equity. By this is meant that the court, after ascertaining the real and originai intention of the parties to a deed or other instrument, (which intention they failed to sufficiently express, through some error, mistake of fact, or inadvertence,) will decree that the instrument be held and construed as if it fully and technically expressed that intention. Churchill v. Meade, 92 Or. 626, 182 P. 368, 371; Gross v. Yeskel, 100 N.J.Eq. 293, 134 A. 737.

See, also, Reformation.

It is to be observed that "reform" is seldom, if ever, used of the correction of defective pleadings, judgments, decrees or other judicial proceedings; "amend" being the proper term for that use. Again, "amend" seems to connote the idea of improving that which may have been well enough before, while "reform" might be considered as properly applicable only to something which before was quite worthless.

REFORM ACTS. A name bestowed on the statutes 2 Wm. IV. c. 45, and 30 & 31 Vict. c. 102, passed to amend the representation of the people in England and Wales; which introduced extended amendments into the system of electing members of the house of commons.

REFORMATION. Remedy, afforded by courts of equity to the parties, to written instruments which import a legal obligation, to reform or rectify such instruments whenever they fail, through fraud or mutual mistake, to express the real agreement or intention of the parties. Greenfield v. Ætna Cas. & Sur. Co., 75 Ohio App. 122, 61 N.E.2d 226, 229. Rubinson v. North American Accident Ins. Co. of Chicago, Ill., 124 Neb. 269, 246 N.W. 349, 350.

See, also, Reform.

REFORMATORY. A place or institution in which efforts are made either to cultivate the intellect or instruct the conscience or improve the conduct where inmates voluntarily submit themselves to its instruction or discipline or are forcibly detained therein. McKinnon v. Second Judicial District Court in and for Washoe County, 35 Nev. 494, 130 P. 465, 468.

REFORMATORY SCHOOLS. In English law. Schools to which convicted juvenile offenders (under sixteen) may be sent by order of the court before which they are tried, if the offense be punishable with penal servitude or imprisonment, and the sentence be to imprisonment for ten days or more. Wharton.

REFRESHER. In English law. A further or additional fee to counsel in a long case, which may be, but is not necessarily, allowed on taxation.

REFRESHING THE MEMORY. The act of a witness who consults his documents, memoranda, or books, to bring more distinctly to his recollection the details of past events or transactions, concerning which he is testifying.

REFUND, *n.* That which is refunded. United States v. Wurts, Pa., 58 S.Ct. 637, 639, 303 U.S. 414, 82 L.Ed. 932.

REFUND, *v.* To repay or restore; to return money in restitution or repayment. Rackliff v. Greenbush, 93 Me. 99, 44 A. 375. City of Long Beach v. Lisenby, 180 Cal. 52, 179 P. 198, 201. United States v. Wurts, Pa., 58 S.Ct. 637, 639, 303 U.S.

414, 82 L.Ed. 932. To fund again or anew; specifically, finance, to borrow, usually by the sale of bonds, in order to pay off an existing loan with the proceeds. Street Improvement Dist. No. 315 v. Arkansas Highway Commission, 190 Ark. 1045, 83 S.W.2d 81, 82.

REFUND ANNUITY CONTRACT. A contract by which an insurance company agrees to repay to the annuitant, in installments during his life, amount paid in by him to company, and if at his death there be a balance unpaid, to pay that balance to person designated by annuitant. In re Atkins' Estate, 129 N.J.Eq. 186, 18 A.2d 45, 49.

REFUNDING BOND. A bond which replaces or pays off outstanding bond which holder surrenders in exchange for new security. Fore v. Alabama State Bridge Corporation, 242 Ala. 455, 6 So.2d 508, 512. Also a bond given to an executor by a legatee, upon receiving payment of the legacy, conditioned to *refund* the same, or so much of it as may be necessary, if the assets prove deficient.

REFUNDS. In the laws of the United States. Sums of money received by the government or its officers which, for any cause, are to be refunded or restored to the parties paying them; such as excessive duties or taxes, duties paid on goods destroyed by accident, duties received on goods which are re-exported, etc.

REFUSAL. The act of one who has, by law, a right and power of having or doing something of advantage, and declines it. Also, the declination of a request or demand, or the omission to comply with some requirement of law, as the result of a positive intention to disobey. In the latter sense, the word is often coupled with "neglect," as if a party shall "neglect or refuse" to pay a tax, file an official bond, obey an order of court, etc. But "neglect" signifies a mere omission of a duty, which may happen through inattention, dilatoriness, mistake, or inability to perform, while "refusal" implies the positive denial of an application or command, or at least a mental determination not to comply. U. S. v. Krafft, C.C.A.N.J., 249 F. 919, 925; American Nat. Bank of Ardmore v. National Bank of Claremore, 119 Okl. 149, 249 P. 424, 428.

An option. Hake v. Groff, 232 Mich. 233, 205 N.W. 145, 146.

REFUSE, *v.* To deny, decline, reject. Burns v. Fox, 113 Ind. 206, 14 N.E. 541. Ex parte Yost, D.C.Cal., 55 F.Supp. 768, 772.

"Fail" is distinguished from "refuse" in that "refuse" involves an act of the will, while "fail" may be an act of inevitable necessity. Maestas v. American Metal Co. of New Mexico, 37 N.M. 203, 20 P.2d 924, 928.

REFUSE, *n.* That which is refused or rejected as useless or worthless. Worthless matter, rubbish, scum, leavings. Stern Holding Co. v. O'Connor, 119 N.J.L. 291, 196 A. 432, 433.

REFUTANTIA. In old records. An acquittance or acknowledgment of renouncing all future claim. Cowell.

REG. GEN. An abbreviation of *"Regula Generalis,"* a general rule, (of court.)

REG. JUD. An abbreviation of *"Registrum Judiciale,"* the register of judicial writs.

REG. LIB. An abbreviation of *"Registrarii Liber,"* the register's book in chancery, containing all decrees.

REG. ORIG. An abbreviation of *"Registrum Originale,"* the register of original writs.

REG. PL. An abbreviation of *"Regula Placitandi,"* rule of pleading.

REGAL FISH. Whales and sturgeons, so called in English law, as belonging to the king by prerogative when cast on shore or caught near the coast. 1 Bl. Comm. 290.

RÉGALE. In old French law. A payment made to the *seigneur* of a fief, on the election of every bishop or other ecclesiastical feudatory, corresponding with the relief paid by a lay feudatory. Steph. Lect. 235.

REGALE EPISCOPORUM. The temporal rights and privileges of a bishop. Cowell.

REGALIA. An abbreviation of *"jura regalia,"* royal rights, or those rights which a king has by virtue of his prerogative. Hence owners of counties palatine were formerly said to have *"jura regalia"* in their counties as fully as the king in his palace. 1 Bl. Comm. 117. The term is sometimes used in the same sense in the Spanish law. Hart v. Burnett, 15 Cal. 566.

Some writers divide the royal prerogative into *majora* and *minora regalia,* the former including the regal dignity and power, the latter the revenue or fiscal prerogatives of the crown. 1 Bl. Comm. 117.

REGALIA FACERE. To do homage or fealty to the sovereign by a bishop when he is invested with the regalia.

REGALITY. A territorial jurisdiction in Scotland conferred by the crown. The lands were said to be given *in liberam regalitatem,* and the persons receiving the right were termed "lords of regality." Bell.

REGARD. In old English law. Inspection; supervision. Also a reward, fee, or perquisite.

REGARD, COURT OF. In forest law. A tribunal held every third year, for the lawing or expeditation of dogs, to prevent them from chasing deer. Cowell.

REGARD OF THE FOREST. In old English law. The oversight or inspection of it, or the office and province of the regarder, who is to go through the whole forest, and every bailiwick in it, before the holding of the sessions of the forest, or justice-seat, to see and inquire after trespassers, and for the survey of dogs. Manwood.

REGARDANT. A term which was applied, in feudal law, to a villein annexed to a manor, and having charge to do all base services within the same, and to see the same freed from all things that might annoy his lord. Such a villein *regardant* was thus opposed to a villein *en gros*, who was transferable by deed from one owner to another. Cowell; 2 Bl. Comm. 93.

REGARDER OF A FOREST. An ancient officer of the forest, whose duty it was to take a view of the forest hunts, and to inquire concerning trespasses, offenses, etc. Manwood.

REGE INCONSULTO. Lat. In English law. A writ issued from the sovereign to the judges, not to proceed in a cause which may prejudice the crown, until advised. Jenk. Cent. 97.

REGENCY. Rule; government; kingship. The man or body of men intrusted with the vicarious government of a kingdom during the minority, absence, insanity, or other disability of the king.

REGENT. A governor or ruler. One who vicariously administers the government of a kingdom, in the name of the king, during the latter's minority or other disability.

A master, governor, director, or superintendent of a public institution, particularly a college or university.

In the canon law, it signifies a master or professor of a college. *Dict. du Dr. Can.*

REGIA DIGNITAS EST INDIVISIBILIS, ET QUÆLIBET ALIA DERIVATIVA DIGNITAS EST SIMILITER INDIVISIBILIS. 4 Inst. 243. The kingly power is indivisible, and every other derivative power is similarly indivisible.

REGIA VIA. Lat. In old English law. The royal way; the king's highway. Co. Litt. 56*a*.

REGIAM MAJESTATEM. A collection of the ancient laws of Scotland. It is said to have been compiled by order of David I., king of Scotland, who reigned from A. D. 1124 to 1153. Hale, Com. Law, 271.

REGICIDE. The murder of a sovereign; also the person who commits such murder.

REGIDOR. In Spanish law. One of a body, never exceeding twelve, who formed a part of the *ayuntamiento*. The office of regidor was held for life; that is to say, during the pleasure of the supreme authority. In most places the office was purchased; in some cities, however, they were elected by persons of the district, called *"capitulares."* 12 Pet. 442, note.

RÉGIME. In French law. A system of rules or regulations.

RÉGIME DOTAL. The *dot*, being the property which the wife brings to the husband as her contribution to the support of the burdens of the marriage, and which may either extend as well to future as to present property, or be expressly confined to the present property of the wife, is subject to certain regulations which are summarized in the phrase *"régime dotal."* The husband has the entire administration during the marriage; but, as a rule, where the *dot* consists of immovables, neither the husband nor the wife, nor both of them together, can either sell or mortgage it. The *dot* is returnable upon the dissolution of the marriage, whether by death or otherwise. Brown.

RÉGIME EN COMMUNAUTÉ. The community of interests between husband and wife which arises upon their marriage. It is either (1) legal or (2) conventional, the former existing in the absence of any "agreement" properly so called, and arising from a mere declaration of community; the latter arising from an "agreement," properly so called. Brown.

REGIMIENTO. In Spanish law. The body of regidores, who never exceeded twelve, forming a part of the municipal council, or *ayuntamiento*, in every capital of a jurisdiction. 12 Pet. 442, note.

REGINA. Lat. The queen.

REGIO ASSENSU. A writ whereby the sovereign gives his assent to the election of a bishop. Reg. Orig. 294.

REGISTER, *v.* To record formally and exactly; to enroll; to enter precisely in a list or the like. Los Angeles County v. Craig, 38 Cal.App.2d 58, 100 P.2d 818, 820. To make correspond exactly one with another; to fit correctly in a relative position; to be in correct alignment one with another. Cover v. Schwartz, Cust. & Pat. App., 28 C.C.P.A. 831, 116 F.2d 512, 515.

REGISTER, *n.* An officer authorized by law to keep a record called a "register" or "registry;" as the register for the probate of wills.

A book containing a record of facts as they occur, kept by public authority; a register of births, marriages, and burials.

REGISTER IN BANKRUPTCY. An officer of the courts of bankruptcy, under the earlier acts of congress in that behalf, having substantially the same powers and duties as the "referees in bankruptcy" under the act of 1898 (11 U.S.C.A.). See Referee.

REGISTER OF DEEDS. The name given in some states to the officer whose duty is to record deeds, mortgages, and other instruments affecting realty in the official books provided and kept for that purpose; more commonly called "recorder of deeds."

REGISTER OF LAND OFFICE. A federal officer appointed for each federal land district, to take charge of the local records and attend to the preliminary matters connected with the sale, preemption, or other disposal of the public lands within the district. Rev.St.U.S. § 2234 (43 U.S.C.A. § 72).

REGISTER OF PATENTS. A book of patents, directed by St. 15 & 16 Vict. c. 83, § 34, passed in

1852, to be kept at the specification office, for public use. 2 Steph. Comm. 29, note *t*.

REGISTER OF SHIPS. A register kept by the collectors of customs, in which the names, ownership, and other facts relative to merchant vessels are required by law to be entered. This register is evidence of the nationality and privileges of an American ship. The certificate of such registration, given by the collector to the owner or master of the ship, is also called the ship's register. Rapalje & Lawrence.

REGISTER OF THE TREASURY. An officer of the United States treasury, whose duty is to keep all accounts of the receipt and expenditure of public money and of debts due to or from the United States, to preserve adjusted accounts with vouchers and certificates, to record warrants drawn upon the treasury, to sign and issue government securities, and take charge of the registry of vessels under United States laws. Rev. St.U.S. § 312 (31 U.S.C.A. § 161) and section 313.

REGISTER OF WILLS. An officer in some of the states, whose function is to record and preserve all wills admitted to probate, to issue letters testamentary or of administration, to receive and file accounts of executors, etc., and generally to act as the clerk of the probate court.

REGISTER OF WRITS. A book preserved in the English court of chancery, in which were entered the various forms of original and judicial writs.

REGISTERED. Entered or recorded in some official register or record or list. State v. McGuire, 183 Iowa 927, 167 N.W. 592, 594.

REGISTERED BOND. The bonds of the United States government (and of many municipal and private corporations) are either registered or "coupon bonds." In the case of a registered bond, the name of the owner or lawful holder is entered in a register or record, and it is not negotiable or transferable except by an entry on the register, and checks or warrants are sent to the registered holder for the successive installments of interest as they fall due. A bond with interest coupons attached is transferable by mere delivery, and the coupons are payable, as due, to the person who shall present them for payment. But the bond issues of many private corporations now provide that the individual bonds "may be registered as to principal," leaving the interest coupons payable to bearer, or that they may be registered as to both principal and interest, at the option of the holder. Benwell v. New York, 55 N.J.Eq. 260, 36 A. 668; Novoprutsky v. Morris Plan Co. of Philadelphia, 319 Pa. 97, 179 A. 218, 219, 98 A.L.R. 1486.

REGISTERED TONNAGE. The registered tonnage of a vessel is the capacity or cubical contents of the ship, or the amount of weight which she will carry, as ascertained in some proper manner and entered on an official register or record. See Reck v. Phœnix Ins. Co., 54 Hun 637, 7 N.Y.S. 492; Wheaton v. Weston, D.C.Pa., 128 F. 153.

REGISTERED TRADE-MARK. A trade-mark filed in the United States patent office, with the necessary description and other statements required by the act of congress, and there duly recorded, securing its exclusive use to the person causing it to be registered. 15 U.S.C.A. § 1051.

REGISTERED VOTERS. In Virginia, this term refers to the persons whose names are placed upon the registration books provided by law as the sole record or memorial of the duly qualified voters of the state. Chalmers v. Funk, 76 Va. 719.

REGISTER'S COURT. In American law. A court in the state of Pennsylvania which has jurisdiction in matters of probate.

REGISTRANT. One who registers; particularly, one who registers anything (*e. g.*, a trade-mark) for the purpose of securing a right or privilege granted by law on condition of such registration.

REGISTRAR. An officer who has the custody or keeping of a registry or register. This word is used in England; "register" is more common in America.

REGISTRAR GENERAL. In English law. An officer appointed by the crown under the great seal, to whom, subject to such regulations as shall be made by a principal secretary of state, the general superintendence of the whole system of registration of births, deaths, and marriages is intrusted. 3 Steph.Comm. 234.

REGISTRAR'S LICENSE. In English law, a license issued by an officer of that name authorizing the solemnization of a marriage without the use of the religious ceremony ordained by the Church of England.

REGISTRARIUS. In old English law. A notary; a registrar or register.

REGISTRATION. Recording; inserting in an official register; enrollment, as registration of voters; the act of making a list, catalogue, schedule, or register, particularly of an official character, or of making entries therein. In re Supervisors of Election, C.C.Del., 1 F. 1.

Any schedule containing a list of voters, the being upon which constitutes a prerequisite to vote.

A method of proof prescribed for ascertaining the electors who shall qualify to cast their votes and being a part of the machinery of elections and safeguards against frauds. O'Brien v. City of Saratoga Springs, 228 N.Y.S. 82, 83, 137 Misc. 728.

A special registration as distinguished from a "general registration" is one designed for a particular election which becomes functus officio when that election has been had. A general registration is one made up under general rules. Cowart v. City of Waycross, 159 Ga. 589, 126 S.E. 476, 479.

REGISTRATION OF STOCK. In the practice of corporations. Recording in the official books of the company of the name and address of the holder of each certificate of stock, with the date of its issue, and, in the case of a transfer of stock from one holder to another, the names of both parties and such other details as will identify the transaction and preserve a memorial or official record of its essential facts. Fisher v. Jones, 82 Ala. 117, 3 So. 13.

REGISTRUM BREVIUM. The register of writs (*q. v.*).

REGISTRY. A register, or book authorized or recognized by law, kept for the recording or registration of facts or documents. The act of recording or writing in the register or depositing in the place of public records. Schneidau v. New Orleans Land Co., 132 La. 264, 61 So. 225, 232.

In commercial law. The registration of a vessel at the custom-house, for the purpose of entitling her to the full privileges of a British or American built vessel. 3 Kent, Comm. 139; Abb. Shipp. 58–96.

REGISTRY OF DEEDS. The system or organized mode of keeping a public record of deeds, mortgages, and other instruments affecting title to real property. Castillero v. U. S., 2 Black, 109, 17 L.Ed. 360.

REGIUS PROFESSOR. A royal professor or reader of lectures founded in the English universities by the king. Henry VIII. founded in each of the universities five professorships, viz., of divinity, Greek, Hebrew, law, and physic. Cowell.

REGLAMENTO. In Spanish colonial law. A written instruction given by a competent authority, without the observance of any peculiar form. Schm. Civil Law, Introd. 93, note.

REGNAL YEARS. Statutes of the British parliament are usually cited by the name and year of the sovereign in whose reign they were enacted, and the successive years of the reign of any king or queen are denominated the "regnal years."

REGNANT. One having authority as a king; one in the exercise of royal authority.

REGNI POPULI. A name given to the people of Surrey and Sussex, and on the sea-coasts of Hampshire. Blount.

REGNUM ECCLESIASTICUM. The ecclesiastical kingdom. 2 Hale, P.C. 324.

REGNUM NON EST DIVISIBILE. Co.Litt. 165. The kingdom is not divisible.

REGRANT. In the English law of real property, when, after a person has made a grant, the property granted comes back to him, (*e. g.*, by escheat or forfeiture,) and he grants it again, he is said to regrant it. The phrase is chiefly used in the law of copyholds.

REGRATING. In old English law. The offense of buying or getting into one's hands at a fair or market any provisions, corn, or other dead victual, with the intention of selling the same again in the same fair or market, or in some other within four miles thereof, at a higher price. The offender was termed a "regrator." 3 Inst. 195. See Forsyth Mfg. Co. v. Castlen, 112 Ga. 199, 37 S.E. 485, 81 Am.St.Rep. 28.

REGRESS. Used principally in the phrase "free entry, egress, and regress" but it is also used to signify the reentry of a person who has been disseised of land. Co.Litt. 318*b*.

REGULA. Lat. In practice. A rule. *Regula generalis,* a general rule; a standing rule or order of a court. Frequently abbreviated *"Reg. Gen."*

REGULA CATONIANA. In Roman law. The rule of Cato. A rule respecting the validity of dispositions by will. See Dig. 34, 7.

REGULA EST, JURIS QUIDEM IGNORANTIAM CUIQUE NOCERE, FACTI VERO IGNORANTIAM NON NOCERE. Cod. 1, 18, 10. It is a rule, that every one is prejudiced by his ignorance of law, but not by his ignorance of fact.

REGULA PRO LEGE, SI DEFICIT LEX. In default of the law, the maxim rules.

REGULÆ GENERALES. Lat. General rules, which the courts promulgate from time to time for the regulation of their practice.

REGULAR. Conformable to law. Steady or uniform in course, practice, or occurrence; not subject to unexplained or irrational variation. Rooney v. City of Omaha, 104 Neb. 260, 177 N.W. 166, 167. Made according to rule, duly authorized, formed after uniform type, built or arranged according to established plan, law, or principle. Merchants' Nat. Bank of Los Angeles v. Continental Nat. Bank of Los Angeles, 98 Cal.App. 523, 277 P. 354, 361. Antonym of "casual" or "occasional." Palle v. Industrial Commission, 79 Utah 47, 7 P.2d 284, 290, 81 A.L.R. 1222.

As to regular "Clergy," "Deposit," "Election," "Indorsement," "Meeting," "Navigation," "Process," "Session," and "Term," see those titles.

REGULAR AND ESTABLISHED PLACE OF BUSINESS. Under Judicial Code, § 48 (28 U.S.C.A. §§ 1400, 1694), permitting patent infringement suits to be brought in the district in which defendant committed acts of infringement and has a regular and established place of business, a "regular" place of business is one where business is carried on regularly, and not temporarily, or for some special work or particular transaction, while an "established" place of business must be a permanent place of business, and a "regular and established place of business" is one where the same business in kind, if not in degree, as that done at the home office or principal place of business, is carried on. Winterbottom v. Casey, D.C.Mich., 283 F. 518, 521; Candas v. Agnini, D.C.N.Y., 14 F. Supp. 21, 22.

A foreign corporation may have a "regular and established place of business" although business therein is merely securing orders and forwarding them to the home office. Shelton v. Schwartz, C.C.A.Ill., 131 F.2d 805, 808.

REGULAR ARMY. Professional permanent soldiery, those who have chosen the military service as a career as distinguished from "militiamen". State ex rel. McGaughey v. Grayston, 349 Mo. 700, 163 S.W.2d 335, 340. In another sense. An army which is comprised of soldiers properly organized as legitimate combatants engaged in war, commanded by a person responsible for his subordinates, having a fixed distinctive emblem, carrying arms openly, and conducting their operations in conformance with the laws and customs of war. Case v. Olson, 234 Iowa 869, 14 N.W.2d 717, 720.

REGULAR COURSE OF BUSINESS. This phrase within Compensation Acts excluding from their benefits person whose employment is not in regular course of business of employer, refers to habitual or regular occupation that party is engaged in with view of winning livelihood or some gain, excluding incidental or occasional operations arising out of transaction of that business; to normal operations which constitute business. Sgattone v. Mulholland & Gotwals, 290 Pa. 341, 138 A. 855, 857, 58 A.L.R. 1463; Passarelli v. Monacelli, 121 Pa.Super. 32, 183 A. 65, 67.

REGULAR ON ITS FACE. Process is "regular on its face" when it proceeds from a court, officer, or body having authority of law to issue process of that nature, and is legal in form and contains nothing to notify or fairly apprise any one that it is issued without authority. Pankewicz v. Jess, 27 Cal.App. 340, 149 P. 997, 998. See, also, Allen v. Cooling, 161 Minn. 10, 200 N.W. 849, 851 (promissory note).

REGULAR RATE. At which employee is employed, within Fair Labor Standards Act, means actual hourly rate of pay of employee computed by dividing his actual weekly wage by number of hours customarily worked. Missel v. Overnight Motor Transp. Co., D.C.Md., 40 F.Supp. 174, 180, 183.

REGULARITER NON VALET PACTUM DE RE MEA NON ALIENANDA. Co. Litt. 223. It is a rule that a compact not to alienate my property is not binding.

REGULARLY. At fixed and certain intervals, regular in point of time. Lamb v. Board of Auditors of Wayne County, 235 Mich. 95, 209 N.W. 195, 196. In accordance with some consistent or periodical rule or practice. Green v. Benedict, 102 Conn. 1, 128 A. 20, 21.

REGULARS. Those who profess and follow a certain rule of life, (*regula,*) belong to a religious order, and observe the three approved vows of poverty, chastity, and obedience. Wharton.

REGULATE. To fix, establish, or control; to adjust by rule, method, or established mode; to direct by rule or restriction; to subject to governing principles or laws. In re Siracusa, 212 N.Y.S. 400, 403, 125 Misc. 882; Southern R. Co. v. Russell, 133 Va. 292, 112 S.E. 700, 703.

The power of Congress to regulate commerce is the power to enact all appropriate legislation for its protection or advancement; to adopt measures to promote its growth and insure its safety; to foster, protect, control, and restrain. Virginian Ry. Co. v. System Federation No. 40, Railway Employees Department of American Federation of Labor, C.C.A.Va., 84 F.2d 641, 650. It is also power to prescribe rule by which commerce is to be governed, and embraces prohibitory regulations. United States v. Darby, U.S.Ga., 61 S.Ct. 451, 456, 312 U.S. 100, 657, 85 L.Ed. 609, 132 A.L.R. 1430.

REGULATION. The act of regulating; a rule or order prescribed for management or government; a regulating principle; a precept. Curless v. Watson, 180 Ind. 86, 102 N.E. 497, 499. Rule of order prescribed by superior or competent authority relating to action of those under its control. State v. Miller, 33 N.M. 116, 263 P. 510, 513.

REGULATION CHARGE. Charge exacted for privilege or as condition precedent to carrying on business. Duff v. Garden City, 122 Kan. 390, 251 P. 1091, 1092.

REGULATION OF AN EXECUTIVE DEPARTMENT. The general rules relating to the subject on which a department acts, made by the head of the department under some act of Congress conferring power to make such regulations, and thereby give to them the force of law. State ex rel. Kaser v. Leonard, 164 Or. 579, 102 P.2d 197, 202, 129 A.L.R. 1125.

REGULUS. Lat. In Saxon law. A title sometimes given to the earl or *comes,* in old charters. Spelman.

REHABERE FACIAS SEISINAM. When a sheriff in the *"habere facias seisinam"* had delivered seisin of more than he ought, this judicial writ lay to make him restore seisin of the excess. Reg. Jud. 13, 51, 54.

REHABILITATE. To invest or clothe again with some right, authority, or dignity; to restore to a former capacity; to reinstate, to qualify again. In re Coleman, D.C.Ky., 21 F.Supp. 923, 924, 925.

In Scotch and French criminal law. To reinstate a criminal in his personal rights which he has lost by a judicial sentence. Brande.

REHABILITATION. Investing or clothing again with some right, authority, or dignity; restoring to a former capacity; reinstating; qualifying again. In re Coleman, D.C.Ky., 21 F.Supp. 923, 924, 925.

French and Scotch criminal law. The reinstatement of a criminal in his personal rights which he has lost by a judicial sentence. Brande.

Of Corporation

Attempt to conserve and administer assets of insolvent corporation in hope of its eventual return from financial stress to solvency. In re Title & Mortgage Guarantee Co. of Buffalo, 274 N.Y.S. 270, 152 Misc. 428. And contemplates continuance of corporate life and activities, and its effort to restore and reinstate corporation to former condition of successful operation and solvency. New York Title & Mortgage Co. v. Friedman, 276 N.Y.S. 72, 153 Misc. 697.

Old English Law

A papal bull or brief for re-enabling a spiritual person to exercise his function, who was formerly disabled; or a *restoring* to a former *ability*. Cowell.

REHEARING. Second consideration of cause for sole purpose of calling to court's attention any error, omission, or oversight in first consideration. Lake v. State, 100 Fla. 373, 129 So. 827, 829. A retrial of issues and presumes notice to parties entitled thereto and opportunity for them to be heard. Yee v. State Board of Equalization of California, 16 Cal.App.2d 417, 60 P.2d 322, 323.

REI INTERVENTUS. Lat. Things intervening; that is, things done by one of the parties to a contract, in the faith of its validity, and with the assent of the other party, and which have so affected his situation that the other will not be allowed to repudiate his obligation, although originally it was imperfect. 1 Bell, Comm. 328, 329.

REI TURPIS NULLUM MANDATUM EST. The mandate of an immoral thing is void. Dig. 17, 1, 6, 3. A contract of mandate requiring an illegal or immoral act to be done has no legal obligation. Story, Bailm. § 158.

REIF. A robbery. Cowell.

REIMBURSE. To pay back, to make restoration, to repay that expended; to indemnify, or make whole. Los Angeles County v. Frisbie, 19 Cal.2d 634, 122 P.2d 526; Askay v. Maloney, 92 Or. 566, 179 P. 899, 901.

REINSTATE. To reinstall; to reestablish; to place again in a former state, condition, or office; to restore to a state or position from which the object or person had been removed. Collins v. U. S., 15 Ct.Cl. 22; Lowry v. Ætna Life Ins. Co., Tex.Civ.App., 120 S.W.2d 505, 507.

To reinstate a policy holder or one who has allowed his policy to lapse does not mean new insurance or taking out a new policy, but does mean that the insured has been restored to all the benefits accruing to him under the policy contract, the original policy. Missouri State Life Ins. Co. v. Jensen, 139 Okl. 130, 281 P. 561, 562.

REINSTATE A CASE. To place case again in same position as before dismissal. United States v. Green, C.C.A.Mont., 107 F.2d 19, 22.

REINSURANCE. A contract by which an insurer procures a third person to insure him against loss or liability by reason of original insurance. A contract that one insurer makes with another to protect the latter from a risk already assumed. Vial v. Norwich Union Fire Ins. Society of Norwich, England, 257 Ill. 355, 100 N.E. 929, 930, 44 L.R.A.,N.S., 317, Ann.Cas.1914A, 1141. It binds the reinsurer to pay to the reinsured the whole loss sustained in respect to the subject of the insurance to the extent to which he is reinsured. Sofia Bros. v. General Reinsurance Corporation, 274 N.Y.S. 565, 153 Misc. 6. Also the substitution, with the consent of the insured, of a second insurer for the first, so that the original insurer is released. People v. American Cent. Ins. Co., 179 Mich. 371, 146 N.W. 235, 236.

RELPUBLICÆ INTEREST VOLUNTATES DEFUNCTORUM EFFECTUM SORTIRI. It concerns the state that the wills of the dead should have their effect.

REISSUABLE NOTES. Bank-notes which, after having been once paid, may again be put into circulation.

REJOIN. In pleading. To answer a plaintiff's replication in an action at law, by some matter of fact.

REJOINDER. In common-law pleading. The second pleading on the part of the defendant, being his answer to the plaintiff's replication.

REJOINING GRATIS. Rejoining voluntarily, or without being required to do so by a rule to rejoin. When a defendant was under terms to rejoin *gratis,* he had to deliver a rejoinder, without putting the plaintiff to the necessity and expense of obtaining a rule to rejoin. 10 Mees. & W. 12; Lush, Pr. 396; Brown.

RELATE. To stand in some relation; to have bearing or concern; to pertain; refer; to bring into association with or connection with; with "to." City of Mitchell v. Western Public Service Co., 124 Neb. 248, 246 N.W. 484, 486; Siano v. Helvering, D.C.N.J., 13 F.Supp. 776, 780.

RELATED. Standing in relation; connected; allied; akin. Nowland Realty Co. v. Commissioner of Internal Revenue, C.C.A.7, 47 F.2d 1018, 1021.

RELATIO EST FICTIO JURIS ET INTENTA AD UNUM. Relation is a fiction of law, and intended for one thing. 3 Coke, 28.

RELATIO SEMPER FIAT UT VALEAT DISPOSITIO. Reference should always be had in such a manner that a disposition in a will may avail. 6 Coke, 76.

RELATION. A relative or kinsman; a person connected by consanguinity. In re Spier's Estate, 224 Mich. 658, 195 N.W. 430, 431; McMenamy v. Kampelmann, 273 Mo. 450, 200 S.W. 1075, 1077. See, also, Relative.

The words "relatives" and "relations," in their primary sense, are broad enough to include any one connected by blood or affinity, even to the remotest degree, but where used in wills, as defining and determining legal succession, are construed to include only those persons who are entitled to share in the estate as next of kin under the statute of distributions. In re Trickett's Estate, 197 Cal. 20, 239 P. 406, 409; Wooten's Trustee v. Hardy, 221 Ky. 338, 298 S.W. 963, 967.

The connection of two persons, or their situation with respect to each other, who are associated, whether by the law, by their own agreement, or by kinship, in some social *status* or union for the purposes of domestic life; as the relation of guardian and ward, husband and wife, master and servant, parent and child; so in the phrase "domestic relations."

The doctrine of "relation" is that principle by which an act done at one time is considered by a fiction of law to have been done at some antecedent period. It is usually applied where several proceedings are essential to complete a particular transaction, such as a conveyance or deed. The last proceeding which consummates the conveyance is held for certain purposes to take effect by relation as of the day when the first proceeding was had. Knapp v. Alexander-Edgar Lumber Co., 237 U.S. 162, 35 S.Ct. 515, 517, 59 L.Ed. 894. And see U. S. v. Anderson, 194 U.S. 394, 24 S.Ct. 716, 48 L.Ed. 1035.

A recital, account, narrative of facts; information given. Thus, suits by *quo warranto* are entitled "on the relation of" a private person, who is called the "relator." But in this connection the word seems also to involve the idea of the suggestion, instigation, or instance of the relator.

In the civil law, the report of the facts and law in a pending case, made by the judges to the emperor, for the purpose of obtaining his opinion on the questions of law involved, in the form of an imperial rescript. This proceeding might be resorted to in cases where no law seemed applicable, or where there were great difficulties in its interpretation, until it was abolished by Justinian. Nov. 125.

RELATION NEVER DEFEATS COLLATERAL ACTS. 18 Vin.Abr. 292.

RELATION SHALL NEVER MAKE GOOD A VOID GRANT OR DEVISE OF THE PARTY. 18 Vin.Abr. 292.

RELATIONS. A term which, in its widest sense, includes all the kindred of the person spoken of. 2 Jarm. Wills, 661.

RELATIVE. A kinsman; a person connected with another by blood or affinity.

When used generically, includes persons connected by ties of affinity as well as consanguinity, and, when used with a restrictive meaning, refers to those only who are connected by blood. Appeal of Schutte, 90 Conn. 529, 97 A. 906, 907.

A person or thing having relation or connection with some other person or thing; as, relative rights, relative powers, *infra.* See also, Relation.

RELATIVE CONFESSION. See Confession.

RELATIVE FACT. In the law of evidence. A fact having relation to another fact; a minor fact; a circumstance.

RELATIVE POWERS. Those which relate to land; so called to distinguish them from those which are collateral to it.

RELATIVE RIGHTS. Those rights of persons which are incident to them as members of society, and standing in various relations to each other. 1 Bl.Comm. 123. Those rights of persons in private life which arise from the civil and domestic relations. 2 Kent, Comm. 1.

RELATIVE WORDS REFER TO THE NEXT ANTECEDENT, UNLESS THE SENSE BE THEREBY IMPAIRED. Noy, Max. 4; Wing. Max. 19; Broom, Max. 606; Jenk. Cent. 180.

RELATIVORUM, COGNITO UNO, COGNOSCITUR ET ALTERUM. Cro. Jac. 539. Of relatives, one being known, the other is also known.

RELATOR. An informer; the person upon whose complaint, or at whose instance certain writs are issued such as information or writ of *quo warranto*, and who is *quasi* the plaintiff in the proceeding. State ex inf. Barker v. Duncan, 265 Mo. 26, 175 S.W. 940, 942, Ann.Cas.1916D, 1.

RELATRIX. In practice. A female relator or petitioner.

RELAXARE. In old conveyancing. To release. *Relaxavi, relaxasse,* have released. Litt. § 445.

RELAXATIO. In old conveyancing. A release; an instrument by which a person relinquishes to another his right in anything.

RELAXATION. In old Scotch practice. Letters passing the signet by which a debtor was relaxed [released] from the horn; that is, from personal diligence. Bell.

RELEASE, *v.* To lease again or grant new lease. Aaron v. Woodcock, 283 Pa. 33, 128 A. 665, 666, 38 A.L.R. 1251. See Accord and Satisfaction.

RELEASE, *n.* The relinquishment, concession, or giving up of a right, claim, or privilege, by the person in whom it exists or to whom it accrues, to the person against whom it might have been demanded or enforced. Miller v. Estabrook, C.C.A. W.Va., 273 F. 143, 148; Coopey v. Keady, 73 Or. 66, 144 P. 99, 101.

In this sense it is a contract and must be supported by lawful and valuable consideration. Hamilton v. Edmundson, 235 Ala. 97, 177 So. 743, 746.

A discharge of a debt by act of party, as distinguished from an extinguishment which is a discharge by operation of law, and, in distinguishing release from receipt, "receipt" is evidence that an obligation has been discharged, but "release" is itself a discharge of it. Glickman v. Weston, 140 Or. 117, 11 P.2d 281, 284.

An *express* release is one directly made in terms by deed or other suitable means. An *implied* release is one which arises from acts of the creditor or owner, without any express agreement. Pothier, Obl. nn. 608, 609. A *release by operation of law* is one which, though not expressly made, the law presumes in consequence of some act of the releasor; for instance, when one of several joint obligors is expressly released, the others are also released by operation of law. 3 Salk. 298; Rowley v. Stoddard, 7 Johns., N.Y., 207.

Liberation, discharge, or setting free from restraint or confinement. Thus, a man unlawfully imprisoned may obtain his *release* on *habeas corpus.* Parker v. U. S., 22 Ct.Cl. 100.

The abandonment to (or by) a person called as a witness in a suit of his interest in the subject-matter of the controversy, in order to qualify him to testify, under the common-law rule.

A receipt or certificate given by a ward to the guardian, on the final settlement of the latter's accounts, or by any other beneficiary on the termination of the trust administration, relinquishing all and any further rights, claims, or demands, growing out of the trust or incident to it.

In admiralty actions, when a ship, cargo, or other property has been arrested, the owner may obtain its release by giving bail, or paying the value of the property into court. Upon this being done he obtains a release, which is a kind of writ under the seal of the court, addressed to the marshal, commanding him to release the property. Sweet.

Estates

The conveyance of a man's interest or right which he hath unto a thing to another that hath the possession thereof or some estate therein. Shep. Touch. 320. The relinquishment of some right or benefit to a person who has already some interest in the tenement, and such interest as qualifies him for receiving or availing himself of the right or benefit so relinquished. Burt. Real Prop. 12; Field v. Columbet, 9 Fed.Cas. 13; Baker v. Woodward, 12 Or. 3, 6 P. 173.

A conveyance of an ulterior interest in lands or tenements to a particular tenant, or of an undivided share to a co-tenant, (the releasee being in either case in privity of estate with the releasor,) or of the right, to a person wrongfully in possession. 1 Steph.Comm. 479.

Deed of release. A deed operating by way of release; but more specifically, in those states where deeds of trust are in use instead of common-law mortgages, as a means of pledging real property as security for the payment of a debt, a "deed of release" is a conveyance in fee, executed by the trustee or trustees, to the grantor in the deed of trust, which conveys back to him the legal title to the estate, and which is to be given on satisfactory proof that he has paid the secured debt in full or otherwise complied with the terms of the deed of trust.

Release by way of enlarging an estate. A conveyance of the ulterior interest in lands to the particular tenant; as, if there be tenant for life or years, remainder to another in fee, and he in remainder releases all his right to the particular tenant and his heirs, this gives him the estate in fee 1 Steph.Comm. 480; 2 Bl.Comm. 324.

Release by way of entry and feoffment. As if there be two joint disseisors, and the disseisee releases to one of them, he shall be sole seised, and shall keep out his former companion; which is the same in effect as if the disseisee had entered and thereby put an end to the disseisin, and afterwards had enfeoffed one of the disseisors in fee. 2 Bl.Comm. 325.

Release by way of extinguishment. As if my tenant for life makes a lease to A. for life, remainder to B. and his heirs, and I release to A., this extinguishes my right to the reversion, and shall inure to the advantage of B.'s remainder, as well as of A.'s particular estate. 2 Bl.Comm. 325.

Release by way of passing a right. As if a man be disseised and releaseth to his disseisor all his right, hereby the disseisor acquires a new right, which changes the quality of his estate, and renders that lawful which before was tortious or wrongful. 2 Bl.Comm. 325.

Release by way of passing an estate. As, where one of two coparceners releases all her right to the other, this passes the fee-simple of the whole. 2 Bl.Comm. 324, 325.

Release of dower. The relinquishment by a married woman of her expectant dower interest or estate in a particular parcel of realty belonging to her husband, as, by joining with him in a conveyance of it to a third person.

Release to uses. The conveyance by a deed of release to one party to the use of another is so termed. Thus, when a conveyance of lands was effected, by those instruments of assurance termed a lease and release, from A. to B. and his heirs, to the use of C. and his heirs, in such case C. at once took the whole fee-simple in such lands; B. by the operation of the statute of uses, being made a mere conduit-pipe for conveying the estate to C. Brown.

RELEASEE. The person to whom a release is made.

RELEASER, or RELEASOR. The maker of a release.

RELEGATIO. Lat. A kind of banishment known to the civil law, which differed from "*deportatio*" in leaving to the person his rights of citizenship.

RELEGATION. In old English law. Banishment for a time only. Co. Litt. 133.

RELEVANCY. Applicability to the issue joined. That quality of evidence which renders it properly applicable in determining the truth and falsity of the matters in issue between the parties to a suit. 1 Greenl.Ev. § 49. Two facts are said to be relevant to each other when so related that according to the common course of events, one either taken by itself or in connection with other facts, proves or renders probable the past, present, or future existence or non-existence of the other. Steph.Dig.Ev. art. 1. Katz v. Delohery Hat Co., 97 Conn. 665, 112 A. 88, 93; Barnett v. State, 104 Ohio St. 298, 135 N.E. 647, 650, 27 A.L.R. 351.

Relevancy is that which conduces to the proof of a pertinent hypothesis; a pertinent hypothesis being one which, if sustained, would logically influence the issue. Whart.Ev. § 20; Hampton v. State, 126 Tex.Cr.R. 211, 70 S.W.2d 1001.

In Scotch law, the relevancy is the justice or sufficiency in law of the allegations of a party. A plea to the relevancy is therefore analogous to the demurrer of the English courts.

A distinction is sometimes taken between "logical" relevancy and "legal" relevancy, the former being judged merely by the standards of ordinary logic or the general laws of reasoning, the latter by the strict and artificial rules of the law with reference to the admissibility of evidence. Hoag v. Wright, 54 N.Y.S. 658, 34 App.Div. 260.

Relevant evidence is such evidence as relates to, or bears directly upon, the point or fact in issue, and proves or has a tendency to prove the proposition alleged; evidence which conduces to prove a pertinent theory in a case. State v. O'Neil, 13 Or. 183, 9 P. 286; Moran v. Abbey, 58 Cal. 163, 168. 1 Whart.Ev. § 20. It does not mean evidence addressed with positive directness to the point but that which according to the common course of events either taken by itself or in connection with other facts, proves or renders probable the past, present or future existence or nonexistence of the other. Seller v. Jenkins, 97 Ind. 430, 438 (quoting Steph.Ev. art. 1, and Best, Principles of Ev. 257, n.). See, also, Relevancy.

Relevancy of evidence does not depend upon the conclusiveness of the testimony offered, but upon its legitimate tendency to establish a controverted fact. Interstate Commerce Commission v. Baird, 24 S.Ct. 563, 194 U.S. 25, 48 L.Ed. 860; State v. Upson, 162 Minn. 9, 201 N.W. 913, 915.

RELEVANT. Applying to the matter in question; affording something to the purpose.

Fact is relevant to another fact when, according to common course of events, existence of one taken alone or in connection with the other fact renders existence of the other certain or more probable. Gulf, C. & S. F. Ry. Co. v. Downs, Tex.Civ.App., 70 S.W.2d 318, 322.

In Scotch law, good in law, legally sufficient; as, a "relevant" plea or defense.

RELEVANT EVIDENCE. See Evidence.

RELIABLE. Trustworthy, worthy of confidence. Quinn v. Daly, 300 Ill. 273, 133 N.E. 290, 291.

RELICT. The survivor of a pair of married people, whether the survivor is the husband or the wife; it means the relict of the united pair, (or of the marriage union,) not the relict of the deceased individual. Spitler v. Heeter, 42 Ohio St. 101.

RELICTA VERIFICATIONE. (Lat. his pleading being abandoned). A confession of judgment made after plea pleaded; viz., a *cognovit actionem* accompanied by a withdrawal of the plea.

RELICTION. An increase of the land by the permanent withdrawal or retrocession of the sea or a river. Hammond v. Shepard, 186 Ill. 235, 57 N.E. 867, 78 Am.St.Rep. 274. Conkey v. Knudsen, 141 Neb. 517, 4 N.W.2d 290, 295.

RELIEF. The assistance or support, pecuniary or otherwise, granted to indigent persons by the proper administrators of the poor-laws.

Also wages paid in cash or in kind for public work because of need. In re Matruski, 8 N.Y.S. 2d 471, 480, 169 Misc. 316.

Deliverance from oppression, wrong, or injustice.

In this sense it is used as a general designation of the assistance, redress, or benefit which a complainant seeks at the hands of a court, particularly in equity. It may be thus used of such remedies as specific performance, or the reformation or rescission of a contract; but it does not seem appropriate to the awarding of money damages.

In feudal law. A sum payable by the new tenant, the duty being incident to every feudal tenure, by way of fine or composition with the lord for taking up the estate which was lapsed or fallen in by the death of the last tenant. At one time the amount was arbitrary, but afterwards the relief of a knight's fee became fixed at one hundred shillings. 2 Bl.Comm. 65.

RELIEF ASSOCIATION. See Railroad Relief Funds.

RELIEVE. To give ease, comfort, or consolation to; to give aid, help, or succor to; alleviate, assuage, ease, mitigate; succor, assist, aid, help; support, sustain; lighten, diminish. Brollier v. Van Alstine, 236 Mo.App. 1233, 163 S.W.2d 109, 115.

To release from a post, station, or duty; to put another in place of, or to take the place of, in the bearing of any burden, or discharge of any duty. Kemp v. Stanley, 204 La. 110, 15 So.2d 1, 11.

In feudal law, to depend; thus, the seigniory of a tenant *in capite* relieves of the crown, meaning that the tenant holds of the crown. The term is not common in English writers. Sweet.

RELIGIO SEQUITUR PATREM. The father's religion is prima facie the infant's religion. Religion will follow the father. [1902] 1 Ch. 688.

RELIGION. Man's relation to Divinity, to reverence, worship, obedience, and submission to mandates and precepts of supernatural or superior beings. In its broadest sense includes all forms of belief in the existence of superior beings exercising power over human beings by volition, imposing rules of conduct, with future rewards and punishments. McMasters v. State, 21 Okl. Cr. 318, 207 P. 566, 568, 29 A.L.R. 292.

One's views of his relations to his Creator and to the obligations they impose of reverence for his being and character, and of obedience to his will. It is often confounded with cultus or form of worship of a particular sect, but is distinguishable from the latter. People ex rel. Fish v. Sandstrom, 3 N.Y.S.2d 1006, 1007, 167 Misc. 436.

Bond uniting man to God, and a virtue whose purpose is to render God worship due him as source of all being and principle of all government of things. Nikulnikoff v. Archbishop, etc., of Russian Orthodox Greek Catholic Church, 255 N.Y.S. 653, 663, 142 Misc. 894.

As used in constitutional provisions forbidding the "establishment of religion," the term means a particular system of faith and worship recognized and practised by a particular church, sect, or denomination. Reynolds v. U. S., 98 U.S. 149, 25 L. Ed. 244; Board of Education v. Minor, 23 Ohio St. 241, 13 Am.Rep. 233

RELIGION, OFFENSES AGAINST. In English law. They are thus enumerated by Blackstone: (1) Apostasy; (2) heresy; (3) reviling the ordinances of the church; (4) blasphemy; (5) profane swearing; (6) conjuration or witchcraft; (7) religious imposture; (8) simony; (9) profanation of the Lord's day; (10) drunkenness; (11) lewdness. 4 Bl.Comm. 43.

RELIGIOUS BOOKS. Those which tend to promote the religion taught by the Christian dispensation, unless by associated words the meaning is so limited to show that some other form of worship is referred to. Simpson v. Welcome, 72 Me. 500, 39 Am.Rep. 349.

RELIGIOUS FREEDOM. Within constitution embraces not only the right to worship God according to the dictates of one's conscience, but also the right to do, or forbear to do, any act, for conscience sake, the doing or forbearing of which is not inimical to the peace, good order, and morals of society. Barnette v. West Virginia State Board of Education, D.C.W.Va., 47 F.Supp. 251, 253, 254; Jones v. City of Moultrie, 196 Ga. 526, 27 S.E.2d 39.

RELIGIOUS CORPORATION See Corporation.

RELIGIOUS HOUSES. Places set apart for pious uses; such as monasteries, churches, hospitals, and all other places where charity was extended to the relief of the poor and orphans, or for the use or exercise of religion.

RELIGIOUS IMPOSTORS. In English law. Those who falsely pretend an extraordinary commission from heaven, or terrify and abuse the people with false denunciations of judgment; they are punishable with fine, imprisonment, and infamous corporal punishment. 4 Broom & H. Comm. 71.

RELIGIOUS LIBERTY. See Liberty.

RELIGIOUS MEN. Such as entered into some monastery or convent. In old English deeds, the vendee was often restrained from aliening to "Jews or religious men" lest the lands should fall into mortmain. Religious men were civilly dead. Blount.

RELIGIOUS SOCIETY. A body of persons associated together for the purpose of maintaining religious worship. The communicants of a denomination who statedly attend services in the church edifice. Fiske v. Beaty, 201 N.Y.S. 441, 444, 206 App.Div. 349.

RELIGIOUS USE. See Charitable Uses.

RELINQUISH. To abandon, to give up, to surrender, to renounce some right or thing. Masser v. London Operating Co., 106 Fla. 474, 145 So. 79, 84; Roy v. Salisbury, Cal.App., 121 P.2d 109, 117.

RELINQUISHMENT. A forsaking, abandoning, renouncing, or giving over a right. Wisconsin-Texas Oil Co. v. Clutter, Tex.Civ.App., 258 S.W. 265, 268.

RELIQUA. The remainder or debt which a person finds himself debtor in upon the balancing or liquidation of an account. Hence *reliquary*, the debtor of a *reliqua;* as also a person who only pays piece-meal. Enc.Lond.

RELIQUES. Remains; such as the bones, etc., of saints, preserved with great veneration as sacred memorials. They have been forbidden to be used or brought into England. St. 3 Jac. I. c. 26.

RELOCATIO. Lat. In the civil law. A renewal of a lease on its determination. It may be either express or tacit; the latter is when the tenant holds over with the knowledge and without objection of the landlord. Mackeld. Rom. Law, § 412.

RELOCATION. In Scotch law. A reletting or renewal of a lease; a *tacit relocation* is permitting a tenant to hold over without any new agreement.

In mining law. A new or fresh location of an abandoned or forfeited mining claim by a stranger, or by the original locator when he wishes to change the boundaries or to correct mistakes in the original location.

REMAINDER. The remnant of an estate in land, depending upon a particular prior estate created at the same time and by the same instrument, and limited to arise immediately on the determination of that estate, and not in abridgement of it. 4 Kent, Comm. 197; Bean v. Atkins, 87 Vt. 376, 89 A. 643, 646; Pinnell v. Dowtin, 224 N.C. 493, 31 S.E.2d 467, 469.

An estate limited to take effect and be enjoyed after another estate is determined. As, if a man seised in fee-simple grants lands to A. for twenty years, and, after the determination of the said term, then to B. and his heirs forever, here A. is tenant for years, *remainder* to B. in fee. 2 Bl.Comm. 164.

An estate in reversion is the residue of an estate, usually the fee left in the grantor and his heirs after the determination of a particular estate which he has granted out of it. The rights of the reversioner are the same as those of a vested remainderman in fee. Sayward v. Sayward, 7 Me. 213, 22 Am.Dec. 191; Glenn v. Holt, Tex.Civ.App., 229 S.W. 684, 685.

In wills. The terms rest, residue, and remainder of estate are usually and ordinarily understood as meaning that part of the estate which is left after all of the other provisions of the will have been satisfied. In re Vail's Estate, 223 Iowa 551, 273 N.W. 107, 110.

Contingent Remainder

An estate in remainder which is limited to take effect either to a dubious and uncertain person, or upon a dubious and uncertain event, by which no present or particular interest passes to the remainder-man, so that the particular estate may chance to be determined and the remainder never take effect. 2 Bl.Comm. 169. A remainder limited so as to depend upon an event or condition which may never happen or be performed, or which may not happen or be performed till after the determination of the preceding estate. Fearne, Rem. 3; Thompson v. Adams, 205 Ill. 552, 69 N.E. 1; Griswold v. Greer, 18 Ga. 545; Price v. Sisson, 13 N.J. Eq. 168.

Cross-Remainder

Where land is devised or conveyed to two or more persons as tenants in common, or where different parts of the same land are given to such persons in severalty, with such limitations that, upon the determination of the particular estate of either, his share is to pass to the other, to the entire exclusion of the ultimate remainder-man or reversioner until all the particular estates shall be exhausted, the remainders so limited are called "cross-remainders." In wills, such remainders may arise by implication; but, in deeds, only by express limitation. 2 Bl.Comm. 381; 2 Washb. Real Prop. 233; 1 Prest.Est. 94.

Executed Remainder

A remainder which vests a present interest in the tenant, though the enjoyment is postponed to the future. 2 Bl.Comm. 168; Fearne, Rem. 31; Hudson v. Wadsworth, 8 Conn. 359.

Executory Remainder

A contingent remainder; one which exists where the estate is limited to take effect either to a dubious and uncertain person or upon a dubious and uncertain event. Temple v. Scott, 143 Ill. 290, 32 N.E. 366.

Vested Remainder

An estate by which a present interest passes to the party, though to be enjoyed *in futuro*, and by which the estate is invariably fixed to remain to a determinate person after the particular estate has been spent. Pinnell v. Dowtin, 224 N.C. 493, 31 S.E.2d 467, 469. One limited to a certain person at a certain time or upon the happening of a necessary event. Ætna Life Ins. Co. v. Hoppin, 214 F. 928, 933, 131 C.C.A. 224.

REMAINDER TO A PERSON NOT OF A CAPACITY TO TAKE AT THE TIME OP APPOINTING IT, IS VOID. Plowd. 27.

REMAINDER VESTED SUBJECT TO BEING DIVESTED. A remainder given to one person, with proviso that it shall go to another under certain contingencies. In re Barnes' Estate, 279 N.Y.S. 117, 155 Misc. 320.

REMAINDERMAN. One who is entitled to the remainder of the estate after a particular estate carved out of it has expired. In re Mawhinney's Will, 261 N.Y.S. 334, 146 Misc. 30.

REMAND. To send back.

Cause

The sending the cause back to the same court out of which it came, for purpose of having some action on it there.

Prisoner

After a preliminary or partial hearing before a court or magistrate, is to send him back to custody, to be kept until the hearing is resumed or the trial comes on. Ex parte Chalfant, 81 W.Va. 93, 93 S.E. 1032, 1033.

When a prisoner is brought before a judge on habeas corpus, for the purpose of obtaining liberty, the judge hears the case, and either discharges him or remands him.

REMANENT PRO DEFECTU EMPTORUM. In practice. The return made by the sheriff to a writ of execution when he has not been able to sell the property seized, that the same *remains unsold for want of buyers.*

REMANENTIA. In old English law. A remainder. Spelman. A perpetuity, or perpetual estate. Glan. lib. 7, c. 1.

REMANET. A remnant; that which remains. Thus the causes of which the trial is deferred from one term to another, or from one sitting to another, are termed *"remanets."* 1 Archb.Pr. 375.

REMEDIAL. Affording a remedy; giving the means of obtaining redress. Of the nature of a remedy; intended to remedy wrongs or abuses, abate faults, or supply defects. Pertaining to or affecting the remedy, as distinguished from that which affects or modifies the right.

REMEDIAL ACTION. One which is brought to obtain compensation or indemnity. Cummings v. Board of Education of Oklahoma City, 190 Okl. 533, 125 P.2d 989, 994.

REMEDIAL STATUTE. One that intends to afford a private remedy to a person injured by the wrongful act. That is designed to correct an existing law, redress an existing grievance, or introduce regulations conducive to the public good. In re School Dist. No. 6, Paris and Wyoming Tps., Kent County, 284 Mich. 132, 278 N.W. 792, 797; Bowles v. Trowbridge, D.C.Cal., 60 F.Supp. 48, 49.

A statute giving a party a mode of remedy for a wrong, where he had none, or a different one, before. 1 Chit.Bl. 86, 87, notes; In re Ungaro's Will, 88 N.J.Eq. 25, 102 A. 244, 246; Cherry v. Kennedy, 144 Tenn. 320, 232 S.W. 661, 662.

The underlying test to be applied in determining whether a statute is penal or remedial is whether it primarily seeks to impose an arbitrary, deterring punishment upon any who might commit a wrong against the public by a violation of the requirements of the statute, or whether the purpose is to measure and define the damages which may accrue to an individual or class of individuals, as just and reasonable compensation for a possible loss having a causal connection with the breach of the legal obligation owing under the statute to such individual or class. Southern Ry. Co. v. Melton, 133 Ga. 277, 291, 307, 65 S.E. 665. In re Engel's Estate, 250 N.Y.S. 648, 653, 140 Misc. 276. *Remedial* statutes are those which are made to supply such defects, and abridge such superfluities, in the common law, as arise either from the general imperfection of all human laws, from change of time and circumstances, from the mistakes and unadvised determinations of unlearned (or even learned) judges, or from any other cause whatsoever. 1 Bl.Comm. 86; Falls v. Key, Tex.Civ.App., 278 S.W. 893, 896; Columbus Trust Co. v. Upper Hudson Electric & R. Co., Sup., 190 N.Y.S. 737, 739. These remedial statutes are themselves divided into *enlarging* statutes, by which the common law is made more comprehensive and extended than it was before, and into *restraining* statutes, by which it is narrowed down to that which is just and proper. A remedial statute is one which not only remedies defects in the common law but defects in civil jurisprudence generally. M. H. Vestal Co. v. Robertson, 277 Ill. 425, 115 N.E. 629, 631; MacDonald v. Hamilton B. Wills & Co., 199 App.Div. 203, 191 N.Y.S. 566, 568.

REMEDIES FOR RIGHTS ARE EVER FAVORABLY EXTENDED. 18 Vin.Abr. 521.

REMEDY. The means by which a right is enforced or the violation of a right is prevented, redressed, or compensated. Remedies are of four kinds: (1) By act of the party injured, the principal of which are defense, recaption, distress, entry, abatement, and seizure; (2) by operation of law, as in the case of retainer and remitter; (3) by agreement between the parties, *e. g.*, by accord and satisfaction and arbitration; and (4) by judicial remedy, *e. g.*, action or suit. Sweet. Berry v. M. F. Donovan & Sons, 120 Me. 457, 115 A. 250, 252, 25 A.L.R. 1021; California Prune & Apricot Growers' Ass'n v. Catz American Co., C.C.A.Cal., 60 F.2d 788, 790, 85 A.L.R. 1117.

The means employed to enforce a right or redress an injury, as distinguished from right, which is a well founded or acknowledged claim. Chelentis v. Luckenbach S. S. Co., 38 S.Ct. 501, 503, 247 U.S. 372, 62 L.Ed. 1171.

Strictly speaking, "remedy" is no part of the action, but is the result thereof, the object for which the action is presented, the end to which all the litigation is directed. Mathews v. Sniggs, 75 Okl. 108, 182 P. 703, 707.

Remedies for the redress of injuries are either public, by indictment, when the injury to the individual or to his property affects the public, or private, when the tort is only injurious to the individual.

That which relieves or cures a disease, including a medicine or remedial treatment. United States v. Natura Co., D.C.Cal., 250 F. 925, 926.

Also a certain allowance to the master of the mint, for deviation from the standard weight and fineness of coins. Enc. Lond.

Adequate Remedy

See Adequate.

Civil Remedy

The remedy afforded by law to a private person in the civil courts in so far as his private and individual rights have been injured by a delict or crime; as distinguished from the remedy by criminal prosecution for the injury to the rights of the public.

Cumulative Remedy

See Cumulative.

Exclusive Remedy

See Exclusive Remedy.

Extraordinary Remedy

See Extraordinary.

Judicial Remedy

See Judicial.

Legal Remedy

A remedy available, under the particular circumstances of the case, in a court of law, as distinguished from a remedy available only in equity. See State v. Sneed, 105 Tenn. 711, 58 S.W. 1070.

Remedy Over

A person who is primarily liable or responsible, but who, in turn, can demand indemnification from another, who is responsible to him, is said to have a "remedy over." For example, a city, being compelled to pay for injuries caused by a defect in the highway, has a "remedy over" against the person whose act or negligence caused the defect, and such person is said to be "liable over" to the city. 2 Black, Judgm. § 575.

REMEMBRANCER. Of the city of London. Parliamentary solicitor to the corporation, and bound to attend all courts of aldermen and common council when required. Pull.Laws & Cust.Lond. 122. See King's Remembrancer.

REMEMBRANCERS. In English law. Officers of the exchequer, whose duty it is to put in remembrance the lord treasurer and the justices of that court of such things as are to be called and dealt in for the benefit of the crown. Jacob.

RÉMÉRÉ. In French law. Redemption; right of redemption.

A sale *à réméré* is a species of conditional sale with right of repurchase. An agreement by which the vendor reserves to himself the right to take back the thing sold on restoring the price paid, with costs and interest. Duverger.

REMISE. To remit or give up. A formal word in deeds of release and quitclaim; the usual phrase being "remise, release, and forever quitclaim." American Mortg. Co. v. Hutchinson, 19 Or. 334, 24 P. 515.

REMISE DE LA DETTE. In French law. The release of a debt.

REMISSION. In civil law. A release of a debt. It is *conventional,* when it is expressly granted to the debtor by a creditor having a capacity to alienate; or *tacit,* when the creditor voluntarily surrenders to his debtor the original title, under private signature constituting the obligation. Civ.Code La. art. 2199. Hall v. Allen Mfg. Co., 133 La. 1079, 63 So. 591, 592.

Forgiveness or condonation of an offense or injury.

At common law. The act by which a forfeiture or penalty is forgiven. United States v. Morris, 10 Wheat. 246, 6 L.Ed. 314.

REMISSIUS IMPERANTI MELIUS PARETUR. 3 Inst. 233. A man commanding not too strictly is better obeyed.

REMISSNESS. The doing of the act in question in a tardy, negligent, or careless manner; but term does not apply to the entire omission or forbearance of the act. Baldwin v. United States Tel. Co., 6 Abb.Prac.N.S., N.Y., 423.

REMIT. To send or transmit; as to *remit* money. Potter v. Morland, 3 Cush. (Mass.) 388; Hollowell v. Life Ins. Co., 35 S.E. 616, 126 N.C. 398. To send back, as to remit a check. Colvin v. Acc. Ass'n, 66 Hun, 543, 21 N.Y.S. 734. To give up; to annul; to relinquish; as to *remit* a fine. People ex rel. Cropsey v. Court of Special Sessions of City of New York, 156 N.Y.S. 61, 62, 170 App.Div. 575.

REMITMENT. The act of sending back to custody; an annulment. Wharton.

REMITTANCE. Money sent by one person to another, either in specie, bill of exchange, check, or otherwise.

REMITTEE. A person to whom a remittance is made. Story, Bailm. § 75.

REMITTER. The relation back of a later defective title to an earlier valid title. *Remitter* occurs where he who has the true property or *jus proprietatis* in lands, but is out of possession thereof, and has no right to enter without recovering possession in an action, has afterwards the freehold cast upon him by some subsequent and of course defective title. In this case he is *remitted,* or sent back by operation of law, to his ancient and more certain title. 3 Bl.Comm. 19.

REMITTIT DAMNA. Lat. An entry on the record, by which the plaintiff declares that he remits a part of the damages which have been awarded him.

REMITTITUR DAMNA. Lat. In practice. An entry made on record, in cases where a jury has given greater damages than a plaintiff has declared for, remitting the excess. 2 Tidd, Pr. 896.

REMITTITUR OF RECORD. The returning or sending back by a court of appeal of the record and proceedings in a cause, after its decision thereon, to the court whence the appeal came, in order that the cause may be tried anew, (where it is so ordered,) or that judgment may be entered in accordance with the decision on appeal, or execution be issued, or any other necessary action be taken in the court below.

REMITTOR. A person who makes a remittance to another.

REMNANT RULE. The rule that width of lot, frontage of which is not specified on plat specifying frontage of all other lots in same block, is length of block, minus total width of other lots. Routh v. Williams, 141 Fla. 334, 193 So. 71, 73.

REMODEL. To model, shape, form, fashion, afresh, or to recast; to model anew; to reconstruct, to reform, reshape, reconstruct, to make over in a somewhat different way. Board of Com'rs of Guadalupe County v. State, 43 N.M. 409, 94 P.2d 515, 520.

REMONSTRANCE. Expostulation; showing of reasons against something proposed; a representation made to a court or legislative body wherein certain persons unite in urging that a contemplated measure be not adopted or passed. Girvin v. Simon, 59 P. 945, 127 Cal. 491; In re Mercer County License Applications, 3 Pa.Co.Ct. R. 45.

REMOTE. At a distance; afar off; inconsiderable; slight. Newsome v. Louisville & N. R. Co., 20 Ala.App. 349, 102 So. 61, 64.

REMOTE CAUSE. In the law of negligence with respect to injury or accident. A cause which would not according to experience of mankind, lead to the event which happened. Miles v. Southeastern Motor Truck Lines, 295 Ky. 156, 173 S.W.2d 990, 994. One where the effect is uncertain, vague, or indeterminate, and where the effect does not necessarily follow. Jaggers v. Southeastern Greyhound Lines, D.C.Tenn., 34 F.Supp. 667, 669. A cause operating mediately through other causes to produce effect. Newsome v. Louisville & N. R. Co., 20 Ala.App. 349, 102 So. 61, 64. Improbable cause. Fitzgerald v. Pennsylvania R. R., 184 A. 299, 301, 121 Pa.Super. 461; Nashville, C. & St. L. Ry. v. Harrell, 21 Tenn.App. 353, 110 S.W.2d 1032, 1038.

To determine whether a given cause is a "proximate cause" or a "remote cause," it must be determined whether the facts constitute a succession of events, so linked together that they become a natural whole, or whether chain of events is so broken that they become independent, and final result cannot be said to be the natural and probable consequence of the primary cause, the negligence of defendants. Fitzgerald v. Pennsylvania R. R., 121 Pa.Super. 461, 184 A. 299.

REMOTE DAMAGE. See Damages.

REMOTE POSSIBILITY. In the law of estates, a double possibility, or a limitation dependent on two or more facts or events both or all of which are contingent and uncertain; as, for example, the limitation of an estate to a given man provided that he shall marry a certain woman and that she shall then die and he shall marry another.

REMOTENESS. Want of close connection between a wrong and the injury which prevents the party injured from claiming compensation from the wrongdoer. Wharton.

REMOTENESS OF EVIDENCE. When the fact or facts proposed to be established as a foundation from which indirect evidence may be drawn, by way of inference, have not a visible, plain, or necessary connection with the proposition eventually to be proved, such evidence is rejected for "remoteness." See 2 Whart.Ev. § 1226, note.

REMOTO IMPEDIMENTO, EMERGIT ACTIO. The impediment being removed, the action rises. When a bar to an action is removed, the action rises up into its original efficacy. Shep.Touch. 150; Wing. 20.

REMOVAL. In a broad sense, the transfer of a person or thing from one place to another. Durrett v. Woods, 155 La. 533, 99 So. 430, 431.

As used in statutes relative to removal from state is often limited to such absence from state as amounts to a change of residence. Smithers v. Smithers, 145 La. 752, 82 So. 879, 880.

REMOVAL FROM OFFICE. Deprivation of office by act of competent superior officer acting within scope of authority. Attorney General ex rel. O'Hara v. Montgomery, 275 Mich. 504, 267 N. W. 550, 553.

"Suspension" is the temporary forced removal from the exercise of office; "removal" is the dismissal from office. Murley v. Township of Raritan, 117 N.J.L. 357, 188 A. 739, 740.

REMOVAL OF CAUSES. The transfer of a cause from one court to another. State ex rel. McNeal v. Avoyelles Parish School Board, 199 La. 859, 7 So.2d 165, 166. Commonly used of the transfer of the jurisdiction and cognizance of an action commenced but not finally determined, with all further proceedings therein, from one trial court to another trial court. More particularly, the transfer of a cause, before trial or final hearing thereof, from a state court to the United States District Court, under the acts of congress in that behalf.

REMOVAL OF PAUPER. The actual transfer of a pauper, by order of a court having jurisdiction, from a poor district in which he has no settlement, but upon which he has become a charge, to the district of his domicile or settlement.

REMOVAL, ORDER OF. An order of court directing the removal of a pauper from the poor district upon which he has illegally become a charge to the district in which he has his settlement. Also an order made by the court *a quo*, directing the transfer of a cause therein depending, with all future proceedings in such cause, to another court.

REMOVAL TO AVOID TAX. Within a statute relating to forfeiture, some transfer of the thing involved from some definite place of manufacture, production, origin, or the like to some other place, whereat or wherefrom collection of tax on it might be less easily effected. U. S. v. One Buick Automobile, D.C.Cal., 300 F. 584, 588; U. S. v. Mangano, C.C.A.Neb., 299 F. 492, 493.

REMOVAL WITHOUT PROPER CAUSE. Of persons in the classified civil service, includes a removal for reasons which are insufficient, frivolous, or irrelevant, and a removal grounded upon evidence which to fair-minded persons appears inadequate to justify the conclusion reached but falling short of an exercise of bad faith. Murray v. Justices of Municipal Court of City of Boston, 233 Mass. 186, 123 N.E. 682, 683. See "Cause."

REMOVER. In practice. A transfer of a suit or cause out of one court into another, which is effected by writ of error, certiorari, and the like. 11 Coke, 41.

REMOVING CLOUD FROM TITLE. Acts or proceedings necessary to render title marketable. Johnston v. Cox, 114 Fla. 243, 154 So. 206.

REMUNERATION. Reward; recompense; salary. Dig. 17, 1, 7.

A *quid pro quo*. If a man gives his services, whatever consideration he gets for giving his services seems to me a remuneration for them. Consequently, I think, if a person was in the receipt of a payment, or in the receipt of a percentage, or any kind of payment which would not be an actual money payment, the amount he would receive annually in respect of this would be "remuneration." 1 Q.B. Div. 663, 664.

RENANT, or RENIANT. In old English law. Denying. 32 Hen. VIII. c. 2.

RENCOUNTER. A sudden hostile collision, as with an enemy; an unexpected encounter or meeting, as of travelers; a contest or debate; a sudden meeting as opposed to a duel which is deliberate. Mulligan v. State, 18 Ga.App. 464, 89 S.E. 541, 544.

RENDER, *v.* To give up; to yield; to return; to surrender. Also to pay or perform; used of rents, services, and the like.

Render an account. Is to present it. Yarbrough v. Armour & Co., 31 Ala.App. 287, 15 So.2d 281, 283.

Render judgment. To pronounce, state, declare, or announce the judgment of the court in a given case or on a given state of facts; not used with reference to judgments by confession, and not synonymous with "entering," "docketing," or "recording" the judgment.

The rendition of a judgment is the judicial act of the court in pronouncing the sentence of the law, while the entry of a judgment is a ministerial act, which consists in spreading upon the record a statement of the final conclusion reached by the court in the matter, thus furnishing external and incontestable evidence of the sentence given and designed to stand as a perpetual memorial of its action. Schuster v. Rader, 13 Colo. 329, 22 P. 505; Farmers' State Bank v. Bales, 64 Neb. 870, 90 N.W. 945; Winstead v. Evans, Tex.Civ.App., 33 S.W. 580; Welch v. Kroger Grocery Co., 177 So. 41, 42, 180 Miss. 89.

Render verdict. To agree on and to report the verdict in due form. S. W. Little Coal Co. v. O'Brien, 63 Ind.App. 504, 113 N.E. 465, 470. To return the written verdict into court and hand it to the trial judge. Kramm v. Stockton Electric R. Co., 22 Cal.App. 737, 136 P. 523, 533.

RENDER, *n.* In feudal law, used in connection with rents and heriots. Goods subject to rent or heriot-service were said to lie in *render*, when the lord might not only seize the identical goods, but might also distrain for them. Cowell.

RENDEZVOUS. Fr. A place appointed for meeting. Especially used of places appointed for the assembling of troops, the coming together of the ships of a fleet, or the meeting of vessels and their convoy.

RENEGADE. One who has changed his profession of faith or opinion; one who has deserted his church or party.

RENEW. To make new again; to restore to freshness; to make new spiritually; to regenerate; to begin again; to recommence; to resume; to restore to existence; to revive; to reestablish; to recreate; to replace; to grant or obtain an extension of. Rayburn v. Guntersville Realty Co., 228 Ala. 662, 154 So. 812, 93 A.L.R. 1055; F. Chafee's Sons v. Blanchard's Estate, 105 Vt. 389, 165 A. 912, 913.

RENEWAL. The act of renewing or reviving. A revival or rehabilitation of an expiring subject; that which is made anew or re-established; in law, meaning an obligation on which time of payment is extended; the substitution of a new right or obligation for another of the same nature, a change of something old to something new; to grant or obtain extension of, to continue in force for a fresh period; as commonly used with reference to notes and bonds importing a postponement of maturity of obligations dealt with; an extension of time in which that obligation may be discharged; an obligation being "renewed" when the same obligation is carried forward by the new paper or undertaking, whatever it may be. Campbell River Timber Co. v. Vierhus, C.C.A.Wash., 86 F.2d 673, 675, 108 A.L.R. 763.

There is clear distinction between stipulation to "renew" lease for additional term and one to "extend," in that stipulation to renew requires making of new lease, while one to extend does not. Sanders v. Wender, 205 Ky. 422, 265 S.W. 939, 941.

RENOUNCE. To make an affirmative declaration of abandonment. Continental Bank & Trust Co. of New York v. Fulton Realty Co., 10 N.J.Misc. 1105, 162 A. 560, 563. To reject; cast off; repudiate; disclaim; forsake; abandon; divest one's self of a right, power, or privilege. Usually it implies an affirmative act of disclaimer or disavowal.

RENOUNCING PROBATE. In English practice. Refusing to take upon one's self the office of executor or executrix. Refusing to take out probate under a will wherein one has been appointed executor or executrix. Holthouse.

RENOVARE. Lat. In old English law. To renew. *Annuatim renovare,* to renew annually. A phrase applied to profits which are taken and the product renewed again. Amb. 131.

RENT. Consideration paid for use or occupation of property. Whiting Paper Co. v. Holyoke Water Power Co., 276 Mass. 542, 177 N.E. 574, 575. Compensation or return of value given at stated times for the possession of lands and tenements corporeal. A sum of money or other consideration, issuing yearly out of lands and tenements corporal; something which a tenant renders out of the profits of the land which he enjoys; a compensation or return, being in the nature of an acknowledgment or recompense given for the possession of some corporeal inheritance. 2 Bl.Comm. 41; In re Perlmutter's Will, 282 N.Y.S. 282, 156 Misc. 571.

Also the payment of royalty under a mineral lease. Robinson v. Horton, 197 La. 919, 2 So.2d 647, 649; Miller v. Carr, 137 Fla. 114, 188 So. 103, 106, 107.

In Louisiana. The contract of *rent of lands* is a contract by which one of the parties conveys and cedes to the other a tract of land, or any other immovable property, and stipulates that the latter shall hold it as owner, but reserving to the former an annual rent of a certain sum of money, or of a certain quantity of fruits, which the other party binds himself to pay him. It is of the essence of this conveyance that it be made in perpetuity. If it be made for a limited time, it is a lease. Civ.Code La. arts. 2779, 2780.

As used in Emergency Price Control Act authorizing recovery of either $50 or treble damages for overcharge of rent, means each separate payment made by tenant to landlord at a specified time for use of landlord's premises, and does not mean a single right to all the payments made on a series of occasions in return for a continuous estate conveyed by landlord. Emergency Price Control Act of 1942, § 205(e), 50 U.S.C.A.Appendix § 925(e). Gilbert v. Thierry, D.C.Mass., 58 F. Supp. 235, 240.

Fair rent. See Fair Rent.

Fee farm rent. A rent charge issuing out of an estate in fee; a perpetual rent reserved on a conveyance of land in fee simple.

Ground rent. See Ground.

Quit rent. Certain established rents of the freeholders and ancient copyholders of manors were so called, because by their payment the tenant was free and "quit" of all other services.

Rack rent. A rent of the full annual value of the tenement or near it. 2 Bl.Comm. 43.

Rent-charge. This arises where the owner of the rent has no future interest or reversion in the land. It is usually created by deed or will, and is accompanied with powers of distress and entry.

Rent-roll. A list of rents payable to a particular person or public body.

Rent seck. Barren rent; a rent reserved by deed, but without any clause of distress. 2 Bl. Comm. 42; 3 Kent, Comm. 461. Kavanaugh v. Cohoes Power & Light Corporation, 114 Misc. 590, 187 N.Y.S. 216, 232.

Rent-service. This consisted of fealty, together with a certain rent, and was the only kind of rent originally known to the common law. It was so called because it was given as a compensation for the services to which the land was originally liable. Brown.

Rents of assize. The certain and determined rents of the freeholders and ancient copyholders of manors. Apparently so called because they were assized or made certain, and so distinguished from a *redditus mobilis,* which was a variable or fluctuating rent. 3 Cruise, Dig. 314; Brown.

Rents resolute. Rents anciently payable to the crown from the lands of abbeys and religious houses; and after their dissolution, notwithstanding that the lands were demised to others, yet the rents were still reserved and made payable again to the crown. Cowell.

RENT MUST BE RESERVED TO HIM FROM WHOM THE STATE OF THE LAND MOVETH. Co.Litt. 143.

RENTAGE. Rent.

RENTAL. (Said to be corrupted from "rent-roll.") In English law. A roll on which the rents of a manor are registered or set down, and by which the lord's bailiff collects the same. It contains the lands and tenements let to each tenant, the names of the tenants, and other particulars. Cunningham; Holthouse.

Payment received periodically for the use of property; rent. Friedbar Realty Corporation v. Sanford, 119 Misc. 621, 198 N.Y.S. 38, 39.

Net Rental

When used with reference to real property, means a rental over and above all expenses. Perkins v. Kirby, 39 R.I. 343, 97 A. 884, 887.

Rental Bolls

In Scotch law. When the tithes (tiends) have been liquidated and settled for so many bolls of corn yearly. Bell.

Rental-Rights

In English law. A species of lease usually granted at a low rent and for life. Tenants under such leases were called "rentalers" or "kindly tenants."

Rental Value

The value of land for use for purpose for which it is adapted in the hands of a prudent occupant. In re Acquiring Lands for an Alley, 147 Minn. 211, 179 N.W. 907, 909. Fair rental value of land, but not the conjectural or probable profits thereof. Maddox v. Yocum, 109 Ind.App. 416, 31 N.E.2d 652, 655.

RENTE. In French law. The annual return which represents the revenue of a capital or of an immovable alienated. The constitution of *rente* is a contract by which one of the parties lends to the other a capital which he agrees not to recall, in consideration of the borrower's paying an annual interest. It is this interest which is called "*rente*." Duverger. The word is therefore nearly synonymous with the English "annuity."

RENTE FONCIÈRE. A rent which issues out of land, and it is of its essence that it be perpetual, for, if it be made but for a limited time, it is a lease. It may, however, be extinguished. Civ. Code La. art. 2780.

RENTE VIAGÈRE. That species of *rente*, the duration of which depends upon the contingency of the death of one or more persons indicated in the contract. The uncertainty of the time at which such death may happen causes the *rente viagère* to be included in the number of aleatory contracts. Duverger. Civ.Code La. art. 2793 defines the contract of annuity as that by which one party delivers to another a sum of money, and agrees not to reclaim it so long as the receiver pays the rent agreed upon.

RENTES. In French law. Government funds. Wharton.

RENTIER. In French law. A fundholder, a person having an income from personal property. Wharton.

RENTS, ISSUES AND PROFITS. The profits arising from property generally. Rents collected by party in possession, the net profits. Phrase does not apply to rental value or value of use and occupation. People v. Gustafson, 53 Cal.App.2d 230, 127 P.2d 627, 632.

RENUNCIATION. The act by which a person abandons a right acquired without transferring it to another. McCormick v. Engstrom, 119 Kan. 698, 241 P. 685, 688.

Under the Negotiable Instruments Law the unilateral act of the holder, usually, without consideration, whereby he expresses the intention of abandoning his rights on the instrument or against one or more parties thereto. McGlynn v. Granstrom, 169 Minn. 164, 210 N.W. 892, 893. See Renounce.

RENVOI. The act of a state in summarily reconducting foreign vagabonds, criminals, etc., to the frontiers of their own state. A doctrine under which the court in resorting to a foreign law adopts the rules of the foreign law as to conflict of laws, which rules may in turn refer the court back to the law of the forum. 31 Harvard Law Rev. 523, 27 Yale Law Journal 509 and In re Tallmadge, 109 Misc. 696, 181 N.Y.S. 336, 341. Also the rule that, in a suit by a nonresident upon a cause arising locally, his capacity to sue is determined by looking to law of his domicile rather than to local law. Gray v. Gray, 87 N.H. 82, 174 A. 508, 511, 94 A.L.R. 1404.

REO ABSENTE. Lat. The defendant being absent; in the absence of the defendant.

REOPENING A CASE. Is to permit the introduction of new evidence and, practically to permit a new trial.

REORGANIZATION. Act or process of organizing again or anew. People ex rel. Barrett v. Halsted Street State Bank, 295 Ill.App. 193, 14 N.E.2d 872, 876.

As applied to corporations. The carrying out, by proper agreements and legal proceedings, of a business plan for winding up the affairs of or foreclosing a mortgage or mortgages upon the property of, insolvent corporations, more frequently railroad companies. It is usually accomplished by the judicial sale of the corporate property and franchises, and the formation by the purchasers of a new corporation. The property and franchises are thereupon vested in the new corporation and its stock and bonds are divided among such of the parties interested in the old company as are parties to the reorganization plan.

In reorganization of corporation, substantially all assets of old corporation are transferred to new, and stockholders hold same proportion of stock in new corporation. Hurst v. D. P. Davis Properties, C.C.A.Fla., 69 F.2d 333, 335.

REPAIR. To mend, remedy, restore, renovate, to restore to a sound or good state after decay, injury, dilapidation, or partial destruction. Mozingo v. Wellsburg Electric Light, Heat & Power Co., 131 S.E. 717, 718, 101 W.Va. 79; Board of Education of Hancock County v. Moorehead, 105 Ohio St. 237, 136 N.E. 913, 914; Weiss v. Mitchell, Tex. Civ.App., 58 S.W.2d 165, 166.

The word "repair" contemplates an existing structure or thing which has become imperfect, and means to supply in the original existing structure that which is lost or destroyed, and thereby restore it to the condition in which it originally existed, as near as may be. Childers v. Speer, 63 Ga.App. 848, 12 S.E.2d 439, 440.

REPAIRS. Restoration to soundness; reparation; work done to property to keep it in good order.

Necessary repairs. For which the master of a ship may lawfully bind the owner are such as are reasonably fit and proper for the ship under the circumstances, and not merely such as are absolutely indispensable for the safety of the ship or the accomplishment of the voyage. The Fortitude, 3 Sumn. 327, F.Cas.No.4,953; Webster v. Seekamp, 4 Barn. & Ald. 352.

REPARATION. The redress of an injury; amends for a wrong inflicted. Jablonowski v. Modern Cap Mfg. Co., 312 Mo. 173, 279 S.W. 89, 95.

REPARATIONE FACIENDA. For making repairs. The name of an old writ which lay in various cases; as if, for instance, there were three tenants in common of a mill or house which had fallen into decay, and one of the three was willing to repair it, and the other two not; in such case the party who was willing to repair might have this writ against the others. Cowell; Fitzh.Nat. Brev. 127.

REPARTIAMENTO. In Spanish law, a judicial proceeding for the partition of property held in common. Steinbach v. Moore, 30 Cal. 505.

REPATRIATION. The regaining nationality after expatriation.

REPAVE. In reference to a street improvement relates generally to a new pavement, either of the same or different material, for the full width of the street theretofore similarly improved, or for some defined section thereof. Cleveland Ry. Co. v. City of Cleveland, 97 Ohio St. 122, 119 N.E. 202, 203.

REPAY. To pay back; refund; restore; return. Harlan Coal & Land Co. v. King Harlan Mining Co., 192 Ky. 111, 232 S.W. 650, 654.

REPEAL. The abrogation or annulling of a previously existing law by the enactment of a subsequent statute which declares that the former law shall be revoked and abrogated, (which is called "express" repeal), or which contains provisions so contrary to or irreconcilable with those of the earlier law that only one of the two statutes can stand in force, (called "implied" repeal.) Oakland Pav. Co. v. Hilton, 69 Cal. 479, 11 P. 3; Pacific Milling & Elevator Co. v. City of Portland, 65 Or. 349, 133 P. 72, 78, 46 L.R.A.,N.S., 363. For "Express Repeal", see that title.

"Repeal" of a law means its complete abrogation by the enactment of a subsequent statute, whereas the "amendment" of a statute means an alteration in the law already existing, leaving some part of the original still standing. State ex inf. Crain ex rel. Peebles v. Moore, 339 Mo. 492, 99 S.W.2d 17, 19.

REPEATERS. Persons who commit crime and are sentenced, and then commit another and are sentenced again. Opolich v. Fluckey, D.C.Ga., 47 F.2d 950.

REPELLITUR A SACRAMENTO INFAMIS. An infamous person is repelled or prevented from taking an oath. Co.Litt. 158; Bract. fol. 185.

REPELLITUR EXCEPTIONE CEDENDARUM ACTIONUM. He is defeated by the plea that the actions have been assigned. Cheesebrough v. Millard, 1 Johns.Ch. (N.Y.) 409, 414.

REPERTORY. In French law. The inventory or minutes which notaries make of all contracts which take place before them. Merl. Repert.

REPETITION. In the civil law. A demand or action for the restoration of money paid under mistake, or goods delivered by mistake or on an unperformed condition. Dig. 12, 6. See Solutio Indebiti.

In Scotch law. The act of reading over a witness' deposition, in order that he may adhere to it or correct it at his choice. The same as *recolement* (*q. v.*) in the French law. 2 Benth.Jud.Ev. 239.

REPETITUM NAMIUM. A repeated, second, or reciprocal distress; withernam. 3 Bl.Comm. 148.

REPETUNDÆ, or PECUNIÆ REPETUNDÆ. In Roman law. The terms used to designate such sums of money as the *socii* of the Roman state, or individuals, claimed to recover from *magistratus, judices,* or *publici curatores,* which they had improperly taken or received in the *provinciæ*, or in the *urbs Roma,* either in the discharge of their *jurisdictio,* or in their capacity of *judices,* or in respect of any other public function. Sometimes the word "*repetundæ*" was used to express the illegal act for which compensation was sought. Wharton.

REPETUNDARUM CRIMEN. In Roman law. The crime of bribery or extortion in a magistrate, or person in any public office. Calvin.

REPLACE. To place again, to restore to a former condition. Illinois Cent. R. Co. v. Franklin County, 387 Ill. 301, 56 N.E.2d 775, 779.

REPLEAD. To plead anew; to file new pleadings.

REPLEADER. When, after issue has been joined in an action, and a verdict given thereon, the pleading is found (on examination) to have miscarried and failed to effect its proper object, viz., of raising an apt and material question between the parties, the court will, on motion of the unsuccessful party, award a *repleader*; that is, will order the parties to plead *de novo* for the purpose of obtaining a better issue. Brown.

Judgment of Repleader

A judgment allowed by the court to do justice between the parties where defect is in form or manner of stating the right, and the issue joined is on an immaterial point, so that court cannot tell for whom to give judgment. 1 Chit.Pl. 687, 688. On the award of a repleader, the parties must recommence their pleadings at the point where the immaterial issue originated. This judgment is interlocutory, *quod partes replacitent.*

REPLEGIARE. To replevy; to redeem a thing detained or taken by another by putting in legal sureties.

REPLEGIARE DE AVERIIS. Replevin of cattle. A writ brought by one whose cattle were distrained, or put in the pound, upon any cause by another, upon surety given to the sheriff to prosecute or answer the action in law. Cowell.

REPLEGIARI FACIAS. You cause to be replevied. In old English law. The original writ in the action of replevin; superseded by the statute of Marlbridge, c. 21. 3 Bl.Comm. 146.

REPLETION. In canon law. Where the revenue of a benefice is sufficient to fill or occupy the whole right or title of the graduate who holds it. Wharton.

REPLEVIABLE, or REPLEVISABLE. Property is said to be repleviable or replevisable when proceedings in replevin may be resorted to for the purpose of trying the right to such property.

REPLEVIN. A personal action *ex delicto* brought to recover possession of goods unlawfully taken, (generally, but not only, applicable to the taking of goods distrained for rent,) the validity of which taking it is the mode of contesting, if the party from whom the goods were taken wishes to have them back *in specie*, whereas, if he prefer to have damages instead, the validity may be contested by action of trespass or unlawful distress. The word means a redelivery to the owner of the pledge or thing taken in distress. Wharton; Sinnott v. Feiock, 165 N.Y. 444, 59 N.E. 265, 53 L.R.A. 565, 80 Am.St.Rep. 736; Healey v. Humphrey, 81 F. 990, 27 C.C.A. 39. A local action to be brought where property is taken or where property is detained, unless statute regulates matter. Miles v. Securities Inv. Co., 171 Tenn. 417, 104 S.W.2d 823. A possessory action, and a plaintiff cannot recover on the weakness of defendant's title, but must recover on the strength of his own title. Hannibal Inv. Co. v. Schmidt, Mo.App., 113 S.W.2d 1048, 1052. Cardinal question in a replevin action is plaintiff's right to immediate possession of the property at the commencement of the action. Warren v. Driscoll, 178 Minn. 344, 227 N.W. 199, 200.

Personal Replevin

A species of action to replevy a man out of prison or out of the custody of any private person. It took the place of the old writ *de homine replegiando*; but, as a means of examining into the legality of an imprisonment, it is now superseded by the writ of *habeas corpus*.

Replevin Bond

A bond executed to indemnify the officer who executed a writ of replevin and to indemnify the defendant or person from whose custody the property was taken for such damages as he may sustain. Imel v. Van Deren, 8 Colo. 90, 5 P. 803.

REPLEVISH. In old English law. To let one to mainprise upon surety. Cowell.

REPLEVISOR. The plaintiff in an action of replevin.

REPLEVY. In reference to the action of replevin, to redeliver goods which have been distrained, to the original possessor of them, on his pledging or giving security to prosecute an action against the distrainor for the purpose of trying the legality of the distress. Also the bailing or liberating a man from prison on his finding bail to answer for his forthcoming at a future time. Brown.

REPLIANT, or REPLICANT. A litigant who replies or files or delivers a replication.

REPLICARE. Lat. In the civil law and old English pleading. To reply; to answer a defendant's plea.

REPLICATIO. Lat. In the civil law and old English pleading. The plaintiff's answer to the defendant's exception or plea; corresponding with and giving name to the *replication* in modern pleading. Inst. 4, 14, pr.

REPLICATION. In pleading. A reply made by the plaintiff in an action to the defendant's plea, or in a suit in chancery to the defendant's answer.

General and Special

In equity practice, a general replication is a general denial of the truth of defendant's plea or answer, and of the sufficiency of the matter alleged in it to bar the plaintiff's suit, and an assertion of the truth and sufficiency of the bill. A special replication is occasioned by the defendant's introducing new matter into his plea or answer, which makes it necessary for the plaintiff to put in issue some additional fact on his part in avoidance of such new matter. James v. Lawson, 103 W.Va. 165, 136 S.E. 851, 853.

REPLY. In its general sense, that what the plaintiff, petitioner, or other person who has instituted a proceeding says in answer to the defendant's case. Sweet. Its office is to join issue or avoid new matter in answer, and not to aid complaint by supplying omission or adding new ground of relief. Teisinger v. Hardy, 91 Mont. 9, 5 P.2d 219, 220.

On trial or argument. When a case is tried or argued in court, the speech or argument of the plaintiff in answer to that of the defendant. Under the practice of the chancery and common-law courts, to reply is to file or deliver a replication, (*q. v.*). Under codes of reformed procedure, the name of the pleading which corresponds to "replication" in common-law or equity practice.

Frivolous or sham reply. For the distinction between these two kinds of replies, see Frivolous.

REPONE. In Scotch practice. To replace; to restore to a former state or right. 2 Alis. Crim. Pr. 351.

REPORT. An official or formal statement of facts or proceedings.

The formal statement in writing made to a court by a master in chancery, a clerk, or referee, as the result of his inquiries into some matter referred to him by the court.

A "report" of a public official is distinguished from a "return" of such official, in that "return" is typically concerned with something done or observed by officer, while "report" embodies result of officer's investigation not originally occurring within his personal knowledge. E. K. Hardison Seed Co. v. Jones, C.C.A.6, 149 F.2d 252, 257.

The name is also applied (usually in the plural) to the published volumes, appearing periodically, containing accounts of the various cases argued and determined in the courts with the decisions thereon.

Lord Coke defines "report" to be "a public relation, or a bringing again to memory cases judicially argued, debated, resolved, or adjudged in any of the king's courts of justice, together with such causes and reasons as were delivered by the judges of the same." Co.Litt. 293.

REPORT FOR INDUCTION. Within the Selective Service Act, to present one's self not only at the appointed place but also in readiness to go through the process which constitutes induction into the army. Selective Training and Service Act of 1940, 50 U.S.C.A. Appendix § 301 et seq. Smith v. U. S., C.C.A.S.C., 148 F.2d 288, 290.

REPORT OF LEGISLATIVE COMMITTEE. That communication which the chairman of the committee makes to the house at the close of the investigation upon which it has been engaged. Brown.

REPORT OFFICE. A department of the English court of chancery. The suitors' account there is discontinued by the 15 & 16 Vict. c. 87, § 36.

REPORTER. A person who reports the decisions upon questions of law in the cases adjudged in the several courts of law and equity. Wharton.

REPORTS, THE. The name given, *par excellence,* to Lord Coke's Reports, from 14 Eliz. to 13 Jac. I., which are cited as "Rep." or "Coke." They are divided into thirteen parts, and the modern editions are in six volumes, including the index.

REPOSITION OF THE FOREST. In old English law. An act whereby certain forest grounds, being made *purlieu* upon view, were by a second view laid to the forest again, put back into the forest. Manwood; Cowell.

REPOSITORIUM. A storehouse or place wherein things are kept; a warehouse. Cro.Car. 555.

REPRESENT. To appear in the character of; personate; to exhibit; to expose before the eyes. To represent a thing is to produce it publicly. Dig. 10, 4, 2, 3; In re Matthews, 57 Idaho, 75, 62 P.2d 578, 580, 111 A.L.R. 13. To represent a person is to stand in his place; to supply his place; to act as his substitute. Plummer v. Brown, 64 Cal. 429, 1 P. 703; Seibert v. Dunn, 216 N.Y. 237, 110 N.E. 447, 449.

REPRESENTATION. Any conduct capable of being turned into a statement of fact. Scandrett v. Greenhouse, 244 Wis. 108, 11 N.W.2d 510, 512.

Contracts

A statement express or implied made by one of two contracting parties to the other, before or at the time of making the contract, in regard to some past or existing fact, circumstance, or state of facts pertinent to the contract, which is influential in bringing about the agreement. Fernandina Shipbuilding & Dry Dock Co. v. Peters, D.C. Fla., 283 F. 621, 627; Kiser v. Richardson, 91 Kan. 812, 139 P. 373, Ann.Cas.1915D, 539.

Insurance

A collateral statement, either by writing not inserted in the policy or by parol, of such facts or circumstances, relative to the proposed adventure, as are necessary to be communicated to the underwriters, to enable them to form a just estimate of the risks. 1 Marsh.Ins. 450; Myers v. Mutual Life Ins. Co. of New York, 83 W.Va. 390, 98 S.E. 424, 426. The allegation of any facts, by the applicant to the insurer, or *vice versa,* preliminary to making the contract, and directly bearing upon it, having a plain and evident tendency to induce the making of the policy. The statements may or may not be in writing, and may be either express or by obvious implication. Augusta Insurance & Banking Co. of Georgia v. Abbott, 12 Md. 348.

In relation to the contract of insurance, there is an important distinction between a representation and a warranty. The former, which precedes the contract of insurance, and is no part of it, need be only materially true; the latter is a part of the contract, and must be exactly and literally fulfilled, or else the contract is broken and inoperative. Glendale Woolen Co. v. Protection Ins. Co., 21 Conn. 19, 54 Am.Dec. 309.

Law of Distribution and Descent

The principle upon which the issue of a deceased person take or inherit the share of an estate which their immediate ancestor would have taken or inherited, if living; the taking or inheriting *per stirpes.* 2 Bl.Comm. 217, 517; In re Paterson's Estate, Cal.App., 76 P.2d 138, 143.

Scotch Law

The name of a plea or statement presented to a lord ordinary of the court of session, when his judgment is brought under review.

General

False representation. See False Representation.

Material representation. In life insurance. One that would influence a prudent insurer in determining whether or not to accept the risk, or in fixing the amount of the premium in the event of such acceptance. Empire Life Ins. Co. v. Jones, 14 Ga.App. 647, 82 S.E. 62, 66. Columbia-Knickerbocker Trust Co. v. Abbot, C.C.A.Mass., 247 F. 833, 857.

Misrepresentation. An intentional false statement respecting a matter of fact, made by one of the parties to a contract, which is material to the contract and influential in producing it.

Promissory representation. A term used chiefly in insurance, and meaning a representation made by the assured concerning what is to happen during the term of the insurance, stated as a matter of expectation or even of contract, and amounting to a promise to be performed after the contract has come into existence. New Jersey Rubber Co. v. Commercial Union Assur. Co., 64 N.J.L. 580, 46 A. 777.

REPRESENTATION OF PERSONS. A fiction of the law, the effect of which is to put the representative in the place, degree, or right of the person represented. Civ.Code La. art. 894.

REPRESENTATION, ESTOPPEL BY. It arises when one by acts, representations, admissions, or silence when he ought to speak out, intentionally or through culpable negligence induces another to believe certain facts to exist and such other rightfully relies and acts on such belief, so that he will be prejudiced if the former is permitted to deny the existence of such facts. Carter v.

Curlew Creamery Co., 16 Wash.2d 476, 134 P.2d 66, 73. It differs from estoppel by record, deed, or contract, in that it is not based on agreement of parties or finding of fact which may not be disputed, and is not mutual, but applies to only one party. Bank of Canton & Trust Co. v. Clark, 198 N.C. 169, 151 S.E. 102, 104.

It is the effect of voluntary conduct of a party whereby he is absolutely precluded, from asserting rights which might perhaps have otherwise existed. Strand v. State, 16 Wash.2d 107, 132 P.2d 1011, 1015.

It is species of "equitable estoppel" or estoppel by matter in pais. Frumin v. Chazen, 153 Tenn. 1, 282 S.W. 199, 201. See, also, Equitable Estoppel and In Pais, Estoppel In.

Elements or essentials of such estoppel include change of position for the worse, Carter v. Curlew Creamery Co., 134 P.2d 66, 73, 16 Wash.2d 476; Campbell v. Salyer, 290 Ky. 493, 161 S.W.2d 596, 599; detriment or injury or prejudice to party claiming estoppel, Blaisdell Automobile Co. v. Nelson, 130 Me. 167, 154 A. 184, 186; Abbott v. Bean, 295 Mass. 268, 3 N.E.2d 762, 768; express or implied representations, Sandifer v. Sandifer's Heirs, La.App., 195 So. 118, 124; false representation, Chicago, R. I. & P. Ry. Co. v. Sawyer, 176 Okl. 446, 56 P.2d 418, 420; Cushing v. United States, D.C.Mass., 18 F.Supp. 83, 85; ignorance of facts by party claiming estoppel, United States v. Dickinson, C.C. A.Mass., 95 F.2d 65, 68; Cain v. Rea, 159 Va. 446, 166 S.E. 478, 483, 85 A.L.R. 945; inducement to action by party claiming estoppel, Rhoads v. Rhoads, 342 Mo. 934, 119 S.W. 2d 247, 252; intent that other party should act on representation or gross and culpable negligence of party sought to be estopped, Cain v. Rea, 159 Va. 446, 166 S.E. 478, 483, 85 A.L.R. 945; Cleaveland v. Malden Sav. Bank, 291 Mass. 295, 197 N.E. 14, 15; knowledge, actual or constructive, of facts by person estopped, Rhoads v. Rhoads, 342 Mo. 934, 119 S.W.2d 247, 252; misleading of person claiming estoppel, Campbell v. Salyer, 290 Ky. 493, 161 S.W.2d 596, 599; Bosen v. Larrabee, 91 N.H. 492, 23 A.2d 331, 332; reliance of one party on conduct of other party, Ouellette v. City of New York Ins. Co., 133 Me. 149, 174 A. 462, 464; Mosley v. Magnolia Petroleum Co., 45 N.M. 230, 114 P.2d 740, 751.

The doctrine ordinarily applies only to representations as to past or present facts. In re Watson's Estate, 30 N.Y. S.2d 577, 586, 177 Misc. 308.

REPRESENTATIVE. One who represents or stands in the place of another. Lee v. Dill, 39 Barb. (N.Y.) 520; Staples v. Lewis, 71 Conn. 288, 41 A. 815.

The definition of a "person" liable for treble damages for overcharges of commodity prices under the Emergency Price Control Act, means the legal successor or representative, such as a receiver, liquidator, executor, administrator, guardian or tutor, but not an agent. Emergency Price Control Act of 1942, § 302(h), 50 U.S.C.A.Appendix, § 942 (h). Husers v. Papania, La.App., 22 So.2d 755, 757.

In constitutional law, a person chosen by the people to represent their several interests in a legislative body. Macrum v. Board of Sup'rs of Suffolk County, 252 N.Y.S. 546, 143 Misc. 358.

Legal Representative

See that title.

Personal Representatives

Executors and administrators of person deceased; but it may have a wider meaning, according to the intention of the person using it, and may include heirs, next of kin, descendants, assignees, grantees, receivers, and trustees in insolvency. In re Wilcox & Howe Co., 70 Conn. 220, 39 A. 163; Shiya v. Erickson, 156 Misc. 738, 282 N.Y.S. 812. See, also, Real Representative, infra.

Real Representative

He who represents or stands in the place of another, with respect to his real property, is so termed, in contradistinction to him who stands in the place of another, with regard to his personal property, and who is termed the "personal representative." Thus the heir is the real representative of his deceased ancestor. Brown.

Representative Action or Suits

See Class or Representative Action.

Representative Democracy

A form of government where the powers of the sovereignty are delegated to a body of men, elected from time to time, who exercise them for the benefit of the whole nation. 1 Bouv.Inst. no. 31.

Representative Peers

Those who, at the commencement of every new parliament, are elected to represent Scotland and Ireland in the British house of lords; sixteen for the former and twenty-eight for the latter country. Brown.

REPRIEVE. In criminal law. The withdrawing of a sentence of death for an interval of time, whereby the execution is suspended. 4 Bl.Comm. 394. Sterling v. Drake, 29 Ohio St. 460, 23 Am. Rep. 762; Gore v. Humphries, 163 Ga. 106, 135 S. E. 481, 485.

Also the withdrawing of any sentence for a period of time. Ex parte Dormitzer, 119 Or. 336, 249 P. 639, 640.

It does no more than stay the execution of a sentence for a time, and it is ordinarily an act of clemency extended to a prisoner to afford him an opportunity to procure some amelioration of the sentence imposed. Palka v. Walker, 124 Conn. 121, 198 A. 265, 267. It cannot be granted until after sentence. State ex rel. Gordon v. Zangerle, 136 Ohio St. 371, 26 N.E.2d 190, 194.

REPRIMAND. A public and formal censure or severe reproof, administered to a person in fault by his superior officer or by a body to which he belongs. Thus, a member of a legislative body may be reprimanded by the presiding officer, in pursuance of a vote of censure, for improper conduct in the house. So a military officer, in some cases, is punished by a reprimand administered by his commanding officer, or by the secretary of war.

REPRISALS. The forcible taking by one nation of a thing that belonged to another, in return or satisfaction for an injury committed by the latter on the former. Vattel, b. 2, c. 18, s. 342.

General Reprisals

Take place by virtue of commissions delivered to officers and citizens of the aggrieved state, directing them to take the persons and property belonging to the offending state wherever found.

Negative Reprisals

Take place when a nation refuses to fulfil a perfect obligation which it has contracted, or to permit another state to enjoy a right which it justly claims.

Positive Reprisals

Consist in seizing the persons and effects belonging to the other nation, in order to obtain satisfaction.

Special Reprisals

Such as are granted in times of peace to particular individuals who have suffered an injury from the citizens or subjects of the other nation.

REPRISES. In English law. Deductions and duties which are yearly paid out of a manor and lands, as rent-charge, rent seck, pensions, corrodies, annuities, etc., so that, when the clear yearly value of a manor is spoken of, it is said to be so much per annum *ultra reprisas,*—besides all *reprises.* Cowell. Delaware & H. Canal Có. v. Von Storch, 196 Pa. 102, 46 A. 375.

REPROBATA PECUNIA LIBERAT SOLVENTEM. Money refused [the refusal of money tendered] releases him who pays, [or tenders it.] 9 Coke, 79*a*.

REPROBATION. In ecclesiastical law. The interposition of objections or exceptions; as to the competency of witnesses, to the due execution of instruments offered in evidence and the like.

REPROBATOR, ACTION OF. In Scotch law. An action or proceeding intended to convict a witness of perjury, to which the witness must be made a party. Bell.

REP-SILVER. In old records. Money paid by servile tenants for exemption from the customary duty of *reaping* for the lord. Cowell.

REPUBLIC. A commonwealth; that form of government in which the administration of affairs is open to all the citizens. In another sense, it signifies the state, independently of its form of government. 1 Toullier 28 and n., 202, note; State v. Harris, 2 Bailey (S.C.) 599; Co.Litt. 303.

REPUBLICAN GOVERNMENT. A government in the republican form; a government of the people; a government by representatives chosen by the people. In re Duncan, 11 S.Ct. 573, 139 U.S. 449, 35 L.Ed. 219; Kadderly v. Portland, 44 Or. 118, 74 P. 710.

REPUBLICATION. The re-execution or re-establishment by a testator of a will which he had once revoked. A second publication of a will, either expressly or by construction. For "Express Republication," see that title.

REPUDIATE. To put away, reject, disclaim, or renounce a right, duty, obligation, or privilege.

REPUDIATION. Rejection; disclaimer; renunciation; the rejection or refusal of an offered or available right or privilege, or of a duty or relation. Iowa State Sav. Bank v. Black, 59 N.W. 283, 91 Iowa, 490; Daley v. Saving Ass'n, 178 Mass. 13, 59 N.E. 452.

Repudiation of contract is in nature of anticipatory breach before performance is due, but does not operate as anticipatory breach unless promisee elects to treat repudiation as breach, and brings suit for damages. Such repudiation is but act or declaration in advance of any actual breach and consists usually of absolute and unequivocal declaration or act amounting to declaration on part of promisor to promisee that he will not make performance on future day at which contract calls for performance. Robinson v. Raquet, 1 Cal.App.2d 533, 36 P.2d 821, 825.

The refusal on the part of a state or government to pay its debts, or its declaration that its obligations, previously contracted, are no longer regarded by it as of binding force.

In the civil law. The casting off or putting away of a woman betrothed; also, but less usually, of a wife; divorcement.

In ecclesiastical law. The refusal to accept a benefice which has been conferred upon the party repudiating.

REPUDIUM. Lat. In Roman law. A breaking off of the contract of espousals, or of a marriage intended to be solemnized. Sometimes translated "divorce;" but this was not the proper sense. Dig. 50, 16, 191.

REPUGNANCY. An inconsistency, opposition, or contrariety between two or more clauses of the same deed, contract, or statute, or between two or more material allegations of the same pleading, or any two writings. Lehman v. U. S., C.C. A.N.Y., 127 F. 45, 61 C.C.A. 577; Swan v. U. S., 9 P. 931, 3 Wyo. 151; Hansen v. Bacher, Tex.Com. App., 299 S.W. 225, 226.

REPUGNANT. That which is contrary to what is stated before, or insensible. A repugnant condition is void. Groenendyk v. Fowler, 204 Iowa, 598, 215 N.W. 718, 720.

REPUTABLE. Worthy of repute or distinction, held in esteem, honorable, praiseworthy. Illinois State Board of Dental Examiners v. People, 123 Ill. 245, 13 N.E. 201.

REPUTABLE CITIZEN. One who is well spoken of by his neighbors and hence presumably of good character. H. L. Shaffer & Co. v. Prosser, 99 Colo. 335, 62 P.2d 1161, 1163.

REPUTATIO EST VULGARIS OPINIO UBI NON EST VERITAS. ET VULGARIS OPINIO EST DUPLEX, SCIL.: OPINIO VULGARIS ORTA INTER GRAVES ET DISCRETOS HOMINES, ET QUÆ VULTUM VERITATIS HABET; ET OPINIO TANTUM ORTA INTER LEVES ET VULGARES HOMINES, ABSQUE SPECIE VERITATIS. Reputation is common opinion where there is not truth. And common opinion is of two kinds, to-wit: Common reputation arising among grave and sensible men, and which has the appearance of truth; and mere opinion arising among foolish and ignorant men, without any appearance of truth. 4 Coke, 107.

REPUTATION. Estimation in which one is held, the character imputed to a person in the neighborhood where he lives. State v. Baldanzo, 106 N.J.L. 498, 148 A. 725, 726, 67 A.L.R. 1207. General opinion, good or bad, held of a person by those of the community in which he resides. State v. Kiziah, 217 N.C. 399, 8 S.E.2d 474, 477; Citizens Bank of Morehead v. Hunt, 287 Ky. 646, 154 S.W. 2d 730, 731; it is necessarily based upon hearsay. Stewart v. State, 148 Tex.Cr.App. 480, 188 S.W. 2d 167, 170.

"Character" is made up of the things an individual actually is and does whereas "reputation" is what people think an individual is and what they say about him. McNaulty v. State, 138 Tex.Cr.R. 317, 135 S.W.2d 987, 989; James v. State, ex rel. Loser, 24 Tenn.App. 453, 145 S.W.2d 1026, 1033.

In the law of evidence, matters of public and general interest, such as the boundaries of counties or towns, rights of common, claims of highway, etc., are allowed to be proved by general reputation; *e. g.*, by the declaration of deceased persons made *ante litem motam*, by old documents, etc., notwithstanding the general rule against secondary evidence. Best, Ev. 632.

REPUTED. Accepted by general, vulgar, or public opinion. Thus, land may be reputed part of a manor, though not really so, and a certain district may be reputed a parish or a manor, or be a parish or a manor in reputation, although it is in reality no parish or manor at all. Brown; Lowell Hardware Co. v. May, 59 Colo. 475, 149 P. 831, 833.

REPUTED OWNER. See Owner.

REQUEST, *v.* To ask for something or for permission or authority to do, see, hear, etc., something; to solicit; and is synonymous with beg, entreat, and beseech. Artificial Ice & Cold Storage Co. v. Martin, 102 Ind.App. 74, 198 N.E. 446, 449.

In its ordinary or natural meaning when used in a will, is precatory and not mandatory. Byars v. Byars, 143 Tex. 10, 182 S.W.2d 363, 364, 366.

REQUEST, *n.* An asking or petition; the expression of a desire to some person for something to be granted or done; particularly for the payment of a debt or performance of a contract; also direction or command in law of wills. Beakey v. Knutson, 90 Or. 574, 174 P. 1149, 1150; Hurley-Tobin Co. v. White, 84 N.J.Eq. 60, 188, 94 A. 52, 53. For "Express Request," see that title.

The two words, "request" and "require," as used in notices to creditors to present claims against an estate, are of the same origin, and virtually synonymous. Prentice v. Whitney, 8 Hun, N.Y., 300.

Pleading

The statement in the plaintiff's declaration that the particular payment or performance, the failure of which constitutes the cause of action, was duly requested or demanded of the defendant.

General

Request, letters of. In English law. Many suits are brought before the Dean of the Arches as original judge, the cognizance of which properly belongs to inferior jurisdictions within the province, but in respect of which the inferior judge has waived his jurisdiction under a certain form of proceeding known in the canon law by the denomination of "letters of request." 3 Steph. Comm. 306.

Request note. In English law. A note requesting permission to remove dutiable goods from one place to another without paying the excise.

Requests, courts of. See Courts of Requests.

Special request. A request actually made, at a particular time and place. This term is used in contradistinction to a general request, which need not state the time when nor place where made. 3 Bouv.Inst. no. 2843.

REQUIRE. To direct, order, demand, instruct, command, claim, compel, request, need, exact. Beakey v. Knutson, 90 Or. 574, 174 P. 1149, 1150. Union Mut. Ins. Co. v. Page, 65 Okl. 101, 164 P. 116, 117, L.R.A.1918C, 1; State ex rel. Frohmiller v. Hendrix, 59 Ariz. 184, 124 P.2d 768, 773.

REQUIREMENT CONTRACT. A contract in writing whereby one agrees to buy, for a sufficient consideration, all the merchandise of a designated type which the buyer may require for use in his own established business. Such contract is not void for uncertainty. Fuchs v. United Motor Stage Co., 135 Ohio St. 509, 21 N.E.2d 669, 672.

REQUISITION. A demand in writing, or formal request or requirement. Atwood v. Charlton, 21 R.I. 568, 45 A. 580.

The taking or seizure of property by government. Benedict v. U. S., D.C.N.Y., 271 F. 714.

In international law. The formal demand by one government upon another, or by the governor of one of the United States upon the governor of a sister state, of the surrender of a fugitive criminal.

In Scotch law. A demand made by a creditor that a debt be paid or an obligation fulfilled. Bell.

REQUISITIONS ON TITLE, in English conveyancing, are written inquiries made by the solicitor of an intending purchaser of land, or of any estate or interest therein, and addressed to the vendor's solicitor, in respect of some apparent insufficiency in the abstract of title. Mozley & Whitley.

REREFIEFS. In Scotch law. Inferior fiefs; portions of a fief or feud granted out to inferior tenants. 2 Bl.Comm. 57.

RERUM ORDO CONFUNDITUR SI UNICUIQUE JURISDICTIO NON SERVETUR. 4 Inst. Proem. The order of things is confounded if every one preserve not his jurisdiction.

RERUM PROGRESSUS OSTENDUNT MULTA, QUÆ IN INITIO PRÆCAVERI SEU PRÆVIDERI NON POSSUNT. 6 Coke, 40. The progress of events shows many things which, at the beginning, could not be guarded against or foreseen.

RERUM SUARUM QUILIBET EST MODERATOR ET ARBITER. Every one is the regulator and disposer of his own property. Co.Litt. 223*a*.

RES. Lat. In the civil law. A thing; an object. As a term of the law, this word has a very wide and extensive signification, including not only things which are objects of property, but also such as are not capable of individual ownership. Inst. 2, 1, pr. And in old English law it is said to have a general import, comprehending both corporeal and incorporeal things of whatever kind, nature, or species. 3 Inst. 182; Bract. fol. 7*b*. By "*res*," according to the modern civilians, is meant everything that may form an *object* of rights, in opposition to "*persona*," which is regarded as a *subject* of rights. "*Res*," therefore, in its general meaning, comprises *actions* of all kinds; while in its restricted sense it comprehends every object of right, except actions. Mackeld. Rom. Law, § 146. This has reference to the fundamental division of the Institutes, that all law relates either to *persons*, to *things*, or to *actions*. Inst. 1, 2, 12.

In modern usage, the term is particularly applied to an object, subject-matter, or *status*, considered as the defendant in an action, or as the object against which, directly, proceedings are taken. Thus, in a prize case, the captured vessel is "the *res*." And proceedings of this character are said to be *in rem*. (See In Personam; In Rem.) "*Res*" may also denote the action or proceeding, as when a cause, which is not between adversary parties, is entitled "*In re* ———."

Classification

Things (res) have been variously divided and classified in law, *e. g.*, in the following ways: (1) Corporeal and incorporeal things; (2) movables and immovables; (3) *res mancipi* and *res nec mancipi*; (4) things real and things personal; (5) things in possession and choses (*i. e.*, things) in action; (6) fungible things and things not fungible, (*fungibiles vel non fungibiles*;) and (7) *res singulæ* (*i. e.*, individual objects) and *universitates rerum*, (*i. e.*, aggregates of things.) Also persons are for some purposes and in certain respects regarded as things. Brown.

General

Res accessoria. In the civil law. An accessory thing; that which belongs to a principal thing, or is in connection with it.

Res adiratæ. The gist of the old action for *res adiratæ* was the fact that the plaintiff had lost his goods, that they had come into the hands of the defendant, and that the defendant, on request, refused to give them up. 3 Holdsw.Hist.E.L. 275.

Res adjudicata. A common but indefensible misspelling of *res judicata*. The latter term designates a point or question or subject-matter which was in controversy or dispute and has been authoritatively and finally settled by the decision of a court; that issuable fact once legally determined is conclusive as between parties in same action or subsequent proceeding. Tiffany Production of California v. Superior Court of California for Los Angeles County, 131 Cal.App. 729, 22 P. 2d 275.

Res adjudicata (if there be such a term) could only mean an article or subject of property "awarded to" a given person by the judgment of a court, which might perhaps be the case in replevin and similar actions.

Res caduca. In the civil law. A fallen or escheated thing; an escheat. Hallifax, Civil Law, b. 2, c. 9, no. 60.

Res communes. In the civil law. Things common to all; that is, those things which are used and enjoyed by every one, even in single parts, but can never be exclusively acquired as a whole, *e. g.*, light and air. Inst. 2, 1, 1; Mackeld. Rom. Law, § 169.

Res controversa. In the civil law. A matter controverted; a matter in controversy; a point in question; a question for determination. Calvin.

Res coronæ. In old English law. Things of the crown; such as ancient manors, homages of the king, liberties, etc. Fleta, lib. 3, c. 6, § 3.

Res corporales. In the civil law. Corporeal things; things which can be touched, or are perceptible to the senses. Dig. 1, 8, 1, 1; Inst. 2, 2; Bract. fols. 7*b*, 10*b*, 13*b*.

Res derelicta. Abandoned property; property thrown away or forsaken by the owner, so as to become open to the acquisition of the first taker or occupant. Rhodes v. Whitehead, 27 Tex. 313, 84 Am.Dec. 631.

Res fungibiles. In the civil law. Fungible things, things of such a nature that they can be replaced by equal quantities and qualities when returning a loan or delivering goods purchased, for example, so many bushels of wheat or so many dollars; but a particular horse or a particular jewel would not be of this character.

Res furtivæ. In Scotch law. Goods which have been stolen. Bell.

Res gestæ. Things done. McClory v. Schneider, Tex.Civ.App., 51 S.W.2d 738, 741. Those circumstances which are the automatic and undesigned incidents of a particular litigated act, which may be separated from act by lapse of time more or less appreciable, and which are admissible when illustrative of such act. The whole of the transaction under investigation and every part of it. Res gestæ is considered as an exception to the hearsay rule. In its operation it renders acts and declarations which constitute a part of the things done and said admissible in evidence, even though they would otherwise come within the rule excluding hearsay evidence or self-serving declarations. The rule is extended to include, not only declarations by the parties to the suit, but includes statements made by bystanders and strangers, under certain circumstances. Edwards v. West Texas Hospital, Tex.Civ.App., 89 S.W.2d 801, 809; Slayback Van Order Co. v. Eiben, 177 A. 671, 673, 115 N.J.L. 17. For evidence to be admissible as res gestæ, there must be an act in itself admissible in the case independently of the declaration that accompanies it; a declaration uttered simultaneously, or almost simultaneously, with the occurrence of the act; and the explanation of the act by what is said when it happens. Staley v. Royal Pines Park, 202 N.C. 155, 162 S.E. 202, 203.

Test as to whether declaration is part of res gestæ depends on whether declaration was facts talking through party or party talking about facts. Batchelor v. Atlantic Coast Line R. Co., 196 N.C. 84, 144 S.E. 542, 544, 60 A.L.R. 1091.

"Res gestae", while often spoken of as an exception to the hearsay rule, is generally not such in fact but ordinarily it relates to statements which because of their intimate relation to facts become a part of those facts and are therefore admitted as such. Industrial Commission of Colorado v. Fotis, 112 Colo. 423, 149 P.2d 657, 659.

Res habiles. In the civil law, things which are prescriptible; things to which a lawful title may be acquired by ordinary prescription.

Res immobiles. In the civil law. Immovable things; including land and that which is connected therewith, either by nature or art, such as trees and buildings. Mackeld. Rom. Law, § 160.

Res incorporales. In the civil law. Incorporeal things; things which cannot be touched; such as those things which consist in right. Inst. 2, 2; Bract. fols. 7*b*, 10*b*. Such things as the mind alone can perceive.

Res integra. A whole thing; a new or unopened thing. The term is applied to those points of law which have not been decided, which are untouched by *dictum* or decision. 3 Mer. 269.

Res inter alios acta. A thing done between others, or between third parties or strangers. Chicago, etc., R. Co. v. Schmitz, 211 Ill. 446, 71 N.E. 1050.

Res ipsa loquitur. The thing speaks for itself. Rebuttable presumption that defendant was negligent, which arises upon proof that instrumentality causing injury was in defendant's exclusive control, and that the accident was one which ordinarily does not happen in absence of negligence. Sliwowski v. New York, N. H. & H. R. Co., 94 Conn. 303, 108 A. 805, 807; Poth v. Dexter Horton Estate, 140 Wash. 272, 248 P. 374, 375; Pearson v. Butts, 224 Iowa 376, 276 N.W. 65, 67.

Res judicata. A matter adjudged; a thing judicially acted upon or decided; a thing or matter settled by judgment. A phrase of the civil law, constantly quoted in the books. Epstein v. Soskin, 86 Misc.Rep. 94, 148 N.Y.S. 323, 324; Rule that final judgment or decree on merits by court of competent jurisdiction is conclusive of rights of parties or their privies in all later suits on points and matters determined in former suit. American S. S. Co. v. Wickwire Spencer Steel Co., D.C.N.Y., 8 F.Supp. 562, 566. And to be applicable, requires identity in thing sued for as well as identity of cause of action, of persons and parties to action, and of quality in persons for or against whom claim is made. Freudenreich v. Mayor and Council of Borough of Fairview, 114 N.J.L. 290, 176 A. 162, 163. The sum and substance of the whole rule is that a matter once judicially decided is finally decided. Massie v. Paul, 263 Ky. 183, 92 S.W.2d 11, 14. See, also, Res Adjudicata, supra.

Estoppel and res judicata distinguished. See Estoppel.

Res litigiosæ. In Roman law, things which are in litigation; property or rights which constitute the subject-matter of a pending action.

Res mancipi. See Mancipi Res.

Res mobiles. In the civil law. Movable things; things which may be transported from one place to another, without injury to their substance and form. Things corresponding with the chattels personal of the common law. 2 Kent, Comm. 347.

Res nova. A new matter; a new case; a question not before decided.

Res nullius. The property of nobody. A thing which has no owner, either because a former owner has finally abandoned it, or because it has never been appropriated by any person, or because (in the Roman law) it is not susceptible of private ownership.

Res periit domino. A phrase used to express that, when a thing is lost or destroyed, it is lost to the person who was the owner of it at the time. Broom, Max. 238.

Res privatæ. In the civil law. Things the property of one or more individuals. Mackeld. Rom. Law, § 157.

Res publicæ. Things belonging to the public; public property; such as the sea, navigable rivers, highways, etc.

Res quotidianæ. Every-day matters; familiar points or questions.

Res religiosæ. Things pertaining to religion. In Roman law, especially, burial-places, which were regarded as sacred, and could not be the subjects of commerce.

Res sacræ. In the civil law. Sacred things. Things consecrated by the pontiffs to the service of God; such as sacred edifices, and gifts or offerings. Inst. 2, 1, 8. Chalices, crosses, censers. Bract. fol. 8.

Res sanctæ. In the civil law. Holy things; such as the walls and gates of a city. Inst. 2, 1, 10. Walls were said to be holy, because any offense against them was punished capitally. Bract. fol. 8.

Res universitatis. In the civil law. Things belonging to a community, (as, to a municipality,) the use and enjoyment of which, according to their proper purpose, is free to every member of the community, but which cannot be appropriated to the exclusive use of any individual; such as the public buildings, streets, etc. Inst. 2, 1, 6; Mackeld. Rom. Law, § 770.

RES ACCENDENT LUMINA REBUS. One thing throws light upon others. Odgen v. Gibbons, 4 Johns.Ch. (N.Y.) 149.

RES ACCESSORIA SEQUITUR REM PRINCIPALEM. Broom, Max. 491. The accessory follows the principal.

RES DENOMINATUR A PRINCIPALI PARTE. 9 Coke, 47. The thing is named from its principal part.

RES EST MISERA UBI JUS EST VAGUM ET INCERTUM. 2 Salk. 512. It is a wretched state of things when law is vague and mutable.

RES GENERALEM HABET SIGNIFICATIONEM QUIA TAM CORPOREA QUAM INCORPOREA CUJUSCUNQUE SUNT GENERIS, NATURÆ, SIVE SPECIEI, COMPREHENDIT. 3 Inst. 182. The word "thing" has a general signification, because it comprehends corporeal and incorporeal objects, of whatever nature, sort, or species.

RES INTER ALIOS ACTA ALTERI NOCERE NON DEBET. Things done between strangers ought not to injure those who are not parties to them. Co.Litt. 132; Broom, Max. 954, 967.

RES INTER ALIOS JUDICATÆ NULLUM ALIIS PRÆJUDICIUM FACIUNT. Matters adjudged in a cause do not prejudice those who were not parties to it. Dig. 44, 2, 1.

RES JUDICATA FACIT EX ALBO NIGRUM; EX NIGRO, ALBUM; EX CURVO, RECTUM; EX RECTO, CURVUM. A thing adjudged [the solemn judgment of a court] makes white, black; black, white; the crooked, straight; the straight, crooked. 1 Bouv. Inst. no. 840.

RES JUDICATA PRO VERITATE ACCIPITUR. A matter adjudged is taken for truth. Dig. 50, 17, 207. A matter decided or passed upon by a court of competent jurisdiction is received as evidence of truth. 2 Kent, Comm. 120.

RES NULLIUS NATURALITER FIT PRIMI OCCUPANTIS. A thing which has no owner naturally belongs to the first finder.

RES PER PECUNIAM ÆSTIMATUR, ET NON PECUNIA PER REM. 9 Coke, 76. The value of a thing is estimated according to its worth in money, but the value of money is not estimated by reference to a thing.

RES PROPRIA EST QUÆ COMMUNIS NON EST. A thing is private which is not common. Le Breton v. Miles, 8 Paige (N.Y.) 261, 270.

RES QUÆ INTRA PRÆSIDIA PERDUCTÆ NONDUM SUNT, QUANQUAM AB HOSTIBUS OCCUPATÆ, IDEO POSTLIMINII NON EGENT, QUIA DOMINUM NONDUM MUTURUNT EX GENTIUM JURE. Things which have not yet been introduced within the enemy's lines, although held by the enemy, do not need the fiction of postliminy on this account, because their ownership by the law of nations has not yet changed. Gro. de Jure B. l. 3, c. 9, § 16; Id. l. 3, c. 6, § 3.

RES SACRA NON RECIPIT ÆSTIMATIONEM. A sacred thing does not admit of valuation. Dig. 1, 8, 9, 5.

RES SUA NEMINI SERVIT. 4 Macq.H.L.Cas. 151. No one can have a servitude over his own property.

RES TRANSIT CUM SUO ONERE. The thing passes with its burden. Where a thing has been incumbered by mortgage, the incumbrance follows it wherever it goes. Bract. fols. 47*b*, 48.

RESALE. Where a person who has sold goods or other property to a purchaser sells them again to some one else. Sometimes a vendor reserves the right of reselling if the purchaser commits default in payment of the purchase money, and in some cases (*e. g.*, on a sale of perishable articles) the vendor may do so without having reserved the right. Sweet.

RESCEIT. In old English practice. An admission or receiving a third person to plead his right in a cause formerly commenced between two others; as, in an action by tenant for life or years, he in the reversion might come in and pray to be received to defend the land, and to plead with the demandant. Cowell.

RESCEIT OF HOMAGE. The lord's receiving homage of his tenant at his admission to the land. Kitch. 148.

RESCIND. To abrogate, annul, avoid, or cancel a contract; particularly, nullifying a contract by the act of a party. Vaughn v. Fey, 47 Cal.App. 485, 190 P. 1041, 1042; Pearson v. Brown, 27 Cal. App. 125, 148 P. 956, 958. To declare a contract void in its inception and to put an end to it as though it never were. Russell v. Stephens, 191 Wash. 314, 71 P.2d 30, 31. Not merely to terminate it and release parties from further obligations to each other but to abrogate it from the beginning and restore parties to relative positions which they would have occupied had no contract ever been made. Wall v. Zynda, 283 Mich. 260, 278 N.W. 66, 68, 114 A.L.R. 1521; Sylvania Industrial Corporation v. Lilienfeld's Estate, C.C.A.Va., 132 F.2d 887, 892, 145 A.L.R. 612.

RESCISSIO. Lat. In the civil law. An annulling; avoiding, or making void; abrogation; rescission. Cod. 4, 44.

In Spanish law, nullity is divided into absolute and relative. The former is that which arises from a law, whether civil or criminal, the principal motive for which is the public interest; and the latter is that which affects only certain individuals. "Nullity" is not to be confounded with "rescission." Nullity takes place when the act is affected by a radical vice, which prevents it from producing any effect; as where an act is in contravention of the laws or of good morals, or where it has been executed by a person who cannot be supposed to have any will, as a child under the age of seven years, or a madman, *(un nino o demente.)* Rescission is where an act, valid in appearance, nevertheless conceals a defect, which may make it null, if demanded by any of the parties; as, for example, mistake, force, fraud, deceit, want of sufficient age, etc. Nullity relates generally to public order, and cannot therefore be made good either by ratification or prescription; so that the tribunals ought, for this reason alone, to decide that the null act can have no effect, without stopping to inquire whether the parties to it have or have not received any injury. Rescission, on the contrary, may be made good by ratification or by the silence of the parties; and neither of the parties can demand it, unless he can prove that he has received some prejudice or sustained some damage by the act. Sunol v. Hepburn, 1 Cal. 281, citing Escriche.

RESCISSION OF CONTRACT. Annulling or abrogation or unmaking of contract and the placing of the parties to it in status quo. Sessions v. Meadows, 13 Cal.App.2d 748, 57 P.2d 548, 549. Kunde v. O'Brian, 214 Iowa 921, 243 N.W. 594, 595. It necessarily involves a repudiation of the contract and a refusal of the moving party to be further bound by it. Wall v. Zynda, 283 Mich. 260, 278 N.W. 66, 68, 114 A.L.R. 1521.

RESCISSORY ACTION. In Scotch law. One to rescind or annul a deed or contract.

RESCOUS. Rescue. The taking back by force goods which had been taken under a distress, or the violently taking away a man who is under arrest, and setting him at liberty, or otherwise procuring his escape, are both so denominated. This was also the name of a writ which lay in cases of rescue. Co.Litt. 160; 3 Bl.Comm. 146; Fitzh.Nat.Brev. 100; 6 Mees. & W. 564.

RESCRIPT. In canon law. A term including any form of apostolical letter emanating from the pope. The answer of the pope in writing. Dict. Droit Can.

At common law. A counterpart, duplicate, or copy.

In American law. A written order from the court to the clerk, giving directions concerning the further disposition of a case. Pub.St.Mass. p. 1295. The written statement by an appellate court of its decision in a case, with the reasons therefor, sent down to the trial court.

In the civil law. A species of imperial constitutions, being the answers of the prince in individual cases, chiefly given in response to inquiries by parties in relation to litigated suits, or to inquiries by the judges, and which became rules for future litigated or doubtful legal questions. Mackeld. Rom. Law, § 46.

RESCRIPTION. In French law. A letter by which one requests some one to pay a certain sum of money, or to account for him to a third person for it. Poth. Cont. de Change, no. 225.

RESCRIPTUM. Lat. In the civil law. A species of imperial constitution, in the form of an answer to some application or petition; a rescript. Calvin.

RESCUE. At common law. Forcibly and knowingly freeing another from arrest or imprisonment without any effort by prisoner to free himself. Merrill v. State, 42 Ariz. 341, 26 P.2d 110. The unlawfully or forcibly taking back goods which have been taken under a distress for rent, damage feasant, etc. Hamlin v. Mack, 33 Mich. 108.

In admiralty and maritime law. The deliverance of property taken as prize, out of the hands of the captors, either when the captured party retake it by their own efforts, or when, pending the pursuit or struggle, the party about to be overpowered receive reinforcements, and so escape capture.

RESCUE DOCTRINE. Under this doctrine, one injured in voluntary attempt to rescue a person whose life is imperiled by negligence of another may recover from the negligent person if the attempted rescue be not an act of extreme recklessness. Rovinski v. Rowe, C.C.A.Mich., 131 F.2d 687, 692, 693.

RESCUSSOR. In old English law. A rescuer; one who commits a rescous. Cro.Jac. 419; Cowell.

RESCYT. L. Fr. Resceit; receipt; the receiving or harboring a felon, after the commission of a crime. Britt. c. 23.

RESEALING WRIT. In English law. The second sealing of a writ by a master so as to continue it, or to cure it of an irregularity.

RESERVANDO. Reserving. In old conveyancing. An apt word of reserving a rent. Co.Litt. 47*a*.

RESERVATIO NON DEBET ESSE DE PROFICUIS IPSIS, QUIA EA CONCEDUNTUR, SED DE REDITU NOVO EXTRA PROFICUA. A reservation ought not to be of the profits themselves, because they are granted, but from the new rent, apart from the profits. Co.Litt. 142.

RESERVATION. A clause in a deed or other instrument of conveyance by which the grantor creates, and reserves to himself, some right, interest, or profit in the estate granted, which had no previous existence as such, but is first called into being by the instrument reserving it; such as rent, or an easement. In re Narragansett Indians, 20 R.I. 715, 40 A. 347; Smith v. Cornell University, 21 Misc. 220, 45 N.Y.S. 640; Johnson v. Peck, 90 Utah 544, 63 P.2d 251.

For exception and reservation distinguished, see Exception.

Public Land Laws of the United States

A reservation is a tract of land, more or less considerable in extent, which is by public authority withdrawn from sale or settlement, and appropriated to specific public uses; such as parks, military posts, Indian lands, etc. Jackson v. Wilcox, 2 Ill. 344; Meehan v. Jones, C.C.Minn., 70 F. 455.

Practice

The reservation of a point of law is the act of the trial court in setting it aside for future consideration, allowing the trial to proceed meanwhile as if the question had been settled one way, but subject to alteration of the judgment in case the court *in banc* should decide it differently.

RESERVE, *v.* To keep back, to retain, to keep in store for future or special use, and to retain or hold over to a future time. Commissioner of Internal Revenue v. Strong Mfg. Co., C.C.A.6, 124 F. 2d 360, 363.

RESERVE, *n.* In insurance law. A sum of money, variously computed or estimated, which, with accretions from interest, is set aside as a fund with which to mature or liquidate by payment or reinsurance with other companies future unaccrued and contingent claims, and claims accrued but contingent and indefinite as to amount or time of payment. Royal Highlanders v. Commissioner of Internal Revenue, C.C.A.8, 138 F.2d 240, 242, 244.

RESERVED LAND. Public land that has been withheld or kept back from sale or disposition. Donley v. Van Horn, 49 Cal.App. 383, 193 P. 514, 516.

RESET. The receiving or harboring an outlawed person. Cowell.

Reset of Theft

In Scotch law. The receiving and keeping stolen goods, knowing them to be stolen, with a design of feloniously retaining them from the real owner. Alis. Crim. Law, 328.

RESETTER. In Scotch law. A receiver of stolen goods knowing them to have been stolen.

RESETTLEMENT. The reopening of an order or decree for the purpose of including therein some recital or provision which should have been included and was initially omitted through inadvertence. In re Bartlett's Will, 299 N.Y.S. 316, 317, 164 Misc. 524.

RESIANCE. Residence, abode, or continuance.

RESIANT. In old English law. Continually dwelling or abiding in a place; resident; a resident. Kitchin, 33; Cowell.

RESIANT ROLLS. Those containing the resiants in a tithing, etc., which are to be called over by the steward on holding courts leet.

RESIDE. Live, dwell, abide, sojourn, stay, remain, lodge. Western-Knapp Engineering Co. v. Gilbank, C.C.A.Cal., 129 F.2d 135, 136.

RESIDENCE. A factual place of abode. Living in a particular locality. Reese v. Reese, 179 Misc. 665, 40 N.Y.S.2d 468, 472; Zimmerman v. Zimmerman, 175 Or. 585, 155 P.2d 293, 295. It requires only bodily presence as an inhabitant of a place. In re Campbell's Guardianship, 216 Minn. 113, 11 N.W.2d 786, 789.

As "domicile" and "residence" are usually in the same place, they are frequently used as if they had the same meaning, but they are not identical terms, for a person may have two places of residence, as in the city and country, but only one domicile. Residence means living in a particular locality, but domicile means living in that locality with intent to make it a fixed and permanent home. Residence simply requires bodily presence as an inhabitant in a given place, while domicile requires bodily presence in that place and also an intention to make it one's domicile. In re Riley's Will, 266 N.Y.S. 209, 148 Misc. 588. "Residence" demands less intimate local ties than "domicile," but "domicile" allows absence for indefinite period if intent to return remains. Immigration Act 1917, § 3, 8 U.S.C.A. § 136 (*e*, *p*). Transatlantica Italiana v. Elting, C.C.A.N.Y., 74 F.2d 732, 733. But see, Ward v. Ward, 115 W.Va. 429, 176 S.E. 708, 709; Southwestern Greyhound Lines v. Craig, 182 Okl. 610, 80 P.2d 221, 224; holding that residence and domicile are synonymous terms. "Residence" has a meaning dependent on context and purpose of statute. In re Jones, 341 Pa. 329, 19 A.2d 280, 282. Words "residence" and "domicile" may have an identical or variable meaning depending on subject-matter and context of statute. Kemp v. Kemp, 16 N.Y.S.2d 26, 34, 172 Misc. 738.

Legal residence. See Legal.

RESIDENT. One who has his residence in a place. See Residence.

Also a tenant, who was obliged to reside on his lord's land, and not to depart from the same; called, also, *"homme levant et couchant,"* and in Normandy, *"resseant du fief."*

RESIDENT FREEHOLDER. A person who resides in the particular place (town, city, county, etc.) and who owns an estate in lands therein amounting at least to a freehold interest. Campbell v. Moran, 71 Neb. 615, 99 N.W. 499.

RESIDENT MINISTER. In international law. A public minister who resides at a foreign court. Resident ministers are ranked in the third class of public ministers. Wheat. Int. Law, 264, 267.

RESIDUAL. Relating to the residue; relating to the part remaining.

RESIDUARY. Pertaining to the residue; constituting the residue; giving or bequeathing the residue; receiving or entitled to the residue. In re Kent's Will, 169 App.Div. 388, 155 N.Y.S. 894, 897.

RESIDUARY ACCOUNT. In English practice. The account which every executor and administrator, after paying the debts and particular legacies of the deceased, and before paying over the residuum, must pass before the board of inland revenue. Mozley & Whitley.

RESIDUARY BEQUEST. A bequest of all of testator's estate not otherwise effectually disposed of. In re Dolan's Estate, Sur., 21 N.Y.S.2d 464, 466.

RESIDUARY CLAUSE. Clause in will by which that part of property is disposed of which remains after satisfying bequests and devises. Sanborn v. Sanborn, 14 N.J.Misc. 260, 184 A. 400, 402.

RESIDUARY DEVISE AND DEVISEE. See Devise.

RESIDUARY ESTATE. That which remains after debts and expenses of administration, legacies, and devises have been satisfied. Nichols v. Swickard, 211 Iowa 957, 234 N.W. 846, 847. It consists of all that has not been legally disposed of by will, other than by residuary clause. In re Cushman's Estate, 257 N.Y.S. 582, 586, 143 Misc. 432.

RESIDUARY LEGACY. See Legacy.

RESIDUARY LEGATEE. See Legatee.

RESIDUE. The surplus of a testator's estate remaining after all the debts and particular legacies have been discharged. 2 Bl.Comm. 514; In re Hamlin, 185 App.Div. 153, 172 N.Y.S. 787, 790; In re Brown v. Hilleary, 147 Or. 185, 32 P.2d 584, 587.

RESIDUUM. That which remains after any process of separation or deduction; a residue or balance. That which remains of a decedent's estate, after debts have been paid and legacies deducted. United States Trust Co. v. Black, 30 N.Y.S. 453, 9 Misc. 653.

RESIGNATIO EST JURIS PROPRII SPONTANEA REFUTATIO. Resignation is a spontaneous relinquishment of one's own right. Godb. 284.

RESIGNATION. Formal renouncement or relinquishment of an office. Steingruber v. City of San Antonio, Tex.Com.App., 220 S.W. 77, 78. It must be made with intention of relinquishing the office accompanied by act of relinquishment. Patten v. Miller, 190 Ga. 123, 8 S.E.2d 757, 770; Sadler v. Jester, D.C.Tex., 46 F.Supp. 737, 740.

In ecclesiastical law. Where a parson, vicar, or other beneficed clergyman voluntarily gives up and surrenders his charge and preferment to those from whom he received the same. It is usually done by an instrument attested by a notary. Phillim.Ecc.Law, 517.

In Scotch law. The return of a fee into the hands of the superior. Bell.

RESIGNATION BOND. A bond or other engagement in writing taken by a patron from the clergyman presented by him to a living, to resign the benefice at a future period. This is allowable in certain cases under St. 9 Geo. IV. c. 94, passed in 1828. 2 Steph.Comm. 721.

RESIGNEE. One in favor of whom a resignation is made. 1 Bell, Comm. 125*n*.

RESILIENCY. In patent law. That quality, as of a metal, which causes it to spring back to its form, inherent in properly tempered metal. Besser v. Merillat Culvert Core Co., D.C.Iowa, 226 F. 783, 786.

RESILIRE. Lat. In old English law. To draw back from a contract before it is made binding. Bract. fol. 38.

RESIST. To oppose. This word properly describes an opposition by direct action and *quasi* forcible means. Powell v. State, 152 Ga. 81, 108 S.E. 464, 465; McAlpine v. State, 19 Ala.App. 391, 97 So. 612, 613.

RESISTANCE. The act of resisting opposition; the employment of forcible means to prevent the execution of an endeavor in which force is employed; standing against; obstructing. U. S. v. Jose, C.C.Wash., 63 F. 954; U. S. v. Huff, C.C. Tenn., 13 F. 639.

RESISTING AN OFFICER. In criminal law, the offense of obstructing, opposing, and endeavoring to prevent (with or without actual force) a peace officer in the execution of a writ or in the lawful discharge of his duty while making an arrest or otherwise enforcing the peace. Jones v. State, 60 Ala. 99.

RESOLUCION. In Spanish colonial law. An opinion formed by some superior authority on matters referred to its decision, and forwarded to inferior authorities for their instruction and government. Schm. Civil Law, 93, note 1.

RESOLUTION. A formal expression of the opinion or will of an official body or a public assembly, adopted by vote; as a legislative resolution. Scudder v. Smith, 331 Pa. 165, 200 A. 601, 604.

Civil Law

The cancellation or annulling, by the act of parties or judgment of a court, of an existing contract which was valid and binding, in consequence of some cause or matter arising after the making of the agreement, and not in consequence of any inherent vice or defect, which, invalidating the contract from the beginning, would be ground for rescission. 7 Toullier, no. 551.

Legislative Practice

The term is usually employed to denote the adoption of a motion, the subject-matter of which would not properly constitute a statute; such as a mere expression of opinion; an alteration of the rules; a vote of thanks or of censure, etc. McDowell v. People, 68 N.E. 379, 204 Ill. 499; Conley v. Texas Division of United Daughters of the Confederacy, Tex.Civ.App., 164 S.W. 24, 26.

The chief distinction between a "resolution" and a "law" is that the former is used whenever the legislative body passing it wishes merely to express an opinion as to some given matter or thing and is only to have a temporary effect on such particular thing, while by a "law" it is intended to permanently direct and control matters applying to persons or things in general. Ex parte Hague, 104 N.J.Eq. 31, 144 A. 546, 559.

Joint resolution. A resolution adopted by both houses of congress or a legislature. When such a resolution has been approved by the president or passed with his approval, it has the effect of a law. 6 Op.Atty.Gen. 680.

The distinction between a joint resolution and a concurrent resolution of congress, is that the former requires the approval of the president while the latter does not. Rep. Sen. Jud. Com. Jan. 1897.

If a resolution originating in one house of the Legislature is passed by that house and is then sent to the other for its concurrence, and is passed by it, signed by the presiding officer of each house and approved by the Governor, it is a "joint resolution" as that term is used in the Constitution and the joint rules of the Legislature. Oklahoma News Co. v. Ryan, 101 Okl. 151, 224 P. 969, 971.

Practice

A solemn judgment or decision of a court.

This word is frequently used in this sense by Coke and some of the more ancient reporters.

RESOLUTIVE. In Scotch conveyancing. Having the quality or effect of resolving or extinguishing a right. Bell.

RESOLUTO JURE CONCEDENTIS RESOLVITUR JUS CONCESSUM. The right of the grantor being extinguished, the right granted is extinguished. Mackeld. Rom. Law, 179; Broom, Max. 467.

RESOLUTORY CONDITION. See Condition.

RESORT, *v.* To go back; as, it resorted to the line of the mother. Hale, Com.Law, c. 11. To frequent; to go, repair, betake one's self, especially to go frequently, customarily, or usually. State v. Poggmeyer, 91 Kan. 633, 138 P. 593, 594.

RESORT, *n.* A place of frequent assembly, a haunt. U. S. ex rel. Dobra v. Lindsey, D.C.Tex., 51 F.2d 141, 142.

Court of last resort. A court whose decision is final and without appeal in reference to the particular case.

RESOURCES. Money or any property that can be converted into supplies; means of raising money or supplies; capabilities of raising wealth or to supply necessary wants; available means or capability of any kind. Shelby County v. Tennessee Centennial Exposition Co., 96 Tenn. 653, 36 S.W. 694, 33 L.R.A. 717. Cerenzia v. Department of Social Security of Washington, 18 Wash.2d 230, 138 P.2d 868, 871.

RESPECTIVE. Relating to particular persons or things, each to each; particular; several; as, their respective homes. Sandford v. Stagg, 106 N.J.Eq. 71, 150 A. 187, 188.

RESPECTU COMPUTI VICECOMITIS HABENDO. A writ for respiting a sheriff's account addressed to the treasurer and barons of the exchequer. Reg. Orig. 139.

RESPECTUS. In old English and Scotch law. Respite; delay; continuance of time; postponement.

RESPICIENDUM EST JUDICANTI NE QUID AUT DURIUS AUT REMISSIUS CONSTITUATUR QUAM CAUSA DEPOSCIT; NEC ENIM AUT SEVERITATIS AUT CLEMENTIÆ GLORIA AFFECTANDA EST. The judge must see that no order be made or judgment given or sentence passed either more harshly or more mildly than the case requires; he must not seek renown, either as a severe or as a tender-hearted judge.

RESPITE. The temporary suspension of the execution of a sentence, a reprieve; a delay, forbearance, or continuation of time. 4 Bl.Comm. 394; State v. District Court of Eighteenth Judicial Dist. in and for Blaine County, 73 Mont. 541, 237 P. 525, 527.

Continuance. In English practice, a jury is said, on the record, to be "respited" till the next term. 3 Bl.Comm. 354.

In the civil law. An act by which a debtor, who is unable to satisfy his debts at the moment, transacts (compromises) with his creditors, and obtains from them time or delay for the payment of the sums which he owes to them. The respite is either voluntary or forced. It is *voluntary* when all the creditors consent to the proposal, which the debtor makes, to pay in a limited time the whole or a part of the debt. It is *forced* when a part of the creditors refuse to accept the debtor's proposal, and when the latter is obliged to compel them by judicial authority to consent to what the others have determined, in the cases directed by law.

RESPITE OF APPEAL. Adjourning an appeal to some future time. Brown.

RESPITE OF HOMAGE. To dispense with the performance of homage by tenants who held their lands in consideration of performing homage to their lords. Cowell.

RESPOND. 1. To make or file an answer to a bill, libel, or appeal, in the character of a respondent, (*q. v.*).

2. To be liable or answerable; to make satisfaction or amends; as, to "respond in damages."

RESPONDE BOOK. In Scotch practice. A book kept by the directors of chancery, in which are entered all non-entry and relief duties payable by heirs who take precepts from chancery. Bell.

RESPONDEAT OUSTER. Upon an issue in law arising upon a dilatory plea, the form of judgment for the plaintiff is that the defendant answer over, which is thence called a judgment of "*respondeat ouster*." This not being a final judgment, the pleading is resumed, and the action proceeds. Steph.Pl. 115; 3 Bl.Comm. 303; Bauer v. Roth, 4 Rawle (Pa.) 91.

RESPONDEAT RAPTOR, QUI IGNORARE NON POTUIT QUOD PUPILLUM ALIENUM ABDUXIT. Hob. 99. Let the ravisher answer, for he cannot be ignorant that he has taken away another's ward.

RESPONDEAT SUPERIOR. Let the master answer. This maxim means that a master is liable in certain cases for the wrongful acts of his servant, and a principal for those of his agent. Broom, Max. 843. Southern Paramount Pictures Co. v. Gaulding, 24 Ga.App. 478, 101 S.E. 311; Delaware, L. & W. R. Co. v. Pittinger, C.C.A.N.J., 293 F. 853, 855. Under this doctrine master is responsible for want of care on servant's part toward those to whom master owes duty to use care, provided failure of servant to use such care occurred in course of his employment. Shell Petroleum Corporation v. Magnolia Pipe Line Co., Tex.Civ.App., 85 S.W.2d 829, 832. Doctrine applies only when relation of master and servant existed between defendant and wrongdoer at time of injury sued for, in respect to very transaction from which it arose. James v. J. S. Williams & Son, 177 La. 1033, 150 So. 9, 11. Hence doctrine is inapplicable where injury occurs while servant is acting outside legitimate scope of authority. Rogers v. Town of Black Mountain, 224 N.C. 119, 29 S.E.2d 203, 205. But if deviation be only slight or incidental, employer may still be liable. Klotsch v. P. F. Collier & Son Corporation, 349 Mo. 40, 159 S.W. 2d 589, 593, 595; Adams v. South Carolina Power Co., 200 S.C. 438, 21 S.E.2d 17, 19, 20.

Doctrine does not apply in relation between state officers and their subordinates, unless superior participates in or directs act. People v. Standard Accident Ins. Co., 42 Cal.App.2d 409, 108 P.2d 923, 925.

Municipalities are exempt from doctrine when officers are acting in exercise of governmental functions. Lemieux v. City of St. Albans, 112 Vt. 512, 28 A.2d 373, 374.

RESPONDENT. In equity practice. The party who makes an answer to a bill or other proceeding in chancery. State ex inf. Barker v. Duncan, 265 Mo. 26, 175 S.W. 940, 942, Ann.Cas.1916D, 1.

In admiralty. The party upon whom a libel in admiralty is served. Brown.

In appellate practice. The party who contends against an appeal. Brown. Brower v. Wellis, 6 Ind.App. 323, 33 N.E. 672.

In the civil law. One who answers or is security for another; a fidejussor. Dig. 2, 8, 6.

RESPONDENTIA. The hypothecation of the cargo or goods on board a ship as security for the repayment of a loan, the term "bottomry" being confined to hypothecations of the ship herself; but now the term "respondentia" is seldom used, and the expression "bottomry" is generally employed, whether the vessel or her cargo or both be the security. Maude & P. Shipp. 433; Smith, Merc. Law, 416. See Maitland v. The Atlantic, 16 F. Cas. 522.

A contract by which a cargo, or some part thereof, is hypothecated as security for a loan, the repayment of which is dependent on maritime risks.

RESPONDERA SON SOVERAIGNE. His superior or master shall answer. Articuli sup. Chart. c. 18.

RESPONDERE NON DEBET. Lat. In pleading. The prayer of a plea where the defendant insists that he ought not to answer, as when he claims a privilege; for example, as being a member of congress or a foreign ambassador. 1 Chit.Pl. 433.

RESPONSA PRUDENTIUM. Lat. Answers of jurists; responses given upon cases or questions of law referred to them, by certain learned Roman jurists, who, though not magistrates, were authorized to render such opinions. These *responsa* constituted one of the most important sources of the earlier Roman law, and were of great value in developing its scientific accuracy. They held much the same place of authority as our modern precedents and reports.

RESPONSALIS. In Old English Law. One who appeared for another.

In ecclesiastical law. A proctor.

RESPONSALIS AD LUCRANDUM VEL PETENDUM. He who appears and answers for another in court at a day assigned; a proctor, attorney, or deputy. 1 Reeve, Eng.Law, 169.

RESPONSIBILITY. The obligation to answer for an act done, and to repair any injury it may have caused.

RESPONSIBILITY OF EVICTION. In a lease the burden of expelling by legal process those in possession, if they wrongfully withhold it. Muller v. Bernstein, 198 Ill.App. 104, 106.

RESPONSIBLE. Liable, legally accountable or answerable. The Mary F. Barrett, C.C.A.Pa., 279 F. 329, 334; Middendorf, Williams & Co. v. Alexander Milburn Co., 113 A. 348, 354, 137 Md. 583. Able to pay a sum for which he is or may become liable, or to discharge an obligation which he may be under. People v. Kent, 160 Ill. 655, 43 N.E. 760.

RESPONSIBLE CAUSE. So as to relieve defendant from liability for injuries. A cause which is the culpable act of a human being who is legally responsible for such act. State, to Use of Schiller, v. Hecht Co., 165 Md. 415, 169 A. 311, 313.

RESPONSIBLE GOVERNMENT. This term generally designates that species of governmental system in which the responsibility for public measures or acts of state rests upon the ministry or executive council, who are under an obligation to resign when disapprobation of their course is expressed by a vote of want of confidence, in the legislative assembly, or by the defeat of an important measure advocated by them.

RESPONSIO UNIUS NON OMNINO AUDIATUR. The answer of one witness shall not be heard at all. A maxim of the Roman law of evidence. 1 Greenl. Ev. § 260.

RESPONSIVE. Answering; constituting or comprising a complete answer. A "responsive allegation" is one which directly answers the allegation it is intended to meet. Picture Plays Theater Co. of Tampa v. Williams, 75 Fla. 556, 78 So. 674, 677, 1 A.L.R. 1.

RESSEISER. The taking of lands into the hands of the crown, where a general livery or *ouster le main* was formerly misused.

REST, *v.* In the trial of an action, a party is said to "rest," or "rest his case," when he intimates that he has produced all the evidence he intends to offer at that stage, and submits the case, either finally, or subject to his right to afterwards offer rebutting evidence.

REST, *n.* Repose, cessation or intermission of motion, exertion or labor; freedom from activity; quiet. Corrugating Machinery Corporation v. Progressive Corrugated Paper Machinery Co., D. C.N.Y., 47 F.2d 273, 275. Also residue (which title see).

RESTAMPING WRIT. Passing it a second time through the proper office, whereupon it receives a new stamp. 1 Chit. Arch. Pr. 212.

RESTAUR, or RESTOR. The remedy or recourse which marine underwriters have against each other, according to the date of their assurances, or against the master, if the loss arise through his default, as through ill loading, want of caulking, or want of having the vessel tight; also the remedy or recourse a person has against his guarantor or other person who is to indemnify him from any damage sustained. Enc. Lond.

RESTAURANT. An establishment where refreshments or meals may be obtained by the public. Donahue v. Conant, 102 Vt. 108, 146 A. 417, 419. It includes cafes, lunchrooms, dairy lunch rooms, cafeterias, tea rooms, waffle houses, fountain lunches, sandwich shops and many others. People, on Complaint of Canniano, v. Kupas, 13 N.Y. S.2d 488, 490, 171 Misc. 480.

RESTITUTIO IN INTEGRUM. Lat. In the civil law. Restoration or restitution to the previous condition. This was effected by the prætor on equitable grounds, at the prayer of an injured party, by rescinding or annulling a contract or transaction valid by the strict law, or annulling a change in the legal condition produced by an omission, and restoring the parties to their previous situation or legal relations. Dig. 4, 1; Mackeld. Rom. Law, § 220.

The restoration of a cause to its first state, on petition of the party who was cast, in order to have a second hearing. Hallifax, Civil Law, b. 3, c. 9, no. 49.

RESTITUTION. Act of restoring; restoration; restoration of anything to its rightful owner; the act of making good or giving equivalent for any loss, damage or injury; and indemnification. State v. Barnett, 110 Vt. 221, 3 A.2d 521, 525, 526.

Equity

Restoration of both parties to their original condition, (when practicable,) upon the rescission of a contract for fraud or similar cause.

Maritime Law

The placing back or restoring articles which have been lost by jettison: This is done, when remainder of the cargo has been saved, at the general charge of the owners of the cargo. Stevens, Av. pt. 1, c. 1, § 1, art. 1, n. 8.

Practice

The return of something to the owner of it or to the person entitled to it, upon the reversal or setting aside of the judgment or order of court under which it was taken from him. Haebler v. Myers, 132 N.Y. 363, 30 N.E. 963, 15 L.R.A. 588, 28 Am.St.Rep. 589; Holloway v. People's Water Co., 100 Kan. 414, 167 P. 265, 269, 2 A.L.R. 161.

If, after money has been levied under a writ of execution, the judgment be reversed by writ of error, or set aside, the party against whom the execution was sued out shall have *restitution*. 2 Tidd, Pr. 1033; 1 Burrill, Pr. 292. So, on conviction of a felon, immediate *restitution* of such of the goods stolen as are brought into court will be ordered to be made to the several prosecutors. 4 Steph. Comm. 434.

General

Restitution of conjugal rights. In English ecclesiastical law. A species of matrimonial cause or suit which is brought whenever either a husband or wife is guilty of the injury of subtraction, or lives separate from the other without any sufficient reason; in which case the ecclesiastical jurisdiction will compel them to come together again, if either be weak enough to desire it, contrary to the inclination of the other. 3 Bl. Comm. 94.

Restitution of minors. In Scotch law. Relief obtained by minor on attaining majority against a deed previously executed by him. Bell.

Restitution of stolen goods. At common law there was no restitution of goods upon an indictment, because it was at the suit of the crown only, therefore the party was compelled to bring an appeal of robbery in order to have his goods again; but a writ of restitution was granted by 21 Hen. VIII. c. 11, and it became the practice of the crown to order, without any writ, immediate restitution of such goods.

Writ of restitution. See that title.

RESTITUTIONE EXTRACTI AB ECCLESIA. A writ to restore a man to the church, which he had recovered for his sanctuary, being suspected of felony. Reg. Orig. 69.

RESTITUTIONE TEMPORALIUM. A writ addressed to the sheriff, to restore the temporalities of a bishopric to the bishop elected and confirmed. Fitzh. Nat. Brev. 169.

RESTRAIN. To limit, confine, abridge, narrow down, restrict, obstruct, impede, hinder, stay, destroy. U. S. v. Keystone Watch Case Co., D.C. Pa., 218 F. 502, 515. To prohibit from action; to put compulsion upon; to restrict; to hold or press back. To enjoin, (in equity.)

RESTRAINING ORDER. An order in the nature of an injunction. See Order.

RESTRAINING POWERS. Restrictions or limitations imposed upon the exercise of a power by the donor thereof.

RESTRAINING STATUTE. A statute which restrains the common law, where it is too lax and luxuriant. 1 Bl. Comm. 87. Statutes restraining the powers of corporations in regard to leases have been so called in England. 2 Bl. Comm. 319, 320.

RESTRAINT. Confinement, abridgment, or limitation. Prohibition of action; holding or pressing back from action. Hindrance, confinement, or restriction of liberty. Obstruction, hindrance or destruction of trade or commerce.

RESTRAINT OF PRINCES AND RULERS. In marine and war risk policies, operation of sovereign power by exercise of vis major, in its sovereign capacity, controlling and divesting for the time, the authority of owner over ship, and clause applies only to acts done in exercise of sovereign power. Baker Castor Oil Co. v. Insurance Co. of North America, D.C.N.Y., 60 F.Supp. 32, 35.

Where the "restraint of princes" clause or similar language is found in the contract, a reasonable apprehension of capture or destruction of the ship or cargo will justify nonperformance of the agreement to carry. The George J. Goulandris, D.C.Me., 36 F.Supp. 827, 830, 834.

RESTRAINT OF MARRIAGE. A contract, covenant, bond, or devise. When conditions unreasonably hamper or restrict the party's freedom to marry, or his choice, or unduly postpone the time of his marriage. "General restraint," as used in the rule invalidating contracts in general restraint of marriage, means restraint binding a competent person not to marry any one at any time. Barnes v. Hobson, Tex.Civ.App., 250 S.W. 238, 242.

RESTRAINT OF TRADE. Contracts or combinations which tend or are designed to eliminate or stifle competition, effect a monopoly, artificially maintain prices, or otherwise hamper or obstruct the course of trade and commerce as it would be carried on if left to the control of natural and economic forces. U. S. v. Reading Co., 40 S.Ct. 425, 429, 253 U.S. 26, 64 L.Ed. 760; U. S. v. Patten, 33 S.Ct. 141, 144, 145, 226 U.S. 525, 57 L.Ed. 333, 44 L.R.A.,N.S., 325.

With reference to contracts between individuals, a restraint of trade is said to be "general" or "special." A contract which forbids a person to employ his talents, industry, or capital in any undertaking within the limits of the state or country is in "general" restraint of trade; if it forbids him to employ himself in a designated trade or business, either for a limited time or within a prescribed area or district, it is in "special" restraint of trade. Holbrook v. Waters, 9 How.Prac. (N.Y.) 337.

"Restraint of trade" at which the Sherman Anti-Trust Act is aimed, are only those which are comparable to restraints deemed illegal at common law. United States v. South-Eastern Underwriters Ass'n, D.C.Ga., 51 F.Supp. 712, 714.

RESTRAINT ON ALIENATION. Restriction of the power of aliening property. See Perpetuity.

In English practice, as applied to counsel, a notice given to a counsel by an attorney on behalf of the plaintiff or defendant in an action, in order to secure his services as advocate when the cause comes on for trial. Holthouse. Blackman v. Webb, 38 Kan. 668, 17 P. 464.

In old English usage. A servant, not menial or familiar,—that is, not continually dwelling in the house of his master, but only wearing his livery, and attending sometimes upon special occasions. Cowell.

RESTRICT. To restrain within bounds; to limit; to confine. State ex rel. Lucey v. Terry, Del.Super., 196 A. 163, 167.

RESTRICTED LANDS. Lands the alienation of which is subject to restrictions imposed by Congress to protect the Indians from their own supposed incompetency. 25 U.S.C.A. § 331 note. Kenny v. Miles, 39 S.Ct. 417, 418, 250 U.S. 58, 63 L.Ed. 841.

RESTRICTION. In the case of land registered under the English land transfer act, 1875, an entry on the register made on the application of the registered proprietor of the land, the effect of which is to prevent the transfer of the land or the creation of any charge upon it, unless notice of the application for a transfer or charge is sent by post to a certain address, or unless the consent of a certain person or persons to the transfer or charge is obtained, or unless some other thing is done. Sweet.

RESTRICTIVE INDORSEMENT. An indorsement so worded as to restrict the further negotiability of the instrument. Thus, "Pay the contents to J. S. only," or "to J. S. for my use," are restrictive indorsements, and put an end to the negotiability of the paper. 1 Daniel, Neg. Inst. § 698.

RESTS, *n.* Periodical balancings of an account, (particularly in mortgage and trust accounts,) made for the purpose of converting interest into principal, and charging the party liable thereon with compound interest. Mozley & Whiteley.

RESULT, *v.* To proceed, to spring, or arise, as a consequence, effect, or conclusion; to come out, or have an issue; to terminate; to end. Abbott v. Prudential Ins. Co. of America, 89 N.H. 149, 195 A. 413, 414.

In law, a thing is said to result when, after having been ineffectually or only partially disposed of, it comes back to its former owner or his representatives. Sweet.

RESULT, *n.* That which results, the conclusion or end to which any course or condition of thing leads, or which is obtained by any process or operation; consequence or effect. Reese v. Dempsey, 48 N.M. 485, 153 P.2d 127, 131.

RESULTING TRUST. See Trust.

RESULTING USE. See Use.

RESUMMONS. In practice. A second summons. The calling a person a second time to answer an action, where the first summons is defeated upon any occasion; as the death of a party, or the like. Cowell.

RESUMPTION. In old English law. The taking again into the king's hands such lands or tenements as before, upon false suggestion, or other error, he had delivered to the heir, or granted by letters patent to any man. Cowell.

RESURRENDER. Where copyhold land has been mortgaged by surrender, and the mortgagee has been admitted, then, on the mortgage debt being paid off, the mortgagor is entitled to have the land reconveyed to him, by the mortgagee surrendering it to the lord to his use. This is called a resurrender. 2 Dav.Conv. 1332*n*.

RETAIL. To sell by small quantities, in broken lots or parcels, not in bulk, to sell direct to consumer. Com. v. Kimball, 7 Metc. (Mass.) 308; Kentucky Consumers' Oil Co. v. Commonwealth, 233 S.W. 892, 893, 192 Ky. 437; Department of Treasury of Indiana v. Ridgely, 211 Ind. 9, 4 N.E. 2d 557, 562, 108 A.L.R. 1067; Guess v. Montague, D.C.S.C., 51 F.Supp. 61, 64, 65.

RETAILER OF MERCHANDISE. A merchant who buys articles in gross or merchandise in large quantities, and sells the same by single articles or in small quantities. Byran v. City of Sparks, 36 Nev. 573, 137 P. 522, 523.

RETAIN. To continue to hold, have, use, recognize, etc., and to keep. Kimbell Trust & Savings Bank v. Hartford Accident & Indemnity Co., 333 Ill. 318, 164 N.E. 661, 662.

In practice. To engage the services of an attorney or counsellor to manage a cause. See Retainer.

RETAINER. The act of withholding what one has in one's own hands by virtue of some right.

Act of the client in employing his attorney or counsel, and also denotes the fee which the client pays when he retains the attorney to act for him, and thereby prevents him from acting for his adversary. Bright v. Turner, 205 Ky. 188, 265 S.W. 627, 628; Devany v. City of South Norfolk, 143 Va. 768, 129 S.E. 672, 674.

General Retainer

Of an attorney or solicitor merely gives a right to expect professional service when requested, but none which is not requested. It binds the person retained not to take a fee from another against his retainer, but to do nothing except what he is asked to do, and for this he is to be distinctly paid. Rhode Island Exch. Bank v. Hawkins, 6 R.I. 206.

Right of Retainer

The right which the executor or administrator of a deceased person has to retain out of the assets sufficient to pay any debt due to him from the deceased in priority to the other creditors whose debts are of equal degree. 3 Steph.Comm. 263. In re Smith's Estate, 179 Wash. 417, 38 P. 2d 244, 245.

Special Retainer

An engagement or retainer of an attorney or solicitor for a special and designated purpose; as, to prepare and try a particular case. Agnew v. Walden, 84 Ala. 502, 4 So. 672.

RETAINER PAY. Compensation paid to enlisted men retained in the service but not rendering active service. French v. French, Cal., 105 P.2d 155, 157.

RETAINING A CAUSE. In English practice, The act of one of the divisions of the high court of justice in retaining jurisdiction of a cause wrongly brought in that division instead of another. Under the judicature acts of 1873 and 1875, this may be done, in some cases, in the discretion of the court or a judge.

RETAINING FEE. A fee given to counsel on engaging his services. Conover v. West Jersey Mortgage Co., 96 N.J.Eq. 441, 126 A. 855, 860.

RETAINING LIEN. See Attorney's Lien.

RETAKING. The taking one's goods, from another, who without right has taken possession thereof. See Recaption.

RETALIATION. See *lex talionis, (q. v.)*.

RETALLIA. In old English law. Retail; the cutting up again, or division of a commodity into smaller parts.

RETENEMENTUM. In old English law. Restraint; detainment; withholding.

RETENTION. In Scotch law. A species of lien; the right to retain possession of a chattel until the lienor is satisfied of his claim upon the article itself or its owner.

RETINENTIA. A retinue, or persons retained by a prince or nobleman. Cowell.

RETIRE. As applied to bills of exchange, this word is ambiguous. It is commonly used of an indorser who takes up a bill by handing the amount to a transferee, after which the indorser holds the instrument with all his remedies intact. But it is sometimes used of an acceptor, by whom, when a bill is taken up or retired at maturity, it is in effect paid, and all the remedies on it extinguished. Byles, Bills, 215. Empire Security Co. v. Berry, 211 Ill.App. 278.

To withdraw from active service as an officer of the army or navy; to separate, withdraw, or remove. State v. Love, 95 Neb. 573, 145 N.W. 1010, 1013, Ann.Cas.1915D, 1078.

RETONSOR. L. Lat. In old English law. A clipper of money. Fleta, lib. 1, c. 20, § 122.

RETORNA BREVIUM. The return of writs. The indorsement by a sheriff or other officer of his doings upon a writ.

RETORNO HABENDO. A writ that lies for the distrainor of goods (when, on replevin brought, he has proved his distress to be a lawful one) against him who was so distrained, to have them returned to him according to law, together with damages and costs. Brown.

RETORSION. In international law. A species of retaliation, which takes place where a government, whose citizens are subjected to severe and stringent regulation or harsh treatment by a foreign government, employs measures of equal severity and harshness upon the subjects of the latter government found within its dominions. Vattel, lib. 2, c. 18, § 341.

RETOUR. In Scotch law. To return a writ to the office in chancery from which it issued.

RETOUR OF SERVICE. In Scotch law. A certified copy of a verdict establishing the legal character of a party as heir to a decedent.

RETOUR SANS FRAIS. Fr. In French law. A formula put upon a bill of exchange to signify that the drawer waives protest, and will not be responsible for costs arising thereon. Arg. Fr. Merc. Law, 573.

RETOUR SANS PROTÊT. Fr. Return without protest. A request or direction by a drawer of a bill of exchange that, should the bill be dishonored by the drawee, it may be returned without protest.

RETRACT. To take back. To retract an offer is to withdraw it before acceptance, which the offerer may always do.

RETRACTATION, in probate practice. A withdrawal of a renunciation, (*q. v.*).

RETRACTO O TANTEO. In Spanish law. The right of revoking a contract of sale; the right of redemption of a thing sold. White, New Recop. b. 2, tit. 13, c. 2, § 4.

RETRACTUS AQUÆ. Lat. The ebb or return of a tide. Cowell.

RETRACTUS FEUDALIS. L. Lat. In old Scotch law. The power which a superior possessed of paying off a debt due to an adjudging creditor, and taking a conveyance to the adjudication. Bell.

RETRAIT. Fr. In old French and Canadian law. The taking back of a fief by the seignior, in case of alienation by the vassal. A right of pre-emption by the seignior, in case of sale of the land by the grantee.

RETRAXIT. Lat. He has withdrawn.

The open, public, and voluntary renunciation by the plaintiff, in open court, of his suit or cause of action, and if this is done by the plaintiff, and a judgment entered thereon by the defendant, the plaintiff's right of action is forever gone. U. S. v. Parker, 7 S.Ct. 454, 120 U.S. 89, 30 L.Ed. 601; Lewis v. Johnson, Cal.App., 80 P.2d 90.

Judgment of Retraxit

One where, after appearance and before judgment, the plaintiff voluntarily enters upon the record that he "withdraws his suit," whereupon judgment is rendered against him.

The difference between a *retraxit* and a *nolle prosequi* is that a *retraxit* is a bar to any future action for the same cause; while a *nolle prosequi* is not, unless made after judgment. Similarly, a *retraxit* differs from a *nonsuit*.

RETREAT TO THE WALL. In the law relating to homicide in self-defense, this phrase means that the party must avail himself of any apparent and reasonable avenues of escape by which his danger might be averted, and the necessity of slaying his assailant avoided. People v. Iams, 57 Cal. 120.

RETRIBUTION. This word is sometimes used in law, though not commonly in modern times, as the equivalent of "recompense," or a payment or compensation for services, property, use of an estate, or other value received.

RETRO. Lat. Back; backward; behind. *Retrofeodum,* a rerefief, or *arriere* fief. Spelman.

RETROACTIVE. Retrospective (*q. v.*). City of Cincinnati v. Bachmann, 51 Ohio App. 108, 199 N.E. 853, 854.

RETROACTIVE INFERENCE. The inferring of a previous fact from present conditions by a trier of facts. Gray v. Kurn, 345 Mo. 1027, 137 S.W. 2d 558, 568.

RETROACTIVE LAW. Retrospective law, which title see.

RETROACTIVE STATUTE. A statute which creates a new obligation on transactions or considerations already past or destroys or impairs vested rights. See, also, Retroactive. London Guarantee & Accident Co. v. Pittman, 69 Ga.App. 146, 25 S.E.2d 60, 65, 66.

RETROCESSION. In the civil law. When the assignee of heritable rights conveys his rights back to the cedent. Ersk. Inst. 3, 5, 1.

RETROSPECTIVE. Looking backward; contemplating what is past; having reference to a state of things existing before the act in question. Walker County Fertilizer Co. v. Napier, 184 Ga. 861, 193 S.E. 770, 773.

RETROSPECTIVE LAW. A law which looks backward or contemplates the past; one which is made to affect acts or facts occurring, or rights accruing, before it came into force. Every statute which takes away or impairs vested rights acquired under existing laws, or creates a new obligation, imposes a new duty, or attaches a new disability in respect to transactions or considerations already past. See Ex Post Facto. Clearwater Tp. v. Board of Sup'rs of Kalkaska County, 187 Mich. 516, 153 N.W. 824, 826; People ex rel. Albright v. Board of Trustees of Firemen's Pension Fund of and for City and County of Denver, Colo., 103 Colo. 1, 82 P.2d 765, 771, 118 A.L.R. 984.

RETTE. L. Fr. An accusation or charge. St. Westm. 1, c. 2.

RETURN. To bring, carry, or send back; to place in the custody of; to restore; to re-deliver; to send back. Tuttle v. City of Boston, 215 Mass. 57, 102 N.E. 350; Johnson v. Curlee Clothing Co., 240 P. 632, 633, 112 Okl. 220.

The act of a sheriff, constable, or other ministerial officer, in delivering back to the court a writ, notice, or other paper, which he was required to serve or execute, with a brief account of his doings under the mandate, the time and mode of service or execution, or his failure to accomplish it, as the case may be. Also the indorsement made by the officer upon the writ or other paper, stating what he has done under it, the time and mode of service, etc. New York, N. H. & H. R. Co. v. Railway Employees' Department,

American Federation of Labor, Federated Shop Crafts, System Federation No. 17, D.C.Conn., 288 F. 588, 591; Smith v. Drake, 174 Ark. 715, 297 S. W. 817.

The report made by the court, body of magistrates, returning board, or other authority charged with the official counting of the votes cast at an election.

In English practice, the election of a member of parliament.

Fair Return

See Fair Return.

False Return

A return to a writ, in which the officer charged with it falsely reports that he served it, when he did not, or makes some other false or incorrect statement, whereby injury results to a person interested. State v. Jenkins, 70 S.W. 152, 170 Mo. 16. In taxation, a return that is incorrect, Du Pont v. Graham, D.C.Del., 283 F. 300, 302, although made in good faith under a mistake of law. Eliot Nat. Bank v. Gill, D.C.Mass., 210 F. 933, 937. Under some statutes, in order to render a return a false return, there must appear, if not a design to mislead or deceive on the part of the taxpayer, at least culpable negligence. Fouts v. State, 149 N.E. 551, 555, 113 Ohio St. 450.

General Return-day

The day for the general return of all writs of summons, subpœna, etc., running to a particular term of the court.

Return-book

The book containing the list of members returned to the house of commons. May, Parl. Pr.

Return-day

The day named in a writ or process, upon which the officer is required to return it. Perry v. John Hancock Mut. Life Ins. Co., C.C.A.Ga., 2 F.2d 250, 251; Wilkinson v. La Combe, 59 Mont. 518, 197 P. 836, 837.

Day on which votes cast are counted and the official result is declared. Landrum v. Centennial Rural High School Dist. No. 2, Tex.Civ.App., 134 S.W.2d 353, 354.

Return Irreplevisable

A writ allowed by the statute of Westm. 2, c. 2, to a defendant who had had judgment upon verdict or demurrer in an action of replevin, or after the plaintiff had, on a writ of second deliverance, become a second time nonsuit in such action. By this writ the goods were returned to the defendant, and the plaintiff was restrained from suing out a fresh replevin. Previously to this statute, an unsuccessful plaintiff might bring actions of replevin *in infinitum,* in reference to the same matter. 3 Bl.Comm. 150.

Return of Premium

The repayment of the whole or a ratable part of the premium paid for a policy of insurance, upon the cancellation of the contract before the time fixed for its expiration. Northwestern Mut. Life Ins. Co. v. Roberts, 177 Cal. 540, 171 P. 313, 315; Equitable Life Assur. Soc. of United States v. Johnson, 53 Cal.App.2d 49, 127 P.2d 95. For special meaning in mutual insurance, see: New York Life Ins. Co. v. Chaves, 21 N.M. 264, 153 P. 303.

Return Unsatisfied

As used in Bankruptcy Act is not equivalent to a return of no property found, but means that the debtor has no property available subject to writ for satisfaction of judgment. In re Toms, C.C.A.Mich., 101 F.2d 617, 619.

Return of Writs

In practice. A short account, in writing, made by the sheriff, or other ministerial officer, of the manner in which he has executed a writ. Steph. Pl. 24.

RETURNABLE. In practice. To be returned; requiring a return. When a writ is said to be "returnable" on a certain day, it is meant that on that day the officer must return it.

RETURNING BOARD. This is the official title in some of the states of the board of canvassers of elections.

RETURNING FROM TRANSPORTATION. Coming back to England before the term of punishment is determined.

RETURNING OFFICER. The official who conducts a parliamentary election in England. The sheriff in counties, and the mayor in boroughs. Wharton.

RETURNUM AVERIORUM. A judicial writ, similar to the *retorno habendo.* Cowell.

RETURNUM IRREPLEGIABILE. A judicial writ addressed to the sheriff for the final restitution or return of cattle to the owner when unjustly taken or distrained, and so found by verdict. It is granted after a nonsuit in a second deliverance. Reg. Jud. 27.

REUS. Lat. In the civil and canon law. The defendant in an action or suit.

A person judicially accused of a crime; a person criminally proceeded against. Hallifax, Civil Law, b. 3, c. 13, no. 7.

A party to a suit, whether plaintiff or defendant; a litigant. This was the ancient sense of the word. Calvin.

A party to a contract. *Reus stipulandi,* a party stipulating; the party who asked the question in the form prescribed for stipulations. *Reus promittendi,* a party promising; the party who answered the question.

REUS EXCIPIENDO FIT ACTOR. The defendant, by excepting or pleading, becomes a plaintiff; that is, where, instead of simply denying the plaintiff's action, he sets up some new matter in defense, he is bound to establish it by proof, just as a plaintiff is bound to prove his cause of action. Bounier, Tr. des Preuves, §§ 152, 320; Best, Ev. p. 294, § 252.

REUS LÆSÆ MAJESTATIS PUNITUR UT PEREAT UNUS NE PEREANT OMNES. A traitor is punished that one may die lest all perish. 4 Coke, 124.

REVE. In old English law. The bailiff of a franchise or manor; an officer in parishes within forests, who marks the commonable cattle. Cowell.

REVE MOTE. In Saxon law. The court of the *reve, reeve,* or *shire reeve.* 1 Reeve, Eng. Law, 6.

REVEL. To behave in a noisy, boisterous manner, like a bacchanal. In re Began, 12 R.I. 309.

REVELAND. The land which in Domesday is said to have been "thane-land," and afterwards converted into "reveland." It seems to have been land which, having reverted to the king after the death of the thane, who had it for life, was not granted out to any by the king, but rested in charge upon the account of the reve or bailiff of the manor. Spel. Feuds, c. 24.

REVELS. Sports of dancing, masking, etc., formerly used in princes' courts, the inns of court, and noblemen's houses, commonly performed by night. There was an officer to order and supervise them, who was entitled the "master of the revels." Cowell.

REVENDICATION. To reclaim or to demand the restoration of; to "reclaim" being to claim something back, which is in the possession of another, but which belongs to the claimant. Witson v. Succession of Staring, La.App., 175 So. 495, 498.

In civil law. The right of a vendor to reclaim goods sold out of the possession of the purchaser, where the price was not paid. Story, Confl. Laws, § 401. Benedict v. Schaettle, 12 Ohio St. 520; Ellis v. Davis, 3 S.Ct. 327, 109 U.S. 485, 27 L.Ed. 1006.

REVENDICATION ACTION. In civil law. One by which a man demands a restoration of a thing of which he claims to be the owner. Cooney v. Blythe Co., La.App., 200 So. 517, 519.

REVENUE. Return, yield, as of land, profit, that which returns or comes back from an investment, the annual or periodical rents, profits, interest or issues of any species of property, real or personal, income. Willoughby v. Willoughby, 66 R.I. 430, 19 A.2d 857, 860.

Also the income of an individual or private corporation. Humphrey v. Lang, 169 N.C. 601, 86 S.E. 526, 527, L.R.A.1916B, 626.

As applied to the income of a government, a broad and general term, including all public moneys which the state collects and receives, from whatever source and in whatever manner. Fletcher v. Oliver, 25 Ark. 295; State ex rel. Thompson v. Board of Regents for Northeast Missouri State Teachers' College, 305 Mo. 57, 264 S.W. 698, 700. The income which a state collects and receives into its treasury, and is appropriated for the payment of its expenses. Public Market Co. of Portland v. City of Portland, 171 Or. 522, 130 P.2d 624, 644.

Land Revenues

See that title.

Public Revenue

The revenue of the government of the state or nation; sometimes, perhaps, that of a municipality.

Revenue Bills

Those that levy taxes in the strict sense of the word. Hart v. Board of Com'rs of Burke County, 192 N.C. 161, 134 S.E. 403, 404.

Revenue Law

Any law which provides for the assessment and collection of a tax to defray the expenses of the government. Such legislation is commonly referred to under the general term "revenue measures," and those measures include all the laws by which the government provides means for meeting its expenditures. The Nashville, 17 Fed.Cas. 1178; Twin City Nat. Bank v. Nebeker, 3 App. D.C. 190; Ard v. People, 66 Colo. 480, 182 P. 892, 893; Colorado Nat. Life Assur. Co. v. Clayton, 54 Colo. 256, 130 P. 330, 332. For "Loss," see that title.

Revenue Side of the Exchequer

That jurisdiction of the court of exchequer, or of the exchequer division of the high court of justice, by which it ascertains and enforces the proprietary rights of the crown against the subjects of the realm. The practice in revenue cases is not affected by the orders and rules under the judicature act of 1875. Mozley & Whitley.

REVERSAL. The annulling or making void a judgment on account of some error or irregularity. Usually spoken of the action of an appellate court.

International Law

A declaration by which a sovereign promises that he will observe a certain order or certain conditions, which have been once established, notwithstanding any changes that might otherwise cause a deviation therefrom. Bouvier.

REVERSE. To overthrow, vacate, set aside, make void, annul, repeal, or revoke, as to reverse a judgment, sentence or decree, or to change to the contrary or to a former condition. Department of Water and Power of City of Los Angeles v. Inyo Chemical Co., Cal.App., 100 P.2d 822, 826. Securities and Exchange Commission v. C. M. Joiner Leasing Corporation, D.C.Tex., 53 F.Supp. 714, 715.

REVERSER. In Scotch law. The proprietor of an estate who grants a wadset (or mortgage) of his lands, and who has a right, on repayment of the money advanced to him, to be replaced in his right. Bell.

REVERSIBLE ERROR. See Error.

REVERSIO. L. Lat. In old English law. The returning of land to the donor. Fleta, lib. 3, cc. 10, 12.

REVERSIO TERRÆ EST TANQUAM TERRA REVERTENS IN POSSESSIONE DONATORI, SIVE HÆREDIBUS SUIS POST DONUM FINITUM. Co. Litt. 142. A reversion of land is, as it were, the return of the land to the possession of the donor or his heirs after the termination of the estate granted.

REVERSION, or ESTATE IN REVERSION. The residue of an estate left by operation of law in the grantor or his heirs, or in the heirs of a testator, commencing in possession on the determination of a particular estate granted or devised. Strong v. Shatto, 45 Cal.App. 29, 187 P. 159, 162; Vantage Mining Co. v. Baker, 170 Mo.App. 457, 155 S.W. 466, 467.

Any future interest left in a transferor or his successor. Miller v. Dierken, 153 Pa.Super. 389, 33 A.2d 804, 805. It is a vested interest or estate, in as much as person entitled to it has a fixed right to future enjoyment. State ex rel. Tozer v. Probate Court of Washington County, 102 Minn. 268, 113 N.W. 888, 893.

The term reversion has two meanings, first, as designating the estate left in the grantor during the continuance of a particular estate and also the residue left in grantor or his heirs after termination of particular estate. Davidson v. Davidson, 350 Mo. 639, 167 S.W.2d 641, 642. Miller v. C. I. R., C.C.A.6, 147 F.2d 189, 193.

It differs from a remainder in that it arises by act of the law, whereas a remainder is by act of the parties. A reversion, moreover, is the remnant left in the grantor, whilst a remainder is the remnant of the whole estate disposed of, after a preceding part of the same has been given away. Copenhaver v. Pendleton, 155 Va. 463, 155 S.E. 802, 806, 77 A.L.R. 324.

Scotch Law

A right of redeeming landed property which has been either mortgaged or adjudicated to secure the payment of a debt. In the former case, the reversion is called "conventional;" in the latter case, it is called "legal;" and the period of seven years allowed for redemption is called the "legal." Bell; Paterson.

Legal reversion. In Scotch law. The period within which a proprietor is at liberty to redeem land adjudged from him for debt.

REVERSIONARY. That which is to be enjoyed in reversion.

REVERSIONARY INTEREST. The interest which a person has in the reversion of lands or other property. A right to the future enjoyment of property, at present in the possession or occupation of another. Holthouse. See, also, Reversion.

REVERSIONARY LEASE. One to take effect *in futuro*. A second lease, to commence after the expiration of a former lease. Wharton.

REVERSIONER. A person who is entitled to an estate in reversion. By an extension of its meaning, one who is entitled to any future estate or any property in expectancy.

REVERT. To turn back, to return to. Reichard v. Chicago, B. & Q. R. Co., 231 Iowa 563, 1 N.W. 2d 721, 727.

With respect to property to go back to and lodge in former owner, who parted with it by creating estate in another which has expired, or to his heirs. Petition of Smith, 291 Pa. 129, 139 A. 832, 835.

In a loose way the term "revert to" is sometimes used in a will as the equivalent of "go to," and, where the language of a will so indicates, it will be construed as used to designate the person to whom the testator wished the land to be given. Mastellar v. Atkinson, 94 Kan. 279, 146 P. 367, 368, Ann.Cas.1917B, 502; In re Owens' Will, 164 Wis. 260, 159 N.W. 906, 907.

REVERTER. Reversion. A possibility of reverter is that species of reversionary interest which exists when the grant is so limited that it may possibly terminate. 1 Washb. Real Prop. 63. See Formedon in the Reverter.

REVEST. To vest again. A seisin is said to *revest*, where it is acquired a second time by the party out of whom it has been divested. 1 Rop. Husb. & Wife, 353. Opposed to "divest." The words "revest" and "divest" are also applicable to the mere right or title, as opposed to the possession. Brown.

REVESTIRE. In old European law. To return or resign an investiture, seisin, or possession that has been received; to reinvest; to re-enfeoff. Spelman.

REVIEW. To re-examine judicially. A reconsideration; second view or examination; revision; consideration for purposes of correction. Used especially of the examination of a cause by an appellate court; and of a second investigation of a proposed public road by a jury of viewers. Swan v. Justices of Superior Court, 222 Mass. 542, 111 N.E. 386, 389; State v. Griffiths, 137 Wash. 448, 242 P. 969, 970.

Bill of Review

In equity practice. A bill, in the nature of a writ of error, filed to procure an examination and alteration or reversal of a decree made upon a former bill, which decree has been signed and enrolled. Story, Eq. Pl. § 403.

Commission of Review

In English ecclesiastical law. A commission formerly sometimes granted, in extraordinary cases, to revise the sentence of the court of delegates, when it was apprehended they had been led into a material error. 3 Bl.Comm. 67.

Court of Review

In England. A court established by 1 & 2 Wm. IV. c. 56, for the adjudicating upon such matters in bankruptcy as before were within the jurisdiction of the lord chancellor. It was abolished in 1847.

Reviewing Taxation

The re-taxing or re-examining an attorney's bill of costs by the master. The courts sometimes order the masters to review their taxation, when, on being applied to for that purpose, it appears that items have been allowed or disallowed on some erroneous principle, or under some mistaken impression. 1 Archb. Pr. K. B. 55.

REVILING CHURCH ORDINANCES. An offense against religion punishable in England by fine and imprisonment. 4 Steph.Comm. 208.

REVISE. To review, re-examine for correction; to go over a thing for the purpose of amending, correcting, rearranging, or otherwise improving it; as, to revise statutes, or a judgment. American Indemnity Co. v. City of Austin, 112 Tex. 239, 246 S.W. 1019, 1023; State ex rel. Taylor v. Scofield, 184 Wash. 250, 50 P.2d 896, 897.

REVISED STATUTES. A body of statutes which have been revised, collected, arranged in order, and re-enacted as a whole. This is the legal title of the collections of compiled laws of several of the states, and also of the United States. Such a volume is usually cited as "Rev. Stat.," "Rev. St.," or "R. S."

REVISING ASSESSORS. In English law. Two officers elected by the burgesses of non-parliamentary municipal boroughs for the purpose of assisting the mayor in revising the parish burgess lists. Wharton.

REVISING BARRISTERS' COURTS. In English law. Courts held in the autumn throughout the country, to revise the list of voters for county and borough members of parliament.

Abolished by the Representation of the People Act, 1918, which repealed the statutes under which they existed. Wharton.

REVISION. A re-examination or careful reading over for correction or improvement. State Road Commission of West Virginia v. West Virginia Bridge Commission, 112 W.Va. 514, 166 S.E. 11, 13.

REVISION OF STATUTES. Is more than a restatement of the substance thereof in different language, but implies a re-examination of them, and may constitute a restatement of the law in a corrected or improved form, in which case the statement may be with or without material change, and is substituted for and displaces and repeals the former law as it stood relating to the subjects within its purview. Maclean v. Brodigan, 41 Nev. 468, 172 P. 375; Elite Laundry Co. v. Dunn, 126 W.Va. 858, 30 S.E.2d 454, 458.

REVIVAL. The process of renewing the operative force of a judgment which has remained dormant or unexecuted for so long a time that execution cannot be issued upon it without new process to reanimate it. Havens v. Sea Shore Land Co., 57 N.J.Eq. 142, 41 A. 755.

The act of renewing the legal force of a contract or obligation, which had ceased to be sufficient foundation for an action, on account of the running of the statute of limitations, by giving a new promise or acknowledgment of it.

REVIVE. To renew, revivify; to make one's self liable for a debt barred by the statute of limitations by acknowledging it; or for a matrimonial offense, once condoned, by committing another. Police Jury of Caddo Parish v. City of Shreveport, 137 La. 1032, 69 So. 828, 831; Maclean v. Brodigan, 41 Nev. 468, 172 P. 375.

REVIVOR, BILL OF. In equity practice. A bill filed for the purpose of reviving or calling into operation the proceedings in a suit when, from some circumstance, (as the death of the plaintiff,) the suit had abated.

REVIVOR, WRIT OF. In English practice. Where it became necessary to revive a judgment, by lapse of time, or change by death, etc., of the parties entitled or liable to execution, the party alleging himself to be entitled to execution might sue out a writ of revivor in the form given in the act, or apply to the court for leave to enter a suggestion upon the roll that it appeared that he was entitled to have and issue execution of the judgment, such leave to be granted by the court or a judge upon a rule to show cause, or a summons, to be served according to the then present practice.

REVOCABLE. Susceptible of being revoked.

REVOCATION. The recall of some power, authority, or thing granted, or a destroying or making void of some deed that had existence until the act of revocation made it void. It may be either *general*, of all acts and things done before; or *special*, to revoke a particular thing. 5 Coke, 90. Ford v. Greenawalt, 292 Ill. 121, 126 N.E. 555, 556; O'Hagan v. Kracke, 300 N.Y.S. 351, 361, 165 Misc. 4.

Revocation by act of the party is an intentional or voluntary revocation. The principal instances occur in the case of authorities and powers of attorney and wills.

A revocation in law, or constructive revocation, is produced by a rule of law, irrespectively of the intention of the parties. Thus, a power of attorney is in general revoked by the death of the principal. Sweet.

REVOCATION OF PROBATE. Is where probate of a will, having been granted, is afterwards recalled by the court of probate, on proof of a subsequent will, or other sufficient cause.

REVOCATION OF WILL. The recalling, annulling or rendering inoperative an existing will, by some subsequent act of the testator, which may be by the making of a new will inconsistent with the terms of the first, or by destroying the old will, or by disposing of the property to which it related, or otherwise. Boudinot v. Bradford, 2 Dall. 268, 1 L.Ed. 375. Cutler v. Cutler, 130 N.C. 1, 40 S.E. 689, 57 L.R.A. 209, 89 Am.St.Rep. 854.

REVOCATIONE PARLIAMENTI. An ancient writ for recalling a parliament. 4 Inst. 44.

REVOCATUR. Lat. It is recalled. This is the term, in English practice, appropriate to signify that a judgment is annulled or set aside for error in fact; if for error in law, it is then said to be *reversed*.

REVOKE. To annul or make void by recalling or taking back, cancel, rescind, repeal, reverse. O'Hagan v. Kracke, 300 N.Y.S. 351, 362, 165 Misc. 4.

REVOLT. The endeavor of the crew of a vessel, or any one or more of them, to overthrow the legitimate authority of her commander, with intent to remove him from his command, or against his will to take possession of the vessel by assuming the government and navigation of her, or by transferring their obedience from the lawful commander to some other person. United States v. Kelly, 11 Wheat. 417, 6 L.Ed. 508; Hamilton v. U. S., C.C.A.Va., 268 F. 15, 18.

REVOLUTION. A complete overthrow of the established government in any country or state by those who were previously subject to it. Gitlow v. Kiely, D.C.N.Y., 44 F.2d 227, 232.

REVOLUTIONARY, *adj.* Pertaining to or connected with, characterized by, or of nature of, revolution. Gitlow v. Kiely, D.C.N.Y., 44 F.2d 227, 233.

REVOLUTIONARY, *n.* One who instigates or favors revolution or one taking part therein. Gitlow v. Kiely, D.C.N.Y., 44 F.2d 227, 233.

REWARD. A recompense or premium offered or bestowed by government or an individual in return for special or extraordinary services to be performed, or for special attainments or achievements, or for some act resulting to the benefit of the public; as, a reward for useful inventions, for the discovery and apprehension of criminals, for the restoration of lost property. Kinn v. First Nat. Bank, 95 N.W. 969, 118 Wis. 537, 99 Am.St. Rep. 1012.

That which is offered or given for some service or attainment; sum of money paid or taken for doing, or forbearing to do, some act. Kirk v. Smith, 48 Mont. 489, 138 P. 1088, 1089.

REWME. In old records. Realm, or kingdom.

REX. Lat. The king. The king regarded as the party prosecuting in a criminal action; as in the form of entitling such actions, "Rex v. Doe."

REX DEBET ESSE SUB LEGE QUIA LEX FACIT REGEM. The king ought to be under the law, because the law makes the king. 1 Bl. Comm. 239.

REX EST LEGALIS ET POLITICUS. Lane, 27. The king is both a legal and political person.

REX EST LEX VIVENS. Jenk. Cent. 17. The king is the living law.

REX EST MAJOR SINGULIS, MINOR UNIVERSIS. Bract. l. 1, c. 8. The king is greater than any single person, less than all.

REX HOC SOLUM NON POTEST FACERE QUOD NON POTEST INJUSTE AGERE. 11 Coke, 72. The king can do everything but an injustice.

REX NON DEBIT ESSE SUB HOMINE, SED SUB DEO ET SUT LEGE, QUIA LEX FACIT REGEM. Bract. fol. 5. The king ought to be under no man, but under God and the law, because the law makes a king. Broom, Max. 47.

REX NON POTEST FALLERE NEC FALLI. The king cannot deceive or be deceived. Grounds & Rud. of Law 438.

REX NON POTEST PECCARE. The king cannot do wrong; the king can do no wrong. 2 Rolle, 304. An ancient and fundamental principle of the English constitution. Jenk. Cent. p. 9, case 16; 1 Bl. Comm. 246.

REX NUNQUAM MORITUR. The king never dies. Broom, Max. 50; Branch, Max. (5th Ed.) 197; 1 Bl. Comm. 249.

RHANDIR. A part in the division of Wales before the Conquest; every township comprehended four gavels, and every gavel had four rhandirs, and four houses or tenements constituted every rhandir. Tayl. Hist. Gav. 69.

RHODIAN LAWS. The earliest code or collection of maritime laws. It was formulated by the people of the island of Rhodes, who, by their commercial prosperity and the superiority of their navies, had acquired the sovereignty of the seas. Its date is very uncertain, but is supposed (by Kent and others) to be about 900 B. C. Nothing of it is now extant except the article on jettison, which has been preserved in the Roman collections or Pandects (Dig. 14, 2; 3 Kent, Comm. 232, 233 "*Lex Rhodia de Jactu.*") The Lex Rhodia de Jactu provided that when the goods of an owner are thrown overboard for the safety of the ship or of the property of other owners, he becomes entitled to a ratable contribution. It has been adopted into the law of all civilized nations. Campbell, Rom. L. 137. Another code, under the same name, was published in more modern times, but is generally considered, by the best authorities, to be spurious. Schomberg, Mar. Laws Rhodes, 37, 38; 3 Kent, Comm. 3, 4; Azuni, Mar. Law, 265–296.

RIAL. A piece of gold coin current for 10s., in the reign of Henry VI., at which time there were half-rials and quarter-rials or rial-farthings. In the beginning of Queen Elizabeth's reign, golden rials were coined at 15s. a piece; and in the time of James I. there were rose-rials of gold at 30s. and spur-rials at 15s. Lown. Essay Coins, 38.

RIBAUD. A rogue; vagrant; whoremonger; a person given to all manner of wickedness. Cowell.

RIBBONMEN. Associations or secret societies formed in Ireland, having for their object the dispossession of landlords by murder and fire-raising. Wharton.

RICHARD ROE, otherwise TROUBLESOME. The casual ejector and fictitious defendant in ejectment, whose services are no longer invoked.

RICOHOME. Span. In Spanish law. A nobleman; a count or baron. 1 White, Recop. 36.

RIDER. A schedule or small piece of parchment annexed to some part of a roll or record. It is frequently familiarly used for any kind of a schedule or writing annexed to a document which cannot well be incorporated in the body of such document. Thus, in passing bills through a legislature, when a new clause is added after the bill has passed through committee, such new clause is termed a "rider." Brown. Cowell; Blount; 2 Tidd, Pr. 730; Com. v. Barnett, 48 A. 976, 199 Pa. 161, 55 L.R.A. 882. An additional paper attached to, and forming a part of, an insurance policy. Hukle v. Great American Ins. Co., 245 N.Y.S. 240, 242, 230 App.Div. 477.

RIDER-ROLL. Rider, which title see.

RIDGLING. A half-castrated horse. Brisco v. State, 4 Tex.App. 221, 30 Am.Rep. 162.

RIDING ARMED. In English law. The offense of riding or going armed with dangerous or unusual weapons is a misdemeanor tending to disturb the public peace by terrifying the good people of the land. 4 Steph. Comm. 357.

The Statute of Northampton, St. 2 Edw. III, c. 3, enacted in 1328, which made this an indictable offense, was in affirmance of the common law, and probably became a part of the common law of the American colonies. 68 C.J. p. 5, n. 35.

RIDING CLERK. In English law. One of the six clerks in chancery who, in his turn for one year, kept the controlment books of all grants that passed the great seal. The six clerks were superseded by the clerks of records and writs.

RIDINGS, (corrupted from *trithings.*) The names of the parts or divisions of Yorkshire, which, of course, are three only, viz., East Riding, North Riding, and West Riding.

RIEN. L. Fr. Nothing. It appears in a few law French phrases.

RIEN CULP. In old pleading. Not guilty.

RIEN DIT. In old pleading. Says nothing, (*nil dicit.*)

RIEN LUY DOIT. In old pleading. Owes him nothing. The plea of *nil debet.*

RIENS EN ARRIÈRE. Nothing in arrear. A plea in an action of debt for arrearages of account. Cowell.

RIENS LOUR DEUST. Not their debt. The old form of the plea of *nil debet.* 2 Reeve, Eng. Law, 332.

RIENS PASSA PER LE FAIT. Nothing passed by the deed. A plea by which a party might avoid the operation of a deed, which had been enrolled or acknowledged in court; the plea of *non est factum* not being allowed in such case.

RIENS PER DESCENT. Nothing by descent. The plea of an heir, where he is sued for his ancestor's debt, and has no land from him by descent, or assets in his hands. Cro. Car. 151; 1 Tidd, Pr. 645; 2 Tidd, Pr. 937.

RIER COUNTY. In old English law. After-county; *i. e.,* after the end of the county court. A time and place appointed by the sheriff for the receipt of the king's money after the end of his county, or county court. Cowell.

RIFFLARE. To take away anything by force.

RIFLETUM. A coppice or thicket. Cowell.

RIGA. In old European law. A species of service and tribute rendered to their lords by agricultural tenants. Supposed by Spelman to be derived from the name of a certain portion of land, called, in England, a "rig" or "ridge," an elevated piece of ground, formed out of several furrows. Burrill.

RIGGING THE MARKET. A term of the stock-exchange, denoting the practice of inflating the price of given stocks, or enhancing their quoted value, by a system of pretended purchases, designed to give the air of an unusual demand for such stocks. L. R. 13 Eq. 447.

RIGHT. As a *noun,* and taken in an *abstract* sense, justice, ethical correctness, or consonance with the rules of law or the principles of morals. In this signification it answers to one meaning of the Latin "*jus,*" and serves to indicate law in the abstract, considered as the foundation of all rights, or the complex of underlying moral principles which impart the character of justice to all positive law, or give it an ethical content.

As a *noun,* and taken in a *concrete* sense, a power, privilege, faculty, or demand, inherent in one person and incident upon another. "Rights" are defined generally as "powers of free action." And the primal rights pertaining to men are undoubtedly enjoyed by human beings purely as such, being grounded in personality, and existing antecedently to their recognition by positive law. But leaving the abstract moral sphere, and giving to the term a juristic content, a "right" is well defined as "a capacity residing in one man of controlling, with the assent and assistance of the state, the actions of others." Holl. Jur. 69.

The noun substantive "a right" signifies that which jurists denominate a "faculty;" that which resides in a determinate person, by virtue of a given law, and which avails against a person (or answers to a duty lying on a person) other than the person in whom it resides. And the noun substantive "rights" is the plural of the noun substantive "a right." But the expression "right," when it is used as an adjective, is equivalent to the adjective "just," as the adverb "rightly" is equivalent to the adverb "justly." And, when used as the abstract name corresponding to the adjective "right," the noun substantive "right" is synonymous with the noun substantive "justice." Aust.Jur. § 264, note.

In a narrower signification, an interest or title in an object of property; a just and legal claim to hold, use, or enjoy it, or to convey or donate it, as he may please. See Co. Litt. 345*a*.

The term "right," in civil society, is defined to mean that which a man is entitled to have, or to do, or to receive from others within the limits prescribed by law. Atchison & N. R. Co. v. Baty, 6 Neb. 40, 29 Am.Rep. 356.

That which one person ought to have or receive from another, it being withheld from him, or not in his possession. In this sense "right" has the force of "claim," and is properly expressed by the Latin "*jus.*" Lord Coke considers this to be the proper signification of the word, especially in writs and pleadings, where an *estate is turned to a right;* as by discontinuance, disseisin, etc. Co. Litt. 345*a*.

See, also, Droit; Jus; Recht.

Classification

Rights may be described as *perfect* or *imperfect*, according as their action or scope is clear, settled, and determinate, or is vague and unfixed.

Rights are either *in personam* or *in rem.* A right *in personam* is one which imposes an obligation on a definite person. A right *in rem* is one which imposes an obligation on persons generally; *i. e.*, either on all the world or on all the world except certain determinate persons. Thus, if I am entitled to exclude all persons from a given piece of land, I have a right *in rem* in respect of that land; and, if there are one or more persons, A., B., and C., whom I am not entitled to exclude from it, my right is still a right *in rem.* Sweet.

Rights may also be described as either *primary* or *secondary. Primary* rights are those which can be created without reference to rights already existing. *Secondary* rights can only arise for the purpose of protecting or enforcing primary rights. They are either preventive (protective) or remedial (reparative.) Sweet.

Preventive or *protective secondary* rights exist in order to prevent the infringement or loss of primary rights. They are judicial when they require the assistance of a court of law for their enforcement, and extrajudicial when they are capable of being exercised by the party himself. *Remedial* or *reparative secondary* rights are also either judicial or extrajudicial. They may further be divided into (1) rights of restitution or restoration, which entitle the person injured to be replaced in his original position; (2) rights of enforcement, which entitle the person injured to the performance of an act by the person bound; and (3) rights of satisfaction or compensation. Sweet.

With respect to the ownership of external objects of property, rights may be classed as *absolute* and *qualified.* An absolute right gives to the person in whom it inheres the uncontrolled dominion over the object at all times and for all purposes. A qualified right gives the possessor a right to the object for certain purposes or under certain circumstances only. Such is the right of a bailee to recover the article bailed when it has been unlawfully taken from him by a stranger.

Rights are also either *legal* or *equitable.* The former is the case where the person seeking to enforce the right for his own benefit has the legal title and a remedy at law. The latter are such as are enforceable only in equity; as, at the suit of *cestui que trust.*

Constitutional Law

There is also a classification of rights, with respect to the constitution of civil society. Thus, according to Blackstone, "the rights of persons, considered in their natural capacities, are of two sorts,—*absolute* and *relative;* absolute, which are such as appertain and belong to particular men, merely as individuals or single persons; relative, which are incident to them as members of society, and standing in various relations to each other." 1 Bl. Comm. 123. Johnson v. Johnson, 32 Ala. 637; People v. Berberrich, 20 Barb. (N. Y.) 224.

Rights are also classified in constitutional law as natural, civil, and political, to which there is sometimes added the class of "personal rights."

Natural rights are those which grow out of the nature of man and depend upon personality, as distinguished from such as are created by law and depend upon civilized society; or they are those which are plainly assured by natural law (Borden v. State, 11 Ark. 519, 44 Am.Dec. 217); or those which, by fair deduction from the present physical, moral, social, and religious characteristics of man, he must be invested with, and which he ought to have realized for him in a jural society, in order to fulfill the ends to which his nature calls him. 1 Woolsey, Polit. Science, p. 26. Such are the rights of life, liberty, privacy, and good reputation. See Black, Const. Law (3d Ed.) 523.

Civil rights are such as belong to every citizen of the state or country, or, in a wider sense, to all its inhabitants, and are not connected with the organization or administration of government. They include the rights of property, marriage, protection by the laws, freedom of contract, trial by jury, etc. Winnett v. Adams, 71 Neb. 817, 99 N.W. 681. Or, as otherwise defined, civil rights are rights appertaining to a person in virtue of his citizenship in a state or community. Rights capable of being enforced or redressed in a civil action. Also a term applied to certain rights secured to citizens of the United States by the thirteenth and fourteenth amendments to the constitution, and by various acts of congress made in pursuance thereof. State of Iowa v. Railroad Co., C.C.Iowa, 37 F. 498, 3 L.R.A. 554; State v. Powers, 51 N.J.L. 432, 17 A. 969.

Political rights consist in the power to participate, directly or indirectly, in the establishment or administration of government, such as the right of citizenship, that of suffrage, the right to hold public office, and the right of petition. Black Const. Law (3d Ed.) 524; Winnett v. Adams, 71 Neb. 817, 99 N.W. 681.

Personal rights is a term of rather vague import, but generally it may be said to mean the right of personal security, comprising those of life, limb, body, health, reputation, and the right of personal liberty.

As an Adjective

The term "right" means just, morally correct, consonant with ethical principles or rules of positive law. It is the opposite of wrong, unjust, illegal.

Old English Law

The term denoted an accusation or charge of crime. Fitzh. Nat. Brev. 66 F.

Other Compound and Descriptive Terms

Base right. In Scotch law, a subordinate right; the right of a subvassal in the lands held by him. Bell.

Bill of rights. See Bill.

Common right. See Common.

Declaration of rights. See *Bill of Rights*, under Bill.

Exclusive right. See Exclusive Right.

Existing right. See Existing Right.

Marital rights. See Marital.

Mere right. In the law of real estate, the mere right of property in land; the right of a proprietor, but without possession or even the right of possession; the abstract right of property.

Patent right. See Patent.

Petition of right. See Petition.

Private rights. Those rights which appertain to a particular individual or individuals, and relate either tc the person, or to personal or real property. 1 Chit. Gen. Pr. 3.

The term "private right," as used with reference to the right of a person to injunctive relief, is used as a mere distinguishing term from "public right," and not as meaning any particular monopolistic right. Long v. Southern Express Co., D.C.Fla., 201 F. 441, 444. "Private rights" of a municipal corporation, as effecting the running of the statute of limitations, are such as only that part of the municipality included within the corporate limits of a municipality are interested in. Board of Com'rs of Woodward County v. Willett, 49 Okl. 254, 152 P. 365, 366, L.R.A. 1916E, 92.

Real right. In Scotch law. That which entitles him who is vested with it to possess the subject as his own, and, if in the possession of another, to demand from him its actual possession. *Real* rights affect the subject itself; *personal* are founded in obligation. Erskine, Inst. 3, 1, 2.

Right heir. See Heir.

Riparian rights. See Riparian.

Vested rights. See Vested.

Writ of right. A procedure for the recovery of real property after not more than sixty years' adverse possession; the highest writ in the law, sometimes called, to distinguish it from others of the droitural class, the "writ of right proper." Abolished by 3 & 4 Wm. IV. c. 27. 3 Steph. Comm. 392.

Writ of right close. An abolished writ which lay for tenants in ancient demesne, and others of a similar nature, to try the right of their lands and tenements in the court of the lord exclusively. 1 Steph. Comm. 224.

RIGHT AND WRONG TEST. Under "this test" if, at the time of committing an act, the party was laboring under such a defect of reason from disease of the mind as not to know the nature and quality of the act he was doing, or if he did know the nature and quality thereof, that he did not know that he was doing what was wrong, he should not be held responsible under the criminal law. State v. Wallace, 170 Or. 60, 131 P.2d 222, 229, 230.

RIGHT IN ACTION. This is a phrase frequently used in place of *chose in action,* and having an identical meaning.

RIGHT IN COURT. See Rectus in Curia.

RIGHT OF ACTION. The right to bring suit; a legal right to maintain an action, growing out of a given transaction or state of facts and based thereon. Hibbard v. Clark, 56 N.H. 155, 22 Am. Rep. 442; Webster v. County Com'rs, 63 Me. 29.

By the old writers the phrase is commonly used to denote that a person has lost a right of entry, and has nothing but a right of action left. Co.Litt. 363*b*.

RIGHT OF DISCUSSION. In Scotch law. The right which the cautioner (surety) has to insist that the creditor shall do his best to compel the performance of the contract by the principal debtor, before he shall be called upon. 1 Bell, Comm. 347.

RIGHT OF DIVISION. In Scotch law. The right which each of several cautioners (sureties) has to refuse to answer for more than his own share of the debt. To entitle the cautioner to this right the other cautioners must be solvent, and there must be no words in the bond to exclude it. 1 Bell, Comm. 347.

RIGHT OF ENTRY. The right of taking or resuming possession of land by entering on it in a peaceable manner.

RIGHT OF HABITATION. In Louisiana. The right to occupy another man's house as a dwelling, without paying rent or other compensation. Civ.Code La. art. 627.

RIGHT OF LOCAL SELF-GOVERNMENT. Power of citizens to govern themselves, as to matters purely local in nature, through officers of their own selection. City of Ardmore v. Excise Board of Carter County, 155 Okl. 126, 8 P.2d 2, 11.

RIGHT OF POSSESSION. Which may reside in one man, while another has the actual possession, being the right to enter and turn out such actual occupant; *e. g.*, the right of a disseisee. An apparent right of possession is one which may be defeated by a better; an actual right of possession, one which will stand the test against all opponents. 2 Bl. Comm. 196; Cahill v. Pine Creek Oil Co., 38 Okl. 568, 134 P. 64, 65.

RIGHT OF PRIVACY. See Privacy.

RIGHT OF PROPERTY. The mere right of property in land; the abstract right which remains to the owner after he has lost the right of possession, and to recover which the writ of right was given. United with possession, and the right of possession, this right constitutes a complete title to lands, tenements, and hereditaments. 2 Bl. Comm. 197.

RIGHT OF REDEMPTION. The right to disincumber property or to free it from a claim or lien; specifically, the right (granted by statute only) to free property from the incumbrance of a foreclosure or other judicial sale, or to recover the title passing thereby, by paying what is due, with interest, costs, etc. Not to be confounded with the "equity of redemption," which exists independently of statute but must be exercised before sale. Mayer v. Farmers' Bank, 44 Iowa 216; Millett v. Mullen, 95 Me. 400, 49 A. 871. Western Land & Cattle Co. v. National Bank of Arizona at Phœnix, 28 Ariz. 270, 236 P. 725, 726.

RIGHT OF RELIEF. In Scotch law. The right of a cautioner (surety) to demand reimbursement from the principal debtor when he has been compelled to pay the debt. 1 Bell, Comm. 347.

RIGHT OF REPRESENTATION AND PERFORMANCE. By the acts 3 & 4 Wm. IV. c. 15, and 5 & 6 Vict. c. 45, the author of a play, opera, or musical composition, or his assignee, has the sole right of representing or causing it to be represented in public at any place in the British dominions during the same period as the copyright in the work exists. The right is distinct from the copyright, and requires to be separately registered. Sweet.

RIGHT OF SEARCH. In international law. The right of one vessel, on the high seas, to stop a vessel of another nationality and examine her papers and (in some cases) her cargo. Thus, in time of war, a vessel of either belligerent has the right to search a neutral ship, encountered at sea, to ascertain whether the latter is carrying contraband goods.

RIGHT OF WAY. The right of passage or of way is a servitude imposed by law or by convention, and by virtue of which one has a right to pass on foot, or horseback, or in a vehicle, to drive beasts of burden or carts, through the estate of another. When this servitude results from the law, the exercise of it is confined to the wants of the person who has it. When it is the result of a contract, its extent and the mode of using it is regulated by the contract. Civ.Code La. art. 722.

"Right of way," in its strict meaning, is the right of passage over another man's ground; and in its legal and generally accepted meaning, in reference to a *railway*, it is a mere easement in the lands of others, obtained by lawful condemnation to public use or by purchase. It would be using the term in an unusual sense, by applying it to an absolute purchase of the fee-simple of lands to be used for a railway or any other kind of a way. Williams v. Western Union Ry. Co., 50 Wis. 76, 5 N.W. 482. And see Kripp v. Curtis, 71 Cal. 62, 11 P. 879; Stuyvesant v. Woodruff, 21 N.J.L. 136, 57 Am.Dec. 156.

"Right of way" has a twofold significance, being sometimes used to mean the mere intangible right to cross, a right of crossing, a right of way, and often used to otherwise indicate that strip of land which a railroad appropriates to its own use, and upon which it builds its roadbed. Marion, B. & E. Traction Co. v. Simmons, 180 Ind. 289, 102 N.E. 132.

The "right of way" is a space of conventional width for one or more railroad tracks, while a "railroad yard" might be extended indefinitely. City of New York v. New York & H. R. Co., Sup., 169 N.Y.S. 12, 14.

RIGHT PATENT. An obsolete writ, which was brought for lands and tenements, and not for an advowson, or common, and lay only for an estate in fee-simple, and not for him who had a lesser estate; as tenant in tail, tenant in frank marriage, or tenant for life. Fitzh. Nat. Brev. 1.

RIGHT TO BEGIN. On the hearing or trial of a cause, or the argument of a demurrer, petition, etc., the right to begin is the right of first addressing the court or jury. The right to begin is frequently of importance, as the counsel who begins has also the right of replying or having the last word after the counsel on the opposite side has addressed the court or jury. Sweet.

RIGHT TO REDEEM. Right of redemption, which title see.

RIGHTS OF PERSONS. Rights which concern and are annexed to the *persons* of men. 1 Bl. Comm. 122.

RIGHTS OF THINGS. Such as a man may acquire over external objects, or things unconnected with his person. 1 Bl. Comm. 122.

RIGHTS, PETITION OF. See Petition.

RIGOR JURIS. Lat. Strictness of law. Latch, 150. Distinguished from *gratia curiæ*, favor of the court.

RIGOR MORTIS. In medical jurisprudence. Cadaveric rigidity; a rigidity or stiffening of the muscular tissue and joints of the body, which sets in at a greater or less interval after death, but usually within a few hours, and which is one of the recognized tests of death.

RING. A clique; an exclusive combination of persons for illegitimate or selfish purposes; as to control elections or political affairs, distribute offices, obtain contracts, control the market or the stock-exchange, etc. Schomberg v. Walker, 132 Cal. 224, 64 P. 290.

RING-DROPPING. In criminal law. A phrase applied in England to a trick frequently practised in committing larcenies.

It is difficult to define it; it will be sufficiently exemplified by the following cases. The prisoner, with some accomplices, being in company with the prosecutor, pretended to find a valuable ring wrapped up in a paper, appearing to be a jeweller's receipt for "a rich brilliant diamond ring." They offered to leave the ring with the prosecutor if he would deposit some money and his watch as a security. The prosecutor, having accordingly laid down his watch and money on a table, was beckoned out of the room by one of the confederates, while the others took away his watch and money. This was held to amount to a larceny; 1 Leach 273. In another case, under similar circumstances, the prisoner procured from the prosecutor twenty guineas, promising to return them the next morning, and leaving the false jewel with him. This was also held to be larceny; 1 Leach 314; 2 East, Pl.Cr. 679.

RINGING THE CHANGES. A larceny effected by tendering a large bill or coin in payment of a small purchase and after correct change has been given, asking for other change and repeating the request until in the confusion of mind created by so many operations, more money is obtained than the thief is entitled to. Howell v. State, 28 Ala. App. 249, 182 So. 96, 97.

RINGING UP. A custom among commission merchants and brokers (not unlike the clearing-house system) by which they exchange contracts for sale against contracts for purchase, or reciprocally cancel such contracts, adjust differences of price between themselves, and surrender margins. Samuels v. Oliver, 130 Ill. 73, 22 N.E. 499; U. S. v. New York Coffee & Sugar Exchange, 44 S.Ct. 225, 226, 263 U.S. 611, 68 L.Ed. 475.

RINGS-GIVING. In English practice. A custom observed by serjeants at law, on being called to that degree or order. The rings are given to the judges, and bear certain mottoes, selected by the serjeant about to take the degree. Brown.

RIOT. In criminal law. A tumultuous disturbance of the peace by three persons or more, assembling together of their own authority, with an intent mutually to assist each other against any who shall oppose them, in the execution of some enterprise of a private nature, and afterwards actually executing the same in a violent and turbulent manner, to the terror of the people, whether the act intended were of itself lawful or unlawful. Hawk. P. C. c. 65, § 1. State v. Stalcup, 23 N.C. 30, 35 Am.Dec. 732. Symonds v. State, 66 Okl.Cr. 49, 89 P.2d 970, 973.

When three or more persons together, and in a violent or tumultuous manner, assemble together to do an unlawful act, or together do a lawful act in an unlawful, violent, or tumultuous manner, to the disturbance of others, they are guilty of a riot. Any use of force or violence, disturbing the public peace, or any threat to use such force or violence, if accompanied by immediate power of execution, by two or more persons acting together, and without authority of law, is a riot.

RIOT ACT. A celebrated English statute, which provides that, if any twelve persons or more are unlawfully assembled and disturbing the peace, any sheriff, under-sheriff, justice of the peace, or mayor may, by proclamation, command them to disperse, (which is familiarly called "reading the riot act,") and that if they refuse to obey, and remain together for the space of one hour after such proclamation, they are all guilty of felony. The act is 1 Geo. I, St. 2, c. 5.

RIOTER. One who encourages, promotes, or takes part in riots. Symonds v. State, 66 Okl.Cr. 49, 89 P.2d 970, 974.

RIOTOSE. L. Lat. Riotously. A formal and essential word in old indictments for riots. 2 Strange, 834.

RIOTOUS ASSEMBLY. In English criminal law. The unlawful assembling of twelve persons or more, to the disturbance of the peace, and not dispersing upon proclamation. 4 Bl. Comm. 142; 4 Steph. Comm. 273. And see Madisonville v. Bishop, 113 Ky. 106, 67 S.W. 269, 57 L.R.A. 130.

RIOTOUSLY. A technical word, properly used in indictments for riot. It of itself implies force and violence. 2 Chit. Crim. Law, 489.

RIPA. Lat. The banks of a river, or the place beyond which the waters do not in their natural course overflow.

RIPARIA. A medieval Latin word, which Lord Coke takes to mean water running between two banks; in other places it is rendered "bank."

RIPARIAN. Belonging or relating to the bank of a river; of or on the bank. Land lying beyond the natural watershed of a stream is not "riparian." Bathgate v. Irvine, 126 Cal. 135, 58 P. 442, 77 Am.St.Rep. 158. Town of Gordonsville v. Zinn, 129 Va. 542, 106 S.E. 508, 513, 14 A.L.R. 318.

The term is sometimes used as relating to the shore of the sea or other tidal water, or of a lake or other considerable body of water not having the character of a watercourse. But this is not accurate. The proper word to be employed in such connections is "littoral."

RIPARIAN NATIONS. In international law. Those who possess opposite banks or different parts of banks of one and the same river.

RIPARIAN OWNER. A riparian proprietor; one who owns land on the bank of a river. Mettler v. Ames Realty Co., 61 Mont. 152, 201 P. 702, 703. See, also, Littoral.

RIPARIAN PROPRIETOR. An owner of land, bounded generally upon a stream of water, and as such having a qualified property in the soil to the thread of the stream with the privileges annexed thereto by law. Potomac Steamboat Co. v. Upper Potomac Steamboat Co., 3 S.Ct. 445, 109 U.S. 672, 27 L.Ed. 1070.

RIPARIAN RIGHTS. The rights of the owners of lands on the banks of watercourses, relating to the water, its use, ownership of soil under the stream, accretions, etc. Mobile Transp. Co. v. Mobile, 128 Ala. 335, 30 So. 645, 64 L.R.A. 333, 86 Am.St.Rep. 143.

Generally speaking such rights are: (1) Use of water for general purposes, as bathing and domestic use; (2) to wharf out to navigability; (3) access to navigable waters. Hilt v. Weber, 252 Mich. 198, 233 N.W. 159, 168, 71 A.L.R. 1238.

RIPARIAN WATER. Water which is below the highest line of normal flow of the river, or stream, as distinguished from flood water. Humphreys-Mexia Co. v. Arseneaux, 116 Tex. 603, 297 S.W. 225, 229, 53 A.L.R. 1147; Motl v. Boyd, 116 Tex. 82, 286 S.W. 458, 468.

RIPARUM USUS PUBLICUS EST JURE GENTIUM, SICUT IPSIUS FLUMINIS. The use of river-banks is by the law of nations public, like that of the stream itself. Dig. 1, 8, 5, pr.; Fleta, l. 3, c. 1, § 5.

RIPE FOR JUDGMENT. A suit, when it is so far advanced, by verdict, default, confession, the determination of all pending motions, or other disposition of preliminary or disputed matters, that nothing remains for the court but to render the appropriate judgment. Hosmer v. Hoitt, 161 Mass. 173, 36 N.E. 835.

RIPTOWELL, or REAPTOWEL. A gratuity or reward given to tenants after they had reaped their lord's corn, or done other customary duties. Cowell.

RIPUARIAN LAW. An ancient code of laws by which the Ripuarii, a tribe of Franks who occupied the country upon the Rhine, the Meuse, and the Scheldt, were governed. They were first reduced to writing by Theodoric, king of Austrasia, and completed by Dagobert. Spelman.

RIPUARIAN PROPRIETORS. Owners of lands bounded by a river or watercourse.

RISCUS. L. Lat. In the civil law. A chest for the keeping of clothing. Calvin.

RISING OF COURT. Properly the final adjournment of the court for the term, though the term is also sometimes used to express the cessation of judicial business for the day or for a recess; it is the opposite of "sitting" or "session." State v. Weaver, 11 Neb. 163, 8 N.W. 385.

RISK. In insurance law; the danger or hazard of a loss of the property insured; the casualty contemplated in a contract of insurance; the degree of hazard; a specified contingency or peril; and, colloquially, the specific house, factory, ship, etc., covered by the policy. People ex rel. Daily Credit Service Corporation v. May, 147 N.Y.S. 487, 489, 162 App.Div. 215; Old Colony Trust Co. v. Commissioner of Internal Revenue, C.C.A.1, 102 F.2d 380, 382.

Assumption of risk. See that title.

Obvious risk. See Obvious.

Perceivable risk. See Perceivable.

RISK INCIDENT TO EMPLOYMENT. Within Workmen's Compensation Acts, one growing out of or connected with what workman must do in fulfilling his contract of service, and may be either ordinary risk, directly connected with employment, or extraordinary risk indirectly connected with employment because of its special nature. Belyus v. Wilkinson, Gaddis & Co., 115 N.J.L. 43, 178 A. 181, 184. Olson Drilling Co. v. Industrial Commission, 386 Ill. 402, 54 N.E.2d 452, 454.

RISK OF NAVIGATION. Not the equivalent of "perils of navigation," but is of more comprehensive import than the latter. Pitcher v. Hennessey, 48 N.Y. 419.

RISTOURNE. Fr. In insurance law; the dissolution of a policy or contract of insurance for any cause. Emerig. Traité des Assur. c. 16.

RITE. Lat. Duly and formally; legally; properly; technically.

RIVAGE. In French law. The shore, as of the sea.

In English law. A toll anciently paid to the crown for the passage of boats or vessels on certain rivers. Cowell.

RIVEARE. To have the liberty of a river for fishing and fowling. Cowell.

RIVER. A natural stream of water, of greater volume than a creek or rivulet, flowing in a more or less permanent bed or channel, between defined banks or walls, with a current which may either be continuous in one direction or affected by the ebb and flow of the tide. Alabama v. Georgia, 23 How. 513, 16 L.Ed. 556; Motl v. Boyd, 116 Tex. 82, 286 S.W. 458, 467.

Rivers are public or private; and of public rivers some are *navigable* and others not. The common-law distinction is that navigable rivers are those only wherein the tide ebbs and flows. But, in modern usage, any river is navigable which affords passage to ships and vessels, irrespective of its being affected by the tide.

Public river. A river capable in its natural state of some useful service to the public because of its existence as such, navigability being not the sole test. St. Regis Paper Co. v. New Hampshire Water Resources Board, 92 N.H. 164, 26 A.2d 832, 838.

RIVER BANKS. The boundaries which confine the water to its channel throughout the entire width when stream is carrying its maximum quantity of water. Mammoth Gold Dredging Co. v. Forbes, 39 Cal.App.2d 739, 104 P.2d 131, 137.

RIXA. Lat. In the civil law. A quarrel; a strife of words. Calvin.

RIXATRIX. In old English law. A scold; a scolding or quarrelsome woman. 4 Bl. Comm. 168.

ROAD. A highway; an open way or public passage; a line of travel or communication extending from one town or place to another; a strip of land appropriated and used for purposes of travel and communication between different places. Shannon v. Martin, 164 Ga. 872, 139 S.E. 671, 672, 54 A.L.R. 1246; San Francisco-Oakland Terminal Rys. v. Alameda County, 66 Cal.App. 77, 225 P. 304, 305. For "Farm-To-Market Roads," see that title.

In maritime law. An open passage of the sea that receives its denomination commonly from some part adjacent, which, though it lie out at sea, yet, in respect of the situation of the land adjacent, and the depth and wideness of the place, is a safe place for the common riding or anchoring of ships; as Dover road, Kirkley road, etc. Hale de Jure Mar. pt. 2, c. 2; The Cuzco, D.C. Wash., 225 F. 169, 176.

Law of the road. Custom or practice which has become crystallized into accepted system of rules regulating travel on highways. Short v. Robinson, 280 Ky. 707, 134 S.W.2d 594, 596. It relates to safety of travel, and is adjustment of rights of travelers using highway at same time. Cofran v. Griffin, 85 N.H. 29, 153 A. 817, 818.

In its specific application, the phrase "law of the road" refers to the rule which requires that vehicles meeting shall turn to the right in passing, or keep to the right of the middle of the highway. Blashfield, Cyc. of Automobile Law and Prac., Perm. Ed., §§ 636, 891.

Private road. This term has various meanings: (1) A road, the soil of which belongs to the owner of the land which it traverses, but which is burdened with a right of way. Morgan v. Livingston, 6 Mart. O. S. (La.) 231. (2) A neighborhood way, not commonly used by others than the people of the neighborhood, though it may be used by any one having occasion. State v. Mobley, 1 McMul. (S.C.) 44. (3) A road intended for the use of one or more private individuals, and not wanted nor intended for general public use, which may be opened across the lands of other persons by statutory authority in some states. Madera County v. Raymond Granite Co., 139 Cal. 128, 72 P. 915. (4) A road which is only open for the benefit of certain individuals to go from and to their homes for the service of their lands and for the use of some estates exclusively.

Public road. A highway; a road or way established and adopted (or accepted as a dedication) by the proper authorities for the use of the general public, and over which every person has a right to pass and to use it for all purposes of travel or transportation to which it is adapted and devoted. State ex rel. Clay County v. Hackmann, 270 Mo. 658, 195 S.W. 706, 708; Schier v. State, 96 Ohio St. 245, 117 N.E. 229.

ROAD DISTRICTS. Public or *quasi* municipal corporations organized or authorized by statutory authority in many of the states for the special purpose of establishing, maintaining, and caring for public roads and highways within their limits, sometimes invested with powers of local taxation, and generally having elective officers styled "overseers" or "commissioners" of roads. Farmer v. Myles, 106 La. 333, 30 So. 858; San Bernardino County v. Southern Pac. R. Co., 137 Cal. 659, 70 P. 782; Madden v. Lancaster County, C.C.A. Neb., 65 F. 191, 12 C.C.A. 566.

ROAD HOG. As applied to automobilists means that they selfishly occupy portions of the road which belong to others. Blue's Truck Line v. Harwell, 59 Ga.App. 305, 200 S.E. 500, 502.

ROAD TAX. A tax for the maintenance and repair of the public roads within the particular jurisdiction, levied either in money or in the form of so many days' labor on the public roads exacted of all the inhabitants of the district. See Lewin v. State, 77 Ala. 46.

ROADBED. The whole material laid in place and ready for travel. Menut & Parks Co. v. Cray, 114 Vt. 41, 39 A.2d 342, 345, 156 A.L.R. 404.

ROADSTEAD. In maritime law. A known general station for ships, notoriously used as such, and distinguished by the name; and not any spot where an anchor will find bottom and fix itself. 1 C. Rob. Adm. 232.

ROB. To take personalty in possession of another from his person or his presence, feloniously and against his will, by violence or by putting him in fear. People v. Flohr, 30 Cal.App.2d 576, 86 P. 2d 862, 864.

ROBBATOR. In old English law. A robber. *Robbatores et burglatores,* robbers and burglars. Bract. fol. 115*b*.

ROBBER. One who commits a robbery. The term is not in law synonymous with "thief," but applies only to one who steals with force or open violence. De Rothschild v. Royal Mail Steam Packet Co., 7 Exch. 742; The Manitoba, D.C.N.Y., 104 F. 151.

ROBBERY. Felonious taking of personal property in the possession of another, from his person or immediate presence, and against his will, accomplished by means of force or fear. 1 Hawk. P. C. 25; 4 Bl. Comm. 243; United States v. Jones, 3 Wash. C. C. 209, F.Cas.No.15,494; Armstrong v. Commonwealth, 190 Ky. 217, 227 S.W. 162, 163; Robards v. State, 37 Okl.Cr. 371, 259 P. 166, 168. Where a person, either with violence or with threats of injury, and putting the person robbed in fear, takes and carries away a thing which is on the body, or in the immediate presence of the person from whom it is taken, under such circumstances that, in the absence of violence or threats, the act committed would be a theft. Steph. Crim. Dig. 208; 2 Russ. Crimes, 78. And see, further, State v. Osborne, 116 Iowa 479, 89 N.W. 1077. Thomas v. State, 91 Ala. 34, 9 So. 81.

Generally speaking, the elements of "robbery" are the taking of personal property or money from the person or presence of another by actual or constructive force without his consent and with the animus furandi or intent to steal. Robbery may thus be said to be a compound larceny, composed of the crime of larceny from the person with the aggravation of force, actual or constructive, used in the taking. Williams v. Mayo, 126 Fla. 871, 172 So. 86, 87.

Highway Robbery. The crime of robbery committed upon or near a public highway. State v. Brown, 113 N.C. 645, 18 S.E. 51; Anderson v. Hartford Accident & Indemnity Co., 247 P. 507, 510, 77 Cal.App. 641; The felonious and forcible taking of property from the person of another on a highway. State v. Holt, 192 N.C. 490, 135 S.E. 324, 325. It differs from robbery in general only in the place where it is committed. Robbery by holdup originally applied to the stopping and robbery of traveling parties, but the term has acquired a broader meaning. It has come to be applied to robbery in general, by the use of force or putting in fear. Duluth St. Ry. Co. v. Fidelity & Deposit Co. of Maryland, 136 Minn. 299, 161 N.W. 595, 596, L.R.A. 1917D, 684. In England, by St. 23 Hen. VIII. c. 1, this was made felony without benefit of clergy, while robbery committed elsewhere was less severely punished. The distinction was abolished by St. 3 & 4 W. & M. c. 9, and in this country it has never prevailed generally.

ROBE. Fr. A word anciently used by sailors for the cargo of a ship. The Italian *"roba"* had the same meaning.

ROBERDSMEN. In old English law. Persons who, in the reign of Richard I., committed great outrages on the borders of England and Scotland. Said to have been the followers of Robert Hood, or Robin Hood. 4 Bl. Comm. 246.

ROD. A lineal measure of sixteen feet and a half, otherwise called a "perch."

ROD KNIGHTS. In feudal law. Certain servitors who held their land by serving their lords on horseback. Cowell.

ROD LICENSE. In Canadian law, a license, granted on payment of a tax or fee, permitting the licensee to angle for fish (particularly salmon) which are otherwise protected or preserved.

ROGARE. Lat. In Roman law. To ask or solicit. *Rogare legem,* to ask for the adoption of a law, *i. e.,* to propose it for enactment, to bring in a bill. In a derivative sense, to vote for a law so proposed; to adopt or enact it.

ROGATIO. Lat. In Roman law. An asking for a law; a proposal of a law for adoption or passage. Derivatively, a law passed by such a form.

ROGATIO TESTIUM. This in making a nuncupative will, is where the testator formally calls upon the persons present to bear witness that he has declared his will. Williams' Ex'rs, 116; Browne, Prob. Pr. 59.

ROGATION WEEK. In English ecclesiastical law. The second week before Whitsunday, thus called from three fasts observed therein, the Monday, Tuesday, and Wednesday, called "Rogation days," because of the extraordinary prayers then made for the fruits of the earth, or as a preparation for the devotion of Holy Thursday. Wharton.

ROGATIONES, QUÆSTIONES, ET POSITIONES DEBENT ESSE SIMPLICES. Hob. 143. Demands, questions, and claims ought to be simple.

ROGATOR. Lat. In Roman law. The proposer of a law or rogation.

ROGATORY LETTERS. A commission from one judge to another requesting him to examine a witness. See Letter.

ROGO. Lat. In Roman law. I ask; I request. A precatory expression often used in wills. Dig. 30, 108, 13, 14.

ROGUE. In English criminal law. An idle and disorderly person; a trickster; a wandering beggar; a vagrant or vagabond. 4 Bl. Comm. 169.

ROLE D'ÉQUIPAGE. In French mercantile law. The list of a ship's crew; a muster roll.

ROLL, *n.* A schedule of parchment which may be turned up with the hand in the form of a pipe or tube. Jacob.

A schedule or sheet of parchment on which legal proceedings are entered. Brown.

In English practice, there were formerly a great variety of these rolls, appropriated to the different proceedings; such as the *warrant of attorney* roll, the *process* roll, the *recognizance* roll, the *imparlance* roll, the *plea* roll, the *issue* roll, the *judgment* roll, the *scire facias* roll, and the roll of proceedings on writs of *error.* 2 Tidd, Pr. 729, 730.

In modern practice, the term is sometimes used to denote a record of the proceedings of a court or public office.

Thus, in English practice, the roll of parchment on which the issue is entered is termed the "issue roll." So the rolls of a manor, wherein the names, rents, and services of the tenants are copied and enrolled, are termed the "court rolls." There are also various other rolls; as those which contain the records of the court of chancery, those which contain the registers of the proceedings of old parliaments, called "rolls of parliament," etc. Brown.

Assessment Roll

In taxation, the list or roll of taxable persons and property, completed, verified, and deposited by the assessors. Bank v. Genoa, 28 Misc. 71, 59 N.Y.S. 829; Adams v. Brennan, 72 Miss. 894, 18 So. 482.

Judgment Roll

In English practice. A roll of parchment containing the entries of the proceedings in an action at law to the entry of judgment inclusive, and which is filed in the treasury of the court. 1 Arch. Pr. K. B. 227, 228; 2 Tidd, Pr. 931; Pettis v. Johnston, 78 Okl. 277, 190 P. 681, 700. A record made of the issue roll (*q. v.*), which, after final judgment has been given in the cause, assumes this name. Steph. Pl. Andr. ed. § 97; 3 Chitty, Stat. 514; Freem. Judg. § 75. The Judicature Act of 1875 requires every judgment to be entered in a book by the proper officer.

It has been abolished, as such, in New Jersey; Jennings v. Philadelphia & R. Co., C.C.N.J., 23 F. 569, 571. There is said to be hopeless confusion in the cases in this country as to what constitutes the judgment roll. All the cases agree that the complaint, the summons and, most of them, the return on the summons, the affidavit for publication in case of constructive service, and papers of that sort are included therein; Terry v. Gibson, 23 Colo.App. 273, 128 P. 1127, 1128, citing many cases, and also 1 Gr. Evid. 511, and Freem.Judg. § 78; Madsen v. Hodson, 69 Utah 527, 256 P. 792, 793. See the title Roll.

Master of the Rolls

See Master.

Oblate Rolls

See that title.

Rolls of Parliament

The manuscript registers of the proceedings of old parliaments; in these rolls are likewise a great many decisions of difficult points of law, which were frequently, in former times, referred to the determination of this supreme court by the judges of both benches, etc.

Rolls of the Exchequer

There are several in this court relating to the revenue of the country.

Rolls of the Temple

In English law. In each of the two Temples is a roll called the "calves-head roll," wherein every bencher, barrister, and student is taxed yearly; also meals to the cook and other officers of the houses, in consideration of a dinner of calves-head, provided in Easter term. Orig. Jur. 199.

Rolls Office of the Chancery

In English law. An office in Chancery Lane, London, which contains rolls and records of the high court of chancery, the master whereof is the second person in the chancery, etc. The rolls court was there held, the master of the rolls sitting as judge; and that judge still sits there as a judge of the chancery division of the high court of justice. Wharton.

Tax Roll

A schedule or list of the persons and property subject to the payment of a particular tax, with the amounts severally due, prepared and authenticated in proper form to warrant the collecting officers to proceed with the enforcement of the tax. Babcock v. Beaver Creek Tp., 64 Mich. 601, 31 N. W. 423; Smith v. Scully, 66 Kan. 139, 71 P. 249.

ROLL, *v.* To rob. Lasecki v. State, 190 Wis. 274, 208 N.W. 868, 869. Long v. State, 141 S.W.2d 349, 350, 139 Tex.Cr.R. 536.

ROLLING. En route; on way to destination; in transit. Sales of goods are often made "rolling" f. o. b. a designated place. Vaccaro Bros. & Co. v. Farris, 92 W.Va. 655, 115 S.E. 830, 831.

ROLLING STOCK. The portable or movable apparatus and machinery of a railroad, particularly such as moves on the road, viz., engines, cars, tenders, coaches, and trucks. Great Northern Ry. Co. v. Flathead County, 61 Mont. 263, 202 P. 198, 200; Black Diamond Coal Mining Co. v. Glover Mach. Works, 212 Ala. 654, 103 So. 853, 854.

ROLLING STOCK PROTECTION ACT. The act of 35 & 36 Vict. c. 50, passed to protect the rolling stock of railways from distress or sale in certain cases.

ROMA PEDITÆ. Lat. Pilgrims that traveled to Rome on foot.

ROMAN CATHOLIC CHARITIES ACT. The statute 23 & 24 Vict. c. 134, providing a method for enjoying estates given upon trust for Roman Catholics, but invalidated by reason of certain of the trusts being superstitious or otherwise illegal. 3 Steph. Comm. 76.

ROMAN CATHOLIC CHURCH. The juristic personality of the Roman Catholic Church, with the right to sue and to take and hold property has been recognized by all systems of European law from the fourth century. It was formally recognized between Spain and the Papacy and by Spanish laws from the beginning of the settlements in the Indies, also by our treaty with Spain in 1898, whereby its property rights were solemnly safeguarded. Municipality of Ponce v. Roman Catholic Church in Porto Rico, 28 S.Ct. 737, 210 U.S. 296, 52 L.Ed. 1068. To the same effect as to the Philippines; Santos v. Roman Catholic Church, 29 S.Ct. 338, 212 U.S. 463, 53 L.Ed. 599.

ROMAN LAW. In a general sense, comprehends all the laws which prevailed among the Romans, without regard to the time of their origin, including the collections of Justinian.

In a more restricted sense, the Germans understand by this term merely the law of Justinian, as adopted by them. Mackeld. Rom. Law, § 18.

In England and America, it appears to be customary to use the phrase, indifferently with "the civil law," to designate the whole system of Roman jurisprudence, including the *Corpus Juris Civilis;* or, if any distinction is drawn, the expression "civil law" denotes the system of jurisprudence obtaining in those countries of continental Europe which have derived their juridical notions and principles from the Justinian collection, while "Roman law" is reserved as the proper appellation of the body of law developed under the government of Rome from the earliest times to the fall of the empire.

ROME-SCOT, or ROME-PENNY. Peter-pence, (*q. v.*). Cowell.

ROMNEY MARSH. A tract of land in the county of Kent, England, containing twenty-four thousand acres, governed by certain ancient and equitable laws of sewers, composed by Henry de Bathe, a venerable judge in the reign of King Henry III.; from which laws all commissioners of sewers in England may receive light and direction. 3 Bl.Comm. 73, note *t;* 4 Inst. 276.

ROOD OF LAND. The fourth part of an acre in square measure, or one thousand two hundred and ten square yards.

ROOM. A space for occupancy or use inclosed on all sides, as in building or apartment, frequently named for use to which it is put as bedroom, dining room, toolroom. Featherstone v. Dessert, 173 Wash. 264, 22 P.2d 1050.

ROOMER. A lodger, one who rents a room or rooms in a house. Atlantic City v. Le Beck, 125 N.J.L. 373, 15 A.2d 653, 654.

ROOT OF DESCENT. The same as "stock of descent."

ROOT OF TITLE. The document with which an abstract of title properly commences. Sweet.

ROS. A kind of rushes, which some tenants were obliged by their tenure to furnish their lords withal. Cowell.

ROSLAND. Healthy ground, or ground full of ling; also watery and moorish land. 1 Inst. 5.

ROSTER. A list of persons who are to perform certain legal duties when called upon in their turn. In military affairs it is a table or plan by which the duty of officers is regulated. Matthews v. Bowman, 25 Me. 167.

ROTA. L. Lat. Succession; rotation. "*Rota* of presentations;" "*rota* of the terms." 2 W.Bl. 772, 773.

A roll or list, as of schoolboys, soldiers, jurors, or the like. Cent. Dict.

In the Roman Catholic Church, an ecclesiastical court, called also "Rota Romana," consisting of 12 "auditors." Webster, Dict. One of its members must be a German, one a Frenchman, two Spaniards, and eight Italians. Encyc. Brit. It has its seat at the papal court, and is divided into two colleges or senates, having jurisdiction of appeals and of all matters beneficiary and patrimonial. There is no appeal from its decisions except to the Pope. Cent. Dict.

Also, a celebrated court at Genoa about the sixteenth century, or before, whose decisions in maritime matters form the first part of *Straccha de Merc.* Ingersoll's Roccus.

ROTA. Span. In Spanish law. Obliterated. White, New Recop. b. 3, tit. 7, c. 5, § 2.

ROTHER-BEASTS. A term which includes oxen, cows, steers, heifers, and such like horned animals. Cowell.

ROTTEN BOROUGHS. Small boroughs in England, which prior to the reform act, 1832, returned one or more members to parliament.

ROTTEN CLAUSE. A clause sometimes inserted in policies of marine insurance to the effect that "if, on a regular survey, the ship shall be declared unseaworthy by reason of being *rotten* or unsound," the insurers shall be discharged. 1 Phil. Ins. § 849. See Steinmetz v. United States Ins. Co., 2 Serg. & R. (Pa.) 296.

ROTULUS WINTONIÆ. The roll of Winton. An exact survey of all England, made by Alfred, not unlike that of Domesday; and it was so called because it was kept at Winchester, among other records of the kingdom; but this roll time has destroyed. Ingulph. Hist. 516.

ROTURE. Fr. In old French and Canadian law. A free tenure without the privilege of nobility; the tenure of a free commoner.

ROTURIER. Fr. In old French and Canadian law. A free tenant of land on services exigible either in money or in kind. Steph. Lect. 229. A free commoner; one who held of a superior, but could have no inferior below him.

ROUND-ROBIN. A circle divided from the center, like Arthur's round table, whence its supposed origin. In each compartment is a signature, so that the entire circle, when filled, exhibits a list, without priority being given to any name. A common form of round-robin is simply to write the names in a circular form. Wharton.

ROUP. In Scotch law. A sale by auction. Bell.

ROUT. A rout is an unlawful assembly which has made a motion towards the execution of the common purpose of the persons assembled. It is, therefore, between an unlawful assembly and a riot. Steph. Crim. Dig. 41. Whenever two or more persons assembled and acting together, make any attempt or advance toward the commission of an act which would be a riot if actually committed. Follis v. State, 37 Tex.Cr.R. 535, 40 S.W. 277.

ROUTE. Course, line of travel, or transit. Louisiana Highway Commission v. Cormier, 13 La.App. 459, 128 So. 56, 61. A trodden or usual way. Tuggle v. Parker, 159 Kan. 572, 156 P.2d 533, 534.

In railroad parlance, a designated course over a way or right of way, irrespective of the singleness or multiplicity of operation thereon. Regenhardt Const. Co. v. Southern Ry. in Kentucky, 297 Ky. 840, 181 S.W.2d 441, 444.

In French insurance law. The way that is taken to make the voyage insured. The direction of the voyage assured.

ROUTOUSLY. In pleading. A technical word in indictments, generally coupled with the word "riotously." 2 Chit. Crim. Law, 488.

ROY. L. Fr. The king.

ROY EST L'ORIGINAL DE TOUTS FRANCHISES. Keilw. 138. The king is the origin of all franchises.

ROY N'EST LIE PER ASCUN STATUTE SI IL NE SOIT EXPRESSMENT NOSME. The king is not bound by any statute, unless expressly named. Jenk. Cent. 307; Broom, Max. 72.

ROY POET DISPENSER OVE MALUM PROHIBITUM, MAIS NON MALUM PER SE. Jenk. Cent. 307. The king can grant a dispensation for a *malum prohibitum*, but not for a *malum per se*.

ROYAL. Of or pertaining to or proceeding from the king or sovereign in a monarchical government.

ROYAL ASSENT. The last form through which a bill goes previously to becoming an act of parliament. It is, in the words of Lord Hale, "the complement and perfection of a law." The royal assent is given either by the king in person or by royal commission by the king himself, signed with his own hand. It is rarely given in person, except when at the end of the session the king attends to prorogue parliament, if he should do so. Brown.

ROYAL BURGHS. Boroughs incorporated in Scotland by royal charter. Bell.

ROYAL COURTS OF JUSTICE. Under the statute 42 & 43 Vict. c. 78, § 28, this is the name given to the buildings, together with all additions thereto, erected under the courts of justice building act, 1865, (28 & 29 Vict. c. 48,) and courts of justice concentration (site) act, 1865, (28 & 29 Vict. c. 49.) Brown.

ROYAL FISH. See Fish.

ROYAL GRANTS. Conveyances of record in England. They are of two kinds: (1) Letters patent; and (2) letters close, or writs close. 1 Steph. Comm. 615–618.

ROYAL HONORS. In the language of diplomacy, the privilege enjoyed by every kingdom in Europe, by the pope, and Swiss confederations, to precedence over all others who do not enjoy the same rank, with the exclusive right of sending to other states public ministers of the first rank, as ambassadors, together with other distinctive titles and ceremonies. Wheat. Int. Law, pt. 2, c. 3, § 2.

ROYAL MINES. Mines of silver and gold belonged to the king of England, as part of his prerogative of coinage, to furnish him with material. 1 Bl.Comm. 294.

ROYAL PREROGATIVE. Those rights and capacities which the king enjoys alone in contradistinction to others and not to those which he enjoys in common with any of his subjects. It is that special pre-eminence which the sovereign has over all other persons, and out of the course of the common law by right of regal dignity. Ætna Casualty & Surety Co. v. Bramwell, D.C. Or., 12 F.2d 307, 309.

ROYAL TITLES ACT, 1901. The title of the sovereign is "By the Grace of God of the United Kingdom of Great Britain and Ireland and of the British Dominions beyond the Seas King, Defender of the Faith, Emperor of India."

ROYALTIES. Regalities; royal property.

ROYALTY. A payment reserved by the grantor of a patent, lease of a mine, or similar right, and payable proportionately to the use made of the right by the grantee. Raynolds v. Hanna, C. C.Ohio, 55 F. 800.

In mining and oil operations, a share of the product or profit paid to the owner of the property. Marias River Syndicate v. Big West Oil Co., 98 Mont. 254, 38 P.2d 599, 601.

A payment which is made to an author or composer by an assignee or licensee in respect of each copy of his work which is sold, or to an inventor in respect of each article sold under the patent. Sweet.

ROYALTY ACRES. That part of the oil that goes to landowner, whether it be in place or after production. Dickens v. Tisdale, 204 Ark. 838, 164 S.W.2d 990, 992.

ROYALTY BONUS. The consideration for oil and gas lease over and above the usual royalty of one-eighth. Sheppard v. Stanolind Oil & Gas Co., Tex.Civ.App., 125 S.W.2d 643, 648.

RUBRIC. The directions in the Book of Common Prayer of the Church of England are so called, being, in the authorized version of 1662, printed in red letters.

RUBRIC OF A STATUTE. Its title, which was anciently printed in red letters. It serves to show the object of the legislature, and thence affords the means of interpreting the body of the act; hence the phrase, of an argument, *"a rubro ad nigrum."* Wharton.

RUDENESS. Roughness; incivility; violence. Touching another with rudeness may constitute a battery.

RUINA. Lat. In the civil law. Ruin, the falling of a house. Dig. 47, 9.

RULE, *v.* To command or require by a rule of court; as, to rule the sheriff to return the writ, to rule the defendant to plead. To settle or decide a point of law arising upon a trial at *nisi prius*; and, when it is said of a judge presiding at such a trial that he "ruled" so and so, it is meant that he laid down, settled, or decided such and such to be the law.

RULE, *n.* An established standard, guide, or regulation; a principle or regulation set up by authority, prescribing or directing action or forbearance; as, the rules of a legislative body, of a company, court, public office, of the law, of ethics. A regulation made by a court of justice or public office with reference to the conduct of business therein.

An order made by a court, at the instance of one of the parties to a suit, commanding a ministerial officer, or the opposite party, to do some act, or to show cause why some act should not be done. It is usually upon some interlocutory matter, and has not the force or solemnity of a decree or judgment.

A rule of law. Thus, we speak of the rule against perpetuities; the rule in Shelley's Case, etc.

Cross–Rules

These were rules where each of the opposite litigants obtained a rule *nisi*, as the plaintiff to increase the damages, and the defendant to enter a nonsuit. Wharton.

General Rules

General or standing orders of a court, in relation to practice, etc.

Rule Absolute

One which commands the subject-matter of the rule to be forthwith enforced. It is usual, when the party has failed to show sufficient cause against a rule *nisi,* to "make the rule absolute," *i. e.,* imperative and final.

Rule Against Perpetuities

See that title.

Rule–Day

In practice. The day on which a rule is returnable, or on which the act or duty enjoined by a rule is to be performed. Cook v. Cook, 18 Fla. 637.

Rule Discharged

A term indicating that the court has refused to take the action sought by the rule, or has decided that the cause shown against the rule is deemed sufficient.

Rule in Shelley's Case

See Shelley's Case, Rule in.

Rule Nisi

A rule which will become imperative and final *unless* cause be shown against it. This rule commands the party to show cause why he should not be compelled to do the act required, or why the object of the rule should not be enforced.

Rule of 1756

A rule of international law, first practically established in 1756, by which neutrals, in time of war, are prohibited from carrying on with a belligerent power a trade which is not open to them in time of peace. 1 Kent, Comm. 82.

Rule of Apportionment

Rule that, where subdivided tract contains more or less than aggregate amount called for, excess or deficiency is apportioned among several tracts. Geiger v. Uhl, 204 Ind. 135, 180 N.E. 10, 12.

Rules of Course

Rules of course are rules which courts authorize their officers to grant without formal application to a judge. Such rules were technically termed in English practice, "side bar rules", because formerly they were moved for by the attorneys at the side bar in court. Brown.

Rules of Court

The rules for regulating the practice of the different courts, which the judges are empowered to frame and put in force as occasion may require. Brown; Goodlett v. Charles, 14 Rich. Law (S. C.) 49.

Rule of Four

The Supreme Court's practice of granting certiorari on vote of four Justices. Rogers v. Missouri Pac. R. Co., Ill., Mo., N.Y., Ohio, 77 S.Ct. 459, 478, 357 U.S. 521, 1 L.Ed.2d 515.

Rule of Kent

Where realty is given by will absolutely to one person, with gift over to another of such portion as may remain undisposed of by first taker at his death, gift over is void, as repugnant to absolute property first given. Andrews v. Andrews, 116 S.E.2d 436, 440, 253 N.C. 139.

Rule of Law

A legal principle, of general application, sanctioned by the recognition of authorities, and usually expressed in the form of a maxim or logical proposition. Called a "rule," because in doubtful or unforeseen cases it is a guide or norm for their decision. Toullier, tit. prel. no. 17.

Rule of Lenity

Where the intention of Congress is not clear from the act itself and reasonable minds might differ as to its intention, the court will adopt the less harsh meaning. U. S. v. Callanan, D.C.Mo., 173 F.Supp. 98, 100.

Rules of Practice

Certain orders made by the courts for the purpose of regulating the practice in actions and other proceedings before them.

Rule of Presumption

Rule changes one of burdens of proof, that is, it declares that main fact will be inferred or assumed from some other fact until evidence to contrary is introduced. Barrett v. U. S., C.A.Ga., 322 F.2d 292, 294.

Rules of Procedure

Rules made by a legislative body concerning the mode and manner of conducting its business. Heiskell v. Baltimore, 65 Md. 125, 4 A. 116, 57 Am. Rep. 308.

Rule of Property

A settled rule or principle, resting usually on precedents or a course of decisions, regulating the ownership or devolution of property. Yazoo & M. V. R. Co. v. Adams, 81 Miss. 90, 32 So. 937.

Rule of the Road

The popular English name for the regulations governing the navigation of vessels in public waters, with a view to preventing collisions. Sweet.

Rule to Plead

A rule of court, taken by a plaintiff as of course, requiring the defendant to plead within a given time, on pain of having judgment taken against him by default.

Rule to Show Cause

A rule commanding the party to appear and show cause why he should not be compelled to do the act required, or why the object of the rule should not be enforced; a rule *nisi,* (*q. v.*).

Special Rule

Rules granted without any motion in court, or when the motion is only assumed to have been made, and is not actually made, are called "common" rules; while the rules granted upon motion actually made to the court in term, or upon a judge's order in vacation, are termed "special" rules. Brown. The term may also be understood as opposed to "general" rule; in which case it means a particular direction, in a matter of practice, made for the purposes of a particular case.

RULE AGAINST PERPETUITIES. Principle that no interest in property is good unless it must vest, if at all, not later than 21 years, plus period of gestation, after some life or lives in being at time of creation of interest. Perkins v. Iglehart, 183 Md. 520, 39 A.2d 672, 676. Bliven v. Borden, 56 R.I. 283, 185 A. 239, 244. St. Louis Union Trust Co. v. Bassett, 85 S.W.2d 569, 575, 337 Mo. 604, 101 A.L.R. 1266.

Some states modified this common law principle by statute.

See, also, Perpetuity.

RULES. In American practice. This term is sometimes used, by metonymy, to denote a time or season in the judicial year when motions may be made and rules taken, as special terms or argument-days, or even the vacations, as distinguished from the regular terms of the courts for the trial of causes; and, by a further extension of its meaning, it may denote proceedings in an action taken out of court. Thus, "an irregularity committed *at rules* may be corrected at the next term of the court." Southall's Adm'r v. Exchange Bank, 12 Grat. (Va.) 312.

RULES OF A PRISON. Certain limits without the walls, within which all prisoners in custody in civil actions were allowed to live, upon giving sufficient security to the marshal not to escape.

RULES OF THE KING'S BENCH PRISON. In English practice. Certain limits beyond the walls of the prison, within which all prisoners in custody in civil actions were allowed to live, upon giving security by bond, with two sufficient sureties, to the marshal, not to escape, and paying him a certain percentage on the amount of the debts for which they were detained. Holthouse.

RUMOR. Flying or popular report; a current story passing from one person to another without any known authority for the truth of it. Webster. It is not generally admissible in evidence. Smith v. Moore, 74 Vt. 81, 52 A. 320; Gaffney v. Royal Neighbors of America, 31 Idaho 549, 174 P. 1014, 1017; State v. Vettere, 76 Mont. 574, 248 P. 179, 183.

RUN, *v.* To have currency or legal validity in a prescribed territory; as, the writ *runs* throughout the county.

To have applicability or legal effect during a prescribed period of time; as, the statute of limitations has *run* against the claim.

To follow or accompany; to be attached to another thing in pursuing a prescribed course or direction; as, the covenant *runs* with the land.

To conduct, manage, carry on. State v. Kamuda, 98 Vt. 466, 129 A. 306, 308.

RUN, *n.* In American law. A watercourse of small size. Webb v. Bedford, 2 Bibb (Ky.) 354.

RUNCARIA. In old records. Land full of brambles and briars. 1 Inst. 5*a*.

RUNCINUS. In old English law. A load-horse; a sumpter-horse or cart-horse.

RUNDLET, or RUNLET. A measure of wine, oil, etc., containing eighteen gallons and a half. Cowell.

RUNNING ACCOUNT. An open unsettled account, as distinguished from a stated and liquidated account. "Running accounts" mean mutual accounts and reciprocal demands between the parties, which accounts and demands remain open and unsettled. Brackenridge v. Baltzell, 1 Ind. 335; Badger Lumber Co. v. W. F. Lyons Ice & Power Co., 174 Mo.App. 414, 160 S.W. 49, 52; Hollingsworth v. Allen, 176 N.C. 629, 97 S.E. 625.

RUNNING A SWITCH. In railroad parlance, going through a switch not properly aligned for the movement made. Benton v. St. Louis-San Francisco R. Co., Mo., 182 S.W.2d 61, 63.

RUNNING AT LARGE. This term is applied to wandering or straying animals. Dixon v. Lewis, 94 Conn. 548, 109 A. 809, 810; Uebele v. State, 21 Ohio App. 459, 153 N.E. 215, 216; Finley v. Barker, 219 Mich. 442, 189 N.W. 197, 200.

RUNNING DAYS. Days counted in their regular succession on the calendar, including Sundays and holidays. Brown v. Johnson, 10 Mees. & W. 334; Crowell v. Barreda, 16 Gray (Mass.) 472; Davis v. Pendergast, 7 F.Cas. 162.

RUNNING LEASE. In old books. A lease which provided that the tenancy should not be confined to any portion of the land granted, and allowed the tenant the use of all the land he could clear, to distinguish it from one confined to a particular division, circumscribed by metes and bounds, within a larger tract. Cowan v. Hatcher, Tenn.Ch. App., 59 S.W. 691.

RUNNING LOOSE. As applied to an engine. Running forward without cars attached to it. Testerman v. Hines, 88 W.Va. 547, 107 S.E. 201.

RUNNING OF THE STATUTE OF LIMITATIONS. A metaphorical expression, by which is meant that the time mentioned in the statute of limitations is considered as passing. United States v. Markowitz, D.C.Cal., 34 F.Supp. 827, 829.

RUNNING POLICY. One which contemplates successive insurances, and which provides that the object of the policy may be from time to time defined, especially as to the subjects of insurance, by additional statements or indorsements. Corporation of London Assurance v. Paterson, 106 Ga. 538, 32 S.E. 650.

RUNNING WITH THE LAND. A covenant is said to run with the land when either the liability to perform it or the right to take advantage of it passes to the assignee of that land. Brown.

RUNNING WITH THE REVERSION. A covenant is said to run with the reversion when either the liability to perform it or the right to take advantage of it passes to the assignee of that reversion. Brown.

RUNRIG LANDS. Lands in Scotland where the ridges of a field belong alternatively to different proprietors. Anciently this kind of possession was advantageous in giving a united interest to tenants to resist inroads. By the act of 1695, c. 23, a division of these lands was authorized, with the exception of lands belonging to corporations. Wharton.

RUPEE. A silver coin of India, rated at 2s. for the current, and 2s. 3d. for the Bombay, rupee.

RUPTUM. Lat. In the civil law. Broken. A term applied to a will. Inst. 2, 17, 3.

RURAL DEANERY. The circuit of an archdeacon's and rural dean's jurisdictions. Every rural deanery is divided into parishes. See 1 Steph. Comm. 117.

RURAL DEANS. In English ecclesiastical law. Very ancient officers of the church, almost grown out of use, until about the middle of the present century, about which time they were generally revived, whose deaneries are as an ecclesiastical division of the diocese or archdeaconry. They are deputies of the bishop, planted all round his diocese, to inspect the conduct of the parochial clergy, to inquire into and report dilapidations, and to examine candidates for confirmation, armed in minuter matters with an inferior degree of judicial and coercive authority. Wharton.

RURAL SERVITUDE. In the civil law. A servitude annexed to a rural estate, (*prædium rusticum.*)

RUSE DE GUERRE. Fr. A trick in war; a stratagem.

RUSTICI. Lat. In feudal law. Natives of a conquered country.

In old English law. Inferior country tenants, churls, or chorls, who held cottages and lands by the services of plowing, and other labors of agriculture, for the lord. Cowell.

RUSTICUM FORUM. Lat. A rude, unlearned, or unlettered tribunal; a term sometimes applied to arbitrators selected by the parties to settle a dispute. Underhill v. Van Cortlandt, 2 Johns.Ch. (N.Y.) 339; Dickinson v. Chesapeake & O. R. Co., 7 W.Va. 429.

RUSTICUM JUDICIUM. Lat. In maritime law. A rough or rude judgment or decision. A judgment in admiralty dividing the damages caused by a collision between the two ships. 3 Kent, Comm. 231; Story, Bailm. § 608*a*. The Victory, C.C.A. Va., 68 F. 400, 15 C.C.A. 490.

RUSTLER. Cattle thief. Galeppi v. C. Swanston and Son, 107 Cal.App. 30, 290 P. 116, 119.

RUTA. Lat. In the civil law. Things extracted from land; as sand, chalk, coal, and such other matters.

RUTA ET CÆSA. In the civil law. Things dug, (as sand and lime,) and things cut, (as wood, coal, etc.) Dig. 19, 1, 17, 6. Words used in conveyancing.

RYOT. In India. A peasant, subject, or tenant of house or land. Wharton.

RYOT–TENURE. A system of land-tenure, where the government takes the place of landowners and collects the rent by means of tax gatherers. The farming is done by poor peasants, (ryots), who find the capital, so far as there is any, and also do the work. The system exists in Turkey, Egypt, Persia, and other Eastern countries, and in a modified form in British India. After slavery, it is accounted the worst of all systems, because the government can fix the rent at what it pleases, and it is difficult to distinguish between rent and taxes.

S

S. As an abbreviation, this letter stands for "section," "statute," and various other words of which it is the initial.

S. B. An abbreviation for "senate bill."

S. B. A. Small Business Administration.

S. C. An abbreviation for "same case." Inserted between two citations, it indicates that the same case is reported in both places. It is also an abbreviation for "supreme court," and for "select cases;" also for "South Carolina."

S. D. An abbreviation for "southern district."

S/D B/L. The abbreviation "S/D B/L" in a contract of sale means sight draft—bill of lading attached. Attalla Oil & Fertilizer Co. v. Goddard, 207 Ala. 287, 92 So. 794, 796.

S. E. C. Securities and Exchange Commission.

S. F. S. An abbreviation in the civil law for *"sine fraude sua,"* (without fraud on his part.) Calvin.

S. L. An abbreviation for "session [or statute] laws."

S. P. An abbreviation of *"sine prole,"* without issue. Also an abbreviation of "same principle," or "same point," indicating, when inserted between two citations, that the second involves the same doctrine as the first.

S. S. A collar formerly worn on state occasions by the Lord Chief Justice of England, and of the Common Pleas and the Lord Chief Baron—now only by the first named of these (*q. v.*).

S. S. A. Social Security Administration.

S. S. S. Selective Service System.

S. V. An abbreviation for *"sub voce,"* under the word; used in references to dictionaries, and other works arranged alphabetically.

These letters also stand for *"sub verbo,"* which has the same meaning as *sub voce*.

SABBATH. One of the names of the first day of the week; more properly called "Sunday," (*q. v.*). Gunn v. State, 89 Ga. 341, 15 S.E. 458; State v. Reade, 98 N.J.L. 596, 121 A. 288.

SABBATH-BREAKING. The offense of violating the laws prescribed for the observance of Sunday. State v. Baltimore & O. R. Co., 15 W.Va. 381, 36 Am.Rep. 803; State v. Popp, 45 Md. 433.

SABBATUM. L. Lat. The Sabbath; also peace. Domesday.

SABBULONARIUM. A gravel pit, or liberty to dig gravel and sand; money paid for the same. Cowell.

SABINIANS. A school or sect of Roman jurists, under the early empire, founded by Ateius Capito, who was succeeded by M. Sabinus, from whom the name.

SABLE. The heraldic term for black. It is called "Saturn," by those who blazon by planets, and "diamond," by those who use the names of jewels. Engravers commonly represent it by numerous perpendicular and horizontal lines, crossing each other. Wharton.

SABOTAGE. A method used by labor revolutionists to force employers to accede to demands made on them. It consists in a willful obstruction and interference with the normal processes of industry. It aims at inconveniencing and tying up all production, but stops short of actual destruction or of endangering human life directly. The original act of sabotage is said to have been the slipping of a wooden shoe, or sabot, of a workman into a loom, in the early days of the introduction of machinery, to impede production. State v. Moilen, 140 Minn. 112, 167 N.W. 345, 347, 1 A.L.R. 331; State v. Tonn, 195 Iowa, 94, 191 N.W. 530, 538.

SABURRA. L. Lat. In old maritime law. Ballast.

SAC. In old English law. A liberty of holding pleas; the jurisdiction of a manor court; the privilege claimed by a lord of trying actions of trespass between his tenants, in his manor court, and imposing fines and amerciaments in the same.

SACABURTH, SACABERE, SAKABERE. In old English law. He that is robbed, or by theft deprived of his money or goods, and puts in surety to prosecute the felon with fresh suit. Bract. fol. 154*b*.

SACCABOR. In old English law. The person from whom a thing had been stolen, and by whom the thief was freshly pursued. Bract. fol. 154*b*. See Sacaburth.

SACCULARII. Lat. In Roman law. Cut-purses. 4 Steph.Comm. 125.

SACCUS. L. Lat. In old English law. A sack. A quantity of wool weighing thirty or twenty-eight stone. Fleta, l. 2, c. 79, § 10.

SACCUS CUM BROCHIA. L. Lat. In old English law. A service or tenure of finding a sack and a broach (pitcher) to the sovereign for the use of the army. Bract. l. 2, c. 16.

SACQUIER. In maritime law. The name of an ancient officer, whose business was to load and unload vessels laden with salt, corn, or fish, to prevent the ship's crew defrauding the merchant by false tale, or cheating him of his merchandise otherwise. Laws Oleron, art. 11; 1 Pet.Adm. Append. 25.

SACRA. Lat. In Roman law. The right to participate in the sacred rites of the city. Butl.Hor. Jur. 27.

SACRAMENTALES. L. Lat. In feudal law. Compurgators; persons who came to purge a defendant by their oath that they believed him innocent.

SACRAMENTI ACTIO. Lat. In the older practice of the Roman law, this was one of the forms of *legis actio,* consisting in the deposit of a stake or juridical wager. See Sacramentum.

SACRAMENTUM. Lat.

Roman Law

An oath, as being a very sacred thing; more particularly, the oath taken by soldiers to be true to their general and their country. Ainsw. Lex.

In one of the formal methods of beginning an action at law (*legis actiones*) known to the early Roman jurisprudence, the *sacramentum* was a sum of money deposited in court by each of the litigating parties, as a kind of wager or forfeit, to abide the result of the suit. The successful party received back his stake; the losing party forfeited his, and it was paid into the public treasury, to be expended for sacred objects, (*in sacris rebus,*) whence the name. See Mackeld. Rom. Law, § 203.

Common Law

An oath. Cowell.

SACRAMENTUM DECISIONIS. The voluntary or decisive oath of the civil law, where one of the parties to a suit, not being able to prove his case, offers to refer the decision of the cause to the oath of his adversary, who is bound to accept or make the same offer on his part, or the whole is considered as confessed by him. 3 Bl.Comm. 342.

SACRAMENTUM FIDELITATIS. In old English law. The oath of fealty. Reg. Orig. 303.

SACRAMENTUM HABET IN SE TRES COMITES,—VERITATEM, JUSTITIAM, ET JUDICIUM; VERITAS HABENDA EST IN JURATO; JUSTITIA ET JUSTICIUM IN JUDICE. An oath has in it three component parts,—truth, justice, and judgment; truth in the party swearing; justice and judgment in the judge administering the oath. 3 Inst. 160.

SACRAMENTUM SI FATUUM FUERIT, LICET FALSUM, TAMEN NON COMMITTIT PERJURIUM. 2 Inst. 167. A foolish oath, though false, makes not perjury.

SACRILEGE. In English criminal law. Larceny from a church. 4 Steph.Comm. 164. The crime of breaking a church or chapel, and stealing therein. 1 Russ. Crimes, 843.

In old English law. The desecration of anything considered holy; the alienation to lay-men or to profane or common purposes of what was given to religious persons and to pious uses. Cowell.

SACRILEGIUM. Lat. In the civil law. The stealing of sacred things, or things dedicated to sacred uses; the taking of things out of a holy place. Calvin.

SACRILEGUS. Lat. In the civil and common law. A sacrilegious person; one guilty of sacrilege.

SACRILEGUS OMNIUM PRÆDONUM CUPIDITATEM ET SCELERA SUPERAT. 4 Coke, 106. A sacrilegious person transcends the cupidity and wickedness of all other robbers.

SACRISTAN. A sexton, anciently called "*sagerson,*" or "*sagiston;*" the keeper of things belonging to divine worship.

SADBERGE. A denomination of part of the county palatine of Durham. Wharton.

SADISM. That state of sexual perversion in man in which the sexual inclination manifests itself by the desire to beat, to maltreat, humiliate and even to kill the person for whom the passion is conceived. 3 Witth. & Beck, Med.Jur. 739.

The opposite of *masochism* (*q. v.*).

SÆMEND. In old English law. An umpire, or arbitrator.

SÆPE CONSTITUTUM EST, RES INTER ALIOS JUDICATAS ALIIS NON PRÆJUDICARE. It has often been settled that matters adjudged between others ought not to prejudice those who were not parties. Dig. 42, 1, 63.

SÆPE VIATOREM NOVA, NON VETUS, ORBITA FALLIT. 4 Inst. 34. A new road, not an old one, often deceives the traveler.

SÆPENUMERO UBI PROPRIETAS VERBORUM ATTENDITUR, SENSUS VERITATIS AMITTITUR. Oftentimes where the propriety of words is attended to, the true sense is lost. Branch, Princ.; 7 Coke, 27.

SÆVITIA. Lat. In the law of divorce. Cruelty; anything which tends to bodily harm, and in that manner renders cohabitation unsafe. 1 Hagg. Const. 458.

SAFE. A metal receptacle for the preservation of valuables.

SAFE-CONDUCT. A guaranty or security granted by the king under the great seal to a stranger, for his safe coming into and passing out of the kingdom. Cowell.

One of the papers usually carried by vessels in time of war, and necessary to the safety of neutral merchantmen. It is in the nature of a license to the vessel to proceed on a designated voyage, and commonly contains the name of the master, the name, description, and nationality of the ship, the voyage intended, and other matters.

A distinction is sometimes made between a *passport,* conferring a general permission to travel in the territory belonging to, or occupied by, the belligerent, and a *safe-conduct,* conferring permission upon an enemy subject or others to proceed to a particular place for a defined object. II Opp. § 218.

SAFE DEPOSIT COMPANY. A company which maintains vaults for the deposit and safe-keeping of valuables in which compartments or boxes are rented to customers who have exclusive access thereto, subject to the oversight and under the rules and regulations of the company.

SAFE LIMIT OF SPEED. As regards limitation on speed of automobiles at crossings, the limit at which one may discern the approaching train and stop before he is in the danger zone. Horton v. New York Cent. R. Co., 200 N.Y.S. 365, 366, 205 App.Div. 763.

SAFE LOADING PLACE. A place where a vessel can be rendered safe for loading by reasonable measures of precaution. 14 Q.B.D. 105; 54 L.J. Q.B. 121.

SAFE PLACE TO WORK. In the law of master and servant, a place in which the master has eliminated all danger which the exercise of reasonable care by the master would remove or guard against. Melody v. Des Moines Union Ry. Co., 161 Iowa, 695, 141 N.W. 438, 439; Blick v. Olds Motor Works, 175 Mich. 640, 141 N.W. 680, 683, 49 L.R.A.,N.S., 883.

Master's duty to provide a "safe place" to work includes places to and from which the employee might be required or expected to go. High Splint Coal Co. v. Ramey's Adm'x, 271 Ky. 532, 112 S.W.2d 1007, 1008.

The rule of furnishing of a "safe place to work" is generally applicable in cases of master and servant or in cases where work is being done on property, vessel, or otherwise, of owner. The Ellenor, D.C.Fla., 39 F.Supp. 576, 580.

SAFE-PLEDGE. A surety given that a man shall appear upon a certain day. Bract. l. 4, c. 1.

SAFEGUARD. In old English law. A special privilege or license, in the form of a writ, under the great seal, granted to strangers seeking their right by course of law within the king's dominions, and apprehending violence or injury to their persons or property from others. Reg. Orig. 26.

A notification by a belligerent commander that buildings or other property upon which the notification is posted up are exempt from interference on the part of his troops. Holland, Laws and Customs of War 44.

The term is likewise used to describe a guard of soldiers who are detailed to accompany enemy subjects or to protect certain enemy property. II Opp. § 219.

SAFETY APPLIANCE ACT. The act of Congress of March 2, 1893 (45 U.S.C.A. §§ 1–7), provides that after January 1, 1898, it shall be unlawful for common carriers in interstate commerce by railroad to use locomotive engines not equipped with power driving-wheel brakes and appliances for operating the train brake system, or to run a train that has not a sufficient number of cars in it so equipped that the engineer on the locomotive can control its speed without requiring hand brakes; and to haul or use on its line any car in interstate traffic "not equipped with couplers coupling automatically by impact, and which can be uncoupled without the necessity of men going between the ends of the cars."

SAFETY ISLAND. A cement sidewalk raised above the street level for the use and protection of pedestrians. Strappelli v. City of Chicago, 371 Ill. 72, 20 N.E.2d 43, 44.

SAGAMAN. A tale-teller; a secret accuser.

SAGES DE LA LEY. L. Fr. Sages of the law; persons learned in the law. A term applied to the chancellor and justices of the king's bench.

SAGIBARO. In old European law. A judge or justice; literally, a man of causes, or having charge or supervision of causes. One who administered justice and decided causes in the *mallum*, or public assembly. Spelman.

SAID. Before mentioned. This word is constantly used in contracts, pleadings, and other legal papers, with the same force as "aforesaid." Murry v. State, 150 Ark. 461, 234 S.W. 485, 486; Greeley Nat. Bank v. Wolf, C.C.A.Colo., 4 F.2d 67, 69.

SAIGA. In old European law. A German coin of the value of a penny, or of three pence.

SAIL. In insurance law. To put to sea; to begin a voyage. To get ship under way in complete readiness for voyage, with purpose of proceeding without further delay. Northland Nav. Co. v. American Merchant Marine Ins. Co. of New York, 212 N.Y.S. 541, 544, 214 App.Div. 571. The least locomotion, with readiness of equipment and clearance, satisfies a warranty to *sail*. Pittegrew v. Pringle, 3 Barn. & Adol. 514.

Vessel "sails" when she has intended cargo on board and is in complete readiness for voyage with stores and crew aboard. Archibald McNeil & Sons Co., of New York, v. Western Maryland Ry. Co., D.C.Pa., 42 F.2d 669, 677.

SAILING. When a vessel quits her moorings, in complete readiness for sea, and it is the actual and real intention of the master to proceed on the voyage, and she is afterwards stopped by head winds and comes to anchor, still intending to proceed as soon as wind and weather will permit, this is a sailing on the voyage within the terms of a policy of insurance. Bowen v. Hope Ins. Co., 20 Pick. (Mass.) 278, 32 Am.Dec. 213.

SAILING INSTRUCTIONS. Written or printed directions, delivered by the commanding officer of a convoy to the several masters of the ships under his care, by which they are enabled to understand and answer his signals, to know the place of rendezvous appointed for the fleet in case of dispersion by storm, by an enemy, or otherwise. Without sailing instructions no vessel can have the protection and benefit of convoy. Marsh. Ins. 368.

SAILORS. Seamen; mariners.

SAINT MARTIN LE GRAND, COURT OF. An ancient court in London, of local importance, formerly held in the church from which it took its name.

SAINT SIMONISM. An elaborate form of non-communistic socialism. It is a scheme which does not contemplate an equal, but an unequal, division of the produce. It does not propose that all should be occupied alike, but differently, according to their vocation or capacity; the function of each being assigned, like grades in a regiment, by the choice of the directing authority, and the remuneration being by salary, proportioned to the importance, in the eyes of that authority, of the function itself, and the merits of the person who fulfills it. 1 Mill.Pol.Econ. 258.

SAIO. In Gothic law. The ministerial officer of a court or magistrate, who brought parties into court and executed the orders of his superior. Spelman.

SAISIE. Fr. In French law. A judicial seizure or sequestration of property, of which there are several varieties. See *infra.*

SAISIE-ARRÊT. An attachment of property in the possession of a third person.

SAISIE-EXÉCUTION. A writ resembling that of *fieri facias;* defined as that species of execution by which a creditor places under the hand of justice (custody of the law) his debtor's movable property liable to seizure, in order to have it sold, so that he may obtain payment of his debt out of the proceeds. Dalloz, Dict.

SAISIE-FORAINE. A permission given by the proper judicial officer to authorize a creditor to seize the property of his debtor in the district which the former inhabits. Dalloz, Dict. It has the effect of an attachment of property, which is applied to the payment of the debt due.

SAISIE-GAGERIE. A conservatory act of execution, by which the owner or principal lessor of a house or farm causes the furniture of the house or farm leased, and on which he has a lien, to be seized; similar to the *distress* of the common law. Dalloz, Dict.

SAISIE-IMMOBILIÈRE. The proceeding by which a creditor places under the hand of justice (custody of the law) the immovable property of his debtor, in order that the same may be sold, and that he may obtain payment of his debt out of the proceeds. Dalloz, Dict.

SAKE. In old English law. A lord's right of amercing his tenants in his court. Keilw. 145.

Acquittance of suit at county courts and hundred courts. Fleta, l. 1, c. 47, § 7.

SALABLE. "Merchantable," fit for sale in usual course of trade, at usual selling prices. Foote v. Wilson, 104 Kan. 191, 178 P. 430; Stevens Tank & Tower Co. v. Berlin Mills Co., 112 Me. 336, 92 A. 180, 181.

SALABLE VALUE. Usual selling price at place where property is situated when its value is to be ascertained. Fort Worth & D. N. Ry. Co. v. Sugg, Tex.Civ.App., 68 S.W.2d 570, 572.

SALADINE TENTH. A tax imposed in England and France, in 1188, by Pope Innocent III., to raise a fund for the crusade undertaken by Richard I. of England and Philip Augustus of France, against Saladin, sultan of Egypt, then going to besiege Jerusalem. By this tax every person who did not enter himself a crusader was obliged to pay a tenth of his yearly revenue and of the value of all his movables, except his wearing apparel, books, and arms. The Carthusians, Bernardines, and some other religious persons were exempt. Gibbon remarks that when the necessity for this tax no longer existed, the church still clung to it as too lucrative to be abandoned, and thus arose the tithing of ecclesiastical benefices for the pope or other sovereigns. Enc.Lond.

SALARIUM. Lat. In the civil law. An allowance of provisions. A stipend, wages, or compensation for services. An annual allowance or compensation. Calvin.

SALARY. A reward or recompense for services performed.

In a more limited sense a fixed periodical compensation paid for services rendered; a stated compensation, amounting to so much by the year, month, or other fixed period, to be paid to public officers and persons in some private employments, for the performance of official duties or the rendering of services of a particular kind, more or less definitely described, involving professional knowledge or skill, or at least employment above the grade of menial or mechanical labor. State v. Speed, 183 Mo. 186, 81 S.W. 1260. A fixed, annual, periodical amount payable for services and depending upon the time of employment and not the amount of services rendered. In re Information to Discipline Certain Attorneys of Sanitary Dist. of Chicago, 351 Ill. 206, 184 N.E. 332, 359. It is synonymous with "wages," except that "salary" is sometimes understood to relate to compensation for official or other services, as distinguished from "wages," which is the compensation for labor. Walsh v. City of Bridgeport, 88 Conn. 528, 91 A. 969, 972, Ann.Cas.1917B, 318. See, also, Fee.

For "Executive Salaries," see that title.

SALE. A contract between two parties, called, respectively, the "seller" (or vendor) and the "buyer," (or purchaser,) by which the former, in consideration of the payment or promise of payment of a certain price in money, transfers to the latter the title and the possession of property. Pard. Droit Commer. § 6; 2 Kent, Comm. 363; Poth. Cont. Sale, § 1; Butler v. Thomson, 92 U.S. 414, 23 L.Ed. 684. In re Frank's Estate, 277 N.Y. S. 573, 154 Misc. 472.

A contract whereby property is transferred from one person to another for a consideration of value, implying the passing of the general and absolute title, as distinguished from a special interest falling short of complete ownership. Arnold v. North American Chemical Co., 232 Mass. 196, 122 N.E. 283, 284; Faulkner v. Town of South Boston, 141 Va. 517, 127 S.E. 380, 381.

An agreement by which one gives a thing for a price in current money, and the other gives the price in order to have the thing itself. Three circumstances concur to the perfection of the contract, to-wit, the thing sold, the price, and the consent. Civ.Code La. art. 2439.

To constitute a "sale," there must be parties standing to each other in the relation of buyer and seller, their minds must assent to the same proposition, and a consideration must pass. Commissioner of Internal Revenue v. Freihofer, C.C.A.3, 102 F.2d 787, 789, 790, 125 A.L.R. 761.

"Sale" consists of two separate and distinct elements: First, contract of sale which is completed when offer is made and accepted and, second, delivery of property which may precede, be accompanied by, or follow, payment of price as may have been agreed on between parties. Inland Refining Co. v. Langworthy, 112 Okl. 280, 240 P. 627, 629.

An essential element of a "sale" is the money price which must either be fixed by agreement or capable of being ascertained therefrom. Puryear-Meyer Grocer Co. v. Cardwell Bank, Mo.App., 4 S.W.2d 489, 490.

"Sale," as applied to relation between landowner and real estate broker working to secure purchaser of land, means procuring purchaser able, ready and willing to buy on terms fixed by seller. T. W. Sandford & Co. v. Waring, 201 Ky. 169, 256 S.W. 9, 10.

Synonyms

The contract of "sale" is distinguished from "barter" (which applies only to goods) and "exchange," (which is used of both land and goods,) in that both the latter terms denote a commutation of property for property; *i. e.*, the price or consideration is always paid in money if the transaction is a sale, but, if it is a barter or exchange, it is paid in specific property susceptible of valuation. Westfall v. Ellis, 141 Minn. 377, 170 N.W. 339, 341; J. I. Case Threshing Mach. Co. v. Loomis, 31 N.D. 27, 153 N.W. 479, 481. "Sale" differs from "gift" in that the latter transaction involves no return or recompense for the thing transferred. But an onerous gift sometimes approaches the nature of a sale, at least where the charge it imposes is a payment of money. "Sale" is also to be discriminated from "bailment;" and the difference is to be found in the fact that the contract of bailment always contemplates the return to the bailor of the specific article delivered, either in its original form or in a modified or altered form, or the return of an article which, though not identical, is of the same class, and is equivalent. But sale never involves the return of the article itself, but only a consideration in money. This contract differs also from "accord and satisfaction;" because in the latter the object of transferring the property is to compromise and settle a claim, while the object of a sale is the price given.

The cardinal difference between the relation of seller and buyer and that of principal and factor is that in a "sale" title passes to the buyer, while in a "consignment" by principal to factor title remains in principal, and only possession passes to factor. McGaw v. Hanway, 120 Md. 197, 87 A. 666, 667, Ann.Cas.1915A, 601, and a "sale" is distinguished from a mortgage, in that the former is a transfer of the absolute property in the goods for a price, whereas a mortgage is at most a conditional sale of property as security for the payment of a debt or performance of some other obligation, subject to the condition that on performance title shall revest in the mortgagor. Waldrep v. Exchange State Bank of Keifer, 81 Okl. 162, 197 P. 509, 511, 14 A.L.R. 747.

An abandonment must be made without any desire that any other person shall acquire the thing abandoned, since if it is made for a consideration it is a "sale" or "barter," and if made without consideration, but with an intention that some other person shall become the possessor, it is a "gift." Del Giorgio v. Powers, 81 P.2d 1006, 1014, 27 Cal.App.2d 668.

General

Absolute and conditional sales. An absolute sale is one where the property in chattels passes to the buyer upon the completion of the bargain. Truax v. Parvis, 7 Houst. (Del.) 330, 32 A. 227. A conditional sale is one in which the transfer of title is made to depend on the performance of a condition, usually the payment of the price; it is a purchase for a price paid or to be paid, to become absolute on a particular event, or a purchase accompanied by an agreement to resell upon particular terms. Poindexter v. McCannon, 16 N.C. 373, 18 Am.Dec. 591; Crimp v. McCormick Const. Co., Ill., 18 C.C.A. 595, 72 F. 366.

Conditional sales are distinguishable from mortgages in that a mortgage assumes the continued existence of a debt and is given as security therefor. Turner v. Kerr, 44 Mo. 429; Crane v. Bonnell, 2 N.J.Eq. 264; Weathersly v. Weathersly, 40 Miss. 462, 90 Am.Dec. 344; Lamborn v. Denison State Bank, 115 Kan. 415, 223 P. 293, 294.

Bill of sale. See Bill.

Cash sale. A transaction whereby payment is to be in full on receipt of the goods. Bernzweig v. Hyman Levin Co., Sup., 172 N.Y.S. 437, 438. A sale where title is not to pass until the price is paid, or where title has passed, but possession is not to be delivered until payment is made. E. L. Welch Co. v. Lahart Elevator Co., 122 Minn. 432, 142 N.W. 828, 830.

Exclusive sale. With respect to a broker. An agreement by the owner that he will not sell the property during the life of the contract to any purchaser not procured by the broker in question. Harris v. McPherson, 97 Conn. 164, 115 A. 723, 724, 24 A.L.R. 1530, but see contra Roberts v. Harrington, 168 Wis. 217, 169 N.W. 603, 10 A.L.R. 810.

Executed and executory sales. An executed sale is one which is final and complete in all its particulars and details, nothing remaining to be done by either party to effect an absolute transfer of the subject-matter of the sale. Fogel v. Brubaker, 15 A. 692, 122 Pa. 7; Martin v. John Clay & Co., Mo.App., 167 S.W.2d 407, 411. An executory sale is one which has been definitely agreed on as to terms and conditions, but which has not yet been carried into full effect in respect to some of its terms or details, as where it remains to determine the price, quantity, or identity of the thing sold, or to pay installments of purchase-money, or to effect a delivery. McFadden v. Henderson, 29 So. 640, 128 Ala. 221; Fogel v. Brubaker, 15 A. 692, 122 Pa. 7; Smith v. Barron County Sup'rs, 44 Wis. 691.

Execution sale. See Execution Sale.

Fair sale. See Fair Sale.

Forced sale. A sale made without the consent or concurrence of the owner of the property, but by virtue of judicial process, such as a writ of execution or an order under a decree of foreclosure.

Fraudulent sale. One made for the purpose of defrauding the creditors of the owner of the property, by covering up or removing from their reach and converting into cash property which would be subject to the satisfaction of their claims.

Judicial sale. One made under the process of a court having competent authority to order it, by an officer duly appointed and commissioned to sell, as distinguished from a sale by an owner in virtue of his right of property. Union Trading Co. v. Drach, 58 Colo. 550, 146 P. 767, 770. Chapman v. Guaranty State Bank, Tex.Com.App., 267 S.W. 690, 693.

Memorandum sale. That form of conditional sale in which the goods are placed in the possession of the vendee subject to his approval, the title remaining in the seller until they are either accepted or rejected by the vendee.

Private sale. One negotiated and concluded privately between buyer and seller, and not made by advertisement and public outcry or auction. Barcello v. Hapgood, 118 N.C. 712, 24 S.E. 124.

Public sale. A sale made in pursuance of a notice, by auction or public outcry. Union & Mercantile Trust Co. v. Harnwell, 158 Ark. 295, 250 S. W. 321, 323.

Sale and return. A species of contract by which the seller (usually a manufacturer or wholesaler) delivers a quantity of goods to the buyer, on the understanding that, if the latter should desire to retain or use or resell any portion of such goods, he will consider such part as having been sold to him, and will pay their price, and the balance he will return to the seller, or hold them, as bailee, subject to his order. Sturm v. Boker, 14 S.Ct. 99, 150 U.S. 312, 37 L.Ed. 1093; Haskins v. Dern, 19 Utah, 89, 56 P. 953; Hickman v. Shimp, 109 Pa. 16; G. A. Soden & Co. v. T. J. Wilkinson & Son, 100 So. 182, 184, 135 Miss. 665.

Under "contract of sale and return" title vests immediately in buyer, who has privilege of rescinding sale, and until privilege is exercised title remains in him. Rio Grande Oil Co. v. Miller Rubber Co. of New York, 31 Ariz. 84, 250 P. 564.

Sale by sample. A sales contract in which it is the understanding of both parties that the goods exhibited constitute the standard with which the goods not exhibited correspond and to which deliveries should conform. M. C. Kiser Co. v. Branan, 31 Ga.App. 241, 120 S.E. 427, 429.

Sale in gross. A sale by the tract, without regard to quantity; it is in that sense a contract of hazard. Miller v. Moore, 45 Cal.App. 283, 187 P. 763, 764; Cox v. Collins, 205 Ala. 491, 88 So. 440, 441.

Sale-note. A memorandum of the subject and terms of a sale, given by a broker or factor to the seller, who bailed him the goods for that purpose, and to the buyer, who dealt with him. Also called "bought and sold notes."

Sale on approval. A species of conditional sale, which is to become absolute only in case the buyer, on trial, approves or is satisfied with the article sold. The approval, however, need not be express; it may be inferred from his keeping the goods beyond a reasonable time. Benj.Sales, § 911; Warren v. Russell, 143 Ark. 516, 220 S.W. 831.

Sale on credit. A sale of property accompanied by delivery of possession, but where payment of the price is deferred to a future day. In re Heinze's Estate, 224 N.Y. 1, 120 N.E. 63, 64.

Sale per aversionem. In the civil law, a sale where the goods are taken in bulk, or not by weight or measure, and for a single price, or where a piece of land is sold for a gross sum, to be paid for the whole premises, and not at a fixed price by the acre or foot. State v. Buck, 46 La. Ann. 656, 15 So. 531.

Sale with all faults. On what is called a "sale with all faults," unless the seller fraudulently and inconsistently represents the article sold to be faultless, or contrives to conceal any fault from the purchaser, the latter must take the article for better or worse. 3 Camp. 154; Brown.

Sale with right of redemption. A sale in which vendor reserves right to take back property by returning price paid. Glover v. Abney, 160 La. 175, 106 So. 735, 739.

Sheriff's sale. A sale of property, conducted by a sheriff, or sheriff's deputy, in virtue of his authority as an officer holding process. Anderson, L. Dict.; Batchelder v. Carter, 2 Vt. 172, 19 Am. Dec. 707.

Tax-sale. A sale of land for unpaid taxes; a sale of property, by authority of law, for the collection of a tax assessed upon it, or upon its owner, which remains unpaid.

Voluntary sale. One made freely, without constraint, by the owner of the thing sold. 1 Bouv. Inst. no. 974.

SALESMAN. One whose occupation is to sell, as goods, merchandise, land, securities, transportation, etc., either in a store or within a given territory; specifically, a commercial traveler. In re Herbert Candy Co., D.C.Pa., 43 F.Supp. 588, 590.

SALET. In old English law. A headpiece; a steel cap or morion. Cowell.

SALFORD HUNDRED COURT OF RECORD. An inferior and local court of record having jurisdiction in personal actions where the debt or damage sought to be recovered does not exceed £50, if the cause of action arise within the hundred of Salford. St. 31 & 32 Vict. c. 130; 2 Exch.Div. 346.

SALIC LAW. A body of law framed by the Salian Franks, a Teutonic race who settled in Gaul about the beginning of the fifth century.

It is the most ancient of the barbarian Codes. It is said to have been compiled about the year 420. It embraced the laws and customs of the Salian Franks. It is of great historical value, in connection with the origins of feudalism and similar subjects. Its most celebrated provision was one which excluded women from the inheritance of landed estates, by an extension of which law females were always excluded from succession to the crown of France. Hence this provision, by itself, is often referred to as the "Salic Law."

In French jurisprudence. The name is frequently applied to that fundamental law of France which excluded females from succession to the crown. Supposed to have been derived from the sixty-second title of the Salic Law, "De Alode." Brande.

SALINE LAND. Land having salt deposits. To fourteen states congress has granted all the salt springs within them; to twelve, a limited grant of them was made. Eighteen states have received no such grant. Montello Salt Co. v. Utah, 31 S. Ct. 706, 221 U.S. 452, 55 L.Ed. 810, Ann.Cas.1912D, 633.

SALMANNUS. A sale-man, found in the Salic Law in the fifth century, who was a third person called in to complete the transfer of property. 12 Harv.L.Rev. 445, Law in Science, etc., by O. W. Holmes, Jr.

SALOON. A place of refreshment. Hinton v. State, 137 Tex.Cr.R. 352, 129 S.W.2d 670, 673. An apartment for a specified public use. Clinton v. Grusendorf, 80 Iowa 117, 45 N.W. 408. In common parlance, a place where intoxicating liquors are sold and consumed. Gibbs v. Arras Bros., 222 N.Y. 332, 118 N.E. 857, 858, L.R.A.1918F, 826, Ann. Cas.1918D, 1141.

SALOON-KEEPER. This expression has a definite meaning, namely, a retailer of cigars, liquors, etc. Cahill v. Campbell, 105 Mass. 40.

SALT DUTY IN LONDON. A custom in the city of London called "granage," formerly payable to the lord mayor, etc., for salt brought to the port of London, being the twentieth part. Wharton.

SALT SILVER. One penny paid at the feast day of St. Martin, by the tenants of some manors, as a commutation for the service of carrying their lord's salt from market to his larder. Paroch.Antiq. 496.

SALUS. Lat. Health; prosperity; safety.

SALUS POPULI SUPREMA LEX. The welfare of the people is the supreme law. Bac. Max. reg. 12; Broom, Max. 1–10; Montesq. Esprit des Lois, lib. 26, c. 23; 13 Coke, 139; Lingo Lumber Co. v. Hayes, Tex.Civ.App., 64 S.W.2d 835, 839.

SALUS REIPUBLICÆ SUPREMA LEX. The welfare of the state is the supreme law. Inhabitants of Springfield v. Connecticut River R. Co., 4 Cush. (Mass.) 71.

SALUS UBI MULTI CONSILIARII. 4 Inst. 1. Where there are many counselors, there is safety.

SALUTE. A gold coin stamped by Henry V. in France, after his conquests there, whereon the arms of England and France were stamped quarterly. Cowell.

In the army and navy an honor paid to a distinguished personage, when troops or squadrons meet, when officers are buried, or to celebrate an event or show respect to a flag and on many other ceremonial occasions. Cent. Dict.

SALVA GARDIA. L. Lat. Safeguard. Reg. Orig. 26.

SALVAGE. In maritime law. A compensation allowed to persons by whose assistance a ship or its cargo has been saved, in whole or in part, from impending danger, or recovered from actual loss, in cases of shipwreck, derelict, or recapture. 3 Kent, Comm. 245; Cope v. Vallette Dry-Dock Co., 7 S.Ct. 336, 119 U.S. 625, 30 L.Ed. 501; J. M. Guffey Petroleum Co. v. Borison, C.C.A.Tex., 211 F. 594, 601.

Elements necessary to valid "salvage" are marine peril, with service voluntarily rendered, when not required as existing duty, or from a special contract, and success in whole or in part, and that service rendered contributed to such success. Robert R. Sizer & Co. v. Chiarello Bros., D. C.N.Y., 32 F.2d 333, 335.

In the older books of the law, (and sometimes in modern writings,) the term is also used to denote the goods or property saved.

Equitable Salvage

By analogy, the term "salvage" is sometimes also used in cases which have nothing to do with maritime perils, but in which property has been preserved from loss by the last of several advances by different persons. In such a case, the person making the last advance is frequently entitled to priority over the others, on the ground that, without his advance, the property would have been lost altogether. This right, which is sometimes called that of "equitable salvage," and is in the nature of a lien, is chiefly of importance with reference to payments made to prevent leases or policies of insurance from being forfeited, or to prevent mines and similar undertakings from being stopped or injured. 1 Fish.Mortg. 149; 3 Ch. Div. 411; L.R. 14 Eq. 4; 7 Ch.Div. 825.

Salvage Charges

This term includes all the expenses and costs incurred in the work of saving and preserving the property which was in danger. The salvage charges ultimately fall upon the insurers.

Salvage Loss

That kind of loss which it is presumed would, but for certain services rendered and exertions made, have become a total loss. In the language of marine underwriters, this term means the difference between the amount of salvage, after deducting the charges, and the original value of the property insured. Koons v. La Fonciere Compagnie, D.C.Cal., 71 F. 981.

Salvage Service

A service voluntarily rendered to a vessel in need of assistance, and is designed to relieve her from distress or danger, either present or to be reasonably apprehended and for which a salvage reward is allowed by the maritime law. The Emanuel Stavroudis, D.C.Md., 23 F.2d 214, 216.

It is distinguished from "towage service," in that the latter is rendered for the mere purpose of expediting a vessel's voyage, without reference to any circumstances of danger, though the service in each case may be rendered in the same way. The Emanuel Stavroudis, D.C.Md., 23 F.2d 214, 216.

SALVIAN INTERDICT. See Interdictum Salvianum.

SALVO. Lat. Saving; excepting; without prejudice to. *Salvo me et hæredibus meis*, except me and my heirs. *Salvo jure cujuslibet*, without prejudice to the rights of any one.

SALVOR. A person who, without any particular relation to a ship in distress, proffers useful service, and gives it as a volunteer adventurer, without any pre-existing covenant that connected him with the duty of employing himself for the preservation of that ship. The Clara, 23 Wall. 16, 23 L.Ed. 150; The Dumper, C.C.A.N.Y., 129 F. 99, 63 C.C.A. 600; Central Stockyard Co. v. Mears, 85 N.Y.S. 795, 89 App.Div. 452.

SALVUS PLEGIUS. L. Lat. A safe pledge; called, also, "*certus plegius*," a sure pledge. Bract. fol. 160*b*.

SAME. The word "same" does not always mean "identical," not different or other. It frequently means of the kind or species, not the specific thing. Crapo v. Brown, 40 Iowa 487, 493. When preceded by the definite article, meaning the one just referred to. In re Conner's Estate, 318 Pa. 150, 178 A. 15, 17.

SAME INVENTION. Within reissue statute, whatever invention was described in original letters patent, and appears therein to have been intended to be secured thereby. 35 U.S.C.A. § 64; Morgan v. Drake, Cust. & Pat.App., 36 F.2d 511, 512. It is not to be determined by the claims of the original patent but from the description and such other evidence as the commissioner may deem relevant. Detrola Radio & Television Corporation v. Hazeltine Corporation, C.C.A.Mich., 117 F.2d 238, 241.

SAME OFFENSE. As used in Constitution, providing that no person shall be twice put in jeopardy for the same offense, does not signify the same offense eo nomine, but the same criminal act, transaction, or omission. State v. Shaver, 197 Iowa 1028, 198 N.W. 329, 336.

SAMPLE. A specimen; a small quantity of any commodity, presented for inspection or examination as evidence of the quality of the whole; as a sample of cloth or of wheat.

SAMPLE, SALE BY. A sale at which only a sample of the goods sold is exhibited to the buyer. See "Sale."

SANATORIUM. A health retreat, or institution for the treatment of disease or care of invalids. People v. Gold, Sp.Sess., 6 N.Y.S.2d 264, 268.

SANÆ MENTIS. Lat. In old English law. Of sound mind. Fleta, lib. 3, c. 7, § 1.

SANCTIO. Lat. In the civil law. That part of a law by which a penalty was ordained against those who should violate it. Inst. 2, 1, 10.

SANCTION, *v.* To assent, concur, confirm, or ratify. U. S. v. Tillinghast, D.C.R.I., 55 F.2d 279, 283.

SANCTION, *n.* In the original sense of the word, a penalty or punishment provided as a means of enforcing obedience to a law. In jurisprudence, a law is said to have a sanction when there is a state which will intervene if it is disobeyed or disregarded. Therefore international law has no legal sanction. Sweet.

In a more general sense, a conditional evil annexed to a law to produce obedience to that law; and, in a still wider sense, an authorization of anything. Occasionally, "sanction" is used (*e. g.*, in Roman law) to denote a statute, the part (penal clause) being used to denote the whole. Brown.

The vindicatory part of a law, or that part which ordains or denounces a penalty for its violation. 1 Bl.Comm. 56.

SANCTUARY. In old English law. A consecrated place which had certain privileges annexed to it, and to which offenders were accustomed to resort for refuge, because they could not be arrested there, nor the laws be executed.

SANDBAG. A tube of strong, flexible material filled with sand, by which a heavy blow may be struck which leaves little or no mark on the skin. Cent. Dict. It is included in the general term *sap* (*q. v.*).

SAND-GAVEL. In old English law. A payment due to the lord of the manor of Rodley, in the county of Gloucester, for liberty granted to the tenants to dig sand for their common use. Cowell.

SANE. Of natural and normal mental condition; healthy in mind.

One who knows the difference between right and wrong, and appreciates the consequences of his acts. State v. Migues, 194 La. 1081, 195 So. 545, 547. Stout v. State, 142 Tex.Civ.R. 537, 155 S.W.2d 374, 377.

SANE MEMORY. Sound mind, memory, and understanding. This is one of the essential elements in the capacity of contracting; and the absence of it in lunatics and idiots, and its immaturity in infants, is the cause of their respective incapacities or partial incapacities to bind themselves. The like circumstance is their ground of exemption in cases of crime. Brown.

SANG, or SANC. In old French. Blood.

SANGUINE, or MURREY. An heraldic term for "blood-color," called, in the arms of princes, "dragon's tail," and, in those of lords, "sardonyx." It is a tincture of very infrequent occurrence, and not recognized by some writers. In engraving, it is denoted by numerous lines in saltire. Wharton.

SANGUINEM EMERE. Lat. In feudal law. A redemption by villeins, of their blood or tenure, in order to become freemen.

SANGUINIS CONJUNCTIO BENEVOLENTIA DEVINCIT HOMINES ET CARITATE. A tie of blood overcomes men through benevolence and family affection. Steere v. Steere, 5 Johns.Ch. (N.Y.) 1, 13, 9 Am.Dec. 256.

SANGUIS. Lat. In the civil and old English law. Blood; consanguinity.

The right or power which the chief lord of the fee had to judge and determine cases where blood was shed. Mon. Aug. t. i. 1021.

SANIPRACTIC. A method of drugless healing. Martin v. Department of Social Security, 12 Wash. 2d 329, 121 P.2d 394, 395.

SANIPRACTORS. Drugless healers. State v. Lydon, 170 Wash. 354, 16 P.2d 848, 851.

SANIS. A kind of punishment among the Greeks; inflicted by binding the malefactor fast to a piece of wood. Enc. Lond.

SANITARIUM. Health station or retreat; boarding-house, or other place where patients are kept and where medical and surgical treatment is given. City of Atlanta v. Blackman Health Resort, 153 Ga. 499, 113 S.E. 545, 548.

SANITARY. That which pertains to health, with especial reference to cleanliness and freedom from infective and deleterious influences. Mayor and City Council of Baltimore v. Bloecher & Schaff, 149 Md. 648, 132 A. 160, 162.

SANITARY AUTHORITIES. In English law. Bodies having jurisdiction over their respective districts in regard to sewerage, drainage, scavenging, the supply of water, the prevention of nuisances and offensive trades, etc., all of which come under the head of "sanitary matters" in the special sense of the word. Sanitary authorities also have jurisdiction in matters coming under the head of "local government." Sweet.

SANITATION. Devising and applying of measures for preserving and promoting public health; removal or neutralization of elements injurious to health; practical application of sanitary science. Smith v. State, 160 Ga. 857, 129 S.E. 542, 544.

SANITY. Sound understanding; the normal condition of the human mind; the reverse of insanity, (*q. v.*). Rust v. Reid, 124 Va. 1, 97 S.E. 324, 331.

The accepted test of "sanity" in criminal cases is whether defendant could distinguish between right and wrong. People v. Dawa, 15 Cal.2d 393, 101 P.2d 498, 499.

SANS CEO QUE. L. Fr. Without this. See Absque Hoc.

SANS FRAIS. Fr. Without expense. See Retour Sans Protêt.

SANS IMPEACHMENT DE WAST. L. Fr. Without impeachment of waste. Litt. § 152. See Absque Impetitione Vasti.

SANS JOUR. Fr. Without day; *sine die.*

SANS NOMBRE. Fr. A term used in relation to the right of putting animals on a common. The term "common *sans nombre*" does not mean that the beasts are to be innumerable, but only indefinite; not certain. Willes, 227.

SANS RECOURS. Fr. Without recourse. See Indorsement.

SAP. A general term which, as applied to weapons, includes a "blackjack," "slung shot," "billy," "sandbag," or "brass knuckles" (see those terms). People v. Mulherin, 35 P.2d 174, 175, 176, 140 Cal. App. 212.

SAPIENS INCIPIT A FINE, ET QUOD PRIMUM EST IN INTENTIONE, ULTIMUM EST IN EXECUTIONE. A wise man begins with the last, and what is first in intention is last in execution. 10 Coke, 25.

SAPIENS OMNIA AGIT CUM CONSILIO. A wise man does everything advisedly. 4 Inst. 4.

SAPIENTIA LEGIS NUMMARIO PRETIO NON EST ÆSTIMANDA. The wisdom of the law cannot be valued by money. Jenk. Cent. 168.

SAPIENTIS JUDICIS EST COGITARE TANTUM SIBI ESSE PERMISSUM, QUANTUM COMMISSUM ET CREDITUM. It is the part of a wise judge to think that a thing is permitted to him, only so far as it is committed and intrusted to him. 4 Inst. 163. That is, he should keep his jurisdiction within the limits of his commission.

SARCULATURA. L. Lat. In old records. Weeding corn. A tenant's service of weeding for the lord. Cowell.

SART. In old English law. A piece of woodland, turned into arable. Cowell.

SARUM. In old records The city of Salisbury in England. Spelman.

SASINE. In Scotch law. The symbolical delivery of land, answering to the livery of seisin of the old English law. 4 Kent, Comm. 459.

SASSE. In old English law. A kind of wear with flood-gates, most commonly in cut rivers, for the shutting up and letting out of water, as occasion required, for the more ready passing of boats and barges to and fro; a lock; a turnpike; a sluice. Cowell.

SASSONS. The corruption of Saxons. A name of contempt formerly given to the English, while they affected to be called "Angles;" they are still so called by the Welsh.

SATIS LIQUET. See Liquet.

SATISDARE. Lat. In the civil law. To guaranty the obligation of a principal.

SATISDATIO. Lat. In the civil law. Security given by a party to an action, as by a defendant, to pay what might be adjudged against him. Inst. 4, 11; 3 Bl.Comm. 291.

SATISFACTION. Act of satisfying; the state of being satisfied. Seago v. New York Cent. R. Co., 349 Mo. 1249, 164 S.W.2d 336, 341. The discharge of an obligation by paying a party what is due to him, (as on a mortgage, lien, or contract,) or what is awarded to him, by the judgment of a court or otherwise. Thus, a judgment is satisfied by the payment of the amount due to the party who has recovered such judgment, or by his levying the amount. Bryant v. Fairfield, 51 Me. 152; Armour Bros. Banking Co. v. Addington, 37 S.W. 100, 1 Ind.T. 304. The execution or carrying into effect of an accord. Barber v. Mallon, Mo.App., 168 S.W.2d 177, 179; R. J. Bearings Corporation v. Warr, 192 Okl. 133, 134 P.2d 355, 357.

Practice

An entry made on the record, by which a party in whose favor a judgment was rendered declares that he has been satisfied and paid.

Equity

The doctrine of satisfaction in equity is somewhat analogous to performance in equity, but differs from it in this respect: that satisfaction is always something given either in whole or in part as a substitute or equivalent for something else, and not (as in performance) something that may be construed as the identical thing covenanted to be done. Brown.

SATISFACTION, CONTRACTS TO. A class of contracts in which one party agrees to perform his promise to the satisfaction of the other. A contract for construction work "to the entire satisfaction of the owners" imports that the construction be to the satisfaction of a reasonable man and not to the personal satisfaction of owners. Waite v. C. E. Shoemaker & Co., 50 Mont. 264, 146 P. 736, 742.

SATISFACTION PIECE. In practice. A memorandum in writing, entitled in a cause, stating that satisfaction is acknowledged between the parties, plaintiff and defendant. Upon this being duly acknowledged and filed in the office where the record of the judgment is, the judgment becomes satisfied, and the defendant discharged from it. 1 Archb.Pr. 722.

SATISFACTION SHOULD BE MADE TO THAT FUND WHICH HAS SUSTAINED THE LOSS. 4 Bouv. Inst. no. 3731.

SATISFACTORY. Where a contract provides that it is to be performed in a manner "satisfactory" to one of the parties, the provision must be construed as meaning that the performance must be such that the party, as a reasonable person, should be satisfied with it. Hoff v. L. Gould & Co., 198 Ill. App. 499, 501.

SATISFACTORY EVIDENCE. Such evidence as is sufficient to produce a belief that the thing is true; credible evidence; such evidence as, in respect to its amount or weight, is adequate or sufficient to justify the court or jury in adopting the conclusion in support of which it is adduced. Walker v. Collins, C.C.A.Kan., 59 F. 74, 8 C.C.A. 1; U. S. v. Lee Huen, D.C.N.Y., 118 F 457.

"Satisfactory evidence," which is sometimes called "sufficient evidence," means that amount of proof which ordinarily satisfies an unprejudiced mind beyond a reasonable doubt. Thayer v. Boyle, 30 Me. 475, 481 (citing 1 Greenl. Ev. § 2); State v. Moss, 95 Or. 616, 188 P. 702, 704. See, also, Sufficient Evidence.

SATISFIED TERM. A term of years in land is thus called when the purpose for which it was created has been satisfied or executed before the expiration of the set period.

SATISFIED TERMS ACT. The statute 8 & 9 Vict. c. 112, passed to abolish satisfied outstanding terms of years in land. By this act, terms which shall henceforth become attendant upon the inheritance, either by express *declaration* or construction of law, are to cease and determine. This, in effect, abolishes outstanding terms. 1 Steph.Comm. 380–382; Williams, Real Prop. pt. 4, c. 1.

SATISFY. To answer or discharge, as a claim, debt, legal demand or the like. Swaner v. Union Mortg. Co., 99 Utah 298, 105 P.2d 342, 345. To comply actually and fully with a demand; to extinguish, by payment or performance.

To convince, as to satisfy a jury. Lawrence v. Goodwill, 44 Cal.App. 440, 186 P. 781, 785.

SATIUS EST PETERE FONTES QUAM SECTARI RIVULOS. Lofft, 606. It is better to seek the source than to follow the streamlets.

SATURDAY'S STOP. In old English law. A space of time from even-song on Saturday till sun-rising on Monday, in which it was not lawful to take salmon in Scotland and the northern parts of England. Cowell.

SAUNKEFIN. L. Fr. End of blood; failure of the direct line in successions. Spelman; Cowell.

SAUVAGINE. L. Fr. Wild animals.

SAUVEMENT. L. Fr. Safely. *Sauvement gardes*, safely kept. Britt. c. 87.

SAVE. To except, reserve, or exempt; as where a statute "saves" vested rights. To toll, or suspend the running or operation of; as to "save" the statute of limitations.

SAVER DEFAULT. L. Fr. In old English practice. To excuse a default. Termes de la Ley.

SAVING. Preservation from danger or loss; economy in outlay; prevention of waste; something laid up or kept from becoming expended or lost; a reservation. Oklahoma Tax Commission v. Sisters of the Sorrowful Mother, 186 Okl. 339, 97 P.2d 888, 892.

SAVING CLAUSE. In a statute an exception of a special thing out of the general things mentioned in the statute. Ordinarily a restriction in a repealing act, which is intended to save rights, pending proceedings, penalties, etc., from the annihilation which would result from an unrestricted repeal. State v. St. Louis, 174 Mo. 125, 73 S.W. 623, 61 L.R.A. 593; Bass v. Albright, Tex.Civ.App., 59 S.W.2d 891, 894.

SAVING THE STATUTE OF LIMITATIONS. A creditor is said to "save the statute of limitations" when he saves or preserves his debt from being barred by the operation of the statute. Thus, in the case of a simple contract debt, if a creditor commence an action for its recovery within six years from the time when the cause of action accrued, he will be in time to save the statute. Brown.

SAVINGS BANK. See Bank.

SAVINGS BANK TRUST. See Trust.

SAVOUR. To partake the nature of; to bear affinity to.

SAVOY. One of the old privileged places, or sanctuaries. 4 Steph.Comm. 227*n.*

SAW LOG. A log of convenient length and otherwise suitable for being manufactured into lumber. Ladnier v. Ingram Day Lumber Co., 135 Miss. 632, 100 So. 369, 370.

SAXON LAGE. The laws of the West Saxons. Cowell.

SAY ABOUT. This phrase, like "more or less," is frequently introduced into conveyances or contracts of sale, to indicate that the quantity of the subject-matter is uncertain, and is only estimated, and to guard the vendor against the implication of having warranted the quantity.

SAYER. In Hindu law. Variable imposts distinct from land, rents, or revenues; consisting of customs, tolls, licenses, duties on goods; also taxes on houses, shops, bazaars, etc. Wharton.

SC. An abbreviation for "scilicet," that is to say.

SCAB. A working man who works for lower wages than or under conditions contrary to those prescribed by a trade union; also one who takes the place of a workingman on a strike. U. S. v. Taliaferro, D.C.Va., 290 F. 214, 218.

SCABINI. In old European law. The judges or assessors of the judges in the court held by the count. Assistants or associates of the count; officers under the count. The permanent selected judges of the Franks. Judges among the Germans, Franks, and Lombards, who were held in peculiar esteem. Spelman.

SCACCARIUM. A chequered cloth resembling a chess-board which covered the table in the exchequer, and on which, when certain of the king's accounts were made up, the sums were marked and scored with counters. Hence the court of exchequer, or *curia scaccarii,* derived its name. 3 Bl. Comm. 44.

SCALAM. At the scale; the old way of paying money into the exchequer. Cowell.

SCALE. In early American law. To adjust, graduate, or value according to a scale. Walden v. Payne, 2 Wash. (Va.) 5, 6.

SCALE TOLERANCE. Nominal variation between different scales in respect of the mass or "weight" of the same goods. Smith v. Louisville & N. R. Co., 202 Iowa, 292, 209 N.W. 465, 466.

SCALER. An expert employed to determine the number of board feet and the percentage of unsound timber in logs. Connecticut Valley Lumber Co. v. Stone, C.C.A.Vt., 212 F. 713, 715.

SCALING LAWS. A term used to signify statutes establishing the process of adjusting the difference in value between depreciated paper money and specie. Such statutes were rendered necessary by the depreciation of paper money necessarily following the establishment of American independence. And, more recently, to discharge those debts which were made payable in Confederate money. The statutes are now obsolete.

SCALPINGS. See Wheat Scalpings.

SCAMNUM CADUCUM. In old records, the cucking-stool, (*q. v.*). Cowell.

SCANDAL. Defamatory reports or rumors; aspersion or slanderous talk, uttered recklessly or maliciously.

Pleading

With reference to necessity of keeping court records free from scandal, an unnecessary statement which bears cruelly upon an individual's moral character, or statement of anything contrary to good manners, or unbecoming court's dignity to hear or which charges some person with a crime not necessary to be shown in the cause. Nadeau v. Texas Co., 104 Mont. 558, 69 P.2d 593, 595, 111 A.L.R. 874; Huffman v. State, 183 Ind. 698, 109 N.E. 401, 402.

SCANDALOUS MATTER. In pleading. Scandal, which title see.

SCANDALUM MAGNATUM. In English law. Scandal or slander of great men or nobles. Words spoken in derogation of a peer, a judge, or other great officer of the realm, for which an action lies, though it is now rarely resorted to. 3 Bl. Comm. 123; 3 Steph.Comm. 473. This offense has not existed in America since the formation of the United States. State v. Shepherd, 177 Mo. 205, 76 S.W. 79, 99 Am.St.Rep. 624.

SCAPELLARE. In old European law. To chop; to chip or haggle. Spelman.

SCAPHA. Lat. In Roman law. A boat; a lighter. A ship's boat.

SCAVAGE, SCHEVAGE, SCHEWAGE, or SHEWAGE. A kind of toll or custom, exacted by mayors, sheriffs, etc., of merchant strangers, for wares showed or offered for sale within their liberties. Prohibited by 19 Hen. VII. c. 7. Cowell.

SCAVAIDUS. The officer who collected the scavage money. Cowell.

SCEATTA. A Saxon coin of less denomination than a shilling. Spelman.

SCEPPA SALIS. An ancient measure of salt, the quantity of which is now not known. Wharton.

SCHAR-PENNY, SHCARN-PENNY, or SCHORN-PENNY. A small duty or compensation. Cowell.

SCHEDULE. A sheet of paper or parchment annexed to a statute, deed, answer in equity, deposition, or other instrument, exhibiting in detail the matters mentioned or referred to in the principal document.

A list or inventory; the paper containing an inventory.

Constitutional Law

A statement annexed to a constitution newly adopted by a state, in which are described at length the particulars in which it differs from the former constitution, or which contains provisions for the adjustment of matters affected by the change from the old to the new constitution.

Practice

When an indictment is returned from an inferior court in obedience to a writ of *certiorari,* the statement of the previous proceedings sent with it. 1 Saund. 309*a,* n. 2.

SCHEME. A design or plan formed to accomplish some purpose—a system. Snider v. Leatherwood, Tex.Civ.App., 49 S.W.2d 1107, 1110.

In English law. A document containing provisions for regulating the management or distribution of property, or for making an arrangement between persons having conflicting rights. Thus, in the practice of the chancery division, where the execution of a charitable trust in the manner directed by the founder is difficult or impracticable, or requires supervision, a scheme for the management of the charity will be settled by the court. Tud. Char. Trusts, 257; Hunt, Eq. 248; Daniell, Ch.Pr. 1765.

SCHETES. Usury. Cowell.

SCHIREMAN. In Saxon law. An officer having the civil government of a *shire,* or county; an earl. 1 Bl.Comm. 398.

SCHIRRENS-GELD. In Saxon law. A tax paid to sheriffs for keeping the shire or county court. Cowell.

SCHISM. In ecclesiastical law. A division or separation in a church or denomination of Christians, occasioned by a diversity of faith, creed, or religious opinions. Lindstrom v. Tell, 131 Minn. 203, 154 N.W. 969, 971.

SCHISM-BILL. In English law. The name of an act passed in the reign of Queen Anne, which restrained Protestant dissenters from educating their own children, and forbade all tutors and schoolmasters to be present at any conventicle or dissenting place of worship. The queen died on the day when this act was to have taken effect, (August 1, 1714,) and it was repealed in the fifth year of Geo. I. Wharton.

SCHOOL. An institution or place for instruction or education. Bastendorf v. Arndt, 290 Mich. 423, 287 N.W. 579, 580, 124 A.L.R. 445. An institution of learning of a lower grade, below a college or a university. A place of primary instruction. The term generally refers to the common or public schools, maintained at the expense of the public. Alexander v. Phillips, 31 Ariz. 503, 254 P. 1056, 1058, 52 A.L.R. 244.

Common Schools

Schools maintained at the public expense and administered by a bureau of the state, district, or municipal government, for the gratuitous education of the children of all citizens without distinction. Board of Education of City of Sapulpa v. Corey, 63 Okl. 178, 163 P. 949, 953; State v. O'Dell, 187 Ind. 84, 118 N.E. 529, 530.

Consolidated School District

A common school district where two or more existing schools have consolidated into one single district. Trustees of Walton School v. Board of Sup'rs of Covington County, 115 Miss. 117, 75 So. 833, 834; Rice v. Gong Lum, 139 Miss. 760, 104 So. 105, 110.

District School

A common or public school for the education at public expense of the children residing within a given district; a public school maintained by a "school district." See *infra.*

Grade School

A school in which the pupils are classified according to progress and taught by different teachers so that a rural school under one teacher is not included within the exception, although various pupils in various stages of progress are classified. Board of County Com'rs of Laramie County v. State, 24 Wyo. 364, 158 P. 801, 804.

High School

A school in which higher branches of learning are taught than in the common schools. Thurman-Watts v. Board of Education of City of Coffeyville, 115 Kan. 328, 222 P. 123, 125. A school in which such instruction is given as will prepare the students to enter a college or university. Whitlock v. State, 30 Neb. 815, 47 N.W. 284.

Normal School

A training school for teachers; one in which instruction is given in the theory and practice of teaching; particularly, in the system of schools generally established throughout the United

States, a school for the training and instruction of those who are already teachers in the public schools or those who desire and expect to become such. Board of Regents v. Painter, 102 Mo. 464, 14 S.W. 938, 10 L.R.A. 493

Private School

One maintained by private individuals or corporations, not at public expense, and open only to pupils selected and admitted by the proprietors or governors, or to pupils of a certain class or possessing certain qualifications, (racial, religious, or otherwise,) and generally supported, in part at least, by tuition fees or charges Quigley v. State, 5 Ohio Cir.Ct.R. 638.

Public Schools

Schools established under the laws of the state (and usually regulated in matters of detail by the local authorities), in the various districts, counties, or towns, maintained at the public expense by taxation, and open with or without charge to the children of all the residents of the town or other district. St. Joseph's Church v. Assessors of Taxes, 12 R.I. 19, 34 Am.Rep. 597. Litchman v. Shannon, 90 Wash. 186, 155 P. 783, 784. Schools belonging to the public and established and conducted under public authority; not schools owned and conducted by private parties, though they may be open to the public generally and though tuition may be free. Gerke v. Purcell, 25 Ohio St. 229.

School Board

A board of municipal officers charged with the administration of the affairs of the public schools. They are commonly organized under the general laws of the state, and fall within the class of *quasi* corporations, sometimes coterminous with a county or borough, but not necessarily so. The members of the school board are sometimes termed "school directors," or the official style may be "the board of school directors." The circuit of their territorial jurisdiction is called a "school district," and each school district is usually a separate taxing district for school purposes.

School Directors

See School Board.

School District

A public and quasi municipal corporation, organized by legislative authority or direction, comprising a defined territory, for the erection, maintenance, government, and support of the public schools within its territory in accordance with and in subordination to the general school laws of the state, invested, for these purposes only, with powers of local self-government and generally of local taxation, and administered by a board of officers, usually elected by the voters of the district, who are variously styled "school directors," or "trustees," "commissioners," or "supervisors" of schools. Hamilton v. San Diego County, 108 Cal. 273, 41 P. 305; Duff v. School Dist. of Perry Tp., 281 Pa. 87, 126 A. 202.

School Lands

Public lands of a state set apart by the state (or by congress in a territory) to create, by the proceeds of their sale, a fund for the establishment and maintenance of public schools.

School-Master

One employed in teaching a school.

SCHOOL PURPOSES. This term in constitutional provision limiting rates of taxation covers ordinary expenses of maintaining and operating schools. Peter v. Kaufmann, 327 Mo. 915, 38 S.W. 2d 1062, 1067.

SCHOUT. In Dutch law. An officer of a court whose functions somewhat resemble those of a sheriff.

SCI. FA. An abbreviation for "*scire facias*," (*q. v.*).

SCIENDUM. Lat. In English law. The name given to a clause inserted in the record by which it is made known that the justice here in court, in this same term, delivered a writ thereupon to the deputy-sheriff of the county aforesaid, to be executed in due form of law. Lee, Dict. "Record."

SCIENDUM EST. Lat. It is to be known; be it remarked. In the books of the civil law, this phrase is often found at the beginning of a chapter or paragraph, by way of introduction to some explanation, or directing attention to some particular rule.

SCIENTER. Lat. Knowingly. The term is used in pleading to signify an allegation (or that part of the declaration or indictment which contains it) setting out the defendant's previous knowledge of the cause which led to the injury complained of, or rather his previous knowledge of a state of facts which it was his duty to guard against, and his omission to do which has led to the injury complained of. The insertion of such an allegation is called "laying the action (or indictment) with a *scienter*." And the term is frequently used to signify the defendant's guilty knowledge. People v. Gould, 237 Mich. 156, 211 N.W. 346, 348. Horton v. Tyree, 104 W.Va. 238, 139 S.E. 737, 738.

SCIENTI ET VOLENTI NON FIT INJURIA. Bract. fol. 20. An injury is not done to one who knows and wills it.

SCIENTIA SCIOLORUM EST MIXTA IGNORANTIA. 8 Coke, 159. The knowledge of smatterers is diluted ignorance.

SCIENTIA UTRIMQUE PAR PARES CONTRAHENTES FACIT. Equal knowledge on both sides makes contracting parties equal. 3 Burrows, 1905. An insured need not mention what the underwriter knows, or what he ought to know. Broom, Max. 772.

SCILICET. Lat. To-wit; that is to say. A word used in pleadings and other instruments, as introductory to a more particular statement of matters previously mentioned in general terms. Hob. 171, 172.

SCINTILLA. Lat. A spark; a remaining particle; the least particle.

SCINTILLA JURIS. In real property law. A spark of right or interest. By this figurative expression was denoted the small particle of interest which, by a fiction of law, was supposed to remain in a feoffee to uses, sufficient to support contingent uses afterwards coming into existence, and thereby enable the statute of uses (27 Hen. VIII. c. 10) to execute them. 2 Washb. Real Prop. 125; 4 Kent, Comm. 238.

SCINTILLA OF EVIDENCE. A spark of evidence. Cunningham v. Union Pac. Ry. Co., 4 Utah, 206, 7 P. 795, 797. A metaphorical expression to describe a very insignificant or trifling item or particle of evidence; used in the statement of the common-law rule that if there is any evidence at all in a case, even a mere *scintilla,* tending to support a material issue, the case cannot be taken from the jury, but must be left to their decision. Offutt v. World's Columbian Exposition, 175 Ill. 472, 51 N.E. 651.

Any material evidence that, if true, would tend to establish issue in mind of reasonable juror. Thackston v. Shelton, 178 S.C. 240, 182 S.E. 436; Lancaster v. South Carolina Power Co., 181 S.C. 244, 186 S.E. 911, 913. Something of substance and relevant consequence and not vague, uncertain, or irrelevant matter not carrying quality of proof or having fitness to induce conviction. City of Houston v. Scanlan, 120 Tex. 264, 37 S.W.2d 718. Wigginton's Adm'r v. Louisville Ry. Co., 256 Ky. 287, 75 S.W.2d 1046, 1051, courts differ as to what constitutes a "scintilla," and some courts do not accept the rule. Sobolovitz v. Lubric Oil Co., 107 Ohio St. 204, 140 N.E. 634, 635.

It is the duty of trial court to instruct a verdict, though there is slight testimony, if its probative force is so weak that it only raises suspicion of existence of facts sought to be established, since such testimony falls short of being "evidence". Texas Pacific Coal & Oil Co. v. Wells, Tex. Civ.App., 151 S.W.2d 927, 929.

Suggestions, if any, from evidence did not amount to "evidence". Cooksey v. McGuire, Tex.Civ.App., 146 S.W.2d 480, 483.

SCIRE DEBES CUM QUO CONTRAHIS. You ought to know with whom you deal. 11 Mees. & W. 405, 632; 13 Mees. & W. 171.

SCIRE ET SCIRE DEBERE ÆQUIPARANTUR IN JURE. To know a thing, and to be bound to know it, are regarded in law as equivalent. Tray. Leg. Max. 551.

SCIRE FACIAS. Lat. In practice. A judicial writ, founded upon some matter of record, such as a judgment or recognizance and requiring the person against whom it is brought to show cause why the party bringing it should not have advantage of such record, or (in the case of a *scire facias* to repeal letters patent) why the record should not be annulled and vacated. 2 Archb.Pr. K.B. 86; Pub. St. Mass. p. 1295. The name is used to designate both the writ and the whole proceeding. City of St. Louis v. Miller, 235 Mo. App. 987, 145 S.W.2d 504, 505.

The most common application of this writ is as a process to revive a judgment, after the lapse of a certain time, or on a change of parties, or otherwise to have execution of the judgment, in which cases it is merely a continuation of the original action. It is used more rarely as a mode of proceeding against special bail on their recognizance, and as a means of repealing letters patent, in which cases it is an original proceeding. 2 Archb. Pr. K. B. 86. American Ry. Express Co. v. F. S. Royster Guano Co., 141 Va. 602, 126 S.E. 678, 679.

SCIRE FACIAS AD AUDIENDUM ERRORES. The name of a writ which is sued out after the plaintiff in error has assigned his errors. Fitzh. Nat.Brev. 20.

SCIRE FACIAS AD DISPROBANDUM DEBITUM. The name of a writ in use in Pennsylvania, which lies by a defendant in foreign attachment against the plaintiff, in order to enable him, within a year and a day next ensuing the time of payment to the plaintiff in the attachment, to disprove or avoid the debt recovered against him. Bouvier.

SCIRE FACIAS AD REHABENDAM TERRAM. Lies to enable a judgment debtor to recover back his lands taken under an *elegit* when the judgment creditor has satisfied or been paid the amount of his judgment. Chit. 692; Fost. on Sci.Fa. 58.

SCIRE FACIAS FOR THE CROWN. In English law. The summary proceeding by extent is only resorted to when a crown debtor is insolvent, or there is good ground for supposing that the debt may be lost by delay. In ordinary cases where a debt or duty appears by record to be owing to the crown, the process for the crown is a writ of *sci. fa. quare executionem non;* but should the defendant become insolvent pending this writ, the crown may abandon the proceeding and resort to an extent. Wharton.

SCIRE FACIAS QUARE RESTITUTIONEM NON. This writ lies where execution on a judgment has been levied, but the money has not been paid over to the plaintiff, and the judgment is afterwards reversed in error or on appeal; in such a case a *scire facias* is necessary before a writ of restitution can issue. Chit. 582; Fost. on Sci. Fa. 64.

SCIRE FACIAS SUR MORTGAGE. A writ issued upon the default of a mortgagor to make payments or observe conditions, requiring him to show cause why the mortgage should not be foreclosed, and the mortgaged property taken and sold in execution.

SCIRE FACIAS SUR MUNICIPAL CLAIM. A writ of *scire facias,* authorized to be issued in Pennsylvania, as a means of enforcing payment of a municipal claim (*q. v.*) out of the real estate upon which such claim is a lien.

SCIRE FECI. Lat. In practice. The name given to the sheriff's return to a writ of *scire facias* that he has caused notice to be given to the party or parties against whom the writ was issued. 2 Archb. Pr. K. B. 98, 99.

SCIRE FIERI INQUIRY. In English law. The name of a writ formerly used to recover the amount of a judgment from an executor.

SCIRE LEGES NON HOC EST VERBA EARUM TENERE, SED VIM AC POTESTATEM. To know the laws is not to observe their mere words, but their force and power; [that is, the essential meaning in which their efficacy resides.] Dig. 1, 3, 17; 1 Kent, Comm. 462.

SCIRE PROPRIE EST REM RATIONE ET PER CAUSAM COGNOSCERE. To know properly is to know a thing in its reason, and by its cause. We are truly said to know anything, where we know the true cause thereof. Co.Litt. 183*b*.

SCIREWYTE. In old English law. A tax or prestation paid to the sheriff for holding the assizes or county courts. Cowell.

SCISSIO. Lat. In old English law. A cutting. *Scissio auricularum*, cropping of the ears. An old punishment. Fleta, lib. 1, c. 38, § 10.

SCITE, or SITE. The sitting or standing on any place; the seat or situation of a capital messuage, or the ground whereon it stands. Jacob.

SCOLD. A troublesome and angry woman, who, by brawling and wrangling among her neighbors, breaks the public peace, increases discord, and becomes a public nuisance to the neighborhood. 4 Steph.Comm. 276.

Common Scold

One who, by the practice of frequent scolding, disturbs the neighborhood. Bish. Crim. Law, § 147. A quarrelsome, brawling, vituperative person. Baker v. State, 53 N.J.Law, 45, 20 A. 858.

SCOPE.

Of Authority

Includes not only actual authorization conferred upon agent by his principal, but also that which has apparently or impliedly been delegated to agent. Angerosa v. White Co., 290 N.Y.S. 204, 208, 248 App.Div. 425.

Of a Patent

The boundaries or limits of the invention protected by the patent, which are not matters of metes and bounds and can never be defined in the definite sense employed in thinking of physical things, but must be determined by methods based upon established principles of patent law. Smith v. Mid-Continent Inv. Co., C.C.A.Mo., 106 F.2d 622, 624.

SCORN, *v.* To hold in extreme contempt, to reject as unworthy of regard; to despise, to contemn, to disdain. U. S. v. Strong, D.C.Wash., 263 F. 789, 796.

SCOT. In old English law. A tax, or tribute; one's *share* of a contribution.

SCOT AND LOT. In English law. The name of a customary contribution, laid upon all subjects according to their ability. Brown.

SCOT AND LOT VOTERS. In English law. Voters in certain boroughs entitled to the franchise in virtue of their paying this contribution. 2 Steph.Comm. 360.

SCOTAL. In old English law. An extortionate practice by officers of the forest who kept alehouses, and compelled the people to drink at their houses for fear of their displeasure. Prohibited by the charter of the forest, c. 7. Wharton.

See *Charta de foresta*.

SCOTCH MARRIAGES. See Gretna Green.

SCOTCH PEERS. Peers of the kindom of Scotland; of these sixteen are elected to parliament by the rest and represent the whole body. They are elected for one parliament only.

SCOTS. In English law. Assessments by commissioners of sewers.

SCOTTARE. To pay scot, tax, or customary dues. Cowell.

SCOUNDREL. An opprobrious epithet, implying rascality, villainy, or a want of honor or integrity. In slander, this word is not actionable *per se*. 2 Bouv.Inst. 2250.

SCRAMBLING POSSESSION. See Possession.

SCRATCHING THE TICKET. Where partisan voters support and vote for one or more of nominees of opposite political party. Swindall v. State Election Board, 168 Okl. 97, 32 P.2d 691, 696.

SCRAWL. Scroll, which title see.

SCREWBALL. Either a peculiar or eccentric person like crackbrain, crackpot, crank, nut, or a stupid or insane person like batty, bug-house, dippy, etc., but it does not connote opprobrium or reprehensibility. Kennedy v. Crouch, Md., 62 A.2d 582, 587.

SCRIBA. Lat. A scribe; a secretary. *Scriba regis*, a king's secretary; a chancellor. Spelman.

SCRIBERE EST AGERE. To write is to act. Treasonable words set down in writing amount to overt acts of treason. 2 Rolle, 89; 4 Bl.Comm. 80; Broom, Max. 312, 967.

SCRIP. Certificates of ownership, either absolute or conditional, of shares in a public company, corporate profits, etc. An acknowledgment by the projectors of a company or the issuers of a loan that the person named therein (or more commonly the holder for the time being of the certificate) is entitled to a certain specified number of shares, debentures, bonds, etc. It is usually given in exchange for the letter of allotment, and in its turn is given up for the shares, debentures, or bonds which it represents. Scrip certificate. Lindl. Partn. 127; Sweet.

The term has also been applied in the United States to warrants or other like orders drawn on a municipal treasury (City of Alma v. Guaranty Sav. Bank, C.C.A.8, 60 F. 207, 8 C.C.A. 564,) to certificates showing the holder to be entitled to a certain portion or allotment of public or state lands, Wait v. State Land Office Com'r, 87 Mich. 353, 49 N.W. 600, and to the fractional paper currency issued by the United States during the period of the Civil War.

SCRIP DIVIDEND. See Dividend.

SCRIPT. Where instruments are executed in part and counterpart, the original or principal is so called.

English Probate Practice

A will, codicil, draft of will or codicil, or written instructions for the same. If the will is destroyed, a copy or any paper embodying its contents becomes a script, even though not made under the direction of the testator. Browne, Prob. Pr. 280.

SCRIPTÆ OBLIGATIONES SCRIPTIS TOLLUNTUR, ET NUDI CONSENSUS OBLIGATIO CONTRARIO CONSENSU DISSOLVITUR. Written obligations are superseded by writings, and an obligation of naked assent is dissolved by assent to the contrary.

SCRIPTORIUM. In old records. A place in monasteries, where writing was done. Spelman.

SCRIPTUM. Lat. A writing; something written. Fleta, l. 2, c. 60, § 25.

SCRIPTUM INDENTATUM. A writing indented; an indenture or deed.

SCRIPTUM OBLIGATORIUM. A writing obligatory. The technical name of a bond in old pleadings. Any writing under seal.

SCRIVENER. A writer; scribe; conveyancer. One whose occupation is to draw contracts, write deeds and mortgages, and prepare other species of written instruments.

Also an agent to whom property is intrusted by others for the purpose of lending it out at an interest payable to his principal, and for a commission or bonus for himself, whereby he gains his livelihood.

Money Scrivener

A money broker. The name was also formerly applied in England to a person (generally an attorney or solicitor) whose business was to find investments for the money of his clients, and see to perfecting the securities, and who was often intrusted with the custody of the securities and the collection of the interest and principal. Williams v. Walker, 2 Sandf.Ch. (N.Y.) 325.

SCROLL. A mark intended to supply the place of a seal, made with a pen or other instrument of writing. Mitch. R. E. and Conv. 454, 455.

A paper or parchment containing some writing, and rolled up so as to conceal it.

SCROOP'S INN. An obsolete law society, also called "Serjeants' Place," opposite to St. Andrew's Church, Holborn, London.

SCRUET-ROLL. In old practice. A species of roll or record, on which the bail on *habeas corpus* was entered.

SCRUTATOR. Lat. In old English law. A searcher or bailiff of a river; a water-bailiff, whose business was to look to the king's rights, as to his wrecks, his flotsam, jetsam, water-strays, royal fishes. Hale, de Jure Mar. par. 1, c. 5.

SCURRILOUS. The low and indecent language of the meaner sort of people, low indecency or abuse; mean; foul; vile, synonymous with vulgar; foul or foul-mouthed. U. S. v. Strong, D.C. Wash., 263 F. 789. 796; U. S. v. Ault, D.C.Wash., 263 F. 800, 810.

SCUSSUS. In old European law. Shaken or beaten out; threshed, as grain. Spelman.

SCUTAGE. In feudal law. A tax or contribution raised by those that held lands by knight's service, towards furnishing the king's army, at the rate of one, two or three marks for every knight's fee.

A pecuniary composition or commutation made by a tenant by knight-service in lieu of actual service. 2 Bl.Comm. 74.

A pecuniary aid or tribute originally reserved by particular lords, instead or in lieu of personal service, varying in amount according to the expenditure which the lord had to incur in his personal attendance upon the king in his wars. Wright, Ten. 121–134.

SCUTAGIO HABENDO. A writ that anciently lay against tenants by knight's service to serve in the wars, or send sufficient persons, or pay a certain sum. Fitzh. Nat. Brev. 83.

SCUTE. A French coin of gold, coined A.D. 1427, of the value of 3s. 4d.

SCUTELLA. A scuttle; anything of a flat or broad shape like a shield. Cowell.

SCUTELLA ELEEMOSYNARIA. An alms-basket.

SCUTIFER. In old records. Esquire; the same as "armiger." Spelman.

SCUTUM ARMORUM. A shield or coat of arms. Cowell.

SCYRA. In old English law. Shire; county; the inhabitants of a county.

SCYREGEMOTE. In Saxon law. The meeting or court of the shire. This was the most important court in the Saxon polity, having jurisdiction of both ecclesiastical and secular causes. Its meetings were held twice in the year. Its Latin name was *"curia comitatis."*

SE DEFENDENDO. Lat. In defending himself; in self-defense. Homicide committed *se defendendo* is excusable.

SEA. The ocean; the great mass of water which surrounds the land. Snowdon v. Guion, 50 N.Y. Super.Ct. 143. In marine insurance "sea" includes not only the high seas but the bays, inlets, and rivers as high up as the tide ebbs and flows. Mannheim Ins. Co. v. Charles Clarke & Co., Tex. Civ.App., 157 S.W. 291, 293.

Beyond Sea

In England, this phrase means beyond the limits of the British Isles; in America, outside the limits of the United States or of the particular state, as the case may be.

High Seas

The ocean; public waters. According to the English doctrine, the high sea begins at the distance of three miles from the coast of any country; according to the American view, at low-water mark, except in the case of small harbors and roadsteads inclosed within the *fauces terræ*. U. S. v. Grush, 26 F.Cas. 50; U. S. v. Rodgers, 14 S.Ct. 109, 150 U.S. 249, 37 L.Ed. 1071. The open ocean outside of the *fauces terræ*, as distinguished from arms of the sea; the waters of the ocean without the boundary of any county. Any waters on the sea-coast which are without the boundaries of low-water mark.

Main Sea

The open, uninclosed ocean; or that portion of the sea which is without the *fauces terræ* on the sea-coast, in contradistinction to that which is surrounded or inclosed between narrow headlands or promontories. U. S. v. Grush, 26 F.Cas. 48; U. S. v. Rodgers, 14 S.Ct. 109, 150 U.S. 249, 37 L.Ed. 1071.

Sea-Batteries

Assaults by masters in the merchant service upon seamen at sea.

Sea-Bed

All that portion of land under the sea that lies beyond the sea-shore.

Sea-Brief

Sea-Letter, which title see.

Sea-Greens

In the Scotch law. Grounds overflowed by the sea in spring tides. Bell.

Sea-Laws

Laws relating to the sea, as the laws of Oleron, etc.

Sea-Letter

A species of manifest, containing a description of the ship's cargo, with the port from which it comes and the port of destination. This is one of the documents necessary to be carried by all neutral vessels, in the merchant service, in time of war, as an evidence of their nationality. 4 Kent, Comm. 157; Sleght v. Hartshorne, 2 Johns. (N.Y.) 540.

The last sea letter was issued at the Port of New York in 1806, and the use of sea letters was discontinued by proclamation of President Madison in 1815. 46 U.S.C.A. §§ 61, 62, note. The words "sea letter," however, are still carried in those sections of the Code, but in 1948 were eliminated from the criminal code as obsolete. 18 U.S.C.A. § 507, note.

Sea-Reeve

An officer in maritime towns and places who took care of the maritime rights of the lord of the manor, and watched the shore, and collected wrecks for the lord. Tomlins.

Sea-Rovers

Pirates and robbers at sea.

Sea-Shore

The margin of the sea in its usual and ordinary state. When the tide is out, low-water mark is the margin of the sea; and, when the sea is full, the margin is high-water mark. The sea-shore is therefore all the ground between the ordinary high-water mark and low-water mark. It cannot be considered as including any ground always covered by the sea, for then it would have no definite limit on the sea-board. Neither can it include any part of the upland, for the same reason. Commonwealth of Massachusetts v. State of New York, 46 S.Ct. 357, 362, 271 U.S. 65, 70 L.Ed. 838; That space of land over which the waters of the sea are spread in the highest water during the winter season. Civ.Code La. art. 442.

Seaworthy, Seaworthiness

See those titles.

SEAL. An impression upon wax, wafer, or some other tenacious substance capable of being impressed. Solon v. Williamsburgh Sav. Bank, 114 N.Y. 132, 21 N.E. 168.

A particular sign, made to attest in the most formal manner, the execution of an instrument.

Merlin defines a seal to be a plate of metal with a flat surface, on which is engraved the arms of a prince or nation, or private individual, or other device, with which an impression may be made on wax or other substance on paper or parchment in order to authenticate them. The impression thus made is also called a "seal." Répert. *mot "Sceau."*

"Seals" serve as an authentication of an instrument and also as the badge of a specialty. Caruthers v. Peninsular Life Ins. Co., 150 Fla. 467, 7 So.2d 841, 842.

Common Seal

A seal adopted and used by a corporation for authenticating its corporate acts and executing legal instruments.

Corporate Seal

The official or common seal of an incorporated company or association.

Great Seal

In English law. A seal by virtue of which a great part of the royal authority is exercised. The office of the lord chancellor, or lord keeper, is created by the delivery of the great seal into his custody. There is one great seal for all public acts of state which concern the United Kingdom. Mozley & Whiteley. In American law, the United

States and also each of the states has and uses a seal, always carefully described by law, and sometimes officially called the "great" seal, though in some instances known simply as "the seal of the United States," or "the seal of the state."

Private Seal

The seal (however made) of a private person or corporation, as distinguished from a seal employed by a state or government or any of its bureaus or departments.

Privy Seal

In English law. A seal used in making out grants or letters patent, preparatory to their passing under the great seal. 2 Bl.Comm. 347.

Public Seal

A seal belonging to and used by one of the bureaus or departments of government, for authenticating or attesting documents, process, or records. An impression made of some device, by means of a piece of metal or other hard substance, kept and used by public authority. Kirksey v. Bates, 7 Port. (Ala.) 534, 31 Am.Dec. 722.

Quarter Seal

In Scotch law. A seal kept by the director of the chancery; in shape and impression the fourth part of the great seal, and called in statutes the "testimonial" of the great seal. Bell.

Seal Days

In English practice. Motion days in the court of chancery, so called because every motion had to be stamped with the seal, which did not lie in court in the ordinary sittings out of term. Wharton.

Seal Office

In English practice. An office for the sealing of judicial writs.

Seal-Paper

In English law. A document issued by the lord chancellor, previously to the commencement of the sittings, detailing the business to be done for each day in his court, and in the courts of the lords justices and vice-chancellors. The master of the rolls in like manner issued a seal-paper in respect of the business to be heard before him. Smith, Ch.Pr. 9.

SEALED. Authenticated by a seal; executed by the affixing of a seal. Also fastened up in any manner so as to be closed against inspection of the contents.

SEALED AND DELIVERED. These words, followed by the signatures of the witnesses, constitute the usual formula for the attestation of conveyances.

SEALED INSTRUMENT. An instrument of writing to which the party to be bound has affixed not only his name, but also his seal, or (in those jurisdictions where it is allowed) a scroll. Leonor v. Ingenio Porvenir C. por A., Sup., 34 N.Y.S.2d 705, 709. And instrument must contain recital to effect that it is given under seal. Marshall v. Walker, 50 Ga.App. 551, 178 S.E. 760.

SEALED VERDICT. When the jury have agreed upon a verdict, if the court is not in session at the time, they are permitted (usually) to put their written finding in a sealed envelope, and then separate. This verdict they return when the court again convenes. The verdict thus returned has the same effect, and must be treated in the same manner, as if returned in open court before any separation of the jury had taken place. Sutliff v. Gilbert, 8 Ohio, 408; Young v. Seymour, 4 Neb. 89. But see Spielter v. North German Lloyd S. S. Co., 249 N.Y.S. 358, 365, 232 App.Div. 104, holding that it is mere agreement reached by jurors, and does not become final until it is read into record and jurors discharged.

SEALING. In matters of succession, the placing, by the proper officer, of seals on the effects of a succession for the purpose of preserving them, and for the interest of third persons. The seals are affixed by order of the judge having jurisdiction. Civ.Code La. art. 1075.

SEALING UP. Where a party to an action has been ordered to produce a document part of which is either irrelevant to the matters in question or is privileged from production, he may, by leave of the court, seal up that part, if he makes an affidavit stating that it is irrelevant or privileged. Daniell, Ch. Pr. 1681. The sealing up is generally done by fastening pieces of paper over the part with gum or wafers. Sweet.

SEALS. In Louisiana. Seals are placed upon the effects of a deceased person, in certain cases, by a public officer, as a method of taking official custody of the succession. See Sealing.

SEAMEN. Sailors; mariners; persons whose business is navigating ships, or who are connected with the ship as such and in some capacity assist in its conduct, maintenance or service. Commonly exclusive of the officers of a ship. The Hurricane, D.C.Pa., 2 F.2d 70, 72; City of Los Angeles v. United Dredging Co., C.C.A.Cal., 14 F 2d 364, 366; The Lillian, D.C.Me., 16 F.2d 146, 148. One whose occupation is to navigate vessels upon the sea including all those on board whose labor contributes to the accomplishment of the main object in which the vessel is engaged. Osland v. Star Fish & Oyster Co., C.C.A.Ala., 107 F.2d 113, 114. One whose duties are maritime in character and are rendered on a vessel in navigable waters. Helena Glendale Ferry Co. v. Walling, C.C.A.Ark. 132 F.2d 616, 619, 620.

A vessel must be in motion or capable of motion and regarded legally as in motion in order that those employed in its use may be regarded as "seamen". Spinner v. Waterways Fuel & Dock Co., 70 Ohio App. 121, 41 N.E. 2d 144, 145, 146.

SEANCE. In French law. A session; as of some public body.

SEARCH.

Criminal Law

An examination of a man's house or other buildings or premises, or of his person, with a view to the discovery of contraband or illicit or stolen property, or some evidence of guilt to be used in the prosecution of a criminal action for some crime or offense with which he is charged. Elliott v. State, 173 Tenn. 203, 116 S.W.2d 1009, 1011. A prying into hidden places for that which is concealed and it is not a search to observe that which is open to view. People v. Exum, 382 Ill. 204, 47 N.E.2d 56, 59.

International Law

The right of search is the right on the part of ships of war to visit and search merchant vessels during war, in order to ascertain whether the ship or cargo is liable to seizure. Resistance to visitation and search by a neutral vessel makes the vessel and cargo liable to confiscation. Numerous treaties regulate the manner in which the right of search must be exercised. Man. Int. Law, 433; Sweet.

Practice

An examination of the official books and dockets, made in the process of investigating a title to land, for the purpose of discovering if there are any mortgages, judgments, tax-liens, or other incumbrances upon it.

General

Unlawful search. Within constitutional immunity from unreasonable searches and seizures, an examination or inspection without authority of law of premises or person with view to discovery of stolen, contraband, or illicit property, or for some evidence of guilt to be used in prosecution of criminal action. Const.U.S. Amend. 4. Bush v. State, 64 Okl.Cr. 161, 77 P.2d 1184, 1187.

Unreasonable search and seizure. At common law, a search which is unreasonably oppressive in its general invasion of the liberty of the citizen. McClannan v. Chaplain, 136 Va. 1, 116 S.E. 495, 498. An examination or inspection, without authority of law, of one's premises or person with a view to the discovery of stolen contraband or illicit property or for some evidence of guilt to be used in prosecution for crime. Graham v. State, 31 Okl.Cr. 125, 237 P. 462, 464. One which is not lawful. United States v. Snyder, D.C.W.Va., 278 F. 650, 658; Hays v. State, 38 Okl.Cr. 331, 261 P. 232, 234.

SEARCH-WARRANT. An order in writing, issued by a justice or other magistrate, in the name of the state, directed to a sheriff, constable, or other officer, commanding him to search a specified house, shop, or other premises, for personal property alleged to have been stolen, or for unlawful goods, and to bring the same, when found, before the magistrate, and usually also the body of the person occupying the premises, to be dealt with according to law. People v. Lavendowsky, 329 Ill. 223, 160 N.E. 582, 585.

SEARCHER. In English law. An officer of the customs, whose duty it is to examine and search all ships outward bound, to ascertain whether they have any prohibited or uncustomed goods on board. Wharton. Jacob.

SEASHORE. That portion of land adjacent to the sea which is alternately covered and left dry by the ordinary flux and reflux of the tides. Wood v. Maitland, 8 N.Y.S.2d 146, 151, 169 Misc. 484. See, also, Sea.

SEASONAL EMPLOYMENT. As used in compensation laws, as basis for determining amount of compensation, refers to occupations which can be carried on only at certain seasons or fairly definite portions of the year, and does not include such occupations as may be carried on throughout entire year. Hiestand v. Ristau, 135 Neb. 881, 284 N.W. 756, 760. Pryor v. Brickley, Del., 5 A.2d 242, 244, 1 Terry 5.

SEATED LAND. Land that is occupied, cultivated, improved, reclaimed, farmed, or used as a place of residence. Residence without cultivation, or cultivation without residence, or both together, impart to land the character of being seated. The term is used, as opposed to "unseated land," in Pennsylvania tax laws. Earley v. Euwer, 102 Pa. 340; Coal Co. v. Fales, 55 Pa. 98.

SEAWAN. The name used by the Algonquin Indians for the shell beads (or wampum) which passed among the Indians as money. Webster.

SEAWORTHINESS. In marine insurance. A warranty of seaworthiness means that the vessel is competent to resist the ordinary attacks of wind and weather, and is competently equipped and manned for the voyage, with a sufficient crew, and with sufficient means to sustain them, and with a captain of general good character and nautical skill. 3 Kent, Comm. 287.

A warranty of seaworthiness extends not only to the condition of the structure of the ship itself, but requires that it be properly laden, and provided with a competent master, a sufficient number of competent officers and seamen, and the requisite appurtenances and equipments, such as ballast, cables and anchors, cordage and sails, food, water, fuel, and lights, and other necessary or proper stores and implements for the voyage. See, also, Seaworthy.

"Seaworthiness" involves no more than reasonable fitness for purpose of a voyage. In re Gravel Products Corporation, C.C.A.N.Y., 24 F.2d 702, 703.

SEAWORTHY. This adjective, applied to a vessel, signifies that she is properly constructed, prepared, manned, equipped, and provided, for the voyage intended. See Seaworthiness.

The term "seaworthy" is somewhat equivocal. In its more literal sense, it signifies capable of navigating the sea; but, more exactly, it implies a condition to be and remain in safety, in the condition she is in, whether at sea, in port, or on a railway, stripped and under repairs. If, when the policy attaches, she is in a suitable place, and capable, when repaired and equipped, of navigating the sea, she is seaworthy. But where a vessel is warranted seaworthy for a specified voyage, the place and usual length being given, something more is implied than mere physical strength and capacity; she must be suitably officered and manned, supplied with provisions and water, and furnished with charts and instruments, and, especially in time of war, with documents necessary to her security against hostile capture. The term "seaworthy," as used in the law and practice of insurance, does not mean, as the term would seem to imply, capable of going to sea or of being navigated on the sea; it imports something very different, and much more, viz., that she is sound, staunch, and strong, in all respects, and equipped, furnished, and provided with officers and men, provisions and documents, for a certain service. In a policy for a definite voyage, the term "seaworthy" means "sufficient for such a vessel and voyage." Newport News Shipbuilding & Dry Dock Co. v. Watson, C.C.A.Va., 19 F.2d 832, 833; The Newport, C.C.A.Cal., 7 F.2d 452, 453.

SEBASTOMANIA. See Insanity.

SECK. A want of remedy by distress. Litt. § 218. See Rent. Want of present fruit or profit, as in the case of the reversion without rent or other service, except fealty. Co.Litt. 151*b*, n. 5.

SECOND. This term, as used in law, may denote either sequence in point of time or inferiority or postponement in respect to rank, lien, order, or privilege.

As to second "Cousin," "Deliverance," "Distress," "Mortgage," and "Surcharge," see those titles. As to "Secondhand Evidence," see Evidence. As to "Second of Exchange," see First.

SECOND LIEN. One which takes rank immediately after a first lien on the same property and is next entitled to satisfaction out of the proceeds.

SECONDARY, *n.* In English practice. An officer of the courts of king's bench and common pleas; so called because he was *second* or next to the chief officer. In the king's bench he was called "Master of the King's Bench Office," and was a deputy of the prothonotary or chief clerk. 1 Archb. Pr. K. B. 11, 12. By St. 7 Wm. IV. and 1 Vict. c. 30, the office of secondary was abolished.

An officer who is next to the chief officer. Also an officer of the corporation of London, before whom inquiries to assess damages are held, as before sheriffs in counties. Wharton.

SECONDARY, *adj.* Of a subsequent, subordinate, or inferior kind or class; generally opposed to "primary."

As to secondary "Conveyances," "Easement," "Franchise," "Meaning," "Use," and "Vein," see those titles.

SECONDARY BOYCOTT. Any combination if its purpose and effect are to coerce customers or patrons, or suppliers through fear of loss or bodily harm, to withhold or withdraw their business relations from employer who is under attack. Wright v. Teamsters' Union Local No. 690, 33 Wash. 905, 207 P.2d 662, 665.

SECONDARY EVIDENCE. That which is inferior to primary. Thus, a copy of an instrument, or oral evidence of its contents, is secondary evidence of the instrument and contents. It is that species of evidence which becomes admissible, as being the next best, when the primary or best evidence of the fact in question is lost or inaccessible; as when a witness details orally the contents of an instrument which is lost or destroyed. Williams v. Davis, 56 Tex. 253; Baucum v. George, 65 Ala. 259; Roberts v. Dixon, 50 Kan. 436, 31 P. 1083.

SECONDARY LIABILITY. A liability which does not attach until or except upon the fulfillment of certain conditions; as that of a surety, or that of an accommodation indorser.

SECOND-HAND EVIDENCE. Evidence which has passed through one or more media before reaching the witness; hearsay evidence.

SECONDS. In criminal law. Those persons who assist, direct, and support others engaged in fighting a duel.

SECRET. Concealed; hidden; not made public; particularly, in law, kept from the knowledge or notice of persons liable to be affected by the act, transaction, deed, or other thing spoken of.

Webster defines "secrete" as "to deposit in a place of hiding, to hide, to conceal"; and defines the adjective "secret" as "hidden, concealed"; and the noun as "something studiously concealed, a thing kept from general knowledge, what is not revealed." The Century Dictionary defines the verb "secrete" as "to make or keep secret, hide, conceal, remove from observation, or the knowledge of others"; and defines the adjective "secret" as "set or kept apart, hidden, concealed"; and the noun as "something studiously hidden or concealed, a thing kept from general knowledge, what is not or should not be revealed." Something known only to one or a few and kept from others. Ferrell v. State, 68 Tex.Cr.R. 487, 152 S.W. 901, 903; Kaumagraph Co. v. Stampagraph Co., 235 N.Y. 1, 138 N.E. 485, 487; Rubner v. Gursky, Sup., 21 N.Y.S.2d 558, 561.

As to secret "Committee," "Equity," "Partnership," and "Trust," see those titles.

SECRET LIEN. A lien reserved by the vendor of chattels, who has delivered them to the vendee, to secure the payment of the price, which is concealed from all third persons.

SECRET SERVICE. A branch of government service concerned with the detection of counterfeiting and other offenses, civil or political, committed or threatened by persons who operate in secrecy. It is under the charge of the treasury department. Its rules and regulations, promulgated by the department, are laws within R. S. U. S. § 753 (28 U.S.C.A. § 2241), authorizing the issuance by a federal court of the writ of *habeas corpus* in case of a prisoner in custody for an act done in pursuance of a law of the United States; U. S. ex rel. Flynn v. Fuellhart, C.C.Pa., 106 F. 911.

SECRETARY. An official scribe, amanuensis, or writer, or person employed to write letters, dispatches, orders, public or private papers, records, and the like. Mauritz v. Schwind, Tex.Civ.App., 101 S.W.2d 1085, 1090.

Of a corporation or association, an officer charged with the direction and management of that part of the business of the company which is concerned with keeping the records, the official correspondence, with giving and receiving notices, countersigning documents, etc.

Also a name given to several of the heads of executive departments in the government of the United States; as the "Secretary of War," "Secretary of the Interior," etc. It is also the style of some of the members of the English cabinet; as the "Secretary of State for Foreign Affairs." There are also secretaries of embassies and legations.

SECRETARY OF DECREES AND INJUNCTIONS. An officer of the English court of chancery. The office was abolished by St. 15 & 16 Vict. c. 87, § 23.

SECRETARY OF EMBASSY. A diplomatic officer appointed as secretary or assistant to an ambassador or minister plenipotentiary.

SECRETARY OF LEGATION. An officer employed to attend a foreign mission and to perform certain duties as clerk.

SECRETARY OF STATE. In American law. Title of the chief of the executive bureau of the United States called the "Department of State." He is a member of the cabinet, and is charged with the general administration of the international and diplomatic affairs of the government. In many of the state governments there is an executive officer bearing the same title and exercising important functions. In English law. The secretaries of state are cabinet ministers attending the sovereign for the receipt and dispatch of letters, grants, petitions, and many of the most important affairs of the kingdom, both foreign and domestic. There are five principal secretaries,—one for the home department, another for foreign affairs, a third for the colonies, a fourth for war, and a fifth for India. Wharton.

SECRETE. To conceal or hide away. Particularly, to put property out of the reach of creditors, either by corporally hiding it, or putting the title in another's name, or otherwise hindering creditors from levying on it or attaching it. Guile v. McNanny, 14 Minn. 522 (Gil. 391) 100 Am.Dec. 244; Sturz v. Fischer, 36 N.Y.S. 894, 15 Misc. 410.

SECRETS OF STATE. The production in court of documents containing secrets of state will not be compelled if it would be injurious to the public interest and if the officer in custody of them claims the privilege. Beatson v. Skene, 5 H. & N. 838, per Pollock, C. B. This is said to include confidential communications made by servants of the Crown to each other. 21 Q. B. D. 512. The question of their production is to be decided by the head of the department having custody of them and not by the court. 5 H. & N. 838; [1900] 1 Ch. 347; 13 Low. Can. 33 (where the cases were fully considered). Appeal of Hartranft, 85 Pa. 433, 27 Am.Rep. 667 (in which Agnew, C. J., vigorously dissented), where a ruling in the trial of Aaron Burr was cited as a precedent. That it is for the judge to pass on the question, see Wigm. Evid. § 2376. In 21 Q. B. D. 515, Field, J., said that if he were sitting, he should consider himself entitled to examine the documents privately, and ascertain the real motive of the refusal to produce.

SECT. As applied to religious bodies. A party or body of persons who unite in holding certain special doctrines or opinions concerning religion, which distinguish them from others holding the same general religious belief. Gerhardt v. Heid, 66 N.D. 444, 267 N.W. 127.

SECTA. In old English law. Suit; attendance at court; the plaintiff's suit or following, *i. e.*, the witnesses whom he was required, in the ancient practice, to bring with him and produce in court, for the purpose of confirming his claim, before the defendant was put to the necessity of answering the declaration. 3 Bl. Comm. 295, 344; Bract. fol. 214*a*. A survival from this proceeding is seen in the formula still used at the end of declarations, "and therefore he brings his suit," (*et inde producit sectam.*) This word, in its secondary meaning, signifies suit in the courts; lawsuit.

SECTA AD CURIAM. A writ that lay against him who refused to perform his suit either to the county court or the court-baron. Cowell.

SECTA AD FURNUM. In old English law. Suit due to a man's public oven or bake-house. 3 Bl. Comm. 235.

SECTA AD JUSTICIAM FACIENDAM. In old English law. A service which a man is bound to perform by his fee.

SECTA AD MOLENDINUM. A writ which lay for the owner of a mill against the inhabitants of a place where such mill is situated, for not doing suit to the plaintiff's mill; that is, for not having their corn ground at it. Brown.

SECTA AD TORRALE. In old English law. Suit due to a man's kiln or malthouse. 3 Bl. Comm. 235.

SECTA CURIÆ. In old English law. Suit of court; attendance at court. The service, incumbent upon feudal tenants, of attending the lord at his court, both to form a jury when required, and also to answer for their own actions when complained of.

SECTA EST PUGNA CIVILIS; SICUT ACTORES ARMANTUR ACTIONIBUS, ET, QUASI, GLADIIS ACCINGUNTUR, ITA REI MUNIUNTUR EXCEPTIONIBUS, ET DEFENDUNTUR, QUASI, CLYPEIS. Hob. 20. A suit is a civil warfare; for as the plaintiffs are armed with actions, and, as it were, girded with swords, so the defendants are fortified with pleas, and are defended, as it were, by shields.

SECTA FACIENDA PER ILLAM QUÆ HABET ENICIAM PARTEM. A writ to compel the heir, who has the elder's part of the co-heirs, to perform suit and services for all the coparceners. Reg. Orig. 177.

SECTA QUÆ SCRIPTO NITITUR A SCRIPTO VARIARI NON DEBET. Jenk. Cent. 65. A suit which is based upon a writing ought not to vary from the writing.

SECTA REGALIS. A suit so called by which all persons were bound twice in the year to attend in the sheriff's tourn, in order that they might be informed of things relating to the public peace. It was so called because the sheriff's tourn was the king's leet, and it was held in order that the people might be bound by oath to bear true allegiance to the king. Cowell.

SECTA UNICA TANTUM FACIENDA PRO PLURIBUS HÆREDITATIBUS. A writ for an heir who was distrained by the lord to do more suits than one, that he should be allowed to do one suit only in respect of the land of divers heirs descended to him. Cowell.

SECTARIAN. Denominational; devoted to, peculiar to, pertaining to, or promotive of, the interest of a sect, or sects; in a broader sense, used to describe the activities of the followers of one faith as related to those of adherents of another. The term is most comprehensive in scope. Gerhardt v. Heid, 66 N.D. 444, 267 N.W. 127, 130.

See, also, Sect.

SECTATORES. Suitors of court who, among the Saxons, gave their judgment or verdict in civil suits upon the matter of fact and law. 1 Reeve, Eng. Law, 22.

SECTION. In text-books, codes, statutes, and other juridical writings, the smallest distinct and numbered subdivisions are commonly called "sections," sometimes "articles," and occasionally "paragraphs." Ex parte Pea River Power Co., 207 Ala. 6, 91 So. 920.

SECTION OF LAND. In American land law. A division or parcel of land, on the government survey, comprising one square mile or 640 acres. Each "township" (six miles square) is divided by straight lines into thirty-six sections, and these are again divided into half-sections and quarter-sections. South Florida Farms Co. v. Goodno, 84 Fla. 532, 94 So. 672, 675.

The general and proper acceptation of the terms "section," "half," and "quarter section," as well as their construction by the general land department, denotes the land in the sectional and subdivisional lines, and not the exact quantity which a perfect admeasurement of an unobstructed surface would declare. Brown v. Hardin, 21 Ark. 327.

SECTIS NON FACIENDIS. A writ which lay for a dowress, or one in wardship, to be free from suit of court. Cowell.

SECTORES. Lat. In Roman law. Purchasers at auction, or public sales.

SECULAR. Not spiritual; not ecclesiastical; relating to affairs of the present world. State v. Smith, 19 Okl.Cr. 184, 198 P. 879, 881.

SECULAR BUSINESS. As used in Sunday laws, this term includes all forms of activity in the business affairs of life, the prosecution of a trade or employment, and commercial dealings, such as the making of promissory notes, lending money, and the like. Lovejoy v. Whipple, 18 Vt. 383, 46 Am.Dec. 157.

SECULAR CLERGY. In ecclesiastical law, the parochial clergy, who perform their ministry *in seculo* (in the world), and who are thus distinguished from the monastic or "regular" clergy. Steph. Comm. 681, note.

SECUNDUM. Lat. In the civil and common law. According to. Occurring in many phrases of familiar use, as follows:

SECUNDUM ÆQUUM ET BONUM. According to what is just and right.

SECUNDUM ALLEGATA ET PROBATA. According to what is alleged and proved; according to the allegations and proofs. 15 East, 81; Cloutman v. Tunison, 1 Sumn. 375, F.Cas.No.2,907.

SECUNDUM ARTEM. According to the art, trade, business, or science.

SECUNDUM BONOS MORES. According to good usages; according to established custom; regularly; orderly.

SECUNDUM CONSUETUDINEM MANERII. According to the custom of the manor.

SECUNDUM FORMAM CHARTÆ. According to the form of the charter, (deed.)

SECUNDUM FORMAM DONI. According to the form of the gift or grant. See Formedon.

SECUNDUM FORMAM STATUTI. According to the form of the statute.

SECUNDUM LEGEM COMMUNEM. According to the common law.

SECUNDUM NATURAM EST COMMODA CUJUSQUE REI EUM SEQUI, QUEM SEQUUNTUR INCOMMODA. It is according to nature that the advantages of anything should attach to him to whom the disadvantages attach. Dig. 50, 17, 10.

SECUNDUM NORMAM LEGIS. According to the rule of law; by the intendment and rule of law.

SECUNDUM REGULAM. According to the rule; by rule.

SECUNDUM SUBJECTAM MATERIAM. According to the subject-matter. 1 Bl. Comm. 229. All agreements must be construed *secundum subjectam materiam* if the matter will bear it. 2 Mod. 80, arg.

SECURE. To give security; to assure of payment, performance, or indemnity; to guaranty or make certain the payment of a debt or discharge of an obligation. Ex parte Reynolds, 52 Ark. 330, 12 S.W. 570.

One "secures" his creditor by giving him a lien, mortgage, pledge, or other security, to be used in case the debtor fails to make payment.

Also, not exposed to danger; safe; so strong, stable or firm as to insure safety. Wenzel & Henoch Const. Co. v. Industrial Commission, 202 Wis. 595, 233 N.W. 777, 779.

SECURED CREDITOR. A creditor who holds some special pecuniary assurance of payment of his debt, such as a mortgage or lien. In re New York Title and Mortgage Co., 160 Misc. 67, 289 N.Y.S. 771, 785, 160 Misc. 67.

SECURITAS. In old English law. Security; surety.

In the civil law. An acquittance or release. Spelman; Calvin.

SECURITATEM INVENIENDI. An ancient writ, lying for the sovereign, against any of his subjects, to stay them from going out of the kingdom to foreign parts; the ground whereof is that every man is bound to serve and defend the commonwealth as the crown shall think fit. Fitzh. Nat. Brev. 115.

SECURITATIS PACIS. In old English law. Security of the peace. A writ that lay for one who was threatened with death or bodily harm by another, against him who so threatened. Reg. Orig. 88.

SECURITIES. Evidences of debts or of property. State v. Allen, 216 N.C. 621, 5 S.E.2d 844, 845, 847. Evidences of obligations to pay money or of rights to participate in earnings and distribution of corporate, trust, and other property. Oklahoma-Texas Trust v. Securities and Exchange Commission, C.C.A.10, 100 F.2d 888, 890.

SECURITY. Protection; assurance; indemnification. The term is usually applied to an obligation, pledge, mortgage, deposit, lien, etc., given by a debtor in order to make sure the payment or performance of his debt, by furnishing the creditor with a resource to be used in case of failure in the principal obligation. The name is also sometimes given to one who becomes surety or guarantor for another. Bissinger & Co. v. Massachusetts Bonding & Ins. Co., 83 Or. 288, 163 P. 592, 593.

Collateral Security

See Collateral.

Counter Security

See Counter.

Marshaling Securities

See Marshaling.

Personal Security

(1) A person's legal and uninterrupted enjoyment of his life, his limbs, his body, his health, and his reputation. 1 Bl. Comm. 129. Sanderson v. Hunt, 76 S.W. 179, 25 Ky.L.Rep. 626. (2) Evidences of debt which bind the person of the debtor, not real property. Merrill v. National Bank, 19 S. Ct. 360, 173 U.S. 131, 43 L.Ed. 640.

Public Securities

Bonds, notes, certificates of indebtedness, and other negotiable or transferable instruments evidencing the public debt of a state or government.

Real Security

The security of mortgages or other liens or incumbrances upon land. See Merrill v. National Bank, 19 S.Ct. 360, 173 U.S. 131, 43 L.Ed. 640.

Security for Costs

See Costs.

Security for Good Behavior

A bond or recognizance which the magistrate exacts from a defendant brought before him on a charge of disorderly conduct or threatening violence, conditioned upon his being of good behavior, or keeping the peace, for a prescribed period, towards all people in general and the complainant in particular.

Treasury Securities

See that title.

SECURITY COUNCIL. The executive body of the United Nations, charged with the duty of preventing or stopping wars by diplomatic, economic or military action. It is composed of five permanent members and six additional members elected at stated intervals.

SECURITY DEPOSIT. Money deposited by tenant with landlord as security for full and faithful performance by tenant of terms of lease. Bowles v. Westbrook Defense Homes, D.C.Conn., 61 F. Supp. 172, 173.

SECURIUS EXPEDIUNTUR NEGOTIA COMMISSA PLURIBUS, ET PLUS VIDENT OCULI QUAM OCULUS. 4 Coke, 46*a*. Matters intrusted to several are more securely dispatched, and eyes see more than eye, [*i. e.*, "two heads are better than one."]

SECUS. Lat. Otherwise; to the contrary. This word is used in the books to indicate the converse of a foregoing proposition, or the rule applicable to a different state of facts, or an exception to a rule before stated.

SED NON ALLOCATUR. Lat. But it is not allowed. A phrase used in the old reports, to signify that the court disagreed with the arguments of counsel.

SED PER CURIAM. Lat. But by the court. This phrase is used in the reports to introduce a statement made by the court, on the argument, at variance with the propositions advanced by counsel, or the opinion of the whole court, where that is different from the opinion of a single judge immediately before quoted.

SED QUÆRE. Lat. But inquire; examine this further. A remark indicating, briefly, that the particular statement or rule laid down is doubted or challenged in respect to its correctness.

SED VIDE. Lat. But see. This remark, followed by a citation, directs the reader's attention to an authority or a statement which conflicts with or contradicts the statement or principle laid down.

SEDATO ANIMO. Lat. With settled purpose. 5 Mod. 291.

SEDE PLENA. Lat. The see being filled. A phrase used when a bishop's see is not vacant.

SEDENTE CURIA. Lat. The court sitting; during the sitting of the court.

SEDERUNT, ACTS OF. In Scotch law. Certain ancient ordinances of the court of session, conferring upon the courts power to establish general rules of practice. Bell.

SEDES. Lat. A see; the dignity of a bishop. 3 Steph. Comm. 65.

SEDGE FLAT. A tract of land below high-water mark. Church v. Meeker, 34 Conn. 421.

SEDITION. An insurrectionary movement tending towards treason, but wanting an overt act; attempts made by meetings or speeches, or by publications, to disturb the tranquillity of the state. Arizona Pub. Co. v. Harris, 181 P. 373, 375, 20 Ariz. 446.

The distinction between "sedition" and "treason" consists in this: that though the ultimate object of sedition is a violation of the public peace, or at least such a course of measures as evidently engenders it, yet it does not aim at direct and open violence against the laws or the subversion of the constitution. Alis.Crim.Law, 580.

In Scotch law. The raising commotions or disturbances in the state. It is a revolt against legitimate authority. Ersk. Inst. 4, 4, 14.

In English law. The offense of publishing, verbally or otherwise, any words or document with the intention of exciting disaffection, hatred, or contempt against the sovereign, or the government and constitution of the kingdom, or either house of parliament, or the administration of justice, or of exciting his majesty's subjects to attempt, otherwise than by lawful means, the alteration of any matter in church or state, or of exciting feelings of ill will and hostility between different classes of his majesty's subjects. Sweet. State v. Shepherd, 177 Mo. 205, 76 S.W. 79, 99 Am. St.Rep. 624.

SEDITIOUS LIBEL. In English law. A written or printed document containing seditious matter or published with a seditious intention, the latter term being defined as "an intention to bring into hatred or contempt, or to excite disaffection against, the king or the government and constitution as by law established, or either house of parliament, or the administration of justice, or to excite British subjects to attempt otherwise than by lawful means the alteration of any matter in church or state by law established, or to promote feelings of ill will and hostility between different classes." Dicey, Const. (4th Ed.) 231, 232. See Black, Const. Law (3d Ed.) p. 654.

SEDUCE. To induce to surrender chastity. State v. Howard, 264 Mo. 386, 175 S.W. 58, 59. To lead away or astray. Mosley v. Lynn, 172 Ga. 193, 157 S.E. 450, 452. See, also, Seduction.

SEDUCING TO LEAVE SERVICE. An injury for which a master may have an action on the case.

SEDUCTION. The act of seducing. Act of man enticing woman to have unlawful intercourse with him by means of persuasion, solicitation, promises, bribes, or other means without employment of force. Van De Velde v. Colle, 8 N.J.Misc. 782, 152 A. 645, 646.

At common law seduction is recognized merely as creating a civil liability, and actions for seduction are based solely upon relation of master and servant and no one but those entitled to services can maintain action. Under statutory provisions in many states the woman is now permitted to recover for her own seduction.

In many states seduction has been made a criminal offense. Previous chaste character of the woman at time of seduction is essential under some statutes.

SEE. The circuit of a bishop's jurisdiction; or his office or dignity, as being bishop of a given diocese.

SEEN. This word, when written by the drawee on a bill of exchange, amounts to an acceptance by the law merchant. Barnet v. Smith, 30 N.H. 256, 64 Am.Dec. 290; Peterson v. Hubbard, 28 Mich. 197.

SEIGNIOR, in its general signification, means "lord," but in law it is particularly applied to the lord of a fee or of a manor; and the fee, dominions, or manor of a seignior is thence termed a "seigniory," *i. e.*, a lordship. He who is a lord, but of no manor, and therefore unable to keep a court, is termed a "seignior in gross." Kitch. 206; Cowell.

Seignior or *Seigneur*. Among the feudists, this name signified lord of the fee. Fitzh.N.B. 23. Seigneur is still used in French Canada. The most extended signification of this word includes not only a lord or peer of parliament, but is applied to the owner or proprietor of a thing, hence the owner of a hawk, and the master of a fishing vessel, is called a seigneur. 37 Edw. III, c. 19; Barrington, Stat. 258.

SEIGNIORAGE. A royalty or prerogative of the sovereign, whereby an allowance of gold and silver, brought in the mass to be exchanged for coin, is claimed. Cowell. Mintage; the charge for coining bullion into money at the mint.

SEIGNIORESS. A female superior.

SEIGNIORY. In English law. A lordship; a manor. The rights of a lord, as such, in lands. Kavanaugh v. Cohoes Power & Light Corporation, 187 N.Y.S. 216, 231, 114 Misc.Rep. 590.

SEISED IN DEMESNE AS OF FEE. This is the strict technical expression used to describe the ownership in "an estate in fee-simple in possession in a corporeal hereditament." The word "seised" is used to express the "seisin" or owner's possession of a freehold property; the phrase "in demesne," or "in his demesne," (*in dominico suo*) signifies that he is seised as owner of the land itself, and not merely of the seigniory or services; and the concluding words, "as of fee," import that he is seised of an estate of inheritance in fee-simple. Where the subject is incorporeal, or the estate expectant on a precedent freehold, the words "in his demesne" are omitted. (Co. Litt. 17*a*; Fleta, l. 5, c. 5, § 18; Bract. l. 4, tr. 5, c. 2, § 2.) Brown.

SEISI. In old English law. Seised; possessed.

SEISIN. The completion of the feudal investiture, by which the tenant was admitted into the feud, and performed the rights of homage and fealty. Stearns, Real Act. 2. Possession with an intent on the part of him who holds it to claim a freehold interest. Deshong v. Deshong, 186 Pa. 227, 40 A. 402, 65 Am.St.Rep. 855. Right to immediate possession according to the nature of the estate. Williams v. Swango, 365 Ill. 549, 7 N.E.2d 306, 309.

Upon the introduction of the feudal law into England, the word "seisin" was applied only to the possession of an estate of freehold, in contradistinction to that precarious kind of possession by which tenants in villeinage held their lands, which was considered to be the possession of those in whom the freehold continued. The word still retains its original signification, being applied exclusively to the possession of land of a freehold tenure, it being inaccurate to use the word as expressive of the possession of leaseholds or terms of years, or even of copyholds. Brown.

Under our law, the word "seisin" has no accurately defined technical meaning. At common law, it imported a feudal investiture of title by actual possession. With us it has the force of possession under some legal title or right to hold. This possession, so far as possession alone is involved, may be shown by parol; but, if it is intended to show possession under a legal title, then the title must be shown by proper conveyance for that purpose. Ford v. Garner, 49 Ala. 603.

Every person in whom a seisin is required by any of the provisions of this chapter shall be deemed to have been seised, if he may have had any right, title, or interest in the inheritance. G.S.N.C. §§ 29-1, rule 12.

Actual Seisin

Possession of the freehold by the *pedis positio* of one's self or one's tenant or agent, or by construction of law, as in the case of a state grant or a conveyance under the statutes of uses, or (probably) of grant or devise where there is no actual adverse possession; it means actual possession as distinguished from constructive possession or possession in law. Carr v. Anderson, 6 App.Div. 6, 39 N.Y.S. 746.

Constructive Seisin

Seisin in law where there is no seisin in fact; as where the state issues a patent to a person who never takes any sort of possession of the lands granted, he has constructive seisin of all the land in his grant, though another person is at the time in actual possession. Garrett v. Ramsey, 26 W.Va. 351.

Covenant of Seisin

See Covenant.

Equitable Seisin

A seisin which is analogous to legal seisin; that is, seisin of an equitable estate in land. Thus a mortgagor is said to have equitable seisin of the land by receipt of the rents. Sweet.

Livery of Seisin

Delivery of possession; called, by the feudists, "investiture."

Primer Seisin

In English law. The right which the king had, when any of his tenants died seised of a knight's fee, to receive of the heir, provided he were of full age, one whole year's profits of the lands, if they were in immediate possession; and half a year's profits, if the lands were in reversion, expectant on an estate for life. 2 Bl. Comm. 66.

Quasi Seisin

A term applied to the possession which a copyholder has of the land to which he has been admitted. The freehold in copyhold lands being in the lord, the copyholder cannot have seisin of them in the proper sense of the word, but he has a customary or *quasi* seisin analogous to that of a freeholder. Williams, Seis. 126; Sweet.

Seisin in Deed

Actual possession of the freehold; the same as actual seisin or seisin in fact. Roetzel v. Beal, 196 Ark. 5, 116 S.W.2d 591, 593.

Seisin in Fact

Possession with intent on the part of him who holds it to claim a freehold interest; the same as actual seisin. Seim v. O'Grady, 42 W.Va. 77, 24 S.E. 994; Savage v. Savage, 19 Or. 112, 23 P. 890, 20 Am.St.Rep. 795.

Seisin in Law

A right of immediate possession according to the nature of the estate. Martin v. Trail, 142 Mo. 85, 43 S.W. 655; Savage v. Savage, 19 Or. 112, 23 P. 890, 20 Am.St.Rep. 795. As the old doctrine of corporeal investiture is no longer in force, the delivery of a deed gives seisin in law. Watkins v. Nugen, 118 Ga. 372, 45 S.E. 262.

Seisin Ox

In Scotch law. A perquisite formerly due to the sheriff when he gave possession to an heir holding crown lands. It was long since converted into a payment in money, proportioned to the value of the estate. Bell.

SEISINA. L. Lat. Seisin.

SEISINA FACIT STIPITEM. Seisin makes the stock. 2 Bl. Comm. 209; Broom, Max. 525, 528.

SEISINA HABENDA. A writ for delivery of seisin to the lord, of lands and tenements, after the sovereign, in right of his prerogative, had had the year, day, and waste on a felony committed, etc. Reg. Orig. 165.

SEIZE. To put in possession, invest with fee simple, be seized of or in, be legal possessor of, or be holder in fee simple. Hanley v. Stewart, 155 Pa. Super. 535, 39 A.2d 323, 326.

SEIZIN. See Seisin.

SEIZING OF HERIOTS. Taking the best beast, etc., where an heriot is due, on the death of the tenant. 2 Bl. Comm. 422.

SEIZURE. To take possession of forcibly, to grasp, to snatch, or to put in possession. Hardie v. State, 140 Tex.Cr.R. 368, 144 S.W.2d 571, 575.

Law of Copyholds

Seizure is where the lord of copyhold lands takes possession of them in default of a tenant. It is either seizure *quousque* or absolute seizure.

Practice

The act performed by an officer of the law, under the authority and exigence of a writ, in taking into the custody of the law the property, real or personal, of a person against whom the judgment of a competent court has passed, condemning him to pay a certain sum of money, in order that such property may be sold, by authority and due course of law, to satisfy the judgment. Or the act of taking possession of goods in consequence of a violation of public law. Carey v. Insurance Co., 54 N.W. 18, 84 Wis. 80, 20 L.R.A. 267, 36 Am.St. Rep. 907.

Seizure, even though hostile, is not necessarily capture, though such is its usual and probable result. The ultimate act or adjudication of the state, by which the seizure has been made, assigns the proper and conclusive quality and denomination to the original proceeding. A condemnation asserts a capture *ab initio;* an award of restitution pronounces upon the act as having been not a valid act of capture, but an act of temporary seizure only. Appleton v. Crowninshield, 3 Mass. 443.

SEIZURE QUOUSQUE. Where the heir on the death of his ancestor postpones claiming admittance from the lord, the lord may, after a reasonable time, and after due proclamation at three successive courts, seize the tenement into his hands *quousque, i. e.* until an heir appears and claims admittance; Jenks, Mod. Land L. 208.

SELDA. A shop, shed, or stall in a market; a wood of sallows or willows; also a sawpit. Co. Litt. 4.

SELECT. To take by preference from among others; to pick out; to cull. Clarke v. Commonwealth, 159 Va. 908, 166 S.E. 541, 543.

SELECT COUNCIL. The name given, in some states, to the upper house or branch of the council of a city.

SELECTI JUDICES. Lat. In Roman law. Judges who were selected very much like our juries. They were returned by the prætor, drawn by lot, subject to be challenged, and sworn. 3 Bl. Comm. 366.

SELECTMEN. The name of certain municipal officers, in the New England states, elected by the towns to transact their general public business, and possessing certain executive powers. Felch v. Weare, 69 N.H. 617, 45 A. 591.

SELF-DEALING. Basically relates to transactions wherein a trustee, acting for himself and also as "trustee," a relation which demands strict fidelity to others, seeks to consummate a deal wherein self-interest is opposed to duty. *Cestui que* trust has in such case the election to affirm or disaffirm, unless countervailing equities have intervened. First Nat. Bank v. Basham, 238 Ala. 500, 191 So. 873, 876, 877, 878, 125 A.L.R. 656; In re Binder's Estate, 137 Ohio St. 26, 27 N.E.2d 939, 947, 129 A.L.R. 130.

SELF-DEFENSE. The protection of one's person or property against some injury attempted by another. The right of such protection. An excuse for the use of force in resisting an attack on the person, and especially for killing an assailant. Whart. Crim. Law, §§ 1019, 1026. The right of a man to repel force by force even to the taking of life in defense of his person, property or habitation, or of a member of his family, against any one who manifests, intends, attempts or endeavors by violence or surprise, to commit a forcible felony. State v. Patterson, 45 Vt. 308, 12 Am.Rep. 200; Logue v. Com., 38 Pa. 265, 80 Am. Dec. 481. Essential elements of "self-defense" are that defendant does not provoke difficulty and that there must be impending peril without convenient or reasonable mode of escape. Hayes v. State, 225 Ala. 253, 142 So. 675, 677. The law of "self-defense" justifies an act done in the reasonable belief of immediate danger, and, if an injury was done by defendant in justifiable self-defense, he can never be punished criminally nor held responsible for damages in a civil action. Baltimore Transit Co. v. Faulkner, 179 Md. 598, 20 A.2d 485, 487.

Accused is not justified in pursuing and killing attacker when danger of death or serious bodily injury has passed. People v. Keys, 62 Cal.App.2d 903, 145 P.2d 589, 596.

SELF-EXECUTING CONSTITUTIONAL PROVISION. Immediately effective without the necessity of ancillary legislation. Cleary v. Kincaid, 23 Idaho, 789, 131 P. 1117, 1118; Stange v. City of Cleveland, 94 Ohio St. 377, 114 N.E. 261, 262.

Constitutional provision is "self-executing" if it supplies sufficient rule by which right given may be enjoyed or duty imposed enforced; constitutional provision is not "self-executing" when it merely indicates principles without laying down rules giving them force of law. Zachary v. City of Wagoner, 146 Okl. 268, 292 P. 345, 348; State v. Perrault, 34 N.M. 438, 283 P. 902, 903.

SELF-EXECUTING JUDGMENTS. Those requiring no affirmative action of the court or action under process issued by the court to execute them. Ætna Casualty & Surety Co. of Hartford, Conn., v. Board of Sup'rs of Warren County, 160 Va. 11, 168 S.E. 617, 629.

SELF-MURDER, SELF-DESTRUCTION, or SELF-SLAUGHTER. See Felo de Se; Suicide.

SELION OF LAND. In old English law. A ridge of ground rising between two furrows, containing no certain quantity, but sometimes more and sometimes less. Termes de la Ley.

SELL. To dispose of by sale (*q. v.*).

SELLER. One who sells anything; the party who transfers property in the contract of sale. The correlative is "buyer," or "purchaser." Though these terms are not inapplicable to the persons concerned in a transfer of real estate, it is more customary to use "vendor" and "purchaser," or "vendee" in that case.

SELLETTE (Fr.). A kind of wooden seat set up in criminal courts in France, on which they placed the accused to undergo his last interrogatory when the conclusions of the counsel for the prosecution went against him with regard to capital punishment or at least penal corporal punishment. It implied moral degradation and was therefore limited to persons accused of crimes entailing corporal punishment. *Ord. Cr. de* 1670, *Tibre* IV, *art.* 21. Abolished by Edict of May 1, 1788. Called a "stool of repentance."

SELLING PUBLIC OFFICES. Buying or selling any office in the gift of the crown, or making any negotiation relating thereto, was deemed a misdemeanor under stats. 5 & 6 Edw. VI. c. 16, and 49 Geo. III. c. 126, 2 Steph. Com., 11th ed. 631.

SELLING STOCKS SHORT. Selling stocks customer does not possess, customer borrowing the number of shares he has sold from some third person to deliver to his vendee expecting to be able to buy the stocks later at a lower figure and return them to the person from whom he borrowed them. Henderson v. Usher, 125 Fla. 709, 170 So. 846, 851.

SEMAYNE'S CASE. This case decided, in 1604, that "every man's house [meaning his dwelling-house only] is his castle," and that an officer executing civil process may not break open outer doors in general, but only inner doors, but that (after request made) he may break open even outer doors to find goods of another wrongfully in the house. Brown. It is reported in 5 Coke, 91.

SEMBLE. L. Fr. It seems; it would appear. This expression is often used in the reports to preface a statement by the court upon a point of law which is not directly decided, when such statement is intended as an intimation of what the decision would be if the point were necessary to be passed upon. It is also used to introduce a suggestion by the reporter, or his understanding of the point decided when it is not free from obscurity.

SEMEL CIVIS SEMPER CIVIS. Once a citizen always a citizen. Tray. Lat. Max. 555.

SEMEL MALUS SEMPER PRÆSUMITUR ESSE MALUS IN EODEM GENERE. Whoever is once bad is presumed to be so always in the same kind of affairs. Cro. Car. 317.

SEMESTRIA. Lat. In the civil law. The collected decisions of the emperors in their councils.

SEMI-MATRIMONIUM. Lat. In Roman law. Half-marriage. Concubinage was so called. Tayl. Civil Law, 273.

SEMI-PLENA PROBATIO. Lat. In the civil law. Half-full proof; half-proof. 3 Bl. Comm. 370. See Half-Proof.

SEMINARIUM. Lat. In the civil law. A nursery of trees. Dig. 7, 1, 9, 6.

SEMINARY. A place of training, an institution of education, a school, academy, college, or university in which young persons are instructed in the several branches of learning which may qualify them for their future employment, and the origin of the word seems to imply a place where the seeds of education are sown and implanted. State v. Northwestern College of Speech Arts, 193 Minn. 123, 258 N.W. 1.

The word is said to have acquired no fixed and definite legal meaning. Maddox v. Adair, Tex.Civ.App., 66 S.W. 811; Warde v. Manchester, 56 N.H. 509, 22 Am.Rep. 504.

SEMINAUFRAGIUM. Lat. In maritime law. Half-shipwreck, as where goods are cast overboard in a storm; also where a ship has been so much damaged that her repair costs more than her worth. Wharton.

SEMITA. In old English law. A path. Fleta, l. 2, c. 52, § 20.

SEMPER. Lat. Always. A word which introduces several Latin maxims, of which some are also used without this prefix.

SEMPER IN DUBIIS BENIGNIORA PRÆFERENDA SUNT. In doubtful cases, the more favorable constructions are always to be preferred. Dig. 50, 17, 56.

SEMPER IN DUBIIS ID AGENDUM EST, UT QUAM TUTISSIMO LOCO RES SIT BONA FIDE CONTRACTA, NISI QUUM APERTE CONTRA LEGES SCRIPTUM EST. In doubtful cases, such a course should always be taken that a thing contracted *bona fide* should be in the safest condition, unless when it has been openly made against law. Dig. 34, 5, 21.

SEMPER IN OBSCURIS, QUOD MINIMUM EST SEQUIMUR. In obscure constructions we always apply that which is the least obscure. Dig. 50, 17, 9; Broom, Max. 687*n*.

SEMPER IN STIPULATIONIBUS, ET IN CETERIS CONTRACTIBUS, ID SEQUIMUR QUOD ACTUM EST. In stipulations and in other contracts we follow that which was done, [we are governed by the actual state of the facts.] Dig. 50, 17, 34.

SEMPER ITA FIAT RELATIO UT VALEAT DISPOSITIO. Reference [of a disposition in a will] should always be so made that the disposition may have effect. 6 Coke, 76*b*.

SEMPER NECESSITAS PROBANDI INCUMBIT EI QUI AGIT. The claimant is always bound to prove, [the burden of proof lies on the actor.]

SEMPER PARATUS. Lat. Always ready. The name of a plea by which the defendant alleges that he has always been ready to perform what is demanded of him. 3 Bl. Comm. 303.

SEMPER PRÆSUMITUR PRO LEGITIMATIONE PUERORUM. The presumption always is in favor of the legitimacy of children. 5 Coke, 98*b;* Co. Litt. 126*a*.

SEMPER PRÆSUMITUR PRO MATRIMONIO. The presumption is always in favor of the validity of a marriage.

SEMPER PRÆSUMITUR PRO NEGANTE. The presumption is always in favor of the one who denies. 10 Clark & F. 534; 3 El. & Bl. 723.

SEMPER PRÆSUMITUR PRO SENTENTIA. The presumption always is in favor of a sentence. 3 Bulst. 42; Branch, Princ.

SEMPER QUI NON PROHIBET PRO SE INTERVENIRE, MANDARE CREDITUR. He who does not prohibit the intervention of another in his behalf is supposed to authorize it. 2 Kent, Comm. 616; Dig. 14, 6, 16; Dig. 46, 3, 12, 4.

SEMPER SEXUS MASCULINUS ETIAM FEMININUM SEXUM CONTINET. The masculine sex always includes the feminine. Dig. 32, 62.

SEMPER SPECIALIA GENERALIBUS INSUNT. Specials are always included in generals. Dig. 50, 17, 147.

SEN. This is said to be an ancient word, which signified "justice." Co. Litt. 61*a*.

SENAGE. Money paid for synodals.

SENATE.

American Law. The name of the upper chamber, or less numerous branch, of the congress of the United States. Also the style of a similar body in the legislatures of several of the states.

Roman Law. The great administrative council of the Roman commonwealth.

SENATOR.

American Law. One who is a member of a senate, either of the United States or of a state.

Old English law. A member of the royal council; a king's councillor.

Roman law. A member of the *senatus*.

SENATORES SUNT PARTES CORPORIS REGIS. Senators are part of the body of the king. Staundef. 72, E.; 4 Inst. 53, in marg.

SENATORS OF THE COLLEGE OF JUSTICE. The judges of the court of session in Scotland are called "Senators of the College of Justice."

SENATUS. Lat. In Roman law. The senate; the great national council of the Roman people.

The place where the senate met. Calvin.

SENATUS CONSULTUM. In Roman law. A decision or decree of the Roman senate, having the force of law, made without the concurrence of the people. These enactments began to take the place of laws enacted by popular vote, when the commons had grown so great in number that they could no longer be assembled for legislative purposes. Mackeld. Rom. Law, § 33; Hunter Rom. Law, xlvii; Inst. 1, 2, 5.

SENATUS CONSULTUM MARCIANUM. A decree of the senate, in relation to the celebration of the Bacchanalian mysteries, enacted in the consulate of Q. Marcius and S. Postumus.

SENATUS CONSULTUM ORFICIANUM. An enactment of the senate (Orficius being one of the consuls and Marcus Antoninus emperor) or admitting both sons and daughters to the succession of a mother dying intestate. Inst. 3, 4, pr.

SENATUS CONSULTUM PEGASIANUM. The The Pegasian decree of the senate. A decree enacted in the consulship of Pegasus and Pusio, in the reign of Vespasian, by which an heir, who was requested to restore an inheritance, was allowed to retain one-fourth of it for himself. Inst. 2, 23, 5.

SENATUS CONSULTUM TREBELLIANUM. A decree of the senate (named from Trebellius, in whose consulate it was enacted) by which it was provided that, if an inheritance was restored under a trust, all actions which, by the civil law, might be brought by or against the heir should be given to and against him to whom the inheritance was restored. Inst. 2, 23, 4; Dig. 36, 1.

SENATUS CONSULTUM ULTIMÆ NESSITATIS. A decree of the senate of the last necessity. The name given to the decree which usually preceded the nomination of a dictator. 1 Bl. Comm. 136.

SENATUS CONSULTUM VELLEIANUM. The Velleian decree of the senate. A decree enacted in the consulship of Velleius, by which married women were prohibited from making contracts. Story, Confl. Laws, § 425.

SENATUS DECRETA. Lat. In the civil law. Decisions of the senate. Private acts concerning particular persons merely.

SENDA. In Spanish law. A path; the right of a path. The right of foot or horse path. White, New Recop. b. 2, tit. 6, § 1.

SENECTUS. Lat. Old age. In the Roman law, the period of *senectus*, which relieved one from the charge of public office, was officially reckoned as beginning with the completion of the seventieth year. Mackeld. Rom. Law, § 138.

SENESCALLUS. In old English law. A seneschal; a steward; the steward of a manor. Fleta, l. 2, c. 72.

SENESCHAL. In old European law. A title of office and dignity, derived from the middle ages, answering to that of steward or high steward in England. Seneschals were originally the lieutenants of the dukes and other great feudatories of the kingdom, and sometimes had the dispensing of justice and high military commands.

SENESCHALLO ET MARESHALLO QUOD NON TENEAT PLACITA DE LIBERO TENEMENTO. A writ addressed to the steward and marshal of England, inhibiting them to take cognizance of an action in their court that concerns freehold. Reg. Orig. 185. Abolished.

SENEUCIA. In old records. Widowhood. Cowell.

SENILE DEMENTIA. That peculiar decay of the mental faculties which occurs in extreme old age, and in many cases much earlier, whereby the person is reduced to second childhood, and becomes sometimes wholly incompetent to enter into any binding contract, or even to execute a will. It is the recurrence of second childhood by mere decay. Byrne v. Fulkerson, 254 Mo. 97, 162 S.W. 171, 178; Guarantee Trust & Safe Deposit Co. v. Waller, 240 Pa. 575, 88 A. 13, 15. See Insanity.

SENILITY. Quality of being senile, an infirmity of old age, trouble proceeding from old age. Kalusch v. Kavli, 185 Minn. 3, 240 N.W. 108, 110. Feebleness of body and mind incident to old age; and an incapacity to contract arising from the impairment of the intellectual faculties by old age. Equitable Life Assur. Soc. of U. S. v. Garrett, 26 Ala.App. 395, 160 So. 776, 777.

SENIOR. The elder. An addition to the name of the elder of two persons in the same family having the same name.

SENIOR COUNSEL. Of two or more counsel retained on the same side of a cause, he is the "senior" who is the elder, or more important in rank or estimation, or who is charged with the more difficult or important parts of the management of the case.

SENIOR JUDGE. Of several judges composing a court, the one who holds the oldest commission, or who has served the longest time under his present commission.

SENIORES. In old English law. Seniors; ancients; elders. A term applied to the great men of the realm. Spelman.

SENIORITY. Represents in the highest degree the right to work, and by seniority the oldest man in point of service, ability and fitness for the job being sufficient, is given choice of jobs, is first promoted within range of jobs subject to seniority, and is the last laid off, proceeding so on down the line to the youngest in point of service. Dooley v. Lehigh Valley R. Co. of Pennsylvania, 130 N.J. Eq. 75, 21 A.2d 334, 338, 339.

SENORIO. In Spanish law. Dominion or property.

SENSUS. Lat. Sense, meaning, signification. *Malo sensu,* in an evil or derogatory sense. *Mitiori sensu,* in a milder, less severe, or less stringent sense. *Sensu honesto,* in an honest sense; to interpret words *sensu honesto* is to take them so as not to impute impropriety to the persons concerned.

SENSUS VERBORUM EST ANIMA LEGIS. 5 Coke, 2. The meaning of the words is the spirit of the law.

SENSUS VERBORUM EST DUPLEX,—MITIS ET ASPER; ET VERBA SEMPER ACCIPIENDA SUNT IN MITIORI SENSU. 4 Coke, 13. The meaning of words is twofold,—mild and harsh; and words are always to be received in their milder sense.

SENSUS VERBORUM EX CAUSA DICENDI ACCIPIENDUS EST; ET SERMONES SEMPER ACCIPIENDI SUNT SECUNDUM SUBJECTAM MATERIAM. The sense of words is to be taken from the occasion of speaking them; and discourses are always to be interpreted according to the subject-matter. 4 Coke, 13*b*. See 2 Kent, Comm. 555.

SENTENCE. The judgment formally pronounced by the court or judge upon the defendant after his conviction in a criminal prosecution, awarding the punishment to be inflicted. Judgment formally declaring to accused legal consequences of guilt which he has confessed or of which he has been convicted. The word is properly confined to this meaning. In *civil* cases, the terms "judgment," "decision," "award," "finding," etc., are used. Archer v. Snook, D.C.Ga., 10 F.2d 567, 569; Hart v. Norman, 92 Misc. 185; 155 N.Y.S 238, 240; State v. Woodbury, 133 Kan. 1, 298 P. 794.

Cumulative sentences. Separate sentences (each additional to the others) imposed upon a defendant who has been convicted upon an indictment containing several counts, each of such counts charging a distinct offense, or who is under conviction at the same time for several distinct offenses; one of such sentences being made to begin at the expiration of another. Carter v. McClaughry, 22 S.Ct. 181, 183 U.S. 365, 46 L.Ed. 236.

Ecclesiastical sentence. In ecclesiastical procedure, analogous to "judgment" (*q. v.*) in an ordinary action. A definite sentence is one which puts an end to the suit, and regards the principal matter in question. An interlocutory sentence determines only some incidental matter in the proceedings. Phillim. Ecc. Law, 1260.

Excessive sentence. See Excessive Sentence.

Final sentence. One which puts an end to a case. Distinguished from interlocutory.

Indeterminate sentence. A form of sentence to imprisonment upon conviction of crime, now authorized by statute in several states, which, instead of fixing rigidly the duration of the imprisonment, declares that it shall be for a period "not less than" so many years "nor more than" so many years, or not less than the minimum period prescribed by statute as the punishment for the particular offense nor more than the maximum period, the exact length of the term being afterwards fixed, within the limits assigned by the court or the statute, by an executive authority, (the governor, board of pardons, etc.,) on consideration of the previous record of the convict, his behavior while in prison or while out on parole, the apparent prospect of reformation and other such considerations.

Interlocutory sentence. In the civil law. A sentence on some indirect question arising from the principal cause. Hallifax, Civil Law, b. 3, ch. 9, no. 40.

Sentence of death recorded. In English practice. The recording of a sentence of death, not actually pronounced, on the understanding that it will not be executed. Such a record has the same effect as if the judgment had been pronounced and the offender reprieved by the court. Mozley & Whitley. The practice is now disused.

Simple sentence. (In rhetoric.) See Simple.

Suspension of sentence. This term may mean either a withholding or postponing the sentencing of a prisoner after the conviction, or a postponing of the execution of the sentence after it has been pronounced. In the latter case, it may, for reasons addressing themselves to the discretion of the court, be indefinite as to time, or during the good behavior of the prisoner. See People v. Webster, 14 Misc. 617, 36 N.Y.S. 745; In re Buchanan, 146 N.Y. 264, 40 N.E. 883.

SENTENCES TO RUN CONCURRENTLY. Merely means that accused is given privilege of serving each day a portion of each sentence. Nishimoto v. Nagle, C.C.A.Cal., 44 F.2d 304, 305.

SENTENTIA. Lat. In the civil law. (1) Sense; import; as distinguished from mere words (2) The deliberate expression of one's will or intention. (3) The sentence of a judge or court.

SENTENTIA A NON JUDICE LATA NEMINI DEBET NOCERE. A sentence pronounced by one who is not a judge should not harm any one. Fleta, l. 6, c. 6, § 7.

SENTENTIA CONTRA MATRIMONIUM NUMQUAM TRANSIT IN REM JUDICATAM. 7 Coke, 43. A sentence against marriage never becomes a matter finally adjudged, *i. e., res judicata.*

SENTENTIA FACIT JUS, ET LEGIS INTERPRETATIO LEGIS VIM OBTINET. Ellesm. Post. N. 55. Judgment creates right, and the interpretation of the law has the force of law.

SENTENTIA FACIT JUS, ET RES JUDICATA PRO VERITATE ACCIPITUR. Ellesm. Post. N. 55. Judgment creates right, and what is adjudicated is taken for truth.

SENTENTIA INTERLOCUTORIA REVOCARI POTEST, DEFINITIVA NON POTEST. Bac. Max. 20. An interlocutory judgment may be recalled, but not a final.

SENTENTIA NON FERTUR DE REBUS NON LIQUIDIS. Sentence is not given upon matters that are not clear. Jenk. Cent. p. 7, case 9.

SEPARABLE. Capable of being separated, disjoined, or divided. In re Babcock, 27 C.C.P.A. 1097, 110 F.2d 665, 667.

SEPARABLE CONTROVERSY. As to removal of causes from state courts to federal courts, this phrase means a separate and distinct cause of action existing in the suit, on which a separate and distinct suit might properly have been brought and complete relief afforded as to such cause of action; or the case must be one capable of separation into parts, so that, in one of the parts, a controversy will be presented, wholly between citizens of different states, which can be fully determined without the presence of any of the other parties to the suit as it has been begun. Fraser v. Jennison, 1 S.Ct. 171, 106 U.S. 191, 27 L. Ed. 131; Gudger v. Western N. C. R. Co., C.C.N. C., 21 F. 81; Steed v. Henry, 180 S.W. 508, 509, 120 Ark. 583; Harrison v. Harrison, D.C.Miss., 5 F.2d 1001, 1003; Mace v. Mayfield, D.C.S.C., 10 F.2d 231, 232. It requires two or more causes of action, one of which is wholly between citizens of different states. Johnson v. Marsh, D.C.Neb., 49 F.Supp. 137, 139, 141, 143.

SEPARALITER. Lat. Separately. Used in indictments to indicate that two or more defendants were charged separately, and not jointly, with the commission of the offense in question. State v. Edwards, 60 Mo. 490.

SEPARATE, *v.* To disunite, divide, disconnect, or sever. Webster; Faucett v. Hensley, 35 Ohio App. 16, 171 N.E. 352, 353.

SEPARATE, *adj.* Individual; distinct; particular; disconnected. Generally used in law as opposed to "joint," though the more usual antithesis of the latter term is "several." Either of these words implies division, distribution, disconnection, or aloofness. Merrill v. Pepperdine, 9 Ind.App. 416, 36 N.E. 921.

As to separate "Acknowledgment" and "Covenant," see those titles.

SEPARATE ACTION. As opposed to a *joint* action, an action brought for himself alone by each of several complainants who are all concerned in the same transaction, but cannot legally join in the suit.

SEPARATE DEMISE IN EJECTMENT. A demise in a declaration in ejectment used to be termed a "separate demise" when made by the lessor separately or individually, as distinguished from a demise made jointly by two or more persons, which was termed a "joint demise." No such demise, either separate or joint, is now necessary in this action. Brown.

SEPARATE ESTATE. The individual property of one of two persons who stand in a social or business relation, as distinguished from that which they own jointly or are jointly interested in. Thus, "separate estate," within the meaning of the bankrupt law, is that in which each partner is separately interested at the time of the bankruptcy. The term can only be applied to such property as belonged to one or more of the partners, to the exclusion of the rest. In re Lowe, 11 Nat. Bankr. Rep. 221, F.Cas.No.8,564. The separate estate of a married woman is that which belongs to her, and over which her husband has no right in equity. It may consist of lands or chattels. Williams v. King, 29 F.Cas. 1,369.

SEPARATE EXAMINATION. The interrogation of a married woman, who appears before an officer for the purpose of acknowledging a deed or other instrument, conducted by such officer in private or out of the hearing of her husband, in order to ascertain if she acts of her own will and without compulsion or constraint of the husband. Also the examination of a witness in private or apart from, and out of the hearing of, the other witnesses in the same cause.

SEPARATE MAINTENANCE. Allowance granted to a wife for support of herself and children while she is living apart from her husband. Cohn v. Cohn, 4 Wash.2d 322, 103 P.2d 366, 367.

Alimony in its strict sense is confined to an allowance made to a wife who is legally separated or divorced from husband, but in many jurisdictions courts have authority to make an allowance to a wife who is living separate and apart from her husband without being legally separated or divorced, and this allowance is often called "separate maintenance." Dyer v. Dyer, 212 N.C. 620, 194 S.E. 278.

SEPARATE PROPERTY. Property owned by married person in his or her own right during marriage. In re Morgan's Estate, 203 Cal. 569, 265 P. 241, 245. See, also, Separate Estate.

Of a married woman. That which she owns in her own right, which is liable only for her own debts, and which she can incumber and dispose of at her own will.

"Separate property" continues to be such as long as it can clearly be traced and identified, and its rents, issues, and profits remain separate property. True v. United States, D.C.Wash., 51 F.Supp. 720, 723, 726.

SEPARATE TRIAL. The separate and individual trial of each of several persons jointly accused of a crime.

SEPARATIM. Lat. In old conveyancing. Severally. A word which made a several covenant. 5 Coke, 23*a*.

SEPARATION. In matrimonial law. A cessation of cohabitation of husband and wife by mutual agreement, or, in the case of "judicial separation," under the decree of a court. Woodruff v. Woodruff, 215 N.C. 685, 3 S.E.2d 5, 6.

SEPARATION A MENSA ET THORO. A partial dissolution of the marriage relation.

SEPARATION OF PATRIMONY. In Louisiana probate law. The creditors of the succession may demand, in every case and against every creditor of the heir, a separation of the property of the succession from that of the heir. This is what is called the "separation of patrimony." The object of a separation of patrimony is to prevent property out of which a particular class of creditors have a right to be paid from being confounded with other property, and by that means made liable to the debts of another class of creditors. Civ.Code La. art. 1444.

SEPARATION ORDER. In England, where a husband is convicted of an aggravated assault upon his wife, the court or magistrate may order that the wife shall be no longer bound to cohabit with him. Such an order has the same effect as a judicial decree of separation on the ground of cruelty. It may also provide for the payment of a weekly sum by the husband to the wife and for the custody of the children. Sweet.

SEPARATISTS. Seceders from the Church of England. They, like Quakers, solemnly affirm, instead of taking the usual oath, before they give evidence.

SEPES. Lat. In old English law. A hedge or inclosure. The inclosure of a trench or canal. Dig. 43, 21, 4.

SEPTENNIAL ACT. In English law. The statute 1 Geo. I. St. 2, c. 38. The act by which a parliament has continuance for seven years, and no longer, unless sooner dissolved; as it always has, in fact, been since the passing of the act. Wharton.

SEPTUAGESIMA. In ecclesiastical law. The third Sunday before *Quadragesima* Sunday, being about the seventieth day before Easter.

SEPTUM. Lat. In old English law. An inclosure or close. Cowell.

Roman law. An inclosure; an inclosed place where the people voted; otherwise called *"ovile."*

SEPTUNX. Lat. In Roman law. A division of the *as*, containing seven *unciæ*, or duodecimal parts; the proportion of seven-twelfths. Tayl. Civil Law, 492.

SEPULCHRE. A grave or tomb. The place of interment of a dead human body. The violation of sepulchres is a misdemeanor at common law.

SEPULTURA. Lat. An offering to the priest for the burial of a dead body.

SEQUAMUR VESTIGIA PATRUM NOSTRORUM. Jenk. Cent. Let us follow the footsteps of our fathers.

SEQUATUR SUB SUO PERICULO. In old English practice. A writ which issued where a sheriff had returned *nihil*, upon a *summoneas ad warrantizandum*, and after an *alias* and *pluries* had been issued. So called because the tenant lost his lands without any recovery in value, unless upon that writ he brought the vouchee into court. Rosc. Real Act. 268; Cowell.

SEQUELA. L. Lat. In old English law. Suit; process or prosecution. *Sequela causæ*, the process of a cause. Cowell.

SEQUELA CURIÆ. Suit of court. Cowell.

SEQUELA VILLANORUM. The family retinue and appurtenances to the goods and chattels of villeins, which were at the absolute disposal of the lord. Par. Antiq. 216.

SEQUELS. Small allowances of meal, or manufactured victual, made to the servants at a mill where corn was ground, by tenure, in Scotland. Wharton.

SEQUESTER, *v.*

Civil Law

To renounce or disclaim, etc. As when a widow came into court and disclaimed having anything to do with her deceased husband's estate, she was said to sequester. The word more commonly signifies the act of taking in execution under a writ of sequestration. Brown.

To deposit a thing which is the subject of a controversy in the hands of a third person, to hold for the contending parties.

To take a thing which is the subject of a controversy out of the possession of the contending parties, and deposit it in the hands of a third person. Calvin.

English Ecclesiastical Practice

To gather and take care of the fruits and profits of a vacant benefice, for the benefit of the next incumbent.

Equity Practice

To take possession of the property of a defendant, and hold it in the custody of the court, until he purges himself of a contempt.

International Law

To confiscate; to appropriate private property to public use; to seize the property of the private citizens of a hostile power, as when a belligerent nation sequesters debts due from its own subjects to the enemy. 1 Kent, Comm. 62.

SEQUESTER, ***n.*** Lat. In the civil law. A person with whom two or more contending parties deposited the subject-matter of the controversy.

SEQUESTRARI FACIAS. In English ecclesiastical practice. A process in the nature of a *levari facias,* commanding the bishop to enter into the rectory and parish church, and to take and sequester the same, and hold them until, of the rents, tithes, and profits thereof, and of the other ecclesiastical goods of a defendant, he have levied the plaintiff's debt. 3 Bl. Comm. 418; 2 Archb. Pr. 1284.

SEQUESTRATIO. Lat. In the civil law. The separating or setting aside of a thing in controversy, from the possession of both parties that contend for it. It is two-fold,—*voluntary,* done by consent of all parties; and *necessary,* when a judge orders it. Brown.

SEQUESTRATION.

Contracts

A species of deposit which two or more persons, engaged in litigation about anything, make of the thing in contest with an indifferent person who binds himself to restore it, when the issue is decided, to the party to whom it is adjudged to belong. Civ. Code La. art. 2973.

Equity Practice

A writ authorizing the taking into the custody of the law of the real and personal estate (or rents, issues, and profits) of a defendant who is in contempt, and holding the same until he shall comply. It is sometimes directed to the sheriff, but more commonly to four commissioners nominated by the complainant. 3 Bl. Comm. 444; Ryan v. Kingsbery, 88 Ga. 361, 14 S.E. 596.

English Ecclesiastical Law

The act of the ordinary in disposing of the goods and chattels of one deceased, whose estate no one will meddle with. Cowell. Or, in other words, the taking possession of the property of a deceased person, where there is no one to claim it.

Also, where a benefice becomes vacant, a sequestration is usually granted by the bishop to the church-wardens, who manage all the profits and expenses of the benefice, plow and sow the glebe, receive tithes, and provide for the necessary cure of souls. Sweet.

International Law

The seizure of the property of an individual, and the appropriation of it to the use of the government.

Louisiana

A mandate of the court, ordering the sheriff, in certain cases, to take in his possession, and to keep, a thing of which another person has the possession, until after the decision of a suit, in order that it be delivered to him who shall be adjudged entitled to have the property or possession of that thing. This is what is properly called a "judicial sequestration." Code Prac. La. art. 269; American Nat. Bank v. Childs, 49 La.Ann. 1359, 22 So. 384.

Mayor's Court

In the mayor's court of London, "an attachment of the property of a person in a warehouse or other place belonging to and abandoned by him. It has the same object as the ordinary attachment, viz., to compel the appearance of the defendant to an action," and, in default, to satisfy the plaintiff's debt by appraisement and execution.

SEQUESTRATOR. One to whom a sequestration is made. One appointed or chosen to perform a sequestration, or execute a writ of sequestration.

SEQUESTRO HABENDO. In English ecclesiastical law. A judicial writ for the discharging a sequestration of the profits of a church benefice, granted by the bishop at the sovereign's command, thereby to compel the parson to appear at the suit of another. Upon his appearance, the parson may have this writ for the release of the sequestration. Reg. Jud. 36.

SEQUI DEBET POTENTIA JUSTITIAM NON PRÆCEDERE. 2 Inst. 454. Power should follow justice, not precede it.

SERF. In the feudal polity, a class of persons whose social condition was servile, and who were bound to labor and onerous duties at the will of their lords. They differed from slaves only in that they were bound to their native soil, instead of being the absolute property of a master.

SERGEANT. In military law. A non-commissioned officer, of whom there are several in each company of infantry, troop of cavalry, etc. The term is also used in the organization of a municipal police force.

Sergeant at arms. See Serjeant.

Sergeant at law. See Serjeant.

Town sergeant. In several states, an officer having the powers and duties of a chief constable or head of the police department of a town or village.

SERIATELY. In series, or following one after another. In re Flint, 32 C.C.P.A. 1116, 150 F.2d 126, 131.

SERIATIM. Lat. Severally; separately; individually; one by one.

SERIOUS. Important; weighty; momentous, grave, great, as in the phrases "serious bodily harm," "serious personal injury," etc. Ward v. State, 70 Tex.Cr.R. 393, 159 S.W. 272, 282; McKee v. State, 93 Tex.Cr.R. 217, 246 S.W. 1035, 1036.

SERIOUS AND WILFUL MISCONDUCT. In Workmen's Compensation Law. The intentional doing of something with the knowledge that it is likely to result in a serious injury, or with a wanton and reckless disregard of its probable consequences. McAdoo v. Industrial Accident Commission, 40 Cal.App. 570, 181 P. 400, 401.

SERIOUS ILLNESS. In life insurance. An illness that permanently or materially impairs, or is likely to permanently or materially impair, the health of the applicant. Not every illness is serious. An illness may be alarming at the time, or thought to be serious by the one afflicted, and yet not be serious in the sense of that term as used in insurance contracts. An illness that is temporary in its duration, and entirely passes away, and is not attended, nor likely to be attended, by a permanent or material impairment of the health or constitution, is not a serious illness. It is not sufficient that the illness was thought serious at the time it occurred, or that it might have resulted in permanently impairing the health. Fishbeck v. New York Life Ins. Co., 179 Wis. 369, 192 N.W. 170, 175; American Nat. Ins. Co. v. Hicks, Tex.Civ. App., 198 S.W. 616, 622.

SERJEANT. The same word etymologically with "sergeant," but the latter spelling is more commonly employed in the designation of military and police officers, (see Sergeant,) while the former is preferred when the term is used to describe certain grades of legal practitioners and certain officers of legislative bodies. See *infra*.

Common Serjeant

A judicial officer attached to the corporation of the city of London, who assists the recorder in disposing of the criminal business at the Old Bailey sessions, or central criminal court. Brown.

Serjeant at Arms

An executive officer appointed by, and attending on, a legislative body, whose principal duties are to execute its warrants, preserve order, and arrest offenders.

Serjeant at Law

A barrister of the common-law courts of high standing, and of much the same rank as a doctor of law is in the ecclesiastical courts. These serjeants seem to have derived their title from the old knights templar, (among whom there existed a peculiar class under the denomination of "*frères sergens*," or "*fratres servientes*,") and to have continued as a separate fraternity from a very early period in the history of the legal profession. The barristers who first assumed the old monastic title were those who practiced in the court of common pleas, and until a recent period (the 25th of April, 1834, 9 & 10 Vict. c. 54) the serjeants at law always had the exclusive privilege of practice in that court. Every judge of a common-law court, previous to his elevation to the bench, used to be created a serjeant at law; but since the judicature act this is no longer necessary. Brown.

Serjeant of the Mace

In English law. An officer who attends the lord mayor of London, and the chief magistrates of other corporate towns. Holthouse.

Serjeants' Inn

The inn to which the serjeants at law belonged, near Chancery lane; formerly called "Faryndon Inn."

SERJEANTIA IDEM EST QUOD SERVITIUM. Co.Litt. 105. Serjeanty is the same as service.

SERJEANTY. A species of tenure by knight service, which was due to the king only, and was distinguished into grand and petit serjeanty. The tenant holding by *grand* serjeanty was bound, instead of attending the king generally in his wars, to do some honorary service to the king in person, as to carry his banner or sword, or to be his butler, champion, or other officer at his coronation. *Petit* serjeanty differed from grand serjeanty, in that the service rendered to the king was not of a personal nature, but consisted in rendering him annually some small implement of war, as a bow, sword, arrow, lance, or the like. Cowell; Brown.

SERMENT. In old English law. Oath; an oath.

SERMO INDEX ANIMI. 5 Coke, 118. Speech is an index of the mind.

SERMO RELATUS AD PERSONAM INTELLIGI DEBET DE CONDITIONE PERSONÆ. Language which is referred to a person ought to be understood of the condition of the person. 4 Coke, 16.

SERMONES SEMPER ACCIPIENDI SUNT SECUNDUM SUBJECTAM MATERIAM, ET CONDITIONEM PERSONARUM. 4 Coke, 14. Language is always to be understood according to its subject-matter, and the condition of the persons.

SERPENT-VENOM REACTION. A test for insanity by means of the breaking up of the red corpuscles of the blood of the suspected person on the injection of the venom of cobras or other serpents; recently employed in judicial proceedings in some European countries and in Japan.

SERRATED. Notched on the edge; cut in notches like the teeth of a saw. This was anciently the method of trimming the top or edge of a deed of indenture. See Indent, *v.*

SERVAGE. In feudal law, where a tenant, besides payment of a certain rent, found one or more workmen for his lord's service. Tomlins.

SERVANDA EST CONSUETUDO LOCI UBI CAUSA AGITUR. The custom of the place where the action is brought is to be observed. Decouche v. Savetier, 3 Johns. Ch. (N. Y.) 190, 219, 8 Am. Dec. 478.

SERVANT. One employed to perform service in master's affairs, whose physical conduct in performance of the service is controlled or is subject to right to control by the master. Brenner v. Socony Vacuum Oil Co., 236 Mo.App. 524, 158 S.W.2d 171, 174, 175; Reiling v. Missouri Ins. Co., 236 Mo.App. 164, 153 S.W.2d 79. A person in the employ of another and subject to his control as to what work shall be done and the means by which it shall be accomplished. Pantell v. Shriver Allison Co., 61 Ohio App. 119, 22 N.E.2d 497, 499. One who is employed to render personal service to another otherwise than in the pursuit of an independent calling, and who, in such service, remains entirely under control and direction of employer. Henley v. State, 59 Ga.App. 595, 2 S.E.2d 139, 142. A person of whatever rank or position in employ and subject to direction or control of another in any department of labor or business. Saums v. Parfet, 270 Mich. 165, 258 N.W. 235, 237. For "Family," see that title.

The term is often given special meanings by statutes and like other words is greatly influenced by context in wills and other documents. Hand v. Cole, 88 Tenn. 400, 12 S.W. 922, 7 L.R.A. 96; In re Thompson's Estate, 126 Misc. Rep. 91, 213 N.Y. S. 426, 429.

SERVE. In Scotch practice. To render a verdict or decision in favor of a person claiming to be an heir; to declare the fact of his heirship judicially. A jury are said to *serve* a claimant *heir,* when they find him to be heir, upon the evidence submitted to them. Bell.

As to serving papers, etc., see Service of Process.

SERVI. Lat. Slaves.

Old English law. Bondmen; servile tenants. Cowell.

Old European law. Persons over whom their masters had absolute dominion.

SERVI REDEMPTIONE. Criminal slaves in the time of Henry I. 1 Kemble, Sax. 197, (1849).

SERVICE. Has a variety of meanings, dependent upon the context or the sense in which used. Central Power & Light Co. v. State, Tex.Civ.App., 165 S.W.2d 920, 925. For "Family," see that title.

Contracts

The being employed to serve another; duty or labor to be rendered by one person to another, the former being bound to submit his will to the direction and control of the latter. Cameron v. State Theater Co., 256 Mass. 466, 152 N.E. 880, 881; Ludwig v. Pacific Fire Ins. Co. of New York, 204 N.Y.S. 465, 466, 123 Misc. 189. The act of serving; the labor performed or the duties required. State ex rel. King v. Board of Trustees of Firemen's Pension Fund of Kansas City, 192 Mo.App. 583, 184 S.W. 929, 930. Occupation, condition, or status of a servant, etc. Performance of labor for benefit of another, or at another's command; attendance of an inferior, hired helper, slave, etc. Claxton v. Johnson County, 194 Ga. 43, 20 S.E.2d 606, 610.

"Service" and "employment" generally imply that the employer, or person to whom the service is due, both selects and compensates the employee, or person rendering the service. Ledvinka v. Home Ins. Co. of New York, 139 Md. 434, 115 A. 596, 597, 19 A.L.R. 167.

The term is used also for employment in one of the offices, departments, or agencies of the government; as in the phrases "civil service," "public service," "military service," etc. Chicago, B. & Q. R. Co. v. School Dist. No. 1 in Yuma County, 63 Colo. 159, 165 P. 260, 263; Miller v. Illinois Bankers' Life Ass'n, 138 Ark. 442, 212 S.W. 310, 311, 7 A.L.R. 378.

Domestic Relations

The "services" of a wife, for the loss of which, occasioned by an injury to the wife, the husband may recover in an action against the tort-feasor, include whatever of aid, assistance, comfort, and society the wife would be expected to render to or bestow upon her husband in the circumstances in which they were situated. Thompson v. Aultman & Taylor Mach. Co., 96 Kan. 259, 150 P. 587, and in all the relations of domestic life, Little Rock Gas & Fuel Co. v. Coppedge, 116 Ark. 334, 172 S.W. 885, 889.

Feudal Law

The consideration which the feudal tenants were bound to render to the lord in recompense for the lands they held of him. The services, in respect of their quality, were either free or base services, and, in respect of their quantity and the time of exacting them, were either certain or uncertain. 2 Bl. Comm. 60.

Practice

The exhibition or delivery of a writ, notice, injunction, etc., by an authorized person, to a person who is thereby officially notified of some action or proceeding in which he is concerned, and is thereby advised or warned of some action or step which he is commanded to take or to forbear. U. S. v. McMahon, 17 S.Ct. 28, 164 U.S. 81, 41 L.Ed. 357; In re Tengwall Co., C.C.A.Ill., 201 F. 82, 84; Martin v. Hawkins, Tex.Civ.App., 238 S.W. 991.

General

Civil service. See that title.

Constructive service of process. Any form of service other than actual personal service; notification of an action or of some proceeding therein, given to a person affected by sending it to him in the mails or causing it to be published in a newspaper.

Personal service. Of a writ or notice is made by delivering it to the person named, in person, Georgia Casualty Co. v. McClure, Tex.Civ.App., 239 S.W. 644, 647; or handing him a copy and informing him of the nature and terms of the original. Leaving a copy at his place of abode is not personal service. Moyer v. Cook, 12 Wis. 336. But where a person named in a summons is of unsound mind, service upon the guardian of such person may be deemed "personal service." Pattison v. Grand Trust & Savings Co., 195 Ind. 313, 144 N.E. 26, 29. Some courts hold to the view that the mailing of a notice is not personal service. State ex rel. Schuhart, 296 Mo. 156, 246 S.W. 196, 200, but others, interpreting the term as it is found in statutes, take a contrary view, United States ex rel. Proctor Mfg. Co. v. Illinois Surety Co., C.C.A.N.Y., 228 F. 304, 305; Hood v. Texas Employers' Ins. Ass'n, Tex.Civ.App., 260 S.W. 243, 245 (registered mail); Kramm v. Stockton Electric R. Co., 22 Cal.App. 737, 136 P. 523, 527 (express).

Public utilities. The furnishing of water, heat, light and power, etc. by them. Claxton v. Johnson County, 194 Ga. 43, 20 S.E.2d 606, 610.

Salvage service. See Salvage.

Secular service. Worldly employment or service, as contrasted with spiritual or ecclesiastical.

Service by publication. Service of a summons or other process upon an absent or nonresident defendant, by publishing the same as an advertisement in a designated newspaper, with such other efforts to give him actual notice as the particular statute may prescribe.

Service of an heir. An old form of Scotch law, fixing the right and character of an heir to the estate of his ancestor. Bell.

Service of process. The service of writs, summonses, rules, etc., signifies the delivering to or leaving them with the party to whom or with whom they ought to be delivered or left; and, when they are so delivered, they are then said to have been served. Usually a copy only is served and the original is shown. Brown.

Special service. In Scotch law. That form of service by which the heir is served to the ancestor who was feudally vested in the lands. Bell.

Substituted service. Any form of service of process other than personal service, such as service by mail or by publication in a newspaper; service of a writ or notice on some person other than the one directly concerned, for example, his attorney of record, who has authority to represent him or to accept service for him.

SERVICE ESTABLISHMENT. Within Fair Labor Standards Act of 1938. An establishment which has ordinary characteristics of retail establishments except that services instead of goods are sold. An establishment the principal activity of which is to furnish service to the consuming public, and includes barber shops, beauty parlors, shoe shining parlors, clothes pressing clubs, laundries and automobile repair shops. Fleming v. A. B. Kirschbaum Co., C.C.A.Pa., 124 F.2d 567, 572.

SERVICES FONCIERS. Fr. In French law. Easements of English law. Brown.

SERVIDUMBRE. In Spanish law. A servitude. The right and use which one man has in the buildings and estates of another, to use them for the benefit of his own. Las Partidas, 3, 31, 1.

SERVIENS AD CLAVAM. Serjeant at mace. 2 Mod. 58.

SERVIENS AD LEGEM. In old English practice. Serjeant at law.

SERVIENS DOMINI REGIS. In old English law. King's serjeant; a public officer, who acted sometimes as the sheriff's deputy, and had also judicial powers. Bract. fols. 145*b*, 150*b*, 330, 358.

SERVIENS NARRATOR. A serjeant-at-law, *q. v.*

SERVIENT. Serving; subject to a service or servitude. A *servient* estate is one which is burdened with a servitude. Burdine v. Sewell, 92 Fla. 375, 109 So. 648, 652; Saratoga State Waters Corporation v. Pratt, 227 N.Y. 429, 125 N.E. 834, 838.

SERVIENT TENEMENT. An estate in respect of which a service is owing, as the *dominant tenement* is that to which the service is due. Northwestern Improvement Co. v. Lowry, 104 Mont. 289, 66 P.2d 792, 795, 110 A.L.R. 605.

SERVIENTIBUS. Certain writs touching servants and their masters violating the statutes made against their abuses. Reg. Orig. 189.

SERVILE EST EXPILATIONIS CRIMEN; SOLA INNOCENTIA LIBERA. 2 Inst. 573. The crime of theft is slavish; innocence alone is free.

SERVITIA PERSONALIA SEQUUNTUR PERSONAM. 2 Inst. 374. Personal services follow the person.

SERVITIIS ACQUIETANDIS. A judicial writ for a man distrained for services to one, when he owes and performs them to another, for the acquittal of such services. Reg. Jud. 27.

SERVITIUM. Lat. In feudal and old English law. The duty of obedience and performance which a tenant was bound to render to his lord, by reason of his fee. Spelman.

SERVITIUM, IN LEGE ANGILÆ, REGULARITER ACCIPITUR PRO SERVITIO QUOD PER TENENTES DOMINIS SUIS DEBETUR RATIONE FEODI SUI. Co. Litt. 65. Service, by the law of England, means the service which is due from the tenants to the lords, by reason of their fee.

SERVITIUM FEODALE ET PRÆDIALE. A personal service, but due only by reason of lands which were held in fee. Bract. l. 2, c. 16.

SERVITIUM FORINSECUM. Forinsec, foreign, or extra service; a kind of service that was due to the king, over and above (*foris*) the service due to the lord.

SERVITIUM INTRINSECUM. Intrainsic or ordinary service; the ordinary service due the chief lord, from tenants within the fee. Bract. fols. 36, 36*b*.

SERVITIUM LIBERUM. A service to be done by feudatory tenants, who were called *"liberi homines,"* and distinguished from vassals, as was their service, for they were not bound to any of the base services of plowing the lord's land, etc., but were to find a man and horse, or go with the lord into the army, or to attend the court, etc. Cowell.

See, also, Liberum Servitium.

SERVITIUM MILITARE. Knight-service; military service. 2 Bl. Comm. 62.

SERVITIUM REGALE. Royal service, or the rights and prerogatives of manors which belong to the king as lord of the same, and which were generally reckoned to be six, viz.: Power of judicature, in matters of property; power of life and death, in felonies and murder; a right to waifs and strays; assessments; minting of money; and assise of bread, beer, weights, and measures. Cowell.

SERVITIUM SCUTI. Service of the shield; that is, knight-service.

SERVITIUM SOCÆ. Service of the plow; that is, socage.

SERVITOR. A serving-man; particularly applied to students at Oxford, upon the foundation, who are similar to sizars at Cambridge. Wharton.

SERVITORS OF BILLS. In old English practice. Servants or messengers of the marshal of the king's bench, sent out with bills or writs to summon persons to that court. Now more commonly called "tipstaves." Cowell.

SERVITUDE.

The Condition of being Bound to Service

The state of a person who is subjected, voluntarily or otherwise, to another person as his servant. Shilling v. State, 143 Miss. 709, 109 So. 737, 739.

A Charge or Burden

A charge or burden resting upon one estate for the benefit or advantage of another; a species of incorporeal right derived from the civil law (see Servitus) and closely corresponding to the "easement" of the common-law, except that "servitude" rather has relation to the burden or the estate burdened, while "easement" refers to the benefit or advantage or the estate to which it accrues. Rowe v. Nally, 81 Md. 367, 32 A. 198; Los Angeles Terminal Land Co. v. Muir, 136 Cal. 36, 68 P. 308.

The term "servitude," in its original and popular sense, signifies the duty of service, or rather the condition of one who is liable to the performance of services. The word, however, in its legal sense, is applied figuratively to things. When the freedom of ownership in land is fettered or restricted, by reason of some person, other than the owner thereof, having some right therein, the land is said to "serve" such person. The restricted condition of the ownership or the right which forms the subject-matter of the restriction is termed a "servitude," and the land so burdened with another's right is termed a "servient tenement," while the land belonging to the person enjoying the right is called the "dominant tenement." The word "servitude" may be said to have both a positive and a negative signification; in the former sense denoting the restrictive right belonging to the entitled party; in the latter, the restrictive duty entailed upon the proprietor or possessor of the servient land. Brown.

Classification

All servitudes which affect lands may be divided into two kinds,—*personal* and *real*. Personal servitudes are those attached to the person for whose benefit they are established, and terminate with his life. This kind of servitude is of three sorts,—usufruct, use, and habitation. Real servitudes, which are also called "predial" or "landed" servitudes, are those which the owner of an estate enjoys on a neighboring estate for the benefit of his own estate. They are called "predial" or "landed" servitudes because, being established for the benefit of an estate, they are rather due to the estate than to the owner personally. Frost-Johnson Lumber Co. v. Salling's Heirs, 150 La. 756, 91 So. 207, 245; Tide-Water Pipe Co. v. Bell, 280 Pa. 104, 124 A. 351, 354, 40 A.L.R. 1516.

Real servitudes are divided, in the civil law, into *rural* and *urban* servitudes. Rural servitudes are such as are established for the benefit of a landed estate; such, for example, as a right of way over the servient tenement, or of access to a spring, a coal-mine, a sand-pit, or a wood that is upon it. Urban servitudes are such as are established for the benefit of one building over another. (But the buildings need not be in the city, as the name would apparently imply.) They are such as the right of support, or of view, or of drip or sewer, or the like. Mackeld. Rom. Law, § 316, et seq.

Servitudes are also classed as *positive* and *negative*. A positive servitude is one which obliges the owner of the servient estate to permit or suffer something to be done on his property by another. A negative servitude is one which does not bind the servient proprietor to permit something to be done upon his property by another, but merely restrains him from making a certain use of his property which would impair the easement enjoyed by the dominant tenement. Rowe v. Nally, 81 Md. 367, 32 A. 198.

Penal servitude. In English criminal law, a punishment which consists in keeping the offender in confinement and compelling him to labor.

Involuntary servitude. See Involuntary.

SERVITUS. Lat. In the civil law. Slavery; bondage; the state of service. An institution of the conventional law of nations, by which one person is subjected to the dominion of another, contrary to natural right. Inst. 1, 3, 2.

Also a service or servitude; an easement.

SERVITUS ACTUS. The servitude or right of walking, riding, or driving over another's ground. Inst. 2, 3, pr. A species of right of way.

SERVITUS ALTIUS NON TOLLENDI. The servitude of not building higher. A right attached to a house, by which its proprietor can prevent his neighbor from building his own house higher. Inst. 2, 3, 4.

SERVITUS AQUÆ DUCENDÆ. The servitude of leading water; the right of leading water to one's own premises through another's land. Inst. 2, 3, pr.

SERVITUS AQUÆ EDUCENDÆ. The servitude of leading off water; the right of leading off the water from one's own onto another's ground. Dig. 8, 3, 29.

SERVITUS AQUÆ HAURIENDÆ. The servitude or right of draining water from another's spring or well. Inst. 2, 3, 2.

SERVITUS CLOACÆ MITTENDÆ. The servitude or right of having a sewer through the house or ground of one's neighbor. Dig. 8, 1, 7.

SERVITUS EST CONSTITUTIO JURE GENTIUM QUA QUIS DOMINO ALIENO CONTRA NATURAM SUBJICITUR. Slavery is an institution by the law of nations, by which a man is subjected to the dominion of another, contrary to nature. Inst. 1, 3, 2; Co. Litt. 116.

SERVITUS FUMI IMMITTENDI. The servitude or right of leading off smoke or vapor through the chimney or over the ground of one's neighbor. Dig. 8, 5, 8, 5–7.

SERVITUS ITINERIS. The servitude or privilege of walking, riding, and being carried over another's ground. Inst. 2, 3, pr. A species of right of way.

SERVITUS LUMINUM. The servitude of lights; the right of making or having windows or other openings in a wall belonging to another, or in a common wall, in order to obtain light for one's building. Dig. 8, 2, 4.

SERVITUS NE LUMINIBUS OFFICIATUR. A servitude not to hinder lights; the right of having one's lights or windows unobstructed or darkened by a neighbor's building, etc. Inst. 2, 3, 4.

SERVITUS NE PROSPECTUS OFFENDATUR. A servitude not to obstruct one's prospect, *i. e.*, not to intercept the view from one's house. Dig. 8, 2, 15.

SERVITUS ONERIS FERENDI. The servitude of bearing weight; the right to let one's building rest upon the building, wall, or pillars of one's neighbor. Mackeld. Rom. Law, § 317.

SERVITUS PASCENDI. The servitude of pasturing; the right of pasturing one's cattle on another's ground; otherwise called *"jus pascendi."* Inst. 2, 3, 2.

SERVITUS PECORIS AD AQUAM ADPULSAM. A right of driving one's cattle on a neighbor's land to water.

SERVITUS PRÆDII RUSTICI. The servitude of a rural or country estate; a rural servitude. Inst. 2, 3, pr., and 3.

SERVITUS PRÆDII URBANI. The servitude of an urban or city estate; an urban servitude. Inst. 2, 3, 1.

SERVITUS PRÆDIORUM. A prædial servitude; a service, burden, or charge upon one estate for the benefit of another. Inst. 2, 3, 3.

SERVITUS PROJICIENDI. The servitude of projecting; the right of building a projection from one's house in the open space belonging to one's neighbor. Dig. 8, 2, 2.

SERVITUS PROSPECTUS. A right of prospect. This may be either to give one a free prospect over his neighbor's land or to prevent a neighbor from having a prospect over one's own land. Dig. 8, 2, 15; Domat, 1, 1, 6.

SERVITUS STILLICIDII. The right of drip; the right of having the water drip from the eaves of one's house upon the house or ground of one's neighbor. Inst. 2, 3, 1, 4; Dig. 8, 2, 2.

SERVITUS TIGNI IMMITTENDI. The servitude of letting in a beam; the right of inserting beams in a neighbor's wall. Inst. 2, 3, 1, 4; Dig. 8, 2, 2.

SERVITUS VIÆ. The servitude or right of way; the right of walking, riding, and driving over another's land. Inst. 2, 3, pr.

SERVUS. Lat. In the civil and old English law. A slave; a bondman. Inst. 1, 3, pr.; Bract. fol. 4*b*.

Servus a manu. (Lat. Literally, a servant *by hand*, or *with the hand.)* A scribe, secretary. Harper's Lat. Dict., citing Suet. Caes. 74 *(i. e.,* the biography of Julius Caesar by Suetonius Tranquillus). This phrase was also written *a manu servus*, and eventually gave rise to the word *amanuensis*, derived from *a manu*, plus *ensis*, and taking the place of *a manu servus*. Cent. Dict. *s. v.* "amanuensis."

SESS. In English law. A tax, rate, or assessment.

SESSIO. Lat. In old English law. A sitting; a session. *Sessio parliamenti*, the sitting of parliament. Cowell.

SESSION. The sitting of a court, Legislature, council, commission, etc., for the transaction of its proper business. Hence, the period of time, within any one day, during which such body is assembled in form, and engaged in the transaction of business, or, in a more extended sense, the whole space of time from its first assembling to its prorogation or adjournment *sine die*. Ralls v. Wyand, 40 Okl. 323, 138 P. 158, 162.

Session of court is time during term in which court sits for transaction of business, after judge arrives and opens court. Carpenter v. City of Birmingham, 221 Ala. 368, 128 So. 899, 900.

Synonyms

Strictly speaking, the word "session," as applied to a court of justice, is not synonymous with the word "term." The "session" of a court is the time during which it actually sits for the transaction of judicial business, and hence terminates each day with the rising of the court. A "term" of court is the period fixed by law, usually embracing many days or weeks, during which it shall be open for the transaction of judicial business and during which it may hold sessions from day to day. But this distinction is not always observed, many authorities using the two words interchangeably. Muse v. Harris, 122 Okl. 250, 254 P. 72, 73; State v. City of Victoria, 97 Kan. 638, 156 P. 705, 708; Nation v. Savely, 127 Okl. 117, 260 P. 32, 35.

General

Court of session. The supreme civil court of Scotland, instituted A. D. 1532, consisting of thirteen (formerly fifteen) judges, viz., the lord president, the lord justice clerk, and eleven ordinary lords.

General sessions. A court of record, in England, held by two or more justices of the peace, for the execution of the authority given them by the commission of the peace and certain statutes. General sessions held at certain times in the four quarters of the year pursuant to St. 2 Hen. V. are properly called "quarter sessions," (*q. v.*,) but intermediate general sessions may also be held. Sweet.

Great session of Wales. A court which was abolished by St. 1 Wm. IV. c. 70. The proceedings now issue out of the courts at Westminster, and two of the judges of the superior courts hold the circuits in Wales and Cheshire, as in other English counties. Wharton.

Joint session. In parliamentary practice, a meeting together and commingling of the two houses of a legislative body, sitting and acting together as one body, instead of separately in their respective houses. Snow v. Hudson, 56 Kan. 378, 43 P. 262.

Petty sessions. In English law. A special or petty session is sometimes kept in corporations and counties at large by a few justices, for dispatching smaller business in the neighborhood between the times of the general sessions; as for licensing alehouses, passing the accounts of the parish officers, etc. Brown.

Quarter sessions. See that title.

Regular session. An ordinary, general, or stated session, (as of a legislative body,) as distinguished from a special or extra session.

Session laws. The name commonly given to the body of laws enacted by a state Legislature at one of its annual or biennial sessions. So called to distinguish them from the "compiled laws" or "revised statutes" of the state.

Session of the peace. In English law. A sitting of justices of the peace for the exercise of their powers. There are four kinds,—petty, special, quarter, and general sessions.

Sessional orders. Certain resolutions which are agreed to by both houses at the commencement of every session of the English parliament, and have relation to the business and convenience thereof; but they are not intended to continue in force beyond the session in which they are adopted. They are principally of use as directing the order of business. Brown.

Sessions. A sitting of justices in court upon their commission, or by virtue of their appointment, and most commonly for the trial of criminal cases. The title of several courts in England and the United States, chiefly those of criminal jurisdiction. Burrill.

Special sessions. In English law. A meeting of two or more justices of the peace held for a special purpose, (such as the licensing of alehouses,) either as required by statute or when specially convoked, which can only be convened after notice to all the other magistrates of the division, to give them an opportunity of attending. Stone, J. Pr. 52, 55.

SET. This word appears to be nearly synonymous with "lease." A lease of mines is frequently termed a "mining set." Brown.

SET ASIDE. A judgment, decree, award, or any proceedings is to cancel, annul, or revoke them at the instance of a party unjustly or irregularly affected by them. Brandt v. Brandt, 40 Or. 477, 67 P. 508.

SET DOWN. A cause for trial or hearing at a given term is to enter its title in the calendar, list, or docket of causes which are to be brought on at that term.

SET OF EXCHANGE. In mercantile law. Foreign bills are usually drawn in duplicate or triplicate, the several parts being called respectively "first of exchange," "second of exchange," etc., and these parts together constitute a "set of exchange." Any one of them being paid, the others become void.

SET OUT. In pleading. To recite or narrate facts or circumstances; to allege or aver; to describe or to incorporate; as, to set out a deed or contract. First Nat. Bank v. Engelbercht, 58 Neb. 639, 79 N.W. 556; Powder Valley State Bank v. Hudelson, 74 Or. 191, 144 P. 494, 497.

SET UP. To bring forward or allege, as something relied upon or deemed sufficient; to propose or interpose, by way of defense, explanation, or justification; as, to set up the statute of limitations, *i. e.*, offer and rely upon it as a defense to a claim.

SETI. As used in mining laws, lease. Brown.

SET-OFF. A counter demand which defendant holds against plaintiff, arising out of a transaction extrinsic of plaintiff's cause of action. Delco Light Co. v. John Le Roy Hutchinson Properties, 128 So. 831, 99 Fla. 410. Counter-demand must be liquidated or capable of liquidation and grow out of a contract or judgment. Marks v. Spitz, D.C. Mass., 4 F.R.D. 348, 350. A money demand independent of and unconnected with plaintiff's cause of action. Otto v. Lincoln Sav. Bank of Brooklyn, 51 N.Y.S.2d 561, 563, 268 App.Div. 400. Only a counter demand upon which defendant at commencement of action might have maintained independent suit. Armstrong v. Marr, 120 Neb. 182, 231 N.W. 758. It generally admits plaintiff's cause of action. Cook v. Soden, 12 N.J.Misc. 337, 171 A. 558, 559.

"Set-off", both at law and in equity, is that right which exists between two parties, each of whom under an independent contract owes an ascertained amount to the other, to set off his respective debt by way of mutual deduction, so that in any action brought for the larger debt the residue only, after such deduction, shall be recovered. John Wills, Inc., v. Citizens Nat. Bank of Netcong, 125 N.J.L. 546, 16 A.2d 804, 806.

A set-off was unknown to the common law; according to which mutual debts were distinct, and inextinguishable except by actual payment, release or agreement. Scarano v. Scarano, 132 N.J.Eq. 362, 28 A.2d 425, 429, 430. A defendant who had a demand against plaintiff was compelled to bring a separate suit or resort to an equity court to have his claim set off. The English statute 2 Geo. II, c. 22, which has been generally adopted in the United States, with some modifications, in cases of mutual debts, however, allowed the defendant to set his debt against the other, either by pleading it in bar, or giving it in evidence, where proper notice had been given of such intention, under the general issue. The statute being made for the benefit of defendant, is not compulsory. The defendant may waive his right, and bring a cross action against plaintiff. Himes v. Barnitz, 8 Watts, Pa., 39; 2 Camp. 594; Hinckly v. Walters, 9 Watts, Pa., 179; Branham v. Johnson, 62 Md. 259.

Independent of statute the right of set-off is of equitable origin and hence power to allow set-offs is inherent in equity courts and courts of equity sometimes allow set-offs where, for some technical reason, it could not be allowed at law under statute. Colton v. Dovers' Perpetual Building and Loan Ass'n, 90 Md. 85, 45 A. 23, 26, 46 L.R.A. 388, 78 Am.St.Rep. 431; Scarano v. Scarano, 132 N.J.Eq. 362, 28 A.2d 425, 429, 430.

It differs from counterclaim, in that a "counterclaim" arises out of the same transaction described in the complaint, while a "set-off" is independent thereof. Savings Bank of New London v. Santaniello, 130 Conn. 206, 33 A.2d 126, 128.

For the distinction between set-off and recoupment, see Recoupment.

"Set-off" differs from a "lien," inasmuch as the former belongs exclusively to the remedy, and is merely a right to insist, if the party think proper to do so, when sued by his creditor on a counter-demand, which can only be enforced through the medium of judicial proceedings; while the latter is, in effect, a substitute for a suit. 2 Op.Attys. Gen. 677.

SETTER. In Scotch law. The granter of a tack or lease. 1 Forb. Inst. pt. 2, p. 153.

SETTLE. A word of equivocal meaning; meaning different things in different connections, and the particular sense in which it is used may be explained by the context or the surrounding circumstances. Accordingly, the term may be employed as meaning to agree, to approve, to arrange, to ascertain, to liquidate, to come to or reach an agreement, to determine, to establish, to fix, to free from uncertainty, to place, or to regulate. Edwards v. Edwards, Tex.Civ.App., 52 S.W. 2d 657, 661; Kocher v. Ricketts, 71 Ohio App. 8, 47 N.E.2d 657, 659.

Parties are said to *settle* an account when they go over its items and ascertain and agree upon the balance due from one to the other. And, when the party indebted pays such balance, he is also said to settle it. M. Zimmerman Co. v. Goldberg, 69 Pa.Super.Ct. 254, 255; State Bank of Stratford v. Young, 159 Iowa, 375, 140 N.W. 376, 380.

Settle a bill of exceptions. To approve it. Kocher v. Ricketts, 71 Ohio App. 8, 47 N.E.2d 657, 659.

When the bill of exceptions prepared for an appeal is not accepted as correct by the respondent, it is *settled* (*i. e.*, adjusted and finally made conformable to the truth) by being taken before the judge who presided at the trial, and by him put into a form agreeing with his minutes and his recollection. Green v. Commonwealth, 181 Ky. 253, 204 S.W. 82, 83.

Settle a document. To make it right in form and in substance. Documents of difficulty or complexity, such as mining leases, settlements by will or deed, partnership agreements, etc., are generally settled by counsel. Sweet.

Settle property. To limit it, or the income of it, to several persons in succession, so that the person for the time being in the possession or enjoyment of it has no power to deprive the others of their right of future enjoyment. Sweet.

Settle up. A term, colloquial rather than legal, which is applied to the final collection, adjustment, and distribution of the estate of a decedent, a bankrupt, or an insolvent corporation. It includes the processes of collecting the property, paying debts and charges, and turning over the balance to those entitled to receive it.

Settled estate. See Estate.

Settled insanity. Habitual insanity. Community Loan & Investment Corporation v. Bowden, 64 Ga.App. 175, 12 S.E.2d 421, 423.

Settling day. The day on which transactions for the "account" are made up on the English stock-exchange. In consols they are monthly; in other investments, twice in the month.

Settling interrogatories. The determination by the court of objections to interrogatories and cross-interrogatories prepared to be used in taking a deposition.

Settling issues. In English practice. Arranging or determining the form of the issues in a cause. Where, in any action, it appears to the judge that the statement of claim or defense or reply does not sufficiently disclose the issues of fact between the parties, he may direct the parties to prepare issues; and such issues shall, if the parties differ, be *settled* by the judge. Judicature Act 1875, schedule, art. 19.

SETTLEMENT. Act or process of adjusting or determining; an adjusting; an adjustment between persons concerning their dealings or difficulties; an agreement by which parties having disputed matters between them reach or ascertain what is coming from one to the other; arrangement of difficulties; composure of doubts or differences; determination by agreement; and liquidation. Sowers v. Robertson, 144 Kan. 273, 58 P.2d 1105, 1107. Payment or satisfaction. Ledbetter v. Hall, 191 Ark. 791, 87 S.W.2d 996, 999. In legal parlance, implies meeting of minds of parties to transaction or controversy. Ezmirlian v. Otto, 139 Cal.App. 486, 34 P.2d 774, 778.

See, also, Settle.

Contracts

Adjustment or liquidation of mutual accounts; the act by which parties who have been dealing together arrange their accounts and strike a balance. Also full and final payment or discharge of an account. Bauer v. National Union Fire Ins. Co. of Pittsburgh, Pa., 51 N.D. 1, 198 N.W. 546, 550; Michael v. Donohoe, 86 W.Va. 34, 102 S.E. 803, 805.

Conveyancing

A disposition of property by deed, usually through the medium of a trustee, by which its enjoyment is limited to several persons in succession, as a wife, children, or other relatives.

Poor Laws

A right acquired by a person, by continued residence for a given length of time in a town or district, to claim aid or relief under the poor-laws in case of his becoming a pauper. Delaware, L. & W. R. Co. v. Petrowsky, C.C.A.N.Y., 250 F. 554, 560, certiorari denied 38 S.Ct. 427, 247 U.S. 508, 62 L. Ed. 1241; Inhabitants of Trenton v. City of Brewer, 134 Me. 295, 186 A. 612, 614.

Settlement once acquired is not necessarily lost or defeated by a voluntary absence for the purpose of obtaining work. State ex rel. Heydenreich v. Lyons, 374 Ill. 557, 30 N.E.2d 46, 51.

Probate Practice

The settlement of an estate consists in its administration by the executor or administrator carried so far that all debts and legacies have been paid and the individual shares of distributees in the corpus of the estate, or the residuary portion, as the case may be, definitely ascertained and determined, and accounts filed and passed, so that nothing remains but to make final distribution. Appeal of Mathews, 72 Conn. 555, 45 A. 170; Pearce v. Pearce, 199 Ala. 491, 74 So. 952, 957.

Public Transactions and Accounts

Administrative determination of the amount due. Illinois Surety Co. v. U. S., 36 S.Ct. 321, 323, 240 U.S. 214, 60 L.Ed. 609; Illinois Surety Co. v. United States, C.C.A.S.C., 215 F. 334, 336; United States, for Use of R. Haas Electric & Mfg. Co., v. Title Guaranty & Surety Co., C.C.A.7, 254 F. 958, 959; U. S., to Use of Crellin, v. George F. Pawling & Co., C.C.A.3, 297 F. 65, 68.

General

Act of settlement. The statute 12 & 13 Wm. III. c. 2, by which the crown of England was limited to the house of Hanover, and some new provisions were added at the same time for the better securing the religion, laws, and liberties.

Deed of settlement. A deed made for the purpose of settling property, *i. e.*, arranging the mode and extent of the enjoyment thereof. The party who settles property is called the "settlor;" and usually his wife and children or his creditors or his near relations are the beneficiaries taking interests under the settlement. Brown.

Equity of settlement. The equitable right of a wife, when her husband sues in equity for the reduction of her equitable estate to his own possession, to have the whole or a portion of such estate settled upon herself and her children. Also a similar right now recognized by the equity courts as directly to be asserted against the husband. Also called the "wife's equity."

Family settlement. See Family Settlement.

Final settlement. This term, as applied to the administration of an estate, is usually understood to have reference to the order of court approving the account which closes the business of the estate, and which finally discharges the executor or administrator from the duties of his trust. Roberts v. Spencer, 112 Ind. 85, 13 N.E. 129.

Strict settlement. This phrase was formerly used to denote a settlement whereby land was limited to a parent for life, and after his death to his first and other sons or children in tail, with trustees interposed to preserve contingent remainders. 1 Steph. Comm. 332, 333. In England, a settlement to the use of the settlor for life, and after his death to the use that his widow may receive a rent charge (or jointure), subject to these life interests, to trustees for a long term of years in trust to raise by mortgage on the term a sum of money for the portions for his younger children, and subject thereto to the use of his first and other sons successively and the heirs male of their bodies, with the ultimate remainder in default of issue to the settlor in fee simple.

Voluntary settlement. A settlement of property upon a wife or other beneficiary, made gratuitously or without valuable consideration.

SETTLER. A person who, for the purpose of acquiring a pre-emption right, has gone upon the land in question, and is actually resident there. Hume v. Gracy, 86 Tex. 671, 27 S.W. 584; McIntyre v. Sherwood, 82 Cal. 139, 22 P. 937.

SETTLOR. The grantor or donor in a deed of settlement.

Also one who creates trust. Ulmer v. Fulton, 129 Ohio St. 323, 195 N.E. 557, 564, 97 A.L.R. 1170. One who furnishes the consideration for the creation of a trust, though in form the trust is created by another. Lehman v. Commissioner of Internal Revenue, C.C.A.2, 109 F.2d 99, 100.

SEVER. To separate, as one from another; to cut off from something; to divide; to part in any way, especially by violence, as by cutting, rending, etc.; as, to sever the head from the body; to cut or break open or apart; to divide into parts; to cut through; to disjoin; as, to sever the arm or leg. Muse v. Metropolitan Life Ins. Co., 193 La. 605, 192 So. 72, 74, 125 A.L.R. 1075. In practice. To insist upon a plea distinct from that of other co-defendants.

SEVERABLE. Admitting of severance or separation, capable of being divided; separable; capable of being severed from other things to which it was joined, and yet maintaining a complete and independent existence. State ex rel. Dolman v. Dickey, 288 Mo. 92, 231 S.W. 582, 585; Lawson v. Muse, 180 Mo.App. 35, 165 S.W. 396, 397.

SEVERABLE CONTRACT. See Contract.

SEVERABLE STATUTE. A statute if after an invalid portion of it has been stricken out, that which remains is self-sustaining and capable of separate enforcement without regard to the stricken portion, in which case that which remains should be sustained. Rutenberg v. City of Philadelphia, 329 Pa. 26, 196 A. 73, 79.

SEVERAL. More than two, often used to designate a number greater than one. First Nat. Trust & Savings Bank of San Diego v. Industrial Accident Commission, 2 P.2d 347, 351, 213 Cal. 322, 78 A.L.R. 1324. Each particular, or a small number, singly taken. Nashville, C. & St. L. Ry. v. Marshall County, 161 Tenn. 236, 30 S.W.2d 268. Separate; individual; independent; severable. In this sense the word is distinguished from "joint." Also exclusive; individual; appropriated. In this sense it is opposed to "common." Townsend v. Roof, 210 Mo.App. 293, 237 S.W. 189, 190; L. L. Satler Lumber Co. v. Exler, 239 Pa. 135, 86 A. 793, 798.

As to several "Counts," "Covenant," "Demise," "Fishery," "Tail," and "Tenancy," see those titles.

SEVERAL ACTIONS. Where a separate and distinct action is brought against each of two or more persons who are all liable to the plaintiff in respect to the same subject-matter, the actions are said to be "several." If all the persons are joined as defendants in one and the same action, it is called a "joint" action.

SEVERAL INHERITANCE. An inheritance conveyed so as to descend to two persons severally, by moieties, etc.

SEVERAL ISSUES. This occurs where there is more than one issue involved in a case. 3 Steph. Comm. 560.

SEVERALLY. Distinctly, separately, apart from others. State Nat. Bk. v. Reilly, 124 Ill. 471, 14 N. E. 657. When applied to a number of persons the expression *severally liable* usually implies that each one is liable alone. Pruyn v. Black, 21 N.Y. 301.

SEVERALTY. A state of separation. An estate in *severalty* is one that is held by a person in his own right only, without any other person being joined or connected with him, in point of interest, during his estate therein. 2 Bl.Comm. 179.

The term "severalty" is especially applied, in England, to the case of adjoining meadows undivided from each other, but belonging, either permanently or in what are called "shifting severalties," to separate owners, and held in severalty until the crops have been carried, when the whole is thrown open as pasture for the cattle of all the owners, and in some cases for the cattle of other persons as well; each owner is called a "severalty owner," and his rights of pasture are called "severalty rights," as opposed to the rights of persons not owners. Cooke, Incl.Acts, 47, 163*n*.

SEVERALTY, ESTATE IN. An estate which is held by the tenant in his own right only, without any other being joined or connected with him in point of interest during the continuance of his estate. 2 Bl.Comm. 179.

SEVERANCE. Act of severing, or state of being severed; partition; separation. Muse v. Metropolitan Life Ins. Co., 193 La. 605, 192 So. 72, 74, 125 A.L.R. 1075.

Pleading

Separation; division. The separation by defendants in their pleas; the adoption, by several defendants, of separate pleas, instead of joining in the same plea. Steph.Pl. 257.

Property

The destruction of any one of the unities of a joint tenancy. It is so called because the estate is no longer a joint tenancy, but is severed. Cutting of the crops, such as corn, grass, etc., or the separating of anything from the realty. Brown.

SEVERANCE DAMAGE. Any element of value arising out of relation of condemned portion to tract of which it was a part. It is to be included in owner's compensation. U. S. v. Miller, 63 S. Ct. 276, 281, 317 U.S. 369, 87 L.Ed. 336, 147 A.L.R. 55.

SEVERE. Sharp, grave, distressing, violent, extreme, torture, rigorous, difficult to be endured. Traders & General Ins. Co. v. Crouch, Tex.Civ. App., 113 S.W.2d 650, 652.

SEVERE ILLNESS. Within life policy. An illness as has, or ordinarily does have, a permanent, detrimental effect upon the physical system. Boos v. Life Ins. Co., 64 N.Y. 236; Pickens v. Security Ben. Ass'n, 231 P. 1016, 1019, 117 Kan. 475, 40 A.L.R. 654.

SEWAGE. Refuse and foul matter, solid or liquid, carried off by sewer. Borough of Wilkinsburg v. School Dist. of Borough of Wilkinsburg, 298 Pa. 193, 148 A. 77, 80.

SEWAGE SYSTEM. A system of sewers for the drainage of foul waters of a community. Pioneer Real Estate Co. v. City of Portland, 247 P. 319, 321, 119 Or. 1.

SEWARD, or SEAWARD. One who guards the sea-coast; *custos maris*.

SEWER. A fresh-water trench or little river, encompassed with banks on both sides, to drain off surplus water into the sea. Cowell. Properly, a trench artificially made for the purpose of carrying water into the sea,* (or a river or pond.) Crabb, Real Prop. § 113; Bennett v. New Bedford, 110 Mass. 433.

In its modern and more usual sense, an artificial (usually under-ground or covered) channel used for the drainage of two or more separate buildings. State Board of Health v. Jersey City, 55 N.J.Eq. 116, 35 A. 835; Aldrich v. Paine, 106 Iowa 461, 76 N.W. 812.

"Sewers" differ from "drains" only in that the former are in cities, and generally covered over, while the latter are in rural communities, and open. Pioneer Real Estate Co. v. City of Portland, 119 Or. 1, 247 P. 319, 321. See, also, Barton v. Drainage Dist. No. 30, 174 Ark. 173, 294 S.W. 418, 419.

Commissioners of Sewers

In English law. The court of commissioners of sewers is a temporary tribunal erected by virtue of a commission under the great seal. Its jurisdiction is to overlook the repairs of sea-banks and sea-walls, and the cleansing of public rivers, streams, ditches, and other conduits whereby any waters are carried off, and is confined to such county or particular district as the commission expressly names. Brown.

Public Sewer

One which serves the public and connects with and receives the discharges from district sewers. Schwabe v. Moore, 187 Mo.App. 74, 172 S.W. 1157, 1159.

Sewer Outlet

As used in a statute, that portion of a sewer which serves no other purpose than to connect the sewer system with the point of discharge. Mogaard v. Robinson, 48 N.D. 859, 187 N.W. 142, 143.

Trunk Sewer

One which bears the same relation to a system of sewers that the trunk of a tree bears to its branches. Rush v. Grandy, 66 Mont. 222, 213 P. 242, 243.

SEX. The sum of the peculiarities of structure and function that distinguish a male from a female organism; the character of being male or female. Webster, Dict.

SEXAGESIMA SUNDAY. In ecclesiastical law. The second Sunday before Lent, being about the sixtieth day before Easter.

SEXHINDENI. In Saxon law. The middle thanes, valued at 600s.

SEXTANS. Lat. In Roman law. A subdivision of the *as*, containing two *unciæ;* the proportion of two-twelfths, or one-sixth. 2 Bl.Comm. 462, note.

SEXTARY. In old records. An ancient measure of liquids, and of dry commodities; a quarter or seam. Spelman.

SEXTERY LANDS. Lands given to a church or religious house for maintenance of a sexton or sacristan. Cowell.

SEXTON. An attendant or care-taker in a church building, usually with care of the attached burying ground.

SEXTUS DECRETALIUM. Lat. The sixth (book) of the decretals; the sext, or sixth decretal. So called because appended, in the body of the canon law, to the five books of the decretals of Gregory IX.; it consists of a collection of supplementary decretals, and was published A. D. 1298. Butl. Hor. Jur. 172; 1 Bl.Comm. 82.

SEXUAL DISEASES. Synonymous with venereal diseases. State v. Hollinshead, 77 Or. 473, 151 P. 710, 711.

SEXUAL INSTINCT, INVERSION AND PERVERSION OF. See Insanity; Pederasty; Sodomy.

SEXUAL INTERCOURSE. Carnal copulation of male and female, implying actual penetration of the organs of the latter. Williams v. State, 92 Fla. 125, 109 So. 305, 306.

SHACK. In English law. The straying and escaping of cattle out of the lands of their owners into other uninclosed land; an intercommoning of cattle. 2 H.Bl. 416.

It sometimes happens that a number of adjacent fields, though held in severalty, *i. e.*, by separate owners, and cultivated separately, are, after the crop on each parcel has been carried in, thrown open as pasture to the cattle of all the owners. "Arable lands cultivated on this plan are called 'shack fields,' and the right of each owner of a part to feed cattle over the whole during the autumn and winter is known in law as 'common of shack,' a right which is distinct in its nature from common because of vicinage, though sometimes said to be nearly identical with it." Elton, Commons, 30; Sweet.

SHAFT. An opening in the ground or in structures. Franklin v. Webber, 93 Or. 151, 182 P. 819, 820.

SHALL. As used in statutes, contracts, or the like, this word is generally imperative or mandatory. McDunn v. Roundy, 191 Iowa, 976, 181 N. W. 453, 454; Bay State St. Ry. Co. v. City of Woburn, 232 Mass. 201, 122 N.E. 268; U. S. v. Two Hundred and Sixty-Seven Twenty-Dollar Gold Pieces, D.C.Wash., 255 F. 217, 218; Baer v. Gore, 79 W.Va. 50, 90 S.E. 530, 531, L.R.A.1917B, 723.

In common or ordinary parlance, and in its ordinary signification, the term "shall" is a word of command, and one which has always or which must be given a compulsory meaning; as denoting obligation. It has a peremptory meaning, and it is generally imperative or mandatory. It has the invariable significance of excluding the idea of discretion, and has the significance of operating to impose a duty which may be enforced, particularly if public policy is in favor of this meaning, or when addressed to public officials, or where a public interest is involved, or where the public or persons have rights which ought to be exercised or enforced, unless a contrary intent appears. People v. O'Rourke, 124 Cal.App. 752, 13 P.2d 989, 992.

But it may be construed as merely permissive or directory, (as equivalent to "may,") to carry out the legislative intention and in cases where no right or benefit to any one depends on its being taken in the imperative sense, and where no public or private right is impaired by its interpretation in the other sense. Spaulding & Kimball v. Ætna Chemical Co., 98 Vt. 169, 126 A. 588, 589; Wisdom v. Board of Sup'rs of Polk County, 236 Iowa 669, 19 N.W.2d 602, 607, 608. Also, as against the government, it is to be construed as "may," unless a contrary intention is manifest. Cairo & Fulton R. Co. v. Hecht, 95 U.S. 170, 24 L.Ed. 423.

Although the word usually denotes an obligation, it also implies an element of futurity. Cunningham v. Long, 125 Me. 494, 135 A. 198, 200; Hemsley v. McKim, 119 Md. 431, 87 A. 506, 511.

SHAM. False;—said of a pleading. Germofert Mfg. Co. v. Castles, 97 S.C. 389, 81 S.E. 665, 666; Segerstrom v. Holland Piano Mfg. Co., 160 Minn. 95, 199 N.W. 897, 898. A sham pleading is therefore one good in form, but false in fact. Bollen v. Woodhams, 68 Colo. 322, 190 P. 427.

For sham "Answer," "Plea," and "Reply," see those titles.

SHANGHAI. To drug, intoxicate, or render insensible and ship as a sailor,—usually to secure advance money or a premium. Webster, Dict.

Under federal law, procuring or inducing, or attempting to do so, by force, or threats, or by representations which one knows or believes to be untrue, or while the person is intoxicated or under the influence of any drug, to go on board of any vessel, or agree to do so, to perform service or labor thereon, such vessel being engaged in interstate or foreign commerce, on the high seas or any navigable water of the United States, or knowingly to detain on board such vessel such person, so procured or induced, or knowingly aiding or abetting such things, is an offense. See 18 U.S.C.A. § 2194.

SHARE, *v.* To partake; enjoy with others; have a portion of. Cook v. Worthington, 116 Ark. 328, 173 S.W. 395, 396; People v. Sigers, 217 Mich. 578, 187 N.W. 373, 374.

SHARE, *n.* A part or definite portion of a thing owned by a number of persons in common and contemplates something owned in common by two or more persons and has reference to that part of the undivided interest which belongs to some one of them. In re Bond & Mortgage Guarantee Co., 157 Misc. 240, 283 N.Y.S. 623, 639.

In the law of corporations and joint-stock companies, a definite portion of the capital of a company.

See, also, Share of Corporate Stock.

SHARE AND SHARE ALIKE. In equal shares or proportions. Jenne v. Jenne, 271 Ill. 526, 111 N.E. 540, 543; Rogers v. Burress, 199 Ky. 766, 251 S.W. 980, 981. The words commonly indicate per capita division; Burton v. Cahill, 192 N.C. 505, 135 S.E. 332, 335; and they may be applied to a division between classes as well as to a division among individuals; Laisure v. Richards, 56 Ind. App. 301, 103 N.E. 679, 682; Tucker v. Nugent, 117 Me. 10, 102 A. 307, 310.

SHARE CERTIFICATE. An instrument under the seal of the company, certifying that the person therein named is entitled to a certain number oi shares; it is *prima facie* evidence of his title thereto. Frank Gilbert Paper Co. v. Prankard, 204 App.Div. 83, 198 N.Y.S. 25, 28; Furr v. Chapman, Tex.Com.App., 286•S.W. 171, 172.

SHARE OF CORPORATE STOCK. A proportional part of certain rights in the management and profits of a corporation during its existence, and in the assets upon dissolution, and evidence of the stockholder's ratable share in the distribution of the assets on the winding up of the corporation's business. Department of Treasury of Indiana v. Crowder, 214 Ind. 252, 15 N.E.2d 89, 91; Commissioner of Internal Revenue v. Scatena, C.C.A.9, 85 F. 729, 732.

SHARE-WARRANT TO BEARER. A warrant or certificate under the seal of the company, stating that the bearer of the warrant is entitled to a certain number or amount of fully paid up shares or stock. Coupons for payment of dividends may be annexed to it. Delivery of the share-warrant operates as a transfer of the shares or stock. Sweet.

SHAREHOLDER. Strictly, a person who has agreed to become a member of a corporation or company, and with respect to whom all the required formalities have been gone through; *e. g.*, signing of deed of settlement, registration, or the like. A shareholder by estoppel is a person who has acted and been treated as a shareholder, and consequently has the same liabilities as if he were an ordinary shareholder. Lindl. Partn. 130. Beal v. Essex Sav. Bank, C.C.A.Mass., 67 F. 816, 15 C.C.A. 128; State v. Mitchell, 104 Tenn. 336, 58 S.W. 365.

SHARP. A "sharp" clause in a mortgage or other security (or the whole instrument described as "sharp") is one which empowers the creditor to take prompt and summary action upon default in payment or breach of other conditions.

SHARPING CORN. A customary gift of corn, which, at every Christmas, the farmers in some parts of England give to their smith for sharpening their plow-irons, harrow-tines, etc. Blount.

SHASTER. In Hindu law. The instrument of government or instruction; any book of instructions, particularly containing Divine ordinances. Wharton.

SHAVE. Sometimes used to denote the act of obtaining the property of another by oppression and extortion. Also used in an innocent sense to denote the buying of existing notes and other securities for money, at a discount. Hence to charge a man with using money for shaving is not libelous *per se.* Trentham v. Moore, 111 Tenn. 346, 76 S.W. 904.

SHAW. In old English law. A wood. Co.Litt. 4*b*.

SHAWATORES. Soldiers. Cowell.

SHEADING. A riding, tithing, or division in the Isle of Man, where the whole island is divided nto six sheadings, in each of which there is a coroner or chief constable appointed by a delivery of a rod at the Tinewald court or annual convention. King, Isle of Man, 7.

SHEEP. A term which ordinarily includes rams, ewes, and lambs. Panhandle & S. F. Ry. Co. v. Bell, Tex.Civ.App., 189 S.W. 1097, 1101. But in the Stat. 7 & 8 Geo. IV, c. 29, § 25, making it a felony to steal any "ram, ewe, sheep, or lamb," the word "sheep" should be used in indictments only when it is intended to refer to a wether more than a year old. Rex v. Birket, 4 Car. & P. 216.

SHEEP–HEAVES. Small plots of pasture, in England, often in the middle of the waste of a manor, of which the soil may or may not be in the lord, but the pasture is private property, and leased or sold as such. They principally occur in the northern counties, (Cooke, Incl. Acts, 44,) and seem to be corporeal hereditaments, (Elton, Commons, 35,) although they are sometimes classed with rights of common, but erroneously, the right being an exclusive right of pasture. Sweet.

SHEEP–SILVER. A service turned into money, which was paid in respect that anciently the tenants used to wash the lord's sheep. Wharton.

SHEEP–SKIN. A deed; so called from the parchment it was written on.

SHEEP–WALK. Right of. Fold-course (*q. v.*) Elton, Commons, 44.

SHEETING. In a technical sense, a form of pile driving, being the lining of timber to a caisson or cofferdam formed of sheet piles or piles with flanking between them. Mazzarisi v. Ward & Tully, 156 N.Y.S. 964, 170 App.Div. 868.

SHELL SHOCK. Not a distinct type of nervous disorder, but a condition produced on certain organisms by sudden fear, or by highly exciting causes; it is a form of neurosis; it is not settled, general insanity, but a functional nervous disease, and not due to organic changes. People v. Gilberg, 197 Cal. 306, 240 P. 1000, 1002. See, also, Shock.

SHELLEY'S CASE, RULE IN. "When the ancestor, by any gift or conveyance, taketh an estate of freehold, and in the same gift or conveyance an estate is limited, either mediately or immediately, to his heirs in fee or in tail, 'the heirs' are words of limitation of the estate, and not words of purchase." 1 Coke, 104; Winchell v. Winchell, 259 Ill. 471, 102 N.E. 823, 824; Gordon v. Cadwalader, 164 Cal. 509, 130 P. 18, 19; McHatton's Estate v. Peale's Estate, Tex.Civ.App., 248 S.W. 103, 105.

This rule is expressed by Chancellor Kent as follows: "Where a person takes an estate of freehold, legally or equitably, under a deed, will, or other writing, and in the same instrument there is a limitation by way of remainder, either with or without the interposition of another estate, of any interest of the same legal or equitable quality to his heirs, or heirs of his body, as a class of persons to take in succession from generation to generation, the limitation to the heirs entitles the ancestor to the whole estate." In re Thorne's Estate, 344 Pa. 503, 25 A.2d 811, 819.

Intimately connected with the quantity of estate which a tenant may hold in realty is the antique feudal doctrine generally known as the "Rule in Shelley's Case," which is reported by Lord Coke in 1 Coke, 93*b* (23 Eliz. in C.B.). This rule was not first laid down or established in that case, but was then simply admitted in argument as a well-founded and settled rule of law, and has always since been quoted as the "Rule in Shelley's Case." Wharton. The rule was adopted as a part of the common law of this country, and in many of the states still prevails. It has been abolished in most of them.

SHELTER. In a statute relating to the provision of food, clothing, and shelter for one's children, a home with proper environments, as well as protection from the weather. Hummel v. State, 73 Ind. App. 12, 126 N.E. 444, 446.

SHEREFFE. The body of the lordship of Cærdiff in South Wales, excluding the members of it. Powel, Hist. Wales, 123.

SHERIFF.

American Law

The chief executive and administrative officer of a county, being chosen by popular election. His principal duties are in aid of the criminal courts and civil courts of record; such as serving process, summoning juries, executing judgments, holding judicial sales and the like. He is also the chief conservator of the peace within his territorial jurisdiction. Harston v. Langston, Tex.Civ. App., 292 S.W. 648, 650. When used in statutes, the term may include a deputy sheriff. Lanier v. Town of Greenville, 174 N.C. 311, 93 S.E. 850, 853.

English Law

The principal officer in every county, who has the transacting of the public business of the county. He is an officer of great antiquity, and was also called the "shire-reeve," "reeve," or "bailiff." He is called in Latin "*vice-comes,*" as being the deputy of the earl or *comes*, to whom anciently the custody of the shire was committed. The duties of the sheriff principally consist in executing writs, precepts, warrants from justices of the peace for the apprehension of offenders, etc. Brown.

Scotch Law

The office of sheriff differs somewhat from the same office under the English law, being, from ancient times, an office of important judicial power, as well as ministerial. The sheriff exercises a jurisdiction of considerable extent, both of civil and criminal character, which is, in a proper sense, judicial, in addition to powers resembling those of an English sheriff. Tomlins; Bell.

General

Deputy sheriff. See Deputy.

High sheriff. One holding the office of sheriff, as distinguished from his deputies or assistants or under sheriffs.

Pocket sheriff. In English law. A sheriff appointed by the sole authority of the crown, without the usual form of nomination by the judges in the exchequer. 1 Bl.Comm. 342; 3 Steph.Comm. 23.

SHERIFF CLERK. The clerk of the sheriff's court in Scotland.

SHERIFF DEPUTE. In Scotch law. The principal sheriff of a county, who is also a judge.

SHERIFF-GELD. A rent formerly paid by a sheriff, and it is prayed that the sheriff in his account may be discharged thereof. Rot. Parl. 50 Edw. III.

SHERIFF-TOOTH. In English law. A tenure by the service of providing entertainment for the sheriff at his county courts. An ancient tax on land in Derbyshire. A common tax formerly levied for the sheriff's diet. Cowell; Wharton.

SHERIFF'S COURT. The court held before the sheriff's deputy, that is, the undersheriff, and wherein actions are brought for recovery of debts under £20. Writs of inquiry are also brought here to be executed. The sheriff's court for the county of Middlesex is that wherein damages are assessed in proper cases after trial at Westminster. Brown.

SHERIFF'S COURT IN LONDON. A tribunal having cognizance of personal actions under the London (city) Small Debts Act of 1852. See 3 Steph.Comm., 11th ed. 30, n., 301, 449, note (1); 3 Bla.Comm. 80, note (j).

The "Sheriffs Court of the City of London" was the name by which the City of London Court was known prior to the County Courts Act, 1867, 30 & 31 Vict. c. 142, § 35. Its procedure was, theretofore, regulated by Acts and Rules peculiar to itself; but by the above enactment, re-enacted by section 185 of the County Courts Act, 1888, it becomes to all intents and purposes a county court. Wharton.

SHERIFF'S JURY. In practice. A jury composed of no determinate number, but which may be more or less than twelve, summoned by the sheriff for the purposes of an inquisition or inquest of office. 3 Bl.Comm. 258.

SHERIFF'S OFFICERS. Bailiffs, who are either bailiffs of hundreds or bound-bailiffs.

SHERIFF'S SALE. See Sale.

SHERIFF'S TOURN. A court of record in England, formerly held twice every year, within a month after Easter and Michaelmas, before the sheriff, in different parts of the county. It was, indeed, only the *turn* or rotation of the sheriff to keep a court-leet in each respective hundred. This was the great court-leet of the county, as the county court is the court-baron; for out of this, for the ease of the sheriff, was taken the court-leet or view of frank-pledge. 4 Bl.Comm. 273. It was obsolete in Coke's time, but was not abolished till 1887. It had a limited criminal jurisdiction.

SHERIFFALTY, or SHRIEVALTY. The time of a man's being sheriff. Cowell. The term of a sheriff's office. Also, the office itself.

SHERIFFWICK. The jurisdiction of a sheriff. Called, in modern law, "bailiwick." The office of a sheriff.

SHERRERIE. A word used by the authorities of the Roman Church, to specify contemptuously the technical parts of the law, as administered by non-clerical lawyers. Wharton.

SHEWER. In the practice of the English high court, when a view by a jury is ordered, persons are named by the court to show the property to be viewed, and are hence called "shewers." There is usually a shewer on behalf of each party. Archb.Pr. 339, et seq.

SHEWING. In English law. To be quit of attachment in a court, in plaints shewed and not avowed. Obsolete.

SHIFT MARRIAGE. When a man died having debts which his widow was unable to pay, she was obliged, if she contracted a second marriage, to leave her clothes in the hands of the creditors, and to go through the ceremony in her shift. Gradually, however, the ceremony was mitigated by the bridegroom lending her clothes for the occasion. Said by Lecky, Hist. of Eng. 18th Cent., IV, p. 23, to be a curious relic of a standard of commercial integrity which had long since passed away.

SHIFTING. Changing; varying; passing from one person to another by substitution.

SHIFTING CLAUSE. In a settlement, a clause by which some other mode of devolution is substituted for that primarily prescribed. Examples of shifting clauses are: The ordinary name and arms clause, and the clause of less frequent occurrence by which a settled estate is destined as the foundation of a second family, in the event of the elder branch becoming otherwise enriched. These shifting clauses take effect under the statute of uses. Sweet.

SHIFTING RISK. In insurance, a risk created by a contract of insurance on a stock of merchandise, or other similar property, which is kept for sale, or is subject to change in items by purchase and sale; the policy being conditioned to cover the goods in the stock at any and all times and not to be affected by changes in its composition. Farmers' etc., Ins. Ass'n v. Kryder, 5 Ind.App. 430, 31 N.E. 851, 51 Am.St.Rep. 284.

SHIFTING SEVERALTY. See Severalty.

SHIFTING STOCK OF MERCHANDISE. A stock of merchandise subject to change from time to time, in the course of trade by purchases, sales, or other transactions. Laderburg v. Miller, C.C.A. Va., 210 F. 614, 617.

SHIFTING THE BURDEN OF PROOF. Transferring it from one party to the other, or from one side of the case to the other, when he upon whom it rested originally has made out a *prima facie* case or defense by evidence, of such a character that it then becomes incumbent upon the other to rebut it by contradictory or defensive evidence.

SHIFTING USE. See Use.

SHILLING. In English law. The name of an English coin, of the value of one-twentieth part of a pound. This denomination of money was also used in America, in colonial times, but was not everywhere of uniform value.

SHIN-PLASTER. Formerly, a jocose term for a bank-note greatly depreciated in value; also for paper money of a denomination less than a dollar. Webster, Dict. See Madison Ins. Co. v. Forsythe, 2 Ind. 483.

SHINNEY. A local name for a homemade whisky. State v. McClinton, 94 So. 141, 142, 152 La. 632.

SHINTO. State religion of Japan.

SHIP, *v.* To put on board a ship; to send by ship. Harrison v. Fortlage, 16 S.Ct. 488, 490, 161 U.S. 57, 40 L.Ed. 616. To place (goods) on board of a vessel for the purchaser or consignee, to be transported at his risk. Krauter v. Menchacatorre, 202 App.Div. 200, 195 N.Y.S. 361, 363.

In a broader sense, to transport. Burton v. State, 135 Ark. 612, 206 S.W. 51, 52. To deliver to a common carrier for transportation. State v. Bayer, 93 Ohio St. 72, 112 N.E. 197, 198; Horner v. Daily, 77 Ind.App. 378, 133 N.E. 585, 587. To send away, to get rid of. Bird v. State, 131 Tenn. 518, 175 S.W. 554, 556, Ann.Cas.1917A, 634. To send by established mode of transportation, as to "carry," "convey," or "transport," which are synonymous and defined, respectively, as "to bear or cause to be borne as from one place to another," "to transport from one place to another," and "to carry or convey from one place to another." Chicago, R. I. & P. Ry. Co. v. Petroleum Refining Co., D.C.Ky., 39 F.2d 629, 630.

SHIP, *n.* A vessel of any kind employed in navigation. In a more restricted and more technical sense, a three-masted vessel navigated with sails. U. S. v. Kelly, 4 Wash.C.C. 528, F.Cas.No.15,516.

Nautical men apply the term "ship" to distinguish a vessel having three masts, each consisting of a lower mast, a topmast, and a topgallant mast, with their appropriate rigging. In familiar language, it is usually employed to distinguish any large vessel, however rigged. Tomlins; Cope v. Vallette Dry-Dock Co., 119 U.S. 625, 7 S.Ct. 336, 30 L.Ed. 501; Swan v. U. S., 19 Ct.Cl. 62; The St. Louis, D.C.Ky., 48 F. 312; Wood v. Two Barges, C.C.La., 46 F. 204, as to what is not a ship.

An agreement to construct an ocean going ship is performed by the construction of an ocean going barge suitable for a cargo carrying steamer, since the hull and spars constitute the ship. Bell v. First Nat. Bank of Rockport, Tex.Civ.App., 226 S.W. 1107.

Ex Ship

These words in a contract of sale are not restricted to any particular ship, and by the usage of merchants simply denote that the property in the goods shall pass to the buyer upon their leaving the ship's tackle, and that he shall be liable for all subsequent charges of landing. They do not constitute a condition of the contract but are inserted for the benefit of the seller. Harrison v. Fortlage, 16 S.Ct. 488, 161 U.S. 57, 40 L.Ed. 616.

General Ship

Where a ship is not chartered wholly to one person, but the owner offers her generally to carry the goods of all comers, or where, if chartered to one person, he offers her to several subfreighters for the conveyance of their goods, she is called a "general" ship, as opposed to a "chartered" one. Brown. One which is employed by the charterer or owner on a particular voyage, and is hired to a number of persons, unconnected with each other to convey their respective goods to the place of destination. Alexander Eccles & Co. v. Strachan Shipping Co., D.C.Ga., 21 F.2d 653, 655; Ward v. Green, 6 Cow., N.Y., 173, 16 Am.Dec. 437.

Ship-Breaking

In Scotch law. The offense of breaking into a ship. Arkley, 461.

Ship-Broker

An agent for the transaction of business between ship-owners and charterers or those who ship cargoes. Little Rock v. Barton, 33 Ark. 444.

Ship-Chandlery

A term of extensive import, and includes everything necessary to furnish and equip a vessel, so as to render her seaworthy for the intended voyage.

Not only stores, stoves, hardware, and crockery have been held to be within the term, but muskets and other arms also, the voyage being round Cape Horn to California, in the course of which voyage arms are sometimes carried for safety. Weaver v. The S. G. Owens, Pa., 29 F.Cas. 17,310; 29 F.Cas. 489.

Ship-Channel

In rivers, harbors, etc., the channel in which the water is deep enough for vessels of large size, usually marked out in harbors by buoys. The Oliver, D.C.Va., 22 F. 848.

Ship-Damage

In the charter-parties with the English East India Company, these words occur. Their meaning is, damage from negligence, insufficiency, or bad stowage in the ship. Abb. Shipp. 204.

Ship-Master

The captain or master of a merchant ship, appointed and put in command by the owner, and having general control of the vessel and cargo, with power to bind the owner by his lawful acts and engagements in the management of the ship.

Ship-Money

In English law. An imposition formerly levied on port-towns and other places for fitting out ships; revived by Charles I., and abolished in the same reign. 17 Car. I. c. 14.

Ship's-Bill

The copy of the bill of lading retained by the master. It is not authoritative as to the terms of the contract of affreightment; the bill delivered to the shipper must control, if the two do not agree. The Thames, 14 Wall. 98, 20 L.Ed. 804.

Ship's Company

A term embracing all the officers of the ship, as well as the mariners or common seamen, but not a passenger. U. S. v. Libby, 26 F.Cas. 928; U. S. v. Winn, 28 F.Cas. 735.

Ship's Husband

In maritime law. A person appointed by the several part-owners of a ship, and usually one of their number, to manage the concerns of the ship for the common benefit. Generally understood to be the general agent of the owners in regard to all the affairs of the ship in the home port. Story, Ag. § 35; 3 Kent, Comm. 151; Webster v. The Andes, 18 Ohio 187; Muldon v. Whitlock, 1 Cow., N.Y., 307, 13 Am.Dec. 533; 1 Y. & C. 326; Gould v. Stanton, 16 Conn. 12. He cannot insure or bind the owners for premiums. Hewett v. Buck, 17 Me. 147, 35 Am.Dec. 243; 2 Maule & S. 485; Foster v. Ins. Co., 11 Pick., Mass., 85; 5 Burr. 2627.

Ship's Papers

The papers which must be carried by a vessel on a voyage, in order to furnish evidence of her national character, the nature and destination of the cargo, and of compliance with the navigation laws. The ship's papers are of two sorts: Those required by the law of a particular country; such as the certificate of registry, license, charter-party, bills of lading and of health, required by the law of England to be on board all British ships. These required by the law of nations to be on board neutral ships, to vindicate their title to that character; these are the pass port, sea-brief, or sea-letter, proofs of property, the muster-roll or *rôle d'equipage*, the charter-party, the bills of lading and invoices, the log-book or ship's journal, and the bill of health. 1 March. Ins. c. 9, § 6. See, also, Grace v. Browne, C.C.A.N.Y., 86 F. 155.

SHIPMENT. The delivery of the goods within the time required on some vessel, destined to the particular port, which the seller has reason to suppose will sail within a reasonable time. It does not mean a clearance of the vessel as well as putting the goods on board where there is nothing to indicate that the seller was expected to exercise any control over the clearance of the vessel or of her subsequent management. Ledon v. Havemeyer, 121 N.Y. 179, 24 N.E. 297, 8 L.R.A. 245. See L.R. 2 App.Cas. 455; Stubbs v. Lund, 7 Mass. 453, 5 Am.Dec. 63; Lamborn & Co. v. Log Cabin Products Co., D.C.Minn., 291 F. 435, 438.

The delivery of goods to a carrier and his issuance of a bill of lading therefor. Goldenberg v. Cutler, 189 App.Div. 489, 178 N.Y.S. 522, 523.

A "shipment" does not consist in loading alone, but consists in complete delivery of goods by the shipper to the carrier for transportation, and shipment is not made until the shipper has parted with all control over the goods and nothing remains to be done by him to complete delivery. National Importing & Trading Co. v. E. A. Bear & Co., 324 Ill. 346, 155 N.E. 343, 346.

The transportation of goods. Pennsylvania R. Co. v. Carolina Portland Cement Co., C.C.A.S.C., 16 F.2d 760, 761.

Also, the property which is the subject of transportation. Pennsylvania R. Co. v. Carolina Portland Cement Co., C.C.A.S.C., 16 F.2d 760, 761. An order. Young v. Flickinger, 75 Cal.App. 171, 242 P. 516, 517. A consignment of goods as delivered by the carrier. Pennsylvania R. Co. v. Kittanning Iron & Steel Mfg. Co., 263 Pa. 205, 106 A. 207, 208.

SHIPPER. A Dutch word, signifying the master of a ship. It is mentioned in some statutes, and is now generally called "skipper." Tomlins.

One who ships goods; one who puts goods on board of a vessel, for carriage to another place during her voyage and for delivery there, by charter-party or otherwise. One who signs a bill of lading as "shipper," unless the contrary appears, is presumably the consignor. New York Cent. R. Co. v. Singer Mfg. Co., 3 N.J.M. 1137, 131 A. 111, 114.

Under federal statutes, one is a "shipper" who, although a consignee, exercises such direct control over shipments of commodities consigned to him by another as enables him, by his own act, to procure for himself discriminations in respect to transportation service. U. S. v. Metropolitan Lumber Co., D.C.N.J., 254 F. 335, 346. Thus, a forwarder of freight, who sends in his own name all the freight he can over a carrier, which, in consideration of the business thus obtained, pays him a commission or salary calculated on the freight moneys received by the carrier from him, is a "shipper," and the payment in form of commission or salary or otherwise is a "rebate" or concession in violation of the Interstate Commerce Act Feb. 4, 1887, c. 104, § 6, 24 Stat. 380 (49 U.S.C.A. § 6), and Elkins Act Feb. 19, 1903, c. 708, 32 Stat. 847, § 1, as amended by Act June 29, 1906, c. 3591, 34 Stat. 587, § 2 (49 U.S.C.A. § 41). U. S. v. Lehigh Valley R. Co., D.C.N.Y., 222 F. 685, 686.

SHIPPER'S ORDER. In bills of lading, is well understood and means that the title remains in the shipper until he orders a delivery of the goods. B. W. McMahan & Co. v. State Nat. Bank of Shawnee, Tex.Civ.App., 160 S.W. 403, 404; Bennett v. Dickinson, 106 Kan. 95, 186 P. 1005.

SHIPPING. Ships in general; ships or vessels of any kind intended for navigation. Relating to ships; as, shipping interests, shipping affairs, shipping business, shipping concerns. Putting on board a ship or vessel, or receiving on board a ship or vessel. Webster, Dict.; Worcester, Dict.

Law of Shipping

A comprehensive term for all that part of the maritime law which relates to ships and the persons employed in or about them. It embraces such subjects as the building and equipment of vessels, their registration and nationality, their ownership and inspection, their employment, (including charter-parties, freight, demurrage, towage, and salvage,) and their sale, transfer, and mortgage; also, the employment, rights, powers, and duties of masters and mariners; and the law relating to ship-brokers, ship-agents, pilots, etc.

SHIPPING ARTICLES. A written agreement between the master of a vessel and the mariners, specifying the voyage or term for which the latter are shipped, and the rate of wages. See 46 U.S.C.A. § 564.

SHIPPING COMMISSIONER. An officer of the United States, appointed by the several circuit courts, within their respective jurisdictions, for each port of entry (the same being also a port of ocean navigation), which, in the judgment of such court, may require the same; his duties being to supervise the engagement and discharge of seamen; to see that men engaged as seamen report on board at the proper time; to facilitate the apprenticing of persons to the marine service; and other similar duties, such as may be required by law. 46 U.S.C.A. §§ 541–549 and notes.

SHIPWRECK. The demolition or shattering of a vessel, caused by her driving ashore or on rocks and shoals in the midseas, or by the violence of winds and waves in tempests. 2 Arn.Ins. p. 734.

SHIRE. A Saxon word which signified a division; it was made up of an indefinite number of hundreds—later called a county (*Comitatus*). 1 Steph.Com. 76.

English Law

A county. So called because every county or shire is divided and parted by certain metes and bounds from another. Co.Litt. 50*a*.

General

Knights of the shire. See that title.

Shire-clerk. He that keeps the county court.

Shire-gemot, scire-gemote, scir-gemot. (From the Saxon *scir* or *scyre*, county, shire, and *gemote*, a court, an assembly.) Variants of *scyregemote* (*q. v.*). See, also, Shire-mote, *infra*.

Shire-man, or scyre-man. Before the Conquest, the judge of the county, by whom trials for land, etc., were determined, Tomlins; Mozley & Whitley.

Shire-mote. The assize of the shire, or the assembly of the people, was so called by the Saxons. It was nearly if not exactly, the same as the *scyregemote*, and in most respects corresponded with what were afterwards called the "county courts." Brown.

Shire-reeve (spelled, also, Shire rieve, or Shire reve). In Saxon law. The reeve or bailiff of the shire. The *viscount* of the Anglo-Normans, and the *sheriff* of later times. Co.Litt. 168*a*.

SHOCK. A sudden agitation of the physical or mental sensibilities. Provident Life and Accident Ins. Co. v. Campbell, 18 Tenn.App. 452, 79 S.W.2d 292, 295.

Mental Shock

A sudden agitation of the mind; startling emotion, as the shock of a painful discovery, a shock of grief or joy. Provident Life and Accident Ins. Co. v. Campbell, 18 Tenn.App. 452, 79 S.W.2d 292, 295.

Physical Shock

A blow, impact, collision, concussion, or violent shake or jar, or a violent collision of bodies, or the concussion caused by it; a sudden striking or dashing together or against something. Provident Life and Accident Ins. Co. v. Campbell, 18 Tenn. App. 452, 79 S.W.2d 292, 295.

Medical Jurisprudence

A sudden depression of the vital forces of the entire body, or a part of it, marking some profound impression produced upon the nervous system, as by severe injury, a surgical operation, profound emotion, or the like, or a prostration of the bodily functions, as from sudden injury or mental disturbance. Provident Life & Accident Ins. Co. v. Campbell, 18 Tenn.App. 452, 79 S.W.2d 292, 295.

SHOOFAA. In Mohammedan law. Pre-emption, or a power of possessing property which has been sold, by paying a sum equal to that paid by the purchaser. Wharton.

SHOOT. To strike with something shot; to hit, wound, or kill, with a missile discharged from a weapon; and the missile meant in such cases is the arrow, bullet, or ball, intended to be discharged and to strike the object aimed at. A person cannot be said to have been shot who was not hit by bullet or ball, but only powder burned by the weapon discharged. State v. Manuel, 153 La. 7, 95 So. 263, 264. The term generally implies the use of firearms. Shumake v. State, 90 Fla. 133, 105 So. 314, 315.

SHOP. A building in which goods and merchandise are sold at retail, or where mechanics work, and sometimes keep their products for sale. State v. Morgan, 98 N.C. 641, 3 S.E. 927; State v. O'Connell, 26 Ind. 267; State v. Sprague, 149 Mo. 409, 50 S.W. 901; Com. v. Riggs, 14 Gray, Mass., 378, 77 Am.Dec. 333; Richards v. Ins. Co., 60 Mich. 426, 27 N.W. 586. There must be some structure of a more or less permanent character. 6 B. & S. 303.

The term is properly applied to a place of manufacture or repair, such as a roundhouse, Koecher v. Minneapolis, St. P. & S. S. M. Ry. Co., 122 Minn. 458, 142 N.W. 874, 876, or a building used for repairing automobiles and for the sale of automobile parts, gas, and oil, State v. Garon, 161 La. 867, 109 So. 530, 532. But it is not strictly applicable to a garage, State v. Garon, 158 La. 1014, 105 So. 47, 48, nor to a restaurant, even though the restaurant also engages in the sale of cigars, Debenham v. Short, Tex.Civ.App., 199 S.W. 1147.

The word "shop" in its popular as well as legal meaning is not confined to a workshop, but is a word of various significance, and "store" and "workshop" are both included in it and do not exhaust its meaning. A place kept and used for the sale of goods may be rightly denominated a "shop". Commonwealth v. Moriarty, 311 Mass. 116, 40 N.E.2d 307, 308.

SHOP RIGHT. In patent law. The right of an employer to use employee's invention in employer's business without payment of royalty. Ashland Oil & Refining Co. v. Dorton, 300 Ky. 385, 189 S.W.2d 394.

It cannot come into existence unless the inventor was an employee of the one claiming the right at the time when the invention was made and reduced to practice. Crom v. Cement Gun Co., D.C.Del., 46 F.Supp. 403, 405.

SHOPA. In old records, a shop. Cowell.

SHOP-BOOK RULE. An exception to the hearsay evidence rule, permitting the introduction in evidence of books of original entry made in the usual course of business, and introduced from proper custody and upon general authentication. Clayton v. Metropolitan Life Ins. Co., 96 Utah 331, 85 P.2d 819, 822, 120 A.L.R. 1117.

SHOP-BOOKS. Books of original entry kept by trademen, shop-keepers, mechanics, and the like, in which are entered their accounts and charges for goods sold, work done, etc., commonly called "account-books," or "books of account." The term does not include the stubs of a check book and entries thereon, McWhorter v. Tyson, 203 Ala. 509, 83 So. 330, 333, nor the book and entries of an express messenger, Rhoades v. New York Cent. & H. R. R. R., 227 Mass. 138, 116 N.E. 244, 245.

SHOPKEEPER. Whether a person who buys and sells commodities as a business is a merchant or a shopkeeper depends on the extent, and not on the character, of his business; if his business is large he is a "merchant," and if it is small he is a "shopkeeper." White Mountain Fur Co. v. Town of Whitefield, 77 N.H. 340, 91 A. 870, 871.

SHORE. Land on the margin of the sea, a lake, or a river,—especially a large river, in which the water ebbs and flows. Galveston v. Menard, 23 Tex. 349; Bell v. Gough, 23 N.J.L. 683.

Strictly and technically, lands adjacent to the sea or other tidal waters; the lands adjoining navigable waters, where the tide flows and reflows, which at high tides are submerged, and at low tides are bare. Shively v. Bowlby, 14 S.Ct. 548, 152 U.S. 1, 38 L.Ed. 331; Mather v. Chapman, 40 Conn. 400, 16 Am.Rep. 46; Axline v. Shaw, 35 Fla. 305, 17 So. 411, 28 L.R.A. 391. The space bounded by the high and low water marks. La Porte v. Menacon, 220 Mich. 684, 190 N.W. 655, 656; Sinford v. Watts, 123 Me. 230, 122 A. 573, 574; Borax Consolidated v. City of Los Angeles, Cal., 56 S.Ct. 23, 296 U.S. 101, 80 L.Ed. 9. And this is also true even though the lands may lie along nonnavigable bodies of water. Hunter v. Van Keuren, 130 Misc. 599, 224 N.Y.S. 153, 160.

Sea-shore is that space of land over which the waters of the sea spread in the highest water, during the winter season. Civ.Code La. art. 451.

Under the civil law the "shore line" boundary of lands adjoining navigable waters is the line marked by the highest tide. Dincans v. Keeran, Tex.Civ.App., 192 S.W. 603, 604.

In connection with salvage, "shore" means the land on which the waters have deposited things which are the subject of salvage, whether below or above ordinary high-water mark. The Gulfport, D.C.Ala., 243 F. 676, 680.

SHORE LANDS. Those lands lying between the lines of high and low water mark. State v. Sturtevant, 76 Wash. 158, 135 P. 1035, 1036. Lands bordering on the shores of navigable lakes and rivers below the line of ordinary high water. Rem. & Bal.Code, Wash., § 6641 (Rem.Rev.Stat. § 7833).

SHORT. Not long; of brief length; brief; not coming up to a measure, standard, requirement, or the like. Webster, Dict.

A term of common use in the stock and produce markets. To say that one is "short," in the vernacular of the exchanges, implies only that one has less of a commodity than may be necessary to meet demands and obligations. It does not imply that commodity cannot or will not be supplied upon demand. Thomas v. McShan, 99 Okl. 88, 225 P. 713, 714.

SHORT CAUSE. A cause which is not likely to occupy a great portion of the time of the court, and which may be entered on the list of "short causes," upon the application of one of the parties, and will then be heard more speedily than it would be in its regular order. This practice obtains in the English chancery and in some of the American states. The time allowed for the hearing varies in the different courts.

SHORT ENTRY. A custom of bankers of entering on the customer's pass-book the amount of notes deposited for collection, in such a manner that the amount is not carried to the latter's general balance until the notes are paid. Giles v. Perkins, 9 East, 12; Blaine v. Bourne, 11 R.I. 121, 23 Am.Rep. 429.

SHORT LEASE. A term applied colloquially, but without much precision, to a lease for a short term, (as a month or a year,) as distinguished from one running for a long period.

SHORT NOTICE. In practice. Notice of less than the ordinary time; generally of half that time. 2 Tidd, Pr. 757. In English Practice, four days' notice of trial. Wharton, Law Dict. *Notice of trial.* 1 Cr. & M. 499.

SHORT RATE. Cancellation of insurance policy. Where insurance policy is mutually rescinded by both parties and new policy contract, identical with original, save for shortened term and lessened earned premium, is re-issued and substituted for original contract. Keehn v. Hi-Grade Coal & Fuel Co., 23 N.J.Misc. 102, 41 A.2d 525, 532.

SHORT SALE. A contract for sale of shares of stock which the seller does not own, or certificates for which are not within his control, so as to be available for delivery at the time when, under rules of the exchange, delivery must be made. Provost v. U. S., 46 S.Ct. 152, 153, 269 U.S. 443, 70 L.Ed. 352; Chandler v. Prince, 221 Mass. 495, 109 N.E. 374, 378. In a "short sale" the broker may make a delivery of bonds or stock, charging the price thereof to the customer, and the account is carried until the customer orders the broker to repurchase the bonds, and an adjustment is made between the broker and customer on the difference between the selling and purchasing price. Brown v. Carpenter, 182 App.Div. 650, 168 N.Y.S. 921, 923.

SHORT SUMMONS. A process, authorized in some of the states, to be issued against an absconding, fraudulent, or nonresident debtor, which is returnable within a less number of days than an ordinary writ of summons.

SHORTFORD. An old custom of the city of Exeter, similar to that of *gavelet* in London, which was a mode of foreclosing the right of a tenant by the chief lord of the fee, in cases of non-payment of rent. Cowell.

SHORTLY AFTER. In point of time, a relative term, meaning in a short or brief time or manner; soon; presently; quickly. Chittenden County Trust Co. v. Hurd, 93 Vt. 71, 106 A. 564, 565.

SHOT. A projectile, particularly a solid ball or bullet that is not intended to fit the bore of a piece; also such prejectiles collectively. Green v. Commonwealth, 122 Va. 862, 94 S.E. 940, 941.

SHOTGUN. A smooth-bore gun, often double-barreled, and now almost universally breach-loading, designed for firing shots at short range and killing small game, especially birds. Henderson v. State, 75 Fla. 464, 78 So. 427, 428.

SHOULD. The past tense of shall, St. Louis & S. F. R. Co. v. Brown, 45 Okl. 143, 144 P. 1075, 1080, ordinarily implying duty or obligation; Scarborough v. Walton, 36 Ga.App. 428, 136 S.E. 830. Kippenbrock v. Wabash R. Co., 270 Mo. 479, 194 S. W. 50, 51; although usually no more than an obligation of propriety or expediency, or a moral obligation, thereby distinguishing it from "ought," U. S. v. Stickrath, D.C.Ohio, 242 F. 151, 153. It is not normally synonymous with "may", Williams v. Mt. Vernon Car Mfg. Co., 197 Ill.App. 271, 272; Elliott v. Maves, 196 Ill.App. 605, 606; and although often interchangeable with the word "would," Barnett v. Savannah Electric Co., 15 Ga.App. 270, 82 S.E. 910, 911, it does not ordinarily express certainty as "will" sometimes does. Hubbard v. Turner Department Store Co., 220 Mo.App. 95, 278 S.W. 1060, 1061.

SHOW, *n.* Something that one views or at which one looks and at the same time hears. Longwell v. Kansas City, 199 Mo.App. 480, 203 S.W. 657, 659.

SHOW, *v.* To make apparent or clear by evidence; to prove. Coyle v. Com., 104 Pa. 133. It may be equivalent to the words "reasonably satisfy," Birmingham Ry., Light & Power Co. v. Cohill, 196 Ala. 278, 72 So. 126, but is not synonymous with "state"; Chapin v. State, 107 Tex.Cr. R. 477, 296 S.W. 1095, 1099; Chumbley v. Courtney, 181 Iowa, 482, 164 N.W. 945, 946.

Although the words "show" and "indicate" are sometimes interchangeable in popular use, they are not always so. To "show" is to make apparent or clear by evidence, to prove; while an "indication" may be merely a symptom; that which points to or gives direction to the mind. Coyle v. Com., 104 Pa. 133. "Show" means to point out, or make known by evidence. Commonwealth v. Delfino, 259 Pa. 272, 102 A. 949, 952.

SHOW CAUSE. Against a rule *nisi*, an order, decree, execution, etc., is to appear as directed, and present to the court such reasons and considerations as one has to offer why it should not be confirmed, take effect, be executed, or as the case may be.

SHOWER. One who accompanies a jury to the scene to call the attention of the jurors to specific objects to be noted. Snyder v. Mass., 54 S.Ct. 330.

SHRUB. A low, small plant, the branches of which grow directly from the earth without any supporting trunk, or stem. Clay v. Tel. Cable Co., 70 Miss. 406, 11 So. 658.

SHUT DOWN. To stop work;—usually said of a factory, etc. Webster, Dict.

Thus, within the meaning of an insurance policy, a saw mill which has stopped running for the winter is shut down, though men are employed about the premises and the machinery has not been dismantled. McKenzie v. Ins. Co., 112 Cal. 548, 44 P. 922.

SHY. To start suddenly aside through fright or suspicion; said especially of horses. San Antonio Machine & Supply Co. v. McKinley, Tex.Civ.App., 239 S.W. 340, 342.

SHYSTER. A trickish knave; one who carries on any business, especially a legal business, in a dishonest way. Gribble v. Press Co., 34 Minn. 343, 25 N.W. 710; Nolan v. Standard Pub. Co., 67 Mont. 212, 216 P. 571, 574. An unscrupulous practitioner who disgraces his profession by doing mean work, and resorts to sharp practice to do it. Bailey v. Kalamazoo Pub. Co., 40 Mich. 251.

SI A JURE DISCEDAS, VAGUS ERIS, ET ERUNT OMNIA OMNIBUS INCERTA. If you depart from the law, you will go astray, and all things will be uncertain to everybody. Co.Litt. 227*b*.

SI ACTIO. Lat. The conclusion of a plea to an action when the defendant demands judgment, if the plaintiff ought to have his action, etc. Obsolete.

SI ALICUJUS REI SOCIETAS SIT ET FINIS NEGOTIO IMPOSITUS EST, FINITUR SOCIETAS. If there is a partnership in any matter, and the business is ended, the partnership ceases. Griswold v. Waddington, 16 Johns, N.Y., 438, 489.

SI ALIQUID EX SOLEMNIBUS DEFICIAT, CUM ÆQUITAS POSCIT, SUBVENIENDUM EST. If any one of certain required forms be wanting, where equity requires, it will be aided. The want of some of a neutral vessel's papers is strong presumptive evidence against the ship's neutrality, yet the want of any one of them is not absolutely conclusive. 1 Kent, Comm. 157.

SI ALIQUID SAPIT. Lat. If he knows anything; if he is not altogether devoid of reason.

SI ASSUETIS MEDERI POSSIS, NOVA NON SUNT TENTANDA. If you can be relieved by accustomed remedies, new ones should not be tried. If an old wall can be repaired, a new one should not be made. 10 Coke, 142*b*.

SI CONSTET DE PERSONA. Lat. If it be certain who is the person meant.

SI CONTINGAT. Lat. If it happen. Words of condition in old conveyances. 10 Coke, 42*a*.

SI DUO IN TESTAMENTO PUGNANTIA REPERIENTUR, ULTIMUM EST RATUM. If two conflicting provisions are found in a will, the last is observed. Lofft 251.

SI FECERIT TE SECURUM. Lat. If he make you secure. In practice. The initial and emphatic words of that description of original writ which directs the sheriff to cause the defendant to appear in court, without any option given him, provided the plaintiff gives the sheriff security effectually to prosecute his claim. 3 Bl.Comm. 274.

SI INGRATUM DIXERIS, OMNIA DIXERIS. If you affirm that one is ungrateful, in that you include every charge. A Roman maxim. Tray. Lat. Max.

SI ITA EST. Lat. If it be so. Emphatic words in the old writ of mandamus to a judge, commanding him, if the fact alleged be truly stated, (*si ita est,*) to affix his seal to a bill of exceptions. Ex parte Crane, 5 Pet. 192, 8 L.Ed. 92.

SI JUDICAS, COGNOSCE. If you judge, understand.

SI MELIORES SUNT QUOS DUCIT AMOR, PLURES SUNT QUOS CORRIGIT TIMOR. If those are better who are led by love, those are the greater number who are corrected by fear. Co.Litt. 392.

SI NON APPAREAT QUID ACTUM EST, ERIT CONSEQUENS UT ID SEQUAMUR QUOD IN REGIONE IN QUA ACTUM EST FREQUENTATUR. If it does not appear what was agreed upon, the consequence will be that we must follow that which is the usage of the place where the agreement was made. Dig. 50, 17, 34.

SI NON OMNES. Lat. In English practice. A writ of association of justices whereby, if all in commission cannot meet at the day assigned, it is allowed that two or more may proceed with the business. Cowell; Fitzh.Nat.Brev. 111 C.

SI NULLA SIT CONJECTURA QUÆ DUCAT ALIO, VERBA INTELLIGENDA SUNT EX PROPRIETATE, NON GRAMMATICA SED POPULARI EX USU. If there be no inference which leads to a different result, words are to be understood according to their proper meaning, not in a grammatical, but in a popular and ordinary, sense, 2 Kent, Comm. 555.

SI PARET. Lat. If it appears. In Roman law. Words used in the formula by which the prætor appointed a judge, and instructed him how to decide the cause.

SI PLURES CONDITIONES ASCRIPTÆ FUERUNT DONATIONI CONJUNCTIM, OMNIBUS EST PARENDUM; ET AD VERITATEM COPULATIVE REQUIRITUR QUOD UTRAQUE PARS SIT VERA, SI DIVISIM, QUILIBET VEL ALTERI EORUM SATIS EST OBTEMPERARE; ET IN DISJUNCTIVIS, SUFFICIT ALTERAM PARTEM ESSE VERAM. If several conditions are conjunctively written in a gift, the whole of them must be complied with; and with respect to their truth, it is necessary that every part be true, taken jointly; if the conditions are separate, it is sufficient to comply with either one or other of them; and being disjunctive, that one or the other be true. Co.Litt. 225.

SI PLURES SINT FIDEJUSSORES, QUOTQUOT ERUNT NUMERO, SINGULI IN SOLIDUM TENENTUR. If there are more sureties than one, how many soever they shall be, they shall each be held for the whole. Inst. 3, 20, 4.

SI PRIUS. Lat. In old practice. If before. Formal words in the old writs for summoning juries. Fleta, l. 2, c. 65, § 12.

SI QUID UNIVERSITATI DEBETUR SINGULIS NON DEBETUR, NEC QUOD DEBET UNIVERSITAS SINGULI DEBENT. If anything be owing to an entire body [or to a corporation], it is not owing to the individual members; nor do the individuals owe that which is owing by the entire body. Dig. 3, 4, 7, 1; 1 Bla.Comm. 484; Lindl. Part. *5.

SI QUIDEM IN NOMINE, COGNOMINE, PRÆNOMINE LEGATARII TESTATOR ERRAVERIT, CUM DE PERSONA CONSTAT, NIHILOMINUS VALET LEGATUM. Although a testator may have mistaken the *nomen, cognomen,* or *prænomen* of a legatee, yet, if it be certain who is the person meant, the legacy is valid. Inst. 2, 20, 29; Broom, Max. 645; 2 Domat b. 2, 1, s. 6, §§ 10, 19.

SI QUIS. Lat. In the civil law. If any one. Formal words in the prætorian edicts. The word *"quis,"* though masculine in form was held to include women. Dig. 50, 16, 1.

SI QUIS CUM TOTUM PETIISSET PARTEM PETAT, EXCEPTIO REI JUDICATÆ VOCET. If a party, when he should have sued for an entire claim, sues only for a part, the judgment is res judicata against another suit. 2 Mart. O. S. (La.) 83.

SI A TUTELA REMOVENDUS EST. Jenk.Cent. 39. If a guardian do fraud to his ward, he shall be removed from his guardianship.

SI QUIS CUSTOS FRAUDEM PUPILLO FECER-SI QUIS PRÆGNANTEM UXOREM RELIQUIT, NON VIDETUR SINE LIBERIS DECESSISSE. If a man dies, leaving his wife pregnant, he shall not be considered to have died without children. A rule of the civil law.

SI QUIS, UNUM PERCUSSERIT, CUM ALIUM PERCUTERE VELLET, IN FELONIA TENETUR. 3 Inst. 51. If a man kill one, meaning to kill another, he is held guilty of felony.

SI RECOGNOSCAT. Lat. If he acknowledge. In old practice. A writ which lay for a creditor against his debtor for money numbered *(pecunia numerata)* or counted; that is, a specific sum of money, which the debtor had acknowledged in the county court, to owe him, as received *in pecuniis numeratis.* Cowell.

SI SUGGESTIO NON SIT VERA, LITERÆ PATENTES VACUÆ SUNT. 10 Coke, 113. If the suggestion be not true, the letters patent are void.

SI TE FECERIT SECURUM. If he make you secure. See Si Fecerit te Securum.

SIB. Sax. A relative or kinsman. Used in the Scotch tongue, but not now in English.

SIC. Lat. Thus; so; in such manner.

SIC ENIM DEBERE QUEM MELIOREM AGRUM SUUM FACERE NE VICINI DETERIOREM FACIAT. Every one ought so to improve his land as not to injure his neighbor's. 3 Kent, Comm. 441. A rule of the Roman law.

SIC INTERPRETANDUM EST UT VERBA ACCIPIANTUR CUM EFFECTU. 3 Inst. 80. [A statute] is to be so interpreted that the words may be taken with effect.

SIC SUBSCRIBITUR. Lat. In Scotch practice. So it is subscribed. Formal words at the end of depositions, immediately preceding the signature. 1 How. State Tr. 1379.

SIC UTERE TUO UT ALIENUM NON LÆDAS. Use your own property in such a manner as not to injure that of another. 9 Coke, 59; 1 Bl.Comm. 306; Broom, Max. 268, 365; Webb, Poll. Torts 153; 2 Bouv.Inst. n. 2379; 5 Exch. 797; 12 Q.B. 739; 4 A. & E. 384; 17 Mass. 334; 4 McCord., S.C., 472. Various comments have been made on this maxim: "Mere verbiage"; El. B. & E. 643. "No help to decision"; L. R. 2 Q.B. 247. "Utterly useless as a legal maxim"; 9 N.Y. 445. It is a mere begging of the question; it assumes the very point in controversy. 13 Lea 507. See 2 Aust.Jurisp. 795, 829.

SICH. A little current of water, which is dry in summer; a water furrow or gutter. Cowell.

SICIUS. A sort of money current among the ancient English, of the value of 2d.

SICK. Affected with disease, ill, indisposed. State v. Douglas, 124 Kan. 482, 260 P. 655, 657. See Sickness.

SICKNESS. Disease; malady; any morbid condition of the body (including insanity) which, for the time being, hinders or prevents the organs from normally discharging their several functions. L. R. 8 Q. B. 295. Any affection of the body which deprives it temporarily of the power to fulfill its usual functions, Martin v. Waycross Coca-Cola Bottling Co., 18 Ga.App. 226, 89 S.E. 495, 496, including injury, Doody v. Davie, 77 Cal. App. 310, 246 P. 339, 340; *contra,* Poole v. Imperial Mut. Life & Health Ins. Co., 188 N.C. 468, 125 S.E. 8. See, also, Beaudoin v. La Societe St. Jean Baptiste de Bienfaisance de Biddeford, 116 Me. 428, 102 A. 234, 235, L.R.A.1918B, 641, limiting the term to those disabilities which are the natural results of disease arising from a pathological condition, and Northwestern Mut. Life Ins. Co. v. Wiggins, C.C.A.Or., 15 F.2d 646, 648, defining sickness as a condition interfering with one's usual avocations.

Illness; an ailment of such a character as to affect the general soundness and health; not a mere temporary indisposition, which does not tend to undermine and weaken the constitution. National Live Stock Ins. Co. v. Bartlow, 60 Ind.App. 233, 110 N.E. 224, 225.

In construing a sickness indemnity policy, there may be said to be three degrees of sickness: First, when the patient is confined to his bed; second, when he is confined to the house, but not to his bed; and, third, when he is too sick to work, but not confined to the house. Rocci v. Massachusetts Acc. Co., 226 Mass. 545, 116 N.E. 477, 479.

SICUT ALIAS. Lat. As at another time, or heretofore. This was a second writ sent out when the first was not executed. Cowell.

SICUT ME DEUS ADJUVET. Lat. So help me God. Fleta, l. 1, c. 18, § 4.

SICUT NATURA NIL FACIT PER SALTUM, ITA NEC LEX. Co.Litt. 238. In the same way as nature does nothing by a bound, so neither does the law.

SIDDI. In the Orient, a name for marihuana. See Mariguana.

SIDE. The margin, edge, verge, or border of a surface; any one of the bounding lines of the surface. Parkman v. Freeman, 121 Me. 341, 117 A. 301, 302.

"Side" may be used in a generic sense so as to include the "front," but it also has a specific meaning which distinguishes it from "front." The word "front" as applied to a house is always specific and speaking of the "side line" of a house as "fronting" toward the street is incorrect. Howland v. Andrus, 81 N.J.Eq. 175, 86 A. 391, 393. The front of a lot is that portion opposite the rear of the lot and facing on the street, and the side is that portion adjacent to the lot or lots on either side of it. Turney v. Shriver, 269 Ill. 164, 109 N.E. 708, 709.

The party or parties collectively to a lawsuit considered in relation to his or their opponents, *i. e.*, the plaintiff side, or the defendant side. Carr v. Davis, 159 Minn. 485, 199 N.W. 237, 239.

A province or field of jurisdiction;—said of courts. Thus, the same court is sometimes said to have different *sides.* An admiralty court may have an "instance side," distinct from its powers as a prize court; the "crown side," (criminal jurisdiction) is to be distinguished from the "plea side," (civil jurisdiction;) the same court may have an "equity side" and a "law side."

SIDE-BAR RULES. In English practice. There are some rules which the courts authorize their officers to grant as a matter of course without formal application being made to them in open court, and these are technically termed "side-bar rules," because formerly they were moved for by the attorneys at the side bar in court; such, for instance, was the rule to plead, which was an order or command of the court requiring a defendant to plead within a specified number of days. Such also were the rules to reply, to rejoin, and many others, the granting of which depended upon settled rules of practice rather than upon the discretion of the courts, all of which have been rendered unnecessary by statutory changes. Brown, voc. "Rule."

SIDE-KICKER. A coined expression without any standing in lexicology, which the court, as a matter of common knowledge, can say is not an uncommon vernacular or colloquial expression which may with equal propriety express a social relationship between the parties to whom it is applied, or convey the idea that they are business partners or have business interests in common. Spoon v. Sheldon, 27 Cal.App. 765, 151 P. 150, 152.

SIDE LINES. In commercial usage, lines of goods sold or businesses followed in addition to one's principal articles or occupation. Merrimac Mfg. Co. v. Bibb, 124 Ark. 189, 186 S.W. 817, Ann. Cas.1918C, 951. In mining law, the side lines of a mining claim are those which measure the extent of the claim on each side of the middle of the vein at the surface. They are not necessarily the side lines as laid down on the ground or on a map or plat; for if the claim, in its longer dimension, crosses the vein, instead of following it, the platted side lines will be treated in law as the end lines, and vice versa. Argentine Min. Co. v. Terrible Min. Co., 7 S.Ct. 1356, 122 U.S. 478, 30 L.Ed. 1140; Del Monte Min. Co. v. Last Chance Min. Co., 18 S.Ct. 895, 171 U.S. 55, 43 L.Ed. 72.

SIDE REPORTS. A term sometimes applied to unofficial volumes or series of reports, as contrasted with those prepared by the official reporter of the court, or to collections of cases omitted from the official reports.

SIDESMEN. In ecclesiastical law. These were originally persons whom, in the ancient episcopal synods, the bishops were wont to summon out of each parish to give information of the disorders of the clergy and people, and to report heretics. In process of time they became standing officers, under the title of "synodsmen," "sidesmen," or "questmen." The whole of their duties seems now to have devolved by custom upon the church-wardens of a parish. 1 Burn. Ecc.Law, 399.

SIDEWALK. That part of a public street or highway designed for the use of pedestrians, City of Birmingham v. Shirley, 209 Ala. 305, 96 So. 214, 215; being exclusively reserved for them, and constructed somewhat differently than other portions of the street used by animals and vehicles generally, Central Life Assur. Soc. of the United States v. City of Des Moines, 185 Iowa 573, 171 N.W. 31, 32. That part of the street of a municipality which has been set apart and used for pedestrians, as distinguished from that portion set apart and used for animals and vehicles. Graham v. Albert Lea, 48 Minn. 201, 50 N.W. 1108; McCormick v. Allegheny County, 263 Pa. 146, 106 A. 203, 204. A way for foot passengers, or a public way especially intended for pedestrians. Russo v. City of Pueblo, 63 Colo. 519, 168 P. 649, 650. A walk for foot passengers at the side of a street or road. Kohlhof v. Chicago, 192 Ill. 249, 61 N.E. 446, 85 Am.St.Rep. 335; Challiss v. Parker, 11 Kan. 391; State v. Berdetta, 73 Ind. 185, 38 Am.Rep. 117; Pequignot v. Detroit, C.C.Mich., 16 F. 212.

Generally the sidewalk is included with the gutters and roadway in the general term *street*. In re Burmeister, 76 N.Y. 174; Warner v. Knox, 50 Wis. 429, 7 N.W. 372; Wiles v. Hoss, 114 Ind. 371, 16 N.E. 800. But in many cases of municipal ordinances and contracts the word street is held not to include sidewalks. Barry v. City of Cloverport, 175 Ky. 548, 194 S.W. 818, 819. See, also, James v. City of Newberg, 101 Or. 616, 201 P. 212.

SIEN. An obsolete form of the word "scion," meaning offspring or descendant. Co.Litt. 123*a*.

SIERVO. Span. In Spanish law. A slave. Las Partidas, pt. 4, tit. 21, l. 1.

SIETE PARTIDAS. Span. Seven parts. See Las Partidas.

SIGHT. The power of seeing; the faculty of vision or of perceiving objects; or the act of seeing, and perception of objects through the eyes. Locomotive Engineers' Mut. Life & Accident Ins. Co. v. Meeks, 157 Miss. 97, 127 So. 699, 703.

Presentment. Bills of exchange are frequently drawn payable at sight or certain number of days or months after sight.

When a bill of exchange is expressed to be payable "at sight," it means on presentment to the drawee. Campbell v. French, 6 Term, 212.

After sight in a bill means after acceptance; in a note, after exhibition to the maker. Dan.Neg.Instr. § 619. A bill drawn payable a certain number of days after sight, acceptance waived, must be presented to fix the time at which the bill is to become due, and the term of the bill begins to run from the date of present. 4 Montreal L. Rep. 249.

SIGHT DRAFTS OR BILLS. Those payable at sight.

SIGIL. In old English law, a seal, or a contracted or abbreviated signature used as a seal.

SIGILLUM. Lat. In old English law. A seal; originally and properly a seal impressed upon wax.

SIGILLUM EST CERA IMPRESSA, QUIA CERA SINE IMPRESSIONE NON EST SIGILLUM. A seal is a piece of wax impressed, because wax without an impression is not a seal. 3 Inst. 169.

SIGLA. Lat. In Roman law. Marks or signs of abbreviation used in writing. Cod. 1, 17, 11, 13.

SIGN. To affix one's name to a writing or instrument, for the purpose of authenticating it, or to give it effect as one's act. McCall v. Textile Industrial Institute, 189 N.C. 775, 128 S.E. 349, 353. To attach a name or cause it to be attached to a writing by any of the known methods of impressing a name on paper. In re Covington Lumber Co., D.C.Wash., 225 F. 444, 446. To affix a signature to; to ratify by hand or seal; to subscribe in one's own handwriting. Webster, Dict.; Knox's Estate, 131 Pa. 230, 18 A. 1021, 6 L.R.A. 353, 17 Am.St.Rep. 798; In re Manchester's Estate, 174 Cal. 417, 163 P. 358, 359, L.R.A.1917D, 629, Ann.Cas. 1918B, 227. See, also, Miner v. Larney, 87 N.J.L. 40, 94 A. 26, 28.

To make any mark, as upon a document, in token of knowledge, approval, acceptance, or obligation. In re Manchester's Estate, 174 Cal. 417, 163 P. 358, 360, L.R.A.1917D, 629, Ann.Cas.1918B,

227; Weiner v. Mullaney, 59 Cal.App.2d 620, 140 P.2d 704, 712. See, also, Pugh v. Jackson, 154 Ky. 772, 159 S.W. 600; and In re Kimmel's Estate, 278 Pa. 435, 123 A. 405, 406, 31 A.L.R. 678, with which compare In re Brennan's Estate, 244 Pa. 574, 91 A. 220, 222. See Signature.

To "sign" is merely to write one's name on paper, or declare assent or attestation by some sign or mark, and does not, like "subscribe," require that one should write at the bottom of the instrument signed. Sheehan v. Kearney, 82 Miss. 688, 21 So. 41, 35 L.R.A. 102; Robins v. Coryell, 27 Barb., N.Y., 560; James v. Patten, 6 N.Y. 9, 55 Am.Dec. 376; In re Phelan's Estate, 82 N.J.Eq. 316, 87 A. 625, 626. But compare in re Manchester's Estate, 174 Cal. 417, 163 P. 358, 359, L.R.A.1917D, 629, Ann.Cas.1918B, 227.

The word "subscribed" is more restricted than the word "signature." The word "signature" in its origin involves merely a sign, the word "subscribed" involves a writing. The signing of a written instrument has a much broader and more extended meaning than attaching one's written signature to it implies. When a person attaches his name or causes it to be attached to a writing by any of the known methods of impressing his name upon paper with the intention of signing it he is regarded as having "signed" in writing. Hagen v. Gresby, 34 N.D. 349, 159 N.W. 3, 5, L.R.A.1917B, 281.

Signing Judgment

In English practice. The signature or allowance of the proper officer of a court, obtained by the party entitled to judgment in an action, expressing generally that judgment is given in his favor, and which stands in the place of its actual delivery by the judges themselves. Steph.Pl. 110, 111; French v. Pease, 10 Kan. 54. In American practice. A signing of the judgment record itself, which is done by the proper officer, on the margin of the record, opposite the entry of the judgment. 1 Burrill, Pr. 268.

SIGN MANUAL. An autograph signature; specifically, the official signature of a sovereign, chief magistrate, or the like, to an official document, as letters patent, to give validity. Webster, Dict.; Wharton, Law Dict.

English Law

The signature of the king to grants or letters patent, inscribed at the top. 2 Sharsw. Bla.Comm. 347*. The sign manual is not good unless countersigned, etc.; 9 Mod. 54. There is this difference between what the sovereign does under the sign manual and what he or she does under the great seal, viz., that the former is done as a personal act of the sovereign; the latter as an act of state. Brown.

SIGNA. The plural of *signum* (*q. v.*).

SIGNAL. A means of communication, as between vessels at sea or between a vessel and the shore. The international code of signals for the use of all nations assigns arbitrary meanings to different arrangements of flags or displays of lights.

SIGNATORIUS ANNULUS. Lat. In the civil law. A signet-ring; a seal-ring. Dig. 50, 16, 74.

SIGNATORY. A term used in diplomacy to indicate a nation which is a party to a treaty.

SIGNATURE. The act of putting down a man's name at the end of an instrument to attest its validity, the name thus written. A "signature" may be written by hand, printed, stamped, typewritten, engraved, photographed, or cut from one instrument and attached to another, and a signature lithographed on an instrument by a party is sufficient for the purpose of signing it; it being immaterial with what kind of instrument a signature is made. Smith v. Greenville County, 188 S.C. 349, 199 S.E. 416, 419. Maricopa County v. Osborn, 60 Ariz. 290, 136 P.2d 270, 274. And whatever mark, symbol, or device one may choose to employ as representative of himself is sufficient. Griffith v. Bonawitz, 73 Neb. 622, 103 N.W. 327, 339. See Sign.

Ecclesiastical Law

The name of a sort of rescript, without seal, containing the supplication, the signature of the pope or his delegate, and the grant of a pardon.

Where one who cannot write directs another to sign for him in his presence, it will be valid with or without a mark. Just v. Wise Tp., 42 Mich. 573, 4 N.W. 298.

The "signature" to a deed may be made either by the grantor affixing his own signature, or by adopting one written for him, or by making his mark, or impressing some other sign or symbol on the paper by which the signature, though written by another for him, may be identified. Lee v. Parker, 171 N.C. 144, 88 S.E. 217, 221.

SIGNET. A seal commonly used for the sign manual of the sovereign. Wharton. In Scotland, a seal by which royal warrants connected with the administration of justice were formerly authenticated.

SIGNIFICATION. In French law. The notice given of a decree, sentence, or other judicial act.

SIGNIFICAVIT. In ecclesiastical law. When this word is used alone, it means the bishop's certificate to the court of chancery in order to obtain the writ of excommunication; but, where the words *"writ of significavit"* are used, the meaning is the same as *"writ de excommunicato capiendo."* Shelf. Mar. & Div. 502. Obsolete.

SIGNIFY. To make known by signs or words; express; communicate; announce; declare. State v. Klein, 94 Wash. 212, 162 P. 52, 53.

SIGNING JUDGMENT. See Sign.

SIGNUM. Lat.

Roman and Civil Law

A sign; a mark; a seal. The seal of an instrument. Calvin.

A species of proof. By *"signa"* were meant those species of *indicia* which come more immediately under the cognizance of the senses; such as stains of blood on the person of one accused of murder, indications of terror at being charged with the offense, and the like. Best, Pres. 13, note *f*.

Saxon Law

The sign of a cross prefixed as a sign of assent and approbation to a charter or deed.

SILENCE. The state of a person who does not speak, or of one who refrains from speaking. In the law of estoppel, "silence" implies knowledge and an opportunity to act upon it. Pence v. Langdon, 99 U.S. 581, 25 L.Ed. 420; Stewart v. Wyoming Cattle Ranch Co., 9 S.Ct. 101, 128 U.S. 383, 32 L. Ed. 439; Chicora Fertilizer Co. v. Dunan, 91 Md. 144, 46 A. 347, 50 L.R.A. 401.

SILENCE, ESTOPPEL BY. It arises where person is under duty to another to speak or failure to speak is inconsistent with honest dealings. In re McArdle's Estate, 250 N.Y.S. 276, 287, 140 Misc. 257; Jones v. Kentucky Glycerine Co., 226 Ky. 676, 11 S.W.2d 713, 716; Tanenbaum Textile Co. v. Schlanger, 287 N.Y. 400, 40 N.E.2d 225, 227.

An agreement inferred from silence rests upon principle of "estoppel." Letres v. Washington Co-op. Chick Ass'n, 8 Wash.2d 64, 111 P.2d 594, 596. Silence, to work "estoppel", must amount to bad faith. Wise v. United States, D.C.Ky., 38 F.Supp. 130, 134.

Elements or essentials of such estoppel include change of position to prejudice of person claiming estoppel, Sherlock v. Greaves, 106 Mont. 206, 76 P.2d 87, 91. Damages if the estoppel is denied, James v. Nelson, C.C.A.Alaska, 90 F.2d 910, 917; duty and opportunity to speak. Codd v. Westchester Fire Ins. Co., 14 Wash.2d 600, 128 P.2d 968, 971, 151 A.L.R. 316; Merry v. Garibaldi, 48 Cal.App.2d 397, 119 P.2d 768, 771. Ignorant of facts by person claiming estoppel, Cushing v. United States, D.C.Mass., 18 F.Supp. 83, 85; Nelson v. Chicago Mill & Lumber Corporation, C.C.A. Ark., 76 F.2d 17, 100 A.L.R. 87; inducing person claiming estoppel to alter his position, Brauch v. Freking, 219 Iowa 556, 258 N.W. 892; Truax, State ex rel. v. Burrows, 136 Neb. 691, 287 N.W. 178, 179; knowledge of facts and of rights by person estopped, Harvey v. Richard, 200 La. 97, 7 So.2d 674, 677; Consolidated Freight Lines v. Groenen, 10 Wash.2d 672, 117 P.2d 966, 968, 137 A.L.R. 1072; misleading of party claiming estoppel, Ridgill v. Clarendon County, 192 S.C. 321, 6 S.E.2d 766, 768; Lincoln v. Bennett, Tex.Civ.App., 135 S.W.2d 632, 636; reliance upon silence of party sought to be estopped, Mosley v. Magnolia Petroleum Co., 45 N.M. 230, 114 P.2d 740, 751. New York Life Ins. Co. v. Talley, C.C.A.Iowa, 72 F.2d 715, 718; willful or culpable silence in absence of duty to speak. Lencioni v. Fidelity Trust & Savings Bank of Fresno, 95 Cal.App. 490, 273 P. 103, 106; Utah State Building Commission for Use and Benefit of Mountain States Supply Co. v. Great American Indemnity Co., 105 Utah 11, 140 P.2d 763, 771, 772.

SILENCE SHOWS CONSENT. 6 Barb. (N.Y.) 28, 35.

SILENT LEGES INTER ARMA. The power of law is suspended during war. Bacon; 4 Inst. 70.

SILENTIARIUS. In English law. One of the privy council; also an usher, who sees good rule and silence kept in court. Wharton.

SILK. Fine, soft thread produced by various species of caterpillars, etc. Lowder v. Union Transfer Co. of San Francisco, 79 Cal.App. 598, 250 P. 703, 704.

Under a statute referring to silk in a manufactured or unmanufactured state, any fabric which contains silk will not necessarily be included. See 28 L.J.C.P. 265; 33 L.J. Ex. 187.

SILK GOWN. Used especially of the gowns worn in England by king's counsel; hence, "to take silk" means to attain the rank of king's counsel. Mozley & Whitley.

SILVA. Lat. In the civil law. Wood; a wood.

SILVA CÆDUA. In the civil law. That kind of wood which was kept for the purpose of being cut.

In English law. Underwood; coppice wood. 2 Inst. 642; Cowell. All small wood and under timber, and likewise timber when cut down, under twenty years' growth; titheable wood. 3 Salk. 347. See, also, Sylva Cædua.

SILVER. Coin made of silver; silver money; money (in general). Webster, Dict.; Cook v. State, 130 Ark. 90, 196 S.W. 922, 924.

SILVER SALT. A name applied commercially to anthraquinone sulphoacid, a coal tar product. Newport Co. v. U. S., 12 Ct.Cust.App. 115, 116.

SIMILAR. Nearly corresponding; resembling in many respects; somewhat like; having a general likeness. Scott v. State, 107 Ohio St. 475, 141 N.E. 19, 23; Greenbaum v. De Jong, 166 N.Y.S. 1042, 1044; People v. Standard Home Co., 59 Colo. 355, 148 P. 869.

Also, sometimes, exactly like; identical; exactly corresponding (at least in all essential particulars). Fletcher v. Interstate Chemical Co., 94 N.J.Law, 332, 110 A. 709; Stowell v. Blanchard, 122 Me. 368, 119 A. 866, 868; Commercial Nat. Bank of Checotah v. Phillips, 61 Okl. 179, 160 P. 920, 921. Thus, a statutory provision in relation to "previous conviction of a *similar* offense" may mean conviction of an offense identical in kind. Com. v. Fontain, 127 Mass. 454.

SIMILAR DESCRIPTION. Such words as used in a tariff act import that the goods are similar in product and adapted to similar uses; not necessarily that they have been produced by similar methods of manufacture. Greenleaf v. Goodrich, 1 Hask. 586, F.Cas. No. 5,778.

SIMILITER. Lat. In pleading. Likewise; the like. The name of the short formula used either at the end of pleadings or by itself, expressive of the acceptance of an issue of fact tendered by the opposite party; otherwise termed a "joinder in issue." Steph.Pl. 57, 237. See Solomons v. Chesley, 57 N.H. 163; 2 Saund. 319*b*; Shaw v. Redmond, 11 Serg. & R. (Pa.) 32. The plaintiff's reply, that, as the defendant has put himself upon the country, he, the plaintiff, does the like. It occurs only when the plea has the conclusion to the country, and its effect is to join the plaintiff in the issue thus tendered by the defendant. Co.Litt. 126*a*.

SIMILITUDO LEGALIS EST CASUUM DIVERSORUM INTER SE COLLATORUM SIMILIS RATIO; QUOD IN UNO SIMILIUM VALET, VALEBIT IN ALTERO. DISSIMILIUM, DISSIMILIS EST RATIO. Legal similarity is a similar reason which governs various cases when compared with each other; for what avails in one similar case will avail in the other. Of things dissimilar, the reason is dissimilar. Co.Litt. 191; Benj.Sales 379.

SIMONIA EST VOLUNTAS SIVE DESIDERIUM EMENDI VEL VENDENDI SPIRITUALIA VEL SPIRITUALIBUS ADHÆRENTIA. CONTRACTUS EX TURPI CAUSA ET CONTRA BONOS MORES. Hob. 167. Simony is the will or desire of buying or selling spiritualities, or things pertaining thereto. It is a contract founded on a bad cause, and against morality.

SIMONY. In English ecclesiastical law. The corrupt presentation of any one to an ecclesiastical benefice for money, gift, or reward. 2 Bl.Comm. 278. An unlawful contract for presenting a clergyman to a benefice. The buying or selling of ecclesiastical preferments or of things pertaining to the ecclesiastical order. Hob. 167. See State v. Buswell, 40 Neb. 158, 58 N.W. 728, 24 L.R.A. 68.

An unlawful agreement to receive a temporal reward for something holy or spiritual. Code 1, 3, 31; Ayliffe, Parerg. 496.

Giving or receiving any material advantage in return for spiritual promotion, whether such advantage be actually received or only stipulated for. Jenks, Mod.Land L. 220.

SIMPLA. Lat. In the civil law. The single value of a thing. Dig. 21, 2, 37, 2.

SIMPLE. Pure; unmixed; not compounded; not aggravated; not evidenced by sealed writing or record.

As to simple "Assault," "Average," "Battery," "Blockade," "Bond," "Confession," "Contract," "Contract Debt," "Deposit," "Imprisonment," "Interest," "Larceny," "Obligation," "Tool," "Trust," and "Warrandice," see those titles.

SIMPLE SENTENCE. In rhetoric, one in which only one principal statement is made, even though there be adverbial phrases modifying the predicate. San Antonio, U. & G. R. Co. v. Dawson, Tex. Civ.App., 201 S.W. 247, 251.

SIMPLEX. Lat. Simple; single; pure; unqualified.

Charta Simplex

A deed-poll or single deed. Jacob, Law Dict.

Simplex Beneficium

In ecclesiastical law. A minor dignity in a cathedral or collegiate church, or any other ecclesiastical benefice, as distinguished from a cure of souls. It may therefore be held with any parochial cure, without coming under the prohibitions against pluralities. Wharton.

Simplex Dictum

In old English practice. Simple averment; mere assertion without proof.

Simplex Justitiarius

In old records. Simple justice. A name sometimes given to a puisne justice. Cowell.

Simplex Loquela

In old English practice. Simple speech; the mere declaration or *plaint* of a plaintiff.

Simplex Obligatio

A single obligation; a bond without a condition. 2 Bl.Comm. 340.

Simplex Peregrinatio

In old English law. Simple pilgrimage. Fleta, l. 4, c. 2, § 2.

SIMPLEX COMMENDATIO NON OBLIGAT. Mere recommendation [of an article] does not bind, [the vendor of it.] Dig. 4, 3, 37; 2 Kent, Comm. 485; Broom, Max. 781; 4 Taunt. 488; 16 Q.B. 282, 283; Cro.Jac. 4; 2 Allen, Mass., 214; 5 Johns, N.Y., 354; 4 Barb., N.Y., 95.

SIMPLEX ET PURA DONATIO DICI POTERIT, UBI NULLA EST ADJECTA CONDITIO NEC MODUS. A gift is said to be pure and simple when no condition or qualification is annexed. Bract. 1.

SIMPLICITA EST LEGIBUS AMICA; ET NIMIA SUBTILITAS IN JURE REPROBATUR. 4 Coke, 8. Simplicity is favorable to the laws; and too much subtlety in law is to be reprobated.

SIMPLICITER. Lat. Simply; without ceremony; in a summary manner.

Directly; immediately; as distinguished from inferentially or indirectly.

By itself; by its own force; *per se*.

SIMUL CUM. Lat. Together with. In actions of tort and in prosecutions, where several persons united in committing the act complained of, some of whom are known and others not, it is usual to allege in the declaration or indictment that the persons therein named did the injury in question, "together with (*simul cum*) other persons unknown." In cases of riots, it is usual to charge that A B, together with others unknown, did the act complained of. 2 Chitty, Cr.Law 488; 2 Salk. 593.

When a party sued with another pleads separately, the plea is generally entitled in the name of the person pleading, adding, "sued with ———," naming the other party. When this occurred, it was, in the old phraseology, called pleading with a *simul cum*.

SIMUL ET SEMEL. Lat. Together and at one time.

SIMULATE. To assume the mere appearance of, without the reality; to assume the signs or indications of, falsely; to counterfeit; feign; imitate; pretend. Harryman v. Harryman, 93 Kan. 223, 144 P. 262, 265, Ann.Cas.1915B, 369. To engage, usually with the co-operation or connivance of another person, in an act or series of acts, which are apparently transacted in good faith, and intended to be followed by their ordinary legal consequences, but which in reality conceal a fraudulent purpose of the party to gain thereby some advantage to which he is not entitled, or to injure, delay, or defraud others. See Cartwright v. Bamberger, 90 Ala. 405, 8 So. 264.

SIMULATED CONTRACT. One which, though clothed in concrete form, has no existence in fact.

It may at any time and at the demand of any person in interest be declared a sham and may be ignored by creditors of the apparent vendor. Hibernia Bank & Trust Co. v. Louisiana Ave. Realty Co., 143 La. 962, 79 So. 554, 556.

SIMULATED FACT. In the law of evidence. A fabricated fact; an appearance given to things by human device, with a view to deceive and mislead. Burrill, Circ.Ev. 131.

SIMULATED JUDGMENT. One which is apparently rendered in good faith, upon an actual debt, and intended to be collected by the usual process of law, but which in reality is entered by the fraudulent contrivance of the parties, for the purpose of giving to one of them an advantage to which he is not entitled, or of defrauding or delaying third persons.

SIMULATED SALE. One which has all the appearance of an actual sale in good faith, intended to transfer the ownership of property for a consideration, but which in reality covers a collusive design of the parties to put the property beyond the reach of creditors, or proceeds from some other fraudulent purpose. Moran v. Johnson, La. App., 151 So. 139, 140.

It results when parties execute a formal act of sale of a thing for which no price is paid or is intended to be paid, and such sale has no legal effect and no title is transferred thereby. If there exists an actual consideration for transfer evidenced by alleged act of sale, no matter how inadequate it be, the transaction is not a "simulated sale", and, even though it be charged to be in fraud of vendor's creditors, such transfer cannot be set aside as a simulation although it may be subject to annulment on the ground of fraud or the giving of undue preference. Caster v. Miller, D.C.La., 39 F.Supp. 120, 123.

SIMULATIO LATENS. Lat. A species of feigned disease, in which disease is actually present, but where the symptoms are falsely aggravated, and greater sickness is pretended than really exists. Beck, Med.Jur. 3.

SIMULATION. Assumption of appearance which was feigned, false, deceptive, or counterfeit. United States v. Peppa, D.C.Cal., 13 F.Supp. 669, 670.

In the civil law. Misrepresentation or concealment of the truth; as where parties pretend to perform a transaction different from that in which they really are engaged. Mackeld.Rom.Law, § 181. A feigned, pretended act, one which assumes the appearance without the reality and, being entirely without effect, it is held not to have existed, and, for that reason, it may be disregarded or attacked collaterally by any interested person. Freeman v. Woods, La.App., 1 So.2d 134, 136.

In French law. Collusion; a fraudulent arrangement between two or more persons to give a false or deceptive appearance to a transaction in which they engage.

SIMULTANEOUS. A word of comparison meaning that two or more occurrences or happenings are identical in time. Brush Electric Co. v. Western Electric Co., C.C.Ill., 69 F. 240, 244.

The word "simultaneous," as used in a patent claim, does not imply absolute synchronism from beginning to end, but has some elasticity. Events may be substantially or relatively simultaneous, although not absolutely so. Westinghouse Mach. Co. v. C. & G. Cooper Co., C.C.A.Ohio, 245 F. 463, 468.

SINCE. This word's proper signification is "after," Keller v. Keller, 121 Kan. 520, 247 P. 433, 435, 49 A.L.R. 113, and in its apparent sense it includes the whole period between the event and the present time. Jones v. Bank, 79 Me. 195, 9 A. 22. "Since" a day named, does not necessarily include that day. Monroe v. Acworth, 41 N.H. 201.

SINDERESIS. "A natural power of the soul, set in the highest part thereof, moving and stirring it to good, and abhorring evil. And therefore *sinderesis* never sinneth nor erreth. And this *sinderesis* our Lord put in man, to the intent that the order of things should be observed. And therefore *sinderesis* is called by some men the 'law of reason,' for it ministereth the principles of the law of reason, the which be in every man by nature, in that he is a reasonable creature." Doct. & Stud. 39.

SINE. Lat. Without.

SINE ANIMO REVERTENDI. Without the intention of returning. 1 Kent, Comm. 78.

SINE ASSENSU CAPITULI. Without the consent of the chapter. In old English practice. A writ which lay where a dean, bishop, prebendary, abbot, prior, or master of a hospital aliened the lands holden in the right of his house, abbey, or priory, without the consent of the chapter; in which cases his successor might have this writ. Fitzh. Nat. Brev. 194, I; Cowell.

SINE CONSIDERATIONE CURIÆ. Without the judgment of the court. Fleta, lib. 2, c. 47, § 13.

SINE DECRETO. Without authority of a judge. 2 Kames, Eq. 115.

SINE DIE. Without day; without assigning a day for a further meeting or hearing.

Hence, a final adjournment; final dismissal of a cause. *Quod eat sine die,* that he go without day; the old form of a judgment for the defendant, *i. e.*, a judgment discharging the defendant from any further appearance in court.

SINE HOC QUOD. Without this, that. A technical phrase in old pleading, of the same import with the phrase *"absque hoc quod."*

SINE NUMERO. Without stint or limit. A term applied to common. Fleta, lib. 4, c. 19, § 8.

SINE PROLE. Without issue. Used in genealogical tables, and often abbreviated into *"s. p."*

SINE QUA NON. Without which not. That without which the thing cannot be. An indispensable requisite or condition.

SINE POSSESSIONE USUCAPIO PROCEDERE NON POTEST. There can be no prescription without possession.

SINECURE. In ecclesiastical law. When a rector of a parish neither resides nor performs duty at his benefice, but has a vicar under him endowed and charged with the cure thereof, this is termed a "sinecure." Brown.

An ecclesiastical benefice without cure of souls.

In popular usage, the term denotes an office which yields a revenue to the incumbent, but makes little or no demand upon his time or attention.

SINGLE. One only; being a unit; alone; one which is abstracted from others. State ex rel. Nelson v. Board of Com'rs of Yellowstone County, 111 Mont. 395, 109 P.2d 1106, 1107.

Unitary; detached; individual; affecting only one person; containing only one part, article, condition, or covenant. State v. Patch, 64 Mont. 565, 210 P. 748, 750. Unmarried. In re Rudman's Estate, 244 Pa. 248, 90 A. 566, 567. The term is applicable to a widow; Crum v. Brock, 136 Miss. 858, 101 So. 704, 705, 12 L.J.W.C. 74; and occasionally even to a married woman living apart from her husband; 12 Q.B.D. 681.

Sometimes, principal; dominating. Attorney General v. Marx, 203 Mich. 331, 168 N.W. 1005, 1006.

As to single "Adultery," "Bill," "Bond," "Combat," "Demise," "Entry," "Escheat," "Obligation," "Original," and "Tract," see those titles.

SINGLE CREDITOR. One having a lien only on a single fund;—distinguished from double creditor, who is one having a lien on two funds. Newby v. Fox, 90 Kan. 317, 133 P. 890, 47 L.R.A.,N.S., 302.

SINGLE JUROR CHARGE. The charge that, if there is any juror who is not reasonably satisfied from the evidence that plaintiff should recover a verdict against the defendant, jury cannot find against defendant. Greyhound Corp. v. Brown, 113 So.2d 916, 919, 269 Ala. 520; Southern Ry. Co. v. Stallings, 107 So.2d 873, 884, 268 Ala. 463.

SINGULAR. Each; as in the expression "all and singular." Also, individual. In grammar, the singular is used to express only one. In law, the singular frequently includes the plural. Under the 13 & 14 Vict. c. 21, § 4, words in acts of parliament importing the singular shall include the plural, and *vice versa,* unless the contrary is expressly provided. Whart. Lex.

As to singular "Successor," and "Title," see those titles.

SINGULI IN SOLIDUM TENENTUR. Each is bound for the whole. 6 Johns.Ch. (N.Y.) 242, 252.

SINKING FUND. See Fund.

SIPESSOCUA. In old English law. A franchise, liberty, or hundred.

SIST, *v.* In Scotch practice. To stay proceedings. Bell.

SIST, *n.* In Scotch practice. A stay or suspension of proceedings; an order for a stay of proceedings. Bell.

SISTER. A woman who has the same father and mother with another, or has one of them only. In the first case, she is called sister, simply; in the second, half-sister. Wood v. Mitchell, 61 How. Prac., N.Y., 48. The word is the correlative of "brother."

SISTER IN LAW. Sister of one's spouse; wife of one's brother.

SIT. To hold court; to do any act of a judicial nature. Russell v. Crook County Court, 75 Or. 168, 146 P. 806, 808. To hold a session, as of a court, grand jury, legislative body, etc. To be formally organized and proceeding with the transaction of business. Allen v. State, 102 Ga. 619, 29 S.E. 470.

SITE. A plot of ground suitable or set apart for some specific use. Victoria v. Our Lord's Church, 22 B.C. 174, 175. A seat or ground plot. Miller v. Alliance Ins. Co. of Boston, C.C.N.Y., 7 F. 649, 651. The term does not of itself necessarily mean a place or tract of land fixed by definite boundaries. Petersburg School Dist. of Nelson County v. Peterson, 14 N.D. 344, 103 N.W. 756, 758. See, also, Scite.

SITHCUNDMAM. In Saxon law. The high constable of a hundred.

SITIO GANADO MAYOR. (Sometimes written, also, *sitio de ganado mayor.)* Sp. In Spanish and Mexican land law, a tract of land in the form of a square, each side of which measures 5,000 varas; the distance from the center of each sitio to each of its sides should be measured directly to the cardinal points of the compass, and should be 2,500 varas. U. S. v. Cameron, 3 Ariz. 100, 21 P. 177. Equivalent to 4338.464 acres. Ainsa v. U. S., 16 S.Ct. 544, 161 U.S. 219, 40 L.Ed. 673. A square league. U. S. v. Sutherland, 19 How. 363, 364, 15 L.Ed. 666.

SITIO DE GANADO MENOR, or sheep ranch, is equivalent to 1928.133 acres. Ainsa v. U. S., 16 S.Ct. 544, 161 U.S. 219, 40 L.Ed. 673.

SITTING. In English law. The part of the year in which judicial business is transacted. A session or term of court; usually plural. People v. Higgins, 173 Misc. 96, 16 N.Y.S.2d 302, 310.

SITTINGS AFTER TERM. Sittings *in banc* after term were held by authority of the St. 1 & 2 Vict. c. 32. The courts were at liberty to transact business at their sittings as in term-time, but the custom was to dispose only of cases standing for argument or judgment. Wharton.

SITTINGS IN BANK, OR BANC. The sittings which the respective superior courts of common law hold during every term for the purpose of hearing and determining the various matters of law agreed before them.

They are so called in contradistinction to the sittings at nisi prius which are held for purpose of trying issues of fact.

In America, the practice is essentially the same, all the judges, or a majority of them usually, sitting in banc and but one holding the court for jury trials; and the term has the same application here as in England.

SITTINGS IN CAMERA. See Chambers.

SITUATE. To give a specific position to; fix a site for; to place in certain position; subject to definite conditions or circumstances; (rare) having a fixed place or a relative position; (archaic) residing; dwelling. Century Ins. Co. v. Glidden Buick Corporation, 174 Misc. 149, 20 N.Y.S.2d 108, 112.

SITUATION. State of being placed; posture. Jones v. Tuck, 48 N.C. 202, 205. Position as regards conditions and circumstances; state; condition. Bellomy v. Bruce, 303 Ill.App. 349, 25 N.E.2d 428, 433.

SITUATION OF DANGER. Within the meaning of the last clear chance rule as applicable to a plaintiff operating a moving vehicle is reached only when plaintiff, in moving toward path of an on-coming train or vehicle has reached a position from which he cannot escape by ordinary care, and it is not enough that plaintiff was merely approaching a position of danger. Johnson v. Sacramento Northern Ry., 54 Cal.App.2d 528, 129 P.2d 503, 506.

SITUS. Lat. Situation; location. Smith v. Bank, 5 Pet. 524, 8 L.Ed. 212; Heston v. Finley, 118 Kan. 717, 236 P. 841, 843; Avery v. Interstate Grocery Co., 118 Okl. 268, 248 P. 340, 341, 52 A.L.R. 528. Site; position; the place where a thing is considered, for example, with reference to jurisdiction over it, or the right or power to tax it. Boyd v. Selma, 96 Ala. 144, 11 So. 393, 16 L.R.A. 729; Bullock v. Guilford, 59 Vt. 516, 9 A. 360; Fenton v. Edwards, 126 Cal. 43, 58 P. 320, 46 L.R.A. 832, 77 Am.St.Rep. 141.

It imports fixedness of location. In its natural signification the term is applicable only to landed estates which are really fixed and immovable. Conventionally, it is applied to personal property as annexing it to the individual to whom it belongs; its situs being primarily in legal contemplation where the owner happens to be at any time. It is the exception that personal property has any other situs than that of the person of its owner. Zanes v. Mercantile Bank & Trust Co. of Texas, Tex.Civ.App., 49 S.W.2d 922, 926.

Generally, personal property has its taxable "situs" in that state where owner of it is domiciled. Smith v. Lummus, 149 Fla. 660, 6 So.2d 625, 627, 628.

"Situs" of a trust means place of performance of active duties of trustee. Campbell v. Albers, 313 Ill.App. 152, 39 N.E.2d 672, 676.

SIVE TOTA RES EVINCATUR, SIVE PARS, HABET REGRESSUM EMPTOR IN VENDITOREM. The purchaser who has been evicted in whole or in part has an action against the vendor. Dig. 21, 2, 1; Broom, Max. 768.

SIX ACTS, THE. The acts passed in 1819, for the pacification of England, are so called. They, in effect, prohibited the training of persons to arms; authorized general searches and seizure of arms; prohibited meetings of more than fifty persons for the discussion of public grievances; repressed with heavy penalties and confiscations seditious and blasphemous libels; and checked pamphleteering by extending the newspaper stamp duty to political pamphlets. Brown.

SIX ARTICLES, LAWS OF. A celebrated act entitled "An act for abolishing diversity of opinion," (31 Hen. VIII, c. 14,) enforcing conformity under the severest penalties on six of the strongest points in the Roman Catholic religion: Transubstantiation, communion in one kind, the celibacy of the clergy, monastic vows, the sacrifice of the mass, and auricular confession. 4 Steph.Com. 183; 4 Reeve, Eng.Law, 378. Repealed by 1 Eliz. c. 1.

SIX CLERKS. In English practice. Officers of the court of chancery, who received and filed all bills, answers, replications, and other papers, signed office copies of pleadings, examined and signed dockets of decrees, etc., and had the care of all records in their office. Holthouse; 3 Bl. Comm. 443. They were abolished by St. 5 Vict. c. 5.

SIX-DAY LICENSE. In English law. A liquor license, containing a condition that the premises in respect of which the license is granted shall be closed during the whole of Sunday, granted under section 49 of the licensing act, 1872 (35 & 36 Vict. c. 94.)

SIXHINDI. Servants of the same nature as rod knights, (*q. v.*) Anc. Inst. Eng.

SKELETON BILL. One drawn, indorsed, or accepted in blank.

SKELETON BILL OF EXCEPTIONS. A bill of exceptions containing calls for the insertion by the clerk of the necessary documents. Padgett v. Gulfport Fertilizer Co., 11 Ala.App. 366, 66 So. 866, 867.

SKID, *n*. A simple contrivance used for handling heavy articles under many conditions. Beckman v. Anheuser Busch Brewing Ass'n, 98 Mo.App. 555, 72 S.W. 710, 711.

SKID, *v*. As used in connection with operation of motor vehicle on roadway means that car slips sideways on road and rear wheels fail to grip roadway. Correira v. Boston Motor Tours, 270 Mass. 88, 169 N.E. 775, 776.

SKILL. Practical and familiar knowledge of the principles and processes of an art, science, or trade, combined with the ability to apply them in practice in a proper and approved manner and with readiness and dexterity. Akridge v. Noble, 114 Ga. 949, 41 S.E. 78; Haworth v. Severs Mfg. Co., 87 Iowa 765, 51 N.W. 68.

Reasonable Skill

Such skill as is ordinarily possessed and exercised by persons of common capacity, engaged in the same business or employment. Mechanics' Bank v. Merchants' Bank, 6 Metc., Mass., 26.

SKILLED WITNESSES. One possessing knowledge and experience as to particular subject which are not acquired by ordinary persons. Firemen's Ins. Co. v. Little, 189 Ark. 640, 74 S.W.2d 777, 780.

Such witness is allowed to give evidence on matters of opinion and abstract fact.

SKINPOP. An intramuscular injection or narcotic drug. Broadway Angels, Inc., v. Wilson, 125 N.Y.S.2d 546, 548, 282 App.Div. 643.

SKIOGRAPHS. Photographs of the interior of the object portrayed. Texas Emp. Ins. Ass'n v. Crow, Tex., 221 S.W.2d 235, 237.

SLACKER. A person who was derelict in the performance of his duty toward his country in the world war. Dimmitt v. Breakey, C.C.A.Tex., 267 F. 792; Choctaw Coal & Mining Co. v. Lillich, 204 Ala. 533, 86 So. 383, 385, 11 A.L.R. 1014.

SLADE. In old records. A long, flat, and narrow piece or strip of ground. Paroch. Antiq. 465.

SLAINS. See Letters of Slains.

SLANDER. The speaking of base and defamatory words tending to prejudice another in his reputation, office, trade, business, or means of livelihood. Little Stores v. Isenberg, 26 Tenn.App. 357, 172 S.W.2d 13, 16. Harbison v. Chicago, R. I. & P. Ry. Co., 327 Mo. 440, 37 S.W.2d 609, 616. Oral defamation; the speaking of false and malicious words concerning another, whereby injury results to his reputation. Pollard v. Lyon, 91 U.S. 227, 23 L.Ed. 308; Fredrickson v. Johnson, 60 Minn. 337, 62 N.W. 388; Johnston v. Savings Trust Co. of St. Louis, Mo., 66 S.W.2d 113, 114; Lloyd v. Commissioner of Internal Revenue, C.C.A.7, 55 F.2d 842, 844. An essential element of "slander" is that slanderous words be spoken in presence of another than person slandered, and publication is always material and issuable fact in action for slander. Tucker v. Pure Oil Co. of Carolinas, 191 S.C. 60, 3 S.E.2d 547, 549. Hence an oral defamation, heard only by one who does not understand the language in which it is spoken, is not "slander". Allen v. American Indemnity Co., 63 Ga. App. 894, 12 S.E.2d 127, 128.

"Libel" and "slander" are both methods of defamation; the former being expressed by print, writing, pictures, or signs; the latter by oral expressions. Ajouelo v. Auto-Soler Co., 61 Ga.App. 216, 6 S.E.2d 415, 418.

SLANDER OF TITLE. A false and malicious statement, oral or written, made in disparagement of a person's title to real or personal property, or of some right of his causing him special damage. Reliable Mfg. Co. v. Vaughan Novelty Mfg. Co., 294 Ill.App. 601, 13 N.E.2d 518; Cawrse v. Signal Oil Co., 164 Or. 666, 103 P.2d 729, 730, 129 A.L.R. 174. "Malice" as essential element of "slander of title" purports an intention to vex, injure or annoy another person. Cawrse v. Signal Oil Co., 164 Or. 666, 103 P.2d 729, 730, 129 A.L.R. 174.

An action for "slander of title" is maintainable only by one who possesses an estate or interest in the property. Allison v. Berry, 316 Ill.App. 261, 44 N.E.2d 929, 934.

SLANDERER. One who maliciously and without reason imputes a crime or fault to another of which he is innocent. See Slander.

SLANDEROUS PER SE. Slanderous in itself. Words falsely spoken of another are slanderous per se only when they impute the commission of a crime involving moral turpitude, impute the existence of a loathsome and infectious disease, impute unfitness to perform the duties of an office or employment, prejudice in a profession or trade, or tend to disinherit him. Smallwood v. York, 163 Ky. 139, 173 S.W. 380, 381, L.R.A.1915D, 578; Nelson v. Rosenberg, 135 Neb. 34, 280 N.W. 229. Words which are slanderous without proof of special damages. Simons v. Harris, 215 Iowa 479, 245 N.W. 875, 876.

To constitute slander "per se," the published statement must be susceptible of but one meaning. Tucker v. Wallace, 90 Mont. 359, 3 P.2d 404, 405.

SLAVE. A person who is wholly subject to the will of another; one who has no freedom of action, but whose person and services are wholly under the control of another. Webster; Anderson v. Salant, 38 R.I. 463, 96 A. 425, 428, L.R.A.1916D, 651.

One who is under the power of a master, and who belongs to him; so that the master may sell and dispose of his person, of his industry, and of his labor, without his being able to do anything, have anything, or acquire anything, but what must belong to his master. Civ.Code La. 1838, art. 35.

SLAVE-TRADE. The traffic in slaves, or the buying and selling of slaves for profit.

SLAVERY. The condition of a slave; that civil relation in which one man has absolute power over the life, fortune, and liberty of another.

SLAY. This word, in an indictment, adds nothing to the force and effect of the word "kill," when used with reference to the taking of human life. It is particularly applicable to the taking of human life in battle; and, when it is not used in this sense, it is synonymous with "kill." State v. Thomas, 32 La.Ann. 351.

SLEDGE. A hurdle to draw traitors to execution. 1 Hale, P. C. 82.

SLEEPING PARTNER. A dormant partner; one whose name does not appear in the firm, and who takes no active part in the business, but who has an interest in the concern, and shares the profits, and thereby becomes a partner, either absolutely, or as respects third persons.

SLEEPING RENT. In English law. An expression frequently used in coal-mine leases and agreements for the same. It signifies a fixed or dead, *i. e.*, certain, rent, as distinguished from a rent or royalty varying with the amount of coals gotten, and is payable although the mine should not be worked at all, but should be sleeping or dead, whence the name. Brown.

SLICE. An indeterminate part or portion. Read v. McKeague, 252 Mass. 162, 147 N.E. 585.

SLICK. Smooth, with a slippery or greasy smoothness. McCall v. B. Nugent Bros. Dry Goods Co., Mo., 236 S.W. 324, 327.

SLIGHT. A word of indeterminate meaning. Moxley v. Hertz, 30 S.Ct. 305, 308, 216 U.S. 344, 54 L.Ed 510. Variously defined as inconsiderable; unimportant; remote; insignificant. Newsome v. Louisville and N. R. Co., 20 Ala.App. 349, 102 So. 61, 64; Moxley v. Hertz, 30 S.Ct. 305, 308, 216 U.S. 344, 356, 54 L.Ed. 510.

As to slight "Care," "Evidence," "Fault," and "Negligence," see those titles.

SLIP. In negotiations for a policy of insurance. In England, the agreement is in practice concluded between the parties by a memorandum called the "slip," containing the terms of the proposed insurance, and initialed by the underwriters. Sweet.

Also that part of a police court which is divided off from the other parts of the court, for the prisoner to stand in. It is frequently called the "dock." Brown.

The intermediate space between two wharves or docks; the opening or vacant space between two piers. Thompson v. New York, 11 N.Y. 120; New York v. Scott, 1 Caines, N.Y., 543.

A break or cleavage in the continuity of the slate structure of the roof of a mine. Edgren v. Scandia Coal Co., 171 Iowa 459, 151 N.W. 519, 522.

SLIPPA. A stirrup. There is a tenure of land in Cambridgeshire by holding the sovereign's stirrup. Wharton.

SLOPE. Within a mining statute, a level or inclined way, passage, or opening used for the same purpose as a shaft. Roberts v. Tennessee Coal, Iron & R. Co., C.C.A.Ala., 255 F. 469, 471.

SLOT MACHINE. Within a statute prohibiting operation of slot machines or similar gambling device, an apparatus by which a person depositing money therein may, by chance, get directly or indirectly money or articles of value worth either more or less than the money deposited. Elder v. Camp, 193 Ga. 320, 18 S.E.2d 622, 624. See also State v. Abbott, 218 N.C. 470, 11 S.E.2d 539, 544.

SLOUGH. An arm of a river, flowing between islands and the main-land, and separating the islands from one another. Sloughs have not the breadth of the main river, nor does the main body of water of the stream flow through them. Dunlieth & D. Bridge Co. v. Dubuque County, 55 Iowa 565, 8 N.W. 443.

SLOUGH SILVER. A rent paid to the castle of Wigmore, in lieu of certain days' work in harvest, heretofore reserved to the lord from his tenants. Cowell.

SLUICEWAY. An artificial channel into which water is let by a sluice. Specifically, a trench constructed over the bed of a stream, so that logs or lumber can be floated down to a convenient place of delivery. Webster. See Anderson v. Munch, 29 Minn. 416, 13 N.W. 192.

SLUM. A squalid, dirty street or quarter of a city, town or village, ordinarily inhabited by the very poor, destitute or criminal classes; overcrowding is usually a prevailing characteristic. Marvin v. Housing Authority of Jacksonville, 133 Fla. 590, 183 So. 145, 150. Spahn v. Stewart, 268 Ky. 97, 103 S.W.2d 651, 658.

SLUNG-SHOT. A small mass of metal or stone fixed on a flexible handle, strap, or the like, used as a weapon. People v. Williams, 100 Cal.App. 149, 279 P. 1040.

SLUSH FUND. Money collected or spent for corrupt purposes such as lobbying or the like. Boehm v. United States, C.C.A.Mo., 123 F.2d 791, 812.

SMAKA. In old records. A small, light vessel; a smack. Cowell.

SMALL DEBTS COURTS. The several county courts established by St. 9 & 10 Vict. c. 95, for the purpose of bringing justice home to every man's door.

SMALL TITHES. All personal and mixed tithes, and also hops, flax, saffrons, potatoes, and sometimes, by custom, wood. Otherwise called "privy tithes." 2 Steph.Comm. 726.

SMART-MONEY. Vindictive or exemplary damages given by way of punishment and example, in cases of gross misconduct of defendant. Brewer v. Jacobs, C.C.Tenn., 22 F. 224; Springer v. Somers Fuel Co., 196 Pa. 156, 46 A. 370; Murphy v. Hobbs, 7 Colo. 541, 5 P. 119, 49 Am.Rep. 366; Cotton v. Fisheries Products Co., 181 N.C. 151, 106 S.E. 487, 488.

SMELLER. In liquor cases. A witness who is shown to know liquor by smell. Mathews v. State, 21 Ala.App. 181, 106 So. 390, 391.

SMELTING. A melting of ores in the presence of some re-agent which operates to separate the metallic element by combining with a non-metallic element. Lowrey v. Smelting & Aluminum Co., C.C.Ohio, 68 F. 354.

SMOKE-FARTHINGS. In old English law. An annual rent paid to cathedral churches; another name for the pentecostals or customary oblations offered by the dispersed inhabitants within a diocese, when they made their processions to the mother cathedral church. Cowell.

SMOKE-SILVER. In English law. A sum paid to the ministers of divers parishes as a modus in lieu of tithe-wood. Blount.

SMUGGLING. The offense of importing prohibited articles, or of defrauding the revenue by the introduction of articles into consumption, without paying the duties chargeable upon them. It may be committed indifferently either upon the excise or customs revenue. Wharton.

Clandestine introduction of goods into United States, importation of which is prohibited without payment of duty, constitutes. Tomplain v. U. S., C.C.A.La., 42 F.2d 203, 204.

The fraudulent taking into a country, or out of it, merchandise which is lawfully prohibited. (Quoted and approved by Brewer, J., in Dunbar v. U. S., 15 S.Ct. 325, 156 U.S. 185, 39 L.Ed. 390.)

"The *bringing on shore*, or carrying from the shore, goods and merchandise, for which the duty has not been paid, or of goods of which the importation or exportation is prohibited." 6 Bac. Abr. 258; Hill v. U. S., C.C.A.Md., 42 F.2d 812, 814.

SMUT. See Obscene.

SNOTTERING SILVER. A small duty which was paid by servile tenants in Wylegh to the abbot of Colchester. Cowell.

SO. In the same manner as has been stated; under this circumstance; in this way, referring to something which is asserted. Blanton v. State, 1 Wash. 265, 24 P. 439, 441. Sometimes the equivalent of "hence," or "therefore," and it is thus understood whenever what follows is an illustration of, or conclusion from, what has gone before. Clem v. State, 33 Ind. 431.

In connection with time, it suggests a period of indefinite duration. Thus, an agreement to pay rent "within a week or so". Marshall v. Partyka, 98 Conn. 778, 120 A. 507, 508.

SO HELP YOU GOD. The formula at the end of a common oath.

SOAKAGE. As used in the laws and regulations relating to withdrawal of liquors from bonded warehouses, the spirits which in course of time in the warehouse had been absorbed by the staves of the barrel containing it. Bernheim Distilling Co. v. Mayes, D.C.Ky., 268 F. 629, 630.

SOBER. Moderate in, or abstinent from, the use of intoxicating liquors. American Cigar Co. v. Fabacher, 156 La. 182, 100 So. 299, 300.

SOBRE. Span. Above; over; upon. Ruis v. Chambers, 15 Tex. 586, 592.

SOBRE-JUEZES. In Spanish law. Superior judges. Las Partidas, pt. 3, tit. 4, l. 1.

SOBRINI and SOBRINÆ. Lat. In the civil law. The children of cousins german in general.

SOC, SOK, or SOKA. In Saxon law. Jurisdiction; a power or privilege to administer justice and execute the laws; also a shire, circuit, or territory. Cowell.

SOCA. A seigniory or lordship, enfranchised by the king, with liberty of holding a court of his *socmen* or *socagers*; *i. e.*, his tenants.

SOCAGE. A species of tenure, in England, whereby the tenant held certain lands in consideration of certain inferior services of husbandry to be performed by him to the lord of the fee. In its most general and extensive signification, a tenure by any certain and determinate service. And in this sense it is by the ancient writers constantly put in opposition to tenure by chivalry or knight-service, where the render was precarious and uncertain. Socage is of two sorts,—free socage, where the services are not only certain, but honorable; and villein socage, where the services, though certain, are of baser nature. Such as hold by the former tenure are also called in Glanvil and other authors by the name of "*liberi sokemanni*," or tenants in free socage. By the statute 12 Car. 2, c. 24, all the tenures by knight-service were, with one or two immaterial exceptions, converted into free and common socage. Cowell; Bract. l. 2, c. 35; 2 Bl.Comm. 79; Fleta, lib. 3, c. 14, § 9; Litt. § 117; Glan. l. 3, c. 7.

SOCAGER. A tenant by socage.

SOCAGIUM IDEM EST QUOD SERVITUM SOCÆ; ET SOCA, IDEM EST QUOD CARUCA. Co. Litt. 86. Socage is the same as service of the soc; and soc is the same thing as a plow.

SOCER. Lat. In the civil law. A wife's father; a father-in-law. Calvin.

SOCIAL CLUBS. Within federal statute imposing tax on dues and initiation fees of such clubs, clubs whose social features are a material part of their activities and necessary to their existence, and not merely incidental. Transportation Club of San Francisco v. United States, Ct.Cl., 17 F.Supp. 201, 205.

SOCIAL CONTRACT, or COMPACT. In political philosophy, a term applied to the theory of the origin of society associated chiefly with the names of Hobbes, Locke and Rousseau, though it can be traced back to the Greek Sophists. Rousseau (Contract Social) held that in the pre-social state man was unwarlike and timid. Laws resulted from the combination of men who agreed, for mutual protection, to surrender individual freedom of action. Government must therefore rest on the consent of the governed. Encycl. Br.

SOCIAL INSURANCE. Covers insurance referred to under the head: Unemployment, old age pensions, mothers' and orphans' pensions, sickness, etc. Smythe v. Home Life & Accident Ins. Co., 134 La. 368, 64 So. 142, 143.

SOCIAL SETTLEMENT. The term as applied to organizations engaged in charitable or philanthropic work, implies a fixed locality to be benefited by supplying moral, physical, and educational help to the poor and needy. In re Young Women's Christian Ass'n, Sup., 141 N.Y.S. 260, 261.

SOCIALISM. Any theory or system of social organization which would abolish, entirely or in great part, the individual effort and competition on which modern society rests, and substitute for it co-operative action, would introduce a more perfect and equal distribution of the products of labor, and would make land and capital, as the instruments and means of production, the joint possession of the members of the community.

SOCIDA. In civil law. The name of a contract by which one man delivers to another, either for a small recompense or for a part of the profits, certain animals on condition that if any of them perish they shall be replaced by the bailee or he shall pay their value.

A contract of hiring, with the condition that the bailee takes upon him the risk of the loss of the thing hired. Wolff § 638.

SOCIEDAD. In Spanish law. Partnership. Schm. Civil Law, 153, 154.

SOCIEDAD ANONIMA. In Spanish and Mexican law. A business corporation. "By the corporate name, the shareholders' names are unknown to the world; and, so far as their connection with the corporation is concerned, their own names may be said to be anonymous, that is, nameless. Hence the derivation of the term 'anonymous' as applied to a body of persons associated together in the form of a company to transact any given business under a company name which does not disclose any of their own." Hall, Mex. Law, § 749.

SOCIEDAD DE GANANCIALES. A Cuban law. It exists between husband and wife and is literally an association for profit. The underlying purpose of such associations is that the spouses may each contribute to a common stock, the wife her dowry, the husband his capital, the gains from those as well as from their joint labors, to be shared equally. On dissolution of the association, ordinarily by death, the distribution is as follows: First the wife gets back her dowry and "parapherna"; second, the debts of the "sociedad" are paid; and the husband's contribution, "capital," is returned. The remainder is profits, "gananciales," and is divided equally between the spouses after restoring any losses to their contributed property. Sanchez v. Bowers, C.C.A.N.Y., 70 F.2d 715, 716, 718.

SOCIETAS. Lat. In the civil law. Partnership; a partnership; the contract of partnership. Inst. 3, 26. A contract by which the goods or labor of two or more are united in a common stock, for the sake of sharing in the gain. Hallifax, Civil Law, b. 2, c. 18, no. 12.

SOCIETAS LEONINA. That kind of society or partnership by which the entire profits belong to some of the partners, in exclusion of the rest. So called in allusion to the fable of the lion, who, having entered into partnership with other animals for the purpose of hunting, appropriated all the prey to himself. Wharton.

SOCIETAS NAVALIS. A naval partnership; an association of vessels; a number of ships pursuing their voyage in company, for purposes of mutual protection.

SOCIÉTÉ. Fr. In French law. Partnership. See Commendam.

SOCIÉTÉ ANONYME. In French law originally a partnership conducted in the name of one of the members; the others were strictly secret partners. To creditors of the firm they came into no relation and under no liability. An association where the liability of all the partners is limited. It had in England until lately no other name than that of "chartered company," meaning thereby a joint-stock company whose shareholders, by a charter from the crown, or a special enactment of the legislature, stood exempted from any liability for the debts of the concern, beyond the amount of their subscriptions. 2 Mill, Pol. Econ. 485.

SOCIÉTÉ D'ACQUETS. A written contract between husband and wife to regard as community property only those things which are acquired during the marriage.

SOCIÉTÉ EN COMMANDITE. In Louisiana. A partnership formed by a contract by which one person or partnership agrees to furnish another person or partnership a certain amount, either in property or money, to be employed by the person or partnership to whom it is furnished, in his or their own name or firm, on condition of receiving a share in the profits, in the proportion determined by the contract, and of being liable to losses and expenses to the amount furnished and no more. Civ.Code La. art. 2839.

SOCIÉTÉ EN NOM COLLECTIF. A partnership in which all the members are jointly and severally liable.

SOCIÉTÉ EN PARTICIPATION. A joint adventure.

SOCIÉTÉ PAR ACTIONS. A joint stock company.

SOCIETY. An association or company of persons (generally unincorporated) united together by mutual consent, in order to deliberate, determine, and act jointly for some common purpose. In a wider sense, the community or public; the people in general. Gilmer v. Stone, 7 S.Ct. 689, 120 U.S. 586, 30 L.Ed. 734.

Within rule that husband is entitled to damages for loss of wife's "society" through wrongful injury means such capacities for usefulness, aid, and comfort as a wife as she possessed at the time of the injuries. Homan v. Missouri Pac. R. Co., 335 Mo. 30, 70 S.W.2d 869.

Civil society—usually, a state, nation, or body politic. Rutherforth, Inst. c. 1, 2.

SOCII MEI SOCIUS MEUS SOCIUS NON EST. The partner of my partner is not my partner. Dig. 50, 17, 47, 1.

SOCIOPATHIC PERSONALITY. See Psychopath.

SOCIUS. Lat. In the civil law. A partner.

SOCMAN. A socager.

Free Socmen. In old English law. Tenants in free socage. Glanv. Lib. 3, c. 7; 2 Bl.Comm. 79.

SOCMANRY. Free tenure by socage.

SOCNA. A privilege, liberty, or franchise. Cowell.

SOCOME. A custom of grinding corn at the lord's mill. Cowell. Bond-socome is where the tenants are bound to it. Blount.

SODOMITE. One who has been guilty of sodomy.

SODOMY. A carnal copulation by human beings with each other against nature, or with a beast. Strum v. State, 168 Ark. 1012, 272 S.W. 359. State v. Young, 140 Or. 228, 13 P.2d 604, 607.

This term is often defined in statutes and judicial decisions as meaning "the crime against nature," the *"crimen innominatum,"* or as carnal copulation, against the order of nature, by man with man, or, in the same unnatural manner, with woman or with a beast. See Code Ga.1882, § 4352 (Penn.Code 1910, § 373); Honselman v. People, 168 Ill. 172, 48 N.E. 304. But, strictly speaking, it should be used only as equivalent to *"pederasty,"* that is, the sexual act as performed by a man upon the person of another man or a boy by penetration of the *anus.* See Ausman v. Veal, 10 Ind. 355, 71 Am.Dec. 331. The term might also, without any great violence to its original meaning, be so extended as to cover the same act when performed in the same manner by a man upon the person of a woman. Another possible method of unilateral sexual connection, by penetration of the mouth *(penem in orem alii immittere, vel penem alii in orem recipere)* is not properly called "sodomy," but "fellation." That this does not constitute sodomy within the meaning of a statute is held in Com. v. Poindexter, Ky., 118 S.W. 943; Lewis v. State, 36 Tex. Cr.R. 37, 35 S.W. 372, 61 Am.St.Rep. 831; but a greater number of jurisdictions hold otherwise. See State v. Farris, 189 Iowa, 505, 178 N.W. 361, 362; Glover v. State, 179 Ind. 459, 101 N.E. 629, 630, L.R.A.,N.S., 473; White v. State, 136 Ga. 158, 71 S.E. 135; State v. Start, 65 Or. 178, 132 P. 512, 46 L.R.A.,N.S., 266. On the other hand *bestiality* is the carnal copulation of a human being with a brute, or animal of the sub-human orders of the opposite sex. It is not identical with sodomy, nor is it a form of sodomy, though the two terms are often confused in legal writings and sometimes in statutes. See Ausman v. Veal, 10 Ind. 355, 71 Am.Dec. 331. *Buggery* is a term rarely used in statutes, but apparently including both sodomy (in the widest sense) and bestiality as above defined. See Ausman v. Veal, 10 Ind. 355, 71 Am.Dec. 331; Com. v. J., 21 Pa.Co. Ct.R. 625.

SOFT DRINK PARLOR. A place where soft drinks are sold and drunk on premises. People v. De Geovanni, 326 Ill. 230, 157 N.E. 195, 197.

SOIL. The surface, or suface-covering of the land, not including minerals beneath it or grass or plants growing upon it. But in a wider (and more usual) sense, the term is equivalent to "land," and includes all that is below, upon, or above the surface.

SOIT. Fr. Let it be; be it so. A term used in several law; French phrases employed in English law, particularly as expressive of the will or assent of the sovereign in formal communications with parliament or with private suitors.

SOIT BAILE AUX COMMONS. Let it be delivered to the commons. The form of indorsement on a bill when sent to the house of commons. Dyer, 93*a*.

SOIT BAILE AUX SEIGNEURS. Let it be delivered to the lords. The form of indorsement on a bill in parliament when sent to the house of lords. Hob. 111*a*.

SOIT DROIT FAIT AL PARTIE. In English law. Let right be done to the party. A phrase written on a petition of right, and subscribed by the king.

SOIT FAIT COMME IL EST DESIRE. Let it be as it is desired. The royal assent to private acts of parliament.

SOJOURNING. This term means something more than "traveling," and applies to a temporary, as contradistinguished from a permanent, residence. Henry v. Ball, 1 Wheat. 5, 4 L.Ed. 21; In re Gahn's Will, 110 Misc. 96, 180 N.Y.S. 262, 266.

SOKEMANRIES. Lands and tenements which were not held by knight-service, nor by grand serjeanty, nor by petit, but by simple services; being, as it were, lands enfranchised by the king or his predecessors from their ancient demesne. Their tenants were *sokemans.* Wharton.

SOKEMANS. In English law. Those who held their lands in socage. 2 Bl. Comm. 100.

SOKE-REEVE. The lord's rent gatherer in the soca. Cowell.

SOLA AC PER SE SENECTUS DONATIONEM TESTAMENTUM AUT TRANSACTIONEM NON VITIAT. Old age does not alone and of itself vitiate a will or gift. Van Alst v. Hunter, 5 Johns. Ch., N.Y., 148, 158.

SOLAR. In Spanish law. Land; the demesne, with a house, situate in a strong or fortified place. White, New Recop. b. 1, tit. 5, c. 3, § 2.

SOLAR DAY. That period of time which begins at sunrise and ends at sunset. Co. Litt. 135*a*.

SOLAR MONTH. A calendar month. See Month.

SOLARES. In Spanish law. Lots of ground. This term is frequently found in grants from the Spanish government of lands in America. 2 White, Recop. 474.

SOLARIUM. Lat. In the civil law. A rent paid for the ground, where a person built on the public land. A ground rent. Spelman; Calvin.

SOLATIUM. Compensation. Damages allowed for injury to the feelings.

SOLD. See "Sale."

SOLD NOTE. A note given by a broker, who has effected a sale of merchandise, to the buyer, stating the fact of sale, quantity, price, etc. Story, Ag. § 28; Saladin v. Mitchell, 45 Ill. 83.

SOLDIER. A military man; a private in the army.

Prior to induction a selectee is subject to Selective Training Act but is not yet a "soldier". Billings v. Truesdell, Kan., 64 S.Ct. 737, 741, 321 U.S. 542, 88 L.Ed. 917.

A member of the Women's Army Corps is a "soldier in the military service." United States v. Willaims, D.C.N.Y., 59 F.Supp. 300, 301.

SOLE. Single; individual; separate; the opposite of joint; as a *sole tenant.* Fort Worth & D. C. Ry. Co. v. Williams, Tex.Civ.App., 275 S.W. 415, 419.

Comprising only one person; the opposite of aggregate; as a *sole corporation.*

Unmarried; as a *feme sole.* See the nouns.

SOLE ACTOR DOCTRINE. Under this doctrine a principal is charged with the knowledge of his agent. It contemplates that agent must have ostensibly endeavored to benefit his principal, and even though he did not do so and his acts were for his personal benefit, possibly through defalcation, the third party who obligated himself must have been under the impression that he was dealing with the principal. General American Life Ins. Co. v. Anderson, D.C.Ky., 46 F.Supp. 189, 195, 196, 198. It is based on the presumption that by reason of the relationship between an agent and his principal the principal is presumed to have been told everything the agent has done and presumed to have known of his actions and promises. Federal Deposit Ins. Corporation v. Pendleton, D.C.Ky., 29 F.Supp. 779, 782, 783.

SOLE AND UNCONDITIONAL OWNER. See Owner.

SOLEMN. Formal; in regular form; with all the forms of a proceeding. As to solemn "Form," see Probate. As to solemn "Oath" and "War," see the nouns.

SOLEMN OCCASION. Within constitutional provision empowering the Legislature to require the opinion of the Justices on important questions of law means occasion when such questions of law are necessary to be determined by the body making the inquiry in the exercise of the power intrusted to it by the Constitution or laws. In re Opinion of the Justices, 217 Mass. 607, 105 N.E. 440, 441.

SOLEMNES LEGUM FORMULÆ. Lat. In the civil law. Solemn forms of laws; forms of forensic proceedings and of transacting legal acts. One of the sources of the unwritten law of Rome. Butl. Hor. Jur. 47.

SOLEMNITAS ATTACHIAMENTORUM. In old English practice. Solemnity or formality of attachments. The issuing of attachments in a certain formal and regular order. Bract. fols. 439, 440; 1 Reeve, Eng. Law, 480.

SOLEMNITATES JURIS SUNT OBSERVANDÆ. The solemnities of law are to be observed. Jenk. Cent. 13.

SOLEMNITY. A rite or ceremony; the formality established by law to render a contract, agreement, or other act valid.

SOLEMNIZE. A marriage, means no more than to enter into a marriage contract, with due publication, before third persons, for the purpose of giving it notoriety and certainty; which may be before any persons, relatives, friends, or strangers, competent to testify to the facts. See Dyer v. Brannock, 66 Mo. 410, 27 Am.Rep. 359; Pearson v. Howey, 11 N.J.L. 19; Bowman v. Bowman, 24 Ill.App. 172.

SOLICIT. To appeal for something; to apply to for obtaining something; to ask earnestly; to ask for the purpose of receiving; to endeavor to obtain by asking or pleading; to entreat, implore, or importune; to make petition to; to plead for; to try to obtain; and though the word implies a serious request, it requires no particular degree of importunity, entreaty, imploration, or supplication. People v. Phillips, 70 Cal.App.2d 449, 160 P. 2d 872, 874. To tempt a person; to lure on, especially into evil. People v. Rice, 383 Ill. 584, 50 N.E. 2d 711, 713. To awake or excite to action, or to invite. In re Winthrop, 135 Wash. 135, 237 P. 3, 4; Briody v. De Kimpe, 91 N.J.Law, 206, 102 A. 688, 689. The term implies personal petition and importunity addressed to a particular individual to do some particular thing. Golden & Co. v. Justice's Court of Woodland Tp., Yolo County, 23 Cal.App. 778, 140 P. 49, 58.

SOLICITATION. Asking; enticing; urgent request. Any action which the relation of the parties justifies in construing into a serious request. State v. Underwood, 79 Or. 338, 155 P. 194. Thus "solicitation of chastity" is the asking or urging a woman to surrender her chastity. State v. Render, 203 Iowa 329, 210 N.W. 911; People v. Murray, 307 Ill. 349, 138 N.E. 649, 653. The word is also used in such phrases as "solicitation to larceny," to bribery, etc.

SOLICITOR. In English law. A legal practitioner in the court of chancery. The words "solicitor" and "attorney" are commonly used indiscriminately, although they are not precisely the same, an attorney being a practitioner in the courts of common law, a solicitor, a practitioner in the courts of equity. Most attorneys take out a certificate to practice in the courts of chancery, and therefore become solicitors also, and, on the other hand, most, if not all, solicitors take out a certificate to practice in the courts of common law, and therefore become attorneys also. Brown.

SOLICITOR GENERAL. In English law. One of the principal law officers of the crown, associated in his duties with the attorney general, holding office by patent during the pleasure of the sovereign, and having a right of preaudience in the courts. 3 Bl. Comm. 27. In American law, an officer of the department of justice, next in rank and authority to the attorney general, whose principal assistant he is. His chief function is to represent the United States in all cases in the supreme court and the court of claims in which the government is interested or to which it is a party, and to discharge the duties of the attorney general in the absence or disability of that officer or when there is a vacancy in the office. Rev.St.U.S. §§ 347, 359 (5 U.S.C.A. §§ 293, 309).

SOLICITOR OF THE SUPREME COURT. The solicitors before the supreme courts, in Scotland, are a body of solicitors entitled to practice in the court of session, etc. Their charter of incorporation bears date August 10, 1797.

SOLICITOR OF THE TREASURY. An officer of the United States attached to the department of justice, having general charge of the law business appertaining to the treasury.

SOLICITOR TO THE SUITORS' FUND. An officer of the English court of chancery, who is appointed in certain cases guardian *ad litem*.

SOLIDARITY. In the civil law, when several persons bind themselves towards another for the same sum, at the same time, and in the same contract; and so obligate themselves that each may be compelled to pay the whole debt, and that payment made by one of them exonerates the others towards the creditor; and the obligation thus contracted is one, in solido, although one of the debtors be obliged differently from the others to the payment of one and the same thing; as if the one be but conditionally bound, while the engagement of the others is pure and simple, or if the one is allowed a term which is not granted to the others. Rex Credit Co. v. Long, La.App., 159 So. 359, 360.

SOLIDARY. A term of civil-law origin, signifying that the right or interest spoken of is joint or common. A "solidary obligation" corresponds to a "joint and several" obligation in the common law; that is, one for which several debtors are bound in such wise that each is liable for the entire amount, and not merely for his proportionate share. But in the civil law the term also includes the case where there are several creditors, as against a common debtor, each of whom is entitled to receive the entire debt and give an acquittance for it.

SOLIDUM. Lat. In the civil law. A whole; an entire or undivided thing.

SOLIDUS LEGALIS. A coin equal to 13s. 4d. of the present standard. 4 Steph. Comm. 119*n*. Originally the "solidus" was a gold coin of the Byzantine Empire, but in medieval times the term was applied to several varieties of coins, or as descriptive of a money of account, and is supposed to be the root from which "shilling" is derived.

SOLINUM. In old English law. Two plowlands, and somewhat less than a half. Co. Litt. 5*a*.

SOLITARY CONFINEMENT. In a general sense, the separate confinement of a prisoner, with only occasional access of any other person, and that only at the discretion of the jailer; in a stricter sense, the complete isolation of a prisoner from all human society, and his confinement in a cell so arranged that he has no direct intercourse with or sight of any human being, and no employment or instruction. See Medley, Petitioner, 10 S.Ct. 384, 134 U.S. 160, 33 L.Ed. 835.

SOLO CEDIT QUOD SOLO IMPLANTATUR. That which is planted in the soil belongs to the soil. The proprietor of the soil becomes also the proprietor of the seed, the plant, and the tree, as soon as these have taken root. Mackeld. Rom. Law, § 275.

SOLO CEDIT QUOD SOLO INÆDIFICATUR. That which is built upon the soil belongs to the soil. The proprietor of the soil becomes also proprietor of the building erected upon it. Mackeld. Rom. Law, § 275.

SOLUM PROVINCIALE. Lat. In Roman law. The *solum italicum* (an extension of the old *Ager Romanus*) admitted full ownership, and of the application to it of *usucapio;* whereas the *solum provinciale* (an extension of the old *Ager Publicus*) admitted of a possessory title only, and of *longi temporis possessio* only. Justinian abolished all distinctions between the two, sinking the *italicum* to the level of the *provinciale.* Brown.

SOLUM REX HOC NON FACERE POTEST, QUOD NON POTEST INJUSTE AGERE. 11 Coke, 72. This alone the king cannot do, he cannot act unjustly.

SOLUS DEUS FACIT HÆREDEM, NON HOMO. Co. Litt. 5. God alone makes the heir, not man.

SOLUTIO. Lat. In civil law. Payment, satisfaction, or release; any species of discharge of an obligation accepted as satisfactory by the creditor. The term refers not so much to the counting out of money as to the substance of the obligation. Dig. 46, 3, 54; Id. 50, 16, 176.

SOLUTIO INDEBITI. In the civil law. Payment of what was not due. From the payment of what was not due arises an obligation *quasi ex contractu.* When one has erroneously given or performed something to or for another, for which he was in no wise bound, he may redemand it, as if he had only lent it. The term "*solutio indebiti*" is here used in a very wide sense, and includes also the case where one performed labor for another, or assumed to pay a debt for which he was not bound, or relinquished a right or released a debt, under the impression that he was legally bound to do so. Mackeld. Rom. Law, § 500.

SOLUTIO PRETII EMPTIONIS LOCO HABETUR. The payment of the price [of a thing] is held to be in place of a purchase, [operates as a purchase.] Jenk. Cent. p. 56, case 2; 2 Kent. Comm. 387.

SOLUTIONE FEODI MILITIS PARLIAMENTI, or FEODI BURGENSIS PARLIAMENTI. Old writs whereby knights of the shire and burgesses might have recovered their wages or allowance if it had been refused. 35 Hen. VIII. c. 11.

SOLUTUS.

In the civil law. Loosed; freed from confinement; set at liberty. Dig. 50, 16, 48.

In Scotch practice. Purged. A term used in old depositions.

SOLVABILITÉ. Fr. In French law. Ability to pay; solvency. Emerig. Traité des Assur. c. 8, § 15.

SOLVENCY. Ability to pay debts as they mature, Vandeventer v. Goss, 116 Mo.App. 316, 91 S.W. 958, 961. Ability to pay debts in the usual and ordinary course of business. Jeck v. O'Meara, 343 Mo. 559, 122 S.W.2d 897, 903. Present ability of debtor to pay out of his estate all his debts. Ring v. Paint and Glass Co., 44 Mo.App. 111, 116. Excess of assets over liabilities. Akin v. Hull, 222 Mo. App. 1022, 9 S.W.2d 688, 690. Also such attitude of a person's property as that it may be reached and subjected by process of law, without his consent, to the payment of such debts. Graf v. Allen, 230 Mo.App. 721, 74 S.W.2d 61, 66. The opposite of *insolvency* (*q. v.*). Marsh v. Dunckel, 25 Hun (N. Y.) 169; Osborne v. Smith, C.C.Minn., 18 F. 130; Larkin v. Hapgood, 56 Vt. 601; Kennedy v. Burr, 101 Wash. 61, 171 P. 1022, 1024.

SOLVENDO. Lat. Paying. An apt word of reserving a rent in old conveyances. Co. Litt. 47*a*.

SOLVENDO ESSE. Lat. To be in a state of solvency; *i. e.*, able to pay.

SOLVENDO ESSE NEMO INTELLIGITUR NISI QUI SOLLDUM POTEST SOLVERE. No one is considered to be solvent unless he can pay all that he owes. Dig. 50, 16, 114.

SOLVENDUM IN FUTURO. (Lat.) To be paid in the future. Used of an indebtedness which is said to be *debitum in presenti* (due now) and *solvendum in futuro* (payable in the future). An interest in an estate may be rested *in presenti*, though it be *solvendum in futuro*, enjoyable in the future.

SOLVENT. See Solvency.

For "solvent debt" and "solvent partner" see "Debt" and "Partner."

SOLVERE. Lat. To pay; to comply with one's engagement; to do what one has undertaken to do; to release one's self from obligation, as by payment of a debt. Calvin.

SOLVERE PŒNAS. To pay the penalty.

SOLVIT. Lat. He paid; paid. 10 East, 206.

SOLVIT AD DIEM. He paid at the day. The technical name of the plea, in an action of debt on bond, that the defendant paid the money *on the day* mentioned in the condition. 1 Archb. N. P. 220, 221.

SOLVIT ANTE DIEM. A plea that the money was paid before the day appointed.

SOLVIT POST DIEM. He paid after the day. The plea in an action of debt on bond that the defendant paid the money *after the day* named for the payment, and before the commencement of the suit. 1 Archb. N. P. 222.

SOLVITUR ADHUC SOCIETAS ETIAM MORTE SOCII. A partnership is moreover dissolved by the death of a partner. Inst. 3, 26, 5; Dig. 17, 2.

SOLVITUR EO LIGAMINE QUO LIGATUR. In the same manner that a thing is bound it is unloosed. Livingston v. Lynch, 4 Johns. Ch. (N. Y.) 582.

SOMERSETT'S CASE. A celebrated decision of the English king's bench, in 1771, (20 How. St. Tr. 1,) that slavery no longer existed in England in any form, and could not for the future exist on English soil, and that any person brought into England as a slave could not be thence removed except by the legal means applicable in the case of any free-born person.

SOMMATION. In French law. A demand served by a *huissier*, by which one party calls upon another to do or not to do a certain thing. This document has for its object to establish that upon a certain date the demand was made. Arg. Fr. Merc. Law, 574.

SOMNAMBULISM. Sleep-walking. Whether this condition is anything more than a co-operation of the voluntary muscles with the thoughts which occupy the mind during sleep is not settled by physiologists. Wharton.

SOMPNOUR. In ecclesiastical law, an officer of the ecclesiastical courts whose duty was to serve citations or process.

SON. An immediate male descendant. The word may be applied also to a distant male descendent. In a broad use, term may be employed as designating any young male person, as a pupil, a ward, an adopted male child or dependent. Lind v. Burke, 56 Neb. 785, 77 N.W. 444, 445.

The description son in wills, means primia facie legitimate son. Flora v. Anderson, C.C.Ohio, 67 F. 182, 185; In re Flood's Estate, 217 Cal. 763, 21 P.2d 579.

SON. Fr. His. See Civ. Code La. art. 3556.

Son assault demesne. His own assault. A plea which occurs in the actions of trespass and trespass on the case, by which the defendant alleges that it was the plaintiff's own original assault that occasioned the trespass for which he has brought the action, and that what the defendant did was merely in his own defense. Steph. Pl. 186; Oliverius v. Wicks, 107 Neb. 821, 187 N.W. 73, 74; Cameron Compress Co. v. Kubecka, Tex. Civ.App., 283 S.W. 285, 287.

SON-IN-LAW. The husband of one's daughter. Diebold v. Diebold, 235 Mo.App. 83, 141 S.W.2d 119, 125.

SONTAGE. A tax of forty shillings anciently laid upon every knight's fee. Cowell.

SONTICUS. Lat. In the civil law. Hurtful; injurious; hindering; excusing or justifying delay. *Morbus sonticus* is any illness of so serious a nature as to prevent a defendant from appearing in court and to give him a valid excuse. Calvin.

SOON. Within a reasonable time. Sanford v. Shephard, 14 Kan. 232.

SOREHON, or SORN. An arbitrary exaction, formerly existing in Scotland and Ireland. Whenever a chieftain had a mind to revel, he came down among the tenants with his followers, by way of contempt called *"Gilliwitfitts,"* and lived on free quarters. Wharton; Bell.

SORNER. In Scotch law. A person who takes meat and drink from others by force or menaces, without paying for it. Bell.

SOROR. Lat. Sister. Inst. 3, 6, 1.

SORORICIDE. The killing or murder of a sister; one who murders his sister. This is not a technical term of the law.

SORS. Lat. In old English law. A principal lent on interest, as distinguished from the interest itself.

A thing recovered in action, as distinguished from the costs of the action.

In the civil law. Lot; chance; fortune; hazard; a lot, made of wood, gold, or other material. Money borrowed, or put out at interest. A principal sum or fund, such as the capital of a partnership. Ainsworth; Calvin.

SORTITIO. Lat. In the civil law. A drawing of lots. *Sortitio judicum* was the process of selecting a number of judges, for a criminal trial, by drawing lots.

SOUGH. In English law. A drain or watercourse. The channels or water-courses used for draining mines are so termed; and those mines which are near to any given sough, and lie within the same level, and are benefited by it, are technically said to lie within the title of that sough. 5 Mees. & W. 228; Brown.

SOUL SCOT. A mortuary, or customary gift due ministers, in many parishes of England, on the death of parishioners. It was originally voluntary and intended as amends for ecclesiastical dues neglected to be paid in the life-time. 2 Bl. Comm. 425.

SOUND, *v.* To have reference or relation to; to aim at. An action is technically said to *sound in damages* where it is brought not for the specific recovery of a thing, but for damages only. Steph. Pl. 105.

SOUND, *adj.* Whole; in good condition; marketable. So used in warranties of chattels. See Brown v. Bigelow, 10 Allen, Mass., 242; Hawkins v. Pemberton, 35 How.Prac., N.Y., 383; Woodbury v. Robbins, 10 Cush. (Mass.) 522. Free from disease. Raney & Hamon v. Hamilton & White, Tex.Civ.App., 234 S.W. 229, 230. The term may also mean free from danger to the life, safety, and welfare. Kuhn v. Cincinnati Traction Co., 109 Ohio St. 263, 142 N.E. 370, 373.

Sound and disposing mind and memory. Testamentary capacity. In re Hudson's Estate, 131 Minn. 439, 155 N.W. 392, 395. Such mind and memory as enables testator to know and understand business in which he is engaged at time of making will. Farmers' Union Bank of Henning v. Johnson, 27 Tenn.App. 342, 181 S.W.2d 369, 374.

Sound judicial discretion. Discretion exercised on full and fair consideration of the facts presented to the judge by the well-known and established mode of procedure. Caldwell v. State, 164 Tenn. 325, 48 S.W.2d 1087, 1089. Discretion exercised not arbitrarily or willfully but with regard to what is right and equitable under the circumstances. Cornwell v. Cornwell, 73 App.D.C. 233, 118 F.2d 396, 398.

Sound health. In insurance law, means that the applicant has no grave impairment or serious disease, and is free from any ailment that seriously affects the general soundness and healthfulness of the system. National Life & Accident Ins. Co. of Nashville, Tenn., v. Martin, 35 Ga.App. 1, 131 S.E. 120, 121; Metropolitan Life Ins. Co. v. Chappell, 151 Tenn. 299, 269 S.W. 21, 24. A state of health unimpaired by any serious malady of which the person himself is conscious. National Life & Accident Ins. Co. v. Ware, 169 Okl. 618, 37 P.2d 905.

Sound mind. The normal condition of the human mind,—that state in which its faculties of perception and judgment are ordinarily well developed, and not impaired by mania, insanity, or dementia. See Daly v. Daly, 183 Ill. 269, 55 N.E. 671; Delafield v. Parish, 25 N.Y. 102; Harrison v. Rowan, 11 Fed.Cas. 661; Yoe v. McCord, 74 Ill. 37; Rodney v. Burton, 4 Boyce (Del.) 171, 86 A. 826, 829. In the law of wills means that testator must have been able to understand and carry in mind, in a general way, nature and situation of his property, his relations to those having claim to his remembrance, and nature of his act. Needham Trust Co. v. Cookson, 251 Mass. 160, 146 N.E. 268; In re Lawrence's Estate, 286 Pa. 58, 132 A. 786, 789; In re Bossom's Will, 195 App.Div. 339, 186 N.Y.S. 782, 786; Rose v. Rose, Mo.Sup., 249 S.W. 605, 607.

Sound value. Of property within fire policy is the cash value of property, making an allowance for depreciation due to use at and immediately preceding the time of the fire. Reliance Ins. Co. v. Bowen, Tex.Civ.App., 54 S.W.2d 597, 598.

SOUNDING IN DAMAGES. When an action is brought, not for the recovery of lands, goods, or sums of money, (as is the case in real or mixed actions or the personal action of debt or detinue,) but for damages only, as in covenant, trespass, etc., the action is said to be "sounding in damages." Steph. Pl. 116. See Collins v. Greene, 67 Ala. 211; Rosser v. Bunn, 66 Ala. 93.

SOUNDNESS. General health; freedom from any permanent disease. 1 Car. & M. 291. See "Sound."

SOURCE. That from which any act, movement, or effect proceeds; a person or thing that originates, sets in motion, or is a primary agency in producing any course of action or result; an originator; creator; origin. A place where something is found or whence it is taken or derived. Jackling v. State Tax Commission, 40 N.M. 241, 58 P.2d 1167, 1171.

The source of income. Place where it is produced. Union Electric Co. v. Coale, 347 Mo. 175, 146 S.W.2d 631, 635.

SOURCES OF THE LAW. The origins from which particular positive laws derive their authority and coercive force. Such are constitutions, treaties, statutes, usages, and customs.

In another sense, the authoritative or reliable works, records, documents, edicts, etc., to which we are to look for an understanding of what constitutes the law. Such, for example, with reference to the Roman law, are the compilations of Justinian and the treatise of Gaius; and such, with reference to the common law, are especially the ancient reports and the works of such writers as Bracton, Littleton, Coke, Fleta, and others.

SOUS. Fr. Under.

SOUS SEING PRIVÉ. Fr. In French law. Under private signature; under the private signature of the parties. A contract or instrument thus signed is distinguished from an "authentic act," which is formally concluded before a notary or judge. Civil Code La. art. 2240.

SOUTH SEA FUND. The produce of the taxes appropriated to pay the interest of such part of the English national debt as was advanced by the South Sea Company and its annuitants. The holders of South Sea annuities have been paid off, or have received other stock in lieu thereof. 2 Steph.Comm. 578.

SOVEREIGN. A person, body, or state in which independent and supreme authority is vested; a chief ruler with supreme power; a king or other ruler with limited power.

In English law. A gold coin of Great Britain, of the value of a pound sterling.

SOVEREIGN IMMUNITY OF STATE FROM LIABILITY. Exists when the state is engaged in a governmental function. Manion v. State, 303 Mich. 1, 5 N.W.2d 527, 528.

SOVEREIGN PEOPLE. The political body, consisting of the entire number of citizens and qualified electors, who, in their collective capacity, possess the powers of sovereignty and exercise them through their chosen representatives. See Scott v. Sandford, 19 How. 404, 15 L.Ed. 691.

SOVEREIGN POWER or SOVEREIGN PREROGATIVE. That power in a state to which none other is superior or equal, and which includes all the specific powers necessary to accomplish the legitimate ends and purposes of government. See Boggs v. Merced Min. Co., 14 Cal. 309; Donnelly v. Decker, 58 Wis. 461, 17 N.W. 389, 46 Am.Rep. 637; Com. v. Alger, 7 Cush., Mass., 81; Ætna Casualty & Surety Co. v. Bramwell, D.C.Or., 12 F.2d 307, 309.

SOVEREIGN RIGHT. A right which the state alone, or some of its governmental agencies, can possess, and which it possesses in the character of a sovereign, for the common benefit, and to enable it to carry out its proper functions; distinguished from such "proprietary" rights as a state, like any private person, may have in property or demands which it owns. See St. Paul v. Chicago, etc., R. Co., 45 Minn. 387, 48 N.W. 17.

SOVEREIGN STATES. States whose subjects or citizens are in the habit of obedience to them, and which are not themselves subject to any other (or paramount) state in any respect. The state is said to be semi-sovereign only, and not sovereign, when in any respect or respects it is liable to be controlled (like certain of the states in India) by a paramount government, (*e. g.*, by the British empire.) Brown. In the intercourse of nations, certain states have a position of entire independence of others, and can perform all those acts which it is possible for any state to perform in this particular sphere. These same states have also entire power of self-government; that is, of independence upon all other states as far as their own territory and citizens not living abroad are concerned. No foreign power or law can have control except by convention. This power of independent action in external and internal relations constitutes complete sovereignty. Wools. Pol. Science, I. 204.

SOVEREIGNTY. The supreme, absolute, and uncontrollable power by which any independent state is governed; supreme political authority; paramount control of the constitution and frame of government and its administration; the self-sufficient source of political power, from which all specific political powers are derived; the international independence of a state, combined with the right and power of regulating its internal affairs without foreign dictation; also a political society, or state, which is sovereign and independent. Chisholm v. Georgia, 2 Dall. 455, 1 L.Ed. 440; Union Bank v. Hill, 3 Cold., Tenn., 325; Moore v. Shaw, 17 Cal. 218, 79 Am.Dec. 123; State v. Dixon, 66 Mont. 76, 213 P. 227.

The power to do everything in a state without accountability,—to make laws, to execute and to apply them, to impose and collect taxes and levy contributions, to make war or peace, to form treaties of alliance or of commerce with foreign nations, and the like. Story, Const. § 207.

"Sovereignty" in government is that public authority which directs or orders what is to be done by each member associated in relation to the end of the association. It is the supreme power by which any citizen is governed and is the person or body of persons in the state to whom there is politically no superior. The necessary existence of the state and that right and power which necessarily follow is "sovereignty." By "sovereignty" in its largest sense is meant supreme, absolute, uncontrollable power, the absolute right to govern. The word which by itself comes nearest to being the definition of "sovereignty" is will or volition as applied to political affairs. City of Bisbee v. Cochise County, 52 Ariz. 1, 78 P.2d 982, 986.

SOVERTIE. In old Scotch law. Surety. Skene.

SOWLEGROVE. February; so called in South Wales. Cowell.

SOWMING AND ROWMING. In Scotch law. Terms used to express the form by which the number of cattle brought upon a common by those having a servitude of pasturage may be justly proportioned to the rights of the different persons possessed of the servitude. Bell.

SOWNE. In old English law. To be leviable. An old exchequer term applied to sheriff's returns. 4 Inst. 107; Cowell; Spelman.

SPADARIUS. Lat. A sword-bearer. Blount.

SPADONES. Lat. In the civil law. Impotent persons. Those who, on account of their temperament or some accident they have suffered, are unable to procreate. Inst. 1, 11, 9; Dig. 1, 7, 2, 1.

SPARSIM. Lat. Here and there; scattered; at intervals. For instance, trespass to realty by cutting timber *sparsim* (here and there) through a tract.

SPATÆ PLACITUM. In old English law. A court for the speedy execution of justice upon military delinquents. Cowell.

SPEAK. In practice. To argue. "The case was ordered to be *spoke to* again." 10 Mod. 107. See Imparlance; Speaking with Prosecutor.

SPEAKER. The official designation of the president or chairman of certain legislative bodies, particularly of the house of representatives in the congress of the United States, of one or both branches of several of the state legislatures, and of the two houses of the British parliament.

The term "speaker," as used in reference to either of the houses of parliament, signifies the functionary acting as chairman. In the commons his duties are to put questions, to preserve order, and to see that the privileges of the house are not infringed; and, in the event of the numbers being even on a division, he has the privilege of giving the casting vote. The speaker of the lords is the lord chancellor or the lord keeper of the great seal of England, or, if he be absent, the lords may choose their own speaker. The duties of the speaker of the lords are principally confined to putting questions, and the lord chancellor has no more to do with preserving order than any other peer. Brown.

SPEAKING DEMURRER. See Demurrer.

SPEAKING ORDER. See Order.

SPEAKING WITH PROSECUTOR. A method of compounding an offense, allowed in the English practice, where the court permits a defendant convicted of a misdemeanor to speak with the prosecutor before judgment is pronounced; if the prosecutor declares himself satisfied, the court may inflict a trivial punishment. 4 Steph.Comm. 261.

SPECIAL. Relating to or designating a species, kind, individual, thing, or sort; designed for a particular purpose; confined to a particular purpose, object, person, or class. Unusual, extraordinary. National Cash Register Co. v. Wall, 58 Mont. 60, 190 P. 135; Steele-Smith Dry Goods Co. v. Birmingham Ry., Light & Power Co., 15 Ala. App. 271, 73 So. 215; People ex rel. City of New York v. Deyo, 158 App.Div. 319, 143 N.Y.S. 334, 335; State ex rel. and to use of Vaught v. Atchison, T. & S. F. Ry. Co., 270 Mo. 251, 192 S.W. 990, 995.

As to special "Acceptance," "Administration," "Agent," "Allocatur," "Allowances," "Appearance," "Assessment," "Assumpsit," "Bail," "Bailiff," "Bastard," "Benefit," "Calendar," "Charge," "Constable," "Contract," "Count," "Covenant," "Custom," "Damage," "Demurrer," "Deposit," "Deputy," "Election," "Finding," "Guaranty," "Guardian," "Imparlance," "Indorsement," "Indorsement of Writ," "Injunction," "Insurance," "Issue," "Jury," "Legacy," "Letter of Credit," "License," "Limitation," "Malice," "Master," "Meeting," "Mortgage," "Motion," "Non Est Factum," "Occupant," "Owner," "Partner," "Partnership," "Plea," "Pleader," "Pleading," "Power," "Privilege," "Proceeding," "Property," "Request," "Replication," "Restraint of Trade," "Retainer," "Rule," "Service," "Sessions," "Statute," "Stock," "Tail," "Term," "Terms," "Traverse," "Trust," "Verdict," and "Warranty," see those titles.

SPECIAL ACT. A private statute; an act which operates only upon particular persons or private concerns. 1 Bl.Comm. 86; Unity v. Burrage, 103 U.S. 454, 26 L.Ed. 405.

SPECIAL CASE. In English practice. When a trial at *nisi prius* appears to the judge to turn on a point of law, the jury may find a general verdict, subject to the opinion of the court above, upon what is termed a "special case" to be made; that is, upon a written statement of all the facts of the case drawn up for the opinion of the court *in banc*, by the counsel and attorneys on either side, under correction of the judge at *nisi prius*. The party for whom the general verdict is so given is in such case not entitled to judgment till the court *in banc* has decided on the special case; and, according to the result of that decision, the verdict is ultimately entered either for him or his adversary. Brown.

SPECIAL CLAIM. In English law. A claim not enumerated in the orders of April 22, 1850, which required the leave of the court of chancery to file it. Such claims are abolished.

SPECIAL COMMISSION. In English law. An extraordinary commission of oyer and terminer and gaol delivery, issued by the crown to the judges when it is necessary that offenses should be immediately tried and punished. Wharton.

SPECIAL ERRORS. Special pleas in error are such as, instead of joining in error, allege some extraneous matter as a ground of defeating the writ of error, *e. g.*, a release of errors, expiration of the time within which error might be brought, or the like. To these, the plaintiff in error may either reply or demur.

SPECIAL EXAMINER. In English law. Some person, not one of the examiners of the court of chancery, appointed to take evidence in a particular suit. This may be done when the state of business in the examiner's office is such that it is impossible to obtain an appointment at a conveniently early day, or when the witnesses may be unable to come to London. Hunt. Eq. pt. I. c. 5, § 2.

SPECIAL EXCEPTION. An objection to the form in which a cause of action is stated. Cochran v. People's Nat. Bank, Tex.Civ.App., 271 S.W. 433, 434.

SPECIAL EXECUTION. A copy of a judgment with a direction to the sheriff indorsed thereon to execute it. Crombie v. Little, 47 Minn. 581, 50 N.W. 823. One that directs a levy upon some special property. Oklahoma Salvage & Supply Co. v. First Nat. Bank, 122 Okl. 128, 251 P. 1006, 1007.

SPECIAL EXECUTOR. One whose power and office are limited, either in respect to the time or place of their exercise, or restricted to a particular portion of the decedent's estate.

One only empowered by will to take charge of a limited portion of the estate, or such part as may lie in one place, or to carry on the administration only to a prescribed point.

SPECIAL FACTS RULE. In corporation law, as respects director's duty of disclosure when dealing with stockholders, is that where special circumstances or facts are present which make it inequitable for the director to withhold information from the stockholder, the duty to disclose arises, and concealment is fraud. Taylor v. Wright, 69 Cal.App.2d 371, 159 P.2d 980, 985.

SPECIAL JURISDICTION. A court authorized to take cognizance of only some few kinds of causes or proceedings expressly designated by statute is called a "court of special jurisdiction."

SPECIAL LAW. One relating to particular persons or things; one made for individual cases or for particular places or districts; one operating upon a selected class, rather than upon the public generally. State v. Irwin, 5 Nev. 120; Sargent v. Union School Dist., 63 N.H. 528, 2 A. 641; Dodge v. Youngblood, Tex.Civ.App., 202 S.W. 116, 118; Ex parte Crane, 27 Idaho 671, 151 P. 1006, 1011, L.R.A.1918A, 942; State v. Daniel, 87 Fla. 270, 99 So. 804, 809. A law is "special" when it is different from others of the same general kind or designed for a particular purpose, or limited in range or confined to a prescribed field of action or operation. State v. Johnson, 170 N.C. 685, 86 S.E. 788, 792.

A law is not special and local in a constitutional sense, if it affects all persons in like circumstances in the same manner. St. Louis-San Francisco Ry. Co. v. Bledsoe, C.C.A.Okl., 7 F.2d 364, 366. Whether an act be local or special is determined by the generality with which it affects the people as a whole, rather than the extent of territory over which it is operative, and, if it equally affects all people coming within its operation, it is not local or special. State ex rel. Garvey v. Buckner, 308 Mo. 390, 272 S.W. 940, 942. In taxation cases, courts make no distinction between "special law" and "local law." Bozarth v. Egg Harbor City, 85 N.J.Law, 412, 89 A. 920, 921. The phrases "special act" and "private act" mean the same thing. Federal Trust Co. v. East Hartford Fire Dist., C.C.A.Conn., 283 F. 95, 98.

SPECIAL LIEN. A special lien is in the nature of a particular lien, being a lien upon particular property; a lien which the holder can enforce only as security for the performance of a particular act or obligation and of obligations incidental thereto. Green v. Coast Line R. Co., 97 Ga. 15, 24 S.E. 814, 33 L.R.A. 806, 54 Am.St.Rep. 379; Civ. Code Cal. § 2875; Marks v. Baum Bldg. Co., 73 Okl. 264, 175 P. 818, 822.

SPECIAL MATTER. Under a plea of the general issue, the defendant is allowed to give special matter in evidence, usually after notice to the plaintiff of the nature of such matter, thus sparing him the necessity of pleading it specially. 3 Bl.Comm. 306.

SPECIAL PAPER. A list kept in the English courts of common law, and now in the king's bench, common pleas, and exchequer divisions of the high court, in which list demurrers, special cases, etc., to be argued are set down. It is distinguished from the new trial paper, peremptory paper, crown paper, revenue paper, etc., according to the practice of the particular division. Wharton.

SPECIAL PLACE. In Negotiable Instruments. A bank, office, or any other place of business, house or residence, usually occupied by people for business, social, or other purposes, without reference to its location, whether within or without a city, town, or village as distinguished from the city, town or village. O'Connor v. Kirby Inv. Co., Tex.Civ.App., 262 S.W. 554, 556; Maddock v. McDonald, 111 Or. 448, 227 P. 463, 464; Corbett v. Ulsaker Printing Co., 49 N.D. 103, 190 N.W. 75, 76, 24 A.L.R. 1047; Harrison v. Beals, 111 Or. 563, 222 P. 728, 731; Moore v. Knemeyer, Tex.Civ.App., 271 S.W. 653, 654.

SPECIAL REGISTRATION. In election laws. Registration for particular election only which does not entitle elector to vote at any succeeding election. Cowart v. City of Waycross, 159 Ga. 589, 126 S.E. 476, 479.

SPECIALIA GENERALIBUS DEROGANT. Special words derogate from general words. A special provision as to a particular subject-matter is to be preferred to general language, which might have governed in the absence of such special provision. L.R. 1 C.P. 546.

SPECIALIST. In stock exchange. Broker who remains at one post of exchange where particular stocks are dealt in and executes orders of other brokers, for which he receives commission; one who specializes in limited group of stocks. In re Brown, 242 N.Y. 1, 150 N.E. 581, 585, 44 A.L.R. 510; People ex rel. Berdan v. Goldfogle, 213 App. Div. 702, 211 N.Y.S. 107.

SPECIALTY. A contract under seal. Furst v. Brady, 375 Ill. 425, 31 N.E.2d 606, 609, 133 A.L.R. 558.

A writing sealed and delivered, containing some agreement. A writing sealed and delivered, which is given as a security for the payment of a debt, in which such debt is particularly specified. Bac. Abr. "Obligation," A.

A corporate seal is not necessary to the contract of a corporation, and hence it is generally deemed that the affixing of a corporate seal to an instrument not required to be executed with that formality indicates that the instrument was intended to be a "specialty", but there is an exception if it appears from the instrument itself that the instrument was not intended to be a specialty. Caruthers v. Peninsular Life Ins. Co., 150 Fla. 467, 7 So.2d 841, 842.

SPECIALTY DEBT. A debt due or acknowledged to be due by deed or instrument under seal. 2 Bl. Comm. 465.

SPECIE. Coin of the precious metals, of a certain weight and fineness, and bearing the stamp of the government, denoting its value as currency. Trebilcock v. Wilson, 12 Wall. 695, 20 L.Ed. 460; Walkup v. Houston, 65 N.C. 501; Henry v. Bank of Salina, 5 Hill, N.Y., 536.

When spoken of a contract, the expression "performance *in specie*" means strictly, or according to the exact terms. As applied to things, it signifies individuality or identity. Thus, on a bequest of a specific picture, the legatee would be said to be entitled to the delivery of the picture *in specie; i. e.,* of the very thing. Whether a thing is due *in genere* or *in specie* depends, in each case, on the will of the transacting parties. Brown.

SPECIES. Lat. In the civil law. Form; figure; fashion or shape. A form or shape given to materials.

SPECIES FACTI. In Scotch law. The particular criminal act charged against a person.

SPECIFIC. Precisely formulated or restricted; definite; explicit; of an exact or particular nature. People v. Thomas, 25 Cal.2d 880, 156 P.2d 7, 17. Having a certain form or designation; observing a certain form; particular; precise; tending to specify, or to make particular, definite, limited or precise. Republic Casualty Co. v. Scandinavian-American Bank, D.C.Wash., 2 F.2d 113, 114; Western Union Telegraph Co. v. South & N. A. R. Co., 184 Ala. 66, 62 So. 788, 793.

As to specific "Denial," "Devise," "Legacy," and "Performance," see those titles.

SPECIFICALLY. In a specific manner; explicitly, particularly, definitely. Straton v. Hodgkins, 109 W.Va. 536, 155 S.E. 902.

SPECIFICATIO. Lat. In the civil law. Literally, a making of form; a giving of form to materials. That mode of acquiring property through which a person, by transforming a thing belonging to another, especially by working up his materials into a new species, becomes proprietor of the same. Mackeld. Rom. Law, § 271.

SPECIFICATION. As used in the law relating to patents, machinery and in building contracts, a particular or detailed statement of the various elements involved. Gilbert v. U. S., 1 Ct.Cl. 34; State v. Kendall, 15 Neb. 262, 18 N.W. 85; Wilson v. Coon, C.C.N.Y., 6 F. 614; State Bank of Freeport v. Cape Girardeau & C. R. Co., 172 Mo.App. 662, 155 S.W. 1111, 1113; R. J. Waddell Inv. Co. v. Hall, 255 Mo. 675, 164 S.W. 541, 544.

Law of Personal Property

The acquisition of title to a thing by working it into new forms or species from the raw material; corresponding to the *specificatio* of the Roman law. See Lampton v. Preston, 1 J. J. Marsh, Ky., 462, 19 Am.Dec. 104.

Right by "specification" can only be acquired when, without the accession of any other material that of another person, which has been used by the operator innocently, has been converted by him into something specifically different in the inherent and characteristic qualities, which identify it. Such is the conversion of corn into meal, of grapes into wine, etc. Bozeman Mortuary Ass'n v. Fairchild, 253 Ky. 74, 68 S.W.2d 756, 92 A.L.R. 419.

Military Law

The clear and particular description of the charges preferred against a person accused of a military offense. Tytler, Mil. Law, 109; Carter v. McClaughry, 22 S.Ct. 181, 183 U.S. 365, 46 L.Ed. 236.

Practice

A detailed and particular enumeration of several points or matters urged or relied on by a party to a suit or proceeding; as, a "specification of errors," or a "specification of grounds of opposition to a bankrupt's discharge." See Railway Co. v. McArthur, 96 Tex. 65, 70 S.W. 317; In re Glass, D.C.Tenn., 119 F. 514; Frank v. Ruzicka, 45 S.D. 49, 185 N.W. 371, 372.

SPECIFY. To mention specifically; to state in full and explicit terms; to point out; to tell or state precisely or in detail; to particularize, or to distinguish by words one thing from another. Independent Highway Dist. No. 2 of Ada County v. Ada County, 24 Idaho 416, 134 P. 542, 545; Roche Valley Land Co. v. Barth, 67 Mont. 353, 215 P. 654, 655; Aleksich v. Industrial Accident Fund, 116 Mont. 127, 151 P.2d 1016, 1021.

SPECIMEN. A sample; a part of something intended to exhibit the kind and quality of the whole. People v. Freeman, 1 Idaho 322.

SPECULATION. Buying or selling with expectation of profiting by a rise or fall in price; also engaging in hazardous business transactions for the chance of unusually large profit. Clucas v. Bank of Montclair, 110 N.J.L. 394, 166 A. 311, 313, 394, 88 A.L.R. 302.

SPECULATIVE DAMAGES. See Damages.

SPECULUM. Lat. Mirror or looking-glass. The title of several of the most ancient lawbooks or compilations. One of the ancient Icelandic books is styled "*Speculum Regale*."

SPEEDY EXECUTION. An execution which, by the direction of the judge at *nisi prius*, issues forthwith, or on some early day fixed upon by the judge for that purpose after the trial of the action. Brown.

SPEEDY REMEDY. One which, having in mind the subject-matter involved, can be pursued with expedition and without essential detriment to the party aggrieved. State v. District Court of Thirteenth Judicial Dist. in and for Yellowstone County, 50 Mont. 289, 146 P. 743, 745, Ann.Cas.1917C, 164.

SPEEDY TRIAL. In criminal law. As secured by constitutional guaranties, a trial conducted according to fixed rules, regulations, and proceedings of law, free from unreasonable delay. People v. Hall, 64 N.Y.S. 433, 51 App.Div. 57; Nixon v. State, 2 Smedes & M., Miss., 507, 41 Am.Dec. 601; Hicks v. Boyne, 236 Mich. 689, 211 N.W. 35; Arrowsmith v. State, 131 Tenn. 480, 175 S.W. 545, 547, L.R.A.1915E, 363; State v. Clark, 86 Or. 464, 168 P. 944, 946. A trial as soon after indictment as prosecution can with reasonable diligence prepare for it. People v. Molinari, 23 Cal.App.2d Supp. 761, 67 P.2d 767, 770.

It does not mean trial immediately after defendant's apprehension and indictment, but trial consistent with court's business. People v. Wilson, 356 Ill. 256, 190 N.E. 270, 272.

SPELLING. The formation of words by letters; orthography. Incorrect spelling does not vitiate a written instrument if the intention clearly appears.

SPEND. To consume by using in any manner, to use up, to exhaust, distribute, as to expend money or any other possession. Levenson v. Wolfson, 42 Ohio App. 332, 182 N.E. 116.

SPENDTHRIFT. One who spends money profusely and improvidently; a prodigal; one who lavishes or wastes his estate. Taylor v. Koenigstein, 128 Neb. 809, 260 N.W. 544.

In some jurisdictions, under statutes, a person who by excessive drinking, gaming, idleness, or debauchery of any kind shall so spend, waste, or lessen his estate as to expose himself or his family to want or suffering, or expose the town to charge or expense for the support of himself or family. Rev.St.Maine, c. 67, § 4, cl. 2 (Rev.St.1930, c. 80, § 4, cl. 2); Pub.Laws N.H.1926, c. 291, § 4; G.L.Mass., c. 201, § 8; Smith-Hurd Rev.St.Ill.1931, c. 86, § 53; Young v. Young, 87 Me. 44, 22 A. 782; Morey's Appeal, 57 N.H. 54; Norton v. Leonard, 12 Pick., Mass., 152, 161; In re Bishop, 149 Ill.App. 491, 498.

Every person who is liable to be put under guardianship on account of excessive drinking, gaming, idleness, or debauchery. Comp.Laws Mich.1929, § 15777; G.L.Vt. 3651.

SPENDTHRIFT TRUST. A trust created to provide a fund for the maintenance of a beneficiary, and at the same time to secure it against his improvidence or incapacity. In re Nicholson's Estate, 104 Colo. 561, 93 P.2d 880, 883. One which provides a fund for benefit of another than settlor, secures it against beneficiary's own improvidence, and places it beyond his creditors' reach. Greenwich Trust Co. v. Tyson, 129 Conn. 211, 27 A.2d 166, 171, 172. Provisions against alienation of the trust fund by the voluntary act of the beneficiary or by his creditors are the usual incidents. Estes v. Estes, Tex.Civ.App., 255 S.W. 649, 650; Newcomb v. Masters, 287 Ill. 26, 122 N.E. 85, 87; Plitt v. Yakel, 129 Md. 464, 99 A. 669, 670; Keating v. Keating, 182 Iowa 1056, 165 N.W. 74, 79; Graham v. More, Mo., 189 S.W. 1186, 1188; Newell v. Tubbs, 103 Colo. 224, 84 P.2d 820, 821.

To constitute valid "spendthrift trust," legal title must be vested in trustee; gift must be only of income to a beneficiary, taking no estate, having no power of alienation, right to possession, nor beneficial interest in property save qualified right to support and equitable interest in income; and trust must be active one. Chinnis v. Cobb, 210 N.C. 104, 185 S.E. 638, 640.

SPERATE. That of which there is hope. Thus a debt which one may hope to recover may be called "sperate," in opposition to "desperate." See 1 Chit. Pr. 520.

SPES ACCRESCENDI. Lat. Hope of surviving. 3 Atk. 762; 2 Kent, Comm. 424.

SPES EST VIGILANTIS SOMNIUM. Hope is the dream of the vigilant. 4 Inst. 203.

SPES IMPUNITATIS CONTINUUM AFFECTUM TRIBUIT DELINQUENDI. The hope of impunity holds out a continual temptation to crime. 3 Inst. 236.

SPES RECUPERANDI. Lat. The hope of recovery or recapture; the chance of retaking property captured at sea, which prevents the captors from acquiring complete ownership of the property until they have definitely precluded it by effectual measures. 1 Kent, Comm. 101.

SPIGURNEL. The sealer of the royal writs.

SPINNING HOUSE. A house of correction to which the authorities of Oxford and Cambridge may send persons (mostly women of frivolous character) not members of the University who are found consorting with the students, to the detriment of their morals. 4 Steph. Comm. 264.

SPINSTER. The addition given, in legal proceedings, and in conveyancing, to a woman who never has been married.

SPIRITUAL. Relating to religious or ecclesiastical persons or affairs, as distinguished from "secular" or lay, worldly, or business matters. Johnson v. State, 107 Miss. 196, 65 So. 218, 220, 51 L.R.A., N.S., 1183.

As to spiritual "Corporation," "Courts," and "Lords," see those titles.

SPIRITUALITIES OF A BISHOP. Those profits which a bishop receives in his ecclesiastical character, as the dues arising from his ordaining and instituting priests, and such like, in contradistinction to those profits which he acquires in his temporal capacity as a baron and lord of parliament, and which are termed his "temporalities," consisting of certain lands, revenues, and lay fees, etc. Cowell.

SPIRITUALITY OF BENEFICES. In ecclesiastical law. The tithes of land, etc. Wharton.

SPIRITUOUS LIQUORS. Inflammable liquids produced by distillation, and forming an article of commerce. Blankenship v. State, 93 Ga. 814, 21 S.E. 130; State v. Munger, 15 Vt. 293; Allred v. State, 89 Ala. 112, 8 So. 56; State v. Dennison, 85 W.Va. 261, 101 S.E. 458, 459; Shaneyfelt v. State, 8 Ala.App. 370, 62 So. 331, 332; Billing v. State, 99 Tex.Cr.R. 653, 271 S.W. 607.

The phrase "spirituous liquor," in a penal statute, cannot be extended beyond its exact literal sense. Spirit is the name of an inflammable liquor produced by distillation. Wine is the fermented juice of the grape, or a preparation of other vegetables by fermentation; hence the term does not include wine. State v. Moore, 5 Blackf., Ind., 118.

SPITAL, or SPITTLE. A charitable foundation; a hospital for diseased people; a hospital. Cowell.

SPITE FENCE. A fence of no beneficial use to person erecting and maintaining it on his land and maintained solely for purpose of annoying owner of adjoining land. Burris v. Creech, 220 N.C. 302, 17 S.E.2d 123. A high and unsightly fence erected to annoy a neighbor or adjoining landowner by obstructing his air, light or view. Kuzniak v. Kozminski, 107 Mich. 444, 65 N.W. 275, 61 Am.St.Rep. 344; Wood, Nuis., 2d Ed., § 6.

SPLIT SENTENCE. One where penalty of fine and imprisonment, as provided by statute, is imposed and imprisonment part is suspended and fine part enforced. Cote v. Cummings, 126 Me. 330, 138 A. 547, 552.

SPLITTING A CAUSE OF ACTION. Dividing a single cause of action, claim, or demand into two or more parts, and bringing suit for one of such parts only. The plaintiff who does this is bound by his first judgment, and can recover no more. 2 Black, Judgm. § 734. Birdville Independent School Dist. v. Deen, Tex.Civ.App., 114 S.W.2d 628, 632. Commencement of an action for only a part of the cause of action. Silber v. James Drug Stores, 124 N.J.L. 401, 11 A.2d 756, 758. Floyd v. C. I. T. Corporation, 191 S.C. 518, 5 S.E.2d 299, 301.

There is no "splitting of causes" where demand which is subject of second action was not due at time of the first action. Glavich v. Industrial Accident Commission of California, 44 Cal.App.2d 517, 112 P.2d 774, 778.

The rule against "splitting causes of action" does not mean that plaintiff cannot sue for less than is his due but means merely that if he does so he may be precluded from maintaining another action for the remainder of the same demand. Scientific & Hospital Supply Corporation v. Board of Education of City of New York, 16 N.Y.S.2d 91, 93, 172 Misc. 770.

The rule against "splitting cause of action" applies only when several actions are between same parties. Warnecke v. Foley, 234 Iowa 348, 11 N.W.2d 457, 459.

SPOLIATION.

English Ecclesiastical Law

An injury done by one clerk or incumbent to another, in taking the fruits of his benefice without any right to them, but under a pretended title. 3 Bl. Comm. 90, 91.

The name of a suit sued out in the spiritual court to recover for the fruits of the church or for the church itself. Fitzh. Nat. Brev. 85.

Torts

Destruction of a thing by the act of a stranger, as the erasure or alteration of a writing by the act of a stranger. This has not the effect to destroy its character or legal effect. 1 Greenl. Ev. § 566; Medlin v. Platt County, 8 Mo. 239, 40 Am. Dec. 135; Edwards v. Thompson, 99 Wash. 188, 169 P. 327, 328; Knox v. Horne, Tex.Civ.App., 200 S.W. 259, 260; Cooper v. Hembree, 194 Okl. 465, 152 P.2d 695, 697.

SPOLIATOR. Lat. A spoiler or destroyer. It is a maxim of law, bearing chiefly on evidence, but also upon the value generally of the thing destroyed, that everything most to his disadvantage is to be presumed against the destroyer, (*spoliator,*) *contra spoliatorem omnia præsumuntur.* 1 Smith, Lead. Cas. 315.

SPOLIATUS DEBET ANTE OMNIA RESTITUI. A party despoiled [forcibly deprived of possession] ought first of all to be restored. 2 Inst. 714; 4 Reeve, Eng. Law, 18.

SPOLIATUS EPISCOPUS ANTE OMNIA DEBET RESTITUI. A bishop despoiled of his see ought, above all, to be restored. See 14 L. Q. R. 27.

SPOLIUM. Lat. In the civil and common law. A thing violently or unlawfully taken from another.

SPONDEO. Lat. In the civil law. I undertake; I engage. Inst. 3, 16, 1.

SPONDES? SPONDEO. Lat. Do you undertake? I do undertake. The most common form of verbal stipulation in the Roman law. Inst. 3, 16, 1.

SPONDET PERITIAM ARTIS. He promises the skill of his art; he engages to do the work in a skillful or workmanlike manner. 2 Kent, Comm. 588. Applied to the engagements of workman for hire. Story, Bailm. § 428.

SPONSALIA, STIPULATIO SPONSALITIA. Lat. In the civil law. Espousal; bethrothal; a reciprocal promise of future marriage.

SPONSIO. Lat. In the civil law. An engagement or undertaking; particularly such as was made in the form of an answer to a formal interrogatory by the other party. Calvin.

An engagement to pay a certain sum of money to the successful party in a cause. Calvin.

SPONSIO JUDICIALIS. In Roman law. A judicial wager corresponding in some respects to the "feigned issue" of modern practice.

SPONSIO LUDICRA. A trifling or ludicrous engagement, such as a court will not sustain an action for. 1 Kames, Eq. Introd. 34. An informal undertaking, or one made without the usual formula of interrogation. Calvin.

SPONSIONS. In international law. Agreements or engagements made by certain public officers (as generals or admirals in time of war) in behalf of their governments, either without authority or in excess of the authority under which they purport to be made, and which therefore require an express or tacit ratification.

SPONSOR. A surety; one who makes a promise or gives security for another, particularly a godfather in baptism.

In the civil law. One who intervenes for another voluntarily and without being requested.

SPONTANEOUS COMBUSTION. The ignition of a body by the internal development of heat without the action of an external agent. Eckman Chemical Co. v. Chicago & N. W. Ry. Co., 107 Neb. 268, 185 N.W. 444, 446.

SPONTANEOUS EXCLAMATION. Within res gestae rule, a statement or exclamation made immediately after some exciting occasion by a participant or spectator and asserting the circumstances of that occasion as it is observed by him. Riley v. State, 50 Ariz. 442, 73 P.2d 96, 101.

SPONTE OBLATA. Lat. A free gift or present to the crown.

SPONTE VIRUM MULIER FUGIENS ET ADULTERA FACTA, DOTE SUA CAREAT, NISI SPONSI SPONTE RETRACTA. Co. Litt. 32*b*. Let a woman leaving her husband of her own accord, and committing adultery, lose her dower, unless taken back by her husband of his own accord.

SPORTING HOUSE. A house of ill-fame. Johnson v. People, 202 Ill. 53, 66 N.E. 877, 881. A house frequented by sportsmen, betting men, gamblers, and the like, but not necessarily a house kept for unlawful sports or practices. White v. Western, Assur. Co. of Toronto, 52 Minn. 352, 54 N.W. 195.

SPORTULA. Lat. In Roman law. A largess, dole, or present; a pecuniary donation; an official perquisite; something over and above the ordinary fee allowed by law. Inst. 4, 6, 24.

SPOUSALS. In old English law. Mutual promises to marry.

SPOT A FREIGHT CAR. To place it at a precise spot where it is to be loaded or unloaded, such as a freight house, a team track, or a shipper's warehouse. Union Pac. R. Co. v. Anderson, 167 Or. 687, 120 P.2d 578, 585.

SPOUSE. One's wife or husband. Rosell v. State Industrial Accident Commission, 164 Or. 173, 95 P.2d 726, 729.

SPOUSE-BREACH. In old English law. Adultery. Cowell.

SPRING. A fountain of water; an issue of water from the earth, or the basin of water at the place of its issue. Webster. A natural chasm in which water has collected, and from which it either is lost by percolation or rises in a defined channel. Furner v. Seabury, 135 N.Y. 50, 31 N.E. 1004; Bloodgood v. Ayers, 108 N.Y. 405, 15 N.E. 433, 2 Am.St.Rep. 443; Proprietors of Mills v. Braintree Water Supply Co., 149 Mass. 478, 21 N.E. 761, 4 L.R.A. 272; Harrison v. Chaboya, 198 Cal. 473, 245 P. 1087, 1088.

SPRING-BRANCH. In American land law. A branch of a stream, flowing from a spring. Wootton v. Redd's Ex'r, 12 Grat. (Va.) 196.

SPRINGING USE. See Use.

SPUILZIE. In Scotch law. The taking away or meddling with movables in another's possession, without the consent of the owner or authority of law. Bell.

SPUR TRACK. A short track leading from a line of railway and connected with it at one end only, and not an adjunct usual or necessary to the operation of main line trains and cars. Simons Brick Co. v. City of Los Angeles, 182 Cal. 230, 187 P. 1066, 1067; Detroit & M. Ry. Co. v. Boyne City, G. & A. R. Co., D.C.Mich., 286 F. 540, 547; Cleveland, C. C. & St. L. Ry. Co. v. Commerce Commission, 315 Ill. 461, 146 N.E. 606, 610; Menasha Woodenware Co. v. Railroad Commission of Wisconsin, 167 Wis. 19, 166 N.W. 435, 438.

SPURIOUS BANK-BILL. A bill which may be a legitimate impression from the genuine plate, but it must have the signatures of persons not the officers of the bank whence it purports to have issued, or else the names of fictitious persons. It may also be an illegitimate impression from a genuine plate, or an impression from a counterfeit plate, but it must have such signatures or names as indicated. A bill, therefore, may be both counterfeit and forged, or both counterfeit and spurious, but it cannot be both forged and spurious. Kirby v. State, 1 Ohio St. 187.

SPURIUS. Lat. In the civil law. A bastard; the offspring of promiscuous cohabitation.

SPY. A person sent into an enemy's camp to inspect their works, ascertain their strength and their intentions, watch their movements, and secretly communicate intelligence to the proper officer. By the laws of war among all civilized nations, a spy is punished with death. Webster. See Vattel, 3, 179; U. S. ex rel. Wessels v. McDonald, D.C.N.Y., 1920, 265 F. 754; Ex parte Milligan, 4 Wall. 2, 44, 18 L.Ed. 281 (argument of counsel).

SQUARE. As used to designate a certain portion of land within the limits of a city or town, this term may be synonymous with "block," that is, the smallest subdivision which is bounded on all sides by principal streets, or it may denote a space (more or less rectangular) not built upon, and set apart for public passage, use, recreation, or ornamentation, in the nature of a "park" but smaller. State v. Natal, 42 La.Ann. 612, 7 South. 781; Rowzee v. Pierce, 75 Miss. 846, 23 South. 307, 40 L.R.A. 402, 65 Am.St.Rep. 625; City of St. Louis v. Pope, 344 Mo. 479, 126 S.W.2d 1201, 1213.

Public Square

In its popular import, the phrase refers almost exclusively to ground occupied by a courthouse owned by a county, Logansport v. Dunn, 8 Ind. 378; but it may be used as synonymous with park; Church of Hoboken v. Council of Hoboken, 33 N. J.L. 13, 97 Am.Dec. 696; Woodward v. City of Des Moines, 182 Iowa 1102, 165 N.W. 313, 314.

Square Block

Territory bounded by four streets. People ex rel. Beinert v. Miller, 100 Misc. 318, 165 N.Y.S. 602, 607; Bernfeld v. Freedenberg, 125 Misc. 645, 211 N.Y.S. 692.

SQUATTER. In American law. One who settles on another's land, particularly on public lands, without legal authority. O'Donnell v. McIntyre, 16 Abb. N. C., N.Y., 84; Parkersburg Industrial Co. v. Schultz, 43 W.Va. 470, 27 S.E. 255. A person entering upon lands, not claiming in good faith the right to do so by virtue of any title of his own or by virtue of some agreement with another whom he believes to hold the title. Mayor and Council of City of Forsyth v. Hooks, 182 Ga. 78, 184 S.E. 724, 728.

A squatter can never gain prescriptive title to land regardless of how long he holds possession, since his possession is never considered as "adverse possession". Conway v. Shuck, 203 Ark. 559, 157 S.W.2d 777, 778.

SQUIRE. A contraction of "esquire."

SS. An abbreviation used in that part of a record, pleading, or affidavit, called the "statement of the venue." Commonly translated or read, "to-wit," and supposed to be a contraction of "*scilicet.*"

Also in ecclesiastical documents, particularly records of early councils, "ss" is used as an abbreviation for *subscripsi.* Occasionally, in Law French, it stands for *sans,* "without," *e. g., "faire feoffment ss son baron."* Bendloe, p. 180.

STAB. A wound inflicted by a thrust with a pointed weapon. State v. Cody, 18 Or. 506, 23 P. 891; Ward v. State, 56 Ga. 410.

STABILIA. A writ called by that name, founded on a custom in Normandy, that where a man in power claimed lands in the possession of an inferior, he petitioned the prince that it might be put into his hands till the right was decided, whereupon he had this writ. Wharton.

STABILIZE. To keep steady, fixed, as distinguished from fluctuating, shifting. McCanless v. Klein, 182 Tenn. 563, 188 S.W.2d 745, 748.

STABILIZE PRICES. Holding prices steady against any and all increases. Philadelphia Coke Co. v. Bowles, Em.App., 139 F.2d 349, 353.

STABIT PRÆSUMPTIO DONEC PROBETUR IN CONTRARIUM. A presumption will stand good till the contrary is proved. Hob. 297; Broom, Max. 949.

STABLE. House, shed, or building for beasts to lodge and feed in. Culp v. Firestone Tire & Rubber Co., 303 Pa. 257, 154 A. 479, 480.

STABLE-STAND. In forest law. One of the four evidences or presumptions whereby a man was convicted of an intent to steal the king's deer in the forest. This was when a man was found at his *standing* in the forest with a cross-bow or long-bow bent, ready to shoot at any deer, or else standing close by a tree with grey-hounds in a leash, ready to slip. Cowell; Manwood.

STABULARIUS. Lat. In the civil law. A stable-keeper. Dig. 4, 9, 4, 1.

STACHIA. In old records. A dam or head made to stop a water-course. Cowell.

STAFF-HERDING. The following of cattle within a forest.

STAGE LINE. A regular line of vehicles for public use operating between distant points or between different cities. Bruce Transfer Co. v. Johnston, 227 Iowa 50, 287 N.W. 278, 280.

STAGE-RIGHT. A word which it has been attempted to introduce as a substitute for "the right of representation and performance," but it can hardly be said to be an accepted term of English or American law. Sweet.

STAGIARIUS. A resident.. Cowell.

STAGNUM. In old English law. A pool, or pond. Co. Litt. 5*a;* Johnson v. Rayner, 6 Gray (Mass.) 110.

STAKE. A deposit made to answer an event, as on a wager. Mohr v. Miesen, 47 Minn. 228, 49 N. W. 862; Pompano Horse Club v. State, 93 Fla. 415, 111 So. 801, 813, 52 A.L.R. 51. Something deposited by two persons with the third on condition that it is to be delivered to the one who shall become entitled to it by the happening of a specified contingency. Baxter v. Deneen, 98 Md. 181, 57 A. 601, 607, 64 L.R.A. 949, 1 Ann.Cas. 147.

STAKEHOLDER. A person with whom money is deposited pending the decision of a bet or wager; (*q. v.*). Sweet. Wabash R. Co. v. Flannigan, 95 Mo.App. 477, 75 S.W. 691; Martin v. Francis, 173 Ky. 529, 191 S.W. 259, 262, L.R.A. 1918F, 966, Ann. Cas.1918E, 289. His function is to receive the sums wagered and hold them against the determining event, whether that event be a horse race or otherwise, and then pay them over to the winner. Also a third person chosen by two or more persons to keep in deposit property the right or possession of which is contested between them, and to be delivered to the one who shall establish his right to it. State v. Dudley, 127 N.J.L. 127, 21 A.2d 209, 210.

STALE, *n.* In Saxon law. Larceny. Wharton.

STALE DEMAND, or CLAIM. A demand or claim that has long remained unasserted, one that is first asserted after an unexplained delay which is so long as to render it difficult or impossible for the court to ascertain the truth of the matters in controversy and do justice between the parties, or as to create a presumption against the existence or validity of the claim, or a presumption that the claim has been abandoned or satisfied. Luschen v. Stanton, 192 Okl. 454, 137 P.2d 567, 572. It implies a greater lapse of time than is necessary to "laches." Bell v. Mackey, 191 S.C. 105, 3 S.E.2d 816, 824, 830. The doctrine is purely an equitable one, and arises only when, from lapse of time and laches of plaintiff, it would be inequitable to allow a party to enforce his legal rights. Wood v. City Board of Plumbing Examiners, 192 Ga. 415, 15 S.E.2d 486, 488; Lamar v. Rivers, 235 Ala. 130, 178 So. 16, 18.

STALLAGE. The liberty or right of pitching or erecting stalls in fairs or markets, or the money paid for the same. 1 Steph. Comm. 664.

STALLARIUS. In Saxon law. The *prœfectus stabuli*, now master of the horse. Sometimes one who has a stall in a fair or market.

STAMP. An impression made by public authority, in pursuance of law, upon paper or parchment, upon which certain legal proceedings, conveyances, or contracts are required to be written, and for which a tax or duty is exacted.

A small label or strip of paper, bearing a particular device, printed and sold by the government, and required to be attached to mail-matter, and to some other articles subject to duty or excise. U. S. v. Skilken, D.C.Ohio, 293 F. 916, 919.

STAMP ACTS. In English law. Acts regulating the stamps upon deeds, contracts, agreements, papers in law proceedings, bills and notes, letters, receipts, and other papers.

STAMP DUTIES. Duties imposed upon and raised from stamps upon parchment and paper, and forming a branch of the perpetual revenue of the kingdom. 1 Bl. Comm. 323.

STANCE. In Scotch law. A resting place; a field or place adjoining a drove-road, for resting and refreshing sheep and cattle on their journey. 7 Bell, App. Cas. 53, 57, 58.

STAND. To cease from movement or progress; to pause, remain stationary or inactive. Jaggers v. Southeastern Greyhound Lines, D.C.Tenn., 34 F.Supp. 667, 668.

To abide; to submit to; as "to *stand* a trial."

To remain as a thing is; to remain in force. Pleadings demurred to and held good are allowed to *stand*.

To appear in court.

STANDARD. Stability, general recognition, and conformity to established practice. Standard Accident Ins. Co. v. Standard Surety & Casualty Co., D.C.N.Y., 53 F.2d 119, 120.

An ensign or flag used in war.

A type, model, or combination of elements accepted as correct or perfect. Ashwell v. Miller, 54 Ind.App. 381, 103 N.E. 37, 40.

STANDARD ESTABLISHED BY LAW. That of a reasonable man under like circumstances. Gulf, C. & S. F. Ry. Co. v. Bell, Tex.Civ.App., 101 S.W. 2d 363, 364.

STANDARD MORTGAGE CLAUSE. In fire policy. Clause providing that in case of loss policy shall be payable to mortgagee, and that his interest as payee shall not be invalidated by act of mortgagor. Rhode Island Ins. Co. v. Wurtman, 265 Ky. 835, 98 S.W.2d 29, 31.

Basic difference in effect between "loss payable clause" and "standard mortgage clause" is that the former is subject to such defenses as insurer may have against the mortgagor, while the latter is not. Overholt v. Reliance Ins. Co. of Philadelphia, 319 Pa. 340, 179 A. 554, 556.

STANDARD OF WEIGHT, or MEASURE. A weight or measure fixed and prescribed by law, to which all other weights and measures are required to correspond.

STANDING. One's place in the community in the estimation of others; his relative position and social, commercial, or moral relations; his repute, grade, or rank. Gross v. State, 186 Ind. 581, 117 N.E. 562, 564, 1 A.L.R. 1151.

STANDING ASIDE JURORS. A practice by which, on the drawing of a jury for a criminal trial, the prosecuting officer puts aside a juror, provisionally, until the panel is exhausted, without disclosing his reasons, instead of being required to challenge him and show cause. The statute 33 Edw. I. deprived the crown of the power to challenge jurors without showing cause, and the practice of standing aside jurors was adopted, in England, as a method of evading its provisions. A similar practice is in use in Pennsylvania. See Warren v. Com., 37 Pa. 54; Zell v. Com., 94 Pa. 272; Haines v. Com., 100 Pa. 322. But in Missouri, it is said that the words "stand aside" are the usual formula, used in impaneling a jury, for rejecting a juror. State v. Hultz, 106 Mo. 41, 16 S.W. 940.

STANDING BY. Used in law as implying knowledge, under such circumstances as rendered it the duty of the possessor to communicate it; and it is such knowledge, and not the mere fact of "standing by," that lays the foundation of responsibility. The phrase does not import an actual presence, "but implies knowledge under such circumstances as to render it the duty of the possessor to communicate it." Anderson v. Hubble, 93 Ind. 573, 47 Am.Rep. 394; Gatling v. Rodman, 6 Ind. 292; Richardson v. Chickering, 41 N.H. 380, 77 Am.Dec. 769; Morrison v. Morrison, 2 Dana, Ky., 16; Piqua State Bank v. Brannum, 103 Kan. 25, 173 P. 1, 2.

STANDING MUTE. A prisoner, arraigned for treason or felony, was said to "stand mute," when he refused to plead, or answered foreign to the purpose, or, after a plea of not guilty, would not put himself upon the country.

STANDING IN LOCO PARENTIS. As required to entitle deceased employee's illegitimate child to compensation under Workmen's Compensation

Act for his death, is voluntary, not court directed, assumption of obligations of parental relation. Smrekar v. Jones & Laughlin Steel Corporation, 137 Pa.Super. 183, 8 A.2d 461, 464.

STANDING ORDERS. Rules and forms regulating the procedure of the two houses of parliament, each having its own. They are of equal force in every parliament, except so far as they are altered or suspended from time to time. Cox, Inst. 136; May, Parl. Pr. 185.

STANDING SEISED TO USES. A covenant to stand seised to uses is one by which the owner of an estate covenants to hold the same to the use of another person, usually a relative, and usually in consideration of blood or marriage. It is a species of conveyance depending for its effect on the statute of uses.

STANDING TO SUE DOCTRINE. Doctrine that in action in federal constitutional court by citizen against a government officer, complaining of alleged unlawful conduct there is no justiciable controversy unless citizen shows that such conduct invades or will invade a private substantive legally protected interest of plaintiff citizen. Associated Industries of New York State v. Ickes, C.C.A.2, 134 F.2d 694, 702.

STANNARIES. A district which includes all parts of Devon and Cornwall where some tin work is situate and in actual operation. The tin miners of the stannaries have certain peculiar customs and privileges.

STANNARY COURTS. Courts of Devonshire and Cornwall for the administration of justice among the miners and tinners. These courts were held before the lord warden and his deputies by virtue of a privilege granted to the workers of the tin-mines there, to sue and be sued in their own courts only, in order that they might not be drawn away from their business by having to attend law-suits in distant courts. Brown.

STAPLE.

English Law

A mart or market. A place where the buying and selling of wool, lead, leather, and other articles were put under certain terms. 2 Reeve, Eng. Law, 393.

International Law

The right of staple, as exercised by a people upon foreign merchants, is defined to be that they may not allow them to set their merchandises and wares to sale but in a certain place. This practice is not in use in the United States. 1 Chit. Com. Law, 103.

General

Law of the staple. Law administered in the court of the mayor of the staple; the law-merchant. 4 Inst. 235. See Staple.

Staple inn. An inn of chancery. See Inns of Chancery.

Statute staple. The statute of the staple, 27 Ed. III. stat. 2, confined the sale of all commodities to be exported to certain towns in England, called *estaple* or *staple,* where foreigners might resort. It authorized a security for money, commonly called statute staple, to be taken by traders for the benefit of commerce; the mayor of the place is entitled to take recognizance of a debt in proper form, which had the effect to convey the lands of the debtor to the creditor till out of the rents and profits of them he should be satisfied. 2 Rolle, Abr. 446; Bac. Abr. *Execution* (B. 1); Co. 4th Inst. 238. A security for a debt acknowledged to be due, so called from its being entered into before the mayor of the *staple,* that is to say, the grand mart for the principal commodities or manufactures of the kingdom, formerly held by act of parliament in certain trading towns. In other respects it resembled the *statute-merchant,* (*q. v.,*) but like that has now fallen into disuse. 2 Bl. Comm. 160; 1 Steph. Comm. 287.

STAR-CHAMBER. A court which originally had jurisdiction in cases where the ordinary course of justice was so much obstructed by one party, through writs, combination of maintenance, or overawing influence that no inferior court would find its process obeyed. The court consisted of the privy council, the common-law judges, and (it seems) all peers of parliament. In the reign of Henry VIII. and his successors, the jurisdiction of the court was illegally extended to such a degree (especially in punishing disobedience to the king's arbitrary proclamations) that it became odious to the nation, and was abolished. 4 Steph. Comm. 310; Sweet.

STAR PAGE. The line and word at which the pages of the first edition of a law book began are frequently marked by a star in later editions, and always should be.

STARBOARD. In maritime law. The righthand side of a vessel when the observer faces forward. "Starboard tack," the course of vessel when she has the wind on her starboard bow. Burrows v. Gower, D.C.Mass., 119 F. 617.

STARE DECISIS. Lat. To abide by, or adhere to, decided cases.

Policy of courts to stand by precedent and not to disturb settled point. Neff v. George, 364 Ill. 306, 4 N.E.2d 338, 390, 391. Doctrine that, when court has once laid down a principle of law as applicable to a certain state of facts, it will adhere to that principle, and apply it to all future cases, where facts are substantially the same. Moore v. City of Albany, 98 N.Y. 396, 410; Regardless of whether the parties and property are the same. Horne v. Moody, Tex.Civ.App., 146 S.W.2d 505, 509, 510. Under doctrine a deliberate or solemn decision of court made after argument on question of law fairly arising in the case, and necessary to its determination, is an authority, or binding precedent in the same court, or in other courts of equal or lower rank in subsequent cases where the very point is again in controversy. State v. Mellenberger, 163 Or. 233, 95 P.2d 709, 719, 720, 128 A.L.R. 1506. Doctrine is one of policy, grounded on theory that security and certainty require that accepted and established legal principle, under which rights may accrue, be recognized and followed, though later found to be not legally sound, but whether previous holding of court shall be adhered to, modified, or overruled is within court's discretion under circumstances of case before it. Otter Tail Power Co. v. Von Bank, 72 N.D. 497, 8 N.W.2d 599, 607, 145 A.L.R. 1343. Under doctrine, when point of law has been settled by decision, it forms precedent which is not afterwards to be departed from, and, while it should ordinarily be strictly adhered to, there are occasions when departure is rendered necessary to vindicate plain, obvious principles of law and remedy continued injustice. McGregor v. Provident Trust Co. of Philadelphia, 119 Fla. 718, 162 So. 323. The doctrine is a salutary one, and should not ordinarily be departed from where decision is of long standing and rights have been acquired under it, unless considerations of public policy demand it. Colonial Trust Co. v. Flanagan, 344 Pa. 556, 25 A.2d 728, 729.

The doctrine is limited to actual determinations in respect to litigated and necessarily decided questions, and is not applicable to dicta or obiter dicta. In re Herle's Estate, 165 Misc. 46, 300 N.Y.S. 103.

Federal courts should in all instances follow the law of the state with respect to the construction of state statutes, and where that law has been determined by the courts of last resort, their decisions are "stare decisis" and must be followed, irrespective of federal courts' opinions concerning what the law ought to be, but with respect to the pronouncement of other state courts, federal courts are not so bound and may conclude that the decision does not truly express the state law. Kehaya v. Axton, D.C.N.Y., 32 F.Supp. 266, 268.

STARE DECISIS ET NON QUIETA MOVERE. To adhere to precedents, and not to unsettle things which are established. 87 Pa. 286; Ballard County v. Kentucky County Debt Commission, 290 Ky. 770, 162 S.W.2d 771, 773. See Stare Decisis.

STARE IN JUDICIO. Lat. To appear before a tribunal, either as plaintiff or defendant.

STARR, or STARRA. The old term for contract or obligation among the Jews, being a corruption from the Hebrew word "*shetar*," a covenant, by an ordinance of Richard I., no starr was allowed to be valid, unless deposited in one of certain repositories established by law, the most considerable of which was in the king's exchequer at Westminster; and Blackstone conjectures that the room in which these chests were kept was thence called the "starr-chamber." 4 Bl. Comm. 266, 267, note *a*.

STAT PRO RATIONE VOLUNTAS. The will stands in place of a reason. Sears v. Shafer, 1 Barb. (N. Y.) 408, 411; Farmers' Loan & Trust Co. v. Hunt, 16 Barb. (N.Y.) 514, 525.

STAT PRO RATIONE VOLUNTAS POPULI. The will of the people stands in place of a reason. People v. Draper, 25 Barb. (N.Y.) 344, 376.

STATE, *v.* To express the particulars of a thing in writing or in words; to set down or set forth in detail; to aver, allege, or declare. People v. Mercado, 59 Cal.App. 69, 209 P. 1035, 1037.

To set down in gross; to mention in general terms, or by way of reference; to refer. Utica v. Richardson, 6 Hill (N.Y.) 300.

STATE, *n.* A people permanently occupying a fixed territory bound together by common-law habits and custom into one body politic exercising, through the medium of an organized government, independent sovereignty and control over all persons and things within its boundaries, capable of making war and peace and of entering into international relations with other communities of the globe. United States v. Kusche, D.C.Cal., 56 F. Supp. 201, 207, 208. The organization of social life which exercises sovereign power in behalf of the people. Delany v. Moraitis, C.C.A.Md., 136 F. 2d 129, 130.

One of the component commonwealths or states of the United States of America. The term is sometimes applied also to governmental agencies authorized by state, such as municipal corporations. George v. City of Portland, 114 Or. 418, 235 P. 681, 683, 39 A.L.R. 341.

The people of a state, in their collective capacity, considered as the party wronged by a criminal deed; the public; as in the title of a cause, "The State *vs.* A. B."

The section of territory occupied by one of the United States.

The circumstances or condition of a being or thing at a given time. State v. Inich, 55 Mont. 1, 173 P. 230, 234.

Foreign State

A foreign country or nation. The several United States are considered "foreign" to each other except as regards their relations as common members of the Union.

State's Evidence

See Evidence.

State Offices

As used in Primary Election Law, offices to be filled by electorate of entire state. Hamilton v. Monroe, Tex.Civ.App., 287 S.W. 304, 305. See "Office."

State Officers

Those whose duties concern the state at large or the general public, or who are authorized to exercise their official functions throughout the entire state, without limitation to any political subdivision of the state. State ex rel. Consolidated School Dist. No. 2 v. Ingram, 317 Mo. 1141, 298 S.W. 37, 38; Ramsay v. Van Meter, 300 Ill. 193, 133 N.E. 193, 195; State v. Jones, 79 Fla. 56, 84 So. 84, 85; McCullough v. Scott, 182 N.C. 865, 109 S.E. 789, 793. In another sense, officers belonging to or exercising authority under one of the states of the Union, as distinguished from the officers of the United States. See In re Police Com'rs, 22 R.I. 654, 49 A. 36; State v. Burns, 38 Fla. 378, 21 So. 290; People v. Nixon, 158 N.Y. 221, 52 N.E. 1117.

State Paper

A document prepared by, or relating to, the political department of the government of a state or nation, and concerning or affecting the administration of its government or its political or international relations. Also, a newspaper, designated by public authority, as the organ for the publication of public statutes, resolutions, notices, and advertisements.

State Revenue

Current income of state from whatever source derived that is subject to appropriation for public uses. State ex rel. McKinley Pub. Co. v. Hackmann, 314 Mo. 33, 282 S.W. 1007, 1011.

State Tax

A tax the proceeds of which are to be devoted to the expenses of the state, as distinguished from taxation for local or municipal purposes. See Youngblood v. Sexton, 32 Mich. 413, 20 Am.Rep. 654; State v. Auditor of State, 15 Ohio St. 482; Society for Establishing Useful Manufactures v. City of Paterson, 89 N.J.Law, 208, 98 A. 440, 441.

State Trial

A trial for a political offense.

State Trials

A work in thirty-three volumes octavo, containing all English trials for offenses against the state and others partaking in some degree of that character, from the ninth year of Hen. II. to the first of Geo. IV.

STATE EXPERIENCE FACTOR. The term as used in Unemployment Compensation Law, means a factor based on factual experience of all employers and their employees operating within the state coming within influence of the act. Broadway v. Alabama Dry Dock & Shipbuilding Co., 246 Ala. 201, 20 So.2d 41, 49.

STATE OF FACTS. Formerly, when a master in chancery was directed by the court of chancery to make an inquiry or investigation into any matter arising out of a suit, and which could not conveniently be brought before the court itself, each party in the suit carried in before the master a statement showing how the party bringing it in represented the matter in question to be; and this statement was technically termed a "state of facts," and formed the ground upon which the evidence was received, the evidence being, in fact, brought by one party or the other, to prove his own or disprove his opponent's state of facts. And so now, a state of facts means the statement made by any one of his version of the facts. Brown.

STATE OF FACTS AND PROPOSAL. In English lunacy practice, when a person has been found a lunatic, the next step is to submit to the master a scheme called a "state of facts and proposal," showing what is the position in life, property, and income of the lunatic, who are his next of kin and heir at law, who are proposed as his committees, and what annual sum is proposed to be allowed for his maintenance, etc. From the state of facts and the evidence adduced in support of it, the master frames his report. Elmer, Lun. 22; Pope, Lun. 79; Sweet.

STATE OF THE CASE. A narrative of the facts upon which the plaintiff relies, substituted for a more formal declaration, in suits in the inferior courts. The phrase is used in New Jersey.

STATE PAPER OFFICE. An office established in London in 1578 for the custody of state papers. The head of it was the "Clerk of the Papers."

STATED. Determined, fixed, or settled. In re McKeon's Estate, 227 Iowa 1050, 289 N.W. 915, 919

Stated Meeting

A meeting of a board of directors, board of officers, etc., held at the time appointed therefor by law, ordinance, by-law, or other regulation; as distinguished from "special" meetings, which are held on call as the occasion may arise, rather than at a regularly appointed time, and from adjourned meetings. See Zulich v. Bowman, 42 Pa. 87; Hanson v. Chicago, B. & Q. R. Co., 32 Wyo. 337, 232 P. 1101, 1104.

Stated Term

A regular or ordinary term or session of a court for the dispatch of its general business, held at the time fixed by law or rule; as distinguished from a *special* term, held out of the due order or for the transaction of particular business.

Stated Times

Occurring at regular intervals or given regularly; fixed, regular in operation or occurrence, not occasional or fluctuating. Zangerle v. State, 115 Ohio St. 168, 152 N.E. 658, 659.

STATEMENT. In a general sense, an allegation; a declaration of matters of fact. The term has come to be used of a variety of formal narratives of facts, required by law in various jurisdictions as the foundation of judicial or official proceedings and in a limited sense is a formal, exact, detailed presentation. Southern Surety Co. v. Schmidt, 117 Ohio St. 28, 158 N.E. 1, 3. For "False and Misleading Statement," and "Foreign Statement," see those titles.

STATEMENT OF AFFAIRS. In English bankruptcy practice, a bankrupt or debtor who has presented a petition for liquidation or composition must produce at the first meeting of creditors a statement of his affairs giving a list of his creditors, secured and unsecured, with the value of the securities, a list of bills discounted, and a statement of his property. Sweet.

STATEMENT OF CLAIM. A written or printed statement by the plaintiff in an action in the English high court, showing the facts on which he relies to support his claim against the defendant, and the relief which he claims. It is delivered to the defendant or his solicitor. The delivery of the statement of claim is usually the next step after appearance, and is the commencement of the pleadings. Sweet.

STATEMENT OF CONFESSION. Oftentimes referred to as a "power of attorney" is written authority of debtor and his direction to enter judgment against debtor as stated therein. Blott v. Blott, 227 Iowa 1108, 290 N.W. 74, 76.

STATEMENT OF DEFENSE. In the practice of the English high court, where the defendant in an action does not demur to the whole of the plaintiff's claim, he delivers a pleading called a "statement of defense." The statement of defense deals with the allegations contained in the statement of claim, (or the indorsement on the writ, if there is no statement of claim,) admitting or denying them, and, if necessary, stating fresh facts in explanation or avoidance of those alleged by the plaintiff. Sweet.

STATEMENT OF PARTICULARS. In English practice, when the plaintiff claims a debt or liquidated demand, but has not indorsed the writ specially, (*i. e.*, indorsed on it the particulars of his claim under Order iii. r. 6,) and the defendant fails to appear, the plaintiff may file a statement of the particulars of his claim, and after eight days enter judgment for the amount, as if the writ had been specially indorsed. Court Rules, xiii. 5; Sweet.

STATE'S EVIDENCE. A popular term for testimony given by an accomplice or joint participant in the commission of a crime tending to criminate or convict the others, and given under an actual or implied promise of immunity for himself.

STATESMAN. A freeholder and farmer in Cumberland. Wharton.

STATIM. Lat. Forthwith; immediately. In old English law, this term meant either "at once," or "within a legal time," *i. e.*, such time as permitted the legal and regular performance of the act in question.

STATING AN ACCOUNT. Exhibiting, or listing in their order, the items which make up an account.

STATING PART OF A BILL. That part of a bill in chancery in which the plaintiff states the facts of his case; it is distinguished from the *charging* part of the bill and from the *prayer*.

STATION. In the civil law. A place where ships may ride in safety. Dig. 50, 16, 59.

A place where military duty is performed or stores are kept or something connected with war is done. McGowan v. United States, 48 Ct.Cl. 95.

A place at which both freight and passengers are received for transportation or delivered after transportation. Daniel v. Doyle, 135 Ark. 547, 204 S.W. 210, 211; Railroad Commission of Texas v. Pecos & N. T. Ry. Co., Tex.Civ.App., 212 S.W. 535, 537.

STATIONER'S COMPANY. A body formed in 1557 in London of 97 London stationers and their successors, to whom was entrusted, in the first instance, and, under Orders in Council, the censorship of the press.

STATIONERS' HALL. In English law. The hall of the stationers' company, at which every person claiming copyright in a book must register his title, in order to be able to bring actions against persons infringing it. 2 Steph.Comm. 37–39.

STATIONERY OFFICE. In Englsh law. A government office established as a department of the treasury, for the purpose of supplying government offices with stationery and books, and of printing and publishing government papers.

STATIST. A statesman; a politician; one skilled in government.

STATISTICS. That part of political science which is concerned in collecting and arranging facts illustrative of the condition and resources of a state. The subject is sometimes divided into (1) historical statistics, or facts which illustrate the former condition of a state; (2) statistics of population; (3) of revenue; (4) of trade, commerce, and navigation; (5) of the moral, social, and physical condition of the people. Wharton.

STATU LIBER. Lat. In Roman law. One who is made free by will under a condition; one who has his liberty fixed and appointed at a certain time or on a certain condition. Dig. 40, 7.

STATU LIBERI. Lat. In Louisiana. Slaves for a time, who had acquired the right of being free at a time to come, or on a condition which was not fulfilled, or in a certain event which had not happened, but who in the meantime remained in a state of slavery. Civ.Code La.1838, art. 37.

STATUS. Standing, state or condition. Reynolds v. Pennsylvania Oil Co., 150 Cal. 629, 89 P. 610, 612. The legal relation of individual to rest of the community. Duryea v. Duryea, 46 Idaho 512, 269 P. 987, 988. The rights, duties, capacities and incapacities which determine a person to a given class. Campb. Austin 137. A legal personal relationship, not temporary in its nature nor terminable at the mere will of the parties, with which third persons and the state are concerned. Holzer v. Deutsche Reichsbahn Gesellschaft, 159 Misc. 830, 290 N.Y.S. 181, 191. While term implies relation it is not a mere relation. De La Montanya v. De La Montanya, 112 Cal. 101, 115, 44 P. 345, 348, 32 L.R.A. 82, 53 Am.St.Rep. 165.

It also means *estate*, because it signifies the condition or circumstances in which one stands with regard to his property. In the Year Books, it was used in this sense; 2 Poll. & Maitl. Hist. E. L. 11.

STATUS DE MANERIO. The assembly of the tenants in the court of the lord of a manor, in order to do their customary suit.

STATUS OF IRREMOVABILITY. In English law. The right acquired by a pauper, after one year's residence in any parish, not to be removed therefrom.

STATUS QUO. The existing state of things at any given date. *Status quo ante bellum,* the state of things before the war.

Last actual, peaceable, noncontested condition which preceded pending controversy. State ex rel. Pay Less Drug Stores v. Sutton, 2 Wash.2d 523, 98 P.2d 680, 683, 684; State on Inf. of McKittrick v. American Ins. Co., 351 Mo. 392, 173 S.W.2d 51, 52.

STATUTA PRO PUBLICO COMMODO LATE INTERPRETANTUR. Jenk.Cent. 21. Statutes made for the public good ought to be liberally construed.

STATUTA SUO CLUDUNTUR TERRITORIO, NEC ULTRA TERRITORIUM DISPONUNT. Statutes are confined to their own territory, and have no extraterritorial effect. Woodworth v. Spring, 4 Allen (Mass.) 324.

STATUTABLE, or STATUTORY. That which is introduced or governed by statute law, as opposed to the common law or equity. Thus, a court is said to have statutory jurisdiction when jurisdiction is given to it in certain matters by act of the legislature.

STATUTE, *n.* An act of the legislature declaring, commanding, or prohibiting something; a particular law enacted and established by the will of the legislative department of government; the written will of the legislature, solemnly expressed according to the forms necessary to constitute it the law of the state. Federal Trust Co. v. East Hartford Fire Dist., C.C.A.Conn., 283 F. 95, 98; In re Van Tassell's Will, 119 Misc. 478, 196 N.Y.S. 491, 494; Washington v. Dowling, 92 Fla. 601, 109 So. 588, 591.

This word is used to designate the written law in contradistinction to the unwritten law. Foster v. Brown, 199 Ga. 444, 34 S.E.2d 530, 535. See Common Law.

Foreign and Civil Law

Any particular municipal law or usage, though resting for its authority on judicial decisions, or the practice of nations. 2 Kent, Comm. 456. The whole municipal law of a particular state, from whatever source arising. Story, Confl. Laws, § 12.

"Statute" also sometimes means a kind of bond or obligation of record, being an abbreviation for "statute merchant" or "statute staple." See *infra.* For mandatory and directory statutes see "Mandatory" and "Directory."

General

Affirmative statute. See Affirmative.

Criminal statute. An act of the Legislature as an organized body relating to crime or its punishment. Washington v. Dowling, 92 Fla. 601, 109 So. 588, 591.

Declaratory statute. See Declaratory.

Enabling statute. See that title.

Expository statute. See that title.

General statute. A statute relating to the whole community, or concerning all persons generally, as distinguished from a private or special statute. 1 Bl.Comm. 85, 86; 4 Coke 75*a*.

Local statute. See Local Law.

Negative statute. A statute expressed in negative terms; a statute which prohibits a thing from being done, or declares what shall *not* be done.

Penal statute. See Penal.

Perpetual statute. One which is to remain in force without limitation as to time; one which contains no provision for its repeal, abrogation, or expiration at any future time.

Personal statutes. In foreign and modern civil law. Those statutes which have principally for their object the *person,* and treat of property only incidentally. Story, Confl. Laws, § 13. A personal statute, in this sense of the term, is a law, ordinance, regulation, or custom, the disposition of which affects the person and clothes him with a capacity or incapacity, which he does not change with every change of abode, but which, upon principles of justice and policy, he is assumed to carry with him wherever he goes. 2 Kent, Comm. 456. The term is also applied to statutes which, instead of being general, are confined in their operation to one person or group of persons. Bank of Columbia v. Walker, 14 Lea (Tenn.) 308; Saul v. Creditors, 5 Mart. N.S. (La.) 591, 16 Am. Dec. 212.

Private statute. A statute which operates only upon particular persons, and private concerns. 1 Bl.Comm. 86. An act which relates to certain individuals, or to particular classes of men. Dwar.St. 629; State v. Chambers, 93 N.C. 600.

Public statute. A statute enacting a universal rule which regards the whole community, as distinguished from one which concerns only particular individuals and affects only their private rights. See Code Civ.Proc.Cal. § 1898.

Punitive statute. See that title.

Real statutes. In the civil law. Statutes which have principally for their object property, and which do not speak of persons, except in relation to property. Story, Confl. Laws, § 13; Saul v. His Creditors, 5 Mart. N.S. (La.) 582, 16 Am.Dec. 212.

Reference statutes. See that title.

Remedial statute. See Remedial.

Revised statutes. A body of statutes which have been revised, collected, arranged in order, and re-enacted as a whole; this is the legal title of the collections of compiled laws of several of the states and also of the United States.

Special statute. One which operates only upon particular persons and private concerns. 1 Bl. Comm. 86. Distinguished from a general or public statute.

Statute fair. In English law. A fair at which laborers of both sexes stood and offered themselves for hire; sometimes called also "Mop."

Statute-merchant. In English law. A security for a debt acknowledged to be due, entered into before the chief magistrate of some trading town, pursuant to the statute 13 Edw. I. *De Mercatoribus,* by which not only the body of the debtor might be imprisoned, and his goods seized in satisfaction of the debt, but also his lands might be delivered to the creditor till out of the rents and profits of them the debt be satisfied. 2 Bl. Comm. 160. Now fallen into disuse. 1 Steph. Comm. 287. See Yates v. People, 6 Johns. (N.Y.) 404.

Statute of accumulations. In English law. The statute 39 & 40 Geo. III. c. 98, forbidding the accumulation, beyond a certain period, of property settled by deed or will.

Statute of allegiance de facto. An act of 11 Hen. VII. c. 1, requiring subjects to give their allegiance to the actual king for the time being, and protecting them in so doing.

Statute of distributions. See Distribution.

Statute of Elizabeth. In English law. The statute 13 Eliz. c. 5, against conveyances made in fraud of creditors.

Statute of frauds. See Frauds, Statute of.

Statute of Gloucester. In English law. The statute 6 Edw. I. c. 1, A.D. 1278. It takes its name from the place of its enactment, and was the first statute giving costs in actions. 3 Bl.Comm. 399.

Statute of laborers. See Laborer.

Statute of limitations. See Limitation.

Statute of uses. See Use.

Statute of wills. In English law. The statute 32 Hen. VIII. c. 1, which enacted that all persons being seised in fee-simple (except *femes covert,* infants, idiots, and persons of non-sane memory might, by will and testament in writing, devise to any other person, except to bodies corporate, two-thirds of their lands, tenements, and hereditaments, held in chivalry, and the whole of those held in socage. 2 Bl.Comm. 375.

Statute roll. A roll upon which an English statute, after receiving the royal assent, was formerly entered.

Statute staple. See Staple.

Statutes at large. Statutes printed in full and in the order of their enactment, in a collected form, as distinguished from any digest, revision, abridgement, or compilation of them. Thus the volumes of "United States Statutes at Large," contain all the acts of congress in their order. The name is also given to an authentic collection of the various statutes which have been passed by the British parliament from very early times to the present day.

Statutes of amendments and jeofailes. Statutes whereby a pleader who perceives any slip in the form of his proceedings, and acknowledges the error (jeofaile), is permitted to amend. State ex rel. Smith v. Trimble, 315 Mo. 166, 285 S.W. 729, 731.

Temporary statute. One which is limited in its duration at the time of its enactment. It continues in force until the time of its limitation has expired, unless sooner repealed. A statute which by reason of its nature has only a single and temporary operation—*e. g.* an appropriation bill—is also called a temporary statute.

Validating statute. See that title.

STATUTE, *v.* In old Scotch law. To ordain, establish, or decree.

STATUTES IN DEROGATION OF COMMON LAW MUST BE STRICTLY CONSTRUED. Cooley, Const. Lim. 75, note; Arthurs, Appeal of, 1 Grant Cas. (Pa.) 57.

STATUTI. Lat. In Roman law. Licensed or registered advocates; members of the college of advocates. The number of these was limited, and they enjoyed special privileges from the time of Constantine to that of Justinian.

STATUTORY. Relating to a statute; created or defined by a statute; required by a statute; conforming to a statute.

STATUTORY BOND. One that either literally or substantially meets requirements of statute. Southern Surety Co. v. United States Cast Iron Pipe & Foundry Co., C.C.A.Mo., 13 F.2d 833, 835.

STATUTORY CRIME. See Crime.

STATUTORY DEDICATION. See Dedication.

STATUTORY EXPOSITION. When the language of a statute is ambiguous, and any subsequent enactment involves a particular interpretation of the former act, it is said to contain a *statutory* exposition of the former act. Wharton.

STATUTORY FORECLOSURE. See Foreclosure.

STATUTORY OBLIGATION. An obligation—whether to pay money, perform certain acts, or discharge certain duties—which is created by or arises out of a statute, as distinguished from one founded upon acts between parties or jural relationships.

STATUTORY RELEASE. A conveyance which superseded the old compound assurance by lease and release. It was created by St. 4 & 5, Vict. c. 21, which abolished the lease for a year.

STATUTORY STAPLE. An ancient writ that lay to take the body of a person and seize the lands and goods of one who had forfeited a bond called statute staple. Reg. Orig. 151. See "Staple."

STATUTUM. Lat. Established; determined.

In the Civil law. A term applied to judicial action. Dig. 50, 16, 46, pr.

In old English law. A statute; an act of parliament.

STATUTUM AFFIRMATIVUM NON DEROGAT COMMUNI LEGI. Jenk. Cent. 24. An affirmative statute does not derogate from the common law.

STATUTUM DE MERCATORIBUS. The statute of Acton Burnell, (*q. v.*).

STATUTUM EX GRATIA REGIS DICITUR, QUANDO REX DIGNATUR CEDERE DE JURE SUO REGIO, PRO COMMODO ET QUIETE POPULI SUI. 2 Inst. 378. A statute is said to be by the grace of the king, when the king deigns to yield some portion of his royal rights for the good and quiet of his people.

STATUTUM GENERALITER EST INTELLIGENDUM QUANDO VERBA STATUTI SUNT SPECIALIA, RATIO AUTEM GENERALIS. When the words of a statute are special, but the reason of it general, the statute is to be understood generally. 10 Coke, 101.

STATUTUM HIBERNIÆ DE COHÆREDIBUS. The statute 14 Hen. III. The third public act in the statute-book. It has been pronounced not to be a statute. In the form of it, it appears to be an instruction given by the king to his justices in Ireland, directing them how to proceed in a certain point where they entertained a doubt. It seems the justices itinerant in that country had a doubt, when land descended to sisters, whether the younger sisters ought to hold of the eldest, and do homage to her for their several portions, or of the chief lord, and do homage to him; and certain knights had been sent over to know what the practice was in England in such a case. 1 Reeve, Eng. Law, 259.

STATUTUM SESSIONUM. In old English law. The statute session; a meeting in every hundred of constables and householders, by custom, for the ordering of servants, and debating of differences between masters and servants, rating of wages, etc. 5 Eliz. c. 4.

STATUTUM SPECIALE STATUTO SPECIALI NON DEROGAT. Jenk. Cent. 199. One special statute does not take from another special statute.

STATUTUM WALLIÆ. The statute of Wales. The title of a statute passed in the twelfth year of Edw. I., being a sort of constitution for the principality of Wales, which was thereby, in a great measure, put on the footing of England with respect to its laws and the administration of justice. 2 Reeve, Eng. Law, 93, 94.

STAURUM. In old records. A store, or stock of cattle. A term of common occurrence in the accounts of monastic establishments. Spelman; Cowell.

STAY, *v.* To stop, arrest, or forbear. State Founders v. Oliver, 165 Md. 360, 169 A. 59, 61.

To "stay" an order or decree means to hold it in abeyance, or refrain from enforcing it. State v. Draney, 57 Utah 14, 176 P. 767, 769.

STAY, *n.* A stopping; the act of arresting a judicial proceeding by the order of a court. In re Schwarz, D.C.N.Y., 14 F. 788.

Also that which holds, restrains, or supports. Armenti v. Brooklyn Union Gas Co., 142 N.Y.S. 420, 425, 157 App.Div. 276; Rookstool v. Cudahy Packing Co., 100 Neb. 118, 158 N.W. 440, 444.

Stay laws. Acts of the legislature prescribing a stay of execution in certain cases, or a stay of foreclosure of mortgages, or closing the courts for a limited period, or providing that suits shall not be instituted until a certain time after the cause of action arose, or otherwise suspending legal remedies; designed for the relief of debtors, in times of general distress or financial trouble.

Stay of execution. The stopping or arresting of execution on a judgment, that is, of the judgment-creditor's right to issue execution, for a limited period. This is given by statute in many jurisdictions, as a privilege to the debtor, usually on his furnishing bail for the debt, costs, and interest. Or it may take place by agreement of the parties. See National Docks, etc., Co. v. Pennsylvania R. Co., 54 N.J.Eq. 167, 33 A. 936; State ex rel. Gray v. Hennings, 194 Mo.App. 545, 185 S.W. 1153, 1154.

Stay of proceedings. The temporary suspension of the regular order of proceedings in a cause, by direction or order of the court, usually to await the action of one of the parties in regard to some omitted step or some act which the court has required him to perform as incidental to the suit; as where a nonresident plaintiff has been ruled to give security for costs. See Wallace v. Wallace, 13 Wis. 226; Lewton v. Hower, 18 Fla. 876; Rossiter v. Ætna L. Ins. Co., 96 Wis. 466, 71 N.W. 898.

"Stay of proceedings" and "abatement", though similar are not identical; abatement being a matter of right, while application for stay of proceedings is addressed to discretion of the court. Evans v. Evans, Tex.Civ.App., 186 S.W.2d 277, 279.

STEADY COURSE. A ship is on a "steady course," not only when her heading does not change, but whenever her future positions are certainly ascertainable from her present position and movements. Commonwealth & Dominion Line v. U. S., C.C.A.N.Y., 20 F.2d 729, 731.

STEAL. This term is commonly used in indictments for larceny, ("take, *steal*, and carry away,") and denotes the commission of theft, that is, the felonious taking and carrying away of the personal property of another, and without right and without leave or consent of owner, People v. Surace, 295 Ill. 604, 129 N.E. 504, 506; State v.

Banoch, 193 Iowa 851, 186 N.W. 436; Alvarado v. State, 38 Okl.Cr. 360, 261 P. 983, 985; and with intent to keep or make use wrongfully. State v. Hillis, 145 Kan. 456, 65 P.2d 251, 252; or it may denote the criminal taking of personal property either by larceny, embezzlement, or false pretenses. Commonwealth v. Farmer, 218 Mass. 507, 106 N.E. 150, 151. But, in popular usage "stealing" may include the unlawful appropriation of things which are not technically the subject of larceny, *e. g.*, immovables. Barnhart v. State, 154 Ind. 177, 56 N.E. 212; Buxton v. International Indemnity Co., 47 Cal.App. 583, 191 P. 84, 86; State v. Blake, 95 W.Va. 467, 121 S.E. 488, 489.

STEALING CHILDREN. See Kidnapping.

STEALTH. Theft is so called by some ancient writers. "Stealth is the wrongful taking of goods without pretense of title." Finch, Law, b. 3, c. 17.

STEAM FITTER. A workman who installs steam pipes, their fittings, etc. Warburton-Beacham Supply Co. v. City of Jackson, 151 Miss. 503, 118 So. 606, 608.

STEAMSHIP. A vessel, the principal motive power of which is steam and not sails. L.R. 7 Q.B. 569. See Western Ins. Co. v. Cropper, 32 Pa. 352, 75 Am.Dec. 561.

STEELBOW GOODS. In Scotch law. Corn, cattle, straw, and implements of husbandry delivered by a landlord to his tenant, by which the tenant is enabled to stock and labor the farm; in consideration of which he becomes bound to return articles equal in quantity and quality, at the expiry of the lease. Bell.

STEERER. One who gains the confidence of the person intended to be fleeced and who may be said to steer or lead the victim to the place where the latter is to be robbed or swindled. Barron v. Board of Dental Examiners of California, 109 Cal. App. 382, 293 P. 144, 145.

STELLIONATAIRE. Fr. In French law. A party who fraudulently mortgages property to which he has no title.

STELLIONATE. In civil law. A name given generally to all species of frauds committed in making contracts but particularly to the crime of aliening the same subject to different persons. 2 Kames, Eq. 40.

STELLIONATUS. Lat. In the civil law. A general name for any kind of fraud not falling under any specific class. But the term is chiefly applied to fraud practiced in the sale or pledging of property; as, selling the same property to two different persons, selling another's property as one's own, placing a second mortgage on property without disclosing the existence of the first, etc.

STENOGRAPHER. One who is skilled in the art of short-hand writing; one whose business is to write in short-hand. See Rynerson v. Allison, 30 S.C. 534, 9 S.E. 656; In re Appropriations for Deputy State Officers, 25 Neb. 662, 41 N.W. 643; Chase v. Vandergrift, 88 Pa. 217.

STENOGRAPHY. Art of writing in shorthand. Harris v. Brockhurst, 119 N.J.L. 187, 194 A. 876, 877.

STEP. When used as prefix in conjunction with a degree of kinship, is repugnant to blood relationship, and is indicative of a relationship by affinity. Grossenbacher v. State, 49 Ohio App. 451, 197 N.E. 382, 383.

STEP-CHILD. The child of one of the spouses by a former marriage. Dangerfield v. Indemnity Ins. Co., La.App., 19 So.2d 598, 600.

STEP-DOWN TRANSFORMER. An induction coil or a transformer so constructed that there is a higher voltage in the primary current than in the secondary current. General Electric Co. v. Butler Light, Heat & Motor Co., D.C.Pa., 205 F. 42, 44.

STEP-FATHER. The husband of one's mother by virtue of a marriage subsequent to that of which the person spoken of is the offspring. Larsen v. Harris Structural Steel Co., 230 App.Div. 280, 243 N.Y.S. 654, 655. The husband of one's mother by virtue of a marriage subsequent to that of which person spoken of is the offspring. Sharp v. Borough of Vineland, 14 N.J.Misc. 256, 183 A. 911, 912.

STEP-MOTHER. The wife of one's father by virtue of a marriage subsequent to that of which the person spoken of is the offspring. Sharp v. Borough of Vineland, 14 N.J.Misc. 256, 183 A. 911, 912.

STEP-SON. The son of one's wife by a former husband, or of one's husband by a former wife.

STEP-UP TRANSFORMER. An induction coil or a transformer so constructed that there is a higher voltage in the secondary current than in the primary current. General Electric Co. v. Butler Light, Heat & Motor Co., D.C.Pa., 205 F. 42, 44.

STERBRECHE, or STREBRICH. The breaking, obstructing, or straitening of a way. Termes de la Ley.

STÈRE. A French measure of solidity, used in measuring wood. It is a cubic meter.

STERILITY. Barrenness; unfruitfulness; incapacity to germinate or reproduce.

STERLING. In English law. Current or standard coin, especially silver coin; a standard of coinage.

STET BILLA. If the plaintiff in a plaint in the mayor's court of London has attached property belonging to the defendant and obtained execution against the garnishee, the defendant, if he wishes to contest the plaintiff's claim, and obtain restoration of his property, must issue a *scire facias ad disprobandum debitum;* if the only question to be tried is the plaintiff's debt, the plaintiff in appearing to the *scire facias* prays *stet billa* "that his bill original," *i. e.*, his original plaint, "may stand, and that the defendant may plead thereto." The action then proceeds in the usual way as if the proceedings in attachment (which are founded on a fictitious default of the defendant in appearing to the plaint) had not taken place. Brand, F. Attachm. 115; Sweet.

STET PROCESSUS. An entry on the roll in the nature of a judgment of a direction that all further proceedings shall be stayed, (*i. e.*, that the process may stand,) and it is one of the ways by which a suit may be terminated by an act of the party, as distinguished from a termination of it by judgment, which is the act of the court. It was used by the plaintiff when he wished to suspend the action without suffering a nonsuit. Brown.

STEVEDORE. A person employed in loading and unloading vessels. The Senator, D.C.Ohio, 21 F. 191; Rankin v. Merchants' & M. Transp. Co., 73 Ga. 232, 54 Am.Rep. 874; Zampiere v. William Spencer & Son Corporation, 194 App.Div. 576, 185 N.Y.S. 639, 640.

STEWARD. A man appointed in the place or stead of another, also a principal officer within his jurisdiction. Brown.

Land Steward

See that title.

Steward of a Manor

An important officer who has the general management of all forensic matters connected with the manor of which he is steward. He stands in much the same relation to the lord of the manor as an under-sheriff does to the sheriff. Cowell.

Steward of all England

In old English law. An officer who was invested with various powers; among others, to preside on the trial of peers.

Steward of Scotland

An officer of the highest dignity and trust. He administered the crown revenues, superintended the affairs of the household, and possessed the privilege of holding the first place in the army, next to the king, in the day of battle. From this office the royal house of Stuart took its name. But the office was sunk on their advancement to the throne, and has never since been revived. Bell.

STEWARTRY. In Scotch law, equivalent to the English "county." See Brown.

STEWS. Certain brothels anciently permitted in England, suppressed by Henry VIII. Also, breeding places for tame pheasants.

STICK. In the old books. To stop; to hesitate; to accede with reluctance. "The court *stuck* a little at this exception." 2 Show. 491.

STICK UP. Rob at the point of a gun. White v. State, 219 Ind. 290, 37 N.E.2d 937, 940.

STICKER. A gummed slip or strip. Crosby v. Libby, 114 Me. 35, 95 A. 329, 330.

STICKLER. (1) An inferior officer who cuts wood within the royal parks of Clarendon. Cowell. (2) An arbitrator. (3) An obstinate contender about anything.

STIFLING A PROSECUTION. Agreeing, in consideration of receiving a pecuniary or other advantage, to abstain from prosecuting a person for an offense not giving rise to a civil remedy; *e. g.*, perjury. Sweet.

STILL. Any device used for separating alcoholic spirits from fermented substances. Moore v. State, 154 Ark. 13, 240 S.W. 1083, 1084; Davis v. State, 102 Tex.Cr.R. 546, 278 S.W. 848, 849. The word is sometimes applied to the whole apparatus for evaporation and condensation used in the manufacture of ardent spirits, but in the description of the parts of the apparatus it is applied merely to the vessel or retort used for boiling and evaporation of the liquid. Hodgkiss v. State, 156 Ark. 340, 246 S.W. 506, 507.

STILL COKE. Coke formed by the distillation of petroleum. Rodman Chemical Co. v. Steel Treating Equipment Co., C.C.A.Mich., 288 F. 471, 473.

STILL WORM. The tube or coil used for condensation of the vapor which is passed through it from boiling mash for the purpose of being distilled into whisky. Rosslot v. State, 162 Ark. 340, 258 S.W. 348.

STILLBORN CHILD. A child born dead or in such an early stage of pregnancy as to be incapable of living, though not actually dead at the time of birth. Children born within the first six months after conception are considered by the civil law as incapable of living, and therefore, though they are apparently born alive, if they do not in fact survive so long as to rebut this presumption of law, they cannot inherit, so as to transmit the property to others. Marsellis v. Thalhimer, 2 Paige (N.Y.) 41, 21 Am.Dec. 66.

STILLICIDIUM. Lat. In the civil law. The drip of water from the eaves of a house. The servitude *stillicidii* consists in the right to have the water drip from one's eaves upon the house or ground of another. The term "*flumen*" designated the rain-water collected from the roof, and carried off by the gutters, and there is a similar easement of having it discharged upon the adjoining estate. Mackeld. Rom. Law, § 317, par. 4.

STINT. In English law. Limit; a limited number. Used as descriptive of a species of common. See Common sans Nombre.

STIPEND. A salary; settled pay. Mangam v. Brooklyn, 98 N.Y. 597, 50 Am.Rep. 705.

In English and Scotch law. A provision made for the support of the clergy.

STIPENDIARY ESTATES. Estates granted in return for services, generally of a military kind. 1 Steph.Comm. 174.

STIPENDIARY MAGISTRATES. In English law. Paid magistrates; appointed in London and some other cities and boroughs, and having in general the powers and jurisdiction of justices of the peace.

STIPENDIUM. Lat. In the civil law. The pay of a soldier; wages; stipend. Calvin.

STIPES. Lat. In old English law. Stock; a stock; a source of descent or title. *Communis stipes*, the common stock. Fleta, lib. 6, c. 2.

STIPITAL. Relating to *stirpes*, roots, or stocks. "Stipital distribution" of property is distribution *per stirpes*; that is, by right of representation.

STIPULATED DAMAGE. Liquidated damage, (*q. v.*).

STIPULATE. Arrange or settle definitely, as an agreement or covenant. Mennen Co. v. Krauss Co., D.C.La., 37 F.Supp. 161, 163.

STIPULATIO. Lat. In the Roman law, *stipulatio* was the verbal contract, (*verbis obligatio,*) and was the most solemn and formal of all the contracts in that system of jurisprudence. It was entered into by question and corresponding answer thereto, by the parties, both being present at the same time, and usually by such words as "*spondes? spondeo,*" "*promittis? promitto,*" and the like. Brown.

STIPULATIO AQUILIANA. A particular application of the *stipulatio*, which was used to collect together into one verbal contract all the liabilities of every kind and quality of the debtor, with a view to their being released or discharged by an *acceptilatio*, that mode of discharge being applicable only to the verbal contract. Brcwn.

STIPULATION. A material article in an agreement.

Practice

The name given to any agreement made by the attorneys engaged on opposite sides of a cause, (especially if in writing,) regulating any matter incidental to the proceedings or trial, which falls within their jurisdiction. Such, for instance, are agreements to extend the time for pleading, to take depositions, to waive objections, to admit certain facts, to continue the cause. See Lewis v. Orpheus, 15 F.Cas. 492; Southern Colonization Co. v. Howard Cole & Co., 185 Wis. 469, 201 N.W. 817, 819.

Practice

An agreement between counsel respecting business before the court. It is not binding unless assented to by the parties or their representatives, and most stipulations are required to be in writing. Holland Banking Co. v. Continental Nat. Bank of Jackson County, Kansas City, Mo., D.C. Mo., 9 F.Supp. 988, 989.

"Stipulations" are of two types: First, those relating to merely precedural matters; and, second, those which have all essential characteristics of mutual contract. Paine v. Chicago & N. W. Ry. Co., 217 Wis. 601, 258 N.W. 846.

Admiralty Practice

A recognizance of certain persons (called in the old law "*fide jussors*") in the nature of bail for the appearance of a defendant. 3 Bl.Comm. 108.

STIPULATOR. In the civil law. The party who asked the question in the contract of stipulation; the other party, or he who answered, being called the "promissor." But, in a more general sense, the term was applied to both the parties. Calvin.

STIRPES. Lat. Descents. The root-stem, or stock of a tree. Figuratively, it signifies in law that person from whom a family is descended, and also the kindred or family. Taking property by right of representation is called "succession *per stirpes,*" in opposition to taking in one's own right, or as a principal, which is termed "taking *per capita.*" Rotmanskey v. Heiss, 86 Md. 633, 39 A. 415. See, also, Per Stirpes and Representation.

STOCK.

Mercantile Law

The goods and wares of a merchant or tradesman, kept for sale and traffic. Schnitzer v. Excelsior Powder Mfg. Co., Mo.App., 160 S.W. 282, 285.

In a larger sense. The capital of a merchant or other person, including his merchandise, money, and credits, or, in other words, the entire property employed in business.

Corporation Law

The term is used in various senses. It may mean the capital or principal fund of a corporation or joint-stock company, formed by the contributions of subscribers or the sale of shares; the aggregate of a certain number of shares severally owned by the members or stockholders of the corporation or the proportional share of an individual stockholder; also the incorporeal property which is represented by the holding of a certificate of stock; and in a wider and more remote sense, the right of a shareholder to participate in the general management of the company and to share proportionally in its net profits or earnings or in the distribution of assets on dissolution, the term "stock" has also been held to embrace not only capital stock of a corporation but all corporate wealth and resources, subject to all corporate liabilities and obligations. Whitman v. Consolidated Gas, Electric Light & Power Co. of Baltimore, 148 Md. 90, 129 A. 22, 27. See also Thayer v. Wathen, 17 Tex.Civ.App. 382, 44 S.W. 906; Harrison v. Vines, 46 Tex. 15; Seawright v. Dickson, 16 Ga.App. 436, 85 S.E. 625, 628; Hood Rubber Co. v. Commonwealth, 238 Mass. 369, 131 N.E. 201, 202.

"Stock" is distinguished from "bonds" and, ordinarily, from "debentures," in that it gives right of ownership in part of assets of corporation and right to interest in any surplus after payment of debt. Carson, Pirie, Scott & Co. v. Duffy-Powers, Inc., D.C.N.Y., 9 F.Supp. 199, 201.

The capital stock of a corporation differs widely in legal import from the aggregate shares into which it is divided by its charter (Farrington v. Tennessee, 95 U.S. 686, 24 L.Ed. 558; People v. Coleman, 126 N.Y. 437, 27 N.E. 818, 12 L.R.A. 762); the former includes only the fund of money or other property derived by it from the sale or exchange of its shares of stock, while the latter represents the totality of the corporate assets and property; Hamor v. Engineering Co., C.C.Del., 84 F. 396. See "Capital Stock."

The funded indebtedness of a state or government, also, is often represented by stocks, shares of which are held by its creditors at interest.

Classes of Corporate Stock

Preferred stock is a separate portion or class of the stock of a corporation, which is accorded, by the charter or by-laws, a preference or priority in respect to dividends, over the remainder of the stock of the corporation, which in that case is called *common stock.* That is, holders of the preferred stock are entitled to receive dividends at a fixed annual rate, out of the net earnings or profits of the corporation, before any distribution of earnings is made to the common stock. If the earnings applicable to the payment of dividends are not more than sufficient for such fixed annual dividend, they will be entirely absorbed by the preferred stock. If they are more than sufficient for the purpose, the remainder may be given entirely to the common stock (which is the more usual custom) or such remainder may be distributed pro rata to both classes of the stock, in which case the preferred stock is said to "participate" with the common. The fixed dividend on preferred stock may be "cumulative" or "non-cumulative." In the former case, if the stipulated dividend on preferred stock is not earned or paid in any one year, it becomes a charge upon the surplus earnings of the next and succeeding years, and all such accumulated and unpaid dividends on the preferred stock must be paid off before the common stock is entitled to receive dividends. In the case of "non-cumulative" preferred stock, its preference for any given year is extinguished by the failure to earn or pay its dividend in that year. If a corporation has no class of preferred stock, all its stock is common stock. The word "common" in this connection signifies that all the holders of such stock are entitled to an equal pro rata division of profits or net earnings, if any there be, without any preference or priority among themselves. *Deferred stock* is rarely issued by American corporations, though it is not uncommon in England. This kind of stock is distinguished by the fact that the payment of dividends upon it is expressly postponed until some other class of stock has received a dividend, or until some certain liability or obligation of the corporation is discharged. If there is a class of "preferred" stock, the common stock may in this sense be said to be "deferred," and the term is sometimes used as equivalent to "common" stock. But it is not impossible that a corporation should have three classes of stock: (1) Preferred, (2) common, and (3) deferred; the latter class being postponed, in respect to participation in profits, until both the preferred and the common stock had received dividends at a fixed rate. See Cook, Corp. § 12; Scott v. Railroad Co., 93 Md. 475, 49 A. 327; Jones v. Railroad Co., 67 N.H. 234, 30 A. 614, 68 Am.St.Rep. 650; General Inv. Co. v. Bethlehem Steel Corp., 87 N.J.Eq. 234, 100 A. 347, 349; Day v. U. S. Cast Iron Pipe & Foundry Co., 96 N.J.Eq. 736, 126 A. 302, 304.

Law of Descent

The term is used, metaphorically, to denote the original progenitor of a family, or the ancestor from whom the persons in question are all descended; such descendants being called "branches." Matter of Samson's Estate, 139 Misc. 490, 249 N.Y.S. 79, 83.

General

Capital stock. See that title.

Certificate of stock. See Certificate.

Exchange of stock. See Exchange.

Guarantied stock. Stock of a corporation which is entitled to receive dividends at a fixed annual rate, the payment of which dividends is guarantied by some outside person or corporation. Field v. Lamson, etc., Mfg. Co., 162 Mass. 388, 38 N.E. 1126, 27 L.R.A. 136.

Public stocks. The funded or bonded debt of a government or state.

Special stock of a corporation, in Massachusetts, is authorized by statute. It is limited in amount to two-fifths of the actual capital. It is subject to redemption by the corporation at par after a fixed time. The corporation is bound to pay a fixed annual dividend on it as a debt. The holders of it are in no event liable for the debts of the corporation beyond their stock; and an issue of special stock makes all the general stockholders liable for all debts and contracts of the corporation until the special stock is fully redeemed. American Tube Works v. Boston Mach. Co., 139 Mass. 5, 29 N.E. 63.

Stock association. A joint-stock company, (*q. v.*).

Stock broker. One who buys and sells stock as the agent of others. Banta v. Chicago, 172 Ill. 204, 50 N.E. 233, 40 L.R.A. 611; Little Rock v. Barton, 33 Ark. 436; Gast v. Buckley, Ky., 64 S.W. 632.

Stock corporation. A corporation having a capital stock divided into shares, and which is authorized by law to distribute to the holders thereof dividends or shares of the surplus profits of the corporation. Buker v. Steele, Co.Ct., 43 N.Y.S. 350.

Stock dividend. See Dividend.

Stock exchange. A voluntary association of persons (not usually a corporation) who, for convenience in the transaction of business with each other, have associated themselves to provide a common place for the transaction of their business; an association of stock-brokers. Dos Passos, Stock-Brok. 14. The building or room used by an association of stock-brokers for meeting for the transaction of their common business.

Stock in trade. Merchandise or goods kept for sale or traffic. Woodworth & Co. v. City of Concord, 78 N.H. 54, 96 A. 296, 297; Shasta Lumber Co. v. McCoy, 85 Cal.App. 468, 259 P. 965, 967, also that form of property owned by a craftsman upon which he exercises his art, skill, or workmanship, and upon which he uses the tools of his trade or business. Armstrong Turner Millinery Co. v. Round, 106 Kan. 146, 186 P. 979, 9 A.L.R. 1255.

Stock jobber. A dealer in stock; one who buys and sells stock on his own account on speculation. State v. Debenture Co., 51 La.Ann. 1874, 26 So. 600.

Stock law district. A district in which stock is by law prohibited from running at large. Griffin v. Fowler, 17 Ala.App. 44, 81 So. 426, 428.

Stock life insurance company. One in which capital stock investment is made by subscribers to stock, and business is thereafter conducted by board of directors elected by its stockholders, and, subject to statutes, distribution of earnings or profits, as between stockholders and policy holders, is determined by board of directors. Atlantic Life Ins. Co. v. Moncure, D.C.Va., 35 F.2d 360, 362.

Stock note. The term has no technical meaning, and may as well apply to a note given on the sale of stock which the bank had purchased or taken in the payment of doubtful debts as to a note given on account of an original subscription to stock. Dunlap v. Smith, 12 Ill. 402.

Stock of merchandise. Goods or chattels which a merchant holds for sale. Swift & Co. v. Tempelos, 178 N.C. 487, 101 S.E. 8, 7 A.L.R. 1581; Meier Electric & Machine Co. v. Dixon, 81 Ind. App. 400, 143 N.E. 363, 364; Balter v. Crum, 199 Mo.App. 380, 203 S.W. 506, 507.

Stock raising. The raising of domestic animals. Krobitzsch v. Industrial Accident Commission of California, 181 Cal. 541, 185 P. 396, 398.

Watered stock. See that title.

STOCKHOLDER. A person who owns shares of stock in a corporation or joint-stock company. Ross v. Knapp, etc., Co., 77 Ill.App. 424; Corwith v. Culver, 69 Ill. 502; Hirshfeld v. Bopp, 145 N.Y. 84, 39 N.E. 817; Ludden & Bates v. Watt, 18 Ala. App. 652, 94 So. 239, 240; Fuller v. Lockhart, 209 N.C. 61, 182 S.E. 733.

Owner of shares in a corporation which has a capital stock. If a corporation has no capital stock, the corporators and their successors are called "members." Civ.Code Dak. § 392 (Comp. Laws N.D.1913, § 4515; Rev.Code 1919, § 247).

STOCKHOLDER'S DERIVATIVE SUIT. An equity proceeding by a stockholder for purpose of sustaining in his own name a right of action existing in corporation itself, where corporation would be an appropriate plaintiff. Felsenheld v. Bloch Bros. Tobacco Co., 119 W.Va. 167, 192 S.E. 545, 546, 123 A.L.R. 334. It is based upon two distinct wrongs: The act whereby corporation was caused to suffer damage, and act of corporation itself in refusing to redress such act. Druckerman v. Harbord, 174 Misc. 1077, 22 N.Y.S.2d 595, 597.

STOCKHOLDER'S LIABILITY. Phrase is frequently employed to denote stockholder's statutory, added or double liability for corporation's debts, notwithstanding full payment for stock, but is often employed where stockholder, agreeing to pay full par value of stock, obtained stock certificate before complete payment or where stock, only partly paid for, is intentionally issued by corporation as fully paid up and all or part of purported consideration therefor is entirely fictitious. Gray Const. Co. v. Fantle, 62 S.D. 345, 253 N.W. 464.

STOCKHOLDERS' REPRESENTATIVE ACTION. An action brought or maintained by a stockholder in behalf of himself and all others similarly situated. New York Cent. R. Co. v. New York & Harlem R. Co., 193 Misc. 795, 85 N.Y.S.2d 112, 115.

STOCKHOLDER'S SUIT. One by the corporation conducted by stockholder as its representative, and the stockholder is only a nominal plaintiff and the corporation is the real party in interest. Rettinger v. Pierpont, 145 Neb. 161, 15 N.W.2d 393, 397. See, also, Derivative Stockholders' Suit.

STOCKS. A machine consisting of two pieces of timber, arranged to be fastened together, and holding fast the legs of a person placed in it. This was an ancient method of punishment.

STOP. Within a statute requiring a motorist striking a person with automobile to stop requires a definite cessation of movement for a sufficient length of time for a person of ordinary powers of observation to fully understand the surroundings of the accident. Moore v. State, 140 Tex.Cr. R. 482, 145 S.W.2d 887, 888.

STOP ORDER. The name of an order grantable in English chancery practice, to prevent drawing out a fund in court to the prejudice of an assignee or lienholder.

A direction by customer to his broker that, if commodity touches price named, broker shall close trade at best available price. Alexas v. Post & Flagg, 129 S.C. 53, 123 S.E. 769, 35 A.L.R. 969; Richter v. Poe, 109 Md. 20, 71 A. 420, 22 L.R.A., N.S., 174.

STOP SIGN. A legally erected and maintained traffic signal requiring all traffic to stop before entering into or crossing an intersection. Sweet v. Awtrey, 70 Ga.App. 334, 28 S.E.2d 154, 161.

STOPPAGE. In the civil law. Compensation or set-off.

STOPPAGE IN TRANSITU. The act by which the unpaid vendor of goods stops their progress and resumes possession of them, while they are in course of transit from him to the purchaser, and not yet actually delivered to the latter.

The right of stoppage *in transitu* is that which the vendor has, when he sells goods on credit to another, of resuming the possession of the goods while they are in the possession of a carrier or middle-man, in the transit to the consignee or vendee, and before they arrive into his actual possession, or the destination he has appointed for them on his becoming bankrupt and insolvent. 2 Kent, Comm. 702.

The right which arises to an unpaid vendor to resume the possession, with which he has parted, of goods sold upon credit, before they come into the possession of a buyer who has become insolvent, bankrupt, or pecuniarily embarrassed. Inslee v. Lane, 57 N.H. 454.

The right of stoppage in transitu continues during the transitus, that is, until the goods are delivered by the carrier to the buyer, or possession, actual or constructive, is taken by the buyer. M. Degaro Co. v. Cleveland, C., C. & St. L. Ry. Co., 123 Ohio St. 179, 174 N.E. 587, 590.

STOPPAGE OF WORK. Within unemployment compensation law denying workman benefits, if his unemployment was due to stoppage of work because of labor dispute in which workman participated means strike. Board of Review v. Mid-Continent Petroleum Corporation, 193 Okl. 36, 141 P.2d 69, 71 72.

STORAGE. Safekeeping of goods in a warehouse or other depository. Lincoln Sav. Bank of Brooklyn v. Brown, Em.App., 137 F.2d 228, 230, 231.

STORE, *v.* To keep merchandise for safe custody, to be delivered in the same condition as when received, where the safe-keeping is the principal object of deposit, and not the consumption or sale. O'Niel v. Buffalo F. Ins. Co., 3 N.Y. 122. Town of Newberry v. Dorrah, 105 S.C. 28, 89 S.E. 402, 403.

STORE, *n.* Any place where goods are deposited and sold by one engaged in buying and selling them. Warburton-Beacham Supply Co. v. City of Jackson, 151 Miss. 503, 118 So. 606, 608. A shop. Midwestern Petroleum Corporation v. State Board of Tax Com'rs, 206 Ind. 688, 187 N.E. 882, 888, 191 N.E. 153. Also Storehouse. Webster; De Wolfe v. Pierce, 196 Ill.App. 360, 361.

Public Store

A government warehouse, maintained for certain administrative purposes, such as the keeping of military supplies, the storing of imported goods under bonds to pay duty, etc.

Stores

The supplies of different articles provided for the subsistence and accommodation of a ship's crew and passengers.

STOREHOUSE. A house in which things are stored; a building for the storing of grain, foodstuffs, or goods of any kind; a magazine; a repository; a warehouse; a store. Moss v. Commonwealth, 271 Ky. 283, 111 S.W.2d 628, 630.

STOREROOM. A room in an apartment or flat house set apart and having conveniences such as shelves, hooks, etc., for storage purposes, and is not, for instance, a bedroom used by the tenant in part for storing his goods. Gardner v. Roosevelt Hotel, 175 Misc. 610, 24 N.Y.S.2d 261, 263.

STORM. Wind outburst of tumultuous force. Schaeffer v. Northern Assur. Co., Mo.App., 177 S.W.2d 688, 691.

STORY OF BUILDING. A habitable space between two floors or a set of rooms on the same floor or level. Biber v. O'Brien, 138 Cal.App. 353, 32 P.2d 425, 429.

STOUTHRIEFF. In Scotch law. Formerly this word included every species of theft accompanied with violence to the person, but of late years it has become the *vox signata* for forcible and masterful depredation within or near the dwelling-house; while robbery has been more particularly applied to violent depredation on the highway, or accompanied by house-breaking. Alis. Prin. Scotch Law, 227.

STOWAGE. In maritime law. The storing, packing, or arranging of the cargo in a ship, in such a manner as to protect the goods from friction, bruising, or damage from leakage.

Money paid for a room where goods are laid; housage. Wharton.

STOWAWAY. One who conceals himself aboard an out-going vessel for the purpose of obtaining free passage. U. S. ex rel. Candreva v. Smith, C.C.A.Ill., 27 F.2d 642, 644.

STOWE. In old English law. A valley. Co.Litt. 4*b*.

STRADDLE. In stock-brokers' parlance the term means the double privilege of a "put" and a "call," and secures to the holder the right to demand of the seller at a certain price within a certain time a certain number of shares of specified stock, or to require him to take, at the same price within the same time, the same shares of stock. Harris v. Tumbridge, 83 N.Y. 95, 38 Am.Rep. 398; Henderson v. Usher, 125 Fla. 709, 170 So. 846, 852. It is not per se a gaming contract, unless intended as a mere cover for a bet or wager on the future price of the stock or commodity. Palmer v. Love, 18 Tenn.App. 579, 80 S.W.2d 100, 106.

STRAGGLER. In Navy Department regulations. One absent without leave, with the probability that he does not intend to desert, but, if his absence continues for 10 days, he becomes a deserter. Reed v. U. S., C.C.A.N.Y., 252 F. 21, 22.

STRAIGHT LINE. The shortest distance between two points. Reed v. Iowa State Highway Commission, 221 Iowa 500, 266 N.W. 47, 50.

STRAIGHT-LINE DEPRECIATION. Division of original cost into as many years as the property would remain in service and deduction of that fraction of the cost for every past year. United

States Industrial Alcohol Co. v. Helvering, C.C.A. 2, 137 F.2d 511, 516.

In estimating deterioration in a plant. Calculation from examination and experience in like constructions the total life period of the constituent parts of the plant, and then deducting from their value that proportion of decrease represented by the ratio of the years which it has been in use in relation to the entire life period as distinguished from the "sinking-fund method" which consists in charging for depreciation an annual sum, which, with compounding interest thereon, will at the termination of the estimated life of the investment replace the original cost, and if cut off at any given period the accumulation will represent the depreciated value to that date. Pacific Gas & Electric Co. v. Devlin, 188 Cal. 33, 203 P. 1058, 1062; People ex rel. Central Hudson Gas & Electric Co. v. State Tax Commission, 218 App.Div. 44, 217 N.Y.S. 707, 712.

STRAMINEUS HOMO. L. Lat. A man of straw, one of no substance, put forward as bail or surety.

STRAND. A shore or bank of the sea or a river. Bell v. Hayes, 60 App.Div. 382, 69 N.Y.S. 898; Harris v. City of St. Helens, 72 Or. 377, 143 P. 941, 944, Ann.Cas.1916D, 1073.

STRANDING. In maritime law. The drifting, driving, or running aground of a ship on a shore or strand. *Accidental* stranding takes place where the ship is driven on shore by the winds and waves. *Voluntary* stranding takes place where the ship is run on shore either to preserve her from a worse fate or for some fraudulent purpose. Marsh. Ins. bk. 1, c. 12, § 1. See Barrow v. Bell, 4 Barn. & C. 736; Strong v. Sun Mut. Ins. Co., 31 N.Y. 106, 88 Am.Dec. 242; London Assur. Co. v. Companhia de Moagens, 17 S.Ct. 785, 167 U.S. 149, 42 L.Ed. 113; Washington Iron Works v. St. Paul Fire & Marine Ins. Co., 128 Wash. 349, 222 P. 487, 489; Lehigh & Wilkes-Barre Coal Co. v. Globe & Rutgers Fire Ins. Co., C.C.A., 6 F.2d 736, 738, 43 A.L.R. 215.

STRANGER. As used with reference to the subject of subrogation, one who, in no event resulting from the existing state of affairs, can become liable for the debt, and whose property is not charged with the payment thereof and cannot be sold therefor. McBride v. McBride, 148 Or. 478, 36 P.2d 175, 177; Home Owners' Loan Corporation v. Crouse, 151 Pa.Super. 259, 30 A.2d 330, 331, 332. See, also, Strangers.

STRANGER IN BLOOD. Any person not within the consideration of natural love and affection arising from relationship.

STRANGERS. By this term is intended third persons generally. Thus the persons bound by a fine are parties, privies, and strangers; the parties are either the cognizors or cognizees; the privies are such as are in any way related to those who levy the fine, and claim under them by any right of blood, or other right of representation; the strangers are all other persons in the world, except only the parties and privies. In its general legal signification the term is opposed to the word "privy." Those who are in no way parties to a covenant, nor bound by it, are also said to be strangers to the covenant. Brown. See Robbins v. Chicago, 4 Wall. 672, 18 L.Ed. 427; Wilson v. Smith, 213 Ky. 836, 281 S.W. 1008, 1010; State v. Mills, 23 N.M. 549, 169 P. 1171, 1173; Gronewold v. Gronewold, 304 Ill. 11, 136 N.E. 489, 490. See, also, Stranger.

STRATAGEM. A deception either by words or actions, in times of war, in order to obtain an advantage over an enemy.

STRATOCRACY. A military government; government by military chiefs of an army.

STRATOR. In old English law. A surveyor of the highways.

STRAW BAIL. See Bail.

STRAY. See Estray.

STREAM. A water course having a source and terminus, banks, and channel, through which waters flow at least periodically, and it usually empties into other streams, lakes, or the ocean, but it does not lose its character as a water course even though it may break up and disappear. Mogle v. Moore, 16 Cal.2d 1, 104 P.2d 785, 789; Everett v. Davis, Cal.App., 107 P.2d 650, 655; Southern Pac. Co. v. Proebstel, 61 Ariz. 412, 150 P.2d 81, 83. A river, brook, or rivulet; anything in fact that is liquid and flows in a line or course. French v. Carhart, 1 N.Y. (1 Comst.) 96, 107. A current of water. A body of water having a continuous flow in one direction. Vandalia R. Co. v. Yeager, 60 Ind.App. 118, 110 N.E. 230, 232. It consists of a bed, banks, and water course. St. Paul Fire & Marine Ins. Co. v. Carroll, Tex.Civ.App., 106 S.W. 2d 757, 758.

Private Stream

A non-navigable creek or water-course, the bed or channel of which is exclusively owned by a private individual. See Adams v. Pease, 2 Conn. 484; Reynolds v. Com, 93 Pa. 461.

STREAMING FOR TIN. The process of working tin in Cornwall and Devon. The right to stream must not be exercised so as to interfere with the rights of other private individuals; *e. g.*, either by withdrawing or by polluting or choking up the water-courses or waters of others; and the statutes 23 Hen. VIII. c. 8, and 27 Hen. VIII. c. 23, impose a penalty of £20 for the offense. Brown.

STREET. An urban way or thoroughfare; a road or public way in a city, town, or village, generally paved, and lined or intended to be lined by houses on each side. U. S. v. Bain, 24 Fed.Cas. 943; Brace v. New York Cent. R. Co., 27 N.Y. 271; Home Laundry Co. v. City of Louisville, 168 Ky. 499, 182 S.W. 645, 648; Chicago, R. I. & P. Ry. Co. v. Redding, 124 Ark. 368, 187 S.W. 651, 652, Ann.Cas.1918D, 183. It includes all urban ways which can be and are generally used for travel. Department of Public Works and Buildings v. Ryan, 357 Ill. 150, 191 N.E. 259, 262. Including sidewalks. Snow v. Johnston, 197 Ga. 146, 28 S.E.2d 270, 276. But does not mean square. Weber v. Chrisamalis, 177 Misc. 772, 30 N.Y.S.2d 874, 875, and normally does not include service entrances or driveways leading off from the street onto adjoining premises. Hill & Combs v. First Nat. Bank of San Angelo, Tex., C.C.A.Tex., 139 F.2d 740, 743.

STREET RAILWAY. See Railway.

STREIGHTEN. In the old books. To narrow or restrict. "The *habendum* should not *streighten* the devise." 1 Leon. 58.

STREPITUS. In old records. Estrepement or strip; a species of waste or destruction of property. Spelman.

STREPITUS JUDICIALIS. Turbulent conduct in a court of justice. Jacob.

STRIA. Curved, crooked and intermitten gouges, of irregular depth and width and rough definition, of certain rock surface, sometimes due to abrasions by icebergs. Imperial Machine & Foundry Corp. v. G. S. Blakeslee & Co., C.C.A.N.Y., 262 F. 419, 421. A furrow, channel or hollow; depression, rut, wrinkle, concave, cup, pocket, dimple. Maxim Mfg. Co. v. Imperial Mach. Co., C.C.A.Ill., 286 F. 79, 83.

STRICT. Exact; accurate; precise; undivating; governed or governing by exact rules.

As to strict "Construction," "Foreclosure," and "Settlement," see those titles.

STRICT LIABILITY. Liability without fault. Case is one of "strict liability" when neither care nor negligence, neither good nor bad faith, neither knowledge nor ignorance will save defendant. Fresno Air Service v. Wood, 43 Cal.Rptr. 276, 279, 232 C.A.2d 801; Anslem v. Travelers Ins. Co., La. App., 192 So.2d 599, 600.

STRICTI JURIS. Lat. Of strict right or law; according to strict law. "A license is a thing *stricti juris;* a privilege which a man does not possess by his own right, but it is conceded to him as an indulgence, and therefore it is to be strictly observed." 2 Rob.Adm. 117.

STRICTISSIMI JURIS. Lat. Of the strictest right or law. "Licenses being matter of special indulgence, the application of them was formerly *strictissimi juris.*" 1 Edw.Adm. 328.

STRICTLY. A strict manner; closely, precisely, rigorously; stringently; positively. Union Ice & Coal Co. v. Town of Ruston, 135 La. 898, 66 So. 262, 263, L.R.A.1915B, 859.

STRICTLY CONSTRUED. Requirement that a penal statute be strictly construed means that the court will not extend punishment to cases not plainly within the language used, but at the same time such statutes are to be fairly and reasonably construed, and will not be given such a narrow and strained construction as to exclude from their operation cases plainly within their scope and meaning. State v. Fleming, 173 Md. 192, 195 A. 392, 393.

STRICTLY MINISTERIAL DUTY. One that is absolute and imperative, requiring neither the exercise of official discretion nor judgment. State ex rel. Heller v. Thornhill, 174 Mo.App. 469, 160 S.W. 558, 559.

STRICTO JURE. Lat. In strict law. 1 Kent, Comm. 65.

STRICTUM JUS. Lat. Strict right or law; the rigor of the law as distinguished from equity.

STRIKE. The act of quitting work by a body of workmen for the purpose of coercing their employer to accede to some demand they have made upon him, and which he has refused. Jeffery-De Witt Insulator Co. v. N. L. R. B., C.C.A.4, 91 F.2d 134, 138. A combination to obtain higher wages, shorter hours of employment, better working conditions or some other concession from employer by the employees stopping work at a preconcerted time, and it involves a combination of persons and not a single individual. Moreland Theatres Corp. v. Portland Moving Picture Mach. Operators' Protective Union, 140 Or. 35, 12 P.2d 333, 338. A cessation of work as a means of enforcing compliance with some demand upon the employer. People v. Tepel, Mag.Ct., 3 N.Y.S.2d 779, 781. A combined effort among workmen to compel the master to the concession of a certain demand, by preventing the conduct of his business until compliance with the demand. Keith Theatre v. Vachon. 134 Me. 392, 187 A. 692, 694.

Mining Law

The strike of a vein or lode is its extension in the horizontal plane, or its lengthwise trend or course with reference to the points of the compass; distinguished from its "dip," which is its slope or slant, away from the perpendicular, as it goes downward into the earth, or the angle of its deviation from the vertical plane. Empire Star Mines Co. v. Butler, 62 Cal.App.2d 49, 145 P.2d 49, 58.

STRIKE OFF. In common parlance, and in the language of the auction-room, property is understood to be "struck off" or "knocked down," when the auctioneer, by the fall of his hammer, or by any other audible or visible announcement, signifies to the bidder that he is entitled to the property on paying the amount of his bid, according to the terms of the sale. Sherwood v. Reade, 7 Hill, N. Y., 439.

A court is said to "strike off" a case when it directs the removal of the case from the record or docket, as being one over which it has no jurisdiction and no power to hear and determine it.

STRIKE SUITS. Shareholder derivative actions begun with hope of winning large attorney fees or private settlements, and with no intention of benefiting corporation on behalf of which suit it theoretically brought. Shapiro v. Magaziner, 210 A.2d 890, 894, 418 Pa. 278.

STRIKEBREAKER. One who takes the place of workman who has left his work in an effort to force the employer to agree to demands made. People, on Complaint of Siegel, v. Kaye, 165 Misc. 663, 1 N.Y.S.2d 354, 355.

STRIKING A DOCKET. In English practice. The first step in the proceedings in bankruptcy, which consists in making affidavit of the debt, and giving a bond to follow up the proceedings with effect. 2 Steph. Comm. 199. When the affidavit and bond are delivered at the bankrupt office, an entry is made in what is called the "docket-book," upon which the petitioning creditor is said to have *struck a docket*. Eden, Bankr. 51, 52.

STRIKING A JURY. The selecting or nominating a jury of twelve men out of the whole number returned as jurors on the panel. It is especially used of the selection of a *special* jury, where a panel of forty-eight is prepared by the proper officer, and the parties, in turn, strike off a certain number of names, until the list is reduced to twelve. A jury thus chosen is called a "struck jury." Wallace v. Railroad Co., 8 Houst., Del., 529, 18 A. 818; Cook v. State, 24 N.J.L. 843.

STRIKING OFF THE ROLL. The disbarring of an attorney or solicitor.

STRIP. The act of spoiling or unlawfully taking away anything from the land, by the tenant for life or years, or by one holding an estate in the land less than the entire fee. Pub.St.Mass.1882, p. 1295.

STRIPPING A MINE. In iron mining. Removal of the earth from the underlying body of iron ore. Bartnes v. Pittsburg Iron Ore Co., 123 Minn. 131, 143 N.W. 117.

STRONG. Cogent, powerful, forcible. Wright v. Austin, Tex.Civ.App., 175 S.W.2d 281, 283.

STRONG HAND. The words "with strong hand" imply a degree of criminal force, whereas the words *vi et armis* ("with force and arms") are mere formal words in the action of trespass, and the plaintiff is not bound to prove any force. The statutes relating to forcible entries use the words "with a strong hand" as describing that degree of force which makes an entry or detainer of lands criminal. Brown.

STRONGLY CORROBORATED. A degree of corroboration amounting to corroboration from independent facts and circumstances which is clear and satisfactory to the court and jury. Wright v. Austin, Tex.Civ.App., 175 S.W.2d 281, 283.

STRUCK. In pleading. A word essential in an indictment for murder, when the death arises from any wounding, beating, or bruising. 1 Bulst. 184; 5 Coke, 122; 3 Mod. 202.

STRUCK JURY. See Striking a Jury.

STRUCTURAL ALTERATION OR CHANGE. One that affects a vital and substantial portion of a thing; that changes its characteristic appearance, the fundamental purpose of its erection, the uses contemplated, one that is extraordinary in scope and effect, or unusual in expenditure. Pross v. Excelsior Cleaning & Dyeing Co., 110 Misc. 195, 179 N.Y.S. 176, 179; Paye v. City of Grosse Pointe, 279 Mich. 254, 271 N.W. 826, 827.

STRUCTURE. Any construction, or any production or piece of work artificially built up or composed of parts joined together in some definite manner. C. K. Eddy & Sons v. Tierney, 276 Mich. 333, 267 N.W. 852, 855. That which is built or constructed; an edifice or building of any kind. Poles connected by wires for the transmission of electricity. Forbes v. Electric Co., 19 Or. 61, 23 P. 670, 20 Am.St.Rep. 793; a mine or pit, Helm v. Chapman, 66 Cal. 291, 5 P. 352; a railroad track, Lee v. Barkhampsted, 46 Conn. 213. Swings or seats are not, McCormack v. Bertschinger, 115 Or. 250, 237 P. 363, 365; Barnes v. Montana Lumber & Hardware Co., 67 Mont. 481, 216 P. 335, 336; Deiner v. Sutermeister, 266 Mo. 505, 178 S.W. 757, 759; Armitage v. Bernheim, 32 Idaho, 594, 187 P. 938, 939.

STRUMPET. A whore, harlot, or courtesan. This word was anciently used for an addition. It occurs as an addition to the name of a woman in a return made by a jury in the sixth year of Henry V. Wharton.

STUFF GOWN. The professional robe worn by barristers of the outer bar; viz., those who have not been admitted to the rank of king's counsel. Brown.

STULTIFY. To make one out mentally incapacitated for the performance of an act.

STULTILOQUIUM. Lat. In old English law. Vicious pleading, for which a fine was imposed by King John, supposed to be the origin of the fines for *beau-pleader*. Crabb, Eng. Law, 135.

STUMP. As respects coal mining operations is the base or remains of a worked-out pillar left after previous mining operations to support the surface. McCormack v. Jermyn, 351 Pa. 161, 40 A. 2d 477, 478.

STUMPAGE. The sum agreed to be paid to an owner of land for trees standing (or lying) upon his land, the purchaser being permitted to enter upon the land and to cut down and remove the trees; in other words, it is the price paid for a license to cut. Blood v. Drummond, 67 Me. 478.

STUPRUM. Lat. In the Roman and civil law. Unlawful sexual intercourse between a man and an unmarried woman;—distinguished from adultery by being committed with a virgin or widow. Inst. 4, 18, 4; Dig. 48, 5, 6; 50, 16, 101.

Any sexual intercourse between a man and an unmarried woman (not a slave), otherwise than in concubinage; illicit intercourse. Webster.

Any union of the sexes forbidden by morality. Cent. Dict.

STURGEON. A royal fish which, when either thrown ashore or caught near the coast, is the property of the sovereign. 2 Steph.Comm. 19*n*, 540.

STYLE. As a verb, to call, name, or entitle one; as a noun, the title or appellation of a person.

SUA SPONTE. Lat. Of his or its own will or motion; voluntarily; without prompting or suggestion.

SUABLE. Capable of being, or liable to be, sued. A suable cause of action is the matured cause of action.

SUAPTE NATURA. Lat. In its own nature. *Suapte natura sterilis,* barren in its own nature and quality; intrinsically barren. 5 Maule & S. 170.

SUB. Lat. Under; upon.

SUB COLORE JURIS. Under color of right; under a show or appearance of right or rightful power.

SUB CONDITIONE. Upon condition. The proper words to express a condition in a conveyance, and to create an estate upon condition. Graves v. Deterling, 120 N.Y. 447, 24 N.E. 655.

SUB CURIA. Lat. Under law.

SUB DISJUNCTIONE. In the alternative. Fleta, lib. 2, c. 60, § 21.

SUB JUDICE. Under or before a judge or court; under judicial consideration; undetermined. 12 East, 409.

SUB MODO. Under a qualification; subject to a restriction or condition.

SUB NOMINE. Under the name; in the name of; under the title of.

SUB PEDE SIGILLI. Under the foot of the seal; under seal. 1 Strange, 521.

SUB POTESTATE. Under, or subject to, the power of another; used of a wife, child, slave, or other person not *sui juris.*

SUB SALVO ET SECURO CONDUCTU. Under safe and secure conduct. 1 Strange, 430. Words in the old writ of *habeas corpus.*

SUB SILENTIO. Under silence; without any notice being taken. Passing a thing *sub silentio* may be evidence of consent.

SUB SPE RECONCILIATIONIS. Under the hope of reconcilement. 2 Kent, Comm. 127.

SUB SUO PERICULO. At his own risk. Fleta, lib, 2, c. 5, § 5.

SUBAGENT. An under-agent; a substituted agent; an agent appointed by one who is himself an agent. 2 Kent, Comm. 633. A person appointed by an agent to perform some duty, or the whole of the business, relating to his agency. A person employed by an agent to assist him in transacting the affairs of his principal. But a mere servant of an agent is not a "subagent." Gulf Refining Co. v. Shirley, Tex.Civ.App., 99 S.W.2d 613, 615.

SUBALTERN. An inferior or subordinate officer. An officer who exercises his authority under the superintendence and control of a superior.

SUB-BALLIVUS. In old English law. An under-bailiff; a sheriff's deputy. Fleta, lib. 2, c. 68, § 2.

SUB-BOIS. Coppice-wood. 2 Inst. 642.

SUBCONTRACT. See Contract.

SUBCONTRACTOR. One who takes portion of a contract from principal contractor or another subcontractor. Hardware Mut. Casualty Co. v. Hilderbrandt, C.C.A.Okl., 119 F.2d 291, 297, 299. One who has entered into a contract, express or implied, for the performance of an act with the person who has already contracted for its performance. Phill. Mech. Liens § 44; Lester v. Houston, 101 N.C. 611, 8 S.E. 366; Gerber v. Sherman, 120 N.J.L. 237, 198 A. 762, 764.

SUBDITUS. Lat. In old English law. A vassal; a dependent; any one under the power of another. Spelman.

SUBDIVIDE. To divide a part into smaller parts; to separate into smaller divisions. As, where an estate is to be taken by some of the heirs *per stirpes,* it is divided and subdivided according to the number of takers in the nearest degree and those in the more remote degree respectively.

SUBDIVISION. Division into smaller parts of the same thing or subject-matter. Kansas City v. Neal, 122 Mo. 232, 26 S.W. 695, 696.

SUBDUCT. In English probate practice, to subduct a *caveat* is to withdraw it.

SUBFLOW. Those waters which slowly find their way through sand and gravel constituting bed of a stream, or lands under or immediately adjacent to stream. Maricopa County Municipal Water Conservation Dist. No. 1 v. Southwest Cotton Co., 39 Ariz. 65, 4 P.2d 369, 380.

SUBHASTARE. Lat. In the civil law. To sell at public auction, which was done *sub hasta,* under a spear; to put or sell under the spear. Calvin.

SUBHASTATIO. Lat. In the civil law. A sale by public auction, which was done *under a spear,* fixed up at the place of sale as a public sign of it. Calvin.

SUBINFEUDATION. The system which the feudal tenants introduced of granting smaller estates out of those which they held of their lord, to be held of themselves as inferior lords. As this system was proceeding downward *ad infinitum,* and depriving the lords of their feudal profits, it was entirely suppressed by the statute *Quia Emptores,* 18 Edw. I. c. 1., and instead of it alienation in the modern sense was introduced, so that thenceforth the alienee held of the same chief lord and by the same services that his alienor before him held. Brown.

SUBIRRIGATE. To irrigate below the surface, as by a system of underground porous pipes, or by natural percolation through the soil. Morrow v. Farmers' Irr. Dist., 117 Neb. 424, 220 N.W. 680, 682.

SUBJACENT SUPPORT. The right of land to be supported by the land which lies under it. See, also, Support.

SUBJECT.

Constitutional Law

One that owes allegiance to a sovereign and is governed by his laws. The natives of Great Britain are *subjects* of the British government. Men in free governments are subjects as well as *citizens*; as citizens they enjoy rights and franchises; as subjects they are bound to obey the laws. Webster. The term is little used, in this sense, in countries enjoying a republican form of government. The Pizarro, 2 Wheat. 245, 4 L.Ed. 226; Swiss Nat. Ins. Co. v. Miller, 267 U.S. 42, 45 S.Ct. 213, 214, 69 L.Ed. 504.

Legislation

The matter of public or private concern for which law is enacted. State ex rel. Jensen v. Kelly, 65 S.D. 345, 274 N.W. 319, 323. Thing legislated about or matters on which Legislature operates to accomplish a definite object or objects reasonably related one to the other. Crouch v. Benet, 198 S.C. 185, 17 S.E.2d 320, 322. The matter or thing forming the groundwork of the act. McCombs v. Dallas County, Tex.Civ.App., 136 S.W.2d 975, 982.

The constitutions of several of the states require that every act of the legislature shall relate to but one *subject*, which shall be expressed in the title of the statute. Ex parte Thomas, 113 Ala. 1, 21 So. 369; In re Mayer, 50 N.Y. 504; State v. County Treasurer, 4 S.C. 528; State v. Laundy, 103 Or. 443, 204 P. 958, 963; Roark v. Prideaux, Tex. Civ.App., 284 S.W. 624, 627; Hoyne v. Ling, 264 Ill. 506, 106 N.E. 349. But term "subject" within such constitutional provisions is to be given a broad and extensive meaning so as to allow legislature full scope to include in one act all matters having a logical or natural connection. Shaw v. State, 76 Okl.Cr. 271, 134 P.2d 999, 1006; Jaffee v. State, 76 Okl.Cr. 95, 134 P.2d 1027, 1032.

Logic

That concerning which the affirmation in a proposition is made; the first word in a proposition. State v. Armstrong, 31 N.M. 220, 243 P. 333, 337.

Scotch Law

The thing which is the object of an agreement.

SUBJECT-MATTER. The subject, or matter presented for consideration; the thing in dispute; the right which one party claims as against the other, as the right to divorce; of ejectment; to recover money; to have foreclosure. Flower Hospital v. Hart, 178 Okl. 447, 62 P.2d 1248, 1252. Nature of cause of action, and of relief sought. Moffatt v. Cassimus, 238 Ala. 99, 190 So. 299, 300.

SUBJECT TO. Liable, subordinate, subservient, inferior, obedient to; governed or affected by; provided that; provided; answerable for. American Mfg. Co. v. Commonwealth, 251 Mass. 329, 146 N.E. 801; Hannibal Trust Co. v. Elzea, 315 Mo. 485, 286 S.W. 371, 377; Allen v. Simmons, 97 W. Va. 318, 125 S.E. 86, 88; Middleton v. Findla, 25 Cal. 76; Manning v. Sams, 143 Ga. 205, 84 S.E. 451; Homan v. Employers Reinsurance Corporation, 345 Mo. 650, 136 S.W.2d 289, 302, 127 A.L.R. 163.

SUBJECTION. The obligation of one or more persons to act at the discretion or according to the judgment and will of others.

SUBLATA CAUSA TOLLITUR EFFECTUS. Co. Litt. 303. The cause being removed the effect ceases.

SUBLATA VENERATIONE MAGISTRATUUM, RES PUBLICA RUIT. When respect for magistrates is taken away, the commonwealth falls. Jenk. Cent. p. 43, case 81.

SUBLATO FUNDAMENTO CADIT OPUS. Jenk. Cent. 106. The foundation being removed, the superstructure falls.

SUBLATO PRINCIPALI, TOLLITUR ADJUNCTUM. When the principal is taken away, the incident is taken also. Co. Litt. 389*a*.

SUBLEASE. See Lease.

SUBLETTING. A leasing by lessee of a whole or part of premises during a portion of unexpired balance of his term. O'Neil v. A. F. Oys & Sons, 216 Minn. 391, 13 N.W.2d 8, 11. See, also, Sublease.

SUBMARINE BASE. See Base.

SUBMERGENCE. As it concerns the proprietorship of land, consists in the disappearance of land under water and the formation of a more or less navigable body over it. Michelsen v. Leskowicz, 269 App.Div. 693, 55 N.Y.S.2d 831, 838.

SUBMISSION. A yielding to authority. A citizen is bound to submit to the laws; a child to his parents.

Maritime Law

Submission on the part of the vanquished, and complete possession on the part of the victor, transfer property as between belligerents. The Alexander, 1 Gall. 532, Fed.Cas.No.164.

Practice

A contract between two or more parties whereby they agree to refer the subject in dispute to others and to be bound by their award. District of Columbia v. Bailey, 171 U.S. 161, 18 S.Ct. 868, 872, 43 L.Ed. 118. Schoolnick v. Finman, 108 Conn. 478, 144 A. 41, 42.

The submission itself implies an agreement to abide the result, even if no such agreement were expressed. Whitcher v. Whitcher, 49 N.H. 176, 180, 6 Am.Rep. 486.

SUBMISSION BOND. The bond by which the parties agree to submit their matters to arbitration, and by which they bind themselves to abide by the award of the arbitrator. Brown.

SUBMIT. To commit to the discretion of another. Board of Education of Cherokee County v. Board of Com'rs of Cherokee County, 150 N.C. 116, 63 S.E. 724, 729. To propound; to present for determination; as an advocate *submits* a proposition for the approval of the court. MacDermot v. Grant, 181 Cal. 332, 184 P. 396; Noland v. Hayward, 69 Colo. 181, 192 P. 657, 658; People ex rel. Kerner v. Huls, 355 Ill. 412, 189 N.E. 346, 348.

SUBMORTGAGE. When a person who holds a mortgage as security for a loan which he has made, procures a loan to himself from a third person, and pledges his mortgage as security, he effects what is called a "submortgage."

SUBNERVARE. To ham-string by cutting the sinews of the legs and thighs.

It was an old custom *meretrices et impudicas mulieres subnervare.* Wharton.

SUBNOTATIONS. In the civil law. The answers of the prince to questions which had been put to him respecting some obscure or doubtful point of law.

SUBORDINATE. Placed in a lower order, class, or rank; occupying a lower position in a regular descending series; inferior in order, nature, dignity, power, importance, or the like; belonging to an inferior order in classification, and having a lower position in a recognized scale; secondary, minor. In re Fidelity Union Title & Mortgage Guaranty Co., 118 N.J.Eq. 155, 177 A. 449, 452.

SUBORDINATE OFFICER. One who performs duties imposed on him under direction of a principal or superior officer or he may be an independent officer subject only to such directions as the statute lays on him. State ex rel. Landis v. Blake, 110 Fla. 178, 148 So. 566, 570.

SUBORN. To prepare. provide, or procure especially in a secret or underhand manner. United States v. Silverman, C.C.A.Pa., 106 F.2d 750, 751.

In criminal law. To procure another to commit perjury. Steph.Crim.Law, 74.

SUBORNATION OF PERJURY. In criminal law. The offense of procuring another to take such a false oath as would constitute perjury in the principal. Stone v. State, 118 Ga. 705, 45 S.E. 630, 98 Am.St.Rep. 145; State v. Fahey, 3 Pennewill, Del., 594, 54 A. 690; State v. Richardson, 248 Mo. 563, 154 S.W. 735, 737, 44 L.R.A.,N.S., 307.

SUBORNER. One who suborns or procures another to commit any crime, particularly to commit perjury.

SUBPOENA. (Lat. Sub, under, poena, penalty). A process to cause a witness to appear and give testimony, commanding him to lay aside all pretenses and excuses, and appear before a court or magistrate therein named at a time therein mentioned to testify for the party named under a penalty therein mentioned. Alexander v. Harrison, 2 Ind.App. 47, 28 N.E. 119, 121.

This is called distinctively a subpœna ad testificandum.

Chancery Practice

A mandatory writ or process directed to and requiring one or more persons to appear at a time to come and answer the matters charged against him or them. Gondas v. Gondas, 99 N.J.Eq. 473, 134 A. 615, 618.

The writ of subpœna was originally proceeding in courts of common law to enforce attendance of witness, but was used in chancery for same purpose as citation in courts of civil and canon law, to compel appearance of defendant and to require him to answer plaintiff's allegations on oath. Gondas v. Gondas, 99 N.J.Eq. 473, 134 A. 615, 618.

SUBPŒNA AD TESTIFICANDUM. Lat. Subpœna to testify. A technical and descriptive term for the ordinary subpœna. Catty v. Brockelbank, 124 N.J.Law 360, 12 A.2d 128, 129. See Subpœna.

SUBPŒNA DUCES TECUM. A process by which the court, at the instances of a suitor, commands a witness who has in his possession or control some document or paper that is pertinent to the issues of a pending controversy, to produce it at the trial. State ex rel. Everglades Cypress Co. v. Smith, 104 Fla. 91, 139 So. 794; Ex parte Hart, 240 Ala. 642, 200 So. 783, 785.

SUBREPTIO. Lat. In the civil law. Obtaining gifts of escheat, etc., from the king by concealing the truth. Bell; Calvin.

SUBREPTION. In French law. The fraud committed to obtain a pardon, title, or grant, by alleging facts contrary to truth.

SUBROGATION. The substitution of one person in the place of another with reference to a lawful claim, demand or right, Whyel v. Smith, 101 Fla. 971, 134 So. 552, 554; so that he who is substituted succeeds to the rights of the other in relation to the debt or claim, and its rights, remedies, or securities. Home Owners' Loan Corporation v. Baker, 299 Mass. 158, 12 N.E.2d 199, 201; Gerken v. Davidson Grocery Co., 57 Idaho 670, 69 P.2d 122, 126. A legal fiction through which a person who, not as a volunteer or in his own wrong, and in absence of outstanding and superior equities, pays debt of another, is substituted to all rights and remedies of the other, and the debt is treated in equity as still existing for his benefit, and the doctrine is broad enough to include every instance in which one party pays the debt for which another is primarily answerable, and which in equity and good conscience should have been discharged by such other. Home Owners' Loan Corporation v. Sears, Roebuck & Co., 123 Conn. 232, 193 A. 769, 772. The principle which lies at the bottom of the doctrine is that the person seeking it must have paid the debt under grave necessity to save himself a loss. The right is never accorded to a volunteer. Callan Court Co. v. Citizens & Southern Nat. Bank, 184 Ga. 87, 190 S.E. 831, 856.

"Subrogation" is equitable remedy borrowed from civil law. Ierardi v. Farmers' Trust Co. of Newark, 4 W.W. Harr. Del., 246, 151 A. 822, 825. And as a matter of right, independently of agreement, takes place only for the benefit of insurers; or of one who, being himself a creditor, has satisfied the lien of a prior creditor; or for the benefit of a purchaser who has extinguished an incumbrance upon the estate which he has purchased; or of a co-obligor or surety who has paid the debt which ought, in whole or in part, to have been met by another. The doctrine of "subrogation" is not applied for the mere stranger or volunteer who has paid the debt of another without any assignment or agreement for subrogation, without being under any legal obligation to make the payment, and without being compelled to do so for the preservation of any rights or property of his own. Harford Bank of Bel Air v. Hopper's Estate, 169 Md. 314, 181 A. 751, 755.

It is also said that its elements are: (1) That party claiming it shall have paid debt; (2) that he was not a volunteer, but had a direct interest in discharge of debt or lien; (3) that he was secondarily liable for debt or discharge of lien; (4) that no injustice would be done to the other party by allowance of the equity. Hampton Loan & Exchange Bank v. Lightsey, 155 S.C. 222, 152 S.E. 425, 427.

Subrogation is of two kinds, either *conventional* or *legal;* the former being where the subrogation is express, by the acts of the creditor and the third person; the latter being (as in the case of sureties) where the subrogation is effected or implied by the operation of the law. Gordon v. Stewart, 4 Neb., Unof., 852, 96 N.W. 628; Connecticut Mut. L. Ins. Co. v. Cornwell, 72 Hun, 199, 25 N.Y.S. 348; French v. Grand Beach Co., 239 Mich. 575, 215 N.W. 13, 14; Meyer v. Florida Home Finders, 90 Fla. 128, 105 So. 267, 268; Combs v. Agee, 148 Va. 471, 139 S.E. 265, 266.

SUBROGEE. A person who is subrogated; one who succeeds to the rights of another by subrogation.

SUBSCRIBE. Literally to write underneath, as one's name; sub, under; scribere, to write; or, to write below a documentary statement, and in its popular meaning is usually limited to a signature at the end of a printed or written instrument. Corporation Commission of North Carolina v. Wilkinson, 201 N.C. 344, 160 S.E. 292, 294. In re Arcowsky's Will, 171 Misc. 41, 11 N.Y.S.2d 853, 854. Also to agree in writing to furnish money or its equivalent. Jefferson County Farm Bureau v. Sherman, 208 Iowa 614, 226 N.W. 182, 185.

SUBSCRIBER. One who writes his name under a written instrument; one who affixes his signature to any document, whether for the purpose of authenticating or attesting it, of adopting its terms as his own expressions, or of binding himself by an engagement which it contains.

One who becomes bound by a subscription to the capital stock of a corporation. Latimer v. Bennett, 37 Ga.App. 246, 139 S.E. 570, 572. A "subscriber" is one who has agreed to take stock from the corporation on the original issue of such stock. Jones v. Rankin, 19 N.M. 56, 140 P. 1120, 1121. "Subscriber," as used in the Workmen's Compensation Act, means an employer who has become a member of the association or insured under the act. In re Cox, 225 Mass. 220, 114 N.E. 281, 283.

SUBSCRIBING WITNESS. He who witnesses or attests the signature of a party to an instrument, and in testimony thereof subscribes his own name to the document.

One who sees a writing executed, or hears it acknowledged, and at the request of the party thereupon signs his name as a witness.

SUBSCRIPTIO. Lat. In the civil law. A writing under, or under-writing; a writing of the name under or at the bottom of an instrument by way of attestation or ratification; subscription.

That kind of imperial constitution which was granted in answer to the prayer of a petitioner who was present. Calvin.

SUBSCRIPTION. The act of writing one's name under a written instrument; the affixing one's signature to any document, whether for the purpose of authenticating or attesting it, of adopting its terms as one's own expressions, or of binding one's self by an engagement which it contains.

Subscription is the act of the hand, while attestation is the act of the senses. To subscribe a paper published as a will is only to write on the same paper the name of the witness; to attest a will is to know that it was published as such, and to certify the facts required to constitute an actual and legal publication. In re Downie's Will, 42 Wis. 66, 76.

A written contract by which one engages to take and pay for capital stock of a corporation, or to contribute a sum of money for a designated purpose, either gratuitously, as in the case of subscribing to a charity, or in consideration of an equivalent to be rendered, as a subscription to a periodical, a forthcoming book, a series of entertainments, or the like. Davis v. Rolley, 124 Kan. 132, 257 P. 746, 747; First Caldwell Oil Co. v. Hunt, 100 N.J.L. 308, 127 A. 209, 210.

SUBSCRIPTION LIST. A list of subscribers to some agreement with each other or a third person.

SUBSELLIA. Lat. In Roman law. Lower seats or benches, occupied by the *judices* and by inferior magistrates when they sat in judgment, as distinguished from the *tribunal* of the prætor. Calvin.

SUBSEQUENS MATRIMONIUM TOLLIT PECCATUM PRÆCEDENS. A subsequent marriage [of the parties] removes a previous fault, *i. e.,* previous illicit intercourse, and legitimates the offspring. A rule of Roman law.

SUBSEQUENT. Following in time; coming or being later than something else; succeeding. Commonwealth v. Ellett, 174 Va. 403, 4 S.E.2d 762, 765.

SUBSEQUENT CONDITION. See Condition.

SUBSEQUENT CREDITOR. One who becomes a creditor after a transfer sought to be impeached as fraudulent is made. Edwards v. Monning, 63 Ohio App. 449, 27 N.E.2d 156, 158.

SUBSIDIARY CORPORATION. One in which another corporation owns at least a majority of the shares, and thus has control. Wheeler v. New York, N. H. & H. R. Co., 112 Conn. 510, 153 A. 159, 160.

See, also, Corporation.

SUBSIDY. Something, usually money, donated or given or appropriated by the government through its proper agencies, in this country by the Congress. Kennecott Copper Corp. v. State Tax Commission, D.C.Utah, 60 F.Supp. 181, 182.

In American law. A grant of money made by government in aid of the promoters of any enterprise, work, or improvement in which the government desires to participate, or which is considered a proper subject for state aid, because likely to be of benefit to the public.

In English law. An aid, tax, or tribute granted by parliament to the king for the urgent occasions of the kingdom, to be levied on every subject of ability, according to the value of his lands or goods. Jacob.

In international law. The assistance given in money by one nation to another to enable it the better to carry on a war, when such nation does not join directly in the war. Vattel, bk. 3, § 82.

SUBSISTENCE. Support. Majors v. Lewis and Clark County, 60 Mont. 698, 201 P. 268, 269. Means of support, provisions, or that which procures provisions or livelihood. Dyer v. Dyer, 212 N.C. 620, 194 S.E. 278.

SUBSOIL. The word includes, *prima facie,* all that is below the actual surface, down to the center of the earth. 17 L.J.C.P. 162. It is a wider term than mines, quarries, or minerals. 2 L.R. Ir. 339.

SUBSTANCE. Essence; the material or essential part of a thing, as distinguished from "form." State v. Burgdoerfer, 107 Mo. 1, 17 S.W. 646, 14 L.R.A. 846; Pierson v. Insurance Co., 7 Houst., Del., 307, 31 A. 966; Metzroth v. City of New York, 241 N.Y. 470, 150 N.E. 519, 520; State v. Gregory, 198 Iowa 316, 198 N.W. 58, 60. That which is essential. Rose v. Osborne, 136 Me. 15, 1 A.2d 225, 226.

It means not merely subject of act, but an intelligible abstract or synopsis of its material and substantial elements, though the "substance" may be stated without recital of any details. State, on Inf. of Murphy, v. Brooks, 241 Ala. 55, 1 So.2d 370, 371.

SUBSTANTIAL. Of real worth and importance; of considerable value; valuable. Tax Commission of Ohio v. American Humane Education Soc., 42 Ohio App. 4, 181 N.E. 557. Belonging to substance; actually existing; real; not seeming or imaginary; not illusive; solid; true; veritable. Seglem v. Skelly Oil Co., 145 Kan. 216, 65 P.2d 553, 554. Something worth while as distinguished from something without value or merely nominal. In re Krause's Estate, 173 Wash. 1, 21 P.2d 268. Synonymous with material. Lewandoski v. Finkel, 129 Conn. 526, 29 A.2d 762, 764.

A claim to bankrupt's property is "substantial" so as to preclude summary proceeding if there are probable facts or circumstances sufficient to support a reasonable legal hypothesis upon which it should be allowed. Atlanta Flooring & Insulation Co. v. Russell, C.C.A.Ga., 146 F.2d 884, 886, 888.

SUBSTANTIAL COMPLIANCE RULE. In like insurance law is that where insured has done substantially all he is required to do under policy to effect change in beneficiary and mere ministerial acts of insurer's officers and agents only remain to be done, change will take effect. Inter-Southern Life Ins. Co. v. Cochran, 259 Ky. 677, 83 S.W. 2d 11, 14.

SUBSTANTIAL DAMAGES. See Damages.

SUBSTANTIAL EQUIVALENT OF PATENTED DEVICE. Same as thing itself, so that if two devices do same work in substantially same way, and accomplish substantially same results, they are equivalent, even though differing in name, form, or shape. Bedell v. Dictograph Products Co., 251 App.Div. 243, 296 N.Y.S. 25, 32; Freeman v. Altvater, C.C.A.Mo., 66 F.2d 506, 511.

SUBSTANTIAL JUSTICE. Justice administered according to the rules of substantive law, notwithstanding errors of procedure. Interstate Bankers Corporation v. Kennedy, D.C.Mun.App., 33 A.2d 165, 166.

SUBSTANTIAL PERFORMANCE. Exists where there has been no willful departure from the terms of the contract, and no omission in essential points, and the contract has been honestly and faithfully performed in its material and substantial particulars, and the only variance from the strict and literal performance consists of technical or unimportant omissions or defects. Cotherman v. Oriental Oil Co., Tex.Civ.App., 272 S.W. 616, 619; Brown v. Aguilar, 202 Cal. 143, 259 P. 735, 737; Cramer v. Esswein, 220 App.Div. 10, 220 N.Y.S. 634; Connell v. Higgins, 170 Cal. 541, 150 P. 769, 774. Performance except as to unsubstantial omissions with compensation therefor. Cassino v. Yacevich, 261 App.Div. 685, 27 N.Y.S. 2d 95, 97, 99.

Equitable doctrine of "substantial performance", protects against forfeiture, for technical inadvertence or trivial variations or omissions in performance. Sgarlat v. Griffith, 349 Pa. 42, 36 A.2d 330, 332.

SUBSTANTIALLY. Essentially; without material qualification; in the main; in substance; materially; in a substantial manner. Kirkpatrick v. Journal Pub. Co., 210 Ala. 10, 97 So. 58, 59; Gibson v. Glos, 271 Ill. 368, 111 N.E. 123, 124; McEwen v. New York Life Ins. Co., 23 Cal.App. 694, 139 P. 242, 243. About, actually, competently, and essentially. Gilmore v. Red Top Cab Co. of Washington, 171 Wash. 346, 17 P.2d 886, 887.

SUBSTANTIATE. To establish the existence or truth of, by true or competent evidence, or to verify. State v. Lock, 302 Mo. 400, 259 S.W. 116, 120; Graves v. School Committee of Wellesley, 299 Mass. 80, 12 N.E.2d 176, 179.

SUBSTANTIVE. An essential part or constituent or relating to what is essential. Stewart-Warner Corporation v. Le Vally, D.C.Ill., 15 F.Supp. 571, 576.

SUBSTANTIVE EVIDENCE. That adduced for the purpose of proving a fact in issue, as opposed to evidence given for the purpose of discrediting a witness, (*i. e.*, showing that he is unworthy of belief,) or of corroborating his testimony. Best, Ev. 246, 773, 803.

SUBSTANTIVE FELONY. An independent felony; one not dependent upon the conviction of another person for another crime. Karakutza v. State, 163 Wis. 293, 156 N.W. 965, 966; Johnson v. State, 68 Fla. 528, 67 So. 100, 103.

SUBSTANTIVE LAW. That part of law which creates, defines, and regulates rights, as opposed to "adjective or remedial law," which prescribes method of enforcing the rights or obtaining redress for their invasion. Maurizi v. Western Coal & Mining Co., 321 Mo. 378, 11 S.W.2d 268, 272; Mix v. Board of Com'rs of Nez Perce County, 18 Idaho, 695, 112 P. 215, 220, 32 L.R.A.,N.S., 534.

SUBSTITUTE, *n.* One who or that which stands in the place of another; that which stands in lieu of something else. State v. Fargo Bottling Works Co., 19 N.D. 396, 124 N.W. 387, 391, 26 L.R.A.,N.S., 872. A person hired by one who has been drafted into the military service of the country, to go to the front and serve in the army in his stead.

SUBSTITUTE, *v.* To put in the place of another person or thing; to exchange. State ex rel. Woolsey v. Morgan, 138 Neb. 635, 294 N.W. 436, 438; Toledo Edison Co. v. McMaken, C.C.A.Ohio, 103 F. 2d 72, 75.

SUBSTITUTE DEFENDANT. One who takes the place of another in the same suit or controversy and not one who is sued upon an entirely different cause of action. McCann v. Bentley Stores Corporation, D.C.Mo., 34 F.Supp. 231, 233.

SUBSTITUTED EXECUTOR. One appointed to act in the place of another executor upon the happening of a certain event; *e. g.*, if the latter should refuse the office.

SUBSTITUTED SERVICE. In American law. Service of process upon a defendant in any manner, authorized by statute, other than personal service within the jurisdiction; as by publication, by mailing a copy to his last known address, or by personal service in another state. See Ruhle v. Caffrey, 115 N.J.L. 517, 180 A. 834, 835.

In English practice. Service of process made under authorization of the court upon some other person, when the person who should be served cannot be found or cannot be reached.

SUBSTITUTES. In Scotch law. The person first called or nominated in a tailzie (entailment of an estate upon a number of heirs in succession) is called the "institute" or "heir-institute;" the rest are called "substitutes."

SUBSTITUTIO HÆREDIS. Lat. In Roman law, is was competent for a testator after instituting a *hæres* (called the "*hæres institutus*") to substitute another (called the "*hæres substitutus*") in his place in a certain event. If the event upon which the substitution was to take effect was the refusal of the instituted heir to accept the inheritance at all, then the substitution was called "*vulgaris,*" (or common;) but if the event was the death of the infant (*pupillus*) after acceptance, and before attaining his majority, (of fourteen years if a male, and of twelve years if a female,) then the substitution was called "*pupillaris,*" (or for minors.) Brown.

SUBSTITUTION. Putting in place of another thing, change of one thing for another, serving in lieu of another, having some of its parts replaced. In re Cooke's Estate, 147 Misc. 528, 264 N.Y.S. 336.

In the civil law. The putting one person in place of another; particularly, the act of a testator in naming a second devisee or legatee who is to take the bequest either on failure of the original devisee or legatee or after him.

"Substitution," with respect to wills, and in view of Civ. Code, art. 1520, prohibiting substitution, is the putting of one person in the place of another so that he may, in default of ability in the former, or after him, have the benefit of the devise or legacy, particularly the act of testator in naming a second devisee or legatee who is to take the bequest on failure of the original devisee or legatee, or after him. In re Courtin, 144 La. 971, 81 So. 457, 459.

In Scotch law. The enumeration or designation of the heirs in a settlement of property. Substitutes in an entail are those heirs who are appointed in succession on failure of others.

SUBSTITUTIONAL, SUBSTITUTIONARY. Where a will contains a gift of property to a class of persons, with a clause providing that on the death of a member of the class before the period of distribution his share is to go to his issue, (if any,) so as to substitute them for him, the gift to the issue is said to be substitutional or substitutionary. A bequest to such of the children of A. as shall be living at the testator's death, with a direction that the issue of such as shall have died shall take the shares which their parents would have taken, if living at the testator's death, is an example. Sweet. Acken v. Osborn, 45 N.J.Eq. 377, 17 A. 767; In re De Laveaga's Estate, 119 Cal. 651, 51 P. 1074.

SUBSTITUTIONARY EVIDENCE. Such as is admitted as a substitute for what would be the original or primary instrument of evidence; as where a witness is permitted to testify to the contents of a lost document.

SUBSTITUTIONARY EXECUTOR. See Executor.

SUBSTRACTION. In French law. The fraudulent appropriation of any property, but particularly of the goods of a decedent's estate.

SUBTENANT. An under-tenant; one who leases all or a part of the rented premises from the original lessee for a term less than that held by the latter. Forrest v. Durnell, 86 Tex. 647, 26 S.W. 481; Peak v. Gaddy, 152 Okl. 138, 3 P.2d 1042, 1043.

SUBTERFUGE. That to which one resorts for escape or concealment. Los Angeles Fisheries v. Crook, C.C.A.Cal., 47 F.2d 1031, 1035.

SUBTERRANEAN WATERS. See Water.

SUBTRACTION. The offense of withholding or withdrawing from another man what by law he is entitled to. There are various descriptions of this offense, of which the principal are as follows: (1) Subtraction of suit and services, which is a species of injury affecting a man's real property, and consists of a withdrawal of (or a neglect to perform or pay) the fealty, suit of court, rent, or services reserved by the lessor of the land. (2) Subtraction of tithes is the withholding from the parson or vicar the tithes to which he is entitled, and this is cognizable in the ecclesiastical courts. (3) Subtraction of conjugal rights is the withdrawing or withholding by a husband or wife of those rights and privileges which the law allows to either party. (4) Subtraction of legacies is the withholding or detaining of legacies by an executor. (5) Subtraction of church rates, in English law, consists in the refusal to pay the amount of rate at which any individual parishioner has been assessed for the necessary repairs of the parish church. Brown.

SUBTRACTION OF CONJUGAL RIGHTS. The act of a husband or wife living separately from the other without a lawful cause. 3 Bl.Comm. 94. See, also, Subtraction.

SUBURBANI. Lat. In old English law. Husbandmen.

SUBVASSORES. In old Scotch law. Base holders; inferior holders; they who held their lands of knights. Skene.

SUCCESSIO. Lat. In the civil law. A coming in place of another, on his decease; a coming into the estate which a deceased person had at the time of his death. This was either by virtue of an express appointment of the deceased person by his *will,* (*ex testamento,*) or by the general appointment of law in case of *intestacy,* (*ab intestato.*) Inst. 2, 9, 7; Heinecc. Elem. lib. 2, tit. 10.

SUCCESSION. The devolution of title to property under the law of descent and distribution. State ex rel. Walker v. Payne, 129 Mo. 468, 31 S.W. 797, 798, 3 L.R.A. 576. The act or right of legal or official investment with a predecessor's office, dignity, possession, or functions; also the legal or actual order of so succeeding from that which is or is to be vested or taken. Glascott v. Bragg, 111 Wis. 605, 87 N.W. 853, 854, 56 L.R.A. 258.

The word when applied to realty denotes persons who take by will or inheritance and excludes those who take by deed, grant, gift, or any form of purchase or contract. Olsan Bros. v. Miller, Tex.Civ.App., 108 S.W.2d 856, 857.

The right by which one set of men may, by succeeding another set, acquire a property in all the goods, movables, and other chattels of a corporation. 2 Bl.Comm. 430. The power of perpetual *succession* is one of the peculiar properties of a corporation. 2 Kent, Comm. 267. See Perpetual.

Civil Law and Louisiana

The *fact* of the transmission of the rights, estate, obligations, and charges of a deceased person to his heir or heirs.

The *right* by which the heir can take possession of the decedent's estate. The right of the heir to step into the place of the deceased, with respect to the possession, control, enjoyment, administration, and settlement of all the latter's property, rights, obligations, charges, etc.

The *estate* of a deceased person, comprising all kinds of property owned or claimed by him, as well as his debts and obligations, and considered as a legal entity (according to the notion of the Roman law) for certain purposes, such as collecting assets and paying debts. Davenport v. Adler, 52 La.Ann. 263, 26 So. 836; Succession of Blumberg, 148 La. 1030, 88 So. 297, 299.

The transmission of the rights and obligations of the deceased to the heirs, also the estates, rights, and charges which a person leaves after his death, whether the property exceeds the charges or the charges exceed the property, or whether he has only left charges without any property. Delaneuville v. Duhe, 114 La. 62, 38 So. 20, 22.

The succession not only includes the rights and obligations of the deceased as they exist at the time of his death, but all that has accrued thereto since the opening of the succession, as also the new charges to which it becomes subject.

The coming in of another to take the property of one who dies without disposing of it by will.

General

Artificial succession. That attribute of a corporation by which, in contemplation of law, the company itself remains always the same though its constituent members or stockholders may change from time to time. See Thomas v. Dakin, 22 Wend., N.Y., 100.

Hereditary succession. Descent or title, by descent at common law; the title whereby a man on the death of his ancestor acquires his estate by right of representation as his heir at law. See In re Donahue's Estate, 36 Cal. 332; Barclay v. Cameron, 25 Tex. 241.

Intestate succession. The succession of an heir at law to the property and estate of his ancestor when the latter has died intestate, or leaving a will which has been annulled or set aside.

Irregular succession. That which is established by law in favor of certain persons, or of the state, in default of heirs, either legal or instituted by testament.

Legal succession. That which the law establishes in favor of the nearest relation of a deceased person.

Natural succession. Succession taking place between natural persons, for example, in descent on the death of an ancestor. Thomas v. Dakin, 22 Wend., N.Y., 100.

SUCCESSION DUTY. An American law. A tax placed on the gratuitous acquisition of property passing on the death of any person by transfer from one person to another. Wachovia Bank & Trust Co. v. Maxwell, 221 N.C. 528, 20 S.E.2d 840, 842.

In English law. A duty, (varying from one to ten per cent.,) payable under the statute 16 & 17 Vict. c. 51, in respect chiefly of real estate and leaseholds, but generally in respect of all property (not already chargeable with legacy duty) devolving upon any one in consequence of any death. Brown.

Succession tax. A tax imposed upon the privilege of receiving property from a decedent by devise or inheritance. See Scholey v. Rew, 23 Wall. 346, 23 L.Ed. 99; State v. Switzler, 143 Mo. 287, 45 S.W. 245, 40 L.R.A. 280; Wonderly v. Tax Commission of Ohio, 112 Ohio St. 233, 147 N.E. 509, 512; Shepard v. State, 184 Wis. 88, 197 N.W. 344, 345; Bankers' Trust Co. v. State, 96 Conn. 361, 114 A. 104, 106.

It is tax on right of succession to property, and not on property itself. Reynolds v. Reynolds, 208 N.C. 578, 182 S.E. 341.

Testamentary succession. In the civil law, that which results from the institution of an heir in a testament executed in the form prescribed by law.

Vacant succession. When no one claims it, or when all the heirs are unknown, or when all the known heirs to it have renounced it. Civ.Code La. art. 1095. Simmons v. Saul, 11 S.Ct. 369, 138 U.S. 439, 34 L.Ed. 1054.

SUCCESSIVE. Following one after another in a line or series. In re Buchholtz, Cust. & Pat.App., 54 F.2d 965, 966.

SUCCESSOR. One that succeeds or follows; one who takes the place that another has left, and sustains the like part or character; one who takes the place of another by succession. Thompson v. North Texas Nat. Bank, Tex.Com.App., 37 S.W.2d 735, 740; Wawak Co. v. Kaiser, C.C.A.Ill., 90 F.2d 694, 697.

One who has been appointed or elected to hold an office after the term of the present incumbent.

Term with reference to corporations, generally means another corporation which, through amalgamation, consolidation, or other legal succession, becomes invested with rights and assumes burdens of first corporation. Schmoele v. Atlantic City R. Co., 110 N.J.Eq. 597, 160 A. 524, 526.

Singular Successor

A term borrowed from the civil law, denoting a person who succeeds to the rights of a former owner in a single article of property, (as by purchase,) as distinguished from a *universal* successor, who succeeds to all the rights and powers of a former owner, as in the case of a bankrupt or intestate estate.

SUCCINCT. Brief, precise, exact. Logan v. Hite, 214 Ind. 233, 13 N.E.2d 702, 703.

SUCCURRITUR MINORI; FACILIS EST LAPSUS JUVENTUTIS. A minor is [to be] aided; a mistake of youth is easy, [youth is liable to err.] Jenk. Cent. p. 47, case 89.

SUCH. Of that kind, having particular quality or character specified. In re Brock, 312 Pa. 92, 166 A. 785, 787. Identical with, being the same as what has been mentioned. In re Watson's Will, 144 Misc. 213, 258 N.Y.S. 755. Alike, similar, of the like kind; "such" represents the object as already particularized in terms which are not mentioned, and is a descriptive and relative word, referring to the last antecedent. Strawberry Hill Land Corporation v. Starbuck, 124 Va. 71, 97 S.E. 362, 366; People ex rel. Kelly v. Public Service Commission, 171 App.Div. 810, 157 N.Y.S. 703, 705.

SUCKEN, SUCHEN. In Scotch law. The whole lands astricted to a mill; that is, the lands of which the tenants are obliged to send their grain to that mill. Bell.

SUDDEN. Happening without previous notice or with very brief notice; coming or occurring unexpectedly; unforeseen; unprepared for. Hagaman v. Manley, 141 Kan. 647, 42 P.2d 946, 949.

SUDDEN AFFRAY. A difficulty or fight suddenly resulting from the mutual agreement of two or more parties. Cavanaugh v. Commonwealth, 172 Ky. 799, 190 S.W. 123, 126; Gibbons v. Commonwealth, 253 Ky. 72, 68 S.W.2d 753.

SUDDEN HEAT OF PASSION. In the common-law definition of manslaughter, this phrase means an access of rage or anger, suddenly arising from a contemporary provocation. It means that the provocation must arise at the time of the killing, and that the passion is not the result of a former provocation, and the act must be directly caused by the passion arising out of the provocation at the time of the homicide. Stell v. State, Tex.Cr. App., 58 S.W. 75; Farrar v. State, 29 Tex.App. 250, 15 S.W. 719; Violett v. Com., 24 Ky.Law Rep. 1720, 72 S.W. 1.

SUDDEN OR VIOLENT INJURY. Injury occurring unexpectedly and not naturally or in the ordinary course of events. State v. District Court of St. Louis County, 138 Minn. 131, 164 N.W. 585, L.R.A.1918C, 116.

SUDDEN PERIL RULE. Under this rule, a defendant who is guilty of primary negligence is not liable in case of sudden peril where the peril or alarm was caused by the negligence of the opposite party, apprehension of peril from the standpoint of defendant seeking to excuse his primary negligence was reasonable, appearance of danger was so imminent as to leave no time for deliberation. White v. Munson, Tex.Civ.App., 162 S.W.2d 429, 432.

But rule cannot be invoked by one bringing emergency on or not using due care, to avoid it. McClelland v. Interstate Transit Lines, 142 Neb. 439, 6 N.W.2d 384, 391.

SUDDER. In Hindu law. The best; the fore-court of a house; the chief seat of government, contradistinguished from "*mofussil,*" or interior of the country; the presidency. Wharton.

SUE. To commence or to continue legal proceedings for recovery of a right; to proceed with as an action, and follow it up to its proper termination; to gain by legal process. Lervold v. Republic Mut. Fire Ins. Co., 142 Kan. 43, 45 P.2d 839, 843, 106 A.L.R. 673. Word includes a proceeding instituted by confession of judgment. Commonwealth ex rel. Bradford County v. Lynch, 146 Pa. Super. 469, 23 A.2d 77, 78.

SUE OUT. To obtain by application; to petition for and take out. Properly the term is applied only to the obtaining and issuing of such process as is only accorded upon an application first made; but conventionally it is also used of the taking out of process which issues of course. The term is occasionally used of instruments other than writs. Thus, we speak of "suing out" a pardon. See South Missouri Lumber Co. v. Wright, 114 Mo. 326, 21 S.W. 811; Kelley v. Vincent, 8 Ohio St. 420; U. S. v. American Lumber Co., 29 C.C.A. 431, 85 F. 830.

SUERTE. In Spanish law. A small lot of ground. Particularly, such a lot within the limits of a city or town used for cultivation or planting as a garden, vineyard or orchard. Building lots in towns and cities are called "solares." Hart v. Burnett, 15 Cal. 554.

SUFFER. To allow, to admit, or to permit. Gregory v. Marks, C.C.Ill., Fed.Cas.No.5,802; 10 Fed.Cas. 1194, 1198; Osborne v. Winter, 133 Cal. App. 664, 24 P.2d 892. It includes knowledge of what is to be done under sufferance. First Nat. Bank & Trust Co. of Port Chester v. New York Title Ins. Co., 171 Misc. 854, 12 N.Y.S.2d 703, 709.

Also to have the feeling or sensation that arises from the action of something painful, distressing or the like; to feel or endure pain; to endure or undergo without sinking; to support; to bear up under; to be affected by; to sustain; to experience; to feel pain, physical or mental. The customary use of the word indicates some experience of conscious pain. New York Life Ins. Co. v. Calhoun, C.C.A.Mo., 97 F.2d 896, 898.

To suffer an act to be done or a condition to exist is to permit or consent to it; to approve of it, and not to hinder it. It implies knowledge, a willingness of the mind and responsible control or ability to prevent. Wilson v. Nelson, 183 U.S. 191, 22 S.Ct. 74, 46 L.Ed. 147; Selleck v. Selleck, 19 Conn. 505; Gregory v. U. S., C.C.N.Y., Fed.Cas. No.5,803; 10 Fed.Cas. 1197; In re Thomas, D.C.Pa., 103 F. 272, 274; Allison v. Commonwealth, 221 Ky. 205, 298 S.W. 680.

SUFFERANCE. Toleration; negative permission by not forbidding; passive consent; license implied from the omission or neglect to enforce an adverse right. See People on Inf. of Price v. Sheffield Farms-Slawson-Decker Co., 225 N.Y. 25, 121 N.E. 474, 476.

SUFFERANCE WHARVES. In English law. Wharves in which goods may be landed before any duty is paid. They are appointed for the purpose by the commissioners of the customs. 2 Steph. Comm. 500, note.

SUFFERENTIA PACIS. Lat. A grant or sufferance of peace or truce.

SUFFERING A RECOVERY. A recovery was effected by the party wishing to convey the land *suffering* a fictitious action to be brought against him by the party to whom the land was to be conveyed, (the demandant,) and allowing the demandant to recover a judgment against him for the land in question. The vendor, or conveying party, in thus assisting or permitting the demandant so to recover a judgment against him, was thence technically said to "suffer a recovery." Brown.

SUFFICIENT. Adequate, enough, as much as may be necessary, equal or fit for end proposed, and that which may be necessary to accomplish an object. Brittain v. Industrial Commission of Ohio, 95 Ohio St. 391, 115 N.E. 110; Galveston, H. & S. A. Ry. Co. v. Enderle, Tex.Civ.App., 170 S.W. 276, 277; Commissioners of Sinking Fund of Louisville v. Anderson, D.C.Ky., 20 F.Supp. 217, 220. Of such quality, number, force, or value as to serve a need or purpose. Nissen v. Miller, 44 N.M. 487, 105 P.2d 324, 326. As to sufficient "Consideration" see that title.

SUFFICIENT CAUSE. With respect to right to remove officers does not mean any cause which removing officer may deem sufficient, but means legal cause, specifically relating to and affecting administration of office, of substantial nature directly affecting public's rights and interests, touching officer's qualifications or his performance of duties, and showing that he is not fit or proper to hold office. Sausbier v. Wheeler, 252 App.Div. 267, 299 N.Y.S. 466, 472; Zurich General Accident & Liability Ins. Co. v. Kinsler, 12 Cal.2d 98, 81 P.2d 913, 915.

SUFFICIENT EVIDENCE. Adequate evidence; such evidence, in character, weight, or amount, as will legally justify the judicial or official action demanded; according to circumstances, it may be "prima facie" or "satisfactory" evidence, according to the definitions of those terms given above. People v. Stern, 33 Misc.Rep. 455, 68 N. Y.S. 732; Mallery v. Young, 94 Ga. 804, 22 S.E. 142; Parker v. Overman, 18 How. 141, 15 L.Ed. 318; State v. Newton, 33 Ark. 284.

Sufficient evidence is that which is satisfactory for the purpose; Mallery v. Young, 94 Ga. 804, 22 S.E. 142, 143; that amount of proof which ordinarily satisfies an unprejudiced mind, beyond a reasonable doubt; Cole v. McClure, 88 Ohio St. 1, 102 N.E. 264, 266. The term is not synonymous with "conclusive." Pensacola & A. R. Co. v. State, 5 So. 833, 835, 25 Fla. 310, 3 L.R.A. 661. But it may be used interchangeably with the term "weight of evidence." Waldron v. New York Cent. Ry. Co., 106 Ohio St. 371, 140 N.E. 161, 163. See, also, Satisfactory Evidence.

SUFFOCATE. To kill by stopping respiration, as by strangling or asphyxiation. Stone v. Physicians Casualty Ass'n of America, 130 Neb. 769, 266 N.W. 605, 607.

SUFFRAGAN. Bishops who in former times were appointed to supply the place of others during their absence on embassies or other business were so termed. They were consecrated as other bishops were, and were anciently called "*chorepiscopi*," or "bishops of the county," in contradistinction to the regular bishops of the city or see. The practice of creating *suffragan* bishops, after having long been discontinued, was recently revived; and such bishops are now permanently "assistant" to the bishops. Brown.

A suffragan is a titular bishop ordained to aid and assist the bishop of the diocese in his spiritual function; or one who supplieth the place instead of the bishop, by whose suffrage ecclesiastical causes or matters committed to him are to be adjudged, acted on, or determined. Some writers call these suffragans by the name of "subsidiary bishops." Tomlins.

SUFFRAGE. A vote; the act of voting; the right or privilege of casting a vote at public elections. The last is the meaning of the term in such phrases as "the extension of the suffrage," "universal suffrage," etc. Spitzer v. Fulton, 33 Misc. 257, 68 N.Y.S. 660; Cofield v. Farrell, 38 Okl. 608, 134 P. 407, 409.

Participation in the suffrage is not of right, but is granted by the state on a consideration of what is most for the interest of the state, Cooley, Const., 2d Ed. 752; Spencer v. Board of Registration, 8 D.C. 169, 29 Am.Rep. 582; U. S. v. Anthony, 11 Blatchf. 200, Fed.Cas.No.14,459. The grant of suffrage makes it a legal right until it is recalled, and it is protected by the law as property is.

SUFFRAGIUM. Lat. In Roman law. A vote; the right of voting in the assemblies of the people.

Aid or influence used or promised to obtain some honor or office; the purchase of office. Cod. 4, 3.

SUGGEST. To introduce indirectly to the thought; to propose with diffidence or modesty; to hint; to intimate. Sims v. Ratcliff, 62 Ind.App. 184, 110 N. E. 122, 123.

SUGGESTIO FALSI. Lat. Suggestion or representation of that which is false; false representation. To recite in a deed that a will was duly executed, when it was not, is *suggestio falsi;* and to conceal from the heir that the will was not duly executed is *suppressio veri.* 1 P. Wms. 240, and see Turney v. Avery, 92 N.J.Eq. 473, 113 A. 710.

SUGGESTION. A suggesting, presentation of an idea especially indirectly, as through association of ideas, bringing before the mind for consideration, action, solution, or the like. Artificial Ice & Cold Storage Co. v. Martin, 102 Ind.App. 74, 198 N.E. 446, 449.

It is in the nature of a hint or insinuation, and lacks the element of probability. Facts which merely suggest do not raise an inference of the existence of the fact suggested, and therefore a suggestion is much less than an inference or presumption. Lopa v. Smith, 37 Ohio App. 346, 174 N.E. 258, 259.

In practice. A statement, formally entered on the record, of some fact or circumstance which will materially affect the further proceedings in the cause, or which is necessary to be brought to the knowledge of the court in order to its right disposition of the action, but which, for some reason, cannot be pleaded. Thus, if one of the parties dies after issue and before trial, his death may be *suggested* on the record. C. J. Huebel Co. v. Mackinnon, 186 Mich. 617, 152 N.W. 1098, 1100.

SUGGESTION OF ERROR. Request for rehearing. White v. State, 190 Miss. 589, 195 So. 479, 482.

SUGGESTIVE INTERROGATION. A phrase used by some writers to signify "leading question." 2 Benth. Jud. Ev. b. 3, c. 3. It is used in the French law.

SUI GENERIS. Lat. Of its own kind or class; *i. e.,* the *only one* of its own kind; peculiar.

SUI HÆREDES. Lat. In the civil law. One's own heirs; proper heirs. Inst. 2, 19, 2.

SUI JURIS. Lat. Of his own right; possessing full social and civil rights; not under any legal disability, or the power of another, or guardianship.

Having capacity to manage one's own affairs; not under legal disability to act for one's self. Story, Ag. § 2.

SUICIDE. Self-destruction; the deliberate termination of one's existence, while in the possession and enjoyment of his mental faculties. See Insurance Co. v. Moore, 34 Mich. 41; Weber v. Supreme Tent, 172 N.Y. 490, 65 N.E. 258, 92 Am.St. Rep. 753; Daniels v. Railroad Co., 183 Mass. 393, 67 N.E. 424, 62 L.R.A. 751.

The term "suicide," as used in insurance policies, has been held to mean death by one's own hand, irrespective of mental condition. Great Southern Life Ins. Co. v. Campbell, 148 Miss. 173, 114 So. 262, 263, 56 A.L.R. 681. But other cases hold that intent is essential. Benard v. Protected Home Circle, 161 App.Div. 59, 146 N.Y.S. 232, 233; American Nat. Ins. Co. v. Anderson, 42 Ga.App. 624, 157 S.E. 112.

SUICIDE, SANE OR INSANE. An exemption from liability for death by "suicide, sane or insane," in a life policy includes self-destruction irrespective of the assured's mental condition at the time of the act. United States Fidelity & Guaranty Co. v. Blum, C.C.A.Wash., 258 F. 897, 899; Power v. Modern Brotherhood of America, 98 Kan. 487, 158 P. 870, 872.

SUING AND LABORING CLAUSE. A clause in an English policy of marine insurance, generally in the following form: "In case of any loss or misfortune, it shall be lawful for the assured, their factors, servants and assigns, to sue, labor, and travel for, in, and about the defense, safeguard, and recovery of the" property insured, "without prejudice to this insurance; to the charges whereof we, the assurers, will contribute." The object of the clause is to encourage the assured to exert themselves in preserving the property from loss. Sweet.

SUIT.

Old English Law

The witnesses or followers of the plaintiff. 3 Bl. Comm. 295. See Secta.

Old books mention the word in many connections which are now disused,—at least, in the United States. Thus, "suit" was used of following any one, or in the sense of pursuit; as in the phrase "making fresh suit." It was also used of a petition to the king or lord. "Suit of court" was the attendance which a tenant owed at the court of his lord. "Suit covenant" and "suit custom" seem to have signified a right to one's attendance, or one's obligation to attend, at the lord's court, founded upon a known covenant, or an immemorial usage or practice of ancestors. "Suit regal" was attendance at the sheriff's tourn or leet, (his court.) "Suit of the king's peace" was pursuing an offender,—one charged with breach of the peace, while *"suithold"* was a tenure in consideration of certain services to the superior lord. Abbott.

Modern Law

A generic term, of comprehensive signification, and applies to any proceeding by one person or persons against another or others in a court of justice in which the plaintiff pursues, in such court, the remedy which the law affords him for the redress of an injury or the enforcement of a right, whether at law or in equity. See Kohl v. U. S., 91 U.S. 375, 23 L.Ed. 449; Weston v. Charleston, 2 Pet. 464, 7 L.Ed. 481; Syracuse Plaster Co. v. Agostini Bros. Bldg. Corporation, 169 Misc. 564, 7 N.Y.S.2d 897. It is, however, seldom applied to a criminal prosecution. And it is sometimes restricted to the designation of a proceeding in equity, to distinguish such proceeding from an action at law. Patterson v. Standard Accident Ins. Co., 178 Mich. 288, 144 N.W. 491, 492, 51 L.R.A., N.S., 583. For "Ancillary" suit and suit "In Rem" see those titles.

General

Class suits. See Class or Representative Action.

Suit against state. Suit in which relief against the state is sought. Louisville & N. R. Co. v. Bosworth, D.C.Ky., 209 F. 380, 401.

Within rule of state immunity from suit without its consent, one in which the subject matter must be an interest of value in a material sense to the state as a distinct entity. American Federation of Labor v. Mann, Tex.Civ. App., 188 S.W.2d 276, 279, 280. And in the determination of whether a suit is one against the state, it is not necessary that the state appear on the record as a party; but, if the state is the real party against which the relief is sought, the suit is a "suit against the state" although nominally it appears on the record as a suit against one of its officers. McKamey v. Aikin, Tex.Civ.App., 118 S.W.2d 482, 483, 484.

Suit money. An allowance, in the nature of temporary alimony, authorized by statute in some states to be made to a wife on the institution of her suit for divorce, intended to cover the reasonable expenses of the suit and to provide her with means for the efficient preparation and trial of her case. See Yost v. Yost, 141 Ind. 584, 41 N.E. 11.

Suit of a civil nature. A suit for the remedy of a private wrong, the test being whether the law is penal in the strict and primary sense, and whether the wrong is to the public or to the individual. City of Montgomery, Ala., v. Postal Telegraph-Cable Co., D.C.Ala., 218 F. 471, 474.

Suit of court. This phrase denoted the duty of attending the lord's court, and, in common with fealty, was one of the incidents of a feudal holding. Brown.

Suit of the king's peace. The pursuing a man for breach of the king's peace by treasons, insurrections, or trespasses. Cowell.

Suits or proceedings at law or in chancery. Suits instituted and carried on in substantial conformity with the forms and modes prescribed by the common law or by the rules in chancery excluding cases instituted and carried on solely in accordance with statutory provisions. Lavin v. Wells Bros. Co., 272 Ill. 609, 112 N.E. 271, 272.

Suit silver. A small sum of money paid in lieu of attendance at the court-baron. Cowell.

SUITABLE. Fit and appropriate for the end in view. U. S. v. American & Patterson, 9 Ct.Cust. App. 244, 245.

SUITAS. Lat. In the civil law. The condition or quality of a *suus hæres,* or proper heir. Hallifax, Civil Law, b. 2, c. 9, no. 11; Calvin.

SUITE. Those persons who by his authority *follow* or attend an ambassador or other public minister.

SUITOR. A party to a suit or action in court. In its ancient sense, "suitor" meant one who was bound to attend the county court; also one who formed part of the *secta.*

SUITORS' DEPOSIT ACCOUNT. Formerly suitors in the English court of chancery derived no income from their cash paid into court, unless it was invested at their request and risk. Now, however, it is provided by the court of chancery (funds) act, 1872, that all money paid into court, and not required by the suitor to be invested, shall be placed on deposit and shall bear interest at two per cent. per annum for the benefit of the suitor entitled to it. Sweet.

SUITORS' FEE FUND. A fund in the English court of chancery into which the fees of suitors in that court were paid, and out of which the salaries of various officers of the court were defrayed. Wharton.

SUITORS' FUND IN CHANCERY. In England. A fund consisting of moneys which, having been paid into the court of chancery, are placed out for the benefit and better security of the suitors, including interest from the same. By St. 32 & 33 Vict. c. 91, § 4, the principal of this fund, amounting to over £3,000,000, was transferred to the commissioners for the reduction of the national debt. Mozley & Whitley.

SULCUS. In old English law. A small brook or stream of water. Cowell.

SULLERY. In old English law. A plowland. 1 Inst. 5.

SUM. In English law. A summary or abstract; a compendium; a collection. Several of the old law treatises are called "sums." Lord Hale applies the term to summaries of statute law.. Burrill.

The sense in which the term is most commonly used is "money"; a quantity of money or currency; any amount indefinitely, a sum of money, a small sum, or a large sum. U. S. v. Van Auken, 96 U.S. 368, 24 L.Ed. 852; Donovan v. Jenkins, 52 Mont. 124, 155 P. 972, 973.

SUM IN GROSS. See In Gross.

SUM PAYABLE. As used within Negotiable Instruments Law is the amount for which, by the terms of the instrument, the maker becomes liable, and which he might tender and pay in full satisfaction of his obligation. First Nat. Bank of Iowa City, Iowa, v. Watson, 56 Okl. 495, 155 P. 1152.

SUMAGE. Toll for carriage on horseback. Cowell.

SUMMA CARITAS EST FACERE JUSTITIAM SINGULIS, ET OMNI TEMPORE QUANDO NECESSE FUERIT. The greatest charity is to do justice to every one, and at any time whenever it may be necessary. 11 Coke, 70.

SUMMA EST LEX QUÆ PRO RELIGIONE FACIT. That is the highest law which favors religion. 10 Mod. 117, 119; Broom, Max. 19.

SUMMA RATIO EST QUÆ PRO RELIGIONE FACIT. That consideration is strongest which determines in favor of religion. Co. Litt. 341*a*; Broom, Max. 19.

SUMMARILY. Without ceremony or delay, short or concise. In re Gabelmann, 136 Misc. 641, 241 N.Y.S. 405, 408.

SUMMARY, *n.* An abridgment; brief; compendium; also a short application to a court or judge, without the formality of a full proceeding. Wharton.

SUMMARY, *adj.* Short, concise. State v. Bettman, 124 Ohio St. 24, 176 N.E. 664, 665. Immediate, peremptory; off-hand; without a jury; provisional; statutory. The term used in connection with legal proceedings means a short, concise, and immediate proceeding. Vance v. Noel, 143 La. 477, 78 So. 741, 742; and trial of a "summary" character is a trial without a jury. State v. King, 137 Tenn. 17, 191 S.W. 352, 354; City of St. Paul v. Robinson, 129 Minn. 383, 152 N.W. 777, Ann.Cas. 1916E, 845.

Summary actions. In Scotch law. Those which are brought into court not by summons, but by petition, corresponding to summary proceedings in English courts. Bell; Brown.

Summary conviction. See Conviction.

Summary jurisdiction. The jurisdiction of a court to give a judgment or make an order itself forthwith; *e. g.*, to commit to prison for contempt; to punish malpractice in a solicitor; or, in the case of justices of the peace, a jurisdiction to convict an offender themselves instead of committing him for trial by a jury. Wharton.

Summary procedure on bills of exchange. This phrase refers to the statute 18 & 19 Vict. c. 67, passed in 1855, for the purpose of facilitating the remedies on bills and notes by the prevention of frivolous or fictitious defenses. By this statute, a defendant in an action on a bill or note, brought within six months after it has become payable, is prohibited from defending the action without the leave of the court or a judge. See 2 Steph. Comm. 118, note; Lush. Pr. 1027.

Summary proceeding. See Proceeding.

SUMMARY PROCESS. See Process.

SUMMER FALLOWING. Plowing and harrowing of grounds preparatory to cropping during next season. Farmers' & Merchants' Bank of Walla Walla v. Small, 131 Wash. 197, 229 P. 531, 533.

SUMMER-HUS SILVER. A payment to the lords of the wood on the Wealds of Kent, who used to visit those places in summer, when their undertenants were bound to prepare little summerhouses for their reception, or else pay a composition in money. Cowell.

SUMMING UP. On the trial of an action by a jury, a recapitulation of the evidence adduced, in order to draw the attention of the jury to the salient points. The counsel for each party has the right of summing up his evidence, if he has adduced any, and the judge sometimes sums up the whole in his charge to the jury. Smith, Act. 157. State v. Ezzard, 40 S.C. 312, 18 S.E. 1025.

SUMMON. In practice. To serve a summons; to cite a defendant to appear in court to answer a suit which has been begun against him; to notify the defendant that an action has been instituted against him, and that he is required to answer to it at a time and place named.

SUMMONEAS. L. Lat. In old practice. A writ of summons; a writ by which a party was summoned to appear in court.

SUMMONERS. Petty officers, who cite and warn persons to appear in any court. Fleta, lib. 9.

SUMMONITIO. L. Lat. In old English practice. A summoning or summons; a writ by which a party was summoned to appear in court, of which there were various kinds. Spelman.

SUMMONITIONES AUT CITATIONES NULLÆ LICEANT FIERI INTRA PALATIUM REGIS. 3 Inst. 141. Let no summonses or citations be served within the king's palace.

SUMMONITORES SCACCARII. Officers who assisted in collecting the revenues by citing the defaulters therein into the court of exchequer.

SUMMONS.

Practice

A writ, directed to the sheriff or other proper officer, requiring him to notify the person named that an action has been commenced against him in the court whence the writ issues, and that he is required to appear, on a day named, and answer the complaint in such action. See Whitney v. Blackburn, 17 Or. 564, 21 P. 874, 11 Am.St.Rep. 857; Horton v. Railway Co., 26 Mo.App. 358.

Under code procedure a summons is not process, but is a notice to defendant that an action against him has been commenced and that judgment will be taken against him if he fails to answer the complaint. Flanary v. Kusha, 143 Minn. 308, 173 N.W. 652; United States v. Van Dusen, C.C. A.Minn., 78 F.2d 121, 124.

Scotch Law

A writ passing under the royal signet, signed by a writer to the signet, and containing the grounds and conclusions of the action, with the warrant for citing the defender. This writ corresponds to the writ of summons in English procedure. Bell; Paters. Comp.

SUMMONS AD RESPONDENDUM. Process issuing in a civil case at law notifying defendant therein named that he must appear on day designated and thereupon make answer to plaintiff's statement of his cause of action. Walker Fertilizer Co. v. Race, 123 Fla. 84, 166 So. 283, 285, 105 A.L.R. 341.

SUMMONS AND ORDER. In English practice. The summons is the application to a common-law judge at chambers in reference to a pending action, and upon it the judge or master makes the order. Mozley & Whitley.

SUMMONS AND SEVERANCE. The proper name of what is distinguished in the books by the name of "summons and severance" is "severance;" for the summons is only a process which must, in certain cases, issue before judgment of severance can be given; while severance is a judgment by which one or more of parties joined in action is enabled to proceed without the other or others. Jacob.

SUMMUM JUS. Lat. Strict right; extreme right. The extremity or rigor of the law. See "Apex Juris."

SUMMUM JUS, SUMMA INJURIA; SUMMA LEX, SUMMA CRUX. Extreme law (rigor of law) is the greatest injury; strict law is great punishment. Hob. 125. That is, insistence upon the full measure of a man's strict legal rights may work the greatest injury to others, unless equity can aid.

SUMNER. See Sompnour.

SUMPTUARY LAWS. Laws made for the purpose of restraining luxury or extravagance, particularly against inordinate expenditures in the matter of apparel, food, furniture, etc.

SUNDAY. The first day of the week is designated by this name; also as the "Lord's Day," and as the "Sabbath." State v. Reade, 98 N.J.L. 596, 121 A. 288, 289.

For Work of Necessity see "Necessity."

SUNDAY SCHOOL. School for religious instruction. Dougherty v. Kentucky Alcoholic Beverage Control Board, 279 Ky. 262, 130 S.W.2d 756, 759; Stubbs v. Texas Liquor Control Board, Tex.Civ. App., 166 S.W.2d 178, 180.

SUNDRIES. Miscellaneous or various items which may be considered together, without being separately specified or identified. People v. Bernstein, 237 App.Div. 270, 261 N.Y.S. 381.

SUNDRY. Separate, divers, or various. Hammond v. State, 173 Ark. 674, 293 S.W. 714, 717.

SUNSTROKE. An inflammatory disease of the brain, brought on by exposure to the too intense heat of the sun's rays, or to overheated air. Mather v. London Guarantee & Accident Co., 125 Minn. 186, 145 N.W. 963; Continental Casualty Co. v. Clark, 70 Okl. 187, 173 P. 453, L.R.A. 1918F, 1007. Though "sunstroke," strictly speaking, is a disease, suddenness of its approach and its catastrophic nature have caused it to be classified as an accident. Lurye v. Stern Bros. Department Store, 275 N.Y. 182, 9 N.E.2d 828, 829.

SUO NOMINE. Lat. In his own name.

SUO PERICULO. Lat. At his own peril or risk.

SUPELLEX. Lat. In Roman law. Household furniture. Dig. 33, 10.

SUPER. Lat. Upon; above; over; higher, as in quantity, quality and degree; more than; as in super-essential, super-natural or super-standard. Fricke v. Braden, 55 Cal.App.2d 266, 130 P.2d 727, 729.

SUPER ALTUM MARE. On the high sea. Hob. 212; 2 Ld. Raym. 1453.

SUPER FIDEM CHARTARUM, MORTUIS TESTIBUS, ERIT AD PATRIAM DE NECESSITATE RECURRENDUM. Co. Litt. 6. The truth of charters is necessarily to be referred to a jury, when the witnesses are dead.

SUPER PRÆROGATIVA REGIS. A writ which formerly lay against the king's tenant's widow for marrying without the royal license. Fitzh. Nat. Brev. 174.

SUPER STATUTO. A writ, upon the statute 1 Edw. III. c. 12, that lay against the king's tenant holding in chief, who aliened the king's land without his license.

SUPER STATUTO DE ARTICULIS CLERI. A writ which lay against a sheriff or other officer who distrained in the king's highway, or on lands anciently belonging to the church.

SUPER STATUTO FACTO POUR SENESCHAL ET MARSHAL DE ROY, ETC. A writ which lay against a steward or marshal for holding plea in his court, or for trespass or contracts not made or arising within the king's household. Wharton.

SUPER STATUTO VERSUS SERVANTES ET LABORATORES. A writ which lay against him who kept any servants who had left the service of another contrary to law.

SUPER VISUM CORPORIS. Upon view of the body. When an inquest is held over a body found dead, it must be *super visum corporis*.

SUPERARE RATIONES. In old Scotch law. To have a balance of account due to one; to have one's expenses exceed the receipts.

SUPERCARGO. In maritime law. A person specially employed by the owner of a cargo to take charge of and sell to the best advantage merchandise which has been shipped, and to purchase returning cargoes and to receive freight, as he may be authorized.

SUPERFICIARIUS. Lat. In the civil law. He who has built upon the soil of another, which he has hired for a number of years or forever, yielding a yearly rent. Dig. 43, 18, 1. In other words, a tenant on ground-rent.

SUPERFICIES. Lat. In the civil law. The alienation by the owner of the surface of the soil of all rights necessary for building on the surface, a yearly rent being generally reserved; also a building or erection. Sandars' Just. Inst. 5th Ed. 133.

SUPERFICIES SOLO CEDIT. Whatever is attached to the land forms part of it. Gaius 2, 73.

SUPERFLUA NON NOCENT. Superfluities do not prejudice. Jenk. Cent. 184. Surplusage does not vitiate.

SUPERFLUOUS LANDS. In English law, lands acquired by a railway company under its statutory powers, and not required for the purposes of its undertaking. The company is bound within a certain time to sell such lands, and, if it does not, they vest in and become the property of the owners of the adjoining lands. Sweet.

SUPERFŒTATION. In medical jurisprudence. The conception of a second embryo during the gestation of the first, or the conception of a child by a woman already pregnant with another, during the time of such pregnancy.

SUPERINDUCTIO. Lat. In the civil law. A species of obliteration. Dig. 28, 4, 1, 1.

SUPERINSTITUTION. The institution of one in an office to which another has been previously instituted; as where A. is admitted and instituted to a benefice upon one title, and B. is admitted and instituted on the title or presentment of another. 2 Cro. Eliz. 463.

A church being full by institution, if a second institution is granted to the same church this is a superinstitution. Wharton.

SUPERINTEND. To have charge and direction of; to direct the course and oversee the details; to regulate with authority; to manage; to oversee with the power of direction; to take care of with authority. Burrell Engineering & Construction Co. v. Grisier, 111 Tex. 477, 240 S.W. 899, 900; State v. First State Bank of Jud, 52 N.D. 231, 202 N.W. 391, 402.

SUPERINTENDENT. One who superintends or has the oversight and charge of something with the power of direction; a manager. Indiana Fibre Products Co. v. Cyclone Mfg. Co., 81 Ind. App. 682, 143 N.E. 169, 171.

SUPERINTENDENT OF SCHOOLS. Officer having the highest authority under the board of education. Eelkema v. Board of Education of City of Duluth, 215 Minn. 590, 11 N.W.2d 76, 77.

SUPERINTENDENT REGISTRAR. In English law. An officer who superintends the registers of births, deaths, and marriages. There is one in every poor-law union in England and Wales.

SUPERIOR, *n.* One who has a right to command; one who holds a superior rank.

SUPERIOR, *adj.* Higher; belonging to a higher grade. People ex rel. McCoy v. McCahey, 296 Ill. App. 310, 15 N.E.2d 988, 993. More elevated in rank or office. Possessing larger power. Entitled to command, influence, or control over another.

In estates, some are superior to others. An estate entitled to a servitude or easement over another estate is called the "superior" or "dominant," and the other, the "inferior" or "servient," estate. 1 Bouv.Inst. no. 1612.

In the feudal law, until the statute *quia emptores* precluded subinfeudations, *(q. v.,)* the tenant who granted part of his estate to be held of and from himself as lord was called a "superior."

Superior and vassal. In Scotch law. A feudal relation corresponding with the English "lord and tenant." Bell.

Superior courts. In English law. The courts of the highest and most extensive jurisdiction, viz., the court of chancery and the three courts of common law, *i. e.,* the King's bench, the common pleas, and the exchequer, which sit at Westminster, were commonly thus denominated. But these courts are now united in the supreme court of judicature. In American law. Courts of general or extensive jurisdiction, as distinguished from the inferior courts. As the *official style* of a tribunal, the term "superior court" bears a different meaning in different states. In some it is a court of intermediate jurisdiction between the trial courts and the chief appellate court; elsewhere it is the designation of the ordinary *nisi prius* courts.

Superior fellow servant. A term introduced into the law of negligence, and meaning one higher in authority than another, and whose commands and directions his inferiors are bound to respect and obey, though engaged at the same manual work. Illinois Cent. R. Co. v. Coleman, 22 Ky.Law Rep. 878, 59 S.W. 14; Knutter v. Telephone Co., 67 N.J.L. 646, 52 A. 565, 58 L.R.A. 808.

Superior force. In the law of bailments and of negligence, an uncontrollable and irresistible force, of human agency, producing results which the person in question could not avoid; equivalent to the Latin phrase *"vis major."* See Vis.

SUPERIORITY. In Scotch law. The *dominium directum* of lands, without the profit. 1 Forb. Inst. pt. 2, p. 97.

SUPER-JURARE. Over-swearing. A term anciently used when a criminal endeavored to excuse himself by his own oath or the oath of one or two witnesses, and the crime objected against him was so plain and notorious that he was convicted on the oaths of many more witnesses. Wharton.

SUPERNUMERARII. Lat. In Roman law. Advocates who were not registered or enrolled and did not belong to the college of advocates. They were not attached to any local jurisdiction. See Statuti.

SUPERONERATIO. Lat. Surcharging a common; *i. e.*, putting in beasts of a number or kind other than the right of common allows.

SUPERONERATIONE PASTURÆ. A judicial writ that lay against him who was impleaded in the county court for the surcharge of a common with his cattle, in a case where he was formerly impleaded for it in the same court, and the cause was removed into one of the superior courts.

SUPERPLUSAGIUM. In old English law. Overplus; surplus; residue or balance. Bract. fol. 301; Spelman.

SUPERSEDE. Obliterate, set aside, annul, replace, make void, inefficacious or useless, repeal. City of Los Angeles v. Gurdane, C.C.A.Cal., 59 F. 2d 161, 163. To set aside, render unnecessary, suspend, or stay. Taylor v. New York Telephone Co., 97 Misc. 160, 160 N.Y.S. 865; Dick v. King, 73 Mont. 456, 236 P. 1093, 1095.

SUPERSEDEAS. In Practice. The name of a writ containing a command to stay the proceedings at law.

A suspension of the power of a trial court to issue an execution on judgment appealed from, or, if writ of execution has issued, it is a prohibition emanating from court of appeal against execution of writ. Stewart v. Hurt, 9 Cal.2d 39, 68 P.2d 726, 727.

An auxiliary process designed to supersede enforcement of trial court's judgment brought up for review, and its application is limited to the judgment from which an appeal is taken. Mascot Pictures Corporation v. Municipal Court of City of Los Angeles, 3 Cal.App.2d 559, 40 P.2d 272.

Originally it was a writ directed to an officer, commanding him to desist from enforcing the execution of another writ which he was about to execute, or which might come in his hands. In modern times the term is often used synonymously with a "stay of proceedings," and is employed to designate the effect of an act or proceeding which of itself suspends the enforcement of a judgment. Dulin v. Coal Co., 98 Cal. 306, 33 P. 123.

SUPERSEDING CAUSE. An act of a third person or other force which by its intervention prevents the actor from being liable for harm to another which his antecedent negligence is a substantial factor in bringing about. Superior Oil Co. v. Richmond, 172 Miss. 407, 159 So. 850, 852. Shuster v. Vecchi, 203 Minn. 76, 279 N.W. 841, 844.

SUPERSTITIOUS USE. In English law. When lands, tenements, rents, goods, or chattels are given, secured, or appointed for and towards the maintenance of a priest or chaplain to say mass, for the maintenance of a priest or other man to pray for the soul of any dead man in such a church or elsewhere, to have and maintain perpetual obits, lamps, torches, etc., to be used at certain times to help to save the souls of men out of purgatory,—in such cases the king, by force of several statutes, is authorized to direct and appoint all such uses to such purposes as are truly charitable. Bac. Abr. "Charitable Uses." The doctrine has no recognition in this country; Appeal of Seibert, 18 Wkly. Notes Cas., Pa., 276; and a bequest to support a Catholic priest, and perhaps other uses void in England, would not be considered as superstitious uses. Harrison v. Brophy, 59 Kan. 1, 51 P. 883, 40 L.R.A. 721.

SUPERVENING CAUSE. A new effective cause which, operating independently of anything else, becomes proximate cause of accident. Chesapeake & O. Ry. Co. v. Crum, 140 Va. 333, 125 S.E. 301, 304.

SUPERVENING NEGLIGENCE. That situations may come within the doctrine of last clear chance or supervening negligence, four conditions must coexist, to wit: (1) That the injured party has already come into a position of peril; (2) that the injuring party then or thereafter becomes, or in the exercise of ordinary prudence ought to have become, aware, not only of that fact, but also that the party in peril either reasonably cannot escape from it or apparently will not avail himself of opportunities open to him for doing so; (3) that the injuring party subsequently has the opportunity by the exercise of reasonable care to save the other from harm; and (4) that he fails to exercise such care. Emmons v. New York and S. R. Co., 108 Conn. 133, 142 A. 676, 677.

See Last Clear Chance.

SUPERVISE. To have general oversight over, to superintend or to inspect. State v. Manning, 220 Iowa 525, 259 N.W. 213.

SUPERVISION. An act of occupation of supervising; inspection. Kemp v. Stanley, 204 La. 110, 15 So.2d 1, 11.

SUPERVISOR. A surveyor or overseer; a highway officer. Also, in some states, the chief officer of a town; one of a board of county officers.

In a broad sense, one having authority over others, to superintend and direct. Cafferty v. Southern Tier Pub. Co., 226 N.Y. 87, 123 N.E. 76, 77.

SUPERVISORS OF ELECTION. Persons appointed and commissioned by the United States circuit judges to supervise the registration of voters and the holding of elections for representatives in congress under Rev. St. §§ 2011–2031; repealed by the act of Feb. 8, 1894, 28 Stat. 36.

SUPERVISORY CONTROL. Control exercised by courts to compel inferior tribunals to act within their jurisdiction, to prohibit them from acting outside their jurisdiction, and to reverse their extrajurisdictional acts. State v. Superior Court of Dane County, 170 Wis. 385, 175 N.W. 927, 928.

SUPPLEMENT, LETTERS OF. In Scotch practice. A process by which a party not residing within the jurisdiction of an inferior court may be cited to appear before it. Bell.

SUPPLEMENTAL. That which is added to a thing to complete it. State v. Day, 189 Ind. 243, 123 N.E. 402, 403; People ex rel. Astor Trust Co. v. State Tax Commission, 174 App.Div. 320, 160 N.Y.S. 854, 858.

SUPPLEMENTAL ACT. That which supplies a deficiency, adds to or completes, or extends that which is already in existence without changing or modifying the original; Act designed to improve an existing statute by adding something thereto without changing the original text. Swanson v. State, 132 Neb. 82, 271 N.W. 264, 268.

SUPPLEMENTAL AFFIDAVIT. An affidavit made in addition to a previous one, in order to supply some deficiency in it. Callan v. Lukens, 89 Pa. 136.

SUPPLEMENTAL ANSWER. One which was filed in chancery for the purpose of correcting, adding to, and explaining an answer already filed. Smith, Ch. Pr. 334. French v. Edwards, 9 Fed. Cas. 780; Yeatman v. Patrician, 144 Wash. 241, 257 P. 622, 624.

SUPPLEMENTAL BILL. In equity pleading. A bill filed in addition to an original bill, in order to supply some defect in its original frame or structure which cannot be supplied by amendment. Story, Eq. Pl. §§ 332–338; Bloxham v. Railroad Co., 39 Fla. 243, 22 So. 697; Thompson v. Schenectady Railroad Co., C.C.N.Y., 119 F. 634; Bartee v. Matthews, 212 Ala. 667, 103 So. 874, 876; Pantaleo v. Colt's Patent Fire Arms Mfg. Co., D.C.N.Y., 13 F.Supp. 989, 990. Also for purpose of bringing into controversy matter occurring after original bill was filed. Snellings v. Builders' Supply Co., 228 Ala. 47, 152 So. 459, 461.

SUPPLEMENTAL BILL IN NATURE OF BILL OF REVIEW. Employed to invoke jurisdiction of court of chancery to recall one of its adjudications made while some fact existed which, if before court, would have prevented rendition of final decree, and which, without negligence of party presenting it, was not earlier presented to chancellor. Brown v. Oehler, 114 Fla. 57, 152 So. 862.

SUPPLEMENTAL CLAIM. A further claim which was filed when further relief was sought after the bringing of a claim. Smith, Ch. Pr. 655.

SUPPLEMENTAL COMPLAINT. Under the codes of practice obtaining in many of the states, a complaint filed in an action to bring to the notice of the court and the opposite party matters occurring after the commencement of action and which may affect the rights asserted. Pouder v. Tate, 132 Ind. 327, 30 N.E. 880; Plumer v. McDonald Lumber Co., 74 Wis. 137, 42 N.W. 250; Title and Trust Co. v. U. S. Fidelity and Guaranty Co., 138 Or. 467, 7 P.2d 805, 812.

It is distinguished from an "amended complaint," in that an "amended complaint" is one which corrects merely faults and errors of a pleading. Pantaleo v. Colt's Patent Fire Arms Mfg. Co., D.C.N.Y., 13 F.Supp. 989, 990.

SUPPLEMENTAL PLEADING. One consisting of facts arising since filing of the original, State v. Patten, 209 Ind. 482, 199 N.E. 577, 579; or of which pleader at time of serving of original pleading had no notice. Fisher v. Bullock, 204 App. Div. 523, 198 N.Y.S. 538, 540.

SUPPLEMENTARY. Added as a supplement; additional; being, or serving as, a supplement. Swanson v. State, 132 Neb. 82, 271 N.W. 264, 268.

SUPPLEMENTARY PROCEEDINGS. Proceedings supplementary to an execution, directed to the discovery of the debtor's property and its application to the debt for which the execution is issued. They are purely statutory, they are in the nature of a creditor's bill for the collection of a judgment or tax, and are proceedings in personam and not in rem. In re Maltbie, 119 N.E. 389, 391, 223 N.Y. 227; Walker v. Staley, 89 Colo. 292, 1 P.2d 924, 925.

SUPPLETORY OATH. See Oath.

SUPPLIANT. The actor in, or party preferring, a petition of right.

SUPPLICATIO. Lat. In the civil law. A petition for pardon of a first offense; also a petition for reversal of judgment; also equivalent to *"duplicatio,"* which corresponds to the common law rejoinder. Calvin.

SUPPLICAVIT. In English law. A writ issuing out of the king's bench or chancery for taking sureties of the peace. It is commonly directed to the justices of the peace, when they are averse to acting in the affair in their judicial capacity. 4 Bl.Comm. 253.

SUPPLICIUM. Lat. In the civil law. Punishment; corporal punishment for crime. Death was called *"ultimum supplicium,"* the last or extreme penalty.

SUPPLIES. In English law. In parliamentary proceedings the sums of money which are annually voted by the house of commons for the maintenance of the crown and the various public services. Jacob; Brown.

Means of provision or relief; stores; available aggregate of things needed or demanded in amount sufficient for a given use or purpose; accumulated stores reserved for distribution; sufficiency for use or need; a quantity of something supplied or on hand. Northern Pac. Ry. Co. v. Sanders County, 66 Mont. 608, 214 P. 596, 599.

In connection with building contracts, things other than labor, which are consumed in, but do not become a physical part of, the structure and is distinguished from the word "materials," which are things becoming a physical part of the structure. Hurley-Mason Co. v. American Bonding Co., 79 Wash. 564, 140 P. 575, 576, L.R.A.1915B, 1131.

SUPPLY. To furnish with what is wanted; available aggregate of things needed or demanded; anything yielded or afforded to meet a want; and the act of furnishing with what is wanted. Clayton v. Bridgeport Mach. Co., Tex.Civ.App., 33 S.W. 2d 787, 789.

SUPPLY, COMMISSIONERS OF. Persons appointed to levy the land-tax in Scotland, and to cause a valuation roll to be annually made up, and to perform other duties in their respective counties. Bell.

SUPPLY, COMMITTEE OF. In English law. All bills which relate to the public income or expenditure must originate with the house of commons, and all bills authorizing expenditure of the public money are based upon resolutions moved in a committee of supply, which is always a committee of the whole house. Wharton.

SUPPORT, *v.* Furnishing funds or means for maintenance; to maintain; to provide for; to enable to continue; to carry on. State v. Hinkle, 161 Wash. 652, 297 P. 1071, 1075. To provide a means of livelihood. Board of Com'rs of Logan County v. State, 122 Okl. 268, 254 P. 710, 711. To vindicate, to maintain, to defend, to uphold with aid or countenance. U. S. v. Schulze, D.C.Cal., 253 F. 377, 379.

To support a rule or order is to argue in answer to the arguments of the party who has shown cause against a rule or order *nisi*.

SUPPORT, *n.* That which furnishes a livelihood; a source or means of living; subsistence, sustenance, or living. Great Western Power Co. of California v. Industrial Accident Commission of California, 191 Cal. 424, 218 P. 1009, 1014.

In a broad sense the term includes all such means of living as would enable one to live in the degree of comfort suitable and becoming to his station of life. Benjamin F. Shaw Co. v. Palmatory, 7 Boyce, Del., 197, 105 A. 417, 419. For "Family," see that title.

It is said to include anything requisite to housing, feeding, clothing, health, proper recreation, vacation, traveling expense, or other proper cognate purposes, In re Vanderbilt's Estate, 223 N.Y.S. 314, 316, 129 Misc. 605; and proper care, nursing, and medical attendance in sickness, and suitable burial at death. McKnight v. McKnight, 212 Mich. 318, 180 N.W. 437, 442.

Support also signifies the right to have one's ground supported so that it will not cave in, when an adjoining owner makes an excavation. This support is of two kinds, *lateral* and *subjacent*. Lateral support is the right of land to be supported by the land which lies next to it. Subjacent support is the right of land to be supported by the land which lies under it.

SUPPOSITION. A conjecture based upon possibility or probability that a thing could or may have occurred, without proof that it did occur. Mitchell's Adm'x v. Harlan Central Coal Co., 263 Ky. 702, 93 S.W.2d 347, 348; Louisville and N. R. Co. v. Mann's Adm'r, 227 Ky. 399, 13 S.W.2d 257, 258.

SUPPRESS. To put a stop to a thing actually existing; to prohibit, put down, to prevent, subdue, or end by force. State v. Mustachia, 152 La. 821, 94 So. 408, 409; State ex rel. Hamilton v. Martin, 173 Wash. 249, 23 P.2d 1.

SUPPRESSIO VERI. Lat. Suppression or concealment of the truth. It is a rule of equity, as well as of law, that a *suppressio veri* is equivalent to a *suggestio falsi*; and where either the suppression of the truth or the suggestion of what is false can be proved, in a fact material to the contract, the party injured may have relief against the contract. Fleming v. Slocum, 18 Johns., N.Y., 405, 9 Am.Dec. 224; Turney v. Avery, 92 N.J.Eq. 473, 113 A. 710.

SUPPRESSIO VERI, EXPRESSIO FALSI. Suppression of the truth is [equivalent to] the expression of what is false. Addington v. Allen, 11 Wend., N.Y., 374, 417.

SUPPRESSIO VERI, SUGGESTIO FALSI. Suppression of the truth is [equivalent to] the suggestion of what is false. Paul v. Hadley, 23 Barb. N.Y. 521, 525.

SUPRA. Lat. Above; upon. This word occurring by itself in a book refers the reader to a previous part of the book, like "*ante*;" it is also the initial word of several Latin phrases.

SUPRA PROTEST. See Protest.

SUPRA-RIPARIAN. Upper riparian; higher up the stream. This term is applied to the estate, rights, or duties of a riparian proprietor whose land is situated at a point nearer the source of the stream than the estate with which it is compared.

SUPREMA POTESTAS SEIPSAM DISSOLVERE POTEST. Supreme power can dissolve itself. Bac. Max.

SUPREMACY. The state of being supreme, or in the highest station of power; paramount authority; sovereignty; sovereign power.

Act of Supremacy

The English statute 1 Eliz. c. 1, whereby the supremacy and autonomy of the crown in spiritual or ecclesiastical matters was declared and established.

Oath of Supremacy

An oath to uphold the supreme power of the kingdom of England in the person of the reigning sovereign.

SUPREME. Superior to all other things.

SUPREME COURT. A court of high powers and extensive jurisdiction, existing in most of the states. In some it is the official style of the chief appellate court or court of last resort. In others (such as New York) the supreme court is a court of general original jurisdiction, possessing also (in New York) some appellate jurisdiction, but not the court of last resort.

Supreme court of errors. In American law. An appellate tribunal, and the court of last resort, in the state of Connecticut.

Supreme court of the United States. The court of last resort in the federal judicial system. It is vested by the constitution with original jurisdiction in all cases affecting ambassadors, public ministers, and consuls, and those in which a state is a party, and appellate jurisdiction over all other cases within the judicial power of the United States, both as to law and fact, with such exceptions and under such regulations as congress may make. Its appellate powers extend to the subordinate federal courts, and also (in certain cases) to the supreme courts of the several states. The court is composed of a chief justice and eight associate justices.

Supreme judicial court. In American law. An appellate tribunal, and the court of last resort, in the states of Maine and Massachusetts.

SUPREME COURT OF JUDICATURE. The court formed by the English judicature act, 1873, (as modified by the judicature act, 1875, the appellate jurisdiction act, 1876, and the judicature acts of 1877, 1879, and 1881,) in substitution for the various superior courts of law, equity, admiralty, probate, and divorce, existing when the act was passed, including the court of appeal in chancery and bankruptcy, and the exchequer chamber. It consists of two permanent divisions, viz., a court of original jurisdiction, called the "high court of justice," and a court of appellate jurisdiction, called the "court of appeal." Its title of "supreme" is now a misnomer, as the superior appellate jurisdiction of the house of lords and privy council, which was originally intended to be transferred to it, has been allowed to remain. Sweet.

High Court of Justice

That branch of the English supreme court of judicature (*q. v.*) which exercises (1) the original jurisdiction formerly exercised by the court of chancery, the courts of queen's bench, common pleas, and exchequer, the courts of probate, divorce, and admiralty, the court of common pleas at Lancaster, the court of pleas at Durham, and the courts of the judges or commissioners of assize; and (2) the appellate jurisdiction of such of those courts as heard appeals from inferior courts. Judicature act, 1873, § 16.

SUPREME POWER. The highest authority in a state, all other powers in it being inferior thereto. State ex rel. Hartley v. Clausen, 146 Wash. 588, 264 P. 403, 405.

SUPREMUS. Lat. Last; the last.

SUPREMUS EST QUEM NEMO SEQUITUR. He is last whom no one follows. Dig. 50, 16, 92.

SUR. Fr. On; upon; over. In the titles of real actions "*sur*" was used to point out what the writ was founded upon. Thus, a real action brought by the owner of a reversion or seigniory, in certain cases where his tenant repudiated his tenure, was called "a writ of right *sur disclaimer*." So, a writ of entry *sur disseisin* was a real action to recover the possession of land from a disseisor. Sweet.

SUR CUI ANTE DIVORTIUM. See Cui Ante Divortium.

SUR CUI IN VITA. A writ that lay for the heir of a woman whose husband had aliened her land in fee, and she had omitted to bring the writ of *cui in vita* for the recovery thereof; in which case her heir might have this writ against the tenant after her decease. Cowell. See Cui in Vita.

SUR DISCLAIMER. A writ in the nature of a writ of right brought by the lord against a tenant who had disclaimed his tenure, to recover the land.

SUR MORTGAGE. Upon a mortgage. In some states the method of enforcing the security of a mortgage, upon default, is by a writ of "*scire facias sur mortgage*," which requires the defendant (mortgagor) to show cause why it should not be foreclosed.

SURCHARGE, *n.* An overcharge; an exaction, impost, or incumbrance beyond what is just and right, or beyond one's authority or power. "Surcharge" may mean a second or further mortgage. Wharton.

SURCHARGE, *v.* To put more cattle upon a common than the herbage will sustain or than the party has a right to do. 3 Bl. Comm. 237.

Equity Practice

To show that a particular item, in favor of the party surcharging, ought to have been included, but was not, in an account which is alleged to be settled or complete. To prove the omission of an item from an account which is before the court as complete, which should be inserted to the credit of the party surcharging. Story, Eq. Jur. § 525; 2 Ves. 565; Perkins v. Hart, 24 U.S. 237, 11 Wheat. 237, 6 L.Ed. 463; Dempsey v. McGinnis, 203 Mo.App. 494, 219 S.W. 148, 150.

General

Second surcharge. In English law. The surcharge of a common a second time, by the same defendant against whom the common was before admeasured, and for which the *writ of second surcharge* was given by the statute of Westminster, 2. 3 Bl. Comm. 239.

Surcharge and falsify. This phrase, as used in the courts of chancery, denotes the liberty which these courts will occasionally grant to a plaintiff, who disputes an account which the defendant alleges to be settled, to scrutinize particular items therein without opening the entire account. The showing an item for which credit ought to have been given, but was not, is to surcharge the account; the proving an item to have been inserted wrongly is to falsify the account. Brown. See Philips v. Belden, 2 Edw. Ch., N.Y., 23; Rehill v. McTague, 114 Pa. 82, 7 A. 224, 60 Am.Rep. 341; Shores-Mueller Co. v. Bell, 21 Ga.App. 194, 94 S.E. 83, 84.

SURDUS. Lat. In the civil law. Deaf; a deaf person. Inst. 2, 12, 3. *Surdus et mutus,* a deaf and dumb person.

SURENCHÈRE. In French law. A party desirous of repurchasing property at auction before the court, can, by offering one-tenth or one-sixth.

according to the case, in addition to the price realized at the sale, oblige the property to be put up once more at auction. This bid upon a bid is called a "*surenchère*." Arg. Fr. Merc. Law, 575.

SURETY. One who undertakes to pay money or to do any other act in event that his principal fails therein. In re Brock, 312 Pa. 92, 166 A. 778, 781. One bound with his principal for the payment of a sum of money or for the performance of some duty or promise and who is entitled to be indemnified by some one who ought to have paid or performed if payment or performance be enforced against him. Anderson v. Trueman, 100 Fla. 727, 130 So. 12, 13. Everyone who incurs a liability in person or estate, for the benefit of another, without sharing in the consideration, stands in the position of a "surety," whatever may be the form of his obligation. Howell v. War Finance Corporation, C.C.A.Ariz., 71 F.2d 237, 243.

A surety and guarantor have this in common, that they are both bound for another person; yet there are points of difference between them. A surety is usually bound with his principal by the same instrument, executed at the same time and on the same consideration. He is an original promisor and debtor from the beginning, and is held ordinarily to every known default of his principal. On the other hand, the contract of guarantor is his own separate undertaking, in which the principal does not join. It is usually entered into before or after that of the principal, and is often founded on a separate consideration from that supporting the contract of the principal. The original contract of the principal is not the guarantor's contract, and the guarantor is not bound to take notice of its nonperformance. The surety joins in the same promise as his principal and is primarily liable; the guarantor makes a separate and individual promise and is only secondarily liable. His liability is contingent on the default of his principal, and he only becomes absolutely liable when such default takes place and he is notified thereof. Georgia Casualty Co. v. Dixie Trust & Security Co., 23 Ga.App. 447, 98 S.E. 414, 416; Stifel Estate Co. v. Cella, 220 Mo.App. 657, 291 S.W. 515, 518; Ricketson v. Lizotte, 90 Vt. 386, 98 A. 801. "Surety" and "guarantor" are both answerable for debt, default, or miscarriage of another, but liability of guarantor is, strictly speaking, secondary and collateral, while that of surety is original, primary, and direct. In case of suretyship there is but one contract, and surety is bound by the same agreement which binds his principal, while in case of guaranty there are two contracts, and guarantor is bound by independent undertaking. Howell v. Commissioner of Internal Revenue, C.C.A.8, 69 F.2d 447, 450.

A surety is an insurer of the debt or obligation; a guarantor is an insurer of the solvency of the principal debtor or of his ability to pay. McClain v. Georgian Co., 17 Ga. App. 648, 87 S.E. 1090; Bishop v. Currie-McGraw Co., 133 Miss. 517, 97 So. 886, 889.

SURETY COMPANY. A company, usually incorporated, whose business is to assume the responsibility of a surety on the bonds of officers, trustees, executors, guardians, etc., in consideration of a fee proportioned to the amount of the security required. See State ex rel. Travelers' Indemnity Co. v. Knott, 114 Fla. 820, 153 So. 304.

SURETY INSURANCE. This phrase is generally used as synonymous with "guaranty insurance." People v. Potts, 264 Ill. 522, 106 N.E. 524, 528.

SURETY OF THE PEACE. A species of preventive justice, and consists in obliging those persons whom there is a probable ground to suspect of future misbehavior, to stipulate with, and to give full assurance to, the public that such offense as is apprehended shall not take place, by finding pledges or securities for keeping the peace, or for their good behavior. Brown. See Hyde v. Greuch, 62 Md. 582.

SURETYSHIP, CONTRACT OF. Contract whereby one party engages to be answerable for debt, default, or miscarriage of another and arises when one is liable to pay debt or discharge obligation, and party is entitled to indemnity from person who should have made the payment in the first instance before surety was so compelled. Bradley v. Bentley, 163 So. 351, 231 Ala. 28. A contract whereby one person engages to be answerable for the debt, default, or miscarriage of another. Pitm. Princ. & Sur. 1, 2; Scandinavian-American Bank of Fargo v. Westby, 41 N.D. 276, 172 N.W. 665, 670. An accessory promise by which a person binds himself for another already bound, and agrees with the creditor to satisfy the obligation, if the debtor does not. Hope v. Board, 43 La.Ann. 738, 9 So. 754. A lending of credit to aid a principal having insufficient credit of his own; the one expected to pay, having the primary obligation, being the "principal," and the one bound to pay, if the principal does not, being the "surety." Rollings v. Gunter, 211 Ala. 671, 101 So. 446, 448.

See Surety.

In contracts of "indemnity" against liability, the engagement is to indemnify another against liability on some obligation which he has incurred, or is about to incur, to a third person, and is not, as in "suretyship," a promise to one to whom another is answerable; in the former there is direct privity between the promisor and promisee and no debt owing by the third person to the promisee and the promisee has no remedy against the third person, whereas in the latter both principal and surety are bound to answer to the promisee. McManus v. Tralles, Mo.App., 253 S.W. 406, 409.

SURFACE. This term, when used in law, is seldom, if ever, limited to mere geometrical superficies, Clinchfield Coal Corporation v. Compton, 148 Va. 437, 139 S.E. 308, 312, 55 A.L.R. 1376; although when used without any qualifying phrase in a deed, it ordinarily signifies only the superficial part of land, Drummond v. White Oak Fuel Co., 104 W.Va. 368, 140 S.E. 57, 58, 56 A.L.R. 303. And when employed in connection with mining, it usually means that part of the earth or geologic section lying over the minerals in question, unless the contract or conveyance otherwise defines it. Marquette Cement Mining Co. v. Oglesby Coal Co., D.C.Ill., 253 F. 107, 111. Thus, where the surface is granted to one and the underlying coal to another, the "surface" includes the soil and waters which lie above and are superincumbent on the coal. Clinchfield Coal Corporation v. Compton, 148 Va. 437, 139 S.E. 308, 312, 55 A.L.R. 1376. Nevertheless, a conveyance of the "surface," except the oil and gas rights in the land, may be deemed, under certain circumstances, to constitute a conveyance of all the land (including coal deposits), except only the oil and gas rights specifically reserved. Ramage v. South Penn Oil Co., 94 W.Va. 81, 118 S.E. 162, 171, 31 A.L.R. 1509.

The term "surface," when used as the subject of a conveyance, is not a definite one capable of a definition of universal application, but is susceptible of limitation according to the intention of the parties using it; and in determining its meaning, regard may be had, not only to the language of the deed in which it occurs, but, also to the situation of the parties, the business in which they were engaged, and to the substance of the transaction. Ramage v. South Penn Oil Co., 94 W.Va. 81, 118 S.E. 162, 171, 31 A.L.R. 1509.

SURFACE WATERS. See Water.

SURGEON. One whose profession or occupation is to cure diseases or injuries of the body by manual operation; one who practices surgery, Webster; which is therapy of a distinctly operative kind, such as cutting operations, the reduction and putting up of fractures and dislocations and similar manual forms of treatment; Napier v. Greenzweig, C.C.A.N.Y., 256 F. 196, 197.

Popularly, one possessing particular knowledge and skill to correct and relieve some unnatural condition of the human body. Maupin v. Southern Surety Co., 205 Mo.App. 81, 220 S.W. 20, 21. One whose occupation is to cure local injuries or disorders, whether by manual operation, or by medication and constitutional treatment. Stewart v. Raab, 55 Minn. 20, 56 N.W. 256; Nelson v. State Board of Health, 108 Ky. 769, 57 S.W. 501, 50 L.R.A. 383; Surgery.

SURGERY. The art or practice of healing by manual operation; that branch of medical science which treats of mechanical or operative measures for healing diseases, deformities or injuries. State v. Eustace, 117 Kan. 746, 233 P. 109, 110; Maryland Casualty Co. v. McCallum, 200 Ala. 154, 75 So. 902, 904. Therapy of a distinctly operative kind, such as cutting operations, the reduction and putting up of fractures and dislocations and similar manual forms of treatment. Napier v. Greenzweig, C.C.A.N.Y., 256 F. 196, 197. As used in statutes, the term does not include osteopathy. Mo. R.S.A. § 10042. Le Grand v. Security Benefit Ass'n, 210 Mo.App. 700, 240 S.W. 852, 853. State v. Eustace, 117 Kan. 746, 233 P. 109, 110.

Greek words signifying the hand and work. Originally, it was part of the profession of barbers, but later was taken up by physicians and now is recognized as that branch of medical science, and more specifically, that branch of medical science which treats of mechanical or operative measures for healing diseases, deformities, or injuries. State ex rel. Beck v. Gleason, 148 Kan. 1, 79 P.2d 911.

The practice of *medicine,* in contradistinction to the practice of *surgery,* denotes the treatment of disease by the administration of drugs or other sanative substances. There cannot be a complete separation between the practice of medicine and surgery; the principles of both are the same throughout, and no one is qualified to practice either who does not properly understand the fundamental principles of both.

SURGICAL OPERATION. An act or series of acts performed on a patient's body by a surgeon to produce a cure. Hartford Live Stock Ins. Co. v. McMillen, C.C.A.Ohio, 9 F.2d 961, 962.

SURMISE. Formerly where a defendant pleaded a local custom, for instance, a custom of the city of London, it was necessary for him to "surmise," that is, to suggest that such custom should be certified to the court by the mouth of the recorder, and without such a surmise the issue was to be tried by the country as other issues of fact are. 1 Burrows, 251; Vin. Abr. 246.

Something offered to a court to move it to grant a prohibition, *audita querela,* or other writ grantable thereon. Jacob.

In ecclesiastical law. An allegation in a libel. A collateral surmise is a surmise of some fact not appearing in the libel. Phillim. Ecc. Law, 1445.

SURNAME. The family name; the name over and above the Christian name. The part of a name which is not given in baptism; the name of a person which is derived from the common name of his parents; In re Faith's Application, 22 N.J. Misc. 412, 39 A.2d 638, 640. The last name; the name common to all members of a family. A patronymic. Riley v. Litchfield, 168 Iowa 187, 150 N.W. 81, 83, Ann.Cas.1917B, 172.

SURPLICE FEES. In English ecclesiastical law. Fees payable on ministerial offices of the church; such as baptisms, funerals, marriages, etc.

SURPLUS. That which remains of a fund appropriated for a particular purpose; the remainder of a thing; the overplus; the residue. Smith v. Cotting, 231 Mass. 42, 120 N.E. 177, 181; People's F. Ins. Co. v. Parker, 35 N.J.L. 577; Towery v. McGaw, 22 Ky.Law.Rep. 155, 56 S.W. 727; Appeal of Coates, 2 Pa. 137; 18 Ves. 466.

The "surplus" of a corporation may mean either the net assets of the corporation in excess of all liabilities including capital stock, Winkelman v. General Motors Corporation, D.C.N.Y., 44 F.Supp. 960, 996; or what remains after making provisions for all liabilities of every kind, except capital stock. Insurance Co. of North America v. McCoach, C.C.A.Pa., 224 F. 657, 658. The term is also defined as the residue of assets after defraying liabilities, Douglas v. Edwards, C.C.A.N.Y., 298 F. 229, 237; Cochrane v. Interstate Packing Co., 139 Minn. 452, 167 N.W. 111, 113; the excess of net assets over the face value of the stock. Sexton v. C. L. Percival Co., 189 Iowa 586, 177 N.W. 83, 86; the excess of gross assets over the outstanding capital stock, without deducting debts or liabilities; State v. State Tax Commission ex rel. Marquette Hotel Inv. Co., 282 Mo. 213, 221 S.W. 721, 722; and as the accumulation of moneys or property in excess of the par value of the stock. Small v. Sullivan, 245 N.Y. 343, 157 N.E. 261, 263.

There is a sharp distinction between the "surplus," as of a bank, and undivided profits. Surplus, like the capital stock, constitutes the working capital of the bank and is, in addition, a fund for the protection of the depositors. First Nat. Bank v. Moon, 102 Kan. 334, 170 P. 33, 34, L.R.A.1918C, 986. The "undivided profits" constitute a temporary fund changing in size from day to day and carried only until dividend periods when it is distributed to the stockholders or transferred to the permanent surplus. It is the fund from which the expenses and losses of the bank are paid. Sarles v. Scandinavian American Bank, 33 N.D. 40, 156 N.W. 556, 557. Willcuts v. Milton Dairy Co., 48 S.Ct. 71, 72, 275 U.S. 215, 72 L.Ed. 247; State ex rel. Payne v. Exchange Bank of Natchitoches, 147 La. 25, 84 So. 481, 482.

As to surplus "Earnings," "Profits," and "Water," see those titles.

SURPLUSAGE. Extraneous, impertinent, superfluous, or unnecessary matter. In re Wolcott's Estate, 54 Utah, 165, 180 P. 169, 170, 4 A.L.R. 727.

Accounts

A greater disbursement than the charge of the accountant amounts unto. In another sense, the remainder or overplus of money left. Jacob. A balance over. 1 Lew. 219.

Pleading

Allegations of matter wholly foreign and impertinent to the cause. All matter beyond the circumstances necessary to constitute the action. 5 East 275; Allaire v. Ouland, 2 Johns. Cas. (N.Y.) 52; Adams v. Capital State Bank, 74 Miss. 307, 20 So. 881; Bradley v. Reynolds, 61 Conn. 271, 23 A. 928; State v. Kavanaugh, 203 La. 1, 13 So.2d 366, 371. Any allegation without which the pleading would yet be adequate. Mathews v. U. S., C.C.A. Neb., 15 F.2d 139, 142; State v. Williams, 94 Vt. 423, 111 A. 701, 708; People v. Osborne, 278 Ill. 104, 115 N.E. 890, 891.

SURPLUSAGIUM NON NOCET. Surplusage does no harm. 3 Bouv. Inst. no. 2949; Broom, Max. 627.

SURPRISE. Act of taking unawares; sudden confusion or perplexity. Davis v. Steuben School Tp., 19 Ind.App. 694, 50 N.E. 1. In its legal acceptation, denotes an unforeseen disappointment against which ordinary prudence would not have afforded protection. Patrick v. Boonville Gas Light Co., 17 Mo.App. 462, 463, 465.

Equity Practice

The act by which a party who is entering into a contract is taken unawares, by which sudden confusion or perplexity is created, which renders it proper that a court of equity should relieve the party so surprised. 2 Brown, Ch. 150.

The situation in which a party is placed without any default of his own, which will be injurious to his interests. Rawle v. Skipwith, 8 Mart. N. S., La., 407.

Anything which happens without the agency or fault of the party affected by it, tending to disturb and confuse the judgment, or to mislead him, of which the opposite party takes an undue advantage, is in equity a surprise, and one species of fraud for which relief is granted. Gidionsen v. Union Depot R. Co., 129 Mo. 392, 31 S.W. 800; Heath v. Scott, 65 Cal. 548, 4 Pac. 557; Zimmerer v. Fremont Nat. Bank, 59 Neb. 661, 81 N.W. 849; Thompson v. Connell, 31 Or. 231, 48 P. 467, 65 Am.St.Rep. 818.

There does not seem anything technical or peculiar in the word "surprise," as used in courts of equity. Where a court of equity relieves on the ground of surprise, it does so upon the ground that the party has been taken unawares, and that he has acted without due deliberation, and under confused and sudden impressions. 1 Story, Eq. Jur. § 120, note. But Jeremy, Eq.Jur. 366, 383, note, seems to think that the word surprise is a technical expression, and nearly synonymous with fraud. It is sometimes used in this sense when it is deemed presumptive of, or approaching to, fraud. 1 Fonbl.Eq. 123; 3 Ch.Cas. 56, 74, 103, 114.

Law

As a ground for a new trial, that situation in which a party is unexpectedly placed without default on his part, which will work injury to his interests. State v. Price, 100 W.Va. 699, 131 S.E. 710, 711. He must show himself to have been diligent at every stage of the proceedings. Henderson v. Hazlett, 75 W.Va. 255, 83 S.E. 907, 908. And that the event was one which ordinary prudence could not have guarded against; Cupples v. Zupan, 35 Idaho, 458, 207 P. 328, 329; Jennings v. American President Lines, 61 Cal.App.2d 417, 143 P.2d 349, 356.

A situation, status, or result produced, having a substantive basis of fact and reason, from which the court may justly deduce, as a legal conclusion, that the party will suffer a judicial wrong if not relieved from his mistake. Levy v. Caledonian Ins. Co., D.C.Cal., 226 F. 336, 337.

The general rule is that when a party or his counsel is "taken by surprise," in a material point or circumstance which could not have been anticipated, and when want of skill, care, or attention cannot be justly imputed, and injustice has been done, a new trial should be granted. Hill. New Trials, 521.

SURREBUTTER. In pleading. The plaintiff's answer of fact to the defendant's rebutter. Steph. Pl. 59. It is governed by the same rules as the replication. See 6 Com. Dig. 185; 7 *id.* 389.

SURREJOINDER. In pleading. The plaintiff's answer of fact to the defendant's rejoinder. Steph. Pl. 59. It is governed in every respect by the same rules as the replication. Steph. Pl. 77, 7 Com. Dig. 389.

SURRENDER. To give back; yield; render up; restore; and in law the giving up of an estate to the person who has it in reversion or remainder, so as to merge it in the larger estate; the giving up of a lease before its expiration; yielding up a tenancy in a copyhold estate to the lord of the manor for a specified purpose; a deed by which surrender is made; the giving up by a bankrupt of his property to his creditors or their assignees; also, his due appearance in the bankruptcy court for examination as formerly required by the bankruptcy acts. In re Emlen's Estate, 333 Pa. 238, 4 A.2d 143, 145; Nolander v. Burns, 48 Minn. 13, 50 N.W. 1016.

A yielding up of an estate for life or years to him who has an immediate estate in reversion or remainder, wherein the estate for life or years may drown by mutual agreement between them. Roberts Inv. Co. v. Hardie Mfg. Co., 142 Or. 179, 19 P.2d 429, 431; Kimberlin v. Hicks, 150 Kan. 449, 94 P.2d 335, 339.

"Surrender" is contractual act and occurs only through consent of both parties. Motch's Adm'r v. Portner, 237 Ky. 25, 34 S.W.2d 744, 745.

Surrender differs from "abandonment," as applied to leased premises, inasmuch as the latter is simply an act on the part of the lessee alone; but to show a surrender, a mutual agreement between lessor and lessee that the lease is terminated must be clearly proved. Noble v. Sturm, 210 Mich. 462, 178 N.W. 99, 106.

A surrender is of a nature directly opposite to a release; for, as the latter operates by the greater estate descending upon the less, the former is the falling of a less estate into a greater, by deed. Shepp.Touchst. 300.

SURRENDER BY BAIL. The act, by bail or sureties in a recognizance, of giving up their principal again into custody, in their own discharge. 1 Burrill, Pr. 394.

SURRENDER BY OPERATION OF LAW. This phrase is properly applied to cases where the tenant for life or years has been a party to some act the validity of which he is by law afterwards estopped from disputing, and which would not be valid if his particular estate continued to exist. Ledsinger v. Burke, 113 Ga. 74, 38 S.E. 313; Brown

v. Cairns, 107 Iowa, 727, 77 N.W. 478. An implied surrender occurs when an estate incompatible with the existing estate is accepted, or the lessee takes a new lease of the same lands. Livingston v. Potts, 16 Johns., N.Y., 28; 1 B. & Ald. 50. See Beall v. White, 94 U.S. 389, 24 L.Ed. 173; Martin v. Stearns, 52 Iowa, 347, 3 N.W. 92.

The rule of law as now settled by recently adjudicated cases is that any acts which are equivalent to an agreement on the part of the tenant to abandon, and on the part of the landlord to resume the possession of the demised premises, amount to a "surrender by operation of law." Carlton Chambers Co. v. Trask, 261 Mass. 264, 158 N.E. 786, 788; 1375–83 Broadway Corporation v. Filler, 267 N.Y.S. 779, 149 Misc. 474. The rule may be safely said to be that a surrender is created by operation of law, when the parties to a lease do some act so inconsistent with the subsisting relation of landlord and tenant as to imply that they have both agreed to consider the surrender as made. Flannagan v. Dickerson, 103 Okl. 206, 229 P. 552, 553; Hodgkiss v. Dayton-Brower Co., 156 N.Y.S. 907, 908, 93 Misc. 109; Triest & Co. v. Goldstone, 173 Cal. 240, 159 P. 715, 716.

SURRENDER OF CHARTER. A corporation created by charter may give up or "surrender" its charter to the people, unless the charter was granted under a statute, imposing indefeasible duties on the bodies to which it applies. Grant, Corp. 45.

SURRENDER OF COPYHOLD. The mode of conveying or transferring copyhold property from one person to another is by means of a surrender, which consists in the yielding up of the estate by the tenant into the hands of the lord for such purposes as are expressed in the surrender. The process in most manors is for the tenant to come to the steward, either in court or out of court, or else to two customary tenants of the same manor, provided there be a custom to warrant it, and there, by delivering up a rod, a glove, or other symbol, as the custom directs, to resign into the hands of the lord, by the hands and acceptance of his steward, or of the said two tenants, all his interest and title to the estate, in trust, to be again granted out by the lord to such persons and for such uses as are named in the surrender, and as the custom of the manor will warrant. Brown.

SURRENDER OF CRIMINALS. The act by which the public authorities deliver a person accused of a crime, and who is found in their jurisdiction, to the authorities within whose jurisdiction it is alleged the crime has been committed.

SURRENDER OF A PREFERENCE. In bankruptcy practice. The surrender to the assignee in bankruptcy, by a preferred creditor, of anything he may have received under his preference and any advantage it gives him, which he must do before he can share in the dividend. In re Richter's Estate, 1 Dill. 544, Fed.Cas.No.11,803. The word as generally defined may denote either compelled or voluntary action. Keppel v. Bank, 197 U.S. 356, 25 S.Ct. 443, 49 L.Ed. 790. In Bankruptcy Act 1898, § 57g (11 U.S.C.A. § 93 (g), providing that creditors must *surrender* preferences before having claims allowed, it is unqualified and generic, and hence embraces both meanings. Keppel v. Bank, *supra*.

SURRENDER TO USES OF WILL. Formerly a copyhold interest would not pass by will unless it had been surrendered to the use of the will. By St. 55 Geo. III. c. 192, this is no longer necessary. 1 Steph. Comm. 639; Mozley & Whitley.

SURRENDEREE. The person to whom a surrender is made.

SURRENDEROR. One who makes a surrender. One who yields up a copyhold estate for the purpose of conveying it.

SURREPTITIOUS. Stealthily or fraudulently done, taken away, or introduced.

SURROGATE. In American law. The name given in some of the states to the judge or judicial officer who has the administration of probate matters, guardianships, etc. See Malone v. Sts. Peter & Paul's Church, 172 N.Y. 269, 64 N.E. 961. In other states he is called judge of probate, register, judge of the orphans' court, etc. He is ordinarily a county officer, with a local jurisdiction limited to his county.

In English law. One that is substituted or appointed in the room of another, as by a bishop, chancellor, judge, etc.; especially an officer appointed to dispense licenses to marry without banns. 2 Steph. Comm. 247.

SURROGATE'S COURT. In the United States. A state tribunal, with similar jurisdiction to the *court of ordinary, court of probate,* etc., relating to matters of probate, etc. 2 Kent, Comm. 409, note *b*. And see Robinson v. Fair, 9 S.Ct. 30, 128 U.S. 53, 32 L.Ed. 415; In re Hawley, 104 N.Y. 250, 10 N.E. 352.

SURROUND. To inclose on all sides; to encompass. In re Creveling, Cust. & Pat.App., 61 F.2d 862, 863.

SURROUNDING CIRCUMSTANCES. Which may permit inference of culpability on part of defendant under res ipsa loquitur rule refers, not to circumstances directly tending to show lack of care, but only to mere neutral circumstances of control and management by defendant, which may, when explained, appear to be entirely consistent with due care. Hepp v. Quickel Auto & Supply Co., 37 N.M. 525, 25 P.2d 197.

SURSISE. L. Fr. In old English law. Neglect; omission; default; cessation.

SURSUM REDDERE. Lat. In old conveyancing. To render up; to surrender.

SURSUMREDDITIO. Lat. A surrender.

SURVEILLANCE. Oversight, superintendence, supervision. People v. Howard, 120 Cal.App. 45, 8 P.2d 176, 179.

SURVEY, *v.* Of land, to ascertain corners, boundaries, divisions, with distances and directions, and not necessarily to compute areas included within defined boundaries. Keer v. Fee, 179 Iowa, 1097, 161 N.W. 545, 547.

SURVEY, *n.* The process by which a parcel of land is measured and its contents ascertained; also a statement of the result of such survey, with the courses and distances and the quantity of the land. Corporation of Frederick Scholes v. Theodore Ficke Warehouses, 213 App.Div. 259, 210 N.Y.S. 341, 343. The land included in field notes. Cross v. Wilkinson, Tex.Civ.App., 187 S.W. 345, 346.

Insurance

An examination. A plan and description of the present existing state, condition, and mode of use of the property. Macatawa Transp. Co. v. Firemen's Fund Ins. Co., 179 Mich. 443, 146 N.W. 396, 398.

In insurance law, the term has acquired a general meaning, inclusive of what is commonly called the "application," which contains the questions propounded on behalf of the company, and the answers of the assured. Albion Lead Works v. Williamsburg City F. Ins. Co., C.C.Mass., 2 F. 484; May v. Buckeye Ins. Co., 25 Wis. 291, 3 Am.Rep. 76.

Sales

An examination.

General

Survey of a vessel. A statement of its present condition. Chicago S. S. Lines v. U. S. Lloyds, C.C.A.Ill., 12 F.2d 733, 737. A public document, looked to both by underwriters and owners, as affording the means of ascertaining, at the time and place, the state and condition of the ship and other property at hazard. Potter v. Ocean Ins. Co., 3 Sumn. 43, 19 Fed.Cas.1,173; Hathaway v. Sun Mut. Ins. Co., 8 Bosw., N.Y., 68.

SURVEYOR. One who makes surveys, determines area of portion of earth's surface, length and direction of boundary lines, and contour of surface. Severance v. Ball, 93 Cal.App. 56, 268 P. 1068, 1070.

SURVEYOR OF HIGHWAYS. In English law. A person elected by the inhabitants of a parish, in vestry assembled, to survey the highways therein. He must possess certain qualifications in point of property; and, when elected, he is compellable, unless he can show some grounds of exemption, to take upon himself the office. Mozley & Whitley.

SURVEYOR OF THE PORT. A revenue officer of the United States appointed for each of the principal ports of entry, whose duties chiefly concern the importations at his station and the determination of their amount and valuation. Rev.St.U.S. § 2627 (19 U.S.C.A. § 40).

SURVIVAL STATUTES. Statutory provision for the survival, after death of the injured person, of certain causes of action for injury to the person whether death results from the injury or from some other cause. The cause of action which survives is for the wrong to the injured person. In re Daniel's Estate, 294 N.W. 465, 208 Minn. 420.

See, also, Wrongful Death Statutes.

SURVIVE. To continue to live or exist beyond the life, or existence of; to continue to live or exist beyond (a specified period or event); to live through in spite of; live on after passing through; to remain alive; exist in force or operation beyond any period specified. Thompson v. New Orleans Ry. & Light Co., 145 La. 805, 83 So. 19, 20.

SURVIVING. Remaining alive. State ex rel. Baker v. Bird, 253 Mo. 569, 162 S.W. 119, 123, Ann. Cas. 1915C, 353.

SURVIVOR. One who survives another; one who outlives another; one who lives beyond some happening; one of two or more persons who lives after the death of the other or others. Baker v. Baker, 182 Ala. 194, 62 So. 284, 286.

The word "survivor," however, in connection with the power of one of two trustees to act, is used not only with reference to a condition arising where one of such trustees dies, but also as indicating a trustee who continues to administer the trust after his cotrustee is disqualified, has been removed, renounces, or refuses to act. Busch v. Schuttler, 216 Ill.App. 212, 217.

SURVIVORSHIP. The living of one of two or more persons after the death of the other or others.

Survivorship is where a person becomes entitled to property by reason of his having survived another person who had an interest in it. In re Conklin's Estate, 20 N.Y.S.2d 59, 62, 259 App.Div. 432; United States v. Jacobs, Ill. & N. Y., 306 U.S. 363, 59 S.Ct. 551, 555, 83 L.Ed. 763.

SUS. PER COLL. An abbreviation of "*suspendatur per collum*," let him be hanged by the neck. Words formerly used in England in signing judgment against a prisoner who was to be executed; being written by the judge in the margin of the sheriff's calendar or list, opposite the prisoner's name. 4 Bl. Comm. 403. Written, also, "sus' per coll'."

SUSCEPTIBLE. Capable. U. S. v. Sischo, D.C. Wash., 262 F. 1001, 1005. And see Bensdorff v. Uihlein, 132 Tenn. 193, 177 S.W. 481, 482, 2 A.L.R. 1364.

SUSPECT. To have a slight or even vague idea concerning;—not necessarily involving knowledge or belief or likelihood. Cheek v. Missouri, K. & T. Ry. Co., 89 Kan. 247, 131 P. 617, 624.

"Suspect" with reference to probable cause as grounds for arrest without warrant is ordinarily used in place of the word believe. U. S. v. Rembert, D.C.Tex., 284 F. 996, 1001. But to "suspect and believe" that a person, claiming to have been falsely imprisoned by a deputy sheriff, is a felon, is not the legal equivalent of belief on probable cause. Hill v. Wyrosdick, 216 Ala. 235, 113 So. 49, 50.

SUSPEND. To interrupt; to cause to cease for a time; to postpone; to stay, delay, or hinder; to discontinue temporarily, but with an expectation or purpose of resumption. To forbid a public officer, attorney, employee, or ecclesiastical person from performing his duties or exercising his functions for a more or less definite interval of time.

Insurance Co. v. Aiken, 82 Va. 428; Stack v. O'Hara, 98 Pa. 232; Reeside v. U. S., 8 Wall. 42, 19 L.Ed. 318; U. S. v. Felder, D.C.N.Y., 13 F.2d 527, 528; Bishop v. Bacon, 130 Pa.Super. 240, 196 A. 918, 921.

To postpone, as a judicial sentence. State v. Anderson, 43 S.D. 630, 181 N.W. 839, 840; People ex rel. Holton v. Hunt, 217 App.Div. 428, 216 N.Y.S. 765, 768, To stay, as a decree;—not synonymous with vacate. Stewart v. Oneal, C.C.A.Ohio, 237 F. 897, 903.

To cause a temporary cessation, as of work by an employee; to lay off;—not synonymous with remove. Thomas v. City of Chicago, 194 Ill.App. 526, 529.

Also, sometimes, to discontinue or dispense with (permanently); to remove permanently from office; to discharge (an employee) permanently. Phelps v. Connellee, Tex.Civ.App., 278 S.W. 939, 941. See Suspension.

SUSPENDER. In Scotch law. He in whose favor a suspension is made.

SUSPENSE. When a rent, profit *à prendre,* and the like, are, in consequence of the unity of possession of the rent, etc., of the land out of which they issue, not *in esse* for a time, they are said to be in suspense, *tunc dormiunt;* but they may be revived or awakened. Co. Litt. 313*a*.

SUSPENSION. A temporary stop, a temporary delay, interruption, or cessation. Hood ex rel. North Carolina Bank & Trust Co. v. Clark, 211 N.C. 693, 191 S.E. 732, 733.

A temporary stop of a right, of a law, and the like. Thus, we speak of a *suspension* of the writ of *habeas corpus,* of a statute, of the power of alienating an estate, of a person in office, etc.

A temporary cutting off or debarring one, as from the privileges of an institution or society. John B. Stetson University v. Hunt, 88 Fla. 510, 102 So. 637, 639.

An ad interim stoppage or arrest of official power and pay;—not synonymous with "removal," which terminates wholly the incumbency of the office or employment. State v. Board of Police & Fire Com'rs of La Crosse, 159 Wis. 295, 150 N.W. 493, 494. Temporary withdrawal or cessation from public work as distinguished from permanent severance accomplished by removal, Bois v. City of Fall River, 257 Mass. 471, 154 N.E. 270; "removal" being, however, the broader term, which may on occasion include suspension. State v. Medler, 19 N.M. 252, 142 P. 376, 379.

Ecclesiastical Law

An ecclesiastical censure, by which a spiritual person is either interdicted the exercise of his ecclesiastical function or hindered from receiving the profits of his benefice. It may be partial or total, for a limited time, or forever, when it is called "deprivation" or "amotion." Ayl. Par. 501.

Scotch Law

A stay of execution until after a further consideration of the cause. Ersk. Inst. 4, 3, 5.

General

Pleas in suspension were those which showed some matter of temporary incapacity to proceed with the action or suit. Steph. Pl. 45.

Suspension of a right. The act by which a party is deprived of the exercise of his right for a time. A temporary stop of a right, a partial extinguishment for a time, as contrasted with a complete extinguishment, where the right is absolutely dead. In re Muser's Estate, 122 Misc. 164, 203 N.Y.S. 619, 621. Suspension of a right in an estate is a temporary or partial withholding of it from use or exercise. It differs from extinguishment, because a suspended right is susceptible of being revived, which is not the case where the right was extinguished. Bac. Abr. *Extinguishment* (A).

Suspension of a statute. A temporary stop. Chicago, R. I. & P. Ry. Co. v. Holliday, 45 Okl. 536, 145 P. 786, 793. The suspension of a statute for a limited time operates so as to prevent its operation for the time; but it has not the effect of a repeal. Brown v. Barry, 3 U.S. 365, 3 Dall. 365, 1 L.Ed. 638.

Suspension of arms. An agreement between belligerents, made for a short time or for a particular place, to cease hostilities between them. See, also, Armistice.

Suspension of business. These words in a statute contemplate an interruption of ordinary business operations, evidenced by some objective features; an interruption of the ordinary course of business, other than a mere failure to meet maturing obligations. Hoover Steel Ball Co. v. Schafer Ball Bearings Co., 89 N.J.Eq. 433, 105 A. 500, 501.

SUSPENSIVE CONDITION. See Condition.

SUSPENSORY CONDITION. See Condition.

SUSPICION. The act of suspecting, or the state of being suspected; imagination, generally of something ill; distrust; mistrust; doubt. McCalla v. State, 66 Ga. 348. The apprehension of something without proof or upon slight evidence. State v. Hall, Mo.App., 285 S.W. 1009, 1011.

Suspicion implies a belief or opinion based upon facts or circumstances which do not amount to proof. Burton v. McNeill, 196 S.C. 250, 13 S.E.2d 10, 11, 133 A.L.R. 603.

SUSPICIOUS CHARACTER. In the criminal laws of some of the states, a person who is known or strongly suspected to be an habitual criminal, or against whom there is reasonable cause to believe that he has committed a crime or is planning or intending to commit one, or whose actions and behavior give good ground for suspicion and who can give no good account of himself, and who may therefore be arrested or required to give security for good behavior. See McFadin v. San Antonio, 22 Tex.Civ.App. 140, 54 S.W. 48; People v. Russell, 35 Misc.Rep. 765, 72 N.Y.Supp. 1; 4 Bl. Comm. 252.

SUSTAIN. To carry on; to maintain. George v. Connecticut Fire Ins. Co., 84 Okl. 172, 201 P. 510, 512, 23 A.L.R. 80.

To support; to warrant;—said of evidence in connection with a verdict, decision, etc. Johnson v. Allispaugh, 58 Ind.App. 83, 107 N.E. 686, 688; Work v. Whittington, 61 Cal.App. 302, 214 P. 474.

To suffer; bear; undergo. To endure or undergo without failing or yielding; to bear up under. Webster.

SUTHDURE. The south door of a church, where canonical purgation was performed, and plaints, etc., were heard and determined. Wharton.

SUTLER. A person who, as a business, follows an army and sells provisions and liquor to the troops. A small trader who follows an army and who is licensed to sell goods, especially edibles, to the soldiers. Keane v. U. S., C.C.A.Va., 272 F. 577, 582.

SUUM CUIQUE TRIBUERE. Lat. To render to everyone his own. One of the three fundamental maxims of the law laid down by Justinian.

SUUS HÆRES. See Hæres.

SUUS JUDEX. Lat. In old English law. A proper judge; a judge having cognizance of a cause. Literally, one's own judge. Bract. fol. 401.

SUZERAIN. In French and feudal law. The immediate vassal of the king; a crown vassal; a tenant *in capite*. A lord who possesses a fief whence other fiefs issue. Note 77 of Butler & Hargrave's notes, Co. Litt. l. 3. Also spelled "suzereign."

International Law

A state that exercises political control over another state, in relation to which it is sovereign. Webster.

The word has no clear or precise signification. It has been extended to the control of European Powers through their colonies over imperfectly civilized people. 12 L. Quart.Rev. 223; 1896, p. 122. See, also, Hershey, Int.L. 106.

In modern times suzerainty is used as descriptive of relations, ill-defined and vague, which exist between powerful and dependent states; its very indefiniteness being its recommendation. While protecting and protected states tend to draw nearer, the reverse is true of suzerain and vassal states; a protectorate is generally the preliminary to incorporation; suzerainty, to separation. Encycl.Br.

It is said that suzerainty is title without corresponding power; protectorate is power without corresponding title. Freund, Pol.Sci.Quart. 1899, p. 28.

SWAIN; SWAINMOTE. See Swein; Sweinmote.

SWAMP. A "swamp" has been defined as wet, spongy land, soft low ground saturated with water, but not usually covered by it, marshy ground away from seashore. Campbell v. Walker, 137 Or. 375, 2 P.2d 912, 914.

SWAMP AND OVERFLOWED LANDS. Lands unfit for cultivation by reason of their swampy character and requiring drainage or reclamation to render them available for beneficial use. Miller v. Eastern Ry. & Lumber Co., 84 Wash. 31, 146 P. 171, 173; Beer v. Whiteville Lumber Co., 170 N.C. 337, 86 S.E. 1024.

Such lands, when constituting a portion of the public domain, have generally been granted by congress to the several states within whose limits they lie. See Miller v. Tobin, C.C.Or., 18 F. 614; Keeran v. Allen, 33 Cal. 546; Hogaboom v. Ehrhardt, 58 Cal. 233; Thompson v. Thornton, 50 Cal. 144; Martin v. Busch, 93 Fla. 535, 112 So. 274, 284.

SWANIMOTE. See Sweinmote.

SWARF-MONEY. Warth-money; or guard-money paid in lieu of the service of castle-ward. Cowell.

SWATCH. Commercially, a small sample of cloth from which suits, etc., are to be ordered. U. S. Fashion & Sample Book Co. v. Montrose Cloak & Suit Co., Mo.Sup., 218 S.W. 867, 869.

SWEAR. To put on oath; to administer an oath to a person.

To take an oath; to become bound by an oath duly administered. To declare on oath the truth (of a petition, etc.). Indiana Quarries Co. v. Simms, 158 Ky. 415, 165 S.W. 422; Landrum v. Landrum, 159 Ga. 324, 125 S.E. 832, 833, 38 A.L.R. 217.

To use profane language;—a punishable offense in many jurisdictions. See Gaines v. State, 7 Lea, Tenn., 410, 40 Am.Rep. 64; State v. Chrisp, 85 N.C. 528, 39 Am.Rep. 713. For "False Swearing," see that title.

SWEARING THE PEACE. Showing to a magistrate that one has just cause to be afraid of another in consequence of his menaces, in order to have him bound over to keep the peace.

SWEATING. The questioning of a person in custody charged with crime with intent to obtain information concerning his connection therewith or knowledge thereof by plying him with questions, or by threats or other wrongful means, extorting information to be used against him. Under the statute mere questioning amounts to "sweating" if done for the purpose of extorting from the accused information to be used against him; that is, inducing him to unwillingly or involuntarily give such information. Commonwealth v. McClanahan, 153 Ky. 412, 155 S.W. 1131, 1132, Ann.Cas. 1915C, 132.

SWEAT SHOP. A plant whose employees are overworked and paid low wages, or a place where employees are required to work to an extent hardly endurable, and in the public mind the term imputes unsavory and illegal business practices. Masters v. Sun Mfg. Co., 237 Mo.App. 240, 165 S.W.2d 701, 703.

SWEEPING. Comprehensive; including in its scope many persons or objects; as, a sweeping objection.

SWEEPSTAKES. In horse racing, the sum of the stakes for which the subscribers agree to pay for each horse nominated. Stone v. Clay, 10 C.C. A. 147, 61 F. 889.

SWEIN. In old English law. A freeman or freeholder within the forest.

SWEINMOTE. In forest law. A court holden before the verderors, as judges, by the stewart of the sweinmote, thrice in every year, the *sweins* or freeholders within the forest composing the jury. Its principal jurisdiction was—*First,* to inquire into the oppressions and grievances committed by the officers of the forest; and, *secondly,* to receive and try presentments certified from the court of attachments in offenses against vert and venison. 3 Bl. Comm. 72.

SWELL. To enlarge or increase. In an action of tort, circumstances of aggravation may "swell" the damages.

SWIFT WITNESS. A term colloquially applied to a witness who is unduly zealous or partial for the side which calls him, and who betrays his bias by his extreme readiness to answer questions or volunteer information.

SWINDLER. A cheat; one guilty of defrauding divers persons. 1 Term, 748.

SWINDLING. Cheating and defrauding grossly with deliberate artifice. Wyatt v. Ayres, 2 Port., Ala., 157; Chase v. Whitlock, 3 Hill, N.Y., 140. Usually applied to a transaction where the guilty party procures the delivery to him, under a pretended contract, of the personal property of another, with the felonious design of appropriating it to his own use. 2 Russ.Cr. 130; Stevenson v. Hayden, 2 Mass. 406; Jones v. State, 97 Ga. 430, 25 S.E. 319.

The acquisition of any personal or movable property, money, or instrument of writing conveying or securing a valuable right, by means of some false or deceitful pretense or device, or fraudulent representation, with intent to appropriate the same to the use of the party so acquiring, or of destroying or impairing the rights of the party justly entitled to the same. May v. State, 15 Tex.App. 436; Cochrain v. State, 93 Tex.Cr.R. 483, 248 S.W. 43, 44.

To make out offense of "cheating" and "swindling" by false representations, state must prove that representations were made, that representations were knowingly and designedly false, that representations were made with intent to defraud, that representations did defraud, that representations related to existing fact or past event, and that party to whom representations were made, relying on their truth, was thereby induced to part with his property. Code 1933, § 26-7401 et seq. Diamond v. State, 52 Ga.App. 184, 182 S.E. 813, 814.

SWITCH. A mechanical device which turns a movable object from one course to another. Jeffery v. Kewaunee, G. B. & W. Ry. Co., 189 Wis. 207, 207 N.W. 283, 284.

As used in railroading, a device for moving a small section of track so that rolling stock may be run or shunted from one line to another. Jeffery v. Kewaunee, G. B. & W. Ry. Co., *supra.* A mechanical arrangement of movable parts of rails for transferring cars from one track to another; also a siding; a turnout. Pittsburgh Rys. Co. v. Borough of Carrick, 259 Pa. 333, 103 A. 106, 108. A track in the nature of a sidetrack adjacent to and used in connection with another line of track. Indiana Rys. & Light Co. v. City of Kokomo, 183 Ind. 543, 108 N.E. 771, 772.

SWITCH LIMITS. Depot or station grounds; yard limits. Atchison, T. & S. F. Ry. Co. v. McCall, 48 Okl. 602, 150 P. 173, 174.

SWITCH-YARD DOCTRINE. The doctrine that there can be no implied license to the public to use the track of a railroad company within the limits of its switch-yard. Binion v. Central of Georgia Ry. Co., 12 Ga.App. 663, 78 S.E. 132.

SWITCHING MOVEMENT or OPERATION. This term becomes of importance in determining whether or not the Safety Appliance Act (45 U.S.C.A. § 1 et seq.) is applicable to a particular set of facts, and is distinguished from "train movement."

Thus, the continuous movement of freight cars, reassembled after switching, from one portion of a railroad yard to another 4,500 feet away, through the business or warehouse part of a city, and crossing several city streets at grade, was held to be a "train movement," and not a "switching operation." Illinois Cent. R. Co. v. U. S., C.C.A.Neb., 14 F.2d 747, 748.

SWITCHING SERVICE. This term is principally used in law in contradistinction to "transportation service," for which different rates may be set. "Transportation service" is one which requires no other service to complete the shipper's object, while "switching service" is one which precedes or follows transportation service. Andrews Steel Co. v. Davis, 210 Ky. 473, 276 S.W. 148, 150; on which legal freight charges have already been earned, or are to be earned. Louisville Water Co. v. Illinois Cent. R. Co., D.C.Ky., 14 F.Supp. 301, 303. The word "switching" in this connection is synonymous with "transferring." J. B. Doppes Sons Lumber Co. v. Cincinnati, N. O. & T. P. Ry. Co., *supra.* The test of distinction between these two services is not only whether the switching service follows transportation, but whether the movement of cars is under the yard-master's direction, in which case it is switching service, or under the trainmaster's direction, in which event it is transportation service. St. Louis, I. M. & S. Ry. Co. v. Clark Pressed Brick Co., 127 Ark. 474, 192 S.W. 382, 384.

"Switching services" may also be distinguished from a "line haul," in that the latter is a definite service rendered between two definite points, to which switching is a mere incident. Cummings Sand & Gravel Co. v. Minneapolis & St. L. Ry. Co., 182 Iowa, 955, 166 N.W. 354, 356, L.R.A.1918C, 797.

SWITCHING TRACKS. Tracks for use in loading, reloading, storing, and switching cars, and other things incidental to railroad's regular train haul. Missouri Pac. R. Co. v. Chicago Great Western R. Co., 137 Kan. 217, 19 P.2d 484, 489.

SWOLING OF LAND. So much land as one's plow can till in a year; a hide of land. Cowell.

SWORN. Frequently used interchangeably with "verified." Francesconi v. Independent School Dist. of Wall Lake, 204 Iowa, 307, 214 N.W. 882, 885. See Swear.

SWORN BROTHERS. In old English law. Persons who, by mutual oaths, covenant to share in each other's fortunes.

SWORN CLERKS IN CHANCERY. Certain officers in the English court of chancery, whose duties were to keep the records, make copies of pleadings, etc. Their offices were abolished by St. 5 & 6 Vict. c. 103.

SYB AND SOM. A Saxon form of greeting, meaning peace and safety.

SYLLABUS. An abstract; a headnote; a note prefixed to the report of an adjudged case, containing an epitome or brief statement of the rulings of the court upon the point or points decided in the case. In West Virginia it is the law of the case, whatever may be the reasoning employed in the opinion of the court. Kuhn v. Coal Co., 215 U.S. 356, 30 S.Ct. 140, 141, 54 L.Ed. 228. The syllabus, however, in that state, is never made up of finding of facts, but is limited to points of law determined. Sometimes the finding of facts is referred to for the purpose of explaining the point of law adjudicated, but only for that purpose. Koonce v. Doolittle, 48 W.Va. 592, 37 S.E. 644, 645. Likewise in Ohio, the authority of decisions of its Supreme Court is limited to points stated in the syllabus. Walsh v. E. G. Shinner & Co., C.C.A. Del., 20 F.2d 586, 588. But ordinarily, where a headnote, even though prepared by the court, is given no special force by statute or rule of court, the opinion is to be looked to for the original and authentic statement of the grounds of decision. Burbank v. Ernst, 232 U.S. 162, 34 S.Ct. 299, 58 L.Ed. 551.

Also, a catalogue or list; specifically (capitalized), a collection of eighty condemned propositions addressed by Pope Pius IX to all the Catholic episcopate, December 8, 1864. It gave rise to the most violent polemics; the Ultramontane party was loud in its praise, while the liberals treated it as a declaration of war by the church on modern society and civilization. Encycl. Br.

SYLLOGISM. In logic. The full logical form of a single argument. It consists of three propositions, (two premises and the conclusion,) and these contain three terms, of which the two occurring in the conclusion are brought together in the premises by being referred to a common class.

SYLVA CÆDUA. Lat. In ecclesiastical law. Wood of any kind which was kept on purpose to be cut, and which, being cut, grew again from the stump or root. Lynd. Prov. 190; 4 Reeve, Eng. Law 90. And see Silva Cædua.

SYMBOLÆOGRAPHY. The art or cunning rightly to form and make written instruments. It is either judicial or extrajudicial; the latter being wholly occupied with such instruments as concern matters not yet judicially in controversy, such as instruments of agreements or contracts, and testaments or last wills. Wharton.

SYMBOLIC DELIVERY. The constructive delivery of the subject-matter of a sale or gift, where it is cumbersome or inaccessible, by the actual delivery of some article which is conventionally accepted as the symbol or representative of it, or which renders access to it possible, or which is evidence of the purchaser's or donee's title to it. Thus, a present gift of the contents of a box in a bank vault, accompanied by a transfer of the key thereto, is valid as a symbolical delivery. In re Leadenham's Estate, 289 Pa. 216, 137 A. 247, 249.

SYMBOLUM ANIMÆ. Lat. A mortuary, or soul scot. See Soul Scot.

SYMMETRY. Due proportion of several parts of a body to each other; adaptation of the form or dimensions of the several parts of a thing to each other; harmonious relation of parts; conformance; consistency; congruity; correspondence or similarity of form, dimensions, or parts on opposite sides of an axis, center, or a dividing plane. Maxwell v. City of Buhl, 40 Idaho, 644, 236 P. 122, 123.

SYMOND'S INN. Formerly an inn of chancery.

SYMPATHETIC STRIKE. A boycott. Booth v. Brown, C.C.Wash., 62 F. 794, 795.

SYNALLAGMATIC CONTRACT. In the civil law. A bilateral or reciprocal contract, in which the parties expressly enter into mutual engagements, each binding himself to the other. Poth. Obl. no. 9. Such are the contracts of sale, hiring, etc. See State ex rel. Waterman v. J. S. Waterman and Co., 178 La. 340, 151 So. 422, 426.

SYNCHRONISM. Two things may be said to be operating in "synchronism," not merely when they operate simultaneously, but also when their cycles of operation bear a timed relation to each other. Diamond Power Specialty Corporation v. Bayer, C.C.A.Mo., 13 F.2d 337, 342.

SYNCHRONIZATION. The operation of two radio broadcasting stations simultaneously upon the same frequency and with identical programs. WGN, Inc., v. Federal Radio Commission, 62 App. D.C. 385, 68 F.2d 432, 433.

SYNCOPARE. To cut short, or pronounce things so as not to be understood. Cowell.

SYNDIC. In the civil law. An advocate or patron; a burgess or recorder; an agent or attorney who acts for a corporation or university; an actor or procurator; an assignee. Wharton.

The word "syndic" in the civil law corresponds very nearly with that of assignee under the common law. Mobile & O. R. Co. v. Whitney, 39 Ala. 468, 471.

In English common law. An agent appointed by a corporation for the purpose of obtaining letters of guardianship and the like, to whom such letters were issued. Minnesota L. & T. Co. v. Beebe, 40 Minn. 7, 41 N.W. 232, 233, 2 L.R.A. 418.

In French law. The person who is commissioned by the courts to administer a bankruptcy. He fulfills the same functions as the trustee or assignee. Also, one who is chosen to conduct the affairs and attend to the concerns of a body corporate or community. In this sense the word corresponds to director or manager. Rodman Notes to *Code de Com.* p. 351; Dalloz, Dict. *Syndic.* See Field v. United States, 9 Pet. 182, 9 L.Ed. 94.

In Louisiana. The assignee of a bankrupt. Also, one of several persons to be elected by the creditors of a succession, for the purpose of administering thereon, whenever a succession has been renounced by the heirs, or has been accepted under the benefit of an inventory, and neither the beneficiary heirs, their attorney in fact, nor tutor will accept the administration and give the security required. Civ.Code. La. art. 1224.

SYNDICALISM. The theory, plan, or practice of trade-union action which aims by the general strike and direct action to establish control by local organizations of workers over the means and processes of production. Webster.

A form or development of trade-unionism, originating in France, which aims at the possession of the means of production and distribution, and ultimately at the control of society and government, by the federated bodies of industrial workers, and which seeks to realize its purposes through the agency of general strikes and of terrorism, sabotage, violence, or other criminal means. New Cent. Dict.

Criminal Syndicalism

Defined by the California Criminal Syndicalism Act as any doctrine or precept advocating, teaching, or aiding and abetting the commission of crime, sabotage (defined in the act as willful and malicious physical damage or injury to physical property), or unlawful acts of force and violence or unlawful methods of terrorism, as a means of accomplishing a change in industrial ownership, or control, or effecting any political change. See People v. Lesse, 52 Cal.App. 280, 199 P. 46, 47; State v. Dingman, 37 Idaho, 253, 219 P. 760, 763.

SYNDICATE. A university committee. A combination of persons or firms united for the purpose of enterprises too large for individuals to undertake; or a group of financiers who buy up the shares of a company in order to sell them at a profit by creating a scarcity. Mozley & Whitley.

An association of individuals, formed for the purpose of conducting and carrying out some particular business transaction, ordinarily of a financial character, in which the members are mutually interested. Hambleton v. Rhind, 84 Md. 456, 36 A. 597, 40 L.R.A. 216. An organization formed for some temporary purpose. Gates v. Megargel, C.C.A.N.Y., 266 F. 811, 817, such as the organization of a real estate trust and the sale of shares to the public. Minot v. Burroughs, 223 Mass. 595, 112 N.E. 620, 623.

Merely "joint adventure," which is special combination in specific venture for profit without partnership or corporate designation. McCausey v. Burnet, 60 App.D.C. 201, 50 F.2d 491, 492.

SYNDICATING. Gathering materials suitable for newspaper publication from writers and artists and distributing the same at regular intervals, in the form of matrices, to newspapers throughout the country for publication on the same day. Star Co. v. Wheeler Syndicate, 91 Misc. Rep. 640, 155 N.Y.S. 782, 784.

SYNDICOS, or SYNDICUS. One chosen by a college, municipality, etc., to defend its cause. Calvin. See Syndic.

SYNGRAPH. The name given by the canonists to deeds or other written instruments of which both parts were written on the same piece of parchment, with some word or letters of the alphabet written between them, through which the parchment was cut in such a manner as to leave half the word on one part and half on the other. It thus corresponded to the chirograph or indenture of the common law. 2 Bl.Comm. 295, 296.

Formerly such writings were attested by the subscription and crosses of the witnesses; afterwards, to prevent frauds and concealments, they made deeds of mutual covenant in a script and rescript, or in a *part* and *counterpart,* and in the middle between the two copies they wrote the word *syngraphus* in large letters, which, being cut through the parchment and one being delivered to each party, on being afterwards put together proved their authenticity.

A deed, bond, or other written instrument under the hand and seal of all the parties. It was so called because the parties *wrote together.*

SYNOD. A meeting or assembly of ecclesiastical persons concerning religion; being the same thing, in Greek, as convocation in Latin. There are four kinds: (1) A general or universal synod or council, where bishops of all nations meet; (2) a national synod of the clergy of one nation only; (3) a provincial synod, where ecclesiastical persons of a province only assemble, being now what is called the "convocation;" (4) a diocesan synod, of those of one diocese. A synod in Scotland is composed of three or more presbyteries. Wharton.

A convention of bishops and elders within a district including at least three presbyteries. Trustees of Pencader Presbyterian Church in Pencader Hundred v. Gibson, Del., 22 A.2d 782, 788.

A meeting of the few adjoining presbyteries,—not the same as an ecumenical council, which is a council of all, and not of a part. Groesbeeck v. Dunscomb, 41 How. Pract., N.Y., 344.

SYNODAL. A tribute or payment in money paid to the bishop or archdeacon by the inferior clergy, at the Easter visitation.

SYNODALES TESTES. L. Lat. Synods-men (corrupted into sidesmen) were the urban and rural deans, now the church-wardens. See Sidesmen.

SYNONYMOUS. Expressing the same or nearly the same idea. McCarthy v. Dunlevy-Franklin Co., 277 Pa. 467, 121 A. 409, 410; Hoffine v. Ewing, 60 Neb. 729, 84 N.W. 93, 95.

SYNOPSIS. A brief or partial statement, less than the whole; an epitome; synonymous with summary. Barker v. Barker, 43 Kan. 91, 22 P. 1000, 1001; State ex rel. Hubbell v. Bettman, 124 Ohio St. 24, 176 N.E. 664, 665.

SYPHILIS. In medical jurisprudence. A venereal disease (vulgarly called "the pox") of peculiar virulence, infectious by direct contact, capable of hereditary transmission, and the source of various other diseases and, directly or indirectly, of insanity.

SYSTEM. Orderly combination or arrangement, as of particulars, parts, or elements into a whole; especially such combination according to some rational principle; any methodic arrangement of parts. State v. Kistler, 119 Neb. 89, 227 N.W. 319, 320. Method; manner; mode. Fosche v. Union Traction Co., 108 Kan. 585; 196 P. 423, 424.

In mining usage, under the principle that a system or plan of development is sufficient to meet the requirements of annual expenditure in development of mining claims, the term "system" or "general system" of work means that work as it is commenced on the ground is such that if continued it will lead to a discovery and development of the veins or ore bodies that are supposed to be in the claims, or if these are known that the work will facilitate the extraction of ores and minerals. Golden Giant Mining Co. v. Hill, 27 N.M. 124, 198 P. 276, 279, 14 A.L.R. 1450.

T

T. As an abbreviation, this letter usually stands for either "Territory," "Trinity," "term," "*tempore*," (in the time of,) or "title."

Every person who was convicted of felony, short of murder, and admitted to the benefit of clergy, was at one time marked with this letter upon the brawn of the thumb. Abolished by 7 & 8 Geo. IV. c. 27. Whart. Dict.

By a law of the Province of Pennsylvania, A. D. 1698, it was provided that a convicted thief should wear a badge in the form of the letter "T.," upon his left sleeve, which badge should be at least four inches long and of a color different from that of his outer garment. Linn, Laws Prov. Pa. 275.

T. R. E. An abbreviation of *"Tempore Regis Edwardi,"* (in the time of King Edward,) of common occurrence in Domesday, when the valuation of manors, as it was in the time of Edward the Confessor, is recounted. Cowell.

TABARD. A short gown; a herald's coat; a surcoat.

TABARDER. One who wears a tabard or short gown; the name is still used as the title of certain bachelors of arts on the old foundation of Queen's College, Oxford. Enc. Lond.

TABELLA. Lat. In Roman law. A tablet. Used in voting, and in giving the verdict of juries and decision of judges; and, when written upon, commonly translated "ballot." The laws which introduced and regulated the mode of voting by ballot were called *"leges tabellariæ."* Calvin.; 1 Kent, Comm. 232, note.

TABELLIO. Lat. In Roman law. An officer corresponding in some respects to a notary. His business was to draw legal instruments, (contracts, wills, etc.,) and witness their execution. Calvin.

Tabelliones differed from notaries in many respects: they had judicial jurisdiction in some cases, and from their judgments there were no appeals. Notaries were then the clerks or aiders of the *tabelliones;* they received the agreements of the parties, which they reduced to short *notes;* and these contracts were not binding until they were written in *extenso,* which was done by the *tabelliones.* Jacob Law Dict. *Tabellion.*

TABERNACULUM. In old records. A public inn, or house of entertainment. Cowell.

TABERNARIUS. Lat. In the civil law. A shopkeeper. Dig. 14, 3, 5, 7.

In old English law. A taverner or tavern keeper. Fleta, lib. 2, c. 12, § 17.

TABES DORSALIS. In medical jurisprudence. Another name for locomotor ataxia. It accompanies attacks of tabetic dementia. See Insanity.

TABETIC DEMENTIA. See Insanity.

TABLE. A synopsis or condensed statement, bringing together numerous items or details so as to be comprehended in a single view; as genealogical tables, exhibiting the names and relationships of all the persons composing a family; life and annuity tables, used by actuaries; interest tables, etc.

TABLE DE MARBRE. Fr. In old French law. Table of Marble; a principal seat of the admiralty, so called. These Tables de Marbre are frequently mentioned in the Ordonnance of the Marine. Burrill.

TABLE OF CASES. An alphabetical list of the adjudged cases cited, referred to, or digested in a legal text-book, volume of reports, or digest, with references to the sections, pages, or paragraphs where they are respectively cited, etc., which is commonly either prefixed or appended to the volume.

TABLE RENTS. In English law. Payments which used to be made to bishops, etc., reserved and appropriated to their table or housekeeping. Wharton.

TABLEAU OF DISTRIBUTION. In Louisiana. A list of creditors of an insolvent estate, stating what each is entitled to. Taylor v. Hollander, 4 Mart.N.S., La., 535.

TABULA. Lat. In the civil law. A table or tablet; a thin sheet of wood, which, when covered with wax, was used for writing.

TABULA IN NAUFRAGIO. Lat. A plank in a shipwreck. This phrase is used metaphorically to designate the power subsisting in a third mortgagee, who took without notice of the second mortgage, to acquire the first incumbrance, attach it to his own, and thus squeeze out and get satisfaction, before the second is admitted to the fund. 1 Story, Eq. Jur. § 414; 2 Ves.Ch. 573. "It may be fairly said that the doctrine survives only in the unjust and much-criticised English rule of tacking." Ames, Lect. Leg. Hist. 269. See Tacking. The use of the expression is attributed to Sir Matthew Hale. See 2 P. Wms. 491.

TABULÆ. Lat. In Roman law. Tables. Writings of any kind used as evidences of a transaction. Brissonius. Contracts and written instruments of all kinds, especially wills. So called because originally written on tablets and with wax. Calvinus.

TABULÆ NUPTIALES. In the civil law. A written record of a marriage; or the agreement as to the *dos.*

TABULARIUS. Lat. A notary, or tabellio. Calvin.

TAC, TAK. In old records. A kind of customary payment by a tenant. Cowell.

TAC FREE. In old records. Free from the common duty or imposition of *tac.* Cowell.

TACHOMETER. A device used on automobiles to record speed. Cooper v. Hoeglund, 221 Minn. 446, 22 N.W.2d 450.

TACIT. Existing, inferred, or understood without being openly expressed or stated, implied by silence or silent acquiescence, understood, implied as a tacit agreement; a tacit understanding. State v. Chadwick, 150 Or. 645, 47 P.2d 232, 234. Done or made in silence, implied or indicated, but not actually expressed. Goree v. Midstates Oil Corporation, 205 La. 988, 18 So.2d 591, 596. Manifested by the refraining from contradiction or objection; inferred from the situation and circumstances, in the absence of express matter.

TACIT ACCEPTANCE. In the civil law, a tacit acceptance of an inheritance takes place when some act is done by the heir which necessarily supposes his intention to accept and which he would have no right to do but in his capacity as heir. Civ. Code La. art. 988.

TACIT DEDICATION. Of property for public use is dedication arising from silence or inactivity, without express contract or agreement. Goree v. Midstates Oil Corporation, 205 La. 988, 18 So.2d 591, 596.

TACIT HYPOTHECATION. In the civil law, a species of lien or mortgage which is created by operation of law without any express agreement of the parties. Mackeld. Rom. Law, § 343. In admiralty law, this term is sometimes applied to a maritime lien, which is not, strictly speaking, an hypothecation in the Roman sense of the term, though it resembles it. See The Nestor, 1 Sumn. 73, 18 Fed.Cas. 9.

TACIT LAW. A law which derives its authority from the common consent of the people without any legislative enactment. 1 Bouv. Inst. no. 120.

TACIT MORTGAGE. In the law of Louisiana. The law alone in certain cases gives to the creditor a mortgage on the property of his debtor, without it being requisite that the parties should stipulate it. This is called "legal mortgage." It is called also "tacit mortgage," because it is established by the law without the aid of any agreement. Civ. Code La. art. 3311.

TACIT RELOCATION. A doctrine borrowed from the Roman law. It is a presumed renovation of the contract from the period at which the former expired, and is held to arise from implied consent of parties, in consequence of their not having signified their intention that agreement should terminate at the period stipulated. Though the original contract may have been for a longer period than one year, the renewed agreement can never be for more than one year, because verbal contract of location can extend longer. Srygley v. City of Nashville, 175 Tenn. 417, 135 S.W.2d 451.

In Scotch law. The tacit or implied renewal of a lease, inferred when the landlord, instead of warning a tenant to remove at the stipulated expiration of the lease, has allowed him to continue without making a new agreement. Bell, "Relocation."

TACIT TACK. In Scotch law. An implied tack or lease; inferred from a tacksman's possessing peaceably after his tack is expired. 1 Forb. Inst. pt. 2, p. 153.

TACITA QUÆDAM HABENTUR PRO EXPRESSIS. 8 Coke, 40. Things unexpressed are sometimes considered as expressed.

TACITE. Lat. Silently; impliedly; tacitly.

TACITURNITY. In Scotch law, laches in not prosecuting a legal claim, or in acquiescing in an adverse one. Mozley & Whitley.

TACK, *v.* To annex some junior lien to a first lien, thereby acquiring priority over an intermediate one. See Tacking.

TACK, *n.* In Scotch law. A term corresponding to the English "lease," and denoting the same species of contract.

Tack duty. Rent reserved upon a lease.

TACKING. The uniting of securities given at different times, so as to prevent any intermediate purchaser from claiming a title to redeem or otherwise discharge one lien, which is prior, without redeeming or discharging the other liens also, which are subsequent to his own title. 1 Story, Eq. Jur. § 412. The term is particularly applied to the action of a third mortgagee who, by buying the first lien and uniting it to his own, gets priority over the second mortgagee.

The source and origin of the English doctrine is the case of Marsh v. Lee, 2 Ventr. 337; 1 Ch.Cas. 162; 1 Wh. & T. L.C.Eq. 611, notes. This case and the doctrine founded upon it has been the subject of severe criticism. Langd. Eq.Pl. 191. Lord Ch. J. Holt is said to have been one of the first to benefit by the right of tacking. Holt v. Mill, 2 Vern. 279. This doctrine is inconsistent with laws which require the recording of mortgages, and in the United States, it does not exist to any extent. Brayee v. Bank, 14 Ohio 318; Dyer v. Graves, 37 Vt. 375; Parkist v. Alexander, 1 Johns.Ch., N.Y., 399; Bisph.Eq. § 159.

The term is also used in a number of other connections, as of possessions, disabilities, or items in accounts or other dealings. In these several cases the purpose of the proposed tacking is to avoid the bar of a statute of limitations. See Davis v. Coblens, 174 U.S. 719, 19 S.Ct. 832, 43 L.Ed. 1147; Knippenberg v. Morris, 80 Ind. 540; Eager v. Com., 4 Mass. 182; Sharp v. Stephens' Committee, 21 Ky.L.Rep. 687, 52 S.W. 977; Graham v. Stanton, 177 Mass. 321, 58 N.E. 1023; Moore v. Blackman, 109 Wis. 528, 85 N.W. 429. The term is applied especially to the process of making out title to land by adverse possession, when the present occupant and claimant has not been in possession for the full statutory period, but adds or "tacks" to his own possession that of previous occupants under whom he claims. See J. B. Streeter Co. v. Fredrickson, 11 N.D. 300, 91 N.W. 692; Frost v. Courtis, 172 Mass. 401, 52 N.E. 515; Murray v. Pannaci, 67 N.J.Eq. 724, 57 A. 1132.

TACKSMAN. In Scotch law. A tenant or lessee; one to whom a *tack* is granted. 1 Forb. Inst. pt. 2, p. 153.

TACTIS SACROSANCTIS. Lat. In old English law. Touching the holy evangelists. Fleta, lib. 3, c. 16, § 21. "A bishop may swear *visis evangeliis,* [looking at the Gospels,] and not *tactis,* and it is good enough." Freem. 133.

TACTO PER SE SANCTO EVANGELIO. Lat. Having personally touched the holy Gospel. Cro. Eliz. 105. The description of a corporal oath.

TAIL. Limited; abridged; reduced; curtailed, as a fee or estate in fee, to a certain order of succession, or to certain heirs.

TAIL, ESTATE IN. An estate of inheritance, which, instead of descending to heirs generally, goes to the heirs of the donee's body, which means his lawful issue, his children, and through them to his grandchildren in a direct line, so long as his posterity endures in a regular order and course of descent, and upon the death of the first owner without issue, the estate determines. 1 Washb. Real Prop. *72. Kolmer v. Miles, 270 Ill. 20, 110 N.E. 407, 408; Tantum v. Campbell, 83 N.J. Eq. 361, 91 A. 120, 121; Harwell v. Harwell, 151 Tenn. 587, 271 S.W. 353, 355.

A freehold of inheritance, limited to a person and the heirs of his body, general or special, male or female, and is the creature of the statute *de Donis.* The estate, provided the entail be not barred, reverts to the donor or reversioner, if the donee die without leaving descendants answering to the condition annexed to the estate upon its creation, unless there be a limitation over to a third person on default of such descendants, when it vests in such third person or remainder-man. Wharton. In re Reeves, 10 Del. Ch. 324, 92 A. 246, 247; 10 Del.Ch. 483, 94 A. 511, 513; Conover v. Cade, 184 Ind. 604, 112 N.E. 7, 11; Gardner v. Anderson, 114 Kan. 778, 227 P. 743, 748; Cox v. Fink, 200 Ky. 219, 254 S.W. 757, 758.

Several Tail

An entail severally to two; as if land is given to two men and their wives, and to the heirs of their bodies begotten; here the donees have a joint estate for their two lives, and yet they have a several inheritance, because the issue of the one shall have his moiety, and the issue of the other the other moiety. Cowell.

Tail after Possibility of Issue Extinct

A species of estate tail which arises where one is tenant in special tail, and a person from whose body the issue was to spring dies without issue, or, having left issue, that issue becomes extinct. In either of these cases the surviving tenant in special tail becomes "tenant in tail after possibility of issue extinct." 2 Bl.Comm. 124.

Tail Female

When lands are given to a person and the *female* heirs of his or her body. The male heirs are not capable of inheriting it.

Tail General

An estate in tail granted to one "and the heirs of his body begotten," which is called "tail general" because, how often soever such donee in tail be married, his issue in general by all and every such marriage is, in successive order, capable of inheriting the estate tail *per formam doni.* 2 Bl.Comm. 113; Tantum v. Campbell, 83 N.J.Eq. 361, 91 A. 120, 122. This is where an estate is limited to a man and the heirs of his body, without any restriction at all; or, according to some authorities, with no other restriction than that in relation to sex. Thus, tail male general is the same thing as tail male; the word "general," in such case, implying that there is no other restriction upon the descent of the estate than that it must go in the male line. So an estate in tail female general is an estate in tail female. The word "general," in the phrase, expresses a purely negative idea, and may denote the absence of any restriction, or the absence of some given restriction which is tacitly understood. Mozley & Whitley.

Tail Male

When certain lands are given to a person and the *male* heirs of his or her body. The female heirs are not capable of inheriting it.

Tail Special

This denotes an estate in tail where the succession is restricted to certain heirs of the donee's body, and does not go to all of them in general; *e. g.,* where lands and tenements are given to a man and "the heirs of his body on Mary, his now wife, to be begotten;" here no issue can inherit but such special issue as is engendered between those two, not such as the husband may have by another wife, and therefore it is called "special tail." 2 Bl.Comm. 113. It is defined by Cowell as the limitation of lands and tenements to a man and his wife and the heirs of their two bodies. But the phrase need not be thus restricted. Tail special, in its largest sense, is where the gift is restrained to certain heirs of the donor's body, and does not go to all of them in general. Mozley & Whitley.

TAIL LIGHT. Red light on the rear of a motor vehicle. Mahar v. Mackay, 55 Cal.App.2d 869, 132 P.2d 42, 47.

TAILAGE. See Tallage.

TAILLE. Fr.

In old English law. The fee which is opposed to fee-simple, because it is so minced or pared that it is not in the owner's free power to dispose of it, but it is, by the first giver, cut or divided from all other, and tied to the issue of the donee,—in short, an estate-tail. Wharton.

In old Franch law. A tax or assessment levied by the king, or by any great lord, upon his subjects, usually taking the form of an imposition upon the owners of real estate. Brande. The equivalent of the English tallage—the typical direct tax in France of the Middle Ages, as tonlieu was the generic term for an indirect tax. See Tallage.

TAILORS TO THE TRADE. Those who cut, make, and trim garments for merchant tailors in different parts of the United States. Magid v. Tannenbaum, 164 App.Div. 142, 149 N.Y.S. 445.

TAILZIE. In Scotch law. An entail. A tailzied fee is that which the owner, by exercising his inherent right of disposing of his property, settles upon others than those to whom it would have descended by law. 1 Forb.Inst. pt. 2, p. 101.

TAINT. A conviction of felony, or the person so convicted. Cowell.

TAKE. To lay hold of; to gain or receive into possession; to seize; to deprive one of the use or possession of; to assume ownership. City of Durham v. Wright, 190 N.C. 568, 130 S.E. 161, 163.

Thus, constitutions generally provide that a man's property shall not be *taken* for public uses without just compensation. Evansville & C. R. Co. v. Dick, 9 Ind. 433; Gas Products Co. v. Rankin, 63 Mont. 372, 207 P. 993, 998, 24 A.L.R. 294; Piper v. Ekern, 180 Wis. 586, 194 N.W. 159, 162, 34 A.L.R. 32. Property may be deemed "taken" within the meaning of these constitutional provisions when it is totally destroyed or rendered valueless, Lund v. Salt Lake County, 58 Utah 546, 200 P. 510, 513; or when it is damaged by a public use in connection with an actual taking by the exercise of eminent domain, City of St. Louis v. St. Louis, I. M. & S. Ry. Co., 272 Mo. 80, 197 S.W. 107, 111; or when there is interference with use of property to owner's prejudice, with resulting diminution in value thereof, Webster County v. Lutz, 234 Ky. 618, 28 S.W.2d 966, 967. But acquisition of title or total destruction of value is not essential to "taking," for which compensation must be made. Cheves v. Whitehead, D.C.Ga., 1 F. Supp. 321, 324.

The word take has many shades of meaning, precise meaning which it is to bear in any case depending on the subject with respect to which it is used. Kennedy v. New York Life Ins. Co., 178 Misc. 258, 172 So. 743, 745.

In the law of larceny, to obtain or assume possession of a chattel unlawfully, and without the owner's consent; to appropriate things to one's own use with felonious intent. Thus, an actual *taking* is essential to constitute larceny. 4 Bl. Comm. 430. A "taking" occurs when a person with a preconceived design to appropriate property to his own use obtains possession of it by means of fraud or trickery. People v. Edwards, 72 Cal.App. 102, 236 P. 944, 948.

In this connection, "take" is not synonymous with "obtain," which embraces many other ways of acquiring property. Allen v. State, 97 Tex.Cr.R. 467, 262 S.W. 502, 503. Nor is "take" necessarily synonymous with "steal." Hunt v. State, 89 Tex.Cr.R. 89, 229 S.W. 869, 871; Louisville & N. R. Co. v. Malone, 200 Ala. 380, 76 So. 296, 297. But the phrase "take by stealth" may have the same meaning as "steal." Roach v. State, 23 Okl.Cr. 280, 214 P. 563, 564.

To seize or apprehend a person; to arrest the body of a person by virtue of lawful process. Thus, a *capias* commands the officer to *take* the body of the defendant. Com. v. Hall, 9 Gray, Mass., 267, 69 Am.Dec. 285.

To acquire the title to an estate; to receive or be entitled to an estate in lands from another person by virtue of some species of title. Thus one is said to "*take* by purchase," "*take* by descent," "*take* a life-interest under the devise," etc. In re Bock, 125 Misc. 653, 211 N.Y.S. 621. 622.

To receive the verdict of a jury; to superintend the delivery of a verdict; to hold a court. The commission of assize in England empowers the judges to *take the assizes*; that is, according to its ancient meaning, to take the verdict of a peculiar species of jury called an "assize;" but, in its present meaning, "to hold the assizes." 3 Bl. Comm. 59, 185. To choose; *e. g., ad capiendas assisas*, to choose a jury.

To procure or to obtain (an appeal). Nessans v. Colomes, 136 La. 1051, 68 So. 122; Cochran v. State, 206 Ala. 74, 89 So. 278.

See, also, Taking.

TAKE AWAY. This term in a statute punishing every person who shall take away any female under 18 from her father for the purpose of prostitution requires only that such person procure or cause her to go away by some persuasion, enticement, or inducement offered, exercised, or held out to the girl, or by furnishing her the means or money with which to go away. State v. Corrigan, 262 Mo. 195, 171 S.W. 51, 54.

TAKE BACK. To revoke; to retract; as, to take back one's promise. Dimock State Bank v. Boehnen, 46 S.D. 50, 190 N.W. 485.

TAKE BY STEALTH. To steal; feloniously to take and carry away the personal goods of another; to take without right, secretly, and without leave or consent of the owner. Roach v. State, 23 Okl.Cr. 280, 214 P. 563, 564.

TAKE CARE OF. To support; maintain; look after (a person). Ballenger v. Ballenger, 208 Ala. 147, 94 So. 127. To pay (a debt). Scranton Mercantile Co. v. E. Schneider & Co., 163 Ark. 536, 260 S.W. 426, 427. To attend to. Southern Surety Co. v. Chicago, R. I. & P. R. Co., 215 Iowa, 525, 245 N.W. 864, 868.

TAKE EFFECT. To become operative or executed. Miller v. Oliver, 54 Cal.App. 495, 202 P. 168, 171. To be in force, or go into operation. Mowery v. Washington Nat. Ins. Co., 289 Ill.App. 443, 7 N.E.2d 334, 335.

TAKE OVER. To assume control or management of;—not necessarily involving the transfer of absolute title. New York Trust Co. v. Farmers' Irr. Dist., C.C.A.Neb., 280 F. 785, 795. See, however, Knight v. First Nat. Bank, C.C.A.Ky., 281 F. 968, 972.

TAKE UP. To pay or discharge (a note). Ashville Sav. Bank v. Lee, 214 Ala. 501, 108 So. 335, 337; McKenzie v. Smith, 18 Ga.App. 626, 89 S.E. 1097, 1098; Dilenbeck v. Herrold, 183 Iowa, 264, 164 N.W. 869, 870. Also, sometimes, to purchase a note. Dilenbeck v. Herrold, *supra*. To retire (a negotiable instrument); to discharge one's liability on it;—said particularly of an indorser or acceptor.

A party to a negotiable instrument, particularly an indorser or acceptor, is said to "take up" the paper, or to "retire" it, when he pays its amount, or substitutes other security for it, and receives it again into his own hands. See Hartzell v. McClurg, 54 Neb. 316, 74 N.W. 626; McKenzie v. Smith, 18 Ga.App. 626, 89 S.E. 1097, 1098.

TAKENOKO. Chopped, cooked, and canned bamboo sprouts from Japan, used as a vegetable in a manner similar to asparagus. Nippon Co. v. U. S., 12 Ct.Cust.App. 548, 549.

TAKEOVER BID. A tender offer, q. v.

TAKER. One who takes or acquires; particularly, one who takes an estate by devise. When an estate is granted subject to a remainder or executory devise, the devisee of the immediate interest is called the "first taker."

TAKING. In criminal law and torts. The act of laying hold upon an article, with or without removing the same. It implies a transfer of possession, dominion, or control. See Take.

Under various statutes relating to sexual offenses, such as the abduction of a girl under the age of 18 years for the purpose of carnal intercourse, to constitute a "taking" no force, actual or constructive, need be exercised. State v. Lauzer, 152 Minn. 279, 188 N.W. 558, 559. The "taking" may be effected by persuasion, enticement, or inducement. State v. Richards, 88 Wash. 160, 152 P. 720. And it is not necessary that the girl be taken from the control or against the will of those having lawful authority over her. State v. Lauzer, 152 Minn. 279, 188 N.W. 558. But the state must prove conduct by defendant indicating a control, complete or partial, of her person, having sexual intercourse as its object. State v. Clough, Del.Gen.Sess., 134 A. 172, 173.

TALC. A mineral compound, known as hydrated silicate of magnesia. U. S. v. R. C. Boeckel & Co., C.C.A.Mass., 221 F. 885, 886.

TALE. The count or counting of money. Said to be derived from the same root as "tally." Cowell. Whence also the modern word "teller."

Old Pleading

The plaintiff's count, declaration, or narrative of his case. 3 Bl.Comm. 293.

TALES. Lat. Such; such men. A number of jurors added to a deficient panel to supply the deficiency. Nesbit v. People, 19 Colo. 441, 36 P. 221. See Shields v. Bank, 3 Hun, N.Y., 477, 479. When, by means of challenges or any other cause, a sufficient number of unexceptionable jurors does not appear at the trial, either party may pray a "tales," as it is termed; that is, a supply of *such* men as are summoned on the first panel in order to make up the deficiency. Brown. See State v. McCrystol, 43 La.Ann. 907, 9 So. 922; Railroad Co. v. Mask, 64 Miss. 738, 2 So. 360.

A list of such jurymen as were of the tales, kept in the king's bench office in England.

TALES DE CIRCUMSTANTIBUS. So many of the by-standers. The emphatic words of the old writ awarded to the sheriff to make up a deficiency of jurors out of the persons present in court. 3 Bl.Comm. 365.

The order of the judge for taking such bystanders as jurors. See Lee v. Evaul, 1 N.J.Law, 283; Fuller v. State, 1 Blackf., Ind., 65.

TALESMAN. A person summoned to act as a juror from among the by-standers in the court. Linehan v. State, 113 Ala. 70, 21 So. 497; Shields v. Niagara County Sav. Bank, 5 Thomp. & C., N.Y., 587. A person summoned as one of the tales added to a jury. Webster.

TALIO. Lat. In the civil law. Like for like; punishment in the same kind; the punishment of an injury by an act of the same kind, as an eye for an eye, a limb for a limb, etc. Calvin.

TALIS INTERPRETATIO SEMPER FIENDA EST, UT EVITETUR ABSURDUM ET INCONVENIENS, ET NE JUDICIUM SIT ILLUSORIUM. 1 Coke, 52. Interpretation is always to be made in such a manner that what is absurd and inconvenient may be avoided, and the judgment be not illusory [or nugatory].

TALIS NON EST EADEM; NAM NULLUM SIMILE EST IDEM. 4 Coke, 18. What is like is not the same; for nothing similar is the same.

TALIS RES, VEL TALE RECTUM, QUÆ VEL QUOD NON EST IN HOMINE ADTUNC SUPERSTITE SED TANTUMMODO EST ET CONSISTIT IN CONSIDERATIONE ET INTELLIGENTIA LEGIS, ET QUOD ALII DIXERUNT TALEM REM VEL TALE RECTUM FORE IN NUBIBUS. Such a thing or such a right as is not vested in a person then living, but merely exists in the consideration and contemplation of law [is said to be in abeyance,] and others have said that such a thing or such a right is in the clouds. Co. Litt. 342.

TALITER PROCESSUM EST. So it has proceeded. Words formerly used in pleading, by which a defendant, in justifying his conduct by the process of an inferior court, alleged the proceedings in such inferior court. Steph.Pl. 5th ed. p. 369. Upon pleading the judgment of an inferior court, the proceedings preliminary to such judgment, and on which the same was founded, must, to some extent, appear in the pleading, but the rule is that they may be alleged with a general allegation that "such proceedings were had," instead of a detailed account of the proceedings themselves, and this general allegation is called the "*taliter processum est.*" A like concise mode of stating former proceedings in a suit is adopted at the present day in chancery proceedings upon petitions and in actions in the nature of bills of revivor and supplement. Brown.

TALLAGE, or TAILAGE. A piece cut out of the whole. Cowell. Used metaphorically for a share of a man's substance paid by way of tribute, toll, or tax, being derived from the French "*tailler,*" which signifies to cut a piece out of the whole. Cowell. See State v. Switzler, 143 Mo. 287, 45 S.W. 245, 40 L.R.A. 280; Lake Shore, etc., R. Co. v. Grand Rapids, 102 Mich. 374, 60 N.W. 767, 29 L.R.A. 195. A term used to denote subsidies, taxes, customs, and, indeed, any imposition whatever by the government for the purpose of raising a revenue. Bacon, Abr. *Smuggling*, etc. (B); Fort. *De Laud.* 26; Madd. Exch. c. 17; Co. 2d Inst. 531. A tax upon cities, townships and boroughs granted to the king as a part of the royal revenue. 2 Steph.Com. 622; 1 Poll. & Maitl. 647.

TALLAGER. A tax or toll gatherer; mentioned by Chaucer (and spelled "talaigier").

TALLAGIUM. L. Lat. A term including all taxes.

TALLAGIUM FACERE. To give up accounts in the exchequer, where the method of accounting was by tallies.

TALLATIO. A keeping account by tallies. Cowell.

TALLEY, or TALLY. A stick cut into two parts, on each whereof is marked, with notches or otherwise, what is due between debtor and creditor. It was the ancient mode of keeping accounts. One part was held by the creditor, and the other by the debtor. The use of tallies in the exchequer was abolished by St. 23 Geo. III. c. 82, and the old tallies were ordered to be destroyed by St. 4 & 5 Wm. IV. c. 15. Wharton. By the custom of London, sealed tallies were effectual as a deed. Liber Albus 191a. They are admissible by the French and Italian Codes as evidence between traders. It is said that they were negotiable. See Penny Encycl.; Hall, Antiq. of Exch. 118.

Tallies of loan. A term originally used in England to describe exchequer bills, which were issued by the officers of the exchequer when a temporary loan was necessary to meet the exigencies of the government, and charged on the credit of the exchequer in general, and made assignable from one person to another. Briscoe v. Bank of Kentucky, 11 Pet. 328, 9 L.Ed. 709.

Tally trade. A system of dealing by which dealers furnish certain articles on credit, upon an agreement for the payment of the stipulated price by certain weekly or monthly installments. McCul. Dict.

TALLIA. L. Lat. A tax or tribute; tallage; a share taken or *cut out* of any one's income or means. Spelman.

TALMUD. A work which embodies the civil and canonical law of the Jewish people.

TALTARUM'S CASE. A case reported in Yearb. 12 Edw. IV. 19–21, which is regarded as having established the foundation of common recoveries.

TALWEG. Germ. (Tal meaning valley, Weg meaning way.) Commonly used by writers on international law in definition of water boundaries between states, meaning the middle or deepest or most navigable channel, and while often styled "fairway" or "midway" or "main channel" the word has been taken over into various languages and the doctrine of Talweg is often applicable in respect of water boundaries to sounds, bays, straits, gulfs, estuaries and other arms of the sea and also applies to boundary lakes and landlocked seas whenever there is a deep water sailing channel therein. State of Louisiana v. State of Mississippi, 26 S.Ct. 408, 421, 202 U.S. 1, 50 L.Ed. 913.

TAM QUAM. A phrase used as the name of a writ of error from inferior courts, when the error is supposed to be as well in giving the judgment as in awarding execution upon it. *(Tam in redditione judicii, quam in adjudicatione executionis.)*

Venire Tam Quam

One by which a jury was summoned, *as well* to try an issue *as* to inquire of the damages on a default. 2 Tidd, Pr. 722, 895.

TAME. Domesticated; accustomed to man; reclaimed from a natural state of wildness. In the Latin phrase, tame animals are described as *domitœ naturœ.*

TAMEN. Lat. Notwithstanding; nevertheless; yet.

TAMPER. To meddle so as to alter a thing, especially to make corrupting or perverting changes; as, to tamper with a document or a text; to interfere improperly; to meddle; to busy oneself rashly; to try trifling or foolish experiments. United States v. Tomicich, D.C.Pa., 41 F.Supp. 33, 35.

TANAMOSHI. Japanese. An association usually consisting of from fourteen to seventeen members. Members are obligated to contribute an agreed amount per month to the association. Each month a drawing is held and the member who bids the highest amount by way of interest and who has not yet received a loan from the association is entitled to take the aggregate of contributions for that particular month, except that at the last meeting of the association no interest is paid. The interest bid each month is returned to each member of the Tanamoshi as his profit on the amount of his contribution to the association. Heylin v. Yil, 30 Haw. 606, 607.

TANGIBLE. Capable of being touched; also, perceptible to the touch; tactile; palpable, and as being capable of being possessed or realized; readily apprehensible by the mind; real; substantial; evidence. Moeller, McPherrin & Judd v. Smith, 127 Neb. 424, 255 N.W. 551.

TANGIBLE PROPERTY. That which may be felt or touched, and is necessarily corporeal, although it may be either real or personal. H. D. & J. K. Crosswell, Inc., v. Jones, D.C.S.C., 52 F.2d 880, 883.

TANISTRY. In old Irish law. A species of tenure, founded on ancient usage, which allotted the inheritance of lands, castles, etc., to the "oldest and worthiest man of the deceased's name and blood." It was abolished in the reign of James I. Jacob; Wharton.

TANK. A receptacle for liquid. American Tank Co. v. Revert Oil Co., 108 Kan. 690, 196 P. 1111, 1112.

TANKAGE. Waste matter from tanks, especially the dried, nitrogenous residue from tanks, in which fat has been rendered, used as a fertilizer. Jenkins v. Springfield Reduction & Chemical Co., 169 Mo.App. 534, 154 S.W. 832, 834. The refuse of meat-packing houses, unfit for human consumption, is known as "tankage" or "liquid stick" according to its water content. Darling & Co. v. U. S., 12 Ct.Cust.App. 86, 87.

TANNERIA. In old English law. Tannery; the trade or business of a tanner. Fleta. lib. 2, c. 52, § 35.

TANTEO. Span. In Spanish law. Pre-emption. White, New Recop. b. 2, tit. 2, c. 3.

TANTO, RIGHT OF. In Mexican law. The right enjoyed by an usufructuary of property, of buying the property at the same price at which the owner offers it to any other person, or is willing to take from another. Civ.Code Mex. art. 992.

TANTUM BONA VALENT, QUANTUM VENDI POSSUNT. Shep. Touch. 142. Goods are worth so much as they can be sold for. 3 Inst. 305.

TANTUM HABENT DE LEGE, QUANTUM HABENT DE JUSTITIA. (Precedents) have value in the law to the extent that they represent justice. Hob. 270.

TARDE VENIT. Lat. In practice. The name of a return made by the sheriff to a writ, when it came into his hands too late to be executed before the return-day.

TARE. A deficiency in the weight or quantity of merchandise by reason of the weight of the box, cask, bag, or other receptacle which contains it and is weighed with it. Also an allowance or abatement of a certain weight or quantity which the seller makes to the buyer, on account of the weight of such box, cask, etc. Napier v. Barney, 5 Blatchf. 191, 17 Fed.Cas. 1149. See Tret.

TARIFF. A cartel of commerce, a book of rates, a table or catalogue, drawn usually in alphabetical order, containing the names of several kinds of merchandise, with the duties or customs to be paid for the same, as settled by authority, or agreed on between the several princes and states that hold commerce together. Enc. Lond.; Railway Co. v. Cushman, 92 Tex. 623, 50 S.W. 1009; Pacific S. S Co. v. Cackette, C.C.A.Or., 8 F.2d 259, 261.

The list or schedule of articles on which a duty is imposed upon their importation into the United States, with the rates at which they are severally taxed. Also the custom or duty payable on such articles. And, derivatively, the system or principle of imposing duties on the importation of foreign merchandise.

TASSUM. In old English law. A heap; a haymow, or hay-stack. *Fœnum in tassis*, hay in stacks. Reg. Orig. 96.

TATH. In the counties of Norfolk and Suffolk, the lords of manors anciently claimed the privilege of having their tenants' flocks or sheep brought at night upon their own demesne lands, there to be folded for the improvement of the ground, which liberty was called by the name of the "tath." Spelman.

TAURI LIBERI LIBERTAS. Lat. A common bull; because he was free to all the tenants within such a manor, liberty, etc.

TAUTOLOGY. Describing the same thing twice in one sentence in equivalent terms; a fault in rhetoric. It differs from repetition or iteration, which is repeating the same sentence in the same or equivalent terms; the latter is *sometimes* either excusable or necessary in an argument or address; the former (tautology) never. Wharton.

TAVERN. A place of entertainment; a house kept up for the accommodation of strangers. Originally, a house for the retailing of liquors to be drunk on the spot. Waitt Const. Co. v. Chase, 197 App.Div. 327, 188 N.Y.S. 589, 592; City of Birmingham v. Bollas, 209 Ala. 512, 96 So. 591, 592.

The word "tavern," in a charter provision authorizing municipal authorities to "license and regulate taverns," includes hotels. "Tavern," "hotel," and "public house" are, in this country, used synonymously; and while they entertain the traveling public, and keep guests, and receive compensation therefor, they do not lose their character, though they may not have the privilege of selling liquors. St. Louis v. Siegrist, 46 Mo. 595. And see Bonner v. Welborn, 7 Ga. 306; Rafferty v. Insurance Co., 18 N.J.L. 484, 38 Am.Dec. 525; In re Brewster, 39 Misc. 689, 80 N.Y.S. 666.

TAVERN KEEPER. One who keeps a tavern. One who keeps an inn; an innkeeper.

TAVERNER. In old English law. A seller of wine; one who kept a house or shop for the sale of wine.

TAX, *v.* To impose a tax; to enact or declare that a pecuniary contribution shall be made by the persons liable, for the support of government. Spoken of an individual, to be taxed is to be included in an assessment made for purposes of taxation.

Practice

A pecuniary burden laid upon individuals or property to support the government, and is a payment exacted by legislative authority. In re Mytinger, D.C.Tex., 31 F.Supp. 977, 978, 979. Annual compensation paid to government for annual protection and for current support of government. Alabama Power Co. v. Federal Power Commission, C.C.A.5, 134 F.2d 602, 608. A ratable portion of the produce of the property and labor of the individual citizens, taken by the nation, in the exercise of its sovereign rights, for the support of government, for the administration of the laws, and as the means for continuing in operation the various legitimate functions of the state. Black, Tax Titles, § 2; New London v. Miller, 60 Conn. 112, 22 A. 499; Graham v. St. Joseph Tp., 67 Mich. 652, 35 N.W. 808; Gibbons v. Ogden, 9 Wheat. 1, 6 L.Ed. 23; Tevander v. Ruysdael, C.C.A.Ill., 299 F. 746, 753; Montgomery County v. City of Montgomery, 190 Ala. 366, 67 So. 311, 313; Strand v. Marin, 30 N.D. 165, 152 N.W. 280. An enforced contribution of money or other property, assessed in accordance with some reasonable rule or apportionment by authority of a sovereign state on persons or property within its jurisdiction for the purpose of defraying the public expenses. Heirs v. Mitchell, 95 Fla. 345, 116 So. 81, 85.

In a general sense, any contribution imposed by government upon individuals, for the use and service of the state, whether under the name of toll, tribute, tallage, gabel, impost, duty, custom, excise, subsidy, aid, supply, or other name. Story, Const. § 950. And in its essential characteristics is not a debt. City of Newark v. Jos. Hollander, Inc., 136 N.J.Eq. 539, 42 A.2d 872, 875.

Synonyms

In a broad sense, *taxes* undoubtedly include *assessments,* and the right to impose assessments has its foundation in the taxing power of the government; and yet, in practice and as generally understood, there is a broad distinction between the two terms. "Taxes," as the term is generally used, are public burdens imposed generally upon the inhabitants of the whole state, or upon some civil division thereof, for governmental purposes, without reference to peculiar benefits to particular individuals or property. "Assessments" have reference to impositions for improvements which are specially beneficial to particular individuals or property, and which are imposed in proportion to the particular benefits supposed to be conferred. They are justified only because the improvements confer special benefits, and are just only when they are divided in proportion to such benefits. Roosevelt Hospital v. New York, 84 N.Y. 112. Flansburg v. Shumway, 117 Neb. 125, 219 N.W. 956, 958. As distinguished from other kinds of taxation, "assessments" are those special and local impositions upon property in the immediate vicinity of municipal improvements which are necessary to pay for the improvement, and are laid with reference to the special benefit which the property is supposed to have derived therefrom. Hale v. Kenosha, 29 Wis. 599; Ridenour v. Saffin, 1 Handy (Ohio) 464; King v. Portland, 2 Or. 146; Witherow v. Board of Drainage Com'rs of Powder Springs Creek Drainage Dist. No. 2, 155 Ga. 476, 117 S.E. 329, 330.

Taxes differ from *subsidies,* in being certain and orderly, and from forced contributions, etc., in that they are levied by authority of law, and by some rule of proportion which is intended to insure uniformity of contribution, and a just apportionment of the burdens of government. Cooley, Tax'n, 2.

To assess or determine; to liquidate, adjust, or settle. Spoken particularly of *taxing costs (q. v.).*

General

Ad valorem tax. See Ad Valorem.

Capitation tax. See that title.

Collateral inheritance tax. See Collateral Inheritance.

Direct tax. One which is demanded from the very persons who, it is intended or desired, should pay it. Indirect taxes are those which are demanded from one person, in the expectation and intention that he shall indemnify himself at the expense of another. Mill, Pol. Econ. Taxes are divided into "direct," under which designation would be included those which are assessed upon the property, person, business, income, etc., of those who are to pay them, and "indirect," or those which are levied on commodities before they reach the consumer, and are paid by those upon whom they ultimately fall, not as taxes, but as part of the market price of the commodity. Cooley, Tax'n, 6.

Historical evidence shows that personal property, contracts, occupations, and the like, have never been regarded as the subjects of direct tax. The phrase is understood to be limited to taxes on land and its appurtenances, and on polls. Veazie Bank v. Fenno, 8 Wall. 533, 19 L.Ed. 482; Railroad Co. v. Morrow, 87 Tenn. 406, 11 S.W. 348, 2 L.R.A. 853; People v. Knight, 174 N.Y. 475, 67 N.E. 65, 63 L.R.A. 87.

Estate tax. A tax upon the right to transfer, while a succession or legacy tax is a tax upon the right to receive. Hazard v. Bliss, 43 R.I. 431, 113 A. 469, 471, 23 A.L.R. 826; Frick v. Lewellyn, D.C.Pa., 298 F. 803, 810; In re Hamlin, 226 N.Y. 407, 124 N.E. 4, 6, 7 A.L.R. 701; In re Sherman's Estate, 179 App.Div. 497, 166 N.Y.S. 19, 23.

Excise and tax distinguished. See Excise.

Floor tax. A tax on all the distilled spirits "on the floor" of a warehouse, *i. e.,* in the warehouse. Greenbrier Distillery Co. v. U. S., D.C.Ky., 288 F. 893, 895.

Franchise tax. See Franchise.

Income tax. See Income.

Indirect taxes are those demanded in the first instance from one person in the expectation and intention that he shall indemnify himself at the expense of another. "Ordinarily all taxes paid primarily by persons who can shift the burden upon some one else, or who are under no legal compulsion to pay them, are considered indirect taxes." Pollock v. Farmers' L. & T. Co., 15 S.Ct. 673, 157 U.S. 429, 39 L.Ed. 759; Thomasson v. State, 15 Ind. 451; Foster & Creighton Co. v. Graham, 154 Tenn. 412, 285 S.W. 570, 572, 47 A.L.R. 971.

Inheritance tax. See Inheritance.

Land tax. See Land Tax.

License tax. See License Fee or Tax.

Local taxes. Those assessments which are limited to certain districts, as poor-rates, parochial taxes, county rates, municipal taxes, etc.

Occupation tax. See Occupation.

Parliamentary taxes. Such taxes as are imposed directly by act of parliament, *i. e.,* by the legislature itself, as distinguished from those which are imposed by private individuals or bodies under the authority of an act of parliament. Thus, a sewers rate, not being imposed directly by act of parliament, but by certain persons termed "commissioners of sewers," is not a parliamentary tax; whereas the income tax, which is directly imposed, and the amount also fixed, by act of parliament, is a parliamentary tax. Brown.

Personal tax. This term may mean either a tax imposed on the person without reference to property, as a capitation or poll tax, or a tax imposed on personal property, as distinguished from one laid on real property. See Jack v. Walker, C.C.Ohio, 79 F. 138, 141; Potter v. Ross, 23 N.J.L. 517.

Poll tax. See that title.

Proportional taxes. Taxes are "proportional" when the proportion paid by each taxpayer bears the same ratio to the amount to be raised that the value of his property bears to the total taxable value, and in the case of a special tax when that is apportioned according to the benefits received. In re Opinion of the Justices, 220 Mass. 613, 108 N.E. 570, 572; Perkins v. Inhabitants of Town of Westwood, 226 Mass. 268, 115 N.E. 411, 412; In re Opinion of the Justices, 77 N.H. 611, 93 A. 311, 312.

Public tax. A tax levied for some general public purpose or for the purposes of the general public revenue, as distinguished from local municipal taxes and assessments. Morgan v. Cree, 46 Vt. 783, 14 Am.Rep. 640; Buffalo City Cemetery v. Buffalo, 46 N.Y. 509.

Sinking fund tax. See Fund.

Specific tax. A tax imposed as a fixed sum on each article or item of property of a given class or kind, without regard to its value; opposed to *ad valorem* tax.

Succession tax. See Succession.

Surtax. An additional tax imposed upon certain kinds of income, such as dividends from corporate stock, royalties, interest from money, notes, credits, bonds and other securities. A surtax is sometimes imposed on incomes exceeding a specified amount.

Tax certificate. A certificate of the purchase of land at a tax sale thereof, given by the officer making the sale, and which is evidence of the holder's right to receive a deed of the land if it is not redeemed within the time limited by law. See Eaton v. Manitowoc County, 44 Wis. 492; Nelson v. Central Land Co., 35 Minn. 408, 29 N.W. 121.

Tax lease. The instrument (or estate) given to the purchaser of land at a tax sale, where the law does not permit the sale of the estate in fee for non-payment of taxes, but instead thereof directs the sale of an estate for years.

Tax levy. The total sum to be raised by a tax. Also the bill, enactment, or measure of legislation by which an annual or general tax is imposed.

Tax purchaser. A person who buys land at a tax-sale; the person to whom land, at a tax-sale thereof, is struck down.

Tax roll. See Roll.

Tax sale. See Sale.

Tax-deed. The conveyance given upon a sale of lands made for non-payment of taxes; the deed whereby the officer of the law undertakes to convey the title of the proprietor to the purchaser at the tax-sale.

Tax-lien. A statutory lien, existing in favor of the state or municipality, upon the lands of a person charged with taxes, binding the same either for the taxes assessed upon the specific tract of land or (in some jurisdictions) for all the taxes due from the individual, and which may be foreclosed for non-payment, by judgment of a court or sale of the land.

Taxing district. The district throughout which a particular tax or assessment is ratably apportioned and levied upon the inhabitants; it may comprise the whole state, one county, a city, a ward, or part of a street.

Taxpayer. A person chargeable with a tax; one from whom government demands a pecuniary contribution towards its support.

Taxpayers' lists. Written exhibits required to be made out by the taxpayers resident in a district, enumerating all the property owned by them and subject to taxation, to be handed to the assessors, at a specified date or at regular periods, as a basis for assessment and valuation.

Tax-title. The title by which one holds land which he purchased at a tax sale. That species of title which is inaugurated by a successful bid for land at a collector's sale of the same for non-payment of taxes, completed by the failure of those entitled to redeem within the specified time, and evidenced by the deed executed to the tax purchaser, or his assignee, by the proper officer.

Tonnage tax. See Tonnage Duty.

Wheel tax. A tax on wheeled vehicles of some or all kinds and bicycles.

Window tax. See that title.

TAX FERRETS. Persons engaged in the business of searching for property omitted from taxation. Their activities when permitted are usually regarded as private rather than as part of a state agency. Pickett v. United States, C.C.A.Mo., 100 F.2d 909, 913.

TAXA. L. Lat. A tax. Spelman.

In old records. An allotted piece of work; a task.

TAXABLE. Subject to taxation; liable to be assessed, along with others, for a share in a tax. Mississippi State Tax Commission v. Brown, 188 Miss. 483, 195 So. 465, 469, 127 A.L.R. 919. Something of value, subject to assessment, and to be levied upon and sold for taxes. Williams v. School Dist. No. 32 in County of Fremont, 56 Wyo. 1, 102 P.2d 48, 52.

Applied to costs in an action, the word means proper to be taxed or charged up; legally chargeable or assessable.

TAXABLE YEAR. This term in internal revenue statutes has different significations, according to its use. Waterman S. S. Corporation v. United States, Ct.Cl., 32 F.Supp. 880, 882; but when used in ordinarily accepted meaning, refers to annual accounting period of taxpayer. American-Hawaiian S. S. Co. v. U. S., Ct.Cl., 46 F.2d 592, 598.

TAXARE. Lat. To rate or value. Calvin.

To tax; to lay a tax or tribute. Spelman.

In old English practice. To assess; to rate or estimate; to moderate or regulate an assessment or rate.

TAXATI. In old European law. Soldiers of a garrison or fleet, assigned to a certain station. Spelman.

TAXATIO. Lat. In Roman law. Taxation or assessment of damages; the assessment, by the judge, of the amount of damages to be awarded to a plaintiff, and particularly in the way of reducing the amount claimed or sworn to by the latter.

TAXATIO ECCLESIASTICA. The value of ecclesiastical benefices made through every diocese in England, on occasion of Pope Innocent IV. granting to King Henry III. the tenth of all spirituals for three years. This taxation was first made by Walter, bishop of Norwich, delegated by the pope to this office in 38 Hen. III., and hence called *"Taxatio Norwicencis."* It is also called "Pope Innocent's Valor." Wharton.

TAXATIO EXPENSARUM. In old English practice. Taxation of costs.

TAXATIO NORWICENSIS. A valuation of ecclesiastical benefices made through every diocese in England, by Walter, bishop of Norwich, delegated by the pope to this office in 38 Hen. III. Cowell.

TAXATION. The process of taxing or imposing a tax. In practice. Adjustment. Fixing the amount; *e. g.* Taxation of costs. 3 Chitty, Gen. Pr. 602. See Tax.

The differences between taxation and taking property in right of eminent domain are that taxation exacts money or services from individuals, as and for their respective shares of contribution to any public burden; while private property taken for public use, by right of eminent domain, is taken, not as the owner's share of contribution to a public burden, but as so much beyond his share, and for which compensation must be made. Moreover, taxation operates upon a community, or upon a class of persons in a community, and by some rule of apportionment; while eminent domain operates upon an individual, and without reference to the amount or value exacted from any other individual, or class of individuals. People v. Brooklyn, 4 N.Y. 419, 55 Am.Dec. 266.

Double Taxation

See Double.

Taxation of Costs

In practice. The process of ascertaining and charging up the amount of costs in an action to which a party is legally entitled, or which are legally chargeable. And, in English practice, the process of examining the items in an attorney's bill of costs and making the proper deductions, if any.

TAXERS. Two officers yearly chosen in Cambridge, England, to see the true gauge of all the weights and measures.

TAXICAB. A motor driven passenger conveyance propelled by electric or gas power, held for public hire, at designated places, charging upon a time or distance basis, carrying passengers to destinations without following any fixed routes. Tuggle v. Parker, 159 Kan. 572, 156 P.2d 533, 534. A conveyance similar to hackney carriage or old-fashioned hack or stage which is held for hire at designated places and has no regular schedule or route, but operates to carry passengers at any time to any point and subject to call. Jarrell v. Orlando Transit Co., 123 Fla. 776, 167 So. 664, 668.

A "taxicab" differs from a jitney bus, street car, or omnibus as a carrier in that it does not follow a well-defined route prescribed by ordinance, but is vehicle subject to contract by person desiring special trip from one point to another, without reference to any prescribed legal route. Jackie Cab Co. v. Chicago Park Dist., 366 Ill. 474, 9 N.E.2d 213, 215, 112 A.L.R. 1410.

TAXING MASTER. See Master.

TAXING OFFICER. Each house of parliament has a taxing officer, whose duty it is to tax the costs incurred by the promoters or opponents of private bills. May, Parl. Pr. 843.

TAXING POWER. The power of any government to levy taxes.

TAXT-WARD. An annual payment made to a superior in Scotland, instead of the duties due to him under the tenure of ward-holding. Abolished. Wharton.

TEA CHEST. A box containing a definite and prescribed amount of tea, otherwise called whole chest (a hundred weight to 140 pounds or more), now seldom shipped, the smaller package being spoken of as half chest (75 to 80 pounds, but the weight varies according to the kind of tea), and quarter chest (from 25 to 30 pounds) and thus a "tea chest" in the language of the trade is understood to be a half chest and not a whole chest. Japan Tea Co. v. Franklin MacVeagh & Co., 142 Minn. 152, 171 N.W. 305, 307.

TEACH. To impart knowledge by means of lessons; to give instruction in; communicating knowledge; introducing into or impressing on the mind as truth or information, and may be done as well through written communications, personal direction, through the public press, or through any means by which information may be disseminated, or it may be done by the adoption of sentiment expressed or arguments made by others which are distributed to others for their adoption and guidance. Ex parte Bernat, D.C.Wash., 255 F. 429, 432.

TEACHER. One who teaches or instructs; especially one whose business or occupation is to teach others; an instructor; preceptor. Ortega

v. Otero, 48 N.M. 588, 154 P.2d 252, 254, 255, 257; Jeu Jo Wan v. Nagle, C.C.A.Cal., 9 F.2d 309, 310.

TEAM. Two or more horses, oxen, or other beasts harnessed together for drawing. Inman v. C., M. & St. P. R. Co., 60 Iowa 462, 15 N.W. 286; with the vehicle to which they are customarily attached; Dains v. Prosser, 32 Barb. (N.Y.) 291; Wilcox v. Hawley, 31 N.Y. 655, in reference to an exemption law. It may mean a vehicle with animals drawing it and used for loads instead of persons. Hotchkiss v. Hoy, 41 Conn. 577. A horse driven with other horses unharnessed; Elliott v. Lisbon, 57 N.H. 29; and a single horse; Hoyt v. Van Alstyne, 15 Barb. (N.Y.) 568; are held teams; Jones v. Holland Furnace Co., 188 Wis. 394, 206 N.W. 57, 59; Tate v. Cody-Henderson Co., 11 Ala.App. 350, 66 So. 837, 838; American Mut. Liability Ins. Co. v. Witham, 124 Me. 240, 127 A. 719. Automobiles may also be included in the meaning of team. Bragdon v. Kellogg, 118 Me. 42, 105 A. 433, 434, 6 A.L.R. 669; Smith v. Howard, 42 R.I. 126, 105 A. 649, 650.

TEAM or THEAME. In old English law. A royalty or privilege granted, by royal charter, to a lord of a manor, for the having, restraining, and judging of bondmen and villeins, with their children, goods, and chattels, etc. Glan. lib. 5, c. 2.

TEAM TRACK. Analogous to freight depot in that it bears the same relation to carload freight that such depot bears to less than carload freight. Shippers have no part in its construction or maintenance. There is a difference between "industrial tracks" and "team tracks." The former are for the handling of carload freight from and to plants. The cost of construction is usually borne in part by the owners of the plants. Carload freight is switched to and from the plants irrespective of whether the carrier performing the switching service participated in the line haul or not. Miller Engineering Co. v. Louisiana Ry. & Nav. Co., 144 La. 786, 81 So. 314, 317.

TEAM WORK. Within the meaning of an exemption law, this term means work done by a team as a substantial part of a man's business; as in farming, staging, express carrying, drawing of freight, peddling, or the transportation of material used or dealt in as a business. Hickok v. Thayer, 49 Vt. 375.

TEAMSTER. One who drives horses and a wagon for the purpose of carrying goods for hire. Elder v. Williams, 16 Nev. 416; Brusie v. Griffith, 34 Cal. 306, 91 Am.Dec. 695. He is liable as a common carrier. Story, Bailm. § 496. A teamster is a laborer; McElwaine v. Hosey, 135 Ind. 481, 35 N.E. 272. See Carrier.

Within an exemption statute, one who habitually makes his living by use of team, harness and wagon or some other form of horse-drawn vehicle. Wertz v. Hale, 212 Iowa, 294, 234 N.W. 534, 535.

TEARING OF WILL. Under statute providing that will may be revoked by tearing, any act of tearing of paper on which will is written, however slight, constitutes an act of "tearing," if done with intent to revoke the will, but no act of tearing or cutting accomplishes such purpose unless done with intent to revoke. Fleming v. Fleming, 367 Ill. 97, 10 N.E.2d 641, 642.

TECHNICAL. Belonging or peculiar to an art or profession. Technical terms are frequently called in the books "words of art."

Immaterial, not affecting substantial rights, without substance. Ætna Ins. Co. v. Waco Co., Tex.Civ.App., 189 S.W. 315, 317; City of Hartselle v. Culver, 216 Ala. 668, 114 So. 58, 60; Englebretson v. Industrial Accident Commission, 170 Cal. 793, 151 P. 421, 422; Jones v. State, 10 Okl.Cr. 216, 137 P. 121, 122.

TECHNICAL MORTGAGE. A true and formal mortgage, as distinguished from other instruments which, in some respects, have the character of equitable mortgages. Harrison v. Annapolis & E. R. R. Co., 50 Md. 514.

TEDDING. Spreading. Tedding grass is spreading it out after it is cut in the swath. 10 East, 5.

TEDING-PENNY. In old English law. A small tax or allowance to the sheriff from each tithing of his county towards the charge of keeping courts, etc. Cowell.

TEEP. In Hindu law. A note of hand; a promissory note given by a native banker or moneylender to *zemindars* and others, to enable them to furnish government with security for the payment of their rents. Wharton.

TEGULA. In the civil law. A tile. Dig. 19, 1, 18.

TEIND COURT. In Scotch law. A court which has jurisdiction of matters relating to *teinds*, or tithes.

TEIND MASTERS. Those entitled to tithes.

TEINDS. In Scotch law. A term corresponding to tithes (*q. v.*) in English ecclesiastical law.

TEINLAND. Sax. In old English law. Land of a thane or Saxon noble; land granted by the crown to a thane or lord. Cowell; 1 Reeve, Eng. Law, 5.

TELEGRAM. A telegraphic dispatch; a message sent by telegraph.

TELEGRAM RACKET. Consists in a fictitious communication such as by radiogram or telephone call authorizing a trustee to pay out money. Cordovano v. State, 61 Ga.App. 590, 7 S.E.2d 45, 47.

TELEGRAPH. In the English telegraph act of 1863, the word is defined as "a wire or wires used for the purpose of telegraphic communication, with any casing, coating, tube, or pipe inclosing the same, and any apparatus connected therewith for the purpose of telegraphic communication." St. 26 & 27 Vict. c. 112, § 3. An apparatus or device for transmitting messages to a distant point. State Public Utilities Com. v. Postal Telegraph-Cable Co., 285 Ill. 411, 120 N.E. 795, 796. Any apparatus for transmitting messages by means of electric currents and signals. Davis v. Pacific Telephone and Telegraph Co., 127 Cal. 312, 315, 316, 59 P. 698, 699.

TELEGRAPHIÆ. A word occasionally used in old English law to describe ancient documents or written evidence of things past. Blount.

TELEPHONE. In a general sense, any instrument or apparatus which transmits sound beyond the limits of ordinary audibility. But, since the recent discoveries in telephony, the name is technically and primarily restricted to an instrument or device which transmits sound by means of electricity and wires similar to telegraphic wires. In a secondary sense, however, being the sense in which it is most commonly understood, the word "telephone" constitutes a generic term, having reference generally to the art of telephony as an institution, but more particularly to the apparatus, as an entirety, ordinarily used in the transmission, as well as in the reception, of telephonic messages. Hockett v. State, 105 Ind. 261, 5 N.E. 178, 55 Am.Rep. 201; State Public Utilities Commission ex rel. Chicago Telephone Co. v. Postal Telegraph-Cable Co., 285 Ill. 411, 120 N.E. 795, 796.

TELETYPE MACHINE. A telegraph machine in general use in telegraph offices, which typewrites the telegram as the message is received instead of requiring an operator to receive it in the Morse code and transcribe it. In re Teletype Mach. No. 33335, 126 Pa.Super. 533, 191 A. 210, 211.

TELEVISION. Seeing at a distance by electrical means while a "motion picture exhibit" is produced by projecting upon a screen with the aid of light rays images recorded upon a film in such rapid and changing succession of exposures as to give the optical effect of a continuous picture of the objects even when in motion. The former directly employs natural phenomena; the latter, mechanics. A notable objective difference is that a motion picture may be re-exhibited as often as desired for the life of the film but a television exhibition once seen is gone forever so far as assembly of the electronic waves upon which the images are carried are concerned. Philadelphia Retail Liquor Dealers Ass'n v. Pennsylvania Liquor Control Bd., 360 Pa. 269, 62 A.2d 53, 55, 4 A.L.R. 1212.

TELLER. One who numbers or counts. An officer of a bank who receives or pays out money. Also one appointed to count the votes cast in a deliberative or legislative assembly or other meeting. The name was also given to certain officers formerly attached to the English exchequer.

A considerable officer in the exchequer, of which officers there are four, whose office is to receive all money due to the king, and to give the clerk of the pells a bill to charge him therewith. They also pay to all persons any money payable by the king, and make weekly and yearly books of their receipts and payments, which they deliver to the lord treasurer. Cowell; Jacob.

TELLERS IN PARLIAMENT. In the language of parliament, the members of the house selected to count the members when a division takes place. In the house of lords a division is effected by the "non-contents" remaining within the bar, and the "contents" going below it, a teller being appointed for each party. In the commons the "ayes" go into the lobby at one end of the house, and the "noes" into the lobby at the other end, the house itself being perfectly empty, and two tellers being appointed for each party. May, Parl. Pr.; Brown.

TELIGRAPHUM. An Anglo-Saxon charter of land. 1 Reeve, Eng. Law, c. 1, p. 10.

TELLTALES. In railroad practice ropes suspended from a wire across the track warning of a low bridge. West v. Chicago, B. & Q. R. Co., 103 C.C.A. 293, 179 F. 801.

TELLWORC. That labor which a tenant was bound to do for his lord for a certain number of days.

TEMENTALE, or TENEMENTALE. A tax of two shillings upon every plow-land, a decennary.

TEMERE. Lat. In the civil law. Rashly; inconsiderately. A plaintiff was said *temere litigare* who demanded a thing out of malice, or sued without just cause, and who could show no ground or cause of action. Brissonius.

TEMPERANCE. Habitual moderation in regard to the indulgence of the natural appetites and passions; restrained or moderate indulgence; moderation; as temperance in eating and drinking; temperance in the indulgence of joy or mirth. People v. Dashaway Ass'n, 84 Cal. 123, 24 P. 277, 12 L.R.A. 117. Not synonymous with abstinence. Mayfield v. Fidelity Casualty Co. of New York, 16 Cal.App.2d 611, 61 P.2d 83, 89.

TEMPEST. A violent or furious storm; a current of wind rushing with extreme violence, and usually accompanied with rain or snow. Stover v. Insurance Co., 3 Phila. (Pa.) 39; Thistle v. Union Forwarding Co., 29 U.C.C.P. 84.

TEMPLARS. A religious order of knighthood, instituted about the year 1119, and so called because the members dwelt in a part of the temple of Jerusalem, and not far from the sepulcher of our Lord. They entertained Christian strangers and pilgrims charitably, and their profession was at first to defend travelers from highwaymen and robbers. The order was suppressed A.D. 1307, and their substance given partly to the knights of St. John of Jerusalem, and partly to other religious orders. Brown.

TEMPLE. Two English inns of court, thus called because anciently the dwelling place of the Knights Templar. On the suppression of the order, they were purchased by some professors of the common law, and converted into *hospitia* or inns of court. They are called the "Inner" and "Middle Temple," in relation to Essex House, which was also a part of the house of the Templars, and called the "Outer Temple," because situated without Temple Bar. Enc. Lond.

TEMPORAL LORDS. The peers of England; the bishops are not in strictness held to be peers, but merely lords of parliament. 2 Steph.Comm. 330, 345.

TEMPORALIS. Lat. In the civil law. Temporary; limited to a certain time.

TEMPORALIS ACTIO. An action which could only be brought within a certain period.

TEMPORALIS EXCEPTIO. A temporary exception which barred an action for a time only.

TEMPORALITIES. In English law. The lay fees of bishops, with which their churches are endowed or permitted to be endowed by the liberality of the sovereign, and in virtue of which they become barons and lords of parliament. Spelman. In a wider sense, the money revenues of a church, derived from pew rents, subscriptions, donations, collections, cemetery charges, and other sources. See Barabasz v. Kabat, 86 Md. 23, 37 A. 720.

TEMPORALITY. The laity; secular people.

TEMPORARILY. Lasting for a time only, existing or continuing for a limited time, not of long duration, not permanent, transitory, changing, but a short time. Young v. Povich, 121 Me. 141, 116 A. 26, 27, 29 A.L.R. 48; Burdine v. Sewell, 92 Fla. 375, 109 So. 648, 653; Vercruysse v. Ulaga, 229 Mich. 49, 201 N.W. 192, 193.

TEMPORARY. That which is to last for a limited time only, as distinguished from that which is perpetual, or indefinite, in its duration. Opposite of permanent. Thus, temporary alimony is granted for the support of the wife pending the action for divorce. Dayton v. Drake, 64 Iowa 714, 21 N.W. 158; Wohlfort v. Wohlfort, 116 Kan. 154, 225 P. 746, 748, 40 A.L.R. 538; Flamm v. City of Passaic, 141 N.J.Misc. 362, 184 A. 748, 750.

A temporary receiver is one appointed to take charge of property until a hearing is had and an adjudication made. Boonville Nat. Bank v. Blakey, 47 C.C.A. 43, 107 F. 895.

As to temporary "Disability", "Insanity", "Injunction", and "Statute" see those titles.

TEMPORE. Lat. In the time of. Thus, the volume called "Cases *tempore* Holt" is a collection of cases adjudged in the king's bench during the time of Lord Holt. Wall.Rep. 398.

TEMPORIS EXCEPTIO. Lat. In the civil law. A plea of time; a plea of lapse of time, in bar of an action. Corresponding to the plea of prescription, or the statute of limitations, in our law. See Mackeld. Rom. Law, § 213.

TEMPUS. Lat. In the civil and old English law. Time in general. A time limited; a season; *e. g., tempus pessonis*, mast time in the forest.

TEMPUS CONTINUUM. In the civil law. A continuous or absolute period of time. A term which begins to run from a certain event, even though he for whom it runs has no knowledge of the event, and in which, when it has once begun to run, all the days are reckoned as they follow one another in the calendar. Dig. 3, 2, 8; Mackeld. Rom. Law, § 195.

TEMPUS ENIM MODUS TOLLENDI OBLIGATIONES ET ACTIONES, QUIA TEMPUS CURRIT CONTRA DESIDES ET SUI JURIS CONTEMPTORES. For time is a means of destroying obligations and actions, because time runs against the slothful and contemners of their own rights. Fleta, l. 4, c. 5, § 12.

TEMPUS SEMESTRE. In old English law. The period of six months or half a year, consisting of one hundred and eighty-two days. Cro.Jac. 166.

TEMPUS UTILE. In the civil law. A profitable or advantageous period of time. A term which begins to run from a certain event, only when he for whom it runs has obtained a knowledge of the event, and in which, when it has once begun to run, those days are not reckoned on which one has no *experiundi potestas; i. e.*, on which one cannot prosecute his rights before a court. Dig. 3, 6, 6; Mackeld. Rom. Law, § 195. A period of time which runs beneficially: *i. e.* feast-days are not included, nor does it run against one absent in a foreign country, or on business of the republic, or detained by stress of weather. But one detained by sickness is not protected from its running; for it runs where there is power to act by an agent as well as where there is power to act personally; and the sick man might have deputed his agent. Calvinus.

TENANCY.

The Estate of a Tenant

The estate of a tenant, as in the expressions "joint tenancy," "tenancy in common."

The Term or Interest of a Tenant

The term or interest of a tenant for years or at will. Sweet; Stone v. City of Los Angeles, 114 Cal.App. 192, 299 P. 838, 841.

It implies a right of possession in tenant exclusive even of landlord. Cleveland v. Milner, 141 Tex. 120, 170 S.W.2d 472, 475.

General Tenancy

A tenancy which is not fixed and made certain in point of duration by the agreement of the parties. Brown v. Bragg, 22 Ind. 122.

Joint Tenancy

An estate in fee-simple, fee-tail, for life, for years, or at will, arising by purchase or grant to two or more persons. Joint tenants have one and the same interest, accruing by one and the same conveyance, commencing at one and the same time, and held by one and the same undivided possession. The grand incident of joint tenancy is survivorship, by which the entire tenancy on the decease of any joint tenant remains to the survivors, and at length to the last survivor. Pub.St. Mass.1882, p. 1292; Simons v. McLain, 51 Kan. 153, 32 P. 919; Thornburg v. Wiggins, 135 Ind. 178, 34 N.E. 999, 22 L.R.A. 42, 41 Am.St.Rep. 422; Van Ausdall v. Van Ausdall, 48 R.I. 106, 135 A. 850,

851; In re Huggins' Estate, 96 N.J.Eq. 275, 125 A. 27, 30. See, also, Tenancy by the Entirety, infra.

Several Tenancy

A tenancy which is separate, and not held jointly with another person.

Tenancy by the Entirety

Is created by a conveyance to husband and wife, whereupon each becomes seized and possessed of the entire estate and after the death of one the survivor takes the whole. Safe Deposit & Trust Co. v. Tait, D.C.Md., 295 F. 429, 431; Dutton v. Buckley, 116 Or. 661, 242 P. 626, 627; Settle v. Settle, 8 F.2d 911, 912, 56 App.D.C. 50, 43 A.L.R. 1079; Raptes v. Cheros, 259 Mass. 37, 155 N.E. 787; Gasner v. Pierce, 286 Pa. 529, 134 A. 494, 495; Smith v. Russell, 172 App.Div. 793, 159 N.Y.S. 169, 170. And is available only to husband and wife. Fairclaw v. Forrest, 76 U.S.App.D.C. 197, 130 F.2d 829, 832, 833, 143 A.L.R. 1154. It is essentially a "joint tenancy," modified by the common-law theory that husband and wife are one person, and survivorship is the predominant and distinguishing feature of each. United States v. Jacobs, Ill. & N. Y., 59 S.Ct. 551, 555, 306 U.S. 363, 83 L.Ed. 763.

The grand characteristic which distinguishes it from a joint tenancy is that it can be terminated only by joint action of husband and wife during their lives, while "joint tenancy" may be terminated by one tenant's conveyance of his interest. Milan v. Boucher, 285 Mass. 590, 189 N.E. 576, 578. In re Cotter's Will, 287 N.Y.S. 670, 673, 159 Misc. 324.

Tenancy in Common

Where property is held by several and distinct titles by unity of possession, neither knowing his own severally, and therefore they all occupy promiscuously. Fullerton v. Storthz Bros. Inv. Co., 190 Ark. 198, 77 S.W.2d 966, 968. The holding of an estate in land by different persons under different titles, but there must be unity of possession and each must have right to occupy the whole in common with his cotenants. Fry v. Dewees, 151 Kan. 488, 99 P.2d 844, 847.

Although "tenancy in common" is generally used with reference to real property, a tenancy in common may exist in personalty as well. Haster v. Blair, 41 Cal.App.2d 896, 107 P.2d 933, 934. See, also, Tenant (Tenant in Common).

TENANT. In the broadest sense, one who holds or possesses lands or tenements by any kind of right or title, whether in fee, for life, for years, at will, or otherwise. Cowell; Young v. Home Telephone Co., Mo.App., 201 S.W. 635, 636; Kavanaugh v. Cohoes Power & Light Corporation, 114 Misc. 590, 187 N.Y.S. 216, 230.

In a more restricted sense, one who holds lands of another; one who has the temporary use and occupation of real property owned by another person, (called the "landlord,") the duration and terms of his tenancy being usually fixed by an instrument called a "lease." Becker v. Becker, 13 App.Div. 342, 43 N.Y.S. 17; Bowe v. Hunking, 135 Mass. 383, 46 Am.Rep. 471; Clift v. White, 12 N.Y. 527; Lightbody v. Truelsen, 39 Minn. 310, 40 N.W. 67; Williams v. Treece, 184 Mo.App. 135, 168 S.W. 209, 211; Minneapolis Iron Store Co. v. Branum, 36 N.D. 355, 162 N.W. 543, 545, L.R.A.1917E, 298. One who occupies another's land or premises in subordination to such other's title and with his assent, express or implied. In re Wilson's Estate, 349 Pa. 646, 37 A.2d 709, 710. One renting land and paying for it either in money or part of crop or equivalent. Wilcox & Co. v. Deines, 119 Neb. 692, 230 N.W. 682, 684.

Strictly speaking, a "tenant" is a person who holds land; but the term is also applied by analogy to personalty. Thus, we speak of a person being tenant for life, or tenant in common, of stock. Sweet.

Feudal Law

One who holds of another (called "lord" or "superior") by some service; as fealty or rent.

Tenant at Will

One who holds possession of premises by permission of owner or landlord, but without fixed term. Wiedemann v. Brown, 190 Minn. 33, 250 N.W. 724; where lands or tenements are let by one man to another, to have and to hold to him at the will of the lessor, by force of which lease the lessee is in possession. In this case the lessee is called "tenant at will," because he hath no certain nor sure estate, for the lessor may put him out at what time it pleaseth him. Litt. § 68; Sweet. Post v. Post, 14 Barb. (N.Y.) 258; Spalding v. Hall, 6 D.C. 125; Freedman v. Gordon, 220 Mass. 324, 107 N.E. 982, 983; Norton v. Averholtzer, 63 Cal.App. 388, 218 P. 637, 640; O'Connor v. Brinsfield, 212 Ala. 68, 101 So. 679, 680.

General

Joint tenants. Two or more persons to whom are granted lands or tenements to hold in fee-simple, fee-tail, for life, for years, or at will. 2 Bl.Comm. 179. Persons who own lands by a joint title created expressly by one and the same deed or will. 4 Kent, Comm. 357. Joint tenants have one and the same interest, accruing by one and the same conveyance, commencing at one and the same time, and held by one and the same undivided possession. 2 Bl.Comm. 180. See, also, Tenancy (Joint Tenancy).

Land tenant. See that title.

Quasi tenant at sufferance. An under-tenant, who is in possession at the determination of an original lease, and is permitted by the reversioner to hold over.

Sole tenant. He that holds lands by his own right only, without any other person being joined with him. Cowell.

Tenant a volunte. L. Fr. A tenant at will.

Tenant at sufferance. One that comes into the possession of land by lawful title, but holds over by wrong, after the determination of his interest. 4 Kent, Comm. 116; 2 Bl.Comm. 150; Fielder v. Childs, 73 Ala. 577; Pleasants v. Claghorn, 2 Miles (Pa.) 304; Bright v. McOuat, 40 Ind. 525; Parker v. Smith, 211 Ky. 624, 277 S.W. 986, 987; Lawer

v. Mitts, 33 Wyo. 249, 238 P. 654, 659; Stanley v. Stembridge, 140 Ga. 750, 79 S.E. 842, 844; Coleman v. State ex rel. Carver, 119 Fla. 653, 161 So. 89, 91.

He has no estate nor title but only naked possession without right and wrongfully, and stands in no privity to landlord and is not entitled to notice to quit, and is a bare licensee to whom landlord owes merely duty not wantonly nor willfully to injure him. Margosian v. Markarian, 288 Mass. 197, 192 N.E. 612, 613; Welch v. Rice, 61 Wyo. 511, 159 P.2d 502, 506, 509.

Tenant by copy of court roll (shortly, "tenant by copy") is the old-fashioned name for a copyholder. Litt. § 73.

Tenant by the curtesy. One who, on the death of his wife seised of an estate of inheritance, after having by her issue born alive and capable of inheriting her estate, holds the lands and tenements for the term of his life. Co.Litt. 30*a*; 2 Bl.Comm. 126.

Tenant by the manner. One who has a less estate than a fee in land which remains in the reversioner. He is so called because in avowries and other pleadings it is specially shown in what manner he is tenant of the land, in contradistinction to the *veray tenant*, who is called simply "tenant." Ham. N.P. 393.

Tenant for life. One who holds lands or tenements for the term of his own life, or for that of any other person, (in which case he is called "*pur auter vie*,") or for more lives than one. 2 Bl.Comm. 120; In re Hyde, 41 Hun (N.Y.) 75.

Tenant for years. One who has the temporary use and possession of lands or tenements not his own, by virtue of a lease or demise granted to him by the owner, for a determinate period of time, as for a year or a fixed number of years. 2 Bl.Comm. 140.

Tenant from year to year. One who holds lands or tenements under the demise of another, where no certain term has been mentioned, but an annual rent has been reserved. See 1 Steph.Comm. 271; 4 Kent, Comm. 111, 114. One who holds over, by consent given either expressly or constructively, after the determination of a lease for years. 4 Kent, Comm. 112. See Shore v. Porter, 3 Term, 16; Rothschild v. Williamson, 83 Ind. 388; Hunter v. Frost, 47 Minn. 1, 49 N.W. 327; Coffman v. Sammons, 76 W.Va. 12, 84 S.E. 1061, 1063; Lawrence v. Goodstein, 91 Misc.Rep. 19, 154 N.Y.S. 229, 231. See, also, Year to Year, Tenancy from.

Tenant in capite. In feudal and old English law. Tenant in chief; one who held immediately under the king, in right of his crown and dignity. 2 Bl.Comm. 60.

Tenant in common. Tenants who hold the same land together by several and distinct titles, but by unity of possession, because none knows his own severalty, and therefore they all occupy promiscuously. 2 Bl.Comm. 191. Where two or more hold the same land, with interests accruing under different titles, or accruing under the same title, but at different periods, or conferred by words of limitation importing that the grantees are to take in distinct shares. 1 Steph.Comm. 323. See Coster v. Lorillard, 14 Wend., N.Y., 336; Taylor v. Millard, 118 N.Y. 244, 23 N.E. 376, 6 L.R.A. 667; Perry v. Jones, 48 Okl. 362, 150 P. 168, 169; Whyman v. Johnston, 62 Colo. 461, 163 P. 76, 77; Stewart v. Young, 212 Ala. 426, 103 So. 44, 45. See, also, Tenancy (Tenancy in Common).

Tenant in dower. This is where the husband of a woman is seised of an estate of inheritance and dies; in this case the wife shall have the third part of all the lands and tenements whereof he was seised at any time during the coverture, to hold to herself for life, as her dower. Co.Litt. 30; 2 Bl.Comm. 129; Combs v. Young, 4 Yerg. (Tenn.) 225, 26 Am.Dec. 225.

Tenant in fee-simple (or tenant in fee). He who has lands, tenements, or hereditaments, to hold to him and his heirs forever, generally, absolutely, and simply; without mentioning *what* heirs, but referring that to his own pleasure, or to the disposition of the law. 2 Bl.Comm. 104; Litt. § 1; Dows v. Board of Com'rs of City of Bayonne, 117 N.J.L. 337, 188 A. 509, 510.

Tenant in severalty. One who holds lands and tenements in his own right only, without any other person being joined or connected with him in point of interest during his estate therein. 2 Bl.Comm. 179.

Tenant in tail. One who holds an estate in fee-tail, that is, an estate which, by the instrument creating it, is limited to some particular heirs, exclusive of others; as to the heirs of *his body* or to the heirs, *male* or *female*, of his body.

Tenant in tail ex provisione viri. Where an owner of lands, upon or previously to marrying a wife, settled lands upon himself and his wife, and the heirs of their two bodies begotten, and then died, the wife, as survivor, became tenant in tail of the husband's lands, in consequence of the husband's provision, (*ex provisione viri.*) Originally, she could bar the estate-tail like any other tenant in tail; but the husband's intention having been merely to provide for her during her widowhood, and not to enable her to bar his children of their inheritance, she was early restrained from so doing, by the statute 32 Hen. VII. c. 36. Brown.

Tenant of the demesne. One who is tenant of a mesne lord; as, where A. is tenant of B., and C. of A., B. is the lord, A. the mesne lord, and C. tenant of the demesne. Ham. N. P. 392, 393.

Tenant paravaile. The under-tenant of land; that is, the tenant of a tenant; one who held of a mesne lord.

Tenant to the præcipe. Before the English fines and recoveries act, if land was conveyed to a person for life with remainder to another in tail, the tenant in tail in remainder was unable to bar the entail without the concurrence of the tenant for life, because a common recovery could only be suffered by the person seised of the land. In such a case, if the tenant for life wished to concur in barring the entail, he usually conveyed his life-estate to some other person, in order that the *præcipe* in the recovery might be issued against the latter, who was therefore called the "tenant to the *præcipe*." Williams, Seis. 169; Sweet.

Tenants by the verge. The "same nature as tenants by copy of court roll, [*i. e.*, copyholders.] But the reason why they be called 'tenants by the verge' is for that, when they will surrender their tenements into the hands of their lord to the use of another, they shall have a little rod (by the custome) in their hand, the which they shall deliver to the steward or to the bailife, * * * and the steward or bailife, according to the custome, shall deliver to him that taketh the land the same rod, or another rod, in the name of seisin; and for this cause they are called 'tenants by the verge,' but they have no other evidence [title-deed] but by copy of court roll." Litt. § 78; Co.Litt. 61*a*.

TENANT–RIGHT. A kind of customary estate in the north of England, falling under the general class of copyhold, but distinguished from copyhold by many of its incidents.

The so-called tenant-right of renewal is the expectation of a lessee that his lease will be renewed, in cases where it is an established practice to renew leases from time to time, as in the case of leases from the crown, from ecclesiastical corporations, or other collegiate bodies. Strictly speaking, there can be no right of renewal against the lessor without an express compact by him to that effect, though the existence of the custom often influences the price in sales.

The Ulster tenant-right may be described as a right on the tenant's part to sell his holding to the highest bidder, subject to the existing or a reasonable increase of rent from time to time, as circumstances may require, with a reasonable veto reserved to the landlord in respect of the incoming tenant's character and solvency. Mozley & Whitley.

TENANT'S FIXTURES. This phrase signifies things which are fixed to the freehold of the demised premises, but which the tenant may detach and take away, provided he does so in season. Wall v. Hinds, 4 Gray (Mass.) 256, 270, 64 Am. Dec. 64.

TENANTABLE REPAIR. Such a repair as will render a house fit for present habitation.

TENCON. L. Fr. A dispute; a quarrel. Kelham.

TEND. To have a leaning; serve, contribute, or conduce in some degree or way, or have a more or less direct bearing or effect; to be directed as to any end, object, or purpose; to have a tendency, conscious or unconscious, to any end, object or purpose. Rogers v. State, 122 Tex.Cr.R. 331, 54 S.W.2d 1010, 1012.

In old English law. To tender or offer. Cowell.

TENDER. An offer of money; the act by which one produces and offers to a person holding a claim or demand against him the amount of money which he considers and admits to be due, in satisfaction of such claim or demand, without any stipulation or condition. Kastens v. Ruland, 94 N.J.Eq. 451, 120 A. 21, 22; Mondello v. Hanover Trust Co., 252 Mass. 563, 148 N.E. 136, 137; Wooton v. Dahlquist, 42 Idaho, 121, 244 P. 407, 409; McCall Co. v. Hobbs-Henderson Co., 138 S.C. 435, 136 S.E. 762, 763.

The offer of performance, not performance itself, and, when unjustifiably refused, places other party in default and permits party making tender to exercise remedies for breach of contract. Walker v. Houston, 215 Cal. 742, 12 P.2d 952, 953, 87 A.L.R. 937.

The actual proffer of money, as distinguished from mere proposal or proposition to proffer it. Caplan v. Shaw, W. Va., 30 S.E.2d 132, 140. Hence mere written proposal to pay money, without offer of cash, is not "tender." Wardlaw v. Woodruff, 175 Ga. 515, 165 S.E. 557, 560.

"Tender," though usually used in connection with an offer to pay money, is properly used in connection with offer of property other than money. Maxwell Implement Co. v. Fitzgerald, 85 Ind.App. 206, 146 N.E. 883, 885; Central Flour Mills Co. v. Gateway Milling Co., Mo.App., 213 S.W. 131, 134; In re Katzowitz, 214 App.Div. 429, 212 N.Y.S. 336, 338; Harrison v. Beals, 111 Or. 563, 222 P. 728, 731; Jose v. Aufderheide, 222 Mo.App. 524, 293 S.W. 476, 479.

Tender, in pleading, is a plea by defendant that he has been always ready to pay the debt demanded, and before the commencement of the action tendered it to the plaintiff, and now brings it into court ready to be paid to him, etc. Brown.

Legal tender is that kind of coin, money, or circulating medium which the law compels a creditor to accept in payment of his debt, when tendered by the debtor in the right amount.

Tender of Amends

An offer by a person who has been guilty of any wrong or breach of contract to pay a sum of money by way of amends. If a defendant in an action make tender of amends, and the plaintiff decline to accept it, the defendant may pay the money into court, and plead the payment into court as a satisfaction of the plaintiff's claim. Mozley & Whitley.

Tender of Issue

A form of words in a pleading, by which a party offers to refer the question raised upon it to the appropriate mode of decision. The common tender of an issue of fact by a defendant is expressed by the words, "and of this he puts himself upon the country." Steph.Pl. 54, 230.

TENEMENT. This term, in its vulgar acceptation, is only applied to houses and other buildings, but in its original, proper, and legal sense it signifies everything that may be *holden*, provided it be of a permanent nature, whether it be of a substantial and sensible, or of an unsubstantial, ideal, kind. Thus, *liberum tenementum*, frank tenement, or freehold, is applicable not only to lands and other solid objects, but also to offices, rents, commons, advowsons, franchises, peerages, etc.

2 Bl.Comm. 16; Mitchell v. Warner, 5 Conn. 517; Oskaloosa Water Co. v. Board of Equalization, 84 Iowa 407, 51 N.W. 18, 15 L.R.A. 296; Field v. Higgins, 35 Me. 341.

Property held by tenant, everything of permanent nature which may be holden, and, in more restrictive sense, house or dwelling. Hughes v. Milby and Dow Coal and Mining Co., 127 Okl. 30, 259 P. 559, 560.

Dominant Tenement

One for the benefit or advantage of which an easement exists or is enjoyed.

Servient Tenement

One which is subject to the burden of an easement existing for or enjoyed by another tenement. See Easement.

TENEMENTAL LAND. Land distributed by a lord among his tenants, as opposed to the demesnes which were occupied by himself and his servants. 2 Bl.Comm. 90.

TENEMENTIS LEGATIS. An ancient writ, lying to the city of London, or any other corporation, (where the old custom was that men might devise by will lands and tenements, as well as goods and chattels,) for the hearing and determining any controversy touching the same. Reg.Orig. 244.

TENENDAS. In Scotch law. The name of a clause in charters of heritable rights, which derives its name from its first words, "*tenendas prœdictas terras;*" it points out the superior of whom the lands are to be holden, and expresses the particular tenure. Ersk. Inst. 2, 3, 24.

TENENDUM. Lat. To be holden. It was used to indicate the lord of whom the land was to be held and the tenure by which it was to be held. but, since all freehold tenures have been converted into socage, the *tenendum* is of no further use, and is therefore joined in the *habendum,*—"to have and to hold." 2 Bl.Comm. 298; 4 Cruise, Dig. 26.

TENENS. A tenant; the defendant in a real action.

TENENTIBUS IN ASSISÂ NON ONERANDIS. A writ that formerly lay for him to whom a disseisor had alienated the land whereof he disseised another, that he should not be molested in assize for damages, if the disseisor had wherewith to satisfy them. Reg. Orig. 214.

TENERE. Lat. In the civil law. To hold; to hold fast; to have in possession; to retain.

In relation to the doctrine of possession, this term expresses merely the fact of manual detention, or the corporal possession of any object, without involving the question of title; while *habere* (and especially *possidere*) denotes the maintenance of possession by a lawful claim; *i. e., civil* possession, as distinguished from mere *natural* possession.

TENERI. The Latin name for that clause in a bond in which the obligor expresses that he is "held and firmly bound" to the obligee, his heirs, etc.

TENET; TENUIT. Lat. He holds; he held. In the Latin forms of the writ of waste against a tenant, these words introduced the allegation of tenure. If the tenancy still existed, and recovery of the land was sought, the former word was used, (and the writ was said to be "in the *tenet.*") If the tenancy had already determined, the latter term was used, (the writ being described as "in the *tenuit,*") and then damages only were sought.

TENHEDED, or TIENHEOFED. In old English law. A dean. Cowell.

TENMENTALE. The number of ten men, which number, in the time of the Saxons, was called a "decennary;" and ten decennaries made what was called a "hundred." Also a duty or tribute paid to the crown, consisting of two shillings for each plowland. Enc.Lond.

TENNE. A term of heraldry, meaning orange color. In engravings it should be represented by lines in bend sinister crossed by others bar-ways. Heralds who blazon by the names of the heavenly bodies, call it "dragon's head," and those who employ jewels, "jacinth." It is one of the colors called "stainand." Wharton.

TENOR. A term used in pleading to denote that an exact copy is set out. 1 Chit.Crim.Law. 235.

By the tenor of a deed, or other instrument in writing, is signified the matter contained therein, according to the true intent and meaning thereof. Cowell.

"Tenor," in pleading a written instrument, imports that the very words are set out. "Purport" does not import this, but is equivalent only to "substance." Com. v. Wright, 1 Cush. (Mass.) 65; Dana v. State, 2 Ohio St. 93; State v. Bonney, 34 Me. 384; State v. Atkins, 5 Blackf. (Ind.) 458; State v. Chinn, 142 Mo. 507, 44 S.W. 245; Saugerties Bank v. Delaware & Hudson Co., 204 App.Div. 211, 198 N.Y.S. 722, 723; State v. Collins, 297 Mo. 257, 248 S.W. 599, 602; Johns v. Rice, 165 Iowa, 233, 145 N.W. 290, 291.

The action of proving the tenor, in Scotland, is an action for proving the contents and purport of a deed which has been lost. Bell.

In Chancery Pleading

A certified copy of records of other courts removed in chancery by *certiorari.* Gres.Eq.Ev. 309.

TENOR EST QUI LEGEM DAT FEUDO. It is the tenor [of the feudal grant] which regulates its effect and extent. Craigius, Jus Feud. (3d Ed.) 66; Broom, Max. 459.

TENORE INDICTAMENTI MITTENDO. A writ whereby the record of an indictment, and the process thereupon, was called out of another court into the queen's bench. Reg.Orig. 69.

TENORE PRÆSENTIUM. By the tenor of these presents, *i. e.,* the matter contained therein, or rather the intent and meaning thereof. Cowell.

TENSERIÆ. A sort of ancient tax or military contribution. Wharton.

TENT. A shelter of flexible material supported by poles stretched by cords that are secured by pegs in the ground. Knowles v. State, 19 Ala.App. 476, 98 So. 207, 208; City of St. Louis v. Nash, 266 Mo. 523, 181 S.W. 1145, 1146, Ann.Cas.1918B, 134; Killman v. State, 2 Tex.App. 222, 28 Am.Rep. 432.

TENTATES PANIS. The essay or assay of bread. Blount.

TENTERDEN'S ACT. In English law. The statute 9 Geo. IV. c. 14, taking its name from Lord Tenterden, who procured its enactment, which is a species of extension of the statute of frauds, and requires the reduction of contracts to writing.

TENTHS. In English law. A temporary aid issuing out of personal property, and granted to the king by parliament; formerly the real tenth part of all the movables belonging to the subject. 1 Bl.Comm. 308.

In English ecclesiastical law. The tenth part of the annual profit of every living in the kingdom, formerly paid to the pope, but by statute 26 Hen. VIII. c. 3, transferred to the crown, and afterwards made a part of the fund called "Queen Anne's Bounty." 1 Bl.Comm. 284–286.

TENUIT. A term used in stating the tenure in an action for waste done after the termination of the tenancy. See Tenet.

TENURA. In old English law. Tenure.

TENURA EST PACTIO CONTRA COMMUNEM FEUDI NATURAM AC RATIONEM, IN CONTRACTU INTERPOSITA. Wright, Ten. 21. Tenure is a compact contrary to the common nature and reason of the fee, put into a contract.

TENURE. The mode or system of holding lands or tenements in subordination to some superior, which, in the feudal ages, was the leading characteristic of real property.

Tenure is the direct result of feudalism, which separated the *dominium directum,* (the dominion of the soil,) which is placed mediately or immediately in the crown, from the *dominion utile,* (the possessory title,) the right to the use and profits in the soil, designated by the term "seisin," which is the highest interest a subject can acquire. Wharton; Kavanaugh v. Cohoes Power & Light Corporation, 187 N.Y.S. 216, 231, 114 Misc. 590.

Wharton gives the following list of tenures which were ultimately developed:

Lay Tenures

I. Frank tenement, or freehold. (1) The military tenures (abolished, except grand serjeanty, and reduced to free socage tenures) were: Knight service proper, or tenure in chivalry; grand serjeanty; cornage. (2) Free socage, or plow-service; either petit serjeanty, tenure in burgage, or gavelkind.

II. Villeinage. (1) Pure villeinage, (whence copyholds at the lord's [nominal] will, which is regulated according to custom). (2) Privileged villeinage, sometimes called "villein socage," (whence tenure in ancient demesne, which is an exalted species of copyhold, held according to custom, and not according to the lord's will,) and is of three kinds: Tenure in ancient demesne; privileged copyholds, customary freeholds, or free copyholds; copyholds of base tenure.

Spiritual Tenures

I. Frankalmoigne, or free alms.

II. Tenure by divine service.

In its general sense, a mode of holding or occupying. Thus, we speak of the tenure of an office, meaning the manner in which it is held, especially with regard to time, (tenure for life, tenure during good behavior,) and of tenure of land in the sense of occupation or tenancy, especially with reference to cultivation and questions of political economy; *e. g.*, tenure by peasant proprietors, cottiers, etc. Sweet. See Bard v. Grundy, 2 Ky. 169; People v. Waite, 9 Wend. (N.Y.) 58; Barrett v. Duff, 114 Kan. 220, 217 P. 918, 922; People ex rel. McCoy v. McCahey, 296 Ill.App. 310, 15 N.E.2d 988, 993.

TENURE BY DIVINE SERVICE. Where an ecclesiastical corporation, sole or aggregate, holds land by a certain divine service; as, to say prayers on a certain day in every year, "or to distribute in almes to an hundred poore men an hundred pence at such a day." Litt. § 137.

TENURE IN OFFICE. Right to perform duties and receive emoluments thereof. State ex rel. Daly v. City of Toledo, 142 Ohio St. 123, 50 N.E.2d 338, 342.

TERCE. In Scotch law. Dower; a widow's right of dower, or a right to a life estate in a third part of the lands of which her husband died seised.

TERCER. In Scotch law. A widow that possesses the third part of her husband's land, as her legal jointure. 1 Kames, Eq. pref.

TERCERONE. A term applied in the West Indies to a person one of whose parents was white and the other a mulatto. See Daniel v. Guy, 19 Ark. 131.

TERM. A word or phrase; an expression; particularly one which possesses a fixed and known meaning in some science, art, or profession.

A fixed period, a determined or prescribed duration. Carpenter v. Okanogan County, 163 Wash. 18, 299 P. 400, 404.

Civil Law

A space of time granted to a debtor for discharging his obligation. Poth. Obl. pt. 2, c. 3, art. 3, § 1; Civ.Code La. art. 2048.

Estates

Bounds, limitation, or extent of time for which an estate is granted; as when a man holds an estate for any limited or specific number of years, which is called his "term," and he himself is called, with reference to the term he so holds, the "termor," or "tenant of the term." Gay Mfg. Co. v. Hobbs, 128 N.C. 46, 38 S.E. 26, 83 Am.St.Rep. 661; Sanderson v. Scranton, 105 Pa. 472; Hurd v. Whitsett, 4 Colo. 84; Rooney v. City of Omaha, 105 Neb. 447, 181 N.W. 143, 144; Curry v. Bacharach Quality Shops, 271 Pa. 364, 117 A. 435, 438.

Of Court

When used with reference to a court, signifies the space of time during which the court holds a session. A *session* signifies the time during the term when the court sits for the transaction of business, and the session commences when the court convenes for the term, and continues until final adjournment, either before or at the expiration of the term. The *term* of the court is the time prescribed by law during which it may be in *session*. The *session* of the court is the time of its actual sitting. Lipari v. State, 19 Tex.App. 431; Conkling v. Ridgely, 112 Ill. 36, 1 N.E. 261, 54 Am.Rep. 204; Lanier v. Shayne, 85 Fla. 212, 95 So. 617, 618; Trower v. Mudd, Mo.App., 242 S.W. 993, 994. But "term" and "session" are often used interchangeably. Nation v. Savely, 127 Okl. 117, 260 P. 32, 35; Muse v. Harris, 122 Okl. 250, 254 P. 72, 73; Lewis County Pub. Co. v. Lewis County Court, 75 W.Va. 305, 83 S.E. 993, 995.

General

General term. A phrase used in some jurisdictions to denote the ordinary session of a court, for the trial and determination of causes, as distinguished from a *special* term, for the hearing of motions or arguments or the despatch of various kinds of formal business, or the trial of a special list or class of cases. Or it may denote a sitting of the court *in banc*. State v. Eggers, 152 Mo. 485, 54 S.W. 498.

Regular term. A term begun at the time appointed by law, and continued, in the discretion of the court, to such time as it may appoint, consistent with the law. Wightman v. Karsner, 20 Ala. 451; Glebe v. State, 106 Neb. 251, 183 N.W. 295, 296; Carter v. State, 14 Ga.App. 242, 80 S.E. 533, 534; State v. Thompson, 100 W.Va. 253, 130 S.E. 456, 460; Ex parte Daly, 66 Fla. 345, 63 So. 834, 835.

Special term. In New York practice, that branch of the court which is held by a single judge for hearing and deciding in the first instance motions and causes of equitable nature is called the "special term," as opposed to the "general term," held by three judges (usually) to hear appeals. Abbott; Gracie v. Freeland, 1 N.Y. 232.

Term attendant on the inheritance. See Attendant Terms.

Term fee. In English practice. A certain sum which a solicitor is entitled to charge to his client, and the client to recover, if successful, from the unsuccessful party; payable for every term in which any proceedings subsequent to the summons shall take place. Wharton.

Term for deliberating. The time given to the beneficiary heir, to examine if it be for his interest to accept or reject the succession which has fallen to him. Civ.Code La. art. 1033.

Term for years. An *estate for years* and the *time* during which such estate is to be held are each called a "term;" hence the term may expire before the time, as by a surrender. Co.Litt. 45.

Term in gross. A term of years is said to be either in gross (outstanding) or attendant upon the inheritance. It is outstanding, or in gross, when it is unattached or disconnected from the estate or inheritance, as where it is in the hands of some third party having no interest in the inheritance; it is attendant, when vested in some trustee in trust for the owner of the inheritance. Brown.

Term of lease. The word "term," when used in connection with a lease, means the period which is granted for the lessee to occupy the premises, and does not include the time between the making of the lease and the tenant's entry. Young v. Dake, 5 N.Y. 463, 55 Am.Dec. 356; De Pauw University v. United Electric Coal Cos., 299 Ill.App. 339, 20 N.E.2d 146, 149.

Term of office. The period during which elected officer or appointee is entitled to hold office, perform its functions, and enjoy its privileges and emoluments. State v. Knight, 76 Mont. 71, 245 P. 267, 268; Wilson v. McCarron, 112 Me. 181, 91 A. 839, 840; State v. Board of Com'rs of Sierra County, 29 N.M. 209, 222 P. 654, 655, 31 A.L.R. 1310; State v. Oklahoma City, 38 Okl. 349, 134 P. 58, 59, 60; Bayley v. Garrison, 190 Cal. 690, 214 P. 871, 872.

Term probatory. The period of time allowed to the promoter of an ecclesiastical suit to produce his witnesses, and prove the facts on which he rests his case. Coote, Ecc.Pr. 240, 241.

Term to conclude. In English ecclesiastical practice. An appointment by the judge of a time at which both parties are understood to renounce all further exhibits and allegations.

Term to propound all things. In English ecclesiastical practice. An appointment by the judge of a time at which both parties are to exhibit all the acts and instruments which make for their respective causes.

In the Law of Contracts and in Court Practice. The word is generally used in the plural, and "terms" are conditions; propositions stated or promises made which, when assented to or accepted by another, settle the contract and bind the parties. Webster. See Hutchinson v. Lord, 1 Wis. 313, 60 Am.Dec. 381; State v. Fawcett, 58 Neb. 371, 78 N.W. 636; Nakdimen v. Ft. Smith & Van Buren Bridge Dist., 115 Ark. 194, 172 S.W. 272, 275.

Special terms. Peculiar or unusual conditions imposed on a party before granting some application to the favor of the court.

Under terms. A party is said to be *under terms* when an indulgence is granted to him by the court in its discretion, on certain conditions. Thus, when an injunction is granted *ex parte*, the party obtaining it is put *under terms* to abide by such order as to damages as the court may make at the hearing. Mozley & Whitley.

TERM INSURANCE. See Insurance.

TERMES DE LA LEY. Terms of the law. The name of a lexicon of the law French words and other technicalities of legal language in old times.

TERMINABLE PROPERTY. This name is sometimes given to property of such a nature that its duration is not perpetual or indefinite, but is limited or liable to terminate upon the happening of an event or the expiration of a fixed term; *e. g.*, a leasehold, a life-annuity, etc.

TERMINATE. To put an end to; to make to cease; to end. Towne v. Towne, 117 Mont. 453, 159 P.2d 352, 357.

TERMINATING BUILDING SOCIETIES. Societies, in England, where the members commence their monthly contributions on a particular day, and continue to pay them until the realization of shares to a given amount for each member, by the advance of the capital of the society to such members as required it, and the payment of interest as well as principal by them, so as to insure such realization within a given period of years. They have been almost superseded by permanent building societies. Wharton.

TERMINATION OF CONDITIONAL CONTRACT. To abrogate so much of it as remains unperformed, doing away with existing agreement under agreed terms and consequences. Sanborn v. Ballanfonte, 98 Cal.App. 482, 277 P. 152, 155. To put an end to all of the unperformed portions thereof. Blodgett v. Merritt Annex Oil Co., 19 Cal.App.2d 169, 65 P.2d 123, 125.

TERMINATION OF EMPLOYMENT. Within policies providing that insurance should cease immediately upon termination of employment, means a complete severance of relationship of employer and employee. Edwards v. Equitable Life Assur. Soc. of United States, 296 Ky. 448, 177 S.W.2d 574, 577, 578; Peters v. Ætna Life Ins. Co. of Hartford, Conn., 279 Mich. 663, 273 N.W. 307, 308.

TERMINER. L. Fr. To determine. See Oyer and Terminer.

TERMINI. Lat. Ends; bounds; limiting or terminating points.

TERMINO. In Spanish law. A common; common land. Common because of vicinage. White, New Recop. b. 2, tit. 1, c. 6, § 1, note.

TERMINUM. A day given to a defendant. Spelman.

TERMINUM QUI PRETERIIT, WRIT OF ENTRY AD. A writ which lay for the reversioner, when the possession was withheld by the lessee, or a stranger, after the determination of a lease for years. Brown.

TERMINUS. Boundary; a limit, either of space or time.

The phrases "*terminus a quo*" and "*terminus ad quem*" are used, respectively, to designate the starting point and terminating point of a private way. In the case of a street, road, or railway, either end may be, and commonly is, referred to as the "terminus."

TERMINUS ANNORUM CERTUS DEBET ESSE ET DETERMINATUS. Co. Litt. 45. A term of years ought to be certain and determinate.

TERMINUS ET FEODUM NON POSSUNT CONSTARE SIMUI IN UNA EADEMQUE PERSONA. Plowd. 29. A term and the fee cannot both be in one and the same person at the same time.

TERMINUS HOMINIS. In English ecclesiastical practice. A time for the determination of appeals, shorter than the *terminus juris*, appointed by the judge. Hallifax, Civil Law, b. 3, c. 11, no. 36.

TERMINUS JURIS. In English ecclesiastical practice. The time of one or two years, allowed by law for the determination of appeals. Hallifax, Civil Law, b. 3, c. 11, no. 38.

TERMOR. He that holds lands or tenements for a term of years or life. But we generally confine the application of the word to a person entitled for a term of years. Mozley & Whitley.

TERMS TO BE UNDER. A party is said to be *under terms,* when an indulgence is granted to him by the court in its discretion, on certain conditions. Thus, when an injunction is granted *ex parte,* the party obtaining it is put *under terms* to abide by such order as to damages as the court may make at the hearing. Moz. & W.

TERRA. Lat. Earth; soil; arable land. Kennett, Gloss.

TERRA AFFIRMATA. Land let to farm.

TERRA BOSCALIS. Woody land.

TERRA CULTA. Cultivated land.

TERRA DEBILIS. Weak or barren land.

TERRA DOMINICA, or INDOMINICATA. The demesne land of a manor. Cowell.

TERRA EXCULTABILIS. Land which may be plowed. Mong. Ang. i. 426.

TERRA EXTENDENDA. A writ addressed to an escheator, etc., that he inquire and find out the true yearly value of any land, etc., by the oath of twelve men, and to certify the extent into the chancery. Reg. Writs, 293.

TERRA FRUSCA, or FRISCA. Fresh land, not lately plowed. Cowell.

TERRA HYDATA. Land subject to the payment of hydage. Selden.

TERRA INSTAURATA. See Instaurum.

TERRA LUCRABILIS. Land gained from the sea or inclosed out of a waste. Cowell.

TERRA NORMANORUM. Land held by a Norman. Paroch. Antiq. 197.

TERRA NOVA. Land newly converted from wood ground or arable. Cowell.

TERRA MANENS VACUA OCCUPANTI CONCEDITUR. 1 Sid. 347. Land lying unoccupied is given to the first occupant.

TERRA PUTURA. Land in forests, held by the tenure of furnishing food to the keepers therein. 4 Inst. 307.

TERRA SABULOSA. Gravelly or sandy ground.

TERRA SALICA. In Salic law. The land of the house; the land within that inclosure which belonged to a German house. No portion of the inheritance of Salic land passes to a woman, but this the male sex acquires; that is, the sons succeed in that inheritance. Lex Salic. tit. 62, § 6.

TERRA TESTAMENTALIS. Gavel-kind land, being disposable by will. Spelman.

TERRA TRANSIT CUM ONERE. Land passes with the incumbrances. Co.Litt. 231; Broom, Max. 437, 630.

TERRA VESTITA. Land sown with corn. Cowell.

TERRA WAINABILIS. Tillable land. Cowell.

TERRA WARRENATA. Land that has the liberty of free-warren.

TERRÆ DOMINICALES REGIS. The demesne lands of the crown.

TERRAGE. In old English law. A kind of tax or charge on land; a boon or duty of plowing, reaping, etc. Cowell.

TERRAGES. An exemption from all uncertain services. Cowell.

TERRARIUS. In old English law. A landholder.

TERRE-TENANT. He who is literally in the occupation or possession of the land, as distinguished from the owner out of possession. But, in a more technical sense, the person who is seised of the land, though not in actual occupancy of it, and locally, in Pennsylvania, one who purchases and takes land subject to the existing lien of a mortgage or judgment against a former owner. See Dengler v. Kiehner, 13 Pa. 38, 53 Am.Dec. 441; Hulett v. Insurance Co., 114 Pa. 142, 6 A. 554; Commonwealth Trust Co. of Pittsburgh v. Harkins, 312 Pa. 402, 167 A. 278, 280.

TERRIER. In English law. A landroll or survey of lands, containing the quantity of acres, tenants' names, and such like; and in the exchequer there is a terrier of all the glebe lands in England, made about 1338. In general, an ecclesiastical terrier contains a detail of the temporal possessions of the church in every parish. Cowell; Tomlins; Mozley & Whitley.

TERRIS BONIS ET CATALLIS REHABENDIS POST PURGATIONEM. A writ for a clerk to recover his lands, goods, and chattels, formerly seized, after he had cleared himself of the felony of which he was accused, and delivered to his ordinary to be purged. Reg. Orig.

TERRIS ET CATALLIS TENTIS ULTRA DEBITUM LEVATUM. A judicial writ for the restoring of lands or goods to a debtor who is distrained above the amount of the debt. Reg. Jud.

TERRIS LIBERANDIS. A writ that lay for a man convicted by attaint, to bring the record and process before the king, and take a fine for his imprisonment, and then to deliver to him his lands and tenements again, and release him of the strip and waste. Reg. Orig. 232. Also it was a writ for the delivery of lands to the heir, after homage and relief performed, or upon security taken that he should perform them. Orig. 293.

TERRITORIAL, TERRITORIALITY. These terms are used to signify connection with, or limitation with reference to, a particular country or territory. Thus, "territorial law" is the correct expression for the law of a particular country or state, although "municipal law" is more common. "Territorial waters" are that part of the sea adjacent to the coast of a given country which is by international law deemed to be within the sovereignty of that country, so that its courts have jurisdiction over offenses committed on those waters, even by a person on board a foreign ship. Sweet.

TERRITORIAL COURTS. The courts established in the territories of the United States.

TERRITORIAL JURISDICTION. Territory over which a government or a subdivision thereof has jurisdiction. State v. Cox, 106 Utah 253, 147 P.2d 858, 861.

Jurisdiction considered as limited to cases arising or persons residing within a defined territory, as, a county, a judicial district, etc. The authority of any court is limited by the boundaries thus fixed. See Phillips v. Thralls, 26 Kan. 781.

TERRITORIAL PROPERTY. The land and water over which the state has jurisdiction and control whether the legal title be in the state itself or in private individuals. Lakes and waters wholly within the state are its property and also the marginal sea within the three-mile limit, but bays and gulfs are not always recognized as state property.

TERRITORY. A part of a country separated from the rest, and subject to a particular jurisdiction.

American Law

A portion of the United States, not within the limits of any state, which has not yet been admitted as a state of the Union, but is organized, with a separate legislature, and with executive and judicial officers appointed by the president. See Ex parte Morgan, D.C.Ark., 20 F. 298, 304; People v. Daniels, 6 Utah, 288, 22 P. 159, 5 L.R.A. 444; Ex parte Heikich Terui, 187 Cal. 20, 200 P. 954, 956, 17 A.L.R. 630.

Const. Amend. 18, prohibiting the transportation of intoxicating liquor within or the importation thereof into the United States and territory subject to its jurisdiction, uses the word "territory" as meaning the regional areas of land and adjacent waters over which the United States claims and exercises dominion and control as a sovereign power. Cunard S. S. Co. v. Mellon, 262 U.S. 100, 43 S.Ct. 504, 507, 67 L.Ed. 894, 27 A.L.R. 1306; International Mercantile Marine v. Stuart, D.C.N.Y., 285 F. 78, 81; State v. Morton, 31 Idaho, 329, 171 P. 495, 496.

TERRITORY OF A JUDGE. The territorial jurisdiction of a judge; the bounds, or district, within which he may lawfully exercise his judicial authority. Phillips v. Thralls, 26 Kan. 781.

TERROR. Alarm; fright; dread; the state of mind induced by the apprehension of hurt from some hostile or threatening event or manifestation; fear caused by the appearance of danger. In an indictment for riot, it must be charged that the acts done were "to the *terror* of the people." See Arto v. State, 19 Tex.App. 136.

TERTIA DENUNCIATIO. Lat. In old English law. Third publication or proclamation of intended marriage.

TERTIUS INTERVENIENS. Lat. In the civil law. A third person intervening; a third person who comes in between the parties to a suit; one who interpleads. Gilbert's Forum Rom. 47.

TEST. To bring one to a trial and examination, or to ascertain the truth or the quality or fitness of a thing.

Something by which to ascertain the truth respecting another thing; a criterion, gauge, standard, or norm.

In public law, an inquiry or examination addressed to a person appointed or elected to a public office, to ascertain his qualifications therefor, but particularly a scrutiny of his political, religious, or social views, or his attitude of past and present loyalty or disloyalty to the government under which he is to act. See Attorney General v. Detroit Common Council, 58 Mich. 213, 24 N.W. 887, 55 Am.Rep. 675; People v. Hoffman, 116 Ill. 587, 5 N.E. 596, 56 Am.Rep. 793; Rogers v. Buffalo, 51 Hun 637, 3 N.Y.S. 674.

TEST ACT. The statute 25 Car. II. c. 2, which directed all civil and military officers to take the oaths of allegiance and supremacy, and make the declaration against transubstantiation, within six months after their admission, and also within the same time receive the sacrament according to the usage of the Church of England, under penalty of £500 and disability to hold the office. 4 Bl.Comm. 58, 59. This was abolished by St. 9 Geo. IV. c. 17, so far as concerns receiving the sacrament, and a new form of declaration was substituted.

TEST ACTION. An action selected out of a considerable number of suits, concurrently depending in the same court, brought by several plaintiffs against the same defendant, or by one plaintiff against different defendants, all similar in their circumstances, and embracing the same questions, and to be supported by the same evidence, the selected action to go first to trial, (under an order of court equivalent to consolidation,) and its decision to serve as a *test* of the right of recovery in the others, all parties agreeing to be bound by the result of the test action.

TEST OATH. An oath required to be taken as a criterion of the fitness of the person to fill a public or political office; but particularly an oath of fidelity and allegiance (past or present) to the established government.

TEST-PAPER. In practice. A paper or instrument shown to a jury as evidence. A term used in the Pennsylvania courts. Depue v. Clare, 7 Pa. 428.

TESTA DE NEVIL. An ancient and authentic record in two volumes, in the custody of the king's remembrancer in the exchequer, said to be compiled by John de Nevil, a justice itinerant, in the eighteenth and twenty-fourth years of Henry III. Cowell. These volumes were printed in 1807, under the authority of the commissioners of the public records, and contain an account of fees held either immediately of the king or of others who held of the king *in capite;* fees holden in frankalmoigne; serjeanties holden of the king; widows and heiresses of tenants *in capite,* whose marriages were in the gift of the king; churches in the gift of the king; escheats, and sums paid for scutages and aids, especially within the county of Hereford. Cowell; Wharton.

TESTABLE. A person is said to be testable when he has capacity to make a will; a man of twenty-one years of age and of sane mind is testable.

TESTACY. The state or condition of leaving a will at one's death. Opposed to "intestacy."

TESTAMENT. A disposition of personal property to take place after the owner's decease, according to his desire and direction. Pluche v. Jones, C.C.A.Tex., 54 F. 860, 865, 4 C.C.A. 622; Aubert's Appeal, 109 Pa. 447, 1 A. 336; Conklin v. Egerton, 21 Wend., N.Y., 436; Ragsdale v. Booker, 2 Strob. Eq. (S.C.) 348; In re Lester's Will, 100 N.J.Eq. 521, 136 P. 322.

The act of last will, clothed with certain solemnities, by which the testator disposes of his property, either universally, or by universal title, or by particular title. Civ.Code La. art. 1571.

The common usage the world over is to employ the words "will," "testament," and "last will and testament" as exactly synonymous. Occidental Life Ins. Co. v. Powers, 192 Wash. 475, 74 P.2d 27, 32, 114 A.L.R. 531. But strictly speaking, the term testament denotes only a will of personal property; a will of land not being called a "testament." Wyers v. Arnold, 347 Mo. 413, 147 S.W.2d 644, 647, 134 A.L.R. 876. The word "testament" is now seldom used, except in the heading of a formal will, which usually begins: "This is the last will and testament of me, A. B.," etc. Sweet.

The true declaration of a man's last will as to that which he would have to be done, after his death. It is compounded, according to Justinian, from *testatio mentis;* but the better opinion is that it is a simple word formed from the Latin *testor,* and not a compound word. Mozley & Whitley.

Military Testament

In English law. A nuncupative will, that is, one made by word of mouth, by which a soldier may dispose of his goods, pay, and other personal chattels, without the forms and solemnities which the law requires in other cases. St. 1 Vict. c. 26, § 11.

Mutual Testaments

Wills made by two persons who leave their effects reciprocally to the survivor.

Mystic Testament

A form of testament made under Spanish law which prevailed in Louisiana and California. See Broutin v. Vassant, 5 Mart. O.S. (La.) 182; Schoul. Wills § 9. In the law of Louisiana. A sealed testament. The mystic or secret testament, otherwise called the "closed testament," is made in the following manner: The testator must sign his dispositions, whether he has written them himself or has caused them to be written by another person. The paper containing those dispositions, or the paper serving as their envelope, must be closed and sealed. The testator shall present it thus closed and sealed to the notary and to seven witnesses, or he shall cause it to be closed and sealed in their presence. Then he shall declare to the notary, in presence of the witnesses, that that paper contains his testament written by himself, or by another by his direction, and signed by him, the testator. The notary shall then draw up the act of superscription, which shall be written on that paper, or on the sheet that serves as its envelope, and that act shall be signed by the testator, and by the notary and the witnesses. Civ.Code La. art. 1584.

TESTAMENTA CUM DUO INTER SE PUGNANTIA REPERIUNTUR, ULTIMUM RATUM EST; SIC EST, CUM DUO INTER SE PUGNANTIA REPERIUNTUR IN EODEM TESTAMENTO. Co.Litt. 112. When two conflicting wills are found, the last prevails; so it is when two conflicting clauses occur in the same will.

TESTAMENTA LATISSIMAM INTERPRETATIONEM HABERE DEBENT. Jenk.Cent. 81. Wills ought to have the broadest interpretation.

TESTAMENTARY. Pertaining to a will or testament; as *testamentary* causes. Derived from, founded on, or appointed by a testament or will; as a *testamentary* guardian, letters *testamentary*, etc.

A paper, instrument, document, gift, appointment, etc., is said to be "testamentary" when it is written or made so as not to take effect until after the death of the person making it, and to be revocable and retain the property under his control during his life, although he may have believed that it would operate as an instrument of a different character. Sweet. See In re Murphy's Estate, 193 Wash. 400, 75 P.2d 916, 920.

Letters Testamentary

The formal instrument of authority and appointment given to an executor by the proper court, upon the admission of the will to probate, empowering him to enter upon the discharge of his office as executor.

Testamentary Capacity

That measure of mental ability which is recognized in law as sufficient for the making a will. See Nicewander v. Nicewander, 151 Ill. 156, 37 N.E. 698; Delafield v. Parish, 25 N.Y. 29; Duffield v. Robeson, 2 Har. (Del.) 379; Lowe v. Williamson, 2 N.J.Eq. 85.

A testator to have such capacity must have sufficient mind and memory to intelligently understand the nature of business in which he is engaged, to comprehend generally the nature and extent of property which constitutes his estate, and which he intends to dispose of, and to recollect the objects of his bounty. In re Larsen's Estate, 191 Wash. 257, 71 P.2d 47, 49. And it depends upon capacity at very time will was executed, and not previously or subsequently. Bishop v. Scharf, 214 Iowa 644, 241 N.W. 3, 7.

Testamentary Causes

In English law. Causes or matters relating to the probate of wills, the granting of administrations, and the suing for legacies, of which the ecclesiastical courts have jurisdiction. 3 Bl.Comm. 95, 98. Testamentary causes are causes relating to the validity and execution of wills. The phrase is generally confined to those causes which were formerly matters of ecclesiastical jurisdiction, and are now dealt with by the court of probate. Mozley & Whitley.

Testamentary Class

Body of persons, uncertain in number at time of gift, ascertainable in future, and each taking in equal or in other definite proportions. Newlin v. Mercantile Trust Co. of Baltimore, 161 Md. 622, 158 A. 51, 57.

Testamentary Disposition

A disposition of property by way of gift, which is not to take effect unless the grantor dies or until that event. Diefendorf v. Diefendorf, 56 Hun 639, 8 N.Y.S. 617; Chestnut St. Nat. Bank v. Fidelity Ins., etc., Co., 40 A. 486, 186 Pa. 333, 65 Am.St.Rep. 860; Patch v. Squires, 105 Vt. 405, 165 A. 919, 921.

Testamentary Guardian

A guardian appointed by the last will of a father for the person and real and personal estate of his child until the latter arrives of full age. 1 Bl.Comm. 462; 2 Kent, Comm. 224; In re De Saulles, 101 Misc. 447, 167 N.Y.S. 445, 453.

Testamentary Paper or Instrument

An instrument in the nature of a will; an unprobated will; a paper writing which is of the character of a will, though not formally such, and, if allowed as a testament, will have the effect of a will upon the devolution and distribution of property. Young v. O'Donnell, 129 Wash. 219, 224 P. 682, 684.

Testamentary Power

A power of appointment exercisable only by will. Restatement, Property, § 321(1).

Testamentary Succession

In Louisiana, that which results from the institution of an heir contained in a testament executed in the form prescribed by law. Civ.Code La. 1900, art. 876.

Testamentary Trustee

See Trustee.

TESTAMENTI FACTIO. Lat. In the civil law. The ceremony of making a testament, either as testator, heir, or witness.

TESTAMENTUM. Lat. In the civil law. A testament; a will, or last will.

In old English law. A testament or will; a disposition of property made in contemplation of death. Bract. fol. 60.

A general name for any instrument of conveyance, including deeds and charters, and so called either because it furnished written *testimony* of the conveyance, or because it was authenticated by witnesses, (*testes.*) Spelman.

TESTAMENTUM EST VOLUNTATIS NOSTRÆ JUSTA SENTENTIA, DE EO QUOD QUIS POST MORTEM SUAM FIERI VELIT. A testament is the just expression of our will concerning that which any one wishes done after his death, [or, as Blackstone translates, "the legal declaration of a man's intentions which he wills to be performed after his death."] Dig. 28, 1, 1; 2 Bl.Comm. 499.

TESTAMENTUM, i. e., TESTATIO MENTIS, FACTA NULLO PRÆSENTE METU PERICULI, SED COGITATIONE MORTALITATIS. Co. Litt. 322. A testament, *i. e.*, the witnessing of one's intention, made under no present fear of danger, but in expectancy of death.

TESTAMENTUM INOFFICIOSUM. Lat. In the civil law. An inofficious testament, (*q. v.*).

TESTAMENTUM OMNE MORTE CONSUMMATUR. Every will is perfected by death. A will speaks from the time of death only. Co. Litt. 232.

TESTARI. Lat. In the civil law. To testify; to attest; to declare, publish, or make known a thing before witnesses. To make a will. Calvin.

TESTATE. One who has made a will; one who dies leaving a will.

If deceased's property passed to the devisees under his will, then he died "testate"; but, if no part of the property of his estate passed by will, but by the statute of descent and distribution, then he died "intestate". Leffler v. Leffler, 151 Fla. 455, 10 So.2d 799, 804.

TESTATION. Witness; evidence.

TESTATOR. One who makes or has made a testament or will; one who dies leaving a will. This term is borrowed from the civil law. Inst. 2, 14, 5, 6.

TESTATORIS ULTIMA VOLUNTAS EST PERIMPLENDA SECUNDUM VERAM INTENTIONEM SUAM. Co. Litt. 322. The last will of a testator is to be thoroughly fulfilled according to his real intention.

TESTATRIX. A woman who makes a will; a woman who dies leaving a will; a female testator.

TESTATUM. The name of a writ which is issued by the court of one county to the sheriff of another county in the same state, when defendant cannot be found in the county where the court is located: for example, after a judgment has been obtained, and a ca. sa. has been issued, which has been returned non est inventus, a testatum ca. sa. may be issued to the sheriff of the county where the defendant is. See Viner, Abr. Testatum 259.

In conveyancing. That part of a deed which commences with the words, "This indenture witnesseth."

TESTATUM WRIT. In practice. A writ containing a *testatum* clause; such as a *testatum capias*, a *testatum fi. fa.*, and a *testatum ca. sa.* See Testatum.

TESTATUS. Lat. In the civil law. Testate; one who has made a will. Dig. 50, 17, 7.

TESTE MEIPSO. Lat. In old English law and practice. A solemn formula of attestation by the sovereign, used at the conclusion of charters, and other public instruments, and also of original writs out of chancery. Spelman.

TESTE OF A WRIT. In practice. The concluding clause, commencing with the word "Witness," etc. A writ which bears the teste is sometimes said to be *tested.*

"Teste" is a word commonly used in the last part of every writ, wherein the date is contained beginning with the words, *"Teste meipso,"* meaning the sovereign, if the writ be an original writ, or be issued in the name of the sovereign; but, if the writ be a judicial writ, then the word "Teste" is followed by the name of the chief judge of the court in which the action is brought, or, in case of a vacancy of such office, in the name of the senior puisne judge. Mozley & Whitley.

TESTED. To be tested is to bear the teste, (*q. v.*).

TESTES. Lat. Witnesses.

TESTES PONDERANTUR, NON NUMERANTUR. Witnesses are weighed, not numbered. That is, in case of a conflict of evidence, the truth is to be sought by weighing the credibility of the respective witnesses, not by the mere numerical preponderance on one side or the other.

TESTES QUI POSTULAT DEBET DARE EIS SUMPTUS COMPETENTES. Whosoever demands witnesses must find them in competent provision.

TESTES, TRIAL PER. A trial had before a judge without the intervention of a jury, in which the judge is left to form in his own breast his sentence upon the credit of the witnesses examined; but this mode of trial, although it was common in the civil law, was seldom resorted to in the practice of the common law, but it is now becoming common when each party waives his right to a trial by jury. Brown.

TESTIBUS DEPONENTIBUS IN PARI NUMERO, DIGNIORIBUS EST CREDENDUM. Where the witnesses who testify are in equal number, [on both sides,] the more worthy are to be believed. 4 Inst. 279.

TESTIFY. To bear witness; to give evidence as a witness; to make a solemn declaration, under oath or affirmation, in a judicial inquiry, for the purpose of establishing or proving some fact. See State v. Robertson, 26 S.C. 117, 1 S.E. 443; Gannon v. Stevens, 13 Kan. 459; Mudge v. Gilbert, 43 How.Prac. (N.Y.) 221; People v. Krotz, 341 Ill. 214, 172 N.E. 135, 137.

TESTIMONIA PONDERANDA SUNT, NON NUMERANDA. Evidence is to be weighed, not enumerated.

TESTIMONIAL. Besides its ordinary meaning of a written recommendation to character, "testimonial" has a special meaning, under St. 39 Eliz. c. 17, § 3, passed in 1597, under which it signified a certificate under the hand of a justice of the peace, testifying the place and time when and where a soldier or mariner landed, and the place of his dwelling or birth, unto which he was to pass, and a convenient time limited for his passage. Every idle and wandering soldier or mariner not having such a testimonial, or willfully exceeding for above fourteen days the time limited thereby, or forging or counterfeiting such testimonial, was to suffer death as a felon, without benefit of clergy. This act was repealed, in 1812, by St. 52 Geo. III. c. 31. Mozley & Whitley.

TESTIMONIAL PROOF. In the civil law. Proof by the evidence of witnesses, *i. e.*, parol evidence, as distinguished from proof by written instruments, which is called "literal" proof.

TESTIMONIO. In Spanish law. An authentic copy of a deed or other instrument, made by a notary and given to an interested party as evidence of his title, the original remaining in the public archives. Guilbeau v. Mays, 15 Tex. 414.

TESTIMONIUM CLAUSE. In conveyancing. That clause of a deed or instrument with which it concludes: "In witness whereof, the parties to these presents have hereunto set their hands and seals."

TESTIMONY. Evidence given by a competent witness, under oath or affirmation; as distinguished from evidence derived from writings, and other sources. Edelstein v. United States, 79 C.C.A. 328, 149 F. 636, 640, 9 L.R.A.,N.S., 236; Grayson v. Durant, 43 Okl. 799, 144 P. 592, 594; Cauble v. Key, Tex.Civ.App., 256 S.W. 654, 655.

Evidence and Testimony as Synonymous or Distinguishable

The words "testimony" and "evidence" are not synonymous. Bednarik v. Bednarik, 18 N.J.Misc. 633, 16 A.2d 80, 89.

Although testimony is evidence, evidence may or may not be testimony or may, and in most cases does, consist of more than testimony. Superior Meat Products v. Holloway, 113 Ill.App. 320, 48 N.E.2d 83, 86.

Anything perceptible to the five senses, constitutes evidence, when submitted to court or jury, if competent. In re Fisher's Estate, 47 Idaho 668, 279 P. 291, 293.

Application for policy, although evidence in suit on policy, was not "testimony," Metropolitan Life Ins. Co. v. Lodzinski, 121 N.J.Eq. 183, 188 A. 681, 688.

"Evidence" is the broader term and includes all testimony. Bednarik v. Bednarik, 18 N.J.Misc. 633, 16 A.2d 80, 89. In re Seigle's Estate, 26 N.Y.S.2d 410, 413, 176 Misc. 15.

"Evidence" of transaction between claimant and decedent, were not "testimony." In re Seigle's Estate, 264 App.Div. 76, 34 N.Y.S.2d 489, 491.

Exhibits are "evidence" but not "testimony". Worland v. McGill, 26 Ohio App. 442, 160 N.E. 478, 480; Madison v. State, 138 Fla. 467, 189 So. 832, 835.

"Testimony" is found in spoken words of witnesses while "evidence" includes documents and other exhibits which may properly be submitted to jury. Madison v. State, 138 Fla. 467, 189 So. 832, 835.

"Testimony" is that species of evidence which is produced through language of witnesses. Weeks v. Bailey, 33 N.M. 193, 263 P. 29, 30.

Testimony is one species of evidence. But the word "evidence" is a generic term which includes every species of it. Gazette Printing Co. v. Morss, 60 Ind. 157. Testimony is the evidence given by witnesses. Evidence is whatever may be given to the jury as tending to prove a case. It includes the testimony of witnesses, documents, admissions of parties, etc. Mann v. Higgins, 83 Cal. 66, 23 P. 206; Carroll v. Bancker, 43 La.Ann. 1078, 10 So. 192; Columbia Nat. Bank v. German Nat. Bank, 56 Neb. 803, 77 N.W. 346; Harris v. Tomlinson, 130 Ind. 426, 30 N.E. 214; Jones v. Gregory, 48 Ill.App. 230; Industrial Commission v. Jasionowski, 24 Ohio App. 66, 156 N.E. 616, 618. What is sworn is testimony; what is the truth deduced therefrom is "evidence." Louisville & N. R. Co. v. Rogers, 21 Ga.App. 324, 94 S.E. 321, 322; Mick v. Mart, N.J.Ch., 65 A. 851.

But in common parlance, "testimony" and "evidence" are synonymous. State v. Winney, 21 N.D. 72, 128 N.W. 680, 681; Jones v. City of Seattle, 51 Wash. 245, 98 P. 743, 745; Fitzgerald v. Benner, 219 Ill. 485, 76 N.E. 709, 716; Grayson v. Durant, 43 Okl. 799, 144 P. 592, 594.

Testimony properly means only such evidence as is delivered by a witness on the trial of a cause, either orally or in the form of affidavits or depositions. Thus, an ancient deed, when offered under proper circumstances, is evidence but it could not strictly be called "testimony."

The words "testimony" and "evidence," are frequently used synonymously. Superior Lloyds of America v. Foxworth, Tex.Civ.App., 178 S.W.2d 724, 726; Roberts v. Carlson, 142 Neb. 851, 857, 8 N.W.2d 175, 179; Wyuta Cattle Co. v. Connell, 43 Wyo. 135, 299 P. 279, 281.

As used in instruction "testimony" was used in the sense of "evidence." In re Burcham's Estate, 211 Iowa 1395, 235 N.W. 764, 766.

The use of the word "testimony" instead of "evidence" in an instruction, where both oral evidence and physical facts and circumstances are defensively interposed, is not prejudicial where it is clear from all the instructions that it was intended that such physical facts should also be considered by the jury. Roberts v. Carlson, 142 Neb. 857, 8 N.W.2d 175, 179.

The word "testimony" as used in statute providing that when any deed, writing, or other document necessary as "testimony" may be in possession of a resident who is not a party subpœna duces tecum shall be issued on application, means "evidence". Ex parte Hart, 240 Ala. 642, 200 So. 783, 786.

Expert Testimony

See Expert Evidence.

Negative Testimony

Testimony not bearing directly upon the immediate fact or occurrence under consideration, but evidencing facts from which it may be inferred that the act or fact in question could not possibly have happened. See Barclay v. Hartman, 43 A. 174, 2 Marv. (Del.) 351; Cinadar v. Detroit, G. H. & M. Ry. Co., 193 Mich. 38, 159 N.W. 312; Heywood v. State, 12 Ga.App. 643, 77 S.E. 1130; Williams v. State, 23 Ga.App. 542, 99 S.E. 43.

Positive Testimony

Direct testimony that a thing did or did not happen. Williams v. State, 23 Ga.App. 542, 99 S.E. 43; Roberts v. State, 90 Fla. 779, 107 So. 242, 244.

TESTIS. Lat. A witness; one who gives evidence in court, or who witnesses a document.

TESTIS DE VISU PRÆPONDERAT ALIIS. 4 Inst. 279. An eye-witness is preferred to others.

TESTIS LUPANARIS SUFFICIT AD FACTUM IN LUPANARI. Moore, 817. A lewd person is a sufficient witness to an act committed in a brothel.

TESTIS NEMO IN SUA CAUSA ESSE POTEST. No one can be a witness in his own cause.

TESTIS OCULATUS UNUS PLUS VALET QUAM AURITI DECEM. 4 Inst. 279. One eye-witness is worth more than ten ear-witnesses.

TESTMOIGNE. An old law French term, denoting evidence or testimony of a witness.

TESTMOIGNES NE POENT TESTIFIER LE NEGATIVE, MES L'AFFIRMATIVE. Witnesses cannot testify to a negative; they must testify to an affirmative. 4 Inst. 279.

TEXT-BOOK. A legal treatise which lays down principles or collects decisions on any branch of the law.

TEXTUS ROFFENSIS. In old English law. The Rochester text. An ancient manuscript containing many of the Saxon laws, and the rights, customs, tenures, etc., of the church of Rochester, drawn up by Ernulph, bishop of that see from A. D. 1114 to 1124. Cowell.

THAINLAND. In old English law. The land which was granted by the Saxon kings to their thains or thanes was so called.

THALWEG. Old German spelling of Talweg, which title see.

THANAGE OF THE KING. A certain part of the king's land or property, of which the ruler or governor was called "thane." Cowell.

THANE. An Anglo-Saxon nobleman; an old title of honor, perhaps equivalent to "baron." There were two orders of thanes,—the king's thanes and the ordinary thanes. Soon after the Conquest this name was disused. Cowell.

THANELANDS. Such lands as were granted by charter of the Saxon kings to their thanes with all immunities, except from the *trinoda necessitas*. Cowell.

THANESHIP. The office and dignity of a thane; the seigniory of a thane.

THAT. A relative pronoun equivalent to who or which, either singular or plural. Dunn v. Bryan, 77 Utah 604, 299 P. 253, 255.

THAT WHICH I MAY DEFEAT BY MY ENTRY I MAKE GOOD BY MY CONFIRMATION. Co. Litt. 300.

THAVIES INN. An inn of chancery. See Inns of Chancery.

THE. An article which particularizes the subject spoken of. "Grammatical niceties should not be resorted to without necessity; but it would be extending liberality to an unwarrantable length to confound the articles 'a' and 'the'. The most unlettered persons understand that 'a' is indefinite, but 'the' refers to a certain object." Per Tilghman, C. J., Sharff v. Com., 2 Bin., Pa., 516; Penn Mut. Life Ins. Co. v. Henderson, D.C.Fla., 244 F. 877, 880; Howell v. State, 138 S.E. 206, 210, 164 Ga. 204; Hoffman v. Franklin Motor Car Co., 32 Ga.App. 229, 122 S.E. 896, 900. "The" house means only one house. Rocci v. Massachusetts Acc. Co., 222 Mass. 336, 110 N.E. 972, 973, Ann. Cas.1918C, 529.

THE FUND WHICH HAS RECEIVED THE BENEFIT SHOULD MAKE THE SATISFACTION. 4 Bouv. Inst. note 3730.

THE LAW ABHORS A MULTIPLICITY OF SUITS.

THE PARTIES BEING IN PARI CASU, JUSTICE IS IN EQUILIBRIO.

THE REPEAL OF THE LAW IMPOSING A PENALTY IS ITSELF A REMISSION.

THEATER. Any edifice used for the purpose of dramatic or operatic or other representations, plays, or performances, for admission to which entrance-money is received, not including halls rented or used occasionally for concerts or theatrical representations. See Bell v. Mahn, 121 Pa. 225, 15 A. 523, 1 L.R.A. 364, 6 Am.St.Rep. 786; Zucarro v. State, 197 S.W. 982, 985, 82 Tex.Cr.R. 1, L.R.A.1918B, 354; City of Ames v. Gerbracht, 189 N.W. 729, 194 Iowa, 267.

THEATER ADMISSION TICKET. Is in nature of a permit to enter place of amusement and use accommodations provided therein for enjoyment of entertainment offered and is evidence of payment of admission fee to proper person, but carries with it no obligation of theater owner to do anything or perform any service. Jordan v. Concho Theatres, Tex.Civ.App., 160 S.W.2d 275, 276.

THEFT. A popular name for larceny. See State v. Stewart, 67 A. 786, 788, 6 Pennewill (Del.) 435. The fraudulent taking of corporeal personal property belonging to another, from his possession, or from the possession of some person holding the same for him, without his consent, with intent to deprive the owner of the value of the same, and to appropriate it to the use or benefit of the person taking. Quitzow v. State, 1 Tex.App. 65, 28 Am.Rep. 396; Mullins v. State, 37 Tex. 338; U. S. v. Thomas, D.C.Cal., 69 F. 588, 590; Fidelity Phœnix Fire Ins. Co. of New York v. Oldsmobile Sales Co., Tex.Civ.App., 261 S.W. 492, 497; Reese v. State, 239 S.W. 619, 620, 91 Tex.Cr.R. 457; Fidelity and Guaranty Fire Corporation v. Ratterman, 262 Ky. 350, 90 S.W.2d 679, 680.

It was also said that it is a wider term than larceny and that it includes swindling and embezzlement and that generally, one who obtains possession of property by lawful means and thereafter appropriates the property to the taker's own use is guilty of a "theft". Kidwell v. Paul Revere Fire Ins. Co., 294 Ky. 833, 172 S.W.2d 639, 640; Whitworth v. State, 11 Tex.App. 414, 428, 429; People v. Pillsbury, 138 P.2d 320, 322, 59 Cal.App.2d 107.

In Scotch law. The secret and felonious abstraction of the property of another for sake of lucre, without his consent. Alis.Crim.Law, 250.

THEFT-BOTE. The offense committed by a party who, having been robbed and knowing the felon, takes back his goods again, or receives other amends, upon an agreement not to prosecute. Farmers' Nat. Bank of Somerset v. Tarter, 256 Ky. 70, 75 S.W.2d 758, 760.

THEFT-BOTE EST EMENDA FURTI CAPTA, SINE CONSIDERATIONE CURIÆ DOMINI REGIS. 3 Inst. 134. Theft-bote is the paying money to have goods stolen returned, without having any respect for the court of the king.

THEFT BY FALSE PRETEXT. Obtaining property by means of false pretext with intent to deprive owner of value of property without his consent and to appropriate it to own use, followed by such appropriation. Vernon's Ann.P.C. art. 1413. Hoovel v. State, 125 Tex.Cr.R. 545, 69 S.W. 2d 104, 106.

THEGN. An Anglo-Saxon term meaning a retainer. Afterwards it came to designate the territorial nobility. At a later period these were king's thegns, who were persons of great importance, and inferior thegns. Military service appears to have run through it all. After the Conquest, they were merged into the class of knights. Encycl. Br.

THEGNAGE TENURE. A kind of tenure in Northumbria in the 13th century and beyond, of which little is known. 2 Holdsw. Hist. E. L. 132.

THELONIO IRRATIONABILI HABENDO. A writ that formerly lay for him that had any part of the king's demesne in fee-farm, to recover reasonable toll of the king's tenants there, if his demesne had been accustomed to be tolled. Reg. Orig. 87.

THELONIUM. An abolished writ for citizens or burgesses to assert their right to exemption from toll. Fitzh. Nat. Brev. 226.

THELONMANNUS. The toll-man or officer who receives toll. Cowell.

THELUSSON ACT. The statute 39 & 40 Geo. III. c. 98, which restricted accumulations to a term of twenty-one years from the testator's death. It was passed in consequence of litigation over the will of one Thelusson.

THEME. In Saxon law. The power of having jurisdiction over naifs or villeins, with their suits or offspring, lands, goods, and chattels. Co. Litt. 116*a*.

THEMMAGIUM. A duty or acknowledgment paid by inferior tenants in respect of theme or team. Cowell.

THEN. This word, as an adverb, means "at that time," referring to a time specified, either past or future. It has no power in itself to fix a time. It simply refers to a time already fixed. Mangum v. Piester, 16 S.C. 329. It may also denote a contingency, and be equivalent to "in that event." Pintard v. Irwin, 20 N.J.L. 505; Western & A. R. Co. v. Smith, 145 Ga. 276, 88 S.E. 983, 985; State ex rel. Hanly v. Montgomery, 132 La. 679, 61 So. 735, 736; In re Swift's Estate, 279 Pa. 424, 124 A. 135, 136; Lermond v. Hyler, 121 Me. 54, 115 A. 546, 551; Roberts v. Wadley, 156 Ga. 35, 118 S.E. 664, 665.

THEN AND THERE. At the time and place last previously mentioned or charged. Context, however, may give the phrase a more remote antecedent than the time and place *last* previously mentioned or charged. Vogrin v. American Steel & Wire Co., 263 Ill. 474, 105 N.E. 332, 333; State v. Mahoney, 115 Me. 251, 98 A. 750, 752; Brogan v. State, 199 Ind. 203, 156 N.E. 515, 516; Bashara v. State, 84 Tex.Cr.R. 263, 206 S.W. 359, 360; State v. Buckwald, 117 Me. 344, 104 A. 520, 521.

THENCE. In surveying, and in descriptions of land by courses and distances, this word, preceding each course given, imports that the following course is continuous with the one before it. Flagg v. Mason, 141 Mass. 66, 6 N.E. 702.

THENCE DOWN THE RIVER. This phrase as used in field notes of a surveyor of a patent, is construed to mean with the meanders of the river, unless there is positive evidence that the meander line as written was where the surveyor in fact ran it; for such lines are to show the general course of the stream and to be used in estimating acreage, and not necessarily boundary lines. Burkett v. Chestnutt, Tex.Civ.App., 212 S.W. 271, 274.

THEOCRACY. Government of a state by the immediate direction of God, (or by the assumed direction of a supposititious divinity,) or the state thus governed.

THEODEN. In Saxon law. A husbandman or inferior tenant; an under-thane. Cowell.

THEODOSIAN CODE. See Codex Theodosianus.

THEOF. In Saxon law. Offenders who joined in a body of seven to commit depredations. Wharton.

THEOPHILUS' INSTITUTES. See Institutes.

THEORETICAL AGRICULTURE. A science comprehending in its scope the nature and properties of soils, the different sorts of plants and seeds fitted for them, the composition and qualities of manures, and the rotation of crops, and involving a knowledge of chemistry, geology, and kindred sciences. State ex rel. Boynton v. Wheat Farming Co., 137 Kan. 697, 22 P.2d 1093.

THEORY OF CASE. Facts on which the right of action is claimed to exist. Pittsburgh, C., C. and St. L. Ry. Co. v. Rogers, 45 Ind.App. 230, 87 N.E. 28, 31. The basis of liability or grounds of defense. Higgins v. Fuller, 48 N.M. 218, 148 P.2d 575, 579.

THEOWES, THEOWMEN, or THEWS. In feudal law. Slaves, captives, or bondmen. Spel. Feuds, c. 5.

THERE. In or at that place. Bedell v. Richardson Lubricating Co., 201 Mo.App. 251, 211 S.W. 104, 106.

THEREABOUT. About that place. Austin v. Bluff City Shoe Co., 176 Mo.App. 546, 158 S.W. 709, 713.

THEREAFTER. After the time last mentioned; after that; after that time; afterward; subsequently; thenceforth. People v. St. Louis, A. & T. H. R. Co., 300 Ill. 519, 133 N.E. 217; Lamoutte v. Title Guaranty & Surety Co., 165 App.Div. 573, 151 N.Y.S. 148, 154; Dauwe v. State, 147 Tex.Cr.R. 384, 180 S.W.2d 925, 927.

THEREBY. By that means; in consequence of that. Fall City Ice & Beverage Co. v. Scanlan Coal Co., 208 Ky. 820, 271 S.W. 1097, 1099.

THEREFOR. For that thing: for it, or them. State v. Dayton Lumber Co., Tex.Civ.App., 159 S. W. 391, 398.

THEREIN. In that place. Mulville v. City of San Diego, 183 Cal. 734, 192 P. 702, 703; City Hospital of Quincy v. Inhabitants of Town of Milton, 232 Mass. 273, 122 N.E. 274.

THEREUPON. Without delay or lapse of time. Putnam v. Langley, 133 Mass. 205. See Hill v. Wand, 47 Kan. 340, 27 P. 988, 27 Am.St.Rep. 288. Immediately. 6 M. & W. 492. See 3 Q. B. 79, where the terms thereupon and thereby are distinguished. Following on; in consequence of. Yuma County Water Users' Ass'n v. Schlecht, 43 S.Ct. 498, 500, 262 U.S. 138, 67 L.Ed. 909; Stephens v. Nacey, 47 Mont. 479, 133 P. 361, 362; Atlanta Gaslight Co. v. Sams, 29 Ga.App. 446, 116 S.E. 21, 25.

THESAURER. Treasurer. 3 State Tr. 691.

THESAURUS, THESAURIUM. The treasury; a treasure.

THESAURUS ABSCONDITUS. In old English law. Treasure hidden or buried. Spelman.

THESAURUS COMPETIT DOMINO REGI, ET NON DOMINO LIBERATIS, NISI SIT PER VERBA SPECIALIA. Fitzh. Coron. 281. A treasure belongs to the king, and not to the lord of a liberty, unless it be through special words.

THESAURUS INVENTUS. In old English law. Treasure found; treasure-trove. Bract. fols. 119*b*, 122.

THESAURUS INVENTUS EST VETUS DISPOSITIO PECUNIÆ, ETC., CUJUS NON EXTAT MODO MEMORIA, ADEO UT JAM DOMINUM NON HABEAT. 3 Inst. 132. Treasure-trove is an ancient hiding of money, etc., of which no recollection exists, so that it now has no owner.

THESAURUS NON COMPETIT REGI, NISI QUANDO NEMO SCIT QUI ABSCONDIT THESAURUM. 3 Inst. 132. Treasure does not belong to the king, unless no one knows who hid it.

THESAURUS REGIS EST VINCULUM PACIS ET BELLORUM NERVUS. Godb. 293. The king's treasure is the bond of peace and the sinews of war.

THESMOTHETE. A law-maker; a law-giver.

THETHINGA. A tithing.

THIA. Lat. In the civil and old European law. An aunt.

THIEF. One who steals; one who commits theft or larceny. Nugent v. Union Automobile Ins. Co., 140 Or. 61, 13 P.2d 343, 344.

THINGS. The objects of dominion or property as contradistinguished from "persons." Western Union Telegraph Co. v. Bush, 191 Ark. 1085, 89 S.W. 2d 723, 725, 103 A.L.R. 367; Gayer v. Whelan, 59 Cal.App.2d 255, 138 P.2d 763, 768. The object of a right; *i. e.*, whatever is treated by the law as the object over which one person exercises a right, and with reference to which another person lies under a duty. Holl. Jur. 83.

The word "estate" in general is applicable to anything of which riches or fortune may consist. The word is likewise relative to the word "things," which is the second object of jurisprudence, the rules of which are applicable to persons, things, and actions. Civ.Code La. art. 448.

Such permanent objects, not being persons, as are sensible, or perceptible through the senses. Aust.Jur. § 452.

Things are distributed into three kinds: (1) Things real or immovable, comprehending lands, tenements, and hereditaments; (2) things personal or movable, comprehending goods and chattels; and (3) things mixed, partaking of the characteristics of the two former, as a title-deed, a term for years. The civil law divided things into corporeal *(tangi possunt)* and incorporeal *(tangi non possunt)*. Wharton.

THINGS IN ACTION. A right to recover money or other personal property by a judicial proceeding. Civ.Code Cal. § 953. See Chose in Action.

THINGS OF VALUE. To be the subject of gaming may be any thing affording the necessary lure to indulge the gambling instinct. Painter v. State, 163 Tenn. 627, 45 S.W.2d 46, 47. Heartley v. State, 178 Tenn. 254, 157 S.W.2d 1, 3.

THINGS PERSONAL. Goods, money, and all other movables, which may attend the owner's person wherever he thinks proper to go. 2 Bl.Comm. 16. Things personal consist of goods, money, and all other movables, and of such rights and profits as relate to movables. 1 Steph. Comm. 156; People v. Brooklyn, 9 Barb. (N.Y.) 546; Castle v. Castle, C.C.A.Hawaii, 267 F. 521, 522. Also all vegetable productions, as the fruit or other parts of a plant when severed from the body of it, or the whole plant itself, when severed from the ground. Western Union Telegraph Co. v. Bush, 191 Ark. 1085, 89 S.W.2d 723, 725, 103 A.L.R. 367.

THINGS REAL. Such things as are permanent, fixed, and immovable, which cannot be carried out of their place; as lands and tenements and hereditaments. 2 Bl. Comm. 16. Western Union Telegraph v. Bush, 191 Ark. 1085, 89 S.W.2d 723, 725, 103 A.L.R. 367.

This definition has been objected to as not embracing incorporeal rights. Mr. Stephen defines *things real* to "consist of things substantial and immovable, and of the rights and profits annexed to or issuing out of these." 1 Steph. Comm. 156. *Things real* are otherwise described to consist of lands, tenements, and hereditaments. People v. Brooklyn, 9 Barb., N.Y., 546; Sox v. Miracle, 35 N.D. 458, 160 N.W. 716, 719.

THINGS ACCESSORY ARE OF THE NATURE OF THE PRINCIPAL. Finch, Law, b. 1, c. 3, n. 25.

THINGS ARE CONSTRUED ACCORDING TO THAT WHICH WAS THE CAUSE THEREOF. Finch, Law, b. 1, c. 3, n. 4.

THINGS ARE DISSOLVED AS THEY BE CONTRACTED. Finch, Law, b. 1, c. 3, n. 7.

THINGS GROUNDED UPON AN ILL AND VOID BEGINNING CANNOT HAVE A GOOD PERFECTION. Finch, Law, b. 1, c. 3, n. 8.

THINGS IN ACTION, ENTRY, OR RE-ENTRY CANNOT BE GRANTED OVER. Van Rensselaer v. Ball, 19 N.Y. 100, 103.

THINGS INCIDENT CANNOT BE SEVERED. Finch, Law, b. 3, c. 1, n. 12.

THINGS INCIDENT PASS BY THE GRANT OF THE PRINCIPAL. Seymour v. Canandaigua & N. F. R. Co., 25 Barb. (N.Y.) 284, 310.

THINGS INCIDENT SHALL PASS BY THE GRANT OF THE PRINCIPAL, BUT NOT THE PRINCIPAL BY THE GRANT OF THE INCIDENT. Co. Litt. 152*a*, 151*b*; Broom, Max. 433.

THINGS SHALL NOT BE VOID WHICH MAY POSSIBLY BE GOOD.

THINGUS. In Saxon law. A thane or nobleman; knight or freeman. Cowell.

THINK. To believe, to consider, to conclude, to esteem; to recollect or call to mind. Martin v. Iowa Ry. Co., 59 Iowa, 414, 13 N.W. 424; Abbott v. Church, 288 Ill. 91, 123 N.E. 306, 308, 4 A.L.R. 975; Trice v. Powell, 168 Va. 397, 191 S.E. 758, 762.

THIRD. Following next after the second; also, with reference to any legal instrument or transaction or judicial proceeding, any outsider or person not a party to the affair nor immediately concerned in it.

Third opposition. In Louisiana, when an execution is levied on property which does not belong to the defendant, but to an outsider, the remedy of the owner is by an intervention called a "third opposition," in which, on his giving security, an injunction or prohibition may be granted to stop the sale. See New Orleans v. Louisiana Const. Co., 9 S.Ct. 223, 129 U.S. 45, 32 L.Ed. 607; Norton v. Walton, C.C.A.La., 288 F. 359, 360.

Third parties. See Party.

Third penny. A portion (one-third) of the amount of all fines and other profits of the county court, which was reserved for the earl, in the early days when the jurisdiction of those courts was extensive, the remainder going to the king.

Third possessor. In Louisiana, a person who buys mortgaged property, but without assuming the payment of the mortgage. Thompson v. Levy, 50 La.Ann. 751, 23 So. 913; New Orleans Land Co. v. Southern States Fair-Pan-American Exposition Co., 143 La. 884, 79 So. 525, 526.

THIRD CONVICTION. Before charge can be considered a "third conviction" of a felony in contemplation of Habitual Criminal Act, accused must have been convicted of a second felony subsequent to his conviction of first one and after he had paid penalty inflicted for it, and third conviction should be subsequent to second, and after he had paid penalty for it. Cobb v. Commonwealth, 267 Ky. 176, 101 S.W.2d 418, 420.

THIRD INTERNATIONAL. Communist International, Moscow International, Red International. An organization founded at Moscow in March, 1919, by delegates from twelve different countries, as a protest against the inactivity and bourgeois character of the Second International and as a call to Communists all over the world to support the Russian Revolution and inaugurate similar movements in other countries. It is still predominantly Russian. Garriga v. Richfield, 174 Misc. 315, 20 N.Y.S.2d 544, 547.

THIRD PARTY BENEFICIARY. In order for one not privy to a contract to maintain an action thereon as a "third party beneficiary", it must appear that the contract was made and intended for his benefit. Fagliarone v. Consolidated Film Industries, 20 N.J.Misc. 193, 26 A.2d 425, 426. And the benefit must be one that is not merely incidental, but must be immediate in such a sense and degree as to indicate the assumption of a duty to make reparation if the benefit is lost. Associated

Flour Haulers & Warehousemen v. Hoffman, 282 N.Y. 173, 26 N.E.2d 7, 10.

Member of union is "third party beneficiary" of contract between employer and union. Helt v. Britten-Fenton Co., 44 N.Y.S.2d 58, 60, 180 Misc. 1077.

THIRD PARTY CLAIM PROCEEDING. A proceeding for the purpose of determining whether the debtor has any right, title or interest in the property upon which the levy has been made and the judgment of the court in such proceedings is only made conclusive as to the right of the plaintiff or other person in whose favor the writ runs to have the property taken and to subject it to payment for other satisfaction of his judgment. Deevy v. Lewis, 54 Cal.App.2d 24, 128 P.2d 577, 579.

THIRDBOROUGH, or THIRDBOROW. An under-constable. Cowell.

THIRDINGS. The third part of the corn growing on the land, due to the lord for a heriot on the death of his tenant, within the manor of Turfat, in Hereford. Blount.

THIRD-NIGHT-AWN-HINDE. By the laws of St. Edward the Confessor, if any man lay a third night in an inn, he was called a "third-night-awn-hinde," and his host was answerable for him if he committed any offense. The first night, forman-night, or uncouth, (unknown,) he was reckoned a stranger; the second night, twa-night, a guest; and the third night, an awn-hinde, a domestic. Bract. l. 3.

THIRDS. The designation, in colloquial language, of that portion of a decedent's personal estate (one-third) which goes to the widow where there is also a child or children. See Yeomans v. Stevens, 2 Allen, Mass., 350; O'Hara v. Dever, 46 Barb. (N.Y.) 614.

THIRLAGE. In Scotch law. A servitude by which lands are astricted or "thirled" to a particular mill, to which the possessors must carry the grain of the growth of the astricted lands to be ground, for the payment of such duties as are either expressed or implied in the constitution of the right. Ersk. Inst. 2, 9, 18.

THIRTY-NINE ARTICLES. See Articles of Religion.

THIS. When "this" and "that" refer to different things before expressed, "this" refers to the thing last mentioned, and "that" to the thing first mentioned. Russell v. Kennedy, 66 Pa. 251. "This" is a demonstrative adjective, used to point out with particularity a person or thing present in place or in thought. Stevens v. Haile, Tex.Civ.App., 162 S.W. 1025, 1028.

THIS DAY SIX MONTHS. Fixing "this day six months," or "three months," for the next stage of a bill, is one of the modes in which the house of lords and the house of commons reject bills of which they disapprove. A bill rejected in this manner cannot be reintroduced in the same session. Wharton.

THISTLE-TAKE. It was a custom within the manor of Halton, in Chester, that if, in driving beasts over a common, the driver permitted them to graze or take but a thistle, he should pay a halfpenny a-piece to the lord of the fee. And at Fiskerton, in Nottinghamshire, by ancient custom, if a native or a cottager killed a swine above a year old, he paid to the lord a penny, which purchase of leave to kill a hog was also called "thistle-take." Cowell.

THOROUGHFARE. The term means, according to its derivation, a street or passage *through* which one can *fare*, (travel;) that is, a street or highway affording an unobstructed exit at each end into another street or public passage. If the passage is closed at one end, admitting no exit there, it is called a *"cul de sac."* Mankato v. Warren, 20 Minn. 150 (Gil. 128); Wiggins v. Tallmadge, 11 Barb. (N.Y.) 462; Morris v. Blunt, 49 Utah, 243, 161 P. 1127, 1130; Burnham v. Holmes, 137 Me. 183, 16 A.2d 476, 477.

THRAVE. In old English law. A measure of corn or grain, consisting of twenty-four sheaves or four shocks, six sheaves to every shock. Cowell.

THREAD. A middle line; a line running through the middle of a stream or road. See Filum; Filum Aquæ; Filum Viæ; Thalweg.

THREAT. A declaration of intention or determination to inflict punishment, loss, or pain on another, or to injure another by the commission of some unlawful act. U. S. v. Daulong, D.C.La., 60 F.Supp. 235, 236. A menace; especially, any menace of such a nature and extent as to unsettle the mind of the person on whom it operates, and to take away from his acts that free and voluntary action which alone constitutes consent. Abbott, United States v. French, D.C.Fla., 243 F. 785, 786; State v. Brownlee, 84 Iowa 473, 51 N.W. 25. Cote v. Murphy, 159 Pa. 420, 28 A. 190, 23 L.R.A. 135, 39 Am.St.Rep. 686. A declaration of one's purpose or intention to work injury to the person, property, or rights of another, with a view of restraining such person's freedom of action. McKenzie v. State, 113 Neb. 576, 204 N.W. 60, 61. Kamenitsky v. Corcoran, 177 App.Div. 605, 164 N.Y.S. 297, 300.

THREATENING LETTERS. Sending threatening letters is the name of the offense of sending letters containing threats of the kinds recognized by the statute as criminal. See People v. Griffin, 2 Barb. (N.Y.) 429.

THREE-DOLLAR PIECE. A gold coin of the United States, of the value of three dollars; authorized by the seventh section of the act of February 21, 1853.

THREE-WEEKS COURT. In the Kentish custom of gavelet, it was the lord's court. 18 Harv.L.R. 40.

THRENGES. Vassals, but not of the lowest degree; those who held lands of the chief lord.

THRITHING. In Saxon and old English law. The third part of a county; a division of a county consisting of three or more hundreds. Cowell. Corrupted to the modern "riding," which is still used in Yorkshire. 1 Bl.Comm. 116.

THROUGH. By means of, in consequence of, by reason of; in, within; over; from end to end, or from one side to the other. Mississippi Cent. R. Co. v. Pace, 109 Miss. 667, 68 So. 926, 927; Hyde Park v. Oakwoods Cemetery Ass'n, 119 Ill. 147, 7 N.E. 627. By the intermediary of; in the name or as agent of; by the agency of; because of. Great Atlantic & Pacific Tea Co. v. City of Richmond, 183 Va. 931, 33 S.E.2d 795, 802.

THROUGH LOT. A lot that abuts upon a street at each end. Illinois Surety Co. v. O'Brien, C.C.A. Ohio, 223 F. 933, 938.

THROW OUT. To ignore (a bill of indictment.)

THROWN FROM AUTOMOBILE. This phrase within accident policy means tossed or hurled out of automobile by some force. Independence Ins. Co. v. Blanford's Adm'x, 276 Ky. 692, 125 S.W.2d 249, 251; Guaranty Trust Co. v. Continental Life Ins. Co., 159 Wash. 683, 294 P. 585, 587.

THRUSTING. Within the meaning of a criminal statute, is not necessarily an attack with a pointed weapon; it means pushing or driving with force, whether the point of the weapon be sharp or not. State v. Lowry, 33 La.Ann. 1224.

THRYMSA. A Saxon coin worth fourpence. Du Fresne.

THUDE-WEALD. A woodward, or person that looks after a wood.

THURINGIAN CODE. One of the "barbarian codes," as they are termed; supposed by Montesquieu to have been given by Theodoric, king of Austrasia, to the Thuringians, who were his subjects. Esprit des Lois, lib. 28, c. 1.

THUS. In the way just indicated. Schrader v. City of Los Angeles, 19 Cal.App.2d 332, 65 P.2d 374, 375.

THWERTNICK. In old English law. The custom of giving entertainments to a sheriff, etc., for three nights.

TICK. A colloquial expression for credit or trust; credit given for goods purchased.

TICKET. In contracts. A slip of paper containing a certificate that the person to whom it is issued, or the holder, is entitled to some right or privilege therein mentioned or described; such, for example, are railroad tickets, theater tickets, pawn tickets, lottery tickets, etc. See Allaire v. Howell Works Co., 14 N.J.L. 24; Interstate Amusement Co. v. Martin, 8 Ala.App. 481, 62 So. 404, 405.

In election law. A list of candidates for particular offices to be submitted to the voters at an election; a ballot. Barr v. Cardell, 173 Iowa 18, 155 N.W. 312, 313; Denny v. Pratt, 104 Conn. 396, 133 A. 107, 109.

TICKET OF LEAVE. In English law. A license or permit given to a convict, as a reward for good conduct, particularly in the penal settlements, which allows him to go at large, and labor for himself, before the expiration of his sentence, subject to certain specific conditions and revocable upon subsequent misconduct.

TICKET-OF-LEAVE MAN. A convict who has obtained a ticket of leave.

TICKET SPECULATOR. One who sells at an advance over the price charged by the management. Speculation of this kind frequently leads to abuse, especially when the theater is full and but few tickets are left, so that extortionate prices may be exacted. Levine v. Brooklyn Nat. League Baseball Club, 179 Misc. 22, 36 N.Y.S.2d 474, 477.

TIDAL. In order that a river may be "tidal" at a given spot, it may not be necessary that the water should be salt, but the spot must be one where the tide, in the ordinary and regular course of things, flows and reflows. 8 Q.B.Div. 630.

TIDE. The ebb and flow of the sea. See Baird v. Campbell, 67 App.Div. 104, 73 N.Y.S. 617.

Neap Tides

Those tides which happen between the full and change of the moon twice in every 24 hours. F. A. Hihn Co. v. City of Santa Cruz, 170 Cal. 430, 150 P. 62, 65.

Tide Land

Land between the lines of the ordinary high and low tides, covered and uncovered successively by the ebb and flow thereof; land covered and uncovered by the ordinary tides; land over which the tide ebbs and flows; land which is daily covered and uncovered by water by the ordinary ebb and flow of normal tides; land usually overflowed by the neap or ordinary tides; such land as is affected by the tide, that lies between ordinary high-water mark and low-water mark, and which is alternately covered and left dry by the ordinary flux and reflux of the tides; that portion of the shore or beach covered and uncovered by the ebb and flow of ordinary tides. Bolsa Land Co. v. Vaqueros Major Oil Co., Cal.App., 76 P.2d 519, 521; Hardy v. California Trojan Powder Co., 109 Or. 76, 219 P. 197, 199.

Tide-Water

Water which falls and rises with the ebb and flow of the tide. The term is not usually applied to the open sea, but to coves, bays, rivers, etc.

Tideway

That land between high and low water mark. In re Inwood Hill Park in Borough of Manhattan, City of New York, 217 App.Div. 587, 217 N.Y.S. 359, 363.

TIDESMEN, in English law, are certain officers of the custom-house, appointed to watch or attend upon ships till the customs are paid; and they are so called because they go aboard the ships at their arrival in the mouth of the Thames, and come up with the tide. Jacob.

TIE, *v.* To bind. "The parson is not tied to find the parish clerk." 1 Leon. 94.

TIE, *n.* When, at an election, neither candidate receives a majority of the votes cast, but each has the same number, there is said to be a "tie." So when the number of votes cast in favor of any measure, in a legislative or deliberative body, is equal to the number cast against it. See Wooster v. Mullins, 64 Conn. 340, 30 A. 144, 25 L.R.A. 694.

TIEL. L. Fr. Such. *Nul tiel record,* no such record.

TIEMPO INHABIL. Span. A time of inability; a time when the person is not able to pay his debts, (when, for instance, he may not alienate property to the prejudice of his creditors.) The term is used in Louisiana. Brown v. Kenner, 3 Mart.O.S. (La.) 270; Thorn v. Morgan, 4 Mart. N.S. (La.) 292, 16 Am.Dec. 173.

TIERCE. L. Fr. Third. *Tierce mein,* third hand. Britt. c. 120.

TIERCE. A liquid measure, containing the third part of a pipe, or forty-two gallons.

TIGH. In old records. A close or inclosure; a croft. Cowell.

TIGHT. As colloquially applied to a note, bond, mortgage, lease, etc., this term signifies that the clauses providing the creditor's remedy in case of default (as, by foreclosure, execution, distress, etc.) are summary and stringent.

TIGNI IMMITTENDI. Lat. In the civil law. The name of a servitude which is the right of inserting a beam or timber from the wall of one house into that of a neighboring house, in order that it may rest on the latter, and that the wall of the latter may bear this weight. Wharton. See Dig. 8, 2, 36.

TIGNUM. Lat. A civil-law term for building material; timber.

TIHLER. In old Saxon law. An accusation.

TILLAGE. A place tilled or cultivated; land under cultivation, as opposed to lands lying fallow or in pasture.

TIMBER. Wood felled for building or other such like use. In a legal sense it generally means (in England) oak, ash, and elm, but in some parts of England, and generally in America, it is used in a wider sense, which is recognized by the law.

The term "timber," as used in commerce, refers generally only to large sticks of wood, squared or capable of being squared for building houses or vessels; and certain trees only having been formerly used for such purposes, namely, the oak, the ash, and the elm, they alone were recognized as timber trees. But the numerous uses to which wood has come to be applied, and the general employment of all kinds of trees for some valuable purpose, has wrought a change in the general acceptation of terms in connection therewith, and we find that Webster defines "timber" to be "that sort of wood which is proper for buildings or for tools, utensils, furniture, carriages, fences, ships, and the like." This would include all sorts of wood from which any useful articles may be made, or which may be used to advantage in any class of manufacture or construction. U. S. v. Stores, C.C., 14 F. 824; Wilson v. State, 17 Tex. App. 393; U. S. v. Soto, 7 Ariz. 230, 64 P. 420; Tuscarora Nation of Indians v. Williams, 141 N.Y.S. 207, 210, 79 Misc. 445; Eagle Coal Co. v. Patrick's Adm'r, 161 Ky. 333, 170 S.W. 960, 961; Nettles v. Lichtman, 228 Ala. 52, 152 So. 450, 453, 91 A.L.R. 1455.

TIMBER CULTURE ENTRY. See Entry.

TIMBER-TREES. Oak, ash, elm, in all places, and, by local custom, such other trees as are used in building. 2 Bl.Comm. 281.

TIMBERLODE. A service by which tenants were bound to carry timber felled from the woods to the lord's house. Cowell.

TIME. The measure of duration.

The word is expressive both of a precise *point* or *terminus* and of an *interval* between two points.

Pleading

A point in or space of duration at or during which some fact is alleged to have been committed.

General

Cooling time. See that title.

Reasonable time. Such length of time as may fairly, properly, and reasonably be allowed or required, having regard to the nature of the act or duty, or of the subject-matter, and to the attending circumstances. It is a maxim of English law that "how long a 'reasonable time' ought to be is not defined in law, but is left to the discretion of the judges." Co. Litt. 50. See Hoggins v. Becraft, 1 Dana (Ky.) 28; Hill v. Hobart, 16 Me. 168; Twin Lick Oil Co. v. Marbury, 91 U.S. 591, 23 L.Ed. 328; Hearne v. Fischer Lime & Cement Co., 220 Ky. 791, 295 S.W. 1012, 1013; Lumbermen's Reciprocal Ass'n v. Warren, Tex.Civ. App., 272 S.W. 826, 827; Simmons v. Western Indemnity Co., Tex.Civ.App., 210 S.W. 713, 715.

Time-bargain. In the language of the stock exchange, an agreement to buy or sell stock at a future time, or within a fixed time, at a certain price. It is in reality nothing more than a bargain to pay differences.

Time check. A certificate signed by a master mechanic or other person in charge of laborers, reciting the amount due to the laborer for labor for a specified time. Burlington Voluntary Relief Dept. v. White, 41 Neb. 547, 59 N.W. 747, 43 Am.St.Rep. 701; Gerlach v. North Texas & S. F. Ry. Co., Tex.Civ.App., 244 S.W. 662, 666.

Time immemorial. Time whereof the memory of a man is not to the contrary.

Time is the essence of contract. Means that performance by one party at time or within period specified in contract is essential to enable him to require performance by other party. Hayes Mfg. Corporation v. McCauley, C.C.A.Ohio, 140 F.2d

187, 190; Williams v. Shamrock Oil and Gas Co., 128 Tex. 146, 95 S.W.2d 1292, 1295, 107 A.L.R. 269.

A contract where the parties evidently contemplated a punctual performance, at the precise time named, as vital to the agreement, and one of its essential elements. Time is *not* of the essence of the contract in any case where a moderate delay in performance would not be regarded as an absolute violation of the contract.

Time of accident. In occupational disease cases, time when disability first occurs. Michigan Quartz Silica Co. v. Industrial Commission, 214 Wis. 492, 253 N.W. 167.

Time of memory. In English law. Time commencing from the beginning of the reign of Richard I. 2 Bl.Comm. 31. Lord Coke defines *time of memory* to be "when no man alive hath had any proof to the contrary, nor hath any conusance to the contrary." Co. Litt. 86*a*, 86*b*.

Time out of memory. Time beyond memory; time out of mind; time to which memory does not extend.

Time-policy. A policy of marine insurance in which the risk is limited, not to a given voyage, but to a certain fixed term or period of time.

TIMOCRACY. An aristocracy of property; government by men of property who are possessed of a certain income.

TIMORES VANI SUNT ÆSTIMANDI QUI NON CADUNT CONSTANTEM VIRUM. 7 Coke, 17. Fears which do not assail a resolute man are to be accounted vain.

TINBOUNDING. A custom regulating the manner in which tin is obtained from wasteland, or land which has formerly been wasteland, within certain districts in Cornwall and Devon. The custom is described in the leading case on the subject as follows: "Any person may enter on the waste-land of another, and may mark out by four corner boundaries a certain area. A written description of the plot of land so marked out with metes and bounds, and the name of the person, is recorded in the local stannaries court, and is proclaimed on three successive court-days. If no objection is sustained by any other person, the court awards a writ to the bailiff to deliver possession of the said 'bounds of tinwork' to the 'bounder,' who thereupon has the exclusive right to search for, dig, and take for his own use all tin and tin-ore within the inclosed limits, paying as a royalty to the owner of the waste a certain proportion of the produce under the name of 'toll-tin.'" 10 Q.B. 26, cited in Elton Commons, 113. The right of tinbounding is not a right of common, but is an interest in land, and, in Devonshire, a corporeal hereditament. In Cornwall tin bounds are personal estate. Sweet.

TINEL. L. Fr. A place where justice was administered. Kelham.

TINEMAN. Sax. In old forest law. A petty officer of the forest who had the care of vert and venison by night, and performed other servile duties.

TINET. In old records. Brush-wood and thorns for fencing and hedging. Cowell; Blount.

TINEWALD. The ancient parliament or annual convention in the Isle of Man, held upon Midsummer-day, at St. John's chapel. Cowell.

TINKERMEN. Fishermen who destroyed the young fry on the river Thames by nets and unlawful engines. Cowell.

TINNELLUS. In old Scotch law. The sea-mark; high-water mark. Tide-mouth. Skene.

TINPENNY. A tribute paid for the liberty of digging in tin-mines. Cowell.

TINSEL OF THE FEU. In Scotch law. The loss of the feu, from allowing two years of feu duty to run into the third unpaid. Bell.

TIP. A sum of money given, as to a servant usually to secure better or more prompt service. Restaurants and Patisseries Longchamps v. Pedrick, D.C.N.Y., 52 F.Supp. 174. A gift. Williams v. Jacksonville Terminal Co., C.C.A.Fla., 118 F.2d 324, 325.

TIPPLING HOUSE. A place where intoxicating drinks are sold in drams or small quantities to be drunk on the premises, and where men resort for drinking purposes. Hussey v. State, 69 Ga. 58; Emporia v. Volmer, 12 Kan. 629; Mohrman v. State, 32 S.E. 143, 105 Ga. 709, 43 L.R.A. 398, 70 Am.St.Rep. 74.

TIPSTAFF. In American law. An officer appointed by the court, whose duty is to wait upon the court when it is in session, preserve order, serve process, guard juries, etc.

In English law. An officer appointed by the marshal of the king's bench to attend upon the judges with a kind of rod or staff tipped with silver, who take into their custody all prisoners, either committed or turned over by the judges at their chambers, etc. Jacob.

TITHER. One who gathers tithes.

TITHES. In English law. The *tenth* part of the increase, yearly arising and renewing from the profits of lands, the stock upon lands, and the personal industry of the inhabitants. 2 Bl.Comm. 24. A species of incorporeal hereditament, being an ecclesiastical inheritance collateral to the estate of the land, and due only to an ecclesiastical person by ecclesiastical law. 1 Crabb, Real Prop. § 133.

Great Tithes

In English ecclesiastical law. Tithes of corn, peas and beans, hay and wood. 2 Chit.Bl.Comm. 24, note; 3 Steph.Comm. 127.

Minute Tithes

Small tithes, such as usually belong to a vicar, as of wool, lambs, pigs, butter, cheese, herbs, seeds, eggs, honey, wax, etc.

Mixed Tithes

Those which arise not immediately from the ground, but from those things which are nourished by the ground, *e. g.*, colts, chickens, calves, milk, eggs, etc. 3 Burn, Ecc. Law, 380; 2 Bl. Comm. 24.

Personal Tithes

Personal tithes are tithes paid of such profits as come by the labor of a man's person; as by buying and selling, gains of merchandise and handicrafts, etc. Tomlins.

Predial Tithes

Such as arise immediately from the ground; as, grain of all sorts, hay, wood, fruits, and herbs.

Tithe-Free

Exempted from the payment of tithes.

Tithe Rent-Charge

A rent-charge established in lieu of tithes, under the tithes commutation act, 1836, (St. 6 & 7 Wm. IV. c. 71.) As between landlord and tenant, the tenant paying the tithe rent-charge is entitled, in the absence of express agreement, to deduct it from his rent, under section 70 of the above act. And a tithe rent-charge unpaid is recoverable by distress as rent in arrear. Mozley & Whitley.

TITHING. One of the civil divisions of England, being a portion of that greater division called a "hundred." It was so called because ten freeholders with their families composed one. It is said that they were all knit together in one society, and bound to the king for the peaceable behavior of each other. In each of these societies there was one chief or principal person, who, from his office, was called "teothing-man," now "tithing-man." Brown.

TITHING–MAN.

Modern Law

A constable. "After the introduction of justices of the peace, the offices of constable and *tithing-man* became so similar that we now regard them as precisely the same." Willc. Const. Introd.

New England

A parish officer annually elected to preserve good order in the church during divine service, and to make complaint of any disorderly conduct. Webster, Dict.

In Saxon Law

The head or chief of a tithing or decennary of ten families; he was to decide all lesser causes between neighbors. Jacob, Law Dict. In modern English law, he is the same as an under-constable or peace-officer.

TITHING–PENNY. In Saxon and old English law. Money paid to the sheriff by the several tithings of his county. Cowell.

TITIUS. In Roman law. A proper name, frequently used in designating an indefinite or fictitious person, or a person referred to by way of illustration. "Titius" and "Seius," in this use, correspond to "John Doe" and "Richard Roe," or to "A. B." and "C. D."

TITLE. The radical meaning of this word appears to be that of a mark, style, or designation; a distinctive appellation; the name by which anything is known. Thus, in the law of persons, a title is an appellation of dignity or distinction, a name denoting the social rank of the person bearing it; as "duke" or "count." So, in legislation, the title of a statute is the heading or preliminary part, furnishing the name by which the act is individually known. It is usually prefixed to the statute in the form of a brief summary of its contents; as "An act for the prevention of gaming." State v. Thomas, 301 Mo. 603, 256 S.W. 1028, 1029. Again, the title of a patent is the short description of the invention, which is copied in the letters patent from the inventor's petition; *e. g.*, "a new and improved method of drying and preparing malt." Johns. Pat. Man. 90.

The title of a book, or any literary composition, is its name; that is, the heading or caption prefixed to it, and disclosing the distinctive appellation by which it is to be known. This usually comprises a brief description of its subject-matter and the name of its author.

"Title" is also used as the name of one of the subdivisions employed in many literary works, standing intermediate between the divisions denoted by the term "books" or "parts," and those designated as "chapters" and "sections."

Law of Trade-Marks

A title may become a subject of property; as one who has adopted a particular title for a newspaper, or other business enterprise, may, by long and prior user, or by compliance with statutory provisions as to registration and notice, acquire a right to be protected in the exclusive use of it. Abbott.

Real Property Law

Title is the means whereby the owner of lands has the just possession of his property. Co. Litt. 345; 2 Bl.Comm. 195; Horney v. Price, 189 N.C. 820, 128 S.E. 321, 323; Hahn v. Fletcher, 189 N.C. 729, 128 S.E. 326, 327; Wimpey v. Ledford, Mo. Sup., 11 A.L.R. 7, 177 S.W. 302, 304; Case v. Mortgage Guarantee and Title Co., 52 R.I. 155, 158 A. 724, 726. The union of all the elements which constitute ownership. Carroll v. City of Newark, 108 N.J.L. 323, 158 A. 458, 461. Full, independent and fee ownership. In re Pelis' Estate, 150 Misc. 918, 271 N.Y.S. 731. The right to or ownership in land. Andrews v. New Britain Nat. Bank, 113 Conn. 467, 155 A. 838, 840.

Title may be defined generally to be the evidence of right which a person has to the possession of property. The word "title" certainly does not merely signify the right which a person has to the possession of property; because there are many instances in which a person may have the right to the possession of property, and at the same time have no title to the same. In its ordinary legal acceptation, however, it generally seems to imply a right of possession also. It, therefore, appears, on the whole, to signify the outward evidence of the right, rather than the mere right itself. Thus, when it is said that the "most imperfect degree of title consists in the mere naked possession or actual occupation of an estate," it means that the mere circumstance of occupying the estate is the weakest species of evidence of the occupier's right to such possession. The word is defined by Sir Edward Coke thus: *Titulus est justa causa possidendi id quod nostrum est,* (1 Inst. 34;) that is to say, the ground whether purchase, gift, or other such ground of acquiring; *"titulus"* being distinguished in this respect from *"modus acquirendi,"* which is the *traditio, i. e.,* delivery or conveyance of the thing. Brown.

Title is when a man hath lawful cause of entry into lands, whereof another is seised; and it signifies also the means whereby a man comes to lands or tenements, as by feoffment, last will and testament, etc. The word "title" includes a right, but is the more general word. Every right is a title, though every title is not a right for which an action lies. Jacob.

The investigation of titles is one of the principal branches of conveyancing and in that practice the word "title" has acquired the sense of "history," rather than of "right." Thus, we speak of an abstract of title, and of investigating a title, and describe a document as forming part of the title to property. Sweet.

Pleading

The right of action which the plaintiff has. The declaration must show the plaintiff's title, and, if such title be not shown in that instrument, the defect cannot be cured by any of the future pleadings. Bac. Abr. "Pleas," etc., B 1.

Procedure

Every action, petition, or other proceeding has a title, which consists of the name of the court in which it is pending, the names of the parties, etc. Administration actions are further distinguished by the name of the deceased person whose estate is being administered. Every pleading, summons, affidavit, etc., commences with the title. In many cases it is sufficient to give what is called the "short title" of an action, namely, the court, the reference to the record, and the surnames of the first plaintiff and the first defendant. Sweet.

General

Absolute title. As applied to title to land, an exclusive title, or at least a title which excludes all others not compatible with it; an absolute title to land cannot exist at the same time in different persons or in different governments. Johnson v. McIntosh, 21 U.S. 543, 8 Wheat. 543, 588, 5 L.Ed. 681.

Abstract of title. See that title.

Adverse title. A title set up in opposition to or defeasance of another title, or one acquired or claimed by adverse possession.

Bond for title. See Bond.

Chain of title. See that title.

Clear title, good title, merchantable title, marketable title, are synonymous; "clear title" meaning that the land is free from incumbrances, "good title" being one free from litigation, palpable defects, and grave doubts, comprising both legal and equitable titles and fairly deducible of record. Ogg v. Herman, 71 Mont. 10, 227 P. 476, 477; Veselka v. Forres, Tex.Civ.App., 283 S.W. 303, 306; Sipe v. Greenfield, 116 Okl. 241, 244 P. 424, 425.

Clear title of record, or clear record title, means freedom from apparent defects, grave doubts, and litigious uncertainties, and is such title as a reasonably prudent person, with full knowledge, would accept. A title dependent for its validity on extraneous evidence, ex parte affidavits, or written guaranties against the results of litigation is not a clear title of record, and is not such title as equity will require a purchaser to accept. Ammerman v. Karnowski, 109 Okl. 156, 234 P. 774, 776; Cleval v. Sullivan, 258 Mass. 348, 154 N.E. 920, 921.

Color of title. See that title.

Covenants for title. Covenants usually inserted in a conveyance of land, on the part of the grantor, and binding him for the completeness, security, and continuance of the title transferred to the grantee. They comprise "covenants for seisin, for right to convey, against incumbrances, for quiet enjoyment, sometimes for further assurance, and almost always of warranty." Rawle, Cov. § 21.

Doubtful title. See that title.

Equitable title. A right in the party to whom it belongs to have the legal title transferred to him; or the beneficial interest of one person whom equity regards as the real owner, although the legal title is vested in another. Wyatt v. Meade County Bank, 40 S.D. 111, 166 N.W. 423, 424; Pogue v. Simon, 47 Or. 6, 81 P. 566, 567, 114 Am. St.Rep. 903, 8 Ann.Cas. 474; Karalis v. Agnew, 111 Minn. 522, 127 N.W. 440, 441; Joy v. Midland State Bank of Omaha, Neb., 28 S.D. 262, 133 N. W. 276, 277; Harris v. Mason, 120 Tenn. 668, 115 S.W. 1146, 25 L.R.A.(N.S.) 1101; Niles v. Anderson, 5 How. (Miss.) 365, 385, quoted in Ayres v. U. S., 42 Ct.Cl. 385, 413. See Equitable Estate.

Examination of title, see Examination.

Imperfect title. One which requires a further exercise of the granting power to pass the fee in land, or which does not convey full and absolute dominion. Paschal v. Perez, 7 Tex. 367; Paschal v. Dangerfield, 37 Tex. 300; Lambert v. Gant, Tex. Civ.App., 290 S.W. 548, 551.

Legal title. See that title.

Lucrative title. In the civil law, title acquired without the giving of anything in exchange for it; the title by which a person acquires anything which comes to him as a clear gain, as, for instance, by gift, descent, or devise. Opposed to "onerous title," as to which see *infra.*

Marketable title. See that title.

Onerous title. In the civil law, title to property acquired by the giving of a valuable consideration for it, such as the payment of money, the rendition of services, the performance of conditions, the assumption of obligations, or the discharge of liens on the property; opposed to "lucrative" title, or one acquired by gift or otherwise without the giving of an equivalent. Scott v. Ward, 13 Cal. 471; Kircher v. Murray, C.C.A.Tex.,

54 F. 617, 624; Yates v. Houston, 3 Tex. 453; Rev. Civ.Code La. 1900, art. 3556, subd. 22.

Paper title. A title to land evidenced by a conveyance or chain of conveyances; the term generally implying that such title, while it has color or plausibility, is without substantial validity.

Passive title. In Scotch law. A title incurred by an heir in heritage who does not enter as heir in the regular way, and therefore incurs liability for all the debts of the decedent, irrespective of the amount of assets. Paterson.

Perfect title. Various meanings have been attached to this term: (1) One which shows the absolute right of possession and of property in a particular person. Henderson v. Beatty, 124 Iowa, 163, 99 N.W. 716; Wilcox Lumber Co. v. Bullock, 109 Ga. 532, 35 S.E. 52; Donovan v. Pitcher, 53 Ala. 411, 25 Am.Rep. 634. (2) A grant of land which requires no further act from the legal authority to constitute an absolute title to the land taking effect at once. Hancock v. McKinney, 7 Tex. 457. (3) A title which does not disclose a patent defect suggesting the possibility of a lawsuit to defend it; a title such as a well-informed and prudent man paying full value for the property would be willing to take. Birge v. Bock, 44 Mo.App. 77. (4) A title which is good both at law and in equity. Warner v. Middlesex Mut. Assur. Co., 21 Conn. 449. (5) One which is good and valid beyond all reasonable doubt. Sheehy v. Miles, 93 Cal. 288, 28 P. 1046; Reynolds v. Borel, 86 Cal. 538, 25 P. 67. (6) A marketable or merchantable title. Ross v. Smiley, 18 Colo.App. 204, 70 P. 766; McCleary v. Chipman, 32 Ind.App. 489, 68 N.E. 320.

Presumptive title. A barely presumptive title, which is of the very lowest order, arises out of the mere occupation or simple possession of property, (*jus possessionis,*) without any apparent right, or any pretense of right, to hold and continue such possession.

Record title. See Record.

Singular title. The title by which a party acquires property as a singular successor.

Tax title. See Tax.

Title by adverse possession or prescription. The right which a possessor acquires to property by reason of his adverse possession during a period of time fixed by law. Walker v. Steffes, 139 Ga. 520, 77 S.E. 580.

The elements of "title by prescription" are open, visible and continuous use under a claim of right, adverse to and with knowledge of owner. Dry Gulch Ditch Co. v. Hutton, 170 Or. 656, 133 P.2d 601, 610.

Such title is equivalent to a "title by deed" and cannot be lost or divested except in the same manner, and mere recognition of title in another after such acquisition will not operate to divest the adverse claimant of that which he has acquired. Maloney v. Bedford, 290 Ky. 647, 162 S.W.2d 198, 199.

Title by descent. That title which one acquires by law as heir to the deceased owner. Stabel v. Gertel, N.J.Sup., 11 N.J.Misc. 247, 165 A. 876, 879.

Title by prescription. See Title by adverse possession, supra.

Title deeds. Deeds which constitute or are the evidence of title to lands.

Title defective in form. Title on face of which some defect appears, not one that may prove defective by circumstances or evidence dehors the instrument. Title defective in form cannot be basis of prescription. Thompson v. Futral, 18 La. App. 685, 136 So. 654.

Title insurance. See Insurance.

Title of a cause. The distinctive appellation by which any cause in court, or other juridical proceeding, is known and discriminated from others.

Title of an act. The heading, or introductory clause, of a statute, wherein is briefly recited its purpose or nature, or the subject to which it relates.

Title of clergymen, (to orders.) Some certain place where they may exercise their functions; also an assurance of being preferred to some ecclesiastical benefice. 2 Steph.Comm. 661.

Title of declaration. That preliminary clause of a declaration which states the name of the court and the term to which the process is returnable.

Title of entry. The right to enter upon lands. Cowell.

Title retention. A form of lien, in the nature of a chattel mortgage, to secure the purchase price. American Indemnity Co. v. Allen, for Use and Benefit of Commerce Union Bank, 176 Tenn. 134, 138 S.W.2d 445, 446.

Title to orders. In English ecclesiastical law, a title to orders is a certificate of preferment or provision required by the thirty-third canon, in order that a person may be admitted into holy orders, unless he be a fellow or chaplain in Oxford or Cambridge, or master of arts of five years' standing in either of the universities, and living there at his sole charges; or unless the bishop himself intends shortly to admit him to some benefice or curacy. 2 Steph.Comm. 661.

Unmarketable title. See that title.

TITULADA. In Spanish law. Title. White, New Recop. b. 1, tit. 5, c. 3, § 2.

TITULARS OF ERECTION. Persons who in Scotland, after the Reformation, obtained grants from the crown of the monasteries and priories then erected into temporal lordships. Thus the titles formerly held by the religious houses, as well as the property of the lands, were conferred on these grantees, who were also called "lords of erection" and "titulars of the teinds." Bell.

TITULUS. Lat. Title. In the civil law. The source or ground of possession; the means whereby possession of a thing is acquired, whether such possession be lawful or not.

In old Ecclesiastical law. A temple or church; the material edifice. So called because the priest in charge of it derived therefrom his name and *title*. Spelman.

TITULUS EST JUSTA CAUSA POSSIDENDI ID QUOD NOSTRUM EST; DICITUR A TUENDO. 8 Coke, 153. A title is the just right of possessing that which is our own; it is so called from *"tuendo,"* defending.

TO. This is ordinarily a word of exclusion, when used in describing premises; it excludes the terminus mentioned. Littlefield v. Hubbard, 120 Me. 226, 113 A. 304, 306; Sinford v. Watts, 123 Me. 230, 122 A. 573, 574; Skeritt Inv. Co. v. City of Englewood, 79 Colo. 645, 248 P. 6, 8. It may be a word of inclusion, and may also mean "into." People v. Poole, 284 Ill. 39, 119 N.E. 916, 917; Thompson v. Reynolds, 59 Utah, 416, 204 P. 516, 518.

TO HAVE AND TO HOLD. The words in a conveyance which show the estate intended to be conveyed. Thus, in a conveyance of land in fee-simple, the grant is to "A. and his heirs, to have and to hold the said [land] unto and to the use of the said A., his heirs and assigns forever." Williams, Real Prop. 198.

Strictly speaking, however, the words "to have" denote the estate to be taken, while the words "to hold" signify that it is to be held of some superior lord, *i. e.*, by way of tenure, *(q. v.)*. The former clause is called the *"habendum;"* the latter, the *"tenendum."* Co.Litt. 6*a*.

TO WIT. That is to say; namely; *scilicet; videlicet*. Spears v. Wise, 187 Ala. 346, 65 So. 786; Williams v. Shows, 187 Ala. 132, 65 So. 839, 840; J. R. Kilgore & Son v. Shannon & Co., 6 Ala.App. 537, 60 So. 520, 525.

TOALIA. In feudal law. A towel. There is a tenure of lands by the service of waiting with a towel at the king's coronation. Cowell.

TOBACCONIST. Any person, firm, or corporation whose business it is to manufacture cigars, snuff, or tobacco in any form. Act of congress of July 13, 1866, § 9 (14 Stat. 120).

TOFT. A place or piece of ground on which a house formerly stood, which has been destroyed by accident or decay. 2 Broom & H.Comm. 17.

TOFTMAN. In old English law. The owner of a toft. Cowell; Spelman.

TOGATI. Lat. In Roman law. Advocates; so called under the empire because they were required, when appearing in court to plead a cause, to wear the *toga,* which had then ceased to be the customary dress in Rome. Vicat.

TOGETHER. In union with, along with. Gilmore v. Mulvihill, 109 Mont. 601, 98 P.2d 335, 341.

TOILET. Act or process of dressing up. Inecto, Inc., v. Higgins, D.C.N.Y., 21 F.Supp. 418, 426. A cleansing and grooming of one's person. Mennen Co. v. Kelly, C.C.A.N.J., 137 F.2d 866, 868.

TOILET PREPARATION. Within statute taxing a "toilet preparation", any preparation which is intended to affect, and conceivably, to improve the bodily appearance. Peroxide Chemical Co. v. Sheehan, C.C.A.Mo., 108 F.2d 306, 308, 309.

TOKEN. A sign or mark; a material evidence of the existence of a fact. Thus, cheating by "false tokens" implies the use of fabricated or deceitfully contrived material objects to assist the person's own fraud and falsehood in accomplishing the cheat. See State v. Green, 18 N.J. Law, 181; State v. Leonard, 73 Or. 451, 144 P. 113, 118; Smith v. State, 74 Fla. 594, 77 So. 274, 277; State v. Whiteaker, 64 Or. 297, 129 P. 534, 537.

TOKEN-MONEY. A conventional medium of exchange consisting of pieces of metal, fashioned in the shape and size of coins, and circulating among private persons, by consent, at a certain value. No longer permitted or recognized as money. 2 Chit.Com.Law, 182.

TOLERATE. To allow so as not to hinder; to permit as something not wholly approved of; to suffer; to endure. Gregory v. U. S., 17 Blatchf. 330, Fed.Cas.No. 5,803.

TOLERATION. The allowance of religious opinions and modes of worship which are contrary to, or different from, those of the established church or belief. Webster.

TOLERATION ACT. The statute 1 W. & M. St. 1, c. 18, for exempting Protestant dissenters from the penalties of certain laws is so called. Brown.

TOLL, *v.* To bar, defeat, or take away; thus, to toll the entry means to deny or take away the right of entry.

To toll the statute of limitations means to show facts which remove its bar of the action.

TOLL, *n.* A sum of money for the use of something, generally applied to the consideration which is paid for the use of a road, bridge, or the like, of a public nature. See Sands v. Manistee River Imp. Co., 8 S.Ct. 113, 123 U.S. 288, 31 L.Ed. 149; Anthony v. Kozer, D.C.Or., 11 F.2d 641, 645; City of Madera v. Black, 181 Cal. 306, 184 P. 397, 400; Rogge v. United States, C.C.A.Alaska, 128 F.2d 800, 802. The price of the privilege of travel over that particular highway and it is a quid pro quo and rests on principle that he who receives the toll does or has done something as an equivalent to him who pays it. State ex rel. Washington Toll Bridge Authority v. Yelle, 195 Wash. 636, 82 P.2d 120, 125.

In English law. An excise of goods; a seizure of some part for permission of the rest. It has two significations: A liberty to buy and sell within the precincts of the manor, which seems to import as much as a fair or market; a tribute or custom paid for passage. Wharton.

A Saxon word signifying, properly, a payment in towns, markets, and fairs for goods and cattle bought and sold. It is a reasonable sum of money due to the owner of the fair or market, upon sale of things tollable within the same. The word is used for a liberty as well to take as to be free from toll. Jacob.

In modern English law. A reasonable sum due to the lord of a fair or market for things sold there which are tollable. 1 Crabb, Real Prop. p. 350, § 683.

Toll and Team

Words constantly associated with Saxon and old English grants of liberties to the lords of manors. Bract. fols. 56, 104*b*, 124*b*, 154*b*. They appear to have imported the privileges of having a market, and jurisdiction of villeins. See Team.

Toll Bridge

A part of the public highway the same as a bridge built by general taxation, the only difference being that it is made at the expense of others, instead of the public, and the cost of construction and maintenance is reimbursed by a toll fixed for the purpose. White River Bridge Co. v. Hurd, 159 Ark. 652, 252 S.W. 917.

Toll Road

A road or highway over which the public has the right to travel upon payment of toll, and on which the parties entitled to such toll have the right to erect gates and bars to insure its payment. In re Newland, C.C.A.Pa., 115 F.2d 165, 166.

Toll Gatherer

The officer who takes or collects toll.

Toll-Thorough

In English law. A toll for passing through a highway, or over a ferry or bridge. Cowell. A toll paid to a town for such a number of beasts, or for every beast that goes through the town, or over a bridge or ferry belonging to it. Com. Dig. "Toll." C. A toll claimed by an individual where he is bound to repair some particular highway. 3 Steph.Comm. 257. And see King v. Nicholson, 12 East, 340; Charles River Bridge v. Warren Bridge, 11 Pet. 582, 9 L.Ed. 773.

Toll Traverse

In English law. A toll for passing over a private man's ground. Cowell. A toll for passing over the private soil of another, or for driving beasts across his ground. Cro.Eliz. 710.

Toll-Turn

In English law. A toll on beasts returning from a market. 1 Crabb, Real Prop. p. 101, § 102. A toll paid at the return of beasts from fair or market, though they were not sold. Cowell.

TOLLAGE. Payment of toll; money charged or paid as toll; the liberty or franchise of charging toll.

TOLLBOOTH. A prison; a customhouse; an exchange; also the place where goods are weighed. Wharton.

TOLLDISH. A vessel by which the toll of corn for grinding is measured.

TOLLE VOLUNTATEM ET ERIT OMNIS ACTUS INDIFFERENS. Take away the will, and every action will be indifferent. Bract. fol. 2.

TOLLER. One who collects tribute or taxes.

TOLLERE. Lat. In the civil law. To lift up or raise; to elevate; to build up.

TOLLS. In a general sense, any manner of customs, subsidy, prestation, imposition, or sum of money demanded for exporting or importing of any wares or merchandise to be taken of the buyer. 2 Inst. 58. For "Fair and Reasonable Tolls," see that title.

TOLLSESTER. An old excise; a duty paid by tenants of some manors to the lord for liberty to brew and sell ale. Cowell.

TOLSEY. The same as "tollbooth." Also a place where merchants meet; a local tribunal for small civil causes held at the Guildhall, Bristol.

TOLT. A writ whereby a cause depending in a court baron was taken and removed into a county court. Old Nat. Brev. 4.

TOLTA. In old English law. Wrong; rapine; extortion. Cowell.

TOLZEY COURT. An inferior court of record having civil jurisdiction, still existing at Bristol, England.

TOMB. An excavation in earth or rock, intended to receive the dead body of a human being. Leaphart v. Harmon, 186 S.C. 362, 195 S.E. 628, 629.

TOMBSTONE. Stone marking place of burial and usually inscribed with memorial of deceased. Anshe Sephard Congregation v. Weisblatt, 170 Md. 390, 185 A. 107, 108.

TON. A measure of weight; differently fixed, by different statutes, at two thousand pounds avoirdupois, (1 Rev.St.N.Y. 609, § 35,) or at twenty hundred-weights, each hundred-weight being one hundred and twelve pounds avoirdupois, [19 U.S.C.A. § 420]); Chemung Iron & Steel Co. v. Mersereau Metal Bed Co., Sup., 179 N.Y.S. 577, 578.

TONNAGE. The capacity of a vessel for carrying freight or other loads, calculated in tons. But the way of estimating the tonnage varies in different countries. In England, tonnage denotes the actual weight in tons which the vessel can safely carry; in America, her carrying capacity estimated from the cubic dimensions of the hold. See Roberts v. Opdyke, 40 N.Y. 259; Kiessig v. San Diego County, 51 Cal.App.2d 47, 124 P.2d 163, 166.

The "tonnage" of a vessel is her capacity to carry cargo, and a charter of "the whole tonnage" of a ship transfers to the charterer only the space necessary for that purpose. Thwing v. Insurance Co., 103 Mass. 405, 4 Am.Rep. 567.

The tonnage of a vessel is her internal cubical capacity, in tons. Inman S. S. Co. v. Tinker, 94 U.S. 238, 24 L.Ed. 118.

TONNAGE–DUTY.

In American law. A tax laid upon vessels according to their tonnage or cubical capacity.

A tonnage duty is a duty imposed on vessels in proportion to their capacity. The vital principle of a tonnage duty is that it is imposed, whatever the subject, solely according to the rule of weight; either as to the capacity to carry or the actual weight of the thing itself. Inman S. S. Co. v. Tinker, 94 U.S. 238, 24 L.Ed. 118; Ross v. Mayor and Council of Borough of Edgewater, 115 N.J.L. 477, 180 A. 866.

A tonnage tax is defined to be a duty levied on a vessel according to the tonnage or capacity. It is a tax upon the boat as an instrument of navigation, and not a tax upon the property of a citizen of the state. The North Cape, 6 Biss. 505. Fed.Cas.No.10,316.

In English law. A duty imposed by parliament upon merchandise exported and imported, according to a certain rate upon every ton. Brown.

TONNAGE-RENT. When the rent reserved by a mining lease or the like consists of a royalty on every ton of minerals gotten in the mine, it is often called a "tonnage-rent." There is generally a dead rent in addition. Sweet.

TONNAGIUM. In old English law. A custom or impost upon wines and other merchandise exported or imported, according to a certain rate per ton. Spelman; Cowell.

TONNETIGHT. In old English law. The quantity of a ton or tun, in a ship's freight or bulk, for which tonnage or tunnage was paid to the king. Cowell.

TONODERACH. In old Scotch law. A thief-taker.

TONSURA. Lat. In old English law. A shaving, or polling; the having the crown of the head shaven; tonsure. One of the peculiar badges of a clerk or clergyman.

TONSURE. In old English law. A being shaven; the having the head shaven; a shaven head. 4 Bl. Comm. 367.

TONTINE. In French law. A species of association or partnership formed among persons who are in receipt of perpetual or life annuities, with the agreement that the shares or annuities of those who die shall accrue to the survivors. This plan is said to be thus named from Tonti, an Italian, who invented it in the seventeenth century. The principle is used in some forms of life insurance. Merl. Repert; Cahn v. Northwestern Mut. Life Ins. Co., 208 Ill.App. 317, 322; Gourley v. Northwestern Nat. Life Ins. Co., 94 Okl. 46, 220 P. 645, 646.

Under the "Tontine" plan of insurance, no accumulation or earnings are credited to the policy unless it remains in force for the Tontine period of a specified number of years. Thus those who survive the period and keep their policies in force share in the accumulated funds and those who die or permit their policies to lapse during period do not; neither do their beneficiaries participate in such accumulation. Commercial Travelers' Ins. Co. v. Carlson, 104 Utah 41, 137 P.2d 656, 660.

TOOK AND CARRIED AWAY. In criminal pleading. Technical words necessary in an indictment for simple larceny.

TOOL. An instrument of manual operation, that is, an instrument to be used and managed by the hand instead of being moved and controlled by machinery. Lovewell v. Westchester F. Ins. Co., 124 Mass. 420, 26 Am.Rep. 671; Reffitt v. Southern Sheet & Tin Plate Co., 170 Ky. 362, 186 S.W. 155, 157; Sturgis Nat. Bank v. Maryland Casualty Co., 252 Mich. 426, 233 N.W. 367, 369.

Simple Tool

In law of Master and Servant. One whose condition can be seen at a glance, or by slightest inspection. Track wrench used to tighten and loosen nuts on railroad track held "simple tool." Allen Gravel Co. v. Yarbrough, 133 Mass. 652, 98 So. 117, 118; Arkansas Cent. R. Co. v. Goad, 136 Ark. 467, 206 S.W. 901, 902; Swaim v. Chicago, R. I. & P. Ry. Co., Iowa, 170 N.W. 296, 299; Kromer v. Minneapolis, St. P. & S. S. M. Ry. Co., 139 Minn. 424, 166 N.W. 1072, 1073; Ronconi v. Northwestern Pac. R. Co., 35 Cal.App. 560, 170 P. 635, 636.

"Simple tool doctrine" is based on the idea that ordinarily an employee has better opportunity than employer to observe defects and guard himself against them and that the employer should not be charged with duty of care or safety of employee with respect to a matter in which the employee is in better position to care for himself. A "tool" is an instrument of manual operation. Tucker v. Holly Hill Lumber Co., 200 S.C. 259, 20 S.E.2d 704, 706.

Tools of Trade, Apparatus of Trade

And like terms under exemption statutes and bankruptcy act cover tools that vary according to the trade, handicraft or art in which they are used. The meaning of the word "tool" dominates the meaning of such terms. Comer v. Powell, Tex.Civ.App., 189 S.W. 88, 91; Lindquist v. Clayton, 54 Utah 79, 179 P. 655, 656; Hooper v. Kennedy, 100 Vt. 314, 137 A. 194, 196; Busse v. Murray Meat & Live Stock Co., 45 Utah 596, 147 P. 626, 628.

TORPEDO DOCTRINE. Attractive nuisance doctrine. Schock v. Ringling Bros. and Barnum & Bailey Combined Shows, 5 Wash.2d 599, 105 P.2d 838, 843.

TORRENS TITLE SYSTEM. A system under which, upon the landowner's application the court may, after appropriate proceedings, direct the issuance of a certificate of title. With exceptions, this certificate is conclusive as to applicant's estate in land. This system is so called, the author being Sir Robert Torrens.

TORT (from Lat. torquere, to twist, tortus, twisted, wrested aside). A private or civil wrong or injury. A wrong independent of contract. 1 Hill, Torts 1. A violation of a duty imposed by general law or otherwise upon all persons occupying the relation to each other which is involved in a given transaction. Coleman v. California Yearly Meeting of Friends Church, 27 Cal.App.2d 579, 81 P.2d 469, 470. There must always be a violation of some duty owing to plaintiff, and generally such duty must arise by operation of law and not by mere agreement of the parties. Diver v. Miller, Del.Super., 148 A. 291, 293.

Three elements of every tort action are: Existence of legal duty from defendant to plaintiff, breach of duty, and damage as proximate result. City of Mobile v. McClure, 221 Ala. 51, 127 So. 832, 835.

A legal wrong committed upon the person or property independent of contract. It may be either (1) a direct invasion of some legal right of the individual; (2) the infraction of some public duty by which special damage accrues to the individual; (3) the violation of some private obligation by which like damage accrues to the individual. In the former case, no special damage is necessary to entitle the party to recover. In the two latter cases, such damage is necessary. Code Ga. 1882, § 2951 (Civ.Code 1910, § 4403). And see Hayes v. Insurance Co., 125 Ill. 626, 18 N.E. 322, 1 L.R.A. 303; Railway Co. v. Hennegan, 33 Tex. Civ.App. 314, 76 S.W. 453. Churchill v. Howe, 186 Mich. 107, 152 N.W. 989, 991; Strachan Shipping Co. v. Hazlip-Hood Cotton Co., 35 Ga.App. 94, 132 S.E. 454, 459; Keiper v. Anderson, 138 Minn. 392, 165 N.W. 237, 239, L.R.A.1918C, 299. A violation of a right in rem which plaintiff has as against all persons with whom he comes in contact or the violation of a right which is created by law and not by any act of parties. Mitchell v. Health Culture Co., 349 Mo. 475, 162 S.W.2d 233, 237.

Maritime Tort

See Maritime.

Personal Tort

One involving or consisting in an injury to the person or to the reputation or feelings, as distinguished from an injury or damage to real or personal property, called a "property tort." Mumford v. Wright, 12 Colo.App. 214, 55 P. 744. Gray v. Blight, C.C.A.Colo., 112 F.2d 696, 699.

Property Tort

See Personal Tort, supra.

Quasi Tort

Though not a recognized term of English law, may be conveniently used in those cases where a man who has not committed a tort is liable as if he had. Thus, a master is liable for wrongful acts done by his servant in the course of his employment. Broom, Com. Law, 690; Underh. Torts, 29.

Willful Tort

See that title.

TORT-FEASOR. A wrong-doer; one who commits or is guilty of a tort. Gordon v. Lee, 133 Me. 361, 178 A. 353, 355.

Joint Tort-Feasors

To be "joint tort-feasors," the parties must either act together in committing the wrong, or their acts, if independent of each other, must unite in causing a single injury. Young v. Dille, 127 Wash. 398, 220 P. 782, 784; Anderson v. Smith, Tex.Civ.App., 231 S.W. 142, 144; Kirkland v. Ensign-Bickford Co., D.C.Conn., 267 F. 472, 475; Verheyen v. Dewey, 27 Idaho 1, 146 P. 1116, 1119; The Ross Coddington, C.C.A.N.Y., 6 F.2d 191, 192; Anderson v. Smith, Tex.Civ.App., 231 S.W. 142, 144.

TORTIOUS. Wrongful; of the nature of a tort. Formerly certain modes of conveyance (*e. g.*, feoffments, fines, etc.) had the effect of passing not merely the estate of the person making the conveyance, but the whole fee-simple, to the injury of the person really entitled to the fee; and they were hence called "tortious conveyances." Litt. § 611; Co. Litt. 271*b*, n. 1; 330*b*, n. 1. But this operation has been taken away. Sweet.

TORTURA LEGUM PESSIMA. The torture or wresting of laws is the worst [kind of torture.] 4 Bacon's Works, 434.

TORTURE. In old criminal law. The question; the infliction of violent bodily pain upon a person, by means of the rack, wheel, or other engine, under judicial sanction and superintendence, in connection with the interrogation or examination of the person, as a means of extorting a confession of guilt, or of compelling him to disclose his accomplices.

TORY. Originally a nickname for the wild Irish in Ulster. Afterwards given to, and adopted by, one of the two great parliamentary parties which have alternately governed Great Britain since the Revolution in 1688. Wharton.

The name was also given, in America, during the struggle of the colonies for independence, to the party of those residents who favored the side of the king and opposed the war.

TOT. In old English practice. A word written by the foreign opposer or other officer opposite to a debt due the king, to denote that it was a *good* debt; which was hence said to be *totted.*

TOTA CURIA. L. Lat. In the old reports. The whole court.

TOTAL. Whole, not divided, lacking no part, entire, full, complete, the whole amount. In re Merritt's Estate, Sur., 180 N.Y.S. 877, 879; Jefferson Standard Life Ins. Co. v. King, 165 S.C. 219, 163 S.E. 653, 656; Utter, absolute. Glaze v. Hart, 225 Mo.App. 1205, 36 S.W.2d 684.

TOTAL DEPENDENCY. Within Workmen's Compensation Acts exist where the dependent subsists entirely on the earnings of the workman. Garbutt v. Stoll, 287 Mich. 396, 283 N.W. 624, 626; Burrows v. Industrial Commission, 246 Wis. 152, 16 N.W.2d 434, 435.

TOTAL DISABILITY. See Disability.

TOTAL EVICTION. That which occurs when the possessor is wholly deprived of his rights in the premises.

TOTAL LOSS.

Fire insurance. The complete destruction of the insured property by fire, so that nothing of value remains from it; as distinguished from a *partial* loss, where the property is damaged, but not entirely destroyed. Springfield Fire & Marine Ins. Co. of Springfield, Mass., v. Shapoff, 179 Ky. 804, 201 S.W. 1116, 1118; Fire Ass'n of Philadelphia v. Strayhorn, Tex.Com.App., 211 S.W. 447, 448, 449; Lowry v. Fidelity-Phœnix Fire Ins. Co., 272 S.W. 79, 80, 219 Mo.App. 121; Roquette v. Farmers Ins. Co., 191 N.W. 772, 774, 49 N.D. 478; Teter v. Franklin Fire Ins. Co., 82 S.E. 40, 42, 74 W.Va. 344.

Test whether building burned is "total loss" is whether substantial portion is left standing in condition reasonably suitable as basis on which to reconstruct building in like condition as to strength, security, and utility as it was before fire. Commerce Ins. Co. v. Sergi, Tex.Civ.App., 60 S.W.2d 1046.

Marine insurance. The entire destruction or loss, to the insured, of the subject-matter of the policy, by the risks insured against. St. Paul Fire & Marine Ins. Co. v. Beacham, 128 Md. 414, 97 A. 708, 709, L.R.A.1916F, 1168.

Actual total loss. The total loss of the vessel covered by a policy of insurance, by its real and substantive destruction, by injuries which leave it no longer existing *in specie*, by its being reduced to a wreck irretrievably beyond repair, or by its being placed beyond the control of the insured and beyond his power of recovery. Distinguished from a *constructive* total loss, which occurs where the vessel, though injured by the perils insured against, remains *in specie* and capable of repair or recovery, but at such an expense, or under such other conditions, that the insured may claim the whole amount of the policy upon abandoning the vessel to the underwriters. In such cases the insured is entitled to indemnity as for a total loss. An exception to the rule requiring abandonment is found in cases where the loss occurs in foreign ports or seas, where it is impracticable to repair. In such cases the master may sell the vessel for the benefit of all concerned, and the insured may claim as for a total loss by accounting to the insurer for the amount realized on the sale.

Constructive total loss. See Actual total loss, supra.

Partial loss. Where an injury results to the vessel from a peril insured against, but where the loss is neither actually nor constructively total. Globe Ins. Co. v. Sherlock, 25 Ohio St. 50, 64; Burt v. Insurance Co., 9 Hun (N.Y.) 383; Carr v. Insurance Co., 109 N.Y. 504, 17 N.E. 369; Wallerstein v. Insurance Co., 3 Rob. (N.Y.) 528.

See, also, Fire Insurance, supra.

TOTIDEM VERBIS. Lat. In so many words.

TOTIES QUOTIES. Lat. As often as occasion shall arise.

TOTIS VIRIBUS. Lat. With all one's might or power; with all his might; very strenuously.

TOTTED. A good debt to the crown, *i. e.*, a debt paid to the sheriff, to be by him paid over to the king. Cowell; Mozley & Whitley.

TOTTEN TRUST. See Trust.

TOTUM PRÆFERTUR UNICUIQUE PARTI. 3 Coke, 41. The whole is preferable to any single part.

TOUCH. In insurance law. To stop at a port. If there be liberty granted by the policy to *touch*, or to *touch and stay*, at an intermediate port on the passage, the better opinion now is that the insured may *trade* there, when consistent with the object and the furtherance of the adventure, by breaking bulk, or by discharging and taking in cargo, provided it produces no unnecessary delay, nor enhances nor varies the risk. 3 Kent, Comm. 314.

TOUCH AND STAY. Words frequently introduced in policies of insurance, giving the party insured the right to stop and stay at certain designated points in the course of the voyage. A vessel which has the power to touch and stay at a place in the course of the voyage must confine herself strictly to the terms of the liberty so given; for any attempt to trade at such a port during such a stay, as, by shipping or landing goods, will amount to a species of deviation which will discharge the underwriters, unless the ship have also liberty to trade as well as to touch and stay at such a place. 1 Marsh. Ins. 275.

TOUCHING A DEAD BODY. It was an ancient superstition that the body of a murdered man would bleed freshly when touched by his murderer. Hence, in old criminal law, this was resorted to as a means of ascertaining the guilt or innocence of a person suspected of the murder.

TOUJOURS ET UNCORE PRIST. L. Fr. Always and still ready. This is the name of a plea of tender.

TOUR D'ECHELLE. In French law. An easement consisting of the right to rest ladders upon the adjoining estate, when necessary in order to repair a party-wall or buildings supported by it.

Also the vacant space surrounding a building left unoccupied in order to facilitate its reparation when necessary. Merl. Repert.

TOURIST. One who makes a tour; one who travels from place to place for pleasure or culture. Jones v. State, 64 Ga.App. 376, 13 S.E.2d 462, 465.

TOURN. In old English law. A court of record, having criminal jurisdiction, in each county, held before the sheriff, twice a year, in one place after another, following a certain circuit or rotation.

TOUT. Fr. All; whole; entirely. *Tout temps prist*, always ready.

TOUT CE QUE LA LOI NE DEFEND PAS EST PERMIS. Everything is permitted which is not forbidden by law.

TOUT TEMPS PRIST. L. Fr. Always ready. The emphatic words of the old plea of tender; the defendant alleging that he has always been ready, and still is ready, to discharge the debt. 3 Bl. Comm. 303; 2 Salk. 622.

TOUT UN SOUND. L. Fr. All one sound; sounding the same; *idem sonans*.

TOUTE EXCEPTION NON SURVEILLÉE TEND À PRENDRE LA PLACE DU PRINCIPE. Every exception not watched tends to assume the place of the principle.

TOWAGE. The act or service of towing ships and vessels, usually by means of a small steamer called a "tug." That which is given for towing ships in rivers.

The drawing a ship or barge along the water by another ship or boat, fastened to her, or by men or horses, etc., on land. It is also money which is given by bargemen to the owner of ground next a river, where they tow a barge or other vessel. Jacob. And see Ryan v. Hook, 34 Hun (N.Y.) 191; The Kingaloch, 26 Eng. Law & Eq. 597; The Egypt, D.C.Va., 17 F. 359, 370.

TOWAGE SERVICE. In admiralty law. A service rendered to a vessel, by towing, for the mere purpose of expediting her voyage, without reference to any circumstances of danger. It is confined to vessels that have received no injury or damage. The Reward, 1 W. Rob. 177; The Athenian, D.C.Mich., 3 F. 248, 249; The Kennebec, C.C.A.Tex., 231 F. 423, 425; The Mercer, C.C.A.N.Y., 297 F. 981, 984.

TOWARD. The word has been held to mean not simply "to" but to include "about." Hudson v. State, 6 Tex.App. 565, 32 Am.Rep. 593. Also, in a course or line leading to, in the direction of. People v. Kreidler, 180 Mich. 654, 147 N.W. 559, 560; State v. Trent, 122 Or. 444, 259 P. 893, 898.

TOWN.

American Law

A civil and political division of a state, varying in extent and importance, but usually one of the divisions of a county. In the New England states, the town is the political unit, and is a municipal corporation. In some other states, where the county is the unit, the town is merely one of its subdivisions, but possesses some powers of local self-government. In still other states, such subdivisions of a county are called "townships," and "town" is the name of a village, borough, or smaller city. See Herrman v. Guttenberg, 62 N.J.Law, 605, 43 A. 703; Van Riper v. Parsons, 40 N.J.Law, 1; State v. Denny, 118 Ind. 449, 21 N.E. 274, 4 L.R.A. 65; Guadalupe County v. Poth (Tex.Civ.App.), 163 S.W. 1050, 1051; People v. Adams State Bank, 272 Ill. 277, 111 N.E. 989, 991; In re Opinion of the Justices, 229 Mass. 601, 119 N.E. 778, 781.

English Law

Originally, a vill or tithing; but now a generic term, which comprehends under it the several species of cities, boroughs, and common towns. 1 Bl. Comm. 114.

The word "town" is quite commonly used as a generic term and as including both cities and villages. Village of Ashley v. Ashley Lumber Co., 40 N.D. 515, 169 N.W. 87, 90; Plainfield-Union Water Co. v. Inhabitants of City of Plainfield, 84 N.J.L. 634, 87 A. 448, 450.

TOWN AGENT. Under the prohibitory liquor laws in force in some of the New England states a town agent is a person appointed in each town to purchase intoxicating liquors for the town and having the exclusive right to sell the same for the permitted purposes, medical, mechanical, scientific, etc. He either receives a fixed salary or is permitted to make a small profit on his sales. The stock of liquors belongs to the town, and is bought with its money. See Black, Intox. Liq. §§ 204, 205.

TOWN CLAUSE. In English practice. A cause tried at the sittings for London and Middlesex, 3 Steph. Comm. 517.

TOWN COLLECTOR. One of the officers of a town charged with collecting the taxes assessed for town purposes.

TOWN COMMISSIONER. In some of the states where the town is the political unit the town commissioners constitute a board of administrative officers charged with the general management of the town's business.

TOWN ORDER OR WARRANT. An official direction in writing by the auditing officers of a town, directing the treasurer to pay a sum of money.

TOWN POUND. A place of confinement maintained by a town for estrays.

TOWN PURPOSE. When it is said that taxation by a town, or the expenditure of the town's money, must be for town purposes, it is meant that the purposes must be public with respect to the town; *i. e.*, concern the welfare and advantage of the town as a whole.

TOWN–REEVE. The reeve or chief officer of a town.

TOWN TAX. Such tax as a town may levy for its peculiar expenses; as distinguished from a county or state tax.

TOWN TREASURER. The treasurer of a town which is an organized municipal corporation.

TOWN–CLERK. In those states where the *town* is the unit for local self-government, the town-clerk is a principal officer who keeps the records, issues calls for town-meetings, and performs generally the duties of a secretary to the political organization. See Seamons v. Fitts, 21 R.I. 236, 42 A. 863.

TOWN–CRIER. An officer in a town whose business it is to make proclamations.

TOWN–HALL. The building maintained by a town for town-meetings and the offices of the municipal authorities.

TOWN–MEETING. Under the municipal organization of the New England states, the town-meeting is a legal assembly of the qualified voters of a town, held at stated intervals or on call, for the purpose of electing town officers, and of discussing and deciding on questions relating to the public business, property, and expenses of the town. See In re Foley, 8 Misc. 57, 28 N.Y.S. 608; Railroad Co. v. Mallory, 101 Ill. 588; Portland Water Co. v. Town of Portland, 97 Conn. 628, 118 A. 84, 86; In re Opinion of the Justices, 229 Mass. 601, 119 N.E. 778, 781.

TOWNSHIP. **1.** In surveys of the public land of the United States, a "township" is a division of territory six miles square, containing thirty-six sections.

2. In some of the states, this is the name given to the civil and political subdivisions of a county. Town, and Liberty Tp. v. Rock Island Tp., 44 Okl. 398, 144 P. 1025, 1026; People v. Stewart, 281 Ill.

365, 118 N.E. 55, 56; City of Hutchinson v. Reno County, 124 Kan. 149, 257 P. 750, 751. Rich v. Industrial Commission, 80 Utah 511, 15 P.2d 641, 645.

TOWNSHIP TRUSTEE. One of a board of officers to whom, in some states, affairs of a township are intrusted.

TOWNSITE. Portion of public domain segregated by proper authority and procedure as site for a town. Metropolitan Life Ins. Co. v. Keating, 191 Minn. 520, 254 N.W. 813.

TOXIC. (Lat. *toxicum*; Gr. *toxikon.*) In medical jurisprudence. Poisonous; having the character or producing the effects of a poison; referable to a poison; produced by or resulting from a poison.

Toxic convulsions. Such as are caused by the action of a poison on the nervous system.

Toxic dementia. Weakness of mind or feeble cerebral activity, approaching imbecility, resulting from continued use or administration of slow poisons or of the more active poisons in repeated small doses, as in cases of lead poisoning and in some cases of addiction to such drugs as opium or alcohol.

Toxanemia. A condition of *anemia* (impoverishment or deficiency of blood) resulting from the action of certain toxic substances or agents.

Toxemia or toxicemia. Blood-poisoning; the condition of the system caused by the presence of toxic agents in the circulation; including both *septicemia* and *pyœmia.*

Toxicosis. A diseased state of the system due to the presence and action of any poison.

TOXICAL. Poisonous; containing poison.

TOXICANT. A poison; a toxic agent; any substance capable of producing toxication or poisoning.

TOXICATE. To poison. Not used to describe the act of one who administers a poison, but the action of the drug or poison itself.

Auto-Intoxication

Self-empoisonment from the absorption of the toxic products of internal metabolism, *e. g.,* ptomaine poisoning.

Intoxication

The state of being poisoned; the condition produced by the administration or introduction into the human system of a poison. This term is popularly used as equivalent to "drunkenness," which, however, is more accurately described as "alcoholic intoxication."

TOXICOLOGY. The science of poisons; that department of medical science which treats of poisons, their effect, their recognition, their antidotes, and generally of the diagnosis and therapeutics of poisoning.

TOXIN. In its widest sense, this term may denote any poison or toxicant; but as used in pathology and medical jurisprudence it signifies, in general, any diffusible alkaloidal substance (as, the ptomaines, abrin, brucin, or serpent venoms), and in particular the poisonous products of pathogenic (disease-producing) bacteria.

Anti-Toxin

A product of pathogenic bacteria which, in sufficient quantities, will neutralize the toxin or poisonous product of the same bacteria. In therapeutics, a preventive remedy (administered by inoculation) against the effect of certain kinds of toxins, venoms, and disease-germs, obtained from the blood of an animal which has previously been treated with repeated minute injections of the particular poison or germ to be neutralized.

Toxicomania

An excessive addiction to the use of toxic or poisonous drugs or other substances; a form of mania or affective insanity characterized by an irresistible impulse to indulgence in opium, cocaine, chloral, alcohol, etc.

Toxiphobia

Morbid dread of being poisoned; a form of insanity manifesting itself by an excessive and unfounded apprehension of death by poison.

TOY. A plaything, often but not necessarily always imaginative of some living or manufactured thing. Steel Stamping Co. v. N. N. Hill Brass Co., D.C.Conn., 17 F.Supp. 18, 20.

TRABES. Lat. In civil law. A beam or rafter of a house. Calvin.

In old English law. A measure of grain, containing twenty-four sheaves; a thrave. Spelman.

TRACEA. In old English law. The track or trace of a felon, by which he was pursued with the hue and cry; a foot-step, hoof-print, or wheel-track. Bract. fols. 116, 121*b*.

TRACING. A tracing is a mechanical copy or *fac simile* of an original, produced by following its lines, with a pen or pencil, through a transparent medium, called tracing paper. Chapman v. Ferry, C.C.Or., 18 F. 539, 540.

TRACKS. A term that may mean rails, or rails and cross-ties, or roadbed according to context. City of Bayonne v. Public Service Ry. Corporation, 98 N.J.L. 255, 119 A. 9. City of Dayton v. South Covington & C. St. Ry. Co., 177 Ky. 202, 197 S.W. 670, 672, L.R.A. 1918B, 476, Ann.Cas.1918E, 229.

Dead Track

A track having a switch to other tracks at one end only with a bumper at the other end. Hoyer v. Central R. Co. of New Jersey, C.C.A.N.Y., 255 F. 493, 494.

Track Delivery Shipments

Carload shipments, as distinguished from ordinary freight unloaded from the cars, known as a "drop shipment" delivery. Boshell v. Receivers of St. Louis & S. F. R. Co., 200 Ala. 366, 76 So. 282, 284.

TRACT. A lot, piece or parcel of land, of greater or less size, the term not importing, in itself, any precise dimension. See Edwards v. Derrickson, 28 N.J.L. 45; Holt v. Wichita County Water Improvement Dist. No. 2, Tex.Civ.App., 48 S.W.2d 527, 529.

As applied to a mineral location the word "tract" implies a surface location. Whildin v. Maryland Gold Quartz Mining Co., 33 Cal.App. 270, 164 P. 908, 910.

TRACTOR. That which draws or is used for drawing as a traction engine, or an automotive vehicle used for drawing or hauling something as a vehicle, plow, harrow, or reaper. State ex rel. Rice v. Louisiana Oil Corporation, 174 Misc. 585, 165 So. 423, 425.

TRACTENT FABRILIA FABRI. Let smiths perform the work of smiths. 3 Co. Epist.

TRADAS IN BALLIUM. You deliver to bail. In old English practice. The name of a writ which might be issued in behalf of a party who, upon the writ *de odio et atia,* had been found to have been maliciously accused of a crime, commanding the sheriff that, if the prisoner found twelve good and lawful men of the county who would be mainpernors for him, he should *deliver* him *in bail* to those twelve, until the next assize. Bract. fol. 123; 1 Reeve, Eng. Law, 252.

TRADE. The act or business of exchanging commodities by barter; or the business of buying and selling for money; traffic; barter. May v. Sloan, 101 U.S. 237, 25 L.Ed. 797; U. S. v. Cassidy, D.C.Cal., 67 F. 698; State v. Deckebach, 113 Ohio St. 347, 149 N.E. 194, 196.

The business which a person has learned and which he carries on for procuring subsistence, or for profit; occupation or employment, particularly mechanical employment; distinguished from the liberal arts and learned professions, and from agriculture. Woodfield v. Colzey, 47 Ga. 124; People v. Warden of City Prison, 144 N.Y. 529, 39 N.E. 686, 27 L.R.A. 718; Detroit Taxicab & Transfer Co. v. Callahan, C.C.A.Mich., 1 F.2d 911, 912. A line of work or a form of occupation pursued as a business or calling, as for a livelihood or for profit; anything practiced as a means of getting a living, money, booty, etc.; mercantile or commercial business in general, or the buying and selling, or exchanging, of commodities, either by wholesale or retail within a country or between countries. Helvering v. Wilmington Trust Co., C.C.A.3, 124 F.2d 156, 158.

All wholesale trade, all buying in order to sell again by wholesale, may be reduced to three sorts: The home trade, the foreign trade of consumption, and the carrying trade. 2 Smith, Wealth Nat. b. 2, c. 5.

TRADE ACCEPTANCE. A draft or bill of exchange drawn by the seller on the purchaser of goods sold and accepted by such purchaser. Luikart v. Massachusetts Bonding & Insurance Co., 129 Neb. 771, 263 N.W. 124, 129.

TRADE AND COMMERCE. The words "trade" and "commerce," when used in juxtaposition impart to each other enlarged signification, so as to include practically every business occupation carried on for subsistence or profit, and into which the elements of bargain and sale, barter, exchange, or traffic, enter. State v. Tagami, 234 P. 102, 105, 195 Cal. 522.

TRADE AGREEMENT. See Collective Labor Agreement.

TRADE COMMISSION, FEDERAL. An act of congress was passed September 26, 1914, creating a Federal Trade Commission, composed of five commissioners appointed by the President with the advice and consent of the Senate. The act provides: "That unfair methods of competition in commerce are hereby declared unlawful," and the commission is "directed to prevent persons, partnerships or corporations, except banks, and common carriers subject to the acts to regulate commerce, from using unfair methods of competition in commerce."

TRADE DISPUTE. Within Unemployment Insurance Act barring benefit payments to persons who leave work because of trade dispute, the term includes controversy over working conditions, American-Hawaiian S. S. Co. v. California Employment Commission, 24 Cal.2d 716, 151 P.2d 213, 215; unwillingness to cross picket lines, Mattson Terminals v. California Employment Commission, 24 Cal.2d 695, 151 P.2d 202, 206.

TRADE DOLLAR. A silver coin of the United States, of the weight of four hundred and twenty grains, troy. Rev.St.U.S. § 3513.

TRADE FIXTURES. See Fixtures.

TRADE-MARK. Generally speaking, a distinctive mark of authenticity, through which the products of particular manufacturers or the vendible commodities of particular merchants may be distinguished from those of others. It may consist in any symbol or in any form of words, but, as its office is to point out distinctively the origin or ownership of the articles to which it is affixed, it follows that no sign or form of words can be appropriated as a valid trade-mark which, from the nature of the fact conveyed by its primary meaning, others may employ with equal truth and with equal right for the same purpose. Jantzen Knitting Mills v. West Coast Knitting Mills, Cust. & Pat.App., 46 F.2d 182, 184.

A distinctive mark, motto, device, or emblem, which a manufacturer stamps, prints, or otherwise affixes to the goods he produces, so that they may be identified in the market, and their origin be vouched for. Trade-Mark Cases, 100 U.S. 87, 25 L.Ed. 550; Buffalo Rubber Mfg. Co. v. Batavia Rubber Co., 90 Misc.Rep. 418, 153 N.Y.S. 779, 783; Iowa Auto Market v. Auto Market & Exchange, 197 Iowa, 420, 197 N.W. 321, 322; Tillman & Bend-el v. California Packing Corporation, C.C.A.Cal., 63 F.2d 498, 503.

"Trade-mark" is created chiefly by use, which must be general, continuous, and exclusive and applied to goods and used in trade under such circumstances of publicity and length of use as to show intention to adopt mark for specific goods. Continental Corporation v. National Union Radio Corporation, C.C.A.Ill., 67 F.2d 938, 942.

A "trade-mark" is merely a protection for good will and is not the subject of property rights except in connection with an existing business. 15 U.S.C.A. § 90. Lazar v. Cecelia Co., D.C.N.Y., 30 F.Supp. 769, 771.

Generally speaking, a "trade-mark" is applicable to a vendible commodity, to which it is affixed, and a "trade-name" to a business and its good will. American Steel Foundries v. Robertson, 46 S.Ct. 160, 162, 269 U.S. 372, 70 L.Ed. 317.

TRADE-MARKS REGISTRATION ACT, 1875. This is the statute 38 & 39 Vict. c. 91, amended by the acts of 1876 and 1877. It provides for the establishment of a register of trade-marks under the superintendence of the commissioners of patents, and for the registration of trade-marks as belonging to particular classes of goods, and for their assignment in connection with the good-will of the business in which they are used. Sweet.

TRADE-NAME. A name used in trade to designate a particular business of certain individuals considered somewhat as an entity, or the place at which a business is located, or of a class of goods, but which is not a technical trade-mark either because not applied or affixed to goods sent into the market or because not capable of exclusive appropriation by anyone as a trade-mark. "Trade-names" may, or may not, be exclusive. Non-exclusive "trade-names" are names that are publici juris in their primary sense, but which in a secondary sense have come to be understood as indicating the goods or business of a particular trader. "Trade-names" are acquired by adoption and user and belong to one who first used them and gave them a value. St. Louis Independent Packing Co. v. Houston, C.C.A.Mo., 215 F. 553, 560; Hartzler v. Goshen Churn & Ladder Co., 55 Ind.App. 455, 104 N.E. 34, 37. See, also, Trade-mark. For "Fanciful Trade-Name," see that title.

A "trade-name" is descriptive of the manufacturer or dealer for protection in trade, to avoid confusion in business, and to secure the advantages of a good reputatfon and is applied more to the good will of a business than as an identification of a product. Mary Muffet, Inc., v. Smelansky, Mo.App., 158 S.W.2d 168, 170.

TRADE-SECRET. A plan or process, tool, mechanism, or compound known only to its owner and those of his employees to whom it is necessary to confide it. Victor Chemical Works v. Iliff, 299 Ill. 532; 132 N.E. 806, 811; Progress Laundry Co. v. Hamilton, 208 Ky. 348, 270 S.W. 834, 835. A secret formula or process not patented, but known only to certain individuals using it in compounding some article of trade having a commercial value. Glucol Mfg. Co. v. Shulist, 239 Mich. 70, 214 N.W. 152, 153; U. S. ex rel. Norwegian Nitrogen Products Co. v. U. S. Tariff Commission, 6 F.2d 491, 495, 55 App.D.C. 366.

TRADE-UNION. A combination of workmen of the same trade or of several allied trades, for the purpose of securing by united action the most favorable conditions regarding wages, hours of labor, etc., for its members. People v. Distributors Division, Smoked Fish Workers Union, Local No. 20377, Sup., 7 N.Y.S.2d 185, 187; Keith Theatre v. Vachon, 134 Me. 392, 187 A. 692, 694.

TRADE-UNION ACT. The statute 34 & 35 Vict. c. 31, passed in 1871, for the purpose of giving legal recognition to trade unions, is known as the "trade-union act," or "trade-union funds protection act." It provides that the members of a trade union shall not be prosecuted for conspiracy merely by reason that the rules of such union are in restraint of trade; and that the agreements of trade unions shall not on that account be void or voidable. Provisions are also made with reference to the registration and registered offices of trade unions, and other purposes connected therewith. Mozley & Whitley.

TRADE USAGE. The usage or customs commonly observed by persons conversant in, or connected with, a particular trade.

TRADER. One who makes it his business to buy merchandise, goods, or chattels to sell the same at a profit. People v. Terkanian, 27 Cal.App.2d 460, 81 P.2d 251, 253. One who sells goods substantially in the form in which they are bought; one who has not converted them into another form of property by his skill and labor. Albuquerque Lumber Co. v. Bureau of Revenue of New Mexico, 42 N.M. 58, 75 P.2d 334, 336.

TRADESMAN. In England, a shopkeeper; in the United States, a mechanic or artificer of any kind, whose livelihood depends on the labor of his hands; Richie v. McCauley, 4 Pa. 472.

TRADICION. Span. In Spanish law. Delivery. White. New Recop. b. 2, tit. 2, c. 9.

TRADING. Engaging in trade, (*q. v.*;) pursuing the business or occupation of trade or of a trader.

TRADING CORPORATION. See Corporation.

TRADING PARTNERSHIP. A firm the nature of whose business, according to the usual modes of conducting it, imports the necessity of buying and selling. Dowling v. National Exch. Bank, 145 U. S. 512, 12 S.Ct. 928, 36 L.Ed. 795; Schumacher v. Sumner Telephone Co., 161 Iowa, 326, 142 N.W. 1034, 1036, Ann.Cas. 1916A, 201; Maasdam v. Blokland, 123 Or. 128, 261 P. 66, 68.

TRADING STAMPS. The name for a method of conducting some kinds of retail business which consists of an agreement between a number of merchants and a corporation that the latter shall print the names of the former in its subscribers' dictionary and circulate a number of copies of the book, and that the merchants shall purchase of the corporation a number of so-called trading stamps, to be given to purchasers with their purchases, and by them preserved and pasted in the books aforesaid until a certain number have been secured, when they shall be presented to the corporation in exchange for the choice of certain articles kept in stock by the corporation. Lansburgh v. D. of Col., 11 App.D.C. 512.

TRADING VOYAGE. One which contemplates the touching and stopping of the vessel at various ports for the purpose of traffic or sale and purchase or exchange of commodities on account of the owners and shippers, rather than the transportation of cargo between terminal points, which is called a "freighting voyage."

TRADITIO. Lat. In the civil law. Delivery; transfer of possession; a derivative mode of acquiring, by which the owner of a corporeal thing, having the right and the will of aliening it, transfers it for a lawful consideration to the receiver. Heinecc. Elem. lib. 2, tit. 1, § 380.

Quasi Traditio

A supposed or implied delivery of property from one to another. Thus, if the purchaser of an article was already in possession of it before the sale, his continuing in possession is considered as equivalent to a fresh delivery of it, delivery being one of the necessary elements of a sale; in other words, a *quasi traditio* is predicated.

Traditio Brevi Manu

A species of constructive or implied delivery. When he who already holds possession of a thing in another's name agrees with that other that thenceforth he shall possess it in his own name, in this case a delivery and redelivery are not necessary. Mackeld. Rom. Law, § 284.

Traditio Clavium

Delivery of keys; a symbolical kind of delivery, by which the ownership of merchandise in a warehouse might be transferred to a buyer. Inst. 2, 1, 44.

Traditio Longa Manu

A species of delivery which takes place where the transferor places the article in the hands of the transferee, or, on his order, delivers it at his house. Mackeld. Rom. Law, § 284.

Traditio Rei

Delivery of the thing. See 5 Maule & S. 82.

TRADITIO LOQUI FACIT CHARTAM. Delivery makes a deed speak. Delivery gives effect to the words of a deed. 5 Coke, 1*a*.

TRADITIO NIHIL AMPLIUS TRANSFERRE DEBET VEL POTEST, AD EUM QUI ACCIPIT, QUAM EST APUD EUM QUI TRADIT. Delivery ought to, and can, transfer nothing more to him who receives than is with him who delivers. Dig. 41, 1, 20, pr.

TRADITION. Delivery. A close translation or formation from the Latin *"traditio."* 2 Bl. Comm. 307.

The tradition or delivery is the transferring of the thing sold into the power and possession of the buyer. Civ. Code La. art. 2477.

In the rule respecting the admission of tradition or general reputation to prove boundaries, questions of pedigree, etc., this word means knowledge or belief derived from the statements or declarations of contemporary witnesses and handed down orally through a considerable period of time. See Westfelt v. Adams, 131 N.C. 379, 42 S.E. 823; In re Hurlburt's Estate, 68 Vt. 366, 35 A. 77, 35 L.R.A. 794.

TRADITIONARY EVIDENCE. Evidence derived from tradition or reputation or the statements formerly made by persons since deceased, in regard to questions of pedigree, ancient boundaries, and the like, where no living witnesses can be produced having knowledge of the facts. Lay v. Neville, 25 Cal. 554.

TRADITOR. In old English law. A traitor; one guilty of high treason. Fleta, lib. 1, c. 21, § 8.

TRADITUR IN BALLIUM. In old practice. Is delivered to bail. Emphatic words of the old Latin bail-piece. 1 Salk. 105.

TRAFFIC. Commerce; trade; sale or exchange of merchandise, bills, money, and the like. The passing of goods or commodities from one person to another for an equivalent in goods or money. Senior v. Ratterman, 44 Ohio St. 673, 11 N.E. 321; Fine v. Moran, 74 Fla. 417, 77 So. 533, 538; Bruno v. U. S., C.C.A.Mass., 289 F. 649, 655; Kroger Grocery and Baking Co. v. Schwer, 36 Ohio App. 512, 173 N.E. 633. The subjects of transportation on a route, as persons or goods; the passing to and fro of persons, animals, vehicles, or vessels, along a route of transportation, as along a street, canal, etc. United States v. Golden Gate Bridge and Highway Dist. of California, D.C.Cal., 37 F. Supp. 505, 512.

TRAFFIC BALANCES. Balances of moneys collected in payment for the transportation of passengers and freight. Chicago & A. R. Co. v. United States & Mexican Trust Co., C.C.A.Kan., 225 F. 940, 946.

TRAFFIC REGULATIONS. Prescribed rules of conduct to promote the orderly and safe flow of traffic. Dembicer v. Pawtucket Cabinet & Builders Finish Co., 58 R.I. 451, 193 A. 622, 625.

TRAHENS. Lat. In French law. The drawer of a bill. Story, Bills, § 12 note.

TRAIL-BASTON. Justices of trail-baston were justices appointed by King Edward I., during his absence in the Scotch and French wars, about the year 1305. They were so styled, says Hollingshed, for trailing or drawing the staff of justice. Their office was to make inquisition, throughout the kingdom, of all officers and others, touching extortion, bribery, and such like grievances, of intruders into other men's lands, barrators, robbers, breakers of the peace, and divers other offenders. Cowell; Tomlins.

TRAILER. A separate vehicle, not driven or propelled by its own power, but drawn by some independent power; a semi-trailer is a separate vehicle which is not driven or propelled by its own power, but, which, to be useful, must be attached to and become a part of another vehicle, and then loses its identity as a separate vehicle. Leamon v. State, 17 Ohio App. 323, 326; Maryland Casualty Co. v. Cross, C.C.A.Tex., 112 F.2d 58, 60.

TRAIN. Continuous or connected line of cars or carriages being transported on railroad from one terminal to another, not merely cars being moved in switchyard for purpose of making up trains or placing them in another part of yard. Squibb v. Elgin, J. & E. Ry. Co., 99 Ind.App. 136, 190 N.E. 879, 881.

TRAIN WRECK. These words, in an accident insurance policy, mean either total or partial destruction of the train. The smashing in of a portion of a passenger car is a "train wreck," though the car is not derailed, and the train soon continues under its own power. Mochel v. Iowa State Traveling Men's Ass'n, 203 Iowa, 623, 213 N.W. 259, 261, 51 A.L.R. 1327.

TRAINBANDS. The militia; the part of a community trained to martial exercises.

TRAISTIS. In old Scotch law. A roll containing the particular dittay taken up upon malefactors, which, with the *porteous,* is delivered by the justice clerk to the coroner, to the effect that the persons whose names are contained in the porteous may be attached, conform to the dittay contained in the traistis. So called, because committed to the *traist,* [trust,] faith, and credit of the clerks and coroner. Skene; Burrill.

TRAITOR. One who, being trusted, betrays; one guilty of treason, (*q. v.*). Vulcan Detinning Co. v. St. Clair, 315 Ill. 140, 145 N.E. 657, 659.

TRAITOROUSLY. In criminal pleading. An essential word in indictments for treason. The offense must be laid to have been committed *traitorously.* Whart.Crim.Law, 100.

TRAJECTITIA PECUNIA. A loan to a shipper to be repaid only in case of a successful voyage. The lender could charge an extraordinary rate of interest, *nauticum fœnus.* Holland, Jurispr. 250.

TRAJECTITIUS. Lat. In the civil law. Sent across the sea.

TRAMMER. A mine laborer shoveling the ore or dirt as it is mined or thrown down into tram cars. Mesich v. Tamarack Mining Co., 184 Mich. 363, 151 N.W. 564, 566.

TRAMP. One who roams about from place to place, begging or living without labor or visible means of support; a vagrant. See State v. Hogan, 63 Ohio St. 202, 58 N.E. 572, 52 L.R.A. 863, 81 Am.St.Rep. 626; Miller v. State, 73 Ind. 92; Railway Co. v. Boyle, 115 Ga. 836, 42 S.E. 242, 59 L.R.A. 104.

TRANSACT. In Scotch law. To compound. Amb. 185.

In common parlance, equivalent to "carry on," when used with reference to business. Territory v. Harris, 8 Mont. 140, 19 P. 286; In re Wellings' Estate, 192 Cal. 506, 221 P. 628, 631.

TRANSACTING BUSINESS. Doing or performing series of acts occupying time, attention, and labor of men for purpose of livelihood, profit or pleasure. Seidenbach's v. A. E. Little Co., 146 Okl. 247, 294 P. 126, 128.

TRANSACTIO. Lat. In the civil law. The settlement of a suit or matter in controversy, by the litigating parties, between themselves, without referring it to arbitration. Hallifax, Civil Law, b. 3, c. 8, no. 14. An agreement by which a suit, either pending or about to be commenced, was forborne or discontinued on certain terms. Calvin.

TRANSACTION. Act of transacting or conducting any business; negotiation; management; proceding; that which is done; an affair. Sheehan v. Pierce, 23 N.Y.S. 1119, 1121, 70 Hun 62, 53 St. R. 438. Something which has taken place, whereby a cause of action has arisen. It must therefore consist of an act or agreement, or several acts or agreements having some connection with each other, in which more than one person is concerned, and by which the legal relations of such persons between themselves are altered. Baker v. S. A. Healy Co., 302 Ill.App. 634, 24 N.E.2d 228, 234.

A broader term than "contract". Hoffman Machinery Corporation v. Ebenstein, 150 Kan. 790, 96 P.2d 661, 663.

A group of facts so connected together as to be referred to by a single legal name; as a crime, a contract, a wrong. Steph.Dig.Evid. art. 3.

Code Practice

"Transaction," as used in statutes permitting cause of action arising out of transaction set forth in complaint to be foundation of counterclaim, properly embraces that combination of acts and events, whether in nature of contract or tort, out of which a legal right springs, or upon which a legal obligation is predicated. Haut v. Gunderson, 54 N.D. 826, 211 N.W. 982, 983; Southeastern Life Ins. Co. v. Palmer, 120 S.C. 490, 113 S.E. 310, 311; Scott v. Waggoner, 48 Mont. 536, 139 P. 454, 456, L.R.A.1916C, 491.

Evidence

A "transaction" between a witness and a decedent, within statutory provisions excluding evidence of such transactions, embraces every variety of affairs which can form the subject of negotiations, interviews, or actions between two persons, and includes every method by which one person can derive impressions or information from the conduct, condition, or language of another. Kentucky Utilities Co. v. McCarty's Adm'r, 169 Ky. 38, 183 S.W. 237, 239; Bright v. Virginia & Gold Hill Water Co., C.C.A.Nev., 270 F. 410, 413; Madero v. Calzado, Tex.Civ.App., 281 S.W. 328, 331. An action participated in by witness and decedent and to which decedent could testify of his own personal knowledge, if alive. Nelson v. Janssen, 144 Neb. 811, 14 N.W.2d 662, 665. A personal or mutual transaction wherein deceased and witness actively participate. Seligman v. Orth, 205 Wis. 199, 236 N.W. 115, 117.

Civil Law

An agreement between two or more persons, who, for preventing or putting an end to a lawsuit, adjust their differences by mutual consent, in the manner which they agree on. This contract must be reduced into writing. Civ.Code La. art. 3071.

TRANSAZIONE. An Italian term which technically refers to an instrument whereby parties agree to put an end to a dispute by means of mutual concessions and is the equivalent of "transactio" under the Roman Law, the principles of which have been carried into the common law and are found in agreements of accord and satisfaction and compromise and settlement. Castelli v. Tolibia, Sup., 83 N.Y.S.2d 554, 562.

TRANSCRIPT. That which has been transcribed; a copy of any kind; a writing made from or after an original; a copy; a copy, particularly of a record; a copy of an original writing or deed and suggests the idea of an original writing. Stephenson v. State, 179 N.E. 633, 637, 205 Ind. 141; O'Quinn v. Tate, Tex.Civ.App., 187 S.W.2d 241, 243.

TRANSCRIPT OF RECORD. The printed record as made up in each case for the supreme court of the United States is so called; also in the Circuit Court of Appeals. If a necessary part has been omitted and is subsequently presented to the appellate court, duly certified, it may be made part of the record by direct order. Jurisdiction attaches upon the filing in the court above of the writ of error and is not defeated by irregularity in the transcript or its certification. Burnham v. North Chicago St. R. Co., 30 C.C.A. 594, 87 F. 168.

TRANSCRIPTIO PEDIS FINIS LEVATI MITTENDO IN CANCELLARIUM. A writ which certified the foot of a fine levied before justices in eyre, etc., into the chancery. Reg.Orig. 669.

TRANSCRIPTIO RECOGNITIONIS FACTÆ CORAM JUSTICIARIIS ITINERANTIBUS, Etc. An old writ to certify a cognizance taken by justices in eyre. Reg.Orig. 152.

TRANSFER, *v*. To convey or remove from one place, person, etc., to another; pass or hand over from one to another; specif., to make over the possession or control of (as, to transfer a title to land); sell or give. Chappell v. State, 216 Ind. 666, 25 N.E.2d 999, 1001.

TRANSFER, *n*. An act of the parties, or of the law, by which the title to property is conveyed from one person to another. Innerarity v. Mims, 1 Ala. 669; Sands v. Hill, 55 N.Y. 18; Wallach v. Stein, 136 A. 209, 210, 103 N.J.L. 470; O'Hagan v. Kracke, 165 Misc. 4, 300 N.Y.S. 351, 361. Alienation; conveyance. 2 Bl.Comm. 294.

TRANSFER OF A CAUSE. The removal of a cause from the jurisdiction of one court or judge to another by lawful authority.

TRANSFER IN CONTEMPLATION OF DEATH. A transfer made under a present apprehension on the part of the transferor, from some existing bodily or mental condition or impending peril, creating a reasonable fear that death is near at hand. This apprehension must be direct and animating and the only cause of the transfer. Rea v. Heiner, D.C.Pa., 6 F.2d 389, 392.

TRANSFER TAX. A tax upon the passing of the title to property or a valuable interest therein out of or from the estate of a decedent, by inheritance, devise, or bequest. In re Hoffman's Estate, 143 N.Y. 327, 38 N.E. 311; In re Brez's Estate, 64 N.E. 958, 172 N.Y. 609. Sometimes also applied to a tax on the transfer of property, particularly of an incorporeal nature, such as bonds or shares of stock, between living persons.

TRANSFER TICKET. An undertaking on the part of a common carrier to continue the carriage further without additional charge if the passenger, in accordance with its terms, again presents himself at the proper place for carriage. It generally designates the point at which the journey is to be renewed, but contains no contract, express or implied, for safety in making the transfer. Anton v. St. Louis Public Service Co., 335 Mo. 188, 71 S.W.2d 702, 706.

TRANSFERABLE. A term used in a *quasi* legal sense, to indicate that the character of assignability or negotiability attaches to the particular instrument, or that it may pass from hand to hand, carrying all rights of the original holder. The words "not transferable" are sometimes printed upon a ticket, receipt, or bill of lading, to show that the same will not be good in the hands of any person other than the one to whom first issued.

TRANSFEREE. He to whom a transfer is made. Kramer v. Spradlin, 148 Ga. 805, 98 S.E. 487, 488.

TRANSFERENCE. In Scotch law. The proceeding to be taken upon the death of one of the parties to a pending suit, whereby the action is transferred or continued, in its then condition, from the decedent to his representatives. Transference is either *active* or *passive*; the former, when it is the pursuer (plaintiff) who dies; the latter, upon the death of the defender. Ersk.Inst. 4, 1, 60.

The transferring of a legacy from the person to whom it was originally given to another; this is a species of ademption, but the latter is the more general term, and includes cases not covered by the former.

TRANSFEROR. One who makes a transfer.

TRANSFERUNTUR DOMINIA SINE TITULO ET TRADITIONE, PER USUCAPTIONEM, SCIL, PER LONGAM CONTINUAM ET PACIFICAM POSSESSIONEM. Co. Litt. 113. Rights of dominion are transferred without title or delivery, by usucaption, to-wit, long and quiet possession.

TRANSFRETATIO. Lat. In old English law. A crossing of the strait, [of Dover;] a passing or sailing over from England to France. The royal passages or voyages to Gascony, Brittany, and other parts of France were so called, and time was sometimes computed from them.

TRANSGRESSIO. In old English law. A violation of law. Also trespass; the action of trespass.

TRANSGRESSIO EST CUM MODUS NON SERVATUR NEC MENSURA, DEBIT ENIM QUILIBET IN SUO FACTO MODUM HABERE ET MENSURAM. Co.Litt. 37. Transgression is when neither mode nor measure is preserved, for every one in his act ought to have a mode and measure.

TRANSGRESSIONE. In old English law. A writ or action of trespass.

TRANSGRESSIONE MULTIPLICATA, CRESCAT PŒNÆ INFLICTIO. When transgression is multiplied, let the infliction of punishment be increased. 2 Inst. 479.

TRANSGRESSIVE TRUST. See Trust.

TRANSHIPMENT. In maritime law. The act of taking the cargo out of one ship and loading it in another.

TRANSIENT, *n.* One who, or that which is temporary. Synonymous with transitory, fugitive, fleeting, momentary. Tilly v. Woodham, La.App., 163 So. 771, 772.

TRANSIENT, *adj.* Passing across, as from one thing or person to another; passing with time of short duration; not permanent; not lasting. Tilly v. Woodham, La.App., 163 So. 771, 772.

TRANSIENT FOREIGNER. One who visits the country, without the intention of remaining. Yates v. Iams, 10 Tex. 170.

TRANSIENT MERCHANT. A merchant who engages in the vending or sale of merchandise at any place in the state temporarily, and who does not intend to become, and does not become, a permanent merchant of such place. State v. Fleming, 24 N.D. 593, 140 N.W. 674.

TRANSIENT PERSON. Within venue statute one who is found in state but who has no fixed place of residence therein. Fagg v. Benners, Tex. Civ.App., 47 S.W.2d 872, 873.

TRANSIRE, *v.* Lat. To go, or pass over; to pass from one thing, person, or place to another.

TRANSIRE, *n.* In English law. A warrant or permit for the custom-house to let goods pass.

TRANSIT. A stop-over privilege on a continuous journey granted by carrier by which a break de facto in continuity of carriage of goods is disregarded and two legs of a journey are treated as though covered without interruption, uniting both legs into a through route for which a joint rate can be published. Galveston Truck Line Corporation v. State, Tex.Civ.App., 123 S.W.2d 797, 802; Baltimore and O. R. Co. v. United States, D.C.N.Y., 24 F.Supp. 734, 735.

TRANSIT IN REM JUDICATAM. It passes into a matter adjudged; it becomes converted into a *res judicata* or judgment. A contract upon which a judgment is obtained is said to pass *in rem judicatam.* United States v. Cushman, 2 Sumn. 436, Fed.Cas.No.14,908; 3 East, 251; Robertson v. Smith, 18 Johns. (N.Y.) 480, 9 Am.Dec. 227.

TRANSIT TERRA CUM ONERE. Land passes subject to any burden affecting it. Co. Litt. 231*a*; Broom, Max. 495, 706.

TRANSITIVE COVENANT. See Covenant.

TRANSITORY. Passing from place to place; that may pass or be changed from one place to another; the opposite of "local." See "Action."

TRANSITUS. Lat. Passage from one place to another; transit. *In transitu,* on the passage, transit, or way. 2 Kent, Comm. 543.

TRANSLADO. Span. A transcript.

TRANSLATION. The reproduction in one language of a book, document, or speech in another language.

The transfer of property; but in this sense it is seldom used. 2 Bl.Comm. 294.

In ecclesiastical law. As applied to a bishop, the term denotes his removal from one diocese to another.

TRANSLATITIUM EDICTUM. Lat. In Roman law. The prætor, on his accession to office, did not usually publish an entirely new edict, but retained the whole or a part of that promulgated by his predecessor, as being of an approved or permanently useful character. The portion thus repeated or handed down from year to year was called the *"edictum translatitium."* See Mackeld. Rom. Law, § 36.

TRANSLATIVE FACT. A fact by means of which a right is transferred or passes from one person to another; one, that is, which fulfills the double function of terminating the right of one person to an object, and of originating the right of another to it.

TRANSMISSION. In the civil law. The right which heirs or legatees may have of passing to their successors the inheritance or legacy to which they were entitled, if they happen to die without having exercised their rights. Domat, liv. 3, t. 1, s. 10; 4 Toullier, no. 186; Dig. 50, 17, 54; Code, 6, 51.

TRANSPORT, *n.* In old New York law. A conveyance of land.

TRANSPORT, *v.* To carry or convey from one place to another. Sacramento Nav. Co. v. Salz, 47 S.Ct. 368, 369, 273 U.S. 326, 71 L.Ed. 663; People v. One 1941 Cadillac Club Coupe, 63 Cal.2d 418, 147 P.2d 49, 51.

TRANSPORTATION. The removal of goods or persons from one place to another, by a carrier. Railroad Co. v. Pratt, 22 Wall. 133, 22 L.Ed. 827; Interstate Commerce Com'n v. Brimson, 14 S.Ct. 1125, 154 U.S. 447, 38 L.Ed. 1047; Gloucester Ferry Co. v. Pennsylvania, 5 S.Ct. 826, 114 U.S. 196, 29 L.Ed. 158.

Criminal Law

A species of punishment consisting in removing the criminal from his own country to another, (usually a penal colony,) there to remain in exile for a prescribed period. Fong Yue Ting v. U. S., 13 S.Ct. 1016, 149 U.S. 698, 37 L.Ed. 905.

TRANSUMPT. In Scotch law, an action of transumpt is an action competent to any one having a partial interest in a writing, or immediate use for it, to support his title or defenses in other actions. It is directed against the custodier of the writing, calling upon him to exhibit it, in order that a transumpt, *i. e.*, a copy, may be judicially made and delivered to the pursuer. Bell.

TRAP. A device, as a pitfall, snare, or machine that shuts suddenly as with a spring, for taking game and other animals; a gin. Hence, any device or contrivance by which one may be caught unawares, strategem; snare; gin. Jones v. C. F. Smith Co., 280 Mich. 514, 273 N.W. 786, 787.

It imports an affirmative intent or design either malicious or mischievous, to cause injury. Gumbart v. Waterbury Club Holding Corporation, D.C.Conn., 27 F.Supp. 228, 229, 230.

The doctrine of "trap" as ground for recovery by trespasser is rested upon theory that owner expected trespasser and prepared an injury. Moseley v. Alabama Power Co., 246 Ala. 416, 21 So.2d 305, 307.

TRASLADO. In Spanish law. A copy; a sight. White, New Recop. b. 3, tit. 7, c. 3.

A copy of a document taken by the notary from the original, or a subsequent copy taken from the protocol, and not a copy taken directly from the matrix or protocol. Downing v. Diaz, 80 Tex. 436, 16 S.W. 54.

TRASSANS. Drawing; one who draws. The drawer of a bill of exchange.

TRASSATUS. One who is drawn, or drawn upon. The drawee of a bill of exchange. Heinecc. de Camb. c. 6, §§ 5, 6.

TRAUMA. In medical jurisprudence. A wound; any injury to the body caused by external violence. Periss v. Nevada Industrial Commission, 55 Nev. 40, 24 P.2d 318.

TRAUMATIC. Caused by or resulting from a wound or any external injury; as, traumatic insanity, produced by an injury to or fracture of the skull with consequent pressure on the brain. Straight Creek Fuel Co. v. Hunt, 221 Ky. 265, 298 S.W. 686, 687.

TRAUMATISM. A diseased condition of the body or any part of it caused by a wound or external injury. Markham v. State Industrial Commission, 85 Okl. 81, 205 P. 163, 169.

TRAVAIL. The act of child-bearing. A woman is said to be in her travail from the time the pains of child-bearing commence until her delivery. Scott v. Donovan, 153 Mass. 378, 26 N.E. 871.

TRAVEL. To go from one place to another at a distance; to journey; spoken of voluntary change of place. White v. Beazley, 1 Barn. & Ald. 171; Hancock v. Rand, 94 N.Y. 1, 46 Am.Rep. 112; State v. Smith, 157 Ind. 241, 61 N.E. 566, 87 Am. St.Rep. 205.

TRAVELED PART OF HIGHWAY. See Traveled Way.

TRAVELED PLACE. A place where the public have, in some manner, acquired the legal right to travel. Sanders v. Southern Ry. Co., Carolina Division, 97 S.C. 423, 81 S.E. 786, 788.

TRAVELED WAY. The traveled path, or the path used for public travel, within located limits of the way. Dupuis v. Town of Billerica, 260 Mass. 210, 157 N.E. 339, 341. Also called "traveled part of highway." Westlund v. Iverson, 154 Minn. 52, 191 N.W. 253; Schnabel v. Kafer, 39 S.D. 70, 162 N.W. 935, 936.

TRAVELER. One who passes from place to place, whether for pleasure, instruction, business or health. Lockett v. State, 47 Ala. 45; 10 C.B.N.S. 429.

TRAVELER'S CHECK. A bill of exchange drawn by the issuing bank upon itself, accepted by the act of issuance, and the right of countermand applied to ordinary checks does not exist as to it. It has the characteristics of a cashier's check of the issuing bank. Pines v. United States, C.C.A. Iowa, 123 F.2d 825, 828.

TRAVELING SALESMAN. A person who travels from town to town and who takes or solicits orders for goods, and forwards them to his principal for approval or rejection. T. C. May Co. v. Menzies Shoe Co., 184 N.C. 150, 113 S.E. 593, 594; Upchurch v. City of La Grange, 159 Ga. 113, 125 S.E. 47, 48.

A traveling salesman is not employed or authorized to fix prices. He cannot pass upon the credit or standing of customers. He does not collect accounts. He is not responsible for the quality, condition or delivery of the goods. He makes no personal contracts and he has no other interest in the sale than his compensation for those which are approved by his employer. The territory assigned to him may be confined to a single city or state, or it may cover cities or states. Commonly, the employer pays the salesman's expenses, but sometimes, especially if he works for a commission, he pays his own expenses. Sometimes he is allotted a certain territory and he receives a commission upon all sales which are sent in from that territory. In some cases the employer may direct the routes he is to travel, and in other cases the salesman chooses his own routes. Sometimes the salesman sends the orders directly to his employer and sometimes the customers themselves send in the orders to the employer. He often sells after exhibiting samples. In re Herbert Candy Co., D.C.Pa., 43 F.Supp. 588, 591.

TRAVELING WAYS. As applied to coal mining, places for the passage of workmen to and from different parts of the mine. Ricardo v. Central Coal & Coke Co., 100 Kan. 95, 163 P. 641, 643.

TRAVERSE. In the language of pleading, a traverse signifies a denial. Thus, where a defendant denies any material allegation of fact in the plaintiff's declaration, he is said to traverse it, and the plea itself is thence frequently termed a "traverse." Brown.

Criminal Practice

To put off or delay the trial of an indictment till a succeeding term. More properly, to deny or take issue upon an indictment. 4 Bl.Comm. 351.

General

Common traverse. A simple and direct denial of the material allegations of the opposite pleading, concluding to the country, and without inducement or *absque hoc.*

General traverse. One preceded by a general inducement, and denying in general terms all that is last before alleged on the opposite side, instead of pursuing the words of the allegations which it denies. Gould.Pl. vii. 5.

Special traverse. A peculiar form of traverse or denial, the design of which, as distinguished from a *common* traverse, is to explain or qualify the denial, instead of putting it in the direct and absolute form. It consists of an affirmative and a negative part, the first setting forth the new affirmative matter tending to explain or qualify the denial, and technically called the "inducement," and the latter constituting the direct denial itself, and technically called the "*absque hoc.*" Steph.Pl. 169–180; Allen v. Stevens, 29 N.J.L. 513; Chambers v. Hunt, 18 N.J.L. 352; People v. Pullman's Car Co., 175 Ill. 125, 51 N.E. 664, 64 L.R.A. 366.

Traverse jury. A petit jury; a trial jury; a jury impaneled to try an action or prosecution, as distinguished from a grand jury. State v. James, 96 N.J.L. 132, 114 A. 553, 555, 16 A.L.R. 1141; De Krasner v. State, 54 Ga.App. 41, 187 S.E. 402, 405.

Traverse of indictment or presentment. The taking issue upon and contradicting or denying some chief point of it. Jacob.

Traverse of office. The proving that an inquisition made of lands or goods by the escheator is defective and untruly made. Tomlins. It is the challenging, by a subject, of an inquest of office, as being defective and untruly made. Mozley & Whitley.

Traverse upon a traverse. One growing out of the same point or subject-matter as is embraced in a preceding traverse on the other side.

TRAVERSER. In pleading. One who traverses or denies. A prisoner or party indicted; so called from his traversing the indictment.

TRAVERSING NOTE. This is a pleading in chancery, and consists of a denial put in by the plaintiff on behalf of the defendant, generally denying all the statements in the plaintiff's bill. The effect of it is to put the plaintiff upon proof of the whole contents of his bill, and is only resorted to for the purpose of saving time, and in a case where the plaintiff can safely dispense with an answer. A copy of the note must be served on the defendant. Brown.

TREACHER, TRECHETOUR, or TREACHOUR. A traitor.

TREAD-MILL, or TREAD-WHEEL. An instrument of prison discipline, being a wheel or cylinder with an horizontal axis, having steps attached to it, up which the prisoners walk, and thus put the axis in motion. The men hold on by a fixed rail, and, as their weight presses down the step upon which they tread, they ascend the next step, and thus drive the wheel. Enc. Brit.

TREASON. The offense of attempting by overt acts to overthrow the government of the state to which the offender owes allegiance; or of betraying the state into the hands of a foreign power. Webster.

"Treason" consists of two elements: Adherence to the enemy, and rendering him aid and comfort. Cramer v. U. S., U.S.N.Y., 65 S.Ct. 918, 932, 325 U.S. 1, 89 L.Ed. 1441.

In England, treason is an offense particularly directed against the person of the sovereign, and consists (1) in compassing or imagining the death of the king or queen, or their eldest son and heir; (2) in violating the king's companion, or the king's eldest daughter unmarried, or the wife of the king's eldest son and heir; (3) in levying war against the king in his realm; (4) in adhering to the king's enemies in his realm, giving to them aid and comfort in the realm or elsewhere, and (5) slaying the chancellor, treasurer, or the king's justices of the one bench or the other, justices in eyre, or justices of assize, and all other justices assigned to hear and determine, being in their places doing their offices. 4 Steph.Comm. 185–193; 4 Bl. Comm. 76–84.

Treason against the United States shall consist only in levying war against them, or in adhering to their enemies, giving them aid and comfort. U.S.Const. art. 3, § 3, cl. 1. See Young v. U. S., 97 U.S. 62, 24 L.Ed. 992; U. S. v. Bollman, 1 Cranch, C.C. 373, Fed.Cas.No.14,622; U. S. v. Pryor, 3 Wash.C.C. 234, Fed.Cas.No.16,096.

Constructive Treason

Treason imputed to a person by law from his conduct or course of actions, though his deeds taken severally do not amount to actual treason. This doctrine is not known in the United States.

High Treason

In English law. Treason against the king or sovereign, as distinguished from petit or petty treason, which might formerly be committed against a subject. 4 Bl.Comm. 74, 75; 4 Steph. Comm. 183, 184, note.

Misprision of Treason

See Misprision.

Petit Treason

In English law. The crime committed by a wife in killing her husband, or a servant his lord or master, or an ecclesiastic his lord or ordinary. 4 Bl.Comm. 75.

Treason-felony

Under the English statute 11 & 12 Vict. c. 12, passed in 1848, is the offense of compassing, devising, etc., to depose her majesty from the crown; or to levy war in order to intimidate either house of parliament, etc., or to stir up foreigners by any printing or writing to invade the kingdom. This offense is punishable with penal servitude for life, or for any term not less than five years, etc., under statutes 11 & 12 Vict. c. 12, § 3; 20 & 21 Vict. c. 3, § 2; 27 & 28 Vict. c. 47, § 2. By the statute first above mentioned, the government is enabled to treat as felony many offenses which must formerly have been treated as high treason. Mozley & Whitley.

TREASONABLE. Having the nature or guilt of treason.

TREASURE. A treasure is a thing hidden or buried in the earth, on which no one can prove his property, and which is discovered by chance. Civil Code La. art. 3423, par. 2. See Treasure-Trove.

TREASURE-TROVE. Literally, treasure found. Money or coin, gold, silver, plate or bullion *found* hidden in the earth or other private place, the owner thereof being unknown. 1 Bl.Comm. 295. Called in Latin "*thesaurus inventus*;" and in Saxon "*fynderinga*." Huthmacher v. Harris, 38 Pa. 499, 80 Am.Dec. 502; Vickery v. Hardin, 77 Ind.App. 558, 133 N.E. 922, 923.

Finder of "treasure trove," is entitled thereto as against owner of land where "treasure trove" is found and all the world save the true owner, in absence of statute. Groover v. Tippins, 51 Ga.App. 47, 179 S.E. 634, 635.

TREASURER. An officer of a public or private corporation, company, or government, charged with the receipt, custody, and disbursement of its moneys or funds. See State v. Eames, 39 La. Ann. 986, 3 So. 93; In re Millward-Cliff Cracker Co.'s Estate, 161 Pa. 167, 28 A. 1072; Jones v. Marrs, 114 Tex. 62, 263 S.W. 570, 574.

TREASURER, LORD HIGH. Formerly the chief treasurer of England, who had charge of the moneys in the exchequer, the chancellor of the exchequer being under him. He appointed all revenue officers and escheaters, and leased crown lands. The office is obsolete, and his duties are now performed by the lords commissioners of the treasury. Stim. Gloss.

TREASURER OF THE UNITED STATES. An officer in the treasury department appointed by the president by and with the advice and consent of the senate. His principal duties are—to receive and keep the moneys of the United States, and disburse the same upon warrants drawn by the secretary of the treasury, countersigned by either comptroller and recorded by the register; to take receipts for all moneys paid by him; to render his account to the first comptroller quarterly, or oftener if required, and transmit a copy thereof, when settled, to the secretary of the treasury; to lay before each house, on the third day of every session of congress, fair and accurate copies of all accounts by him from time to time rendered to and settled with the first comptroller, and a true and perfect account of the state of the treasury; to submit at all times to the secretary of the treasury and the comptroller, or either of them, the inspection of the moneys in his hands. (31 U.S.C.A. § 141 et seq.).

The office of the Treasurer of the United States and certain other offices and agencies and their functions were consolidated into the Fiscal Service of the Treasury Department, the function of said office to be administered by the Treasurer of the United States by Reorg. Plan No. III, § 1(a), eff. June 30, 1940, set out in note under 5 U.S.C.A. § 133t.

TREASURER'S REMEMBRANCER. In English law. He whose charge was to put the lord treasurer and the rest of the judges of the exchequer in remembrance of such things as were called on and dealt in for the sovereign's behoof. There is still one in Scotland. Wharton.

TREASURY. A place or building in which stores of wealth are reposited; particularly, a place where the public revenues are deposited and kept, and where money is disbursed to defray the expenses of government. Webster.

That department of government which is charged with the receipt, custody, and disbursement (pursuant to appropriations) of the public revenues or funds.

TREASURY, FIRST LORD OF. A high office of state in Great Britain, usually held by the Prime Minister.

TREASURY BENCH. In the English house of commons, the first row of seats on the right hand of the speaker is so called, because occupied by the first lord of the treasury or principal minister of the crown. Brown.

TREASURY CHEST FUND. A fund, in England, originating in the unusual balances of certain grants of public money, which is used for banking and loan purposes by the commissioners of the treasury. Wharton.

TREASURY NOTE. A note or bill issued by the treasury department by the authority of the United States government, and circulating as money. See Brown v. State, 120 Ala. 342, 25 So. 182.

TREASURY SECURITIES. Such as have been lawfully issued and thereafter have been bought by corporation for a consideration out of corporate funds or otherwise acquired from owners, and not retired but placed as an asset of the corporation in its treasury for future use as such. Miners Nat. Bank of Pottsville v. Frackville Sewerage Co., 157 Pa.Super. 167, 42 A.2d 177, 179.

TREASURY STOCK. Ordinarily stock which has been issued as fully paid to stockholders and subsequently acquired by the corporation to be used by it in furtherance of its corporate purposes, and stock which is merely to be held as unsubscribed for and unissued is not usually regarded as "treasury stock". In re Public Service Holding Corporation, Del., 24 A.2d 584, 586.

TREATMENT. A broad term covering all the steps taken to effect a cure of an injury or disease; the word including examination and diagnosis as well as application of remedies. Kirschner v. Equitable Life Assur. Soc. of U. S., 157 Misc. 635, 284 N.Y.S. 506, 510; Hester v. Ford, 221 Ala. 592, 130 So. 203, 206.

TREATY.

International Law

A compact made between two or more independent nations with a view to the public welfare. Louis Wolf & Co. v. United States, Cust. & Pat.App., 107 F.2d 819, 827; United States v. Belmont, N.Y., 57 S.Ct. 758, 761, 301 U.S. 324, 81 L. Ed. 1134.

An agreement, league, or contract between two or more nations or sovereigns, formally signed by commissioners properly authorized, and solemnly ratified by the several sovereigns or the supreme power of each state. Edye v. Robertson, 5 S.Ct. 247, 112 U.S. 580, 28 L.Ed. 798; Ex parte Ortiz, C.C.Minn., 100 F. 962; Charlton v. Kelly, 33 S.Ct. 945, 954, 29 S.Ct. 447, 57 L.Ed. 1274, 46 L.R.A., N.S., 397.

A "treaty" is not only a law but also a contract between two nations and must, if possible, be so construed as to give full force and effect to all its parts. United States v. Reid, C.C.A.Or., 73 F.2d 153, 155.

Personal treaties relate exclusively to the persons of the contracting sovereigns, such as family alliances, and treaties guaranteeing the throne to a particular sovereign and his family. As they relate to the persons, they expire of course on the death of the sovereign or the extinction of his family. With the advent of constitutional government in Europe these treaties have lost their importance. *Real* treaties relate solely to the subject-matters of the convention, independently of the persons of the contracting parties, and continue to bind the state, although there may be changes in its constitution or in the persons of its rulers. Boyd's Wheat. Int. Law § 29.

Private Law

The discussion of terms which immediately precedes the conclusion of a contract or other transaction. A warranty on the sale of goods, to be valid, must be made during the "treaty" preceding the sale. Chit. Cont. 419; Sweet.

TREATY OF PEACE. An agreement or contract made by belligerent powers, in which they agree to lay down their arms, and by which they stipulate the conditions of peace and regulate the manner in which it is to be restored and supported. Vattel, b. 4, c. 2, § 9.

TREBELLANIC PORTION. In consequence of this article, the trebellanic portion of the civil law—that is to say, the portion of the property of the testator which the instituted heir had a right to detain when he was charged with a *fidei commissa* or fiduciary bequest—is no longer a part of our law. Civ.Code La. art. 1520, par. 3.

TREBLE COSTS. See Costs.

TREBLE DAMAGES. In practice. Damages given by statute in certain cases, consisting of the single damages found by the jury, actually tripled in amount. The usual practice has been for the jury to find the single amount of the damages, and for the court, on motion, to order that amount to be trebled. 2 Tidd, Pr. 893, 894.

TREBUCKET. A tumbrel, castigatory, or cucking stool. See James v. Comm., 12 Serg. & R. (Pa.) 227.

TREE. A woody plant, the branches of which spring from, and are supported upon, a trunk or body. Nettles v. Lichtman, 228 Ala. 52, 152 So. 450, 452, 91 A.L.R. 1455.

TREET. In old English law. Fine wheat.

TREMAGIUM, TREMESIUM. In old records. The season or time of sowing summer corn, being about March, the third month, to which the word may allude. Cowell.

TRES FACIUNT COLLEGIUM. Three make a corporation; three members are requisite to constitute a corporation. Dig. 50, 16, 8; 1 Bl.Comm. 469.

TRESAEL. L. Fr. A great-great-grandfather. Britt. c. 119. Otherwise written *"tresaiel,"* and *"tresayle."* 3 Bl.Comm. 186; Litt. § 20.

TRESAYLE. An abolished writ sued on ouster by abatement, on the death of the grandfather's grandfather.

TRESPASS. Doing of unlawful act or of lawful act in unlawful manner to injury of another's person or property. Waco Cotton Oil Mill of Waco v. Walker, Tex.Civ.App., 103 S.W.2d 1071, 1072. An unlawful act committed with violence, actual or implied, causing injury to the person, property, or relative rights of another; an injury or misfeasance to the person, property, or rights of another, done with force and violence, either actual or implied in law. Grunson v. State, 89 Ind. 536, 46 Am.Rep. 178; Southern Ry. Co. v. Harden, 101 Ga. 263, 28 S.E. 847; Brown v. Walker, 188 N.C. 52, 123 S.E. 633, 636. It comprehends not only forcible wrongs, but also acts the consequences of which make them tortious. Mawson v. Vess Beverage Co., Mo.App., 173 S.W.2d 606, 612, 613, 614.

Trespass, in its most comprehensive sense, signifies any transgression or offense against the law of nature, of society, or of the country in which we live; and this, whether it relates to a man's person or to his property. In its more limited and ordinary sense, it signifies an injury committed with violence, and this violence may be either actual or implied; and the law will imply violence though none is actually used, when the injury is of a direct and immediate kind, and committed on the person or tangible and corporeal property of the plaintiff. Of actual violence, an assault and battery is an instance; of implied, a peaceable but wrongful entry upon a person's land. Brown.

In practice a form of action, at the common law, which lies for redress in the shape of money damages for any unlawful injury done to the plaintiff, in respect either to his person, property, or rights, by the immediate force and violence of the defendant.

Continuing trespass. One which is in its nature a permanent invasion of the rights of another; as, where a person builds on his own land so that a part of the building overhangs his neighbor's land. H. H. Hitt Lumber Co. v. Cullman Property Co., 189 Ala. 13, 66 So. 720, 721.

Joint trespass. Where two or more persons unite in committing it, or where some actually commit the tort, the others command, encourage or direct it. Stephens v. Schadler, 182 Ky. 833, 207 S.W. 704.

Permanent trespass. One which consists of a series of acts, done on successive days, which are of the same nature, and are renewed or continued from day to day, so that, in the aggregate, they make up one indivisible wrong. 3 Bl.Comm. 212.

Trespass de bonis asportatis. (Trespass for goods carried away.) In practice. The technical name of that species of action of trespass for injuries to personal property which lies where the injury consists in *carrying away* the goods or property. See 3 Bl.Comm. 150, 151.

Trespass for mesne profits. A form of action supplemental to an action of ejectment, brought against the tenant in possession to recover the profits which he has wrongfully received during the time of his occupation. 3 Bl.Comm. 205.

Trespass on the case. The form of action, at common law, adapted to the recovery of damages for some injury resulting to a party from the wrongful act of another, unaccompanied by direct or immediate force, or which is the indirect or secondary consequence of defendant's act. Commonly called, by abbreviation, "Case." Munal v. Brown, C.C.Colo., 70 F. 968; Nolan v. Railroad Co., 70 Conn. 159, 39 A. 115, 43 L.R.A. 305; New York Life Ins. Co. v. Clay County, 221 Iowa 966, 267 N.W. 79, 80.

Trespass quare clausum fregit. "Trespass wherefore he broke the close." The common-law action for damages for an unlawful entry or trespass upon the plaintiff's land. In the Latin form of the writ, the defendant was called upon to show why he broke the plaintiff's close; *i. e.*, the real or imaginary structure inclosing the land, whence the name. It is commonly abbreviated to *"trespass qu. cl. fr."* See Kimball v. Hilton, 92 Me. 214, 42 A. 394. See, also, Trespass to try title, infra.

Trespass to try title. The name of the action used in several of the states for the recovery of the possession of real property, with damages for any trespass committed upon the same by the defendant.

A procedure by which rival claims to title or right to possession of land may be adjudicated, and as an incident partition may also be had when the controversy concerning title or right to possession is settled. Tide Water Oil Co. v. Bean, Tex.Civ.App., 148 S.W.2d 184, 187, 188.

It is different from "trespass quare clausum fregit," in that title must be proved. Bethea v. Home Furniture Co., 185 S.C. 271, 194 S.E. 10, 11.

Trespass vi et armis. Trespass with force and arms. The common-law action for damages for any injury committed by the defendant with direct and immediate force or violence against the plaintiff or his property. See Mawson v. Vess Beverage Co., Mo.App., 173 S.W.2d 606, 613.

TRESPASSER. One who has committed trespass.

Joint Trespassers

Two or more who unite in committing a trespass. Kansas City v. File, 60 Kan. 157, 55 P. 877; Bonte v. Postel, 109 Ky. 64, 58 S.W. 536, 51 L.R.A. 187.

Trespasser Ab Initio

Trespasser from the beginning. A term applied to a tort-feasor whose acts relate back so as to make a previous act, at the time innocent, unlawful; as if he enter peaceably, and subsequently commit a breach of the peace, his entry is considered a trespass. Stim. Gloss. See Wright v. Marvin, 59 Vt. 437, 9 A. 601.

TRESTORNARE. In old English law. To turn aside; to divert a stream from its course. Bract. fols. 115, 234*b*. To turn or alter the course of a road. Cowell.

TRESVIRI. Lat. In Roman law. Officers who had the charge of prisons, and the execution of condemned criminals. Calvin.

TRET. An allowance made for the water or dust that may be mixed with any commodity. It differs from *tare*, (*q. v.*).

TRETHINGA. In old English law. A trithing; the court of a trithing.

TREYT. Withdrawn, as a juror. Written also *treat*. Cowell.

TRIA CAPITA, in Roman law, were *civitas, libertas,* and *familia; i. e.*, citizenship, freedom, and family rights.

TRIAL. A judicial examination, in accordance with law of the land, of a cause, either civil or criminal, of the issues between the parties, whether of law or fact, before a court that has jurisdiction over it. People v. Vitale, 364 Ill. 589, 5 N.E. 2d 474, 475. Gulf, C. & S. F. Ry. Co. v. Muse, 109 Tex. 352, 207 S.W. 897, 899, 4 A.L.R. 613; State v. Dubray, 121 Kan. 886, 250 P. 316, 319; Photo Cines Co. v. American Film Mfg. Co., 190 Ill.App. 124, 128. For purpose of determining such issue. City of Pasadena v. Superior Court in and for Los Angeles County, 212 Cal. 309, 298 P. 968, 970; State ex rel. Stokes v. Second Judicial Dist. Court, in and for Washoe County, 55 Nev. 115, 127 P.2d 534.

It includes all proceedings from time when issue is joined, or, more usually, when parties are called to try their case in court, to time of its final determination. Molen v. Denning & Clark Livestock Co., 56 Idaho 57, 50 P.2d 9, 11.

And in its strict definition, the word "trial" in criminal procedure means the proceedings in open court after the pleadings are finished and the prosecution is otherwise ready, down to and including the rendition of the verdict. Thomas v. Mills, 117 Ohio St. 114, 157 N.E. 488, 489, 54 A. L.R. 1220.

Fair and Impartial Trial

See Fair and Impartial Trial.

Fair Trial

See Fair Trial.

Mistrial

See that title.

New Trial

A re-examination of an issue of fact in the same court after a trial and decision by a jury or court or by referees. Code Civ.Proc.Cal. § 656. A re-examination of the issue in the same court, before another jury, after a verdict has been given. Pen.Code Cal. § 1179. A re-examination in the same court of an issue of fact, or some part or portions thereof, after the verdict by a jury, report of a referee, or a decision by the court. Rev. Code Iowa 1880, § 2837 (Code 1931, § 11549). And see Oxford v. State, 80 Okl. 103, 194 P. 101; Warner v. Goding, 91 Fla. 260, 107 So. 406, 408.

New Trial Paper

In English practice. A paper containing a list of causes in which rules *nisi* have been obtained for a new trial, or for entering a verdict in place of a nonsuit, or for entering judgment *non obstante veredicto,* or for otherwise varying or setting aside proceedings which have taken place at *nisi prius.* These are called on for argument in the order in which they stand in the paper, on days appointed by the judges for the purpose. Brown.

Public Trial

A trial held in public, in the presence of the public, or in a place accessible and open to the attendance of the public at large, or of persons who may properly be admitted. "The requirement of a public trial is for the benefit of the accused; that the public may see he is fairly dealt with and not unjustly condemned, and that the presence of interested spectators may keep his triers keenly alive to a sense of their responsibility and to the importance of their functions; and the requirement is fairly observed if, without partiality or favoritism, a reasonable proportion of the public is suffered to attend, notwithstanding that those persons whose presence could be of no service to the accused, and who would only be drawn thither by a prurient curiosity, are excluded altogether." Cooley, Const.Lim. *312. And see People v. Hall, 64 N.Y.S. 433, 51 App.Div. 57; Commonwealth v. Trinkle, 124 A. 191, 192, 279 Pa. 564; People v. Greeson, 203 N.W. 141, 149, 230 Mich. 124.

Separate Trial

See Separate.

Speedy Trial

See that title.

State Trial

See State.

Trial Amendment

Pleading that a litigant files during progress of actual trial of case, office of which is to meet some situation that is developed by evidence. Texas Electric Service Co. v. Kinkead, Tex.Civ. App., 84 S.W.2d 567, 570.

Trial at Bar

A species of trial now seldom resorted to, excepting in cases where the matter in dispute is one of great importance and difficulty. It takes place before all the judges at the bar of the court in which the action is brought. Brown. See 2 Tidd, Pr. 747; Steph.Pl. 84.

Trial at Nisi Prius

In practice. The ordinary kind of trial which takes place at the sittings, assizes, or circuit, before a single judge. 2 Tidd, Pr. 751, 819.

Trial by Certificate

A form of trial allowed in cases where the evidence of the person certifying was the only proper criterion of the point in dispute. Under such circumstances, the issue might be determined by the certificate alone, because, if sent to a jury, it would be conclusive upon them, and therefore their intervention was unnecessary. Tomlins.

Trial by Fire

See Ordeal.

Trial by Grand Assize

A peculiar mode of trial allowed in writs of right. See Assize; Grand Assize.

Trial by Inspection or Examination

A form of trial in which the judges of the court, upon the testimony of their own senses, decide the point in dispute.

Trial by Jury

A trial in which the issues of fact are to be determined by the verdict of a jury of twelve men, duly selected, impaneled, and sworn. The terms "jury" and "trial by jury" were used at the adoption of the constitution, and always, it is believed, before that time, and almost always since, in a single sense. A jury for the trial of a cause was a body of twelve men, described as upright, well-qualified, and lawful men, disinterested and impartial, not of kin nor personal dependents of either of the parties, having their homes within the jurisdictional limits of the court, drawn and selected by officers free from all bias in favor of or against either party, duly impaneled under the direction of a competent court, sworn to render a true verdict according to the law and the evidence given them, who, after hearing the parties and their evidence, and receiving the instructions of the court relative to the law involved in the trial, and deliberating, when necessary, apart from all extraneous influences, must return their unanimous verdict upon the issue submitted to them. State v. McClear, 11 Nev. 60. And see Gunn v. Union R. Co., 23 R.I. 289, 49 A. 999; State v. Hamey, 168 Mo. 167, 67 S.W. 620, 57 L.R.A. 846; Branham v. Commonwealth, 209 Ky. 734, 273 S.W. 489, 490; Davis v. Central States Fire Ins. Co., 121 Kan. 69, 245 P. 1062, 1063; N. Wagman & Co. v. Schafer Motor Freight Service, 167 Misc. 681, 4 N.Y.S.2d 526, 529.

In a federal court a trial by jury as understood and applied at common law and includes all the essential elements as they were recognized in this country and England when the constitution was adopted, including a jury of 12 men, neither more nor less. U.S.C.A.Const. art. 3, § 2, cl. 3; Amend. 6. Coates v. Lawrence, D.C.Ga., 46 F.Supp. 414, 423.

The Seventh Amendment to Federal Constitution declaring the right of "trial by jury" applies only to suits at common law. U.S.C.A.Const.Amend. 7. Ransom v. Staso Milling Co., D.C.Vt., 2 F.R.D. 128, 130, 131.

A right to a "trial by jury" when given by a constitution means a trial by a jury of 12, but where the right to a jury trial is not given by the constitution, the legislature may fix the number of jurors at less than 12. Doyle v.

Police Court of City of Niagara Falls, 177 Misc. 359, 30 N.Y.S.2d 324, 325. And is right to a jury trial in such cases as it existed at time of adoption of constitution. Blum v. Fresh Grown Preserve Corporation, N.Y., 292 N.Y. 241, 54 N.E.2d 809, 810.

Trial by Proviso

A proceeding allowed where the plaintiff in an action desists from prosecuting his suit, and does not bring it to trial in convenient time. The defendant, in such case, may take out the *venire facias* to the sheriff, containing these words, *"proviso quod,"* etc., *i. e.*, provided that. If plaintiff take out any writ to that purpose, the sheriff shall summon but one jury on them both. This is called "going to trial by proviso." Jacob, tit. "Proviso."

Trial by the Record

A form of trial resorted to where issue is taken upon a plea of *nul tiel record*, in which case the party asserting the existence of a record as pleaded is bound to produce it in court on a day assigned. If the record is forthcoming, the issue is tried by inspection and examination of it. If the record is not produced, judgment is given for his adversary. 3 Bl.Comm. 330.

Trial by Wager of Battel

See Wager of Battel.

Trial by Wager of Law

In old English law. A method of trial, where the defendant, coming into court, made oath that he did not owe the claim demanded of him, and eleven of his neighbors, as compurgators, swore that they believed him to speak the truth. 3 Bl. Comm. 343. See Wager of Law.

Trial by Witnesses

The name "trial *per testes*" has been used for a trial without the intervention of a jury, is the only method of trial known to the civil law, and is adopted by depositions in chancery. The judge is thus left to form, in his own breast, his sentence upon the credit of the witnesses examined. But it is very rarely used at common law. Tomlins.

Trial De Novo

A new trial or retrial had in an appellate court in which the whole case is gone into as if no trial whatever had been had in the court below. See Karcher v. Green, 32 A. 225, 8 Houst. (Del.) 163; Ex parte Morales, Tex.Cr.App., 53 S.W. 108; Carlson v. Avery Co., 196 Ill.App. 262, 272; Bardwell v. Riverside Oil and Refining Co., 139 Okl. 26, 280 P. 1083, 1085.

Trial Jury

See Jury.

Trial List

A list of cases marked down for trial for any one term.

Trial With Assessors

Admiralty actions involving nautical questions, *e. g.*, actions of collision, are generally tried in England before a judge, with Trinity Masters sitting as assessors. Rosc.Adm. 179.

TRIATIO IBI SEMPER DEBET FIERI, UBI JURATORES MELIOREM POSSUNT HABERE NOTITIAM. Trial ought always to be had where the jurors can have the best information. 7 Coke, 1.

TRIBAL LANDS. Lands of Indian reservation which are not occupied by individual Indians and are the unallotted or common lands of the nation. Tuscarora Nation of Indians v. Williams, 79 Misc. 445, 141 N.Y.S. 207, 208.

Land allotted in severalty to a restricted Indian is no longer part of the "reservation" nor is it "tribal land" but the virtual fee is in the allottee with certain restrictions on the right of alienation. United States v. Oklahoma Gas & Electric Co., C.C.A.Okl., 127 F.2d 349, 353.

TRIBUERE. Lat. In the civil law. To give; to distribute.

TRIBUNAL. The seat of a judge; the place where he administers justice. The whole body of judges who compose a jurisdiction; a judicial court; the jurisdiction which the judges exercise. See Foster v. Worcester, 16 Pick. (Mass.) 81.

Roman Law

An elevated seat occupied by the prætor, when he judged, or heard causes in form. Originally a kind of stage made of wood in the form of a square, and movable, but afterwards built of stone in the form of a semicircle. Adams, Rom. Ant. 132, 133.

TRIBUNAUX DE COMMERCE. In French law. Certain courts composed of a president, judges, and substitutes, which take cognizance of all cases between merchants, and of disagreements among partners. Appeals lie from them to the courts of justice. Brown.

TRIBUTARY, *n.* Any stream flowing directly or indirectly into a river. [1895] 1 Q.B. 237; Bull v. Siegrist, 169 Or. 180, 126 P.2d 832, 834.

TRIBUTARY, *adj.* Paying or yielding tribute, taxed or assessed by tribute. Amsbary v. City of Twin Falls, 34 Idaho 313, 200 P. 723, 724.

TRIBUTE. A contribution which is raised by a prince or sovereign from his subjects to sustain the expenses of the state.

A sum of money paid by an inferior sovereign or state to a superior potentate, to secure the friendship or protection of the latter. Brande.

TRICESIMA. An ancient custom in a borough in the county of Hereford, so called because thirty burgesses paid 1d. rent for their houses to the bishop, who was lord of the manor. Wharton.

TRIDING-MOTE. The court held for a triding or trithing. Cowell.

TRIDUUM. In old English law. The space of three days. Fleta, lib. 1, c. 31, § 7.

TRIENNIAL ACT. An act of parliament of 1641, which provided that if in every third year parliament was not summoned and assembled before September 3, it should assemble on the second Monday of the next November.

Also an act of 1694, which provided that a parliament be called within three years after dissolution, and that the utmost limit of a parliament be three years. This was followed by the Septennial Act of 1716.

TRIENS. Lat.

In feudal law. Dower or third. 2 Bl.Comm. 129.

In Roman law. A subdivision of the *as,* containing four *unciæ;* the proportion of four-twelfths or one-third. 2 Bl.Comm. 462, note *m.* A copper coin of the value of one-third of the *as.* Brande.

TRIGAMUS. In old English law. One who has been thrice married; one who, at different times and successively, has had three wives; a trigamist. 3 Inst. 88.

TRIGILD. In Saxon law. A triple gild, geld, or payment; three times the value of a thing, paid as a composition or satisfaction. Spelman.

TRINEPOS. (Lat.) In Roman law. Great-grandson of a grandchild.

TRINEPTIS. (Lat.) Great-granddaughter of a grandchild.

TRINITY HOUSE. In English law. A society at Deptford Strond, Incorporated by Hen. VIII. in 1515, for the promotion of commerce and navigation by licensing and regulating pilots, and ordering and erecting beacons, light-houses, buoys, etc. Wharton.

TRINITY MASTERS. Elder brethren of the Trinity House. If a question arising in an admiralty action depends upon technical skill and experience in navigation, the judge or court is usually assisted at the hearing by two Trinity Masters, who sit as assessors, and advise the court on questions of a nautical character. Williams & B. Adm. Jur. 271; Sweet.

TRINITY SITTINGS. Sittings of the English court of appeal and of the high court of justice in London and Middlesex, commencing on the Tuesday after Whitsun week, and terminating on the 8th of August.

TRINITY TERM. One of the four terms of the English courts of common law, beginning on the 22d day of May, and ending on the 12th of June. 3 Steph.Comm. 562.

TRINIUMGELDUM. In old European law. An extraordinary kind of composition for an offense, consisting of *three times nine,* or twenty-seven times the single geld or payment. Spelman.

TRINKETS. Small articles of personal adornment or use when the object is essentially ornamental. 28 L.J.C.P. 626.

TRINODA NECESSITAS. Lat. In Saxon law. A threefold necessity or burden. A term used to denote the three things from contributing to the performance of which no lands were exempted, viz., *pontis reparatio* (the repair of bridges,) *arcis constructio,* (the building of castles,) *et expeditio contra hostem,* (military service against an enemy.) 1 Bl.Comm. 263, 357.

TRIORS. In practice. Persons who are appointed to try challenges to jurors, *i. e.,* to hear and determine whether a juror challenged for favor is or is not qualified to serve.

The lords chosen to try a peer, when indicted for felony, in the court of the lord high steward, are also called "triors." Mozley & Whitley.

TRIP, *n.* A journey or going from one place to another. F. S. Royster Guano Co. v. Globe & Rutgers Fire Ins. Co., 252 N.Y. 75, 168 N.E. 834, 837.

In mining, a number of cars attached together and drawn by a mule. Maize v. Big Creek Coal Co., Mo.App., 203 S.W. 633, 634.

TRIP, *v.* To make a false step; to catch the foot; to stumble; to cause to stumble, or take a false step; to cause to lose the footing, as by suddenly checking the motion of a foot or leg; to throw off balance. Johnston v. City of St. Louis, Mo.App., 138 S.W.2d 666, 671.

TRIPARTITE. In conveyancing. Of three parts; a term applied to an indenture to which there are three several parties, (of the first, second, and third parts,) and which is executed in triplicate.

TRIPLE ALLIANCE. A treaty between Germany, Austria-Hungary and Italy, formed at the close of the Franco-Prussian War (1870–71).

TRIPLE ENTENTE. A treaty between Russia, France and Great Britain, formed early in the 20th century.

TRIPLICACION. L. Fr. In old pleading. A rejoinder in pleading; the defendant's answer to the plaintiff's replication. Britt. c. 77.

TRIPLICATIO. Lat. In the civil law. The reply of the plaintiff to the rejoinder of the defendant. It corresponds to the surrejoinder of common law. Inst. 4, 14; Bract. l. 5, t. 5, c. 1.

TRISTRIS. In old forest law. A freedom from the duty of attending the lord of a forest when engaged in the chase. Spelman.

TRITAVIA. Lat. In the civil law. A great-grandmother's great-grandmother; the female ascendant in the sixth degree.

TRITAVUS. Lat. In the civil law. A great-grandfather's great-grandfather; the male ascendant in the sixth degree.

TRITHING. In Saxon law. One of the territorial divisions of England, being the *third* part of a county, and comprising three or more hundreds. Within the trithing there was a court held (called "trithing-mote") which resembled the court-leet, but was inferior to the county court.

TRITHING–MOTE. The court held for a trithing or riding.

TRITHING–REEVE. The officer who superintended a trithing or riding.

TRIUMVIR. Lat. In old English law. A trithing man or constable of three hundred. Cowell.

TRIUMVIRI CAPITALES. Lat. In Roman law. Officers who had charge of the prison, through whose intervention punishments were inflicted. They had eight lictors to execute their orders. Vicat, Voc.Jur.

TRIVERBIAL DAYS. In the civil law. Juridical days; days allowed to the prætor for deciding causes; days on which the prætor might speak the *three* characteristic *words* of his office, viz., *do, dico, addico.* Calvin. Otherwise called *"dies fasti."* 3 Bl.Comm. 424, and note *u.*

TRIVIAL. Trifling; inconsiderable; of small worth or importance. In equity, a demurrer will lie to a bill on the ground of the *triviality* of the matter in dispute, as being below the dignity of the court. 4 Bouv.Inst. no. 4237.

TRONAGE. In English law. A customary duty or toll for weighing wool; so called because it was weighed by a common *trona,* or beam. Fleta, lib. 2, c. 12.

TRONATOR. A weigher of wool. Cowell.

TROOPS. Within railroad land grant acts, requiring the railroads to transport free from toll or other charge troops of the United States, and in the land grant equalization agreements, whereby the railroads were to transport such troops at half rates, means soldiers collectively, a body of soldiers, and does not include discharged soldiers or military prisoners, rejected applicants for enlistment returning home from recruiting depots, accepted applicants for enlistment going to recruiting depots, retired soldiers or soldiers on furloughs, traveling as individuals and not as a body. United States v. Union Pac. R. Co., 39 S.Ct. 294, 295, 249 U.S. 354, 63 L.Ed. 643; Southern Pac. Co. v. U. S., 52 S.Ct. 324, 325, 285 U.S. 240, 76 L.Ed. 736. Or army engineers, engaged in improvement of rivers and harbors. Southern Pac. Co. v. U. S., 52 S.Ct. 324, 326, 285 U.S. 240, 76 L.Ed. 736.

TROPHY. Anything taken from an enemy and shown or treasured up in proof of victory; a price or token of victory in any contest; hence, a memento of victory or success; an ornamental group of objects hung together on a wall, or any collection of objects typical of some event, art, industry, or branch of knowledge; a memento or memorial. In re Vortex Cup Co., Cust. & Pat.App., 83 F.2d 821, 822.

TROPHY MONEY. Money formerly collected and raised in London, and the several counties of England, towards providing harness and maintenance for the militia, etc.

TROVER. In common-law practice, the action of trover (or trover and conversion) is a species of action on the case, and originally lay for the recovery of damages against a person who had *found* another's goods and wrongfully converted them to his own use. Subsequently the allegation of the loss of the goods by the plaintiff and the finding of them by the defendant was merely fictitious, and the action became the remedy for any wrongful interference with or detention of the goods of another. 3 Steph.Comm. 425. Sweet. See Burnham v. Pidcock, 33 Misc. 65, 66 N.Y.S. 806; Spellman v. Richmond & D. R. Co., 35 S.C. 475, 14 S.E. 947, 28 Am.St.Rep. 858; Daisy-Belle Petroleum Co. v. Thomas, 151 Okl. 94, 1 P.2d 700, 702. In form a fiction; in substance, a remedy to recover the value of personal chattels *wrongfully* converted by another to his own use. 1 Burr. 31; Athens & Pomeroy Coal & Land Co. v. Tracy, 22 Ohio App. 21, 153 N.E. 240, 243; Siverson v. Clanton, 88 Or. 261, 170 P. 933, 935. See Conversion.

A possessory action wherein plaintiff must show that he has either a general or special property in thing converted and the right to its possession at the time of the alleged conversion. Patten v. Dennison, 137 Me. 1, 14 A.2d 12. And lies only for wrongful appropriation of goods, chattels, or personal property which is specific enough to be identified. Olschewski v. Hudson, 87 Cal.App. 282, 262 P. 43, 46.

TROY WEIGHT. A weight of twelve ounces to the pound, having its name from Troyes, a city in Aube, France.

TRUCE. In international law. A suspension or temporary cessation of hostilities by agreement between belligerent powers; an armistice. Wheat. Int.Law, 442.

TRUCE OF GOD. In medieval law. A truce or suspension of arms promulgated by the church, putting a stop to private hostilities at certain periods or during certain sacred seasons.

TRUCK. Wheeled vehicle for carrying heavy weight; an automobile for transporting heavy loads. Paltani v. Sentinel Life Ins. Co., 121 Neb. 447, 237 N.W. 392.

TRUCK ACTS. Acts in England, 1 & 2 Wm. IV, amended in 1887 and 1896, which provide that workmen shall not have unreasonable deductions made from their wages (as for fines, damaged goods, materials, or tools), nor have their wages paid otherwise than in current coin, nor be obliged to spend them in any particular place or manner.

TRUE. Conformable to fact; correct; exact; actual; genuine; honest. See First State Bank of Teague v. Hadden, Tex.Civ.App., 158 S.W. 1168, 1170.

In one sense, that only is "true" which is conformable to the actual state of things. In that sense, a statement is "untrue" which does not express things exactly as they are. But in another and broader sense the word "true" is often used as a synonym of "honest", "sincere", not "fraudulent." Zolintakis v. Equitable Life Assur. Soc. of United States, C.C.A.Utah, 108 F.2d 902, 905; Moulor v. American Life Ins. Co., 4 S.Ct. 466, 111 U.S. 335, 28 L.Ed. 447.

TRUE ADMISSION. A formal act done in course of judicial proceedings which waives or dispenses with production of evidence by conceding for purposes of litigation that proposition of fact alleged by opponent is true. Maltz v. Jackoway-Katz Cap Co., 336 Mo. 1000, 82 S.W.2d 909, 917.

TRUE BILL. In criminal practice. The indorsement made by a grand jury upon a bill of indictment, when they find it sustained by the evidence laid before them, and are satisfied of the truth of the accusation. 4 Bl.Comm. 306.

TRUE COPY. A true copy, does not mean an absolutely exact copy but means that the copy shall be so true that anybody can understand it. It may contain an error or omission. 51 L.J.Ch. 905.

TRUE, PUBLIC, AND NOTORIOUS. These three qualities used to be formally predicated in the libel in the ecclesiastical courts, of the charges which it contained, at the end of each article severally. Wharton.

TRUE VALUE RULE. Under this rule, one who subscribes for and receives corporate stock must pay therefor the par value thereof either in money or in money's worth, so that the real assets of the corporation shall at least square with its books, and whenever, whether by fraud, accident or mistake, the true value of property, labor or services received in payment does not equal par value, stock is deemed unpaid for to the full extent of the difference, and holders are liable to creditors for the difference, notwithstanding good faith of directors. Johansen v. St. Louis Union Trust Co., 345 Mo. 135, 131 S.W.2d 599, 603.

TRUE VERDICT. The voluntary conclusion of the jury after deliberate consideration, and it is none the less a true verdict because the respective jurors may have been liberal in concessions to each other, if conscientiously and freely made. A verdict is not a "true verdict," the result of any arbitrary rule or order, whether imposed by themselves, or by the court or officer in charge. Mann v. State, 26 Ala.App. 558, 163 So. 821.

TRUNK RAILWAY. See Railway.

TRUST.

1. In General

A right of property, real or personal, held by one party for the benefit of another. See Goodwin v. McMinn, 193 Pa. 646, 44 A. 1094, 74 Am.St. Rep. 703; Boyce v. Mosely, 102 S.C. 361, 86 S.E. 771, 773; King v. Richardson, C.C.A.N.C., 136 F.2d 849, 856, 857. A confidence reposed in one person, who is termed trustee, for the benefit of another, who is called the cestui que trust, respecting property which is held by the trustee for the benefit of the cestui que trust. State ex rel. Wirt v. Superior Court for Spokane County, 10 Wash.2d 362, 116 P.2d 752, 755. Any arrangement whereby property is transferred with intention that it be administered by trustee for another's benefit. Raffo v. Foltz, 106 Cal.App. 51, 288 P. 884, 886.

A fiduciary relation with respect to property, subjecting person by whom the property is held to equitable duties to deal with the property for the benefit of another person which arises as the result of a manifestation of an intention to create it. Goodenough v. Union Guardian Trust Co., 267 N.W. 772, 773, 774, 275 Mich. 698. An obligation on a person arising out of confidence reposed in him to apply property faithfully and according to such confidence; as being in nature of deposition by which proprietor transfers to another property of subject intrusted, not that it should remain with him, but that it should be applied to certain uses for the behoof of third party. MacKenzie v. Union Guardian Trust Co., 262 Mich. 563, 247 N.W. 914, 919; Gurnett v. Mutual Life Ins. Co. of New York, 356 Ill. 612, 191 N.E. 250, 252.

A "trust" can be created for any purpose which is not illegal, and which is not against public policy. Collins v. Lyon, Inc., 181 Va. 230, 24 S.E.2d 572, 579.

Essential elements of "trust" are designated beneficiary and trustee, fund sufficiently identified to enable title to pass to trustee, and actual delivery to trustee with intention of passing title. City Bank Farmers' Trust Co. v. Charity Organization Soc. of City of New York, 238 App. Div. 720, 265 N.Y.S. 267.

Accessory trust. In Scotch law, equivalent to "active" or "special" trust. See *infra*.

Active trust. One which imposes upon the trustee the duty of taking active measures in the execution of the trust, as, where property is conveyed to trustees with directions to sell and distribute the proceeds among creditors of the grantor; distinguished from a "passive" or "dry" trust. In re Buch's Estate, 278 Pa. 185, 122 A. 239, 240; Welch v. Northern Bank & Trust Co., 100 Wash. 349, 170 P. 1029, 1032.

Cestui que trust. The person for whose benefit a trust is created or who is to enjoy the income or the avails of it.

Charitable trusts. Trusts designed for the benefit of a class or the public generally. They are essentially different from private trusts in that the beneficiaries are uncertain. Bauer v. Myers, C. C.A.Kan., 244 F. 902, 911.

Complete voluntary trust. One completely created, the subject-matter being designated, the trustee and beneficiary being named, and the limitations and trusts being fully and perfectly declared. In re Leigh's Estate, 186 Iowa 931, 173 N.W. 143, 146.

Constructive trust. A trust raised by construction of law, or arising by operation of law, as distinguished from an express trust. Wherever the circumstances of a transaction are such that the person who takes the legal estate in property cannot also enjoy the beneficial interest without necessarily violating some established principle of equity, the court will immediately raise a *constructive trust*, and fasten it upon the conscience of the legal owner, so as to convert him into a trustee for the parties who in equity are entitled to the beneficial enjoyment. Hill, Trustees, 116; 1 Spence, Eq.Jur. 511; Nester v. Gross, 66 Minn. 371,

69 N.W. 39; Porter v. Shaffer, 147 Va. 921, 133 S.E. 614, 616; Misamore v. Berglin, 197 Ala. 111, 72 So. 347, 349, L.R.A.1916F, 1024.

See, also, Involuntary Trust infra.

"Constructive trusts" do not arise by agreement or from intention, but by operation of law, and fraud, active or constructive, is their essential element. Actual fraud is not necessary, but such a trust will arise whenever circumstances under which property was acquired made it inequitable that it should be retained by him who holds the legal title. Constructive trusts have been said to arise through the application of the doctrine of equitable estoppel, or under the broad doctrine that equity regards and treats as done what in good conscience ought to be done, and such trusts are also known as "trusts ex maleficio" or "ex delicto" or "involuntary trusts" and their forms and varieties are practically without limit, being raised by courts of equity whenever it becomes necessary to prevent a failure of justice. Union Guardian Trust Co. v. Emery, 292 Mich. 394, 290 N.W. 841, 845.

Contingent trust. An express trust depending for its operation upon a future event. Civ.Code Ga.1910, § 3734.

Direct trust. An express trust, as distinguished from a constructive or implied trust. Currence v. Ward, 43 W.Va. 367, 27 S.E. 329.

Directory trust. One which is not completely and finally settled by the instrument creating it, but only defined in its general purpose and to be carried into detail according to later specific directions.

Dry trust. One which merely vests the legal title in the trustee, and does not require the performance of any active duty on his part to carry out the trust. In re Shaw's Estate, 198 Cal. 352, 246 P. 48, 52; Blackburn v. Blackburn, 167 Ky. 113, 180 S.W. 48, 49.

Educational trusts. Trusts for the founding, endowing, and supporting schools for the advancement of all useful branches of learning, which are not strictly private. Richards v. Wilson, 185 Ind. 335, 112 N.E. 780, 794.

Executed trust. A trust of which the scheme has in the outset been completely declared. Adams, Eq. 151. A trust in which the estates and interest in the subject-matter of the trust are completely limited and defined by the instrument creating the trust, and require no further instruments to complete them. Bisp.Eq. 20; Pillot v. Landon, 46 N.J.Eq. 310, 19 A. 25; Egerton v. Brownlow, 4 H.L.Cas. 210; Mattsen v. U. S. Ensilage Harvester Co., 171 Minn. 237, 213 N.W. 893, 895.

Executory trust. One which requires the execution of some further instrument, or the doing of some further act, on the part of the creator of the trust or of the trustee, towards its complete creation or full effect. Martling v. Martling, 55 N.J.Eq. 771, 39 A. 203; Carradine v. Carradine, 33 Miss. 729; In re Fair's Estate, 132 Cal. 523, 60 P. 442, 84 Am.St.Rep. 70; Pillot v. Landon, 46 N.J.Eq. 310, 19 A. 25.

Express active trust. Where will confers upon executor authority to generally manage property of estate and pay over net income to devisees or legatees, such authority creates an "express active trust." In re Thomas' Estate, 17 Wash.2d 674, 136 P.2d 1017, 1020, 147 A.L.R. 598.

Express private passive trust has been defined as existing where land is conveyed to or held by one person in trust for another, without any power being expressly or impliedly given trustee to take actual possession of land or exercise acts of ownership over it, except by beneficiary's direction. Elvins v. Seestedt, 141 Fla. 266, 193 So. 54, 57, 126 A.L.R. 1001.

Express trust. A trust created or declared in express terms, and usually in writing, as distinguished from one inferred by the law from the conduct or dealings of the parties. State v. Campbell, 59 Kan. 246, 52 P. 454; Kaphan v. Toney, Tenn.Ch., 58 S.W. 913; Sanford v. Van Pelt, 314 Mo. 175, 282 S.W. 1022, 1030; Holsapple v. Schrontz, 65 Ind.App. 390, 117 N.E. 547, 549.

Imperfect trust. An executory trust, (which see;) and see Executed Trust.

Implied trust. A trust raised or created by implication of law; a trust implied or presumed from circumstances. Wilson v. Welles, 79 Minn. 53, 81 N.W. 549; Holsapple v. Schrontz, 65 Ind. App. 390, 117 N.E. 547, 549; Springer v. Springer, 144 Md. 465, 125 A. 162, 166.

Instrumental trust. See Ministerial Trusts, infra.

Involuntary trust. "Involuntary" or "constructive" trusts embrace all those instances in which a trust is raised by the doctrines of equity, for the purpose of working out justice in the most efficient manner, when there is no intention of the parties to create a trust relation. This class of trusts may usually be referred to fraud, either actual or constructive, as an essential element. Bank v. Kimball Milling Co., 1 S.D. 388, 47 N.W. 402, 36 Am.St.Rep. 739.

Massachusetts or business trusts. See "Trust Estates as Business Companies."

Ministerial trusts. (Also called "instrumental trusts.") Those which demand no further exercise of reason or understanding than every intelligent agent must necessarily employ; as to convey an estate. They are a species of special trusts, distinguished from discretionary trusts, which necessarily require much exercise of the understanding. 2 Bouv.Inst. no. 1896.

Naked trust. A dry or passive trust; one which requires no action on the part of the trustee, beyond turning over money or property to the *cestui que trust*. Cerri v. Akron-People's Telephone Co., D.C.Ohio, 219 F. 285, 292.

Passive trust. A trust as to which the trustee has no active duty to perform. Holmes v. Walter, 118 Wis. 409, 95 N.W. 380, 62 L.R.A. 986; Dixon v. Dixon, 123 Me. 470, 124 A. 198, 199.

Precatory trust. Where words employed in a will or other instrument do not amount to a positive command or to a distinct testamentary disposition, but are terms of entreaty, request, recommendation, or expectation, they are termed "precatory words," and from such words the law will raise a trust, called a "precatory trust," to carry out the wishes of the testator or grantor. See Bohon v. Barrett, 79 Ky. 378; Hunt v. Hunt, 18 Wash. 14, 50 P. 578; Aldrich v. Aldrich, 172 Mass. 101, 51 N.E. 449.

Private trust. One established or created for the benefit of a certain designated individual or individuals, or a known person or class of persons, clearly identified or capable of identification by the terms of the instrument creating the trust, as distinguished from trusts for public institutions or charitable uses. See Pennoyer v. Wadhams, 20 Or. 274, 25 P. 720, 11 L.R.A. 210; Doyle v. Whalen, 87 Me. 414, 32 A. 1022, 31 L.R.A. 118; Brooks v. Belfast, 90 Me. 318, 38 A. 222; Bauer v. Myers, C.C.A.Kan., 244 F. 902, 911.

Proprietary trust. In Scotch law, a naked, dry, or passive trust. See *supra*.

Public trust. One constituted for the benefit either of the public at large or of some considerable portion of it answering a particular description; public trusts and charitable trusts may be considered in general as synonymous expressions. Lewin, Trusts, 20; Bauer v. Myers, C.C.A.Kan., 244 F. 902, 911.

Resulting trust. One that arises by implication of law, or by the operation and construction of equity, and which is established as consonant to the presumed intention of the parties as gathered from the nature of the transaction. It arises where the legal estate in property is disposed of, conveyed, or transferred, but the intent appears or is inferred from the terms of the disposition, or from the accompanying facts and circumstances, that the beneficial interest is not to go or be enjoyed with the legal title. Lafkowitz v. Jackson, C.C.A.Mo., 13 F.2d 370, 372. See Sanders v. Steele, 124 Ala. 415, 26 So. 882. Farwell v. Wilcox, 73 Okl. 230, 175 P. 936, 938, 4 A.L.R. 156; Cummings v. Cummings, 55 Cal.App. 433, 203 P. 452, 455.

Savings bank trust. A Totten trust.

Secret trusts. Where a testator gives property to a person, on a verbal promise by the legatee or devisee that he will hold it in trust for another person. Sweet.

Shifting trust. An express trust which is so settled that it may operate in favor of beneficiaries additional to, or substituted for, those first named, upon specified contingencies. Civ.Code Ga.1910, § 3734.

Simple trust. A simple trust corresponds with the ancient use, and arises where property is simply vested in one person for the use of another, and the nature of the trust, not being qualified by the settlor, is left to the construction of law. Perkins v. Brinkley, 133 N.C. 154, 45 S.E. 541; Dodson v. Ball, 60 Pa. 500, 100 Am.Dec. 586.

Special trust. One in which a trustee is interposed for the execution of some purpose particularly pointed out, and is not, as in case of a simple trust, a mere passive depositary of the estate, but is required to exert himself actively in the execution of the settlor's intention; as, where a conveyance is made to trustees upon trust to reconvey, or to sell for the payment of debts. Lew.Tr. 3, 16.

Special trusts have been divided into (1) ministerial (or instrumental) and (2) discretionary. The former, such as demand no further exercise of reason or understanding than every intelligent agent must necessarily employ; the latter, such as cannot be duly administered without the application of a certain degree of prudence and judgment. 2 Bouv.Inst. no. 1896; Perkins v. Brinkley, 133 N.C. 154, 45 S.E. 541.

Spendthrift trust. See Spendthrift.

Totten trust. A trust created by the deposit by one person of his own money in his own name as a trustee for another and it is a tentative trust revocable at will until the depositor dies or completes the gift in his lifetime by some unequivocal act or declaration such as delivery of the pass book or notice to the beneficiary and if the depositor dies before the beneficiary without revocation or some decisive act or declaration of disaffirmance the presumption arises that an absolute trust was created as to the balance on hand at the death of the depositor. Murray v. Brooklyn Sav. Bank, 258 App.Div. 132, 15 N.Y.S.2d 915, 917; In re Totten, 179 N.Y. 112, 71 N.E. 748, 70 L.R.A. 711, 1 Ann. Cas. 900.

Transgressive trust. A name sometimes applied to a trust which transgresses or violates the rule against perpetuities. See Pulitzer v. Livingston, 89 Me. 359, 36 A. 635.

Trust allotments. Allotments to Indians, in which a certificate or trust patent is issued declaring that the United States will hold the land for a designated period in trust for the allottee. U. S. v. Bowling, 41 S.Ct. 561, 562, 256 U.S. 484, 65 L.Ed. 1054.

Trust company. A corporation formed for the purpose of taking, accepting, and executing all such trusts as may be lawfully committed to it, and acting as testamentary trustee, trustee under deeds of settlement or for married women, executor, guardian, etc. To these functions are sometimes (but not necessarily) added the business of acting as fiscal agent for corporations, attending to the registration and transfer of their stock and bonds, serving as trustee for their bond or mortgage creditors, and transacting a general banking and loan business. See Venner v. Farmers' L. & T. Co., 54 App.Div. 271, 66 N.Y.Supp. 773; Mercantile Nat. Bank v. New York, 7 S.Ct. 826, 121 U.S. 138, 30 L.Ed. 895; Loudoun Nat. Bank of Leesburg v. Continental Trust Co., 164 Va. 536, 180 S. E. 548, 551.

Trust deed. (1) A species of mortgage given to a trustee for the purpose of securing a numerous class of creditors, as the bondholders of a railroad corporation, with power to foreclose and sell on failure of the payment of their bonds, notes, or other claims. (2) In some of the states, and in the District of Columbia, a trust deed or deed of trust is a security resembling a mortgage, being a conveyance of lands to trustees to secure the payment of a debt, with a power of sale upon default, and upon a trust to apply the net proceeds to paying the debt and to turn over the surplus to the grantor. Dean v. Smith, 53 N.D. 123, 204 N.W. 987, 994; Guaranty Title & Trust Co. v. Thompson, 93 Fla. 983, 113 So. 117, 120.

A "trust deed" on real estate as security for a bond issue is, in effect, a mortgage on property executed by the mortgagor to a third person as trustee to hold as security for the mortgage debt as evidenced by the bonds, for the benefit of the purchasers of the bonds as lenders. Marden v. Elks Club, 138 Fla. 707, 190 So. 40, 42.

Trust deposit. Where money or property is deposited to be kept intact and not commingled with other funds or property of bank and is to be returned in kind to depositor or devoted to particular purpose or requirement of depositor or payment of particular debts or obligations of depositor. Also called "special deposit". Maurello v. Broadway Bank & Trust Co. of Paterson, 114 N.J.L. 167, 176 A. 391, 394. See, also "Deposit."

Trust estate. This term may mean either the estate of the trustee,—that is, the legal title,—or the estate of the beneficiary, or the corpus of the property which is the subject of the trust. See Cooper v. Cooper, 5 N.J.Eq. 9; Farmers' L. & T. Co. v. Carroll, 5 Barb. (N.Y.) 643.

Trust ex delicto. Trust ex maleficio, which title see, infra.

Trust ex maleficio. A species of constructive trust arising out of some fraud, misconduct, or breach of faith on the part of the person to be charged as trustee, which renders it an equitable necessity that a trust should be implied. See Rogers v. Richards, 67 Kan. 706, 74 P. 255; Kent v. Dean, 128 Ala. 600, 30 So. 543; Chanowsky v. Friedman, Tex.Civ.App., 108 S.W.2d 752, 754. See, also, Constructive Trust, supra.

Trust fund. A fund held by a trustee for the specific purposes of the trust; in a more general sense, a fund which, legally or equitably, is subject to be devoted to a particular purpose and cannot or should not be diverted therefrom. In this sense it is often said that the assets of a corporation are a "trust fund" for the payment of its debts. See Henderson v. Indiana Trust Co., 143 Ind. 561, 40 N.E. 516; In re Beard's Estate, 7 Wyo. 104, 50 Pac. 226, 38 L.R.A. 860, 75 Am.St. Rep. 882; Spencer v. Smith, C.C.A.Colo., 201 F. 647, 652; Terhune v. Weise, 132 Wash. 208, 231 P. 954, 955, 38 A.L.R. 94.

Trust fund doctrine. In substance, that where corporation transfers all its assets with a view to going out of business and nothing is left with which to pay debts, transferee is charged with notice of the circumstances of the transaction, and takes the assets subject to an equitable lien for the unpaid debts of the transferring company; the property of a corporation being a fund subject to be first applied to the payment of debts. Meikle v. Export Lumber Co., C.C.A.Or., 67 F.2d 301, 304.

Under such doctrine, if insolvent corporation's assets are distributed among its stockholders before its debts are paid, each stockholder is liable to creditors for full amount received by him. Scott v. Commissioner of Internal Revenue, C.C.A.8, 117 F.2d 36, 39.

Trust in invitum. A constructive trust imposed by equity, contrary to the trustee's intention and will, upon property in his hands. Sanford v. Hamner, 115 Ala. 406, 22 So. 117.

Trust legacy. See Legacy.

Trust receipt. Document in which is expressed security transaction, whereunder the lender having no prior title in the goods on which the lien is to be given, and not having possession which remains in the borrower, lends his money to the borrower on security of the goods, which the borrower is privileged to sell clear of the lien on agreement to pay all or part of the proceeds of the sale to the lender. In re Boswell, C.C.A.Cal., 96 F.2d 239, 242.

A term specifically applied to a written instrument whereby banker having advanced money for purchase of imported merchandise and having taken title in his own name, delivers possession to importer on agreement in writing to hold merchandise in trust for banker till he is paid. Simons v. Northeastern Finance Corporation, 271 Mass. 285, 171 N.E. 643, 644.

Voluntary trust. An obligation arising out of a personal confidence reposed in, and voluntarily accepted by, one for the benefit of another, as distinguished from an "involuntary" trust, which is created by operation of law. Civ.Code Cal. §§ 2216, 2217. According to another use of the term, "voluntary" trusts are such as are made in favor of a volunteer, that is, a person who gives nothing in exchange for the trust, but receives it as a pure gift; and in this use the term is distinguished from "trusts for value," the latter being such as are in favor of purchasers, mortgagees, etc. A "voluntary trust" is an equitable gift, and in order to be enforceable by the beneficiaries must be complete. Cameron v. Cameron, 96 Okl. 98, 220 P. 889, 890; Logan v. Ryan, 68 Cal.App. 448, 229 P. 993, 996.

The difference between a "gift inter vivos" and a "voluntary trust" is that, in a gift, the thing itself with title passes to the donee, while, in a voluntary trust, the actual title passes to a cestui que trust while the legal title is retained by the settlor, to be held by him for the purposes of the trust or is by the settlor transferred to another to hold for the purposes of the trust. Allen v. Hendrick, 104 Or. 202, 206 P. 733, 740.

Voting trust. See that title.

2. Constitutional and Statutory Law

An association or organization of persons or corporations having the intention and power, or the tendency, to create a monopoly, control production, interfere with the free course of trade or transportation, or to fix and regulate the supply and the price of commodities.

In the history of economic development, the "trust" was originally a device by which several corporations engaged in the same general line of business might combine for their mutual advantage, in the direction of eliminating destructive competition, controlling the output of their commodity, and regulating and maintaining its price, but at the same time preserving their separate individual existence, and without any consolidation or merger. This device was the erection of a central committee or board, composed, perhaps, of the presidents or general managers of the different corporations, and the transfer to them of a majority of the stock in each of the corporations, to be held "in trust" for the several stockholders so assigning their holdings. These stockholders received in return "trust certificates" showing that they were entitled to receive the dividends on their assigned stock, though the voting power of it had passed to the trustees. This last feature enabled the trustees or committee to elect all the directors of all the corporations, and through them the officers, and thereby to exercise an absolutely controlling influence over the policy and operations of each constituent company, to the ends and with the purposes above mentioned. Though the "trust," in this sense, is now seldom if ever resorted to as a form of corporate organization, having given place to the "holding corporation" and other devices, the word has become current in statute laws as well as popular speech, to designate almost any form of combination of a monopolistic character or tendency. See Black, Const. Law (3d Ed.) p. 428; Northern Securities Co. v. U. S., 193 U.S. 197, 24 Sup.Ct. 436, 48 L.Ed. 679; MacGinniss v. Mining Co., 29 Mont. 428, 75 P. 89; Georgia Fruit Exchange v. Turnipseed, 9 Ala.App. 123, 62 So. 542, 546; Mallinckrodt Chemical Works v. State of Missouri, 35 S.Ct. 671, 673, 238 U.S. 41, 59 L.Ed. 1192.

In a looser sense the term "trust" is applied to any combination of establishments in the same line of business for securing the same ends by holding the individual interests of each subservient to a common authority for the common interests of all. Mallinckrodt Chemical Works v. State of Missouri, 35 S.Ct. 671, 673, 238 U.S. 41, 59 L.Ed. 1192.

TRUST ESTATES AS BUSINESS COMPANIES. A practice originating in Massachusetts of vesting a business or certain real estate in a group of trustees, who manage it for the benefit of the beneficial owners; the ownership of the latter is evidenced by negotiable (or transferable) shares. The trustees are elected by the shareholders, or, in case of a vacancy, by the board of trustees. Provision is made in the agreement and declaration of trust to the effect that when new trustees are elected, the trust estate shall vest in them without further conveyance. The declaration of trust specifies the powers of the trustees. They have a common seal; the board is organized with the usual officers of a board of trustees; it is governed by by-laws; the officers have the usual powers of like corporate officers; so far as practicable, the trustees in their collective capacity, are to carry on the business under a specified name. The trustees may also hold shares as beneficiaries. Provision may be made for the alteration or amendment of the agreement or declaration in a specified manner. In Eliot v. Freeman, 31 Sup.Ct. 360, 220 U.S. 178, 55 L.Ed. 424, it was held that such a trust was not within the corporation tax provisions of the tariff act of Aug. 5, 1909. See also Zonne v. Minneapolis Syndicate, 31 S.Ct. 361, 220 U.S. 187, 55 L.Ed. 428.

TRUSTEE. The person appointed, or required by law, to execute a trust; one in whom an estate, interest, or power is vested, under an express or implied agreement to administer or exercise it for the benefit or to the use of another called the cestui que trust. Pioneer Mining Co. v. Tyberg, C.C.A.Alaska, 215 F. 501, 506, L.R.A.1915B, 442; Kaehn v. St. Paul Co-op. Ass'n, 156 Minn. 113, 194 N.W. 112; Catlett v. Hawthorne, 157 Va. 372, 161 S.E. 47, 48. Person who holds title to res and administers it for others' benefit. Reinecke v. Smith, Ill., 53 S.Ct. 570, 289 U.S. 172, 77 L.Ed. 1109.

In a strict sense, a "trustee" is one who holds the legal title to property for the benefit of another, while, in a broad sense, the term is sometimes applied to anyone standing in a fiduciary or confidential relation to another, such as agent, attorney, bailee, etc. State ex rel. Lee v. Sartorius, 344 Mo. 912, 130 S.W.2d 547, 549, 550.

"Trustee" is also used in a wide and perhaps inaccurate sense, to denote that a person has the duty of carrying out a transaction, in which he and another person are interested, in such manner as will be most for the benefit of the latter, and not in such a way that he himself might be tempted, for the sake of his personal advantage, to neglect the interests of the other. In this sense, directors of companies are said to be "trustees for the shareholders." Sweet.

Conventional Trustee

One appointed by a decree of court to execute a trust, as distinguished from one appointed by the instrument creating the trust. Gilbert v. Kolb, 85 Md. 627, 37 Atl. 423.

Joint Trustees

Two or more persons who are intrusted with property for the benefit of one or more others.

Judicial Trustee

A "judicial trustee," as distinguished from a conventional trustee, is an officer of a chancery court whose acts are generally limited and defined by familiar and settled rules and procedure. Kramme v. Mewshaw, 147 Md. 535, 128 A. 468, 472.

Public Trustee

An act of 1906 referring to England and Wales provides for the appointment of a public trustee to administer estates of small value, to act as custodian trustee, or as ordinary trustee or judicial trustee, or to administer the property of a convict under the Forfeiture Act.

Quasi Trustee

A person who reaps a benefit from a breach of trust, and so becomes answerable as a trustee. Lewin, Trusts (4th Ed.) 592, 638.

Testamentary Trustee

A trustee appointed by or acting under a will; one appointed to carry out a trust created by a will. The term does not ordinarily include an executor or an administrator with the will annexed, or a guardian, except when they act in the execution of a trust created by the will and which is separable from their functions as executors, etc. See In re Hazard, 51 Hun, 201, 4 N.Y.Supp. 701; In re Valentine's Estate, 1 Misc. 491, 23 N.Y. Supp. 289; In re Hawley, 104 N.Y. 250, 10 N.E. 352.

Trustee Acts

The statutes 13 & 14 Vict. c. 60, passed in 1850, and 15 & 16 Vict. c. 55, passed in 1852, enabling the court of chancery, without bill filed, to appoint new trustees in lieu of any who, on account of death, lunacy, absence, or otherwise, are unable or unwilling to act as such; and also to make vesting orders by which legal estates and rights may be transferred from the old trustee or trustees to the new trustee or trustees so appointed. Mozley & Whitley.

Trustee Ex Maleficio

A person who, being guilty of wrongful or fraudulent conduct, is held by equity to the duty and liability of a trustee, in relation to the subject-matter, to prevent him from profiting by his own wrong. Rice v. Braden, 243 Pa. 141, 89 A. 877, 880. Alabama Water Co. v. City of Anniston, 227 Ala. 579, 151 So. 457, 458.

Trustee in Bankruptcy

A person in whom the property of a bankrupt is vested in trust for the creditors.

Trustee Process

The name given, in the New England states, to the process of garnishment or foreign attachment.

Trustee Relief Acts

The statute 10 & 11 Vict. c. 96, passed in 1847, and statute 12 & 13 Vict. c. 74, passed in 1849, by which a trustee is enabled to pay money into court, in cases where a difficulty arises respecting the title to the trust fund. Mozley & Whiteley.

TRUSTER. In Scotch law. The maker or creator of a trust.

TRUSTIS. In old European law. Trust; faith; confidence; fidelity.

TRUSTOR. One who creates a trust. Also called settlor. Ulmer v. Fulton, 129 Ohio St. 323, 195 N.E. 557, 564, 97 A.L.R. 1170.

TRUTH. There are three conceptions as to what constitutes "truth": Agreement of thought and reality; eventual verification; and consistency of thought with itself. Memphis Telephone Co. v. Cumberland Telephone & Telegraph Co., C.C.A. Tenn., 231 F. 835, 842.

For "Fact" and "truth" distinguished, see Fact.

TRY. To examine judicially; to examine and investigate a controversy, by the legal method called "trial," for the purpose of determining the issues it involves.

TSAR. The better, though perhaps less common spelling of "czar" (*q. v.*).

TUAS RES TIBI HABETO. Lat. Have or take your things to yourself. The form of words by which, according to the old Roman law, a man divorced his wife. Calvin.

TUB. In mercantile law. A measure containing sixty pounds of tea, and from fifty-six to eighty-six pounds of camphor. Jacob.

TUB-MAN. In English law. A barrister who has a preaudience in the exchequer, and also one who has a particular place in court, is so called. Brown.

TUCHAS. In Spanish law. Objections or exceptions to witnesses. White, New Recop. b. 3, tit. 7, c. 10.

TUCKER ACT. The act of March 3, 1887, relating to the jurisdiction of the court of claims. Garl. & Ralston, Fed. Pr. 413.

TUERTO. In Spanish law. Tort. Las Partidas, pt. 7, tit. 6, 1, 5.

TUG. A steam vessel built for towing; synonymous with "tow-boat."

TUITION. The act or business of teaching the various branches of learning. State ex rel. Veeder v. State Board of Education, 97 Mont. 121, 33 P.2d 516, 522.

TULLIANUM. Lat. In Roman law. That part of a prison which was under ground. Supposed to be so called from Servius Tullius, who built that part of the first prison in Rome. Adams, Rom. Ant. 290.

TUMBREL. A castigatory, trebucket, or ducking-stool, anciently used as a punishment for common scolds.

TUMULTUOUS PETITIONING. Under St. 13 Car. II. St. 1, c. 5, this was a misdemeanor, and consisted in more than twenty persons signing any petition to the crown or either house of parliament for the alteration of matters established by law in church or state, unless the contents thereof had been approved by three justices, or the majority of the grand jury at assizes or quarter sessions. No petition could be delivered by more than ten persons. 4 Bl.Comm. 147; Mozley & Whitley.

TUN. A measure of wine or oil, containing four hogsheads.

TUNING. The term as used with reference to signaling by electro-magnetic waves, or wireless telegraphy, means the bringing of two or more electrical circuits into resonance, or the adjustment of capacity and inductance to secure the time-period vibration or wave length desired. The wave length assigned to a station might be called its "tune." National Electric Signaling Co. v. Telefunken Wireless Telegraph Co. of United States, C.C.A.Pa., 208 F. 679, 695.

TUNGREVE. A town-reeve or bailiff. Cowell.

TUNNAGE. A duty in England anciently due upon all wines imported, over and above the prisage and butlerage. 2 Steph.Com. 628.

TURBA. Lat. In the civil law. A multitude; a crowd or mob; a tumultuous assembly of persons. Said to consist of ten or fifteen, at the least. Calvin.

TURBARY. Turbary, or common of turbary, is the right or liberty of digging turf upon another man's ground. Brown.

TURF AND TWIG. A piece of turf, or a twig or a bough, were delivered by the feoffer to the feoffee in making livery of seisin. 2 Bla.Com. 315.

TURN, or TOURN. The great court-leet of the county, as the old county court was the court-baron. Of this the sheriff is judge, and the court is incident to his office; wherefore it is called the "sheriff's tourn;" and it had its name originally from the sheriff making a turn of circuit about his shire, and holding this court in each respective hundred. Wharton.

TURN KEY JOB. In oil drilling industry a job wherein driller of oil well undertakes to furnish everything and does all work required to complete well, place it on production, and turn it over ready to turn the key and start oil running into tanks. Retsal Drilling Co. v. Commissioner of Internal Revenue, C.C.A.Tex., 127 F.2d 355, 357.

TURNED TO A RIGHT. This phrase means that a person whose estate is divested by usurpation cannot expel the possessor by mere entry, but must have recourse to an action, either possessory or droitural. Mozley & Whiteley.

TURNKEY. A person, under the superintendence of a jailer, who has the charge of the keys of the prison, for the purpose of opening and fastening the doors.

TURNOUT. A short side-track on a railroad which may be occupied by one train while another is passing on the main track; a siding. Philadelphia v. R. Co., 133 Pa. 134, 19 A. 356; Indiana Rys. & Light Co. v. City of Kokomo, 183 Ind. 543, 108 N.E. 771, 772.

TURNPIKE. A gate set across a road, to stop travelers and carriages until toll is paid for the privilege of passage thereon.

TURNPIKE ROADS. These are roads on which parties have by law a right to erect gates and bars, for the purpose of taking toll, and of refusing the permission to pass along them to all persons who refuse to pay. Northam Bridge Co. v. London Ry. Co., 6 Mees. & W. 428. A public highway, established by public authority for public use, and is to be regarded as a public easement, and not as private property. The only difference between this and a common highway is that, instead of being made at the public expense in the first instance, it is authorized and laid out by public authority, and made at the expense of individuals in the first instance; and the cost of construction and maintenance is reimbursed by a toll, levied by public authority for the purpose. Com. v. Wilkinson, 16 Pick. (Mass.) 175, 26 Am. Dec. 654.

TURNTABLE DOCTRINE. Also termed attractive nuisance doctrine. This doctrine requires the owner of premises not to attract or lure children into unsuspected danger or great bodily harm, by keeping thereon attractive machinery or dangerous instrumentalities in an exposed and unguarded condition, and where injuries have been received by a child so enticed the entry is not regarded as unlawful, and does not necessarily preclude a recovery of damages; the attractiveness of the machine or structure amounting to an implied invitation to enter. Heller v. New York N. H. & H. R. Co., C.C.A.N.Y., 265 F. 192, 194. It imposes a liability on a property owner for injuries to a child of tender years, resulting from something on his premises that can be operated by such a child and made dangerous by him, and which is attractive to him and calculated to induce him to use it, where he fails to protect the thing so that a child of tender years cannot be hurt by it. Barnhill's Adm'r v. Mt. Morgan Coal Co., D.C. Ky., 215 F. 608, 609.

Doctrine is that who maintains or creates upon his premises or upon the premises of another in any public place an instrumentality or condition which may reasonably be expected to attract children of tender years and to constitute a danger to them is under duty to take the precautions that a reasonably prudent person would take under similar circumstance, to prevent injury to such children. Schock v. Ringling Bros. and Barnum & Bailey Combined Shows, 5 Wash.2d 599, 105 P.2d 838, 843.

The dangerous and alluring qualities of a railroad turntable gave the "attractive nuisance rule" the name of "Turntable Doctrine." Louisville & N. R. Co. v. Vaughn, 292 Ky. 120, 166 S.W.2d 43, 46.

TURPIS. Lat. In the civil law. Base; mean; vile; disgraceful; infamous; unlawful. Applied both to things and persons. Calvin.

TURPIS CAUSA. A base cause; a vile or immoral consideration; a consideration which, on account of its immorality, is not allowed by law to be sufficient either to support a contract or found an action; *e. g.*, future illicit intercourse.

TURPIS CONTRACTUS. An immoral or iniquitous contract.

TURPIS EST PARS QUÆ NON CONVENIT CUM SUO TOTO. The part which does not agree with its whole is of mean account, [entitled to small or no consideration.] Plowd. 101; Shep. Touch. 87.

TURPITUDE. In its ordinary sense, inherent baseness or vileness of principle or action; shameful wickedness; depravity. In its legal sense, everything done contrary to justice, honesty, modesty, or good morals. State v. Anderson, 117 Kan. 117, 230 P. 315, 317; Hughes v. State Board of Medical Examiners, 162 Ga. 246, 134 S.E. 42, 46. An action showing gross depravity. Traders & General Ins. Co. v. Russell, Tex.Civ.App., 99 S.W.2d 1079, 1084.

Moral Turpitude

A term of frequent occurrence in statutes, especially those providing that a witness' conviction of a crime involving moral turpitude may be shown as tending to impeach his credibility. In general, it means neither more nor less than "turpitude," *i. e.*, anything done contrary to justice, honesty, modesty, or good morals. In re Williams, 64 Okl. 316, 167 P. 1149, 1152; In re Humphrey, 174 Cal. 290, 163 P. 60, 62. Indeed, it is sometimes candidly admitted that the word "moral" in this phrase does not add anything to the meaning of the term other than that emphasis which may result from a tautological expression. Hughes v. State Board of Medical Examiners, 162 Ga. 246, 134 S.E. 42, 46. It is also commonly defined as an act of baseness, vileness, or depravity in the private and social duties which a man owes to his fellow man or to society in general, contrary to the accepted and customary rule of right and duty between man and man. Moore v. State, 12 Ala. App. 243, 67 So. 789, 791; United States v. Uhl, C.C.A.N.Y., 210 F. 860, 862.

Although a vague term, it implies something immoral in itself, regardless of its being punishable by law. Pippin v. State, 197 Ala. 613, 73 So. 340, 342; Coykendall v. Skrmetta, C.C.A.Ga., 22 F.2d 120; Thus excluding unintentional wrong, or an improper act done without unlawful or improper intent. Drazen v. New Haven Taxicab Co., 95 Conn. 500, 111 A., 861, 863. It is also said to be restricted to the gravest offenses, consisting of felonies, infamous crimes, and those that are malum in se and disclose a depraved mind. Bartos v. United States District Court for District of Nebraska, C.C.A.Neb., 19 F.2d 722, 724.

TURPITUDO. Lat. Baseness; infamy; immorality; turpitude.

TUTA EST CUSTODIA QUÆ SIBIMET CREDITUR. Hob. 340. That guardianship is secure which is intrusted to itself alone.

TUTELA. Lat. In the civil law. Tutelage; that species of guardianship which continued to the age of puberty; the guardian being called "*tutor*," and the ward, "*pupillus*." 1 Dom. Civil Law, b. 2, tit. 1, p. 260. A power given by the civil law over a free person to defend him when by reason of his age he is unable to defend himself. A child under the power of his father was not subject to tutelage, because not a free person, *caput liberum*.

TUTELA LEGITIMA. Legal tutelage; tutelage created by act of law, as where none had been created by testament. Inst. 1, 15, pr.

TUTELA TESTAMENTARIA. Testamentary tutelage or guardianship; that kind of tutelage which was created by will. Calvin.

TUTELÆ ACTIO. Lat. In the civil law. An action of tutelage; an action which lay for a ward or pupil, on the termination of tutelage, against the *tutor* or guardian, to compel an account. Calvin.

TUTELAGE. Guardianship; state of being under a guardian. See Tutela.

TUTELAM REDDERE. Lat. In the civil law. To render an account of tutelage. Calvin. *Tutelam reposcere*, to demand an account of tutelage.

TUTEUR. In French law. A kind of guardian.

TUTEUR OFFICIEUX. A person over fifty years of age may be appointed a tutor of this sort to a child over fifteen years of age, with the consent of the parents of such child, or, in their default, the *conseil de famille*. The duties which such a tutor becomes subject to are analogous to those in English law of a person who puts himself *in loco parentis* to any one. Brown.

TUTEUR SUBROGÉ. The title of a second guardian appointed for an infant under guardianship. His functions are exercised in case the interests of the infant and his principal guardian conflict. Code Nap. 420; Brown.

TUTIUS ERRATUR EX PARTE MITIORE. 3 Inst. 220. It is safer to err on the gentler side [or on the side of mercy].

TUTIUS SEMPER EST ERRARE ACQUIETANDO, QUAM IN PUNIENDO, EX PARTE MISERICORDIÆ QUAM EX PARTE JUSTITIÆ. It is always safer to err in acquitting than punishing, on the side of mercy than on the side of justice. Branch, Princ.; 2 Hale, P. C. 290; Broom, Max. 326; Com. v. York, 9 Metc. (Mass.) 116, 43 Am.Dec. 373.

TUTOR. One who teaches, usually a private instructor. State ex rel. Veeder v. State Board of Education, 97 Mont. 121, 33 P.2d 516, 522.

In the civil law. This term corresponds nearly to "guardian," (*i. e.*, a person appointed to have the care of the person of a minor and the administration of his estate,) except that the guardian of a minor who has passed a certain age is called "curator," and has powers and duties differing somewhat from those of a tutor. See Washington Bank and Trust Co. v. Magee, 187 Miss. 198, 192 So. 438.

TUTOR ALIENUS. In English law. The name given to a stranger who enters upon the lands of an infant within the age of fourteen, and takes the profits. He may be called to an account by the infant and be charged as guardian in socage. Littleton, § 124; Co.Litt. 89*b*, 90*a*.

TUTOR PROPRIUS. The name given to one who is rightly a guardian in socage, in contradistinction to a *tutor alienus*.

TUTORSHIP. The office and power of a tutor. The power which an individual, *sui juris*, has to take care of the person of one who is unable to take care of himself.

There are four sorts of tutorships: Tutorship by nature; tutorship by will; tutorship by the effect of the law; tutorship by the appointment of the judge. Civ.Code La. art. 247.

TUTORSHIP BY NATURE. Upon the death of either parent, the tutorship of minor children belongs of right to the other. Upon divorce or judicial separation from bed and board of parents, the tutorship of each minor child belongs of right to the parent under whose care he or she has been placed or to whose care he or she has been entrusted. All those cases are called tutorship by nature. Civ.Code La. art. 250.

TUTORSHIP BY WILL. The right of appointing a tutor, whether a relation or a stranger, belongs exclusively to the father or mother dying last. This is called "tutorship by will," because generally it is given by testament; but it may likewise be given by any declaration by the surviving father or mother, executed before a notary and two witnesses. Civ.Code La. art. 257.

TUTRIX. A female tutor.

TWA NIGHT GEST. In Saxon law. A guest on the second night. By the laws of Edward the Confessor it was provided that a man who lodged at an inn, or at the house of another, should be considered, on the first night of his being there, a stranger, (*uncuth;*) on the second night, a guest; on the third night, a member of the family. This had reference to the responsibility of the host or entertainer for offenses committed by the guest.

TWELFHINDI. The highest rank of men in the Saxon government, who were valued at 1200s. If any injury were done to such persons, satisfaction was to be made according to their worth. Cowell.

TWELVE TABLES. The earliest statute or code of Roman law, framed by a commission of ten men, B.C. 450, upon the return of a commission of three who had been sent abroad to study foreign laws and institutions. The Twelve Tables consisted partly of laws transcribed from the institutions of other nations, partly of such as were altered and accommodated to the manners of the Romans, partly of new provisions, and mainly, perhaps, of laws and usages under their ancient kings. They formed the source and foundation for the whole later development of Roman jurisprudence. They exist now only in fragmentary form. See 1 Kent, Comm. 520. These laws were substantially a codification, and not merely an incorporation, of the customary law of the people. There were Greek elements in them, but still they were essentially Roman. Hunter, Rom.L. 16. See Stephenson, Hist.Rom.L. 120; Sohm's Inst.Rom.L.

TWELVE-DAY WRIT. A writ issued under the St. 18 & 19 Vict. c. 67, for summary procedure on bills of exchange and promissory notes, abolished by rule of court in 1880. Wharton.

TWELVEMONTH. This term (in the singular number), includes all the year; but *twelve months* are to be computed according to twenty-eight days for every month. 6 Coke, 62.

TWELVE-MONTH BOND. "Twelve-month bond," under statute effective Jan. 20, 1837 (Hartley's Dig. art. 1277), had a double character, first as an obligation known to the Spanish civil law, and second, as a summary statutory judgment, with the force and effect of any other judgment of a court of competent jurisdiction; it being also a consent judgment. Clements v. Texas Co., Tex.Civ.App., 273 S.W. 993, 1001.

TWENTY PER CENT RULE. In election contests is that votes of entire precinct will be thrown out when such large proportion of votes cast was illegal, and it is impossible to determine for whom illegal votes were cast. Johnson v. Caddell, 251 Ky. 14, 64 S.W.2d 441.

TWENTY-FOUR CALENDAR MONTHS. Two years; a period of exactly 730 days. Carey v. Deems, 101 N.J.L. 419, 129 A. 191, 193.

TWICE IN JEOPARDY. See Jeopardy; Once in Jeopardy.

TWISTING. Colloquially, in insurance, the misrepresentation or misstatements of fact or incomplete comparison of policies to induce the insured to give up a policy in one company for the purpose of taking insurance in another. Brandt v. Beha, 217 App.Div. 644, 216 N.Y.S. 178, 179.

TWO ISSUE RULE. Error in charge dealing exclusively with one of two or more complete and independent issues required to be presented to jury in civil action will be disregarded, if charge in respect to another independent issue which will support verdict is free from prejudicial error, unless it is disclosed that verdict is in fact based upon issue to which erroneous instruction related. Asteri v. City of Youngstown, Ohio App., 121 N.E.2d 143, 145.

TWO YEARS. A period of exactly 730 days; identical with twenty-four calendar months. Carey v. Deems, 101 N.J.L. 419, 129 A. 191, 193. Thus, it is held that an accusation filed on March 16, 1912, and charging the commission of an offense on March 16, 1910, was not filed "within two years" after the commission of the offense. McLendon v. State, 14 Ga.App. 274, 80 S.E. 692.

TWYHINDI. The lower order of Saxons, valued at 200s. in the scale of pecuniary mulcts inflicted for crimes. Cowell. See Twelfhindi.

TYBURN TICKET. In English law. A certificate which was given to the prosecutor of a felon to conviction. By the 10 & 11 Will. III. c. 23, the original proprietor or first assignee of such certificate is exempted from all parish and ward offices within the parish or ward where the felony was committed. Bacon, Abr. *Constable* (C).

TYHTLAN. In Saxon law. An accusation, impeachment, or charge of any offense.

TYING. A term which, as used in a contract of lease of patented machinery means that the lessee has secured only limited rights of use, and that if he exceeds such limited rights by agreeing not to use the machines of others he may lose his lease. United States v. United Shoe Machinery Co. of New Jersey, D.C.Mass., 222 F. 349, 388, 394.

TYING WIRE. In concrete construction, No. 16 black fencing wire used to fasten the steel together. Soule v. Northern Const. Co., 33 Cal.App. 300, 165 P. 21, 22.

TYLWITH. Brit. A tribe or family branching or issuing out of another. Cowell.

TYMBRELLA. In old English law, a tumbrel, castigatory, or ducking stool, anciently used as an instrument of punishment for common scolds.

TYPEWRITING. The process of printing letter by letter by the use of a typewriter, Acme Coal

Co. v. Northrup Nat. Bank of Iola, Kan., 23 Wyo. 66, 146 P. 593, L.R.A.1915D, 1084, an instrument operated by hand, and used largely in business requiring much correspondence with others, or in connection with commercial transactions. Hooper v. Kennedy, 100 Vt. 314, 137 A. 194, 196. Typewriting, for certain purposes and under different statutes, is sometimes deemed to be included within the term "writing," and sometimes within the term "printing."

TYRANNY. Arbitrary or despotic government; the severe and autocratic exercise of sovereign power, either vested constitutionally in one ruler, or usurped by him by breaking down the division and distribution of governmental powers.

TYRANT. A despot; a sovereign or ruler, legitimate or otherwise, who uses his power unjustly and arbitrarily, to the oppression of his subjects.

TYROTOXICON. In medical jurisprudence. A poisonous ptomaine produced in milk, cheese, cream, or ice-cream by decomposition of albuminous constituents.

TYRRA, or TOIRA. A mount or hill. Cowell.

TYTHE. Tithe, or tenth part.

TYTHING. A company of ten; a district; a tenth part. See Tithing.

TZAR, TZARINA. Formerly, the emperor and empress of Russia. See Czar.

U

U. B. An abbreviation for "Upper Bench."

U. C. An abbreviation for "Upper Canada," used in citing the reports.

U. R. Initials of *"uti rogas,"* be it as you desire, a ballot thus inscribed, by which the Romans voted in favor of a bill or candidate. Tayl.Civil Law, 191.

U. S. An abbreviation for "United States."

U. S. E. S. United States Employment Service.

UBERRIMA FIDES. Lat. The most abundant good faith; absolute and perfect candor or openness and honesty; the absence of any concealment or deception, however slight. A phrase used to express the perfect good faith, concealing nothing, with which a contract must be made; for example, in the case of insurance, the insured must observe the most perfect good faith towards the insurer. 1 Story, Eq.Jur. § 317.

Contracts of life insurance are said to be "uberrimæ fidæ" when any material misrepresentation or concealment is fatal to them. Equitable Life Assur. Soc. v. McElroy, 28 C.C.A. 365, 83 F. 631, 636.

UBI ALIQUID CONCEDITUR, CONCEDITUR ET ID SINE QUO RES IPSA ESSE NON POTEST. When anything is granted, that also is granted without which the thing granted cannot exist. Broom, Max. 483; 13 Mees. & W. 706.

UBI ALIQUID IMPEDITUR PROPTER UNUM, EO REMOTO, TOLLITUR IMPEDIMENTUM. Where anything is impeded by one single cause, if that be removed, the impediment is removed. Branch, Princ., citing 5 Coke, 77*a*.

UBI CESSAT REMEDIUM ORDINARIUM, IBI DECURRITUR AD EXTRAORDINARIUM. Where the ordinary remedy fails, recourse must be had to an extraordinary one. 4 Coke, 92*b*.

UBI CULPA EST, IBI PŒNA SUBESSE DEBET. Where the crime is committed, there ought the punishment to be undergone. Jenk.Cent. 325.

UBI DAMNA DANTUR, VICTUS VICTORI IN EXPENSIS CONDEMNARI DEBET. Where damages are given, the vanquished party ought to be condemned in costs to the victor. 2 Inst. 289; 3 Sharsw. Bla. Comm. 399.

UBI EADEM RATIO, IBI EADEM LEX; ET DE SIMILIBUS IDEM EST JUDICIUM. 7 Coke, 18. Where the same reason exists, there the same law prevails; and, of things similar, the judgment is similar. Where there is the same reason, there is the same law, and the same judgment should be rendered on the same state of facts. Broom, Max. 103, n. 153, 155.

UBI EST FORUM, IBI ERGO EST JUS. The law of the forum governs. 31 Law Mag. & Rev. 471.

UBI EST SPECIALIS, ET RATIO GENERALIS GENERALITER ACCIPIENDA EST. See Ubi lex est specialis, etc.

UBI ET DANTIS ET ACCIPIENTIS TURPITUDO VERSATUR, NON POSSE REPETI DICIMUS; QUOTIENS AUTEM ACCIPIENTIS TURPITUDO VERSATUR, REPETI POSSE. Where there is turpitude on the part of both giver and receiver, we say it cannot be recovered back; but as often as the turpitude is on the side of the receiver [alone] it can be recovered back. Mason v. Waite, 17 Mass. 562.

UBI FACTUM NULLUM, IBI FORTIA NULLA. Where there is no principal fact, there can be no accessory. 4 Coke, 426. Where there is no act, there can be no force.

UBI JUS, IBI REMEDIUM. Where there is a right, there is a remedy. Broom, Max. 191, 204; 1 Term R. 512; Co.Litt. 197*b*; 7 Gray (Mass.) 197; Henry v. Cherry & Webb, 73 A. 97, 101, 30 R.I. 13, 24 L.R.A. 991, 136 Am.St.Rep. 928, 18 Ann. Cas. 1006. It is said that the rule of primitive law was the reverse: Where there is a remedy, there is a right. Salmond, Jurispr. 645.

UBI JUS INCERTUM, IBI JUS NULLUM. Where the law is uncertain, there is no law.

UBI LEX ALIQUEM COGIT OSTENDERE CAUSAM, NECESSE EST QUOD CAUSA SIT JUSTA ET LEGITIMA. Where the law compels a man to show cause, it is necessary that the cause be just and lawful. 2 Inst. 289.

UBI LEX EST SPECIALIS, ET RATIO EJUS GENERALIS, GENERALITER ACCIPIENDA EST. 2 Inst. 43. Where the law is special, and the reason of it general, it ought to be taken as being general. When the reason for a particular legislative act and acts of the same general character is the same, they should have the same effect. Guile v. La Crosse Gas & Electric Co., 145 Wis. 157, 130 N.W. 234, 241.

UBI LEX NON DISTINGUIT, NEC NOS DISTINGUERE DEBEMUS. Where the law does not distinguish, neither ought we to distinguish. 7 Coke, 5*b*.

UBI MAJOR PARS EST, IBI TOTUM. Where the greater part is, there the whole is. That is, majorities govern. Moore, 578.

UBI MATRIMONIUM, IBI DOS. Where there is marriage, there is dower. Bract. 92.

UBI NON ADEST NORMA LEGIS, OMNIA QUASI PRO SUSPECTIS HABENDA SUNT. When the law fails to serve as a rule, almost everything ought to be suspected. Bac. Aphorisms, 25.

UBI NON EST ANNUA RENOVATIO, IBI DECIMÆ NON DEBENT SOLVI. Where there is no annual renovation, there tithes ought not to be paid.

UBI NON EST CONDENDI AUCTORITAS, IBI NON EST PARENDI NECESSITAS. Dav. Ir. K. B. 69. Where there is no authority for establishing a rule, there is no necessity of obeying it.

UBI NON EST DIRECTA LEX, STANDUM EST ARBITRIO JUDICIS, VEL PROCEDENDUM AD SIMILIA. Ellesm. Post. N. 41. Where there is no direct law, the opinion of the judge is to be taken, or references to be made to similar cases.

UBI NON EST LEX, IBI NON EST TRANSGRESSIO, QUOAD MUNDUM. Where there is no law, there is no transgression, so far as relates to the world. 4 Coke, 16*b*.

UBI NON EST MANIFESTA INJUSTITIA, JUDICES HABENTUR PRO BONIS VIRIS, ET JUDICATUM PRO VERITATE. Where there is no manifest injustice, the judges are to be regarded as honest men, and their judgment as truth. Goix v. Low, 1 Johns. Cas. (N.Y.) 341, 345.

UBI NON EST PRINCIPALIS, NON POTEST ESSE ACCESSORIUS. 4 Coke, 43. Where there is no principal, there cannot be an accessory.

UBI NULLA EST CONJECTURA QUÆ DUCAT ALIO, VERBA INTELLIGENDA SUNT EX PROPRIETATE, NON GRAMMATICA, SED POPULARI EX USU. Where there is nothing to call for a different construction, [the] words [of an instrument] are to be understood, not according to their strict grammatical meaning, but according to their popular and ordinary sense. Grot. de Jure B. lib. 2, c. 16.

UBI NULLUM MATRIMONIUM, IBI NULLA DOS. Where there is no marriage, there is no dower. Bract. fol. 92; 2 Bl.Comm. 130; Co.Litt. 32*a*.

UBI PERICULUM, IBI ET LUCRUM COLLOCATUR. He at whose risk a thing is, should receive the profits arising from it.

UBI PUGNANTIA INTER SE IN TESTAMENTO JUBERENTUR, NEUTRUM RATUM EST. Where repugnant or inconsistent directions are contained in a will, neither is valid. Dig. 50, 17, 188, pr.

UBI QUID GENERALITER CONCEDITUR INEST HÆC EXCEPTIO, SI NON ALIQUID SIT CONTRA JUS FASQUE. 10 Coke, 78. Where a thing is conceded generally [or granted in general terms], this exception is implied: that there shall be nothing contrary to law and right.

UBI QUIS DELINQUIT, IBI PUNIETUR. Where a man offends, there he shall be punished. In cases of felony, the trial shall be always by the common law in the same place where the offense was, and shall not be supposed in any other place. 6 Coke 47b

UBI RE VERA. Where in reality; when in truth or in point of fact. Cro. Eliz. 645; Cro. Jac. 4.

UBI SUPRA. Lat. Where above mentioned. Webster, Dict.

UBI VERBA CONJUNCTA NON SUNT SUFFICIT ALTERUTRUM ESSE FACTUM. Dig. 50, 17, 110, 3. Where words are not conjoined, it is enough if one or other be complied with. Where words are used disjunctively, it is sufficient that either one of the things enumerated be performed.

UBICUNQUE EST INJURIA, IBI DAMNUM SEQUITUR. Wherever there is a wrong, there damage follows. 10 Co. 116.

UBIQUITY. Omnipresence; presence in several places, or in all places, at one time. A fiction of English law is the "legal ubiquity" of the sovereign, by which he is constructively present in all the courts. 1 Bl.Comm. 270.

UDAL. A term mentioned by Blackstone as used in Finland to denote that kind of right in real property which is called, in English law, "allodial." 2 Bl.Comm. 45, note *f*.

UFFER. See Huisserium.

UKAAS, UKASE. Originally, a law or ordinance made by the czar of Russia.

Hence, any official decree or proclamation. Webster, Dict.

ULLAGE. In commercial law. The amount wanting when a cask, on being gauged, is found not to be completely full.

ULNA FERREA. L.Lat. In old English law. The iron ell; the standard ell of iron, kept in the exchequer for the rule of measure.

ULNAGE. Alnage. See Alnager.

ULTERIOR. Beyond what is manifest, seen or avowed, intentionally kept concealed. Harding v. McCullough, 236 Iowa 556, 19 N.W.2d 613, 616.

ULTIMA RATIO. Lat. The last argument; the last resort; the means last to be resorted to.

ULTIMA VOLUNTAS TESTATORIS EST PERIMPLENDA SECUNDUM VERAM INTENTIONEM SUAM. The last will of a testator is to be fulfilled according to his true intention. Co.Litt. 322; Broom, Max. 566.

ULTIMATE. At last, finally, or at the end; the last in the train of progression or sequence tended toward by all that precedes; arrived at as the last result; final. Texas Employers Ins. Ass'n v. Reed, Tex.Civ.App., 150 S.W.2d 858, 862.

ULTIMATE FACTS. In practice and pleading. Averments in pleadings. Oliver v. Coffman, 113 Ind.App. 507, 45 N.E.2d 351, 354, 355; Issuable facts. Maxwell Steel Vault Co. v. National Casket Co., D.C.N.Y., 205 F. 515, 524. Facts essential to the right of action or matter of defense. Wichita Falls & Oklahoma Ry. Co. v. Pepper, 134 Tex. 360, 135 S.W.2d 79, 84. Facts necessary and essential for decision by court. People ex rel. Hudson & M. R. Co. v. Sexton, Sup., 44 N.Y.S.2d 884, 885. Those facts which it is expected evidence will support. McDuffie v. California Tehama Land Corporation, 138 Cal.App. 245, 32 P.2d 385, 386. The issuable, constitutive, or traversable facts essential to statement of cause of action. Johnson v. Johnson, 92 Mont. 512, 15 P.2d 842, 844. The logical conclusions deduced from certain primary evidentiary facts. Mining Securities Co. v. Wall, 99 Mont. 596, 45 P.2d 302, 306.

Those facts found in that vaguely defined field lying between evidential facts on the one side and the primary issue or conclusion of law on the other, being but the logical results of the proofs, or, in other words, mere conclusions of fact. Christmas v. Cowden, 44 N.M. 517, 105 P.2d 484, 487.

The final or resulting fact reached by processes of logical reasoning from the detached or successive facts in evidence, and which is fundamental and determinative of the whole case. Levins v. Rovegno, 71 Cal. 273, 12 P. 161; Kahn v. Central Smelting Co., 2 Utah, 371; Caywood v. Farrell, 175 Ill. 480, 51 N.E. 775; Maeder Steel Products Co. v. Zanello, 109 Or. 562, 220 P. 155, 159. The final resulting effect reached by processes of legal reasoning from the evidentiary facts. Oregon Home Builders v. Montgomery Inv. Co., 94 Or. 349, 184 P. 487, 489. See, also, Ultimate Facts.

ULTIMATUM. Lat. The last. The final and ultimate proposition made in negotiating a treaty, a contract, or the like. The word also means the result of a negotiation, and it comprises the final determination of a party concerned in the matter in dispute.

ULTIMUM SUPPLICIUM. Lat. The last or extreme punishment; the extremity of punishment; the punishment of death. 4 Bl.Comm. 17.

ULTIMUM SUPPLICIUM ESSE MORTEM SOLAM INTERPRETAMUR. The extremest punishment we consider to be death alone. Dig. 48, 19, 21.

ULTIMUS HÆRES. Lat. The last or remote heir; the lord. So called in contradistinction to the *hæres proximus* and the *hæres remotior*. Dalr. Feud. Prop. 110.

ULTRA. Lat. Beyond; outside of; in excess of.

Damages Ultra

Damages beyond a sum paid into court.

Ultra Mare

Beyond sea. One of the old essoins or excuses for not appearing in court at the return of process. Bract. fol. 338.

Ultra Reprises

After deduction of drawbacks; in excess of deductions or expenses.

Ultra Vires

The modern technical designation, in the law of corporations, of acts beyond the scope of the powers of a corporation, as defined by its charter or act of incorporation. State ex rel. v. Holston Trust Co., 168 Tenn. 546, 79 S.W.2d 1012, 1016. The term has a broad application and includes not only acts prohibited by the charter, but acts which are in excess of powers granted and not prohibited. State ex rel. Supreme Temple of Pythian Sisters v. Cook, 234 Mo.App. 898, 136 S.W.2d 142, 146, and generally applied either when a corporation has no power whatever to do an act, or when the corporation has the power but exercises it irregularly. People ex rel. Barrett v. Bank of Peoria, 295 Ill.App. 543, 15 N.E.2d 333, 335. Act is "ultra vires" when corporation is without authority to perform it under any circumstances or for any purpose. Orlando Orange Groves Co. v. Hale, 107 Fla. 304, 144 So. 674, 676.

By doctrine of "ultra vires" a contract made by a corporation beyond the scope of its corporate powers is unlawful. Community Federal Sav. & Loan Ass'n of Independence, Mo., v. Fields, C.C.A.Mo., 128 F.2d 705, 708.

While the phrase "ultra vires" has been used to designate, not only acts beyond the express and implied powers of a corporation, but also acts contrary to public policy or contrary to some express statute prohibiting them, the latter class of acts is now termed illegal, and the "ultra vires" confined to the former class. In re Grand Union Co., C.C.A.N.Y., 219 F. 353, 363; Staacke v. Routledge, 111 Tex. 489, 241 S.W. 994, 998; Pennsylvania R. Co. v. Minis, 120 Md. 461, 496, 87 A. 1062, 1072.

ULTRA POSSE NON POTEST ESSE, ET VICE VERSA. What is beyond possibility cannot exist, and the reverse, [what cannot exist is not possible.] Wing. Max. 100.

ULTRONEOUS WITNESS. In Scotch law. A volunteer witness; one who appears to give evidence without being called upon. 2 Alis.Crim.Pr. 393.

UMPIRAGE. The decision of an umpire. Powell v. Ford, 4 Lea (Tenn.) 288. The word "Umpirage," in reference to an umpire, is the same as the word "award," in reference to arbitrators; but "award" is commonly applied to the decision of the umpire also.

UMPIRE. One clothed with authority to act alone in rendering a decision where arbitrators have disagreed. Hughes v. National Fuel Co., 121 W.Va. 392, 3 S.E.2d 621, 626.

When matters in dispute are submitted to two or more arbitrators, and they do not agree in their decision, it is usual for another person to be called in as "umpire," to whose sole judgment it is then referred. Brown. And see Ingraham v. Whitmore, 75 Ill. 30; Tyler v. Webb, 10 B. Mon. (Ky.) 123; Lyon v. Blossom, 4 Duer (N.Y.) 325. An "umpire," strictly speaking, makes his award independently of that of the arbitrators. Dennis v. Standard Fire Ins. Co., 90 N.J.Eq. 419, 107 A. 161, 163.

UN-. A prefix used indiscriminately, and may mean simply "not." Thus, "unlawful" means "not authorized by law." State v. Sanders, 136 La. 1059, 68 So. 125, 126, Ann.Cas.1916E, 105.

UN NE DOIT PRISE ADVANTAGE DE SON TORT DEMESNE. 2 And. 38, 40. One ought not to take advantage of his own wrong.

UNA PERSONA VIX POTEST SUPPLERE VICES DUARUM. 7 Coke, 118. One person can scarcely supply the place of two. See 9 H.L.Cas. 274.

UNA VOCE. Lat. With one voice; unanimously; without dissent.

UNABLE. This term, as used in a statute providing that evidence given in a former trial may be proved in a subsequent trial, where the witness is unable to testify, means mentally and physically unable. Hansen-Rynning v. Oregon-Washington R. & Nav. Co., 105 Or. 67, 209 P. 462, 464.

UNACCRUED. Not become due, as rent on a lease. Elms Realty Co. v. Wood, 285 Mo. 130, 225 S.W. 1002, 1005.

UNADJUSTED. Uncertain; not agreed upon. Richardson v. Woodbury, 43 Me. 214.

UNALIENABLE. Inalienable; incapable of being aliened, that is, sold and transferred.

UNAMBIGUOUS. Susceptible of but one meaning. Lawrie v. Miller, Tex.Com.App., 45 S.W.2d 172, 173.

UNANIMITY. Agreement of all the persons concerned, in holding one and the same opinion or determination of any matter or question; as the concurrence of a jury in deciding upon their verdict. See Unanimous.

UNANIMOUS. To say that a proposition was adopted by a "unanimous" vote does not always mean that every one present voted for the proposition, but it may, and generally does, mean, when a viva voce vote is taken, that no one voted in the negative. State v. Stephens, 195 Mo.App. 34, 189 S.W. 630, 631.

UNASCERTAINED. Not certainly known or determined. Commissioner of Internal Revenue v. Owens, C.C.A.10, 78 F.2d 768, 773.

UNASCERTAINED DUTIES. Payment in gross, on an estimate as to amount, and where the merchant, on a final liquidation, will be entitled by law to allowances or deductions which do not depend on the rate of duty charged, but on the ascertainment of the quantity of the article subject to duty. Moke v. Barney, 5 Blatchf. 274, Fed. Cas.No.9,698.

UNAVOIDABLE. Not avoidable, incapable of being shunned or prevented, inevitable, and necessary. Day Wood Heel Co. v. Rover, 123 Ohio St. 349, 175 N.E. 588, 590.

UNAVOIDABLE ACCIDENT. An inevitable accident. Leland v. Empire Engineering Co., 135 Md. 208, 108 A. 570, 575, which could not have been foreseen and prevented by using ordinary diligence, and resulting without fault. U. S. v. Kansas City Southern Ry. Co., D.C.Ark., 189 F. 471. Not necessarily an accident which it was physically impossible, in the nature of things, for the person to have prevented, but one not occasioned in any degree, either remotely or directly, by the want of such care or skill as the law holds every man bound to exercise. An accident which could not be prevented by the exercise of ordinary care and prudence. Wollaston v. Stiltz, 114 A. 198, 200, 1 W.W.Harr. (Del.) 273; Atlantic Coast Line R. Co. v. Cook, 34 Ga.App. 1, 128 S.E. 75, 76. A casualty which occurs without negligence of either party and when all means which common prudence suggests have been used to prevent it. Bucktrot v. Partridge, 130 Okl. 122, 265 P. 768, 771.

The term is sometimes defined, however, as synonymous with "act of God,"—any accident produced by physical causes which are inevitable, such as lightnings, storms, perils of the sea, earthquakes, inundations, sudden death, or illness. Early v. Hampton, 15 Ga.App. 95, 82 S.E. 669, 671.

UNAVOIDABLE CASUALTY. An event or accident which human prudence, foresight, and sagacity cannot prevent, happening against will and without negligence. Fernwood Mining Co. v. Pluma, 211 S.W. 159, 163, 138 Ark. 193; Sabin v. Sunset Garden Co., 184 Okl. 106, 85 P.2d 294, 295. Welles v. Castles, 3 Gray (Mass.) 325. Within the meaning of statutes in several states relating to the vacation of judgments, means some casualty or misfortune growing out of conditions or circumstances that prevented the party or his attorney from doing something that, except therefor, would have been done, and does not include mistakes or errors of judgment growing out of misconstruction or understanding of the law, or the failure of parties or counsel through mistake to avail themselves of remedies, which if resorted to would have prevented the casualty or misfortune.

If by any care, prudence, or foresight a thing could have been guarded against, it is not unavoidable. Central Line of Boats v. Lowe, 50 Ga. 509; E. P. Barnes & Bro. v. Eastin, 190 Ky. 392, 227 S.W. 578, 580. The term is not ordinarily limited to an act of God. Kirby v. Davis, 210 Ala. 192, 97 So. 655, 656.

The term refers to events which human prudence or foresight cannot prevent (but see Kohlman v. Moore, 175 Ky. 710, 194 S.W. 933, 935), such as disease and death, miscarriage of the mails, or mistake in the wording of a telegram. Wagner v. Lucas, 79 Okl. 231, 193 P. 421, 422. It may include the sickness. Thweatt v. Grand Temple and Tabernacle of International Order of Twelve Knights and Daughters of Tabor, of Arkansas, 128 Ark. 269, 193 S. W. 508, 509, or death of an attorney, Columbia County v. England, 151 Ark. 465, 236 S.W. 625, 626, or his failure, through some oversight or misunderstanding, to defend. Krause v. Hobart, 173 Iowa, 330, 155 N.W. 279, but it does not apply to the neglect of an attorney or his client; Gavin v. Heath, 125 Okl. 118, 256 P. 745, 746; McGuire v. Mishawaka Woolen Mills, 218 Ky. 530, 291 S.W. 747, 749.

UNAVOIDABLE CAUSE. A cause which reasonably prudent and careful men under like circumstances do not and would not ordinarily anticipate, and whose effects, under similar circumstances, they do not and would not ordinarily avoid. Chicago, B. & Q. R. Co. v. U. S., 114 C.C.A. 334, 194 F. 342.

UNAVOIDABLE DANGERS. This term in a marine policy covering unavoidable dangers of the river includes the unexplained capsizing of a vessel, though human intervention existed in the operation of the vessel, for "unavoidable dangers" mean those unpreventable by persons operating the vessel, and, like the term perils of the sea, include all kinds of marine casualties, thus including accidents in which there is human intervention. A river vessel's tendency to turn over, due to topheavy construction, necessary on account of the shallowness of rivers, is an "unavoidable danger" within the policy. Hillman Transp. Co. v. Home Ins. Co. of New York, 268 Pa. 547, 112 A. 108, 111.

UNBOLTED CORN MEAL. The courts judicially know that corn meal is an unmixed meal made from entire grains of corn, and that "unbolted corn meal" is simply meal not bolted, or from which the bran has not been sifted or separated. Miller Grain & Commission Co. v. International Sugar Feed No. 2 Co., 197 Ala. 100, 72 So. 368.

UNBROKEN. Continuous, as adverse possession. Panhandle & S. F. Ry. Co. v. Hoffman, Tex.Civ. App., 250 S.W. 246, 248.

UNCEASESATH. In Saxon law. An oath by relations not to avenge a relation's death. Blount.

UNCERTAINTY. The state or quality of being unknown or vague. Such vagueness, obscurity, or confusion in any written instrument, *e. g.*, a will, as to render it unintelligible to those who are called upon to execute or interpret it, so that no definite meaning can be extracted from it.

UNCHASTITY. Impurity in mind and conduct, which may exist without actually engaging in unlawful sexual intercourse. State v. Valvoda, 170 Iowa 102, 152 N.W. 21, 23; Cooper v. State, 15 Ala.App. 657, 74 So. 753, 754.

UNCIA. Lat. In Roman law. An ounce; the twelfth of the Roman "*as*," or pound. The twelfth part of anything; the proportion of one-twelfth. 2 Bl. Comm. 462, note *m*.

UNCIA AGRI, UNCIA TERRÆ. These phrases often occur in the charters of the British kings, and signify some measure or quantity of land. It is said to have been the quantity of twelve *modii;* each *modius* being possibly one hundred feet square. Jacob; Mon. Ang. tom. 3, pp. 198, 205.

UNCIARIUS HÆRES. Lat. In Roman law. An heir to one-twelfth of an estate or inheritance. Calvin.

UNCLE. The brother of one's father or mother. State v. Reedy, 44 Kan. 190, 24 P. 66; State v. Guiton, 51 La.Ann. 155, 24 So. 784; Capps v. State, 87 Fla. 388, 100 So. 172, 173.

UNCLEAN HANDS PRINCIPLE. Principle that one who has unclean hands is not entitled to relief in equity. Van Antwerp v. Van Antwerp, 242 Ala. 92, 5 So.2d 73, 78, 79, 80. The doctrine has no application unless party's wrongdoing has some proximate relation to the subject matter in controversy. Fritz v. Jungbluth, 141 Neb. 770, 4 N.W. 2d 911, 913, 914. Vercesi v. Petri, 334 Pa. 385, 5 A. 2d 563, 565.

UNCONDITIONAL. Not limited or affected by any condition;—applied especially to the quality of an insured's estate in the property insured. Libby Lumber Co. v. Pacific States Fire Ins. Co., 79 Mont. 166, 255 P. 340, 344, 60 A.L.R. 1; Rochester German Ins. Co. v. Schmidt, 89 C.C.A. 333, 162 F. 447. See the subtitle "Sole and unconditional owner" under the main title Owner.

UNCONSCIONABLE BARGAIN. An unconscionable bargain or contract is one which no man in his senses, not under delusion, would make, on the one hand, and which no fair and honest man would accept, on the other. Hume v. U. S., 10 S.Ct. 134, 132 U.S. 406, 33 L.Ed. 393; Edler v. Frazier, 174 Iowa 46, 156 N.W. 182, 187; Hall v. Wingate, 159 Ga. 630, 126 S.E. 796, 813; 2 Ves. 125; 4 Bouv. Inst. n. 3848.

UNCONSCIONABLE CONDUCT. Conduct that is monstrously harsh and shocking to the conscience. Domus Realty Corporation v. 3440 Realty Co., 179 Misc. 749, 40 N.Y.S.2d 69, 73.

UNCONSCIOUS. Not possessed of mind. Wilson v. Ray, 64 Ga.App. 540, 13 S.E.2d 848, 852.

UNCONSTITUTIONAL. That which is contrary to the constitution. The opposite of "constitutional." See State v. McCann, 4 Lea (Tenn.) 10; In re Rahrer, C.C.Kan., 43 F. 558, 10 L.R.A. 444; Norton v. Shelby County, 6 S.Ct. 1121, 118 U.S. 425, 30 L.Ed. 178. The word does not necessarily mean that the act assailed is contrary to sound principles of legislation. Ketterer v. Lederer, D. C.Pa., 269 F. 153, 154.

This word is used in two different senses. One, which may be called the English sense, is that the legislation conflicts with some recognized general principle. This is no more than to say that it is unwise, or is based upon a wrong or unsound principle, or conflicts with a generally accepted policy. The other, which may be called the American sense, is that the legislation conflicts with some provision of our written Constitution, which it is beyond the power of the Legislature to change. U. S. v. American Brewing Co., D.C.Pa., 1 F.2d 1001, 1002.

This expression as applied to an act of parliament means simply that it is, in the opinion of the speaker, opposed to the spirit of the English constitution; it cannot mean that the act is either a breach of the law or is void. When applied to a law passed by the French parliament, it means that the law is opposed to the articles of the constitution; it does not necessarily mean that the law in question is void, for it is by no means certain that any French court will refuse to enforce a law because it is unconstitutional. It would probably, though not of necessity, be, when employed by a Frenchman, a term of censure. Dicey, Const. 516.

UNCONTROLLABLE. Incapable of being controlled or ungovernable. Alford v. Zeigler, 65 Ga. App. 294, 16 S.E.2d 69, 72.

UNCONTROLLABLE IMPULSE. As an excuse for the commission of an act otherwise criminal, this term means an impulse towards its commission of such fixity and intensity that it cannot be resisted by the person subject to it, in the enfeebled condition of his will and moral sense resulting from derangement or mania. See Insanity. And see State v. O'Neil, 51 Kan. 651, 33 P. 287, 24 L.R.A. 555.

UNCORE PRIST. L. Fr. Still ready. A species of plea or replication by which the party alleges that he is still ready to pay or perform all that is justly demanded of him. In conjunction with the phrase *"tout temps prist,"* it signifies that he has always been and still is ready to do what is required, thus saving costs where the whole cause is admitted, or preventing delay where it is a replication, if the allegation is made out. 3 Bl. Comm. 303.

UNCUTH. In Saxon law. Unknown; a stranger. A person entertained in the house of another was, on the first night of his entertainment, so called. Bract. fol. 124*b*. See Twa Night Gest.

UNDE NIHIL HABET. Lat. In old English law. The name of the writ of dower, which lay for a widow, where *no dower* at all had been assigned her within the time limited by law. 3 Bl. Comm. 183.

UNDEFENDED. A term sometimes applied to one who is obliged to make his own defense when on trial, or in a civil cause. A cause is said to be undefended when the defendant makes default, in not putting in an appearance to the plaintiff's action; in not putting in his statement of defense; or in not appearing at the trial either personally or by counsel, after having received due notice. Mozley & Whitley.

UNDER. Sometimes used in its literal sense of below in position, beneath, but more frequently in its secondary meaning of "inferior" or "subordinate." Mills v. Stoddard, Mo., 49 U.S. 345, 8 How. 356, 12 L.Ed. 1107; Biordi v. Yanosevich, 93 Pa.Super. 578, 582.

Also according to; as, "under the testimony." Boughan v. State, 193 Ind. 66, 138 N.E. 87.

UNDER AND SUBJECT. Words frequently used in conveyances of land which is subject to a mortgage, to show that the grantee takes subject to such mortgage. See Walker v. Physick, 5 Pa. 203; Lavelle v. Gordon, 15 Mont. 515, 39 P. 740, 27 A.L. R.,N.S., 337, 401.

UNDER CONTROL. This phrase does not necessarily mean the ability to stop instanter under any and all circumstances, an automobile being "under control" within the meaning of the law if it is moving at such a rate, and the mechanism and power under such control, that it can be brought to a stop with a reasonable degree of celerity. Esponette v. Wiseman, 130 Me. 297, 155 A. 650, 653. And motorist is only bound to use that degree of care, caution, and prudence that an ordinarily careful, cautious, and prudent man would have used at the time under same or similar circumstances in operation of said automobile. Gregory v. Suhr, 221 Iowa 1283, 268 N.W. 14, 17. In general, as applied to street cars or railroad trains, the term denotes the control and preparation appropriate to probable emergencies. Lincoln v. Pacific Electric Ry. Co., 33 Cal.App. 83, 164 P. 412, 415; Torantolla v. Kansas City Rys. Co., Mo. App., 226 S.W. 617, 618. It is such control as will enable a train to be stopped promptly if need should arise. Missouri K. & T. Ry. Co. v. Missouri Pac. Ry. Co., 103 Kan. 1, 175 P. 97, 102. It implies the ability to stop within the distance the track is seen to be clear. Fuller v. Oregon-Washington R. & Nav. Co., 93 Or. 160, 181 P. 338, 341.

UNDER HERD. A term conveying the idea that a considerable number of domestic animals are gathered together and held together by herders in constant attendance and in control of their movements from place to place on a public range or within certain areas. Schreiner v. Deep Creek Stock Ass'n, 68 Mont. 104, 217 P. 663, 665.

UNDER THE INFLUENCE OF INTOXICATING LIQUOR. Phrase as used in statutes or ordinances prohibiting the operation of motor vehicle by a party under the influence of intoxicating liquor covers not only all well-known and easily recognized conditions and degrees of intoxication, but any abnormal mental or physical condition which is the result of indulging in any degree in intoxicating liquors, and which tends to deprive one of that clearness of intellect and control of himself which he would otherwise possess. Commonwealth v. Long, 131 Pa.Super. 28, 198 A. 474, 477. Any condition where intoxicating liquor has so far affected the nervous system, brain or muscles of the driver as to impair, to an appreciable degree, his ability to operate his automobile in the manner that an ordinary, prudent and cautious man, in full possession of his faculties, using reasonable care, would operate or drive under like conditions. Luellen v. State, 64 Okl.Cr. 382, 81 P.2d 323, 328.

UNDER WAY. Not being at anchor, or made fast to the shore, or aground;—said of vessels subject to the navigation rules embraced in Act June 7, 1897, c. 4, 30 Stat. 96 (33 U.S.C.A. § 154 et seq., 46 U.S.C.A. § 381 note). The George W. Elder, C.C.A.Or., 249 F. 956, 958; Kaseroff v. Petersen, C.C.A.Cal., 136 F.2d 184, 186.

Thus, a vessel lying with her nose against the bank of a stream and holding her position against the current by the movement of her wheel is a vessel under way, and not entitled to the rights of an anchored vessel. The Ruth, 108 C.C.A. 199, 186 F. 87. And a steamer being towed down stream by tugs without any steam on her boilers, except for steering purposes, is nevertheless "under way." The Scandinavia, D.C.N.Y., 11 F.2d 542, 543.

UNDER-CHAMBERLAINS OF THE EXCHEQUER. Two officers who cleaved the tallies written by the clerk of the tallies, and read the same, that the clerk of the pell and comptrollers thereof might see their entries were true. They also made searches for records in the treasury, and had the custody of Domesday Book. Cowell. The office is now abolished.

UNDERCURRENT OR UNDERFLOW OF SURFACE STREAM. Those waters which slowly find their way through sand and gravel constituting bed of a stream, or lands under or immediately adjacent to stream, and are themselves part of surface stream. Maricopa County Municipal Water Conservation Dist. No. 1 v. Southwest Cotton Co., 39 Ariz. 65, 4 P.2d 369, 380.

UNDERFLOW. See Undercurrent.

UNDERGROUND WATERS. See Water, subtitle Subterranean Waters.

UNDERGROWTH. A term applicable to plants growing under or below other greater plants. Clay v. Telegraph Co., 70 Miss. 411, 11 So. 658.

UNDER-LEASE. Where lessee lets premises for less time than period of his unexpired term, Marathon Oil Co. v. Lambert, Tex.Civ.App., 103 S.W. 2d 176, 181. Also the transfer of a part only of the lands, though for the whole term. Fulton v. Stuart, 2 Ohio 216, 15 Am.Dec. 542; *contra,* Cox v. Fenwick, 4 Bibb, Ky., 538.

See, also, that title under main title Lease.

UNDERLIE THE LAW. In Scotch criminal procedure, an accused person, in appearing to take his trial, is said "to compear and underlie the law." Mozley & Whiteley.

UNDER-SHERIFF. An officer who acts directly under the sheriff, and performs all the duties of the sheriff's office, a few only excepted where the personal presence of the high-sheriff is necessary. The sheriff is civilly responsible for the acts or omissions of his under-sheriff. Mozley & Whiteley. See Delfelder v. Teton Land and Investment Co., 46 Wyo. 142, 24 P.2d 702.

A sheriff's deputy, who, being designated by the sheriff as an "under sheriff," becomes his chief deputy with authority by virtue of his appointment to execute all the ordinary duties of the office of sheriff. Shirran v. Dallas, 21 Cal.App. 405, 132 P. 454, 458. A distinction is sometimes made between this officer and a *deputy,* the latter being appointed for a special occasion or purpose, while the former discharges, in general, all the duties required by the sheriff's office.

UNDERSIGNED, THE. The person whose name is signed or the persons whose names are signed at the end of a document; the subscriber or subscribers. Farmers' Exchange Bank of Elvaston v. Sollars, 353 Ill. 224, 187 N.E. 289, 290, 89 A.L.R. 398.

UNDERSTAND. To know; to apprehend the meaning; to appreciate; as, to understand the nature and effect of an act. Western Indemnity Co. v. MacKechnie, Tex.Civ.App., 214 S.W. 456, 460; International-Great Northern R. Co. v. Pence, Tex. Civ.App., 113 S.W.2d 206, 210. To have a full and clear knowledge of; to comprehend. Fox v. Schaeffer, 131 Conn. 439, 41 A.2d 46, 49.

Thus, to invalidate a deed on the ground that the grantor did not understand the nature of the act, the grantor must be incapable of comprehending that the effect of the act would divest him of the title to the land set forth in the deed. Miller v. Folsom, 49 Okl. 74, 149 P. 1185, 1188. As used in connection with the execution of wills and other instruments, the term includes the realization of the practical effects and consequences of the proposed act. Tillman v. Ogren, 99 Misc. 539, 166 N.Y.S. 39, 40.

UNDERSTANDING. In the law of contracts. An agreement. Southern Ry. Co. v. Powell, 124 Va. 65, 97 S.E. 357, 358. An implied agreement resulting from the express terms of another agreement, whether written or oral. United States v. United Shoe Machinery Co., D.C.Mo., 234 F. 127, 148. An informal agreement, or a concurrence as to its terms. Barkow v. Sanger, 47 Wis. 507, 3 N.W. 16. A valid contract engagement of a somewhat informal character. Winslow v. Lumber Co., 32 Minn. 238, 20 N.W. 145. This is a loose and ambiguous term, unless it be accompanied by some expression to show that it constituted a meeting of the minds of parties upon something respecting which they intended to be bound. Camp v. Waring, 25 Conn. 529.

The term may also import simply a wish or hope, as in a will bequeathing property to another with the "understanding" that at the legatee's death, all property derived under the will should be given to the testatrix's sister. Vincent v. Rix, 127 Misc. 639, 217 N.Y.S. 393, 399.

UNDERSTOOD. The phrase "it is understood," when employed as a word of contract in a written agreement, has the same force as the words "it is agreed." Phœnix Iron & Steel Co. v. Wilkoff Co., C.C.A.Ohio, 253 F. 165, 167; Mertz v. Fleming, 185 Wis. 58, 200 N.W. 655, 656.

UNDERTAKE. To take on oneself; to engage in; to enter upon; to take in hand; set about; attempt; as, to undertake a task; a journey; and, specifically, to take upon oneself solemnly or expressly; to lay oneself under obligation or to enter into stipulation; to perform or to execute; to covenant; contract; hence to guarantee; be surety for; promise; to accept or take over as a charge; to accept responsibility for the care of; to engage to look after or attend to; as to undertake a patient or guest. Lowe v. Poole, 235 Ala. 441, 179 So. 536, 540. To endeavor to perform, try, to promise, engage, or agree, assume an obligation. Torelle v. Templeman, 94 Mont. 149, 21 P.2d 60.

UNDERTAKER. One who undertakes (to do something). In a mechanic's lien statute, the word has been held not to include a mere furnisher of material in connection with the erection of the building. In re American Lime Co., D.C.Tenn., 201 F. 433, 435.

One whose business is to prepare the dead for burial and to take the charge and management of funerals. Anderson v. State, 19 Ala.App. 606, 99 So. 778, 779; State v. Whyte, 177 Wis. 541, 188 N.W. 607, 608, 23 A.L.R. 67.

UNDERTAKING. A promise, engagement, or stipulation. An engagement by one of the parties to a contract to the other, as distinguished from the mutual engagement of the parties to each other. 5 East 17; 4 B. & Ald. 595, followed in Alexander v. State, 28 Tex.App. 186, 12 S.W. 595. It does not necessarily imply a consideration. Thompson v. Blanchard, 3 N.Y. 335.

In a somewhat special sense, a promise given in the course of legal proceedings by a party or his counsel, generally as a condition to obtaining some concession from the court or the opposite party. Sweet.

A promise or security in any form. Code, Iowa, § 48, par. 20.

An official undertaking, such as one by a county clerk or other officer under statutes, unlike an official bond, is not required to be signed by the principal. Fleischner v. Florey, 111 Or. 35, 224 P. 831, 832.

UNDER-TENANT. A tenant under one who is himself a tenant; one who holds by under-lease. See, also, Under-Lease.

UNDERTOOK. Agreed; promised; assumed. This is the technical word to be used in alleging the promise which forms the basis of an action of *assumpsit*. Bacon, Abr. *Assumpsit* (F).

UNDER-TREASURER OF ENGLAND. He who transacted the business of the lord high treasurer.

UNDER-TUTOR. In Louisiana. In every tutorship there shall be an under-tutor, whom it shall be the duty of the judge to appoint at the time letters of tutorship are certified for the tutor. It is the duty of the under-tutor to act for the minor whenever the interest of the minor is in opposition to the interest of the tutor. Civ. Code La. arts. 273, 275.

UNDERWRITE. To insure life or property. See Underwriter.

To insure the sale of corporate bonds or similar securities to the public by agreeing to buy those which are not sold. Busch v. Stromberg-Carlson Tel. Mfg. Co., C.C.A. Mo., 217 F. 328, 330; Stewart v. G. L. Miller & Co., 161 Ga. 919, 132 S.E. 535, 538, 45 A.L.R. 559. To agree to sell bonds, etc., to the public, or to furnish the necessary money for such securities, and to buy those which cannot be sold. Minot v. Burroughs, 223 Mass. 595, 112 N.E. 620, 623; Rauer's Law & Collection Co. v. Harrell, 32 Cal. App. 45, 162 P. 125, 131.

An underwriting contract, aside from its use in insurance, is an agreement, made before corporate shares are brought before the public, that in the event of the public not taking all the shares or the number mentioned in the agreement, the underwriter will take the shares which the public do not take; "underwriting" being a purchase, together with a guaranty of a sale of the bonds. Fraser v. Home Telephone & Telegraph Co., 91 Wash. 253, 157 P. 692, 694; In re Hackett, Hoff and Thiermann, C.C.A.Wis., 70 F.2d 815, 819.

UNDERWRITER. The person who insures another, as in a fire or life policy; the insurer. See Childs v. Firemen's Ins. Co., 66 Minn. 393, 69 N. W. 141, 35 L.R.A. 99. Especially, a person who joins with others in entering into a marine policy of insurance as insurer.

One who underwrites corporate bonds or stocks. Fraser v. Home Telephone & Telegraph Co., 91 Wash. 253, 157 P. 692, 694. One who agrees with others to purchase an entire issue of bonds or other securities, usually at the end of a certain period. By reason of such underwriting, the bonds, etc., obtain a market value or a value as collateral security. See Underwrite.

UNDISCLOSED PRINCIPAL. If, at time of transaction conducted by agent, other party thereto has no notice that agent is acting for a principal, the principal is "undisclosed principal." Dodge v. Blood, 299 Mich. 364, 300 N.W. 121, 123.

UNDISPUTED. Meaning "uncontested," rather than "uncontradicted." Pennsylvania R. Co. v. Stallings, 165 Md. 615, 170 A. 163, 164.

UNDISPUTED FACT. Within the meaning of a statute, an admitted fact, which the court has not deemed sufficiently material to add to the finding, or has inadvertently omitted from it; a fact not found by the court does not become an "undisputed fact," merely because one or more witnesses testify to it without direct contradiction. Dexter Yarn Co. v. American Fabrics Co., 102 Conn. 529, 129 A. 527, 532.

UNDIVIDED PROFITS. Profits which have not in fact been divided or distributed, English & Mersick Co. v. Eaton, D.C.Conn., 299 F. 646, 649; or otherwise used, Douglas v. Edwards, C.C.A.N. Y., 298 F. 229, 237. Current undistributed earnings. Edwards v. Douglas, 46 S.Ct. 85, 89, 269 U. S. 204, 70 L.Ed. 235. Winkelman v. General Motors Corporation, D.C.N.Y., 44 F.Supp. 960, 966. Profits not set aside as surplus or distributed in dividends. First Nat. Bank v. Moon, 102 Kan. 334, 170 P. 33, 34, L.R.A.1918C, 986; Phillips v. U. S., D.C.Pa., 12 F.2d 598, 600.

The terms "surplus" and "undivided profits" have different meanings in banking circles. State ex rel. Payne v. Exchange Bank of Natchitoches, 84 So. 481, 482, 147 La. 25. Surplus, like the capital stock, constitutes the working capital of the bank and is, in addition, a fund for the protection of the depositors. The "undivided profits" constitute a temporary fund changing in size from day to day and carried only until dividend periods when it is distributed to the stockholders or transferred to the permanent surplus. It is the fund from which the expenses and losses of the bank are paid. Sarles v. Scandinavian American Bank, 33 N.D. 40, 156 N.W. 556, 557.

"Surplus" and "undivided profits," as commonly employed in corporate accounting, denote an excess in the aggregate value of the assets of the corporation over the sum of liabilities, including capital stock; "surplus" describing such part of the excess in the value of the corporate assets as is treated by the corporation as part of the permanent capital, while the term "undivided profits" designates such part of the excess as consists of profits neither distributed as dividends nor carried to the surplus account. Willcuts v. Milton Dairy Co., 48 S.Ct. 71, 72, 275 U.S. 215, 72 L.Ed. 247.

UNDIVIDED RIGHT. An undivided right or title, or a title to an undivided portion of an estate, is that owned by one of two or more tenants in common or joint tenants before partition. Held by the same title by two or more persons, whether their rights are equal as to value or quantity, or unequal. See In re Wellington, 16 Pick. (Mass.) 98, 26 Am.Dec. 631.

UNDRES. In old English law. Minors or persons under age not capable of bearing arms. Fleta, l. 1, c. 9; Cowell.

UNDUE. More than necessary; not proper; illegal. Webb v. Superior Court in and for Del Norte County, 28 Cal.App. 391, 152 P. 957, 958. See, also, Elk Hotel Co. v. United Fuel Gas Co., 75 W.Va. 200, 83 S.E. 922, 924, L.R.A.1917E, 970.

It denotes something wrong, according to the standard of morals which the law enforces in relations of men, and in fact illegal, and qualifies the purpose with which influence is exercised or result which it accomplishes. Morris v. Morris, 192 Miss. 518, 6 So.2d 311, 312.

UNDUE INFLUENCE. Any improper or wrongful constraint, machination, or urgency of persuasion whereby the will of a person is overpowered and he is induced to do or forbear an act which he would not do or would do if left to act freely. Powell v. Betchel, 340 Ill. 330, 172 N.E. 765, 768. Influence which deprives person influenced of free agency or destroys freedom of his will and renders it more the will of another than his own. Conner v. Brown, Del., 3 A.2d 64, 71, 9 W.W.Harr. 529; In re Velladao's Estate, 31 Cal.App.2d 355, 88 P.2d 187, 190.

"Undue influence" is not necessarily physical injury or threat of it, but is a species of duress, or at least often indistinguishable from it. Trigg v. Trigg, 37 N.M. 296, 22 P.2d 119. And although there is no coercion amounting to duress, but transaction is result of moral, social, or domestic force, consciously and designedly exerted on party, peculiarly susceptible to external pressure on account of mental weakness, old age, ignorance, and the like, controlling the free action of the will, and preventing a true consent, equity may relieve against the transaction on the ground of "undue influence." In re Null's Estate, 302 Pa. 64, 153 A. 137, 139. But modest persuasion or arguments addressed to the understanding or the appeal of affection cannot be deemed "undue influence". Calveard v. Reynolds, 281 Ky. 518, 136 S.W.2d 795, 799.

Undue influence consists (1) in the use, by one in whom a confidence is reposed by another, or who holds a real or apparent authority over him, of such confidence or authority, for the purpose of obtaining an unfair advantage over him; (2) in taking an unfair advantage of another's weakness of mind; or (3) in taking a grossly oppressive and unfair advantage of another's necessities or distress. Buchanan v. Prall, 39 N.D. 423, 167 N.W. 488, 489; Dolliver v. Dolliver, 94 Cal. 642, 30 P. 4.

"Undue influence," such as will invalidate a will, must be something which destroys the free agency of the testator at the time when the instrument is made, and which, in effect, substitutes the will of another for that of the testator. It is not sufficient that the testator was influenced by the beneficiaries in the ordinary affairs of life, or that he was surrounded by them and in confidential relations with them at the time of its execution. Mere general influence, not brought to bear on the testamentary act, is not undue influence; but in order to constitute undue influence, it must be used directly to procure the will, and must amount to coercion destroying the free agency of the testator. Mere suspicion that undue influence was brought to bear is not sufficient to justify the setting aside of the will. Myers v. Myers, 130 Okl. 184, 266 P. 452, 455. To constitute "undue influence," justifying denial or revocation of probate of will, testator's mind must have been so controlled or affected by persuasion or pressure, artful or fraudulent contrivances, or by influences of persons in close confidential relations with him, that he is not left to act intelligently, understandingly, and voluntarily, but subject to will or purposes of another. In re Starr's Estate, 125 Fla. 536, 170 So. 620. Solicitation, importunity, argument, advice, and persuasion are not "undue influence" sufficient to avoid a contract or will. Influence obtained by persuasion and argument, or gained by kindness and affection, is not prohibited, where no imposition or fraud is practiced, and where the person's will is not overcome. Barron v. Reardon, 137 Md. 308, 113 A. 283, 285; Stump v. Sturn, C.C.A.W.Va., 254 F. 535, 538.

Undue influence at elections occurs where any one interferes with the free exercise of a voter's franchise, by violence, intimidation, or otherwise. It is a misdemeanor. 1 Russ.Crimes, 321; Steph. Crim. Dig. 79.

UNEARNED INCREMENT. Value due to no labor or expenditure on the part of an owner but to natural causes making an increased demand for it, such as increase of population or the general progress of society. Miller v. Huntington & Ohio Bridge Co., 123 W.Va. 320, 15 S.E.2d 687, 699.

UNEDUCATED. Not synonymous with illiterate. A man might be able to read and write, carry on a business correspondence, understand business transactions, and be bound by all his contracts, and yet be an "uneducated" man. Baker v. Patton, 144 Ga. 502, 87 S.E. 659, 660.

UNEMPLOYMENT. State of being not employed, lack of employment. A. J. Meyer & Co. v. Unemployment Compensation Commission, 348 Mo. 147, 152 S.W.2d 184, 189.

UNEQUAL. Not uniform. Los Angeles County v. Ransohoff, 24 Cal.App.2d 238, 74 P.2d 828, 830. Ill-balanced; uneven; partial; unfair;—not synonymous with inappropriate, which means unsuitable, unfit, or improper. Lane v. St. Denis Catholic Church of Benton, Mo.App., 274 S.W. 1103, 1106.

UNEQUIVOCAL. Clear; plain; capable of being understood in only one way, or as clearly demonstrated; free from uncertainty, or without doubt; and, when used with reference to the burden of proof, it implies proof of the highest possible character and it imports proof of the nature of mathematical certainty. Berry v. Maywood Mut. Water Co. No. 1, 11 Cal.App.2d 479, 53 P.2d 1032; Molyneux v. Twin Falls Canal Co., 54 Idaho 619, 35 P.2d 651, 656, 94 A.L.R. 1264.

UNERRING. Incapable of error or failure; certain; sure; infallible. Gardner v. State, 27 Wyo. 316, 196 P. 750, 752, 15 A.L.R. 1040.

UNETHICAL. Not ethical; hence, colloquially, not according to business or professional standards. Kraushaar v. La Vin, 181 Misc. 508, 42 N.Y.S.2d 857, 859.

UNETHICAL CONDUCT. Authorizing recovery of broker's commission for sale completed by another broker means a purpose to obtain profits from broker's exertions without payment, and exists where employer revokes the broker's authority and makes the sale through other means when the broker has performed all he has undertaken or is plainly or evidently approaching success. Kacavas v. Diamond, 303 Mass. 88, 20 N.E.2d 936, 938.

UNEXCEPTIONABLE. Without any fault; not subject to any objection or criticism. Washam v. Beaty, 210 Ala. 635, 99 So. 163, 167.

UNEXPECTED. Not expected, coming without warning, sudden. Bachus v. Ronnebaum, 98 Ind. App. 603, 186 N.E. 386, 387.

UNEXPIRED TERM. Remainder of a period prescribed by law after a portion of such time has passed, and phrase is not synonymous with "vacancy." State ex rel. Sanchez v. Dixon, La.App., 4 So.2d 591, 596.

UNFAIR. In the labor movement, unfriendly to organized labor; refusing to recognize its rules and regulations;—applied particularly to employers, *e. g.*, one who refuses to employ members of a trade union. Steffes v. Motion Picture Mach. Operators' Union, 136 Minn. 200, 161 N.W. 524. A characterization of an employer who refuses to conduct his business in manner desired by union. John R. Thompson Co. v. Delicatessen and Cafeteria Workers Union Local 410, 126 N.J. Eq. 119, 8 A.2d 130, 133; Blossom Dairy Co. v.

International Brotherhood of Teamsters, 125 W. Va. 165, 23 S.E.2d 645, 650.

UNFAIR COMPETITION. A term which may be applied generally to all dishonest or fraudulent rivalry in trade and commerce, but is particularly applied in the courts of equity (where it may be restrained by injunction) to the practice of endeavoring to substitute one's own goods or products in the markets for those of another, having an established reputation and extensive sale, by means of imitating or counterfeiting the name, title, size, shape, or distinctive pecularities of the article, or the shape, color, label, wrapper, or general appearance of the package, or other such simulations, the imitation being carried far enough to mislead the general public or deceive an unwary purchaser, and yet not amounting to an absolute counterfeit or to the infringement of a trade-mark or trade-name. Called in France *"concurrence deloyale"* and in Germany *"unlauterer Wettbewerb."* Reddaway v. Banham, [1896] App.Cas. 199; Singer Mfg. Co. v. June Mfg. Co., 16 S.Ct. 1002, 163 U.S. 169, 41 L.Ed. 118; Dennison Mfg. Co. v. Thomas Mfg. Co., C.C.Del., 94 F. 651; Sterling Remedy Co. v. Eureka Chemical Co., 25 C.C.A. 314, 80 F. 108.

The simulation by one person of the name, materials, color scheme, symbols, patterns, or devices employed by another for purpose of deceiving the public, or substitution of goods, or wares of one person for those of another, thus falsely inducing purchase of goods and obtaining benefits belonging to competitor. Mathews Conveyor Co. v. Palmer-Bee Co., C.C.A.Mich., 135 F.2d 73, 84; Esskay Art Galleries v. Gibbs, 205 Ark. 1157, 172 S.W.2d 924, 926. American Fork & Hoe Co. v. Stampit Corporation, C.C.A.Ohio, 125 F.2d 472, 474, 475. Passing off, or attempting to pass off upon the public the goods or business of one person as the goods or business of another. Westminister Laundry Co. v. Hesse Envelope Co., 174 Mo.App. 238, 156 S.W. 767, 768; Sayre v. McGill Ticket Punch Co., D.C.Ill., 200 F. 771, 773; Socony-Vacuum Oil Co. v. Oil City Refiners, C.C.A.Ohio, 136 F.2d 470, 474. The selling of another's product as one's own. A. L. A. Schechter Poultry Corporation v. United States, N.Y., 55 S.Ct. 837, 844, 295 U.S. 495, 79 L.Ed. 1570, 97 A.L.R. 947. The sale of goods by means which shock judicial sensibilities. Margarete Steiff v. Bing, D.C.N.Y., 215 F. 204, 206. See, however, Federal Trade Commission v. Gratz, 40 S.Ct. 572, 575, 253 U.S. 421, 64 L.Ed. 993. Also deceitful advertising which injures a competitor, bribery of employees, secret rebates and concessions, and other devices of unfair trade. In re Northern Pigment Co., Cust. & Pat. App., 71 F.2d 447, 453.

Fraudulent intent is a necessary ingredient of unfair competition. Queen Mfg. Co. v. Isaac Ginsberg & Bros., C.C.A.Mo., 25 F.2d 284, 288.

The equitable doctrine of "unfair competition" is not confined to cases of actual market competition between similar products of different parties, but extends to all cases in which one party fraudulently seeks to sell his goods as those of another. Wisconsin Electric Co. v. Dumore Co., C.C.A.Ohio, 35 F.2d 555, 557.

Test of "unfair competition" is, not whether distinction between two competing products can be recognized when placed alongside each other, but whether, when the two products are not viewed together, a purchaser of ordinary prudence would be induced by reason of the marked resemblance in general effect to mistake one for the other despite differences in matters of detail. Ralston Purina Co. v. Checker Food Products Co., Mo.App., 80 S.W.2d 717, 719, 720.

UNFAIR HEARING. Where the defect, or the practice complained of, was such as might have led to a denial of justice, or where there was absent one of the elements deemed essential to due process. Ex parte Bridges, D.C.Cal., 49 F.Supp. 292, 302, 306; Bufalino v. Irvine, C.C.A.Kan., 103 F.2d 830, 832; Kielema v. Crossman, C.C.A.Tex., 103 F.2d 292, 293.

UNFAIR LABOR PRACTICE. Within National Labor Relations Act for an employer: (1) To interfere with, restrain, or coerce employees in the exercise of their rights to self-organization, to form, join or assist labor organizations, to bargain collectively through representatives of their own choosing, and to engage in concerted activities, for the purpose of collective bargaining or other mutual aid or protection. (2) To dominate or interfere with the formation or administration of any labor organization or contribute financial or other support to it. (3) By discrimination in regard to hire or tenure of employment or any term or condition of employment to encourage or discourage membership in any labor organization. (4) To discharge or otherwise discriminate against an employee because he has filed charges or given testimony under the Act. (5) To refuse to bargain collectively with the representatives of his employees. National Labor Relations Act, §§ 7, 8, 29 U.S.C.A. §§ 102.1 et seq., 157, 158.

The following has been held to be "unfair labor practice" under National Relations Act:

Failure to re-employ striking employees. Western Cartridge Co. v. National Labor Relations Board, C.C.A.7, 139 F.2d 855, 858. Refusal of employer to reinstate union members who were evicted from plant unless members would withdraw from union. National Labor Relations Board v. J. G. Boswell Co., C.C.A.9, 136 F.2d 585, 590, 592, 596. Refusal of employer to bargain collectively in good faith. National Labor Relations Board v. Griswold Mfg. Co., C.C.A.3, 106 F.2d 713, 724; National Labor Relations Board v. Somerset Shoe Co., C.C.A.1, 111 F.2d 681, 688, 689. Threats by employer to close if union gained a foothold in plant. National Labor Relations Board v. J. G. Boswell Co., C.C.A.9, 136 F.2d 585, 590, 592, 596. Anti-union statements made by employer's supervisory employees during and after strike, together with statement to one of the strikers that he would never get a job in that town anymore. N. L. R. B. v. Indiana Desk Co., C.C.A.7, 149 F.2d 987, 992, 996. Refusal of employer to permit posting of a notice that employer would not discriminate against employees who wished to join union. National Labor Relations Board v. J. G. Boswell Co., C.C.A.9, 136 F.2d 585, 590, 592, 596. Discharge of an employee because of membership in or activity on behalf of a labor organization. National Labor Relations Board v. Newark Morning Ledger, C.C.A. 3, 120 F.2d 262, 268; National Labor Relations Board v. Bank of America Trust & Savings Ass'n, C.C.A.9, 130 F.2d 624, 628, 629. Employer's interference with and his dominating formation and administration of new labor organization. National Labor Relations Board v. Swift & Co., C.C. A.8, 116 F.2d 143, 145 146; National Labor Relations Board v. Blossom Products Corporation, C.C.A.3, 121 F.2d 260, 262; National Labor Relations Board v. Stackpole Carbon Co., C.C.A.3, 105 F.2d 167, 173, 175. Refusal of employer which had refused to bargain with union which had been certified as the exclusive bargaining agent. National Labor

Relations Board v. John Engelhorn & Sons, C.C.A.3, 134 F.2d 553, 558. Assault by persons employed by manufacturer upon union organizers or sympathizers. National Labor Relations Board v. Ford Motor Co., C.C.A.6, 114 F.2d 905, 911, 915. Discharge of employee because he would not become member of union in accordance with closed shop agreement. Virginia Electric & Power Co. v. National Labor Relations Board, C.C.A.4, 132 F.2d 390, 396.

UNFAIR METHODS OF COMPETITION. This phrase within Federal Trade Commission Act has broader meaning than common-law term "unfair competition," but its scope cannot be precisely defined, and what constitutes "unfair methods of competition" must be determined in particular instances, upon evidence, in light of particular competitive conditions and of what is found to be a specific and substantial public interest. Federal Trade Commission Act § 5, 15 U.S.C.A. § 45. A.L. A. Schechter Poultry Corporation v. United States, N.Y., 55 S.Ct. 837, 844, 295 U.S. 495, 79 L.Ed. 1570, 97 A.L.R. 947.

The term though not defined by the statute is clearly inapplicable to practices never heretofore regarded as opposed to good morals because characterized by deception, bad faith, fraud, or oppression, or as against public policy because of their dangerous tendency unduly to hinder competition or create monopoly. The act was not intended to fetter free and fair competition as commonly understood and practiced by honorable opponents in trade. In re Amtorg Trading Corporation, Cust & Pat.App., 75 F.2d 826, 830. But a method was said to be an unfair method if it does not leave to each actual or potential competitor a fair opportunity for play of his contending force engendered by an honest desire for gain. California Rice Industry v. Federal Trade Commission, C.C.A.9, 102 F.2d 716, 721.

UNFAIR TRADE, DOCTRINE OF. The doctrine that one person has no right to sell goods as goods of another, nor to do other business as the business of another. Foster Canning Co. v. Lardan Packing Co., Sup., 17 N.Y.S.2d 583, 585.

UNFAITHFUL. Characterized by bad faith;—not synonymous with "illegal," which means unlawful or contrary to law, nor with "improper," which, as applied to conduct, implies such conduct as a man of ordinary and reasonable prudence would not, under the circumstances, have been guilty of. State v. American Surety Co. of New York, 26 Idaho 652, 145 P. 1097, 1104, Ann.Cas. 1916E, 209.

UNFINISHED. Not completed; not brought to an end; imperfect; the last effort, as a final touch is given to a work. Bell & Graddy v. O'Brien, Tex. Civ.App., 113 S.W.2d 560, 562.

UNFIT. Unsuitable, incompetent, not adapted or qualified for a particular use or service, having no fitness. Morse v. Caldwell, 55 Ga.App. 804, 191 S.E. 479, 488.

UNFIT FOR USE AS A BEVERAGE. This language in a statute is not necessarily applicable to an alcoholic compound or preparation merely because it may be drunk in sufficient quantities to produce death. Thamann v. Merritt, 111 Neb. 639, 197 N.W. 413, 414.

UNFORESEEN. Not foreseen, not expected. Pampel v. Board of Examiners, 114 Mont. 380, 136 P.2d 991, 994.

UNFORESEEN CAUSE. With reference to causes excusing delay, under the Workmen's Compensation Act, in giving notice of injury, a cause which could not have been reasonably foreseen as likely to arise or occur, and yet is of such a nature as to have substantially interfered with the giving of the notice. Wardwell's Case, 121 Me. 216, 116 A. 447, 448. A reasonable cause. Donahue v. R. A. Sherman's Sons Co., 39 R.I. 373, 98 A. 109, L.R.A. 1917A, 76.

UNFORESEEN EVENT. In the civil law. A vis major; an uncontrollable force;—so used in Civ. Code La. art. 2697, relating to the termination of a lease by the total destruction of the property. Knapp v. Guerin, 144 La. 754, 81 So. 302, 305.

UNGELD. In Saxon law. An outlaw; a person whose murder required no composition to be made, or *weregeld* to be paid, by his slayer.

UNHARMED. Within provision of Federal Kidnapping Act that death sentence shall not be imposed if kidnapped person has been liberated unharmed, means uninjured. Federal Kidnapping Act § 1 et seq., as amended, 18 U.S.C.A. § 1201 et seq. Robinson v. U. S., Ky., 65 S.Ct. 666, 668, 324 U.S. 282, 89 L.Ed. 944.

UNIATE CHURCH. One united with Rome and subject to control by local ecclesiastical authority representing the Vatican. Drozda v. Bassos, 260 App.Div. 408, 23 N.Y.S.2d 544, 547.

UNICA TAXATIO. The obsolete language of a special award of *venire*, where, of several defendants, one pleads, and one lets judgment go by default, whereby the jury, who are to try and assess damages on the issue, are also to assess damages against the defendant suffering judgment by default. Wharton.

UNIFACTORAL OBLIGATION. See Contract.

UNIFIED. Made one. Adams v. Salt River Valley Water Users' Ass'n, 53 Ariz. 374, 89 P.2d 1060, 1071.

UNIFORM, *n.* Within the meaning of an ordinance requiring a traction company to give free transportation to members of the police force and fire department when in uniform, a plain clothes man, whose only prescribed uniform was a metal badge which might be worn concealed, while wearing such badge was "in uniform." Montgomery Light & Traction Co. v. Avant, 202 Ala. 404, 80 So. 497, 498, 3 A.L.R. 384.

UNIFORM, *adj.* Conforming to one rule, mode, or unvarying standard; not different at different times or places; applicable to all places or divisions of a country. People v. Vickroy, 266 Ill. 384, 107 N.E. 638, 640. Equable; applying alike to all within a class. Bufkin v. Mitchell, 106 Miss. 253, 63 So. 458, 459, 50 L.R.A.,N.S., 428.

A statute is general and uniform in its operation when it operates equally upon all persons who are brought within the relations and circumstances provided for, McAunich v. Mississippi & M. R. Co., 20 Iowa, 342. Stevens v. Village of

Nashwauk, 161 Minn. 20, 200 N.W. 927, 929, when all persons under the same conditions and in the same circumstances are treated alike, and classification is reasonable and naturally inherent in the subject-matter. Kelly v. Finney, 207 Ind. 557, 194 N.E. 157, 166.

The words "general" and "uniform" as applied to laws have a meaning antithetical to special or discriminatory laws. Ex parte Nowak, 184 Cal. 701, 195 P. 402, 404. The term "uniform," however, does not mean universal. Watson v. Greely, 67 Cal.App. 328, 227 P. 664, 670.

The burdens of taxation, to be uniform, must have the essential of equality, and must bear alike upon all the property within the limits of the unit wherein it is lawful to levy taxes for a purpose, whether that unit be the state, county, or a municipality. Lang v. Commonwealth, 190 Ky. 29, 226 S.W. 379, 382. See, also, Jordan v. Duval County, 68 Fla. 48, 66 So. 298, 299. And requirement is met when tax is equal on all persons belonging to descibed class on which tax is imposed. Hilton v. Harris, 207 N.C. 465, 177 S.E. 411.

With reference to locality, a tax is "uniform" when it operates with equal force and effect in every place where the subject of it is found, and with reference to classification, it is uniform when it operates without distinction or discrimination upon all persons composing the described class. Hart v. Board of Comrs. of Burke County, 192 N.C. 161, 134 S.E. 403, 405; City of Cape Girardeau v. Fred A. Groves Motor Co., 346 Mo. 762, 142 S.W.2d 1040, 1042.

UNIFORM LAWS. A considerable number of laws have been approved by the National Conference of Commissioners on Uniform State Laws, and many of them have been adopted in one or more jurisdictions in the United States and its possessions. Among the more important of these laws are the Uniform Negotiable Instruments Act which has been adopted in all the states as well as in the District of Columbia, Alaska, Hawaii, the Philippine Islands, and Porto Rico; the Uniform Sales Act, which in 1950 had been adopted in 37 jurisdictions; the Uniform Bills of Lading Act, in 32 jurisdictions; the Uniform Stock Transfer Act, in all the states as well as in the District of Columbia, Alaska and Hawaii; and the Uniform Partnership Act, in 32. Others which may be mentioned include the Uniform Warehouse Receipts, Declaratory Judgments, Fiduciaries, Fraudulent Conveyance, Desertion and Nonsupport, Veterans' Guardianship, Conditional Sales and Limited Partnership Acts.

UNIFORMITY. Conformity to one pattern; sameness. Naill v. Order of United Commercial Travelers of America, 103 Okl. 179, 229 P. 833, 837.

"Uniformity of operation" of laws does not require "universality of operation." The former term relates to similarity of conditions affecting subjects or localities of the state that are appropriately classified. The latter term relates to the whole and every part of the state. State v. Daniel, 87 Fla. 270, 99 So. 804, 809.

The constitutional requirement of "uniformity" is complied with when the law operates uniformly upon all persons brought within the relations and circumstances provided by it. Abbott v. Commissioners of Roads and Revenues of Fulton County, 160 Ga. 657, 129 S.E. 38, 41.

Uniformity in taxation implies equality in the burden of taxation, which cannot exist without uniformity in the mode of assessment, as well as in the rate of taxation. Further, the uniformity must be coextensive with the territory to which it applies. And it must be extended to all property subject to taxation, so that all property may be taxed alike and equally. Exchange Bank v. Hines, 3 Ohio St. 15. And see Edye v. Robertson, 5 S.Ct. 247, 112 U.S. 580, 28 L.Ed. 798; People v. Auditor General, 7 Mich. 90; Hilger v. Moore, 56 Mont. 146, 182 P. 477, 481. Department of Justice v. A. Overholt and Co., 331 Pa. 182, 200 A. 849, 853.

The rule of "uniformity" does not require that all subjects be taxed, nor taxed alike, but is complied with when the tax is levied equally and uniformly on all subjects of the same class and kind. Sims v. Ahrens, 167 Ark. 557, 271 S.W. 720, 729. The uniformity required in taxation is limited to a uniformity in rate, assessment, and valuation of the particular tax involved, and has no reference to a uniformity of the sum total of taxes which a citizen is required to pay. King v. Sullivan County, 128 Tenn. 393, 160 S.W. 847, 848, and does not require uniformity of collection, but only uniformity of assessment. Mississippi State Tax Commission v. Flora Drug Co., 167 Miss. 1, 148 So. 373, 378.

Uniformity in taxation means equality in burden and not equality in method. Ewert v. Taylor, 38 S.D. 124, 160 N. W. 797, 803.

See, also, "Uniform, *adj.*"

UNIFORMITY, ACT OF. An act which regulates the terms of membership in the Church of England and the colleges of Oxford and Cambridge, (St. 13 & 14 Car. II. c. 4.) See St. 9 & 10 Vict. c. 59. The act of uniformity has been amended by the St. 35 & 36 Vict. c. 35, which *inter alia* provides a shortened form of morning and evening prayer. Wharton.

UNIFORMITY OF PROCESS ACT. The English statute of 2 Wm. IV. c. 39, establishing a uniform process for the commencement of actions in all the courts of law at Westminster. 3 Steph. Comm. 566. The improved system thus established was more fully amended by the Procedure Acts of 1852, 1854, and 1860, and by the Judicature Acts of 1873 and 1875.

UNIFY. To cause to be one; to make into a unit; to unite; to become one; to consolidate. Adams v. Salt River Valley Water Users' Ass'n, 53 Ariz. 374, 89 P.2d 1060, 1071.

UNIGENITURE. The state of being the only begotten.

UNILATERAL. One-sided; ex parte; having relation to only one of two or more persons or things.

UNILATERAL CONTRACT. See Contract.

UNILATERAL MISTAKE. A mistake or misunderstanding as to the terms or effect of a contract, made or entertained by one of the parties to it but not by the other. Green v. Stone, 54 N.J. Eq. 387, 34 A. 1099, 55 Am.St.Rep. 577; Kant v. Atlanta, B. & A. R. Co., 189 Ala. 48, 66 So. 598, 599.

UNILATERAL RECORD. Records are unilateral when offered to show a particular fact, as a *prima facie* case, either for or against a stranger. Colligan v. Cooney, 107 Tenn. 214, 64 S.W. 31.

UNIMPEACHABLE WITNESS. Within a statute requiring proof of a holographic will by the unimpeachable evidence of at least three disinterested witnesses to the testator's handwriting, one whom the jury finds to speak truthfully and whose conclusion they find to be correct, notwithstanding the presence of other evidence contradicting him. Sneed v. Reynolds, 166 Ark. 581, 266 S.W. 686, 689; Murphy v. Murphy, 144 Ark. 429, 222 S.W. 721, 723.

UNIMPROVED LAND. A statutory term which includes lands, once improved, that have reverted to a state of nature, as well as lands that have never been improved. Moore v. Morris, 118 Ark. 516, 177 S.W. 6, 8.

UNINCLOSED PLACE. A place not entirely inclosed, an "inclosed" place being a place inclosed on all sides by some sort of material. Ex parte Wisner, 32 Cal.App. 637, 163 P. 868, 869.

UNINFECTED. Untainted or uncontaminated, not affected unfavorably, not impregnated or permeated with that which is bad or harmful. Leonardi v. A. Habermann Provision Co., 143 Ohio St. 623, 56 N.E.2d 232, 237.

UNINTELLIGIBLE. That which cannot be understood.

UNIO. Lat. In canon law. A consolidation of two churches into one. Cowell.

UNIO PROLIUM. Lat. Uniting of offspring. A method of adoption, chiefly used in Germany, by which step-children (on either or both sides of the house) are made equal, in respect to the right of succession, with the children who spring from the marriage of the two contracting parties. See Heinecc. Elem. § 188.

UNION. A league; a federation; an unincorporated association of persons for a common purpose; as, a trade or labor union. Hughes v. State, 109 Ark. 403, 160 S.W. 209. A joinder of separate entities. State ex rel. Dawson v. Dinwiddie, 186 Okl. 63, 95 P.2d 867, 869.

Ecclesiastical Law

Two or more benefices which have been united into one benefice. Sweet.

English Poor-Law

Two or more parishes which have been consolidated for the better administration of the poor-law therein.

Public Law

A popular term in America for the United States; also, in Great Britain, for the consolidated governments of England and Scotland, or for the political tie between Great Britain and Ireland.

Scotch Law

A "clause of union" is a clause in a feoffment by which two estates, separated or not adjacent, are united as one, for the purpose of making a single seisin suffice for both.

UNION-JACK. The national flag of Great Britain and Ireland, which combines the banner of St. Patrick with the crosses of St. George and St. Andrew. The word "jack" is most probably derived from the surcoat, charged with a red cross, anciently used by the English soldiery. This appears to have been called a "jacque," whence the word "jacket," anciently written "jacquit." Some, however, without a shadow of evidence, derive the word from "*Jacques*," the first alteration having been made in the reign of King James I. Wharton.

UNION MORTGAGE CLAUSE. A clause, as in a fire policy (together with the rider making the loss, if any, payable to the mortgagee), which provides that if the policy is made payable to a mortgagee of the insured real estate, no act or default of any person other than such mortgagee, or his agents or those claiming under him, shall affect his right to recover in case of loss on such real estate. Bankers' Joint Stock Land Bank of Milwaukee, Wis., v. St. Paul Fire & Marine Ins. Co., 158 Minn. 363, 197 N.W. 749. Prudential Ins. Co. of America v. German Mut. Fire Ins. Ass'n of Lohman, 231 Mo.App. 699, 105 S.W.2d 1001.

Such clause creates independent contract between insurer and mortgagee. Conard v. Moreland, 230 Iowa 520, 298 N.W. 628, 629. And is distinguished from "open mortgage clause" in that latter clause simply provides that policy is payable to mortgagee as his interest may appear. Prudential Ins. Co. of America v. German Mut. Fire Ins. Ass'n of Lohman, 231 Mo.App. 699, 105 S.W.2d 1001. And mortgagee under such latter clause is merely an appointee to receive fund recoverable in case of loss to extent of his interest. Capital Fire Ins. Co. of Cal. v. Langhorne, C.C.A.Minn., 146 F.2d 237, 241.

UNION OF CHURCHES. A combining and consolidating of two churches into one. Also it is when one church is made subject to another, and one man is rector of both; and where a conventual church is made a cathedral. Tomlins.

UNION SHOP. One in which none but members of labor union are engaged as workmen. People v. Fisher, 3 N.Y.S. 786, 788, 50 Hun, 552.

It was also said that "union shop" exists where employer is permitted to employ a non-union worker, but such worker is required to join the union as a requisite to his continuing work. And that it is distinguished from "closed shop" where the worker must be a member of the union as a condition precedent to his employment. Miners in General Group v. Hix, 123 W.Va. 637, 17 S.E.2d 810, 813.

UNION SOLDIERS. Those who fought in the American Civil War in support of the Union, in contradistinction to Confederate soldiers, who fought for the establishment of the new confederacy. Keely v. Board of Sup'rs of Dubuque County, 158 Iowa 205, 139 N.W. 473, 474.

UNIT. A single thing of any kind. State ex rel. S. Monroe & Son Co. v. Tracy, 129 Ohio St. 550, 196 N.E. 650. A term sometimes used in the sense of a share, as in an oil syndicate, Chew v. U. S., C.C.A.Ark., 9 F.2d 348, 351, or as equivalent to an investment security. State v. Summerland, 150 Minn. 266, 185 N.W. 255, 256.

UNIT CF PRODUCTION. The "unit of production" method of determining the taxable net income or profit in the oil or gas business is accomplished by a system of accounting by which is ascertained, as nearly as science will permit, the total amount of recoverable oil in the property, and to each barrel of this oil is assigned its part of the capital investment, and from the sale price of each barrel produced and sold there is deducted the expenses of producing it, and its proportion of the capital investment, leaving the balance as profit, and thus, when the property is exhausted, the operator has received back his capital and expenses, and accounted for his net income or loss. Carter v. Phillips, 88 Okl. 202, 212 P. 747, 750.

UNIT RULE. A method of valuing securities by multiplying the total number of shares held by the sale price of one share sold on a licensed stock exchange, ignoring all other facts regarding value. Citizens Fidelity Bank & Trust Co. v. Reeves, Ky., 259 S.W.2d 432, 434.

UNITAS PERSONARUM. Lat. The unity of persons, as that between husband and wife, or ancestor and heir.

UNITE. To join in an act, to concur, to act in concert. Bowling v. Wilkerson, D.C.Ky., 19 F. Supp. 584, 587.

UNITED GREEK CATHOLIC CHURCH. All the churches of the Byzantine Rite in communion with the See of Rome. The term is synonymous with "Uniate Greek Catholic Church" or "Uniat Greek Catholic Church," and signifies an ecclesiastical body in union with the Roman Catholic Church and acknowledging the primacy and supremacy of the pope. Morris v. Featro, 340 Pa. 354, 17 A.2d 403, 405.

UNITED IN INTEREST. A statutory term applicable to codefendants only when they are similarly interested in and will be similarly affected by the determination of the issues involved in the action; McCord v. McCord, 104 Ohio St. 274, 135 N.E. 548, 549; *e. g.*, joint obligors upon a guaranty; Columbia Graphophone Co. v. Slawson, 100 Ohio St. 473, 126 N.E. 890, 891.

UNITED KINGDOM OF GREAT BRITAIN AND IRELAND. The official title of the kingdom composed of England, Scotland, Ireland, and Wales, and including the colonies and possessions beyond the seas, under the act of January 1, 1801, effecting the union betwen Ireland and Great Britain.

UNITED NATIONS. An organization started by the allied powers in World War II for the stated purposes of preventing war, providing justice and promoting welfare and human rights of peoples. It consists of a Security Council and a General Assembly and subordinate agencies.

UNITED STATES. This term has several meanings. It may be merely the name of a sovereign occupying the position analogous to that of other sovereigns in family of nations, it may designate territory over which sovereignty of United States extends, or it may be collective name of the states which are united by and under the Constitution. Hooven & Allison Co. v. Evatt, U. S. Ohio, 65 S.Ct. 870, 880, 324 U.S. 652, 89 L.Ed. 1252.

UNITED STATES BONDS. Obligations for payment of money which have been at various times issued by the government of the United States.

UNITED STATES COMMISSIONER. Whose powers in federal matters, are in most respects the same as those of justices of the peace in felony offenses against laws of state, is not a judge or court, and does not hold court, but is an adjunct of court, possessing independent, though subordinate, judicial powers of his own. U. S. v. Napela, D.C.N.Y., 28 F.2d 898, 899.

UNITED STATES COURTS. Except in the case of impeachments the judicial power of the United States is vested by the Constitution in a supreme court and such other inferior courts as may be from time to time established by congress. All the judges are appointed by the president, with the advice and consent of the senate, to hold office during good behavior, and their compensation cannot be diminished during their terms of office. The judges, other than those of the supreme court, are circuit judges and district judges. The circuit judges compose the courts of appeals and the district judges hold the district courts, and also at times sit in the circuit courts of appeal. For a detailed statement of the territorial boundaries of the several districts and divisions of districts, see 28 U.S.C.A. § 81 et seq. and various special acts.

It shall be the duty of the district court of each judicial district to appoint such number of persons, to be known as United States commissioners, at such places in the district as may be designated by the district court. Rev.St.U.S. § 627 (28 USCA § 631). Austill v. United States, 58 Ct.Cl. 232; United States v. Maresca, D.C.N.Y., 266 F. 713.

In statutes, the words "court of the district", Prieto v. U. S. Shipping Board Emergency Fleet Corporation, 117 Misc. 703, 193 N.Y.S. 342, and "courts of the United States," are commonly deemed to refer to federal courts and not to state courts. General Inv. Co. v. Lake Shore & M. S. Ry. Co., C.C.A.Ohio, 269 F. 235, 237.

UNITED STATES CURRENCY. Commonly understood to include every form of currency authorized by the United States government, whether issued directly by it or under its authority. Appel v. State, 28 Ariz. 416, 237 P. 190, 191.

UNITED STATES NOTES. Promissory notes, resembling bank-notes, issued by the government of the United States.

UNITED STATES OFFICER. Usually and strictly, in United States statutes, a person appointed in the manner declared under Const. art. 2, § 2, McGrath v. U. S., C.C.A.N.Y., 275 F. 294, 300, providing for the appointment of officers, either by the President and the Senate, the President alone, the courts of law, or the heads of departments, Steele v. U. S., 45 S.Ct. 417, 418, 267 U.S. 505, 69 L.Ed. 761. Dropps v. U. S., C.C.A.Minn., 34 F.2d 15, 17.

UNITY. In the law of estates. The peculiar characteristic of an estate held by several in joint tenancy, and which is fourfold, viz., unity of interest, unity of title, unity of time, and unity of possession. In other words, joint tenants have one and the same interest, accruing by one and the same conveyance, commencing at one and the same time, and held by one and the same undivided possession. 2 Bl. Comm. 180.

UNITY OF INTEREST. Required in case of joint tenancy means that interests must accrue by one and same conveyance. Hernandez v. Becker, C.C. A.N.M., 54 F.2d 542, 547. It also signifies that no one of joint tenants can have a greater interest in the property than each of the others, while, in the case of tenants in common, one of them may have a larger share than any of the others. Williams, Real Prop. 134, 139.

UNITY OF POSSESSION. Joint possession of two rights by several titles. As if I take a lease of land from a person at a certain rent, and afterwards I buy the fee-simple of such land, by this I acquire unity of possession, by which the lease is extinguished. Cowell; Brown. It is also one of the essential properties of a joint estate, requiring that the joint tenants must hold the same undivided possession of the whole and enjoy same rights until death of one. Hernandez v. Becker, C.C.A.N.M., 54 F.2d 542, 547.

UNITY OF SEISIN. Where a person seised of land which is subject to an easement, *profit à prendre*, or similar right, also becomes seised of the land to which the easement or other right is annexed. Sweet.

UNITY OF TIME. One of the essential properties of a joint estate; the estates of the tenants being vested at one and the same period. 2 Bl. Comm. 181; Hernandez v. Becker, C.C.A.N.M., 54 F.2d 542, 547.

UNITY OF TITLE. Applied to joint tenants, signifies that they hold their property by one and the same title, while tenants in common may take property by several titles. Williams, Real Prop. 134.

Legal requirements of easement of "right of way of necessity" are unity of title, by which is meant that owner of dominant estate must show that his land and that of owner of servient estate once belonged to same person, severance of title, and necessity. Brasington v. Williams, 143 S.C. 223, 141 S.E. 375, 382.

UNIUS OMNINO TESTIS RESPONSIO NON AUDIATUR. The answer of one witness shall not be heard at all; the testimony of a single witness shall not be admitted under any circumstances. A maxim of the civil and canon law. Cod. 4, 20, 9; 3 Bl. Comm. 370; Best, Ev. p. 426, § 390, and note.

UNIUSCUJUSQUE CONTRACTUS INITIUM SPECTANDUM EST, ET CAUSA. The commencement and cause of every contract are to be regarded. Dig. 17, 1, 8; Story, Bailm. § 56.

UNIVERSAL. Having relation to the whole or an entirety; pertaining to all without exception; a term more extensive than "general," which latter may admit of exceptions. See Blair v. Howell, 68 Iowa, 619, 28 N.W. 199; Koen v. State, 35 Neb. 676, 53 N.W. 595, 17 L.R.A. 821.

UNIVERSAL AGENT. One who is appointed to do all the acts which the principal can personally do, and which he may lawfully delegate the power to another to do. Story, Ag. 18; Baldwin v. Tucker, 112 Ky. 282, 65 S.W. 841, 57 L.R.A. 451.

UNIVERSAL LEGACY. See Legacy.

UNIVERSAL PARTNERSHIP. See Partnership.

UNIVERSAL REPRESENTATION. In Scotch law. A term applied to the representation by an heir of his ancestor. Bell.

UNIVERSAL SUCCESSION. In the civil law. Succession to the entire estate of another, living or dead, though generally the latter, importing succession to the entire property of the predecessor as a juridical entirety, that is, to all his active as well as passive legal relations. Mackeld. Rom. Law, § 649.

UNIVERSALIA SUNT NOTIORA SINGULARIBUS. 2 Rolle, 294. Things universal are better known than things particular.

UNIVERSITAS. Lat. In the civil law. A corporation aggregate. Dig. 3, 4, 7. Literally, a whole formed out of many individuals. 1 Bl. Comm. 469.

UNIVERSITAS FACTI. In the civil law. A plurality of corporeal things of the same kind, which are regarded as a whole; *e. g.*, a herd of cattle, a stock of goods. Mackeld. Rom. Law, § 162.

UNIVERSITAS JURIS. In the civil law. A quantity of things of all sorts, corporeal as well as incorporeal, which, taken together, are regarded as a whole; *e. g.*, an inheritance, an estate. Mackeld. Rom. Law, § 162.

UNIVERSITAS RERUM. In the civil law. Literally, a whole of things. Several single things, which, though not mechanically connected with one another, are, when taken together, regarded as a whole in any legal respect. Mackeld. Rom. Law, § 162.

UNIVERSITAS VEL CORPORATIO NON DICITUR ALIQUID FACERE NISI ID SIT COLLEGIALITER DELIBERATUM, ETIAMSI MAJOR PARS ID FACIAT. A university or corporation is not said to do anything unless it be deliberated upon as a body, although the majority should do it. Dav. 48.

UNIVERSITY. An institution of higher learning, consisting of an assemblage of colleges united under one corporate organization and government, affording instruction in the arts and sciences and the learned professions, and conferring degrees. See Com. v. Banks, 198 Pa. 397, 48 A. 277.

Whole body of teachers and scholars, engaged at particular place in giving and receiving instruction in higher branches of learning; also such persons, associated together as society or corporate body with definite organization and acknowledged powers and privileges, especially of conferring degrees, and forming institution for promotion of education in higher and more important branches of learning. West v. Board of Trustees of Miami University and Miami Normal School, 41 Ohio App. 367, 181 N.E. 144, 149.

UNIVERSITY COURT. See Chancellor's Courts in the Two Universities.

UNIVERSUS. Lat. The whole; all together. Calvin.

UNJUST. Contrary to right and justice, or to the enjoyment of his rights by another, or to the standards of conduct furnished by the laws. U. S. v. Oglesby Grocery Co., D.C.Ga., 264 F. 691, 695; Komen v. City of St. Louis, 316 Mo. 9, 289 S.W. 838, 841.

UNJUST ENRICHMENT, DOCTRINE OF. Doctrine that person shall not be allowed to profit or enrich himself inequitably at another's expense. American University v. Forbes, 88 N.H. 17, 183 A. 860, 862. Under this doctrine a defendant has something of value at the plaintiff's expense under circumstances which impose a legal duty of restitution. Herrmann v. Gleason, C.C.A.Mich., 126 F.2d 936, 940. Doctrine permits recovery in certain instances where person has received from another a benefit retention of which would be unjust. Seekins v. King, 66 R.I. 105, 17 A.2d 869, 871, 134 A.L.R. 1060. Doctrine is not contractual but is equitable in nature. State v. Martin, 59 Ariz. 438, 130 P.2d 48, 52.

"Unjust enrichment" of a person occurs when he has and retains money or benefits which in justice and equity belong to another. Hummel v. Hummel, 133 Ohio St. 520, 14 N.E.2d 923, 927. Thus one who has conferred a benefit upon another solely because of a basic mistake of fact induced by a nondisclosure is entitled to restitution on above doctrine. Conkling's Estate v. Champlin, 193 Okl. 79, 141 P.2d 569, 570.

UNKOUTH. Unknown. The law French form of the Saxon "uncouth." Britt. c. 12.

UNLAGE. Sax. An unjust law.

UNLARICH. In old Scotch law. That which is done without law or against law. Spelman.

UNLAW. In Scotch law. A witness was formerly inadmissible who was not worth the king's *unlaw; i. e.,* the sum of £10 Scots, then the common fine for absence from court and for small delinquencies. Bell.

UNLAWFUL. That which is contrary to law or unauthorized by law. State v. Chenault, 20 N.M. 181, 147 P. 283, 285. That which is not lawful. State v. Bulot, 175 La. 21, 142 So. 787, 788. The acting contrary to, or in defiance of the law; disobeying or disregarding the law. While necessarily not implying the element of criminality, it is broad enough to include it. Sturgeon v. Crosby Mortuary, 140 Neb. 82, 299 N.W. 378, 383.

"Unlawful" and "illegal" are frequently used as synonymous terms, but, in the proper sense of the word, "unlawful," as applied to promises, agreements, considerations, and the like, denotes that they are ineffectual in law because they involve acts which, although not illegal, *i. e.,* positively forbidden, are disapproved of by the law, and are therefore not recognized as the ground of legal rights, either because they are immoral or because they are against public policy. It is on this ground that contracts in restraint of marriage or of trade are generally void. Sweet. And see Hagerman v. Buchanan, 45 N.J.Eq. 292, 17 A. 946, 14 Am.St.Rep. 732; Tatum v. State, 66 Ala. 467. People v. Chicago Gas Trust Co., 130 Ill. 268, 22 N.E. 798, 8 L.R.A. 497, 17 Am.St.Rep. 319.

UNLAWFUL ACT. Act contrary to law, and presupposes that there must be an existing law. State v. Campbell, 217 Iowa 848, 251 N.W. 717, 92 A.L.R. 1176.

In criminal jurisprudence, a violation of some prohibitory law and includes all willful, actionable violations of civil rights, and is not confined to criminal acts. State v. Hailey, 350 Mo. 300, 165 S.W.2d 422, 427.

The "unlawful acts" within manslaughter statutes consist of reckless conduct or conduct evincing marked disregard for safety of others. State v. Newton, 105 Utah 561, 144 P.2d 290, 293; State v. Thatcher, 108 Utah 63, 157 P.2d 258, 261.

UNLAWFUL ASSEMBLY. At common law. The meeting together of three or more persons, to the disturbance of the public peace, and with the intention of co-operating in the forcible and violent execution of some unlawful private enterprise. If they take steps towards the performance of their purpose, it becomes a *rout;* and, if they put their design into actual execution, it is a *riot.* 4 Bl. Comm. 146. To constitute offense it must appear that there was common intent of persons assembled to attain purpose, whether lawful or unlawful, by commission of acts of intimidation and disorder likely to produce danger to peace of neighborhood, and actually tending to inspire courageous persons with well-grounded fear of serious breaches of public peace. State v. Butterworth, 104 N.J.L. 579, 142 A. 57, 60, 58 A.L.R. 744.

Three or more persons who assemble peaceably without violent or tumultuous manner to do lawful act, but who thereafter make attempt or motion to do any act whether lawful or unlawful, in either tumultuous, violent, or unful manner to the terror or disturbance of others, become an "unlawful assembly." Koss v. State, 217 Wis. 325, 258 N.W. 860, 862.

UNLAWFUL BELLIGERENTS. Enemies passing the boundaries of the United States for purpose of destroying war industries and supplies without a uniform or other emblem signifying their belligerent status or discarding that means of identification after entry. Ex parte Quirin, App.D.C., 63 S.Ct. 2, 15, 317 U.S. 1, 87 L.Ed. 3.

UNLAWFUL DETAINER. The unjustifiable retention of the possession of lands by one whose original entry was lawful and of right, but whose right to the possession has terminated and who refuses to quit, as in the case of a tenant holding over after the termination of the lease and in spite of a demand for possession by the landlord. McDevitt v. Lambert, 80 Ala. 536, 2 So. 438; Silva v. Campbell, 84 Cal. 420, 24 Pac. 316; Brandley v. Lewis, 97 Utah 217, 92 P.2d 338, 339.

Actions of "unlawful detainer" concern only right of possession of realty, and differ from ejectment in that no ultimate question of title or estate can be determined. McCracken v. Wright, 159 Kan. 615, 157 P.2d 814, 817.

Where an entry upon lands is unlawful, whether forcible or not, and the subsequent conduct is forcible and tortious, the offense committed is a "forcible entry and detainer;" but where the original entry is lawful, and the subsequent holding forcible and tortious, the offense is an "unlawful detainer" only. Pullen v. Boney, 4 N.J.L. 129.

UNLAWFUL ENTRY. An entry upon lands effected peaceably and without force, but which is without color of title and is accomplished by means of fraud or some other willful wrong. Blaco v. Haller, 9 Neb. 149, 1 N.W. 978.

UNLAWFUL PICKETING. Picketing which is not honest or truthful. Park & Tilford Import Corporation v. International Brotherhood of Teamsters, Chauffeurs, Warehousemen and Helpers of America, Local No. 848, A. F. of L., Cal. App., 139 P.2d 963, 971; Magill Bros. v. Building Service Employees' International Union, 20 Cal.2d 506; 127 P.2d 542, 543. Picketing which involves false statements or misrepresentations of facts. Wiest v. Dirks, 215 Ind. 568, 20 N.E.2d 969, 971. Picketing when it ceases to serve the purpose it seeks to accomplish. E. M. Loew's Enterprises v. International Alliance of Theatrical Stage Employees, 125 Conn. 391, 6 A.2d 321, 323, 122 A.L.R. 1287. When force or violence is used to persuade or prevent workmen from continuing their employment. Ex parte Bell, 37 Cal.App.2d 582, 100 P.2d 339, 343.

UNLAWFUL TOUCHING OF PERSON'S BODY. Constituting physical injury to person may be indirect, as by precipitation on body of person of any material substance. Christy Bros. Circus v. Turnage, 38 Ga.App. 581, 144 S.E. 680, 681.

UNLAWFUL TRANSPORTATION OF INTOXICATING LIQUORS. To constitute this offense there must be a substantial movement or transporting of the liquor from one place or vicinity to another. Nelson v. State, 116 Neb. 219, 216 N.W. 556, 557.

UNLAWFULLY. Illegally; wrongfully. Dickinson v. New York, 92 N.Y. 584; Dameron v. Hamilton, 264 Mo. 103, 174 S.W. 425, 430; See State v. Massey, 97 N.C. 465, 2 S.E. 445.

This word is frequently used in indictments in the description of the offence; it is necessary when the crime did not exist at common law, and when a statute, in describing an offence which it creates, uses the word; 1 Mood.C.C. 339; but is unnecessary whenever the crime existed at common law and is manifestly illegal; 1 Chit. Cr.L. *241.

UNLESS. If it be not that, if it be not the case that, if not, supposing not, if it be not, except. West Lumber Co. v. Keen, Tex.Com.App., 237 S. W. 236; Ward v. Interstate Business Men's Acc. Ass'n, 185 Iowa, 674, 169 N.W. 451, 452. A reservation or option to change one's mind provided a certain event happens, a conditional promise. Federal Sign System v. Amavet, 7 La.App. 680, 682.

UNLESS LEASE. An oil and gas lease which provides that lease will be rendered null and void and lessee will automatically be relieved from liability, upon failure to commence operations or to pay rent. It must be expressly stipulated in the lease that lease shall become null and void at a certain time "unless" the lessee begins operations or pays the rental stipulated. Brunson v. Carter Oil Co., D.C.Okl., 259 F. 656, 663.

Where the word "unless" precedes the description of the act to be performed under an oil lease, no obligation to perform that act is imposed by the lease. McCrabb v. Moulton, C.C.A.Mo., 124 F.2d 689, 691.

UNLIMITED. Without confines, unrestricted, boundless. Flynn v. Caplan, 234 Mass. 516, 126 N.E. 776, 777.

UNLIQUIDATED. Not ascertained in amount; not determined; remaining unassessed or unsettled; as unliquidated damages; Davies v. Turner, 61 Ga.App. 531, 6 S.E.2d 356, 358.

A debt is spoken of as "unliquidated," if the amount thereof cannot be ascertained at the trial by a mere computation, based on the terms of the obligation or on some other accepted standard. Hettrick Mfg. Co. v. Barish, 120 Misc. 673, 199 N.Y.S. 755, 767.

Under the law of accord and satisfaction, a claim or debt will be regarded as unliquidated if it is in dispute as to the proper amount. Paulsen Estate v. Naches-Selah Irr. Dist., 190 Wash. 205, 67 P.2d 856, 858.

A claim in bankruptcy is "unliquidated" until final fixation of amount of liability. United States v. Sullivan, D.C. N.Y., 19 F.Supp. 695, 698. See, also, Damages.

UNLIQUIDATED DEMAND. Where it is admitted that one of two specific sums is due, but there is a dispute as to which is proper amount. Perryman Burns Coal Co. v. Seaboard Coal Co. of Connecticut, 128 Conn. 70, 20 A.2d 404, 405.

UNLIVERY. A term used in maritime law to designate the unloading of cargo of a vessel at the place where it is properly to be delivered. The Two Catharines, 24 F.Cas. 429.

UNLOADING. Act of discharging a cargo, taking a load from, disburdening or removing from. American Oil & Supply Co. v. United States Casualty Co., 19 N.J.Misc. 7, 18 A.2d 257, 259.

An unloading clause in an automobile liability policy covers the entire process involved in the movement of articles by and from a motor vehicle to the place where they are turned over to the one to whom the insured is to make delivery, if the clause is construed in accordance with what may be called the "complete operation" rule. Pacific Auto. Ins. Co. v. Commercial Cas. Ins. Co. of N. Y., 161 P.2d 423, 108 Utah 500, 160 A.L.R. 1251. There are, however, two other rules or doctrines used by various courts in applying the unloading clause of such a policy. One is known as the "coming to rest" rule, and the other is the "continuous passage" rule. Blashfield, Cyc. of Automobile Law and Prac., Perm. Ed., § 3972.5. But the complete operation rule is said to be the modern doctrine, supported by the trend of the later cases. London Guarantee & Acc. Co. v. C. B. White & Bros., 49 S.E.2d 254, 188 Va. 195.

UNLOOKED FOR MISHAP OR UNTOWARD EVENT. One occurring unexpectedly and not naturally or in ordinary course of events. Fogg v. Van Saun Coal Co., 12 N.J.Misc. 680, 174 A. 419, 421.

UNMARKETABLE TITLE. When for vendee to accept title proffered would lay him open to fair probability of vexatious litigation with possibility of serious loss. Schoenberg v. O'Connor, 14 N.J. Misc. 412, 185 A. 377, 381. It being sufficient to render it so if ordinarily prudent man with knowledge of the facts and aware of legal questions involved would not accept it in the ordinary course of business but title need not be bad in fact; Barrett v. McMannis, 153 Kan. 420, 110 P.2d 774, 777, 778; Ayers v. Graff, 153 Kan. 209, 109 P.2d 202, 203; Ghormley v. Kleeden, 155 Kan. 319, 124 P.2d 467, 470.

Where some defect of substantial character exists and facts are known which fairly raise reasonable doubt as to title. Schul v. Clapp, 154 Kan. 372, 118 P.2d 570, 574. And mere quibbles and pecadilloes which the ingenuity of counsel can raise against a title do not render it an "unmarketable title". Barrett v. McMannis, 153 Kan. 420, 110 P.2d 774, 778.

UNMARRIED. Its primary meaning is never having been married; but it is a word of flexible meaning and it may be construed as not having a husband or wife at the time in question. 9 H.L. Cas. 601; People v. Weinstock, Mag.Ct., 140 N.Y.S. 453, 458.

A divorced woman has been held an unmarried woman. In re Giles, 85 C.C.A. 418, 158 F. 596; State v. Wallace, 79 Or. 129, 154 P. 430, L.R.A.1916D, 457. Douglas v. Board of Foreign Missions of Presbyterian Church in U. S. of America, 110 N.J.Eq. 331, 160 A. 37, 39.

UNNATURAL OFFENSE. The infamous crime against nature; *i. e.*, sodomy or buggery.

UNNATURAL WILL. An expression applied to disposition of estate or large portion thereof to strangers, to exclusion of natural objects of testator's bounty without apparent reason. In re Shay's Estate, 196 Cal. 355, 237 P. 1079, 1083.

UNNECESSARY. Not required by the circumstances of the case. Hickman v. Ohio State Life Ins. Co., 92 Ohio St. 87, 110 N.E. 542, 543.

UNNECESSARY HARDSHIP. Within zoning ordinance so as to authorize granting of variance on such ground if land cannot yield a reasonable return if used only for a purpose allowed in zone, the plight of owner is due to unique circumstances not to general conditions in the neighborhood and use to be authorized will not alter essential character of the locality. Calcagno v. Town Board of Town of Webster, 265 App.Div. 687, 41 N.Y.S.2d 140, 142.

It has also been said that test whether terms of zoning ordinance impose an "unnecessary hardship", depends on whether use restriction is so unreasonable as to constitute an arbitrary interference with basic right of private property. Scaduto v. Town of Bloomfield, 127 N.J.L. 1, 20 A.2d 649, 650.

UNO ABSURDO DATO, INFINITA SEQUUNTUR. 1 Coke, 102. One absurdity being allowed, an infinity follows.

UNO ACTU. Lat. In a single act; by one and the same act.

UNO FLATU. Lat. In one breath. 3 Man. & G. 45. *Uno flatu, et uno intuitu*, at one breath, and in one view. Pope v. Nickerson, 3 Story, 504, F. Cas.No. 11,274.

UNOCCUPIED. Within fire policy exempting insurer from liability in case dwelling is "unoccupied," means when it is not used as a residence, when it is no longer used for the accustomed and ordinary purposes of a dwelling or place of abode, or when it is not the place of usual return and habitual stoppage. Vinton v. Atlas Assur. Co., 107 Vt. 272, 178 A. 909, 911. Hence a mere temporary absence of occupants of dwelling house from such premises, with intention to return thereto does not render dwelling "unoccupied". Foley v. Sonoma County Farmers' Mut. Fire Ins. Co., 18 Cal.2d 232, 115 P.2d 1, 2, 3.

See Occupation.

UNPRECEDENTED. Having no precedent or example, novel, new, unexampled. State v. Malone, Tex.Civ.App., 168 S.W.2d 292, 300. Unusual and extraordinary; affording no reasonable warning or expectation of recurrence. Nashville, C. & St. L. Ry. v. Yarbrough, 194 Ala. 162, 69 So. 582, 584.

UNPRECEDENTED RAINFALL. An unusual and extraordinary rainfall as has no example or parallel in the history of rainfall in the vicinity affected, or as affords no reasonable warning or expectation that it will likely occur again. City of Birmingham v. Jackson, 229 Ala. 133, 155 So. 527. Trout Brook Co. v. Willow River Power Co., 221 Wis. 616, 267 N.W. 302, 305.

UNPROFESSIONAL CONDUCT. That which is by general opinion considered to be grossly unprofessional because immoral or dishonorable. State Board of Dental Examiners v. Savelle, 90 Colo. 177, 8 P.2d 693, 697. That which violates ethical code of profession or such conduct which is unbecoming member of profession in good standing. People v. Gorman, 346 Ill. 432, 178 N.E. 880, 885. It involves breach of duty which professional ethics enjoin. People v. Johnson, 344 Ill. 132, 176 N.E. 278, 282.

UNQUES. L. Fr. Ever; always. *Ne unques*, never.

UNQUES PRIST. L. Fr. Always ready. Cowell. Another form of *tout temps prist*.

UNREASONABLE. Irrational; foolish; unwise; absurd; silly; preposterous; senseless; stupid. Southern Kansas State Lines Co. v. Public Service Commission, 135 Kan. 657, 11 P.2d 985, 987. Not reasonable; immoderate; exorbitant. Cass v. State, 124 Tex.Cr.R. 208, 61 S.W.2d 500. Capricious; arbitrary; confiscatory. Harris v. State Corporation Commission, 46 N.M. 352, 129 P.2d 323, 328.

UNREASONABLE REFUSAL TO SUBMIT TO OPERATION. An injured employee's refusal to submit to an operation is unreasonable, so as to deprive him of right to workmen's compensation if it appears that an operation of a simple character not involving serious suffering or danger will result in substantial physical improvement. Black Star Coal Co. v. Surgener, 297 Ky. 653, 181 S.W.2d 53, 54.

UNREASONABLE RESTRAINT OF TRADE. Within Sherman Anti-Trust Act agreements for price maintenance of articles moving in interstate commerce. Sherman Anti-Trust Act, § 1, 15 U.S.C.A. § 1. American Tobacco Co. v. U. S., C. C.A.Ky., 147 F.2d 93, 108. Any combination or conspiracy that operates directly on prices or price structure and has for its purpose the fixing of prices. United States v. Waltham Watch Co., D.C.N.Y., 47 F.Supp. 524, 531.

UNREASONABLE RESTRAINT ON ALIENATION. Brought about by gift of absolute ownership in property followed by such condition as takes away incidents of such ownership. Bliven v. Borden, 56 R.I. 283, 185 A. 239, 244.

UNREASONABLE SEARCH. See Search.

UNRULY AND DANGEROUS ANIMALS. Within the meaning of the law, such as are likely to injure other domestic animals and persons. Fink v. United States Coal & Coke Co., 72 W.Va. 507, 78 S.E. 702, 703.

UNSAFE. Dangerous. Hanson v. City of Anamosa, 158 N.W. 591, 595, 177 Iowa 101; Houston & T. C. R. Co. v. Smallwood, Tex.Civ.App., 171 S.W. 292, 293.

UNSEATED LAND. A phrase used in the Pennsylvania tax laws to describe land which, though owned by a private person, has not been reclaimed, cultivated, improved, occupied, or made a place of residence. See Seated Land, *supra*. And see Stoetzel v. Jackson, 105 Pa. 567; McLeod v. Lloyd, 43 Or. 260, 71 P. 799. A tract of land ceases to be unseated as soon as it is actually occupied with a view to permanent residence. Wallace v. Scott, 7 Watts & S. (Pa.) 248.

UNSEAWORTHY. Of a vessel, unable to withstand the perils of an ordinary voyage at sea. Fireman's Fund Ins. Co. v. Compania de Navegacion, Interior, S. A., C.C.A.La., 19 F.2d 493, 495; Or if she could not reasonably have been expected to make the voyage. Interlake Iron Corporation v. Gartland S. S. Co., C.C.A.Mich., 121 F.2d 267, 269, 270. Or if not manned by a competent crew. Peninsular & Occidental S. S. Co. v. National Labor Relations Board, C.C.A.5, 98 F. 2d 411, 414. But a ship is not "unseaworthy" where defect in ship is such that defect can be remedied on the spot in a short time by materials available. Middleton & Co. (Canada) Limited v. Ocean Dominion Steamship Corporation, C.C.A. N.Y., 137 F.2d 619, 622.

UNSOLEMN WAR. War denounced without a declaration; war made not upon general but special declaration; imperfect war. People v. McLeod, 1 Hill, N.Y., 409, 37 Am.Dec. 328.

UNSOLEMN WILL. In the Civil law. One in which an executor is not appointed. Swimb. Wills 29.

UNSOUND MIND. A person of unsound mind is one who from infirmity of mind is incapable of managing himself or his affairs. The term, therefore, includes insane persons, idiots, and imbeciles. Sweet. See Insanity. And see Cheney v. Price, 90 Hun 238, 37 N.Y.S. 117; In re Black's Estate, 1 Myr.Prob. (Cal.) 24. Stewart v. Lispenard, 26 Wend. (N.Y.) 300; Ray v. State, 32 Ga.App. 513, 124 S.E. 57. It exists where there is an essential privation of the reasoning faculties, or where a person is incapable of understanding and acting with discretion in the ordinary affairs of life. Oklahoma Natural Gas Corporation v. Lay, 175 Okl. 75, 51 P.2d 580, 582.

But eccentricity, uncleanliness, slovenliness, neglect of person and clothing, and offensive and disgusting personal habits do not constitute unsoundness of mind. Pendarvis v. Gibb, 328 Ill. 282, 159 N.E. 353, 357.

UNTHRIFT. A prodigal; a spendthrift. 1 Bl. Comm. 306.

UNTIL. Up to time of. A word of limitation, used ordinarily to restrict that which precedes to what immediately follows it, and its office is to fix some point of time or some event upon the arrival or occurrence of which what precedes will cease to exist. State v. Kehoe, 144 P. 162, 164, 49 Mont. 582; Irwin v. Irwin, 167 N.Y.S. 76, 78, 179 App.Div. 871; Empire Oil and Refining Co. v. Babson, 182 Okl. 336, 77 P.2d 682, 684.

UNTOWARD EVENT. See Unlooked for Mishap.

UNTRUE. *Prima facie* inaccurate, but not necessarily wilfully false. 3 B. & S. 929.

A statement is "untrue" which does not express things exactly as they are. Zolintakis v. Equitable Life Assur. Soc. of United States, C.C.A.Utah, 108 F.2d 902, 905.

UNUMQUODQUE DISSOLVITUR EODEM LIGAMINE QUO LIGATUR. Every obligation is dissolved by the same solemnity with which it is created. Broom, Max. 884.

UNUMQUODQUE EODEM MODO QUO COLLIGATU EST, DISSOLVITUR,—QUO CONSTITUITUR, DESTRUITUR. Everything is dissolved by the same means by which it is put together,—destroyed by the same means by which it is established. 2 Rolle, 39; Broom, Max. 891.

UNUMQUODQUE EST ID QUOD EST PRINCIPALIUS IN IPSO. Hob. 123. That which is the principal part of a thing is the thing itself.

UNUMQUODQUE PRINCIPIORUM EST SIBIMETIPSI FIDES; ET PERSPICUA VERA NON SUNT PROBANDA. Every general principle [or maxim of law] is its own pledge or warrant; and things that are clearly true are not to be proved. Branch; Co. Litt. 11.

UNUS NULLUS RULE, THE. The rule of evidence which obtains in the civil law, that the testimony of *one* witness is equivalent to the testimony of *none*. Wharton.

UNUSUAL. Uncommon; not usual, rare. Thompson v. Anderson, 107 Utah 331, 153 P.2d 665, 666.

UNUSUAL CIRCUMSTANCE. Requiring apportionment between life tenants and remaindermen of dividends declared upon stock held in corpus of trust is not one set up by fiduciary or court, but comes from some administrative or corporate act within corporation or some break down within corporate structure. In re Knox' Estate, 328 Pa. 177, 195 A. 28, 30, 113 A.L.R. 1185.

UNVALUED POLICY. One where the value of property insured is not settled in policy, and in case of loss must be agreed on or proved. Hartford Live Stock Ins. Co. v. Gibson, 256 Ky. 338, 76 S.W.2d 17, 18.

UNWHOLESOME FOOD. Food not fit to be eaten; food which if eaten would be injurious.

UNWORTHY. Unbecoming, discreditable, not having suitable qualities or value. Alsup v. State, 91 Tex.Cr.R. 224, 238 S.W. 667, 669.

UNWRITTEN LAW. All that portion of the law, observed and administered in the courts, which has not been enacted or promulgated in the form of a statute or ordinance, including the unenacted portions of the common law, general and particular customs having the force of law, and the rules, principles, and maxims established by judicial precedents or the successive like decisions of the courts. See Code Civ. Proc. Cal. § 1899; B. & C. Comp. Or. 1901, § 736 (Code 1930, § 9-609).

A popular expression to designate a supposed rule of law that a man who takes the life of his wife's paramour or daughter's seducer is not guilty of a criminal offence. Almerigi v. State, 17 Okl.Cr. 458, 188 P. 1094, 1096. A trial judge is said to have expressed to a jury his approval of a verdict based upon such a theory; see 43 Canada L. J. 764; see 19 Green Bag 721, an article from the London L. J.; see also 12 Law Notes 224.

The rule was much urged upon a jury in the common pleas of Philadelphia: Biddle, J., said to counsel: "In this court the 'unwritten law' is not worth the paper it *isn't* written on." It was held that such defense is not available to one accused of homicide in Wehenkel v. State, 116 Neb. 493, 218 N.W. 137, 138, and in People v. Young, 70 Cal. App.2d 28, 160 P.2d 132, 136.

UPKEEP. The act of keeping up or maintaining; maintenance, repair. Central Hanover Bank & Trust Co. v. Nisbet, 121 Conn. 682, 186 A. 643, 645.

UPLANDS. Lands bordering on bodies of waters. Martin v. Busch, 93 Fla. 535, 112 So. 274, 285.

UPLIFTED HAND. The hand raised towards the heavens, in one of the forms of taking an oath, instead of being laid upon the Gospels.

UPPER BENCH. The court of king's bench, in England, was so called during the interval between 1649 and 1660, the period of the commonwealth, Rolle being then chief justice. See 3 Bl. Comm. 202.

UPSET PRICE. The price at which any subject, as lands or goods, is exposed to sale by auction, below which it is not to be sold. In a final decree in foreclosure, the decree should name an upset price large enough to cover costs and all allowances made by the court, receiver's certificates and interest, liens prior to the bonds, amounts diverted from the earnings, and all undetermined claims which will be settled before the confirmation and sale. Blair v. St. Louis, H. & K. R. Co., C.C.Mo., 25 F. 232; Brinckley v. Sager, 232 Wis. 88, 286 N.W. 570, 573.

UPSUN. In Scotch law. Between the hours of sunrise and sunset. Poinding must be executed with *upsun*. 1 Forb. Inst. pt. 3, p. 32.

URBAN. Of or belonging to a city or town. Derived from the Latin "urbanis," which in that language imports the same meaning. City of South Pasadena v. City of San Gabriel, 134 Cal.App. 403, 25 P.2d 516.

URBAN HOMESTEAD. See Homestead.

URBAN SERVITUDE. City servitudes, or servitudes of houses, are called "urban." They are the easements appertaining to the building and construction of houses; as, for instance, the right to light and air, or the right to build a house so as to throw the rain-water on a neighbor's house. Mozley & Whitley; Civ. Code La. § 711.

URBS. Lat. In Roman law. A city, or a walled town. Sometimes it is put for *civitas,* and denotes the inhabitants, or both the city and its inhabitants; *i. e.,* the municipality or commonwealth. By way of special pre-eminence, *urbs* meant the city of Rome. Ainsworth.

URE. L. Fr. Effect; practice. *Mis en ure,* put in practice; carried into effect. Kelham.

USAGE. A reasonable and lawful public custom in a locality concerning particular transactions which is either known to the parties, or so well established, general, and uniform that they must be presumed to have acted with reference thereto. Milroy v. Railway Co., 98 Iowa 188, 67 N.W. 276; Barnard v. Kellogg, 10 Wall. 388, 19 L.Ed. 987; Barreda v. Milmo Nat. Bank, Tex.Civ.App., 241 S.W. 743, 745. Gerseta Corporation v. Silk Ass'n of America, 220 App.Div. 293, 222 N.Y.S. 11, 13. Practice in fact. Electrical Research Products v. Gross, C.C.A.Alaska, 120 F.2d 301, 305. Uniform practice or course of conduct followed in certain lines of business or professions or some procedure or phase thereof. Turner v. Donovan, 3 Cal.App.2d 485, 39 P.2d 858, 859.

"Usage" cannot be proved by isolated instances, but must be certain, uniform and notorious. Unkovich v. New York Cent. R. Co., 128 N.J.Eq. 377, 16 A.2d 558, 561. It is distinguished from "custom" in that "usage" derives its efficacy from assent of parties to transaction, and hence is important only in consensual agreements, while "custom" derives its efficacy from its adoption into the law, is binding irrespective of any manifestation of assent by parties concerned, and may be of importance in any department of law. Gulf Refining Co. v. Universal Ins. Co., C.C.A.N.Y., 32 F.2d 555, 557.

"Usage," in French law, is the *"usus"* of Roman law, and corresponds very nearly to the tenancy at will or on sufferance of English law. Brown.

"Usage," in its most extensive meaning, includes both custom and prescription; but, in its narrower signification, the term refers to a general habit, mode, or course of procedure. A usage differs from a custom, in that it does not require that the usage should be immemorial to establish it; but the usage must be known, certain, uniform, reasonable, and not contrary to law. Lowry v. Read, 3 Brewst. (Pa.) 452.

Fair Usage

See Fair Usage.

General Usage

One which prevails generally throughout the country, or is followed generally by a given profession or trade, and is not local in its nature or observance.

Usage of Trade

A course of dealing; a mode of conducting transactions of a particular kind. Haskins v. Warren, 115 Mass. 535. A mode of dealing generally observed in a particular trade. United States v. Stanolind Crude Oil Purchasing Co., C. C.A.Okl., 113 F.2d 194, 200; Codd v. Westchester Fire Ins. Co., 14 Wash.2d 600, 128 P.2d 968, 973.

USANCE. In mercantile law. The common period fixed by the usage or custom or habit of dealing between the country where a bill is drawn, and that where it is payable, for the payment of bills of exchange. It means, in some countries, a month, in others two or more months, and in others half a month. Story, Bills, §§ 50, 144, 332.

USE, *v.* To make use of, to convert to one's service, to avail one's self of, to employ. Hopkins v. Howard's Ex'x, 266 Ky. 685, 99 S.W.2d 810, 812. To leave no capacity of force or use in. Bridgeport Mach. Co. v. McKnab, 136 Kan. 781, 18 P.2d 186, 187.

USE, *n.* Act of employing everything, or state of being employed; application; employment, as the use of a pen, or his machines are in use. Also the fact of being used or employed habitually; usage, as, the wear and tear resulting from ordinary use. Berry-Kofron Dental Laboratory Co. v. Smith, 345 Mo. 922, 137 S.W.2d 452, 454, 455, 456. The purpose served, a purpose, object or end for useful or advantageous nature. Brown v. Kennedy, Ohio App., 49 N.E.2d 417, 418.

A confidence reposed in another, who was made tenant of the land, or terre-tenant, that he would dispose of the land according to the intention of the *cestui que use,* or him to whose use it was granted, and suffer him to take the profits. 2 Bl. Comm. 328.

A right in one person, called the *"cestui que use,"* to take the profits of land of which another has the legal title and possession, together with the duty of defending the same, and of making estates thereof according to the direction of the *cestui que use.* Bouvier.

Uses and *trusts* are not so much different things as different aspects of the same subject. A use regards principally the beneficial interest; a trust regards principally the nominal ownership. The usage of the two terms is, however, widely different. The word "use" is employed to denote either an estate vested since the statute of uses, and by force of that statute, or to denote such an estate created before the statute as, had it been created since, would have become a legal estate by force of the statute. The word "trust" is employed since that statute to denote the relation between the party invested with the legal estate (whether by force of that statute or independently of it) and the party beneficially entitled, who has hitherto been said to have the equitable estate. Mozley & Whiteley.

Civil Law

A right of receiving so much of the natural profits of a thing as is necessary to daily sustenance. It differs from "usufruct," which is a right not only to use, but to enjoy. 1 Browne, Civil & Adm. Law, 184.

Right given to any one to make a gratuitous use of a thing belonging to another, or to exact such a portion of the fruit it produces as is necessary for his personal wants and those of his family. Civ.Code La. art. 626.

Conveyancing

"Use" literally means "benefit;" thus, in an ordinary assignment of chattels, the assignor transfers the property to the assignee for his "absolute use and benefit." In the expressions "separate use," "superstitious use," and "charitable use," "use" has the same meaning Sweet.

Non-technical Sense

The "use" of a thing means that one is to enjoy, hold, occupy, or have some manner of benefit thereof. Bryson v. Hicks, 78 Ind.App. 111, 134 N.E. 874, 875. Use also means usefulness, utility, advantage, productive of benefit. Williams v. City of Norman, 85 Okl. 230, 205 P. 144, 148; National Surety Co. v. Jarrett, 95 W.Va. 420, 121 S.E. 291, 295, 36 A.L.R. 1171.

General

Cestui que use. A person for whose use and benefit lands or tenements are held by another. The latter, before the statute of uses, was called the "feoffee to use," and held the nominal or legal title.

Charitable use. See Charitable.

Contingent use. A use limited to take effect upon the happening of some future contingent event; as where lands are conveyed to the use of A. and B., after a marriage shall be had between them. 2 Bl.Comm. 334; Haywood v. Shreve, 44 N.J.L. 94; Jemison v. Blowers, 5 Barb. (N.Y.) 692.

Exclusive use. See Exclusive Use.

Executed use. The first use in a conveyance upon which the statute of uses operates by bringing the possession to it, the combination of which, *i. e.,* the use and the possession, form the legal estate, and thus the statute is said to execute the use. Wharton.

Executory uses. These are springing uses, which confer a legal title answering to an executory devise; as when a limitation to the use of A. in fee is defeasible by a limitation to the use of B., to arise at a future period, or on a given event.

Existing use. See Existing Use.

Feoffee to uses. A person to whom (before the statute of uses) land was conveyed "for the use" of a third person. He held the nominal or legal title, while the third person, called the *"cestui que use,"* was entitled to the beneficial enjoyment of the estate.

Official use. An active use before the statute of uses, which imposed some duty on the legal owner or feoffee to uses; as a conveyance to A. with directions for him to sell the estate and distribute the proceeds among B., C., and D. To enable A. to perform this duty, he had the legal possession of the estate to be sold. Wharton.

Passive use. A permissive use (*q. v.*).

Permissive use. A passive use which was resorted to before the statute of uses, in order to avoid a harsh law; as that of mortmain or a feudal forfeiture. It was a mere invention in order to evade the law by secrecy; as a conveyance to A. to the use of B. A. simply held the possession, and B. enjoyed the profits of the estate. Wharton.

Resulting use. A use raised by equity for the benefit of a feoffor who has made a voluntary conveyance to uses without any declaration of the use. 2 Washb.Real Prop. 100. A resulting use arises where the legal seisin is transferred, and no use is expressly declared, nor any consideration or evidence of intent to direct the use. The use then remains in the original grantor, for it cannot be supposed that the estate was intended to be given away, and the statute immediately transfers the legal estate to such resulting use. Wharton.

Secondary use. A use limited to take effect in derogation of a preceding estate, otherwise called a "shifting use," as a conveyance to the use of A. and his heirs, with a proviso that, when B. returns from India, then to the use of C. and his heirs. 1 Steph.Comm. 546.

Shifting use. A use which is so limited that it will be made to shift or transfer itself, from one beneficiary to another, upon the occurrence of a certain event after its creation. For example, an estate is limited to the use of A. and his heirs, provided that, upon the return of B. from Rome, it shall be to the use of C. and his heirs; this is a shifting use, which transfers itself to C. when the event happens. 1 Steph.Comm. 503; 2 Bl. Comm. 335. These shifting uses are common in all settlements; and, in marriage settlements, the first use is always to the owner in fee till the marriage, and then to other uses. The fee remains with the owner until the marriage, and then it *shifts* as uses arise. 4 Kent, Comm. 297.

Springing use. A use limited to arise on a future event where no preceding use is limited, and which does not take effect in derogation of any other interest than that which results to the grantor, or remains in him in the meantime. 2 Washb.Real.Prop. 281; Smith v. Brisson, 90 N.C. 288.

Statute of uses. An English statute enacted in 1536, (27 Hen. VIII, c. 10,) directed against the practice of creating uses in lands, and which converted the purely equitable title of persons entitled to a use into a legal title or absolute ownership with right of possession. The statute is said to "execute the use," that is, it abolishes the intervening estate of the feoffee to uses, and makes the beneficial interest of the *cestui que use* an absolute legal title. See Ohio & Colorado Smelting & Refining Co. v. Barr, 58 Colo. 116, 144 P. 552, 554.

Superstitious uses. See that title.

Use and habitation. Within a grant does not mean the exclusive use and habitation, but the necessities of the grantee are determinative of extent of privileges to be enjoyed. Barrett v. Barrett, La.App., 5 So.2d 381, 383.

Use and occupation. This is the name of an action, being a variety of *assumpsit*, to be maintained by a landlord against one who has had the occupation and enjoyment of an estate, under a contract to pay therefor, express or implied, but not under such a lease as would support an action specifically for rent. Thackray v. Ritz, 130 Misc. 403, 223 N.Y.S. 668, 669.

Use plaintiff. One for whose use (benefit) an action is brought in the name of another. Thus, where the assignee of a chose in action is not allowed to sue in his own name, the action would be entitled "A. B. (the assignor) for the Use of C. D. (the assignee) against E. F." In this case, C. D. is called the "use plaintiff."

USED FOR ILLEGAL CONVEYING OF LIQUOR. Automobile is so used, if liquor is in or on the car and is being intentionally conveyed by its movements, though it is upon the person of an occupant of the car while he is conveyed by it. Morris v. State, 220 Ala. 418, 125 So. 655.

USEE. A person for whose use a suit is brought; otherwise termed the "use plaintiff."

USEFUL. The term as used in the patent law, when applied to a machine, means that the machine will accomplish its purpose practically when applied in industry. Besser v. Merrilat Culvert Core Co., C.C.A.Iowa, 243 F. 611.

By "useful" is meant such an invention as may be applied to some beneficial use in society, in contradistinction to an invention which is injurious to the morals, the health, or the good order of society. Bedford v. Hunt, 1 Mason, 302, F.Cas.No.1,217.

USEFULNESS. Capabilities for use. The word pertains to the future as well as to the past. Chesapeake, O. & S. W. R. Co. v. Dyer Co., 87 Tenn. 712, 11 S.W. 943.

USER. The actual exercise or enjoyment of any right or property. It is particularly used of franchises.

Adverse User

Such a use of the property under claim of right as the owner himself would make, asking no permission, and disregarding all other claims to it, so far as they conflict with this use. Blanchard v. Moulton, 63 Me. 434; Murray v. Scribner, 74 Wis. 602, 43 N.W. 549; Thorworth v. Scheets, 269 Ill. 573, 110 N.E. 42, 45; Cummins v. Dumas, 147 Miss. 215, 113 So. 332, 334.

USER DE ACTION. L. Fr. In old practice. The pursuing or bringing an action. Cowell.

USHER. This word is said to be derived from "*huissier*," and is the name of a subordinate officer in some English courts of law. Archb.Pr. 25.

USHER OF THE BLACK ROD. The gentleman usher of the black rod is an officer of the house of lords appointed by letters patent from the crown. His duties are, by himself or deputy, to desire the attendance of the commons in the house of peers when the royal assent is given to bills, either by the king in person or by commission, to execute orders for the commitment of persons guilty of breach of privilege, and also to assist in the introduction of peers when they take the oaths and their seats. Brown.

USING MAIL TO DEFRAUD. The elements of this offense are the formation of a scheme or artifice to defraud, and use of mails for purpose of executing or attempting to execute such scheme or artifice; the latter element being gist of the offense. 18 U.S.C.A. § 1341. Stryker v. United States, C.C.A.Colo., 95 F.2d 601, 604, 605. The crime is complete when mails are used in such scheme, and what happened subsequently is not controlling. United States v. Ames, D.C.N.Y., 39 F.Supp. 885, 886.

USING THE SERVICE OF ANOTHER FOR PAY. This phrase as used in Compensation Act defining employer means right to control the means and manner of that service, as distinguished from results of such service, the word "service" meaning the performance of labor for the benefit of another. Rutherford v. Tobin Quarries, 336 Mo. 1171, 82 S.W.2d 918, 923.

USO. In Spanish law. Usage; that which arises from certain things which men say and do and practice uninterruptedly for a great length of time, without any hindrance whatever. Las Partidas, pt. 1, tit. 2, l. 1.

USQUE. Lat. Up to; until. This is a word of exclusion, and a release of all demands *usque ad* a certain day does not cover a bond made on that day. 2 Mod. 28.

Usually applied to ownership of property. Applied to right to air it has been held that ownership extends "*usque ad coelum.*" Romano v. Birmingham Ry. Light & Power Co., 182 Ala. 335, 62 So. 677, 46 L.R.A.,N.S., 642, Ann.Cas.1915D, 776. See A Coelo Usque Ad Centrum.

USQUE AD FILUM AQUÆ, OR VIÆ. Up to the middle of the stream or road.

USUAL. Habitual; ordinary; customary; according to usage or custom; commonly established, observed, or practiced. Such as is in common use or occurs in ordinary practice or course of events. See Chicago & A. R. Co. v. Hause, 71 Ill.App. 147; Kellogg v. Curtis, 69 Me. 214, 31 Am.Rep. 273; Oilmen's Reciprocal Ass'n v. Gilleland, Tex.Com. App., 291 S.W. 197, 199; Roberts Coal Co. v. Corder Coal Co., 143 Va. 133, 129 S.E. 341, 344; Webb v. New Mexico Pub. Co., 47 N.M. 279, 141 P.2d 333, 335. Synonymous with custom, common, wonted, regular. Dancy v. Abraham Bros. Packing Co., 171 Tenn. 311, 102 S.W.2d 526, 528.

USUAL COURSE. These words in statute excepting from application of Compensation Act employment not in usual course of employer's trade or business, refer to normal operations constituting regular business of employer. Longshoremen's and Harbor Workers' Compensation Act, 33 U.S.C.A. §§ 901–950; D.C.Code 1929, T. 19, §§ 11, 12, 33 U.S.C.A. § 901 note. Hoage v. Hartford Accident & Indemnity Co., 64 App.D.C. 258, 77 F.2d 381.

USUAL COVENANTS. See Covenant.

USUAL PLACE OF ABODE. Within meaning of statute relating to service of process is place where defendant is actually living at time of service. State ex rel. Merritt v. Heffernan, 142 Fla. 496, 195 So. 145, 147, 127 A.L.R. 1263; Caskey v. Peterson, 220 Wis. 690, 263 N.W. 658, 660.

USUAL TERMS. A phrase in the common-law practice, which meant pleading issuably, rejoining *gratis*, and taking short notice of trial. When a defendant obtained further time to plead, these were the terms usually imposed. Wharton.

USUARIUS. Lat. In the civil law. One who had the mere use of a thing belonging to another for the purpose of supplying his daily wants; a usuary. Dig. 7, 8, 10, pr.; Calvin.

USUCAPIO, or USUCAPTIO. A term of Roman law used to denote a mode of acquisition of property. It corresponds very nearly to the term "prescription." But the prescription of Roman law differed from that of the English law, in this: that no *mala fide* possessor (*i. e.*, person in possession knowingly of the property of another) could, by however long a period, acquire title by possession merely. The two essential requisites to *usucapio* were *justa causa* (*i. e.*, title) and *bona fides*, (*i. e.*, ignorance.) The term "*usucapio*" is sometimes, but erroneously, written "*usucaptio.*" Brown. See Pavey v. Vance, 56 Ohio St. 162, 46 N.E. 898.

As to "lucrativa usucapio," see that title.

USUCAPIO CONSTITUTA EST UT ALIQUIS LITIUM FINIS ESSET. Prescription was instituted that there might be some end to litigation. Dig. 41, 10, 5; Broom, Max. 894, note.

USUFRUCT. In the civil law. The right of enjoying a thing, the property of which is vested in another, and to draw from the same all the profit, utility, and advantage which it may produce, provided it be without altering the substance of the thing. Civ.Code La. art. 533. Mulford v. Le Franc, 26 Cal. 102; Modern Music Shop v. Concordia Fire Ins. Co. of Milwaukee, 131 Misc. 305, 226 N.Y.S. 630, 635.

Under Greek Law. A right attached to the person which may not be inherited. New England Trust Co. v. Wood, Mass., 93 N.E.2d 547, 549.

Imperfect Usufruct

An imperfect or quasi usufruct is that which is of things which would be useless to the usufructuary if he did not consume or expend them or change the substance of them; as, money, grain, liquors. Civ.Code La. art. 534.

See Quasi Usufruct infra.

Legal Usufruct

See that title.

Perfect Usufruct

An usufruct in those things which the usufructuary can enjoy without changing their substance, though their substance may be diminished or deteriorate naturally by time or by the use to which they are applied, as, a house, a piece of land, furniture, and other movable effects. Civ.Code La. art. 534.

Quasi Usufruct

In the civil law. Originally the usufruct gave no right to the substance of the thing, and consequently none to its consumption; hence only an inconsumable thing could be the object of it, whether movable or immovable. But in later times the right of usufruct was, by analogy, extended to consumable things, and therewith arose the distinction between true and *quasi* usufructs. See Mackeld. Rom. Law, § 307; Civ.Code La. art. 534. See Imperfect Usufruct, *supra*.

USUFRUCTUARY. In the civil law. One who has the usufruct or right of enjoying anything in which he has no property, Cartwright v. Cartwright, 18 Tex. 628.

USUFRUIT. In French law. The same as the *usufruct* of the English and Roman law.

USURA. Lat. In the civil law. Money given for the use of money; interest. Commonly used in the plural, "*usuræ.*" Dig. 22, 1.

USURA EST COMMODUM CERTUM QUOD PROPTER USUM REI MUTUATÆ RECIPITUR. SED SECUNDARIO SPIRARE DE ALIQUA RETRIBUTIONE, AD VOLUNTATEM EJUS QUI MUTUATUS EST, HOC NON EST VITIOSUM. Usury is a certain benefit which is received for the use of a thing lent. But to have an understanding [literally, to breathe or whisper,] in an incidental way, about some compensation to be made at the pleasure of the borrower, is not lawful. Branch, Princ.; 5 Coke, 70*b*; Glan. lib. 7, c. 16.

USURA MANIFESTA. Manifest or open usury; as distinguished from *usura velata*, veiled or concealed usury, which consists in giving a bond for the loan, in the amount of which is included the stipulated interest.

USURA MARITIMA. Interest taken on bottomry or respondentia bonds, which is proportioned to the risk, and is not affected by the usury laws.

USURARIUS. In old English law. A usurer. Fleta, lib. 2, c. 52, § 14.

USURIOUS. Pertaining to usury; partaking of the nature of usury; involving usury; tainted with usury; as, a usurious contract.

USURIOUS CONTRACT. A contract if interest contracted to be paid exceeds the rate established by statute. Commerce Farm Credit Co. v. Ramp, Tex.Civ.App., 116 S.W.2d 1144, 1149. It being sufficient when there is contingency whereby lender may get more than lawful rate of interest. Reynolds Mortg. Co. v. Thomas, Tex.Civ.App., 61 S.W.2d 1011, 1013. See, also, Usury.

USURP. To seize and hold any office by force, and without right; applied to seizure of office, place, functions, powers, rights, etc. State ex rel. Scanes v. Babb, 124 W.Va. 428, 20 S.E.2d 683, 686.

USURPATIO. Lat. In the civil law. The interruption of a usucaption, by some act on the part of the real owner. Calvin.

USURPATION. The unlawful assumption of the use of property which belongs to another; an interruption or the disturbing a man in his right and possession. Tomlins.

The unlawful seizure or assumption of sovereign power; the assumption of government or supreme power by force or illegally, in derogation of the constitution and of the rights of the lawful ruler.

"Usurpation" for which writ of prohibition may be granted involves attempted exercise of power not possessed by inferior officer. Ex parte Wilkinson, 220 Ala. 529, 126 So. 102, 104.

USURPATION OF ADVOWSON. An injury which consists in the absolute ouster or dispossession of the patron from the advowson or right of presentation, and which happens when a stranger who has no right presents a clerk, and the latter is thereupon admitted and instituted. Brown.

USURPATION OF FRANCHISE OR OFFICE. The unjustly intruding upon or exercising any office, franchise, or liberty belonging to another. See, also, Usurpation.

"Usurpation" of public office authorizing quo warranto action under statute may be with or without forcible seizure of office and prerogatives thereof, and may consist of mere unauthorized assumption and exercise of power in performing duties of office upon claim of right thereto. State ex rel. Kirk v. Wheatley, 133 Ohio St. 164, 12 N.E.2d 491, 493.

USURPED POWER. In insurance. An invasion from abroad, or an internal rebellion, where armies are drawn up against each other, when the laws are silent, and when the firing of towns becomes unavoidable. These words cannot mean the power of a common mob. 2 Marsh.Ins. 791.

USURPER. One who assumes the right of government by force, contrary to and in violation of the constitution of the country. Toul, *Droit. Civ.* n. 32.

USURPER OF A PUBLIC OFFICE. One who either intrudes into a vacant office or ousts the incumbent without any color of title. Neal v. Parker, 200 Ark. 10, 139 S.W.2d 41, 44. One who intrudes on office and assumes to exercise its functions without legal title or color of right thereto. Alleger v. School Dist. No. 16, Newton County, Mo.App., 142 S.W.2d 660, 663; State ex rel. City of Republic v. Smith, 345 Mo. 1158, 139 S.W.2d

929, 933. Any person attempting to fill pretended office attempted to be created by an unconstitutional law. Bodcaw Lumber Co. of Louisiana v. Jordan, La.App., 14 So.2d 98, 101.

USURY.

Modern Law

An illegal contract for a loan or forbearance of money, goods, or things in action, by which illegal interest is reserved, or agreed to be reserved or taken. Midland Loan Finance Co. v. Lorentz, 209 Minn. 278, 296 N.W. 911, 914, 915. An unconscionable and exorbitant rate or amount of interest. Heilos v. State Land Co., 113 N.J.Eq. 239, 166 A. 330, 332. An unlawful contract upon the loan of money, to receive the same again with exorbitant increase. 4 Bl.Comm. 156. The reserving and taking, or contracting to reserve and take, either directly or by indirection, a greater sum for the use of money than the lawful interest. See Henry v. Bank of Salina, 5 Hill. (N.Y.) 528; In re Elmore Cotton Mills (D.C.) 217 F. 810, 814. See, also, Usurious Contract.

"Usury" does not depend on question whether the lender actually gets more than the legal rate of interest or not; but on whether there was a purpose in his mind to make more than legal interest for the use of money, and whether, by the terms of the transaction, and the means used to effect the loan, he may by its enforcement be enabled to get more than the legal rate. American Nat. Ins. Co. v. Schenck, Tex.Civ.App., 85 S.W.2d 833, 837.

A profit greater than the lawful rate of interest, intentionally exacted as a bonus, for the forbearance of an existing indebtedness or a loan of money, imposed upon the necessities of the borrower in a transaction where the money is to be returned at all events. Monk v. Goldstein, 172 N.C. 516, 90 S.E. 519, 520; Anderson v. Beadle, 35 N.M. 654, 5 P.2d 528, 529.

Old English Law

Interest of money; increase for the loan of money; a reward for the *use* of money. 2 Bl.Comm. 454. The taking of any compensation whatever for the use of money. Marshall v. Beeler, 104 Kan. 32, 178 P. 245, 246; Schlesinger v. State, 195 Wis. 366, 218 N.W. 440, 442, 57 A.L.R. 352.

USUS. Lat. In Roman law. A precarious enjoyment of land, corresponding with the right of *habitatio* of houses, and being closely analogous to the tenancy at sufferance or at will of English law. The *usuarius* (*i. e.*, tenant by *usus*) could only hold on so long as the owner found him convenient, and had to go so soon as ever he was in the owner's way, (*molestus.*) The *usuarius* could not have a friend to share the produce. It was scarcely permitted to him (Justinian says) to have even his wife with him on the land; and he could not let or sell, the right being strictly personal to himself. Brown.

USUS BELLICI. Lat. In international law. Warlike uses or objects. It is the *usus bellici* which determine an article to be contraband. 1 Kent, Comm. 141.

USUS EST DOMINIUM FIDUCIARIUM. Bac. St. Uses. Use is a fiduciary dominion.

USUS ET STATUS SIVE POSSESSIO POTIUS DIFFERUNT SECUNDUM RATIONEM FORI, QUAM SECUNDUM RATIONEM REI. Bac. St. Uses. Use and estate, or possession, differ more in the rule of the court than in the rule of the matter.

USUS FRUCTUS. Lat. In Roman law. Usufruct; usufructuary right or possession. The temporary right of using a thing, without having the ultimate property, or full dominion, of the substance. 2 Bl.Comm. 327.

UT CURRERE SOLEBAT. Lat. As it was wont to run; applied to a water-course.

UT DE FEODO. L. Lat. As of fee.

UT HOSPITES. Lat. As guests. 1 Salk. 25, pl. 10.

UT PŒNE AD PAUCOS, METUS AD OMNES PERVENIAT. That the punishment may reach a few, but the fear of it affect all. A maxim in criminal law, expressive of one of the principal objects of human punishment. 4 Inst. 6; 4 Bl. Comm. 11.

UT RES MAGIS VALEAT QUAM PEREAT. That the thing may rather have effect than be destroyed. Simonds v. Walker, 100 Mass. 113; National Pemberton Bank v. Lougee, 108 Mass. 373, 11 Am. Rep. 367. Charitable bequests are also governed by this maxim. King v. Richardson, C.C.A.N.C., 136 F.2d 849, 858.

UT SUMMÆ POTESTATIS REGIS EST POSSE QUANTUM VELIT, SIC MAGNITUDINIS EST VELLE QUANTUM POSSIT. 3 Inst. 236. As the highest power of a king is to be able to do all he wishes, so the highest greatness of him is to wish all he is able to do.

UTAS. In old English practice. Octave; the octave; the eighth day following any term or feast. Cowell.

UTENSIL. A much broader term than "tool," though it may be applicable to many implements designated tools in common parlance. Murphy v. Continental Ins. Co., 178 Iowa, 375, 157 N.W. 855, 857, L.R.A. 1917B, 934. For "Farm Utensils," see that title.

UTERINE. Born of the same mother. A uterine brother or sister is one born of the same mother, but by a different father.

UTERO-GESTATION. Pregnancy.

UTERQUE. Lat. Both; each. "The justices, being in doubt as to the meaning of this word in an indictment, demanded the opinions of grammarians, who delivered their opinions that this word doth aptly signify *one of them.*" 1 Leon. 241.

UTFANGTHEF, or UTFANGENETHEF. In Saxon and old English law. The privilege of a lord of a manor to judge and punish a thief dwelling out of his liberty, and committing theft without the same, if he were caught within the lord's jurisdiction. Cowell.

The right of the lord of a manor to hang a thief caught with the stolen goods, whether or not the capture was made on the manor. 1 Holdsw. Hist. E. L. 11. See Infangenthef.

UTI. Lat. In the civil law. To use. Strictly, to use for necessary purposes; as distinguished from *"frui,"* to enjoy. Heinecc. Elem. lib. 2, tit. 4, § 415.

UTI FRUI. Lat. In the civil law. To have the full use and enjoyment of a thing, without damage to its substance. Calvin.

UTI POSSIDETIS. Lat.

The Civil Law

A species of interdict for the purpose of retaining possession of a thing, granted to one who, at the time of contesting suit, was in possession of an immovable thing, in order that he might be declared the legal possessor. Hallifax, Civil Law, b. 3, c. 6, no. 8. See Utrubi.

International Law

A phrase used to signify that the parties to a treaty are to retain possession of what they have acquired by force during the war. Wheat. Int. Law, 627.

A treaty which terminates a war may adopt this principle or that of the *status quo ante bellum,* or a combination of the two. In default of any treaty stipulation, the former doctrine prevails. Guillermo Alvarez y Sanches v. U. S., 42 Ct.Cl. 458.

UTI ROGAS. Lat. In Roman law. The form of words by which a vote in favor of a proposed law was orally expressed. *Uti rogas, volo vel jubeo,* as you ask, I will or order; I vote as you propose; I am for the law. The letters "U. R." on a ballot expressed the same sentiment. Adams, Rom. Ant. 98, 100.

UTILE PER INUTILE NON VITIATUR. The useful is not vitiated by the useless. Surplusage does not spoil the remaining part if that is good in itself. Dyer, 392; Broom, Max. 627; 2 Wheat. 221, 4 L.Ed. 224.

UTILIDAD. Span. In Spanish law. The profit of a thing. White, New Recop. b. 2, tit. 2, c. 1.

UTILIS. Lat. In the civil law. Useful; beneficial; equitable; available. *Actio utilis,* an equitable action. Calvin. *Dies utilis,* an available day.

UTILITY. In patent law. Industrial value; the capability of being so applied in practical affairs as to prove advantageous in the ordinary pursuits of life, or add to the enjoyment of mankind. Callison v. Dean, C.C.A.Okl., 70 F.2d 55, 58. The absence of frivolity and mischievousness, and utility for some beneficial purpose. Rob. Pat. § 339. But there is no utility if the invention can be used only to commit a fraud with, Klein v. Russell, 19 Wall. 433, 22 L.Ed. 116; or for some immoral purpose, Lowell v. Lewis, 1 Mason, 182, F. Cas.No.8,568; or can be used only for gambling purposes in saloons, Schultze v. Holtz, C.C.Cal., 82 F. 448; or if the invention is dangerous in its use, Mitchell v. Tilghman, 19 Wall. 287, 22 L.Ed. 125.

"Utility" is established if only partial success is attained. Emery Industries v. Schumann, C.C.A.Ill., 111 F.2d 209, 211.

The "utility" which an infringing defendant is estopped to deny means sufficient practical utility to make a device useful in the sense of the patent statute. The estoppel does not forbid him to deny that there is any useful function, or new result serving to give inventive character to the slight step which a patentee has taken in differentiation from prior art. Sandy MacGregor Co. v. Vaco Grip Co., C.C.A.Ohio, 2 F.2d 655, 656.

UTLAGATUS, or UTLAGATUM. In old English law. An outlawed person; an outlaw.

UTLAGATUS EST QUASI EXTRA LEGEM POSITUS. CAPUT GERIT LUPINUM. 7 Coke, 14. An outlaw is, as it were, put out of the protection of the law. He bears the head of a wolf.

UTLAGATUS PRO CONTUMACIA ET FUGA, NON PROPTER HOC CONVICTUS EST DE FACTO PRINCIPALI. Fleta. One who is outlawed for contumacy and flight is not on that account convicted of the principal fact.

UTLAGE. L. Fr. An outlaw. Britt. c. 12.

UTLESSE. An escape of a felon out of prison.

UTMOST CARE. Substantially synonymous with "highest care." Brogan v. Union Traction Co., 76 W.Va. 698, 86 S.E. 753, 756.

The "utmost care" which is required of a carrier of persons for reward, means the highest degree of care, but does not mean that in point of fact the same degree or quantum of care should be applied in every case, since the necessary degree of care varies with the dangers to be anticipated by a man of the utmost degree of prudence from the surrounding circumstances and conditions of each case. Chicago, R. I. & P. Ry. Co. v. Shelton, 135 Okl. 53, 273 P. 988, 990.

UTMOST RESISTANCE. This term, under the rule that to constitute rape there must be utmost resistance by the woman, is a relative rather than a positive term, and means that greatest effort of which she is capable must be used to foil assailant. State v. Brewster, 208 Iowa, 122, 222 N.W. 6. McLain v. State, 159 Wis. 204, 149 N.W. 771, 772.

UTRUBI.

Civil Law

The name of a species of interdict for retaining a thing, granted for the purpose of protecting the possession of a movable thing, as the *uti possidetis* was granted for an immovable. Inst. 4, 15, 4; Mackeld. Rom. Law, § 260.

Scotch Law

An interdict as to movables, by which the colorable possession of a *bona fide* holder is continued until the final settlement of a contested right; corresponding to *uti possidetis* as to heritable property. Bell.

UTRUMQUE NOSTRUM. Both of us. Words used formerly in bonds.

UTTER, *v.* To put or send (as a forged check) into circulation; Smith v. Commonwealth, 151 Ky. 517, 152 S.W. 574, 575; To publish or put forth; Barron v. State, 12 Ga.App. 342, 77 S.E. 214, 215; Valley Dry Goods Co. v. Buford, 114 Miss. 414, 75 So. 252, 254. To offer. Bish. Cr. L. § 607.

To utter and publish an instrument, as a counterfeit note, is to declare or assert, directly or indirectly, by words or actions, that it is good; uttering it is a declaration that it is good, with an intention or offer to pass it. Whart.Crim.Law, § 703; Com. v. Searle, 2 Binn., Pa., 338, 4 Am.Dec. 446; Terry v. State, 29 Ala.App. 340, 197 So. 44, 45.

To utter, as used in a statute against forgery and counterfeiting, means to offer, whether accepted or not, a forged instrument, with the representation, by words or actions, that the same is genuine. See State v. Horner, 48 Mo. 522; People v. Rathbun, 21 Wend., N.Y., 521; People v. Caton, 25 Mich. 392; Commonwealth v. Fenwick, 177 Ky. 685, 198 S.W. 32, 34, L.R.A.1918B, 1189; Jones v. State, 69 Okl.Cr. 244, 101 P.2d 860, 863; 2 Bish.Cr.L. § 605.

"Uttering" or "publishing" a check consists in presenting it for payment, and the act is then done although no money may be obtained. State v. Hobl, 108 Kan. 261, 194 P. 921, 924.

UTTER, *adj.* Entire; complete; absolute; total. Bell v. Commonwealth, 170 Va. 597, 195 S.E. 675, 683.

In a statute making utter desertion for three years a ground for divorce, it suggests an abnegation of all the duties and obligations resulting from the marriage contract. Moody v. Moody, 118 Me. 454, 108 A. 849.

UTTER BAR. In English law. The bar at which those barristers, usually junior men, practice who have not yet been raised to the dignity of king's counsel. These junior barristers are said to plead without the bar; while those of the higher rank are admitted to seats within the bar, and address the court or a jury from a place reserved for them, and divided off by a bar. Brown. Also called "outer bar."

UTTER BARRISTER. In English law. Those barristers who plead without the bar, and are distinguished from benchers, or those who have been readers, and who are allowed to plead within the bar, as the king's counsel are. Cowell. See Outer Bar.

UXOR. Lat. In the civil law. A wife; a woman lawfully married.

Et Uxor

And his wife. A term used in indexing, abstracting, and describing conveyances made by a man and his wife as grantors, or to a man and his wife as grantees. Often abbreviated *"et ux."* Thus, "John Doe *et ux.* to Richard Roe."

Jure Uxoris

In right of his wife. A term used of a husband who joins in a deed, is seised of an estate, brings a suit, etc., in the right or on the behalf of his wife. 3 Bl. Comm. 210.

UXOR ET FILIUS SUNT NOMINA NATURÆ. Wife and son are names of nature. 4 Bac. Works, 350.

UXOR NON EST SUI JURIS, SED SUB POTESTATE VIRI. A wife is not her own mistress, but is under the power of her husband. 3 Inst. 108.

UXOR SEQUITUR DOMICILIUM VIRI. A wife follows the domicile of her husband. Tray. Lat. Max. 606.

UXORICIDE. The killing of a wife by her husband; one who murders his wife. Not a technical term of the law.

V

V. As an abbreviation, this letter may stand for "Victoria," "volume," or "verb;" also "*vide*" (see) and "*voce*" (word).

It is also a common abbreviation of "*versus*," in the titles of causes, and reported cases.

V. A. Veterans Administration.

V. C. An abbreviation for "vice-chancellor."

V. C. C. An abbreviation for "vice-chancellor's court."

V. E. An abbreviation for "*venditioni exponas*," (*q. v.*).

V. G. An abbreviation for "*verbi gratia*," for the sake of example.

V. I. S. T. A. Volunteers in Service to America.

VACANCY. A place which is empty. Wallace v. Payne, 197 Cal. 539, 241 P. 879. State v. Young, 137 La. 102, 68 So. 241, 247.

A strip of unsurveyed and unsold public lands. Hughes v. Rhodes, Tex.Civ.App., 137 S.W.2d 820, 821.

An unoccupied or unfilled post, position, or office. Alcorn ex rel. Hendrick v. Keating, 120 Conn. 427, 181 A. 340. An existing office, etc., without an incumbent. State v. Board of Election Com'rs of City of Tipton, 196 Ind. 472, 149 N.E. 69, 71. The state of being destitute of an incumbent, or a proper or legally qualified officer. Ashcroft v. Goodman, 139 Tenn. 625, 202 S.W. 939. The term is principally applied to an interruption in the incumbency of an office, or to cases where the office is not occupied by one who has a legal right to hold it and to exercise the rights and perform the duties pertaining thereto. Frantz v. Davis, 131 S.E. 784, 785, 144 Va. 320. State ex rel. Plunkett v. Miller, 162 Miss. 149, 137 So. 737, 739. See, also, Vacant.

The word "vacancy," when applied to official positions, means, in its ordinary and popular sense, that an office is unoccupied, and that there is no incumbent who has a lawful right to continue therein until the happening of a future event, though the word is sometimes used with reference to an office temporarily filled. Futrell v. Oldham, 107 Ark. 386, 155 S.W. 502, 504, Ann.Cas.1915A, 571; State v. Caulk, 3 W.W.Harr., Del., 344, 138 A. 354, 357.

Misconduct in office does not create a "vacancy". State ex rel. Brister v. Weston, 241 Wis. 584, 6 N.W.2d 648, 651. And though "suspension" becomes imperative pending trial of a public officer for malfeasance or nonfeasance in office, "vacancy" does not occur until the officer is removed following trial. State ex rel. Carlson v. Strunk, 219 Minn. 529, 18 N.W.2d 457, 460. But annulment of election creates a "vacancy" in office. Killian v. Wilkins, 203 S.C. 74, 26 S.E.2d 246, 248.

A person by entering armed forces of the United States does not create a vacancy of a civil office formerly held by such person. State ex rel. Thomas v. Wysong, 125 W.Va. 369, 24 S.E.2d 463, 467; Gullickson v. Mitchell, 113 Mont. 359, 126 P.2d 1106, 1110, 1111, 1114; In re Advisory Opinion to Governor, 150 Fla. 556, 8 So.2d 26, 32, 140 A.L.R. 1481.

VACANT. Empty; unoccupied; as, "vacant" office. Shaffner v. Shaw, 191 Iowa 1047, 180 N.W. 853, 854. Deprived of contents, without inanimate objects. It implies entire abandonment, nonoccupancy for any purpose. Foley v. Sonoma County Farmers' Mut. Fire Ins. Co. of Sonoma, Cal. App., 108 P.2d 939, 942.

"Vacant" and "unoccupied," as used together in rider to fire policy, have different meanings; term "vacant" meaning "empty," while term "unoccupied" means lack of habitual presence of human beings. Jelin v. Home Ins. Co., C.C.A.N.J., 72 F.2d 326, 327.

Absolutely free, unclaimed, and unoccupied; as, "vacant" land. Donley v. Van Horn, 49 Cal.App. 383, 193 P. 514, 516. See, also, War Fork Land Co. v. Llewellyn, 199 Ky. 607, 251 S.W. 663, 665. But land which is partially cultivated may still be "vacant land" within the meaning of a statute. Di Legge v. Peper, 148 Md. 268, 129 A. 292, 293.

See, also, Vacancy, and as to vacant "Possession" and "Succession," see those titles.

VACANTIA BONA. Lat. In the civil law. Goods without an owner, or in which no one claims a property; escheated goods. Inst. 2, 6, 4; 1 Bl. Comm. 298.

VACATE. To annul; to set aside; to cancel or rescind; to render an act void; as, to vacate an entry of record, or a judgment. Stewart v. Oneal, C.C.A.Ohio, 237 F. 897, 903.

As applied to a judgment or decree it is not synonymous with "suspend" which means to stay enforcement of judgment or decree. Ohio Fuel Gas Co. v. City of Mt. Vernon, 37 Ohio App. 159, 174 N.E. 260, 262.

To put an end to; as, to vacate a street. McCarl v. Clarke County, 167 Iowa, 14, 148 N.W. 1015, 1017.

To move out; to make vacant or empty; to leave; especially, to surrender possession by removal; to cease from occupancy. Ruble v. Ruble, Tex.Civ.App., 264 S.W. 1018, 1020; Polich v. Severson, 68 Mont. 225, 216 P. 785, 787.

See, also, Vacancy.

VACATIO. Lat. In the civil law. Exemption; immunity; privilege; dispensation; exemption from the burden of office. Calvin.

VACATION. A recess or leave of absence, a respite or time of respite from active duty, an intermission or rest period during which activity or work is suspended. It is a period of freedom from duty, but not the end of employment. In re Dauber, 151 Pa.Super. 293, 30 A.2d 214, 216. The act or result of vacating. An intermission of procedure. Kettlekamp v. Watkins, 70 Mont. 391, 225 P. 1003, 1006. It is not a termination of the relation of master and servant. Gutzwiller v. American Tobacco Co., 97 Vt. 281, 122 A. 586, 588. In schools, there are customary vacations at Christmas, Easter, and during the summer. Duffey v. School Committee of Town of Hopkinton, 236 Mass. 5, 127 N.E. 540.

That period of time between the end of one term of court and the beginning of another.

O'Neal v. State, 35 Ga.App. 665, 134 S.E. 332, 333; Conkling v. Ridgely, 112 Ill. 36, 1 N.E. 261, 54 Am. Rep. 204; Brayman v. Whitcomb, 134 Mass. 525.

Sometimes, any time when the court is not in session. St. Louis, I. M. & S. Ry. Co. v. Ingram, 118 Ark. 377, 176 S.W. 692, 693.

Under practice statutes the intermission between the calls of the equity docket. West v. State ex rel. Matthews, 233 Ala. 588, 173 So. 46, 47.

Ecclesiastical Law

Vacation signifies that a church or benefice is vacant; *e. g.*, on the death or resignation of the incumbent, until his successor is appointed. 2 Inst. 359; Phillim.Ecc.Law, 495.

VACATION BARRISTER. See Barrister.

VACATUR. Lat. Let it be vacated. In practice, a rule or order by which a proceeding is vacated; a vacating.

VACATURA. An avoidance of an ecclesiastical benefice. Cowell.

VACCARIA. In old English law. A dairyhouse. Co. Litt. 5*b*.

VACCINATION. Inoculation with vaccine or the virus of cowpox as a preventive against the smallpox; frequently made compulsory by statute. Daniel v. Putnam County, 113 Ga. 570, 38 S.E. 980, 54 L.R.A. 292; Zucht v. King, Tex.Civ.App., 225 S.W. 267.

VACUA POSSESSIO. Lat. The vacant possession, *i. e.*, free and unburdened possession, which (*e. g.*,) a vendor had and has to give to a purchaser of lands.

VACUITY. Emptiness; vacancy; want of reality; nihility. McQueen v. Ahbe, 99 W.Va. 650, 130 S.E. 261, 262.

VACUUM. Practically synonymous with suction, although suction may be the result of vacuum. Pennsylvania Rubber Co. v. Dreadnaught Tire & Rubber Co., D.C.Del., 225 F. 138, 141.

VACUUS. Lat. In the civil law. Empty; void; vacant; unoccupied. Calvin.

VADES. Lat. In the civil law. Pledges; sureties; bail; security for the appearance of a defendant or accused person in court. Calvin.

VADIARE DUELLUM. L. Lat. In old English law. To wage or gage the *duellum*; to wage battel; to give pledges mutually for engaging in the trial by combat.

VADIMONIUM. Lat. In Roman law. Bail or security; the giving of bail for appearance in court; a recognizance. Calvin. An ancient form of suretyship. Hunter, Rom.L. 526.

VADIUM. Lat. A pledge; security by pledge of property. Coggs v. Bernard, 2 Ld.Raym. 913.

VADIUM MORTUUM. A mortgage or *dead pledge;* a security given by the borrower of a sum of money, by which he grants to the lender an estate in fee, on condition that, if the money be not repaid at the time appointed, the estate so put in pledge shall continue to the lender as dead or gone from the mortgagor. 2 Bl.Comm. 157.

VADIUM PONERE. To take bail for the appearance of a person in a court of justice. Tomlins.

VADIUM VIVUM. A species of security by which the borrower of a sum of money made over his estate to the lender until he had received that sum out of the issues and profits of the land. It was so called because neither the money nor the lands were lost, and were not left in dead pledge, but this was a *living* pledge, for the profits of the land were constantly paying off the debt. Litt. § 206; 1 Pow.Mortg. 3; Termes de la Ley; Spect v. Spect, 88 Cal. 437, 26 P. 203, 13 L.R.A. 137, 22 Am.St.Rep. 314; O'Neill v. Gray, 39 Hun (N.Y.) 566; Kortright v. Cady, 21 N.Y. 344, 78 Am.Dec. 145.

VADLET. In old English law. The king's eldest son; hence the valet or knave follows the king and queen in a pack of cards. Bar.Obs.St. 344.

VADELET. See Valec.

VADUM. In old records, a ford, or wading place. Cowell.

VAGABOND. A vagrant or homeless wanderer without means of honest livelihood. Neering v. Illinois Cent. R. Co., 383 Ill. 366, 50 N.E.2d 497, 502. One who wanders from place to place, having no fixed dwelling, or, if he has one, not abiding in it; a wanderer, especially such a person who is lazy and generally worthless and without means of honest livelihood. Goodman v. Eggers, 11 N.J.Misc. 811, 168 A. 317, 318.

Vagabonds are described in old English statutes as "such as wake on the night and sleep on the day, and haunt customable taverns and ale-houses and routs about; and no man wot from whence they came, nor whither they go." 4 Bl.Comm. 169. See Forsyth v. Forsyth, 46 N.J.Eq. 400, 19 A. 119; Johnson v. State, 28 Tex.App. 562, 13 S.W. 1005.

VAGABUNDUM NUNCUPAMUS EUM QUI NULLIBI DOMICILIUM CONTRAXIT HABITATIONIS. We call him a "vagabond" who has acquired nowhere a domicile of residence. Phillim. Dom. 23, note.

VAGRANCY. At common law, the act of going about from place to place by a person without visible means of support, who is idle, and who, though able to work for his or her maintenance, refuses to do so, but lives without labor or on the charity of others. Ex parte Hudgins, 86 W. Va. 526, 103 S.E. 327, 328, 9 A.L.R. 1361. See Vagrant.

Ordinarily, a course of conduct or manner of life, rather than a single act, is necessary to give rise to charge of "vagrancy". State v. Suman, 216 Minn. 293, 12 N.W.2d 620, 621.

Under some statutes, however, a single act may be sufficient. 66 C.J. p. 401. Thus, it has been held that the act of prowling about and creeping up on parked automobiles and their occupants at night, under circumstances indicating an intent to commit a crime, constitutes vagrancy. Smith v. Drew, 26 P.2d 1040, 175 Wash. 11. It has also been held that, although traveling by automobile, a person may nevertheless be a vagrant, and, even though he travels without stop or hesitation for a considerable distance, he may still come within a statute punishing one who "wanders about" at late hours. Blashfield, Cyc. of Automobile Law and Prac., Perm. Ed., § 5528.84.

VAGRANT. At common law, wandering or going about from place to place by idle person who had no lawful or visible means of support and who subsisted on charity and did not work, though able to do so. State v. Harlowe, 174 Wash. 227, 24 P.2d 601.

A general term, including, in English law, the several classes of idle and disorderly persons, rogues, and vagabonds, and incorrigible rogues. 4 Steph.Comm. 308, 309.

One who strolls from place to place, an idle wanderer, specifically, one who has no settled habitation, a vagabond. Neering v. Illinois Cent. R. Co., 383 Ill. 366, 50 N.E.2d 497, 502. A person able to work who spends his time in idleness or immorality, having no property to support him and without some visible and known means of fair, honest and reputable livelihood. State v. Oldham, 224 N.C. 415, 30 S.E.2d 318, 319. One who is apt to become a public charge through his own laziness. People, on Complaint of McDonough, v. Gesino, Sp.Sess., 22 N.Y.S.2d 284, 285. See Vagrancy.

A person who lives without employment is not a "vagrant" if he has sufficient means belonging to himself or means provided for him in a legitimate way. People v. Banwer, Mag.Ct., 22 N.Y.S.2d 566, 569, 571.

VAGRANT ACT. In English law. The statute 5 Geo. IV. c. 83, which is an act for the punishment of idle and disorderly persons. 2 Chit.St. 145. The act of 17 Geo. II divided vagrants into idle and disorderly persons; rogues and vagabonds; and incorrigible rogues. Other statutes were passed as late at 32 Geo. III bearing on this subject. See Jacob's Law Dict. *s. v. Vagrant.*

VAGUE. Indefinite. City of Cincinnati v. Schill, 125 Ohio St. 57, 180 N.E. 545, 547. Uncertain; not susceptible of being understood. 5 B. & C. 583.

Vague and unsatisfactory testimony is that which is dim and shadowy and fails to relieve the mind of the trier of facts from doubt or uncertainty. Weliska's Case, 125 Me. 147, 131 A. 860, 861.

VALE. In Spanish law. A promissory note. White, New Recop. b. 3, tit. 7, c. 5, § 3. See Govin v. De Miranda, 140 N.Y. 662, 35 N.E. 628.

VALEAT QUANTUM VALERE POTEST. It shall have effect as far as it can have effect. Cowp. 600; 4 Kent, Comm. 493; Shep.Touch. 87.

VALEC, VALECT, or VADELET. In old English law. A young gentleman; also a servitor or gentleman of the chamber. Cowell.

VALENTIA. L. Lat. The value or price of anything.

VALESHERIA. In old English law. The proving by the kindred of the slain, one on the father's side, and another on that of the mother, that a man was a Welshman. Wharton. See Engleshire.

VALET. Anciently, a name denoting young gentlemen of rank and family, but afterwards applied to those of lower degree; now used for a menial servant, more particularly occupied about the person of his employer. Cab.Lawy. 800.

VALID. Having legal strength or force, executed with proper formalities, incapable of being rightfully overthrown or set aside. Edwards v. O'Neal, Tex.Civ.App., 28 S.W.2d 569, 572. Of binding force; legally sufficient or efficacious; authorized by law. Anderson, L.Dict.; Morrison v. Farmers' & Traders' State Bank, 70 Mont. 146, 225 P. 123, 125. Good or sufficient in point of law; efficacious; executed with the proper formalities; incapable of being rightfully overthrown or set aside; sustainable and effective in law, as distinguished from that which exists or took place in fact or appearance, but has not the requisites to enable it to be recognized and enforced by law. Thompson v. Town of Frostproof, 89 Fla. 92, 103 So. 118; United States v. McCutchen, D.C.Cal., 234 F. 702, 709.

A deed, will, or other instrument, which has received all the formalities required by law, is said to be valid.

Meritorious; as a *valid* defense. Berringer v. Stevens, 145 Ark. 293, 225 S.W. 14, 15.

VALID REASON. These words, in a statute providing for the withdrawal of the names of petitioners for a road improvement district when valid reasons therefor are presented, mean a sound sufficient reason, such as fraud, deceit, misrepresentation, duress, etc., a reason upon which the petitioner could support or justify his change in attitude. The word "valid" necessarily possesses an element of legal strength and force, and inconsistent positions have no such force. Echols v. Trice, 130 Ark. 97, 196 S.W. 801, 802.

VALIDATE. To test the validity of; to make valid; to confirm. Thompson v. Town of Frostproof, 89 Fla. 92, 103 So. 118. To sanction, to affirm. Peck v. Tugwell, 199 La. 125, 5 So.2d 524, 529.

VALIDATING STATUTE. A statute, purpose of which is to cure past errors and omissions and thus make valid what was invalid, but it grants no indulgence for the correction of future errors. Petition of Miller, 149 Pa.Super. 142, 28 A.2d 257, 258.

VALIDITY. Legal sufficiency, in contradistinction to mere regularity. Home Ins. Co. of New York v. Gaines, 74 Colo. 62, 218 P. 907, 908.

VALIDITY OF A STATUTE. This phrase, within the meaning of a constitutional provision relating to the jurisdiction of the Supreme Court, refers to the power to enact the particular statute, and not merely to its judicial construction or application. Boehringer v. Yuma County, 15 Ariz. 546, 140 P. 507, 508.

VALIDITY OF A TREATY. The term "validity," as applied to treaties, admits of two descriptions—necessary and voluntary. By the former is meant that which results from the treaties having been made by persons authorized by, and for purposes consistent with, the constitution. By voluntary validity is meant that validity which a treaty, voidable by reason of violation by the other party, still continues to retain by the silent acquiescence and will of the nation. It is voluntary, because it is at the will of the nation to let it remain or to extinguish it. The principles which govern and decide the necessary validity of a treaty are of a judicial nature, while those on which its voluntary validity depends are of a political nature. 2 Paine 688, as paraphrased in 5 Moore, Int.L. Dig. 183.

VALIDITY OF A WILL. As used in will contest statute has reference only to the genuineness or legal sufficiency of will under attack. In re Elliott's Estate, 22 Wash.2d 334, 156 P.2d 427, 438, 157 A.L.R. 1335.

VALLEY. As applied to a mountainous country, lowlands, in contradistinction to mountain slopes and ridges. Whaley v. Northern Pac. R. Co., C.C. Mont., 167 F. 664.

VALOR BENEFICIORUM. L. Lat. The value of every ecclesiastical benefice and preferment, according to which the first fruits and tenths are collected and paid. It is commonly called the "king's books," by which the clergy are at present rated. 2 Steph.Comm. 533; Wharton.

VALOR MARITAGII. Lat. Value of the marriage. The amount forfeited under the ancient tenures by a ward to a guardian who had offered her a marriage without disparagement, which she refused. In feudal law, the guardian in chivalry had the right of tendering to his infant ward a suitable match, without "disparagement," (inequality,) which, if the infants refused, they forfeited the value of the marriage (*valor maritagii*) to their guardian; that is, so much as a jury would assess, or any one would *bona fide* give, to the guardian for such an alliance. 2 Bl.Comm. 70; Litt. § 110.

A writ which lay against the ward, on coming of full age, for that he was not married, by his guardian, for the *value of the marriage,* and this though no convenient marriage had been offered. Termes de la Ley.

VALUABLE. Of financial or market value; commanding or worth a good price; of considerable worth in any respect; estimable. Webster, Dict.

VALUABLE CONSIDERATION. A class of consideration upon which a promise may be founded, which entitles the promisee to enforce his claim against an unwilling promisor. Cockrell v. McKenna, 103 N.J.L. 166, 134 A. 687, 688, 48 A.L.R. 234, some right, interest, profit, or benefit accruing to one party, or some forbearance, detriment, loss, or responsibility given, suffered, or undertaken by the other. Onsrud v. Paulsen, 219 Wis. 1, 261 N.W. 541, 542. Industrial Loan & Investment Bank v. Dardine, 207 N.C. 509, 177 S.E. 635. A gain or loss to either party is not essential, it is sufficient if the party in whose favor the contract is made parts with a right which he might otherwise exert. Miller Ice Co. v. Crim, 299 Ill. App. 615, 20 N.E.2d 347. It need not be translatable into dollars and cents, but is sufficient if it consists of performance, or promise thereof, which promisor treats and considers of value to him. Asmus v. Longenecker, 131 Neb. 608, 269 N.W. 117, 119. It is not essential that the person to whom the consideration moves should be benefited, provided the person from whom it moves is, in a legal sense, injured. The injury may consist of a compromise of a disputed claim or forbearance to exercise a legal right, the alteration in position being regarded as a detriment that forms a consideration independent of the actual value of the right forborne. Boston Excelsior Co. v. Amerio, 147 Misc. 1, 263 N.Y.S. 174. Mutual promises in contract is sufficient. Adams, Payne & Gleaves v. Indiana Wood Preserving Co., 155 Va. 18, 154 S.E. 558, 562. For "Fair and Valuable Consideration," see that title.

The following was said to be a valuable consideration: Extension of time for payment of an obligation. C. I. T. Corporation v. Furrow, 227 Iowa 961, 289 N.W. 697, 698; Farmers & Merchants State Bank of Cawker City v. Higgins, 149 Kan. 783, 89 P.2d 916. Marriage. Rutland v. Norris, 154 Fla. 894, 19 So.2d 418, 419. Release of property subject to execution. Bradley v. DeLoach, 176 Ga. 142, 167 S.E. 301, 303. Pre-existing debt. Yale Oil Corporation v. Sedlacek, 99 Mont. 411, 43 P.2d 887, 890. (Contra Duncan v. Jones, Tex.Civ.App., 153 S.W.2d 214, 216.) The distinction between a *good* and a *valuable* consideration is that the former consists of blood, or of natural love and affection; as when a man grants an estate to a near relation from motives of generosity, prudence, and natural duty; and the latter consists of such a consideration as money, marriage which is to follow, or the like, which the law esteems an equivalent given for the grant. 2 Bl.Comm. 297; Exum v. Lynch, 188 N.C. 392, 125 S.E. 15, 18; Gay v. Fricks, 211 Ala. 119, 99 So. 846, 847; Barton v. Wilson, 116 Ark. 400, 172 S.W. 1032, 1034.

VALUABLE IMPROVEMENTS. As used in a statute relating to the specific performance of a parol contract for the purchase of real estate, improvements of such character as add permanent value to the freehold, and such as would not likely be made by one not claiming the right to the possession and enjoyment of the freehold estate. Improvements of a temporary and unsubstantial character will not amount to such part performance as, when accompanied by possession alone, will take the contract out of the operation of the statute of frauds. Farr v. West, 152 Ga. 595, 110 S.E. 724. The valuable improvements may, however, be slight and of small value, provided they are substantial and permanent in their nature, beneficial to the freehold, and such as none but an owner would ordinarily make. Vickers v. Robinson, 157 Ga. 731, 122 S.E. 405, 408.

VALUABLE PAPERS. This term as used in statute requiring that a holographic will devising realty be found among the "valuable papers" of decedent, in order to be effective, refers to such papers as are regarded by the testator as worthy of preservation and therefore in his estimation of some value. Fransioli v. Podesta, 21 Tenn.App. 554, 113 S.W.2d 769, 773, 777. And does not refer only to papers having money value. Pulley v. Cartwright, 23 Tenn.App. 690, 137 S.W.2d 336, 340.

VALUABLE THING. This phrase, as used in statutes relating to cheating and defrauding by means of false pretenses, does not embrace a mere pecuniary advantage devoid of any physical attribute possessed by money, chattels, or valuable securities. State v. Tower, 122 Kan. 165, 251 P. 401, 402, 52 A.L.R. 1160. The words include everything of value, State v. Thatcher, 35 N.J.L. 452; as a promissory note, State v. Tomlin, 29 N.J.L. 13; or a physician's services; State v. Ball, 114 Miss. 505, 75 So. 373, 374, L.R.A.1917E, 1046.

Within gaming statutes, anything which affords the lure to indulge the gambling instinct. State v. Betti, 21 N.J.Misc. 345, 34 A.2d 91, 94.

VALUATION. The act of ascertaining the worth of a thing. The estimated worth of a thing. Lowenstein v. Schiffer, 38 App.Div. 178, 56 N.Y.S. 674; State v. Central Pac. R. Co., 7 Nev. 104. Soniat v. Board of State Affairs, 146 La. 450, 83 So. 760, 762.

"Valuation" of itself does not levy tax upon person or property, but is necessary step preliminary thereto. Johnson v. Board of Park Com'rs of Ft. Wayne, 202 Ind. 282, 174 N.E. 91, 94. For "Fair Valuation", see that title.

VALUATION LIST. In English law. A list of all the ratable hereditaments in a parish, showing the names of the occupier, the owner, the property, the extent of the property, the gross estimated rental, and the ratable value; prepared by the overseers of each parish in a union under section 14 of the union assessment committee act, 1862 (St. 25 & 26 Vict. c. 103,) for the purposes of the poor rate. Wharton.

VALUE. The utility of an object in satisfying, directly or indirectly, the needs or desires of human beings, called by economists "value in use;" or its worth consisting in the power of purchasing other objects, called "value in exchange." Joint Highway Dist. No. 9 v. Ocean Shore R. Co., 128 Cal.App. 743, 18 P.2d 413, 417. Also the estimated or appraised worth of any object or property, calculated in money.

Any consideration sufficient to support a simple contract. Fowler v. Smith, 24 Ohio App. 324, 156 N.E. 913, 914; Veigel v. Johnson, 163 Minn. 288, 204 N.W. 36, 37; Wilbour v. Hawkins, 38 R.I. 116, 94 A. 856, 857.

The term is often used as an abbreviation for "valuable consideration," especially in the phrases "purchaser for value," "holder for value," etc. See Mays v. First State Bank of Keller, Tex.Civ.App., 233 S.W. 326, 328; Farr-Barnes Lumber Co. v. Town of St. George, 128 S.C. 67, 122 S.E. 24, 26.

In economic consideration, the word "value," when used in reference to property, has a variety of significations, according to the connection in which the word is employed. It may mean the cost of a production or reproduction of the property in question, when it is sometimes called "sound value"; or it may mean the purchasing power of the property, or the amount of money which the property will command in exchange, if sold, this being called its "market value," which in the case of any particular property may be more or less than either the cost of its production or its value measured by its utility to the present or some other owner; or the word may mean the subjective value of property, having in view its profitableness for some particular purpose, sometimes termed its "value for use." William H. Low Estate Co. v. Lederer Realty Corporation, 35 R.I. 352, 86 A. 881, 883, Ann.Cas. 1916A, 341. See Agency of Canadian Car & Foundry Co. v. Pennsylvania Iron Works Co., C.C.A.Pa., 256 F. 339, 344; Babbitt v. Read, C.C.A.N.Y., 236 F. 42, 46; James v. Speer, 69 Mont. 100, 220 P. 535, 537; Burroughs v. School Dist. No. 2, Town of Richland, 155 Wis. 426, 144 N.W. 977, 978.

Salable value, actual value, market value, fair value, reasonable value, and cash value may all mean the same thing and may be designed to effect the same purpose. Burr. Tax. 227. See Cummings v. Bank, 101 U.S. 162, 25 L.Ed. 903; Wood v. Syracuse School Dist. No. 1, 108 Kan. 1, 193 P. 1049, 1050; Gulf Compress Co. v. Insurance Co. of Pennsylvania, 129 Tenn. 586, 167 S.W. 859, 863; In re Woolsey's Estate, 109 Neb. 138, 190 N.W. 215, 24 A.L.R. 1038.

"Value," as used in Const.U.S. art. 1, § 8, giving Congress power to coin money and regulate the value thereof, is the true, inherent, and essential value, not depending upon accident, place, or person, but the same everywhere and to every one, and in this sense regulating the value of the coinage is merely determining and maintaining coinage composed of certain coins within certain limitations at a certain specific composition and weight. Klattenburg v. Qualsett, 114 Neb. 18, 205 N.W. 577, 578.

"Value" of land for purpose of taxation is represented by price that would probably be paid therefor after fair negotiations between willing seller and buyer. Thaw v. Town of Fairfield, 132 Conn. 173, 43 A.2d 65, 67, 160 A.L.R. 679.

"Values," as used in tax statutes, are valuations of officials whose duty it is to make them. Wymore v. Markway, 338 Mo. 46, 89 S.W.2d 9, 13.

"Value" as it relates to stolen property is the market value at the time and place of the taking, or, in case of property without a market value, the cost of replacing it. Patterson v. State, 138 Tex.Cr.R. 551, 137 S.W.2d 1030; Givens v. State, 143 Tex.Cr.R. 277, 158 S.W.2d 535, 536.

As respects whether value of stolen property equals or exceeds jurisdictional amount fixed by the National Stolen Property Act, "value" of stolen property is market value at time and place of taking, if it has a market value. National Stolen Property Act, §§ 1–7, 18 U.S.C.A. § 413 et seq. Husten v. United States, C.C.A.Minn., 95 F.2d 168.

In action to recover chattel, "value" means value at time of trial, not at time of seizure thereof. Spear v. Auto Dealers' Discount Corporation, 154 Misc. 801, 278 N.Y.S. 561.

"Value" as used in eminent domain proceeding means market value, (which title see infra). Epstein v. Boston Housing Authority, 317 Mass. 297, 58 N.E.2d 135, 137.

Under the Uniform Sales Act, "value" is any consideration sufficient to support a simple contract. Blumberg v. Taggart, 213 Minn. 39, 5 N.W.2d 388, 392.

For purposes of corporate reorganization, "value" is a reasonable capitalization of future earnings as reasonably foreseeable at date of reorganization. Commissioner of Internal Revenue v. Marshall, C.C.A.2, 125 F.2d 943, 946.

Clear Value

Of an estate for the purpose of an inheritance tax is what remains after all claims against it have been paid. In re Hildebrand's Estate, 262 Pa. 112, 104 A. 866.

Face Value

See Face Value.

Fair and Equitable Value

See Fair and Equitable Value.

Fair and Reasonable Market Value

See Fair and Reasonable Market Value

Fair and Reasonable Value

See Fair and Reasonable Value.

Fair Cash Market Value

See Fair Cash Market Value.

Fair Cash Value

See Fair Cash Value.

Fair Value

See Fair Value.

Market Value

Fair value of property as between one who wants to purchase it and another who desires to sell it. Lincoln Joint Stock Land Bank v. Board of Review of Sioux City, 227 Iowa, 1136, 290 N.W. 94, 95; People ex rel. Pennsylvania Tunnel & Terminal R. Co. v. Miller, Sup., 26 N.Y.S.2d 232, 236. What willing purchaser will give for property under fair market conditions. People v. F. H. Smith Co., 230 App.Div. 268, 243 N.Y.S. 446, 451. Not what the owner could realize at a forced sale, but the price he could obtain after reasonable and ample time, such as would ordinarily be taken by an owner to make a sale of like property. Wade v. Rathbun, 23 Cal.App.2d Supp. 758, 67 P.2d 765, 766.

Net Value

The "reserve" or "net value" of a life insurance policy is the fund accumulated out of the net premiums during the earlier years of the policy while the premium uniform throughout life or a term of years exceeds the actual value of the risk, and with the net premiums to be received in the future is the exact mathematical equivalent of the obligation incurred by the company. Hay v. Meridian Life & Trust Co., 57 Ind.App. 536, 101 N.E. 651, 654. The "net value" of a policy is equivalent to "reserve," and means that part of the annual premium paid by insured which, according to the American Experience Table of Mortality, must be set apart to meet or mature the company's obligations to insured, the net value of a policy on a given date being its actual value, its reserve. Jefferson v. New York Life Ins. Co., 151 Ky. 609, 152 S.W. 780, 783.

True Value

At which property must be assessed is price which would be paid therefor on assessing date to willing seller, not compelled to sell, by willing purchaser, not compelled to purchase. New York Bay R. Co. v. Kelly, 22 N.J.Misc. 204, 37 A.2d 624, 628.

Value of Matter in Controversy

As used in the Judicial Code, § 24 (28 U.S.C.A. § 1331, et seq.), the pecuniary result to either party which a judgment entered in the case would directly produce, either at once or in the future. Elliott v. Empire Natural Gas Co., C.C.A.Kan., 4 F.2d 493, 497.

Value of Plant in Successful Operation

Synonymous with "going value," or "going concern value," meaning the additional value that a purchaser will give for the properties and business of the companies because they are going concerns with established businesses; the additional value, over and above the fair and reasonable value of the physical properties plus the working capital, which a customer would pay for the property because it is a going concern. Pacific Telephone & Telegraph Co. v. Whitcomb, D.C.Wash., 12 F.2d 279, 284.

Value Received

A phrase usually employed in a bill of exchange or promissory note, to denote that a lawful consideration has been given for it. Baker v. Thomas, 102 Neb. 401, 167 N.W. 407; Clayton v. Clayton, 125 N.J.L. 537, 17 A.2d 496, 497. It is prima facie evidence of consideration; Palmer v. Blanchard, 113 Me. 380, 94 A. 220, 223, Ann.Cas.1917A, 809; Moses v. Bank, 13 S.Ct. 900, 149 U.S. 298, 37 L.Ed. 743; although not necessarily in money, Osgood v. Bringolf, 32 Iowa, 265.

The phrase when put in a bill of exchange, will bear two interpretations: The drawer of the bill may be presumed to acknowledge the fact that he has received value from the payee, 3 Maule & S. 351; Benjamin v. Tillman, 2 McLean 213, Fed.Cas.No.1,304; or when the bill has been made payable to the order of the drawer and accepted, it implies that value has been received by the acceptor. 5 Maule & S. 65; Thurman v. Van Brunt, 19 Barb., N.Y., 409. The words are not required by the Uniform Negotiable Instruments Act.

VALUED POLICY. One in which a definite valuation is by agreement of both parties put on the subject-matter of the insurance and written in the face of the policy and such value, in the absence of fraud or mistake, is conclusive on the parties. Lee v. Hamilton Fire Ins. Co., 130 Misc.Rep. 165, 223 N.Y.S. 441, 442. One in which both property insured and loss are valued. Hight v. Maryland Ins. Co., 69 S.D. 320, 10 N.W.2d 285, 288.

It is distinguished from an "open policy", which is one where the value of the property insured is not settled in the policy. Ellis v. Hartford Livestock Ins. Co., 293 Ky. 683, 170 S.W.2d 51, 53.

VALUELESS. Worthless. Central of Georgia Ry. Co. v. Cooper, 14 Ga.App. 738, 82 S.E. 310, 311.

VALUER. A person whose business is to appraise or set a value upon property.

VALVASORS, or VIDAMES. An obsolete title of dignity next to a peer. 2 Inst. 667; 2 Steph. Comm. 612.

VANA EST ILLA POTENTIA QUÆ NUNQUAM VENIT IN ACTUM. That power is vain [idle or useless] which never comes into action, [which is never exercised.] 2 Coke, 51.

VANDALIC. Willfully or ignorantly destructive. Unkelsbee v. Homestead Fire Ins. Co. of Baltimore, D.C.Mun.App., 41 A.2d 168, 170.

VANDALISM. Willful or ignorant destruction of artistic or literary treasures; hostility to or contempt for what is beautiful or venerable. Unkelsbee v. Homestead Fire Ins. Co. of Baltimore, D.C.Mun.App., 41 A.2d 168, 170, 172.

VANI TIMORES SUNT ÆSTIMANDI, QUI NON CADUNT IN CONSTANTEM VIRUM. Those are to be regarded as idle fears which do not affect a steady [firm or resolute] man. 7 Coke, 27.

VANI TIMORIS JUSTA EXCUSATIO NON EST. A frivolous fear is not a legal excuse. Dig. 50, 17, 184; 2 Inst. 483; Broom, Max. 256, n.

VANTARIUS. L. Lat. In old records. A forefootman. Spelman; Cowell.

VARA. A Spanish-American measure of length, equal to 33 English inches or a trifle more or less, varying according to local usage. See U. S. v. Perot, 98 U.S. 428, 25 L.Ed. 251.

A measure used in Mexican land grants equal to 32.9927 inches. Ainsa v. U. S., 16 S.Ct. 544, 161 U.S. 219, 40 L.Ed. 673.

VARDA. In old Scotch law. Ward; custody; guardianship. Answering to "*warda*," in old English law. Spelman.

VARENNA. In old Scotch law. A warren. Answering to "*warenna*," in old English law. Spelman.

VARIANCE. In pleading and practice. A discrepancy or disagreement between two instruments or two steps in the same cause, which ought by law to be entirely consonant. Thus, if the evidence adduced by the plaintiff does not agree with the allegations of his declaration, it is a variance; and so if the statement of the cause of action in the declaration does not coincide with that given in the writ. See Keiser v. Topping, 72 Ill. 229; Mulligan v. U. S., 56 C.C.A. 50, 120 F. 98; State v. Wadsworth, 30 Conn. 57; Mathews v. U. S., C.C.A.Neb., 15 F.2d 139, 142. For "Fatal Variance," see that title.

A disagreement between the allegations and the proof in some matter which, in point of law, is essential to the charge or claim. Franks v. Reeder, 101 Okl. 18, 223 P. 126, 127; State v. Brozich, 108 Ohio St. 559, 141 N.E. 491. A substantial departure in the evidence adduced from the issue as made by the pleadings. Sposedo v. Merriman, 111 Me. 530, 90 A. 387, 392; Davidson Grocery Co. v. Johnston, 24 Idaho, 336, 133 P. 929, 931, Ann.Cas.1915C, 1129. The test of materiality of "variance" in an information is whether the pleading so fully and correctly informs a defendant of offense with which he is charged that, taking into account proof which is introduced against him, he is not misled in making his defense. People v. Guerrero, 22 Cal.2d 183, 137 P.2d 21, 24.

To constitute a "variance," there must be a real and tangible difference between the allegations in the pleading and the proof offered in its support. James A. C. Tait & Co. v. Stryker, 117 Or. 338, 243 P. 104, 106. The difference must be substantial and material. Epstein v. Waas, 28 N.M. 608, 216 P. 506, 508; Johnson v. Doubleday, 92 Vt. 267, 102 A. 1038, 1040. It must be one that actually misleads the adverse party to his prejudice in maintaining his action or defense on the merits, German-American Bank of Seattle v. Wright, 85 Wash. 460, 148 P. 769, 771, Ann.Cas. 1917D, 381; or, in criminal cases, one which might mislead the defense or expose a defendant to being put twice in jeopardy for the same offense, Brashears v. State, 38 Okl.Cr. 175, 259 P. 665, 667; McCallister v. State, 217 Ind. 65, 26 N.E.2d 391, 393.

A "variance" in criminal case is an essential difference between accusation and proof, best illustrated where one crime is alleged and another proved, and test of material variance is whether offense alleged in a second indictment is the same as that alleged in the first, and accordingly a plea of autrefois acquit must be upon a prosecution for the identical offense. U. S. v. Wills, C.C.A.Pa., 36 F.2d 855, 856.

"Variance," *i. e.*, a disagreement between allegations and proof in some matter which, in point of law, is essential to the claim or charge, differs from "repugnancy," which consists of two inconsistent allegations in one pleading. Fowler v. State, 20 Okl.Cr. 410, 203 P. 900, 901.

"Variance" also differs from failure of proof. Gordon v. Pollock, 124 Okl. 64, 253 P. 1021, 1023. A variance occurs when, though the pleading and proof do not exactly correspond, they may be made to do so by amendment in the discretion of the court and upon such terms and conditions as may be just. Deligny v. Tate Furniture Co., 170 N.C. 189, 86 S.E. 980, 984.

VARIATION. Difference in degrees between the direction of the true pole and the magnetic pole; it is comparatively fixed for any one locality, but is not the same in different localities. The Aakre, C.C.A.N.Y., 122 F.2d 469, 472.

VARIOUS. Separate. Simmons v. Ramsbottom, 51 Wyo. 419, 68 P.2d 153, 156.

VARRANTIZATIO. In old Scotch law. Warranty.

VAS. Lat. In the civil law. A pledge; a surety; bail or surety in a criminal proceeding or civil action. Calvin.

VASECTOMY. A comparatively simple and painless operation, performed by section (cutting) of the *vas deferens* or spermatic cord, or by a tying off or ligaturing thereof;—sometimes performed on rapists and other criminals (especially sexual offenders), and on persons who are mentally defective. Laws Iowa 1911, c. 129; Rem. & Bal. Code (Wash.) § 2287 (Rem.Rev.Stat. § 2287); Rev. Laws Nev. § 6293 (Comp.Laws 1929, § 9977). Some of these and similar statutes have been declared unconstitutional; Williams v. Smith, 190 Ind. 526, 131 N.E. 2; Mickle v. Henrichs, D.C.Nev., 262 F. 687; Smith v. Bd. of Examiners, 85 N.J.L. 46, 88 A. 963; but in 1927, the validity of a Virginia statute (Laws 1924, c. 394) providing for vasectomy in the case of males and for salpingectomy in the case of females was sustained in Buck v. Bell, 47 S.Ct. 584, 274 U.S. 200, 71 L.Ed. 1000, affirming 143 Va. 310, 130 S.E. 516, 51 A.L.R. 855. Sterilization of the female may also be accomplished by an operation known as oöphorectomy or ovariotomy. Acts Conn.1909, c. 209.

VASSAL. In feudal law. A feudal tenant or grantee; a feudatory; the holder of a fief on a feudal tenure, and by the obligation of performing feudal services. The correlative term was "lord." The vassal himself might be lord of some other vassal.

In after-times, this word was used to signify a species of slave who owed servitude and was in a state of dependency on a superior lord. 2 Bla. Comm. 53.

VASSAL STATES. In international law. States which are supposed to possess only those rights and privileges which have been expressly granted to them, but actually they seem to be well-nigh independent. Hershey, Int. L. 106. Egypt was such; also Crete.

VASSALAGE. The state or condition of a vassal.

VASSELERIA. The tenure or holding of a vassal. Cowell.

VASTUM. L. Lat. A waste or common lying open to the cattle of all tenants who have right of commoning. Cowell.

VASTUM FORESTÆ VEL BOSCI. In old records. Waste of a forest or wood. That part of a forest or wood wherein the trees and underwood were so destroyed that it lay in a manner waste and barren. Paroch. Antiq. 351, 497; Cowell.

VAUDERIE. In old European law. Sorcery; witchcraft; the profession of the Vaudois.

VAUDEVILLE. A species of theatrical entertainment, composed of isolated acts forming a balanced show. Hart v. B. F. Keith Vaudeville Exchange, C.C.A.N.Y., 12 F.2d 341, 342. And see Princess Amusement Co. v. Wells, C.C.A.Tenn., 271 F. 226, 231.

VAVASORY. The lands that a vavasour held. Cowell.

VAVASOUR. One who was in dignity next to a baron. Britt. 109; Bract. lib. 1, c. 8. One who held of a baron. Enc.Brit.

VEAL-MONEY. The tenants of the manor of Bradford, in the county of Wilts, paid a yearly rent by this name to their lord, in lieu of veal paid formerly in kind. Wharton.

VECORIN. In old Lombardic law. The offense of stopping one on the way; forestalling. Spelman.

VECTIGAL, ORIGINE IPSA, JUS CÆSARUM ET REGUM PATRIMONIALE EST. Dav. 12. Tribute, in its origin, is the patrimonial right of emperors and kings.

VECTIGAL JUDICIARIUM. Lat. Fines paid to the crown to defray the expenses of maintaining courts of justice. 3 Salk. 33.

VECTIGALIA. In Roman law. Customs-duties; taxes paid upon the importation or exportation of certain kinds of merchandise. Cod. 4, 61. They differed from tribute, which was a tax paid by each individual.

Rent from state lands. Hunter, Rom.L. 901.

VECTURA. In maritime law. Freight.

VEGETABLE. A plant cultivated for food. State v. Hurst, 149 Or. 519, 41 P.2d 1079, 1081.

A part or the whole of a herb used chiefly for culinary purposes, but also frequently for feeding domestic animals. In a comprehensive sense, any living organism not possessed of animal life; a plant of any kind. There is no well-drawn distinction between vegetables and fruits in the popular sense; but it has been held by the courts that all those which, like potatoes, carrots, peas, celery, lettuce, tomatoes, etc., are eaten (whether cooked or raw) during the principal part of a meal are to be regarded as "vegetables," while those used for dessert are fruits. State v. Hurst, 149 Or. 519, 41 P.2d 1079, 1080.

VEHICLE. That in or on which a person or thing is or may be carried from one place to another, especially along the ground, also through the air; any moving support or container fitted or used for the conveyance of bulky objects; a means of conveyance. Moffitt v. State Automobile Ins. Ass'n, 140 Neb. 578, 300 N.W. 837, 838. Any carriage moving on land, either on wheels or runners; a conveyance; that which is used as an instrument of conveyance, transmission or communication. Burford-Toothaker Tractor Co. v. Curry, 241 Ala. 350, 2 So.2d 420, 421; People v. Curnuch, 177 Misc. 606, 31 N.Y.S.2d 105, 107.

Any carriage, conveyance, or other artificial contrivance used, or capable of being used, as a means of transportation on land;—not ordinarily including locomotives, cars, and street cars which run and are operated only over and upon a permanent track or fixed way, unless the context of the ordinance or statute in question clearly indicates an intention to the contrary. Conder v. Griffith, 61 Ind. App. 218, 111 N.E. 816, 818; Rev.St.U.S. § 4 (1 U.S.C.A. § 4). The word includes a street sprinkler, St. Louis v. Woodruff, 71 Mo. 92; but not a ferry boat, Duckwall v. Albany, 25 Ind. 286; nor a domestic animal, unattached to a vehicle or a conveyance. State v. One Black Horse Mule, 207 Ala. 277, 92 So. 548. It has also been held to include a scraper used to remove snow from ice which was to be cut, particularly since the scraper had facilities for dumping and unloading and was horse-drawn. Berg v. Hetzler Bros., 166 N.Y.S. 830, 179 App.Div. 551. A combined thresher and cleaner, mounted on axles and wheels, while being drawn from farm to farm. Vincent v. Taylor Bros., 180 App.Div. 818, 168 N.Y.S. 287, 288. A bicycle; Sharkey v. Herman Bros., 3 N.J.Misc. 126, 127 A. 525, 526; Tulsa Ice Co. v. Wilkes, 54 Okl. 519, 153 P. 1169, 1171. A motorcycle; Knight v. Savannah Electric Co., 20 Ga.App. 314, 93 S.E. 17. And it includes an automobile; Shepard v. Findley, 204 Iowa, 107, 214 N.W. 676, 678; Stanley v. Tomlin, 143 Va. 187, 129 S.E. 379, 382; even though, at the time of the enactment of the legislation involved, automobiles were not in use, U. S. v. One Cadillac Automobile, D.C.Tenn., 2 F.2d 886, 888; City of Henderson v. Lockett, 157 Ky. 366, 163 S.W. 199, 201; White v. District of Columbia, 4 F.2d 163, 164, 55 App.D.C. 197. The term was held not to include a street car in the following cases: City of Chicago v. Keogh, 291 Ill. 188, 125 N.E. 881, 882; Harris v. Johnson, 174 Cal. 55, 161 P. 1155, 1156, L.R.A.1917C, 477, Ann. Cas.1918E, 560; Reed v. Public Service Ry. Co., 89 N.J.L. 431, 99 A. 100; Monongahela Bridge Co. v. R. Co., 114 Pa. 484, 8 A. 233. *Contra*, Bradley v. Minneapolis St. Ry. Co., 161 Minn. 322, 201 N.W. 606, 608, 46 A.L.R. 993.

As used in various statutes, however, the word is often given a somewhat narrower meaning than that which might be indicated by the above definition. Thus, it has been held that the term is inapplicable to a hand sled, Idell v. Day, 273 Pa. 34, 116 A. 506, 507, 20 A.L.R. 1429; to a child's coaster, Wright v. Salzberger & Sons, 81 Cal.App. 690, 254 P. 671, 676; and to an elevator, Wilson v. C. Dorflinger & Sons, 218 N.Y. 84, 112 N.E. 567, 568, Ann.Cas. 1917D, 38, reversing Wilson v. C. Dorflinger & Sons, 170 App.Div. 119, 155 N.Y.S. 857, 858.

But as defined in the Tariff Act, it has a much broader meaning, and includes any sort of conveyance used in the transportation of passengers and merchandise either by land or by water or through the air. Mellon v. Minneapolis, St. P. & S. S. M. Ry. Co., 56 App.D.C. 160, 11 F.2d 332, 334. United States v. One Pitcairn Biplane, Registration No. N.C.-5062, Engine No. A.D.-8285, D.C.N.Y., 11 F. Supp. 24, 26.

VEHMGERICHT. See Fehmgericht.

VEIES. L. Fr. Distresses forbidden to be replevied; the refusing to let the owner have his cattle which were distrained. Kelham.

VEILINGS. As used in the tariff act, a material chiefly or exclusively used for the making of veils. A veil is a piece of cloth or other material, usually thin and light, designed to be worn over the head and face as an ornament or to protect or wholly or partly conceal the face from view. The textile material which is used to mask or screen the features resting beneath the face panels of caskets would be commonly and popularly regarded as veiling. Tiedeman & Sons v. U. S., 8 Ct. Cust.App. 134, 135.

VEIN. In mining law. A continuous body of mineral or mineralized rock, filling a seam or fissure in the earth's crust, within defined boundaries in the general mass of the mountain (which boundaries clearly separate it from the neighboring rock), and having a general character of continuity in the direction of its length. San Francisco Chemical Co. v. Duffield, C.C.A.Wyo., 201 F. 830, 835; McMullin v. Magnuson, 102 Colo. 230, 78 P.2d 964, 968. It includes all deposits of mineral matter found through a mineralized zone or belt coming from the same source, impressed with the same forms, and appearing to have been created by the same processes. Inyo Marble Co. v. Loundagin, 7 P.2d 1067, 1072, 120 Cal.App. 298.

A requirement that a miner shall locate his claim "along the vein" means along the out-crop or course of the apex, and not along the strike. Stewart Mining Co. v. Bourne, C.C.A.Idaho, 218 F. 327, 329.

The terms "principal," "original," and "primary," as well as "secondary," "accidental," and "incidental," have all been employed to describe the different veins found within the same surface boundaries, but their meaning is not entirely clear in all cases. They may refer to the relative importance or value of the different veins, or the relations to each other, or to the time of discovery, but the words "secondary," "accidental," and "incidental" are most frequently used to distinguish between the discovery vein and other veins within the same surface boundaries. Northport Smelting & Refining Co. v. Lone Pine-Suprise Consol. Mines Co., D.C.Wash., 271 F. 105, 111.

Discovery Vein

That vein which served as a basis of the location, in contradistinction to secondary, accidental, and incidental veins. Northport Smelting & Refining Co. v. Long Pine-Surprise Consol. Mines Co., D.C.Wash., 271 F. 105, 113. The primary vein for the purpose of locating a mining claim and determining which are the end and which the side lines. Where the discovery vein crosses the opposite side lines of the claim as located, the side lines become end lines, not only with respect to such vein, but for determination of extralateral rights in any other vein which apexes within the claim. Northport Smelting & Refining Co. v. Lone Pine-Surprise Consol. Mines Co., C.C.A. Wash., 278 F. 719, 720.

VEJOURS. Viewers; persons sent by the court to take a view of any place in question, for the better decision of the right. It signifies, also, such as are sent to view those that *essoin* themselves *de malo lecti*, (*i. e.*, excuse themselves on ground of illness) whether they be in truth so sick as that they cannot appear, or whether they do counterfeit. Cowell.

VEL NON. Or not.

These words appear in the phrase "devisavit vel non" (*q. v.*), meaning, literally, "did he devise or not." 26 C. J.S. p. 1296. Examples of their use by the courts may be seen in the following quotations: "So the sufficiency vel non of the order of publication is important" (Cone v. Benjamin, 27 So.2d 90, 97, 157 Fla. 800); "the negligence vel non of the owner was * * * for the jury" (Johnson v. Wood, 21 So.2d 353, 355, 155 Fla. 753); and "We come at last to the merits vel non of this appeal" (Hollywood, Inc., v. Clark, 15 So.2d 175, 185, 153 Fla. 501).

VELABRUM. In old English law. A tollbooth. Cro.Jac. 122.

VELITIS JUBEATIS QUIRITES? Lat. Is it your will and pleasure, Romans? The form of proposing a law to the Roman people. Tayl.Civil Law, 155.

VELLE NON CREDITUR QUI OBSEQUITUR IMPERIO PATRIS VEL DOMINI. He is not presumed to consent who obeys the orders of his father or his master. Dig. 50, 17, 4.

VELTRARIA. The office of dog-leader, or courser. Cowell.

VELTRARIUS. One who leads greyhounds. Blount.

VELVET. In a secondary meaning, soft; smooth. Chapin-Sacks Mfg. Co. v. Hendler Creamery Co., D.C.Md., 231 F. 550, 551; Chapin-Sacks Mfg. Co. v. Hendler Creamery Co., C.C.A.Md., 254 F. 553, 555.

VENAL. Pertaining to something that is bought; capable of being bought; offered for sale; mercenary. Used usually in an evil sense, such purchase or sale being regarded as corrupt and illegal.

VENARIA. Beasts caught in the woods by hunting.

VENATIO. Hunting. Cowell.

VEND. To transfer to another for a pecuniary equivalent; to make an object of trade, especially by hawking or peddling; to sell. Goins v. State, 194 Ark. 598, 108 S.W.2d 1082, 1083.

The term is not commonly applied to the sale of real estate, although its derivatives "vendor" and "vendee" are.

VENDEE. A purchaser or buyer; one to whom anything is sold. Generally used of the purchaser of real property, one who acquires chattels by sale being called a "buyer."

VENDENS EANDEM REM DUOBUS FALSARIUS EST. He is fraudulent who sells the same thing twice. Jenk.Cent. 107.

VENDETTA. A private blood feud, in which a family seeks to avenge one of its members on the offender or his family. Stephens v. Howells Sales Co., D.C.N.Y., 16 F.2d 805, 808.

VENDIBLE. Fit or suitable to be sold; capable of transfer by sale; merchantable.

VENDITÆ. In old European law. A tax upon things sold in markets and public fairs. Spelman.

VENDITIO. Lat. In the civil law. In a strict sense, sale; the act of selling; the contract of sale, otherwise called *"emptio venditio."* Inst. 3, 24. Calvin.

In a large sense, any mode or species of alienation; any contract by which the property or ownership of a thing may be transferred. Inst. 3, 24. Calvin.

VENDITION. Sale; the act of selling.

VENDITIONI EXPONAS. Lat. You expose to sale. Richmond Cedar Works v. Stringfellow, D. C.N.C., 236 F. 264, 272. The name of a writ of execution, requiring a sale to be made, directed to a sheriff when he has levied upon goods under a *fieri facias,* but returned that they remained unsold for want of buyers; and in some jurisdictions it is issued to cause a sale to be made of lands, seized under a former writ, after they have been condemned or passed upon by an inquisition. Frequently abbreviated to *"vend. ex."* Beebe v. U. S., 16 S.Ct. 532, 161 U.S. 104, 40 L.Ed. 633; Ritchie v. Higginbotham, 26 Kan. 648; W. T. Carter & Bro. v. Bendy, Tex.Civ.App., 251 S.W. 265, 272; State ex rel. First Nat. Bank v. Ogden, 173 Okl. 285, 49 P.2d 565, 567.

The writ gives no new authority to the sheriff but only directs him to perform his duty under the execution. Fannin's Ex'r v. Haney, 283 Ky. 68, 140 S.W.2d 630, 632.

VENDITOR. Lat. A seller; a vendor. Inst. 3, 24; Bract. fol. 41.

VENDITOR REGIS. In old English law. The king's seller or salesman; the person who exposed to sale those goods and chattels which were seized or distrained to answer any debt due to the king. Cowell.

VENDITRIX. Lat. A female vendor. Cod. 4, 51, 3.

VENDOR. The person who transfers property by sale, particularly real estate, "seller" being more commonly used for one who sells personalty. The latter may, however, with entire propriety, be termed a vendor; Atlantic Refining Co. v. Van Valkenburg, 265 Pa. 456, 109 A. 208, 210; *e. g.,* a merchant; a retail dealer; Edgin v. Bell-Wayland Co., Okl.Cr.App., 149 P. 1145, L.R.A.1915F, 916; sometimes, one who buys to sell; Commonwealth v. Thorne, Neal & Co., 70 Pa.Super.Ct. 599, 602.

One who negotiates the sale, and becomes the recipient of the consideration, though the title comes to the vendee from another source, and not from the vendor. Rutland v. Brister, 53 Miss. 685; Canavan v. Coleman, 204 Iowa 901, 216 N.W. 292, 293.

VENDOR AND PURCHASER ACT. The act of 37 & 38 Vict. c. 78, which substitutes forty for sixty years as the root of title, and amends in other ways the law of vendor and purchaser. Mozley & Whiteley.

VENDOR'S LIEN. A creature of equity, a lien implied to belong to a vendor for the unpaid purchase price of land, where he has not taken any other lien or security beyond the personal obligation of the purchaser. Special Tax School Dist. No. 1 of Orange County v. Hillman, 131 Fla. 725, 179 So. 805, 809. An equitable security which arises from the fact that a vendee has received from his vendor property for which he has not paid the full consideration, and such lien exists independently of any express agreement. Sturdy v. Smith, Mo.App., 132 S.W.2d 1033, 1037; Causer v. Wilmoth, Mo.App., 142 S.W.2d 777, 779; Mollett v. Beckman, Mo.App., 78 S.W.2d 886. 890.

Also, a lien existing in the unpaid vendor of chattels, the same remaining in his hands, to the extent of the purchase price, where the sale was for cash, or on a term of credit which has expired, or on an agreement by which the seller is to retain possession. See Morgan v. Dalrymple, 59 N. J.Eq. 22, 46 A. 664; Lee v. Murphy, 119 Cal. 364, 51 P. 549.

In English and American law a vendor's lien is exceptional in character, and is an importation from the civil law, which found its recognition through courts of chancery, on the equitable principle that the person who had secured the estate of another ought not in conscience to be allowed to keep it and not pay full consideration money, and that to enforce that payment it was just that the vendor should have a lien upon the property. Martin v. Becker, 169 Cal. 301, 146 P. 665, 671, Ann.Cas.1916D, 171.

VENDUE. A sale; generally a sale at public auction; and more particularly a sale so made under authority of law, as by a constable, sheriff, tax collector, administrator, etc.

VENDUE MASTER. An auctioneer.

VENEREAL. Sexual; as, *venereal* diseases. State v. Hollinshead, 77 Or. 473, 151 P. 710, 711.

VENEREAL DISEASE. One of several diseases identified with sexual intercourse. Collective term for gonorrhea, chancroid, and syphilis. Coleman v. National Life & Accident Ins. Co., La.App., 145 So. 298, 299.

VENIA. A kneeling or low prostration on the ground by penitents; pardon.

VENIA ÆTATIS. A privilege granted by a prince or sovereign, in virtue of which a person is entitled to act, *sui juris,* as if he were of full age. Story, Confl. Laws, § 74.

VENIÆ FACILITAS INCENTIVUM EST DELINQUENDI. 3 Inst. 236. Facility of pardon is an incentive to crime.

VENIRE. Lat. To come; to appear in court. Sometimes used as the name of the writ for summoning a jury, more commonly called a *"venire facias."*

VENIRE DE NOVO. Venire facias de novo, which title see.

VENIRE FACIAS. Lat. In practice. A judicial writ, directed to the sheriff of the county in which a cause is to be tried, commanding him that he "cause to come" before the court, on a certain day therein mentioned, twelve good and lawful men of the body of his county, qualified according to law, by whom the truth of the matter may be the better known, and who are in no wise of kin either to the plaintiff or to the defendant, to make a jury of the county between the parties in the action, because as well the plaintiff as the defendant, between whom the matter in variance is, have put themselves upon that jury, and that he return the names of the jurors, etc. 2 Tidd, Pr. 777, 778; 3 Bl.Comm. 352.

VENIRE FACIAS AD RESPONDENDUM. A writ to summon a person, against whom an indictment for a misdemeanor has been found, to appear and be arraigned for the offense. A justice's warrant is now more commonly used. Archb. Crim. Pl. 81; Sweet.

VENIRE FACIAS DE NOVO. A fresh or new *venire*, which the court grants when there has been some impropriety or irregularity in returning the jury, or where the verdict is so imperfect or ambiguous that no judgment can be given upon it, or where a judgment is reversed on error, and a new trial awarded. See Bosseker v. Cramer, 18 Ind. 44; Maxwell v. Wright, 160 Ind. 515, 67 N.E. 267. "The ancient common-law mode of proceeding to a new trial was by a writ of venire facias de novo. The new trial is a modern invention, intended to mitigate the severity of the proceeding to attaint. While a venire de novo and new trial are quite different, they are alike in that a new trial takes place in both. The material difference between them is that a venire de novo must be granted upon matters appearing upon the face of the record, but a new trial may be granted for things out of the record. Lowry v. Indianapolis Traction & Terminal Co., 77 Ind.App. 138, 126 N.E. 223, 225. See, also, 1 Wils. 48; 47 Am.L.Rev. 377.

The terms "venire facias de novo" and "venire de novo" are now used interchangeably to denote a new trial. Brodie v. State, 202 Ind. 40 171 N.E. 585.

VENIRE FACIAS JURATORES. A judicial writ directed to the sheriff, when issue was joined in an action, commanding him to cause to come to Westminster, on such a day, twelve free and lawful men of his county by whom the truth of the matter at issue might be better known. This writ was abolished by section 104 of the common-law procedure act, 1852, and by section 105 a precept issued by the judges of assize is substituted in its place. The process so substituted is sometimes loosely spoken of as a "*venire.*" Brown. See, also, Steph.Pl. 104; Cridland v. Floyd, 6 Serg. & R. (Pa.) 414; 3 Chitty, Pr. 797.

VENIRE FACIAS TOT MATRONAS. A writ to summon a jury of matrons to execute the writ *de ventre inspiciendo.*

VENIREMAN. A member of a panel of jurors; a juror summoned by a writ of *venire facias.*

VENIT ET DEFENDIT. L. Lat. In old pleading. Comes and defends. The proper words of appearance and defense in an action. 1 Ld. Raym. 117.

VENIT ET DICIT. Lat. In old pleading. Comes and says. 2 Salk. 544.

VENTE. In French law. Sale; contract of sale.

VENTE À RÉMÉRÉ. A conditional sale, in which the seller reserves the right to redeem or repurchase at the same price. The term is used in Canada and Louisiana.

VENTE ALEATOIRE. A sale subject to an uncertain event.

VENTE AUX ENCHÈRES. An auction.

VENTER. Lat. (ventre, Fr.) The belly; the womb; the wife. Used in law as designating the maternal parentage of children. Thus, where in ordinary phraseology we should say that A. was B.'s child by his first wife, he would be described in law as "by the first *venter.*" Brown. A child is said to be *en ventre sa mere* before it is born; while it is a fœtus.

VENTRE INSPICIENDO. See De Ventre Inspiciendo; Venire facias tot matronas.

VENTURE, *v.* To take (the) chances. Allan v. Hargadine-McKittrick Dry Goods Co., 315 Mo. 254, 286 S.W. 16, 19.

VENTURE, *n.* An undertaking attended with risk, especially one aiming at making money; business speculation. McRee v. Quitman Oil Co., 16 Ga.App. 12, 84 S.E. 487.

VENUE. Formerly spelled *visne.* Co.Litt. 125*a*. In pleading and practice. A neighborhood; the neighborhood, place, or county in which an injury is declared to have been done, or fact declared to have happened. 3 Bl.Comm. 294; Jackson v. State, 187 Ind. 694, 121 N.E. 114, 115; 4 C. & P. 363; Heikes v. Com., 26 Pa. 513; Searcy v. State, 4 Tex. 450; People v. Lafuente, 6 Cal. 202.

Also, the county (or geographical division) in which an action or prosecution is brought for trial, and which is to furnish the panel of jurors. Armstrong v. Emmet, 41 S.W. 87, 16 Tex.Civ.App. 242; Paige v. Sinclair, 130 N.E. 177, 178, 237 Mass. 482; Commonwealth v. Reilly, 324 Pa. 558, 188 A. 574, 579; Heckler Co. v. Incorporated Village of Napoleon, 56 Ohio App. 110, 10 N.E.2d 32, 35. It relates only to place where or territory within which either party may require case to be tried. Cushing v. Doudistal, 278 Ky. 779, 129 S.W.2d 527, 528, 530. It has relation to convenience of litigants and may be waived or laid by consent of parties. Iselin v. La Coste, C.C.A.La., 147 F. 2d 791, 795.

"Venue," as a matter of procedure, does not arise until an action is started. State ex rel. Helmes v. District Court of Ramsey County, 206 Minn. 357, 287 N.W. 875.

"Venue" does not refer to jurisdiction at all. Arganbright v. Good, 46 Cal.App.2d Super. 877, 116 P.2d 186. "Jurisdiction" of the court means the inherent power to decide a case, whereas "venue" designates the particular county or city in which a court with jurisdiction may hear and determine the case. Southern Sand & Gravel Co. v. Massaponax Sand & Gravel Corporation, 145 Va. 317, 133 S.E. 812, 813. Stanton Trust and Savings Bank v. Johnson, 104 Mont. 235, 65 P.2d 1188, 1189.

In the common-law practice, that part of the declaration in an action which designates the county in which the action is to be tried. Sweet.

Local Venue

In pleading. A venue which must be laid in a particular county. When the action could have arisen only in a particular county, it is local, and the venue must be laid in that county. 1 Tidd, Pr. 427; Deacon v. Shreve, 23 N.J.L. 204.

VENUE FACTS. Facts to be established at hearing on plea of privilege. Central Motor Co. v. Roberson, Tex.Civ.App., 139 S.W.2d 287, 289. Facts which by statute constitute an exception to the general right of a defendant to be sued in the county of his residence. Crawford v. Sanger, Tex Civ.App., 160 S.W.2d 115, 116.

VENUE JURISDICTION. Power of the particular court to function. Brand v. Pennsylvania R. Co., D.C.Pa., 22 F.Supp. 569, 571.

VERANDA. A porch; a portico; a covered place of entrance to a building, differentiated from its principal mass. Hieronimus v. Moran, 272 Ill. 254, 111 N.E. 1022, 1025.

VERAY. L. Fr. True. An old form of *vrai.* Thus, *veray,* or true *tenant,* is one who holds in fee-simple; *veray tenant by the manner,* is the same as tenant by the manner, (*q. v.,*) with this difference only: that the fee-simple instead of remaining in the lord, is given by him or by the law to another. Ham. N.P. 393, 394.

VERBA. Lat. (Plural of *verbum.*) Words.

VERBA ACCIPIENDA SUNT CUM EFFECTU, UT SORTIANTUR EFFECTUM. Words are to be received with effect, so that they may produce effect. Bac.Max.

VERBA ACCIPIENDA SUNT SECUNDUM SUBJECTAM MATERIAM. 6 Coke, 62. Words are to be understood with reference to the subject-matter.

VERBA ACCIPIENDA UT SORTIANTUR EFFECTUM. Words are to be taken so that they may have some effect. 4 Bacon, Works 258.

VERBA ÆQUIVOCA, AC IN DUBIO SENSU POSITA, INTELLIGUNTUR DIGNIORI ET POTENTIORI SENSU. Equivocal words, and such as are put in a doubtful sense, are [to be] understood in the more worthy and effectual sense [in their best and most effective sense]. 6 Coke, 20*a.*

VERBA ALIQUID OPERARI DEBENT; DEBENT INTELLIGI UT ALIQUID OPERENTUR. 8 Coke, 94. Words ought to have some operation; they ought to be interpreted in such a way as to have some operation.

VERBA ALIQUID OPERARI DEBENT, VERBA CUM EFFECTU SUNT ACCIPIENDA. Words are to be taken so as to have effect. Bacon, Max. Reg. 3, p. 47. See 1 Duer, Ins. 210, 211, 216.

VERBA ARTIS EX ARTE. Terms of art should be explained from the art. 2 Kent, Comm. 556, note.

VERBA CANCELLARIÆ. Words of the chancery. The technical style of writs framed in the office of chancery. Fleta, lib. 4, c. 10, § 3.

VERBA CHARTARUM FORTIUS ACCIPIUNTUR CONTRA PROFERENTEM. The words of charters are to be received more strongly against the grantor [or the person offering them]. Co. Litt. 36; Broom, Max. 594; Bacon, Max.Reg. 3; Noy, Max., 9th ed. p. 48; 8 Term 605; 15 East 546; 1 Ball. & B. 335; 2 Pars. Con. 22.

VERBA CUM EFFECTU ACCIPIENDA SUNT. Bac. Max. 3. Words ought to be used so as to give them their effect.

VERBA CURRENTIS MONETÆ, TEMPUS SOLUTIONIS DESIGNANT. Dav. 20. The words "current money" designate current at the time of payment.

VERBA DEBENT INTELLIGI CUM EFFECTU, UT RES MAGIS VALEAT QUAM PEREAT. Words ought to be understood with effect, that a thing may rather be preserved than destroyed. 2 Smith, Lead. Cas. 530.

VERBA DEBENT INTELLIGI UT ALIQUID OPERENTUR. Words ought to be understood so as to have some operation. 8 Coke, 94*a.*

VERBA DICTA DE PERSONA INTELLIGI DEBENT DE CONDITIONE PERSONÆ. Words spoken of a person are to be understood of the condition of the person. 2 Rolle, 72.

VERBA FORTIUS ACCIPIUNTUR CONTRA PROFERENTEM. Words are to be taken most strongly against him who uses them. Bac. Max. 11, reg. 3.

VERBA GENERALIA GENERALITER SUNT INTELLIGENDA. 3 Inst. 76. General words are to be generally understood.

VERBA GENERALIA RESTRINGUNTUR AD HABILITATEM REI VEL APTITUDINEM PERSONÆ. General words must be narrowed either to the nature of the subject-matter or to the aptitude of the person. Broom, Max. 646; Bacon, Max.Reg. 10; 11 C.B. 254, 356.

VERBA ILLATA (RELATA) INESSE VIDENTUR. Words referred to are to be considered as if incorporated. Broom, Max. 674, 677; 11 Mees. & W. 183; 10 C.B. 261, 263, 266.

VERBA IN DIFFERENTI MATERIA PER PRIUS, NON PER POSTERIUS, INTELLIGENDA SUNT. Words on a different subject are to be understood by what precedes, not by what comes after. A maxim of the civil law. Calvin.

VERBA INTELLIGENDA SUNT IN CASU POSSIBILI. Words are to be understood in [or "of," or "in reference to"] a possible case. A maxim of the civil law. Calvin.

VERBA INTENTIONI, NON E CONTRA, DEBENT INSERVIRE. 8 Coke, 94. Words ought to be made subservient to the intent, not the intent to the words. 6 Allen (Mass.) 324; Bailey v. Abington, 201 Ark. 1072, 148 S.W.2d 176, 179.

VERBA ITA SUNT INTELLIGENDA, UT RES MAGIS VALEAT QUAM PEREAT. The words [of an instrument] are to be so understood, that the subject-matter may rather be of force than perish, [rather be preserved than destroyed; or, in other words, that the instrument may have effect, if possible.] Bac. Max. 17, in reg. 3; Plowd. 156; 2 Bl.Comm. 380; 2 Kent, Comm. 555.

VERBA MERE ÆQUIVOCA, SI PER COMMUNEM USUM LOQUENDI IN INTELLECTU CERTO SUMMUNTUR, TALIS INTELLECTUS PRÆFERENDUS EST. [In the case of] words merely equivocal, if they are taken by the common usage of speech in a certain sense, such sense is to be preferred. A maxim of the civil law. Calvin.

VERBA NIHIL OPERARI MELIUS EST QUAM ABSURDE. It is better that words should have no operation at all than [that they should operate] absurdly. A maxim of the civil law. Calvin.

VERBA NON TAM INTUENDA, QUAM CAUSA ET NATURA REI, UT MENS CONTRAHENTIUM EX EIS POTIUS QUAM EX VERBIS APPAREAT. The words [of a contract] are not so much to be looked at as the cause and nature of the thing, [which is the subject of it,] in order that the intention of the contracting parties may appear rather from them than from the words. Calvin.

VERBA OFFENDI POSSUNT, IMO AB EIS RECEDERE LICET, UT VERBA AD SANUM INTELLECTUM REDUCANTUR. Words may be opposed, [taken in a contrary sense,] nay, we may disregard them altogether, in order that the [general] words [of an instrument] may be restored to a sound meaning. A maxim of the civilians. Calvin.

VERBA ORDINATIONIS QUANDO VERIFICARI POSSUNT IN SUA VERA SIGNIFICATIONE, TRAHI AD EXTRANEUM INTELLECTUM NON DEBENT. When the words of an ordinance can be carried into effect in their own true meaning, they ought not to be drawn to a foreign intendment. A maxim of the civilians. Calvin.

VERBA POSTERIORA PROPTER CERTITUDINEM ADDITA, AD PRIORA QUÆ CERTITUDINE INDIGENT, SUNT REFERENDA. Subsequent words, added for the purpose of certainty, are to be referred to the preceding words which require the certainty. Wing. Max. 167, max. 53; Broom, Max. 586; 6 Coke, 236.

VERBA PRECARIA. In the civil law. Precatory words; words of trust, or used to create a trust.

VERBA PRO RE ET SUBJECTA MATERIA ACCIPI DEBENT. Words ought to be understood in favor of the thing and subject-matter. A maxim of the civilians. Calvin.

VERBA QUÆ ALIQUID OPERARI POSSUNT NON DEBENT ESSE SUPERFLUA. Words which can have any kind of operation ought not to be [considered] superfluous. Calvin.

VERBA, QUANTUMVIS GENERALIA, AD APTITUDINEM RESTRINGANTUR, ETIAMSI NULLAM ALIAM PATERENTUR RESTRICTIONEM. Words, howsoever general, are restrained to fitness, (*i. e.*, to harmonize with the subject-matter,) though they would bear no other restriction. Spiegelius.

VERBA RELATA HOC MAXIME OPERANTUR PER REFERENTIAM, UT IN EIS INESSE VIDENTUR. Related words [words connected with others by reference] have this particular operation by the reference, that they are considered as being inserted in those [clauses which refer to them.] Co. Litt. 9*b*, 359*a*. Words to which reference is made in an instrument have the same effect and operation as if they were inserted in the clauses referring to them. Broom, Max. 673; 14 East 568.

VERBA RELATA INESSE VIDENTUR. Words to which reference is made seem to be incorporated. 11 Cush. (Mass.) 137.

VERBA SECUNDUM MATERIAM SUBJECTAM INTELLIGI NEMO EST QUI NESCIAT. There is no one who does not know that words are to be understood according to their subject-matter. Calvin.

VERBA SEMPER ACCIPIENDA SUNT IN MITIORI SENSU. Words are always to be taken in the milder sense. 4 Coke, 13*a*.

VERBA STRICTÆ SIGNIFICATIONIS AD LATAM EXTENDI POSSUNT, SI SUBSIT RATIO. Words of a strict or narrow signification may be extended to a broad meaning, if there be ground in reason for it. A maxim of the civilians. Calvin; Spiegelius.

VERBA SUNT INDICES ANIMI. Words are the indices or indicators of the mind or thought. Latch, 106.

VERBAL. Strictly, of or pertaining to words; expressed in words, whether spoken or written, but commonly in spoken words; hence, by confusion, spoken; oral. Webster, Dict. Parol; by word of mouth; as, verbal agreement, verbal evidence; or written, but not signed, or not executed with the formalities required for a deed or prescribed by statute in particular cases. Musgrove v. Jackson, 59 Miss. 390.

VERBAL ACT DOCTRINE. Under this doctrine, utterances accompanying some act or conduct to which it is desired to give legal effect are admissible where conduct to be characterized by words is material to issue and equivocal in its nature, and words accompany conduct and aid in giving it legal significance. Keefe v. State, 50 Ariz. 295, 72 P.2d 425, 427.

Under doctrine, where declarations of an individual are so connected with his acts as to derive a degree of credit from such connection, independently of the declaration, the declaration becomes part of the transaction and is admissible. American Employers Ins. Co. v. Wentworth, 90 N.H. 112, 5 A.2d 265, 269.

The "verbal act doctrine" and the "res gestæ doctrine" coincide practically and serve equally to admit certain sorts of statements, but they are nevertheless wholly distinct in their nature and in their right to exist. American Employers Ins. Co. v. Wentworth, 90 N.H. 112, 5 A.2d 265, 269.

VERBAL NOTE. A memorandum or note, in diplomacy, not signed, sent when an affair has continued a long time without any reply, in order to avoid the appearance of an urgency which perhaps is not required; and, on the other hand, to guard against the supposition that it is forgotten, or that there is an intention of not prosecuting it any further. Wharton.

VERBAL PROCESS. In Louisiana. *Procès verbal, (q. v.).*

VERBIS STANDUM UBI NULLA AMBIGUITAS. One must abide by the words where there is no ambiguity. Tray. Lat. Max. 612.

VERBUM IMPERFECTI TEMPORIS REM ADHUC IMPERFECTAM SIGNIFICAT. The imperfect tense of the verb indicates an incomplete matter. Mactier v. Frith, 6 Wend. (N.Y.) 103, 120, 21 Am.Dec. 262.

VERDERER, or VERDEROR. An officer of the king's forest, who is sworn to maintain and keep the assizes of the forest, and to view, receive, and enroll the attachments and presentments of all manner of trespasses of vert and venison in the forest. Manw. c. 6, § 5.

VERDICT. From the Latin "veredictum," a true declaration. State v. Blue, 134 La. 561, 64 So. 411, 413; Clark v. State, 170 Tenn. 499, 97 S.W.2d 644, 646. In practice. The formal and unanimous decision or finding made by a jury, impaneled and sworn for the trial of a cause, and reported to the court (and accepted by it), upon the matters or questions duly submitted to them upon the trial. Sitterson v. Sitterson, 191 N.C. 319, 131 S.E. 641, 642, 51 A.L.R. 760; Roth v. East Connellsville Coke Co., 242 Pa. 23, 88 A. 781. A declaration of the truth as to matters of fact submitted to jury. Groves v. State, 162 Ga. 161, 132 S.E. 769, 770; Arcadia Timber Co. v. Evans, 304 Mo. 674, 264 S.W. 810. The definitive answer given by the jury to the court concerning the matters of fact committed to the jury for their deliberation and determination. Ralston v. Stump, 75 Ohio App. 375, 62 N.E.2d 293, 294.

A true response of 12 men to the issues in the case, arrived at after a consideration of all the evidence in the case, by each juror acting independently and voluntarily in forming his conclusion, or the concurrent coincident conclusion of the 12. Roberts v. State, 26 Ala.App. 331, 159 So. 373, 374.

Explanations or comments in a written verdict are no part of the "verdict" of the jury but are mere "surplusage". Anderson v. Penn Hall Co., D.C.Pa., 47 F.Supp. 691, 692.

Until accepted by the court, a finding of the jury is not a "verdict." Schulman v. Stock, 89 Conn. 237, 93 A. 531. Anderson v. Penn Hall Co., D.C.Pa., 47 F.Supp. 691, 692. The only "verdict" is that which the jury announces orally to the court, and which is received and recorded at direction of court as the jury's finding.

Although in common language, the word may be used in a more extended sense, it has a well-defined signification in law. It means the decision of a jury, and not the decision of a court or a referee or a commissioner. Kerner v. Petigo, 25 Kan. 656. "Decision" bears the same relation to nonjury cases as "verdict" to jury cases, and a "verdict" is a conclusion upon the facts, and in effect a direction for judgment, while a "decision" is an order for judgment, and determines the judgment to be entered. Schofield v. Baker, D.C.Wash., 242 F. 657, 658.

Adverse Verdict

Where a party, appealing from an allowance of damages by commissioners, recovers a verdict in his favor, but for a less amount of damages than had been originally allowed, such verdict is *adverse* to him, within the meaning of his undertaking to pay costs if the verdict should be adverse to him. Hamblin v. Barnstable County, 16 Gray (Miss.) 256.

Chance Verdict

One determined by hazard or lot, and not by the deliberate understanding and agreement of the jury. Goodman v. Cody, 1 Wash.T. 335, 34 Am.Rep. 808; Improvement Co. v. Adams, 1 Colo. App. 250, 28 P. 662.

A verdict is not a "chance verdict" merely because, in arriving at the amount, the jury took each juror's estimate of what should be assessed as the damages and divided the total by the number of jurors, and afterward knowingly and understandingly agreed that such quotient should be the amount of the verdict. Great Northern Ry. Co. v. Lenton, 31 N.D. 555, 154 N.W. 275, 277. See, also, Foley v. Hornung, 35 Cal.App. 304, 169 P. 705, 709. See Quotient Verdict, infra.

Compromise Verdict

One which is the result, not of justifiable concession of views, but of improper compromise of the vital principles which should have controlled the decision. Goelet v. Matt J. Ward Co., 155 C. C.A. 9, 242 F. 65, 67. Although it is proper for jurors to harmonize their views and reach a verdict with proper regard for each other's opinions, it is not proper for any juror to surrender his conscientious convictions on any material issue in return for a relinquishment by others of their like settled opinions on another issue, producing a result which does not command the approval of the whole panel. Snyder v. Portland Ry., Light & Power Co., 107 Or. 673, 215 P. 887, 889.

Excessive Verdict

See Excessive Verdict.

False Verdict

One obviously opposed to the principles of right and justice; an untrue verdict. Formerly, if a jury gave a false verdict, the party injured by it might sue out and prosecute a writ of attaint against them, either at common law or on the statute 11 Hen. VII. c. 24, at his election, for the purpose of reversing the judgment and punishing the jury for their verdict; but not where the jury erred merely in point of law, if they found according to the judge's direction. The practice of setting aside verdicts and granting new trials, however, so superseded the use of attaints that there is no instance of one to be found in the books or reports later than in the time of Elizabeth, and it was altogether abolished by 6 Geo. IV. c. 50, § 60. Wharton.

General Verdict

A verdict whereby the jury find either for the plaintiff or for the defendant in general terms; the ordinary form of a verdict. Glenn v. Sumner, 10 S.Ct. 41, 132 U.S. 152, 33 L.Ed. 301; Childs v. Carpenter, 87 Me. 114, 32 A. 780. A finding by the jury in the terms of the issue referred to them. Settle v. Alison, 52 Am.Dec. 393, 8 Ga. 208. Tidd, Pr. 798. That by which the jury pronounces generally on all of the issues in favor of plaintiff or defendant. Skelton v. City of Newberg, 76 Or. 126, 148 P. 53, 55; Cleveland, C. C. & St. L. Ry. Co. v. Wolf, 189 Ind. 585, 128 N.E. 38, 40. That by which they pronounce generally upon all or any of the issues, either in favor of the plaintiff or defendant;—distinguished from a special verdict, which is that by which the jury finds facts only. Comp.Stat. Okl.1921, § 551 (Code 1931, § 369).

A "general verdict" is one by which the jury pronounces at the same time on the facts and the law, either in favor of the plaintiff or the defendant. Schofield v. Baker, D.C. Wash., 242 F. 657, 658; Co.Litt. 228; 4 Bla.Comm. 461. A general verdict of guilty in a criminal case means guilty on every count. Simmons v. State, 162 Ga. 316, 134 S.E. 54, 55.

Open Verdict

A verdict of a coroner's jury which finds that the subject "came to his death by means to the jury unknown," or "came to his death at the hands of a person or persons to the jury unknown," that is, one which leaves open either the question whether any crime was committed or the identity of the criminal.

Partial Verdict

In criminal law, a verdict by which the jury acquit the defendant as to a part of the accusation and find him guilty as to the residue. State v. McGee, 33 S.E. 353, 55 S.C. 247, 74 Am.St.Rep. 741; U. S. v. Watkins, 28 F.Cas. 419.

Privy Verdict

One given after the judge has left or adjourned the court, and the jury, being agreed, in order to be delivered from their confinement, obtain leave to give their verdict privily to the judge out of court. Such a verdict is of no force unless afterwards affirmed by a public verdict given openly in court. This practice is now superseded by that of rendering a sealed verdict. See Young v. Seymour, 4 Neb. 89.

Public Verdict

A verdict openly delivered by the jury in court. Withee v. Rowe, 45 Me. 571.

Quotient Verdict

A money verdict the amount of which is fixed by the following process: Each juror writes down the sum he wishes to award by the verdict, and these amounts are all added together, and the total is divided by twelve, (the number of jurors,) the quotient being the verdict of the jury by their agreement. Speer v. State, 130 Ark. 457, 198 S.W. 113, 115; St. Louis & S. F. R. Co. v. Brown, 45 Okl. 143, 144 P. 1075, 1077; Hamilton v. Owego Water Works, 22 App.Div. 573, 48 N.Y.S. 106. To invalidate a verdict of this kind, it must appear that, in advance of the computation, there was an agreement to be bound by the result. In re Havenmaier's Estate, 163 Minn. 218, 203 N.W. 958, 959; Great Northern Ry. Co. v. Lenton, 154 N.W. 275, 277, 31 N.D. 555; Carter v. Marshall Oil Co., 185 Iowa 416, 170 N.W. 798, 800.

Sealed Verdict

See Sealed.

Special Verdict

A special finding of the facts of a case by a jury, leaving to the court the application of the law to the facts thus found. 1 Archb.Pr.K.B. 213; 3 Bl.Comm. 377; Statler v. U. S., 15 S.Ct. 616, 157 U.S. 277, 39 L.Ed. 700; Samlin v. U. S., C.C.A., 278 F. 170, 172. A special finding by the jury on each material issue of the case. Ford v. Brown, 45 Nev. 202, 200 P. 522, 525.

A "special verdict" exhibits the legitimate facts and leaves the legal conclusions to the court, and must cover all the issues in the case, while an answer to a special interrogatory may respond to but a single inquiry pertaining merely to one issue essential to the general verdict. Childress v. Lake Erie & W. R. Co., 182 Ind. 251, 105 N.E. 467, 470.

Verdict by Lot

This type of verdict was formerly held to be legitimate, 1 Keble 811; but such verdicts are now held to be illegal. See Barnard v. State, 221 S.W. 293, 294, 87 Tex.Cr.R. 365; Chance Verdict, *supra*.

Verdict Contrary to Law

A verdict which law does not authorize jury to render on evidence because conclusion drawn is not justified thereby. Gruhn v. J. H. Taylor Const. Co., 180 Misc. 956, 40 N.Y.S.2d 765, 770. One which is contrary to the principles of law as applied to the facts which the jury were called upon to try and contrary to the principles of law which should govern the cause. Piepho v. Gesse, 106 Ind.App. 450, 18 N.E.2d 468, 471.

Verdict of Guilty But Insane

A special verdict which amounts to an acquittal of the person tried. Rex v. Taylor, [1915] 2 K. B. 709, 712.

Verdict of No Cause of Action

A verdict for defendant. Felter v. Mulliner, 2 Johns. 181.

Verdict of Not Guilty

Simply a verdict of not proven in the particular case tried; it is not a verdict of innocence, and hence is not conclusive against the state in favor of any other person than the defendant who was actually acquitted. Woody v. State, 10 Okl.Cr. 322, 136 P. 430, 432, 49 L.R.A.,N.S., 479.

Verdict Subject to Opinion of Court

A verdict returned by the jury, the entry of judgment upon which is subject to the determination of points of law reserved by the court upon the trial.

VERDICT, ESTOPPEL BY. The term is sometimes applied to the estoppel arising from a former adjudication of the same fact or issue between the same parties or their privies. Chicago Theological Seminary v. People, 189 Ill. 439, 59 N.E. 977; Swank v. Railway Co., 61 Minn. 423, 63 N.W. 1088. But this use is not correct, as it is not the verdict which creates an estoppel, but the judgment, and it is immaterial whether a jury participated in the trial or not. The doctrine of estoppel by verdict is but another branch of the doctrine of res judicata. Chicago Title & Trust Co. v. National Storage Co., 260 Ill. 485, 103 N.E. 227, 231; Citizen's Loan & Trust Co. of Washington, Ind. v. Sanders, 99 Ind.App. 77, 187 N.E. 396, 398. See, however, Coffman v. Hope Natural Gas Co., 74 W.Va. 57, 81 S.E. 575. See, also, Judgment, Estoppel By.

A former adjudication is conclusive in subsequent proceeding between same parties but on a different cause of action as to facts actually decided. Kimpton v. Spellman, 351 Mo. 674, 173 S.W.2d 886, 891; Holtz v. Beighley, 211 Minn. 153, 300 N.W. 445, 446.

It arises when material fact has been determined in former suit between same parties or those in privity with them, in which such fact was also material. Little v. Blue Goose Motor Coach Co., 346 Ill. 266, 178 N.E. 496, 497; Citizen's Loan & Trust Co. of Washington, Ind. v. Sanders, 187 N.E. 396, 99 Ind.App. 77. It is limited to matters actually or by necessary implication found and determined in prior action. Missouri District Telegraph Co. v. Southwestern Bell Telephone Co., 338 Mo. 692, 93 S.W.2d 19, 22. It operates only as to issues actually litigated. Gustafson v. Gustafson, 178 Minn. 1, 226 N.W. 412, 413.

It is not a decision on the law that concludes the parties, but the determination of a controlling fact or matter in issue. People v. Louisville & N. R. Co., 350 Ill. 274, 183 N.E. 233, 235.

The rules of "estoppel by verdict" apply to some fact or issue necessarily determined by the previous litigation. Skolnik v. Petella, 376 Ill. 500, 34 N.E.2d 825, 827.

To operate as "estoppel by verdict," it is necessary that there shall have been a finding of a specific fact in former judgment or record that was material and controlling in case, or was necessarily involved in verdict or judgment, and also material and controlling in pending case. Brown v. Brown, 286 Ill.App. 471, 3 N.E.2d 945, 946.

Where controlling fact or question material to determination of both causes is decided in a former suit and is again in issue in a subsequent suit between same parties, first adjudication will, if properly presented, be conclusive. Brown v. Brown, 286 Ill.App. 471, 3 N.E.2d 945, 946; McKee v. Producers' & Refiners' Corporation, 170 Okl. 559, 41 P.2d 466, 469.

VEREBOT. Sax. In old records. A packet-boat or transport vessel. Cowell.

VEREDICTUM. L. Lat. In old English law. A verdict; a declaration of the truth of a matter in issue, submitted to a jury for trial.

VEREDICTUM, QUASI DICTUM VERITATIS; UT JUDICIUM QUASI JURIS DICTUM. Co. Litt. 226. The verdict is, as it were, the *dictum* [saying] of truth; as the judgment is the *dictum* of law.

VERGE, or VIRGE. In English law. The compass of the royal court, which bounds the jurisdiction of the lord steward of the household; it seems to have been twelve miles about. Britt. 68. An uncertain quantity of land from fifteen to thirty acres. 28 Edw. I. Also a stick, or rod, whereby one is admitted tenant to a copyhold estate. Old Nat. Brev. 17.

VERGELT. In Saxon law. A mulct or fine for a crime. See Weregild.

VERGENS AD INOPIAM. L. Lat. In Scotch law. Verging towards poverty; in declining circumstances. 2 Kames, Eq. 8.

VERGERS. In English law. Officers who carry white wands before the justices of either bench. Cowell. Mentioned in Fleta, as officers of the king's court, who oppressed the people by demanding exorbitant fees. Fleta, lib. 2, c. 38.

VERIFICATION. Confirmation of correctness, truth, or authenticity by affidavit, oath, or deposition. McNamara v. Powell, Sup., 52 N.Y.S.2d 515, 527.

Pleading

A certain formula with which all pleadings containing new affirmative matter must conclude, being in itself an averment that the party pleading is ready to establish the truth of what he has set forth.

The usual form of verification of a plea containing matter of fact is, *"And this he is ready to verify,"* etc. See 3 Bla.Comm. 309.

Practice

The examination of a writing for the purpose of ascertaining its truth. A certificate or affidavit that it is true.

"Verification" is not identical with "authentication." A notary may verify a mortgagee's written statement of the actual amount of his claim, but need not authenticate the act by his seal. Ashley v. Wright, 19 Ohio St. 291.

Confirmation of the correctness, truth, or authenticity of a pleading, account, or other paper, by an affidavit, oath, or deposition. Herbert v. Roxana Petroleum Corporation, D.C.Ill., 12 F.2d 81, 83; McDonald v. Rosengarten, 134 Ill. 126, 25 N.E. 429; Summerfield v. Phœnix Assur. Co., C.C. Va., 65 F. 296; Patterson v. Brooklyn, 6 App.Div. 127, 40 N.Y.S. 581.

VERIFY. To confirm or substantiate by oath. S. B. McMaster, Inc., v. Chevrolet Motor Co., D.C. S.C., 3 F.2d 469, 471; Francesconi v. Independent School Dist. of Wall Lake, 204 Iowa 307, 214 N.W. 882, 885; Marshall v. State, 116 Neb. 45, 215 N.W. 564, 566. Particularly used of making formal oath to accounts, petitions, pleadings, and other papers.

The word "verified," when used in a statute, ordinarily imports a verity attested by the sanctity of an oath. Bristol v. Buck, 201 App.Div. 100, 194 N.Y.S. 53, 55. It is frequently used interchangeably with "sworn." Francesconi v. Independent School Dist. of Wall Lake, 204 Iowa, 307, 214 N.W. 882, 885.

To prove to be true; to establish the truth of; to confirm; to confirm the truth or truthfulness of; to check or test the accuracy or exactness of; to confirm or establish the authenticity of; to authenticate; to prove; to maintain; to affirm; to support; second; back as a friend. MacNeill v. Maddox, 194 Ga. 802, 22 S.E.2d 653, 654.

The word "verify" sometimes means to confirm and substantiate by oath, and sometimes by argument. When used in legal proceedings it is generally employed in the former sense. De Witt v. Hosmer, 3 How.Prac., N.Y., 284.

VERIFIED COPY. A copy, if successive witnesses trace the original into the hands of a witness who made or compared the copy. Nu Car Carriers v. Traynor, 75 U.S.App.D.C. 174, 125 F.2d 47, 48.

VERIFIED NAMES. Names verified by county clerk in accordance with his duty to check names of signers against official registration lists. Allan v. Rasmussen, 101 Utah 33, 117 P.2d 287, 289.

VERILY. In very truth; beyond doubt or question; in fact; certainly; truly; confidently; really. Gregg v. Sigurdson, 67 Mont. 272, 215 P. 662.

VERITAS, A QUOCUNQUE DICITUR, A DEO EST. 4 Inst. 153. Truth, by whomsoever pronounced, is from God.

VERITAS DEMONSTRATIONIS TOLLIT ERROREM NOMINIS. The truth of the description removes an error in the name. 1 Ld.Raym. 303.

VERITAS HABENDA EST IN JURATORE; JUSTITIA ET JUDICIUM IN JUDICE. Truth is the desideratum in a juror; justice and judgment in a judge. Bract. fol. 185*b*.

VERITAS NIHIL VERETUR NISI ABSCONDI. Truth fears nothing but to be hid. 9 Coke, 20*b*.

VERITAS NIMIUM ALTERCANDO AMITTITUR. Truth is lost by excessive altercation. Hob. 344.

VERITAS NOMINIS TOLLIT ERROREM DEMONSTRATIONIS. The truth of the name takes away the error of description. Bacon, Max. Reg. 25; Broom, Max. 637, 641; 8 Taunt. 313; 2 Jones, Eq. (N.C.) 72.

VERITAS, QUÆ MINIME DEFENSATUR OPPRIMITUR; ET QUI NON IMPROBAT, APPROBAT. 3 Inst. 27. Truth which is not sufficiently defended is overpowered; and he who does not disapprove, approves.

VERITATEM QUI NON LIBERE PRONUNCIAT PRODITOR EST VERITATIS. 4 Inst. Epil. He who does not freely speak the truth is a betrayer of truth.

VERITY. Truth; truthfulness; conformity to fact. The records of a court "import uncontrollable verity." 1 Black, Judgm. § 276.

VERNA. Lat. In the civil law. A slave born in his master's house.

VERSARI. Lat. In the civil law. To be employed; to be conversant. *Versari male in tutela,* to misconduct one's self in a guardianship. Calvin.

VERSUS. Lat. Against. In the title of a cause, the name of the plaintiff is put first, followed by the word *"versus,"* then the defendant's name. Thus, "Fletcher *versus* Peck," or "Fletcher *against* Peck." The word is commonly abbreviated *"vs."* or *"v."* *Vs.* and *versus* have become ingrafted upon the English language; their meaning is as well understood and their use quite as appropriate as the word *against* could be. Smith v. Butler, 25 N.H. 523.

VERT. Everything bearing green leaves in a forest. Manwood, For. Law 146.

Also that power which a man has, by royal grant, to cut green wood in a forest.

In heraldry, green color, called "venus" in the arms of princes, and "emerald" in those of peers, and expressed in engravings by lines in bend. Wharton.

VERTICAL PRICE-FIXING CONTRACT. A contract between producers and wholesalers or distributors, between producers and retailers, or between wholesalers or distributors and retailers, and not between producers themselves, between wholesalers themselves, or between retailers themselves as to sale or retail prices. Pazen v. Silver Rod Stores, 130 N.J.Eq. 407, 22 A.2d 237, 239; Seagram Distillers Corporation v. Old Dearborn Distributing Co., 363 Ill. 610, 2 N.E.2d 940, 942.

VERTIGO. A term quite commonly used in the sense of dizziness, giddiness—a condition in which the individual or the objects around him appear to be whirling about. Post v. Grand Lodge, A. O. U. W., 211 Iowa 786, 232 N.W. 140, 144.

VERUS. Lat. True; truthful; genuine; actual; real; just.

VERY. As an adjective means real, actual, or true, but as an adverb means in a high degree, exceedingly, extremely; to no small extent. Benoist v. Driveaway Co. of Missouri, Mo.App., 122 S.W. 2d 86, 90; Shriver v. Union Stockyards Nat. Bank, 117 Kan. 638, 232 P. 1062, 1066.

VERY HIGH DEGREE OF CARE. That degree of care that would be used by a very cautious, prudent, and competent person under like or similar circumstances. Wichita Valley Ry. Co. v. Williams, Tex.Civ.App., 3 S.W.2d 141, 142.

VERY LORD AND VERY TENANT. They that are immediate lord and tenant one to another. Cowell.

VESSEL. A ship, brig, sloop, or other craft used in navigation. The word in its broadest sense is more comprehensive than "ship."

Any structure which is made to float upon the water, for purposes of commerce or war, whether impelled by wind, steam, or oars. Chaffe v. Ludeling, 27 La.Ann. 607. Any structure, especially a hollow one, made to float upon the water for purposes of navigation; a craft for navigation of the water, often, specifically, one larger than a common row boat; as, a war vessel; a passenger vessel. City of Tampa v. Tampa Shipbuilding & Engineering Co., 136 Fla. 216, 186 So. 411, 412; Massman Const. Co. v. Bassett, D.C.Mo., 30 F. Supp. 813, 815.

Every description of water-craft or other artificial contrivances used, or capable of being used, as a means of transportation on water. Rev.St.U.S. § 3 (1 U.S.C.A. § 3); Maryland Casualty Co. v. Lawson, C.C.A.Fla., 94 F.2d 190, 192. Under this definition, the term has been held to include a large barge, without motive power of its own. Norton v. Warner Co., Pa., 64 S.Ct. 747, 751, 321 U.S. 565, 88 L.Ed. 931; and likewise a house boat, not permanently attached to the shore, though without motive power, The Ark, D.C.Fla., 17 F.2d 446, 447; but not a wharfboat, secured to the shore by cables and used as an office, warehouse, and wharf, and having water and electric light connections and telephone system, Evansville & Bowling Green Packet Co. v. Chero Cola Bottling Co., 271 U.S. 19, 46 S.Ct. 379, 380, 70 L.Ed. 805; nor a dry dock used for the repair of vessels, though capable of being floated and towed from place to place; Berton v. Tietjen & Lang Dry Dock Co., D.C.N.J., 219 F. 763, 771.

As used in various other statutes, the word "vessel" has been held applicable to a ferryboat, Port Huron & Sarnia Ferry Co. v. Lawson, D.C.Mich., 292 F. 216, 219; a pile driver scow, George Leary Const. Co. v. Matson, C.C.A.Va., 272 F. 461, 462; a derrick boat, carrying a derrick used for loading logs from the river bank upon boats, Patton-Tully Transp. Co. v. Turner, C.C.A.Tenn., 269 F. 334, 336; a hydro-aeroplane while moving on the water, Reinhardt v. Newport Flying Service Corporation, 232 N.Y. 115, 133 N.E. 37, 372, 18 A.L.R. 1324; and even to a log raft. The Libby Maine, D.C.Wash., 3 F.2d 79, 80. The term is broad enough to include a vessel's tackle, apparel, furniture, chronometer and appurtenances. The Frolic, D.C.R.I., 148 F. 921.

The word has also been held to include a new ship as soon as its hull has been launched, The Pinthis, C.C.A. N.J., 286 F. 122; and any structure which is so far completed as to be capable of being used as a means of transportation on water, R. R. Ricou & Sons Co. v. Fairbanks, Morse & Co., C.C.A.Fla., 11 F.2d 103, 104; but not an old hull built of timber taken from an old dry dock. The Dredge A, D.C.N.C., 217 F. 617, 630. *Contra,* Moores v. Underwriters, C.C.Tenn., 14 F. 236.

The words "boat," "craft," and "water craft" are usually applied to small vessels, while larger vessels, especially in the case of large iron steamships, are usually referred to by the term "steamer," or "steamship," or "vessel." The Saxon, D.C.S.C., 269 F. 639, 641.

A utensil, such as a bottle, designed to hold liquids, etc. Old Tavern Farm v. Fickett, 125 Me. 123, 131 A. 305, 306.

Foreign Vessel

A vessel owned by residents in, or sailing under the flag of, a foreign nation. "Foreign vessel," under the embargo act of January, 1808, means a vessel under the flag of a foreign power, and not a vessel in which foreigners domiciled in the United States have an interest. The Sally, 1 Gall. 58, F. Cas.No.12,257.

Public Vessel

One owned and used by a nation or government for its public service, whether in its navy, its revenue service, or otherwise.

VEST. To give an immediate, fixed right of present or future enjoyment. Baldwin v. Fleck, Tex. Civ.App., 168 S.W.2d 904, 909. To accrue to; to be fixed; to take effect.

To clothe with possession; to deliver full possession of land or of an estate; to give seisin; to enfeoff. Spelman.

The normal sense of the word is to indicate a present and immediate interest, as distinguished from one that is contingent. In re Stocker's Estate, 260 Pa. 385, 103 A. 885, 886; Crawford v. Carlisle, 206 Ala. 379, 89 So. 565, 571.

Under Executive Order empowering Alien Property Custodian to "vest" any property of enemy national in the process of administration, the term is equivalent to "seize" and gives the Custodian the right to the immediate possession of the property for the benefit of the United States. Executive Order March 11, 1942, No. 9095, as amended, 50 U.S.C.A.Appendix § 6; Trading With the Enemy Act § 5 (b), as amended, 50 U.S.C.A.Appendix § 5(b). In re Oneida Nat. Bank & Trust Co. of Utica, 53 N.Y.S.2d 416, 419, 183 Misc. 374.

VESTA. The crop on the ground. Cowell.

VESTED. Fixed; accrued; settled; absolute. Orthwein v. Germania Life Ins. Co. of City of New York, 261 Mo. 650, 170 S.W. 885, 888. Having the character or giving the rights of absolute ownership; not contingent; not subject to be defeated by a condition precedent. Scott v. West, 63 Wis. 529, 24 N.W. 161; McGillis v. McGillis, 11 App. Div. 359, 42 N.Y.S. 924; Smith v. Proskey, 39 Misc. 385, 79 N.Y.S. 851.

VESTED DEVISE. See Devise.

VESTED ESTATE. An interest clothed with a present, legal, and existing right of alienation. Anderson v. Menefee, Tex.Civ.App., 174 S.W. 904, 908; Chaison v. Chaison, Tex.Civ.App., 154 S.W.2d 961, 964. Any estate, whether in possession or not, which is not subject to any condition precedent and unperformed. The interest may be either a present and immediate interest, or it may be a future but uncontingent, and therefore transmissible, interest. Brown. See Tayloe v. Gould, 10 Barb. (N.Y.) 388; estate by which present interest is invariably fixed to remain to determinate person on determination of preceding freehold estate. Story v. First Nat. Bank & Trust Co. in Orlando, 115 Fla. 436, 156 So. 101. An estate, when the person or the class which takes the remainder is in existence or is capable of being ascertained when the prior estate vests. Commissioner of Internal Revenue v. Kellogg, C.C.A.3, 119 F.2d 54, 57; or when there is an immediate right of present enjoyment or a present right of future enjoyment. In re Kelly's Estate, 167 Misc. 751, 4 N.Y.S.2d 675, 678.

A vested estate, whether present or future, may be absolutely or defeasibly vested. L'Etourneau v. Henquenet, 89 Mich. 428, 50 N.W. 1077, 28 Am.St.Rep. 310. If a present right exists to future possession, the estate is "vested," even though actual possession may be defeated by a future event. Wheaton Coal Co. v. Harris, 288 Pa. 294, 135 A. 637, 638. See, also, Vest.

VESTED GIFT. A gift if it is immediate, notwithstanding that its enjoyment may be postponed. Bankers Trust Co. v. Garver, 222 Iowa 196, 268 N. W. 568, 571. A future gift when the right to receive it is not subject to a condition precedent. First & American Nat. Bank of Duluth v. Higgins, 208 Minn. 295, 293 N.W. 585, 594. Where future gift is postponed to let in some other interest. Barrett v. Barrett, 134 N.J.Eq. 138, 34 A.2d 579, 590.

VESTED IN INTEREST. A legal term applied to a present fixed right of future enjoyment; as reversions, vested remainders, such executory devises, future uses, conditional limitations, and other future interests as are not referred to, or made to depend on, a period or event that is uncertain. Wharton. See Smith v. West, 103 Ill. 337; Hawley v. James, 5 Paige (N.Y.) 466; Gates v. Seibert, 157 Mo. 254, 57 S.W. 1065, 80 Am.St.Rep. 625.

VESTED IN POSSESSION. A legal term applied to a right of present enjoyment actually existing. See Vest.

VESTED INTEREST. A present right or title to a thing, which carries with it an existing right of alienation, even though the right to possession or enjoyment may be postponed to some uncertain time in the future, as distinguished from a future right, which may never materialize or ripen into title, and it matters not how long or for what length of time the future possession or right of enjoyment may be postponed, if the present right exists to alienate and pass title. Fugazzi v. Fugazzi's Committee, 275 Ky. 62, 120 S.W.2d 779, 781. A future interest not dependent on an uncertain period or event, or a fixed present right of future enjoyment. In re Whiting, D.C.N.C., 3 F.2d 440, 441; McMannis v. Peerless Casualty Co., 114 Me. 98, 95 A. 510. When a person has a right to immediate possession on determination of preceding or particular estate. In re Clark's Estate, Orph., 13 N.J.Misc. 393, 178 A. 574, 575. One in which there is a present fixed right, either of present enjoyment or of future enjoyment. Painter v. Herschberger, 340 Mo. 347, 100 S.W.2d 532, 535.

It is not the uncertainty of enjoyment in the future, but the uncertainty of the right of enjoyment, which makes the difference between a "vested" and a "contingent" interest. Mahoney v. Mahoney, 98 Conn. 525, 120 A. 342, 345; Grant v. Grant, 187 Ga. 807, 2 S.E.2d 421, 427. A future interest is vested when there is a person in being who would have a right, defeasible or indefeasible, to the immediate possession of the property, upon the ceasing of the intermediate or precedent interest. Civil Code Cal. § 694. See Allison v. Allison, 101 Va. 537, 44 S.E. 904, 63 L.R.A. 920; Hawkins v. Bohling, 168 Ill. 214, 48 N.E. 94; Stewart v. Harriman, 56 N.H. 25, 22 Am.Rep. 408; Bunting v. Speek, 41 Kan. 424, 21 P. 288, 3 L.R.A. 690.

VESTED LEGACY. A legacy given in such terms that there is a fixed, indefeasible right to its payment. In re Central Union Trust Co. of New York, 183 N.Y.S. 671, 673, 193 App.Div. 292. A legacy payable at a future time, certain to arrive, and not subject to conditions precedent, is vested, where there is a person in esse at the testator's death capable of taking when the time arrives, though his interest may be altogether defeated by his own death. In re Youngblood's Estate, 117 Pa. Super. 550, 178 A. 517, 518. A legacy is said to be vested when the words of the testator making the bequest convey a transmissible interest, whether present or future, to the legatee in the legacy. Thus a legacy to one to be paid when he attains the age of twenty-one years is a vested legacy, because it is given unconditionally and absolutely, and therefore vests an immediate interest in the legatee, of which the enjoyment only is deferred or postponed. Brown. See Magoffin v. Patton, 4 Rawle (Pa.) 113; Talmadge v. Seaman, 85 Hun 242, 32 N.Y.S. 906; Rubencane v. McKee, 6 Del.Ch. 40, 6 A. 639.

VESTED REMAINDER. See Remainder.

VESTED RIGHTS. In constitutional law. Rights which have so completely and definitely accrued to or settled in a person that they are not subject to be defeated or canceled by the act of any other private person, and which it is right and equitable that the government should recognize and protect, as being lawful in themselves, and settled according to the then current rules of law, and of which the individual could not be deprived arbitrarily without injustice, or of which he could not justly be deprived otherwise than by the established methods of procedure and for the public welfare. Cassard v. Tracy, 52 La.Ann. 835, 27 So. 368, 49 L.R.A. 272; Stimson Land Co. v. Rawson, C.C. Wash., 62 F. 429; Parker v. Schrimsher, Tex.Civ. App., 172 S.W. 165, 168. Which cannot be interfered with by retrospective laws, are interests which it is proper for state to recognize and protect and of which individual cannot be deprived arbitrarily without injustice. American States Water Service Co. of California v. Johnson, 31 Cal.App.2d 606, 88 P.2d 770, 774. Immediate or fixed right to present or future enjoyment and one that does not depend on an event that is uncertain. Dunham Lumber Co. v. Gresz, 71 N.D. 491, 2 N.W.2d 175, 179, 141 A.L.R. 60; Massa v. Nastri, 125 Conn. 144, 3 A.2d 839, 840, 120 A.L.R. 939; Wylie v. City Commission of Grand Rapids, 293 Mich. 571, 292 N.W. 668, 674. A right complete and consummated, and of such character that it cannot be divested without the consent of the person to whom it belongs, and fixed or established, and no longer open to controversy. State ex rel. Milligan v. Ritter's Estate, Ind.App., 46 N.E.2d 736, 743.

VESTIGIAL WORDS. Those contained in a statute which by reason of a succession of statutes on the same subject-matter, amending or modifying previous provisions of the same, are rendered useless or meaningless by such amendments. They should not be permitted to defeat the fair meaning of the statute. Saltonstall v. Birtwell, 17 S.Ct. 19, 164 U.S. 70, 41 L.Ed. 348.

VESTIGIUM. Lat. In the law of evidence, a vestige, mark, or sign; a trace, track, or impression left by a physical object. Fleta, l. 1, c. 25, § 6.

VESTING ORDER. In English law. An order which may be granted by the chancery division of the high court of justice, (and formerly by chancery,) passing the legal estate in lieu of a conveyance. Commissioners also, under modern statutes, have similar powers. St. 15 & 16 Vict. c. 55; Wharton.

VESTRY. In ecclesiastical law. The place in a church where the priest's vestures are deposited. Also an assembly of the minister, church-wardens, and parishioners, usually held in the vestry of the church, or in a building called a "vestry-hall," to act upon business of the church. Mozley & Whiteley.

VESTRY-CESS. A rate levied in Ireland for parochial purposes, abolished by St. 27 Vict. c. 17.

VESTRY-CLERK. An officer appointed to attend vestries, and take an account of their proceedings, etc.

VESTRY-MEN. A select number of parishioners elected in large and populous parishes to take care of the concerns of the parish; so called because they used ordinarily to meet in the vestry of the church. Cowell.

VESTURA. A crop of grass or corn. Also a garment; metaphorically applied to a possession or seisin.

VESTURA TERRÆ. In old English law. The vesture of the land; that is, the corn, grass, underwood, sweepage, and the like. Co. Litt. 4*b*. See Simpson v. Coe, 4 N.H. 301.

VESTURE. In old English law. Profit of land. "How much the *vesture* of an acre is worth." Cowell.

VESTURE OF LAND. A phrase including all things, trees excepted, which grow upon the surface of the land, and clothe it externally. Ham. N.P. 151.

VETERA STATUTA. Lat. Ancient statutes. The English statutes from *Magna Charta* to the end of the reign of Edward II. are so called; those from the beginning of the reign of Edward III. being contradistinguished by the appellation of "*Nova Statuta.*" 2 Reeve, Eng. Law, 85.

VETERAN. Within Civil Service Laws giving preference to veterans, any honorably discharged soldier, sailor, marine, nurse, or army field clerk, who has served in military service of the United States in any war. Ryan v. Civil Service Commission of New Jersey, 115 N.J.L. 316, 179 A. 848, 849.

VETERINARIAN. One who practices the art of treating diseases and injuries of domestic animals, surgically or medically. Tucker v. Williamson, D.C.Ohio, 229 F. 201, 210.

VETITUM NAMIUM. L. Lat. Where the bailiff of a lord distrains beasts or goods of another, and the lord forbids the bailiff to deliver them when the sheriff comes to make replevin, the owner of the cattle may demand satisfaction in *placitum de vetito namio.* 2 Inst. 140; 2 Bl.Comm. 148.

VETO (Lat. I forbid). The refusal of assent by the executive officer whose assent is necessary to perfect a law which has been passed by the legislative body, and the message which is usually sent to such body by the executive, stating such refusal and the reasons therefor. It is either absolute or qualified, according as the effect of its exercise is either to destroy the bill finally, or to prevent its becoming law unless again passed by a stated proportion of votes or with other formalities. Or the veto may be merely suspensive. See People v. Board of Councilmen (Super. Buff.) 20 N.Y. Supp. 51.

A statement by the Governor that he objects to certain items of an appropriation bill, without stating his reasons therefor, is insufficient to constitute an effective veto of such items. State v. French, 133 Kan. 579, 300 P. 1082, 1083. And where Governor returned resolution to the house in which it originated for purpose of correction of typographical error only, such communication was also held not to constitute a "veto". In re Block 1, Donly Heights Addition, Oklahoma City, 194 Okl. 221, 149 P.2d 265, 267.

Pocket Veto

Non-approval of a legislative act by the president or state governor, with the result that it fails to become a law, not by a written disapproval, (a veto in the ordinary form,) but by remaining silent until the adjournment of the legislative body, when that adjournment takes place before the expiration of the period allowed by the constitution for the examination of the bill by the executive.

VETO POWER. Executive's power conditionally to prevent acts passed by Legislature which have not yet become law. Fitzsimmons v. Leon, C.C.A. Puerto Rico, 141 F.2d 886, 888.

VETUS JUS. Lat. The old law. A term used in the civil law, sometimes to designate the law of the Twelve Tables, and sometimes merely a law which was in force previous to the passage of a subsequent law. Calvin.

VEX. To harass, disquiet, annoy; as by repeated litigation upon the same facts.

VEXARI. Lat. To be harassed, vexed, or annoyed; to be prosecuted; as in the maxim, *Nemo debet bis vexari pro una et eadem causa,* no one should be twice prosecuted for one and the same cause.

VEXATA QUÆSTIO. Lat. A vexed question; a question often agitated or discussed, but not determined or settled; a question or point which has been differently determined, and so left doubtful. 7 Coke, 45*b*; 3 Burrows, 1547.

VEXATION. The injury or damage which is suffered in consequence of the tricks of another.

VEXATIOUS. Without reasonable or probable cause or excuse. Gardner v. Queen Ins. Co. of America, 232 Mo.App. 1101, 115 S.W.2d 4, 7.

VEXATIOUS ACTIONS ACT. An act of parliament of 1896, authorizing the High Court to make an order, on the application of the attorney-general, that a person shown to be habitually and vexatiously litigious, without reasonable ground, shall not institute legal proceedings in that or any other court, without leave of the High Court judge thereof, upon satisfactory proof that such legal proceedings are not an abuse of the process of the court and that there is a *prima facie* ground therefor. The order when made is published in the Gazette. See 76 L.T. 351; [1913] W.N. 274 (Div.Ct.).

VEXATIOUS DELAY OR REFUSAL TO PAY. Under statute permitting recovery of damages for "vexatious delay" of an insurer in payment of a policy, no penalty can be inflicted unless it appears to a reasonable and prudent man before the trial that refusal was willful and without reasonable cause, and penalty will not be inflicted because of adverse outcome of trial. New York Life Ins. Co. v. Calhoun, C.C.A.Mo., 114 F.2d 526, 537.

An insurer is allowed an honest difference of opinion regarding its liability under a policy and so long as it acts in good faith, may contest either an issue of fact or an issue of law. Camp v. John Hancock Mut. Life Ins. Co. of Boston, Mass., Mo.App., 165 S.W.2d 277, 283.

VEXATIOUS PROCEEDING. Proceeding instituted maliciously and without probable cause. Paramount Pictures v. Blumenthal, 256 App.Div. 756, 11 N.Y.S.2d 768, 772. Kind of malicious prosecution differing principally because based on civil action. Calvo v. Bartolotta, 112 Conn. 396, 152 A. 311. When the party bringing proceeding is not acting *bona fide*, and merely wishes to annoy or embarrass his opponent, or when it is not calculated to lead to any practical result. Such a proceeding is often described as "frivolous and vexatious," and the court may stay it on that ground. Sweet.

VEXATIOUS REFUSAL TO PAY. See Vexatious Delay.

VEXED QUESTION. A question or point of law often discussed or agitated, but not determined or settled.

VI AUT CLAM. Lat. In the civil law. By force or covertly. Dig. 43, 24.

VI BONORUM RAPTORUM. Lat. In the civil law. Of goods taken away by force. The name of an action given by the prætor as a remedy for the violent taking of another's property. Inst. 4, 2; Dig. 47, 8.

VI ET ARMIS. Lat. With force and arms. See Trespass.

VIA. Lat. Way, road.

In the civil law. Way; a road; a right of way. The right of walking, riding, and driving over another's land. Inst. 2, 3, pr. A species of rural servitude, which included *iter* (a footpath) and *actus*, (a driftway.)

In old English law. A way; a public road; a foot, horse, and cart way. Co. Litt. 56*a*.

VIA ANTIQUA VIA EST TUTA. The old way is the safe way. Manning v. Manning's Ex'rs, 1 Johns. Ch. (N.Y.) 527, 530.

VIA ORDINARIA; VIA EXECUTIVA. In the law of Louisiana, the former phrase means in the ordinary way or by ordinary process, the latter means by executory process or in an executory proceeding. A proceeding in a civil action is "ordinary" when a citation takes place and all the delays and forms of law are observed; "executory" when seizure is obtained against the property of the debtor, without previous citation, in virtue of an act or title importing confession of judgment, or in other cases provided by law. Code Prac. La. art. 98.

VIA PUBLICA. In the civil law. A public way or road, the land itself belonging to the public. Dig. 43, 8, 2, 21.

VIA REGIA. In English law. The king's highway for all men. Co.Litt. 56*a*. The highway or common road, called "the king's" highway, because authorized by him and under his protection. Cowell.

VIA TRITA EST TUTISSIMA. The trodden path is the safest. Broom, Max. 134; 10 Coke, 142.

VIABILITY. Capability of living. A term used to denote the power a new-born child possesses of continuing its independent existence.

VIABLE. Livable, having the appearance of being able to live. Wehrman v. Farmers' & Merchants' Sav. Bank of Durant, 221 Iowa 249, 259 N.W. 564. Capable of life. This term is applied to a newly-born infant, and especially to one prematurely born, which is not only born alive, but in such a state of organic development as to make possible the continuance of its life.

VIÆ SERVITUS. Lat. A right of way over another's land.

VIAGÈRE RENTE. In French law. A rent-charge or annuity payable for the life of the annuitant.

VIANDER. In old English law. A returning officer. 7 Mod. 13.

VIATOR. Lat. In Roman law. A summoner or apparitor; an officer who attended on the tribunes and ædiles.

VICAR. One who performs the functions of another; a substitute. Also the incumbent of an appropriated or impropriated ecclesiastical benefice, as distinguished from the incumbent of a non-appropriated benefice, who is called a "rector." Wharton. See Pinder v. Barr, 4 El. & Bl. 115.

VICAR GENERAL. An ecclesiastical officer who assists the archbishop in the discharge of his office.

VICARAGE. In English ecclesiastical law. The living or benefice of a vicar, as a parsonage is of a parson. 1 Bl.Comm. 387, 388.

VICARIAL TITHES. Petty or small tithes payable to the vicar. 2 Steph.Comm. 681.

VICARIO, etc. An ancient writ for a spiritual person imprisoned, upon forfeiture of a recognizance, etc. Reg. Orig. 147.

VICARIUS APOSTOLICUS. An officer through whom the Pope exercises authority in parts remote, and who is sometimes sent with episcopal functions into provinces where there is no bishop resident or there has been a long vacancy in the see, or into infidel or heretical countries. 2 Phill. Int.L. 529.

VICARIUS NON HABET VICARIUM. A deputy has not [cannot have] a deputy. A delegated power cannot be again delegated. Broom, Max. 839.

VICE. A fault, defect, or imperfection.

As applied to an animal a bad habit or failing. F. Giovannozzi & Sons v. Luciani, Del.Super., 2 Terry 211, 18 A.2d 435, 437.

In the civil law, redhibitory vices are such faults or imperfections in the subject-matter of a sale as will give the purchaser the right to return the article and demand back the price.

VICE. Lat. In the place or stead. *Vice mea,* in my place.

Vice-admiral. An officer in the navy ranking below an admiral.

Vice-admiral of the coast. A county officer in England appointed by the admiral "to be answerable to the high admiral for all the coasts of the sea, when need and occasion shall be." He also had power to arrest ships, when found within a certain district, for the use of the king. His office was judicial as well as ministerial. The appointment to the office is still made for a few countries of England.

Vice-admiralty courts. In English law. Courts established in the king's possessions beyond the seas, with jurisdiction over maritime causes, including those relating to prize. 3 Steph.Comm. 435; 3 Bl.Comm. 69.

Vice-chamberlain. A great officer under the lord chamberlain, who, in the absence of the lord chamberlain, has the control and command of the officers appertaining to that part of the royal household which is called the "chamber." Cowell.

Vice-chancellor. See Chancellor.

Vice-comes. A title formerly bestowed on the sheriff of a county, when he was regarded as the deputy of the count or earl. Co.Litt. 168.

Vice-comitissa. In old English law. A viscountess. Spelman.

Vice-commercial agent. In the consular service of the United States, this was formerly the title of a consular officer who was substituted temporarily to fill the place of a commercial agent when the latter was absent or relieved from duty. See Commercial Agent.

Vice-constable of England. An ancient officer in the time of Edward IV.

Vice-consul. In the consular service of the United States a consular officer who is substituted temporarily to fill the place of a consul who is absent or relieved from duty. 22 U.S.C.A. § 938. Schunior v. Russell, 83 Tex. 83, 18 S.W. 484. In international law generally the term designates a commercial agent who acts in the place or stead of a consul or who has charge of a portion of his territory. In old English law, it meant the deputy or substitute of an earl (*comes*), who was anciently called "consul," answering to the more modern "*vice-comes.*" Burrill.

Vice-dominus. A sheriff.

Vice-dominus episcopi. The vicar general or commissary of a bishop. Blount.

Vice-gerent. A deputy or lieutenant.

Vice-judex. In old Lombardic law. A deputy judge.

Vice-marshal. An officer who was appointed to assist the earl marshal.

Vice-president of the United States. The title of the second officer, in point of rank, in the executive branch of the government of the United States.

Vice-principal. See Principal.

Vice-versa. Conversely; in inverted order; in reverse manner.

VICE-COMES NON MISIT BREVE. The sheriff hath not sent the writ. The form of continuance on the record after issue and before trial. 7 Mod. 349; 11 Mod. 231.

VICEROY. A person clothed with authority to act in place of the king; hence, the usual title of the governor of a dependency.

VICINAGE. Neighborhood; near dwelling; vicinity. 2 Bl.Comm. 33; Cowell. In modern usage, it means the county where a trial is had, a crime committed, etc. State v. Crinklaw, 40 Neb. 759, 59 N.W. 370; Convers v. Railway Co., 18 Mich. 468; Ex parte MacDonald, 20 Cal.App. 641, 129 P. 957. Also a jury of the county wherein trial is had. People v. Richardson, 138 Cal.App. 404, 32 P.2d 433, 435.

VICINETUM. The neighborhood; vicinage; the venue. Co.Litt. 185*b*.

VICINI VICINIORA PRÆSUMUNTUR SCIRE. 4 Inst. 173. Persons living in the neighborhood are presumed to know the neighborhood.

VICINITY. Quality or state of being near, or not remote; nearness; propinquity; proximity; a region about, near or adjacent; adjoining space or country. Casper v. City and County of San Francisco, 6 Cal.2d 376, 57 P.2d 920, 922. Neighborhood; etymologically, by common understanding, it admits of a wider latitude than proximity or contiguity, and may embrace a more extended space than that lying contiguous to the place in question; and, as applied to towns and other territorial divisions, may embrace those not adjacent. Haley v. Ins. Co., 12 Gray (Mass.) 545; Langley v. Barnstead, 63 N.H. 246; Chandler, Gardner & Williams v. Reynolds, 250 Mass. 309, 145 N.E. 476, 478.

VICIOUS INTROMISSION. In Scotch law. A meddling with the movables of a deceased, without confirmation or probate of his will or other title. Wharton.

VICIOUS PROPENSITY. A propensity or tendency of animal to do any act which might endanger the safety of persons and property of others in a given situation. Hartman v. Aschaffenburg, La.App., 12 So.2d 282, 286.

VICIS ET VENELLIS MUNDANDIS. An ancient writ against the mayor or bailiff of a town, etc., for the clean keeping of their streets and lanes. Reg.Orig. 267.

VICOUNTIEL, or VICONTIEL. Anything that belongs to the sheriffs, as *vicontiel writs*; *i. e.*, such as are triable in the sheriff's court. As to vicontiel rents, see St. 3 & 4 Wm. IV. c. 99, §§ 12, 13, which places them under the management of the commissioners of the woods and forests. Cowell.

VICOUNTIEL JURISDICTION. That jurisdiction which belongs to the officers of a county; as sheriffs, coroners, etc.

VICTUALLER. In English law. A person authorized by law to keep a house of entertainment for the public; a publican. 9 Adol. & E. 423. One who serves food or drink prepared for consumption on the premises. Friend v. Childs Dining Hall Co., 231 Mass. 65, 120 N.E. 407, 409, 5 A.L.R. 1100.

VICTUALS. Food ready to eat. Friend v. Childs Dining Hall Co., 231 Mass. 65, 120 N.E. 407, 5 A.L.R. 1100.

VICTUS. Lat. In the civil law. Sustenance; support; the means of living.

VICTUS, VICTORI IN EXPENSIS CONDEMNANDUS EST. The vanquished is to be condemned in costs to the conqueror, or he who loses the suit pays costs to his adversary. State ex rel. Macri v. City of Bremerton, 8 Wash.2d 93, 111 P.2d 612, 620.

VIDAME. In French feudal law. Originally, an officer who represented the bishop, as the viscount did the count. In process of time, these dignitaries erected their offices into fiefs, and became feudal nobles, such as the *vidame* of Chartres, Rheims, etc., continuing to take their titles from the seat of the bishop whom they represented, although the lands held by virtue of their fiefs might be situated elsewhere. Brande; Burrill.

VIDE. Lat. A word of reference. *Vide ante*, or *vide supra*, refers to a previous passage, *vide post*, or *vide infra*, to a subsequent passage, in a book.

VIDEBIS EA SÆPE COMMITTI QUÆ SÆPE VINDICANTUR. 3 Inst. Epil. You will see those things frequently committed which are frequently punished.

VIDELICET. Lat. The words "to-wit," or "that is to say," so frequently used in pleading, are technically called the "*videlicet*" or "*scilicet*;" and when any fact alleged in pleading is preceded by, or accompanied with these words, such fact is, in the language of the law, said to be "laid under a *videlicet*." The use of the *videlicet* is to point out, particularize, or render more specific that which has been previously stated in general language only; also to explain that which is doubtful or obscure. Brown. See Stukeley v. Butler, Hob. 171; Gleason v. McVickar, 7 Cow. (N.Y.) 43; Com. v. Quinlan, 27 N.E. 8, 153 Mass. 483; People v. Shaver, 367 Ill. 339, 11 N.E.2d 400, 402. Its common office is to state time, place, or manner which are of the essence of the matter in issue. Board of Sup'rs, Warren County, v. Vicksburg Hospital, 173 Miss. 805, 163 So. 382.

VIDETUR QUI SURDUS ET MUTUS NE POET FAIRE ALIENATION. It seems that a deaf and dumb man cannot alienate. Brower v. Fisher, 4 Johns.Ch. (N.Y.) 444; Brooke, Abr. "Eschete," pl. 4.

VIDIMUS. An *inspeximus*, (*q. v.*). Barring, Ob. St. 5.

VIDUA REGIS. Lat. In old English law. A king's widow. The widow of a tenant *in capite*. So called, because she was not allowed to marry a second time without the king's permission; obtaining her dower also from the assignment of the king, and having the king for her patron and defender. Spelman.

VIDUITATIS PROFESSIO. Lat. The making a solemn profession to live a sole and chaste woman.

VIDUITY. Widowhood.

VIE. Fr. Life; occurring in the phrases *cestui que vie*, *pur autre vie*, etc.

VIEW. The right of prospect; the outlook or prospect from the windows of one's house. A species of urban servitude which prohibits the obstruction of such prospect. 3 Kent, Comm. 448.

At common law, the proceeding by which tribunal goes to an object which cannot be produced in court because it is immovable or inconvenient to remove, and there observes it. Conner v. Parker, Tex.Civ.App., 181 S.W.2d 873, 874. An inspection by the jury previously to the trial of property in controversy, or of a place where a crime has been committed. See Garbarsky v. Simkin, 36 Misc. 195, 73 N.Y.S. 199; Wakefield v. Railroad Co., 63 Me. 385; Lancaster County v. Holyoke, 37 Neb. 328, 55 N.W. 950, 21 L.R.A. 394; Commonwealth v. Dascalakis, 246 Mass. 12, 140 N.E. 470, 477.

Offense is taking place within "view" of officer, so as to authorize arrest without warrant when officer's senses afford him knowledge that offense is being committed. Bass v. State, 182 Md. 496, 35 A.2d 155, 159; Kennington-Saenger, Inc. v. Wicks, 168 Miss. 566, 151 So. 549, 551.

Evidence

A "view" is not technically "evidence". Berlandi v. Commonwealth, 314 Mass. 424, 50 N.E.2d 210, 226.

Effect of jury's view of scene of murder without accused's presence in person is evidence. Snyder v. Commonwealth of Massachusetts, Mass., 54 S.Ct. 330, 291 U.S. 97, 78 L.Ed. 674, 90 A.L.R. 575.

Object of jury in viewing scene of crime is to clarify situation, and information thus obtained constitutes "evidence." Watson v. State, 166 Tenn. 400, 61 S.W. 476.

The jury's viewing of land, claimed by plaintiff to have been greatly damaged by overflow of river allegedly caused by railroad's reconstruction of bridge, although not in all respects "evidence", was proper to enable jury to understand better testimony given. Doman v. Baltimore & O. R. Co., 125 W.Va. 8, 22 S.E.2d 703, 705.

What was seen by master, in suits to enjoin commonwealth's interference with outdoor advertising, who traveled to view billboards, etc., was in a sense "evidence." General Outdoor Advertising Co. v. Department of Public Works, 289 Mass. 149, 193 N.E. 799, 812.

Where trial judge visited premises what he saw and observed was "evidence" in plaintiff's personal injury action. Lee v. Dawson, 44 Cal.App.2d 362, 112 P.2d 683, 685.

VIEW AND DELIVERY. When a right of common is exercisable not over the whole waste, but only in convenient places indicated from time to time by the lord of the manor or his bailiff, it is said to be exercisable after "view and delivery." Elton, Commons, 233.

VIEW, DEMAND OF. In real actions, the defendant was entitled to demand a *view*, that is, a sight of the thing, in order to ascertain its identity and other circumstances. As, if a real action were brought against a tenant, and such tenant did not exactly know what land it was that the demandant asked, then he might pray the view, which was that he might see the land which the demandant claimed. Brown.

VIEW OF AN INQUEST. A view or inspection taken by a jury, summoned upon an inquisition or inquest, of the place or property to which the inquisition or inquiry refers. Brown.

VIEW OF FRANK-PLEDGE. In English law. An examination to see if every freeman above twelve years of age within the district had taken the oath of allegiance, and found nine freeman pledges for his peaceable demeanor. 1 Reeve, Eng. Law, 7.

VIEWERS. Persons appointed by a court to make an investigation of certain matters, or to examine a particular locality, (as, the proposed site of a new road,) and to report to the court the result of their inspection, with their opinion on the same.

Old Practice

Persons appointed under writs of view to testify the view. Rosc. Real Act. 253.

VIF-GAGE. L. Fr. In old English law. A *vivum vadium* or living pledge, as distinguished from a *mortgage* or dead pledge. Properly, an estate given as security for a debt, the debt to be satisfied out of the rents, issues, and profits.

VIGIL. In ecclesiastical law. The eve or next day before any solemn feast.

VIGILANCE. Watchfulness; precaution; a proper degree of activity and promptness in pursuing one's rights or guarding them from infraction, or in making or discovering opportunities for the enforcement of one's lawful claims and demands.

It is the opposite of *laches*. Wynne v. Conrad, 220 N.C. 355, 17 S.E.2d 514, 518.

VIGILANT. Watchful, awake, and on the alert; attentive to discover and avoid danger, or to provide for safety; circumspect; cautious; wary. City Ice & Fuel Co. v. Center, 54 Ohio App. 116, 6 N.E.2d 580, 583.

VIGILANTIBUS ET NON DORMIENTIBUS JURA SUBVENIUNT. The laws aid those who are vigilant, not those who sleep upon their rights. 2 Inst. 690; Merchants' Bank of Newburyport, President, etc., of, v. Stevenson, 7 Allen (Mass.) 493; Broom, Max. 892.

VIGOR. Lat. Strength; virtue; force; efficiency. *Proprio vigore*, by its own force.

VIIS ET MODIS. Lat. In the ecclesiastical courts, service of a decree or citation *viis et modis, i. e.*, by all "ways and means" likely to affect the party with knowledge of its contents, is equivalent to substituted service in the temporal courts, and is opposed to personal service. Phillim. Ecc. Law, 1258, 1283.

VILL. In old English law, this word was used to signify the parts into which a hundred or wapentake was divided. It also signifies a town or city.

Demi-vill

A town consisting of five freemen, or frankpledges. Spelman.

VILLA EST EX PLURIBUS MANSIONIBUS VICINATA, ET COLLATA EX PLURIBUS VICINIS, ET SUB APPELLATIONE VILLARUM CONTINENTUR BURGI ET CIVITATES. Co. Litt. 115. Vill is a neighborhood of many mansions, a collection of many neighbors, and under the term of "vills" boroughs and cities are contained.

VILLA REGIA. Lat. In Saxon law. A royal residence. Spelman.

VILLAGE. A collection of houses collocated after something like regular plan regarding streets and lanes, without intervening farm land, but with convenient curtilages attached, an assemblage of houses, less than a town or city, but urban or semiurban in character, or any small assemblage of houses for dwellings, business, or both, in country, whether situated on regularly laid out streets and alleys or not. Supervisors of Manheim Tp., Lancaster County, v. Workman, 154 Pa.Super. 146, 35 A.2d 747, 750.

In some states, this is the legal description of a class of municipal corporations of smaller population than "cities" and having a simpler form of government, and corresponding to "towns" and "boroughs," as these terms are employed elsewhere.

So it was held that a "village" is a municipal corporation invested with particular franchises, and it may take and hold real and personal estate absolutely or in trust for any public use, and its corporate powers extend beyond the field of local government and the administration of local affairs. Village of Kenmore v. Erie County, 252 N.Y. 437, 169 N.E. 637, 639.

VILLAIN. An opprobrious epithet, implying great moral delinquency, and equivalent to knave, rascal, or scoundrel. The word is libelous. 1 Bos. & P. 331.

VILLANIS REGIS SUBTRACTIS REDUCENDIS. A writ that lay for the bringing back of the king's bondmen, that had been carried away by others out of his manors whereto they belonged. Reg. Orig. 87.

VILLANUM SERVITIUM. In old English law. Villein service. Fleta, lib. 3, c. 13, § 1.

VILLEIN. A person attached to a manor, who was substantially in the condition of a slave, who performed the base and servile work upon the manor for the lord, and was, in most respects, a subject of property belonging to him. 1 Washb. Real Prop. 26.

VILLEIN IN GROSS. A villein who was annexed to the person of the lord, and transferable by deed from one owner to another. 2 Bl. Comm. 93.

VILLEIN REGARDANT. A villein annexed to the manor of land; a serf.

VILLEIN SERVICES. Base services, such as villeins performed. 2 Bl. Comm. 93. They were not, however, exclusively confined to villeins, since they might be performed by freemen, without impairing their free condition. Bract. fol. 24*b*.

VILLEIN SOCAGE. In feudal and old English law. A species of tenure in which the services to be rendered were certain and determinate, but were of a base or servile nature; *i. e.*, not suitable to a man of free and honorable rank. This was also called "privileged villeinage," to distinguish it from "pure villeinage," in which the services were not certain, but the tenant was obliged to do whatever he was commanded. 2 Bl. Comm. 61.

VILLENAGE. A servile kind of tenure belonging to lands or tenements, whereby the tenant was bound to do all such services as the lord commanded, or were fit for a villein to do. Cowell. See Villein.

Pure Villenage

A base tenure, where a man holds upon terms of doing whatsoever is commanded of him, nor knows in the evening what is to be done in the morning, and is always bound to an uncertain service. 1 Steph. Comm. (7th Ed.) 188.

VILLENOUS JUDGMENT. A judgment which deprived one of his *libera lex*, whereby he was discredited and disabled as a juror or witness; forfeited his goods and chattels and lands for life; wasted the lands, razed the houses, rooted up the trees, and committed his body to prison. It has become obsolete. 4 Bl. Comm. 136; 4 Steph. Comm. 230; 4 Broom & H. Comm. 153. Wharton.

VIM VI REPELLERE LICET, MODO FIAT MODERAMINE INCULPATÆ TUTELÆ, NON AD SUMENDAM VINDICTAM, SED AD PROPULSANDAM INJURIAM. It is lawful to repel force by force, provided it be done with the moderation of blameless defense, not for the purpose of taking revenge, but to ward off injury. Co. Litt. 162*a*.

VINAGIUM. A payment of a certain quantity of wine instead of rent for a vineyard. 2 Mon. Ang. p. 980.

VINCULACION. In Spanish law. An entail. Schm. Civil Law, 308.

VINCULO. In Spanish law. The bond, chain, or tie of marriage. White, New Recop. b. 1, tit. 6, c. 1, § 2.

VINCULO MATRIMONII. See A Vinculo Matrimonii; Divorce.

VINCULUM JURIS. In the Roman law, an obligation is defined as a *vinculum juris, i. e.*, "a bond of law," whereby one party becomes or is bound to another to do something according to law.

VINDEX. Lat. In the civil law. A defender.

VINDICARE. Lat. In the civil law. To claim, or challenge; to demand one's own; to assert a right in or to a thing; to assert or claim a property in a thing; to claim a thing as one's own. Calvin.

VINDICATIO. Lat. In the civil law. The claiming a thing as one's own; the asserting of a right or title in or to a thing.

VINDICATORY PARTS OF LAWS. The sanction of the laws, whereby it is signified what evil or penalty shall be incurred by such as commit any public wrongs, and transgress or neglect their duty. 1 Steph. Comm. 37.

VINDICTA. In Roman law. A rod or wand; and, from the use of that instrument in their course, various legal acts came to be distinguished by the term; *e. g.*, one of the three ancient modes of manumission was by the *vindicta;* also the rod or wand intervened in the progress of the old action of *vindicatio*, whence the name of that action. Brown.

VINDICTIVE DAMAGES. See Damages.

VINOUS LIQUORS. This term includes all alcoholic beverages made from the juice of the grape by the process of fermentation, and perhaps similar liquors made from apples and from some species of berries; but not pure alcohol nor distilled liquors nor malt liquors such as beer and ale. See Adler v. State, 55 Ala. 23; Reyfelt v. State, 73 Miss. 415, 18 So. 925; Lemly v. State, 70 Miss. 241, 12 So. 22, 20 L.R.A. 645; Com. v. Reyburg, 122 Pa. 299, 16 A. 351, 2 L.R.A. 415; Feldman v. Morrison, 1 Ill.App. 462; Hinton v. State, 132 Ala. 29, 31 So. 563.

VINTNER. One who sells wine. A covenant prohibiting the trade of a vintner includes a person selling wines not to be drunk on the premises. 25 L. T. (N. S.) 312.

VIOL. Fr. In French law. Rape. Barring. Ob. St. 139.

VIOLATION. Injury; infringement; breach of right, duty or law; ravishment; seduction. The statute 25 Edw. III. St. 5, c. 2, enacts that any person who shall *violate* the king's companion shall be guilty of high treason.

VIOLENCE. Unjust or unwarranted exercise of force, usually with the accompaniment of vehemence, outrage or fury. People v. McIlvain, 55 Cal. App.2d 322, 130 P.2d 131, 134. Force, physical force, force unlawfully exercised, the abuse of force, that force which is employed against common right, against the laws, and against public liberty. Merl. Répert; Anderson-Berney Bldg. Co. v. Lowry, Tex.Civ.App., 143 S.W.2d 401, 403.

"Violence" in labor disputes is not limited to physical contact or injury, but may include picketing conducted with misleading signs, false statements, publicity, and veiled threats by words and acts. Esco Operating Corporation v. Kaplan, 258 N.Y.S. 303, 144 Misc. 646.

VIOLENT. Moving, acting, or characterized, by physical force, especially by extreme and sudden or by unjust or improper force; furious, vehement; as a violent storm or wind; a violent attack: marked by, or due to, strong mental excitement; vehement, passionate; as, violent speech; violent reproaches: produced or effected by force; not spontaneous or natural; unnatural; abnormal; as, a violent death: acting with or exerting great force on the mind, or as evidence; nearly conclusive, as in the phrase, often used in legal contention, violent presumption: great; extreme; used intensively; as a violent contrast in colors, violent pain, passion, etc. Provident Life & Accident Ins. Co. v. Campbell, 18 Tenn.App. 452, 79 S. W.2d 292, 296.

VIOLENT DEATH. Death caused by violent external means, as distinguished from natural death, caused by disease or the wasting of the vital forces.

Death is "violent" within accident policy if it results from external agency and is not in ordinary course of nature. Caffaro v. Metropolitan Life Ins. Co., 14 N.J.Misc. 167, 183 A. 200.

VIOLENT PRESUMPTION. In the law of evidence. Proof of a fact by the proof of circumstances which necessarily attend it. 3 Bl. Comm. 371. Violent presumption is many times equal to full proof. 3 Bl. Comm. 371. See Davis v. Curry, 2 Bibb (Ky.) 239; Shealy v. Edwards, 75 Ala. 419. Something more than a mere "presumption". Hughes v. State, 212 Ind. 577, 10 N.E.2d 629, 633.

VIOLENT PROFITS. Mesne profits in Scotland. "They are so called because due on the tenant's forcible or unwarrantable detaining the possession after he ought to have removed." Ersk. Inst. 2, 6, 54; Bell.

VIOLENTA PRÆSUMPTIO ALIQUANDO EST PLENA PROBATIO. Co. Litt. 6*b*. Violent presumption is sometimes full proof.

VIOLENTLY. By the use of force; forcibly; with violence. The term is used in indictments for certain offenses. State v. Blake, 39 Me. 324; State v. Crawford, 60 Utah 6, 206 P. 717, 718.

VIPERINA EST EXPOSITIO QUÆ CORRODIT VISCERA TEXTUS. 11 Coke, 34. It is a poisonous exposition which destroys the vitals of the text.

VIR. Lat. A man, especially as marking the sex. In the Latin phrases and maxims of the old English law, this word generally means "husband," the expression *vir et uxor* corresponding to the law French *baron et feme*.

VIR ET UXOR CENSENTUR IN LEGE UNA PERSONA. Jenk. Cent. 27. Husband and wife are considered one person in law.

VIR ET UXOR SUNT QUASI UNICA PERSONA, QUIA CARO ET SANGUIS UNUS; RES LICET SIT PROPRIA UXORIS, VIR TAMEN EJUS CUSTOS, CUM SIT CAPUT MULIERIS. Co. Litt. 112. Man and wife are, as it were, one person, because only one flesh and blood; although the property may be the wife's, the husband is keeper of it, since he is the head of the wife.

VIR MILITANS DEO NON IMPLICETUR SECULARIBUS NEGOTIIS. Co. Litt. 70. A man fighting for God must not be involved in secular business.

VIRES. Lat. (The plural of *"vis."*) Powers; forces; capabilities; natural powers; powers granted or limited. See Ultra Vires.

VIRES ACQUIRIT EUNDO. It gains strength by continuance. Mann v. Mann's Ex'rs, 1 Johns. Ch. (N.Y.) 231, 237.

VIRGA. In old English law. A rod or staff; a rod or ensign of office. Cowell.

VIRGA TERRÆ, (or VIRGATA TERRÆ.) In old English law. A yard-land; a measure of land of variable quantity, containing in some places twenty, in others twenty-four, in others thirty, and in others forty, acres. Cowell; Co. Litt. 5*a*.

VIRGATA. A quarter of an acre of land. It might also be used to express a quarter of a hide of land.

VIRGATA REGIA. In old English law. The verge; the bounds of the king's household, within which the court of the steward had jurisdiction. Crabb, Eng. Law, 185.

VIRGATE. A yard-land.

VIRGE, TENANT BY. A species of copyholder, who holds by the virge or rod.

VIRGO INTACTA. Lat. A pure virgin.

VIRIDARIO ELIGENDO. A writ for choice of a verderer in the forest. Reg. Orig. 177.

VIRILIA. The privy members of a man, to cut off which was felony by the common law, though the party consented to it. Bract. l. 3, 144; Cowell.

VIRTUAL REPRESENTATION, DOCTRINE OF. Under this doctrine, where parties interested are numerous and the suit is for an object common to all of them, some of the body may maintain a bill on behalf of themselves and of the others. Padway v. Pacific Mut. Life Ins. Co. of California, D.C. Wis., 42 F.Supp. 569, 576; Waybright v. Columbian

Mut. Life Ins. Co., D.C.Tenn., 30 F.Supp. 885, 888; Lightle v. Kirby, 194 Ark. 535, 108 S.W.2d 896, 897.

VIRTUOUS. A woman is a "virtuous female" if her body be pure and if she has never had sexual intercourse with another, though both her mind and heart be impure. Thomas v. State, 19 Ga.App. 104, 91 S.E. 247, 250.

VIRTUTE CUJUS. Lat. By virtue whereof. This was the clause in a pleading justifying an entry upon land, by which the party alleged that it was in virtue of an order from one entitled that he entered. Wharton.

VIRTUTE OFFICII. Lat. By virtue of his office. By the authority vested in him as the incumbent of the particular office.

An officer acts "virtute officii" when he acts by the authority vested in him as the incumbent of the particular office. Aldridge v. Wooten, 68 Ga.App. 887, 24 S.E.2d 700, 701. Where acts done are within the authority of the officer, but in doing them he exercises that authority improperly, or abuses the confidence which the law reposes in him, whilst acts done "colore officii" are where they are of such a nature that his office gives him no authority to do them. State v. Roy, 41 N.M. 308, 68 P.2d 162, 165; Yuma County v. Wisener, 45 Ariz. 475, 46 P.2d 115, 118, 99 A.L.R. 642.

VIS. Lat. Any kind of force, violence, or disturbance relating to a man's person or his property.

The plural is *vires (q. v.)*.

VIS ABLATIVA. In the civil law. Ablative force; force which is exerted in taking away a thing from another. Calvin.

VIS ARMATA. In the civil and old English law. Armed force; force exerted by means of arms or weapons.

VIS CLANDESTINA. In old English law. Clandestine force; such as is used by night. Bract. fol. 162.

VIS COMPULSIVA. In the civil and old English law. Compulsive force; that which is exerted to compel another to do an act against his will; force exerted by menaces or terror.

VIS DIVINA. In the civil law. Divine or superhuman force; the act of God.

VIS ET METUS. In Scotch law. Force and fear. Bell.

VIS EXPULSIVA. In old English law. Expulsive force; force used to expel another, or put him out of his possession. Bracton contrasts it with *"vis simplex,"* and divides it into expulsive force with arms, and expulsive force without arms. Bract. fol. 162.

VIS EXTURBATIVA. In the civil law. Exturbative force; force used to thrust out another. Force used between two contending claimants of possession, the one endeavoring to thrust out the other. Calvin.

VIS FLUMINIS. In the civil law. The force of a river; the force exerted by a stream or current; water-power.

VIS IMPRESSA. The original act of force out of which an injury arises, as distinguished from *"vis proxima,"* the proximate force, or immediate cause of the injury. 2 Greenl. Ev. § 224.

VIS INERMIS. In old English law. Unarmed force; the opposite of *"vis armata."* Bract. fol. 162.

VIS INJURIOSA. In old English law. Wrongful force; otherwise called *"illicita,"* (unlawful.) Bract. fol. 162.

VIS INQUIETATIVA. In the civil law. Disquieting force. Calvin. Bracton defines it to be where one does not permit another to use his possession quietly and in peace. Bract. fol. 162.

VIS LAICA. In old English law. Lay force; an armed force used to hold possession of a church. Reg. Orig. 59, 60.

VIS LEGIBUS EST INIMICA. 3 Inst. 176. Violence is inimical to the laws.

VIS LICITA. In old English law. Lawful force. Bract. fol. 162.

VIS MAJOR. A greater or superior force; an irresistible force. A loss that results immediately from a natural cause without the intervention of man, and could not have been prevented by the exercise of prudence, diligence, and care. The George Shiras, 9 C.C.A. 511, 61 F. 300, 17 U.S.App. 528; National Carbon Co. v. Bankers Mortg. Co. of Topeka, C.C.A.Kan., 77 F.2d 614, 617. A natural and inevitable necessity, and one arising wholly above the control of human agencies, and which occurs independently of human action or neglect. The Adventuress, D.C.Mass., 214 F. 834, 839. In the civil law, this term is sometimes used as synonymous with *"vis divina,"* or the act of God. Calvin. Noel Bros. v. Texas and P. Ry. Co., 16 La. App. 622, 133 So. 830, 831.

VIS PERTUBATIVA. In old English law. Force used between parties contending for a possession.

VIS PROXIMA. Immediate force. See Vis Impressa.

VIS SIMPLEX. In old English law. Simple or mere force. Distinguished by Bracton from *"vis armata,"* and also from *"vis expulsiva."* Bract. fol. 162.

VISA. An official indorsement upon a document, passport, commercial book, etc., to certify that it has been examined and found correct or in due form. See also Visé.

VISCOUNT. A decree of English nobility, next below that of earl.

An old title of the sheriff.

VISÉ. An indorsement made on a passport by the proper authorities, denoting that it has been examined, and that the person who bears it is permitted to proceed on his journey. Webster. See also Visa.

VISIBLE. Perceptible, discernible, clear, distinct, evident, open, conspicuous. Mutual Trust & Deposit Co. v. Travelers' Protective Ass'n of America, 57 Ind.App. 329, 104 N.E. 880, 883; Branch v. State, 73 Tex.Cr.R. 471, 165 S.W. 605, 606.

VISIT. In international law. The right of visit or visitation is the right of a cruiser or war-ship to stop a vessel sailing under another flag on the high seas, and send an officer to such vessel to ascertain whether her nationality is what it purports to be. It is exercisable only when suspicious circumstances attend the vessel to be visited; as when she is suspected of a piratical character.

VISITATION. Inspection; superintendence; direction; regulation. Bank of America Nat. Trust & Savings Ass'n v. Douglas, 70 App.D.C. 221, 105 F.2d 100, 105, 123 A.L.R. 1266.

As applied to corporations, means, in law, the act of a superior or superintending officer who visits a corporation to examine into its manner of conducting business and to enforce an observance of its laws and regulations. Kawfield Oil Co. v. Illinois Refining Co., 169 Okl. 75, 35 P.2d 961, 963. Also a power given by law to the founders of all eleemosynary corporations. 2 Kent, Comm. 300–303; 1 Bl. Comm. 480, 481. In England, the visitation of ecclesiastical corporations belongs to the ordinary. 1 Bl.Comm. 480, 481. See Trustees of Union Baptist Ass'n v. Hunn, 7 Tex. Civ.App. 249, 26 S.W. 755; Thompson v. Southern Connellsville Coke Co., 269 Pa. 500, 112 A. 533, 534.

VISITATION BOOKS. In English law. Books compiled by the heralds, when progresses were solemnly and regularly made into every part of the kingdom, to inquire into the state of families, and to register such marriages and descents as were verified to them upon oath; they were allowed to be good evidence of pedigree. 3 Bl. Comm. 105; 3 Steph.Comm. 724.

VISITOR. An inspector of the government of corporations, or bodies politic. 1 Bl.Comm. 482.

The ordinary is visitor of spiritual corporations. But corporations instituted for private charity, if they are lay, are visitable by the founder, or whom he shall appoint; and from the sentence of such visitor there lies no appeal. By implication of law, the founder and his heirs are visitors of lay foundations, if no particular person is appointed by him to see that the charity is not perverted. Jacob.

The term "visitor" is also applied to an official appointed to see and report upon persons found lunatics by inquisition, and to a person appointed by a school board to visit houses and see that parents are complying with the provisions in reference to the education of their children. Mozley & Whitley.

VISITOR OF MANNERS. The regarder's office in the forest. Manw. i. 195.

VISNE. L. Fr. The neighborhood; vicinage; venue. The district from which juries were drawn at common law. Ex parte McNeeley, 36 W.Va. 84, 14 S.E. 436, 15 L.R.A. 226, 32 Am.St.Rep. 831; State v. Kemp, 34 Minn. 61, 24 N.W. 349.

VISUS. Lat. In old English practice. View; inspection, either of a place or person.

VITAL STATISTICS. Public records kept by a state, city or other governmental subdivision, under a statutory provision, of births, marriages and deaths, and disease.

VITAMIN. Nitrogenous substance found in some nucleic acids in the form of pyrimidine bases, as cytosin, minute quantities of which are essential to the diet of man, birds, and other animals. In re Wallerstein, Cust. & Pat. App., 53 F.2d 530, 531.

"Vitamin D" functions in regulating the metabolism of calcium and phosphorus in the body and is, therefore, concerned with the proper formation of bones and teeth. It is recognized as especially beneficial in the infant and growing child as a preventative and therapy of rickets and the building of strong bones and teeth. It is also an essential vitamin for adults. Vitamin D in nature is found almost exclusively in sunshine and certain fish livers which are unavailable to humans in the normal diet. Quaker Oats Co. v. Federal Security Administrator, C.C.A.7, 129 F.2d 76, 80.

VITIATE. To impair; to make void or voidable; to cause to fail of force or effect; to destroy or annul, either entirely or in part, the legal efficacy and binding force of an act or instrument; as when it is said that fraud *vitiates a contract.*

VITILIGATE. To litigate cavilously, vexatiously, or from merely quarrelsome motives.

VITIOUS INTROMISSION. In Scotch law. An unwarrantable intermeddling with the movable estate of a person deceased, without the order of law. Ersk.Prin. b. 3, tit. 9, § 25. The irregular intermeddling with the effects of a deceased person, which subjects the party to the whole debts of the deceased. 2 Kames, Eq. 327.

VITIUM CLERICI. In old English law. The mistake of a clerk; a clerical error.

VITIUM CLERICI NOCERE NON DEBET. Jenk. Cent. 23. A clerical error ought not to hurt.

VITIUM EST QUOD FUGI DEBET, NISI, RATIONEM NON INVENIAS, MOX LEGEM SINE RATIONE ESSE CLAMES. Ellesm. Post. N. 86. It is a fault which ought to be avoided, that if you cannot discover the reason you should presently exclaim that the law is without reason.

VITIUM SCRIPTORIS. In old English law. The fault or mistake of a writer or copyist; a clerical error. Gilb. Forum Rom. 185.

VITREOUS. Consisting of or resembling glass in its important characteristics. Vantine & Co. v. U. S., 9 Ct.Cust.App. 291, 292.

VITRICUS. Lat. In the civil law. A stepfather; a mother's second husband. Calvin.

VIVA AQUA. Lat. In the civil law. Living water; running water; that which issues from a spring or fountain. Calvin.

VIVA PECUNIA. Lat. Cattle, which obtained this name from being received during the Saxon period as money upon most occasions, at certain regulated prices. Cowell.

VIVA VOCE. Lat. With the living voice; by word of mouth. As applied to the examination of witnesses, this phrase is equivalent to "orally." It is used in contradistinction to evidence on affidavits or depositions. As descriptive of a species of voting, it signifies voting by speech or outcry, as distinguished from voting by a written or printed ballot.

The word "ballot" is used as a symbol of secrecy, while "viva voce" is used as a symbol of publicity. Day v. Walker, 124 Neb. 500, 247 N.W. 350, 351.

VIVARIUM. Lat. In the civil law. An inclosed place, where live wild animals are kept. Calvin.; Spelman.

VIVARY. In English law. A place for keeping wild animals alive, including fishes; a fish pond, park, or warren.

VIVUM VADIUM. See Vadium.

VIX ULLA LEX FIERI POTEST QUÆ OMNIBUS COMMODA SIT, SED SI MAJORI PARTI PROSPICIAT, UTILIS EST. Scarcely any law can be made which is adapted to all, but, if it provide for the greater part, it is useful. Plowd. 369.

VIZ. A contraction for *videlicet*, to-wit, namely, that is to say.

VOCABULA ARTIS. Lat. Words of art; technical terms.

VOCABULA ARTIUM EXPLICANDA SUNT SECUNDUM DEFINITIONES PRUDENTUM. Terms of arts are to be explained according to the definitions of the learned or skilled [in such arts.] Bl. Law Tracts, 6.

VOCARE AD CURIAM. In feudal law. To summon to court. Feud. Lib. 2, tit. 22.

VOCATIO IN JUS. Lat. A summoning to court. In the earlier practice of the Roman law, (under the *legis actiones*,) the creditor orally called upon his debtor to go with him before the prætor for the purpose of determining their controversy, saying, *"In jus eamus; in jus te voco."* This was called *"vocatio in jus."*

VOCATION. One's regular calling or business. Mutual Life Ins. Co. of New York v. Enecks, 41 Ga.App. 644, 154 S.E. 198, 199. The activity on which one spends major portion of his time and out of which he makes his living. Employers' Liability Assur. Corporation v. Accident & Casualty Ins. Co. of Winterthur, Switzerland, C.C.A. Ohio, 134 F.2d 566, 568.

VOCIFERATIO. Lat. In old English law. Outcry; hue and cry. Cowell.

VOCIFEROUS. In a statute forbidding the use of loud and vociferous language, making a loud outcry; clamorous; noisy. Webst.; Anderson v. State, Tex.Cr.App., 20 S.W. 359; Thomason v. State, 98 Tex.Cr.R. 312, 265 S.W. 579.

VOCO. Lat. In the civil and old English law. I call; I summon; I vouch. *In jus voco te*, I summon you to court; I summon you before the prætor. The formula by which a Roman action was anciently commenced. Adams, Rom. Ant. 242.

VOID. Null; ineffectual; nugatory; having no legal force or binding effect; unable, in law, to support the purpose for which it was intended. McGarry v. Village of Wilmette, 303 Ill. 147, 135 N.E. 96, 98; Hardison v. Gledhill, Ga.App., 33 S.E.2d 921, 924.

There is this difference between the two words "void" and "voidable:" *void* in the strict sense, means that an instrument or transaction is nugatory and ineffectual so that nothing can cure it; *voidable*, when an imperfection or defect can be cured by the act or confirmation of him who could take advantage of it. Wharton. The term "void," however, as applicable to conveyances or other agreements, has not at all times been used with technical precision, nor restricted to its peculiar and limited sense, as contradistinguished from "voidable;" it being frequently introduced, even by legal writers and jurists, when the purpose is nothing further than to indicate that a contract was invalid, and not binding in law. But the distinction between the terms "void" and "voidable," in their application to contracts, is often one of great practical importance; and, whenever entire technical accuracy is required, the term "void" can only be properly applied to those contracts that are of no effect whatsoever, such as are a mere nullity, and incapable of confirmation or ratification. Allis v. Billings, 6 Metc., Mass., 415, 39 Am.Dec. 744.

The word "void," in its strictest sense, means that which has no force and effect, is without legal efficacy, is incapable of being enforced by law, or has no legal or binding force, but frequently the word is used and construed as having the more liberal meaning of "voidable." In re Validation of $50,000 Serial Funding Bonds of Clarke County, 187 Miss. 512, 193 So. 449, 452.

The word "void" is used in statutes in the sense of utterly void so as to be incapable of ratification, and also in the sense of voidable and resort must be had to the rules of construction in many cases to determine in which sense the Legislature intended to use it. An act or contract neither wrong in itself nor against public policy, which has been declared void by statute for the protection or benefit of a certain party, or class of parties, is voidable only. U. S. v. New York & Porto Rico S. S. Co., 239 U.S. 88, 36 S.Ct. 41, 42, 60 L.Ed. 161; Weede v. Iowa Southern Utilities Co. of Delaware, 231 Iowa 784, 2 N.W.2d 372, 397, 398.

VOID CONTRACT. One which never had any legal existence or effect, and such contract cannot in any manner have life breathed into it. National Union Indemnity Co. v. Bruce Bros., Inc., 44 Ariz. 454, 38 P.2d 648, 652. Expression denotes that the parties to the transaction have gone through the form of making a contract, but that none has been made in law because of lack of some essential element of a contract, and such contract creates no legal rights and either party thereto may ignore it at his pleasure, in so far as it is executory. Griffin v. Smith, C.C.A.Ind., 101 F.2d 348, 350.

VOID IN PART, VOID IN TOTO. Curtis v. Leavitt, 15 N.Y. 9, 96.

VOID JUDGMENT. One which has no legal force or effect, invalidity of which may be asserted by any person whose rights are affected at any time and at any place directly or collaterally. Reynolds v. Volunteer State Life Ins. Co., Tex.Civ.App., 80 S.W.2d 1087, 1092. One which, from its inception is and forever continues to be absolutely null, without legal efficacy, ineffectual to bind parties or support a right, of no legal force and effect whatever, and incapable of confirmation, ratification, or enforcement in any manner or to any degree. Ex parte Myers, 121 Neb. 56, 236 N.W. 143,

144. One that has merely semblance without some essential elements, as want of jurisdiction or failure to serve process or have party in court. Wellons v. Lassiter, 200 N.C. 474, 157 S.E. 434, 436. It is subject to collateral attack. Owens v. Cocroft, 14 Ga.App. 322, 80 S.E. 906, 907.

VOID MARRIAGE. One not good for any legal purpose, the invalidity of which may be maintained in any proceeding between any parties, while a "voidable marriage" is one where there is an imperfection which can be inquired into only during the lives of both of the parties in a proceeding to obtain a sentence declaring it void. State v. Smith, 101 S.C. 293, 85 S.E. 958, 959, Ann. Cas.1917C, 149.

"Voidable marriage" is valid for all civil puposes until annulled in direct proceedings, but "void marriage" is nullity and may be impeached at any time. Pridgen v. Pridgen, 203 N.C. 533, 166 S.E. 591, 593.

VOID PROCESS. One which fails in some material respect to comply with the requisite form of legal process. United States v. Van Dusen, C. C.A.Minn., 78 F.2d 121, 124.

VOID THINGS ARE AS NO THINGS. People v. Shall, 9 Cow. (N.Y.) 778, 784.

VOIDABLE. That may be avoided, or declared void; not absolutely void, or void in itself. 2 Kent, Comm. 234. That which operates to accomplish the thing sought to be accomplished, until the fatal vice in the transaction has been judicially ascertained and declared. Slaughter v. Qualls, Tex., 162 S.W.2d 671, 674. It imports a valid act which may be avoided rather than an invalid act which may be confirmed. Paulson v. McMillan, 8 Wash.2d 295, 111 P.2d 983, 985. See Void.

VOIDABLE CONTRACT. One which is void as to wrongdoer but not void as to wronged party, unless he elects to so treat it. Depner v. Joseph Zukin Blouses, 13 Cal.App.2d 124, 56 P.2d 574, 575. See, also, Void.

VOIDABLE JUDGMENT. One apparently valid, but in truth wanting in some material respect. Reynolds v. Volunteer State Life Ins. Co., Tex.Civ. App., 80 S.W.2d 1087, 1092. One rendered by a court having jurisdiction but which is irregularly and erroneously rendered. Tanton v. State Nat. Bank of El Paso, Tex., 43 S.W.2d 957, 960; Gehret v. Hetkes, Tex., 36 S.W.2d 700, 701; Easterline v. Bean, Tex., 49 S.W.2d 427, 429.

VOIDABLE MARRIAGE. See Void Marriage.

VOIDABLE PREFERENCE. Under Bankruptcy Act, where person while insolvent and within four months of bankruptcy transferred property, effect of which will be to enable one creditor to obtain greater percentage of his debt than other creditors of same class and person receiving it or to be benefited thereby has reasonable cause to believe that enforcement of transfer will result in preference. Bankr.Act §§ 60a, 60b, 11 U.S.C.A. § 96 (a, b). Haas v. Sachs, C.C.A.Ark., 68 F.2d 623, 625. But it is unnecessary that bankrupt should have intended to prefer person receiving or benefited by transfer. Sams v. First Nat. Bank of Meridian, Miss., 181 So. 320, 321.

VOIDANCE. The act of emptying; ejection from a benefice.

VOIR DIRE. L. Fr. To speak the truth. This phrase denotes the preliminary examination which the court may make of one presented as a witness or juror, where his competency, interest, etc., is objected to. State v. McRae, 200 N.C. 149, 156 S.E. 800, 803.

VOITURE. Fr. Carriage; transportation by carriage.

VOLENS. Lat. Willing. He is said to be willing who either expressly consents or tacitly makes no opposition. Calvin.

VOLENTI NON FIT INJURIA. He who consents cannot receive an injury. Broom, Max. 268, 269, 271, 395; Shelf. Mar. & Div. 449; Poole v. Lutz and Schmidt, 273 Ky. 586, 117 S.W.2d 575, 576.

VOLITIONAL INSANITY. Which means that although accused can distinguish between right and wrong, still he is unable because of mental disease to resist the impulse to commit the criminal act. State v. Jackson, 346 Mo. 474, 142 S.W.2d 45, 49.

VOLUIT, SED NON DIXIT. He willed, but he did not say. He may have intended so, but he did not say so. A maxim frequently used in the construction of wills, an answer to arguments based upon the supposed intention of a testator. 2 Pow.Dev. 625; 4 Kent, Comm. 538.

VOLUMEN. Lat. In the civil law. A volume; so called from its form, being *rolled* up.

VOLUMUS. Lat. We will; it is our will. The first word of a clause in the royal writs of protection and letters patent. Cowell.

VOLUNTARILY. Done by design or intention, intentional, proposed, intended, or not accidental. Louisville & N. R. Co. v. Hall, 223 Ala. 338, 135 So. 466, 471. Intentionally and without coercion. Young v. Young, 148 Kan. 876, 84 P.2d 916, 917.

VOLUNTARILY LEAVING WORK. So as to render employee ineligible for unemployment compensation exists where employee, without action by the employer, resigns, leaves, or quits his employment. Department of Labor and Industry v. Unemployment Compensation Board of Review, 133 Pa.Super. 518, 3 A.2d 211, 214, 215.

VOLUNTARIUS DÆMON. A voluntary madman. A term applied by Lord Coke to a drunkard, who has voluntarily contracted madness by intoxication. Co.Litt. 247; 4 Bl.Comm. 25.

VOLUNTARY. Unconstrained by interference; unimpelled by another's influence; spontaneous; acting of oneself. Coker v. State, 199 Ga. 20, 33 S.E.2d 171, 174. Done by design or intention, purpose, intended. Nelson County v. Williams County, N.D., 276 N.W. 265, 269. Proceeding from the free and unrestrained will of the person. Brown v. McCulloch, Tenn.App., 144 S.W.2d 1, 4. Produced in or by an act of choice. Hartingh v. Bay Circuit Judge, 176 Mich. 289, 142 N.W. 585, 587, Ann.Cas.1915B, 520. Resulting from choosing. Travelers' Protective Ass'n v. Jones, 75 Ind.App. 29, 127 N.E. 783, 784. The word, especially in statutes, often implies knowledge of essential facts. Sweeney v. Sweeney, 96 Vt. 196, 118 A. 882, 26 A.L.R. 1066; Choate v. State, 19 Okl.Cr. 169, 197 P. 1060, 1063.

Without consideration; without valuable consideration; gratuitous, as a *voluntary* conveyance. London v. G. L. Anderson Brass Works, 197 Ala. 16, 72 So. 359, 363. Also, having a merely nominal consideration; as, a *voluntary* deed. Russ v. Blackshear, 88 Fla. 573, 102 So. 749, 750.

As to voluntary "Answer," "Assignment," "Bankruptcy," "Confession," "Conveyance," "Deposit," "Escape," "Indebtedness," "Manslaughter," "Nonsuit," "Oath," "Payment," "Redemption," "Sale," "Settlement," "Trust," and "Waste," see those titles.

VOLUNTARY ABANDONMENT. As ground for divorce within statutes is constituted, if there is a final departure, without consent of other party, without sufficient reason and without intent to return. Nelson v. Nelson, 244 Ala. 421, 14 So.2d 155, 156.

VOLUNTARY COURTESY. A voluntary act of kindness; an act of kindness performed by one man towards another, of the free will and inclination of the doer, without any previous request or promise of reward made by him who is the object of the courtesy; from which the law will not imply a promise of remuneration. Holthouse.

VOLUNTARY DISCONTINUANCE. Voluntary action on part of plaintiff, whereby his case goes out of court without decision on merits. Ferber v. Brueckl, 322 Mo. 892, 17 S.W.2d 524, 527.

VOLUNTARY EXPOSURE TO UNNECESSARY DANGER. An intentional act which reasonable and ordinary prudence would pronounce dangerous. Archibald v. Order of United Commercial Travelers, 117 Me. 418, 104 A. 792, 793; Federal Sav. & Ins. Co. v. Rager, 75 Ind.App. 295, 128 N.E. 773, 774. Intentional exposure to unnecessary danger, implying a conscious knowledge of the danger. Empire Life Ins. Co. v. Allen, 111 Ga. 413, 81 S.E. 120, 122. The voluntary doing of an act which is not necessary to be done, but which requires exposure to known danger to which one would not be exposed if unnecessary act is not done. Landau v. Travelers' Ins. Co., 315 Mo. 760, 287 S.W. 346, 351. The term implies a conscious, intentional exposure, something of which one is conscious but willing to take the risk.

VOLUNTARY IGNORANCE. This exists where a party might, by taking reasonable pains, have acquired the necessary knowledge, but has neglected to do so.

VOLUNTARY JURISDICTION. In English law. A jurisdiction exercised by certain ecclesiastical courts, in matters where there is no opposition. 3 Bl.Comm. 66. The opposite of *contentious* jurisdiction, (*q. v.*). In Scotch law. One exercised in matters admitting of no opposition or question, and therefore cognizable by any judge, and in any place, and on any lawful day. Bell.

VOLUNTAS. Lat. Properly, volition, purpose, or intention, or a design or the feeling or impulse which prompts the commission of an act; but in old English law the term was often used to denote a will, that is, the last will and testament of a decedent, more properly called *testamentum*.

VOLUNTAS DONATORIS IN CHARTA DONI SUI MANIFESTE EXPRESSA OBSERVETUR. Co.Litt. 21. The will of the donor manifestly expressed in his deed of gift is to be observed.

VOLUNTAS EST JUSTA SENTENTIA DE EO QUOD QUIS POST MORTEM SUAM FIERI VELIT. A will is an exact opinion or determination concerning that which each one wishes to be done after his death.

VOLUNTAS ET PROPOSITUM DISTINGUUNT MALEFICIA. The will and the proposed end distinguish crimes. Bract. fols. 2*b*, 136*b*.

VOLUNTAS FACIT QUOD IN TESTAMENTO SCRIPTUM VALEAT. Dig. 30, 1, 12, 3. It is intention which gives effect to the wording of a will.

VOLUNTAS IN DELICTIS, NON EXITUS SPECTATUR. 2 Inst. 57. In crimes, the will, and not the consequence, is looked to.

VOLUNTAS REPUTATUR PRO FACTO. The intention is to be taken for the deed. 3 Inst. 69; Broom, Max. 311.

VOLUNTAS TESTATORIS EST AMBULATORIA USQUE AD EXTREMUM VITÆ EXITUM. 4 Coke, 61. The will of a testator is ambulatory until the latest moment of life.

VOLUNTAS TESTATORIS HABET INTERPRETATIONEM LATAM ET BENIGNAM. Jenk. Cent. 260. The intention of a testator has a broad and benignant interpretation.

VOLUNTAS ULTIMA TESTATORIS EST PERIMPLENDA SECUNDUM VERAM INTENTIONEM SUAM. Co.Litt. 322. The last will of the testator is to be fulfilled according to his true intention.

VOLUNTEER. A person who gives his services without any express or implied promise of remuneration. Chicago & E. I. R. Co. v. Argo, 82 Ill. App. 667. One who intrudes himself into a matter which does not concern him, or one who pays the debt of another without request, when he is not legally or morally bound to do so, and when he has no interest to protect in making such payment. Missouri, K. & T. Ry. Co. of Texas v. Hood (Tex.Civ.App.) 172 S.W. 1120. See Irvine v. Angus, 35 C.C.A. 501, 93 F. 633; Arnold v. Green, 116 N.Y. 566, 23 N.E. 1; In re Welton's Estate, 141 Misc. 674, 253 N.Y.S. 128, 140. One who, acting on his own initiative, pays debt of another without invitation, compulsion, or the necessity of self-protection. In re Farmers' & Merchants' State Bank of Nooksack, 175 Wash. 78, 26 P.2d 631. One who merely offers his service on his own free will, as opposed to one who is conscripted. Gooden v. Mitchell, 2 Terry 301, 21 A.2d 197, 202. Also an attorney, as to any persons other than those by whom he was retained. In re Greenberg, 174 Misc. 182, 20 N.Y.S.2d 432, 433.

Conveyancing

One who holds a title under a voluntary conveyance, *i. e.*, one made without consideration, good or valuable, to support it.

Law of Master and Servant

The term "Volunteer" includes one who, without the assent of the master and without justification arising from a legitimate personal interest, unnecessarily assists a servant in the performance of the master's business. Kalmich v. White, 95 Conn. 568, 111 A. 845, 846; Goshen Furnace Corporation v. Tolley's Adm'r, 134 Va. 404, 114 S.E. 728, 730.

Military Law

One who freely and voluntarily offers himself for service in the army or navy; as distinguished from one who is compelled to serve by draft or conscription, and also from one entered by enlistment in the standing army.

VOTE. Suffrage; the expression of his will, preference, or choice, formally manifested by a member of a legislative or deliberative body, or of a constituency or a body of qualified electors, in regard to the decision to be made by the body as a whole upon any proposed measure or proceeding or in passing laws, rules or regulations, or the selection of an officer or representative. And the aggregate of the expressions of will or choice, thus manifested by individuals, is called the "vote of the body." See Maynard v. Board of Canvassers, 84 Mich. 228, 47 N.W. 756, 11 L.R.A. 332; Gillespie v. Palmer, 20 Wis. 546; Commonwealth v. Baker, 237 Ky. 380, 35 S.W.2d 548, 549; Sawyer Stores v. Mitchell, 103 Mont. 148, 62 P.2d 342, 348.

Casting Vote

See that title.

Cumulative Voting

See Cumulative.

Voting Trust

A term applied to the accumulation in a single hand or in a few hands of shares of corporate stock, belonging to several or many owners, in trust for purpose of voting the shares in order, thereby, to control the business of the company through selection of directors. Manson v. Curtis, 223 N.Y. 313, 119 N.E. 559, 561, Ann.Cas.1918E, 247; Groub v. Blish, 88 Ind.App. 309, 152 N.E. 609, 611. See Voting Trust, *infra.*

VOTER. The word has two meanings—a person who performs act of voting, and a person who has the qualifications entitling him to vote. Its meaning depends on the connections in which it is used, and is not always equivalent to electors. Board of Education of Oklahoma City v. Woodworth, 89 Okl. 192, 214 P. 1077, 1079; State v. Williams, 100 Fla. 996, 130 So. 428, 430.

When used in apposition to or in contrast with the word "elector," it has but one meaning. A voter in this sense is an elector who exercises the privilege conferred upon him by the Constitution and laws of voting. He is an elector who does vote. State v. Williams, 100 Fla. 996, 130 So. 428, 432.

In a limited sense a voter is a person having the legal right to vote, sometimes called a legal voter. Aczel v. United States, C.C.A., 232 F. 652, 657; State v. Stewart, 57 Mont. 397, 188 P. 904, 907.

VOTES AND PROCEEDINGS. In the houses of parliament the clerks at the tables make brief entries of all that is actually done; and these minutes, which are printed from day to day for the use of members, are called the "votes and proceedings of parliament." From these votes and proceedings the journals of the house are subsequently prepared, by making the entries at greater length. Brown.

VOTING BY BALLOT. The term is used to distinguish open voting from secret voting. The privilege of secrecy is of the essence of "voting by ballot." Smith & Son v. MacAulay, Vt., 196 A. 281, 283.

VOTING TRUST. One created by an agreement between a group of the stockholders of a corporation and the trustee, or by a group of identical agreements between individual stockholders and a common trustee, whereby it is provided that for a term of years, or for a period contingent upon a certain event, or until the agreement is terminated, control over the stock owned by such stockholders, either for certain purposes or for all, shall be lodged in the trustee, with or without a reservation to the owner or persons designated by them of the power to direct how such control shall be used. Alderman v. Alderman, 178 S.C. 9, 181 S.E. 897, 105 A.L.R. 102. A device whereby two or more persons, owning stock with voting powers, divorce voting rights thereof from ownership, retaining to all intents and purposes the latter in themselves and transferring the former to trustees in whom voting rights of all depositors in the trust are pooled. Peyton v. William C. Peyton Corporation, Del.Ch., 194 A. 106, 111.

Agreement accumulating several owners' stock in hands of one or more persons in trust for voting purposes in order to control corporate business and affairs. It differs from proxy or reciprocal proxy in that it does not make either party the other's agent. Bankers' Fire & Marine Ins. Co. v. Sloss, 229 Ala. 26, 155 So. 371.

VOTUM. Lat. A vow or promise. *Dies votorum*, the wedding day. Fleta l. 1, c. 4.

VOUCH. To call upon; to call in to warranty; to call upon the grantor or warrantor to defend the title to an estate.

To vouch is to call upon, rely on, or quote as an authority. Thus, in the old writers, to vouch a case or report is to quote it as an authority. Co.Litt. 70*a*.

VOUCHEE. In common recoveries, the person who is called to warrant or defend the title is called the "vouchee." 2 Bouv. Inst. no. 2093.

Common Vouchee

In common recoveries, the person who is vouched to warranty. In this fictitious proceeding the crier of the court usually performs the office of a common vouchee. 2 Bl.Comm. 358; 2 Bouv. Inst. n. 2093.

VOUCHER. A receipt, acquittance, or release, which may serve as evidence of payment or discharge of a debt, or to certify the correctness of accounts. An account-book containing the acquittances or receipts showing the accountant's discharge of his obligations. Whitwell v. Willard, 1 Metc. (Mass.) 218. When used in connection with disbursement of money, a written or printed instrument in the nature of a bill of particulars, account, receipt, or acquittance, that shows on its face the fact, authority, and purpose of disbursement. Robertson's Guardian v. Fidelity & Casualty Co. of New York, 227 Ky. 114, 12 S.W.2d 298, 300.

In Old Conveyancing

The person on whom the tenant calls to defend the title to the land, because he warranted the title to him at the time of the original purchase.

VOUCHER TO WARRANTY. The calling one who has warranted lands, by the party warranted, to come and defend the suit for him. Co.Litt. 101*b*.

VOX EMISSA VOLAT; LITERA SCRIPTA MANET. The spoken word flies; the written letter remains. Broom, Max. 666.

VOX SIGNATA. In Scotch practice. An emphatic or essential word. 2 Alis.Crim.Pr. 280.

VOYAGE. In maritime law. The passing of a vessel by sea from one place, port, or country to another. The term is held to include the enterprise entered upon, and not merely the route. Friend v. Insurance Co., 113 Mass. 326.

A voyage commences only when the vessel breaks ground or leaves her moorings in complete readiness for sailing and proceeding out to sea destined for her next port of call. The Willowpool, D.C.N.Y., 12 F.Supp. 96, 100.

Foreign Voyage

A voyage to some port or place within the territory of a foreign nation. The *terminus* of a voyage determines its character. If it be within the limits of a foreign jurisdiction, it is a foreign voyage, and not otherwise. Taber v. United States, 1 Story, 1, Fed.Cas.No.13,722; The Three Brothers, 23 Fed.Cas. 1,162.

Voyage Insured

In insurance law. A transit at sea from the *terminus a quo* to the *terminus ad quem*, in a prescribed course of navigation, which is never set out in any policy, but virtually forms parts of all policies, and is as binding on the parties thereto as though it were minutely detailed. 1 Arn. Ins. 333.

Voyage Policy

See Policy of Insurance.

VRAIC. Seaweed. It is used in great quantities by the inhabitants of Jersey and Guernsey for manure, and also for fuel by the poorer classes.

VS. An abbreviation for *versus*, (against,) constantly used in legal proceedings, and especially in entitling cases.

VULGAR. Lack of cultivation or refinement. Darnell v. State, 72 Tex.Cr.R. 271, 161 S.W. 971.

VULGARIS OPINIO EST DUPLEX, VIZ., ORTA INTER GRAVES ET DISCRETOS, QUÆ MULTUM VERITATIS HABET, ET OPINIO ORTA INTER LEVES ET VULGARES HOMINES ABSQUE SPECIE VERITATIS. 4 Coke 107. Common opinion is of two kinds, viz., that which arises among grave and discreet men, which has much truth in it, and that which arises among light and common men, without any appearance of truth.

VULGARIS PURGATIO. Lat. In old English law. Common purgation; a name given to the trial by *ordeal*, to distinguish it from the canonical purgation, which was by the oath of the party. 4 Bl.Comm. 342.

VULGO CONCEPTI. Lat. In the civil law. Spurious children; bastards.

VULGO QUÆSITI. Lat. In the civil law. Spurious children; literally, gotten from the people; the offspring of promiscuous cohabitation, who are considered as having no father. Inst. 3, 4, 3; Inst. 3, 5, 4.

W

W. As an abbreviation, this letter frequently stands for "William," (king of England,) "Westminster," "west," or "western."

W. D. An abbreviation for "Western District."

WABBLE. To vacillate or sway unsteadily from side to side; to vacillate or show unsteadiness; to move or move along with an irregular rocking or staggering motion or unsteadily from one side to the other. Meadows v. State, 186 Ga. 592, 199 S.E. 133, 135.

WACREOUR. L. Fr. A vagabond, or vagrant. Britt. c. 29.

WADIA. A pledge. See Vadium; Fides Facta.

WADSET. In Scotch law. The old term for a mortgage. A right by which lands or other heritable subjects are impignorated by the proprietor to his creditor in security of his debt. Wadsets are usually drawn in the form of mutual contracts, in which one party sells the land, and the other grants the right of reversion. Ersk. Inst. 2, 8, 3.

WADSETTER. In Scotch law. A creditor to whom a wadset is made, corresponding to a mortgagee.

WAFTORS. Conductors of vessels at sea. Cowell.

WAGA. In old English law. A weight; a measure of cheese, salt, wool, etc., containing two hundred and fifty-six pounds avoirdupois. Cowell; Spelman.

WAGE. In old English practice. To give security for the performance of a thing. Cowell.

WAGE EARNER. Within Bankruptcy Act exempting wage earners from involuntary bankruptcy proceedings must have as his paramount occupation the earning of salary or wages, indicia of wage earning being whether earner depends on his wages for his subsistence and whether wage earning is his paramount occupation. Bankr.Act §§ 1(27), 4b, 11 U.S.C.A. §§ 1(27), 22(b). In re Gainfort, D.C.Cal., 14 F.Supp. 788, 791.

WAGER. A contract by which two or more parties agree that a certain sum of money or other thing shall be paid or delivered to one of them or that they shall gain or lose on the happening of an uncertain event or upon the ascertainment of a fact in dispute, where the parties have no interest in the event except that arising from the possibility of such gain or loss. H. Seay & Co. v. Moore, Tex.Com.App., 261 S.W. 1013, 1014; Young v. Stephenson, 82 Okl. 239, 200 P. 225, 228, 24 A.L.R. 978; Odle v. State, 139 Tex.Cr.R. 288, 139 S.W.2d 595, 597. See, also, Bet.

It was said that contract giving one party or the other an option to carry out the transaction or not at pleasure is not invalid as a "wager." Palmer v. Love, 18 Tenn. App. 579, 80 S.W.2d 100, 105; but if, under guise of contract of sale, real intent of both parties is merely to speculate in rise or fall of prices and property is not to be delivered, but at time fixed for delivery one party is to pay difference between contract price and market price, transaction is invalid as "wager." Baucum & Kimball v. Garrett Mercantile Co., 188 La. 728, 178 So. 256, 259, 260.

WAGER OF BATTEL. The trial by wager of battel was a species of trial introduced into England, among other Norman customs, by William the Conqueror, in which the person accused fought with his accuser, under the apprehension that Heaven would give the victory to him who was in the right. 3 Bl.Comm. 337. It was abolished by St. 59 Geo. III., c. 46.

WAGER OF LAW. In old practice. The giving of *gage* or sureties by a defendant in an action of debt that at a certain day assigned he would *make his law*; that is, would take an oath in open court that he did not owe the debt, and at the same time bring with him eleven neighbors, (called "compurgators,") who should avow upon their oaths that they believed in their consciences that he said the truth. Glanv. lib. 1, c. 9, 12; Bract. fol. 156*b*; Britt. c. 27; 3 Bl.Comm. 343; Cro.Eliz. 818.

WAGER POLICY. See Policy of Insurance.

WAGERING CONTRACT. One in which the parties stipulate that they shall gain or lose, upon the happening of an uncertain event, in which they have no interest except that arising from the possibility of such gain or loss. Fareira v. Gabell, 89 Pa. 89.

WAGERING GAIN. The share of each, where individuals carrying on business in partnership make gains in wagering transactions. Jennings v. Commissioner of Internal Revenue, C.C.A.Tex., 110 F.2d 945, 946.

WAGES. A compensation given to a hired person for his or her services; the compensation agreed upon by a master to be paid to a servant, or any other person hired to do work or business for him. Ciarla v. Solvay Process Co., 172 N.Y.S. 426, 428, 184 App.Div. 629; Cookes v. Lymperis, 178 Mich. 299, 144 N.W. 514, 515; Phœnix Iron Co. v. Roanoke Bridge Co., 169 N.C. 512, 86 S.E. 184, 185. Every form of remuneration payable for a given period to an individual for personal services, including salaries, commissions, vacation pay, dismissal wages, bonuses and reasonable value of board, rent, housing, lodging, payments in kind, tips, and any other similar advantage received from the individual's employer or directly with respect to work for him. Ernst v. Industrial Commission, 246 Wis. 205, 16 N.W.2d 867.

In a limited sense the word "wage" means pay given for labor usually manual or mechanical at short stated intervals as distinguished from salary, but in general the word means that which is pledged or paid for work or other services; hire; pay. In its legal sense, the word "wages" means the price paid for labor, reward of labor, specified sum for a given time of service or a fixed sum for a specified piece of work. In re Hollingsworth's Estate, 37 Cal. App.2d 432, 99 P.2d 599, 600, 602.

Maritime Law

The compensation allowed to seamen for their services on board a vessel during a voyage.

Political Economy

The reward paid, whether in money or goods, to human exertion, considered as a factor in the production of wealth, for its co-operation in the process.

"Three factors contribute to the production of commodities,—nature, labor, and capital. Each must have a share of the product as its reward, and this share, if it is just, must be proportionate to the several contributions. The share of the natural agents is rent; the share of labor, *wages*; the share of capital, interest. The clerk receives a salary; the lawyer and doctor, fees; the manufacturer, profits. Salary, fees, and profits are so many forms of wages for services rendered." De Laveleye, Pol. Econ.

WAGON. A kind of four-wheel vehicle, especially one used for carrying freight or merchandise. McMullen v. Shields, 96 Mont. 191, 29 P.2d 652, 654. A vehicle moving on wheels and usually drawn by horses. The word wagon is a generic term and includes other species of vehicle by whatever name they may be called. An automobile is a vehicle propelled by power generated within itself, used to convey passengers or materials, and in a general sense is a wagon. Strycker v. Richardson, 77 Pa.Super.Ct. 252, 255, but see contra United States v. One Automobile, D.C. Mont., 237 F. 891, 892; Whitney v. Welnitz, 153 Minn. 162, 190 N.W. 57, 28 A.L.R. 68. For "Farm Wagon," see that title.

WAGONAGE. Money paid for carriage in a wagon.

WAGONWAY. That part of a street ordinarily used for the passage of vehicles within the curb lines. Delaware, L. & W. R. Co. v. Chiara, C.C.A. N.J., 95 F.2d 663, 666.

WAIF. Waifs are goods found, but claimed by nobody; that of which every one waives the claim. Also, goods stolen and waived, or thrown away by the thief in his flight, for fear of being apprehended. Wharton.

Waifs are to be distinguished from *bona fugitiva*, which are the goods of the felon himself, which he abandons in his flight from justice. Brown. See People v. Kaatz, 3 Parker, Cr.R. (N.Y.) 138; Hall v. Gildersleeve, 36 N.J.L. 237.

WAINABLE. In old records. That may be plowed or manured; tillable. Cowell; Blount.

WAINAGE. In old English law. The team and instruments of husbandry belonging to a countryman, and especially to a villein who was required to perform agricultural services.

WAINAGIUM. What is necessary to the farmer for the cultivation of his land. Barring. Ob.St. 12; Magna Carta, c. 14. Instruments of husbandry. 1 Poll. & Maitl. 399.

WAIN-BOTE. In feudal and old English law. Timber for wagons or carts.

WAITING CLERKS. Officers whose duty it formerly was to wait in attendance upon the court of chancery. The office was abolished in 1842 by St. 5 & 6 Vict. c. 103. Mozley & Whitley.

WAIVE, *v.* To abandon or throw away; as when a thief, in his flight, throws aside the stolen goods, in order to facilitate his escape, he is technically said to *waive* them.

In modern law, to abandon, throw away, renounce, repudiate, or surrender a claim, a privilege, a right, or the opportunity to take advantage of some defect, irregularity, or wrong. See Brigham Young University v. Industrial Commission of Utah, 74 Utah 349, 279 P. 889, 893, 65 A.L.R. 152.

A person is said to waive a benefit when he renounces or disclaims it, and he is said to waive a tort or injury when he abandons the remedy which the law gives him for it. Sweet.

In order for one to "waive" a right, he must do it knowingly and be possessed of the facts. Barnhill v. Rubin, D.C.Tex., 46 F.Supp. 963, 966.

WAIVE, *n.* In old English law. A woman outlawed. The term is, as it were, the feminine of "outlaw," the latter being always applied to a man; "waive," to a woman. Cowell.

WAIVER. The intentional or voluntary relinquishment of a known right, Lehigh Val. R. Co. v. Ins. Co., 172 F. 364, 97 C.C.A. 62; Vermillion v. Prudential Ins. Co. of America, 230 Mo.App. 993, 93 S.W.2d 45, 51; or such conduct as warrants an inference of the relinquishment of such right, Rand v. Morse, C.C.A.Mo., 289 F. 339, 344; Dexter Yarn Co. v. American Fabrics Co., 102 Conn. 529, 129 A. 527, 537; Gibbs v. Bergh, 51 S.D. 432, 214 N.W. 838, 841; or when one dispenses with the performance of something he is entitled to exact or when one in possession of any right, whether conferred by law or by contract, with full knowledge of the material facts, does or forbears to do something the doing of which or the failure of forbearance to do which is inconsistent with the right, or his intention to rely upon it. Estoup Signs v. Frank Lower, Inc., La.App., 10 So.2d 642, 645. The renunciation, repudiation, abandonment, or surrender of some claim, right, privilege, or of the opportunity to take advantage of some defect, irregularity, or wrong. Christenson v. Carleton, 37 A. 226, 69 Vt. 91; Shaw v. Spencer, 100 Mass. 395, 97 Am.Dec. 107, 1 Am.Rep. 115; Smiley v. Barker, 28 C.C.A. 9, 83 F. 684; Boos v. Ewing, 17 Ohio 523, 49 Am.Dec. 478. A doctrine resting upon an equitable principle, which courts of law will recognize. Atlas Life Ins. Co. v. Schrimsher, 179 Okl. 643, 66 P.2d 944, 948. See, also, Estoppel.

"Waiver" is essentially unilateral, resulting as legal consequence from some act or conduct of party against whom it operates, and no act of party in whose favor it is made is necessary to complete it. Coleman Production Credit Ass'n v. Mahan, Tex.Civ.App., 168 S.W.2d 903, 904. And may be shown by acts and conduct and sometimes by nonaction. Concrete Engineering Co. v. Grande Bldg. Co., 230 Mo.App. 443, 86 S.W.2d 595, 608.

Waiver is distinguished from "estoppel" in that in "waiver" the essential element is an actual intent to abandon or surrender a right, while in "estoppel" such intent is immaterial; the necessary condition being the deception to his injury of the other party by the conduct of the one estopped. Insurance Co. of North America v. Williams, 42 Ariz. 331, 26 P.2d 117, 119. And "estoppel," may result though party estopped did not intend to lose any existing rights. Boyce v. Toke Point Oyster Co., 145 Or. 114, 25 P.2d 930.

Insurance Law

Substance of doctrine of "waiver" in insurance law is that if insurer, with knowledge of facts which would bar existing primary liability, recognizes such primary liability by treating policy as in force, it will not thereafter be allowed to plead such facts to avoid its primary liability. Protective Life Ins. Co. v. Cole, 230 Ala. 450, 161 So. 818, 819.

Express Waiver

The voluntary, intentional relinquishment of a known right. Dickert v. Aetna Life Ins. Co., 176 S.C. 476, 180 S.E. 462.

Implied Waiver

A waiver is implied where one party has pursued such a course of conduct with reference to the other party as to evidence an intention to waive his rights or the advantage to which he may be entitled, or where the conduct pursued is inconsistent with any other honest intention than an intention of such waiver, provided that the other party concerned has been induced by such conduct to act upon the belief that there has been a waiver, and has incurred trouble or expense thereby. Astritch v. German-American Ins. Co., C.C.A.Pa., 131 F. 20, 65 C.C.A. 251; Roumage v. Insurance Co., 13 N.J.L. 124.

To make out a case of implied "waiver" of a legal right, there must be a clear, unequivocal and decisive act of the party showing such purpose, or acts amounting to an estoppel on his part. Rosenthal v. New York Life Ins. Co., C.C.A.Mo., 99 F.2d 578, 579.

Waiver by Election of Remedies, Doctrine of

Doctrine applies if there exist two or more coexisting remedies between which there is right of election, inconsistency as to such available remedies, and actual bringing of action or doing some other decisive act, with knowledge of facts, whereby party electing indicates his choice between such inconsistent remedies. Hertz v. Mills, D.C.Md., 10 F.Supp. 979, 981.

Waiver of Exemption

A clause inserted in a note, bond, lease, etc., expressly waiving the benefit of the laws exempting limited amounts of personal property from levy and sale on judicial process, so far as concerns the enforcement of the particular debt or obligation. Mitchell v. Coates, 47 Pa. 203; Wyman v. Gay, 90 Me. 36, 37 A. 325, 60 Am.St.Rep. 238; Howard B. & L. Ass'n v. Philadelphia & R. R. Co., 102 Pa. 223.

Waiver of Immunity

A means authorized by statutes by which a witness, in advance of giving testimony or producing evidence, may renounce the fundamental right guaranteed to him by constitutions, that no person shall be compelled in any criminal case to be a witness against himself. In re Grae, 282 N.Y. 428, 26 N.E.2d 963, 966.

Waiver of Protest

An agreement by the indorser of a note or bill to be bound in his character of indorser without the formality of a protest in case of non-payment, or, in the case of paper which cannot or is not required to be protested, dispensing with the necessity of a demand and notice. First Nat. Bank v. Falkenhan, 94 Cal. 141, 29 P. 866; Coddington v. Davis, 1 N.Y. 190.

Waiver of Tort

The election, by an injured party, for purposes of redress, to treat the facts as establishing an implied contract, which he may enforce, instead of an injury by fraud or wrong, for the committing of which he may demand damages, compensatory or exemplary. Harway v. Mayor, etc., of City of New York, 1 Hun (N.Y.) 630.

WAKEMAN. The chief magistrate of Ripon, in Yorkshire.

WAKENING. In Scotch law. The revival of an action. A process by which an action that has lain over and not been insisted in for a year and a day, and thus technically said to have "fallen asleep," is wakened, or put in motion again. 1 Forb. Inst. pt. 4, p. 170; Ersk. Prin. 4, 1, 33.

WALAPAUZ. In old Lombardic law. The disguising the head or face, with the intent of committing a theft.

WALENSIS. In old English law. A Welshman.

WALESCHERY. The being a Welshman. Spelman.

WALISCUS. In Saxon law. A servant, or any ministerial officer. Cowell.

WALKERS. Foresters who have the care of a certain space of ground assigned to them. Cowell.

WALL. An erection of stone, brick, or other material, raised to some height, and intended for purposes of security or inclosure. In law, this term occurs in such compounds as "ancient wall," "party-wall," "division-wall," etc.

Common Wall

A party wall; one which has been built at the common expense of the two owners whose properties are contiguous, or a wall built by one party in which the other has acquired a common right. Campbell v. Mesier, 4 Johns. Ch. (N.Y.) 342, 8 Am. Dec. 570.

WALLIA. In old English law. A wall; a sea-wall; a mound, bank, or wall erected in marshy districts as a protection against the sea. Spelman.

WAMPUM. Beads made of shells, used as money by the North American Indians, and which continued current in New York as late as 1693.

WAND OF PEACE. In Scotch law. A wand or staff carried by the messenger of a court, and which, when deforced, (that is, hindered from executing process,) he breaks, as a symbol of the deforcement, and protest for remedy of law. 2 Forb.Inst. 207.

WANDER. To ramble here and there without any certain course. Guidoni v. Wheeler, C.C.A. Alaska, 230 F. 93, 96; Ex parte Karnstrom, 297 Mo. 384, 249 S.W. 595, 596.

WANLASS. An ancient customary tenure of lands; *i. e.*, to drive deer to a stand that the lord may have a shot. Blount, Ten. 140.

WANT OF CONSIDERATION. Embraces transactions or instances where no consideration was intended to pass. In re Conrad's Estate, 333 Pa. 561, 3 A.2d 697, 699. Ranschenbach v. McDaniel's Estate, 122 W.Va. 632, 11 S.E.2d 852, 854. For distinction between "failure of consideration" and "want of consideration," see Failure of Consideration.

WANT OF JURISDICTION. A want of authority to exercise in a particular manner a power which the board or tribunal has, the doing of something in excess of authority possessed. Evans v. Superior Court in and for City and County of San Francisco, 14 Cal.2d 563, 96 P.2d 107, 116.

WANT OF REPAIR. As to highways, anything in the state or condition of the highway which renders it unsafe or inconvenient for ordinary travel. Adams v. Town of Bolton, Mass., 297 Mass. 459, 9 N.E.2d 562, 565, 111 A.L.R. 856.

WANTAGE. In marine insurance. Ullage; deficiency in the contents of a cask or vessel caused by leaking. Cory v. Boylston Fire & Marine Ins. Co., 107 Mass. 140, 9 Am.Rep. 14.

WANTON. Reckless, heedless, malicious, characterized by extreme recklessness, foolhardiness, recklessly disregardful of the rights or safety of others or of consequences. In re Wegner, C.C.A. Ill., 88 F.2d 899, 902; Cover v. Hershey Transit Co., 290 Pa. 551, 139 A. 266, 268.

WANTON ACT. One done in reckless disregard of the rights of others, evincing a reckless indifference to consequences to the life, or limb, or health, or reputation or property rights of another, and is more than negligence, more than gross negligence, and is such conduct as indicates a reckless disregard of the just rights or safety of others or of the consequences of action, equivalent in its results to willful misconduct. Ziman v. Whitley, 110 Conn. 108, 147 A. 370, 372.

Ill will is not a necessary element of a wanton act, but to constitute an act "wanton" party doing act or failing to act must be conscious of his conduct and, though having no intent to injure, must be conscious from his knowledge of surrounding circumstances and conditions that his conduct will naturally and probably result in injury. Proud v. Adelberg, 290 Ill.App. 319, 8 N.E.2d 678, 681.

WANTON ACTS AND OMISSIONS. Those of such character or done in such manner or under such circumstances as to indicate that a person of ordinary intelligence actuated by normal and natural concern for the welfare and safety of his fellowmen who might be affected by them could not be guilty of them unless wholly indifferent to their probable injurious effect or consequences. Pupke v. Pupke, 102 Colo. 337, 79 P.2d 290, 292.

WANTON AND FURIOUS DRIVING. An offence against public health, which under the stat. 24 & 25 Vict. c. 100, s. 56, is punishable as a misdemeanor by fine or imprisonment. In this country the offence is usually provided for by state, county, or municipal legislation.

WANTON AND RECKLESS MISCONDUCT. Occurs when a person, with no intent to cause harm, intentionally performs an act so unreasonable and dangerous that he knows, or should know, that it is highly probable that harm will result. Donnelly v. Southern Pac. Co., 18 Cal.2d 863, 118 P.2d 465, 469, 470.

WANTON INJURY. Injury produced by conscious and intentional wrongful act, or omission of known duty with reckless indifference to consequences. Duke v. Gaines, 224 Ala. 519, 140 So. 600, 601. It must be predicated upon actual knowledge of another's peril and a failure to take available preventative action knowing that such failure will probably result in injury. Rainey v. State, 31 Ala.App. 271, 17 So.2d 683, 686.

WANTON MISCONDUCT. Act or failure to act, when there is a duty to act, in reckless disregard of rights of another, coupled with a consciousness that injury is a probable consequence of act or omission. Swain v. American Mut. Liability Ins. Co., C.C.A.La., 134 F.2d 886, 887. A conduct manifesting disposition to perversity. Universal Concrete Pipe Co. v. Bassett, 130 Ohio St. 567, 200 N.E. 843, 846, 119 A.L.R. 646.

WANTON NEGLIGENCE. Heedless and reckless disregard for another's rights with consciousness that act or omission to act may result in injury to another. Craig v. Stagner, 159 Tenn. 511, 19 S.W.2d 234, 236.

WANTONNESS. Conscious doing of some act or the omission of some duty with knowledge of existing conditions and consciousness that, from the act or omission, injury will likely result to another. Bedwell v. De Bolt, 221 Ind. 600, 50 N.E.2d 875, 877. First Nat. Bank v. Sanders, 227 Ala. 313, 149 So. 848, 849. Conscious failure by one charged with a duty to exercise due care and diligence to prevent an injury after the discovery of the peril, or under circumstances where he is charged with a knowledge of such peril, and being conscious of the inevitable or probable results of such failure. Stout v. Gallemore, 138 Kan. 385, 26 P.2d 573. A reckless or intentional disregard of the property, rights, or safety of others, implying, actively, a willingness to injure and disregard of the consequences to others, and, passively, more than mere negligence, that is, a conscious and intentional disregard of duty. Brasington v. South Bound R. Co., 40 S.E. 665, 62 S.C. 325, 89 Am.St.Rep. 905; Louisville & N. R. Co. v. Webb, 12 So. 374, 97 Ala. 308; Walldren Express & Van Co. v. Krug, 291 Ill. 472, 126 N.E. 97, 98.

WAPENTAKE. In English law. A local division of the country; the name is in use north of the Trent to denote a hundred. The derivation of the name is said to be from "weapon" and "take," and indicates that the division was originally of a military character. Cowell; Brown.

Also a hundred court.

WAR. Hostile contention by means of armed forces, carried on between nations, states, or rulers, or between parties in the same nation or state. Gitlow v. Kiely, D.C.N.Y., 44 F.2d 227, 233. A contest by force between two or more nations, carried on for any purpose or armed conflict of sovereign powers or declared and open hostilities, or the state of nations among whom there is an interruption of pacific relations, and a general contention by force, authorized by the sovereign. West v. Palmetto State Life Ins. Co., 202 S.C. 422, 25 S.E. 2d 475, 477, 478, 145 A.L.R. 1461.

"War" does not exist merely because of an armed attack by the military forces of another nation until it is a condition recognized or accepted by political authority of government which is attacked, either through an actual declaration of war or other acts demonstrating such position. Savage v. Sun Life Assur. Co. of Canada, D.C.La., 57 F.Supp. 620, 621.

Articles of War

See Article.

Civil War

An internecine war. A war carried on between opposing masses of citizens of the same country or nation. Before the declaration of independence, the war between Great Britain and the United Colonies was a civil war; but instantly on that event the war changed its nature, and became a public war between independent states. Hubbard v. Exp. Co., 10 R.I. 244; Brown v. Hiatt, 4 F.Cas. 387; Prize Cases, 2 Black, 667, 17 L.Ed. 459; Central R. & B. Co. v. Ward, 37 Ga. 515.

Imperfect War

See Perfect War.

Laws of War

This term denotes a branch of public international law, and comprises the body of rules and principles observed by civilized nations for the regulation of matters inherent in, or incidental to, the conduct of a public war; such, for example, as the relations of neutrals and belligerents, blockades, captures, prizes, truces and armistices, capitulations, prisoners, and declarations of war and peace.

Mixed War

A mixed war is one which is made on one side by public authority, and on the other by mere private persons. People v. McLeod, 1 Hill (N.Y.) 377, 415, 37 Am.Dec. 328.

Perfect War

Where whole nation is at war with another whole nation, but when the hostilities are limited as respects places, persons, and things, the war is termed "imperfect war." Bas v. Tingy, 4 Dall. 37, 40, 1 L.Ed. 731.

Private War

One between private persons, lawfully exerted by way of defense, but otherwise unknown in civil society. People v. McLeod, 25 Wend. (N.Y.) 576, 37 Am.Dec. 328.

Public War

Every contention by force, between two nations, in external matters, under the authority of their respective governments. Prize Cases, 2 Black, 666, 17 L.Ed. 459; People v. McLeod, 25 Wend. (N.Y.) 483, 37 Am.Dec. 328.

Solemn War

A war made in form by public declaration; a war solemnly declared by one state against another. Bas v. Tingy, 4 Dall. 37, 40, 1 L.Ed. 731.

War Office

In England. A department of state from which the sovereign issues orders to his forces. Wharton.

WAR POWER of federal government is the power to wage war successfully. Brown v. Wright, C. C.A.W.Va., 137 F.2d 484, 489; United States v. Maviglia, D.C.N.J., 52 F.Supp. 946, 947. It embraces every aspect of national defense, including protection of war materials as well as members of armed forces from injury and danger. Schueller v. Drum, D.C.Pa., 51 F.Supp. 383, 387; but direct interference with liberty and property and abridgement of constitutional guaranties of freedom can be justified under the "war power" only where the danger to the government is real, impending and imminent. Schueller v. Drum, D.C. Pa., 51 F.Supp. 383, 387.

WARABI. Dried wild ferns from Japan, used as a vegetable in a manner similar to spinach. Nippon Co. v. U. S., 12 Ct.Cust.App. 548, 549.

WARD. Guarding; care; charge; as, the ward of a castle; so in the phrase "watch and ward."

A division in the city of London committed to the special ward (guardianship) of an alderman.

A territorial division is adopted in most American cities by which the municipality is separated into a number of precincts or districts called "wards" for purposes of police, sanitary regulations, prevention of fires, elections, etc. See State ex rel. Witkowski v. Gora, 195 Wis. 515, 218 N.W. 837, 839.

A corridor, room, or other division of a prison, hospital, or asylum.

A person, especially an infant, placed by authority of law under the care of a guardian.

Ward-corn. In old English law. The duty of keeping watch and *ward*, with a *horn* to blow upon any occasion of surprise. 1 Mon.Ang. 976.

Ward-fegh. Sax. In old records. Ward-fee; the value of a ward, or the money paid to the lord for his redemption from wardship. Blount.

Ward-holding. In old Scotch law. Tenure by military service; the proper feudal tenure of Scotland. Abolished by St. 20 Geo. II. c. 50. Ersk. Prin. 2, 4, 1.

Ward-in-chancery. An infant who is under the superintendence of the chancellor.

Ward-mote. In English law. A court kept in every ward in London, commonly called the "ward-mote court," or "inquest." Cowell.

Ward-patient. One who pays for his hospital care but receives free of charge medical and surgical care from members of the hospital staff. Sheridan v. Quarrier, 127 Conn. 279, 16 A.2d 479, 480.

Ward-penny. In old English law. Money paid to the sheriff or castellains, for the duty of watching and warding a castle. Spelman.

Ward-staff. In old records. A constable's or watchman's staff. Cowell.

Ward-wit. In old English law. Immunity or exemption from the duty or service of ward, or from contributing to such service. Spelman. Exemption from amercement for not finding a man to do ward. Fleta, lib. 1, c. 47, § 16.

Wardage. Money paid and contributed to watch and ward. Domesday.

Wards of admiralty. Seamen are sometimes thus designated, because, in view of their general improvidence and rashness, and though they are not technically incapable of contracting, their contracts are treated like those of fiduciaries and beneficiaries, and if there is any inequality in terms or any disproportion in the bargain or any sacrifice of rights of seamen which are not compensated by extraordinary benefits, the judicial interpretation of the transaction is that the bargain is unjust and that pro tanto, the bargain ought to be set aside as inequitable. See Garrett v. Moore-McCormack Co., Pa., 63 S.Ct. 246, 251, 317 U.S. 239, 87 L.Ed. 239.

Wards of court. Infants and persons of unsound mind. Davis' Committee v. Loney, 290 Ky. 644, 162 S.W.2d 189, 190. Their rights must be guarded jealously. Montgomery v. Erie R. Co., C.C.A.N.J., 97 F.2d 289, 292.

Wardship. In military tenures, the right of the lord to have custody, as guardian, of the body and lands of the infant heir, without any account of profits, until he was twenty-one or she sixteen. In socage the guardian was accountable for profits; and he was not the lord, but the nearest relative to whom the inheritance could not descend, and the wardship ceased at fourteen. In copyholds, the lord was the guardian, but was perhaps accountable for profits. Stim. Gloss. See 2 Bl. Comm. 67.

Wardship in chivalry. An incident to the tenure of knight-service.

Wardship in copyholds. The lord is guardian of his infant tenant by special custom.

WARDA. L. Lat.

In old English law. Ward; guard; protection; keeping; custody. Spelman.

A ward; an infant under wardship. Spelman.

In old Scotch law. An award; the judgment of a court.

WARDEN. A guardian; a keeper. This is the name given to various officers.

WARDEN OF THE CINQUE PORTS. In English law. The title of the governor or presiding officer of the Cinque Ports, (*q. v.*).

WARDS AND LIVERIES. In English law. The title of a court of record, established in the reign of Henry VIII. See Court of Wards and Liveries.

WARECTARE. L. Lat. In old English law. To fallow ground; or plow up land (designed for wheat) in the spring, in order to let it lie fallow for the better improvement. Fleta, lib. 2, c. 33; Cowell.

WAREHOUSE. A place adapted to the reception and storage of goods and merchandise. State v. Huffman, 136 Mo. 58, 37 S.W. 797; Owen v. Boyle, 22 Me. 47; Carter v. Bauman, C.C.A.Cal., 19 F.2d 855, 856. The term may include any structure used to hold goods, stores or wares temporarily or for a length of time. In re Miller Land & Livestock Co., D.C.Mont., 56 F.Supp. 34, 35.

WAREHOUSE BOOK. A book used by merchants to contain an account of the quantities of goods received, shipped, and remaining in stock.

WAREHOUSE RECEIPT. A receipt given by a warehouseman for goods received by him on storage in his warehouse. Merchants' Warehouse Co. v. McClain, C.C.Pa., 112 F. 789; Collins v. Ralli, 20 Hun (N.Y.) 255; Vannett v. Reilly-Herz Automobile Co., 42 N.D. 607, 173 N.W. 466, 467. It is evidence of title to goods thereby represented. Woldson v. Davenport Mill & Elevator Co., 169 Wash. 298, 13 P.2d 478, 480.

WAREHOUSE SYSTEM. A system of public stores or warehouses, established or authorized by law, called "bonded warehouses," in which an importer may deposit goods imported, in the custody of the revenue officers, paying storage, but not being required to pay the customs duties until the goods are finally removed for consumption in the home market, and with the privilege of withdrawing the goods from store for the purpose of re-exportation without paying any duties.

WAREHOUSEMAN. One engaged in business of receiving and storing goods of others for compensation or profit; person who receives goods and merchandise to be stored in his warehouse for hire; one who, as a business and for hire, keeps and stores goods of others. State ex rel. and for Use and Benefit of Cawrse v. American Surety Co. of New York, 148 Or. 1, 35 P.2d 487, 491.

The business is public or private as it may be conducted for storage of goods of general public or for those of certain persons. Tobacco Growers' Co-op. Ass'n v. Danville Warehouse Co., 144 Va. 456, 132 S.E. 482, 486; State, to Use of Hubbard & Moffitt Commission Co. v. Cochrane, 264 Mo. 581, 175 S.W. 599, 600.

WARNING. A pointing out of danger. Also a protest against incurring it. Keller v. Banks, 130 Me. 397, 156 A. 817, 821.

The purpose of a "warning" is to apprise a party of the existence of danger of which he is not aware to enable him to protect himself against it, and where the party is aware of the danger, the warning will serve no useful purpose and is unnecessary, and there is no duty to warn against risks which are open and obvious. Wiseman v. Northern Pac. Ry. Co., 214 Minn. 101, 7 N.W.2d 672, 675.

Under the old practice of the English court of probate, was a notice given by a registrar of the principal registry to a person who had entered a *caveat*, warning him, within six days after service, to enter an appearance to the *caveat* in the principal registry, and to set forth his interest, concluding with a notice that in default of his doing so the court would proceed to do all such acts, matters, and things as should be necessary. By the rules under the judicature acts, a writ of summons has been substituted for a warning. Sweet.

WARNISTURA. In old records. Garniture; furniture; provision. Cowell.

WARNOTH. In old English law. An ancient custom, whereby, if any tenant holding of the Castle of Dover failed in paying his rent at the day, he should forfeit double, and, for the second failure, treble, etc. Cowell.

WARP. A rope attached to some fixed point, used for moving a ship. Pub. St. Mass. 1882, p. 1297.

WARRANDICE. In Scotch law. Warranty; a clause in a charter or deed by which the grantor obliges himself that the right conveyed shall be effectual to the receiver. Ersk. Prin. 2, 3, 11. A clause whereby the grantor of a charter obliges himself to warrant or make good the thing granted to the receiver. 1 Forb. Inst. pt. 2, p. 113.

Absolute Warrandice

A warranting or assuring of property against all mankind. It is, in effect, a covenant of title.

Real Warrandice

An infeoffment of one tenament given in security of another.

Simple Warrandice

An obligation to warrant or secure from all subsequent or future deeds of the grantor. A simple warranty against the grantor's own acts. Whishaw.

WARRANT, ***v.***

In contracts. To engage or promise that a certain fact or state of facts, in relation to the subject-matter, is, or shall be, as it is represented to be.

In conveyancing. To assure the title to property sold, by an express covenant to that effect in the deed of conveyance. To stipulate by an express covenant that the title of a grantee shall be good, and his possession undisturbed.

WARRANT, ***n.*** 1. A writ or precept from a competent authority in pursuance of law, directing the doing of an act, and addressed to an officer or person competent to do the act, and affording him protection from damage, if he does it. People v. Wood, 71 N.Y. 376.

2. Particularly, a writ or precept issued by a magistrate, justice, or other competent authority, addressed to a sheriff, constable, or other officer, requiring him to arrest the body of a person therein named, and bring him before the magistrate or court, to answer, or to be examined, touching some offense which he is charged with having committed. See People v. Baxter, City Ct., 32 N.Y.S.2d 325, 327. See, also, Bench-Warrant; Search-Warrant.

3. An order by which the drawer authorizes one person to pay a particular sum of money. Shawnee County v. Carter, 2 Kan. 130.

4. An authority issued to a collector of taxes, empowering him to collect the taxes extended on the assessment roll, and to make distress and sale of goods or land in default of payment.

5. A command of a council, board, or official whose duty it is to pass upon the validity and determine the amount of a claim against the municipality, to the treasurer to pay money out of any funds in the municipal treasury, which are or may become available for the purpose specified, to a designated person whose claim therefor has been duly adjusted and allowed. Roe v. Roosevelt Water Conservation Dist., 41 Ariz. 197, 16 P.2d 967, 970; State v. State Board of Examiners, 74 Mont. 1, 238 P. 316, 328.

A "warrant" differs from a "bond" in that a bond is a "negotiable instrument", whereas a warrant is nonnegotiable and is subject at all times to the defenses it would be were it in the hands of the original payee, which is not the case with a negotiable bond. Adams v. McGill, Tex.Civ.App., 146 S.W.2d 332, 334.

6. In England, a dividend warrant or coupon. See Coupons.

Bench warrant. See Bench.

Death warrant. A warrant issued generally by the chief executive authority of a state, directed to the sheriff or other proper local officer or the warden of a jail, commanding him at a certain time to proceed to carry into execution a sentence of death imposed by the court upon a convicted criminal.

Distress warrant. See Distress.

Dividend warrant. In England, a coupon. See Coupons.

General warrant. A process which formerly issued from the state secretary's office in England to take up (without naming any persons) the author, printer, and publisher of such obscene and seditious libels as were specified in it. It was declared illegal and void for uncertainty by a vote of the house of commons on the 22d April, 1766. Wharton.

Land warrant. See that title.

Landlord's warrant. See Landlord.

Search warrant. See that title.

Warrant creditor. See Creditor.

Warrant in bankruptcy. A warrant issued, upon an adjudication in bankruptcy, directing the marshal to take possession of the bankrupt's property, notify creditors, etc.

Warrant of arrest. See Arrest.

Warrant of attorney. In practice. An instrument in writing, addressed to one or more attorneys therein named, authorizing them, generally, to appear in any court, or in some specified court, on behalf of the person giving it, and to confess judgment in favor of some particular person therein named, in an action of debt. It usually contains a stipulation not to bring any writ of error, or file a bill in equity, so as to delay him. 2 Burrill, Pr. 239; Treat v. Tolman, 51 C.C.A. 522, 113 F. 892. Such writing usually being given as security for obligation on which judgment was authorized, and in such procedure service of process was not essential. Bonnett-Brown Corporation v. Coble, 195 N.C. 491, 142 S.E. 772, 774.

Warrant of commitment. A written authority committing a person to custody.

Warrant of merchantability. Warranty that goods are reasonably fit for general purpose for which sold. Sperry Flour Co. v. De Moss, 141 Or. 440, 18 P.2d 242, 243, 90 A.L.R. 406.

Warrant officers. In the United States army, navy, coast and geodetic survey, coast guard, marine corps and air force, these are a class of inferior officers who hold their rank by virtue of a written warrant instead of a commission.

Warrant to sue and defend. In old practice. A special warrant from the crown, authorizing a party to appoint an attorney to sue or defend for him. 3 Bl.Comm. 25. A special authority given by a party to his attorney, to commence a suit, or to appear and defend a suit, in his behalf. These warrants are now disused, though formal entries of them upon the record were long retained in practice. 1 Burrill, Pr. 39.

WARRANTEE. A person to whom a warranty is made.

WARRANTIA CHARTÆ. In old practice. Warranty of charter. A writ which lay for one who, being enfeoffed of lands or tenements, with a clause of warranty, was afterwards impleaded in an assize or other action in which he could not vouch to warranty. In such case, it might be brought against the warrantor, to compel him to assist the tenant with a good plea or defense, or else to render damages and the value of the land, if recovered against the tenant. Cowell; 3 Bl. Comm. 300.

WARRANTIA CUSTODIÆ. An old English writ, which lay for him who was challenged to be a ward to another, in respect to land said to be holden by knight-service; which land, when it was bought by the ancestors of the ward, was warranted free from such thraldom. The writ lay against the warrantor and his heirs. Cowell.

WARRANTIA DIEI. A writ which lay for a man who, having had a day assigned him personally to appear in court in any action in which he was sued, was in the mean time, by commandment, employed in the king's service, so that he could not come at the day assigned. It was directed to the justices that they might not record him in default for that day. Cowell.

WARRANTIZARE. In old conveyancing. To warrant; to bind one's self, by covenant in a deed of conveyance, to defend the grantee in his title and possession.

WARRANTIZARE EST DEFENDERE ET ACQUIETARE TENENTEM, QUI WARRANTUM VOCAVIT, IN SEISINA SUA; ET TENENS DE RE WARRANTI EXCAMBIUM HABEBIT AD VALENTIAM. Co.Litt. 365. To warrant is to defend and insure in peace the tenant, who calls for warranty, in his seisin; and the tenant in warranty will have an exchange in proportion to its value.

WARRANTOR. One who makes a warranty. Shep. Touch. 181.

WARRANTOR POTEST EXCIPERE QUOD QUERENS NON TENET TERRAM DE QUA PETIT WARRANTIAM, ET QUOD DONUM FUIT INSUFFICIENS. Hob. 21. A warrantor may object that the complainant does not hold the land of which he seeks the warranty, and that the gift was insufficient.

WARRANTY. A promise that a proposition of fact is true. The Fred Smartley, Jr., C.C.A.Va., 108 F.2d 603, 606.

Real Property Law

A real covenant by the grantor of lands, for himself and his heirs, to warrant and defend the title and possession of the estate granted, to the grantee and his heirs, whereby, either upon voucher, or judgment in the writ of *warrantia chartæ*, and the eviction of the grantee by paramount title, the grantor was bound to recompense him with other lands of equal value. Co.Litt. 365*a*. See "Covenant."

Sales of Personal Property

A statement or representation made by the seller of goods, contemporaneously with and as a part of the contract of sale, though collateral to the express object of it, having reference to the character, quality, or title of the goods, by which he promises or undertakes that certain facts are or shall be as he then represents them. Schley v. Zalis, 172 Md. 336, 191 A. 563, 564; Great Atlantic & Pacific Tea Co. v. Walker, Tex.Civ.App., 104 S.W.2d 627, 632. A promise or agreement by seller that article sold has certain qualities or that seller has good title thereto. Chanin v. Chevrolet Motor Co., D.C.Ill., 15 F.Supp. 57, 58. A statement of fact respecting the quality or character of goods sold, made by the seller to induce the sale, and relied on by the buyer. Hercules Powder Co. v. Rich, C.C.A.Ark., 3 F.2d 12, 14; Van Horn v. Stautz, 297 Ill. 530, 131 N.E. 153, 154.

"Warranty" in sale of personalty ordinarily applies only between seller and immediate buyer, and does not give such buyer right to sue original seller. Timberland Lumber Co. v. Climax Mfg. Co., C.C.A.Pa., 61 F.2d 391, 392.

Contracts

An undertaking or stipulation, in writing, or verbally, that a certain fact in relation to the subject of a contract is or shall be as it is stated or promised to be. United Iron Works Co. v. Henryetta Coal & Mining Co., 62 Okl. 99, 162 P. 209, 210; Hurley-Mason Co. v. Stebbins, Walker & Spinning, 79 Wash. 366, 140 P. 381, 384, L.R.A.1915B, 1131, Ann.Cas.1916A, 948. An express or implied statement of something undertaken as part of contract but collateral to its object. Pauls Valley Milling Co. v. Gabbert, 182 Okl. 500, 78 P.2d 685, 686.

A warranty differs from a representation in that a warranty must always be given contemporaneously with, and as part of, the contract; whereas a representation precedes and induces to the contract. And, while that is their difference in nature, their difference in consequence or effect is this: that, upon breach of warranty, (or false warranty,) the contract remains binding, and damages only are recoverable for the breach; whereas, upon a false representation, the defrauded party may elect to avoid the contract, and recover the entire price paid. Brown. And see Griswold v. Morrison, 53 Cal.App. 93, 200 P. 62, 65.

The same transaction cannot be characterized as a warranty and a fraud at the same time. A warranty rests upon contract, while fraud, or fraudulent representations have no element of contract in them, but are essentially a tort. When judges or law-writers speak of a fraudulent warranty, the language is neither accurate nor perspicuous. If there is a breach of warranty, it cannot be said that the warranty was fraudulent, with any more propriety than any other contract can be said to have been fraudulent, because there has been a breach of it. On the other hand, to speak of a false representation as a contract or warranty, or as tending to prove a contract or warranty, is a perversion of language and of correct ideas. Rose v. Hurley, 39 Ind. 81; Boysen v. Petersen, 203 Iowa 1073, 211 N.W. 894, 895.

Insurance

A "warranty" in the law of insurance consists of a statement by insured upon the literal truth of which the validity of the contract depends. Braddock, by Smith, v. Pacific Woodmen Life Ass'n, 89 Utah 75, 54 P.2d 1189, 1192. Statement, made in insurance contract by insured, which is susceptible of no construction other than that parties mutually intended that policy should not be binding, unless such statement be literally true. Brotherhood of Railroad Trainmen v. Wood, Tex. Civ.App., 79 S.W.2d 665, 668.

It is in the nature of a condition precedent and must appear on face of policy; or, if on another part of it, or on a paper physically attached to it, it must appear that the statements were intended to form part of policy; or, if on another paper, they must be so referred to in policy as clearly to indicate that the parties intended them to form a part of it, but it is not necessary that the statements in an application be set forth in the policy. City Bank & Trust Co. v. Commercial Casualty Co., La.App., 176 So. 27.

Warranty may be either "affirmative" or "promissory." The former affirms the existence of a fact at the time the policy is entered into, while the latter requires that something be done or not done after the policy has taken effect. Sentinel Life Ins. Co. v. Blackmer, C.C.A.Colo., 77 F.2d 347, 350.

General

Affirmative warranty. In the law of insurance, warranties may be either affirmative or promissory. Affirmative warranties may be either express or implied, but they usually consist of positive representations in the policy of the existence of some fact or state of things at the time, or previous to the time, of the making of the policy; they are, in general, conditions precedent, and if untrue, whether material to the risk or not, the policy does not attach, as it is not the contract of the insurer. Maupin v. Insurance Co., 53 W.Va. 557, 45 S.E. 1003; Orient Ins. Co. v. Van Zandt-Bruce Drug Co., 50 Okl. 558, 151 P. 323, 324. See, also, Insurance.

Collateral warranty. Existed when the heir's title was not derived from the warranting ancestor, and yet it barred the heir from claiming the land by any collateral title, upon the presumption that he might thereafter have assets by descent from or through the ancestor; and it imposed upon him the obligation of giving the warrantee other lands in case of eviction, provided he had assets. 2 Bl.Com. 301.

Continuing warranty. One which applies to the whole period during which the contract is in force; *e. g.*, an undertaking in a charter-party that a vessel shall continue to be of the same class that she was at the time the charter-party was made.

Covenant of warranty. See Covenant.

Executory warranties. See Executory Warranties.

Express warranty. In contracts and sales, one created by the apt and explicit statements of the seller or person to be bound. Borrekins v. Bevan, 3 Rawle (Pa.) 36, 23 Am.Dec. 85; White v. Stelloh, 74 Wis. 435, 43 N.W. 99; Hausken v. Hodson-Feenaughty Co., 109 Wash. 606, 187 P. 319, 321. In the law of insurance, an agreement expressed in a policy, whereby the assured stipulates that certain facts relating to the risk are or shall be true, or certain acts relating to the same subject have been or shall be done. 1 Phil.Ins. (4th Ed.) p. 425; Petit v. German Ins. Co., C.C.W.Va., 98 F. 802; Insurance Co. v. Morgan, 90 Va. 290, 18 S.E. 191.

General warranty. The name of a covenant of warranty inserted in deeds, by which the grantor binds himself, his heirs, etc., to "warrant and forever defend" to the grantee, his heirs, etc., the title thereby conveyed, against the lawful claims of all persons whatsoever. Where the warranty is only against the claims of persons claiming "by, through, or under" the grantor or his heirs, it is called a "special warranty."

Implied warranty. When the law derives it by implication or inference from the nature of the transaction or the relative situation or circumstances of the parties. Great Atlantic & Pacific Tea Co. v. Walker, Tex.Civ.App., 104 S.W.2d 627, 632.

Lineal warranty. In old conveyancing, the kind of warranty which existed when the heir derived title to the land warranted either from or through the ancestor who made the warranty.

Personal warranty. One available in personal actions, and arising from the obligation which one has contracted to pay the whole or part of a debt due by another to a third person. Flanders v. Seelye, 105 U.S. 718, 26 L.Ed. 1217.

Promissory warranty. In the law of insurance, a warranty which requires the performance or omission of certain things or the existence of certain facts after the beginning of the contract of insurance and during its continuance, and the breach of which will avoid the policy. See King v. Relief Ass'n, 35 App.Div. 58, 54 N.Y.S. 1057; McKenzie v. Insurance Co., 112 Cal. 548, 44 P. 922.

Special warranty. A clause of warranty inserted in a deed of lands, by which the grantor covenants, for himself and his heirs, to "warrant and forever defend" the title to the same, to the grantee and his heirs, etc., against all persons claiming "by, through, or under" the grantor or his heirs. If the warranty is against the claims of all persons whatsoever, it is called a "general" warranty.

Warranty deed. One which contains a covenant of warranty.

Warranty of fitness. Warranty by seller that goods sold are suitable for special purpose of buyer. Sperry Flour Co. v. De Moss, 141 Or. 440, 18 P.2d 242, 243, 90 A.L.R. 406.

Warranty, voucher to. In old practice. The calling a warrantor into court by the party warranted, (when tenant in a real action brought for recovery of such lands,) to defend the suit for him. Co.Litt. 101*b*.

WARREN. A term in English law for a place in which birds, fishes, or wild beasts are kept.

A franchise or privilege, either by prescription or grant from the king, to keep beasts and fowls of warren, which are hares, coneys, partridges, pheasants, etc.

Also any place to which such privilege extends. Mozley & Whiteley.

Free Warren

A franchise for the preserving and custody of beasts and fowls of warren. 2 Bl.Comm. 39, 417; Co.Litt. 233. This franchise gave the grantee sole right of killing, so far as his warren extended, on condition of excluding other persons. 2 Bl. Comm. 39.

WARSCOT. In Saxon law. A customary or usual tribute or contribution towards armor, or the arming of the forces.

WARTH. In old English law. A customary payment, supposed to be the same with *ward-penny*. Spelman; Blount.

WASH. A shallow part of a river or arm of the sea.

The sandy, rocky, gravelly, boulder-bestrewn part of a river bottom deposited on level land near mouth of a canyon representing rocks and gravel washed down by a mountain stream. Haack v. San Fernando Mission Land Co., 177 Cal. 140, 169 P. 1021, 1022.

A fermented wort from which spirit is distilled. Neal v. State, 154 Ark. 324, 242 S.W. 578, 579; Pack v. State, 116 Or. 416, 241 P. 390, 392.

WASH BANK. A bank composed of such substance that it is liable to be washed away by the action of the water thereon, so as to become unsafe to travelers on highway. Kerr v. Bougher, 16 Ohio App. 434, 437.

WASH SALE or WASHED SALE. In the language of the stock exchange, this term is applied to the operation of simultaneously buying and selling the same stock. In re Wettengel, C.C.A.3, 238 F. 798, 799. Also a fictitious kind of sale, disallowed on stock and other exchanges, in which a broker who has received orders from one person to buy and from another person to sell a particular amount or quantity of some particular stock or commodity simply transfers the stock or commodity from one principal to the other and pockets the difference, instead of executing both orders separately to the best advantage in each case, as is required by the rules of the different exchanges. U. S. v. Keough, D.C.Nev., 48 F.2d 246, 252.

WASHING–HORN. The sounding of a horn for washing before dinner. The custom was formerly observed in the Temple.

WASHINGTON, TREATY OF. A treaty signed on May 8, 1871, between Great Britain and the United States of America, with reference to certain differences arising out of the war between the northern and southern states of the Union, the Canadian fisheries, and other matters. Wharton.

WASHOUT SIGNAL. In railroad parlance. Emergency signal meaning to stop immediately. Stinson v. Aluminum Co. of America, C.C.A.Tenn., 141 F.2d 682, 684.

WASTE. An abuse or destructive use of property by one in rightful possession. Halifax Drainage Dist. of Volusia County v. Gleaton, 137 Fla. 397, 188 So. 374, 379. Spoil or destruction, done or permitted, to lands, houses, gardens, trees, or other corporeal hereditaments, by the tenant thereof, to the prejudice of the heir, or of him in reversion or remainder. 2 Bl.Comm. 281. Camden Trust Co. v. Handle, 132 N.J.Eq. 97, 26 A.2d 865, 869, 154 A.L.R. 602. A destruction or material alteration or deterioration of the freehold, or of the improvements forming a material part thereof, by any person rightfully in possession, but who has not the fee title or the full estate. Hayman v. Rownd, 82 Neb. 598, 118 N.W. 328, 45 L.R.A.(N.S.) 623; Thomas v. Thomas, 166 N.C. 627, 82 S.E. 1032, 1033, L.R.A.1915B, 219. An unreasonable or improper use, abuse, mismanagement, or omission of duty touching real estate by one rightfully in possession, which results in its substantial injury. Thayer v. Shorey, 287 Mass. 76, 191 N.E. 435, 437, 94 A.L.R. 307. Any unlawful act or omission of duty on the part of the tenant which results in permanent injury to the inheritance. It is the violation of an obligation to treat the premises in such manner that no harm be done to them, and that the estate may revert to those having an underlying interest, undeteriorated by any willful or negligent acts. Camden Trust Co. v. Handle, 130 N.J.Eq. 125, 21 A.2d 354, 358.

The early English doctrine was to the effect that anything which changed the character or nature of the land, notwithstanding the fact that it was an improvement thereto, constituted "waste." Whitehead v. Whitehead, Del.Orph., 181 A. 684, 685.

The primary distinction between "waste" and "trespass" is that in waste the injury is done by one rightfully in possession. Camden Trust Co. v. Handle, 132 N.J.Eq. 97, 26 A.2d 865, 867, 869.

Old English Criminal Law

A prerogative or liberty, on the part of the crown, of committing *waste* on the lands of felons, by pulling down their houses, extirpating their gardens, plowing their meadows, and cutting down their woods. 4 Bl.Comm. 385.

General

Commissive waste. Active or positive waste; waste done by acts of spoliation or destruction, rather than by mere neglect; the same as voluntary waste. See *infra*.

Double waste. See Double.

Equitable waste. Injury to a reversion or remainder in real estate, which is not recognized by the courts of law as waste, but which equity will interpose to prevent or remedy. Gannon v. Peterson, 193 Ill. 372, 62 N.E. 210, 55 L.R.A. 701; Crowe v. Wilson, 65 Md. 479, 5 A. 427, 57 Am.Rep. 343. Otherwise defined as an unconscientious abuse of the privilege of non-impeachability for waste at common law, whereby a tenant for life, without impeachment of waste, will be restrained from committing willful, destructive, malicious, or extravagant waste, such as pulling down houses, cutting timber of too young a growth, or trees planted for ornament, or for shelter of premises. Wharton.

Impeachment of waste. Liability for waste committed, or a demand or suit for compensation for waste committed upon lands or tenements by a tenant thereof who has no right to commit waste. On the other hand, a tenure "without impeachment of waste" signifies that the tenant cannot be called to account for waste committed.

Nul waste. "No waste." The name of a plea in an action of waste, denying the commission of waste, and forming the general issue.

Permissive waste. That kind of waste which is a matter of omission only, as by suffering a house to fall for want of necessary reparations. 2 Bl. Comm. 281; Willey v. Laraway, 64 Vt. 559, 25 A. 436; White v. Wagner, 4 Har. & J. (Md.) 391, 7 Am.Dec. 674.

Voluntary waste. Active or positive waste; waste done or committed, in contradistinction to that which results from mere negligence, which is called "permissive" waste. 2 Bouv. Inst. no. 2394. "Voluntary waste" is the willful destruction or carrying away of something attached to the freehold, and "permissive waste" is the failure to take reasonable care of the premises. Fisher's Ex'r v. Haney, 180 Ky. 257, 202 S.W. 495, 496. Voluntary or commissive waste consists of injury to the demised premises or some part thereof, when occasioned by some deliberate or voluntary act, as, for instance, the pulling down of a house or removal of floors, windows, doors, furnaces, shelves, or other things affixed to and forming part of the freehold. Regan v. Luthy, 11 N.Y.S. 709, 16 Daly 413. Contrasted with "permissive" waste.

Writ of waste. See that title.

WASTE-BOOK. A book used by merchants, to receive rough entries or memoranda of all transactions in the order of their occurrence, previous to their being posted in the journal. Otherwise called a "blotter."

WASTE WATER. Water that is actually wasted or not needed by the claimant thereto; water which, after it has served the purpose of the lawful claimant thereto, has been permitted to run to waste or to escape; and water which from unavoidable causes escapes from the ditches, canals, or other works of the lawful claimants. Rock Creek Ditch & Flume Co. v. Miller, 93 Mont. 248, 17 P.2d 1074, 1077, 89 A.L.R. 200. But water is not "waste water" so long as it remains on the land of the original appropriator. Barker v. Sonner, 135 Or. 75, 294 P. 1053, 1054.

WASTEL. A standard of quality of bread, made of the finest white flour. *Cocket* bread was slightly inferior in quality. The statute of 1266 mentions seven kinds of bread. See Assisa; Studer, Oak Book of Southhampton, Vol. II.

WASTING PROPERTY. Includes such property as leasehold interests; royalties; patent rights; interests in things the substance of which is consumed, such as mines, oil and gas wells, quarries and timber lands; interests in things which are consumed in the using or are worn out by use, such as machinery and farm implements. In re Pennock's Will, 285 N.Y. 475, 35 N.E.2d 177, 178.

WASTING TRUST. A trust in which the trustee may apply a part of the principal to make good a deficiency of income.

WASTORS. In old statutes. A kind of thieves.

WATCH, *v.* To keep guard; to stand as sentinel; to be on guard at night, for the preservation of the peace and good order.

WATCH, *n.* A body of constables on duty on any particular night.

A division of a ship's crew. At sea, the ship's company is divided into two watches, larboard and starboard, with a mate to command each. O'Hara v. Luckenbach S. S. Co., 46 S.Ct. 157, 160, 269 U.S. 364, 70 L.Ed. 313. Also the division of the day into time periods of service of the officers and crew, and, by immemorial Anglo-Saxon maritime custom, the time period of a watch never exceeds four hours. The Denali, C.C.A.Wash., 105 F.2d 413, 416.

WATCH AND WARD. "Watch" denotes keeping guard during the night; "ward," by day.

WATCHMAN. An officer in cities and towns having duty to watch and care for inhabitants' property; he possesses generally the common-law authority of a constable to arrest on reasonable ground to suspect felony, though without proof of commission of felony. Harris v. Sevier, 19 La. App. 165, 138 So. 459, 460. Also one whose services are constant watching or patrolling of the particular building or contiguous group of buildings. Bartholome v. Baltimore Fire Patrol & Despatch Co., D.C.Md., 48 F.Supp. 98, 103.

WATER. As designating a commodity or a subject of ownership, this term has the same meaning in law as in common speech; but in another sense, and especially in the plural, it may designate a body of water, such as a river, a lake, or an ocean, or an aggregate of such bodies of water, as in the phrases "foreign waters," "waters of the United States," and the like.

Water is neither land nor tenement nor susceptible of absolute ownership. It is a movable thing and must of necessity continue common by the law of nature. It admits only of a transient usufructuary property, and if it escapes for a moment, the right to it is gone forever, the qualified owner having no legal power of reclamation. It is not capable of being sued for by the name of "water," nor by a calculation of its cubical or superficial measure; but the suit must be brought for the land which lies at the bottom covered with water. As water is not land, neither is it a tenement, because it is not of a permanent nature, nor the subject of absolute property. It is not in any possible sense real estate, and hence is not embraced in a covenant of general warranty. Mitchell v. Warner, 5 Conn. 518.

Coast Waters

See that title.

Developed Water

Water which is brought to the surface and made available for use by the party claiming the water. Mountain Lake Mining Co. v. Midway Irr. Co., 47 Utah 346, 149 P. 929, 933.

Flood Waters

Waters which escape from a water course in great volume and flow over adjoining lands in no regular channel. The fact that such errant waters make for themselves a temporary channel or follow some natural channel, gully, or depression does not affect their character as "flood waters" or give to the course which they follow the character of a natural "water course." Mogle v. Moore, Cal.App., 96 P.2d 147, 150, 151; Everett v. Davis, Cal.App., 107 P.2d 650, 654, 655.

Foreign Waters

Those belonging to another nation or country or subject to another jurisdiction, as distinguished from "domestic" waters. The Pilot, 1 C.C.A. 523, 50 F. 437.

Inland Waters

See Inland.

Navigable Waters

See Navigable.

Percolating Waters

Those which pass through the ground beneath the surface of the earth without any definite channel, and do not form a part of the body or flow, surface or subterranean, of any water-course. They may be either rain waters which are slowly infiltrating through the soil or waters seeping through the banks or the bed of a stream, and which have so far left the bed and the other waters as to have lost their character as a part of the flow of that stream. Vineland Irr. Dist. v. Azusa Irr. Co., 126 Cal. 486, 58 P. 1057, 46 L.R.A. 820; Los Angeles v. Pomeroy, 124 Cal. 597, 57 Pac. 585; Clinchfield Coal Corporation v. Compton, 148 Va. 437, 139 S.E. 308, 311, 55 A.L.R. 1376; Flanigan v. State, 113 Misc. 91, 183 N.Y.S. 934, 935.

Private Waters

Non-navigable streams, or bodies of water not open to the resort and use of the general public, but entirely owned and controlled by one or more individuals. Piazzek v. Drainage Dist. No. 1 of Jefferson County, 119 Kan. 119, 237 P. 1059, 1060.

Public Waters

Such as are adapted for the purposes of navigation, or those to which the general public have a right of access, as distinguished from artificial lakes, ponds, and other bodies of water privately owned, or similar natural bodies of water owned exclusively by one or more persons. See Lamprey v. Metcalf, 52 Minn. 181, 53 N.W. 1139, 18 L.R.A. 670, 38 Am.St.Rep. 541; State v. Theriault, 70 Vt. 617, 41 A. 1030, 43 L.R.A. 290, 67 Am.St. Rep. 648.

Subterranean Waters

Waters which lie wholly beneath the surface of the ground, and which either ooze and seep through the subsurface strata without pursuing any defined course or channel, (percolating waters,) or flow in a permanent and regular but invisible course, or lie under the earth in a more or less immovable body, as a subterranean lake.

Surface Waters

As distinguished from the waters of a natural stream, lake, or pond, surface waters are such as diffuse themselves over the surface of the ground, following no defined course or channel, and not gathering into or forming any more definite body of water than a mere bog or marsh. They generally originate in rains and melting snows, but the flood waters of a river may also be considered as surface waters if they become separated from the main current, or leave it never to return, and spread out over lower ground. See Schaefer v. Marthaler, 34 Minn. 487, 26 N.W. 726, 57 Am.Rep. 40; Crawford v. Rambo, 44 Ohio St. 279, 7 N.E. 429; San Gabriel Valley Country Club v. Los Angeles County, 182 Cal. 392, 188 P. 554, 556, 9 A.L.R. 1200; Thompson v. New Haven Water Co., 86 Conn. 597, 86 A. 585, 588, 45 L.R.A.,N.S., 457.

Water derived from rains and melting snows that is diffused over surface of the ground, and it continues to be such and may be impounded by the owner of the land until it reaches some well-defined channel in which it is accustomed to, and does, flow with other waters, or until it reaches some permanent lake or pond, whereupon it ceases to be "surface water" and becomes a "water course" or a "lake" or "pond," as the case may be. State v. Hiber, 48 Wyo. 172, 44 P.2d 1005, 1008, 1011.

Surplus Water

Water running off from ground which has been irrigated; water not consumed by the process of irrigation; water which the land irrigated will not take up. Wedgworth v. Wedgworth, 20 Ariz. 518, 181 P. 952, 954.

Tide Waters

See Tide.

Water Course

See that title *infra*.

Water Front

Land or land with buildings fronting on a body of water. City of Long Beach v. Lisenby, 175 Cal. 575, 166 P. 333, 335.

Water Power

The water power to which a riparian owner is entitled consists of the fall in the stream when in its natural state, as it passes through his land, or along the boundary of it; or, in other words, it consists of the difference of level between the surface where the stream first touches his land, and the surface where it leaves it. McCalmont v. Whitaker, 3 Rawle (Pa.) 90, 23 Am.Dec. 102.

The use of water for power according to common understanding means its application to a water wheel to the end that its energy under the specified head and fall may be utilized and converted into available force. Holyoke Water Power Co. v. American Writing Paper Co., D.C.Mass., 17 F.Supp. 895, 898.

Water Right

A legal right, in the nature of a corporeal hereditament, to use the water of a natural stream or water furnished through a ditch or canal, for general or specific purposes, such as irrigation, mining, power, or domestic use, either to its full capacity or to a measured extent or during a defined portion of the time. See Hill v. Newman, 5 Cal. 445, 63 Am.Dec. 140; Murphy v. Kerr, D.C. N.M., 296 F. 536, 541; City of Los Angeles v. City of Glendale, Cal.App., 132 P.2d 574, 584. A usufruct in a stream consisting in the right to have the water flow so that some portion of it may be reduced to possession and be made private property of individual, and it is therefore the right to divert water from natural stream by artificial means and apply the same to beneficial use. Ronzio v. Denver & R. G. W. R. Co., C.C.A.Utah, 116 F.2d 604, 605. It includes right to change the place of diversion, storage, or use of water if rights of other water users will not be injured. Lindsey v. McClure, C.C.A.N.M., 136 F.2d 65, 70.

It was also said to be real property which may be sold and transferred separately from land on which it has been used. Federal Land Bank of Spokane v. Union Cent. Life Ins. Co., 54 Idaho 161, 29 P.2d 1009, 1011.

Water Right Claim

A "water right claim," as filed with the state engineer, is merely a declaration of intention to create a water right. Washington State Sugar Co. v. Goodrich, 27 Idaho 26, 147 P. 1073, 1076.

Water-Bailiff

The title of an officer, in port towns in England, appointed for the searching of ships. Also of an officer belonging to the city of London, who had the supervising and search of the fish brought thither. Cowell.

Water-Bayley

In American law. An officer mentioned in the colony laws of New Plymouth, (A. D. 1671,) whose duty was to collect dues to the colony for fish taken in their waters. Probably another form of *water-bailiff*. Burrell.

Water-Gage

A sea-wall or bank to restrain the current and overflowing of the water; also an instrument to measure water. Cowell.

Water-Gang

A Saxon word for a trench or course to carry a stream of water, such as are commonly made to drain water out of marshes. Cowell.

Water-Gavel

In old records. A gavel or rent paid for fishing in or other benefit received from some river or water. Cowell; Blount.

Water-Logged

A vessel is "water-logged" when she becomes heavy and unmanageable on account of the leakage of water into the hold. Fireman's Fund Ins. Co. v. Globe Nav. Co., C.C.A.Wash., 236 F. 618, 625.

Water-Mark

See that title *infra*.

Water-Measure

In old statutes. A measure greater than Winchester measure by about three gallons in the bushel. Cowell.

Water-Packed

A "water-packed" bale of cotton is one to the lint of which water is added in such a manner that the weight is increased, or in which water-damaged cotton is placed, or the sampling sides of which are packed with lint cotton not so wet or water-damaged. Wallace v. Crosthwait, 196 Ala. 356, 71 So. 666, 667.

Waters of the United States

All waters within the United States which are navigable for the purposes of commerce, or whose navigation successfully aids commerce, are included in this term. The Daniel Ball, 6 F.Cas. 1161.

Waterscape

An aqueduct or passage for water.

WATER COURSE. A running stream of water; a natural stream fed from permanent or natural sources, including rivers, creeks, runs, and rivulets. There must be a stream, usually flowing in a particular direction, though it need not flow continuously. It may sometimes be dry. It must flow in a definite channel, having a bed or banks, and usually discharges itself into some other stream or body of water. It must be something more than a mere surface drainage over the entire face of the tract of land, occasioned by unusual freshets or other extraordinary causes. Leader v. Matthews, 192 Ark. 1049, 95 S.W.2d 1138, 1139; Los Angeles v. Pomeroy, 124 Cal. 597, 57 P. 587; Walt v. Phillips, 166 Ark. 163, 266 S.W. 71, 73; Turner v. Big Lake Oil Co., Tex.Civ.App., 62 S.W.2d 491, 493.

A "water course," in the legal meaning of the word, does not consist merely of the stream as it flows within the banks which form its channel in ordinary stages of water, but the stream still retains its character as a water course when, in times of ordinary high water, the stream extending beyond its own banks, is accustomed to flow down over the adjacent lowlands in a broader but still definable stream. Atchison, T. & S. F. Ry. Co. v. Hadley, 168 Okl. 588, 35 P.2d 463, 466.

Water flowing underground in a known and well defined channel is not "percolating water", but constitutes a "water course", and is governed by law applicable to "surface streams", rather than by law applicable to percolating waters. Bull v. Siegrist, 169 Or. 180, 126 P.2d 832, 834.

Natural Water Course

A natural stream flowing in a defined bed or channel; one formed by the natural flow of the water, as determined by the general superficies or conformation of the surrounding country, as distinguished from an "artificial" water course, formed by the work of man, such as a ditch or canal. See Barkley v. Wilcox, 86 N.Y. 140, 40 Am. Rep. 519; Hawley v. Sheldon, 64 Vt. 491, 24 Atl. 717, 33 Am.St.Rep. 941; Porter v. Armstrong, 129 N.C. 101, 39 S.E. 799; Gaskill v. Barnett, 52 Ind. App. 654, 101 N.E. 40, 42; Williams v. Bass, 179 Wis. 364, 191 N.W. 499, 500.

WATER-MARK. A mark indicating the highest point to which water rises, or the lowest point to which it sinks.

High-Water Mark

This term is properly applicable to tidal waters, and designates the line on the shore reached by the water at the high or flood tide. With reference to the waters of artificial ponds or lakes, created by dams in unnavigable streams, it denotes the highest point on the shores to which the dams can raise the water in ordinary circumstances. Howard v. Ingersoll, 13 How. 423, 14 L.Ed. 189; Storer v. Freeman, 6 Mass. 437, 4 Am.Dec. 155; Brady v. Blackinton, 113 Mass. 245; Cook v. McClure, 58 N.Y. 444, 17 Am.Rep. 270. The high-water mark of a river, not subject to tide, is the line which the river impresses on the soil by covering it for sufficient periods to deprive it of vegetation, and to destroy its value for agriculture. Raide v. Dollar, 34 Idaho 682, 203 P. 469, 471; Union Sand & Gravel Co. v. Northcott, 102 W.Va. 519, 135 S.E. 589, 592; Tilden v. Smith, 94 Fla. 502, 113 So. 708, 712.

Low-Water Mark

That line on the shore of the sea which marks the edge of the waters at the lowest point of the ordinary ebb tide. See Stover v. Jack, 60 Pa. 342, 100 Am.Dec. 566; Gerrish v. Prop'rs of Union Wharf, 26 Me. 395, 46 Am.Dec. 568. The "low-water mark," of a river is the point to which the water recedes at its lowest stage. Union Sand & Gravel Co. v. Northcott, 102 W.Va. 519, 135 S.E. 589, 593; Joyce-Watkins Co. v. Industrial Commission, 325 Ill. 378, 156 N.E. 346, 348.

WATER ORDEAL. See Ordeal.

WATERED STOCK. Stock which is issued by a corporation as fully paid-up stock, when in fact the whole amount of the par value thereof has not been paid in. Harn v. Smith, 85 Okl. 137, 204 P. 642, 644; Bank of Commerce v. Goolsby, 129 Ark. 416, 196 S.W. 803, 807; Loud v. Solomon, 188 Mich. 7, 154 N.W. 73, 75. Stock issued as bonus or otherwise without consideration or issued for a less sum of money than par value, or issued for labor, services, or property which at a fair valuation is less than the par value. Thomason v. Miller, Tex.Civ.App., 4 S.W.2d 668, 670.

WATERWAY. Water course. Smith v. Cameron, 123 Or. 501, 262 P. 946, 948. See Water Course.

WAVESON. In old records. Such goods as, after a wreck, swim or float on the waves. Jacob.

WAX SCOT. A duty anciently paid twice a year towards the charge of wax candles in churches. Spelman.

WAY. A passage, path, road, or street. In a technical sense, a *right* of passage over land.

"Ways are appendant or appurtenant" when they are incident to an estate, one terminus being on the land of the party claiming it; while "way in gross" must be a personal right, not assignable nor inheritable. Safety Building & Loan Co. v. Lyles, 131 S.C. 540, 128 S.E. 724, 725. See "Easement."

Private Way

A right which a person has of passing over the land of another. Jones v. Venable, 120 Ga. 1, 47 S.E. 549; Kister v. Reeser, 98 Pa. 1, 42 Am.Rep. 608; Kripp v. Curtis, 71 Cal. 62, 11 P. 879. In another sense (chiefly in New England) a private way is one laid out by the local public authorities for the accommodation of individuals and wholly or chiefly at their expense, but not restricted to their exclusive use, being subject, like highways, to the public easement of passage. Clark v. Boston, C. & M. R. Co., 24 N.H. 118; Butchers', etc., Ass'n v. Boston, 139 Mass. 290, 30 N.E. 94.

Right of Way

See that title.

Way of Necessity

Exists where land granted is completely environed by land of the grantor, or partially by his land and the land of strangers. The law implies from these facts that a private right of way over the grantor's land was granted to the grantee as appurtenant to the estate. Gwinn v. Gwinn, 77 W.Va. 281, 87 S.E. 371, 373; Violet v. Martin, 62 Mont. 335, 205 P. 221, 223. It is not merely one of convenience, and never exists where person may reach highway over his own land. Backhausen v. Mayer, 204 Wis. 286, 234 N.W. 904, 905, 74 A.L.R. 1245. And it cannot legally exist where neither the party claiming the way nor owner of land over which it is claimed, nor anyone under whom either of them claim, was ever seized of both tracts of land at same time. Bowles v. Chapman, 180 Tenn. 232, 175 S.W.2d 313, 314. It is not based on continuous adverse user, but arises by implication of law from necessities of case, and ceases when necessity therefor ceases. Waubun Beach Ass'n v. Wilson, 274 Mich. 598, 265 N.W. 474, 478, 103 A.L.R. 983.

The extent of a "way of necessity" is a way such as is required for complete and beneficial use of land to which the way is impliedly attached. New York Cent. R. Co. v. Yarian, Ind., 219 Ind. 477, 39 N.E.2d 604, 606, 139 A.L.R. 455.

WAY-BILL. A writing in which is set down the names of passengers who are carried in a public conveyance, or the description of goods sent with a common carrier by land. Wharton.

WAY-GOING CROP. A crop of grain sown by a tenant for a term certain, during his tenancy, but which will not ripen until after the expiration of his lease. In the absence of an express agreement to the contrary tenant is entitled thereto. Commonwealth v. Peterman, 130 Pa.Super. 497, 198 A. 687, 688.

WAYLEAVE. A right of way over or through land for the carriage of minerals from a mine or quarry. It is an easement, being a species of the class called "rights of way," and is generally created by express grant or reservation. Sweet.

WAYNAGIUM. Implements of husbandry. 1 Reeve, Eng.Law, c. 5, p. 268.

WAYS AND MEANS. In a legislative body, the "committee on ways and means" is a committee appointed to inquire into and consider the methods and sources for raising revenue, and to propose means for providing the funds needed by the government.

WAYWARDENS. The English highway acts provide that in every parish forming part of a highway district there shall annually be elected one or more waywardens. The waywardens so elected, and the justices for the county residing within the district, form the highway board for the district. Each waywarden also represents his parish in regard to the levying of the highway rates, and in questions arising concerning the liability of his parish to repairs, etc. Sweet.

WEALD. Sax. A wood; the woody part of a country.

WEALREAF. In old English law. The robbing of a dead man in his grave.

WEALTH. All material objects, capable of satisfying human wants, desires, or tastes, having a value in exchange, and upon which human labor has been expended; *i. e.*, which have, by such labor, been either reclaimed from nature, extracted or gathered from the earth or sea, manufactured from raw materials, improved, adopted, or cultivated.

"The aggregate of all the things, whether material or immaterial, which contribute to comfort and enjoyment, which cannot be obtained without more or less labor, and which are objects of frequent barter and sale, is what we usually call 'wealth.'" Bowen, Pol. Econ. See Branham v. State, 96 Ga. 307, 22 S.E. 957.

WEAPON. An instrument of offensive or defensive combat, or anything used, or designed to be used, in destroying, defeating or injuring an enemy. Perry v. Commonwealth, 286 Ky. 587, 151 S.W.2d 377, 379; People ex rel. Griffin v. Hunt, 150 Misc. 163, 270 N.Y.S. 248. Something to fight with. Highsaw v. Creech, 17 Tenn.App. 573, 69 S.W.2d 249.

The term is chiefly used, in law, in the statutes prohibiting the carrying of "concealed" or "deadly" weapons. See those titles. And see also "Offensive."

WEAR, or WEIR. A great dam or fence made across a river, or against water, formed of stakes interlaced by twigs of osier, and accommodated for the taking of fish, or to convey a stream to a mill. Cowell; Jacob.

WEAR AND TEAR. "Natural wear and tear" means deterioration or depreciation in value by ordinary and reasonable use of the subject-matter. Green v. Kelly, 20 N.J.L. 548.

WEARING APPAREL. As generally used in statutes, refers not merely to a person's outer clothing, but covers all articles usually worn, and includes underclothing. Arnold v. U. S., 13 S.Ct. 406, 147 U.S. 494, 37 L.Ed. 253. All articles of dress generally worn by persons in the calling and condition of life and in the locality of the person in question. In re Steimes' Estate, 150 Misc. 279, 270 N.Y.S. 339.

WEATHERING. Consists in subjecting raw natural gasoline to the atmosphere in open tanks until by evaporation, sometimes accelerated by steam coils, the required vapor pressure or vapor tension of the remaining liquid is had. Carbide & Carbon Chemicals Co. v. Phillips Petroleum Co., D.C.Del., 28 F.2d 218.

WED. Sax. A covenant or agreement. Cowell. A pledge. Jenks, Hist. E. L. 13.

WEDBEDRIP. Sax. In old English law. A customary service which tenants paid to their lords, in cutting down their corn, or doing other harvest duties; as if a *covenant* to *reap* for the lord at the time of his *bidding* or commanding. Cowell.

WEDLOCK. As used in the phrase "born out of wedlock" in Uniform Illegitimacy Act, means the ceremony or state of marriage or status of husband and wife and is equivalent to matrimony but does not include status of wife and her paramour. State v. Coliton, N.D., 73 N.D. 582, 17 N.W.2d 546, 549, 156 A.L.R. 1403.

WEEK. A period of seven consecutive days of time; and, in some uses, the period beginning with Sunday and ending with Saturday. See Leach v. Burr, 23 S.Ct. 393, 188 U.S. 510, 47 L.Ed. 567; Ronkendorff v. Taylor, 4 Pet. 361, 7 L.Ed. 882; United States v. Southern Pac. Co., C.C.A. Utah, 209 F. 562, 567; Progressive Building and Loan Ass'n v. McIntyre, 169 Tenn. 491, 89 S.W.2d 336, 337.

Words "two weeks" mean fourteen days. Fisher v. Booher, 269 Ky. 501, 107 S.W.2d 307, 309.

WEEK-WORK. In early English times, the obligation of a tenant to work two or three days in every week for his lord, during the greater part of the year, and four or five during the summer months. 1 Poll. & Maitl. 349.

WEHADING. In old European law. The judicial combat, or duel; the trial by battel.

WEIGHAGE. In English law. A duty or toll paid for weighing merchandise. It is called *"tronage"* for weighing wool at the king's beam, or *"pesage"* for weighing other avoirdupois goods. 2 Chit. Com.Law, 16.

WEIGHT. A measure of heaviness or ponderosity; and in a metaphorical sense influence, effectiveness, or power to influence judgment or conduct. The quantity of heaviness, the quality of being heavy, the degree or extent of downward pressure under the influence of gravity, or the quantity of matter as estimated by the balance or scale. Dwight & Lloyd Sintering Co. v. American Ore Reclamation Co., C.C.A.N.Y., 263 F. 315, 316.

Gross Weight

The whole weight of goods and merchandise, including the dust and dross, and also the chest or bag, etc., upon which tare and tret are allowed.

Miner's Weight

Such quantity of mine-run material, as operators and miners may, from time to time, agree as being necessary or sufficient to produce a ton of prepared coal. Drake v. Berry, 259 Pa. 8, 102 A. 315, 320.

WEIGHT OF EVIDENCE. The balance of preponderance of evidence; the inclination of the greater amount of credible evidence, offered in a trial, to support one side of the issue rather than the other.

The "weight" or "preponderance of proof" is a phrase constantly used, the meaning of which is well understood and easily defined. It indicates clearly to the jury that the party having the burden of proof will be entitled to their verdict, if, on weighing the evidence in their minds, they shall find the greater amount of credible evidence sustains the issue which is to be established before them. Haskins v. Haskins, 9 Gray, Mass., 393. Weight is not a question of mathematics, but depends on its effect in inducing belief. It often happens that an uncorroborated witness may tell a story so natural and reasonable, and in manner so sincere and honest, as to command belief, though contradicted by others. Braunschweiger v. Waits, 179 Pa. 47, 36 A. 155, 156. "Weight of proof" means greater amount of credible evidence and is synonymous with "preponderance of proof." Haskins v. Haskins, 75 Mass. (9 Gray) 390, 393. For a contrary holding, see Shinn v. Tucker, 37 Ark. 580, 588. Sec, also, Preponderance.

WEIR. A fence or an inclosure of twigs, set in a stream to catch fish. Pub.St.Mass. p. 1297; Treat v. Chipman, 35 Me. 38.

WELDING. The art, practiced immemorially, of uniting two pieces of metal in one piece by heating those portions which are to be welded to a temperature at which they become plastic, and then pressing them strongly together, so as to effect a union. Thomson Spot Welder Co. v. Ford Motor Co., 44 S.Ct. 533, 534, 265 U.S. 445, 68 L.Ed. 1098.

WELFARE. Well-doing or well-being in any respect; the enjoyment of health and common blessings of life; exemption from any evil or calamity; prosperity; happiness. Wiseman v. Tanner, D.C. Wash., 221 F. 694, 698.

WELFARE OF CHILD. Under statutes requiring in awarding custody of minor that "welfare of child," be guide, parents need only be honest and respectable, with disposition and capacity to maintain and educate child. In re Bourquin, 88 Mont. 118, 290 P. 250, 251. The "welfare of a child", is gauged by father's means and station in life and does not contemplate that child be taken from father because another can give child more in a material way. Starr v. Gorman, 136 N.J.L. 105, 40 A.2d 564, 565.

WELL, *adj.*

Marine Insurance

A term used as descriptive of the safety and soundness of a vessel, in a warranty of her condition at a particular time and place; as, "warranted *well* at ——— on ———."

Old Reports

Good, sufficient, unobjectionable in law; the opposite of "ill."

WELL, *n.* A hole or shaft sunk into the earth in order to obtain a fluid, such as water, oil, brine, or natural gas, from a subterranean supply. Loosely, any shaft or pit dug or bored in earth, or any space so constructed as to suggest or be likened to, a well for water; a pit or hole in the ground or a hollow cylinder built in such hole; or a shaft or excavation in mining. Seismograph Service Corporation v. Mason, 193 Okl. 623, 145 P.2d 967, 970.

Completed Well

In oil prospecting leases, a well drilled to the formation or sand in which oil in district in question is usually and commonly found. Kies v. Williams, 190 Ky. 596, 228 S.W. 40, 41.

WELL-BORN MEN. A tribunal in New Amsterdam (New York). 1 Fiske, Dutch and Quaker Colonies 238.

WELL KNOWING. A phrase used in pleading as the technical expression in laying a *scienter,* (*q. v.*).

WELSH MORTGAGE. See Mortgage.

WELSHING. Receiving a sum of money or valuable thing, undertaking to return the same or the value thereof together with other money, if an event (for example, the result of a horse-race) shall be determined in a certain manner, and at the time of receiving the deposit intending to cheat and defraud the depositor. Coldr. & Hawks. Gambling 303. The crime is larceny at common law.

WELSHER. One who at a race track makes bets or receives money to be bet and absconds without paying his losses or returning money entrusted to him. People v. Monroe, 349 Ill. 270, 182 N.E. 439, 443, 85 A.L.R. 605.

WEN. An indolent encysted tumor of the skin, especially a sebaceous cyst. Life & Casualty Ins. Co. v. King, 137 Tenn. 685, 195 S.W. 585, 589.

WEND. In old records. A large extent of ground, comprising several *juga*; a perambulation; a circuit. Spelman; Cowell.

WEOTUMA. The purchase price of a wife among the heathen Germans. 2 Holdsw.Hist.E.L. 77.

WERA, or WERE. The estimation or price of a man, especially of one slain. In the criminal law of the Anglo-Saxons, every man's life had its value, called a "were," or "*capitis œstimatio.*"

WEREGELT THEF. Sax. In old English law. A robber who might be ransomed. Fleta, lib. 1, c. 47, § 13.

WEREGILD, or WERGILD. This was the price of homicide, or other atrocious personal offense, paid partly to the king for the loss of a subject, partly to the lord for the loss of a vassal, and partly to the next of kin of the injured person. In the Anglo-Saxon laws, the amount of compensation varied with the degree or rank of the party slain. Brown. See Angild; Angylde; Assithment.

WERELADA. A purging from a crime by the oaths of several persons, according to the degree and quality of the accused. Cowell.

WERGELT. In old Scotch law. A sum paid by an offender as a compensation or satisfaction for the offense; a weregild, or wergild.

WERP-GELD. Belg. In European law. Contribution for jettison; average.

WEST SAXON LAGE. The laws of the West Saxons, which obtained in the counties to the south and west of England, from Kent to Devonshire. Blackstone supposes these to have been much the same with the laws of Alfred, being the municipal law of the far most considerable part of his dominions, and particularly including Berkshire, the seat of his peculiar residence. 1 Bl.Comm. 65.

See Mercen-Lage.

WESTMINSTER. A city immediately adjoining London, and forming a part of the metropolis; formerly the seat of the superior courts of the kingdom.

WESTMINSTER CONFESSION. A document containing a statement of religious doctrine, concocted at a conference of British and continental Protestant divines at Westminster, in the year 1643, which subsequently became the basis of the Scotch Presbyterian Church. Wharton.

WESTMINSTER THE FIRST, STATUTE OF. The statute 3 Edw. I., A. D. 1275. This statute, which deserves the name of a code rather than an act, is divided into fifty-one chapters. Without extending the exemption of churchmen from civil jurisdiction, it protects the property of the church from the violence and spoliation of the king and the nobles, provides for freedom of popular elections, because sheriffs, coroners, and conservators of the peace were still chosen by the freeholders in the county court, and attempts had been made to influence the election of knights of the shire, from the time when they were instituted. It contains a declaration to enforce the enactment of *Magna Charta* against excessive fines, which might operate as perpetual imprisonment; enumerates and corrects the abuses of tenures, particularly as to marriage of wards; regulates the levying of tolls, which were imposed arbitrarily by the barons and by cities and boroughs; corrects and restrains the powers of the king's escheator and other officers; amends the criminal law, putting the crime of rape on the footing to which it has been lately restored, as a most grievous, but not capital, offense; and embraces the subject of procedure in civil and criminal matters, introducing many regulations to render it cheap, simple, and expeditious. 1 Camp. Lives Ld. Ch. p. 167; 2 Reeve, Eng. Law, c. 9, p. 107. Certain parts of this act are repealed by St. 26 & 27 Vict. c. 125. Wharton.

WESTMINSTER THE SECOND, STATUTE OF. The statute 13 Edw. I. St. 1, A. D. 1285, otherwise called the "Statute *de Donis Conditionalibus.*" See 2 Reeve, Eng. Law, c. 10, p. 163. Certain parts of this act are repealed by St. 19 & 20 Vict. c. 64, and St. 26 & 27 Vict. c. 125. Wharton.

WESTMINSTER THE THIRD, STATUTE OF. A statute passed in the eighteenth year of Edward I. More commonly known as the "Statute of *Quia Emptores,*" (*q. v.*). See Barring. Ob. St. 167–169.

WET. A term used to designate one in favor of allowing the sale of intoxicating liquors. State v. Shumaker, 200 Ind. 623, 157 N.E. 769, 778.

WET GAS. Natural gas as it flows from the earth, requiring separation of gasoline therefrom to make it salable. Atlas Milling Co. v. Jones, D.C.Okl., 29 F.Supp. 942, 945.

WET OIL. Oil which carries in cohesion with it more than 3 per cent. by volume of water and sediment. In re Great Western Petroleum Corporation, D.C.Cal., 16 F.Supp. 247, 252.

WETHER. A castrated ram, at least one year old. In an indictment it may be called a "sheep." Rex v. Birket, 4 Car. & P. 216.

WHACK. To divide into shares, apportion, parcel out, make a division settlement, square accounts, or to pay. Schook v. Zimmerman, 188 Mich. 617, 155 N.W. 526, 531.

WHALE. A royal fish, the head being the king's property, and the tail the queen's. 2 Steph.Comm. 19, 448, 540.

WHALER. A vessel employed in the whale fishery.

WHARF. A structure on the margin of navigable waters, alongside of which vessels can be brought for the sake of being conveniently loaded or unloaded, or a space of ground, artificially prepared, for the reception of merchandise from a ship or vessel, so as to promote the discharge of such vessel. State v. Louisiana Terminal Co., 179 La. 671, 154 So. 731.

A broad, plain place near a river, canal, or other water, to lay wares on that are brought to or from the water. Cowell.

Private Wharf

One whose owner or lessee has the exclusive enjoyment or use thereof. Hamilton v. Portland State Pier Site Dist., 120 Me. 15, 112 A. 836, 840; The M. L. C. No. 10, C.C.A.N.Y., 10 F.2d 699, 702.

Public Wharf

One to which vessels and the public can resort, either at will or on assignment of a berth by a harbor authority. Kafline v. Brooklyn Eastern Dist. Terminal Co., 168 N.Y.S. 120, 121, 180 App. Div. 858.

Sufferance Wharves

Such as may be appointed by the commissioners for the purpose of customs, under the British act of 1876.

WHARFAGE. The money paid for landing goods upon, or loading them from, a wharf. Manhattan Lighterage Corporation v. Moore McCormack Line, D.C.N.Y., 45 F.Supp. 271, 273. Charge for use of wharf by way of rent or compensation. Marine Lighterage Corporation v. Luckenbach S. S. Co., 139 Misc. 612, 248 N.Y.S. 71, 72.

WHARFING OUT, RIGHT OF. A right to the exclusive use of submerged lands as by the affixing thereto or the establishment thereon of a permanent structure to some point within the navigable body of water, deep and wide enough to dock ocean-going vessels, and it presupposes exclusive use and to that extent may interfere with fishing or navigation. City of Oakland v. Hogan, 41 Cal. App.2d 333, 106 P.2d 987, 994.

WHARFINGER. The owner or occupier of a wharf, one who for hire receives merchandise on his wharf, either for the purpose of forwarding or for delivery to the consignee on such wharf. Teahan v. Industrial Accident Commission, 210 Cal. 342, 292 P. 120, 121.

WHEEL. An engine of torture used in medieval Europe, on which a criminal was bound while his limbs or bones were broken one by one till he died.

WHEELAGE. Duty or toll paid for carts, etc., passing over certain ground. Cowell.

WHEELERS. Persons employed by a motor carrier to load freight on outgoing truck or trailer bodies and to report physical defects in and need for repairs to such bodies. Crean v. M. Moran Transp. Lines, D.C.N.Y., 57 F.Supp. 212, 216.

WHELPS. The young of certain animals of a base nature or *feræ naturæ.*

WHEN. At what time; at the time that; at which time; at that time. Gehrung v. Collister, 52 Ohio App. 314, 3 N.E.2d 700, 701. At, during, or after the time that; at or just after the moment that. In re Morrow's Will, 41 N.M. 723, 73 P.2d 1360, 1364. In the event that, on condition that, in virtue of the circumstances that. Frequently employed as equivalent to the word "if" in legislative enactments and in common speech. Collins v. Atlantic Coast Line R. Co., 183 S.C. 284, 190 S.E. 817, 825.

WHEN AND WHERE. Technical words in pleading, formerly necessary in making *full defense* to certain actions.

WHEN MANY JOIN IN ONE ACT, THE LAW SAYS IT IS THE ACT OF HIM WHO COULD BEST DO IT; AND THINGS SHOULD BE DONE BY HIM WHO HAS THE BEST SKILL. Nov. Max.

WHEN NO TIME IS LIMITED, THE LAW APPOINTS THE MOST CONVENIENT.

WHEN THE COMMON LAW AND STATUTE LAW CONCUR, THE COMMON LAW IS TO BE PREFERRED. 4 Co. 71.

WHEN THE FOUNDATION FAILS, ALL FAILS.

WHEN THE LAW GIVES ANYTHING, IT GIVES A REMEDY FOR THE SAME.

WHEN THE LAW PRESUMES THE AFFIRMATIVE, THE NEGATIVE IS TO BE PROVED. 1 Rolle 83.

WHEN TWO TITLES CONCUR, THE BEST IS PREFERRED. Finch, Law. b. 1, c. 4, n. 82.

WHENEVER. At whatever time; at what time soever. Williams v. Potter, D.C.N.Y., 210 F. 318, 325; People v. Merhige, 221 Mich. 601, 180 N.W. 418, 422. In any or every instance in which. Chiapetta v. Jordan, 153 Fla. 788, 16 So.2d 641, 644. As long as. Moore v. Johnson, 85 N.J.Law, 40, 88 A. 699, 701. As soon as; upon which; where; in case; if. People v. Merhige, 212 Mich. 601, 180 N.W. 418, 422.

WHERE. At the place. Girl v. U. S. Railroad Administration, 194 Iowa 1382, 189 N.W. 834, 835; Shearer v. Farmers' Life Ins. Co., 106 Kan. 574, 189 P. 648, 650. As used in the statutory language, "where the prosecution is held," the word does not refer to the geographical location of the place of hearing, but rather to the tribunal or official before whom the case is tried. Barth v. State, 107 Ohio St. 154, 140 N.E. 650, 651.

If; in the case of; in the event that. Graham v. Standard Fire Ins. Co., 119 S.C. 218, 112 S.E. 88, 89.

WHERE THERE IS EQUAL EQUITY, THE LAW MUST PREVAIL. Bisp.Eq. § 40; 4 Bouv.Inst. n. 3727.

WHERE TWO RIGHTS CONCUR, THE MORE ANCIENT SHALL BE PREFERRED.

WHEREAS. When in fact. Stoltz v. People, 59 Colo. 342, 148 P. 865, 866. Although. Hill v. Smith, 95 Conn. 579, 111 A. 840, 842.

A "whereas" clause of a contract is but an introductory or prefatory statement meaning "considering that" or "that being the case", and is not an essential part of the operating portions of the contract. Jones v. City of Paducah, 283 Ky. 628, 142 S.W.2d 365, 367.

WHEREBY. By or through which; by the help of which; in accordance with which. State ex rel. Finnegan v. Lincoln Dairy Co., 221 Wis. 1, 265 N.W. 197, 200.

WHEREUPON. Upon which; after which. Lee v. Cook, 1 Wyo. 419.

WHEREVER. As often as. Moore v. Johnson, 85 N.J.Law, 40, 88 A. 699, 701.

WHICH. A clause introduced by the relative pronoun "which" is a sufficient allegation of the fact stated in it, if, when read in connection with its context, it plainly manifests an intent on the part of the pleader to set up such fact and rely upon it. Bishop v. Wheeling Mold & Foundry Co., 82 W.Va. 637, 96 S.E. 1020, 1022.

WHIG. This name was applied in Scotland, A. D. 1648, to those violent Covenanters who opposed the Duke of Hamilton's invasion of England in order to restore Charles I. The appellation of "Whig" and "Tory" to political factions was first heard of in A. D. 1679, and, though as senseless as any cant terms that could be devised, they became instantly as familiar in use as they have since continued. 2 Hall. Const. Hist. c. 12; Wharton.

WHILE. Pending or during the time that. Fireman's Fund Ins. Co. v. Jackson, 161 Ga. 559, 131 S.E. 359, 360. Often used adversatively and to imply contrast, and in some constructions introduces a parenthetical clause. Jackson v. Texas Co., C.C. A.Okl., 75 F.2d 549, 553.

WHIPLASH INJURY. A snapping of the neck when a person gets his head thrown forward or back or from side to side. Breitenberg v. Parker, 372 S.W.2d 828, 832, 237 Ark. 261. It is caused by a sudden and unexpected forced movement of the neck of an individual while he is in a relaxed position and against which he cannot protect himself. Hanover Fire Ins. Co. v. Sides, C.A.La., 320 F.2d 437, 441. It may result in several types of pathological findings, such as sprain, fracture, dislocation and so forth. Self v. Johnson, La.App., 124 So.2d 324, 325; Luquette v. Bouillion, La.App., 184 So.2d 766, 768.

WHIPPING. A mode of punishment, by the infliction of stripes, occasionally used in England and in a few of the American states. See Act of February 28, 1839, § 5 (18 U.S.C.A. § 3564).

WHIPPING-POST. A post or stake to which a criminal is tied to undergo the punishment of whipping.

WHIPPING STRAP. Device to warn employees on train of approach to tunnel. Southern Ry. Co. v. Crawley, 229 Ala. 162, 155 So. 568.

See, also, Telltales.

WHISKY. An alcoholic liquid obtained by the distillation of the mash of fermented grain. Ramsey v. State, 132 Tex.Cr.R. 411, 104 S.W.2d 858, 859. Containing many times one-half of one per cent. of alcohol. Allshouse v. U. S., C.C.A.Pa., 38 F.2d 234, 235.

Within the pure food act of 1906, it is the product of sound grain distilled at a low temperature so as to retain in the distillate the congeneric properties of the grain which gives to the liquor when matured by aging in charred casks its desirable potable character. Neutral spirits which are distilled at a high temperature may be made from different materials and do not contain such properties, and which are not rendered potable by aging although reduced by water to potable strength, and from which most of the fusel oil has been removed, are not whisky, nor a like substance with whisky. Woolner & Co. v. Rennick, C.C.Ill., 170 F. 662.

WHITE ACRE. A fictitious name given to a piece of land, in the English books, for purposes of illustration.

WHITE BONNET. In Scotch law. A fictitious offerer or bidder at a roup or auction sale. Bell.

WHITE MEATS. In old English law. Milk, butter, cheese, eggs, and any composition of them. Cowell.

WHITE METAL. In a special technical sense, the copper sulphide remaining when, in smelting copper ore, copper matte is treated to break up and remove iron sulphide. United Verde Copper Co. v. Peirce-Smith Converter Co., C.C.A.Del., 7 F.2d 13, 14.

WHITE MULE. Corn whisky. State v. Johnson, Mo.Sup., 292 S.W. 41. Contraband whisky. Sloan v. State, 193 Ind. 625, 141 N.E. 321.

WHITE PERSONS. As used in Rev.St.U.S. § 2169 (Naturalization Act March 26, 1790, c. 3, 1 Stat. 103, as amended by Act Feb. 18, 1875, c. 80, § 1, 18 Stat. 318 [8 U.S.C.A. § 703]), members of the white or Caucasian race, as distinct from the black, red, yellow, and brown races. Petition of Easurk Emsen Charr, D.C.Mo., 273 F. 207, 209; Takao Ozawa v. U. S., 43 S.Ct. 65, 68, 260 U.S. 178, 67 L.Ed. 199; In re Ah Yup, 5 Sawy. 155, F.Cas. No. 104.

Whether applicant for United States citizenship is a "white person" eligible for citizenship under statute enumerating classes of people eligible therefor depends, not upon ethnological classification of group to which he belongs, but upon whether members of such group with characteristics existing in 1790 when statute was first enacted were intended by Congress to be classified as white persons. In re Ahmed Hassan, D.C.Mich., 48 F.Supp. 843, 845. And statute uses the words "white persons" as meaning primarily the European peoples who constituted the class from which virtually all of immigration to United States has come and who readily become assimilated into our civilization. In re Ahmed Hassan, D.C.Mich., 48 F.Supp. 843, 845.

The term excludes: a Hindu, U. S. v. Ali, D.C.Mich., 7 F.2d 728, 731; a Mongolian, In re Ah Yup, 5 Sawy. 155, F. Cas.No.104; In re Fisher, D.C.Cal., 21 F.2d 1007; Terrace v. Thompson, D.C.Wash., 274 F. 841, 843; In re Lampitoe, D.C.N.Y., 232 F. 382; a native born Filipino, In re Cariaga, D.C.Mich., 47 F.2d 609; a native of Afghanistan, In re Feroz Din, D.C.Cal., 27 F.2d 568, an Arab, In re Ahmed Hassan, D.C.Mich., 48 F.Supp. 843, 845. (Contra In re Moriez, D.C.Mass., 54 F.Supp. 941, 942.) It has been held to include a Syrian; Dow v. United States, C.C.A.S.C., 226 F. 145; In re Ellis, D.C.Or., 179 F. 1002; Bessho v. U. S., C.C.A.Va., 178 F. 245, 101 C.C.A. 605; and an Armenian; In re Halladjian, C.C.Mass., 174 F. 834.

In the legislation of the slave period, persons without admixture of colored blood, whatever the actual complexion might be. Du Val v. Johnson, 39 Ark. 192. See, also, White Race.

In South Africa, persons of European descent. [1905] T. S. 621.

WHITE RACE. Within the meaning of the Mississippi Constitution of 1890, § 207, providing that there shall be separate schools for the white and colored races, the Caucasian race;—the term "colored races," being used in contradistinction to the white race, and embracing all other races. Rice v. Gong Lum, 139 Miss. 760, 104 So. 105, 107. See, also, White Persons.

WHITE RENTS. In English law. Rents paid in silver, and called "white rents," or "*redditus albi*," to distinguish them from rents payable in corn, labor, provisions, etc., called "black-rent" or "black-mail." Co. 2d Inst. 19. See Alba Firma.

WHITE SLAVE. A term used in the United States statutes and in common talk (though not very appropriately) to indicate a female with reference to whom an offense is committed under the so-called Mann White Slave Traffic Act of June 25, 1910 (18 U.S.C.A. §§ 2421–2424), prohibiting the transportation in interstate and foreign commerce for immoral purposes of women and girls.

WHITE SPURS. A kind of esquires. Cowell.

WHITECAPS. The name of an unlawful organization against which Tennessee in 1897 enacted a statute (Acts 1897, c. 52) entitled, "An act to prevent and punish the formation or continuance of conspiracies and combinations for certain unlawful purposes," etc., commonly known as the "Law against Whitecaps." Persons guilty of any offense under the act were rendered incompetent for jury service. Jenkins v. State, 99 Tenn. 569, 42 S.W. 263.

WHITEFRIARS. A place in London between the Temple and Blackfriars, which was formerly a sanctuary, and therefore privileged from arrest. Wharton.

WHITEHART SILVER. A mulct on certain lands in or near to the forest of Whitehart, paid into the exchequer, imposed by Henry III. upon Thomas de la Linda, for killing a beautiful white hart which that king before had spared in hunting. Camd. Brit. 150.

WHITSUN FARTHINGS. Pentecostals, (*q. v.*).

WHITSUNTIDE. The feast of Pentecost, being the fiftieth day after Easter, and the first of the four cross-quarter days of the year. Wharton.

WHITTANWARII. In old English law. A class of offenders who whitened stolen ox-hides and horse-hides so that they could not be known and identified.

WHOEVER. This word in statutes may be construed as including corporations and partnerships. American Socialist Soc. v. U. S., C.C.A.N.Y., 266 F. 212, 213; U. S. v. American Socialist Soc., D.C. N.Y., 260 F. 885, 887.

WHOLE. Hale, hearty, strong, sound; also, entire, complete. Clark v. Commercial Casualty Ins. Co., 107 W.Va. 380, 148 S.E. 319, 320.

WHOLE BLOOD. See Blood.

WHOLE CHEST. In the tea trade, a chest containing 100 to 140 pounds or more. Japan Tea Co. v. Franklin MacVeagh & Co., 142 Minn. 152, 171 N.W. 305, 307.

WHOLE GALE. A wind from 55 to 75 miles per hour. The President Madison, C.C.A.Wash., 91 F.2d 835, 841.

WHOLESALE. Selling to retailers or jobbers rather than to consumers. Stolze Lumber Co. v. Stratton, 386 Ill. 334, 54 N.E.2d 554, 558. A sale in large quantity to one who intends to resell. Guess v. Montague, D.C.S.C., 51 F.Supp. 61, modified on other grounds, C.C.A.S.C., 140 F.2d 500. A sale of goods by the piece or in large quantities. Fleming v. American Stores Co., D.C.Pa., 42 F.Supp. 511, 522.

WHOLESALE BAKERY. A business or industry where food products composed principally of flour or meal are prepared and sold in gross to the retail dealer and vendor. Continental Baking Co. v. Campbell, 176 Okl. 218, 55 P.2d 114, 117.

WHOLESALE DEALER. One whose business is the selling of goods in gross to retail dealers, and not by the small quantity or parcel to consumers thereof. Veazey Drug Co. v. Bruza, 169 Okl. 418, 37 P.2d 294.

WHOLESALE PRICE. That which retailer pays in expectation of obtaining higher price by way of profit from ultimate consumer. Guess v. Montague, D.C.S.C., 51 F.Supp. 61, 65.

WHOLESALER. One who buys in comparatively large quantities, and who sells, usually in smaller quantities, but never to the ultimate consumer of an individual unit. He sells either to a "jobber," a sort of middleman, or to a "retailer," who sells to the consumer. Great Atlantic & Pacific Tea Co. v. Cream of Wheat Co., C.C.A.N.Y., 227 F. 46, 47; Fischbach Brewing Co. v. City of St. Louis, 95 S.W.2d 335, 340, 231 Mo.App. 793.

WHOLESOME. Sound, tending to promote health. Leonardi v. A. Habermann Provision Co., 143 Ohio St. 623, 56 N.E.2d 232, 237.

WHOLLY. Not partially. Corsaut v. Equitable Life Assur. Soc. of the United States, 203 Iowa, 741, 211 N.W. 222, 224, 51 A.L.R. 1035; McCormick v. Central Coal & Coke Co., 117 Kan. 686, 232 P. 1071, 1074. In a whole or complete manner; entirely; completely; perfectly. Knox v. Washer, 153 Tenn. 630, 284 S.W. 888, 889. Exclusively; to the exclusion of other things. Commonwealth v. City of Richmond, 116 Va. 69, 81 S.E. 69, 73, L.R.A. 1915A, 1118. Equally. The Canadian Farmer, D.C.Cal., 290 F. 601, 603. Totally; fully. Chicago & Calumet Dist. Transit Co. v. Mueller, 213 Ind. 530, 12 N.E.2d 247, 249.

WHOLLY AND PERMANENTLY DISABLED. Term within disability clause of life policy does not mean "partial" or "temporary," and is not to be construed literally so as to require condition of complete helplessness or utter hopelessness to be entitled to benefits. Duhaime v. Prudential Ins. Co. of America, 86 N.H. 307, 167 A. 269, 270, but must be given rational meaning. Clarkson v. New York Life Ins. Co., D.C.Fla., 4 F.Supp. 791, 793.

WHOLLY DEPENDENT. A person is to be regarded as "wholly dependent" upon a workman, within meaning of compensation acts, when his support is derived wholly from the workman's wages. Baker v. Western Power & Light Co., 147 Kan. 571, 78 P.2d 36, 40; Central Surety and Insurance Corporation v. Industrial Commission, 94 Colo. 341, 30 P.2d 253, 255.

Person may be "wholly dependent" on workman though he may have some slight savings of his own, or some other slight property, or be able to make something by his own service. United States Coal & Coke Co. v. Sutton, 268 Ky. 405, 105 S.W.2d 173, 177.

WHOLLY DESTROYED. A building is "wholly destroyed" within the meaning of statutes permitting recovery of the full amount of a fire insurance policy, when, although some part remains standing, it can no longer be designated as a building. Eck v. Netherlands Ins. Co., 203 Wis. 515, 234 N.W. 718, 719. The words mean totally destroyed as a building, although there is not an absolute extinction of all its parts. Hart v. North British & Mercantile Ins. Co., 182 La. 551, 162 So. 177.

WHOLLY DISABLED. These words within accident policy do not mean a state of complete physical and mental incapacity or utter helplessness but mean rather inability to do all the substantial and material acts necessary to carry on a certain business or occupation or any business or occupation in a customary and usual manner and which acts the insured would be able to perform in such manner but for the disability. Jacobson v. Mutual Ben. Health & Accident Ass'n, 70 N.D. 566, 296 N.W. 545, 552, 553. Total disability. Maryland Assur. Corporation v. Smith, 786 Ky. 513, 151 S.W. 409, 412. See, also, Disability.

WHORE. A woman who practices illicit sexual intercourse, either for hire or to gratify a depraved passion. Rowe v. Myers, 204 Mich. 374, 169 N.W. 823, 825. A woman given to promiscuous intercourse. Barnett v. Phelps, 97 Or. 242, 191 P. 502, 503, 11 A.L.R. 663. A woman who practices unlawful commerce with men, particularly one who does so for hire; a harlot; a concubine; a prostitute. Sheehey v. Cokley, 43 Iowa 183, 22 Am.Rep. 236.

WHOREMASTER. Ordinarily, one who practices lewdness; also, one who keeps or procures whores for others; a pimp; a procurer. Hickerson v. Masters, 190 Ky. 168, 226 S.W. 1072, 1073.

WIC. A place on the sea-shore or the bank of a river.

WICA. A country house or farm. Cowell.

WICK. Sax. A village, town, or district. Hence, in composition, the territory over which a given jurisdiction extends. Thus, "bailiwick" is the territorial jurisdiction of a bailiff or sheriff or constable. "Sheriff-wick" was also used in the old books.

WIDEN. To increase in width; to extend. In re Day, 109 A. 573, 7 Boyce (Del.) 556.

WIDOW. A woman whose husband is dead, and who has not remarried. In re Embiricos' Estate, 184 Misc. 453, 52 N.Y.S.2d 425, 427.

Grass Widow

See that title.

King's Widow

One whose deceased husband had been the king's tenant *in capite*; she could not marry again without the royal permission.

Widow-bench

The share of her husband's estate which a widow is allowed besides her jointure.

Widow's Chamber

See Chamber, Widow's.

Widow's Quarantine

In old English law. The space of forty days after the death of a man who died seised of lands, during which his widow might remain in her husband's capital mansion-house, without rent, and during which time her dower should be assigned. 2 Bl.Comm. 135. See Vannoy v. Green, 206 N.C. 77, 173 S.E. 277.

Widow's Terce

In Scotch law. The right which a wife has after her husband's death to a third of the rents of lands in which her husband died infeft; dower. Bell.

Year of Mourning

See that title, and Annus Luctus.

WIDOWER. A man who has lost his wife by death and has not married again. Abrams v. Unknown Heirs of Rice, 317 Mo. 216, 295 S.W. 83, 85.

WIDOWHOOD. The state or condition of being a widow, or, sometimes, a widower. An estate is sometimes settled upon a woman "during widowhood," which is expressed in Latin, "*durante viduitate.*"

WIENER. A small sausage of unknown content commonly called a "hot dog." State v. Shoaf, 179 N.C. 744, 102 S.E. 705, 9 A.L.R. 426.

WIFA. L. Lat. In old European law. A mark or sign; a mark set up on land, to denote an exclusive occupation, or to prohibit entry. Spelman.

WIFE. A woman united to a man by marriage; a woman who has a husband living and undivorced. The correlative term is "husband." Davis v. Bass, 188 N.C. 200, 124 S.E. 566, 568; Estes v. Merrill, 121 Ark. 361, 181 S.W. 136, 137; Ex parte Suzanna, D.C.Mass., 295 F. 713, 714.

Workmen's Compensation Laws should be strictly interpreted where rights of legal wife as against putative wife would be defeated or lessened by liberal interpretation, and, as so interpreted, terms "wife" and "widow" within compensation law do not include wife of putative marriage. Fulton Bag & Cotton Mills v. Fernandez, La. App., 159 So. 339, 345.

"Examination of wife," see Private Examination.

WIFE AND CHILDREN. A conveyance or devise by a man to his wife and children will be presumed, in the absence of language indicating a contrary purpose, to be to wife for life, with remainder to her and grantor's or testator's children. Sower v. Lillard, 207 Ky. 283, 269 S.W. 330, 331.

WIFE'S EQUITY. When a husband is compelled to seek the aid of a court of equity for the purpose of obtaining the possession or control of his wife's estate, that court will recognize the right of the wife to have a suitable and reasonable provision made, by settlement or otherwise, for herself and her children, out of the property thus brought within its jurisdiction. This right is called the "wife's equity," or "equity to a settlement." See 2 Kent, Comm. 139.

WIFE'S PART. See Legitime.

WIGREVE. In old English law. The overseer of a wood. Cowell.

WILD ANIMALS (or animals *feræ naturæ*). Animals of an untamable disposition; animals in a state of nature.

WILD FOWL. Any large eatable bird of a wild nature. Crabtree v. State, 123 Ark. 68, 184 S.W. 430.

WILD LAND. Land in a state of nature, as distinguished from improved or cultivated land. Clark v. Phelps, 4 Cow., N.Y., 203. Land in a wilderness state, not used in connection with improved estates. Central Maine Power Co. v. Rollins, 126 Me. 299, 138 A. 170, 174. When land is contiguous to improved and cultivated land, and commonly used therewith for fuel, fencing, repairs, or pasturing, it no longer has the character of "wild land." Holden v. Page, 107 A. 492, 494, 118 Me. 242.

WILD WELL. In the parlance of men in the gas industry, a gas well wherein the gas pipe develops a leak at a point beneath the surface of ground with the result that large amounts of gas escape. Mitchell v. Mitchell Drilling Co., 154 Kan. 117, 114 P.2d 841, 842.

WILD'S CASE, RULE IN. A devise to B. and his children or issue, B. having no issue at the time of the devise, gives him an estate tail; but, if he have issue at the time, B. and his children take joint estates for life. 6 Coke, 16*b*; Tudor, Lead. Cas. Real Prop. 542, 581.

WILL, *v.* An auxiliary verb commonly having the mandatory sense of "shall" or "must." Tennessee Cent. R. Co. v. Morgan, 132 Tenn. 1, 175 S. W. 1148, 1153. State v. Summers, Mo.App., 281 S.W. 123, 124. It is a word of certainty, while the word "may" is one of speculation and uncertainty. Carson v. Turrish, 140 Minn. 445, 168 N.W. 349, 352, L.R.A.1918F, 154.

WILL, *n.* Wish; desire; pleasure; inclination; choice; the faculty of conscious, and especially of deliberate, action. State v. Schwab, 109 Ohio St. 532, 143 N.E. 29, 31. When a person expresses his "will" that a particular disposition be made of his property, his words are words of command, Temple v. Russell, 251 Mass. 231, 146 N.E. 679, 680, 49 A.L.R. 1, and the word "will" as so used is mandatory, comprehensive, and dispositive in nature, Mastellar v. Atkinson, 94 Kan. 279, 146 P. 367, 368, Ann.Cas.1917B, 502.

Law of Wills

The legal expression or declaration of a person's mind or wishes as to the disposition of his property, to be performed or take effect after his death. Swinb. Wills, § 2; Thomas v. House, 145 Va. 742, 134 S.E. 673, 674; In re McCune's Estate, 265 Pa. 523, 109 A. 156, 157; Krause v. Krause, 113 Neb. 22, 201 N.W. 670, 673. A revocable instrument by which a person makes disposition of his property to take effect after his death. Howard's Ex'r v. Dempster, 246 Ky. 153, 54 S.W.2d 660, 661. Any instrument whereby a person makes a disposition of his property to take effect after his death. Todd v. Williams' Adm'x, 264 Ky. 788, 95 S.W.2d 593, 596. A written instrument executed with the formalities of law, whereby a person makes a disposition of his property to take effect after his death. Tax Commission of Ohio v. Parker, 117 Ohio St. 215, 158 N.E. 89, 90.

To constitute "will," intention must appear that writer by document itself intended to make disposition of property effective only after death. In re Button's Estate, 209 Cal. 325, 287 P. 964, 967.

A "will" is not a sheet of paper, nor a number of sheets or pages, but consists of the words written thereon. In re Golden's Will, 165 Misc. 205, 300 N.Y.S. 737, 738. And the form of an instrument is of little consequence in determining whether it is a will, but if it is executed with formalities required by statute, and if it is to operate only after death of maker, it is a "will". In re Fowle's Estate, 292 Mich. 500, 290 N.W. 883, 885.

Instruments conveying a present interest are deeds, and not wills, Jung v. Petermann, Tex.Civ.App., 194 S.W. 202, 205; Moss v. Hodges, 294 Ky. 677, 172 S.W.2d 584, 585; for wills pass no interest until after the death of the maker; Willis v. Fiveash, Tex.Civ.App., 297 S.W. 509, 510; Sims v. Brown, 252 Mo. 58, 158 S.W. 624, 627. An instrument, although in form of a bill or note, which is intended to have no operation until death of maker, is not "contractual" but is of the nature of a "will." In re Murphy's Estate, 193 Wash. 400, 75 P.2d 916, 924.

"Codicil" to will is distinguished from new "will," in that the latter revokes the first in its entirety unless otherwise provided therein. In re Bissell's Estate, 302 Pa. 27, 153 A. 692, 694.

The distinction between a "will" and a "power of appointment" is that a will concerns the estate of the testator, while an appointment under a power concerns that of the donor of the power. Thompson v. Pew, 214 Mass. 520, 102 N.E. 122.

The difference between a will and a trust is that a will operates from the moment of death, while a trust operates in præsenti to a certain extent. Allen v. Hendrick, 104 Or. 202, 206 P. 733, 740.

A gift inter vivos is distinguishable from a will in that such a gift may be made by parol and, upon the acceptance of the gift by the donee, the gift is irrevocable by the donor, while ordinarily a will is required to be in writing, and usually is made in view of the fact of death, and is ineffective until the death of the testator and the admission of the will to probate. York v. Trigg, 87 Okl. 214, 209 P. 417, 423.

The term will, as an expression of the final disposition of one's property, is confined to the English laws and those countries which derive their jurisprudence from that source. The term *testamentum*, or *testament*, is exclusively used in the Roman civil law and by the continental writers upon that subject.

A will, when it operates upon personal property, is sometimes called a "testament," and when upon real estate, a "devise;" but the more general and the more popular denomination of the instrument embracing equally real and personal estate is that of "last will and testament." 4 Kent, Comm. 501; In re Kiltz's Will, 125 Misc.Rep. 475, 211 N.Y.S. 450, 461.

Criminal Law

The power of the mind which directs the action of a man.

Scotch Practice

That part or clause of a process which contains the mandate or command to the officer. Bell.

General

Ambulatory will. A changeable will (*ambulatoria voluntas*), the phrase merely denoting the power which a testator possesses of altering his will during his life-time. See Hattersley v. Bissett, 50 N.J.Eq. 577, 25 A. 332.

Conditional will. A conditional disposition is one which depends upon the occurrence of some uncertain event, by which it is either to take effect or to be defeated. Rogers v. Mosier, 121 Okl. 213, 245 P. 36, 38. If the happening of an event named in a will is the reason for making the will, it is "unconditional"; but, if the testator intends to dispose of his property in case the event happens, the will is "conditional." Ferguson v. Ferguson, Tex.Civ.App., 288 S.W. 833, 835.

Conjoint will. See Joint Will, *infra.*

Counter wills. Another name for "double," "mutual," or "reciprocal" wills. Wright v. Wright, 215 Ky. 394, 285 S.W. 188, 189.

Double will. Called also a "counter," "mutual," or "reciprocal" will. Wright v. Wright, 215 Ky. 394, 285 S.W. 188, 189. See Double.

Estate at will. This estate entitles the grantee or lessee to the possession of land during the pleasure of both the grantor and himself, yet it creates no sure or durable right, and is bounded by no definite limits as to duration. It must be at the reciprocal will of both parties, (for, if it be at the will of the lessor only, it is a lease for life,) and the dissent of either determines it. Wharton.

Holographic will. One that is entirely written, dated, and signed by the hand of the testator himself. In re Hail's Estate, 106 Okl. 124, 235 P. 916, 917; In re Cole's Will, 171 N.C. 74, 87 S.E. 962; Civ.Code La. art. 1588. Sometimes spelled "olographic." Succession of Cunningham, 142 La. 701, 77 So. 506, 510. The statutes in the different states differ to some extent, but agree substantially with the English statute of Charles II. Compliance with the precise terms of the statutory definition or requirements is commonly insisted upon with the utmost meticulosity. In re Thorn's Estate, 183 Cal. 512, 192 P. 19, 20.

Joint and mutual will. One executed jointly by two persons with reciprocal provisions, which shows on its face that the devises are made one in consideration of the other. Wright v. Wright, 215 Ky. 394, 285 S.W. 188, 189; Bright v. Cox, 147 Ga. 474, 94 S.E. 572, 573.

Joint will. One where the same instrument is made the will of two or more persons and is jointly signed by them. Such wills are usually executed to make testamentary disposition of joint property. Bright v. Cox, 147 Ga. 474, 94 S.E. 572, 573; Campbell v. Dunkelberger, 172 Iowa 385, 153 N.W. 56, 58. A joint or conjoint will is a testamentary instrument executed by two or more persons, in pursuance of a common intention, for the purpose of disposing of their several interests in property owned by them in common, or of their separate property treated as a common fund, to a third person or persons. Ginn v. Edmundson, 173 N.C. 85, 91 S.E. 696.

Mutual will. One in which two or more persons make mutual or reciprocal provisions in favor of each other. Ginn v. Edmundson, 173 N.C. 85, 91 S.E. 696. "Mutual wills" are the separate wills of two persons which are reciprocal in their provisions, and such a will may be both joint and mutual. Campbell v. Dunkelberger, 172 Iowa 385, 153 N.W. 56, 58; Carle v. Miles, 89 Kan. 540, 132 P. 146, Ann.Cas.1915A, 363; Bright v. Cox, 147 Ga. 474, 94 S.E. 572, 573. Sometimes called a "reciprocal," "double," or "counter" will. Wright v. Wright, 215 Ky. 394, 285 S.W. 188, 189.

Mystic will. See Testament.

Non-intervention will. In some jurisdictions, one authorizing the executor to act without bond and to manage, control, and settle the estate without the intervention of any court whatsoever. In re MacDonald's Estate, 29 Wash. 422, 428, 69 P. 1111.

Nuncupative will. See that title.

Reciprocal will. One in which two or more persons make mutual or reciprocal provisions in favor of each other. Ginn v. Edmundson, 173 N.C. 85, 91 S.E. 696. Also known as a "mutual," "double," or "counter" will. Wright v. Wright, 215 Ky. 394, 285 S.W. 188, 189.

Self-proved wills. A will which eliminates some of the formalities of proof by execution in compliance with statute. It is made self-proved by affidavit of attesting witnesses in the form prescribed by statute. Most statutes provide that, unless contested, such a will may be admitted to probate without testimony of subscribing witnesses.

Statute of wills. See Wills Act, *infra*.

Unofficious will. In the civil law, *testamentum inofficium*. One made in disregard of natural obligations as to inheritance. Stein v. Wilzinski, 4 Redf.Sur. (N.Y.) 450; 2 Bla.Comm. 502; Hadley, Rom.L. 317. It has no place in the common law; 1 Fost. & F. 578.

WILL CONTEST. A proceeding sui generis, a suit in rem, having for its purpose determination of question of whether there is or is not a will. McCrary v. Michael, 233 Mo.App. 797, 109 S.W.2d 50, 51. Any kind of litigated controversy concerning the eligibility of an instrument to probate as distinguished from validity of the contents of the will. In re Hesse's Estate, 62 Ariz. 273, 157 P.2d 347, 349.

WILLA. In Hindu law. The relation between a master or patron and his freedman, and the relation between two persons who had made a reciprocal testamentary contract. Wharton.

WILLFUL. Proceeding from a conscious motion of the will; voluntary. Nashville, C. & St. L. Ry. Co. v. Commonwealth, 160 Ky. 50, 169 S.W. 511, 513.

Intractable; having a headstrong disposition to act by the rule of contradiction. Bersch v. Morris & Co., 106 Kan. 800, 189 P. 934, 935, 9 A.L.R. 1374. Obstinate; perverse. Lynch v. Commonwealth, 131 Va. 762, 109 S.E. 427, 428; Jones v. State, 7 Ala.App. 180, 62 So. 306, 307.

Intending the result which actually comes to pass; designed; intentional; not accidental or involuntary. Garrett v. Commonwealth, 215 Ky. 484, 285 S.W. 203, 204; State v. Muzzy, 87 Vt. 267, 88 A. 895, 896; Roseville Trust Co. v. American Surety Co. of New York, 91 N.J.Law, 588, 103 A. 182; State v. Lehman, 131 Minn. 427, 155 N.W. 399, Ann.Cas.1917D, 615; United States v. Illinois Cent. R. Co., La., 58 S.Ct. 533, 535, 303 U.S. 239, 82 L.Ed. 773.

The word "wilful" is a word of many meanings depending on the context in which it is used. Zimberg v. United States, C.C.A.Mass., 142 F.2d 132, 137.

A "willful" act may be described as one done intentionally, knowingly, and purposely, without justifiable excuse, as distinguished from an act done carelessly, thoughtlessly, heedlessly, or inadvertently. Lobdell Car Wheel Co. v. Subielski, 125 A. 462, 464, 2 W.W.Harr. (Del.) 462.

A willful differs essentially from a negligent act. The one is positive and the other negative. Sturm v. Atlantic Mut. Ins. Co., 38 N.Y.Super.Ct. 317; Thayer v. Denver & R. G. R. Co., 21 N.M. 330, 154 P. 691, 694. Simple negligence arises merely from heedlessness, and consists simply of facts of nonfeasance, and is therefore incompatible with willfulness, which comprises acts of aggressive wrong, Stauffer v. Schlegel, 74 Ind.App. 431, 129 N.E. 44, 46; and presupposes a conscious purpose to injure, In re Cunningham, D.C.N.Y., 253 F. 663, 665; Ft. Wayne & Wabash Valley Traction Co. v. Justus, 180 Ind. 464, 115 N.E. 585, 587; Brittain v. Southern Ry. Co., 167 N.C. 642, 83 S.E. 702, 703.

"Willfulness" implies an act done intentionally and designedly; "wantonness" implies action without regard to the rights of others, a conscious failure to observe care, a conscious invasion of the rights of others, willful, unrestrained action; and "recklessness" a disregard of consequences, an indifference whether a wrong or injury is done or not, and an indifference to natural and probable consequences. Jensen v. Denver & R. G. R. Co., 44 Utah, 100, 138 P. 1185, 1188. See, also, Evans v. Illinois Cent. R. Co., 289 Mo. 493, 233 S.W. 397, 399; Cover v. Hershey Transit Co., 290 Pa. 551, 139 A. 266, 268; Feore v. Trammel, 212 Ala. 325, 102 So. 529, 533; Crosman v. Southern Pac. Co., 44 Nev. 286, 194 P. 839, 843.

The word "reckless," as applied to negligence, is the legal equivalent of "willful" or "wanton." Heller v. New York, N. H. & H. R. Co., C.C.A.N.Y., 265 F. 192, 194. And see Strough v. Central R. Co. of New Jersey, C.C.A.N.J., 209 F. 23, 26.

Conscious; knowing; done with stubborn purpose, but not with malice. Bundy v. State, 206 N.W. 21, 22, 114 Neb. 121; American Surety Co. of New York v. Sullivan, C.C.A.N.Y., 7 F.2d 605,

606; Helme v. Great Western Milling Co., 43 Cal. App. 416, 185 P. 510, 512; Gray v. Alabama Fuel & Iron Co., 216 Ala. 416, 113 So. 35, 39.

Premeditated; malicious; done with evil intent, or with a bad motive or purpose, or with indifference to the natural consequences; unlawful; without legal justification. State v. Vanderveer, 115 Wash. 184, 196 P. 650; State v. Johnson, 194 N.C. 378, 139 S.E. 697, 698; Boyce v. Greeley Square Hotel Co., 228 N.Y. 106, 126 N.E. 647, 649; State v. Palmer, 94 Vt. 278, 110 A. 436, 437.

Words which import an exercise of the will, such as "feloniously," "maliciously," and "unlawfully," will supply the place of the word "willfully" in an indictment. Howenstine v. U. S., C.C.A.Cal., 263 F. 1, 3; Chapman v. Com., 5 Whart. (Pa.) 427, 34 Am.Dec. 565. *Contra,* State v. Waters, Mo.App., 189 S.W. 624; State v. Hyman, 116 Me. 419, 102 A. 231, 232.

WILLFUL AND MALICIOUS INJURY. The word "willful," as used in this phrase in the Bankruptcy Act July 1, 1898, c. 541, § 17(2), 30 Stat. 550, as amended by the Act of Feb. 5, 1903, c. 487, 32 Stat. 797 (11 U.S.C.A. § 35), means intentional though not necessarily deliberate. Nunn v. Drieborg, 235 Mich. 383, 209 N.W. 89, 90; Wellman v. Mead, 93 Vt. 322, 107 A. 396, 404. Mere negligence is not enough; In re Roberts, D.C. Mich., 290 F. 257, 259; In re Byrne, C.C.A.N.Y., 296 F. 98, 100; there must be an intent to commit a wrong either through actual malice or from which malice will be implied; McClellan v. Schmidt, D. C.N.J., 235 F. 986, 987. Such an injury does not necessarily involve hatred or ill will, as a state of mind, but arises from intentional wrong committed without just cause or excuse. In re Wernecke, D.C.N.Y., 1 F.Supp. 127, 168. It may involve merely a willful disregard of what one knows to be his duty, an act which is against good morals and wrongful in and of itself, and which necessarily causes injury and is done intentionally. In re Stenger, D.C.Mich., 283 F. 419, 420; In re Phillips, D.C.Ohio, 298 F. 135, 138.

WILLFUL AND WANTON INJURY. To constitute such injury, act producing injury must have been knowingly and intentionally committed, or committed under circumstances evincing reckless disregard of safety of person injured. Price v. Gabel, 162 Wash. 275, 298 P. 444, 447.

WILLFUL INDIFFERENCE TO THE SAFETY OF OTHERS. Imports an intentional lack of regard concerning the safety of others, or an intentional doing of something with knowledge that serious injury is a probable result. People v. Murray, 58 Cal.App.2d 239, 136 P.2d 389, 391.

WILLFUL MISCONDUCT OF EMPLOYEE. Under Workmen's Compensation Acts, precluding compensation, means more than mere negligence, and contemplates the intentional doing of something with knowledge that it is likely to result in serious injuries, or with reckless disregard of its probable consequences. Carroll v. Ætna Life Ins. Co., 39 Ga.App. 78, 146 S.E. 788, 789; Black Mountain Corporation v. Higgins, 226 Ky. 7, 10 S.W.2d 463, 464.

WILLFUL OR WANTON MISCONDUCT. Failure to exercise ordinary care to prevent injury to a person who is actually known to be or reasonably expected to be within the range of a dangerous act being done. Georgia Power Co. v. Deese, 78 Ga.App. 704, 51 S.E.2d 724, 728.

WILLFUL OR WANTON NEGLIGENCE. Failure to exercise ordinary care to prevent injury to a person who is actually known to be, or reasonably is expected to be, within range of a known danger. Barall Food Stores v. Bennett, 194 Okl. 508, 153 P.2d 106, 109, 110.

WILLFUL TORT. Implies intent or purpose to injure. Cousins v. Booksbaum, 51 Ohio App. 150, 200 N.E. 133, 135; American Casualty Co. v. Brinsky, 51 Ohio App. 298, 200 N.E. 654, 655.

It involves elements of intent or purpose and malice or ill will, but malice or ill will may be shown by indifference to safety of others, with knowledge of their danger, or failure to use ordinary care to avoid injury after acquiring such knowledge. Hillard v. Western & Southern Life Ins. Co., 68 Ohio App. 426, 34 N.E.2d 75, 77.

WILLFUL MURDER. The unlawful and intentional killing of another without excuse or mitigating circumstances. State v. Dalton, 178 N.C. 779, 101 S.E. 548, 549.

WILLFUL NEGLIGENCE. See Negligence.

WILLINGLY. Voluntarily; unreluctantly; without reluctance, and of one's own free choice. Edwards v. State, 21 Ala.App. 375, 108 So. 639, 640. See State v. Schwab, 109 Ohio St. 532, 143 N.E. 29, 31. As used in an instruction that one cannot invoke the doctrine of self-defense if he enters a fight willingly, it means voluntarily, aggressively, and without legal excuse. State v. Evans, 194 N.C. 121, 138 S.E. 518, 519.

WILLS ACT. In England. The statute 32 Hen. VIII. c. 1, passed in 1540, by which persons seized in fee-simple of lands holden in socage tenure were enabled to devise the same at their will and pleasure, except to bodies corporate; and those who held estates by the tenure of chivalry were enabled to devise two-third parts thereof.

Also, the statute 7 Wm. IV. & 1 Vict. c. 26, passed in 1837, and also called "Lord Langdale's Act." This act permits of the disposition by will of every kind of interest in real and personal estate, and provides that all wills, whether of real or of personal estate, shall be attested by two witnesses, and that such attestation shall be sufficient. Other important alterations are effected by this statute in the law of wills. Mozley & Whiteley.

WINCHESTER MEASURE. The standard measure of England, originally kept at Winchester. 1 Bl.Comm. 274.

WINCHESTER, STATUTE OF. A statute passed in the thirteenth year of the reign of Edward I., by which the old Saxon law of police was enforced, with many additional provisions. 2 Reeve, Eng.Law, 163; Crabb, Hist.Eng.Law, 189. It required every man to provide himself with armor to aid in keeping the peace; and if it did not create the offices of high and petty constables, it recognized and regulated them, and charged them with duties answering somewhat to those of our militia officers. The statute took its name from the ancient capital of the kingdom. It was repealed by the Statute of 7 & 8 Geo. IV. c. 27. See 1 Seld.Essays 153.

WIND SHIELD. On automobiles, the glass between the two front standards or posts;—not ordinarily including wind deflectors placed outside of such standards. Hammond v. Benzer Corporation, D.C.N.Y., 295 F. 908, 912.

WIND UP. To settle the accounts and liquidate the assets of a partnership or corporation, for the purpose of making distribution and dissolving the concern. State v. Norman, 86 Okl. 36, 206 P. 522, 527; State v. Quigley, 93 Okl. 296, 220 P. 918; Barret v. Skalsky, 118 Kan. 162, 233 P. 1043.

WINDING–UP ACTS. In English law. General acts of parliament, regulating settlement of corporate affairs on dissolution.

WINDOW. An opening made in the wall of a building to admit light and air, and to furnish a view or prospect. Hale v. Ins. Co., 46 Mo.App. 508; Benner v. Benner, 119 Me. 79, 109 A. 376, 377. The use of this word in law is chiefly in connection with the doctrine of ancient lights and other rights of adjacent owners.

WINDOW ENVELOPE. One which has on its face a patch of transparent paper forming a window through which an address written upon an inclosure can be seen. Outlook Envelope Co. v. Samuel Cupples Envelope Co., C.C.A.N.Y., 223 F. 327, 329.

WINDOW TAX. A tax on windows, levied on houses which contained more than six windows, and were worth more than £5 per annum; established by St. 7 Wm. III. c. 18. St. 14 & 15 Vict. c. 36, substituted for this tax a tax on inhabited houses. Wharton.

WINDSHAKES. Cracks in timber that are due to the wind when the timber stood, or to drying in the center after the timber is cut. Swartz v. Bergendahl-Knight Co., 259 Pa. 421, 103 A. 220, 221.

WINDSOR FOREST. A royal forest founded by Henry VIII.

WINDSTORM. A storm characterized by high wind, with little or no precipitation. George A. Hoagland & Co. v. Insurance Co. of North America, 131 Neb. 105, 267 N.W. 239, 241. A violent wind. Clark v. Fidelity & Guaranty Fire Corporation, City Ct., 39 N.Y.S.2d 377, 379, 380.

WINDY SHOTS. In blasting operations, explosions which cause pieces of rock to fly up in the air. Brede v. Minnesota Crushed Stone Co., 146 Minn. 406, 178 N.W. 820, 821.

WINE. The fermented juice of the grape. State v. Moore, 5 Blackf. (Ind.) 118; Tux Ginger Ale Co. v. Davis, 12 Cal.App.2d 73, 54 P.2d 1122. A vinous liquor, Peretto v. State, 31 Okl.Cr. 319, 238 P. 870, containing more than 1 per cent. of alcohol, People v. Mueller, 168 Cal. 526, 143 P. 750, 751. Sometimes loosely used as to unfermented juice of the grape or any fruit used as a beverage. State v. Rosasco, 103 Or. 343, 205 P. 290, 295. But see State v. Dennison, 85 W.Va. 261, 101 S.E. 458, 460.

WINTER. A period of three months, whether reckoned astronomically from the winter solstice, on December 21, to the vernal equinox, on March 21, or according to the conventional method used in the United States as including December, January, and February. Saarela v. Hoglund, 198 Ill. App. 485, 487. In a popular sense, the cold months. Whitney v. Aronson, 21 Cal.App. 9, 130 P. 700.

WINTER CIRCUIT. An occasional circuit appointed for the trial of prisoners, in England, and in some cases of civil causes, between Michaelmas and Hilary terms.

WINTER HEYNING. The season between 11th November and 23d April, which is excepted from the liberty of commoning in certain forests. St. 23 Car. II. c. 3.

WINZE. A vertical or steeply inclined passageway driven to connect a mine working with another. Empire Star Mines Co. v. Butler, 62 Cal. App.2d 49, 145 P.2d 49, 63.

WISBY, LAWS OF. The name given to a code of maritime laws promulgated at Wisby, then the capital of Gothland, in Sweden, in the latter part of the thirteenth century. This compilation resembled the laws of Oleron in many respects, and was early adopted, as a system of sea laws, by the commercial nations of Northern Europe. It formed the foundation for the subsequent code of the Hanseatic League. A translation of the Laws of Wisby may be seen in the appendix to 1 Pet. Adm. And see 3 Kent, Comm. 13. They are also printed in 30 F.Cas. 1189.

WISH. Eager desire; longing; expression of desire; a thing desired; an object of desire. Noice v. Schnell, 101 N.J.Eq. 252, 137 A. 582, 589, 52 A.L. R. 965. As used in wills, it is sometimes merely directory or precatory; Colonial Trust Co. v. Brown, 105 Conn. 261, 135 A. 555, 563; Schill v. Schill, 101 N.J.Eq. 482, 138 A. 530, 531; and sometimes mandatory; Strout v. Strout, 117 Me. 357, 104 A. 577, 578; being equivalent to "will," Tzeses v. Tenez Const. Co., 97 N.J.Eq. 501, 128 A. 388, or to "give" or "devise," Brown v. Brown, 180 N.C. 433, 104 S.E. 889, 890.

WISTA. In Saxon law. Half a hide of land, or sixty acres.

WIT. To know; to learn; to be informed. Used only in the infinitive, *to wit*, which term is equivalent to "that is to say," "namely," or "*videlicet*."

WITAM. The purgation from an offense by the oath of the requisite number of witnesses.

WITAN. In Saxon law. Wise men; persons of information, especially in the laws; the king's advisers; members of the king's council; the optimates, or principal men of the kingdom. 1 Spence, Eq. Jur. 11, note.

WITCHCRAFT. Under Sts. 33 Hen. VIII. c. 8, and 1 Jac. I. c. 12, the offense of witchcraft, or supposed intercourse with evil spirits, was punishable with death. These acts were not repealed till 1736. 4 Bl.Comm. 60, 61. In Salem, in 1692, 20 persons were put to death by hanging. The last victims in England were executed in 1716, and the last in Scotland in 1722. 29 Encyc. Americana, 430, 431; 1 Beard, Rise of Amer. Civilization, 150.

WITE. Sax. A punishment, pain, penalty, mulct, or criminal fine. Cowell.

An atonement among the early Germans by a wrong-doer to the king or the community. It is said to be the germ of the idea that wrong is not simply the affair of the injured individual, and is therefore a condition precedent to the growth of a criminal law. 2 Holdsw. Hist. E. L. 37. See 1 Sel.Essays, Anglo-Amer. L. H. 100.

WITEKDEN. A taxation of the West Saxons, imposed by the public council of the kingdom.

WITENA DOM. In Saxon law. The judgment of the county court, or other court of competent jurisdiction, on the title to property, real or personal. 1 Spence, Eq.Jur. 22.

WITENAGEMOTE. (Spelled, also, *witenagemot, wittenagemot, witanagemote*, etc.) "The assembly of wise men." This was the great national council or parliament of the Saxons in England, comprising the noblemen, high ecclesiastics, and other great thanes of the kingdom, advising and aiding the king in the general administration of government.

It was the grand council of the kingdom, and was held, generally, in the open air, by public notice or particular summons, in or near some city or populous town. These notices or summonses were issued upon determination by the king's select council, or the body met without notice, when the throne was vacant, to elect a new king. Subsequently to the Norman Conquest it was called *commune concilium regni, curia regis* and finally *parliament;* but its character had become considerably changed. It was a court of last resort, more especially for determining disputes between the king and his thanes, and, ultimately, from all inferior tribunals. Great offenders, particularly those who were members of or might be summoned to the king's court, were here tried. The casual loss of title-deeds was supplied, and a very extensive equity jurisdiction exercised. 1 Spence, Eq.Jur. 73; 1 Bla.Comm. 147; 1 Reeve, Hist.Eng.Law 7; 9 Co.Pref. It passed out of existence with the Norman Conquest, and the subsequent Parliament was a separate growth, and not a continuation of the Witenagemot. 29 Encyc. Americana, 432.

WITENS. The chiefs of the Saxon lords or thanes, their nobles, and wise men.

WITH. A word denoting a relation of proximity, contiguity, or association. White v. White, 183 Va. 239, 31 S.E.2d 558, 561. Sometimes equivalent to the words, "in addition to," but not synonymous with "including," as in a complaint demanding a specified sum, "with interest." Halpern v. Langrock Bros. Co., 169 App.Div. 464, 155 N.Y.S. 167, 168.

WITH ALL FAULTS. This phrase, used in a contract of sale, implies that the purchaser assumes the risk of all defects and imperfections, provided they do not destroy the identity of the thing sold.

WITH CONSENT. Phrase within a Constitution providing that Governor shall appoint officers with consent of senate, requires confirmation by senate and appointment under such provision is ineffective until confirmed. State, ex rel. Nagle v. Stafford, 97 Mont. 275, 34 P.2d 372, 379.

WITH PREJUDICE. The term, as applied to judgment of dismissal is as conclusive of rights of parties as if action had been prosecuted to final adjudication adverse to the plaintiff. Fenton v. Thompson, 352 Mo. 199, 176 S.W.2d 456, 460.

WITH STRONG HAND. In pleading. A technical phrase indispensable in describing a forcible entry in an indictment. No other word or circumlocution will answer the same purpose. Rex v. Wilson, 8 Term R. 357.

WITHDRAW. To take away what has been enjoyed; to take from. Central R. & B. Co. v. State, 54 Ga. 409. To remove. Hamilton v. Kentucky Distilleries & Warehouse Co., C.C.A.Ky., 288 F. 326, 327.

WITHDRAWAL. Removal of money or securities from a bank or other place of deposit. Hensch v. Metropolitan Savings & Loan Co., 50 Ohio App. 25, 197 N.E. 416, 418.

WITHDRAWING A JUROR. In practice. The withdrawing of one of the twelve jurors from the box, with the result that, the jury being now found to be incomplete, no further proceedings can be had in the cause. The withdrawing of a juror is always by the agreement of the parties, and is frequently done at the recommendation of the judge, where it is doubtful whether the action will lie; and in such case the consequence is that each party pays his own costs (in Pennsylvania it is held that the costs abide the event of the suit). It is, however, no bar to a future action for the same cause. 2 Tidd, Pr. 861, 862; 1 Archb. Pr.K.B. 196; Wabash R. Co. v. McCormick, 23 Ind.App. 258, 55 N.E. 251; People v. Judges of New York, 8 Cow. (N.Y.) 127; Glendenning v. Canary, 64 N.Y. 636; Wolcott v. Studebaker, C.C. Ill., 34 F. 8; 3 Term 657; 1 Cr. M. & R. 64; Tr. & H. Pr. § 689; Ry. & M. 402; 3 B. & Ad. 349; 3 Chitty, Pr. 917. In American practice, it is usually a mere method of continuing a case, for some good reason. The cases are collected in a note in 48 L. R.A. 432.

WITHDRAWAL OF CHARGES. A failure to prosecute by the person preferring charges;—distinguished from a dismissal, which is a determination of their invalidity by the tribunal hearing them. Butler v. McSweeney, 222 Mass. 5, 109 N.E. 653, 655.

WITHDRAWING RECORD. In practice. The withdrawing by a plaintiff of the *nisi prius* or trial record filed in a cause, just before the trial is entered upon, for the purpose of preventing the cause from being tried. This may be done before the jury are sworn, and afterwards, by consent of the defendant's counsel. 2 Tidd, Pr. 851; 1 Archb. Pr. K. B. 189; 3 Chit.Pr. 870; 2 C. & P. 185; 3 Camp. 333.

WITHERNAM. In practice. A taking by way of reprisal; a taking or a reprisal of other goods, in lieu of those that were formerly taken and eloigned or withholden. 2 Inst. 141. A reciprocal distress, in lieu of a previous one which has been eloigned. 3 Bl.Comm. 148.

The name of a writ which issues on the return of *elongata* to an alias or pluries writ of replevin, by which the sheriff is commanded to take the defendant's own goods which may be found in his bailiwick, and keep them safely, not to deliver them to the plaintiff until such time as the defendant chooses to submit himself and allow the distress, and the whole of it to be replevied; and he is thereby further commanded that he do return to the court in what manner he shall have executed the writ. Hamm.N.P. 453; 2 Inst. 140; Fitzh.N.B. 68, 69.

WITHERSAKE. An apostate, or perfidious renegade. Cowell.

WITHHOLD. To retain in one's possession that which belongs to or is claimed or sought by another. Fitzpatrick v. Garver, 253 Mo. 189, 161 S.W. 714, 715. To omit to disclose upon request; as, to withhold information. State v. Sharp, 121 Minn. 381, 141 N.W. 526, 527, 528. To refrain from paying that which is due. Dupuy v. Board of Education of City and County of San Francisco, 106 Cal.App. 533, 289 P. 689, 691.

Withholding means of support from dependents. Made felony by a statute, presupposes existence or ability to obtain means of support by accused, and need by alleged dependents from whom support is withheld. McBrayer v. State, 112 Fla. 415, 150 So. 736, 737.

WITHIN. Into. State v. Warburton, 97 Wash. 242, 166 P. 615, 617. In inner or interior part of, or not longer in time than. In re White's Estate, 130 Kan. 714, 288 P. 764, 765. Through. Mississippi Cent. R. Co. v. Pace, 109 Miss. 667, 68 So. 926, 927. Inside the limits of. Sacks v. Legg, 219 Ill.App. 144, 148; Ex parte Watson, 82 W.Va. 201, 95 S.E. 648. On. Continental Life Ins. Co. v. Wilson, 36 Ga.App. 540, 137 S.E. 403.

When used relative to time, has been defined variously as meaning any time before; at or before; at the end of; before the expiration of; not beyond; not exceeding; not later than. Glenn v. Garrett, Tex.Civ.App., 84 S.W.2d 515, 516.

The use of the word "within" as a limit of time, or degree, or space, embraces the last day, or degree, or entire distance, covered by the limit fixed. Rice v. J. H. Beavers & Co., 196 Ala. 355, 71 So. 659; Ardery v. Dunn, 181 Ind. 225, 104 N.E. 299, 300; Laws N.Y. 1910, c. 347.

WITHOUT. Outside; beyond. Welton v. Missouri, 91 U.S. 277, 23 L.Ed. 347; Ainslie v. Martin, 9 Mass. 456; Collins v. Morgan, C.C.A.Kan., 243 F. 495, 498. In excess of. Milwaukee Western Fuel Co. v. Industrial Commission of Wisconsin, 159 Wis. 635, 150 N.W. 998, 999.

WITHOUT DAY. A term used to signify that an adjournment or continuance is indefinite or final, or that no subsequent time is fixed for another meeting, or for further proceedings. See Sine Die.

WITHOUT DELAY. Instantly; at once. Rathbun v. Globe Indemnity Co., 107 Neb. 18, 184 N.W. 903, 908, 24 A.L.R. 191. Also, within the time allowed by law. See State v. Dolan, Mo.App., 216 S.W. 334.

WITHOUT GIVING COMPENSATION THEREFOR. This phrase within automobile guest statute indicates an intention to exclude application of "guest" designation not only to one who has paid cash or equivalent for his transportation but also to one who pays such recompense as makes it worth the other's while to furnish the ride. Duclos v. Tashjian, 32 Cal.App.2d 444, 90 P.2d 140, 143.

WITHOUT HER CONSENT. This phrase, as used in the law of rape, is equivalent to "against the will," and signifies the manifestation of the utmost reluctance and greatest resistance on the woman's part. State v. Catron, 317 Mo. 894, 296 S.W. 141, 143.

WITHOUT IMPEACHMENT OF WASTE. The effect of the insertion of this clause in a lease for life is to give the tenant the right to cut timber on the estate, without making himself thereby liable to an action for waste. When a tenant for life holds the land without impeachment of waste, he is, of course, dispunishable for waste, whether wilful or otherwise. But still this right must not be wantonly abused so as to destroy the estate; and he will be enjoined from committing malicious waste. Bac.Abr. Waste (N); 2 Eq.Cas. Abr. *Waste* (A, pl. 8). And see Derham v. Hovey, 195 Mich. 243, 161 N.W. 883, 884, 21 A.L.R. 999.

WITHOUT JUSTIFICATION. In a statute punishing any parent who willfully or without justification deserts a child under 16 years of age in destitute or necessitous circumstances, the term "without justification" is equivalent to "willfully." Ex parte Strong, 95 Tex.Cr.R. 250, 252 S.W. 767, 769.

WITHOUT NOTICE. As used of purchasers, etc., equivalent to "in good faith." Hunt v. Gragg, 19 N.M. 450, 145 P. 136, 138.

WITHOUT PREJUDICE. Where an offer or admission is made "without prejudice," or a motion is denied or a suit dismissed "without prejudice," it is meant as a declaration that no rights or privileges of the party concerned are to be considered as thereby waived or lost except in so far as may be expressly conceded or decided. See Genet v. Delaware & H. Canal Co., 170 N.Y. 278, 63 N.E. 350; O'Keefe v. Irvington Real Estate Co., 87 Md. 196, 39 Atl. 428; Olson v. Coalfield School Dist. No. 16 of Divide County, 54 N.D. 657, 210 N.W. 180, 181.

A dismissal "without prejudice" allows a new suit to be brought on the same cause of action. Freidenbloom v. McAfee, Tex.Civ.App., 167 S.W. 28; McIntyre v. McIntyre, 205 Mich. 496, 171 N.W. 393, 394.

The words "without prejudice" import into any transaction that the parties have agreed that as between themselves the receipt of money by one and its payment by the other shall not of themselves have any legal effect on the rights of the parties, but they shall be open to settlement by legal controversy as if the money had not been paid. In re Bell, 344 Pa. 223, 25 A.2d 344, 350.

The words "without prejudice", as used in judgment, ordinarily import the contemplation of further proceedings, and, when they appear in an order or decree, it shows that the judicial act is not intended to be res judicata of the merits of the controversy. Fiumara v. American Surety Co. of New York, 346 Pa. 584, 31 A.2d 283, 287.

WITHOUT RECOURSE. This phrase, used in making a qualified indorsement of a negotiable instrument, signifies that the indorser means to save himself from liability to subsequent holders, and is a notification that, if payment is refused by the parties primarily liable, recourse cannot be had to him. See Thompson v. First State Bank, 102 Ga. 696, 29 S.E. 610; Binswanger v. Hewitt, 79 Misc. 425, 140 N.Y.S. 143, 145.

An indorser "without recourse" specially declines to assume any responsibility for payment. Arthur v. Rosier, 217 Mo.App. 382, 266 S.W. 737, 738. He assumes no contractual liability by virtue of the indorsement itself, Kaill v. Bell, 88 Kan. 666, 129 P. 1135, 1136; and becomes a mere assignor of the title to the paper, Cameron v. Ham, 23 Ohio App. 359, 155 N.E. 655, 656; but such an indorsement does not indicate that the indorsee takes with notice of defects, or that he does not take on credit of the other parties to the note, Robertson v. American Inv. Co., 170 Ark. 413, 279 S.W. 1008, 1010.

Where a note and mortgage are transferred without recourse, legal effect of words "without recourse" constitutes indorser a mere assignor subject to no liability except as an implied guarantor that instruments are genuine, that he has good title to them, and that he is not aware of any illegality in them. Home Ins. Co. v. Citizens Bank, 181 Miss. 181, 178 So. 589, 590.

WITHOUT RESERVE. A term applied to a sale by auction, indicating that no price is reserved.

WITHOUT STINT. Without limit; without any specified number.

WITHOUT THE STATE. This phrase, in a statute providing that in computing limitations, the time during which the defendant shall be without the state shall be excluded, has no relation to mere temporary absence from domicile or residence in the state. Clegg v. Bishop, 105 Conn. 564, 136 A. 102, 104.

WITHOUT THIS, THAT. In pleading. Formal words used in pleadings by way of *traverse,* particularly by way of *special* traverse, (*q. v.*,) importing an express denial of some matter of fact alleged in a previous pleading, including the declaration, plea, replication, etc. Steph.Pl. 168, 169, 179, 180. The Latin term is *absque hoc.* Com.Dig. *Pleader* (G 1); 1 Chitty, Pl. 576, note *a.*

WITNESS, *v.* To subscribe one's name to a deed, will, or other document, for the purpose of attesting its authenticity, and proving its execution, if required, by bearing witness thereto.

To see the execution of, as an instrument, and subscribe it for the purpose of establishing its authenticity. In re Harter's Estate, 229 Iowa 238, 294 N.W. 357, 360, 362.

WITNESS, *n.* In general, one who, being present, personally sees or perceives a thing; a beholder, spectator, or eyewitness. In re Harter's Estate, 229 Iowa 238, 294 N.W. 357, 362.

One who testifies to what he has seen, heard, or otherwise observed. Wigginton v. Order of United Commercial Travelers of America, C.C.A.Ind., 126 F.2d 659, 666.

A person whose declaration under oath (or affirmation) is received as evidence for any purpose, whether such declaration be made on oral examination or by deposition or affidavit. Code Civ.Proc.Cal. § 1878.

A person attesting genuineness of signature to document by adding his signature. In re Gorrell's Estate, 19 N.J.Misc. 168, 19 A.2d 334, 335.

One who is called upon to be present at a transaction, as a wedding, or the making of a will, that he may thereafter, if necessary, testify to the transaction.

Accused, by availing himself of statute providing that accused shall be a competent witness at his own request but not otherwise, assumes position of "witness". State v. McKinnon, 223 N.C. 160, 25 S.E.2d 606, 609; State v. Auston, 223 N.C. 203, 25 S.E.2d 613, 614.

Adverse witness. A witness whose mind discloses a bias hostile to the party examining him. Brown; Greenough v. Eccles, 5 C.B.(N.S.) 801.

Attesting witness. See Attestation.

Competent witness. See Competent.

Credible witness. See Credible.

Expert witnesses. See Expert Witnesses.

Hostile witness. See that title.

Prosecuting witness. See that title.

Subscribing witness. See that title.

Swift witness. See that title.

Witness to will. One who has attested the will by subscribing his name thereto. In re Johnson's Will, 175 Wis. 1, 183 N.W. 888, 889.

WITNESS AGAINST HIMSELF. The federal constitutional provision that no person shall be compelled in any criminal case, to be a "witness against himself" must be applied in a broad spirit to secure to citizen immunity from self-accusation and provision applies to all proceedings wherein defendant is acting as a witness in any investigation that requires him to give testimony that might tend to show him guilty of crime. U.S.C.A.Const. Amend. 5. United States v. Goodner, D.C.Colo., 35 F.Supp. 286, 290.

WITNESSING PART. In a deed or other formal instrument, is that part which comes after the recitals, or, where there are no recitals, after the parties. It usually commences with a reference to the agreement or intention to be effectuated, then states or refers to the consideration, and concludes with the operative words and parcels, if any. Where a deed effectuates two distinct objects, there are two witnessing parts. 1 Dav.Prec. Conv. 63, et seq.; Sweet.

WITTINGLY. With knowledge and by design, excluding only cases which are the result of accident or forgetfulness, and including cases where one does an unlawful act through an erroneous belief of his right. Osborne v. Warren, 44 Conn. 357.

WITWORD. A legally allowed claim, more especially the right to vindicate ownership or possession by one's affirmation under oath. Vinogradoff, Engl. Soc. in 11th Cent. 9.

WOLD. Sax. In England. A down or champaign ground, hilly and void of wood. Cowell; Blount.

WOLF'S HEAD. In old English law. This term was used as descriptive of the condition of an outlaw. Such persons were said to carry a wolf's head, (*caput lupinum;*) for if caught alive they were to be brought to the king, and if they defended themselves they might be slain and their heads carried to the king, for they were no more to be accounted of than wolves. Termes de la Ley, "Woolferthfod."

WOMEN. All the females of the human species. All such females who have arrived at the age of puberty. Dig. 50, 16, 13.

WONG. Sax. In old records. A field. Spelman; Cowell.

WOOD. The tough, hard substance of all trees and shrubs. It includes not only the hard fiber bundles of trees and shrubs in general, but also the tougher fibrous components of some herbaceous plants. It is a very broad term and includes not only material obtained from exogenous plants, but also like substances obtained from palms, from bamboo (which is a giant grass), and from some ferns (which are herbaceous plants). Steinhardt & Bro. v. U. S., 9 Ct.Cust.App. 62, 63.

WOOD LEAVE. A license or right to cut down, remove, and use standing timber on a given estate or tract of land. Osborne v. O'Reilly, 42 N.J.Eq. 467, 9 A. 209.

WOOD PLEA COURT. A court held twice in the year in the forest of Clun, in Shropshire, for determining all matters of wood and agistments. Cowell.

WOOD-CORN. In old records. A certain quantity of oats or other grain, paid by customary tenants to the lord, for liberty to pick up dead or broken wood. Cowell.

WOOD-GELD. In old English law. Money paid for the liberty of taking wood in a forest. Cowell.

Immunity from such payment. Spelman.

WOOD-MOTE. In forest law. The old name of the court of attachments; otherwise called the "Forty-Days Court." Cowell; 3 Bl.Comm. 71.

WOODS. A forest; land covered with a large and thick collection of natural forest trees. The old books say that a grant of "all his woods" (*omnes boscos suos*) will pass the land, as well as the trees growing upon it. Co.Litt. 4*b*. See Averitt v. Murrell, 49 N.C. 323; Hall v. Cranford, 50 N.C. 3; Achenbach v. Johnston, 84 N.C. 264.

WOODSRIDER. This term has been applied to an overseer of work in the woods for a private turpentine operator. Griffith v. Hulion, 90 Fla. 582, 107 So. 354, 355.

WOOD-STREET COMPTER. The name of an old prison in London.

WOODWARDS. Officers of the forest, whose duty consists in looking after the wood and vert and venison, and preventing offenses relating to the same. Manw. 189.

WOODWORK. Objects made of wood and things produced by the carpenter or joiner's art. Smith v. National Fire Ins. Co., 175 N.C. 314, 95 S.E. 562, 564.

WOODWORKER. A worker in wood, as a carpenter, joiner, or cabinetmaker. Smith v. National Fire Ins. Co., 175 N.C. 314, 95 S.E. 562, 564.

WOOL-SACK. The seat of the lord chancellor of England in the house of lords, being a large square bag of wool, without back or arms, covered with red cloth. Webster; Brande.

WORDS. Symbols indicating ideas and subject to contraction and expansion to meet the idea sought to be expressed. Association for Protection of Adirondacks v. MacDonald, 253 N.Y. 234, 170 N.E. 902, 903. But labels whose content and meaning are continually shifting with the times. Massachusetts Protective Ass'n v. Bayersdorfer, C.C.A.Ohio, 105 F.2d 595, 597.

As used in law, this term generally signifies the technical terms and phrases appropriate to particular instruments, or aptly fitted to the expression of a particular intention in legal instruments. See the subtitles following.

WORDS ACTIONABLE IN THEMSELVES. In libel and slander, impute the guilt of some offense for which the party, if guilty, might be indicted and punished by the criminal courts. Parker v. Kirkland, 298 Ill.App. 340, 18 N.E.2d 709, 718.

WORDS OF ART. The vocabulary or terminology of a particular art or science, and especially those expressions which are idiomatic or peculiar to it. See Cargill v. Thompson, 57 Minn. 534, 59 N.W. 638.

WORDS OF LIMITATION. See Limitation.

WORDS OF PROCREATION. To create an estate tail by deed, it is necessary that words of procreation should be used in order to confine the estate to the descendants of the first grantee, as in the usual form of limitation,—"to A. and the heirs of his body." Sweet.

WORDS OF PURCHASE. See Purchase.

WORK. To exert one's self for a purpose, to put forth effort for the attainment of an object, to be engaged in the performance of a task, duty, or the like. The term covers all forms of physical or mental exertions, or both combined, for the attainment of some object other than recreation or amusement. Leathers & Martin v. Conley, La. App., 157 So. 607, 609. Tennessee Coal, Iron & R. Co. v. Muscoda Local No. 123, Ala., 64 S.Ct. 698, 703, 705, 321 U.S. 590, 88 L.Ed. 949, 152 A.L.R. 1014.

"Work," so far as it refers to a provision regulating street trades for children, means selling, exposing or offering articles for sale, regardless of whether such activity is carried on under technical employment or for a wage. Commonwealth v. Prince, 313 Mass. 223, 46 N.E.2d 755, 757.

WORK AND LABOR. The name of one of the common counts in actions of *assumpsit*, being for work and labor done and materials furnished by the plaintiff for the defendant.

WORK FLOATS. Used to recover sunken logs, are rafts made of logs with boards nailed across on which men stand to work. Ledoux v. Joncas, 163 Minn. 498, 204 N.W. 635, 636.

WORK OF ART. As used in section 5 of the Copyright Act of 1919, 17 U.S.C.A. § 5, relating to the registration of models or designs for work of art, does not necessarily mean something displaying artistic merit, but means "objet d'art," that is, something upon which the labors of an artist as such may have been employed. Jones Bros. Co. v. Underkoffler, D.C.Pa., 16 F.Supp. 729, 730.

WORK OF NATIONAL IMPORTANCE. Under the Selective Service Act providing that conscientious objectors should be assigned to such work means work of value to the nation for the common defense and general welfare. 50 U.S.C.A. Appendix § 305 (g). United States ex rel. Zucker v. Osborne, D.C.N.Y., 54 F.Supp. 984, 986, 987.

WORK OF NECESSITY. Excepted from operation of Sunday statutes embraces all work reasonably essential to the economic, social or moral welfare of the people, viewed in light of the habits and customs of the age in which they live and of the community in which they reside. Francisco v. Commonwealth, 180 Va. 371, 23 S.E.2d 234, 238, 239.

WORK PRODUCT. This concept embraces matter representing work done by attorney in his professional capacity in the course of attorney-client relationship. Lundberg v. Welles, D.C.N.Y., 11 F.R.D. 136, 138.

WORK RELIEF. Wages paid by a city or town from money specifically appropriated for the purpose or from money provided by the federal government, or any agency thereof, to persons unemployed or whose employment is inadequate to provide the necessities of life. In re Youngs, 172 Misc. 155, 14 N.Y.S.2d 800, 802.

WORK WEEK. Within Fair Labor Standards Act, a week during which work is performed. 29 U.S.C.A. § 207. Plourde v. Massachusetts Cities Realty Co., D.C.Mass., 47 F.Supp. 668, 671.

WORKAWAY. Extra man employed on vessel as an accommodation to himself. The Tashmoo, D.C.N.Y., 48 F.2d 366, 368.

WORK-BEAST, or WORK-HORSE. These terms mean an animal of the horse kind, which can be rendered fit for service, as well as one of maturer age and in actual use. Winfrey v. Zimmerman, 8 Bush (Ky.) 587.

WORK-HOUSE. A place where convicts (or paupers) are confined and kept at labor.

WORKING CAPITAL. Cash and other quick assets. Crocker v. Waltham Watch Co., 315 Mass. 397, 53 N.E.2d 230, 237.

WORKING DAYS.

Construction Contracts

The term "working days" may exclude not only Sundays and holidays, but also days upon which no work can be done because of weather conditions. Christopher & Simpson Architectural Iron & Foundry Co. v. E. A. Steininger Const. Co., 200 Mo.App. 33, 205 S.W. 278, 283; F. J. Mumm Contracting Co. v. Village of Kenmore, 104 Misc. 268, 171 N.Y.S. 673.

Maritime Law

Running or calendar days on which law permits work to be done, excluding Sundays and legal holidays. Sherwood v. American Sugar Refining Co., C.C.A.N.Y., 8 F.2d 586, 588; The Olaf, D.C. Pa., 248 F. 807, 809.

WORKING FACE. Place in a mine where the miners actually drill and load ore. Tennessee Coal, Iron & R. Co. v. Muscoda Local No. 123, Ala., 64 S.Ct. 698, 700, 321 U.S. 590, 88 L.Ed. 949.

WORKING FOREMAN. Performs same type of work as those whom he supervises. Zaetz v. General Instrument Corporation, 21 N.J.Misc. 76, 30 A.2d 504, 506.

WORKING INTEREST. See Royalty.

WORKMAN. One who labors; one employed to do business for another. Harris v. City of Baltimore, 151 Md. 11, 133 A. 888, 889; Europe v. Addison Amusements, 231 N.Y. 105, 131 N.E. 750. One employed in manual labor, skilled or unskilled, an artificer, mechanic, or artisan. Cohen v. Rosalsky, 230 App.Div. 604, 246 N.Y.S. 299, 301.

The word workmen in provision of Bankruptcy Act regarding priority of wage claims must be construed in accordance with its common and popular meaning, in which sense it would not include professional persons. Bankr.Act § 64, sub. a(2), 11 U.S.C.A. § 104, sub. a(2). In re Paradise Catering Corporation, D.C.N.Y., 36 F.Supp. 974, 975.

Workmen's Compensation Act

The term "workman" in the Workmen's Compensation Act means, as the act states, one who engages to furnish services subject to the control of an employer, and the relation necessary to constitute one an employer and another a workman under the act is the relation of master and servant originating in a contract for personal services, subject to complete control of the details of the work and the mode of its performance. Landberg v. State Industrial Accident Commission, 107 Or. 498, 215 P. 594, 596.

WORKMEN'S COMPENSATION. Name commonly used to designate the method and means created by statutes for giving greater protection and security to the workman and his dependents against injury and death occurring in the course of employment. United Air Lines Transport Corporation v. Industrial Commission, 107 Utah 52, 151 P.2d 591, 594. It is not health insurance, and was not intended to compensate for disability through sickness or disease not caused by accidental injury arising out of and in course of employment. Gumtow v. Kalamazoo Motor Express, 266 Mich. 16, 253 N.W. 198.

WORKMEN'S COMPENSATION ACTS. Laws passed in most of the states of the Union which provide for fixed awards to employees or their dependents in case of industrial accidents and dispense with proof of negligence and legal actions. Some of the acts go beyond the simple determination of the right to compensation, and provide insurance systems, either under state supervision or otherwise.

Under the acts, methods are usually prescribed for the expression by employers and workmen of their preference as to the acceptance or rejection of the compensation system. This ranges from each workman filing a written rejection to a presumed acceptance in the absence of formal rejection.

Under the elective system in most of the states, it is made an inducement, that where employers refuse to come within the provisions of the compensation law, the customary defenses to actions for injuries shall not be allowed them.

WORKMEN'S COMPENSATION LOSS. See Loss.

WORKS. Sometimes, a mill, factory, or other establishment for performing industrial labor of any sort (South St. Joseph Land Co. v. Pitt, 114 Mo. 135, 21 S.W. 449); also, a building, structure, or erection of any kind upon land, as in the civil-law phrase "new works."

New Works

A term of the civil law comprehending every sort of edifice or other structure which is newly commenced on a given estate or lot. Its importance lies chiefly in the fact that a remedy is given ("denunciation of new works") to an adjacent proprietor whose property would be injured or subjected to a more onerous servitude if such a work were allowed to proceed to completion.

Public Works

Works, whether of construction or adaptation, undertaken and carried out by the national, state, or municipal authorities, and designed to subserve some purpose of public necessity, use, or convenience; such as public buildings, roads, aqueducts, parks, etc. Ellis v. Common Council, 123 Mich. 567, 82 N.W. 244; Chattanooga & Tennessee River Power Co. v. U. S., C.C.A.Tenn., 209 F. 28, 29. All fixed works constructed for public use. State v. A. H. Read Co., 33 Wyo. 387, 240 P. 208, 211. The term usually relates to the construction of public improvements and not to their maintenance or operation. State v. Peters, 112 Ohio St. 249, 147 N.E. 81, 83.

WORKSHOP. Within Workmen's Compensation Acts, a room or place wherein power-driven machinery is employed and manual labor is exercised by way of trade for gain or otherwise. Remsnider v. Union Savings & Trust Co., 89 Wash. 87, 154 P. 135, 136, Ann.Cas.1917D, 40.

It must be one provided or operated by the employer or one over which he has control or supervision. City of Hobart v. Wagoner, 191 Okl. 689, 132 P.2d 926, 927.

WORLD. This term sometimes denotes all persons whatsoever who may have, claim, or acquire an interest in the subject-matter; as in saying that a judgment *in rem* binds "all the world."

WORLDLY. Of or pertaining to the world or the present state of existence; temporal; earthly; devoted to, interested in, or connected with this present life, and its cares, advantages, or pleasures, to the exclusion of those of a future life. Anderson v. Gibson, 116 Ohio St. 684, 157 N.E. 377, 379, 54 A.L.R. 92. Concerned with enjoyment of this present existence; secular; not religious, spiritual, or holy. Commonwealth v. American Baseball Club of Philadelphia, 290 Pa. 136, 138 A. 497, 499, 53 A.L.R. 1027.

WORLDLY EMPLOYMENT OR BUSINESS, which, on Sunday, is prohibited by statutes in some states, includes the operation of a motion picture show under the New Jersey Vice and Immorality Act, § 1 (4 Comp.St.1910, p. 5712), Rosenberg v. Arrowsmith, 82 N.J.Eq. 570, 89 A. 524, 525, and one who does this habitually is guilty of keeping a disorderly house. State v. Rosenberg, N.J.Sup., 115 A. 203. The words also include, in Delaware, under Rev.Code 1915, § 4784, the playing of football on Sunday, knowing that tickets of admission were being offered for sale and sold to the public, Walsh v. State, Del.Super., 136 A. 160, 163, and, in Pennsylvania, professional baseball, Commonwealth v. American Baseball Club of Philadelphia, 200 Pa. 136, 138 A. 497, 499, 53 A.L.R. 1027. But in the latter state it has been thought, at least by the lower courts, that notwithstanding Act April 22, 1794 (3 Smith's Laws, p. 177), § 1 (18 P.S. § 1991) one may lawfully purchase a cigar on Sunday. Commonwealth v. Hoover, 25 Pa. Super.Ct. 133, 134.

WORRYING CATTLE OR SHEEP. Within statutes providing that any one finding a dog, not on the premises of its owner, worrying cattle or sheep, may kill the dog, means to run after; to chase; to bark at. Bass v. Nofsinger, 222 Wis. 480, 269 N.W. 303, 304; Failing v. People, 105 Colo. 399, 98 P.2d 865, 867.

WORSHIP. Any form of religious service showing reverence for Divine Being, or exhortation to obedience to or following of the mandates of such Being. People on Complaint of Doyle v. Smith, 259 N.Y. 48, 180 N.E. 891. Religious exercises participated in by a number of persons assembled for that purpose, the disturbance of which is a statutory offense in many states. Hamsher v. Hamsher, 132 Ill. 273, 22 N.E. 1123, 8 L.R.A. 556; State v. District Board, 76 Wis. 177, 44 N.W. 967, 7 L.R.A. 330, 20 Am.St.Rep. 41; State v. Buswell, 40 Neb. 158, 58 N.W. 728, 24 L.R.A. 68; State v. Norris, 59 N.H. 536; Woodall v. State, 4 Ga.App. 783, 62 S.E. 485.

English Law

A title of honor or dignity used in addresses to certain magistrates and other persons of rank or office. Co. 2d Inst. 666; Bacon, Abr. *Misnomer* (A 2).

Public Worship

This term may mean the worship of God, conducted and observed under public authority; or it may mean worship in an open or public place, without privacy or concealment; or it may mean the performance of religious exercises, under a provision for an equal right in the whole public to participate in its benefits; or it may be used in contradistinction to worship in the family or the closet. In this country, what is called "public worship" is commonly conducted by voluntary societies, constituted according to their own notions of ecclesiastical authority and ritual propriety, opening their places of worship, and admitting to their religious services such persons, and upon such terms, and subject to such regulations, as they may choose to designate and establish. A church absolutely belonging to the public, and in which all persons without restriction have equal rights, such as the public enjoy in highways or public landings, is certainly a very rare institution. Attorney General v. Merrimack Mfg. Co., 14 Gray (Mass.) 586.

WORSTED. Primarily and popularly, a yarn or fabric made wholly of wool. Federal Trade Commission v. Winsted Hosiery Co., 42 S.Ct. 384, 385, 258 U.S. 483, 66 L.Ed. 729.

WORT. Mash; wash; specifically, the mash after the malt, or other active ingredient, has been added, either before or during fermentation. Pack v. State, 116 Or. 416, 241 P. 390, 392.

WORT or WORTH. A curtilage or country farm.

WORTH. The quality of a thing which gives it value. McLane v. Pittsburg Rys. Co., 230 Pa. 29, 79 A. 237, 238. Although "worth" in some connections may mean more than pecuniary value, in law it means that sum of valuable qualities which renders a thing valuable and useful expressed in the current medium of the country; value. Duke v. City of Anniston, 5 Ala.App. 348, 60 So. 447. Furnishing an equivalent for. Herb v. Hallowell, 304 Pa. 128, 154 A. 582, 585.

WORTHIER TITLE. At common law where testator undertook to devise to an heir exactly same interest in land as such heir would take by descent, descent was regarded as the "worthier title" and heir took by descent rather than by devise. Jones v. Petrie, 156 Kan. 241, 132 P.2d 396, 398.

WORTHIEST OF BLOOD. In the English law of descent. A term applied to males, expressive of the preference given to them over females. See 2 Bl.Comm. 234–240. See some singular reasons given for this in Plowd. 305.

WORTHING OF LAND. A certain quantity of land so called in the manor of Kingsland, in Hereford. The tenants are called "worthies." Wharton.

WORTHLESS. Destitute of worth, of no value or use. Spring City Foundry Co. v. Commissioner of Internal Revenue, 54 S.Ct. 644, 292 U.S. 182, 78 L.Ed. 1200.

WORTHY. Having worth; possessing merit; valuable; deserving of honor, or the like; of high station; of high social position; deserved, merited. Woodstown Nat. Bank and Trust Co. v. Snelbaker, 136 N.J.Eq. 62, 40 A.2d 222, 227.

WOULD. A word sometimes expressing what might be expected. Taylor v. Metropolitan St. Ry. Co., 256 Mo. 191, 165 S.W. 327, 331. Often interchangeable with the word "should," Barnett v. Savannah Electric Co., 15 Ga.App. 270, 82 S.E. 910, 911, but not with "could," Gehrig v. Chicago & A. R. Co., 201 Ill.App. 287, 293.

WOUND. An injury to the body of a person or animal, especially one caused by violence, by which the continuity of the covering, as skin, mucous membrane, or conjunctiva, is broken. Gasperino v. Prudential Ins. Co. of America, Mo.App., 107 S.W.2d 819, 827. Any breaking up or dispersion, or disintegration of the natural continuity of a tissue of the body. Gasperino v. Prudential Ins. Co. of America, Mo.App., 107 S.W.2d 819, 827. Also injuries of every kind which affect the body, whether they are cuts, lacerations, fractures, or bruises. State v. Hammerli, Kan.Sup., 58 P. 559; Gatlin v. State, 18 Ga.App. 9, 89 S.E. 345. Also, any lesion of the body, Robinson v. Masonic Protective Ass'n, 87 Vt. 138, 88 A. 531, 47 L.R.A.,N.S., 924, a "lesion" being a hurt, loss, or injury. People v. Durrand, 307 Ill. 611, 139 N.E. 78, 83.

WOUNDED FEELINGS. Such as result from indignities to self-respect, sensibilities, or pride of a person, as distinguished from usual mental pain and suffering consequent to physical injury. Interstate Life & Accident Co. v. Brewer, 56 Ga.App. 599, 193 S.E. 458, 464.

WOUNDING. An aggravated species of assault and battery, consisting in one person giving another some dangerous hurt. 3 Bl.Comm. 121.

WRATH. Not merely anger, but violent anger. Jerald v. Houston, 124 Kan. 657, 261 P. 851, 856.

WRECCUM MARIS SIGNIFICAT ILLA BONA QUÆ NAUFRAGIO AD TERRAM PELLUNTUR. A wreck of the sea signifies those goods which are driven to shore from a shipwreck.

WRECK. To destroy, disable, or seriously damage. Zohner v. Sierra Nevada Life and Casualty Co., 114 Cal.App. 85, 299 P. 749, 751. To reduce to a wreck or ruinous state by any kind of violence; to overthrow, shatter, or destroy; to cause to crash or suffer ruin, synonymous with ruin, smash, and demolish. Its antonyms are save, salvage, and preserve. Star Mfg. Co. v. Quarrles, 172 Okl. 550, 46 P.2d 497, 498. Destruction, disorganization, or serious injury of anything, especially by violence. Houston Printing Co. v. Hunter, Tex.Civ.App., 105 S.W.2d 312, 317.

Goods cast ashore by the sea, and not claimed by the owner within a year, or other specified period; which, in such case, become the property of the state. 2 Kent, Comm. 322; Proctor v. Adams, 113 Mass. 376, 18 Am.Rep. 500. The term applies to property cast upon land by the sea. Baker v. Hoag, 7 N.Y. 555, 59 Am.Dec. 431. To jetsam, flotsam, and ligan. Murphy v. Dunham, D.C.Mich., 38 F. 503.

Common Law

Goods cast ashore from a wrecked vessel, where no living creature has escaped from the wreck alive; and which are forfeited to the crown, or to persons having the franchise of wreck. Cowell. But if claimed by the true owner within a year and a day the goods, or their proceeds, must be restored to him, by virtue of stat. Westm. I., 3 Edw. I. c. 4.

Maritime Law

A ship becomes a wreck when, in consequence of injuries received, she is rendered absolutely unnavigable, or unable to pursue her voyage, without repairs exceeding the half of her value. Wood v. Insurance Co., 6 Mass. 479, 4 Am.Dec. 163; Collard v. Eddy, 17 Mo. 355; Baker v. Hoag, 7 N.Y. 558, 59 Am.Dec. 431; Peele v. Insurance Co., 19 F. Cas. 104; Lacaze v. State, 1 Add., Pa., 99.

A "wrecked vessel," however, in common phraseology, includes a sunken vessel. See Gilchrist v. Godman, D.C. Ill., 79 F. 970; Act March 3, 1899, § 15 (33 USCA § 409); The R. J. Moran, C.C.A.N.Y., 299 F. 500; Thames Towboat Co. v. Fields, D.C.N.Y., 287 F. 155.

Wreck Commissioners

Persons appointed by the English lord chancellor under the merchant shipping act, 1876, (section 29,) to hold investigations at the request of the board of trade into losses, abandonments, damages, and casualties of or to ships on or near the coast of the United Kingdom, whereby loss of life is caused. Sweet.

WRECKER. Motor vehicles equipped for removing wrecked or disabled vehicles. Gossett v. Van Egmond, 176 Or. 134, 155 P.2d 304, 312.

WRECKFREE. Exempt from the forfeiture of shipwrecked goods and vessels to the king. Cowell.

WRENCH. Violent twist; a sprain and injury by twisting as in a joint. Traders & General Ins. Co. v. Lincecum, Tex.Civ.App., 126 S.W.2d 692, 695.

WRESTLING. Engaging in a contest, usually between two persons, who seek to throw each other to the ground or floor, commonly in such a manner that one contestant's shoulders are held against the ground or floor. Jacobs v. Loyal Protective Ins. Co., 97 Vt. 516, 124 A. 848, 852.

WRINKLE. A stria; furrow; channel; hollow; depression; rut; cup; pocket; dimple. Maxim Mfg. Co. v. Imperial Mach. Co., C.C.A.Ill., 286 F. 79, 83.

WRIST-DROP. A form of paralysis of the hand and wrist resulting from an affection of the nerve which supplies the muscles of the forearm, wrist, and hand. Freeman v. Chicago, M. & St. P. Ry. Co., 52 Mont. 1, 154 P. 912, 913.

WRIT. A precept in writing, couched in the form of a letter, running in the name of the king, president, or state, issuing from a court of justice, and sealed with its seal, addressed to a sheriff or other officer of the law, or directly to the person whose action the court desires to command, either as the commencement of a suit or other proceeding or as incidental to its progress, and requiring the performance of a specified act, or giving authority and commission to have it done.

A mandatory precept issuing from court of justice. Poirier v. East Coast Realty Co., 84 N.H. 461, 152 A. 612, 613. Process. State ex rel. Walling v. Sullivan, 245 Wis. 180, 13 N.W.2d 550, 555.

For the names and description of various particular writs, see the titles below.

Old English Law

An instrument in the form of a letter; a letter or letters of attorney. This is a very ancient sense of the word.

In the old books, "writ" is used as equivalent to "action;" hence writs are sometimes divided into real, personal, and mixed.

Scotch Law

A writing; an instrument in writing, as a deed, bond, contract, etc. 2 Forb. Inst. pt. 2, pp. 175–179.

General

Alias writ. A second writ issued in the same cause, where a former writ of the same kind has been issued without effect.

Close writ. In English law, a name given to certain letters of the sovereign, sealed with his great seal and directed to particular persons and for particular purposes, which, not being proper for public inspection, were closed up and sealed on the outside; also, a writ directed to the sheriff instead of to the lord. 2 Bl.Comm. 346; 3 Reeve, Eng. Law. 45.

Concurrent writs. Duplicate originals, or several writs running at the same time for the same purpose, for service on or arrest of a person, when it is not known where he is to be found; or for service on several persons, as when there are several defendants to an action. Mozley & Whitley.

Judicial writs. In English practice. The capias and all other writs subsequent to the original writ not issuing out of chancery, but from the court to which the original was returnable. Being grounded on what had passed in that court in consequence of the sheriff's return, they were called *judicial* writs, in contradistinction to the writs issued out of chancery, which were called *original* writs. 3 Bl.Comm. 282. Such writs as issue under the private seal of the courts, and not under the great seal of England, and are tested or witnessed, not in the king's name, but in the name of the chief judge of the court out of which they issue. The word "judicial" is used in contradistinction to "original;" original writs being such as issue out of chancery under the great seal, and are witnessed in the king's name. See 3 Bl. Comm. 282. Pullman's Palace-Car Co. v. Washburn, C.C.Mass., 66 F. 792.

Junior writ. One which is issued, or comes to the officer's hands, at a later time than a similar writ, at the suit of another party, or on a different claim, against the same defendant.

Original writ. In English practice. An original writ was the process formerly in use for the commencement of personal actions. It was a mandatory letter from the king, issuing out of chancery, sealed with the great seal, and directed to the sheriff of the county wherein the injury was committed, or was supposed to have been committed, requiring him to command the wrong-doer or accused party either to do justice to the plaintiff or else to appear in court and answer the accusation against him. This writ is now disused, the writ of summons being the process prescribed by the uniformity of process act for commencing personal actions; and under the judicature act, 1873, all suits, even in the court of chancery, are to be commenced by such writs of summons. Brown.

Patent writ. In old practice, an open writ; one not closed or sealed up.

Peremptory writ. An original writ, called from the words of the writ a "*si te fecerit securum*," and which directed the sheriff to cause the defendant to appear in court without any option given him, provided the plaintiff gave the sheriff security effectually to prosecute his claim. The writ was very occasionally in use, and only where nothing was specifically demanded, but only a satisfaction in general; as in the case of writs of trespass on the case, wherein no debt or other specific thing was sued for, but only damages to be assessed by a jury. Brown.

Prerogative writs. Those issued by the exercise of the extraordinary power of the crown (the court, in modern practice) on proper cause shown; namely, the writs of *procedendo, mandamus, prohibition, quo warranto, habeas corpus,* and *certiorari.*

WRIT DE BONO ET MALO. See De Bono et Malo; Assize.

WRIT DE EJECTIONE FIRMÆ. See Ejectione Firmæ.

WRIT DE HÆRETICO COMBURENDO. See De Hæretico Comburendo.

WRIT DE HOMINE REPLEGIANDO. See De Homine Replegiando.

WRIT DE ODIO ET ATIA. See De Odio et Atia.

WRIT DE RATIONABILI PARTE BONORUM. See De Rationabili Parte Bonorum.

WRIT OF AD QUOD DAMNUM. See Ad Quod Damnum.

WRIT OF ASSISTANCE. The name of a writ which issues from the court of chancery, in aid of the execution of a judgment at law, to put the complainant into possession of lands adjudged to him, when the sheriff cannot execute the judgment. Emerick v. Miller, Ind.App., 62 N.E. 285; Hagerman v. Heltzel, 21 Wash. 444, 58 P. 580; Marblehead Land Co. v. Los Angeles County, D.C. Cal., 276 F. 305.

A form of process issued by an equity court to transfer the possession of lands, title or possession to which it has previously adjudicated, as a means of enforcing its decree, and performs the same office in a suit in equity as an execution in an action at law. Burney v. Lee, 57 Ariz. 41, 110 P.2d 554, 556. Its office is confined to lend aid to original equity jurisdiction, and the writ cannot be employed as a substitute for other common-law or statutory actions. Patterson v. McKay, 202 Ark. 241, 150 S.W.2d 196. It is essentially a mandatory injunction, effect of which is to bring about a change in the possession of realty—it dispossesses the occupant and gives possession to one adjudged entitled thereto by the court. Dusbabek v. Local Building & Loan Ass'n, 178 Okl. 592, 63 P.2d 756, 759.

A "writ of assistance" is equivalent to the writ of habere facias possessionem at law, and issues as of course without notice, so far as the parties to the record are concerned, when necessary to execute a decree. Gardner v. Duncan, 104 Miss. 477, 61 So. 545, 546.

While the office of both a writ of assistance and a writ of possession is to put the party entitled thereto into the possession of property, the former issues from equity and the latter from law. Southern State Bank v. Leverette, 187 N.C. 743, 123 S.E. 68, 70.

An ancient writ issuing out of the exchequer. Moz. & W. A writ issuing from the court of exchequer to the sheriff commanding him to be in aid of the king's tenants by knight's service, or the king's collectors, debtors, or accountants, to enforce payment of their own dues, in order to enable them to pay their own dues to the king. 1 Madox, Hist. Exch. 675.

WRIT OF ASSOCIATION. In English practice. A writ whereby certain persons (usually the clerk of assize and his subordinate officers) are directed to associate themselves with the justices and serjeants; and they are required to admit the said persons into their society in order to take the assizes. 3 Bl.Comm. 59.

WRIT OF ATTACHMENT. A writ employed to enforce obedience to an order or judgment of the court. It may take the form of commanding the sheriff to attach the disobedient party and to have him before the court to answer his contempt. Smith, Act. 176.

In its generic sense, any mesne civil process in the nature of a writ on which property may be attached, including trustee process. Smith v. Smith, 120 Me. 379, 115 A. 87, 88. See, also, Attachment.

WRIT OF CONSPIRACY. A writ which anciently lay against persons who had conspired to injure the plaintiff, under the same circumstances which would now give him an action on the case. It did not lie at common law, in any case, except when the conspiracy was to indict the party either of treason or felony; all the other cases of conspiracy in the books were but actions on the case. Hutchins v. Hutchins, 7 Hill (N.Y.) 104.

WRIT OF COVENANT. A writ which lies where a party claims damages for breach of covenant; *i. e.*, of a promise under seal.

WRIT OF DEBT. A writ which lies where the party claims the recovery of a debt; *i. e.*, a liquidated or certain sum of money alleged to be due to him.

This is debt *in the debet*, which is the principal and only common for. There is another species mentioned in the books, called the debt *in the detinet*, which lies for the specific recovery of *goods* under a contract to deliver them. 1 Chitty, Pl. 101.

WRIT OF DECEIT. The name of a writ which lies where one man has done anything in the name of another, by which the latter is damnified and deceived. Fitzh.Nat.Brev. 95, E.

WRIT OF DELIVERY. A writ of execution employed to enforce a judgment for the delivery of chattels. It commands the sheriff to cause the chattels mentioned in the writ to be returned to the person who has obtained the judgment; and, if the chattels cannot be found, to distrain the person against whom the judgment was given until he returns them. Smith, Act. 175; Sweet.

WRIT OF DETINUE. A writ which lies where a party claims the specific recovery of goods and chattels, or deeds and writings, detained from him. This is seldom used; trover is the more frequent remedy, in cases where it may be brought.

WRIT OF DOWER. This is either a writ of dower *unde nihil habet*, which lies for a widow, commanding the tenant to assign her dower, no part of which has yet been set off to her; or a writ of *right of dower*, whereby she seeks to recover the remainder of the dower to which she is entitled, part having been already received from the tenant. This latter writ is seldom used.

WRIT OF EJECTMENT. The writ in an action of ejectment, for the recovery of lands. See Ejectment.

WRIT OF ENTRY. A real action to recover the possession of land where the tenant (or owner) has been disseised or otherwise wrongfully dispossessed. If the disseisor has aliened the land, or if it has descended to his heir, the writ of entry is said to be in the *per*, because it alleges that the defendant (the alienee or heir) obtained possession *through* the original disseisor. If two alienations (or descents) have taken place, the writ is in the *per* and *cui*, because it alleges that the defendant (the second alienee) obtained possession *through* the first alienee, *to whom* the original disseisor had aliened it. If more than two alienations (or descents) have taken place, the writ is in the *post*, because it simply alleges that the defendant acquired possession *after* the original disseisin. Co.Litt. 238*b*; 3 Bl.Comm. 180. The writ of entry was abolished, with other real actions, in England, by St. 3 & 4 Wm. IV. c. 27, § 36, but is still in use in a few of the states of the Union. Sweet. See, also, Entry, Writ of.

WRIT OF ERROR. A writ issued from a court of appellate jurisdiction, directed to the judge or judges of a court of record, requiring them to remit to the appellate court the record of an action before them, in which a final judgment has been entered, in order that examination may be made of certain errors alleged to have been committed, and that the judgment may be reversed, corrected, or affirmed, as the case may require. Siegelschiffer v. Penn Mut. Life Ins. Co., C.C.A.N.Y., 248 F. 226, 228; Ward v. Williams, 270 Ill. 547, 110 N.E. 821, 823; Board of County Com'rs of Harford County v. Jay, 122 Md. 324, 89 A. 715, 717. It is brought for supposed error in law apparent on record and takes case to higher tribunal, which affirms or reverses. Chambers v. State, 117 Fla. 642, 158 So. 153. It is commencement of new suit to set aside judgment, and is not continuation of suit to which it relates. Winchester v. Winn, 225 Mo.App. 288, 29 S.W.2d 188, 190. And unless abolished by statute, is writ of right applicable to all cases in which jurisdiction is exercised according to course of common law, but is inapplicable to cases not known to or in derogation of common law, unless otherwise provided by statute. Freeport Motor Casualty Co. v. Madden, 354 Ill. 329, 188 N.E. 415, 416.

"Appeal" is a process of civil law origin that entirely removes cause to appellate court subjecting facts as well as law to review and retrial, while "writ of error" is a process of common-law origin and removes nothing to appellate court for re-examination except the law. Whidden v. Abbott, 119 Fla. 25, 160 So. 475.

WRIT OF ERROR CORAM NOBIS. A common-law writ, the purpose of which is to correct a judgment in the same court in which it was rendered, on the ground of error of fact. Washington v. State, 92 Fla. 740, 110 So. 259, 262; People v. Black, 89 Cal.App. 225, 264 P. 346; for which the statute provides no other remedy, which fact did not appear of record, Ernst v. State, 181 Wis. 155,

193 N.W. 978; or was unknown to the court when judgment was pronounced, and which, if known, would have prevented the judgment, and which was unknown, and could not have been known to the party by the exercise of reasonable diligence in time to have been otherwise presented to the court, unless he was prevented from so presenting them by duress, fear, or other sufficient cause, Nickels v. State, 86 Fla. 208, 98 So. 502, 504; Smulski v. H. Feinberg Furniture Co., Del.Super., 193 A. 585, 587; as where judgment is rendered against a party after his death, or an infant not properly represented by guardian, or a feme covert where common-law disability still exists, or where some defect exists in the process or the execution thereof. Schneider v. Schneider, Mo.App., 273 S.W. 1081, 1083; 1 Saund. 101; Steph.Pl. *119; Day v. Hamburgh, 1 Browne, Pa. 75.

An ordinary "writ of error" is brought for a supposed error in law apparent on the record, and takes the case to a higher tribunal where the question is to be decided and the judgment, sentence or decree is to be affirmed or reversed, while the "writ of error coram nobis" is brought for an alleged error in fact not appearing on the record and lies to the same court in order that it may correct the error, which it is presumed would not have been committed had the fact been brought to the court's notice in the first instance. State v. Wagner, 232 Wis. 138, 286 N.W. 544, 545.

At common law in England, it issued from the Court of King's Bench to a judgment of that court. Its principal aim is to afford the court in which an action was tried an opportunity to correct its own record with reference to a vital fact not known when the judgment was rendered. Lamb v. State, 91 Fla. 396, 107 So. 535, 537, 538; Rhodes v. State, 199 Ind. 183, 156 N.E. 389, 392. It is also said that at common law it lay to correct purely ministerial errors of the officers of the court. Cramer v. Illinois Commercial Men's Ass'n, 260 Ill. 516, 103 N.E. 459, 461.

WRIT OF ERROR CORAM VOBIS. This writ, at the English common law, is distinguished from "writ of error coram nobis," in that the former issued from the Court of King's Bench to a judgment of the Court of Common Pleas, whereas the latter issued from the Court of King's Bench to a judgment of that court. Lamb v. State, 107 So. 535, 537, 91 Fla. 396.

WRIT OF EXECUTION. A writ to put in force the judgment or decree of a court.

WRIT OF EXIGI FACIAS. See Exigent.

WRIT OF FALSE JUDGMENT. A writ which appears to be still in use to bring appeals to the English high court from inferior courts not of record proceeding according to the course of the common law. Archb.Pr. 1427.

WRIT OF FORMEDON. A writ which lies for the recovery of an estate by a person claiming as issue in tail, or by the remainder-man or reversioner after the termination of the entail. See Formedon.

WRIT OF INQUIRY. In common-law practice. A writ which issues after the plaintiff in an action has obtained a judgment by default, on an unliquidated claim, directing the sheriff, with the aid of a jury, to inquire into the amount of the plaintiff's demand and assess his damages. Lennon v. Rawitzer, 57 Conn. 583, 19 A. 334; Havens v. Hartford & N. R. Co., 28 Conn. 70; McGowin v. Dickson, 182 Ala. 161, 62 So. 685, 688.

WRIT OF MAINPRIZE, or MAINPRISE. In English law. A writ directed to the sheriff, (either generally, when any man is imprisoned for a bailable offense and bail has been refused, or specially, when the offense or cause of commitment is not properly bailable below,) commanding him to take sureties for the prisoner's appearance, commonly called "mainpernors," and to set him at large. 3 Bl.Comm. 128. See, also, Mainprise.

WRIT OF MANDAMUS. See Mandamus.

WRIT OF MESNE. In old English law. A writ which was so called by reason of the words used in the writ, namely, "*Unde idem A. qui medius est inter C. et prœfatum B.*"; that is, A., who is mesne between C., the lord paramount, and B., the tenant paravail. Co.Litt. 100*a*.

WRIT OF POSSESSION. This is the writ of execution employed to enforce a judgment to recover the possession of land. It commands the sheriff to enter the land and give possession of it to the person entitled under the judgment. Smith, Act. 175. For a distinction between this writ and the "Writ of Assistance," see that title.

WRIT OF PRÆCIPE. This writ is also called a "writ of covenant," and is sued out by the party to whom lands are to be conveyed by fine, the foundation of which is a supposed agreement or covenant that the one shall convey the land to the other. 2 Bl.Comm. 349.

WRIT OF PREVENTION. This name is given to certain writs which may be issued in anticipation of suits which may arise. Co.Litt. 100. See Quia Timet.

WRIT OF PROBABLE CAUSE. An auxiliary process designed to supersede enforcement of judgment of trial court brought up for review. Martin v. Rosen, 2 Cal.App.2d 450, 38 P.2d 855, 857.

WRIT OF PROCESS. See Process; Action.

WRIT OF PROCLAMATION. In English law. By the statute 31 Eliz. c. 3, § 1, when an *exigent* is sued out, a writ of proclamation shall issue at the same time, commanding the sheriff of the county where the defendant dwells to make three proclamations thereof, in places the most notorious, and most likely to come to his knowledge, a month before the outlawry shall take place. 3 Bl.Comm. 284.

When it is not directed to the same sheriff as the *exigent* is, it is called a foreign writ of proclamation. 4 Reeve, Hist. Eng. Law 261.

WRIT OF PROHIBITION. See Prohibition.

WRIT OF PROTECTION. In England, the king may, by his writ of protection, privilege any person in his service from arrest in civil proceedings during a year and a day; but this prerogative is seldom, if ever, exercise. Archb.Pr. 687. See Co. Litt. 130*a*.

WRIT OF QUARE IMPEDIT. See Quare Impedit.

WRIT OF RECAPTION. If, pending an action of replevin for a distress, the defendant distrains again for the same rent or service, the owner of the goods is not driven to another action of replevin, but is allowed a writ of recaption, by which he recovers the goods and damages for the defendant's contempt of the process of the law in making a second distress while the matter is *sub judice.* Woodf. Landl. & Ten. 484.

WRIT OF REPLEVIN. See Replevin.

WRIT OF RESTITUTION. A writ which is issued on the reversal of a judgment commanding the sheriff to restore to the defendant below the thing levied upon, if it has not been sold, and, if it has been sold, the proceeds. Bac.Abr. "Execution," Q. A writ which lies, after the reversal of a judgment, to restore a party to all that he has lost by occasion of the judgment. 2 Tidd, Pr. 1186.

WRIT OF REVIEW. A general designation of any form of process issuing from an appellate court and intended to bring up for review the record or decision of the court below. Hopkins v. Benson, 21 Me. 401; West v. De Moss, 50 La.Ann. 1349, 24 So. 325. In Code practice, a substitute for, or equivalent of, the writ of certiorari. California & O. Land Co. v. Gowen, C.C.Or., 48 F. 775; Burnett v. Douglas County, 4 Or. 389; In re Winegard, 78 Hun, 58, 28 N.Y.S. 1039.

WRIT OF RIGHT. A writ which lay for one who had the right of property, against another who had the right of possession and the actual occupation. The writ properly lay only to recover corporeal hereditaments for an estate in fee-simple; but there were other writs, said to be "in the nature of a writ of right," available for the recovery of incorporeal hereditaments or of lands for a less estate than a fee-simple. Brown; Fitzh. N. B. 1 (B); 3 Bl.Comm. 391.

"Originally a writ of right is so called because it orders the feudal lord to do full right to the demandant, *plenum rectum tenere.* . . . But when possessory actions have been established in the king's court, 'right' is contrasted with 'seisin,' and all writs originating proprietary actions for land . . . come to be known as writs of right." Maitland, in 2 Sel.Essays, Anglo-Am.Leg. Hist. 563.

In another sense, a writ which is grantable as a matter of right, as opposed to a "prerogative writ," which is issued only as a matter of grace or discretion.

WRIT OF SUMMONS. The writ by which, under the English judicature acts, all actions are commenced.

WRIT OF SUPERSEDEAS. See Supersedeas.

WRIT OF SUPERVISORY CONTROL. A writ which is issued only to correct erroneous rulings made by the lower court within its jurisdiction, where there is no appeal, or the remedy by appeal cannot afford adequate relief, and gross injustice is threatened as the result of such rulings. State v. District Court of First Judicial Dist. in and for Lewis and Clark County, 50 Mont. 428, 147 P. 612, 613. It is in nature of summary appeal to control course of litigation in trial court when necessary to prevent miscarriage of justice, and may be employed to prevent extended and needless litigation. State ex rel. Regis v. District Court of Second Judicial Dist. in and for Silver Bow County, 102 Mont. 74, 55 P.2d 1295.

Function of "writ of supervisory control" is to enable Supreme Court to control course of litigation in inferior courts where such courts are proceeding within their jurisdiction, but by mistake of law, or willful disregard of it, are doing gross injustice, and there is no appeal or remedy by appeal is inadequate. State ex rel. State Bank of Townsend v. District Court of First Judicial Dist. in and for Lewis and Clark County, 94 Mont. 551, 25 P.2d 396.

WRIT OF TOLT. In old English law. The name of a writ to remove proceedings on a writ of right patent from the court-baron into the county court.

WRIT OF TRIAL. In English law. A writ directing an action brought in a superior court to be tried in an inferior court or before the undersheriff, under St. 3 & 4 Wm. IV, c. 42. It is now superseded by the county courts act of 1867, c. 142, § 6, by which a defendant, in certain cases, is enabled to obtain an order that the action be tried in a county court. 3 Steph.Comm. 515, n.; Mozley & Whitley.

WRIT OF WASTE. The name of a writ to be issued against a tenant who has committed waste of the premises. There were anciently several forms of this writ, adapted to the particular circumstances. Fitzh.Nat.Brev. 125.

WRIT PRO RETORNO HABENDO. A writ commanding the return of the goods to the defendant, upon a judgment in his favor in replevin, upon the plaintiff's default.

WRITER OF THE TALLIES. In England, An officer of the exchequer whose duty it was to write upon the tallies the letters of tellers' bills.

WRITER TO THE SIGNET. In Scotch law. An officer nearly corresponding to an attorney at law, in English and American practice. "Writers to the signet," called also "clerks to the signet," derive their name from the circumstance that they were anciently clerks in the office of the secretary of state, by whom writs were prepared and issued under the royal *signet* or seal; and, when the signet became employed in judicial proceedings, they obtained a monopoly of the privileges of acting as agents or attorneys before the court of session. Brande, voc. "Signet."

WRITING. The expression of ideas by letters visible to the eye. Clason v. Bailey, 14 Johns. (N. Y.) 491. The giving an outward and objective form to a contract, will, etc., by means of letters or marks placed upon paper, parchment, or other material substance.

In the most general sense of the word, "writing" denotes a document, whether manuscript or printed, as opposed to mere spoken words. Writing is essential to the validity of certain contracts and other transactions. Sweet. See "Instrument."

WRITING OBLIGATORY. The technical name by which a *bond* is described in pleading. Denton v. Adams, 6 Vt. 40.

WRITTEN CONTRACT. See Contract.

WRITTEN INSTRUMENT. Something reduced to writing as a means of evidence, and as the means of giving formal expression to some act or contract. Curlee Clothing Co. v. Lowery, Tex.Civ. App., 275 S.W. 730, 732.

WRITTEN LAW. One of the two leading divisions of the Roman law, comprising the *leges, plebiscita, senatus-consulta, principum placita, magistratuum edicta,* and *responsa prudentum.* Inst. 1, 2, 3.

Statute law. 1 Steph.Comm. 40. Law deriving its force from express legislative enactment. 1 Bl.Comm. 62, 85.

WRONG. A violation of the legal rights of another; an invasion of right to the damage of the parties who suffer it, especially a tort. State ex rel. and to Use of Donelon v. Deuser, 345 Mo. 628, 134 S.W.2d 132, 133. It usually signifies injury to person, property or relative noncontractual rights of another than wrongdoer, with or without force, but, in more extended sense, includes violation of contract. Daurizio v. Merchants' Despatch Transp. Co., 152 Misc. 716, 274 N.Y.S. 174.

The idea of *rights* naturally suggests the correlative one of *wrongs;* for every right is capable of being violated. A right to receive payment for goods sold (for example) implies a wrong on the part of him who owes, but withholds the price; a right to live in personal security, a wrong on the part of him who commits personal violence. And therefore, while, in a general point of view, the law is intended for the establishment and maintenance of *rights,* we find it, on closer examination, to be dealing both with rights and wrongs. It first fixes the character and definition of rights, and then, with a view to their effectual security, proceeds to define wrongs, and to devise the means by which the latter shall be prevented or redressed. 1 Steph.Comm. 126.

Private Wrong

The violation of public or private rights, when considered in reference to the injury sustained by the individual, and consequently as subjects for civil redress or compensation. 3 Steph.Comm. 356; Huntington v. Attrill, 13 S.Ct. 224, 146 U.S. 657, 36 L.Ed. 1123; Tomlin v. Hildreth, 65 N.J.Law, 438, 47 A. 649; State v. Magee Pub. Co., 29 N.M. 455, 224 P. 1028, 1031, 38 A.L.R. 142.

Public Wrongs

Violations of public rights and duties which affect the whole community, considered as a community; crimes and misdemeanors. 3 Bl.Comm. 2; 4 Bl.Comm. 1.

Real Wrong

In old English law. An injury to the freehold.

WRONGDOER. One who commits an injury; a *tort-feasor.* The term ordinarily imports an invasion of right to the damage of the party who suffers such invasion. Merrill v. Comstock, 154 Wis. 434, 143 N.W. 313, 317.

WRONGFUL. Injurious, heedless, unjust, reckless, unfair. Infringement of some right. Mathes v. Williams, Tex.Civ.App., 134 S.W.2d 853, 858.

WRONGFUL ACT. Any act which in the ordinary course will infringe upon the rights of another to his damage, unless it is done in the exercise of an equal or superior right. Victor v. Lewis, La.App., 157 So. 293, 295; Louis Kamm, Inc., v. Flink, 113 N.J.Law 582, 175 A. 62, 67, 99 A.L.R. 1.

No act is "wrongful" unless the probability of injury to some determinate person or class of persons raises the duty as to those persons to refrain from such act. Harper v. Remington Arms Co., 156 Misc. 53, 280 N.Y.S. 862.

WRONGFUL CONDUCT. Conduct which contravenes some duty which law attaches to relation between parties affected. Duncan v. Lumbermen's Mut. Casualty Co., 91 N.H. 349, 23 A.2d 325, 326.

WRONGFUL DEATH STATUTES. Statutory provision which operates upon the common-law rule that the death of a human being may not be complained of as an injury in a civil court. The cause of action for wrongful death is for the wrong to the beneficiaries. In re Daniel's Estate, 294 N.W. 465, 470, 208 Minn. 420.

See, also, Survival Statutes.

WRONGFUL LEVY. Which will entitle the owner of property levied on to damages for wrongful execution, has been made where there has been done to a third person's personalty those acts that would constitute a valid and complete levy if the debtor's property had been seized. Farris v. Castor, 186 Okl. 668, 99 P.2d 900, 902, 903.

WRONGFULLY. In a wrong manner; unjustly; in a manner contrary to the moral law, or to justice. Board of Com'rs of Howard County v. Armstrong, 91 Ind. 536.

WRONGFULLY INTENDING. In the language of pleading, this phrase is appropriate to be used in alleging the malicious motive of the defendant in committing the injury which forms the cause of action.

WRONGOUS. In Scotch law. Wrongful; unlawful; as *wrongous* imprisonment. Ersk.Prin. 4, 4, 25.

WURTH. In Saxon law. Worthy; competent; capable. *Atheswurthe,* worthy of oath; admissible or competent to be sworn. Spelman.

WYE. As applied to a street railway, a "wye" means a track with two branches, one joining the main track from one direction and the other joining the main track from another direction. Falls v. Grand Rapids, G. H. & M. Ry. Co., 189 Mich. 644, 155 N.W. 548, 549.

WYTE. In old English law. Acquittance or immunity from amercement.

X

X. In the written terminology of various arts and trades, where two or more dimensions of the same piece or article are to be stated, this letter is a well-known symbol equivalent to the word "by." Thus, the formula "3 x 5 in." will be understood, or may be explained by parol evidence, to mean "three by five inches," that is, measuring three inches in one direction and five in another. See Jaqua v. Witham & A. Co., 106 Ind. 547, 7 N.E. 314.

XENODOCHIUM. In the civil and old English law. An inn allowed by public license, for the entertainment of strangers, and other guests. Calvin.; Cowell.

A hospital; a place where sick and infirm persons are taken care of. Cowell.

XENODOCHY. Reception of stranger; hospitality. Enc. Lond.

XYLON. A punishment among the Greeks answering to our stocks. Wharton.

Y

YA ET NAY. In old records. Mere assertion and denial, without oath.

YACHT. Vessel larger than a rowboat used for private pleasure. Barker v. Inhabitants of Town of Fairhaven, 265 Mass. 333, 163 N.E. 901, 902.

YACHT BASIN. A system of channels, docks and wharves suitable for carrying, floating, anchoring, landing, loading and unloading yachts and other like sea-going craft. State v. City of Clearwater, 135 Fla. 148, 184 So. 790, 794.

YAHRZEIT. In the Orthodox Jewish faith an annual prayer for repose of soul of dead person. In re Fleishfarb's Will, 151 Misc. 399, 271 N.Y.S. 736.

YARD. A measure of length, containing three feet, or thirty-six inches.

A piece of land inclosed for the use and accommodation of the inhabitants of a house.

An enclosure, with or without buildings, devoted to some work or business. Grace Iron & Steel Corporation v. Ackerman, 123 N.J.L. 54, 7 A.2d 820, 822.

YARDLAND, or *virgata terræ*, is a quantity of land, said by some to be twenty acres, but by Coke to be of uncertain extent.

YARDMAN. Employee who takes care of or assists in care of yards and grounds. Statter v. Herring, 217 Iowa 410, 251 N.W. 715.

YEA AND NAY. Yes and no. According to a charter of Athelstan, the people of Ripon were to be believed in all actions or suits upon their yea and nay, without the necessity of taking any oath. Brown.

See, also, Yeas and Nays.

YEAR. The period in which the revolution of the earth round the sun, and the accompanying changes in the order of nature, are completed. Generally, when a statute speaks of a year, twelve calendar, and not lunar, months are intended. Cro.Jac. 166. The year is either astronomical, ecclesiastical, or regnal, beginning on the 1st of January, or 25th of March, or the day of the sovereign's accession. Wharton.

The civil year differs from the astronomical, the latter being composed of three hundred and sixty-five days, five hours, forty-eight minutes, forty-six seconds and a fraction, while the former consists sometimes of three hundred and sixty-five days, and at others, in leap-years, of three hundred and sixty-six days.

When the period of a "year" is named, a calendar year is generally intended, but the subject-matter or context of statute or contract in which the term is found or to which it relates may alter its meaning. J. L. Hammett Co. v. Alfred Peates Co., 105 N.E. 370, 217 Mass. 520, L.R.A.1915A, 334; United States Trust Co. v. Commissioner of Corporations and Taxation, 299 Mass. 296, 13 N.E.2d 6, 299 Mass. 296.

Natural Year

In old English law. That period of time in which the sun was supposed to revolve in its orbit, consisting of 365 days and one-fourth of a day, or six hours. Bract. fol. 359*b*.

Year and Day

This period was fixed for many purposes in law. Thus, in the case of an estray, if the owner did not claim it within that time, it became the property of the lord. So the owners of wreck must claim it within a year and a day. Death must follow upon wounding within a year and a day if the wounding is to be indicted as murder. Also, a year and a day were given for prosecuting or avoiding certain legal acts; *e. g.*, for bringing actions after entry, for making claim for avoiding a fine, etc. Brown.

Year Books

Books of reports of cases in a regular series from the reign of the English King Edward **I.**, inclusive, to the time of Henry VIII., which were taken by the prothonotaries or chief scribes of the courts, at the expense of the crown, and published annually; whence their name, "Year Books." Brown.

Year, Day, and Waste

In English law. An ancient prerogative of the king, whereby he was entitled to the profits, for a year and a day, of the lands of persons attainted of petty treason or felony, together with the right of wasting the tenements, afterwards restoring the property to the lord of the fee. Abrogated by St. 54 Geo. III., c. 145. Wharton.

See An, Jour, et Waste.

Year of Our Lord

In England the time of an offense may be alleged as that of the sovereign's reign, or as that of the year of our Lord. The former is the usual mode. Hence there "year" alone might not indicate the time intended, but as we have no other era, therefore, any particular year must mean that year in our era. Com. v. Doran, 14 Gray (Mass.) 38. The abbreviation A. D. may be omitted; and the word year is not fatal; State v. Bartlett, 47 Me. 393; *contra*, Com. v. McLoon, 5 Gray (Mass.) 92, 66 Am.Dec. 354.

Year to Year, Tenancy from

This estate arises either expressly, as when land is let from year to year; or by a general parol demise, without any determinate interest, but reserving the payment of an annual rent; or impliedly, as when property is occupied generally under a rent payable yearly, half-yearly, or quarterly; or when a tenant holds over, after the expiration of his term, without having entered into any new contract, and pays rent, (before which he is tenant on sufferance.) Wharton. See, also, Tenant, subtitle Tenant from Year to Year.

Years, Estate for

See Estate for Years.

YEAR OF MOURNING. The Roman "annus luctus" (*q. v.*).

The reason for the widow's year of mourning has been stated as follows: "But if a man dies, and his widow soon after marries again, and a child is born within such a time as by the course of nature it might have been the child of either husband, in this case he is said to be more than ordinarily legitimate; for he may, when he arrives at years of discretion, choose which of the fathers he pleases. To prevent this, the civil law ordained that no widow should marry for one year, and the same constitution was probably transmitted to our ancestors from the Romans, during their stay in Britain, for we find it established under the Saxon and Danish governments." 1 Bl. Comm. 456 (quoted from Browne's Abr., p. 151 [Gavit's Ed., p. 198]).

YEARLING. A young animal past its first year and not yet two years old. Moran v. State, 160 Miss. 598, 135 So. 209.

YEAS AND NAYS. The affirmative and negative votes on a bill or measure before a legislative assembly. "Calling the yeas and nays" is calling for the individual and oral vote of each member, usually upon a call of the roll.

YEAST. A small cellular micro-organism. In its ordinary significance, it is a conglomerate mass of infinitesimally small cells. Standard Brands v. National Grain Yeast Corporation, N.J., 60 S.Ct. 27, 28, 308 U.S. 34, 84 L.Ed. 17.

YELLOW DOG CONTRACT. A contract by which employer requires employee to sign an instrument promising as condition that he will not join a union during its continuance, and will be discharged if he does join. Denver Local Union No. 13 of International Brotherhood of Teamsters, Chauffeurs, Stablemen, and Helpers of America v. Perry Truck Lines, 101 P.2d 436, 443, 106 Colo. 25.

YEME. In old records. Winter; a corruption of the Latin "*hiems*." See Hyems.

YEN HOCK. A piece of metal sharpened at one end and blunt on the other end, used to cook an opium pill or yen pock. People v. Graves, 84 Cal. App.2d 531, 191 P.2d 32, 33.

YEN POCK. An opium pill. People v. Graves, 84 Cal.App.2d 531, 191 P.2d 32, 33.

YEN SHEE. A carbonized opium and a black granular substance. People v. Graves, 84 Cal. App.2d 531, 191 P.2d 32, 33.

YEOMAN. In English law. A commoner; a freeholder under the rank of gentleman. Cowell. A man who has free land of forty shillings by the year; who was anciently thereby qualified to serve on juries, vote for knights of the shire, and do any other act, where the law requires one that is *probus et legalis homo*. 1 Bl.Comm. 406, 407.

This term is occasionally used in American law, but without any definite meaning, except in the United States navy, where it designates an appointive petty officer. Who performs clerical duties usually associated with office workers.

YEOMANRY. The collected body of yeomen.

YEOMEN OF THE GUARD. Properly called "yeomen of the guard of the royal household;" a body of men of the best rank under the gentry, and of a larger stature than ordinary, every one being required to be six feet high. Enc. Lond.

YEVEN, or YEOVEN. Given; dated. Cowell.

YIDDISH. A Middle High German dialect, or number of dialects, spoken by Jews, containing a large number of Germanized Hebrew words, and using Hebrew characters for its literature. U. S. ex rel. Engel v. Tod, C.C.A.2, 294 F. 820, 822.

YIELD. In the law of real property. To perform a service due by a tenant to his lord. Hence the usual form of reservation of a rent in a lease begins with the words "yielding and paying." Sweet.

In patent law. The word "yielding," as used in a patent claim, is not the equivalent of "resilient," or "spring-supported," but may be applied to a part which is retractable at will. Mergenthaler Linotype Co. v. International Typesetting Mach. Co., D.C.N.Y., 229 F. 168, 192.

YIELD UPON INVESTMENT Proportionate rate which the income upon an investment bears to the total cost interest excepted on that investment, taking into consideration the time when the investment may be outstanding before being paid off. Baltimore Mail S. S. Co. v. United States, D.C. Md., 7 F.Supp. 651, 653.

YIELDING AND PAYING In conveyancing. The initial words of that clause in leases in which the rent to be paid by the lessee is mentioned and reserved.

YOKELET. A little farm, requiring but a yoke of oxen to till it.

YOM KIPPUR. Day of Atonement, is the most sacred and solemn holiday in the Jewish calendar, a day on which Jews throughout the world, after a period of fasting, congregate together at their respective synagogues to worship and pray and ask divine forgiveness for sins committed during the year. Hoffman v. Graber, Mo.App., 153 S.W. 2d 817, 818.

YORK-ANTWERP RULES. Certain rules relating to uniform bills of lading formulated by the Association for the Reform and Codification of the Laws of Nations, now the International Law Association.

These rules are commonly incorporated in contracts of affreightment. They are the result of conferences of representatives of mercantile interests from several countries, in the interest of uniformity of law. They have no statutory authority. The text is in Maclachlan's Mercht. Shipping. For a history of them, see Lowndes, Gen. Av.

YORK, CUSTOM OF. A custom of the province of York in England, by which the effects of an intestate, after payment of his debts, are in general divided according to the ancient universal doctrine of the *pars rationabilis*; that is, one-third each to the widow, children, and administrator. 2 Bl.Comm. 518.

YORK, STATUTE OF. An important English statute passed at the city of York, in the twelfth year of Edward II., containing provisions on the subject of attorneys, witnesses, the taking of inquests by *nisi prius*, etc. 2 Reeve, Eng. Law, 299–302.

YOUNGER CHILDREN. This phrase, when used in English conveyancing with reference to settlements of land, signifies all such children as are not entitled to the rights of an eldest son. It therefore includes daughters, even those who are older than the eldest son. Mozley & Whiteley.

YOUTH. This word may include children and young persons of both sexes. Nelson v. Cushing, 2 Cush. (Mass.) 519, 528.

YULE. The times of Christmas and Lammas.

YVERNAIL BLE. L. Fr. Winter grain. Kelham.

Z

ZAMINDAR. See Zemindar.

ZANJA. Span. A water ditch or artificial canal, and particularly one used for purposes of irrigation. See Pico v. Colimas, 32 Cal. 578.

ZANJERO. Span. A water commissioner or superintendent, or supervisor of an irrigation system. See Pico v. Colimas, 32 Cal. 578; Everett v. Standard Acc. Ins. Co., 45 Cal.App. 332, 187 P. 996, 1000.

ZEALOT. This word is commonly taken in a bad sense, as denoting a separatist from the Church of England, or a fanatic. Brown.

ZEALOUS WITNESS. An untechnical term denoting a witness, on the trial of a cause, who manifests a partiality for the side calling him, and an eager readiness to tell anything which he thinks may be of advantage to that side.

ZEIR. O. Sc. Year. "*Zeir* and day." Bell.

ZEMINDAR. In Hindu law. Landkeeper. An officer who under the Mohammedan government was charged with the financial superintendence of the lands of a district, the protection of the cultivators, and the realization of the government's share of its produce, either in money or kind. Wharton.

ZEOLITE PROCESS. The "zeolite process" of softening water consists in passing hard water through a filter bed of granular sodium zeolites, which exchange their sodium base for the calcium and magnesium in the water. Permutit Co. v. Wadham, D.C.Mich., 294 F. 370, 371.

ZEOLITES. Chemical compounds existing in nature, and also produced chemically, possessing the unique and valuable property of being able, when saturated with solution of sodium chloride, to take up from water passed through them such hardening elements as calcium or magnesium, and to exchange the same for salt when brought in contact therewith. Permutit Co. v. Graver Corporation, D.C.Ill., 37 F.2d 385, 386.

ZETETICK. Proceeding by inquiry. Enc. Lond.

ZIGARI, or ZINGARI. Rogues and vagabonds in the middle ages; from Zigi, now Circassia.

ZOLL-VEREIN. A union of German states for uniformity of customs, established in 1819. It continued until the unification of the German empire, including Prussia, Saxony, Bavaria, Wurtemberg, Baden, Hesse-Cassel, Brunswick, and Mecklenburg-Strelitz, and all intermediate principalities. It was subsequently superseded by the German empire; and the federal council of the empire took the place of that of the Zoll-Verein. Wharton.

ZONE OF EMPLOYMENT. Within which injuries to employees are compensable under Workmen's Compensation Acts is the place of employment and the area thereabout, including the means of ingress thereto and egress therefrom under the control of the employer. Merz v. Industrial Commission of Ohio, 134 Ohio St. 36, 15 N.E. 2d 632, 633. It implies reasonable proximity to place of employment. Evans v. Workmen's Compensation Commissioner, 124 W.Va. 336, 20 S.E.2d 172, 173.

ZONING. The division of a city by legislative regulation into districts and the prescription and application in each district of regulations having to do with structural and architectural designs of buildings and of regulations prescribing use to which buildings within designated districts may be put. Miller v. Board of Public Works of City of Los Angeles, 195 Cal. 477, 234 P. 381, 384, 38 A. L.R. 1479; Elizabeth City v. Aydlett, 201 N.C. 602, 161 S.E. 78, 79.

ZYGOCEPHALUM. In the civil law. A measure or quantity of land. Nov. 17, c. 8. As much land as a yoke of oxen could plow in a day. Calvin.

ZYGOSTATES. In the civil law. A weigher; an officer who held or looked to the balance in weighing money between buyer and seller; an officer appointed to determine controversies about the weight of money. Spelman.

ZYTHUM. Lat. A liquor or beverage made of wheat or barley. Dig. 33, 6, 9, pr.

A TABLE

OF

BRITISH REGNAL YEARS

Sovereign	Accession	Length of reign
William I	Oct. 14, 1066	21
William II	Sept. 26, 1087	13
Henry I	Aug. 5, 1100	36
Stephen	Dec. 26, 1135	19
Henry II	Dec. 19, 1154	35
Richard I	Sept. 23, 1189	10
John	May 27, 1199	18
Henry III	Oct. 28, 1216	57
Edward I	Nov. 20, 1272	35
Edward II	July 8, 1307	20
Edward III	Jan. 25, 1326	51
Richard II	June 22, 1377	23
Henry IV	Sept. 30, 1399	14
Henry V	March 21, 1413	10
Henry VI	Sept. 1, 1422	39
Edward IV	March 4, 1461	23
Edward V	April 9, 1483	—
Richard III	June 26, 1483	3
Henry VII	Aug. 22, 1485	24
Henry VIII	April 22, 1509	38
Edward VI	Jan. 28, 1547	7
Mary	July 6, 1553	6
Elizabeth	Nov. 17, 1558	45
James I	March 24, 1603	23
Charles I	March 27, 1625	24
The Commonwealth	Jan. 30, 1649	11
Charles II	May 29, 1660	37
James II	Feb. 6, 1685	4
William and Mary	Feb. 13, 1689	14
Anne	March 8, 1702	13
George I	Aug. 1, 1714	13
George II	June 11, 1727	34
George III	Oct. 25, 1760	60
George IV	Jan. 29, 1820	11
William IV	June 26, 1830	7
Victoria	June 20, 1837	64
Edward VII	Jan. 22, 1901	9
George V	May 6, 1910	25
Edward VIII	Jan. 20, 1936	1
George VI	Dec. 11, 1936	15
Elizabeth II	Feb. 6, 1952	—

ABBREVIATIONS

A

A. Alabama;—Arkansas;—Abbott (see Abb.);—Annuals (Louisiana);—Atlantic Reporter.

A.2d. Atlantic Reporter, Second Series.

A.B. Anonymous Reports at the end of Bendloe.

A.B.A.Jour. American Bar Association Journal.

A.B.R. American Bankruptcy Reports.

A'B.R.J.N.S.W. A'Beckett's Reserved (Equity) Judgments, New South Wales.

A'B.R.J.P.P. A'Beckett's Reserved Judgments, Port Philip.

A.B.R.N.S. American Bankruptcy Reports, New Series.

A.C. Appellate Court;—Case on Appeal;—Appeal Cases;—Advance California Reports.

[1891] A.C. Law Reports, Appeal Cases, from 1891 onward.

1917, A.C. 1917, Appeal Cases, Canada.

1918, A.C. Law Reports, 1918, Appeal Cases, Eng.

A.C.A. Advance California Appellate Reports.

A.C.C. American Corporation Cases (Withrow's).

A.C.L.J. American Civil Law Journal.

A.C.R. American Criminal Reports.

A.D. American Decisions;—Appellate Division, New York Supreme Court.

A.E.C. American Electrical Cases.

A.G. (or A.G.Op.) Attorney General's Opinions.

A.G.Dec. Attorney General's Decisions.

A.Ins.R. American Insolvency Reports.

A.K.Marsh. A. K. Marshall's Kentucky Reports.

A.L.C. American Leading Cases.

A.L.R. American Law Reports.

A.M.C. American Maritime Cases.

A.M. & O. Armstrong, Macartney & Ogle's Irish Nisi Prius Reports.

A.Moo. A. Moore's Reports, in vol. 1 Bosanquet & Puller.

A.N.C. Abbott's New Cases, New York;—American Negligence Cases.

A.N.R. American Negligence Reports, Current Series.

A.P.B. Ashurst's Paper Books (MSS. in Lincoln's Inn Library).

A.R. American Reports;—Atlantic Reporter;—Appeal Reports, Ontario.

A.R.C. American Ruling Cases;—American Railway Cases.

A.R.S. Arizona Revised Statutes.

A.R.R. American Railway Reports.

A.R.V.R. 22. Anno Regni Victoriæ Regina Vicesimo Secundo.

A.Rep. American Reports;—Atlantic Reporter (commonly cited Atl. or A.).

A.S.R. American State Reports.

A. & E. Adolphus & Ellis' English Queen's Bench Reports;—Admiralty and Ecclesiastical.

A. & E.Cas. American & English Annotated Cases.

A. & E.Corp.Cas. American and English Corporation Cases.

A. & E.Ency.Law (or A. & E.Enc.L. & Pr.). American & English Encyclopædia of Law & Practice.

A. & E.N.S. Adolphus & Ellis' English Queen's Bench Reports, New Series.

A. & E.P. & P. American and English Pleading and Practice.

A. & E.R.R.C. (or A. & E.R.Cas.). American & English Railroad Cases.

A. & H. Arnold & Hodges' English Queen's Bench Reports.

A. & N. Alcock & Napier's Irish King's Bench Reports.

Ab.Eq.Cas. Equity Cases Abridged (English).

Abb. Abbott. See below.

Abb.Ad. (or Abb.Adm.). Abbott's Admiralty Reports.

Abb.App.Dec. Abbott's New York Court of Appeals Decisions.

Abb.Beech.Tr. Abbott's Report of the Beecher Trial.

Abb.C.C. Abbott's Circuit Court, United States.

Abb.Ct.App. Abbott's New York Court of Appeals Decisions.

Abb.Dec. Abbott's New York Court of Appeals Decisions.

Abb.Dig. Abbott's New York Digest.

Abb.Dig.Corp. Abbott's Digest Law of Corporations.

Abb.Law Dict. Abbott's Law Dictionary.

Abb.Mo.Ind. Abbott's Monthly Index.

Abb.N.C. Abbott's New Cases, New York.

Abb.N.S. Abbott's Practice Reports, New Series.

Abb.N.Y.App. Abbott's New York Court of Appeals Decisions.

Abb.N.Y.Dig. Abbott's New York Digest.

Abb.Nat.Dig. Abbott's National Digest.

Abb.Pr. (or Prac.). Abbott's New York Practice Reports.

Abb.Pr.N.S. Abbott's New York Practice Reports, New Series.

Abb.Ship. Abbott (Lord Tenterden) on Shipping.

Abb.Tr.Ev. Abbott's Trial Evidence.

Abb.U.S. Abbott's United States Circuit Court Reports.

Abb.Y.Bk. Abbott's Year Book of Jurisprudence.

Abbott. Abbott's Dictionary.

A'Beck.R.J.N.S.W. A'Beckett's Reserved (Equity) Judgments. New South Wales.

A'Beck.R.J.P.P. A'Beckett's Reserved Judgments. (Port Phillip).

A'Beck.Res.Judgm. (or A'Beck.Judg.Vict.) A'Beckett's Reserved Judgments of Victoria.

Abr. Abridgment;—Abridged.

Abr.Case. Crawford & Dix's Abridged Cases, Ireland.

Abr.Case.Eq. Equity Cases Abridged (English).

Act. (or Act.Pr.C.). Acton's English Privy Council Reports.

Acta Cancellariae. English Chancery Reports.

Acton. Acton, Eng.

Ad.Jus. Adam's Justiciary Reports (Scotch).

Ad. & E. (or Ad. & Ell.). Adolphus & Ellis' English King's Bench Reports.

Ad. & Ell.N.S. Adolphus & Ellis' Reports, New Series;—English Queen's Bench (commonly cited Q.B.).

Adams. Adams' Reports, vols. 41, 42 Maine;—Adams' Reports, vol. 1 New Hampshire.

Adams, Eq. Adams' Equity.

Adams, Rom.Ant. Adams, Roman Antiquities.

Add. Addison's Reports, Pennsylvania;—Addams' English Ecclesiastical Reports.

Add.Cont. Addison on Contracts.

Add.Ecc. Addams' Ecclesiastical Reports.

Add.Rep. Addison's Pennsylvania Reports.

Add.Torts. Addison on Torts.

Addams. Addams' Ecclesiastical Reports, English.

Addis. (or Add.Pa.). Addison's (Pennsylvania County Court) Reports.

Adj.Sess. Adjourned Session.

Adm. & Ecc. Admiralty and Ecclesiastical;—English Law Reports, Admiralty and Ecclesiastical.

Adol. & El. Adolphus & Ellis' Reports, English King's Bench.

Adol. & El.N.S. Adolphus & Ellis' Reports, New Series, English Queen's Bench.

Adolph. & E. Adolphus & Ellis' English King's Bench Reports.

Adolph. & E.N.S. Adolphus & Ellis' New Series (usually cited as Queen's Bench).

Adv.Ops. Advance Opinions.

Agra, F.B. Agra High Court, Full Bench (India).

Agra H.C. Agra High Court Reports (India).

Aik. Aikens' Vermont Reports.

Aik.Dig. Aikin's Digest of Laws, Ala.

Aikens (Vt.). Aikens' Reports, Vermont.

Ainsw. (or Ainsworth). Ainsworth's Lexicon.

Air L.Rev. Air Law Review.

Al. Aleyn's Select Cases, King's Bench;—Alabama;—Allen.

Al.Tel.Ca. Allen's Telegraph Cases.

Al. & Nap. Alcock & Napier's Irish King's Bench Reports.

Ala. Alabama;—Alabama Reports.

Ala.App. Alabama Appellate Court.

Ala.L.J. Alabama Law Journal.

Ala.L.Rev. Alabama Law Review.

Ala.Law. Alabama Lawyers.

Ala.N.S. Alabama Reports, New Series.

Ala.Sel.Cas. Alabama Select Cases, by Shepherd, see Alabama Reports, vols. 37, 38 and 39.

Ala.St.Bar Ass'n. Alabama State Bar Association.

Alaska. Alaska Reports.

Alaska Co. Alaska Codes, Carter.

Alb.Arb. Albert Arbitration (Lord Cairns' Decisions).

Alb.Law J. Albany Law Journal.

Alberta L.Q. Alberta Law Quarterly.

Alc. (or Alc.Reg. or Alc.Reg.Cas.). Alcock's Irish Registry Cases.

Alc. & Nap. Alcock & Napier's Irish King's Bench Reports.

Ald. Alden's Condensed Reports, Pennsylvania.

Alex.Cas. Report of the Alexandria Case by Dudley.

Alex.Ins. Alexander on Life Insurance in New York.

Alexander. Alexander's Reports, vols. 66–72 Mississippi.

Aleyn. Aleyn's Select Cases, English King's Bench.

Alger's Law Promoters & Prom.Corp. Alger's Law in Relation to Promoters and Promotion of Corporations.

Alis.Princ.Scotch Law. Alison's Principles of the Criminal Law of Scotland.

Alison Pr. Alison's Practice, Scotch.

All. Allen's Massachusetts Reports.

All.N.B. Allen's New Brunswick Reports.

All.Ser. Allahabad Series, Indian Law Reports.

All.Tel.Cas. Allen's Telegraph Cases.

Allen. Allen's Massachusetts Reports;—Allen's Reports, New Brunswick;—Allen's Reports, Washington.

Allen Tel.Cas. Allen's Telegraph Cases.

Allin (or Allinson). Allinson, Pennsylvania Superior and District Court.

Allison's Am.Dict. Allison's American Dictionary.

Alta.L. Alberta Law.

Am.Bank.R. (or Am.B'kc'y Rep.). American Bankruptcy Reports.

Am.Bankr.Reg. National Bankruptcy Register, U.S.

Am.Bankr.Rep.N.S. American Bankruptcy Reports, New Series.

Am.Bankr.Rev. American Bankruptcy Review.

Am.C.L.J. American Civil Law Journal, N.Y.

Am.Cent.Dig. American Digest (Century Edition).

Am.Corp.Cas. American Corporation Cases (Withrow's).

Am.Cr. American Criminal.

Am.Cr.Rep. American Criminal Reports.

Am.Cr.Tr. American Criminal Trials. Chandler's.

Am.Dec. American Decisions.

Am.Dig. American Digest.

Am.Dig.Cent.Ed. American Digest (Century Edition).

Am.Dig.Dec.Ed. (or Decen.Ed.). American Digest (Decennial Edition).

Am.Ed. American Edition.

Am.El.Ca. (or Am.Elec.Ca. or Am.Electr.Cas.). American Electrical Cases.

Am.Enc.Dict. American Encyclopedic Dictionary.

Am.Fed.Tax R. American Federal Tax Reports.

Am.Ins. Arnold on Marine Insurance.

Am.Ins.Rep. (or Am.Insol.Rep.). American Insolvency Reports.

Am.J.Int.L. American Journal of International Law.

Am.Jour.Pol. American Journal of Politics.

Am.Jour.Soc. American Journal of Sociology.

Am.Jud.Soc. American Judicature Society.

Am.Jur. American Jurisprudence;—American Jurist, Boston.

Am.L.C.R.P. Sharswood and Budd's Leading Cases on Real Property.

Am.L.Cas. American Leading Cases.

Am.L.J. (or Am.Law J.). American Law Journal; American Law Journal (Hall's) Philadelphia.

Am.L.J. (N.S.) American Law Journal (Clark's).

Am.L.J.N.S. American Law Journal, New Series, Philadelphia.

Am.L.J. (O) American Law Journal (Ohio).

Am.L.J. (O.S.) American Law Journal (Hall's).

Am.L.Reg. (N.S.) (or Am.Law Reg.N.S.) American Law Register, New Series.

Am.L.Reg. (O.S.) (or Am.Law Reg.O.S.) American Law Register, Old Series.

Am.L.Rev. American Law Review, Boston.

Am.L.S.Rev. American Law School Review.

Am.L.T.Bankr. American Law Times Bankruptcy Reports.

Am.L.T.R. (or Am.Law T.Rep.) American Law Times Reports.

Am.L.T.R.N.S. American Law Times Reports, New Series.

Am.Lab.Leg.Rev. American Labor Legislation Review.

Am.Law Inst. American Law Institute Restatement of the Law.

Am.Law Mag. American Law Magazine.

Am.Law Rec. American Law Record (Cincinnati).

Am.Law Reg. American Law Register.

Am.Law Rev. American Law Review.

Am.Law S.Rev. American Law School Review.

Am.Lead.Cas. American Leading Cases (Hare & Wallace's).

Am.Leg.N. American Legal News.

Am.Neg.Ca. (or Am.Negl.Cas.) American Negligence Cases.

Am.Neg.Rep. (or Am.Negl.R.) American Negligence Reports.

Am.Pol.Sci.Rev. American Political Science Review.

Am.Pr. American Practice.

Am.Pr.Rep. American Practice Reports, Washington, D.C.

Am.Prob. American Probate.

Am.Prob.N.S. American Probate, New Series.

Am.Prob.Rep. American Probate Reports.

Am.R. (or Am.Rep.) American Reports.

Am.R.R.Cas. American Railway Cases (Smith & Bates').

Am.R.R.Rep. (or Am.R.Rep.). American Railway Reports.

Am.R.R. & C.Rep. (or Am.R. & Corp.) American Railroad & Corporation Reports.

Am.Rep. American Reports (Selected Cases).

Am.Ry.Ca. American Railway Cases.

Am.Ry.Rep. American Railway Reports.

Am.St.Rep. American State Reports.

Am.St.Ry.Dec. American Street Railway Decisions.

Am.St.Ry.Rep. American Street Railway Reports.

Am.Tr.-M.Cas. American Trade-Mark Cases (Cox's).

Am. & Eng.Corp.Cas. American and English Corporation Cases.

Am. & Eng.Corp.Cas.N.S. American & English Corporation Cases, New Series.

Am. & Eng.Dec. in Eq. American and English Decisions in Equity.

Am. & Eng.Ency.Law (or Am. & Eng.Enc.Law). American and English Encyclopedia of Law.

Am. & Eng.Enc.Law Sup. American and English Encyclopedia of Law, Supplement.

Am. & Eng.Pat.Cas. (or Am. & Eng.Pat.Ca.). American and English Patent Cases.

Am. & Eng.R.R.Ca. American and English Railroad Cases.

Am. & Eng.Ry.Cas. (or Am. & Eng.Ry.Ca.). American and English Railway Cases.

Am. & Eng.Ry.Cas.N.S. American & English Railroad Cases, New Series.

Amb. (or Ambl.) Ambler's English Chancery Reports.

Amend. Amendment.

Amer. American;—Amerman, vols. 111-115 Pennsylvania.

Amer.Jur. American Jurist.

Amer.Law. American Lawyer, New York.

Amer.Law Reg. (N.S.). American Law Register, New Series.

Amer.Law Reg. (O.S.). American Law Register, Old Series.

Amer.Law Rev. American Law Review.

Amer. & Eng.Enc.Law. American & English Encyclopædia of Law.

Ames. Ames' Reports, vols. 4-8 Rhode Island;—Ames' Reports, vol. 1 Minnesota.

Ames Cas.B. & N. Ames' Cases on Bills and Notes.

Ames Cas.Par. Ames' Cases on Partnership.

Ames Cas.Pl. Ames' Cases on Pleading.

Ames Cas.Sur. Ames' Cases on Suretyship.

Ames Cas.Trusts. Ames' Cases on Trusts.

Ames, K. & B. Ames, Knowles & Bradley's Reports, vol. 8 Rhode Island.

Amos & F.Fixt. Amos & Ferrard on Fixtures.

Anc.Charters. Ancient Charters, 1692.

And. Andrews' Reports, vols. 63-72 Connecticut;—Andrews' English King's Bench Reports;—Anderson, England.

And.Law Dict. Anderson's Law Dictionary.

Anders. (or Anderson). Anderson's Reports, English Court of Common Pleas.

Andr. (or Andrews). Andrews' English King's Bench Reports. See also And.

Ang. Angell's Reports, Rhode Island.

Ang.Car. Angell on Carriers.

Ang.Highw. Angell & Durfee on Highways.

Ang.Ins. Angell on Insurance.

Ang.Lim. Angell on Limitations.

Ang.Waters (or Ang.Tide Waters). Angell on Tide Waters.

Ang.Water Courses. Angell on Water Courses.

Ang. & A.Corp. Angell & Ames on Corporations.

Ang. & Dur. Angell & Durfee's Reports, vol. 1 Rhode Island.

Ann. Queen Anne, as 8 Ann. c. 19;—Annally's Reports, K.B.

Ann.Cal.Codes. West's Annotated California Codes.

Ann.Cas. American & English Annotated Cases;—New York Annotated Cases.

Ann.Cas.1912A. American Annotated Cases 1912A, et seq.

Ann.Code. Annotated Code.

Ann.Codes & St. Bellinger and Cotton's Annotated Codes and Statutes, Or.

Ann.Law Reg. Annual Law Register of the U. S.

Ann.Reg. Annual Register, London.

Ann.St. Annotated Statutes.

Ann.St.Ind.T. Annotated Statutes of Indian Territory.

Annally. Annally's Reports, K.B.

Annaly. Annaly's edition of Lee *tempore* Hardwicke.

Anne. Queen Anne (thus "1 Anne," denotes the first year of the reign of Queen Anne).

Anson, Cont. Anson on Contracts.

Anstr. Anstruther's Reports, English Exchequer.

Anth. Anthon's New York Nisi Prius Reports;—Anthony's Illinois Digest.

Anth.N.P. Anthon's New York Nisi Prius Reports.

Anth.Shep. Anthony's edition of Shephard's Touchstone.

Ap.Justin. Apud Justinianum;—In Justinian's Institutes.

App. Appleton's Reports, vols. 19, 20 Maine.

App.Cas. Appeal Cases, English Law Reports;—Appeal Cases, United States;—Appeal Cases of the different States;—Appeal Cases, District of Columbia.

[1891] App.Cas. Law Reports, Appeal Cases, from 1891 onward.

App.Cas.Beng. Sevestre and Marshall's Bengal Reports.

App.Ct.Rep. Bradwell's Illinois Appeal Court Reports.

App.D. South African Law Reports, Appellate Division.

App.D.C. Appeals, District of Columbia.

App.Div. Appellate Division, New York.

App.Jur.Act 1876. Appellate Jurisdiction Act, 1876, 39 & 40 Vict. c. 59.

App.R., N.Z. (or App.N.Z.). Appeal Reports, New Zealand.

App.Rep.Ont. Appeal Reports, Ontario.

Appe.Bre. Appendix to Breese's Reports.

Append. Appendix.

Appleton. Appleton's Reports, vols. 19, 20 Maine.

Ar.Rep. Argus Reports, Victoria.

Arabin. Decisions of Seargeant Arabin.

Arb.J. Arbitration Journal.

Arbuth. Arbuthnot's Select Criminal Cases, Madras.

Arch. Court of Arches, England.

Arch.Cr.Pl. (or Archb.Crim.Pl.). Archbold's Criminal Pleading.

Arch.N.P. Archbold's Law of Nisi Prius.

Arch.P.L.Cas. Archbold's Abridgment of Poor Law Cases.

Arch.Sum. Archbold's Summary of Laws of England.

Archb.Civil Pl. Archbold's Civil Pleading.

Archb.Cr.Law. Archbold's Pleading and Evidence in Criminal Cases.

Archb.Cr.Prac. & Pl. Archbold's Pleading and Evidence in Criminal Cases.

Archb.Crim.Pl. Archbold's Criminal Pleading.

Archb.Landl. & Ten. Archbold's Landlord and Tenant.

Archb.N.P. Archbold's Nisi Prius Law.

Archb.New Pr. (or N.Prac.). Archbold's New Practice.

Archb.Pr. Archbold's Practice.

Archb.Pr.K.B. Archbold's Practice King's Bench.

Archer. Archer's Reports, Florida.

Archer & Hogue. Archer & Hogue's Reports, vol. 2 Florida.

Architects' L.R. Architects' Law Reports (Eng.).

Arg.Fr.Merc.Law. Argles (Napoleon), Treatise Upon French Mercantile Law, etc.

Arg.Rep. Reports printed in Melbourne Argus, Australia.

Ariz. Arizona;—Arizona Reports.

Ark. Arkansas;—Arkansas Reports;—Arkley's Justiciary Reports, Scotland.

Ark.Just. Arkley's Justiciary Reports, Scotland.

Ark.L.J. Arkansas Law Journal, Fort Smith.

Ark.L.Rev. Arkansas Law Review.

Arkl. (or Arkley). Arkley's Justiciary Reports, Scotland.

Arms.Br.P.Cas. Armstrong's Breach of Privilege Cases, New York.

Arms.Con.Elec. Armstrong's New York Contested Elections.

Arms.Elect.Cas. Armstrong's Cases of Contested Elections, New York.

Arms.M. & O. (or Arms.Mac. & Og.). Armstrong, Macartney, & Ogle's Irish Nisi Prius Reports.

Arms.Tr. Armstrong's Limerick Trials, Ireland.

Arn. Arnold's English Common Pleas Reports;—Arnot's Criminal Trials, Scotland.

Arn.El.Cas. Arnold's Election Cases. English.

Arn.Ins. Arnould on Marine Insurance.

Arn. & H. (or Arn. & Hod.). Arnold & Hodges' English Queen's Bench Reports.

Arn. & Hod.B.C. Arnold & Hodges' English Bail Court Reports.

Arn. & Hod.Pr.Cas. Arnold & Hodges' Practice Cases, English.

Arnold. Arnold's Common Pleas Reports, English.

Arnot Cr.C. Arnot's Criminal Cases, Scotland.

Artic.Cleri. Articles of the clergy.

Articuli sup.Chart. Articles upon the charters.

Ashe. Ashe's Tables to the Year Books (or to Coke's Reports;—or to Dyer's Reports).

Ashm. Ashmead's Pennsylvania Reports.

Ashton. Ashton's Reports, vols. 9–12 Opinions of the United States Attorneys General.

Ashurst MS. Ashurst's Paper Books, Lincoln's Inn Library;—Ashurst's Manuscript Reports, printed in vol. 2 Chitty.

Asp. Aspinall, English Admiralty.

Asp.Cas. (or Rep.). English Maritime Law Cases, new series by Aspinall.

Asp.M.C. Aspinall's Maritime Cases.

Aspin. Aspinall's Maritime Cases, Eng.

Ass. Book of Assizes.

Ass.Jerus. Assizes of Jerusalem.

Assem. Assembly, State Legislature.

Assiz. Assizes.

Ast.Ent. Aston's Entries.

Atch. Atchison's English Navigation and Trade Reports.

Ath.Mar.Sett. Atherly on Marriage Settlements.

Atk. Atkyn's English Chancery Reports.

Atk.P.T. Atkyn's Parliamentary Tracts.

Atk.Sher. Atkinson on Sheriffs.

Atl. Atlantic Reporter.

Atl.Mo. Atlantic Monthly.

Atl.R. (or Rep.). Atlantic Reporter.

Atty.Gen.Op. Attorney-Generals' Opinions, United States.

Atty.Gen.Op.N.Y. Attorney-Generals' Opinions, New York.

Atwater. Atwater's Reports, vol. 1 Minnesota.

Auch. Auchinleck's Manuscript Cases, Scotch Court of Session.

Auct.Reg. & L.Chron. Auction Register and Law Chronicle.

Aul.Gel.Noctes Atticæ. Aulus Gellius, Noctes Atticæ.

Aust. Austin's English County Court Cases;—Australia.

Aust.Jur. Austin's Province of Jurisprudence.

Aust.Jur.Abr. Austin's Lectures on Jurisprudence, abridged.

Aust.L.J. Australian Law Journal.

Aust.L.T. Australian Law Times.

Austin (Ceylon). Austin's Ceylon Reports.

Austin C.C. Austin's English County Court Reports.

Austr.C.L.R. Commonwealth Law Reports, Australia.

Austr.Jur. Australian Jurist.

Austr.L.T. Australian Law Times.

Ayl.Pan. See Ayliffe.

Ayl.Pand. See Ayliffe.

Ayl.Par. See Ayliffe.

Ayliffe. Ayliffe's Pandects;—Ayliffe's Parergon Juris Canonici Angelicani.

Ayliffe Parerg. See Ayliffe.

Azuni, Mar.Law. Azuni on Maritime Law.

B

BAJI. California Jury Instructions, Civil.

B.C. Bankruptcy Cases;—British Columbia.

B.C.C. Bail Court Reports (Saunders & Cole);—Bail Court Cases (Lowndes & Maxwell);—Brown's Chancery Cases.

B.C.R. (or B.C.Rep.). Saunders & Cole's Bail Court Reports, English;—British Columbia Reports.

B.Ch. Barbour's Chancery Reports, New York.

B.D. & O. Blackham, Dundas & Osborne's Nisi Prius Reports, Ireland.

B.L.R. Bengal Law Reports.

B.M. Burrow's Reports *tempore* Mansfield;—Ben Monroe's Reports, Kentucky;—Moore's Reports, English.

B.Mon. (or B.Monr.). Ben Monroe's Reports, Kentucky.

B.Moore. Moore's Reports, English.

B.N.A. Bureau of National Affairs.

B.N.C. Bingham's New Cases, English Common Pleas;—Brooke's New Cases, English King's Bench;—Busbee's North Carolina Law Reports.

B.N.P. Buller's Nisi Prius.

B.P.B. Buller's Paper Book, Lincoln's Inn Library.

B.P.C. Brown's Cases in Parliament.

B.P.L.Cas. Bott's Poor Law Cases.

B.P.N.R. Bosanquet & Puller's New Reports, English Common Pleas.

B.P.R. Brown's Parliamentary Reports.

B.R. Bancus Regis, or King's Bench;—Bankruptcy Reports;—Bankruptcy Register, New York;—National Bankruptcy Register Reports.

B.R.C. British Ruling Cases.

B.R.H. Cases in King's Bench *tempore* Hardwicke.

B.T.A. Board of Tax Appeals, U. S.

B.U.L.Rev. Boston University Law Review.

B.W.C.C. Butterworth's Workmen's Compensation Cases, Eng.

B. & A. Barnewall & Adolphus' English King's Bench Reports;—Barnewall & Alderson's English King's Bench Reports;—Baron & Arnold's English Election Cases;—Baron & Austin's English Election Cases;—Banning & Arden's Patent Cases.

B. & Ad. (or Adol.). Barnewall & Adolphus' English King's Bench Reports.

B. & Ald. Barnewall & Alderson's English King's Bench Reports.

B. & Arn. Barron & Arnold's Election Cases.

B. & Aust. Barron & Austin's English Election Cases.

B. & B. Broderip & Bingham's English Common Pleas Reports;—Ball & Beatty's Irish Chancery Reports;—Bowler & Bowers, vols. 2, 3 United States Comptroller's Decisions.

B. & Bar. Bench and Bar.

B. & C. Barnewall & Cresswell's English King's Bench Reports.

B. & C.Comp. Bellinger and Cotton's Annotated Codes and Statutes, Or.

B. & D. Benloe & Dalison, English.

B. & F. Broderip & Fremantle's English Ecclesiastical Reports.

B. & H. Blatchford & Howland's United States District Court Reports.

B. & H.Cr.Cas. (or B. & H.Lead.Cas.). Bennett & Heard Leading Criminal Cases, Eng.

B. & H.Dig. Bennett & Heard's Massachusetts Digest.

B. & H.Lead.Cas. Bennett & Heard's Leading Criminal Cases.

B. & I. Bankruptcy and Insolvency Cases.

B. & L. Browning & Lushington's English Admiralty Reports.

B. & M. (or B. & Macn.). Browne & Macnamara's Reports, English.

B. & P. Bosanquet & Puller's English Common Pleas Reports.

B. & P.N.R. Bosanquet & Puller's New Reports.

B. & S. Best & Smith's English Queen's Bench Reports.

B. & V. Beling & Vanderstraaten's Reports, Ceylon.

Ba. & Be. Ball & Beatty's Irish Chancery Reports.

Bab.Auct. Babington on Auctions.

Bac.Abr. Bacon's Abridgment.

Bac.Aph. (or Bac.Aphorisms). Bacon's (Sir Francis) Aphorisms.

Bac.Ben.Soc. Bacon on Benefit Societies and Life Insurance.

Bac.Dig. Bacon's Georgia Digest.

Bac.Ins. Bacon on Benefit Societies and Life Insurance.

Bac.Law Tracts (or Bac.Ir.). Bacon's (Sir Francis) Law Tracts.

Bac.Max. Bacon's (Sir Francis) Maxims.

Bac.Read.Uses. Bacon (Sir Francis), Reading upon the Statute of Uses.

Bac.St.Uses. Bacon (Sir Francis), Reading upon the Statute of Uses.

Bac.Works. Bacon's (Sir Francis), Works.

Bach. Bach's Reports, vols. 19–21 Montana.

Bacon. Bacon's Abridgment;—Bacon's Aphorisms;—Bacon's Complete Arbitrator;—Bacon's Elements of the Common Law;—Bacon on Government;—Bacon's Law Tracts;—Bacon on Leases and Terms of Years;—Bacon's Maxims;—Bacon on Uses.

Bagl. Bagley's Reports, vols. 16–19 California.

Bagl. & H. Bagley and Harmen's California Reports.

Bail. Bailey's Law Reports, South Carolina.

Bail Ct.Cas. Lowndes & Maxwell's English Bail Court Cases.

Bail Ct.Rep. Saunders & Cole's English Bail Court Reports;—Lowndes & Maxwell's English Bail Court Cases.

Bail.Dig. Bailey's North Carolina Digest.

Bail.Eq. Bailey's Equity Reports, South Carolina.

Bail.L. Bailey's Law, South Carolina.

Baild. Baildon's Select Cases in Chancery (Selden Society, vol. X.) England.

Bailey. Bailey's Law Reports, South Carolina Court of Appeals.

Bailey, Ch. Bailey's Chancery Reports, South Carolina.

Bailey Eq. Bailey's Equity Reports, South Carolina Court of Appeals.

Bailey, Dict. Nathan Bailey's English Dictionary.

Bailey, Mast.Liab. Bailey's Law of Master's Liability for Injuries to Servant.

Baill.Dig. Baillie's Digest of Mohammedan Law.

Bainb.Mines. Bainbridge on Mines and Minerals.

Baker, Quar. Baker's Law of Quarantine.

Bald.App.11 Pet. Baldwin's Appendix to 11 Peters.

Bald. (or Bald.C.C. or Baldw.). Baldwin's United States Circuit Court Reports;—Baldus (Commentator on the Code);—Baldasseroni (on Maritime Law).

Baldw.Dig. Baldwin's Connecticut Digest.

Balf. (or Balf.Pr.). Balfour's Practice, Laws of Scotland.

Ball & B. Ball & Beatty's Irish Chancery Reports.

Ballinger's Ann.Codes & St. Ballinger's Annotated Codes and Statutes, Wash.

Balt.L.Tr. Baltimore Law Transcript.

Ban. & A. Banning & Arden's Patent Cases, U. S.

Bank.and Ins.R. Bankruptcy and Insolvency Reports, English.

Bank.Cas. Banking Cases.

Bank.Ct.Rep. Bankrupt Court Reports, New York;—The American Law Times Bankruptcy Reports are sometimes thus cited.

Bank.Gaz. Bankruptcy Gazette.

Bank.I. (or Bank.Inst.). Bankter's Institutes of Scottish Law.

Bank.L.J. Banking Law Journal.

Bank.Reg. Bankruptcy Register.

Bank.Rep. American Law Times Bankruptcy Reports.

Bank. & Ins. (or Bank. & Ins.R.). Bankruptcy and Insolvency Reports, Eng.

Banker's Law J. Banker's Law Journal.

Bankr.Act. Bankruptcy Act.

Bankr.Form. Bankruptcy Forms.

Banks. Banks' Reports, vols. 1–5 Kansas.

Bann. Bannister's Reports, English Common Pleas.

Bann.Br. Bannister's edition of O. Bridgman's English Common Pleas Reports.

Bann. & A. Banning & Arden (U. S.).

Bann. & A.Pat.Cas. Banning & Arden's Patent Cases.

Bar. Barnardiston's English King's Bench Reports;—Barnardiston's Chancery;—Bar Reports in all the Courts, English;—Barbour's Supreme Court Reports, New York;—Barrows' Reports, vol. 18 Rhode Island.

Bar.Ch. (or Chy.). Barnardiston's English Chancery Reports.

Bar Ex.Jour. Bar Examination Journal (London).

Bar.Mag. Barrington's Magna Charta.

Bar.N. Barnes' Notes, English Common Pleas Reports.

Bar.Obs.St. Barrington's Observations upon the Statutes from Magna Charta to 21 James I.

Bar. & Ad. Barnewall & Adolphus' English King's Bench Reports.

Bar. & Al. Barnewall & Alderson's English King's Bench Reports.

Bar. & Arn. Barron & Arnold's English Election Cases.

Bar. & Aust. (or Au.). Barron & Austin's English Election Cases.

Bar. & Cr. Barnewall & Cresswell's English King's Bench Reports.

Barb. Barbour's Supreme Court Reports, New York;—Barber's Reports, vols. 14–24 Arkansas.

Barb.Abs. Barbour's Abstracts of Chancellor's Decisions, New York.

Barb.App.Dig. Barber's Digest, New York.

Barb.Ark. Barber's Reports, vols. 14–24 Arkansas.

Barb.Ch. Barbour's New York Chancery Reports.

Barb.Ch.Pr. Barbour's Chancery Practice (Text Book).

Barb.Cr.Law. Barbour's Criminal Law.

Barb.Dig. Barber's Digest of Kentucky.

Barb.G.L. Barber's Gold Law, South Africa.

Barb.S.C. Barbour's Supreme Court Reports, New York.

Barb. & C.Ky.St. Barbour and Carroll's Kentucky Statutes.

Barbe. Barber's Reports, Arkansas. See Barb. Ark.

Barc.Dig. Barclay's Missouri Digest.

Barn. Barnardiston's English King's Bench Reports;—Barnes' English Common Pleas Reports;—Barnfield's Reports, vols. 19–20 Rhode Island.

Barn.Ch. Barnardiston's English Chancery Reports.

Barn.No. Barnes' Note of Cases, English Common Pleas.

Barn. & A. Barnewall & Alderson's English King's Bench Reports.

Barn. & Ad. (or Adol.). Barnewall & Adolphus' English King's Bench Reports.

Barn. & Ald. Barnewall & Alderson's English King's Bench Reports.

Barn. & C. (or Cr., Cress.). Barnewall & Cresswell's English King's Bench Reports.

Barnard.Ch. Barnardiston's Chancery Reports.

Barnard.K.B. Barnardiston's King's Bench Reports.

Barnes. Barnes' Practice Cases, English.

Barnes, N.C. Barnes' Notes of Cases in Common Pleas.

Barnes Notes. Barnes' Notes, Eng.

Barnes's Fed.Code. Barnes's Federal Code.

Barnet. Barnet's Reports, vols. 27–29 English Central Criminal Courts Reports.

Barnf. & S. Barnfield and Stiness' Reports, vol. 20 Rhode Island.

Barnw.Dig. Barnwall's Digest of the Year Books.

Barr. Barr's Reports, vols. 1–10 Pennsylvania State;—Barrows' Reports, vol. 18 Rhode Island.

Barr.MSS. Barradall's Manuscript Reports, Virginia.

Barr.St. Barrington's Observations upon the Statutes from Magna Charta to 21 James I.

Barr. & Arn. Barron & Arnold's English Election Cases.

Barr. & Aus. Barron & Austin's English Election Cases.

Barring.Obs.St. (or Barring.St.). Barrington's Observations upon the Statutes from Magna Charta to 21 James I.

Barrows. Barrows' Reports, vol. 18 Rhode Island.

Bart.El.Cas. Bartlett's Congressional Election Cases.

Bat.Dig. Battle's Digest, North Carolina.

Bat.Rev.St. Battle's Revisal of the Public Statutes of North Carolina.

Bates (or Bates Ch.). Bates's Chancery Reports, Del.

Bates' Ann.St. Bates' Annotated Revised Statutes, Ohio.

Bates' Dig. Bates' Digest, Ohio.

Bates, Part. Bates' Law of Partnership.

Batt. (or Batty.). Batty's Irish King's Bench Reports.

Battle's Revisal. Battle's Revisal of the Public Statutes of North Carolina.

Batts' Ann.St.Batts' Rev.St. Batts' Annotated Revised Civil Statutes, Tex.

Bax. (or Baxt.). Baxter's Reports, vols. 60–68 Tennessee.

Bay. Bay's South Carolina Reports;—Bay's Reports, vols. 1–3 and 5–8 Missouri.

Bayley, Bills. Bayley on Bills.

Baylies, Sur. Baylies on Sureties and Guarantors.

Beach, Contrib.Neg. Beach on Contributory Negligence.

Beach, Eq.Prac. Beach's Modern Practice in Equity.

Beach, Inj. Beach on Injunctions.

Beach, Mod.Eq.Jur. Beach's Commentaries on Modern Equity Jurisprudence.

Beach, Priv.Corp. Beach on Private Corporations.

Beach, Pub.Corp. Beach on Public Corporations.

Beach, Rec. Beach on the Law of Receivers.

Beas. Beasley's New Jersey Chancery Reports.

Beasl. Beasley, N.J.; Beasley, New Jersey Equity Reports.

Beat. (or Beatt.; Beatty). Beatty's Irish Chancery Reports.

Beav. Beavan's English Rolls Court Reports.

Beav.R. & C.Cas. English Railway and Canal Cases, by Beavan and others.

Beav. & Wal.Ry.Cas. Beavan & Walford's Railway and Canal Cases, England.

Beavan, Ch. Beavan's English Rolls Court Reports.

Beaw. (or Beaw.Lex Merc.). Beawes' Lex Mercatoria.)

Beck. Beck's Reports, vols. 12–16 Colorado; also vol. 1 Colorado Court of Appeals.

Beck, Med.Jur. Beck's Medical Jurisprudence.

Bedell. Bedell's Reports, vol. 163 New York.

Bee. Bee's United States District Court Reports.

Bee Adm. Bee's Admiralty. An Appendix to Bee's District Court Reports.

Bee C.C.R. Bee's Crown Cases Reserved, English.

Beebe Cit. Beebe's Ohio Citations.

Bel. Bellewe's English King's Bench Reports;—Bellasis' Bombay Reports;—Beling's Ceylon Reports;—Bellinger's Reports, vols. 4–8 Oregon.

Beling. Beling's Ceylon Reports.

Beling & Van. Beling & Vanderstraaten's Ceylon Reports.

Bell. Bell's Dictionary and Digest of the Laws of Scotland;—Bell's English Crown Cases Reserved;—Bell's Scotch Appeal Cases;—Bell's Scotch Session Cases;—Bell's Calcutta Reports, India;—Bellewe's English King's Bench Reports;—Brooke's New Cases, by Bellewe;—Bellinger's Reports, vols. 4–8 Oregon;—Bellasis' Bombay Reports.

Bell Ap.Ca. Bell's Scotch Appeals.

Bell App.Cas. Bell's Scotch House of Lords (Appeal) Cases.

Bell C.C. Bell's English Crown Cases Reserved;—Bellasis' Civil Cases, Bombay;—Bellasis' Criminal Cases, Bombay.

Bell C.H.C. Bell's Reports, Calcutta High Court.

Bell Cas. Bell's Cases, Scotch Court of Session.

Bell.Cas.t.Hen.VIII. Brooke's New Cases (collected by Bellewe).

Bell.Cas.t.Rich.II. Bellewe's English King's Bench Reports (time of Richard II).

Bell, Comm. Bell's Commentaries on the Law of Scotland.

Bell Cr.C. Bell's English Crown Cases;—Beller's Criminal Cases, Bombay.

Bell, Dict. Bell's Dictionary and Digest of the Laws of Scotland.

Bell fol. Bell's folio Reports, Scotch Court of Session.

Bell H.C. Bell's Reports, High Court of Calcutta.

Bell H.L. (or Bell, H.L.Sc.). Bell's House of Lord's Cases, Scotch Appeals.

Bell Med.L.J. Bell's Medico Legal Journal.

Bell Oct. (or 8vo.). Bell's octavo Reports, Scotch Court of Session.

Bell P.C. Bell's Cases in Parliament, Scotch Appeals.

Bell Put.Mar. Bell's Putative Marriage Case, Scotland.

Bell Sc.App. Bell's Appeals to House of Lords from Scotland.

Bell Sc.Cas. Bell's Scotch Court of Session Cases.

Bell Sc.Dig. Bell's Scottish Digest.

Bell Ses.Cas. Bell's Cases in the Scotch Court of Session.

Bellas. 'Bellasis' Criminal (or Civil) Cases, Bombay.

Bellewe. Bellewe's English King's Bench Reports.

Bellewe t.Hen.VIII. Brooke's New Cases (collected by Bellewe).

Bellinger. Bellinger's Reports, vols. 4–8 Oregon.

Bellingh.Tr. Report of Bellingham's Trial.

Belt Bro. Belt's edition of Brown's Chancery Reports.

Belt Sup. (or Belt Sup.Ves.). Belt's Supplement to Vesey Senior's English Chancery Reports.

Belt Ves.Sen. Belt's edition of Vesey Senior's English Chancery Reports.

Ben. Benedict's United States District Court Reports.

Ben.Adm. Benedict's Admiralty Practice.

Ben.F.I.Cas. Bennett's Fire Insurance Cases.

Ben.Ins.Cas. Bennett's Insurance Cases.

Ben Mon. Ben Monroe's Reports, Kentucky.

Ben. & Dal. Benloe & Dalison's English Common Pleas Reports.

Ben. & H.L.C. Bennett & Heard's Leading Criminal Cases.

Ben. & S.Dig. Benjamin & Slidell's Louisiana Digest.

Bench & B. Bench and Bar (periodical), Chicago.

Bench & Bar. Bench and Bar.

Bendl. Bendloe (see Benl.).

Bendloe. Bendloe's or New Benloe's Reports, English Common Pleas, Edition of 1661.

Bened. Benedict's United States District Court Reports.

Beng.L.R. Bengal Law Reports, India.

Beng.L.R.App.Cas. Bengal Law Reports, Appeal Cases (India).

Beng.L.R.P.C. Bengal Law Reports, Privy Council (India).

Beng.L.R.Supp. Bengal Law Reports, Supp. (India).

Beng.S.D.A. Bengal Sudder Dewanny Adawlut Reports.

Benj. Benjamin. New York Annotated Cases, 6 vols.

Benj.Sales. Benjamin on Sales.

Benj.Chalm.Bills & N. Benjamin's Chalmer's Bills and Notes.

Benl. Benloe's or Bendloe's English King's Bench Reports.

Benl.K.B. Benloe's King Bench Reports, England.

Benl. & D. Benloe & Dallison, Eng.

Benl. in Ashe. Benloe at the end of Ashe's Tables.

Benl. in Keil. Benloe or Bendloe in Keilway's Reports.

Benl.New. Benloe's Reports, English King's Bench.

Benl.Old. Benloe of Benloe & Dalison English Common Pleas Reports.

Benl. & Dal. Benloe & Dalison's Common Pleas Reports.

Benn. Bennett, Cal.

Benn.Cal. Bennett's Reports, vol. 1 California.

Benn. (Dak.) Bennett's Dakota Cases.

Benn.F.I.Cas. Bennett's Fire Insurance Cases.

Benn. (Mo.) Bennett's Missouri Cases.

Benn. & H.Cr.Cas. Bennett & Heard's Leading Criminal Cases.

Benn. & H.Dig. Bennett & Herard Massachusetts Digest.

Benne. Reporter of vol. 7, Modern Reports.

Bennett. Bennett's Reports, vol. 1 California;—Bennett's Reports, vol. 1 Dakota;—Bennett's Reports, vols. 16–21 Missouri.

Bent. Bentley's Reports, Irish Chancery.

Benth.Ev. (or Benth.Jud.Ev.). Bentham on Rationale of Judicial Evidence.

Bentl.Atty.-Gen. Bentley's Reports, vols. 13–19 Attorneys-General's Opinions.

Beor. Queensland Law Reports.

Ber. Berton's New Brunswick Reports.

Berk Co.L.J. (or Berks). Berk County Law Journal, Pa.

Bern. Bernard's Church Cases, Ireland.

Berry. Berry's Reports, vols. 1–28 Missouri Court of Appeals.

Bert. Berton's New Brunswick Reports.

Best, Ev. Best on Evidence.

Best, Pres. (or Best, Presumptions). Best on Presumptions of Law and Fact.

Best & S. (or Best & Sm.). Best & Smith's English Queen's Bench Reports.

Bett's Dec. Blatchford and Howland's United States District Court Reports;—Olcott's United States District Court Reports.

Bev. (Ceylon), (or Beven). Beven's Ceylon Reports.

Bev.Pat. Bevill's Patent Cases, English.

Bev. & M. Bevin & Mill's Reports, Ceylon.

Bibb. Bibb's Reports, Kentucky.

Bick. (or Bick. & Hawl.). Bicknell & Hawley's Reports, vols. 10–20 Nevada.

Bick. (In.) Bicknell's Reports, India.

Bid.Ins. Biddle on Insurance.

Bid.War.Sale Chat. Biddle on Warranties in Sale of Chattels.

Big. Bignell's Reports, India.

Big.Cas. Bigelow's Cases, William I to Richard I.

Bigg.L.I.Cas. (or Big.L. & A.Ins.Cas.). Bigelow's Life and Accident Insurance Cases.

Big.Ov.Cas. Bigelow's Overruled Cases.

Big.Plac. Bigelow's Placita Anglo-Normannica.

Big.Torts. Bigelow on Torts.

Bigelow, Estop. Bigelow on Estoppel.

Bigelow, Lead.Cas. Bigelow's Leading Cases on Bills and Notes, Torts, or Wills.

Bign. Bignell's Indian Reports.

Bi-Mo.L.Rev. Bi-Monthly Law Review.

Bin. Binney's Pennsylvania Reports.

Bin.Dig. Binmore's Digest, Michigan.

Bing. Bingham's English Common Pleas Reports.

Bing.N.C. Bingham's New Cases, English Common Pleas.

Binn. Binney's Pennsylvania Reports.

Binns' Just. Binns' Justice (Pa.).

Birds.St. Birdseye's Statutes, New York.

Biret, Vocab. Biret, Vocabularie des Cinq Codes, ou definitions simplifées des termes de droit et de jurisprudence exprimés dan ces codes.

Bis. (or Biss.). Bissell's United States Circuit Court Reports.

Bish.Cont. Bishop on Contracts.

Bish.Cr.Law. Bishop on Criminal Law.

Bish.Cr.Proc. (or Bich.Crim.Proc.). Bishop on Criminal Procedure.

Bish.Mar. & Div. (or Bish.Mar., Div. & Sep.) Bishop on Marriage, Divorce, and Separation.

Bish.New Cr.Law. Bishop's New Criminal Law.

Bish.New Cr.Proc. Bishop's New Criminal Procedure.

Bish.Non-Cont.Law. Bishop on Non-Contract Law, Rights and Torts.

Bish.St.Crimes. Bishop on Statutory Crimes.

Bishop Dig. Bishop's Digest, Montana.

Bisp.Eq. (or Bisph.Eq.). Bispham's Equity.

Biss. (or Bis.). Bissell's United States Circuit Court Reports.

Bissett, Est. Bissett on Estates for Life.

Bit. & Wise. Bittleston and Wise, New Magistrate Cases, English.

Bitt. Bittleston's Reports in Chambers, Q. B.

Bitt.Chamb.Rep. Bittleston's Chamber Reports, England.

Bitt.Pr.Cas. (or Bit.Prac.Cas.) Bittleston's Practice Cases, English.

Bitt.W. & P. Bittleson, Wise & Parnell's Reports, vols. 2, 3 New Practice Cases.

Bk. Black's United States Supreme Court Reports.

Bl. Black's United States Supreme Court Reports;—Blatchford's United States Circuit Court Reports;—Blackford's Indiana Reports;—Henry Blackstone's English Common Pleas Reports;—W. Blackstone's English King's Bench Reports;—Blackstone.

Bl.C.C. Blatchford's United States Circuit Court Reports.

Bl.Com. (or Bl. Comm.). Blackstone's Commentaries.

Bl.Dict. Black's Dictionary.

Bl.D. & O. Blackham, Dundas & Osborne's Irish Nisi Prius Reports.

Bl.H. Henry Blackstone's English Common Pleas Reports.

Bl.Judgm. Black on Judgments.

Bl.Law Tracts. Blackstone's Law Tracts.

Bl.Prize (or Bl.Pr.Cas.). Blatchford's Prize Cases.

Bl.R. (or Bl.W.). Sir William Blackstone's English King's Bench Reports.

Bl. & H. (or Bl. & How.). Blatchford & Howland's United States District Court Reports;—Blake & Hedges' Reports, vols. 2–3 Montana.

Bl. & W.Mines. Blanchard & Weeks' Leading Cases on Mines.

Bla.Ch. Bland's Maryland Chancery Reports.

Bla.Com. Blackstone's Commentaries.

Bla.H. Henry Blackstone's English Common Pleas Reports.

Bla.R. William Blackstone's English Reports.

Bla.W. Sir William Blackstone's Reports English King's Bench.

Black. Black's United States Supreme Court Reports;—Black's Reports, vols. 30–53 Indiana;—H. Blackstone's English Common Pleas Reports;—W. Blackstone's English King's Bench Reports;—Blackford's Indiana Reports.

Black.Cond.Rep. Blackwell's Condensed Illinois Reports.

Black, Const.Law. Black on Constitutional Law.

Black, Const.Prohib. Black's Constitutional Prohibitions.

Black.D. & O. Blackham, Dundas & Osborne's Irish Nisi Prius Reports.

Black Dict. Black's Law Dictionary.

Black.H. Henry Blackstone's English Common Pleas Reports.

Black, Interp.Laws. Black on Interpretation of Laws.

Black, Intox.Liq. Black on Intoxicating Liquors.

Black, Judg. (or Black, Judgm.). Black on Judgments.

Black.Jus. Blackerby's Justices' Cases.

Black, Law Dict. Black's Law Dictionary.

Black R. Black's United States Supreme Court Reports;—W. Blackstone's English King's Bench Reports. See Black.

Black Ship.Ca. Black's Decisions in Shipping Cases.

Black, St.Const. Black on Construction and Interpretation of Laws.

Black, Tax Titles. Black on Tax Titles.

Black.W. W. Blackstone's English King's Bench Reports.

Blackb.Sales. Blackburn on Sales.

Blackerby. Blackerby (Eng.).

Blackf. Blackford's Indiana Reports.

Blackst.R. Wm. Blackstone's Reports, English.

Blackw.Cond. Blackwell's Condensed Reports, Illinois.

Blackw.Tax Titles. Blackwell's Tax Titles.

Blair Co. (or Blair). Blair County Law Reports, Pa.

Blake. Blake's Reports, vols. 1–3 Montana.

Blake & H. Blake and Hedges' Reports, vols. 2–3 Montana.

Blan. & W.Lead.Cas. Blanchard & Weeks' Leading Cases, Mines.

Blanc. & W.L.C. Blanchard & Weeks' Leading Cases on Mines, etc.

Bland (or Bland's Ch.). Bland's Maryland Chancery Reports.

Blatchf. (or Blatchf.C.C.). Blatchford's United States Circuit Court Reports—United States Appeals.

Blatchf.Pr.Cas. Blatchford's Prize Cases.

Blatchf. & H. Blatchford & Howland's United States District Court Reports.

Bleck (or Bleckley). Bleckley's Reports, vols. 34, 35 Georgia.

Bli. (or Bligh). Bligh's English House of Lords Reports.

Bli.N.S. (or Bligh N.S.). Bligh's English House of Lords Reports, New Series.

Bliss. Delaware County Reports, Pennsylvania.

Bliss, Code Pl. Bliss on Code Pleading.

Bliss Ins. Bliss on Life Insurance.

Bliss N.Y.Co. Bliss's New York Code.

Bloom.Man. (or Neg.) Cas. Bloomfield's Manumission (or Negro) Cases, New Jersey.

Blount. Blount's Law Dictionary.

Blount Tr. Blount's Impeachment Trial.

Bluett. Bluett's Isle of Man Cases.

Bomb.H.Ct. Bombay High Court Reports.

Bomb.L.R. Bombay Law Reporter.

Bomb.Sel.Cas. Bombay Select Cases.

Bomb.Ser. Bombay Series, Indian Law Reports.

Bond. Bond's United States Circuit Reports.

Boor. (or Booraem). Booraem's Reports, vols. 6–8 California.

Boote, Suit at Law. Boote's Suit at Law.

Booth, Real Act. Booth on Real Actions.

Borr. Borradaile's Reports, Bombay.

Bos. Bosworth's New York Superior Court Reports.

Bos. & P. Bosanquet and Puller's English Common Pleas Reports.

Bos. & P.N.R. Bosanquet & Puller's New Reports, English Common Pleas.

Bos. & P. (or Bos. & Pul.). Bosanquet & Puller's English Common Pleas Reports.

Bos. & P.N.R. (or Bos. & Pul.N.R.). Bosanquet & Puller's New Reports, English Common Pleas.

Bost.L.R. Boston Law Reporter.

Bost.Pol.Rep. Boston Police Court Reports.

Boston U.L.Rev. Boston University Law Review.

Bosw. Bosworth's New York Superior Court Reports;—Boswell's Reports, Scotch.

Bott P.L. Bott's Poor Laws.

Bott P.L.Cas. Bott's Poor Law Cases.

Bott P.L.Const. Const's Edition of Bott's Poor Law Cases.

Bott Set.Cas. Bott's Poor Law (Settlement) Cases.

Bould. Bouldin's Reports, vol. 119 Alabama.

Bouln (or Boulnois). Boulnois' Reports, Bengal.

Bourke. Bourke's Reports, Calcutta High Court.

Bouv.Inst. Bouvier's Institutes of American Law.

Bouv.Law Dict. (or Bouv.L.D. or Bouvier). Bouvier's Law Dictionary.

Bov.Pat.Ca. Bovill's Patent Cases.

Bow. Bowler & Bowers, vols. 2, 3, United States Comptroller's Decisions.

Bowen, Pol.Econ. Bowen's Political Economy.

Bowyer, Mod.Civil Law. Bowyer's Modern Civil Law.

Boyce. Boyce's Reports, Delaware.

Br. Bracton;— Bradford;— Bradwell;— Brayton;—Breese;— Brevard;— Brewster;— Bridgman;— Brightly;— British;— Britton;— Brockenbrough;— Brooke;— Broom;— Brown;— Brownlow;—Bruce. See below, especially under Bro.

Br.C.C. British (or English) Crown Cases (American reprint);—Brown's Chancery Cases, England.

Br.Cr.Ca. British (or English) Crown Cases.

Br.Fed.Dig. Brightly's Federal Digest.

Br.N.C. Brooke's New Cases, English King's Bench.

Br.P.C. (or Bro.P.C.). Brown's English Parliamentary Cases.

Br.Reg. Braithwaite's Register.

Br.Sup. Brown's Supplement to Morrison's Dictionary, Sessions Cases, Scotland.

Br.Syn. (or Bro.Syn. or Bro.Synop. Brown's Synopsis of Decisions, Scotch Court of Sessions.

Br. & B. Broderip & Bingham, English Common Pleas.

Br. & Fr. (or Br. & F.Ecc.) Broderick & Fremantle's Ecclesiastical Cases, English.

Br. & Gold. Brownlow & Goldesborough's English Common Pleas Reports.

Br. & L. (or Br. & Lush.). Brownlow & Lushington's English Admiralty Reports.

Br. & R. Brown & Rader's Missouri Reports.

Brac. (or Bract. or Bracton). Bracton de Legibus et Consuetudinibus Angliæ.

Brad. Bradford's Surrogate Reports, New York;—Bradford's Iowa Reports;—Bradwell's Illinois Appeal Reports;—Bradley's Reports, Rhode Island.

Bradb. Bradbury's Pleading and Practice Reports, N. Y.

Bradf. Bradford's New York Surrogate Reports;—Bradford's Reports, Iowa.

Bradf.Sur. Bradford's Surrogate Court Reports, New York.

Bradw. Bradwell's Appellate Reports, Illinois.

Brady Ind. Brady's Index, Arkansas Reports.

Brame. Brame's Reports, vols. 66–72 Mississippi.

Branch. Branch's Reports, vol. 1 Florida.

Branch, Max. Branch's Maxims.

Branch, Princ. Branch's Principia Legis et Equitatis.

Brand. Brandenburg's Reports, vol. 21, Opinions Attorneys-General.

Brand.F.Attachm. (or Brand. For Attachm.). Brandon on Foreign Attachment.

Brande. Brande's Dictionary of Science.

Brandt, Sur. Brandt on Suretyship and Guaranty.

Brans.Dig. Branson's Digest, Bombay.

Brant. Brantly's Reports, vols. 80–90 Maryland.

Brayt. Brayton's Vermont Reports.

Breese. Breese's Reports, vol. 1 Illinois.

Brett Ca.Eq. Brett's Cases in Modern Equity.

Brev. Brevard's South Carolina Reports.

Brev.Dig. Brevard's Digest.

Brev.Ju. Brevia Judicialia (Judicial Writs).

Brew. Brewer's Reports, vols. 19–26 Maryland.

Brewst. Brewster's Pennsylvania Reports.

Brick.Dig. Brickell's Digest, Alabama.

Bridg.Dig.Ind. Bridgman's Digested Index.

Bridg.J. Sir J. Bridgman's English Common Pleas Reports.

Bridg.O. Sir Orlando Bridgman's English Common Pleas Reports—(sometimes cited as Carter).

Brief of Phi Delta Phi. Brief of Phi Delta Phi.

Bright. (Pa.) (or Brightly). Brightly's Nisi Prius Reports, Pennsylvania.

Bright.Dig. (or Brightly, Dig.). Brightly's Digest, N. Y.; Brightly's Digest, Penn.;—Brightly's Analytical Digest of the Laws of the United States.

Bright.Elec.Cas. (or Bright.E.C. or Brightly, Elect. Cas.). Brightly's Leading Election Cases, Pa.

Bright.N.P. (or Brightly, N.P.). Brightly's Nisi Prius Reports, Pa.

Bright.Purd. (or Brightly's Purd.Dig.). Brightly's Edition of Purdon's Digest of Laws of Pennsylvania.

Brightly. Brightly, Pa.

Brisb. (or Brisbin) Minn. Reporter, vol. 1 Minnesota.

Brissonius. De verborum quæ ad jus civile pertinent significatione.

Brit. Britton's Ancient Pleas of the Crown.

Brit.Cr.Cas. British (or English) Crown Cases.

Brit.Quar.Rev. British Quarterly Review.

Britt. Britton on Ancient Pleading.

Bro. See, also, Brown and Browne. Browne's Pennsylvania Reports;—Brown's Michigan Nisi Prius Reports;—Brown's English Chancery Reports;—Brown's Parliamentary Cases;—Brown's Reports, vols. 53–65 Mississippi;—Brown's Reports, vols. 80–137 Missouri.

Bro. (Pa.). Browne's Pennsylvania Reports.

Bro.Abr. in Eq. Browne's New Abridgment of Cases in Equity.

Bro.Adm. Brown's United States Admiralty Reports.

Bro.A. & R. Brown's United States District Court Reports (Admiralty and Revenue Cases).

Bro.C.C. Brown's English Chancery Cases, or Reports.

Bro.Ch. (or Bro.Ch.Cas. or Bro.Ch.R.). Brown's English Chancery Reports.

Bro.Civ.Law. Browne's Civil and Admiralty Law.

Bro.Ecc. Brooke's Six Judgments in Ecclesiastical Cases (English).

Bro.Just. Broun's Justiciary, Scotland.

Bro.N.C. Brooke's New Cases, English King's Bench.

Bro.N.P. Brown's Michigan Nisi Prius Reports;—Brown's Nisi Prius Cases, English.

Bro.P.C. (or Br.P.C.). Brown's English Parliamentary Cases.

Bro.Supp. Brown's Supplement to Morrison's Dictionary of the Court of Session, Scotland.

Bro.Syn. (or Bro.Synop.). Brown's Synopsis of Decisions, Scotch Court of Session.

Bro.V.M. Brown's Vade Mecum.

Bro. & F. (or Bro. & Fr.). Broderick & Fremantle's English Ecclesiastical Cases.

Bro. & G. Brownlow & Goldesborough's English Common Pleas Reports.

Bro. & Lush. Browning & Lushington's English Admiralty Reports.

Brock. (or Brock. C.C. or Brock.Marsh.). Brockenbrough's Marshall's Decisions, United States Circuit Court.

Brock.Cas. Brockenbrough's Virginia Cases.

Brock. & H. (or Brock. & Hol.). Brockenbrough & Holmes, Virginia Cases.

Brod.Stair. Brodie's Notes to Stair's Institutes, Scotch.

Brod. & B. (or Brod. & Bing.). Broderip & Bingham's English Common Pleas Reports.

Brod. & F. (or Brod. & Fr.). Broderick & Fremantle's Ecclesiastical Cases.

Brodix Am. & E.Pat.Cas. Brodix's American & English Patent Cases.

Brook N.Cas. Brook's New Cases, Eng.

Brooke (or Brooke [Petit]). Brooke's New Cases, English King's Bench.

Brooke, Abr. Brooke's Abridgment.

Brooke Eccl. (or Brooke Eccl.Judg.). Brooke's Six Ecclesiastical Judgments.

Brooke N.C. Brooke's New Cases, English King's Bench Reports. (Bellewe's Cases *tempore* Henry VIII.)

Brooke Six Judg. Brooke's Six Ecclesiastical Judgments (or Reports).

Brooklyn Daily Rec. Brooklyn Daily Record.

Brooklyn L.Rev. Brooklyn Law Review.

Brooks. Brooks' Reports, vols. 106–119 Michigan.

Broom, Com.Law. Broom's Commentaries on the Common Law.

Broom, Leg.Max. (or Broom, Max.). Broom's Legal Maxims.

Broom & H.Comm. Broom & Hadley's Commentaries on the Law of England.

Broun (or Broun Just.). Broun's Reports, Scotch Justiciary Court.

Brown. Brown's Reports, vols. 53–65 Mississippi;—Brown's English Parliamentary Cases;—Brown's English Chancery Reports;—Brown's Law Dictionary;—Brown's Scotch Reports;—Brown's United States District Court Reports;—Brown's U. S. Admiralty Reports;—Brown's Michigan Nisi Prius Reports;—Brown's Reports, vols. 4–25 Nebraska;—Brownlow (& Goldesborough's) English Common Pleas Reports;—Brown's Reports, vols. 80–137 Missouri. See, also, Bro. and Browne.

Brown A. & R. Brown's United States District Court Reports (Admiralty and Revenue Cases).

Brown, Adm. Brown's United States Admiralty Reports.

Brown, C.C. (or Brown, Ch. or Brown Ch.Cas. or Brown Ch.R.). Brown's English Chancery Cases or Reports.

Brown, Civ. & Adm.Law. Brown's Civil and Admiralty Law.

Brown Ecc. Brown's Ecclesiastical Reports, English.

Brown N.P. (or Brown N.P. [Mich.]). Brown's Michigan Nisi Prius Reports.

Brown N.P.Cas. Brown's Nisi Prius Cases, English.

Brown P.C. Brown's Parliamentary Cases, English House of Lords.

Brown, Parl.Cas. Brown's Parliamentary Cases, English House of Lords.

Brown, Sup. (or Brown Sup.Dec.). Brown's Supplement to Morrison's Dictionary, Session Cases, Scotland.

Brown Syn. Brown's Synopsis of Decisions, Scotch.

Brown's Roman Law. Brown's Epitome and Analysis of Savigny's Treatise on Obligations in Roman Law.

Brown. & Gold. Brownlow & Goldesborough's English Common Pleas Reports.

Brown & H. Brown & Hemingway's Reports, vols. 53–58 Mississippi.

Brown. & L. (or Brown. & Lush.). Browning & Lushington's English Admiralty Reports.

Browne Bank Cas. (or Browne N.B.C.). Browne's National Bank Cases.

Browne, Civ.Law. Browne's Civil and Admiralty Law.

Browne. Browne's Pennsylvania Reports;—Browne's Reports, vols. 97–114 Massachusetts;—Browne, New York Civil Procedure. See also Bro. and Brown.

Browne, Div. Browne's Divorce Court Practice.

Browne, Jud.Interp. Browne's Judicial Interpretation of Common Words and Phrases.

Browne, Prob.Pr. Browne's Probate Practice.

Browne, St.Frauds. Browne on Statute of Frauds.

Browne & G. (or Browne & Gray). Browne & Gray's Reports, vols. 110–111 Massachusetts.

Browne & Macn. Browne & Macnamara's English Railway and Canal Cases.

Brownl. (or Brownl. & G. or Brownl. & Gold.). Brownlow and Goldesborough, English Common Pleas Reports.

Bru. (or Bruce). Bruce's Scotch Court of Session Reports.

Brun. (or Brunner, Col.Cas.). Brunner's Collective Cases, United States.

Brunk.Ir.Dig. Brunker's Irish Common Law Digest.

Brunner Sel.Cas. Brunner's Selected Cases United States Circuit Courts.

Bt. Benedict's United States District Court Reports.

Buch. (or Buch.Rep.). Buchanan's (Eben J. or James) Reports, Cape of Good Hope.

Buch.Cas. (or Tr.). Buchanan's Remarkable Criminal Cases, Scotland.

Buch.Ct.Ap.Cape G.H. Buchanan's Court of Appeals Reports, Cape of Good Hope.

Buch.E.Cape G.H. E. Buchanan's Reports, Cape of Good Hope.

Buch.E.D.Cape G.H. Buchanan's Eastern District Reports, Cape of Good Hope.

Buch.J.Cape G.H. J. Buchanan's Reports, Cape of Good Hope.

Buck. Buck's English Cases in Bankruptcy;—Buck's Reports, vols. 7–8 Montana.

Buck.Cooke. Bucknill's Cooke's Cases of Practice, Common Pleas.

Buck.Dec. Buckner's Decisions (in Freeman's Mississippi Chancery Reports).

Buff.Super.Ct. (N.Y.). Sheldon's Superior Court Reports, Buffalo, New York.

Bull.N.P. Buller's Law of Nisi Prius, English.

Bull. & C.Dig. Bullard & Curry's Louisiana Digest.

Buller MSS. J. Buller's Paper Books, Lincoln's Inn Library.

Bulletin Comp.L. Bulletin, Comparative Law Bureau.

Bulst. Bulstrode's English King's Bench Reports.

Bump, Fraud.Conv. Bump on Fraudulent Conveyances.

Bump's Int.Rev.Law. Bump's Internal Revenue Laws.

Bump N.C. Bump's Notes on Constitutional Decisions.

Bunb. Bunbury's English Exchequer Reports.

Bur. Burnett's Reports, Wisconsin.

Bur. (or Burr.). Burrow's English King's Bench Reports.

Bur.M. Burrow's Reports *tempore* Mansfield.

Burf. Burford's Reports, vols. 6–9 Oklahoma.

Burg.Dig. Burgwyn's Digest Maryland Reports.

Burge, Confl.Law. Burge on the Conflict of Laws.

Burge, Sur. Burge on Suretyship.

Burgess. Burgess' Reports, vols. 46–49 Ohio State.

Burke Tr. Burke's Celebrated Trials.

Burks. Burks' Reports, vols. 91–97 Virginia.

Burlamaqui (or Burl.Natural & Pol.Law). Burlamaqui's Natural and Political Law.

Burlesque Reps. Skillman's New York Police Reports.

Burm.L.R. Burmah Law Reports.

Burn. Burnett's Reports, Wis.

Burn, Dict. Burn's Law Dictionary.

Burn, Ecc.Law. Burn's Ecclesiastical Law.

Burn, J.P. Burn's Justice of the Peace.

Burnet. Burnet's Manuscript Decisions, Scotch Court of Session.

Burnett. Burnett's Wisconsin Reports;—Burnett's Reports, vols. 20–22 Oregon.

Burns' Ann.St. Burns' Annotated Statutes, Ind.

Burns' Rev.St. Burns' Annotated Statutes, Ind.

Burr. Burrow's English King's Bench Reports.

Burr.Law Dict. Burrill's Law Dictionary.

Burr.S.C. (or Burr.S.Cas. or Burr.Sett.Cas.). Burrows' English Settlement Cases.

Burr Tr.Rob. (or Burr, Tr.). Burr's Trial, reported by Robertson.

Burrill (or Burr.Dict.). Burrill's Law Dictionary.

Burrill, Assignm. Burrill on Assignments.

Burrill, Circ.Ev. Burrill on Circumstantial Evidence.

Burrill, Pr. Burrill's Practice.

Burrow. Burrow's Reports, English King's Bench.

Burrow, Sett.Cas. Burrow's English Settlement Cases.

Burt.Cas. Burton's Collection of Cases and Opinions.

Burt.Real Prop. Burton on Real Property.

Burt.Sc.Tr. Burton's Scotch Trials.

Bus.L.J. Business Law Journal.

Busb. Busbee's Law Reports, North Carolina.

Busb.Cr.Dig. Busbee's Criminal Digest, North Carolina.

Busb.Eq. Busbee's Equity Reports, North Carolina.

Bush. Bush, Ky.

Bush. Bush's Reports, Kentucky.

Butl.Co.Litt. Butler's Notes to Coke on Littleton.

Butl.Hor.Jur. Butler's Horæ Juridicæ Subsecivæ.

Butt's Sh. Butt's Edition of Shower's English King's Bench Reports.

Buxton. Buxton's Reports, vols. 123–126 North Carolina.

Byles, Bills. Byles on Bills.

Bynk. Bynkershoek on the Law of War.

Bynk.Obs.Jur.Rom. Bynkershoek, Observationum Juris Romani Libri.

C

C. Cowen's Reports, New York;—Connecticut;—California;—Colorado;—Canada (Province).

C.2d (or Cal.2d). California Reports, Second Series.

C.A. Court of Appeals.

C.A. (or Cal.App.). California Appellate Reports.

C.A.2d (or Cal.App.2d). California Appellate Reports, Second Series.

C.A.Supp. (or Cal.App.Supp.). California Appellate Reports Supplement.

C.A.2d Supp. (or Cal.App.2d Supp.). California Appellate Reports Second Series Supplement.

C.B. Chief Baron of the Exchequer;—Common Bench;—English Common Bench Reports by Manning, Granger & Scott.

C.B.Dig. Customs Bureau Digest.

C.B.N.S. Common Bench Reports, New Series.

C.B.R. Cour de Blanc de la Reine, Quebec.

C.C.A. United States Circuit Court of Appeals Reports.

C.C.C. Choice Cases in Chancery.

C.C.Chr. (or C.C.Chron.). Chancery Cases Chronicle, Ontario.

C.C.E. Caines' Cases in Error, New York;—Cases of Contested Elections.

C.C.L.C. Civil Code, Quebec.

C.C.P. Code of Civil Procedure.

C.C.P.A. United States Court of Customs and Patent Appeals.

C.C.Supp. City Court Reports, Supplement New York.

C.D. Commissioner's Decisions, United States Patent Office;—Century Digest;—Current Digest.

C.E.Gr. (or C.E.Green). C. E. Green's New Jersey Equity Reports.

C.F.R. Code of Federal Regulations.

C.G.S.A. Connecticut General Statutes Annotated.

C.H. & A. Carrow, Hamerton & Allen's New Sessions Cases, English.

C.I.R. Commissioner of Internal Revenue.

C.J. Corpus Juris.

C.J.Ann. Corpus Juris Annotations.

C.J.C. Couper's Judiciary Cases, Scotland.

C.J.Can. Corpus Juris Canonici.

C.J.Civ. Corpus Juris Civilis.

C.J.S. Corpus Juris Secundum.

C.L. English Common Law Reports, American Reprint.

C.L.Ch. (or C.L.Chamb.Rep.). Common Law Chamber Reports, Ontario.

C.L.Chamb. Chamber's Common Law, U.C.

C.L.J. California Law Journal.

C.L.J. & Lit.Rev. California Law Journal and Literary Review.

C.L.P.Act. English Common Law Procedure Act.

C.L.R. Common Law Reports, printed by Spottiswoode;—"English Common Law Reports" (1853–1855;—California Law Review.

C.Leg.Rec. California Legal Record.

C.M. & R. (or C.M.R.). Crompton, Meeson & Roscoe, English Exchequer Reports.

C.N. Code Napoléon.

C.N.Conf. Cameron & Norwood's North Carolina Conference Reports.

C.N.P. Cases at Nisi Prius.

C.N.P.C. Campbell's Nisi Prius Cases.

C.O. Common Orders.

C. of C.E. Cases of Contested Elections, United States.

C.P.C. Code of Civil Procedure, Quebec.

C.P.C. (or Coop.). C. P. Cooper's English Chancery Practice Cases.

C.P.C.t.Br. C. P. Cooper's English Chancery Reports *tempore* Brougham.

C.P.C.t.Cott. C. P. Cooper's English Chancery Reports *tempore* Cottenham.

C.P.Cooper. Cooper's English Chancery.

C.P.D. (or C.P.Div.). Common Pleas Division, English Law Reports (1875–1880).

C.P.Q. Code of Civil Procedure, Quebec (1897).

C.P.Rep. Common Pleas Reporter, Scranton, Pennsylvania.

C.P.U.C. Common Pleas Reports, Upper Canada.

C.Pr. Code of Procedure;—Code de Procédure Civile.

C.R. Chancery Reports;—Code Reporter, New York.

C.R.N.S. Code Reports, New Series, New York.

C.Rob. C. Robinson, English Admiralty.

C.Rob. (or C.Rob.Adm.). Christopher Robinson's Reports on English Admiralty.

C.S. Court of Session, Scotland.

C.S.B.C. Consolidated Statutes, British Columbia.

C.S.C. Consolidated Statutes of Canada, 1859.

C.S.L.C. Consolidated Statutes, Lower Canada.

C.S.M. Consolidated Statutes of Manitoba.

C.S.N.B. Consolidated Statutes of New Brunswick.

C.S.U.C. Consolidated Statutes of Upper Canada, 1859.

C.S. & J. Cushing, Storey & Josselyn's Election Cases. See vol. 1 Cushing's Election Cases, Massachusetts.

C.S. & P. Craigie, Stewart & Paton's Scotch Appeal Cases.

C.t.K. Cases *tempore* King (Macnaghten's Select Chancery Cases, English).

C.t.N. Cases *tempore* Northington (Eden's English Chancery Reports).

C.t.T. Cases *tempore* Talbot, English Chancery.

C.Theod. Codex Theodosiani.

C.U. California Unreported Cases.

C.W.Dud. C. W. Dudley's Law or Equity Reports, South Carolina.

C. & A. Cooke & Alcock's Irish King's Bench Reports.

C. & C. Coleman & Caine's Cases, New York.

C. & D. Corbett & Daniel's English Election Cases;—Crawford & Dix's Abridged Cases, Irish.

C. & D.A.C. Crawford & Dix's Abridged Cases, Irish.

C. & D.C.C. Crawford & Dix's Irish Circuit Cases.

C. & E. Cababé & Ellis, English.

C. & F. Clark & Finnelly's English House of Lords Reports.

C. & H.Dig. Coventry & Hughes' Digest.

C. & J. Crompton & Jervis' English Exchequer Reports.

C. & K. Carrington & Kirwan's English Nisi Prius Reports.

C. & L. Connor & Lawson's Irish Chancery Reports.

C. & L.C.C. Cane & Leigh's Crown Cases.

C. & L.Dig. Cohen & Lee's Maryland Digest.

C. & M. Crompton & Meeson's English Exchequer Reports;—Carrington & Marshman's English Nisi Prius Reports.

C. & N. Cameron & Norwood's North Carolina Conference Reports.

C. & O.R.Cas. English Railway and Canal Cases, by Carrow & Oliver et al.

C. & P. Carrington & Payne's English Nisi Prius Reports;—Craig & Phillips' Chancery Reports.

C. & R. Cockburn & Rowe's English Election Cases.

C. & S.Dig. Connor & Simonton's South Carolina Digest.

Ca. Case or Placitum;—Cases (see Cas.).

Ca.t.Hard. Cases *tempore* Hardwicke.

Ca.t.K. Cases *tempore* King;—Cases *tempore* King, Chancery.

Ca.t.Talb. Cases *tempore* Talbot, Chancery.

Ca.temp.F. Cases *tempore* Finch.

Ca.temp.H. Cases *tempore* Hardwicke, King's Bench.

Ca.temp.Holt. Cases *tempore* Holt, King's Bench.

Cab.Lawy. The Cabinet Lawyer.

Cab. & E. (or Cab. & El.). Cababé & Ellis, English.

Cadw.Dig. Cadwalader's Digest of Attorney-General's Opinions.

Cai. Caines' Term Reports, New York Supreme Court.

Cai.Cas. (or Cai.Cas.Err.). Caines' New York Cases in Error.

Cai.T.R. Caines' Term Reports, New York Supreme Court.

Cain. Caines, New York.

Caines. Caines' Reports, New York Supreme Court.

Caines Cas. Caines' Cases, Court of Errors, New York.

Cairn's Dec. Cairn's Decisions in the Albert Arbitration.

Cal. California;—California Reports;—Calthrop's English King's Bench Reports;—Caldecott's English Settlement Cases.

Cal.2d (or C.2d). California Reports, Second Series.

Cal.App. (or C.A.). California Appellate Reports.

Cal.App. California Appellate Reports.

Cal.App.2d (or C.A.2d). California Appellate Reports, Second Series.

Cal.App.Supp. (or C.A.Supp.). California Appellate Reports Supplement.

Cal.App.2d Supp. (or C.A.2d Supp.). California Appellate Reports, Second Series Supplement.

Cal.App.Dec. California Appellate Decisions.

Cal.App.Supp. California, Appellate Department of the Superior Court.

Cal.Dec. California Decisions.

Cal.J.I.C. California Jury Instructions, Criminal.

Cal.Jur. California Jurisprudence.

Cal.L.J. California Law Journal; California Law Journal, San Francisco.

Cal.L.R. Calcutta Law Reporter (Ind.).

Cal.L.Rev. California Law Review.

Cal.Leg.Rec. California Legal Record, San Francisco.

Cal.Rep. California Reports;—Calthrop's English King's Bench Reports.

Cal.Rptr. West's California Reporter.

Cal.S.B.J. State Bar Journal of California.

Cal.S.D.A. Calcutta Sudder Dewanny Adawlut Reports.

Calc.Ser. (or Cal.Ser.). Calcutta Series Indian Law Reports.

Cal.Unrep. California Unreported Cases.

Calcutta L.J. Calcutta Law Journal.

Cald. Caldwell's Reports, vols. 25-36 West Virginia.

Cald. (or Cald.J.P. or Cald.M.Cas. or Cald.S.C.). Caldecott's English Magistrate's (Justice of the Peace) and Settlement Cases.

Call. Call's Virginia Reports.

Call.Sew. Callis on Sewers.

Callis, Sew. Callis on Sewers.

Calth. Calthrop's English King's Bench Reports.

Calthr. Calthrop, Eng.

Calv.Parties. Calvert's Parties to Suits in Equity.

Calvin (or Calvin.Lex.Jurid.). Calvinus Lexicon Juridicum.

Cam. Cameron's Reports, Upper Canada, Queen's Bench.

Cam.Cas. Cameron's Cases, Can.

Cam.Duc. Camera Ducata (Duchy Chamber).

Cam.Op. Cameron's Legal Opinions, Toronto.

Cam.Scac. Camera Scaccaria (Exchequer Chamber).

Cam.Stell. Camera Stellata (Star Chamber).

Cam. & N. (or Cam. & Nor.). Cameron & Norwood's North Carolina Conference Reports.

Cambria. Cambria County Legal Journal (Pa.).

Cambridge L.J. Cambridge Law Journal.

Camd.Brit. (or Camden). Camden's Britannia.

Camp. Camp's Reports, vol. 1 North Dakota;—Campbell's English Nisi Prius Reports;—Campbell's Reports, vols. 27-58 Nebraska. See also Campbell.

Camp.Dec. (or Campb.Dec.). Campbell's Decisions.

Camp.Lives Ld.Ch. Campbell's Lives of the Lord Chancellors.

Camp.N.P. Campbell's English Nisi Prius Reports.

Campbell (or Campb. or Camp.). Campbell's English Nisi Prius Reports;—Campbell's Reports of Taney's United States Circuit Court Decisions;—Campbell's Legal Gazette Reports, Pennsylvania;—Campbell's Reports, vols. 27-58 Nebraska.

Can.App.Cas. Canadian Appeal Cases.

Can.B.R. Canadian Bar Review.

Can.Cr.Cas. Canadian Criminal Cases.

Can.Exch. Canada Exchequer Reports.

Can.Gaz. Canadian Gazette.

Can.L.J. Canada Law Journal.

Can.L.J.N.S. Canada Law Journal, New Series.

Can.L.R. Canada Law Reports, Exchequer Court and Supreme Court.

Can.L.T.Occ.Notes. Canadian Law Times Occasional Notes.

Can.Leg.N. Canada Legal News.

Can.Mun.J. Canadian Municipal Journal.

Can.R.Cas. (or Can.Ry.Cas.). Canadian Railway Cases.

Can.S.C. Canada Supreme Court.

Can.S.C.Rep. Canada Supreme Court Reports.

Canada L.T. or (Can.L.T.). Canadian Law Times.

Canal Zone Sup.Ct. Canal Zone Supreme Court.

Cane & L. Cane & Leigh's Crown Cases Reserved.

Cape L.J. Cape Law Journal (South Africa).

Car. Carolus (as 4 Car. II.);—Carolina.

Car., H. & A. Carrow, Hamerton & Allen's New Sessions Cases, English.

Car.L.J. Carolina Law Journal.

Car.Law Repos. Carolina Law Repository, N.C.

Car., O. & B. English Railway & Canal Cases, by Carrow, Oliver, Bevan et al.

Car. & K. (or Kir.). Carrington & Kirwan's English Nisi Prius Reports.

Car. & M. (or Mar.). Carrington & Marshman's English Nisi Prius Reports.

Car. & Ol. (or Car. & O.). English Railway & Canal Cases, by Carrow, Oliver et al.

Car. & P. Carrington's & Payne's English Nisi Prius Reports.

Carl. Carleton, New Brunswick.

Carp.P.C. Carpmael's English Patent Cases.

Carpenter. Carpenter's Reports, vols. 52-53 California.

Carr.Cas. Carran's Summary Cases, India.

Carr., Ham. & Al. Carrow, Hamerton & Allen's New Sessions Cases, English.

Carr. & K. Carrington & Kirwan.

Carr. & M. Carrington and Marshman's English Nisi Prius Reports.

Carrau. Carrau's edition of "Summary Cases," Bengal.

Cart. Cartwright's Cases, Canada.

Carter. Carter's English Common Pleas Reports, same as Orlando Bridgman;—Carter's Reports, vols. 1, 2, Indiana.

Carth. Carthew's English King's Bench Reports.

Cartwr.Cas. Cartwright's Cases, Can.

Carv.Carr. Carver's Treatise on the Law Relating to the Carriage of Goods by Sea.

Cary. Cary's English Chancery Reports.

Cas. Casey's Reports, vols. 25–36 Pennsylvania State.

Cas.App. Cases of Appeal to the House of Lords.

Cas.Arg. & Dec. Cases Argued and Decreed in Chancery, English.

Cas.B.R. Cases Banco Regis *tempore* William III. (12 Modern Reports).

Cas.B.R.Holt. Cases and Resolutions (of settlements; not Holt's King's Bench Reports).

Cas.C.L. Cases in Crown Law.

Cas.Ch. Cases in Chancery, English;—Select Cases in Chancery;—Cases in Chancery (9 Modern Reports).

Cas.Eq. Cases in Equity, Gilbert's Reports;—Cases and Opinions in Law, Equity, and Conveyancing.

Cas.Eq.Abr. Cases in Equity, Abridged, English.

Cas.F.T. Cases *tempore* Talbot, by Forrester, English Chancery.

Cas.H.L. (or Cas.H. of L.). Cases in the House of Lords.

Cas. In C. Cases in Chancery;—Select Cases in Chancery.

Cas.K.B. Cases in King's Bench (8 Modern Reports).

Cas.K.B.t.H. (or Cas.K.B.t.Hardw.). Cases *tempore* Hardwicke (W. Kelynge's English King's Bench Reports).

Cas.L. & Eq. Cases in Law and Equity (10 Modern Reports);—Gilbert's Cases in Law and Equity, English.

Cas.P. (or Parl.). Cases in Parliament.

Cas.Pr. Cases of Practice, English King's Bench.

Cas.Pr.C.P. Cases of Practice, English Common Pleas (Cooke's Reports).

Cas.Pr.K.B. Cases of Practice in the King's Bench.

Cas.R. Casey's Reports, vols. 25–36 Pennsylvania State.

Cas.S.C. (Cape G.H.). Cases in the Supreme Court, Cape of Good Hope.

Cas.Self Def. Horrigan & Thompson's Cases on Self-Defense.

Cas.Sett. Cases of Settlement, King's Bench.

Cas.Six Cir. Cases on the Six Circuits, Ireland.

Cas.t.Ch.II. Cases *tempore* Charles II., in vol. 3 of Reports in Chancery.

Cas.t.F. Cases *tempore* Finch, English Chancery.

Cas.t.Geo.I. Cases *tempore* George I., English Chancery (8, 9 Modern Reports).

Cas.t.H. (or Cas.t.Hardwicke or Hardw.). Cases *tempore* Hardwicke, English King's Bench (Ridgway, Lee, or Annaly); West's Chancery Reports, *tempore* Hardwicke.

Cas.t.Holt (or H.). Cases *tempore* Holt, English King's Bench;—Holt's Reports.

Cas.t.K. (or King). Select Cases *tempore* King, English Chancery (edited by Macnaghten);—Moseley's Chancery Reports, *tempore* King.

Cas.t.Lee. (Phillimore's) Cases *tempore* Lee, English Ecclesiastical.

Cas.t.Mac. Cases *tempore* Macclesfield (10 Modern Reports).

Cas.t.Nap. Cases *tempore* Napier, by Drury, Irish Chancery.

Cas.t.North. Cases *tempore* Northington (Eden's English Chancery Reports).

Cas.t.Plunk. Cases *tempore* Plunkett, by Lloyd & Gould, Irish Chancery.

Cas.t.Q.A. Cases *tempore* Queen Anne (11 Modern Reports).

Cas.t.Sugd. Cases *tempore* Sugden, Irish Chancery.

Cas.t.Tal. (or Talb.). Cases *tempore* Talbot, English Chancery.

Cas.t.Wm.III. Cases *tempore* William III. (12 Modern Reports).

Cas.Tak. & Adj. Cases Taken and Adjudged (first edition of Reports in Chancery).

Cas.w.Op. Cases, with Opinions, by Eminent Counsel.

Cas.Wm.I. Bigelow's Cases, William I. to Richard I.

Case & Com. Case and Comment.

Casey. Casey's Reports, vols. 25–36 Pennsylvania State.

Cass.Dig. Cassel's Digest, Canada.

Cass.Sup.C.Prac. Cassel's Supreme Court Practice, 2d edition by Masters.

Cates. Cates Reports, Tenn.

Cel.Tr. Burke's Celebrated Trials.

Cent. Central Reporter (Pa.).

Cent.Dict. Century Dictionary.

Cent.Dict. & Ency. Century Dictionary and Encyclopedia.

Cent.Dig. Century Digest.

Cent.L.J. (or Cent.Law J.). Central Law Journal, St. Louis, Mo.

Cent.L.Mo. Central Law Monthly.

[1891] Ch. Law Reports, Chancery Division, from 1891 onward.

Ch.App. Chancery Appeal Cases, English Law Reports.

Ch.App.Cas. Chancery Appeal Cases, English Law Reports.

Ch.Cas. Cases in Chancery.

Ch.Cas.Ch. Choyce Cases in Chancery.

Ch.Cham. (or Ch.Ch.). Chancery Chamber Reports, Ontario.

Ch.Chamb. Chancery Chambers, U.C.

Ch.Col.Op. Chalmers' Colonial Opinions.

Ch.Dig. Chaney's Digest, Michigan Reports.

Ch.Div. (or D.). Chancery Division, English Law Reports (1876–1890).

Ch.Pl. Chitty on Pleading.

Ch.Prec. Precedents in Chancery.

Ch.R.M. R. M. Charlton's Georgia Reports.

Ch.Rep. (or Ch.R. or Ch.Repts.). Reports in Chancery;—Irish Chancery Reports.

Ch.Rep.Ir. Irish Chancery Reports.

Ch.Sent. Chancery Sentinel, Saratoga, New York.

Ch.T.U.P. T. U. P. Charlton's Georgia Reports.

Ch. & Cl.Cas. Cripp's Church and Clergy Cases.

Chal.Op. Chalmers' Colonial Opinions.

Cham. (or Chamb.). Chamber Reports, Upper Canada.

Chamb.Dig.P.H.C. Chambers' Digest of Public Health Cases.

Chamb.Rep. Chancery Chamber Reports, Ontario.

Chamber. Chamber Reports, Upper Canada.

Chambers' Cyclopædia. Ephraim Chambers' English Cyclopædia.

Chan. Chaney's Reports, vols. 37–58 Michigan;—Chancellor;—Chancery (see Ch.).

Chan.Sentinel. Chancery Sentinel, N.Y.

Chanc. Chancery (see Ch.).

Chand. Chandler's Reports, Wisconsin;—Chandler's Reports, vols. 20, 38–44 New Hampshire.

Chand.Cr.Tr. (or Chand.Crim.Tr.). Chandler's American Criminal Trials.

Chaney. Chaney's Reports, vols. 37–58 Michigan.

Charl.Pr.Cas. Charley's English Practice Cases.

Charlt.R.M. R. M. Charlton's Georgia Reports.

Charlt. (or Charlt.T.U.P.). T. U. P. Charlton's Georgia Reports.

Chase. Chase's United States Circuit Court Decisions.

Chase, Steph.Dig.Ev. Chase on Stephens' Digest of Evidence.

Chase's St. Chase's Statutes at Large, Ohio.

Chest.Co.Rep. (or Chester Co.Rep.). Chester County Reports, Pa.

Chev. Cheves' South Carolina Law Reports.

Chev.Ch. (or Eq.). Cheves' South Carolina Equity Reports.

Cheves. Cheves' Law Reports, South Carolina.

Chi.Bar Rec. Chicago Bar Record.

Chi.-Kent Rev. Chicago-Kent Review.

Chi.Leg.N. Chicago Legal News, Ill.

Chicago L.B. Chicago Law Bulletin, Ill.

Chicago, L.J. Chicago Law Journal.

Chicago L.Rec. Chicago Law Record.

Chicago L.T. Chicago Law Times.

Chip. Chipman's Reports, New Brunswick.

Chip.D. D. Chipman's Vermont Reports.

Chip.MS. Reports printed from Chipman's Manuscript, New Brunswick.

Chip.N. N. Chipman's Vermont Reports.

Chip.W. Chipman's New Brunswick Reports.

Chit. (or Chitt.). Chitty's English Bail Court Reports.

Chit.Archb.Pr. Chitty's Archbold's Practice.

Chit.Bills. Chitty on Bills.

Chit.Bl.Comm. Chitty's Blackstone's Commentaries.

Chit.Com.Law. Chitty on Commercial Law.

Chit.Cont. Chitty on Contracts.

Chit.Cr.Law (or Chit.Crim.Law). Chitty's Criminal Law.

Chit.Gen.Pr. Chitty's General Practice.

Chit.Med.Jur. Chitty on Medical Jurisprudence.

Chit.Pl. Chitty on Pleading.

Chit.Pr. Chitty's General Practice.

Chit.St. Chitty's Statutes of Practical Utility.

Chitt. Chitty's English Bail Court Reports.

Chitty. Chitty on Bills.

Chitty, Bl.Comm. Chitty's Edition of Blackstone's Commentaries.

Chitty, Com.Law. Chitty on Commercial Law.

Choyce Cas.Ch. Choyce Cases in Chancery, Eng.

Chr.Rep. Chamber Reports, Upper Canada.

Chr.Rob. Christopher Robinson's English Admiralty Reports.

Chute, Eq. Chute's Equity under the Judicature Act.

Cic.Frag.de Repub. Cicero, Fragmenta de Republica.

Cin.Law Bull. Cincinnati Law Bulletin, Ohio.

Cin.Law Rev. Univ. of Cincinnati Law Review.

Cin.R. (or Cin.Rep. or Chinc. [Ohio]). Cincinnati Superior Court Reports, Ohio.

Cin.Sup.Ct.Rep. (or Cin.Super.Ct.Rep'r.). Cincinnati Superior Court Reporter, Ohio.

Cinc.L.Bull. Weekly Law Bulletin, Ohio.

Cir.Ct.Dec. Circuit Court Decisions, Ohio.

Cir.Ct.R. Circuit Court Reports, Ohio.

Cir.Ct.Rule. Circuit Court Rule.

City Ct.R. (or City Ct.Rep.). City Court Reports, New York.

City Ct.R.Supp. (or City Ct.Rep.Supp.). City Court Reports, Supplement, N.Y.

City Hall Rec. (or City H.Rec.). City Hall Recorder, N.Y.

City Hall Rep. City Hall Reporter, Lomas, N.Y.

Civ.Code. Civil Code.

Civ.Code Prac. Civil Code of Practice.

Civ.Prac.Act. Civil Practice Act.

Civ.Proc.R. (or Civ.Pro., Civ.Pro.R., Civ.Proc.Rep.). Civil Procedure Reports, N.Y.

Cl.App. Clark's Appeal Cases, House of Lords.

Cl.Ch. Clarke's Chancery Reports, New York.

Cl.Home. Clerk Home, Scotch Session Cases.

Cl. & Fin. (or F.). Clark & Finnelly's House of Lords Cases.

Cl. & Fin.N.S. House of Lords Cases, by Clark.

Cl. & H. Clarke & Hall's Contested Elections in Congress.

Clancy, Husb. & W. (or Clancy Rights). Clancy's Treatise of the Rights, Duties and Liabilities of Husband and Wife.

Clark. Clark, Pa.

Clark. English House of Lords Cases, by Clark;—Clark's Reports, vol. 58 Alabama; Clark's Pennsylvania Law Journal Reports. See, also, Clarke.

Clark Dig. Clark's Digest, House of Lords Reports.

Clark's Code. Clark's Annotated Code of Civil Procedure, N.C.

Clark & F. (or Fin.). Clark & Finnelly's Reports, English House of Lords.

Clark & Fin.N.S. Clark's House of Lords Cases.

Clarke. Clarke's New York Chancery Reports;—Clarke's edition of vols. 1–8 Iowa;—Clarke's Reports, vols. 19–22 Michigan;—Clarke's Notes of Cases, Bengal. See, also, Clark.

Clarke Ch. (or Ch.R.). Clarke's New York Chancery Reports.

Clarke Not. (or R. & O.). Clarke's Notes of Cases, in his "Rules and Orders," Bengal.

Clarke & H.Elec.Cas. Clarke & Hall's Cases of Contested Elections in Congress.

Clarke & S.Dr.Cas. Clarke & Scully's Drainage Cases, Ont.

Clayt. Clayton's English Reports, York Assizes.

Clem. Clemens' Reports, vols. 57–59 Kansas.

Clerk Home. Clerk Home's Decisions, Scotch Court of Session.

Clay's Dig. Clay's Digest of Laws of Alabama.

Clev.Insan. Clevenger's Medical Jurisprudence of Insanity.

Cleve.Law Rec. Cleveland Law Recorder, Ohio.

Cleve.Law Rep. Cleveland Law Reporter, Ohio.

Clif. Clifford's United States Circuit Court Reports.

Clif. (South.) El.Cas. Clifford's Southwick Election Cases.

Clif. & Rick. (or Clif. & R.). Clifford & Rickard's English Locus Standi Reports.

Clif. & St. Clifford & Stephens' English Locus Standi Reports.

Cliff. Clifford's Reports, United States, First Circuit.

Clin.Dig. Clinton's Digest, New York.

Clk.Mag. Clerk's Magazine, London;—Rhode Island Clerk's Magazine.

Clow L.C. on Torts. Clow's Leading Cases on Torts.

Co. Coke's English King's Bench Reports.

Co.Ent. Coke's Entries.

Co.G. Reports and Cases of Practice in Common Pleas *tempore* Anne, Geo. I., and Geo. II., by Sir G. Coke. (Same as Cooke's Practice Reports.)

Co.Inst. Coke's Institutes.

Co.Litt. The First Part of the Institutes of the Laws of England, or a Commentary on Littleton, by Sir Edward Coke.

Co.P.C. Coke's Reports, English King's Bench.

Co.Pl. Coke's Pleadings (sometimes published separately).

Co.R.(N.Y.). Code Reporter, New York.

Co.R.N.S. Code Reporter, New Series.

Co.Rep. Coke's Reports, King's Bench.

Cobb. Cobb's Reports, vols. 4–20 Georgia;—Cobb's Reports, vol. 121 Alabama.

Cobb, Dig. Cobb's Digest of Statute Laws, Ga.

Cobb.St.Tr. Cobbett's (afterwards Howell's) State Trials.

Cobbey, Repl. Cobbey's Practical Treatise on the Law of Replevin.

Cobbey's Ann.St. Cobbey's Annotated Statutes, Neb.

Cochr. Cochran's Nova Scotia Reports;—Cochrane's Reports, vols. 3–7 North Dakota.

Cock.Tich.Ca. Cockburn's Charge in the Tichborne Case.

Cock. & Rowe (or Cock. & R.). Cockburn & Rowe's Election Cases.

Cocke. Cocke's Reports, vols. 16–18 Alabama;—Cocke's Reports, vols. 14, 15 Florida.

Cod. Codex Justinianus.

Cod.Jur.Civ. Codex Juris Civilis;—Justinian's Code.

Cod.St. Codified Statutes.

Cod.Theodos. Codex Theodorianus.

Code. Criminal Code of Canada, 1892.

Code Civ.Pro. (or Proc.). Code of Civil Procedure.

Code Civil. Code Civil or Civil Code of France.

Code Cr.Pro. (or Proc.). Code of Criminal Procedure.

Code d'Instr.Crim. Code d'Instruction Criminelle.

Code de Com. Code de Commerce.

Code Gen.Laws. Code of General Laws.

Code La. Civil Code of Louisiana.

Code N. (or Nap.). Code Napoléon, French Civil Code.

Code Prac. Code of Practice.

Code Pro. Code of Procedure.

Code Pub.Gen.Laws. Code of Public General Laws.

Code Pub.Loc.Laws. Code of Public Local Laws.

Code R.N.S. Code Reports, New Series.

Code Rep. New York Code Reporter.

Code Rep.N.S. New York Code Reports, New Series.

Code Supp. Supplement to the Code.

Cof. (or Coff.Prob., or Coffey Prob.Dec.). Coffey's Probate, Cal.

Cof.Dig. Cofer's Digest, Kentucky.

Coffey Prov.Dec. Coffey's Probate Decisions.

Cogh.Epit. Coghlan's Epitome of Hindu Law Cases.

Cohen, Adm.Law. Cohen's Admiralty Jurisdiction, Law, and Practice.

Coke. Coke's English King's Bench Reports (cited by parts and not by volume).

Coke Inst. Coke's Institutes.

Coke Lit. Coke on Littleton.

Col. Colorado;—Colorado Reports;—Coldwell's Reports, Tennessee;—Coleman's Reports, vols. 99, 101, 106, 110–129 Alabama.

Col.App. Colorado Appeals.

Col.C.C. Collyer's English Chancery Cases.

Col.Cas. Coleman's Cases (of Practice), New York.

Col.L.J. Colonial Law Journal (N.S.).

Col.L.Rep. Colorado Law Reporter.

Col.Law Review. Columbia Law Review.

Col. & Cal.Cas. (or Colem. & C.Cas.). Coleman & Caines' Cases, N.Y.

Cold. (or Coldw.). Coldwell's Tennessee Reports.

Cole. Cole's edition of Iowa Reports;—Coleman's Reports, vols. 99, 101–106, 110–129 Alabama.

Cole.Cas.Pr. Coleman's Cases, New York.

Colem.Cas. Coleman's Cases, N.Y.

Coll. Colles' Parliamentary Cases.

Coll. (or C.C.). Collyer's English Chancery Cases.

Coll.P.C. (or Coll.Parl.Cas.). Colles' English Parliamentary (House of Lords) Cases.

Coll. & E.Bank. Collier and Eaton's American Bankruptcy Reports.

Colles. Colles' English Parliamentary Cases.

Colly. Collyer's English Vice Chancellors' Reports.

Colly.Partn. Collyer on Partnerships.

Colo. Colorado Reports.

Colo.App. Colorado Appeals Reports.

Colo.Law Rep. Colorado Law Reporter.

Colq. Colquit's Reports (1 Modern).

Colq.Rom.Civil Law. Colquhoun's Roman Civil Law.

Colt. (Reg.Ca.). Coltman's Registration Cases.

Coltm. Coltman, Eng.

Colum.Jur. Columbia Jurist, New York.

Colum.L.Rev. Columbia Law Review.

Colum.L.T. Columbia Law Times, New York.

Colvil. Colvil's Manuscript Decisions, Scotch Court of Session.

Com. Comyn's Reports, English King's Bench;—Comberbach's English King's Bench Reports;—Comstock's Reports, vols. 1–4 New York Court of Appeals.

Com.B. Common Bench Reports (Manning, Granger, and Scott).

Com.B.N.S. English Common Bench Reports, New Series.

Com.Cas. Commercial Cases, England.

Com.Dig. Comyns' Digest.

Com.Jour. Journals of the House of Commons.

Com.L. Commercial Law, Can.

Com.L.J. Commercial Law Journal.

Com.L.R. (or Com.Law R.). English Common Law Reports.

Com.Law Rep. English Common Law Reports;—Common Law Reports, published by Spottiswoode.

Com. on Con. Comyn's Law of Contracts.

Com.Pl. Common Pleas, English Law Reports.

Com.Pl.Div. (or P.Div. or Pl.Div.). Common Pleas Division, English Law Reports.

Comb. Comberbach's English King's Bench Reports.

Comm. Commentaries.

Comp.Dec. Comptroller's Decisions.

Comp.Laws. Compiled Laws.

Comp.St. (or Comp.Stat.). Compiled Statutes.

Comptr.Treas.Dec. Comptroller Treasury Decisions.

Comst. (or Coms.). Comstock's Reports, vols. 1–4 New York Court of Appeals.

Comyn, Usury. Comyn on Usury.

Comyns. Comyns' English King's Bench Reports.

Comyns' Dig. Comyns' Digest, English.

Con. Conover's Reports, Wisconsin;—Continuation of Rolle's Reports (2 Rolle);—Connoly, New York Criminal.

Con.Cus. Conroy's Custodian Reports.

Con.St. Consolidated Statutes.

Con.Sur. Connoly's Surrogate, N.Y.

Con. & Law. Connor & Lawson's Irish Chancery Reports.

Cond.Ch.R. (or Cond.Eng.Ch.). Condensed English Chancery Reports.

Cond.Eccl. (or Cond.Ecc.R.). Condensed Ecclesiastical Reports.

Cond.Ex.R. (or Cond.Exch.R.). Condensed Exchequer Reports.

Cond.Rep.U.S. Peters' Condensed United States Reports.

Conf. Conference Reports (by Cameron and Norwood), North Carolina.

Conf.R. Conference Reports, N.C.

Cong. Congress.

Cong.El.Cas. (or Elect.Cas.). Congressional Election Cases.

Cong.Rec. Congressional Record, Washington.

Conk.Adm. Conkling's Admiralty.

Conn. Connecticut;—Connecticut Reports;—Connoly, New York, Surrogate.

Conn.B.J. Connecticut Bar Journal.

Conover. Conover's Reports, vols. 16–106 Wisconsin.

Conr. (or Conroy). Conroy's Custodian Reports.

Consist. (or Consist.Rep.). English Consistorial Reports, by Haggard.

Consolid.Ord. Consolidated General Orders in Chancery.

Const. Constitutional Reports, South Carolina, by Mill;—Constitutional Reports, South Carolina, by Treadway;—Constitutional Reports, vol. 1 South Carolina, by Harper.

Const.Amend. Amendment to Constitution.

Const.Hist. Hallam's Constitutional History of England.

Const.N.S. Constitutional Reports (Mill), South Carolina, New Series.

Const.Oth. Constitutiones Othoni (found at the end of Lyndewood's Provinciale).

Const.Rep. Constitutional Reports, S.C.

Const.Rev. Constitutional Review.

Const.S.C. Constitutional Reports, South Carolina, printed by Treadway.

Const.S.C.N.S. South Carolina Constitutional Reports, New Series, printed by Mill.

Const.U.S. Constitution of the United States.

Const.U.S.Amend. Amendment to the Constitution of the United States.

Cont.Elect.Case. Contested Election Cases (U.S.).

Coo. & Al. Cooke & Alcock's Irish King's Bench Reports.

Cook, Corp. Cook on Corporations.

Cook, Stock, Stockh. & Corp.Law. Cook on Stock, Stockholders, and General Corporation Law.

Cook Vice-Adm. (or Cook V. Adm.). Cook's Vice-Admiralty, L.C.;—Cook's Vice-Admiralty Reports, Nova Scotia.

Cook's Pen.Code. Cook's Penal Code, N.Y.

Cooke. Cooke's Cases of Practice, English Common Pleas;—Cooke's Reports, Tennessee.

Cooke, Incl.Acts. Cooke's Inclosure Acts.

Cooke, Ins. Cooke on Life Insurance.

Cooke Pr.Cas. Cooke's Practice Reports, English Common Pleas.

Cooke Pr.Reg. Cooke's Practical Register of the Common Pleas.

Cooke & A. (or Al., Alc.). Cooke & Alcock's Reports, Irish.

Cooley. Cooley's Reports, vols. 5–12 Michigan.

Cooley, Bl.Comm. Cooley's Edition of Blackstone's Commentaries.

Cooley, Const.Law. Cooley's Constitutional Law.

Cooley, Const.Lim. Cooley on Constitutional Limitations.

Cooley, Tax'n (or Cooley, Tax.). Cooley on Taxation.

Cooley, Torts. Cooley on Torts.

Coop. Cooper's Tennessee Chancery Reports;—Cooper's Reports, vols. 21–24 Florida;—Cooper's English Chancery Reports *tempore* Eldon;—Cooper's English Chancery Reports *tempore* Cottenham;—Cooper's English Chancery Reports *tempore* Brougham;—Cooper's English Practice Cases, Chancery.

Coop.C.C. (or Cas.). Cooper's Chancery Cases *tempore* Cottenham.

Coop.C. & P.R. Cooper's Chancery and Practice Reporter, Upper Canada.

Coop.Ch. Cooper's Tennessee Chancery Reports.

Co-op.Dig. Co-operative Digest, United States Reports.

Coop.Eq.Pl. Cooper's Equity Pleading.

Coop.Pr.Cas. Cooper's Practice Cases, English Chancery.

Coop.Sel.Cas. Cooper's Select Cases *tempore* Eldon, English Chancery.

Coop.t.Br. (or Coop.t.Brough.). Cooper's Cases *tempore* Brougham.

Coop.t.Cott. (or Coop.t.Cotten.). Cooper's Cases *tempore* Cottenham, English Chancery.

Coop.t.Eld. Cooper's Cases *tempore* Eldon, English Chancery.

Coop.Tenn.Ch. Cooper's Tennessee Chancery Reports.

Cooper. Cooper's English Chancery.

Coote, Ecc.Pr. Coote's Ecclesiastical Practice.

Coote, Mortg. Coote on Mortgages.

Coote, Prob.Pr. Coote's Probate Practice.

Cope. Cope's Reports, vols. 63–72 California.

Copp L.L. Copp's Public Land Laws.

Copp Land. Copp's Land Office Decisions.

Copp Min.Dec. Copp's United States Mining Decisions.

Copp, Pub.Land Laws. Copp's United States Public Land Laws.

Cor. Coram;—Coryton's Bengal Reports.

Corb. & D. (or Corb. & Dan.). Corbett & Daniell's English Election Cases.

Corn.Deeds. Cornish on Purchase Deeds.

Cornell L.Q. Cornell Law Quarterly.

Cornish, Purch.Deeds. Cornish on Purchase Deeds.

Corp. Pennsylvania Corporation Reporter.

Corp.Jur.Can. Corpus Juris Canonici.

Corp.Jur.Civ. Corpus Juris Civilis.

Corp.Reorg. Corporate Reorganizations.

Cory. Coryton's Reports, Calcutta.

Cou. Couper's Justiciary Reports, Scotland.

Coup. (or Coup.Just. or Couper). Couper's Justiciary Reports, Scotland.

Court Sess.Ca. Court of Sessions Cases, Scotch.

Court. & Macl. Courtnay & Maclean's Scotch Appeals (6 and 7 Wilson and Shaw).

Cont.Dig. Coutlée's Digest, Canada Supreme Court.

Cow. Cowen's New York Reports;—Cowper's English King's Bench Reports.

Cow.Cr.Dig. Cowen's Criminal Digest.

Cow.Cr.R. (or Cow.Cr.Rep.). Cowen's Criminal Reports, N.Y.

Cow.Dic. (or Dict.). Cowell's Law Dictionary.

Cow.Dig. Cowell's East India Digest.

Cow.Int. Cowell's Interpreter.

Cow.N.Y. Cowen's New York Reports.

Cowell. Cowell's Law Dictionary;—Cowell's Interpreter.

Cowp. Cowper's English King's Bench Reports.

Cowp.Cas. Cowper's Cases (in the third volume of Reports in Chancery).

Cox. Cox's English Chancery Reports;—Cox's English Criminal Cases;—Cox's Reports, vols. 25–27 Arkansas.

Cox Am.T.M.Cas. (or Am.Tr.M.Cas.). Cox's American Trade-Mark Cases.

Cox C.C. Cox's English Criminal Cases;—Cox's Crown Cases;—Cox's County Court Cases.

Cox Ch. Cox's English Chancery Cases.

Cox Cr.Cas. Cox's English Criminal Cases.

Cox Cr.Dig. Cox's Criminal Law Digest.

Cox, Inst. Cox's Institutions of the English Government.

Cox J.S.Cas. Cox's Joint Stock Cases.

Cox, M. & H. (or Mc. & H. or McC. & H.). Cox, McCrae & Hertslet's English County Court Reports.

Cox Mag.Ca. Cox's Magistrate Cases.

Cox Man.Tr.M. Cox's Manual of Trade-Mark Cases.

Cox Tr.M. Cox's Manual of Trade-Mark Cases.

Cox.Tr.M.Cas. Cox's American Trade-Mark Cases.

Cox & Atk. Cox & Atkinson, English Registration Appeal Reports.

Coxe. Coxe's Reports, New Jersey.

Cr. Cranch's Reports, United States Supreme Court;—Cranch's United States Circuit Court Reports.

Cr.Act. Criminal Act.

Cr.App. Criminal Appeals, Eng.

Cr.C.C. (or Cra. or Cra.C.C.). Cranch's United States Circuit Court Cases (Reports).

Cr.Cas.Res. Crown Cases Reserved.

Cr.Cir.Comp. Crown Circuit Companion, Irish.

Cr.Code. Criminal Code.

Cr.Code Prac. Criminal Code of Practice.

Cr.Law Mag. Criminal Law Magazine, N.J.

Cr.Law Rec. Criminal Law Recorder.

Cr.Law Rep. Criminal Law Reporter.

Cr.M. & R. Crompton, Meeson & Roscoe's English Exchequer Reports.

Cr.Pat.Dec. Cranch's Decisions on Patent Appeals.

Cr.Prac.Act. Criminal Practice Act.

Cr.Proc.Act. Criminal Procedure Act.

Cr.S. & P. Craigie, Stewart & Paton's Scotch Appeal Cases (same as Paton).

Cr.St. Criminal Statutes.

Cr. & Dix. Crawford & Dix's Irish Circuit Court Cases.

Cr. & Dix Ab.Cas. Crawford & Dix's (Irish) Abridged Notes of Cases.

Cr. & Dix C.C. Crawford & Dix's Irish Circuit Court Cases.

Cr. & J. Crompton & Jervis.

Cr. & M. Crompton & Meeson's English Exchequer Reports.

Cr. & Ph. Craig & Phillips' English Chancery Reports.

Crab. Crabbe's United States District Court Reports.

Crabb, Com.Law. Crabb on the Common Law.

Crabb, Eng. Crabb's English Synonyms.

Crabb, Eng.Law. Crabb's History of the English Law.

Crabb, Hist.Eng.Law. Crabb's History of the English Law.

Crabb, Real Prop. Crabb on the Law of Real Property.

Crabb, Technol.Dict. Crabb's Technological Dictionary.

Crabbe (or Crab.). Crabbe's United States District Court Reports.

Craig, Dict. Craig's Etymological, Technological, and Pronouncing Dictionary.

Craig & P. Craig and Phillips' English Chancery Reports.

Craig & Ph. Craig and Phillips' English Chancery Reports.

Craig. & St. (or S. & P.). Craigie, Stewart & Paton's Scotch Appeals Cases (same as Paton).

Craigius, Jus Feud. Craigius Jus Feudale.

Craik C.C. Craik's English Causes Célèbres.

Cranch. Cranch's United States Supreme Court Reports.

Cranch C.C. (or D.C.). Cranch's U. S. Circuit Court Reports, District of Columbia.

Cranch Pat.Dec. Cranch's Patent Decisions.

Crane. Crane's Reports, vol. 22 Montana.

Craw. Crawford's Reports, vols. 53–67 Arkansas.

Craw. & D. (or Crawf. & D.). Crawford & Dix's Circuit Court Cases, Ireland.

Craw. & D.Ab.Cas. (or Crawf. & D.Abr.Cas. or Craw. & D.Abr.C.). Crawford & Dix's Abridged Cases, Ireland.

Creasy. Creasy's Ceylon Reports.

Cress.Ins.Cas. (or Cressw.Ins.Cas.). Cresswell's English Insolvency Cases.

Crim.L.Mag. Criminal Law Magazine, Jersey City, New Jersey.

Crim.L.Rep. Criminal Law Reporter.

Crim.Rec. Criminal Recorder, Philadelphia;—Criminal Recorder, London;—Criminal Recorder, vol. 1 Wheeler's New York Criminal Reports.

Cripp's Ch.Cas. (or Cripp Ch.Cas.). Cripp's Church and Clergy Cases.

Critch. Critchfield's Reports, vols. 5–21 Ohio State.

Cro. Croke's English King's Bench Reports;—Keilway's English King's Bench Reports.

Cro.Cas. (or Cro.Car.). Croke's English King's Bench Reports *tempore* Charles I, 3 Cro.

Cro.Eliz. Croke's English King's Bench Reports *tempore* Elizabeth (1 Cro.).

Cro.Jac. Croke's English King's Bench Reports *tempore* James (Jacobus) I. (2 Cro.).

Crockford. English Maritime Law Reports, published by Crockford.

Cromp. Star Chamber Cases, by Crompton.

Cromp.Exch.R. Crompton's Exchequer Reports, English.

Cromp.Jur. Crompton's Jurisdiction of Courts.

Cromp.Just. Crompton's Office of Justice of the Peace.

Cromp.M. & R. Crompton, Meeson and Roscoe's English Exchequer Reports.

Cromp.R. & C.Pr. Crompton's Rules and Cases of Practice.

Cromp. & J. (or Cromp. & Jerv.). Crompton & Jervis' English Exchequer Reports.

Cromp. & M. (or Mees.). Crompton & Meeson's English Exchequer Reports.

Crompt. Star Chamber Cases by Crompton.

Crosw.Pat.Cas. (or Crosw.Pat.Ca.). Croswell's Collection of Patent Cases, U. S.

Crounse. Crounse's Reports, vol. 3 Nebraska.

Crowth. (or Crowther). Crowther's Ceylon Reports.

Cruise Dig. Cruise's Digest of the Law of Real Property.

Crump Ins. Crump on Marine Insurance.

Crumrine. Crumrine's Reports, vols. 116–146 Pennsylvania.

Ct.App.N.Z. (or Rep.N.Z.). Court of Appeals Reports, New Zealand.

Ct.Cl. Court of Claims, United States.

Ct.Cust. & Pat.App. Court of Customs and Patent Appeals.

Cujacius. Cujacius, Opera, quæ de Jure fecit, etc.

Cum. & Dun.Rem.Tr. Cummins & Dunphy's Remarkable Trials.

Cummins. Cummins' Idaho Reports.

Cun. (or Cunn.). Cunningham's English King's Bench Reports.

Cun.Dict. Cunningham's Dictionary.

Cunn. Cunningham's English Bench Reports.

Cunningham. Cunningham's Reports, English King's Bench.

Cur. Curtis' United States Circuit Court Reports;—Curia.

Cur.Com. Current Comment and Legal Miscellany.

Cur.Dec. Curtis' Decisions, United States Supreme Court.

Cur.Ov.Ca. Curwen's Overruled Cases, Ohio.

Current Ct.Dec. Current Court Decisions.

Curry. Curry's Reports, vols. 6–19 Louisiana.

Curt. Curtis' United States Circuit Court Reports;—Curteis' English Ecclesiastical Reports.

Curt.Adm.Dig. Curtis' Admiralty Digest.

Curt.C.C. Curtis' United States Circuit Court Decisions.

Curt.Cond. Curtis' (Condensed) Decisions, United States Supreme Court.

Curt.Dec. Curtis' United States Supreme Court Decisions.

Curt.Dig. Curtis' Digest, United States.

Curt.Ecc. Curteis' English Ecclesiastical Reports.

Curt.Pat. Curtis on Patents.

Curtis. Curtis' United States Circuit Court Reports.

Curw. Curwen's Overruled Cases;—Curwen's Statutes of Ohio.

Curw.L.O. Curwen's Laws of Ohio 1854, 1 vol.

Curw.R.S. Curwen's Revised Statutes of Ohio.

Cush. Cushing's Massachusetts Reports;—Cushman's Mississippi Reports.

Cush.Elec.Cas. Cushing's Election Cases in Massachusetts.

Cush.Law & Prac.Leg.Assem. Cushing's Law and Practice of Legislative Assemblies.

Cush.Man. Cushing's Manual.

Cushing. Cushing's Massachusetts Reports.

Cushm. (or Cushman). Cushman's Reports, vols. 23–29 Mississippi.

Cust.A. United States Customs Appeals.

Cust.Rep. Custer's Ecclesiastical Reports.

Cyc. Cyclopædia of Law and Procedure.

Cyc.Ann. Cyclopedia of Law & Procedure Annotations.

Cyc.Law & Proc. Cyclopedia of Law and Procedure.

Cyclop.Dict. Shumaker & Longsdorf's Cyclopedic Dictionary.

D

D. Delaware;—Dallas' United States and Pennsylvania Reports;—Denio's Reports, New York;—Dunlop, Bell & Murray's Reports, Scotch Session Cases (Second Series);—Digest of Justinian, 50 books, never been translated into English;—Disney, Ohio;—Divisional Court;—Dowling, English;—Dominion of Canada.

D.(N.S.). Dowling's Practice Cases, New Series, English.

D.B. Domesday Book.

D.B. & M. Dunlop, Bell & Murray, Scotland.

D.C. District of Columbia;—United States District Court.

D.C.App. District of Columbia Appeals.

D.C.C.E. District of Columbia Code Encyclopedia.

D.Chip. D. Chipman's Reports, Vermont.

D.G. De Gex;—De Gex's English Bankruptcy Reports.

D.G.F. & J. De Gex, Fisher, & Jones' English Chancery Reports.

D.G.F. & J.B. De Gex, Fisher, & Jones' English Bankruptcy Reports.

D.G.J. & S. De Gex, Jones, & Smith's English Chancery Reports.

D.G.J. & S.B. De Gex, Jones, & Smith's English Bankruptcy Reports.

D.G.M. & G. De Gex, Macnaghten, & Gordon's English Chancery Reports.

D.G.M. & G.B. De Gex, Macnaghten, & Gordon's English Bankruptcy Reports.

D.N.S. Dowling's Reports, New Series, English Bail Court;—Dow, New Series (Dow & Clark, English House of Lords Cases).

D.P.C. Dowling's English Practice Cases.

D.W.I. Descriptive-Word Index.

D. & B. (or D. & B.C.C.). Dearsly & Bell's English Crown Cases.

D. & C. Dow & Clark's English House of Lords (Parliamentary) Cases;—District and County Reports.

D. & C. (or D. & Ch. or D. & Chit.). Deacon & Chitty's English Bankruptcy Reports.

D. & E. Durnford & East's (Term) Reports, English King's Bench.

D. & J. De Gex & Jones' English Chancery Reports.

D. & J.B. De Gex & Jones' English Bankruptcy Reports.

D. & L. Dowling & Lowndes' English Bail Court Reports.

D. & M. Davison & Merivale's English Queen's Bench Reports.

D. & P. Denison & Pearce, English.

D. & R. Dowling & Ryland's English King's Bench Reports.

D. & R.M.C. (or D. & R.Mag.Cas.). Dowling & Ryland's Magistrate Cases, Eng.

D. & R.N.P. (or D. & R.N.P.C.). Dowling & Ryland's English Nisi Prius Cases.

D. & S. Drewry & Smale's Chancery Reports;—Doctor and Student;—Deane and Swabey.

D. & Sw. Deane & Swabey, Eng.

D. & W. Drury & Walsh's Irish Chancery Reports;—Drury & Warren's Irish Chancery Reports.

D. & War. Drury & Warren's Reports, Irish Chancery.

Daily L.N. Daily Legal News, Pa.

Daily L.R. Daily Legal Record, Pa.

Daily Transc. Daily Transcript.

Dak. Dakota;—Dakota Territory Reports.

Dak.Law Rev. Dakota Law Review.

Dal. Dallas' United States Reports;—Dalison's English Common Pleas Reports (bound with Benloe);—Dalrymple's Scotch Session Cases.

Dal.C.P. Dalison's Common Pleas, Eng.

Dal.Coop. Dallas' Report of Cooper's Opinion on the Sentence of a Foreign Court of Admiralty.

Dale. Dale's Reports, vols. 2–3 Oklahoma.

Dale Eccl. (or Dale Ecc.). Dale's Ecclesiastical Reports, Eng.

Dale Leg.Rit. Dale's Legal Ritual (Ecclesiastical) Reports.

Dalison. Dalison's English Common Pleas Reports (bound with Benloe).

Dall. Dallam's Decisions, Tex;—Dallas' Pennsylvania and United States Reports.

Dall.Dec. (or Dall.Dig.). Dallam's Texas Decisions, printed originally in Dallam's Digest.

Dall. in Keil. Dallison in Keilway's Reports, English King's Bench.

Dall.Laws. Dallas' Laws, Pa.

Dall.S.C. Dallas' United States Supreme Court Reports.

Dallas. Dallas' Pennsylvania and United States Reports.

Dalloz. Dictionnaire général et raisonné de legislation, de doctrine, et de jurisprudence, en matière civile, commerciale, criminelle, administrative, et de droit public.

Dalr. Dalrymple's Decisions, Scotch Court of Session;—(Dalrymple of) Stair's Decisions, Scotch Court of Session;—(Dalrymple of) Hailes' Scotch Session Cases.

Dalr.Dec. Dalrymple's Decisions, Scotland.

Dalr.Feud.Prop. Dalrymple on Feudal Property.

Dalrymple. (Sir Hew) Dalrymple's Scotch Session Cases; (Sir David Dalrymple of) Hailes' Scotch Session Cases;—(Sir James Dalrymple of) Stair's Scotch Session Cases. See, also, Dal. and Dalr.

Daly. Daly's New York Common Pleas Reports.

Dampier MSS. Dampier's Paper Book, Lincoln's Inn Library.

Dan. Daniell's Exchequer and Equity Reports;—Dana's Kentucky Reports;—Danner's Reports, vol. 42 Alabama.

Dan. & Ll. Danson & Lloyd's Mercantile Cases.

Dana. Dana's Kentucky Reports.

Dane Abr. Dane's Abridgment.

Daniel, Neg.Inst. Daniel's Negotiable Instruments.

Daniell, Ch.Pl. & Prac. Daniell's Chancery Pleading and Practice.

Daniell, Ch.Prac. (or Daniell, Ch.Pr.). Daniell's Chancery Pleading and Practice.

Dann. Dann's Arizona Reports;—Danner's Reports, vol. 42 Alabama;—Dann's California Reports.

Dans. & L. (or Dans. & Lld.). Danson & Lloyd's English Mercantile Cases.

D'Anv.Abr. D'Anver's Abridgment, Eng.

Darl.Pr.Ct.Sess. Darling, Practice of the Court of Session (Scotch).

Dart, Vend. Dart on Vendors and Purchasers.

Das. Dasent's Bankruptcy and Insolvency Reports;—Common Law Reports, vol. 3.

Dass.Dig. Dassler's Kansas Digest.

Dass.Ed. Dassler's Edition, Kansas Reports.

Dauph.Co. Dauphin County, Pa.

Dauph.Co.Rep. (or Dauph.). Dauphin County Reporter, Pennsylvania.

Dav. Daveis' United States District Court Reports (now republished as 2 Ware);—Davy's or Davies' Irish King's Bench and Exchequer Reports;—Davies' English Patent Cases;—Davis' Reports (Abridgment of Sir Edward Coke's Reports);—Davis' Reports, vol. 2 Hawaii;—Davis' United States Supreme Court Reports.

Dav.Coke. Davis' Abridgment of Coke's Reports.

Dav.Conv. Davidson's Conveyancing.

Dav.Dig. Davis' Indiana Digest.

Dav.Ir. Davies' Irish Reports.

Dav.Ir.K.B. Davies' Reports, Irish King's Bench.

Dav.Pat.Cas. Davies' English Patent Cases.

Dav.Prec.Conv. Davidson's Precedents in Conveyancing.

Dav.Rep. Davies' (Sir John) Reports, King's Bench, Ireland.

Dav. & M. (or Dav. & Mer.). Davison & Merivale, Eng.

Daveis. Daveis' United States District Court Reports (republished as 2 Ware).

Davidson. Davidson's Reports, vols. 92–111 North Carolina.

Davies. Davies' (or Davis' or Davys') Irish King's Bench Reports.

Davis. Davis' Hawaiian Reports;—Davies' (or Davys') Irish King's Bench Reports;—Davis' Reports, vols. 108–176 United States Supreme Court.

Davis (J.C.B.). Davis' United States Supreme Court Reports.

Davis, Bldg.Soc. Davis' Law of Building Societies.

Davis, Cr.Law. Davis Criminal Law.

Davys. Davys, Ireland.

Dawson's Code. Dawson's Code of Civil Procedure, Colo.

Day. Day's Connecticut Reports;—Connecticut Reports, proper, reported by Day.

Dayt.Term Rep. Dayton Term Reports, Dayton, Ohio.

Dayton. Dayton Ohio Reports.

Dea. Deady's United States District Court Reports.

Dea. & Chit. Deacon & Chitty's English Bankruptcy Reports.

Dea. & Sw. Deane & Swabey's Reports, Probate and Divorce.

Deac. Deacon's English Bankruptcy Reports.

Deac.Cr.Law. Deacon on Criminal Law of England.

Deac. & C. Deacon & Chitty's English Bankruptcy Reports.

Deady. Deady's United States Circuit Reports.

Deane. Deane (& Swabey's) English Probate and Divorce Reports;—Deane's Reports vols. 24–26 Vermont.

Deane Ecc.Rep. Deane & Swabey's English Ecclesiastical Reports.

Deane & Sw. Deane & Swabey's English Ecclesiastical Reports.

Dears.C.C. Dearsly's English Crown Cases.

Dears. & B. Dearsley & Bell, Eng.

Dears. & B.C.C. (or Dears. & B.Crown Cas.). Dearsley and Bell's English Crown Cases.

Deas & A. Deas & Anderson, Eng.

Deas & And. Deas & Anderson's Reports, Scotch Court of Session.

Dec.Com.Pat. Decisions of the Commissioner of Patents.

Dec.Dig. American Digest, Decennial Edition.

Dec.O. Ohio Decisions.

Dec.t.H. & M. Decisions of Admiralty *tempore* Hay and Marriott.

Dec.U.S.Comp.Gen. Decisions of U.S. Comptroller General.

Decen.Dig. American Digest, Decennial Edition.

De G.F. & J. De Gex, Fisher, & Jones' English Chancery Reports.

De G.F. & J.By. De Gex, Fisher, & Jones' English Bankruptcy Appeals.

De G.J. & S. De Gex, Jones, & Smith's English Chancery Reports.

De G.J. & S.By. De Gex, Jones, & Smith's English Bankruptcy Appeals.

De G.M. & G. De Gex, Macnaghten, & Gordon's English Bankruptcy Reports;—De Gex, Macnaghten, & Gordon's English Chancery Reports.

De G.M. & G.By. De Gex, Macnaghten, & Gordon's English Bankruptcy Appeals.

De G. & J. De Gex & Jones' English Chancery Reports.

De G. & J.By. De Gex & Jones' English Bankruptcy Appeals.

De G. & Sm. De Gex & Smale's English Chancery Reports.

De Gex. De Gex's English Bankruptcy Reports.

De Gex, F. & J. De Gex, Fisher & Jones' English Chancery Reports.

De Gex, J & S. De Gex, Jones, and Smith's English Chancery Reports.

De Gex, M. & G. De Gex, Macnaghten & Gordon's Reports, English.

De Hart, Mil.Law. De Hart on Military Law.

De Jure Mar. Malloy's De Jure Maritimo.

Del. Delaware;—Delaware Reports;—Delane's English Revision Cases;—Delaware County Reports, Pennsylvania.

Del.C.Ann. Delaware Code Annotated.

Del.Ch. Delaware Chancery Reports, by Bates.

Del.Co. (or Del.Co.R.). Delaware County Reports, Pa.

Del.Cr.Cas. Delaware Criminal Cases, by Houston.

Del.El.Cas. Delane's English Election (Revision) Cases.

Del.Term R. Delaware Term Reports.

Delehanty. Miscellaneous Reports, New York.

De Lolme, Eng.Const. De Lolme on the English Constitution.

Dem.Sur. (or Dem.Surr.). Demarest's Surrogate, N. Y.

Demol. Demolombe's Code Napoléon.

Den. Denio's New York Reports;—Denis' Reports, vol. 32 Louisiana Annual;—Denied.

Den.C.C. Denison's English Crown Cases.

Den. & P. Denison & Pearce's English Crown Cases, vol. 2 Denison.

Denio. Denio's New York Reports.

Denis. Denis' Reports, vols. 32–46 Louisiana.

Denison, Cr.Cas. Denison's English Crown Cases.

Dens. Denslow's Notes to second edition, vols. 1–3 Michigan Reports.

Denver L.J. Denver Law Journal.

Denver L.N. Denver Legal News.

De Orat. Cicero, De Oratore.

Des. Desaussure's South Carolina Equity Reports.

Desaus. (or Desaus.Eq.). Desaussure's Equity, S.C.

Dest.Cal.Dig. Desty's California Digest.

Desty, Tax'n. Desty on Taxation.

Detroit L.Rev. Detroit Law Review.

Detroit Leg.N. Detroit Legal News, Mich.

Dev. Devereux's North Carolina Law Reports;—Devereux's Reports, United States Court of Claims.

Dev.C.C. Devereux's Reports, United States Court of Claims.

Dev.Ct.Cl. Devereux's Reports, United States Court of Claims.

Dev.Eq. Devereux's North Carolina Equity.

Dev.L. Devereux's North Carolina Law Reports.

Dev. & B. (or Dev. & Bat.). Devereux & Battle, N.C.

Dev. & B.Eq. (or Dev. & Bat.Eq.). Devereux & Battle's Equity, N.C.

Devl.Deeds. Devlin on Deeds.

Dew. Dewey's Reports, vols. 60–61 Kansas;—Dewey's Kansas Court of Appeals Reports.

De Witt. De Witt's Reports, vols. 24–42 Ohio State.

Di. (or Dy.) . Dyer's English Reports, King's Bench.

Dice. Dice's Reports, vols. 79–91 Indiana.

Dicey, Confl.Laws. Dicey on Conflict of Laws.

Dicey, Dom. Dicey's Law of Domicil.

Dicey, Const. Dicey, Lectures Introductory to the Study of the Law of the English Constitution.

Dick. Dickens, Scotland;—Dickinson, N.J.;—Dickens' English Chancery Reports;—Dickinson's Reports, vols. 46–58 New Jersey Equity.

Dict. Dictionary.

Dict.Droit Civil. Dictionnaire Droit Civil.

Dicta. Dicta, Denver Bar Association.

Dig. Digest;—Digest of Justinian;—Digest of Writs.

Dig.Fla. Thompson's Digest of Laws, Fla.

Dig.Proem. Digest of Justinian, Proem.

Dig.St. English's Digest of the Statutes, Ark.

Dill. (or Dil.). Dillon's United States Circuit Court Reports.

Dill.Laws Eng. & Am. Dillon's Laws and Jurisprudence of England and America.

Dill.Mun.Corp. Dillon on Municipal Corporations.

Dirl. Dirleton's Decisions, Court of Session.

Dirl.Dec. Dirleton's Decisions, Scotland.

Disn. (or Dis.). Disney's Superior Court Reports, Cincinnati.

Dist. (or Dist.Rep.). District Reports.

Docket. The Docket, Pa.

Doct. & Stud. Doctor and Student.

Dod. (or Dods.). Dodson's English Admiralty Reports.

Dod.Adm. Dodson's Reports, English Admiralty Courts.

Dom.Book. Domesday Book.

Dom.Civ.Law. Domat's Civil Law.

Dom.L.R. Dominion Law Reports, Canada.

Dom.Proc. Domus Procerum. In the House of Lords.

Domat. Domat on Civil Law.

Domat Supp. au Droit Public. Domat, Les Lois Civiles, Le Droit Public, etc. Augmentée des 3e et 4e livres du Droit Public, par M. de Hericourt, etc.

Domes. Domesday Book.

Domesday. Domesday Book.

Donaker. Donaker's Reports, vol. 154 Indiana.

Donn. Donnelly's Reports, English Chancery;—Donnelly's Irish Land Cases.

Donnelly. Donnelly, Eng.

Dor.Q.B. (or Dorion). Dorion's Quebec Queen's Bench Reports;—(Dec. de la Cour D'Appel).

Dorion. Dorion, Lower Canada.

Dos Passos, Stock-Brok. Dos Passos on Stock-Brokers and Stock Exchanges.

Doug. Douglas' Michigan Reports;—Douglas' English King's Bench Reports;—Douglas' English Election Cases.

Doug. (Mich.). Douglas' Law Reports, Michigan.

Doug.El.Ca. (or Dougl.El.Cas.). Douglas' Election Cases, Eng.

Dow (or Dow P.C.). Dow's House of Lords (Parliamentary) Cases, same as Dow's Reports;—Dowling's English Practice Cases.

Dow N.S. Dow & Clark's English House of Lords Cases.

Dow P.C. Dow's Parliamentary Cases;—Dowling's English Practice Cases.

Dow & C. Dow & Clark's English House of Lords Cases.

Dow. & L. Dowling & Lowndes' English Bail Court Reports.

Dow. & Ry. Dowling & Ryland's English King's Bench Reports;—Dowling & Ryland's English Nisi Prius Cases.

Dow. & Ry.M.C. Dowling & Ryland's English Magistrates' Cases.

Dow. & Ry.N.P. Dowling & Ryland's English Nisi Prius Cases. (Often bound at end of vol. 1 Dowling & Ryland's King's Bench Reports.)

Dowl. (or Dowl.P.C.). Dowling's English Bail Court (Practice) Cases.

Dowl.N.S. Dowling's English Bail Court Reports, New Series.

Dowl.P.C. Dowling's English Bail Court (Practice) Cases.

Dowl.P.C.N.S. Dowling's Practice Cases, New Series, Eng.

Dowl.Pr.C.N.S. Dowling's Reports, New Series, English Practice Cases.

Dowl. & L. Dowling & Lowndes' English Bail Court Reports.

Dowl. & Lownd. Dowling & Lowndes' English Practice Cases.

Dowl. & R. (or Dowl. & Ryl.). Dowling & Ryland's English King's Bench Reports.

Dowl. & Ryl.M.C. Dowling & Ryland's English Magistrates' Cases.

Dowl. & Ryl.N.P. Dowling & Ryland's English Nisi Prius Cases.

Down. & Lud. Downton & Luder's English Election Cases.

Dr. Drewry's English Vice Chancellor's Reports;—Drury's Irish Chancery Reports *tempore* Sugden; —Drury's Irish Chancery Reports *tempore* Napier.

Dr.R.t.Nap. Drury's Irish Chancery Reports *tempore* Napier.

Dr.R.t.Sug. Drury's Irish Chancery Reports *tempore* Sugden.

Dr. & Sm. Drewry & Smale's English Vice Chancellors' Reports.

Dr. & Wal. Drury & Walsh's Irish Chancery Reports.

Dr. & War. Drury & Warren's Irish Chancery Reports.

Drake, Attachm. Drake on Attachments.

Draper. Draper's Upper Canada King's Bench Reports, Ontario.

Drew. Drewry's English Vice Chancellors' Reports;—Drew's Reports, vol. 13 Florida.

Drew. & Sm. Drewry & Smale's English Vice Chancellors' Reports.

Drink. Drinkwater's English Common Pleas Reports.

Drinkw. Drinkwater, Eng.

Drone, Copyr. Drone on Copyrights.

Dru. Drury's Irish Chancery Reports *tempore* Sugden.

Dru.t.Nap. Drury's Irish Chancery Reports *tempore* Napier.

Dru. & Wal. Drury & Walsh's Irish Chancery Reports.

Dru. & War. Drury & Warren's Irish Chancery Reports.

Drury. Drury, Ireland.

Drury t.Sug. Drury's Irish Chancery Reports *tempore* Sugden.

Dub. *Dubitatur;—Dubitante.*

Dub.Rev. Dublin Review, Dublin, Ireland.

Du Cange. Du Cange's Glossarium.

Dud. (Ga.). Dudley's Georgia Reports.

Dud. (S.C.). Dudley's Law Reports, South Carolina.

Dud.Ch. (or Eq.). Dudley's South Carolina Equity Reports.

Dud.Eq. (S.C.). Dudley's Equity Reports, South Carolina.

Dud.L. (or Dud.Law or Dud.L.S.C.). Dudley's Law, S.C.

Duer. Duer's New York Superior Court Reports.

Duer, Ins. Duer on Insurance.

Dufresne. Dufresne's [Law] Glossary.

Duke B.A.J. Duke Bar Association Journal.

Dun. Duncan (see Dunc.);—Dunlap (see Dunl.).

Dun. & Cum. Dunphy & Cummins' Remarkable Trials.

Dunc.Ent.Cas. Duncan's Scotch Entail Cases.

Dunc.N.P. Duncombe's Nisi Prius.

Dungl.Med.Dict. Dunglison, Dictionary of Medical Science and Literature.

Dunl.Abr. Dunlap's Abridgment of Coke's Reports.

Dunl.Adm.Pr. Dunlop's Admiralty Practice.

Dunl.B. & M. Dunlop, Bell & Murray, Scotland.

Dunlop. Dunlop, Scotland.

Dunlop (Dunl.B. & M.). Dunlop, Bell & Murray's Reports, Second Series, Scotch Session Cases.

Dunn. Dunning's English King's Bench Reports.

Dup.Jur. Duponceau on Jurisdiction of United States Courts.

Durf. Durfee's Reports, vol. 12 Rhode Island.

Durie. Durie's Scottish Court of Session Cases.

Durn. & E. Durnford & East's English King's Bench Reports (Term Reports).

Dutch. Dutcher's New Jersey Reports.

Duv. Duvall's Kentucky Reports;—Duval's Reports, Canada Supreme Court.

Duval. Duval's Reports, Canada Supreme Court.

Dwar.St. Dwarris on Statutes.

Dy. (or Dyer). Dyer's English King's Bench Reports.

E

E. East's Reports.

E.B. & E. Ellis, Blackburn & Ellis' English Queen's Bench Reports.

E.B. & S. (Ellis) Best & Smith's English Queen's Bench Reports.

E.C. English Cases;—English Chancery;—English Chancery Reports;—Election Cases, Ontario.

E.C.L. English Common Law Reports.

E.D.C. Eastern District Court, South Africa.

E.D.S. E. D. Smith's New York Common Pleas Reports.

E.D.Smith (N.Y.). E. D. Smith's New York Common Pleas Reports.

E.E. English Exchequer Reports.

E.E.R. English Ecclesiastical Reports.

E.L. & Eq. English Law and Equity Reports.

E.O. Executive Orders.

E.P.C. East's Pleas of the Crown.

E.R. East's King's Bench Reports;—Election Reports.

E.R.C. English Ruling Cases.

E. & A. Ecclesiastical and Admiralty;—Error and Appeal;—Spink's Ecclesiastical and Admiralty Reports;—Upper Canada Error and Appeal Reports.

E. & A.R. Error and Appeal Reports, Ontario.

E. & A.W.C. Grant's Error and Appeal Reports, Ontario.

E. & B. Ellis & Blackburn's Queen's Bench Reports.

E. & E. Ellis & Ellis' English Queen's Bench Reports.

E. & I. English and Irish Appeals, House of Lords.

E. & Y. Eagle & Younge's English Tithe Cases.

Ea. East's English King's Bench Reports.

Eag. & Y. (or Eag. & Yo.). Eagle & Young's Tithe Cases, Eng.

East. East's King's Bench Reports;—East's Notes of Cases in Morley's Indian Digest;—Eastern Reporter.

East.L.R. Eastern Law Reporter, Canada.

East N. of C. East's Notes of Cases (in Morley's East Indian Digest).

East, P.C. (or Pl.Cr.). East's Pleas of the Crown.

East.Rep. Eastern Reporter.

East.T. Eastern Term, Eng.

Ebersole. Ebersole's Reports, vols. 59-80 Iowa.

Eccl.R. English Ecclesiastical Reports.

Eccl.Stat. Ecclesiastical Statutes.

Eccl. & Ad. Ecclesiastical and Admiralty;—Spink's Ecclesiastical and Admiralty Reports.

Ed. Edition;—Eden's English Chancery Reports.

Ed.Bro. Eden's edition of Brown's English Chancery Reports.

Ed.Cr. Edwards' New York Chancery Reports.

Ed. et Ord. Edits et Ordonnances (Lower Canada).

Eden. Eden's Reports, High Court of Chancery, England.

Eden, Bankr. Eden's Bankrupt Law.

Eden, Pen.Law. Eden's Principles of Penal Law.

Eden's Prin.P.L. Eden's Principles of Penal Law.

Edg. Edgar's Reports, Court of Session. Scotland.

Edgar. Edgar, Scotland.

Edict. Edicts of Justinian.

Edinb.L.J. Edinburgh Law Journal.

Edm.Sel.Cas. Edmonds' New York Select Cases.

Edmonds' St. at Large. Edmonds' Statutes at Large, N.Y.

Edw. Edwards' New York Chancery Reports;—Edwards' English Admiralty Reports;—Edwards' Reports, vols. 2, 3 Missouri.

Edw. (Tho.). Edwards' English Admiralty Reports.

Edw.Abr. Edwards' Abridgment of Prerogative Court Cases.

Edw.Adm. Edwards' English Admiralty Reports.

Edw.Bailm. Edwards on the Law of Bailments.

Edw.Bills & N. Edwards on Bills and Notes.

Edw.Brok. & F. Edwards on Factors and Brokers.

Edw.Ch. Edwards' New York Chancery Reports.

Edw.Lead.Dec. Edwards' Leading Decisions in Admiralty (Edwards' Admiralty Reports).

Edw.Pr.Cas. Edwards' Prize Cases (English Admiralty Reports).

Edw.Pr.Ct.Cas. Edwards' Abridgment of Prerogative Court Cases.

Edw.Rec. Edwards on Receivers in Equity.

Efird. Efird's Reports, vols. 45-56 South Carolina.

El. Queen Elizabeth;—Elchies' Decisions, Scotch Court of Session.

El.B. & E. Ellis, Blackburn, & Ellis' English Queen's Bench Reports.

El., Bl. & El. Ellis, Blackburn & Ellis' English Queen's Bench Reports.

El.Cas. Election Cases.

El.Dict. Elchies' Dictionary of Decisions, Court of Session, Scotland.

El. & B. (or Bl). Ellis & Blackburn's English Queen's Bench Reports.

El. & El. Ellis & Ellis' English Queen's Bench Reports.

Elchies' Dict. Elchies' (Dictionary of) Decisions, Scotch Court of Session.

Elec.Cas.N.Y. New York Election Cases (Armstrong's).

Eliz. Queen Elizabeth, as 13 Eliz.

Ell.Bl. & Ell. Ellis, Blackburn, & Ellis' English Queen's Bench Reports.

Ell.Dig. Eller's Digest, Minnesota.

Ell. & Bl. Ellis & Blackburn's English Queen's Bench Reports.

Ell. & Ell. Ellis & Ellis' English Queen's Bench Reports.

Ellesm.Post N. Ellesmere's Post Nati.

Elliot, Deb.Fed.Const. Elliot's Debates on the Federal Constitution.

Elliott, App.Proc. Elliott's Appellate Procedure.

Elliott, R.R. Elliott on Railroads.

Elliott, Roads & S. Elliott on Roads and Streets.

Elliott, Supp. Elliott Supplement to the Indiana Revised Statutes.

Ellis & Bl. Ellis and Blackburn's English Queen's Bench Reports.

Elm.Dig. Elmer's Digest, New Jersey.

Elmer, Lun. Elmer's Practice in Lunacy.

Elph.Interp.Deeds. Elphinstone's Rules for Interpretation of Deeds.

Els.W.Bl. Elsley's edition of Wm. Blackstone's English King's Bench Reports.

Elton, Com. Elton on Commons and Waste Lands.

Elton, Copyh. Elton on Copyholds.

Emerig.Assur. Emerigon, Traité des Assurances et des Contrats à la Grosse.

Emerig.Ins. Emerigon on Insurance.

Emerig.Mar.Loans. Emerigon on Maritime Loans.

Emerig.Tr. des Ass. Emerigon, Traité des Assurances.

Emerig.Traité des Assur. Emerigon, Traité des Assurances.

Enc. Encyclopædia.

Enc.Amer. Encyclopædia Americana.

Enc.Arch. Gwilt's Encyclopedia of Architecture.

Enc.Brit. Encyclopædia Britannica.

Enc.Dict. Encyclopædic Dictionary, Edited by Robert Hunter 1879–1888.

Enc.Forms. Encyclopædia of Forms.

Enc.Ins.U.S. Insurance Year-Book.

Enc.Law (or Ency.Law). American and English Encyclopædia of Law.

Enc.Pl. & Prac. (or Enc.Pl. & Pr.). Encyclopedia of Pleading and Practice.

Ency.U.S.Sup.Ct.Rep. Encyclopedia of United States Supreme Court Reports.

Encyc. Encyclopædia.

End.Bldg.Ass'ns. Endlich on Building Associations.

End.Interp.St. Endlich's Commentaries on the Interpretation of Statutes.

Eng. English;—English's Reports, vols. 6–13 Arkansas;—English Reports by N. C. Moak.

Eng.Ad. English Admiralty;—English Admiralty Reports.

Eng.C.C. (or Cr.Cas.). English Crown Cases.

Eng.C.L. English Common Law Reports.

Eng.Ch. English Chancery;—English Chancery Reports;—Condensed English Chancery Reports.

Eng.Ecc.R. English Ecclesiastical Reports.

Eng.Eccl. English Ecclesiastical Reports.

Eng.Exch. English Exchequer Reports.

Eng.Ir.App. Law Reports, English and Irish Appeal Cases.

Eng.Judg. Scotch Court of Session Cases, decided by the English Judges.

Eng.L. & Eq. (or Eng.Law & Eq.). English Law and Equity Reports, American Reprint.

Eng.R. & C.Cas. English Railway and Canal Cases.

Eng.Rep. Moak's English Reports;—English's Reports, vols. 6–13 Arkansas; English Reports.

Eng.Rep.R. (or Re.). English Reports, Full Reprint.

Eng.Ru.Ca. English Ruling Cases.

Eng.Ry. & C.Cas. English Railway and Canal Cases.

Eng.Sc.Ecc. English and Scotch Ecclesiastical Reports.

Eng. & Ir.App. Law Reports, English and Irish Appeal Cases.

English. English's Reports, vols. 6–13 Arkansas.

Ent. Coke's Entries;—Rastell's Entries.

Entries, Ancient. Rastell's Entries (cited in Rolle's Abridgment).

Eq. Equity.

Eq.Cas. Equity Cases in vol. 9 Modern Reports.

Eq.Cas.Abr. Equity Cases Abridged (English).

Eq.Judg. Equity Judgments (by A'Beckett) New South Wales.

Eq.Rep. Equity Reports;—Gilbert's Equity Reports;—Harper's South Carolina Equity Reports;—The Equity Reports, published by Spottiswoode.

Erie (or Erie Co.L.J.). Erie County Law Journal, Pa.

Err. & App. Error and Appeals Reports, Upper Canada.

Ersk. Erskine's Institutes of the Law of Scotland;—Erskine's Principles of the Law of Scotland.

Ersk.Dec. Erskine's United States Circuit Court, etc., Decisions, in vol. 35 Georgia.

Ersk.Inst. Erskine's Institutes of the Law of Scotland.

Ersk.Prin. Erskine's Principles of the Law of Scotland.

Ersk.Speeches. Erskine's Speeches.

Erskine, Inst. Erskine's Institutes of the Law of Scotland.

Escriche. Escriche, Diccionario Razonado de Legislacion y Jurisprudencia.

Escriche, Dic.Leg. Escriche, Diccionario Razonado de Legislacion y Jurisprudencia.

Escriche, Dict. Escriche's Dictionary of Jurisprudence.

Esp. (or Esp.N.P.) Espinasse's English Nisi Prius Reports.

Esprit des Lois. Montesquieu, Esprit des Lois.

Eth.Nic. Aristotle, Nicomachean Ethics.

Euer. Euer, Eng.

Ev. Evidence.

Ev.Tr. Evans' Trial.

Ewell L.C. Ewell's Leading Cases on Infancy, etc.

Ex. English Exchequer Reports, Welsby, Hurlstone & Gordon.

Ex.C.R. Exchequer Court of Canada Reports.

Ex.D. (or Ex.Div.). Exchequer Division, English Law Reports.

Ex.Sess. Extra Session.

Exch. Exchequer;—Exchequer Reports (Welsby, Hurlstone, & Gordon);—English Law Reports, Exchequer;—English Exchequer Reports.

Exch.Can. Exchequer Reports, Canada.

Exch.Cas. Exchequer Cases (Legacy Duties, etc.), Scotland.

Exch.Div. Exchequer Division, English Law Reports.

Exch.Rep. Exchequer Reports.

Eyre. Eyre's Reports, English.

F

F. Federal Reporter;—Fitzherbert's Abridgment.

F.2d. Federal Reporter, Second Series.

F.Abr. Fitzherbert's Abridgment is commonly referred to by the other law writers by the title and number of the placita only, e. g. "coron, 30."

F.B.C. Fonblanque's Bankruptcy Cases.

F.B.R. Full Bench Rulings, Bengal.

F.B.R.N.W.P. Full Bench Rulings, Northwest Provinces, India.

F.C. Federal Cases.

F.C.C. Federal Communications Commission.

F.Ct.Sess. Fraser's Court of Sessions Cases, Scotland.

F.N.B. Fitzherbert's Natura Brevium.

F.P.C. Federal Power Commission.

F.R. Federal Register;—Federal Reporter.

F.R.D. Federal Rules Decisions.

F.S.A. Federal Statutes Annotated;—Florida Statutes Annotated.

F.Supp. Federal Supplement.

F.T.C. Federal Trade Commission.

F.& F. Foster & Finlason's English Nisi Prius Reports.

F.& Fitz. Falconer & Fitzherbert's English Election Cases.

F.& J.Bank.De Gex. Fisher & Jones' English Bankruptcy Reports.

F.& S. Fox and Smith's Irish King's Bench Reports.

Fairf. Fairfield, Me.

Fairfield. Fairfield's Reports, vols. 10–12 Maine.

Falc. Falconer's Scotch Court of Session Cases.

Falc.Marine Dict. Falconer's Marine Dictionary.

Falc.& F. (or Falc.& Fitz.). Falconer & Fitzherbert, Eng.

Fam.Cas.Cir.Ev. Famous Cases of Circumstantial Evidence, by Phillips.

Far. (or Farr.). Farresley (see Farresley).

Farresley. Farresley's Reports, vol. 7 Modern Reports;—Farresley's Cases in Holt's King's Bench Reports.

Faust. Faust's Compiled Laws, S.C.

Fay.L.J. Fayette Law Journal, Pa.

Fearne, Rem. Fearne on Contingent Remainders.

Fed. Federal Reporter.

Fed.B.A.J. Federal Bar Association Journal.

Fed.Ca. (or Cas.). Federal Cases.

Fed.Cas.No. Federal Case Number.

Fed.L.Q. Federal Law Quarterly (Indianapolis).

Fed.R. (or Rep.). Federal Reporter.

Fed.Reg. Federal Register.

Fed.Rules Civ.Proc. Federal Rules of Civil Procedure.

Fed.Rules Cr.Proc. Federal Rules of Criminal Procedure.

Fent.Imp.Judg. Fenton's Important Judgments, New Zealand.

Fent.N.Z. Fenton's New Zealand Reports.

Ferard, Fixt. Amos & Ferard on Fixtures.

Ferg.Cons. Fergusson's (Scotch) Consistorial Reports.

Fergusson. (Fergusson of) Kilgerran's Scotch Session Cases.

Fernald, Eng. Synonyms. Fernald's English Synonyms.

Ferriere. Ferriere's Dictionnaire de Droit et de Pratique.

Fessen, Pat. Fessenden on Patents.

Fett.Carr. Fetter's Treatise on Carriers of Passengers.

Feud.Lib. The Book of Feuds. See this dictionary, *s. v.* "Liber Feudorum."

Ff. Pandectæ (Juris Civilis).

Field, Corp. Field on Corporations.

Fin. Finch's English Chancery Reports;—Finlason (see Finl.).

Finch. English Chancery Reports *tempore* Finch.

Finch Ins.Dig. Finch's Insurance Digest.

Finch L.C. Finch's Land Cases.

Finch, Law. Finch, Sir Henry; a Discourse of Law, 1759.

Finl.L.C. Finlason's Leading Cases on Pleading.

Finl.Rep. Finlason's Report of the Gurney Case.

First pt.Edw.III. Part II of the Year Books.

First pt.H.VI. Part VII of the Year Books.

Fish. Fisher's United States Patent Cases;—Fisher's United States Prize Cases.

Fish.Cas. Fisher's Cases, United States District Courts.

Fish.Dig. Fisher's English Common Law Digest.

Fish.Mortg. Fisher on Mortgages.

Fish.Pat. (or Fish.Pat.Cas.). Fisher's United States Patent Cases.

Fish.Pat.Rep. Fisher's United States Patent Reports.

Fish.Prize (or Pr.Cas.). Fisher's United States Prize Cases.

Fisher (or Fish.Prize Cas.). Fisher's Prize Cases, U. S.

Fitz. Fitzherbert's Abridgment (see F. & Fitz.).

Fitz.Abridg. Fitzherbert's Abridgment.

Fitzg. Fitzgibbon's English King's Bench Reports.

Fitzh.Abr. Fitzherbert's Abridgment.

Fitzh.N.B. (or Nat.Brev.). Fitzherbert's New Natura Brevium.

Fitzh.N.Br. Fitzherbert's Natura Brevium, Eng.

Fl. Fleta;—Flanders (see Fland.).

Fl. & K. (or Fl. & Kel.). Flanagan & Kelly's Irish Rolls Court Reports.

Fla. Florida;—Florida Reports.

Fla.L.J. Florida Law Journal.

Fla.L.Rev. Florida Law Review.

Flan. & Kel. Flanagan & Kelly's Irish Rolls Court Reports.

Fleta. Fleta, Commentarius Juris Anglicani.

Flip. Flippin's United States Circuit Court Reports.

Flor. Florida;—Florida Reports.

Fogg. Fogg's Reports, vols. 32–37 New Hampshire.

Fol.P.L.Cas. Foley's Poor Law Cases.

Fonbl. Fonblanque's Equity;—Fonblanque on Medical Jurisprudence;—Fonblanque's New Reports, English Bankruptcy.

Fonbl.Eq. Fonblanque's Equity.

Fonbl.R. Fonblanque's English Cases (or New Reports) in Bankruptcy.

Foote & E.Incorp.Co. Foote and Everett's Law of Incorporated Companies Operating under Municipal Franchises.

For. Forrest's Exchequer Reports;—Forrester's Chancery Reports (Cases *tempore* Talbot).

For.Cas. & Op. Forsyth's Cases and Opinions.

For.de Laud. Fortescue's De Laudibus Legum Angliæ.

Forb. Forbes' Decisions in the Scotch Court of Session.

Forb.Inst. Forbes' Institutes of the Law of Scotland.

Forbes. Forbes, Eng.

Fordham L.Rev. Fordham Law Review.

Forman. Forman's Reports, Illinois.

Forr. Forrest's English Exchequer Reports;—Forrester's English Chancery Cases (commonly cited, Cases *tempore* Talbot).

Forrest. Forrest's Reports, English Exchequer.

Forrester. Forrester's Cases, Eng.

Fors.Cas. & Op. Forsyth's Cases and Opinions on Constitutional Law.

Fort. Fortescue's English King's Bench Reports.

Fortes. Fortescue's Reports, English Courts.

Fortes.de Laud. Fortescue, De Laudibus Legum Angliæ.

Fortesc. Fortescue, Eng.

Fortnightly L.J. Fortnightly Law Journal.

Forum. Forum (periodical). Baltimore and New York.

Foss, Judg. Foss' Judges of England.

Fost. Foster's English Crown Law or Crown Cases;—Foster's New Hampshire Reports;—Foster's Legal Chronicle Reports, Pennsylvania;—Foster's Reports, vols. 5, 6 and 8 Hawaii.

Fost.Cr.Law (or Fost.Crown Law). Foster's English Crown Law or Crown Cases.

Fost.Fed.Prac. Foster's Treatise on Pleading and Practice in Equity in Courts of United States.

Fost. on Sci.Fa. Foster on the Writ of Scire Facias.

Fost. & F. (or Fost. & Fin.). Foster and Finlason's English Nisi Prius Reports.

Foster. Foster's English Crown Law;—Legal Chronicle Reports (Pennsylvania), edited by Foster;—Foster's New Hampshire Reports.

Fount. Fountainhall's Decisions, Scotch Court of Session.

Fount.Dec. Fountainhall's Decisions, Scotland.

Fowl.L.Cas. Fowler's Leading Cases on Collieries.

Fox. Fox's Reports, English.

Fox Reg.Ca. Fox's Registration Cases.

Fox & S. (or Fox & Sm.). Fox & Smith's Irish King's Bench Reports.

Fr. Freeman's English King's Bench and Chancery Reports;—Fragment.

Fr.Ch. Freeman's English Chancery Reports;—Freeman's Mississippi Chancery Reports.

Fr.E.C. Fraser's Election Cases.

Fran.Max. Francis' Maxims of Equity.

Franc.Judg. Francillon's Judgments, County Courts.

France. France's Reports, vols. 3–11 Colorado.

Fras.Dom.Rel. Fraser on Personal and Domestic Relations, Scotland.

Fras.Elec.Cas. Fraser's English Election Cases.

Fraser. Fraser's English Cases of Controverted Elections.

Fraz. (or Fraz.Adm.). Frazer's Admiralty Cases, etc., Scotland.

Free. Freeman's English King's Bench Reports, vol. 1 Freeman's King's Bench Reports and vol. 2 Freeman's Chancery Reports. See also Freem.

Free.Ch. Freeman's English Chancery Reports;—Freeman's Mississippi Chancery Reports.

Freem. (Ill.). Freeman's Reports, Illinois.

Freem.C.C. Freeman's English Chancery Cases.

Freem.Compar.Politics. Freeman, Comparative Politics.

Freem.Judgm. Freeman on Judgments.

Freem.K.B. Freeman's English King's Bench Reports.

Fries Tr. Trial of John Fries (Treason).

Frith. Opinions Attorneys-General, pt. 2, vol. 21.

Full B.R. Full Bench Rulings, Bengal (or Northwestern Provinces).

Fuller. Fuller's Reports, vols. 59–105 Michigan.

Fulton. Fulton's Reports, Bengal.

G

G. King George, as 15 Geo. II;—Gale's English Exchequer Reports.

G.Coop. (or Cooper). G. Cooper's English Chancery.

G.Gr. G. Greene's Iowa Reports.

G.M.Dudl. G. M. Dudley's Georgia Reports.

G.O. General Orders, Court of Chancery, Ontario.

G. & D. Gale & Davidson's English Queen's Bench Reports.

G. & G. Goldsmith & Guthrie, Missouri.

G. & J. Gill & Johnson's Maryland Reports;—Glyn & Jameson's English Bankruptcy Reports.

G. & T. Gould & Tucker's Notes on Revised Statutes of United States.

Ga. Georgia;—Georgia Reports.

Ga.App. Georgia Appeals.

Ga.B.J. Georgia Bar Journal.

Ga.Dec. Georgia Decisions.

Ga.L.J. Georgia Law Journal.

Ga.L.Rep. Georgia Law Reporter.

Ga.L.Rev. Georgia Law Review.

Ga.Supp. Lester's Supplement, vol. 33 Georgia.

Gabb.Cr.Law. Gabbett's Criminal Law.

Gaius. Gaius' Institutes.

Gal. (or Gall.). Gallison's Reports, United States Circuit Courts.

Galb. & M. Galbraith & Meek's Reports, vol. 12 Florida.

Galbraith. Galbraith's Reports, vols. 9–12 Florida.

Gale. Gale's English Exchequer Reports.

Gale, Easem. Gale on Easements.

Gale's St. Gale's Statutes, Ill.

Gale & Dav. Gale & Davison's Queen's Bench Reports.

Gale & Whatley Easem. Gale and Whatley, afterwards Gale, on Easements.

Gall. Gallison's Reports, United States Circuit Courts.

Gall.Cr.Cas. Gallick's Reports (French Criminal Cases).

Gamb. & Barl. Gamble & Barlow's Digest, Irish.

Gantt Dig. Gantt's Digest Statutes, Arkansas.

Gard.N.Y.Rept. (or Rep.). Gardenier's New York Reporter.

Gardenhire. Gardenhire's Reports, vols. 14, 15 Missouri.

Gardn.P.C. Gardner Peerage Case, reported by Le Marchant.

Gaspar. Gaspar's Small Cause Court Reports, Bengal.

Gav. & H.Rev.St. Gavin and Hord's Revised Statutes, Ind.

Gayarré. Gayarré's Reports, vols. 25–28 Louisiana Annual.

Gaz.Bank. Gazette of Bankruptcy, London.

Gaz.Dig. Gazzam's Digest of Bankruptcy Decisions.

Gaz. & B.C.Rep. Gazette & Bankrupt Court Reporter, New York.

Gear, Landl. & T. Gear on Landlord and Tenant.

Geld. & M. Geldart & Maddock's English Chancery Reports, vol. 6 Maddock's Reports.

Geld. & Ox. Nova Scotia Decisions, by Geldert & Oxley.

Geld. & R. Geldert & Russell, Nova Scotia.

Geldart. Geldart & Maddock's English Chancery Reports, vol. 6 Maddock's Reports.

Gen.Abr.Cas.Eq. General Abridgment of Cases in Equity (Equity Cases Abridged).

Gen.Assem. General Assembly.

Gen.Dig. General Digest American and English Reports.

Gen.Dig.U.S. General Digest of the United States.

Gen.Laws. General Laws.

Gen.Ord. General Orders, Ontario Court of Chancery.

Gen.Ord.Ch. General Orders of the English High Court of Chancery.

Gen.R.R.Act. General Railroad Act.

Gen.St. General Statutes.

Geo. Georgia;—Georgia Reports;—King George (as 13 Geo. II.).

Geo.Coop. George Cooper's English Chancery Cases, time of Eldon.

Geo.Dec. Georgia Decisions.

Geo.Dig. George's Digest, Mississippi.

Geo.Wash.L.Rev. George Washington Law Review.

George. George's Reports, vols. 30–39 Mississippi.

George, Partn. George on Partnership.

Georgetown L.J. Georgetown Law Journal.

Gib.Cod. Gibson's Codex Juris Ecclesiastical Anglicani.

Gib.Dec. Gibson's Scottish Decisions.

Gibb.Sur. Gibbon's Surrogate, N.Y.

Gibbon. Gibbon on Nuisances.

Gibbon, Rom.Emp. Gibbon, History of the Decline and Fall of the Roman Empire.

Gibbs. Gibbs' Reports, vols. 2–4 Michigan.

Gibbs' Jud.Chr. Gibbs' Judicial Chronicle.

Gibs.Camd. Gibson's [edition of] Camden's Britannia.

Gibson. (Gibson of) Durie's Decisions, Scotch Court of Session.

Gif. (or Giff.). Giffard's English Vice-Chancellors' Reports.

Giff. & H. Giffard and Hemming's Reports, English Chancery.

Giffard. Giffard, Eng.

Gil. Gilfillan's Edition, vols. 1–20 Minnesota;—Gilman's Reports, vols. 6–10 Illinois;—Gilmer's Virginia Reports;—Gilbert's English Chancery Reports;—Gilbert's English Cases in Law and Equity.

Gil. & Fal. Gilmour & Falconer's Scotch Session Cases.

Gilb. Gilbert's Reports, English Chancery.

Gilb.C.P. (or Gilb.Com.Pl.). Gilbert's Common Pleas, Eng.

Gilb.Cas. Gilbert's English Cases in Law and Equity.

Gilb.Ch. Gilbert's English Chancery Reports.

Gilb.Com.Pl. Gilbert's Common Pleas.

Gilb.Eq. Gilbert's English Equity or Chancery Reports.

Gilb.Exch. Gilbert's Exchequer, Eng.

Gilb.Forum Rom. Gilbert's Forum Romanum.

Gilb.Rents. Gilbert's Treatise on Rents.

Gilb.Rep. Gilbert's English Chancery Reports.

Gilb.Repl. Gilbert on Replevin.

Gilb.Ten. Gilbert on Tenure.

Gilb.Uses. Gilbert on Uses and Trusts.

Gilbert, Ev. Gilbert's Law of Evidence.

Gilbert, Tenures. Gilbert on Tenures.

Gilbert, Uses, by Sugd. Gilbert's Uses and Trusts by Sugden.

Gild. Gildersleeve's Reports, vols. 1–8 New Mexico.

Gilfillan. Gilfillan's Edition of Minnesota Reports.

Gill. Gill's Maryland Reports.

Gill Pol.Rep. Gill's Police Court Reports, Boston, Massachusetts.

Gill. & J. (Md.). Gill & Johnson's Reports, Maryland.

Gill & Johns. Gill & Johnson's Maryland Reports.

Gillet, Cr.Law. Gillett's Treatise on Criminal Law and Procedure in Criminal Cases.

Gilm. Gilman's Reports, vols. 6–10 Illinois;—Gilmer's Reports, Virginia;—Gilmour's Reports, Scotch Court of Session.

Gilm.Dig. Gilman's Digest, Illinois and Indiana.

Gilm. & Falc. Gilmour & Falconer's Reports, Scotch Court of Session.

Gilman. Gilman, Ill.

Gilmer. Gilmer, Va.

Gilp. Gilpin's United States District Court Reports.

Gilp.Opin. Gilpin's Opinions of the United States Attorneys-General.

Gl. & J. Glyn & Jameson's English Bankruptcy Reports.

Glan.lib. Glanville, De Legibus et Consuetudinibus Angliæ.

Glanv. (or Glanvil.). Glanville, De Legibus et Consuetudinibus Angliæ.

Glanv.El.Cas. Glanville's English Election Cases.

Glas. (or Glasc.). Glascock's Reports in all the Courts of Ireland.

Glenn. Glenn's Reports, vols. 16–18 Louisiana Annual.

Glov.Mun.Corp. Glover on Municipal Corporations.

Glyn & J. (or Glyn & Jam.). Glyn & Jameson English Reports, English Bankruptcy.

Go. Goebel's Probate Court Cases.

Godb. Godbolt's English King's Bench Reports.

Godd.Easem. Goddard on Easements.

Godo. Godolphin's Abridgment of Ecclesiastical Law;—Godolphin on Admiralty Jurisdiction;—Godolphin's Orphan's Legacy;—Godolphin's Repertorium Canonicum.

Godol.Ecc.Law. Godolphin's Abridgment of Ecclesiastical Law.

Goeb. Goebel's Probate Court Cases.

Gold. (or Goldes.). Goldesborough's or Gouldsborough's English King's Bench Reports.

Gold. & G. Goldsmith & Guthrie's Reports, vols. 36–67 Missouri Appeals.

Good.Pat. Goodeve's Abstract of Patent Cases.

Good. & Wood. Full Bench Rulings, Bengal, edited by Goodeve & Woodman.

Gordon. Gordon's Reports, vols. 24–26 Colorado and vols. 10–13 Colorado Appeals.

Gosf. Gosford's Manuscript Reports, Scotch Court of Session.

Gould. Gouldsborough's English King's Bench Reports.

Gould, Pl. Gould on Pleading.

Gould, Wat. Gould on Waters.

Gould's Dig. Gould's Digest of Laws, Ark.

Gould & T. Gould & Tucker's Notes on Revised Statutes of United States.

Gouldsb. Gouldsborough, Eng.

Gow (or Gow N.P.). Gow's English Nisi Prius Cases.

Gr. Grant's Cases, Pennsylvania;—Green's New Jersey Reports;—Greenleaf's Maine Reports;—Grant's Cases, Canada;—Grant's Chancery Reports, Ontario.

Gr.Ca. Grant's Cases.

Gr.Eq. (or Ch.). (H. W.) Green's New Jersey Equity Reports;—Gresley's Equity Evidence.

Gra. Grant (see Grant);—Graham's Reports, vols. 98–107 Georgia.

Grah. & W.New Trials. Graham and Waterman on New Trials.

Grand Cou. Grand Coutumier de Normandie.

Granger. Granger's Reports, vols. 22–23 Ohio State.

Grant. Grant's Upper Canada Chancery Reports;—Grant's Pennsylvania Cases;—(Grant of) Elchies' Scotch Session Cases;—Grant's Jamaica Reports.

Grant, Bank. Grant on Banking.

Grant Cas. Grant's Pennsylvania Cases.

Grant Ch. Grant's Upper Canada Chancery Reports.

Grant, Corp. Grant on Corporations.

Grant E. & A. Grant's Error and Appeal Reports, Ontario.

Grant Err. & App. Grant's Error & Appeal, Upper Canada.

Grant, Jamaica. Grant's Jamaica Reports.

Grant Pa. Grant's Pennsylvania Cases.

Grant U.C. Grant's Upper Canada Chancery Reports.

Grat. (or Gratt.). Grattan's Virginia Reports.

Grav. de Jur.Nat.Gent. Gravina, De Jure Naturale Gentium, etc.

Gravin. Gravina, Originum Juris Civilis.

Gray. Gray's Massachusetts Reports;—Gray's Reports, vols. 112–122 North Carolina.

Green. Green's New Jersey Law or Equity Reports;—Green's Reports, vols. 11–17 Rhode Island;—G. Greene's Iowa Reports;—Greenleaf's Reports, vols. 1–9 Maine;—Green's Reports, vol. 1 Oklahoma.

Green Bag. Green Bag, A Legal Journal, Boston.

Green (C.E.). C. E. Green's Chancery Reports, New Jersey.

Green Ch. H. W. Green's New Jersey Chancery Reports, vols. 2–4 New Jersey Equity.

Green Cr. Green's Criminal Law, Eng.

Green, Cr.Law R. (or Green Cr.L.Rep.). Green's Criminal Law Reports.

Green, H.W. H. W. Green, N.J.

Green, J.S. J. S. Green, N.J.

Green L. (or N.J.). J. S. Green's Law Reports, vols. 13–15 New Jersey Law.

Green.Ov.Cas. Greenleaf's Overruled Cases.

Green Sc.Tr. Green's Scottish Trials for Treason.

Greene. G. Greene's Iowa Reports;—C. E. Green's New Jersey Equity Reports, vols. 16–27 New Jersey Equity;—Greene's Reports, vol. 7 New York Annotated Cases.

Greene. G. Greene's Iowa Reports.

Greenh.Pub.Pol. Greenhood's Doctrine of Public Policy in the Law of Contracts.

Greenl. Greenleaf's Reports, vols. 1–9 Maine.

Greenl.Cruise (or Greenl.Cruise, Real Prop.). Greenleaf's Edition of Cruise's Digest of Real Property.

Greenl.Ev. Greenleaf on Evidence.

Greenl.Ov.Cas. Greenleaf's Overruled Cases.

Green's Brice, Ultra Vires. Green's Edition of Brice's Ultra Vires.

Gren. Grenier's Ceylon Reports.

Gres.Eq.Ev. Gresley's Equity Evidence.

Grif.L.Reg. Griffith's Law Register, Burlington, New Jersey.

Grif.P.R.Cas. Griffith's English Poor Rate Cases.

Griffith. Griffith's Reports, vols. 1–5 Indiana Appeals and vols. 117–132 Indiana.

Grisw. Griswold's Reports, vols. 14–19 Ohio.

Gro. Grotius, De Jure Belli et Pacis.

Gro. de J.B. Grotius, De Jure Belli et Pacis.

Gross, St. Gross' Illinois Compiled Laws, or Statutes.

Grot. de Jur.B. Grotius, De Jure Belli et Pacis.

Grotius. Grotius' Latin Law.

Guizot, Hist.Civilization. Guizot, General History of Civilization in Europe.

Guizot, Rep.Govt. Guizot, History of Representative Government.

Gunby's Dec. Gunby's Decisions, La.

Gundry. Gundry Manuscript, Lincoln's Inn Library.

Guth.Sh.Cas. Guthrie's Sheriff Court Cases, Scotland.

Guthrie. Guthrie's Reports, vols. 33–83 Missouri Appeals.

Guy, Med.Jur. Guy, Medical Jurisprudence.

Guyot, Inst.Feod. Guyot, Institutes Feodales.

Gwill.T.Cas. (or Gwil.Ti.Cas.). Gwillim's Tithe Cases, Eng.

H

H. Howard's United States Supreme Court Reports;—Hill's New York Reports.

H.Bl. Henry Blackstone's English Common Pleas Reports.

H.C.R. High Court Reports, India.

H.C.R.N.W.P. High Court Reports, Northwest Provinces, India.

H.E.C. Hodgin's Election Cases, Ontario.

H.L. (or H.L.Cas.). House of Lords Cases.

H.L.Rep. English House of Lords Reports.

H.P.C. Hale's Pleas of the Crown;—Hawkins' Pleas of the Crown.

H.W.Gr. H. W. Green's New Jersey Equity Reports.

H. & B. Hudson & Brooke's Irish King's Bench Reports.

H. & C. Hurlstone & Coltman's English Exchequer Reports.

H. & D. Lalor's Supplement to Hill & Denio's New York Reports.

H. & G. Harris & Gill's Maryland Reports;—Hurlstone & Gordon's English Reports.

H. & H. Horn & Hurlstone's English Exchequer Reports;—Harrison & Hodgin's Municipal Reports, Upper Canada.

H. & J. Harris & Johnson's Maryland Reports;—Hayes & Jones' Exchequer Reports, Ireland.

H. & M. Hening & Munford's Virginia Reports;—Hemming & Miller's English Vice-Chancellors' Reports.

H. & M.Ch. Hemming & Miller's English Vice-Chancellors' Reports.

H. & McH. Harris & McHenry's Maryland Reports.

H. & N. Hurlstone & Norman's English Exchequer Reports.

H. & P. Hopwood & Philbrick's English Election Cases.

H. & R. Harrison & Rutherford's English Common Pleas Reports.

H. & S. Harris & Simrall, Mississippi.

H. & T. Hall & Twell's English Chancery Reports.

H. & T.Self-Def. Horrigan & Thompson's Cases on the Law of Self-Defense.

H. & W. Harrison & Wollaston's English King's Bench Reports;—Hurlstone & Walmsley's English Exchequer Reports.

Ha. Hare's Chancery Reports;—Hall;—Haggard.

Ha. & Tw. Hall & Twell's English Chancery Reports.

Had. Haddington;—Hadley's Reports, vols. 45–48 New Hampshire.

Hadd. Haddington, Eng.

Haddington. Haddington's Manuscript Reports, Scotch Court of Session.

Hadl. Hadley's Reports, vols. 45–48 New Hampshire.

Hadl.Rom.Law. Hadley's Introduction to the Roman Law.

Hadley. Hadley's Reports, vols. 45–48 New Hampshire.

Hag. (or Hagg.) Adm. Haggard's English Admiralty Reports.

Hag. (or Hagg.) Con. Haggard's English Consistory Reports.

Hag. (or Hagg.) Ecc. Haggard's English Ecclesiastical Reports.

Hagan. Hagan's Reports, vols. 1–2 Utah.

Hagans. Hagans' Reports, vols. 1–5 West Virginia.

Hagg. See Hag.

Hagg.Adm. Haggard's English Admiralty Reports.

Hagg.Cons. (or Hagg.Consist.). Haggard's English Consistory Reports.

Hagg.Ecc. Haggard's English Ecclesiastical Reports.

Hagn. & Mill. Hagner & Miller's Reports, vol. 2 Maryland Chancery.

Hailes (or Hailes Dec.). Hailes' Decisions, Scotch Court of Sessions.

Hal.Law. Halsted's New Jersey Law Reports.

Halc.Min.Cas. Halcomb's Mining Cases, London, 1826.

Hale. Hale's Reports, vols. 33–37 California;—Hale's Common Law, Eng.

Hale, Anal. Hale's Analysis of the Law.

Hale C.L. (or Com.Law). Hale's History of the Common Law.

Hale, De Jure Mar. Hale, De Jure Maris.

Hale Ecc. Hale's Ecclesiastical Reports, English.

Hale, Hist.Eng.Law. Hale's History of the English Law.

Hale P.C. Hale's Pleas of the Crown.

Hale Prec. Hale's Precedents in (Ecclesiastical) Criminal Cases.

Hale, Torts. Hale on Torts.

Halk. Halkerston's Compendium of Scotch Faculty Decisions;—Halkerston's Digest of the Scotch Marriage Law;—Halkerston's Latin Maxims.

Halk.Comp. Halkerston's Compendium of Scotch Faculty Decisions.

Halk.Lat.Max. Halkerston's Latin Maxims.

Hall. Hall's New York Superior Court Reports;—Hall's Reports, vols. 56, 57 New Hampshire;—Hallett's Reports, vols. 1, 2 Colorado.

Hall.Const.Hist. Hallam's Constitutional History of England.

Hall, Émerig.Mar.Loans. Hall, Essay on Maritime Loans from the French of Émerigon.

Hall, Int.Law. Hall on International Law.

Hall, Marit.Loans. Hall, Essay on Maritime Loans from the French of Émerigon.

Hall, Mex.Law. Hall, Laws of Mexico Relating to Real Property, etc.

Hall. Middle Ages. Hallam's Middle Ages.

Hall, Profits à Prendre. Hall, Treatise on the Law Relating to Profits à Prendre, etc.

Hall's Am.L.J. Hall's American Law Journal.

Hall & T. (or Hall & Tw.). Hall & Twells, Eng.

Hallam, Mid.Ages. Hallam's Middle Ages.

Halleck, Int.Law. Halleck's International Law.

Hallett. Hallett's Reports, vols. 1, 2 Colorado.

Hallifax, Anal. (or Civil Law). Hallifax's Analysis of the Civil Law.

Hals. Halsted's New Jersey Law Reports.

Hals.Ch. (or Eq.). Halsted's New Jersey Equity Reports.

Halsbury L.Eng. Halsbury's Law of England.

Halst. Halsted, N. J.

Halst.Ch. Halsted's Chancery, N.J.

Ham. Hammond's Nisi Prius;—Hammond's Reports, vols. 1–9 Ohio.

Ham.A. & O. Hammerton, Allen & Otter, English Magistrates' Cases, vol. 3 New Sessions Cases.

Ham.Cont. Hammon on Contracts.

Ham.N.P. Hammond's Nisi Prius.

Ham.Parties. Hammond on Parties to Action.

Hamel, Cust. Hamel's Laws of the Customs.

Hamilton. (Hamilton of) Haddington's Manuscript Cases, Scotch Court of Session;—Hamilton, American Negligence Cases.

Hamlin. Hamlin's Reports, vols. 81–93 Maine.

Hammond. Hammond's Reports, vols. 1–9 Ohio;—Hammond's Reports, vols. 36–45 Georgia.

Hammond & Jackson. Hammond & Jackson's Reports, vol. 45 Georgia.

Han. Handy's Ohio Reports.

Han. (or Han. [N.B.]). Hannay's Reports, vols. 12, 13 New Brunswick.

Hand. Hand's Reports, vols. 40–45 New York;—Handy's Ohio Reports.

Handy. Handy's Ohio Reports.

Hanes. Hanes' English Chancery.

Hanmer. Lord Kenyon's Notes (English King's Bench Reports), edited by Hanmer.

Hann. Hannay's Reports, vols. 12, 13 New Brunswick.

Hansb. Hansbrough's Reports, vols. 76–90 Virginia.

Har. Harmonized;—Harrison (see Harr.);—Harrington's Chancery Reports, Michigan.

Har. (Del.). Harrington's Reports, vols. 1–5 Delaware.

Har.St.Tr. Hargrave's State Trials.

Har. & G. (or Har. & Gill). Harris & Gill's Maryland Reports.

Har. & J. (Md.). Harris & Johnson's Maryland Reports.

Har. & John. Harris & Johnson's Maryland Reports.

Har. & McH. Harris & McHenry's Maryland Reports.

Har. & Ruth. Harrison & Rutherford's English Common Pleas Reports.

Har. & Woll. Harrison & Wollaston's English King's Bench Reports.

Harc. Harcarse's Decisions, Scotch Court of Session.

Hard. (or Hardin). Hardin's Kentucky Reports.

Hard. (or Hardres). Hardres' English Exchequer Reports.

Hardes. Hardesty, Delaware Term Reports.

Hardr. (or Hardres). Hardres' English Exchequer Reports.

Hardw. Cases *tempore* Hardwicke, by Ridgeway;—Cases *tempore* Hardwicke, by Lee.

Hare. Hare's English Vice-Chancellors' Reports.

Hare, Const.Law. Hare's American Constitutional Law.

Hare & Wal.L.C. American Leading Cases, edited by Hare & Wallace.

Harg. Hargrave's State Trials;—Hargrove's Reports, vols. 68–75 North Carolina.

Harg.Co.Litt. Hargrave's Notes to Coke on Littleton.

Harg.Law Tracts. Hargrave's Law Tracts.

Harg.St.Tr. (or State Tr.). Hargrave's State Trials.

Hargrave & Butler's Notes on Co.Litt. Hargrave and Butler's Notes on Coke on Littleton.

Hargrove. Hargrove's Reports, vols. 68–75 North Carolina.

Harm. Harmon's Reports, vols. 13–15 California;—Harmon's Upper Canada Common Pleas Reports.

Harp. Harper's South Carolina Law Reports.

Harp.Con.Cas. Harper's Conspiracy Cases, Maryland.

Harp.Eq. Harper's Equity Reports, South Carolina.

Harp.L. (or S.C.). Harper's Law Reports, South Carolina.

Harr. Harrison's Reports, New Jersey;—Harrington's Reports, Delaware;—Harrington's Chancery Reports, Michigan;—Harris' Reports, vols. 13–24 Pennsylvania;—Harrison's Reports, vols. 15–17 and 23–29 Indiana.

Harr. (Mich.). Harrington's Michigan Chancery Reports.

Harr. (N.J.). Harrison's Reports, vols. 16–19 New Jersey Law.

Harr.Ch. Harrison's Chancery, Eng.

Harr.Con.La.R. Harrison's Condensed Louisiana Reports.

Harr.Dig. Harrison's Digest, English.

Harr. & G. Harris & Gill's Maryland Reports.

Harr. & H. (or Harr. & Hodg.). Harrison & Hodgin's Upper Canada Municipal Reports.

Harr. & J. Harris & Johnson's Maryland Reports.

Harr. & McH. Harris & McHenry's Maryland Reports.

Harr. & R. (or Harr. & Ruth.). Harrison & Rutherford's English Common Pleas Reports.

Harr. & Sim. Harris & Simrall's Reports, vols. 49–52 Mississippi.

Harr. & W. (or Harr. & Woll.). Harrison & Wollaston's English King's Bench Reports.

Harring. Harrington's Delaware Reports;—Harrington's Michigan Chancery Reports.

Harris. Harris' Reports, vols. 13–24 Pennsylvania.

Harris Dig. Harris' Digest, Georgia.

Harris & Simrall. Harris & Simrall's Reports, vols. 49–52 Mississippi.

Harrison. Harrison's Reports, vols. 15–17 and 23–29 Indiana.

Harrison, Ch. Harrison's Chancery Practice.

Hart. Hartley's Reports, vols. 4–10 Texas;—Hartley's Digest of Texas Laws.

Hart.Dig. Hartley's Digest of Laws, Tex.

Hartley. Hartley's Reports, vols. 4–10 Texas.

Hartley & Hartley. Hartley & Hartley's Reports, vols. 11–21 Texas.

Harv.L.Rev. Harvard Law Review.

Hasb. Hasbrouck's Reports, Idaho.

Hask. Haskell's United States Circuit Court Reports.

Hast. Hastings' Reports, vols. 69–70 Maine.

Hats. Hatsell's Parliamentary Precedents.

Hav.Ch.Rep. Haviland's Chancery Reports, Prince Edward Island.

Hav.P.E.I. Haviland's Reports, Prince Edward Island.

Havil. Haviland, Pr.Edw.Isl.

Haw. Hawkins (see Hawk.);—Hawaiian Reports;—Hawley's Reports, vols. 10–20 Nevada.

Haw.Cr.Rep. Hawley's American Criminal Reports.

Haw.W.C. Hawes' Will Case.

Hawaii (or Hawaiian Rep.). Hawaii (Sandwich Islands) Reports.

Hawaii.Fed. Hawaiian Federal.

Hawes, Jur. Hawes on Jurisdiction of Courts.

Hawk. (or Hawk.P.C. [or Pl.Cr.]). Hawkins' Pleas of the Crown.

Hawk.Co.Litt. Hawkins' Coke upon Littleton.

Hawk.Wills. Hawkins' Construction of Wills.

Hawkins. Hawkins' Reports, vols. 19–24 Louisiana Annual.

Hawks. Hawks' North Carolina Reports.

Hawl.Cr.R. Hawley's American Criminal Reports.

Hawley. Hawley's Reports, vols. 10–20 Nevada.

Hay. Haywood's North Carolina Reports;—Haywood's Tennessee Reports (Haywood's Reports are sometimes referred to as though numbered consecutively from North Carolina through Tennessee);—Hayes' Irish Exchequer Reports. See also Hayes;—Hayes' Reports, Calcutta;—Hay's Scotch Decisions.

Hay Acc. (or Dec.). Hay's Decisions on Accidents and Negligence.

Hay.Exch. Hayes' Irish Exchequer Reports.

Hay P.L. Hay's Poor Law Decisions.

Hay. & H. Hayward & Hazelton's United States Circuit Court Reports.

Hay. & Haz. Hayward & Hazelton, Circuit Court, District of Columbia.

Hay. & J. Hayes & Jones, Irish.

Hay & M. (or Marr.). Hay & Marriott's Admiralty Reports (usually cited, Marriott's Reports).

Hayes (or Hayes Exch.). Hayes' Irish Exchequer Reports.

Hayes, Conv. Hayes on Conveyancing.

Hayes & J. (or Hayes & Jo. [or Jon.]). Hayes & Jones' Irish Exchequer Reports.

Hayn.Lead.Cas. Haynes' Students' Leading Cases.

Haynes, Eq. Haynes' Outlines of Equity.

Hayw. Haywood's North Carolina Reports;—Haywood's Tennessee Reports (see Hay.).

Hayw.L.R. Hayward's Law Register, Boston.

Hayw. & H. Hayward & Hazelton's United States Circuit Court Reports.

Haz.Reg. (or Haz.Pa.Reg.). Hazard's Register, Pa.

Haz.U.S.Reg. Hazard's United States Register.

Head. Head's Tennessee Reports.

Heard's Shortt, Extr.Rem. Heard's Edition of Shortt on Extraordinary Legal Remedies.

Heath. Heath's Reports, vols. 36–40 Maine.

Heck.Cas. Hecker's Cases on Warranty.

Hedges. Hedges' Reports, vols. 2–6 Montana.

Heinecc.Ant.Rom. Heineccius (J. G.) Antiquitatum Romanarum (Roman Antiquities).

Heinecc. de Camb. Heineccius (J. G.) Elementa Juris Cambialis.

Heinecc.Elem. Heineccius (J. G.) Elementa Juris Civilis (Elements of the Civil Law.)

Heisk. Heiskell's Tennessee Reports.

Helm. Helm's Reports, vols. 2–9 Nevada.

Hem. Hempstead, United States;—Hemmingway, Mississippi.

Hem. & M. Hemming & Miller's English Vice-Chancellors' Reports.

Hemp. (or Hempst.). Hempstead's United States Circuit Court Reports.

Hen. King Henry, as 8 Hen. VI.

Hen.Bl. Henry Blackstone's English Common Pleas Reports.

Hen.Man.Cas. Henry's Manumission Cases.

Hen.St. Hening's Statutes, Va.

Hen. & M. (Va.). Hening & Munford's Virginia Reports.

Hen. & Mun. Hening & Munford's Virginia Reports.

Hepb. Hepburn's Reports, vols. 3, 4 California;—Hepburn's Reports, vol. 13 Pennsylvania.

Herm.Estop. Herman's Law of Estoppel.

Herm.Ex'ns. Herman's Law of Executions.

Het. (or Hetl. or Het.C.P.). Hetley's Common Pleas, Eng.

Heyw.Ca. Heywood's Table of Cases, Georgia.

Hibb. Hibbard's Reports, vol. 20 Opinions Attorneys-General;—Hibbard's Reports, vol. 67 New Hampshire.

High Ct. High Court Reports, Northwest Provinces of India.

High, Extr.Leg.Rem. High on Extraordinary Legal Remedies.

High, Inj. High on Injunctions.

High, Rec. High on Receivers.

Hight. Hight's Reports, vols. 57–58 Iowa.

Hil.Abr. Hilliard's American Law.

Hil.T. Hilary Term, Eng.

Hil.Term 4, Will. IV. Hilary Term 4, William IV.

Hil.Torts. Hilliard on the Law of Torts.

Hill. Hill's New York Reports;—Hill's Law Reports, South Carolina.

Hill.Am.Law. Hilliard's American Law.

Hill.Cont. Hilliard on Contracts.

Hil.Elem.Law. Hilliard's Elements of Law.

Hill Eq. (or Ch.). Hill's Equity, South Carolina Reports.

Hill, Law. Hill's Law, S.C.

Hill.Mortg. Hilliard's Law of Mortgages.

Hill N.Y. Hill's New York Reports.

Hill.New Trials. Hilliard on New Trials.

Hill.Real Prop. Hilliard on Real Property.

Hill S.C. Hill's South Carolina Reports (Law or Equity).

Hill's Ann.Codes & Laws. Hill's Annotated Codes and General Laws, Or.

Hill's Ann.St. & Codes. Hill's Annotated General Statutes and Codes, Wash.

Hill's Code. Hill's Annotated Codes and General Laws, Or.;—Hill's Annotated General Statutes and Codes, Wash.

Hill & Den. Hill & Denio, New York.

Hill & D.Supp. (or Hill & Den.Supp.). Lalor's Supplement to Hill & Denio's Reports, N.Y.

Hilliard, R.P. Hilliard on Real Property.

Hillyer. Hillyer's Reports, vols. 20–22 California.

Hilt. Hilton's New York Common Pleas Reports.

Hinde Ch.Pr. Hinde, Modern Practice of the High Court of Chancery.

Hines. Hines' Reports, vols. 83–96 Kentucky.

Hittell's Laws. Hittell's General Laws, Cal.

Ho.Lords Cas. House of Lords Cases (Clark's).

Hob. Hobart's English King's Bench Reports.

Hodg. Hodges' English Common Pleas Reports.

Hodg.Can.Elec.Cas. Hodgin's Canada Election Cases.

Hodg.El. Hodgins' Election, Upper Canada.

Hodge, Presb.Law. Hodge on Presbyterian Law.

Hodges. Hodges, Eng.

Hoff. Hoffman's Land Cases, United States District Court;—Hoffman's New York Chancery Reports.

Hoff.Ch. Hoffman's New York Chancery Reports.

Hoff.Dec. Hoffman's Decisions.

Hoff.Land (or Hoff.L.Cas.). Hoffman's Land Cases, United States District Court.

Hoff.Lead.Cas. Hoffman's Leading Cases on Commercial Law.

Hoff.Mast. Hoffman's Master in Chancery.

Hoff.N.Y. (or Hoffm.Ch.). Hoffman's New York Chancery Reports.

Hoff.Op. Hoffman's Opinions.

Hog. Hogan's Irish Rolls Court Reports;—(Hogan of) Harcarse's Scotch Session Cases.

Hog.St.Tr. Hogan's State Trials, Pennsylvania.

Hogue. Hogue's Reports, vols. 1–4 Florida.

Holc.L.Cas. Holcombe's Leading Cases of Commercial Law.

Holl.Jur. Holland's Elements of Jurisprudence.

Hollinshead. Hollinshead's Reports, vol. 1 Minnesota.

Holm. (or Holmes). Holmes' United States Circuit Court Reports;—Holmes' Reports, vols. 15–17 Oregon.

Holt. Holt's English King's Bench Reports;—Holt's English Nisi Prius Reports;—Holt's English Equity Reports.

Holt Adm.Cas. Holt's English Admiralty Cases (Rule of the Road).

Holt Eq. Holt's English Equity Reports.

Holt K.B. Holt's English King's Bench Reports.

Holt N.P. Holt's English Nisi Prius Reports.

Holt R. of R. Holt's Rule of the Road Cases.

Holt, Shipp. Holt on Shipping.

Holthouse (or Holthouse, Law Dict.). Holthouse's Law Dictionary.

Holtz.Enc. Holtzendorff. Encyclopädie der Rechtswissenschaft. (Encyclopedia of Jurisprudence.)

Home (or Home H.Dec.). Home's Manuscript Decisions, Scotch Court of Session. See also Kames.

Hooker. Hooker's Reports, vols. 25–62 Connecticut.

Hoon. Hoonahan's Sind Reports, India.

Hop. & C. Hopwood & Coltman's English Registration Appeal Cases.

Hop. & Ph. Hopwood & Philbrick's English Registration Appeal Cases.

Hope. Hope (of Kerse) Manuscript Decisions, Scotch Court of Session.

Hope Dec. Hope's Decisions, Scotland.

Hopk.Adm. (or Judg.). Hopkinson's Pennsylvania Admiralty Judgments.

Hopk.Adm.Dec. Admiralty Decisions of Hopkinson in Gilpin's Reports.

Hopk.Ch. Hopkins' New York Chancery Reports.

Hopk.Dec. Hopkins' Decisions, Pa.

Hopk.Wks. Hopkinson's Works, Pa.

Hopw. & C. (or Hopw. & Colt.). Hopwood & Coltman's English Registration Appeal Cases.

Hopw. & P. (or Hopw. & Phil.). Hopwood & Philbrick's English Registration Appeal Cases.

Hor. & Th.Cas. Horrigan & Thompson's Cases on Self-Defense.

Horn & H. Horn & Hurlstone's English Exchequer Reports.

Horne, M.J. Horne's Mirror of Justice.

Horner. Horner's Reports, vols. 11–23 South Dakota.

Horner's Ann.St. Horner's Annotated Revised Statutes, Ind.

Horner's Rev.St. Horner's Annotated Revised Statutes, Ind.

Horr & B.Mun.Ord. Horr and Bemis' Treatise on Municipal Police Ordinances.

Horr. & Th. (or Horr. & T.Cas.Self-Def.). Horrigan and Thompson's Cases on Self-Defense.

Horw.Y.B. Horwood's Year Books of Edward I.

Hosea. Hosea, Ohio.

Hoskins. Hoskins' Reports, vol. 2 North Dakota.

Hough C.-M.Cas. Hough's Court-Martial Case Book, London, 1821.

Houghton. Houghton's Reports, vol. 97 Alabama.

Hous. Houston's Delaware Reports.

House of L. House of Lords Cases.

Houst. Houston's Delaware Reports.

Houst.Cr.Cas. Houston's Delaware Criminal Cases.

Hov. Hovenden on Frauds;—Hovenden's Supplement to Vesey, Jr.'s, English Chancery Reports.

Hov.Sup. Hovenden's Supplement to Vesey, Jr.'s, English Chancery Reports.

Hoved. Hoveden, Chronica.

How. Howard's United States Supreme Court Reports;—Howard's Mississippi Reports;—Howard's New York Practice Reports;—Howell's Reports, vols. 22–23 Nevada.

How. (Miss.). Howard's Mississippi Reports.

How.Ann.St. Howell's Annotated Statutes, Mich.

How.App. (or How.App.Cas.). Howard's Appeal Cases, N.Y.

How.Cas. Howard's New York Court of Appeals Cases;—Howard's Popery Cases.

How.Ch.—Howard's Chancery, Ireland.

How.Cr.Tr. Howison's Criminal Trials, Virginia.

How.Eq.Exch. Howard's Equity Exchequer.

How.L.Rev. Howard Law Review.

How.N.S. Howard's New York Practice Reports, New Series.

How.Pr. Howard's New York Practice Reports.

How.Pr.N.S. (or How.Prac.,N.S.). Howard's Practice, New Series, N.Y.

How.Prac. (N.Y.). Howard's New York Practice Reports.

How.S.C. (or U.S.), Howard's United States Supreme Court Reports.

How.St. Howell's Annotated Statutes, Mich.

How.St.Tr. (or State Tr.). Howell's English State Trials.

How. & Beat. Howell & Beatty's Reports, vol. 22 Nevada.

How. & H.St. Howard and Hutchinson's Statutes, Miss.

How. & Nor. Howell & Norcross' Reports, vols. 23, 24 Nevada.

Howell N.P. Howell's Nisi Prius Reports, Michigan.

Howell, St.Tr. Howell's English State Trials.

Hu. Hughes' United States Circuit Court Reports;—Hughes' Kentucky Reports.

Hub.Leg.Direc. Hubbell's Legal Directory.

Hub.Præl.J.C. Huber, Prælectiones Juris Civilis.

Hubb.Succ. Hubback's Evidence of Succession.

Hubbard. Hubbard's Reports, vols. 45–51 Maine.

Hud. & B. (or Hud. & Br.). Hudson & Brooke's Irish King's Bench Reports.

Hugh. Hughes' United States Circuit Court Reports;—Hughes' Kentucky Reports.

Hugh.(Ky.). Hughes' Kentucky Reports.

Hughes. Hughes' United States Circuit Court Reports.

Hughes Fed.Prac. Hughes Federal Practice.

Hugo, Hist. du Droit Rom. Hugo, Histoire du Droit Romain.

Hum. Humphrey's Tennessee Reports.

Hume. Hume's Scotch Session Cases.

Hume, Hist.Eng. Hume's History of England.

Humph. (or Humph. [Tenn.]). Humphrey's Tennessee Reports.

Hun. Hun's New York Supreme Court Reports, also Appellate Division Supreme Court, New York.

Hunt, Bound. Hunt's Law of Boundaries and Fences.

Hunt Cas. Hunt's Annuity Cases.

Hunt, Eq. Hunt's Suit in Equity.

Hunter, Rom.Law. Hunter on Roman Law.

Hunter, Suit Eq. Hunter's Proceeding in a Suit in Equity.

Hur. Hurlstone (see Hurl.).

Hurd's Rev.St. Hurd's Revised Statutes, Ill.

Hurl. & C. (or Colt.). Hurlstone & Coltman's English Exchequer Reports.

Hurl.Bonds. Hurlstone on Bonds.

Hurl. & G. (or Hurl. & Gord.). Hurlstone and Gordon's Reports, 10, 11, English Exchequer Reports.

Hurl. & N. (or Nor.). Hurlstone & Norman's English Exchequer Reports.

Hurl. & W. (or Hurl. & Walm.). Hurlstone & Walmsley's English Exchequer Reports.

Hut. Hutton's English Common Pleas Reports.

Hutch. Hutcheson's Reports, vols. 81–84 Alabama.

Hutch.Carr. Hutchinson on Carriers.

Hutch.Code. Hutchinson's Code, Miss.

Hutch.Dig.St. Hutchinson's Code, Miss.

Hutt. Hutton's English Common Pleas Reports.

Hyde. Hyde's Reports, Bengal.

I

I. Idaho;—Illinois;—Indiana;—Iowa;—Irish (see Ir.).

I.C.A. Iowa Code Annotated.

I.C.C. Interstate Commerce Commission.

I.C.L.R. Irish Common Law Reports.

I.C.R. Irish Chancery Reports;—Irish Circuit Reports.

I.E.R. Irish Equity Reports.

I.J.Cas. Irvine's Justiciary Cases, Scotland.

I.R. Irish Reports.

I.R.C. Internal Revenue Code.

I.R.C.L. Irish Reports, Common Law Series.

I.R.Eq. Irish Reports, Equity Series.

I.R.R. International Revenue Record, New York City.

I.T.R. Irish Term Reports, by Ridgeway, Lapp & Schoales.

Ia. Iowa;—Iowa Reports.

Ida. (or Idaho). Idaho;—Idaho Reports.

Idaho L.J. Idaho Law Journal.

Iddings D.R.D. Iddings Dayton Term Reports.

Iddings T.R.D. Iddings' Dayton Term Reports.

Ill. Illinois;—Illinois Reports.

Ill.App. Illinois Appeal Reports.

Ill.B.J. Illinois Bar Journal.

Ill.C.C. Illinois Circuit Court.

Ill.L.B. Illinois Law Bulletin.

Ill.L.Q. Illinois Law Quarterly.

Ill.L.Rev. Illinois Law Review.

Ill.Rev.Stat. Illinois Revised Statutes State Bar Association Edition.

Imp.Dict. Imperial Dictionary.

Imp.Fed. Imperial Federation, London.

Ind. Indiana;—Indiana Reports;—India;—(East) Indian.

Ind.App. Law Reports, Indian Appeals;—Indiana Appeals.

Ind.App.Supp. Supplemental Indian Appeals, Law Reports.

Ind.Jur. Indian Jurist, Calcutta;—Indian Jurist, Madras.

Ind.L.J. Indiana Law Journal.

Ind.L.R. (East) Indian Law Reports.

Ind.L.R.Alla. Indian Law Reports, Allahabad.

Ind.L.R.Bomb. Indian Law Reports, Bombay Series.

Ind.L.R.Calc. Indian Law Reports, Calcutta Series.

Ind.L.R.Mad. Indian Law Reports, Madras Series.

Ind.L.Reg. Indiana Legal Register.

Ind.L.Rep. Indiana Law Reporter.

Ind.Rep. Indiana Reports;—Index Reporter.

Ind.Super. Indiana Superior Court Reports (Wilson's).

Ind.T. Indian Territory;—Indian Territory Reports.

Ind.T.Ann.St. Indian Territory Annotated Statutes.

Ing.Ves. Ingraham's edition of Vesey, Jr.

1, 2, Inst. (1, 2) Coke's Inst.

Ins.Law J. Insurance Law Journal, Pa.

Ins.Rep. Insurance Reporter, Phila., Pa.

Inst., 1, 2, 3. Justinian's Inst. lib. 1, tit. 2, § 3.

Inst., 1, 2, 31. Justinian's Institutes, lib. 1, tit. 2, § 31.

The Institutes of Justinian are divided into four books,—each book is divided into titles, and each title into paragraphs, of which the first, described by the letters *pr.*, or *princip.*, is not numbered. The old method of citing the Institutes was to give the commencing words of the paragraph and of the title; *e. g.*, § *si adversus, Inst. de Nuptiis.* Sometimes the number of the paragraph was introduced, *e.g* ., § 12, *si adversus, Inst. de Nuptiis.* The modern way is to give the number of the book, title, and paragraph, thus;—*Inst. I.* 10, 12; would be read *Inst., Lib. I.* tit. 10, § 12.

Inst.Epil. Epilogue to [a designated part or volume of] Coke's Institutes.

Inst.Proem. *Proeme* [introduction] to [a designated part or volume of] Coke's Institutes.

Instr.Cler. Instructor Clericalis.

Int.Case. Rowe's Interesting Cases, English and Irish.

Int.Com.Commn. Interstate Commerce Commission.

Int.L.N. International Law Notes.

Int.Private Law. Westlake's Private International Law.

Int.Rev.Manual. Internal Revenue Manual.

Int.Rev.Rec. Internal Revenue Record.

Internat.Dict. Webster's International Dictionary.

Interst.Com.R. Interstate Commerce Reports.

Iowa. Iowa Reports.

Iowa L.B. Iowa Law Bulletin.

Iowa L.Rev. Iowa Law Review.

Ir. Irish;—Ireland;—Iredell's North Carolina Law or Equity Reports.

1891 Ir. Law Reports, 1891, Irish.

Ir.C.L. Irish Common Law Reports.

Ir.Ch. Irish Chancery Reports.

Ir.Cir. (or Ir.Cir.Rep.). Irish Circuit Reports.

Ir.Com.Law Rep. Irish Common Law Reports.

Ir.Eccl. Irish Ecclesiastical Reports, by Milward.

Ir.Eq. Irish Equity Reports.

Ir.Jur. Irish Jurist.

Ir.L. Irish Law Reports.

Ir.L.N.S. Irish Common Law Reports.

Ir.L.R. Irish Law Reports;—The Law Reports, Ireland, now cited by the year.

Ir.L.T. Irish Law Times (Dublin).

Ir.L.T.Jour. Irish Law Times Journal.

Ir.L.T.Rep. Irish Law Times Reports.

Ir.Law Rec. Irish Law Recorder.

Ir.Law Rep. Irish Law Reports.

Ir.Law Rep.N.S. Irish Common Law Reports.

Ir.Law & Ch. Irish Common Law and Chancery Reports (New Series).

Ir.Law & Eq. Irish Law and Equity Reports (Old Series).

Ir.R.1894. Irish Law Reports for year 1894.

Ir.R.C.L. Irish Reports, Common Law Series.

Ir.R.Eq. Irish Reports, Equity Series.

Ir.R.Reg.App. Irish Reports, Registration Appeals.

Ir.R.Reg. & L. Irish Reports, Registry and Land Cases.

Ir.St.Tr. Irish State Trials (Ridgeway's).

Ir.T.R. (or Term Rep.). Irish Term Reports (by Ridgeway, Lapp & Schoales).

Ired. Iredell's North Carolina Law Reports.

Ired.Eq. Iredell's North Carolina Equity Reports.

Irv. Irvine's Scotch Justiciary Reports.

Irv.Just. Irvine's Justiciary Cases, Eng.

Irwin's Code. Clark, Cobb and Irwin's Code, Ga.

J

J. Johnson's New York Reports.

J.Air L. Journal of Air Law.

J.B.A.Dist.Colum. Journal of the Bar Association of the District of Columbia.

J.B.A.Kan. Journal of the Bar Association of Kansas.

J.Bridgm. John Bridgman, Eng.

J.C. Johnson's Cases, New York Supreme Court.

J.C.P. Justice of the Common Pleas.

J.Ch. (or J.C.R.). Johnson's New York Chancery Reports.

J. d'Ol. Les Jugemens d'Oleron.

J.H. Journal of the House.

J.J.Mar. J. J. Marshall's Kentucky Reports.

J.J.Marsh. (Ky.). J. J. Marshall's Kentucky Reports.

J.Kel. Sir John Kelyng's English Crown Cases.

J.Mo.B. Journal of the Missouri Bar.

J.N.A.Referees Bank. Journal of the National Association of Referees in Bankruptcy.

J.P. Justice of the Peace;—The Justice of the Peace, London, periodical.

J.P.Sm. (or J.P.Smith). J. P. Smith's English King's Bench Reports.

J.Pat.Office Soc. Journal of the Patent Office Society.

J.R. Johnson's New York Reports.

J.Radio L. Journal of Radio Law.

J.S.Gr. J. S. Green's New Jersey Reports.

J.Scott. Reporter English Common Bench Reports.

J.Scott, N.S. English Common Bench Reports, New Series, by John Scott.

J.Soc.Pub.Teach.Law. Journal of the Society of Pub. Teachers of Law.

J.Voet, Com. ad Pand. Voet (Jan), Commentarius ad Pandectas.

J. & C. Jones & Carey, Ireland.

J. & H. Johnson & Hemming's English Vice-Chancellors' Reports.

J. & L. (or J. & La T.). Jones & La Touche's Irish Chancery Reports.

J. & S. Jones & Spencer's New York Superior Court Reports.

J. & S.Jam. Judah & Swan's Jamaica Reports.

J. & W. Jacob & Walker's English Chancery Reports.

Jac. Jacobus (King James);—Jacob's English Chancery Reports;—Jacob's Law Dictionary.

Jac.Law Dict. Jacob's Law Dictionary.

Jac.Sea Laws. Jacobsen's Law of the Sea.

Jac. & W. (or Walk.). Jacob & Walker's English Chancery Reports.

Jack. & G.Landl. & Ten. Jackson & Gross, Treatise on the Law of Landlord and Tenant in Pennsylvania.

Jackson. Jackson's Reports, vols. 43–66 Georgia;—Jackson's Reports, vols. 1–29 Texas Court of Appeals.

Jackson & Lumpkin. Jackson & Lumpkin's Georgia Reports.

Jacob. Jacob's Law Dictionary.

Jagg.Torts. Jaggard on Torts.

James (N.Sc.). James' Reports, Nova Scotia.

James Sel.Cases. James' Select Cases, Nova Scotia.

James. & Mont. Jameson & Montagu's English Bankruptcy Reports (in vol. 2 Glyn & Jameson).

Jar.Cr.Tr. Jardine's Criminal Trials.

Jarm.Wills. Jarman on Wills.

Jebb (or Jebb C.C.). Jebb's Irish Crown Cases.

Jebb Cr. & Pr.Cas. Jebb's Irish Crown and Presentment Cases.

Jebb & B. Jebb & Bourke's Irish Queen's Bench Reports.

Jebb & S. (or Sym.). Jebb & Symes' Irish Queen's Bench Reports.

Jeff. Jefferson's Virginia Reports.

Jeff.Man. Jefferson's Manual of Parliamentary Law.

Jenk. (or Jenk.Cent.). Jenkins' Eight Centuries of Reports, English Exchequer.

Jenks. Jenks' Reports, vol. 58 New Hampshire.

Jenn. Jennison's Reports, vols. 14–18 Michigan.

Jeremy, Eq.Jur. Jeremy's Equity Jurisdiction.

Jo.T. Sir T. Jones' Reports.

Jo. & La.T. Jones & La Touche's Irish Chancery Reports.

John. (or Johns.). Johnson's New York Reports;—Johnson's Reports of Chase's Decisions;—Johnson's Maryland Chancery Decisions;—Johnson's English Vice-Chancellors' Reports;—Johnson, N. M.

John.Dict. Johnson's English Dictionary.

John Marshall L.Q. The John Marshall Law Quarterly.

Johns.Cas. Johnson's New York Cases.

Johns.Ch. Johnson's New York Chancery Reports;—Johnson's English Vice-Chancellors' Report;—Johnson's Maryland Chancery Decisions;—Johnston's Reports, New Zealand.

Johns.Ct.Err. Johnson's Reports, New York Court of Errors.

Johns.Dec. Johnson's Maryland Chancery Decisions.

Johns.Eng.Ch. Johnson's English Chancery Reports.

Johns.Pat.Man. Johnson's Patent Manual.

Johns.Rep. Johnson's Reports, New York Supreme Court.

Johns.Tr. Johnson's Impeachment Trial.

Johns.U.S. Johnson's Reports of Chase's United States Circuit Court Decisions.

Johns.V.C. Johnson's English Vice-Chancellors' Reports.

Johns. & H. (or Johns. & Hem.). Johnson & Hemming's English Chancery Reports.

Johnson. Johnson's Reports, New York;—Johnson's English Vice-Chancellors' Reports;—Johnson's Maryland Chancery Decisions.

Johnson's Quarto Dict. Johnson's Quarto Dictionary.

Johnst. (N.Z.). Johnston's Reports, New Zealand.

Jon.Exch. (or Jon.Ir.Exch.). Jones' Irish Exchequer Reports.

Jon. & Car. Jones & Cary's Irish Exchequer Reports.

Jon. & L. Jones & La Touche's Irish Chancery Reports.

Jones. Jones' Reports, vols. 43–48, 52–57, 61, 62 Alabama;—Jones' Reports, vols. 11, 12 Pennsylvania;—Jones' Reports, vols. 22–31 Missouri;—Jones' Law or Equity Reports, North Carolina;—Jones' Irish Exchequer Reports;—Jones' Upper Canada Common Pleas Reports;—Jones & Spencer's New York Superior Court Reports.

Jones (Pa.). Jones Reports, vols. 11, 12 Pennsylvania.

Jones 1. Sir William Jones' English King's Bench Reports.

Jones 2. Sir Thomas Jones' English King's Bench Reports.

Jones, Bailm. Jones' Law of Bailments.

Jones, Barclay & Whittelsey. Jones, Barclay, & Whittelsey's Reports, vol. 31 Missouri.

Jones, Chat.Mortg. Jones on Chattel Mortgages.

Jones, Easem. Jones' Treatise on Easements.

Jones Eq. Jones' North Carolina Equity Reports.

Jones Exch. Jones Exchequer, Ireland.

Jones, French Bar. Jones' History of the French Bar.

Jones Ir. Jones' Irish Exchequer Reports.

Jones Law (or Jones N.C.). Jones' North Carolina Law Reports.

Jones, Liens. Jones on Liens.

Jones, Mortg. Jones on Mortgages.

Jones, Pledges. Jones on Pledges and Collateral Securities.

Jones, Securities. Jones on Railroad Securities.

Jones T. Sir Thomas Jones' English King's Bench Reports.

Jones U.C. Jones' Reports, Upper Canada.

Jones W. Sir William Jones' English King's Bench Reports.

Jones & C. Jones & Cary's Irish Exchequer Reports.

Jones & La T. Jones & La Touche's Irish Chancery Reports.

Jones & McM. (Pa.). Jones & McMurtrie's Pennsylvania Supreme Court Reports.

Jones & S. (or Jones & Spen.). Jones & Spencer's New York Superior Court Reports.

Jones & V.Laws. Jones and Varick's Laws, N.Y.

Josephs. Josephs' Reports, vol. 21 Nevada.

Jour.Am.Jud.Soc. Journal of the American Judicature Society.

Jour.Comp.Leg. Journal of the Society of Comparative Legislation.

Jour.Conat.Law. Journal of Conational Law.

Jour.Crim.L. Journal of Criminal Law and Criminology.

Jour.Juris. Journal of Jurisprudence.

Jour.Law. Journal of Law.

Jour.Ps.Med. Journal of Psychological Medicine and Medical Jurisprudence.

Joyce, Ins. Joyce on Insurance.

Jud.Repos. Judicial Repository, N.Y.

Jud. & Sw. Judah & Swan's Reports, Jamaica.

Judd. Judd's Reports, vol. 4 Hawaii.

Jur. The Jurist, London.

Jur. (N.S.). The Jurist (New Series) Reports in all the Courts, London.

Jur. (N.S.) Ex. Jurist (New Series) Exchequer.

Jurid.Rev. Juridical Review.

Just. (or Just.L.R.). Justices' Law Reporter, Pa.

Just.Dig. Digest of Justinian, 50 books. Never translated into English.

Just.Inst. Justinian's Institutes. See note following "Inst. 1, 2, 31."

Juta. Juta's Cape of Good Hope Reports.

K

K. Keyes' New York Court of Appeals Reports;—Kenyon's English King's Bench Reports;—Kansas (see Kan.).

K.B. King's Bench Reports.

[1901] K.B. Law Reports, King's Bench Division, from 1901 onward.

1917 K.B. Law Reports, 1917, King's Bench, Eng.

K.C.R. Reports in the time of Chancellor King.

K. & F.N.S.W. Knox & Fitzhardinge's New South Wales Reports.

K. & G. Keane & Grant, Eng.

K. & G.R.C. Keane & Grant's English Registration Appeal Cases.

K. & J. Kay & Johnston's English Vice-Chancellors' Reports.

K. & O. Knapp & Ombler's English Election Cases.

K. & R. Kent and Radcliff's Law of New York, Revision of 1801.

Kam. Kames' Decisions of the Scottish Court of Session.

Kam.Rem.Dec. Kames' Remarkable Decisions, Scotch Court of Session.

Kam.Sel.Dec. Kames' Select Decisions, Scotch Court of Session.

Kames Dec. Kames' Decisions, Scotland.

Kames Elucid. Kames' Elucidation, Scotland.

Kames, Eq. Kames' Principles of Equity.

Kames Rem.Dec. Kames' Remarkable Decisions, Scotland.

Kames Sel.Dec. Kames' Select Decisions, Scotland.

Kan. (or Kans.). Kansas;—Kansas Reports.

Kan.C.L.Rep. Kansas City Law Reporter.

Kan.City L.Rev. Kansas City Law Review.

Kan.Jud.Council Bull. Kansas Judicial Council Bulletin.

Kan.L.J. Kansas Law Journal.

Kan.Law. Kansas Lawyer.

Kan.St.L.J. Kansas State Law Journal.

Kans.App. Kansas Appeals Reports.

Kay. Kay's English Vice-Chancellors' Reports.

Kay & J. (or Kay & Johns.). Kay and Johnson's English Vice Chancellors' Reports.

Ke. Keen's English Rolls Court Reports.

Keane & Gr. Keane & Grant's English Registration Appeal Cases.

Keb. (or Kebl.). Keble's English King's Bench Reports.

Keen (or Keen, Ch.). Keen's English Rolls Court Reports.

Keener, Quasi Contr. Keener's Cases on Quasi Contracts.

Keil. (or Keilw. or Keilway). Keilway's English King's Bench Reports.

Kel. Sir John Kelyng's English Crown Cases.

Kel. I. Sir John Kelyng's English Crown Cases.

Kel. 2. William Kelynge's English Chancery Reports.

Kel.Ga. Kelly's Reports, vols. 1–3 Georgia.

Kel.J. Sir John Kelyng's English Crown Cases.

Kel.W. Wm. Kelynge's English Chancery Reports.

Kelham. Kelham's Norman French Law Dictionary.

Kellen. Kellen's Reports, vols. 146–155 Massachusetts.

Kelly. Kelly's Reports, vols. 1–3 Georgia.

Kelly & Cobb. Kelly & Cobb's Reports, vols. 4, 5 Georgia.

Kelyng, J. Kelyng's English Crown Cases.

Kelynge, W. Kelynge's English Chancery Reports.

Kemble, Sax. Kemble, The Saxons in England.

Ken. Kentucky (see Ky.);—Kenyon English King's Bench Reports.

Ken.Dec. Kentucky Decisions, by Sneed.

Ken.L.Rep. Kentucky Law Reporter.

Kenan. Kenan's Reports, vols. 76–91 North Carolina.

Kenn.Par.Antiq. Kennett, Parochial Antiquities.

Kennett. Kennett's Glossary;—Kennett upon Impropriations.

Kennett, Gloss. Kennett's Glossary.

Kent. Kent's Commentaries on American Law.

Kent, Com. (or Comm.). Kent's Commentaries on American Law.

Kent & R.St. Kent and Radcliff's Law of New York, Revision of 1801.

Keny. Kenyon's English King's Bench Reports.

Keny.C.H. (or 3 Keny.). Chancery Reports at the end of 2 Kenyon.

Kern. Kern's Reports, vols. 100–116 Indiana;—Kernan's Reports, vols. 11–14 New York Court of Appeals.

Kerr. Kerr's New Brunswick Reports;—Kerr's Reports;—J. M. Kerr's Reports, vols. 27–29 New York Civil Procedure.

Kerr, Inj. Kerr on Injunctions.

Kerr (N.B.). Kerr's New Brunswick Reports.

Kerr, Rec. Kerr on Receivers.

Kerse. Kerse's Manuscript Decisions, Scotch Court of Session.

Kersey, Dict. John Kersey's English Dictionary, 1708.

Key. (or Keyes). Keyes' New York Court of Appeals Reports.

Keyl. Keilwey's (or Keylway's) English King's Bench Reports.

Kilk. Kilkerran's Decisions, Scotch Court of Session.

King. King's Reports, vols. 5, 6 Louisiana Annual.

King.Cas. temp. Select Cases *tempore* King, English Chancery.

King's Conf.Ca. (or King's Con.Cs.). King's Conflicting Cases (Texas).

Kinney, Law Dict. & Glos. Kinney's Law Dictionary and Glossary.

Kir. (Kirb. or Kirby). Kirby's Connecticut Reports.

Kitch. (or Kitch.Courts). Kitchin on Jurisdictions of Courts-Leet, Courts-Baron, etc.

Kitchin. Kitchin on Jurisdictions of Courts-Leet, Courts-Baron, etc.

Kn. (or Kn.A.C.). Knapp's Appeal Cases (English Privy Council).

Kn.N.S.W. Knox, New South Wales Reports.

Kn. & Moo. Knapp & Moore's Reports, vol. 3 Knapp's Privy Council.

Kn. & O. Knapp & Ombler's English Election Reports.

Knapp. Knapp's Privy Council Reports, England.

Knapp & O. Knapp & Ombler, Eng.

Knight, Mech.Dict. Knight's American Mechanical Dictionary.

Knowles. Knowles' Reports, vol. 3 Rhode Island.

Knox. Knox, New South Wales Reports.

Knox & F. (or Knox & Fitz.). Knox & Fitzhardinge, N. S.Wales.

Kolze. Transvaal Reports by Kolze.

Kreider. Kreider's Reports, vols. 1–21 Washington.

Kress. Kress' Reports, vols. 166–194 Pennsylvania;—Kress' Pennsylvania Superior Court.

Kulp. Kulp's Luzerne Legal Register Reports, Pennsylvania.

Ky. Kentucky;—Kentucky Reports.

Ky.Dec. Sneed's Kentucky Decisions.

Ky.L.J. Kentucky Law Journal.

Ky.L.R. (or Ky.Law Rep.). Kentucky Law Reporter.

Ky.Op. Kentucky Opinions.

Ky.S.B.J. Kentucky State Bar Journal.

Ky.St.Law. Morehead and Brown Digest of Statute Laws, Ky.

Kyd. Kyd on Bills of Exchange.

Kyd, Corp. Kyd on Corporations.

L

L. Lansing's Supreme Court Reports, New York.

L.A. Lawyers' Reports Annotated.

L.C. Lord Chancellor;—Lower Canada;—Leading Cases.

L.C.B. Lord Chief Baron.

L.C.D. Lower Court Decisions, Ohio.

L.C.Eq. White & Tudor's Leading Cases in Equity.

L.C.G. Lower Courts Gazette, Toronto.

L.C.Jur. Lower Canada Jurist.

L.C.L.J. Lower Canada Law Journal.

L.C.R. Lower Canada Reports.

L.C.Rep.S.Qu. Lower Canada Reports Seignorial Questions.

L.D. Law Dictionary.

L.D. (or Dec.). Land Office Decisions, United States.

L.Ed. Lawyers' Edition Supreme Court Reports.

L.G. Law Glossary.

L.I. Legal Intelligencer, Pa.

L.J. Law Journal.

L.J.Adm. Law Journal Admiralty, New Series, Eng.

L.J.App. Law Journal, New Series, Appeals.

L.J.Bank. (or L.J.Bankr.). Law Journal Bankruptcy, New Series, Eng.

L.J.Bk. Law Journal, New Series, Bankruptcy (1831 onward).

L.J.C.C.R. Law Journal, New Series, Crown Cases Reserved.

L.J.C.P. (or L.J.C.P.D.). Law Journal, New Series, Common Pleas Decisions.

L.J.C.P.O.S. Law Journal Common Pleas, Old Series, Eng.

L.J.Ch. Law Journal, New Series, Chancery Division (1831 on).

L.J.Ch. (O.S.). Law Journal, Old Series, 1822, 1831.

L.J.D. & M. Law Journal, New Series, Divorce and Matrimonial.

L.J.Ecc. Law Journal Reports, Ecclesiastical (1831 on).

L.J.Eccl. Law Journal Ecclesiastical, New Series, Eng.

L.J.Ex. Law Journal, New Series, Exchequer Division (1831 on).

L.J.Exch. Law Journal, New Series, Exchequer.

L.J.Exch.O.S. Law Journal Exchequer, Old Series, Eng.

L.J.H.L. Law Journal, New Series, House of Lords.

L.J.K.B. Law Journal, King's Bench.

L.J.K.B.O.S. Law Journal King's Bench, Old Series, Eng.

L.J.L.C. Law Journal, Lower Canada.

L.J.L.T. Law Journal, Law Tracts.

L.J.M.C. (or L.J.M.Cas.). Law Journal, New Series, Divorce and Matrimonial;—Law Journal, Magistrates' Cases.

L.J.M.C.O.S. Law Journal Magistrate Cases, Old Series, Eng.

L.J.M.P.A. Law Journal, Matrimonial, Probate and Admiralty.

L.J.M. & W. Morgan & Williams' Law Journal, London.

L.J.N.C. Law Journal, Notes of Cases.

L.J.N.S. The Law Journal, New Series, London (1831 onwards).

L.J.O.S. The Law Journal, Old Series, London (1822–1831).

L.J.P. (or P.C.). Law Journal, New Series, Privy Council;—Law Journal, Probate, Divorce and Admiralty.

L.J.P. (D. & A.). Law Journal, New Series, Probate, Divorce and Admiralty.

L.J.P.D. & Adm. Law Journal Probate Divorce & Admiralty, New Series, Eng.

L.J.P. & M. (or L.J.Prob. & Mat.). Law Journal, New Series, Probate and Matrimonial (1831 onward).

L.J.Prob.N.S. Law Journal Probate, Divorce and Admiralty Reports, N.Y.

L.J.Q.B. Law Journal, New Series, Queen's Bench (1831 on).

L.J.Q.B.D. Law Journal, New Series, Queen's Bench Division.

L.J.Rep. Law Journal Reports.

L.J.Rep.N.S. Law Journal Reports, New Series (1831 onward).

L.J. (U.C.). Law Journal, Upper Canada.

L.M. & P. Lowndes, Maxwell & Pollock's English Bail Court Reports.

L.N. Liber Niger, or the Black Book.

L.P.R. Lilly's Practical Register.

L.R. Law Reports (English);—Law Reporter (Law Times Reports, New Series);—(Irish) Law Recorder;—Louisiana Reports.

L.R.A. Lawyers' Reports, Annotated.

L.R.A.1915A. Lawyers' Reports Annotated 1915A, et seq.

L.R.A. (N.S.). Lawyers' Reports Annotated, New Series.

L.R.A. & E. English Law Reports, Admiralty and Ecclesiastical (1866–1875).

L.R.App. (or L.R.App.Cas.). English Law Reports, Appeal Cases, House of Lords.

L.R.Burm. Law Reports, British Burmah.

L.R.C.C. English Law Reports, Crown Cases Reserved (1866–1875).

L.R.C.P. English Law Reports, Common Pleas (1866–1875).

L.R.C.P.D. English Law Reports, Common Pleas Division.

L.R.Ch. English Law Reports, Chancery Appeal Cases (1866–1875).

L.R.Ch.D. (or Div.). Law Reports, Chancery Division, English Supreme Court of Judicature.

L.R.E. & I.App. English Reports, English and Irish Appeals.

L.R.Eq. English Law Reports, Equity (1866–1875).

L.R.Ex. (or L.R.Exch. or L.R.Ex.Cas.). English Law Reports, Exchequer (1866–1875).

L.R.Ex.Div. English Law Reports, Exchequer Division.

L.R.H.L. English Law Reports, House of Lords, English and Irish Appeal Cases.

L.R.H.L.Sc. English Law Reports, House of Lords, Scotch and Divorce Appeal Cases (1866–1875).

L.R.Ind.App. (or L.R.Indian App.). Law Reports Indian Appeals, Eng.

L.R.Ir. Law Reports, Ireland (1879–1893).

L.R.Misc.D. Law Reports, Miscellaneous Division.

L.R.N.S. Irish Law Recorder, New Series.

L.R.N.S.W. Law Reports, New South Wales.

L.R.P.C. English Law Reports, Privy Council, Appeal Cases (1866–1875).

L.R.P.Div. (or L.R.Prob.Div.). English Law Reports, Probate, Divorce and Admiralty Division.

L.R.P. & D. (or L.R.Prob. & Div.). English Law Reports, Probate and Divorce.

L.R.P. & M. Law Reports, Probate and Matrimonial (1866–1875).

L.R.Q.B. English Law Reports, Queen's Bench (1866–1875).

L.R.Q.B.Div. English Law Reports, Queen's Bench Division.

L.R.S.A. Law Reports, South Australia.

L.R.Sc. & D. English Law Reports, Scotch and Divorce Cases, before the House of Lords.

L.R.Sess.Cas. English Law Reports, Sessions Cases.

L.R.Stat. English Law Reports, Statutes.

LSA–R.S. West's Louisiana Revised Statutes.

L.T. Law Times, Pa.

L.T.N.S. (or L.T.R.N.S.). Law Times (New Series) Reports, London;—American Law Times Reports.

L.T.O.S. Law Times, Old Series.

L.T.Rep.N.S. Law Times Reports, New Series, Eng.

L. & B.Bull. Law and Bank Bulletin.

L. & C. (or L. & C.C.C.). Leigh & Cave's English Crown Cases, Reserved.

L. & E. English Law and Equity Reports.

L. & E.Rep. Law and Equity Reporter New York.

L. & G.t.Plunk. Lloyd & Gould's Irish Chancery Reports *tempore* Plunkett.

L. & G.t.Sug. Lloyd & Gould's Irish Chancery Reports *tempore* Sugden.

L. & M. Lowndes & Maxwell's English Practice Cases.

L. & T. Longfield & Townsend's Irish Exchequer Reports.

L. & W. Lloyd & Welsby's English Mercantile Cases.

La. Louisiana;—Louisiana Reports;—Lane's English Exchequer Reports.

La.A. (Orleans). Court of Appeal, Parish of Orleans.

La.Ann. (or La.An.). Louisiana Annual Reports;—Lawyers' Reports. Annotated.

La.App. Louisiana Court of Appeals;—Louisiana Appeal Reports.

La.L.J. Louisiana Law Journal, Schmidt's.

La.Law Review. Louisiana Law Review.

La.T.R. Louisiana Term Reports, vols. 3–12 Martin, Louisiana.

La Thém.L.C. La Thémis (Periodical) Lower Canada.

Lab. Labatt's California District Court Reports.

Lab.Rel.Rep. Labor Relations Reporter.

Lacey Dig. Lacey's Digest Railway Decisions.

Lack.Bar. Lackawanna Bar, Pa.

Lack.Bar.R. Lackawanna Bar Reporter, Pa.

Lack.Jur. Lackawanna Jurist, Pa.

Lack.L.N. (or Lack.Leg.N.). Lackawanna Legal News, Pa.

Lack.L.R. (or Lack.Leg.Rec.). Lackawanna Legal Record, Pa.

Ladd. Ladd's Reports, vols. 59–64 New Hampshire.

Lalor. Lalor's Supplement to Hill & Denio's New York Reports.

Lalor, Pol.Econ. Lalor, Cyclopædia of Political Science, Political Economy, etc.

Lalor, Supp. Lalor's Supplement to Hill & Denio's Reports, N. Y.

Lamar. Lamar's Reports, vols. 25–40 Florida.

Lamb. Lamb's Reports, vols. 103–105 Wisconsin.

Lamb.Arch. Lambard's Archaionomia.

Lamb.Const. Lambard, Duties of Constables, etc.

Lamb.Eir. Lambard's Eirenarcha.

Lanc.Bar. Lancaster Bar, Pa.

Lanc.Law Rev. Lancaster Law Review.

Lanc.Rev. Lancaster Review, Pa.

Land Com.Rep. Land Commissioners Reports, Ireland.

Land Dec. Land Decisions, U.S.

Lane. Lane's English Exchequer Reports.

Langd.Cont. Langdell's Cases on Contracts;—Langdell's Summary of the Law of Contracts.

Lans. Lansing's New York Supreme Court Reports.

Lans.Ch. Lansing's Chancery Decisions, New York.

Las Partidas. Las Siete Partidas.

Latch. Latch's English King's Bench Reports.

Lath. Lathrop's Reports, vols. 115–145 Massachusetts.

Lauder. (Lauder of) Fountainhall's Scotch Session Cases.

Laur.H.C.Ca. Lauren's High Court Cases (Kimberly).

Law Bull. Law Bulletin, San Francisco.

Law Ex.J. Law Examination Journal (London).

Law.Guild Rev. Lawyers Guild Review.

Law J.Ch. Law Journal, New Series, Chancery.

Law J.Exch. Law Journal, New Series, Exchequer.

Law J.I.B. Law Journal, New Series, English Queen's Bench.

Law J.P.D. Law Journal, Probate Division.

Law J.R., Q.B. (or Law J.Q.B.). Law Journal, New Series, Queen's Bench, Eng.

Law Lib. Law Library, Philadelphia.

Law Lib.J. Law Library Journal.

Law Mag. & Rev. Law Magazine and Review.

Law Notes. Law Notes.

Law of Trusts, Tiff. & Bul. Tiffany and Bullard on Trusts and Trustees.

Law Q.Rev. Law Quarterly Review.

Law Rep. Monthly Law Reporter, Boston, Mass.

Law Rep.A. & E. Law Reports, Admiralty and Ecclesiastical.

Law Rep.App.Cas. Law Reports, Appeal Cases.

Law Rep.C.C. Law Reports, Crown Cases.

Law Rep.C.P. Law Reports, Common Pleas.

Law Rep.C.P.D. Law Reports, Common Pleas Division.

Law Rep.Ch. Law Reports, Chancery Appeal Cases.

Law Rep.Ch.D. Law Reports, Chancery Division.

Law Rep.Eq. Law Reports, Equity Cases.

Law Rep.Ex. Law Reports, Exchequer.

Law Rep.Ex.D. Law Reports, Exchequer Division.

Law Rep.H.L. Law Reports, House of Lords, English and Irish Appeal Cases.

Law Rep.H.L.Sc. Law Reports, Scotch and Divorce Appeal Cases, House of Lords.

Law Rep.Ind.App. Law Reports, Indian Appeals.

Law Rep.Ir. Law Reports, Irish.

Law Rep.Misc.D. Law Reports, Miscellaneous Division.

Law Rep.N.S. Law Reports, New Series, N.Y.

Law Rep.P.C. Law Reports, Privy Council, Appeal Cases.

Law Rep.P. & D. Law Reports, Probate and Divorce Cases.

Law Rep.Q.B. Law Reports, Queen's Bench.

Law Rep.Q.B.D. Law Reports, Queen's Bench Division.

Law Repos. Carolina Law Repository, North Carolina.

Law Ser.Mo.Bull. University of Missouri Bulletin, Law Series.

Law Soc.J. Law Society Journal.

Law Stud.H. Law Students' Helper.

Law Stud.Mag.N.S. Law Students Magazine, New Series.

Law T. English Law Times Reports.

Law T., N.S. English Law Times Reports, New Series.

Law Times (N.S.). Law Times, New Series, Lackawanna, Pa.

Law Times (O.S.). Law Times, Old Series, Luzerne, Pa.

Law. & Bank. Lawyer and Banker.

Law & Contem.Prob. Law and Contemporary Problems.

Lawes, Pl. Lawes on Pleading.

Lawrence. Lawrence's Reports, vol. 20 Ohio.

Lawrence Comp.Dec. Lawrence's First Comptroller's Decisions.

Lawson, Exp.Ev. Lawson on Expert and Opinion Evidence.

Lawson, Pres.Ev. Lawson on Presumptive Evidence.

Lawson, Rights, Rem. & Pr. Lawson on Rights, Remedies and Practice.

Lawson, Usages & Cust. Lawson on the Law of Usages and Customs.

Lawy.Rev. The Lawyers' Review, Seattle, Wash.

Ld.Ken. Lord Kenyon's English King's Bench Reports.

Ld.Raym. Lord Raymond's English King's Bench Reports.

Le Mar. Le Marchant's Gardner Peerage Case.

Lea. Lea's Tennessee Reports;—Leach.

Leach. Leach's English Crown Cases.

Leach C.L. Leach, Cases in Crown Law.

Leach Cl.Cas. Leach's Club Cases, London.

Leach, Cr.Cas. Leach's English Crown Cases.

Lead.Cas.Am. American Leading Cases, by Hare & Wallace.

Lead.Cas.Eq. Leading Cases in Equity, by White & Tudor.

Leake. Leake on Contracts;—Leake's Digest of the Law of Property in Land.

Leake, Cont. Leake on Contracts.

Leam. & Spic. Leaming and Spicer's Laws, Grants, Concessions and Original Constitutions, N.J.

Lebanon. Lebanon County Law Journal, Pa.

Leç.El.Dr.Civ.Rom. Leçons Elémentaries du Droit Civil Romain.

Lee. Lee's English Ecclesiastical Reports;—Lee's Reports, vols. 9–12 California.

Lee, Dict. Lee's Dictionary of Practice.

Lee Eccl. Lee's Ecclesiastical, Eng.

Lee G. Sir George Lee's English Ecclesiastical Reports.

Lee t.Hardw. Lee *tempore* Hardwicke, Eng.

Leese. Leese's Reports, vol. 26 Nebraska.

Lef.Dec. Lefevre's Parliamentary Decisions, reported by Bourke.

Leg.Canut. Leges Canuti (laws of King Canute or Knut.)

Leg.Alfred. Leges Alfredi (laws of King Alfred.)

Leg.Edm. Leges Edmundi (laws of King Edmund.)

Leg.Ethel. Leges Ethelredi.

Leg.H.I. Laws of [King] Henry the First.

Leg.Gaz. (or Leg.Gaz.R. [Pa.]). Legal Gazette Reports, Pennsylvania.

Leg.Op. Legal Opinion, Pa.

Leg.Rec. Legal Record Reports, Pa.

Leg. & Ins.Rep. Legal and Insurance Reports (Pa.).

Legg. Leggett's Reports, Sind, India.

Legge. Legge's Supreme Court Cases, New South Wales.

Leh.L.J. Lehigh County Law Journal, Pa.

Lehigh. Lehigh Valley Law Reporter, Pa.

Leigh. Leigh's Virginia Reports.

Leigh & C. Leigh & Cave's English Crown Cases.

Leo. (or Leon.). Leonard's English King's Bench Reports.

Lest.P.L. Lester's Decisions in Public Land Cases.

Lester. Lester's Reports, vols. 31–33 Georgia.

Lester Supp. (or Lest. & But.). Lester & Butler's Supplement to Lester's Georgia Reports.

Lev. Levinz's English King's Bench Reports.

Lew. Lewin's English Crown Cases Reserved;—Lewis, Missouri;—Lewis, Nevada.

Lew.C.C. Lewin's English Crown Cases.

Lew.C.L. Lewis' Criminal Law.

Lew.L.Cas. Lewis Leading Cases on Public Land Law.

Lewis. Lewis' Reports, vols. 29–35 Missouri Appeals; —Lewis' Reports, vol. 1 Nevada;—Lewis' Kentucky Law Reporter.

Lewis, Perp. Lewis on the Law of Perpetuity.

Lex.Jurid. Calvinus, Lexicon Juridicum Juris Cæsari simul et Canonici, etc.

Lex Salic. Lex Salica.

Ley. Ley's English King's Bench Reports.

Lib. Liber (book);—Library.

Lib.Ass. Liber Assisarum (Year Books, Part V).

Lib.L. & Eq. Library of Law and Equity.

Lib.Reg. Register Books.

Liberian L. Liberian Law.

Lieb.Herm. Lieber's Hermeneutics.

Lieber Civ.Lib. Lieber on Civil Liberty and Self Government.

Life and Acc.Ins.R. Bigelow's Life and Accident Insurance Reports.

Lil. Lilly's English Assize Reports.

Lil.Abr. Lilly's Abridgment.

Lil.Conv. Lilly's Conveyancer.

Lil.Reg. Lilly's Practical Register.

Lilly, Abr. Lilly's Abridgment, or Practical Register.

Lincoln L.Rev. Lincoln Law Review.

Lindl.Copartn. Lindley on Partnership.

Lindl.Partn. Lindley on Partnerships.

Linn Ind. Linn's Index of Pennsylvania Reports.

Linn, Laws Prov.Pa. Linn on the Laws of the Province of Pennsylvania.

Lit. (or Litt.). Littell's Kentucky Reports;—Littleton's English Common Pleas Reports;—Coke on Littleton.

Lit. (or Litt.) Sel.Ca. Littell's Select Kentucky Cases.

Lit. & Bl.Dig. Littleton & Blatchley's Insurance Digest.

Litt.Ten. Littleton's Tenures.

Littell. Littell's Kentucky Reports.

Littleton. Littleton's English Common Pleas and Exchequer Reports.

Liverm.Ag. Livermore on Principal and Agent.

Liz.Sc.Exch. Lizars' Exchequer Cases, Scotch.

Ll. & G.t.P. (or Ll. & G.t.Pl.). Lloyd & Goold's Irish Chancery Reports *temp.* Plunkett.

Ll. & G.t.S. Lloyd & Goold's Irish Chancery Reports *tempore* Sugden.

Ll. & W. (or Lloyd & W.). Lloyd & Welsby's English Mercantile Cases.

Loc.Acts. Local Acts.

Loc.Code. Local Code.

Loc.Ct.Gaz. Local Courts and Municipal Gazette, Toronto.

Loc.Gov. Local Government, Eng.

Loc.Laws. Local Laws.

Locc. de Jur.Mar. Loccenius, De Jure Maritimo et Navali.

Lock.Rev.Ca. Lockwood's New York Reversed Cases.

Locus Standi. Locus Standi Reports, English.

Lofft. Lofft's English King's Bench Reports.

Lofft, Append. Lofft's Maxims, appended to Lofft's Reports.

Lom.C.H.Rep. Lomas's City Hall Reporter, N.Y.

Lom.Dig. Lomax's Digest of Real Property.

Lomax, Ex'rs. Lomax on Executors.

Lond. London Encyclopedia.

London L.Mag. London Law Magazine.

Long, Irr. Long on Irrigation.

Long Q. Long Quinto (Year Books, Part X).

Longf. & T. (or Long. & Town.). Longfield & Townsend's Irish Exchequer Reports.

Lor. & Russ. Loring & Russell's Election Cases, Mass.

Lorenz. Lorenz's Ceylon Reports.

Loring & Russell. Loring & Russell's Massachusetts Election Cases.

Lou. (or Louis.). Louisiana (see La.).

Low. (or Low.Dis.). Lowell's United States District Court Reports.

Low.Can. (or Can.R.). Lower Canada Reports.

Low.Can.Seign. Lower Canada Seignorial Reports.

Lowell. Lowell's United States District Court Reports.

Lower Ct.Dec. Lower Court Decisions, Ohio.

Lown.Leg. Lowndes on Legacies.

Lown. & M. Lowndes & Maxwell's English Bail Court Reports.

Lown.M. & P. Lowndes, Maxwell, & Pollock's English Bail Court Reports.

Loyola Law Rev. Loyola Law Review.

Luc. (or Lucas). Lucas' Reports, Part X Modern Reports.

Lud.El.Cas. Luder's English Election Cases.

Ludden. Ludden's Reports, vols. 43, 44 Maine.

Lum.P.L.Cas. Lumley's Poor Law Cases.

Lumpkin. Lumpkin's Reports, vols. 59–77 Georgia.

Lush. (or Lush.Adm.). Lushington's English Admiralty Reports.

Lush Pr. Lush's Common Law Practice.

Lut. Lutwyche's English Common Pleas Reports.

Lut.Elec.Cas. Lutwyche's Election Cases, England.

Lut.R.C. Lutwyche's English Registration Appeal Cases.

Lutw.E. Lutwyche's English Common Pleas Reports.

Lutw.Reg.Cas. Lutwyche's Registration Cases, Eng.

Luz.L.J. Luzerne Law Journal, Pa.

Luz.L.O. (or Luz.Leg.Obs.). Luzerne Legal Observer, Pa.

Luz.L.R. (or Luz.Leg.Reg.). Luzerne Legal Register, Pa.

Luz.L.Reg.Rep. Luzerne Legal Register Reports (Continuation of Kulp) Pa.

Luz.L.T. (N.S.). Luzerne Law Times, New Series, Pa.

Luz.L.T. (O.S.) Luzerne Law Times, Old Series, Pa.

Luz.Law T. Luzerne Law Times, Pa.

Lynd.Prov. Lyndwood's Provinciales.

M

M. Massachusetts;—Maryland;—Maine;—Michigan; — Minnesota;— Mississippi;— Missouri;— Montana.

M.A. Missouri Appeals.

M.C.C. Moody's English Crown Cases, Reserved.

M.C.L.A. Michigan Compiled Laws Annotated.

M.D. & D. (or De G.). Montagu, Deacon & De Gex's English Bankruptcy Reports.

M.G.L.A. Massachusetts General Laws Annotated.

M.G. & S. Manning, Granger, & Scott's English Common Pleas Reports.

M.P.C. Moore's English Privy Council Cases.

M.R.S.A. Maine Revised Statutes Annotated.

M.S.A. Minnesota Statutes Annotated.

M. & A. Montagu & Ayrton's English Bankruptcy Reports.

M. & B. Montagu & Bligh's English Bankruptcy Reports.

M. & C. Mylne & Craig's English Chancery Reports; —Montagu & Chitty's English Bankruptcy Reports.

M. & C.Partidas. Moreau-Lislet and Carleton's Laws of Las Sièté Partidas in force in Louisiana.

M. & Cht.Bankr. Montagu & Chitty's English Bankruptcy Reports.

M. & G. Manning & Granger's English Common Pleas Reports;—Maddock & Geldart's English Chancery Reports, vol. 6 Maddock's Reports.

M. & Gel. Maddock & Geldart's English Chancery Reports, vol. 6 Maddock's Reports.

M. & Gord. Macnaghten & Gordon's English Chancery Reports.

M. & H. Murphy & Hurlstone's English Exchequer Reports.

M. & K. Mylne & Keen's English Chancery Reports.

M. & M. Moody & Malkin's English Nisi Prius Reports.

M. & McA. Montagu & McArthur's English Bankruptcy Reports.

M. & P. Moore & Payne's English Common Pleas Reports.

M. & R. Manning & Ryland's English King's Bench Reports;—Moody & Robinson's English Nisi Prius Reports;—Maclean & Robinson's Scotch Appeal Cases.

M. & R.M.C. Manning & Ryland's English Magistrate Cases.

M. & Rob. Moody & Robinson, Eng.

M. & S. Maule & Selwyn's English King's Bench Reports;—Moore & Scott's English Common Pleas Reports;—Manning & Scott's Reports, vol. 9 Common Bench.

M. & W. Meeson & Welsby's English Exchequer Reports.

M. & Y. Martin & Yerger's Tennessee Reports.

Mac. See also Mc.

Mac. Macnaghten's English Chancery Reports.

Mac.N.Z. Macassey's New Zealand Reports.

Mac.Pat.Cas. Macrory's Patent Cases.

Mac. & G. Macnaghten & Gordon's English Chancery Reports.

Mac. & Rob. Maclean & Robinson's Scotch Appeal Cases.

MacAr. (or MacArth., MacArthur). MacArthur's District of Columbia Reports;—MacArthur's Patent Cases.

MacAr.Pat.Cas. MacArthur's Patent Cases.

MacAr. & M. MacArthur & Mackey's District of Columbia Reports.

Macas. Macassey's Reports, New Zealand.

Macaulay, Hist.Eng. Macaulay's History of England.

Macc.Cas. Maccala's Breach of Promise Cases.

Maccl. Macclesfield's Reports, 10 Modern Reports.

Maccl.Tr. Macclesfield's Trial (Impeachment), London, 1725.

Macd.Jam. Macdougall's Jamaica Reports.

Macf. (or Macfar. or MacFarl.). Macfarlane's Reports, Jury Courts, Scotland.

Mackeld. Mackeldey on Modern Civil Law;—Mackeldey on Roman Law.

Mackeld.Civil Law. Mackeldey on Modern Civil Law.

Mackeld.Rom.Law. Mackeldey on Roman Law.

Mackey. Mackey's Reports, District of Columbia.

Macl. McLean's United States Circuit Court Reports;—Maclaurin's Scotch Criminal Decisions.

Macl.Dec. Maclaurin's Scotch Criminal Decisions.

Macl.Shipp. Maclachlan on Merchant Shipping.

Macl. & R. Maclean & Robinson's Scotch Appeal Cases.

Macn. Macnaghten's Select Cases in Chancery *tempore* King;—W. H. Macnaghten's Reports, India.

Macn. (Fr.). Sir Francis Macnaghten's Bengal Reports.

Macn.N.A.Beng. Macnaghten's Nizamut Adawlut Reports, Bengal.

Macn.S.D.A.Beng. (W. H.) Macnaghten's Sudder Dewanny Adawlut Reports, Bengal.

Macn. & G. Macnaghten & Gordon's English Chancery Reports.

Macph. Macpherson, Lee & Bell's (Third Series) Scotch Court of Session Cases.

Macph.Jud.Com. Macpherson, Practice of the Judicial Committee of the Privy Council.

Macph.Priv.Coun. Macpherson's Privy Council Practice.

Macph.S. & L. Macpherson, Shirreff & Lee, Scotland.

Macq. (or Macq.H.L.Cas.). Macqueen's Scotch Appeal Cases (House of Lords).

Macr.P.Cas. Macrory's Patent Cases.

Macr. & H. Macrae & Hertslet's Insolvency Cases.

MacSwin.Mines. MacSwinney, Law of Mines, Quarries, and Minerals.

Mad. Maddock's English Chancery Reports;—Madras;—Maddox's Reports, vols. 9–19 Montana.

Mad.H.C. Madras High Court Reports.

Mad.S.D.A.R. Madras Sudder Dewanny Adawlut Reports.

Mad.Sel.Dec. Madras Select Decrees.

Mad.Ser. Madras Series (East) India Law Reports.

Mad. & B. Maddox & Bach's Reports, vol. 19 Montana.

Mad. & Gel. Maddock & Geldart's English Chancery Reports, vol. 6 Maddock's Reports.

Madd. Maddock's English Chancery Reports;—Maddox's Reports, vols. 9–19 Montana.

Madd.Ch.Pr. Maddock's Chancery Practice.

Madras L.J. Madras Law Journal.

Mag.Cas. Magistrates' Cases, especially the series edited by Bittleston, Wise, & Parnell.

Mag.Char. Magna Carta or Charta. See Barrington's Revised Statutes of England, 1870, vol. 1, p. 84, and Coke's Second Institute, vol. 1, first 78 pages.

Mag.Dig. Magrath's South Carolina Digest.

Mag.Rot. Magus Rotulus (the Great Roll of the Exchequer).

Mag. & Con. Magistrate and Constable.

Mag. & M. & P.L. Magistrate and Municipal and Parochial Lawyer.

Magruder. Magruder's Reports, vols. 1, 2 Maryland.

Maine, Anc.Law. Maine on Ancient Law.

Maine L.Rev. Maine Law Review.

Maine, Popular Govt. Maine, Popular Government.

Maitland. Maitland's Manuscript Scotch Session Cases.

Malloy. Malloy's Irish Chancery Reports.

Malone. Editor, vols. 6, 9, and 10, Heiskell's Tennessee Reports.

Man. Manning's Reports (English Court of Revision);—Manitoba;—Manning's Reports, vol. 1 Michigan;—Manuscript;—Manson's English Bankruptcy Cases.

Man.Cas. Manumission Cases in New Jersey, by Bloomfield.

Man.El.Cas. Manning's English Election Cases (Court of Revision).

Man.Exch.Pr. Manning's Exchequer Practice.

Man.Gr. & S. (or Man., G. & S). Manning, Granger, and Scott's English Common Pleas Reports.

Man.Int.Law. Manning, Commentaries on the Law of Nations.

Man.L.J. Manitoba Law Journal.

Man.L.R. Manitoba Law Reports.

Man.t.Wood. Manitoba *tempore* Wood.

Man.Unrep.Cas. Manning's Unreported Cases, La.

Man. & G. Manning & Granger's English Common Pleas Reports.

Man. & Ry. Manning & Ryland's English King's Bench Reports.

Man. & Ry.Mag.Cas. (or Man. & R.). Manning & Ryland's English Magistrates' Cases.

Man. & S. Manning & Scott's Reports, vol. 9 Common Bench.

Manb.Coke. Manby's Abridgment of Coke's Reports.

Manitoba. Armour's Queen's Bench and County Court Reports *tempore* Wood, Manitoba;—Manitoba Law Reports.

Manning (or Man.Unrep.Cas.). Manning's Unreported Cases, Louisiana;—Manning's Reports, vol. 1 Michigan.

Manning, La. Unreported Cases, Louisiana.

Mans. Mansfield's Reports, vols. 49–52 Arkansas;—Manson, English Bankruptcy Cases.

Manson. Manson, Eng.

Manson, Bankr.Cas. Manson's Bankruptcy and Winding-Up Cases.

Manum.Cases. Manumission Cases, New Jersey (Bloomfield's).

Manw. (or Manw.For.Laws). Manwood's Forest Laws.

Mar. March's English King's Bench Reports;— Marshall's United States Circuit Court Reports;—Marshall's Kentucky Reports;—Martin's Louisiana Reports;—Martin's North Carolina Reports;—Marshall's Reports, Bengal;—Maryland.

Mar.Br. March's Translation of Brooke's New Cases.

Mar.L.C. English Maritime Law Cases (Crockford).

Mar.L.C.N.S. English Maritime Law Cases, New Series (Aspinall).

Mar.La. Martin's Louisiana Reports.

Mar.N.C. Martin's North Carolina Reports.

Mar.N.S. (or Mart. [N.S.]). Martin's Louisiana Reports, New Series.

Mar.Prov. Maritime Province Reports, Canada.

Mar.R. English Maritime Law Reports.

Mar.Reg. Mitchell's Maritime Register, London.

March. March's Translation of Brooke's New Cases, King's Bench.

March N.C. March's New Cases, English King's Bench.

Marine Ct.R. Marine Court Reporter (McAdam's) New York.

Marks & Sayre. Marks & Sayre's Reports, vol. 108 Alabama.

Marquette L.Rev. Marquette Law Review.

Marr. Marriott's English Admiralty Decisions;—Marrack's European Assurance Cases.

Marr.Adm. Marriott's Reports, English Admiralty.

Mars. Marsden's English Admiralty Reports.

Mars.Adm. Marsden's Admiralty, Eng.

Marsh. Marshall's United States Circuit Court Decisions;—Marshall's English Common Pleas Reports;—Marshall's Bengal Reports;—Marshall, Kentucky;—Marshall's Reports, vol. 4 Utah.

Marsh. (A.K.). A. K. Marshall's Kentucky Reports.

Marsh. (J.J.). J. J. Marshall's Kentucky Reports.

Marsh.Beng. (or Calc.). Marshall's Reports, Bengal.

Marsh.C.P. Marshall's English Common Pleas Reports.

Marsh.Ceylon. Marshall's Ceylon Reports.

Marsh.Dec. Marshall's United States Circuit Court Decisions (Brockenbrough);—Marshall on the Federal Constitution.

Marsh.Ins. Marshall on Marine Insurance.

Marsh.Op. Marshall's Constitutional Opinions.

Mart. Martin (see Martin).

Mart. (La.). Martin's Louisiana Reports.

Mart. (N.C.). Martin's North Carolina Reports.

Mart.Cond.La. Martin's Condensed Louisiana Reports.

Mart.Dec. United States Decisions in Martin's North Carolina Reports.

Martin, Dict. Edward Martin's English Dictionary.

Mart.N.S. (La.). Martin's Louisiana Reports, New Series.

Mart.O.S. (La.). Martin's Louisiana Reports, Old Series.

Mart.U.S.C.C. Martin's United States Circuit Court Reports.

Mart. & Y. (Tenn.). Martin & Yerger's Tennessee Reports.

Mart. & Yerg. Martin & Yerger's Tennessee Reports.

Marth.W.Ca. Martha Washington Case, see United States v. Cole, 5 McLean, 513, Fed.Cas.No.14,832.

Martin. Martin's Louisiana Reports;—Martin's North Carolina Reports;—Martin's Reports, vols. 21–30 Georgia;—Martin's Reports, vols. 54–70 Indiana.

Martin Index. Martin's Index to Virginia Reports.

Marv. Marvel's Reports, Delaware.

Mas. (or Mason [U.S.]). Mason's United States Circuit Court Reports.

Mason's Code. Mason's United States Code Annotated.

Mass. Massachusetts;—Massachusetts Reports.

Mass.Elec.Ca. Massachusetts Election Cases.

Mass.L.Q. Massachusetts Law Quarterly.

Mass.L.R. Massachusetts Law Reporter, Boston.

Massey v. Headford. An Irish Criminal Conversation Case, 1804. Originally printed in Ireland and reprinted both in New York and Philadelphia.

Mast. Master's Reports, vols. 25–28 Canada Supreme Court.

Mat. Mathews.

Mat.Par. (or Paris). Matthew Paris, Historia Minor.

Math.Pres.Ev. Mathews on Presumptive Evidence.

Mathews. Mathews' Reports, vols. 6–9 West Virginia.

Mats. (or Matson). Matson's Reports, vols. 22–24 Connecticut.

Matthews. Matthew's Reports, vol. 75 Virginia.

Maude & P.Shipp. Maude & Pollock's Law of Merchant Shipping.

Maude & P.Mer.Shipp. Maude & Pollock's Law of Merchant Shipping.

Maul. & Sel. (or Maule & S.). Maule & Selwyn's English King's Bench Reports.

Maur.Dec. Mauritius Decisions.

Max.Dig. Maxwell's Nebraska Digest.

Maxw.Adv.Gram. W. H. Maxwell's Advanced Lessons in English Grammar.

Maxw.Cr.Proc. Maxwell's Treatise on Criminal Procedure.

Maxw.Interp.St. Maxwell on the Interpretation of Statutes.

May, Ins. May on Insurance.

May, Parl.Law. May's Parliamentary Law.

May, Parl.Pr. May's Parliamentary Practice.

Mayn. Maynard's Reports, Edward II. (Year Books, Part I).

Mc. See also Mac.

McAdam, Landl. & T. McAdam on Landlord and Tenant.

McAll. (or McAl.) McAllister's United States Circuit Court Reports.

McBride. McBride's Reports, vol. 1 Missouri.

McCah. McCahon's Reports (United States District Court for the District of Kansas).

McCahon. McCahon, Kan.

McCar. McCarter's New Jersey Equity Reports;—McCarty's New York Civil Procedure Reports.

McCart. McCarter, N.J.

McCarty, Civ.Proc. McCarty's Civil Procedure Reports, N.Y.

McCl. McClelland's English Exchequer Reports.

McCl. & Y. McClelland & Younge's English Exchequer Reports.

McClain's Code. McClain's Annotated Code and Statutes, Iowa.

McClain, Cr.Law. McClain's Criminal Law.

McClell. McClelland, Eng.

McClell. & Y. McClelland & Younge, Eng.

McCook. McCook's Reports, vol. 1 Ohio State.

McCord. McCord's South Carolina Law Reports.

McCord Eq. (or Ch.). McCord's South Carolina Equity Reports.

McCorkle. McCorkle's Reports, vol. 65 North Carolina.

McCr. (or McCrary). McCrary's United States Circuit Court Reports.

McCrary, Elect. McCrary's American Law of Elections.

McCul.Dict. McCullough's Commercial Dictionary.

McCul.Pol.Econ. McCulloch, Political Economy.

McDevitt. McDevitt's Land Commissioner's Reports, Ireland.

McFar. McFarlane's Reports (Scotch Jury Court).

McGill. McGill's Manuscript Scotch Session Cases.

McGl. (or McGloin). McGloin's Louisiana Reports.

McKelvey, Ev. McKelvey on Evidence.

McL. (or McLean). McLean's United States Circuit Court Reports.

McL. & R. McLean & Robinson's Scotch Appeal Cases.

McM.Com.Dec. McMaster's Commercial Decisions.

McMul. McMullan's South Carolina Law Reports.

McMul.Eq. McMullan's South Carolina Equity Reports.

McNagh. McNaghten (see Macn.).

McPherson. McPherson, Lee, & Bell's (Third Series) Scotch Session Cases.

McWillie. McWillie's Reports, vols. 73–76 Mississippi.

Md. Maryland;—Maryland Reports;—Harris & McHenry's Maryland Reports.

Md.Ch. Maryland Chancery Decisions.

Md.L.Rec. Maryland Law Record, Baltimore.

Md.L.Rep. Maryland Law Reporter, Baltimore.

Md.L.Rev. Maryland Law Review.

Me. Maine;—Maine Reports.

Means. Means' Kansas Reports.

Mechem, Ag. Mechem on Agency.

Mechem, Pub.Off. Mechem on Public Offices and Officers.

Med.L.J. (or Med.Leg.J.). Medico-Legal Journal, New York.

Med.L.N. (or Med.Leg.N.). Medico Legal News, New York.

Med.L.P. Medico Legal Papers, New York.

Medd. Meddaugh's Reports, vol. 13 Michigan.

Mees. & Ros. Meeson & Roscoe's English Exchequer Reports.

Mees. & W. (or Wels.). Meeson & Welsby's English Exchequer Reports.

Meg. Megone's Company Case.

Meigs. Meigs' Tennessee Reports.

Meigs, Dig. Meigs' Digest of Decisions of the Courts of Tennessee.

Melv.Tr. Melville's Trial (Impeachment), London.

Mem. in Scacc. Memorandum or memoranda in the Exchequer.

Mem.L.J. Memphis Law Journal, Tennessee.

Memphis L.J. Memphis Law Journal, Tenn.

Menken. Menken's Reports, vol. 30 New York Civil Procedure Reports.

Menz. (or Menzies Cape of Good Hope.). Menzies' Reports, Cape of Good Hope.

Mer. Merivale's Chancery Reports.

Mercer, Beasley L.Rev. Mercer, Beasley Law Review.

Mercer L.Rev. Mercer Law Review.

Meriv. Merivale's English Chancery Reports.

Merl.Quest. Merlin, Questions de Droit.

Merl. Répert. Merlin, Répertoire de Jurisprudence.

Met. (or Metc.). Metcalf's Massachusetts Reports;—Metcalfe's Kentucky Reports;—Metcalf's Reports, vol. 3 Rhode Island.

Metc.Ky. Metcalfe's Kentucky Reports.

Meth.Ch.Ca. Report of Methodist Church Case.

Miami L.Q. Miami Law Quarterly.

Mich. Michigan;—Michigan Reports;—Michaelmas.

Mich.C.C.R. Michigan Circuit Court Reporter, Marquette.

Mich.L.J. Michigan Law Journal.

Mich.L.Rev. Michigan Law Review.

Mich.Lawyer. Michigan Lawyer.

Mich.Leg.News. Michigan Legal News.

Mich.N.P. Michigan Nisi Prius Reports.

Mich.Pol.Soc. Michigan Political Science Association.

Mich.S.B.J. Michigan State Bar Journal.

Mich.T. Michaelmas Terms.

Mich.Vac. Michaelmas Vacation.

Middx.Sit. Sittings for Middlesex at Nisi Prius.

Mil. Miles' Pennsylvania Reports;—Miller (see Mill.).

Miles. Miles' District Court Reports, City and County of Philadelphia, Pennsylvania.

Mill. Mill's South Carolina Constitutional Reports;—Miller's Reports, vols. 1–5 Louisiana;—Miller's Reports, vols. 3–18 Maryland;—Miller's Decisions, United States.

Mill, Const. (S.C.). Mill's South Carolina Constitutional Reports.

Mill.Dec. Miller's Decisions (Woolworth's Reports) United States Circuit Court;—Miller's Decisions United States Supreme Court.

Mill.La. Miller's Reports, vols. 1–5 Louisiana.

Mill, Log. Mill's Logic.

Mill.Md. Miller's Reports, vols. 3–18 Maryland.

Mill, Pol.Ec. Mill's Political Economy.

Mill. & V.Code. Milliken & Vertrees' Code, Tenn.

Miller. Miller's Reports, vols. 1–5 Louisiana;—Miller's Reports, vols. 3–18 Maryland.

Miller, Const. Miller on the Constitution of the United States.

Miller's Code. Miller's Revised and Annotated Code, Iowa.

Mills. Mills Surrogate, N.Y.

Mills' Ann.St. Mills' Annotated Statutes, Colo.

Mills, Em.Dom. Mills on Eminent Domain.

Milw. Milward's Irish Ecclesiastical Reports.

Min. Minor;—Minor's Alabama Reports.

Min.Inst. Minor's Institutes Statute Law.

Minn. Minnesota;—Minnesota Reports.

Minn.Ct.Rep. Minnesota Court Reporter.

Minn.L.Rev. Minnesota Law Review.

Minn.Law J. Minnesota Law Journal.

Minor. Minor's Alabama Reports;—Minor's Institutes.

Minor, Inst. Minor's Institutes of Common and Statute Law.

Minshew. Minshew (John), "The Guide into the Tongues also the Exposition of the Terms of the Laws of this Land." (England.)

Mirr. Horne's Mirror of Justices.

Misc.Laws. Miscellaneous Laws, Or.

Miscel. (or Misc.Rep.). Miscellaneous Reports, N.Y.

Miss. Mississippi;—Mississippi Reports;—Missouri.

Miss.Dec. Mississippi Decisions, Jackson.

Miss.L.J. Mississippi Law Journal.

Miss.St.Ca. Mississippi State Cases.

Mister. Mister's Reports, vols. 17–32 Missouri Appeals.

Mitch.M.R. Mitchell's Maritime Register, London.

Mitch.Mod.Geog. Mitchell's Modern Geography.

Mitf.Eq.Pl. Mitford on Equity Pleading.

McMul. McMullan, South Carolina.

Mo. Missouri;—Missouri Reports;—Moore's English King's Bench Reports;—Moore's English Common Pleas Reports;—Moore's English Privy Council Reports;—Modern Reports, English;—English King's Bench, etc., (see Mod.);—Monthly;—Moore's Indian Appeal Cases.

Mo. (F.). Sir Francis Moore's English King's Bench Reports.

Mo. (J.B.). J. B. Moore's English Common Pleas Reports.

Mo.App. Missouri Appeal Reports.

Mo.App.Rep. Missouri Appellate Reporter.

Mo.I.A. Moore's Indian Appeals.

Mo.L.Rev. Missouri Law Review.

Mo.P.C. Moore's English Privy Council Reports.

Mo.St.Ann. Missouri Statutes Annotated.

Mo. & P. Moore & Payne's English Common Pleas Reports.

Mo. & R. Moody & Robinson's English Nisi Prius Reports.

Mo. & S. Moore & Scott's English Common Pleas Reports.

Moak, Eng.R. Moak's English Reports.

Moak, Underh.Torts. Moak's Edition of Underhill on Torts.

Moak & Eng.Rep. Moak's English Reports.

Mob. Mobley's Election Cases.

Mod. Modern Reports, English King's Bench, etc;—Modified.

Mod.Cas. Modern Cases, vol. 6 Modern Reports.

Mod.Cas.L. & Eq. Modern Cases at Law and Equity, vols. 8, 9 Modern Reports.

Mod.Cas.per Far. (or t.Holt). Modern Cases *tempore* Holt, by Farresley, vol. 7 Modern Reports.

Mod.Rep. The Modern Reports, English King's Bench, etc.;—Modern Reports by Style (Style's King's Bench Reports).

Mol. (or Moll.). Molloy's Irish Chancery Reports.

Mol.de Jure Mar. Molloy, De Jure Maritimo et Navali.

Molloy. Molloy, Ireland.

Moly. Molyneau's Reports, English Courts.

Mon. Montana;—T. B. Monroe's Kentucky Reports;—Ben Monroe's Kentucky Reports.

Mon. (B.). Ben Monroe's Kentucky Reports.

Mon. (T.B.). T. B. Monroe's Kentucky Reports.

Mon.Angl. Monasticon Anglicanum.

Mona. (or Monaghan). Monaghan's Reports, vols. 147–165 Pennsylvania.

Monag. Monaghan, Pa.

Monr. Monroe (see Mon.).

Monroe L.R. Monroe Legal Reporter, Pa.

Mont. Montana;—Montana Reports;—Montagu's English Bankruptcy Reports;—Montriou's Bengal Reports.

Mont.Bank.Rep. Montagu's English Bankruptcy Reports.

Mont.Co.L.R. Montgomery County Law Reporter, Pennsylvania.

Mont.Cond.Rep. Montreal Condensed Reports.

Mont.D. & De G. Montagu, Deacon & De Gex's English Bankruptcy Reports.

Mont.Ind. Monthly Index to Reporters (National Reporter System).

Mont.L.R. Montreal Law Reports, Queen's Bench;—Montreal Law Reports, Superior Court.

Mont.L.R.Q.B. Montreal Law Reports, Queen's Bench.

Mont.L.R.S.C. Montreal Law Reports, Superior Court.

Mont.Law Rev. Montana Law Review.

Mont. & A. (Mont. & Ayr.). Montagu & Ayrton, Eng.

Mont. & B. (Mont. & Bl.). Montagu & Bligh's English Bankruptcy Reports.

Mont. & C. Montagu & Chitty's English Bankruptcy Reports.

Mont. & M. (or Mont. & Mac A.). Montagu and MacArthur's English Bankruptcy Reports.

Montesq. (or Montesq.Esprit des Lois). Montesquieu, Esprit des Lois.

Montg. (or Montg.Co.Law Rep'r) (Pa.). Montgomery County Law Reporter, Pennsylvania.

Month.Jur. Monthly Jurist, Bloomington, Ill.

Month.L.J. Monthly Journal of Law, Wash.

Month.L.Mag. Monthly Law Magazine (London).

Month.L.Rep. Monthly Law Reporter, Boston.

Month.L.Rev. Monthly Law Review.

Month.Law Bul. Monthly Law Bulletin, N.Y.

Month.Leg.Exam. Monthly Legal Examiner, N.Y.

Month.West.Jur. Monthly Western Jurist, Bloomington, Ill.

Montr. Montriou's Reports, Bengal;—Montriou's Supplement to Morton's Reports.

Montr.Cond.Rep. Montreal Condensed Reports.

Montr.Leg.N. Montreal Legal News.

Montr.Q.B. Montreal Law Reports, Queen's Bench.

Montr.Super. Montreal Law Reports, Superior Court.

Moo. Francis Moore's English King's Bench Reports;—J. M. Moore's English Common Pleas Reports;—Moody's English Crown Cases.

Moo.A. Moore's Reports, vol. 1 Bosanquet & Puller, after page 470.

Moo.C.C. (or Moo.Cr.C.). Moody's English Crown Cases Reserved.

Moo.C.P. Moore's English Common Pleas Reports.

Moo.Ind.App. Moore's Reports, Privy Council, Indian Appeals.

Moo.J.B. Moore's English Common Pleas Reports.

Moo.K.B. Moore's English King's Bench Reports.

Moo.P.C. Moore's Privy Council Cases, Old and New Series.

Moo.Tr. Moore's Divorce Trials.

Moo. & Mal. Moody & Malkin's English Nisi Prius Reports.

Moo. & Pay. Moore & Payne's English Common Pleas Reports.

Moo. & Rob. Moody & Robinson's English Nisi Prius Reports.

Moo. & Sc. Moore & Scott's English Common Pleas Reports.

Mood. (or Moody). Moody's English Crown Cases, Reserved.

Mood. & Malk. Moody & Malkin's English Nisi Prius Reports.

Mood. & R. Moody & Robinson's English Nisi Prius Reports.

Mood. & Rob. Moody & Robinson, English.

Moody, Cr.Cas. Moody's English Crown Cases.

Moody & M. Moody & Mackin's English Nisi Prius Reports.

Moody & R. Moody and Robinson's English Nisi Prius Reports.

Moon. Moon's Reports, vols. 133–144 Indiana and vols. 6–14 Indiana Appeals.

Moore. Moore's English King's Bench Reports;—Moore's English Common Pleas Reports;—Moore's English Privy Council Reports;—Moore's Reports, vols. 28–34 Arkansas;—Moore's Reports, vol. 67 Alabama;—Moore's Reports, vols. 22–24 Texas.

Moore (A.). A. Moore's Reports in 1 Bosanquet & Puller, after page 470.

Moore C.P. Moore's English Common Pleas Reports.

Moore, Cr.Law. Moore's Criminal Law and Procedure.

Moore E.I. Moore's East Indian Appeals.

Moore G.C. Moore's Gorham Case (English Privy Council).

Moore Indian App. Moore's Indian Appeals, Eng.

Moore K.B. Sir F. Moore's English King's Bench Reports.

Moore P.C. Moore's English Privy Council Reports

Moore P.C.N.S. Moore's English Privy Council Reports, New Series.

Moore, Presby.Dig. Moore's Presbyterian Digest.

Moore & P. Moore & Payne's English Common Pleas Reports.

Moore & S. Moore & Scott's English Common Pleas Reports.

Moore & W. (or Moore & Walker). Moore & Walker's Reports, vols. 22–24 Texas.

Mor. Morison's Dictionary of Decisions in the Court of Session, Scotland;—Morris (see Morr.).

Mor.Corp. Morawetz on Private Corporations.

Mor.Dic. Morison's Dictionary, Scotch Decisions and Supplement.

Mor.Ia. Morris' Iowa Reports.

Mor.Min.Rep. Morrison's Mining Reports.

Mor.Priv.Corp. Morawetz on Private Corporations.

Mor.St.Cas. Morris' Mississippi State Cases.

Mor.Supp. Supplement to Morison's Dictionary, Scotch Court of Session.

Mor.Syn. Morison's Synopsis, Scotch Session Cases.

Mor.Tran. Morrison's Transcript of United States Supreme Court Decisions.

Moreau & Carleton's Partidas. Moreau-Lislet and Carleton's Laws of Las Siètè Partidas in force in Louisiana.

Morg. & W.L.J. Morgan & Williams' Law Journal, London.

Morl.Dig. Morley's East Indian Digest.

Morr. Morris' Iowa Reports (see, also, Morris and Mor.);—Morrow's Reports, vols. 23–36 Oregon;—Morrell's English Bankruptcy Reports.

Morr.Jam. Morris' Jamaica Reports.

Morr.M.R. (or Morr.Min.Rep.). Morrison's Mining Reports, Chicago.

Morr.St.Cas. Morris' State Cases, Mississippi.

Morr.Trans. Morrison's Transcript, United States Supreme Court Decisions.

Morrell, Bankr.Cas. Morrell's English Bankruptcy Cases.

Morris. Morris' Iowa Reports;—Morris' Reports, vol. 5 California;—Morris' Reports, vols. 43–48 Mississippi;—Morris' Jamaica Reports;—Morris' Bombay Reports;—Morrissett's Reports, vols. 80, 98 Alabama.

Morris Repl. Morris on Replevin.

Morris & Har. Morris & Harrington's Sudder Dewanny Adawlut Reports, Bombay.

Morse, Banks. Morse on the Law of Banks and Banking.

Morse Tr. Morse's Famous Trials.

Morton. Morton's Reports, Bengal.

Mos. Mosely's English Chancery Reports.

Moult.Ch.P. Moulton's Chancery Practice, New York.

Mozley & Whiteley. Mozley & Whiteley's Law Dictionary.

Mu.Corp.Ca. Withrow's Corporation Cases, vol. 2.

Mulford, Nation. Mulford, The Nation.

Mum.Jam. Mumford's Jamaica Reports.

Mumf. Mumford's Jamaica Reports.

Mun. (or Mun.L.Rep.). Municipal Law Reporter.

Mun. (or Munf.). Munford's Virginia Reports.

Mun.Code. Municipal Code.

Mun.Corp.Cas. Municipal Corporation Cases.

Mun.L.J. Municipal Law Journal.

Mur. Murphey's North Carolina Reports;—Murray's Scotch Jury Court Reports;—Murray's Ceylon Reports;—Murray's New South Wales Reports.

Mur.U.S.Ct. Murray's Proceedings in the United States Courts.

Mur. & Hurl. Murphy & Hurlstone's English Exchequer Reports.

Murfree, Off.Bonds. Murfree on Official Bonds.

Murph. Murphey's North Carolina Reports.

Murr. Murray's Scotch Jury Trials;—Murray's Ceylon Reports;—Murray's New South Wales Reports.

Murray. Murray's Scotch Jury Court Reports.

Murray (Ceylon). Murray's Ceylon Reports.

Murray's Eng.Dict. Murray's English Dictionary.

Mutukisna. Mutukisna's Ceylon Reports.

Myer Dig. Myer's Texas Digest.

Myer Fed.Dec. Myer's Federal Decisions.

Myl. & C. (or Cr.). Mylne & Craig's English Chancery Reports.

Myl. & K. (or Mylne & K.). Mylne & Keen's English Chancery Reports.

Myr. Myrick's California Probate Court Reports.

Myr.Prob. (Cal.). Myrick's California Probate Court Reports.

N

N. Nebraska;—Nevada;—Northeastern Reporter (properly cited N. E.);—Northwestern Reporter (properly cited N. W.).

N.Am.Rev. North American Review.

N.B. New Brunswick Reports.

N.B.Eq. New Brunswick Equity.

N.B.Eq.Ca. New Brunswick Equity Cases.

N.B.Eq.Rep. New Brunswick Equity Reports.

N.B.N.R. (or N.B.N.Rep.). National Bankruptcy News and Reports.

N.B.R. National Bankruptcy Register, New York;—New Brunswick Reports.

N.B.Rep. New Brunswick Reports.

N.B.V.Ad. New Brunswick Vice Admiralty Reports.

N.Benl. New Benloe, English King's Bench Reports.

N.C. North Carolina;—North Carolina Reports;—Notes of Cases (English, Ecclesiastical, and Maritime);—New Cases (Bingham's New Cases).

N.C.C. New Chancery Cases (Younge & Collyer).

N.C.C.A. Negligence & Compensation Cases Annotated (U.S.).

N.C.Conf. North Carolina Conference Reports.

N.C.Ecc. Notes of Cases in the Ecclesiastical and Maritime Courts.

N.C.L.Rep. North Carolina Law Repository.

N.C.L.Rev. North Carolina Law Review.

N.C.Str. Notes of Cases, by Strange, Madras.

N.C.T.Rep. (or N.C.Term R.). North Carolina Term Reports.

N.Car. North Carolina;—North Carolina Reports.

N.Chip. (or N.Chip. [Vt.]). N. Chipman's Vermont Reports.

N.D. North Dakota;—North Dakota Reports.

N.D.L.Rev. North Dakota Law Review.

N.E. New England;—New edition;—North Eastern Reporter.

N.E.2d. North Eastern Reporter, Second Series.

N.E.R. North Eastern Reporter (commonly cited N. E.);—New England Reporter.

N.E.Rep. North Eastern Reporter.

N.F. Newfoundland;—Newfoundland Reports.

N.H. New Hampshire;—New Hampshire Reports.

N.H.L.Rep. New Hamphire Law Reporter.

N.H.R. New Hampshire Reports.

N.H. & C. English Railway and Canal Cases, by Nicholl, Hare, Carrow, etc.

N.J. New Jersey;—New Jersey Reports.

N.J.Eq. (or Ch.). New Jersey Equity Reports.

N.J.L. New Jersey Law Reports.

N.J.L.J. (or N.J.Law J.). New Jersey Law Journal.

N.J.L.Rev. New Jersey Law Review.

N.J.Misc. New Jersey Miscellaneous.

N.J.S.A. New Jersey Statutes Annotated.

N.J.Super. New Jersey Superior Court Reports.

N.L. Nelson's Lutwyche, English Common Pleas Reports.

N.L.L. New Library of Law and Equity, English.

N.L.R.B. National Labor Relations Board Reports.

N.M. New Mexico;—New Mexico Reports.

N.M.St.Bar Assn. New Mexico State Bar Association.

N.Mag.Ca. New Magistrates' Cases.

N. of Cas. Notes of Cases, English Ecclesiastical and Maritime Courts;—Notes of Cases at Madras (by Strange).

N. of Cas.Madras. Notes of Cases at Madras (by Strange).

N.P. Nisi Prius.

N.P.C. Nisi Prius Cases.

N.P.R. Nisi Prius Reports.

N.R. New Reports (English, 1862–1865);—Bosanquet & Puller's New Reports;—Not Reported.

N.R.B.P. New Reports of Bosanquet & Puller.

N.R.L. Revised Laws 1813, N.Y.

N.S. New Series;—Nova Scotia.

N.S.Dec. Nova Scotia Decisions.

N.S.L.R. Nova Scotia Law Reports.

N.S.R. Nova Scotia Reports.

N.S.W. New South Wales Reports, Old and New Series.

N.S.W.Eq.Rep. (or N.S.Wales L.R.Eq.). New South Wales Law Reports Equity.

N.S.Wales L. New South Wales Law.

N.S.W.L.R. New South Wales Law Reports.

N.S.W.St.R. New South Wales State Reports.

N.Sc.Dec. Nova Scotia Decisions.

N.W. North Western Reporter.

N.W.2d. North Western Reporter, Second Series.

N.W.L.Rev. North Western Law Review, Chicago.

N.W.R. (or Rep.). North Western Reporter.

N.W.T. (or N.W.T.Rep.). Northwest Territories Reports, Canada.

N.Y. New York;—New York Court of Appeals Reports.

N.Y.Ann.Ca. New York Annotated Cases.

N.Y.App.Dec. New York Court of Appeals Decisions.

N.Y.Cas.Err. New York Cases in Error (Caines' Cases).

N.Y.Ch.Sent. New York Chancery Sentinel.

N.Y.City Ct. New York City Court.

N.Y.City Ct.Suppl. New York City Court Supplement.

N.Y.City H.Rec. New York City Hall Recorder.

N.Y.Civ.Pr.Rep. New York Civil Procedure Reports.

N.Y.Civ.Proc. New York Civil Procedure.

N.Y.Civ.Proc.R., N.S. New York Civil Procedure Reports, New Series.

N.Y.Code Rep. (or N.Y.Code Report.). New York Code Reporter.

N.Y.Code Reports, N.S. New York Code Reports, New Series.

N.Y.Cond. New York Condensed Reports.

N.Y.Cr.R. (or Rep.). New York Criminal Reports.

N.Y.Ct.App. New York Court of Appeals.

N.Y.Daily L.Gaz. New York Daily Law Gazette.

N.Y.Daily Reg. New York Daily Register.

N.Y.El.Cas. (or N.Y.Elect.Cas.). New York Election Cases.

N.Y.Jur. New York Jurist.

N.Y.L.C.Ann. New York Leading Cases Annotated.

N.Y.L.Gaz. New York Law Gazette, N. Y.

N.Y.L.Rec. New York Law Record.

N.Y.L.Rev. New York Law Review.

N.Y.L.S.Rev. New York Law School Review.

N.Y.Law J. New York Law Journal.

N.Y.Leg.N. New York Legal News.

N.Y.Leg.Obs. New York Legal Observer, New York City (Owen's).

N.Y.Leg.Reg. New York Legal Register.

N.Y.Misc. New York Miscellaneous Reports.

N.Y.Mo.L.R. New York Monthly Law Reports.

N.Y.Month.L.Bul. New York Monthly Law Bulletin.

N.Y.Month.L.R. New York Monthly Law Reports.

N.Y.Mun.Gaz. New York Municipal Gazette.

N.Y.Op.Att.-Gen. Sickels' Opinions of the Attorney-General of New York.

N.Y.P.R. New York Practice Reports.

N.Y.Pr.Rep. New York Practice Reports.

N.Y.Rec. New York Record.

N.Y.Reg. New York Daily Register.

N.Y.Rep. New York Court of Appeals Reports.

N.Y.Reptr. New York Reporter (Gardenier's).

N.Y.S. New York Supplement;—New York State;—New York State Reporter.

N.Y.S.2d New York Supplement Reporter, Second Series.

N.Y.S.B.A.Bull. New York State Bar Association Bulletin.

N.Y.Spec.Term R. Howard's Practice Reports.

N.Y.St.Dept.Rep. New York State Department Reports.

N.Y.St.Rep. New York State Reporter.

N.Y.Sup. New York Supreme Court Reports.

N.Y.Super.Ct. New York Superior Court Reports.

N.Y.Supp. New York Supplement.

N.Y.Supr. New York Supreme Court Reports.

N.Y.T.R. New York Term Reports (Caines' Reports).

N.Y.Them. New York Themis.

N.Y.U.L.Q.Rev. New York University Law Quarterly Review.

N.Y.Wkly.Dig. New York Weekly Digest.

N.Z. New Zealand;—New Zealand Reports.

N.Z.Jur. New Zealand Jurist.

N.Z.Jur.N.S. New Zealand Jurist, New Series.

N.Z.Rep. New Zealand Reports, Court of Appeals.

N. & H. (or Hop.). Nott & Huntington's United States Court of Claims Reports.

N. & M. Nevile & Manning's English King's Bench Reports.

N. & M.Mag. Nevile & Manning's English Magistrates' Cases.

N. & Mc. Nott & McCord's South Carolina Reports.

N. & P. Nevile & Perry's English King's Bench Reports.

N. & P.Mag. Nevile & Perry's English Magistrates' Cases.

Nal.St.P. Nalton's Collection of State Papers.

Nap. Napier.

Napton. Napton's Reports, vol. 4 Missouri.

Narr.Mod. Narrationes Modernæ, or Style's King's Bench Reports.

Nat.B.C. National Bank Cases.

Nat.B.J. National Bar Journal.

Nat.B.R. (or Nat.Bank.Reg.). National Bankruptcy Register Reports.

Nat.Bankr.Law. National Bankruptcy Law.

Nat.Bankr.R. National Bankruptcy Register, U.S.

Nat.Corp.Rep. National Corporation Reporter, Chicago.

Nat.L.Rec. National Law Record.

Nat.L.Rep. National Law Reporter.

Nat.L.Rev. National Law Review, Philadelphia.

Nat.Mun.Rev. National Municipal Review.

Nat.Reg. National Register, edited by Mead, 1816.

Nat.Rept.Syst. National Reporter System.

Nat.Rev. National Review, London.

Nat.U.L.Rev. National University Law Review.

Natl.Rep.Sys. National Reporter System.

Nd. Newfoundland Reports.

Neb. Nebraska;—Nebraska Reports.

Neb.L.B. Nebraska Law Bulletin.

Neb., Unoff. Nebraska Unofficial.

Neg.Cas. Bloomfield's Manumission or Negro Cases, New Jersey.

Neg.Inst.Law. Negotiable Instrument Law.

Nel. Nelson's English Chancery Reports.

Nell. Nell's Ceylon Reports.

Nels. Nelson's English Chancery Reports.

Nels.Abr. Nelson's Abridgment of the Common Law.

Nels.Fol.Rep. Finch's Chancery Reports, edited by Nelson.

Nev. Nevada;—Nevada Reports.

Nev.S.B.J. Nevada State Bar Journal.

Nev. & M. (or Man.). Nevile & Manning's English King's Bench Reports.

Nev. & Mac. Neville & Macnamara's English Railway and Canal Cases.

Nev. & Macn. Neville & Macnamara's English Railway and Canal Cases.

Nev. & Man.Mag.Cas. Nevile & Manning's English Magistrate's Cases.

Nev. & P. Nevile & Perry's English King's Bench Reports.

Nev. & P.Mag.Cas. Nevile & Perry's English Magistrates' Cases.

New. Newell, Illinois Appeal Reports.

New Ann.Reg. New Annual Register, London.

New B.Eq.Ca. New Brunswick Equity Cases.

New B.Eq.Rep. New Brunswick Equity Reports, vol. 1.

New Benl. New Benloe's Reports, English King's Bench.

New Br. New Brunswick Reports.

New Cas. New Cases (Bingham's New Cases).

New Cas.Eq. New Cases in Equity, vols. 8, 9 Modern Reports.

New Eng.Hist. New England Historical and Genealogical Register.

New Mag.Cas. New Magistrates' Cases (Bittleston, Wise & Parnell).

New Nat.Brev. New Natura Brevium.

New Pr.Cases. New Practice Cases, English.

New Rep. New Reports in all the Courts, London;—Bosanquet & Puller's New Reports, vols. 4, 5 Bosanquet & Puller.

New Sess.Cas. Carrow, Hammerton & Allen's New Session Cases, English.

New So.W. New South Wales.

New Term Rep. New Term Reports;—Dowling & Ryland's King's Bench Reports.

New York City B.A.Bul. Bulletin of Ass'n of the Bar of the City of N. Y.

New York Supp. New York Supplement.

New Zeal.L. New Zealand Law.

Newb. (or Newb.Adm.). Newberry's United States District Court, Admiralty Reports.

Newbyth. Newbyth's Manuscript Decisions, Scotch Session Cases.

Newell. Newell's Reports, vols. 48–90 Illinois Appeals.

Newell, Defam. Newell on Defamation, Slander and Libel.

Newell, Eject. Newell's Treatise on the Action of Ejectment.

Newell, Mal.Pros. Newell's Treatise on Malicious Prosecution.

Newell, Sland. & L. Newell on Slander and Libel.

Newf.Sel.Cas. Newfoundland Select Cases.

Newfoundl. Newfoundland.

Newl.Ch.Prac. Newland's Chancery Practice.

Nich.H. & C. (or Nicholl). Nicholl, Hare & Carrow's English Railway and Canal Cases.

Nicholson. Nicholson's Manuscript Decisions, Scotch Session Cases.

Niebh.Hist.Rom. Niebuhr, Roman History.

Nient cul. *Nient culpable* (not guilty).

Nil.Reg. (or Niles Reg.). Niles' Weekly Register.

Nisbet. (Nisbet of) Dirleton's Scotch Session Cases.

Nisi Prius & Gen.T.Rep. Nisi Prius & General Term Reports, Ohio.

Nix.Dig. Nixon's Digest of Laws. N.J.

No.Ca.Ecc. & Mar. Notes of Cases (English), Ecclesiastical and Maritime.

No.East.Rep. North Eastern Reporter (commonly cited N. E.).

No.West.Rep. North Western Reporter (commonly cited N. W.).

Nol.Mag. (or Just. or Sett.Cas.). Nolan's English Magistrates' Cases.

Nolan. Nolan, Eng.

Non cul. *Non culpabilis* (not guilty).

Norc. Norcross' Reports, vols. 23–24 Nevada.

Norr. Norris' Reports, vols. 82–96 Pennsylvania.

Norris. Norris, Pa.

North. Reports *tempore* Northington (Eden's English Chancery Reports).

North.Co. Northampton County Reporter, Pa.

North W.L.J. North Western Law Journal.

North & G. North & Guthrie's Reports, vols. 68–80 Missouri Appeals.

Northam. (or Northam.Law Rep.). Northampton County Law Reporter, Pa.

Northum. (or Northumb.Co. or Northumb.Co.Leg.N.). Northumberland County Legal News, Pa.

Northumb.L.J. Northumberland Legal Journal, Pa.

Northw.Pr. Northwest Provinces, India.

Northw.Rep. Northwestern Reporter (commonly cited N. W.).

Not.Cas. Notes of Cases in the English Ecclesiastical and Maritime Courts;—Notes of Cases at Madras (Strange).

Not.Cas.Madras. Notes of Cases at Madras (Strange).

Not.Dec. Notes of Decisions (Martin's North Carolina Reports).

Not.J. Notaries Journal.

Not.Op. Wilmot's Notes of Opinions and Judgments.

Notes of Ca. Notes of Cases, English.

Notes on U.S. Notes on United States Reports.

Notre Dame Law. Notre Dame Lawyer.

Nott & Hop. Nott & Hopkins' United States Court of Claims Reports.

Nott & Hunt. Nott & Huntington's Reports, vols. 1–7 United States Court of Claims.

Nott & McC. Nott & McCord's South Carolina Reports.

Nov. Novellæ. The Novels or New Constitutions.

Nov.Sc. Nova Scotia.

Nov.Sc.Dec. Nova Scotia Decisions.

Nov.Sc.L.R. Nova Scotia Law Reports.

Noy. Noy's English King's Bench Reports.

Noy, Max. Noy's Maxims.

Nye. Nye's Reports, vols. 18–20 Utah.

O

O. Ohio Reports;—Ontario;—Ontario Reports;—Oregon Reports;—Otto's United States Supreme Court Reports.

O.B. Old Bailey;—Old Benloe;—Orlando Bridgman.

O.B.S. Old Bailey's Sessions Papers.

O.B. & F.N.Z. Ollivier, Bell & Fitzgerald's New Zealand Reports.

O.Ben. Old Benloe's Reports, English Common Pleas.

O.Bridg. (or O.Bridgm.). Orlando Bridgman's English Common Pleas Reports;—Carter's Reports, *tempore* Bridgman's English Common Pleas.

O.C. Orphans' Court.

O.C.C. Ohio Circuit Court Reports.

O.C.C.N.S. Ohio Circuit Court Reports, New Series.

O.C.D. Ohio Circuit Decisions.

O.D. Ohio Decisions.

O.D.C.C. Ohio Decisions, Circuit Court (properly cited Ohio Circuit Decisions).

O.J.Act. Ontario Judicature Act.

O.L.D. Ohio Lower Court Decisions.

O.L.J. Olwines Law Journal, Pa.

O'M. & H. O'Malley & Hardcastle, Ireland.

O.N.B. Old Natura Brevium.

O.O. Ohio Opinions.

O.R. Ontario Reports.

O.S. Ohio State Reports;—Old Series;—Old Series King's & Queen's Bench Reports, Ontario (Upper Canada);—Oklahoma Statutes.

O.S.A. Oklahoma Statutes Annotated.

O.S.C.D. (or O.S.U.). Ohio Supreme Court Decisions, Unreported Cases.

O.S.Supp. Oklahoma Statutes Supplement.

O.S. & C.P.Dec. Ohio Superior and Common Pleas Decisions.

O.St. Ohio State Reports.

O.S.U. Ohio Supreme Court Decisions, Unreported Cases.

O. & T. Oyer and Terminer.

O. & W.Dig. Oldham and White's Digest of Laws, Tex.

O'Brien. O'Brien's Upper Canada Reports.

O'Callaghan, New Neth. O'Callaghan's History of New Netherland.

Oct.Str. Octavo Strange, Select Cases on Evidence.

Odeneal. Odeneal's Reports, vols. 9–11 Oregon.

Off.Exec. Wentworth's Office of Executors.

Off.Gaz. Official Gazette.

Off.Gaz.Pat.Off. Official Gazette, United States Patent Office.

Officer. Officer's Reports, vols. 1–9 Minnesota.

Ogden. Ogden's Reports, vols. 12–15 Louisiana.

Ogilvie, Dict. Ogilvie's Imperial Dictionary of the English Language.

Ohio. Ohio;—Ohio Reports.

Ohio App. Ohio Appellate Reports.

Ohio Bar. Ohio State Bar Association Report.

Ohio Cir.Ct.R. Ohio Circuit Court Reports.

Ohio Cir.Ct.R.N.S. Ohio Circuit Court Reports, New Series.

Ohio Cir.Dec. Ohio Circuit Decisions.

Ohio Dec. Ohio Decisions.

Ohio Dec.Reprint. Ohio Decisions, Reprint.

Ohio F.Dec. Ohio Federal Decisions.

Ohio Jur. Ohio Jurisprudence.

Ohio Law Abst. Ohio Law Abstract.

Ohio Law Bul. Ohio Law Bulletin.

Ohio Law J. Ohio Law Journal.

Ohio Law Rep. Ohio Law Reporter.

Ohio Leg.N. Ohio Legal News.

Ohio N.P. Ohio Nisi Prius.

Ohio N.P.N.S. Ohio Nisi Prius, New Series.

Ohio O. Ohio Opinions.

Ohio Prob. Ohio Probate.

Ohio St. Ohio State Reports.

Ohio St.L.J. Law Journal of Student Bar Association of Ohio State Univ.

Ohio Sup. & C.P.Dec. (or Ohio S. & C.P.Dec.). Ohio Superior and Common Pleas Decisions.

O'Keefe Ord. O'Keefe's Orders in Chancery, Ireland.

Okl. Oklahoma;—Oklahoma Reports.

Okl.Cr. Oklahoma Criminal Reports.

Okl.L.J. Oklahoma Law Journal.

Okl.St.Ann. Oklahoma Statutes Annotated.

Okla. Oklahoma;—Oklahoma Reports.

Okla.L.Rev. Oklahoma Law Review.

Okla.S.B.J. Oklahoma State Bar Journal.

Olc. (or Olc.Adm., Olcott). Olcott's United States District Court, Admiralty.

Olcott. Olcott, U.S.

Old Ben. Benloe in Benloe & Dalison, English Common Pleas Reports.

Old.Nat.Brev. Old Natura Brevium.

Oldr. Oldright's Reports, Nova Scotia.

Oliv.B. & L. Oliver, Beavan & Lefroy's Reports, vols. 5–7, English Railway and Canal Cases.

Oll.B. & F. Ollivier, Bell, & Fitzgerald, New Zealand.

O'Mal. & H. O'Malley & Hardcastle's English Election Cases.

Onsl.N.P. Onslow's Nisi Prius.

Ont. Ontario;—Ontario Reports.

Ont.A. (or Ont.App.R.). Ontario Appeals Reports.

Ont.El.Ca. Ontario Election Cases.

Ont.L.J. Ontario Law Journal.

Ont.L.J.N.S. Ontario Law Journal New Series.

Ont.P.R. (or Ont.Pr.Rep.). Ontario Practice Reports.

Ont.Pr. Ontario Practice.

Ont.W.N. Ontario Weekly Notes.

Ont.W.R. Ontario Weekly Reporter.

Op.Attys.Gen. Opinions of the United States Attorneys General.

Op.N.Y.Atty.Gen. Sickels' Opinions of Attorneys-General of New York.

Op.Sol.Dept.Labor. Opinions of the Solicitor for the Department of Labor dealing with Workmen's Compensation.

Or. Oregon;—Oregon Reports.

Or.T.Rep. Orleans Term Reports, vols. 1, 2 Martin, Louisiana.

Ord. Ordinance.

Ord.de la Mar. (or Ord.Mar.). Ordonnance de la Marine de Louis XIV.

Oreg. Oregon;—Oregon Reports.

Oreg.L.Rev. (or Or.L.Rev.). Oregon Law Review.

Orl.Bridgman. Orlando Bridgman's English Common Pleas Reports.

Orl.T.R. Orleans Term Reports, vols. 1, 2 Martin, Louisiana.

Orleans App. Orleans Court of Appeals, La.

Orleans T.R. Orleans Term Reports, 1 and 2 Martin's Reports, La.

Ormond. Ormond's Reports, vols. 12–15 Alabama.

Ort.Inst. Ortolan's Institutes of Justinian.

Ot. Otto's United States Supreme Court Reports.

Out. Outerbridge's Reports, vols. 97–110 Pennsylvania State.

Outerbridge. Outerbridge, Pa.

Over. (or Overton). Overton's Tennessee Reports.

Overt. Overton, Tenn.

Ow. Owen's English King's Bench Reports;—New South Wales Reports.

Owen. Owen's English King's Bench Reports.

Oxley. Young's Vice-Admiralty Decisions, Nova Scotia, edited by Oxley.

P

P. Easter (Paschal) Term;—Pennsylvania;—Peters;—Pickering's Massachusetts Reports;—Probate;—Pacific Reporter.

P.2d. Pacific Reporter, Second Series.

[1891] P. Law Reports, Probate Division, from 1891 onward.

P.A.D. Peters' Admiralty Decisions.

P.C. Pleas of the Crown;—Parliamentary Cases;—Practice Cases;—Prize Cases;—Patent Cases;—Privy Council;—Prize Court;—Probate Court;—Precedents in Chancery.

P.C.App. Privy Council Appeals.

P.C.C. Privy Cases;—Peters' Circuit Court Reports.

P.C.L.J. Pacific Coast Law Journal.

P.Cl.R. Parker's Criminal Reports, New York;—Privy Council Reports.

P.D. Probate Division, English Law Reports (1876–1890).

P.E.I. (or P.E.I.Rep.). Prince Edward Island Reports (Haviland's).

P.F.S. P. F. Smith's Reports, vols. 51–81½ Pennsylvania State.

P.F.Smith. P. F. Smith, Pa.

P.Jr. & H. (or P. & H.). Patton, Jr., & Heath's Virginia Reports.

P.L. Public Laws.

P.L.J. Pittsburgh Law Journal, Pa.

P.L.M. Pacific Law Magazine.

P.L.R. Pacific Law Reporter.

P.N.P. Peake's English Nisi Prius Cases.

P.O.Cas. Perry's Oriental Cases, Bombay.

P.O.G. Patent Office Gazette.

P.O.R. Patent Office Reports.

P.P. Parliamentary Papers.

P.R. Parliamentary Reports;—Pennsylvania Reports, by Penrose & Watts;—Pacific Reporter;—Probate Reports.

P.R.C.P. Practical Register in Common Pleas.

P.R.Ch. Practical Register in Chancery.

P.R.R. Puerto Rico Supreme Court Reports.

P.R.U.C. Practical Reports, Upper Canada.

P.R. & D. (or P.R. & D.El.Cas.). Power, Rodwell & Dew's Election Cases, Eng.

P.S. Purdon's Pennsylvania Statutes Annotated.

P.S.C.U.S. Peters' United States Supreme Court Reports.

P.S.R. Pennsylvania State Reports.

P.U.Fort. Public Utilities Fortnightly.

P.U.R. Public Utilities Reports.

P.W. (or P.Wms.). Peere Williams' English Chancery Reports.

P. & B. Pugsley & Burbridge's Reports, New Brunswick.

P. & C. Prideaux & Cole's Reports, English Courts, vol. 4 New Session Cases.

P. & D. Perry & Davison's English Queen's Bench Reports;—Probate and Divorce.

P. & H. Patton, Jr., & Heath's Virginia Reports.

P. & K. Perry & Knapp's English Election Cases.

P. & L.Dig.Laws. Pepper & Lewis' Digest of Laws, Pa.

P. & L.Laws. Private and Local Laws.

P. & M. Philip & Mary;—Pollock and Maitland's History of English Law.

P. & R. Pigott & Rodwell's Election Cases, English.

P. & W. Penrose & Watts' Pennsylvania Reports.

Pa. Pennsylvania;—Pennsylvania Reports, by Penrose & Watts;—Pennsylvania State Reports;—Paine, United States.

Pa.Bk.Cas. Pennsylvania Bank Cases.

Pa.C.C. (or Pa.Co.Ct. or Pa.Co.Ct.R.). Pennsylvania County Court Reports.

Pa.Cas. Pennsylvania Supreme Court Cases, Sadler.

Pa.Com.Pl. Pennsylvania Common Pleas Reporter.

Pa.Dist. (or Pa.Dist.R.). Pennsylvania District Court Reports.

Pa.Dist. & Co. Pennsylvania District and County.

Pa.L.J. Pennsylvania Law Journal Reports (Clark's);—Pennsylvania Law Journal, Philadelphia.

Pa.L.J.R. Clark's Pennsylvania Law Journal Reports.

Pa.L.M. Pennsylvania Law Magazine.

Pa.L.Rec. Pennsylvania Law Record, Philadelphia.

Pa.Law J. Pennsylvania Law Journal.

Pa.Law Ser. (or Pa.L.S.). Pennsylvania Law Series.

Pa.Leg.Gaz. Legal Gazette Reports (Campbell) Pa.

Pa.N.P. Brightly's Nisi Prius Reports, Pennsylvania.

Pa.Rep. Pennsylvania Reports.

Pa.St. Pennsylvania State Reports.

Pa.St.Tr. Pennsylvania State Trials (Hogan's).

Pa.Super. (or Pa.Super.Ct. or Penn.Super.). Pennsylvania Superior Court Reports.

Pac. Pacific Reporter.

Pac.R. (or Rep.). Pacific Reporter (commonly cited Pac. or P.).

Pacific C.L.J. Pacific Coast Law Journal, San Francisco.

Pacific Law Mag. Pacific Law Magazine.

Pai. Paine's United States Circuit Court Reports;—Paige's New York Chancery Reports.

Pai.Ch. (or Paige). Paige's New York Chancery Reports.

Paine (or Paine C.C.). Paine's United States Circuit Court Reports.

Paine, Elect. Paine on Elections.

Paley, Mor.Ph. Wm. Paley's Moral Philosophy, Eng.

Paley, Prin. & Ag. (or Paley, Ag.). Paley on Principal and Agent, or Agency.

Palgrave. Palgrave's Proceedings in Chancery;—Palgrave's Rise and Progress of the English Commonwealth.

Palm. Palmer's English King's Bench Reports;—Palmer's Reports, vols. 53–60 Vermont.

Pamphl.Laws. Pamphlet Laws, Acts.

Pand. Pandects.

Panel. The Panel.

Papy. Papy's Reports, vols. 5, 6 Florida.

Par. Parker's English Exchequer Reports;—Parsons' Reports, vols. 65–66 New Hampshire;—Parker's New York Criminal Reports.

Par.Dec. Parsons' Decisions, Massachusetts.

Par.Eq.Cas. (or Pars.). Parsons' Select Equity Cases, Pennsylvania.

Pard.Droit Commer. Pardessus, Cours de Droit Commercial.

Pardessus. Pardessus, Cours de Droit Commercial;—Pardessus, Lois Maritimes;—Pardessus, Traites des Servitudes.

Park. Parker's New York Criminal Reports;—Parker's English Exchequer Reports.

Park.Cr.Cas. Parker's New York Criminal Reports.

Park.Dig. Parker's California Digest.

Park.Exch. Parker's English Exchequer Reports.

Park, Ins. Park on Insurance.

Park.Ins. Parker's Insurance, Eng.

Park.Rev.Cas. Parker's English Exchequer Reports (Revenue Cases).

Parker. Parker's English Exchequer Reports;—Parker's New York Criminal Reports;—Parker's New Hampshire Reports.

Parker, Cr.Cas. (N.Y.). Parker's New York Criminal Reports.

Parker, Cr.R. (N.Y.). Parker's New York Criminal Reports.

Parl.Cas. Parliamentary Cases (House of Lords Reports).

Parl.Reg. Parliamentary Register.

Paroch.Ant. Kennett's Parochial Antiquities.

Pars. Parsons (see Par.).

Pars.Ans. Parsons' Answer to the Fifth Part of Coke's Reports.

Pars.Bills & N. Parsons on Bills and Notes.

Pars.Cont. Parson on Contracts.

Pars.Eq.Cas. Parsons' Select Equity Cases, Pennsylvania.

Pars.Mar.Ins. Parsons on Marine Insurance.

Pars.Mar.Law. Parsons on Maritime Law.

Pars.Merc.Law. Parsons on Mercantile Law.

Pars.Shipp. & Adm. Parsons on Shipping and Admiralty.

Partidas. Moreau-Lislet and Carleton's Laws of Las Siété Partidas in force in Louisiana.

Pas. (Terminus Paschae) Easter Term.

Pasch.Dig. Paschal's Texas Digest of Decisions.

Paschal. Paschal's Reports, vols. 28–31 Texas and Supplement to vol. 25.

Paschal's Ann.Const. Paschal's United States Constitution, Annotated.

Pat. Patent;—Paton's Scotch Appeal Cases;—Paterson's Scotch Appeal Cases;—Paterson's New South Wales Reports.

Pat.App.Cas. Paton's Scotch Appeal Cases (Craigie, Stewart & Paton);—Paterson's Scotch Appeal Cases.

Pat.Comp. Paterson's Compendium of English and Scotch Law.

Pat.Dec. Patent Decisions.

Pat.Law Rev. Patent Law Review, Washington, D.C.

Pat.Off.Gaz. Patent Office Gazette.

Pat.Off.Rep. Patent Office Reports.

Pat. & H. Patton, Jr., & Heath's Virginia Reports.

Pat. & Mur. Paterson & Murray's Reports, New South Wales.

Pater. Paterson's Scotch Appeal Cases;—Paterson's New South Wales Reports.

Paters.Comp. Paterson's Compendium of English and Scotch Law.

Paterson. Paterson's Compendium of English and Scotch Law;—Paterson on the Game Laws;—Paterson's Liberty of the Press;—Paterson on the Liberty of the Subject;—Paterson's Law and Usages of the Stock Exchange;—Paterson's Scotch Appeal Cases.

Paton. Craigie, Stewart, & Paton's Scotch Appeal Cases.

Paton App.Cas. Paton's Appeal Cases, Scotland.

Patr.Elect.Cas. Patrick's Election Cases, Upper Canada.

Patrick El.Cas. Patrick's Election Cases, Canada.

Patt. & H. Patton, Jr., & Heath's Virginia Reports.

Paulus. Julius Paulus, Sententiæ Receptæ.

Pea. Peake's English Nisi Prius Reports.

Peabody L.Rev. Peabody Law Review.

Peake Add.Cas. Peake's Additional Cases, vol. 2 of Peake.

Peake N.P. Peake's English Nisi Prius Cases.

Pearce C.C. Pearce's Reports in Dearsly's Crown Cases. English.

Pears. Pearson's Reports, Pennsylvania.

Peck. Peck's Tennessee Reports;—Peck's Reports, vols. 11–30 Illinois;—Peckwell's English Election Cases.

Peck (Tenn.). Peck's Tennessee Reports.

Peck.El.Cas. Peckwell's English Election Cases.

Peck Tr. Peck's Trial (Impeachment).

Peckw. Peckwell's English Election Cases.

Peeples. Peeples' Reports, vols. 77–97 Georgia.

Peeples & Stevens. Peeples & Stevens Reports, vols. 80–97 Georgia.

Peere Wms. Peere-Williams' Reports, English Chancery.

Pen.Code. Penal Code.

Pen.Laws. Penal Laws.

Pen.N.J. Pennington's New Jersey Reports.

Pen. & W. Penrose & Watts' Pennsylvania Reports.

Penn. Pennsylvania;—Pennsylvania State Reports;—Pennypacker's Unreported Pennsylvania Cases;—Pennington's New Jersey Reports;—Pennewill's Delaware Reports.

Penn.B.A.Q. Pennsylvania Bar Association Quarterly.

Penn.Co.Ct.Rep. Pennsylvania County Court Reports.

Penn.Del. Pennewill's Delaware Reports.

Penn.Dist.Rep. Pennsylvania District Reports.

Penn.L.Rev. Pennsylvania Law Review.

Penn.Rep. Pennsylvania State Reports.

Penn.St. (or St.R.). Pennsylvania State Reports.

Pennewill. Pennewill Reports, Del.

Penning. Pennington's New Jersey Reports.

Penny. Pennypacker's Unreported Pennsylvania Cases;—Pennypacker's Pennsylvania Colonial Cases.

Penny.Col.Cas. Pennypacker Colonial Cases, Pa.

Penr. & W. Penrose & Watts' Pennsylvania Reports.

Peo.L.Adv. People's Legal Adviser, Utica, New York.

Pepper & L.Dig.Laws. Pepper and Lewis' Digest of Laws, Pa.

Per.Or.Cas. Perry's Oriental Cases, Bombay.

Per. & Dav. Perry & Davison's English King's Bench Reports.

Per. & Kn. Perry & Knapp's English Election Reports.

Perk. Perkins on Conveyancing;—Perkins on Pleading;—Perkins' Profitable Book (Conveyancing).

Perry. Sir Erskine Perry's Reports, in Morley's (East) Indian Digest;—Perry's Oriental Cases, Bombay.

Perry, Trusts. Perry on Trusts.

Perry & D. Perry & Davison's English King's Bench Reports.

Perry & Kn. Perry & Knapp's English Election Cases.

Pet. Peters' United States Supreme Court Reports;—Peters' United States Circuit Court Reports;—Peters' United States District Court Reports (Admiralty Decisions);—Peters' Prince Edward Island Reports.

Pet.Ab. Petersdorff's Abridgment.

Pet.Ad. (or Pet.Adm.). Peters' United States District Court Reports (Admiralty Decisions).

Pet.Br. Petit Brooke, or Brooke's New Cases, English King's Bench.

Pet.C.C. Peters' United States Circuit Court Reports.

Pet.Cond. Peters' Condensed Reports, United States Supreme Court.

Pet.Dig. Peters' United States Digest;—Peticolas' Texas Digest.

Pet.S.C. Peters' United States Supreme Court Reports.

Peters Adm. Peters' United States District Court Reports (Admiralty Decisions).

Petersd.Ab. Petersdorff's Abridgment.

Petit Br. Petit Brooke, or Brooke's New Cases, English King's Bench.

Ph. Phillips' English Chancery Reports;—Phillimore's English Ecclesiastical Reports (see Phil.).

Ph.Ch. Phillips' English Chancery Reports.

Ph.St.Tr. Phillipps' State Trials.

Phal.C.C. Phalen's Criminal Cases.

Pheney Rep. Pheney's New Term Reports.

Phil. Phillips' English Chancery Reports;—Phillips' North Carolina Reports;—Phillips' English Election Cases;—Phillimore's English Ecclesiastical Reports;—Philadelphia Reports;—Phillips' Illinois Reports;—Phillips' Treatise on Insurance.

Phil.Ch. Phillips' English Chancery Reports.

Phil.Ecc.Judg. Phillimore's Ecclesiastical Judgments.

Phil.Ecc.R. Phillimore's English Ecclesiastical Reports.

Phil.El.Cas. Phillips' English Election Cases.

Phil.Eq. Phillips' North Carolina Equity Reports.

Phil.Ev. Phillips on Evidence.

Phil.Ev.Cow. & H. & Edw.Notes. Phillipps' on Evidence, Notes by Cowen, Hill and Edwards.

Phil.Fam.Cas. Phillipps' Famous Cases in Circumstantial Evidence.

Phil.Ins. Phillips on Insurance.

Phil.Law (or Phil.N.C.). Phillips' North Carolina Law Reports.

Phil.Mech.Liens. Phillips on Mechanics' Liens.

Phil.Pat. Phillips on Patents.

Phil.St.Tr. Phillipps' State Trials.

Phil. & M. Philip and Mary, as 4 & 5 Phil. & M.

Phila. (Pa.). Philadelphia Reports, Common Pleas of Philadelphia County.

Phila.Law Lib. Philadelphia Law Library.

Phila.Leg.Int. Philadelphia Legal Intelligencer, Pa.

Philippine Co. Philippine Code.

Philippine. Philippine Reports.

Philippine L.J. Philippine Law Journal.

Phill. Phillips (see Phil. and Phillips).

Phill.Ins. Phillips on Insurance.

Phillim. Phillimore's English Ecclesiastical Reports. See, also, Phil.

Phillim.Dom. Phillimore on the Law of Domicil.

Phillim.Ecc.Law. Phillimore's Ecclesiastical Law.

Phillim.Int.Law. Phillimore's International Law.

Phillips. Phillips' English Chancery Reports;—Phillips' North Carolina Reports, Law and Equity;—Phillips' Reports, vols. 152–187 Illinois.

Pick. Pickering's Massachusetts Reports.

Pickle. Pickle's Reports, vols. 85–103 Tennessee.

Pierce, R.R. Pierce on Railroad Law.

Pig.Rec. Pigott's Recoveries, Eng.

Pig. & R. Pigott & Rodwell's English Registration Appeal Cases.

Pike. Pike's Reports, vols. 1–5 Arkansas.

Pin. (or Pinn.). Pinney's Wisconsin Reports.

Ping.Chat.Mortg. Pingrey's Treatise of Chattel Mortgages.

Piston (or Pist.). Piston's Mauritius Reports.

Pitc.Crim.Tr. Pitcairn's Ancient Criminal Trials, Scotland.

Pitc.Tr. Pitcairn's Ancient Criminal Trials, Scotland.

Pitm.Prin. & Sur. Pitman on Principal and Surety.

Pitts (or Pittsb. or Pitts.Rep.). Pittsburg Reports;—Pittsburgh, Pa.

Pittsb.L.Rev. Pittsburgh Law Review.

Pittsb.Leg.J.N.S. Pittsburgh Legal Journal New Series, Pa.

Pittsb.Leg.J.(O.S.). Pittsburg Legal Journal, Old Series.

Pittsb.R.(Pa.). Pittsburg Reports, Pennsylvania Courts (reprinted from the Journal).

Pl. (or Pl.Com.). Plowden's Commentaries or Reports, English King's Bench, etc.

Pl.C. Placita Coronæ (Pleas of the Crown).

Platt, Cov. Platt on the Law of Covenants.

Platt, Leas. Platt on Leases.

Plow. Plowden's English King's Bench Reports.

Plowd. Plowden's English King's Bench Commentaries or Reports.

Poe, Pl. Poe on Pleading and Practice.

Pol. Pollexfen's English King's Bench Reports, etc.;—Police.

Pol.Code. Political Code.

Pol.Cont. Pollock on Contracts.

Pol.Sci.Q. (or Pol.Sci.Quar.). Political Science Quarterly.

Poll. Pollexfen's English King's Bench Reports.

Poll.C.C.Pr. Pollock's Practice of the County Courts.

Pollex. Pollexfen's English King's Bench Reports, etc.

Pollexf. Pollexfen, Eng.

Pom.Const.Law. Pomeroy's Constitutional Law of the United States.

Pom.Code Rem. Pomeroy on Code Remedies.

Pom.Eq.Jur. Pomeroy's Equity Jurisprudence.

Pom.Rem. Pomeroy on Civil Remedies.

Pom.Rem. & Rem.Rights. Pomeroy on Civil Remedies & Remedial Rights.

Pom.Spec.Perf. Pomeroy on Specific Performance of Contracts.

Pomeroy. Pomeroy's Reports, vols. 73–128 California.

Pop. Popham's English King's Bench Reports.

Pop.Sci.Mo. Popular Science Monthly.

Pope. (Pope) Opinions Attorney General, pt. 1, vol. 22.

Pope, Lun. Pope on Lunacy.

Poph. Popham's English King's Bench Reports.

Poph. (2). Cases at the end of Popham's Reports.

Port. (Ala.). Porter's Alabama Reports.

Port.Ins. Porter's Laws of Insurance.

Porter. Porter's Alabama Reports;—Porter's Reports, vols. 3–7 Indiana.

Posey. Posey's Unreported Cases, Texas.

Posey, Unrep.Cas. Posey's Unreported Cases, Tex.

Post. Post's Reports, vols. 23–26 Michigan;—Post's Reports, vols. 42–64 Missouri.

Poste's Gaius Inst. Poste's Translation of Gaius.

Pot.Dwar. Potter's Dwarris on Statutes.

Poth.Bail à Rente. Pothier, Traité du Contrat de Bail à Rente.

Poth.Cont. Pothier's Contracts.

Poth.Cont.de Change. Pothier, Traité du Contrat de Change.

Poth.Cont.Sale (or Poth.Contr.Sale). Pothier, Treatise on the Contract of Sale.

Poth.de Change. Pothier, Traité due Contrat de Change.

Poth.de l'Usure. Pothier, Traité de l'Usure.

Poth.de Société App. Pothier, Traité du Contrat de Société.

Poth.du Depot. Pothier, Traité du Dépôt.

Poth.Louage. Pothier, Traité du Contrat de Louage.

Poth.Mar.Cont. Pothier's Treatise on Maritime Contracts.

Poth.Mar.Louage. Pothier, Traité du Contrat de Louage.

Poth.Obl. (or Poth.Oblig.). Pothier on Obligations.

Poth.Pand. Pothier's Pandects.

Poth.Proc.Civil. Pothier, Traité de la Procédure Civile.

Poth.Proc.Crim. Pothier, Traité de la Procédure Criminale.

Poth.Société. Pothier, Traité due Contrat de Société.

Poth.Traité de Change. Pothier, Traité du Contrat de Change.

Poth.Vente. Pothier, Traité du Contrat de Vente.

Pothier, Pand. Pothier, Pandectæ Justinianeæ, etc.

Potter. Potter's Reports, vols. 4–7 Wyoming.

Pow.Cont. Powell on Contracts.

Pow.Dev. Powell, Essay upon the Learning of Devises, etc.

Pow.Mortg. Powell on Mortgages.

Pow.R. & D. Power, Rodwell & Drew's English Election Cases.

Pow.Surr. Powers' Surrogate, N.Y.

Power's Sur. Power's Surrogate, N.Y.

Pr. Price's English Exchequer Reports;—*Principium* (the beginning of a title, law, or section);—Practice Reports (Ontario).

Pr.C.K.B. Practice Cases in the King's Bench.

Pr.Ch. Precedents in Chancery, by Finch;—Practice in the High Court of Chancery.

Pr.Dec. Printed Decisions (Sneed's), Kentucky.

Pr.Div. Probate Division, Law Reports;—Pritchard's Divorce and Matrimonial Cases.

Pr.Edw.Isl. Prince Edward Island.

Pr.Exch. Price's English Exchequer Reports.

Pr.Falc. President Falconer's Reports, Scotch Court of Session.

Pr.Min. Printed Minutes of Evidence.

Pr.R. (or Pr.Rep.). Practice Reports, Eng.

Pr.Reg.B.C. Practical Register in the Bail Court.

Pr.Reg.C.P. Practical Register in the Common Pleas.

Pr.Reg.Ch. Practical Register in Chancery.

Pr. & Div. Probate and Divorce, English Law Reports.

Pra.Cas. Prater's Cases on Conflict of Laws.

Prac.Act. Practice Act.

Pratt Cont.Cas. Pratt's Contraband-of-War Cases.

Prec.Ch. Precedents in Chancery.

Prer. Prerogative Court.

Pres.Falc. President Falconer's Scotch Session Cases (Gilmour & Falconer).

Prest.Conv. Preston on Conveyancing.

Prest.Est. Preston on Estates.

Prest.Merg. Preston on Merger.

Pri. (or Price). Price's Exchequer Reports.

Price. Price, Eng.

Price Min.Cas. Price's Mining Cases.

Price Notes P.P. Price's Notes of Points of Practice, English Exchequer Cases.

Price Pr.Cas. Price's Practice Cases, Eng.

Prickett. Prickett's Reports, Idaho.

Prid. & C. Prideaux & Cole's English Reports, vol. 4 New Sessions Cases.

Prin.Dec. Printed Decisions (Sneed's), Kentucky.

Pritch.Quar.Sess. Pritchard, Quarter Sessions.

Priv.Counc.App. Privy Council Appeals.

Priv.Laws. Private Laws.

Priv.St. Private Statutes.

Prob. English Probate and Admiralty Reports for year cited.

[1891] Prob. Law Reports, Probate Division, from 1891 onward.

Prob.1917. Law Reports, Probate Division, Eng.

Prob.Code. Probate Code.

Prob.Ct.Rep. Probate Court Reporter, Ohio.

Prob.Div. Probate Division, English Law Reports.

Prob.Pr.Act. Probate Practice Act.

Prob.R. (or Prob.Rep.). Probate Reports.

Prob.Rep.Ann. Probate Reports Annotated.

Prob. & Adm.Div. Probate and Admiralty Division, Law Reports.

Prob. & Div. Probate and Divorce, English Law Reports.

Prob. & Mat. Probate and Matrimonial Cases.

Proc.Prac. Proctor's Practice.

Prop.Lawyer N.S. Property Lawyer, New Series (periodical), England.

Prouty. Prouty's Reports, vols. 61–68 Vermont.

Prov.St. Statutes, Laws, of the Province of Massachusetts.

Prt.Rep. Practice Reports.

Psych. & M.L.J. Psychological and Medico-Legal Journal, New York.

Pub.Acts. Public Acts.

Pub.Gen.Laws. Public General Laws.

Pub.Laws. Public Laws.

Pub.Loc.Laws. Public Local Laws.

Pub.St. Public Statutes.

Pub. & Loc.Laws. Public and Local Laws.

Puerto Rico. Puerto Rico.

Puerto Rico Fed. Puerto Rico Federal.

Puffendorf. Puffendorf's Law of Nature and Nations.

Pugs. Pugsley's Reports, New Brunswick.

Pugs. & Burb. Pugsley & Burbridge's Reports, New Brunswick.

Pull.Accts. Pulling's Law of Mercantile Accounts.

Pull.Laws & Cust.Lond. Pulling, Treatise on the Laws, Customs, and Regulations of the City and Port of London.

Pull.Port of London. Pulling, Treatise on the Laws, Customs, and Regulations of the City and Port of London.

Pulsifer. Pulsifer's Reports, vols. 65–68 Maine.

Pump Ct. Pump Court (London).

Punj.Rec. Punjab Record.

Purd.Dig. (or Purd.Dig.Laws). Purdon's Digest of Laws, Pa.

Purple's St. Purple's Statutes, Scates' Compilation.

Pyke. Pyke's Lower Canada King's Bench Reports.

Q

Q. Quadragesms (Year Books, Part IV);—Quebec;—Queensland.

Q.B. Queen's Bench;—Queen's Bench Reports (Adolphus & Ellis, New Series);—English Law Reports, Queen's Bench (1841–1852);—Queen's Bench Reports, Upper Canada;—Queen's Bench Reports, Quebec.

[1891] Q.B. Law Reports, Queen's Bench, from 1891 onward.

Q.B.Div. (or Q.B.D.). Queen's Bench Division, English Law Reports (1876–1890).

Q.B.R. Queen's Bench Reports, by Adolphus & Ellis (New Series).

Q.B.U.C. Queen's Bench Reports, Upper Canada.

Q.L.R. Quebec Law Reports;—Queensland Law Reports.

Q.P.R. Quebec Practice Reports.

Q.R. Official Reports, Province of Quebec.

Q.R.Q.B. Quebec Queen's Bench Reports.

Quadr. Quadragesms (Year Books, Part IV).

Quart.L.J. Quarterly Law Journal (Richmond, Va.).

Quart.L.Rev. Quarterly Law Review (Richmond, Va.).

Quart.Rev. Quarterly Law Review, Richmond, Virginia.

Que.K.B. Quebec, King's Bench, Canada.

Que.L. Quebec Law.

Que.Pr. Quebec Practice.

Que.Q.B. Quebec Official Reports Queen's Bench.

Que.Rev.Jud. Quebec Revised Judicial.

Que.Super. Quebec Official Reports Superior Court.

Queb.L.R. Quebec Law Reports, two series, Queen's Bench or Superior Court.

Queb.Q.B. Quebec Queen's Bench Reports.

Queens.L.R. Queensland Law Reports.

Queensl.J.P. Queensland Justice of the Peace.

Queensl.L. Queensland Law.

Queensl.L.J. Queensland Law Journal.

Queensl.S.C.R. Queensland Supreme Court Reports.

Quin. (or Quincy). Quincy's Massachusetts Reports.

Quinti, Quinto. Year Book, 5 Henry V.

R

R.A. Registration Appeals;—Regular Appeals.

R.C. Rolls of Court;—Record Commissioners;—Railway Cases;—Registration Cases;—Revue Critique, Montreal;—Revised Statutes 1855, Mo.

R.C.L. Ruling Case Law.

R.C.W.A. Revised Code of Washington Annotated.

R.C. & C.R. Revenue, Civil, and Criminal Reporter, Calcutta.

R.G. Regulæ Generales, Ontario.

R.I. Rhode Island;—Rhode Island Reports.

R.J. & P.J. Revenue, Judicial, and Police Journal, Calcutta.

R.L. Revised Laws;—Revue Legale.

R.L. & S. Ridgeway, Lapp & Schoales' Irish King's Bench Reports.

R.L. & W. Roberts, Leaming & Wallis' English County Court Reports.

R.M.Ch. R. M. Charlton's Georgia Reports.

R.M.Charlt. R. M. Charlton, Ga.

R.P.C. Real Property Cases, English;—Reports Patent Cases.

R.P. & W. (Rawle) Penrose & Watts' Pennsylvania Reports.

R.R.Rep. Railroad Reports.

R.R. & Can.Cas. Railway and Canal Cases, English.

R.S. Revised Statutes.

R.S.Comp. Statutes of Connecticut, Compilation of 1854.

R.t.F. Reports *tempore* Finch, English Chancery.

R.t.H. Reports *tempore* Hardwicke (Lee) English King's Bench;—Reports *tempore* Holt (Cases Concerning Settlement).

R.t.Hardw. Reports *tempore* Hardwicke, English King's Bench.

R.t.Holt. Reports *tempore* Holt, English King's Bench.

R.t.Q.A. Reports *tempore* Queen Anne, vol. 11 Modern Reports.

R. & C.Cas. (or R. & Can.Cas.). Railway & Canal Cases, Eng.

R. & C.N.Sc. Russell & Chesley's Reports, Nova Scotia.

R. & Can.Tr.Cas. Railway & Canal Traffic Cases, Eng.

R. & G.N.Sc. Russell & Geldert's Reports, Nova Scotia.

R. & H.Dig. Robinson & Harrison's Digest, Ontario.

R. & J.Dig. Robinson & Joseph's Digest, Ontario.

R. & M. Russell & Mylne's English Chancery Reports;—Ryan & Moody's English Nisi Prius Reports.

R. & M.C.C. Ryan & Moody's Crown Cases Reserved, English.

R. & M.Dig. Rapalje & Mack's Digest of Railway Law.

R. & M.N.P. Ryan & Moody's Nisi Prius Cases, English.

R. & R. Russell & Ryan Crown Cases, Eng.

R. & R.C.C. Russell & Ryan's English Crown Cases, Reserved.

R. & Ry.C.C. Russell and Ryan's English Crown Cases.

Ra.Ca. English Railway and Canal Cases.

Rader. Rader's Reports, vols. 137–156 Missouri.

Rag. California Superior Court Decisions (Ragland).

Rail. & Can.Cas. English Railway and Canal Cases;—Railway and Canal Traffic Cases.

Railway Cas. Railway Cases.

Railway & Corp.Law J. Railway and Corporation Law Journal.

Ram Cas.P. & E. Ram's Cases of Pleading and Evidence.

Ram Leg.Judgm. (Towns.Ed.). Ram's Science of Legal Judgment, Notes by Townshend.

Ram. & Mor. Ramsey & Morin's Montreal Law Reporter.

Ramsay, App.Cas. Ramsay, Appeal Cases, Canada.

Rand. Randolph's Virginia Reports;—Randolph's Reports, vols. 21–56 Kansas;—Randolph's Reports, vols. 7–11 Louisiana Annual;—Randall's Reports, vols. 52–71 Ohio State.

Rand.Com.Paper. Randolph on Commercial Paper.

Rand.Em.Dom. Randolph on Eminent Domain.

Rand.Perp. Randall on Perpetuities.

Raney. Raney's Reports, vols. 16–20 Florida.

Rang.Dec. Sparks' Rangoon Decisions, British Burmah.

Rap.Contempt. Rapalje on Contempt.

Rap.Fed.Ref.Dig. Rapalje's Federal.Reference Digest.

Rap.Jud.Q.B.R. Rapport's Judiciaries de Quebec Cour du Banc de la Reine.

Rap.Jud.Q.C.S. Rapport's Judiciaries de Quebec Cour Superieure.

Rap.Lar. Rapalje on Larceny.

Rap.N.Y.Dig. Rapalje's New York Digest.

Rap.Wit. Rapalje's Treatise on Witnesses.

Rap. & L. (or Law.). Rapalje & Lawrence, American and English Cases.

Rap. & L.Law Dict. Rapalje and Lawrence Law Dictionary.

Rapal. & L. Rapalje & Lawrence, American and English Cases.

Ratt.L.C. Rattigan's Leading Cases on Hindoo Law.

Raw. (or Rawle). Rawle's Pennsylvania Reports.

Rawle, Const.U.S. Rawle on the Constitution of the United States.

Rawle, Cov. Rawle on Covenants for Title.

Rawle Pen. & W. (Rawle) Penrose & Watts, Pennsylvania.

Ray, Med.Jur. Ray's Medical Jurisprudence of Insanity.

Raym. (or Raym.Ld.). Lord Raymond's English King's Bench Reports.

Raym.Sir T. Sir Thomas Raymond's English King's Bench Reports.

Raym.T. Sir Thomas Raymond, Eng.

Raymond. Raymond's Reports, vols. 81–89 Iowa.

Rayn. Rayner's English Tithe Cases.

Re-af. Re-affirmed.

Re.de J. Revue de Jurisprudence, Montreal.

Re.de L. Revue de Jurisprudence et Legislation, Montreal.

Real Est.Rec. Real Estate Record, New York.

Real Pr.Cas. Real Property Cases (English).

Rec. Records;—Recorder;—American Law Record.

Rec.Dec. Vaux's Recorder's Decisions, Philadelphia.

Red. Redfield's New York Surrogate Reports;—Reddington, Maine.

Red.Am.R.R.Cas. Redfield's Leading American Railway Cases.

Red.Cas.R.R. Redfield's Leading American Railway Cases.

Red.Cas.Wills. Redfield's Leading Cases on Wills.

Red.R.R.Cas. Redfield's Leading American Railway Cases.

Red. & Big.Cas.B. & N. Redfield & Bigelow's Leading Cases on Bills and Notes.

Redf. (or Redf.Surr.). Redfield's New York Surrogate Reports.

Redf.Carr. Redfield on Carriers and Bailments.

Redf.R.Cas. Redfield's Railway Cases, Eng.

Redf.Railways. Redfield on Railways.

Redf.Sur. (N.Y.) Redfield's New York Surrogate Court Reports.

Redf.Wills. Redfield's Leading Cases on Wills.

Redf. & B. Redfield & Bigelow's Leading Cases, Eng.

Redington. Redington's Reports, vols. 31–35 Maine.

Reed Fraud. Reed's Leading Cases on Statute of Frauds.

Rees' Cyclopædia. Abraham Rees' English Cyclopædia.

Reese. Reporter, vols. 5, 11 Heiskell's Tennessee Reports.

Reeve, Eng.Law (or Reeve, Hist.Eng.Law). Reeve's History of the English Law.

Ref.n.r.e. Refused, not reversible error.

Ref.w.m. Refused, want of merit.

Reg.App. Registration Appeals.

Reg.Brev. Register of Writs.

Reg.Cas. Registration Cases.

Reg.Gen. Regulæ Generales.

Reg.Jud. Registæm Judicale.

Reg.Om.Brev. Registrum Omnium Brevium.

Reg.Orig. Registrum Originale.

Reg.Writ. Register of Writs.

Reilly. Reilly's English Arbitration Cases.

Rem.Cr.Tr. Remarkable Criminal Trials.

Rem.Tr. Cummins & Dunphy's Remarkable Trials.

Rem.Tr.No.Ch. Benson's Remarkable Trials and Notorious Characters.

Remy. Remy's Reports, vols. 145–154 Indiana; also Indiana Appellate Court Reports.

Rep. Report;—Reports;—Reporter;—Repealed;—Wallace's The Reporters;—Coke's English King's Bench Reports.

Rep. (1, 2, etc.). Coke's English King's Bench Reports.

Rep.Ass.Y. Clayton's Reports of Assizes at Yorke.

Rep.Cas.Eq. Gilbert's Chancery Reports.

Rep.Cas.Madr. Reports of Cases, Dewanny Adawlut, Madras.

Rep.Cas.Pr. Reports of Cases of Practice (Cooke's).

Rep.Ch. Reports in Chancery, English.

Rep.Ch.Pr. Reports on Chancery Practice.

Rep..Com.Cas. Reports on Commercial Cases, Bengal.

Rep.Const.Ct. Reports of the Constitutional Court, South Carolina (Treadway, Mill, or Harper).

Rep.Cr.L.Com. Reports of Criminal Law Commissioners.

Rep.Eq. Gilbert's English Reports in Equity.

Rep. in Ch. Reports in Chancery, English.

Rep.Q.A. Report *tempore* Queen Anne, vol. 11 Modern.

Rep.Sel.Cas.Ch. Kelynge's (W) English Chancery Reports.

Rep.t.Finch. Reports *tempore* Finch, English Chancery.

Rep.t.Hard. Lee's Reports *tempore* Hardwicke, English King's Bench Reports.

Rep.t.Holt. Reports *tempore* Holt (English Cases of Settlement).

Rep.t.O.Br. Carter's English Common Pleas Reports *tempore* O. Bridgman.

Rep.t.Q.A. Reports *tempore* Queen Anne, vol. 11 Modern Reports.

Rep.t.Talb. Reports *tempore* Talbot, English Chancery.

Rep.Yorke Ass. Clayton's Reports of Assizes at Yorke.

Reports. The Reports;—Coke's English King's Bench Reports.

Reprint. English Reprint.

Res. & Eq.Judgm. Reserved & Equity Judgments, N. S.Wales.

Rettie. Rettie, Crawford & Melville's Scotch Session Cases (4th series).

Rev. Revision of the Statutes Revised.

Rev.C. & C.Rep. Revenue, Civil, and Criminal Reporter, Bengal.

Rev.Civ.Code. Revised Civil Code.

Rev.Civ.St. Revised Civil Statutes.

Rev.Code. Revised Code.

Rev.Code Civ.Proc. Revised Code Civil Procedure.

Rev.Code Cr.Proc. Revised Code of Criminal Procedure.

Rev.Cr.Code. Revised Criminal Code.

Rev.Crit. Revue Critique, Canada.

Rev.de Jur. Revue de Jurisprudence, Canada.

Rev.de Legis. Revue de Legislation, Canada.

Rev.Laws. Revised Laws.

Rev.Leg. Revue Legale, Canada.

Rev.Leg.N.S. Revue Legale, New Series, Canada.

Rev.Mun.Code. Revised Municipal Code.

Rev.Ord. Revised Ordinances.

Rev.Ord.N.W.T. Revised Ordinances, Northwest Territories (Canada) 1888.

Rev.Pen.Code. Revised Penal Code.

Rev.Pol.Code. Revised Political Code.

Rev.Rep. Revised Reports, Eng.

Rev.St. Revised Statutes.

Reyn. Reynolds' Reports, vols. 40–42 Mississippi.

Reynolds' Land Laws. Reynolds' Spanish and Mexican Land Laws.

Rice. Rice's South Carolina Law Reports.

Rice's Code. Rice's Code of Practice, Colo.

Rice Eq. (or Ch.). Rice's South Carolina Equity Reports.

Rice, Ev. Rice's Law of Evidence.

Rich. Richardson's South Carolina Law Reports;—Richardson's Reports, vols. 2–5 New Hampshire.

Rich.C.P. Richardson's Practice Common Pleas, Eng.

Rich.Ch. Richardson's South Carolina Equity Reports.

Rich.Ct.Cl. Richardson's Court of Claims Reports.

Rich.Dict. Richardson's New Dictionary of the English Language.

Rich Eq. Richardson's South Carolina Equity Reports.

Rich.Eq. (or Ch.) Cas. Richardson's South Carolina Equity Reports.

Rich.Law (S.C.). Richardson's South Carolina Law Reports.

Rich.N.S. Richardson's South Carolina Reports, New Series.

Rich.Pr.Reg. Richardson's Practical Register, English Common Pleas.

Rich. & H. Richardson & Hook's Street Railway Decisions.

Rich. & W. Richardson & Woodbury's Reports, vol. 2 New Hampshire.

Riddle's Lex. Riddle's Lexicon.

Ridg. Ridgeway's Reports *tempore* Hardwicke, Chancery and King's Bench.

Ridg.Ap. Ridgeway's Irish Appeal (or Parliamentary) Cases.

Ridg.Cas. Ridgeway's Reports *tempore* Hardwicke, Chancery and King's Bench.

Ridg.L. & S. Ridgeway, Lapp & Schoales' Irish Term Reports.

Ridg.P.C. (or Ridg.Parl.). Ridgeway's Irish Appeal (or Parliamentary) Cases.

Ridg.Rep. (or St.Tr.). Ridgeway's (Individual) Reports of State Trials in Ireland.

Ridg.t.Hard. (or Ridg.t.Hardw. or Ridg. & Hard.). Ridgeway's Reports *tempore* Hardwicke, Chancery and King's Bench.

Ridgew. Ridgeway (see Ridg.).

Ridley, Civil & Ecc.Law. Ridley's Civil and Ecclesiastical Law.

Ried. Riedell's Reports, vols. 68, 69 New Hampshire.

Ril. (or Riley). Riley's South Carolina Law Reports;—Riley's Reports, vols. 37–42 West Virginia.

Ril. (or Riley) Ch. (or Eq.). Riley's South Carolina Chancery Reports.

Ril.Harp. Riley's Edition of Harper's South Carolina Reports.

Riley. Riley's South Carolina Chancery Reports;—Riley's South Carolina Law Reports;—Riley's Reports, vols. 37–42 West Virginia.

Riner. Riner's Reports, vol. 2 Wyoming.

Riv.Ann.Reg. Rivington's Annual Register.

Rob. Robinson's Virginia Reports;—Robinson's Louisiana Reports;—Robinson's Reports, vols. 2–9 and 17–23 Colorado Appeals;—Robertson's New York Superior Court Reports;—Robinson's English Ecclesiastical Reports;—Chr. Robinson's English Admiralty Reports;—W. Robinson's English Admiralty Reports;—Robinson's Scotch Appeal Cases;—Robertson's Scotch Appeal Cases;—Robinson's Reports, vol. 38 California;—Robinson's Reports, vols. 1–4 Louisiana Annual;—Roberts' Reports, vols. 29–31 Louisiana Annual;—Robards' Reports, vols. 12, 13 Missouri;—Robards' Conscript Cases, Texas;—Chr. Robinson's Upper Canada Reports;—J. L. Robinson's Upper Canada Reports;—Robertson's Reports, vol. 1 Hawaii;—Robinson's Reports, vol. 1 Nevada.

Rob.Adm. Chr. Robinson's English Admiralty Reports.

Rob.Adm. & Pr. Roberts on Admiralty and Prize.

Rob.App. Robertson's Scotch Appeal Cases.

Rob.Car.V. Robertson's History of the Reign of the Emperor Charles V.

Rob.Cas. Robertson's Scotch Appeal Cases.

Rob.Chr. Chr. Robinson's English Admiralty Reports.

Rob.Consc.Cas. Robards' Conscript Cases, Texas.

Rob.Ecc. (or Rob.Eccl.). Robertson's English Ecclesiastical Reports.

Rob.Eq. Roberts' Principles of Equity.

Rob.Jun. William Robertson's English Admiralty Reports.

Rob.L. & W. Roberts, Leaming & Wallis' County Court Reports.

Rob.La. Robinson's Louisiana Reports.

Rob.Pat. Robinson on Patents.

Rob.S.I. Robertson's Sandwich Island (Hawaiian) Reports.

Rob.Sc.App. Robinson's Scotch Appeals, English House of Lords.

Rob.Sr.Ct. Robertson's New York Superior Court Reports.

Rob.U.C. Robinson's Reports, Upper Canada.

Rob.Va. Robinson's Virginia Reports.

Rob.Wm.Adm. William Robinson's English Admiralty Reports.

Robards. Robards' Reports, vols. 12, 13 Missouri;—Robards' Texas Conscript Cases.

Robards & Jackson. Robards & Jackson's Reports, vols. 26–27 Texas.

Robb (or Robb Pat.Cas.). Robb's United States Patent Cases.

Robert.App.Cas. Robertson's Appeal Cases, Scotland.

Roberts. Roberts' Reports, vols. 29–31 Louisiana Annual.

Robertson. Robertson's Scotch Appeal Cases;—Robertson's New York Superior Court Reports;—Robertson's New York Marine Court Reports;—Robertson's English Ecclesiastical Reports;—Robertson's Hawaiian Reports. See, also, Rob.

Robin.App. (or Robin.App.Cas.). Robinson's Appeal Cases, Scotland.

Robinson. Chr. Robinson's English Admiralty Reports;—W. Robinson's English Admiralty Reports;—Robinson's Virginia Reports;—Robinson's Louisiana Reports;—Robinson's Scotch Appeal Cases;—Robinson's Reports, vol. 38 California;—Chr. Robinson's Reports, Upper Canada;—J. L. Robinson's Reports, Upper Canada;—Robinson's Reports, Colorado;—Robinson's Reports, vol. 1 Nevada.

Robs.Bankr. Robson's Bankrupt Practice;—Robertson's Handbook of Bankers' Law.

Robt. Robert;—Robertson.

Roccus, Ins. Roccus on Insurance.

Rocky Mt.L.Rev. Rocky Mountain Law Review.

Rodman. Rodman's Reports, vols. 78–82 Kentucky.

Rog.Ecc.Law. Rogers' Ecclesiastical Law.

Rogers. Rogers' Reports, vols. 47–51 Louisiana Annual.

Rol. (or Roll.). Rolle's English King's Bench Reports.

Roll. Roll of the Term.

Rolle (or Roll.Rep.). Rolle's English King's Bench Reports.

Rolle Abr. Rolle's Abridgment.

Rolle R. Rolle's English King's Bench Reports.

Rolls Ct.Rep. Rolls' Court Reports.

Rom. (or Rom.Cas.). Romilly's Notes of Cases, Eng.

Rom.Law. Mackeldy's Handbook of the Roman Law.

Root. Root's Connecticut Reports.

Rop.Husb. & Wife. Roper on Husband and Wife.

Rop.Leg. Roper on Legacies.

Rorer, Jud.Sales. Rorer on Void Judicial Sales.

Rorer, R.R. Rorer on Railways.

Rosc.Adm. Roscoe's Admiralty Jurisdiction and Practice.

Rosc.Crim.Ev. Roscoe on Criminal Evidence.

Rosc.Jur. Roscoe's Jurist, London.

Rosc.N.P. Roscoe's Nisi Prius.

Rosc.Real Act. Roscoe on Real Actions.

Roscoe. Roscoe's Reports of Supreme Court of Cape of Good Hope (South Africa).

Roscoe, Bldg.Cas. Roscoe, Digest of Building Cases, Eng.

Roscoe, Cr.Ev. (or Rosc.Crim.Ev.). Roscoe on Criminal Evidence.

Rose (or Rose B.C.). Rose's Reports, English Bankruptcy.

Rose Notes. Rose's Notes on United States Reports.

Rose W.C. Rose Will Case, New York.

Ross, Cont. Ross on Contracts.

Ross, Conv. Ross' Lectures on Conveyancing, etc., Scotland.

Ross Lead.Cas. Ross' Leading Cases, Eng.

Ross Ldg.Cas. Ross' Leading Cases on Commercial Law.

Rot.Flor. Rotæ Florentine (Reports of the Supreme Court, or Rota, of Florence).

Rot.Parl. Rotulæ Parliamentariæ.

Rowe. Rowe's Interesting Parliamentary and Military Cases.

Rowe Rep. Rowe's Reports (Irish).

Rowell. Rowell's Reports, vols. 45–52 Vermont.

Rowell, El.Cas. Rowell's Contested Election Cases, U. S. House of Representatives.

Roy.Dig. Royall's Digest Virginia Reports.

R.S. Revised Statutes.

Rt.Law Repts. (or Rt.Law Rep.). Rent Law Reports, India.

Rucker. Rucker's Reports, vols. 43–46 West Virginia.

Ruff. (or Ruff. & H.). Ruffin & Hawks' North Carolina Reports.

Rul.Cas. Campbell's Ruling Cases, Eng.

Rules Sup.Ct. Rules of the Supreme Court.

Runn. (or Runnells). Runnell's Reports, Iowa.

Rus. Russell.

Russ. Russell's English Chancery Reports.

Russ.Arb. Russell on Arbitrators.

Russ.Ch. Russell's English Chancery Reports.

Russ.Cr. (or Russ.Crimes). Russell on Crimes and Misdemeanors.

Russ.Elec.Cas. (or Russ.Elect.Cas.). Russell's Election Cases, Mass., Nova Scotia;—Russell's Election Reports, Canada.

Russ.Eq.Cas. Russell's Equity Cases, Nova Scotia.

Russ.Eq.Rep. Russell's Equity Decisions, Nova Scotia.

Russ.Fact. Russell on Factors and Brokers.

Russ.Merc.Ag. Russell on Mercantile Agency.

Russ.N.Sc. Russell's Equity Cases, Nova Scotia.

Russ.t.Eld. Russell's English Chancery Reports *tempore* Elden.

Russ. & C.Eq.Cas. Russell's & Chesley's Equity Cases, Nova Scotia.

Russ. & Ches. Russell & Chesley's Reports, Nova Scotia.

Russ. & Ches.Eq. Russell & Chesley's Equity Reports, Nova Scotia.

Russ. & Geld. Russell & Geldert's Reports, Nova Scotia.

Russ. & M. Russell & Mylne's English Chancery Reports.

Russ. & R.Cr.Cas. Russell and Ryan's English Crown Cases Reserved.

Russ. & Ry. Russell & Ryan's English Crown Cases Reserved.

Russell. Russell's Equity Decisions, Nova Scotia.

Rutg.Cas. Rutger-Waddington Case, New York City, 1784.

Rutgers L.Rev. Rutgers Law Review.

Ruth.Inst. Rutherford's Institutes of Natural Law.

Ry.Cas. Reports of Railway Cases.

Ry.Med.Jur. Ryan's Medical Jurisprudence.

Ry. & Can.Cas. Railway and Canal Cases, England.

Ry. & Can.Traf.Ca. Railway and Canal Traffic Cases.

Ry. & Corp.Law J. (or Ry. & Corp.Law Jour.). Railway and Corporation Law Journal.

Ry. & M. (or Ry. & M.N.P.). Ryan & Moody's Nisi Prius Reports, English.

Ry. & M.C.C. Ryan and Moody's Crown Cases Reserved, Eng.

Ryde, Rat.App. Ryde's Rating Appeals, Eng.

Rymer. Rymer's Fœdera.

S

S. Shaw, Dunlop, & Bell's Scotch Court of Session Reports (1st Series);—Shaw's Scotch House of Lords Appeal Cases;—Southeastern Reporter (properly cited S.E.);—Southwestern Reporter (properly cited S. W.);—New York Supplement;—Supreme Court Reporter.

S.A.L.R. South Australian Law Reports.

S.Af.L.J. South African Law Journal.

S.App. Shaw's Scotch House of Lords Appeal Cases.

S.Austr.L. South Australia Law.

S.Aust.L.R. South Australian Law Reports.

S.B. Upper Bench, or Supreme Bench.

S.Bar J. State Bar Journal of California.

S.C. South Carolina;—South Carolina Reports, New Series;—Same Case;—Superior Court;—Supreme Court;—Sessions Cases;—Samuel Carter (see Orlando Bridgman).

1907 S.C. Court of Session Cases, Scotland.

S.C.A. Supreme and Exchequer Courts Act, Canada.

S.C.Bar Assn. South Carolina Bar Association.

S.C.C. Select Chancery Cases (part 3 of Cases in Chancery);—Small Cause Court, India.

S.C.Dig. Cassell's Supreme Court Digest, Canada.

S.C.E. Select Cases Relating to Evidence, Strange.

S.C.Eq. South Carolina Equity.

1907 S.C., J. Court of Justiciary Cases, Scotland.

S.C.L. South Carolina Law.

S.C.R. South Carolina Reports, New Series;—Harper's South Carolina Reports;—Supreme Court Reports;—Supreme Court Rules;—Supreme Court of Canada Reports.

S.Car. South Carolina;—South Carolina Reports, New Series.

S.Ct. Supreme Court Reporter.

S.D. South Dakota;—South Dakota Reports.

S.D.A. Sudder Dewanny Adawlut Reports, India.

S.D. & B. Shaw, Dunlop & Bell's Scotch Court of Session Reports (1st Series).

S.D. & B.Sup. Shaw, Dunlop & Bell's Supplement, containing House of Lords Decisions.

S.E. South Eastern Reporter.

S.E.2d. South Eastern Reporter, Second Series.

S.E.C. Securities and Exchange Commission Decisions.

S.F. Used by the West Publishing Company to locate place where decision is from, as, "S. F. 59," San Francisco Case No. 59 on Docket.

S.F.A. Sudder Foujdaree Adawlut Reports, India.

S.H.A. Smith-Hurd Illinois Annotated Statutes.

S.Just. Shaw's Justiciary Cases, Scotland.

S.L.C. Smith's Leading Cases.

S.L.C.App. Stuart's Lower Canada Appeal Cases.

S.L.J. Scottish Law Journal, Edinburgh.

S.R. State Reporter, New York.

S.S. Synopsis Series of United States Treasury Decisions.

S.S.C. Sandford's New York City Superior Court Reports.

S.T. (or St.Tri.) State Trials.

S.T.D. Synopsis Treasurer's Decisions.

S.Teind. Shaw's Teind Cases, Scotland.

S.V.A.R. Stuart's Vice-Admiralty Reports, Quebec.

S.W. South Western;—South Western Reporter.

S.W.2d. South Western Reporter, Second Series.

S.W.L.J. South Western Law Journal, Nashville, Tenn.

S.W.L.Rev. South Western Law Review.

S.W.Rep. South Western Reporter (commonly cited S.W.).

S. & B. Smith & Batty's Irish King's Bench Reports.

S. & C. Saunders & Cole's English Bail Court Reports;—Swan & Critchfield, Revised Statutes, Ohio.

S. & C.Rev.St. Swan and Critchfield's Revised Statutes, Ohio.

S. & D. Shaw, Dunlop, & Bell's Scotch Court of Session Reports (1st series).

S. & G. Smale & Giffard, English.

S. & L. Schoales & Lefroy's Irish Chancery Reports.

S. & M. Shaw & Maclean's Appeal Cases, House of Lords;—Smedes & Marshall's Mississippi Reports.

S. & M.Ch. Smedes & Marshall's Mississippi Chancery Reports.

S. & R. Sergeant & Rawle's Pennsylvania Reports.

S. & R. on Neg. Shearman and Redfield on Negligence.

S. & S. Sausse & Scully's Irish Rolls Court Reports;—Simons & Stuart, English Vice-Chancellors' Reports;—Swan & Sayler, Revised Statutes of Ohio.

S. & Sm. Searle & Smith's English Probate and Divorce Reports.

S. & T. Swabey & Tristram's English Probate and Divorce Reports.

Sadler. Sadler's Cases, Pa.

Sal. Salinger's Reports, vols. 90–108 Iowa.

Salk. Salkeld's English King's Bench Reports.

Salm.Abr. Salmon's Abridgment of State Trials.

Salm.St.R. Salmon's Edition of the State Trials.

San Fran.L.B. San Francisco Law Bulletin.

San Fran.L.J. or San.F.L.J.). San Francisco Law Journal.

Sanb. & B.Ann.St. Sanborn and Berryman's Annotated Statutes, Wis.

Sand. Sandford's New York Superior Court Reports.

Sand.Ch. Sandford's New York Chancery Reports.

Sand.I.Rep. Sandwich Island (Hawaiian) Reports.

Sand.Uses and Trusts. Sanders on Uses and Trusts.

Sand. & H.Dig. Sandels and Hill's Digest of Statutes, Ark.

Sandars, Just.Inst. (or Sand.Inst.Just.Introd.). Sandars' Edition of Justinian's Institutes.

Sandf. Sandford's New York Superior Court Reports.

Sandf.Ch. Sandford's New York Chancery Reports.

Sandl.St.Pap. Sandler's State Papers.

Sanf. Sanford's Reports, vol. 59 Alabama.

Sar.Ch.Sen. Saratoga Chancery Sentinel.

Sask.L. Saskatchewan Law.

Sau. & Sc. Sausse & Scully's Irish Rolls Court Reports.

Sauls. Saulsbury's Reports, vols. 5–6 Delaware.

Saund. Saunders' English King's Bench Reports.

Saund.Pl. & Ev. Saunders' Pleading and Evidence.

Saund. & C. Saunders & Cole's English Bail Court Reports.

Saund. & Mac. Saunders & Macrae's English County Court Cases.

Sausse & Sc. Sausse & Scully's Irish Rolls Court Reports.

Sav. Savile's English Common Pleas Reports.

Sav.Dr.Rom. Savigny Droit Romaine.

Sav.Priv. Trial of the Savannah Privateers.

Sav.Syst. Savigny, System des Heutigen Römischen Richts.

Saw. (or Sawy.). Sawyer's United States Circuit Court Reports.

Sax. (or Saxt.). Saxton's New Jersey Chancery Reports.

Say. (or Sayer). Sayer's English King's Bench Reports.

Sayles' Ann.Civ.St. Sayles' Annotated Civil Statutes, Tex.

Sayles' Civ.St. Sayles' Revised Civil Statutes, Tex.

Sayles' Rev.Civ.St. Sayles' Revised Civil Statutes, Tex.

Sayles' St. Sayles' Revised Civil Statutes, Tex.

Sayles' Supp. Supplement to Sayles' Annotated Civil Statutes, Tex.

Sc. *Scilicet* (that is to say);—Scaccaria (Exchequer);—Scott's Reports, English Common Pleas;—Scotch;—Scammon's Reports, vols. 2–5 Illinois.

Sc.Jur. Scottish Jurist.

Sc.L.Rep. (or Sc.L.R.). Scottish Law Reporter, Edenburgh.

Sc.N.R. Scott's New Reports.

Sc.Sess.Cas. Scotch Court of Session Cases.

Sc. & Div.App. Scotch and Divorce Appeals (Law Reports).

Scac. Scaccaria Curia (Court of Exchequer).

Scam. Scammon's Reports, vols. 2–5 Illinois.

Scates' Comp.St. Treat, Scates & Blackwell Compiled Statutes, Ill.

Sch.L.R. Schuylkill Legal Record, Pa.

Sch. & Lef. Schoales & Lefroy's Irish Chancery Reports.

Schalk. Schalk's Jamaica Reports.

Scher. Scherer, New York Miscellaneous Reports.

Schm.Civil Law. Schmidt's Civil Law of Spain and Mexico.

Schmidt, Civ.Law. Schmidt on the Civil Law of Spain and Mexico.

Schoales & L. Schoales and Lefroy's Irish Chancery Reports.

Schomberg, Mar.Laws Rhodes. Schomberg, Treatise on the Maritime Laws of Rhodes.

Schouler, Bailm. Schouler on Bailments.

Schouler, Dom.Rel. Schouler on Domestic Relations.

Schouler, Pers.Prop. Schouler on Personal Property.

Schouler, U.S.Hist. Schouler's History of the United States under the Const.1783–1847.

Schouler, Wills. Schouler on Wills.

Schuyl.Leg.Reg. Schuylkill Legal Record, Pottsville, Pa.

Sci.fa.ad dis.deb. *Scire facias ad disprobandum debitum.*

Sco. Scott's English Common Pleas Reports.

Sco.N.R. Scott's New Reports, English Common Pleas.

Scot. Scotland;—Scottish.

Scot.Jur. Scottish Jurist, Edinburgh.

Scot.L.R. Scottish Law Reporter, Edinburgh;—Scottish Law Review, Glasgow.

Scot L.T. Scot Law Times, Edinburgh.

Scot.Law J. Scottish Law Journal (Glasgow).

Scott. Scott's English Common Pleas Reports;—Scott's New York Civil Procedure.

Scott J. Reporter, English Common Bench Reports.

Scott N.R. Scott's New Reports, English Common Pleas.

Scr.L.T. Scranton Law Times, Pennsylvania.

Searle & Sm. Searle & Smith's English Probate and Divorce Reports.

Seb.Trade-Marks. Sebastian on Trade-Marks.

Sec.leg. *Secundum legum* (according to law).

Sec.reg. *Secundum regulam* (according to rule).

Secd.pt.Edw.III. Part 3 of the Year Books.

Secd.pt.H.VI. Part 8 of the Year Books.

Sedg.Dam. Sedgwick on the Measure of Damage.

Sedg.L.Cas. Sedgwick's Leading Cases on Damages;—Sedgwick's Leading Cases on Real Property.

Sedg.St. & Const.Law. Sedgwick on Statutory and Constitutional Law.

Sedg. & W.Tr.Title Land. Sedgwick and Wait on the Trial of Title to Land.

Seign.Rep. Seigniorial Reports, Lower Canada.

Sel.Cas.Ch. Select Cases in Chancery (part 3 of Cases in Chancery).

Sel.Cas.D.A. Select Cases (Sudder), Dewanny Adawlut, India.

Sel.Cas.Ev. Select Cases in Evidence (Strange).

Sel.Cas.N.F. Select Cases, Newfoundland.

Sel.Cas.N.W.P. Selected Cases, Northwest Provinces, India.

Sel.Cas.N.Y. Yates' Select Cases, New York.

Sel.Cas.t.Br. Cooper's Select Cases *tempore* Brougham.

Sel.Cas.t.King. Select Cases in Chancery *tempore* King.

Sel.Cas.t.Nap. (Drury's) Select Cases *tempore* Napier, Irish Chancery.

Sel.Cas.with Opin. Select Cases with Opinions, by a Solicitor.

Sel.Dec.Bomb. Selected Decisions, Sudder Dewanny Adawlut, Bombay.

Sel.Dec.Madr. Select Decrees, Sudr Udawlut, Madras.

Sel.L.Cas. Select Law Cases, Eng.

Sel.Pr. Sellon's Practice.

Seld. Selden's Reports, vol. 5–10 New York Court of Appeals.

Seld.Notes. Selden's Notes, New York Court of Appeals.

Seld.Tit.Hon. Selden's Titles of Honor.

Selden. Selden's Reports, New York Court of Appeals.

Sell.Prac. (or Sell.Pr.). Sellon's Practice in the King's Bench.

Selw. Selwyn's Nisi Prius, Eng.

Selw.N.P. Selwyn's Law of Nisi Prius.

Selw. & Barn. The First Part of Barnewall & Alderson's English King's Bench Reports.

Serg.Land Laws Pa. Sergeant on the Land Laws of Pennsylvania.

Serg. & Lowb.Rep. English Common Law Reports, American reprints edited by Sergeant & Lowber.

Serg. & R. Sergeant & Rawle's Pennsylvania Reports.

Sess. Session.

Sess.Acts. Session Acts.

Sess.Cas. Sessions Cases (English King's Bench Reports);—Scotch Court of Session Cases.

Sess.Cas.Sc. Scotch Court of Session Cases.

Sess.Laws. Session Laws.

Sess.Pap.C.C.C. Session Papers, Central Criminal Court.

Sess.Pap.O.B. Session Papers, Old Bailey.

Set. (or Sett. & Rem.) Cas. English Settlement and Removal Cases (Burrow's Settlement Cases).

Sev.H.C. Sevestre's High Court Reports, Bengal.

Sev.S.D.A. Sevestre's Sudder Dewanny Adawlut Reports, Bengal.

Sewell, Sheriffs. Sewell on the Law of Sheriffs.

Sh. Shower's English Parliamentary Cases;—Shower's English King's Bench Reports;—Shepley's Reports, vols. 13–18 and 21–30 Maine;—Shaw's Scotch Appeal Cases;—Shaw's, etc., Decisions in the Scotch Court of Session (1st Series);—Shaw's Scotch Justiciary Cases;—Shaw's Scotch Teind Court Reports;—G. B. Shaw's Reports, vols. 10, 11 Vermont;—W. G. Shaw's Reports, vols. 30–35 Vermont;—Shirley's Reports, vols. 49–55 New Hampshire;—Sheldon's Buffalo, New York, Superior Court Reports;—Shepherd's Reports, Alabama;—Shipp's Reports, vols. 66, 67 North Carolina;—Shand's Reports, vols. 11–44 South Carolina;—Shadforth's Reserved Judgments, Victoria.

Sh.App. Shaw's Scotch Appeal Cases.

Sh.Crim.Cas. Shaw's Criminal Cases (Justiciary Court).

Sh.Dig. Shaw's Digest of Decisions, Scotland.

Sh.Jus. Shaw's Justiciary Cases, Scotland.

Sh.W. & C. Shaw, Wilson & Courtenay's Scotch Appeals Reports (Wilson & Shaw's Reports).

Sh. & Dunl. Shaw & Dunlop's Scotch Court of Session Reports (1st Series).

Sh. & Macl. Shaw & Maclean's Scotch Appeal Cases.

Shad. Shadford's Victoria Reports.

Shan. (or Shan.Cas.). Shannon's Tennessee Cases.

Shand. Shand's Reports, vols. 11–44 South Carolina.

Shankland's St. Shankland's Public Statutes, Tenn.

Shannon's Code. Shannon's Annotated Code, Tenn.

Shars.Bl.Comm. Sharswood's Blackstone's Commentaries.

Shars.Tab.Ca. Sharswood's Table of Cases, Connecticut.

Shars. & B.Lead.Cas.Real Prop. Sharswood and Budd's Leading Cases of Real Property.

Shaw. Shaw's Scotch Appeal Cases;—Shaw's, etc., Decisions in the Scotch Court of Session (1st Series);—Shaw's Scotch Justiciary Cases;—Shaw's Scotch Teind Court Reports;—G. B. Shaw's Reports, vols. 10, 11 Vermont;—W. G. Shaw's Reports, vols. 30–35 Vermont.

Shaw (G.B.). G. B. Shaw's Reports, vols. 10, 11 Vermont.

Shaw (W.G.). W. G. Shaw's Reports, 30–35 Vermont.

Shaw App. Shaw's Appeal Cases, Scotland.

Shaw Crim.Cas. Shaw's Criminal Cases, Scotland.

Shaw.Dec. Shaw's, etc., Decisions in the Scotch Court of Session (1st Series).

Shaw, Dunl. & B. Shaw, Dunlop & Bell's (1st Series) Scotch Session Cases.

Shaw, H.L. Shaw's Scotch Appeal Cases, House of Lords.

Shaw Jus. Shaw's (John) Scotch Justiciary Cases.

Shaw T.Cas. Shaw's Scotch Teind Court Reports.

Shaw, W. & C. Shaw, Wilson & Courtenay, Scotch (same as Wilson & Shaw).

Shaw & D. Shaw & Dunlop, Scotland.

Shaw & M. (or Shaw & Macl.). Shaw & MacLean, Scotland.

Shear. & R.Neg. Shearman and Redfield on Negligence.

Shel. Sheldon (see Sheld.).

Shel.Ca. Shelley's Case in vol. 1 Coke's Reports.

Sheld. (or Sheldon). Sheldon's Reports, Superior Court of Buffalo, New York.

Sheld.Subr. Sheldon on Subrogation.

Shelf.Lun. Shelford on Lunacy.

Shelf.Mar. & Div. Shelford on Marriage and Divorce.

Shep. Shepley's Reports, vols. 13–18 and 21–39 Maine;—Shepherd's Reports, Alabama.

Shep.Abr. Sheppard's Abridgment.

Shep.Sel.Cas. Shepherd's Select Cases, Alabama.

Shep.Touch. Sheppard's Touchstone.

Sheph.Sel.Cas. Shepherd's Select Cases, Ala.

Sher.Ct.Rep. Sheriff Court Reports, Scotland;—Sheriff Court Reporter.

Shiel. Shiel's Reports, Cape Colony.

Shinn, Repl. Shinn's Treatise on American Law of Replevin.

Shipp. Shipp's Reports, vols. 66, 67 North Carolina.

Shirl. Shirley's Reports, vols. 49–55 New Hampshire.

Shirl.L.C. Shirley's Leading Crown Cases, Eng.

Shortt, Inform. Shortt on Informations, Criminal, Quo Warranto, Mandamus, and Prohibition.

Show. Shower's English Parliamentary Cases;—Shower's English King's Bench Reports.

Show.K.B. Shower's English King's Bench Reports.

Show.P.C. Shower's English Parliamentary Cases.

Si De Ka Quarterly. Si De Ka Quarterly.

Sick. Sickels' Reports, vols. 46–146 New York Court of Appeals.

Sick.Min.Dec. Sickels' Mining Laws and Decisions.

Sick.Op. Sickels' Opinions of the New York Attorneys-General.

Sid. Siderfin's English King's Bench Reports.

Silv. Silvernail's Unreported Cases, New York Court of Appeals;—Unreported Cases, New York Supreme Court;—Criminal Reports, New York.

Silv.App. Silvernail's Appeals, N. Y.

Silv.Sup. Silvernail's Supreme, N. Y.

Silv.Cit. Silvernail's New York Citations.

Silvernail. Silvernail, N. Y.

Sim. Simons' English Vice-Chancery Reports;—Simmons' Reports, vols. 95–97, 99 Wisconsin.

Sim.N.S. Simons' English Vice-Chancery Reports, New Series.

Sim. & C. Simmons & Conover's Reports, vols. 95–97, 99 Wisconsin.

Sim. & Stu. (or Sim. & S.). Simons & Stuart's English Vice-Chancery Reports.

Sinclair. Sinclair's Manuscript Decisions, Scotch Session Cases.

Singers. Singers Probate Court, Pa.

Sir T.J. Sir Thomas Jones' Reports.

Six Circ. Cases on the Six Circuits, Irish.

Skene. Skene's De Verborum Significatione.

Skill.Pol.Rep. Skillman's New York Police Reports.

Skin. Skinner's English King's Bench Reports.

Skinker. Skinker's Reports, vols. 65–79 Missouri.

Slade. Slade's Reports, vol. 15 Vermont.

Slade's St. Slade's Laws, Vt.

Sm.Ac. Smith's Actions at Law.

Sm.C.C.M. Smith's Circuit Courts-Martial Reports, Maine.

Sm.Cond.Ala. Smith's Condensed Alabama Reports.

Sm.E.D. E. D. Smith's Reports, New York.

Sm.Eq. Smith's (J. W.) Manual of Equity;—Smith's Principles of Equity.

Sm.L.C. Smith's Leading Cases.

Sm.L.Cas.Com.L. Smith's Leading Cases on Commercial Law.

Sm. & B.R.R.Cas. Smith & Bates' American Railway Cases.

Sm. & Bat. Smith & Batty's Irish King's Bench Reports.

Sm. & G. Smale & Giffard's English Vice-Chancellors' Reports;—Smith & Guthrie's Reports, vols. 81–83 Missouri Appeals.

Sm. & M. Smedes & Marshall's Mississippi Reports.

Sm. & M.Ch. Smedes & Marshall's Mississippi Chancery Reports.

Sma. & Giff. Smale & Giffard's English Vice-Chancellors' Reports.

Smale & G. Smale & Giffard, Eng.

Smed. & M. Smedes & Marshall's Mississippi Reports.

Smed. & M.Ch. Smedes & Marshall's Mississippi Chancery Reports.

Smedes & M. (Miss.). Smedes & Marshall's Mississippi Reports.

Smedes & M.Ch. Smedes & Marshall's Chancery, Miss.

Smi. & Bat. Smith & Batty's Irish King's Bench Reports.

Smith. Smith's New Hampshire Reports; Smith's Reports, vols. 2–4 Dakota;—J. P. Smith's English King's Bench Reports;—Smith, in continuation of Fox & Smith;—Smith, English Registration;—P. F. Smith's Pennsylvania State Reports;—E. P. Smith's Reports, vols. 15–27 New York Court of Appeals;—E. D. Smith's New York Common Pleas Reports;—E. H. Smith's Reports, vols. 147–162 New York Court of Appeals;—Smith's Reports, vols. 54–62 California;—Smith's Indiana Reports;—Smith's Reports, vols. 61–64 Maine;—Smith's Reports, vols. 1–11 Wisconsin;—E. B. Smith's Reports, vols. 21–47 Illinois Appeals;—Smith, Reporter, vols. 7, 12 Heiskell's Tennessee Reports;—Smith's Reports, vols. 81–83 Missouri Appeals.

Smith, Act. Smith's Actions at Law.

Smith, C.C.M. Smith's Circuit Courts-Martial Reports, Me.

Smith C.P. (or E.D.). E. D. Smith's Common Pleas Reports, New York.

Smith, Ch.Pr. Smith's Chancery Practice.

Smith, Com.Law. Smith's Manual of Common Law.

Smith Cond.Rep. Smith's Condensed Reports, Ala.

Smith, Cont. Smith on Contracts.

Smith de Rep.Angl. Smith (Sir Thomas), De Republica Anglica [The Commonwealth of England and the Manner of Government Thereof. 1621].

Smith, Dict.Antiq. Smith's Dictionary of Greek and Roman Antiquities.

Smith, E.D. E. D. Smith, N.Y.

Smith E.H. Smith's (E. H.) Reports, vols. 147–162 New York Court of Appeals.

Smith E.P. (or Ct.App.). E. P. Smith's Reports, vols. 15–27 New York Court of Appeals.

Smith, Ex.Int. Smith on Executory Interest.

Smith-Hurd Ann.St. Smith-Hurd Illinois Annotated Statutes.

Smith Ind. Smith's Indiana Reports.

Smith J.P. J. P. Smith's English King's Bench Reports.

Smith K.B. Smith's King's Bench, Eng.

Smith L.C. Smith's Leading Cases.

Smith, L.J. Smith's Law Journal.

Smith, Laws Pa. Smith's Laws of Pennsylvania.

Smith, Lead.Cas. Smith's Leading Cases.

Smith, Man.Eq.Jur. Smith's Manual of Equity Jurisprudence.

Smith Me. Smith's Reports, vols. 61–64 Maine.

Smith, Merc.Law. Smith on Mercantile Law.

Smith N.H. Smith's New Hampshire Reports.

Smith N.Y. Smith's Reports, vols. 15–27 and 147–162 New York Court of Appeals.

Smith P.F. (or Pa.). P. F. Smith's Pennsylvania State Reports.

Smith Reg. Smith's Registration, Eng.

Smith, Wealth Nat. Smith, Inquiry into the Nature and Causes of the Wealth of Nations.

Smith Wis. Smith's Reports, vols. 1–11 Wisconsin.

Smith's Laws. Smith's Laws, Pa.

Smith's Lead.Cas. Smith's Leading Cases.

Smith & B. Smith & Batty's Irish King's Bench Reports;—Smith & Bates' American Railway Cases.

Smith & B.R.R.C. Smith & Bates' American Railway Cases.

Smith & G. Smith & Guthrie's Missouri Appeals Reports.

Smoult. Notes of Cases in Smoult's Collection of Orders, Calcutta.

Smy. (or Smythe). Smythe's Irish Common Pleas Reports.

Smythe. Smythe, Ir.

Sneed. Sneed's Tennessee Reports;—Sneed's Kentucky Decisions.

Sneed Dec. Sneed's Kentucky Decisions.

Snell, Eq. Snell's Principles in Equity.

Snow. Snow's Reports, vol. 3 Utah.

Snyder, Mines. Snyder on Mines and Mining.

So. Southern Reporter.

So.2d. Southern Reporter, Second Series.

So.Aus.L.R. South Australian Law Reports.

So.Calif.L.Rev. (or So.Cal.L.R.). Southern California Law Review.

So.Car. South Carolina;—South Carolina Reports.

So.Car.Const. South Carolina Constitutional Reports (by Treadway, by Mill, or by Harper).

So.Car.L.J. South Carolina Law Journal, Columbia.

So.East.Rep. South Eastern Reporter.

So.L.J. Southern Law Journal & Reporter, Nashville, Tenn.

So.L.Q. Southern Law Quarterly.

So.L.Rev. Southern Law Review, Nashville, Tenn;—Southern Law Review, St. Louis.

So.L.Rev.N.S. Southern Law Review, New Series, St. Louis, Mo.

So.L.T. Southern Law Times.

So.Law. Southern Lawyer.

So.Rep. Southern Reporter (commonly cited South. or So.).

So.West.Rep. South Western Reporter (commonly cited S.W.).

Soc.Econ. Social Economist.

Sol.J. Solicitors' Journal, London.

Sol.J. & R. Solicitors' Law Journal and Reporter, London.

Som. (or Som.L.J.). Somerset Legal Journal, Pa.

Somn.Gavelkind (or Somner). Somner on Gavelkind.

Sou.Aus.L.R. South Australian Law Reports.

Soule, Syn. Soule's Dictionary of English Synonymes.

South. Southern Reporter.

South Car. South Carolina.

Southard. Southard's New Jersey Reports.

Southw.L.J. Southwestern Law Journal and Reporter.

Sp. Spink's English Ecclesiastical and Admiralty Reports;—Spears' South Carolina Law Reports.

Sp.Acts. Special Acts.

Sp.Eq. (or Ch.). Spears' South Carolina Equity Reports.

Sp.Laws. Special Laws.

Sp.Pr.Cas. Spink's Prize Cases.

Sp.Sess. Special Session.

Sp.St. Private and Special Laws.

Sp. & Sel.Cas. Special and Selected Law Cases.

Sparks. Sparks' Reports, British Burmah.

Spaulding. Spaulding's Reports, vols. 71–80 Maine.

Spears (or Speers). Spears' (or Speers') South Carolina Law Reports.

Spears (or Speers) Eq. Spears' (or Speers') South Carolina Equity Reports.

Spel.Feuds. Spelman, Feuds.

Spel.Rep. Spelman's Reports, Manuscript, English King's Bench.

Spell.Extr.Rel. Spelling on Extraordinary Relief in Equity and in Law.

Spell.Extr.Rem. Spelling's Treatise on Injunctions and Other Extraordinary Remedies.

Spelman. Spelman, Glossarium Archaiologicum.

Spence, Ch. Spence's Equitable Jurisdiction of the Court of Chancery.

Spence, Eq.Jur. Spence's Equitable Jurisdiction of the Court of Chancery.

Spencer. Spencer's New Jersey Reports;—Spencer's Reports, vols. 10–20 Minnesota.

Spinks. Spinks' English Ecclesiastical and Admiralty Reports.

Spinks, P.C. Spinks' English Prize Cases.

Spinks, Prize Cas. Spinks' Admiralty Prize Cases.

Spooner. Spooner's Reports, vols. 12–15 Wisconsin.

Spottis. Sir R. Spottiswoode's Reports, Scotch Court of Session.

Spottis.C.L. & Eq.Rep. Common Law and Equity Reports, published by Spottiswoode.

Spottisw. Spottiswoode, Scotland.

Spottisw.Eq. Spottiswoode's Equity, Scotland.

Spr. (or Sprague). Sprague's United States District Court (Admiralty) Decisions.

St. State;—Story's United States Circuit Court Reports (see Sto.);—Stair's Scotch Court of Session Reports;—Stuart's (Milne & Peddie) Scotch Session Cases;—Statutes;—Laws or Acts, in some states.

St. at Large. South Carolina Session Laws.

St.Cas. Stillingfleet's Ecclesiastical Cases, English.

St.Ch.Cas. Star Chamber Cases.

St.Clem. St. Clement's Church Case, Philadelphia.

St.Eccl.Cas. Stillingfleet's Ecclesiastical Cases.

St.John's L.Rev. St. John's Law Review.

St.Law. Loughborough's Digest of Statute Law, Ky.

St.Lim. Statute of Limitations.

St.Louis L.Rev. St.Louis Law Review.

St.M. & P. Stuart, Milne & Peddie, Scotch.

St.Mark. St. Mark's Church Case, Philadelphia.

St.Marlb. Statute of Marlbridge.

St.Mert. Statute of Merton.

St.Rep. State Reports;—State Reporter.

St.Tr. The State Trials, English.

St.Westm. Statute of Westminster.

Stafford. Stafford's Reports, vols. 69–71 Vermont.

Stair. Stair's Reports, Scotch Court of Session.

Stair, Inst. Stair's Institutes of the Laws of Scotland.

Stan.L.R. (or Stanford L.Rev.). Stanford Law Review.

Stand.Dict. Standard Dictionary.

Stanton. Stanton's Reports, vols. 11–13 Ohio.

Stanton's Rev.St. Stanton's Revised Statutes, Ky.

Star. (or Starkie). Starkie's English Nisi Prius Reports.

Star Ch.Ca. Star Chamber Cases.

Stark.N.P. Starkie's English Nisi Prius Reports.

Starkie, Ev. Starkie on Evidence.

Starkie, Sland. & L. Starkie, on Slander and Libel.

Starr & C.Ann.St. Starr and Curtis' Annotated Statutes, Ill.

Stat. (or Stat. at L.). United States Statutes at Large.

State Tr. State Trials, English.

Staundef. Staundeforde, Exposition of the King's Prerogative.

Staundef.P.C. Staundeforde, Les Plees del Coron.

Stearns, Real Act. Stearns' Real Actions.

Steph.Comm. Stephen's Commentaries on English Law.

Steph.Cr.Law. Stephen's General View of the Criminal Law.

Steph.Dig. Stephen's Quebec Law Digest.

Steph.Dig.Cr.Law (or Steph.Crim.Dig.). Stephen's Digest of the Criminal Law.

Steph.Dig.Ev. (or Steph.Ev.). Stephen's Digest of the Law of Evidence.

Steph.Lect. Stephen, Lectures on History of France.

Steph.Pl. Stephen on Pleading.

Stev.Dig. Stevens' New Brunswick Digest.

Stevens & G. Stevens & Graham's Reports, vols. 80–111 Georgia.

Stew. Stewart's Alabama Reports;—Stewart's New Jersey Equity Reports;—Stewart's (R. W.) Reports, vols. 1–10 South Dakota; Stewart's Reports, N.S.

Stew. (N.J.). Stewart's New Jersey Equity Reports.

Stew.Adm. Stewart's Vice-Admiralty Reports, Nova Scotia.

Stew.Dig. Stewart's Digest of Decisions of the Courts of Law and Equity, N. J.

Stew.Eq. Stewart's Reports, vols. 28–45 New Jersey Equity.

Stew.N.Sc. Stewart's Admiralty Reports, Nova Scotia.

Stew.V.A. Stewart's Vice-Admiralty Reports, Nova Scotia.

Stew. & P. Stewart & Porter's Alabama Reports.

Stiles. Stiles' Reports, vols. 22–29 Iowa.

Still.Eccl.Cas. Stillingfleet's Ecclesiastical Cases.

Stim.Gloss. (or Stim.Law Gloss.). Stimson's Law Glossary.

Stimson. Stimson's Law Glossary.

Stiness. Stiness' Reports, vols. 20–21 Rhode Island.

Sto. (or Sto.C.C.). Story's United States Circuit Court Reports.

Sto.Const. Story's Commentaries on the Constitution of the United States.

Stock. Stockton's New Jersey Equity Reports;—Stockton, New Brunswick (same as Berton's Reports).

Stockett. Stockett's Reports, vols. 27–79 Maryland.

Stockt. Stockton's Equity, N.J.

Stockt.Ch. Stockton's New Jersey Chancery Reports.

Stockt.Vice-Adm. Stockton's Vice-Admiralty, New Brunswick.

Stor.Dict. Stormouth's Dictionary of the English Language.

Story. Story's United States Circuit Court Reports. See, also, Sto.

Story, Ag. Story on Agency.

Story, Bailm. Story on Bailments.

Story, Bills. Story on Bills.

Story, Comm.Const. Story's Commentaries on the Constitution of the United States.

Story, Confl.Laws. Story on Conflict of Laws.

Story, Const. Story on the Constitution.

Story, Cont. Story on Contracts.

Story, Eq.Jur. Story's Equity Jurisprudence.

Story, Eq.Pl. Story's Equity Pleading.

Story, Laws. Story's Laws of the United States.

Story, Merchants. Abbott's Merchant Ships and Seamen by Story.

Story, Partn. Story on Partnership.

Story, Prom.Notes. Story on Promissory Notes.

Story, Sales. Story on Sales of Personal Property.

Story, U.S.Laws. Story's Laws of the United States.

Story's Laws. Story's United States Laws.

Str. Strange's English King's Bench Reports.

Str.Cas.Ev. (or Str.8vo.). Strange's Cases of Evidence ("Octavo Strange").

Str.N.C. Sir T. Strange's Notes of Cases, Madras.

Stra. Strange.

Strahan. Strahan's Reports, vol. 19 Oregon.

Stran. Strange.

Strange. Strange's Reports, English Courts.

Strange, Madras. Strange's Notes of Cases, Madras.

Stratton. Stratton's Reports, vols. 12–14 Oregon.

Stringfellow. Stringfellow's Reports, vols. 9–11 Missouri.

Strob. Strobhart's South Carolina Law Reports.

Strob.Eq. (or Ch.). Strobhart's South Carolina Equity Reports.

Struve. Struve's Reports, vol. 3 Washington Territory.

Stu.Adm. (or V.A.). Stuart's Lower Canada Vice-Admiralty Reports.

Stu.Ap. Stuart's Appeal Cases (Lower Canada King's Bench Reports).

Stu.K.B. (or L.C.). Stuart's Lower Canada King's Bench Reports.

Stu.M. & P. (or Stu.Mil. & Ped.). Stuart, Milne & Peddie's Scotch Court of Sessions Reports.

Stuart. Stuart's Lower Canada King's Bench Reports;—Stuart's Lower Canada Vice-Admiralty Reports;—Stuart, Milne & Peddie's Scotch Court of Session Reports.

Stuart L.C.K.B. Stuart's Lower Canada King's Bench Reports.

Stuart L.C.V.A. Stuart's Lower Canada Vice-Admiralty Reports.

Stuart Vice-Adm. Stuart's Vice-Admiralty, Lower Canada.

Stud.Hist. Studies in History, Economics and Public Law.

Sty. Style's English King's Bench Reports.

Sty.Pr.Reg. Style's Practical Register.

Style. Style's English King's Bench Reports.

Sud.Dew.Ad. Sudder Dewanny Adawlut Reports, India.

Sud.Dew.Rep. Sudder Dewanny's Reports, Northwest Provinces, India.

Sugd.Powers. Sugden on Powers.

Sugd.Vend. Sugden on Vendors and Purchasers.

Sull.Lect. Sullivan's Lectures on Constitution and Laws of England.

Sum. Sumner's United States Circuit Court Reports.

Summ.Dec. Summary Decisions, Bengal.

Summerfield, S. Summerfield's (S.) Reports, vol. 21 Nevada.

Sumn. Sumner's United States Circuit Court Reports.

Sumn.Ves. (or Sum.Ves.). Sumner's Edition of Vesey's Reports.

Sup. Supreme.

Sup.Ct. Supreme Court Reporter.

Sup.Ct.Rep. Supreme Court Reporter of Decisions of United States Supreme Court.

Super. Superior Court;—Superior Court Reports.

Super.Ct. Superior Court Reports, Pa.

Supp. New York Supplement Reports.

Supp.Code. Supplement to Code.

Supp.Gen.St. Supplement to the General Statutes.

Supp.Rev. Supplement to the Revision.

Supp.Rev.Code. Supplement to the Revised Code.

Supp.Rev.St. Supplement to the Revised Statutes.

Supp.Ves.Jun. Supplement to Vesey, Jr.'s, Reports.

Supr. Supreme;—Superior Court Reports.

Surr. Surrogate.

Sus.Leg.Chron. Susquehanna Legal Chronical, Pa.

Susq.L.C. Susquehanna Leading Chronicle.

Susq.L.Chron. Susquehanna Legal Chronicle, Pa.

Suth. Sutherland's Reports.

Suth.Bengal. Sutherland's High Court Reports, Bengal.

Suth.Dam. Sutherland on the Law of Damages.

Suth.F.B.R. Sutherland's Full Bench Rulings, Bengal.

Suth.P.C.J. (or A.). Sutherland's Privy Council Judgments or Appeals.

Suth.St.Const. Sutherland on Statutes and Statutory Construction.

Suth.W.R. Sutherland's Weekly Reporter, Calcutta.

Sw. Swanston's English Chancery Reports;—Swabey's English Admiralty Reports;—Sweeney's New York Superior Court Reports;—Swan's Tennessee Reports;—Swinton's Scotch Justiciary Cases;—Swan;—Sweet;—Swift.

Sw. (or Swab.) & Tr. Swabey & Tristram's English Probate and Divorce Reports.

Swab. (or Swab.Admr.). Swabey's English Admiralty Reports.

Swan. Swan's Tennessee Reports;—Swanston's English Chancery Reports.

Swan.Ch. Swanston's English Chancery Reports.

Swan Tr. Swan's Treatise, Ohio.

Swan '41. Swan's Revised Statutes of Ohio, 1841.

Swan '54. Swan's Revised Statutes of Ohio, 1854.

Swan & C.R.St. Swan and Critchfield's Revised Statutes, Ohio.

Swan & S.St. Swan and Sayler's Supplement to the Revised Statutes, Ohio.

Swans. (or Swanst.). Swanston's English Chancery Reports.

Swan's St. Swan's Statutes, Ohio.

Sween. Sweeney's New York Superior Court Reports.

Sweeny. Sweeny, N.Y.

Sweet. Sweet's Law Dictionary;—Sweet on the Limited Liability Act;—Sweet's Marriage Settlement Cases;—Sweet's Precedents in Conveyancing;—Sweet on Wills.

Sweet M.Sett.Cas. Sweet's Marriage Settlement Cases.

Swift, Dig. Swift's Digest, Connecticut.

Swin. Swinton's Scotch Justiciary Reports.

Swin.Jus.Cas. Swinton's Scotch Justiciary Cases.

Swin.Reg.App. Swinton's Scotch Registration Appeal Cases.

Swinb.Wills. Swinburne on Wills.

Swint. Swinton's Justiciary Cases, Scotland.

Syme. Syme's Scotch Justiciary Reports.

Syn.Ser. Synopsis Series of the United States Treasury Decisions.

T

T. Territory;—Texas Reports;—Tappan's Ohio Reports.

T.B.Mon. T. B. Monroe's Kentucky Reports.

T.B. & M. Tracewell, Bowers & Mitchell, United States Comptroller's Decisions, 1898.

T.C. Tax Court of the United States.

T.D. U. S. Treasury Decisions.

T.Jones (or 2 Jones). T. Jones' English King's Bench Reports.

T.L.R. Times Law Reports.

T.M. Tax Magazine.

T.M.R. Trade Mark Reports.

T.R. Term Reports, Durnford & East;—Teste Rege;—Dayton Term Reports.

T.R. (N.Y.). Caines' (Term) Reports, New York.

T.R.E. (or T.E.R.). Tempore Regis Edwardi.

T.R.N.S. Term Reports, New Series (East's Reports).

T.Raym. Sir T. Raymond's English King's Bench Reports.

T.T. Trinity Term.

T.T.R. Tarl Town Reports, New South Wales.

T.U.P.Charlt. T. U. P. Charlton's Reports, Georgia.

T. & C. Thompson & Cook's New York Supreme Court Reports.

T. & G. Tyrwhitt & Granger's English Exchequer Reports.

T. & H.Prac. Troubat and Haly's Pennsylvania Practice.

T. & M. Temple & Mew's Crown Cases, English.

T. & P. Turner & Phillips' Reports, English Chancery.

T. & R. Turner & Russell's English Chancery Reports.

Tait. Tait's Manuscript Decisions, Scotch Session Cases.

Tal. (or Talb.). Cases *tempore* Talbot, English Chancery.

Tam. Tamlyn's English Rolls Court Reports.

Taml. Tamlyn, Eng.

Tan. (or Taney). Taney's United States Circuit Court Reports.

Tanner. Tanner's Reports, vols. 8–14 Indiana;—Tanner's Reports, vols. 13–17 Utah.

Tap. (or Tapp.). Tappan's Ohio Reports.

Tapping. Tapping on the Writ of Mandamus.

Tariff Ind., New. New's Tariff Index.

Tarl.Term R. Tarleton's Term Reports, New South Wales.

Tasm.L.R. Tasmanian Law Reports.

Tate's Dig. Tate's Digest of Laws, Va.

Taun. (or Taunt.). Taunton's English Common Pleas Reports.

Tax L.Rev. Tax Law Review.

Tax Law Rep. Tax Law Reporter.

Tay. Taylor (see Taylor);—Taylor's Reports, Ontario.

Tay.J.L. (or Tay.N.C.). J. L. Taylor's North Carolina Reports.

Tay.U.C. Taylor's Upper Canada Reports.

Tay. & B. Taylor & Bell's Bengal Reports.

Tayl. Taylor, N. C.

Tayl.Civil Law. Taylor on Civil Law.

Tayl.Corp. Taylor on Private Corporations.

Tayl.Ev. Taylor on Evidence.

Tayl.Gloss. Taylor's Law Glossary.

Tayl.Hist.Gav. Taylor (Silas), History of Gavelkind.

Tayl.Landl. & Ten. Taylor's Landlord and Tenant.

Tayl.Med.Jur. Taylor's Medical Jurisprudence.

Tayl.Priv.Corp. Taylor on Private Corporations.

Tayl.St. Taylor's Revised Statutes, Wis.

Taylor. Taylor's North Carolina Reports;—Taylor's Upper Canada Reports;—Taylor's Bengal Reports.

Taylor U.C. Taylor's King's Bench Reports, Upper Canada (now Ontario).

Techn.Dict. Crabb's Technological Dictionary.

Temp. *Tempore* (in the time of).

Temp.Geo.II. Cases in Chancery *tempore* George II.

Temp.L.Q. Temple Law Quarterly.

Temp. & M. Temple & Mew's English Crown Cases.

Temple & M. Temple & Mew Crown Cases, Eng.

Ten.Cas. Thompson's Unreported Cases, Tennessee;—Shannon's Cases, Tennessee.

Tenn. Tennessee;—Tennessee Reports (Overton's).

Tenn.App. Tennessee Appeals.

Tenn.Cas. Shannon's Tennessee Cases;—Unreported Tennessee Cases.

Tenn.Ch. Cooper's Tennessee Chancery Reports.

Tenn.Ch.A. Tennessee Chancery Appeals.

Tenn.Civ.A. Tennessee Civil Appeals.

Tenn.L.Rev. Tennessee Law Review.

Tenn.Leg.Rep. Tennessee Legal Reporter, Nashville.

Ter.Laws. Territorial Laws.

Term. Term Reports, English King's Bench (Durnford & East's Reports).

Term N.C. Term Reports, North Carolina, by Taylor.

Term R. Term Reports, English King's Bench (Durnford & East's Reports).

Termes de la Ley. Terms of the Common Laws and Statutes Expounded and Explained by John Rastell.

Terr. Territory;—Terrell's Reports, vols. 38–71 Texas.

Terr. & Walk. Terrell & Walker's Reports, vols. 38–51 Texas.

Terry. Terry, Del.

Tex. Texas;—Texas Reports.

Tex.A.Civ.Cas. White & Wilson's Civil Cases, Tex.

Tex.A.Civ.Cas. (Wilson). Texas Court of Appeal Civil Cases.

Tex.App. Texas Court of Appeals Reports (Criminal Cases);—Texas Civil Appeals Cases.

Tex.Civ.App. (or Tex.Civ.Rep.). Texas Civil Appeals Reports.

Tex.Com.App. Texas Commission of Appeals.

Tex.Cr.R. (or Tex.Crim.Rep.). Texas Criminal Reports.

Tex.Ct.Rep. Texas Court Reporter.

Tex.Dec. Texas Decisions.

Tex.Jur. Texas Jurisprudence.

Tex.L.J. Texas Law Journal, Tyler.

Tex.L.Rev. Texas Law Review.

Tex.Law & Leg. Texas Law and Legislation.

Tex.Supp. Supplement to vol. 25, Texas Reports;—Texas Supplement.

Tex.Unrep.Cas. Posey's Unreported Cases.

Th. Thomas (see Thom.);—Thomson (see Thom.);—Thompson (see Thomp.).

Th.C.C. Thatcher's Criminal Cases, Massachusetts.

Th.C.Const.Law. Thomas' Leading Cases in Constitutional Law.

Th. & C. Thompson & Cook's New York Supreme Court Reports.

Thac.Cr.Cas. Thacher's Massachusetts Criminal Reports.

Thacher, Cr.Cas. Thacher's Criminal Cases, Mass.

Thayer. Thayer's Reports, vol. 18 Oregon.

Thayer, Prelim.Treatise Ev. Thayer's Preliminary Treatise on Evidence.

The Rep. The Reporter;—The Reports (Coke's Reports).

Them. La Themis, Montreal, Quebec;—The American Themis, New York.

Theob. on Wills. Theobald on Wills.

Tho. Thomas (see Thom.);—Thomson (see Thom.);—Thompson (see Thomp.).

Thom. Thomson's Reports, Nova Scotia;—Thomas' Reports, vol. 1 Wyoming.

Thom.Co.Litt. Thomas' Edition of Coke upon Littleton.

Thom.Const.L. (or L.C.). Thomas' Leading Cases on Constitutional Law.

Thom.Dec. 1 Thomson, Nova Scotia Reports.

Thom.Rep. 2 Thomson, Nova Scotia Reports.

Thom.Sel.Dec. Thomson's Select Decisions, Nova Scotia.

Thom. & Fr. Thomas & Franklin's Reports, vol. 1 Maryland Chancery.

Thomas. Thomas' Reports, Wyoming Territory.

Thomas, Mortg. Thomas on Mortgages.

Thomas, Negl. Thomas on Negligence.

Thomp.Cal. Thompson's Reports, vols. 39, 40 California.

Thomp.Cit. Thompson's Citations, Ohio;—Indiana.

Thomp.Dig. Thompson's Digest of Laws, Fla.

Thomp.Liab.Stockh. Thompson on Liability of Stockholders.

Thomp.N.B.Cas. Thompson's National Bank Cases.

Thomp.Neg. Thompson's Cases on Negligence.

Thomp.Tenn.Cas. Thompson's Unreported Tennessee Cases.

Thomp.Trials. Thompson on Trials.

Thomp. & C. Thompson & Cook's New York Supreme Court Reports.

Thomp. & St.Code. Thompson and Steger's Code, Tenn.

Thomps.Cas. Thompson's Cases, Tenn.

Thompson. Thompson's Reports, vols. 39, 40 California;—Thompson's Nova Scotia Reports.

Thor. Thorington's Reports, vol. 107 Alabama.

Thorn. Thornton's Notes of Cases, Ecclesiastical and Maritime.

Thornt. & Bl.Bldg. & Loan Ass'ns. Thornton and Blackledge's Law Relating to Building and Loan Associations.

Thornton, Gifts. Thornton on Gifts and Advancements.

Thorpe. Thorpe's Reports, vol. 52 Louisiana Annual.

Thos. Thomas (see Thom.).

Throop, Pub.Off. Throop's Treatise on Public Officers.

Tich.Tr. Report of the Tichborne Trial, London.

Tidd. Tidd's Costs;—Tidd's Practice.

Tidd, Prac. (or Tidd Pr.). Tidd's Practice.

Tied.Lim.Police Power. Tiedeman's Treatise on the Limitations of Police Power in the United States.

Tied.Mun.Corp. Tiedeman's Treatise on Municipal Corporations.

Tiedeman, Real Prop. Tiedeman on Real Property.

Tiff. (or Tiffany). Tiffany's Reports, vols. 28–39 New York Court of Appeals.

Till. & Yates App. Tillinghast & Yates on Appeals.

Tillman. Tillman's Reports, vols. 68, 69, 71, 73, 75 Alabama.

Times L.R. (or Times L.Rep.). Times Law Reports.

Tinw. Tinwald's Reports, Scotch Court of Sessions.

Title News. Title News.

To.Jo. Sir Thomas Jones' English King's Bench Reports.

Tobey. Tobey's Reports, vols. 9–10 Rhode Island.

Toller. Toller on Executors.

Tomkins & J.Mod.Rom.Law. Tomkins & Jencken, Compendium of the Modern Roman Law.

Toml. (or Toml. [Cas.]). Tomlins' Election Evidence Cases.

Toml.Law Dict. Tomlins' Law Dictionary.

Toml.Supp.Br. Tomlins' Supplement to Brown's Parliamentary Cases.

Tot. (or Toth.). Tothill's English Chancery Reports.

Touch. Sheppard's Touchstone.

Toull. Toullier's Droit Civil Français.

Toull.Droit Civil Fr. (or Toullier, Dr.Civ.Fr.). Toullier's Droit Civil Français.

Town.St.Tr. Townsend's Modern State Trials.

Townsh.Pl. Townshend's Pleading.

Townsh.Sland. & L. Townshend on Slander and Libel.

Tr. & H.Pr. Troubat & Haly's Practice, Pa.

Tr.App. New York Transcript Appeals.

Tr.Ch. Transactions of the High Court of Chancery (Tothill's Reports).

Trace. & M. Tracewell and Mitchell, United States Comptroller's Decisions.

Traité du Mar. Pothier, Traité du Contrat de Mariage.

Trans.App. Transcript Appeals, New York.

Transcr.A. Transcript Appeals, N. Y.

Tray.Lat.Max. (or Leg.Max.). Trayner, Latin Maxims and Phrases, etc.

Tread. (or Tread.Const. [S.C.]). Treadway's South Carolina Constitutional Reports.

Treas.Dec. Treasury Decisions, U. S.

Tred. Tredgold's Reports, Cape Colony.

Tri.Bish. Trial of the Seven Bishops.

Tri.E. of Cov. Trial of the Earl of Coventry.

Trint.T. Trinity Term, Eng.

Tripp. Tripp's Reports, vols. 5–6 Dakota.

Tristram. Tristram's Supplement to vol. 4 Swabey & Tristram.

Troub.Lim.Partn. Troubat on Limited Partnership.

Troub. & H.Prac. Troubat & Haly's Practice, Pa.

Tru.Railw.Rep. Truman's American Railway Reports.

True. Trueman's New Brunswick Reports and Equity Cases.

Truem, Eq.Cas. Trueman's Equity Cases, New Brunswick.

Trust Bull. Trust Bulletin.

Tuck. Tucker's New York Surrogate Reports;—Tucker's Select Cases, Newfoundland;—Tucker's Reports, vols. 156–175 Massachusetts;—Tucker's District of Columbia Appeals Reports.

Tuck.Sel.Cas. Tucker's Select Cases, Newfoundland.

Tuck.Sur. (or Tuck.Surr.). Tucker's Surrogate, Reports, City of New York.

Tucker's Blackstone. Tucker's Blackstone's Commentaries.

Tud.Cas.Merc.Law. Tudor's Leading Cases on Mercantile Law.

Tud.Cas.R.P. Tudor's Leading Cases on Real Property.

Tud.Char.Trusts. Tudor on Charitable Trusts.

Tudor, Lead.Cas.Real Prop. Tudor's Leading Cases on Real Property.

Tul.L.Rev. Tulane Law Review.

Tupper. Tupper's Reports, Ontario Appeals;—Tupper's Upper Canada Practice Reports.

Tur. Turner & Russell's English Chancery Reports.

Turn. Turner's Reports, vols. 99–101 Kentucky;—Turner's Reports, vols. 35, 48 Arkansas.

Turn.Anglo Sax. Turner, History of the Anglo Saxons.

Turn. & P. (or Turn. & Ph.). Turner & Phillips' Reports, English Chancery.

Turn. & R. Turner & Russell's English Chancery Reports.

Turn. & Rus. (or Russ.). Turner & Russell's English Chancery Reports.

Tuttle. Tuttle's Reports, vols. 23–32 and 41–52 California.

Tuttle & Carpenter. Tuttle & Carpenter's Reports, vol. 52 California.

Ty. Tyler.

Tyl. (or Tyler). Tyler's Vermont Reports.

Tyler, Ej. Tyler on Ejectment and Adverse Enjoyment.

Tyler, Steph.Pl. Tyler's Edition of Stephen on Principles of Pleading.

Tyng. Tyng's Reports, vols. 2–17 Massachusetts.

Tyr. (or Tyrw.). Tyrwhitt & Granger's English Exchequer Reports.

Tyr. & Gr. (or Tyrw. & G.). Tyrwhitt & Granger's English Exchequer Reports.

Tytler, Mil.Law. Tytler on Military Law and Courts-Martial.

U

U. Utah;—Utah Reports.

U.B. Upper Bench.

U.B.Pr. Upper Bench Precedents *tempore* Car. I.

U.C. Upper Canada.

U.C.App. Upper Canada Appeals.

U.C.C.P. Upper Canada Common Pleas Reports.

U.C.Ch. Upper Canada Chancery Reports.

U.C.Cham. Upper Canada Chamber Reports.

U.C.E. & A. Upper Canada Error and Appeal Reports.

U.C.Jur. Upper Canada Jurist.

U.C.K.B. (or U.C.O.S.). Upper Canada King's Bench Reports, Old Series.

U.C.Pr. (or P.R.). Upper Canada Practice Reports.

U.C.Q.B. Upper Canada Queen's Bench Reports.

U.C.Q.B.O.S. (or U.C.O.S.). Upper Canada Queen's (King's) Bench Reports, Old Series.

U.C.R. Queen's Bench Reports, Ontario.

U.C.Rep. Upper Canada Reports.

U.Chi.L.Rev. University of Chicago Law Review.

U.Cin.L.Rev. University of Cincinnati Law Review.

U.Detroit L.J. University of Detroit Law Journal.

U.K. United Kingdom.

U.Kan.City L.Rev. University of Kansas City Law Review.

U.L.A. Uniform Laws Annotated.

U.Mo.B., Law Ser. University of Missouri Bulletin, Law Series.

U.Newark L.Rev. University of Newark Law Review.

U. of Pitts.L.Rev. University of Pittsburgh Law Review.

U.Pa.L.Rev. University of Pennsylvania Law Review.

U.S. United States;—United States Reports.

U.S.Ap. (or U.S.App.). United States Appeals Reports.

U.S.App.D.C. United States Court of Appeals for the District of Columbia.

U.S.Aviation Rep. Aviation Reports, U. S.

U.S.C. United States Code.

U.S.C.A. United States Code Annotated.

U.S.C.C. United States Circuit Court;—United States Court of Claims.

U.S.C.S. United States Civil Service Commission.

U.S.C.Supp. United States Code Supplement.

U.S.Code Cong.Serv. U.S.Code Congressional Service.

U.S.Comp.St. United States Compiled Statutes.

U.S.Comp.St.Supp. United States Compiled Statutes Supplement.

U.S.Cong. & Adm.Serv. U.S.Congressional and Administrative Service.

U.S.Ct.Cl. Reports of the United States Court of Claims.

U.S.D.C. United States District Court;—United States District of Columbia.

U.S.Jur. United States Jurist, Washington, D. C.

U.S.L.Ed. Lawyers' Ed. Supreme Court Reports.

U.S.L.J. United States Law Journal, New Haven and New York.

U.S.L.Rev. United States Law Review.

U.S.Law Mag. United States Law Magazine, N. Y.

U.S.Month.Law Mag. United States Monthly Law Magazine.

U.S.Pat.Q. U. S. Patent Quarterly.

U.S.R. United States Supreme Court Reports.

U.S.R.S. United States Revised Statutes.

U.S.Reg. United States Register, Philadelphia.

U.S.Rev.St. United States Revised Statutes.

U.S.S.C.Rep. United States Supreme Court Reports.

U.S.St. at L. United States Statutes at Large.

U.S.St.Tr. United States State Trials (Wharton's).

U.S.Sup.Ct.Rep. United States Supreme Court Reporter.

U.Toronto L.J. University of Toronto Law Journal.

Udal. Fiji Law Reports (Udal) (Fiji).

Ulm.L.Rec. Ulman's Law Record, New York.

Underh.Torts. Underhill on Torts.

Underhill, Ev. Underhill on Evidence.

Unof. Unofficial, Reports.

Up.Ben.Pre. Upper Bench Precedents, *tempore* Car. I.

Up.Can. Upper Canada (see U. C.).

Utah. Utah.

V

V. Vermont;—Vermont Reports;—Victoria;—Virginia;—Virginia Reports.

V.A.M.S. Vernon's Annotated Missouri Statutes.

V.A.T.S. Vernon's Annotated Texas Statutes.

V.C.C. Vice-Chancellor's Court.

V.C.Rep. Vice-Chancellor's Reports.

V.L.R. Victorian Law Reports, Australia. (For Victorian see Vict.).

V.N. Van Ness' Prize Cases.

V.R. Vermont Reports.

V.S. Vermont Statutes.

V. & B. Vesey & Beames' English Chancery Reports.

V. & S. Vernon & Scriven's Irish King's Bench Reports.

Va. Virginia;—Virginia Reports;—Gilmer's Virginia Reports.

Va.Bar.Assn. Virginia State Bar Association.

Va.Cas. Virginia Cases (by Brockenbrough & Holmes).

Va.Ch.Dec. Chancery Decisions, Virginia.

Va.Dec. Virginia Decisions.

Va.L.Reg. Virgina Law Register.

Va.L.Reg.N.S. Virginia Law Register, New Series.

Va.L.Rev. Virginia Law Review.

Va.Law J. Virginia Law Journal, Richmond.

Va.R. Virginia Reports;—Gilmer's Virginia Reports.

Val.Com. Valen's Commentaries.

Van Fleet, Coll.Attack. Van Fleet on Collateral Attack.

Van K. Van Koughnet's Reports, vols. 15–21 Upper Canada Common Pleas.

Van.L. Vander Linden's Practice, Cape Colony.

Van.N. (or Van Ness, Prize Cas.). Van Ness' Prize Cases, U. S.

Vand.L.Rev. Vanderbilt Law Review.

Vanderstr. Vanderstraaten's Ceylon Reports.

Vatt. Vattel's Law of Nations.

Vatt.Law Nat. (or Vattel). Vattel's Law of Nations.

Vaug. (or Vaugh.). Vaughan's English Common Pleas Reports.

Vaughan. Vaughan's English Common Pleas Reports.

Vaux. Vaux's Recorder's Decisions, Philadelphia.

Vaux Rec.Dec. Vaux's Recorder's Decisions, Phila., Pa.

Ve. (or Ves.). Vesey's English Chancery Reports.

Ve. (or Ves.) & B. Vesey & Beames' English Chancery Reports.

Veazey. Veazey's Reports, vols. 36–46 Vermont.

Vent. Ventris' English Common Pleas Reports.

Ventr. Ventris' English King's Bench Reports.

Ver. (or Verm.). Vermont Reports.

Vern. Vernon's English Chancery Reports.

Vern. & Scr. (or S. or Scriv.). Vernon & Scriven's Irish King's Bench Reports.

Vernon's Ann.C.C.P. Vernon's Annotated Texas Code of Criminal Procedure.

Vernon's Ann.Civ.St. Vernon's Annotated Texas Civil Statutes.

Vernon's Ann.P.C. Vernon's Annotated Texas Penal Code.

Ves. Vesey's English Chancery Reports.

Ves.Jr. Vesey, Jr.'s, English Chancery Reports.

Ves.Jr.Suppl. Vesey Junior Supplement, Eng.

Ves.Jun.Supp. Supplement to Vesey, Jr.'s, Reports, by Hovenden.

Ves.Sen. (or Sr.). Vesey, Sr.'s, English Chancery Reports.

Ves.Suppl. Vesey Senior Supplement, Eng.

Ves. & B. (or Bea.). Vesey & Beames' English Chancery Reports.

Vet.Na.B. Old Natura Brevium.

Vez. Vezey's (Vesey's) English Chancery Reports.

Vicat. (or Vicat.Voc.Jur.). Vocabularium jurisutriusque, ex variis editis.

Vict. Queen Victoria.

Vict.L. Victorian Law.

Vict.L.R. Victorian Law Reports, Australia.

Vict.L.R.Min. Victorian Mining Law Reports.

Vict.L.T. Victorian Law Times, Melbourne.

Vict.Rep. Victorian Reports.

Vict.Rep. (Adm.). Victorian Reports (Admiralty) (Australia).

Vict.Rep. (Eq.). Victorian Reports (Equity) (Australia).

Vict.Rep. (Law). Victorian Reports (Law) (Australia).

Vict.Rev. Victorian Review.

Vict.St.Tr. Victorian State Trials.

Vil. & Br. Vilas & Bryant's Edition of the Wisconsin Reports.

Vilas. Vilas' New York Criminal Reports.

Vin.Abr. Viner's Abridgment.

Virg. Virginia (see Va.);—Virgin.

Virgin. Virgin's Reports, vols. 52–60 Maine;—Virginia (see Va.).

Virgin Islands. Virgin Islands.

Viz. *Videlicet* (that is to say).

Vo. Verbo.

Voet, Com.ad Pand. Voet, Commentarius ad Pandectas.

Vr. Vroom's New Jersey Reports.

Vroom (G.D.W.). G. D. W. Vroom's Reports, vols. 36–63 New Jersey Law.

Vroom (P.D.). P. D. Vroom's Reports, vols. 30–35 New Jersey Law.

Vt. Vermont;—Vermont Reports.

W

W. King William;—Wheaton's United States Supreme Court Reports;—Wendell's New York Reports;—Watt's Reports, Pennsylvania;—Weekly;—Wisconsin;—Wyoming;—Wright's Ohio Reports.

W.A. Western Australia.

W.Bl. Sir William Blackstone's English King's Bench Reports.

W.C.C. Washington's United States Circuit Court Reports;—Minton-Senhouse's Workmen's Compensation Cases, Eng.

W.C. & Ins.Rep. Workmen's Compensation & Insurance Reports.

W.H.Chron. Westminster Hall Chronicle, London.

W.H. & G. Welsby, Hurlstone & Gordon's English Exchequer Reports.

W.Jo. Sir William Jones' English King's Bench Reports.

W.Jones. William Jones, Eng.

W.Kel. William Kelynge's English Chancery Reports.

W.N. Weekly Notes, London.

W.N.C. Weekly Notes of Cases, Pa.

W.P.Cas. Wollaston's English Bail Court (Practice) Cases.

W.R. Weekly Reporter, London;—Weekly Reporter, Bengal;—Wendell's New York Reports;—Wisconsin Reports;—West's Reports (English Chancery).

W.Rep. West's Reports *tempore* Hardwicke, English Chancery.

W.Rob. (or W.Rob.Adm.). W. Robinson's English Admiralty Reports.

W.S. Wagner's Statutes, Mo.

W.S.A. Wisconsin Statutes Annotated.

W.T.R. Weekly Transcript Reports, New York.

W.Ty.R. Washington Territory Reports.

W.Va. West Virginia;—West Virginia Reports.

W.Va.L.Q. West Virginia Law Quarterly;—West Virginia Law Quarterly and The Bar.

W.W.Harr. W. W. Harrington, Del.

W.W. & A'B. Vict. Wyatt, Webb, & A'Beckett's Reports, Victoria.

W.W. & D. Willmore, Wollaston & Davison.

W.W. & H. Willmore, Wollaston, & Hodges' English Queen's Bench Reports.

W. & B.Dig. Walker & Bates' Digest, Ohio.

W. & C. Wilson & Courtenay's Scotch Appeal Cases (see Wilson & Shaw).

W. & L.Dig. Wood & Long's Digest, Illinois.

W. & M. Woodbury & Minot's United States Circuit Court Reports;—William & Mary.

W. & S. Watts & Sergeant's Pennsylvania Reports;—Wilson & Shaw's Scotch Appeal Cases.

W. & S.App. Wilson & Shaw's Scotch Appeals, English House of Lords.

W. & T.Eq.Ca. (or L.C.). White & Tudor's Leading Cases in Equity.

W. & W. White & Wilson's Texas Court of Appeals, Civil Cases.

W. & W.Vict. Wyatt & Webb's Victorian Reports.

Wa. Watts' Reports, Pennsylvania;—Wales.

Wade, Am.Mining Law. Wade on American Mining Law.

Wade, Attachm. Wade on Attachment and Garnishment.

Wag.St. Wagner's Statutes, Mo.

Wait, Act. & Def. Wait's Actions and Defences.

Wait Dig. Wait's Digest, New York.

Wait St.Pap. Wait's State Papers of the United States.

Wait's Prac. Wait's New York Practice.

Wal. Wallace (see Wall.).

Wal. by L. Wallis' Irish Reports, by Lyne.

Wal.Jr. (or Wall.Jr.). Wallace's (J. W.) United States Circuit Court Reports.

Walk. (or Walker). Walker's Mississippi Reports;—Walker's Michigan Chancery Reports;—Walker's Reports, vols. 25, 72–88 Texas;—Walker's Reports, vols. 1–10 Texas Civil Appeals;—Walker's Reports, vols. 96, 109 Alabama;—Walker's Pennsylvania Reports.

Walk. (Pa.). Walker's Pennsylvania Reports.

Walk.Am.Law. Walker's American Law.

Walk.Ch. (or Mich.). Walker's Michigan Chancery Reports.

Walk.Miss. Walker's Mississippi Reports.

Walk.Pat. Walker on Patents.

Wall. Wallace's United States Supreme Court Reports;—Wallace's (Sr.) United States Circuit Court Reports;—Wallace's Philadelphia Reports;—Wallis' Irish Chancery Reports.

Wall.C.C. Wallace's United States Circuit Court Reports, Third Circuit.

Wall.Jr. (or Wall.Jr.C.C.). Wallace, Junior's Reports, U. S.

Wall.Rep. Wallace on the Reporters;—Wallace's United States Supreme Court Reports.

Wall.S.C. Wallace's United States Supreme Court Reports.

Wall.Sen. (or Wal.Sr.). Wallace's (J. B.) United States Circuit Court Reports.

Wallis. Wallis' Irish Chancery Reports.

Wallis by L. Wallis' Irish Chancery Reports, by Lyne.

Walsh. Walsh's Registry Cases, Ireland.

War.Op. (or Warwick's Op.). Warwick's Opinions (City Solicitor of Philadelphia, Pa.)

Ward. Warden's Reports, Ohio;—Warden & Smith's Reports, Ohio.

Ward, Leg. Ward on Legacies.

Warden. Warden's Reports, vols. 2, 4 Ohio State.

Warden & Smith. Warden & Smith's Reports, vol. 3 Ohio State.

Ware. Ware's United States District Court Reports.

Warth Code. West Virginia Code, 1899.

Warv.Abst. Warvelle on Abstracts of Title.

Wash. Washington;—Washington's Reports;—Washington's United States Circuit Court Reports;—Washington's Virginia Reports;—Washburn's Reports, vols. 16–23 Vermont;—Washington County Reports, Pa.

Wash.C.C. Washington's United States Circuit Court Reports.

Wash.Co.R. Washington County Reports, Pa.

Wash.L.Rev. Washington Law Review.

Wash.Law Rep. Washington Law Reporter, D. C.

Wash.St. Washington State Reports.

Wash.T. Washington Territory.

Wash.Ter. Washington Territory Reports.

Wash.Ter.N.S. Allen's Washington Territory Reports, New Series.

Wash.U.L.Q. Washington University Law Quarterly.

Wash.Va. Washington's Virginia Reports.

Wash. & Haz.P.E.I. Washburton & Hazard's Reports, Prince Edward Island.

Wash. & Lee L.Rev. Washington and Lee Law Review.

Washb. Washburn, Vt.

Washb.Easem. Washburn on Easements and Servitudes.

Washb.Real Estate. Washburn on Real Property.

Washb.Real Prop. Washburn on Real Property.

Washburn. Washburn's Reports, vols. 16–23 Vermont.

Wat. Watkins;—Watson.

Wat.C.G.H. Watermeyer's Cape of Good Hope Reports.

Wat.Cr.Dig. Waterman's Criminal Digest, United States.

Wat.Set-Off. Waterman on Set-Off.

Watermeyer. Watermeyer's Cape of Good Hope Reports.

Watk.Conv. Watkins' Conveyancing.

Watk.Copyh. Watkins' Copyholds.

Wats.Arb. Watson on Arbitration.

Wats.Cler.Law. Watson's Clergyman's Law.

Wats.Comp.Eq. Watson's Compendium of Equity.

Watts. Watts' Pennsylvania Reports;—Watts' Reports, vols. 16–24 West Virginia.

Watts & S. (or Serg.). Watts & Sergeant's Pennsylvania Reports.

Web.Pat.Cas. Webster's Patent Cases.

Web.Tr. The Trial of Professor Webster for Murder.

Webb. Webb's Reports, vols. 6–20 Kansas;—Webb's Reports, vols. 11–20 Texas Civil Appeals.

Webb, A'B. & W. Webb, A'Beckett, & Williams' Victorian Reports, Australia.

Webb, A'B. & W.Eq. Webb, A'Beckett, & Williams' Equity Reports, Victoria.

Webb, A'B. & W.I.P. & M. Webb, A'Beckett, & Williams' Insolvency, Probate, and Matrimonial Reports, Victoria.

Webb, A'B. & W.Min. Webb, A'Beckett, & Williams' Mining Cases, Victoria.

Webb & Duval. Webb & Duval's Reports, vols. 1–3 Texas.

Webs. Webster.

Webst.Dict. (or Webster). Webster's Dictionary.

Webst.Dict.Unab. Webster's Unabridged Dictionary.

Webst.Int.Dict. Webster's International Dictionary.

Webster in Sen.Doc. Webster in Senate Documents.

Wedgw.Dict.Eng.Etymology. Wedgwood's Dictionary of English Etymology.

Week.Jur. Weekly Jurist, Ill.

Week.L.Rec. Weekly Law Record.

Week.L.Rev. Weekly Law Review, San Francisco.

Week.Law & Bk. Bull. Weekly Law & Bank Bulletin.

Week.Reptr. Weekly Reporter, London;—Weekly Reporter, Bengal.

Week.Trans.Rep. (or Week.Trans.Repts.). Weekly Transcript Reports, N. Y.

Weeks, Attys. at Law. Weeks on Attorneys at Law.

Weight.Med.Leg.Gaz. Weightman's Medico-Legal Gazette, London.

Wel. Welsh's Irish Registry Cases.

Wells, Repl. Wells on Replevin.

Welsb., H. & G. Welsby, Hurlstone, & Gordon's English Exchequer Reports.

Welsb., Hurl. & G. Welsby, Hurlstone, and Gordon's Reports, 1–9 English Exchequer Reports.

Welsh. Welsh's Registry Cases, Ireland;—Welsh's Irish Cases at Sligo;—Welsh's (Irish) Case of James Feighny, 1838.

Welsh Reg.Cas. Welsh's Irish Registry Cases.

Wend. Wendell's New York Reports.

Wenz. Wenzell's Reports, vols. 60—Minnesota.

Wesk.Ins. Weskett on Insurance.

Weskett, Ins. Weskett's Complete Digest of the Theory, Laws and Practice of Insurance.

West. West's Reports, English House of Lords;—West's Reports, English Chancery;—Western Tithe Cases;—Weston's Reports, vols. 11–14 Vermont;—Westmoreland Law Journal (Pa.).

West.Aus. Western Australia.

West Ch. West's English Chancery Cases.

West Co.Rep. West Coast Reporter.

West Coast Rep. West Coast Reporter.

West H.L. West's Reports, English House of Lords.

West.Jur. Western Jurist, Des Moines, Iowa.

West.L.Gaz. Western Law Gazette, Cincinnati, Ohio.

West.L.M. Western Law Monthly, Ohio.

West.L.R. Western Law Reporter, Canada.

West.L.T. Western Law Times, Canada.

West.Law J. Western Law Journal, Cincinnati, Ohio.

West.Law Month. Western Law Monthly, Ohio.

West's Op. West's Opinions (City Solicitor of Philadelphia, Pa.).

West.R. Western Reporter.

West Symb. West's Symboleographie.

West t.H. West's English Chancery Reports *tempore* Hardwicke.

West t.Hardw. West *temp.* Hardwicke, Eng.

West Va. West Virginia;—West Virginia Reports.

West.Wkly. Western Weekly, Canada.

1917 West.Wkly. 1917 Western Weekly, Canada.

Western Reserve L.N. Western Reserve Law Notes.

Westl.Priv.Int.Law (or Westlake Int.Private Law). Westlake's Private International Law.

Westm. Statute of Westminster;—Westmoreland Law Journal, Pa.

Westm.Rev. Westminster Review.

Weston. Weston's Reports, vols. 11–14 Vermont.

Weth. Wethey's Reports, Canada.

Wh. Wheaton's United States Supreme Court Reports;—Wharton's Pennsylvania Reports;—Wheeler's New York Criminal Reports.

Wh.Cr.Cas. Wheeler's New York Criminal Cases.

Wh. & T.L.C. White & Tudor's Leading Cases in Equity.

Whar. Wharton's Pennsylvania Reports.

Whar.Dig. Wharton's Digest, Pennsylvania.

Whar.St.Tr. Wharton's State Trials, United States.

Whart. Wharton.

Whart. (Pa.). Wharton's Pennsylvania Reports.

Whart.Ag. Wharton on Agency.

Whart.Am.Cr.Law (or Whart.Crim.Law). Wharton's American Criminal Law.

Whart.Confl.Laws. Wharton's Conflict of Laws.

Whart.Cr.Ev. Wharton on Criminal Evidence.

Whart.Cr.Law (or Whart.Crim.Law). Wharton's American Criminal Law.

Whart.Cr.Pl. & Prac. Wharton's Criminal Pleading & Practice.

Whart.Ev. Wharton on Evidence in Civil Issues.

Whart.Hom. (or Whart.Homicide). Wharton's Law of Homicide.

Whart.Law Dict. Wharton's Law Dictionary, or Law Lexicon.

Whart.Law Lexicon. Wharton's Law Dictionary (or Law Lexicon).

Whart.Lex. Wharton's Law Lexicon.

Whart.Neg. Wharton on Negligence.

Whart.St.Tr. (or Whart.State Tr.). Wharton's State Trials, U. S.

Whart. & S.Med.Jur. Wharton & Stillé's Medical Jurisprudence.

Wheat. Wheaton's United States Supreme Court Reports.

Wheat.El.Int.Law. Wheaton's Elements of International Law.

Wheat.Hist.Law Nat. Wheaton's History of the Law of Nations.

Wheat.Int.Law. Wheaton's International Law.

Wheel. Wheeler's New York Criminal Cases;—Wheelock's Reports, vols. 32–37 Texas.

Wheel.Br.Cas. Wheeling Bridge Case.

Wheel.Cr.C. Wheeler's New York Criminal Cases.

Wheel.Cr.Rec. Wheeler's Criminal Recorder, New York, vol. 1 Wheeler's Criminal Cases.

Wheeler, Cr.Cas. Wheeler's New York Criminal Cases.

Whishaw. Whishaw's Law Dictionary.

Whit.Pat.Cas. Whitman's Patent Cases, United States.

Whitak.Liens. Whitaker on Liens.

White. White's Reports, vols. 10–15 West Virginia;—White's Reports, vols. 30–40 Texas Court of Appeals;—White, Scotch Justiciary Reports.

White, Coll. White's New Collection of the Laws, etc., of Great Britain, France and Spain.

White, New Recop. (or Nov.Recop.). See White, Recop.

White, Recop. White, New Recopilacion. A New Collection of Laws and Local Ordinances of Great Britain, France, and Spain, Relating to the Concessions of Land in Their Respective Colonies, with the Laws of Mexico and Texas on the Same Subjects.

White's Ann.Pen.Code. White's Annotated Penal Code, Tex.

White & T.L.Cas. (or White & T.Lead Cas.Eq.). White and Tudor's Leading Cases in Equity.

White & W. White & Willson's Reports, vol. 142 Texas Civil Appeals.

White & W.Civ.Cas.Ct.App. White & Willson's Civil Cases Court of Appeals, Tex.

Whitm.Lib.Cas. Whitman's Massachusetts Libel Cases.

Whitm.Pat.Cas. Whitman's Patent Cases.

Whitm.Pat.Law Rev. Whitman's Patent Law Review, Washington, D. C.

Whitney. Whitney's Land Laws, Tennessee.

Whitt. Whittelsey's Reports, vols. 31–41 Missouri.

Whitt.Co. Whittaker's Codes, Ohio.

Wig.Wills. Wigram on Wills.

Wight. (or Wightw.). Wightwick's English Exchequer Reports.

Wight El.Cas. Wight's Election Cases (Scotch).

Wil. Williams (see Will.);—Wilson (see Wils.).

Wilcox. Wilcox's Reports, vol. 10 Ohio;—Wilcox, Pennsylvania.

Wilcox Cond. Wilcox, Condensed Ohio Reports.

Wildm.Int.Law. Wildman's International Law.

Wilk. Wilkinson's Texas Court of Appeals and Civil Appeals;—Wilkinson's Reports, Australia.

Wilk. & Ow. (or Wilk. & Pat. or Wilk. & Mur.). Wilkinson, Owen, Paterson & Murray's New South Wales Reports.

Will. Willes' English Common Pleas Reports;—Willson's Reports, vols. 29–30 Texas Appeals, also vols. 1, 2 Texas Civil Appeals;—William, as 1 Will. IV. See, also, Williams.

Will.Ann.Reg. Williams' Annual Register, New York.

Will.-Bund St.Tr. Willis-Bund's Cases from State Trials.

Will.Eq.Jur. Willard's Equity Jurisprudence.

Will.Mass. Williams' Reports, vol. 1 Massachusetts.

Will.P. Peere-Williams' English Chancery Reports.

Will.Saund. Williams' Notes to Saunders' Reports.

Will.Vt. Williams' Reports, vols. 27–29 Vermont.

Will., Woll. & Dav. Willmore, Wollaston & Davison's English Queen's Bench Reports.

Will., Woll. & Hodg. Willmore, Wollaston & Hodges, English Queen's Bench Reports.

Willc.Const. Willcock, The Office of Constable.

Willcock, Mun.Corp. Willcock's Municipal Corporation.

Willes. Willes' English King's Bench and Common Pleas Reports.

Williams. Peere-Williams' English Chancery Reports; —Williams' Reports, vols. 27-29 Vermont;—Williams' Reports, vol. 1 Massachusetts;—Williams' Reports, vols. 10-12 Utah.

Williams, Common. Williams on Rights of Common.

Williams, Ex'rs. Williams on Executors.

Williams, Ex'rs, R. & T.Ed. Williams on Executors, Randolph and Talcott Edition.

Williams P. Peere-Williams' English Chancery Reports.

Williams, Pers.Prop. Williams on Personal Property.

Williams, Real Prop. Williams on Real Property.

Williams, Saund. Williams' Notes to Saunders' Reports.

Williams, Seis. Williams on Seisin.

Williams & B.Adm.Jur. Williams & Bruce on Admiralty Jurisdiction.

Willis, Trustees. Willis on Trustees.

Willm. W. & D. Willmore, Wollaston & Davison's English Queen's Bench Reports.

Willm.W. & H. Willmore, Wollaston & Hodges' English Queen's Bench Reports.

Wills, Cir.Ev. (or Wills, Circ.Ev.). Wills on Circumstantial Evidence.

Willson. Willson's Reports, vols. 29-30 Texas Appeals, also vols. 1, 2 Texas Court of Appeals, Civil Cases.

Willson, Civ.Cas.Ct.App. Willson's Civil Cases Court of Appeals, Tex.

Willson, Tex.Cr.Law. Willson's Revised Penal Code, Code of Criminal Procedure, and Penal Laws of Texas.

Wilm. Wilmot's Notes of Opinions, English King's Bench.

Wilm.Op. (or Judg.). Wilmot's Notes of Opinions.

Wils. Wilson's English Common Pleas Reports.

Wils. (Ind.). Wilson's Indiana Superior Court Reports.

Wils.C.P. Wilson's Common Pleas, Eng.

Wils.Ch. Wilson's English Chancery Reports.

Wils.Ent. Wilson's Entries and Pleadings (same as vol. 3 Lord Raymond).

Wils.Exch. Wilson's English Exchequer Reports.

Wils.Ind.Gloss. Wilson, Glossary of Indian Terms.

Wils.K.B. Sergeant Wilson's English King's Bench Reports.

Wils.P.C. Wilson's Privy Council, Eng.

Wils. & Court. Wilson & Courtenay's Scotch Appeals Cases (see Wilson & Shaw).

Wils. & S. (or Wils. & Sh.). Wilson & Shaw's Scotch Appeals Cases (Shaw, Wilson & Courtenay).

Wilson. Wilson's English Common Pleas Reports;—Wilson's English Chancery Reports;—Wilson's English Exchequer Equity Reports;—Wilson's Indiana Superior Court Reports;—Wilson's Reports, vols. 1, 3 Oregon;—Wilson's Reports, vols. 48-59 Minnesota.

Wilson's Rev. & Ann.St. Wilson's Revised and Annotated Statutes, Okl.

Win. Winston's Law Reports, North Carolina;—Winch's English Common Pleas Reports.

Win.Eq. Winston's Equity Reports, North Carolina.

Winch. Winch's English Common Pleas Reports;—Winch's Entries.

Winfield, Words & Phrases. Winfield's Adjudged Words and Phrases, with Notes.

Wing. (or Wing.Max.). Wingate's Maxims.

Wins.Eq. Winston's Equity Reports, North Carolina.

Winst. (or Winst.Eq.). Winston's Law or Equity Reports, North Carolina.

Wis. Wisconsin;—Wisconsin Reports.

Wis.Bar Assn. Wisconsin State Bar Association.

Wis.L.N. (or Wis.Leg.N.). Wisconsin Legal News, Milwaukee.

Wis.L.Rev. Wisconsin Law Review.

Wis.S.B.A.Bull. Wisconsin State Bar Association Bulletin.

With.Corp.Cas. Withrow's American Corporation Cases.

Withrow. Withrow's Reports, vols. 9-21 Iowa.

Witthaus & Becker's Med.Jur. Witthaus and Becker's Medical Jurisprudence.

Wkly.Dig. Weekly Digest, N.Y.

Wkly.Law Bul. Weekly Law Bulletin, Ohio.

Wkly.Law Gaz. Weekly Law Gazette, Ohio.

Wkly.Notes Cas. (Pa.). Weekly Notes of Cases, Philadelphia, Pennsylvania.

Wkly.Rep. Weekly Reporter, London, Eng.

Wm. William, as 9 Wm. III.

Wm.Bl. William Blackstone's English King's Bench Reports.

Wm.Rob. (or Wm.Rob.Adm.). William Robinson's English Admiralty Reports.

Wm. & Mary. William and Mary, as 2 Wm. & Mary, c. 1.

Wms. Williams (see Will.).

Wms.Ann.Reg. Williams' Annual Register, New York.

Wms.Ex'rs. Williams on Executors.

Wms.Mass. Williams' Reports, vol. 1 Massachusetts.

Wms.Notes. Williams' Notes to Saunders' Reports.

Wms.Peere. Peere-Williams' English Chancery Reports.

Wms.Saund. Williams' Notes to Saunders' Reports.

Wms.Vt. Williams' Reports, vols. 27-29 Vermont.

Woerner, Adm'n. Woerner's Treatise on the American Law of Administration.

Wol. Wollaston's English Bail Court Reports;—Wolcott's Reports, vol. 7 Delaware Chancery.

Wolf. & B. Wolferstan & Bristow's English Election Cases.

Wolf. & D. Wolferstan & Dew, English.

Wolff. Dr. de la Nat. Wolffius, Droit de la Nature.

Wolff. Inst. (or Wolff. Inst. Nat.). Wolffius, Institutiones Juris Naturæ et Gentium.

Wolffius (or Wolffius, Inst.). Wolffius, Institutiones Juris Naturæ et Gentium.

Woll. (or Woll. P.C.). Wollaston's English Bail Court Reports (Practice Cases).

Women Law.J. Women Lawyers Journal.

Wood. Woods' United States Circuit Court Reports; —Wood's English Tithe Cases.

Wood Conv. Wood on Conveyancing.

Wood Decr. Wood's (Decrees in) Tithe Cases.

Wood H. Hutton's Wood's Decrees in Tithe Cases.

Wood, Ins. Wood on Fire Insurance;—Wood's Institutes of English Law.

Wood, Inst. Wood's Institutes of English Law.

Wood, Inst.Com.Law. Wood's Institutes of the Common Law.

Wood, Landl. & Ten. Wood on Landlord and Tenant.

Wood.Lect. Wooddeson's Lectures on Laws of England.

Wood, Lim. Wood on Limitation of Actions.

Wood, Mast. & Serv. Wood on Master and Servant.

Wood, Nuis. Wood on Nuisances.

Wood, Ry.Law. Wood's Law of Railroads.

Wood Ti.Cas. Wood's Tithe Cases.

Wood's Civ.Law. Wood's Institutes of the Civil Law of England.

Wood's Dig. Wood's Digest of Laws, Cal.

Wood. & M. (or Woodb. & M.). Woodbury & Minot's United States Circuit Court Reports.

Woodd.Lect. Wooddeson's Lectures on the Laws of England.

Woodf.Cel.Tr. Woodfall's Celebrated Trials.

Woodf.Landl. & T. (or Woodf.Landl. & Ten.). Woodfall on Landlord and Tenant.

Woodm.Cr.Cas. Woodman's Reports of Thacher's Criminal Cases, Massachusetts.

Woods (or Woods' C.C.). Woods' United States Circuit Court Reports.

Woods, St.Frauds. Wood's Treatise on the Statutes of Frauds.

Woodw.Dec. Woodward's Decisions, Pa.

Woodw.Dec.Pa. Woodward's Common Pleas Decisions, Pennsylvania.

Wool. Woolworth's United States Circuit Court Reports;—Woolrych.

Wool.C.C. Woolworth's Reports, United States Circuit Courts, 8th Circuit (Fuller's Opinions).

Woolr.Waters. Woolrych's Law of Waters.

Wools.Pol.Science (or Woolsey, Polit.Science). Woolsey's Political Science.

Woolw. (or Woolw.Rep.). Woolworth's United States Circuit Court Reports;—Woolworth's Reports, vol. 1 Nebraska.

Wor.Dict. (or Worcest.Dict.). Worcester's Dictionary.

Worcester. Worcester, Dictionary of the English Language.

Words.Elect.Cas. Wordsworth's Election Cases.

Work.Comp. Workmen's Compensation Law of Pennsylvania.

Works, Courts. Works on Courts and Their Jurisdiction.

Works, Pr. Works' Practice, Pleading, and Forms.

Wr. Wright (see Wright);—Wright's Reports, vols. 37–50 Pennsylvania State.

Wr.Ch. (or Wr.Ohio). Wright's Reports, Ohio.

Wr.Pa. Wright's Reports, vols. 37–50 Pennsylvania State.

Wright (or Wri.). Wright's Reports, vols. 37–50 Pennsylvania State;—Wright's Ohio Reports.

Wright N.P. Wright's Nisi Prius Reports, Ohio.

Wright, Ten. Wright on Tenures.

Wy. Wyoming;—Wyoming Reports;—Wythe's Virginia Chancery Reports.

Wy.Dic. Wyatt's Dickens' Chancery Reports.

Wy.W. & A'Beck. Wyatt, Webb & A'Beckett, Vict.

Wy. & W. Wyatt & Webb, Vict.

Wyatt, Prac.Reg. Wyatt's Practical Register in Chancery.

Wyatt, W. & A'B. Wyatt, Webb & A'Beckett's Reports, Victoria.

Wyatt, W. & A'B.Eq. Wyatt, Webb & A'Beckett's Equity Reports, Victoria.

Wyatt, W. & A'B.I.P. & M. Wyatt, Webb & A'Beckett's Insolvency, Probate and Matrimonial Reports, Victoria.

Wyatt, W. & A'B.Min. Wyatt, Webb & A'Beckett's Mining Cases, Victoria.

Wyatt & W.Eq. Wyatt & Webb's Equity Reports, Victoria.

Wyatt & W.I.P. & M. Wyatt & Webb's Insolvency, Probate, and Matrimonial Reports, Victoria.

Wyatt & W.Min. Wyatt & Webb's Mining Cases, Victoria.

Wyatt & Webb. Wyatt & Webb's Reports, Victoria.

Wyman. Wyman's Reports, India.

Wynne Bov. Wynne's Bovill's Patent Cases.

Wyo. Wyoming;—Wyoming Reports.

Wyo.L.J. Wyoming Law Journal.

Wyo.T. Wyoming Territory.

Wythe. Wythe's Virginia Chancery Reports.

Y

Y. Yeates' Pennsylvania Reports.

Y.B. Year Book, English King's Bench, etc.

Y.B.Ed.I. Year Books of Edward I.

Y.B.P.1, Edw.II. Year Books, Part 1, Edward II.

Y.B.S.C. Year Books, Selected Cases, 1.

Y.L.R. York Legal Record.

Y. & C. Younge & Collyer's English Chancery Reports and Exchequer.

Y. & C.Exch. Younge & Collyer's Exchequer, Eng.

Y. & Coll. Younge & Collyer's Chancery, Eng.

Y. & J. Younge & Jervis' English Exchequer Reports.

Yale L.J. Yale Law Journal.

Yates Sel.Cas. Yates' New York Select Cases.

Yea. (or Yeates). Yeates' Pennsylvania Reports.

Yearb. Year Book, English King's Bench, etc.

Yearb.P.7, Hen.VI. Year Books, Part 7, Henry VI.

Yearbook School Law. Yearbook of School Law.

Yeates. Yeates, Pa.

Yel. Yelverton's English King's Bench Reports.

Yelv. Yelverton, English.

Yerg. Yerger's Tennessee Reports.

Yo. Young (see You.).

York Ass. Clayton's Reports (York Assizes).

York Leg.Rec. (or York). York Legal Record.

You. Younge's English Exchequer Equity Reports.

You. & Coll.Ch. Younge & Collyer's English Chancery Reports.

You. & Coll.Ex. Younge & Collyer's English Exchequer Equity Reports.

You. & Jerv. Younge & Jervis' English Exchequer Reports.

Young. Young's Reports, vols. 31–47 Minnesota.

Young Adm. Young's Nova Scotia Admiralty Cases.

Young Adm.Dec. Young's Admiralty Decisions.

Young M.L.Cas. Young's Maritime Law Cases.

Young, Naut.Dict. Young, Nautical Dictionary.

Younge. Younge's English Exchequer Equity Reports.

Younge & C.Ch. (or Younge & Coll.Ch.). Younge & Collyer's English Chancery Reports.

Younge & Coll.Ex. Younge & Collyer's English Exchequer Equity Reports.

Younge & J. Younge & Jervis, English.

Yuk. Yukon Territory.

Z

Zab. Zabriskie's New Jersey Reports.

Zane. Zane's Reports, vols. 4–9 Utah.

Zinn Ca.Tr. Zinn's Select Cases in the Law of Trusts.